I thank my God every time I remember you,
constantly praying with joy
in every one of my prayers for all of you.

Philippians 1:3-4

Presented To

____

By

____

On

____

This book can change your life.

The Bible's essential message is this: God loves us and wants to be in a lifelong **friendship** with us. The Bible tells the story of God's love, revealed most perfectly in Jesus' **life**, death, and Resurrection. Through Christ, God offers us forgiveness, freedom, companionship, and **new** life. It is a wonderful gift, but we must choose to accept it. How will you respond to that invitation?

Lord God, here I am!
You created me and know me completely.
You know all about my life—my joys and my
sufferings, my questions and my dreams.
I know you love me, even when I feel my sins
and mistakes make me unlovable.
Help me to love you, God, with all my heart,
mind, and soul, and to love all people,
even as I love myself.

Jesus, thank you for showing me how to live.
I know you want only the best for my life,
and I believe following you is the way to a
full and abundant life.

Holy Spirit, give me the courage and wisdom
to be Jesus' follower, even when it isn't easy.
Fill me with the joy and peace that comes
from doing your will.

Amen.

THE Catholic Youth Bible®
Third Edition

Pray It! Study It! Live It!®
resources offer a holistic approach
to learning, living, and passing on the
Catholic faith.

For the text of the articles and introductions

Nihil Obstat: Rev. William M. Becker, STD
Censor Librorum
June 14, 2011

Imprimatur: † Most Rev. John M. Quinn
Bishop of Winona
June 14, 2011

For the text of the New American Bible, Revised Edition (NABRE)

RESCRIPT

In accord with canon 825 §1 of the Code of Canon Law, the United States Conference of Catholic Bishops hereby approves for publication The New American Bible, Revised Old Testament, a translation of the Sacred Scriptures authorized by the Confraternity of Christian Doctrine, Inc.

The translation was approved by the Administrative Committee of the United States Conference of Catholic Bishops in November 2008 and September 2010. It is permitted by the undersigned for private use and study.

Given in the city of Washington, the District of Columbia, on the Feast of Saint Jerome, Priest and Doctor of the Church, the 30th day of September, in the year of our Lord 2010.

† Francis Cardinal George, O.M.I.
Archbishop of Chicago
President, USCCB

The Revised New Testament

Nihil Obstat: Stephen J. Hartdegen, O.F.M., S.S.L.
Censor Deputatus

Imprimatur: † James A. Hickey, S.T.D., J.C.D.
Archbishop of Washington
August 27, 1986

The *Nihil Obstat* and *Imprimatur* are official declarations that a book is free of doctrinal and moral error. No implication is contained therein that those who have granted the *Nihil Obstat* and *Imprimatur* agree with the content, opinions, or statements expressed. Nor do they assume any legal responsibility associated with publication.

Third edition reviewers and article writers: Catherine Cory, Marissa Esparza-Garcia, Dennis Kurtz, Paula Norbert, Margaret Nutting Ralph, Larry Schatz, FSC, James Spillman, Alan Talley, Michael Theisen

Interior Design: Laurie Nelson; Illustrations: Vicki Shuck; Typesetting: Blue Heron Bookcraft; Proofreading: Peachtree Editorial and Proofreading Services

The acknowledgments continue on page 1831.

The publishing team included Virginia Halbur, development editor; prepress and manufacturing coordinated by the production departments of Saint Mary's Press.

Catholic Youth Bible®, Third Edition

Printed in the United States of America
4133 (PO3366)
ISBN 978-1-59982-141-2, paper
ISBN 978-1-59982-142-9, hardcover
ISBN 978-1-59982-143-6, leatherette
Library of Congress Cataloging-in-Publication Data
Bible. English. New American. 2012.
The Catholic youth Bible : New American Bible, revised edition : translated from the original languages with critical use of all the ancient sources. — 3rd ed.
p. cm.
Includes index.
ISBN 978-1-59982-141-2 (pbk.) — ISBN 978-1-59982-142-9 (hardbound) — ISBN 978-1-59982-143-6 (leatherette)
I. Title.
BS192.3.A12012 W56 2012
220.5'2054—dc23

2011038270

THE Catholic Youth Bible®

Third Edition

NEW AMERICAN BIBLE, REVISED EDITION

TRANSLATED FROM THE ORIGINAL LANGUAGES
WITH CRITICAL USE OF ALL THE ANCIENT SOURCES

AUTHORIZED BY THE BOARD OF TRUSTEES OF THE
CONFRATERNITY OF CHRISTIAN DOCTRINE
AND APPROVED BY THE ADMINISTRATIVE COMMITTEE
OF THE UNITED STATES CONFERENCE OF CATHOLIC BISHOPS

saint mary's press

Contents

The Old Testament

The New Testament

Welcome!

This Unique Bible Is for YOU!

***The Catholic Youth Bible*® (*CYB*)** is filled with things that will make it easier for you to understand the Bible's message. The authors, editors, designers, and artists involved in creating its special features were focused on you — a young person seeking answers to life's important questions. The *CYB* can be a true companion, helping you find the answers you seek and perhaps raising new questions along the way. It will help you see yourself in God's image and likeness...

a vital part of God's saving work in the world.

What Makes this Youth Bible CATHOLIC?

For starters, its introductions and articles reflect Catholic interpretation of the Bible and make connections to Catholic beliefs and traditions. In addition, this Bible contains all seventy-three books and letters that form a complete Catholic Bible, seven more than most other Bibles (see "The Case of the Missing Books," near Tb 1:16). Does this mean that other Christians cannot use ***The Catholic Youth Bible***? Not at all. When it comes to the Scriptures, Christians from all cultures and denominations have more in common than they have differences.

As You Use this Bible, keep in mind two important points. The first is that the Bible is for everyone. Wherever you are in your relationship with God, ***the Bible can speak to you.*** The articles in the ***CYB*** invite you to consider what the church teaches about God's message in the Bible, whether you are a committed Christian or a searcher with lots of questions.

The second point is that all the special features in ***The Catholic Youth Bible*** are designed to encourage you ***to read the Bible itself.*** It is the Bible's stories, poems, prophecies, and letters that carry this central message: ***God desires a loving relationship with us.*** The special features of this Bible can help you understand God's message. **But it is God's word in the Bible that can CHANGE YOUR LIFE!**

Special Features

The Catholic Youth Bible is loaded with special features to help make it easier for you to read and understand the Bible. Here is a list of some of those features and where to find them.

SECTION INTRODUCTIONS

Each major section of the Bible (the Pentateuch, the historical books, the biblical novellas, the wisdom books, the prophetic books, the Gospels and the Acts of the Apostles, and the Letters and Revelation) begins with background on the books in that section.

BOOK INTRODUCTIONS

Introductions at the beginning of most books (sometimes two or three books share a single introduction) give insight into each book's central message and an overview of its contents.

COLOR INSERTS

The five sections of color inserts cover how to read and study the Bible; how to pray with the Scriptures; how to apply biblical principles to daily life and six saints who illustrate the principles, including a list of the seven principles of Catholic social teaching; photos and charts highlighting biblical people, places, and events; and an overview of Catholic practices and prayers.

The **"Live It!"** articles apply the Bible's messages to situations you may be facing now or will face in the future.

The **"Pray It!"** articles can help you use the Bible for personal prayer. They show the biblical basis for the prayer and sacramental life of the Catholic Church.

The **"Did You Know?"** articles provide background from biblical scholars to help you understand the culture and traditions of biblical times, or the Church's interpretation of certain passages.

The **"Introducing . . ."** articles give a quick introduction to the lives of important biblical people.

The **"Catholic Connection"** articles are full-page articles that show the biblical basis for many Catholic Christian beliefs and practices.

The **"Cultural Connection"** articles explain how people in different cultures have understood and lived out God's revelation in the Bible. The articles represent many of the diverse cultures that have found their home in the United States.

These articles focus on the seven principles of Catholic social teaching and help the reader to understand their biblical basis.

WHERE DO I FIND IT?

Several indexes are located at the back of the Bible. The first index helps you locate Bible passages on events, people, and teachings of Jesus. The second index helps you find Bible passages related to Catholic teaching. The third index helps you find Bible passages related to each sacrament. The fourth index helps you find articles on the seven themes of Catholic social teaching. The fifth index helps you find Bible passages related to life and faith issues. The sixth index leads you to articles on specific topics.

STUDY AIDS

A calendar of the Church year and Sunday readings, a glossary of Scripture-related terms, color maps, pictures, and a timeline are found at the back of the Bible. The timeline and maps will help you locate where and when different biblical events occurred.

The Bible Is Multicultural

The Bible developed in the midst of great cultural diversity. In fact, the Bible was originally written in at least two languages, Hebrew and Greek. The people of the Old Testament were influenced by Arabic, Egyptian, and other Middle Eastern cultures that surrounded them. Later, they and the early Christian church were influenced by the Greek and Roman cultures. In the Bible, God is revealed as the God of all nations and all cultures.

As the word of God, the Bible's core message of God's love for human beings speaks to people of any culture. That is one reason the Bible has been translated into more languages than any other book in the world. Christians also believe that God is at work in the lives of people of every culture, whether or not they have been formally introduced to the Christian message. Listening to other cultures' experience of God can deepen Christian people's appreciation of God's message present in the Bible.

We also live in a multicultural world. ***The Catholic Youth Bible*** responds to this reality in two main ways. First, all the articles attempt to speak in a way that people of all cultures can appreciate and understand. Second, some articles have been specially written to represent distinct cultural perspectives. Most of these articles represent African American, Asian American, Hispanic and Latino, and Native American perspectives. The revised edition of ***The Catholic Youth Bible, Third Edition*** also includes additional articles representing cultural perspectives from around the world.

All the articles share cultural experiences and traditions, religious symbols, prayers, and poetry, and they connect all these elements to the Bible. If you would like to read articles from one of the four major cultural perspectives mentioned above, the subject index contains entries for those.

The cultural perspectives represented in ***The Catholic Youth Bible*** are a small sampling of the many unique cultures in the world. Because of space restrictions, articles on many cultures could not be included. Despite these limitations, the multicultural articles can deepen your appreciation of the Bible's message and of the rich ways different cultures live that message.

Navigating
The Catholic Youth Bible

The Catholic Youth Bible has several aids to help you locate references to Bible books and the Bible's special features. The contents on pages iv–v will be your main guide in locating the different books and features. However, the last page in the color section (facing the back cover) lists all the Bible books alphabetically and gives their abbreviations and beginning page numbers. You will find this a useful and easy-to-locate guide. Also, the section "Where Do I Find It?" offers several types of indexes to help you locate specific passages and articles.

Throughout ***The Catholic Youth Bible,*** there are many references to specific Bible passages. These references are given in shorthand form, such as Jn 3:16–17. The initial letters are the abbreviation for (or, in a few cases, the full name of) the Bible book. The number before the colon stands for the chapter, and the number(s) after the colon stands for the verse(s). So Jn 3:16–17 refers to the Gospel According to John, chapter 3, verses 16 to 17.

Name of Book Verse(s)

Jn 3:16–17

Chapter

Most of the articles end with a citation identifying the Bible passage the article is based on. It is important to read the passage before reading the article.

In addition to the Bible text, you will find footnotes and Scripture cross-references printed along the bottom of each page. Every time you see an obelisk (†) in the Bible text, you will find a corresponding footnote labeled with the same chapter and verse numbers at the bottom of the page. The footnotes provide you with added information about words and phrases mentioned in the Bible. Every time you see an asterisk (*) in the Bible text, you will find a corresponding cross-reference labeled with the same chapter and verse numbers at the bottom of the page. The cross-references direct you to similar Scripture passages.

Preface to the New American Bible
The Old Testament

On September 30, 1943, His Holiness Pope Pius XII issued his now famous encyclical on scripture studies, *Divino afflante Spiritu*. He wrote: "We ought to explain the original text which was written by the inspired author himself and has more authority and greater weight than any, even the very best, translation whether ancient or modern. This can be done all the more easily and fruitfully if to the knowledge of languages be joined a real skill in literary criticism of the same text."

Early in 1944, in conformity with the spirit of the encyclical, and with the encouragement of Archbishop Cicognani, Apostolic Delegate to the United States, the Bishops' Committee of the Confraternity of Christian Doctrine requested members of The Catholic Biblical Association of America to translate the sacred scriptures from the original languages or from the oldest extant form of the text, and to present the sense of the biblical text in as correct a form as possible.

The first English Catholic version of the Bible, the Douay-Rheims (1582–1609/10), and its revision by Bishop Challoner (1750) were based on the Latin Vulgate. In view of the relative certainties more recently attained by textual and higher criticism, it has become increasingly desirable that contemporary translations of the sacred books into English be prepared in which due reverence for the text and strict observance of the rules of criticism would be combined.

The New American Bible has accomplished this in response to the need of the church in America today. It is the achievement of some fifty biblical scholars, the greater number of whom, though not all, are Catholics. In particular, the editors-in-chief have devoted twenty-five years to this work. The collaboration of scholars who are not Catholic fulfills the directive of the Second Vatican Council, not only that "correct translations be made into different languages especially from the original texts of the sacred books," but that, "with the approval of the church authority, these translations be produced in cooperation with separated brothers" so that "all Christians may be able to use them."

The text of the books contained in *The New American Bible* is a completely new translation throughout. From the original and the oldest available texts of the sacred books, it aims to convey as directly as possible the thought and individual style of the inspired writers. The better understanding of Hebrew and Greek, and the steady development of the science of textual criticism, the fruit of patient study since the time of St. Jerome, have allowed the translators and editors in their use of all available materials to approach more closely than ever before the sense of what the sacred authors actually wrote.

Where the translation supposes the received text—Hebrew, Aramaic, or Greek, as the case may be—ordinarily contained in the best-known editions, as the original or the oldest extant form, no additional remarks are necessary. But for those who are happily able to study the original text of the scriptures at firsthand, a supplementary series of textual notes pertaining to the Old Testament was added originally in an appendix to the typical edition. (It is now obtainable in a separate booklet from The Catholic Biblical Association of America, The Catholic University of America, Washington, DC 20064.) These notes furnish a guide in those cases in which the editorial board judges that the manuscripts in the original languages, or the evidence of the ancient versions, or some similar source, furnish the correct reading of a passage, or at least a reading more true to the original than that customarily printed in the available editions.

The Massoretic text of 1 and 2 Samuel has in numerous instances been corrected by the more ancient manuscripts Samuel a, b, and c from Cave 4 of Qumran, with the aid of important evidence from the Septuagint in both its oldest form and its Lucianic recension. Fragments of the lost Book of Tobit in Aramaic and in Hebrew, recovered from Cave 4 of Qumran, are in substantial agreement with the Sinaiticus Greek recension used for the translation of this book. The lost original Hebrew text of 1 Maccabees is replaced by its oldest extant form in Greek. Judith, 2 Maccabees, and parts of Esther are also translated from the Greek.

The basic text for the Psalms is not the Masoretic but one which the editors considered closer to the original inspired form, namely the Hebrew text underlying the new Latin Psalter of the Church, the *Liber Psalmorum* (1944[1], 1945[2]). Nevertheless they retained full liberty to establish the reading of the original text on sound critical principles.

The translation of Sirach, based on the original Hebrew as far as it is preserved and corrected from the ancient versions, is often interpreted in the light of the traditional Greek text. In the Book of Baruch the basic text is the Greek of the Septuagint, with some readings derived from an underlying Hebrew form no longer extant. In the deuterocanonical sections of Daniel (3:24–91, chapter 13 and chapter 14 [these are Azariah, Susanna, and Bel and the Dragon respectively in WORDsearch]), the basic text is the Greek text of Theodotion, occasionally revised according to the Greek text of the Septuagint.

In some instances in the Book of Job, in Proverbs, Sirach, Isaiah, Jeremiah, Ezekiel, Hosea, Amos, Micah, Nahum, Habakkuk, and Zechariah there is good reason to believe that the original order of lines was accidentally disturbed in the transmission of the text. The verse numbers given in such cases are always those of the current Hebrew text, though the arrangement differs. In these instances the textual notes advise the reader of the difficulty. Cases of exceptional dislocation are called to the reader's attention by footnotes.

The Books of *Genesis* to *Ruth* were first published in 1952; the Wisdom Books, *Job* to *Sirach,* in 1955; the Prophetic Books, *Isaiah* to *Malachi,* in 1961; and the Historical Books, *Samuel* to *Maccabees,* in 1969. In the present edition of *Genesis* to *Ruth* there are certain new features: a general introduction to the Pentateuch, a retranslation of the text of Genesis with an introduction, cross-references, and revised textual notes, besides new and expanded exegetical notes which take into consideration the various sources or literary traditions.

The revision of *Job* to *Sirach* includes changes in strophe division in Job and Proverbs and in titles of principal parts and sections of Wisdom and Ecclesiastes. Corrections in the text of Sirach are made in Sir 39:27—44:17 on the basis of the Masada text, and in 51:13–30 on the basis of the occurrence of this canticle in the Psalms scroll from Qumran Cave 11. In this typical edition, new corrections are reflected in the textual notes of Job, Proverbs, Wisdom, and Sirach. In the Psalms, the enumeration found in the Hebrew text is followed instead of the double enumeration, according to both the Hebrew and the Latin Vulgate texts, contained in the previous edition of this book.

In the Prophetic Books *Isaiah* to *Malachi,* only minor revisions have been made in the structure and wording of the texts, and in the textual notes.

The spelling of proper names in *The New American Bible* follows the customary forms found in most English Bibles since the Authorized Version.

The work of translating the Bible has been characterized as "the sacred and apostolic work of interpreting the word of God and of presenting it to the laity in translations as clear as the difficulty of the matter and the limitations of human knowledge permit" (A. G. Cicognani, Apostolic Delegate, in *The Catholic Biblical Quarterly,* 6, [1944], 389–90). In the appraisal of the present work, it is hoped that the words of the encyclical *Divino afflante Spiritu* will serve as a guide: "Let all the sons of the church bear in mind that the efforts of these resolute laborers in the vineyard of the Lord should be judged not only with equity and justice but also with the greatest charity; all moreover should abhor that intemperate zeal which imagines that whatever is new should for that very reason be opposed or suspected."

Conscious of their personal limitations for the task thus defined, those who have prepared this text cannot expect that it will be considered perfect; but they can hope that it may deepen in its readers "the right understanding of the divinely given Scriptures," and awaken in them "that piety by which it behooves us to be grateful to the God of all providence, who from the throne of his majesty has sent these books as so many personal letters to his own children" *(Divino afflante Spiritu).*

Preface to the New American Bible
Revised Old Testament

The first step in the genesis of *The New American Bible* was taken in 1936 when His Excellency, the Most Reverend Edwin V. O'Hara, D.D., chairman of the Episcopal Committee of the Confraternity of Christian Doctrine, invited a group of Catholic Scripture scholars to plan for a revised edition of the Challoner-Rheims New Testament, primarily on the basis of the Vulgate; the plans soon expanded to include the revision of the Old Testament. Archbishop O'Hara's initiative resulted in the formation of the Catholic Biblical Association, whose principal activity in its early years was this work of revision and translation. (For information on the work done on the New Testament, see the "Preface to *The New American Bible*: First Edition of the New Testament" and "Preface to the Revised Edition.") In 1943 His Holiness Pope Pius XII issued the encyclical *Divino afflante spiritu*, which encouraged Scripture scholars to translate the Scriptures from the original languages. He wrote: "We ought to explain the original text which was written by the inspired author himself and has more authority and greater weight than any, even the very best, translation whether ancient or modern. This can be done all the more easily and fruitfully if to the knowledge of languages be joined a real skill in literary criticism of the same text." Although at this point work on almost twenty of the Old Testament books was completed or near completion, that work was abandoned and the new project of translating from the Hebrew, Greek, and Aramaic was undertaken.

The completed books of the Old Testament were initially published, as they became available, in four volumes: Genesis–Ruth (1952), Job–Sirach (1955), Isaiah–Malachi (1961), and Samuel–Maccabees (1969). Some fifty scholars collaborated on this project; these were mainly Catholics, but, in accord with the suggestion of Vatican II that "with the approval of the church authority, these translations be produced in cooperation with separated brothers" so that "all Christians may be able to use them" (*Dei Verbum*, No. 22), non-Catholics also participated in the work. To this point the translation had been known under the name of the "Confraternity of Christian Doctrine" or CCD for short, but when these parts of the Old Testament were combined with the New Testament in a single volume, it was given the name "New American Bible," in part to reflect its ecumenical character. In producing the new volume certain changes were made from the original four volumes: a retranslation of the Book of Genesis, cross-references, new and expanded exegetical notes.

New translations and revision of existing translations are required from time to time for various reasons. For example, it is important to keep pace with the discovery and publication of new and better ancient manuscripts (e.g., the Dead Sea scrolls) so that the best possible textual tradition will be followed, as required by *Divino afflante spiritu*. There are advances in linguistics of the biblical languages which make possible a better understanding and more accurate translation of the original languages. And there are changes and developments in vocabulary and the cultural background of the receptor language. An obvious example of this is the abandonment in English of the second person singular (use of "thee," "thou," "sayest," "hearest"), which had a major impact on Bible translations. Other changes are less obvious but are nevertheless present. There have been changes in vocabulary; for example, the term "holocaust" is now normally reserved for the sacrilegious attempt to destroy the Jewish people by the Third Reich. Concerns such as these are reflected in what Pope John Paul II spoke of as the "three pillars" of good biblical translation: "A good translation is based on three pillars that must contemporaneously support the entire work. First, there must be a deep knowledge of the language and the cultural world at the point of origin. Next, there must be a good familiarity with the language and cultural context at the point where the work will arrive. Lastly, to crown the work with success, there must be an adequate mastery of the contents and meaning of what one is translating"—and he praised the translation that "utilizes the vocabulary and idioms of everyday speech" ("le parole e le forme della lingua di tutti i giorni"). (From an address to the United Bible Societies, November 26, 2001.)

This new edition is a thorough revision of the already excellent *New American Bible* Old Testament of 1970. Work on most books of the Old Testament, begun in 1994 and completed in 2001, was done by forty revisers and a board of eight editors. The 1991 revision of the Psalter, the work of thirty revisers and six editors, was further revised by seven revisers and two editors between 2009 and 2010. As suggested in the comments above, the revision aimed at making use of the best manuscript traditions available (see below), translating as accurately as possible, and rendering the result in good contemporary English. In many ways it is a more literal translation than the original NAB and has attempted to be more consistent in rendering Hebrew (or Greek) words and idioms, especially in technical contexts, such as regulations for sacrifices. In translating the Psalter special effort was made to provide a smooth, rhythmic translation for easy singing or recitation, and to retain the concrete imagery of the Hebrew.

Where the Old Testament translation supposes the received text—Hebrew, Aramaic, or Greek, as the case may be—ordinarily contained in the best-known editions, as the original or the oldest extant form, no additional remarks are necessary. Where the translators have departed from those received texts, e.g., by following the Septuagint rather than the Masoretic text, accepting a reading of what is judged to be a better textual tradition, as from a Qumran manuscript, or by emending a reading apparently corrupted in transmission, such changes are recorded in the revised edition of the *Textual Notes on The New American Bible*. Additional information on the textual tradition for some books may be found in the introduction to the book in the same *Textual Notes*.

In particular, important manuscripts from Cave 4 of Qumran, as well as the most useful recensions of the Septuagint, have been consulted in the preparation of 1 and 2 Samuel. Fragments of the lost Book of Tobit in Aramaic and in Hebrew, recovered from Cave 4 of Qumran, are in substantial agreement with the Sinaiticus Greek recension used for the translation of this book. The lost original Hebrew text of 1 Maccabees is replaced by its oldest extant form in Greek. Judith, 2 Maccabees, and parts of Esther are also translated from the Greek. The translation of The Wisdom of Ben Sira is based on the original Hebrew as far as it is preserved, with corrections from the ancient versions; otherwise, the Greek of the Septuagint is followed. In the Book of Baruch the basic text is the Greek of the Septuagint, with some readings derived from an underlying Hebrew form no longer extant. In the deuterocanonical sections of Daniel (3:24–90; 13:1–14:42), the basic text is the Greek text of so-called Theodotion, occasionally revised according to the Greek text of the Septuagint.

The Old Testament

Introduction to the Pentateuch

Have you ever been late to a movie? You probably spent a few minutes trying to figure out what you missed and hoped it wasn't too important to the plot. Like the first crucial minutes of a movie, the five books of the Pentateuch set the stage for much of what happens in the rest of the Bible. If you don't know the people involved and their wonderful stories, when you read later books, you might find yourself asking: What's going on? Why is he doing this? What does she mean by that?

In Depth

The name *Pentateuch* literally means "five-part writing." Thus, the Pentateuch is the first five books of the Old Testament: Genesis, Exodus, Leviticus, Numbers, and Deuteronomy. These books are special to Jewish and Christian believers because they are God's word, reveal who God is, and tell of the origins of God's People and their unique relationship with God—sometimes called salvation history. They are the blueprint needed for properly understanding the rest of the Bible. The Pentateuch introduces the idea of a single God who is responsible for all creation. It also tells that this God is active in the world and in the lives of its people, and that the Israelites have been called into a special relationship with this God.

One of the central elements of the special relationship between God and the Israelites described in the Pentateuch is the Sinai Covenant. A covenant establishes a new relationship between two parties and is marked by a solemn promise, where both parties agree to fulfill certain obligations. The Sinai Covenant is the most famous one between God and Israel, with Moses as the mediator, which you will read about in Exodus. In Genesis, you will read about the covenant God makes with Noah, Abraham, and Jacob, which lead to the Sinai Covenant.

Reading the Pentateuch is like appreciating a fine tapestry. When you view a tapestry from the front, all the threads combine to make a beautiful, coherent image. In the same way, an overall look at the covenant, stories, and laws in the Pentateuch combines them to form a picture of the love relationship between God and the people of Israel. A close look at the back of a tapestry shows a more chaotic mix of colors and yarn. So too a closer look at the writings in the Pentateuch reveals not one story but many.

Biblical scholars speak of four primary sources for the stories and traditions in the Pentateuch. The sources reflect four different schools of thought about Israel's relationship with God. For convenience, each source is referred to as an individual author.

- The Yahwist used Yahweh as God's name. This source is also referred to as J, taken from the German spelling of the divine name. This writer focused on the southern kingdom of Judah, used lots of stories, emphasized God's closeness to humanity, and portrayed God acting as a human person.

- The Elohist (E) referred to God as Elohim or Lord. The Elohist wrote about the northern kingdom of Israel and was concerned about idolatry and morality. The writings of the Elohist present God's presence as mediated, such as through a burning bush.
- After the fall of the Northern Kingdom, E and J combined to form the Priestly writing (P). The Priestly writer emphasized religious rituals and the role of the priesthood. This writer portrayed God as more distant and used a more formal style. This source was written after the Babylonian Exile.
- Finally, the Deuteronomist (D) emphasized the Law as the foundation of the kingdom of Judah. Deuteronomy is the fifth book of the Pentateuch and the first book in the Deuteronomistic history.

Knowing that these four sources contributed to the final form of the Pentateuch can help us understand that the Pentateuch books are not simply records of events as they occurred but rather faith accounts about the Israelites' growing relationship with God, inspired by God and told from different perspectives.

In the Pentateuch, God reveals how much God loves the human race collectively and how much God loves us personally. God wishes to be in a relationship with us today just as much as God did back then. The Pentateuch reminds us that we are all children of God and are waiting for the full realization of God's reign.

Other Background

- Some of the most familiar stories and people of the Old Testament are found in Genesis and Exodus. Genesis includes the stories of Creation, Adam and Eve, Noah and the Flood, Abraham and Sarah, and Joseph and his brothers. Exodus contains the stories of Moses and the burning bush, Pharaoh and the ten plagues, the parting of the Red Sea, the Exodus out of Egypt, and the Ten Commandments.
- The Jewish people also refer to the five books of the Pentateuch as the Torah, meaning "teaching" or "instruction."
- An ancient tradition named Moses as the original writer of the Pentateuch. This was no doubt due to Moses' importance in the Pentateuch itself. But evidence suggests that most of the Pentateuch was written hundreds of years after Moses' death.
- There are different types of writing in the Pentateuch. Genesis is all inspired narrative, Leviticus and Deuteronomy are mostly laws, and Exodus and Numbers are approximately half narratives and half laws. Deuteronomy is unique in that it uses preaching rather than narrative.

Displays of awesome cosmic power, tender love stories, tearful family reunions, and tales of deceit, rape, murder, and worldwide destruction. Does this sound like the script for next summer's blockbuster movie? No, it's the Book of Genesis! It is the story of how a world created for love and harmony goes astray because of human sin. Through it all, God is at work, forming a people to restore what was lost.

In Depth

Genesis gathers together inspired stories and traditions that reveal Israel's understanding of God's nature and purpose, and the beginning of the Israelites' special relationship with God. Genesis has two main sections. The first section (1:1—11:26) contains some of the Bible's most memorable stories about Creation and the effect of sin. Chapters 1–2 tell two accounts of Creation that portray the beauty and wonder of the natural world and emphasize the goodness and harmony that God intended in Creation. Creation culminates in human beings, made in God's own image. Those human beings, symbolic of us all, live in a wonderful garden in harmony with God, Creation, and each other. But in chapter 3, sin enters the world, and as a result, Adam and Eve will experience separation, suffering, and ultimately death.

And the first sin spreads, first to the family (Cain and Abel in chapter 4), then to all society (Noah and the Flood in chapters 6–9). Even after the Flood and God's covenant with Noah, the story of the tower of Babel demonstrates that sin pits nation against nation. As you read these chapters, remember that they were written not as historical accounts or scientific explanations but as inspired stories that share a faith perspective and teach important religious truths.

The second section of Genesis (11:27—50:26) tells the story of the origins of the Israelite people. The story begins with Abraham and Sarah (originally called Abram and Sarai) and continues with Ishmael and Isaac and with Isaac and Rebekah's children, Esau and Jacob. Genesis ends with Joseph, one of Jacob's twelve sons, cleverly saving Egypt and Israel from famine. These sections introduce the covenant God makes with Abraham and the Israelite people and remind the reader that God's plans will overcome human sin and weakness.

At a Glance

Preamble. The Creation of the World (1:1—2:3).

I. The Story of the Nations (2:4—11:26).

A. The Creation of the Man and the Woman, Their Offspring, and the Spread of Civilization (2:4—4:26).

B. The Pre-flood Generations (5:1—6:8).

C. The Flood and the Renewed Blessing (6:9—9:29).

D. The Populating of the World and the Prideful City (10:1—11:9).

E. The Genealogy from Shem to Terah (11:10—26).

II. The Story of the Ancestors of Israel (11:27—50:26).

A. The Story of Abraham and Sarah (11:27—25:18).

B. The Story of Isaac and Jacob (25:19—36:43).

C. The Story of Joseph (37:1—50:26).

Quick Facts

Period Covered: The stories in the first eleven chapters are primeval history. Genesis 11:27—50:26 covers the period of the ancestors or patriarchs.

Themes: the goodness of Creation, human responsibility, the effects of sin, covenant, God's bringing good out of evil

The Book of **Genesis**

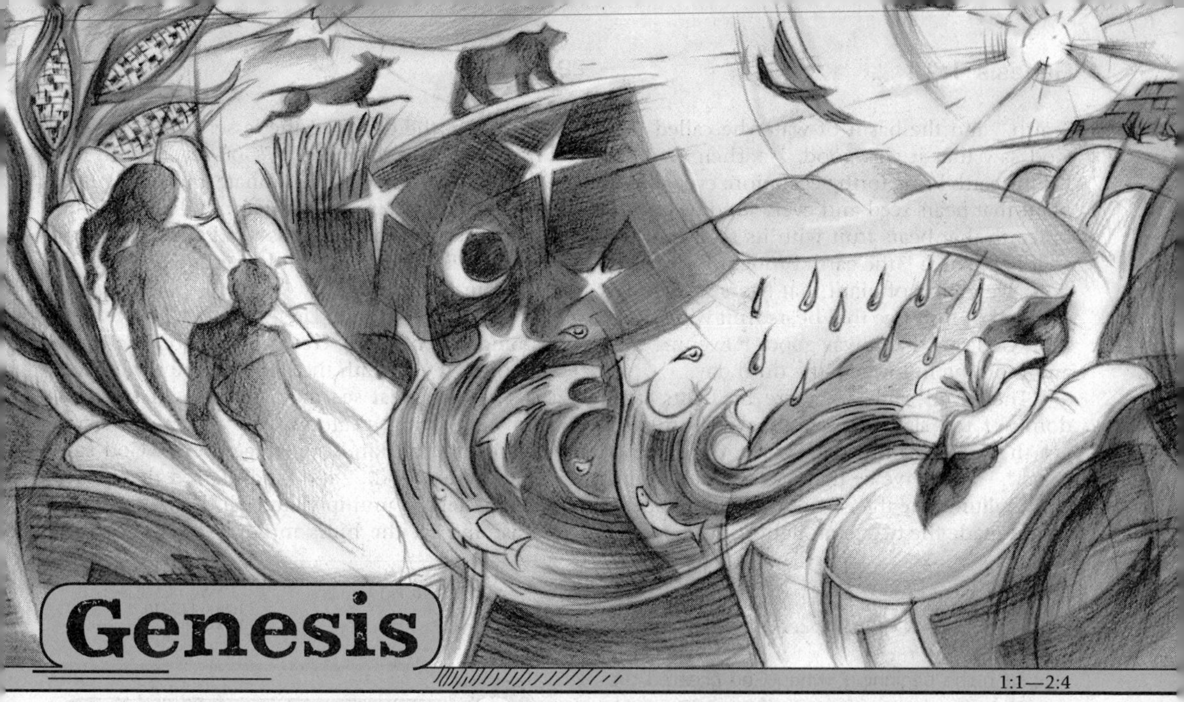

Genesis

Preamble. The Creation of the World

The Story of Creation†

1 [1]In the beginning, when God created the
heavens and the earth*— [2]† and the earth
was without form or shape, with darkness over
the abyss and a mighty wind sweeping over the
waters—*
[3]Then God said: Let there be light, and there
was light.* [4]God saw that the light was good. God
then separated the light from the darkness. [5]God
called the light "day," and the darkness he called
"night." Evening came, and morning followed—
the first day.†
[6]Then God said: Let there be a dome in the
middle of the waters, to separate one body of
water from the other. [7]God made the dome,†
and it separated the water below the dome from
the water above the dome. And so it happened.*
[8]God called the dome "sky." Evening came, and
morning followed—the second day.
[9]Then God said: Let the water under the sky
be gathered into a single basin, so that the dry
land may appear. And so it happened: the water
under the sky was gathered into its basin, and the
dry land appeared.* [10]God called the dry land

†

1:1–2:3 This section, from the Priestly source, functions as an introduction, as ancient stories of the origin of the world (cosmogonies) often did. It introduces the primordial story (2:4–11:26), the stories of the ancestors (11:27–50:26), and indeed the whole Pentateuch. The chapter highlights the goodness of creation and the divine desire that human beings share in that goodness. God brings an orderly universe out of primordial chaos merely by uttering a word. In the literary structure of six days, the creation events in the first three days are related to those in the second three.

1. light (day)/darkness (night)	=	4.	sun/moon
2. arrangement of water	=	5.	fish + birds from waters
3. a) dry land	=	6.	a) animals
b) vegetation			b) human beings: male/female

The seventh day, on which God rests, the climax of the account, falls outside the six-day structure.

Until modern times the first line was always translated, "In the beginning God created the heavens and the earth." Several comparable ancient cosmogonies, discovered in recent times, have a "when . . . then" construction, confirming the translation "when . . . then" here as well. "When" introduces the pre-creation state and "then" introduces the creative act affecting that state. The traditional translation, "In the beginning," does not reflect the Hebrew syntax of the clause.

1:2 This verse is parenthetical, describing in three phases the pre-creation state symbolized by the chaos out of which God brings order: "earth," hidden beneath the encompassing cosmic waters, could not be seen, and thus had no "form"; there was only darkness; turbulent wind swept over the waters. Commencing with the last-named elements (darkness and water), vv. 3–10 describe the rearrangement of this chaos: light is made (first day) and the water is divided into water above and water below the earth so that the earth appears and is no longer "without outline." *The abyss*: the primordial ocean according to the ancient Semitic cosmogony. After God's creative activity, part of this vast body forms the salt-water seas (vv. 9–10); part of it is the fresh water under the earth (Ps 33:7; Ez 31:4), which wells forth on the earth as springs and fountains (Gn 7:11; 8:2; Prv 3:20). Part of it, "the upper water" (Ps 148:4; Dn 3:60), is held up by the dome of the sky (vv. 6–7), from which rain descends on the earth (Gn 7:11; 2 Kgs 7:2, 19; Ps 104:13). *A mighty wind*: literally, "spirit or breath [*ruah*] of God"; cf. Gn 8:1.

1:5 In ancient Israel a day was considered to begin at sunset.

1:7 *The dome*: the Hebrew word suggests a gigantic metal dome. It was inserted into the middle of the single body of water to form dry space within which the earth could emerge. The Latin Vulgate translation *firmamentum*, "means of support (for the upper waters); firmament," provided the traditional English rendering.

*

1:1 Gn 2:1, 4; 2 Mc 7:28; Ps 8:4; 33:6; 89:12; 90:2; Wis 11:17; Sir 16:24; Jer 10:12; Acts 14:15; Col 1:16–17; Heb 1:2–3; 3:4; 11:3; Rev 4:11.
1:2 Jer 4:23.
1:3 2 Cor 4:6.
1:7 Prv 8:27–28; 2 Pt 3:5.
1:9 Jb 38:8; Ps 33:7; Jer 5:22.

"earth," and the basin of water he called "sea."
God saw that it was good. 11 * Then God said:
Let the earth bring forth vegetation: every kind of
plant that bears seed and every kind of fruit tree
on earth that bears fruit with its seed in it. And
so it happened: 12 the earth brought forth vegeta-
tion: every kind of plant that bears seed and ev-
ery kind of fruit tree that bears fruit with its seed
in it. God saw that it was good. 13 Evening came,
and morning followed—the third day.
14 Then God said: Let there be lights in the
dome of the sky, to separate day from night.
Let them mark the seasons, the days and the
years,* 15 and serve as lights in the dome of the
sky, to illuminate the earth. And so it happened:
16 God made the two great lights, the greater one
to govern the day, and the lesser one to govern
the night, and the stars.* 17 God set them in the
dome of the sky, to illuminate the earth, 18 to
govern the day and the night, and to separate
the light from the darkness. God saw that it was
good. 19 Evening came, and morning followed—
the fourth day.
20 * Then God said: Let the water teem with an
abundance of living creatures, and on the earth
let birds fly beneath the dome of the sky. 21 God
created the great sea monsters and all kinds of
crawling living creatures with which the water
teems, and all kinds of winged birds. God saw
that it was good, 22 and God blessed them, say-
ing: Be fertile, multiply, and fill the water of the
seas; and let the birds multiply on the earth.*

1:11 Ps 104:14.
1:14 Jb 26:10; Ps 19:2–3; Bar 3:33.
1:16 Dt 4:19; Ps 136:7–9; Wis 13:2–4; Jer 31:35.
1:20 Jb 12:7–10.
1:22 Gn 8:17.

In The Beginning

"In the beginning, when God created the heavens and the earth . . ." (Gn 1:1). This simple verse is one of the foundational beliefs of Christianity. We are not a random collection of atoms. The world is not a lucky combination of cosmic circumstances. The universe did not just accidentally happen.

The beginning of wisdom is acknowledging that a higher power is at work in our lives, that the universe has purpose, and that everything was created by God. The ancient writers and editors of Genesis expressed these ideas in the Creation stories. The Church affirms these beliefs. They are expressed in a prayer called the Apostles' Creed, which begins, "I believe in God, the Father almighty, Creator of heaven and earth."

Genesis expresses another foundational belief: God created everything good! Read the story in chapter 1, and see how this belief is constantly repeated: And humankind is "very good," created in God's own image. This is God's message to you in the first chapter of the Bible: You carry God's image within you. You are very good! Don't let anyone try to convince you otherwise.

▶ Gn 1:1—2:4

Did You Know?

Literary Genres

Some Christians believe that God actually created the world in seven twenty-four-hour days. Such a belief comes from a literal reading of the first chapter of Genesis, as though it were a scientific textbook. However, Genesis was written not as a science article but as a series of symbolic stories, sometimes called mythic stories, that convey great moral and spiritual truths. We should not try to come to any scientific conclusions about the creation of the world from reading these stories.

Mythic stories are one literary type, or genre. You just have to look in a newspaper to see examples of different literary genres: news stories, advice columns, editorials, and comics. Each genre has different rules for interpreting its meaning. The Bible also contains many types of literary genres, including hero stories, poetry, laws, legends, fictional satire, debates, and letters. To properly understand the Bible, pay attention to the literary genre—otherwise, you might believe the Bible is saying something God doesn't intend.

▶ Gn 1:1—2:4

GN

Catholic Social Teaching

Coworkers with God

In the opening chapters of the Book of Genesis, we read the wonderful story of God's creation of the universe. With each new day, God creates the light and darkness, the earth and sea, the plants and animals, and ultimately humankind. On the seventh day, God observes the amazing creation and we read, "God looked at everything he had made, and he found it very good" (Gn 1:31).

After God creates the man and woman, he commands them to "fill the earth and subdue it" (Gn 1:28). In other words, human beings are to cooperate with God in the completion and care of creation. With God's grace, we participate in laying the foundation for God's reign on earth.

Catholic social teaching tells us that as coworkers with God in caring for and sustaining the world, we have a responsibility to protect both the dignity of the human person as well as the planet. Amazing breakthroughs are happening in our world all the time, and yet, as Christians, we are asked to consider whether such developments are in keeping with the teachings of our Church. For example, we now have the ability to clone animals and genetically alter agricultural products, but will these practices sustain our world or ultimately destroy it? Do these practices really revere and value human life and the created order?

God has given us the amazing gift of intellectual inquiry, which can lead to wonderful advancements for our world, but we must always ask ourselves how we might help promote ethical approaches to research so that future generations may continue to enjoy the beauty of creation and thrive in the universe.

- As a coworker with God, how do I sustain and care for God's creation?
- How might I use my gifts of knowledge and education to really improve the world and help bring about God's reign on earth?

Genesis, chapters 1–2
Caring for God's Creation

23 Evening came, and morning followed—the
fifth day.
24 * Then God said: Let the earth bring forth every kind of living creature: tame animals, crawling
things, and every kind of wild animal. And so it
happened: 25 God made every kind of wild animal,
every kind of tame animal, and every kind of thing
that crawls on the ground. God saw that it was
good. 26 * Then God said: Let us make† human
beings in our image, after our likeness. Let them
have dominion over the fish of the sea, the birds
of the air, the tame animals, all the wild animals,
and all the creatures that crawl on the earth.

27 God created mankind in his image;
in the image of God he created them;
male and female† he created them.

28 God blessed them and God said to them: Be
fertile and multiply; fill the earth and subdue it.†
Have dominion over the fish of the sea, the birds
of the air, and all the living things that crawl on

†

1:26 *Let us make*: in the ancient Near East, and sometimes in the Bible, God was imagined as presiding over an assembly of heavenly beings who deliberated and decided about matters on earth (1 Kgs 22:19–22; Is 6:8; Ps 29:1–2; 82; 89:6–7; Jb 1:6; 2:1; 38:7). This scene accounts for the plural form here and in Gn 11:7 ("Let us then go down . . ."). Israel's God was always considered "Most High" over the heavenly beings. *Human beings*: Hebrew *'ādām* is here the generic term for humankind; in the first five chapters of Genesis it is the proper name Adam only at 4:25 and 5:1–5. *In our image, after our likeness*: "image" and "likeness" (virtually synonyms) express the worth of human beings who have value in themselves (human blood may not be shed in 9:6 because of this image of God) and in their task, dominion (1:28), which promotes the rule of God over the universe.

1:27 *Male and female*: as God provided the plants with seeds (vv. 11, 12) and commanded the animals to be fertile and multiply (v. 22), so God gives sexuality to human beings as their means to continue in existence.

1:28 *Fill the earth and subdue it*: the object of the verb "subdue" may be not the earth as such but earth as the territory each nation must take for itself (chaps. 10–11), just as Israel will later do (see Nm 32:22, 29; Jos 18:1). The two divine commands define the basic tasks of the human race—to continue in existence through generation and to take possession of one's God-given territory. The dual command would have had special meaning when Israel was in exile and deeply anxious about whether they would continue as a nation and return to their ancient territory. *Have dominion*: the whole human race is made in the "image" and "likeness" of God and has "dominion." Comparable literature of the time used these words of kings rather than of human beings in general; human beings were invariably thought of as slaves of the gods created to provide menial service for the divine world. The royal language here does not, however, give human beings unlimited power, for kings in the Bible had limited dominion and were subject to prophetic critique.

*

1:24 Sir 16:27–28.
1:26–27 Gn 5:1, 3; 9:6; Ps 8:5–6; Wis 2:23; 10:2; Sir 17:1, 3–4; Mt 19:4; Mk 10:6; Jas 3:7; Eph 4:24; Col 3:10.
1:28 Gn 8:17; 9:1; Ps 8:6–9; 115:16; Wis 9:2.

GN

Cultural Connection

God Is Our Creator

According to Genesis, chapters 1–2, God created the universe and is the source of order in all creation. Creation is good, and its goodness is reflected in the harmony, peace, and love between the Creator and his creatures, and among the creatures themselves. In Hispanic theological traditions, this ideal relationship—symbolized by the way God and Adam and Eve relate in the Garden of Eden—is considered the foundation in which salvation history is rooted.

- How are your relationships with God, your friends, your family, and nature characterized by harmony, peace, and love?
- Reflect on how you can improve some of your strained relationships, and ask God's help to do it.

Human beings are created in God's image and likeness and share God's attributes: freedom, love, knowledge, and the ability to create. With these gifts comes the responsibility of caring for all creation.

- Give thanks and praise to God for creation, especially for your own life and the lives of the people around you.
- Think of how you, your family, and your community can take better care of all creation. Pray that you fully develop your capacity to love, to know the truth, and to use your freedom wisely.

God established a covenant with us at the moment of our creation, and we keep this covenant by freely placing ourselves in God's hands and being responsive to God's invitation to live in communion with God and people.

- How do you use your freedom to respond to God's invitation?
- Think about the aspects of your life for which you most need God's wisdom to live in harmony and love. Put yourself in God's hands, and let God help and direct you.

▶ **Genesis, chapters 1–2**

the earth.* 29 † * God also said: See, I give you ev-
ery seed-bearing plant on all the earth and every
tree that has seed-bearing fruit on it to be your
food; 30 and to all the wild animals, all the birds
of the air, and all the living creatures that crawl
on the earth, I give all the green plants for food.
And so it happened. 31 God looked at everything
he had made, and found it very good. Evening
came, and morning followed—the sixth day.*

2 1 Thus the heavens and the earth and all their
array were completed.* 2 † On the seventh
day God completed the work he had been doing;
he rested on the seventh day from all the work he
had undertaken.* 3 God blessed the seventh day
and made it holy, because on it he rested from all
the work he had done in creation.*

I. The Story of the Nations

The Garden of Eden

4 This is the story† of the heavens and the
earth at their creation. When the LORD God made
the earth and the heavens— 5 there was no field

†

1:29 According to the Priestly tradition, the human race was originally intended to live on plants and fruits as were the animals (see v. 30), an arrangement that God will later change (9:3) in view of the human inclination to violence.

2:2 The mention of the seventh day, repeated in v. 3, is outside the series of six days and is thus the climax of the account. The focus of the account is God. The text does not actually institute the practice of keeping the Sabbath, for it would have been anachronistic to establish at this point a custom that was distinctively Israelite (Ex 31:13, 16, 17), but it lays the foundation for the later practice. Similarly, ancient creation accounts often ended with the construction of a temple where the newly created human race provided service to the gods who created them, but no temple is mentioned in this account. As was the case with the Sabbath, it would have been anachronistic to institute the temple at this point, for Israel did not yet exist. In Ex 25–31 and 35–40, Israel builds the tabernacle, which is the precursor of the Temple of Solomon.

2:4 *This is the story*: the distinctive Priestly formula introduces older traditions, belonging to the tradition called Yahwist, and gives them a new setting. In the first part of Genesis, the formula "this is the story" (or a similar phrase) occurs five times (2:4; 5:1; 6:9; 10:1; 11:10), which corresponds to the five occurrences of the formula in the second part of the book (11:27; 25:12, 19; 36:1[9]; 37:2). Some interpret the formula here as retrospective ("Such is the story"), referring back to chap. 1, but all its other occurrences introduce rather than summarize. It is introductory here; the Priestly source would hardly use the formula to introduce its own material in chap. 1.

The cosmogony that begins in v. 4 is concerned with the nature of human beings, narrating the story of the essential institutions and limits of the human race through their first ancestors. This cosmogony, like 1:1–3 (see note there), uses the "when . . . then" construction

*

1:29–30 Gn 9:3; Ps 104:14–15. **1:31** 1 Tm 4:4. **2:1** Is 45:12; Jn 1:3. **2:2** Ex 20:9–11; 31:17; Heb 4:4, 10. **2:3** Ex 20:11; Dt 5:14; Neh 9:14.

shrub on earth and no grass of the field had
sprouted, for the LORD God had sent no rain
upon the earth and there was no man† to till
the ground, 6 but a stream† was welling up out
of the earth and watering all the surface of the
ground— 7 then the LORD God formed the man†
out of the dust of the ground and blew into his
nostrils the breath of life, and the man became
a living being.*
8 The LORD God planted a garden in Eden, in
the east,† and placed there the man whom he
had formed.* 9 † Out of the ground the LORD

G N

† common in ancient cosmogonies. The account is generally attributed to the Yahwist, who prefers the divine name "Yhwh" (here rendered LORD) for God. God in this story is called "the LORD God" (except in 3:1–5); "LORD" is to be expected in a Yahwist account but the additional word "God" is puzzling.

2:5 *Man*: the Hebrew word *'adam* is a generic term meaning "human being." In chaps. 2–3, however, the archetypal human being is understood to be male (Adam), so the word *'adam* is translated "man" here.

2:6 *Stream*: the water wells up from the vast flood below the earth. The account seems to presuppose that only the garden of God was irrigated at this point. From this one source of all the fertilizing water on the earth, water will be channeled through the garden of God over the entire earth. It is the source of the four rivers mentioned in vv. 10–14. Later, with rain and cultivation, the fertility of the garden of God will appear in all parts of the world.

2:7 God is portrayed as a potter molding the human body out of earth. There is a play on words in Hebrew between *'adam* ("human being," "man") and *'adama* ("ground"). It is not enough to make the body from earth; God must also breathe into the man's nostrils. A similar picture of divine breath imparted to human beings in order for them to live is found in Ez 37:5, 9–10; Jn 20:22. The Israelites did not think in the (Greek) categories of body and soul.

2:8 *Eden, in the east*: the place names in vv. 8–14 are mostly derived from Mesopotamian geography (see note on vv. 10–14). Eden may be the name of a region in southern Mesopotamia (modern Iraq), the term derived from the Sumerian word *eden*, "fertile plain." A similar-sounding Hebrew word means "delight," which may lie behind the Greek translation, "The Lord God planted a paradise [= pleasure park] in Eden." It should be noted, however, that the garden was not intended as a paradise for the human race, but as a pleasure park for God; the man tended it for God. The story is not about "paradise lost."

The garden in the precincts of Solomon's Temple in Jerusalem seems to symbolize the garden of God (like gardens in other temples); it is apparently alluded to in Ps 1:3; 80:10; 92:14; Ez 47:7–12; Rev 22:1–2.

2:9 The second tree, the tree of life, is mentioned here and at the end of the story (3:22, 24). It is identified with Wisdom in Prv 3:18; 11:30; 13:12; 15:4, where the pursuit of wisdom gives back to human beings the life that is made inaccessible to them in Gn 3:24. In

* **2:7** Gn 3:19; 18:27; Tb 8:6; Jb 34:15; Ps 103:14; 104:29; Eccl 3:20; 12:7; Wis 7:1; Sir 33:10; 1 Cor 15:45.
2:8 Is 51:3; Ez 31:9.

Live It!

In God's Image

God does not make mistakes; people do. Some people might be tempted to deny their racial heritage, even to change their physical appearance in order to conform to the latest fad or fit the dominant cultural image of beauty. We must remember that physical features are not accidents. God planned for them—we are all made in God's image, inside and out.

If we are to authentically love ourselves, we must love our whole selves. This includes a love for dark skin or light skin, straight hair or curly hair, wide nose or pug nose, and all the variations in between. Whatever our appearance, we are all blessed by God.

▶ **Gn 1:26–27**

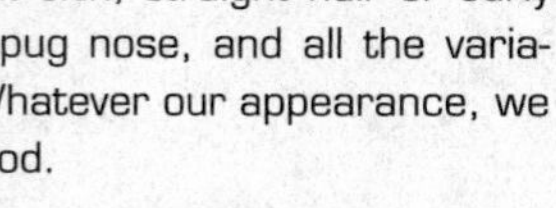

Pray It!

The Sabbath

Even God needed to take a rest. The writer of Genesis makes this point to remind readers to set aside a day for rest and prayer, which Jewish people call the Sabbath. Honoring the Sabbath is an act of trust in God. It means we believe that the world will not fall apart if we stop our activity. The world is in God's hands. We can hear this truth echoed in Jesus' words:

> Notice how the flowers grow. They do not toil or spin. But I tell you, not even Solomon in all his splendor was dressed like one of them. If God so clothes the grass in the field that grows today and is thrown into the oven tomorrow, will he not much more provide for you, O you of little faith? (Lk 12:27–28)

Traditionally, Christians rest and pray on Sunday because it is the day on which Jesus was resurrected. In our culture today, it seems that many people are losing this practice.

- What could we gain if we recommitted ourselves to a day of rest, celebration, and prayer?
- What can you do personally to more fully honor the concept of Sabbath rest?

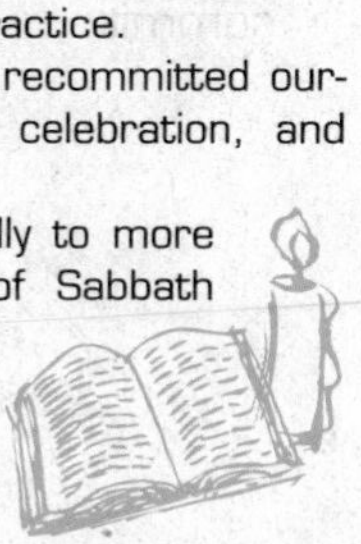

▶ **Gn 2:1–3**

GN

Catholic Connection

Original Sin

Before the Fall, Adam and Eve had it all. God gave them freedom and established a close friendship with them. They could simply walk about the garden tending to it alongside of God. They lived in perfect harmony with each other and all of creation without fear, suffering, or death. Yet, Adam and Eve wanted more. By believing the serpent's lie, Adam and Eve sought to make themselves equal to God. They distrusted God's goodness, directly disobeyed God, and abused the freedom God had given them. The results were tragic. Adam and Eve's friendship with God turned into fear as they hid in the garden. After being expelled from the garden, tension and strife entered Adam and Eve's once harmonious relationship. The creation they once helped tend with God became hazardous and difficult to manage. Ultimately, through their sin, death became a reality for Adam and Eve. Though this account in chapter three of Genesis uses figurative language, it points to the reality that all of humanity has been affected by the sin our first parents freely chose to commit.

This original sin and its consequences have been handed down to every generation throughout all of history, with the exception of Jesus and his mother, Mary. Although we are not personally responsible for it, our nature also has been wounded by this sin. As a result, we do not have the original holiness and justice God intended for us, but are inclined to sin and subject to death. Fortunately, Jesus Christ, unlike Adam and Eve, came in total obedience to the will of God. As a result, the sin brought into the world by Adam and Eve has been overcome by the Passion, death, and Resurrection of Jesus Christ. (Read Romans 5:12–21 to learn more about the relationship between Adam and Jesus.) Through the grace of the sacrament of Baptism, we are freed from original sin and turned back toward God. And the graces we receive through Christ will surpass those that Adam and Eve ever knew before the Fall!

Gn 3:1–24

Catechism, nos. 369–421

God made grow every tree that was delightful to
look at and good for food, with the tree of life
in the middle of the garden and the tree of the
knowledge of good and evil.*
10 A river rises in Eden† to water the gar-
den; beyond there it divides and becomes four
branches. 11 The name of the first is the Pishon;
it is the one that winds through the whole land
of Havilah, where there is gold. 12 The gold of
that land is good; bdellium and lapis lazuli are
also there. 13 The name of the second river is the
Gihon; it is the one that winds all through the
land of Cush.* 14 The name of the third river is
the Tigris; it is the one that flows east of Asshur.
The fourth river is the Euphrates.
15 The LORD God then took the man and settled
him in the garden of Eden, to cultivate and care
for it.* 16 The LORD God gave the man this order:
You are free to eat from any of the trees of the
garden* 17 except the tree of knowledge of good
and evil. From that tree you shall not eat; when
you eat from it you shall die.†*
18 The LORD God said: It is not good for the man
to be alone. I will make a helper suited to him.†*
19 So the LORD God formed out of the ground
all the wild animals and all the birds of the air,
and he brought them to the man to see what he
would call them; whatever the man called each
living creature was then its name. 20 The man
gave names to all the tame animals, all the birds
of the air, and all the wild animals; but none
proved to be a helper suited to the man.
21 So the LORD God cast a deep sleep on the
man, and while he was asleep, he took out one of
his ribs and closed up its place with flesh.* 22 The
LORD God then built the rib that he had taken
from the man into a woman. When he brought
her to the man, 23 the man said:

"This one, at last, is bone of my bones
and flesh of my flesh;
This one shall be called 'woman,'
for out of man this one has been taken."†

24 * That is why a man leaves his father and
mother and clings to his wife, and the two of
them become one body.†
25 The man and his wife were both naked, yet
they felt no shame.†

Expulsion from Eden

3 1 Now the snake was the most cunning† of
all the wild animals that the LORD God had
made. He asked the woman, "Did God really say,
'You shall not eat from any of the trees in the
garden'?" 2 The woman answered the snake: "We
may eat of the fruit of the trees in the garden;
3 * it is only about the fruit of the tree in the mid-
dle of the garden that God said, 'You shall not eat
it or even touch it, or else you will die.'" 4 But
the snake said to the woman: "You certainly will
not die!* 5 God knows well that when you eat of
it your eyes will be opened and you will be like
gods, who know† good and evil." 6 The woman
saw that the tree was good for food and pleasing
to the eyes, and the tree was desirable for gaining
wisdom. So she took some of its fruit and ate it;
and she also gave some to her husband, who was

---

the new creation described in the Book of Revelation, the tree of life is once again made available to human beings (Rev 2:7; 22:2, 14, 19). *Knowledge of good and evil*: the meaning is disputed. According to some, it signifies moral autonomy, control over morality (symbolized by "good and evil"), which would be inappropriate for mere human beings; the phrase would thus mean refusal to accept the human condition and finite freedom that God gives them. According to others, it is more broadly the knowledge of what is helpful and harmful to humankind, suggesting that the attainment of adult experience and responsibility inevitably means the loss of a life of simple subordination to God.

2:10–14 *A river rises in Eden*: the stream of water mentioned in v. 6, the source of all water upon earth, comes to the surface in the garden of God and from there flows out over the entire earth. In comparable religious literature, the dwelling of god is the source of fertilizing waters. The four rivers represent universality, as in the phrase "the four quarters of the earth." In Ez 47:1–12; Zec 14:8; Rev 22:1–2, the waters that irrigate the earth arise in the temple or city of God. The place names in vv. 11–14 are mainly from southern Mesopotamia (modern Iraq), where Mesopotamian literature placed the original garden of God. The Tigris and the Euphrates, the two great rivers in that part of the world, both emptied into the Persian Gulf. Gihon is the modest stream issuing from Jerusalem (2 Sm 5:8; 1 Kgs 1:9–10; 2 Chr 32:4), but is here regarded as one of the four great world rivers and linked to Mesopotamia, for Cush here seems to be the territory of the Kassites (a people of Mesopotamia) as in Gn 10:8. The word Pishon is otherwise unknown but is probably formed in imitation of Gihon. Havilah seems, according to Gn 10:7 and 1 Chr 1:9, to be in Cush in southern Mesopotamia though other locations have been suggested.

2:17 *You shall die*: since they do not die as soon as they eat from the forbidden tree, the meaning seems to be that human beings have become mortal, destined to die by virtue of being human.

2:18 *Helper suited to him*: lit., "a helper in accord with him." "Helper" need not imply subordination, for God is called a helper (Dt 33:7; Ps 46:2). The language suggests a profound affinity between the man and the woman and a relationship that is supportive and nurturing.

2:23 The man recognizes an affinity with the woman God has brought him. Unlike the animals who were made from the ground, she is made from his very self. There is a play on the similar-sounding Hebrew words *'ishsha* ("woman," "wife") and *'ish* ("man," "husband").

2:24 *One body*: lit., "one flesh." The covenant of marriage establishes kinship bonds of the first rank between the partners.

2:25 *They felt no shame*: marks a new stage in the drama, for the reader knows that only young children know no shame. This draws the reader into the next episode, where the couple's disobedience results in their loss of innocence.

3:1 *Cunning*: there is a play on the words for "naked" (2:25) and "cunning/wise" (Heb. *'arum*). The couple seek to be "wise" but end up knowing that they are "naked."

3:5 *Like gods, who know*: or "like God who knows."

2:9 Gn 3:22; Prv 3:18; Rev 2:7; 22:2, 14.
2:13 Sir 24:25.
2:15 Sir 7:15.
2:16 Ps 104:14–15.
2:17 Gn 3:2–3; Rom 6:23.
2:18 Tb 8:6; Sir 36:24; 1 Cor 11:9; 1 Tm 2:13.
2:21 Sir 17:1; 1 Cor 11:8–9; 1 Tm 2:13.
2:24 Mt 19:5; Mk 10:7; 1 Cor 7:10–11; Eph 5:31.
3:3 Gn 2:17; Rom 6:23.
3:4–5 Wis 2:24; Sir 25:14; Is 14:14; Jn 8:44; 2 Cor 11:3.

GN

with her, and he ate it.* 7 Then the eyes of both
of them were opened, and they knew that they
were naked; so they sewed fig leaves together and
made loincloths for themselves.
8 When they heard the sound of the LORD God
walking about in the garden at the breezy time
of the day,† the man and his wife hid themselves
from the LORD God among the trees of the gar-
den.* 9 The LORD God then called to the man and
asked him: Where are you? 10 He answered, "I
heard you in the garden; but I was afraid, because
I was naked, so I hid." 11 Then God asked: Who
told you that you were naked? Have you eaten
from the tree of which I had forbidden you to
eat? 12 The man replied, "The woman whom you
put here with me—she gave me fruit from the
tree, so I ate it." 13 The LORD God then asked the
woman: What is this you have done? The woman
answered, "The snake tricked me, so I ate it."*
14 Then the LORD God said to the snake:

Because you have done this,
  cursed are you
  among all the animals, tame or wild;
On your belly you shall crawl,
  and dust you shall eat
  all the days of your life.†*
15 I will put enmity between you and the woman,
  and between your offspring and hers;
They will strike at your head,
  while you strike at their heel.†*

16 To the woman he said:

I will intensify your toil in childbearing;
  in pain† you shall bring forth children.
Yet your urge shall be for your husband,
  and he shall rule over you.

17 To the man he said: Because you listened to
your wife and ate from the tree about which I
commanded you, You shall not eat from it,

Cursed is the ground† because of you!
  In toil you shall eat its yield
  all the days of your life.*
18 Thorns and thistles it shall bear for you,
  and you shall eat the grass of the
  field.
19 By the sweat of your brow
  you shall eat bread,
Until you return to the ground,
  from which you were taken;
For you are dust,
  and to dust you shall return.*

20 The man gave his wife the name "Eve," be-
cause she was the mother of all the living.†
21 The LORD God made for the man and his
wife garments of skin, with which he clothed
them. 22 Then the LORD God said: See! The man
has become like one of us, knowing good and
evil! Now, what if he also reaches out his hand
to take fruit from the tree of life, and eats of it
and lives forever?* 23 The LORD God therefore
banished him from the garden of Eden, to till the
ground from which he had been taken. 24 He ex-
pelled the man, stationing the cherubim and the
fiery revolving sword east of the garden of Eden,
to guard the way to the tree of life.

Cain and Abel

4 1 The man had intercourse with his wife Eve,
and she conceived and gave birth to Cain,
saying, "I have produced a male child with the
help of the LORD."† 2 Next she gave birth to his
brother Abel. Abel became a herder of flocks,

---

† **3:8** *The breezy time of the day*: lit., "the wind of the day." Probably shortly before sunset.

3:14 Each of the three punishments (the snake, the woman, the man) has a double aspect, one affecting the individual and the other affecting a basic relationship. The snake previously stood upright, enjoyed a reputation for being shrewder than other creatures, and could converse with human beings as in vv. 1–5. It must now move on its belly, is more cursed than any creature, and inspires revulsion in human beings (v. 15).

3:15 *They will strike . . . at their heel*: the antecedent for "they" and "their" is the collective noun "offspring," i.e., all the descendants of the woman. Christian tradition has seen in this passage, however, more than unending hostility between snakes and human beings. The snake was identified with the devil (Wis 2:24; Jn 8:44; Rev 12:9; 20:2), whose eventual defeat seemed implied in the verse. Because "the Son of God was revealed to destroy the works of the devil" (1 Jn 3:8), the passage was understood as the first promise of a redeemer for fallen humankind, the protoevangelium. Irenaeus of Lyons (ca. A.D. 130–200), in his *Against Heresies* 5.21.1, followed by several other Fathers of the Church, interpreted the verse as referring to Christ, and cited Gal 3:19 and 4:4 to support the reference. Another interpretive translation is *ipsa*, "she," and is reflected in Jerome's Vulgate. "She" was thought to refer to Mary, the mother of the messiah. In Christian art Mary is sometimes depicted with her foot on the head of the serpent.

3:16 *Toil . . . pain*: the punishment affects the woman directly by increasing the toil and pain of having children. *He shall rule over you*: the punishment also affects the woman's relationship with her husband. A tension is set up in which her urge (either sexual urge or, more generally, dependence for sustenance) is for her husband but he rules over her. But see Sg 7:11.

3:17–19 *Cursed is the ground*: the punishment affects the man's relationship to the ground (*'adam* and *'adamah*). *You are dust*: the punishment also affects the man directly insofar as he is now mortal.

3:20 The man gives his wife a more specific name than "woman" (2:23). The Hebrew name *hawwa* ("Eve") is related to the Hebrew word *hay* ("living"); "mother of all the living" points forward to the next episode involving her sons Cain and Abel.

4:1 The Hebrew name *qayin* ("Cain") and the term *qaniti* ("I have produced") present a wordplay that refers to metalworking; such wordplays are frequent in Genesis.

---

* **3:6** Gn 3:22; 1 Tm 2:14.
3:8 Jer 23:24.
3:13 2 Cor 11:3.
3:14 Is 65:25; Mi 7:17; Rev 12:9.
3:15 Rom 16:20; 1 Jn 3:8; Rev 12:17.
3:17 Gn 5:29; Rom 5:12; 8:20; Heb 6:8.
3:19 Gn 2:7; Jb 10:9; 34:15; Ps 90:3; 103:14; Eccl 3:20; 12:7; Wis 15:8; Sir 10:9; 17:2; Rom 5:12; 1 Cor 15:21; Heb 9:27.
3:22 Gn 2:9; Rev 22:2, 14.

and Cain a tiller of the ground.† 3 In the course of
time Cain brought an offering to the LORD from
the fruit of the ground, 4 while Abel, for his part,
brought the fatty portion† of the firstlings of his
flock.* The LORD looked with favor on Abel and
his offering, 5 but on Cain and his offering he
did not look with favor. So Cain was very angry
and dejected. 6 Then the LORD said to Cain: Why
are you angry? Why are you dejected? 7 If you act
rightly, you will be accepted;† but if not, sin lies
in wait at the door: its urge is for you, yet you
can rule over it.*

8 Cain said to his brother Abel, "Let us go out
in the field."† When they were in the field, Cain
attacked his brother Abel and killed him.* 9 Then
the LORD asked Cain, Where is your brother
Abel? He answered, "I do not know. Am I my
brother's keeper?" 10 God then said: What have
you done? Your brother's blood cries out to me
from the ground! 11 Now you are banned from
the ground† that opened its mouth to receive
your brother's blood from your hand.* 12 If you
till the ground, it shall no longer give you its pro-
duce. You shall become a constant wanderer on
the earth. 13 Cain said to the LORD: "My punish-
ment is too great to bear. 14 Look, you have now
banished me from the ground. I must avoid you
and be a constant wanderer on the earth. Anyone
may kill me at sight." 15 Not so! the LORD said to
him. If anyone kills Cain, Cain shall be avenged
seven times. So the LORD put a mark† on Cain, so
that no one would kill him at sight. 16 Cain then
left the LORD's presence and settled in the land of
Nod,† east of Eden.

Descendants of Cain and Seth

17 † Cain had intercourse with his wife, and
she conceived and bore Enoch. Cain also became
the founder of a city, which he named after his
son Enoch. 18 To Enoch was born Irad, and Irad
became the father of Mehujael; Mehujael became
the father of Methusael, and Methusael became
the father of Lamech. 19 Lamech took two
wives; the name of the first was Adah, and the
name of the second Zillah. 20 Adah gave birth
to Jabal, who became the ancestor of those who
dwell in tents and keep livestock. 21 His brother's
name was Jubal, who became the ancestor of all
who play the lyre and the reed pipe. 22 Zillah, on

Live It!

Brothers and Sisters

"Am I my brother's keeper?" (Gn 4:9). With that famous question, Cain pretends he does not know where his brother is. God does not answer Cain's question directly, but each of us knows the response. We are—each of us and all of us—responsible for one another: family, friends, and strangers. We are brothers and sisters because God has created us that way. We cannot avoid our obligation to watch out for one another.

- Are there people in your life who need you to be a brother or sister to them? How can you reach out to them?

▶ Gn 4:9

4:2 Some suggest the story reflects traditional strife between the farmer (Cain) and the nomad (Abel), with preference for the latter reflecting the alleged nomadic ideal of the Bible. But there is no disparagement of farming here, for Adam was created to till the soil. The story is about two brothers (the word "brother" occurs seven times) and God's unexplained preference for one, which provokes the first murder. The motif of the preferred younger brother will occur time and again in the Bible, e.g., Isaac, Jacob, Joseph, and David (1 Sm 16:1–13).

4:4 *Fatty portion*: it was standard practice to offer the fat portions of animals. Others render, less satisfactorily, "the choicest of the firstlings." The point is not that Abel gave a more valuable gift than Cain, but that God, for reasons not given in the text, accepts the offering of Abel and rejects that of Cain.

4:7 *You will be accepted*: the text is extraordinarily condensed and unclear. "You will be accepted" is a paraphrase of one Hebrew word, "lifting." God gives a friendly warning to Cain that his right conduct will bring "lifting," which could refer to acceptance (*lifting*) of his future offerings or of himself (as in the Hebrew idiom "*lifting* of the face") or *lifting* up of his head in honor (cf. note on 40:13), whereas wicked conduct will make him vulnerable to sin, which is personified as a force ready to attack. In any case, Cain has the ability to do the right thing. *Lies in wait*: sin is personified as a power that "lies in wait" (Heb. *robes*) at a place. In Mesopotamian religion, a related word (*rabisu*) refers to a malevolent god who attacks human beings in particular places like roofs or canals.

4:8 *Let us go out in the field*: to avoid detection. The verse presumes a sizeable population which Genesis does not otherwise explain.

4:11 *Banned from the ground*: lit., "cursed." The verse refers back to 3:17 where the ground was cursed so that it yields its produce only with great effort. Cain has polluted the soil with his brother's blood and it will no longer yield any of its produce to him.

4:15 *A mark*: probably a tattoo to mark Cain as protected by God. The use of tattooing for tribal marks has always been common among the Bedouin of the Near Eastern deserts.

4:16 *The land of Nod*: a symbolic name (derived from the verb *nûd*, to wander) rather than a definite geographic region.

4:17–24 Cain is the first in a seven-member linear genealogy ending in three individuals who initiate action (Jabal, Jubal, and Tubalcain). Other Genesis genealogies also end in three individuals initiating action (5:32 and 11:26). The purpose of this genealogy is to explain the origin of culture and crafts among human beings. The names in this genealogy are the same (some with different spellings) as those in the ten-member genealogy (ending with Noah), which has a slightly different function. See note on 5:1–32.

4:4 Ex 34:19; Heb 11:4.
4:7 Sir 7:1; Jude 11.
4:8 Wis 10:3; Mt 23:35; Lk 11:51; 1 Jn 3:12; Jude 11.
4:11 Dt 27:24.

GN

Catholic Social Teaching

The Cycle of Violence

Cain was a murderer. Some might say that he deserved the death penalty. But in Genesis 4:15, God marks Cain so that he is protected from being killed. God seeks to stop the cycle of violence. Why kill someone to show that it is wrong to kill someone?

Catholic social teaching echoes this sentiment, asserting that all life—even the life of a violent criminal—has a God-given sense of dignity that must be protected at all times. This can sometimes be a difficult teaching to understand. It's easy to see why we should work to protect the dignity of the poor, the dying, and the unborn—but murderers too? Why should we respect someone whose actions have not shown any concern for life?

The Scriptures have taught us to believe that justice cannot be achieved through vengeance and that forgiveness, reconciliation, and conversion are always possible, even for the greatest of sinners. Capital punishment has proven to be unnecessary, ineffective, and unacceptable in today's world, given the alternative options that are available for achieving retribution. When we choose to support capital punishment, we feed the cycle of violence and risk becoming less sensitive to the preciousness of every human life; we forget that all of us—even grave sinners—have been created in the image and likeness of God.

▶ **Gn 4:15**

Life and Dignity of the Human Person

---

her part, gave birth to Tubalcain, the ancestor of
all who forge instruments of bronze and iron.
The sister of Tubalcain was Naamah. 23 † Lamech
said to his wives:

"Adah and Zillah, hear my voice;
wives of Lamech, listen to my utterance:
I have killed a man for wounding me,
a young man for bruising me.
24 If Cain is avenged seven times,
then Lamech seventy-seven times."

25 † Adam again had intercourse with his wife,
and she gave birth to a son whom she called
Seth. "God has granted me another offspring
in place of Abel," she said, "because Cain killed
him." 26 To Seth, in turn, a son was born, and he
named him Enosh.

At that time people began to invoke the LORD
by name.*

Generations: Adam to Noah†

5 1 * This is the record of the descendants of
Adam. When God created human beings, he
made them in the likeness of God; 2 he created
them male and female. When they were created,
he blessed them and named them humankind.
3 * Adam was one hundred and thirty years

†

4:23–24 Lamech's boast shows that the violence of Cain continues with his son and has actually increased. The question is posed to the reader: how will God's creation be renewed?

4:25–26 The third and climactic birth story in the chapter, showing that this birth, unlike the other two, will have good results. The name Seth (from the Hebrew verb *shat,* "to place, replace") shows that God has replaced Abel with a worthy successor. From this favored line Enosh ("human being/humankind"), a synonym of Adam, authentic religion began with the worship of Yhwh; this divine name is rendered as "the LORD" in this translation. The Yahwist source employs the name Yhwh long before the time of Moses. Another ancient source, the Elohist (from its use of the term *Elohim,* "God," instead of *Yhwh,* "LORD," for the pre-Mosaic period), makes Moses the first to use Yhwh as the proper name of Israel's God, previously known by other names as well; cf. Ex 3:13–15.

5:1–32 The second of the five Priestly formulas in Part I ("This is the record of the descendants . . ."; see 2:4a; 6:9; 10:1; 11:10) introduces the second of the three linear genealogies in Gn 1–11 (4:17–24 and 11:10–26). In each, a list of individuals (six in 4:17–24, ten in 5:1–32, or nine in 11:10–26) ends in three people who initiate action. Linear genealogies (father to son) in ancient societies had a communicative function, grounding the authority or claim of the last-named individual in the first-named. Here, the genealogy has a literary function as well, advancing the story by showing the expansion of the human race after Adam, as well as the transmission to his descendant Noah of the divine image given to Adam. Correcting the impression one might get from the genealogy in 4:17–24, this genealogy traces the line through Seth rather than through Cain. Most of the names in the series are the same as the names in Cain's line in 4:17–19 (Enosh, Enoch, Lamech) or spelled with variant spellings (Mahalalel, Jared, Methuselah). The genealogy itself and its placement before the flood shows the influence of ancient Mesopotamian literature, which contains lists of cities and kings before and after the flood. Before the flood, the ages of the kings ranged from 18,600 to 36,000 years, but after it were reduced to between 140 and 1,200 years. The biblical numbers are much smaller. There are some differences in the numbers in the Hebrew and Greek manuscripts.

*

4:26 1 Chr 1:1; Lk 3:38.
5:1 Gn 1:27; Wis 2:23; Sir 17:1; Jas 3:9.
5:3–32 1 Chr 1:1–4; Lk 3:36–38.

old when he begot a son in his likeness, after his image; and he named him Seth.* 4 Adam lived eight hundred years after he begot Seth, and he had other sons and daughters. 5 The whole lifetime of Adam was nine hundred and thirty years; then he died.

6 When Seth was one hundred and five years old, he begot Enosh. 7 Seth lived eight hundred and seven years after he begot Enosh, and he had other sons and daughters. 8 The whole lifetime of Seth was nine hundred and twelve years; then he died.

9 When Enosh was ninety years old, he begot Kenan. 10 Enosh lived eight hundred and fifteen years after he begot Kenan, and he had other sons and daughters. 11 The whole lifetime of Enosh was nine hundred and five years; then he died.

12 When Kenan was seventy years old, he begot Mahalalel. 13 Kenan lived eight hundred and forty years after he begot Mahalalel, and he had other sons and daughters. 14 The whole lifetime of Kenan was nine hundred and ten years; then he died.

15 When Mahalalel was sixty-five years old, he begot Jared. 16 Mahalalel lived eight hundred and thirty years after he begot Jared, and he had other sons and daughters. 17 The whole lifetime of Mahalalel was eight hundred and ninety-five years; then he died.

18 When Jared was one hundred and sixty-two years old, he begot Enoch. 19 Jared lived eight hundred years after he begot Enoch, and he had other sons and daughters. 20 The whole lifetime of Jared was nine hundred and sixty-two years; then he died.

21 When Enoch was sixty-five years old, he begot Methuselah. 22 Enoch walked with God after he begot Methuselah for three hundred years, and he had other sons and daughters. 23 The whole lifetime of Enoch was three hundred and sixty-five years. 24 Enoch walked with God,† and he was no longer here, for God took him.*

25 When Methuselah was one hundred and eighty-seven years old, he begot Lamech. 26 Methuselah lived seven hundred and eighty-two years after he begot Lamech, and he had other sons and daughters. 27 The whole lifetime of Methuselah was nine hundred and sixty-nine years; then he died.

28 When Lamech was one hundred and eighty-two years old, he begot a son 29 * and named him Noah, saying, "This one shall bring us relief from our work and the toil of our hands, out of the very ground that the LORD has put under a curse."† 30 Lamech lived five hundred and ninety-five years after he begot Noah, and he had other sons and daughters. 31 The whole lifetime of Lamech was seven hundred and seventy-seven years; then he died.

32 When Noah was five hundred years old, he begot Shem, Ham, and Japheth.† *

Origin of the Nephilim†

6 1 When human beings began to grow numerous on the earth and daughters were born to them, 2 the sons of God† saw how beautiful the daughters of human beings were, and so they took for their wives whomever they pleased.* 3 Then the LORD said: My spirit shall not remain in human beings forever, because they are only flesh. Their days shall comprise one hundred and twenty years.

4 The Nephilim appeared on earth in those days, as well as later,† after the sons of God had intercourse with the daughters of human beings, who bore them sons. They were the heroes of old, the men of renown.*

†

5:24 Enoch is in the important seventh position in the ten-member genealogy. In place of the usual formula "then he died," the change to "Enoch walked with God" implies that he did not die, but like Elijah (2 Kgs 2:11–12) was taken alive to God's abode. This mysterious narrative spurred much speculation and writing (beginning as early as the third century B.C.) about Enoch the sage who knew the secrets of heaven and who could communicate them to human beings (see Sir 44:16; 49:14; Heb 11:5; Jude 14–15 and the apocryphal work 1 Enoch).

5:29 The sound of the Hebrew word *noah*, "Noah," is echoed in the word *yenahamenu*, "he will bring us relief"; the latter refers both to the curse put on the soil because of human disobedience (3:17–19) and to Noah's success in agriculture, especially in raising grapes for wine (9:20–21).

5:32 *Shem, Ham, and Japheth*: like the genealogies in 4:17–24 and 11:10–26, the genealogy ends in three individuals who engage in important activity. Their descendants will be detailed in chap. 10, where it will be seen that the lineage is political-geographical as well as "ethnic."

6:1–4 These enigmatic verses are a transition between the expansion of the human race illustrated in the genealogy of chap. 5 and the flood depicted in chaps. 6–9. The text, apparently alluding to an old legend, shares a common ancient view that the heavenly world was populated by a multitude of beings, some of whom were wicked and rebellious. It is incorporated here, not only in order to account for the prehistoric giants, whom the Israelites called the Nephilim, but also to introduce the story of the flood with a moral orientation—the constantly increasing wickedness of humanity. This increasing wickedness leads God to reduce the human life span imposed on the first couple. As the ages in the preceding genealogy show, life spans had been exceptionally long in the early period, but God further reduces them to something near the ordinary life span.

6:2 *The sons of God*: other heavenly beings. See note on 1:26.

6:4 *As well as later*: the belief was common that human beings of gigantic stature once lived on earth. In some cultures, such heroes could make positive contributions, but the Bible generally regards them in a negative light (cf. Nm 13:33; Ez 32:27). The point here is that even these heroes, filled with vitality from their semi-divine origin, come under God's decree in v. 3.

*

5:3 Gn 4:25.
5:24 Wis 4:10–11; Sir 44:16; 49:14; Heb 11:5.
5:29 Gn 3:17–19.
5:32 Gn 6:10; 10:1.
6:2 Mt 24:38; Lk 17:26–27.
6:4 Wis 14:6; Bar 3:26.

Did You Know?

The Flood

The sin of Adam and Eve in the garden starts a disastrous trend in which each generation adds to sin in the world. This sin leads to the corruption of the world and the destruction of human beings. The Great Flood illustrates the ancient belief that God washed the world clean of this sinfulness and gave another chance to those who were faithful to God.

Other ancient cultures had stories about great floods. But in those stories, vindictive gods caused the floods for petty reasons. These gods had no real love for humanity. The Bible's Flood story is unique because it insists that God acted out of justice and in response to great evil.

God takes great care to save Noah and his family because they are faithful to God. After the Flood, God makes a covenant with Noah, promising never to destroy the earth by flood again—another unique element not found in the stories of other cultures.

Gn 6:1—9:17

Warning of the Flood

5 † When the LORD saw how great the wicked-
ness of human beings was on earth, and how
every desire that their heart conceived was always
nothing but evil,* 6 the LORD regretted making
human beings on the earth, and his heart was
grieved.†
7 So the LORD said: I will wipe out from the
earth the human beings I have created, and not
only the human beings, but also the animals and
the crawling things and the birds of the air, for I
regret that I made them.† 8 But Noah found favor
with the LORD.
9 These are the descendants of Noah. Noah
was a righteous man and blameless in his gen-
eration;* Noah walked with God. 10 Noah begot
three sons: Shem, Ham, and Japheth.
11 But the earth was corrupt† in the view of God
and full of lawlessness.* 12 When God saw how
corrupt the earth had become, since all mortals
had corrupted their ways on earth,* 13 God said to
Noah: I see that the end of all mortals has come,
for the earth is full of lawlessness because of them.
So I am going to destroy them with the earth.*

Preparation for the Flood

14 Make yourself an ark of gopherwood,† equip
the ark with various compartments, and cover it
inside and out with pitch. 15 This is how you shall
build it: the length of the ark will be three hun-
dred cubits, its width fifty cubits, and its height
thirty cubits.† 16 Make an opening for daylight†
and finish the ark a cubit above it. Put the ark's
entrance on its side; you will make it with bot-
tom, second and third decks. 17 I, on my part, am
about to bring the flood waters on the earth, to
destroy all creatures under the sky in which there
is the breath of life; everything on earth shall
perish.* 18 I will establish my covenant with you.
You shall go into the ark, you and your sons,

† **6:5–8:22** The story of the great flood is commonly regarded as a composite narrative based on separate sources woven together. To the Yahwist source, with some later editorial additions, are usually assigned 6:5–8; 7:1–5, 7–10, 12, 16b, 17b, 22–23; 8:2b–3a, 6–12, 13b, 20–22. The other sections are usually attributed to the Priestly writer. There are differences between the two sources: the Priestly source has two pairs of every animal, whereas the Yahwist source has seven pairs of clean animals and two pairs of unclean; the floodwater in the Priestly source is the waters under and over the earth that burst forth, whereas in the Yahwist source the floodwater is the rain lasting forty days and nights. In spite of many obvious discrepancies in these two sources, one should read the story as a coherent narrative. The biblical story ultimately draws upon an ancient Mesopotamian tradition of a great flood, preserved in the Sumerian flood story, the eleventh tablet of the Gilgamesh Epic, and (embedded in a longer creation story) the Atrahasis Epic.

6:6 *His heart was grieved*: the expression can be misleading in English, for "heart" in Hebrew is the seat of memory and judgment rather than emotion. The phrase is actually parallel to the first half of the sentence ("the LORD regretted . . .").

6:7 Human beings are an essential part of their environment, which includes all living things. In the new beginning after the flood, God makes a covenant with human beings and every living creature (9:9–10). The same close link between human beings and nature is found elsewhere in the Bible; e.g., in Is 35, God's healing transforms human beings along with their physical environment, and in Rom 8:19–23, all creation, not merely human beings, groans in labor pains awaiting the salvation of God.

6:11 *Corrupt*: God does not punish arbitrarily but simply brings to its completion the corruption initiated by human beings.

6:14 *Gopherwood*: an unidentified wood mentioned only in connection with the ark. It may be the wood of the cypress, which in Hebrew sounds like "gopher" and was widely used in antiquity for shipbuilding.

6:15 Hebrew "cubit," lit., "forearm," is the distance from the elbow to the tip of the middle finger, about eighteen inches (a foot and a half). The dimensions of Noah's ark were approximately 440 × 73 × 44 feet. The ark of the Babylonian flood story was an exact cube, 120 cubits (180 feet) in length, width, and height.

6:16 *Opening for daylight*: a conjectural rendering of the Hebrew word *sohar*, occurring only here. The reference is probably to an open space on all sides near the top of the ark to admit light and air. The ark also had a window or hatch, which could be opened and closed (8:6).

6:5 Ps 14:2–3.
6:9 Wis 10:4; Sir 44:17.
6:11 Jb 22:15–17.
6:12 Ps 14:2.
6:13 Sir 40:9–10; 44:17; Mt 24:37–39.
6:17 Gn 7:4, 21; 2 Pt 2:5.

your wife and your sons' wives with you.* 19 Of
all living creatures you shall bring two of every
kind into the ark, one male and one female,† to
keep them alive along with you. 20 Of every kind
of bird, of every kind of animal, and of every
kind of thing that crawls on the ground, two of
each will come to you, that you may keep them
alive. 21 Moreover, you are to provide yourself
with all the food that is to be eaten, and store it
away, that it may serve as provisions for you and
for them. 22 Noah complied; he did just as God
had commanded him.†

7 1 Then the LORD said to Noah: Go into the ark,
you and all your household, for you alone
in this generation have I found to be righteous
before me.* 2 Of every clean animal, take with
you seven pairs, a male and its mate; and of the
unclean animals, one pair, a male and its mate;
3 likewise, of every bird of the air, seven pairs, a
male and a female, to keep their progeny alive
over all the earth. 4 For seven days from now I will
bring rain down on the earth for forty days and
forty nights, and so I will wipe out from the face
of the earth every being that I have made.* 5 Noah
complied, just as the LORD had commanded.

The Great Flood

6 Noah was six hundred years old when the
flood came upon the earth. 7 Together with his
sons, his wife, and his sons' wives, Noah went
into the ark because of the waters of the flood.*
8 Of the clean animals and the unclean, of the
birds, and of everything that crawls on the
ground, 9 two by two, male and female came to
Noah into the ark, just as God had commanded
him.* 10 When the seven days were over, the wa-
ters of the flood came upon the earth.
11 In the six hundredth year of Noah's life, in
the second month, on the seventeenth day of the
month: on that day

All the fountains of the great abyss† burst
forth,
and the floodgates of the sky were opened.

12 For forty days and forty nights heavy rain
poured down on the earth.
13 On the very same day, Noah and his sons
Shem, Ham, and Japheth, and Noah's wife, and
the three wives of Noah's sons had entered the
ark, 14 together with every kind of wild animal,
every kind of tame animal, every kind of crawl-
ing thing that crawls on the earth, and every kind
of bird. 15 Pairs of all creatures in which there

Live It!

Sin Has Social Consequences

At the beginning of the Noah story, sin has continued to spread so that it has become an accepted part of society. The Great Flood, which wipes out a whole civilization, symbolizes the consequences of widespread sin. Later in Genesis, the story of the tower of Babel (11:1–9) symbolizes another consequence of the institutionalized sin of disobedience and pride.

When sin becomes part of our social systems and our institutions, the Church calls it social sin. Social sin is a result of personal sin, but it is bigger than any one person's choice. Examples of social sin are the unequal distribution of the world's wealth, the exploitation of workers by corporations, and discrimination based on race or gender. The good news is that God's saving power is greater than social sin!

- What are the effects of social sin in your community? in your country? in the world?
- How are Christians in your church or community organizing to stand against social sin?

Gn 6:1—9:17

---

† **6:19–21** *You shall bring two of every kind . . . , one male and one female*: For the Priestly source (P), there is no distinction between clean and unclean animals until Sinai (Lv 11), no altars or sacrifice until Sinai, and all diet is vegetarian (Gn 1:29–30); even after the flood P has no distinction between clean and unclean, since "any living creature that moves about" may be eaten (9:3). Thus P has Noah take the minimum to preserve all species, one pair of each, without distinction between clean and unclean, but he must also take on provisions for food (6:21). The Yahwist source (J), which assumes the clean-unclean distinction always existed but knows no other restriction on eating meat (Abel was a shepherd and offered meat as a sacrifice), requires additional clean animals ("seven pairs") for food and sacrifice (7:2–3; 8:20).

6:22 *Just as God had commanded him*: as in the creation of the world in chap. 1 and in the building of the tabernacle in Ex 25–31, 35–40 (all from the Priestly source), everything takes place by the command of God. In this passage and in Exodus, the commands of God are carried out to the letter by human agents, Noah and Moses. Divine speech is important. God speaks to Noah seven times in the flood story.

7:11 *Abyss*: the subterranean ocean; see note on 1:2.

---

* **6:18** Gn 9:9; Wis 14:6; Heb 11:7; 1 Pt 3:20.
7:1 Wis 10:4; Sir 44:17; 2 Pt 2:5.
7:4 Gn 6:17; 2 Pt 2:5.
7:7 Wis 14:6; 1 Pt 3:20; 2 Pt 2:5.
7:9 Gn 6:19.

Did You Know?

GN

Water in the Bible

For the ancient Hebrews, although water often represented a source of life, it also represented forces of destruction over which God triumphs. In the story of Creation, God is portrayed as mastering the waters that represent chaos (see Gn 1:1–2)—God constructs the upper and lower firmaments to hold back the waters. At the time of the Great Flood, God releases the waters, and they destroy life on the earth. At the time of the Exodus, God will once again display the divine mastery of the waters, as will Jesus Christ later on.

was the breath of life came to Noah into the ark.
16 Those that entered were male and female; of
all creatures they came, as God had commanded
Noah. Then the LORD shut him in.
17 The flood continued upon the earth for
forty days. As the waters increased, they lifted
the ark, so that it rose above the earth. 18 The
waters swelled and increased greatly on the
earth, but the ark floated on the surface of
the waters. 19 Higher and higher on the earth the
waters swelled, until all the highest mountains
under the heavens were submerged. 20 The waters
swelled fifteen cubits higher than the submerged
mountains. 21 All creatures that moved on earth
perished: birds, tame animals, wild animals,
and all that teemed on the earth, as well as all
humankind.* 22 Everything on dry land with
the breath of life in its nostrils died. 23 The LORD
wiped out every being on earth: human beings
and animals, the crawling things and the birds of
the air; all were wiped out from the earth. Only
Noah and those with him in the ark were left.
24 And when the waters had swelled on the

8 earth for one hundred and fifty days, 1 God
remembered Noah and all the animals, wild
and tame, that were with him in the ark. So
God made a wind sweep over the earth, and the
waters began to subside. 2 The fountains of the
abyss and the floodgates of the sky were closed,
and the downpour from the sky was held back.
3 Gradually the waters receded from the earth. At
the end of one hundred and fifty days, the waters
had so diminished 4 that, in the seventh month,
on the seventeenth day of the month, the ark
came to rest on the mountains of Ararat.† 5 The
waters continued to diminish until the tenth
month, and on the first day of the tenth month
the tops of the mountains appeared.
6 At the end of forty days Noah opened the
hatch of the ark that he had made, 7 † and he
released a raven. It flew back and forth until the
waters dried off from the earth. 8 Then he re-
leased a dove, to see if the waters had lessened
on the earth. 9 But the dove could find no place
to perch, and it returned to him in the ark, for
there was water over all the earth. Putting out
his hand, he caught the dove and drew it back
to him inside the ark. 10 He waited yet seven days
more and again released the dove from the ark.
11 In the evening the dove came back to him, and
there in its bill was a plucked-off olive leaf! So
Noah knew that the waters had diminished on
the earth. 12 He waited yet another seven days
and then released the dove; but this time it did
not come back.
13 † In the six hundred and first year, in the
first month, on the first day of the month, the
water began to dry up on the earth. Noah then
removed the covering of the ark and saw that the
surface of the ground had dried. 14 In the second
month, on the twenty-seventh day of the month,
the earth was dry.
15 Then God said to Noah: 16 Go out of the
ark, together with your wife and your sons and
your sons' wives. 17 Bring out with you every liv-
ing thing that is with you—all creatures, be they
birds or animals or crawling things that crawl on
the earth—and let them abound on the earth,
and be fertile and multiply on it.* 18 So Noah
came out, together with his sons and his wife
and his sons' wives; 19 and all the animals, all the
birds, and all the crawling creatures that crawl on
the earth went out of the ark by families.
20 Then Noah built an altar to the LORD, and
choosing from every clean animal and every
clean bird, he offered burnt offerings on the al-
tar. 21 When the LORD smelled the sweet odor, the

†

8:4 *The mountains of Ararat*: the mountain country of ancient Arartu in northwest Iraq, which was the highest part of the world to the biblical writer. There is no Mount Ararat in the Bible.

8:7–12 In the eleventh tablet of the Gilgamesh Epic, Utnapishtim (the equivalent of Noah) released in succession a dove, a swallow, and a raven. When the raven did not return, Utnapishtim knew it was safe to leave the ark. The first century A.D. Roman author Pliny tells of Indian sailors who release birds in order to follow them toward land.

8:13–14 On the first day of the first month, the world was in the state it had been on the day of creation in chap. 1. Noah had to wait another month until the earth was properly dry as in 1:9.

*

7:21–23 Jb 22:16; Mt 24:39; Lk 17:27; 2 Pt 3:6.

8:17 Gn 1:22, 28.

LORD said to himself: Never again will I curse the
ground because of human beings, since the de-
sires of the human heart are evil from youth; nor
will I ever again strike down every living being,
as I have done.*

22 All the days of the earth,
seedtime and harvest,
cold and heat,
Summer and winter,
and day and night
shall not cease.*

Covenant with Noah

9 1 † God blessed Noah and his sons and said
to them: Be fertile and multiply and fill the
earth.* 2 † Fear and dread of you shall come
upon all the animals of the earth and all the
birds of the air, upon all the creatures that move
about on the ground and all the fishes of the sea;
into your power they are delivered. 3 * Any living
creature that moves about shall be yours to eat;
I give them all to you as I did the green plants.
4 * Only meat with its lifeblood still in it you
shall not eat.† 5 Indeed for your own lifeblood I
will demand an accounting: from every animal I
will demand it, and from a human being, each
one for the blood of another, I will demand an
accounting for human life.*

6† Anyone who sheds the blood of a human
being,
by a human being shall that one's blood be
shed;
For in the image of God
have human beings been made.*

7 Be fertile, then, and multiply; abound on earth
and subdue it.*

8 † God said to Noah and to his sons with him:
9 See, I am now establishing my covenant with
you and your descendants after you* 10 and with
every living creature that was with you: the birds,

8:11

the tame animals, and all the wild animals that
were with you—all that came out of the ark. 11 I
will establish my covenant with you, that never
again shall all creatures be destroyed by the wa-
ters of a flood; there shall not be another flood to
devastate the earth.* 12 God said: This is the sign
of the covenant that I am making between me
and you and every living creature with you for all
ages to come: 13 * I set my bow in the clouds to
serve as a sign of the covenant between me and
the earth. 14 When I bring clouds over the earth,
and the bow appears in the clouds, 15 I will re-
member my covenant between me and you and
every living creature—every mortal being—so
that the waters will never again become a flood
to destroy every mortal being.* 16 When the bow
appears in the clouds, I will see it and remember
the everlasting covenant between God and every
living creature—every mortal being that is on
earth. 17 God told Noah: This is the sign of the

†

9:1 God reaffirms without change the original blessing and mandate of 1:28. In the Mesopotamian epic Atrahasis, on which the Genesis story is partly modeled, the gods changed their original plan by restricting human population through such means as childhood diseases, birth demons, and mandating celibacy among certain groups of women.

9:2–3 Pre-flood creatures, including human beings, are depicted as vegetarians (1:29–30). In view of the human propensity to violence, God changes the original prohibition against eating meat.

9:4 Because a living being dies when it loses most of its blood, the ancients regarded blood as the seat of life, and therefore as sacred. Jewish tradition considered the prohibition against eating meat with blood to be binding on all, because it was given by God to Noah, the new ancestor of all humankind; therefore the early Christian Church retained it for a time (Acts 15:20, 29).

9:6 The image of God, given to the first man and woman and transmitted to every human being, is the reason that no violent attacks can be made upon human beings. That image is the basis of the dignity of every individual who, in some sense, "represents" God in the world.

9:8–17 God makes a covenant with Noah and his descendants and, remarkably, with all the animals who come out of the ark: never again shall the world be destroyed by flood. The sign of this solemn promise is the appearance of a rainbow.

*

8:21 Sir 44:18; Is 54:9; Rom 7:18.
8:22 Jer 33:20, 25.
9:1 Gn 1:22, 28; 8:17.
9:3 Gn 1:29–30; Dt 12:15.
9:4 Lv 7:26–27; 17:4; Dt 12:16, 23; 1 Sm 14:33; Acts 15:20.
9:5 Gn 4:10–11; Ex 21:12.
9:6 Gn 1:26–27; Lv 24:17; Nm 35:33; Jas 3:9.
9:7 Gn 1:28; 8:17; 9:2; Jas 3:7.
9:9 Gn 6:18.
9:11 Sir 44:18; Is 54:9.
9:13 Sir 43:12.
9:15 Is 54:9.

GN

Pray It!

The Rainbow

What do you see when you see a rainbow? Do you see a multicolored arc caused by the refraction of sunlight through droplets of water? or do you see a wonder of nature that causes you to stop and stare in awe? Something as remarkable as a rainbow is more than just science. It's no wonder the writer of Genesis used it as a symbol of God's covenant promise—a sign of God's faithfulness and love. When God and Israel see the rainbow in the clouds, they will recall their covenant together.

God of imagination and color, only you could come up with the idea of a rainbow! Rainstorm and sunshine, harmony and diversity, mercy and hope, promise and joy, wonder and awe, faithfulness and love. Are these inside me, the wondrous creation you delight in? Guide me to the rainbows in my life!

▶ **Gn 9:8–17**

covenant I have established between me and ev-
ery mortal being that is on earth.

Noah and His Sons

18 † The sons of Noah who came out of the
ark were Shem, Ham and Japheth. Ham was the
father of Canaan.* 19 These three were the sons
of Noah, and from them the whole earth was
populated.
20 Noah, a man of the soil, was the first to plant
a vineyard. 21 He drank some of the wine, became
drunk, and lay naked inside his tent.* 22 Ham,
the father of Canaan, saw his father's nakedness,
and he told his two brothers outside. 23 Shem
and Japheth, however, took a robe, and holding
it on their shoulders, they walked backward and
covered their father's nakedness; since their faces
were turned the other way, they did not see their
father's nakedness. 24 When Noah woke up from
his wine and learned what his youngest son had
done to him, 25 he said:

"Cursed be Caanan!
The lowest of slaves
shall he be to his brothers."*

26 He also said:

"Blessed be the LORD, the God of Shem!
Let Canaan be his slave.
27 May God expand Japheth,†
and may he dwell among the tents of
Shem;
and let Canaan be his slave."

28 Noah lived three hundred and fifty years af-
ter the flood. 29 The whole lifetime of Noah was
nine hundred and fifty years; then he died.

Table of the Nations†

10 1 These are the descendants of Noah's
sons, Shem, Ham and Japheth, to whom
children were born after the flood.
2 * The descendants of Japheth: Gomer,†

---

† **9:18–27** The character of the three sons is sketched here. The fault is not Noah's (for he could not be expected to know about the intoxicating effect of wine) but Ham's, who shames his father by looking on his nakedness, and then tells the other sons. Ham's conduct is meant to prefigure the later shameful sexual practices of the Canaanites, which are alleged in numerous biblical passages. The point of the story is revealed in Noah's curse of Ham's son Canaan and his blessing of Shem and Japheth.

9:27 In the Hebrew text there is a play on the words *yapt* ("expand") and *yepet* ("Japheth").

10:1–32 Verse 1 is the fourth of the Priestly formulas (2:4; 5:1; 6:9; 11:10) that structure Part I of Genesis; it introduces 10:2–11:9, the populating of the world and the building of the city. In a sense, chaps. 4–9 are concerned with the first of the two great commands given to the human race in 1:28, "Be fertile and multiply!" whereas chaps. 10–11 are concerned with the second command, "Fill the earth and subdue it!" ("Subdue it" refers to each nation's taking the land assigned to it by God.) Gn 9:19 already noted that all nations are descended from the three sons of Noah; the same sentiment is repeated in 10:5, 18, 25, 32; 11:8. The presupposition of the chapter is that every nation has a land assigned to it by God (cf. Dt 32:8–9). The number of the nations is seventy (if one does not count Noah and his sons, and counts Sidon [vv. 15, 19] only once), which is a traditional biblical number (Jgs 8:30; Lk 10:1, 17). According to Gn 46:27 and Ex 1:5, Israel also numbered seventy persons, which shows that it in some sense represents the nations of the earth.

This chapter classifies the various peoples known to the ancient Israelites; it is theologically important as stressing the basic family unity of all peoples on earth. It is sometimes called the Table of the Nations. The relationship between the various peoples is based on linguistic, geographic, or political grounds (v. 31). In general, the descendants of Japheth (vv. 2–5) are the peoples of the Indo-European languages to the north and west of Mesopotamia and Syria; the descendants of Ham (vv. 6–20) are the Hamitic-speaking peoples of northern Africa; and the descendants of Shem (vv. 21–31) are the Semitic-speaking peoples of Mesopotamia, Syria and Arabia. But there are many exceptions to this rule; the Semitic-speaking peoples of Canaan are considered descendants of Ham, because at one time they were subject to Hamitic Egypt (vv. 6, 15–19). This chapter is generally considered to be a composite from the Yahwist source (vv. 8–19, 21, 24–30) and the Priestly source (vv. 1–7, 20, 22–23, 31–32). Presumably that is why certain tribes of Arabia are listed under both Ham (v. 7) and Shem (vv. 26–28).

10:2 *Gomer*: the Cimmerians; *Madai*: the Medes; *Javan*: the Greeks.

---

* **9:18** Gn 5:32; 10:1.
9:21 Lam 4:21; Hb 2:15.
9:25 Dt 27:16; Wis 12:11.
10:2–8 1 Chr 1:5–10.

Magog, Madai, Javan, Tubal, Meshech and Ti-
ras.* [3]The descendants of Gomer: Ashkenaz,†
Diphath and Togarmah. [4]The descendants of
Javan: Elishah,† Tarshish, the Kittim and the
Rodanim. [5]From these branched out the mari-
time nations.

These are the descendants of Japheth by their
lands, each with its own language, according to
their clans, by their nations.

[6]The descendants of Ham: Cush,† Mizraim,
Put and Canaan. [7]The descendants of Cush:
Seba, Havilah, Sabtah, Raamah and Sabteca. The
descendants of Raamah: Sheba and Dedan.

[8]Cush† became the father of Nimrod, who
was the first to become a mighty warrior on
earth. [9]He was a mighty hunter in the eyes of the
LORD; hence the saying, "Like Nimrod, a mighty
hunter in the eyes of the LORD." [10]His kingdom
originated in Babylon, Erech and Accad, all of
them in the land of Shinar.† [11]From that land he
went forth to Assyria, where he built Nineveh,
Rehoboth-Ir† and Calah, [12]as well as Resen, be-
tween Nineveh and Calah,† the latter being the
principal city.

[13]* Mizraim became the father of the Ludim,
the Anamim, the Lehabim, the Naphtuhim,
[14]the Pathrusim,† the Casluhim, and the Caph-
torim from whom the Philistines came.

[15]Canaan became the father of Sidon, his first-
born, and of Heth;† [16]also of the Jebusites, the
Amorites, the Girgashites, [17]the Hivites, the Ar-
kites, the Sinites, [18]the Arvadites, the Zemarites,
and the Hamathites. Afterward, the clans of the
Canaanites spread out, [19]so that the Canaanite
borders extended from Sidon all the way to Ge-
rar, near Gaza, and all the way to Sodom, Go-
morrah, Admah and Zeboiim, near Lasha.

[20]These are the descendants of Ham, accord-
ing to their clans, according to their languages,
by their lands, by their nations.

[21]To Shem also, Japheth's oldest brother and
the ancestor of all the children of Eber,† children
were born. [22]* The descendants of Shem: Elam,
Asshur, Arpachshad, Lud and Aram. [23]The de-
scendants of Aram: Uz, Hul, Gether and Mash.

[24]Arpachshad became the father of Shelah,
and Shelah became the father of Eber. [25]To Eber
two sons were born: the name of the first was Pe-
leg, for in his time the world was divided;† and
the name of his brother was Joktan.

[26]Joktan became the father of Almodad, She-
leph, Hazarmaveth, Jerah, [27]Hadoram, Uzal,
Diklah, [28]Obal, Abimael, Sheba, [29]Ophir, Hav-
ilah and Jobab. All these were descendants of
Joktan. [30]Their settlements extended all the way
from Mesha to Sephar, the eastern hill country.

[31]These are the descendants of Shem, accord-
ing to their clans, according to their languages,
by their lands, by their nations.

[32]These are the clans of Noah's sons, accord-
ing to their origins and by their nations. From
these the nations of the earth branched out after
the flood.

Tower of Babel†

11 [1]The whole world had the same language
and the same words. [2]When they were
migrating from the east, they came to a valley
in the land of Shinar† and settled there. [3]They
said to one another, "Come, let us mold bricks
and harden them with fire." They used bricks for
stone, and bitumen for mortar. [4]Then they said,
"Come, let us build ourselves a city and a tower
with its top in the sky,† and so make a name for
ourselves; otherwise we shall be scattered all over
the earth."

[5]The LORD came down to see the city and the
tower that the people had built. [6]Then the LORD
said: If now, while they are one people and all
have the same language, they have started to do
this, nothing they presume to do will be out of
their reach. [7]Come, let us go down and there
confuse their language, so that no one will un-
derstand the speech of another. [8]So the LORD

†

10:3 *Ashkenaz*: an Indo-European people, which later became the medieval rabbinic name for Germany. It now designates one of the great divisions of Judaism, Eastern European Yiddish-speaking Jews.

10:4 *Elishah*: Cyprus; *the Kittim*: certain inhabitants of Cyprus; *the Rodanim*: the inhabitants of Rhodes.

10:6 *Cush*: biblical Ethiopia, modern Nubia. *Mizraim*: Lower (i.e., northern) Egypt; *Put*: either Punt in East Africa or Libya.

10:8 *Cush*: here seems to be Cossea, the country of the Kassites; see note on 2:10–14. *Nimrod*: possibly Tukulti-Ninurta I (thirteenth century B.C.), the first Assyrian conqueror of Babylonia and a famous city-builder at home.

10:10 *Shinar*: the land of ancient Babylonia, embracing Sumer and Akkad, present-day southern Iraq, mentioned also in 11:2; 14:1.

10:11 *Rehoboth-Ir*: lit., "wide-streets city," was probably not the name of another city, but an epithet of Nineveh; cf. Jon 3:3.

10:12 *Calah*: Assyrian Kalhu, the capital of Assyria in the ninth century B.C.

10:14 *The Pathrusim*: the people of Upper (southern) Egypt; cf. Is 11:11; Jer 44:1; Ez 29:14; 30:13. *Caphtorim*: Crete; for Caphtor as the place of origin of the Philistines, cf. Dt 2:23; Am 9:7; Jer 47:4.

10:15 *Heth*: the biblical Hittites; see note on 23:3.

10:21 *Eber*: the eponymous ancestor of the Hebrews, that is, the one to whom they traced their name.

10:25 In the Hebrew text there is a play on the name *Peleg* and the word *niplega*, "was divided."

11:1–9 This story illustrates increasing human wickedness, shown here in the sinful pride that human beings take in their own achievements apart from God. Secondarily, the story explains the diversity of languages among the peoples of the earth.

11:2 *Shinar*: see note on 10:10.

11:4 *Tower with its top in the sky*: possibly a reference to the chief ziggurat of Babylon, *E-sag-ila*, lit., "the house that raises high its head."

*

10:2 Ez 38:2. **10:22–29** 1 Chr 1:17–23.

10:13–18 1 Chr 1:11–16.

GN

Live It!

A Barrier or a Bridge?

Language can be either a barrier or a bridge. Through our speech, we connect with other people. And we often hear that love, music, and a smile are universal languages. Yet, languages also separate, symbolizing differences between cultures and nations, which can cause wars and other atrocities to erupt.

The story of the tower of Babel is an ancient explanation of why the separation between people, symbolized by different languages, occurs. The people ignore God's command to "fill the earth" (Gn 1:28). Instead, they gather in one place to try to build a tower reaching to heaven, a sin of pride and arrogance. God confuses their language to foil their plan. It is not language but pride that separates us.

In the Acts of the Apostles, chapter 2, language serves as a bridge. The Holy Spirit enables the people from many different lands to hear the Apostles speaking in their own languages. The Spirit serves to unify us, no matter what earthly language we speak. Anyone who has attended a World Youth Day knows that when we live by the Spirit, we can rise above the differences of language and culture. The Good News is universal and unites us!

▶ Gn 11:1–9

scattered them from there over all the earth, and
they stopped building the city. 9 That is why it
was called Babel,† because there the LORD con-
fused the speech of all the world. From there the
LORD scattered them over all the earth.

Descendants from Shem to Abraham†

10 * These are the descendants of Shem. When
Shem was one hundred years old, he begot Ar-
pachshad, two years after the flood. 11 Shem lived
five hundred years after he begot Arpachshad,
and he had other sons and daughters. 12 When
Arpachshad was thirty-five years old, he begot
Shelah.† 13 Arpachshad lived four hundred and
three years after he begot Shelah, and he had
other sons and daughters.
14 When Shelah was thirty years old, he begot
Eber. 15 Shelah lived four hundred and three
years after he begot Eber, and he had other sons
and daughters.
16 When Eber† was thirty-four years old, he
begot Peleg. 17 Eber lived four hundred and thirty
years after he begot Peleg, and he had other sons
and daughters.
18 When Peleg was thirty years old, he begot
Reu. 19 Peleg lived two hundred and nine years
after he begot Reu, and he had other sons and
daughters.
20 When Reu was thirty-two years old, he begot
Serug. 21 Reu lived two hundred and seven years
after he begot Serug, and he had other sons and
daughters.
22 When Serug was thirty years old, he begot
Nahor. 23 Serug lived two hundred years after he
begot Nahor, and he had other sons and daugh-
ters.
24 When Nahor was twenty-nine years old, he
begot Terah. 25 Nahor lived one hundred and
nineteen years after he begot Terah, and he had
other sons and daughters.
26 When Terah was seventy years old, he begot
Abram,† Nahor and Haran.*

II. The Story of the Ancestors of Israel

Terah

27 These are the descendants of Terah.† Terah
begot Abram, Nahor, and Haran, and Haran
begot Lot. 28 Haran died before Terah his father,

---

† **11:9** *Babel*: the Hebrew form of the name "Babylon"; the Babylonians interpreted their name for the city, *Bab-ili*, as "gate of god." The Hebrew word *balal*, "he confused," has a similar sound.

11:10–26 The second Priestly genealogy goes from Shem to Terah and his three sons Abram, Nahor, and Haran, just as the genealogy in 5:3–32 went from Adam to Noah and his three sons Shem, Ham, and Japheth. This genealogy marks the important transition in Genesis between the story of the nations in 1:1–11:26 and the story of Israel in the person of its ancestors (11:27–50:26). As chaps. 1–11 showed the increase and spread of the nations, so chaps. 12–50 will show the increase and spread of Israel. The contrast between Israel and the nations is a persistent biblical theme. The ages given here are from the Hebrew text; the Samaritan and Greek texts have divergent sets of numbers in most cases. In comparable accounts of the pre-flood period, enormous life spans are attributed to human beings. It may be an attempt to show that the pre-flood generations were extraordinary and more vital than post-flood human beings.

11:12 The Greek text adds Kenan (cf. 5:9–10) between Arpachshad and Shelah. The Greek listing is followed in Lk 3:36.

11:16 *Eber*: the eponymous ancestor of the Hebrews, "descendants of Eber" (10:21, 24–30); see note on 14:13.

11:26 Abram is a dialectal variant of Abraham. God will change his name in view of his new task in 17:4.

11:27 *Descendants of Terah*: elsewhere in Genesis the story of the son is introduced by the name of the father (25:12, 19; 36:1; 37:2).

---

* **11:10–26** 1 Chr 1:24–27; Lk 3:34–36. **11:26** Jos 24:2; 1 Chr 1:26–27.

in his native land, in Ur of the Chaldeans.†
29 Abram and Nahor took wives; the name of
Abram's wife was Sarai,† and the name of Na-
hor's wife was Milcah, daughter of Haran, the
father of Milcah and Iscah.* 30 Sarai was barren;
she had no child.
31 Terah took his son Abram, his grandson Lot,
son of Haran, and his daughter-in-law Sarai, the
wife of his son Abram, and brought them out
of Ur of the Chaldeans, to go to the land of Ca-
naan. But when they reached Haran, they settled
there.* 32 The lifetime of Terah was two hundred
and five years; then Terah died in Haran.†

Abram's Call and Migration

12 1 The LORD said to Abram: Go forth† from
your land, your relatives, and from your
father's house to a land that I will show you.*
2 † I will make of you a great nation, and I will
bless you; I will make your name great, so that
you will be a blessing.* 3 * I will bless those who
bless you and curse those who curse you. All the
families of the earth will find blessing in you.†
4 * Abram went as the LORD directed him, and
Lot went with him. Abram was seventy-five years
old when he left Haran. 5 † Abram took his wife
Sarai, his brother's son Lot, all the possessions
that they had accumulated, and the persons they
had acquired in Haran, and they set out for the
land of Canaan. When they came to the land of
Canaan, 6 † Abram passed through the land as far
as the sacred place at Shechem, by the oak of Mo-
reh. The Canaanites were then in the land.
7 The LORD appeared to Abram and said: To
your descendants I will give this land. So Abram
built an altar there to the LORD who had appeared
to him.* 8 From there he moved on to the hill
country east of Bethel, pitching his tent with
Bethel to the west and Ai to the east. He built an
altar there to the LORD and invoked the LORD by
name. 9 Then Abram journeyed on by stages to
the Negeb.†

Abram and Sarai in Egypt†

10 There was famine in the land; so Abram
went down to Egypt to sojourn there, since the
famine in the land was severe.* 11 When he was
about to enter Egypt, he said to his wife Sarai: "I
know that you are a beautiful woman. 12 When
the Egyptians see you, they will say, 'She is his
wife'; then they will kill me, but let you live.
13 Please say, therefore, that you are my sister,† so

---

† The Abraham-Sarah stories begin (11:27–32) and end with genealogical notices (25:1–18), which concern, respectively, the families of Terah and of Abraham. Most of the traditions in the cycle are from the Yahwist source. The so-called Elohist source (E) is somewhat shadowy, denied by some scholars but recognized by others in passages that duplicate other narratives (20:1–18 and 21:22–34). The Priestly source consists mostly of brief editorial notices, except for chaps. 17 and 23.

11:28 *Ur of the Chaldeans*: Ur was an extremely ancient city of the Sumerians (later, of the Babylonians) in southern Mesopotamia. The Greek text has "the land of the Chaldeans." After a millennium of relative unimportance, Ur underwent a revival during the Neo-Babylonian/Chaldean empire (625–539 B.C.). The sixth-century author here identified the place by its contemporary name. As chap. 24 shows, Haran in northern Mesopotamia is in fact the native place of Abraham. In the Genesis perspective, the human race originated in the East (3:24; 4:16) and migrated from there to their homelands (11:2). Terah's family moved from the East (Ur) and Abraham will complete the journey to the family's true homeland in the following chapters.

11:29 *Sarai*: like Abram, a dialectal variant of the more usual form of the name Sarah. In 17:15, God will change it to Sarah in view of her new task.

11:32 Since Terah was seventy years old when his son Abraham was born (v. 26), and Abraham was seventy-five when he left Haran (12:4), Terah lived in Haran for sixty years after Abraham's departure. According to the tradition in the Samaritan text, Terah died when he was one hundred and forty-five years old, therefore, in the same year in which Abraham left Haran. This is the tradition followed in Stephen's speech: Abraham left Haran "after his father died" (Acts 7:4).

12:1–3 *Go forth . . . find blessing in you*: the syntax of the Hebrew suggests that the blessings promised to Abraham are contingent on his going to Canaan.

12:2 The call of Abraham begins a new history of blessing (18:18; 22:15–18), which is passed on in each instance to the chosen successor (26:2–4; 28:14). This call evokes the last story in the primeval history (11:1–9) by reversing its themes: Abraham goes forth rather than settle down; it is God rather than Abraham who will make a name for him; the families of the earth will find blessing in him.

12:3 *Will find blessing in you*: the Hebrew conjugation of the verb here and in 18:18 and 28:14 can be either reflexive ("shall bless themselves by you" = people will invoke Abraham as an example of someone blessed by God) or passive ("by you all the families of earth will be blessed" = the religious privileges of Abraham and his descendants ultimately will be extended to the nations). In 22:18 and 26:4, another conjugation of the same verb is used in a similar context that is undoubtedly reflexive ("bless themselves"). Many scholars suggest that the two passages in which the sense is clear should determine the interpretation of the three ambiguous passages: the privileged blessing enjoyed by Abraham and his descendants will awaken in all peoples the desire to enjoy those same blessings. Since the term is understood in a passive sense in the New Testament (Acts 3:25; Gal 3:8), it is rendered here by a neutral expression that admits of both meanings.

12:5 The ancestors appear in Genesis as pastoral nomads living at the edge of settled society, and having occasional dealings with the inhabitants, sometimes even moving into towns for brief periods. Unlike modern nomads such as the Bedouin, however, ancient pastoralists fluctuated between following the herds and sedentary life, depending on circumstances. Pastoralists could settle down and farm and later resume a pastoral way of life. Indeed, there was a symbiotic relationship between pastoralists and villagers, each providing goods to the other. *Persons*: servants and others who formed the larger household under the leadership of Abraham; cf. 14:14.

12:6 Abraham's journey to the center of the land, Shechem, then to Bethel, and then to the Negeb, is duplicated in Jacob's journeys (33:18; 35:1, 6, 27; 46:1) and in the general route of the conquest under Joshua (Jos 7:2; 8:9, 30). Abraham's journey is a symbolic "conquest" of the land he has been promised. In building altars here (vv. 7, 8) and elsewhere, Abraham acknowledges his God as Lord of the land.

12:9 *The Negeb*: the semidesert land south of Judah.

12:10–13:1 Abraham and Sarah's sojourn in Egypt and encounter with Pharaoh foreshadow their descendants' experience, suggesting a divine design in which they must learn to trust. The story of Sarah, the ancestor in danger, is told again in chap. 20, and also in 26:1–11 with Rebekah instead of Sarah. Repetition of similar events is not unusual in literature that has been orally shaped.

12:13 *You are my sister*: the text does not try to excuse Abraham's deception, though in 20:12 a similar deception is somewhat excused.

---

* **11:29** Gn 17:15.
11:31 Jos 24:3; Neh 9:7; Jdt 5:6–9; Acts 7:4.
12:1 Acts 7:3; Heb 11:8.
12:2 Gn 17:6; Sir 44:20–21; Rom 4:17–22.
12:3 Gn 18:18; 22:18; Acts 3:25; Gal 3:8.
12:4–5 Gn 11:31; Jos 24:3; Acts 7:4.
12:7 Ex 33:1; Dt 34:4; Acts 7:5.
12:10 Gn 26:1.

GN

Introducing...

Abraham and Sarah

Abraham, whose name was originally Abram, is an important figure for three major world religions: Judaism, Christianity, and Islam. Abraham is regarded as the great example of faith in God. He first appears in Genesis 11:26. For many years, Abram lives in Haran in northern Mesopotamia (see map 1, "The World of the Patriarchs") with his wife, Sarai. God calls Abram and Sarai to leave their home, seals a covenant with them, and changes their names to Abraham and Sarah. God's covenant promises that they will be the parents "of a multitude of nations" (17:5) and their descendants will be as numerous as the "stars of the sky" (22:17).

Later, God requests that Abraham sacrifice his son Isaac. God stops him from going through with it, but Abraham's willingness to cooperate with God and his complete trust in God become the foundation for Israel's faith. Not surprisingly, in the Old Testament, when a prophet or teacher needed an example of someone with unwavering trust in God, Abraham was often cited.

In the New Testament, Abraham is revered as the first patriarch to enter into a covenant with God (see Mt 1:1, Lk 16:19–31) and the great pioneer of Israel's faith (see Acts 7:2–50, Rom 4:1–25, Heb 7:1–10).

▶ Gn 12:1—25:11

that I may fare well on your account and my life
may be spared for your sake."* 14 When Abram
arrived in Egypt, the Egyptians saw that the
woman was very beautiful. 15 When Pharaoh's
officials saw her they praised her to Pharaoh,
and the woman was taken into Pharaoh's house.
16 Abram fared well on her account, and he
acquired sheep, oxen, male and female servants,
male and female donkeys, and camels.†
17 But the LORD struck Pharaoh and his
household with severe plagues because of Sarai, Abram's wife.* 18 Then Pharaoh summoned
Abram and said to him: "How could you do this
to me! Why did you not tell me she was your
wife? 19 Why did you say, 'She is my sister,' so
that I took her for my wife? Now, here is your
wife. Take her and leave!"
20 Then Pharaoh gave his men orders concerning Abram, and they sent him away, with his wife
and all that belonged to him.

Abram and Lot Part

13 1 From Egypt Abram went up to the Negeb
with his wife and all that belonged to him,
and Lot went with him.* 2 † Now Abram was
very rich in livestock, silver, and gold.* 3 From
the Negeb he traveled by stages toward Bethel,
to the place between Bethel and Ai where his
tent had formerly stood, 4 the site where he had
first built the altar; and there Abram invoked the
LORD by name.*
5 Lot, who went with Abram, also had flocks
and herds and tents, 6 so that the land could
not support them if they stayed together; their
possessions were so great that they could not
live together. 7 There were quarrels between the
herders of Abram's livestock and the herders of
Lot's livestock. At this time the Canaanites and
the Perizzites were living in the land.
8 So Abram said to Lot: "Let there be no strife
between you and me, or between your herders
and my herders, for we are kindred. 9 Is not the
whole land available? Please separate from me.
If you prefer the left, I will go to the right; if
you prefer the right, I will go to the left." 10 Lot
looked about and saw how abundantly watered
the whole Jordan Plain was as far as Zoar, like the
LORD's own garden, or like Egypt. This was before
the LORD had destroyed Sodom and Gomorrah.
11 Lot, therefore, chose for himself the whole
Jordan Plain and set out eastward. Thus they
separated from each other. 12 Abram settled in
the land of Canaan, while Lot settled among the
cities of the Plain, pitching his tents near Sodom.

†

12:16 *Camels*: domesticated camels did not come into common use in the ancient Near East until the end of the second millennium B.C. Thus the mention of camels here (24:11–64; 30:43; 31:17, 34; 32:8, 16; 37:25) is seemingly an anachronism.

13:2–18 In this story of Abraham and Lot going their separate ways, Abraham resolves a family dispute by an act that shows both trust in God and generosity toward his nephew. The story suggests Lot rather than Abraham is the natural choice to be the ancestor of a great family; he is young and he takes the most fertile land (outside the land of Canaan). In contrast to Lot, who lifts his eyes to choose for himself (vv. 10–11), Abraham waits for God to tell him to lift his eyes and see the land he will receive (v. 14). Chaps. 18–19 continue the story of Abraham and Lot. Abraham's visionary possession of the land foreshadows that of Moses (Dt 3:27; 34:4).

*

12:13 Gn 20:12–13; 26:7.
12:17 Ps 105:14.
13:1 Gn 12:9.
13:2 Ps 112:1–3; Prv 10:22.
13:4 Gn 12:8.

13 Now the inhabitants of Sodom were wicked,
great sinners against the LORD.*
14 After Lot had parted from him, the LORD said
to Abram: Look about you, and from where you
are, gaze to the north and south, east and west;*
15 all the land that you see I will give to you and
your descendants forever.* 16 I will make your
descendants like the dust of the earth; if anyone
could count the dust of the earth, your descen-
dants too might be counted.* 17 Get up and walk
through the land, across its length and breadth,
for I give it to you. 18 Abram moved his tents and
went on to settle near the oak of Mamre, which is
at Hebron. There he built an altar to the LORD.*

The Four Kings

14 1 † When Amraphel king of Shinar, Ari-
och king of Ellasar, Chedorlaomer king
of Elam, and Tidal king of Goiim 2 made war
on Bera king of Sodom, Birsha king of Gomor-
rah, Shinab king of Admah, Shemeber king of
Zeboiim, and the king of Bela (that is, Zoar),
3 all the latter kings joined forces in the Valley
of Siddim (that is, the Salt Sea†). 4 For twelve
years they had served Chedorlaomer, but in the
thirteenth year they rebelled. 5 In the fourteenth
year Chedorlaomer and the kings allied with him
came and defeated the Rephaim in Ashteroth-
karnaim, the Zuzim in Ham, the Emim in
Shaveh-kiriathaim, 6 and the Horites in the hill
country of Seir, as far as El-paran, close by the
wilderness.* 7 They then turned back and came
to En-mishpat (that is, Kadesh), and they sub-
dued the whole country of both the Amalekites
and the Amorites who lived in Hazazon-tamar.
8 Thereupon the king of Sodom, the king of Go-
morrah, the king of Admah, the king of Zeboiim,
and the king of Bela (that is, Zoar) marched
out, and in the Valley of Siddim they went into
battle against them: 9 against Chedorlaomer king
of Elam, Tidal king of Goiim, Amraphel king of
Shinar, and Arioch king of Ellasar—four kings
against five. 10 Now the Valley of Siddim was full
of bitumen pits; and as the king of Sodom and
the king of Gomorrah fled, they fell into these,
while the rest fled to the mountains. 11 The vic-
tors seized all the possessions and food supplies
of Sodom and Gomorrah and then went their
way. 12 They took with them Abram's nephew
Lot, who had been living in Sodom, as well as
his possessions, and departed.*
13 A survivor came and brought the news to
Abram the Hebrew,† who was camping at the
oak of Mamre the Amorite, a kinsman of Eshcol
and Aner; these were allies of Abram. 14 When
Abram heard that his kinsman had been cap-
tured, he mustered three hundred and eighteen
of his retainers,† born in his house, and went
in pursuit as far as Dan. 15 He and his servants
deployed against them at night, defeated them,
and pursued them as far as Hobah, which is
north of Damascus. 16 He recovered all the pos-
sessions. He also recovered his kinsman Lot and
his possessions, along with the women and the
other people.
17 When Abram returned from his defeat of
Chedorlaomer and the kings who were allied
with him, the king of Sodom went out to greet
him in the Valley of Shaveh (that is, the King's
Valley).
18 Melchizedek, king of Salem,† brought out
bread and wine. He was a priest of God Most
High. 19 He blessed Abram with these words:*

"Blessed be Abram by God Most High,
the creator of heaven and earth;
20 And blessed be God Most High,
who delivered your foes into your hand."

†

14:1 Abraham plays a role with other world leaders. He defeats a coalition of five kings from the east (where, later, Israel's enemies lived) and is recognized by a Canaanite king as blessed by God Most High. The historicity of the events is controverted; apart from Shinar (Babylon), Tidal (Hittite Tudhaliya), and Elam, the names and places cannot be identified with certainty. The five cities were apparently at the southern end of the Dead Sea, and all but Bela (i.e., Zoar) were destined for destruction (19:20–24; Hos 11:8). The passage belongs to none of the traditional Genesis sources; it has some resemblance to reports of military campaigns in Babylonian and Assyrian royal annals.

14:3 *The Salt Sea*: the Dead Sea.

14:13 *Abram the Hebrew*: "Hebrew" was used by biblical writers for the pre-Israelite ancestors. Linguistically, it is an ethnic term; it may be built on the root Eber, who is the eponymous ancestor of the Israelites, that is, the one to whom they traced their name (10:21, 24–25; 11:14–17), or it may reflect the tradition that the ancestors came from beyond (*eber*) the Euphrates. It is used only by non-Israelites, or by Israelites speaking to foreigners.

14:14 *Retainers*: the Hebrew word *hanik* is used only here in the Old Testament. Cognate words appear in Egyptian and Akkadian texts, signifying armed soldiers belonging to the household of a local leader.

14:18 Melchizedek, king of Salem (Jerusalem, cf. Ps 76:3), appears with majestic suddenness to recognize Abraham's great victory, which the five local kings were unable to achieve. He prepares a feast in his honor and declares him blessed or made powerful by God Most High, evidently the highest God in the Canaanite pantheon. Abraham acknowledges the blessing by giving a tenth of the recaptured spoils as a tithe to Melchizedek. The episode is one of several allusions to David, king at Jerusalem, who also exercised priestly functions (2 Sm 6:17). Heb 7 interprets Melchizedek as a prefiguration of Christ. *God Most High*: in Heb. *El Elyon*, one of several "El names" for God in Genesis, others being *El Olam* (21:33), *El* the God of Israel (33:20), *El Roi* (16:13), *El Bethel* (35:7), and *El Shaddai* (the usual P designation for God in Genesis). All the sources except the Yahwist use El as the proper name for God used by the ancestors. The god El was well-known across the ancient Near East and in comparable religious literature. The ancestors recognized this God as their own when they encountered him in their journeys and in the shrines they found in Canaan.

*

13:13 Gn 18:20; Ez 16:49; 2 Pt 2:6–8; Jude 7.
13:14 Gn 28:14.
13:15 Gn 12:7; Mt 5:5; Lk 1:55, 73; Acts 7:5; Rom 4:13; Gal 3:16.
13:16 Gn 22:17; Nm 23:10.
13:18 Gn 14:13.
14:6 Dt 2:12.
14:12 Gn 13:10–12.
14:19 Ps 110:4; Heb 5:6, 10; 7:1.

Catholic Connection

Sacramental Symbols

Sometimes words alone are not enough. Consider the inexpressible joy and relief of Abram in Genesis 14:17–20. Abram's nephew Lot has been captured by foreign invaders and Abram takes his men to battle and returns Lot safely. Upon Abram's return, Melchizedek, a king and priest, meets with Abram to rejoice in their great victory. As part of their celebration, Melchizedek uses not only words but the everyday objects of bread and wine in a ritual to offer a blessing on Abram and to give praise to God.

The use of symbols, like bread and wine, even today enable us to express and deepen our relationship with God. In the Catholic Church, this is most evident when we celebrate the sacraments. The symbols used in the sacraments find their roots in three areas.

The first area is from Creation. Because God created the world, it is natural that we can find and express meaning through symbols like fire and water. For example, during the sacrament of Baptism, we use water as a sign of purification and new birth and a lit candle as a sign of our desire to walk in the light of Christ.

The second area from which sacramental symbols come is everyday human life. These are things we commonly do, like rubbing oils or lotion on our bodies or placing a reassuring hand on a friend. For example, in the sacrament of the Anointing of the Sick, the priest uses oil to bless and strengthen the sick and places or lays a hand upon them as a sign of blessing.

The third source of sacramental symbols is from events in the history of God's people, especially the Passover. We see this most clearly when we celebrate the Eucharist; we use the symbols of bread and wine along with words and gestures that Jesus used when he celebrated the Passover with his disciples on the eve of his Crucifixion.

When the Church celebrates the sacraments, it combines words with symbols; through faith and the power of the Holy Spirit, the sacraments express and make present to us the graces offered by Christ.

▶ **Gn 14:17–20**

Catechism, nos. 1145–1152

Then Abram gave him a tenth of everything.
21 The king of Sodom said to Abram, "Give
me the captives; the goods you may keep." 22 But
Abram replied to the king of Sodom: "I have
sworn to the LORD, God Most High,† the creator
of heaven and earth, 23 that I would not take so
much as a thread or a sandal strap from anything
that is yours, so that you cannot say, 'I made
Abram rich.' 24 Nothing for me except what my
servants have consumed and the share that is due
to the men who went with me—Aner, Eshcol and
Mamre; let them take their share."

The Covenant with Abram†

15 1 Some time afterward, the word of the
LORD came to Abram in a vision: Do not
fear, Abram! I am your shield; I will make your
reward very great.
2 But Abram said, "Lord GOD, what can you
give me, if I die childless and have only a servant
of my household, Eliezer of Damascus?" 3 Abram
continued, "Look, you have given me no off-
spring, so a servant of my household will be my
heir." 4 Then the word of the LORD came to him:
No, that one will not be your heir; your own off-
spring will be your heir.* 5 He took him outside
and said: Look up at the sky and count the stars, if
you can. Just so, he added, will your descendants
be.* 6 * Abram put his faith in the LORD, who at-
tributed it to him as an act of righteousness.†
7 He then said to him: I am the LORD who
brought you from Ur of the Chaldeans to give you
this land as a possession.* 8 "Lord GOD," he asked,
"how will I know that I will possess it?" 9 † He
answered him: Bring me a three-year-old heifer, a
three-year-old female goat, a three-year-old ram,
a turtledove, and a young pigeon.* 10 He brought
him all these, split them in two, and placed each
half opposite the other; but the birds he did not
cut up. 11 Birds of prey swooped down on the
carcasses, but Abram scared them away. 12 As the
sun was about to set, a deep sleep fell upon Abram,
and a great, dark dread descended upon him.
13 † Then the LORD said to Abram: Know for
certain that your descendants will reside as aliens
in a land not their own, where they shall be en-
slaved and oppressed for four hundred years.*
14 But I will bring judgment on the nation they
must serve, and after this they will go out with
great wealth.* 15 You, however, will go to your
ancestors in peace; you will be buried at a ripe
old age. 16 In the fourth generation† your descen-
dants will return here, for the wickedness of the
Amorites is not yet complete.*
17 When the sun had set and it was dark, there

Did You Know?

Fire in the Bible

Fire appears frequently throughout the Old Testament, symbolizing two aspects of God: presence and holiness. Fire symbolizes a special presence of God in the sealing of the covenant with Abraham (see Gn 15:17), in the burning bush (see Ex 3:2), and in the pillar of fire leading Israel through the desert (see Ex 13:21). Fire also symbolizes God's holiness appearing to purge and purify those who deviate from God's ways, as in Sodom and Gomorrah (see Gn 19:24) and the seventh plague against Egypt (see Ex 9:23).

▶ Gn 15:17

---

† **14:22** In vv. 22–24, Abraham refuses to let anyone but God enrich him. Portrayed with the traits of a later Israelite judge or tribal hero, Abraham acknowledges that his victory is from God alone.

15:1–21 In the first section (vv. 1–6), Abraham is promised a son and heir, and in the second (vv. 7–21), he is promised a land. The structure is similar in both: each of the two promises is not immediately accepted; the first is met with a complaint (vv. 2–3) and the second with a request for a sign (v. 8). God's answer differs in each section—a sign in v. 5 and an oath in vv. 9–21. Some scholars believe that the Genesis promises of progeny and land were originally separate and only later combined, but progeny and land are persistent concerns especially of ancient peoples and it is hard to imagine one without the other.

15:6 Abraham's act of faith in God's promises was regarded as an act of righteousness, i.e., as fully expressive of his relationship with God. St. Paul (Rom 4:1–25; Gal 3:6–9) makes Abraham's faith a model for Christians.

15:9–17 Cutting up animals was a well-attested way of making a treaty in antiquity. Jer 34:17–20 shows the rite is a form of self-imprecation in which violators invoke the fate of the animals upon themselves. The eighth-century B.C. Sefire treaty from Syria reads, "As this calf is cut up, thus Matti'el shall be cut up." The smoking fire pot and the flaming torch (v. 17), which represent God, pass between the pieces, making God a signatory to the covenant.

15:13–16 The verses clarify the promise of the land by providing a timetable of its possession: after four hundred years of servitude, your descendants will actually possess the land in the fourth generation (a patriarchal generation seems to be one hundred years). The iniquity of the current inhabitants (called here the Amorites) has not yet reached the point where God must intervene in punishment. Another table is given in Ex 12:40, which is not compatible with this one.

15:16 *Generation*: the Hebrew term *dor* is commonly rendered as "generation," but it may signify a period of varying length. A "generation" is the period between the birth of children and the

---

* **15:4** Gn 17:16.
15:5 Gn 22:17; 28:14; Ex 32:13; Dt 1:10; Sir 44:21; Rom 4:18; Heb 11:12.
15:6 1 Mc 2:52; Rom 4:3, 9, 22; Gal 3:6–7; Jas 2:23.
15:7 Gn 11:31; 12:1; Ex 32:13; Neh 9:7–8; Acts 7:2–3.
15:9 Lv 1:14.
15:13 Ex 12:40; Nm 20:15; Jdt 5:9–10; Is 52:4; Acts 13:20; Gal 3:17.
15:14 Ex 3:8, 21–22.
15:16 1 Kgs 21:26.

Live It!

Love and Jealousy

A love triangle in the Bible! The relationship between Abram, Sarai, and Hagar is shocking by Christian moral standards but would not have been unusual in their time. A patriarch like Abram would often have children by several wives, slaves, and concubines (something like mistresses who lived with the household). It's not surprising that such relationships would have fostered jealousy and tension. The conflict between Hagar and Sarai must have been fierce, to cause Hagar to leave the security of Abram's household.

Today, we encourage victims of abuse and harassment to speak out and take action, so it may seem strange to us that God's angel seeks out Hagar and asks her to return to a place where she is likely to be mistreated. When we encounter people who have been abused or harassed, we need to help them seek justice and set things right. Remember the larger message in Genesis—that every person is created in God's image and is to be treated with the utmost dignity and respect. Carrying out this message is our responsibility as brothers and sisters to one another.

▶ **Gn 16:1–16**

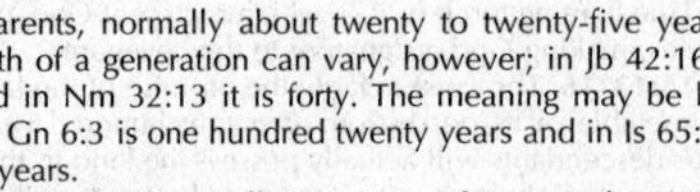

appeared a smoking fire pot and a flaming torch,
which passed between those pieces. 18 † On that
day the LORD made a covenant with Abram, say-
ing: To your descendants I give this land, from
the Wadi of Egypt to the Great River, the Euphra-
tes,* 19 * the land of the Kenites, the Kenizzites,
the Kadmonites, 20 the Hittites, the Perizzites, the
Rephaim, 21 the Amorites, the Canaanites, the
Girgashites, and the Jebusites.

Birth of Ishmael†

16 1 Abram's wife Sarai had borne him no
children. Now she had an Egyptian maid-
servant named Hagar.* 2 Sarai said to Abram:
"The LORD has kept me from bearing children.
Have intercourse with my maid; perhaps I will
have sons through her." Abram obeyed Sarai.† *
3 Thus, after Abram had lived ten years in the
land of Canaan, his wife Sarai took her maid,
Hagar the Egyptian, and gave her to her husband
Abram to be his wife. 4 He had intercourse with
her, and she became pregnant. As soon as Hagar
knew she was pregnant, her mistress lost stature
in her eyes.† * 5 * So Sarai said to Abram: "This
outrage against me is your fault. I myself gave
my maid to your embrace; but ever since she
knew she was pregnant, I have lost stature in
her eyes. May the LORD decide between you and
me!" 6 Abram told Sarai: "Your maid is in your
power. Do to her what you regard as right." Sa-
rai then mistreated her so much that Hagar ran
away from her.
7 The LORD's angel† found her by a spring in
the wilderness, the spring on the road to Shur,*
8 and he asked, "Hagar, maid of Sarai, where have
you come from and where are you going?" She
answered, "I am running away from my mistress,
Sarai." 9 But the LORD's angel told her: "Go back
to your mistress and submit to her authority.
10 I will make your descendants so numerous,"

† birth of their parents, normally about twenty to twenty-five years. The actual length of a generation can vary, however; in Jb 42:16 it is thirty-five and in Nm 32:13 it is forty. The meaning may be life spans, which in Gn 6:3 is one hundred twenty years and in Is 65:20 is one hundred years.

15:18–21 The *Wadi,* i.e., a gully or ravine, *of Egypt* is the Wadi-el-'Arish, which is the boundary between the settled land and the Sinai desert. Some scholars suggest that the boundaries are those of a Davidic empire at its greatest extent; others that they are idealized boundaries. Most lists of the ancient inhabitants of the promised land give three, six, or seven peoples, but vv. 19–21 give a grand total of ten.

16:1–16 In the previous chapter Abraham was given a timetable of possession of the land, but nothing was said about when the child was to be born. In this chapter, Sarah takes matters into her own hands, for she has been childless ten years since the promise (cf. 12:4 with 16:16). The story is about the two women, Sarah the infertile mistress and Hagar the fertile slave; Abraham has only a single sentence. In the course of the story, God intervenes directly on the side of Hagar, for she is otherwise without resources.

16:2 The custom of an infertile wife providing her husband with a concubine to produce children is widely attested in ancient Near Eastern law; e.g., an Old Assyrian marriage contract states that the wife must provide her husband with a concubine if she does not bear children within two years.

16:4 Because barrenness was at that time normally blamed on the woman and regarded as a disgrace, it is not surprising that Hagar looks down on Sarah. Ancient Near Eastern legal practice addresses such cases of insolent slaves and allows disciplining of them. Prv 30:23 uses as an example of intolerable behavior "a maidservant when she ousts her mistress."

16:7 *The LORD's angel*: a manifestation of God in human form; in v. 13 the messenger is identified with God. See note on Ex 3:2.

*

15:18 Ex 32:13; Neh 9:8; Ps 105:11; Sir 44:21.
15:19–20 Dt 7:1.
16:1 Gn 11:30.
16:2 Gn 21:8–9; Gal 4:22.
16:4 1 Sm 1:6; Prv 30:23.
16:5–16 Gn 21:10–19.
16:7 Ex 15:22.

added the LORD's angel, "that they will be too
many to count."* 11 Then the LORD's angel said
to her:

"You are now pregnant and shall bear a son;
you shall name him Ishmael,†
For the LORD has heeded your affliction.
12 He shall be a wild ass of a man,
his hand against everyone,
and everyone's hand against him;
Alongside† all his kindred
shall he encamp."*

13 To the LORD who spoke to her she gave a
name, saying, "You are God who sees me";† she
meant, "Have I really seen God and remained
alive after he saw me?"* 14 That is why the well
is called Beer-lahai-roi.† It is between Kadesh
and Bered.
15 Hagar bore Abram a son, and Abram named
the son whom Hagar bore him Ishmael.*
16 Abram was eighty-six years old when Hagar
bore him Ishmael.

Covenant of Circumcision†

17 1 When Abram was ninety-nine years old,
the LORD appeared to Abram and said:
I am God the Almighty. Walk in my presence
and be blameless.* 2 Between you and me I will
establish my covenant, and I will multiply you
exceedingly.*
3 Abram fell face down and God said to him:
4 For my part, here is my covenant with you:
you are to become the father of a multitude of
nations.* 5 No longer will you be called Abram;
your name will be Abraham,† for I am making
you the father of a multitude of nations.* 6 I
will make you exceedingly fertile; I will make
nations of you; kings will stem from you. 7 I will
maintain my covenant between me and you and
your descendants after you throughout the ages

Live It!

Covenant

Covenant is a powerful word in the Bible, with deep religious significance because it expresses the intimate relationship between God and God's people. At its most basic level, a covenant is a promise, made by both parties involved, to do certain things. In the covenant God makes with Noah, God promises never to destroy the earth again, and Noah's family promises to fill the earth and subdue it (see Gn 9:1–17). In the covenant with Abraham, God promises that Abram's descendants will be numerous and become a great nation. In return, Abram and all the male members of his household and their male descendants are circumcised as a sign that they belong to God (see 17:1–27). In the covenant made at Mount Sinai with Moses (see Ex 19:1–9) and the Hebrew people, God promises to give them the Promised Land. In return, they promise to follow the laws God gives to them.

We are, each of us, part of these ancient promises. Like the many faithful people who have gone before us, we too are the descendants of Abraham and Sarah, believers in the one God and members of God's family. We too are heirs to a special, intimate relationship with the Holy One through Jesus.

▶ **Gn 17:1–27**

†

16:11 *Ishmael*: in Hebrew the name means "God has heard." It is the same Hebrew verb that is translated "heeded" in the next clause. In other ancient Near Eastern texts, the name commemorated the divine answer to the parents' prayer to have a child, but here it is broadened to mean that God has "heard" Hagar's plight. In vv. 13–14, the verb "to see" is similarly broadened to describe God's special care for those in need.

16:12 *Alongside*: lit., "against the face of"; the same phrase is used of the lands of Ishmael's descendants in 25:18. It can be translated "in opposition to" (Dt 21:16; Jb 1:11; 6:28; 21:31), but here more likely means that Ishmael's settlement was near but not in the promised land.

16:13 *God who sees me*: Hebrew *el-ro'i* is multivalent, meaning either "God of seeing," i.e., extends his protection to me, or "God sees," which can imply seeing human suffering (29:32; Ex 2:25; Is 57:18; 58:3). It is probable that Hagar means to express both of these aspects. *Remained alive*: for the ancient notion that a person died on seeing God, see Gn 32:31; Ex 20:19; Dt 4:33; Jgs 13:22.

16:14 *Beer-lahai-roi*: possible translations of the name of the well include: "spring of the living one who sees me"; "the well of the living sight"; or "the one who sees me lives." See note on v. 13.

17:1–27 The Priestly source gathers the major motifs of the story so far and sets them firmly within a covenant context; the word "covenant" occurs thirteen times. There are links to the covenant with Noah (v. 1 = 6:9; v. 7 = 9:9; v. 11 = 9:12–17). In this chapter, vv. 1–8 promise progeny and land; vv. 9–14 are instructions about circumcision; vv. 15–21 repeat the promise of a son to Sarah and distinguish this promise from that to Hagar; vv. 22–27 describe Abraham's carrying out the commands. *The Almighty*: traditional rendering of Hebrew *El Shaddai*, which is P's favorite designation of God in the period of the ancestors. Its etymology is uncertain, but its root meaning is probably "God, the One of the Mountains."

17:5 Abram and Abraham are merely two forms of the same name, both meaning, "the father is exalted"; another variant form is

*

16:10 Gn 17:20; 21:13, 18; 25:12–18.
16:12 Gn 21:20; 25:18.
16:13 Gn 24:62.
16:15 Gn 16:2; Gal 4:22.
17:1 Gn 35:11; Ex 6:3.
17:2 Gn 12:2; 13:16; Ex 32:13.
17:4 Sir 44:21; Rom 4:17.
17:5 Neh 9:7.

Did You Know?

Circumcision

Circumcision, the removal of the foreskin of the penis, was practiced by many peoples in the ancient world. In Israel circumcision was performed shortly after birth. It symbolized that this person belonged to the people of God, and was required by the Covenant that God made first with Abraham and then with Moses and all of Israel. Today most Jews continue circumcision as a religious practice, and other people may be circumcised for personal reasons.

In the early Church, circumcision became the center of a controversy about whether Gentiles who wanted to become Christians had to first become Jews (see Acts of the Apostles, chapter 15; Phil 3:2–9).

▶ Gn 17:9–14

as an everlasting covenant, to be your God and
the God of your descendants after you.* 8 I will
give to you and to your descendants after you the
land in which you are now residing as aliens, the
whole land of Canaan, as a permanent posses-
sion; and I will be their God.* 9 God said to Abra-
ham: For your part, you and your descendants
after you must keep my covenant throughout the
ages. 10 This is the covenant between me and you
and your descendants after you that you must
keep: every male among you shall be circum-
cised.† * 11 Circumcise the flesh of your foreskin.
That will be the sign of the covenant between
me and you.* 12 Throughout the ages, every male
among you, when he is eight days old, shall be
circumcised, including houseborn slaves and
those acquired with money from any foreigner
who is not of your descendants.* 13 Yes, both
the houseborn slaves and those acquired with
money must be circumcised. Thus my covenant
will be in your flesh as an everlasting covenant.
14 If a male is uncircumcised, that is, if the flesh
of his foreskin has not been cut away, such a one
will be cut off from his people; he has broken
my covenant.
15 God further said to Abraham: As for Sarai
your wife, do not call her Sarai; her name will be
Sarah.† 16 I will bless her, and I will give you a
son by her. Her also will I bless; she will give rise
to nations, and rulers of peoples will issue from
her.* 17 Abraham fell face down and laughed† as
he said to himself, "Can a child be born to a man
who is a hundred years old? Can Sarah give birth
at ninety?"* 18 So Abraham said to God, "If only
Ishmael could live in your favor!" 19 God replied:
Even so, your wife Sarah is to bear you a son, and
you shall call him Isaac. It is with him that I will
maintain my covenant as an everlasting covenant
and with his descendants after him.* 20 Now
as for Ishmael, I will heed you: I hereby bless
him. I will make him fertile and will multiply
him exceedingly. He will become the father of
twelve chieftains, and I will make of him a great
nation.* 21 But my covenant I will maintain with
Isaac, whom Sarah shall bear to you by this time
next year.* 22 When he had finished speaking
with Abraham, God departed from him.
23 Then Abraham took his son Ishmael and all
his slaves, whether born in his house or acquired
with his money—every male among the members
of Abraham's household—and he circumcised
the flesh of their foreskins on that same day, as
God had told him to do. 24 Abraham was ninety-
nine years old when the flesh of his foreskin was
circumcised,* 25 and his son Ishmael was thirteen
years old when the flesh of his foreskin was cir-
cumcised. 26 Thus, on that same day Abraham
and his son Ishmael were circumcised; 27 and all
the males of his household, including the slaves
born in his house or acquired with his money
from foreigners, were circumcised with him.

Abraham's Visitors

18 1 † The LORD appeared to Abraham by the
oak of Mamre, as he sat in the entrance

† Abiram (Nm 16:1; 1 Kgs 16:34). The additional *-ha-* in the form Abraham is explained by popular etymology as coming from *ab-hamon goyim*, "father of a multitude of nations."

17:10 *Circumcised*: circumcision was widely practiced in the ancient world, usually as an initiation rite for males at puberty. By shifting the time of circumcision to the eighth day after birth, biblical religion made it no longer a "rite of passage" but the sign of the eternal covenant between God and the community descending from Abraham.

17:15 Sarai and Sarah are variant forms of the same name, both meaning "princess."

17:17 *Laughed*: *yishaq*, which is also the Hebrew form of the name "Isaac"; similar explanations of the name are given in Gn 18:12 and 21:6.

18:1 Chapters 18 and 19 combined form a continuous narrative, concluding the story of Abraham and his nephew Lot that began in 13:2–18. The mysterious men visit Abraham in Mamre to promise him and Sarah a child the following year (18:1–15) and then visit Lot

17:7 Ps 105:42; Lk 1:72–73; Gal 3:16.
17:8 Ex 32:13; Dt 1:8; 14:2; Lk 1:55; Acts 7:5.
17:10 Jn 7:22; Acts 7:8; Rom 4:11.
17:11 Sir 44:20.
17:12 Lv 12:3; Lk 1:59; 2:21.
17:16 Gn 18:10; Gal 4:23.
17:17 Rom 4:19; Heb 11:11–12.
17:19 Gn 11:30; 21:2; Ex 32:13; Sir 44:22.
17:20 Gn 16:10; 21:13, 18; 25:12–16.
17:21 Gn 18:14; 21:2; 26:2–5; Rom 9:7.
17:24 Gn 17:10; Rom 4:11.

of his tent, while the day was growing hot.
[2] Looking up, he saw three men standing near
him. When he saw them, he ran from the en-
trance of the tent to greet them; and bowing to
the ground,* [3] he said: "Sir,† if it please you, do
not go on past your servant. [4] Let some water be
brought, that you may bathe your feet, and then
rest under the tree. [5] Now that you have come to
your servant, let me bring you a little food, that
you may refresh yourselves; and afterward you
may go on your way." "Very well," they replied,
"do as you have said."
[6] Abraham hurried into the tent to Sarah and
said, "Quick, three measures† of bran flour!
Knead it and make bread." [7] He ran to the herd,
picked out a tender, choice calf, and gave it to a
servant, who quickly prepared it. [8] Then he got
some curds† and milk, as well as the calf that had
been prepared, and set these before them, wait-
ing on them under the tree while they ate.
[9] "Where is your wife Sarah?" they asked him.
"There in the tent," he replied. [10] One of them†
said, "I will return to you about this time next
year, and Sarah will then have a son." Sarah was
listening at the entrance of the tent, just behind
him.* [11] Now Abraham and Sarah were old, ad-
vanced in years, and Sarah had stopped having
her menstrual periods.* [12] So Sarah laughed† to
herself and said, "Now that I am worn out and
my husband is old, am I still to have sexual plea-
sure?" [13] But the LORD said to Abraham: "Why did
Sarah laugh and say, 'Will I really bear a child, old
as I am?' [14] Is anything too marvelous for the LORD
to do? At the appointed time, about this time next
year, I will return to you, and Sarah will have a
son."* [15] Sarah lied, saying, "I did not laugh," be-
cause she was afraid. But he said, "Yes, you did."

Abraham Intercedes for Sodom

[16] With Abraham walking with them to see
them on their way, the men set out from there
and looked down toward Sodom. [17] The LORD
considered: Shall I hide from Abraham what I
am about to do, [18] now that he is to become a
great and mighty nation, and all the nations of
the earth are to find blessing in him?* [19] Indeed, I
have singled him out that he may direct his chil-
dren and his household in the future to keep the
way of the LORD by doing what is right and just,
so that the LORD may put into effect for Abra-
ham the promises he made about him. [20] * So
the LORD said: The outcry against Sodom and
Gomorrah is so great, and their sin so grave,†
[21] that I must go down to see whether or not their

Live It!

What's So Funny?

Laughter is not a word we usually associate with the Bible, and certainly not with the Old Testament. Most of the stories are serious, filled with accounts of sacrifice, battles, and the Covenant. But here is Sarah, an old woman, long past childbearing age. She overhears one of Abraham's mysterious guests tell him that in a year he and Sarah will have a son (see Gn 18:10). How can she help but laugh? She and Abraham do produce, of course, a son called Isaac, whose Hebrew name, *Yishaq*, means "laughed." Sarah's cynical chuckles must have turned to joyful laughs at the birth of her beloved son. Laughter is a wonderful response to the gift of life and is a natural and often spontaneous response to God's presence within us and around us.

"Is anything too marvelous for the LORD to do?" (verse 14). We are all tempted to laugh at the notion that miracles can happen to us. As we grow in faith and open ourselves to God's goodness, our laughter will change from skeptical laughter to joyful laughter.

▶ **Gn 18:9–15**

† in Sodom to investigate and then to punish the corrupt city (19:1–29). Between the two visits, Abraham questions God about the justice of punishing Sodom (18:16–33). At the end of the destruction of Sodom, there is a short narrative about Lot as the ancestor of Moab and the Ammonites (19:30–38).

18:3 Abraham addresses the leader of the group, whom he does not yet recognize as the Lord; in the next two verses he speaks to all three men. The other two are later (Gn 19:1) identified as angels. The shifting numbers and identification of the visitors are a narrative way of expressing the mysterious presence of God.

18:6 *Three measures*: Hebrew *seah*; three seahs equal one ephah, about half a bushel.

18:8 *Curds*: a type of soft cheese or yogurt.

18:10 *One of them*: i.e., the Lord.

18:12 *Sarah laughed*: a play on the verb "laugh," which prefigures the name of Isaac; see note on 17:17.

18:20 The immorality of the cities was already hinted at in 13:13, when Lot made his choice to live there. The "outcry" comes from the victims of the injustice and violence rampant in the city, which will shortly be illustrated in the treatment of the visitors. The outcry of the Hebrews under the harsh treatment of Pharaoh (Ex 3:7) came up to God who reacts in anger at mistreatment of the poor

* **18:2** Heb 13:1–2.
18:10 Gn 17:19; 21:1; 2 Kgs 4:16; Rom 9:9.
18:11 Gn 17:17; Rom 4:19; Heb 11:11–12.
18:14 Mt 19:26; Mk 10:27; Lk 1:37; 18:27; Rom 4:21.
18:18 Lk 1:55.
18:20 Gn 19:13; Is 3:9; Lk 17:28; Jude 7.

GN

Pray It!

Get Close to God

Our prayers reveal what we believe about God and what we value. Abraham's bargaining for the inhabitants of Sodom and Gomorrah shows his faith, his care for others, and his closeness with God. Although he is humble, he deals with God as a friend whom he is not afraid to be honest with.

We too must be honest with God in our prayer. Many Christians simply do not trust God enough to be completely themselves with God. They are afraid to share their doubts, anger, grief, and frustrations. But God is big enough to handle it all. Find a way in your prayer time to share your innermost thoughts and feelings with God. For some people, journaling helps; others yell and shout aloud at the Lord. Remember that love requires freedom and God wants to be invited in. Tell God what is on your mind right now. Don't hold back.

▶ **Gn 18:22–33**

actions are as bad as the cry against them that comes to me. I mean to find out.

[22]As the men turned and walked on toward Sodom, Abraham remained standing before the LORD. [23]Then Abraham drew near and said: "Will you really sweep away the righteous with the wicked? [24]Suppose there were fifty righteous people in the city; would you really sweep away and not spare the place for the sake of the fifty righteous people within it? [25]Far be it from you to do such a thing, to kill the righteous with the wicked, so that the righteous and the wicked are treated alike! Far be it from you! Should not the judge of all the world do what is just?"* [26]The LORD replied: If I find fifty righteous people in the city of Sodom, I will spare the whole place for their sake. [27]Abraham spoke up again: "See how I am presuming to speak to my Lord, though I am only dust and ashes!* [28]What if there are five less than fifty righteous people? Will you destroy the whole city because of those five?" I will not destroy it, he answered, if I find forty-five there. [29]But Abraham persisted, saying, "What if only forty are found there?" He replied: I will refrain from doing it for the sake of the forty. [30]Then he said, "Do not let my Lord be angry if I go on. What if only thirty are found there?" He replied: I will refrain from doing it if I can find thirty there. [31]Abraham went on, "Since I have thus presumed to speak to my Lord, what if there are no more than twenty?" I will not destroy it, he answered, for the sake of the twenty. [32]But he persisted: "Please, do not let my Lord be angry if I speak up this last time. What if ten are found there?" For the sake of the ten, he replied, I will not destroy it.*

[33]The LORD departed as soon as he had finished speaking with Abraham, and Abraham returned home.

Destruction of Sodom and Gomorrah†

19 [1]The two angels reached Sodom in the evening, as Lot was sitting at the gate of Sodom. When Lot saw them, he got up to greet them; and bowing down with his face to the ground, [2]he said, "Please, my lords,† come aside into your servant's house for the night, and bathe your feet; you can get up early to continue your journey." But they replied, "No, we will pass the night in the town square."* [3]He urged them so strongly, however, that they turned aside to his place and entered his house. He prepared a banquet for them, baking unleavened bread, and they dined.

[4]* Before they went to bed, the townsmen of Sodom, both young and old—all the people to the last man—surrounded the house. [5]They called to Lot and said to him, "Where are the men who came to your house tonight? Bring them out to us that we may have sexual relations with them." [6]Lot went out to meet them at the entrance. When he had shut the door behind him, [7]he said, "I beg you, my brothers, do not do this wicked thing! [8]I have two daughters who have never had sexual relations with men. Let me bring them out to you,† and you may do to

---

(cf. Ex 22:21–23; Is 5:7). Sodom and Gomorrah became types of sinful cities in biblical literature. Is 1:9–10; 3:9 sees their sin as lack of social justice, Ez 16:46–51, as disregard for the poor, and Jer 23:14, as general immorality. In the Genesis story, the sin is violation of the sacred duty of hospitality by the threatened rape of Lot's guests.

19:1–29 The story takes place in one day (counting a day from the previous evening): evening (v. 1), dawn (v. 15), and sunrise (v. 23). The passage resembles Jgs 19:15–25, which suggests dependence of one story on the other.

19:2 *My lords*: Lot does not yet know that the men are God's messengers; cf. 18:3.

19:8 *Let me bring them out to you*: the authority of a patriarch

---

18:25 Dt 32:4; Jb 8:3, 20; Wis 12:15.
18:27 Sir 10:9; 17:27.
18:32 Jer 5:1; Ez 22:30.
19:2 Heb 13:1–2.
19:4–9 Jgs 19:22–25; Jude 7.

them as you please. But do not do anything to
these men, for they have come under the shelter
of my roof." [9]They replied, "Stand back! This
man," they said, "came here as a resident alien,
and now he dares to give orders! We will treat
you worse than them!" With that, they pressed
hard against Lot, moving in closer to break down
the door.* [10]But his guests put out their hands,
pulled Lot inside with them, and closed the
door; [11]they struck the men at the entrance of
the house, small and great, with such a blinding
light† that they were utterly unable to find the
doorway.

[12]Then the guests said to Lot: "Who else be-
longs to you here? Sons-in-law, your sons, your
daughters, all who belong to you in the city—
take them away from this place!* [13]We are about
to destroy this place, for the outcry reaching the
LORD against those here is so great that the LORD
has sent us to destroy it."* [14]So Lot went out and
spoke to his sons-in-law, who had contracted
marriage with his daughters.† "Come on, leave
this place," he told them; "the LORD is about to
destroy the city." But his sons-in-law thought he
was joking.

[15]As dawn was breaking, the angels urged Lot
on, saying, "Come on! Take your wife with you
and your two daughters who are here, or you will
be swept away in the punishment of the city."
[16]When he hesitated, the men, because of the
LORD's compassion for him, seized his hand and
the hands of his wife and his two daughters and
led them to safety outside the city. [17]As soon as
they had brought them outside, they said: "Flee
for your life! Do not look back or stop anywhere
on the Plain. Flee to the hills at once, or you will
be swept away."* [18]"Oh, no, my lords!" Lot re-
plied to them. [19]"You have already shown favor
to your servant, doing me the great kindness of
saving my life. But I cannot flee to the hills, or
the disaster will overtake and kill me. [20]Look,
this town ahead is near enough to escape to. It is
only a small place.† Let me flee there—is it not
a small place?—to save my life." [21]"Well, then,"
he replied, "I grant you this favor too. I will
not overthrow the town you have mentioned.
[22]Hurry, escape there! I cannot do anything until
you arrive there." That is why the town is called
Zoar.*

[23]The sun had risen over the earth when Lot
arrived in Zoar, [24]and the LORD rained down sul-
fur upon Sodom and Gomorrah, fire from the
LORD out of heaven.* [25]He overthrew† those cit-
ies and the whole Plain, together with the inhab-
itants of the cities and the produce of the soil.*
[26]But Lot's wife looked back, and she was turned
into a pillar of salt.*

[27]The next morning Abraham hurried to the
place where he had stood before the LORD. [28]As
he looked down toward Sodom and Gomor-
rah and the whole region of the Plain,† he saw
smoke over the land rising like the smoke from
a kiln.*

Live It!

Be Kind to Strangers

If our first gesture to outsiders were one of respect, kindness, and gracious hospitality, what might our world be like? The story of Sodom and Gomorrah shows us the results of disrespect, inhospitality, and the attempted sexual abuse of strangers. Like Abraham, Lot is a wonderful host. But the people of Sodom want Lot's visitors for their own sexual pleasure; being welcoming and hospitable is clearly the last thing on their minds.

As children of God, we have a responsibility to extend our kindness to stranger and friend alike. So how are visitors or new students treated in your school? How are guests treated in your home?

▶ **Gn 19:1–11**

---

† within his house was virtually absolute. Lot's extreme response of offering his daughters to a violent mob seems to be motivated by the obligation of hospitality.

19:11 *Blinding light*: an extraordinary flash that temporarily dazed the wicked men and revealed to Lot the true nature of his guests.

19:14 It is uncertain whether Lot's sons-in-law were fully married to his daughters or only "engaged" to them (Israelite "engagement" was the first part of the marriage ceremony), or even whether the daughters involved were the same as, or different from, the two daughters who were still in their father's house.

19:20 *A small place*: the Hebrew word *misar*, lit., "a little thing," has the same root consonants as the name of the town Zoar in v. 22.

19:25 *Overthrew*: this term, lit., "turned upside down," is used consistently to describe the destruction of the cities of the Plain. The imagery of earthquake and subsequent fire fits the geology of this region.

19:28–29 In a deft narrative detail, Abraham looks down from the height east of Hebron, from which he could easily see the region at

* **19:9** Gn 13:12; 2 Pt 2:7–8.
19:12 2 Pt 2:7–9.
19:13 Is 1:7, 9; Ez 16:49–50; Zep 2:9.
19:17 Wis 10:6.
19:22 Wis 10:6.
19:24 Ps 9:6; 11:6; 107:34; Wis 10:7; Sir 16:8; Is 1:9; Lk 17:29; 2 Pt 2:6.
19:25 Dt 29:22; Is 13:19; Jer 50:40; Lam 4:6; Am 4:11.
19:26 Wis 10:7; Lk 17:32.
19:28 Rev 9:2; 14:10–11.

29 When God destroyed the cities of the Plain,
he remembered Abraham and sent Lot away
from the upheaval that occurred when God over-
threw the cities where Lot had been living.

Moabites and Ammonites†

30 Since Lot was afraid to stay in Zoar, he and
his two daughters went up from Zoar and settled
in the hill country, where he lived with his two
daughters in a cave. 31 The firstborn said to the
younger: "Our father is getting old, and there is
not a man in the land to have intercourse with us
as is the custom everywhere. 32 Come, let us ply
our father with wine and then lie with him, that
we may ensure posterity by our father." 33 So that
night they plied their father with wine, and the
firstborn went in and lay with her father; but he
was not aware of her lying down or getting up.
34 The next day the firstborn said to the younger:
"Last night I lay with my father. Let us ply him
with wine again tonight, and then you go in and
lie with him, that we may ensure posterity by
our father." 35 So that night, too, they plied their
father with wine, and then the younger one went
in and lay with him; but he was not aware of her
lying down or getting up.
36 Thus the two daughters of Lot became preg-
nant by their father. 37 The firstborn gave birth
to a son whom she named Moab, saying, "From
my father."† He is the ancestor of the Moabites
of today.* 38 The younger one, too, gave birth to
a son, and she named him Ammon, saying, "The
son of my kin."† He is the ancestor of the Am-
monites of today.*

Abraham at Gerar†

20 1 From there Abraham journeyed on to
the region of the Negeb, where he settled
between Kadesh and Shur.† While he resided
in Gerar as an alien, 2 Abraham said of his wife
Sarah, "She is my sister." So Abimelech, king
of Gerar, sent and took Sarah. 3 But God came
to Abimelech in a dream one night and said to
him: You are about to die because of the woman
you have taken, for she has a husband. 4 Abim-
elech, who had not approached her, said: "O
Lord, would you kill an innocent man? 5 Was
he not the one who told me, 'She is my sister'?
She herself also stated, 'He is my brother.' I acted
with pure heart and with clean hands." 6 † God
answered him in the dream: Yes, I know you did
it with a pure heart. In fact, it was I who kept
you from sinning against me; that is why I did
not let you touch her. 7 So now, return the man's
wife so that he may intercede for you, since he
is a prophet,† that you may live. If you do not
return her, you can be sure that you and all who
are yours will die.
8 Early the next morning Abimelech called all
his servants and informed them of everything
that had happened, and the men were filled
with fear. 9 Then Abimelech summoned Abra-
ham and said to him: "What have you done to
us! What wrong did I do to you that you would
have brought such great guilt on me and my
kingdom? You have treated me in an intolerable
way. 10 What did you have in mind," Abimelech
asked him, "that you would do such a thing?"
11 Abraham answered, "I thought there would be
no fear of God† in this place, and so they would
kill me on account of my wife. 12 Besides, she
really is my sister,† but only my father's daugh-
ter, not my mother's; and so she became my
wife. 13 When God sent me wandering from my
father's house, I asked her: 'Would you do me
this favor? In whatever place we come to, say: He
is my brother.' "*
14 Then Abimelech took flocks and herds and
male and female slaves and gave them to Abra-
ham; and he restored his wife Sarah to him.
15 Then Abimelech said, "Here, my land is at your
disposal; settle wherever you please." 16 To Sarah

---

† the southern end of the Dead Sea, where the cities of the Plain were probably located.

19:30–38 This Israelite tale about the origin of Israel's neighbors east of the Jordan and the Dead Sea was told partly to ridicule these ethnically related but rival nations and partly to give popular etymologies for their names. The stylized nature of the story is seen in the names of the daughters ("the firstborn" and "the younger"), the ease with which they fool their father, and the identical descriptions of the encounters.

19:37 *From my father*: in Hebrew, *me'abi*, similar in sound to the name "Moab."

19:38 *The son of my kin*: in Hebrew, *ben-ammi*, similar in sound to the name "Ammonites."

20:1–18 Abraham again passes off his wife Sarah as his sister to escape trouble in a foreign land (cf. 12:10–13:1, the J source). The story appears to be from a different source (according to some, E) and deals with the ethical questions of the incident. Gn 26:6–11 is yet another retelling of the story, but with Isaac and Rebekah as characters instead of Abraham and Sarah.

20:1 *Kadesh and Shur*: Kadesh-barnea was a major oasis on the southernmost border of Canaan, and Shur was probably the "way to Shur," the road to Egypt. Gerar was a royal city in the area, but has not been identified with certainty.

20:6 Abimelech is exonerated of blame, but by that fact not cleared of the consequences of his act. He is still under the sentence of death for abducting another man's wife; the consequences result from the deed not the intention.

20:7 *Prophet*: only here is Abraham explicitly called "prophet," Hebrew *nabi* (cf. Ps 105:15).

20:11 *Fear of God* is the traditional though unsatisfactory rendering of Hebrew *yir'at YHWH*, literally, "revering Yahweh." The phrase refers neither to the emotion of fear nor to religious reverence of a general kind. Rather it refers to adherence to a single deity (in a polytheistic culture), honoring that deity with prayers, rituals, and obedience. The phrase occurs again in 26:24; 43:23; and 50:19. It is very common in the wisdom literature of the Bible.

20:12 *My sister*: marrying one's half sister was prohibited later in Israel's history.

---

* **19:37** Dt 2:9. **19:38** Dt 2:19. **20:13** Gn 12:13.

he said: "I hereby give your brother a thousand shekels of silver. This will preserve your honor before all who are with you and will exonerate you before everyone." 17 Abraham then interceded with God, and God restored health to Abimelech, to his wife, and his maidservants, so that they bore children; 18 for the LORD had closed every womb in Abimelech's household on account of Abraham's wife Sarah.

Birth of Isaac†

21 1 The LORD took note of Sarah as he had said he would; the LORD did for her as he had promised.* 2 Sarah became pregnant and bore Abraham a son in his old age, at the set time that God had stated.* 3 Abraham gave the name Isaac to this son of his whom Sarah bore him.* 4 When his son Isaac was eight days old, Abraham circumcised him, as God had commanded.* 5 Abraham was a hundred years old when his son Isaac was born to him. 6 Sarah then said, "God has given me cause to laugh,† and all who hear of it will laugh with me.* 7 Who would ever have told Abraham," she added, "that Sarah would nurse children! Yet I have borne him a son in his old age." 8 The child grew and was weaned, and Abraham held a great banquet on the day of the child's weaning.

9 Sarah noticed the son whom Hagar the Egyptian had borne to Abraham playing with her son Isaac; 10 so she demanded of Abraham: "Drive out that slave and her son! No son of that slave is going to share the inheritance with my son Isaac!"* 11 Abraham was greatly distressed because it concerned a son of his.† 12 But God said to Abraham: Do not be distressed about the boy or about your slave woman. Obey Sarah, no matter what she asks of you; for it is through Isaac that descendants will bear your name.* 13 As for the son of the slave woman, I will make a nation of him also,† since he too is your offspring.

14 Early the next morning Abraham got some bread and a skin of water and gave them to Hagar. Then, placing the child on her back,† he sent her away. As she roamed aimlessly in the wilderness of Beer-sheba, 15 the water in the skin was used up. So she put the child down under one of the bushes, 16 and then went and sat down opposite him, about a bowshot away; for she said to herself, "I cannot watch the child die." As she sat opposite him, she wept aloud. 17 God

Pray It!

Hagar's Rescue

Genesis 21:9–21 is part two of the Hagar and Ishmael story begun in 16:1–16. Once again, Hagar is the victim of Sarah's jealousy. But this time God does not send her back. Seemingly facing certain death, Hagar receives from God the ability to see the opportunity for life in front of her. This time the writer of Genesis makes the point that God rescues the oppressed and abandoned. Hagar and Ishmael survive, and from their descendants, a great people emerges.

Hagar's story reminds us that God wants to rescue us from oppression and injustice. Often we want to ask God to magically take these things away. But because God has given human beings free will, we cannot always be spared from the injustice of others. In your prayer, you can always ask God to rescue you, to give you the vision to see the healthy choices you can make to improve your situation. Do that right now if you are in an unjust situation. God's grace can be found in all things, even during our darkest times.

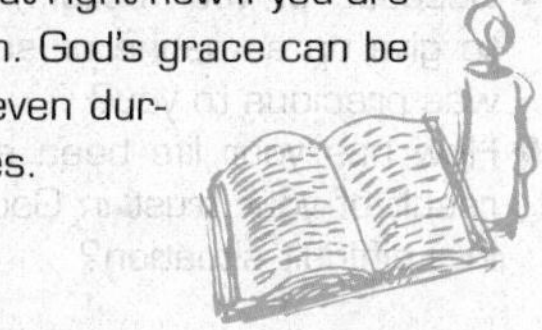

► Gn 21:9–21

† 21:1–21 The long-awaited birth of Isaac parallels the birth of Ishmael in chap. 16, precipitating a rivalry and expulsion as in that chapter. Though this chapter is unified, the focus of vv. 1–7 is exclusively on Sarah and Isaac, and the focus of vv. 8–21 is exclusively on Hagar and Ishmael. The promise of a son to the barren Sarah and elderly Abraham has been central to the previous chapters and now that promise comes true with the birth of Isaac. The other great promise, that of land, will be resolved, at least in an anticipatory way, in Abraham's purchase of the cave at Machpelah in chap. 23. The parallel births of the two boys has influenced the Lucan birth narratives of John the Baptist and Jesus (Lk 1–2).

21:6 *Laugh*: for the third time (cf. 17:17 and 18:12) there is laughter, playing on the similarity in Hebrew between the pronunciation of the name Isaac and words associated with laughter.

21:11 *A son of his*: Abraham is the father of both boys, but Sarah is the mother only of Isaac. Abraham is very concerned that Ishmael have a sufficient inheritance.

21:13 *I will make a nation of him also*: Ishmael's descendants are named in 25:12–18.

21:14 *Placing the child on her back*: a reading based on an emendation of the traditional Hebrew text. In the traditional Hebrew text, Abraham put the bread and the waterskin on Hagar's back, while her son apparently walked beside her. In this way the traditional Hebrew text harmonizes the data of the Priestly source, in which Ishmael would have been at least fourteen years old when Isaac was born; compare 16:16 with 21:5; cf. 17:25. But in the present Elohist (?) story, Ishmael is obviously a little boy, not much older than Isaac; cf. vv. 15, 18.

* **21:1** Gn 17:19; 18:10.
21:2 Gal 4:23; Heb 11:11.
21:3 Mt 1:2; Lk 3:34.
21:4 Gn 17:10–14; Acts 7:8.
21:6 Gn 17:17.
21:10 Jgs 11:2; Gal 4:30.
21:12 Rom 9:7; Heb 11:18.

GN

Pray It!

Ultimate Trust in God!

To us it seems horrible that God would ask Abraham to sacrifice his son Isaac. But this story is meant to be a sign of Abraham's complete trust in God. Ultimately, God prevented the sacrifice because God wanted not Isaac's death but Abraham's faith. Because of his willingness to respond to God's demand, Abraham is recognized as the father of our faith. Our trust in God should be as total as Abraham's trust was.

We probably won't ever be faced with the test of Abraham, but perhaps we will be faced with different, though equally difficult, tests of faith in our own lives. The story of Abraham shows us the power of faith. Because of Abraham's faith in God's promise, Isaac lived and became the father of Jacob, whose twelve sons became the twelve Tribes of Israel. In your prayer time, reflect or journal on the following questions:

- Because of your beliefs, have you ever had to give up someone or something that was precious to you?
- How has your life been enriched as a result of your trust in God in a difficult situation?

Gn 22:1–19

heard the boy's voice, and God's angel called to
Hagar from heaven: "What is the matter, Hagar?
Do not fear; God has heard the boy's voice in this
plight of his.* 18 Get up, lift up the boy and hold
him by the hand; for I will make of him a great
nation." 19 Then God opened her eyes, and she
saw a well of water. She went and filled the skin
with water, and then let the boy drink.
20 God was with the boy as he grew up. He lived
in the wilderness and became an expert bowman.
21 He lived in the wilderness of Paran. His mother
got a wife for him from the land of Egypt.

The Covenant at Beer-sheba

22 † At that time Abimelech, accompanied by
Phicol, the commander of his army, said to Abra-
ham: "God is with you in everything you do. 23 So
now, swear to me by God at this place† that you
will not deal falsely with me or with my progeny
and posterity, but will act as loyally toward me
and the land in which you reside as I have acted
toward you." 24 Abraham replied, "I so swear."
25 Abraham, however, reproached Abimelech
about a well that Abimelech's servants had seized
by force. 26 "I have no idea who did that," Abime-
lech replied. "In fact, you never told me about it,
nor did I ever hear of it until now."
27 Then Abraham took sheep and cattle and
gave them to Abimelech and the two made a
covenant. 28 Abraham also set apart seven ewe
lambs of the flock, 29 and Abimelech asked him,
"What is the purpose of these seven ewe lambs
that you have set apart?" 30 Abraham answered,
"The seven ewe lambs you shall accept from me
that you may be my witness that I dug this well."
31 This is why the place is called Beer-sheba; the
two of them took an oath there. 32 When they
had thus made the covenant in Beer-sheba,
Abimelech, along with Phicol, the commander
of his army, left to return to the land of the Phi-
listines.†
33 Abraham planted a tamarisk at Beer-sheba,
and there he invoked by name the LORD, God the
Eternal.† 34 Abraham resided in the land of the
Philistines for a long time.

The Testing of Abraham†

22 1 Some time afterward, God put Abraham
to the test and said to him: Abraham!
"Here I am!" he replied.* 2 Then God said: Take
your son Isaac, your only one, whom you love,
and go to the land of Moriah. There offer him up
as a burnt offering on one of the heights that I
will point out to you.* 3 Early the next morning
Abraham saddled his donkey, took with him two
of his servants and his son Isaac, and after cutting

† **21:22** Of the two related promises of progeny and land, that of progeny has been fulfilled in the previous chapter. Now the claim on the land begins to be solidified by Abimelech's recognition of Abraham's claim on the well at Beer-sheba; it will be furthered by Abraham's purchase of the cave at Machpelah in chap. 23. Two levels of editing are visible in the story: (1) vv. 22–24, 27, 32, the general covenant with Abimelech; (2) vv. 25–26, 28–30, 31, Abraham's claim on the well. Both versions play on the root of the Hebrew word *sheba'*, which means "seven" and "swear," and the place name Beer-sheba.

21:23 *This place*: Beer-sheba (v. 31). Abimelech had come from Gerar (20:2), about thirty miles west of Beer-sheba.

21:32 *Philistines*: one of the Sea Peoples, who migrated from Mycenaean Greece around 1200 B.C. and settled on the coastland of Canaan, becoming a principal rival of Israel. Non-biblical texts do not use the term "Philistine" before ca. 1200 B.C.; it is probable that this usage and those in chap. 26 are anachronistic, perhaps applying a later ethnic term for an earlier, less-known one.

21:33 *God the Eternal*: in Hebrew, *'el 'olam*, perhaps the name of the deity of the pre-Israelite sanctuary at Beer-sheba, but used by Abraham as a title of God; cf. Is 40:28.

22:1–19 The divine demand that Abraham sacrifice to God the son of promise is the greatest of his trials; after the successful completion of the test, he has only to buy a burial site for Sarah and find a wife for

* **21:17** Gn 16:7. **22:1** Sir 44:20. **22:2** 2 Chr 3:1; 1 Mc 2:52; Heb 11:17.

the wood for the burnt offering, set out for the
place of which God had told him.
4 On the third day Abraham caught sight of the
place from a distance. 5 Abraham said to his ser-
vants: "Stay here with the donkey, while the boy
and I go on over there. We will worship and then
come back to you." 6 So Abraham took the wood
for the burnt offering and laid it on his son Isaac,
while he himself carried the fire and the knife.
As the two walked on together, 7 Isaac spoke to
his father Abraham. "Father!" he said. "Here I
am," he replied. Isaac continued, "Here are the
fire and the wood, but where is the sheep for the
burnt offering?" 8 "My son," Abraham answered,
"God will provide the sheep for the burnt offer-
ing." Then the two walked on together.
9 When they came to the place of which God
had told him, Abraham built an altar there and
arranged the wood on it. Next he bound† his son
Isaac, and put him on top of the wood on the al-
tar.* 10 Then Abraham reached out and took the
knife to slaughter his son.* 11 But the angel of
the LORD called to him from heaven, "Abraham,
Abraham!" "Here I am," he answered. 12 "Do not
lay your hand on the boy," said the angel. "Do
not do the least thing to him. For now I know
that you fear God, since you did not withhold
from me your son, your only one."* 13 Abraham
looked up and saw a single ram caught by its
horns in the thicket. So Abraham went and took
the ram and offered it up as a burnt offering in
place of his son.† 14 Abraham named that place
Yahweh-yireh;† hence people today say, "On the
mountain the LORD will provide."
15 † A second time the angel of the LORD called
to Abraham from heaven 16 * and said: "I swear
by my very self—oracle of the LORD—that because
you acted as you did in not withholding from me
your son, your only one, 17 I will bless you and
make your descendants as countless as the stars
of the sky and the sands of the seashore; your
descendants will take possession of the gates of
their enemies,* 18 and in your descendants all the
nations of the earth will find blessing, because
you obeyed my command."*
19 Abraham then returned to his servants, and
they set out together for Beer-sheba, where Abra-
ham lived.

Nahor's Descendants†

20 Some time afterward, the news came to
Abraham: "Milcah too has borne sons to your
brother Nahor: 21 Uz, his firstborn, his brother
Buz, Kemuel the father of Aram, 22 Chesed, Hazo,
Pildash, Jidlaph, and Bethuel." 23 Bethuel became
the father of Rebekah. These eight Milcah bore
to Nahor, Abraham's brother. 24 His concubine,
whose name was Reumah, also bore children:
Tebah, Gaham, Tahash, and Maacah.

Purchase of a Burial Plot†

23 1 The span of Sarah's life was one hun-
dred and twenty-seven years. 2 She died
in Kiriath-arba—now Hebron—in the land of
Canaan, and Abraham proceeded to mourn
and weep for her. 3 Then he left the side of his
deceased wife and addressed the Hittites:† 4 "Al-
though I am a resident alien† among you, sell

Isaac. The story is widely recognized as a literary masterpiece, depicting in a few lines God as the absolute Lord, inscrutable yet ultimately gracious, and Abraham, acting in moral grandeur as the great ancestor of Israel. Abraham speaks simply, with none of the wordy evasions of chaps. 13 and 21. The style is laconic; motivations and thoughts are not explained, and the reader cannot but wonder at the scene. In vv. 15–18, the angel repeats the seventh and climactic promise. *Moriah*: the mountain is not given a precise geographical location here, though 2 Chr 3:1 identifies Moriah as the mountain of Jerusalem where Solomon built the Temple; Abraham is thus the first to worship there. The word "Moriah" is a play on the verb "to see" (Heb. *ra'ah*); the wordplay is continued in v. 8, "God will provide (lit., "see")" and in v. 14, Yahweh-yireh, meaning "the Lord will see/provide."

22:9 *Bound*: the Hebrew verb is *'aqad*, from which is derived the noun Akedah, "the binding (of Isaac)," the traditional Jewish name for this incident.

22:13 While the Bible recognizes that firstborn males belong to God (Ex 13:11–16; 34:19–20), and provides an alternate sacrifice to redeem firstborn sons, the focus here is on Abraham's being tested by God (v. 1). But the widely attested practice of child sacrifice underscores, for all its horror today, the realism of the test.

22:14 *Yahweh-yireh*: a Hebrew expression meaning "the Lord will see/provide." See note on vv. 1–19.

22:15–19 The seventh and climactic statement of the blessings to Abraham. Unlike the other statements, which were purely promissory, this one is presented as a reward for Abraham's extraordinary trust.

22:20–24 The descendants to the second generation of Nahor, Abraham's brother, who married Milcah. Of Terah's three sons (11:27), the oldest, Abraham, fathered Isaac (21:1–7), and the youngest, Haran (who died in Ur), fathered Lot. Abraham is now told that Nahor had eight children by Milcah and four by his concubine Reumah. Apart from the notice about the children born to Abraham by his second wife, Keturah (25:1–6), all the information about Terah's family to the second generation is now complete. It is noteworthy that Jacob will, like Nahor, have eight children by his wives and four by his concubines.

23:1–20 The occasion for purchasing the land is the need for a burial site for Sarah, for it would be unthinkable to bury Sarah outside of the promised land. One of the two great promises to Abraham, that of progeny, has been fulfilled (21:1–7). And now the promise of land is to be fulfilled, through a kind of down payment on the full possession that will take place only with the conquest under Joshua and during the reign of David. This purchase has been prepared for by Abimelech's recognition of Abraham's claim to the well at Beer-sheba (21:22–34). Among the ancestral stories this narrative is one of two that are entirely from the P source (chap. 17 being the other). The Priestly writers may have intended to encourage the generation of the exile to a renewed hope of repossessing their land.

23:3 *The Hittites*: in the Bible the term is applied to several different groups—inhabitants of the second-millennium Hittite empire in Asia Minor and northern Syria, residents of the Neo-Hittite kingdoms in northern Syria in the first part of the first millennium, and (following Assyrian terminology) the inhabitants of Syria and Palestine. The third group is meant here.

23:4 *A resident alien*: such a one would normally not have the

---

22:9 Jas 2:21.
22:10 Wis 10:5.
22:12 Rom 8:32; 1 Jn 4:9.
22:16–17 Gn 15:5; Ex 32:13; Lk 1:73; Rom 4:13; Heb 6:13–14; 11:12.
22:17 Gn 24:60.
22:18 Gn 12:3; 18:18; 26:4; Sir 44:21; Acts 3:25; Gal 3:16.

me from your holdings a burial place, that I
may bury my deceased wife."* 5 The Hittites an-
swered Abraham: "Please, 6 sir, listen to us! You
are a mighty leader among us. Bury your dead
in the choicest of our burial sites. None of us
would deny you his burial ground for the burial
of your dead." 7 Abraham, however, proceeded
to bow low before the people of the land, the
Hittites, 8 and said to them: "If you will allow
me room for burial of my dead, listen to me!
Intercede for me with Ephron, son of Zohar, 9 so
that he will sell me the cave of Machpelah that
he owns; it is at the edge of his field. Let him
sell it to me in your presence at its full price for
a burial place."

10 Now Ephron was sitting with the Hittites.
So Ephron the Hittite replied to Abraham in the
hearing of the Hittites, all who entered the gate
of his city: 11 "Please, sir, listen to me! I give you
both the field and the cave in it; in the presence
of my people I give it to you. Bury your dead!"
12 But Abraham, after bowing low before the
people of the land, 13 addressed Ephron in the
hearing of these men: "If only you would please
listen to me! I will pay you the price of the field.
Accept it from me, that I may bury my dead
there." 14 Ephron replied to Abraham, "Please,
15 sir, listen to me! A piece of land worth four
hundred shekels† of silver—what is that between
you and me? Bury your dead!" 16 * Abraham ac-
cepted Ephron's terms; he weighed out to him
the silver that Ephron had stipulated in the hear-
ing of the Hittites, four hundred shekels of silver
at the current market value.†

17 * Thus Ephron's field in Machpelah, facing
Mamre, together with its cave and all the trees
anywhere within its limits, was conveyed 18 to
Abraham by purchase in the presence of the
Hittites, all who entered the gate of Ephron's city.
19 After this, Abraham buried his wife Sarah in
the cave of the field of Machpelah, facing Mam-
re—now Hebron—in the land of Canaan. 20 Thus
the field with its cave was transferred from the
Hittites to Abraham as a burial place.

Isaac and Rebekah†

24 1 Abraham was old, having seen many
days, and the LORD had blessed him in
every way. 2 * Abraham said to the senior servant
of his household, who had charge of all his pos-
sessions: "Put your hand under my thigh,† 3 and
I will make you swear by the LORD, the God of
heaven and the God of earth, that you will not
take a wife for my son from the daughters of the
Canaanites among whom I live,* 4 but that you
will go to my own land and to my relatives to get
a wife for my son Isaac." 5 The servant asked him:
"What if the woman is unwilling to follow me
to this land? Should I then take your son back
to the land from which you came?" 6 Abraham
told him, "Never take my son back there for any
reason! 7 The LORD, the God of heaven, who took
me from my father's house and the land of my
relatives, and who confirmed by oath the prom-
ise he made to me, 'I will give this land to your
descendants'—he will send his angel before you,
and you will get a wife for my son there.* 8 If the
woman is unwilling to follow you, you will be
released from this oath to me. But never take my
son back there!" 9 So the servant put his hand un-
der the thigh of his master Abraham and swore
to him concerning this matter.

10 The servant then took ten of his master's
camels, and bearing all kinds of gifts from his
master, he made his way to the city of Nahor†
in Aram Naharaim. 11 Near evening, at the time

---

† right to own property. The importance of Abraham's purchase of the field in Machpelah, which is worded in technical legal terms, lies in the fact that it gave his descendants their first, though small, land rights in the country that God had promised the patriarch they would one day inherit as their own. Abraham therefore insists on purchasing the field and not receiving it as a gift.

23:15 *Four hundred shekels*: probably an exorbitant sum; Jeremiah (32:9) paid only seventeen shekels for his field in Anathoth, though the Babylonian invasion no doubt helped to reduce the price.

23:16 *The current market value*: the standard weight called a shekel varied according to time and place.

24:1–67 The story of Abraham and Sarah is drawing to a close. The promises of progeny (21:1–7) and land (chap. 23) have been fulfilled and Sarah has died (23:1–2). Abraham's last duty is to ensure that his son Isaac shares in the promises. Isaac must take a wife from his own people (vv. 3–7), so the promises may be fulfilled. The extraordinary length of this story and its development of a single theme contrast strikingly with the spare style of the preceding Abraham and Sarah stories. It points ahead to the Jacob and Joseph stories.

The length of the story is partly caused by its meticulous attention to the sign (vv. 12–14), its fulfillment (vv. 15–20), and the servant's retelling of sign and fulfillment to Rebekah's family to win their consent (vv. 34–49).

24:2 *Put your hand under my thigh*: the symbolism of this act was apparently connected with the Hebrew concept of children issuing from their father's "thigh" (the literal meaning of "direct descendants" in 46:26; Ex 1:5). Perhaps the man who took such an oath was thought to bring the curse of sterility on himself if he did not fulfill his sworn promise. Jacob made Joseph swear in the same way (Gn 47:29). In both these instances, the oath was taken to carry out the last request of a man upon his death.

24:10 *Nahor*: it is uncertain whether this is the place where Abraham's brother Nahor (11:27) had lived or whether it is the city Nahur, named in the Mari documents (nineteenth and eighteenth centuries B.C.), near the confluence of the Balikh and Middle Euphrates rivers. *Aram Naharaim*: lit., "Aram between the two rivers," is the Yahwist designation for Terah's homeland. The two rivers are the Habur and the Euphrates. The Priestly designation for the area is Paddan-aram, which is from the Assyrian *padana*, "road or garden," and Aram, which refers to the people or land of the Arameans.

---

* **23:4** Gn 33:19; Acts 7:16; Heb 11:9.
23:16 Acts 7:16.
23:17–18 Gn 49:29–30.
24:2–3 Gn 47:29.
24:3 Gn 24:37; 28:1–2; Jgs 14:3; Tb 4:12.
24:7 Gn 12:7; Ex 6:8; Tb 5:17; Gal 3:16.

when women go out to draw water, he made the
camels kneel by the well outside the city. 12 Then
he said: "LORD, God of my master Abraham, let it
turn out favorably for me† today and thus deal
graciously with my master Abraham. 13 While I
stand here at the spring and the daughters of the
townspeople are coming out to draw water, 14 if
I say to a young woman, 'Please lower your jug,
that I may drink,' and she answers, 'Drink, and I
will water your camels, too,' then she is the one
whom you have decided upon for your servant
Isaac. In this way I will know that you have dealt
graciously with my master."

15 * He had scarcely finished speaking when
Rebekah—who was born to Bethuel, son of Mil-
cah, the wife of Abraham's brother Nahor—came
out with a jug on her shoulder. 16 The young
woman was very beautiful, a virgin, untouched
by man. She went down to the spring and filled
her jug. As she came up, 17 the servant ran to-
ward her and said, "Please give me a sip of water
from your jug." 18 "Drink, sir," she replied, and
quickly lowering the jug into her hand, she gave
him a drink. 19 When she had finished giving
him a drink, she said, "I will draw water for your
camels, too, until they have finished drinking."
20 With that, she quickly emptied her jug into the
drinking trough and ran back to the well to draw
more water, until she had drawn enough for all
the camels. 21 The man watched her the whole
time, silently waiting to learn whether or not the
LORD had made his journey successful. 22 When
the camels had finished drinking, the man took
out a gold nose-ring weighing half a shekel, and
two gold bracelets weighing ten shekels for her
wrists. 23 Then he asked her: "Whose daughter are
you? Tell me, please. And is there a place in your
father's house for us to spend the night?" 24 She
answered: "I am the daughter of Bethuel the son
of Milcah, whom she bore to Nahor. 25 We have
plenty of straw and fodder," she added, "and also
a place to spend the night." 26 The man then knelt
and bowed down to the LORD, 27 saying: "Blessed
be the LORD, the God of my master Abraham,
who has not let his kindness and fidelity toward
my master fail. As for me, the LORD has led me
straight to the house of my master's brother."

28 Then the young woman ran off and told
her mother's household what had happened.
29 * Now Rebekah had a brother named Laban.
Laban rushed outside to the man at the spring.
30 † When he saw the nose-ring and the bracelets
on his sister's arms and when he heard Rebekah
repeating what the man had said to her, he went
to him while he was standing by the camels at
the spring. 31 He said: "Come, blessed of the
LORD! Why are you standing outside when I have
made the house ready, as well as a place for the
camels?" 32 The man then went inside; and while
the camels were being unloaded and provided
with straw and fodder, water was brought to
bathe his feet and the feet of the men who were
with him. 33 But when food was set before him,
he said, "I will not eat until I have told my story."
"Go ahead," they replied.

34 "I am Abraham's servant," he began. 35 "The
LORD has blessed my master so abundantly that
he has become wealthy; he has given him flocks
and herds, silver and gold, male and female
slaves, and camels and donkeys. 36 My master's
wife Sarah bore a son to my master in her old
age, and he has given him everything he owns.
37 My master put me under oath, saying: 'You
shall not take a wife for my son from the daugh-
ters of the Canaanites in whose land I live; 38 in-
stead, you must go to my father's house, to my
own family, to get a wife for my son.' 39 When I
asked my master, 'What if the woman will not
follow me?' 40 he replied: 'The LORD, in whose
presence I have always walked, will send his an-
gel with you and make your journey successful,
and so you will get a wife for my son from my
own family and my father's house.* 41 Then you
will be freed from my curse. If you go to my fam-
ily and they refuse you, then, too, you will be free
from my curse.'†

42 "When I came to the spring today, I said:
'LORD, God of my master Abraham, please make
successful the journey I am on. 43 While I stand
here at the spring, if I say to a young woman who
comes out to draw water, 'Please give me a little
water from your jug,' 44 and she answers, 'Drink,
and I will draw water for your camels, too—then
she is the woman whom the LORD has decided
upon for my master's son.'

45 "I had scarcely finished saying this to myself
when Rebekah came out with a jug on her shoul-
der. After she went down to the spring and drew
water, I said to her, 'Please let me have a drink.'
46 She quickly lowered the jug she was carrying

†

24:12 *Let it turn out favorably for me*: let me have a favorable sign; cf. end of v. 14.

24:30 Laban becomes hospitable only when he sees the servant's rich gifts, which is in humorous contrast to his sister's spontaneous generosity toward the servant. Laban's opportunism points forward to his behavior in the Jacob stories (31:14–16).

24:41 *Curse*: this would be the consequence of failing to carry out the oath referred to in v. 3.

*

24:15 Gn 22:23.
24:29 Gn 27:43.
24:40 Tb 5:17; 10:13.

GN

and said, 'Drink, and I will water your camels,
too.' So I drank, and she watered the camels
also. 47 When I asked her, 'Whose daughter are
you?' she answered, 'The daughter of Bethuel,
son of Nahor, borne to Nahor by Milcah.' So I
put the ring on her nose and the bracelets on her
wrists. 48 Then I knelt and bowed down to the
LORD, blessing the LORD, the God of my master
Abraham, who had led me on the right road to
obtain the daughter of my master's kinsman for
his son. 49 Now, if you will act with kindness and
fidelity toward my master, let me know; but if
not, let me know that too. I can then proceed
accordingly."

50 * Laban and Bethuel said in reply: "This
thing comes from the LORD; we can say nothing
to you either for or against it. 51 Here is Rebekah,
right in front of you; take her and go, that she
may become the wife of your master's son, as the
LORD has said." 52 When Abraham's servant heard
their answer, he bowed to the ground before the
LORD. 53 Then he brought out objects of silver
and gold and clothing and presented them to Re-
bekah; he also gave costly presents to her brother
and mother. 54 After he and the men with him
had eaten and drunk, they spent the night there.
When they got up the next morning, he said,
"Allow me to return to my master."* 55 Her
brother and mother replied, "Let the young
woman stay with us a short while, say ten days;
after that she may go." 56 But he said to them,
"Do not detain me, now that the LORD has made
my journey successful; let me go back to my
master." 57 They answered, "Let us call the young
woman and see what she herself has to say about
it." 58 So they called Rebekah and asked her,
"Will you go with this man?" She answered, "I
will."† 59 At this they sent off their sister Rebekah
and her nurse with Abraham's servant and his
men. 60 They blessed Rebekah and said:

"Sister, may you grow
    into thousands of myriads;
And may your descendants gain possession
    of the gates of their enemies!"*

61 Then Rebekah and her attendants started out;
they mounted the camels and followed the man.
So the servant took Rebekah and went on his
way.

62 Meanwhile Isaac had gone from Beer-lahai-
roi and was living in the region of the Negeb.*
63 One day toward evening he went out to walk
in the field, and caught sight of camels ap-
proaching. 64 Rebekah, too, caught sight of Isaac,
and got down from her camel. 65 She asked the
servant, "Who is the man over there, walking
through the fields toward us?" "That is my mas-
ter," replied the servant. Then she took her veil
and covered herself.

66 The servant recounted to Isaac all the things
he had done. 67 Then Isaac brought Rebekah into
the tent of his mother Sarah. He took Rebekah as
his wife. Isaac loved her and found solace after
the death of his mother.

Abraham's Sons by Keturah

25 1 † * Abraham took another wife, whose
name was Keturah. 2 She bore him Zim-
ran, Jokshan, Medan, Midian, Ishbak, and
Shuah.† 3 Jokshan became the father of Sheba
and Dedan. The descendants of Dedan were the
Asshurim, the Letushim, and the Leummim.*
4 The descendants of Midian were Ephah, Epher,
Hanoch, Abida, and Eldaah. All of these were
descendants of Keturah.

5 Abraham gave everything that he owned to
his son Isaac.† 6 To the sons of his concubines,
however, he gave gifts while he was still living,
as he sent them away eastward, to the land of
Kedem,† away from his son Isaac.

Death of Abraham

7 The whole span of Abraham's life was one
hundred and seventy-five years. 8 Then he
breathed his last, dying at a ripe old age, grown
old after a full life; and he was gathered to his
people. 9 His sons Isaac and Ishmael buried him
in the cave of Machpelah, in the field of Ephron,
son of Zohar the Hittite, which faces Mamre,*
10 the field that Abraham had bought from the

†

24:58 Marriages arranged by the woman's father did not require the woman's consent, but marriages arranged by the woman's brother did. Laban is the brother and Rebekah is therefore free to give her consent or not.

25:1–11 As with the story of Terah in 11:27–32, this section lists all the descendants of Abraham as a means of concluding the story. The Jacob story ends similarly with the listing of the twelve sons (35:22–26), the death of Isaac (35:27–29), and the descendants of Esau (chap. 36). *Abraham took another wife*: though mentioned here, Abraham's marriage to a "concubine," or wife of secondary rank, is not to be understood as happening chronologically after the events narrated in the preceding chapter.

25:2 Three of the six names can be identified: the Midianites are a trading people, mentioned in the Bible as dwelling east of the Gulf of Aqaba in northwest Arabia; Ishbak is a north Syrian tribe; Shuah is a city on the right bank of the Middle Euphrates. The other names are probably towns or peoples on the international trade routes.

25:5 Amid so many descendants, Abraham takes steps that Isaac will be his favored heir.

25:6 *The land of Kedem*: or "the country of the East," the region inhabited by the Kedemites or Easterners (29:1; Jgs 6:3, 33; Jb 1:3; Is 11:14). The names mentioned in vv. 2–4, as far as they can be identified, are those of tribes in the Arabian desert.

*

24:50–51 Tb 7:11–12.
24:54 Tb 7:14; 8:20.
24:60 Gn 22:17.
24:62 Gn 16:13–14; 25:11.
25:1–4 1 Chr 1:32–33.
25:3 Is 21:13.
25:9–10 Gn 23:3–20.

Hittites; there he was buried next to his wife
Sarah. 11 After the death of Abraham, God blessed
his son Isaac, who lived near Beer-lahai-roi.

Descendants of Ishmael

12 † These are the descendants of Abraham's
son Ishmael, whom Hagar the Egyptian, Sar-
ah's slave, bore to Abraham. 13 * These are the
names of Ishmael's sons, listed in the order of
their birth: Ishmael's firstborn Nebaioth, Kedar,
Adbeel, Mibsam,* 14 Mishma, Dumah, Massa,
15 Hadad, Tema, Jetur, Naphish, and Kedemah.
16 These are the sons of Ishmael, their names by
their villages and encampments; twelve chief-
tains of as many tribal groups.*
17 The span of Ishmael's life was one hundred
and thirty-seven years. After he had breathed
his last and died, he was gathered to his people.
18 The Ishmaelites ranged from Havilah, by Shur,
which is on the border of Egypt, all the way to
Asshur; and they pitched camp† alongside their
various kindred.*

Birth of Esau and Jacob

19 † These are the descendants of Isaac, son of
Abraham; Abraham begot Isaac. 20 Isaac was forty
years old when he married Rebekah, the daughter
of Bethuel the Aramean of Paddan-aram† and the
sister of Laban the Aramean.* 21 Isaac entreated the
LORD on behalf of his wife, since she was sterile.
The LORD heard his entreaty, and his wife Rebekah
became pregnant. 22 But the children jostled each
other in the womb so much that she exclaimed, "If
it is like this,† why go on living!" She went to con-
sult the LORD, 23 and the LORD answered her:

Two nations are in your womb,
two peoples are separating while still
within you;
But one will be stronger than the other,
and the older will serve the younger.† *

24 When the time of her delivery came, there were
twins in her womb.* 25 The first to emerge was red-
dish,† and his whole body was like a hairy mantle;
so they named him Esau. 26 Next his brother came
out, gripping Esau's heel;† so he was named Jacob.
Isaac was sixty years old when they were born.*

Did You Know?

Abraham's Descendants

God promised Hagar that her son Ishmael would be made "a great nation" (Gn 21:18). The Old Testament lists twelve princely tribes that descended from Abraham's older son (see 25:13–16), tribes traditionally associated with the people of ancient Edom. A much later Islamic tradition identifies Muhammad and his descendants—the Muslims—as "children of Ishmael."

Abraham's younger son, Isaac, was the father of Jacob. The Jewish people trace their lineage to Jacob and his twelve sons. Because Jesus was a Jew, Christians ultimately trace their ancestry through Jacob to Abraham as well.

Thus, three major world religions—Judaism, Christianity, and Islam—all see Abraham as their "father in faith."

▶ **Gn 25:12–18**

---

†

25:12 Like the conclusion of the Jacob story (chap. 36), where the numerous descendants of the rejected Esau are listed, the descendants of the rejected Ishmael conclude the story.

25:18 *Pitched camp*: lit., "fell"; the same Hebrew verb is used in Jgs 7:12 in regard to the hostile encampment of desert tribes. The present passage shows the fulfillment of the prediction contained in Gn 16:12.

25:19–36:43 The Jacob cycle is introduced as the family history of Isaac (Jacob's father), just as the Abraham stories were introduced as the record of the descendants of Terah (Abraham's father, 11:27). The cycle, made up of varied stories, is given unity by several recurring themes: birth, blessing and inheritance, which are developed through the basic contrasts of barrenness/fertility, non-blessing/blessing, and inheritance/exile/homeland. The large story has an envelope structure in which Jacob's youth is spent in Canaan striving with his older brother Esau (25:19–28:22), his early adulthood in Paddan-aram building a family and striving with his brother-in-law Laban (chaps. 29–31), and his later years back in Canaan (chaps. 32–36).

25:20 *Paddan-aram*: the name used by the Priestly tradition for the northwest region of Mesopotamia, between the Habur and the Euphrates rivers. In Assyrian, *padana* is a road or a garden, and Aram refers to the people or the land of the Arameans. The equivalent geographical term in the Yahwist source is Aram Naharaim, "Aram between two rivers."

25:22 *If it is like this*: in Hebrew, the phrase *lamah zeh* is capable of several meanings; it occurs again in v. 32 ("What good . . . ?"), 32:30 ("Why do you want . . . ?"), and 33:15 ("For what reason?"). It is one of several words and motifs that run through the story, suggesting that a divine pattern (unknown to the actors) is at work.

25:23 *The older will serve the younger*: Rebekah now knows something that no one else knows, that God favors Jacob over Esau. The text does not say if she shared this knowledge with anyone or kept it to herself, but, from their actions, it seems unlikely that either Isaac or Esau knew. That fact must be borne in mind in assessing Rebekah's role in chap. 27, the theft of Esau's blessing.

25:25 *Reddish*: in Hebrew, *'admoni*, a reference to Edom, another name for Esau (v. 30; 36:1). Edom was also the name of the country south of Moab (southeast of the Dead Sea) where the descendants of Esau lived. It was called the "red" country because of its reddish sandstone. Moreover, "red" points ahead to the red stew in the next scene. *Hairy*: in Hebrew, *se'ar*, a reference to Seir, another name for Edom (36:8).

25:26 *Heel*: in Hebrew *'aqeb*, a wordplay on the name Jacob;

---

*

25:13–16 1 Chr 1:29–31.
25:13 Is 60:7.
25:16 Gn 17:20.
25:18 Gn 16:12.
25:20 Gn 24:67.
25:23 Gn 27:29; Nm 24:18; Mal 1:2–5; Rom 9:10–13.
25:24 Hos 12:4.
25:26 Mt 1:2.

Pray It!

G N

Sibling Rivalry

It is common for siblings to have conflict in their relationship, but with Jacob and Esau, the conflict becomes extreme. Follow their story in Genesis, chapters 27–28, 33.

For another story of extreme sibling rivalry, see Genesis 37:12–36. Joseph's brothers (all sons of Jacob) are so jealous of him that they plot to kill him. But instead, he gets sold as a slave—and that turns out to be a great career move for him.

The story of the prodigal son in Luke 15:11–32 is yet another example of sibling rivalry.

Do you have any brothers or sisters? If so, how do you treat them? Do you ever pray for them? Do you ever tell them that you care about them—even if they drive you crazy at times?

If you don't have any brothers or sisters, how about cousins, neighbors, or friends? All relationships get better with prayer and care. Take a moment to pray for your siblings, a close cousin, or friend by name.

▶ **Gn 25:19–34**

27 When the boys grew up, Esau became a skill-
ful hunter, a man of the open country; whereas
Jacob was a simple† man, who stayed among
the tents.* 28 Isaac preferred Esau, because he
was fond of game; but Rebekah preferred Jacob.
29 Once, when Jacob was cooking a stew, Esau
came in from the open country, famished. 30 He
said to Jacob, "Let me gulp down some of that
red stuff;† I am famished." That is why he was
called Edom. 31 But Jacob replied, "First sell me
your right as firstborn."† * 32 "Look," said Esau, "I
am on the point of dying. What good is the right
as firstborn to me?" 33 But Jacob said, "Swear to
me first!" So he sold Jacob his right as firstborn
under oath.* 34 Jacob then gave him some bread
and the lentil stew; and Esau ate, drank, got up,
and went his way. So Esau treated his right as
firstborn with disdain.

Isaac and Abimelech

26 1 † * There was a famine in the land,
distinct from the earlier one that had oc-
curred in the days of Abraham, and Isaac went
down to Abimelech, king of the Philistines in
Gerar.* 2 The LORD appeared to him and said:
Do not go down to Egypt, but camp in this land
wherever I tell you. 3 Sojourn in this land, and I
will be with you and bless you; for to you and
your descendants I will give all these lands, in
fulfillment of the oath that I swore to your father
Abraham.* 4 I will make your descendants as
numerous as the stars in the sky, and I will give
them all these lands, and in your descendants
all the nations of the earth will find blessing—*
5 this because Abraham obeyed me, keeping my
mandate, my commandments, my ordinances,
and my instructions.
6 † So Isaac settled in Gerar. 7 When the men
of the place asked questions about his wife, he
answered, "She is my sister." He was afraid that,
if he called her his wife, the men of the place
would kill him on account of Rebekah, since she
was beautiful. 8 But when they had been there for
a long time, Abimelech, king of the Philistines,
looked out of a window and saw Isaac fondling
his wife Rebekah. 9 He called for Isaac and said:
"She must certainly be your wife! How could
you have said, 'She is my sister'?" Isaac replied,
"I thought I might lose my life on her account."
10 "How could you have done this to us!" ex-
claimed Abimelech. "It would have taken very
little for one of the people to lie with your wife,
and so you would have brought guilt upon us!"
11 Abimelech then commanded all the people:

cf. 27:36. The first of three scenes of striving with Esau. The second is vv. 27–34, and the third, chap. 27. In all the scenes, Jacob values the blessing more than his ardent but unreflective brother Esau does.

25:27 *Simple*: the Hebrew word denotes soundness, integrity, health, none of which fit here. Whatever its precise meaning, it must be opposite to the qualities of Esau.

25:30 *Red stuff*: in Hebrew, *'adom;* another play on the word Edom, the "red" land.

25:31 *Right as firstborn*: the privilege that entitled the firstborn son to a position of honor in the family and to a double share in the possessions inherited from the father. There is a persistent wordplay between *bekorah*, "right of the firstborn," and *berakah*, "the blessing." Contrary to custom, the preference here is for the younger son, as it was in the choice of Isaac over Ishmael.

26:1 The promise of land and numerous descendants given to Abraham (12:1–3; 15; 17; 22:17–18) is renewed for his son Isaac. The divine blessing to Isaac is mentioned also in vv. 12, 24, and 29.

26:6–11 This scene is the third version of the wife-in-danger story (cf. chaps. 12 and 20). The mention of the famine in 26:1 recalls the famine in 12:10; the name Abimelech, king of the Philistines in Gerar, recalls 20:2. The deception, according to all the stories, is the claim that the wife is a sister. This story (from the Yahwist source) departs from the two previous accounts in that the wife is not taken into the harem of the foreign king.

*
25:27 Gn 27:6–7.
25:31 Dt 21:17.
25:33 Heb 12:16.
26:1–14 Gn 12:10–20.
26:1 Gn 12:10.
26:3 Gn 12:7; 15:18; Ex 32:13; Ps 105:9; Sir 44:22; Heb 11:9.
26:4 Gn 12:3; 22:17–18; 28:14; Ex 32:13.

"Anyone who maltreats this man or his wife shall be put to death."

12 † Isaac sowed a crop in that region and reaped a hundredfold the same year. Since the LORD blessed him, 13 * he became richer and richer all the time, until he was very wealthy. 14 He acquired flocks and herds, and a great work force, and so the Philistines became envious of him. 15 * The Philistines had stopped up and filled with dirt all the wells that his father's servants had dug back in the days of his father Abraham. 16 So Abimelech said to Isaac, "Go away from us; you have become far too numerous for us." 17 Isaac left there and camped in the Wadi Gerar where he stayed. 18 Isaac reopened the wells which his father's servants had dug back in the days of his father Abraham and which the Philistines had stopped up after Abraham's death; he gave them names like those that his father had given them. 19 But when Isaac's servants dug in the wadi and reached spring water in their well, 20 the shepherds of Gerar argued with Isaac's shepherds, saying, "The water belongs to us!" So he named the well Esek,† because they had quarreled there. 21 Then they dug another well, and they argued over that one too; so he named it Sitnah.† 22 So he moved on from there and dug still another well, but over this one they did not argue. He named it Rehoboth,† and said, "Because the LORD has now given us ample room, we shall flourish in the land."

23 From there Isaac went up to Beer-sheba. 24 The same night the LORD appeared to him and said: I am the God of Abraham, your father. Do not fear, for I am with you. I will bless you and multiply your descendants for the sake of Abraham, my servant.* 25 So Isaac built an altar there and invoked the LORD by name. After he had pitched his tent there, Isaac's servants began to dig a well nearby.

26 * Then Abimelech came to him from Gerar, with Ahuzzath, his councilor, and Phicol, the general of his army. 27 Isaac asked them, "Why have you come to me, since you hate me and have driven me away from you?" 28 They answered: "We clearly see that the LORD has been with you, so we thought: let there be a sworn agreement between our two sides—between you and us. Let us make a covenant with you: 29 you shall do no harm to us, just as we have not maltreated you, but have always acted kindly toward you and have let you depart in peace. So now, may you be blessed by the LORD!" 30 Isaac then made a feast for them, and they ate and drank. 31 Early the next morning they exchanged oaths. Then Isaac sent them on their way, and they departed from him in peace.

32 That same day Isaac's servants came and informed him about the well they had been digging; they told him, "We have reached water!" 33 He called it Shibah;† hence the name of the

Introducing...

Jacob

According to the Bible, Abraham was the father of Isaac, and Isaac was the father of Jacob, and Jacob was the father of twelve sons who became the leaders of the twelve Tribes of Israel. Jacob, like his ancestors, participated in the covenant with God that promised a great land and many descendants. He is portrayed as a very human character with a wide range of emotions and actions, both good and bad. Jacob is a repentant brother, a kind father, and a successful herder, but he is also a trickster who steals his brother Esau's birthright and his father's blessing (see Gn 25:29–34, 27:1–29). It is no wonder that Jacob's name means "supplanter" or "heel grabber."

In a dream, God renews the covenant promises to Jacob (see Gn 28:10–17), and in another dream (see 35:9–15), God changes Jacob's name to Israel (see 32:22–32). Jacob's descendants become known as the Israelites. His story reveals that God's blessing continues to work even through flawed human beings.

▶ Gn 25:19—50:14

† **26:12–33** The dispute is over water rights. In a sparsely watered land, wells were precious and claims on water could function as a kind of claim on the land. Scholars generally judge the account of the dispute over water rights and its settlement by a legal agreement between Isaac and Abimelech to be a Yahwist version of the similar story about Abraham in 21:22–34. Here, Abimelech realizes that Isaac has brought blessing to his people and thus desires a covenant with him. The feast in v. 30 is part of the covenant ceremony.

26:20 *Esek*: "quarrel."

26:21 *Sitnah*: "opposition."

26:22 *Rehoboth*: "wide spaces," i.e., ample room to live; site is probably SW of modern day Beer-sheba.

26:33 *Shibah*: the place name Shibah is a play on two Hebrew words, *shebu'ah*, "oath," and *shwebaa'*, "seven." In v. 31, they exchanged oaths.

26:13–14 Jb 1:3.
26:15–24 Gn 21:25–31.
26:24 Gn 46:3.
26:26–33 Gn 21:22–31; Prv 16:7.

Did You Know?

God's Surprising Choice

In most ancient cultures, including Israel's, the oldest son of the family was expected to inherit his father's property (the birthright) and authority (the blessing). In the story of Esau and Jacob, Jacob tricks Esau (the oldest son) out of his birthright (see Gn 25:29–34) and deceives his blind father into giving him the blessing (see 27:1–29).

It is surprising that Genesis makes no comment on Jacob's actions. Ultimately, the story is not a commentary on Jacob's morality but about God's justice. God is not bound by cultural expectations. Again and again in the Old Testament, God defies human norms by choosing the "little ones" for big responsibilities: Jacob, Joseph, Ruth, David, and Esther, for example. Even the Israelites themselves were an unlikely choice on God's part. Why didn't God choose a nation of great wealth and power instead of a group that was enslaved?

The story of Jacob and Esau reminds us that God does not bow to human expectations or plans. God's ways are often surprising!

▶ Gn 27:1–40

city is Beer-sheba to this day. 34 † When Esau
was forty years old, he married Judith, daughter
of Beeri the Hittite, and Basemath, daughter of
Elon the Hivite.* 35 But they became a source of
bitterness to Isaac and Rebekah.

Jacob's Deception†

27 1 When Isaac was so old that his eyesight
had failed him, he called his older son
Esau and said to him, "My son!" "Here I am!" he
replied. 2 Isaac then said, "Now I have grown old.
I do not know when I might die. 3 So now take
your hunting gear—your quiver and bow—and
go out into the open country to hunt some game
for me. 4 Then prepare for me a dish in the way I
like, and bring it to me to eat, so that I may bless
you† before I die."
5 Rebekah had been listening while Isaac was
speaking to his son Esau. So when Esau went out
into the open country to hunt some game for his
father,* 6 Rebekah said to her son Jacob, "Listen!
I heard your father tell your brother Esau, 7 'Bring
me some game and prepare a dish for me to eat,
that I may bless you with the LORD's approval be-
fore I die.' 8 Now, my son, obey me in what I am
about to order you. 9 Go to the flock and get me
two choice young goats so that with these I might
prepare a dish for your father in the way he likes.
10 Then bring it to your father to eat, that he may
bless you before he dies." 11 But Jacob said to his
mother Rebekah, "But my brother Esau is a hairy
man and I am smooth-skinned!* 12 Suppose my
father feels me? He will think I am making fun of
him, and I will bring on myself a curse instead of
a blessing." 13 His mother, however, replied: "Let
any curse against you, my son, fall on me! Just
obey me. Go and get me the young goats."
14 So Jacob went and got them and brought
them to his mother, and she prepared a dish in
the way his father liked. 15 Rebekah then took
the best clothes of her older son Esau that she
had in the house, and gave them to her younger
son Jacob to wear; 16 and with the goatskins she
covered up his hands and the hairless part of his
neck. 17 Then she gave her son Jacob the dish and
the bread she had prepared.
18 Going to his father, Jacob said, "Father!"
"Yes?" replied Isaac. "Which of my sons are
you?" 19 Jacob answered his father: "I am Esau,
your firstborn. I did as you told me. Please sit up
and eat some of my game, so that you may bless
me." 20 But Isaac said to his son, "How did you
get it so quickly, my son?" He answered, "The
LORD, your God, directed me." 21 Isaac then said
to Jacob, "Come closer, my son, that I may feel
you, to learn whether you really are my son Esau

---

† **26:34–35** These verses from the Priestly source introduce the next section on Esau's loss of his right as firstborn by suggesting a motivation for this in Isaac's and Rebekah's dislike for Esau's Canaanite wives.

27:1–45 The chapter, a literary masterpiece, is the third and climactic wresting away of the blessing of Esau. Rebekah manages the entire affair, using perhaps her privileged information about Jacob's status (25:23); Jacob's only qualm is that if his father discovers the ruse, he will receive a curse instead of a blessing (vv. 11–12). Isaac is passive as he was in chaps. 22 and 24. The deception is effected through clothing (Jacob wears Esau's clothing), which points ahead to a similar deception of a patriarch by means of clothing in the Joseph story (37:21–33). Such recurrent acts and scenes let the reader know a divine purpose is moving the story forward even though the human characters are unaware of it.

27:4 *I may bless you*: Isaac's blessing confers fertility (vv. 27–28) and dominion (v. 29). The "dew of heaven" is rain that produces grain and wine, two of the principal foodstuffs of the ancient Near East. The "fertility of the earth" may allude to oil, the third basic foodstuff. The full agricultural year may be implied here: the fall rains are followed by the grain harvests of the spring and the grape harvest of late summer, and then the olive harvest of the fall (cf. Dt 11:14; Ps 104:13–15).

26:34–35 Gn 27:46.
27:5 Gn 25:28.
27:11 Gn 25:25.

or not." 22 So Jacob moved up closer to his father.
When Isaac felt him, he said, "Although the voice
is Jacob's, the hands are Esau's." 23 (He failed to
identify him because his hands were hairy, like
those of his brother Esau; so he blessed him.)
24 Again Isaac said, "Are you really my son Esau?"
And Jacob said, "I am." 25 Then Isaac said, "Serve
me, my son, and let me eat of the game so that I
may bless you." Jacob served it to him, and Isaac
ate; he brought him wine, and he drank. 26 Fi-
nally his father Isaac said to him, "Come closer,
my son, and kiss me." 27 As Jacob went up to kiss
him, Isaac smelled the fragrance of his clothes.
With that, he blessed him, saying,

"Ah, the fragrance of my son
  is like the fragrance of a field
  that the LORD has blessed!*
28 May God give to you
  of the dew of the heavens
And of the fertility of the earth
  abundance of grain and wine.
29 *May peoples serve you,
  and nations bow down to you;
Be master of your brothers,
  and may your mother's sons bow down to
    you.
Cursed be those who curse you,
  and blessed be those who bless you."

30 Jacob had scarcely left his father after Isaac
had finished blessing him, when his brother Esau
came back from his hunt. 31 Then he too prepared
a dish, and bringing it to his father, he said, "Let
my father sit up and eat some of his son's game,
that you may then give me your blessing." 32 His
father Isaac asked him, "Who are you?" He said,
"I am your son, your firstborn son, Esau." 33 Isaac
trembled greatly. "Who was it, then," he asked,
"that hunted game and brought it to me? I ate it all
just before you came, and I blessed him. Now he
is blessed!" 34 As he heard his father's words, Esau
burst into loud, bitter sobbing and said, "Father,
bless me too!" 35 When Isaac said, "Your brother
came here by a ruse and carried off your bless-
ing," 36 Esau exclaimed, "He is well named Jacob,
is he not! He has supplanted me† twice! First he
took away my right as firstborn, and now he has
taken away my blessing." Then he said, "Have you
not saved a blessing for me?"* 37 Isaac replied to
Esau: "I have already appointed him your master,
and I have assigned to him all his kindred as his
servants; besides, I have sustained him with grain
and wine. What then can I do for you, my son?"
38 But Esau said to his father, "Have you only one
blessing, father? Bless me too, father!" and Esau
wept aloud.* 39 His father Isaac said in response:

"See, far from the fertile earth
  will be your dwelling;
  far from the dew of the heavens above!*
40 By your sword you will live,
  and your brother you will serve;
But when you become restless,
  you will throw off his yoke from your
    neck."*

41 Esau bore a grudge against Jacob because of
the blessing his father had given him. Esau said
to himself, "Let the time of mourning for my fa-
ther come, so that I may kill my brother Jacob."*
42 When Rebekah got news of what her older son
Esau had in mind, she summoned her younger
son Jacob and said to him: "Listen! Your brother
Esau intends to get his revenge by killing you.
43 So now, my son, obey me: flee at once to my
brother Laban in Haran, 44 and stay with him a
while until your brother's fury subsides— 45 until
your brother's anger against you subsides and he
forgets what you did to him. Then I will send for
you and bring you back. Why should I lose both
of you in a single day?"

Jacob Sent to Laban

46 Rebekah said to Isaac: "I am disgusted with
life because of the Hittite women. If Jacob also
should marry a Hittite woman, a native of the
land, like these women, why should I live?"*

28 1 † Isaac therefore summoned Jacob and
blessed him, charging him: "You shall
not marry a Canaanite woman!* 2 Go now to

†

27:36 *He has supplanted me*: in Hebrew, *wayyaqebeni*, a word-play on the name Jacob, *ya'aqob*; see Jer 9:3 and Gn 25:26. There is also a play between the Hebrew words *bekorah* ("right of the first-born") and *berakah* ("blessing").

28:1–9 A glimpse of Rebekah's shrewdness is provided by 27:42–28:2. She is aware of Esau's murderous plot against Jacob (27:42–45) but realizes the episode of the stolen blessing is still painful to Isaac; she therefore uses another motive to persuade Isaac to send Jacob away—he must marry within the family (endogamy), unlike Esau. Esau, unreflective as usual, realizes too late he also should marry within the family but, significantly, marries from Abraham's rejected line. At this point in the story, Jacob (and his mother) have taken the blessing for themselves. Their actions have put Jacob in a precarious position: he must flee the land because of his brother's murderous intent and find a wife in a far country. One might ask how God's blessing can be given to such an unworthy schemer. There is a biblical pattern of preferring the younger brother or sister over

*

27:27 Gn 22:17–18; Heb 11:20.
27:29 Gn 25:23; 49:8; Nm 24:9.
27:36 Gn 25:26, 29–34; Hos 12:4.
27:38 Heb 12:17.
27:39 Heb 11:20.
27:40 2 Kgs 8:20, 22; 2 Chr 21:8.
27:41 Wis 10:10; Ob 10.
27:46 Gn 26:34–35.
28:1 Gn 24:3–4; 26:35.

Pray It!

G
N

Friendship with God

Just as Jacob is leaving his home and everything he knows, God establishes a personal relationship with him through a dream. In this relationship, God and Jacob interact personally, are accountable to each other, and trust each other. Jacob will need this relationship to help him through the tough times ahead. See Genesis 32:23–33 for further developments in Jacob's relationship with God.

God, I want to know your presence. Use my dreams and my waking thoughts; use my family, friends, and neighbors; use your holy word. Use them all to reach me. For I know your presence will sustain me on my most difficult journeys, as it did Jacob.

▶ Gn 28:10–22

Paddan-aram, to the home of your mother's
father Bethuel, and there choose a wife for your-
self from among the daughters of Laban, your
mother's brother.* 3May God Almighty bless
you and make you fertile, multiply you that you
may become an assembly of peoples. 4May God
extend to you and your descendants the blessing
of Abraham, so that you may gain possession of
the land where you are residing, which he as-
signed to Abraham."* 5Then Isaac sent Jacob on
his way; he went to Paddan-aram, to Laban, son
of Bethuel the Aramean, and brother of Rebekah,
the mother of Jacob and Esau.*

6Esau noted that Isaac had blessed Jacob when
he sent him to Paddan-aram to get himself a wife
there, and that, as he gave him his blessing, he
charged him, "You shall not marry a Canaanite
woman," 7and that Jacob had obeyed his father
and mother and gone to Paddan-aram. 8Esau
realized how displeasing the Canaanite women
were to his father Isaac, 9so Esau went to Ish-
mael, and in addition to the wives he had, mar-
ried Mahalath, the daughter of Abraham's son
Ishmael and sister of Nebaioth.*

Jacob's Dream at Bethel†

10Jacob departed from Beer-sheba and pro-
ceeded toward Haran. 11When he came upon
a certain place,† he stopped there for the night,
since the sun had already set. Taking one of the
stones at the place, he put it under his head and
lay down in that place. 12Then he had a dream:
a stairway† rested on the ground, with its top
reaching to the heavens; and God's angels were
going up and down on it.* 13And there was the
LORD standing beside him and saying: I am the
LORD, the God of Abraham your father and
the God of Isaac; the land on which you are lying
I will give to you and your descendants.* 14Your
descendants will be like the dust of the earth, and
through them you will spread to the west and
the east, to the north and the south. In you
and your descendants all the families of the earth
will find blessing.* 15I am with you and will pro-
tect you wherever you go, and bring you back to
this land. I will never leave you until I have done
what I promised you.*

16When Jacob awoke from his sleep, he said,
"Truly, the LORD is in this place and I did not
know it!" 17He was afraid and said: "How awe-
some this place is! This is nothing else but the
house of God, the gateway to heaven!" 18Early
the next morning Jacob took the stone that he
had put under his head, set it up as a sacred pil-
lar,† and poured oil on top of it.* 19He named

the older—Isaac over Ishmael, Jacob over Esau, Rachel over Leah, Joseph over his older brothers, Ephraim over Manasseh (Gn 48:14), David over his older brothers.

28:10–22 As Jacob is leaving the land on his way to an uncertain future in Paddan-aram, God appears to him at a sacred place that Jacob had visited only to take a night's rest. Jacob's unawareness of the holiness of the place underscores the graciousness of the gift. On his return to Canaan, he will again encounter a divine visitor in the form of the mysterious attacker (32:23–33) and, after his return and reconciliation with Esau, he will again go to Bethel (35:1–15).

28:11 *Place*: the Hebrew word is often used specifically of a sacred site. The ambiguous word "place" is used here, for the text emphasizes that Jacob has no idea the place he has come upon is sacred; only when he wakes up does he realize it is sacred. The place was Bethel (v. 19), a sacred site as early as the time of Abraham (12:8).

28:12 *Stairway*: in Hebrew, *sullam*, traditionally but inaccurately translated as "ladder." The corresponding verb, *salal*, means "to heap up" something, such as dirt for a highway or a ramp. The imagery in Jacob's dream may be derived from the Babylonian ziggurat or temple tower, "with its top in the sky" (11:4), and with brick steps leading up to a small temple at the top.

28:18 *Sacred pillar*: in Hebrew, *masseba*, a stone which might vary in shape and size, set upright and usually intended for some religious purpose. The custom of erecting such sacred pillars in Palestine went back to its pre-Israelite period; but since their polytheistic associations were often retained, later Israelite religion forbade their erection (Lv 26:1; Dt 16:22) and ordered the destruction of those that were associated with other religions (Ex 34:13; Dt 12:3).

28:2 Gn 22:22.
28:4 Ex 32:13.
28:5 Jdt 8:26.
28:9 Gn 36:2–3.
28:12 Jn 1:51.
28:13 Dt 1:8; Mi 7:20.
28:14 Gn 12:3; 13:14–15; 15:5–6; 18:18; 22:17–18; 26:4; Dt 19:8; Sir 44:21.
28:15 Gn 31:3.
28:18 Gn 31:13; 35:14–15.

that place Bethel,† whereas the former name of
the town had been Luz.*
20 Jacob then made this vow:† "If God will be
with me and protect me on this journey I am
making and give me food to eat and clothes to
wear, 21 and I come back safely to my father's
house, the LORD will be my God. 22 This stone
that I have set up as a sacred pillar will be the
house of God. Of everything you give me, I will
return a tenth part to you without fail."

Arrival in Haran†

29 1 *After Jacob resumed his journey,
he came to the land of the Kedemites.
2 Looking about, he saw a well in the open coun-
try, with three flocks of sheep huddled near it,
for flocks were watered from that well. A large
stone covered the mouth of the well.* 3 When all
the shepherds were assembled there they would
roll the stone away from the mouth of the well
and water the sheep. Then they would put the
stone back again in its place over the mouth of
the well.
4 Jacob said to them, "My brothers, where are
you from?" "We are from Haran," they replied.
5 Then he asked them, "Do you know Laban,
son of Nahor?" "We do," they answered.* 6 He
inquired further, "Is he well?" "He is," they an-
swered; "and here comes his daughter Rachel
with the sheep." 7 Then he said: "There is still
much daylight left; it is hardly the time to bring
the animals home. Water the sheep, and then
continue pasturing them." 8 They replied, "We
cannot until all the shepherds are here to roll the
stone away from the mouth of the well; then can
we water the flocks."
9 While he was still talking with them, Rachel
arrived with her father's sheep, for she was the
one who tended them. 10 As soon as Jacob saw
Rachel, the daughter of his mother's brother
Laban, and the sheep of Laban, he went up,
rolled the stone away from the mouth of the
well, and watered Laban's sheep. 11 Then Jacob
kissed Rachel and wept aloud. 12 Jacob told Ra-
chel that he was her father's relative, Rebekah's
son. So she ran to tell her father. 13 When Laban
heard the news about Jacob, his sister's son, he
ran to meet him. After embracing and kissing
him, he brought him to his house. Jacob then
repeated to Laban all these things, 14 and Laban
said to him, "You are indeed my bone and my
flesh."†

Marriage to Leah and Rachel

After Jacob had stayed with him a full month,
15 † Laban said to him: "Should you serve me for
nothing just because you are a relative of mine?
Tell me what your wages should be." 16 Now
Laban had two daughters; the older was called
Leah, the younger Rachel. 17 Leah had dull eyes,†
but Rachel was shapely and beautiful. 18 Because
Jacob loved Rachel, he answered, "I will serve
you seven years for your younger daughter Ra-
chel."† 19 Laban replied, "It is better to give her
to you than to another man. Stay with me." 20 So
Jacob served seven years for Rachel, yet they
seemed to him like a few days because of his
love for her.*
21 Then Jacob said to Laban, "Give me my
wife, that I may consummate my marriage with
her, for my term is now completed." 22 So Laban
invited all the local inhabitants and gave a ban-
quet. 23 At nightfall he took his daughter Leah
and brought her to Jacob, and he consummated
the marriage with her. 24 Laban assigned his
maidservant Zilpah to his daughter Leah as her
maidservant. 25 In the morning, there was Leah!
So Jacob said to Laban: "How could you do this
to me! Was it not for Rachel that I served you?
Why did you deceive me?" 26 Laban replied, "It is

†

28:19 *Bethel*: i.e., "house of God"; the reference is to the house of God in v. 17.

28:20 *This vow*: knowing well that Esau's murderous wrath stands between him and the possession of the land promised him, Jacob makes his vow very precise. He vows to make the God who appeared to him his own if the God guides him safely to Paddan-aram and back to this land.

29:1–14 Jacob's arrival in Haran. The sight of Rachel inspires Jacob to the superhuman feat of rolling back the enormous stone by himself. The scene evokes the meeting of Abraham's steward and Jacob's mother Rebekah at a well (24:11–27).

The verse begins the story of Jacob's time in Mesopotamia (29:1–31:54), which is framed on either side by Jacob's time in Canaan, 25:19–28:22 and 32:1–36:43. In these chapters, Jacob suffers Laban's duplicity as Esau had to suffer his, though eventually Jacob outwits Laban and leaves Mesopotamia a wealthy man. An elaborate chiastic (or envelope) structure shapes the diverse material: (A) Jacob's arrival in Haran in 29:1–4; (B) contract with Laban in 29:15–20; (C) Laban's deception of Jacob in 29:21–30; (D) the center, the birth of Jacob's children in 29:31–30:24; (C') Jacob's deception of Laban in 30:25–43; (B') dispute with Laban in 31:17–42; (A') departure from Laban in 31:43–54. As the chiasm reverses, so do the fortunes of Laban and Jacob. *Kedemites*: see note on 25:6.

29:14 *Bone and . . . flesh*: the Hebrew idiom for English "flesh and blood" (cf. 2:23; Jgs 9:2; 2 Sm 5:1 = 1 Chr 11:1).

29:15–30 Laban's deception and Jacob's marriages. There are many ironies in the passage. Jacob's protest to Laban, "How could you do this to me?" echoes the question put to Abraham (20:9) and Isaac (26:10) when their deceptions about their wives were discovered. The major irony is that Jacob, the deceiver of his father and brother about the blessing (chap. 27), is deceived by his uncle (standing in for the father) about his wife.

29:17 *Dull eyes*: in the language of beauty used here, "dull" probably means lacking in the luster that was the sign of beautiful eyes, as in 1 Sm 16:12 and Sg 4:1.

29:18 Jacob offers to render service (Jos 15:16–17; 1 Sm 17:25; 18:17) to pay off the customary bridal price (Ex 22:15–16; Dt 22:29).

28:19 Gn 35:6; 48:3; Jos 18:13; Jgs 1:23; Hos 12:5.
29:1 Wis 10:10.
29:2 Gn 24:11–12.
29:5 Tb 7:4.
29:20 Hos 12:13.

Live It!

When Lies Boomerang

Predictably, Jacob becomes upset when he finds out he has been deceived by Laban (see Gn 29:25). Yet, the very reason Jacob is working for his uncle Laban is because he has fled from his brother Esau, whom he deceived several years earlier (see 27:1–40). Jacob's lies and deceit have boomeranged, so now he is the victim.

Just as the good deeds we do often come back to us, sometimes in surprising ways, so it is with the bad deeds. Think about your bad deeds as slow-moving boomerangs. Sooner or later, they will come back to you and the situation probably won't be too pleasant. Is that what you want? Reflect on a lie you told that has come back to haunt you.

▶ **Gn 29:15–30**

not the custom in our country to give the youn-
ger daughter before the firstborn. 27 Finish the
bridal week† for this one, and then the other will
also be given to you in return for another seven
years of service with me."*
28 Jacob did so. He finished the bridal week for
the one, and then Laban gave him his daughter
Rachel as a wife. 29 Laban assigned his maid-
servant Bilhah to his daughter Rachel as her
maidservant. 30 Jacob then consummated his
marriage with Rachel also, and he loved her
more than Leah. Thus he served Laban another
seven years.*

Jacob's Children†

31 When the LORD saw that Leah was unloved,
he made her fruitful, while Rachel was barren.
32 Leah conceived and bore a son, and she named
him Reuben;† for she said, "It means, 'The LORD
saw my misery; surely now my husband will love
me.' "* 33 She conceived again and bore a son,
and said, "It means, 'The LORD heard that I was
unloved,' and therefore he has given me this one
also"; so she named him Simeon.† 34 Again she
conceived and bore a son, and she said, "Now
at last my husband will become attached to me,
since I have now borne him three sons"; that
is why she named him Levi.† 35 Once more she
conceived and bore a son, and she said, "This
time I will give thanks to the LORD"; therefore
she named him Judah.† Then she stopped bear-
ing children.*

30 1 When Rachel saw that she had not borne
children to Jacob, she became envious of
her sister. She said to Jacob, "Give me children
or I shall die!"* 2 Jacob became angry with Ra-
chel and said, "Can I take the place of God, who
has denied you the fruit of the womb?"* 3 She
replied, "Here is my maidservant Bilhah. Have
intercourse with her, and let her give birth on my
knees,† so that I too may have children through
her."* 4 So she gave him her maidservant Bilhah
as wife,† and Jacob had intercourse with her.
5 When Bilhah conceived and bore a son for
Jacob, 6 Rachel said, "God has vindicated me;
indeed he has heeded my plea and given me a
son." Therefore she named him Dan.† 7 Rachel's
maidservant Bilhah conceived again and bore a

†

29:27 *The bridal week*: an ancient wedding lasted for seven days; cf. Jgs 14:12, 17.

29:31–30:24 The note of strife, first sounded between Jacob and Esau in chaps. 25–27, continues between the two wives, since Jacob loved Rachel more than Leah (29:30). Jacob's neglect of Leah moves God to make her fruitful (29:31). Leah's fertility provokes Rachel. Leah bears Jacob four sons (Reuben, Levi, Simeon, and Judah) and her maidservant Zilpah, two (Gad and Asher). Rachel's maidservant Bilhah bears two (Dan and Naphtali). After the mandrakes (30:14–17), Leah bears Issachar and Zebulun and a daughter Dinah. Rachel then bears Joseph and, later in the land of Canaan, Benjamin (35:18).

29:32 *Reuben*: the literal meaning of the Hebrew name is disputed. One interpretation is *re'u ben*, "look, a son!", but here in Genesis (as also with the names of all the other sons of Jacob), it is given a symbolic rather than an etymological interpretation. Name and person were regarded as closely interrelated. The symbolic interpretation of Reuben's name, according to the Yahwist source, is based on the similar-sounding *ra'a be'onyi*, "he saw my misery." In the Elohist source, the name is explained by the similar-sounding *ye'ehabani*, "he will love me."

29:33 *Simeon*: in popular etymology, related to *shama'*, "he heard."

29:34 *Levi*: related to *yillaweh*, "he will become attached."

29:35 *Judah*: related to *'odeh*, "I will give thanks, praise."

30:3 *On my knees*: in the ancient Near East, a father would take a newborn child in his lap to signify that he acknowledged it as his own; Rachel uses the ceremony in order to adopt the child and establish her legal rights to it.

30:4 *As wife*: in 35:22 Bilhah is called a "concubine" (Heb. *pilegesh*). In v. 9, Zilpah is called "wife," and in 37:2 both women are called wives. The basic difference between a wife and a concubine was that no bride price was paid for the latter. The interchange of terminology shows that there was some blurring in social status between the wife and the concubine.

30:6 *Dan*: explained by the term *dannanni*, "he has vindicated me."

*

29:27 Hos 12:13.
29:30 Dt 21:15–17.
29:32 Gn 49:3.
29:35 Mt 1:2; Lk 3:33.
30:1 Prv 30:16.
30:2 2 Kgs 5:7.
30:3 Gn 16:2–4.

second son for Jacob, [8] and Rachel said, "I have wrestled strenuously with my sister, and I have prevailed." So she named him Naphtali.†

[9] When Leah saw that she had ceased to bear children, she took her maidservant Zilpah and gave her to Jacob as wife. [10] So Leah's maidservant Zilpah bore a son for Jacob. [11] Leah then said, "What good luck!" So she named him Gad.† [12] Then Leah's maidservant Zilpah bore a second son to Jacob; [13] and Leah said, "What good fortune, because women will call me fortunate!" So she named him Asher.†

[14] One day, during the wheat harvest, Reuben went out and came upon some mandrakes† in the field which he brought home to his mother Leah. Rachel said to Leah, "Please give me some of your son's mandrakes." [15] Leah replied, "Was it not enough for you to take away my husband, that you must now take my son's mandrakes too?" Rachel answered, "In that case Jacob may lie with you tonight in exchange for your son's mandrakes." [16] That evening, when Jacob came in from the field, Leah went out to meet him. She said, "You must have intercourse with me, because I have hired you with my son's mandrakes." So that night he lay with her, [17] and God listened to Leah; she conceived and bore a fifth son to Jacob. [18] Leah then said, "God has given me my wages for giving my maidservant to my husband"; so she named him Issachar.† [19] Leah conceived again and bore a sixth son to Jacob; [20] and Leah said, "God has brought me a precious gift. This time my husband will honor me, because I have borne him six sons"; so she named him Zebulun.† [21] Afterwards she gave birth to a daughter, and she named her Dinah.

[22] Then God remembered Rachel. God listened to her and made her fruitful. [23] She conceived and bore a son, and she said, "God has removed my disgrace."* [24] She named him Joseph,† saying, "May the LORD add another son for me!"

Jacob Outwits Laban†

[25] After Rachel gave birth to Joseph, Jacob said to Laban: "Allow me to go to my own region and land. [26] Give me my wives and my children for whom I served you and let me go, for you know the service that I rendered you." [27] Laban answered him: "If you will please! I have learned through divination that the LORD has blessed me because of you." [28] He continued, "State the wages I owe you, and I will pay them." [29] Jacob replied: "You know what work I did for you and how well your livestock fared under my care; [30] the little you had before I came has grown into an abundance, since the LORD has blessed you in my company. Now, when can I do something for my own household as well?" [31] Laban asked, "What should I give you?" Jacob answered: "You do not have to give me anything. If you do this thing for me, I will again pasture and tend your sheep. [32] Let me go through your whole flock today and remove from it every dark animal among the lambs and every spotted or speckled one among the goats.† These will be my wages. [33] In the future, whenever you check on my wages, my honesty will testify for me: any animal that is not speckled or spotted among the goats, or dark among the lambs, got into my possession by theft!" [34] Laban said, "Very well. Let it be as you say."

[35] That same day Laban removed the streaked and spotted he-goats and all the speckled and spotted she-goats, all those with some white on them, as well as every dark lamb, and he put them in the care of his sons.† [36] Then he put a three days' journey between himself and Jacob, while Jacob was pasturing the rest of Laban's flock.

[37] Jacob, however, got some fresh shoots of

---

† **30:8** *Naphtali*: explained by the Hebrew term *naftulim*, lit., "contest" or "struggle."

30:11 *Gad*: explained by the Hebrew term *begad*, lit., "in luck," i.e., "what good luck!"

30:13 *Asher*: explained by the term *be'oshri*, lit., "in my good fortune," i.e., "what good fortune," and by the term *ye'ashsheruni*, "they call me fortunate."

30:14 *Mandrakes*: an herb whose root was thought to promote conception. The Hebrew word for mandrakes, *duda'im*, has erotic connotations, since it sounds like the words *daddayim* ("breasts") and *dodim* ("sexual pleasure").

30:18 *Issachar*: explained by the terms, *sekari*, "my reward," and in v. 16, *sakor sekartika*, "I have hired you."

30:20 *Zebulun*: explained by the terms, *zebadani . . .zebed tob*, "he has brought me a precious gift," and *yizbeleni*, "he will honor me."

30:24 *Joseph*: explained by the words *yosep*, "may he add," and in v. 23, *'asap*, "he has removed."

30:25–43 Jacob's deception of Laban. Jacob has been living in Laban's household as an indentured worker paying off the bride price. Having paid off all his obligations, he wants to settle his accounts with Laban. His many children attest to the fulfillment of the Lord's promise of numerous progeny; the birth of Joseph to his beloved Rachel signals the fulfillment in a special way. To enter into the Lord's second promise, the land, he must now return to Canaan.

30:32 *Dark . . . lambs . . . spotted or speckled . . . goats*: in the Near East the normal color of sheep is light gray, whereas that of goats is dark brown or black. A minority of sheep in that part of the world have dark patches, and a minority of goats, white markings. Laban is quick to agree to the offer, for Jacob would have received only a few animals. But Jacob gets the better of him, using two different means: (1) he separates out the weaker animals and then provides visual impressions to the stronger animals at mating time (a folkloric belief); (2) in 31:8–12, he transmits the preferred characteristics through controlled propagation. It should be noted that Jacob has been told what to do in a dream (31:10) and that God is behind the increase in his flocks.

30:35 By giving the abnormally colored animals to his sons, Laban not only deprived Jacob of his first small wages, but he also schemed to prevent the future breeding of such animals in the flock entrusted to Jacob.

30:23 Lk 1:25.

GN

poplar, almond and plane† trees, and he peeled white stripes in them by laying bare the white core of the shoots. 38 The shoots that he had peeled he then set upright in the watering troughs where the animals came to drink, so that they would be in front of them. When the animals were in heat as they came to drink, 39 the goats mated by the shoots, and so they gave birth to streaked, speckled and spotted young. 40 The sheep, on the other hand, Jacob kept apart, and he made these animals face the streaked or completely dark animals of Laban. Thus he produced flocks of his own, which he did not put with Laban's flock. 41 Whenever the hardier animals were in heat, Jacob would set the shoots in the troughs in full view of these animals, so that they mated by the shoots; 42 but with the weaker animals he would not put the shoots there. So the feeble animals would go to Laban, but the hardy ones to Jacob. 43 So the man grew exceedingly prosperous, and he owned large flocks, male and female servants, camels, and donkeys.

Flight from Laban

31 1 † Jacob heard that Laban's sons were saying, "Jacob has taken everything that belonged to our father, and he has produced all this wealth from our father's property." 2 Jacob perceived, too, that Laban's attitude toward him was not what it had previously been. 3 Then the LORD said to Jacob: Return to the land of your ancestors, where you were born, and I will be with you.*

4 So Jacob sent for Rachel and Leah to meet him in the field where his flock was. 5 There he said to them: "I have noticed that your father's attitude toward me is not as it was in the past; but the God of my father has been with me. 6 You know well that with all my strength I served your father; 7 yet your father cheated me and changed my wages ten times. God, however, did not let him do me any harm.* 8 Whenever your father said, 'The speckled animals will be your wages,' the entire flock would bear speckled young; whenever he said, 'The streaked animals will be your wages,' the entire flock would bear streaked young. 9 So God took away your father's livestock and gave it to me. 10 Once, during the flock's mating season, I had a dream in which I saw he-goats mating that were streaked, speckled and mottled. 11 In the dream God's angel said to me, 'Jacob!' and I replied, 'Here I am!' 12 Then he said: 'Look up and see. All the he-goats that are mating are streaked, speckled and mottled, for I have seen all the things that Laban has been doing to you. 13 I am the God of Bethel, where you anointed a sacred pillar and made a vow to me. Get up now! Leave this land and return to the land of your birth.' "*

14 Rachel and Leah answered him: "Do we still have an heir's portion in our father's house? 15 Are we not regarded by him as outsiders?† He not only sold us; he has even used up the money that he got for us! 16 All the wealth that God took away from our father really belongs to us and our children. So do whatever God has told you."* 17 Jacob proceeded to put his children and wives on camels, 18 and he drove off all his livestock and all the property he had acquired in Paddan-aram, to go to his father Isaac in the land of Canaan.

19 Now Laban was away shearing his sheep, and Rachel had stolen her father's household images.† * 20 Jacob had hoodwinked† Laban the Aramean by not telling him that he was going to flee. 21 Thus he fled with all that he had. Once he was across the Euphrates, he headed for the hill country of Gilead.

22 On the third day, word came to Laban that Jacob had fled. 23 Taking his kinsmen with him, he pursued him for seven days† until he caught up with him in the hill country of Gilead. 24 But that night God appeared to Laban the Aramean in a dream and said to him: Take care not to say anything to Jacob.*

---

†

30:37 *Plane*: also called the Oriental Plane, a deciduous tree found in riverine forests and marshes.

31:1–54 Jacob flees with his family from Laban. The strife that has always accompanied Jacob continues as Laban's sons complain, "he has taken everything that belonged to our father"; the brothers' complaint echoes Esau's in 27:36. Rachel and Leah overcome their mutual hostility and are able to leave together, a harbinger of the reconciliation with Esau in chap. 33.

31:15 *Outsiders*: lit., "foreign women"; they lacked the favored legal status of native women. *Used up*: lit., "eaten, consumed"; the bridal price that a man received for giving his daughter in marriage was legally reserved as her inalienable dowry. Perhaps this is the reason that Rachel took the household images belonging to Laban.

31:19 *Household images*: in Hebrew, *teraphim*, figurines used in divination (Ez 21:26; Zec 10:2). Laban calls them his "gods" (v. 30). The traditional translation "idols" is avoided because it suggests false gods, whereas Genesis seems to accept the fact that the ancestors did not always live according to later biblical religious standards and laws.

31:20 *Hoodwinked*: lit., "stolen the heart of," i.e., lulled the mind of. *Aramean*: the earliest extra-biblical references to the Arameans date later than the time of Jacob, if Jacob is dated to the mid-second millennium; to call Laban an Aramean and to have him speak Aramaic (Jegar-sahadutha, v. 47) is an apparent anachronism. The word may have been chosen to underscore the growing estrangement between the two men and the fact that their descendants will be two different peoples.

31:23 *For seven days*: lit., "a way of seven days," a general term to designate a long distance; it would actually have taken a camel caravan many more days to travel from Haran to Gilead, the region east of the northern half of the Jordan. The mention of camels in this passage is apparently anachronistic since camels were not domesticated until the late second millennium.

*

31:3 Gn 26:3; 28:15; 32:10.
31:7 Jdt 8:26.
31:13 Gn 28:18.
31:16 Wis 10:10–11.
31:19 Gn 31:34; 1 Sm 19:13.
31:24 Wis 10:12.

Jacob and Laban in Gilead

25 When Laban overtook Jacob, Jacob's tents
were pitched in the hill country; Laban also
pitched his tents in the hill country of Gilead.
26 Laban said to Jacob, "How could you hood-
wink me and carry off my daughters like prison-
ers of war?† 27 Why did you dupe me by stealing
away secretly? You did not tell me! I would have
sent you off with joyful singing to the sound
of tambourines and harps. 28 You did not even
allow me a parting kiss to my daughters and
grandchildren! Now what you have done makes
no sense. 29 I have it in my power to harm all of
you; but last night the God of your father said
to me, 'Take care not to say anything to Jacob!'
30 Granted that you had to leave because you
were longing for your father's house, why did
you steal my gods?" 31 Jacob replied to Laban,
"I was frightened at the thought that you might
take your daughters away from me by force. 32 As
for your gods, the one you find them with shall
not remain alive! If, with our kinsmen looking
on, you identify anything here as belonging to
you, take it." Jacob had no idea that Rachel had
stolen the household images.

33 Laban then went in and searched Jacob's tent
and Leah's tent, as well as the tents of the two
maidservants; but he did not find them. Leaving
Leah's tent, he went into Rachel's. 34 † Mean-
while Rachel had taken the household images,
put them inside the camel's saddlebag, and
seated herself upon them. When Laban had rum-
maged through her whole tent without finding
them,* 35 she said to her father, "Do not let my
lord be angry that I cannot rise in your presence;
I am having my period." So, despite his search,
he did not find the household images.

36 Jacob, now angered, confronted Laban and
demanded, "What crime or offense have I com-
mitted that you should hound me? 37 Now that
you have rummaged through all my things,
what have you found from your household be-
longings? Produce it here before your kinsmen
and mine, and let them decide between the two
of us.
38 "In the twenty years that I was under you,
no ewe or she-goat of yours ever miscarried, and
I have never eaten rams of your flock. 39 * I never
brought you an animal torn by wild beasts; I
made good the loss myself. You held me respon-
sible for anything stolen by day or night.† 40 Of-
ten the scorching heat devoured me by day, and
the frost by night, while sleep fled from my eyes!
41 Of the twenty years that I have now spent in
your household, I served you fourteen years for
your two daughters and six years for your flock,
while you changed my wages ten times. 42 If the
God of my father, the God of Abraham and the
Fear of Isaac, had not been on my side, you
would now have sent me away empty-handed.
But God saw my plight and the fruits of my toil,
and last night he reproached you."*

43 † Laban replied to Jacob: "The daughters are
mine, their children are mine, and the flocks are
mine; everything you see belongs to me. What
can I do now for my own daughters and for the
children they have borne? 44 † Come, now, let
us make a covenant, you and I; and it will be a
treaty between you and me."

45 Then Jacob took a stone and set it up as a sa-
cred pillar.* 46 Jacob said to his kinsmen, "Gather
stones." So they got stones and made a mound;
and they ate there at the mound. 47 Laban called
it Jegar-sahadutha,† but Jacob called it Galeed.
48 Laban said, "This mound will be a witness
from now on between you and me." That is why
it was named Galeed— 49 and also Mizpah,† for
he said: "May the LORD keep watch between you
and me when we are out of each other's sight.
50 If you mistreat my daughters, or take other
wives besides my daughters, know that even
though no one else is there, God will be a wit-
ness between you and me."

51 Laban said further to Jacob: "Here is this
mound, and here is the sacred pillar that I have
set up between you and me. 52 This mound will
be a witness, and this sacred pillar will be a

---

†

31:26 *Prisoners of war*: lit., "women captured by the sword"; the women of a conquered people were treated as part of the victor's spoil; cf. 1 Sm 30:2; 2 Kgs 5:2.

31:34 As in chap. 27, a younger child (Rachel) deceives her father to gain what belongs to him.

31:39 Jacob's actions are more generous than the customs suggested in the Code of Hammurabi: "If in a sheepfold an act of god has occurred, or a lion has made a kill, the shepherd shall clear himself before the deity, and the owner of the fold must accept the loss" (par. 266); cf. Ex 22:12.

31:43–54 In this account of the non-aggression treaty between Laban and Jacob, the different objects that serve as witness (sacred pillar in v. 45, cairn of stones in v. 46), their different names (Jegar-sahadutha in v. 47, Mizpah in v. 49), and the two references to the covenant meal (vv. 46, 54) suggest that two versions have been fused. One version is the Yahwist source, and another source has been used to supplement it.

31:44–54 The treaty is a typical covenant between two parties: Jacob was bound to treat his wives (Laban's daughters) well, and Laban was bound not to cross Jacob's boundaries with hostile intent.

31:47–48 *Jegar-sahadutha*: an Aramaic term meaning "mound of witness." *Galeed*: in Hebrew, "the mound of witness."

31:49 *Mizpah*: a town in Gilead; cf. Jgs 10:17; 11:11, 34; Hos 5:1. The Hebrew name *mispa* ("lookout") is allied to *yisep yhwh* ("may the Lord keep watch"), and also echoes the word *masseba* ("sacred pillar").

*

31:34 Gn 31:19.
31:39 Ex 22:12.
31:42 Gn 31:24, 29.
31:45 Gn 28:18; 35:14.

witness, that, with hostile intent, I may not pass
beyond this mound into your territory, nor may
you pass beyond it into mine. 53 May the God of
Abraham and the God of Nahor, the God of their
father, judge between us!" Jacob took the oath by
the Fear of his father Isaac.† 54 He then offered a
sacrifice on the mountain and invited his kins-
men to share in the meal. When they had eaten,
they passed the night on the mountain.

32 1 † Early the next morning, Laban kissed
his grandchildren and his daughters and
blessed them; then he set out on his journey back
home. 2 Meanwhile Jacob continued on his own
way, and God's angels encountered him. 3 When
Jacob saw them he said, "This is God's encamp-
ment." So he named that place Mahanaim.†

Envoys to Esau

4 Jacob sent messengers ahead to his brother
Esau in the land of Seir, the country of Edom,*
5 ordering them: "Thus you shall say to my lord
Esau: 'Thus says your servant Jacob: I have been
residing with Laban and have been delayed until
now. 6 I own oxen, donkeys and sheep, as well
as male and female servants. I have sent my lord
this message in the hope of gaining your favor.' "
7 When the messengers returned to Jacob, they
said, "We found your brother Esau. He is now
coming to meet you, and four hundred men are
with him."
8 Jacob was very much frightened. In his anxiety,
he divided the people who were with him, as well
as his flocks, herds and camels, into two camps.
9 "If Esau should come and attack one camp," he
reasoned, "the remaining camp may still escape."
10 Then Jacob prayed: "God of my father Abraham
and God of my father Isaac! You, LORD, who said
to me, 'Go back to your land and your relatives,
and I will be good to you.'* 11 I am unworthy of all
the acts of kindness and faithfulness that you have
performed for your servant: although I crossed the
Jordan here with nothing but my staff, I have now
grown into two camps. 12 Save me from the hand
of my brother, from the hand of Esau! Otherwise I
fear that he will come and strike me down and the
mothers with the children. 13 You yourself said, 'I
will be very good to you, and I will make your de-
scendants like the sands of the sea, which are too
numerous to count.' "*
14 After passing the night there, Jacob selected
from what he had with him a present for
his brother Esau: 15 two hundred she-goats and
twenty he-goats; two hundred ewes and twenty
rams; 16 thirty female camels and their young;
forty cows and ten bulls; twenty female donkeys
and ten male donkeys. 17 He put these animals in
the care of his servants, in separate herds, and he
told the servants, "Go on ahead of me, but keep
some space between the herds." 18 He ordered
the servant in the lead, "When my brother Esau
meets you and asks, 'To whom do you belong?
Where are you going? To whom do these ani-
mals ahead of you belong?' 19 tell him, 'To your
servant Jacob, but they have been sent as a gift to
my lord Esau. Jacob himself is right behind us.' "
20 He also ordered the second servant and the
third and all the others who followed behind the
herds: "Thus and so you shall say to Esau, when
you reach him; 21 and also tell him, 'Your servant
Jacob is right behind us.' " For Jacob reasoned,
"If I first appease him with a gift that precedes
me, then later, when I face him, perhaps he will
forgive me." 22 So the gifts went on ahead of him,
while he stayed that night in the camp.

Jacob's New Name†

23 That night, however, Jacob arose, took his
two wives, with the two maidservants and his
eleven children, and crossed the ford of the
Jabbok. 24 After he got them and brought them
across the wadi and brought over what belonged
to him, 25 Jacob was left there alone. Then a
man† wrestled with him until the break of dawn.
26 When the man saw that he could not prevail
over him, he struck Jacob's hip at its socket, so
that Jacob's socket was dislocated as he wrestled
with him.* 27 The man then said, "Let me go, for

† **31:53** *Fear of . . . Isaac*: an archaic title for Jacob's God of the Father.

32:1–22 Jacob's negotiations with Esau. Laban kisses his daughters and grandchildren good-bye but not Jacob. On leaving Mesopotamia, Jacob has an encounter with angels of God (vv. 2–3), which provokes him to exclaim, "This is God's encampment," just as he exclaimed upon leaving Canaan, "This is the house of God, the gateway to heaven" (28:11–17).

32:3 *Mahanaim*: a town in Gilead (Jos 13:26, 30; 21:38; 2 Sm 2:8; etc.). The Hebrew name means "two camps." There are other allusions to the name in vv. 8, 11.

32:23–33 As Jacob crosses over to the land promised him, worried about the impending meeting with Esau, he encounters a mysterious adversary in the night with whom he wrestles until morning. The cunning Jacob manages to wrest a blessing from the night stranger before he departs. There are folkloric elements in the tale—e.g., the trial of the hero before he can return home, the nocturnal demon's loss of strength at sunrise, the demon protecting its river, the power gained by knowledge of an opponent's name—but these have been worked into a coherent though elliptical narrative. The point of the tale seems to be that the ever-striving, ever-grasping Jacob must eventually strive with God to attain full possession of the blessing.

32:25 *A man*: as with Abraham's three visitors in chap. 18, who appear sometimes as three, two, and one (the latter being God), this figure is fluid; he loses the match but changes Jacob's name (v. 29), an act elsewhere done only by God (17:5, 15). A few deft narrative touches manage to express intimate contact with Jacob while preserving the transcendence proper to divinity.

* **32:4** Gn 36:6.
32:10 Gn 31:3.
32:13 Gn 28:14; 48:16; Ex 32:13; Heb 11:12.
32:26 Hos 12:5.

it is daybreak." But Jacob said, "I will not let you
go until you bless me." 28 "What is your name?"
the man asked. He answered, "Jacob."* 29 Then
the man said, "You shall no longer be named
Jacob, but Israel,† because you have contended
with divine and human beings and have pre-
vailed." 30 Jacob then asked him, "Please tell me
your name." He answered, "Why do you ask for
my name?" With that, he blessed him. 31 Jacob
named the place Peniel,† "because I have seen
God face to face," he said, "yet my life has been
spared."*
32 At sunrise, as he left Penuel, Jacob limped
along because of his hip. 33 That is why, to this
day, the Israelites do not eat the sciatic muscle
that is on the hip socket, because he had struck
Jacob's hip socket at the sciatic muscle.

Jacob and Esau Meet†

33 1 Jacob looked up and saw Esau coming,
and with him four hundred men. So he
divided his children among Leah, Rachel, and
the two maidservants, 2 putting the maidservants
and their children first, Leah and her children
next, and Rachel and Joseph last. 3 He himself
went on ahead of them, bowing to the ground
seven times, until he reached his brother. 4 Esau
ran to meet him, embraced him, and flinging
himself on his neck, kissed him as he wept.
5 Then Esau looked up and saw the women
and children and asked, "Who are these with
you?" Jacob answered, "They are the children
with whom God has graciously favored your
servant." 6 Then the maidservants and their chil-
dren came forward and bowed low; 7 next, Leah
and her children came forward and bowed low;
lastly, Joseph and Rachel came forward and
bowed low. 8 Then Esau asked, "What did you
intend with all those herds that I encountered?"
Jacob answered, "It was to gain my lord's favor."
9 Esau replied, "I have plenty; my brother, you
should keep what is yours." 10 "No, I beg you!"
said Jacob. "If you will do me the favor, accept
this gift from me, since to see your face is for
me like seeing the face of God—and you have
received me so kindly. 11 Accept the gift I have
brought you. For God has been generous toward
me, and I have an abundance." Since he urged
him strongly, Esau accepted.
12 Then Esau said, "Let us break camp and be
on our way; I will travel in front of you." 13 But
Jacob replied: "As my lord knows, the children
are too young. And the flocks and herds that
are nursing are a concern to me; if overdriven
for even a single day, the whole flock will die.
14 Let my lord, then, go before his servant, while

Pray It!

Wrestling with God

Even after twenty years, Jacob is anxious about meeting Esau again. This time Jacob uses his craftiness not to deceive Esau but to gain Esau's good graces. Then, while on the way home, he has an amazing religious experience. Many Scripture scholars believe the strange wrestling encounter is a symbol that Jacob has become a changed person. He finally realizes that in all his troubles, God was his true opponent.

Perhaps at times you have wrestled with yourself or with God. It is not so much that God is your opponent or that you are in a contest. It is the wrestling itself that matters. When you face challenges, especially the big ones, you wrestle between the person you are now and the person God is calling you to be.

In your prayer time, reflect or journal on the following questions:

- When does it seem like God is trying to wrestle with you? What does it feel like?
- Is God challenging you about something in your life right now?
- What blessings might you gain in accepting God's challenge and changing your life?

▶ **Gn 32:23–33**

† **32:29** *Israel*: the first part of the Hebrew name *Yisrael* is given a popular explanation in the word *saritha*, "you contended"; the second part is the first syllable of *'elohim*, "divine beings." The present incident, with a similar allusion to the name Israel, is referred to in Hos 12:5, where the mysterious wrestler is explicitly called an angel.

32:31 *Peniel*: a variant of the word Penuel (v. 32), the name of a town on the north bank of the Jabbok in Gilead (Jgs 8:8–9, 17; 1 Kgs 12:25). The name is explained as meaning "the face of God," *peni-'el. Yet my life has been spared*: see note on 16:13.

33:1–20 The truly frightening confrontation seems to have already occurred in Jacob's meeting the divine stranger in the previous chapter. In contrast, this meeting brings reconciliation. Esau, impulsive but largehearted, kisses the cunning Jacob and calls him brother (v. 9). Jacob in return asks Esau to accept his blessing (*berakah*, translated "gift," v. 11), giving back at least symbolically what he had taken many years before and responding to Esau's erstwhile complaint ("he has taken away my blessing," 27:36). Verses 12–17 show that the reconciliation is not total and, further, that Jacob does not intend to share the ancestral land with his brother.

* **32:28** Gn 35:10; 1 Kgs 18:31; 2 Kgs 17:34. **32:31** Jgs 13:22.

Live It!

Letting Go of the Past

Jacob is understandably apprehensive as he approaches his long-estranged twin brother. How will Esau react? But Esau, who was wronged by Jacob, runs to meet him and gives him a hug. All is forgiven, and the two are reconciled at last. This story is like the parable of the prodigal son in Luke 15:11–32.

All of us have wronged others, especially the people we care about most. All of us have also experienced forgiveness. Nothing is quite like the freedom that comes with genuine forgiveness and reconciliation. A burden is lifted. A heavy heart is made lighter. A vengeful attitude is transformed into a feeling of inner peace and harmony. This is the work of God's grace. Forgiveness and reconciliation are powerful signs of the presence of God. We can almost feel the enormous sense of relief Jacob experiences as he realizes that his brother holds no grudge.

- Does a relationship in your life need forgiveness and reconciliation? If so, what can you do to bring about healing in this relationship?

Gn 33:1–17

I proceed more slowly at the pace of the livestock
before me and at the pace of my children, until
I join my lord in Seir." 15 Esau replied, "Let me
at least put at your disposal some of the people
who are with me." But Jacob said, "Why is this
that I am treated so kindly, my lord?" 16 So on
that day Esau went on his way back to Seir, 17 and
Jacob broke camp for Succoth.† There Jacob built
a home for himself and made booths for his live-
stock. That is why the place was named Succoth.
18 Jacob arrived safely at the city of Shechem,
which is in the land of Canaan, when he came
from Paddan-aram. He encamped in sight of
the city.* 19 The plot of ground on which he had
pitched his tent he bought for a hundred pieces
of money† from the descendants of Hamor, the
father of Shechem.* 20 He set up an altar there
and invoked "El, the God of Israel."*

The Rape of Dinah

34 1 † Dinah, the daughter whom Leah had
borne to Jacob, went out to visit some of
the women of the land. 2 When Shechem, son
of Hamor the Hivite,† the leader of the region,
saw her, he seized her and lay with her by force.
3 He was strongly attracted to Dinah, daughter of
Jacob, and was in love with the young woman.
So he spoke affectionately to her. 4 Shechem said
to his father Hamor, "Get me this young woman
for a wife."
5 Meanwhile, Jacob heard that Shechem had de-
filed his daughter Dinah; but since his sons were
out in the field with his livestock, Jacob kept quiet
until they came home. 6 Now Hamor, the father
of Shechem, went out to discuss the matter with
Jacob, 7 just as Jacob's sons were coming in from
the field. When they heard the news, the men
were indignant and extremely angry. Shechem
had committed an outrage in Israel by lying with
Jacob's daughter; such a thing is not done.* 8 Ha-
mor appealed to them, saying: "My son Shechem
has his heart set on your daughter. Please give her
to him as a wife. 9 Intermarry with us; give your
daughters to us, and take our daughters for your-
selves. 10 Thus you can live among us. The land is
open before you. Settle and move about freely in
it and acquire holdings here."† 11 Then Shechem
appealed to Dinah's father and brothers: "Do me
this favor, and whatever you ask from me, I will
give. 12 No matter how high you set the bridal price
and gift, I will give you whatever you ask from me;
only give me the young woman as a wife."

Revenge of Jacob's Sons

13 Jacob's sons replied to Shechem and his
father Hamor with guile, speaking as they did

†

33:17 *Succoth*: an important town near the confluence of the Jabbok and the Jordan (Jos 13:27; Jgs 8:5–16; 1 Kgs 7:46). *Booths*: in Hebrew, *sukkot*, of the same sound as the name of the town.

33:19 *Pieces of money*: in Hebrew, *qesita*, a monetary unit of which the value is unknown. *Descendants of Hamor*: Hamorites, "the people of Hamor"; cf. Jgs 9:28. Hamor was regarded as the eponymous ancestor of the pre-Israelite inhabitants of Shechem.

34:1–31 The story of the rape of Dinah and the revenge of Jacob's sons on the men of the city of Shechem may reflect the relations of the tribes of Simeon and Levi to their Canaanite neighbors around Shechem; the tribes are represented by their eponymous ancestors. Jacob's farewell testament (49:5–7) cites this incident as the reason for the decline of the tribes of Simeon and Levi. Ominously, vv. 30–31 leave the situation unresolved, with Jacob concerned about the welfare of the whole family, and Simeon and Levi concerned only about the honor of their full sister. The danger to the family from narrow self-interest will continue in the Joseph story.

34:2 *Hivite*: the Greek text has "Horite"; the terms were apparently used indiscriminately to designate the Hurrian or other non-Semitic elements in Palestine.

34:10 Hamor seems to be making concessions to Jacob's family in the hope of avoiding warfare between the two families.

*

33:18 Gn 12:6; Jn 4:5.
33:19 Jos 24:32; Jn 4:5; Acts 7:16.
33:20 Jgs 6:24.
34:7 2 Sm 13:12.

because he had defiled their sister Dinah. [14]They said to them, "We are not able to do this thing: to give our sister to an uncircumcised man. For that would be a disgrace for us. [15]Only on this condition will we agree to that: that you become like us by having every male among you circumcised. [16]Then we will give you our daughters and take your daughters in marriage; we will settle among you and become one people. [17]But if you do not listen to us and be circumcised, we will take our daughter and go."

[18]Their proposal pleased Hamor and his son Shechem. [19]The young man lost no time in acting on the proposal, since he wanted Jacob's daughter. Now he was more highly regarded than anyone else in his father's house. [20]So Hamor and his son Shechem went to the gate of their city and said to the men of their city: [21]"These men are friendly toward us. Let them settle in the land and move about in it freely; there is ample room in the land for them. We can take their daughters in marriage and give our daughters to them. [22]But only on this condition will the men agree to live with us and form one people with us: that every male among us be circumcised as they themselves are. [23]Would not their livestock, their property, and all their animals then be ours? Let us just agree with them, so that they will settle among us."

[24]All who went out of the gate of the city listened to Hamor and his son Shechem, and all the males, all those who went out of the gate of the city,† were circumcised. [25]On the third day, while they were still in pain, two of Jacob's sons, Simeon and Levi, brothers of Dinah, each took his sword, advanced against the unsuspecting city and massacred all the males.* [26]After they had killed Hamor and his son Shechem with the sword, they took Dinah from Shechem's house and left.* [27]Then the other sons of Jacob followed up the slaughter and sacked the city because their sister had been defiled. [28]They took their sheep, cattle and donkeys, whatever was in the city and in the surrounding country. [29]They carried off all their wealth, their children, and their women, and looted whatever was in the houses.*

[30]Jacob said to Simeon and Levi: "You have brought trouble upon me by making me repugnant to the inhabitants of the land, the Canaanites and the Perizzites. I have so few men that, if these people unite against me and attack me, I and my household will be wiped out." [31]But they retorted, "Should our sister be treated like a prostitute?"

Live It!

No Way, Shechem!

Every now and then there will be a news story about someone being attacked by another person or one ethnic group attacking another group, and sometimes part of their domination and victory includes rape. This is an especially evil act because it combines brutal violence with sex. Any time a woman is raped, she is violated against her will, and she can never be the same. Males can also be victims of rape.

The story in Genesis, chapter 34, tells us of Shechem, a local prince, who rapes Dinah. Because of his power, Shechem figures he can do what he wants to her. But in the end, his life is taken.

Rape is a violent and sinful act, no matter what the context. We are to respect one another, no matter what. Position or power does not give us the right to commit sexual violence. Rape and any other sexual abuse are an outrage to God.

Gn 34:1–31

Bethel Revisited

35 [1]† God said to Jacob: Go up now to Bethel. Settle there and build an altar there to the God who appeared to you when you were fleeing from your brother Esau.* [2]So Jacob told his household and all who were with him: "Get rid of the foreign gods† among you; then purify yourselves and change your clothes.

†

34:24 *All those who went out of the gate of the city*: apparently meaning all the residents. By temporarily crippling the men through circumcision, Jacob's sons deprived the city of its defenders.

35:1–7 Jacob returns to Bethel and founds the sanctuary, an event that forms a "bookend" to the first visit to Bethel in 28:10–22. To enter the Lord's sanctuary, one must purify oneself and get rid of all signs of allegiance to other gods (Jos 24:23; Jgs 10:16). Jacob also seems to initiate the custom of making a pilgrimage to Bethel (see Ps 122:1 and Is 2:3, 5).

35:2 *Foreign gods*: divine images, including those of household deities (see note on 31:19), that Jacob's people brought with them from Paddan-aram.

34:25 Gn 49:6.
34:26 Jdt 9:2.
34:29 Jdt 9:3–4.
35:1 Gn 28:12–13.

GN

3 Let us now go up to Bethel so that I might
build an altar there to the God who answered
me in the day of my distress and who has been
with me wherever I have gone." 4 They gave Ja-
cob all the foreign gods in their possession and
also the rings they had in their ears† and Jacob
buried them under the oak that is near Shechem.
5 Then, as they set out, a great terror fell upon the
surrounding towns, so that no one pursued the
sons of Jacob.
6 Thus Jacob and all the people who were with
him arrived in Luz (now Bethel) in the land of
Canaan.* 7 There he built an altar and called the
place El-Bethel,† for it was there that God had re-
vealed himself to him when he was fleeing from
his brother.*
8 Deborah, Rebekah's nurse, died. She was
buried under the oak below Bethel, and so it was
named Allon-bacuth.†
9 On Jacob's arrival from Paddan-aram, God
appeared to him again and blessed him. 10 God
said to him:

Your name is Jacob.
You will no longer be named Jacob,
but Israel will be your name.*

So he was named Israel. 11 Then God said to
him: I am God Almighty; be fruitful and mul-
tiply. A nation, indeed an assembly of nations,
will stem from you, and kings will issue from
your loins. 12 The land I gave to Abraham and
Isaac I will give to you; and to your descendants
after you I will give the land.*
13 Then God departed from him. 14 In the place
where God had spoken with him, Jacob set up a
sacred pillar, a stone pillar, and upon it he made
a libation and poured out oil.* 15 Jacob named
the place where God spoke to him Bethel.

Jacob's Family

16 Then they departed from Bethel; but while
they still had some distance to go to Ephrath,
Rachel went into labor and suffered great dis-
tress. 17 When her labor was most intense, the
midwife said to her, "Do not fear, for now you
have another son." 18 With her last breath—for
she was at the point of death—she named him
Ben-oni;† but his father named him Benjamin.
19 Thus Rachel died; and she was buried on the
road to Ephrath (now Bethlehem).† * 20 Jacob
set up a sacred pillar on her grave, and the same
pillar marks Rachel's grave to this day.
21 Israel moved on and pitched his tent beyond
Migdal-eder. 22 While Israel was encamped in
that region, Reuben went and lay with Bilhah,
his father's concubine. When Israel heard of it,
he was greatly offended.† *
The sons of Jacob were now twelve. 23 The
sons of Leah: Reuben, Jacob's firstborn, Simeon,
Levi, Judah, Issachar, and Zebulun; 24 † the sons
of Rachel: Joseph and Benjamin; 25 the sons of
Rachel's maidservant Bilhah: Dan and Naphtali;
26 the sons of Leah's maidservant Zilpah: Gad
and Asher. These are the sons of Jacob who were
born to him in Paddan-aram.
27 Jacob went home to his father Isaac at
Mamre, in Kiriath-arba (now Hebron), where
Abraham and Isaac had resided. 28 The length of
Isaac's life was one hundred and eighty years;
29 then he breathed his last. He died as an old
man and was gathered to his people. After a full
life, his sons Esau and Jacob buried him.

Edomite Lists†

36 1 These are the descendants of Esau (that
is, Edom). 2 † Esau took his wives from
among the Canaanite women: Adah, daughter

---

†

35:4 *Rings . . . their ears*: the earrings may have belonged to the gods because earrings were often placed on statues.

35:7 *El-Bethel*: probably to be translated "the god of Bethel." This is one of several titles of God in Genesis that begin with *El* (= God), e.g., *El Olam* (21:33), *El Elyon* (14:18), *El* the God of Israel (33:20), *El Roi* (16:13), and *El Shaddai*. Most of these (except *El Shaddai*) are tied to specific Israelite shrines.

35:8 *Allon-bacuth*: the Hebrew name means "oak of weeping."

35:18 *Ben-oni*: means either "son of my vigor" or, more likely in the context, "son of affliction." *Benjamin*: "son of the right hand," meaning a son who is his father's help and support.

35:19 *Bethlehem*: the gloss comes from a later tradition that identified the site with Bethlehem, also called Ephrath or Ephratha (Jos 15:59; Ru 4:11; Mi 5:1). But Rachel's grave was actually near Ramah (Jer 31:15), a few miles north of Jerusalem, in the territory of Benjamin (1 Sm 10:2).

35:22 The genealogy in vv. 23–29 is prefaced by a notice about Reuben's sleeping with Bilhah, his father's concubine. Such an act is a serious challenge to the authority of the father (cf. 2 Sm 3:7 and 16:21). In his final testament in chap. 49, Jacob cites this act of Reuben as the reason for Reuben's loss of the authority he had as firstborn son (49:4). Reuben's act is one more instance of strife in the family and of discord between father and son.

35:24–26 Benjamin is here said to have been born in Paddan-aram, apparently because all twelve sons of Jacob are considered as a unit.

36:1–43 The line of Esau. In the preceding chapter (35:22–26), the list of Jacob's children completes the narrative of Jacob; in this chapter, the narrative of Esau is complete when his descendants are listed. The notice of Abraham's death and burial in 25:7–10 was followed by a list of the line of his elder son Ishmael (25:12–18) and here Isaac's death and burial are followed by the line of Esau. The lines of both Ishmael and Esau are introduced by the same double formula, "These are the descendants of . . ." (25:12; 36:9) and "These are the names of the sons of . . ." (25:13; 36:10). The chapter consists of diverse material: vv. 1–3, Esau's wives; vv. 9–14, Esau's descendants; vv. 15–19, the clans of Esau; vv. 20–30, the Horites of Seir; vv. 31–39, the Edomite kings; vv. 40–43, the Edomites.

36:2–14 The names of Esau's wives and of their fathers given here

---

*

35:6 Gn 28:19; Jos 18:13; Jgs 1:22–23.
35:7 Gn 28:12–13.
35:10 1 Kgs 18:31; 2 Kgs 17:34.
35:12 Ex 32:13; Heb 11:9.
35:14 Gn 28:18; 31:45.
35:19 Gn 48:7; 1 Sm 10:2; Mi 5:1.
35:22 Gn 49:4; 1 Chr 5:1.

of Elon the Hittite; Oholibamah, the daughter of
Anah the son of Zibeon the Hivite;* 3and Base-
math, daughter of Ishmael and sister of Neba-
ioth. 4Adah bore Eliphaz to Esau; Basemath bore
Reuel;* 5and Oholibamah bore Jeush, Jalam and
Korah. These are the sons of Esau who were born
to him in the land of Canaan.*

6Esau took his wives, his sons, his daughters,
and all the members of his household, as well
as his livestock, all his cattle, and all the prop-
erty he had acquired in the land of Canaan, and
went to the land of Seir, away from his brother
Jacob.* 7Their possessions had become too great
for them to dwell together, and the land in which
they were residing could not support them be-
cause of their livestock. 8So Esau settled in the
highlands of Seir. (Esau is Edom.)* 9These are
the descendants of Esau,† ancestor of the Edom-
ites, in the highlands of Seir.

10These are the names of the sons of Esau:
Eliphaz, son of Adah, wife of Esau, and Reuel,
son of Basemath, wife of Esau. 11* The sons of
Eliphaz were Teman, Omar, Zepho, Gatam, and
Kenaz. 12Timna was a concubine of Eliphaz, the
son of Esau, and she bore Amalek to Eliphaz.
Those were the sons of Adah, the wife of Esau.
13These were the sons of Reuel: Nahath, Zerah,
Shammah, and Mizzah. Those were the sons of
Basemath, the wife of Esau.* 14These were the
sons of Esau's wife Oholibamah—the daugh-
ter of Anah, son of Zibeon—whom she bore to
Esau: Jeush, Jalam, and Korah.*

15These are the clans of the sons of Esau. The
sons of Eliphaz, Esau's firstborn: the clans of Te-
man, Omar, Zepho, Kenaz, 16Korah, Gatam, and
Amalek. These are the clans of Eliphaz in the
land of Edom; they are the sons of Adah. 17These
are the sons of Reuel, son of Esau: the clans of
Nahath, Zerah, Shammah, and Mizzah. These
are the clans of Reuel in the land of Edom; they
are the sons of Basemath, wife of Esau. 18These
were the sons of Oholibamah, wife of Esau:
the clans of Jeush, Jalam, and Korah. These are
the clans of Esau's wife Oholibamah, daughter
of Anah. 19These are the sons of Esau—that is,
Edom—according to their clans.

20These are the sons of Seir the Horite,† the
inhabitants of the land: Lotan, Shobal, Zibeon,
Anah,* 21Dishon, Ezer, and Dishan; those are the
clans of the Horites, sons of Seir in the land of
Edom. 22* The sons of Lotan were Hori and He-
mam, and Lotan's sister was Timna. 23These are
the sons of Shobal: Alvan, Mahanath, Ebal, She-
pho, and Onam. 24These are the sons of Zibeon:
Aiah and Anah. He is the Anah who found water
in the desert while he was pasturing the donkeys
of his father Zibeon. 25These are the children
of Anah: Dishon and Oholibamah, daughter of
Anah. 26These are the sons of Dishon: Hemdan,
Eshban, Ithran, and Cheran. 27These are the sons
of Ezer: Bilhan, Zaavan, and Akan. 28These are
the sons of Dishan: Uz and Aran. 29These are the
clans of the Horites: the clans of Lotan, Shobal,
Zibeon, Anah, 30Dishon, Ezer, and Dishan; those
are the clans of the Horites, clan by clan, in the
land of Seir.

31* These are the kings who reigned in the
land of Edom before any king reigned over the
Israelites.† 32Bela, son of Beor, became king
in Edom; the name of his city was Dinhabah.
33When Bela died, Jobab, son of Zerah, from
Bozrah, succeeded him as king. 34When Jobab
died, Husham, from the land of the Temanites,
succeeded him as king. 35When Husham died,
Hadad, son of Bedad, succeeded him as king. He
is the one who defeated Midian in the country of
Moab; the name of his city was Avith. 36When
Hadad died, Samlah, from Masrekah, succeeded
him as king. 37When Samlah died, Shaul, from
Rehoboth-on-the-River, succeeded him as king.
38When Shaul died, Baal-hanan, son of Achbor,
succeeded him as king. 39When Baal-hanan, son
of Achbor, died, Hadad succeeded him as king;
the name of his city was Pau. His wife's name
was Mehetabel, the daughter of Matred, son of
Mezahab.

40These are the names of the clans of Esau
identified according to their families and locali-
ties: the clans of Timna, Alvah, Jetheth, 41Ohol-
ibamah, Elah, Pinon, 42Kenaz, Teman, Mibzar,
43Magdiel, and Iram. Those are the clans of the
Edomites, according to their settlements in their
territorial holdings—that is, of Esau, the ancestor
of the Edomites.

† differ considerably from their names cited from other old sources in 26:34 and 28:9. *Zibeon the Hivite*: in v. 20 he is called a "Horite"; see note on 34:2.

36:9 *These are the descendants of Esau*: the original heading of the genealogy is preserved in v. 10 ("These are the names of the sons of Esau"). This use of the Priestly formula is secondary and should not be counted in the list of ten such formulas in Genesis.

36:20 *Seir the Horite*: according to Dt 2:12, the highlands of Seir were inhabited by Horites before they were occupied by the Edomites.

36:31 *Before any king reigned over the Israelites*: obviously this statement was written after the time of Saul, Israel's first king. According to 1 Sm 14:47, Saul waged war against the Edomites; according to 2 Sm 8:2, 13–14 and 1 Kgs 11:14–17, David made Edom a vassal state and nearly wiped out the royal line. These events reflect the words of the Lord to Rebekah at the birth of the boys, "the older shall serve the younger" (25:23).

* **36:2** Gn 26:34.
36:4 1 Chr 1:35.
36:5 1 Chr 1:35.
36:6 Gn 32:4.
36:8 Dt 2:4–5; Jos 24:4.
36:11–12 1 Chr 1:36.
36:13 1 Chr 1:37.
36:14 1 Chr 1:35.
36:20–21 1 Chr 1:38.
36:22–28 1 Chr 1:39–42.
36:31–43 1 Chr 1:43–54.

G
N

Introducing...

Joseph

The timeless power of Joseph's story is reaffirmed by the long and successful run of the Broadway play *Joseph and the Amazing Technicolor Dreamcoat.* (In other Bible versions, the "long ornamented tunic" in Genesis 37:3 is translated as a "coat of many colors.") The play is based on chapters 37–50 of Genesis, which contain one of the world's greatest stories of family, jealousy, betrayal, and forgiveness.

A son of Jacob and Rachel, Joseph carries to Egypt the divine promises of land and descendants, and eventually becomes the link with the story of Moses and the Exodus. As Jacob's favorite son, Joseph experiences the jealousy of his brothers, who sell him to Egyptian merchants. In Egypt, Joseph rises to power, becoming second in command to the pharaoh. Later, when Joseph's brothers come to Egypt looking for food, he forgives them and becomes reconciled with them.

Joseph's story encourages us to forgive others, even when we have been unjustly treated by them. Whenever we have been greatly wronged, remembering Joseph will offer us hope and courage.

▶ Gn 37:1—50:26

Joseph Sold into Egypt

37 1 Jacob settled in the land where his fa-
ther had sojourned, the land of Canaan.†
2 This is the story of the family of Jacob.† When
Joseph was seventeen years old, he was tending
the flocks with his brothers; he was an assistant
to the sons of his father's wives Bilhah and Zil-
pah, and Joseph brought their father bad reports
about them. 3 Israel loved Joseph best of all his
sons, for he was the child of his old age; and he
had made him a long ornamented tunic.† 4 When
his brothers saw that their father loved him best
of all his brothers, they hated him so much that
they could not say a kind word to him.
5 † Once Joseph had a dream, and when he
told his brothers, they hated him even more.*
6 He said to them, "Listen to this dream I had.
7 There we were, binding sheaves in the field,
when suddenly my sheaf rose to an upright po-
sition, and your sheaves formed a ring around
my sheaf and bowed down to it." 8 His brothers
said to him, "Are you really going to make your-
self king over us? Will you rule over us?" So they
hated him all the more because of his dreams
and his reports.*
9 Then he had another dream, and told it to his
brothers. "Look, I had another dream," he said;
"this time, the sun and the moon and eleven
stars were bowing down to me." 10 When he
told it to his father and his brothers, his father
reproved him and asked, "What is the meaning
of this dream of yours? Can it be that I and your
mother and your brothers are to come and bow
to the ground before you?" 11 So his brothers
were furious at him but his father kept the mat-
ter in mind.
12 One day, when his brothers had gone to
pasture their father's flocks at Shechem, 13 Israel
said to Joseph, "Are your brothers not tending
our flocks at Shechem? Come and I will send
you to them." "I am ready," Joseph answered.
14 "Go then," he replied; "see if all is well with
your brothers and the flocks, and bring back
word." So he sent him off from the valley of He-
bron. When Joseph reached Shechem, 15 a man
came upon him as he was wandering about in

†

37:1 The statement points ahead to 47:27, "Thus Israel settled in the land of Egypt, in the region of Goshen." These two statements frame the Joseph narrative; the later material (47:28–49:33) is about Jacob; chap. 50 brings to a conclusion themes remaining from the earlier story. One aim of the Joseph story is to explain how Israel came to Egypt after sojourning so long in Canaan.

37:2 The Joseph story is great literature not only in its themes but in its art. The stories show an interest in the psychology of the characters; everyone acts "in character" yet there is never a doubt that a divine purpose is bringing events to their conclusion. According to a literary analysis, vv. 1–4 set the scene; vv. 5–36 introduce the dramatic tension in the form of a conflict within the family; chaps. 38–41 describe the journeys away from their family of the eponymous ancestors of the two great tribes of later times, Judah (chap. 38) and Joseph (chaps. 39–41) and their preliminary conclusions; chaps. 42–44 detail the famine and journeys for food (chaps. 42, 43) that bring the brothers and (indirectly) the father into fresh contact with a mature Joseph who now has the power of life and death over them; 45:1–47:27 is the resolution (reconciliation of Joseph to his brothers) and the salvation of the family.

37:3 Jacob's favoring Joseph over his other sons is a cause of the brothers' attempt on his life. Throughout the story, Jacob is unaware of the impact of his favoritism on his other sons (cf. vv. 33–35; 42:36). *Long ornamented tunic*: the meaning of the Hebrew phrase is unclear. In 2 Sm 13:18–19, it is the distinctive dress of unmarried royal daughters. The "coat of many colors" in the Septuagint became the traditional translation. Ancient depictions of Semites in formal dress show them with long, ornamented robes and that is the most likely meaning here. Possibly, the young Joseph is given a coat that symbolizes honor beyond his years. Later, Pharaoh will clothe Joseph in a robe that symbolizes honor (41:42).

37:5–10 Joseph's dreams of ruling his brothers appear at first glance to be merely adolescent grandiosity, and they bring him

*

37:5 Gn 42:9. **37:8** Gn 50:17–18.

the fields. "What are you looking for?" the man
asked him. 16 "I am looking for my brothers," he
answered. "Please tell me where they are tend-
ing the flocks." 17 The man told him, "They have
moved on from here; in fact, I heard them say,
'Let us go on to Dothan.' " So Joseph went after
his brothers and found them in Dothan. 18 They
saw him from a distance, and before he reached
them, they plotted to kill him. 19 They said to
one another: "Here comes that dreamer! 20 Come
now, let us kill him and throw him into one of
the cisterns here; we could say that a wild beast
devoured him. We will see then what comes of
his dreams."*

21 † But when Reuben heard this, he tried to
save him from their hands, saying: "We must
not take his life." 22 Then Reuben said, "Do not
shed blood! Throw him into this cistern in the
wilderness; but do not lay a hand on him." His
purpose was to save him from their hands and
restore him to his father.*

23 So when Joseph came up to his brothers,
they stripped him of his tunic, the long orna-
mented tunic he had on; 24 then they took him
and threw him into the cistern. The cistern was
empty; there was no water in it.

25 Then they sat down to eat. Looking up,
they saw a caravan of Ishmaelites coming from
Gilead, their camels laden with gum, balm, and
resin to be taken down to Egypt.* 26 Judah said
to his brothers: "What is to be gained by killing
our brother and concealing his blood?* 27 Come,
let us sell him to these Ishmaelites, instead of
doing away with him ourselves. After all, he is
our brother, our own flesh." His brothers agreed.
28 Midianite traders passed by, and they pulled
Joseph up out of the cistern. They sold Joseph
for twenty pieces of silver† to the Ishmaelites,
who took him to Egypt.* 29 When Reuben went
back to the cistern and saw that Joseph was not
in it, he tore his garments,† 30 and returning to
his brothers, he exclaimed: "The boy is gone!
And I—where can I turn?" 31 They took Joseph's
tunic, and after slaughtering a goat, dipped the
tunic in its blood. 32 Then they sent someone to
bring the long ornamented tunic to their father,
with the message: "We found this. See whether
it is your son's tunic or not." 33 He recognized it
and exclaimed: "My son's tunic! A wild beast has
devoured him! Joseph has been torn to pieces!"*
34 Then Jacob tore his garments, put sackcloth
on his loins, and mourned his son many days.
35 Though his sons and daughters tried to console
him, he refused all consolation, saying, "No, I
will go down mourning to my son in Sheol."†
Thus did his father weep for him.*

Did You Know?

Dreams

In the ancient world, belief in the reality and significance of dreams was widespread. The ancients believed that dreams and visions revealed messages, prophecies, and healing from their gods. Israel shared this view of the importance of dreams. Joseph is described as an interpreter of dreams, and this skill earns him Pharaoh's respect (see Gn 41:37–45), as well as his brothers' jealousy (see 37:5–11).

In the Old Testament, the prophets are often referred to as seers because the word of God so often comes to them through dreams and visions. The focus, however, is always on the word of God and its meaning, not on the dream itself. In fact, a character in the story, inspired by God, usually interprets the dream, which aims to lead the people to more faithful observance of the covenant. If the dream does not do this, it is to be considered a false dream. (See other references to dreams in Genesis 28:10–22; Deuteronomy 13:2–6; Sirach 34:1–4; Jeremiah 27:9–10, 29:8–9; Joel 2:28; Zechariah 1:8; and Matthew 1:20, 2:13.)

▶ **Gn 37:1–11, 40:1—41:36**

GN

only trouble. His later successes make it clear, however, that they were from God. Another confirmation of their divine source is the doubling of dreams (cf. 41:32).

37:21–36 The chapter thus far is from the Yahwist source, as are also vv. 25–28a. But vv. 21–24 and 28b–36 are from another source (sometimes designated the Elohist source). In the latter, Reuben tries to rescue Joseph, who is taken in Reuben's absence by certain Midianites; in the Yahwist source, it is Judah who saves Joseph's life by having him sold to certain Ishmaelites. Although the two variant forms in which the story was handed down in early oral tradition differ in these minor points, they agree on the essential fact that Joseph was brought as a slave into Egypt because of the jealousy of his brothers.

37:28 *They sold Joseph . . . silver*: editors tried to solve the confusion, created by different sources, by supposing that it was the Midianite traders who pulled Joseph out of the pit and sold him to Ishmaelites. In all probability, one source had the brothers selling Joseph to Ishmaelites, whereas the other had them cast him into the pit whence he was taken by Midianite traders.

37:29 *Tore his garments*: the traditional sign of mourning in the ancient Near East.

37:35 *Sheol*: see note on Ps 6:6.

37:20 Gn 44:28.
37:22 Gn 42:22.
37:25 Gn 43:11.
37:26 Jb 16:18.
37:28 Ps 105:17; Wis 10:13; Acts 7:9.
37:33 Gn 44:28.
37:35 Gn 42:38.

G
N

Did You Know?

Levirate Marriage

Why does Onan have to marry his dead brother's wife and have a son by her? One of the laws specified in Deuteronomy 25:5–10 regulates what is called levirate marriage. *Levirate* means "brother-in-law." When a man's married brother dies without a son, that man is obligated to marry the wife who was left, and the first son whom she bears shall "continue the line of the deceased" (verse 6). This marriage practice seems to have developed in Israel for several reasons:

- A male child was needed to be heir to the dead man's property because women generally did not own property.
- The dead man's widow needed support and protection.
- A male heir ensured that the family property was kept within the immediate family.

▶ Gn 38:8

36 The Midianites, meanwhile, sold Joseph in
Egypt to Potiphar, an official of Pharaoh and his
chief steward.*

Judah and Tamar†

38 1 About that time Judah went down, away
from his brothers, and pitched his tent
near a certain Adullamite named Hirah. 2 There
Judah saw the daughter of a Canaanite named
Shua; he married her, and had intercourse with
her.* 3 She conceived and bore a son, whom she
named Er. 4 Again she conceived and bore a son,
whom she named Onan. 5 Then she bore still
another son, whom she named Shelah. She was
in Chezib† when she bore him.*
6 Judah got a wife named Tamar for his first-
born, Er. 7 But Er, Judah's firstborn, greatly of-
fended the LORD; so the LORD took his life.*
8 * Then Judah said to Onan, "Have intercourse
with your brother's wife, in fulfillment of your
duty as brother-in-law, and thus preserve your
brother's line."† 9 Onan, however, knew that the
offspring would not be his; so whenever he had
intercourse with his brother's wife, he wasted his
seed on the ground, to avoid giving offspring to
his brother. 10 What he did greatly offended the
LORD, and the LORD took his life too. 11 Then Ju-
dah said to his daughter-in-law Tamar, "Remain
a widow in your father's house until my son
Shelah grows up"—for he feared that Shelah also
might die like his brothers. So Tamar went to live
in her father's house.
12 Time passed, and the daughter of Shua,
Judah's wife, died. After Judah completed the
period of mourning, he went up to Timnah, to
those who were shearing his sheep, in company
with his friend Hirah the Adullamite. 13 Then Ta-
mar was told, "Your father-in-law is on his way
up to Timnah to shear his sheep." 14 So she took
off her widow's garments, covered herself with a
shawl, and having wrapped herself sat down at
the entrance to Enaim, which is on the way to
Timnah; for she was aware that, although Shelah
was now grown up, she had not been given to him
in marriage.* 15 When Judah saw her, he thought
she was a harlot, since she had covered her face.
16 So he went over to her at the roadside and said,
"Come, let me have intercourse with you," for he
did not realize that she was his daughter-in-law.
She replied, "What will you pay me for letting
you have intercourse with me?" 17 He answered,
"I will send you a young goat from the flock."
"Very well," she said, "provided you leave me a
pledge until you send it." 18 Judah asked, "What
pledge should I leave you?" She answered, "Your
seal and cord,† and the staff in your hand." So he

† **38:1–30** This chapter has subtle connections to the main Joseph story. It tells of the eponymous founder of the other great tribe of later times, Judah. Having already been introduced as one of the two good brothers in 37:26–27, he appears here as the father-in-law of the twice-widowed Tamar; he has reneged on his promise to provide his son Shelah to her in a levirate marriage. Unjustly treated, Tamar takes matters into her own hands and tricks Judah into becoming the father of her children, Perez and Zerah. Judah ultimately acknowledges that his daughter-in-law was right ("She is in the right rather than I," v. 26). In contrast to Judah's expectations, the family line does not continue through his son Shelah, but through the children of Tamar. Similarities relate this little story to the main narrative: the deception involving an article of clothing (the widow's garments of Tamar, Judah's seal, cord, and staff) point back to the bloody tunic that deceives Jacob in 37:31–33; a woman attempts the seduction of a man separated from his family, for righteous purposes in chap. 38, for unrighteous purposes in chap. 39.

38:5 *Chezib*: a variant form of Achzib (Jos 15:44; Mi 1:14), a town in the Judean Shephelah.

38:8 *Preserve your brother's line*: lit., "raise up seed for your brother": an allusion to the law of levirate, or "brother-in-law," marriage; see notes on Dt 25:5; Ru 2:20. Onan's violation of this law brought on him God's punishment (vv. 9–10).

38:18 *Seal and cord*: the cylinder seal, through which a hole was bored lengthwise so that it could be worn from the neck by a cord, was a distinctive means of identification. Apparently one's staff could also be marked with some sign of identification (cf. Nm 17:17–18).

* **37:36** Ps 105:17. **38:2** 1 Chr 2:3. **38:5** 1 Chr 4:21. **38:7** 1 Chr 2:3. **38:8** Dt 25:5; Mt 22:24; Mk 12:19; Lk 20:28. **38:14** Prv 7:10.

gave them to her and had intercourse with her,
and she conceived by him. 19 After she got up and
went away, she took off her shawl and put on her
widow's garments again.
20 Judah sent the young goat by his friend
the Adullamite to recover the pledge from the
woman; but he did not find her. 21 So he asked
the men of that place, "Where is the prostitute,†
the one by the roadside in Enaim?" But they
answered, "No prostitute has been here." 22 He
went back to Judah and told him, "I did not find
her; and besides, the men of the place said, 'No
prostitute has been here.' " 23 "Let her keep the
things," Judah replied; "otherwise we will be-
come a laughingstock. After all, I did send her
this young goat, but you did not find her."
24 About three months later, Judah was told,
"Your daughter-in-law Tamar has acted like a
harlot and now she is pregnant from her har-
lotry." Judah said, "Bring her out; let her be
burned." 25 But as she was being brought out, she
sent word to her father-in-law, "It is by the man
to whom these things belong that I am preg-
nant." Then she said, "See whose seal and cord
and staff these are." 26 Judah recognized them
and said, "She is in the right rather than I, since
I did not give her to my son Shelah." He had no
further sexual relations with her.
27 When the time of her delivery came, there
were twins in her womb.* 28 While she was giv-
ing birth, one put out his hand; and the midwife
took and tied a crimson thread on his hand,
noting, "This one came out first." 29 * But as he
withdrew his hand, his brother came out; and
she said, "What a breach you have made for
yourself!" So he was called Perez.† 30 Afterward
his brother, who had the crimson thread on his
hand, came out; he was called Zerah.† *

Joseph's Temptation

39 1 When Joseph was taken down to Egypt,
an Egyptian, Potiphar, an official of Phar-
aoh and his chief steward, bought him from the
Ishmaelites who had brought him there. 2 * The
LORD was with Joseph and he enjoyed great suc-
cess and was assigned to the household of his
Egyptian master. 3 When his master saw that the
LORD was with him and brought him success
in whatever he did, 4 he favored Joseph and
made him his personal attendant; he put him
in charge of his household and entrusted to him
all his possessions.* 5 From the moment that
he put him in charge of his household and all
his possessions, the LORD blessed the Egyptian's
house for Joseph's sake; the LORD's blessing was
on everything he owned, both inside the house
and out. 6 Having left everything he owned in
Joseph's charge, he gave no thought, with Joseph
there, to anything but the food he ate.
Now Joseph was well-built and handsome.
7 After a time, his master's wife looked at him
with longing and said, "Lie with me." 8 But he
refused and said to his master's wife, "Look, as
long as I am here, my master does not give a
thought to anything in the house, but has en-
trusted to me all he owns. 9 He has no more au-
thority in this house than I do. He has withheld
from me nothing but you, since you are his wife.
How, then, could I do this great wrong and sin
against God?" 10 Although she spoke to him day
after day, he would not agree to lie with her, or
even be near her.*
11 One such day, when Joseph came into the
house to do his work, and none of the house-
hold servants were then in the house, 12 she laid
hold of him by his cloak, saying, "Lie with me!"
But leaving the cloak in her hand, he escaped
and ran outside. 13 When she saw that he had
left his cloak in her hand as he escaped outside,
14 she cried out to her household servants and
told them, "Look! My husband has brought us
a Hebrew man to mock us! He came in here to
lie with me, but I cried out loudly. 15 When he
heard me scream, he left his cloak beside me and
escaped and ran outside."
16 She kept the cloak with her until his master
came home. 17 Then she told him the same story:
"The Hebrew slave whom you brought us came
to me to amuse himself at my expense. 18 But
when I screamed, he left his cloak beside me
and escaped outside." 19 When the master heard
his wife's story in which she reported, "Thus and
so your servant did to me," he became enraged.
20 Joseph's master seized him and put him into
the jail where the king's prisoners were con-
fined.* And there he sat, in jail.

†

38:21 *Prostitute*: the Hebrew term *qedesha*, lit., "consecrated woman," designates a woman associated with a sanctuary whose activities could include prostitution; cf. Dt 23:18; Hos 4:14, where the same Hebrew word is used. In 38:15 and 24 the common word for prostitute, *zona*, is used.

38:29 *He was called Perez*: the Hebrew word means "breach."

38:30 *He was called Zerah*: a name connected here by popular etymology with a Hebrew word for the red light of dawn, alluding apparently to the crimson thread.

*

38:27 1 Chr 2:4.
38:29 Ru 4:12; Mt 1:3; Lk 3:33.
38:30 Nm 26:20; 1 Chr 2:4; Mt 1:3.
39:2 1 Sm 3:19; 10:7; 18:14; 2 Sm 5:10; 2 Kgs 18:7; Acts 7:9.
39:4 Dn 1:9.
39:10 1 Mc 2:53.
39:20 Ps 105:18.

21 But the LORD was with Joseph, and showed
him kindness by making the chief jailer well-
disposed toward him.* 22 The chief jailer put
Joseph in charge of all the prisoners in the jail.
Everything that had to be done there, he was the
one to do it. 23 The chief jailer did not have to
look after anything that was in Joseph's charge,
since the LORD was with him and was bringing
success to whatever he was doing.

The Dreams Interpreted

40 1 † Some time afterward, the royal cup-
bearer and baker offended their lord, the
king of Egypt. 2 Pharaoh was angry with his two
officials, the chief cupbearer and the chief baker,
3 and he put them in custody in the house of the
chief steward, the same jail where Joseph was
confined. 4 The chief steward assigned Joseph to
them, and he became their attendant.

After they had been in custody for some time,
5 the cupbearer and the baker of the king of Egypt
who were confined in the jail both had dreams
on the same night, each his own dream and
each dream with its own meaning. 6 When Jo-
seph came to them in the morning, he saw that
they looked disturbed. 7 So he asked Pharaoh's
officials who were with him in custody in his
master's house, "Why do you look so troubled
today?" 8 They answered him, "We have had
dreams, but there is no one to interpret them."
Joseph said to them, "Do interpretations not
come from God? Please tell me the dreams."*

9 Then the chief cupbearer told Joseph his
dream. "In my dream," he said, "I saw a vine
in front of me, 10 and on the vine were three
branches. It had barely budded when its blossoms
came out, and its clusters ripened into grapes.
11 Pharaoh's cup was in my hand; so I took the
grapes, pressed them out into his cup, and put it
in Pharaoh's hand." 12 Joseph said to him: "This
is its interpretation. The three branches are three
days; 13 within three days Pharaoh will single
you out† and restore you to your post. You will
be handing Pharaoh his cup as you formerly did
when you were his cupbearer. 14 Only think of
me when all is well with you, and please do me
the great favor of mentioning me to Pharaoh, to
get me out of this place. 15 The truth is that I was
kidnapped from the land of the Hebrews, and I
have not done anything here that they should
have put me into a dungeon."

16 When the chief baker saw that Joseph had
given a favorable interpretation, he said to him:
"I too had a dream. In it I had three bread
baskets on my head; 17 in the top one were all
kinds of bakery products for Pharaoh, but the
birds were eating them out of the basket on my
head." 18 Joseph said to him in reply: "This is its
interpretation. The three baskets are three days;
19 within three days Pharaoh will single you out
and will impale you on a stake, and the birds will
be eating your flesh."

20 And so on the third day, which was Phar-
aoh's birthday, when he gave a banquet to all his
servants, he singled out the chief cupbearer and
chief baker in the midst of his servants. 21 He re-
stored the chief cupbearer to his office, so that he
again handed the cup to Pharaoh; 22 but the chief
baker he impaled—just as Joseph had told them
in his interpretation. 23 Yet the chief cupbearer
did not think of Joseph; he forgot him.

Pharaoh's Dream

41 1 † After a lapse of two years, Pharaoh had
a dream. He was standing by the Nile,
2 when up out of the Nile came seven cows, fine-
looking and fat; they grazed in the reed grass.
3 Behind them seven other cows, poor-looking
and gaunt, came up out of the Nile; and standing
on the bank of the Nile beside the others, 4 the
poor-looking, gaunt cows devoured the seven
fine-looking, fat cows. Then Pharaoh woke up.

5 He fell asleep again and had another dream.
He saw seven ears of grain, fat and healthy, grow-
ing on a single stalk. 6 Behind them sprouted
seven ears of grain, thin and scorched by the east
wind; 7 and the thin ears swallowed up the seven
fat, healthy ears. Then Pharaoh woke up—it was
a dream!

8 Next morning his mind was agitated. So
Pharaoh had all the magicians† and sages of
Egypt summoned and recounted his dream to
them; but there was no one to interpret it for
him. 9 Then the chief cupbearer said to Pharaoh:
"Now I remember my negligence! 10 Once, when
Pharaoh was angry with his servants, he put me

---

†

40:1 Joseph interprets the dreams of the Pharaoh's two officials. His ability to interpret the dreams shows that God is still with him and points forward to his role of dream interpreter for Pharaoh in chap. 41.

40:13 *Single you out*: lit., "lift up your head" (see also vv. 19, 20).

41:1–57 Joseph correctly interprets Pharaoh's dream and becomes second in command over all Egypt.

41:8 *Magicians*: one of the tasks of the "magicians" was interpreting dreams. The interpretation of dreams was a long-standing practice in Egypt. A manual of dream interpretation has been found, written in the early second millennium and re-published later in which typical dreams are given ("If a man sees himself in a dream . . .") followed by a judgment of "good" or "bad." Interpreters were still needed for dreams, however, and Pharaoh complains that none of his dream interpreters can interpret his unprecedented dream. The same term will be used of Pharaoh's magicians in Exodus.

*

39:21 Acts 7:9–10. **40:8** Gn 41:16.

and the chief baker in custody in the house of
the chief steward. 11 Later, we both had dreams
on the same night, and each of our dreams had
its own meaning. 12 There was a Hebrew youth
with us, a slave of the chief steward; and when
we told him our dreams, he interpreted them for
us and explained for each of us the meaning of
his dream.* 13 Things turned out just as he had
told us: I was restored to my post, but the other
man was impaled."
14 Pharaoh therefore had Joseph summoned,
and they hurriedly brought him from the dun-
geon. After he shaved and changed his clothes,
he came to Pharaoh.* 15 Pharaoh then said to
Joseph: "I had a dream but there was no one to
interpret it. But I hear it said of you, 'If he hears a
dream he can interpret it.' " 16 "It is not I," Joseph
replied to Pharaoh, "but God who will respond
for the well-being of Pharaoh."*
17 Then Pharaoh said to Joseph: "In my dream,
I was standing on the bank of the Nile, 18 when
up from the Nile came seven cows, fat and well-
formed; they grazed in the reed grass. 19 Behind
them came seven other cows, scrawny, most
ill-formed and gaunt. Never have I seen such
bad specimens as these in all the land of Egypt!
20 The gaunt, bad cows devoured the first seven
fat cows. 21 But when they had consumed them,
no one could tell that they had done so, because
they looked as bad as before. Then I woke up.
22 In another dream I saw seven ears of grain, full
and healthy, growing on a single stalk. 23 Behind
them sprouted seven ears of grain, shriveled and
thin and scorched by the east wind; 24 and the
seven thin ears swallowed up the seven healthy
ears. I have spoken to the magicians, but there is
no one to explain it to me."
25 Joseph said to Pharaoh: "Pharaoh's dreams
have the same meaning. God has made known
to Pharaoh what he is about to do. 26 The seven
healthy cows are seven years, and the seven
healthy ears are seven years—the same in each
dream. 27 The seven thin, bad cows that came
up after them are seven years, as are the seven
thin ears scorched by the east wind; they are
seven years of famine. 28 Things are just as I told
Pharaoh: God has revealed to Pharaoh what he
is about to do. 29 Seven years of great abundance
are now coming throughout the land of Egypt;
30 but seven years of famine will rise up after
them, when all the abundance will be forgotten
in the land of Egypt. When the famine has ex-
hausted the land, 31 no trace of the abundance
will be found in the land because of the famine
that follows it, for it will be very severe. 32 That
Pharaoh had the same dream twice means that
the matter has been confirmed by God and
that God will soon bring it about.
33 "Therefore, let Pharaoh seek out a discern-
ing and wise man and put him in charge of the
land of Egypt. 34 Let Pharaoh act and appoint
overseers for the land to organize it during the
seven years of abundance. 35 They should collect
all the food of these coming good years, gather-
ing the grain under Pharaoh's authority, for food
in the cities, and they should guard it. 36 This
food will serve as a reserve for the country against
the seven years of famine that will occur in the
land of Egypt, so that the land may not perish in
the famine."
37 This advice pleased Pharaoh and all his
servants.* 38 "Could we find another like him,"
Pharaoh asked his servants, "a man so endowed
with the spirit of God?" 39 So Pharaoh said to Jo-
seph: "Since God has made all this known to you,
there is no one as discerning and wise as you are.
40 You shall be in charge of my household, and
all my people will obey your command. Only
in respect to the throne will I outrank you."*
41 Then Pharaoh said to Joseph, "Look, I put you
in charge of the whole land of Egypt." 42 With
that, Pharaoh took off his signet ring† and put
it on Joseph's finger. He dressed him in robes of
fine linen and put a gold chain around his neck.
43 He then had him ride in his second chariot,
and they shouted "Abrek!"† before him.
Thus was Joseph installed over the whole land
of Egypt. 44 "I am Pharaoh," he told Joseph, "but
without your approval no one shall lift hand or
foot in all the land of Egypt." 45 Pharaoh also be-
stowed the name of Zaphenath-paneah† on Jo-
seph, and he gave him in marriage Asenath, the
daughter of Potiphera, priest of Heliopolis. And
Joseph went out over the land of Egypt. 46 Joseph
was thirty years old when he entered the service
of Pharaoh, king of Egypt.

†

41:42 *Signet ring*: a finger ring in which was set a stamp seal, different from the cylinder seal such as Judah wore; see note on 38:18. By receiving Pharaoh's signet ring, Joseph was made vizier of Egypt (v. 43); the vizier was known as "seal-bearer of the king of Lower Egypt." The gold chain was a symbol of high office in ancient Egypt.

41:43 *Abrek*: apparently a cry of homage, though the word's derivation and actual meaning are uncertain.

41:45 *Zaphenath-paneah*: a Hebrew transcription of an Egyptian name meaning "the god speaks and he (the newborn child) lives." *Asenath*: means "belonging to (the Egyptian goddess) Neith." *Potiphera*: means "he whom Ra (the Egyptian god) gave"; a shorter form of the same name was borne by Joseph's master (37:36). *Heliopolis*: in Hebrew, *On*, a city seven miles northeast of modern Cairo, site of the chief temple of the sun god; it is mentioned also in v. 50; 46:20; Ez 30:17.

*

41:12 Dn 1:17.
41:14 Ps 105:20.
41:16 Gn 40:8.
41:37 Acts 7:10.
41:40 1 Mc 2:53; Ps 105:21; Wis 10:14; Acts 7:10.

GN

After Joseph left Pharaoh, he went throughout
the land of Egypt. 47 During the seven years of
plenty, when the land produced abundant crops,
48 he collected all the food of these years of plenty
that the land of Egypt was enjoying and stored it
in the cities, placing in each city the crops of the
fields around it. 49 Joseph collected grain like the
sands of the sea, so much that at last he stopped
measuring it, for it was beyond measure.

50 Before the famine years set in, Joseph be-
came the father of two sons, borne to him by
Asenath, daughter of Potiphera, priest of Heliop-
olis.* 51 Joseph named his firstborn Manasseh,†
meaning, "God has made me forget entirely my
troubles and my father's house"; 52 and the sec-
ond he named Ephraim,† meaning, "God has
made me fruitful in the land of my affliction."

53 When the seven years of abundance enjoyed
by the land of Egypt came to an end, 54 the seven
years of famine set in, just as Joseph had said.
Although there was famine in all the other coun-
tries, food was available throughout the land of
Egypt.* 55 When all the land of Egypt became
hungry and the people cried to Pharaoh for food,
Pharaoh said to all the Egyptians: "Go to Jo-
seph and do whatever he tells you." 56 When the
famine had spread throughout the land, Joseph
opened all the cities that had grain and rationed
it to the Egyptians, since the famine had gripped
the land of Egypt. 57 Indeed, the whole world
came to Egypt to Joseph to buy grain, for famine
had gripped the whole world.

The Brothers' First Journey to Egypt†

42 1 When Jacob learned that grain rations
were for sale in Egypt, he said to his sons:
"Why do you keep looking at one another?" 2 He
went on, "I hear that grain is for sale in Egypt.
Go down there and buy some for us, that we
may stay alive and not die."* 3 So ten of Joseph's
brothers went down to buy grain from Egypt.
4 But Jacob did not send Joseph's brother Ben-
jamin with his brothers, for he thought some
disaster might befall him. 5 And so the sons of
Israel were among those who came to buy grain,
since there was famine in the land of Canaan.*

6 Joseph, as governor of the country, was the
one who sold grain to all the people of the land.
When Joseph's brothers came, they bowed down
to him with their faces to the ground.* 7 He rec-
ognized them as soon as he saw them. But he
concealed his own identity from them and spoke
harshly to them. "Where do you come from?" he
asked them. They answered, "From the land of
Canaan, to buy food."

8 When Joseph recognized his brothers, al-
though they did not recognize him, 9 he was
reminded of the dreams he had about them. He
said to them: "You are spies.* You have come
to see the weak points† of the land." 10 "No,
my lord," they replied. "On the contrary, your
servants have come to buy food. 11 All of us are
sons of the same man. We are honest men; your
servants have never been spies." 12 But he an-
swered them: "Not so! It is the weak points of
the land that you have come to see." 13 "We your
servants," they said, "are twelve brothers, sons
of a certain man in Canaan; but the youngest
one is at present with our father, and the other
one is no more."* 14 "It is just as I said," Joseph
persisted; "you are spies. 15 This is how you shall
be tested: I swear by the life of Pharaoh that you
shall not leave here unless your youngest brother
comes here. 16 So send one of your number to
get your brother, while the rest of you stay here
under arrest. Thus will your words be tested for
their truth; if they are untrue, as Pharaoh lives,
you are spies!" 17 With that, he locked them up
in the guardhouse for three days.

18 On the third day Joseph said to them: "Do
this, and you shall live; for I am a God-fearing
man. 19 If you are honest men, let one of your
brothers be confined in this prison, while the rest
of you go and take home grain for your starving
families. 20 But you must bring me your youn-
gest brother. Your words will thus be verified,
and you will not die." To this they agreed.* 21 To
one another, however, they said: "Truly we are
being punished because of our brother. We saw
the anguish of his heart when he pleaded with
us, yet we would not listen. That is why this an-
guish has now come upon us."* 22 Then Reuben
responded, "Did I not tell you, 'Do no wrong to
the boy'? But you would not listen! Now comes

†

41:51 *Manasseh*: an allusion to this name is in the Hebrew expression, *nishshani*, "he made me forget."

41:52 *Ephraim*: related to the Hebrew expression *hiphrani*, "(God) has made me fruitful." The name originally meant something like "fertile land."

42:1–38 The first journey of the brothers to Egypt. Its cause is famine, which was also the reason Abraham and Sarah undertook their dangerous journey to Egypt. The brothers bow to Joseph in v. 6, which fulfills Joseph's dream in 37:5–11. Endowed with wisdom, Joseph begins a process of instruction or "discipline" for his brothers that eventually forces them to recognize the enormity of their sin against him and the family. He controls their experience of the first journey with the result that the second journey in chaps. 43–44 leads to full acknowledgment and reconciliation.

42:9, 12 *Weak points*: lit., "the nakedness of the land"; the military weakness of the land, like human nakedness, should not be seen by strangers.

*

41:50 Gn 46:20; 48:5.
41:54 Ps 105:16; Acts 7:11.
42:2 Acts 7:12.
42:5 Jdt 5:10; Acts 7:11.
42:6 Ps 105:21.
42:9 Gn 37:5.
42:13 Gn 44:20.
42:20 Gn 43:5.
42:21 Gn 37:18–27.

the reckoning for his blood."* 23 They did not
know, of course, that Joseph understood what
they said, since he spoke with them through an
interpreter. 24 But turning away from them, he
wept. When he was able to speak to them again,
he took Simeon from among them and bound
him before their eyes. 25 Then Joseph gave orders
to have their containers filled with grain, their
money replaced in each one's sack, and provi-
sions given them for their journey. After this had
been done for them, 26 they loaded their donkeys
with the grain and departed.
27 At the night encampment, when one of them
opened his bag to give his donkey some fodder,
he saw his money there in the mouth of his bag.
28 He cried out to his brothers, "My money has
been returned! Here it is in my bag!" At that their
hearts sank. Trembling, they asked one another,
"What is this that God has done to us?"
29 When they got back to their father Jacob in
the land of Canaan, they told him all that had
happened to them. 30 "The man who is lord of
the land," they said, "spoke to us harshly and
put us in custody on the grounds that we were
spying on the land. 31 But we said to him: 'We
are honest men; we have never been spies. 32 We
are twelve brothers, sons of the same father; but
one is no more, and the youngest one is now
with our father in the land of Canaan.' 33 Then
the man who is lord of the land said to us: 'This
is how I will know if you are honest men: leave
one of your brothers with me, then take grain for
your starving families and go. 34 When you bring
me your youngest brother, and I know that you
are not spies but honest men, I will restore your
brother to you, and you may move about freely
in the land.' "
35 When they were emptying their sacks, there
in each one's sack was his moneybag! At the sight
of their moneybags, they and their father were
afraid. 36 Their father Jacob said to them: "Must
you make me childless? Joseph is no more, Sim-
eon is no more, and now you would take Ben-
jamin away! All these things have happened to
me!" 37 Then Reuben told his father: "You may
kill my own two sons if I do not return him to
you! Put him in my care, and I will bring him
back to you." 38 But Jacob replied: "My son shall
not go down with you. Now that his brother
is dead, he is the only one left. If some disas-
ter should befall him on the journey you must
make, you would send my white head down to
Sheol in grief."*

The Second Journey to Egypt†

43 1 Now the famine in the land grew severe.
2 So when they had used up all the grain
they had brought from Egypt, their father said to
them, "Go back and buy us a little more food."
3 But Judah replied: "The man strictly warned
us, 'You shall not see me unless your brother is
with you.'* 4 If you are willing to let our brother
go with us, we will go down to buy food for
you. 5 But if you are not willing, we will not go
down, because the man told us, 'You shall not
see me unless your brother is with you.' "* 6 Is-
rael demanded, "Why did you bring this trouble
on me by telling the man that you had another
brother?" 7 They answered: "The man kept asking
about us and our family: 'Is your father still liv-
ing? Do you have another brother?' We answered
him accordingly. How could we know that he
would say, 'Bring your brother down here'?"
8 Then Judah urged his father Israel: "Let the
boy go with me, that we may be off and on our
way if you and we and our children are to keep
from starving to death.* 9 I myself will serve as a
guarantee for him. You can hold me responsible
for him. If I fail to bring him back and set him
before you, I will bear the blame before you for-
ever.* 10 Had we not delayed, we could have been
there and back twice by now!"
11 Israel their father then told them: "If it must
be so, then do this: Put some of the land's best
products in your baggage and take them down to
the man as gifts: some balm and honey, gum and
resin, and pistachios and almonds.* 12 Also take
double the money along, for you must return the
amount that was put back in the mouths of your
bags; it may have been a mistake. 13 Take your
brother, too, and be off on your way back to the
man. 14 May God Almighty grant you mercy in
the presence of the man, so that he may let your
other brother go, as well as Benjamin. As for me,
if I am to suffer bereavement, I shall suffer it."
15 So the men took those gifts and double
the money and Benjamin. They made their way
down to Egypt and presented themselves before
Joseph. 16 When Joseph saw them and Benja-
min, he told his steward, "Take the men into
the house, and have an animal slaughtered and
prepared, for they are to dine with me at noon."

G N

†

43:1–34 The second journey to Egypt. Joseph the sage has carefully prepared the brothers for a possible reconciliation. In this chapter and the following one Judah steps forward as the hero, in contrast to chaps. 37 and 42 where Reuben was the hero. Here Judah serves as guarantee for Benjamin.

*

42:22 Gn 37:22.
42:38 Gn 37:35.
43:3 Gn 44:23.
43:5 Gn 42:20.
43:8 Gn 42:37.
43:9 Gn 44:32.
43:11 Gn 45:23.

17 Doing as Joseph had ordered, the steward conducted the men to Joseph's house. 18 But they became apprehensive when they were led to his house. "It must be," they thought, "on account of the money put back in our bags the first time, that we are taken inside—in order to attack us and take our donkeys and seize us as slaves." 19 So they went up to Joseph's steward and talked to him at the entrance of the house. 20 "If you please, sir," they said, "we came down here once before to buy food.* 21 But when we arrived at a night's encampment and opened our bags, there was each man's money in the mouth of his bag—our money in the full amount! We have now brought it back.* 22 We have brought other money to buy food. We do not know who put our money in our bags." 23 He replied, "Calm down! Do not fear! Your God and the God of your father must have put treasure in your bags for you. As for your money, I received it." With that, he led Simeon out to them.

24 The steward then brought the men inside Joseph's house. He gave them water to wash their feet, and gave fodder to their donkeys. 25 Then they set out their gifts to await Joseph's arrival at noon, for they had heard that they were to dine there. 26 When Joseph came home, they presented him with the gifts they had brought inside, while they bowed down before him to the ground. 27 After inquiring how they were, he asked them, "And how is your aged father, of whom you spoke? Is he still alive?"* 28 "Your servant our father is still alive and doing well," they said, as they knelt and bowed down. 29 Then Joseph looked up and saw Benjamin, his brother, the son of his mother. He asked, "Is this your youngest brother, of whom you told me?" Then he said to him, "May God be gracious to you, my son!"* 30 With that, Joseph hurried out, for he was so overcome with affection for his brother that he was on the verge of tears. So he went into a private room and wept there.

31 After washing his face, he reappeared and, now having collected himself, gave the order, "Serve the meal." 32 It was served separately to him,† to the brothers, and to the Egyptians who partook of his board. Egyptians may not eat with Hebrews; that is abhorrent to them. 33 When they were seated before him according to their age, from the oldest to the youngest, they looked at one another in amazement; 34 and as portions were brought to them from Joseph's table, Benjamin's portion was five times as large as† anyone else's. So they drank freely and made merry with him.

Final Test†

44 1 Then Joseph commanded his steward: "Fill the men's bags with as much food as they can carry, and put each man's money in the mouth of his bag. 2 In the mouth of the youngest one's bag put also my silver goblet, together with the money for his grain." The steward did as Joseph said. 3 At daybreak the men and their donkeys were sent off. 4 They had not gone far out of the city when Joseph said to his steward: "Go at once after the men! When you overtake them, say to them, 'Why did you repay good with evil? Why did you steal my silver goblet? 5 Is it not the very one from which my master drinks and which he uses for divination?† What you have done is wrong.'"

6 When the steward overtook them and repeated these words to them, 7 they said to him: "Why does my lord say such things? Far be it from your servants to do such a thing! 8 We even brought back to you from the land of Canaan the money that we found in the mouths of our bags. How could we steal silver or gold from your master's house? 9 If any of your servants is found to have the goblet, he shall die, and as for the rest of us, we shall become my lord's slaves." 10 But he replied, "Now what you propose is fair enough, but only the one who is found to have it shall become my slave, and the rest of you can go free." 11 Then each of them quickly lowered his bag to the ground and opened it; 12 and when a search was made, starting with the oldest and ending with the youngest, the goblet turned up in Benjamin's bag. 13 At this, they tore their garments. Then, when each man had loaded his donkey again, they returned to the city.

---

† **43:32** *Separately to him*: that Joseph did not eat with the other Egyptians was apparently a matter of rank.

43:34 *Five times as large as*: probably an idiomatic expression for "much larger than." Cf. 45:22.

44:1–34 Joseph's pressure on his brothers and Judah's great speech. Judah has the longest speech in the Book of Genesis; it summarizes the recent past (vv. 18–29), shows the pain Joseph's actions have imposed on their aged father (vv. 30–32), and ends with the offer to take the place of Benjamin as servant of Joseph (vv. 33–34). The role of Judah in the entire story is exceedingly important and is easily underrated: he tries to rescue Joseph (37:26–27), his "going down away from the brothers" is parallel to Joseph's (chap. 38) and prepares him (as it prepares Joseph) for the reconciliation, his speech in chap. 44 persuades Joseph to reveal himself and be reconciled to his brothers. Here, Judah effectively replaces Reuben as a spokesman for the brothers. Jacob in his testament (chap. 49) devotes the most attention to Judah and Joseph. In one sense, the story can be called the story of Joseph and Judah.

44:5 *Divination*: seeking omens through liquids poured into a cup or bowl was a common practice in the ancient Near East; cf. v. 15. Even though divination was frowned on in later Israel (Lv 19:31), it is in this place an authentic touch which is ascribed to Joseph, the wisest man in Egypt.

---

* **43:20** Gn 42:3. **43:21** Gn 42:27–28. **43:27** Tb 7:4. **43:29** Gn 42:13.

14 When Judah and his brothers entered Joseph's house, he was still there; so they flung themselves on the ground before him. 15 "How could you do such a thing?" Joseph asked them. "Did you not know that such a man as I could discern by divination what happened?" 16 Judah replied: "What can we say to my lord? How can we plead or how try to prove our innocence? God has uncovered your servants' guilt.† Here we are, then, the slaves of my lord—the rest of us no less than the one in whose possession the goblet was found." 17 Joseph said, "Far be it from me to act thus! Only the one in whose possession the goblet was found shall become my slave; the rest of you may go back unharmed to your father."

18 Judah then stepped up to him and said: "I beg you, my lord, let your servant appeal to my lord, and do not become angry with your servant, for you are the equal of Pharaoh. 19 My lord asked his servants,† 'Have you a father, or another brother?' 20 So we said to my lord, 'We have an aged father, and a younger brother, the child of his old age. This one's full brother is dead, and since he is the only one by his mother who is left, his father is devoted to him.'* 21 Then you told your servants, 'Bring him down to me that I might see him.' 22 We replied to my lord, 'The boy cannot leave his father; his father would die if he left him.' 23 But you told your servants, 'Unless your youngest brother comes down with you, you shall not see me again.'* 24 When we returned to your servant my father, we reported to him the words of my lord.

25 "Later, our father said, 'Go back and buy some food for us.' 26 So we reminded him, 'We cannot go down there; only if our youngest brother is with us can we go, for we may not see the man if our youngest brother is not with us.' 27 Then your servant my father said to us, 'As you know, my wife bore me two sons. 28 One of them, however, has gone away from me, and I said, "He must have been torn to pieces by wild beasts!" I have not seen him since.* 29 If you take this one away from me too, and a disaster befalls him, you will send my white head down to Sheol in grief.'

30 "So now, if the boy is not with us when I go back to your servant my father, whose very life is bound up with his, he will die as soon as he sees that the boy is missing; 31 and your servants will thus send the white head of your servant our father down to Sheol in grief. 32 Besides, I, your servant, have guaranteed the boy's safety for my father by saying, 'If I fail to bring him back to you, father, I will bear the blame before you forever.'* 33 So now let me, your servant, remain in place of the boy as the slave of my lord, and let the boy go back with his brothers. 34 How could I go back to my father if the boy were not with me? I could not bear to see the anguish that would overcome my father."

The Truth Revealed†

45 1 Joseph could no longer restrain himself in the presence of all his attendants, so he cried out, "Have everyone withdraw from me!" So no one attended him when he made himself known to his brothers. 2 But his sobs were so loud that the Egyptians heard him, and so the news reached Pharaoh's house. 3 * "I am Joseph," he said to his brothers. "Is my father still alive?" But his brothers could give him no answer, so dumbfounded were they at him.

4 "Come closer to me," Joseph told his brothers. When they had done so, he said: "I am your brother Joseph, whom you sold into Egypt. 5 But now do not be distressed, and do not be angry with yourselves for having sold me here. It was really for the sake of saving lives that God sent me here ahead of you.* 6 The famine has been in the land for two years now, and for five more years cultivation will yield no harvest. 7 God, therefore, sent me on ahead of you to ensure for you a remnant on earth and to save your lives in an extraordinary deliverance. 8 So it was not really you but God who had me come here; and he has made me a father to Pharaoh,† lord of all his household, and ruler over the whole land of Egypt.

9 † "Hurry back, then, to my father and tell him: 'Thus says your son Joseph: God has made me lord of all Egypt; come down to me without delay.* 10 You can settle in the region of Goshen,† where you will be near me—you and your

†

44:16 *Guilt*: in trying to do away with Joseph when he was young.

44:19 *My lord asked his servants*: such frequently repeated expressions in Judah's speech show the formal court style used by a subject in speaking to a high official.

45:1–28 Joseph reveals his identity and the family is reconciled.

45:8 *Father to Pharaoh*: a term applied to a vizier in ancient Egypt.

45:9–15 In these verses, as in 46:31–47:5a, all from the Yahwist source, Joseph in his own name invites his father and brothers to come to Egypt. Only after their arrival is Pharaoh informed of the fact. On the other hand, in 45:16–20, which scholars have traditionally attributed to the Elohist source, it is Pharaoh himself who invites Joseph's family to migrate to his domain.

45:10 *The region of Goshen*: the meaning of the term is unknown. It is found in no Egyptian source. It is generally thought to be in the modern Wadi Tumilat in the eastern part of the Nile Delta.

*

44:20 Gn 42:13.
44:23 Gn 43:3.
44:28 Gn 37:20, 33.
44:32 Gn 43:9.
45:3–4 Acts 7:13.
45:5 Gn 50:20.
45:9 Acts 7:14.

Live It!

God's Master Plan

After Joseph's tearful reconciliation with his brothers, he tells them that their past treatment of him enabled him to save them from the famine. Because he ended up in Egypt and rose to power, he can now invite them to stay as guests of the pharaoh.

Joseph realizes that good has come out of an evil act. He sees the events of his family's life as part of God's plan to preserve life and to make sure the Covenant continues. Joseph's insight does not justify what his brothers did, but it does help us realize that good can come out of a tragic event. It is often hard for us to understand why something bad is happening, but as time passes, we often gain perspective and insight. These are the rewards of trust and faith. Joseph remained faithful, despite many difficulties. Let us strive to do the same, assured that not even our sinfulness can thwart God's saving plans.

- When have you experienced good things coming out of a bad situation?
- Has it ever seemed like God has upset part of your life, only to result in something better than you expected?

Gn 45:5–8

children and children's children, your flocks and
herds, and everything that you own. 11 I will pro-
vide for you there in the five years of famine that
lie ahead, so that you and your household and
all that are yours will not suffer want.' 12 Surely,
you can see for yourselves, and Benjamin can see
for himself, that it is I who am speaking to you.
13 Tell my father all about my high position in
Egypt and all that you have seen. But hurry and
bring my father down here." 14 Then he threw his
arms around his brother Benjamin and wept on
his shoulder. 15 Joseph then kissed all his broth-
ers and wept over them; and only then were his
brothers able to talk with him.

16 The news reached Pharaoh's house: "Jo-
seph's brothers have come." Pharaoh and his
officials were pleased. 17 So Pharaoh told Joseph:
"Say to your brothers: 'This is what you shall do:
Load up your animals and go without delay to
the land of Canaan. 18 There get your father and
your households, and then come to me; I will
assign you the best land in Egypt, where you
will live off the fat of the land.'* 19 Instruct them
further: 'Do this. Take wagons from the land of
Egypt for your children and your wives and bring
your father back here. 20 Do not be concerned
about your belongings, for the best in the whole
land of Egypt shall be yours.' "

21 The sons of Israel acted accordingly. Joseph
gave them the wagons, as Pharaoh had ordered,
and he supplied them with provisions for the
journey. 22 He also gave to each of them a set of
clothes, but to Benjamin he gave three hundred
shekels of silver and five sets of clothes. 23 More-
over, what he sent to his father was ten donkeys
loaded with the finest products of Egypt and
another ten loaded with grain and bread and
provisions for his father's journey. 24 As he sent
his brothers on their way, he told them, "Do not
quarrel on the way."

25 So they went up from Egypt and came to the
land of Canaan, to their father Jacob. 26 When
they told him, "Joseph is still alive—in fact, it is
he who is governing all the land of Egypt," he
was unmoved, for he did not believe them. 27 But
when they recounted to him all that Joseph had
told them, and when he saw the wagons that Jo-
seph had sent to transport him, the spirit of their
father Jacob came to life. 28 "Enough," said Israel.
"My son Joseph is still alive! I must go and see
him before I die."

Migration to Egypt

46 1 † Israel set out with all that was his.
When he arrived at Beer-sheba, he of-
fered sacrifices to the God of his father Isaac.
2 There God, speaking to Israel in a vision by
night, called: Jacob! Jacob! He answered, "Here I
am." 3 Then he said: I am God,† the God of your
father. Do not be afraid to go down to Egypt,
for there I will make you a great nation. 4 I will
go down to Egypt with you and I will also bring
you back here, after Joseph has closed your eyes.
5 So Jacob departed from Beer-sheba, and the
sons of Israel put their father and their wives and
children on the wagons that Pharaoh had sent to

† **46:1–47:26** Jacob and his family settle in Egypt. Joseph's economic policies.

46:3 *I am God*: more precisely according to the Hebrew text, "I am El." "El" is here a divine name, not the common noun "god."

* **45:18** Acts 7:14.

transport him. 6 They took with them their live-
stock and the possessions they had acquired in
the land of Canaan. So Jacob and all his descen-
dants came to Egypt.* 7 His sons and his grand-
sons, his daughters and his granddaughters—all
his descendants—he took with him to Egypt.
8 These are the names of the Israelites, Jacob
and his children, who came to Egypt.
Reuben, Jacob's firstborn,* 9 † and the sons of
Reuben: Hanoch, Pallu, Hezron, and Carmi.*
10 The sons of Simeon: Jemuel, Jamin, Ohad,
Jachin, Zohar, and Shaul, son of a Canaanite
woman.* 11 The sons of Levi: Gershon, Kohath,
and Merari.* 12 The sons of Judah: Er, Onan,
Shelah, Perez, and Zerah—but Er and Onan
had died in the land of Canaan; and the sons
of Perez were Hezron and Hamul.* 13 The sons
of Issachar: Tola, Puah, Jashub, and Shimron.*
14 The sons of Zebulun: Sered, Elon, and Jah-
leel.* 15 These were the sons whom Leah bore to
Jacob in Paddan-aram, along with his daughter
Dinah—thirty-three persons in all, sons and
daughters.
16 The sons of Gad: Zephon, Haggi, Shuni, Ez-
bon, Eri, Arod, and Areli.* 17 The sons of Asher:
Imnah, Ishvah, Ishvi, and Beriah, with their sister
Serah; and the sons of Beriah: Heber and Mal-
chiel.* 18 These are the children of Zilpah, whom
Laban had given to his daughter Leah; these she
bore to Jacob—sixteen persons in all.
19 The sons of Jacob's wife Rachel: Joseph and
Benjamin. 20 In the land of Egypt Joseph became
the father of Manasseh and Ephraim, whom
Asenath, daughter of Potiphera, priest of Heli-
opolis, bore to him.* 21 The sons of Benjamin:
Bela, Becher, Ashbel, Gera, Naaman, Ahiram,
Shupham, Hupham, and Ard.* 22 These are the
sons whom Rachel bore to Jacob—fourteen per-
sons in all.
23 The sons of Dan: Hushim.* 24 The sons of
Naphtali: Jahzeel, Guni, Jezer, and Shillem.*
25 These are the sons of Bilhah, whom Laban had
given to his daughter Rachel; these she bore to
Jacob—seven persons in all.
26 Jacob's people who came to Egypt—his

† **46:9–27** This genealogical list is based on the clan lists (Nm 26:5–50) from the Mosaic period.

* **46:6** Ex 1:1; Jos 24:4; Jdt 5:10; Acts 7:15.
46:8 Ex 1:2.
46:9 Ex 6:14; Nm 26:5; 1 Chr 5:3.
46:10 Ex 6:15; Nm 26:12; 1 Chr 4:24.
46:11 Ex 6:16; Nm 3:17; 26:57; 1 Chr 6:1.
46:12 Gn 38:3–10, 29–30; Nm 26:19; Ru 4:12; 1 Chr 2:5.
46:13 Nm 26:23–24; 1 Chr 7:1.
46:14 Nm 26:26.
46:16 Nm 26:15–16.
46:17 Nm 26:44; 1 Chr 7:30–31.
46:20 Gn 41:50; Nm 26:28, 35.
46:21 Nm 26:38; 1 Chr 7:6; 8:1–4.
46:23 Nm 26:42.
46:24 Nm 26:48–49; 1 Chr 7:13.

Did You Know?

Israel's Ancestry

Although the Israelites descended from many different kin, the Book of Genesis traces their origins back to a series of common ancestors, which served to unite them as a people. Genesis tells the stories of those great ancestors, men and women called patriarchs and matriarchs, who were the founders of what later became the people of Israel. The twelve Tribes of Israel are understood to be descendants of Jacob's twelve sons (see Jacob's last words in Genesis, chapter 49, for a description of those tribes). Twelve becomes an important number that comes up again and again in the Bible. For example, the twelve Apostles are Jesus' closest followers in the New Testament.

It can be confusing to remember who is related to whom, so here's a chart to keep everyone straight:

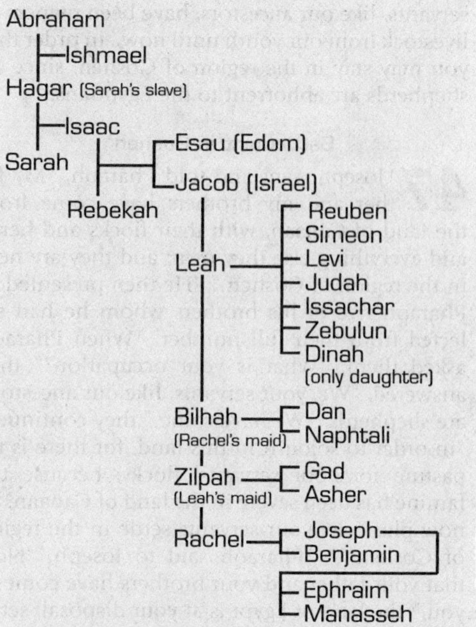

- Levi's tribe was set aside as priests and was not assigned land after the conquest of Canaan.
- Because Jacob adopted Joseph's sons Ephraim and Manasseh, Joseph is the father of two tribes.

direct descendants, not counting the wives of
Jacob's sons—numbered sixty-six persons in all.*
27 Together with Joseph's sons who were born to
him in Egypt—two persons—all the people com-
prising the household of Jacob who had come to
Egypt amounted to seventy persons† in all.*
28 Israel had sent Judah ahead to Joseph, so
that he might meet him in Goshen. On his ar-
rival in the region of Goshen, 29 Joseph prepared
his chariot and went up to meet his father Israel
in Goshen. As soon as Israel made his appear-
ance, Joseph threw his arms around him and
wept a long time on his shoulder. 30 And Israel
said to Joseph, "At last I can die, now that I have
seen for myself that you are still alive."
31 Joseph then said to his brothers and his
father's household: "I will go up and inform
Pharaoh, telling him: 'My brothers and my
father's household, whose home is in the land
of Canaan, have come to me. 32 The men are
shepherds, having been owners of livestock;†
and they have brought with them their flocks
and herds, as well as everything else they own.'
33 So when Pharaoh summons you and asks what
your occupation is, 34 you must answer, 'We your
servants, like our ancestors, have been owners of
livestock from our youth until now,' in order that
you may stay in the region of Goshen, since all
shepherds are abhorrent to the Egyptians."

Settlement in Goshen

47 1 Joseph went and told Pharaoh, "My fa-
ther and my brothers have come from
the land of Canaan, with their flocks and herds
and everything else they own; and they are now
in the region of Goshen." 2 He then presented to
Pharaoh five of his brothers whom he had se-
lected from their full number. 3 When Pharaoh
asked them, "What is your occupation?" they
answered, "We, your servants, like our ancestors,
are shepherds. 4 We have come," they continued,
"in order to sojourn in this land, for there is no
pasture for your servants' flocks, because the
famine has been severe in the land of Canaan. So
now please let your servants settle in the region
of Goshen."* 5 Pharaoh said to Joseph, "Now
that your father and your brothers have come to
you, 6 the land of Egypt is at your disposal; settle
your father and brothers in the pick of the land.
Let them settle in the region of Goshen. And
if you know of capable men among them, put
them in charge of my livestock." 7 Then Joseph
brought his father Jacob and presented him to
Pharaoh. And Jacob blessed Pharaoh. 8 Then
Pharaoh asked Jacob, "How many years have you
lived?" 9 Jacob replied: "The years I have lived as
a wayfarer amount to a hundred and thirty. Few
and hard have been these years of my life, and
they do not compare with the years that my an-
cestors lived as wayfarers."† 10 Then Jacob blessed
Pharaoh and withdrew from his presence.
11 Joseph settled his father and brothers and
gave them a holding in Egypt on the pick of the
land, in the region of Rameses,† as Pharaoh had
ordered. 12 And Joseph provided food for his fa-
ther and brothers and his father's whole house-
hold, down to the youngest.

Joseph's Land Policy

13 Since there was no food in all the land be-
cause of the extreme severity of the famine, and
the lands of Egypt and Canaan were languishing
from hunger, 14 Joseph gathered in, as payment
for the grain that they were buying, all the money
that was to be found in Egypt and Canaan, and
he put it in Pharaoh's house. 15 When all the
money in Egypt and Canaan was spent, all the
Egyptians came to Joseph, pleading, "Give us
food! Why should we perish in front of you?
For our money is gone." 16 "Give me your live-
stock if your money is gone," replied Joseph. "I
will give you food in return for your livestock."
17 So they brought their livestock to Joseph, and
he gave them food in exchange for their horses,
their flocks of sheep and herds of cattle, and their
donkeys. Thus he supplied them with food in ex-
change for all their livestock in that year. 18 That
year ended, and they came to him in the next one
and said: "We cannot hide from my lord that,
with our money spent and our livestock made
over to my lord, there is nothing left to put at my
lord's disposal except our bodies and our land.
19 Why should we and our land perish before
your very eyes? Take us and our land in exchange
for food, and we will become Pharaoh's slaves
and our land his property; only give us seed, that

†

46:27 *Seventy persons*: it is difficult to get this exact number by adding up the persons mentioned in the preceding genealogies. One might assume it refers to Jacob and sixty-nine descendants, excluding Er and Onan but including Dinah. Ex 1:5 repeats the number but excludes Jacob. Dt 10:22 refers to seventy persons descending to Egypt. The best solution is to take the number as expressing totality. Since there are seventy nations in chap. 10, it is likely that the text is drawing a parallel between the two entities and suggesting that Israel "represents" the nations before God.

46:32 *Owners of livestock*: the phrase occurs only here and in v. 34. The difference between this term and "shepherds" is not clear, for the brothers do not mention it to Pharaoh in 47:3.

47:9 *Wayfarer . . . wayfarers*: human beings are merely sojourners on earth; cf. Ps 39:13.

47:11 *The region of Rameses*: same as the region of Goshen; see note on 45:10.

*

46:26 Ex 1:5.
46:27 Ex 1:5; Dt 10:22; Acts 7:14.
47:4 Ex 23:9; Dt 23:8.

we may survive and not perish, and that our land
may not turn into a waste."
20 So Joseph acquired all the land of Egypt for
Pharaoh. Each of the Egyptians sold his field,
since the famine weighed heavily upon them.
Thus the land passed over to Pharaoh, 21 and the
people were reduced to slavery, from one end of
Egypt's territory to the other. 22 Only the priests'
lands Joseph did not acquire. Since the priests
had a fixed allowance from Pharaoh and lived
off the allowance Pharaoh had granted them,
they did not have to sell their land.
23 Joseph told the people: "Now that I have
acquired you and your land for Pharaoh, here is
your seed for sowing the land. 24 But when the
harvest is in, you must give a fifth of it to Phar-
aoh, while you keep four-fifths as seed for your
fields and as food for yourselves and your house-
holds and as food for your children." 25 "You
have saved our lives!" they answered. "We have
found favor with my lord; now we will be Phar-
aoh's slaves." 26 Thus Joseph made it a statute for
the land of Egypt, which is still in force, that a
fifth of its produce should go to Pharaoh. Only
the land of the priests did not pass over to Phar-
aoh.

Israel Blesses Ephraim and Manasseh

27 Thus Israel settled in the land of Egypt, in
the region of Goshen. There they acquired hold-
ings, were fertile, and multiplied greatly.* 28 † Ja-
cob lived in the land of Egypt for seventeen years;
the span of his life came to a hundred and forty-
seven years. 29 When the time approached for
Israel to die, he called his son Joseph and said to
him: "If it pleases you, put your hand under my
thigh as a sign of your enduring fidelity to me;
do not bury me in Egypt. 30 When I lie down with
my ancestors, take me out of Egypt and bury me
in their burial place."* "I will do as you say," he
replied. 31 But his father demanded, "Swear it to
me!" So Joseph swore to him. Then Israel bowed
at the head of the bed.†

48

1 † Some time afterward, Joseph was in-
formed, "Your father is failing." So he
took along with him his two sons, Manasseh and
Ephraim. 2 When Jacob was told, "Your son Jo-
seph has come to you," Israel rallied his strength
and sat up in bed.
3 * Jacob then said to Joseph: "God Almighty
appeared to me at Luz† in the land of Canaan,
and blessing me, 4 he said, 'I will make you fertile
and multiply you and make you into an assem-
bly of peoples, and I will give this land to your
descendants after you as a permanent posses-
sion.' 5 So now your two sons who were born to
you in the land of Egypt before I joined you here,
shall be mine; Ephraim and Manasseh shall be
mine as much as Reuben and Simeon are mine.
6 Progeny born to you after them shall remain
yours; but their heritage shall be recorded in the
names of their brothers. 7 * I do this because,
when I was returning from Paddan, your mother
Rachel died, to my sorrow, during the journey
in Canaan, while we were still a short distance
from Ephrath; and I buried her there on the way
to Ephrath [now Bethlehem]."†
8 When Israel saw Joseph's sons, he asked,
"Who are these?" 9 "They are my sons," Joseph
answered his father, "whom God has given me
here." "Bring them to me," said his father, "that
I may bless them." 10 Now Israel's eyes were dim
from age; he could not see well. When Joseph
brought his sons close to him, he kissed and em-
braced them. 11 Then Israel said to Joseph, "I never
expected to see your face again, and now God has
allowed me to see your descendants as well!"
12 Joseph removed them from his father's knees
and bowed down before him with his face to the
ground. 13 Then Joseph took the two, Ephraim
with his right hand, to Israel's left, and Manasseh
with his left hand, to Israel's right, and brought
them up to him. 14 But Israel, crossing his hands,
put out his right hand and laid it on the head of
Ephraim, although he was the younger, and his
left hand on the head of Manasseh, although he

†

47:28–50:26 Supplements to the Joseph story. Most of the material in this section centers on Jacob—his blessing of Joseph's sons, his farewell testament, and his death and burial in Canaan. Only the last verses (50:15–26) redirect attention to Jacob's sons, the twelve brothers; they are assured that the reconciliation will not collapse after the death of the patriarch.

47:31 *Israel bowed at the head of the bed*: meaning perhaps that he gave a nod of assent and appreciation as he lay on his bed. The oath and gesture are the same as Abraham's in 24:2. Israel's bowing here suggests the fulfillment of Joseph's dreams in 37:9–10, when parents and brothers bowed down to Joseph (cf. 42:6; 43:26). By using different vowels for the Hebrew word for "bed," the Greek version translated it as "staff," and understood the phrase to mean that he bowed in worship, leaning on the top of his staff; it is thus quoted in Heb 11:21.

48:1–22 Jacob continues his preparations for death. In a scene that evokes the nearly blind Isaac blessing Jacob and Esau (chap. 27), Jacob blesses Joseph's two sons. He adopts them, elevating them to a status equal to that of Jacob's first sons Reuben and Simeon (cf. 1 Chr 5:1). The adoption is one more instance of Jacob's favoring Rachel and those born of her. The mention of Jacob's failing eyesight and his selection of the younger son over the older evokes the great deathbed scene in chap. 27. He reaffirms to Joseph the ancient divine promise of progeny and land.

48:3 *Luz*: an older name of Bethel (28:19).

48:7 Since her early death prevented Rachel from bearing more than two sons, Jacob feels justified in treating her two grandsons as if they were her own offspring.

*

47:27 Ex 1:7.
47:30 Gn 50:5.
48:3–4 Gn 28:12–15; 35:6.
48:7 Gn 35:19.

Cultural Connection

Assemble and Hear!

Genesis 49:1–2 is the first reading at Mass on the ninth day before Christmas. This is an important day for Filipino Catholics because it marks the beginning of Simbang Gabi, or Dawn Worship.

On the nine days before Christmas, people gather to celebrate Mass in the dark of the predawn—usually between four and five o'clock in the morning. Mass ends with chocolate and buns and socializing. In fact, this is such a popular custom that even people who don't come to Mass all year will make it for the nine Masses of Simbang Gabi! It is a special celebration of thankfulness for the gift of their Catholic faith.

This Philippine tradition is an example of a Catholic custom called a novena. A novena is a public or private prayer repeated nine times. It can be a prayer said every day for nine days, one day a week for nine weeks, one day a month for nine months, or in any other pattern of nine. Why not make up your own personal novena? Just think of a prayer in a form you find meaningful (journaling, singing, reading the Scriptures, or even praying silently), and repeat it once a day for nine days or once a week for nine weeks. Happy praying!

► Gn 49:1–2

was the firstborn. 15Then he blessed them with
these words:

"May the God in whose presence
my fathers Abraham and Isaac walked,
The God who has been my shepherd
from my birth to this day,*
16 The angel who has delivered me from all
harm,
bless these boys
That in them my name be recalled,
and the names of my fathers, Abraham and
Isaac,
And they may become teeming multitudes
upon the earth!"

17When Joseph saw that his father had laid
his right hand on Ephraim's head, this seemed
wrong to him; so he took hold of his father's
hand, to remove it from Ephraim's head to Ma-
nasseh's, 18saying, "That is not right, father; the
other one is the firstborn; lay your right hand
on his head!" 19But his father refused. "I know
it, son," he said, "I know. That one too shall
become a people, and he too shall be great. Nev-
ertheless, his younger brother shall surpass him,
and his descendants shall become a multitude of
nations." 20So he blessed them that day and said,
"By you shall the people of Israel pronounce
blessings, saying, 'God make you like Ephraim
and Manasseh.' " Thus he placed Ephraim before
Manasseh.*
21Then Israel said to Joseph: "I am about to
die. But God will be with you and will restore
you to the land of your ancestors. 22* As for me,
I give to you, as to the one above his brothers,
Shechem, which I captured from the Amorites
with my sword and bow."†

Jacob's Testament†

49 1Jacob called his sons and said: "Gather
around, that I may tell you what is to
happen to you in days to come.

2 "Assemble and listen, sons of Jacob,
listen to Israel, your father.

† **48:22** Both the meaning of the Hebrew and the historical reference in this verse are obscure. By taking the Hebrew word for Shechem as a common noun meaning shoulder or mountain slope, some translators render the verse, "I give you one portion more than your brothers, which I captured . . ." The reference may be to the capture of Shechem by the sons of Jacob (34:24–29). Shechem lay near the border separating the tribal territory of Manasseh from that of Ephraim (Jos 16:4–9; 17:1–2, 7).

49:1–27 The testament, or farewell discourse, of Jacob, which has its closest parallel in Moses' farewell in Dt 33:6–25. From his privileged position as a patriarch, he sees the future of his children (the eponymous ancestors of the tribes) and is able to describe how they will fare and so gives his blessing. The dense and archaic poetry is obscure in several places. The sayings often involve wordplays (explained in the notes). The poem begins with the six sons of Leah (vv. 2–15), then deals with the sons of the two secondary wives, and ends with Rachel's two sons, Joseph and Benjamin. Reuben, the oldest son, loses his position of leadership as a result of his intercourse with Bilhah (35:22), and the words about Simeon and Levi allude to their

* **48:15** Heb 11:21.
48:20 Heb 11:21.
48:22 Jos 17:14, 17–18; Jn 4:5.

3 "You, Reuben, my firstborn,
my strength and the first fruit of my vigor,
excelling in rank and excelling in power!
4 Turbulent as water, you shall no longer excel,
for you climbed into your father's bed
and defiled my couch to my sorrow.*

5† "Simeon and Levi, brothers indeed,
weapons of violence are their knives.†
6 Let not my person enter their council,
or my honor be joined with their company;
For in their fury they killed men,
at their whim they maimed oxen.*
7 Cursed be their fury so fierce,
and their rage so cruel!
I will scatter them in Jacob,
disperse them throughout Israel.

8 "You, Judah, shall your brothers praise
—your hand on the neck of your enemies;
the sons of your father shall bow down to you.
9 Judah is a lion's cub,
you have grown up on prey, my son.
He crouches, lies down like a lion,
like a lioness—who would dare rouse him?*
10 The scepter shall never depart from Judah,
or the mace from between his feet,
Until tribute comes to him,†
and he receives the people's obedience.
11 He tethers his donkey to the vine,
his donkey's foal to the choicest stem.
In wine he washes his garments,
his robe in the blood of grapes.†
12 His eyes are darker than wine,
and his teeth are whiter than milk.

13 "Zebulun shall dwell by the seashore;
he will be a haven for ships,
and his flank shall rest on Sidon.

14 "Issachar is a rawboned donkey,
crouching between the saddlebags.
15 When he saw how good a settled life was,
and how pleasant the land,
He bent his shoulder to the burden
and became a toiling serf.

16 "Dan shall achieve justice† for his people
as one of the tribes of Israel.
17 Let Dan be a serpent by the roadside,
a horned viper by the path,
That bites the horse's heel,
so that the rider tumbles backward.

18 "I long for your deliverance, O LORD!†

19 "Gad shall be raided by raiders,
but he shall raid at their heels.†

20 "Asher's produce is rich,
and he shall furnish delicacies for kings.

21 "Naphtali is a hind let loose,
which brings forth lovely fawns.

22 "Joseph is a wild colt,
a wild colt by a spring,
wild colts on a hillside.
23 Harrying him and shooting,
the archers opposed him;
24 But his bow remained taut,
and his arms were nimble,
By the power of the Mighty One of Jacob,
because of the Shepherd, the Rock of Israel,
25 The God of your father, who helps you,†
God Almighty, who blesses you,
With the blessings of the heavens above,
the blessings of the abyss that crouches below,
The blessings of breasts and womb,
26 the blessings of fresh grain and blossoms,
the blessings of the everlasting mountains,
the delights of the eternal hills.
May they rest on the head of Joseph,
on the brow of the prince among his brothers.

† taking revenge for the rape of Dinah (chap. 34). The preeminence of Judah reflects his rise in the course of the narrative (mirroring the rise of Joseph). See note on 44:1–34.

49:5–7 This passage probably refers to their attack on the city of Shechem (Gn 34). Because there is no indication that the warlike tribe of Levi will be commissioned as a priestly tribe (Ex 32:26–29; Dt 33:11), this passage reflects an early, independent tradition.

49:5 *Knives*: if this is the meaning of the obscure Hebrew word here, the reference may be to the knives used in circumcising the men of Shechem (34:24; cf. Jos 5:2).

49:10 *Until tribute comes to him*: this translation is based on a slight change in the Hebrew text, which, as it stands, would seem to mean, "until he comes to Shiloh." A somewhat different reading of the Hebrew text would be, "until he comes to whom it belongs." This last has been traditionally understood in a messianic sense. In any case, the passage aims at the supremacy of the tribe of Judah and of the Davidic dynasty.

49:11 *In wine . . . the blood of grapes*: Judah's clothes are poetically pictured as soaked with grape juice from trampling in the wine press, the rich vintage of his land; cf. Is 63:2.

49:16 In Hebrew the verb for "achieve justice" is from the same root as the name Dan.

49:18 This short plea for divine mercy has been inserted into the middle of Jacob's testament.

49:19 In Hebrew there is assonance between the name Gad and the words for "raided," "raiders," and "raid."

49:25–26 A very similar description of the agricultural riches of the tribal land of Joseph is given in Dt 33:13–16.

49:4 Gn 35:22; 1 Chr 5:1–2. **49:6** Gn 34:25. **49:9** 1 Chr 5:2.

27 "Benjamin is a ravenous wolf;
mornings he devours the prey,
and evenings he distributes the spoils."

Farewell and Death

28 All these are the twelve tribes of Israel, and
this is what their father said about them, as he
blessed them. To each he gave a suitable bless-
ing. 29 Then he gave them this charge: "Since I
am about to be gathered to my people, bury me
with my ancestors in the cave that lies in the
field of Ephron the Hittite, 30 the cave in the field
of Machpelah, facing on Mamre, in the land of
Canaan, the field that Abraham bought from
Ephron the Hittite for a burial ground.* 31 There
Abraham and his wife Sarah are buried, and so
are Isaac and his wife Rebekah, and there, too, I
buried Leah— 32 the field and the cave in it that
had been purchased from the Hittites."

33 When Jacob had finished giving these in-
structions to his sons, he drew his feet into the
bed, breathed his last, and was gathered to his
people.

Jacob's Funeral

50 1 Joseph flung himself upon his father
and wept over him as he kissed him.
2 Then Joseph ordered the physicians in his ser-
vice to embalm his father. When the physicians
embalmed Israel, 3 they spent forty days at it, for
that is the full period of embalming; and the
Egyptians mourned him for seventy days. 4 When
the period of mourning was over, Joseph spoke
to Pharaoh's household. "If you please, appeal
to Pharaoh, saying: 5 My father made me swear:
'I am dying. Bury me in my grave that I have pre-
pared for myself in the land of Canaan.' So now
let me go up to bury my father. Then I will come
back."* 6 Pharaoh replied, "Go and bury your fa-
ther, as he made you promise on oath."

7 So Joseph went up to bury his father; and
with him went all of Pharaoh's officials who
were senior members of his household and all
the other elders of the land of Egypt, 8 as well
as Joseph's whole household, his brothers, and
his father's household; only their children and
their flocks and herds were left in the region of
Goshen. 9 Chariots, too, and horsemen went up
with him; it was a very imposing retinue.

10 When they arrived at Goren-ha-atad,† which
is beyond the Jordan, they held there a very
great and solemn memorial service; and Joseph
observed seven days of mourning for his father.
11 When the Canaanites who inhabited the land
saw the mourning at Goren-ha-atad, they said,
"This is a solemn funeral on the part of the Egyp-
tians!" That is why the place was named Abel-
mizraim. It is beyond the Jordan.

12 Thus Jacob's sons did for him as he had in-
structed them. 13 They carried him to the land of
Canaan and buried him in the cave in the field
of Machpelah, facing on Mamre, the field that
Abraham had bought for a burial ground from
Ephron the Hittite.*

14 After Joseph had buried his father he re-
turned to Egypt, together with his brothers and
all who had gone up with him for the burial of
his father.

Plea for Forgiveness

15 † Now that their father was dead, Joseph's
brothers became fearful and thought, "Suppose
Joseph has been nursing a grudge against us and
now most certainly will pay us back in full for
all the wrong we did him!" 16 So they sent to Jo-
seph and said: "Before your father died, he gave
us these instructions: 17 'Thus you shall say to
Joseph: Please forgive the criminal wrongdoing
of your brothers, who treated you harmfully.'
So now please forgive the crime that we, the
servants of the God of your father, committed."
When they said this to him, Joseph broke into
tears. 18 Then his brothers also proceeded to fling
themselves down before him and said, "We are
your slaves!" 19 But Joseph replied to them: "Do
not fear. Can I take the place of God? 20 Even
though you meant harm to me, God meant it for
good, to achieve this present end, the survival
of many people.* 21 So now, do not fear. I will
provide for you and for your children." By thus
speaking kindly to them, he reassured them.*

22 Joseph remained in Egypt, together with his

---

† **50:10–11** *Goren-ha-atad*: "Threshing Floor of the Brambles." *Abel-mizraim*: although the name really means "watercourse of the Egyptians," it is understood here, by a play on the first part of the term, to mean "mourning of the Egyptians." The site has not been identified through either reading of the name. But it is difficult to see why the mourning rites should have been held in the land beyond the Jordan when the burial was at Hebron. Perhaps an earlier form of the story placed the mourning rites beyond the Wadi of Egypt, the traditional boundary between Canaan and Egypt (Nm 34:5; Jos 15:4, 47).

50:15–26 The final reconciliation of the brothers. Fearful of what may happen after the death of their father, the brothers engage in a final deception, inventing the dying wish of Jacob. Again, Joseph weeps, and, again, his brothers fall down before him, offering to be his slaves (44:16, 33). Joseph's assurance is also a summation of the story: "Even though you meant harm to me, God meant it for good, to achieve this present end, the survival of many people" (v. 20). Joseph's adoption of the children of Manasseh's son Machir recalls Jacob's adoption of his grandchildren (48:5, 13–20); the adoptions reflect tribal history (cf. Jgs 5:14).

* **49:30** Gn 23:17. **50:5** Gn 47:30. **50:13** Gn 23:16; Jos 24:32; Acts 7:16. **50:20** Gn 45:5. **50:21** Gn 47:12.

father's household. He lived a hundred and ten
years. 23 He saw Ephraim's children to the third
generation, and the children of Manasseh's son
Machir were also born on Joseph's knees.*

Death of Joseph

24 Joseph said to his brothers: "I am about to
die. God will surely take care of you and lead
you up from this land to the land that he prom-
ised on oath to Abraham, Isaac and Jacob."*
25 Then, putting the sons of Israel under oath, he
continued, "When God thus takes care of you,
you must bring my bones up from this place."*
26 Joseph died at the age of a hundred and ten.
He was embalmed and laid to rest in a coffin in
Egypt.*

50:23 Nm 32:39; Jos 17:1.
50:24 Ex 3:8; Heb 11:22.
50:25 Ex 13:19; Heb 11:22.
50:26 Sir 49:15.

Exodus

Click! Chains snap shut around your ankles. Crack! The tip of a whip whistles past your head. Bang! A door shuts, leaving you in darkness. These are the sounds of slavery, and they come as a surprise at the beginning of the Book of Exodus. What happened after the happy ending in Genesis? Like an action-packed drama, Exodus tells a story of deceit and broken promises, and of how God's miraculous interventions delivered the Israelites from their slavery in Egypt.

At a Glance

I. **Introduction: The Oppression of the Israelites in Egypt (1:1—2:22).**

II. **The Call and Commission of Moses (2:23—7:7).**

III. **The Contest with Pharaoh (7:8—13:16).**

IV. **The Deliverance of the Israelites from Pharaoh and Victory at the Sea (13:17—15:21).**

V. **The Journey in the Wilderness to Sinai (15:22—18:27).**

VI. **Covenant and Legislation at Mount Sinai (19:1—31:18).**

VII. **Israel's Apostasy and God's Renewal of the Covenant (32:1—34:35).**

VIII. **The Building of the Tabernacle and the Descent of God's Glory upon It (35:1—40:38).**

Quick Facts

Period Covered: sometime from 1500 to 1250 BC

Inspired Author: unknown author gathering oral tradition and stories from various tribal peoples

Themes: God liberates people from slavery and oppression. God sustains the Israelites in the wilderness. God forms a covenant marked by laws and rituals.

In Depth

The Book of Exodus is the ultimate story of Israel's liberation. *Exodus* literally means "departure," and this book's central event tells how God liberates the Israelite people from slavery in Egypt (an event called the Exodus). Its central character is Moses, who is chosen by God to become God's messenger and the instrument of God's power. Exodus was written hundreds of years after these events, using oral tradition that described the origin of many of the Israelites' beliefs and religious rituals.

Exodus is divided into eight sections. The first five sections, chapters 1–18, begin with the Israelites enslaved in Egypt and prohibited from worshiping their God. Israel cries out to God, and God answers by sending Moses. When Pharaoh refuses to let the Israelites go, God sends ten devastating plagues, and Pharaoh finally gives in. Later, Pharaoh changes his mind and chases the Israelites, only to have his army destroyed after the Israelites' escape through the Red Sea. This section ends with the people wandering through the wilderness, sustained by food and water miraculously provided by God.

Sections six through eight of Exodus, chapters 19–40, occur at Mount Sinai. There God enters into a covenant with all the people. God's part of the Sinai Covenant is to guarantee continued protection. Israel's part is to be faithful to God alone, a faithfulness marked by special laws (see chapters 20–23) and special worship (see chapters 24–31) that unite them as a people. Exodus ends with Israel still encamped at Mount Sinai, struggling to become a people of the Covenant.

The stories and laws in Exodus are at the heart of both Jewish and Christian belief in a God who saves, a God of freedom. You cannot fully appreciate the meaning of Jesus' life, death, and Resurrection without knowing these stories.

Chapters 19–20

Exodus

I. Introduction: The Oppression of the Israelites in Egypt

Jacob's Descendants in Egypt

1 [1]These are the names of the sons of Israel†
who, accompanied by their households, en-
tered into Egypt with Jacob: [2]† Reuben, Simeon,
Levi and Judah; [3]Issachar, Zebulun and Benja-
min; [4]Dan and Naphtali; Gad and Asher. [5]The
total number of Jacob's direct descendants† was
seventy.* Joseph was already in Egypt.
[6]Now Joseph and all his brothers and that
whole generation died.* [7]But the Israelites were
fruitful and prolific. They multiplied and became
so very numerous that the land was filled with
them.†

The Oppression

[8]* Then a new king, who knew nothing of Jo-
seph,† rose to power in Egypt. [9]He said to his
people, "See! The Israelite people have multi-
plied and become more numerous than we are!
[10]Come, let us deal shrewdly with them to stop
their increase;† otherwise, in time of war they too
may join our enemies to fight against us, and so
leave the land."
[11]Accordingly, they set supervisors over the Is-
raelites to oppress them with forced labor.* Thus
they had to build for Pharaoh† the garrison cities
of Pithom and Raamses. [12]Yet the more they were
oppressed, the more they multiplied and spread,
so that the Egyptians began to loathe the Israel-
ites. [13]So the Egyptians reduced the Israelites to

†

1:1 *Sons of Israel*: here literally the first-generation sons of Jacob/Israel. Cf. v. 5. However, beginning with v. 7 the same Hebrew phrase refers to Jacob's more remote descendants; hence, from there on, it is ordinarily rendered "the Israelites." *Households*: the family in its fullest sense, including wives, children and servants.

1:2 Jacob's sons are listed here according to their respective mothers. Cf. Gn 29:31; 30:20; 35:16–26.

1:5 *Direct descendants*: lit., "persons coming from Jacob's loins"; hence, wives of Jacob's sons and servants are not included. Cf. Gn 46:26. *Seventy*: Gn 46:26, along with the Septuagint for the verse, agrees on a total of sixty-six coming down to Egypt with Jacob, but in v. 27 the Hebrew text adds the two sons born to Joseph in Egypt and presupposes Jacob himself and Joseph for a total of seventy; the Septuagint adds "nine sons" born to Joseph to get a total of seventy-five. This is the figure the Septuagint and 4QEx[a] have here in Ex 1:5.

1:7 *Fruitful . . . multiplied . . . the land was filled with them*: the language used here to indicate the fecundity of the Israelite population echoes the divine blessing bestowed upon humanity at creation (Gn 1:28) and after the flood (Gn 9:1) as well as suggesting fulfillment of the promises to the ancestors Abraham, Isaac, and Jacob (Gn 12:2; 13:16; 15:5; 28:14; passim).

1:8 *Who knew nothing of Joseph*: the nuance intended by the Hebrew verb "know" here goes beyond precise determination. The idea may be not simply that a new king came to power who had not heard of Joseph but that this king ignored the services that Joseph had rendered to Egypt, repudiating the special relationship that existed between Joseph and his predecessor on the throne.

1:10 *Increase*: Pharaoh's actions thereby immediately pit him against God's will for the Israelites to multiply; see note on v. 7 above.

1:11 *Pharaoh*: not a personal name, but a title common to all the kings of Egypt.

*

1:5 Gn 46:26–27; Dt 10:22; Acts 7:14.
1:6 Gn 50:26.
1:8–10 Acts 7:18–19.
1:11 Dt 26:6.

Live It!

Saving Lives

In the story of the birth of Moses, Pharaoh orders the Egyptian midwives to kill all the male Israelite babies at birth. The midwives recognize such killing as an atrocity and refuse to obey Pharaoh. Their actions might be considered civil disobedience against unjust laws.

Some people claim that the right to have an abortion is a just law. Most of us have seen the images of an unborn baby resting within its mother's womb, thanks to the technology of ultrasounds. Clearly, there is a living human being there, who only needs a safe and protective environment in which to grow. Doesn't society have an obligation to protect this completely defenseless life? Where is the justice for the unborn child?

As the Egyptian midwives knew, all human life is sacred, no matter where or in what stage of development it exists.

▶ Ex 1:15–22

cruel slavery, 14 making life bitter for them with
hard labor, at mortar† and brick and all kinds of
field work—cruelly oppressed in all their labor.

Command to the Midwives

15 The king of Egypt told the Hebrew mid-
wives, one of whom was called Shiphrah and the
other Puah, 16 "When you act as midwives for the
Hebrew women, look on the birthstool:† if it is
a boy, kill him; but if it is a girl, she may live."
17 The midwives, however, feared God; they did
not do as the king of Egypt had ordered them,
but let the boys live. 18 So the king of Egypt sum-
moned the midwives and asked them, "Why
have you done this, allowing the boys to live?"
19 The midwives answered Pharaoh, "The Hebrew
women are not like the Egyptian women. They
are robust and give birth before the midwife ar-
rives." 20 Therefore God dealt well with the mid-
wives; and the people multiplied and grew very
numerous. 21 And because the midwives feared
God, God built up families for them. 22 Pharaoh
then commanded all his people, "Throw into the
Nile every boy that is born,* but you may let all
the girls live."

Birth and Adoption of Moses

2 1 Now a man† of the house of Levi married a
Levite woman,* 2 and the woman conceived
and bore a son. Seeing what a fine child he was,
she hid him for three months.* 3 But when she
could no longer hide him, she took a papyrus
basket,† daubed it with bitumen and pitch, and
putting the child in it, placed it among the reeds
on the bank of the Nile. 4 His sister stationed
herself at a distance to find out what would hap-
pen to him.
5 Then Pharaoh's daughter came down to bathe
at the Nile, while her attendants walked along
the bank of the Nile. Noticing the basket among
the reeds, she sent her handmaid to fetch it. 6 On
opening it, she looked, and there was a baby boy
crying! She was moved with pity for him and
said, "It is one of the Hebrews' children." 7 Then
his sister asked Pharaoh's daughter, "Shall I go
and summon a Hebrew woman to nurse the
child for you?" 8 Pharaoh's daughter answered
her, "Go." So the young woman went and called
the child's own mother. 9 Pharaoh's daughter
said to her, "Take this child and nurse him for
me, and I will pay your wages."† So the woman
took the child and nursed him. 10 When the child
grew,† she brought him to Pharaoh's daughter,
and he became her son.* She named him Moses;
for she said, "I drew him out of the water."

† **1:14** *Mortar*: either the wet clay with which the bricks were made, as in Na 3:14, or the cement used between the bricks in building, as in Gn 11:3.

1:16 *Birthstool*: apparently a pair of stones on which the mother is seated for childbirth opposite the midwife. The Hebrew word elsewhere is used to refer to the stones of a potter's wheel.

2:1 *Now a man*: the chapter begins abruptly, without names for the man or woman (in contrast to the midwives of 1:15), who in 6:20 are identified as Amram and Jochebed.

2:3 *Basket*: the same Hebrew word is used in Gn 6:14 and throughout the flood narrative for Noah's ark, but nowhere else in the Bible. Here, however, the "ark" or "chest" was made of papyrus stalks. Presumably the allusion to Genesis is intentional. Just as Noah and his family were preserved safe from the threatening waters of the flood in the ark he built, so now Moses is preserved from the threatening waters of the Nile in the ark prepared by his mother. *Among the reeds*: the Hebrew noun for "reed" is overwhelmingly used in the phrase "Reed Sea," traditionally translated "Red Sea."

2:9 *And I will pay your wages*: the idea that the child's mother will be paid for nursing her child—and by Pharaoh's own daughter—heightens the narrative's irony.

2:10 *When the child grew*: while v. 9 implies that the boy's mother cared for him as long as he needed to be nursed (presumably, between two and four years), the same verb appears in v. 11 to describe the attainment of adulthood. *And he became her son*: Pharaoh's daughter adopts Moses, thus adding to the irony of the account. The king of Egypt had ordered the killing of all the sons of the Hebrews, and one now becomes the son of his own daughter! *Moses*: in Hebrew, *mosheh*. There is a play on words here: Hebrew

* **1:22** Acts 7:19.
2:1 Ex 6:20; Nm 26:59.
2:2 Acts 7:20; Heb 11:23.
2:10 Acts 7:21; Heb 11:24.

Moses' Flight to Midian

11 * On one occasion, after Moses had grown
up,† when he had gone out to his kinsmen and
witnessed their forced labor, he saw an Egyp-
tian striking a Hebrew, one of his own kinsmen.
12 Looking about and seeing no one, he struck
down the Egyptian and hid him in the sand.
13 The next day he went out again, and now two
Hebrews were fighting! So he asked the culprit,
"Why are you striking your companion?" 14 But
he replied, "Who has appointed you ruler and
judge over us? Are you thinking of killing me as
you killed the Egyptian?" Then Moses became
afraid and thought, "The affair must certainly be
known." 15 When Pharaoh heard of the affair, he
sought to kill Moses. But Moses fled from Phar-
aoh and went to the land of Midian.† * There he
sat down by a well.

16 Now the priest of Midian had seven daugh-
ters, and they came to draw water and fill the
troughs to water their father's flock. 17 But shep-
herds came and drove them away. So Moses
rose up in their defense and watered their flock.
18 When they returned to their father Reuel,† he
said to them, "How is it you have returned so
soon today?" 19 They answered, "An Egyptian†
delivered us from the shepherds. He even drew
water for us and watered the flock!" 20 "Where is
he?" he asked his daughters. "Why did you leave
the man there? Invite him to have something to
eat." 21 Moses agreed to stay with him, and the
man gave Moses his daughter Zipporah in mar-
riage. 22 She conceived and bore a son, whom he
named Gershom;† for he said, "I am a stranger
residing in a foreign land."*

II. The Call and Commission of Moses

The Burning Bush

23 A long time passed, during which the king
of Egypt died. The Israelites groaned under their
bondage and cried out, and from their bondage
their cry for help went up to God.* 24 God heard
their moaning and God was mindful of his cov-
enant* with Abraham, Isaac and Jacob. 25 God
saw the Israelites, and God knew . . . .†

3 1 † Meanwhile Moses was tending the flock of
his father-in-law Jethro, the priest of Midian.
Leading the flock beyond the wilderness, he came
to the mountain of God, Horeb.† 2 There the an-
gel of the LORD† appeared to him as fire flaming
out of a bush.* When he looked, although the
bush was on fire, it was not being consumed. 3 So

† *mosheh* echoes *meshithihu* ("I drew him out"). However, the name Moses actually has nothing to do with that Hebrew verb, but is probably derived from Egyptian "beloved" or "has been born," preserved in such Pharaonic names as Thutmoses (meaning approximately "Beloved of the god Thoth" or "The god Thoth is born, has given birth to [the child]"). The original meaning of Moses' name was no longer remembered (if it was Egyptian, it may have contained an Egyptian divine element as well, perhaps the name of the Nile god Hapi), and a secondary explanation was derived from this story (or gave rise to it, if the drawing from the water of the Nile was intended to foreshadow the Israelites' escape from Egypt through the Red Sea).

2:11 *After Moses had grown up*: cf. 7:7, where Moses is said to be eighty years old at the time of his mission to Pharaoh. *Striking*: probably in the sense of "flogging"; in v. 12, however, the same verb is used in the sense of "killing."

2:15 *Land of Midian*: the territory under the control of a confederation made up, according to Nm 31:8, of five Midianite tribes. According to Gn 25:1–2, Midian was a son of Abraham by Keturah. In view of the extreme hostility in later periods between Israel and Midian (cf. Nm 31; Jgs 6–8), the relationship is striking, as is the account here in Exodus of good relations between Moses and no less than a Midianite priest.

2:18 *Reuel*: also called Jethro. Cf. 3:1; 4:18; 18:1.

2:19 *An Egyptian*: Moses was probably wearing Egyptian dress, or spoke Egyptian to Reuel's daughters.

2:22 *Gershom*: the name is explained unscientifically as if it came from the Hebrew word *ger*, "sojourner, resident alien," and the Hebrew word *sham*, "there." *Stranger residing*: Hebrew *ger*, one who seeks and finds shelter and a home away from his or her own people or land.

2:25 *God knew*: in response to the people's cry, God, mindful of the covenant, looks on their plight and acknowledges firsthand the depth of their suffering (see 3:7). In vv. 23–25, traditionally attributed to the Priestly writer, God is mentioned five times, in contrast to the rest of chaps. 1–2, where God is rarely mentioned. These verses serve as a fitting transition to Moses' call in chap. 3.

3:1–4:17 After the introduction to the narrative in 2:23–25, the commissioning itself falls into three sections: God's appearance under the aspect of a burning bush (3:1–6); the explicit commission (3:7–10); and an extended dialogue between Moses and God, in the course of which Moses receives the revelation of God's personal name. Although in the J source of the Pentateuch people have known and invoked God's personal name in worship since the time of Seth (Gn 4:26), for the E and P sources (see 6:2–4) God first makes this name publicly available here through Moses.

3:1 *The mountain of God, Horeb*: traditionally, "Horeb" is taken to be an alternate name in E source material and Deuteronomy (e.g., Dt 1:2) for what in J and P is known as Mount Sinai, the goal of the Israelites' journey after leaving Egypt and the site of the covenant God makes with Israel. However, it is not clear that originally the two names reflect the same mountain, nor even that "Horeb" refers originally to a mountain and not simply the dry, ruined region (from Hebrew *horeb*, "dryness, devastation") around the mountain. Additionally, the position of "Horeb" at the end of the verse may indicate that the identification of the "mountain of God" with Horeb (= Sinai?) represents a later stage in the evolution of the tradition about God's meeting with Moses. The phrase "mountain of God" simply anticipates the divine apparitions which would take place there, both on this occasion and after the Israelites' departure from Egypt; alternatively, it means that the place was already sacred or a place of pilgrimage in pre-Israelite times. In any case, the narrative offers no indications of its exact location.

3:2 *The angel of the LORD*: Hebrew *mal'ak* or "messenger" is regularly translated *angelos* by the Septuagint, from which the English word "angel" is derived, but the Hebrew term lacks connotations now popularly associated with "angel" (such as wings). Although angels frequently assume human form (cf. Gn 18–19), the term is also used to indicate the visual form under which God occasionally appeared and spoke to people, referred to indifferently in some Old Testament texts either as God's "angel," *mal'ak*, or as God. Cf. Gn 16:7, 13; Ex 14:19, 24–25; Nm 22:22–35; Jgs 6:11–18. *The bush*: Hebrew *seneh*, perhaps "thorny bush," occurring only here in vv. 2–4 and in Dt 33:16. Its use here is most likely a wordplay on Sinai

2:11–14 Acts 7:23–28.
2:15 Acts 7:29; Heb 11:27.
2:22 Ex 18:3.
2:23 Ex 3:7, 9; Dt 26:7.
2:24 Ex 6:5; Ps 105:8–9; 106:44–45.
3:2–10 Acts 7:30–35.

Cultural Connection

Holy Ground

EX

In many Asian cultures, before people enter a home, they remove their shoes. People do this before entering a mosque too. Perhaps you remove your shoes before entering your home as well. Removing one's shoes is a common sign of respect. Moses is commanded to remove his sandals in Exodus 3:5. Why? Because he is standing on holy ground. Why is the ground holy? Because God is present.

Moses is awestruck and humbled by his experience of God's presence. In today's multimedia culture, we are rarely awed by anything. Even the burning bush would be just another special effect. How can we regain our sense of awe at God's majesty? Some people experience it in nature, looking at a star-filled sky or the waves rolling in on the ocean. Others experience it in getting to know other people deeply. Still others find it in the amazing patterns that science reveals. The one common element to experiencing awe seems to be the ability to slow down, look closely, and appreciate what we discover.

So, slow down, find your own holy ground, take your shoes off, and let God fill you with awe!

Ex 3:1–6

Moses decided, "I must turn aside to look at this
remarkable sight. Why does the bush not burn
up?" 4 When the LORD saw that he had turned
aside to look, God called out to him from the
bush: Moses! Moses! He answered, "Here I am."
5 God said: Do not come near! Remove your
sandals from your feet, for the place where you
stand is holy ground.* 6 I am the God of your
father,† he continued, the God of Abraham, the
God of Isaac, and the God of Jacob.* Moses hid
his face, for he was afraid to look at God.

The Call and Commission of Moses

7 But the LORD said: I have witnessed the affliction of my people in Egypt and have heard their
cry against their taskmasters, so I know well what
they are suffering. 8 Therefore I have come down†
to rescue them from the power of the Egyptians
and lead them up from that land into a good
and spacious land, a land flowing with milk and
honey, the country of the Canaanites, the Hittites, the Amorites, the Perizzites, the Girgashites,
the Hivites and the Jebusites.* 9 Now indeed
the outcry of the Israelites has reached me, and
I have seen how the Egyptians are oppressing
them. 10 Now, go! I am sending you to Pharaoh
to bring my people, the Israelites, out of Egypt.
11 But Moses said to God, "Who am I† that I
should go to Pharaoh and bring the Israelites out
of Egypt?" 12 God answered: I will be with you;
and this will be your sign† that I have sent you.
When you have brought the people out of Egypt,

† (Hebrew *sinay*), implying a popular etymology for the name of the sacred mountain.

3:6 *God of your father*: a frequently used epithet in Genesis (along with the variants "my father" and "your father") for God as worshiped by the ancestors. As is known from its usage outside of the Bible in the ancient Near East, it suggests a close, personal relationship between the individual and the particular god in question, who is both a patron and a protector, a god traditionally revered by the individual's family and whose worship is passed down from father to son. *The God of Abraham . . . Jacob*: this precise phrase (only here and in v. 15; 4:5) stresses the continuity between the new revelation to Moses and the earlier religious experience of Israel's ancestors, identifying the God who is now addressing Moses with the God who promised land and numerous posterity to the ancestors. Cf. Mt 22:32; Mk 12:26; Lk 20:37. *Afraid to look at God*: the traditions about Moses are not uniform in regard to his beholding or not being able to look at God (cf. 24:11; 33:11, 18–23; 34:29–35). Here Moses' reaction is the natural and spontaneous gesture of a person suddenly confronted with a direct experience of God. Aware of his human frailty and the gulf that separates him from the God who is holy, he hides his face. To encounter the divine was to come before an awesome and mysterious power unlike any other a human being might experience and, as such, potentially threatening to one's very identity or existence (see Gn 32:30).

3:8 *I have come down*: cf. Gn 11:5, 7; 18:21. *Flowing with milk and honey*: an expression denoting agricultural prosperity, which seems to have been proverbial in its application to the land of Canaan. Cf. Ex 13:5; Nm 13:27; Jos 5:6; Jer 11:5; 32:22; Ez 20:6, 15.

3:11 *Who am I*: this question is always addressed by an inferior to a superior (to the ruler in 1 Sm 18:18; to God in 2 Sm 7:18 and its parallel, 1 Chr 17:16; 1 Chr 29:14; 2 Chr 2:5). In response to some special opportunity or invitation, the question expresses in a style typical of the ancient Near East the speaker's humility or gratitude or need of further assistance, but never unwillingness or an outright refusal to respond. Instead the question sets the stage for further support from the superior should that be needed (as here).

3:12 *Sign*: a visible display of the power of God. The ancient notion of a sign from God does not coincide with the modern understanding of "miracle," which suggests some disruption in the

* **3:5** Jos 5:15.
3:6 Ex 4:5; Mt 22:32; Mk 12:26; Lk 20:37.
3:8 Gn 15:19–21.

you will serve God at this mountain. 13 "But,"
said Moses to God, "if I go to the Israelites and
say to them, 'The God of your ancestors has sent
me to you,' and they ask me, 'What is his name?'
what do I tell them?" 14 God replied to Moses: I
am who I am.† Then he added: This is what you
will tell the Israelites: I AM has sent me to you.
15 God spoke further to Moses: This is what
you will say to the Israelites: The LORD, the God
of your ancestors, the God of Abraham, the God
of Isaac, and the God of Jacob, has sent me to
you.

> This is my name forever;*
> this is my title for all generations.

16 Go and gather the elders of the Israelites,
and tell them, The LORD, the God of your ances-
tors, the God of Abraham, Isaac, and Jacob, has
appeared to me and said: I have observed you
and what is being done to you in Egypt; 17 so I
have decided to lead you up out of your afflic-
tion in Egypt into the land of the Canaanites,
the Hittites, the Amorites, the Perizzites, the
Girgashites, the Hivites and the Jebusites, a land
flowing with milk and honey. 18 They will listen
to you. Then you and the elders of Israel will go
to the king of Egypt and say to him:* The LORD,
the God of the Hebrews, has come to meet us.
So now, let us go a three days' journey in the
wilderness to offer sacrifice to the LORD, our God.
19 Yet I know that the king of Egypt will not allow
you to go unless his hand is forced. 20 So I will
stretch out my hand and strike Egypt with all the
wondrous deeds I will do in its midst. After that
he will let you go. 21 * I will even make the Egyp-
tians so well-disposed toward this people that,
when you go, you will not go empty-handed.
22 Every woman will ask her neighbor and the
resident alien in her house for silver and gold
articles† and for clothing, and you will put them
on your sons and daughters. So you will plunder
the Egyptians.

Did You Know?

God's Mysterious Name

"I am who I am"—one possible translation of *Yahweh* from Exodus 3:14—seems more like a definition than a name. Some scholars have suggested *Yahweh* might be better translated "he causes to be what exists." In any case, the four Hebrew letters *YHWH* (or *Yahweh* in English) are difficult to translate. Over the centuries, the Jewish people stopped pronouncing the four letters out of reverence for God and replaced them with the word *Adonai*, meaning "my Lord." Most English translations of the Bible respect this long-standing tradition, translating the original *YHWH* as "LORD." This mysterious name of God reminds us that no name or symbol can fully express who God is.

▶ Ex 3:13–15

EX

4 1 "But," objected Moses, "suppose they do
not believe me or listen to me? For they may
say, 'The LORD did not appear to you.' " 2 The
LORD said to him: What is in your hand? "A staff,"
he answered. 3 God said: Throw it on the ground.
So he threw it on the ground and it became a
snake,* and Moses backed away from it. 4 Then
the LORD said to Moses: Now stretch out your
hand and take hold of its tail. So he stretched
out his hand and took hold of it, and it became

† laws governing nature. While most any phenomenon can become a vehicle for displaying the purposes and providence of God, here the sign intended to confirm Moses' commission by God seems to be the burning bush itself. Since normally the giving of such a sign would follow the commission rather than precede it (see Jgs 6:11–24), some see Israel's service of God at Sinai after the exodus from Egypt as the confirmatory sign, albeit retroactively. It is more likely, however, that its mention here is intended to establish the present episode with Moses alone as a prefigurement of God's fiery theophany to all Israel on Mount Sinai. *Serve God*: Hebrew *'-b-d*, "serve," includes among its meanings both the notion of "serving or working for another" and the notion of "worship." The implication here is that the Israelites' service/worship of God is incompatible with their service to Pharaoh.

3:14 *I am who I am*: Moses asks in v. 13 for the name of the One speaking to him, but God responds with a wordplay which preserves the utterly mysterious character of the divine being even as it appears to suggest something of the inner meaning of God's name: *'ehyeh* "I am" or "I will be(come)" for "*Yhwh*," the personal name of the God of Israel. While the phrase "I am who I am" resists unraveling, it nevertheless suggests an etymological linking between the name "Yhwh" and an earlier form of the Hebrew verbal root *h-y-h* "to be." On that basis many have interpreted the name "Yhwh" as a third-person form of the verb meaning "He causes to be, creates," itself perhaps a shortened form of a longer liturgical name such as "(God who) creates (the heavenly armies)." Note in this connection the invocation of Israel's God as "LORD (*Yhwh*) of Hosts" (e.g., 1 Sm 17:45). In any case, out of reverence for God's proper name, the term *Adonai*, "my Lord," was later used as a substitute. The word LORD (in small capital letters) indicates that the Hebrew text has the sacred name (*Yhwh*), the tetragrammaton. The word "Jehovah" arose from a false reading of this name as it is written in the current Hebrew text. The Septuagint has *egō eimi ho ōn*, "I am the One who is" (*ōn* being the participle of the verb "to be"). This can be taken as an assertion of God's aseity or self-existence, and has been understood as such by the Church, since the time of the Fathers, as a true expression of God's being, even though it is not precisely the meaning of the Hebrew.

3:22 *Articles*: probably jewelry.

* **3:15** Ps 135:13. **3:18** Ex 5:3. **3:21–22** Ex 11:2–3; 12:35–36. **4:3** Ex 7:10.

Catholic Connection

God the Father

Have you ever asked your parents what your name means or why they chose it for you? Generally, behind each name is a story or a meaning that says something about the individual. The same is true about God's own name, which was revealed to Moses from the burning bush. God tells Moses that his name in Hebrew is "Yahweh," which can be translated as "I AM WHO AM" or "he causes to be what exists." From this name we learn that God alone is the source of all things.

But the meaning from one name alone cannot be enough to truly encompass all that God is. Perhaps that is why, along with Yahweh, the Old Testament has many descriptive names for God, such as "God the Almighty" (Gn 17:1), "God from old" (Is 40:28) and "the Most High" (Is 14:14).

One name the Israelites often used was Father (see Dt 32:6) in reference to God as the creator of all things. But it was not until Jesus came into the world that we learned the true meaning of the name "Father" for God. By revealing himself as God's only Son, Jesus also revealed his relationship with God as Father. (See "The Trinity," near Jn 17:20–26, for more information about the relationship between God the Father and Jesus.) From the name Father, we are reminded of our role as God's adopted daughters and sons and the endless love the Father has for each one of us. The name Father also helps us to remember God's authority and power over us and all of creation. Jesus taught us to pray calling God Father, and so we are able to address God intimately and realize that God desires a loving and personal relationship with us.

Ex 3:13–15

Catechism, nos. 232–242

Cultural Connection

The Name of God

Many Native American peoples, such as the Lakota and the Sioux, have several names for God. *Wakan-Tanka* and *Tun-ka-shi-la* are still commonly used today. These words for God are often translated as "Great Spirit."

This is a good translation because *Wakan* is a word that brings together the concepts of mystery, sacredness, holiness, awe, and inspiration. *Tanka* describes something that is great.

Tun-ka-shi-la is often used the same way as *Wakan-Tanka*, but its meaning is slightly different. *Tun-ka-shi-la* is often translated as "Grandfather or Great Grandfather," but it means the "one who is the oldest, so old that nothing or no one is older." *Tun-ka-shi-la* is a name that reflects the Great Spirit as the source of all things, the one who has existed from the beginning.

▶ Ex 3:13–15

a staff in his hand. 5 That is so they will believe
that the LORD, the God of their ancestors, the God
of Abraham, the God of Isaac, and the God of
Jacob, did appear to you.
6 Again the LORD said to him: Put your hand
into the fold of your garment. So he put his hand
into the fold of his garment, and when he drew it
out, there was his hand covered with scales, like
snowflakes. 7 Then God said: Put your hand back
into the fold of your garment. So he put his hand
back into the fold of his garment, and when he
drew it out, there it was again like his own flesh.
8 If they do not believe you or pay attention to
the message of the first sign, they should believe
the message of the second sign. 9 And if they do
not believe even these two signs and do not listen to you, take some water from the Nile and
pour it on the dry land. The water you take from
the Nile will become blood on the dry land.*

Aaron's Office as Assistant

10 Moses, however, said to the LORD, "If you
please, my Lord, I have never been eloquent,
neither in the past nor now that you have spoken to your servant; but I am slow of speech and
tongue."* 11 The LORD said to him: Who gives one
person speech? Who makes another mute or deaf,
seeing or blind? Is it not I, the LORD? 12 Now go, I
will assist you in speaking† and teach you what you
are to say. 13 But he said, "If you please, my Lord,
send someone else!"† 14 Then the LORD became
angry with Moses and said: I know there is your
brother, Aaron the Levite, who is a good speaker;
even now he is on his way to meet you. When he
sees you, he will truly be glad. 15 You will speak to
him and put the words in his mouth. I will assist
both you and him in speaking and teach you both
what you are to do. 16 He will speak to the people
for you: he will be your spokesman,† and you will
be as God to him.* 17 Take this staff† in your hand;
with it you are to perform the signs.

Moses' Return to Egypt

18 After this Moses returned to Jethro† his
father-in-law and said to him, "Let me return to
my kindred in Egypt, to see whether they are still
living." Jethro replied to Moses, "Go in peace."
19 Then the LORD said to Moses in Midian: Return
to Egypt, for all those who sought your life are
dead. 20 So Moses took his wife and his sons,
mounted them on the donkey, and started back
to the land of Egypt. Moses took the staff of God
with him. 21 The LORD said to Moses: On your return to Egypt, see that you perform before Pharaoh all the wonders I have put in your power.
But I will harden his heart† and he will not let

†

4:12 *Assist you in speaking*: lit., "be with your mouth"; cf. v. 15, lit., "be with your mouth and with his mouth."

4:13 *Send someone else*: lit., "send by means of him whom you will send," that is, "send whom you will."

4:16 *Spokesman*: lit., "mouth"; Aaron was to serve as a mouthpiece for Moses, as a prophet does for God; hence the relation between Moses and Aaron is compared to that between God and his prophet: Moses "will be as God to," i.e., lit., "will become God for him." Cf. 7:1.

4:17 *This staff*: probably the same as that of vv. 2–4; but some understand that a new staff is now given by God to Moses.

4:18 *Jethro*: the Hebrew text has "Jether," apparently a variant form of "Jethro" found in the same verse. *To see whether they are still living*: Moses did not tell his father-in-law his main reason for returning to Egypt.

4:21 *Harden his heart*: in the biblical view, the heart, whose actual function in the circulation of blood was unknown, typically

*

4:9 Ex 7:17, 19–20.
4:10 Ex 6:12.
4:16 Ex 7:1.

Cultural Connection

God Sends Prophets to Liberate His People

God responded to the cry of his people, choosing Moses as a prophet and commissioning him to lead the Israelites to freedom. Despite Moses' first doubts, with God's assistance, Moses became an effective and powerful leader. God would not let Moses' excuses stand in the way of God's mission of liberation.

Christians share in Jesus Christ's prophetic work as well. We too need to speak out against injustice and help the victims of oppression. Like the prophets before us, we can succeed only with God's help.

In our time, great spiritual leaders have risen up to lead people to freedom: Mohandas Gandhi, Martin Luther King Jr., Dorothy Day, Archbishop Oscar Romero, and César Chávez are just a few. As in the case of Moses, God inspired these leaders to see their people experiencing injustice and to seek to liberate them from oppressive powers. You can be sure that these people also had their doubts and relied on God for their strength and hope.

- Are you aware of any group that is being oppressed today? How might God be calling you to help?
- Ask God for wisdom, strength, and help in your mission.

▶ Ex 4:1–17

the people go. 22 * So you will say to Pharaoh,
Thus says the LORD: Israel is my son, my firstborn.
23 I said to you: Let my son go, that he may serve
me. Since you refused to let him go, I will kill
your son, your firstborn.*
24 † On the journey, at a place where they
spent the night, the LORD came upon Moses and
sought to put him to death. 25 * But Zipporah
took a piece of flint and cut off her son's foreskin
and, touching his feet,† she said, "Surely you are
a spouse of blood to me." 26 So God let Moses
alone. At that time she said, "A spouse of blood,"
in regard to the circumcision.
27 The LORD said to Aaron: Go into the wilderness to meet Moses. So he went; when meeting
him at the mountain of God, he kissed him.
28 Moses told Aaron everything the LORD had sent
him to say, and all the signs he had commanded
him to do. 29 Then Moses and Aaron went and
gathered all the elders of the Israelites. 30 Aaron
told them everything the LORD had said to Moses,
and he performed the signs before the people.
31 The people believed, and when they heard that
the LORD had observed the Israelites and had seen
their affliction,† they knelt and bowed down.

Pharaoh's Hardness of Heart

5 1 Afterwards, Moses and Aaron went to Pharaoh and said, "Thus says the LORD, the God
of Israel: Let my people go, that they may hold
a feast† for me in the wilderness." 2 Pharaoh answered, "Who is the LORD, that I should obey him

† performs functions associated today more with the brain than with the emotions. Therefore, while it may be used in connection with various emotional states ranging from joy to sadness, it very commonly designates the seat of intellectual and volitional activities. For God to harden Pharaoh's heart is to harden his resolve against the Israelites' desire to leave. In the ancient world, actions which are out of character are routinely attributed not to the person but to some "outside" superhuman power acting upon the person (Jgs 14:16; 1 Sm 16:10). Uncharacteristically negative actions or states are explained in the same way (1 Sm 16:14). In this instance, the opposition of Pharaoh, in the face of God's displays of power, would be unintelligible to the ancient Israelites unless he is seen as under some divine constraint. But this does not diminish Pharaoh's own responsibility. In the anthropology of the ancient Israelites there is no opposition between individual responsibility and God's sovereignty over all of creation. Cf. Rom 9:17–18.

4:24–26 This story continues to perplex commentators and may have circulated in various forms before finding its place here in Exodus. Particularly troublesome is the unique phrase "spouse of blood." Nevertheless, v. 26, which apparently comes from the hand of a later commentator on the original story, is intended to offer some clarification. It asserts that when Zipporah used the problematic expression (addressing it either to Moses or her son), she did so with reference to the circumcision performed on her son—the only place in the Bible where this rite is performed by a woman. Whatever the precise meaning of the phrase "spouse of blood," circumcision is the key to understanding it as well as the entire incident. One may conclude, therefore, that God was angry with Moses for having failed to keep the divine command given to Abraham in Gn 17:10–12 and circumcise his son. Moses' life is spared when his wife circumcises their son.

4:25 *Touching his feet*: a euphemism most probably for the male sexual organ (see 2 Kgs 18:27; Is 7:20); whether the genitals of the child (after Zipporah circumcised him) or of Moses (after the circumcision of his son) is not clear.

4:31 *Observed . . . their affliction*: the same phrases used in God's dialogue with Moses in 3:16–17.

5:1 *Hold a feast*: the Hebrew verb used here, *hagag* ("to celebrate a feast or a festival"; see 12:14; 23:14), refers to a community cele-

* **4:22** Sir 36:11.
4:23 Ex 11:5; 12:29.
4:25 Is 6:2; 7:20.

Catholic Social Teaching

Slave Labor

Demanding bosses. Long hours. Poor working conditions. Although this story details Pharaoh's unjust treatment of the Israelites almost 3,500 years ago, it is a story that is unfortunately and remarkably similar to the work lives of many laborers throughout the world today. The word *sweatshop* is commonly used to describe a working environment with dangerous and unjust working conditions. Workers in sweatshops typically have very few rights and are often made to work long hours for low wages. The companies that use sweatshops to produce their goods are familiar names to us all. You may even be wearing clothes right now that have been manufactured under unjust conditions, without even knowing it!

Catholic social teaching, however, demands that we become more aware of the origins of the things we buy. If we ignore the conditions under which these products were produced, then in a small way, we contribute to the injustice. But if we refuse to buy these products and stand up in a unified way against those companies that continue to use sweatshop labor, we will emphatically assert that all workers deserve to be treated with dignity and that low wages, unfair labor practices, and dangerous working conditions are unjust and unacceptable in our world today.

Exodus, chapter 5

The Dignity of Work and the Rights of Workers

and let Israel go? I do not know the LORD,† and
I will not let Israel go." 3 They replied, "The God
of the Hebrews has come to meet us. Let us go a
three days' journey in the wilderness, that we may
offer sacrifice to the LORD, our God,* so that he
does not strike us with the plague or the sword."
4 The king of Egypt answered them, "Why, Moses
and Aaron, do you make the people neglect their
work? Off to your labors!" 5 Pharaoh continued,
"Look how they are already more numerous†
than the people of the land, and yet you would
give them rest from their labors!"
6 That very day Pharaoh gave the taskmasters
of the people and their foremen† this order:
7 "You shall no longer supply the people with
straw for their brickmaking† as before. Let them
go and gather their own straw! 8 Yet you shall
levy upon them the same quota of bricks as
they made previously. Do not reduce it. They
are lazy; that is why they are crying, 'Let us go
to offer sacrifice to our God.' 9 Increase the work
for the men, so that they attend to it and not to
deceitful words."
10 So the taskmasters of the people and their
foremen went out and told the people, "Thus
says Pharaoh,† 'I will not provide you with straw.
11 Go and get your own straw from wherever you
can find it. But there will not be the slightest
reduction in your work.'" 12 The people, then,
scattered throughout the land of Egypt to gather
stubble for straw, 13 while the taskmasters kept
driving them on, saying, "Finish your work, the
same daily amount as when the straw was supplied to you." 14 The Israelite foremen, whom the
taskmasters of Pharaoh had placed over them,
were beaten, and were asked, "Why have you not
completed your prescribed amount of bricks yesterday and today, as before?"

† bration marked above all by a procession to the sanctuary. It is used especially of three major feasts: Unleavened Bread, Pentecost (in 23:16, "the Feast of Harvest," but customarily "the Feast of Weeks" [*Shavuot*]), and Succoth/Sukkoth (in 34:16, "the Feast of Ingathering," but more frequently "of Booths, or Tabernacles," as in Dt 16:13, 16; 31:10; Lv 23:34; Zec 14:16; passim) and—along with the related noun *hag*—the Passover in 12:14. See 23:14–18; 34:18–25.

5:2 *I do not know the LORD*: whether or not he had heard of the Lord, the God of Israel, Pharaoh here refuses to acknowledge the Lord's authority. See note on 1:8.

5:5 *They are already more numerous*: a recollection of Pharaoh's earlier words to his subjects in 1:9.

5:6 *The taskmasters of the people and their foremen*: the former were higher officials and probably Egyptians; the latter were lower officials (perhaps recordkeepers or clerks), chosen from the Israelites themselves. Cf. v. 14.

5:7 Straw was mixed with clay to give sun-dried bricks greater cohesion and durability.

5:10 *Thus says Pharaoh*: the standard formula for prophetic oracles, but with Pharaoh rather than the Lord as the subject. This heightens the sense of personal conflict between Pharaoh, who acts as if he were God, and the Lord, whose claims are spurned by Pharaoh.

* **5:3** Ex 3:18.

Complaint of the Foremen

[15]Then the Israelite foremen came and cried
out to Pharaoh:† "Why do you treat your ser-
vants in this manner? [16]No straw is supplied to
your servants, and still we are told, 'Make bricks!'
Look how your servants are beaten! It is you who
are at fault." [17]He answered, "Lazy! You are lazy!
That is why you keep saying, 'Let us go and of-
fer sacrifice to the LORD.' [18]Now off to work! No
straw will be supplied to you, but you must sup-
ply your quota of bricks."
[19]The Israelite foremen realized they were in
trouble, having been told, "Do not reduce your
daily amount of bricks!" [20]So when they left
Pharaoh they assailed Moses and Aaron, who
were waiting to meet them, [21]and said to them,
"The LORD look upon you and judge! You have
made us offensive to Pharaoh and his servants,
putting a sword into their hands to kill us."

Renewal of God's Promise

[22]Then Moses again had recourse to the LORD
and said, "LORD, why have you treated this peo-
ple badly? And why did you send me? [23]From
the time I went to Pharaoh to speak in your
name, he has treated this people badly, and you
have done nothing to rescue your people."

6 [1]The LORD answered Moses: Now you will
see what I will do to Pharaoh. For by a strong
hand, he will let them go; by a strong hand,† he
will drive them from his land.

Confirmation of the Promise to the Ancestors

[2]† Then God spoke to Moses, and said to
him: I am the LORD. [3]As God the Almighty† I
appeared* to Abraham, Isaac, and Jacob, but by
my name, LORD, I did not make myself known
to them. [4]I also established my covenant with
them, to give them the land of Canaan, the land
in which they were residing as aliens.* [5]Now
that I have heard the groaning of the Israelites,
whom the Egyptians have reduced to slavery, I

Pray It!

Why Me?

Read Exodus 5:22–23. Can you imagine how Moses must have felt? He did what God told him to do, and things only got worse for the Israelites. But Moses was still able to talk to God, even if only to say, "Why did you send me?" (verse 22).

Thomas Merton, a famous Trappist monk and spiritual writer, knew that Christians sometimes feel like Moses did:

The Christian
must have the courage
to follow Christ.
The Christian
who is risen in Christ
must dare
to be like Christ:
he must dare
to follow conscience
even in unpopular causes.
He must, if necessary,
be able to disagree with the majority
and make decisions
that he knows
to be according to the Gospel
and teaching of Christ,
even when others
do not understand
why he is acting this way.

(*He Is Risen*, p. 22)

The next time you are feeling a little like Moses and wondering, Why me? try this prayer:

Faithful God, help me to trust in you during times of disappointment and disillusion. I want to believe you are working in ways I cannot see. Please help my disbelief, for I know that you will honor my best efforts and make things come out right in the end. Amen.

▶ Ex 5:22–23

† **5:15** *Cried out to Pharaoh*: the Hebrew verb translated "cry out" and its related noun are normally used of appeals to God by Moses (8:8; 14:15; 15:25; 17:4), the people (3:7, 9; 14:10), or an oppressed individual (22:22, 26). Here, by implication, these minor Israelite officials appeal to Pharaoh as if he were their God. See v. 10.

6:1 *By a strong hand*: by God's hand or Pharaoh's hand? The Hebrew is ambiguous; although it may be an allusion to God's hand of 3:19–20, both interpretations are possible.

6:2–7:7 According to the standard source criticism of the Pentateuch, 6:2–7:7 represents a Priestly version of the JE call narrative in 3:1–4:17. But in context the present account does more than simply repeat the earlier passage. See note below.

6:3 *God the Almighty*: in Hebrew, *El Shaddai.* This traditional translation does not have a firm philological basis. *But by my name . . . I did not make myself known to them*: although the text implies that the name LORD was unknown previously, in context the emphasis in the passage falls on the understanding of God that comes with knowledge of the name. In this way God responds to the worsening plight of the Israelites and Moses' complaint in 5:23 that God has done nothing at all to rescue them.

* **6:3** Gn 17:1; 35:11. **6:4** Gn 15:18; 17:4–8.

am mindful of my covenant.* 6 Therefore, say to
the Israelites: I am the LORD. I will free you from
the burdens of the Egyptians and will deliver
you from their slavery. I will redeem you by my
outstretched arm and with mighty acts of judg-
ment. 7 I will take you as my own people, and I
will be your God;* and you will know that I, the
LORD, am your God who has freed you from the
burdens of the Egyptians 8 and I will bring you
into the land which I swore to give to Abraham,
Isaac, and Jacob. I will give it to you as your own
possession—I, the LORD! 9 But when Moses told
this to the Israelites, they would not listen to him
because of their dejection and hard slavery.
10 Then the LORD spoke to Moses: 11 Go, tell
Pharaoh, king of Egypt, to let the Israelites leave
his land. 12 However, Moses protested to the
LORD, "If the Israelites did not listen to me, how
is it possible that Pharaoh will listen to me, poor
speaker† * that I am!" 13 But the LORD spoke to
Moses and Aaron regarding the Israelites and
Pharaoh, king of Egypt, and charged them to
bring the Israelites out of the land of Egypt.

Genealogy of Moses and Aaron

14 These are the heads of their ancestral
houses.† The sons of Reuben,* the firstborn of
Israel: Hanoch, Pallu, Hezron and Carmi; these
are the clans of Reuben. 15 The sons of Simeon:*
Jemuel, Jamin, Ohad, Jachin, Zohar and Shaul,
the son of a Canaanite woman; these are the
clans of Simeon. 16 These are the names of the
sons of Levi,* in their genealogical order: Ger-
shon, Kohath and Merari. Levi lived one hun-
dred and thirty-seven years.
17 The sons of Gershon,* by their clans: Libni
and Shimei. 18 The sons of Kohath:* Amram,
Izhar, Hebron and Uzziel. Kohath lived one
hundred and thirty-three years. 19 The sons of
Merari:* Mahli and Mushi. These are the clans of
Levi in their genealogical order.
20 Amram married his aunt† Jochebed,* who
bore him Aaron, Moses, and Miriam. Amram
lived one hundred and thirty-seven years. 21 The
sons of Izhar: Korah, Nepheg and Zichri. 22 The
sons of Uzziel: Mishael, Elzaphan and Sithri.

Pray It!

You Promised, God

The Israelite people had been slaves for so long, they were discouraged and did not believe Moses' liberating message in Exodus 6:1–9. Moses probably sounded crazy to them. The writer of Exodus reminds us of God's faithfulness to God's promises and that God's plans cannot be stopped by human weakness. We too may find it hard to believe in God's power in our lives when we feel burdened and oppressed, especially over a long time.

In your prayer time, reflect or journal on the following questions and suggestion:

- When do you find it hard to believe in God's promises?
- What people do you know who find it hard to accept God's power in their lives?
- What barriers are keeping them from accepting God?
- Make up your own prayer expressing your desire to count on God's promises.

▶ **Ex 6:1–9**

23 Aaron married Elisheba, Amminadab's*
daughter, the sister of Nahshon; she bore him
Nadab, Abihu, Eleazar and Ithamar. 24 The sons
of Korah: Assir, Elkanah and Abiasaph. These are
the clans of the Korahites. 25 Eleazar, Aaron's son,
married one of Putiel's daughters, who bore him
Phinehas.† These are the heads of the ancestral
houses of the Levites by their clans. 26 These are
the Aaron and the Moses to whom the LORD said,
"Bring the Israelites out from the land of Egypt,
company by company." 27 They are the ones
who spoke to Pharaoh, king of Egypt, to bring
the Israelites out of Egypt—the same Moses and
Aaron.

6:12 *Poor speaker*: lit., "uncircumcised of lips": a metaphor expressing the hindrance of good communication expressed as "slow of speech and tongue" (4:10). Also used as a metaphor for impeded "heart" (Lv 26:41; Dt 10:16).

6:14 The purpose of the genealogy here is to give the line from which Moses and Aaron sprang, with special emphasis placed on the line of Aaron. Reuben and Simeon are mentioned first because, as older brothers of Levi, their names occur before his in the genealogy.

6:20 *His aunt*: more exactly, "his father's sister." Later on such a marriage was forbidden. Cf. Lv 18:12. Hence, the Greek and Latin versions render here, "his cousin."

6:25 *Phinehas*: according to Nm 25:13, Phinehas was given by God "the covenant of an everlasting priesthood" because of his zeal for God when the Israelites committed apostasy by worshiping the Baal of Peor in the plains of Moab (see Nm 25:1–18).

*

6:5 Ex 2:24.
6:7 Lv 26:12.
6:12 Ex 4:10.
6:14 Nm 26:5–6; 1 Chr 5:3.
6:15 Nm 26:12; 1 Chr 4:24.
6:16 Nm 3:17; 1 Chr 6:1; 23:6.
6:17 Nm 3:21; 1 Chr 6:2; 23:7.
6:18 Nm 3:27; 1 Chr 6:3, 18.
6:19 Nm 3:20; 1 Chr 6:4, 14; 23:21.
6:20 Nm 26:59.
6:23 Ru 4:19–20; 1 Chr 2:10.

Did You Know?

Plagues and the Crossing of the Red Sea

The writer of Exodus combines several versions of what happened in describing the ten plagues and the crossing of the Red Sea. Like in a fine tapestry, the different strands are carefully woven together to produce a suspenseful story. When Pharaoh refuses to let the Israelites go, God sends ten plagues to convince Pharaoh to cooperate. The first nine plagues are religious interpretations of naturally occurring events. For example, Exodus says that the first plague is the water of the Nile turning to blood. At times silt and microbes pollute and redden the Nile, making the water undrinkable. The Israelite people see God at work in the miraculous timing of these natural events.

Finally, God must resort to drastic measures. For the tenth plague, God sends the angel of death to kill the firstborn children of the Egyptians. Moses has the Israelites mark their doorposts with the blood of a lamb so that the angel of death "passes over" their homes. Pharaoh is now eager to get rid of the Israelites and releases them from service. They gladly begin their journey to God's Promised Land.

After the Israelites leave, Pharaoh regrets his decision and sends his army after them. As the Egyptians close in, the Israelites seem to be trapped at the marshlands by the Red Sea (see map 2, "The Exodus from Egypt"). Although the prose version of this situation in Exodus, chapter 14, and the poetic version in chapter 15 differ in many details, both stress that the Israelites are able to pass through a section of wetlands that was made nearly dry by a strong east wind. The chariot wheels of the Egyptians get stuck in the mud, and as the water returns, they drown. Again, it is the timing of God's help that enables the miraculous escape. God hears God's people and sets them free!

Ex 7:1—14:31

28 When the LORD spoke to Moses in the land
of Egypt 29 the LORD said to Moses: I am the LORD.
Say to Pharaoh, king of Egypt, all that I tell you.
30 But Moses protested to the LORD, "Since I am a
poor speaker, how is it possible that Pharaoh will
listen to me?"

7 1 The LORD answered Moses: See! I have made
you a god to Pharaoh,* and Aaron your
brother will be your prophet.† 2 You will speak
all that I command you. In turn, your brother
Aaron will tell Pharaoh to let the Israelites go out
of his land. 3 Yet I will make Pharaoh so head-
strong that, despite the many signs and wonders
that I work in the land of Egypt, 4 Pharaoh will
not listen to you. Therefore I will lay my hand
on Egypt and with mighty acts of judgment I will
bring my armies, my people the Israelites, out of
the land of Egypt. 5 All Egyptians will know that I
am the LORD, when I stretch out my hand against
Egypt and bring the Israelites out of their midst.
6 This, then, is what Moses and Aaron did.
They did exactly as the LORD had commanded
them. 7 Moses was eighty years old, and Aaron
eighty-three, when they spoke to Pharaoh.

III. The Contest with Pharaoh

The Staff Turned into a Serpent

8 The LORD spoke to Moses and Aaron: 9 When
Pharaoh demands of you, "Produce a sign or
wonder," you will say to Aaron: "Take your staff
and throw it down before Pharaoh, and it will
turn into a serpent."* 10 Then Moses and Aaron
went to Pharaoh and did just as the LORD had
commanded. Aaron threw his staff down before
Pharaoh and his servants, and it turned into a
serpent. 11 Pharaoh, in turn, summoned the wise
men and the sorcerers, and they also, the ma-
gicians* of Egypt, did the same thing by their
magic arts. 12 Each one threw down his staff, and
they turned into serpents. But Aaron's staff swal-
lowed their staffs. 13 Pharaoh, however, hardened
his heart and would not listen to them, just as
the LORD had foretold.

First Plague: Water Turned into Blood†

14 Then the LORD said to Moses: Pharaoh is ob-
stinate† in refusing to let the people go. 15 In the

†

7:1 *Prophet*: Hebrew *nabi*, one who can legitimately speak for God and in God's name to another or others. Just as God spoke to Moses, so Moses will speak to Aaron, who will be a "prophet" to Pharaoh. Cf. 4:16.

7:14–12:30 After a brief preface (vv. 8–13) drawn from the

*

7:1 Ex 4:15–16. **7:9** Ex 4:3. **7:11** 2 Tm 3:8.

morning, just when he sets out for the water, go to
Pharaoh and present yourself by the bank of the
Nile, holding in your hand the staff that turned
into a snake.† [16]Say to him: The LORD, the God of
the Hebrews, sent me to you with the message:
Let my people go to serve me in the wilderness.
But as yet you have not listened. [17]Thus says the
LORD: This is how you will know that I am the
LORD. With the staff here in my hand, I will strike
the water in the Nile and it will be changed into
blood.* [18]The fish in the Nile will die, and the
Nile itself will stink so that the Egyptians will be
unable to drink water from the Nile.

[19]The LORD then spoke to Moses: Speak to
Aaron: Take your staff and stretch out your hand
over the waters of Egypt—its streams, its canals,
its ponds, and all its supplies of water—that they
may become blood. There will be blood through-
out the land of Egypt, even in the wooden pails
and stone jars.

[20]This, then, is what Moses and Aaron did, ex-
actly as the LORD had commanded. Aaron raised
his staff and struck the waters in the Nile in full
view of Pharaoh and his servants, and all the wa-
ter in the Nile was changed into blood. [21]The fish
in the Nile died, and the Nile itself stank so that
the Egyptians could not drink water from it. There
was blood throughout the land of Egypt. [22]But the
Egyptian magicians did the same† by their magic
arts. So Pharaoh hardened his heart and would not
listen to them, just as the LORD had said. [23]Pharaoh
turned away and went into his house, with no con-
cern even for this. [24]All the Egyptians had to dig
round about the Nile for drinking water, since they
could not drink any water from the Nile.

Second Plague: the Frogs

[25]Seven days passed after the LORD had struck
the Nile. [26]Then the LORD said to Moses: Go to
Pharaoh and tell him:* Thus says the LORD: Let
my people go to serve me. [27]If you refuse to let
them go, then I will send a plague of frogs over
all your territory. [28]The Nile will teem with frogs.
They will come up and enter into your palace
and into your bedroom and onto your bed, into
the houses of your servants, too, and among your
people, even into your ovens and your kneading
bowls. [29]The frogs will come up over you and
your people and all your servants.

8 [1]The LORD then spoke to Moses: Speak to
Aaron: Stretch out your hand with your staff
over the streams, the canals, and the ponds, and
make frogs overrun the land of Egypt. [2]So Aaron
stretched out his hand over the waters of Egypt,
and the frogs came up and covered the land of
Egypt. [3]But the magicians did the same by their
magic arts and made frogs overrun the land of
Egypt.

[4]Then Pharaoh summoned Moses and Aaron
and said, "Pray to the LORD to remove the frogs
from me and my people, and I will let the peo-
ple go to sacrifice to the LORD." [5]Moses answered
Pharaoh, "Please designate for me the time when
I am to pray for you and your servants and your
people, to get rid of the frogs from you and your
houses. They will be left only in the Nile." [6]"To-
morrow," he said. Then Moses replied, "It will
be as you have said, so that you may know that
there is none like the LORD, our God. [7]The frogs
will leave you and your houses, your servants
and your people; they will be left only in the
Nile."

[8]After Moses and Aaron left Pharaoh's pres-
ence, Moses cried out to the LORD on account of
the frogs that he had inflicted on Pharaoh; [9]and
the LORD did as Moses had asked. The frogs died
off in the houses, the courtyards, and the fields.
[10]Heaps of them were piled up, and the land
stank. [11]But when Pharaoh saw there was a re-
spite, he became obstinate and would not listen
to them, just as the LORD had said.

Third Plague: the Gnats

[12]Thereupon the LORD spoke to Moses: Speak
to Aaron: Stretch out your staff and strike the
dust of the earth, and it will turn into gnats†*
throughout the land of Egypt. [13]They did so.

Priestly source, a narrative depicting the series of ten disasters that God brings upon Pharaoh because of his stubbornness ensues. Although most of these disasters, known traditionally as the "ten plagues of Egypt," could be interpreted as naturally occurring phenomena, they are clearly represented by the biblical authors as extraordinary events indicative of God's intervention on behalf of Israel and as occurring exactly according to Moses' commands. See Ps 78:43–51 and 105:27–36 for poetic versions of these plagues, which also differ significantly from the account here.

7:14 *Pharaoh is obstinate*: lit., "Pharaoh's heart is heavy" (*kabed*); thus not precisely the same Hebrew idiom as found in vv. 13 and 22, "stubborn," lit., "Pharaoh's heart was hard(ened)" (*hazaq*) (cf. the related idiom with Pharaoh as the object, e.g., 4:21).

7:15 *The staff that turned into a snake*: the allusion is to 4:2–4 rather than 7:9–12. The latter comes from the hand of the Priestly writer and features Aaron—with his staff—as the principal actor.

7:22 *The Egyptian magicians did the same*: this is an exaggeration, presumably influenced by the similar statement in v. 11; whereas the magicians could turn their staffs into snakes after Aaron had done so, after Aaron's sign there should not have been any water in Egypt still unchanged to blood for the magicians "to do the same" with it (cf. v. 24).

8:12, 17 *Gnats, flies*: it is uncertain what species of troublesome insects are meant here in vv. 12–14 and then in vv. 17–27, the identification as "gnat" (vv. 12–14) and as "fly" (vv. 17–27) being based on the rendering of the Septuagint. Others suggest "lice" in vv. 12–14, while rabbinic literature renders Hebrew *'arob* in vv. 17–27 as a "mixture of wild animals." In the Hebrew of the Old Testament, the word occurs only in the context of the plagues (see also Ps 78:45 and 105:31).

7:17–21 Ex 4:9; Ps 78:44; 105:29; Wis 11:5–7.
7:26–29 Ps 78:45; 105:30.
8:12–13 Ps 105:31.

Aaron stretched out his hand with his staff and struck the dust of the earth, and gnats came upon human being and beast alike. All the dust of the earth turned into gnats throughout the land of Egypt. [14]Though the magicians did the same thing to produce gnats by their magic arts, they could not do so.* The gnats were on human being and beast alike, [15]and the magicians said to Pharaoh, "This is the finger of God."† Yet Pharaoh hardened his heart and would not listen to them, just as the LORD had said.

Fourth Plague: the Flies

[16]Then the LORD spoke to Moses: Early tomorrow morning present yourself to Pharaoh when he sets out toward the water, and say to him: Thus says the LORD: Let my people go to serve me. [17]For if you do not let my people go, I will send swarms of flies upon you and your servants and your people and your houses. The houses of the Egyptians and the very ground on which they stand will be filled with swarms of flies. [18]But on that day I will make an exception of the land of Goshen, where my people are, and no swarms of flies will be there, so that you may know that I the LORD am in the midst of the land. [19]I will make a distinction† between my people and your people. This sign will take place tomorrow. [20]This the LORD did. Thick swarms of flies entered the house of Pharaoh and the houses of his servants; throughout Egypt the land was devastated on account of the swarms of flies.*

[21]Then Pharaoh summoned Moses and Aaron and said, "Go sacrifice to your God within the land." [22]But Moses replied, "It is not right to do so, for what we sacrifice to the LORD, our God, is abhorrent to the Egyptians.† If we sacrifice what is abhorrent to the Egyptians before their very eyes, will they not stone us? [23]We must go a three days' journey in the wilderness and sacrifice to the LORD, our God, as he commands us." [24]Pharaoh said, "I will let you go to sacrifice to the LORD, your God, in the wilderness, provided that you do not go too far away. Pray for me." [25]Moses answered, "As soon as I leave you I will pray to the LORD that the swarms of flies may depart tomorrow from Pharaoh, his servants, and his people. Pharaoh, however, must not act deceitfully again and refuse to let the people go to sacrifice to the LORD." [26]When Moses left Pharaoh, he prayed to the LORD; [27]and the LORD did as Moses had asked, removing the swarms of flies from Pharaoh, his servants, and his people. Not one remained. [28]But once more Pharaoh became obstinate and would not let the people go.

Fifth Plague: the Pestilence

9 [1]Then the LORD said to Moses: Go to Pharaoh and tell him: Thus says the LORD, the God of the Hebrews: Let my people go to serve me. [2]For if you refuse to let them go and persist in holding them, [3]the hand of the LORD will strike your livestock in the field—your horses, donkeys, camels, herds and flocks—with a very severe pestilence. [4]But the LORD will distinguish between the livestock of Israel and that of Egypt, so that nothing belonging to the Israelites will die. [5]And the LORD set a definite time, saying: Tomorrow the LORD will do this in the land. [6]And on the next day the LORD did it. All the livestock of the Egyptians died,* but not one animal belonging to the Israelites died. [7]But although Pharaoh found upon inquiry that not even so much as one of the livestock of the Israelites had died, he remained obstinate and would not let the people go.

Sixth Plague: the Boils

[8]So the LORD said to Moses and Aaron: Each of you take handfuls of soot from a kiln, and in the presence of Pharaoh let Moses scatter it toward the sky. [9]It will turn into fine dust over the whole land of Egypt and cause festering boils† on human being and beast alike throughout the land of Egypt.

[10]So they took the soot from a kiln and appeared before Pharaoh. When Moses scattered it toward the sky, it caused festering boils on human being and beast alike. [11]Because of the boils the magicians could not stand in Moses' presence, for there were boils on the magicians as well as on the rest of the Egyptians. [12]But the LORD hardened Pharaoh's heart, and he would

---

† **8:15** *The finger of God*: previously the magicians had, for the most part, been able to replicate the signs and wonders Moses performed to manifest God's power—turning their staffs into snakes (7:11–12), turning water into blood (7:22), and producing frogs to overrun the land of Egypt (8:3). But now for the first time they are unable to compete, and confess a power greater than their own is at work. Cf. Lk 11:20.

8:19 *A distinction*: while some uncertainty surrounds the Hebrew here rendered as "distinction," it is clear that now the Israelites begin to be set apart from the Egyptians, a separation that reaches a climax in the death of the Egyptian firstborn (11:7).

8:22 Perhaps Moses is deceiving the Pharaoh much like the "God-fearing" midwives (1:16–20), although ancient historians writing about Egypt some time after the period in which the exodus is set do note Egyptian prohibitions on sacrificing cattle or slaughtering sacred animals. As such, the Egyptians might well have fiercely resented certain sacrificial practices of the Israelites. Certain animals were held sacred in Egypt, as the representations of various deities.

9:9 *Boils*: the exact nature of the disease is not clear. Semitic cognates, for example, suggest the Hebrew root means "to be hot" and thus point to some sort of inflammation. The fact that soot taken from the kiln is the agent of the disease would point in the same direction. See further Lv 13:18–23; Dt 28:35; 2 Kgs 20:7.

---

* **8:14** Wis 17:7. **8:20** Ps 78:45; 105:31; Wis 16:9. **9:6** Ps 78:48.

not listen to them, just as the LORD had said to
Moses.

Seventh Plague: the Hail

13 Then the LORD spoke to Moses: Early tomor-
row morning present yourself to Pharaoh and
say to him: Thus says the LORD, the God of the
Hebrews: Let my people go to serve me, 14 for this
time I will unleash all my blows upon you and
your servants and your people, so that you may
know that there is none like me anywhere on
earth. 15 For by now I should have stretched out
my hand and struck you and your people with
such pestilence that you would have vanished
from the earth. 16 But this is why I have let you
survive: to show you† my power and to make my
name resound throughout the earth!* 17 Will you
continue to exalt yourself over my people and
not let them go? 18 At this time tomorrow, there-
fore, I am going to rain down such fierce hail
as there has never been in Egypt from the day it
was founded up to the present. 19 Therefore, or-
der your livestock and whatever else you have in
the open fields to be brought to a place of safety.
Whatever human being or animal is found in
the fields and is not brought to shelter will die
when the hail comes down upon them. 20 Those
of Pharaoh's servants who feared the word of the
LORD hurried their servants and their livestock off
to shelter. 21 But those who did not pay attention
to the word of the LORD left their servants and
their livestock in the fields.

22 The LORD then said to Moses: Stretch out
your hand toward the sky, that hail may fall
upon the entire land of Egypt, on human being
and beast alike and all the vegetation of the fields
in the land of Egypt. 23 So Moses stretched out
his staff toward the sky, and the LORD sent forth
peals of thunder and hail.* Lightning flashed
toward the earth, and the LORD rained down hail
upon the land of Egypt. 24 There was hail and
lightning flashing here and there through the
hail, and the hail was so fierce that nothing like it
had been seen in Egypt since it became a nation.
25 Throughout the land of Egypt the hail struck
down everything in the fields, human being and
beast alike; it struck down all the vegetation of
the fields and splintered every tree in the fields.
26 Only in the land of Goshen, where the Israel-
ites were, was there no hail.

27 Then Pharaoh sent for Moses and Aaron and
said to them, "I have sinned this time! The LORD
is the just one, and I and my people are the ones
at fault. 28 Pray to the LORD! Enough of the thun-
der† and hail! I will let you go; you need stay no
longer." 29 Moses replied to him, "As soon as I
leave the city I will extend my hands to the LORD;
the thunder will cease, and there will be no more
hail so that you may know that the earth belongs
to the LORD. 30 But as for you and your servants, I
know that you do not yet fear the LORD God."

31 Now the flax and the barley were ruined, be-
cause the barley was in ear and the flax in bud.
32 But the wheat and the spelt were not ruined,
for they grow later.

33 When Moses had left Pharaoh and gone out
of the city, he extended his hands to the LORD.
The thunder and the hail ceased, and the rain
no longer poured down upon the earth. 34 But
Pharaoh, seeing that the rain and the hail and
the thunder had ceased, sinned again and be-
came obstinate, both he and his servants. 35 In
the hardness of his heart, Pharaoh would not
let the Israelites go, just as the LORD had said
through Moses.

Eighth Plague: the Locusts

10 1 Then the LORD said to Moses: Go to Phar-
aoh, for I have made him and his servants
obstinate in order that I may perform these signs
of mine among them 2 and that you may recount
to your son and grandson how I made a fool of
the Egyptians and what signs I did among them,
so that you may know that I am the LORD.*

3 So Moses and Aaron went to Pharaoh and
told him, "Thus says the LORD, the God of the
Hebrews: How long will you refuse to submit to
me? Let my people go to serve me. 4 For if you
refuse to let my people go, tomorrow I will bring
locusts into your territory. 5 They will cover the
surface of the earth, so that the earth itself will
not be visible. They will eat up the remnant you
saved undamaged from the hail, as well as all the
trees that are growing in your fields. 6 They will
fill your houses and the houses of your servants
and of all the Egyptians—something your par-
ents and your grandparents have not seen from
the day they appeared on this soil until today."
With that he turned and left Pharaoh.

7 But Pharaoh's servants said to him, "How
long will he be a snare for us? Let the people go
to serve the LORD, their God. Do you not yet re-
alize that Egypt is being destroyed?" 8 So Moses
and Aaron were brought back to Pharaoh, who
said to them, "Go, serve the LORD, your God. But
who exactly will go?" 9 Moses answered, "With

---

† **9:16** *To show you*: some ancient versions such as the Septuagint read, "to show through you." Cf. Rom 9:17.
9:28 *Thunder*: lit., "divine voices," "voices of God," or the like.

* **9:16** Rom 9:17. **9:23–24** Ps 78:47; 105:32–33. **10:2** Dt 6:20–25.

our young and old we must go; with our sons
and daughters, with our flocks and herds we
must go. It is a pilgrimage feast of the LORD for
us." 10 "The LORD help you,"† Pharaoh replied,
"if I let your little ones go with you! Clearly, you
have some evil in mind. 11 By no means! Just
you men go and serve the LORD.† After all, that is
what you have been asking for." With that they
were driven from Pharaoh's presence.
12 * The LORD then said to Moses: Stretch out
your hand over the land of Egypt for the lo-
custs, that they may come upon it and eat up
all the land's vegetation, whatever the hail has
left. 13 So Moses stretched out his staff over the
land of Egypt, and the LORD drove an east wind†
over the land all that day and all night. When it
was morning, the east wind brought the locusts.
14 The locusts came up over the whole land of
Egypt and settled down over all its territory.
Never before had there been such a fierce swarm
of locusts, nor will there ever be again. 15 They
covered the surface of the whole land, so that it
became black. They ate up all the vegetation in
the land and all the fruit of the trees the hail had
spared. Nothing green was left on any tree or
plant in the fields throughout the land of Egypt.
16 Pharaoh hurriedly summoned Moses and
Aaron and said, "I have sinned against the LORD,
your God, and against you. 17 But now, do for-
give me my sin only this once, and pray to the
LORD, your God, only to take this death from
me." 18 When Moses left Pharaoh, he prayed to
the LORD, 19 and the LORD caused the wind to shift
to a very strong west wind, which took up the
locusts and hurled them into the Red Sea.† Not
a single locust remained within the whole terri-
tory of Egypt. 20 Yet the LORD hardened Pharaoh's
heart, and he would not let the Israelites go.

Ninth Plague: the Darkness

21 * Then the LORD said to Moses: Stretch out
your hand toward the sky, that over the land of
Egypt there may be such darkness† that one can
feel it. 22 So Moses stretched out his hand toward
the sky, and there was dense darkness through-
out the land of Egypt for three days. 23 People
could not see one another, nor could they get up
from where they were, for three days. But all the
Israelites had light where they lived.
24 Pharaoh then summoned Moses and Aaron
and said, "Go, serve the LORD. Only your flocks
and herds will be detained. Even your little ones
may go with you." 25 But Moses replied, "You
also must give us sacrifices and burnt offerings
to make to the LORD, our God. 26 Our livestock
also must go with us. Not an animal must be
left behind, for some of them we will select for
service† to the LORD, our God; but we will not
know with which ones we are to serve the LORD
until we arrive there." 27 But the LORD hardened
Pharaoh's heart, and he was unwilling to let
them go. 28 Pharaoh said to Moses, "Leave me,
and see to it that you do not see my face again!
For the day you do see my face you will die!"
29 Moses replied, "You are right! I will never see
your face again."

Tenth Plague: the Death of the Firstborn

11 1 Then the LORD spoke to Moses: One more
plague I will bring upon Pharaoh and upon
Egypt. After that he will let you depart. In fact,
when he finally lets you go, he will drive you
away. 2 * Instruct the people that every man is to
ask his neighbor, and every woman her neigh-
bor, for silver and gold articles and for clothing.
3 The LORD indeed made the Egyptians well-
disposed toward the people; Moses himself was
very highly regarded by Pharaoh's servants and
the people in the land of Egypt.
4 Moses then said, "Thus says the LORD: About
midnight I will go forth through Egypt.* 5 * Every
firstborn in the land of Egypt will die, from the
firstborn of Pharaoh who sits on his throne to
the firstborn of the slave-girl who is at the hand-
mill,† as well as all the firstborn of the animals.
6 Then there will be loud wailing throughout

†

10:10 *The LORD help you . . .*: lit., "May the Lord be with you in the same way as I let you . . ."; a sarcastic blessing intended as a curse.

10:11 Pharaoh realized that if the men alone went they would have to return to their families. He suspected that the Hebrews had no intention of returning.

10:13 *East wind*: coming across the desert from Arabia, the strong east wind brings Egypt the burning sirocco and, at times, locusts. Cf. 14:21.

10:19 *The Red Sea*: the traditional translation, cf. Septuagint and other Versions; but the Hebrew literally means "sea of reeds" or "reedy sea," which could probably be applied to a number of bodies of shallow water, most likely somewhat to the north of the present deep Red Sea.

10:21 *Darkness*: commentators note that at times a storm from the south, called the *khamsin*, blackens the sky of Egypt with sand from the Sahara; the dust in the air is then so thick that the darkness can, in a sense, "be felt." But such observations should not obscure the fact that for the biblical author what transpires in each of the plagues is clearly something extraordinary, an event which witnesses to the unrivaled power of Israel's God.

10:26 *Service*: as is obvious from v. 25, the service in question here is the offering of sacrifice. The continued use of the verb *'bd* "to serve" and related nouns for both the people's bondage in Egypt and their subsequent service to the Lord dramatizes the point of the conflict between Pharaoh and the God of Israel, who demands from the Israelites an attachment which is exclusive. See Lv 25:55.

11:5 *Handmill*: two pieces of stone were used to grind grain. A smaller upper stone was moved back and forth over a larger stationary stone. This menial work was done by slaves and captives.

*

10:12–15 Ps 78:46; 105:34–35. **10:21–22** Ps 105:28. **11:2–3** Ex 3:21–22; 12:35–36. **11:4** Ex 12:12. **11:5–6** Ex 12:29–30.

the land of Egypt, such as has never been, nor
will ever be again. 7 But among all the Israelites,
among human beings and animals alike, not
even a dog will growl, so that you may know
that the LORD distinguishes between Egypt and
Israel. 8 All these servants of yours will then come
down to me and bow down before me, saying:
Leave, you and all your followers!* Then I will
depart." With that he left Pharaoh's presence in
hot anger.
9 The LORD said to Moses: Pharaoh will not
listen to you so that my wonders may be mul-
tiplied in the land of Egypt. 10 Thus, although
Moses and Aaron performed all these wonders
in Pharaoh's presence, the LORD hardened Phar-
aoh's heart, and he would not let the Israelites go
from his land.

The Passover Ritual Prescribed†

12 1 The LORD said to Moses and Aaron in the
land of Egypt: 2 † This month will stand at
the head of your calendar; you will reckon it the
first month of the year.* 3 Tell the whole commu-
nity of Israel: On the tenth of this month every
family must procure for itself a lamb, one apiece
for each household. 4 If a household is too small
for a lamb, it along with its nearest neighbor will
procure one, and apportion the lamb's cost† in
proportion to the number of persons, according
to what each household consumes. 5 Your lamb
must be a year-old male and without blemish.
You may take it from either the sheep or the
goats. 6 You will keep it until the fourteenth day
of this month, and then, with the whole com-
munity of Israel assembled, it will be slaughtered
during the evening twilight. 7 They will take some
of its blood and apply it to the two doorposts
and the lintel of the houses in which they eat it.
8 They will consume its meat that same night, eat-
ing it roasted with unleavened bread and bitter
herbs. 9 Do not eat any of it raw or even boiled
in water, but roasted, with its head and shanks
and inner organs. 10 You must not keep any of it
beyond the morning; whatever is left over in the
morning must be burned up.
11 This is how you are to eat it: with your loins
girt, sandals on your feet and your staff in hand,
you will eat it in a hurry. It is the LORD's Passover.
12 For on this same night I will go through Egypt,
striking down every firstborn in the land, human
being and beast alike, and executing judgment
on all the gods of Egypt—I, the LORD!* 13 But
for you the blood will mark the houses where
you are. Seeing the blood, I will pass over you;
thereby, when I strike the land of Egypt, no de-
structive blow will come upon you.*
14 This day will be a day of remembrance for
you, which your future generations will celebrate
with pilgrimage to the LORD; you will celebrate it
as a statute forever. 15 For seven days you must
eat unleavened bread. From the very first day
you will have your houses clear of all leaven.
For whoever eats leavened bread from the first
day to the seventh will be cut off† from Israel.
16 On the first day you will hold a sacred assem-
bly, and likewise on the seventh. On these days
no sort of work shall be done, except to prepare
the food that everyone needs. 17 Keep, then, the
custom of the unleavened bread,* since it was
on this very day that I brought your armies out
of the land of Egypt. You must observe this day
throughout your generations as a statute forever.
18 From the evening of the fourteenth day of the
first month until the evening of the twenty-first
day of this month you will eat unleavened bread.
19 For seven days no leaven may be found in your
houses; for anyone, a resident alien or a native,
who eats leavened food will be cut off from the
community of Israel. 20 You shall eat nothing
leavened; wherever you dwell you may eat only
unleavened bread.

Promulgation of the Passover

21 Moses summoned all the elders of Israel and
said to them, "Go and procure lambs for your
families, and slaughter the Passover victims.
22 * Then take a bunch of hyssop,† and dipping
it in the blood that is in the basin, apply some
of this blood to the lintel and the two doorposts.
And none of you shall go outdoors until morn-
ing. 23 For when the LORD goes by to strike down
the Egyptians, seeing the blood on the lintel and

†

12:1–20 This section, which interrupts the narrative of the exodus, contains later legislation concerning the celebration of Passover.

12:2 As if to affirm victory over Pharaoh and sovereignty over the Israelites, the Lord proclaims a new calendar for Israel. *This month*: Abib, the month of "ripe grain." Cf. 13:4; 23:15; 34:18; Dt 16:1. It occurred near the vernal equinox, March–April. Later it was known by the Babylonian name of Nisan. Cf. Neh 2:1; Est 3:7.

12:4 *The lamb's cost*: some render the Hebrew, "reckon for the lamb the number of persons required to eat it." Cf. v. 10.

12:15 *Cut off*: a common Priestly term, not easily reduced to a simple English equivalent, since its usage appears to involve a number of associated punishments, some or all of which may come into play in any instance of the term's use. These included the excommunication of the offender from the Israelite community, the premature death of the offender, the eventual eradication of the offender's posterity, and finally the loss by the offender of all ancestral holdings.

12:22 *Hyssop*: a plant with many small woody branches that was convenient for a sprinkling rite.

*

11:8 Ex 12:31–33.
12:2–20 Lv 23:5–8; Nm 9:2–5; 28:16–25; Dt 16:1–8.
12:12 Nm 33:4.
12:13 Heb 11:28.
12:17 Ex 13:3.
12:22–23 Ex 12:7, 13.

Did You Know?

The Passover

"Why is this night so different from all other nights?" This question, asked by the youngest member of the family, is part of the Jewish celebration of the Passover. Jewish people continue to celebrate the Passover today in fulfillment of Moses' command, "You will keep this practice forever as a statute for yourselves and your descendants" (Ex 12:24).

The Passover is celebrated around a meal including lamb and unleavened bread. The lamb recalls the Passover lamb whose blood was placed on the doorpost to protect the firstborn from the angel of death. The unleavened bread recalls the haste with which the people prepared to depart. Retelling the ancient story, generations of Jews have remembered that "night of nights" when the angel of death passed over the Israelites' houses and struck down the firstborn of the Egyptians. On that night, the people of God were finally released from slavery. Thus, Passover is a celebration of God's gift of freedom—a religious Independence Day, so to speak.

It was during the Passover celebration that Jesus had his farewell dinner (see Lk 22:7–20), placing himself as the Paschal sacrifice. Christians see Jesus as the new Passover; through his death and Resurrection, we are finally liberated from all bondage, including sin and death.

▶ Ex 12:14–28

the two doorposts, the LORD will pass over that
door and not let the destroyer come into your
houses to strike you down.
24 "You will keep this practice forever as a stat-
ute for yourselves and your descendants. 25 Thus,
when you have entered the land which the LORD
will give you as he promised, you must observe
this rite. 26 * When your children ask you, 'What
does this rite of yours mean?' 27 you will reply, 'It
is the Passover sacrifice for the LORD, who passed
over the houses of the Israelites in Egypt; when
he struck down the Egyptians, he delivered our
houses.'"
Then the people knelt and bowed down, 28 and
the Israelites went and did exactly as the LORD
had commanded Moses and Aaron.

Death of the Firstborn

29 * And so at midnight the LORD struck down
every firstborn in the land of Egypt, from the
firstborn of Pharaoh sitting on his throne to the
firstborn of the prisoner in the dungeon, as well
as all the firstborn of the animals. 30 Pharaoh
arose in the night, he and all his servants and
all the Egyptians; and there was loud wailing
throughout Egypt, for there was not a house
without its dead.

Permission to Depart

31 During the night Pharaoh summoned Moses
and Aaron and said, "Leave my people at once,
you and the Israelites! Go and serve the LORD as
you said. 32 Take your flocks, too, and your herds,
as you said, and go; and bless me, too!"†
33 The Egyptians, in a hurry to send them away
from the land, urged the people on, for they
said, "All of us will die!" 34 The people, there-
fore, took their dough before it was leavened, in
their kneading bowls wrapped in their cloaks on
their shoulders. 35 * And the Israelites did as Mo-
ses had commanded: they asked the Egyptians
for articles of silver and gold and for clothing.
36 Indeed the LORD had made the Egyptians so
well-disposed toward the people that they let
them have whatever they asked for. And so they
despoiled the Egyptians.

Departure from Egypt

37 The Israelites set out from Rameses* for Suc-
coth, about six hundred thousand men on foot,
not counting the children. 38 A crowd of mixed
ancestry† also went up with them, with livestock
in great abundance, both flocks and herds. 39 The
dough they had brought out of Egypt they baked
into unleavened loaves. It was not leavened,
because they had been driven out of Egypt and
could not wait. They did not even prepare food
for the journey.
40 The time the Israelites had stayed in Egypt†

---

†

12:32 *Bless me, too*: in a final and humiliating admission of defeat, once again Pharaoh asks Moses to intercede for him (cf. 8:24). However, Pharaoh may be speaking sarcastically.

12:38 *Mixed ancestry*: not simply descendants of Jacob; cf. Nm 11:4; Lv 24:10–11.

12:40 *In Egypt*: according to the Septuagint and the Samaritan Pentateuch "in Canaan and Egypt," thus reckoning from the time of Abraham. Cf. Gal 3:17.

---

*

12:26–27 Ex 13:8, 14–15; Dt 6:20–25.
12:29–30 Ex 11:4–6; Nm 33:4; Ps 78:51; 105:36; 136:10; Wis 18:10–16.
12:35–36 Ex 3:21–22; 11:2–3; Ps 105:37–38.
12:37 Nm 33:3–5.

was four hundred and thirty years.* 41 At the end
of four hundred and thirty years, on this very
date, all the armies of the LORD left the land of
Egypt. 42 This was a night of vigil for the LORD,
when he brought them out of the land of Egypt;
so on this night all Israelites must keep a vigil for
the LORD throughout their generations.

12:22

Law of the Passover

43 The LORD said to Moses and Aaron: This is
the Passover statute. No foreigner may eat of it.
44 However, every slave bought for money you
will circumcise; then he may eat of it. 45 But no
tenant or hired worker may eat of it. 46 It must be
eaten in one house; you may not take any of its
meat outside the house.* You shall not break any
of its bones.† 47 The whole community of Israel
must celebrate this feast. 48 If any alien* residing
among you would celebrate the Passover for the
LORD, all his males must be circumcised, and
then he may join in its celebration just like the
natives. But no one who is uncircumcised may
eat of it. 49 There will be one law† for the native
and for the alien residing among you.
50 All the Israelites did exactly as the LORD had
commanded Moses and Aaron. 51 On that same
day the LORD brought the Israelites out of the
land of Egypt company by company.

Consecration of Firstborn

13 1 The LORD spoke to Moses and said: 2 Con-
secrate to me every firstborn; whatever
opens the womb among the Israelites,* whether
of human being or beast, belongs to me.
3 * Moses said to the people, "Remember this
day on which you came out of Egypt, out of a
house of slavery. For it was with a strong hand
that the LORD brought you out from there. Noth-
ing made with leaven may be eaten. 4 This day
on which you are going out is in the month of
Abib.† 5 Therefore, when the LORD, your God,
has brought you into the land of the Canaan-
ites, the Hittites, the Amorites, the Perrizites, the
Girgashites, the Hivites, and the Jebusites, which
he swore to your ancestors to give you, a land
flowing with milk and honey, you will perform
the following service† in this month. 6 For seven
days you will eat unleavened bread, and the
seventh day will also be a festival to the LORD.
7 Unleavened bread may be eaten during the
seven days, but nothing leavened and no leaven
may be found in your possession in all your ter-
ritory. 8 And on that day you will explain to your
son, 'This is because of what the LORD did for me
when I came out of Egypt.' 9 It will be like a sign†
on your hand and a reminder on your forehead,*
so that the teaching of the LORD will be on your
lips: with a strong hand the LORD brought you
out of Egypt. 10 You will keep this statute at its
appointed time from year to year.
11 "When the LORD, your God, has brought you
into the land of the Canaanites, just as he swore
to you and your ancestors, and gives it to you,
12 * you will dedicate to the LORD every newborn
that opens the womb; and every firstborn male
of your animals will belong to the LORD. 13 Ev-
ery firstborn of a donkey you will ransom with
a sheep. If you do not ransom it, you will break
its neck. Every human firstborn of your sons you

†

12:46 *You shall not break any of its bones*: the application of these words to Jesus on the cross (Jn 19:36) sees the Paschal lamb as a prophetic type of Christ, sacrificed to free men and women from the bondage of sin. Cf. also 1 Cor 5:7; 1 Pt 1:19.

12:49 *One law*: the first appearance of the word torah, traditionally translated as "law," though it can have the broader meaning of "teaching" or "instruction." Elsewhere, too, it is said that the "alien" is to be accorded the same treatment as the Israelite (e.g., Lv 19:34).

13:4 *Abib*: lit., "ear (of grain)," the old Canaanite name for this month; Israel later called it "Nisan." It was the first month in their liturgical calendar (cf. Ex 12:2).

13:5 *The following service*: the celebration of the feast of Unleavened Bread now constitutes the Israelites' service, in contrast to the "service" they performed for Pharaoh as his slaves.

13:9 *Sign*: while here observance of the feast of Unleavened Bread is likened only metaphorically to a physical sign of one's piety that can be worn as a kind of badge in commemoration of the exodus, from ancient times Jews have seen in this verse also the basis for the wearing of phylacteries. These are small receptacles for copies of biblical verses which Jewish men bind to the arms and forehead as a kind of mnemonic device for the observance of the Law.

*

12:40 Gn 15:13; Acts 7:6; Gal 3:17.
12:46 Nm 9:12; Jn 19:36.
12:48 Nm 9:14.
13:2 Ex 13:12–15.
13:3–10 Ex 12:2–20.
13:9 Ex 13:16; Dt 6:8; 11:18.
13:12–15 Ex 13:2; 22:28–29; 34:19–20; Nm 3:12–13; 8:16–17; 18:15; Dt 15:19.

EX

Cultural Connection

Look to the Hills

An African American theology professor tells a story about two Israelites who, while crossing the Red Sea, kept looking down at their feet. One said: "Look at my feet. They're covered with mud. This is some fine mess that Moses led us into." They crossed the sea without ever looking up. They never saw the sea parted on either side. As they wiped the mud from their feet and garments, they completely missed the sea's closing and the Egyptians' being swallowed up at God's command!

Although it seems like it would have been impossible to miss something so fantastic as the parting of the Red Sea, it is sometimes easy to focus so much on the negative that we miss the positive. Some people—especially when life is difficult—keep looking down and miss seeing God's power and their own talents and gifts. Looking down can almost become second nature, poisoning a person's whole attitude. People can waste a lot of time looking down at life's struggles and never looking up.

Brothers and sisters, the resurrected Christ has won victory for all, for people of every race and culture—so look up! Keep your eyes on the high calling of God in Christ Jesus. Remember the hopeful words in Psalm 121:1–2:

> I raise my eyes toward the mountains.
> From whence shall come my help?
> My help comes from the Lord,
> the maker of heaven and earth.

- What do you do when self-doubt and negativity tempt you to keep looking down?
- How can you encourage others when it seems that the injustices and struggles of life have beaten them down?

▶ Ex 14:1-31

must ransom. 14 And when your son asks you
later on, 'What does this mean?' you will tell
him, 'With a strong hand the Lord brought us
out of Egypt, out of a house of slavery. 15 When
Pharaoh stubbornly refused to let us go, the Lord
killed every firstborn in the land of Egypt, the
firstborn of human being and beast alike. That is
why I sacrifice to the Lord every male that opens
the womb, and why I ransom every firstborn of
my sons.' 16 It will be like a sign on your hand
and a band on your forehead that with a strong
hand the Lord brought us out of Egypt."*

IV. The Deliverance of the Israelites from Pharaoh and Victory at the Sea

Toward the Red Sea

17 Now, when Pharaoh let the people go, God
did not lead them by way of the Philistines'
land,† though this was the nearest; for God said:
If the people see that they have to fight, they
might change their minds and return to Egypt.
18 Instead, God rerouted them toward the Red
Sea by way of the wilderness road, and the Isra-
elites went up out of the land of Egypt arrayed
for battle. 19 Moses also took Joseph's bones*
with him, for Joseph had made the Israelites take
a solemn oath, saying, "God will surely take care
of you, and you must bring my bones up with
you from here."
20 Setting out from Succoth, they camped at
Etham* near the edge of the wilderness.
21 * The Lord preceded them, in the daytime
by means of a column of cloud to show them the
way, and at night by means of a column of fire†
to give them light. Thus they could travel both
day and night. 22 Neither the column of cloud by
day nor the column of fire by night ever left its
place in front of the people.

14 1 Then the Lord spoke to Moses: 2 Speak
to the Israelites: Let them turn about and
camp before Pi-hahiroth, between Migdol and

†

13:17 *By way of the Philistines' land*: the most direct route from Egypt to Palestine, along the shore of the Mediterranean.

13:21 *A column of cloud . . . a column of fire*: probably one and the same extraordinary phenomenon, a central nucleus of fire surrounded by smoke; only at night was its luminous nature visible; cf. 40:38.

*

13:16 Ex 13:9.
13:19 Gn 50:25; Jos 24:32.
13:20 Nm 33:6.
13:21–22 Ex 40:38; Nm 9:15–22; Dt 1:33; Neh 9:19; Ps 78:14; 105:39; Wis 10:17.

the sea.* Camp in front of Baal-zephon,† just
opposite, by the sea. 3 Pharaoh will then say,
"The Israelites are wandering about aimlessly in
the land. The wilderness has closed in on them."
4 I will so harden Pharaoh's heart that he will
pursue them. Thus I will receive glory through
Pharaoh and all his army, and the Egyptians will
know that I am the LORD.

This the Israelites did. 5 * When it was reported
to the king of Egypt that the people had fled,
Pharaoh and his servants had a change of heart
about the people. "What in the world have we
done!" they said. "We have released Israel from
our service!" 6 So Pharaoh harnessed his chariots
and took his army with him. 7 He took six hun-
dred select chariots and all the chariots of Egypt,
with officers† on all of them. 8 The LORD hard-
ened the heart of Pharaoh, king of Egypt, so that
he pursued the Israelites while they were going
out in triumph. 9 The Egyptians pursued them—
all Pharaoh's horses, his chariots, his horsemen,†
and his army—and caught up with them as they
lay encamped by the sea, at Pi-hahiroth, in front
of Baal-zephon.

Crossing the Red Sea

10 Now Pharaoh was near when the Israelites
looked up and saw that the Egyptians had set out
after them. Greatly frightened, the Israelites cried
out to the LORD. 11 To Moses they said, "Were
there no burial places in Egypt that you brought
us to die in the wilderness? What have you done
to us, bringing us out of Egypt? 12 Did we not tell
you this in Egypt, when we said, 'Leave us alone
that we may serve the Egyptians'? Far better for us
to serve the Egyptians than to die in the wilder-
ness." 13 But Moses answered the people, "Do not
fear! Stand your ground and see the victory the
LORD will win for you today. For these Egyptians
whom you see today you will never see again.
14 The LORD will fight for you; you have only to
keep still."

15 Then the LORD said to Moses: Why are you
crying out to me? Tell the Israelites to set out.
16 And you, lift up your staff and stretch out your
hand over the sea, and split it in two, that the
Israelites may pass through the sea on dry land.
17 But I will harden the hearts of the Egyptians
so that they will go in after them, and I will re-
ceive glory through Pharaoh and all his army,
his chariots and his horsemen. 18 The Egyptians
will know that I am the LORD, when I receive
glory through Pharaoh, his chariots, and his
horsemen.

19 The angel of God,† who had been leading

Live It!

God Liberates Us from Oppression

The crossing of the Red Sea is one of the most famous stories in the Bible. It is ultimately a story that graphically illustrates that God frees us from oppression. The Israelites were free to return once again to the homeland they had left many centuries before. Like so many people before them and since, they became migrants searching for a better place to call home.

Hundreds of thousands of people are migrating at this very moment. Some are fleeing war or political persecution. Many others, like the ancient Israelites when they first went to Egypt, are simply trying to keep their families from starving. Yet, so often, migrants, immigrants, and refugees are treated with disdain. Some people claim that foreigners are "overrunning our country" or "taking our jobs." They forget that the United States, at least, is a nation of immigrants. Their story is very often our own story as well.

- What situations are you aware of where people are being oppressed or exploited because of their immigrant status, their educational level, or their need for food and shelter?
- How can you stand up to unjust situations and welcome the stranger living in your midst?

▶ **Ex 14:1–31**

EX

14:2 *Pi-hahiroth . . . Migdol . . . Baal-zephon*: these places have not been definitively identified. Even the relative position of Pi-hahiroth and Baal-zephon is not clear; perhaps the former was on the west shore of the sea, where the Israelites were, and the latter on the opposite shore.

14:7 *Officers*: cf. 1 Kgs 9:22; Ez 23:15. The Hebrew word *shalish*, rendered in 1 Kgs 9:22 as "adjutant," has yet to have its meaning convincingly established. Given the very possible etymological connection with the number "three," others suggest the translation "three-man crew" or, less likely, the "third man in the chariot" although Egyptian chariots carried two-man crews. The author of the text may have been describing the chariots of his experience without direct historical knowledge of Egyptian ways.

14:9 *Horsemen*: the usage here may be anachronistic, since horsemen, or cavalry, play a part in warfare only at the end of the second millennium B.C.

14:19 *Angel of God*: Hebrew *mal'ak ha'elohim* (Septuagint *ho angelos tou theou*) here refers not to an independent spiritual being but

14:2 Nm 33:7–8. **14:5–8** Wis 19:3; 1 Mc 4:9.

Did You Know?

Song at the Sea

The Song at the Sea in Exodus 15:1–21 is probably the oldest writing in the Bible. It is an example of how the Israelite people put stories of God's mighty deeds into song so that they could be remembered and passed on from generation to generation.

Verses 20–21 tell us that the prophetess Miriam led the prayer—singing and dancing. Miriam was Moses and Aaron's sister. It is most likely Miriam who watched over her younger brother Moses when their mother placed him in the basket amid the reeds (see Ex 2:4,7–8; Nm 26:59).

The prophet Micah describes Moses, Aaron, and Miriam as a leadership team sent by God (see Mi 6:4). Many biblical scholars believe that Miriam may be the author of the Song at the Sea. This is one of the few biblical stories that clearly shows a woman serving as a prayer leader.

▶ Ex 15:1–21

Israel's army, now moved and went around be-
hind them. And the column of cloud, moving
from in front of them, took up its place behind
them, [20]so that it came between the Egyptian
army and that of Israel. And when it became
dark, the cloud illumined the night; and so the
rival camps did not come any closer together all
night long.† [21]* Then Moses stretched out his
hand over the sea; and the LORD drove back the
sea with a strong east wind all night long and
turned the sea into dry ground. The waters were
split, [22]so that the Israelites entered into the
midst of the sea on dry land, with the water as a
wall to their right and to their left.

Rout of the Egyptians

[23]The Egyptians followed in pursuit after
them—all Pharaoh's horses and chariots and
horsemen—into the midst of the sea. [24]But dur-
ing the watch just before dawn, the LORD looked
down from a column of fiery cloud upon the
Egyptian army and threw it into a panic; [25]and
he so clogged their chariot wheels that they could
drive only with difficulty. With that the Egyp-
tians said, "Let us flee from Israel, because the
LORD is fighting for them against Egypt."

[26]Then the LORD spoke to Moses: Stretch out
your hand over the sea, that the water may flow
back upon the Egyptians, upon their chariots
and their horsemen. [27]So Moses stretched out
his hand over the sea, and at daybreak the sea
returned to its normal flow. The Egyptians were
fleeing head on toward it when the LORD cast the
Egyptians into the midst of the sea. [28]* As the
water flowed back, it covered the chariots and
the horsemen. Of all Pharaoh's army which had
followed the Israelites into the sea, not even one
escaped. [29]But the Israelites had walked on dry
land through the midst of the sea, with the water
as a wall to their right and to their left. [30]Thus the
LORD saved Israel on that day from the power of
Egypt. When Israel saw the Egyptians lying dead
on the seashore [31]and saw the great power that
the LORD had shown against Egypt, the people
feared the LORD. They believed in the LORD* and
in Moses his servant.

15 [1]Then Moses and the Israelites sang* this
song to the LORD:†

I will sing to the LORD, for he is gloriously
triumphant;
horse and chariot he has cast into the sea.
2 My strength and my refuge is the LORD,
and he has become my savior.*
This is my God, I praise him;

† to God's power at work in the world; corresponding to the column of cloud/fire, the expression more clearly preserves a sense of distance between God and God's creatures. The two halves of the verse are parallel and may come from different narrative sources.

14:20 The reading of the Hebrew text here is uncertain. The image is of a darkly glowing storm cloud, ominously bright, keeping the two camps apart.

15:1–21 This poem, regarded by many scholars as one of the oldest compositions in the Bible, was once an independent work. It has been inserted at this important juncture in the large narrative of Exodus to celebrate God's saving power, having miraculously delivered the people from their enemies, and ultimately leading them to the promised land.

Although the victory it describes over the Egyptians at the sea bears a superficial resemblance in v. 8 to the preceding depiction of the water standing like a wall (14:22), the poem (as opposed to the following prose verse, v. 19) suggests a different version of the victory at sea than that found in chap. 14. There is no splitting of the sea in an act reminiscent of the Lord's combat at creation with the sea monsters Rahab and Leviathan (Jb 9:13; 26:12; Ps 74:13–14; 89:11; Is 51:9–10); nor is there mention of an east wind driving the waters back so that the Israelites can cross. In this version it is by means of a storm at sea, caused by a ferocious blast from his nostrils, that the Lord achieves a decisive victory against Pharaoh and his army (vv. 1–12). The second half of the poem (vv. 13–18) describes God's guidance into the promised land.

* **14:21–22** Ex 15:19; Ps 66:6; 78:13; 136:13–14; Wis 10:18; 19:7–8; Is 63:12–13; Heb 11:29.
14:28–29 Dt 11:4; Ps 106:11.
14:31 Ex 4:31; Ps 106:12; Wis 10:20.
15:1 Ex 15:21.
15:2 Ps 118:14; Is 12:2.

the God of my father, I extol him.
3 The LORD is a warrior,
LORD is his name!
4 Pharaoh's chariots and army he hurled into the sea;
the elite of his officers were drowned in the Red Sea.†
5 The flood waters covered them,
they sank into the depths like a stone.*
6 Your right hand, O LORD, magnificent in power,
your right hand, O LORD, shattered the enemy.
7 In your great majesty you overthrew your adversaries;
you loosed your wrath to consume them like stubble.
8 At the blast of your nostrils the waters piled up,
the flowing waters stood like a mound,
the flood waters foamed in the midst of the sea.
9 The enemy boasted, "I will pursue and overtake them;
I will divide the spoils and have my fill of them;
I will draw my sword; my hand will despoil them!"
10 When you blew with your breath, the sea covered them;
like lead they sank in the mighty waters.
11 Who is like you among the gods, O LORD?
Who is like you, magnificent among the holy ones?
Awe-inspiring in deeds of renown, worker of wonders,
12 when you stretched out your right hand,
the earth swallowed them!
13 In your love† you led the people you redeemed;
in your strength you guided them to your holy dwelling.
14 The peoples heard and quaked;
anguish gripped the dwellers in Philistia.
15 Then were the chieftains of Edom dismayed,
the nobles of Moab seized by trembling;
All the inhabitants of Canaan melted away;
16 *terror and dread fell upon them.
By the might of your arm they became silent like stone,

Introducing...

Moses

Moses is, without doubt, the most important character in the Pentateuch, if not the entire Old Testament. Struggling to find language to describe his greatness, Deuteronomy 34:10 says, "Since then no prophet has arisen in Israel like Moses, whom the LORD knew face to face." Born to a couple from the tribe of Levi and raised as an Egyptian by the Pharaoh's daughter, Moses was perfectly suited to negotiate Israel's freedom from slavery in Egypt. In event after event, the author of Exodus shows us Moses' wonder-working power, his prophetic skill, and his intimacy with God.

Despite all of Moses' great accomplishments, he never loses his humanness. He lacks confidence in his ability to speak (see Ex 4:10); he is angry and frustrated with his people (see 17:4), and he bargains with God out of love for his people (see 32:11–14). Moses, noble but also knowing sadness, is elegantly portrayed in the passage where he dies within sight of the Promised Land (see Deuteronomy, chapter 34). These qualities paint a picture of someone whose perseverance and trust allow God to work through him.

A prophet is literally God's voice, and Moses was indeed God's voice, which shaped Israel to be a people of the Covenant. All other leaders and figures in the Old Testament are compared with Moses. In the New Testament, even Jesus is compared with Moses.

EX

while your people, LORD, passed over,
while the people whom you created passed over.†
17 You brought them in, you planted them
on the mountain that is your own—
The place you made the base of your throne, LORD,

†

15:4 *Red Sea*: the traditional translation of the Hebrew *yam suph*, which actually means "Sea of Reeds" or "reedy sea." The location is uncertain, though in view of the route taken by the Israelites from Egypt to Sinai, it could not have been the Red Sea, which is too far south. It was probably a smaller body of water south of the Gulf of Suez. The term occurs also in Exodus at 10:19; 13:18; and 23:31.

15:13 *Love*: the very important Hebrew term *hesed* carries a variety of nuances depending on context: love, kindness, faithfulness. It is often rendered "steadfast love." It implies a relationship that generates an obligation and therefore is at home in a covenant context. Cf. 20:6.

15:16 *Passed over*: an allusion to the crossing of the Jordan River (cf. Jos 3–5), written as if the entry into the promised land had already occurred. This verse suggests that at one time there was a ritual enactment of the conquest at a shrine near the Jordan River which included also a celebration of the victory at the sea.

*

15:5 Neh 9:11. **15:16–17** Ps 78:53–55.

Live It!

Those Whiny Israelites

It's so easy to complain, isn't it? As soon as things aren't quite the way we would like, we start fussing and whining and grumbling. We have all done it. We are no different from the Israelites who, despite having just been miraculously delivered from slavery, start complaining after a few days in the wilderness. "Why," they ask, "would God lead us through the Red Sea only to let us die of hunger?"

The next time we hear ourselves complaining about something, let's pause and try to see a bigger picture, perhaps the one that God sees. Then we can ask ourselves, Is this really worth complaining about?

▶ Ex 16:1–3

the sanctuary, LORD, your hands established.
18 May the LORD reign forever and ever!

19 When Pharaoh's horses and chariots and horsemen entered the sea, the LORD made the waters of the sea flow back upon them, though the Israelites walked on dry land through the midst of the sea.* 20 Then the prophet Miriam, Aaron's sister, took a tambourine in her hand, while all the women went out after her with tambourines, dancing; 21 and she responded† to them:

Sing to the LORD, for he is gloriously triumphant;
horse and chariot he has cast into the sea.*

V. The Journey in the Wilderness to Sinai

At Marah and Elim

22 * Then Moses led Israel forward from the Red Sea,† and they marched out to the wilderness of Shur. After traveling for three days through the wilderness without finding water, 23 they arrived at Marah, where they could not drink its water, because it was too bitter. Hence this place was called Marah. 24 As the people grumbled against Moses, saying, "What are we to drink?" 25 he cried out to the LORD, who pointed out to him a piece of wood. When he threw it into the water, the water became fresh.*

It was here that God, in making statutes and ordinances for them, put them to the test. 26 He said: If you listen closely to the voice of the LORD, your God, and do what is right in his eyes: if you heed his commandments and keep all his statutes, I will not afflict you with any of the diseases with which I afflicted the Egyptians;* for I, the LORD, am your healer.

27 Then they came to Elim, where there were twelve springs of water and seventy palm trees, and they camped there near the water.*

The Wilderness of Sin

16 1 Having set out from Elim, the whole Israelite community came into the wilderness of Sin, which is between Elim and Sinai, on the fifteenth day of the second month† after their departure from the land of Egypt. 2 Here in the wilderness the whole Israelite community grumbled against Moses and Aaron. 3 The Israelites said to them, "If only we had died at the LORD's hand in the land of Egypt, as we sat by our kettles of meat and ate our fill of bread! But you have led us into this wilderness to make this whole assembly die of famine!"

The Quail and the Manna

4 Then the LORD said to Moses:* I am going to rain down bread from heaven† for you. Each day the people are to go out and gather their daily portion; thus will I test them, to see whether they follow my instructions or not. 5 On the sixth day, however, when they prepare what they bring in, let it be twice as much as they gather on the other days. 6 So Moses and Aaron told all the Israelites,* "At evening you will know that it was the LORD who brought you out of the land of Egypt; 7 and in the morning you will see the glory of the LORD, when he hears your grumbling against him. But who are we that you should grumble

†

15:21 *She responded*: Miriam's refrain echoes the first verse of this song and was probably sung as an antiphon after each verse.

15:22 *Red Sea*: see note on Ex 15:4.

16:1 *On the fifteenth day of the second month*: just one full month after their departure from Egypt. Cf. 12:2, 51; Nm 33:3–4. The Septuagint takes the date to be the beginning of the Israelites' grumbling.

16:4 *Bread from heaven*: as a gift from God, the manna is said to come down from the sky. Cf. Ps 78:24–25; Wis 16:20. Perhaps it was similar to a natural substance that is still found in small quantities on

*

15:19 Ex 14:21–29.
15:21 Ex 15:1.
15:22–23 Nm 33:8.
15:25 Sir 38:5.
15:26 Dt 7:15.
15:27 Nm 33:9.
16:4 Ps 78:24–25; 105:40; Jn 6:31–32; 1 Cor 10:3.
16:6–7 Ex 16:12.

Cultural Connection

Manna and Rice

Rice is the symbol of our life
We eat rice daily
There are different kinds of rice
But we are one
as the rice-eating community
Rice is the symbol of celebration
We express our joy of harvest with it
There are many sufferings in Asia
but we anticipate the time of cosmic
celebration.

(From Maren C. Tirabassi and Kathy Wonson Eddy, editors, *Gifts of Many Cultures*, p. 186)

This poem from Japan, by Masao and Fumiko Takenaka, expresses their appreciation for rice, the most basic food of the Japanese. It unites them as a people and reminds them to be joyful. In a similar way, Exodus tells how the gift of manna united the Israelites and gave them a reason for celebration despite their many trials.

What foods unite you and your friends? your family? your culture? What connections do you see between manna, rice, and the Eucharist?

▶ **Ex 16:1–36**

EX

against us?" 8 And Moses said, "When the LORD
gives you meat to eat in the evening and in the
morning your fill of bread, and hears the grum-
bling you utter against him, who then are we?
Your grumbling is not against us, but against
the LORD."
9 Then Moses said to Aaron, "Tell the whole
Israelite community: Approach the LORD, for he
has heard your grumbling." 10 But while Aaron
was speaking to the whole Israelite community,
they turned in the direction of the wilderness,
and there the glory of the LORD appeared in the
cloud! 11 The LORD said to Moses: 12 I have heard
the grumbling of the Israelites. Tell them: In the
evening twilight you will eat meat, and in the
morning you will have your fill of bread, and
then you will know that I, the LORD, am your
God.
13 In the evening, quail* came up and covered
the camp. In the morning there was a layer of
dew all about the camp, 14 and when the layer of
dew evaporated, fine flakes were on the surface
of the wilderness, fine flakes like hoarfrost on the
ground. 15 On seeing it, the Israelites asked one
another, "What is this?"† for they did not know
what it was. But Moses told them, "It is the bread
which the LORD has given you to eat.*

Regulations Regarding the Manna

16 "Now, this is what the LORD has com-
manded. Gather as much of it as each needs
to eat, an omer† for each person for as many
of you as there are, each of you providing for
those in your own tent." 17 The Israelites did so.
Some gathered a large and some a small amount.
18 † But when they measured it out by the omer,
the one who had gathered a large amount did
not have too much, and the one who had gath-
ered a small amount did not have too little. They
gathered as much as each needed to eat. 19 Moses
said to them, "Let no one leave any of it over un-
til morning." 20 But they did not listen to Moses,
and some kept a part of it over until morning,
and it became wormy and stank. Therefore Mo-
ses was angry with them.
21 Morning after morning they gathered it, as
much as each needed to eat; but when the sun
grew hot, it melted away. 22 On the sixth day they
gathered twice as much food, two omers for each
person. When all the leaders of the community

---

the Sinai peninsula—probably the honey-like resin from the tamarisk tree—but here it is, at least in part, clearly an extraordinary sign of God's providence. With reference to Jn 6:32, 49–52, the Christian tradition has regarded the manna as a type of the Eucharist. *Test*: as the text stands, it seems to leave open the question whether the test concerns trusting in God to provide them with the daily gift of food or observing the sabbath instructions.

16:15 *What is this*: the Hebrew *man hu* is thus rendered by the ancient versions, which understood the phrase as a popular etymology of the Hebrew word *man*, "manna"; but some render *man hu*, "This is manna."

16:16 *Omer*: a dry measure of approximately two quarts.

16:18 Paul cites this passage as an example of equitable sharing (2 Cor 8:15).

16:13 Nm 11:31; Ps 78:27–28. **16:15** Dt 8:3.

Pray It!

Prayer in Support of Others

During the battle against Amalek, Moses' outstretched arms could be understood as a prayer of support for the Israelites. It was an effective prayer too, because as long as he was able to maintain it, the Israelites were winning. When he could not maintain the prayer by himself, Aaron and Hur helped.

Prayer makes a difference. Research has shown that prayer helps people's emotional and physical health and healing, though it cannot explain why. Spiritual energy is a proven, powerful force.

Prayer doesn't even need words. To hold someone in prayer, just think of the person, and quietly take his or her pain or joy into your heart. Who in your life right now needs to be held in prayer? Take a moment to pray for those people.

▶ Ex 17:8–16

came and reported this to Moses, 23 he told them, "That is what the LORD has prescribed. Tomorrow is a day of rest, a holy sabbath of the LORD. Whatever you want to bake, bake; whatever you want to boil, boil; but whatever is left put away and keep until the morning." 24 When they put it away until the morning, as Moses commanded, it did not stink nor were there worms in it. 25 Moses then said, "Eat it today, for today is the sabbath of the LORD. Today you will not find any in the field. 26 Six days you will gather it, but on the seventh day, the sabbath, it will not be there." 27 Still, on the seventh day some of the people went out to gather it, but they did not find any. 28 Then the LORD said to Moses: How long will you refuse to keep my commandments and my instructions? 29 Take note! The LORD has given you the sabbath. That is why on the sixth day he gives you food for two days. Each of you stay where you are and let no one go out on the seventh day. 30 After that the people rested on the seventh day.

31 The house of Israel named this food manna.* It was like coriander seed,† white, and it tasted like wafers made with honey.

32 Moses said, "This is what the LORD has commanded. Keep a full omer of it for your future generations, so that they may see the food I gave you to eat in the wilderness when I brought you out of the land of Egypt." 33 Moses then told Aaron, "Take a jar† and put a full omer of manna in it. Then place it before the LORD to keep it for your future generations." 34 As the LORD had commanded Moses, Aaron placed it in front of the covenant† to keep it.

35 The Israelites ate the manna for forty years, until they came to settled land;* they ate the manna until they came to the borders of Canaan. 36 (An omer is one tenth of an ephah.)†

Water from the Rock

17 1 From the wilderness of Sin the whole Israelite community journeyed by stages, as the LORD directed, and encamped at Rephidim.*

But there was no water for the people to drink, 2* and so they quarreled with Moses and said, "Give us water to drink." Moses replied to them, "Why do you quarrel with me? Why do you put the LORD to a test?" 3 Here, then, in their thirst for water, the people grumbled against Moses, saying, "Why then did you bring us up out of Egypt? To have us die of thirst with our children and our livestock?" 4 So Moses cried out to the LORD, "What shall I do with this people? A little more and they will stone me!" 5 The LORD answered Moses: Go on ahead of the people, and take along with you some of the elders of Israel, holding in your hand, as you go, the staff with which you struck the Nile. 6 I will be standing there in front of you on the rock in Horeb. Strike the rock, and the water will flow from it for the people to drink.* Moses did this, in the sight of the elders of Israel. 7 The place was named Massah and Meribah,† because the Israelites quarreled there and tested the LORD, saying, "Is the LORD in our midst or not?"*

†

16:31 *Coriander seed*: small, round, aromatic seeds of bright brown color; the comparison, therefore, refers merely to the size and shape, not to the taste or color of the manna.

16:33 *Jar*: according to the Greek translation, which is followed in Heb 9:4, this was a golden vessel.

16:34 *The covenant*: i.e., the ark of the covenant, in which were placed the two tablets of the Ten Commandments. Cf. 25:16, 21–22.

16:36 *Omer . . . ephah*: see note on Is 5:10.

17:7 *Massah . . . Meribah*: Hebrew words meaning, respectively, "the place of the test" and "the place of strife, of quarreling."

*

16:31 Nm 11:7.
16:35 Jos 5:12.
17:1 Nm 33:12–14.
17:2–7 Nm 20:2–13.
17:5–6 Dt 8:15; Ps 78:15–16; 105:41; Wis 11:4; Is 43:20; 48:21.
17:7 Ps 95:8–9.

Battle with Amalek

8 Then Amalek† came and waged war against
Israel in Rephidim.* 9 So Moses said to Joshua,
"Choose some men for us, and tomorrow go out
and engage Amalek in battle. I will be standing
on top of the hill with the staff of God in my
hand." 10 Joshua did as Moses told him: he en-
gaged Amalek in battle while Moses, Aaron, and
Hur climbed to the top of the hill. 11 As long as
Moses kept his hands raised up, Israel had the
better of the fight, but when he let his hands
rest, Amalek had the better of the fight. 12 Moses'
hands, however, grew tired; so they took a rock
and put it under him and he sat on it. Meanwhile
Aaron and Hur supported his hands, one on one
side and one on the other, so that his hands
remained steady until sunset. 13 And Joshua de-
feated Amalek and his people with the sword.

14 Then the LORD said to Moses: Write this
down in a book as something to be remem-
bered, and recite it to Joshua:* I will completely
blot out the memory of Amalek from under the
heavens. 15 Moses built an altar there, which he
named Yahweh-nissi;† 16 for he said, "Take up
the banner of the LORD!† The LORD has a war
against Amalek through the ages."

Meeting with Jethro

18 1 Now Moses' father-in-law Jethro, the
priest of Midian, heard of all that God had
done for Moses and for his people Israel: how
the LORD had brought Israel out of Egypt. 2 So
his father-in-law Jethro took along Zipporah,
Moses' wife—now this was after Moses had sent
her back—† 3 and her two sons. One of these was
named Gershom;* for he said, "I am a resident
alien in a foreign land." 4 The other was named
Eliezer; for he said, "The God of my father is my
help; he has rescued me from Pharaoh's sword."
5 Together with Moses' wife and sons, then, his
father-in-law Jethro came to him in the wilder-
ness where he was encamped at the mountain
of God,† 6 and he sent word to Moses, "I, your
father-in-law Jethro, am coming to you, along
with your wife and her two sons."

7 Moses went out to meet his father-in-law,
bowed down, and then kissed him. Having
greeted each other, they went into the tent. 8 Mo-
ses then told his father-in-law of all that the
LORD had done to Pharaoh and the Egyptians for
the sake of Israel, and of all the hardships that
had beset them on their journey, and how the
LORD had rescued them. 9 Jethro rejoiced over all
the goodness that the LORD had shown Israel in
rescuing them from the power of the Egyptians.
10 "Blessed be the LORD," he said, "who has res-
cued you from the power of the Egyptians and of
Pharaoh. 11 Now I know that the LORD is greater
than all the gods; for he rescued the people from
the power of the Egyptians when they treated
them arrogantly." 12 Then Jethro, the father-in-
law of Moses, brought a burnt offering† and
sacrifices for God, and Aaron came with all the
elders of Israel to share with Moses' father-in-law
in the meal before God.

Appointment of Minor Judges

13 The next day Moses sat in judgment for
the people, while they stood around him from
morning until evening. 14 When Moses' father-
in-law saw all that he was doing for the people,
he asked, "What is this business that you are
conducting for the people? Why do you sit alone
while all the people have to stand about you
from morning till evening?" 15 Moses answered
his father-in-law, "The people come to me to
consult God. 16 Whenever they have a disagree-
ment, they come to me to have me settle the
matter between them and make known to them
God's statutes and instructions."

17 "What you are doing is not wise," Moses'
father-in-law replied. 18 "You will surely wear
yourself out, both you and these people with
you. The task is too heavy for you;* you cannot
do it alone. 19 † Now, listen to me, and I will give

17:8 *Amalek*: the Amalekites appear in the Bible as early inhabitants of southern Palestine and the Sinai peninsula prior to the appearance of the Israelites in the region. Cf. Nm 24:20.

17:15 *Yahweh-nissi*: meaning, "the Lord is my banner."

17:16 *Take up the banner of the LORD*: lit., "a hand on the LORD's banner," apparently a war cry for the Israelite troops in the conduct of Holy War; however, the Hebrew text is difficult to interpret.

18:2 *Moses had sent her back*: a later gloss which attempts to harmonize Zipporah's presence with Jethro here in this story and the account of Moses' return to Egypt with Zipporah in 4:20.

18:5 The allusion to meeting Moses encamped at the mountain of God, prior to the arrival of the Israelites at Sinai in chap. 19, might well suggest a different narrative context for this story from an earlier stage of the biblical tradition's development. It is noteworthy that immediately after the Sinai pericope (Ex 19:1–Nm 10:28), recounting the theophany at Sinai and the giving of the law, the narrative of Israel's march through the wilderness resumes with an apparent doublet of the visit by Moses' father-in-law (Nm 10:29–32).

18:12 That a non-Israelite, such as Jethro, should bless Israel's God by way of acknowledging what God had done for Israel (v. 10) is not entirely surprising; but the Midianite priest's sacrifice to the God of Israel, including his presiding over a sacrificial meal with Aaron and the elders of Israel, is unusual, suggesting that he was himself already a worshiper of Yhwh, Israel's God. Note further in this connection the role Jethro takes in the following narrative (vv. 13–27) in instituting a permanent judiciary for the Israelites. *Burnt offering*: a sacrifice wholly burnt up as an offering to God.

18:19–20 By emphasizing Moses' mediatorial role for the people before God in regard to God's statutes and instructions, this story

17:8 Dt 25:17–19; 1 Sm 15:2. **17:14** Nm 24:20; 1 Sm 15:3, 20. **18:3** Ex 2:22. **18:18** Nm 11:14.

Live It!

Sharing Responsibility

Was Moses a workaholic (see Ex 18:18)? Maybe he just found himself suddenly overwhelmed by too many responsibilities. Fortunately for Moses, he had a wise father-in-law, Jethro, who offered some advice to help lighten his load. Moses heeded his advice and asked others to help him. In the process, Moses empowered others to take responsibility and was relieved of his burden as well. It was truly a win-win situation.

When leaders share responsibility, they are saying to other people, "I trust you, we're in this together, and you are needed." When you are in a leadership position, remember Jethro's advice to Moses, and don't be a lone ranger; ask others to help!

▶ **Ex 18:13–26**

you some advice, and may God be with you. Act
as the people's representative before God, and
bring their disputes to God. 20 Enlighten them in
regard to the statutes and instructions, showing
them how they are to conduct themselves and
what they are to do. 21 But you should also look
among all the people for able and God-fearing
men, trustworthy men who hate dishonest gain,
and set them over the people as commanders of
thousands, of hundreds, of fifties, and of tens.*
22 Let these render decisions for the people in all
routine cases. Every important case they should
refer to you, but every lesser case they can settle
themselves. Lighten your burden by letting them
bear it with you! 23 If you do this, and God so
commands you,† you will be able to stand the
strain, and all these people, too, will go home
content."
24 Moses listened to his father-in-law and did
all that he had said. 25 He picked out able men
from all Israel and put them in charge of the peo-
ple as commanders of thousands, of hundreds,
of fifties, and of tens. 26 They rendered decisions
for the people in all routine cases. The more diffi-
cult cases they referred to Moses, but all the lesser
cases they settled themselves. 27 Then Moses said
farewell to his father-in-law, who went off to his
own country.

VI. Covenant and Legislation at Mount Sinai

Arrival at Sinai

19 1* In the third month after the Israelites'
departure from the land of Egypt, on the
first day, they came to the wilderness of Sinai.
2 After they made the journey from Rephidim
and entered the wilderness of Sinai, they then
pitched camp in the wilderness.†
While Israel was encamped there in front of
the mountain, 3 Moses went up to the mountain
of God. Then the LORD called to him from the
mountain, saying: This is what you will say to the
house of Jacob; tell the Israelites: 4 You have seen
how I treated the Egyptians and how I bore you
up on eagles' wings and brought you to myself.*
5 Now, if you obey me completely and keep my
covenant,† you will be my treasured possession
among all peoples,* though all the earth is mine.
6 You will be to me a kingdom of priests,† a holy
nation.* That is what you must tell the Israel-
ites. 7 So Moses went and summoned the elders
of the people. When he set before them all that
the LORD had ordered him to tell them, 8 all the
people answered together, "Everything the LORD
has said, we will do." Then Moses brought back
to the LORD the response of the people.
9 The LORD said to Moses: I am coming to you
now in a dense cloud,* so that when the people

---

† about the institution of Israel's judiciary prepares for Moses' role in the upcoming revelation of the law at Sinai.

18:23 *And God so commands you*: i.e., and God approves.

19:2 Apparently from a different source (P) than v. 1, which notes the date, v. 2 from the J source includes a second notice of the arrival in the wilderness of Sinai. The Israelites now will be camped at Sinai from this point on all the way to Nm 10:10. This is a striking indication of the centrality and importance of the Sinai narrative in the overall composition of the Pentateuch.

19:5 *Covenant*: while covenants between individuals and between nations are ubiquitous in the ancient Near East, the adaptation of this concept to express the relationship that will henceforth characterize God's relationship to Israel represents an important innovation of biblical faith. Other gods might "choose" nations to fulfill a special destiny or role in the world; but only Israel's God is bound to a people by covenant. Thereby Israel's identity as a people is put upon a foundation that does not depend upon the vicissitudes of Israelite statehood or the normal trappings of national existence. Israel will be a covenant people.

19:6 *Kingdom of priests*: inasmuch as this phrase is parallel to "holy nation," it most likely means that the whole Israelite nation is set apart from other nations and so consecrated to God, or holy, in the way priests are among the people (cf. Is 61:6; 1 Pt 2:5, 9).

---

* **18:21, 25** Dt 1:15; 16:18. **19:1–2** Nm 33:15. **19:4** Dt 32:11–12. **19:5** Dt 7:6; 14:2; 26:18–19; 32:8–9. **19:6** 1 Pt 2:9. **19:9** Ex 20:21; 24:15–18.

hear me speaking with you, they will also remain
faithful to you.
When Moses, then, had reported the response
of the people to the LORD, 10 the LORD said to
Moses: Go to the people and have them sanc-
tify themselves today and tomorrow. Have them
wash their garments 11 and be ready for the third
day; for on the third day the LORD will come
down on Mount Sinai in the sight of all the
people. 12 Set limits for the people all around,*
saying: Take care not to go up the mountain,
or even to touch its edge. All who touch the
mountain must be put to death. 13 No hand shall
touch them, but they must be stoned to death
or killed with arrows. Whether human being or
beast, they must not be allowed to live. Only
when the ram's horn sounds may they go up on
the mountain.† 14 Then Moses came down from
the mountain to the people and had them sanc-
tify themselves, and they washed their garments.
15 He said to the people, "Be ready for the third
day. Do not approach a woman."

The Great Theophany

16 * On the morning of the third day there
were peals of thunder and lightning, and a heavy
cloud over the mountain, and a very loud blast
of the shofar,† so that all the people in the camp
trembled. 17 But Moses led the people out of the
camp to meet God, and they stationed them-
selves at the foot of the mountain. 18 Now Mount
Sinai was completely enveloped in smoke, be-
cause the LORD had come down upon it in fire.
The smoke rose from it as though from a kiln,
and the whole mountain trembled violently.
19 The blast of the shofar grew louder and louder,
while Moses was speaking and God was answer-
ing him with thunder.
20 † When the LORD came down upon Mount
Sinai, to the top of the mountain, the LORD sum-
moned Moses to the top of the mountain, and
Moses went up. 21 Then the LORD told Moses: Go
down and warn the people not to break through
to the LORD in order to see him; otherwise many
of them will be struck down. 22 For their part,
the priests, who approach the LORD must sanc-
tify themselves; else the LORD will break out in
anger against them. 23 But Moses said to the
LORD, "The people cannot go up to Mount
Sinai, for you yourself warned us, saying: Set
limits around the mountain to make it sacred."
24 So the LORD said to him: Go down and come
up along with Aaron. But do not let the priests
and the people break through to come up to the
LORD; else he will break out against them." 25 So
Moses went down to the people and spoke to
them.

The Ten Commandments†

20 1 Then God spoke all these words:
2 * I am the LORD your God, who brought
you out of the land of Egypt,* out of the house

The Ten Commandments

(listed in the traditional order, using the words of Exodus)

1. I am the LORD your God, . . . you shall not have other gods besides me.
2. You shall not invoke the name of the LORD, your God, in vain.
3. Remember the sabbath day—keep it holy.
4. Honor your father and your mother.
5. You shall not kill.
6. You shall not commit adultery.
7. You shall not steal.
8. You shall not bear false witness against your neighbor.

9. & 10. You shall not covet your neighbor's house. You shall not covet your neighbor's wife . . . or anything that belongs to your neighbor.

Ex 20:2–17

† **19:13** *May they go up on the mountain*: in vv. 12–13a, a later Priestly reshaping of an earlier version of the instructions governing how the people are to prepare for the encounter with God (vv. 10–11, 13b), the people are to be restrained from ascending the mountain, which is suffused with the holiness of God and too dangerous for their approach. In the earlier version, as v. 13b suggests, the sanctified people must come near, in order to hear God speaking with Moses (v. 9) and in this way receive confirmation of his special relationship with God.

19:16 *Shofar*: a ram's horn used like a trumpet for signaling both for liturgical and military purposes.

19:20–25 At this point the Priestly additions of vv. 12–13a are elaborated with further Priestly instructions, which include the priests' sanctifying themselves apart from the people (v. 22) and Aaron accompanying Moses to the top of the mountain (v. 24).

20:1–17 The precise numbering and division of these precepts into "ten commandments" is somewhat uncertain. Traditionally among Catholics and Lutherans vv. 1–6 are considered as only one commandment, and v. 17 as two. The Anglican, Greek Orthodox,

* **19:12–13** Ex 34:3; Heb 12:18–19. **19:16–19** Dt 4:10–12. **20:2–17** Dt 5:6–21. **20:2** Lv 26:13; Ps 81:11; Hos 13:4.

Did You Know?

The Ten Commandments

The covenant God made with the Israelites is often called the Sinai Covenant. The Ten Commandments are a handy summary of the Sinai Covenant—literally handy because they can be counted off on one's fingers. Because the commandments are short (so short that they are sometimes called the Ten Words) and most of them begin with a similar phrase ("You shall not"), they are easily committed to memory. The ancient Israelites believed that everyone had to know and observe these basic rules if God's people were to live together in peace and security. Today, three major world religions—Jewish, Christian, and Islamic—continue to revere the Ten Commandments as basic building blocks of human community.

For the ancient Israelites, the Ten Commandments covered specific behaviors that made them different from the neighboring cultures. Over the centuries, Christians have applied the moral principles of the Ten Commandments to many other moral questions. In fact, the *Catechism of the Catholic Church* presents the Ten Commandments as the structure for teaching about many moral issues. For Jesus' teaching on the commandments, see Matthew 5:1–7:29, 22:34–40; and Mark 12:28–34.

▶ Ex 20:1–17

of slavery. 3 You shall not have other gods be-
side me.† 4 You shall not make for yourself an
idol* or a likeness of anything† in the heavens
above or on the earth below or in the waters
beneath the earth; 5 you shall not bow down be-
fore them or serve them.* For I, the LORD, your
God, am a jealous God, inflicting punishment
for their ancestors' wickedness on the children
of those who hate me, down to the third and
fourth generation†; 6 but showing love down to
the thousandth generation of those who love me
and keep my commandments.
7 You shall not invoke the name of the LORD,
your God, in vain.† * For the LORD will not leave
unpunished anyone who invokes his name in
vain.
8 Remember the sabbath day—keep it holy.†
9 Six days you may labor and do all your work,
10 but the seventh day is a sabbath of the LORD
your God.* You shall not do any work, either
you, your son or your daughter, your male or
female slave, your work animal, or the resident
alien within your gates. 11 For in six days the
LORD made the heavens and the earth, the sea
and all that is in them; but on the seventh day
he rested.* That is why the LORD has blessed the
sabbath day and made it holy.†

† and Reformed churches count vv. 1–6 as two, and v. 17 as one. Cf. Dt 5:6–21. The traditional designation as "ten" is not found here but in 34:28 (and also Dt 4:13 and 10:4), where these precepts are alluded to literally as "the ten words." That they were originally written on two tablets appears in Ex 32:15–16; 34:28–29; Dt 4:13; 10:2–4.

The present form of the commands is a product of a long development, as is clear from the fact that the individual precepts vary considerably in length and from the slightly different formulation of Dt 5:6–21 (see especially vv. 12–15 and 21). Indeed they represent a mature formulation of a traditional morality. Why this specific selection of commands should be set apart is not entirely clear. None of them is unique in the Old Testament and all of the laws which follow are also from God and equally binding on the Israelites. Even so, this collection represents a privileged expression of God's moral demands on Israel and is here set apart from the others as a direct, unmediated communication of God to the Israelites and the basis of the covenant being concluded on Sinai.

20:3 *Beside me*: this commandment is traditionally understood as an outright denial of the existence of other gods except the God of Israel; however, in the context of the more general prohibitions in vv. 4–5, v. 3 is, more precisely, God's demand for Israel's exclusive worship and allegiance. The Hebrew phrase underlying the translation "beside me" is, nonetheless, problematic and has been variously translated, e.g., "except me," "in addition to me," "in preference to me," "in defiance of me," and "in front of me" or "before my face." The latter translation, with its concrete, spatial nuances, has suggested to some that the prohibition once sought to exclude from the Lord's sanctuary the cult images or idols of other gods, such as the asherah, or stylized sacred tree of life, associated with the Canaanite goddess Asherah (34:13). Over the course of time, as vv. 4–5 suggest, the original scope of v. 3 was expanded.

20:4 *Or a likeness of anything*: compare this formulation to that found in Dt 5:8, which understands this phrase and the following phrases as specifications of the prohibited idol (Hebrew *pesel*), which usually refers to an image that is carved or hewn rather than cast.

20:5 *Jealous*: demanding exclusive allegiance. *Inflicting punishment . . . the third and fourth generation*: the intended emphasis is on God's mercy by the contrast between punishment and mercy ("to the thousandth generation"—v. 6). Other Old Testament texts repudiate the idea of punishment devolving on later generations (cf. Dt 24:16; Jer 31:29–30; Ez 18:2–4). Yet it is known that later generations may suffer the punishing effects of sins of earlier generations, but not the guilt.

20:7 *In vain*: i.e., to no good purpose, a general framing of the prohibition which includes swearing falsely, especially in the context of a legal proceeding, but also goes beyond it (cf. Lv 24:16; Prv 30:8–9).

20:8 *Keep it holy*: i.e., to set it apart from the other days of the week, in part, as the following verse explains, by not doing work that is ordinarily done in the course of a week. The special importance of this command can be seen in the fact that, together with vv. 9–11, it represents the longest of the Decalogue's precepts.

20:11 Here, in a formulation which reflects Priestly theology, the veneration of the sabbath is grounded in God's own hallowing of the sabbath in creation. Compare 31:13; Dt 5:15.

20:4 Ex 34:17; Lv 26:1; Dt 4:15–19; 27:15.
20:5 Ex 34:7, 14; Nm 14:18; Dt 4:24; 6:15.
20:7 Lv 19:12; 24:16.
20:8–11 Ex 23:12; 31:13–16; 34:21; 35:2; Lv 23:3.
20:11 Ex 31:17; Gn 2:2–3.

[12]† * Honor your father and your mother, that
you may have a long life in the land the LORD
your God is giving you.*
[13]You shall not kill.† *
[14]You shall not commit adultery.*
[15]You shall not steal.*
[16]You shall not bear false witness against your
neighbor.*
[17]You shall not covet your neighbor's house.
You shall not covet your neighbor's wife, his
male or female slave, his ox or donkey, or any-
thing that belongs to your neighbor.*

Moses Accepted as Mediator

[18]Now as all the people witnessed the thun-
der and lightning, the blast of the shofar and
the mountain smoking, they became afraid and
trembled.* So they took up a position farther
away [19]and said to Moses, "You speak to us, and
we will listen; but do not let God speak to us,
or we shall die." [20]Moses answered the people,
"Do not be afraid, for God has come only to test
you and put the fear of him upon you so you do
not sin." [21]So the people remained at a distance,
while Moses approached the dark cloud where
God was.

The Covenant Code

[22]† The LORD said to Moses: This is what you
will say to the Israelites: You have seen for your-
selves that I have spoken to you from heaven.
[23]You shall not make alongside of me gods of
silver, nor shall you make for yourselves gods
of gold.* [24]An altar of earth make for me, and
sacrifice upon it your burnt offerings and com-
munion sacrifices, your sheep and your oxen.*
In every place where I cause my name to be in-
voked† I will come to you and bless you. [25]But if
you make an altar of stone for me,* do not build
it of cut stone, for by putting a chisel to it you
profane it. [26]You shall not ascend to my altar by
steps, lest your nakedness be exposed.

Live It!

Living the Ten Commandments

If there is any part of the Old Testament that most people have heard of, it is probably the Ten Commandments. They are so basic and so familiar to us, primarily because they make so much sense. Disobeying authority, stealing, lying, killing, committing adultery: these actions happen all around us today, just as they did four thousand years ago. The bottom line is that the Ten Commandments still make sense; they are still valid, because human nature hasn't really changed, and God knows that. So, look them over carefully, commit them to memory, and ask God to help you with the ones that are the most challenging.

▶ **Ex 20:2–17**

Laws Regarding Slaves

21 [1]These are the ordinances† you shall lay
before them. [2]* When you purchase a
Hebrew slave,† he is to serve you for six years,
but in the seventh year he shall leave as a free
person without any payment. [3]If he comes into
service alone, he shall leave alone; if he comes
with a wife, his wife shall leave with him. [4]But
if his master gives him a wife and she bears him

20:12–17 The Decalogue falls into two parts: the preceding precepts refer to God, the following refer primarily to one's fellow Israelites.

20:13 *Kill*: as frequent instances of killing in the context of war or certain crimes (see vv. 12–18) demonstrate in the Old Testament, not all killing comes within the scope of the commandment. For this reason, the Hebrew verb translated here as "kill" is often understood as "murder," although it is in fact used in the Old Testament at times for unintentional acts of killing (e.g., Dt 4:41; Jos 20:3) and for legally sanctioned killing (Nm 35:30). The term may originally have designated any killing of another Israelite, including acts of manslaughter, for which the victim's kin could exact vengeance. In the present context, it denotes the killing of one Israelite by another, motivated by hatred or the like (Nm 35:20; cf. Hos 6:9).

20:22–23:33 This collection consists of the civil and religious laws, both apodictic (absolute) and casuistic (conditional), which were given to the people through the mediation of Moses. They will be written down by Moses in 24:4.

20:24 *Where I cause my name to be invoked*: i.e., at the sacred site where God wishes to be worshiped. Dt 12 will demand the centralization of all sacrificial worship in one place chosen by God.

21:1 *Ordinances*: judicial precedents to be used in settling questions of law and custom. More than half of the civil and religious laws in this collection (20:22–23:33), designated in 24:7 as "the book of the covenant," have parallels in the cuneiform laws of the ancient Near East. It is clear that Israel participated in a common legal culture with its neighbors.

21:2 *Slave*: an Israelite could become a slave of another Israelite as a means of paying a debt, or an Israelite could be born into slavery due to a parent's status as a slave. Here a time limit is prescribed for such slavery; other stipulations (vv. 20–21, 26–27) tried to reduce the evils of slavery, but slavery itself is not condemned in the Old Testament.

20:12–16 Mt 19:18–19; Mk 10:19; Lk 18:20; Rom 13:9.
20:12 Lv 20:9; Mt 15:4; Mk 7:10; Eph 6:2–3.
20:13 Mt 5:21.
20:14 Lv 18:20; 20:10; Dt 22:22; Mt 5:27.
20:15 Lv 19:11.
20:16 Ex 23:1; Dt 19:16–19; Prv 19:5, 9; 24:28.
20:17 Rom 7:7.
20:18–21 Dt 4:11; 5:22–27; 18:16; Heb 12:18–19.
20:23 Ex 20:3–4.
20:24 Dt 12:5, 11; 14:23; 16:6.
20:25 Dt 27:5; Jos 8:31.
21:2–6 Lv 25:39–55; Dt 15:12–18; Jer 34:14.

sons or daughters, the woman and her children
belong to her master and the man shall leave
alone. 5 If, however, the slave declares, 'I love my
master and my wife and children; I will not leave
as a free person,' 6 his master shall bring him to
God† and there, at the door or doorpost, he shall
pierce his ear with an awl, thus keeping him as
his slave forever.

7 When a man sells his daughter as a slave, she
shall not go free as male slaves do. 8 But if she
displeases her master, who had designated her†
for himself, he shall let her be redeemed. He has
no right to sell her to a foreign people, since he
has broken faith with her. 9 If he designates her
for his son, he shall treat her according to the or-
dinance for daughters. 10 If he takes another wife,
he shall not withhold her food, her clothing, or
her conjugal rights. 11 If he does not do these
three things for her, she may leave without cost,
without any payment.

Personal Injury

12 † Whoever strikes someone a mortal blow
must be put to death.* 13 However, regarding
the one who did not hunt another down, but
God caused death to happen by his hand, I will
set apart for you a place to which that one may
flee. 14 But when someone kills a neighbor after
maliciously scheming to do so, you must take
him even from my altar and put him to death.
15 Whoever strikes father or mother shall be put
to death.†

16 A kidnaper, whether he sells the person or
the person is found in his possession, shall be
put to death.*

17 Whoever curses† father or mother shall be
put to death.*

18 When men quarrel and one strikes the other
with a stone or with his fist, not mortally, but
enough to put him in bed, 19 the one who struck
the blow shall be acquitted, provided the other
can get up and walk around with the help of
his staff. Still, he must compensate him for his
recovery time and make provision for his com-
plete healing.

20 When someone strikes his male or female
slave with a rod so that the slave dies under his
hand, the act shall certainly be avenged. 21 If,
however, the slave survives for a day or two, he
is not to be punished, since the slave is his own
property.

22 † When men have a fight and hurt a preg-
nant woman, so that she suffers a miscarriage,
but no further injury, the guilty one shall be
fined as much as the woman's husband demands
of him, and he shall pay in the presence of the
judges. 23 * But if injury ensues, you shall give life
for life, 24 eye for eye, tooth for tooth, hand for
hand, foot for foot, 25 burn for burn, wound for
wound, stripe for stripe.

26 When someone strikes his male or female
slave in the eye and destroys the use of the eye,
he shall let the slave go free in compensation for
the eye. 27 If he knocks out a tooth of his male or
female slave, he shall let the slave go free in com-
pensation for the tooth.

28 When an ox gores a man or a woman to
death, the ox must be stoned; its meat may not be
eaten. The owner of the ox, however, shall be free
of blame. 29 But if an ox was previously in the habit
of goring people and its owner, though warned,
would not watch it; should it then kill a man or
a woman, not only must the ox be stoned, but its
owner also must be put to death. 30 If, however, a
fine is imposed on him, he must pay in ransom†
for his life whatever amount is imposed on him.
31 This ordinance applies if it is a boy or a girl that
the ox gores. 32 But if it is a male or a female slave
that it gores, he must pay the owner of the slave
thirty shekels of silver, and the ox must be stoned.

†

21:6 *To God*: the ritual of the piercing of the slave's ear, which signified a lifetime commitment to the master, probably took place at the door of the household, where God as protector of the household was called upon as a witness. Another possible location for the ritual would have been the door of the sanctuary, where God or judges would have witnessed the slave's promise of lifetime obedience to his master.

21:8 *Designated her*: intended her as a wife of second rank.

21:12–14 Unintentional homicide is to be punished differently from premeditated, deliberate murder. One who kills unintentionally can seek asylum by grasping the horns of the altar at the local sanctuary. In later Israelite history, when worship was centralized in Jerusalem, cities throughout the realm were designated as places of refuge. Apparently the leaders of the local community were to determine whether or not the homicide was intentional.

21:15 The verb used most often signifies a violent, sometimes deadly, attack. The severe penalty assigned is intended to safeguard the integrity of the family.

21:17 *Curses*: not merely an angrily uttered expletive at one's parents, but a solemn juridical formula of justifiable retribution which was considered to be legally binding and guaranteed by God.

21:22–25 This law of talion is applied here in the specific case of a pregnant woman who, as an innocent bystander, is injured by two fighting men. The law of talion is not held up as a general principle to be applied throughout the book of the covenant. (But see note on Lv 24:19–20.) Here this principle of rigorous accountability aimed to prevent injury to a woman about to give birth by apparently requiring the assailant to have his own wife injured as she was about to bring new life into his family. However, it is debatable whether talion was ever understood or applied literally in Israel. In his Sermon on the Mount, Jesus challenges his audience to find a deeper form of justice than the supposed equilibrium offered by talion (Mt 5:38–40).

21:30 *Ransom*: the amount of money or material goods required to restore the relationship between the relatives of the victim and the negligent owner of the goring ox.

*

21:12 Lv 24:17; Nm 35:15–29; Dt 4:41–42; 19:2–5.
21:16 Dt 24:7.
21:17 Lv 20:9; Prv 20:20; Mt 15:4; Mk 7:10.
21:23–25 Lv 24:18–21; Dt 19:21; Mt 5:38.

Property Damage

33 When someone uncovers or digs a cistern
and does not cover it over again, should an ox
or a donkey fall into it, 34 the owner of the cis-
tern must make good by restoring the value of
the animal to its owner, but the dead animal he
may keep.
35 When one man's ox hurts another's ox and
it dies, they shall sell the live ox and divide this
money as well as the dead animal equally be-
tween them. 36 But if it was known that the ox
was previously in the habit of goring and its
owner would not watch it, he must make full
restitution, an ox for an ox; but the dead animal
he may keep.
37 When someone steals an ox or a sheep and
slaughters or sells it, he shall restore five oxen for
the one ox, and four sheep for the one sheep.*

22 1 [If a thief is caught† in the act of house-
breaking and beaten to death, there is no
bloodguilt involved. 2 But if after sunrise he is
thus beaten, there is bloodguilt.] He must make
full restitution. If he has nothing, he shall be sold
to pay for his theft. 3 If what he stole is found
alive in his possession, be it an ox, a donkey or a
sheep, he shall make twofold restitution.
4 When someone causes a field or a vineyard
to be grazed over, by sending his cattle to graze
in another's field, he must make restitution with
the best produce of his own field or vineyard.
5 If a fire breaks out, catches on to thorn bushes,
and consumes shocked grain, standing grain, or
the field itself, the one who started the fire must
make full restitution.

Trusts and Loans

6 When someone gives money or articles to
another for safekeeping and they are stolen from
the latter's house, the thief, if caught, must make
twofold restitution. 7 If the thief is not caught, the
owner of the house shall be brought to God,† to
swear that he himself did not lay hands on his
neighbor's property. 8 In every case of dishonest
appropriation, whether it be about an ox, or a
donkey, or a sheep, or a garment, or anything else
that has disappeared, where another claims that
the thing is his, the claim of both parties shall be
brought before God; the one whom God convicts
must make twofold restitution to the other.
9 When someone gives an ass, or an ox, or a
sheep, or any other animal to another for safekeep-
ing, if it dies, or is maimed or snatched away, with-
out anyone witnessing the fact, 10 there shall be an
oath before the LORD between the two of them that
the guardian did not lay hands on his neighbor's
property; the owner must accept the oath, and no
restitution is to be made. 11 But if the guardian has
actually stolen from it, then he must make restitu-
tion to the owner. 12 If it has been killed by a wild
beast, let him bring it as evidence; he need not
make restitution for the mangled animal.*
13 When someone borrows an animal from a
neighbor, if it is maimed or dies while the owner
is not present, that one must make restitution.
14 But if the owner is present, that one need not
make restitution. If it was hired, this was covered
by the price of its hire.

Social Laws

15 * When a man seduces a virgin who is not
betrothed, and lies with her, he shall make her
his wife by paying the bride price. 16 If her father
refuses to give her to him, he must still pay him
the bride price for virgins.†
17 You shall not let a woman who practices
sorcery live.*
18 Anyone who lies with an animal shall be put
to death.*
19 Whoever sacrifices to any god, except to the
LORD alone, shall be put under the ban.*
20 You shall not oppress or afflict a resident
alien, for you were once aliens residing in the
land of Egypt.* 21 You shall not wrong any
widow or orphan. 22 If ever you wrong them and
they cry out to me, I will surely listen to their cry.
23 My wrath will flare up, and I will kill you with
the sword; then your own wives will be widows,
and your children orphans.
24 * If you lend money to my people, the
poor among you, you must not be like a money
lender; you must not demand interest from
them. 25 If you take your neighbor's cloak as a
pledge, you shall return it to him before sunset;
26 for this is his only covering; it is the cloak for
his body. What will he sleep in? If he cries out to
me, I will listen; for I am compassionate.*

† **22:1–2** *If a thief is caught*: this seems to be a fragment of what was once a longer law on housebreaking, which has been inserted here into the middle of a law on stealing animals. At night the householder would be justified in killing a burglar outright, but not so in the daytime, when the burglar could more easily be caught alive. *He must make full restitution*: this stood originally immediately after 21:37.

22:7 *Brought to God*: either within the household or at the sanctuary, the owner of the house is required to take an oath before God.

22:16 *The bride price for virgins*: fifty shekels according to Dt 22:29.

* **21:37** 2 Sm 12:6.
22:12 Gn 31:39.
22:15–16 Dt 22:28–29.
22:17 Lv 19:26, 31; 20:6, 27; Dt 18:10–11.
22:18 Lv 18:23; Dt 27:21.
22:19 Dt 13; 17:2–7.
22:20–23 Ex 23:9; Lv 19:33–34; Dt 10:18–19; 24:17–18; 27:19; Zec 7:10.
22:24 Lv 25:35–38; Dt 23:19–20; 24:10–13; Ez 18:7–8, 17–18.
22:25–26 Dt 24:10–13; Jb 22:6; Prv 20:16; 27:13; Am 2:8.

EX

Catholic Social Teaching

Caring for the Poor and Vulnerable

"You shall not oppress or afflict a resident alien. . . . You shall not wrong any widow or orphan" (Ex 22:20–21). This section of the Sinai laws reminds the Israelites to take care of the poor and vulnerable in their midst. One of the key principles of Catholic social teaching is the *Option for the Poor and Vulnerable.* This means that as a society we are obliged to always be mindful of how policies and laws affect those who are poorest and most vulnerable. Policies and laws that affect how we develop the land, grow and sell our food, provide health care, price prescription drugs, and make education accessible can either increase or reduce poverty.

The Church tells us that a basic moral test of a society is how it treats its most vulnerable members. So, how do you think we are doing? Does everyone in our society have access to the basic rights of nutrition, housing, education, and health care? If not, what are we doing about it?

Ex 22:21–27
Option for the Poor and Vulnerable

27 You shall not despise God,† nor curse a
leader of your people.*
28 You shall not delay the offering of your
harvest and your press. You shall give me the
firstborn of your sons. 29 You must do the same
with your oxen and your sheep; for seven days
the firstling may stay with its mother, but on the
eighth day you must give it to me.*
30 You shall be a people sacred to me. Flesh
torn to pieces in the field you shall not eat; you
must throw it to the dogs.*

23 1 You shall not repeat a false report. Do
not join your hand with the wicked to be
a witness supporting violence.* 2 You shall not
follow the crowd in doing wrong. When testify-
ing in a lawsuit, you shall not follow the crowd
in perverting justice. 3 You shall not favor the
poor in a lawsuit.*
4 When you come upon your enemy's ox or
donkey going astray, you must see to it that it
is returned.* 5 When you notice the donkey of
one who hates you lying down under its burden,
you should not desert him; you must help him
with it.
6 You shall not pervert justice for the needy
among you in a lawsuit. 7 You shall keep away
from anything dishonest. The innocent and the
just you shall not put to death, for I will not ac-
quit the guilty. 8 Never take a bribe, for a bribe
blinds the clear-sighted and distorts the words
of the just.* 9 You shall not oppress a resident
alien; you well know how it feels to be an alien,
since you were once aliens yourselves in the land
of Egypt.*

Religious Laws

10 * For six years you may sow your land and
gather in its produce. 11 But the seventh year you
shall let the land lie untilled and fallow, that
the poor of your people may eat of it and their
leftovers the wild animals may eat. So also shall
you do in regard to your vineyard and your ol-
ive grove.
12 For six days you may do your work, but on
the seventh day you must rest,* that your ox
and your donkey may have rest, and that the
son of your maidservant and the resident alien
may be refreshed. 13 Give heed to all that I have
told you.
You shall not mention the name of any other
god; it shall not be heard from your lips.
14 * Three times a year you shall celebrate a
pilgrim feast to me.† 15 You shall keep the feast
of Unleavened Bread. As I have commanded you,
you must eat unleavened bread for seven days

†

22:27 *Despise God*: a turning away from God's authority and so failing to honor God (cf. 1 Sm 2:30).

23:14 These three feasts—Passover/Unleavened Bread, Weeks (Pentecost), and Booths (Tabernacles or Succoth/Sukkoth)—are also listed in 34:18–26; Lv 23; Dt 16.

*

22:27 Acts 23:5.
22:29 Ex 13:2; 34:19; Lv 22:27; Dt 15:19.
22:30 Lv 7:24; 17:15; 22:8.
23:1–2 Dt 19:16–21.
23:3 Lv 19:15.
23:4 Dt 22:1–4.
23:8 Dt 16:19; 27:25; Sir 20:28.
23:9 Ex 22:20.
23:10–11 Lv 25:3–7.
23:12 Ex 20:8–10.
23:14–17 Ex 34:18, 22–24; Lv 23; Dt 16:1–17.

at the appointed time in the month of Abib, for
it was then that you came out of Egypt. No one
shall appear before me† empty-handed. 16You
shall also keep the feast of the grain harvest with
the first fruits of the crop that you sow in the
field; and finally, the feast of Ingathering at the
end of the year, when you collect your produce
from the fields. 17Three times a year shall all your
men appear before the LORD God.
18You shall not offer the blood of my sacrifice
with anything leavened;* nor shall the fat of my
feast be kept overnight till the next day. 19The
choicest first fruits of your soil you shall bring to
the house of the LORD, your God.
You shall not boil a young goat in its mother's
milk.†

Reward of Fidelity

20See, I am sending an angel* before you, to
guard you on the way and bring you to the place
I have prepared. 21Be attentive to him and obey
him. Do not rebel against him, for he will not
forgive your sin. My authority is within him.†
22If you obey him and carry out all I tell you, I
will be an enemy to your enemies and a foe to
your foes.
23My angel will go before you and bring you
to the Amorites, Hittites, Perizzites, Canaanites,
Hivites and Jebusites; and I will wipe them out.
24Therefore, you shall not bow down to their
gods and serve them, nor shall you act as they
do; rather, you must demolish them and smash
their sacred stones.† * 25You shall serve the LORD,
your God; then he will bless your food and drink,
and I will remove sickness from your midst; 26no
woman in your land will be barren or miscarry;
and I will give you a full span of life.
27I will have the terror of me precede you, so
that I will throw into panic every nation you
reach.* I will make all your enemies turn from
you in flight, 28and ahead of you I will send
hornets† to drive the Hivites, Canaanites and
Hittites out of your way. 29But I will not drive
them all out before you in one year, lest the land
become desolate and the wild animals multiply
against you. 30Little by little I will drive them
out before you, until you have grown numerous
enough to take possession of the land. 31* I will
set your boundaries from the Red Sea to the sea
of the Philistines,† and from the wilderness to
the Euphrates; all who dwell in this land I will
hand over to you and you shall drive them out
before you. 32You shall not make a covenant
with them or their gods. 33They must not live in
your land. For if you serve their gods, this will
become a snare to you.*

Ratification of the Covenant

24 1Moses himself was told: Come up to the
LORD, you and Aaron, with Nadab, Abihu,
and seventy of the elders of Israel. You shall bow
down at a distance. 2Moses alone is to come
close to the LORD; the others shall not come close,
and the people shall not come up with them.
3When Moses came to the people and related
all the words and ordinances of the LORD, they
all answered with one voice, "We will do every-
thing that the LORD has told us."* 4Moses then
wrote down all the words of the LORD and, rising
early in the morning, he built at the foot of the
mountain an altar and twelve sacred stones† for
the twelve tribes of Israel. 5* Then, having sent
young men of the Israelites to offer burnt offer-
ings and sacrifice young bulls as communion
offerings to the LORD, 6Moses took half of the
blood and put it in large bowls; the other half
he splashed on the altar. 7Taking the book of the
covenant, he read it aloud to the people, who an-
swered, "All that the LORD has said, we will hear
and do." 8Then he took the blood and splashed
it on the people, saying, "This is the blood of the
covenant which the LORD has made with you ac-
cording to all these words."
9Moses then went up with Aaron, Nadab,
Abihu, and seventy elders of Israel, 10and they
beheld the God of Israel. Under his feet there

EX

†

23:15 *Appear before me*: the original expression was "see my face"; so also in several other places, as 23:17; 34:23–24; Dt 16:16; 31:11.

23:19 *Boil a young goat in its mother's milk*: this command, repeated in 34:26 and Dt 14:21, is difficult to understand. It may originate from a taboo that forbade killing the young that were still nursing from the mother, or that forbade the mixing of life and death: the slaughtered young goat with the milk that previously had nourished its life. The Jewish dietary custom of keeping meat and dairy products separate is based on this command.

23:21 *My authority is within him*: lit., "My name is within him."

23:24 *Sacred stones*: objects that symbolized the presence of Canaanite deities. In general, standing stones served as memorials for deities, persons, or significant events such as military victories or covenant-making. See 24:4.

23:28 *Hornets*: the Hebrew *sir'ah* is a disputed term, but according to ancient interpreters it refers to hornets that were unleashed against the enemy to sting them and cause panic (cf. Dt 7:20; Jos 24:12; Wis 12:8). Others associate the word with plagues or troublesome afflictions.

23:31 *The sea of the Philistines*: the Mediterranean. Only in the time of David and Solomon did the territory of Israel come near to reaching such distant borders.

24:4 *Sacred stones*: stone shafts or slabs, erected as symbols of the fact that each of the twelve tribes had entered into this covenant with God; see 23:24; Gn 28:18.

*

23:18–19 Ex 34:25–26.
23:20 Ex 14:19; 32:34; 33:2.
23:23–24 Ex 34:10–16; Nm 33:51–52; Dt 7:24–26.
23:27–30 Dt 2:25; 7:20–22.
23:31 Gn 15:18; Dt 11:24; Jos 1:4.
23:32–33 Ex 34:12–16; Dt 7:2–6.
24:3 Ex 19:8.
24:5–8 Heb 9:18–20.

Did You Know?

Sacrifice and the Eucharist

Sacrifice is defined as an offering made to God that becomes holy by being set apart, blessed, and burned or consumed. Just as food and gifts were brought to a king as a form of tribute and worship, so too in Israel animals were brought to God and sacrificed, their blood splattered on the altar, and their meat cooked and eaten as a form of worship that brought communion with God. The blood symbolized God's gift of life, and when the blessed sacrifice was eaten, communion occurred between God and people. In Exodus, chapter 24, when Israel is about to ratify the covenant with God, Moses smears the blood of the animal on the altar to assert the Israelites' union with God through the observance of the covenant.

In the New Testament, the language Jesus uses at his Last Supper seems to reflect this sacrificial understanding. Jesus shares bread and wine as his body and blood and speaks about a New Covenant that will be ratified by the giving of his body and the shedding of his blood. Even today, Catholics celebrating the Eucharist in Jesus' memory encounter the real presence of Jesus in the sacred food of bread and wine, recalling the New Covenant of love he established through giving his body and shedding his blood.

▶ Ex 24:1–8

appeared to be sapphire tilework, as clear as the
sky itself. 11 Yet he did not lay a hand on these
chosen Israelites. They saw God,† and they ate
and drank.

Moses on the Mountain

12 The LORD said to Moses: Come up to me
on the mountain and, while you are there, I
will give you the stone tablets* on which I have
written the commandments intended for their
instruction. 13 So Moses set out with Joshua, his
assistant, and went up to the mountain of God.
14 He told the elders, "Wait here for us until we
return to you. Aaron and Hur are with you. Any-
one with a complaint should approach them."
15 Moses went up the mountain. Then the cloud
covered the mountain. 16 The glory of the LORD
settled upon Mount Sinai. The cloud covered it
for six days, and on the seventh day he called
to Moses from the midst of the cloud.* 17 To the
Israelites the glory of the LORD was seen as a con-
suming fire on the top of the mountain.* 18 But
Moses entered into the midst of the cloud and
went up on the mountain. He was on the moun-
tain for forty days and forty nights.*

Collection of Materials

25 1 The LORD spoke to Moses:* 2 Speak to the
Israelites: Let them receive contributions
for me. From each you shall receive the contri-
bution that their hearts prompt them to give me.
3 These are the contributions you shall accept
from them: gold, silver, and bronze;* 4 violet,
purple, and scarlet yarn; fine linen and goat hair;
5 rams' skins dyed red, and tahash† skins; acacia
wood; 6 oil for the light; spices for the anointing
oil and for the fragrant incense; 7 onyx stones and
other gems for mounting on the ephod and the
breastpiece. 8 They are to make a sanctuary for
me, that I may dwell in their midst.* 9 According
to all that I show you regarding the pattern of the
tabernacle and the pattern of its furnishings, so
you are to make it.*

Plan of the Ark

10 You shall make an ark of acacia wood,* two
and a half cubits† long, one and a half cubits
wide, and one and a half cubits high. 11 Plate
it inside and outside with pure gold, and put a
molding of gold around the top of it. 12 Cast four
gold rings and put them on the four supports of
the ark, two rings on one side and two on the
opposite side. 13 Then make poles of acacia wood
and plate them with gold. 14 These poles you are
to put through the rings on the sides of the ark,
for carrying it; 15 they must remain in the rings of
the ark and never be withdrawn. 16 In the ark you
are to put the covenant which I will give you.

24:11 *They saw God*: the ancients thought that the sight of God would bring instantaneous death. Cf. 33:20; Gn 16:13; 32:31; Jgs 6:22–23; 13:22. *Ate and drank*: partook of the sacrificial meal.

25:5 *Tahash*: perhaps a kind of specially finished leather. The Greek and Latin versions took it for the color hyacinth.

25:10 *Cubits*: the distance between the elbow and tip of the middle finger of an average-size person, about eighteen inches. The dimensions of the ark of the covenant were approximately 3 3/4 feet long, 2 1/4 feet wide, and 2 1/4 feet high.

24:12 Ex 31:18; 32:15–16; Dt 5:22.
24:16 Sir 45:5.
24:17 Ex 19:18; Heb 12:18.
24:18 Ex 34:28; Dt 9:9.
25:1–7 Ex 35:4–9, 20–29.
25:3 Ex 35:4–9.
25:8–9 Ex 26:1–30; 36:8–38.
25:9 Acts 7:44.
25:10–22 Ex 37:1–9; Heb 9:1–5.

[17]You shall then make a cover† of pure gold,
two and a half cubits long, and one and a half cu-
bits wide. [18]Make two cherubim† of beaten gold
for the two ends of the cover; [19]make one cherub
at one end, and the other at the other end, of one
piece with the cover, at each end. [20]The cherubim
shall have their wings spread out above, sheltering
the cover with them; they shall face each other,
with their faces looking toward the cover. [21]This
cover you shall then place on top of the ark. In
the ark itself you are to put the covenant which I
will give you. [22]There I will meet you and there,
from above the cover, between the two cherubim
on the ark of the covenant, I will tell you all that
I command you regarding the Israelites.

The Table

[23]You shall also make a table of acacia* wood,
two cubits long, a cubit wide, and a cubit and a
half high. [24]Plate it with pure gold and make a
molding of gold around it. [25]Make a frame† for it,
a handbreadth high, and make a molding of gold
around the frame. [26]You shall also make four
rings of gold for it and fasten them at the four cor-
ners, one at each leg. [27]The rings shall be along-
side the frame as holders for the poles to carry
the table. [28]These poles for carrying the table you
shall make of acacia wood and plate with gold.
[29]You shall make its plates† and cups, as well as
its pitchers and bowls for pouring libations; make
them of pure gold. [30]On the table you shall al-
ways keep showbread set before me.*

The Menorah

[31]You shall make a menorah† of pure beaten
gold*—its shaft and branches—with its cups
and knobs and petals springing directly from it.
[32]Six branches are to extend from its sides, three
branches on one side, and three on the other.
[33]† On one branch there are to be three cups,

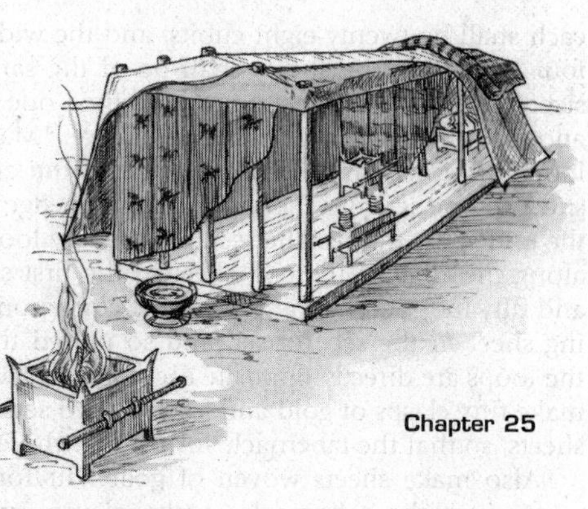

Chapter 25

shaped like almond blossoms, each with its
knob and petals; on the opposite branch there
are to be three cups, shaped like almond blos-
soms, each with its knob and petals; and so for
the six branches that extend from the menorah.
[34]On the menorah there are to be four cups,†
shaped like almond blossoms, with their knobs
and petals. [35]The six branches that go out from
the menorah are to have a knob under each
pair. [36]Their knobs and branches shall so spring
from it that the whole will form a single piece
of pure beaten gold. [37]† You shall then make
seven lamps* for it and so set up the lamps that
they give their light on the space in front of the
menorah. [38]These, as well as the trimming shears
and trays,† must be of pure gold. [39]Use a talent†
of pure gold for the menorah and all these uten-
sils. [40]See that you make them according to the
pattern shown you on the mountain.*

The Tent Cloth

26 [1]The tabernacle itself you shall make out
of ten sheets† woven of fine linen twined
and of violet, purple, and scarlet yarn, with cher-
ubim embroidered on them.* [2]The length of

†

25:17 *Cover*: the Hebrew term, *kapporet*, has been connected with *kippur*, as in the feast of Yom Kippur or Day of Atonement (Lv 16; 23:26–32): hence, influenced by the Greek and Latin versions, and Luther's German, English translations have rendered it "propitiatory," "mercy seat," and the like.

25:18–20 *Cherubim*: probably in the form of human-headed winged lions. The cherubim over the ark formed the throne for the invisible Lord. Cf. Ps 80:2. For a more detailed description of the somewhat different cherubim in the Temple of Solomon, see 1 Kgs 6:23–28; 2 Chr 3:10–13.

25:25 *A frame*: probably placed near the bottom of the legs to keep them steady. The golden table of Herod's Temple is pictured thus on the Arch of Titus.

25:29–30 The plates held the showbread, that is, the holy bread which was placed upon the table every sabbath as an offering to God, and was later eaten by the priests. The cups held the incense which was strewn upon the bread. Cf. Lv 24:5–9. The libation wine was poured from the pitchers into the bowls. All these vessels were kept on the golden table.

25:31 *Menorah*: this traditional lampstand is still used today in Jewish liturgy.

25:33 In keeping with the arrangement of the ornaments on the shaft, the three sets of ornaments on each branch were probably so placed that one was at the top and the other two equally spaced along the length of the branch. *Knob*: the cup-shaped seed capsule at the base of a flower.

25:34–35 Of the four ornaments on the shaft, one was at the top and one was below each of the three sets of side branches.

25:37 The lamps were probably shaped like small boats, with the wick at one end; the end with the wick was turned toward the front of the menorah.

25:38 *Trays*: small receptacles for the burnt-out wicks.

25:39 *Talent*: Heb. *kikkar*. The largest unit of weight used in the Bible, equivalent to 3,000 shekels (see 38:24). It is difficult to be precise about biblical weights; the Israelite talent may have weighed between 75–80 pounds.

26:1 *Sheets*: strips of tapestry, woven of white linen, the colored threads being used for the cherubim which were embroidered on

*

25:23–30 Ex 37:10–16.
25:30 Lv 24:5–9.
25:31–40 Ex 37:17–24.
25:37 Lv 24:2–4; Nm 8:2.
25:40 Heb 8:5.
26:1–14 Ex 36:8–19.

each shall be twenty-eight cubits, and the width four cubits; all the sheets shall be of the same size. 3 Five of the sheets are to be joined one to another; and the same for the other five. 4 Make loops of violet yarn along the edge of the end sheet in one set, and the same along the edge of the end sheet in the other set. 5 Make fifty loops along the edge of the end sheet in the first set, and fifty loops along the edge of the corresponding sheet in the second set, and so placed that the loops are directly opposite each other. 6 Then make fifty clasps of gold and join the two sets of sheets, so that the tabernacle forms one whole.

7 Also make sheets woven of goat hair for a tent† over the tabernacle. Make eleven such sheets; 8 the length of each shall be thirty cubits, and the width four cubits: all eleven sheets shall be of the same size. 9 Join five of the sheets into one set, and the other six sheets into another set. Use the sixth sheet double at the front of the tent.† 10 Make fifty loops along the edge of the end sheet in one set, and fifty loops along the edge of the end sheet in the second set. 11 Also make fifty bronze clasps and put them into the loops, to join the tent into one whole. 12 There will be an extra half sheet of tent covering, which shall be allowed to hang down over the rear of the tabernacle. 13 Likewise, the sheets of the tent will have an extra cubit's length to be left hanging down on either side of the tabernacle to cover it. 14 Over the tent itself make a covering of rams' skins dyed red, and above that, a covering of tahash skins.

The Framework

15 * You shall make frames for the tabernacle, acacia-wood uprights. 16 The length of each frame is to be ten cubits, and its width one and a half cubits. 17 Each frame shall have two arms† joined one to another; so you are to make all the frames of the tabernacle. 18 Make the frames of the tabernacle as follows: twenty frames on the south side, 19 with forty silver pedestals under the twenty frames, two pedestals under each frame for its two arms; 20 twenty frames on the other side of the tabernacle, the north side, 21 with their forty silver pedestals, two pedestals under each frame. 22 At the rear of the tabernacle, to the west, six frames, 23 and two frames for the corners of the tabernacle, at its rear. 24 These two shall be double at the bottom, and likewise double at the top, to the first ring. That is how both corner frames are to be made. 25 Thus, there shall be eight frames, with their sixteen silver pedestals, two pedestals under each frame. 26 Also make bars of acacia wood: five for the frames on one side of the tabernacle, 27 five for those on the other side, and five for those at the rear, to the west. 28 The center bar, at the middle of the frames, shall reach across from end to end. 29 Plate the frames with gold, and make gold rings on them as holders for the bars, which are also to be plated with gold. 30 You shall set up the tabernacle according to its plan, which you were shown on the mountain.

The Veils

31 You shall make a veil woven of violet, purple, and scarlet yarn,* and of fine linen twined, with cherubim embroidered on it.* 32 It is to be hung on four gold-plated columns of acacia wood, which shall have gold hooks† and shall rest on four silver pedestals. 33 Hang the veil from clasps. The ark of the covenant you shall bring inside, behind this veil which divides the holy place from the holy of holies. 34 Set the cover on the ark of the covenant in the holy of holies.

35 Outside the veil you shall place the table and the menorah, the latter on the south side of the tabernacle, opposite the table, which is to be put on the north side. 36 For the entrance of the tent make a variegated† curtain of violet, purple, and scarlet yarn and of fine linen twined. 37 Make five columns of acacia wood for this curtain; plate them with gold, with their hooks of gold; and cast five bronze pedestals for them.

The Altar for Burnt Offerings

27 1 You shall make an altar* of acacia wood, on a square, five cubits long and five cubits wide; it shall be three cubits high. 2 At the four corners make horns† that are of one piece with the altar. You shall then plate it with bronze. 3 Make pots for removing the ashes, as

† them. These sheets were stretched across the top of the tabernacle to form a roof, their free ends hanging down inside the framework that formed the walls.

26:7 *Tent*: the cloth made of sheets of goat hair to cover the tabernacle.

26:9 Half the width of the end strip was folded back at the front of the tabernacle, thus leaving another half-strip to hang down at the rear. Cf. v. 12.

26:17 *Arms*: lit., "hands." According to some, they served as "tongue and groove" to mortise the structural elements; according to others, they were pegs that fitted into sockets in the pedestals.

26:32 *Hooks*: probably placed near the tops of the columns, to hold the rope from which the veils and curtains hung.

26:36 *Variegated*: without definite designs such as the cherubim on the inner veil.

27:2 *Horns*: the horn of a ram, goat or ox is a common Old Testament figure for strength and dignity; they represent the divine character of the altar itself or the deity worshiped there.

* **26:15–30** Ex 36:20–34. **26:31** Ex 36:35–38. **26:31** 2 Chr 3:14. **27:1–8** Ex 38:1–7.

well as shovels, basins, forks, and fire pans; all
these utensils you shall make of bronze. 4 Make
for it a grating,† a bronze network; make four
bronze rings for it, one at each of its four corners.
5 Put it down around the altar, on the ground.
This network is to be half as high as the altar.
6 You shall also make poles of acacia wood for
the altar, and plate them with bronze. 7 These
poles are to be put through the rings, so that they
are on either side of the altar when it is carried.
8 Make the altar itself in the form of a hollow†
box. Just as it was shown you on the mountain,
so it is to be made.

Court of the Tabernacle

9 * You shall also make a court for the taberna-
cle. On the south side the court shall have hang-
ings, of fine linen twined, a hundred cubits long,
10 with twenty columns and twenty pedestals of
bronze; the hooks and bands on the columns
shall be of silver. 11 On the north side there shall
be similar hangings, a hundred cubits long, with
twenty columns and twenty pedestals of bronze;
the hooks and bands on the columns shall be of
silver. 12 On the west side, across the width of the
court, there shall be hangings, fifty cubits long,
with ten columns and ten pedestals. 13 The width
of the court on the east side shall be fifty cubits.
14 On one side there shall be hangings to the
extent of fifteen cubits, with three columns and
three pedestals; 15 on the other side there shall
be hangings to the extent of fifteen cubits, with
three columns and three pedestals.
16 At the gate of the court there shall be a
variegated curtain, twenty cubits long, woven of
violet, purple, and scarlet yarn and of fine linen
twined. It shall have four columns and four
pedestals.
17 All the columns around the court shall have
bands and hooks of silver, and pedestals of
bronze. 18 The court is to be one hundred cubits
long, fifty cubits wide, and five cubits high. Fine
linen twined must be used, and the pedestals
must be of bronze. 19 All the fittings of the taber-
nacle, whatever be their use, as well as all its tent
pegs and all the tent pegs of the court, must be
of bronze.

Oil for the Lamps

20 You shall command the Israelites to bring
you clear oil of crushed olives, to be used for
the light, so that you may keep lamps burning
always.* 21 From evening to morning Aaron and
his sons shall maintain them before the LORD in
the tent of meeting, outside the veil which hangs
in front of the covenant. This shall be a perpetual
statute for the Israelites throughout their gener-
ations.

The Priestly Vestments

28 1 * Have your brother Aaron, and with
him his sons, brought to you, from
among the Israelites, that they may be my priests:
Nadab and Abihu, Eleazar and Ithamar, Aar-
on's sons. 2 For the glorious adornment of your
brother Aaron you shall have sacred vestments
made. 3 Therefore, tell the various artisans whom
I have endowed with skill† to make vestments
for Aaron to consecrate him as my priest. 4 These
are the vestments they shall make: a breastpiece,
an ephod, a robe, a brocade tunic, a turban, and
a sash. In making these sacred vestments which
your brother Aaron and his sons are to wear in
serving as my priests, 5 they shall use gold, violet,
purple, and scarlet yarn and fine linen.

The Ephod and Breastpiece

6 The ephod† they shall make of gold thread
and of violet, purple, and scarlet yarn, embroi-
dered on cloth of fine linen twined.* 7 It shall
have a pair of shoulder straps joined to its two
upper ends. 8 The embroidered belt of the ephod
shall extend out from it and, like it, be made of
gold thread, of violet, purple, and scarlet yarn,
and of fine linen twined.
9 Get two onyx stones and engrave on them the
names of the sons of Israel: 10 six of their names
on one stone, and the names of the remaining
six on the other stone, in the order of their birth.
11 As a gem-cutter engraves a seal, so shall you
have the two stones engraved with the names of
the sons of Israel and then mounted in gold fili-
gree work. 12 Set these two stones on the shoulder
straps of the ephod as memorial stones of the

†

27:4 *Grating*: it is not clear whether this was flush with the altar or at some small distance from it; in the latter case the space between the altar and the grating would be filled with stones and serve as a platform around the altar, which would otherwise be too high for the priest to reach conveniently.

27:8 *Hollow*: probably filled with earth or stones when in use. Cf. 20:24–25.

28:3 *Artisans . . . endowed with skill*: lit., "wise of heart," and "filled with a spirit of wisdom." In Hebrew wisdom includes practical skills. Cf. 35:35; 36:1–2.

28:6 *Ephod*: this Hebrew word is retained in the translation because it is the technical term for a peculiar piece of the priestly vestments, the exact nature of which is uncertain. It seems to have been a sort of apron that hung from the shoulders of the priest by shoulder straps (v. 7) and was tied around his waist by the loose ends of the attached belt (v. 8).

*

27:9–19 Ex 38:9–20.
27:20–21 Lv 24:1–4.
28:1–5 Ex 39:1; Sir 45:7.
28:6–12 Ex 39:2–7; Sir 45:8–14.

sons of Israel. Thus Aaron shall bear their names
on his shoulders as a reminder before the LORD.
13 Make filigree rosettes of gold,* 14 as well as two
chains of pure gold, twisted like cords, and fasten
the cordlike chains to the filigree rosettes.
15 * The breastpiece† of decision you shall
also have made, embroidered like the ephod
with gold thread and violet, purple, and scarlet
yarn on cloth of fine linen twined. 16 It is to be
square when folded double, a span high and a
span wide. 17 † On it you shall mount four rows
of precious stones: in the first row, a carnelian,
a topaz, and an emerald; 18 in the second row,
a garnet, a sapphire, and a beryl; 19 in the third
row, a jacinth, an agate, and an amethyst; 20 in
the fourth row, a chrysolite, an onyx, and a jas-
per. These stones are to be mounted in gold fili-
gree work, 21 twelve of them to match the names
of the sons of Israel, each stone engraved like a
seal with the name of one of the twelve tribes.
22 When the chains of pure gold, twisted like
cords, have been made for the breastpiece, 23 you
shall then make two rings of gold for it and
fasten them to the two upper ends of the breast-
piece. 24 The gold cords are then to be fastened to
the two rings at the upper ends of the breastpiece,
25 the other two ends of the cords being fastened
in front to the two filigree rosettes which are
attached to the shoulder straps of the ephod.
26 Make two other rings of gold and put them on
the two lower ends of the breastpiece, on its edge
that faces the ephod. 27 Then make two more
rings of gold and fasten them to the bottom
of the shoulder straps next to where they join
the ephod in front, just above its embroidered
belt. 28 Violet ribbons shall bind the rings of the
breastpiece to the rings of the ephod, so that the
breastpiece will stay right above the embroidered
belt of the ephod and not swing loose from it.
29 Whenever Aaron enters the sanctuary, he
will thus bear the names of the sons of Israel
on the breastpiece of decision over his heart as
a constant reminder before the LORD. 30 In this
breastpiece of decision* you shall put the Urim
and Thummim,† that they may be over Aaron's
heart whenever he enters the presence of the
LORD. Thus he shall always bear the decisions
for the Israelites over his heart in the presence
of the LORD.

Other Vestments

31 The robe of the ephod* you shall make
entirely of violet material. 32 It shall have an
opening for the head in the center, and around
this opening there shall be a selvage, woven as
at the opening of a shirt, to keep it from being
torn. 33 At the hem at the bottom you shall make
pomegranates, woven of violet, purple, and scar-
let yarn and fine linen twined, with gold bells
between them; 34 a gold bell, a pomegranate, a
gold bell, a pomegranate, all around the hem
of the robe. 35 Aaron shall wear it when minis-
tering, that its sound may be heard as he enters
and leaves the LORD's presence in the sanctuary;
else he will die.
36 You shall also make a plate of pure gold and
engrave on it, as on a seal engraving, "Sacred to
the LORD." 37 This plate is to be tied over the tur-
ban with a violet ribbon in such a way that it rests
on the front of the turban,* 38 over Aaron's fore-
head. Since Aaron bears whatever guilt the Israel-
ites may incur in consecrating any of their sacred
gifts, this plate must always be over his forehead,
so that they may find favor with the LORD.
39 * The tunic of fine linen shall be brocaded.
The turban shall be made of fine linen. The sash
shall be of variegated work.
40 Likewise, for the glorious adornment of Aar-
on's sons you shall have tunics and sashes and
skullcaps made, for glorious splendor. 41 With
these you shall clothe your brother Aaron and
his sons. Anoint and install them,† consecrating
them as my priests. 42 You must also make linen
pants for them, to cover their naked flesh from
their loins to their thighs.* 43 Aaron and his sons
shall wear them whenever they go into the tent
of meeting or approach the altar to minister in
the sanctuary, lest they incur guilt and die. This
shall be a perpetual ordinance for him and for
his descendants.

Consecration of the Priests

29 1 This is the rite you shall perform in con-
secrating them as my priests.* Procure a

†

28:15–30 *Breastpiece*: an approximately nine-inch square, pocket-like receptacle for holding the Urim and Thummim (v. 30). It formed an integral part of the ephod, to which it was attached by an elaborate system of rings and chains. Both the ephod and its breastpiece were made of brocaded linen. *Span*: Heb. *zeret*, the distance between the top of the little finger and the thumb; one half a cubit, approximately nine inches.

28:17–20 The translation of the Hebrew names of some of these gems is quite conjectural.

28:30 *Urim and Thummim*: both the meaning of these Hebrew words and the exact nature of the objects so designated are uncertain. They were apparently lots of some kind which were drawn or cast by the priest to ascertain God's decision on particular questions. Hence, the pocket in which they were kept was called "the breastpiece of decision."

28:41 *Install them*: lit., "fill their hands," a technical expression used for the installation of priests.

*

28:13–14 Ex 28:22, 25; 39:15, 18. **28:15–21** Ex 39:15–21. **28:30** Lv 8:8; Sir 45:11. **28:31–35** Ex 39:20–25; Lv 8:9; Sir 45:10. **28:37** Ex 39:31; Lv 8:9. **28:39–43** Ex 39:27–31. **28:42** Ez 44:18. **29:1–8** Lv 8:1–9.

young bull and two unblemished rams. 2 With bran flour make unleavened cakes mixed with oil, and unleavened wafers spread with oil, 3 and put them in a basket. Take the basket of them along with the bull and the two rams. 4 Aaron and his sons you shall also bring to the entrance of the tent of meeting, and there wash them with water. 5 Take the vestments and clothe Aaron with the tunic, the robe of the ephod, the ephod itself, and the breastpiece, fastening the embroidered belt of the ephod around him. 6 Put the turban on his head, the sacred diadem on the turban. 7 Then take the anointing oil and pour it on his head, and anoint him. 8 Bring forward his sons also and clothe them with the tunics, 9 gird them with the sashes, and tie the skullcaps on them.* Thus shall the priesthood be theirs by a perpetual statute, and thus shall you install Aaron and his sons.

Installation Sacrifices

10 * Now bring forward the bull in front of the tent of meeting. There Aaron and his sons shall lay their hands on its head. 11 Then slaughter the bull before the LORD, at the entrance of the tent of meeting. 12 Take some of its blood and with your finger put it on the horns of the altar. All the rest of the blood you shall pour out at the base of the altar. 13 All the fat that covers its inner organs, as well as the lobe of its liver and its two kidneys, together with the fat that is on them, you shall take and burn on the altar. 14 But the meat and hide and dung of the bull you must burn up outside the camp, since this is a purification offering.*

15 Then take one of the rams, and after Aaron and his sons have laid their hands on its head, 16 slaughter it. The blood you shall take and splash on all the sides of the altar. 17 Cut the ram into pieces; you shall wash its inner organs and shanks and put them with the pieces and with the head. 18 Then you shall burn the entire ram on the altar, since it is a burnt offering, a sweet-smelling oblation to the LORD.

19 After this take the other ram, and when Aaron and his sons have laid their hands on its head, 20 slaughter it. Some of its blood you shall take and put on the tip of Aaron's right ear and on the tips of his sons' right ears and on the thumbs of their right hands and the great toes of their right feet. Splash the rest of the blood on all the sides of the altar. 21 Then take some of the blood that is on the altar, together with some of the anointing oil, and sprinkle this on Aaron and his vestments, as well as on his sons and their vestments, that he and his sons and their vestments may be sacred.

22 Now, from this ram you shall take its fat: its fatty tail,† the fat that covers its inner organs, the lobe of its liver, its two kidneys with the fat that is on them, and its right thigh, since this is the ram for installation; 23 then, out of the basket of unleavened food that you have set before the LORD, you shall take one of the loaves of bread, one of the cakes made with oil, and one of the wafers. 24 All these things you shall put into the hands of Aaron and his sons, so that they may raise them as an elevated offering† before the LORD. 25 After you receive them back from their hands, you shall burn them on top of the burnt offering on the altar as a sweet-smelling oblation to the LORD. 26 Finally, take the brisket of Aaron's installation ram and raise it as an elevated offering before the LORD; this is to be your own portion.

27 † Thus shall you set aside the brisket of whatever elevated offering is raised,* as well as the thigh of whatever contribution is raised up, whether this be the installation ram or anything else belonging to Aaron or to his sons. 28 Such things are due to Aaron and his sons from the Israelites by a perpetual statute as a contribution. From their communion offerings, too, the Israelites shall make a contribution, their contribution to the LORD.

29 The sacred vestments* of Aaron shall be passed down to his sons after him, that in them they may be anointed and installed. 30 The son who succeeds him as priest and who is to enter the tent of meeting to minister in the sanctuary shall be clothed with them for seven days.

31 * You shall take the installation ram and boil its meat in a holy place. 32 At the entrance of the tent of meeting Aaron and his sons shall eat the meat of the ram and the bread that is in the basket. 33 They themselves are to eat of these things by which atonement was made at their installation and consecration; but no unauthorized person may eat of them, since they are sacred. 34 If some of the meat of the installation sacrifice or some of the bread remains over on the next

†

29:22 *Fatty tail*: the thick layer of fat surrounding the tails of sheep and rams bred in the Middle East. It is regarded as a choice food. Cf. Lv 3:9.

29:24–26 *Elevated offering*: the portions of a communion offering, brisket and right thigh, which the officiating priest raised in the presence of the Lord. They were reserved for Aaron and his sons.

29:27–30 These verses are a parenthetical interruption of the installation ritual; v. 31 belongs logically immediately after v. 26.

*

29:9 Lv 8:13.
29:10–26 Lv 8:14–30.
29:14 Heb 13:11.
29:27–28 Lv 7:31–34; 10:14–15; Nm 18:18–19; Dt 18:3.
29:29 Nm 20:26, 28.
29:31–34 Lv 8:31–32.

day, this remnant you must burn up; it is not to be eaten, since it is sacred.

[35]Carry out all these commands in regard to Aaron and his sons just as I have given them to you.* Seven days you shall spend installing them, [36]* sacrificing a bull each day as a purification offering, to make atonement. Thus you shall purify the altar† by purging it, and you shall anoint it in order to consecrate it. [37]Seven days you shall spend in purging the altar and in consecrating it. Then the altar will be most sacred, and whatever touches it will become sacred.

[38]† Now, this is what you shall regularly offer on the altar: two yearling lambs* as the sacrifice established for each day; [39]one lamb in the morning and the other lamb at the evening twilight. [40]With the first lamb there shall be a tenth of an ephah of bran flour mixed with a fourth of a hin† of oil of crushed olives and, as its libation, a fourth of a hin of wine. [41]The other lamb you shall offer at the evening twilight, with the same grain offering and libation as in the morning. You shall offer this as a sweet-smelling oblation to the LORD. [42]Throughout your generations this regular burnt offering shall be made before the LORD at the entrance of the tent of meeting, where I will meet you and speak to you.

[43]There, at the altar, I will meet the Israelites; hence, it will be made sacred by my glory.* [44]Thus I will consecrate the tent of meeting and the altar, just as I also consecrate Aaron and his sons to be my priests. [45]I will dwell in the midst of the Israelites and will be their God. [46]They shall know that I, the LORD, am their God who brought them out of the land of Egypt, so that I, the LORD, their God, might dwell among them.

Altar of Incense

30 [1]For burning incense you shall make an altar of acacia wood,* [2]with a square surface, a cubit long, a cubit wide, and two cubits high, with horns that are of one piece with it. [3]Its grate on top, its walls on all four sides, and its horns you shall plate with pure gold. Put a gold molding around it. [4]Underneath the molding you shall put gold rings, two on one side and two on the opposite side, as holders for the poles used in carrying it. [5]Make the poles, too, of acacia wood and plate them with gold. [6]This altar you are to place in front of the veil that hangs before the ark of the covenant where I will meet you.*

[7]On it Aaron shall burn fragrant incense. Morning after morning, when he prepares the lamps, [8]and again in the evening twilight, when he lights the lamps, he shall burn incense. Throughout your generations this shall be the regular incense offering before the LORD. [9]On this altar you shall not offer up any profane incense, or any burnt offering or grain offering; nor shall you pour out a libation upon it. [10]Once a year Aaron shall purge its horns.* Throughout your generations he is to purge it once a year with the blood of the atoning purification offering. This altar is most sacred to the LORD.

Census Tax

[11]The LORD also told Moses: [12]When you take a census* of the Israelites who are to be enrolled, each one, as he is enrolled, shall give the LORD a ransom for his life, so that no plague may come upon them for being enrolled. [13]This is what everyone who is enrolled must pay: a half-shekel, according to the standard of the sanctuary shekel—twenty gerahs to the shekel—a half-shekel contribution to the LORD.* [14]Everyone who is enrolled, of twenty years or more, must give the contribution to the LORD. [15]The rich need not give more, nor shall the poor give less, than a half-shekel in this contribution to the LORD to pay the ransom for their lives. [16]* When you receive this ransom money from the Israelites, you shall donate it to the service of the tent of meeting, that there it may be a reminder of the Israelites before the LORD of the ransom paid for their lives.

The Basin

[17]The LORD told Moses: [18]For ablutions you shall make a bronze basin with a bronze stand. Place it between the tent of meeting and the altar, and put water in it.* [19]Aaron and his sons shall use it in washing their hands and feet.* [20]When they are about to enter the tent of meeting, they must wash with water, lest they die. Likewise when they approach the altar to minister, to offer an oblation to the LORD, [21]they must wash their hands and feet, lest they die. This shall be

---

† **29:36–37** *Purify the altar*: the purpose of the purification offering here is to cleanse, or purify, the newly constructed altar of any defilement resulting from presumably minor and inadvertent sins, but the text is not explicit about what the offenses were or who committed them. So various theories have been proposed to explain the cause of the altar's contamination. Note, however, that the offering appears to be demanded of Aaron and his sons; they are the ones who lay hands upon it (v. 10).

29:38–42 A parenthesis inserted into the rubrics for consecrating the altar; v. 43 belongs directly after v. 37.

29:40 *Hin*: see note on Ez 45:24.

---

* **29:35** Lv 8:36. **29:36–37** Lv 8:33–35. **29:38–42** Nm 28:3–8. **29:43** Ex 25:22. **30:1–5** Ex 37:25–28. **30:6** Ex 40:26. **30:10** Lv 16:18. **30:12** Nm 1:2–3; 26:2. **30:13** Mt 17:24–27. **30:16** Ex 38:25. **30:18** Ex 38:8; 40:7, 30. **30:19–21** Ex 40:31–32.

a perpetual statute for him and his descendants throughout their generations.

The Anointing Oil

[22] The LORD told Moses: [23] Take the finest spices: five hundred shekels of free-flowing myrrh; half that amount, that is, two hundred and fifty shekels, of fragrant cinnamon; two hundred and fifty shekels of fragrant cane; [24] five hundred shekels of cassia—all according to the standard of the sanctuary shekel; together with a hin of olive oil; [25] and blend them into sacred anointing oil,* perfumed ointment expertly prepared.* With this sacred anointing oil [26] you shall anoint the tent of meeting and the ark of the covenant, [27] the table and all its utensils, the menorah and its utensils, the altar of incense [28] and the altar for burnt offerings with all its utensils, and the basin with its stand. [29] When you have consecrated them, they shall be most sacred; whatever touches them shall be sacred. [30] Aaron and his sons you shall also anoint and consecrate as my priests.* [31] Tell the Israelites: As sacred anointing oil this shall belong to me throughout your generations. [32] It may not be used in any ordinary anointing of the body, nor may you make any other oil of a like mixture. It is sacred, and shall be treated as sacred by you. [33] Whoever prepares a perfume like this, or whoever puts any of this on an unauthorized person, shall be cut off from his people.

The Incense

[34] * The LORD told Moses: Take these aromatic substances: storax and onycha and galbanum, these and pure frankincense in equal parts; [35] and blend them into incense. This fragrant powder, expertly prepared, is to be salted and so kept pure and sacred. [36] Grind some of it into fine dust and put this before the covenant in the tent of meeting where I will meet you. This incense shall be treated as most sacred by you. [37] You may not make incense of a like mixture for yourselves; you must treat it as sacred to the LORD. [38] Whoever makes an incense like this for his own enjoyment of its fragrance, shall be cut off from his people.

Choice of Artisans

31 [1] * The LORD said to Moses: [2] See, I have singled out† Bezalel, son of Uri, son of Hur, of the tribe of Judah, [3] and I have filled him with a divine spirit of skill and understanding and knowledge in every craft: [4] in the production of embroidery, in making things of gold, silver, or bronze, [5] in cutting and mounting precious stones, in carving wood, and in every other craft. [6] As his assistant I myself have appointed Oholiab, son of Ahisamach, of the tribe of Dan. I have also endowed all the experts with the necessary skill to make all the things I have commanded you: [7] * the tent of meeting, the ark of the covenant with its cover, all the furnishings of the tent, [8] the table with its utensils, the pure gold menorah with all its utensils, the altar of incense, [9] the altar for burnt offerings with all its utensils, the basin with its stand, [10] the service cloths,† the sacred vestments for Aaron the priest, the vestments for his sons in their ministry, [11] the anointing oil, and the fragrant incense for the sanctuary. According to all I have commanded you, so shall they do.

Sabbath Laws

[12] * The LORD said to Moses: [13] You must also tell the Israelites: Keep my sabbaths, for that is to be the sign between you and me throughout the generations, to show that it is I, the LORD, who make you holy. [14] † Therefore, you must keep the sabbath for it is holiness for you. Whoever desecrates it shall be put to death. If anyone does work on that day, that person must be cut off from the people. [15] Six days there are for doing work, but the seventh day is the sabbath of complete rest, holy to the LORD. Anyone who does work on the sabbath day shall be put to death. [16] So shall the Israelites observe the sabbath, keeping it throughout their generations as an everlasting covenant. [17] Between me and the Israelites it is to be an everlasting sign; for in six days the LORD made the heavens and the earth, but on the seventh day he rested at his ease.

[18] When the LORD had finished speaking to Moses on Mount Sinai, he gave him the two tablets of the covenant, the stone tablets inscribed by God's own finger.*

VII. Israel's Apostasy and God's Renewal of the Covenant

The Golden Calf

32 [1] When the people saw that Moses was delayed in coming down from the mountain, they gathered around Aaron and said to

---

31:2 *Singled out*: lit., "called by name"; cf. 35:30.

31:10 *The service cloths*: so the Greek. They were perhaps the colored cloths mentioned in Nm 4:4–15.

31:14–15 For the distinction between work proscribed on certain festivals and weekly Sabbaths, see note on Lv 23:3.

30:25 Ex 37:29.
30:25–29 Ex 40:9–11; Lv 8:10; Nm 7:1.
30:30 Ex 29:7; Lv 8:12.
30:34–38 Ex 25:6; 37:29.
31:1–6 Ex 35:30–35.
31:7–11 Ex 35:10–19.
31:12–17 Ex 20:8–11; 35:1–3.
31:18 Ex 24:12; 32:15–16; Dt 5:22.

Live It!

Caught Up in the Moment

Now that I think about it, it was a stupid thing to do. But it is so hard to be objective when you are caught up in the excitement of the moment. We had been waiting a long time for Moses—too long, it seems. We got bored and restless. You know how it is. Someone came up with the idea of the golden calf. It sounded like fun, something to pass the time and remind us of the old gods. And I have to admit, that calf did look pretty good!

I do feel sorry for Aaron. Moses saw what we had done and hurled the stone tablets to the ground in a fit of rage. Aaron tried to explain how it was, but Moses would hear none of it. He was upset. He had a right to be. There is no valid excuse for what we did. Aaron tried to pretend that the calf sort of formed itself, but it was a feeble excuse. We all knew it. And when we learned what was on the stone tablets, we knew we had done wrong. Moses had brought those tablets from the hands of God. This was to have been a solemn moment, followed by a great celebration. But instead, we had to face the wrath of Moses and pick up the shattered pieces of stone.

It is so easy to lose sight of what we are all about. It is so easy to do something stupid when we are bored and tired of waiting. And then we wonder how we could have let ourselves get so far off track. It is too easy, isn't it? We are all too human at times.

No, I don't blame Moses for losing his temper. He had every right. We let him down. We let ourselves down. But most of all, we let God down.

▶ Ex 32:1–35

him, "Come, make us a god who will go before
us; as for that man Moses who brought us out
of the land of Egypt, we do not know what has
happened to him."* 2 Aaron replied, "Take off
the golden earrings that your wives, your sons,
and your daughters are wearing, and bring them
to me." 3 So all the people took off their earrings
and brought them to Aaron. 4 He received their
offering, and fashioning it with a tool, made a
molten calf. Then they cried out, "These are your
gods, Israel, who brought you† up from the land
of Egypt."* 5 On seeing this, Aaron built an altar
in front of the calf and proclaimed, "Tomorrow
is a feast of the LORD." 6 Early the next day the
people sacrificed burnt offerings and brought
communion sacrifices. Then they sat down to eat
and drink, and rose up to revel.*

7 * Then the LORD said to Moses: Go down at
once because your people, whom you brought
out of the land of Egypt, have acted corruptly.
8 They have quickly turned aside from the way I
commanded them, making for themselves a molten calf and bowing down to it, sacrificing to it
and crying out, "These are your gods, Israel, who
brought you up from the land of Egypt!" 9 * I have
seen this people, how stiff-necked they are, continued the LORD to Moses. 10 Let me alone, then,
that my anger may burn against them to consume
them. Then I will make of you a great nation.

11 † But Moses implored the LORD, his God,
saying,* "Why, O LORD, should your anger burn
against your people, whom you brought out of
the land of Egypt with great power and with a
strong hand? 12 Why should the Egyptians say,
'With evil intent he brought them out, that he
might kill them in the mountains and wipe them
off the face of the earth'? Turn from your burning
wrath; change your mind about punishing your
people. 13 Remember your servants Abraham,
Isaac, and Israel, and how you swore to them by
your own self, saying,* 'I will make your descendants as numerous as the stars in the sky; and all
this land that I promised, I will give your descendants as their perpetual heritage.' " 14 So the LORD
changed his mind about the punishment he had
threatened to inflict on his people.

15 Moses then turned and came down the
mountain with the two tablets of the covenant

† **32:4–5** *Who brought you . . . a feast of the LORD*: it seems that the golden calf was intended as an image, not of another god, but of the Lord, whose strength was symbolized by the strength of a young bull. The Israelites, however, had been forbidden to represent the Lord under any visible form. Cf. 20:4. In the tenth century Jeroboam made golden calves for the shrines at Bethel and Dan, presumably to function as thrones for the Lord as the ark did in Jerusalem (see 1 Kgs 12:27–30).

32:11–13 Moses uses three arguments to persuade the Lord to remain faithful to the Sinai covenant even though the people have broken it: (1) they are God's own people, redeemed with God's great power; (2) God's reputation will suffer if they are destroyed; (3) the covenant with Abraham still stands. The Lord's change of mind is a testimony to Israel's belief in the power of intercessory prayer.

32:1 Ex 32:23; Acts 7:40.
32:4 Ex 32:8; 1 Kgs 12:28.
32:6 1 Cor 10:7.
32:7–8 Dt 9:12, 16.
32:9–10 Dt 9:13.
32:11–12 Nm 14:13–19; Dt 9:28–29; Ps 106:23.
32:13 Gn 22:16–17.

in his hands,* tablets that were written on both
sides, front and back. 16 The tablets were made
by God; the writing was the writing of God,
engraved on the tablets.* 17 Now, when Joshua
heard the noise of the people shouting, he
said to Moses, "That sounds like a battle in the
camp." 18 But Moses answered,

"It is not the noise of victory,
it is not the noise of defeat;
the sound I hear is singing."

19 As he drew near the camp, he saw the calf and
the dancing. Then Moses' anger burned, and he
threw the tablets down and broke them on the
base of the mountain.* 20 Taking the calf they
had made, he burned it in the fire and then
ground it down to powder, which he scattered on
the water† and made the Israelites drink.*
21 † Moses asked Aaron, "What did this people
do to you that you should lead them into a grave
sin?" 22 Aaron replied, "Do not let my lord be an-
gry. You know how the people are prone to evil.
23 They said to me, 'Make us a god to go before
us; as for this man Moses who brought us out
of the land of Egypt, we do not know what has
happened to him.' 24 So I told them, 'Whoever is
wearing gold, take it off.' They gave it to me, and
I threw it into the fire, and this calf came out."
25 Moses saw that the people were running wild
because Aaron had lost control—to the secret de-
light of their foes. 26 Moses stood at the gate of
the camp and shouted, "Whoever is for the LORD,
come to me!" All the Levites* then rallied to him,
27 and he told them, "Thus says the LORD, the God
of Israel: Each of you put your sword on your
hip! Go back and forth through the camp, from
gate to gate, and kill your brothers, your friends,
your neighbors!" 28 The Levites did as Moses had
commanded, and that day about three thousand
of the people fell. 29 Then Moses said, "Today you
are installed as priests† for the LORD, for you went
against your own sons and brothers, to bring a
blessing upon yourselves this day."

The Atonement

30 On the next day Moses said to the people,*
"You have committed a grave sin. Now I will go
up to the LORD; perhaps I may be able to make
atonement for your sin." 31 So Moses returned
to the LORD and said, "Ah, this people has com-
mitted a grave sin in making a god of gold for
themselves! 32 Now if you would only forgive
their sin! But if you will not, then blot me out
of the book that you have written."† 33 The LORD
answered Moses: Only the one who has sinned
against me will I blot out of my book. 34 Now, go
and lead the people where I have told you. See,
my angel will go before you. When it is time for
me to punish, I will punish them for their sin.
35 Thus the LORD struck the people for making
the calf, the one that Aaron made.

33 1 The LORD spoke to Moses: Go! You and
the people whom you have brought up
from the land of Egypt are to go up from here to
the land about which I swore to Abraham, Isaac,
and Jacob: I will give it to your descendants.*
2 Driving out the Canaanites, Amorites, Hittites,
Perizzites, Hivites and Jebusites, I will send an
angel before you* 3 to a land flowing with milk
and honey. But I myself will not go up in your
company, because you are a stiff-necked people;
otherwise I might consume you on the way.
4 When the people heard this painful news, they
mourned, and no one wore any ornaments.
5 The LORD spoke to Moses: Speak to the Isra-
elites: You are a stiff-necked people. Were I to go
up in your company even for a moment, I would
destroy you. Now off with your ornaments! Let
me think what to do with you. 6 So, from Mount
Horeb onward, the Israelites stripped off their
ornaments.

Moses' Intimacy with God

7 Moses used to pitch a tent* outside the camp
at some distance. It was called the tent of meet-
ing. Anyone who wished to consult the LORD
would go to the tent of meeting outside the camp.
8 Whenever Moses went out to the tent, the people
would all rise and stand at the entrance of their
own tents, watching Moses until he entered the
tent. 9 As Moses entered the tent, the column of
cloud would come down and stand at its entrance
while the LORD spoke with Moses. 10 On seeing
the column of cloud stand at the entrance of the

EX

†

32:20 *The water*: according to Dt 9:21, this was the stream that flowed down Mount Sinai.

32:21–24 Aaron attempts to persuade Moses not to act in anger, just as Moses persuaded the Lord. He also shifts the blame from himself to the people.

32:29 *Installed as priests*: lit., "fill your hands," a term for the ordination of priests (see 28:41; 29:9, 29, 33, 35; Nm 3:3). Because of their zeal for the true worship of the Lord, the Levites were chosen to be special ministers of the ritual service.

32:32 *The book that you have written*: a symbolic reference to the list of God's faithful people.

*

32:15 Dt 9:15.
32:16 Ex 31:18.
32:19 Dt 9:16–17.
32:20 Dt 9:21.
32:26–29 Dt 33:8–9.
32:30–34 Dt 9:18–19.
33:1 Gn 12:7.
33:2 Ex 23:23.
33:7 Ex 29:42–43.

Pray It!

God Passing By

How close can we get to God without actually seeing God's face? If anyone would know, it is Moses. His rather amazing encounter with God is recorded in Exodus 33:17–23.

We too can experience, as many saints and mystics have, a deep intimacy with God. It is significant that God and Moses most often met in nature. If you are lucky, you have a favorite outdoor spot. Perhaps it is a place where you can simply sit and ponder as you gaze at the scenery before you. Perhaps during a sunset on a lovely summer evening or while gazing at the sea or a flowing stream, you somehow connect with God. You may not actually see or feel the hand of God, but somehow you know that God is with you and you are catching a glimpse of God's glory. You feel yourself held in the palm of God's gracious hand. And sometimes, like Moses (see 34:29), you are transformed by the power of God's presence.

Where do you most fully experience the presence of God? Close your eyes and call to mind that place; spend some time in prayer there for awhile.

▶ Ex 33:18–23

tent, all the people would rise and bow down at
the entrance of their own tents. 11 The LORD used
to speak to Moses face to face,* as a person speaks
to a friend. Moses would then return to the camp,
but his young assistant, Joshua, son of Nun, never
left the tent. 12 Moses said to the LORD, "See, you
are telling me: Lead this people.* But you have
not let me know whom you will send with me.
Yet you have said: You are my intimate friend;†
You have found favor with me. 13 Now, if I have
found favor with you, please let me know your
ways so that, in knowing you, I may continue
to find favor with you. See, this nation is indeed
your own people. 14 The LORD answered: I myself†
will go along, to give you rest. 15 Moses replied, "If
you are not going yourself, do not make us go up
from here. 16 For how can it be known that I and
your people have found favor with you, except
by your going with us? Then we, your people and
I, will be singled out from every other people on
the surface of the earth." 17 The LORD said to Mo-
ses: This request, too, which you have made, I
will carry out, because you have found favor with
me and you are my intimate friend.
18 Then Moses said, "Please let me see your
glory!" 19 The LORD answered: I will make all my
goodness pass before you, and I will proclaim
my name, "LORD," before you; I who show fa-
vor to whom I will, I who grant mercy to whom
I will.* 20 But you cannot see my face,* for no
one can see me and live.† 21 Here, continued the
LORD, is a place near me where you shall station
yourself on the rock. 22 When my glory passes I
will set you in the cleft of the rock and will cover
you with my hand until I have passed by. 23 Then
I will remove my hand, so that you may see my
back; but my face may not be seen.

Renewal of the Tablets

34 1 The LORD said to Moses: "Cut two stone
tablets like the former,* that I may write on
them the words† which were on the former tablets
that you broke. 2 Get ready for tomorrow morn-
ing, when you are to go up Mount Sinai and there
present yourself to me on the top of the mountain.
3 No one shall come up with you, and let no one
even be seen on any part of the mountain;* even
the sheep and the cattle are not to graze in front
of this mountain." 4 Moses then cut two stone tab-
lets like the former, and early the next morning he
went up Mount Sinai as the LORD had commanded
him, taking in his hand the two stone tablets.
5 The LORD came down in a cloud and stood
with him there and proclaimed the name, "LORD."
6 So the LORD passed before him and proclaimed:
The LORD, the LORD, a God gracious and merci-
ful, slow to anger and abounding in love and
fidelity,† 7 continuing his love for a thousand

† 33:12 *Intimate friend*: lit., "know by name." The root word meaning "know" or "make known" appears four times in vv. 12–13.

33:14 *I myself*: lit., "my face," that is, "my presence." The making of the calf (32:1–4) is an attempt to control the Lord's presence. In response the Lord refuses to accompany the people (33:3) until Moses persuades him.

33:20 *No one can see me and live*: reflecting the tradition that to see God meant instant death. This is contradicted by the statements that Hagar (Gn 16:13), Jacob (Gn 32:31), and Manoah and his wife (Jgs 13:22) all "see God" and yet live (see also Ex 24:10–11).

34:1 *Words*: a common term for commandments, especially the Decalogue (see v. 28). In v. 27 "words" connotes the commands given in vv. 11–26.

34:6 *Gracious . . . fidelity*: this succinct poetic description of God is an often-repeated statement of belief (see Nm 14:18; Ps 103:8;

* **33:11** Nm 12:8; Dt 34:10; Sir 45:4–5.
33:12 Ex 32:34.
33:19 Rom 9:15.
33:20 Jn 1:18; 1 Tm 6:16.
34:1 Dt 10:1–2.
34:3 Ex 19:12–13, 21.

generations, and forgiving wickedness, rebellion,
and sin; yet not declaring the guilty guiltless, but
bringing punishment for their parents' wicked-
ness on children and children's children to the
third and fourth generation!* 8 Moses at once
knelt and bowed down to the ground. 9 Then he
said, "If I find favor with you, Lord, please, Lord,
come along in our company. This is indeed a
stiff-necked people; yet pardon our wickedness
and sins, and claim us as your own."

Religious Laws

10 The LORD said: Here is the covenant I will
make. Before all your people I will perform
marvels never before done† in any nation any-
where on earth, so that all the people among
whom you live may see the work of the LORD.
Awe-inspiring are the deeds I will perform with
you! 11 As for you, observe what I am command-
ing you today.*

See, I am about to drive out before you the
Amorites, Canaanites, Hittites, Perizzites, Hi-
vites and Jebusites. 12 * Take care not to make a
covenant with the inhabitants of the land that
you are to enter; lest they become a snare among
you. 13 Tear down their altars; smash their sacred
stones, and cut down their asherahs.† 14 You
shall not bow down to any other god, for the
LORD—"Jealous"† his name—is a jealous God.
15 Do not make a covenant with the inhabitants
of the land; else, when they prostitute themselves
with their gods and sacrifice to them, one of
them may invite you and you may partake of the
sacrifice. 16 And when you take their daughters as
wives for your sons, and their daughters prosti-
tute themselves with their gods, they will make
your sons do the same.

17 You shall not make for yourselves molten
gods.*

18 You shall keep the festival of Unleavened
Bread.* For seven days at the appointed time

Did You Know?

Major Jewish Feasts

The joyful anticipation we feel before a major holiday seems to be shared by people of all cultures and religious traditions. Certainly, the Israelites had that feeling before the three festivals described in Exodus 34:18–26 (and in 23:14–17). They looked forward to them the way we might look forward to Christmas or Easter.

The *feast of Unleavened Bread*, which began on the day after Passover and lasted a week, marked the beginning of the barley harvest. This feast probably originated in a pre-Passover agricultural holiday. Originally, unleavened bread—bread made without yeast—was eaten during this week to symbolize a fresh start. Later, the feast was connected to the Passover celebration, and the custom of eating unleavened bread came to be seen as a reminder of the haste with which the people had left Egypt—before having time to leaven their bread.

The *feast of Weeks*, or Pentecost, began seven weeks after the barley harvest, to celebrate the start of the wheat harvest. Later, the feast of Weeks took on added significance. Because the Israelites had arrived at Mount Sinai in the third month after their departure from Egypt (see 19:1), this weeklong feast came to be seen as a celebration of God's covenant with Israel.

The third weeklong festival, the *feast of Booths*, also called the festival of Tabernacles, was celebrated as the produce of the land was gathered. Much like our own Thanksgiving Day, it was a time set aside to thank God for the bounty of the earth. It is the most popular of these feasts. Because booths are tents, this feast reminded the Israelites of the time they spent wandering in the desert. In Exodus it is called the feast of the Ingathering, and in other places, simply the festival (see 1 Kgs 8:2).

▶ Ex 34:18–26

145:8; Jl 2:13; Jon 4:2). All the terms describe God's relationship to the covenant people.

34:10 *Never before done*: lit., "created." The verb used here (Heb. *bara'*) is predicated only of God (see Gn 1:1, 21, 27; Ps 51:12). These wonders are a new creation and can be performed only by God.

34:13 Asherah was the name of a Canaanite goddess. In her honor wooden poles (*asherot*) were erected, just as stone pillars (*massebot*) were erected in honor of the god Baal. Both were placed near the altar in a Canaanite shrine.

34:14 *Jealous*: see note on 20:5. Some, by a slight emendation, render, "The Lord is jealous for his name." Cf. Ez 39:25.

34:6–7 Ex 20:5–6; Nm 14:18; Dt 5:9–10; Jer 32:18.
34:11 Ex 13:5; 33:2.
34:12–16 Ex 23:32–33; Dt 7:1–5; 12:2–3.
34:17 Lv 19:4; Dt 5:8–9.
34:18 Ex 12:15–20; 13:3–4.

in the month of Abib you are to eat unleavened
bread, as I commanded you; for in the month of
Abib you came out of Egypt.
19 To me belongs every male that opens the
womb among all your livestock, whether in the
herd or in the flock.* 20 The firstling of a donkey
you shall redeem with a lamb; if you do not re-
deem it, you must break its neck. The firstborn
among your sons you shall redeem.
No one shall appear before me empty-handed.
21 Six days you may labor,* but on the seventh
day you shall rest; even during the seasons of
plowing and harvesting you must rest.
22 * You shall keep the feast of Weeks with
the first fruits of the wheat harvest, likewise, the
feast of the Ingathering at the close of the year.†
23 Three times a year all your men shall appear
before the Lord, the LORD God of Israel. 24 Since I
will drive out the nations before you and enlarge
your territory, no one will covet your land when
you go up three times a year to appear before the
LORD, your God.
25 You shall not offer me the blood of sacrifice
with anything leavened, nor shall the sacrifice
of the Passover feast be kept overnight for the
next day.
26 The choicest first fruits of your soil you shall
bring to the house of the LORD, your God.
You shall not boil a young goat in its mother's
milk.*

Radiance of Moses' Face

27 Then the LORD said to Moses: Write down
these words, for in accordance with these words
I have made a covenant with you and with Israel.
28 So Moses was there with the LORD for forty days
and forty nights,* without eating any food or
drinking any water, and he wrote on the tablets
the words of the covenant, the ten words.
29 As Moses came down from Mount Sinai with
the two tablets of the covenant in his hands, he
did not know that the skin of his face had be-
come radiant† while he spoke with the LORD.
30 When Aaron, then, and the other Israelites
saw Moses and noticed how radiant the skin of
his face had become, they were afraid to come
near him. 31 Only after Moses called to them
did Aaron and all the leaders of the community
come back to him. Moses then spoke to them.
32 Later, all the Israelites came up to him, and
he enjoined on them all that the LORD had told
him on Mount Sinai. 33 When Moses finished
speaking with them, he put a veil over his face.
34 Whenever Moses entered the presence of the
LORD to speak with him, he removed the veil
until he came out again.* On coming out, he
would tell the Israelites all that he had been
commanded. 35 Then the Israelites would see that
the skin of Moses' face was radiant; so he would
again put the veil over his face until he went in
to speak with the LORD.

VIII. The Building of the Tabernacle and the Descent of God's Glory upon It

Sabbath Regulations

35 1 Moses assembled the whole Israelite
community and said to them,* "These are
the words the LORD has commanded to be ob-
served. 2 On six days work may be done, but the
seventh day shall be holy to you as the sabbath
of complete rest to the LORD. Anyone who does
work on that day shall be put to death. 3 You
shall not even light a fire in any of your dwellings
on the sabbath day."

Collection of Materials

4 Moses said to the whole Israelite community,
"This is what the LORD has commanded: 5 * Re-
ceive from among you contributions for the
LORD. Everyone, as his heart prompts him, shall
bring, as a contribution to the LORD, gold, silver,
and bronze; 6 violet, purple, and scarlet yarn;
fine linen and goat hair; 7 rams' skins dyed red,
and tahash skins; acacia wood; 8 oil for the light;
spices for the anointing oil and for the fragrant
incense; 9 onyx stones and other gems for mount-
ing on the ephod and on the breastpiece.

Call for Artisans

10 * "Let every artisan among you come and
make all that the LORD has commanded: 11 the
tabernacle, with its tent, its covering, its clasps,
its frames, its bars, its columns, and its pedestals;
12 the ark, with its poles, the cover, and the cur-
tain veil; 13 the table, with its poles and all its
utensils, and the showbread; 14 the menorah,

---

† **34:22** *Feast of Weeks*: the festival of thanksgiving for the harvest, celebrated seven weeks or fifty days after the beginning of the harvest. It was also called Pentecost (fiftieth) and coincided with the giving of the law on Mount Sinai, fifty days after the offering of the first fruits; cf. Lv 23:10–11; Dt 16:9. *Feast of the Ingathering*: feast of Booths.

34:29 *Radiant*: the Hebrew word translated "radiant" is spelled like the term for "horns." Thus the artistic tradition of portraying Moses with horns.

* **34:19–20** Ex 13:2, 12–13; 23:15. **34:21** Ex 20:9–10. **34:22–23** Ex 23:16–17; Dt 16:10, 13, 16. **34:25–26** Ex 23:18–19. **34:28** Ex 24:18; Dt 9:9, 18; 10:2, 4. **34:33–34** 2 Cor 3:13, 16. **35:1–3** Ex 31:13–17. **35:5–9** Ex 25:2–7. **35:10–19** Ex 31:6–11.

with its utensils, the lamps, and the oil for the light; [15]the altar of incense, with its poles; the anointing oil, and the fragrant incense; the entrance curtain for the entrance of the tabernacle; [16]the altar for burnt offerings, with its bronze grating, its poles, and all its utensils; the basin, with its stand; [17]the hangings of the court, with their columns and pedestals; the curtain for the gate of the court; [18]the tent pegs for the tabernacle and for the court, with their ropes; [19]the service cloths for use in the sanctuary; the sacred vestments for Aaron, the priest, and the vestments for his sons in their ministry."

The Contribution

[20]When the whole Israelite community left Moses' presence, [21]all, as their hearts moved them and their spirit prompted, brought a contribution to the LORD for the work of the tent of meeting, for all its services, and for the sacred vestments. [22]Both the men and the women, all as their heart prompted them, brought brooches, earrings, rings, necklaces, and various other gold articles.* Everyone who could presented an offering of gold to the LORD. [23]Everyone who happened to have violet, purple, or scarlet yarn, fine linen or goat hair, rams' skins dyed red or tahash skins, brought them. [24]Whoever could make a contribution of silver or bronze offered it to the LORD; and everyone who happened to have acacia wood for any part of the work, brought it. [25]All the women who were expert spinners brought hand-spun violet, purple, and scarlet yarn and fine linen thread. [26]All the women, as their hearts and skills moved them, spun goat hair. [27]The tribal leaders brought onyx stones and other gems for mounting on the ephod and on the breastpiece; [28]as well as spices, and oil for the light, anointing oil, and fragrant incense. [29]Every Israelite man and woman brought to the LORD such voluntary offerings as they thought best, for the various kinds of work which the LORD, through Moses, had commanded to be done.

The Artisans

[30]Moses said to the Israelites:* "See, the LORD has singled out Bezalel, son of Uri, son of Hur, of the tribe of Judah, [31]and has filled him with a divine spirit of skill and understanding and knowledge in every craft: [32]in the production of embroidery, in making things of gold, silver, or bronze, [33]in cutting and mounting precious stones, in carving wood, and in every other craft. [34]He has also given both him and Oholiab, son of Ahisamach, of the tribe of Dan, the ability to teach others. [35]He has endowed them with skill to execute all types of work: engraving, embroidering, the making of variegated cloth of violet, purple, and scarlet yarn and fine linen thread, weaving, and all other arts and crafts.

36 [1]"Bezalel, therefore, will set to work with Oholiab and with all the artisans whom the LORD has endowed with skill and understanding in knowing how to do all the work for the service of the sanctuary, just as the LORD has commanded."*

EX

[2]Moses then called Bezalel and Oholiab and all the other artisans whom the LORD had endowed with skill, men whose hearts moved them to come and do the work. [3]They received from Moses all the contributions which the Israelites had brought for the work to be done for the sanctuary service. Still, morning after morning the people continued to bring their voluntary offerings to Moses. [4]Thereupon all the artisans who were doing the work for the sanctuary came from the work each was doing, [5]and told Moses, "The people are bringing much more than is needed to carry out the work which the LORD has commanded us to do." [6]Moses, therefore, ordered a proclamation to be made throughout the camp: "Let neither man nor woman make any more contributions for the sanctuary." So the people stopped bringing their offerings; [7]there was already enough at hand, and more than enough, to complete the work to be done.

The Tent Cloth and Coverings

[8]* The various artisans who were doing the work made the tabernacle with its ten sheets woven of fine linen twined, having cherubim embroidered on them with violet, purple, and scarlet yarn. [9]The length of each sheet was twenty-eight cubits, and the width four cubits; all the sheets were the same size. [10]Five of the sheets were joined together, edge to edge; and the other five sheets likewise, edge to edge. [11]Loops of violet yarn were made along the edge of the end sheet in the first set, and the same along the edge of the end sheet in the second set. [12]Fifty loops were thus put on one inner sheet, and fifty loops on the inner sheet in the other set, with the loops directly opposite each other. [13]Then fifty clasps of gold were made, with which the sheets were joined so that the tabernacle formed one whole.

[14]Sheets of goat hair were also woven as a tent over the tabernacle. Eleven such sheets were made. [15]The length of each sheet was thirty cubits

35:22–28 Ex 25:3–7.
35:30–35 Ex 31:1–6.
36:1–2 Ex 31:1, 6.
36:8–19 Ex 26:1–14.

Did You Know?

The Ark of the Covenant

The ark of the Covenant, which Bezalel made in fulfillment of God's command, was a portable box in which the Israelites kept the tablets of the Law (see Dt 10:1–5, 1 Kgs 8:9) and possibly other sacred items. The large box was made of gold-plated wood, with four rings attached to its lower corners; through these rings, gold-plated poles were inserted for carrying the ark in procession. On top of the ark sat two golden angels facing each other, their wings touching over their heads.

The ark of the Covenant was a symbol of God's saving presence among the Israelites. It accompanied them during their forty years in the desert (see Nm 10:33–36) and was solemnly carried through the Jordan River when they entered the Promised Land (see Jos 3:1–17). Later, the Israelite soldiers took the ark into battle, invoking God's strength against their enemies (see 1 Sm 4:1–11). After the ark was lost in battle to the Philistines, David retrieved it and brought it to Jerusalem (see 2 Sm 6:1–23), where his son Solomon eventually enthroned it in the Temple, in the holy of holies (see 1 Kgs 8:1–11). The ark remained there until the destruction of Jerusalem in 587 BC, when it was lost to history.

▶ Ex 37:1–9

and the width four cubits; all eleven sheets were the same size. 16 Five of these sheets were joined into one set, and the other six sheets into another set. 17 Fifty loops were made along the edge of the end sheet in one set, and fifty loops along the edge of the corresponding sheet in the other set. 18 Fifty bronze clasps were made with which the tent was joined so that it formed one whole. 19 A covering for the tent was made of rams' skins dyed red and, above that, a covering of tahash skins.

The Framework

20 * Frames were made for the tabernacle, acacia-wood uprights. 21 The length of each frame was ten cubits, and the width one and a half cubits. 22 Each frame had two arms, fastening them one to another. In this way all the frames of the tabernacle were made. 23 The frames for the tabernacle were made as follows: twenty frames on the south side, 24 with forty silver pedestals under the twenty frames, two pedestals under each frame for its two arms; 25 twenty frames on the other side of the tabernacle, the north side, 26 with their forty silver pedestals, two pedestals under each frame. 27 At the rear of the tabernacle, to the west, six frames were made, 28 and two frames were made for the corners of the tabernacle, at its rear. 29 These were double at the bottom, and likewise double at the top, to the first ring. That is how both corner frames were made. 30 Thus, there were eight frames, with their sixteen silver pedestals, two pedestals under each frame. 31 Bars of acacia wood were also made, five for the frames on one side of the tabernacle, 32 five for those on the other side, and five for those at the rear, to the west. 33 The center bar, at the middle of the frames, was made to reach across from end to end. 34 The frames were plated with gold, and gold rings were made on them as holders for the bars, which were also plated with gold.

The Veil

35 * The veil was made of violet, purple, and scarlet yarn, and of fine linen twined, with cherubim embroidered on it. 36 Four gold-plated columns of acacia wood, with gold hooks, were made for it, and four silver pedestals were cast for them.

37 The curtain for the entrance of the tent was made of violet, purple, and scarlet yarn, and of fine linen twined, woven in a variegated manner. 38 Its five columns, with their hooks as well as their capitals and bands, were plated with gold; their five pedestals were of bronze.

The Ark

37 1 Bezalel made the ark of acacia wood, two and a half cubits long, one and a half cubits wide, and one and a half cubits high. 2 The inside and outside were plated with gold, and a molding of gold was put around it. 3 Four gold rings were cast for its four supports, two rings on one side and two on the opposite side. 4 Poles of acacia wood were made and plated with gold; 5 these poles were put through the rings on the sides of the ark, for carrying it.

6 The cover was made of pure gold, two and a half cubits long and one and a half cubits wide. 7 Two cherubim of beaten gold were made for the two ends of the cover; 8 one cherub was at one end, the other at the other end, made of one

---

* **36:20–34** Ex 26:15–29. **36:35–38** Ex 26:31–37.

piece with the cover, at each end. 9 The cherubim had their wings spread out above, sheltering the cover. They faced each other, with their faces looking toward the cover.*

The Table

10 * The table was made of acacia wood, two cubits long, a cubit wide, and a cubit and a half high. 11 It was plated with pure gold, and a molding of gold was put around it. 12 A frame a handbreadth high was also put around it, with a molding of gold around the frame. 13 Four rings of gold were cast for it and fastened at the four corners, one at each leg. 14 The rings were alongside the frame as holders for the poles to carry the table. 15 These poles for carrying the table were made of acacia wood and plated with gold. 16 The vessels that were set on the table, its plates and cups, as well as its pitchers and bowls for pouring libations, were made of pure gold.

The Menorah

17 * The menorah was made of pure beaten gold—its shaft and branches—with its cups and knobs and petals springing directly from it. 18 Six branches extended from its sides, three branches on one side and three on the other. 19 On one branch there were three cups, shaped like almond blossoms, each with its knob and petals; on the opposite branch there were three cups, shaped like almond blossoms, each with its knob and petals; and so for the six branches that extended from the menorah. 20 On the menorah there were four cups, shaped like almond blossoms, with their knobs and petals. 21 The six branches that went out from the menorah had a knob under each pair. 22 The knobs and branches so sprang from it that the whole formed but a single piece of pure beaten gold. 23 Its seven lamps, as well as its trimming shears and trays, were made of pure gold. 24 A talent of pure gold was used for the menorah and its various utensils.

The Altar of Incense

25 * The altar of incense was made of acacia wood, on a square, a cubit long, a cubit wide, and two cubits high, having horns that sprang directly from it. 26 Its grate on top, its walls on all four sides, and its horns were plated with pure gold; and a gold molding was put around it. 27 Underneath the molding gold rings were placed, two on one side and two on the opposite

37:1–9

side, as holders for the poles used in carrying it. 28 The poles, too, were made of acacia wood and plated with gold.

29 The sacred anointing oil and the fragrant incense were prepared in their pure form by a perfumer.*

The Altar for Burnt Offerings

38 1 The altar for burnt offerings* was made of acacia wood, on a square, five cubits long and five cubits wide; its height was three cubits. 2 At the four corners horns were made that sprang directly from the altar. It was then plated with bronze. 3 All the utensils of the altar, the pots, shovels, basins, forks and fire pans, were likewise made of bronze. 4 A grating, a bronze network, was made for the altar and placed around it, on the ground, half as high as the altar itself. 5 Four rings were cast for the four corners of the bronze grating, as holders for the poles, 6 which were made of acacia wood and plated with bronze. 7 The poles were put through the rings on the sides of the altar for carrying it. The altar was made in the form of a hollow box.

8 The bronze basin,* with its bronze stand, was made from the mirrors of the women who served† at the entrance of the tent of meeting.

The Court of the Tabernacle

9 * The court was made as follows. On the south side the hangings of the court were of

† 38:8 The reflecting surface of ancient mirrors was usually of polished bronze. *The women who served:* cf. 1 Sm 2:22.

37:1–9 Ex 25:10–22.
37:10–16 Ex 25:23–30.
37:17–24 Ex 25:31–39.
37:25–28 Ex 30:1–5.
37:29 Ex 30:23–25, 34–36.
38:1–7 Ex 27:1–8; 2 Chr 1:5.
38:8 Ex 30:18–21.
38:9–20 Ex 27:9–19.

fine linen twined, a hundred cubits long, 10 with
twenty columns and twenty pedestals of bronze,
the hooks and bands of the columns being of
silver. 11 On the north side there were similar
hangings, a hundred cubits long, with twenty
columns and twenty pedestals of bronze; the
hooks and bands of the columns were of silver.
12 On the west side there were hangings, fifty cu-
bits long, with ten columns and ten pedestals;
the hooks and bands of the columns were of sil-
ver. 13 On the east side the court was fifty cubits.
14 On one side there were hangings to the extent
of fifteen cubits, with three columns and three
pedestals; 15 on the other side, beyond the gate
of the court, there were likewise hangings to the
extent of fifteen cubits, with three columns and
three pedestals. 16 The hangings on all sides of
the court were woven of fine linen twined. 17 The
pedestals of the columns were of bronze, while
the hooks and bands of the columns were of
silver; the capitals were silver-plated, and all the
columns of the court were banded with silver.
18 At the gate of the court there was a variegated
curtain, woven of violet, purple, and scarlet yarn
and of fine linen twined, twenty cubits long and
five cubits wide, in keeping with the hangings of
the court. 19 There were four columns and four
pedestals of bronze for it, while their hooks were
of silver, and their capitals and their bands silver-
plated. 20 All the tent pegs for the tabernacle and
for the court around it were of bronze.

Amount of Metal Used

21 The following is an account of the various
amounts used on the tabernacle, the tabernacle of
the covenant, drawn up at the command of Mo-
ses by the Levites under the direction of Ithamar,
son of Aaron the priest. 22 However, it was Bezalel,
son of Uri,* son of Hur, of the tribe of Judah, who
made all that the LORD commanded Moses, 23 and
he was assisted by Oholiab, son of Ahisamach, of
the tribe of Dan, who was an engraver, an embroi-
derer, and a weaver of variegated cloth of violet,
purple, and scarlet yarn and of fine linen.
24 All the gold used in the entire construction
of the sanctuary, having previously been given as
an offering, amounted to twenty-nine talents and
seven hundred and thirty shekels, according to
the standard of the sanctuary shekel. 25 The silver
of those of the community who were enrolled
was one hundred talents and one thousand
seven hundred and seventy-five shekels, accord-
ing to the standard of the sanctuary shekel; 26 one
bekah apiece, that is, a half-shekel, according to
the standard of the sanctuary shekel, was received
from everyone who was enrolled, of twenty years
or more, namely, six hundred and three thou-
sand five hundred and fifty men.* 27 One hun-
dred talents of silver were used for casting the
pedestals of the sanctuary and the pedestals of
the veil, one talent for each pedestal, or one hun-
dred talents for the one hundred pedestals. 28 The
remaining one thousand seven hundred and
seventy-five shekels were used for making the
hooks on the columns, for plating the capitals,
and for banding them with silver. 29 The bronze,
given as an offering, amounted to seventy talents
and two thousand four hundred shekels. 30 With
this were made the pedestals at the entrance of
the tent of meeting, the bronze altar with its
bronze gratings, and all the utensils of the altar,
31 the pedestals around the court, the pedestals at
the gate of the court, and all the tent pegs for the
tabernacle and for the court around it.

The Priestly Vestments

39 1 With violet, purple, and scarlet yarn
were woven the service cloths for use in
the sanctuary, as well as the sacred vestments*
for Aaron, as the LORD had commanded Moses.
2 * The ephod was woven of gold thread and of
violet, purple, and scarlet yarn and of fine linen
twined. 3 Gold was first hammered into gold leaf
and then cut up into threads, which were woven
with the violet, purple, and scarlet yarn into an
embroidered pattern on the fine linen. 4 Shoul-
der straps were made for it and joined to its two
upper ends. 5 The embroidered belt on the ephod
extended out from it, and like it, was made of
gold thread, of violet, purple, and scarlet yarn,
and of fine linen twined, as the LORD had com-
manded Moses. 6 The onyx stones were prepared
and mounted in gold filigree work; they were
engraved like seal engravings with the names of
the sons of Israel. 7 These stones were set on the
shoulder straps of the ephod as memorial stones
of the sons of Israel, just as the LORD had com-
manded Moses.
8 * The breastpiece was embroidered like the
ephod, with gold thread and violet, purple, and
scarlet yarn on cloth of fine linen twined. 9 It was
square and folded double, a span high and a span
wide in its folded form. 10 Four rows of precious
stones were mounted on it: in the first row a carne-
lian, a topaz, and an emerald; 11 in the second row,
a garnet, a sapphire, and a beryl; 12 in the third
row a jacinth, an agate, and an amethyst; 13 in the
fourth row a chrysolite, an onyx, and a jasper.
They were mounted in gold filigree work. 14 These

38:22–23 Ex 31:2, 6; 35:30, 34; 36:1.
38:26 Nm 1:46.
39:1 Ex 31:10.
39:2–10 Ex 28:6–12.
39:8–14 Ex 28:15–21.

stones were twelve, to match the names of the sons of Israel, and each stone was engraved like a seal with the name of one of the twelve tribes.

15 * Chains of pure gold, twisted like cords, were made for the breastpiece, 16 together with two gold filigree rosettes and two gold rings. The two rings were fastened to the two upper ends of the breastpiece. 17 The two gold chains were then fastened to the two rings at the ends of the breastpiece. 18 The other two ends of the two chains were fastened in front to the two filigree rosettes, which were attached to the shoulder straps of the ephod. 19 Two other gold rings were made and put on the two lower ends of the breastpiece, on the edge facing the ephod. 20 Two more gold rings were made and fastened to the bottom of the two shoulder straps next to where they joined the ephod in front, just above its embroidered belt. 21 Violet ribbons bound the rings of the breastpiece to the rings of the ephod, so that the breastpiece stayed right above the embroidered belt of the ephod and did not swing loose from it. All this was just as the LORD had commanded Moses.

Other Vestments

22 The robe of the ephod was woven entirely of violet yarn, 23 with an opening in its center like the opening of a shirt, with selvage around the opening to keep it from being torn. 24 At the hem of the robe pomegranates were made of violet, purple, and scarlet yarn and of fine linen twined; 25 bells of pure gold were also made and put between the pomegranates all around the hem of the robe: 26 a bell, a pomegranate, a bell, a pomegranate, all around the hem of the robe which was to be worn in performing the ministry—all this, just as the LORD had commanded Moses.

27 For Aaron and his sons there were also woven tunics of fine linen;* 28 the turban of fine linen; the ornate skullcaps of fine linen; linen pants of fine linen twined; 29 and sashes of variegated work made of fine linen twined and of violet, purple, and scarlet yarn, as the LORD had commanded Moses. 30 * The plate of the sacred diadem was made of pure gold and inscribed, as on a seal engraving: "Sacred to the LORD." 31 It was tied over the turban with a violet ribbon, as the LORD had commanded Moses.

Presentation of the Work to Moses

32 Thus the entire work of the tabernacle of the tent of meeting was completed. The Israelites did the work just as the LORD had commanded Moses; so it was done. 33 They then brought to Moses the tabernacle, the tent with all its furnishings, the clasps, the frames, the bars, the columns, the pedestals, 34 the covering of rams' skins dyed red, the covering of tahash skins, the curtain veil; 35 the ark of the covenant with its poles, the cover, 36 the table with all its utensils and the showbread, 37 the pure gold menorah with its lamps set up on it and with all its utensils, the oil for the light, 38 the golden altar, the anointing oil, the fragrant incense; the curtain for the entrance of the tent, 39 the altar of bronze with its bronze grating, its poles and all its utensils, the basin with its stand, 40 the hangings of the court with their columns and pedestals, the curtain for the gate of the court with its ropes and tent pegs, all the equipment for the service of the tabernacle of the tent of meeting; 41 the service cloths for use in the sanctuary, the sacred vestments for Aaron the priest, and the vestments to be worn by his sons in their ministry. 42 Just as the LORD had commanded Moses, so the Israelites had carried out all the work. 43 So when Moses saw that all the work was done just as the LORD had commanded, he blessed them.

Setting up the Tabernacle

40 1 Then the LORD said to Moses: 2 * On the first day of the first month† you shall set up the tabernacle of the tent of meeting.* 3 Put the ark of the covenant in it, and screen off the ark with the veil.* 4 Bring in the table and set it. Then bring in the menorah and set up the lamps on it. 5 Put the golden altar of incense in front of the ark of the covenant, and hang the curtain at the entrance of the tabernacle. 6 Put the altar for burnt offerings in front of the entrance of the tabernacle of the tent of meeting. 7 Place the basin between the tent of meeting and the altar, and put water in it. 8 Set up the court round about, and put the curtain at the gate of the court.

9 * Take the anointing oil and anoint the tabernacle and everything in it, consecrating it and all its furnishings, so that it will be sacred. 10 Anoint the altar for burnt offerings and all its utensils, consecrating it, so that it will be most sacred. 11 Likewise, anoint the basin with its stand, and thus consecrate it.

12 * Then bring Aaron and his sons to the entrance of the tent of meeting, and there wash them with water. 13 Clothe Aaron with the sacred vestments and anoint him, thus consecrating him as

EX

†

40:2 *On the first day of the first month*: almost a year after the departure of the Israelites from Egypt. Cf. v. 17.

*

39:15–21 Ex 28:31–35.
39:27–29 Ex 28:39–42.
39:30–31 Ex 28:36–37.
40:2–8 Ex 40:16–33.
40:2 Ex 26:30.
40:3–8 Ex 26:33–37.
40:9–11 Ex 30:26–29.
40:12–15 Ex 28:41; 29:4–9; Lv 8:1–13.

Cultural Connection

Umbrellas, Arks, and Tents

Umbrellas offer protection from the sun or rain. In Asian cultures, servants would hold umbrellas over emperors and kings. Catholics in Indonesia have adapted this custom for their worship. Often an umbrella is set up over the tabernacle. Umbrellas are held over a priest when he carries the Blessed Sacrament or over the statue of Jesus' Sacred Heart when it is carried in a procession. The umbrella has become a sign of reverence for something that symbolizes God's presence.

The ark of the Covenant was built to act like an umbrella, to protect and revere the tablets of the Law (the Commandments). When the ark was not being carried, it rested in the tabernacle in the holy of holies, which was a special tent at the center of the Israelites' camp. The ark and the tent served the same practical purpose as an umbrella and had the same deeper meaning of revering God's presence.

The next time you use an umbrella, remember how umbrellas are used to show respect for that which is holy: the body of Christ, the Ten Commandments, and one of God's greatest creations—*you!*

Ex 40:1–15

my priest. 14 Bring forward his sons also, and clothe
them with the tunics. 15 As you have anointed their
father, anoint them also as my priests. Thus, by be-
ing anointed, shall they receive a perpetual priest-
hood throughout all future generations.
16 Moses did just as the LORD had commanded
him. 17 On the first day of the first month of the
second year the tabernacle was set up. 18 It was
Moses who set up the tabernacle. He placed its
pedestals, set up its frames, put in its bars, and
set up its columns. 19 He spread the tent over the
tabernacle and put the covering on top of the
tent, as the LORD had commanded him. 20 * He
took the covenant and put it in the ark; he placed
poles alongside the ark and set the cover upon
it. 21 He brought the ark into the tabernacle and
hung the curtain veil, thus screening off the ark
of the covenant, as the LORD had commanded
him. 22 He put the table in the tent of meeting, on
the north side of the tabernacle, outside the veil,
23 and arranged the bread on it before the LORD,
as the LORD had commanded him.* 24 He placed
the menorah in the tent of meeting, opposite
the table, on the south side of the tabernacle,
25 and he set up the lamps before the LORD, as
the LORD had commanded him. 26 He placed the
golden altar in the tent of meeting, in front of
the veil, 27 and on it he burned fragrant incense,
as the LORD had commanded him. 28 He hung the
curtain at the entrance of the tabernacle. 29 He
put the altar for burnt offerings in front of the
entrance of the tabernacle of the tent of meeting,
and sacrificed burnt offerings and grain offerings
on it, as the LORD had commanded him. 30 * He
placed the basin between the tent of meeting
and the altar, and put water in it for washing.
31 Moses and Aaron and his sons used to wash
their hands and feet there, 32 for they washed
themselves whenever they went into the tent of
meeting or approached the altar, as the LORD had
commanded Moses. 33 Finally, he set up the court
around the tabernacle and the altar and hung the
curtain at the gate of the court.
Thus Moses finished all the work.

God's Presence in the Tabernacle

34 * Then the cloud covered the tent of meet-
ing, and the glory of the LORD filled the taberna-
cle. 35 Moses could not enter the tent of meeting,
because the cloud settled down upon it and the
glory of the LORD filled the tabernacle. 36 Whenever
the cloud rose from the tabernacle, the Israelites
would set out on their journey. 37 But if the cloud
did not lift, they would not go forward; only when
it lifted did they go forward. 38 The cloud of the
LORD was over the tabernacle by day, and fire in
the cloud at night, in the sight of the whole house
of Israel in all the stages of their journey.

* **40:20–29** Ex 25:16, 21; 26:33–37. **40:23** Ex 25:30. **40:30–32** Ex 30:18–21. **40:34–38** Nm 9:15–22.

When approaching a stop sign, come to a complete stop before proceeding. No shoes, no shirt, no service. The line forms here. Sometimes it seems that life is just made up of a bunch of rules and laws. But when we really think about it, we realize that rules and laws are designed to help society work smoothly and to make sure we respect one another's rights. The Book of Leviticus has a similar function. It is primarily a list of laws, rules, and instructions to ensure holiness and order in worship and the people's way of life.

The Book of Leviticus

At a Glance

I. Ritual of Sacrifices (1:1—7:38).

A. Instructions for the Israelites (1:1—5:26).

B. Instructions for the Priests (6:1—7:38).

II. Ceremony of Ordination (8:1—10:20).

III. Laws regarding Legal Purity (11:1—16:34).

IV. Holiness Laws (17:1—26:46).

V. Redemption of Offerings (27:1–34).

Quick Facts

Period Covered: after the Exodus, during the Israelites' encampment at Mount Sinai

Inspired Author: the Priestly writer writing after the Babylonian Exile

Theme: to teach the way of holiness through observance of the Law and religious ritual

In Depth

Leviticus, the third book of the Pentateuch, or Torah, is named after the tribe of Levi, whose male members were designated priests in Israel. It was their responsibility to conduct appropriate worship of God. For that reason, the book has often been referred to as the Torah (Law) of the Priests.

Most Scripture scholars believe that the laws and regulations in Leviticus developed over hundreds of years after the people entered the Promised Land. The book was compiled at a time when the priests were struggling to unify Israel as it lay in ruins from its Babylonian conquerors. They wished to gather the various traditions and regulations that governed Israel's way of life. The author of Leviticus, referred to as the Priestly writer, writes as if these gathered traditions and regulations were given by God to Moses at Mount Sinai as part of the original Law. The author wishes to show that these laws are an extension of the Sinai Covenant.

If the goal of Israel's existence is to "be holy, because I [the Lord] am holy" (Lev 11:45), then the Book of Leviticus records how holiness becomes part of every aspect of Israel's existence. Chapters 17–26 are described as the Holiness Laws. The words on love of neighbor in 19:18 are quoted several times in the New Testament. The purpose of Leviticus is to call Israel to follow the Law, and thus become a holy people and make its land a suitable place for God to dwell.

The customs and rites in Jesus' time are observances of the laws in Leviticus. Many of those customs and rites were left behind as Christianity emerged as a distinct religion.

Leviticus

25:9

I. Ritual of Sacrifices

A. Instructions for the Israelites

Burnt Offerings

1 [1]The LORD called Moses, and spoke to him from
the tent of meeting:* [2]Speak to the Israelites
and tell them: When any one of you† brings an
offering of livestock to the LORD, you shall bring
your offering from the herd or from the flock.*
[3]† * If a person's offering is a burnt offering†
from the herd, the offering must be a male with-
out blemish.* The individual shall bring it to the
entrance of the tent of meeting to find favor with
the LORD, [4]and shall lay a hand† on the head* of
the burnt offering, so that it may be acceptable*
to make atonement* for the one who offers it.
[5]The bull shall then be slaughtered† before the
LORD, and Aaron's sons, the priests, shall offer its
blood by splashing it on all the sides of the altar
which is at the entrance of the tent of meeting.*
[6]Then the burnt offering shall be flayed and cut
into pieces. [7]After Aaron's sons, the priests, have
put burning embers on the altar and laid wood
on them, [8]they shall lay the pieces of meat, to-
gether with the head and the suet, on top of the
wood and the embers on the altar; [9]but the inner
organs and the shanks shall be washed with wa-
ter. The priest shall then burn all of it on the altar
as a burnt offering, a sweet-smelling oblation to
the LORD.*
[10]If a person's burnt offering is from the flock,
that is, a sheep or a goat, the offering must be a
male without blemish. [11]It shall be slaughtered
on the north side of the altar before the LORD, and

1:2 *Any one of you*: women as well as men bring sacrifices (see 12:6–8; 15:28–30) and are explicitly obligated in other ritual matters (e.g., 13:29, 38; Nm 5:6; 6:2; Lk 2:24). Thus, though the Hebrew formulates sacrificial and other law with male reference, the translation reflects the inclusion of women in ritual requirements. *From the herd or from the flock*: the only animals which could be used as sacrificial victims were domestic animals either of the bovine class (bulls, cows and calves) or the ovine class (sheep and lambs, goats and kids). Excluded, therefore, were not only all wild animals, but also such "unclean" domestic animals as the camel and the donkey (cf. 11:1–47; 27:26–27).

1:3–5 *Entrance of the tent of meeting . . . before the LORD*: probably the forecourt from the entrance of the court to the entrance of the tent (cf. Ex 27). Thus the altar in front of the tent was entirely accessible to the laity.

1:3 The burnt offering is used for regular daily (6:1–6) offerings, public festivals (Nm 28–29), purification rituals (Lv 12:6–8; 14:19–20; 15:15, 30), and individuals' vows and voluntary offerings (22:18–20).

1:4 *Lay a hand*: the imposition of a single hand for the sacrifices in chaps. 1–5 may be a means of designating the animal as belonging to the offerer. See note on 16:21. *Atonement*: see note on 16:6.

1:5 *Shall then be slaughtered*: lit., "he shall slaughter the bull." Slaughtering is not something the offerer must do (as opposed to, for example, hand placement [v. 4] or the presentation of sacrificial portions as an elevated offering [7:29–34]). Thus the verb is construed impersonally here.

1:1 Ex 40.
1:2 Lv 1:3, 10; 3:1, 6, 12.
1:3 Lv 6:1–6; 22:18–19.
1:3 Lv 22:17–25; Ex 12:5.
1:4 Lv 3:2, 8, 13; 4:4, 15, 24, 29, 33; 8:14, 18, 22; Nm 8:12; 2 Chr 29:23; cf. Lv 16:21; 24:14; Nm 27:18, 23; Dt 34:9.
1:4 Lv 19:5; 22:19–29; Gn 4:3–5; Mal 1:8–14.
1:4 Lv 9:7; 14:20; Jb 1:5; 42:8; cf. Gn 32:21; Ex 29:36–37; 30:15; Lv 16:16–20; 17:11; Ez 43:20, 26.
1:5 Lv 1:11, 15; 3:2, 8, 13; cf. Lv 4:5–7, 25.
1:9 Lv 2:2; 3:5; 4:31; 26:31; Gn 8:20–21; Nm 28:2; cf. Lv 3:11; 21:6, 21; 22:25.

Aaron's sons, the priests, shall splash its blood on all the sides of the altar. 12 When it has been cut into pieces, the priest shall lay these, together with the head and suet, on top of the wood and the embers on the altar; 13 but the inner organs and the shanks shall be washed with water. The priest shall then offer all of it, burning it on the altar. It is a burnt offering, a sweet-smelling oblation to the LORD.

14 If a person offers a bird as a burnt offering to the LORD, the offering brought must be a turtledove or a pigeon.* 15 Having brought it to the altar, the priest shall wring its head off and burn it on the altar. The blood shall be drained out against the side of the altar.* 16 He shall remove its crissum† by means of its feathers and throw it on the ash heap at the east side of the altar. 17 Then, having torn the bird open by its wings without separating the halves, the priest shall burn it on the altar, on the wood and the embers. It is a burnt offering, a sweet-smelling oblation to the LORD.

Grain Offerings

2 1 †* When anyone brings a grain offering to the LORD, the offering must consist of bran flour. The offerer shall pour oil on it and put frankincense* over it, 2 and bring it to Aaron's sons, the priests. A priest shall take a handful of the bran flour and oil, together with all the frankincense, and shall burn it on the altar as a token of the offering,† a sweet-smelling oblation to the LORD.* 3 The rest of the grain offering belongs to Aaron and his sons,* a most holy* portion from the oblations to the LORD.

4 When you offer a grain offering baked in an oven, it must be in the form of unleavened cakes made of bran flour mixed with oil, or of unleavened wafers spread with oil.* 5 If your offering is a grain offering that is fried on a griddle,* it must be of bran flour mixed with oil and unleavened. 6 Break it into pieces, and pour oil over it. It is a grain offering. 7 If your offering is a grain offering that is prepared in a pan, it must be made of bran flour, fried in oil. 8 A grain offering that is made in any of these ways you shall bring to the LORD.

Did You Know?

The Covenant Laws

Even though Christians are not bound by the Jewish religion—see the Letters to the Hebrews and to the Romans—the laws in Leviticus help us understand the meaning of life for the Israelites. These laws developed out of their experience of striving to be faithful to God and were interpreted and taught by the priests of the tribe of Levi.

The purity laws may seem the strangest to us today. They defined who or what was pure—that is, free from contamination—and therefore acceptable to God for the purpose of liturgical worship. They included laws on sickness, especially leprosy, because physical disease was understood as a symptom of sin or spiritual contamination. Purity laws also covered food, animals, bodily discharges, and corpses.

Other laws described proper relationships between people. These laws reflected more the intentions of the heart. Later, the prophets and Jesus would emphasize that impurity comes from the heart, not from something outside the person (see Mk 7:1–23). Other laws regulated priestly ministry, and still others regulated social institutions. Nothing was left to chance. The laws of the covenant made it clear that God was present in every aspect of the people's lives.

LV

It shall be presented to the priest, who shall take it to the altar. 9 The priest shall then remove from the grain offering a token and burn it on the altar as a sweet-smelling oblation to the LORD. 10 The rest of the grain offering belongs to Aaron and his sons, a most holy portion from the oblations to the LORD.

11 † Every grain offering that you present to

†

1:16 *Crissum*: the area around the anus of the bird, lying beneath the bird's tail.

2:1 Grain offerings are used as independent offerings (those in this chapter and cf. 6:12–16; 8:26–27; 23:10–11), as substitutes for other offerings in a case of poverty (5:11–13), and as accompaniments to animal offerings (cf. Nm 15:1–12; 28:1–29:39; Lv 14:20; 23:12, 18, 37). Chapter 2 describes two basic types of grain offering: uncooked (vv. 1–3) and cooked (vv. 4–10). The flour (*sōlet*) used was made of wheat (Ex 29:2) and Jewish tradition and Semitic cognates indicate that it is a coarse rather than a fine flour.

2:2 *Token of the offering*: lit., "reminder." Instead of burning the whole grain offering, only this part is burned on the altar.

2:11–12 No grain offering that is leavened can be offered on the altar. Those in 7:13 and 23:17 are leavened but not offered on the altar. The Hebrew word for "honey" may refer to fruit syrup as well as to bee honey.

*

1:14 Lv 5:7; 12:8; 15:14–15; Lk 2:24.
1:15 Lv 5:8–9.
2:1 Lv 5:11–13; 6:7–16; 7:9–14; 24:5–9; Nm 15:1–21; cf. Gn 4:3–5.
2:1 Cf. Ex 30:1–10; Lv 16:11–13; Prv 27:9.
2:2 Lv 1:9.
2:3 Lv 6:9; 7:9–10.
2:3 Lv 6:10, 18, 22; 10:12, 17; 24:9.
2:4 1 Chr 23:29.
2:5 Lv 6:14.

the LORD shall be unleavened, for you shall not burn any leaven or honey as an oblation to the LORD.* 12 Such you may present to the LORD in the offering of the first produce that is processed,* but they are not to be placed on the altar for a pleasing odor. 13 You shall season all your grain offerings with salt. Do not let the salt of the covenant with your God† be lacking from your grain offering. On every offering you shall offer salt.*

14 If you offer a grain offering of first ripe fruits to the LORD, you shall offer it in the form of fresh early grain, roasted by fire and crushed as a grain offering of your first ripe fruits. 15 You shall put oil on it and set frankincense on it. It is a grain offering. 16 The priest shall then burn some of the groats and oil, together with all the frankincense, as a token of the offering, an oblation to the LORD.

Communion Sacrifices

3 1†* If a person's offering is a communion sacrifice, if it is brought from the herd, be it a male or a female animal, it must be presented without blemish* before the LORD. 2 The one offering it shall lay a hand on the head* of the offering. It shall then be slaughtered at the entrance of the tent of meeting. Aaron's sons, the priests, shall splash its blood on all the sides of the altar. 3* From the communion sacrifice the individual shall offer as an oblation to the LORD the fat† that covers the inner organs, and all the fat that adheres to them, 4 as well as the two kidneys, with the fat on them near the loins, and the lobe of the liver, which is removed with the kidneys. 5 Aaron's sons shall burn this on the altar with the burnt offering that is on the wood and the embers, as a sweet-smelling oblation to the LORD.*

6 If the communion sacrifice one offers to the LORD is from the flock, be it a male or a female animal, it must be presented without blemish. 7 If one presents a lamb as an offering, that person shall bring it before the LORD, 8 and after laying a hand on the head of the offering, it shall then be slaughtered before the tent of meeting. Aaron's sons shall splash its blood on all the sides of the altar. 9 From the communion sacrifice the individual shall present as an oblation to the LORD its fat: the whole fatty tail, which is removed close to the spine, the fat that covers the inner organs, and all the fat that adheres to them, 10 as well as the two kidneys, with the fat on them near the loins, and the lobe of the liver, which is removed with the kidneys. 11 The priest shall burn this on the altar as food,* an oblation to the LORD.

12 If a person's offering is a goat, the individual shall bring it before the LORD, 13 and after laying a hand on its head, it shall then be slaughtered before the tent of meeting. Aaron's sons shall splash its blood on all the sides of the altar. 14 From this the one sacrificing shall present an offering as an oblation to the LORD: the fat that covers the inner organs, and all the fat that adheres to them, 15 as well as the two kidneys, with the fat on them near the loins, and the lobe of the liver, which is removed with the kidneys. 16 The priest shall burn these on the altar as food, a sweet-smelling oblation.

All the fat belongs to the LORD. 17 This shall be a perpetual ordinance for your descendants wherever they may dwell. You shall not eat any fat or any blood.†*

Purification Offerings

4 1 The LORD said to Moses: 2* Tell the Israelites: When a person inadvertently† does wrong by violating any one of the LORD's prohibitions—

For the Anointed Priest

3 If it is the anointed priest† who thus does wrong and thereby makes the people guilty, he

---

† **2:13** *The salt of the covenant with your God*: partaking of salt in common was an ancient symbol of friendship and alliance. Cf. Mark 9:49–50 and Col 4:6.

3:1 The exact meaning of Hebrew *shelamim*, "communion sacrifice," is not clear. It has also been rendered "gift," "(re)payment," "peace," "well-being," or "covenant" offering. This offering may be brought for a vow or voluntary offering (cf. 22:21). A distinct version of the communion sacrifice is the thanksgiving offering (7:11–15 vis-à-vis vv. 16–18).

3:3–5 *Fat*: only part of the offering is devoted to God, as opposed to the burnt offering (chap. 1), which is wholly burnt (except for the skin). The meat is distributed among the offerer (and the offerer's party) and the priests (cf. 7:11–36).

3:17 *Any fat or any blood*: this prohibition is mentioned here because portions of this offering could be eaten by lay Israelites, who may not be entirely familiar with the prohibition (cf. 7:22–27; 19:26). The fat prohibited is only the visceral fat mentioned in 3:9–10, 14–15, not muscular fat.

4:2 *Inadvertently*: the concern in this chapter, and much of chap. 5, is wrongs done unintentionally. Intentional ("high-handed") sins are punished with being "cut off" from the people (Nm 15:30–31). See note on Lv 7:20. *LORD's prohibitions*: not included in the faults figured here is failure to perform positive commandments. Failing to perform positive commands, however, still renders the individual liable to other punishment (e.g., failing to observe the Passover, Nm 9:13). Cf. Nm 15:22–31.

4:3 *The anointed priest*: the chapter presents four cases of inadvertent wrong, arranged in descending order according to the status of the wrongdoer: high priest (vv. 3–12), entire community (vv. 13–21), tribal leader (vv. 22–26), and general populace (vv. 27–35).

---

* **2:11** Mt 16:12; Mk 8:15; Lk 12:1; 1 Cor 5:7; Gal 5:9.
2:12 Nm 18:12–13, 27; 15:20–21.
2:13 Nm 18:19; Ezr 6:9; 7:22; Ez 43:24.
3:1 Lv 7:11–36.
3:1 Lv 22:21.
3:2 Lv 1:4.
3:3–5 Lv 3:9–10, 14–16; 4:8–9, 31, 35; 6:5; 7:3–4, 30–31; 8:16, 25; 16:25; 17:6; Ex 29:13, 22; cf. Ez 44:15.
3:5 Lv 1:9.
3:11 Lv 9:19.
3:17 Lv 17:10.
4:2 Lv 6:17–23; Nm 15:22–31.

shall offer to the LORD an unblemished bull of
the herd as a purification offering for the wrong
he committed. 4 Bringing the bull to the entrance
of the tent of meeting, before the LORD, he shall
lay his hand on its head* and slaughter it be-
fore the LORD. 5 † The anointed priest shall then
take some of the bull's blood and bring it into
the tent of meeting, 6 where, dipping his finger
in the blood, he shall sprinkle some of it seven
times before the LORD, toward the veil of the
sanctuary.* 7 The priest shall also put some of
the blood on the horns of the altar of fragrant
incense which stands before the LORD in the
tent of meeting. The rest of the bull's blood he
shall pour out at the base of the altar for burnt
offerings which is at the entrance of the tent of
meeting. 8 He shall remove all the fat of the bull
of the purification offering: the fat that covers the
inner organs, and all the fat that adheres to them,
9 as well as the two kidneys, with the fat on them
near the loins, and the lobe of the liver, which is
removed with the kidneys, 10 just as the fat pieces
are removed from the ox of the communion sac-
rifice.* The priest shall burn these on the altar for
burnt offerings. 11 † But the hide of the bull and
its meat, with its head, shanks, inner organs and
dung, 12 that is, the whole bull, shall be brought
outside the camp to a clean place† where the
ashes are deposited and there be burned in a
wood fire. At the place of the ash heap, there it
must be burned.*

For the Community

13 If the whole community of Israel errs† inad-
vertently and without even being aware of it vio-
lates any of the LORD's prohibitions, and thus are
guilty, 14 when the wrong that was committed be-
comes known, the community shall offer a bull
of the herd as a purification offering. They shall
bring it before the tent of meeting. 15 The elders
of the community shall lay their hands on the
bull's head before the LORD. When the bull has
been slaughtered before the LORD, 16 the anointed
priest shall bring some of its blood into the
tent of meeting, 17 and dipping his finger in the
blood, he shall sprinkle it seven times before
the LORD, toward the veil. 18 He shall also put
some of the blood on the horns of the altar

Pray It!

Sin Offering

The sin offering laws probably seem strange to you. The Israelites understood that sin affects not only the sinner but also those whose lives the sinner touches. They understood sin as incurring a debt that must be repaid. The sinner made a guilt offering to atone for the sin.

Christians believe that Jesus became the sin offering who took on the debt of the sins of the whole world, once and for all. However, Christians still have an obligation to recognize and confess their sins. For Catholics this occurs formally in the sacrament of Penance and Reconciliation. Catholics admit their sinfulness and receive God's forgiveness by participating in this sacrament.

Take a moment to thank God for the great gift of Jesus and for the forgiveness of our sins.

► Lv 4:1—5:26

which is before the LORD in the tent of meeting.
The rest of the blood he shall pour out at the base
of the altar for burnt offerings which is at the en-
trance of the tent of meeting. 19 He shall remove
all of its fat and burn it on the altar, 20 doing
with this bull just as he did with the other bull
of the purification offering; he will do the same
thing. Thus the priest shall make atonement* on
their behalf, that they may be forgiven. 21 This
bull shall also be brought outside the camp and
burned,* just as the first bull. It is a purification
offering for the assembly.

For the Tribal Leader

22 Should a tribal leader* do wrong inadver-
tently by violating any one of the prohibitions
of the LORD his God, and thus be guilty, 23 when
he learns of the wrong he committed, he shall

† The higher one's position, the more deeply the sin affects the sanctuary (vv. 5–7, 17–18 versus vv. 25, 29, 34). See note on 16:6. *Purification offering*: the Hebrew verb *ḥiṭṭēʾ* means "remove sin, purify" (Lv 8:15; Ez 43:20–23; 45:18–19; cf. Ex 29:36). The offering cleansed the various places to which the blood was applied or the rooms in which it was sprinkled.

4:5–7 On the structure of the sanctuary, see Ex 26–27.

4:11–12 See note on 6:17–23.

4:12 *Clean place*: i.e., ritually "clean" or pure. It has nothing to do with the presence of dirt or waste. See 6:4.

4:13 *Whole community . . . errs*: this case probably complements that of vv. 3–12. There the high priest sins so that the people become guilty. Those verses deal with his requirements for atonement; vv. 13–21 deal with the people's requirements.

* **4:4** Lv 1:4. **4:6–7** Lv 4:17–18; 16:16; cf. 4:25. **4:10** Lv 3:3. **4:12** Lv 6:23. **4:20** Lv 1:4. **4:21** Lv 6:23. **4:22** Nm 10:4; 25:14.

bring as his offering an unblemished male goat.
24 He shall lay his hand on its head and it shall be
slaughtered in the place where the burnt offering
is slaughtered, before the LORD. It is a purification
offering. 25 The priest shall then take some of the
blood of the purification offering on his finger
and put it on the horns* of the altar for burnt
offerings. The rest of the blood he shall pour out
at the base of the altar. 26 All of its fat he shall
burn on the altar like the fat of the communion
sacrifice. Thus the priest shall make atonement
on the tribal leader's behalf for his wrong, that
he may be forgiven.

For the General Populace

27 If anyone of the general populace does wrong
inadvertently by violating one of the LORD's pro-
hibitions, and thus is guilty, 28 upon learning of
the wrong committed, that person shall bring
an unblemished she-goat as the offering for the
wrong committed. 29 The wrongdoer shall lay a
hand on the head of the purification offering, and
the purification offering shall be slaughtered at
the place of the burnt offerings. 30 The priest shall
then take some of its blood on his finger and put
it on the horns of the altar for burnt offerings. The
rest of the blood he shall pour out at the base of
the altar. 31 He shall remove all the fat, just as the
fat is removed from the communion sacrifice. The
priest shall burn it on the altar for a sweet odor to
the LORD. Thus the priest shall make atonement,
so that the individual may be forgiven.
32 If, however, a person brings a lamb as a
purification offering, that person shall bring an
unblemished female, and 33 lay a hand on its
head. It shall be slaughtered as a purification
offering in the place where the burnt offering is
slaughtered. 34 The priest shall then take some of
the blood of the purification offering on his fin-
ger and put it on the horns of the altar for burnt
offerings. The rest of the blood he shall pour out
at the base of the altar. 35 He shall remove all its
fat just as the fat is removed from the lamb of
the communion sacrifice. The priest shall burn
these on the altar with the other oblations for
the LORD. Thus the priest shall make atonement
on the person's behalf for the wrong committed,
that the individual may be forgiven.

Special Cases for Purification Offerings†

5 1 If a person, either having seen or come to
know something, does wrong by refusing
as a witness under oath to give information,*
that individual shall bear the penalty; 2 or if
someone, without being aware of it, touches any
unclean thing, such as the carcass of an unclean
wild animal, or an unclean domestic animal, or
an unclean swarming creature,† and thus is un-
clean and guilty;* 3 or if someone, without being
aware of it, touches some human uncleanness,*
whatever kind of uncleanness this may be, and
then subsequently becomes aware of guilt; 4 or
if someone, without being aware of it, rashly ut-
ters an oath with bad or good intent,* whatever
kind of oath this may be, and then subsequently
becomes aware of guilt in regard to any of these
matters— 5 when someone is guilty in regard to
any of these matters, that person shall confess
the wrong committed, 6 and make reparation
to the LORD for the wrong committed: a female
animal from the flock, a ewe lamb or a she-goat,
as a purification offering. Thus the priest shall
make atonement on the individual's behalf for
the wrong.
7 If, however, the person cannot afford an an-
imal of the flock,* that person shall bring to the
LORD as reparation for the wrong committed two
turtledoves or two pigeons, one for a purifica-
tion offering and the other for a burnt offering.
8 The guilty party shall bring them to the priest,
who shall offer the one for the purification of-
fering first.* Wringing its head at the neck, yet
without breaking it off, 9 he shall sprinkle some
of the blood of the purification offering against
the side of the altar. The rest of the blood shall
be drained out against the base of the altar. It is
a purification offering. 10 The other bird he shall
offer as a burnt offering according to procedure.
Thus the priest shall make atonement on the
person's behalf for the wrong committed, so that
the individual may be forgiven.
11 If the person is unable to afford even two
turtledoves or two pigeons, that person shall
bring as an offering for the wrong committed
one tenth of an ephah† of bran flour for a purifi-
cation offering. The guilty party shall not put oil

---

† **5:1–13** This differs from the prescriptions for purification offerings in chap. 4 by listing four specific wrongs for which a purification offering is brought and allowing the substitution of birds and grain offerings in the case of poverty.

5:2 *Swarming creature*: a rather imprecise categorization that includes various small creatures in the seas, such as fish that go about in large groups or swarms (Gn 1:20; Lv 11:10); or, similarly, various winged insects that mass in the skies (Lv 11:20; Dt 14:19); and, finally, various small creatures that move in swarms on land, whether crawlers, quadrupeds, or of the multilegged variety (Lv 11:41–42). According to 11:29–30, even various rodents and lizards can be included in this category.

5:11 *Ephah*: see note on Is 5:10.

---

* **4:25** Lv 4:30, 34; 8:15; 9:9; 16:18; Ex 29:12; Ez 43:20; cf. Lv 4:7.
5:1 Jgs 17:2–3; Prv 29:24.
5:2 Lv 11:1–45; 15:31; 17:15–16.
5:3 Lv 12:4; 13:35–36; 15:2–12, 19–27; Nm 19:14–22.
5:4 Nm 30:3; Jgs 11:30–36; 1 Sm 14:24–30; Mk 6:23–26; Acts 23:12.
5:7 Cf. Lv 5:11; 12:8; 14:21.
5:8 Lv 1:14–17.

or place frankincense on it, because it is a puri-
fication offering.* 12 The individual shall bring it
to the priest, who shall take a handful as a token
of the offering and burn it on the altar with the
other oblations for the LORD. It is a purification
offering. 13 Thus the priest shall make atonement
on the person's behalf for the wrong committed
in any of the above cases, so that the individual
may be forgiven. The rest of the offering, like the
grain offering, shall belong to the priest.

Reparation Offerings†

14 The LORD said to Moses: 15 * When a person
commits sacrilege by inadvertently misusing any
of the LORD's sacred objects,* the wrongdoer shall
bring to the LORD as reparation an unblemished
ram from the flock, at the established value† in
silver shekels according to the sanctuary shekel,
as a reparation offering. 16 The wrongdoer shall
also restore what has been misused of the sa-
cred objects, adding a fifth of its value,* and
give this to the priest. Thus the priest shall make
atonement for the person with the ram of the
reparation offering, so that the individual may
be forgiven.
17 If someone does wrong and violates one
of the LORD's prohibitions without realizing it,
that person is guilty* and shall bear the penalty.
18 The individual shall bring to the priest an un-
blemished ram of the flock, at the established
value, for a reparation offering. The priest shall
then make atonement on the offerer's behalf for
the error inadvertently and unknowingly com-
mitted so that the individual may be forgiven.
19 It is a reparation offering. The individual must
make reparation to the LORD.
20 The LORD said to Moses: 21 When someone
does wrong and commits sacrilege against the
LORD by deceiving* a neighbor about a deposit
or a pledge or a stolen article, or by otherwise
retaining a neighbor's goods unjustly;* 22 or if,
having found a lost article, the person lies about
it, swearing falsely about any of the things that
a person may do wrong— 23 when someone
has thus done wrong and is guilty, that person
shall restore the thing that was stolen, the item
unjustly retained, the item left as deposit, or the
lost article that was found 24 or whatever else the
individual swore falsely about. That person shall
make full restitution of the thing itself, and add
one fifth of its value to it, giving it to its owner at
the time of reparation. 25 Then that person shall
bring to the priest as reparation to the LORD an
unblemished ram of the flock, at the established
value, as a reparation offering. 26 The priest shall
make atonement on the person's behalf before
the LORD, so that the individual may be forgiven
for whatever was done to incur guilt.

B. Instructions for the Priests

The Daily Burnt Offering

6 1 The LORD said to Moses: 2 † * Give Aaron
and his sons the following command: This
is the ritual† for the burnt offering—the burnt
offering that is to remain on the hearth of the al-
tar all night until the next morning, while the fire
is kept burning on the altar. 3 The priest, clothed
in his linen robe and wearing linen pants under-
neath, shall take away the ashes to which the fire
has reduced the burnt offering on the altar, and
lay them at the side of the altar. 4 Then, having
taken off these garments and put on other gar-
ments, he shall carry the ashes to a clean place
outside the camp. 5 The fire on the altar is to be
kept burning; it must not go out. Every morning
the priest shall put firewood on it. On this he
shall lay out the burnt offering* and burn the
fat of the communion offering. 6 The fire is to be
kept burning continuously on the altar; it must
not go out.

The Grain Offering†

7 This is the ritual of the grain offering. Aaron's
sons shall offer it before the LORD, in front of the
altar. 8 A priest shall then take from the grain of-
fering a handful of bran flour and oil, together
with all the frankincense that is on it,* and this
he shall burn on the altar as a token of the of-
fering, a sweet aroma to the LORD. 9 The rest of it

† **5:14–26** This last half of the chapter deals with a distinct sacrifice, the reparation offering (Heb. *'asham*). The Hebrew root for this term has a basic meaning of "be guilty." The noun can have a consequential sense of "that which is due from guilt," i.e., "compensation, indemnification, reparation"; hence the translation "reparation offering," rather than the alternatives "guilt offering" or "trespass offering." This offering is brought most often in cases of sacrilege.

5:15 *At the established value*: the Hebrew term *'erkĕkā*, which in context means "(established) value," may indicate that a person could bring the monetary equivalent of a ram instead of an actual animal. See vv. 18, 25.

6:2–6 This passage may have reference to the burnt offering that is offered in the morning and late afternoon each day (cf. Ex 29:38–42; Nm 28:3–8).

6:2 *Ritual*: Hebrew *torah*, which also has the broader meaning of "instruction." The treatment of sacrifices in chaps. 6–7 recapitulates the offerings treated in 1–5 but now with more emphasis on priestly duties and prerogatives.

6:7–11 The passage is apparently concerned with the raw grain offering of 2:1–3.

* **5:11** Lv 2:1–3; Nm 5:15.
5:15 Lv 7:1–6; Nm 5:5–8.
5:15 Lv 22:14.
5:16 Lv 22:14; 27:13, 15, 19, 27.
5:17 Ps 19:13; Jb 1:5.
5:21 Ps 59:13; Hos 4:2.
5:21 Ex 22:6–12.
6:2 Lv 1.
6:5 Lv 9:17.
6:8 Lv 2:1–3.

Aaron and his sons may eat; but it must be eaten unleavened in a sacred place:* in the court of the tent of meeting they shall eat it. 10 It shall not be baked with leaven. I have given it to them as their portion from the oblations for the LORD; it is most holy,* like the purification offering and the reparation offering. 11 Every male of Aaron's descendants may eat of it perpetually throughout your generations as their rightful due from the oblations for the LORD. Whatever touches the oblations becomes holy.

High Priest's Daily Grain Offering†

12 The LORD said to Moses: 13 This is the offering that Aaron and his sons shall present to the LORD on the day he is anointed: one tenth of an ephah of bran flour for the regular grain offering, half of it in the morning and half of it in the evening. 14 You shall bring it well kneaded and fried in oil on a griddle.* Having broken the offering into pieces, you shall present it as a sweet aroma to the LORD. 15 The anointed priest descended from Aaron who succeeds him shall do likewise. This is the LORD's due forever. The offering shall be wholly burned.* 16 Every grain offering of a priest shall be a whole offering; it may not be eaten.

Purification Offerings†

17 The LORD said to Moses: 18 * Tell Aaron and his sons: This is the ritual for the purification offering. At the place where the burnt offering is slaughtered, there also, before the LORD, shall the purification offering be slaughtered. It is most holy.* 19 The priest who offers the purification offering shall eat of it; it shall be eaten in a sacred place,* in the court of the tent of meeting. 20 Whatever touches its flesh becomes holy. If any of its blood spatters on a garment, the stained part must be washed in a sacred place. 21 A clay vessel in which it has been boiled shall be broken; if it is boiled in a copper vessel, this shall be scoured afterward and rinsed with water.* 22 Every male of the priestly line may eat it. It is most holy. 23 But no purification offering of which some blood has been brought into the tent of meeting* to make atonement in the sanctuary shall be eaten; it must be burned with fire.*

Reparation Offerings

7 1 †* This is the ritual for the reparation offering. It is most holy. 2 At the place where the burnt offering is slaughtered, the reparation offering shall also be slaughtered.* Its blood shall be splashed on all the sides of the altar. 3 * All of its fat shall be offered: the fatty tail, the fat that covers the inner organs, and all the fat that adheres to them, 4 as well as the two kidneys with the fat on them near the loins, and the lobe of the liver, which is removed with the kidneys. 5 The priest shall burn these on the altar as an oblation to the LORD. It is a reparation offering. 6 Every male of the priestly line may eat of it; but it must be eaten in a sacred place.* It is most holy.*

7 Because the purification offering and the reparation offering are alike, both have the same ritual. The reparation offering belongs to the priest who makes atonement with it. 8 As for the priest who offers someone's burnt offering, to him belongs the hide of the burnt offering that is offered. 9 † * Also, every grain offering that is baked in an oven or made in a pan or on a griddle shall belong to the priest who offers it, 10 whereas all grain offerings* that are mixed with oil or are dry shall belong to all of Aaron's sons without distinction.

Communion Sacrifices†

11 * This is the ritual for the communion sacrifice that is offered to the LORD. 12 † If someone

---

† **6:12–16** This seems to refer to a grain offering offered twice daily by the high priest, perhaps identical to the regular grain offering in Nm 4:16 (cf. Neh 10:34). This offering is distinct from the grain offering that accompanies the daily burnt offering.

6:17–23 There are two types of purification offering: one whose blood is used inside the tent sanctuary (4:1–12, 13–21) and another whose blood was only used at the outer sacrificial altar (4:22–26, 27–31, 32–35). The carcasses of the former, as well as of purification offerings brought by the priests themselves (cf. 8:14–17; 9:8–11), are not eaten by priests but disposed of at the ash heap outside the camp, which itself is set up around the sanctuary (Ex 29:14; Lv 4:11–12, 21; 6:23; 8:17; 9:11; 16:27). The Letter to the Hebrews compares Jesus' suffering "outside the gate" to the disposal of purification offering carcasses outside the camp (Heb 13:11–13).

7:1–6 These prescriptions may appear here rather than in 5:14–26 where this offering is first treated because the monetary equivalent of the offering might have been brought instead of an actual animal. See note on 5:15.

7:9–10 For the distinction between uncooked and cooked grain offerings, see 2:1–10 and note on 2:1. The contradiction between v. 9 and 2:10 may reflect a development in custom, with the distribution in v. 9 coming from earlier times, when sanctuary personnel was more limited.

7:11–36 This section discusses three types of communion sacrifice: the thanksgiving offering (vv. 12–15), a votive offering, and a voluntary offering (vv. 16–18). The latter two are similar and are thus mentioned together. Verses 19–36 apply to all types of communion sacrifice.

7:12–13 Four types of breads accompany the thanksgiving offering. Three types are cooked grain offerings comparable to those in 2:4–10. Also required are loaves of leavened bread (see 2:11).

---

* **6:9** Lv 6:19; 7:6; 10:13, 17; 24:9.
6:10 Lv 2:3.
6:14 Lv 2:5.
6:15 Lv 2:9.
6:18 Lv 4:1–5:13.
6:18 Lv 2:3.
6:19 Lv 6:9.
6:21 Lv 11:32–33; 15:12.
6:23 Lv 4:5; Heb 13:11.
6:23 Lv 4:11–12, 21; 8:17; 9:11; 16:27.
7:1 Lv 5:14–26.
7:2 Lv 6:18.
7:3 Lv 3:4.
7:6 Lv 6:9.
7:6 Lv 2:3.
7:9 Lv 2:3–10; Nm 18:9; Ez 44:29.
7:10 Lv 2:14–15.
7:11 Lv 3.

offers it for thanksgiving, that person shall offer it with unleavened cakes mixed with oil, unleavened wafers spread with oil, and cakes made of bran flour mixed with oil and well kneaded. 13 One shall present this offering together with loaves of leavened bread along with the thanksgiving communion sacrifice. 14 From this the individual shall offer one bread of each type of offering as a contribution† to the LORD; this shall belong to the priest who splashes the blood of the communion offering.

15 †* The meat of the thanksgiving communion sacrifice shall be eaten on the day it is offered; none of it may be kept till the next morning.* 16 However, if the sacrifice offered is a votive or a voluntary offering,† it shall be eaten on the day the sacrifice is offered, and on the next day what is left over may be eaten.* 17 But what is left over of the meat of the sacrifice on the third day must be burned in the fire. 18 If indeed any of the flesh of the communion sacrifice is eaten on the third day, it shall not be accepted; it will not be reckoned to the credit of the one offering it. Rather it becomes a desecrated meat. Anyone who eats of it shall bear the penalty.†

19 † Should the meat touch anything unclean, it may not be eaten, but shall be burned in the fire.* As for other meat, all who are clean may eat of it. 20 If, however, someone in a state of uncleanness eats the meat of a communion sacrifice belonging to the LORD, that person shall be cut off†* from the people. 21 Likewise, if someone touches anything unclean, whether it be human uncleanness or an unclean animal or an unclean loathsome creature, and then eats the meat of the communion sacrifice belonging to the LORD, that person, too, shall be cut off from the people.

Prohibition Against Blood and Fat

22 The LORD said to Moses: 23 Tell the Israelites: You shall not eat the fat of any ox or sheep or goat.* 24 Although the fat of an animal that has died a natural death or has been killed by wild beasts may be put to any other use, you may not eat it.* 25 If anyone eats the fat of an animal from which an oblation is made to the LORD, that person shall be cut off from the people. 26 * Wherever you dwell, you shall not eat any blood, whether of bird or of animal. 27 Every person who eats any blood shall be cut off from the people.

Portions from the Communion Sacrifice for Priests

28 The LORD said to Moses: 29 Tell the Israelites: The person who offers a communion sacrifice to the LORD shall be the one to bring from it the offering to the LORD. 30 The offerer's own hands shall carry the oblations for the LORD: the person shall bring the fat together with the brisket, which is to be raised as an elevated* offering† before the LORD. 31 The priest shall burn the fat on the altar,* but the brisket belongs to Aaron and his sons. 32 Moreover, from your communion sacrifices you shall give to the priest the right leg as a contribution. 33 The one among Aaron's sons who offers the blood and the fat of the communion offering shall have the right leg as his portion, 34 for from the communion sacrifices of the Israelites I have taken the brisket that is elevated and the leg that is a contribution, and I have given them to Aaron, the priest, and to his sons as their due from the Israelites forever.*

35 This is the priestly share from the oblations for the LORD, allotted to Aaron and his sons on the day they were brought forth to be the priests of the LORD, 36 which the LORD ordered to be given them from the Israelites on the day they were anointed, as their due throughout their generations forever.

Summary

37 This is the ritual for the burnt offering, the grain offering, the purification offering, the

L
V

†

7:14 *Contribution*: Hebrew *terumah*. This does not indicate a particular ritual action. The word simply means "gift, something set apart."

7:15–18 Sacrifices must be properly consumed for them to be effective (cf. also 19:5–8; 22:30). Similar rules obtain for the Passover offering (Ex 12:10; Nm 9:12; cf. Ex 23:18; 34:25; Dt 16:4) and the ordination offering (Ex 29:34; Lv 8:32).

7:16 *Votive or a voluntary offering*: these are not specific types of offerings but rather motivations for bringing the communion sacrifice (cf. 22:18). A votive offering is brought as the consequence of a promise (vow) made to God. A voluntary offering is a spontaneous gift to God independent of a prior promise. See note on 27:2–13.

7:18 *Bear the penalty*: this refers in many cases to punishment by God (cf. 17:16; 19:8; 20:17, 19; Nm 18:1, 23; 30:16).

7:19–21 For ritual impurity, see note on 11:1–15:33.

7:20 *Cut off*: a common term in the Priestly source that cannot always be reduced to a simple English equivalent, since its usage appears to involve a number of associated punishments, some or all of which may come into play in any one instance (see Ex 12:15 and note). All the same, as a punishment from God, to be "cut off" (from one's people) frequently appears to refer to termination of the offender's family line (and perhaps in some cases an early death); see Lv 20:2–3, 20–21; Ru 4:10; Ps 109:13; Mal 2:12.

7:30 *Raised as an elevated offering*: these portions of the sacrifices were specially dedicated by lifting them in presentation before God's abode. The sanctifying effect of this action is clearly seen in 23:17–20; Nm 6:19–20.

*

7:15 Lv 19:6–7.
7:15 Lv 22:29–30.
7:16 Lv 19:5–8.
7:19 Lv 12:4.
7:20 Lv 17:4, 9–10, 14; 18:29; 20:3, 5–6, 17–18; Gn 17:14; Ex 30:33; Nm 15:31; Ps 37:9, 28, 34; 109:13.
7:23 Lv 3:17.
7:24 Lv 22:8.
7:26 Lv 17:10.
7:30 Lv 8:27, 29; 9:21; 10:15; 14:12, 21, 24; 23:17, 20; Nm 6:20; 8:13; 18:18.
7:31 Lv 3:11, 16.
7:34 Ex 29:27–28.

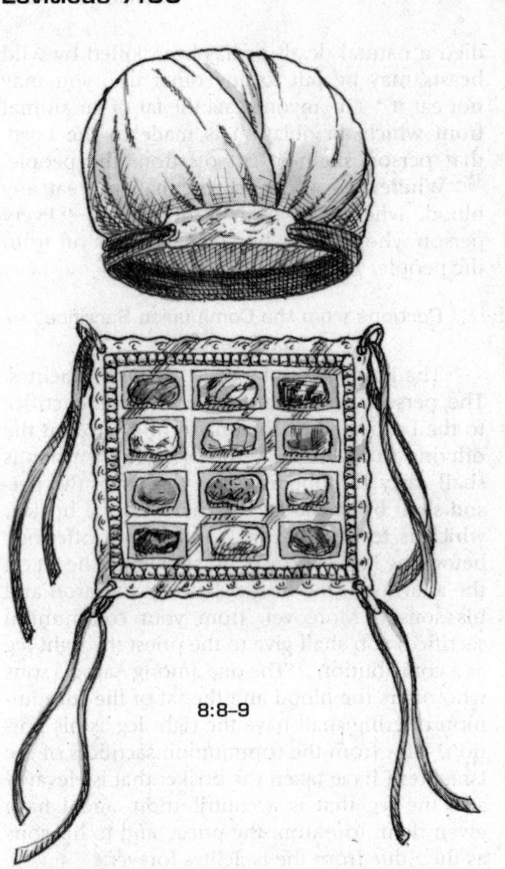

8:8–9

reparation offering, the ordination offering,* and
the communion sacrifice, 38 which the LORD en-
joined on Moses at Mount Sinai at the time when
he commanded the Israelites in the wilderness of
Sinai to bring their offerings to the LORD.*

II. Ceremony of Ordination

Ordination of Aaron and His Sons†

8 1 * The LORD said to Moses: 2 Take Aaron along
with his sons, the vestments, the anointing
oil, the bull for a purification offering, the two
rams, and the basket of unleavened bread, 3 then
assemble the whole community† at the entrance
of the tent of meeting. 4 Moses did as the LORD had
commanded. When the community* had assem-
bled at the entrance of the tent of meeting, 5 Moses
told them: "This is what the LORD has ordered to
be done." 6 Bringing forward Aaron and his sons,
Moses first washed them with water. 7 † Then he
put the tunic on Aaron,* girded him with the
sash, clothed him with the robe, placed the ephod
on him, and girded him with the ephod's embroi-
dered belt, fastening the ephod on him with it.
8 He then set the breastpiece on him, putting the
Urim and Thummim† in it. 9 He put the turban
on his head, attaching the gold medallion, the
sacred headband,† on the front of the turban, as
the LORD had commanded Moses to do.
10 † Taking the anointing oil, Moses anointed
and consecrated the tabernacle and all that was
in it.* 11 Then he sprinkled some of the oil seven
times on the altar, and anointed the altar, with
all its utensils, and the laver, with its base, to
consecrate them. 12 He also poured some of the
anointing oil on Aaron's head and anointed him,
to consecrate him.* 13 Moses likewise brought
forward Aaron's sons, clothed them with tunics,
girded them with sashes, and put skullcaps on
them, as the LORD had commanded him to do.

Ordination Sacrifices

14 He brought forward the bull for a purifica-
tion offering, and Aaron and his sons laid their
hands on its head. 15 When it was slaughtered,
Moses took the blood† and with his finger he put
it on the horns around the altar, thus purifying
the altar.* He poured out the rest of the blood
at the base of the altar. Thus he consecrated it so
that atonement could be made on it. 16 Taking
all the fat that was over the inner organs, as well
as the lobe of the liver and the two kidneys with
their fat,* Moses burned them on the altar. 17 The
bull, however, with its hide and flesh and dung
he burned in the fire outside the camp, as the
LORD had commanded Moses to do.*

†

8:1–2 This chapter presents the fulfillment of the commands in Ex 28–29; 30:26–30; and 40:9–15.

8:3–4 *Community*: this word (Heb. *'edah*) may refer to tribal leaders, all adult males, or the entire nation. The last is probably intended here.

8:7–9, 13 On the priestly clothing, see Ex 28–29. *Ephod*: according to Ex 28:6–14, the term for one of Aaron's special vestments made of gold thread, with multicolored woolen thread woven into it as well as fine linen. In appearance it resembled a kind of apron, hung on the priest by shoulder straps and secured by an embroidered belt. A somewhat simpler "apron" was presumably worn by other priests (1 Sm 22:18).

8:8 *The Urim and Thummim*: see Ex 28:30 and note there. Although these terms and the object(s) they refer to are still unexplained, they appear to be small objects that functioned like dice or lots to render a decision for those making an inquiry of God, perhaps originally in legal cases where the guilt of the accused could not otherwise be determined (cf. Ex 28:30; Nm 27:21; Dt 33:8; 1 Sm 28:6; Ezr 2:63; Neh 7:65).

8:9 *Headband*: see Ex 39:30–31. The gold medallion, together with its cords, comprises the sacred headband.

8:10–12 Anointing with the specially prepared oil (cf. Ex 30:22–33) is one of the means of making objects and persons holy by setting them apart for a special function or purpose.

8:15 *Moses took the blood*: Moses is acting as a priest in this chapter.

*

7:37 Lv 8:22.
7:38 Lv 26:46; 27:34.
8:1 Cf. Ex 28–29; 39; 40:12–15.
8:4 Nm 27:19.
8:7–9 Sir 45:8–13; Heb 5:1–4; 7:1–28.
8:10 Ex 30:26.
8:12 Sir 45:15.
8:15 Heb 9:22.
8:16–17 Lv 3:4–5; 4:8–11.
8:17 Lv 6:23.

18 He next brought forward the ram of the burnt offering,* and Aaron and his sons laid their hands on its head. 19 When it was slaughtered, Moses splashed the blood on all sides of the altar. 20 After the ram was cut up into pieces, Moses burned the head, the cut-up pieces and the suet. 21 After the inner organs and the shanks were washed with water, Moses burned these remaining parts of the ram on the altar. It was a burnt offering for a sweet aroma, an oblation to the LORD, as the LORD had commanded Moses.

22 † Then he brought forward the second ram, the ordination ram,* and Aaron and his sons laid their hands on its head. 23 When it was slaughtered, Moses took some of its blood and put it on the lobe of Aaron's right ear, on the thumb of his right hand, and on the big toe† of his right foot.* 24 Moses had the sons of Aaron also come forward, and he put some of the blood on the lobes of their right ears, on the thumbs of their right hands, and on the big toes of their right feet. The rest of the blood he splashed on all the sides of the altar. 25 He then took the fat: the fatty tail and all the fat over the inner organs, the lobe of the liver and the two kidneys with their fat, and likewise the right thigh; 26 from the basket of unleavened bread that was set before the LORD he took one unleavened cake, one loaf of bread made with oil, and one wafer; these he placed on top of the portions of fat and the right thigh. 27 He then put all these things upon the palms of Aaron and his sons, whom he had raise them as an elevated offering before the LORD.* 28 When Moses had removed them from their palms, he burned them on the altar with the burnt offering. They were an ordination offering for a sweet aroma, an oblation to the LORD. 29 He then took the brisket and raised it as an elevated offering before the LORD; this was Moses' own portion of the ordination ram, as the LORD had commanded Moses. 30 Taking some of the anointing oil and some of the blood that was on the altar, Moses sprinkled it upon Aaron and his vestments, as well as his sons and their vestments, thus consecrating both Aaron and his vestments and his sons and their vestments.*

31 Moses said to Aaron and his sons, "Boil the meat at the entrance of the tent of meeting, and there eat it with the bread that is in the basket of the ordination offering, in keeping with the command I have received: 'Aaron and his sons shall eat of it.' 32 What is left over of the meat and the bread you shall burn in the fire. 33 Moreover, you are not to depart† from the entrance of the tent of meeting for seven days, until the days of your ordination are completed; for your ordination is to last for seven days. 34 What has been done today the LORD has commanded be done, to make atonement for you. 35 You must remain at the entrance of the tent of meeting day and night for seven days, carrying out the prescriptions of the LORD, so that you do not die, for this is the command I have received."* 36 So Aaron and his sons did all that the LORD had commanded through Moses.

Octave of the Ordination

9 1 On the eighth day†* Moses summoned Aaron and his sons, together with the elders of Israel, 2 and said to Aaron, "Take a calf of the herd for a purification offering and a ram for a burnt offering, both without blemish, and offer them before the LORD. 3 † Tell the Israelites, too: Take a he-goat for a purification offering, a calf and a lamb, both unblemished yearlings, for a burnt offering, 4 and an ox and a ram for a communion sacrifice, to sacrifice before the LORD, along with a grain offering mixed with oil; for today the LORD will appear to you." 5 So they brought what Moses had ordered before the tent of meeting. When the whole community had come forward and stood before the LORD, 6 † Moses said, "This is what the LORD orders you to do, that the glory of the LORD may appear to you. 7 Approach the altar," Moses then told Aaron, "and make your purification offering and your burnt offering in atonement for yourself and for your household;† then make the offering of the people in atonement for them, as the LORD has commanded."*

8 Approaching the altar, Aaron first slaughtered

---

† **8:22–32** The priestly ordination offering is a unique type of sacrifice but similar in many respects to the communion sacrifice (chap. 3; 7:11–34).

8:23–24 *Lobe . . . thumb . . . toe*: these parts of the body are meant to represent the body as a whole. The application of the blood symbolizes the priests' passing from a profane to a holy state. Cf. 14:14–17.

8:33–35 *You are not to depart*: the tenor and context of this requirement in vv. 33 and 35 seem to indicate that the priests are not to leave the sanctuary precincts for any reason. *Your ordination is to last for seven days . . . what has been done today . . . be done*: the consecration rites in Exodus are to be performed every day for seven days (cf. Ex 29:30, 35–37).

9:1 *Eighth day*: this is the conclusion of the priestly initiation ceremony.

9:3–4 The seven-day consecration of the priests in chap. 8 did not require sacrifices from the community. Now communal sacrifices as well as priestly sacrifices are required.

9:6–21 Aaron and his sons now perform the offerings, instead of Moses (see note on 8:15).

9:7 *For your household*: unlike the Septuagint, the Hebrew reads *be'ad ha'am*, "for the people."

---

* **8:18** Lv 1:10–13.
8:22 Lv 7:37.
8:23 Lv 14:14, 17.
8:27 Lv 7:30.
8:30 Ex 40:15.
8:35 Lv 10:7.
9:1 Lv 8:33.
9:7 Lv 16:3–5.

the calf of the purification offering that was his own offering. 9 When his sons presented the blood to him, he dipped his finger in the blood and put it on the horns of the altar.* The rest of the blood he poured out at the base of the altar. 10 He then burned on the altar the fat, the kidneys and the lobe of the liver from the purification offering, as the LORD had commanded Moses; 11 but the flesh and the hide he burned in the fire outside the camp.* 12 Then Aaron slaughtered the burnt offering. When his sons brought him the blood, he splashed it on all sides of the altar. 13 They then brought him the pieces and the head of the burnt offering, and he burned them on the altar. 14 Having washed the inner organs and the shanks, he burned these also with the burnt offering on the altar.*

15 Then he had the people's offering brought. Taking the goat that was for the people's purification offering, he slaughtered it and offered it as a purification offering as before. 16 Then he brought forward the burnt offering and offered it according to procedure. 17 He then presented the grain offering; taking a handful of it, he burned it on the altar, in addition to the morning burnt offering.* 18 Finally he slaughtered the ox and the ram, the communion sacrifice of the people. When his sons brought him the blood, Aaron splashed it on all sides of the altar.* 19 The portions of fat from the ox and from the ram, the fatty tail, the covering fat, the kidneys, and the lobe of the liver 20 they placed on top of the briskets. Aaron burned the fat pieces on the altar, 21 but the briskets and the right thigh he raised as an elevated offering* before the LORD, as the LORD had commanded Moses.

Revelation of the Lord's Glory

22 † Aaron then raised his hands over the people and blessed* them. When he came down from offering the purification offering, the burnt offering, and the communion offering, 23 Moses and Aaron went into the tent of meeting. On coming out they blessed the people. Then the glory of the LORD appeared to all the people. 24 † Fire came forth from the LORD's presence and consumed the burnt offering and the fat on the altar.* Seeing this, all the people shouted with joy and fell prostrate.

Nadab and Abihu

10 1 † Aaron's sons Nadab and Abihu took their censers and, putting incense on the fire they had set in them,* they offered before the LORD unauthorized fire, such as he had not commanded. 2 Fire therefore came forth from the LORD's presence and consumed them,* so that they died in the LORD's presence. 3 Moses then said to Aaron, "This is as the LORD said:

Through those near to me I will be sanctified;
in the sight of all the people I will obtain glory."† *

But Aaron said nothing. 4 † Then Moses summoned Mishael and Elzaphan, the sons of Aaron's uncle Uzziel, with the order, "Come, carry your kinsmen from before the sanctuary to a place outside the camp." 5 So they drew near and carried them by means of their tunics outside the camp, as Moses had commanded.

Conduct of the Priests

6 Moses said to Aaron and his sons Eleazar and Ithamar, "Do not dishevel your hair* or tear your garments,* lest you die and bring God's wrath also on the whole community. While your kindred, the rest of the house of Israel, may mourn for those whom the LORD's fire has burned up, 7 you shall not go beyond the entrance of the tent of meeting,* else you shall die; for the anointing oil of the LORD is upon you." So they did as Moses told them.

8 The LORD said to Aaron: 9 When you are to go to the tent of meeting, you and your sons are forbidden, by a perpetual statute throughout your generations, to drink any wine or strong drink, lest you die.* 10 You must be able to distinguish between what is sacred and what is profane, and

---

9:22–23 The people are blessed twice. For the possible content of the blessing, compare the priestly blessing in Nm 6:22–27. Solomon offers a double blessing at the dedication of the Temple (1 Kgs 8:14–21, 55–61).

9:24 The theophany consists of a fire that apparently comes from the tent of meeting. God's fiery glory is also manifested in the pillar of cloud and fire that led the Israelites and rested over the tent of meeting (Ex 13:21; 40:38; Nm 9:15–23; 10:11). On God's fiery glory, see also Ex 24:17; Ez 1:27–28.

10:1–2 Nadab and Abihu are the older sons of Aaron (Ex 6:23–24). Their sin apparently involves using embers from an unapproved source instead of the altar (cf. 16:12). The fire that destroys them is the same type found in 9:24.

10:3 The explanation for the divine reaction indicates that improper cultic actions desecrate God and compromise God's glory. Desecration evokes divine punishment (cf. Ex 28:43; Nm 4:15, 19–20). *Those near to me*: i.e., cultic officials.

10:4–5 Moses has lay people remove the bodies so that the priests can continue their cultic activities free of contamination by a corpse (cf. Nm 19).

9:9 Lv 4:25, 30, 34.
9:11 Lv 6:23.
9:14 Lv 1:5–9.
9:17 Nm 28:23; 2 Kgs 16:15; Ez 46:13–15.
9:18 Lv 3:2.
9:21 Lv 7:30–34.
9:22 Nm 6:22–27.
9:24 1 Kgs 18:38; 2 Chr 7:1; 2 Mc 2:10; cf. Ex 24:16–17.
10:1 Lv 16:1; Nm 3:4; 26:61; 1 Chr 24:2.
10:2 Nm 16:35; cf. Lv 9:24.
10:3 Lv 21:17, 21; Nm 20:12.
10:6 Lv 13:45.
10:6 Lv 21:5–6, 10–12.
10:7 Lv 8:33–35; 21:12.
10:9 Ez 44:21.

between what is clean and what is unclean;† * [11]and you must be able to teach the Israelites all the statutes that the LORD has given them through Moses.

The Eating of the Priestly Portions

[12]Moses said to Aaron and his surviving sons, Eleazar and Ithamar, "Take the grain offering† left over from the oblations to the LORD, and eat it beside the altar in the form of unleavened cakes, since it is most holy. [13]You must eat it in a sacred place because it is your and your sons' due from the oblations to the LORD; such is the command I have received. [14]* The brisket of the elevated offering and the leg† of the contribution, however, you and your sons and daughters may eat, in a clean place; for these have been assigned to you and your children as your due from the communion sacrifices of the Israelites. [15]The leg of the contribution and the brisket of the elevated offering shall be brought in with the oblations of fat to be raised as an elevated offering before the LORD. They shall belong to you and your children as your due forever, as the LORD has commanded."

[16]Moses inquired closely about the goat of the purification offering† and discovered that it had all been burned. So he was angry with the surviving sons of Aaron, Eleazar and Ithamar, and said, [17]* "Why did you not eat the purification offering in the sacred place, since it is most holy? It has been given to you that you might remove the guilt of the community and make atonement for them before the LORD. [18]Since its blood was not brought inside the sanctuary, you should certainly have eaten the offering in the sanctuary, as I was commanded." [19]Aaron answered Moses, "Even though they presented their purification offering and burnt offering before the LORD today, still this misfortune has befallen me. Had I then eaten of the purification offering today, would it have been pleasing to the LORD?" [20]On hearing this, Moses was satisfied.

III. Laws Regarding Ritual Purity†

Clean and Unclean Meats†

11 [1]* The LORD said to Moses and Aaron: [2]Speak to the Israelites and tell them: Of all land animals these are the ones you may eat: [3]Any animal that has hoofs you may eat, provided it is cloven-footed and chews the cud. [4]But you shall not eat* any of the following from among those that only chew the cud or only have hoofs: the camel, which indeed chews the cud, but does not have hoofs and is therefore unclean for you; [5]the rock hyrax,† which indeed chews the cud, but does not have hoofs and is therefore unclean for you; [6]the hare, which indeed chews the cud, but does not have hoofs and is therefore unclean for you; [7]and the pig,* which does indeed have hoofs and is cloven-footed, but does not chew the cud and is therefore unclean for you. [8]You shall not eat their meat, and you shall not touch their carcasses; they are unclean for you.

[9]Of the various creatures that live in the water, you may eat the following: whatever in the seas or in river waters that has both fins and scales you may eat.* [10]But of the creatures that swarm in the water or of animals that otherwise live in the water, whether in the sea or in the rivers, all those that lack either fins or scales are loathsome for you, [11]and shall always be loathsome to you. Their meat you shall not eat, and their carcasses

†

10:10 *Sacred and . . . profane . . . clean and . . . unclean*: something or someone may be either sacred or profane (i.e., ordinary, not set apart), and at the same time clean or unclean. Priests would be particularly concerned about keeping what is unclean away from the sacred.

10:12–13 *Grain offering*: this is the grain offering of the people of 9:4, 17. Only the token offering had been offered; the rest was for the priests' consumption.

10:14 *Brisket . . . leg*: these are from the Israelites' communion sacrifices in 9:4, 18–21.

10:16–20 *Goat of the purification offering*: this is the people's purification offering of 9:3, 15. Since its blood is not brought into the sanctuary, then, according to 6:17–23, this is the type of purification offering which is to be eaten by the priests in a holy place. *Eleazar and Ithamar*: they burned the entire goat of the people's purification offering (9:15) instead of eating it in a sacred place (6:19) to remove ritually the sin of the community by the ingestion of the meat of the offering. Aaron's defense of this action of his sons is somewhat vague: he merely alludes to the loss suffered in the death of Nadab and Abihu, without giving an explicit reason for Eleazar and Ithamar's not eating the people's purification offering, as required.

11:1–15:33 Priestly legislation manifests two types of impurity or uncleanness: tolerated and prohibited. Prohibited impurity arises from various sins (e.g., 4:1–5; 5:2–3; 18:6–23; 20:2–5; Nm 5:13–14; 6:6–7). Tolerated impurity has three main sources: certain dead bodies (animal and human; cf. Lv 11 and Nm 19), various regular and abnormal genital discharges (Lv 12; 15), and diseases (specifically "scaly infection," chaps. 13–14). An additional tolerated impurity is that generated by the cult in order to rectify the effect of these impurities or sins (cf. chap. 4; 16:26, 28).

11:1–47 Apart from the introduction and conclusion (vv. 1–2a, 46–47), this chapter has three sections: (1) prohibitions against eating certain land, water, and air animals (vv. 2b–23); (2) consequences of contact with various animals (vv. 24–41); (3) a prohibition against eating small land animals, which is motivated by the requirement that Israel be holy as God is holy (vv. 41–45). These animals are impure only when dead. Cf. Dt 14:3–21.

11:5–6 According to modern zoology, *the rock hyrax* (*Hyrax syriacus*) is classified as an ungulate, and *the hare* as a rodent; neither is a ruminant. They appear to chew their food as the true ruminants do, and it is upon this appearance that the classification in the text is based.

*

10:10 Lv 11:47; 20:25; Ez 22:26; 44:23.
10:14 Lv 7:34.
10:17 Lv 6:18–19.
11:1 Lv 27:11, 27; Gn 7:2–3, 8–9; Dt 14:3–21.
11:4 Jgs 13:4, 7; Is 66:17; Ez 4:12–14.
11:7 Prv 11:22; Is 65:4; 66:17; Mt 7:6; 8:30–32; Mk 5:11–16; Lk 8:32–33; 15:15–16.
11:9 Jn 21:9–13.

you shall loathe. [12] Every water creature that lacks
fins or scales is loathsome for you.
[13] Of the birds,† these you shall loathe; they
shall not be eaten, they are loathsome: the
griffon vulture, the bearded vulture, the black
vulture, [14] the kite, the various species of fal-
cons, [15] the various species of crows, [16] the eagle
owl, the kestrel, the long-eared owl, the various
species of hawks, [17] the little owl, the cormorant,
the screech owl, [18] the barn owl, the horned owl,
the osprey, [19] the stork, the various species of her-
ons, the hoopoe, and the bat.
[20] The various winged insects that walk on all
fours are loathsome for you. [21] But of the various
winged insects that walk on all fours you may eat
those that have legs jointed above their feet for
leaping on the ground; [22] hence of these you may
eat the following: the various kinds of locusts,
the various kinds of bald locusts, the various
kinds of crickets, and the various kinds of grass-
hoppers.* [23] All other winged insects that have
four legs are loathsome for you.
[24] You become unclean by the following—any-
one who touches their carcasses shall be unclean
until evening,* [25] and anyone who carries any part
of their carcasses shall wash his garments and be
unclean until evening— [26] by all hoofed animals
that are not cloven-footed or do not chew the cud;
they are unclean for you; anyone who touches
them becomes unclean. [27] Also by the various
quadrupeds that walk on paws; they are unclean
for you; anyone who touches their carcasses shall
be unclean until evening, [28] and anyone who car-
ries their carcasses shall wash his garments and be
unclean until evening. They are unclean for you.
[29] Of the creatures that swarm on the ground,
the following are unclean for you: the rat, the
mouse, the various kinds of lizards, [30] the gecko,
the spotted lizard, the agama, the skink, and
the chameleon. [31] Among the various swarming
creatures, these are unclean for you. Everyone
who touches them when they are dead shall be
unclean until evening. [32] Everything on which
one of them falls when dead becomes unclean,
including any article of wood, cloth, leather or
goat hair—any article of which use can be made.
It must be immersed in water and remain un-
clean until evening, when it again becomes clean.
[33] Should any of these creatures fall into a clay
vessel, everything in it becomes unclean, and the
vessel itself you must break. [34] Any food that can
be eaten which makes contact with water, and
any liquid that may be drunk, in any such vessel
become unclean. [35] Any object on which any part
of their carcasses falls becomes unclean; if it is an
oven or stove, this must be broken to pieces; they
are unclean and shall always be unclean to you.
[36] However, a spring or a cistern for collecting

Did You Know?

The Israelite Diet

The diet of the ancient Israelites consisted mainly of breads, cereals, fruits, vegetables, and dairy products. Meat was served only on special occasions because it was expensive. A typical family meal was made up of barley or wheat bread, grapes, figs, olive oil, beans, cucumbers, onions, and cheese. On festive occasions, beef or lamb might grace the table.

The laws in Leviticus, chapter 11, contain many restrictions regarding the eating of animals. The reasons for these restrictions are not clear, although many scholars believe one purpose was to keep the Israelites from consuming animals used in pagan worship (for example, the pig offered in Babylonian services). Hygiene was likely another consideration.

The basic "meat laws" were as follows:

- Of the larger animals, those that chewed their cud and had split hooves could be eaten. Therefore, lamb was acceptable, but pork was not.
- Sea creatures only with both fins and scales could be eaten. Thus, catfish and eels were to be avoided.
- Eagles, vultures, buzzards, and many other birds were excluded from the table.
- Rodents, reptiles, and insects (except locusts and grasshoppers) were spurned altogether.
- The blood from all animals had to be drained completely before cooking because blood was seen as the life force and therefore as belonging to God alone.
- It was unlawful to touch or eat any animal found dead; contact with any dead body made one impure.

▶ Lv 11:1–47

LV

† **11:13–23, 30** *Birds*: the term is broader, including all animals that fly (including bats, v. 19, and flying insects, vv. 20–23). The identification of the various Hebrew names for these birds and reptiles is in many cases uncertain.

* **11:22** Mt 3:4; Mk 1:6. **11:24** Lv 5:2; 7:21.

Cultural Connection

A Mother's Prayer at Childbirth

Sun, moon, stars,
you that move in the heavens,
hear this mother!
A new life has come among you.
Make its path smooth that it may reach
the brow of the first hill.

Winds, clouds, rain, mist,
all that move in the air,
hear this mother!
A new life has come among you.
Make its path smooth that it may reach
the brow of the second hill.

Hills, valleys, rivers, lakes, trees, grasses,
all of the earth, hear this mother!
A new life has come among you.
Make its path smooth that it may reach
the brow of the third hill.

Birds that fly in the air,
animals that dwell in the forest,
insects that creep in the grasses and burrow in
the ground,
hear this mother!
A new life has come among you.
Make its path smooth that it may reach
the brow of the fourth hill.
All the heavens, air and earth,
hear this mother!
A new life has come among you.
Make its path smooth—then shall it travel
beyond the four hills!

Like the Israelites, with their purification ritual described in Leviticus, chapter 12, most cultures have rituals and prayers associated with childbirth. In this mother's prayer of the Omaha tribe, the four hills refer to the four parts of human life—childhood, youth, adulthood, and old age. What a wonderful reminder that life is a journey and that all creation is invited to celebrate new life!

▶ Lv 12:1–8

water remains clean; but whoever touches such an
animal's carcass becomes unclean. 37 If any part of
their carcasses falls on any sort of grain that is to
be sown, it remains clean; 38 but if the grain has
become moistened, it becomes unclean to you
when any part of their carcasses falls on it.
39 † * When one of the animals that you could
otherwise eat dies of itself, anyone who touches
its carcass shall be unclean until evening; 40 and
anyone who eats any part of its carcass shall wash
his garments and be unclean until evening;* so
also, anyone who carries its carcass shall wash
his garments and be unclean until evening.
41 All the creatures that swarm on the ground
are loathsome and shall not be eaten. 42 Whether
it crawls on its belly, goes on all fours, or has
many legs—any creature that swarms on the
earth—you shall not eat them; they are loath-
some. 43 Do not make yourselves loathsome by
any swarming creature nor defile yourselves with
them and so become unclean by them.* 44 For
I, the LORD, am your God. You shall make and
keep yourselves holy,† because I am holy.* You
shall not make yourselves unclean, then, by any
swarming creature that crawls on the ground.
45 Since I, the LORD, am the one who brought you
up from the land of Egypt that I might be your
God, you shall be holy, because I am holy.
46 This is the instruction for land animals, birds,
and all the creatures that move about in the wa-
ter, as well as any animal that swarms on the
ground, 47 that you may distinguish between the
clean and the unclean, and between creatures that
may be eaten and those that may not be eaten.*

Uncleanness of Childbirth

12 1 The LORD said to Moses: 2 Tell the Israel-
ites: When a woman has a child, giving

†

11:39–40 These animals create uncleanness, but are not prohibited as food (cf. 17:15–16). Priests who have a higher degree of holiness than other Israelites may not eat these animals (22:8; cf. Ez 44:31). Cf. Ex 22:30; Dt 14:21.

11:44–45 *Keep yourselves holy . . . you shall be holy*: a similar idea is expressed in 20:25–26. There, distinguishing between the animals is compared to God's distinguishing between the peoples and choosing Israel.

*

11:39 Lv 17:15–16; 22:8; Ex 22:30; Ez 4:12–14; 44:31.
11:40 Lv 17:15; 22:8.
11:43–44 Lv 20:25–26.
11:44 Lv 19:2; 20:7, 26; Mt 5:48; 1 Pt 1:16.
11:47 Lv 10:10.

birth to a boy, she shall be unclean† for seven
days, with the same uncleanness as during her
menstrual period.* 3 On the eighth day, the flesh
of the boy's foreskin shall be circumcised,†*
4 and then she shall spend thirty-three days more
in a state of blood purity; she shall not touch
anything sacred nor enter the sanctuary till the
days of her purification are fulfilled. 5 If she gives
birth to a girl, for fourteen days she shall be as
unclean as during her menstrual period, after
which she shall spend sixty-six days† in a state
of blood purity.

6 † When the days of her purification for a son
or for a daughter are fulfilled,* she shall bring to
the priest at the entrance of the tent of meeting a
yearling lamb for a burnt offering and a pigeon
or a turtledove for a purification offering. 7 The
priest shall offer them before the LORD to make
atonement for her, and thus she will be clean
again after her flow of blood. Such is the ritual
for the woman who gives birth to a child, male or
female. 8 If, however, she cannot afford a lamb,*
she may take two turtledoves or two pigeons,*
the one for a burnt offering and the other for a
purification offering. The priest shall make atone-
ment for her, and thus she will again be clean.

LV

Scaly Infection†

13 1 The LORD said to Moses and Aaron:
2 * When someone has on the skin a mark,
lesion, or blotch which appears to develop into
a scaly infection, the person shall be brought to
Aaron, the priest, or to one of the priests among
his sons. 3 If the priest, upon examination of the
skin's infection, finds that the hair on the infec-
tion has turned white and the infection itself
appears to be deeper than the skin,† it is indeed
a scaly infection; the priest, on seeing this, shall
declare the person unclean. 4 † If, however, the
blotch on the skin is white, but does not seem to
be deeper than the skin, nor has the hair turned
white, the priest shall quarantine the afflicted
person for seven days.† 5 Should the priest,
upon examination on the seventh day, find that
the infection has remained unchanged in color
and has not spread on the skin, the priest shall
quarantine the person for another seven days.
6 Should the priest, upon examination again on
the seventh day, find that the infection is now
faded and has not spread on the skin, the priest
shall declare the person clean; it was merely a
scab. The person shall wash his garments† and
so become clean. 7 But if, after the person was
examined by the priest and declared clean, the
scab spreads at all on the skin, the person shall
once more be examined by the priest. 8 Should
the priest, upon examination, find that the scab
has indeed spread on the skin, he shall declare
the person unclean; it is a scaly infection.

9 When someone is afflicted with a scaly infec-
tion, that person shall be brought to the priest.
10 Should the priest, upon examination, find
that there is a white mark on the skin which has
turned the hair white and that there is raw flesh
in it, 11 it is a chronic scaly infection on the skin.
The priest shall declare the person unclean with-
out quarantine, since the individual is certainly
unclean. 12 † If the scaly infection breaks out on

†

12:2–5 The mother has two stages of uncleanness or impurity: the first where her uncleanness is as severe as during her menstrual period and is contagious to profane persons and objects (cf. 15:19–24), and the second where she does not contaminate persons and objects but is still impure to what is holy, such as the sanctuary (12:4) or sacrifices. The implication is that in the second stage she may resume sexual relations with her husband (which would be prohibited in the first stage according to 18:19).

12:3 Circumcision is the sign of the covenant between God and Israel (Gn 17:1–27) and allows full participation in the religious community (Ex 12:43–49; Jos 5:2–10). This command was fulfilled after Jesus' birth (Lk 2:21).

12:5 *If she gives birth to a girl . . . sixty-six days*: while the longer period of uncleanness following the birth of a girl, compared to that following the birth of a boy, might reflect the relative disparity in social status between men and women in ancient Israel (and attested in other cultures), this is by no means certain. There is no simple correlation in the Bible between the worth of something and the degree of impurity it can occasion.

12:6–8 Certain tolerated impurities (see note on 11:1–15:33) are strong enough to pollute the sanctuary and require purification offerings, including the parturient (see also 14:10–32; 15:13–15, 28–30). Cf. note on 4:3. Mary fulfilled the command of bringing sacrifices after the birth of Jesus (Lk 2:22–24).

13:1–14:57 These chapters deal with scaly or fungal infections (Hebrew *ṣāra'at*). The older translation "leprosy" is misleading because *ṣāra'at* refers to not just one but several chronic and enduring skin diseases in human beings. The disease known as "leprosy" (Hansen's disease) is probably not included among the conditions described in the chapter. Also the term *ṣāra'at* refers to fungal growths in fabrics and on the walls of houses. The reason why these conditions, and not other diseases, were considered unclean may be that they were quite visible, associated with death (cf. Nm 12:9–12), and traditionally connected with punishment by the deity (Lv 14:34; Dt 28:27, 35; 2 Sm 3:29; 2 Kgs 5:26–27; 2 Chr 26:16–21).

13:3 The symptoms of white hair and depth (perhaps a subcutaneous lesion) do not clearly correlate with known skin diseases or lesions. It may be that the symptoms are a hybrid ideal that do not reflect reality and are the result of priestly systematization. The same judgment applies to the conditions in vv. 10–11, 20, 25; cf. note on vv. 12–17.

13:4–8 The symptoms here involve a flaky patch of skin that spreads after one week or stays the same after two. This correlates with many skin diseases, such as psoriasis, seborrhoeic dermatitis, certain mycotic infections, patchy eczema, and pityriasis rosea.

13:4 *Quarantine . . . seven days*: unless lesions have unmistakable symptoms of scaly infection, time is needed to distinguish disease from a condition which is following the natural course of healing and remission. Cf. vv. 5, 21, 26, 27, 31, 33, 50, 54; 14:38.

13:6 *Wash his garments*: even suspected scaly infections create some impurity, not just diagnosed infections (vv. 45–46).

13:12–17 This is not a paradox, namely where a limited lesion is impure but one that covers the whole body is pure. Rather, a white lesion that lacks ulcerated skin ("raw flesh") is pure, even if

*

12:2 Lv 15:19.
12:3 Gn 17:12; Jn 7:22.
12:6 Lk 2:22–24.
12:8 Lv 14:21–22.
12:8 Lv 1:14; Lk 2:24.
13:2 Lv 22:4; Ex 4:6; Nm 5:2–3; Dt 24:8; 2 Sm 3:29; 2 Kgs 5:1, 3–7, 11, 27; Mk 1:40–45.

the skin and, as far as the priest can see, covers all the skin of the afflicted person from head to foot, 13 should the priest then, upon examination, find that the scaly infection does cover the whole body, he shall declare the afflicted person clean; since the person has turned completely white; that individual is clean. 14 But as soon as raw flesh appears, the individual is unclean; 15 on observing the raw flesh, the priest shall declare the person unclean, because raw flesh is unclean; it is a scaly infection. 16 If, however, the raw flesh again turns white, the person shall return to the priest; 17 should the latter, upon examination, find that the infection has indeed turned white, he shall declare the afflicted person clean; the individual is clean.

18 If a boil appeared on a person's skin which later healed, 19 should now in the place of the boil a white mark or a reddish white blotch develop, the person shall be examined by the priest. 20 If the latter, upon examination, finds that it is deeper than the skin and that the hair has turned white, he shall declare the person unclean; it is a scaly infection that has broken out in the boil. 21 But if the priest, upon examination, finds that there is no white hair in it and that it is not deeper than the skin and is faded, the priest shall quarantine the person for seven days. 22 If it has then spread on the skin, the priest shall declare the person unclean; it is an infection. 23 But if the blotch remains the same without spreading, it is merely the scar of the boil; the priest shall therefore declare the person clean.

24 If there was a burn on a person's skin, and the burned area now becomes a reddish white or a white blotch, 25 when the priest, upon examination, finds that the hair has turned white in the blotch and this seems to be deeper than the skin, it is a scaly infection that has broken out in the burn; the priest shall therefore declare the person unclean; it is a scaly infection. 26 But if the priest, upon examination, finds that there is no white hair in the blotch and that this is not deeper than the skin and is faded, the priest shall quarantine the person for seven days. 27 Should the priest, upon examination on the seventh day, find that it has spread at all on the skin, he shall declare the person unclean; it is a scaly infection. 28 But if the blotch remains the same without spreading on the skin and is faded, it is merely the spot of the burn; the priest shall therefore declare the person clean, since it is only the scar of the burn.

29 † When a man or a woman has an infection on the head or in the beard, 30 should the priest, upon examination, find that the infection appears to be deeper than the skin and that there is fine yellow hair in it, the priest shall declare the person unclean; it is a scall. It is a scaly infection of the head or beard. 31 But if the priest, upon examining the scall infection, finds that it does not appear to be deeper than the skin, though the hair in it may not be black, the priest shall quarantine the scall-stricken person for seven days. 32 Should the priest, upon examining the infection on the seventh day find that the scall has not spread and has no yellow hair in it and does not seem to be deeper than the skin, 33 the person shall shave, but not the scall spot. Then the priest shall quarantine the scall-diseased person for another seven days. 34 If the priest, upon examining the scall on the seventh day, finds that it has not spread on the skin and that it does not appear to be deeper than the skin, he shall declare the person clean; the latter shall wash his garments, and will thus be clean. 35 But if the scall spreads at all on the skin after the person has been declared clean— 36 should the priest, upon examination, find that the scall has indeed spread on the skin, he need not look for yellow hair; the individual is unclean. 37 If, however, the scall has remained unchanged in color and black hair has grown in it, the disease has been healed; the person is clean, and the priest shall declare the individual clean.

38 † When the skin of a man or a woman is spotted with several white blotches, 39 if the priest, upon examination, finds that the blotches on the skin are pale white, it is only tetter that has broken out on the skin, and the person therefore is clean.

40 When a man loses the hair of his head, he is simply bald on the crown and not unclean.* 41 So too, if he loses the hair on the front of his head, he is simply bald on the forehead and not unclean. 42 But when there is a reddish white infection on his bald crown or bald forehead, it is a scaly infection that is breaking out there. 43 If the priest, upon examination, finds that the infection spot on the bald area on the crown or forehead has the same reddish white appearance as that of a scaly infection of the skin, 44 the man has a scaly

† it covers the whole body. This formulation reflects priestly interest in systematization.

13:29–37 The symptoms in this unit may include either favus (a mycotic infection) or a protein deficiency syndrome (Kwashiorkor) where the hair may be fine and copper-red to yellow.

13:38–39 This may refer to vitiligo, where patches of the skin and hair lose pigmentation.

13:40 2 Kgs 2:23.

infection and is unclean. The priest shall declare
him unclean; his infection is on his head.
45 † The garments of one afflicted with a scaly
infection shall be rent and the hair disheveled,*
and the mustache covered.* The individual shall
cry out, "Unclean, unclean!" 46 As long as the
infection is present, the person shall be unclean.
Being unclean, that individual shall dwell apart,
taking up residence outside the camp.*

Fungal Infection of Fabrics and Leather

47 When a fungal infection is on a garment of
wool or of linen, 48 or on the warp and woof† of
linen or wool, or on a hide or anything made of
leather, 49 if the infection on the garment or hide,
or on the warp or woof, or on any leather article
is greenish or reddish, the thing is indeed a fun-
gal infection and must be examined by the priest.
50 Having examined the infection, the priest shall
quarantine the infected article for seven days. 51 If
the priest, upon inspecting the infection on the
seventh day, finds that it has spread on the gar-
ment, or on the warp or woof, or on the leather,
whatever be its use, the infection is a harmful
fungus; the article is unclean. 52 He shall there-
fore burn up the garment, or the warp or woof,
be it of wool or linen, or any leather article which
is infected; since it is a harmful fungus, it must be
destroyed by fire. 53 But if the priest, upon exami-
nation, finds that it has not spread on the gar-
ment, or on the warp or woof, or on the leather
article, 54 he shall give orders to have the infected
article washed and then quarantined for another
seven days. 55 If the priest, upon examination af-
ter the infection was washed, finds that it has not
changed its color, even though it may not have
spread, the article is unclean. You shall burn it
with fire. It is a fray, be it on its inner or outer
side. 56 But if the priest, upon examination, finds
that the infection has faded after the washing,
he shall cut it out of the garment, or the leather,
or the warp or woof. 57 If, however, the infection
again appears on the garment, or on the warp or
woof, or on the leather article, it is still virulent
and you shall burn the thing infected with fire.
58 But if, after the washing, the infection has dis-
appeared from the garment, or the warp or woof,
or the leather article, the thing shall be washed a
second time, and thus it will be clean. 59 This is
the instruction for a fungal* infection on a gar-
ment of wool or linen, or on a warp or woof, or
on any leather article, to determine whether it is
clean or unclean.

Purification After Scaly Infection

14 1 † The LORD said to Moses: 2 * This is the
ritual for someone that had a scaly infec-
tion at the time of that person's purification.*
The individual shall be brought to the priest,
3 who is to go outside the camp.* If the priest,
upon inspection, finds that the scaly infection
has healed in the afflicted person, 4 he shall or-
der that two live, clean birds,† as well as some
cedar wood, scarlet yarn, and hyssop be obtained
for the one who is to be purified.* 5 † The priest
shall then order that one of the birds be slaugh-
tered over an earthen vessel with fresh water in it.
6 Taking the living bird with the cedar wood, the
scarlet yarn and the hyssop, the priest shall dip
them, including the live bird, in the blood of the
bird that was slaughtered over the fresh water,
7 and then sprinkle seven times on the person to
be purified from the scaly infection. When he has
thus purified that person, he shall let the living
bird fly away over the countryside.* 8 The per-
son being purified shall then wash his garments,
shave off all hair, and bathe in water,† and so
become clean. After this the person may come
inside the camp, but shall still remain outside his
or her tent for seven days.* 9 On the seventh day
this individual shall again shave off all hair, of
the head, beard, and eyebrows—all hair must be
shaved—and also wash his garments and bathe
the body in water, and so become clean.

†

13:45–46 The symbolic association with death is found in the mourning activities in which those diagnosed with these afflictions engage: rending clothes, disheveling the hair, and covering the mouth. They are also excluded from the camp. Cf. examples of exclusion in Nm 5:1–4; 12:14–15; 2 Kgs 7:3–10; 15:5; 2 Chr 26:21. Persons with scaly infections must have been able to pollute others in the priestly system, though this is not stated. Hence, they must cry out "Unclean, unclean!" to warn others of their presence.

13:48 *Warp and woof*: it is possible that the nature of the weave allowed fungus to grow separately along warp or woof. Otherwise, this may refer to the yarns before they are woven together.

14:1–32 The rites here are for purification from human scaly infections after recovery, not for healing (but cf. 2 Kgs 5:10–14).

14:4–7 The bird rite is also found for purifying a house from a fungus (vv. 49–53). The rite apparently removes impurity from the individual and, by means of the live bird, sends it away to unpopulated areas (v. 7). This is similar to the dispatch of a goat laden with sins on the Day of Atonement (16:21–22).

14:5–7 The blood from the bird serves as a ritual detergent, much like the blood from the purification offering (see notes on 4:3). It is not a sacrifice, however, since it is not performed at the sanctuary. *Fresh water*: lit., "living water," taken from some source of running water, not from a cistern.

14:8 *Bathe in water*: This phrase occurs frequently in Lv 14–16 and is imprecise. It can refer to both ordinary and cultic washing. The context will determine the meaning. At this early period in Israel's history it is probably not a reference to cultic immersion in a Mikveh—a Second Temple period ritual.

*

13:45 Lv 10:6.
13:45 Mi 3:7.
13:46 Lv 14:3; Nm 5:2; 12:14–15; 2 Kgs 7:3–10; 15:5; 2 Chr 26:21; Mt 26:6; Mk 14:3; Lk 17:11–19.
13:59 Lv 14:54–57.
14:2 2 Kgs 5:10, 14; Mt 8:4; 10:8; Mk 1:44; Lk 4:27; 5:14.
14:2 Lv 14:48–53.
14:3 Lv 13:46.
14:4 Nm 19:6.
14:7 Lv 16:21–22.
14:8 Lv 15:13, 28.

10 On the eighth day the individual shall take two unblemished male lambs, one unblemished yearling ewe lamb, three tenths of an ephah of bran flour mixed with oil for a grain offering, and one log† of oil. 11 The priest who performs the purification ceremony shall place the person who is being purified, as well as all these offerings, before the LORD at the entrance of the tent of meeting. 12 Taking one of the male lambs, the priest shall present it as a reparation offering,* along with the log of oil, raising them as an elevated* offering before the LORD. 13 This lamb shall be slaughtered in the sacred place where the purification offering and the burnt offering are slaughtered, because the reparation offering is like the purification offering; it belongs to the priest and is most holy. 14 † * Then the priest shall take some of the blood of the reparation offering and put it on the lobe of the right ear, the thumb of the right hand, and the big toe of the right foot of the person being purified. 15 The priest shall also take the log of oil and pour some of it into the palm of his own left hand; 16 then, dipping his right finger in the oil on his left palm, he shall sprinkle some of it with his finger seven times before the LORD. 17 Of the oil left in his hand the priest shall put some on the lobe of the right ear, the thumb of the right hand, and the big toe of the right foot of the person being purified, over the blood of the reparation offering. 18 The rest of the oil in his hand the priest shall put on the head* of the one being purified. Thus shall the priest make atonement for the individual before the LORD. 19 The priest shall next offer the purification offering,* thus making atonement on behalf of the one being purified from the uncleanness. After this the burnt offering shall be slaughtered. 20 The priest shall offer the burnt offering* and the grain offering on the altar before the LORD. Thus shall the priest make atonement for the person, and the individual will become clean.

Poor Person's Sacrifices

21 If a person is poor and cannot afford so much,* that person shall take one male lamb for a reparation offering, to be used as an elevated offering in atonement, one tenth of an ephah of bran flour mixed with oil for a grain offering, a log of oil, 22 and two turtledoves or pigeons, which the individual can more easily afford, the one as a purification offering and the other as a burnt offering. 23 On the eighth day of purification the person shall bring them to the priest, at the entrance of the tent of meeting before the LORD. 24 Taking the lamb of the reparation offering, along with the log of oil, the priest shall raise them as an elevated offering before the LORD. 25 When the lamb of the reparation offering has been slaughtered, the priest shall take some of its blood, and put it on the lobe of the right ear, on the thumb of the right hand, and on the big toe of the right foot of the person being purified. 26 The priest shall then pour some of the oil into the palm of his own left hand 27 and with his right finger sprinkle some of the oil in his left palm seven times before the LORD. 28 Some of the oil in his hand the priest shall also put on the lobe of the right ear, the thumb of the right hand, and the big toe of the right foot of the person being purified, where he had sprinkled the blood of the reparation offering. 29 The rest of the oil in his hand the priest shall put on the head of the one being purified. Thus shall he make atonement for the individual before the LORD. 30 Then, of the turtledoves or pigeons, such as the person can afford, 31 the priest shall offer one as a purification offering and the other as a burnt offering,* along with the grain offering. Thus shall the priest make atonement before the LORD for the person who is being purified. 32 This is the ritual for one afflicted with a scaly infection who has insufficient means for purification.

Fungal Infection of Houses

33 †The LORD said to Moses and Aaron: 34 When you come into the land of Canaan, which I am giving you to possess, if I put* a fungal infection in any house of the land you occupy, 35 the owner of the house shall come and report to the priest, "Something like an infection has appeared in my house." 36 The priest shall then order the house to be cleared out before he goes in to examine the infection, lest everything in the house become unclean. Only after this is he to go in to examine the house. 37 If the priest, upon inspection, finds that the infection on the walls of the house consists of greenish or reddish spots* which seem to

LV

†

14:10 *Log*: a liquid measure of capacity attested in the Bible only here. It is apparently equal in capacity to one-half liter.

14:14–17 The application of blood and oil here facilitates the movement of the person from the severely impure to the pure profane sphere; it reintegrates him or her into the community. Cf. 8:23–24.

14:33–53 Discussion of fungi in houses is probably delayed until here because it deals with a case pertaining to living in the land (v. 34) as opposed to the foregoing cases which apply even in the wilderness. The rules on fabrics (13:47–58) apply to the tent dwellings in the wilderness.

*

14:12 Lv 7:1–10.
14:12 Lv 7:30.
14:14 Lv 8:23–24.
14:18 Lv 8:12, 30.
14:19 Lv 4.
14:20 Lv 1.
14:21 Lv 5:7, 11; 12:8.
14:31 Lv 1:14–17; 5:7–10.
14:34 Nm 12:9–15; 2 Kgs 15:4–5; 2 Chr 26:16–21.
14:37 Lv 13:49.

go deeper than the surface of the wall, [38]he shall
go out of the house to the doorway and quaran-
tine the house for seven days. [39]On the seventh
day the priest shall return. If, upon inspection, he
finds that the infection has spread on the walls,
[40]he shall order the infected stones to be pulled
out and cast in an unclean place outside the city.
[41]The whole inside of the house shall then be
scraped, and the mortar that has been scraped off
shall be dumped in an unclean place outside the
city. [42]Then other stones shall be brought and
put in the place of the old stones, and new mor-
tar obtained and plastered on the house. [43]If the
infection breaks out once more in the house after
the stones have been pulled out and the house
has been scraped and replastered, [44]the priest
shall come; and if, upon inspection, he finds that
the infection has spread in the house, it is a cor-
rosive fungus in the house, and it is unclean. [45]It
shall be pulled down, and all its stones, beams
and mortar shall be hauled away to an unclean
place outside the city. [46]* Whoever enters a
house while it is quarantined shall be unclean
until evening. [47]Whoever sleeps or eats in such a
house shall also wash his garments.

[48]* If the priest finds, when he comes to the
house, that the infection has in fact not spread in
the house after the plastering, he shall declare the
house clean, since the infection has been healed.
[49]To purify the house, he shall take two birds,
as well as cedar wood, scarlet yarn, and hyssop.
[50]One of the birds he shall slaughter over an
earthen vessel with fresh water in it. [51]Then, taking
the cedar wood, the hyssop and the scarlet yarn,
together with the living bird, he shall dip them all
in the blood of the slaughtered bird and the fresh
water, and sprinkle the house seven times. [52]Thus
he shall purify the house with the bird's blood
and the fresh water, along with the living bird,
the cedar wood, the hyssop, and the scarlet yarn.
[53]He shall then let the living bird fly away over the
countryside outside the city. Thus he shall make
atonement for the house, and it will be clean.

[54]This is the ritual for every kind of human
scaly infection and scall, [55]and for fungus dis-
eases in garments and houses— [56]for marks,
lesions and blotches— [57]to give direction when
there is a state of uncleanness and when a state of
cleanness. This is the ritual for scaly infection.

Sexual Uncleanness†

15 [1]The LORD said to Moses and Aaron:
[2]† Speak to the Israelites and tell them:
When any man has a genital discharge, he is
thereby unclean.* [3]Such is his uncleanness from
this discharge, whether his body† drains freely
with the discharge or is blocked up from the dis-
charge. His uncleanness is on him all the days
that his body discharges or is blocked up from
his discharge; this is his uncleanness. [4]Any bed
on which the man with the discharge lies is un-
clean, and any article on which he sits is unclean.
[5]Anyone who touches his bed shall wash his
garments, bathe in water, and be unclean until
evening. [6]Whoever sits on an article on which
the man with the discharge was sitting shall wash
his garments, bathe in water, and be unclean un-
til evening. [7]Whoever touches the body of the
man with the discharge shall wash his garments,
bathe in water, and be unclean until evening. [8]If
the man with the discharge spits on a clean per-
son, the latter shall wash his garments, bathe in
water, and be unclean until evening. [9]Any saddle
on which the man with the discharge rides is un-
clean. [10]Whoever touches anything that was un-
der him shall be unclean until evening; whoever
carries any such thing shall wash his garments,
bathe in water, and be unclean until evening.*
[11]Anyone whom the man with the discharge
touches with his unrinsed hands shall wash his
garments, bathe in water, and be unclean until
evening. [12]Earthenware touched by the man with
the discharge shall be broken; and every wooden
article shall be rinsed with water.

[13]When a man with a discharge becomes
clean† of his discharge, he shall count seven
days* for his purification. Then he shall wash his
garments and bathe his body in fresh water, and
so he will be clean. [14]On the eighth day he shall
take two turtledoves or two pigeons,* and going
before the LORD, to the entrance of the tent of
meeting, he shall give them to the priest, [15]who
shall offer them up, the one as a purification
offering and the other as a burnt offering. Thus
shall the priest make atonement before the LORD
for the man because of his discharge.

[16]† When a man has an emission of semen,
he shall bathe his whole body in water and be

---

†

15:1–33 Sexual discharges may be unclean partly because they involve the loss of life fluids or are otherwise involved with phenomena at the margins of life and death.

15:2–3 The uncleanness here is perhaps a discharge of pus because of urethritis (often but not solely associated with gonorrhea).

15:3 *Body*: here a euphemism in the Hebrew for "penis."

15:13 *Becomes clean*: i.e., when his discharge ceases. The rite that follows is for purification, not a cure; see note on 14:1–32.

15:16–18 Menstrual blood, semen, and other impurities in Lv 11–15 are considered "impure" either because they are force of life whose "loss" represents death or because, as uniquely human con-

---

*

14:46–47 cf. Lv 15:10.
14:48 Lv 14:2–9.
15:2 Nm 5:2.
15:10 Lv 11:24–25, 27–28, 39–40; 14:46–47.
15:13 Lv 14:8.
15:14 Lv 12:8; 14:22.

unclean until evening.* 17 Any piece of cloth or
leather with semen on it shall be washed with
water and be unclean until evening.
18 If a man has sexual relations with a woman,
they shall both bathe in water and be unclean
until evening.
19 † When a woman has a flow of blood from
her body, she shall be in a state of menstrual un-
cleanness for seven days. Anyone who touches
her shall be unclean until evening.* 20 Anything
on which she lies or sits during her menstrual pe-
riod shall be unclean. 21 Anyone who touches her
bed shall wash his garments, bathe in water, and
be unclean until evening. 22 Whoever touches
any article on which she was sitting shall wash
his garments, bathe in water, and be unclean un-
til evening. 23 Whether an object† is on the bed
or on something she sat upon, when the person
touches it, that person shall be unclean until eve-
ning. 24 If a man lies with her, he contracts her
menstrual uncleanness and shall be unclean for
seven days;* every bed on which he then lies also
becomes unclean.
25 † When a woman has a flow of blood for sev-
eral days outside her menstrual period, or when
her flow continues beyond the ordinary period,
as long as she suffers this unclean flow she shall
be unclean, just as during her menstrual period.*
26 Any bed on which she lies during such a flow
becomes unclean, as it would during her men-
strual period, and any article on which she sits
becomes unclean just as during her menstrual pe-
riod. 27 Anyone who touches them becomes un-
clean; that person shall wash his garments, bathe
in water, and be unclean until evening.
28 * When she becomes clean from her flow,
she shall count seven days; after this she becomes
clean. 29 On the eighth day she shall take two
turtledoves or two pigeons and bring them to
the priest at the entrance of the tent of meeting.
30 The priest shall offer one of them as a purifi-
cation offering and the other as a burnt offering.
Thus shall the priest make atonement before the
LORD for her because of her unclean flow.
31 You shall warn the Israelites of their un-
cleanness, lest they die through their uncleanness
by defiling my tabernacle,* which is in their
midst.
32 This is the ritual for the man with a dis-
charge, or who has an emission of semen, and
thereby becomes unclean; 33 as well as for the
woman who has her menstrual period; or one
who has a discharge, male or female; and also for
the man who lies with an unclean woman.

Did You Know?

Monthly Periods

Not every woman suffers pain and swelling as part of her menstrual cycle, but many do. Imagine the life of women in Old Testament days. No sanitary supplies, just strips of cloth. Not much privacy. Not much sympathy from men. No understanding of human biology. Just the monthly flow of blood and the trouble and discomfort of dealing with it.

And on top of the discomfort, women were seen as unclean during their menstrual period. How uncaring this may seem today! How did this unclean concept in Leviticus 15:19–33 develop, anyway? It probably had to do with blood's being a powerful sign of life, implying that a loss of blood meant someone was not healthy and could possibly be a danger to the community.

Thankfully, we do not apply all the Mosaic laws to life today. We have grown in our understanding of human biology and of human dignity. Let's never stop growing.

▶ Lv 15:19–33

The Day of Atonement

16 1 † After the death of Aaron's two sons,*
who died when they encroached on the
LORD's presence, the LORD spoke to Moses 2 and

† ditions, they are symbolically incompatible with the deity and the divine abode, the sanctuary. Lv 15:16 refers to a spontaneous nocturnal emission, and either because this marks life and death boundaries or because of its uniquely human (versus divine) character, any contact with it renders the object or person ritually unclean. Thus, in 15:18 it is not the marital act itself that is polluting, but only semen.

15:19–24 This is normal menstruation.

15:23 *An object*: the Hebrew is unclear. This translation means that even an object on the woman's unclean bed or chair can mediate uncleanness to another, but only if all the object touched is still on the bed or article sat upon, thus forming a chain of simultaneous contact.

15:25–30 This is menstruation outside the normal cycle or for periods longer than normal. A woman with a chronic blood flow was healed by touching the tassel of Jesus' cloak (Mt 9:20–22; Mk 5:25–34; Lk 8:43–48).

16:1–34 This is the narrative sequel of the story in chap. 10. The ritual in chapter 16 originally may have been an emergency rite in response to unexpected pollution of the sanctuary.

* **15:16** Ex 19:15; Dt 23:11–12; 1 Sm 21:6. **15:19** Lv 12:2, 5; 2 Sm 11:4; Ez 36:17. **15:24** Lv 18:19; 20:18; Ez 18:6. **15:25** Mt 9:20–22; Mk 5:25–34; Lk 8:43–48. **15:28** Lv 15:13–15. **15:31** Lv 5:2–3; 22:9; Nm 19:13, 20. **16:1** Lv 10:1–5.

Live It!

The Scapegoat

What an interesting tradition! In the Israelite ritual described in Leviticus 16:20–21, the leader symbolically transfers all the people's sins onto a goat and drives it away. It is a liberating act that allows a fresh start.

But today, the idea of a scapegoat conveys oppression rather than freedom. A person becomes the scapegoat when other people blame him or her for their problems. Here is an example:

Suppose you are on a soccer team that expects this week's game to be easy, so no one works hard at practice. On game day, the score is tied near the end of the game. While your team is consumed in thoughts of going home, the other team scores a goal and wins the game. Everyone gets mad at the goalie for not preventing the goal. The goalie is the scapegoat, but you all should share in the fault for the loss because none of you practiced well or played your best.

- Have you ever been the scapegoat for someone else's problems? If so, how did that feel? What did you do?
- Have you ever scapegoated someone else when you were partly to blame for some situation? What happened? How will you prevent scapegoating in the future?

▶ **Lv 16:20–21**

said to him: Tell your brother Aaron that he is
not to come whenever he pleases† into the in-
ner sanctuary, inside the veil,* in front of the
cover on the ark, lest he die, for I reveal myself
in a cloud above the ark's cover. [3]Only in this
way may Aaron enter the inner sanctuary. He
shall bring a bull of the herd for a purification
offering and a ram for a burnt offering. [4]He shall
wear the sacred linen tunic, with the linen pants
underneath, gird himself with the linen sash and
put on the linen turban.* But since these vest-
ments are sacred, he shall not put them on until
he has first bathed his body in water.* [5]From the
Israelite community he shall receive two male
goats for a purification offering and one ram for
a burnt offering.
[6]Aaron shall offer the bull, his purification
offering, to make atonement† for himself and
for his household. [7]Taking the two male goats
and setting them before the LORD at the entrance
of the tent of meeting, [8]he shall cast lots* to de-
termine which one is for the LORD and which for
Azazel.† * [9]The goat that is determined by lot for
the LORD, Aaron shall present and offer up as a
purification offering. [10]But the goat determined
by lot for Azazel he shall place before the LORD
alive, so that with it he may make atonement by
sending it off to Azazel in the desert.
[11]Thus shall Aaron offer his bull for the puri-
fication offering, to make atonement for himself
and for his family. When he has slaughtered it,
[12]he shall take a censer full of glowing embers
from the altar before the LORD, as well as a dou-
ble handful of finely ground fragrant incense,
and bringing them inside the veil, [13]there before
the LORD he shall put incense on the fire, so that a
cloud of incense may shield the cover that is over
the covenant, else he will die. [14]Taking some of
the bull's blood, he shall sprinkle it with his fin-
ger on the front of the ark's cover and likewise
sprinkle some of the blood with his finger seven
times in front of the cover.
[15]Then he shall slaughter the goat of the people's
purification offering, and bringing its blood inside
the veil, he shall do with it as he did with the
bull's blood, sprinkling it on the ark's cover and in
front of it. [16]Thus he shall purge the inner sanctu-
ary† of all the Israelites' impurities and trespasses,
including all their sins. He shall do the same for
the tent of meeting,* which is set up among them
in the midst of their uncleanness. [17]No one else

†

16:2 *Not to come whenever he pleases*: access to the various parts of the sanctuary is strictly controlled. Only the high priest can enter the most holy place, and only once a year. *The veil*: the Letter to the Hebrews makes use of the imagery of the Day of Atonement (in Hebrew *Yom Kippur*) to explain Jesus' sacrifice (Heb 9:1–14, 23–28). *Ark's cover*: the meaning of *kappōret* is not certain. It may be connected with the verb *kipper* "to atone, purge" (see note on v. 6) and thus refer to this part of the ark as a focus of atonement or purification.

16:6 *Make atonement*: the Hebrew verb *kipper* refers specifically to the removal of sin and impurity (cf. Ex 30:10; Lv 6:23; 8:15; 16:16, 18, 20, 27, 33; Ez 43:20, 26; 45:20), thus "to purge" in vv. 16, 18, 20, and 33, and more generally to the consequence of the sacrificial procedure, which is atonement (cf. Lv 17:11). "Atonement" is preeminently a function of the purification sacrifice, but other sacrifices, except apparently for the communion sacrifice, achieve this as well.

16:8 *Azazel*: a name for a demon (meaning something like "angry/fierce god"). See note on 17:7.

16:16 *Inner sanctuary*: this refers to the most holy room (vv. 2, 11–15). *Trespasses, including all their sins*: the term for "trespasses" (Heb. *pesha'im*), which has overtones of rebellion, and the phrase

*

16:2 Lv 23:26–32; Nm 29:7–11; Heb 9:6–28.
16:4 Lv 8:7; Ex 28:1–40.
16:4 Lv 8:6.
16:8 Jos 7:14–20; Acts 1:26.
16:8 Lv 17:7.
16:16 Lv 4:5–7, 16–18.

may be in the tent of meeting from the time he enters the inner sanctuary to make atonement until he departs. When he has made atonement for himself and his household, as well as for the whole Israelite assembly, [18] † he shall come out to the altar before the LORD and purge it also. Taking some of the bull's and the goat's blood, he shall put it on the horns around the altar, [19] and with his finger sprinkle some of the blood on it seven times.* Thus he shall purify it and sanctify it from the impurities of the Israelites.

The Scapegoat

[20] When he has finished purging the inner sanctuary, the tent of meeting and the altar, Aaron shall bring forward the live goat. [21] Laying both hands† on its head, he shall confess over it all the iniquities of the Israelites and their trespasses, including all their sins, and so put them on the goat's head.* He shall then have it led into the wilderness by an attendant. [22] The goat will carry off all their iniquities to an isolated region.*

When the goat is dispatched into the wilderness, [23] Aaron shall go into the tent of meeting, strip off the linen vestments he had put on when he entered the inner sanctuary, and leave them in the tent of meeting. [24] After bathing his body with water in a sacred place, he shall put on his regular vestments, and then come out and offer his own and the people's burnt offering, in atonement for himself and for the people, [25] and also burn the fat of the purification offering on the altar.

[26] The man who led away the goat for Azazel shall wash his garments and bathe his body in water; only then may he enter the camp. [27] The bull and the goat of the purification offering whose blood was brought to make atonement in the inner sanctuary, shall be taken outside the camp,* where their hides and flesh and dung shall be burned in the fire. [28] The one who burns them shall wash his garments and bathe his body in water; only then may he enter the camp.

The Fast

[29] * This shall be an everlasting statute for you: on the tenth day of the seventh month every one

16:20–22

of you, whether a native or a resident alien, shall humble yourselves† and shall do no work. [30] For on this day atonement is made for you to make you clean; of all your sins you will be cleansed before the LORD. [31] It shall be a sabbath of complete rest for you, on which you must humble yourselves—an everlasting statute.

[32] This atonement is to be made by the priest who has been anointed and ordained to the priesthood in succession to his father. He shall wear the linen garments, the sacred vestments, [33] and purge the most sacred part of the sanctuary, as well as the tent of meeting, and the altar. He shall also make atonement for the priests and all the people of the assembly. [34] This, then, shall be an everlasting statute for you: once a year atonement shall be made on behalf of the Israelites for all their sins. And Moses did as the LORD had commanded him.

† "all their sins" indicate that even sins committed intentionally are included (such as when the sinner "acts defiantly," as in Nm 15:30–31). This complements the scheme found in Lv 4 (see note on 4:3): intentional sins pollute the sanctuary more and penetrate even further than inadvertent sins, namely to the most holy place. *The same for the tent of meeting*: this rite may be that found in 4:5–7, 16–18 where blood is sprinkled in the anterior room and blood is placed on the horns of the incense altar there. Cf. Ex 30:10.

16:18–19 Thus a third locale in the sanctuary complex, the open-air altar, is purified. See the summaries in 16:20, 33.

16:21 *Both hands*: this gesture is for transferring sins to the head of the goat and is apparently different in meaning from the one-handed gesture that precedes the slaughtering of sacrificial animals (1:4; 3:2; 4:4; see note on 1:4).

16:29 *Humble yourselves*: also v. 31. The idiom used here (Heb. *'innâ nephesh*) involves mainly fasting (Ps 35:13), but probably prohibits other activities such as anointing (Dn 10:3) and sexual intercourse (2 Sm 12:15–24). Such acts of self-denial display the need for divine favor. Fasting is often undertaken in times of emergency and mourning (cf. 1 Sm 14:24; 2 Sm 1:12; 3:35; cf. Mk 2:18–22).

* **16:19** Lv 4:25, 30, 34. **16:21** Is 53:6; 2 Cor 5:21. **16:22** Lv 14:7, 53; Is 53:11–12; Jn 1:29; 1 Pt 2:24. **16:27** Lv 4:11–12; 6:23; Heb 13:11–13. **16:29** Lv 23:27, 32; Nm 29:7.

IV. Holiness Laws

Sacredness of Blood

17 1 The LORD said to Moses: 2 Speak to Aaron and his sons, as well as to all the Israelites, and tell them: This is what the LORD has commanded: 3 † Any Israelite who slaughters an ox or a sheep or a goat, whether in the camp or outside of it, 4 without first bringing it to the entrance of the tent of meeting to present it as an offering to the LORD in front of the LORD's tabernacle, shall be judged guilty of bloodshed† *—that individual has shed blood, and shall be cut off* from the people. 5 This is so that such sacrifices as they used to offer in the open field the Israelites shall henceforth bring to the LORD at the entrance of the tent of meeting, to the priest, and sacrifice them there as communion sacrifices to the LORD.* 6 The priest will splash the blood on the altar of the LORD at the entrance of the tent of meeting and burn the fat for an odor pleasing to the LORD. 7 No longer shall they offer their sacrifices to the demons† with whom they prostituted themselves.* This shall be an everlasting statute for them and their descendants.

8 Tell them, therefore: Anyone, whether of the house of Israel or of the aliens residing among them, who offers a burnt offering or sacrifice 9 without bringing it to the entrance of the tent of meeting to offer it to the LORD, shall be cut off from the people. 10 * As for anyone, whether of the house of Israel or of the aliens residing among them, who consumes any blood, I will set myself against that individual and will cut that person off from among the people, 11 since the life of the flesh is in the blood,* and I have given it to you to make atonement† on the altar for yourselves, because it is the blood as life that makes atonement. 12 That is why I have told the Israelites: No one among you, not even a resident alien, may consume blood.

13 Anyone hunting,† whether of the Israelites or of the aliens residing among them, who catches an animal or a bird that may be eaten, shall pour out its blood and cover it with earth,* 14 since the life of all flesh is its blood. I have told the Israelites: You shall not consume the blood of any flesh. Since the life of all flesh is its blood, anyone who consumes it shall be cut off.

15 Everyone, whether a native or an alien, who eats of an animal that died of itself or was killed by a wild beast, shall wash his garments, bathe in water, and be unclean until evening, and then become clean.* 16 If one does not wash his garments and bathe, that person shall bear the penalty.

Laws Concerning Sexual Behavior

18 1 The LORD said to Moses: 2 Speak to the Israelites and tell them: I, the LORD, am your God.† 3 You shall not do as they do in the land of Egypt, where you once lived, nor shall you do as they do in the land of Canaan, where I am bringing you; do not conform to their customs.* 4 My decrees you shall carry out, and my statutes you shall take care to follow. I, the LORD, am your God. 5 Keep, then, my statutes and decrees, for the person who carries them out will find life† through them. I am the LORD.*

6 † None of you shall approach a close relative† to have sexual intercourse. I am the LORD. 7 † You shall not disgrace your father by having intercourse with your mother.* She is your own mother; you shall not have intercourse with her. 8 You shall not have intercourse with your father's wife, for that would be a disgrace to your father. 9 You shall not have intercourse with your sister,† * your father's daughter or your mother's

LV

†

17:3–4 Any animal slaughtered must be brought to the tent of meeting as an offering. This differs from Dt 12:15–28, which allows those living too far from the temple to slaughter an animal for food at home without offering it as a sacrifice.

17:4 *Guilty of bloodshed*: human beings and animals can incur blood guilt for killing human beings (cf. Gn 9:5–6); human beings can incur blood guilt for killing animals (see note on Lv 24:17–22).

17:7 *Demons*: for Hebrew *śeʿîrîm*, lit., "goats." Like the demon Azazel (cf. 16:8, 10, 21–22), they dwell in the open country (17:5). Cf. Is 13:21; 34:14.

17:11 *To make atonement*: this is probably to be understood in the context of liability for shedding animal blood (cf. v. 4). Placing the blood on the altar exonerates the slaughterer from guilt for the killing. See note on 16:6.

17:13 *Hunting*: game animals are not permitted as offerings. One nonetheless has to treat the blood of these animals carefully by covering it with earth. Cf. Dt 12:16, 24.

18:2 *I, the LORD, am your God*: this declaration appears frequently elsewhere throughout chaps. 17–26, sometimes with a statement of God's holiness or his sanctifying activity. It emphasizes the importance of the laws and the relationship of the divine lawgiver to the people.

18:5 *Find life*: in Dt 30:15–20 Moses sets before the people life and death. The alternatives are set out in detail in Lv 26 and Dt 28. Cf. Ez 20:11, 13, 21.

18:6–23 These laws deal with illicit sexual behavior. Lv 20:10–21 reiterates most of these cases, with penalties. Cf. also Dt 27:15–26; Ez 22:7–12. The ordering of the cases in Lv 18 seems to be: blood relatives (vv. 6–13), those related by marriage (vv. 14–18), then other cases (vv. 19–23).

18:6 *Close relative*: this refers to a blood relative and includes those not specifically mentioned in the list, such as one's own daughter and a full sister. *Have sexual intercourse*: lit., "to uncover nakedness."

18:7–8 Cf. the story of Reuben lying with Bilhah, his father's concubine and Rachel's maid (Gn 35:22; 49:4).

18:9, 11 Cf. actual or possible marriage to a half sister in Gn 20:12 and 2 Sm 13:13.

*

17:4 Lv 24:18.
17:4 Lv 7:20.
17:5 Lv 3:1–2, 7–8, 13.
17:7 Ex 34:15; Dt 32:17; 2 Chr 11:15; 1 Cor 10:20.
17:10–14 Lv 3:17; 7:26–27; Gn 9:4; Dt 12:16, 23–24.
17:11 Gn 9:4.
17:13 Dt 12:15–16.
17:15 Lv 11:39–40; 22:8.
18:3 Lv 20:22–23.
18:5 Ez 20:11, 13, 21; Gal 3:12.
18:7 Lv 20:11; Dt 23:1; 27:20; 1 Cor 5:1.
18:9 Lv 20:17; Dt 27:22.

daughter, whether she was born in your own
household or born elsewhere. 10 You shall not
have intercourse with your son's daughter or with
your daughter's daughter,† for that would be a
disgrace to you. 11 You shall not have intercourse
with the daughter whom your father's wife bore
to him in his household,* since she, too, is your
sister. 12 You shall not have intercourse with your
father's sister,* since she is your father's relative.
13 You shall not have intercourse with your moth-
er's sister, since she is your mother's relative.
14 You shall not disgrace your father's brother
by having sexual relations with his wife,* since
she, too, is your aunt. 15 You shall not have inter-
course with your daughter-in-law;† * she is your
son's wife; you shall not have intercourse with
her. 16 You shall not have intercourse with your
brother's wife;† * that would be a disgrace to your
brother. 17 You shall not have intercourse with a
woman and also with her daughter, nor shall you
marry and have intercourse with her son's daugh-
ter or her daughter's daughter;* they are related
to her. This would be shameful. 18 While your
wife is still living you shall not marry her sister as
her rival and have intercourse with her.*

19 You shall not approach a woman to have
intercourse with her while she is in her men-
strual uncleanness.* 20 You shall not have sexual
relations with your neighbor's wife,† * defiling
yourself with her. 21 * You shall not offer any
of your offspring for immolation to Molech,†
thus profaning the name of your God. I am the
LORD. 22 You shall not lie with a male as with a
woman;* such a thing is an abomination. 23 You
shall not have sexual relations with an animal,
defiling yourself with it; nor shall a woman set
herself in front of an animal to mate with it; that
is perverse.*

24 Do not defile yourselves by any of these
things, because by them the nations whom I am
driving out of your way have defiled themselves.

Live It!

A Very Special Gift

The laws about sexual relations in Leviticus, chapter 18, are another example of how holiness extended to all aspects of life for the Israelites. The people had experienced the sexual promiscuity of other cultures (see Genesis, chapter 19). To become a great nation, the children of God, they had to abandon unhealthy and unholy sexual practices and follow God's way.

Young people today also receive many confusing cultural messages about when it is okay to have sex. In movies, television, and music, sex happens all the time between unmarried people, with no consequences. But the Church, parents, and teachers are saying to wait until marriage. What is a person to believe?

Think about this: Suppose you are receiving a special gift for Christmas. The gift has been wrapped and hidden, not to come out until Christmas Day. How would you feel if you discovered the present and opened it before Christmas? You probably would initially feel some excitement and pleasure in opening the gift. But the special meaning of opening it on the right day would be lost—for both you and the one presenting it to you.

Sex is a wonderful gift from God, meant for that day when you say, "I do," to someone you are committed to in marriage. Only in marriage can sex unite a couple as God intended. Marriage provides the place where children can be properly raised. That is why the Bible tells us to wait until we are married to have sex—so this gift will be as special as it is meant to be.

► Lv 18:1–30

†

18:10 Daughter incest is found in the story of Lot (Gn 19:30–38).

18:15 Judah had intercourse with his daughter-in-law Tamar (Gn 38), but did not know her true identity until her pregnancy was discovered.

18:16 This refers to cohabiting with one's sister-in-law not only while the brother is alive, but also after he is dead. Dt 25:5–10 allows for the marriage to the wife of a brother when that brother died without a male heir. Cf. Gn 38:6–14. It was the violation of this law of Leviticus which aroused the wrath of John the Baptist against Herod Antipas (Mt 14:4; Mk 6:18).

18:20 Adultery in the Hebrew Bible and the ancient Near East is intercourse between a married or betrothed woman and any male. In the Bible it is generally punishable by the death of both individuals (20:10; cf. Dt 22:22–27). Intercourse with an unmarried or unbetrothed woman is not prohibited but carries responsibilities and fines (cf. Ex 22:15–16; Dt 22:28–29). Cf. Lv 19:20–22.

18:21 *Immolation to Molech*: the reference is to the custom of sacrificing children to the god Molech. Cf. Ez 16:20–21; 20:26, 31; 23:37. See note on Lv 20:1–5.

*

18:11 Lv 20:17.
18:12 Lv 20:19.
18:14 Lv 20:20.
18:15 Lv 20:12.
18:16 Lv 20:21; Dt 25:5–10; Mt 14:3–4; Mk 6:18.
18:17 Lv 20:14; Dt 27:23.
18:18 Gn 29:27–28.
18:19 Lv 15:24, 33; 20:18; Ez 18:6; 22:10.
18:20 Lv 20:10; Ex 20:14; Dt 5:18; 22:22; Mt 5:27–30; Jn 8:4–5.
18:21 Lv 20:2–5; Dt 18:10; 1 Kgs 11:7; 2 Kgs 16:3.
18:22 Lv 20:13; Gn 19:4–11; Jgs 19:22–30; Rom 1:27; 1 Cor 6:9.
18:23 Lv 20:15–16; Ex 22:18; Dt 27:21.

You Shall Be Holy

As the Israelites' image of God developed, so did their sense of how they needed to live as God's people. As God's Chosen People, they felt called to behave according to God's plan for them by keeping themselves pure as individuals and as a community. The laws in the Book of Leviticus are examples of how they lived out the call to be holy. For them, holiness was not just for the Sabbath or the Temple but for every day and everything.

Think about the choices you make in your own life. How do your choices help you to be holy in today's world? Ponder these questions for a bit:

- How do you treat your friends?
- How do you spend your money?
- How much time do you spend alone with God?

Being holy has a lot to do with how we live out the moments of our day and how often we remember that we are in God's presence.

► **Leviticus, chapters 19–20**

25 And so the land has become defiled, and I have
punished it for its wickedness, and the land has
vomited out its inhabitants.* 26 You, however,
must keep my statutes and decrees, avoiding all
these abominations, both the natives and the
aliens resident among you— 27 because the pre-
vious inhabitants did all these abominations and
the land became defiled; 28 otherwise the land
will vomit you out also for having defiled it, just
as it vomited out the nations before you. 29 For
whoever does any of these abominations shall be
cut off from the people. 30 Heed my charge, then,
not to observe the abominable customs that have
been observed before your time, and thus become
impure by them.* I, the LORD, am your God.

Various Rules of Conduct

19 1 The LORD said to Moses: 2 Speak to the
whole Israelite community and tell them:
Be holy, for I, the LORD your God, am holy.† *
3 † Each of you revere your mother and father,*
and keep my sabbaths.* I, the LORD, am your
God.

4 Do not turn aside to idols, nor make molten
gods for yourselves.* I, the LORD, am your God.

5 When you sacrifice your communion sacri-
fice to the LORD, you shall sacrifice it so that it is
acceptable on your behalf. 6 It must be eaten on
the day of your sacrifice or on the following day.
Whatever is left over until the third day shall be
burned in fire. 7 If any of it is eaten on the third
day, it will be a desecrated offering and not be
accepted;* 8 whoever eats of it then shall bear
the penalty for having profaned what is sacred
to the LORD. Such a one shall be cut off* from
the people.

9 † When you reap the harvest of your land,
you shall not be so thorough that you reap the
field to its very edge, nor shall you gather the
gleanings of your harvest.* 10 Likewise, you shall
not pick your vineyard bare, nor gather up the
grapes that have fallen. These things you shall
leave for the poor and the alien. I, the LORD, am
your God.

11 † You shall not steal. You shall not deceive
or speak falsely to one another.* 12 You shall not
swear falsely by my name, thus profaning the
name of your God.* I am the LORD.

13 You shall not exploit your neighbor. You
shall not commit robbery. You shall not with-
hold overnight the wages of your laborer.*
14 † You shall not insult the deaf, or put a stum-
bling block in front of the blind, but you shall
fear your God. I am the LORD.

15 You shall not act dishonestly in render-
ing judgment. Show neither partiality to the
weak nor deference to the mighty, but judge
your neighbor justly.* 16 You shall not go about

19:2 *Be holy, for I . . . am holy*: in the writings commonly attributed to the Priestly collection, Israel is called to be holy through obeying God's precepts (11:44–45; 20:7–8, 24–26; Nm 15:40–41). Cf. Dt 14:2, 21; 26:19; and Ex 19:6.

19:3–4 Cf. the Decalogue laws on revering parents (Ex 20:12; Dt 5:16), keeping sabbaths (Ex 20:8–11; Dt 5:12–15), and not making or worshiping idols (Ex 20:2–6; Dt 5:7–10).

19:9–10 The Israelites maintain the poor in part by letting them gather unharvested portions of fields and vineyards. Cf. 23:22; Ru 2:1–10.

19:11–13 Cf. the Decalogue commandments against stealing (Ex 20:15; Dt 5:19), wrongly using God's name (Ex 20:7; Dt 5:11), and swearing falsely against another (Ex 20:16; Dt 5:20).

19:14 In Dt 27:18 a curse falls on the head of the one who misleads the blind.

18:25 Lv 20:22.
18:30 Lv 20:23; Dt 18:9.
19:2 Lv 11:44.
19:3 Lv 20:9; Ex 20:12.
19:3 Lv 23:3.
19:4 Lv 26:1; Ex 20:3–5; 34:17; Dt 5:8; 27:15.
19:7 Lv 7:15–18.
19:8 Lv 7:20.
19:9 Lv 23:22; Dt 24:19–22.
19:11 Ex 20:15–16.
19:12 Ex 20:7; Mt 5:33–37.
19:13 Dt 24:14–15.
19:15 Ex 23:2–3; Dt 1:17; 16:19; Ps 82:2; Prv 24:23.

spreading slander among your people; nor shall
you stand by idly when your neighbor's life is at
stake. I am the LORD.
17 † You shall not hate any of your kindred in
your heart. Reprove your neighbor openly so that
you do not incur sin because of that person.*
18 Take no revenge and cherish no grudge against
your own people. You shall love your neighbor
as yourself. I am the LORD.*
19 † Keep my statutes: do not breed any of your
domestic animals with others of a different spe-
cies; do not sow a field of yours with two differ-
ent kinds of seed; and do not put on a garment
woven with two different kinds of thread.*
20 † * If a man has sexual relations with a fe-
male slave who has been acquired by another
man but has not yet been redeemed or given
her freedom, an investigation shall be made.
They shall not be put to death, because she has
not been freed. 21 The man shall bring to the en-
trance of the tent of meeting as his reparation to
the LORD a ram as a reparation offering.* 22 With
the ram of the reparation offering the priest shall
make atonement before the LORD for the wrong
the man has committed, so that he will be for-
given for the wrong he has committed.
23 When you come into the land and plant
any fruit tree there,* first look upon its fruit as
if it were uncircumcised. For three years, it shall
be uncircumcised for you; it may not be eaten.
24 In the fourth year, however, all of its fruit shall
be dedicated to the LORD in joyous celebration.
25 Not until the fifth year may you eat its fruit, to
increase the yield for you. I, the LORD, am your
God.
26 Do not eat anything with the blood still in
it.* Do not recite charms or practice soothsay-
ing.† * 27 Do not clip your hair at the temples,
nor spoil the edges of your beard. 28 Do not
lacerate your bodies for the dead, and do not tat-
too yourselves.† * I am the LORD.
29 You shall not degrade your daughter by
making a prostitute of her;* otherwise the land
will prostitute itself and become full of lewdness.
30 Keep my sabbaths, and reverence my sanctu-
ary.* I am the LORD.
31 Do not turn to ghosts or consult spirits, by
which you will be defiled.* I, the LORD, am your
God.
32 Stand up in the presence of the aged, show
respect for the old, and fear your God. I am the
LORD.
33 When an alien resides with you in your land,
do not mistreat such a one.* 34 You shall treat the
alien who resides with you no differently than
the natives born among you; you shall love the
alien as yourself; for you too were once aliens in
the land of Egypt.* I, the LORD, am your God.
35 Do not act dishonestly in using measures of
length or weight or capacity. 36 You shall have a
true scale and true weights, an honest ephah and
an honest hin.† * I, the LORD, am your God, who
brought you out of the land of Egypt. 37 Be care-
ful, then, to observe all my statutes and decrees.
I am the LORD.

Penalties for Various Sins

20 1 † The LORD said to Moses: 2 Tell the Is-
raelites: Anyone, whether an Israelite or
an alien residing in Israel, who gives offspring to
Molech shall be put to death.* The people of the
land shall stone that person. 3 * I myself will turn
against and cut off* that individual from among
the people; for in the giving of offspring to Mo-
lech, my sanctuary was defiled* and my holy
name was profaned. 4 If the people of the land
condone the giving of offspring to Molech, by
failing to put the wrongdoer to death, 5 I myself

19:17–18 These verses form a unit and describe different attitudes and actions towards one's fellow Israelites. A separate passage is necessary to advise a similar attitude toward aliens (vv. 33–34). Cf. 25:39–46. The admonition at the end of v. 18 came to be viewed in Judaism and Christianity as one of the central commandments. (See Mt 22:34–40; Mk 12:28–34; Lk 10:25–28; cf. Mt 19:19; Rom 13:8–10; Gal 5:14). The New Testament urges love for enemies as well as neighbors (Mt 5:43–48; Lk 6:27–36; cf. Prv 25:21–22).

19:19 One reason why mixtures are prohibited seems to be that they are holy (see Dt 22:9, 10–11). Israelites are allowed mixtures in the wearing of fringes on the edges or corners of their clothing (Nm 15:37–41; Dt 22:12). Some mixtures are considered abominations (cf. Lv 18:23; Dt 22:5).

19:20–22 On adultery, see note on 18:20. Here it is not adultery in the technical sense since the woman is not free. A reparation offering is required as a penalty (see 5:14–26).

19:26 *Recite charms . . . soothsaying*: methods of divination (cf. Gn 44:5, 15; Is 2:6; Ez 21:26–28). Legitimate means of learning the future or God's will were through the Urim and Thummim stones (see Lv 8:8), lots (see Lv 16:8) and prophets (cf. Dt 18:9–22; 1 Sm 28:6–7).

19:28 *Do not tattoo yourselves*: see note on Gn 4:15. This prohibition probably refers only to the common ancient Near Eastern practice of branding a slave with its owner's name as well as branding the devotees of a god with its name.

19:36 *Ephah*: see note on Is 5:10; *hin*: see note on Ez 45:24.

20:1–5 The term Molech may refer to a deity, perhaps with an underworld association, and the activity forbidden here may be connected with divination. Cf. Dt 18:10; 2 Kgs 17:17; 21:6. In the kingdom of Judah the cult appears to have been practiced in the Valley of Hinnom, just outside Jerusalem on the west and south (2 Kgs 23:10; Jer 32:35).

19:17 Mt 18:15; Lk 17:3; Gal 6:1.
19:18 Mt 5:43; 19:19; 22:39; Mk 12:31; Rom 13:9; Gal 5:14; Jas 2:8; 1 Jn 3:14.
19:19 Dt 22:9–12.
19:20 Dt 22:22–29.
19:21 Lv 5:14–26.
19:23 Dt 20:19–20.
19:26 Lv 17:10.
19:26 Dt 18:10; 2 Kgs 17:17; 21:6; 2 Chr 33:6.
19:28 Lv 21:5.
19:29 Lv 21:7, 14.
19:30 Lv 19:3.
19:31 Lv 20:6, 27; Dt 18:11; Is 8:19.
19:33 Ex 22:20; 23:9; Jer 22:3; Mal 3:5.
19:34 Dt 10:19.
19:36 Dt 25:13–16; Prv 16:11; Am 8:5; Mi 6:10–11.
20:2 Lv 18:21; Dt 12:31; 18:10; 2 Kgs 16:3; 17:17; 21:6; 23:10; Jer 32:35.
20:3 Ez 23:39.
20:3 Lv 7:20.
20:3 Lv 15:31.

will turn against that individual and his or her family, and I will cut off from their people both the wrongdoer and all who follow this person by prostituting themselves with Molech.

6 Should anyone turn to ghosts and spirits and prostitute oneself with them,* I will turn against that person and cut such a one off from among the people. 7 Sanctify yourselves, then, and be holy; for I, the LORD, your God,* am holy. 8 Be careful, therefore, to observe my statutes. I, the LORD, make you holy.

9 Anyone who curses father or mother shall be put to death;† * and having cursed father or mother, such a one will bear the bloodguilt.† 10 † If a man commits adultery with his neighbor's wife,* both the adulterer and the adulteress shall be put to death. 11 If a man disgraces his father by lying with his father's wife,* the two of them shall be put to death; their bloodguilt is upon them. 12 If a man lies with his daughter-in-law,* both of them shall be put to death; they have done what is perverse; their bloodguilt is upon them. 13 If a man lies with a male as with a woman,* they have committed an abomination; the two of them shall be put to death; their bloodguilt is upon them. 14 If a man marries a woman and her mother also,* that is shameful conduct; the man and the two women as well shall be burned to death, so that shamefulness may not be found among you. 15 If a man has sexual relations with an animal,* the man shall be put to death, and you shall kill the animal. 16 If a woman goes up to any animal to mate with it,* you shall kill the woman and the animal; they shall both be put to death; their bloodguilt is upon them. 17 If a man marries his sister,* his father's daughter or his mother's daughter, and they have intercourse with each other, that is disgraceful; they shall be publicly cut off† from the people; the man shall bear the penalty of having had intercourse with his own sister. 18 If a man lies with a woman during her menstrual period and has intercourse with her, he has laid bare the source of her flow and she has uncovered it.* The two of them shall be cut off from the people. 19 You shall not have intercourse with your mother's sister or your father's sister,* because that dishonors one's own flesh; they shall bear their penalty. 20 If a man lies with his uncle's wife, he disgraces his uncle;* they shall bear the penalty; they shall die childless. 21 If a man takes his brother's wife, it is severe defilement and he has disgraced his brother;* they shall be childless.

22 Be careful to observe all my statutes and all my decrees; otherwise the land where I am bringing you to dwell will vomit you out.* 23 Do not conform, therefore, to the customs of the nations* whom I am driving out of your way, because all these things that they have done have filled me with disgust for them. 24 But to you I have said:* You shall take possession of their land. I am giving it to you to possess, a land flowing with milk and honey. I, the LORD, am your God, who have set you apart from other peoples. 25 * You, too, must set apart, then, the clean animals from the unclean, and the clean birds from the unclean, so that you do not make yourselves detestable through any beast or bird or any creature which creeps on the ground that I have set apart for you as unclean. 26 To me, therefore, you shall be holy; for I, the LORD, am holy,* and I have set you apart from other peoples to be my own.

27 A man or a woman who acts as a medium or clairvoyant* shall be put to death. They shall be stoned to death; their bloodguilt is upon them.

Sanctity of the Priesthood

21 1 † The LORD said to Moses: Speak to the priests, Aaron's sons, and tell them: None of you shall make himself unclean for any dead person among his kindred,* 2 except for his

†

20:9 *Curses father or mother . . . put to death*: this is more than a simple expletive uttered in anger against one's parents. See note on Ex 21:17.

20:9–21 *Bloodguilt*: these penalties, beginning with cursing one's parents, reflect the concerns of a patriarchal society that the breakdown of one's relations with one's parents can lead to the breakdown of all other familial relationships, resulting in the breakdown of society.

20:10–21 See 18:6–23 and notes there. It appears that the inclusion of various penalties in 20:10–21 accounts for the different order of the cases here compared to the order found in 18:6–23. The reason why the offenses in 20:10–21 carry different penalties, however, is not clear. Perhaps the cases in vv. 17–21 were considered slightly less serious, being condemned but not criminally prosecuted.

20:17 *Cut off*: see note on 7:20.

21:1–12 While off duty the regular priests are not to become corpse-contaminated except for the close relatives listed in vv. 2–3. While on duty they presumably could not become impure at all. The high priest is restricted from all corpse contamination, on or off duty (vv. 11–12). Lay Israelites are not restricted from corpse contamination, except when in contact with what is holy (cf. Dt 26:14). See note on Lv 11:39–40. Israelites who undertake a nazirite vow enter into a sanctified state and cannot contact corpses (Nm 6:6–12). Cf. Ez 44:25–27.

*

20:6 Lv 19:31.
20:7 Lv 11:44.
20:9 Lv 19:3; Ex 21:17; Dt 21:18–21; Prv 20:20; Mt 15:4; Mk 7:10.
20:10 Lv 18:20.
20:11 Lv 18:8.
20:12 Lv 18:15.
20:13 Lv 18:22.
20:14 Lv 18:17.
20:15 Lv 18:23.
20:16 Lv 18:23.
20:17 Lv 18:9.
20:18 Lv 18:19.
20:19 Lv 18:12–13.
20:20 Lv 18:14.
20:21 Lv 18:16.
20:22 Lv 18:25, 28.
20:23 Lv 18:30.
20:24 Ex 3:8, 17.
20:25 Lv 11:2–47; Dt 14:4–20.
20:26 Lv 11:44.
20:27 Lv 19:31; Ex 22:17; Dt 18:11.
21:1 Ez 44:25–27.
21:2 Lv 10:6–7.

nearest relatives, his mother or father, his son or
daughter, his brother* 3 or his unmarried sister,
who is of his own family while she remains sin-
gle; for these he may make himself unclean. 4 But
as a husband among his kindred† he shall not
make himself unclean and thus profane himself.
5 The priests shall not make bald the crown of
their head, nor shave the edges of their beard,
nor lacerate their body.* 6 They shall be holy
to their God, and shall not profane their God's
name, since they offer the oblations of the LORD,
the food of their God; so they must be holy.
7 † A priest shall not marry a woman debased
by prostitution, nor a woman who has been di-
vorced by her husband; for the priest is holy to
his God.* 8 Honor him as holy for he offers the
food* of your God; he shall be holy to you, be-
cause I, the LORD, am holy who make you holy.
9 If a priest's daughter debases herself by pros-
titution, she thereby debases her father; she shall
be burned with fire.*
10 The most exalted of the priests, upon whose
head the anointing oil has been poured and who
has been ordained to wear the special vestments,
shall not dishevel his hair or rend his garments,
11 nor shall he go near any dead person.* Not
even for his father or mother may he thus be-
come unclean; 12 nor shall he leave the sanctuary
and profane the sanctuary of his God, for the
consecration of the anointing oil of his God is
upon him.* I am the LORD.
13 He shall marry only a woman who is a vir-
gin. 14 He shall not marry a widow or a woman
who has been divorced or one who has been
debased by prostitution, but only a virgin, taken
from his kindred, he shall marry,* 15 so that he
not profane his offspring among his kindred. I,
the LORD, make him holy.

Priestly Blemishes†

16 The LORD said to Moses: 17 Say to Aaron:
None of your descendants, throughout their
generations, who has any blemish shall come
forward to offer the food of his God. 18 Anyone
who has any of the following blemishes may not
come forward:* he who is blind, or lame, or who
has a split lip, or a limb too long, 19 or a broken
leg or arm, 20 or who is a hunchback or dwarf
or has a growth in the eye, or who is afflicted
with sores, scabs, or crushed testicles. 21 No de-
scendant of Aaron the priest who has any such
blemish may draw near to offer the oblations
of the LORD; on account of his blemish he may
not draw near to offer the food of his God. 22 He
may, however, eat the food of his God: of the
most sacred as well as sacred offerings.* 23 Only,
he may not enter through the veil nor draw near
to the altar on account of his blemish; he shall
not profane my sacred precincts, for it is I, the
LORD, who make them holy.
24 Moses, therefore, told this to Aaron and his
sons and to all the Israelites.

Priestly Purity†

22 1 The LORD said to Moses: 2 Tell Aaron and
his sons to treat with respect the sacred
offerings which the Israelites consecrate to me;
otherwise they will profane my holy name. I am
the LORD.
3 † Tell them: If any one of you, or of your de-
scendants in any future generation, dares, while
he is in a state of uncleanness, to draw near the
sacred offerings which the Israelites consecrate
to the LORD, such a one shall be cut off from my
presence.* I am the LORD.
4 No descendant of Aaron who is stricken
with a scaly infection,* or who suffers from a
genital discharge,* may eat of the sacred offer-
ings, until he again becomes clean. Moreover, if
anyone touches a person who has become un-
clean by contact with a corpse,* or if anyone has
had an emission of semen,* 5 or if anyone touches
any swarming creature* whose uncleanness is
contagious or any person whose uncleanness, of
whatever kind it may be, is contagious—* 6 the
one who touches such as these shall be unclean
until evening and may not eat of the sacred por-
tions until he has first bathed his body in water.*
7 Then, when the sun sets, he shall be clean.*
Only then may he eat of the sacred offerings, for

LV

†

21:4 *Husband among his kindred*: this probably refers to relatives by marriage and may even include his wife.

21:7 The ideal seems to be that a priest marry a virgin. This is explicitly stated for the high priest (cf. vv. 13–14; so also Ez 44:22, except there priests may marry widows of priests). The high priest has the added limitation that his wife must come from his kindred, i.e., the priestly family (cf. Ez 44:22).

21:16–23 Though priests with certain bodily imperfections cannot serve at the altar (vv. 18–20), they are not impure, since they may still eat of the offerings, which are holy, and do so within the sanctuary precincts since it is there the most holy offerings are to be eaten (v. 22).

22:1–16 While priests with bodily imperfections may eat the holy sacrifices (21:16–23), those impure and those not of the priestly household may not.

22:3–8 On uncleanness, see chaps. 11–15 and notes there.

21:5 Lv 19:27–28; Ez 44:20.
21:7 Lv 19:29; Ez 44:22.
21:8 Lv 1:9.
21:9 Gn 38:24.
21:11 Lv 10:4–7.
21:12 Lv 10:7.
21:14 Ez 44:22.
21:18 Lv 22:19–25; Dt 23:2–9.
21:22 Lv 2:3, 10; 6:29; 7:6, 34.
22:3 Lv 7:20–21.
22:4 Lv 13–14.
22:4 Lv 15:2–18.
22:4 Nm 19:14–22.
22:4 Lv 15:16.
22:5 Lv 11:29–31.
22:5 Lv 15:2–12, 18–27.
22:6 Lv 17:15; Nm 19:7–8, 19; Heb 10:22.
22:7 Dt 23:12.

they are his food. 8 † He shall not make himself
unclean by eating of any animal that has died
of itself or has been killed by wild beasts.* I am
the LORD.
9 They shall keep my charge so that they will
not bear the punishment in this matter and die*
for their profanation. I am the LORD who makes
them holy.
10 Neither an unauthorized person nor a
priest's tenant or laborer may eat of any sacred
offering.* 11 But a slave† whom a priest acquires
by purchase or who is born in his house may
eat of his food. 12 † A priest's daughter who is
married to an unauthorized person may not eat
of the sacred contributions. 13 But if a priest's
daughter is widowed or divorced and, having no
children, returns to her father's house, she may
then eat of her father's food as in her youth. No
unauthorized person, however, may eat of it.
14 * If such a one eats of a sacred offering through
inadvertence, that person shall make restitution
to the priest for the sacred offering, with an in-
crement of one fifth of the amount. 15 The priests
shall not allow the sacred offerings which the
Israelites contribute to the LORD to be profaned*
16 nor make them incur a penalty when they eat
their sacred offerings. For I, the LORD, make them
holy.

Unacceptable Victims

17 † The LORD said to Moses: 18 Speak to Aaron
and his sons and to all the Israelites, and tell
them: When anyone of the house of Israel, or any
alien residing in Israel, who presents an offering,
brings a burnt offering* as a votive offering or as
a voluntary offering to the LORD, 19 if it is to be
acceptable for you, it must be an unblemished
male of the herd, of the sheep or of the goats.*
20 You shall not offer one that has any blemish,
for such a one would not be acceptable on your
behalf.* 21 When anyone presents a communion
sacrifice* to the LORD from the herd or the flock
in fulfillment of a vow, or as a voluntary offering,
if it is to find acceptance, it must be unblem-
ished; it shall not have any blemish. 22 One that
is blind or lame or maimed, or one that has run-
ning lesions or sores or scabs, you shall not offer
to the LORD; do not put such an animal on the
altar as an oblation to the LORD. 23 † An ox or a
sheep that has a leg that is too long or is stunted
you may indeed present as a voluntary offering,
but it will not be acceptable as a votive offering.
24 One that has its testicles bruised or crushed or
torn out or cut off you shall not offer to the LORD.
You shall neither do this in your own land 25 nor
receive from a foreigner any such animals to offer
up as the food of your God; since they are de-
formed or blemished, they will not be acceptable
on your behalf.
26 † The LORD said to Moses: 27 When an ox or
a lamb or a goat is born, it shall remain with its
mother for seven days; only from the eighth day
onward will it be acceptable, to be offered as an
oblation to the LORD.* 28 You shall not slaughter
an ox or a sheep on one and the same day with
its young. 29 Whenever you offer a thanksgiving
sacrifice to the LORD, so offer it that it may be
acceptable on your behalf; 30 it must be eaten on
the same day; none of it shall be left over until
morning.* I am the LORD.
31 Be careful to observe my commandments. I
am the LORD. 32 Do not profane my holy name,
that in the midst of the Israelites I may be hal-
lowed. I, the LORD, make you holy, 33 who led
you out of the land of Egypt to be your God. I
am the LORD.

Holy Days†

23 1 The LORD said to Moses: 2 Speak to the
Israelites and tell them: The following are
the festivals* of the LORD, which you shall declare
holy days. These are my festivals:
3 For six days work may be done; but the sev-
enth day is a sabbath of complete rest,† a de-
clared holy day; you shall do no work. It is the
LORD's sabbath wherever you dwell.*

22:8 See note on 11:39–40.

22:11 *Slave*: in contrast to the tenant or hired worker of v. 10, the slave, who is by definition a foreigner, is part of the priest's household and therefore may eat of sacrifices.

22:12–13 A priest's daughter, when a dependent of her father, may eat of the lesser holy offerings.

22:17–25 This passage complements the section on the bodily imperfections of priests in 21:16–23. The laws taken together indicate that whoever and whatever approaches and contacts the altar needs to be physically unimpaired.

22:23 Burnt offerings and communion sacrifices brought as voluntary offerings may have slight defects, probably because they are freely given and do not depend upon a prior promise as do votive offerings.

22:26–30 Other activities and procedures that would impair sacrifice are appended here. The rules in vv. 27–28 are reminiscent of the rule not to boil a young goat in its mother's milk (Ex 23:19; 34:26; Dt 14:21) and not to take a bird and its eggs (Dt 22:6–7), all of which have a humanitarian tenor.

23:1–44 This is paralleled by another calendar from the Priestly tradition, in Nm 28–29. Non-Priestly resumes of festal and holy observances are found in Ex 23:10–17; 34:18–24 and Dt 16:1–17.

23:3 *Sabbath of complete rest*: the sabbath and the Day of Atonement are called "sabbaths of complete rest" (Ex 16:23; 31:15; 35:2; Lv 16:31; 23:32). Work of any sort is prohibited on these days

---

22:8 Lv 11:39–40; Ez 44:31.
22:9 Lv 15:31.
22:10 Mt 12:4.
22:14 Lv 5:15–16.
22:15 Lv 19:8; Nm 18:32.
22:18 Lv 1:3.
22:19 Lv 21:16–23.
22:20 Dt 15:21; 17:1; Mal 1:7–14.
22:21 Lv 3:1; 7:11.
22:27 Ex 22:29; 23:19.
22:30 Lv 7:15.
23:2 Nm 28–29; Dt 16:1–17.
23:3 Lv 19:3; 26:2; Ex 20:8–11; 23:12; 31:14–15; 34:21; Nm 28:9–10; Dt 5:12–15; Lk 13:14.

Cultural Connection

Korean Festival Customs

In preparation for the Lunar New Year (in January or February) and for the Moon Festival (a feast of thanksgiving in August), Korean families follow some traditional customs. These customs are similar to those of the Israelite festivals described in Leviticus, chapter 23.

In Korea, the day before each feast is used for purification. People take ceremonial baths, symbolizing the total cleansing of their body, their spirit, and their attitudes. The baths wash away meanness, carelessness, and other faults. The people also wear new clothes and often get a haircut.

Before sunrise on the day of the feast, the people bow before a table holding name cards of their ancestors. They use incense, pour out wine, and pray to their ancestors, asking for their intercession and help. Family members pray silently for all their individual and family needs. During the day, families visit the homes of their extended family. During these visits, the prayer ritual is often repeated.

After a day of visiting, families return home for a feast of the best food and drink possible. The sharing of food is the most significant part of the meal. Neighbors exchange portions of food with one another and bring food to poor families. Families set food on a small table near the door as an offering of thanks to the Creator and sprinkle rice on the ground around their house in gratitude for the crops.

Lv 23:4–44

Passover

4 These are the festivals of the LORD, holy days
which you shall declare at their proper time.*
5 The Passover of the LORD† falls on the four-
teenth day of the first month, at the evening
twilight.* 6 The fifteenth day of this month is the
LORD's feast of Unleavened Bread. For seven days
you shall eat unleavened bread.* 7 On the first of
these days you will have a declared holy day; you
shall do no heavy work. 8 On each of the seven
days you shall offer an oblation to the LORD.
Then on the seventh day you will have a declared
holy day; you shall do no heavy work.
9 † The LORD said to Moses: 10 Speak to the Is-
raelites and tell them: When you come into the
land which I am giving you, and reap its harvest,
you shall bring the first sheaf of your harvest to
the priest, 11 who shall elevate* the sheaf before
the LORD that it may be acceptable on your be-
half.* On the day after the sabbath† the priest
shall do this. 12 On this day, when your sheaf is
elevated, you shall offer to the LORD for a burnt
offering an unblemished yearling lamb. 13 Its
grain offering shall be two tenths of an ephah
of bran flour mixed with oil, as a sweet-smelling
oblation to the LORD; and its libation shall be a
fourth of a hin of wine. 14 You shall not eat any
bread or roasted grain or fresh kernels until this
day, when you bring the offering for your God.
This shall be a perpetual statute throughout your
generations wherever you dwell.

Pentecost

15 Beginning with the day after the sabbath, the
day on which you bring the sheaf for elevation, you
shall count seven full weeks;* 16 you shall count to
the day after the seventh week, fifty days.† * Then

(Lv 23:3, 28; Nm 29:7) as opposed to other holy days where only laborious work is prohibited but light work, such as preparing food, is allowed (Ex 12:16; cf. Lv 23:7, 8, 21, 25, 35, 36; Nm 28:18, 25, 26; 29:1, 12, 35).

23:5–6 *The Passover of the LORD . . .feast of Unleavened Bread*: the two occasions were probably separate originally. Combined they celebrate the exodus from Egypt. Cf. Ex 12:1–20, 43–49; Nm 28:16–25.

23:9–14 Around Passover a first fruits offering is to be brought (see 2:14), consisting of a sheaf of barley, the crop that matures at this time of year.

23:11 *Day after the sabbath*: the singular term *shabbat* "sabbath" may mean "week" here and refer to the seven-day period of the feast of Unleavened Bread. According to this interpretation, the barley sheaf is offered the day after the week of Unleavened Bread. Others understand it as referring to the first or last day of Unleavened Bread.

23:16–21 *Fifty days*: Pentecost. This festival occurs on a single day, fifty days after the feast of Unleavened Bread, elsewhere called the "feast of the Harvest" (Ex 23:16), "Day of First Fruits" (Nm 28:26),

---

23:4 Ex 23:14–19.
23:5 Ex 12:1–51; Nm 9:1–8; 28:16–25; Dt 16:1–8.
23:6 Ex 12:18; 13:3–10; 23:15; 34:18.
23:11 Lv 7:30.
23:11 Dt 26:2.
23:15 Ex 23:16; 34:22; Nm 28:26–31; Dt 16:9–12.
23:16 Acts 2:1.

you shall present a new grain offering to the LORD.
17 For the elevated offering of your first-ripened
fruits to the LORD, you shall bring with you from
wherever you live two loaves of bread made of
two tenths of an ephah of bran flour and baked
with leaven. 18 Besides the bread, you shall offer
to the LORD a burnt offering of seven unblemished
yearling lambs, one bull of the herd, and two rams,
along with their grain offering and libations, as a
sweet-smelling oblation to the LORD. 19 One male
goat shall be sacrificed as a purification offering,
and two yearling lambs as a communion sacrifice.
20 The priest shall elevate them—that is, the two
lambs—with the bread of the first-ripened fruits as
an elevated offering before the LORD; these shall be
sacred to the LORD and belong to the priest. 21 On
this same day you shall make a proclamation:
there shall be a declared holy day for you; no heavy
work may be done. This shall be a perpetual statute
through all your generations wherever you dwell.
22 * When you reap the harvest of your land,
you shall not be so thorough that you reap the
field to its very edge, nor shall you gather the
gleanings of your harvest. These things you shall
leave for the poor and the alien. I, the LORD, am
your God.

New Year's Day

23 The LORD said to Moses: 24 Tell the Israelites:
On the first day of the seventh month† * you
will have a sabbath rest, with trumpet blasts as
a reminder, a declared holy day; 25 you shall do
no heavy work, and you shall offer an oblation
to the LORD.

The Day of Atonement

26 The LORD said to Moses: 27 Now the tenth
day of this seventh month is the Day of Atone-
ment.† * You will have a declared holy day. You
shall humble yourselves and offer an oblation
to the LORD. 28 On this day you shall not do any
work, because it is the Day of Atonement, when
atonement is made for you before the LORD, your
God. 29 Those who do not humble themselves on
this day shall be cut off from the people. 30 If any-
one does any work on this day, I will remove that
person from the midst of the people. 31 You shall
do no work; this is a perpetual statute through-
out your generations wherever you dwell; 32 it is a
sabbath of complete rest for you. You shall hum-
ble yourselves. Beginning on the evening of the
ninth of the month, you shall keep your sabbath
from evening to evening.

The Feast of Booths

33 The LORD said to Moses: 34 Tell the Israelites:
The fifteenth day of this seventh month is the
LORD's feast of Booths,† * which shall continue
for seven days. 35 On the first day, a declared holy
day, you shall do no heavy work. 36 For seven
days you shall offer an oblation to the LORD, and
on the eighth day you will have a declared holy
day. You shall offer an oblation to the LORD. It is
the festival closing. You shall do no heavy work.
37 † These, therefore, are the festivals of the
LORD which you shall declare holy days, in order
to offer as an oblation to the LORD burnt offer-
ings and grain offerings, sacrifices and libations,
as prescribed for each day, 38 in addition to the
LORD's sabbaths, your donations, your various
votive offerings, and the voluntary offerings that
you present to the LORD.
39 On the fifteenth day, then, of the seventh
month, when you have gathered in the produce
of the land, you shall celebrate the feast of the
LORD† for a whole week. The first and the eighth
day shall be days of rest. 40 On the first day you
shall gather fruit of majestic trees, branches of
palms, and boughs† of leafy trees and valley
willows. Then for a week you shall make merry
before the LORD, your God. 41 You shall keep this
feast of the LORD for one whole week in the year.
By perpetual statute throughout your generations
in the seventh month of the year, you shall keep
it. 42 You shall dwell in booths for seven days;
every native-born Israelite shall dwell in booths,
43 that your descendants may realize that, when
I led the Israelites out of the land of Egypt, I

† and "feast of Weeks" (Ex 34:22; Dt 16:10, 16). The name Pentecost comes from the later Greek term for the holy day (cf. Acts 2:1; 20:16; 1 Cor 16:8), referring to the fiftieth day. This is the occasion for bringing the first fruits of the wheat harvest.

23:24 *First day of the seventh month*: the seventh new moon is counted from a new year beginning in the spring (cf. v. 5). Like the seventh day in the week, it is preeminent among the new moon days (cf. Nm 28:11–15; 29:1–6).

23:27 *Day of Atonement*: see chap. 16 and notes there.

23:34 *Feast of Booths*: this is the final harvest festival of the year celebrating the remaining harvest. It is called the "feast of Ingathering" (Ex 23:16; 34:22), the "feast of Booths" (Lv 23:34; Dt 16:13), or simply the "feast" (1 Kgs 8:65). It is a seven-day festival with an eighth closing day. The first and eighth days are rest days (see note on v. 3).

23:37–38 This appears to be the original conclusion of the chapter.

23:39–43 *The feast of the LORD*: the feast of Booths, the preeminent festival. This section supplements vv. 33–36 by prescribing the popular activities for the festival.

23:40–43 *Fruit . . . branches . . . boughs*: the fruit and/or foliage from these trees is to be gathered, but it is not said how they are used. The command to make merry suggests they may have been used in a procession or even circumambulation of the altar (cf. Ps 26:6). Later tradition understood these prescriptions as referring to making the booths out of the foliage (Neh 8:15).

23:22 Lv 19:9–10.
23:24 Nm 29:1–6.
23:27 Lv 16:1–34; 25:9; Nm 29:7–11.
23:34 Ex 23:16; 34:22; Dt 16:13–15; 31:10; 2 Mc 1:9, 18; Jn 7:2.

made them dwell in booths. I, the LORD, am your
God.
44 Thus did Moses announce to the Israelites
the festivals of the LORD.

The Sanctuary Light†

24 1 The LORD said to Moses: 2 Order the Isra-
elites to bring you clear oil of crushed ol-
ives for the light, so that you may keep the lamp
burning regularly.* 3 In the tent of meeting, out-
side the veil that hangs in front of the covenant,
Aaron shall set up the lamp to burn before the
LORD regularly, from evening till morning, by a
perpetual statute throughout your generations.
4 He shall set up the lamps on the pure gold me-
norah to burn regularly before the LORD.

The Showbread†

5 You shall take bran flour and bake it into
twelve cakes,* using two tenths of an ephah of
flour for each cake. 6 These you shall place in
two piles, six in each pile, on the pure gold table
before the LORD. 7 With each pile put some pure
frankincense, which shall serve as an oblation
to the LORD, a token of the bread offering. 8 Reg-
ularly on each sabbath day the bread* shall be
set out before the LORD on behalf of the Israelites
by an everlasting covenant. 9 It shall belong to
Aaron and his sons, who must eat it in a sacred
place, since it is most sacred,* his as a perpetual
due from the oblations to the LORD.

Punishment of Blasphemy†

10 A man born of an Israelite mother and an
Egyptian father went out among the Israelites,
and in the camp a fight broke out between the
son of the Israelite woman and an Israelite man.
11 The son of the Israelite woman uttered the
LORD's name in a curse and blasphemed. So he
was brought to Moses—now his mother's name
was Shelomith, daughter of Dibri, of the tribe
of Dan— 12 and he was kept in custody till a de-
cision from the LORD should settle the case for
them.* 13 The LORD then said to Moses: 14 Take the
blasphemer outside the camp, and when all who
heard him have laid their hands† on his head,*
let the whole community stone him. 15 Tell the
Israelites: Anyone who blasphemes God shall
bear the penalty; 16 whoever utters the name of
the LORD in a curse shall be put to death.* The
whole community shall stone that person; alien
and native-born alike must be put to death for
uttering the LORD's name in a curse.
17 † Whoever takes the life of any human being
shall be put to death;* 18 whoever takes the life
of an animal shall make restitution of another
animal, life for a life.* 19 † Anyone who inflicts
a permanent injury on his or her neighbor shall
receive the same in return: 20 fracture for fracture,
eye for eye, tooth for tooth. The same injury that
one gives another shall be inflicted in return.*
21 Whoever takes the life of an animal shall make
restitution, but whoever takes a human life shall
be put to death. 22 You shall have but one rule,
for alien and native-born alike.* I, the LORD, am
your God.
23 When Moses told this to the Israelites, they
took the blasphemer outside the camp and
stoned him;* they did just as the LORD com-
manded Moses.

The Sabbatical Year

25 1 The LORD said to Moses on Mount Sinai:
2 † Speak to the Israelites and tell them:
When you enter the land that I am giving you,
let the land, too, keep a sabbath for the LORD.
3 For six years you may sow your field, and for
six years prune your vineyard, gathering in their
produce.* 4 But during the seventh year the land
shall have a sabbath of complete rest, a sabbath

†

24:1–4 On the lamp, see Ex 25:31–40; 26:35; 27:20–21; 37:17–24; 40:24–25; Nm 8:1–4. It occupies the south side of the anterior room of the sanctuary tent and provides light for that room.

24:5–9 On the bread table, see Ex 25:23–29; 26:35; 37:10–16; 40:22–23. It occupies the north side of the anterior room of the sanctuary tent. The bread is a type of grain offering (see note on 2:1).

24:10–22 This is a narrative where an offense leads to clarifying revelation similar to the cases in Lv 10:1–7 and 16:1–34; Nm 9:6–14 and 15:32–36.

24:14 *Laid their hands*: see notes on 1:4 and 16:21. It may be that blasphemy generated a type of pollution which the hearers return to the culprit by this gesture.

24:17–22 A digression dealing with bodily injury follows the blasphemy rules. It may have been appended since the first case is another example of the death penalty. But the section develops according to its own logic. All legal traditions require death for homicide: Gn 9:5–6; Ex 21:12–14; Nm 35:9–34; Dt 19:1–13; cf. Ex 20:13 and Dt 5:17.

24:19–20 The phrase "life for a life" in v. 18 leads to introducing the law of talion in vv. 19–20. Some have interpreted the law here and the similar expressions in Ex 21:23–25 and Dt 19:21 to mean that monetary compensation equal to the injury is to be paid, though the wording of the law here and the context of Dt 19:21 indicate an injury is to be inflicted upon the injurer.

25:2–7 As every seventh day is to be a day of rest (cf. 23:3), so every seventh year is a year of rest (cf. 26:34–35, 43). The rest consists in not doing agricultural work. The people are to live off what grows naturally in the fields (vv. 6–7). Verses 19–22 add insurance by saying that God will make the sixth-year crop abundant such that its excess will stretch over the seventh sabbatical year as well as the eighth year when new crops are not yet harvested (cf. 26:10). Cf. Ex 23:10–11.

*

24:2 Ex 25:31–40; 27:20–21.
24:5 Ex 25:23–30; 1 Kgs 7:48; 2 Chr 13:11; Heb 9:2.
24:8 1 Chr 9:32.
24:9 1 Sm 21:5.
24:12 Nm 15:34.
24:14 Lv 16:21.
24:16 Ex 22:27; 1 Kgs 21:10, 13; Mt 26:65–66; Jn 10:33.
24:17 Gn 9:5–6; Ex 21:12–14; Nm 35:9–34; Dt 19:11–13.
24:18 Ex 21:33–34; cf. Lv 17:4.
24:20 Ex 21:23–25; Dt 19:21; Mt 5:38.
24:22 Lv 19:34; Ex 12:49; Nm 15:16.
24:23 Acts 7:57–58.
25:3 Ex 23:10–11.

25:9

for the LORD,* when you may neither sow your field nor prune your vineyard. 5 The aftergrowth of your harvest you shall not reap, nor shall you pick the grapes of your untrimmed vines. It shall be a year of rest for the land. 6 While the land has its sabbath, all its produce will be food to eat for you yourself and for your male and female slave, for your laborer and the tenant who live with you, 7 and likewise for your livestock and for the wild animals on your land.

The Jubilee Year

8 † You shall count seven weeks of years—seven times seven years—such that the seven weeks of years amount to forty-nine years. 9 Then, on the tenth day of the seventh month† let the ram's horn resound; on this, the Day of Atonement,* the ram's horn blast shall resound throughout your land. 10 You shall treat this fiftieth year as sacred. You shall proclaim liberty in the land for all its inhabitants.* It shall be a jubilee for you, when each of you shall return to your own property, each of you to your own family. 11 This fiftieth year is your year of jubilee; you shall not sow, nor shall you reap the aftergrowth or pick the untrimmed vines, 12 since this is the jubilee. It shall be sacred for you. You may only eat what the field yields of itself.

13 In this year of jubilee, then, each of you shall return to your own property. 14 Therefore, when you sell any land to your neighbor or buy any from your neighbor, do not deal unfairly with one another. 15 On the basis of the number of years since the last jubilee you shall purchase the land from your neighbor;* and so also, on the basis of the number of years of harvest, that person shall sell it to you. 16 When the years are many, the price shall be so much the more; when the years are few, the price shall be so much the less. For it is really the number of harvests that the person sells you. 17 Do not deal unfairly with one another, then; but stand in fear of your God. I, the LORD, am your God.

18 Observe my statutes and be careful to keep my ordinances, so that you will dwell securely in the land. 19 The land will yield its fruit and you will eat your fill, and live there securely.* 20 And if you say, "What shall we eat in the seventh year, if we do not sow or reap our crop?"* 21 I will command such a blessing for you in the sixth year that there will be crop enough for three years, 22 and when you sow in the eighth year, you will still be eating from the old crop; even into the ninth year, until the crop comes in, you will still be eating from the old crop.*

Redemption of Property†

23 The land shall not be sold irrevocably; for the land is mine, and you are but resident aliens and under my authority. 24 Therefore, in every part of the country that you occupy, you must permit the land to be redeemed. 25 When one of your kindred is reduced to poverty and has to sell some property, that person's closest relative,† who has the duty to redeem it, shall come and redeem what the relative has sold.* 26 If, however, the person has no relative to redeem it, but later on acquires sufficient means to redeem it, 27 the person shall calculate the years since the sale, return the balance to the one to whom it was sold, and thus regain the property.* 28 But if the person does not acquire sufficient means to buy back the land, what was sold shall remain in the possession of the purchaser until the year of the jubilee, when it must be released and returned to the original owner.*

29 † When someone sells a dwelling in a walled town, it can be redeemed up to a full year after its sale—the redemption period is one year. 30 But if such a house in a walled town has not been redeemed at the end of a full year, it shall belong irrevocably to the purchaser throughout the generations; it shall not be released in the jubilee.

†

25:8–17 The fiftieth year is the jubilee, determined by counting off "seven weeks of years." It is sacred, like the sabbath day. Specifically, in it indentured Israelites return to their own households and land that has been sold returns to its original owner. Different laws are found in Ex 21:1–6; Dt 15:1–3, 12–18 (cf. Jer 34:8–22).

25:9 *Seventh month*: the priestly laws reflect the use of two calendars, one starting in the spring (cf. chap. 23) and one in the fall. The jubilee is calculated on the basis of the latter. *Ram's horn*: Hebrew *shophar*. The name for the year, jubilee (Heb. *yobel*), also means "ram's horn" and comes from the horn blown to announce the occasion.

25:23–55 This is a series of laws dealing mainly with situations of poverty in which one has to sell land, obtain a loan, or become indentured. Many of the laws are connected with the release of debts in the jubilee year.

25:25 A close family member is responsible for redemption. Some of these are specified in v. 49.

25:29–31 Not being able to redeem a house in a walled city after one year is probably due to the demographic and economic situation of large towns as opposed to small villages and open agricultural areas. The agricultural lands associated with the latter were the foundation for the economic viability of the Israelite family, and as such, God—who is the ultimate owner of the land (25:23)—has assigned them to the Israelites as permanent holdings.

*

25:4 Lv 26:34; 1 Mc 6:49, 53.
25:9 Lv 16:29.
25:10 Nm 36:4; Is 61:2; Jer 34:8–22; Ez 46:17; Lk 4:19.
25:15 Lv 27:18, 23.
25:19 Lv 26:5–6.
25:20 Mt 6:25, 31–34; Lk 12:22, 29.
25:22 Lv 26:10.
25:25 Ru 2:20; 4:4, 6; Jer 32:7–8.
25:27 Lv 27:18, 23.
25:28 Lv 27:24.

31 However, houses in villages that are not en-
circled by walls shall be reckoned as part of the
surrounding farm land; they may be redeemed,
and in the jubilee they must be released.
32 † In levitical cities* the Levites shall always
have the right to redeem the houses in the cities
that are in their possession. 33 As for levitical prop-
erty that goes unredeemed—houses sold in cities
of their possession shall be released in the jubilee;
for the houses in levitical cities are their posses-
sion in the midst of the Israelites. 34 Moreover, the
pasture land* belonging to their cities shall not be
sold at all; it must always remain their possession.
35 When one of your kindred is reduced to
poverty and becomes indebted to you, you shall
support that person like a resident alien; let your
kindred live with you. 36 Do not exact interest in
advance or accrued interest,† but out of fear of
God let your kindred live with you. 37 * Do not
give your money at interest or your food at a
profit. 38 I, the LORD, am your God, who brought
you out of the land of Egypt to give you the land
of Canaan and to be your God.
39 † When your kindred with you, having been
so reduced to poverty, sell themselves to you,
do not make them work as slaves.* 40 Rather,
let them be like laborers or like your tenants,
working with you until the jubilee year, 41 when,
together with any children, they shall be released
from your service and return to their family and
to their ancestral property. 42 Since they are my
servants, whom I brought out of the land of
Egypt, they shall not sell themselves as slaves
are sold. 43 Do not lord it over them harshly, but
stand in fear of your God.
44 † The male and female slaves that you pos-
sess—these you shall acquire from the nations
round about you.* 45 You may also acquire them
from among the resident aliens who reside with
you, and from their families who are with you,
those whom they bore in your land. These you
may possess, 46 and bequeath to your children
as their hereditary possession forever. You may
treat them as slaves. But none of you shall lord it
harshly over any of your fellow Israelites.*

Did You Know?

7 x 7 + 1 = Jubilee!

In the Bible, seven is a special number. Just as the seventh day of the week was set aside as a day of rest in ancient Israel, so the seventh year was set aside as a year of rest for the land. Fields were to remain uncultivated during the seventh year; whatever fruits or grains grew on their own were to be left for those who were poor. The "sabbatical year" was a reminder to the people that the land actually belonged to God, not to them.

Seven may be a special number, but seven times seven plus one is very special. The fiftieth year—the year after seven times seven years—was declared the Jubilee year, and God's law demanded some very special things to happen. The people were to take a year of vacation from their normal routine. This meant no planting for a farmer, no lending for a banker, and no big sales for a merchant. Why this break? Because God wanted the Jubilee year to be a time when everyone started over with a clean slate. During the Jubilee, all land was to be returned to its original owners, and all Israelite slaves were to be set free. Debts were to be forgiven and justly settled. The year of Jubilee was like the reset button on a computer, stopping everything and returning it to its original setting. It was a check against the unjust distribution of property and wealth.

The Catholic Church has continued the custom of celebrating the fiftieth year, especially when it marks the end of a century. Faithful to its Jewish roots, the Church sees the Jubilee year as a special time for renewal. In preparation for a Jubilee year, it asks individuals and communities to commit themselves to following Jesus more faithfully.

▶ Leviticus, chapter 25

†

25:32–34 An exception to the rule in vv. 29–31 is made for levitical cities (Nm 35:1–8), since the Levites have no broad land holdings. Their houses can be redeemed and are to be released in the jubilee year.

25:36 *Interest in advance or accrued interest*: two types of interest are mentioned here. The former may refer to interest subtracted from the loaned amount in advance, and the latter, to interest or a payment in addition to the loaned amount.

25:39–43 Here the individual Israelite has no assets and must become indentured to another Israelite for economic survival. No provision is given for redemption before the jubilee year, though such is probably allowed.

25:44–46 While Israelites may not be held as permanent slaves (vv. 39–43, 47–55), foreigners may be. They are not released in the jubilee, but may be bequeathed to one's children. They may be treated as "slaves," i.e., harshly (cf. Ex 21:20–21).

*

25:32 Nm 35:1–8.
25:34 Nm 35:3.
25:37 Ex 22:24; Dt 23:20.
25:39 Ex 21:2–11; Dt 15:12–18; 1 Kgs 9:22; Jer 34:8–22.
25:44 Dt 21:10–14.
25:46 Is 14:1–2.

47 When your kindred, having been so reduced to poverty, sell themselves to a resident alien who has become wealthy or to descendants of a resident alien's family, 48 even after having sold themselves, they still may be redeemed by one of their kindred, 49 by an uncle or cousin, or by some other relative from their family; or, having acquired the means, they may pay the redemption price themselves. 50 With the purchaser they shall compute the years from the sale to the jubilee, distributing the sale price over these years as though they had been hired as laborers. 51 The more years there are, the more of the sale price they shall pay back as the redemption price; 52 the fewer years there are before the jubilee year, the more they have as credit; in proportion to the years of service they shall pay the redemption price. 53 The tenant alien shall treat those who sold themselves as laborers hired on an annual basis, and the alien shall not lord it over them harshly before your very eyes. 54 And if they are not redeemed by these means, they shall nevertheless be released, together with any children, in the jubilee year. 55 For the Israelites belong to me as servants; they are my servants, whom I brought out of the land of Egypt, I, the LORD, your God.

The Reward of Obedience

26 1 † Do not make idols for yourselves. You shall not erect a carved image or a sacred stone for yourselves, nor shall you set up a carved stone for worship in your land;* for I, the LORD, am your God. 2 Keep my sabbaths,* and reverence my sanctuary. I am the LORD.

3 † * If you live in accordance with my statutes and are careful to observe my commandments, 4 I will give you your rains in due season, so that the land will yield its crops, and the trees their fruit;* 5 your threshing will last till vintage time, and your vintage till the time for sowing, and you will eat your fill of food, and live securely in your land.* 6 I will establish peace in the land, and you will lie down to rest with no one to cause you anxiety. I will rid the country of ravenous beasts, and no sword shall sweep across your land. 7 You will rout your enemies, and they shall fall before your sword. 8 Five of you will put a hundred of your foes to flight, and a hundred of you will put to flight ten thousand, till your enemies fall before your sword.* 9 I will look with favor upon you, and make you fruitful and numerous,* as I carry out my covenant with you. 10 You shall eat the oldest stored harvest, and have to discard it to make room for the new.* 11 * I will set my tabernacle in your midst, and will not loathe you. 12 Ever present in your midst, I will be your God, and you will be my people; 13 I, the LORD, am your God, who brought you out of the land of Egypt to be their slaves no more, breaking the bars of your yoke and making you walk erect.*

The Punishment of Disobedience†

14 * But if you do not heed me and do not keep all these commandments, 15 if you reject my statutes and loathe my decrees, refusing to obey all my commandments and breaking my covenant, 16 then I, in turn, will do this to you: I will bring terror upon you—with consumption and fever to dim the eyes and sap the life. You will sow your seed in vain, for your enemies will consume the crop. 17 I will turn against you, and you will be beaten down before your enemies* and your foes will lord it over you. You will flee though no one pursues you.

18 If even after this you do not obey me, I will increase the chastisement for your sins sevenfold,* 19 to break your proud strength. I will make the sky above you as hard as iron, and your soil as hard as bronze, 20 so that your strength will be spent in vain; your land will bear no crops, and its trees no fruit.

21 If then you continue hostile, unwilling to obey me, I will multiply my blows sevenfold, as your sins deserve. 22 I will unleash wild beasts against you, to rob you of your children and wipe out your livestock, till your population dwindles away and your roads become deserted.

23 If, with all this, you still do not accept my discipline and continue hostile to me, 24 * I, too, will continue to be hostile to you and I, for my part, will smite you for your sins sevenfold. 25 I will bring against you the sword, the avenger of

---

† **26:1–46** This chapter concludes the revelation of laws at Mount Sinai (cf. v. 46). Blessings and curses are also found at the end of Deuteronomy's law collection (Dt 28). Similar lists of blessings and curses appear in the conclusions of ancient Near Eastern treaties.

26:3–13 The blessings are concerned with the well-being of the nation and its land and involve agricultural bounty, national security, military success and population growth.

26:14–46 To encourage obedience, the list of punishments is longer than the blessings (cf. a similar proportion in Dt 28). The punishments are presented in waves (vv. 14–17, 18–20, 21–22, 23–26, 27–39), one group following another if the people do not return to obedience. Punishments involve sickness, pestilence, agricultural failure and famine, attack of wild animals, death of the people's children, destruction of illicit and even licit cults, military defeat, panic, and exile.

---

* **26:1** Lv 19:4; Nm 33:52.
26:2 Lv 23:3.
26:3 Dt 28:1–69.
26:4 Dt 11:14; Ps 85:13; Ez 34:26–27.
26:5 Lv 25:18–19; Dt 12:10.
26:8 Dt 32:30; Jos 23:10.
26:9 Gn 1:28; Ex 1:7.
26:10 Lv 25:22.
26:11–12 Ex 29:45; Ez 37:26–28; 2 Cor 6:16.
26:13 Ez 34:27; Na 1:13.
26:14 Dt 28:15–69.
26:17 2 Kgs 8:33–34.
26:18 Ps 79:12; Prv 6:31.
26:24–25 Jer 2:30; Ez 5:17; 14:17.

my covenant. Though you then huddle together
in your cities, I will send pestilence among you,
till you are delivered to the enemy. 26 When I
break your staff of bread, ten women will need
but one oven for baking your bread, and they
shall dole it out to you by weight;* and though
you eat, you shall not be satisfied.
27 If, despite all this, you disobey and continue
hostile to me, 28 I will continue in my hostile
rage toward you, and I myself will discipline you
for your sins sevenfold, 29 till you begin to eat
the flesh of your own sons and daughters.* 30 I
will demolish your high places, overthrow your
incense stands, and cast your corpses upon the
corpses of your idols.* In my loathing of you, 31 I
will lay waste your cities and desolate your sanc-
tuaries, refusing your sweet-smelling offerings.
32 So devastated will I leave the land that your
enemies who come to live there will stand aghast
at the sight of it.* 33 And you I will scatter among
the nations* at the point of my drawn sword,
leaving your countryside desolate and your cities
deserted. 34 Then shall the land, during the time
it lies waste, make up its lost sabbaths, while
you are in the land of your enemies; then shall
the land have rest and make up for its sabbaths*
35 during all the time that it lies desolate, enjoy-
ing the rest that you would not let it have on
your sabbaths when you lived there.
36 Those of you who survive in the lands of
their enemies, I will make so fainthearted that
the sound of a driven leaf will pursue them,
and they shall run as if from the sword, and
fall though no one pursues them; 37 stumbling
over one another as if to escape a sword, while
no one is after them—so helpless will you be to
take a stand against your foes! 38 You shall per-
ish among the nations, swallowed up in your
enemies' country. 39 Those of you who survive
will waste away in the lands of their enemies, for
their own and their ancestors' guilt.*
40 † They will confess* their iniquity and the in-
iquity of their ancestors in their treachery against
me and in their continued hostility toward me,
41 so that I, too, had to be hostile to them and
bring them into their enemies' land. Then, when
their uncircumcised hearts are humbled and
they make amends for their iniquity, 42 I will re-
member my covenant with Jacob, and also my
covenant with Isaac; and also my covenant with
Abraham I will remember.* The land, too, I will
remember. 43 The land will be forsaken by them,
that in its desolation without them, it may make
up its sabbaths, and that they, too, may make
good the debt of their guilt for having spurned
my decrees and loathed my statutes. 44 Yet even
so, even while they are in their enemies' land,
I will not reject or loathe them to the point of
wiping them out, thus making void my covenant
with them; for I, the LORD, am their God. 45 I will
remember for them the covenant I made with
their forebears, whom I brought out of the land
of Egypt before the eyes of the nations,* that I
might be their God. I am the LORD.
46 These are the statutes, decrees and laws
which the LORD established between himself and
the Israelites through Moses on Mount Sinai.*

V. Redemption of Offerings

Votive Offerings and Dedications

27 1 The LORD said to Moses: 2 † Speak to the
Israelites and tell them: When anyone
makes a vow to the LORD* with respect to the
value of a human being, 3 the value for males be-
tween the ages of twenty and sixty shall be fifty
silver shekels, by the sanctuary shekel; 4 and for
a female, the value shall be thirty shekels. 5 For
persons between the ages of five and twenty, the
value for a male shall be twenty shekels, and for
a female, ten shekels. 6 For persons between the
ages of one month and five years, the value for a
male shall be five silver shekels, and for a female,
three shekels. 7 For persons of sixty or more, for
a male the value shall be fifteen shekels, and ten
shekels for a female. 8 However, if the one who
made the vow is too poor to meet the sum,*
the person must be set before the priest, who
shall determine a value; the priest will do this in
keeping with the means of the one who made
the vow.
9 If the offering vowed to the LORD is an animal

†

26:40–45 Even though the people may be severely punished, God will remember the covenant when the people repent.

27:2–13 Vows are conditional promissory oaths. One covenants to do something for the benefit of God, usually to make a dedication, if God fulfills the individual's accompanying request (cf. Gn 28:20–21; Jgs 11:30–31; 1 Sm 1:11; 2 Sm 15:7–8; Ps 56:13–14). Vows must be fulfilled (Nm 30:3; Dt 23:22; cf. Ps 66:13–15). Verses 2–8 deal with votive offerings involving human beings. Actual dedication of human beings (cf. Jgs 11:30–31, 34–40; 1 Sm 1:11, 24–28) is obviated by payment of the person's value (mentioned in the temple income in 2 Kgs 12:5). The values reflect the different economic and administrative roles of people in different age and gender groups within ancient Israelite society. Verses 9–13 concern the bringing of animals for a vow.

*

26:26 Is 9:19; Ez 4:16; 5:16; 14:13; Mi 6:14.
26:29 Lam 2:20.
26:30 2 Chr 14:5; 34:3–4, 7; Ez 6:3–6.
26:32 1 Kgs 9:8; Jer 9:11; 18:16; 19:8; 25:18.
26:33 Ps 44:12; Jer 15:7; Ez 6:8.
26:34 Lv 25:2; 2 Chr 36:21.
26:39 Ez 4:17; 24:23; 33:10.
26:40 Lv 16:21; Nm 5:7; Neh 1:6.
26:42 Ex 6:5; 2 Kgs 13:23; Ps 106:45; Ez 16:60.
26:45 Ex 12:51.
26:46 Lv 7:38; Nm 36:13.
27:2 Dt 23:22–24; Jgs 11:30–31; Eccl 5:3–4.
27:8 Lv 5:7, 11.

LV

that may be sacrificed, every such animal given
to the LORD becomes sacred.* 10 The offerer shall
not substitute or exchange another for it, either
a worse or a better one. If the offerer exchanges
one animal in place of another, both the origi-
nal and its substitute shall become sacred. 11 If
any unclean animal which is unfit for sacri-
fice* to the LORD is vowed, it must be set before
the priest, 12 who shall determine its value† in
keeping with its good or bad qualities, and the
value set by the priest shall stand. 13 If the offerer
wishes to redeem the animal, the person shall
pay one fifth more than this valuation.*

14 † When someone dedicates a house as sa-
cred to the LORD,† the priest shall determine its
value in keeping with its good or bad qualities,
and the value set by the priest shall stand. 15 A
person dedicating a house who then wishes to
redeem it shall pay one fifth more than the price
thus established, and then it will again belong to
that individual.*

16 If someone dedicates to the LORD a portion
of hereditary land, its valuation shall be made
according to the amount of seed required to sow
it, the acreage sown with a homer† of barley
seed being valued at fifty silver shekels. 17 If the
dedication of a field is made at the beginning of
a jubilee period, the full valuation shall hold;
18 but if it is some time after this, the priest shall
estimate its money value according to the num-
ber of years left until the next jubilee year, with
a corresponding reduction on the valuation.*
19 A person dedicating a field who then wishes
to redeem† * it shall pay one fifth more than
the price thus established, and so reclaim it. 20 If,
instead of redeeming such a field, one sells it†
to another, it may no longer be redeemed; 21 but
at the jubilee it shall be released* as sacred† to
the LORD; like a field that is put under the ban, it
shall become priestly property.

22 If someone dedicates to the LORD a field that
was purchased and was not part of hereditary
property, 23 the priest shall compute its value in
proportion to the number of years until the next
jubilee, and on the same day the person shall pay
the price thus established, a sacred donation to
the LORD; 24 at the jubilee the field shall revert
to the hereditary owner of this land from whom
it had been purchased.†

25 Every valuation shall be made according to
the standard of the sanctuary shekel. There are
twenty gerahs to the shekel.

Irredeemable Offerings

26 † Note that a firstborn animal,* which as
such already belongs to the LORD, may not be
dedicated. Whether an ox or a sheep, it is the
LORD's. 27 But if it is an unclean animal,† it may
be redeemed by paying one fifth more than its
value. If it is not redeemed, it shall be sold at
its value.

28 Note, also, that any possession which some-
one puts under the ban† for the LORD, whether
it is a human being, an animal, or a hereditary
field, shall be neither sold nor redeemed; every-
thing that is put under the ban becomes most
holy to the LORD.* 29 All human beings that are
put under the ban cannot be redeemed; they
must be put to death.*

30 † All tithes of the land, whether in grain
from the fields or in fruit from the trees, belong
to the LORD; they are sacred to the LORD.* 31 If

†

27:12 *Determine its value*: in contrast to human beings (vv. 3–7) there are no set values for unclean animals, and the condition of the animal is taken into consideration (cf. vv. 14, 27).

27:14–24 These verses deal with dedications. They take effect when uttered and, unlike vows, they are not conditional. They are related to the jubilee year laws in 25:23–31.

27:14 *House as sacred to the LORD*: the house becomes sanctuary property and presumably may be sold to another if the owner does not redeem it (cf. notes on vv. 20 and 21). While 25:31 requires that unredeemed houses in unwalled towns be returned to the original owners at the jubilee, in the laws here such houses apparently become the property of the sanctuary (cf. v. 21). It is likely that dedicated houses in a walled city needed to be redeemed within one year, following 25:29–30.

27:16 *Homer*: see note on Is 5:10.

27:19 *Redeem*: the person apparently can redeem the land up to the jubilee year, following 25:23–28. See note on v. 21.

27:20 *If . . . one sells it*: the verse is difficult since the person should not be able to sell the land after it is dedicated. The verb "sells" may be construed impersonally here: "If . . . it is sold," i.e., by the sanctuary.

27:21 *Released as sacred*: the dedication changes the ownership of the land. It now belongs to the sanctuary. It returns to the sanctuary's possession after leasing it out (v. 20). Presumably if the land remained in the sanctuary's possession until the jubilee, and it was not redeemed, the land would belong permanently to the sanctuary and priests.

27:24 In contrast to the cases in vv. 14–15 and 16–21, this land returns to the original owner since that individual did not personally make the dedication. The principle is that one cannot permanently dedicate what one does not own. Cf. 2 Sm 24:22–25.

27:26 Firstborn animals and human beings already belong to God (cf. Ex 13:1–2, 12; 34:19); they cannot be vowed or dedicated. Cf. Nm 18:15–18; Dt 15:19–23.

27:27 *An unclean animal*: such as the firstborn of a donkey, which was unfit for sacrifice. According to Ex 13:13; 34:20, a firstborn donkey was to be redeemed by offering a sheep in its stead, or was to have its neck broken.

27:28 *Puts under the ban*: this is a higher form of dedication to God than that found in vv. 14–24. Anything so dedicated is beyond redemption and cannot be sold by the sanctuary and priests (contrast vv. 15, 19, 20). This type of dedication is found mostly in contexts of war (e.g., Jos 6:17–21; 8:26; 10:1, 28). Lv 27:28 shows that the ban can apply to one's own property.

27:30–33 On the regulation concerning the tithes see Dt 14:22–29.

*

27:9 Lv 27:11, 27.
27:11 Lv 11:2–8; Ex 13:13; 34:20.
27:13 Lv 5:16, 24.
27:15 Lv 22:14.
27:18 Lv 25:15–16, 26–27, 50–52.
27:19 Lv 25:25.
27:21 Lv 25:28, 31.
27:26 Ex 13:2.
27:28 Nm 18:14; Dt 7:26; Jos 7:1; 1 Sm 15:21; Ez 44:29.
27:29 1 Kgs 20:42.
27:30 Nm 18:25–32; Dt 14:22–24; Mal 3:8, 10.

someone wishes to redeem any of the tithes, the
person shall pay one fifth more than their value.
32 The tithes of the herd and the flock, every tenth
animal that passes under the herdsman's rod,
shall be sacred to the LORD. 33 It shall not matter
whether good ones or bad ones are thus chosen,
and no exchange may be made. If any exchange
is made, both the original animal and its substi-
tute become sacred and cannot be redeemed.
34 These are the commandments which the LORD
gave Moses on Mount Sinai for the Israelites.*

* **27:34** Lv 7:38.

Numbers

Sound the trumpet, beat the drum, we are going to war! The call to arms brings out the best and the worst in people—courage and cowardice, love and hate, hope and fear. The Book of Numbers records the varied experiences of the Israelites as they prepare for the armed conquest of the Promised Land. But most important, it tells of God's insistence that they maintain their purity and holiness to be worthy recipients of God's promises.

In Depth

Although the Book of Numbers is named for the two censuses mentioned in it (see chapters 1 and 26), the book's original Hebrew name, meaning "in the desert," describes it better. Numbers picks up the story of the Israelites where Exodus leaves off. The first section begins with a census at Mount Sinai to determine who is eligible for military service. As the people prepare to enter the Promised Land, their leaders review the laws and regulations with them.

In the second section, the Israelites begin their journey to the Promised Land. Unfortunately, they have not learned to put their faith in God, and their journey is marked by grumbling, rebellion, and even idolatry. When the first army refuses to enter the Promised Land because of reports that it is inhabited by a race of giants (see Nm 13:32–33), God decrees that none of the older generation who left Egypt shall enter the Promised Land. So, the Israelites begin their desert wandering, which lasts thirty-eight years (see map 2, "The Exodus from Egypt").

The third section of Numbers paints a more hopeful picture. The people of the new generation are faithful and obedient as they prepare to enter the Promised Land. They experience victory against the Midianites (see chapter 31) and conquer the land east of the Jordan (see chapter 32). The God who liberated their ancestors from Egypt and sustained and led them through the wilderness with Moses is the same God who now makes ready to fulfill the promise of the Land to Israel.

Numbers was compiled and edited by priestly scribes hundreds of years after these events, after the people had lost the Promised Land to the Babylonians. They fully appreciated the gift of the Land only after they had lost it. For the Israelites in the Babylonian Exile, Numbers portrayed the hopeful, grateful, and faithful hearts required of those whom God blesses.

At a Glance

I. **Census and Preparation for the Departure from Sinai (1:1—10:10).**

II. **Departure, Rebellion, and Wandering in the Wilderness for Forty Years (10:11—25:18).**

III. **Second Census of a New Generation and Preparation to Enter the Promised Land (25:19—36:13).**

Quick Facts

Period Covered: the thirty-eight years of wandering in the desert after the Exodus

Inspired Authors: priestly scribes writing during the Babylonian Exile (587–538 BC)

Theme: Faithfulness and gratefulness to God are necessary for Israel to obtain the Promised Land.

Numbers

13:23

I. Census and Preparation for the Departure from Sinai

The Census

1 1 In the second year after the Israelites' depar-
ture from the land of Egypt, on the first day of
the second month, the LORD said to Moses at the
tent of meeting in the wilderness of Sinai: 2 † Take
a census of the whole community of the Israel-
ites,* by clans and ancestral houses, registering
by name each male individually. 3 You and Aaron
shall enroll in companies all the men in Israel
of twenty years or more who are fit for military
service.

Moses' Assistants

4 With you there shall be a man from each tribe,
each the head of his ancestral house. 5 * These are
the names of those who are to assist you:

from Reuben: Elizur, son of Shedeur;
6 from Simeon: Shelumiel, son of Zurishaddai;
7 from Judah:* Nahshon, son of Amminadab;
8 from Issachar: Nethanel, son of Zuar;
9 from Zebulun: Eliab, son of Helon;
10 for the descendants of Joseph: from Ephraim:
Elishama, son of Ammihud; and from
Manasseh: Gamaliel, son of Pedahzur;
11 from Benjamin: Abidan, son of Gideoni;
12 from Dan: Ahiezer, son of Ammishaddai;
13 from Asher: Pagiel, son of Ochran;
14 from Gad: Eliasaph, son of Reuel;
15 from Naphtali: Ahira, son of Enan.

16 * These were the elect of the community,
leaders of their ancestral tribes, heads of the clans
of Israel. 17 So Moses and Aaron took these men
who had been designated by name, 18 and assem-
bled the whole community on the first day of
the second month. Every man of twenty years or
more then registered individually his name and
lineage according to clan and ancestral house,
19 as the LORD had commanded Moses. So he en-
rolled them in the wilderness of Sinai.

Count of the Twelve Tribes

20 Of the descendants of Reuben, the firstborn
of Israel, registered individually by name and
lineage according to their clans and ancestral
houses, every male of twenty years or more, ev-
eryone fit for military service: 21 those enrolled
from the tribe of Reuben were forty-six thousand
five hundred.

22 Of the descendants of Simeon, registered in-
dividually by name and lineage according to their
clans and ancestral houses, every male of twenty
years or more, everyone fit for military service:
23 those enrolled from the tribe of Simeon were
fifty-nine thousand three hundred.

† **1:2** All Israel was divided into tribes, each tribe into clans, and each clan into ancestral houses.

* **1:2–3** Nm 14:29; 26:2–51. **1:5–15** Nm 10:14–28. **1:7** Mt 1:4; Lk 3:32–33. **1:16** Ex 18:21, 25.

24 Of the descendants of Gad, registered by
name and lineage according to their clans and
ancestral houses, every male of twenty years or
more, everyone fit for military service: 25 those
enrolled from the tribe of Gad were forty-five
thousand six hundred and fifty.

26 Of the descendants of Judah, registered by
name and lineage according to their clans and
ancestral houses, every male of twenty years or
more, everyone fit for military service: 27 those
enrolled from the tribe of Judah were seventy-
four thousand six hundred.

28 Of the descendants of Issachar, registered by
name and lineage according to their clans and
ancestral houses, every male of twenty years or
more, everyone fit for military service: 29 those
enrolled from the tribe of Issachar were fifty-four
thousand four hundred.

30 Of the descendants of Zebulun, registered by
name and lineage according to their clans and
ancestral houses, every male of twenty years or
more, everyone fit for military service: 31 those
enrolled from the tribe of Zebulun were fifty-
seven thousand four hundred.

32 Of the descendants of Joseph:

Of the descendants of Ephraim, registered by
name and lineage according to their clans and
ancestral houses, every male of twenty years or
more, everyone fit for military service: 33 those
enrolled from the tribe of Ephraim were forty
thousand five hundred.

34 Of the descendants of Manasseh, registered
by name and lineage according to their clans
and ancestral houses, every male of twenty years
or more, everyone fit for military service: 35 those
enrolled from the tribe of Manasseh were thirty-
two thousand two hundred.

36 Of the descendants of Benjamin, registered
by name and lineage according to their clans
and ancestral houses, every male of twenty years
or more, everyone fit for military service: 37 those
enrolled from the tribe of Benjamin were thirty-
five thousand four hundred.

38 Of the descendants of Dan, registered by
name and lineage according to their clans and
ancestral houses, every male of twenty years or
more, everyone fit for military service: 39 those
enrolled from the tribe of Dan were sixty-two
thousand seven hundred.

40 Of the descendants of Asher, registered by
name and lineage according to their clans and
ancestral houses, every male of twenty years or
more, everyone fit for military service: 41 those
enrolled from the tribe of Asher were forty-one
thousand five hundred.

42 Of the descendants of Naphtali, registered
by name and lineage according to their clans
and ancestral houses, every male of twenty years
or more, everyone fit for military service: 43 those

Did You Know?

Holy War

The Book of Numbers begins with a census of "all the men in Israel of twenty years or more who are fit for military service" (1:3). The people of Israel are preparing to take over the land God had promised to them, the Chosen People. This is no ordinary war but a Holy war, a war that they believe is divinely inspired, even a war God commands. In 31:2 God says to Moses, "Avenge the Israelites on the Midianites." The Israelites go on to kill every Midianite except for the young girls who are virgins.

How are we to understand this? Does God really order the killing of innocent people? To answer this, let's first remember that the writers of the Bible were influenced by their own cultural background and understanding of God. Three main things were probably on the mind of the writer of Numbers. First, the early Israelites viewed God as a warrior god fighting for them. Second, they believed the Canaanites were a wicked and idolatrous people who deserved punishment. And finally, they believed the Midianites deserved special punishment because they had led the Israelites into idolatry and sin at Shittim (see 25:1–5).

Holy wars are dangerous. Throughout history people have committed atrocities in the name of God. Christians must interpret the Old Testament in the light of Jesus' teachings in the New Testament. Jesus clearly taught that we are to love our enemies because they too are God's beloved children. Jesus was teaching an insight learned by the Israelites hundreds of years after the conquering of Canaan, an insight understood after the Babylonian Exile and taught in the Book of Jonah. This is one area where the New Testament teaching replaces an earlier Old Testament understanding. Holy wars have no place in the lives of Christians.

enrolled from the tribe of Naphtali were fifty-
three thousand four hundred.
44 It was these who were enrolled, each accord-
ing to his ancestral house, by Moses and Aaron
and the twelve leaders of Israel. 45 The total en-
rollment of the Israelites of twenty years or more,
according to their ancestral houses, everyone fit
for military service in Israel— 46 the total enroll-
ment was six hundred and three thousand, five
hundred and fifty.

Levites Omitted in the Census

47 Now the Levites were not enrolled* by their
ancestral tribe with the others.† 48 For the LORD
had told Moses, 49 The tribe of Levi alone you shall
not enroll nor include in the census along with
the other Israelites. 50 You are to give the Levites
charge of the tabernacle of the covenant with all
its equipment and all that belongs to it. It is they
who shall carry the tabernacle with all its equip-
ment and who shall be its ministers;* and they
shall camp all around the tabernacle. 51 When the
tabernacle is to move on, the Levites shall take it
down; when the tabernacle is to be pitched, it is
the Levites who shall set it up. Any unauthorized
person who comes near† it shall be put to death.*
52 The other Israelites shall camp according to
their companies, each in their own divisional
camps,* 53 but the Levites shall camp around the
tabernacle of the covenant to ensure that God's
wrath will not fall upon the Israelite community.
The Levites shall keep guard over the tabernacle of
the covenant.* 54 The Israelites complied; they did
just as the LORD had commanded Moses.

Arrangement of the Tribes

2 1 The LORD said to Moses and Aaron: 2 The
Israelites shall camp, each in their own
divisions, under the ensigns of their ancestral
houses.* They shall camp at some distance all
around the tent of meeting.
3 † Encamped on the east side, toward the
sunrise, shall be the divisional camp of Judah,
arranged in companies. The leader of the Judah-
ites is Nahshon, son of Amminadab, 4 and the
enrollment of his company is seventy-four thou-
sand six hundred. 5 Encamped beside it is the
tribe of Issachar. The leader of the Issacharites
is Nethanel, son of Zuar, 6 and the enrollment
of his company is fifty-four thousand four hun-
dred. 7 Also the tribe of Zebulun. The leader of
the Zebulunites is Eliab, son of Helon, 8 and the
enrollment of his company is fifty-seven thou-
sand four hundred. 9 The total enrollment of the
camp of Judah by companies is one hundred and
eighty-six thousand four hundred. They shall be
first on the march.
10 The divisional camp of Reuben shall be on
the south side, by companies. The leader of the
Reubenites is Elizur, son of Shedeur, 11 and the
enrollment of his company is forty-six thou-
sand five hundred. 12 Encamped beside it is the
tribe of Simeon. The leader of the Simeonites is
Shelumiel, son of Zurishaddai, 13 and the enroll-
ment of his company is fifty-nine thousand three
hundred. 14 Next is the tribe of Gad. The leader of
the Gadites is Eliasaph, son of Reuel, 15 and the
enrollment of his company is forty-five thousand
six hundred and fifty. 16 The total enrollment of
the camp of Reuben by companies is one hun-
dred and fifty-one thousand four hundred and
fifty. They shall be second on the march.
17 Then the tent of meeting and the camp of
the Levites shall set out in the midst of the di-
visions. As they camp, so also they will march,
each in place, by their divisions.
18 The divisional camp of Ephraim shall be
on the west side, by companies. The leader of
the Ephraimites is Elishama, son of Ammihud,
19 and the enrollment of his company is forty
thousand five hundred. 20 Beside it shall be the
tribe of Manasseh. The leader of the Manassites is
Gamaliel, son of Pedahzur, 21 and the enrollment
of his company is thirty-two thousand two hun-
dred. 22 Also the tribe of Benjamin. The leader
of the Benjaminites is Abidan, son of Gideoni,
23 and the enrollment of his company is thirty-
five thousand four hundred. 24 The total enroll-
ment of the camp of Ephraim by companies is
one hundred and eight thousand one hundred.
They shall be third on the march.
25 The divisional camp of Dan shall be on
the north side, by companies. The leader of the
Danites is Ahiezer, son of Ammishaddai, 26 and
the enrollment of his company is sixty-two thou-
sand seven hundred. 27 Encamped beside it shall
be the tribe of Asher. The leader of the Asherites
is Pagiel, son of Ochran, 28 and the enrollment

NM

†

1:47 The Levites were not enrolled in this census, which was principally for military purposes, but a separate census was made of them. Cf. 3:15–16, 39.

1:51 *Comes near*: here and in 3:10, 38; 17:5; 18:4, 7 the Hebrew word rendered "comes near" is very nearly a technical term for someone who intrudes upon or violates a space set apart as holy and for which they have not been qualified by priesthood.

2:3–31 A similar arrangement of the tribes around the central sanctuary in the ideal Israel is given in Ez 48.

*

1:47 Nm 2:33; 3:14–39; 26:57–62.
1:50 Nm 3:7–8; 4:2–49; 1 Chr 6:33.
1:51 Nm 3:10, 38; 18:7; 2 Sm 6:6–7; 1 Chr 13:10.
1:52 Nm 2:2, 34.
1:53 Nm 3:7–8, 38; 8:19; 18:4–5.
2:2 Nm 1:52.

of his company is forty-one thousand five hundred. [29]Also the tribe of Naphtali. The leader of the Naphtalites is Ahira, son of Enan, [30]and the enrollment of his company is fifty-three thousand four hundred. [31]The total enrollment of the camp of Dan is one hundred and fifty-seven thousand six hundred. They shall be the last on the march, by divisions.

[32]* These are the enrollments of the Israelites according to their ancestral houses. The total enrollment of the camps by companies is six hundred and three thousand five hundred and fifty. [33]The Levites, however, were not enrolled with the other Israelites, just as the LORD had commanded Moses. [34]The Israelites did just as the LORD had commanded Moses; both in camp and on the march they were in their own divisions, everyone by clan and according to ancestral house.

The Sons of Aaron

3 [1]These are the offspring of Aaron and Moses at the time the LORD spoke to Moses on Mount Sinai. [2]These are the names of Aaron's sons: Nadab, the firstborn, Abihu, Eleazar, and Ithamar.* [3]These are the names of Aaron's sons, the anointed priests whom he ordained to serve as priests. [4]But Nadab and Abihu died* in the presence of the LORD when they offered unauthorized fire before the LORD in the wilderness of Sinai; and they left no sons. So only Eleazar and Ithamar served as priests during the lifetime of their father Aaron.

Levites in Place of the Firstborn

[5]Now the LORD said to Moses: [6]Summon the tribe of Levi and station them before Aaron the priest to serve him.* [7]They shall discharge his obligations and those of the whole community before the tent of meeting* by maintaining the tabernacle. [8]They shall have responsibility for all the furnishings of the tent of meeting and discharge the obligations of the Israelites by maintaining the tabernacle. [9]You shall assign the Levites to Aaron and his sons;* they have been assigned unconditionally to him from among the Israelites. [10]But you will appoint only Aaron and his descendants to exercise the priesthood.* Any unauthorized person who comes near shall be put to death.

[11]The LORD said to Moses: [12]I hereby take the Levites from the Israelites in place of every firstborn that opens the womb among the Israelites.* The Levites, therefore, are mine, [13]because every firstborn is mine. When I struck down all the firstborn in the land of Egypt, I consecrated to me every firstborn in Israel, human being and beast alike. They belong to me; I am the LORD.

Census of the Levites

[14]The LORD said to Moses in the wilderness of Sinai: [15]Enroll the Levites by their ancestral houses and clans, enrolling every male of a month or more.* [16]Moses, therefore, enrolled them at the direction of the LORD, just as the LORD had charged.

[17]* These were the sons of Levi by name: Gershon, Kohath and Merari. [18]These were the names of the sons of Gershon, by their clans: Libni and Shimei. [19]The sons of Kohath, by their clans, were Amram, Izhar, Hebron and Uzziel. [20]The sons of Merari, by their clans, were Mahli and Mushi. These were the clans of the Levites by their ancestral houses.

Duties of the Levitical Clans

[21]To Gershon belonged the clan of the Libnites and the clan of the Shimeites; these were the clans of the Gershonites. [22]Their enrollment, registering every male of a month or more, was seven thousand five hundred. [23]The clans of the Gershonites camped behind the tabernacle, to the west. [24]The leader of the ancestral house of the Gershonites was Eliasaph, son of Lael. [25]* At the tent of meeting their responsibility was the tabernacle:† the tent and its covering, the curtain at the entrance of the tent of meeting, [26]the hangings of the court, the curtain at the entrance of the court enclosing both the tabernacle and the altar, and the ropes—whatever pertained to their maintenance.

[27]To Kohath belonged the clans of the Amramites, the Izharites, the Hebronites, and the Uzzielites; these were the clans of the Kohathites. [28]Their enrollment, registering every male of a month or more, was eight thousand three hundred. They were the ones who performed the duties of the sanctuary. [29]The clans of the Kohathites camped on the south side of the tabernacle. [30]And the leader of their ancestral house

†

3:25–26 The Gershonites had two wagons for transporting these things; cf. 7:7. For a description of the tabernacle, see Ex 26:1–6; the tent, Ex 26:7–13; its covering, Ex 26:14; the curtain at the entrance, Ex 26:36; the hangings of the court, Ex 27:9–15; the curtain at the entrance of the court, Ex 27:16; the ropes of the tabernacle, Ex 35:18.

2:32–33 Nm 1:44–49.
3:2 Ex 6:23; 1 Chr 24:1.
3:4 Nm 26:61; Lv 10:1–2; 1 Chr 24:2.
3:6 Nm 18:2.
3:7 Nm 8:24.
3:9 Nm 8:19.
3:10 Nm 1:51; 18:7.
3:12–13 Nm 3:41; 8:16–18; Ex 13:2, 12, 15.
3:15 Nm 3:39; 26:62.
3:17–20 Nm 26:57; Gn 46:11; Ex 6:16–19; 1 Chr 6:1–2, 16–19.
3:25–26 Ex 26:7, 14, 36; 36:14.

of the clan of the Kohathites was Elizaphan, son of Uzziel. [31]Their responsibility was the ark, the table, the menorah, the altars, the utensils of the sanctuary with which the priests minister, the veil, and everything pertaining to their maintenance.† [32]The chief of the leaders of the Levites, however, was Eleazar, son of Aaron the priest; he was in charge of those who performed the duties of the sanctuary.

[33]To Merari belonged the clans of the Mahlites and the Mushites; these were the clans of Merari. [34]Their enrollment, registering every male of a month or more, was six thousand two hundred. [35]The leader of the ancestral house of the clans of Merari was Zuriel, son of Abihail. They camped at the north side of the tabernacle. [36] † The Merarites were assigned responsibility for the boards of the tabernacle, its bars, columns, pedestals, and all its fittings—and everything pertaining to their maintenance, [37] as well as the columns of the surrounding court with their pedestals, pegs and ropes.

[38]East of the tabernacle, that is, in front of the tent of meeting, toward the sunrise, were camped Moses and Aaron and the latter's sons, performing the duties of the sanctuary incumbent upon the Israelites. Any unauthorized person who came near was to be put to death.

[39]The total enrollment of the Levites whom Moses and Aaron enrolled at the direction of the LORD, by clans, every male a month old or more, was twenty-two thousand.

Census and Ransom of Firstborn

[40]The LORD then said to Moses: Enroll every firstborn male of the Israelites a month old or more, and count the number of their names. [41]Then take the Levites for me—I am the LORD—in place of all the firstborn of the Israelites, as well as the Levites' cattle, in place of all the firstborn among the cattle of the Israelites. [42]So Moses enrolled all the firstborn of the Israelites, as the LORD had commanded him. [43]All the firstborn males, registered by name, of a month or more, numbered twenty-two thousand two hundred and seventy-three.

[44]The LORD said to Moses: [45]Take the Levites in place of all the firstborn of the Israelites, and the Levites' cattle in place of their cattle, that the Levites may belong to me. I am the LORD. [46]As a redemption-price for the two hundred and seventy-three firstborn of the Israelites over and above the number of the Levites, [47]you shall take five shekels for each individual, according to the sanctuary shekel, twenty gerahs to the shekel.* [48]Give this money to Aaron and his sons as a redemption-price for the extra number. [49]So Moses took the redemption money for those over and above the ones redeemed by the Levites. [50]From the firstborn of the Israelites he took the money, one thousand three hundred and sixty-five shekels according to the sanctuary shekel. [51]He then gave this redemption money to Aaron and his sons, at the direction of the LORD, just as the LORD had commanded Moses.

Duties Further Defined

4 [1]The LORD said to Moses and Aaron: [2]Take a census among the Levites of the Kohathites, by clans and ancestral houses, [3]all between thirty† and fifty years of age, who will join the personnel for doing tasks in the tent of meeting.*

[4]This is the task of the Kohathites in the tent of meeting: the most sacred objects. [5]In breaking camp, Aaron and his sons shall go in and take down the screening curtain† and cover the ark of the covenant with it. [6]Over these they shall put a cover of yellow-orange skin, and on top of this spread an all-violet cloth and put the poles in place. [7]On the table of the Presence they shall spread a violet cloth and put on it the plates and cups, as well as the bowls and pitchers for libations; the established bread offering shall remain on the table. [8]Over these they shall spread a scarlet cloth and cover it with a covering of yellow-orange skin, and put the poles in place. [9]They shall use a violet cloth to cover the menorah of the light with its lamps, tongs, and trays, as well as the various containers of oil from which it is supplied. [10]The menorah with all its utensils they shall then put in a covering of yellow-orange skin, and place on a litter. [11]Over the golden altar† they shall spread a violet cloth, and cover this also with a covering of yellow-orange skin, and put the poles in place. [12]Taking

†

3:31 The Kohathites had to carry these sacred objects on their shoulders; cf. 7:9. For a description of the ark, see Ex 25:10–22; the table, Ex 25:23–30; the menorah, Ex 25:31–40; the altars, Ex 27:1–8; 30:1–10.

3:36–37 The Merarites had four wagons for transporting this heavy material; cf. 7:8. For a description of the boards, bars, etc., of the tabernacle, see Ex 26:15–30; the columns, pedestals, etc., of the court, Ex 27:9–19.

4:3 *Thirty*: according to other passages the Levites began to serve when they were twenty-five (8:24) or even only twenty years old (1 Chr 23:24, 27; 2 Chr 31:17; Ezr 3:8; but cf. 1 Chr 23:3).

4:5 *The screening curtain*: the veil between the inner and the outer rooms of the sanctuary. Cf. Ex 26:31–33.

4:11 *The golden altar*: the altar of incense. Cf. Ex 30:1–6.

*

3:47 Nm 18:16; Ex 30:13; Lv 27:25; Ez 45:12. **4:3** Nm 8:24; 1 Chr 23:24–27.

the utensils of the sanctuary service, they shall
put them all in violet cloth and cover them with
a covering of yellow-orange skin. They shall then
place them on a litter. 13 After cleansing the altar†
of its ashes, they shall spread a purple cloth over
it. 14 On this they shall put all the utensils with
which it is served: the fire pans, forks,† shovels,
basins, and all the utensils of the altar. They shall
then spread a covering of yellow-orange skin
over this, and put the poles in place.
15 Only after Aaron and his sons have finished
covering the sacred objects and all their utensils
on breaking camp, can the Kohathites enter to
carry them. But they shall not touch the sacred
objects; if they do they will die.* These, then, are
the objects in the tent of meeting that the Ko-
hathites shall carry.
16 Eleazar, son of Aaron the priest, shall be
in charge of the oil for the light, the fragrant
incense, the established grain offering, and the
anointing oil. He shall be in charge of the whole
tabernacle with all the sacred objects and utensils
that are in it.
17 The LORD said to Moses and Aaron: 18 Do
not let the group of Kohathite clans perish from
among the Levites. 19 That they may live and not
die when they approach the most sacred objects,
this is what you shall do for them: Aaron and his
sons shall go in and assign to each of them his
task and what he must carry; 20 but the Kohath-
ites shall not go in to look upon the sacred ob-
jects even for an instant, or they will die.*
21 The LORD said to Moses: 22 Take a census of
the Gershonites also, by ancestral houses and
clans, 23 enrolling all between thirty and fifty
years of age who will join the personnel to do
the work in the tent of meeting. 24 This is the task
of the clans of the Gershonites, what they must
do and what they must carry: 25 they shall carry
the curtains of the tabernacle, the tent of meet-
ing with its covering and the outer wrapping of
yellow-orange skin, the curtain at the entrance of
the tent of meeting, 26 the hangings of the court,
the curtain at the entrance to the gate of the court
that encloses both the tabernacle and the altar,
together with their ropes and all other objects
necessary for their use. Whatever is to be done
to maintain these things, they shall do. 27 The
service of the Gershonites shall be entirely under
the direction of Aaron and his sons, with regard
to what they must carry and what they must do;
you shall list for them by name what they are
to carry. 28 This, then, is the task of the clans of
the Gershonites in the tent of meeting; and they
shall be under the supervision of Ithamar, son of
Aaron the priest.
29 The Merarites, too, you shall enroll by clans
and ancestral houses, 30 enrolling all between
thirty and fifty years of age who will join the per-
sonnel to maintain the tent of meeting. 31 * This
is what they shall be responsible for carrying,
with respect to all their service in the tent of
meeting: the boards of the tabernacle with its
bars, columns and pedestals, 32 and the columns
of the surrounding court with their pedestals,
pegs and ropes, including all their accessories
and everything for their maintenance. You shall
list by name the objects they shall be responsible
for carrying. 33 This, then, is the task of the clans
of the Merarites with respect to all their service
in the tent of meeting under the supervision of
Ithamar, son of Aaron the priest.

Number of Adult Levites

34 So Moses and Aaron and the leaders of the
community enrolled the Kohathites, by clans
and ancestral houses, 35 all between thirty and
fifty years of age who will join the personnel to
work in the tent of meeting; 36 their enrollment
by clans was two thousand seven hundred and
fifty. 37 Such was the enrollment of the clans of
the Kohathites, everyone who was to serve in the
tent of meeting, whom Moses enrolled, together
with Aaron, as the LORD directed through Moses.
38 As for the enrollment of the Gershonites, by
clans and ancestral houses, 39 all between thirty
and fifty years of age who will join the person-
nel to work in the tent of meeting— 40 their en-
rollment by clans and ancestral houses was two
thousand six hundred and thirty. 41 Such was the
enrollment of the clans of the Gershonites, ev-
eryone who was to serve in the tent of meeting,
whom Moses enrolled, together with Aaron, as
the LORD directed.
42 As for the enrollment of the clans of the
Merarites, by clans and ancestral houses, 43 all
from thirty up to fifty years of age who will join
the personnel to work in the tent of meeting—
44 their enrollment by clans was three thousand
two hundred. 45 Such was the enrollment of the
clans of the Merarites, whom Moses enrolled, to-
gether with Aaron, as the LORD directed through
Moses.
46 As for the total enrollment of the Levites,

†

4:13 *The altar*: the bronze altar for animal sacrifices. Cf. Ex 27:1–8.

4:14 *Forks*: used in turning over the sacrificed animal on the fire of the altar. *Basins*: to receive the sacrificial blood; cf. Zec 9:15.

*

4:15 2 Sm 6:6–7; 1 Chr 13:9–10.

4:20 1 Sm 6:19–20.

4:31 Nm 3:36–37.

which Moses and Aaron and the Israelite leaders
had made, by clans and ancestral houses, 47 all
between thirty and fifty years of age who were
to undertake tasks of service or transport for the
tent of meeting— 48 their total enrollment was
eight thousand five hundred and eighty. 49 As the
LORD directed through Moses, they gave each of
them their assignments for service and for trans-
port; just as the LORD had commanded Moses.

The Unclean Expelled

5 1 The LORD said to Moses: 2 Order the Israel-
ites to expel from camp everyone with a scaly
infection, and everyone suffering from a dis-
charge, and everyone who has become unclean
by contact with a corpse.† * 3 Male and female
alike, you shall expel them. You shall expel them
from the camp so that they do not defile their
camp, where I dwell in their midst.* 4 This the
Israelites did, expelling them from the camp;
just as the LORD had commanded Moses, so the
Israelites did.

Unjust Possession†

5 The LORD said to Moses: 6 * Tell the Israel-
ites: If a man or a woman commits any offense
against another person, thus breaking faith with
the LORD, and thereby becomes guilty, 7 that per-
son shall confess the wrong that has been done,
make restitution in full, and in addition give
one fifth of its value to the one that has been
wronged. 8 However, if there is no next of kin,†
one to whom restitution can be made, the resti-
tution shall be made to the LORD and shall fall
to the priest; this is apart from the ram of atone-
ment with which the priest makes atonement for
the guilty individual. 9 Likewise, every contribu-
tion among the sacred offerings that the Israelites
present to the priest will belong to him.* 10 Each
shall possess his own sacred offerings; what is
given to a priest shall be his.*

Ordeal for Suspected Adultery

11 The LORD said to Moses: 12 Speak to the Isra-
elites and tell them: If a man's wife goes astray
and becomes unfaithful to him 13 by virtue of a
man having intercourse with her* in secret from
her husband and she is able to conceal the fact
that she has defiled herself for lack of a witness
who might have caught her in the act; 14 or if a
man is overcome by a feeling of jealousy that
makes him suspect his wife, and she has defiled
herself; or if a man is overcome by a feeling of
jealousy that makes him suspect his wife and she
has not defiled herself— 15 then the man shall
bring his wife to the priest as well as an offering
on her behalf, a tenth of an ephah† of barley
meal. However, he shall not pour oil on it nor
put frankincense over it, since it is a grain offer-
ing of jealousy, a grain offering of remembrance
which recalls wrongdoing.
16 The priest shall first have the woman come
forward and stand before the LORD. 17 In an
earthen vessel he shall take holy water,† as well
as some dust from the floor of the tabernacle
and put it in the water.* 18 Making the woman
stand before the LORD, the priest shall uncover
her head and place in her hands the grain offer-
ing of remembrance, that is, the grain offering
of jealousy, while he himself shall hold the wa-
ter of bitterness that brings a curse. 19 Then the
priest shall adjure the woman, saying to her, "If
no other man has had intercourse with you, and
you have not gone astray by defiling yourself
while under the authority of your husband, be
immune to this water of bitterness that brings
a curse. 20 But if you have gone astray while un-
der the authority of your husband, and if you
have defiled yourself and a man other than your
husband has had intercourse with you"— 21 so
shall the priest adjure the woman with this
imprecation—"may the LORD make you a curse
and malediction† among your people by caus-
ing your uterus to fall and your belly to swell!
22 May this water, then, that brings a curse, enter
your bowels to make your belly swell and your
uterus fall!"* And the woman shall say, "Amen,
amen!"† 23 The priest shall put these curses in
writing and shall then wash them off into the wa-
ter of bitterness, 24 and he will have the woman
drink the water of bitterness that brings a curse,
so that the water that brings a curse may enter

†

5:2 For the laws regarding victims of skin disease, see Lv 13–14; those suffering from a discharge, Lv 15; those unclean by contact with a corpse, Nm 19:11–22; Lv 21:1–4.

5:5–10 The basic law on unjust possession is given in Lv 5:14–26. The new item here concerns the case where the injured party has died and left no heirs, in which case the restitution must be made to the priest.

5:8 *Next of kin*: Hebrew *go'el* ("redeemer"), a technical term denoting the nearest relative, upon whom devolved the obligation of "redeeming" the family property, in order to keep it within the family. Cf. Lv 25:25; Ru 4:1–6.

5:15 *Ephah*: see note on Is 5:10.

5:17 *Holy water*: water from the basin that stood in the court of the tabernacle.

5:21 *Curse and malediction*: the woman's name would be used in curses and oaths to invoke a similar misfortune on another person or on oneself. Cf. Is 65:15; Jer 29:22.

5:22 *Amen*: a Hebrew word meaning "certainly, truly," used to give assent to a statement, a curse, a blessing, a prayer, or the like, in the sense of "so be it."

*

5:2 Nm 19:11, 13; Lv 13:46; 21:1; 22:4.
5:3 Nm 35:34.
5:6–10 Lv 5:21–25.
5:9 Dt 18:3–4; Ez 44:29–30.
5:10 Lv 10:12–15.
5:13 Lv 18:20; Jn 8:4.
5:17 Nm 19:17.
5:22 Ps 109:18.

into her to her bitter hurt. [25]But first the priest
shall take the grain offering of jealousy from the
woman's hand, and having elevated the grain of-
fering before the LORD, shall bring it to the altar,
[26]where he shall take a handful of the grain offer-
ing as a token offering and burn it on the altar.*
Only then shall he have the woman drink the
water. [27]Once he has had her drink the water, if
she has defiled herself and been unfaithful to her
husband, the water that brings a curse will enter
into her to her bitter hurt, and her belly will swell
and her uterus will fall, so that she will become
a curse among her people. [28]If, however, the
woman has not defiled herself, but is still pure,
she will be immune and will still be fertile.

[29]This, then, is the ritual for jealousy when a
woman goes astray while under the authority of
her husband and defiles herself, [30]or when such
a feeling of jealousy comes over a man that he
becomes suspicious of his wife; he shall have her
stand before the LORD, and the priest shall per-
form this entire ritual for her. [31]The man shall
be free from punishment,† but the woman shall
bear her punishment.

Laws Concerning Nazirites

6 [1]The LORD said to Moses: [2]Speak to the Isra-
elites and tell them: When men or women
solemnly take the nazirite† vow to dedicate
themselves to the LORD, [3]they shall abstain from
wine and strong drink;* they may neither drink
wine vinegar, other vinegar, or any kind of grape
juice, nor eat either fresh or dried grapes. [4]As
long as they are nazirites they shall not eat any-
thing of the produce of the grapevine; not even
the seeds or the skins. [5]While they are under the
nazirite vow, no razor shall touch their hair.*
Until the period of their dedication to the LORD
is over, they shall be holy, letting the hair of their
heads grow freely. [6]As long as they are dedicated
to the LORD, they shall not come near a dead per-
son.* [7]Not even for their father or mother, sister
or brother, should they defile themselves, when
these die, since their heads bear their dedication
to God. [8]As long as they are nazirites they are
holy to the LORD.

[9]If someone dies very suddenly in their pres-
ence, defiling their dedicated heads, they shall
shave their heads on the day of their purifica-
tion, that is, on the seventh day. [10]On the eighth
day they shall bring two turtledoves or two pi-
geons to the priest at the entrance of the tent of
meeting. [11]The priest shall offer up the one as a
purification offering and the other as a burnt of-
fering, thus making atonement for them for the
sin they committed with respect to the corpse.
On the same day they shall reconsecrate their
heads [12]and rededicate themselves to the LORD
for the period of their dedication, bringing a
yearling lamb as a reparation offering. The previ-
ous period is not valid, because they defiled their
dedicated heads.

[13]This is the ritual for the nazirites:* When
the period of their dedication is complete they
shall go to the entrance of the tent of meeting,
[14]bringing their offerings to the LORD, one un-
blemished yearling lamb for a burnt offering,
one unblemished yearling ewe lamb for a pu-
rification offering, one unblemished ram as a
communion offering, [15]and a basket of unleav-
ened cakes of bran flour mixed with oil and of
unleavened wafers spread with oil, along with
their grain offerings and libations. [16]The priest
shall present them before the LORD, and shall
offer up the purification offering and the burnt
offering for them. [17]He shall then offer up the
ram as a communion sacrifice to the LORD, along
with the basket of unleavened cakes, and the
priest will offer the grain offering and libation.
[18]Then at the entrance of the tent of meeting the
nazirite shall shave his or her dedicated head,
take the hair of the dedicated head, and put it in
the fire under the communion sacrifice. [19]After
the nazirite has shaved off the dedicated hair,
the priest shall take a boiled shoulder of the ram,
as well as one unleavened cake from the basket
and one unleavened wafer, and shall put them
in the hands of the nazirite. [20]The priest shall
then elevate them as an elevated offering before
the LORD. They are an offering belonging to the
priest, along with the brisket of the elevated of-
fering and the leg of the contribution. Only after
this may the nazirite drink wine.

[21]This, then, is the law for the nazirites, that is,
what they vow as their offering to the LORD in ac-
cord with their dedication, apart from anything

---

†

5:31 *Free from punishment*: the point is that a husband will not suffer a harmful consequence if his accusation is not borne out by the ordeal; if he's right, his wife's punishment vindicates him. For her part, the woman (if guilty) must bear her punishment.

6:2–21 *Nazirite*: from the Hebrew word *nazir*, meaning "set apart as sacred, dedicated, vowed." The nazirite vow could be either for a limited period or for life. Those bound by this vow had to abstain from all the products of the grapevine, from cutting or shaving their hair, and from contact with a corpse. They were regarded as men and women of God like the prophets; cf. Am 2:11–12. Examples of lifelong nazirites were Samson (Jgs 13:4–5, 7; 16:17), Samuel (1 Sm 1:11), and John the Baptist (Lk 1:15). At the time of Jesus the practice of taking the nazirite vow for a limited period seems to have been quite common, even among the early Christians; cf. Acts 18:18; 21:23–24, 26.

---

*

5:26 Lv 5:12.
6:3–4 Jgs 13:7, 14.
6:5 Jgs 13:5; 16:17; 1 Sm 1:11.
6:6 Nm 19:11, 16; Lv 21:11.
6:13 Acts 21:24, 26.

else which their means may allow. In keeping
with the vow they take so shall they do, accord-
ing to the law of their dedication.

The Priestly Blessing

22 The LORD said to Moses: 23 Speak to Aaron
and his sons and tell them: This is how you shall
bless the Israelites. Say to them:

24 The LORD bless you and keep you!
25 The LORD let his face shine upon you, and be
gracious to you!
26 The LORD look upon you kindly and give you
peace!†

27 So shall they invoke my name upon the Israel-
ites, and I will bless them.

Offerings of the Tribal Leaders

7 1 Now, when Moses had completed the erec-
tion of the tabernacle, he anointed and con-
secrated it with all its equipment,* as well as the
altar with all its equipment. After he anointed
and consecrated them, 2 an offering was made by
the tribal leaders of Israel, who were heads of an-
cestral houses, the same leaders of the tribes who
supervised those enrolled. 3 The offering they
brought before the LORD consisted of six wagons
for baggage and twelve oxen, that is, a wagon
for every two tribal leaders, and an ox for each.
These they presented before the tabernacle.
4 The LORD then said to Moses: 5 Accept their
offering, that these things may be put to use to
maintain the tent of meeting. Assign them to the
Levites, to each according to his duties. 6 So Mo-
ses accepted the wagons and oxen, and assigned
them to the Levites. 7 He gave two wagons and
four oxen to the Gershonites* according to their
duties, 8 and four wagons and eight oxen to the
Merarites according to their duties, under the
supervision of Ithamar, son of Aaron the priest.
9 He gave none to the Kohathites, because they
were responsible for maintenance of the sacred
objects that had to be carried on their shoul-
ders.*
10 For the dedication of the altar also, the tribal
leaders brought offerings when it was anointed;*
the leaders presented their offering before the al-
tar. 11 But the LORD said to Moses: Let one leader
each day present his offering for the dedication
of the altar.

Pray It!

God Bless You

A very old blessing in Numbers 6:22–27 (some of which is repeated in Pss 4:7 and 67:2) was not originally a Christian blessing, but its three parts remind us of Christian blessings calling on the Trinity.

This blessing is a good one for special occasions. You could write it on a card for a birthday, Mother's Day or Father's Day, a wedding anniversary, or any other special event. Or you could use it to make a poster or an engraving for a first Communion, a wedding, or a Confirmation.

If this blessing sounds familiar, maybe it's because on New Year's Day (the feast of Mary, mother of God), we hear it as the first reading. It's the perfect way to start the new year.

▶ **Nm 6:22–27**

12 † The one who presented his offering on the
first day was Nahshon, son of Amminadab, of
the tribe of Judah. 13 His offering consisted of one
silver plate weighing a hundred and thirty shek-
els and one silver basin weighing seventy shekels
according to the sanctuary shekel, both filled
with bran flour mixed with oil for a grain offer-
ing; 14 one gold cup of ten shekels' weight filled
with incense; 15 one bull from the herd, one ram,
and one yearling lamb for a burnt offering; 16 one
goat for a purification offering; 17 and two bulls,
five rams, five he-goats, and five yearling lambs
for a communion sacrifice. This was the offering
of Nahshon, son of Amminadab.
18 On the second day Nethanel, son of Zuar,
tribal leader of Issachar, made his offering. 19 He
presented as his offering one silver plate weigh-
ing a hundred and thirty shekels and one silver
basin weighing seventy shekels according to the
sanctuary shekel, both filled with bran flour
mixed with oil for a grain offering; 20 one gold
cup of ten shekels' weight filled with incense;

†

6:26 *Peace*: the Hebrew word *Shalom* includes the idea of happiness, good health, prosperity, friendship, and general well-being. To use this term as a greeting was to pray for all these things upon the one greeted.

7:12–88 The repetitious account of the same offerings brought by each of the twelve tribal leaders and the summary of them are characteristic of an official registration.

7:1 Ex 40:17.
7:7–8 Nm 4:24–33.
7:9 Nm 3:31; 4:4–15.
7:10 Nm 7:84.

21 one bull from the herd, one ram, and one yearling lamb for a burnt offering; 22 one goat for a purification offering; 23 and two bulls, five rams, five he-goats, and five yearling lambs for a communion sacrifice. This was the offering of Nethanel, son of Zuar.

24 On the third day it was the turn of the tribal leader of the Zebulunites, Eliab, son of Helon. 25 His offering consisted of one silver plate weighing a hundred and thirty shekels and one silver basin weighing seventy shekels according to the sanctuary shekel, both filled with bran flour mixed with oil for a grain offering; 26 one gold cup of ten shekels' weight filled with incense; 27 one bull from the herd, one ram, and one yearling lamb for a burnt offering; 28 one goat for a purification offering; 29 and two bulls, five rams, five he-goats, and five yearling lambs for a communion sacrifice. This was the offering of Eliab, son of Helon.

30 On the fourth day it was the turn of the tribal leader of the Reubenites, Elizur, son of Shedeur. 31 His offering consisted of one silver plate weighing a hundred and thirty shekels and one silver basin weighing seventy shekels according to the sanctuary shekel, both filled with bran flour mixed with oil for a grain offering; 32 one gold cup of ten shekels' weight filled with incense; 33 one bull from the herd, one ram, and one yearling lamb for a burnt offering; 34 one goat for a purification offering; 35 and two bulls, five rams, five he-goats, and five yearling lambs for a communion sacrifice. This was the offering of Elizur, son of Shedeur.

36 On the fifth day it was the turn of the tribal leader of the Simeonites, Shelumiel, son of Zurishaddai. 37 His offering consisted of one silver plate weighing a hundred and thirty shekels and one silver basin weighing seventy shekels according to the sanctuary shekel, both filled with bran flour mixed with oil for a grain offering; 38 one gold cup of ten shekels' weight filled with incense; 39 one bull from the herd, one ram, and one yearling lamb for a burnt offering; 40 one goat for a purification offering; 41 and two bulls, five rams, five he-goats, and five yearling lambs for a communion sacrifice. This was the offering of Shelumiel, son of Zurishaddai.

42 On the sixth day it was the turn of the tribal leader of the Gadites, Eliasaph, son of Reuel. 43 His offering consisted of one silver plate weighing a hundred and thirty shekels and one silver basin weighing seventy shekels according to the sanctuary shekel, both filled with bran flour mixed with oil for a grain offering; 44 one gold cup of ten shekels' weight filled with incense; 45 one bull from the herd, one ram, and one yearling lamb for a burnt offering; 46 one goat for a purification offering; 47 and two bulls, five rams, five he-goats, and five yearling lambs for a communion sacrifice. This was the offering of Eliasaph, son of Reuel.

48 On the seventh day it was the turn of the tribal leader of the Ephraimites, Elishama, son of Ammihud. 49 His offering consisted of one silver plate weighing a hundred and thirty shekels and one silver basin weighing seventy shekels according to the sanctuary shekel, both filled with bran flour mixed with oil for a grain offering; 50 one gold cup of ten shekels' weight filled with incense; 51 one bull from the herd, one ram, and one yearling lamb for a burnt offering; 52 one goat for a purification offering; 53 and two bulls, five rams, five he-goats, and five yearling lambs for a communion sacrifice. This was the offering of Elishama, son of Ammihud.

54 On the eighth day it was the turn of the tribal leader of the Manassites, Gamaliel, son of Pedahzur. 55 His offering consisted of one silver plate weighing a hundred and thirty shekels and one silver basin weighing seventy shekels according to the sanctuary shekel, both filled with bran flour mixed with oil for a grain offering; 56 one gold cup of ten shekels' weight filled with incense; 57 one bull from the herd, one ram, and one yearling lamb for a burnt offering; 58 one goat for a purification offering; 59 and two bulls, five rams, five he-goats, and five yearling lambs for a communion sacrifice. This was the offering of Gamaliel, son of Pedahzur.

60 On the ninth day it was the turn of the tribal leader of the Benjaminites, Abidan, son of Gideoni. 61 His offering consisted of one silver plate weighing a hundred and thirty shekels and one silver basin weighing seventy shekels according to the sanctuary shekel, both filled with bran flour mixed with oil for a grain offering; 62 one gold cup of ten shekels' weight filled with incense; 63 one bull from the herd, one ram, and one yearling lamb for a burnt offering; 64 one goat for a purification offering; 65 and two bulls, five rams, five he-goats, and five yearling lambs for a communion sacrifice. This was the offering of Abidan, son of Gideoni.

66 On the tenth day it was the turn of the tribal leader of the Danites, Ahiezer, son of Ammishaddai. 67 His offering consisted of one silver plate weighing a hundred and thirty shekels and one silver basin weighing seventy shekels according to the sanctuary shekel, both filled with bran flour mixed with oil for a grain offering; 68 one gold cup of ten shekels' weight filled with

incense; [69] one bull from the herd, one ram, and one yearling lamb for a burnt offering; [70] one goat for a purification offering; [71] and two bulls, five rams, five he-goats, and five yearling lambs for a communion sacrifice. This was the offering of Ahiezer, son of Ammishaddai.

[72] On the eleventh day it was the turn of the tribal leader of the Asherites, Pagiel, son of Ochran. [73] His offering consisted of one silver plate weighing one hundred and thirty shekels and one silver basin weighing seventy shekels according to the sanctuary shekel, both filled with bran flour mixed with oil for a grain offering; [74] one gold cup of ten shekels' weight filled with incense; [75] one bull from the herd, one ram, and one yearling lamb for a burnt offering; [76] one goat for a purification offering; [77] and two bulls, five rams, five he-goats, and five yearling lambs for a communion sacrifice. This was the offering of Pagiel, son of Ochran.

[78] On the twelfth day it was the turn of the tribal leader of the Naphtalites, Ahira, son of Enan. [79] His offering consisted of one silver plate weighing a hundred and thirty shekels and one silver basin weighing seventy shekels according to the sanctuary shekel, both filled with bran flour mixed with oil for a grain offering; [80] one gold cup of ten shekels' weight filled with incense; [81] one bull from the herd, one ram, and one yearling lamb for a burnt offering; [82] one goat for a purification offering; [83] and two bulls, five rams, five he-goats, and five yearling lambs for a communion sacrifice. This was the offering of Ahira, son of Enan.

[84] These were the offerings for the dedication of the altar, given by the tribal leaders of Israel on the occasion of its anointing: twelve silver plates, twelve silver basins, and twelve gold cups. [85] Each silver plate weighed a hundred and thirty shekels, and each silver basin seventy, so that all the silver of these vessels amounted to two thousand four hundred shekels, according to the sanctuary shekel. [86] The twelve gold cups that were filled with incense weighed ten shekels apiece, according to the sanctuary shekel, so that all the gold of the cups amounted to one hundred and twenty shekels. [87] The animals for the burnt offerings were, in all, twelve bulls, twelve rams, and twelve yearling lambs, with their grain offerings; those for the purification offerings were twelve goats. [88] The animals for the communion sacrifices were, in all, twenty-four bulls, sixty rams, sixty he-goats, and sixty yearling lambs. These, then, were the offerings for the dedication of the altar after it was anointed.

The Voice

[89] When Moses entered the tent of meeting to speak with God, he heard the voice addressing him from above the cover* on the ark of the covenant, from between the two cherubim; and so it spoke to him.

The Menorah

8 [1] The LORD said to Moses: [2] Speak to Aaron and say: "When you set up the menorah-lamps,* have the seven lamps throw their light in front of the menorah."† [3] Aaron did so, setting up the menorah-lamps to face the area in front of the menorah, just as the LORD had commanded Moses. [4] This is the construction of the menorah: hammered gold,* from its base to its bowls† it was hammered; according to the pattern which the LORD had shown Moses, so he made the menorah.

Purification of the Levites

[5] The LORD said to Moses: [6] Take the Levites from among the Israelites and cleanse them.† [7] This is what you shall do to them to cleanse them. Sprinkle them with the water of purification, have them shave their whole bodies and wash their garments, and so cleanse themselves. [8] Then they shall take a bull from the herd, along with its grain offering of bran flour mixed with oil; and you shall take another bull from the herd for a purification offering. [9] Bringing the Levites before the tent of meeting, you shall assemble also the whole community of the Israelites. [10] When you have brought the Levites before the LORD, the Israelites shall lay their hands upon them. [11] Aaron shall then present the Levites before the LORD as an elevated offering from the Israelites, that they may perform the service of the LORD. [12] The Levites in turn shall lay their hands on the heads of the bulls, offering one as a purification offering and the other as a burnt offering to the LORD, to make atonement for the Levites. [13] Then you shall have the Levites stand before Aaron and his sons, and you shall present

N
M

†

8:2 *Menorah*: a seven-branched lampstand; see Ex 25:31–40; 37:17–24.

8:4 *Bowls*: lit., "blossom," a designation for the blossom-shaped cups holding the lamps of the menorah.

8:6 *Cleanse them*: in the language of the Pentateuch only the priests were "consecrated," that is, made sacred or set aside for the Lord, in an elaborate ceremony described in Ex 29 and in this chapter. The Levites were "cleansed," that is, made ritually clean for their special work.

*

7:89 Ex 25:22.
8:2 Ex 25:37.
8:4 Ex 25:31, 40.

them as an elevated offering to the LORD; 14 thus you shall separate the Levites from the rest of the Israelites, and the Levites shall belong to me.*

15 Only then shall the Levites enter upon their service in the tent of meeting, when you have cleansed them and presented them as an elevated offering. 16 For they, among the Israelites, are totally dedicated to me; I have taken them for myself in place of everyone that opens the womb, the firstborn of all the Israelites.* 17 Indeed, all the firstborn among the Israelites, human being and beast alike, belong to me; I consecrated them to myself on the day I killed all the firstborn in the land of Egypt.* 18 But I have taken the Levites in place of all the firstborn Israelites; 19 and from among the Israelites I have given to Aaron and his sons these Levites, who are to be dedicated,* to perform the service of the Israelites in the tent of meeting and to make atonement for them, so that no plague may strike among the Israelites should they come too near the sanctuary.

20 This, then, is what Moses and Aaron and the whole community of the Israelites did with respect to the Levites; the Israelites did exactly as the LORD had commanded Moses concerning them. 21 When the Levites had purified themselves† and washed their garments, Aaron presented them as an elevated offering before the LORD, and made atonement for them to cleanse them. 22 Only then did they enter upon their service in the tent of meeting under the supervision of Aaron and his sons. Exactly as the LORD had commanded Moses concerning the Levites, so it was done with regard to them.

Age Limits for Levitical Service

23 The LORD said to Moses: 24 This is the rule for the Levites. Everyone twenty-five years old or more shall join the personnel in the service of the tent of meeting.* 25 But everyone fifty on up shall retire from the work force and serve no more. 26 They shall assist their fellow Levites in the tent of meeting in performing their duties, but they shall not do the work. This, then, is how you are to regulate the duties of the Levites.

Second Passover

9 1 The LORD said to Moses in the wilderness of Sinai, in the first month of the second year following their departure from the land of Egypt: 2 Tell the Israelites to celebrate the Passover at the prescribed time. 3 In the evening twilight of the fourteenth day of this month* you shall celebrate it at its prescribed time, in accord with all its statutes and regulations. 4 So Moses told the Israelites to celebrate the Passover, 5 and they did celebrate the Passover on the fourteenth day of the first month during the evening twilight in the wilderness of Sinai. Just as the LORD had commanded Moses, so the Israelites did.

6 There were some, however, who were unclean because of a human corpse and so could not celebrate the Passover that day. These men came up to Moses and Aaron that same day 7 and they said to them, "Although we are unclean because of a human corpse, why should we be deprived of presenting the LORD's offering at its prescribed time along with other Israelites?" 8 Moses answered them, "Wait so that I can learn what the LORD will command in your regard."

9 The LORD then said to Moses: 10 Speak to the Israelites: "If any one of you or of your descendants is unclean because of a human corpse, or is absent on a journey, you may still celebrate the LORD's Passover. 11 But you shall celebrate it in the second month,* on the fourteenth day of that month during the evening twilight, eating it with unleavened bread and bitter herbs, 12 and not leaving any of it over till morning, nor breaking any of its bones,* but observing all the statutes of the Passover. 13 However, anyone who is clean and not away on a journey, who yet fails to celebrate the Passover, shall be cut off from the people, for not presenting the LORD's offering at the prescribed time. That person shall bear the consequences of this sin.

14 "If an alien† who lives among you would celebrate the LORD's Passover, it shall be celebrated according to the statutes and regulations for the Passover. You shall have the same law for the resident alien as for the native of the land."*

The Fiery Cloud

15 On the day when the tabernacle was erected, the cloud† covered the tabernacle, the tent of the covenant; but from evening until morning it took on the appearance of fire over the tabernacle.* 16 It was always so: during the day the cloud covered the tabernacle and at night had the appearance of fire. 17 Whenever the cloud rose

---

†

8:21 *Purified themselves*: by having the "water of purification" sprinkled on them as prescribed in v. 7.

9:14 *An alien*: compare this passage with the Passover legislation in Ex 12:48, where circumcision is required of the alien who would celebrate the feast.

9:15 *The cloud*: already mentioned at the departure from Egypt; cf. Ex 13:21–22.

*

8:14 Nm 3:45.
8:16 Nm 3:12, 45.
8:17 Nm 3:13; Lk 2:23.
8:19 Nm 3:9–10.
8:24 Nm 4:3, 23.
9:3 Ex 12:6; Lv 23:5.
9:11 2 Chr 30:2–15.
9:12 Ex 12:46; Jn 19:36.
9:14 Ex 12:48–49.
9:15 Ex 13:21.

from the tent, the Israelites would break camp;
wherever the cloud settled, the Israelites would
pitch camp.* 18 At the direction of the LORD the
Israelites broke camp, and at the LORD's direction
they pitched camp.* As long as the cloud stayed
over the tabernacle, they remained in camp.
19 Even when the cloud lingered many days
over the tabernacle, the Israelites kept the charge
of the LORD and would not move on. 20 Yet if
it happened the cloud was over the tabernacle
only for a few days, at the direction of the LORD
they stayed in camp; and at the LORD's direction
they broke camp. 21 If it happened the cloud re-
mained there only from evening until morning,
when the cloud rose in the morning, they would
break camp. Whether the cloud lifted during the
day or the night they would then break camp.
22 Whether the cloud lingered over the tabernacle
for two days or for a month or longer, the Israel-
ites remained in camp and did not break camp;
but when it lifted, they broke camp. 23 At the
direction of the LORD they pitched camp, and at
the LORD's direction they broke camp; they kept
the charge of the LORD, as the LORD directed them
through Moses.

The Silver Trumpets

10 1 The LORD said to Moses: 2 Make two
trumpets of silver, making them of ham-
mered silver, for you to use in summoning the
community and in breaking camp. 3 When both
are blown, the whole community shall gather
round you at the entrance of the tent of meeting;
4 but when one of them is blown, only the tribal
leaders, the heads of the clans of Israel, shall
gather round you. 5 When you sound the signal,
those encamped on the east side shall break
camp; 6 when you sound a second signal, those
encamped on the south side shall break camp;
when you sound a third signal, those encamped
on the west side shall break camp; when you
sound a fourth signal, those encamped on the
north side shall break camp. Thus shall the sig-
nal be sounded for them to break camp. 7 But in
calling forth an assembly you are to blow a blast,
without sounding the signal.
8 The sons of Aaron, the priests, shall blow the
trumpets; this is prescribed forever for you and
your descendants. 9 * When in your own land
you go to war against an enemy that is attacking
you, you shall sound the alarm on the trumpets,
and you shall be remembered before the LORD,
your God, and be saved from your foes. 10 And
when you rejoice† on your festivals, and your
new-moon feasts, you shall blow the trumpets
over your burnt offerings and your communion
sacrifices,* so that this serves as a reminder of
you before your God. I, the LORD, am your God.

II. Departure, Rebellion, and Wandering in the Wilderness for Forty Years

Departure from Sinai

11 In the second year, on the twentieth day
of the second month, the cloud rose from the
tabernacle of the covenant, 12 and the Israelites
moved on from the wilderness of Sinai by stages,
until the cloud came to rest in the wilderness of
Paran.
13 The first time that they broke camp at the
direction of the LORD through Moses, 14 * the
divisional camp of the Judahites, arranged in
companies, was the first to set out. Over its
whole company was Nahshon, son of Ammin-
adab, 15 with Nethanel, son of Zuar, over the
company of the tribe of Issacharites, 16 and Eliab,
son of Helon, over the company of the tribe of
Zebulunites. 17 Then, after the tabernacle was dis-
mantled, the Gershonites and Merarites who car-
ried the tabernacle set out. 18 The divisional camp
of the Reubenites, arranged in companies, was
the next to set out. Over its whole company was
Elizur, son of Shedeur, 19 with Shelumiel, son of
Zurishaddai, over the company of the tribe of
Simeonites, 20 and Eliasaph, son of Reuel, over
the company of the tribe of Gadites. 21 The Ko-
hathites, who carried the sacred objects, then set
out. Before their arrival the tabernacle would be
erected. 22 The divisional camp of the Ephraim-
ites set out next, arranged in companies. Over its
whole company was Elishama, son of Ammihud,
23 with Gamaliel, son of Pedahzur, over the com-
pany of the tribe of Manassites, 24 and Abidan,
son of Gideoni, over the company of the tribe of
Benjaminites. 25 Finally, as rear guard for all the
camps, the divisional camp of the Danites set
out, arranged in companies. Over its whole com-
pany was Ahiezer, son of Ammishaddai, 26 with
Pagiel, son of Ochran, over the company of the
tribe of Asherites, 27 and Ahira, son of Enan, over
the company of the tribe of Naphtalites. 28 This
was the order of march for the Israelites, com-
pany by company, when they set out.

† **10:10** *When you rejoice*: cf. Dt 16:14. *Festivals*: the great annual feasts of the Passover, Pentecost and Booths described in Lv 23; Nm 28–29.

9:17 Wis 18:3.
9:18 1 Cor 10:1.
10:9 2 Chr 13:14.
10:10 Nm 29:1; 2 Chr 29:26–28.
10:14–16 Nm 2:3, 5, 7.

Hobab as Guide

29 Moses said to Hobab,† son of Reuel the
Midianite, Moses' father-in-law, "We are setting
out for the place concerning which the LORD has
said, 'I will give it to you.' Come with us, and
we will be generous toward you, for the LORD
has promised prosperity to Israel." 30 But he an-
swered, "No, I will not come. I am going instead
to the land of my birth." 31 Moses said, "Please,
do not leave us; you know where we can camp
in the wilderness, and you can serve as our guide.
32 If you come with us, we will share with you the
prosperity the LORD will bestow on us."

Into the Wilderness

33 * From the mountain of the LORD† they
made a journey of three days, and the ark of the
covenant of the LORD went before them for the
three-day journey to seek out a resting place for
them. 34 And the cloud of the LORD was over them
by day when they set out from camp.

35 Whenever the ark set out, Moses would say,

"Arise, O LORD, may your enemies be scattered,
and may those who hate you flee before
you."

36 And when it came to rest, he would say,

"Bring back, O LORD, the myriads of Israel's
troops!"

Discontent of the People

11 1 Now the people complained bitterly in the
hearing of the LORD;* and when he heard it
his wrath flared up, so that the LORD's fire burned
among them and consumed the outskirts of the
camp. 2 But when the people cried out to Mo-
ses, he prayed to the LORD and the fire died out.
3 Hence that place was called Taberah,† because
there the fire of the LORD burned among them.

4 The riffraff among them were so greedy for
meat that even the Israelites lamented again,* "If
only we had meat for food! 5 We remember the
fish we used to eat without cost in Egypt, and
the cucumbers, the melons, the leeks, the on-
ions, and the garlic. 6 But now we are famished;
we have nothing to look forward to but this
manna."*

7 * Manna was like coriander seed† and had
the appearance of bdellium. 8 When they had
gone about and gathered it up, the people would
grind it between millstones or pound it in a mor-
tar, then cook it in a pot and make it into loaves,
with a rich creamy taste. 9 At night, when the dew
fell upon the camp, the manna also fell.*

10 When Moses heard the people, family after
family, crying at the entrance of their tents, so
that the LORD became very angry, he was grieved.
11 "Why do you treat your servant so badly?" Mo-
ses asked the LORD. "Why are you so displeased
with me that you burden me with all this people?
12 Was it I who conceived all this people? or was
it I who gave them birth, that you tell me to carry
them at my breast, like a nurse carrying an infant,
to the land you have promised under oath to
their fathers? 13 Where can I get meat to give to all
this people? For they are crying to me, 'Give us
meat for our food.' 14 I cannot carry all this peo-
ple by myself, for they are too heavy for me. 15 If
this is the way you will deal with me, then please
do me the favor of killing me at once, so that I
need no longer face my distress."

The Seventy Elders

16 Then the LORD said to Moses: Assemble for
me seventy of the elders of Israel, whom you
know to be elders and authorities among the
people, and bring them to the tent of meeting.
When they are in place beside you, 17 I will come
down and speak with you there. I will also take
some of the spirit that is on you and will confer
it on them, that they may share the burden of the
people with you. You will then not have to bear
it by yourself.

18 To the people, however, you shall say: "Sanc-
tify yourselves for tomorrow, when you shall
have meat to eat. For in the hearing of the LORD
you have cried, 'If only we had meat for food!
Oh, how well off we were in Egypt!' Therefore
the LORD will give you meat to eat, 19 and you will
eat it, not for one day, or two days, or five, or ten,
or twenty days, 20 but for a whole month—until
it comes out of your very nostrils and becomes
loathsome to you. For you have rejected the LORD

---

†

10:29–32 *Hobab*: one of three names for the father-in-law of Moses (see Ex 2:18; 4:18; 18:6; Jgs 4:11). Here perhaps Hobab's initial refusal indicates he wished to be coaxed before granting the favor. From Jgs 1:16 it seems probable that he did accede to Moses' request. However, Ex 18:27 suggests Moses' father-in-law returned to his own land. Indeed, to the extent Nm 10:29–32 appears to repeat Ex 18:27, it may indicate a resumption of the narrative of Israel's march through the wilderness after the "digression" formed by the Israelite sojourn at Sinai, Ex 19:1–Nm 10:28.

10:33 *The mountain of the LORD*: Sinai (Horeb), elsewhere always called "the mountain of God."

11:3 *Taberah*: means "the burning."

11:7 *Coriander seed*: see note on Ex 16:31. *Bdellium*: a transparent, amber-colored gum resin, which is also mentioned in Gn 2:12.

*

10:33 Dt 1:33.
11:1 Dt 9:22.
11:4 Ps 78:18.
11:5–6 Nm 21:5; Ex 16:3; Acts 7:39.
11:7–8 Ex 16:14–15, 31; Ps 78:24; Wis 16:20; Jn 6:31.
11:9 Ex 16:14–15.

who is in your midst, and in his presence you
have cried, 'Why did we ever leave Egypt?' "
[21] But Moses said, "The people around me in-
clude six hundred thousand soldiers; yet you say,
'I will give them meat to eat for a whole month.'
[22] Can enough sheep and cattle be slaughtered
for them? If all the fish of the sea were caught
for them, would they have enough?" [23] The LORD
answered Moses: Is this beyond the LORD's reach?
You shall see now whether or not what I have
said to you takes place.

The Spirit on the Elders

[24] So Moses went out and told the people what
the LORD had said. Gathering seventy elders of
the people, he had them stand around the tent.
[25] The LORD then came down in the cloud and
spoke to him. Taking some of the spirit that was
on Moses, he bestowed it on the seventy elders;
and as the spirit came to rest on them, they
prophesied† but did not continue.
[26] Now two men, one named Eldad and the
other Medad, had remained in the camp, yet
the spirit came to rest on them also. They too
had been on the list, but had not gone out to
the tent; and so they prophesied in the camp.
[27] So, when a young man ran and reported to
Moses, "Eldad and Medad are prophesying in
the camp," [28] Joshua, son of Nun, who from his
youth had been Moses' aide, said, "My lord, Mo-
ses, stop them." [29] But Moses answered him, "Are
you jealous for my sake? If only all the people of
the LORD were prophets! If only the LORD would
bestow his spirit on them!" [30] Then Moses retired
to the camp, along with the elders of Israel.

The Quail

[31] There arose a wind* from the LORD that drove
in quail from the sea and left them all around the
camp site, to a distance of a day's journey and at
a depth of two cubits upon the ground.† [32] * So
all that day, all night, and all the next day the
people set about to gather in the quail. Even the
one who got the least gathered ten homers† of
them. Then they spread them out all around the
camp. [33] But while the meat was still between
their teeth, before it could be chewed, the LORD's

Live It!

The Jealousy of Miriam and Aaron

It isn't very hard to identify with the feelings Miriam and Aaron have toward their brother Moses. After all, God speaks directly to Moses, so why can't God speak to them as well? What makes Moses so special?

Jealousy is a sneaky vice that slowly grows and makes itself apparent without us realizing it. Soon we begin to feel a sense of resentment at how someone else seems to be getting all the breaks. We know we've crossed the line when we actually feel glad that something didn't work out for that person or even that something bad happened. Jealousy is like a dangerous cancer, growing until it affects our whole outlook on life (see what happens to Miriam in Nm 12:10).

- Think of a time when you felt jealous of another. How did that affect your attitude toward that person?

▶ **Numbers, chapter 12**

wrath flared up against the people, and the LORD
struck them with a very great plague. [34] So that
place was named Kibroth-hattaavah,† because it
was there that the greedy people were buried.
[35] From Kibroth-hattaavah the people set out
for Hazeroth, where they stayed.

Jealousy of Aaron and Miriam

12 [1] Miriam and Aaron spoke against Moses
on the pretext of the Cushite woman he
had married; for he had in fact married a Cush-
ite woman.† [2] They complained,† "Is it through
Moses alone that the LORD has spoken? Has he
not spoken through us also?" And the LORD heard

† **11:25** *They prophesied*: in the sense, not of foretelling the future, but of speaking in enraptured enthusiasm. Such manifestations are mentioned in the early days of Hebrew prophecy (1 Sm 10:10–12; 19:20–21; Jl 3:1) and in the first years of the Church (Acts 2:6–11, 17; 19:6; 1 Cor 12–14).

11:31 The heaps of quail lying upon the ground all around the Israelites' camp suggest the ambiguity of God's response to the people's lament for meat in v. 4 and foreshadow the plague which God will now bring upon Israel (v. 33). Their request had been nothing less than a rejection of what God has done for them (v. 20).

11:32 *Homers*: see note on Is 5:10. *They spread them out*: to cure by drying.

11:34 *Kibroth-hattaavah*: means "graves of greed."

12:1 *Cushite woman*: apparently Zipporah, the Midianite, is meant; cf. Ex 2:21.

12:2 The apparent reason for Miriam's and Aaron's quarrel with their brother Moses was jealousy of his authority; his Cushite wife served only as an occasion for the dispute.

* **11:31** Ps 78:26–28. **11:32–33** Ps 78:26–31.

this. 3 * Now the man Moses was very humble,
more than anyone else on earth. 4 So at once
the LORD said to Moses and Aaron and Miriam:
Come out, you three, to the tent of meeting. And
the three of them went. 5 Then the LORD came
down in a column of cloud, and standing at the
entrance of the tent, called, "Aaron and Miriam."
When both came forward, 6 the LORD said: Now
listen to my words:

If there are prophets among you,
in visions I reveal myself to them,
in dreams I speak to them;
7 Not so with my servant Moses!
Throughout my house he is worthy of trust:† *
8 face to face I speak to him,*
plainly and not in riddles.
The likeness of the LORD he beholds.

Why, then, do you not fear to speak against my
servant Moses? 9 And so the LORD's wrath flared
against them, and he departed.

NM

Miriam's Punishment

10 Now the cloud withdrew from the tent,
and there was Miriam,* stricken with a scaly
infection, white as snow!† When Aaron turned
toward Miriam and saw her stricken with snow-
white scales, 11 he said to Moses, "Ah, my lord!
Please do not charge us with the sin that we
have foolishly committed! 12 Do not let her be
like the stillborn baby that comes forth from its
mother's womb with its flesh half consumed."
13 Then Moses cried to the LORD, "Please, not
this! Please, heal her!" 14 But the LORD answered
Moses: Suppose her father had spit in her face,
would she not bear her shame for seven days?
Let her be confined outside the camp for seven
days; afterwards she may be brought back. 15 So
Miriam was confined outside the camp for seven
days, and the people did not start out again until
she was brought back.
16 After that the people set out from Hazeroth
and encamped in the wilderness of Paran.

The Twelve Scouts

13 1 The LORD said to Moses: 2 Send men to
reconnoiter the land of Canaan, which I
am giving the Israelites. You shall send one man
from each ancestral tribe, every one a leader
among them. 3 * So Moses sent them from the
wilderness of Paran, at the direction of the LORD.
All of them were leaders among the Israelites.
4 These were their names:

from the tribe of Reuben, Shammua, son of Zaccur;
5 from the tribe of Simeon, Shaphat, son of Hori;
6 from the tribe of Judah, Caleb, son of Jephunneh;
7 from the tribe of Issachar, Igal;
8 for the Josephites, from the tribe of Ephraim, Hoshea, son of Nun;
9 from the tribe of Benjamin, Palti, son of Raphu;
10 from the tribe of Zebulun, Gaddiel, son of Sodi;
11 for the Josephites, from the tribe of Manasseh, Gaddi, son of Susi;
12 from the tribe of Dan, Ammiel, son of Gemalli;
13 from the tribe of Asher, Sethur, son of Michael;
14 from the tribe of Naphtali, Nahbi, son of Vophsi;
15 from the tribe of Gad, Geuel, son of Machi.

16 These are the names of the men whom Moses
sent to reconnoiter the land. But Hoshea, son of
Nun, Moses called Joshua.†
17 In sending them to reconnoiter the land of
Canaan, Moses said to them, "Go up there in the
Negeb, up into the highlands, 18 and see what
kind of land it is and whether the people living
there are strong or weak, few or many. 19 Is the
country in which they live good or bad? Are the
towns in which they dwell open or fortified? 20 Is
the soil fertile or barren, wooded or clear? And
do your best to get some of the fruit of the land."
It was then the season for early grapes.
21 So they went up and reconnoitered the land
from the wilderness of Zin† as far as where Re-
hob adjoins Lebo-hamath. 22 * Going up by way
of the Negeb, they reached Hebron, where Ahi-
man, Sheshai and Talmai, descendants of the

†

12:7 *Worthy of trust*: the text is open to a variety of interpretations. Thus, the word of Moses may be relied upon by Israel because God speaks to him directly; or, Moses alone is worthy of God's trust in God's household (heavenly or earthly). An alternative translation, however, is: "with all my house he is entrusted."

12:10 *Stricken with a scaly infection, white as snow*: see note on Lv 13:1–14:47. The point of the simile lies either in the flakiness or the whiteness of snow.

13:16 *Joshua*: in Hebrew, "Jehoshua," which was later modified to "Jeshua," the Hebrew name for "Jesus." Hoshea and Joshua are variants of one original name meaning "the LORD saves." Cf. Mt 1:21.

13:21 *The wilderness of Zin*: north of Paran and southwest of the Dead Sea. It is quite distinct from "the wilderness of Sin" near the border of Egypt (Ex 16:1; 17:1; Nm 33:11). *Lebo-hamath*: a town near

*

12:3 Sir 45:1–2.
12:7 Heb 3:2, 5.
12:8 Ex 33:1; Dt 34:10; Sir 45:3.
12:10 Dt 24:9.
13:3–33 Dt 1:22–28.
13:22 Jos 11:21–22.

Anakim,† were. (Now Hebron had been built seven years before Zoan in Egypt.) 23 They also reached the Wadi Eshcol,† where they cut down a branch with a single cluster of grapes on it, which two of them carried on a pole, as well as some pomegranates and figs. 24 It was because of the cluster the Israelites cut there that they called the place Wadi Eshcol.*

Their Report

25 They returned from reconnoitering the land forty days later. 26 * Proceeding directly to Moses and Aaron and the whole community of the Israelites in the wilderness of Paran at Kadesh, they made a report to them and to the whole community, showing them the fruit of the land. 27 They told Moses: "We came to the land to which you sent us. It does indeed flow with milk and honey, and here is its fruit. 28 However, the people who are living in the land are powerful, and the towns are fortified and very large.* Besides, we saw descendants of the Anakim there. 29 Amalekites live in the region of the Negeb; Hittites, Jebusites and Amorites dwell in the highlands, and Canaanites along the sea and the banks of the Jordan."

30 Caleb, however, quieted the people before Moses and said, "We ought to go up and seize the land, for we can certainly prevail over it." 31 But the men who had gone up with him said, "We cannot attack these people; they are too strong for us." 32 They spread discouraging reports* among the Israelites about the land they had reconnoitered, saying, "The land that we went through and reconnoitered is a land that consumes its inhabitants. And all the people we saw there are huge. 33 * There we saw the Nephilim† (the Anakim are from the Nephilim); in our own eyes we seemed like mere grasshoppers, and so we must have seemed to them."

Threats of Revolt

14 1 At this, the whole community broke out with loud cries, and the people wept into the night. 2 * All the Israelites grumbled against Moses and Aaron, the whole community saying to them, "If only we had died in the land of Egypt," or "If only we would die here in the wilderness! 3 Why is the LORD bringing us into this land only to have us fall by the sword? Our wives and little ones will be taken as spoil. Would it not be better for us to return to Egypt?" 4 So they said to one another, "Let us appoint a leader and go back to Egypt."

5 But Moses and Aaron fell prostrate before the whole assembled community of the Israelites; 6 while Joshua, son of Nun, and Caleb, son of Jephunneh, who had been among those that reconnoitered the land, tore their garments 7 and said to the whole community of the Israelites,* "The land which we went through and reconnoitered is an exceedingly good land. 8 If the LORD is pleased with us, he will bring us in to this land and give it to us, a land which flows with milk and honey. 9 * Only do not rebel against the LORD! You need not be afraid of the people of the land, for they are but food for us!† Their protection has left them, but the LORD is with us. Do not fear them."

The Lord's Sentence

10 The whole community threatened to stone them. But the glory of the LORD appeared at the tent of meeting to all the Israelites. 11 And the LORD said to Moses: How long will this people spurn me? How long will they not trust me, despite all the signs I have performed among them?* 12 I will strike them with pestilence and disown them. Then I will make of you a nation greater and mightier than they.*

13 * But Moses said to the LORD: "The Egyptians will hear of this, for by your power you brought out this people from among them. 14 They will tell the inhabitants of this land, who have heard that you, LORD, are in the midst of this people; you, LORD, who directly revealed yourself! Your cloud stands over them, and you go before them by day in a column of cloud and by night in a column of fire.* 15 If now you slay this people all at once, the nations who have heard such reports of you will say, 16 'The LORD was not able to bring this people into the land he swore to give them; that is why he slaughtered them in the wilder-

NM

---

† Riblah (Jer 39:5–6) at the southern border of Hamath, an independent kingdom in southern Syria. David's conquests extended as far as Hamath (2 Sm 8:9–11), and Lebo-hamath thus formed the northern border of the ideal extent of Israel's possessions (Nm 34:7–9; Ez 47:15; 48:1). This may suggest that this verse was inserted precisely to extend the scope of the reconnaisance; cf. Dt 1:24.

13:22, 28 *Anakim*: an aboriginal race in southern Palestine, largely absorbed by the Canaanites. Either because of their tall stature or because of the massive stone structures left by them, the Israelites regarded them as giants.

13:23 *Eshcol*: means "cluster."

13:33 *Nephilim*: i.e., "fallen ones" (in the Septuagint, "giants"), a reference to fallen heroes of old. Cf. Gn 6:4.

14:9 *They are but food for us*: lit., "for they are our bread." "Bread" (Heb. *lechem*) is here used in the sense of "prey, spoils" to be consumed by an invader. This is the answer to the pessimistic report that this land "consumes its inhabitants" (13:32).

---

* **13:24** Nm 32:9; Dt 1:24–25.
13:26–27 Ex 3:8, 17.
13:28–29 Dt 9:1–2.
13:32 Nm 32:9; Jos 14:8.
13:33 Dt 2:10.
14:2 Ex 16:3; Ps 106:25.
14:7–8 Dt 1:25.
14:9 Dt 7:18.
14:11 Ps 78:22, 32.
14:12 Ex 32:10.
14:13–16 Ex 32:12; Dt 9:26–29; Ps 106:23.
14:14 Ex 13:21; Jos 2:9–10.

ness.'* 17 Now then, may my Lord's forbearance
be great, even as you have said, 18 * 'The LORD
is slow to anger and abounding in kindness,
forgiving iniquity and rebellion; yet certainly
not declaring the guilty guiltless, but punishing
children to the third and fourth generation for
their parents' iniquity.' 19 Pardon, then, the in-
iquity of this people in keeping with your great
kindness, even as you have forgiven them from
Egypt until now."*

20 The LORD answered: I pardon them as you
have asked. 21 Yet, by my life and the LORD's glory
that fills the whole earth, 22 of all the people who
have seen my glory and the signs I did in Egypt
and in the wilderness,* and who nevertheless
have put me to the test ten times already and
have not obeyed me, 23 not one shall see the land
which I promised on oath to their ancestors.
None of those who have spurned me shall see
it. 24 But as for my servant Caleb, because he has
a different spirit and follows me unreservedly,*
I will bring him into the land which he entered,
and his descendants shall possess it. 25 But now,
since the Amalekites and Canaanites are living
in the valleys,† turn away tomorrow and set out
into the wilderness by way of the Red Sea road.

26 The LORD also said to Moses and Aaron:
27 How long will this wicked community grum-
ble against me?* I have heard the grumblings
of the Israelites against me. 28 Tell them:† "By
my life"—oracle of the LORD—"I will do to you
just what I have heard you say. 29 Here in the
wilderness* your dead bodies shall fall. Of all
your men of twenty years or more, enrolled in
your registration, who grumbled against me,
30 not one of you shall enter the land where I sol-
emnly swore to settle you, except Caleb, son of
Jephunneh, and Joshua, son of Nun. 31 Your little
ones, however, who you said would be taken as
spoil, I will bring in, and they shall know the
land you rejected.* 32 But as for you, your bod-
ies shall fall here in the wilderness, 33 while your
children will wander for forty years, suffering for
your infidelity, till the last of you lies dead in the
wilderness.* 34 Corresponding to the number of
days you spent reconnoitering the land—forty
days—you shall bear your punishment one year
for each day: forty years. Thus you will realize
what it means to oppose me. 35 I, the LORD, have
spoken; and I will surely do this to this entire
wicked community that conspired against me:
here in the wilderness they shall come to their
end and there they will die."

36 And the men whom Moses had sent to re-
connoiter the land* and who on returning had
set the whole community grumbling against
him by spreading discouraging reports about the
land— 37 these men who had spread discourag-
ing reports about the land were struck down by
the LORD and died. 38 Only Joshua, son of Nun,
and Caleb, son of Jephunneh, survived of all the
men who had gone to reconnoiter the land.*

Unsuccessful Invasion

39 When Moses repeated these words to all the
Israelites, the people mourned greatly. 40 Early
the next morning they started up high into the
hill country, saying, "Here we are, ready to go up
to the place that the LORD spoke of:* for we did
wrong." 41 But Moses said, "Why are you now
transgressing the LORD's order? This cannot suc-
ceed. 42 Do not go up, because the LORD is not in
your midst; do not allow yourself to be struck
down by your enemies.* 43 For there the Amalek-
ites and Canaanites will face you, and you will
fall by the sword. You have turned back from
following the LORD; therefore the LORD will not
be with you."

44 Yet they dared to go up high into the hill
country,* even though neither the ark of the cov-
enant of the LORD nor Moses left the camp. 45 And
the Amalekites and Canaanites who dwelt in that
hill country came down and defeated them, beat-
ing them back as far as Hormah.†

Secondary Offerings

15 1 The LORD spoke to Moses: 2 † Speak to
the Israelites and say to them: When you
enter the land that I am giving you for your set-
tlements, 3 if you make to the LORD an oblation
from the herd or from the flock—either a burnt
offering or a sacrifice, to fulfill a vow, or as a

†

14:25 *The valleys*: the low-lying plains in the Negeb and along the seacoast and in the Jordan depression, as well as the higher valleys in the mountains farther north: cf. v. 45.

14:28–29 God punished the grumblers by giving them their wish; cf. v. 2. Their lack of trust in God is cited in 1 Cor 10:10 and Heb 3:12–18 as a warning for Christians.

14:45 *Hormah*: one of the Canaanite royal cities in southern Judah, according to the tradition attested in Jos 12:14, although Nm 21:1–3 gives it as the new name for the city of Arad when it was destroyed by Israel. According to the list of conquered cities preserved in Jgs 1, the earlier name for the city of Hormah was Zephath. The precise location is unknown.

15:2–16 These laws on sacrifice are complementary to those of Lv 1–3. Since the food of the Israelites consisted not only of meat but also of bread, oil and wine, they offered flour, wine and oil in sacrifice to the Lord besides the animal oblations.

*

14:16 Ex 32:12; Dt 9:28.
14:18 Ex 20:5; 34:6–7; Ps 103:8; 145:8.
14:19 Ps 78:38.
14:22–23 Dt 1:35.
14:24 Jos 14:8–9.
14:27 Ex 16:7, 12.
14:29 Dt 1:35; Heb 3:17.
14:31 Dt 1:39.
14:33–34 Nm 13:26; 32:13; Ps 95:10; Ez 4:6.
14:36–37 Nm 13:17, 32–33; 1 Cor 10:10.
14:38 Nm 26:65.
14:40 Nm 13:18; Dt 1:41.
14:42 Dt 1:42.
14:44 Dt 1:43.

voluntary offering, or for one of your festivals—to produce a pleasing aroma for the LORD, 4 the one presenting the offering shall also present to the LORD a grain offering, a tenth of a measure† of bran flour mixed with a fourth of a hin of oil, 5 as well as wine for a libation, a fourth of a hin. You will do this with the burnt offering or the sacrifice, for each lamb. 6 Alternatively for a ram you shall make a grain offering of two tenths of a measure of bran flour mixed with a third of a hin of oil, 7 and for a libation, a third of a hin of wine, thereby presenting a pleasing aroma to the LORD. 8 If you make an offering from the herd—either a burnt offering, or a sacrifice, to fulfill a vow, or as a communion offering to the LORD, 9 with it a grain offering of three tenths of a measure of bran flour mixed with half a hin of oil will be presented; 10 and you will present for a libation, half a hin of wine—a sweet-smelling oblation to the LORD. 11 The same is to be done for each ox, ram, lamb or goat. 12 Whatever the number you offer, do the same for each of them.

13 All the native-born shall make these offerings in this way, whenever they present a sweet-smelling oblation to the LORD. 14 Likewise, in any future generation, any alien residing with you or anyone else in your midst, who presents an oblation of pleasing aroma to the LORD, must do as you do. 15 There is but one statute for you and for the resident alien, a perpetual statute throughout your generations. You and the resident alien will be alike before the LORD; 16 you and the alien residing with you will have the same rule and the same application of it.

17 The LORD spoke to Moses: 18 Speak to the Israelites and say to them: When you enter the land into which I am bringing you 19 and eat of the bread of the land, you shall offer the LORD a contribution. 20 A round loaf from your first batch of dough† you shall offer as a contribution. Just like a contribution from the threshing floor you shall offer it.* 21 Throughout your generations you shall give a contribution to the LORD from your first batch of dough.

Purification Offerings†

22 If through inadvertence you fail to do any of these commandments which the LORD has given to Moses—* 23 anything the LORD commanded you through Moses from the time the LORD first gave the command down through your generations— 24 if it was done inadvertently without the community's knowledge, the whole community shall sacrifice one bull from the herd as a burnt offering of pleasing aroma to the LORD, along with its prescribed grain offering and libation, as well as one he-goat as a purification offering. 25 * Then the priest shall make atonement for the whole Israelite community; and they will be forgiven, since it was inadvertence, and for their inadvertence they have brought their offering: an oblation to the LORD as well as their purification offering before the LORD. 26 Not only the whole Israelite community but also the aliens residing among you shall be forgiven, since the inadvertent fault affects all the people.

27 If it is an individual who sins inadvertently,* this person shall bring a yearling she-goat as a purification offering. 28 And the priest shall make atonement before the LORD for the one who erred, since the sin was inadvertent, making atonement for the person to secure forgiveness. 29 You shall have but one rule for the person who sins inadvertently, whether a native-born Israelite or an alien residing among you.

30 But anyone who acts defiantly,* whether a native or an alien, reviles the LORD, and shall be cut off from among the people. 31 * For having despised the word of the LORD and broken his commandment, he must be cut off entirely and bear the punishment.

The Sabbath-breaker

32 While the Israelites were in the wilderness, a man was discovered gathering wood on the sabbath day. 33 Those who caught him at it brought him to Moses and Aaron and the whole community. 34 But they put him in custody, for there was no clear decision† as to what should be done with him.* 35 Then the LORD said to Moses: This man shall be put to death; let the whole community stone him outside the camp. 36 So the whole community led him outside the camp and stoned him to death, as the LORD had commanded Moses.

†

15:4 *Measure*: the word, supplied from the context, does not appear in the Hebrew (as also in vv. 6, 9; 28:9, 12, 20, 28; 29:3, 9, 14). Probably the ephah (which is named in 5:15; 28:5) is intended. *Hin*: see note on Ez 45:24.

15:20 *Dough*: the meaning of the Hebrew term is uncertain; some render, "baking utensils." This word is used elsewhere only in Ez 44:30 and Neh 10:33; a related Hebrew word is used in Lv 2:14.

15:22–31 See note on Lv 4:2. Although Lv 4–5 and Nm 15:22–31 both concern inadvertent sins, the emphasis here, as opposed to Lv 4–5, is on the failure of the community to perform "positive commands" rather than on doing what is prohibited.

15:34 *No clear decision*: either it was not clear that gathering wood constituted "work" and as such a willful violation of the sabbath and a capital offense; or they did not yet know how the death penalty was to be inflicted.

*

15:19–20 Ez 44:30.
15:22–23 Lv 4:13–14.
15:25 Lv 4:20.
15:27–28 Lv 4:27–28.
15:30 Dt 17:12.
15:31 Prv 13:13.
15:34 Lv 24:12.

Tassels on the Cloak

37 The LORD said to Moses: 38 Speak to the Isra-
elites and tell them that throughout their gener-
ations they are to make tassels† for the corners
of their garments, fastening a violet cord to each
corner.* 39 When you use these tassels, the sight
of the cord will remind you of all the command-
ments of the LORD and you will do them, without
prostituting yourself going after the desires of
your hearts and your eyes. 40 Thus you will re-
member to do all my commandments and you
will be holy to your God. 41 I, the LORD, am your
God who brought you out of the land of Egypt to
be your God: I, the LORD your God.*

Rebellion of Korah

16 1 † Korah, son of Izhar, son of Kohath, son
of Levi, and the Reubenites Dathan and
Abiram, sons of Eliab, and On, son of Peleth,†
son of Reuben took 2 two hundred and fifty Is-
raelites who were leaders in the community,
members of the council and men of note, and
confronted Moses. 3 Holding an assembly against
Moses and Aaron, they said,* "You go too far!
The whole community, all of them, are holy; the
LORD is in their midst. Why then should you set
yourselves over the LORD's assembly?"
4 When Moses heard this, he fell prostrate.
5 Then he said to Korah and to all his faction,
"May the LORD make known tomorrow morning
who belongs to him and who is the holy one
and whom he will have draw near to him! The
one whom he chooses, he will have draw near
to him. 6 Do this: take your censers, Korah and
all his faction, 7 and put fire in them and place
incense in them before the LORD tomorrow. He
whom the LORD then chooses is the holy one.
You Levites go too far!"
8 Moses also said to Korah, "Hear, now, you
Levites! 9 * Are you not satisfied that the God of
Israel has singled you out from the community
of Israel, to have you draw near him to maintain
the LORD's tabernacle, and to attend upon the
community and to serve them? 10 He has allowed
you and your Levite kinsmen with you to ap-
proach him, and yet you seek the priesthood too.
11 It is therefore against the LORD that you and all
your faction are conspiring. As for Aaron, what
has he done that you should grumble against
him?"

Rebellion of Dathan and Abiram

12 Moses summoned Dathan and Abiram, sons
of Eliab, but they answered, "We will not go.†
13 Are you not satisfied that you have brought us
here from a land flowing with milk and honey
to have us perish in the wilderness, that now you
must also lord it over us? 14 Far from bringing us
to a land flowing with milk and honey, or giving
us fields and vineyards for our inheritance, will
you gouge out our eyes?† No, we will not go."
15 Then Moses became very angry and said to
the LORD, "Pay no attention to their offering. I
have never taken a single donkey from them, nor
have I wronged any one of them."*

Korah

16 Moses said to Korah, "You and all your fac-
tion shall appear before the LORD tomorrow—you
and they and Aaron too. 17 Then each of you take
his own censer, put incense in it, and present it
before the LORD, two hundred and fifty censers;
and you and Aaron, each with his own censer,
do the same." 18 So each of them took their cen-
sers, and laying incense on the fire they had put
in them, they took their stand by the entrance of
the tent of meeting along with Moses and Aaron.
19 Then, when Korah had assembled all the com-
munity against them at the entrance of the tent
of meeting, the glory of the LORD appeared to the
entire community, 20 and the LORD said to Moses
and Aaron: 21 Stand apart from this community,
that I may consume them at once. 22 But they fell
prostrate and exclaimed, "O God, God of the
spirits of all living creatures, if one man sins will
you be angry with the whole community?" 23 The
LORD answered Moses: 24 Speak to the community

†

15:38 *Tassels*: at the time of Jesus these tassels were worn by all pious Jews, including Jesus (Mt 9:20–21; Mk 6:56); some Pharisees wore very large ones in a display of their zeal for the law (Mt 23:5).

16:1–3 The evidence seems to show that accounts of two, if not more, distinct rebellions have been combined in this chapter. The most obvious are the rebellions of Korah and his faction (Nm 27:3) and of Dathan and Abiram (Dt 11:6); cf. Ps 106. The present account combines both events into one narrative; but even here it is rather easy to separate the two. The rebellion of the Reubenites, Dathan and Abiram, was more political in character, against Moses alone as the civil leader (cf. v. 13); these rebels were punished by being swallowed alive in an earthquake. The rebellion of Korah was more religious in character, directed primarily against the religious leadership of Aaron (though in vv. 19–22 it is Korah and the whole community against both Moses and Aaron). About two hundred and fifty malcontents joined Korah's faction, and they are punished by fire. The parts of the present section which refer to the rebellion of Dathan and Abiram are vv. 12–15 and vv. 25–34 of chap. 16; the rest of chap. 16 and all of chap. 17 chiefly concern the rebellion of Korah.

16:1 *The Reubenites . . . son of Peleth*: some suggest on the basis of 26:5, 8 and Gn 46:9 reading instead of the traditional Hebrew text: "son of Levi, and Dathan and Abiram, sons of Eliab, son of Pallu, son of Reuben."

16:12 *We will not go*: to appear before Moses' "tribunal."

16:14 *Gouge out our eyes*: blind us to the real state of affairs.

*

15:38 Dt 22:12.
15:41 Lv 22:32–33.
16:3 Ps 106:16–18; Sir 45:19.
16:9 Dt 10:8.
16:15 1 Sm 12:3.

and tell them: Withdraw from the area around
the tent† of Korah, Dathan and Abiram.

Punishment of Dathan and Abiram

25 Moses, followed by the elders of Israel, arose
and went to Dathan and Abiram.† 26 Then he
spoke to the community, "Move away from the
tents of these wicked men and do not touch
anything that is theirs: otherwise you too will
be swept away because of all their sins." 27 So
they withdrew from the area around the tents of
Korah, Dathan and Abiram. When Dathan and
Abiram had come out and were standing at the
entrance of their tents with their wives, their chil-
dren, and their little ones, 28 Moses said, "This is
how you shall know that the LORD sent me to do
all I have done, and that it was not of my own
devising: 29 if these die an ordinary death, merely
suffering the fate common to all humanity, the
LORD has not sent me. 30 But if the LORD makes a
chasm, and the ground opens its mouth and swal-
lows them with all belonging to them, and they
go down alive to Sheol,† then you will know that
these men have spurned the LORD." 31 * No sooner
had he finished saying all this than the ground
beneath them split open, 32 and the earth opened
its mouth and swallowed them and their families
and all of Korah's people† with all their posses-
sions. 33 They went down alive to Sheol with all
belonging to them; the earth closed over them,
and they disappeared from the assembly. 34 But
all the Israelites near them fled at their shrieks,
saying, "The earth might swallow us too!"

Punishment of Korah

35 And fire from the LORD came forth which
consumed the two hundred and fifty men who
were offering the incense.

17 1 The LORD said to Moses: 2 Tell Eleazar, son
of Aaron the priest, to remove the censers
from the embers; and scatter the fire some dis-
tance away, for they have become holy— 3 † the
censers of those who sinned at the cost of their
lives. Have them hammered into plates to cover
the altar, because in being presented before the
LORD they have become holy. In this way they
shall serve as a sign to the Israelites. 4 So taking
the bronze censers which had been presented by
those who were burned, Eleazar the priest had
them hammered into a covering for the altar,
5 just as the LORD had directed him through Mo-
ses. This was to be a reminder to the Israelites
that no unauthorized person, no one who was
not a descendant of Aaron, should draw near to
offer incense before the LORD, lest he meet the
fate of Korah and his faction.

6 The next day the whole Israelite community
grumbled against Moses and Aaron, saying, "You
have killed the people of the LORD." 7 But while
the community was assembling against them,
Moses and Aaron turned toward the tent of meet-
ing, and the cloud now covered it and the glory
of the LORD appeared. 8 Then Moses and Aaron
came to the front of the tent of meeting, 9 and
the LORD said to Moses: 10 Remove yourselves
from this community, that I may consume them
at once. But they fell prostrate.

11 Then Moses said to Aaron, "Take your censer,
put fire from the altar in it, lay incense on it, and
bring it quickly to the community to make atone-
ment for them; for wrath has come forth from
the LORD and the plague has begun."* 12 Aaron
took his censer just as Moses directed and ran in
among the assembly, where the plague had al-
ready begun among the people. Then he offered
the incense and made atonement for the people,
13 while standing there between the living and
the dead. And so the scourge was checked.
14 There were fourteen thousand seven hundred
dead from the scourge, in addition to those who
died because of Korah. 15 When the scourge had
been checked, Aaron returned to Moses at the
entrance of the tent of meeting.

Aaron's Staff

16 The LORD now said to Moses: 17 Speak to the
Israelites and get from them a staff† for each
ancestral house, twelve staffs in all, from all
the leaders of their ancestral houses. Write each

†

16:24 *Withdraw from the area around the tent*: the word for "tent," *mishkan*, here and in v. 27, is otherwise used in the singular only for the tent of meeting, suggesting possibly the erection of a rival sanctuary by the rebels. Note further, as an indication of the fact that various accounts of rebellion have been fused here, that in v. 19 the entire community had been assembled by Korah at the tent of meeting.

16:25 Since Dathan and Abiram had refused to go to Moses (vv. 12–14), he, with the elders as witnesses, was obliged to go to their tents.

16:30 *Sheol*: see note on Ps 6:6.

16:32 *And all of Korah's people*: the implication of this secondary addition to the text is, on the one hand, that Korah met his death elsewhere, presumably with the two hundred and fifty offering incense (vv. 16–17, 35); or, on the other hand, he died along with Dathan and Abiram in the splitting of the earth.

17:3 Whatever was brought into intimate contact with something holy shared in its holiness. See note on 19:20.

17:17 The staff was not merely an article of practical use, but also a symbol of authority; cf. Gn 49:10; Nm 24:17; Jer 48:17. Therefore, the staff of a leader of a tribe was considered the emblem of the tribe; in fact, certain Hebrew words such as *matteh*, the word for "staff" here, also mean "tribe." Perhaps for this reason, to avoid confusion, the author here uses the term *bet'ab*, "ancestral house," for "tribe" instead of one of the ordinary words for "tribe."

*

16:31–34 Nm 26:10; Lv 10:2; Dt 11:6; Ps 106:17–18.

17:11 Wis 18:20–21.

man's name on his staff; [18]and write Aaron's
name on Levi's staff.† For each head of an ances-
tral house shall have a staff. [19]Then deposit them
in the tent of meeting, in front of the covenant,
where I meet you. [20]The staff of the man whom I
choose shall sprout. Thus I will rid myself of the
Israelites' grumbling against you.
[21]So Moses spoke to the Israelites, and all
their leaders gave him staffs, twelve in all, one
from each leader of their ancestral houses; and
Aaron's staff was among them. [22]Then Moses
deposited the staffs before the LORD in the tent
of the covenant. [23]The next day, when Moses
entered the tent of the covenant, Aaron's staff,
representing the house of Levi, had sprouted. It
had put forth sprouts, produced blossoms, and
borne ripe almonds! [24]So Moses brought out all
the staffs from the LORD's presence to all the Isra-
elites, and each one identified his own staff and
took it. [25]Then the LORD said to Moses: Put back
Aaron's staff in front of the covenant, for safe
keeping as a sign to the rebellious, so that their
grumbling against me may cease and they might
not die. [26]Moses did this. Just as the LORD had
commanded him, so he did.

Charge of the Sacred Things

[27]† Then the Israelites exclaimed to Moses,
"We will perish; we are lost, we are all lost! [28]Any-
one who approaches the tabernacle of the LORD
will die! Will there be no end to our perishing?"

18 [1]The LORD said to Aaron:† You and your
sons as well as your ancestral house with
you† shall be responsible for any sin with respect
to the sanctuary; but only you and your sons
with you shall be responsible for any sin with re-
spect to your priesthood. [2]You shall also present
with you your kinsmen of the tribe of Levi, your
ancestral tribe, that they may be joined to you†
and assist you, while you and your sons with you
are in front of the tent of the covenant. [3]They
shall discharge your obligations and those with
respect to the whole tent; however, they shall not
come near the utensils of the sanctuary or the al-
tar, or else both they and you will die. [4]They will
be joined to you to perform the duties associated
with the tent of meeting, all the labor pertaining
to the tent. But no unauthorized person† shall
come near you. [5]You shall perform the duties of
the sanctuary and of the altar, that wrath may not
fall again upon the Israelites.
[6]I hereby take your kinsmen, the Levites, from
among the Israelites; they are a gift to you,* ded-
icated to the LORD for the labor they perform for
the tent of meeting. [7]* But you and your sons
with you must take care to exercise your priest-
hood in whatever concerns the altar and the area
within the veil.† I give you your priesthood as a
gift. Any unauthorized person who comes near
shall be put to death.

The Priests' Share of the Sacrifices

[8]The LORD said to Aaron:† I hereby give to
you charge of the contributions made to me,
including the various holy offerings of the Isra-
elites;* I assign them to you and to your sons as
a perquisite, a perpetual due. [9]This is what you
shall have from the oblations that are most holy:
every offering of theirs—namely, all their grain
offerings, purification offerings, and reparation
offerings which they must return to me—shall be
most holy for you and for your sons. [10]You shall
eat them in a most holy place;† every male may
partake of them. As holy, they belong to you.
[11]This also you shall have: the contributions
that are their gifts, including the elevated offer-
ing† of the Israelites; I assign them to you and to
your sons and daughters with you as a perpetual
due.* All in your household who are clean may
eat them. [12]I also assign to you all the best* of
the new oil and of the new wine and grain that
they give to the LORD as their first produce that
has been processed. [13]The first-ripened fruits of
whatever is in their land, which they bring to the
LORD, shall be yours; all of your household who

17:18 *Levi's staff*: it is not clear whether this is considered as one of the twelve mentioned in the preceding verse, or as a thirteenth staff. Sometimes Levi is reckoned as one of the twelve tribes (e.g., Dt 27:12–13), but more often the number twelve is arrived at by counting the two sub-tribes of Joseph, i.e., Ephraim and Manasseh, as distinct tribes. In this passage also it seems probable that the tribe of Levi is considered apart from the other twelve tribes.

17:27–28 The people's distress here echoes their panic in 16:34, and may be heightened further by the death of the two hundred and fifty leaders offering incense in 16:35.

18:1–3 This law, which kept unqualified persons from contact with holy things, is in response to the Israelites' cry in 17:28. It is followed by other laws concerning priests and Levites.

18:1 *With you*: not only in the present but also those of his house in the future.

18:2 *Be joined to you*: in Hebrew a pun on the popular etymology of the name "Levi." Cf. Gn 29:34.

18:4 *Unauthorized person*: here, "one who is not a Levite"; in v. 7, "one who is not a priest."

18:7 *Veil*: the outer veil, or "curtain," is probably meant.

18:8–10 Two classes of offerings are here distinguished: the most holy offering, which only the male members of the priestly families could eat (vv. 8–10), and the other offerings, which the women of the priestly families could eat (vv. 11–19).

18:10 *In a most holy place*: in the court of the tabernacle, according to Lv 6:9, 19.

18:11 *Elevated offering*: this included the brisket and right thigh (v. 18), the shoulder of the peace offering (Lv 7:30–34), and portions of the nazirite sacrifice (Nm 6:19–20). *With you*: see note on v. 1. Aaron had no daughters; see also v. 19.

18:6 Nm 3:9; 8:19.
18:7 Nm 3:10.
18:8 Nm 5:9.
18:11 Ex 29:27–28; Lv 7:34; 10:14.
18:12–13 Dt 18:4; 26:2.

are clean may eat them. [14]Whatever is under the ban† in Israel shall be yours. [15]Every living thing that opens the womb, human being and beast alike, such as are to be offered to the LORD, shall be yours;* but you must redeem the firstborn of human beings, as well as redeem the firstborn of unclean animals. [16]For the redemption price of a son, when he is a month old, you shall pay the equivalent of five silver shekels according to the sanctuary shekel, that is, twenty gerahs. [17]But the firstborn of cattle, or the firstborn of sheep or the firstborn of goats you shall not redeem; they are holy. Their blood you must splash on the altar and their fat you must burn as an oblation of pleasing aroma to the LORD. [18]* Their meat, however, shall be yours, just as the brisket of the elevated offering and the right thigh belong to you. [19]As a perpetual due I assign to you and to your sons and daughters with you all the contributions of holy things which the Israelites set aside for the LORD; this is a covenant of salt† to last forever before the LORD, for you and for your descendants with you. [20]* Then the LORD said to Aaron:† You shall not have any heritage in their land nor hold any portion among them; I will be your portion and your heritage among the Israelites.

Tithes Due the Levites

[21]To the Levites, however, I hereby assign all tithes in Israel as their heritage in recompense for the labor they perform, the labor pertaining to the tent of meeting.* [22]The Israelites may no longer approach the tent of meeting, thereby incurring the penalty of death. [23]Only the Levites are to perform the labor pertaining to the tent of meeting, and they shall incur the penalty for the Israelites' sin;† this is a permanent statute for all your generations. But they shall not have any heritage among the Israelites, [24]for I have assigned to the Levites as their heritage the tithes which the Israelites put aside as a contribution to the LORD. That is why I have said, they will not have any heritage among the Israelites.

Tithes Paid by the Levites

[25]The LORD said to Moses: [26]Speak to the Levites and say to them: When you take from the Israelites the tithes I have assigned you from them as your heritage, you are to make a contribution from them to the LORD, a tithe of the tithe; [27]and your contribution will be credited to you as if it were grain from the threshing floor or new wine from the vat. [28]Thus you too shall make a contribution to the LORD from all the tithes you take from the Israelites, handing over to Aaron the priest the contribution to the LORD. [29]From all the gifts to you, you shall make every contribution due to the LORD—from their best parts, that is the part to be consecrated from them.

[30]Say to them also: Once you have made your contribution from the best part, the rest of the tithe will be credited to the Levites as if it were produce of the threshing floor or the produce of the vat. [31]You and your households may eat it anywhere, since it is your recompense in exchange for labor in the tent of meeting. [32]You will incur no punishment when you contribute the best part of it. But do not profane the holy offerings of the Israelites or else you shall die.

Ashes of the Red Heifer

19 [1]The LORD spoke to Moses and Aaron: [2]This is the statute for the ritual which the LORD has commanded. Tell the Israelites to procure for you a red heifer without defect and free from every blemish and on which no yoke has ever been laid. [3]You will give it to Eleazar the priest, and it will be led outside the camp† and slaughtered in his presence. [4]Eleazar the priest will take some of its blood on his finger and sprinkle it seven times toward the front of the tent of meeting.† [5]Then the heifer will be burned in his sight; it will be burned with its hide and flesh, its blood and dung; [6]and the priest will take cedar wood, hyssop and scarlet yarn and throw them into the fire in which the heifer is being burned. [7]The priest shall then

†

18:14 *Under the ban*: in Hebrew, *herem*, which means here "set aside from profane use and made sacred to the Lord." Cf. Lv 27:21, 28.

18:19 *A covenant of salt*: cf. 2 Chr 13:5. The reference may perhaps be to the preservative power of salt (cf. Mt 5:13); but more likely the phrase refers to the custom of eating salt together to render a contract unbreakable. See note on Lv 2:13.

18:20 The priests and Levites were forbidden to own hereditary land such as the other Israelites possessed; therefore in the allotment of the land (chap. 34) they did not receive any portion of it. Certain cities, however, were assigned to them for their residence; cf. 35:1–8.

18:23 *Incur the penalty for the Israelites' sin*: the Levites are responsible for protecting the sanctuary from illegitimate encroachment and in this sense pay the penalty for the Israelites' iniquity. This responds further to the fears of the people expressed in 17:27–28.

19:3 *Outside the camp*: several early Christian writers saw in this a prefiguring of the sacrificial death of Jesus outside the walls of Jerusalem; cf. Jn 19:20; Heb 13:12; in the purifying water, into which the ashes of the red heifer were put, they saw a type of the water of Baptism.

19:4 *Toward the front of the tent of meeting*: since the tabernacle faced the east (Ex 26:15–30), the killing of the heifer would take place east of the camp; in later times it was done on the Mount of Olives, east of the Temple.

*

18:15 Ex 13:2.
18:18 Lv 7:31–34.
18:20 Dt 10:9; 18:1–2; Jos 13:33; Ez 44:28.
18:21 Heb 7:5.

wash his garments and bathe his body in water, afterward he may enter the camp. The priest remains unclean until the evening. [8]Likewise, the one who burned the heifer shall wash his garments in water, bathe his body in water, and be unclean until evening. [9]Then somebody who is clean shall gather up the ashes of the heifer and deposit them in a clean place outside the camp. There they are to be kept to prepare purification water for the Israelite community. This is a purification offering. [10]The one who has gathered up the ashes of the heifer shall also wash his garments and be unclean until evening. This is a permanent statute, both for the Israelites and for the alien residing among them.

Use of the Ashes

[11]Those who touch the corpse of any human being will be unclean for seven days; [12]they shall purify themselves with the water on the third and on the seventh day, and then be clean. But if they fail to purify themselves on the third and on the seventh day, they will not become clean. [13]* Those who touch the corpse of a human being who dies and who fail to purify themselves defile the tabernacle of the LORD and these persons shall be cut off from Israel. Since the purification water has not been splashed over them, they remain unclean: their uncleanness is still on them.

[14]This is the ritual: When someone dies in a tent, everyone who enters the tent, as well as everyone already in it, will be unclean for seven days; [15]and every open vessel with its lid unfastened will be unclean. [16]Moreover, everyone who in the open country touches a person who has been slain by the sword or who has died naturally, or who touches a human bone or a grave, will be unclean for seven days. [17]For anyone who is thus unclean, ashes shall be taken from the burnt purification offering, and spring water will be poured on them from a vessel.* [18]Then someone who is clean will take hyssop, dip it in this water, and sprinkle it on the tent and on all the vessels and persons that were in it, or on the one who touched the bone, the slain person or the other corpse, or the grave. [19]The clean will sprinkle the unclean on the third and on the seventh day, and thus purify them on the seventh day. Then they will wash their garments and bathe in water, and in the evening be clean. [20]† Those who become unclean and fail to purify themselves—those people will be cut off from the assembly, because they defile the sanctuary of the LORD. The purification water has not been splashed over them; they remain unclean. [21]This will be a permanent statute for you.

Those who sprinkle the purification water will wash their garments, and those who come in contact with the purification water will be unclean until evening. [22]Moreover, anything that the unclean person touches becomes unclean itself, and the one who touches such a person becomes unclean until evening.

Death of Miriam

20 † [1]The Israelites, the whole community, arrived in the wilderness of Zin† in the first month, and the people stayed at Kadesh. It was here that Miriam died, and here that she was buried.

Need for Water at Kadesh

[2]Since the community had no water, they held an assembly against Moses and Aaron. [3]The people quarreled with Moses, exclaiming, "Would that we had perished when our kindred perished before the LORD! [4]Why have you brought the LORD's assembly into this wilderness for us and our livestock to die here? [5]Why have you brought us up out of Egypt, only to bring us to this wretched place? It is not a place for grain nor figs nor vines nor pomegranates! And there is no water to drink!" [6]But Moses and Aaron went away from the assembly to the entrance of the tent of meeting, where they fell prostrate.

Sin of Moses and Aaron

Then the glory of the LORD appeared to them, [7]and the LORD said to Moses: [8]Take the staff and assemble the community, you and Aaron your brother, and in their presence command the rock to yield its waters. Thereby you will bring forth water from the rock for them, and supply the community and their livestock with water. [9]So Moses took the staff from its place before the LORD, as he was ordered. [10]Then Moses and Aaron gathered the assembly in front of the rock, where he said to them,* "Just listen, you rebels!

†

19:20 Ritual uncleanness is, as it were, contagious; so also sacredness; see note on 17:3.

20:1–29 In this chapter the deaths of the three wilderness leaders are either intimated or explicitly reported: Miriam, v. 1; Moses, v. 12; Aaron, vv. 12, 22–29.

20:1 *The wilderness of Zin*: a barren region with a few good oases, southwest of the Dead Sea. See note on 13:21. *The first month*: we would expect the mention also of the day and of the year (after the exodus) when this took place; cf. similar dates in 1:1; 10:11; 33:38; Dt 1:3. Here the full date is left unspecified. According to one chronology, the Israelites arrived in Kadesh in the third year after the exodus (cf. Dt 1:46). But the itinerary in chap. 33 would suggest the fortieth year, the year in which Aaron died (33:38).

*

19:13 Lv 15:31. **19:17–19** Heb 9:13–14. **20:10** Ex 17:5–6.

Are we to produce water for you out of this
rock?" 11 * Then, raising his hand, Moses struck
the rock twice† with his staff, and water came out
in abundance, and the community and their live-
stock drank. 12 † But the LORD said to Moses and
Aaron: Because you did not have confidence in
me, to acknowledge my holiness before the Isra-
elites, therefore you shall not lead this assembly
into the land I have given them.
13 These are the waters of Meribah,* where the
Israelites quarreled with the LORD, and through
which he displayed his holiness.

Edom's Refusal

14 From Kadesh Moses sent messengers to the
king of Edom: "Thus says your brother Israel:†
You know of all the hardships that have befallen
us, 15 how our ancestors went down to Egypt, and
we stayed in Egypt a long time, and the Egyptians
treated us and our ancestors harshly. 16 When we
cried to the LORD,* he heard our cry and sent an
angel who led us out of Egypt. Now here we are
at Kadesh, a town at the edge of your territory.
17 Please let us pass through your land. We will
not cross any fields or vineyards, nor drink any
well water, but we will go straight along the King's
Highway† without turning to the right or to the
left, until we have passed through your territory."
18 But Edom answered him, "You shall not
pass through here; if you do, I will advance
against you with the sword." 19 The Israelites said
to him, "We will go up along the highway. If we
or our livestock drink any of your water, we will
pay for it. It is nothing—just let us pass through
on foot." 20 But Edom replied, "You shall not
pass through,"* and advanced against them with
a large and heavily armed force. 21 Therefore,
since Edom refused to let Israel pass through
their territory, Israel turned away from them.

Death of Aaron

22 * Setting out from Kadesh, the Israelites,
the whole community, came to Mount Hor.†
23 There at Mount Hor, on the border of the land
of Edom, the LORD said to Moses and Aaron:
24 Let Aaron be gathered to his people, for he
shall not enter the land I have given to the Is-
raelites, because you both rebelled against my
directions at the waters of Meribah. 25 Take Aaron
and Eleazar his son and bring them up on Mount
Hor.* 26 Then strip Aaron of his garments and
put them on Eleazar, his son; but there Aaron
shall be gathered up in death.
27 Moses did as the LORD commanded. When
they had climbed Mount Hor in view of the
whole community, 28 Moses stripped Aaron of
his garments and put them on Eleazar his son.
Then Aaron died there on top of the mountain.*
When Moses and Eleazar came down from the
mountain, 29 all the community understood that
Aaron had breathed his last; and for thirty days
the whole house of Israel mourned Aaron.

Victory over Arad

21 1 When the Canaanite, the king of Arad,†
who ruled over the Negeb,* heard that the
Israelites were coming along the way of Atharim,
he engaged Israel in battle and took some of
them captive. 2 Israel then made this vow to the
LORD: "If you deliver this people into my hand, I
will put their cities under the ban."* 3 The LORD
paid attention to Israel and delivered up the
Canaanites,* and they put them and their cit-
ies under the ban. Hence that place was named
Hormah.†

The Bronze Serpent

4 From Mount Hor they set out by way of the
Red Sea, to bypass the land of Edom, but the peo-
ple's patience was worn out by the journey; 5 so
the people complained* against God and Moses,
"Why have you brought us up from Egypt to die
in the wilderness, where there is no food or water?
We are disgusted with this wretched food!"†
6 So the LORD sent among the people seraph†
serpents, which bit* the people so that many

---

†

20:11 *Twice*: perhaps because he did not have sufficient faith to work the wonder with the first blow. Cf. v. 12.

20:12–13 What lay behind Moses and Aaron's lack of confidence is not made explicit in the text. *Holiness*: an allusion to the name of the place, Kadesh, which means "holy, sanctified, sacred." Meribah means "contention." Cf. Ex 17:7.

20:14 *Your brother Israel*: according to biblical tradition, the Edomites were descended from Esau, the brother of Jacob. Their country, to the southeast of the Dead Sea, was also known as Seir; cf. Gn 25:24–26; 36:1, 8–9.

20:17 *The King's Highway*: an important highway, running north and south along the plateau east of the Dead Sea. In ancient times it was much used by caravans and armies; later it was improved by the Romans, and large stretches of it are still clearly recognizable.

20:22 *Mount Hor*: not definitively identified, but probably to be sought in the vicinity of Kadesh. According to Dt 10:6, Aaron died at Moserah (cf. "Moseroth" in Nm 33:30–31), which is apparently the name of the region in which Mount Hor is situated.

21:1–3 The account of this episode seems to be a later insertion here, since logically v. 4 belongs immediately after 20:29. Perhaps this is the same event as that mentioned in Jgs 1:16–17.

21:3 *Hormah*: related to the Hebrew word *herem*, meaning "put under the ban." See notes on 14:45; 18:14.

21:5 *This wretched food*: apparently the manna is meant.

21:6 *Seraph*: the Hebrew name for a certain species of venomous snake; etymologically the word might signify "the fiery one." Compare the winged throne guardians in Is 6:2, 6; see also Is 14:29; 30:6.

---

*

20:11 Ps 78:15–16; Wis 11:4; 1 Cor 10:4.
20:13 Nm 27:14; Ex 17:7.
20:16 Ex 2:23.
20:20 Jgs 11:17.
20:21–22 Nm 33:37.
20:25–26 Dt 32:50.
20:28 Nm 33:38.
21:1 Nm 33:40.
21:2 Jos 6:17; Jgs 1:17.
21:3 Nm 14:45.
21:5 Nm 11:6; Ex 16:3.
21:6 Dt 8:15; Wis 16:5; 1 Cor 10:9.

of the Israelites died. 7 Then the people came to Moses and said, "We have sinned in complaining against the LORD and you. Pray to the LORD to take the serpents from us." So Moses prayed for the people, 8 and the LORD said to Moses: Make a seraph and mount it on a pole, and everyone who has been bitten will look at it and recover.† 9 Accordingly Moses made a bronze serpent† and mounted it on a pole, and whenever the serpent bit someone, the person looked at the bronze serpent and recovered.*

Journey Around Moab

10 The Israelites moved on and encamped in Oboth.* 11 Then they moved on from Oboth and encamped in Iye-abarim† in the wilderness facing Moab on the east. 12 Moving on from there, they encamped in the Wadi Zered. 13 Moving on from there, they encamped on the other side of the Arnon, in the wilderness that extends from the territory of the Amorites; for the Arnon forms Moab's boundary, between Moab and the Amorites. 14 Hence it is said in the "Book of the Wars of the LORD":†

"Waheb in Suphah and the wadies,
15 Arnon and the wadi gorges
That reach back toward the site of Ar†
and lean against the border of Moab."

16 From there they went to Beer,† which is the well of which the LORD said to Moses, Gather the people together so that I may give them water. 17 Then Israel sang this song:

Spring up, O well!—so sing to it—
18 The well that the princes sank,
that the nobles of the people dug,
With their scepters and their staffs—
from the wilderness, a gift.

19 From Beer to Nahaliel, from Nahaliel to Bamoth, 20 from Bamoth to the valley in the country of Moab at the headland of Pisgah that overlooks Jeshimon.†

Victory over Sihon

21 Now Israel sent messengers to Sihon, king of the Amorites, with the message, 22 "Let us pass through your land. We will not turn aside into any field or vineyard, nor will we drink any well water, but we will go straight along the King's Highway until we have passed through your territory." 23 Sihon,* however, would not permit Israel to pass through his territory, but mustered all his forces and advanced against Israel into the wilderness. When he reached Jahaz, he engaged Israel in battle. 24 But Israel put him to the sword, and took possession of his land from the Arnon to the Jabbok and as far as Jazer of the Ammonites, for Jazer is the boundary of the Ammonites. 25 * Israel seized all the towns here, and Israel settled in all the towns of the Amorites, in Heshbon and all its dependencies. 26 For Heshbon was the city of Sihon, king of the Amorites, who had fought against the former king of Moab and had taken all his land from him as far as the Arnon. 27 That is why the poets say:

"Come to Heshbon, let it be rebuilt,
let Sihon's city be firmly constructed.
28 For fire went forth from Heshbon
and a blaze from the city of Sihon;
It consumed Ar of Moab
and swallowed up the high places of the Arnon.
29 Woe to you, Moab!
You are no more, people of Chemosh!†
He let his sons become fugitives
and his daughters be taken captive by the Amorite king Sihon.
30 From Heshbon to Dibon their dominion is no more;
Ar is laid waste; fires blaze as far as Medeba."

31 So Israel settled in the land of the Amorites. 32 Moses sent spies to Jazer; and the Israelites captured it with its dependencies and dispossessed the Amorites who were there.

21:8 *Everyone who has been bitten will look at it and recover*: in the Gospel of John this scene is regarded as a type for the crucifixion of Jesus (Jn 3:14–15).

21:9 King Hezekiah, in his efforts to reform Israelite worship, "smashed the bronze serpent Moses had made" (2 Kgs 18:4).

21:11 *Iye-abarim*: probably means "the ruins in the Abarim (Mountains)." See note on 27:12.

21:14 *The "Book of the Wars of the LORD"*: an ancient collection of Israelite songs, now lost. *Waheb in Suphah*: since neither place is mentioned elsewhere, it is uncertain whether these Hebrew words are to be considered as place names; some Hebrew words, now lost, must have preceded this phrase.

21:15 *Ar*: a city or district in Moab, located on the Arnon; see v. 28; Dt 2:18.

21:16 *Beer*: "a well," here used as a place name.

21:20 *Jeshimon*: "the wasteland"; in 1 Sm 23:19, 24 and 26:1, 3, this is the wilderness of Judah on the western side of the Dead Sea, but here and in Nm 23:28, it seems to refer to the southern end of the Jordan valley where Beth-jeshimoth was situated.

21:29 *Chemosh*: the chief god of the Moabites, mentioned in the famous inscription of Mesha, king of Moab, who ruled at the same time as the Omrides in Israel. Cf. 1 Kgs 11:7, 33; 2 Kgs 23:13; Jer 48:7, 13.

21:9 Wis 16:6–7, 10; Jn 3:14–15.
21:10 Nm 33:43–44.
21:23 Dt 2:32; Jgs 11:20.
21:25–26 Jos 21:39; Jgs 11:26.

Victory over Og

33 * Then they turned and went up along the
road to Bashan. But Og, king of Bashan, ad-
vanced against them with all his forces to give
battle at Edrei. 34 The LORD, however, said to Mo-
ses: Do not fear him; for into your hand I deliver
him with all his forces and his land. You will do
to him as you did to Sihon, king of the Amorites,
who reigned in Heshbon.* 35 So they struck him
down with his sons and all his forces, until not
a survivor was left to him, and they took posses-
sion of his land.

22 1 Then the Israelites moved on and en-
camped in the plains of Moab† on the
other side of the Jordan opposite Jericho.

Balaam Summoned

2 Now Balak, son of Zippor, saw all that Israel
did to the Amorites, 3 and Moab feared the Isra-
elites greatly because they were numerous. Moab
was in dread of the Israelites. 4 So Moab said to
the elders of Midian, "Now this horde will devour
everything around us as an ox devours the grass
of the field." At that time Balak, son of Zippor,
was king of Moab; 5 and he sent messengers to
Balaam, son of Beor, at Pethor on the river, in the
land of the Ammonites,† to summon him with
these words, "A people has come out of Egypt!
They have covered up the earth and are settling
down opposite me! 6 Now come, curse this peo-
ple for me,† since they are stronger than I am. Per-
haps I may be able to defeat them and drive them
out of the land. For I know that whoever you
bless is blessed and whoever you curse is cursed."
7 So the elders of Moab and the elders of Midian,
themselves experts in divination,† left and went
to Balaam, to whom they gave Balak's message.
8 He said to them, "Stay here overnight, and I will
give you whatever answer the LORD gives me." So
the princes of Moab lodged with Balaam.
9 Then God came to Balaam and said: Who are
these men with you? 10 Balaam answered God,
"Balak, son of Zippor, king of Moab, sent me
the message: 11 'This people that has come out of
Egypt has covered up the earth. Now come, lay
a curse on them for me; perhaps I may be able
to fight them and drive them out.'" 12 But God
said to Balaam: Do not go with them and do
not curse this people, for they are blessed. 13 The
next morning Balaam arose and told the princes
of Balak, "Go back to your own country, for the
LORD has refused to let me go with you." 14 So the
princes of Moab went back to Balak with the re-
port, "Balaam refused to come with us."

Second Appeal to Balaam

15 Balak yet again sent princes, who were more
numerous and more distinguished than the
others. 16 On coming to Balaam they told him,
"Thus says Balak, son of Zippor: Please do not
refuse to come to me. 17 I will reward you very
handsomely and will do anything you ask of me.
Come, lay a curse on this people for me." 18 * But
Balaam replied to Balak's servants, "Even if Balak
gave me his house full of silver and gold, I could
not do anything, small or great, contrary to the
command of the LORD, my God. 19 But, you too
stay here overnight, so that I may learn what else
the LORD may say to me." 20 That night God came
to Balaam and said to him: If these men have
come to summon you, go back with them; yet
only on the condition that you do exactly as I tell
you. 21 So the next morning when Balaam arose,
he saddled his donkey,† and went off with the
princes of Moab.

The Talking Donkey

22 But now God's anger flared up† at him for
going, and the angel of the LORD took up a posi-
tion on the road as his adversary. As Balaam was
riding along on his donkey, accompanied by two
of his servants, 23 the donkey saw the angel of the
LORD standing in the road with sword drawn. The
donkey turned off the road and went into the
field, and Balaam beat the donkey to bring her
back on the road. 24 Then the angel of the LORD
stood in a narrow lane between vineyards with a
stone wall on each side. 25 When the donkey saw

†

22:1 *The plains of Moab*: the lowlands to the northeast of the Dead Sea, between the Jordan and the foothills below Mount Nebo. Here the Israelites remained until they crossed the Jordan, according to Jos 1–4. Jericho lay to the west of the Jordan.

22:5 *In the land of the Ammonites*: the translation rests on a slight emendation of the traditional Hebrew text in accordance with the tradition represented by the Vulgate. While Pethor remains unidentified, this verse supports an identification of Balaam's homeland in the Transjordan (cf. the Deir 'Alla Inscriptions), over against other traditions in the text which connect Balaam with Syria (23:7; Dt 23:5).

22:6 *Curse this people for me*: Balak believed that Balaam, known in the tradition as a diviner (cf. Jos 13:22), could utter a curse upon Israel which would come to pass.

22:7 *Experts in divination*: lit., "divination was in their hand," i.e., "in their possession"; cf. Ezr 7:25.

22:21 *Donkey*: technically a she-donkey; Heb. *aton*.

22:22 *God's anger flared up*: God's apparent change of mind became a source of much speculation in the tradition. So, for example, God was angry, not merely because Balaam was going to Balak, for he had God's permission for the journey (v. 20), but perhaps because he was tempted by greed to curse Israel against God's command (cf. 2 Pt 2:15; Jude 11; compare Nm 22:32). *Adversary*: Heb. *satan*; see also v. 32; cf. 1 Sm 29:4; 2 Sm 19:22; 1 Kgs 11; Jb 1–2; Ps 109:6; Zec 3:1–2; 1 Chr 21:1.

*

21:33 Dt 3:1–7.
21:34 Ps 136:17–22.
22:18 Nm 24:13.

Pray It!

The Talking Donkey

Balaam is an interesting biblical character. He is not an Israelite and seems to be a sort of prophet for hire. Balak, the king of Moab, hires him to prophesy against Israel. But Balaam, hearing a message from God through his donkey, instead of cursing the Israelites, blesses them four times. Even though the Israelites were unfaithful, God continues to be with them, to bless them.

Balaam is a sign of the universal character of God's call, and the donkey is a symbol of the poor and oppressed. The complaining and whining donkey represents those who usually are not heard but are given a voice through the prophets.

This story gives us two insights into prayer. First, if God can use a donkey to talk to Balaam, God can use anything to talk to us. God speaks to us in many ways—through our experiences, the Scriptures, poetry and music, our relationship with nature, and more. Are we paying attention? Second, God wants us to hear the often unheard voice of those who are poor and oppressed. Do you hear God's voice expressed through them?

▶ **Nm 22:22–35**

NM

the angel of the LORD there, she pressed against
the wall; and since she squeezed Balaam's leg
against the wall, he beat her again. 26 Then the an-
gel of the LORD again went ahead, and stood next
in a passage so narrow that there was no room
to move either to the right or to the left. 27 When
the donkey saw the angel of the LORD there, she
lay down under Balaam. Balaam's anger flared up
and he beat the donkey with his stick.
28 * Then the LORD opened the mouth of the
donkey, and she asked Balaam, "What have I
done to you that you beat me these three times?"
29 "You have acted so willfully against me," said
Balaam to the donkey, "that if I only had a sword
at hand, I would kill you here and now." 30 But
the donkey said to Balaam, "Am I not your don-
key, on which you have always ridden until now?
Have I been in the habit of treating you this way
before?" "No," he replied.
31 Then the LORD opened Balaam's eyes, so that
he saw the angel of the LORD standing on the
road with sword drawn; and he knelt and bowed
down to the ground. 32 But the angel of the LORD
said to him: "Why have you beaten your donkey
these three times? I have come as an adversary
because this rash journey of yours is against my
will. 33 When the donkey saw me, she turned
away from me these three times. If she had not
turned away from me, you are the one I would
have killed, though I would have spared her."
34 Then Balaam said to the angel of the LORD, "I
have sinned. Yet I did not know that you took
up a position to oppose my journey. Since it has
displeased you, I will go back home." 35 But the
angel of the LORD said to Balaam: "Go with the
men; but you may say only what I tell you." So
Balaam went on with the princes of Balak.
36 When Balak heard that Balaam was com-
ing, he went out to meet him at Ar-Moab on the
border formed by the Arnon, at its most distant
point. 37 And Balak said to Balaam, "Did I not
send an urgent summons to you? Why did you
not come to me? Did you think I could not re-
ward you?" 38 Balaam answered Balak, "Well, I
have come to you after all. But what power have I
to say anything? I can speak only what God puts
in my mouth." 39 Then Balaam went with Balak,
and they came to Kiriath-huzoth. 40 Here Balak
sacrificed oxen and sheep, and sent portions to
Balaam and to the princes who were with him.

The First Oracle

41 The next morning Balak took Balaam up on
Bamoth-baal, and from there he could see some
of the people.

23 1 Then Balaam said to Balak, "Build me
seven altars here, and here prepare seven
bulls and seven rams for me." 2 So Balak did as
Balaam had ordered, and Balak and Balaam of-
fered a bull and a ram on each altar. 3 Balaam
said to Balak, "Stand here by your burnt offering
while I go over there. Perhaps the LORD will meet
me, and then I will tell you whatever he lets me
see." And so he went out on the barren height.
4 Then God met Balaam, and Balak said to him:
"I have erected the seven altars, and have offered
a bull and a ram on each altar." 5 The LORD put an
utterance in Balaam's mouth, and said: Go back
to Balak, and speak accordingly. 6 So he went
back to Balak, who was still standing by his burnt

22:28 2 Pt 2:15–16.

offering together with all the princes of Moab.
7 Then Balaam recited his poem:

From Aram† Balak has led me here,
Moab's king, from the mountains of Qedem:*
"Come, curse for me Jacob,
come, denounce Israel."
8 How can I lay a curse on the one whom God has not cursed?
How denounce the one whom the LORD has not denounced?
9 For from the top of the crags I see him,
from the heights I behold him.
Here is a people that lives apart†
and does not reckon itself among the nations.
10 Who has ever counted the dust of Jacob,
who numbered Israel's dust-cloud?†
May I die the death of the just,
may my end be like theirs!

11 "What have you done to me?" cried Balak to
Balaam. "It was to lay a curse on my foes that I
brought you here; but instead, you have blessed
them!" 12 Balaam replied, "Is it not what the LORD
puts in my mouth that I take care to repeat?"

The Second Oracle

13 Then Balak said to him, "Please come with
me to another place† from which you can see
them; but you will see only some, not all of
them, and from there lay a curse on them for
me." 14 So he brought him to a lookout post on
the top of Pisgah, where he built seven altars
and offered a bull and a ram on each of them.
15 Balaam then said to Balak, "Stand here by
your burnt offering, while I seek a meeting over
there." 16 Then the LORD met Balaam, and, hav-
ing put an utterance in his mouth, said to him:
Return to Balak, and speak accordingly. 17 So
he went to Balak, who was still standing by his
burnt offering together with the princes of Moab.
When Balak asked him, "What did the LORD say?"
18 Balaam recited his poem:

Rise, Balak, and listen;
give ear to my testimony, son of Zippor!
19 God is not a human being who speaks falsely,
nor a mortal, who feels regret.
Is God one to speak and not act,
to decree and not bring it to pass?
20 I was summoned to bless;
I will bless; I cannot revoke it!
21 Misfortune I do not see in Jacob,
nor do I see misery† in Israel.
The LORD, their God, is with them;
among them is the war-cry of their King.
22 They have the like of a wild ox's horns:†
God who brought them out of Egypt.*
23 No, there is no augury against Jacob,
nor divination against Israel.
Now it is said of Jacob,
of Israel, "Look what God has done!"
24 Here is a people that rises up like a lioness,
and gets up like a lion;
It does not rest till it has devoured its prey
and has drunk the blood of the slain.*

25 "Neither lay a curse on them nor bless
them," said Balak to Balaam. 26 But Balaam an-
swered Balak, "Did I not tell you, 'Everything the
LORD tells me I must do'?"

The Third Oracle

27 Then Balak said to Balaam, "Come, let me
bring you to another place; perhaps God will ap-
prove of your laying a curse on them for me from
there." 28 So he took Balaam to the top of Peor,
that overlooks Jeshimon. 29 Balaam then said to
Balak, "Build me seven altars here; and here pre-
pare for me seven bulls and seven rams." 30 And
Balak did as Balaam had ordered, offering a bull
and a ram on each altar.

24 1 Balaam, however, perceiving that the
LORD was pleased to bless Israel, did not
go aside as before to seek omens, but turned
his gaze toward the wilderness. 2 When Balaam
looked up and saw Israel encamped, tribe by
tribe, the spirit of God came upon him, 3 and he
recited his poem:

The oracle of Balaam, son of Beor,
the oracle of the man whose eye is true,

† **23:7** *Aram*: the ancient name of the region later known as Syria. *The mountains of Qedem*: Qedem is the name for a region in northern Syria. Qedem also means "eastern." Perhaps this designates the low ranges in the Syrian desert. The "mountains of old" is also a possible translation.

23:9 *A people that lives apart*: that is, "securely"; cf. Dt 33:28.

23:10 *The dust of Jacob . . . Israel's dust-cloud*: the Israelites will be as numerous as the dust kicked up by Israel in its march through the wilderness.

23:13 *To another place*: Balak thought that if Balaam would view Israel from a different site, he could deliver a different kind of omen.

23:21 *Misfortune . . . misery*: Balaam states that he is unable to see any evils for Israel.

23:22 *A wild ox's horns*: Israel possesses the strength of a wild ox because of God's presence among them. Compare the claim by the psalmist, the Lord is "my rock . . . my saving horn" (Ps 18:3).

* **23:7** Nm 22:6. **23:22** Nm 24:8. **23:24** Nm 24:9; Gn 49:9.

4 The oracle of one who hears what God says,
and knows what the Most High knows,
Of one who sees what the Almighty sees,
in rapture† and with eyes unveiled:
5 How pleasant are your tents, Jacob;
your encampments, Israel!
6 Like palm trees spread out,
like gardens beside a river,
Like aloes the LORD planted,
like cedars beside water;
7 Water will drip from their buckets,
their seed will have plentiful water;
Their king will rise higher than Agag†
and their dominion will be exalted.
8 They have the like of a wild ox's horns:
God who brought them out of Egypt.
They will devour hostile nations,
break their bones, and crush their loins.*
9 Crouching, they lie like a lion,
or like a lioness; who will arouse them?
Blessed are those who bless you,
and cursed are those who curse you!*

N
M

10 In a blaze of anger at Balaam, Balak clapped
his hands† and said to him, "It was to lay a
curse on my foes that I summoned you here;
yet three times now you have actually blessed
them!* 11 Now flee to your home. I promised to
reward you richly, but the LORD has withheld the
reward from you!" 12 Balaam replied to Balak,
"Did I not even tell the messengers whom you
sent to me, 13 'Even if Balak gave me his house
full of silver and gold, I could not of my own
accord do anything, good or evil, contrary to
the command of the LORD'? Whatever the LORD
says I must say.*

The Fourth Oracle

14 "But now that I am about to go to my own
people, let me warn you what this people will do
to your people in the days to come." 15 Then he
recited his poem:

The oracle of Balaam, son of Beor,
the oracle of the man whose eye is true,
16 The oracle of one who hears what God says,
and knows what the Most High knows,
Of one who sees what the Almighty sees,
in rapture and with eyes unveiled.
17 I see him, though not now;
I observe him, though not near:
A star shall advance from Jacob,
and a scepter† shall rise from Israel,
That will crush the brows of Moab,*
and the skull of all the Sethites,
18 Edom will be dispossessed,
and no survivor is left in Seir.
Israel will act boldly,
19 and Jacob will rule his foes.

20 Upon seeing Amalek, Balaam recited his
poem:

First† of the nations is Amalek,
but their end is to perish forever.*

21 Upon seeing the Kenites,† he recited his poem:

Though your dwelling is safe,
and your nest is set on a cliff;
22 Yet Kain will be destroyed
when Asshur† takes you captive.

† **24:4** *In rapture*: lit., "falling," therefore possibly "in a trance." However, this interpretation is uncertain.

24:7 *Agag*: during Saul's reign, king of Amalek (1 Sm 15:8), fierce enemy of Israel during the wilderness period; see v. 20 (Ex 17:8–16).

24:10 *Balak clapped his hands*: a gesture suggesting contempt or derision, apparently made in anger (cf. Jb 27:23; Lam 2:15).

24:17 *A star . . . a scepter*: some early Christian writers, as well as rabbinic interpreters, understood this prophecy in messianic terms. So, for example, Rabbi Akiba designates Bar Kosiba the messiah in the early second century A.D. by calling him Bar Kokhba, i.e., son of the star, alluding to this passage. Although this text is not referred to anywhere in the New Testament, in a Christian messianic interpretation the star would refer to Jesus, as also the scepter from Israel; cf. Is 11:1. But it is doubtful whether this passage is to be connected with the "star of the Magi" in Mt 2:1–12. *The brows of Moab, and the skull of all the Sethites*: under the figure of a human being, Moab is specified as the object of conquest by a future leader of Israel. The personification of peoples or toponyms is common enough in the Old Testament; see, e.g., Hos 11:1; Ps 98:8. In Jer 48:45, which paraphrases the latter part of our verse, Moab is depicted as someone whose boasting warrants its ruin. In view of the use of Heb. *pe'ah* (here "brows") in Nm 34:3 to indicate a boundary, some see in the "brows" of Moab and the "skull" of the Sethites a representation of features of Moab's topography, i.e., the borderlands and the interior plateau. *The Sethites*: cf. Gn 4:25; here probably a general designation for nomadic/tribal groups on the borders of Palestine, unless they are to be identified with the Shutu mentioned in Execration texts of the early second millennium B.C. and the fourteenth century Amarna tablets from Egypt; however, the Shutu are not attested in Moab. On the basis of Gn 4:25 and Gn 25, one might also think of a reference to humanity in general.

24:20 *First*: lit., "the beginning." In the Bible, Amalek is a people indigenous to Palestine and therefore considered as of great antiquity. There is a deliberate contrast here between the words "first" and "end."

24:21 *The Kenites* lived in high strongholds in the mountains of southern Palestine and the Sinai Peninsula, and were skilled in working the various metals found in their territory. Their name is connected, at least by popular etymology, with the Hebrew word for "smith"; of similar sound to *qayin*, i.e., "Kain" or "smith," is the Hebrew word for "nest," *qen*—hence the play on words in the present passage.

24:22 *Asshur*: the mention of Asshur, i.e., Assyria, is not likely before the ninth or eighth centuries B.C.

24:8 Nm 23:22.
24:9 Nm 23:24; Gn 12:3; 27:29; 49:9.
24:10 Nm 23:11.
24:13 Nm 22:18.
24:17 2 Sm 8:2.
24:20 Ex 17:14; 1 Sm 15:3.

23 Upon seeing† [the Ishmaelites?] he recited his
poem:

Alas, who shall survive of Ishmael,
24 to deliver them from the hands of the
Kittim?
When they have conquered Asshur and
conquered Eber,
They too shall perish forever.

25 Then Balaam set out on his journey home;
and Balak also went his way.

Worship of Baal of Peor

25 1 While Israel was living at Shittim,† the
people profaned themselves by prosti-
tuting themselves with the Moabite women.*
2 These then invited the people to the sacrifices
of their god, and the people ate of the sacrifices*
and bowed down to their god. 3 Israel thereby at-
tached itself to the Baal of Peor,* and the LORD's
anger flared up against Israel. 4 * The LORD said to
Moses: Gather all the leaders of the people, and
publicly execute them† before the LORD, that the
blazing wrath of the LORD may turn away from
Israel. 5 So Moses told the Israelite judges, "Each
of you kill those of his men who have attached
themselves to the Baal of Peor."†

Zeal of Phinehas

6 At this a certain Israelite came and brought in
a Midianite woman† to his kindred in the view
of Moses and of the whole Israelite community,
while they were weeping at the entrance of the
tent of meeting. 7 * When Phinehas, son of El-
eazar, son of Aaron the priest, saw this, he rose
up from the assembly, and taking a spear in his
hand, 8 followed the Israelite into the tent where
he pierced the two of them, the Israelite and the
woman. Thus the plague upon the Israelites was
checked; 9 but the dead from the plague were
twenty-four thousand.
10 Then the LORD said to Moses: 11 Phinehas,
son of Eleazar, son of Aaron the priest, has
turned my anger from the Israelites by his being
as jealous among them as I am; that is why I did
not put an end to the Israelites in my jealousy.†
12 * Announce, therefore, that I hereby give him
my covenant of peace,† 13 which shall be for him
and for his descendants after him the covenant of
an everlasting priesthood, because he was jealous
on behalf of his God and thus made expiation
for the Israelites.
14 † The name of the slain Israelite, the one
slain with the Midianite woman, was Zimri, son
of Salu, prince of a Simeonite ancestral house.
15 The name of the slain Midianite woman was
Cozbi, daughter of Zur, who was head of a clan,
an ancestral house, in Midian.

Vengeance on the Midianites

16 † The LORD then said to Moses: 17 * Treat the
Midianites as enemies and strike them, 18 for they
have been your enemies by the deceitful deal-
ings they had with you regarding Peor and their
kinswoman Cozbi, the daughter of a Midianite
prince, who was slain at the time of the plague
because of Peor.

III. Second Census of a New Generation and Preparation to Enter the Promised Land

The Second Census

26 25:19 After the plague 1 the LORD said to Mo-
ses and Eleazar, son of Aaron the priest:
2 Take a census, by ancestral houses, throughout
the community of the Israelites of all those of
twenty years or more who are eligible for mili-
tary service in Israel.* 3 So on the plains of Moab

† **24:23–24** *Upon seeing*: this phrase, lacking the Hebrew text, is found in the Septuagint, but without "the Ishmaelites" designated as the subject of the oracle. The Hebrew text of the oracle itself shows considerable disarray; the translation therefore relies on reconstruction of the putative original and is quite uncertain.

25:1 *Shittim*: the full name was Abel-shittim, a locality at the foot of the mountains in the northeastern corner of the plains of Moab (33:49). *Prostituting themselves*: the application to men of such traditional language for apostasy clearly suggests apostasy was taken to be an inevitable consequence of intermarriage with the Midianite women.

25:4 *Publicly execute them*: the same phrase occurs in 2 Sm 21:6–14, where the context shows that at least a part of the penalty consisted in being denied honorable burial. In both passages, dismemberment or impalement (perhaps subsequent to the actual execution) as a punishment for the breaking of covenant pledges, is a possible interpretation of the Hebrew phrase.

25:5 Thereby Moses apparently alters the Lord's command to execute all the leaders.

25:6 *Midianite woman*: according to 22:4, 7, the Midianites were allied with the Moabites in opposing Israel, while 31:16 claims that Balaam had induced the Midianite women to lure the Israelites away from the Lord. *They were weeping*: on account of the plague that had struck them; cf. v. 8.

25:11 *My jealousy*: God's desire to maintain an exclusive hold on the allegiance of the Israelites.

25:12 *Covenant of peace*: by means of this covenant between God and Phinehas, Phinehas can expect God's protection, especially from any threat of reprisal for his action; cf. Is 54:10; Ez 34:25; 37:26.

25:14–15 The noble lineage of the slain couple is mentioned in order to stress the courage of Phinehas in punishing them. The zeal of Phinehas became proverbial; cf. Ps 106:30; Sir 45:23; 1 Mc 2:26, 54.

25:16–18 The account of the execution of this command is given in 31:1–18.

* **25:1** Nm 31:16.
25:2 Ex 34:15–16.
25:3 Ps 106:28; Hos 9:10.
25:4 Dt 4:3.
25:7 Ps 106:30.
25:12–13 1 Mc 2:26, 54; Ps 106:31; Sir 45:23–24.
25:17–18 Nm 31:2–12.
26:2 Nm 1:2–3.

along the Jordan at Jericho, Moses and Eleazar the priest enrolled them, 4 those of twenty years or more, as the LORD had commanded Moses.

The Israelites who came out of the land of Egypt were as follows:†

5 * Reuben, the firstborn of Israel. The descendants of Reuben by their clans were: through Hanoch, the clan of the Hanochites; through Pallu, the clan of the Palluites; 6 through Hezron, the clan of the Hezronites; through Carmi, the clan of the Carmites. 7 These were the clans of the Reubenites, and those enrolled numbered forty-three thousand seven hundred and thirty.

8 From Pallu descended Eliab. 9 The sons of Eliab were Nemuel, Dathan, and Abiram*—the same Dathan and Abiram, ones designated by the community, who contended with Moses and Aaron as part of Korah's faction when they contended with the LORD. 10 The earth opened its mouth and swallowed them, along with Korah, as a warning. The faction was destroyed when the fire consumed two hundred and fifty men. 11 The descendants of Korah, however, did not die out.

NM

12 The descendants of Simeon by clans were: through Nemuel,† the clan of the Nemuelites; through Jamin, the clan of the Jaminites; through Jachin, the clan of the Jachinites; 13 through Zerah, the clan of the Zerahites; through Shaul, the clan of the Shaulites. 14 These were the clans of the Simeonites, twenty-two thousand two hundred.

15 The descendants of Gad by clans were: through Zephon, the clan of the Zephonites; through Haggi, the clan of the Haggites; through Shuni, the clan of the Shunites; 16 through Ozni, the clan of the Oznites; through Eri, the clan of the Erites; 17 through Arod, the clan of the Arodites; through Areli, the clan of the Arelites. 18 These were the clans of the descendants of Gad, of whom there were enrolled forty thousand five hundred.

19 The sons of Judah were Er and Onan. Er and Onan died in the land of Canaan.* 20 The descendants of Judah by their clans were: through Shelah, the clan of the Shelahites; through Perez, the clan of the Perezites; through Zerah, the clan of the Zerahites. 21 The descendants of Perez were: through Hezron, the clan of the Hezronites; through Hamul, the clan of the Hamulites. 22 These were the clans of Judah, of whom there were enrolled seventy-six thousand five hundred.

23 The descendants of Issachar by their clans were: through Tola, the clan of the Tolaites; through Puvah, the clan of the Puvahites; 24 through Jashub, the clan of the Jashubites; through Shimron, the clan of the Shimronites. 25 These were the clans of Issachar, of whom there were enrolled sixty-four thousand three hundred.

26 The descendants of Zebulun by their clans were: through Sered, the clan of the Seredites; through Elon, the clan of the Elonites; through Jahleel, the clan of the Jahleelites. 27 These were the clans of the Zebulunites, of whom there were enrolled sixty thousand five hundred.

28 The sons of Joseph were Manasseh and Ephraim. 29 The descendants of Manasseh by clans were: through Machir, the clan of the Machirites. Now Machir begot Gilead: through Gilead, the clan of the Gileadites. 30 The descendants of Gilead were: through Iezer, the clan of the Iezrites; through Helek, the clan of the Helekites; 31 through Asriel, the clan of the Asrielites; through Shechem, the clan of the Shechemites; 32 through Shemida, the clan of the Shemidaites; through Hepher, the clan of the Hepherites. 33 * As for Zelophehad, son of Hepher—he had no sons, but only daughters. The names of the daughters of Zelophehad were Mahlah, Noah, Hoglah, Milcah and Tirzah. 34 These were the clans of Manasseh, and those enrolled numbered fifty-two thousand seven hundred.

35 These were the descendants of Ephraim by their clans: through Shuthelah, the clan of the Shuthelahites; through Becher, the clan of the Becherites; through Tahan, the clan of the Tahanites. 36 These were the descendants of Shuthelah: through Eran, the clan of the Eranites. 37 These were the clans of the Ephraimites, of whom there were enrolled thirty-two thousand five hundred.

These were the descendants of Joseph by their clans.

38 The descendants of Benjamin by their clans were: through Bela, the clan of the Belaites; through Ashbel, the clan of the Ashbelites; through Ahiram, the clan of the Ahiramites; 39 through Shupham, the clan of the Shuphamites; through Hupham, the clan of the Huphamites. 40 The sons of Bela were Ard and Naaman:

†

26:4 This introduction to the census seems to contradict vv. 64–65 by including those who came out of Egypt.

26:12 *Nemuel*: so also in 1 Chr 4:24. In Gn 46:10 and Ex 6:15, a son of Simeon with the same position in the genealogy bears the name "Jemuel"; it is uncertain which form is correct. See above, v. 9, where the name "Nemuel" occurs for a person descended from Pallu. Some speculate this name was inserted from v. 12 to provide a continuing line for Pallu.

*

26:5–6 1 Chr 5:3.
26:9–10 Nm 16:1, 32.
26:19 Gn 38:7, 10; 46:12; 1 Chr 2:3.
26:33 Nm 27:1; 36:11; Jos 17:3.

through Ard, the clan of the Ardites; through
Naaman, the clan of the Naamites. 41 These were
the descendants of Benjamin by their clans, of
whom there were enrolled forty-five thousand
six hundred.
42 These were the descendants of Dan by their
clans: through Shuham the clan of the Shuham-
ites. These were the clans of Dan, 43 of whom
there were enrolled sixty-four thousand four
hundred.
44 The descendants of Asher by their clans were:
through Imnah, the clan of the Imnites; through
Ishvi, the clan of the Ishvites; through Beriah, the
clan of the Beriites; 45 through Heber, the clan of
the Heberites; through Malchiel, the clan of the
Malchielites. 46 The name of Asher's daughter was
Serah. 47 These were the clans of the descendants
of Asher, of whom there were enrolled fifty-three
thousand four hundred.
48 The descendants of Naphtali by their clans
were: through Jahzeel, the clan of the Jahzeelites;
through Guni, the clan of the Gunites; 49 through
Jezer, the clan of the Jezerites; through Shillem,
the clan of the Shillemites. 50 These were the
clans of Naphtali, of whom there were enrolled
forty-five thousand four hundred.
51 These were the Israelites who were enrolled:
six hundred and one thousand seven hundred
and thirty.

Allotment of the Land†

52 The LORD said to Moses: 53 * Among these the
land shall be divided as their heritage in keeping
with the number of people named. 54 * To a large
tribe you shall assign a large heritage, to a small
tribe a small heritage, each receiving its heritage
in proportion to the number enrolled in it. 55 But
the land shall be divided by lot, all inheriting ac-
cording to the lists of their ancestral tribes. 56 As
the lot falls the heritage of each tribe, large or
small, will be assigned.

Census of the Levites

57 These were the Levites enrolled by clans:
through Gershon, the clan of the Gershon-
ites; through Kohath, the clan of the Kohath-
ites; through Merari, the clan of the Merarites.
58 These were clans of Levi: the clan of the
Libnites, the clan of the Hebronites, the clan of
the Mahlites, the clan of the Mushites, the clan
of the Korahites.†
Now Kohath begot Amram, 59 whose wife was
named Jochebed. She was the daughter of Levi,
born to Levi in Egypt. To Amram she bore Aaron
and Moses and Miriam their sister. 60 To Aaron
were born Nadab and Abihu, Eleazar and Ith-
amar. 61 But Nadab and Abihu died when they
offered unauthorized fire before the LORD. 62 The
Levites enrolled were twenty-three thousand, ev-
ery male one month or more of age.* They were
not enrolled with the other Israelites, however,
for no heritage was given them among the Isra-
elites.
63 These, then, were those enrolled by Moses
and Eleazar the priest, when they enrolled the
Israelites on the plains of Moab along the Jor-
dan at Jericho. 64 Among them there was not
one of those who had been enrolled by Moses
and Aaron the priest, when they enrolled the
Israelites in the wilderness of Sinai. 65 * For
the LORD had told them that they would surely
die in the wilderness, and not one of them
was left except Caleb, son of Jephunneh, and
Joshua, son of Nun.

Zelophehad's Daughters

27 1 The daughters of Zelophehad, son of
Hepher, son of Gilead, son of Machir, son
of Manasseh, came forward. (Zelophehad be-
longed to the clans of Manasseh, son of Joseph.)
The names of his daughters were Mahlah, Noah,
Hoglah, Milcah and Tirzah.* 2 Standing before
Moses, Eleazar the priest, the princes, and the
whole community at the entrance of the tent of
meeting, they said: 3 "Our father died in the wil-
derness. Although he did not join the faction of
those who conspired against the LORD,† Korah's
faction, he died for his own sin without leaving
any sons. 4 But why should our father's name be
cut off from his clan merely because he had no
son? Give us land among our father's kindred."

Laws Concerning Heiresses†

5 So Moses laid their case before the LORD, 6 and
the LORD said to him: 7 The plea of Zelophehad's
daughters is just; you shall give them hereditary

†

26:52–56 The division of Canaan among the various tribes and clans and families was determined not only by the size of each group but also by lot. Perhaps the lots determined the respective locality of each tribal land and the section reserved for each clan, while the relative size of the allotted locality and section depended on the numerical strength of each group. The Israelites considered the outcome of the drawing of lots as an expression of God's will; cf. Lv 16:8–10; Jos 14:2; 15:1; etc.; Acts 1:23–26.

26:58 Compare 3:18–20 for a different listing.

27:3 *He did not join . . . against the LORD*: had he done so, he and his heirs could have been deprived of a portion in the promised land.

27:5–11 The purpose of this law, as also that of the related laws in 36:2–10 (marriage within the same tribe), Dt 25:5–10 (levirate marriage), and Lv 25:10 (return of property in the jubilee year), was to keep the landed property within the proper domain of each tribe.

*

26:53 Jos 11:23.
26:54 Nm 33:54; 35:8.
26:62 Nm 3:39.
26:65 Nm 14:22–24, 29.
27:1 Nm 26:33; Jos 17:3.

land among their father's kindred and transfer
their father's heritage to them. 8 Tell the Israelites:
If a man dies without leaving a son, you shall
transfer his heritage to his daughter; 9 if he has
no daughter, you shall give his heritage to his
brothers; 10 if he has no brothers, you shall give
his heritage to his father's brothers; 11 if his father
had no brothers, you shall give his heritage to his
nearest relative in his clan, who shall then take
possession of it.

This will be the statutory procedure for the Israelites, as the LORD commanded Moses.*

Joshua to Succeed Moses

12 The LORD said to Moses: Go up into this
mountain of the Abarim range† and view the
land that I have given to the Israelites.* 13 When
you have viewed it, you will be gathered to your
people, as was Aaron your brother.* 14 For in the
rebellion of the community in the wilderness of
Zin you both rebelled against my order to acknowledge my holiness before them by means
of the water.* (These were the waters of Meribah
of Kadesh in the wilderness of Zin.)

15 Then Moses said to the LORD, 16 "May the
LORD, the God of the spirits of all humanity,† set
over the community someone 17 who will be their
leader in battle and who will lead them out and
bring them in, that the LORD's community may
not be like sheep without a shepherd." 18 And the
LORD replied to Moses: Take Joshua, son of Nun,*
a man of spirit,† and lay your hand upon him.
19 Have him stand before Eleazar the priest and
the whole community, and commission him in
their sight. 20 Invest him with some of your own
power, that the whole Israelite community may
obey him. 21 He shall present himself to Eleazar
the priest, who will seek for him the decision of
the Urim† in the LORD's presence; and as it directs, Joshua, all the Israelites with him, and the
whole community will go out for battle; and as
it directs, they will come in.

22 Moses did as the LORD had commanded
him. Taking Joshua and having him stand before
Eleazar the priest and the whole community,
23 he laid his hands on him and commissioned
him, as the LORD had directed through Moses.

NM

General Sacrifices

28 1 The LORD said to Moses: 2 Give the Israelites this commandment: At their prescribed times, you will be careful to present to me the food offerings that are due me, oblations of pleasing aroma to me.

Each Morning and Evening

3 * You will tell them therefore: This is the obla-
tion which you will offer to the LORD: two unblemished yearling lambs each day as the regular burnt
offering,† 4 offering one lamb in the morning and
the other during the evening twilight, 5 each with
a grain offering of one tenth of an ephah of bran
flour mixed with a fourth of a hin of oil of crushed
olives.† 6 This is the regular burnt offering that was
made at Mount Sinai for a pleasing aroma, an
oblation to the LORD. 7 And as the libation for the
first lamb, you will make a libation to the LORD in
the sanctuary† of a fourth of a hin of strong drink.
8 The other lamb you will offer during the evening
twilight, making the same grain offering and the
same libation as in the morning, as an oblation of
pleasing aroma to the LORD.

On the Sabbath

9 On the sabbath day: two unblemished yearling lambs, with a grain offering of two tenths of
an ephah of bran flour mixed with oil, and its libation. 10 This is the sabbath burnt offering each
sabbath, in addition to the regular burnt offering
and its libation.

At the New Moon Feast

11 On your new moons† you will offer as a
burnt offering to the LORD two bulls of the herd,
one ram, and seven unblemished yearling lambs,
12 with three tenths of an ephah of bran flour
mixed with oil as the grain offering for each bull,
two tenths of an ephah of bran flour mixed with

† **27:12** *The Abarim range*: the mountains on the eastern side of the Dead Sea. The peak of this chain is Mount Nebo where Moses views the promised land before he dies (Dt 32:49).

27:16 *The God of the spirits of all humanity*: the sense is that God knows the character and abilities of all people and therefore knows best whom to appoint (cf. Jgs 6:34; 11:29; 1 Sm 16:13); see the same phrase in Nm 16:22, where "spirit" evidently means the life principle.

27:18 *A man of spirit*: lit., "a man in whom there is spirit," that is, probably one who is endowed with a courageous spirit (Jos 2:11); compare Gn 41:38; Dt 34:9.

27:21 *The Urim*: certain sacred objects which Israelite priests employed to discern the divine will, probably by obtaining a positive or negative answer to a given question. The full expression was "the Urim and Thummim"; cf. Ex 28:30; Lv 8:8; Dt 33:8; Ezr 2:63; Neh 7:65. Joshua ordinarily did not receive direct revelations from God as Moses had received them.

28:3 *The regular burnt offering*: "the *tamid* burnt offering," the technical term for the daily sacrifice. The lambs—as well as the goats for the purification offering (vv. 15, 22, 30)—are all specified as males.

28:5 *Oil of crushed olives*: this oil, probably made in a mortar, was purer and more expensive than oil extracted in the olive press.

28:7 *In the sanctuary*: i.e., the tent of meeting. But according to Sir 50:15, the libation was poured at the base of the outer altar.

28:11 *On your new moons*: beginning on the evening when the crescent of the new moon first appeared. The beginning of the month is reckoned according to the new moon.

27:11 Jer 32:6–9.
27:12 Dt 3:27; 32:49; 34:1.
27:13–14 Nm 20:12, 24.
27:14 Dt 32:51.
27:18 Dt 34:9.
28:3–8 Ex 29:38–42.

oil as the grain offering for the ram, 13 and one tenth of an ephah of bran flour mixed with oil as the grain offering for each lamb, a burnt offering with a pleasing aroma, an oblation to the LORD. 14 Their libations will consist of a half a hin of wine for each bull, a third of a hin for the ram, and a fourth of a hin for each lamb. This is the burnt offering for the new moon, for every new moon through the months of the year. 15 Moreover, there will be one goat for a purification offering to the LORD; it will be offered in addition to the regular burnt offering and its libation.

At the Passover

16 The fourteenth day† of the first month is the Passover of the LORD,* 17 and the fifteenth day of this month is the pilgrimage feast. For seven days unleavened bread is to be eaten. 18 On the first day you will declare a holy day, and you shall do no heavy work.† * 19 You will offer an oblation, a burnt offering to the LORD: two bulls of the herd, one ram, and seven yearling lambs that you are sure are unblemished. 20 Their grain offerings will be of bran flour mixed with oil; you will offer three tenths of an ephah for each bull and two tenths for the ram. 21 You will offer one tenth for each of the seven lambs; 22 and one goat as a purification offering to make atonement for yourselves. 23 These offerings you will make in addition to the morning burnt offering which is part of the regular burnt offering. 24 You will make exactly the same offerings each day for seven days as food offerings, oblations of pleasing aroma to the LORD; they will be offered in addition to the regular burnt offering with its libation. 25 On the seventh day you will declare a holy day: you shall do no heavy work.*

At Pentecost

26 On the day of first fruits,† on your feast of Weeks,* when you present to the LORD an offering of new grain, you will declare a holy day: you shall do no heavy work. 27 You will offer burnt offering for a pleasing aroma to the LORD: two bulls of the herd, one ram, and seven yearling lambs that you are sure are unblemished. 28 Their grain offerings will be of bran flour mixed with oil: three tenths of an ephah for each bull, two tenths for the ram, 29 and one tenth for each of the seven lambs. 30 One goat will be for a purification offering to make atonement for yourselves. 31 You will make these offerings, together with their libations, in addition to the regular burnt offering with its grain offering.

Did You Know?

Other Jewish Feasts

In chapter 29 of Numbers, we find the instructions for two more Jewish festivals. (For other Jewish festivals, see Ex 34:18–26.) The *feast of Trumpets* is a fall celebration prescribed for "the seventh month on the first day" (Nm 29:1). This day of rest, marked by trumpet blasts and sacrifices, came to be called Rosh Hashanah (head of the year), the beginning of the Jewish New Year.

On the tenth day of the seventh month, the Israelites celebrated the Day of Atonement (Yom Kippur). On this solemn day of penance and fasting, the high priest laid the sins of the people on a so-called scapegoat (see Lv 16:20–21), then ran the beast into the wilderness, thus symbolically purifying the nation.

▶ Nm 29:1–11

On New Year's Day

29 1 In the seventh month on the first day† you will declare a holy day, and do no heavy work; it shall be a day on which you sound the trumpet.* 2 You will offer a burnt offering for a pleasing aroma to the LORD: one bull of the herd, one ram, and seven unblemished yearling lambs. 3 Their grain offerings will be of bran flour mixed with oil: three tenths of an ephah for the bull, two tenths for the ram, 4 and one tenth for each of the seven lambs. 5 One goat will be a purification offering to make atonement for

NM

† **28:16** *The fourteenth day*: toward evening at the end of this day; cf. Ex 12:6, 18.

28:18 *Heavy work*: apparently, some sorts of activity are permitted on a day such as this, whereas "any work" is prohibited by 29:7 on the Day of Atonement. See note on Lv 23:3.

28:26 *The day of first fruits*: a unique term for this feast, which is usually called "the feast of Weeks"; it was celebrated as a thanksgiving for the wheat harvest seven weeks after the barley harvest (Passover). In the time of Jesus it was commonly known by the Greek word "Pentecost," that is, "fiftieth" (day after the Passover); see note on Lv 23:16–21.

29:1 *In the seventh month on the first day*: (about September–October) now the Jewish New Year's Day. In the older calendar the year began with the first of Nisan (March–April), which is still known as the first month; cf. Ex 12:2.

* **28:16** Ex 12:18; Lv 23:5; Dt 16:1.
28:18 Ex 12:16; Lv 23:7.
28:25 Ex 12:16; 13:6; Lv 23:8.
28:26 Ex 34:22.
29:1 Nm 10:10; Lv 23:24.

yourselves. 6 These are in addition to the burnt offering for the new moon with its grain offering, and in addition to the regular burnt offering with its grain offering, together with the libations prescribed for them, for a pleasing aroma, an oblation to the LORD.

On the Day of Atonement

7 On the tenth day of this seventh month† you will declare a holy day, humble yourselves, and do no sort of work.* 8 You will offer a burnt offering to the LORD, a pleasing aroma: one bull of the herd, one ram, and seven yearling lambs that you are sure are unblemished. 9 Their grain offerings of bran flour mixed with oil: three tenths of an ephah for the bull, two tenths for the one ram, 10 and one tenth for each of the seven lambs. 11 One goat will be a purification offering. These are in addition to the purification offering for purging,† the regular burnt offering with its grain offering, and their libations.

On the Feast of Booths

12 † On the fifteenth day of the seventh month you will declare a holy day:* you shall do no heavy work. For the following seven days you will celebrate a pilgrimage feast to the LORD. 13 You will offer a burnt offering, an oblation of pleasing aroma to the LORD: thirteen bulls† of the herd, two rams, and fourteen yearling lambs that are unblemished. 14 Their grain offerings will be of bran flour mixed with oil: three tenths of an ephah for each of the thirteen bulls, two tenths for each of the two rams, 15 and one tenth for each of the fourteen lambs. 16 One goat will be a purification offering. These are in addition to the regular burnt offering with its grain offering and libation.

17 On the second day: twelve bulls of the herd, two rams, and fourteen unblemished yearling lambs, 18 with the grain offerings and libations for the bulls, rams and lambs in their prescribed number, 19 as well as one goat as a purification offering, besides the regular burnt offering with its grain offering and libation.

20 On the third day: eleven bulls, two rams, and fourteen unblemished yearling lambs, 21 with the grain offerings and libations for the bulls, rams and lambs in their prescribed number, 22 as well as one goat for a purification offering, besides the regular burnt offering with its grain offering and libation.

23 On the fourth day: ten bulls, two rams, and fourteen unblemished yearling lambs, 24 the grain offerings and libations for the bulls, rams and lambs in their prescribed number, 25 as well as one goat as a purification offering, besides the regular burnt offering, its grain offering and libation.

26 On the fifth day: nine bulls, two rams, and fourteen unblemished yearling lambs, 27 * with the grain offerings and libations for the bulls, rams and lambs in their prescribed number, 28 as well as one goat as a purification offering, besides the regular burnt offering with its grain offering and libation.

29 On the sixth day: eight bulls, two rams, and fourteen unblemished yearling lambs, 30 with the grain offerings and libations for the bulls, rams and lambs in their prescribed number, 31 as well as one goat as a purification offering, besides the regular burnt offering, its grain offering and libation.

32 On the seventh day: seven bulls, two rams, and fourteen unblemished yearling lambs, 33 with the grain offerings and libations for the bulls, rams and lambs in their prescribed number, 34 as well as one goat as a purification offering, besides the regular burnt offering, its grain offering and libation.

35 On the eighth day* you will hold a public assembly:† you shall do no heavy work. 36 You will offer a burnt offering, an oblation of pleasing aroma to the LORD: one bull, one ram, and seven unblemished yearling lambs, 37 with the grain offerings and libations for the bulls, rams and lambs in their prescribed number, 38 as well as one goat as a purification offering, besides the regular burnt offering with its grain offering and libation.

39 These are the offerings you will make to the LORD on your festivals, besides your votive or voluntary offerings of burnt offerings, grain offerings, libations, and communion offerings.

30 1 So Moses instructed the Israelites exactly as the LORD had commanded him.

†

29:7 *The tenth day of this seventh month*: the Day of Atonement. *Humble yourselves*: that is, with fasting.

29:11 *The purification offering for purging*: the bull prescribed in Lv 16:11–12 for the purging of the tent sanctuary.

29:12 This feast of Booths (Tabernacles or Sukkot) celebrating the vintage harvest was the most popular of all and therefore had the most elaborate ritual. See note on Lv 23:34.

29:13 *Thirteen bulls*: the number of bulls sacrificed before the octave day was seventy, arranged on a descending scale so that the number on the seventh day was the sacred number seven.

29:35 *A public assembly*: the Hebrew word is the technical term for the closing celebration of the three major feasts of the Passover, Pentecost and Booths, or of other special feasts that lasted for a week. Cf. Lv 23:36; Dt 16:8; 2 Chr 7:9; Neh 8:18.

29:7 Lv 16:29; 23:27–28, 32. **29:27** Nm 29:30, 37.
29:12 Lv 23:34–35. **29:35** Lv 23:36; Jn 7:37.

Validity and Annulment of Vows

2 Moses said to the heads of the Israelite tribes,
"This is what the LORD has commanded: 3 When
a man makes a vow to the LORD or binds himself
under oath to a pledge,† he shall not violate his
word, but must fulfill exactly the promise he has
uttered.*
4 "When a woman makes a vow to the LORD,
or binds herself to a pledge, while still in her fa-
ther's house in her youth, 5 and her father learns
of her vow or the pledge to which she bound
herself and says nothing to her about it, then any
vow or any pledge to which she bound herself re-
mains valid. 6 But if on the day he learns of it her
father opposes her, then any vow or any pledge
to which she bound herself becomes invalid; and
the LORD will release her from it, since her father
opposed her.
7 "If she marries while under a vow or under a
rash pledge to which she bound herself, 8 and her
husband learns of it, yet says nothing to her on
the day he learns it, then the vows or the pledges
to which she bound herself remain valid. 9 But if
on the day her husband learns of it he opposes
her, he thereby annuls the vow she had made or
the rash pledge to which she had bound herself,
and the LORD will release her from it. 10 (The vow
of a widow or of a divorced woman, however,
any pledge to which such a woman binds her-
self, is valid.)
11 "If it is in her husband's house† that she
makes a vow or binds herself under oath to a
pledge, 12 and her husband learns of it yet says
nothing to her to oppose her, then all her vows
remain valid or any pledge to which she has
bound herself. 13 But if on the day he learns of
them her husband annuls them, then whatever
she has expressly promised in her vows or in her
pledge becomes invalid; since her husband has
annulled them, the LORD will release her from
them.
14 "Any vow or any pledge that she makes un-
der oath to humble herself, her husband may ei-
ther confirm or annul. 15 But if her husband, day
after day, says nothing at all to her, he thereby
confirms all her vows or all the pledges incum-
bent upon her; he has confirmed them, because
on the day he learned of them he said nothing to
her. 16 If, however, he annuls them† some time
after he first learned of them, he will be respon-
sible for her guilt."
17 These are the statutes which the LORD com-
manded Moses concerning a husband and his
wife, as well as a father and his daughter while
she is still in her youth in her father's house.

Did You Know?

Making a Vow

Vow. Such a simple word, really. Three letters. One syllable. But its simplicity masks its meaning. If a word's length were directly related to its significance, *vow* would have to become a long word indeed. It is a heavy word, one that we use sparingly. We tend to associate it with marriage or the life commitment of priests and religious sisters and brothers. Vows can be public or private, solemn or simple.

From a faith perspective, a person making a vow is making a deep, binding promise before God. A vow cannot really be captured on paper. A vow must be lived out. It must be internalized. It is the foundation for a life choice. We know, deep in our heart, that God is part of our vows.

The Israelites also took vows seriously. Numbers, chapter 30, is devoted to laws about vows. The laws were sexist by our standards. For example, a father or a husband could veto a woman's vows. Such laws were deemed acceptable in the Israelites' patriarchal society, but they are not in ours.

Nm 30:2–6

Campaign Against the Midianites

31 1 The LORD said to Moses:† 2 Avenge the Isra-
elites on the Midianites, and then you will
be gathered to your people. 3 So Moses told the
people, "Arm some men among you for
the campaign, to attack Midian and to execute
the LORD's vengeance on Midian. 4 From each
of the tribes of Israel you will send a thousand

† **30:3** *A vow . . . a pledge*: here the former signifies the promise to dedicate either a person, an animal, or a thing or their equivalent to the sanctuary upon the fulfillment of some specified conditions (Lv 27:1–13); the latter signifies the assumption of either a positive or a negative obligation—that is, the promise either to do something or to abstain from something; cf. v. 14.

30:11 *In her husband's house*: after her marriage. This contrasts with the case given in vv. 7–9.

30:16 *He annuls them*: he prevents their fulfillment. Since he has first allowed the vows to remain valid, he can no longer annul them.

31:1–3 The narrative of Israel's campaign against Midian, which was interrupted after 25:18, is now resumed.

* **30:3** Dt 23:22; Eccl 5:3–4.

men to the campaign." [5]From the contingents of Israel, therefore, a thousand men of each tribe were levied, so that there were twelve thousand men armed for war. [6]Moses sent them out on the campaign, a thousand from each tribe, with Phinehas, son of Eleazar, the priest for the campaign, who had with him the sacred vessels and the trumpets for sounding the alarm. [7]They waged war against the Midianites, as the LORD had commanded Moses, and killed every male. [8]Besides those slain in battle, they killed the kings of Midian: Evi, Rekem, Zur, Hur and Reba, the five kings of Midian;† and they also killed Balaam, son of Beor, with the sword. [9]But the Israelites took captive the women of the Midianites with their children, and all their herds and flocks and wealth as loot, [10]while they set on fire all the towns where they had settled and all their encampments. [11]Then they took all the plunder, with the people and animals they had captured, and brought the captives, together with the spoils and plunder, [12]to Moses and Eleazar the priest and to the Israelite community at their camp on the plains of Moab by the Jordan opposite Jericho.

Treatment of the Captives

[13]When Moses and Eleazar the priest, with all the leaders of the community, went outside the camp to meet them, [14]Moses became angry with the officers of the army, the commanders of thousands and the commanders of hundreds, who were returning from the military campaign. [15]"So you have spared all the women!" he exclaimed. [16]"These are the very ones who on Balaam's advice were behind the Israelites' unfaithfulness to the LORD in the affair at Peor,* so that plague struck the LORD's community. [17]† Now kill, therefore, every male among the children and kill every woman who has had sexual relations with a man. [18]But you may spare for yourselves all the girls who have not had sexual relations.

Purification After Combat

[19]"Moreover, remain outside the camp for seven days; every one of you who has killed anyone or touched someone killed will purify yourselves on the third and on the seventh day—both you and your captives. [20]You will also purify every garment, every article of leather, everything made of goats' hair, and every article of wood."

[21]Eleazar the priest told the soldiers who had taken part in the battle: "This is the prescribed ritual which the LORD has commanded Moses: [22]gold, silver, bronze, iron, tin and lead—[23]whatever can stand fire—you shall put into the fire, that it may become clean; however, it must also be purified with water of purification.† But whatever cannot stand fire you must put into the water. [24]On the seventh day you will wash your garments, and then you will again be clean. After that you may enter the camp."

Division of the Spoils

[25]The LORD said to Moses: [26]With the help of Eleazar the priest and of the heads of the ancestral houses of the community, inventory all the spoils captured, human being and beast alike; [27]then divide the spoils† between the warriors who went on the campaign and the whole community. [28]You will levy a tax for the LORD on the soldiers who went on the campaign: one out of every five hundred persons, oxen, donkeys, and sheep. [29]From their half you will take it and give it to Eleazar the priest as a contribution to the LORD. [30]From the Israelites' half you will take one captive from every fifty human beings, oxen, donkeys, and sheep—all the animals—and give them to the Levites, who perform the duties of the LORD's tabernacle. [31]So Moses and Eleazar the priest did this, as the LORD had commanded Moses.

Amount of the Plunder

[32]This plunder, what was left of the loot which the troops had taken, amounted to six hundred and seventy-five thousand sheep, [33]seventy-two thousand oxen, [34]sixty-one thousand donkeys, [35]and thirty-two thousand women who had not had sexual relations.

[36]The half-share that fell to those who had gone out on the campaign was in number: three hundred and thirty-seven thousand five hundred sheep, [37]of which six hundred and seventy-five fell as tax to the LORD; [38]thirty-six thousand oxen, of which seventy-two fell as tax to the LORD; [39]thirty thousand five hundred donkeys, of which sixty-one fell as tax to the LORD; [40]and sixteen thousand persons, of whom thirty-two

†

31:8 *The five kings of Midian*: they are called Midianite princes, Sihon's vassals, in Jos 13:21.

31:17 There are later references to Midian in Jgs 6–8; 1 Kgs 11:18; Is 60:6. The present raid was only against those Midianites who were dwelling at this time near the encampment of the Israelites.

31:23 *Water of purification*: water mixed with the ashes of the red heifer as prescribed in 19:9.

31:27 *Divide the spoils*: for a similar division of the plunder into two equal parts, between those who engaged in the battle and those who stayed with the baggage, cf. 1 Sm 30:24. But note that here the tax on the plunder of the noncombatants is ten times as much as that on the soldiers' plunder.

*

31:16 2 Pt 2:15; Rev 2:14.

persons fell as tax to the LORD. 41 Moses gave
the taxes contributed to the LORD to Eleazar
the priest, exactly as the LORD had commanded
Moses.
42 As for the Israelites' half, which Moses had
taken from the men who had fought— 43 the
community's half was three hundred and thirty-
seven thousand five hundred sheep, 44 thirty-six
thousand oxen, 45 thirty thousand five hundred
donkeys, 46 and sixteen thousand persons. 47 From
the Israelites' half, Moses took one captive from
every fifty, from human being and beast alike,
and gave them to the Levites, who performed
the duties of the LORD's tabernacle, exactly as the
LORD had commanded Moses.

Gifts of the Officers

48 Then those who were officers over the con-
tingents of the army, commanders of thousands
and commanders of hundreds, came up to Moses
49 and said to him, "Your servants have counted
the soldiers under our command, and not one of
us is missing. 50 † So, we have brought as an offer-
ing to the LORD articles of gold that each of us has
picked up—anklets, bracelets, rings, earrings, or
pendants—to make atonement for ourselves be-
fore the LORD." 51 Moses and Eleazar the priest ac-
cepted the gold from them, all fashioned pieces.
52 The gold that was given as a contribution to
the LORD—from the commanders of thousands
and the commanders of hundreds—amounted
in all to sixteen thousand seven hundred and
fifty shekels. 53 What the common soldiers had
looted each one kept for himself.† 54 So Moses
and Eleazar the priest accepted the gold from the
commanders of thousands and of hundreds, and
put it in the tent of meeting as a reminder on be-
half of the Israelites before the LORD.

Request of Gad and Reuben

32 1 Now the Reubenites and Gadites had a
very large number of livestock. Noticing
that the land of Jazer and of Gilead† was a place
suited to livestock, 2 the Gadites and Reubenites
came to Moses and Eleazar the priest and to the
leaders of the community and said, 3 † "The re-
gion of Ataroth, Dibon, Jazer, Nimrah, Heshbon,
Elealeh, Sebam, Nebo and Baal-meon— 4 the
land which the LORD has laid low before the
community of Israel, is a land for livestock, and
your servants have livestock." 5 They continued,
"If we find favor with you, let this land be given
to your servants as their possession. Do not make
us cross the Jordan."

Moses' Rebuke

6 But Moses answered the Gadites and Reuben-
ites: "Are your kindred, then, to go to war, while
you remain here? 7 Why do you wish to discour-
age the Israelites from crossing to the land the
LORD has given them? 8 That is just what your an-
cestors did when I sent them from Kadesh-barnea
to reconnoiter the land.* 9 They went up to the
Wadi Eshcol and reconnoitered the land, then
so discouraged the Israelites that they would not
enter the land the LORD had given them. 10 * At
that time the anger of the LORD flared up, and
he swore: 11 None of the men twenty years old
or more who have come up from Egypt will see
the land I promised under oath to Abraham and
Isaac and Jacob, because they have not followed
me unreservedly— 12 * except the Kenizzite† Ca-
leb, son of Jephunneh, the Kenizzite, and Joshua,
son of Nun, since they have followed the LORD
unreservedly. 13 So the anger of the LORD flared
up against the Israelites and he made them wan-
der in the wilderness forty years, until the whole
generation that had done evil in the sight of the
LORD had disappeared. 14 And now here you are,
offspring of sinful stock, rising up in your ances-
tors' place to add still more to the LORD's blazing
anger against the Israelites. 15 If you turn away
from following him, he will again abandon them
in the wilderness, and you will bring about the
ruin of this entire people."

Counter Proposal

16 But they approached him and said: "We will
only build sheepfolds here for our flocks and
towns for our families; 17 but we ourselves will
march as troops in the vanguard before the Isra-
elites,* until we have led them to their destina-
tion. Meanwhile our families will remain in the
fortified towns because of the land's inhabitants.
18 We will not return to our homes until all the
Israelites have taken possession of their heritage.

NM

†

31:50 The precise nature and use of some of these articles of gold is not certain.

31:53 Apparently because of the commanders' generosity the common troops were under no sort of obligation to make their own offerings and could keep their loot.

32:1 *Gilead*: the name of the western part of the plateau east of the Jordan, sometimes signifying the whole region from the Yarmuk to the Jordan, sometimes only the northern part of this region, and sometimes, as here, only its southern part. Jazer lay to the east of southern Gilead.

32:3 The places named in this verse, as well as the additional ones given in vv. 34–38, were all in the former kingdom of Sihon, that is, in the region between the Jabbok and the Arnon. Cf. 21:23–24; Jos 13:19–21, 24–27.

32:12 *Kenizzite*: a member of the clan of Kenaz, which, according to Gn 36:11, 15, 42, was Edomite; but, according to Nm 13:6; 34:19, Caleb belonged to the tribe of Judah; cf. also Jos 14:6, 14.

*

32:8–9 Nm 13:31–33; Dt 1:22.
32:10–11 Dt 1:34–35.
32:12 Nm 14:24; Dt 1:36.
32:17 Jos 4:12–13.

19 * But we will not claim any heritage with them across the Jordan and beyond, because we have received a heritage for ourselves on the eastern side of the Jordan."

Agreement Reached

20 † Moses said to them in reply: "If you do this—if you march as troops before the LORD into battle 21 and cross the Jordan in full force before the LORD until he has driven his enemies out of his way 22 and the land is subdued before the LORD, then you may return here, free from every obligation to the LORD and to Israel, and this land will be your possession before the LORD.* 23 But if you do not do this, you will have sinned against the LORD, and you can be sure that the consequences of your sin will overtake you. 24 Build the towns, then, for your families, and the folds for your flocks, but fulfill what you have promised."

25 The Gadites and Reubenites answered Moses, "Your servants will do as my lord commands. 26 * While our wives and children, our livestock and other animals remain there in the towns of Gilead, 27 all your servants will go across as armed troops before the LORD to battle, just as my lord says."

28 So Moses gave this command in their regard to Eleazar the priest, to Joshua, son of Nun, and to the heads of the ancestral houses of the Israelite tribes: 29 He said to them, "If all the Gadites and Reubenites cross the Jordan with you in full force before the LORD into battle, the land will be subdued before you, and you will give them Gilead as a possession. 30 But if they will not go across in force with you before the LORD, you will bring their wives and children and livestock across before you into Canaan, and they will possess a holding among you in the land of Canaan."

31 To this the Gadites and Reubenites replied, "We will do what the LORD has ordered your servants. 32 We ourselves will go across in force before the LORD into the land of Canaan, but we will retain our hereditary property on this side of the Jordan."† 33 So Moses gave them—†the Gadites and Reubenites, as well as half the tribe of Manasseh, son of Joseph—the kingdom of Sihon, king of the Amorites, and the kingdom of Og, king of Bashan, the land with its towns, and the districts of the surrounding towns.*

34 The Gadites rebuilt the cities of Dibon, Ataroth, Aroer, 35 Atroth-shophan, Jazer, Jogbehah, 36 Beth-nimrah and Beth-haran—fortified cities—and sheepfolds. 37 The Reubenites rebuilt Heshbon, Elealeh, Kiriathaim, 38 Nebo, Baal-meon (names to be changed!),† and Sibmah. These towns, which they rebuilt, they called by their old names.

Other Conquests

39 The descendants of Machir, son of Manasseh, went to Gilead and captured it, dispossessing the Amorites who were there. 40 (Moses gave Gilead to Machir,* son of Manasseh, and he settled there.) 41 Jair,* a descendant of Manasseh, went and captured their tent villages, and called them Havvoth-jair.† 42 Nobah went and captured Kenath with its dependencies and called it Nobah after his own name.

Stages of the Journey

33 1 The following are the stages by which the Israelites went out by companies from the land of Egypt under the guidance of Moses and Aaron.† 2 Moses recorded the starting points of the various stages at the direction of the LORD. These are the stages according to their starting points: 3 They set out from Rameses in the first month, on the fifteenth day of the first month. On the day after the Passover the Israelites went forth in triumph, in view of all Egypt, 4 while the Egyptians buried those whom the LORD had struck down, every firstborn; on their gods, too, the LORD executed judgments.*

†

32:20–22 Since the ark of the Lord was carried into battle with the Israelite army, the vanguard was said to march before the Lord (see Jos 6:6–9).

32:32 *This side of the Jordan*: lit., "beyond the Jordan"; the perspective in Hebrew is from the west bank looking toward the east bank where the Reubenites and Gadites finally settled.

32:33 The preceding is concerned solely with the two tribes of Gad and Reuben and with the land of the former kingdom of Sihon; it seems probable that the sudden reference here to the half-tribe of Manasseh and to their territory in Bashan, the former kingdom of Og, is a later addition to the text.

32:38 The phrase in parentheses is probably a gloss, warning the reader perhaps to substitute some other word for Nebo and Baal, the names of foreign deities mentioned in the last two city names. *They called by their old names*: lit., "they called by their names"; however, some understand the current Hebrew text to mean, "they called by new names," or "their own names."

32:41 *Havvoth-jair*: that is, "villages of Jair."

33:1–3 According to v. 2, this list of camping sites was drawn up by Moses as an itinerary recording Israel's trek through the wilderness. Comparison with the more detailed accounts of the journey as given elsewhere suggests that the list is not necessarily comprehensive. It records just forty camping sites, not counting the starting place, Rameses, and the terminus, the plains of Moab. This number, which corresponds exactly to the forty years of wandering in the wilderness, is probably a schematic device. Moreover, it seems that in its present form the order of some of the names here has been disturbed. Several names listed here are not recorded elsewhere.

*

32:19 Jos 13:8.
32:22 Jos 1:15.
32:26 Jos 1:14.
32:33 Dt 3:12; 29:7; Jos 12:6; 13:8.
32:40 Dt 3:15.
32:41 Dt 3:14.
33:4–5 Ex 12:12, 29, 37.

From Egypt to Sinai

5 Setting out from Rameses, the Israelites
camped at Succoth. 6 Setting out from Succoth,
they camped at Etham near the edge of the wil-
derness. 7 Setting out from Etham, they turned
back to Pi-hahiroth, which is opposite Baal-
zephon, and they camped opposite Migdol.*
8 Setting out from Pi-hahiroth, they crossed over
through the sea into the wilderness,* and after
they traveled a three days' journey in the wilder-
ness of Etham, they camped at Marah. 9 Setting
out from Marah, they came to Elim; at Elim
there were twelve springs of water and seventy
palm trees, and they camped there.* 10 Setting
out from Elim, they camped beside the Red Sea.
11 Setting out from the Red Sea, they camped
in the wilderness of Sin. 12 Setting out from the
wilderness of Sin, they camped at Dophkah.
13 Setting out from Dophkah, they camped at
Alush. 14 Setting out from Alush, they camped at
Rephidim, where there was no water for the peo-
ple to drink.* 15 Setting out from Rephidim, they
camped in the wilderness of Sinai.*

From Sinai to Kadesh

16 Setting out from the wilderness of Sinai,
they camped at Kibroth-hattaavah. 17 Setting out
from Kibroth-hattaavah, they camped at Haze-
roth.* 18 Setting out from Hazeroth, they camped
at Rithmah. 19 Setting out from Rithmah, they
camped at Rimmon-perez. 20 Setting out from
Rimmon-perez, they camped at Libnah. 21 Setting
out from Libnah, they camped at Rissah. 22 Set-
ting out from Rissah, they camped at Kehelathah.
23 Setting out from Kehelathah, they camped
at Mount Shepher. 24 Setting out from Mount
Shepher, they camped at Haradah. 25 Setting out
from Haradah, they camped at Makheloth. 26 Set-
ting out from Makheloth, they camped at Tahath.
27 Setting out from Tahath, they camped at Terah.
28 Setting out from Terah, they camped at Mith-
kah. 29 Setting out from Mithkah, they camped at
Hashmonah. 30 † Setting out from Hashmonah,
they camped at Moseroth. 31 Setting out from
Moseroth, they camped at Bene-jaakan. 32 Setting
out from Bene-jaakan, they camped at Mount
Gidgad. 33 Setting out from Mount Gidgad, they
camped at Jotbathah. 34 Setting out from Jotba-
thah, they camped at Abronah. 35 Setting out
from Abronah, they camped at Ezion-geber.†
36 Setting out from Ezion-geber, they camped in
the wilderness of Zin, that is, Kadesh.*

From Kadesh to the Plains of Moab

37 Setting out from Kadesh, they camped at
Mount Hor on the border of the land of Edom.

38 Aaron the priest ascended Mount Hor* at
the LORD's direction, and there he died in the
fortieth year after the departure of the Israelites
from the land of Egypt, on the first day of the
fifth month. 39 Aaron was a hundred and twenty-
three years old when he died on Mount Hor.

40 † When the Canaanite, the king of Arad,
who ruled over the Negeb in the land of Canaan,
heard that the Israelites were coming . . . .

41 † Setting out from Mount Hor, they camped
at Zalmonah. 42 Setting out from Zalmonah,
they camped at Punon. 43 Setting out from Pu-
non, they camped at Oboth. 44 Setting out from
Oboth, they camped at Iye-abarim on the border
of Moab. 45 Setting out from Iye-abarim, they
camped at Dibon-gad. 46 Setting out from Dibon-
gad, they camped at Almon-diblathaim. 47 Setting
out from Almon-diblathaim, they camped in the
Abarim range opposite Nebo. 48 Setting out from
the Abarim range, they camped on the plains
of Moab by the Jordan opposite Jericho. 49 They
camped by the Jordan on the plains of Moab ex-
tended from Beth-jeshimoth to Abel-shittim.

Conquest and Division of Canaan

50 The LORD spoke to Moses on the plains of
Moab by the Jordan opposite Jericho: 51 Speak
to the Israelites and say to them: When you go
across the Jordan into the land of Canaan, 52 dis-
possess all the inhabitants of the land before
you; destroy all their stone figures, destroy all
their molten images, and demolish all their high
places.*

53 You will take possession of the land and set-
tle in it, for I have given you the land to possess.
54 You will apportion the land among yourselves
by lot, clan by clan, assigning a large heritage to

†

33:30–36 Moseroth is mentioned in Dt 10:6 (in the form of "Moserah") as the place where Aaron died, apparently a variant of the tradition here in v. 38 regarding the place of Aaron's death; so also Nm 20:22–24 and Dt 32:50. Perhaps Moseroth was close to Mount Hor.

33:35 *Ezion-geber*: Solomon conducted sea trade with Ophir from this port (1 Kgs 9:26), today probably identified on the northern coast of the Gulf of Elath between the Jordanian city of Aqabah and the Israeli city of Elath.

33:40 The verse repeats almost verbatim the same introduction to the account of the victory over Arad as is given in 21:1–3, where it also follows the account of Aaron's death. Perhaps the isolated verse here is intended by the editor(s) of Numbers to point the reader to the fuller account given there.

33:41b–49 It seems that this section stood originally immediately after v. 36a.

*

33:7 Ex 14:2.
33:8 Ex 15:22.
33:9 Ex 15:27.
33:14 Ex 17:1.
33:15 Ex 19:2.
33:17–18 Nm 11:34–35.
33:36–37 Nm 20:1, 22.
33:38 Nm 20:25; Dt 32:50.
33:52 Ex 23:31; 34:13; Dt 7:5; 12:3.

a large clan and a small heritage to a small clan.*
Wherever anyone's lot falls, there will his posses-
sion be; you will apportion these shares within
your ancestral tribe.
55 But if you do not dispossess the inhabitants
of the land before you, those whom you allow
to remain will become barbs in your eyes and
thorns in your sides, and they will harass you in
the land where you live,* 56 and I will treat you as
I had intended to treat them.

The Boundaries

34 1 The LORD spoke to Moses: 2 Give the Isra-
elites this order: When you enter the land
of Canaan, this is the territory that shall fall to
you as your heritage—the land of Canaan with
its boundaries:
3 Your southern boundary will be at the wilder-
ness of Zin along the border of Edom;* on the
east your southern boundary will begin at the
end of the Salt Sea. 4 Then your boundary will
turn south of the Akrabbim Pass and cross Zin.
Terminating south of Kadesh-barnea, it extends
to Hazar-addar and crosses to Azmon.* 5 Then
the boundary will turn from Azmon to the Wadi
of Egypt and terminate at the Sea.*
6 For your western boundary you will have the
Great Sea† with its coast; this will be your west-
ern boundary.
7 This will be your boundary on the north:
from the Great Sea you will draw a line to
Mount Hor,† 8 and draw it from Mount Hor to
Lebo-hamath, with the boundary terminating at
Zedad. 9 Then the boundary extends to Ziphron
and terminates at Hazar-enan. This will be your
northern boundary.
10 For your eastern boundary you will draw a
line from Hazar-enan to Shepham. 11 From She-
pham the boundary will go down to Riblah, east
of Ain, and descending further, the boundary will
strike the ridge on the east side of the Sea of Chin-
nereth;† 12 then the boundary will descend along
the Jordan and terminate with the Salt Sea.
This will be your land, with the boundaries
that surround it.
13 Moses also gave this order to the Israelites:
"This is the land, to be apportioned among you
by lot, which the LORD has commanded to be
given to the nine and a half tribes. 14 For the tribe
of the Reubenites according to their ancestral
houses, and the tribe of the Gadites according to
their ancestral houses, as well as half of the tribe
of Manasseh, have already received their heri-
tage; 15 these two and a half tribes have received
their heritage across the Jordan opposite Jericho,
in the east, toward the sunrise."

Supervisors of the Allotment

16 The LORD spoke to Moses: 17 These are the
names of the men who shall apportion the land
among you: Eleazar the priest, and Joshua, son of
Nun; 18 * and you will designate one leader from
each of the tribes to apportion the land. 19 These
are the names of the men:

from the tribe of Judah: Caleb, son of Jephunneh,
20 from the tribe of the Simeonites: Samuel, son of Ammihud;
21 from the tribe of Benjamin: Elidad, son of Chislon;
22 from the tribe of the Danites: a leader, Bukki, son of Jogli;
23 for the descendants of Joseph: from the tribe of the Manassites: a leader, Hanniel, son of Ephod; and
24 from the tribe of the Ephraimites: a leader, Kemuel, son of Shiphtan;
25 from the tribe of the Zebulunites: a leader, Elizaphan, son of Parnach;
26 from the tribe of the Issacharites: a leader, Paltiel, son of Azzan;
27 from the tribe of the Asherites: a leader, Ahihud, son of Shelomi;
28 from the tribe of the Naphtalites: a leader, Pedahel, son of Ammihud.

29 These are the ones whom the LORD commanded
to apportion to the Israelites their heritage in the
land of Canaan.

Cities for the Levites

35 1 The LORD spoke to Moses on the plains
of Moab by the Jordan opposite Jericho:
2 * Command the Israelites out of the heritage
they possess to give the Levites cities to dwell in;
you will also give the Levites the pasture lands
around the cities. 3 The cities will be for them to
dwell in, and the pasture lands will be for their
cattle, their flocks, and all their other animals.
4 The pasture lands of the cities to be assigned
the Levites shall extend a thousand cubits out

NM

---

† 34:6 *The Great Sea*: the Mediterranean.

34:7–8 *Mount Hor*: different from the one where Aaron died; cf. 20:22; 33:37–38.

34:11 *Sea of Chinnereth*: in the New Testament known as the Sea of Galilee; today called Lake Kinneret.

* 33:54 Nm 26:53–56.
33:55 Jos 23:13; Jgs 2:3.
34:3 Jos 15:1–2.
34:4 Jos 15:3.
34:5 Jos 15:4.
34:18 Nm 1:4.
35:2 Jos 14:3–4; 21:2.

from the city walls in every direction. 5 You will measure out two thousand cubits outside the city along the east side, two thousand cubits along the south side, two thousand cubits along the west side, and two thousand cubits along the north side, with the city lying in the center. These will be the pasture lands of their cities.

6 * Now these are the cities you will give to the Levites: the six cities of asylum which you must establish for the homicide to run to, and in addition forty-two other cities— 7 a total of forty-eight cities with their pasture lands which you will assign to the Levites. 8 † In assigning the cities from what the Israelites possess, take more from a larger group and fewer from a smaller one, so that each will cede cities to the Levites in proportion to the heritage which it receives.

Cities of Asylum

9 * The LORD spoke to Moses: 10 Speak to the Israelites and say to them: When you go across the Jordan into the land of Canaan, 11 select for yourselves cities to serve as cities of asylum, where a homicide who has killed someone inadvertently may flee. 12 These cities will serve you as places of asylum from the avenger of blood,† so that a homicide will not be put to death until tried before the community. 13 As for the cities you assign, you will have six cities of asylum: 14 you will designate three cities beyond the Jordan, and you will designate three cities in the land of Canaan. These will be cities of asylum. 15 These six cities will serve as places of asylum for the Israelites, and for the resident or transient aliens among them, so that anyone who has killed a person inadvertently may flee there.

Murder and Manslaughter

16 † If someone strikes another with an iron instrument and causes death, that person is a murderer, and the murderer must be put to death.* 17 If someone strikes another with a death-dealing stone in the hand and death results, that person is a murderer, and the murderer must be put to death. 18 Or if someone strikes another with a death-dealing club in the hand and death results, that person is a murderer, and the murderer must be put to death. 19 The avenger of blood is the one who will kill the murderer, putting the individual to death on sight.

20 If someone pushes another out of hatred, or throws something from an ambush, and death results,* 21 or strikes another with the hand out of enmity and death results, the assailant must be put to death as a murderer. The avenger of blood will kill the murderer on sight.

22 * However, if someone pushes another without malice aforethought, or without lying in ambush throws some object at another, 23 or without seeing drops upon another some death-dealing stone and death results, although there was neither enmity nor malice— 24 then the community will judge between the assailant and the avenger of blood in accordance with these norms. 25 The community will deliver the homicide from the avenger of blood and the community will return the homicide to the city of asylum where the latter had fled;* and the individual will stay there until the death of the high priest who has been anointed with sacred oil. 26 If the homicide leaves at all the bounds of the city of asylum to which flight had been made, 27 and is found by the avenger of blood beyond the bounds of the city of asylum, and the avenger of blood kills the homicide, the avenger incurs no bloodguilt; 28 for the homicide was required to stay in the city of asylum until the death of the high priest. Only after the death of the high priest may the homicide return to the land of the homicide's possession.

29 This is the statute for you throughout all your generations, wherever you live, for rendering judgment.

Judgment

30 Whenever someone kills another, the evidence of witnesses is required to kill the murderer.* A single witness does not suffice for putting a person to death.

No Indemnity

31 You will not accept compensation in place of the life of a murderer who deserves to die, but that person must be put to death. 32 Nor will you accept compensation to allow one who has fled to a city of asylum to return to live in the land before the death of the high priest. 33 You will not pollute the land where you live. For bloodshed pollutes the land, and the land can have no expiation for the blood shed on it except through

†

35:8 This provision was hardly observed in the actual assignment of the levitical cities as narrated in Jos 21.

35:12 *The avenger of blood*: Hebrew, *go'el*, often translated as "redeemer," one who, as next of kin to the slain (2 Sm 14:7), and here, as executor of public justice, had the right and duty to take the life of the murderer; cf. Dt 19:6, 12; Jos 20:3, 5, 9.

35:16–25 Here, as also in Dt 19:1–13, there is a casuistic development of the original law as stated in Ex 21:12–14.

*

35:6 Dt 4:41–42; Jos 20:2.
35:9–15 Dt 19:2; Jos 20:2–6.
35:16 Ex 21:12; Lv 24:17.
35:20 Ex 21:14; Dt 19:11.
35:22 Jos 20:3.
35:25 Jos 20:6.
35:30 Dt 17:6; 19:15; Jn 8:17; 2 Cor 13:1; 1 Tm 5:19.

the blood of the one who shed it. 34 Do not defile
the land in which you live and in the midst of
which I dwell;* for I the LORD dwell in the midst
of the Israelites.

Inheritance of Daughters

36 1 The heads of the ancestral houses in a
clan of the descendants of Gilead, son of
Machir, son of Manasseh—one of the Josephite
clans—came up and spoke before Moses and El-
eazar the priest and before the leaders who were
the heads of the ancestral houses of the Israelites.
2 They said: "The LORD commanded my lord to
apportion the land by lot for a heritage among
the Israelites;* and my lord was commanded by
the LORD to give the heritage of Zelophehad our
kinsman to his daughters. 3 But if they marry into
one of the other Israelite tribes, their heritage will
be withdrawn from our ancestral heritage and
will be added to that of the tribe into which they
marry; thus the heritage that fell to us by lot will
be diminished. 4 When the Israelites celebrate
the jubilee year,† the heritage of these women
will be added to that of the tribe into which they
marry and their heritage will be withdrawn from
that of our ancestral tribe."
5 † So Moses commanded the Israelites at the
direction of the LORD: "The tribe of the Josephites
are right in what they say. 6 This is what the LORD
commands with regard to the daughters of Ze-
lophehad: They may marry anyone they please,
provided they marry into a clan of their ances-
tral tribe, 7 so that no heritage of the Israelites
will pass from one tribe to another, but all the
Israelites will retain their own ancestral heritage.
8 Every daughter who inherits property in any of
the Israelite tribes will marry someone belonging
to a clan of her own ancestral tribe, in order that
all the Israelites may remain in possession of their
own ancestral heritage. 9 Thus, no heritage will
pass from one tribe to another, but all the Israel-
ite tribes will retain their own ancestral heritage."
10 The daughters of Zelophehad did exactly
as the LORD commanded Moses. 11 Mahlah, Tir-
zah, Hoglah, Milcah and Noah, Zelophehad's
daughters, married sons of their uncles on their
father's side. 12 They married within the clans
of the descendants of Manasseh, son of Joseph;
hence their heritage remained in the tribe of their
father's clan.

Conclusion

13 These are the commandments and deci-
sions which the LORD commanded the Israelites
through Moses, on the plains of Moab beside the
Jordan opposite Jericho.

† 36:4 Before the jubilee year various circumstances, such as divorce, could make such property revert to its original tribal owners; but in the jubilee year it became irrevocably attached to its new owners.

36:5–9 This is a supplement to the law given in 27:5–11.

35:34 Ex 29:45. 36:2 Nm 26:55; 27:6; Jos 17:3–4.

Imagine this touching scene: You are standing at the bedside of your aging grandparent with all your cousins and family members. Your grandfather or grandmother begins to speak, sharing stories about the lessons he or she has learned from life. You listen to the familiar stories as if for the first time, and you are awed by the wisdom and love they contain. This is the scene Deuteronomy sets up—Moses is like the wise, aging grandparent, sharing his instructions and encouragement before dying.

The Book of Deuteronomy

At a Glance

- **I. First Address (1:1—4:43).**
- **II. Second Address (4:44—28:69).**
  - **A. The Lord's Covenant with Israel (4:44—11:32).**
  - **B. The Deuteronomic Code (12:1—28:69).**
- **III. Third Address (29:1—33:29).**
- **IV. The Death of Moses (34:1–12)**

Quick Facts

Period Covered: just before the Israelites enter the Promised Land

Inspired Authors: scribes from the eighth century BC adapting the earlier Covenant Law to Israel's changing situation

Theme: the importance of the covenant, the total commitment required by God's law

In Depth

The word *Deuteronomy* means "second law" in Greek. The first Law given on Mount Sinai was proposed by God to guide Israel in its wilderness journey. Written at a time when Israel was settled in the Promised Land and in need of religious reformation, Deuteronomy is a "second Law," adapted to the new situation of a people that needs to be reminded of its covenant with God.

Deuteronomy has four divisions:

- In the first address (1:1—4:43), Moses addresses Israel by reviewing its history since Mount Horeb (Deuteronomy's term for Mount Sinai). Moses calls Israel to faithfulness and loyalty.
- In the second address (4:44—28:69), Moses reviews the Ten Commandments and the essence of the Law. He reminds the Israelites of the rewards for obeying and the consequences of disobeying the Law.

  Chapters 12–26 are the most important part of this section of Deuteronomy, Moses spells out a law to shape and govern the Israelites' new life as they settle in the Land.
- In the third address (chapters 29–33), Moses gives his last will and testament, offers a final blessing, and dies.
- The last section (chapter 34) describes Moses death. His death is portrayed as the "sealing" of the second Law.

More than anything else, Deuteronomy stresses Israel as one people, with one God, one sanctuary, and now one Land. These elements not only make Israel a unique people but also bind it together in unity and solidarity. The Land of Promise now becomes a symbol of God's blessing and favor, the fulfillment of God's promises in the covenant.

Deuteronomy

I. First Address

Introduction

1 1 † These are the words that Moses spoke to all
Israel beyond the Jordan in the wilderness, in
the Arabah, opposite Suph, between Paran and
Tophel, Laban, Hazeroth, and Dizahab. 2 It is a
journey of eleven days from Horeb† to Kadesh-
barnea by way of the highlands of Seir.
3 In the fortieth year,† on the first day of the
eleventh month, Moses spoke to the Israelites ac-
cording to all that the LORD had commanded him
to speak to them, 4 after he had defeated Sihon,
king of the Amorites, who reigned in Heshbon,*
and Og, king of Bashan, who reigned in Ashtaroth
and in Edrei. 5 Beyond the Jordan, in the land of
Moab, Moses undertook to explain this law:

Departure from Horeb

6 † * The LORD, our God, said to us at Horeb:†
You have stayed long enough at this mountain.
7 Leave here and go to the hill country of the Am-
orites† and to all the surrounding regions, the
Arabah, the mountains, the Shephelah, the Negeb
and the seacoast—the land of the Canaanites and
the Lebanon as far as the Great River, the Euphra-
tes. 8 See, I have given that land over to you.* Go
now and possess the land that the LORD swore to
your ancestors, Abraham, Isaac, and Jacob, to give
to them and to their descendants after them.

Appointment of Elders

9 * At that time I said to you, "I am unable to
carry you by myself.* 10 The LORD, your God, has
made you numerous, and now you are as numer-
ous as the stars of the heavens.* 11 May the LORD,
the God of your ancestors, increase you a thou-
sand times over, and bless you as he promised!
12 But how can I, by myself, bear the weight, the
contentiousness of you? 13 Provide wise, discern-
ing, and reputable persons for each of your tribes,
that I may appoint them as your leaders." 14 You
answered me, "What you have proposed is good."

†

1:1 The entire book of Deuteronomy is set "beyond the Jordan," in the land of Moab (cf. v. 5; Nm 36:13), on the eve of the Israelites' crossing of the Jordan (Jos 3). *The Arabah*: the valley of the Jordan and the depression south of the Dead Sea.

1:2 *Horeb*: an alternative name for Mount Sinai, the wilderness mountain where the Israelites received revelation from God (cf. Ex 3; 19). *Kadesh-barnea*: the southern gateway to the land of Canaan, from which Moses sent spies to reconnoiter the land (cf. Nm 13:26; 32:8). *Seir*: Edom, the land just south of Moab.

1:3 *Fortieth year*: counting from the exodus from Egypt (cf. Ex 12:2; 13:20–22).

1:6–3:29 Throughout this section Moses is reviewing the events following the departure from Horeb, as a basis for the exhortation beginning in 4:1. Most of these events are narrated with some variation in the Book of Numbers.

1:6 *Horeb*: the name given to the mountain of revelation in the Elohist and Deuteronomic traditions; this mountain is called Sinai in the Yahwist and Priestly traditions.

1:7 *The hill country of the Amorites*: the central mountain range of Palestine. *The Negeb*: the arid land in southern Palestine. *The Lebanon*: the mountain range of Phoenicia, north of Palestine. This is

*

1:4 Dt 2:24–3:11; Nm 21:21–35.
1:6–8 Ex 32:34–33:3.
1:8 Dt 6:10, 23; 9:5, 27; 29:13; 30:20; 34:4; Gn 12:7; 13:14–15; 15:18–21; 17:8; 26:3–5; 28:13–14.
1:9–18 Ex 18:13–26; Nm 11:16–30.
1:9 Dt 1:31.
1:10 Dt 10:22; Gn 15:5; 22:17; 26:3–4; Ex 32:13.

15 So I took the leaders of your tribes, wise and
reputable, and set them as leaders over you, com-
manders over thousands, over hundreds, over
fifties and over tens, and other tribal officers.
16 * I charged your judges at that time, "Listen to
complaints among your relatives, and administer
true justice to both parties even if one of them is
a resident alien. 17 In rendering judgment, do not
consider who a person is; give ear to the lowly
and to the great alike, fearing no one, for the
judgment is God's. Any case that is too difficult
for you bring to me and I will hear it." 18 Thus I
charged you, at that time, with all the things you
were to do.

The Twelve Scouts

19 * Then we set out from Horeb and jour-
neyed through that whole vast and fearful wil-
derness that you have seen, in the direction of
the hill country of the Amorites, as the LORD, our
God, had commanded; and we came to Kadesh-
barnea.* 20 I said to you, "You have come to the
hill country of the Amorites, which the LORD,
our God, is giving us. 21 See, the LORD, your God,
has given this land over to you. Go up and take
possession of it, as the LORD, the God of your an-
cestors, has promised you. Do not fear or be dis-
mayed." 22 Then all of you approached me and
said, "Let us send men ahead to spy out the land
for us and report to us on the road we should fol-
low and the cities we will come upon." 23 Agree-
ing with the proposal, I took twelve men from
your number, one from each tribe. 24 They set
out into the hill country as far as the Wadi Esh-
col, and explored it. 25 Then, taking along some
of the fruit of the land, they brought it down to
us and reported, "The land the LORD, our God, is
giving us is good."

Threats of Revolt

26 * But you refused to go up;* you defied
the command of the LORD, your God. 27 You set
to murmuring in your tents, "Out of hatred for
us the LORD has brought us out of the land of
Egypt,* to deliver us into the power of the Amo-
rites and destroy us. 28 What shall we meet with
up there? Our men have made our hearts melt by
saying, 'The people are bigger and taller than we,
and their cities are large and fortified to the sky;
besides, we saw the Anakim† there.' "*
29 But I said to you, "Have no dread or fear of
them. 30 * The LORD, your God, who goes before
you, is the one who will fight for you, just as he
acted with you before your very eyes in Egypt,
31 as well as in the wilderness, where you saw
how the LORD, your God, carried you, as one
carries his own child, all along your journey un-
til you arrived at this place." 32 Despite this, you
would not trust the LORD, your God, 33 who jour-
neys before you to find you a place to camp—by
night in the fire, and by day in the cloud, to show
you the way to go.* 34 When the LORD heard your
words, he was angry, and took an oath: 35 Not a
single one of this evil generation shall look upon
the good land I swore to give to your ancestors,
36 except Caleb,† son of Jephunneh. He shall see
it, for to him and to his descendants I will give
the land he trod upon,* because he has fully fol-
lowed the LORD.
37 The LORD was angered against me also on
your account, and said, You shall not enter there
either,* 38 but Joshua,* son of Nun, your atten-
dant, shall enter. Encourage him, for he is the
one who is to give Israel its possession. 39 Your
little ones, who you said would become plunder,
and your children, who as yet do not know good
from evil—they shall enter there; to them I will
give it, and they shall take possession of it. 40 But
as for yourselves: turn back and proceed into the
wilderness on the Red Sea road.

Unsuccessful Invasion

41 * In reply you said to me, "We have sinned
against the LORD. We will go up ourselves and
fight, just as the LORD, our God, commanded us."
And each of you girded on his weapons, making
light of going up into the hill country. 42 But the
LORD said to me, Warn them: Do not go up and
fight—for I will not be in your midst—lest you be
beaten down before your enemies. 43 I gave you
this warning but you would not listen. You de-
fied the LORD's command and arrogantly went off
into the hill country. 44 Then the Amorites living
in that hill country came out against you and put

---

† an idealized presentation of the land the Israelites were to occupy; Israel never held power as far as the "Great River" (the Euphrates). The Amorites and the Canaanites were only two of several different peoples occupying the land (cf. 7:1).

1:28 *Anakim*: a people proverbially notable for height, mentioned in pre-Israelite Egyptian texts, and in the biblical tradition associated with the region of Hebron and the hill country of Judah (Nm 13:22, 28, 33; Jos 11:21; 14:12, 15).

1:36 *Except Caleb*: and Joshua (v. 38).

*

1:16–17 Dt 10:17–18; 16:18–20.
1:19–25 Nm 13:1–27.
1:19 Nm 11:11–36.
1:26–40 Nm 13:28–14:38.
1:26 Dt 9:23.
1:27 Dt 9:28.
1:28 Dt 1:28; 2:10–11, 21; 9:2; Nm 13:22, 28, 33; Jos 11:21–22; 14:12, 15; 15:13–14; 21:11; Jgs 1:20.
1:30–31 Dt 3:22; 8:15; 32:10; Ex 14:13–14.
1:33 Ex 13:21; 40:38; Nm 9:15–16; 10:33–34; 14:14.
1:36 Jos 14:6–14.
1:37 Dt 4:21; 34:4; Nm 20:12.
1:38 Dt 31:3, 7–8; Nm 27:18–23; 34:17; Jos 1:1–9.
1:41–46 Nm 14:39–45.

DT

you to flight the way bees do, cutting you down
in Seir as far as Hormah. 45 On your return you
wept before the LORD, but the LORD did not listen
to your voice or give ear to you. 46 That is why you
had to stay as long as you did at Kadesh.

Northward Along Edom

2 1 * Then we turned and proceeded into the
wilderness on the Red Sea road,* as the LORD
had told me, and circled around the highlands
of Seir for a long time. 2 Finally the LORD said to
me, 3 You have wandered round these highlands
long enough; turn and go north. 4 Command
the people: You are now about to pass through
the territory of your relatives, the descendants
of Esau, who live in Seir. Though they are afraid
of you, be very careful 5 not to come in conflict
with them, for I will not give you so much as a
foot of their land, since I have already given Esau
possession of the highlands of Seir.* 6 You shall
purchase from them with money the food you
eat; even the water you drink you shall buy from
them with money. 7 Surely, the LORD, your God,
has blessed you in all your undertakings; he has
been concerned† about your journey through
this vast wilderness. It is now forty years that
the LORD, your God, has been with you, and you
have lacked nothing.* 8 So we passed by our rel-
atives, the descendants of Esau who live in Seir,
leaving behind us the Arabah route, Elath, and
Ezion-geber.

Along Moab

Then we turned and passed on toward the
wilderness of Moab. 9 * And the LORD said to me,
Do not show hostility to the Moabites or engage
them in battle, for I will not give you possession
of any of their land, since I have given Ar to the
descendants of Lot as their possession.* 10 (For-
merly the Emim lived there, a people great and
numerous and as tall as the Anakim;* 11 like the
Anakim they are considered Rephaim, though
the Moabites call them Emim.* 12 In Seir, how-
ever, the former inhabitants were the Horites;*
the descendants of Esau dispossessed them,
clearing them out of the way and dwelling in
their place, just as Israel has done in the land of
its possession which the LORD gave it.) 13 Now get
ready to cross the Wadi Zered.
So we crossed the Wadi Zered. 14 * Now thirty-
eight years had elapsed between our departure
from Kadesh-barnea and the crossing of the
Wadi Zered; in the meantime the whole genera-
tion of soldiers had perished from the camp, as
the LORD had sworn they should. 15 Indeed the
LORD's own hand was against them, to rout them
from the camp completely.

Along Ammon

16 * When at length death had put an end to all
the soldiers among the people, 17 the LORD said to
me, 18 You are now about to leave Ar and the ter-
ritory of Moab behind. 19 As you come opposite
the Ammonites,* do not show hostility or come
in conflict with them, for I will not give you
possession of any land of the Ammonites, since
I have given it to the descendants of Lot as their
possession. 20 (This also is considered a country
of the Rephaim; formerly the Rephaim dwelt
there. The Ammonites call them Zamzummim,*
21 a people great and numerous and as tall as the
Anakim. But these, too, the LORD cleared out of
the way for the Ammonites, so that they dispos-
sessed them and dwelt in their place.* 22 He did
the same for the descendants of Esau, who live
in Seir, by clearing the Horites out of their way,
so that they dispossessed them and dwelt in
their place down to the present.* 23 As for the Av-
vim, who once lived in villages in the vicinity of
Gaza,† the Caphtorim, migrating from Caphtor,
cleared them away and dwelt in their place.)*

Defeat of Sihon

24 * Advance now across the Wadi Arnon. I
now deliver into your power Sihon, the Amorite
king of Heshbon, and his land. Begin to take
possession; engage him in battle.* 25 This day I
will begin to put a fear and dread of you into
the peoples everywhere under heaven, so that at
the mention of your name they will quake and
tremble before you.
26 So I sent messengers from the wilderness
of Kedemoth to Sihon, king of Heshbon, with
this offer of peace: 27 "Let me pass through your
country. I will travel only on the road. I will not
turn aside either to the right or to the left. 28 The
food I eat you will sell me for money, and the
water I drink, you will give me for money. Only

† **2:7** *Concerned*: lit., "known"; cf. Ex 2:25.
2:23 *Gaza*: later a stronghold of the Philistines (cf. Jos 13:3). *Caphtor*: the island of Crete.

* **2:1–8** Nm 20:14–21; Jgs 11:15–17.
2:1 Dt 1:40; Nm 14:25.
2:5 Gn 36:6–8.
2:7 Dt 8:2–5.
2:9–13 Nm 21:12–15; Jgs 11:17–18.
2:9 Gn 19:36–38.
2:10 Dt 1:28.
2:11 Dt 2:20; 3:11, 13; Gn 14:5; 15:20; Jos 12:4; 13:12; 17:15.
2:12 Gn 14:6; 36:20–30.
2:14–15 Nm 14:28–35.
2:16–19 Nm 21:24.
2:19 Gn 19:36–38.
2:20 Dt 2:11; 3:11, 13; Gn 14:5; 15:20; Jos 12:4; 13:12; 17:15.
2:21 Dt 1:28.
2:22 Gn 14:6; 36:6–8, 20–30.
2:23 Gn 10:14; Jos 13:3; 18:23; 1 Chr 1:12; Jer 47:4; Am 9:7.
2:24–3:11 Dt 1:4; 29:7; 31:4; Jos 2:10; 9:10; 12:1–6; Neh 9:22; Ps 135:10–12; 136:17–22.
2:24–37 Nm 21:21–32; Jgs 11:19–22.

let me march through, 29 as the descendants of
Esau who dwell in Seir and the Moabites who
dwell in Ar have done, until I cross the Jordan
into the land the LORD, our God, is about to give
us."* 30 But Sihon, king of Heshbon, refused to
let us pass through his land, because the LORD,
your God, made him stubborn in mind and obstinate in heart that he might deliver him into
your power, as indeed he has now done.

31 Then the LORD said to me, Now that I have
already begun to give over to you Sihon and his
land, begin to take possession. 32 So Sihon and
all his people advanced against us to join battle at Jahaz; 33 but since the LORD, our God, had
given him over to us, we defeated him and his
sons and all his people. 34 * At that time we captured all his cities and put every city under the
ban,† men, women and children; we left no survivor. 35 Our only plunder was the livestock and
the spoils of the captured cities. 36 From Aroer on
the edge of the Wadi Arnon and from the town
in the wadi itself, as far as Gilead,* no city was
too well fortified for us. All of them the LORD,
our God, gave over to us. 37 However, just as the
LORD, our God, commanded us, you did not encroach upon any of the Ammonite land, neither
the region bordering on the Wadi Jabbok, nor
the cities of the highlands.*

Defeat of Og

3 1 Then we turned and proceeded up the road
to Bashan. But Og, king of Bashan,* came
out against us with all his people to give battle
at Edrei. 2 The LORD said to me, Do not be afraid
of him, for I have delivered him into your power
with all his people and his land. Do to him as
you did to Sihon, king of the Amorites, who
reigned in Heshbon. 3 And thus the LORD, our
God, delivered into our power also Og, king of
Bashan, with all his people. We defeated him
so completely that we left him no survivor. 4 At
that time we captured all his cities; there was no
town we did not take: sixty cities in all, the whole
region of Argob, the kingdom of Og in Bashan—
5 all these cities were fortified with high walls
and gates and bars—besides a great number of
unwalled towns. 6 * As we had done to Sihon,
king of Heshbon, so also here we put all the
towns under the ban, men, women and children;
7 but all the livestock and the spoils of each city
we took as plunder for ourselves.

8 And so at that time we took from the two
kings of the Amorites beyond the Jordan the
territory from the Wadi Arnon to Mount Hermon 9 (the Sidonians call Hermon Sirion and
the Amorites call it Senir), 10 all the towns of the
plateau, all of Gilead, and all of Bashan as far as
Salecah and Edrei, towns of the kingdom of Og
in Bashan. 11 (Og, king of Bashan, was the last
remaining survivor of the Rephaim. He had a
bed of iron,† nine regular cubits long and four
wide, which is still preserved in Rabbah of the
Ammonites.)*

Allotment of the Conquered Lands

12 * As for the land we took possession of at
that time, I gave Reuben and Gad the territory
from Aroer, on the edge of the Wadi Arnon,
halfway up into the highlands of Gilead, with
its cities. 13 The rest of Gilead and all of Bashan,
the kingdom of Og, I gave to the half-tribe of
Manasseh. (The whole Argob region, all that part
of Bashan, was once called a land of the Rephaim.* 14 Jair, a Manassite,* took all the region of
Argob as far as the border of the Geshurites and
Maacathites, and named them—Bashan, that
is—after himself, Havvoth-jair, the name it bears
today.) 15 To Machir† I gave Gilead, 16 and to
Reuben and Gad the territory from Gilead to the
Wadi Arnon—the middle of the wadi being its
boundary—and to the Wadi Jabbok, which is the
border of the Ammonites, 17 as well as the Arabah
with the Jordan and its banks from Chinnereth†
to the Salt Sea of the Arabah, under the slopes of
Pisgah on the east.

18 * At that time I charged you: The LORD, your
God, has given you this land as your possession.
But all your troops equipped for battle must
cross over in the vanguard of your fellow Israelites. 19 But your wives and children, as well as
your livestock, of which I know you have a large
number, shall remain behind in the towns I have

†

2:34 *Under the ban*: in Hebrew, *herem*, which means to devote to the Lord (cf. 7:1–5; 20:10–18). The biblical text often presents *herem* as the total extermination of a population as a manifestation of the will of the Lord. It is historically doubtful that Israel ever literally carried out this theological program.

3:11 *Bed of iron*: some translate, "a sarcophagus of basalt"; its dimensions would be approximately thirteen and a half feet by six feet.

3:15 *Machir*: a clan of the tribe of Manasseh (cf. Gn 50:23).

3:17 *Chinnereth*: later known as the Lake of Gennesaret and the Sea of Galilee. *The Salt Sea*: the Dead Sea. *Pisgah*: a mountain range to the northeast of the Salt Sea; Mount Nebo, from which Moses viewed the promised land, is in this range (cf. v. 27; 34:1).

*

2:29 Dt 2:4–9.
2:34–35 Dt 3:6; 7:2, 26; 13:16, 18; 20:16–18; Jos 10:40; 11:11–12.
2:36 Dt 3:12–13; Jos 13:8–13, 15–23.
2:37 Nm 21:24; Jos 12:2.
3:1–11 Nm 21:33–35.
3:6–7 Dt 2:34–35; 7:2, 26; 13:16, 18; 20:16–18; Jos 10:40; 11:11–12.
3:11 Dt 2:11, 20; 3:13; Gn 14:5; 15:20; Jos 12:4; 13:12; 17:15.
3:12–22 Nm 32:1–42; Jos 13:8–33.
3:13 Dt 2:11, 20; 3:11; Gn 14:5; 15:20; Jos 12:4; 13:12; 17:15.
3:14 Nm 32:41; Jgs 10:4; 1 Chr 2:23.
3:18–20 Jos 1:12–15; 4:12; 22:1–4.

DT

given you, 20 until the LORD has settled your rela-
tives as well, and they too possess the land which
the LORD, your God, will give them on the other
side of the Jordan. Then you may all return to the
possessions I have given you.
21 And I charged Joshua as well, "Your own
eyes have seen all that the LORD, your God, has
done to both these kings; so, too, will the LORD
do to all the kingdoms into which you will cross
over. 22 Do not fear them, for it is the LORD, your
God, who will fight for you."*

Moses Excluded from the Promised Land

23 * It was then that I entreated the LORD,
24 "Lord GOD, you have begun to show to your
servant your greatness and your mighty hand.
What god in heaven or on earth can perform
deeds and powerful acts like yours? 25 Ah, let
me cross over and see the good land beyond the
Jordan, that fine hill country, and the Lebanon!"
26 But the LORD was angry with me on your ac-
count† and would not hear me.* The LORD said
to me, Enough! Speak to me no more of this.
27 Go up to the top of Pisgah and look out to the
west, and to the north, and to the south, and to
the east. Look well, for you shall not cross this
Jordan.* 28 Commission Joshua,* and encourage
and strengthen him, for it is he who will cross
at the head of this people and he who will give
them possession of the land you are to see.
29 So we remained in the valley opposite Beth-
peor.

DT

Advantages of Fidelity

4 1 Now therefore, Israel, hear the statutes and
ordinances I am teaching you to observe, that
you may live, and may enter in and take posses-
sion of the land which the LORD, the God of your
ancestors, is giving you.* 2 In your observance
of the commandments of the LORD, your God,*
which I am commanding you, you shall not add
to what I command you nor subtract from it.
3 You have seen with your own eyes what the LORD
did at Baal-peor:* the LORD, your God, destroyed
from your midst everyone who followed the Baal
of Peor; 4 but you, who held fast to the LORD,
your God, are all alive today. 5 See, I am teaching
you the statutes and ordinances as the LORD, my
God, has commanded me, that you may observe
them in the land you are entering to possess.
6 Observe them carefully, for this is your wisdom
and discernment in the sight of the peoples, who
will hear of all these statutes and say, "This great
nation is truly a wise and discerning people."*
7 * For what great nation is there that has gods so
close to it as the LORD, our God, is to us whenever
we call upon him? 8 Or what great nation has stat-
utes and ordinances that are as just as this whole
law which I am setting before you today?*

Revelation at Horeb

9 However, be on your guard and be very care-
ful not to forget the things your own eyes have
seen, nor let them slip from your heart as long
as you live, but make them known to your chil-
dren* and to your children's children, 10 that day
you stood before the LORD, your God, at Horeb,
when the LORD said to me: Assemble the people
for me, that I may let them hear my words, that
they may learn to fear† me as long as they live in
the land and may so teach their children. 11 * You
came near and stood at the foot of the mountain,
while the mountain blazed to the heart of the
heavens with fire and was enveloped in a dense
black cloud. 12 Then the LORD spoke to you from
the midst of the fire.* You heard the sound of the
words, but saw no form; there was only a voice.
13 He proclaimed to you his covenant, which he
commanded you to keep: the ten words,† which
he wrote on two stone tablets.* 14 At that time
the LORD charged me to teach you the statutes
and ordinances for you to observe in the land
you are about to cross into and possess.

Danger of Idolatry

15 Because you saw no form at all on the day
the LORD spoke to you at Horeb from the midst
of the fire, be strictly on your guard 16 not to act
corruptly by fashioning an idol for yourselves to
represent any figure, whether it be the form of a
man or of a woman,* 17 the form of any animal
on the earth, the form of any bird that flies in
the sky, 18 the form of anything that crawls on
the ground, or the form of any fish in the waters

†

3:26 *On your account*: that Moses saw but never entered the promised land is attested by every Pentateuchal tradition, but different reasons are given in different places. Nm 20:12 and Dt 32:51 present Moses as being at fault. Here, as in 1:37 and 4:21, the fault lies in the people but affects Moses.

4:10 *Fear*: not in the sense of "be terrified," but rather "manifest reverence or awe."

4:13 *Ten words*: the ten commandments, or decalogue (cf. 5:22; Ex 34:28).

3:22 Dt 1:30; Ex 14:13–14.
3:23–29 Nm 27:12–23.
3:26 Dt 4:21.
3:27 Dt 3:17; 32:48–52; 34:1–4.
3:28 Dt 1:38; 31:7–8.
4:1 Dt 4:45; 5:1, 31; 6:1, 17, 20; 11:32; 12:1; 26:16.
4:2 Dt 13:1.
4:3 Nm 25:1–13; Ps 106:28; Hos 9:10.
4:6 Dt 26:5; Gn 12:2; 18:18; 46:3; Ex 32:10.
4:7–8 2 Sm 7:23.
4:8 Dt 4:44.
4:9 Dt 6:7, 20–25; 11:19–21; 29:29; 31:12–13; Ps 78:3–6.
4:11–13 Ex 19:7–20:21.
4:12 Dt 4:33, 36; 5:4.
4:13 Dt 5:6–21; 10:4; Ex 20:1–17; 24:12; 31:18; 34:27–28.
4:16 Dt 5:8; Ex 20:4.

under the earth. 19 And when you look up to the
heavens and behold the sun or the moon or the
stars, the whole heavenly host, do not be led
astray into bowing down to them and serving
them.* These the LORD, your God, has appor-
tioned to all the other nations under the heav-
ens; 20 but you the LORD has taken and led out
of that iron foundry, Egypt, that you might be
his people, his heritage, as you are today.* 21 But
the LORD was angry with me on your account*
and swore that I should not cross the Jordan nor
enter the good land which the LORD, your God,
is giving you as a heritage. 22 I myself shall die
in this country; I shall not cross the Jordan; but
you are going to cross over and take possession
of that good land.* 23 Be careful, therefore, lest
you forget the covenant which the LORD, your
God, has made with you, and fashion for your-
selves against his command an idol in any form
whatsoever.* 24 For the LORD, your God, is a con-
suming fire, a jealous God.† *

God's Fidelity and Love

25 * When you have children and children's
children, and have grown old in the land, should
you then act corruptly by fashioning an idol in
the form of anything, and by this evil done in
his sight provoke the LORD, your God, 26 I call
heaven and earth this day to witness against you,
that you shall all quickly perish from the land
which you are crossing the Jordan to possess.
You shall not live in it for any length of time
but shall be utterly wiped out.* 27 The LORD will
scatter you among the peoples, and there shall
remain but a handful of you among the nations
to which the LORD will drive you. 28 There you
shall serve gods that are works of human hands,
of wood and stone, gods which can neither see
nor hear, neither eat nor smell.* 29 Yet when you
seek the LORD, your God, from there, you shall
indeed find him if you search after him with all
your heart and soul.* 30 In your distress, when
all these things shall have come upon you, you
shall finally return to the LORD, your God, and
listen to his voice. 31 Since the LORD, your God, is
a merciful God, he will not abandon or destroy
you, nor forget the covenant with your ancestors
that he swore to them.*

32 Ask now of the days of old, before your time,
ever since God created humankind upon the
earth; ask from one end of the sky to the other:
Did anything so great ever happen before? Was
it ever heard of? 33 Did a people ever hear the
voice of God speaking from the midst of fire, as
you did, and live?* 34 Or did any god venture to
go and take a nation for himself from the midst
of another nation, by testings, by signs and won-
ders,* by war, with strong hand and outstretched
arm, and by great terrors, all of which the LORD,
your God, did for you in Egypt before your very
eyes? 35 All this you were allowed to see that you
might know that the LORD is God; there is no
other.* 36 Out of the heavens he let you hear his
voice to discipline you; on earth he let you see
his great fire, and you heard him speaking out
of the fire. 37 For love of your ancestors he chose
their descendants after them and by his presence
and great power led you out of Egypt, 38 dispos-
sessing before you nations greater and mightier
than you, so as to bring you in and to give their
land to you as a heritage, as it is today. 39 This is
why you must now acknowledge, and fix in your
heart, that the LORD is God in the heavens above
and on earth below, and that there is no other.*
40 And you must keep his statutes and command-
ments which I command you today, that you
and your children after you may prosper, and
that you may have long life on the land which
the LORD, your God, is giving you forever.*

Cities of Refuge

41 * Then Moses set apart three cities in the
region east of the Jordan, 42 to which a homicide
might flee who killed a neighbor unintention-
ally, where there had been no hatred previously,
so that the killer might flee to one of these cities
and live: 43 Bezer in the wilderness, in the region
of the plateau, for the Reubenites; Ramoth in

DT

† **4:24** *A jealous God*: Hebrew *'el qanna*. The root of the adjective *qanna* expresses the idea of intense feeling focused on solicitude for someone or something; see, e.g., Ps 69:10; Sg 8:6; Is 9:6; 37:32; Ez 39:25. The Septuagint translated the adjective as *zelotes*, and the Vulgate followed suit; hence the traditional English rendering "jealous" (and sometimes "zealous") found in the Douai-Rheims and King James versions. In modern usage, however, "jealous" denotes unreasonable, petty possessiveness, a meaning, even as nuance, wanting in the Hebrew. In the first commandment (5:6–10; Ex 20:2–6) and passages derived from it (like 4:24; 6:15; Ex 34:14; Jos 24:19; Na 1:2), Israel's God is represented as totally committed to his purpose, and Israel is put on notice to take him and his directives for their life as a people with equal seriousness.

* **4:19** Dt 17:3; Jb 31:26–28.
4:20 1 Kgs 8:51; Is 48:10; Jer 11:4.
4:21 Dt 1:37; 3:26.
4:22 Dt 3:27; 34:1–12; Jos 1–12.
4:23 Dt 4:16; 9:12–14; Ex 32:1–10.
4:24 Dt 5:9; 6:15; 9:3; Ex 24:17; 34:14.
4:25–27 Dt 28:64–67.
4:26 Dt 30:19; 31:28; 32:1; Is 1:2.
4:28 Dt 28:64; 29:17; Lv 26:30–39; Ps 115:4–8; 135:15–18; Is 44:9–20.
4:29 Dt 6:5; Jer 29:13–14.
4:31 Dt 31:8; Gn 9:9–17; 15:18–21; 17:1–21; Ex 34:6–7.
4:33 Dt 4:36; 5:24, 26; Ex 20:19.
4:34 Dt 7:19; 26:8; 29:2; Ex 7:3; 15:3–10; Jer 32:21.
4:35 Dt 4:39; 32:39; 1 Kgs 8:60; Is 43:10–13; Jl 2:27.
4:39 Dt 4:35; 32:39; 1 Kgs 8:60; Is 43:10–13; Jl 2:27.
4:40 Dt 6:3; 12:28.
4:41–43 Dt 19:1–13; Nm 35:10–28; Jos 20:1–9.

Cultural Connection

The Lakota Code

See how similar these guidelines from a Native American tribal code are to the Ten Commandments (Dt 5:1–21), not to mention our own civil laws, school policies, and even family rules. What can we learn from them?

- Love one another.
- Pity orphan children. Be kind to them because they are poor; feed them and clothe them.
- Do not kill one another.
- Do not steal anything from anyone, especially from your own people.
- Do not tell lies to anyone, or lie about anyone.
- Respect your brothers and sisters. Do not marry in your own family.
- The ability to make good speech is a great gift from the maker, owner of all things, to the people. This is why you should not talk badly about anyone. Bad talk can hurt one's family or everyday life.
- Never quarrel among one another. Be good to others and always be friendly to whomever you meet, wherever you meet them.
- Do not brag about yourself, or try to hurt another's feelings. The generous person is the one who is respected.

(Ron Zeilinger, *Sacred Ground*, pp. 74–75)

▶ Dt 5:1–21

Gilead for the Gadites; and Golan in Bashan for
the Manassites.

D
T

II. Second Address

A. The Lord's Covenant with Israel

Introduction

44 This is the law† which Moses set before the
Israelites.* 45 These are the decrees, and the stat-
utes and ordinances† which Moses proclaimed
to the Israelites after they came out of Egypt,*
46 * beyond the Jordan in the valley opposite
Beth-peor, in the land of Sihon, king of the Am-
orites, who reigned in Heshbon, whom Moses
and the Israelites defeated after they came out of
Egypt.* 47 They took possession of his land and
the land of Og, king of Bashan, as well—the land
of these two kings of the Amorites in the region
beyond the Jordan to the east: 48 from Aroer on
the edge of the Wadi Arnon to Mount Sion†
(that is, Hermon) 49 and all the Arabah beyond
the Jordan to the east, as far as the Arabah Sea†
under the slopes of Pisgah.

The Covenant at Horeb

5 1 Moses summoned all Israel and said to
them, Hear, O Israel, the statutes and ordi-
nances which I proclaim in your hearing this day,
that you may learn them and take care to observe
them.* 2 The LORD, our God, made a covenant
with us at Horeb; 3 not with our ancestors† did
the LORD make this covenant, but with us, all of
us who are alive here this day. 4 * Face to face, the
LORD spoke with you on the mountain from the
midst of the fire,* 5 while I was standing between
the LORD and you at that time, to announce to you
these words of the LORD, since you were afraid of
the fire and would not go up the mountain:

The Decalogue

6 * I am the LORD your God, who brought you
out of the land of Egypt,* out of the house of
slavery. 7 * You shall not have other gods beside

† **4:44** *Law*: Hebrew *torah*, meaning "instruction," "law," "teaching"; the standard translation "law" comes from the influence of the Septuagint's *nomos*, "law," and the extensive legislation in Ex 20–Nm 10.

4:45 *Statutes and ordinances*: terms referring to the legal corpus in 12:1–26:19.

4:48 *Sion*: another name for Mount Hermon, besides those mentioned in 3:9 (to be distinguished from the Mount Zion of Jerusalem).

4:49 *The Arabah Sea*: the Dead Sea, cf. 3:17.

5:3 *Not with our ancestors*: in fact, the covenant was made with the ancestors, but these had died out during the "forty" years. The covenant is considered to be ongoing—for Israel in Moab and beyond.

* **4:44** Dt 4:8; 17:18–19; 30:10; 31:11–12.
4:45 Dt 4:1; 5:1, 31; 6:1, 17, 20; 11:32; 12:1; 26:16; Ps 25:10.
4:46–49 Dt 2:24–3:29.
4:46 Dt 3:29; 34:6.
5:1 Dt 4:1, 45; 5:31; 6:1, 17, 20; 11:32; 12:1; 26:16.
5:4–5 Ex 19:3–25; 20:18–19; 24:2.
5:4 Dt 34:10; Nm 12:8.
5:6–21 Ex 20:2–17.
5:6 Ex 20:2; Ps 81:11.
5:7–10 Dt 4:23–24, 31; 6:4–5; 7:9–10; 12:2–13:18; 17:3; 18:20; 24:16; 27:15; Ex 20:3–6; 34:6–7, 14; Lv 26:1; Nm 14:18; Ps 81:10; 97:7; Jer 7:9; 31:29–30; 32:18–19; Ez 18:1–24.

Catholic Connection

The Ten Commandments

After a thrilling escape from Egypt and forty long years wandering in the desert, Moses and the Israelites find themselves on the threshold of completing their journey. Unfortunately, Moses has grown old and knows he will not finish the journey with his people. He therefore gathers them together and reminds them of their past and their responsibilities. Most importantly, Moses reminds them of the covenant they made with God on Mount Sinai and of their responsibility to follow the Ten Commandments.

It was through God's offer of love and friendship that the Israelites entered into the covenant relationship with God. As a natural part of that relationship, God gave the Israelites the Ten Commandments as a path to the new life they were about to begin. These commandments were God's own words and provided a list of moral responsibilities that revealed God's will for each individual and all the Israelites as part of their new relationship with God. As a sign of the commandments' importance, the Israelites built the ark of the Covenant and kept the two stone tablets with them on their journey to the Promised Land. The Ten Commandments showed the Israelites how to live not only free from slavery, but free from the slavery of sin.

Jesus himself lived and taught the importance of the Ten Commandments. He summed them up in his two-fold command to love God and to love our neighbor. Following Jesus' affirmation of the Ten Commandments and their importance throughout the Sacred Scriptures, the Church uses the Ten Commandments as an important part of its moral teachings. The section on morality in the *Catechism of the Catholic Church* even follows the structure of the Ten Commandments as a way to convey Catholic moral teachings.

As followers of Jesus, all Christians are obligated to always live by the Ten Commandments. The Ten Commandments can be divided into two groups. The first three commandments focus on our responsibilities toward God, and the remaining seven focus on our responsibilities toward one another. Together the two groups unite our spiritual life and our social life, where one is incomplete without the other. By following the Ten Commandments, we unite ourselves to Christ and to one another.

Try putting a copy of the Ten Commandments up on your mirror. That way each morning you too can be reminded of your responsibilities as a child of God and follower of Jesus. And remember, God never gives us a responsibility without giving us the grace to fulfill it.

Dt 5:1–21

Catechism, nos. 2052–2082

DT

me. [8]You shall not make for yourself an idol or
a likeness of anything in the heavens above or
on the earth below or in the waters beneath the
earth; [9]† you shall not bow down before them
or serve them. For I, the LORD, your God, am a
jealous† God, bringing punishment for their
parents' wickedness on the children of those
who hate me, down to the third and fourth gen-
eration, [10]but showing love down to the thou-
sandth generation of those who love me and
keep my commandments.
[11]You shall not invoke the name of the LORD,
your God, in vain.* For the LORD will not leave
unpunished anyone who invokes his name in
vain.
[12]* Observe the sabbath day—keep it holy, as
the LORD, your God, commanded you. [13]Six days
you may labor and do all your work, [14]but the
seventh day is a sabbath of the LORD your God.
You shall not do any work, either you, your son
or your daughter, your male or female slave, your
ox or donkey or any work animal, or the resident
alien within your gates, so that your male and fe-
male slave may rest as you do. [15]Remember that
you too were once slaves in the land of Egypt,
and the LORD, your God, brought you out from
there with a strong hand and outstretched arm.
That is why the LORD, your God, has commanded
you to observe the sabbath day.
[16]* Honor your father and your mother, as the
LORD, your God, has commanded you, that you
may have a long life and that you may prosper in
the land the LORD your God is giving you.
[17]* You shall not kill.†
[18]* You shall not commit adultery.
[19]* You shall not steal.
[20]* You shall not bear dishonest witness
against your neighbor.
[21]* You shall not covet your neighbor's wife.
You shall not desire your neighbor's house or
field, his male or female slave, his ox or donkey,
or anything that belongs to your neighbor.

Moses as Mediator

[22]These words the LORD spoke with a loud
voice to your entire assembly on the moun-
tain from the midst of the fire and the dense
black cloud, and added no more. He inscribed
them on two stone tablets and gave them to
me.* [23]But when you heard the voice from the
midst of the darkness, while the mountain was
ablaze with fire, you came near to me, all your
tribal heads and elders, [24]and said, "The LORD,
our God, has indeed let us see his glory and his
greatness, and we have heard his voice from the
midst of the fire.* Today we have found out that
God may speak to a mortal and that person may
still live. [25]Now, why should we die? For this
great fire will consume us. If we hear the voice
of the LORD, our God, any more, we shall die.*
[26]For what mortal has heard the voice of the liv-
ing God speaking from the midst of fire, as we
have, and lived? [27]You go closer and listen to all
that the LORD, our God, will say, and then tell us
what the LORD, our God, tells you; we will listen
and obey."*
[28]The LORD heard your words as you were
speaking to me and said to me, I have heard the
words these people have spoken to you, which
are all well said.* [29]Would that they might al-
ways be of such a mind, to fear me and to keep
all my commandments! Then they and their
descendants would prosper forever. [30]Go, tell
them: Return to your tents. [31]Then you stand
here near me and I will give you all the com-
mandments, the statutes and the ordinances; you
must teach them, that they may observe them in
the land I am giving them to possess.*
[32]Be careful, therefore, to do as the LORD, your
God, has commanded you, not turning aside to

†

5:9–10 Israel is confronted with a choice, to "love" or to "hate" the Lord, and with the consequences of each choice. "Wickedness" works destruction not only on those who do it but also down the generations, in a sort of ripple effect. Yet, if Israel keeps the commandments, they will experience the Lord's *hesed* ("love") down to the thousandth generation. Thus the Lord's merciful love is disproportionate to the evil results of iniquity ("down to the third and fourth generation"). *To the thousandth generation*: lit., "to thousands"; cf. 7:9.

5:9 *Jealous*: see note on 4:24.

5:17 *Kill*: see note on Ex 20:13.

*

5:11 Dt 6:13; 10:20; 18:20; 23:21–23; Ex 20:7; Lv 19:12; 24:10–23; Ps 24:4; Jer 29:23; Mt 5:33–37.
5:12–15 Dt 14:22–16:17; 24:18, 22; Ex 20:8–11; 23:12; 31:12–17; 34:21; Is 58:13–14; Jer 17:21–27; Mt 12:1–14; Mk 2:23–3:6; Lk 6:1–11; 13:10–17; 14:1–6; Jn 5:2–18; 7:22–23.
5:16 Dt 21:18–21; 27:16; Ex 20:12; 21:15, 17; Sir 3:1–16; Mt 10:34–39; 12:46–50; 15:4; 19:19; Mk 3:31–35; 7:10; 10:19; Lk 8:19–21; 14:26; 18:20, 28–30; Eph 6:1–4.
5:17 Dt 4:41–43; 19:1–13; 20:1–21:9; 21:18–23; Gn 4:8–16; Ex 20:13; 21:12–14; Nm 35:16–34; Jer 7:9; Hos 4:2; Mt 5:21–26; 19:18; Mk 10:19; Lk 18:20; Jas 2:11.
5:18 Dt 22:13–23:1; Gn 20:1–18; 39:7–20; Ex 20:14; Lv 18:20; 20:10; 2 Sm 11:1–12:25; Jer 7:9; Hos 4:2; Mt 5:27–30; 19:18; Mk 10:19; Lk 18:20; Jas 2:11.
5:19 Dt 23:24; 24:7; Gn 40:15; Ex 20:15; 21:16, 37; 22:1–3, 12; Lv 19:11, 13; 1 Kgs 21:1–19; Jer 7:9; Hos 4:2; Mt 19:18; Mk 10:19; Lk 18:20.
5:20 Dt 19:15–19; Ex 20:16; 23:1–3; Lv 19:11, 15–16; 1 Kgs 21:1–19; Ps 5:6–10; 10:7–9; 27:12; Prv 25:18; 30:8–10; Jer 7:9; Hos 4:2; Mt 19:18; 26:59–60; Mk 10:19; Lk 18:20.
5:21 Dt 7:25; Ex 20:17; Jos 7:21; 2 Sm 11:1–12:25; 1 Kgs 21:1–19; Is 5:8; Mi 2:2; Mt 5:27–30; Lk 12:13–21; Eph 5:5; Col 3:5.
5:22 Dt 4:13; 9:9–11, 17; 10:1–5; Ex 24:12; 31:18; 32:15–20; 34:1–5.
5:24 Dt 4:33, 36; Ex 20:19.
5:25 Dt 18:16.
5:27 Ex 20:19.
5:28 Dt 18:17.
5:31 Dt 4:1, 45; 5:1; 6:1, 17, 20; 11:32; 12:1; 26:16.

the right or to the left, 33 but following exactly
the way that the LORD, your God, commanded
you that you may live and prosper, and may have
long life in the land which you are to possess.*

6 1 This then is the commandment, the statutes
and the ordinances,* which the LORD, your
God, has commanded that you be taught to ob-
serve in the land you are about to cross into to
possess, 2 so that you, that is, you, your child, and
your grandchild, may fear the LORD, your God, by
keeping, as long as you live, all his statutes and
commandments* which I enjoin on you, and
thus have long life. 3 Hear then, Israel, and be
careful to observe them, that it may go well with
you and that you may increase greatly; for the
LORD, the God of your ancestors, promised you a
land flowing with milk and honey.*

The Great Commandment†

4 * Hear, O Israel!† The LORD is our God, the
LORD alone! 5 Therefore, you shall love the LORD,
your God, with your whole heart, and with your
whole being, and with your whole strength.*
6 * Take to heart these words which I command
you today.* 7 Keep repeating them to your chil-
dren. Recite them when you are at home and
when you are away, when you lie down and
when you get up.* 8 Bind them on your arm as
a sign† and let them be as a pendant on your
forehead.* 9 Write them on the doorposts of your
houses and on your gates.*

Fidelity in Prosperity

10 * When the LORD, your God, brings you into
the land which he swore to your ancestors, to
Abraham, Isaac, and Jacob, that he would give
you, a land with fine, large cities that you did not
build,* 11 with houses full of goods of all sorts
that you did not garner, with cisterns that you
did not dig, with vineyards and olive groves that

Did You Know?

The Shema: Putting God First

Deuteronomy 6:4 is the most famous declaration of faith in the Old Testament: "Hear, O Israel! The LORD is our God, the LORD alone!" This short verse, part of a prayer called the Shema, is uttered daily by faithful Jews. It has been so important that the commands of verses 8–9 often have been interpreted literally. The Pharisees of Jesus' day, for example, wore miniature copies of the prayer on their bodies and attached other copies to their doorposts. Orthodox Jews today continue this tradition. Keeping the law of God is a privilege—something to be "worn" with pride!

The Shema reminds Jewish people to put God first and to love God with all their heart, soul, and might. Think about people who seem to carry God in their heart all the time. Are they lost and frustrated? Do they seem angry and hate filled? Chances are they seem more relaxed and sure of themselves than most people do. Having God in your sights at all times will help in more ways than you could ever imagine!

Dt 6:4–9

you did not plant; and when, therefore, you eat
and are satisfied,* 12 * be careful not to forget the
LORD, who brought you out of the land of Egypt,
that house of slavery. 13 * The LORD, your God,
shall you fear; him shall you serve,† and by his
name shall you swear. 14 * You shall not go after

†

6:4–5 This passage, an expansion of the first commandment (5:6–10), contains the basic principle of the whole Mosaic law, the keynote of the Book of Deuteronomy: since the Lord alone is God, Israel must love him with an undivided heart. Jesus cited these words as "the greatest and the first commandment," embracing in itself the whole law of God (Mt 22:37–38; Mk 12:29–30; Lk 10:27).

6:4 *Hear, O Israel!*: in Hebrew, *shema yisra'el*; hence this passage (vv. 4–9), containing the Great Commandment, is called the Shema. In later Jewish tradition, 11:13–21 and Nm 15:37–41 were added to form a prayer recited every evening and morning. *The LORD is our God, the LORD alone*: other possible translations are "the Lord our God is one Lord"; "the Lord our God, the Lord is one"; "the Lord is our God, the Lord is one."

6:8 *Bind them . . . as a sign*: these injunctions were probably meant merely in a figurative sense; cf. Ex 13:9, 16. In the late postexilic period, they were taken quite literally, and devout Jews tied on their arms and foreheads "phylacteries," boxes containing strips of parchment on which these words were inscribed; cf. Mt 23:5.

6:13 *Him shall you serve*: the verb could be translated as either "serve" or "worship" (cf. 5:9).

*

5:33 Dt 4:40.
6:1 Dt 4:1, 45; 5:1, 31; 6:17, 20; 11:32; 12:1; 26:16.
6:2 Dt 4:10, 40; 5:29; 6:24; 10:12–13.
6:3 Ex 3:8.
6:4–5 Dt 4:35, 39; 5:6–10; 6:13–14; 10:17; 1 Kgs 8:60; 18:39; 2 Kgs 5:15; 19:15, 19; Is 44:6; 45:5–6; Mt 22:37–38; Mk 12:29–30; Lk 10:27.
6:5 Dt 4:29; 10:12; 11:13; 13:4; 26:16; 30:2, 10; 1 Sm 7:3; 2 Kgs 23:3, 25.
6:6–9 Dt 11:18–21.
6:6 Dt 11:18; 30:14; 32:46; Ps 37:31; Prv 3:3; Is 51:7; Jer 31:33.
6:7 Dt 4:9–10; 6:20–25; 11:1–7, 19; 31:13; 32:46; Prv 6:22.
6:8 Dt 11:18; Ex 13:9, 16; Prv 3:3; 6:21.
6:9 Dt 11:20.
6:10–19 Dt 5:6–10.
6:10 Dt 1:8.
6:10–11 Dt 8:7–14; 32:11–14; Jos 24:13; Neh 9:25.
6:12 Dt 5:6.
6:13 Dt 10:20; Is 48:1; Jer 4:2; 12:16; Mt 4:10; Lk 4:8.
6:14–15 Dt 4:23–26; 8:19–20; 11:16–17, 28; 29:18–28; 30:17–18; 2 Kgs 17:7–18.

DT

Cultural Connection

Don't Lose Your Language!

"*Qui perd sa langue, perd sa foi.*" This French Canadian proverb means, "Lose your language, lose your faith."

As Canada was being settled, the French were afraid that the English culture would dominate the land and culture. Most of the French were Catholic, and most of the English were Protestant. The French believed their faith was so tied to their language that the loss of their language would mean a loss to their faith and how they expressed it culturally.

This same fear is present in the Bible. Peter was afraid to eat with the Gentiles—those who were not Jews (see Gal 2:12). The Samaritan woman at the well knew that Jesus, a Jew, should have nothing to do with her because Samaritans were considered "half-Jews" due to intermarriage (see Jn 4:9).

Chapter 7 of Deuteronomy portrays this fear in a frightening way. Israelites were told not just to avoid pagans but to destroy them. Intermarriage would mean losing Jewish language, culture, and faith—and sooner or later would lead to worshiping false gods (see also Ex 23:23–26).

Yet Jesus treated the Samaritan woman with dignity. Paul challenged Peter to eat with the uncircumcised and to let them become Christians without first becoming Jews. We need not be afraid of those who are different from us. We can treat others with dignity and even build friendship without the fear of losing our language or our faith.

▶ Dt 7:1–5

DT

other gods, any of the gods of the surrounding
peoples—[15] for the LORD, your God who is in
your midst, is a passionate God—lest the anger
of the LORD, your God, flare up against you and
he destroy you from upon the land.
[16] You shall not put the LORD, your God, to
the test, as you did at Massah.* [17] But keep the
commandments of the LORD, your God, and the
decrees and the statutes he has commanded you.
[18] Do what is right and good in the sight of the
LORD, that it may go well with you, and you may
enter in and possess the good land which the
LORD promised on oath to your ancestors, [19] driv-
ing all your enemies out of your way, as the LORD
has promised.*

Instruction to Children

[20] * Later on, when your son asks you, "What
do these decrees and statutes and ordinances
mean?"* which the LORD, our God, has enjoined
on you, [21] * you shall say to your son, "We were
once slaves of Pharaoh in Egypt, but the LORD
brought us out of Egypt with a strong hand*
[22] and wrought before our eyes signs and won-
ders, great and dire, against Egypt and against
Pharaoh and his whole house. [23] He brought us
from there to bring us in and give us the land he
had promised on oath to our ancestors.* [24] * The
LORD commanded us to observe all these statutes
in fear of the LORD, our God, that we may always
have as good a life as we have today. [25] This is
our justice before the LORD, our God: to observe
carefully this whole commandment he has en-
joined on us."

Destruction of the Nations in the Land

7 [1] * When the LORD, your God, brings you into
the land which you are about to enter to pos-
sess, and removes many nations before you—the
Hittites, Girgashites, Amorites, Canaanites, Periz-
zites, Hivites, and Jebusites,* seven nations more
numerous and powerful than you—[2] and when
the LORD, your God, gives them over to you and
you defeat them, you shall put them under the
ban. Make no covenant with them* and do not
be gracious to them. [3] * You shall not intermarry

6:16 Ex 17:1–7; Ps 95:8–9; Mt 4:7; Lk 4:12.
6:19 Ex 23:27; 34:11; Jos 1–12.
6:20–25 Dt 6:6–9.
6:20 Ex 12:26; 13:14; Jos 4:6, 21.
6:21–23 Dt 26:5–10.
6:21 Dt 5:3, 6.
6:23 Dt 1:8.
6:24–25 Dt 4:1–4; 30:15–20.
7:1–11 Ex 23:23–33; 34:11–16; Nm 33:51–56.
7:1 Dt 1:7; Gn 10:16–17; 13:7; 15:19–21; 23:3–20; 34:2, 30; 49:29–30; Ex 3:8; 23:23; 33:2; Nm 13:29; Jos 1:4; 3:10; 9:1–7; 15:63; 17:15; 24:11; Jgs 1:4–5; 3:3, 5; 2 Sm 5:6–10; 1 Kgs 9:20; Ez 16:3, 45.
7:2 Dt 2:34–35; 3:6; 7:26; 13:16, 18; 20:16–18; Ex 23:32–33; 34:12, 15; Jos 9:3–27; 10:40; 11:11–12; Jgs 2:2.
7:3–4 Gn 34:9–10; Ex 34:16; Jos 23:12–13; Jgs 3:5–6; 1 Kgs 11:1–6.

with them, neither giving your daughters to their sons nor taking their daughters for your sons. 4 For they would turn your sons from following me to serving other gods, and then the anger of the LORD would flare up against you and he would quickly destroy you.

5 But this is how you must deal with them:* Tear down their altars, smash their sacred pillars, chop down their asherahs,† and destroy their idols by fire. 6 For you are a people holy to the LORD, your God; the LORD, your God, has chosen you from all the peoples on the face of the earth to be a people specially his own.* 7 It was not because you are more numerous than all the peoples that the LORD set his heart on you and chose you; for you are really the smallest of all peoples.* 8 It was because the LORD loved you and because of his fidelity to the oath he had sworn to your ancestors, that the LORD brought you out with a strong hand and redeemed you from the house of slavery, from the hand of Pharaoh, king of Egypt.* 9 * Know, then, that the LORD, your God, is God: the faithful God who keeps covenant mercy to the thousandth generation toward those who love him and keep his commandments,* 10 but who repays with destruction those who hate him; he does not delay with those who hate him, but makes them pay for it. 11 Therefore carefully observe the commandment, the statutes and the ordinances which I command you today.

Blessings of Obedience

12 * As your reward for heeding these ordinances and keeping them carefully, the LORD, your God, will keep with you the covenant mercy he promised on oath to your ancestors. 13 He will love and bless and multiply you; he will bless the fruit of your womb and the produce of your soil, your grain and wine and oil, the young of your herds and the offspring of your flocks, in the land which he swore to your ancestors he would give you. 14 You will be blessed above all peoples; no man or woman among you shall be childless nor shall your livestock be barren. 15 The LORD will remove all sickness from you; he will not afflict you with any of the malignant diseases that you know from Egypt, but will leave them with all those who hate you.

16 You shall consume all the peoples which the LORD, your God, is giving over to you. You are not to look on them with pity, nor serve their gods, for that would be a snare to you.* 17 * If you say to yourselves, "These nations are more numerous than we. How can we dispossess them?" 18 do not be afraid of them. Rather, remember clearly what the LORD, your God, did to Pharaoh and to all Egypt: 19 the great testings which your own eyes have seen, the signs and wonders, the strong hand and outstretched arm with which the LORD, your God, brought you out. The same also will he do to all the peoples of whom you are now afraid. 20 Moreover, the LORD, your God, will send hornets among them, until those who are left and those who are hiding from you are destroyed.* 21 Therefore, do not be terrified by them, for the LORD, your God, who is in your midst, is a great and awesome God. 22 He will remove these nations before you little by little. You cannot finish with them quickly, lest the wild beasts become too numerous for you.* 23 The LORD, your God, will give them over to you and throw them into utter panic until they are destroyed.* 24 He will deliver their kings into your power, that you may make their names perish from under the heavens. No one will be able to stand up against you,* till you have destroyed them. 25 * The images of their gods you shall destroy by fire. Do not covet the silver or gold on them, nor take it for yourselves, lest you be ensnared by it; for it is an abomination to the LORD, your God.* 26 You shall not bring any abominable thing into your house, so as to be, like it, under the ban; loathe and abhor it utterly for it is under the ban.†

God's Care

8 1 Be careful to observe this whole commandment* that I enjoin on you today, that you may live and increase, and may enter in and

DT

†

7:5 *Sacred pillars . . . asherahs*: cut or uncut stones and wooden poles or trees (cf. 16:21) that had some cultic function. Fairly common religious artifacts, their association with the non-Israelite cults of Canaan and perhaps with Canaanite gods and goddesses, specifically the goddess Asherah, led to their condemnation in the Deuteronomic reform and possibly earlier.

7:26 *Under the ban*: and therefore doomed to destruction; see note on 2:34.

*

7:5 Dt 12:2–3, 29–31; 16:21–22; Ex 34:13; 2 Kgs 18:4; 23:4–24.
7:6 Dt 14:2, 21; 26:18–19; 32:8–14; Ex 19:5–6; Ps 135:4; Mal 3:17.
7:7 Dt 10:15.
7:8 Dt 5:6; 9:26; 13:5; 15:15; 21:8; 24:18; Ps 78:42.
7:9–10 Dt 4:31; 5:9–10; 24:16; Ex 20:5–6; 34:6–7; Nm 14:18; Jer 31:29–30; 32:18–19; Ez 18:1–24; Jn 9:1–3.
7:9 Dt 5:9–10; 7:12; 32:4; 1 Kgs 8:23–24; Neh 1:5; 9:32; Ps 89:1–2, 24, 28, 33–34; 98:3; Is 49:7; 54:10; 55:3; Dn 9:4; Jon 4:2; Mi 7:20.
7:12–15 Dt 15:6; 28:1–14; 30:1–10; Ex 23:22–33; Lv 26:3–13.
7:16 Dt 5:7–10.
7:17–19 Dt 1:28–31; 3:22; 4:34, 37–38; 9:1–3; 20:1; 29:2–3; Jos 23:3, 9–10.
7:20 Ex 23:28.
7:22 Ex 23:29–30; Jgs 3:1–6.
7:23 Dt 7:2.
7:24 Dt 11:25; Jos 12:7–24.
7:25–26 Dt 5:8–9; 9:21; Jos 6:18–19; 7:1, 20–21; Jgs 8:24–27; 17:2–4; 1 Kgs 15:13; 2 Kgs 23:4.
7:25 Dt 12:31; 17:1; 18:12; 22:5; 23:18; 24:4; 25:16; Prv 6:16; 15:8–9, 26.
8:1 Dt 4:1; 6:1.

Cultural Connection

The Principle of *Ujima*

Decades before the Civil War, the Underground Railroad helped thousands of African slaves find their way to freedom. The Underground Railroad was not a real railroad but a loose network of antislavery northerners—mostly African Americans—who helped escaped slaves reach safety in the free states or Canada. People called conductors guided groups of fugitive slaves through isolated areas at night so that they wouldn't be spotted. Others opened their homes and farms to give them safe places to stay during the day. It was dangerous work because professional slave catchers and local officials were always looking for escaped slaves to return for financial rewards.

The Underground Railroad is just one example of what can be accomplished through the Kwanzaa principle of *ujima* (see "Kwanzaa as a Way of Life," near Dt 10:12–22), which is collective work and responsibility. Our African American ancestors in this country worked together bravely for the common good. Many members of the Underground Railroad were former slaves themselves and took responsibility for freeing others as they had been freed. Today, we need young people with the same sense of responsibility and the willingness to work together to free others from poverty, violence, and addiction.

Martin Luther King Jr. did this. In his last speech, he said to you and me: "I've been to the Mountain top, and I've seen the Promised Land. I may not get there with you, but I want you to know that we as a people will get to the Promised Land." He knew he would not live to see his people freed from prejudice and discrimination. But he spent his whole life working with others toward that goal.

The author of Deuteronomy wrote long after Moses' time. Many of the Chosen People had indeed become wealthy, so he used Moses' authority to remind them of how they had gotten to where they were. Their ancestors—escaped, impoverished slaves—trusted in God and worked together over a long time to bring prosperity to the nation. This is the mentality we too must cultivate to bring success to ourselves and our people.

▶ Dt 8:11–18

D
T

possess the land which the LORD promised on oath
to your ancestors. 2 Remember how for these forty
years the LORD, your God, has directed all your
journeying in the wilderness,* so as to test you by
affliction, to know what was in your heart: to keep
his commandments, or not. 3 He therefore let you
be afflicted with hunger, and then fed you with
manna,* a food unknown to you and your ancestors, so you might know that it is not by bread
alone† that people live, but by all that comes forth
from the mouth of the LORD. 4 The clothing did
not fall from you in tatters, nor did your feet swell
these forty years.* 5 So you must know in your
heart that, even as a man disciplines his son, so
the LORD, your God, disciplines you.* 6 Therefore,
keep the commandments of the LORD, your God,
by walking in his ways and fearing him.

Cautions About Prosperity

7 * For the LORD, your God, is bringing you into
a good country, a land with streams of water, with
springs and fountains welling up in the hills and
valleys, 8 a land of wheat and barley, of vines and
fig trees and pomegranates, of olive trees and of
honey, 9 a land where you will always have bread
and where you will lack nothing, a land whose
stones contain iron and in whose hills you can
mine copper. 10 But when you have eaten and are
satisfied, you must bless the LORD, your God, for
the good land he has given you. 11 * Be careful not
to forget the LORD, your God, by failing to keep
his commandments and ordinances and statutes
which I enjoin on you today: 12 lest, when you
have eaten and are satisfied, and have built fine

† **8:3** *Not by bread alone*: Deuteronomic theology puts the good things promised faithful Israel into the context of the Lord's gratuitous love. As in 6:10–12, the goods of life must be seen as gift. Israel is to seek what really matters; all else will be added (cf. Mt 6:33).

* **8:2** Dt 1:3; 2:7; 29:4; Ps 95:10; Am 2:10.
8:3 Ex 16:11–36; Nm 11:5–9; Jos 5:12; Mt 4:4; Lk 4:4.
8:4 Dt 29:4; Neh 9:21.
8:5 Dt 4:36; 11:2; 21:18–21; Ps 94:12; Prv 3:11–12.
8:7–9 Dt 1:25; 11:10–12; 32:13–14; 33:28.
8:11–14 Dt 6:10–12.

houses and lived in them, 13 and your herds and
flocks have increased, your silver and gold has
increased, and all your property has increased,
14 you then become haughty of heart and forget
the LORD, your God, who brought you out of the
land of Egypt, that house of slavery; 15 he guided
you through the vast and terrible wilderness with
its saraph† serpents and scorpions, its parched
and waterless ground; he brought forth water for
you from the flinty rock* 16 and fed you in the wil-
derness with manna, a food unknown to your an-
cestors, that he might afflict you and test you, but
also make you prosperous in the end. 17 Other-
wise, you might say in your heart,* "It is my own
power and the strength of my own hand that has
got me this wealth." 18 Remember then the LORD,
your God, for he is the one who gives you the
power to get wealth, by fulfilling, as he has now
done, the covenant he swore to your ancestors.
19 But if you do forget the LORD, your God, and
go after other gods, serving and bowing down to
them,* I bear witness to you this day that you will
perish utterly. 20 Like the nations which the LORD
destroys before you, so shall you too perish for
not listening to the voice of the LORD, your God.

Unmerited Success

9 1 Hear, O Israel! You are now about to cross
the Jordan to enter in and dispossess nations
greater and stronger than yourselves, having large
cities fortified to the heavens,* 2 the Anakim, a
people great and tall.* You yourselves know of
them and have heard it said of them, "Who can
stand up against the Anakim?" 3 Know, then, to-
day that it is the LORD, your God, who will cross
over before you as a consuming fire; he it is who
will destroy them and subdue them before you, so
that you can dispossess and remove them quickly,
as the LORD promised you.* 4 After the LORD, your
God, has driven them out of your way, do not say
in your heart, "It is because of my justice the LORD
has brought me in to possess this land,* and be-
cause of the wickedness of these nations the LORD
is dispossessing them before me."† 5 No, it is not
because of your justice or the integrity of your
heart that you are going in to take possession of
their land; but it is because of their wickedness
that the LORD, your God, is dispossessing these
nations before you and in order to fulfill the
promise he made on oath to your ancestors, Abra-
ham, Isaac, and Jacob.* 6 Know this, therefore: it
is not because of your justice that the LORD, your
God, is giving you this good land to possess, for
you are a stiff-necked people.*

The Golden Calf

7 Remember and do not forget how you an-
gered the LORD, your God, in the wilderness. From
the day you left the land of Egypt until you came
to this place, you have been rebellious toward
the LORD.* 8 * At Horeb you so provoked the LORD
that he was angry enough to destroy you,* 9 when
I had gone up the mountain to receive the stone
tablets of the covenant which the LORD made with
you.* Meanwhile I stayed on the mountain forty
days and forty nights; I ate no food and drank no
water. 10 The LORD gave me the two stone tablets
inscribed, by God's own finger,* with a copy of
all the words that the LORD spoke to you on the
mountain from the midst of the fire on the day
of the assembly. 11 Then, at the end of the forty
days and forty nights, when the LORD had given
me the two stone tablets, the tablets of the cov-
enant, 12 * the LORD said to me, Go down from
here now, quickly, for your people whom you
have brought out of Egypt are acting corruptly;
they have already turned aside from the way I
commanded them and have made for themselves
a molten idol. 13 I have seen now how stiff-necked
this people is, the LORD said to me. 14 Let me be,
that I may destroy them and blot out their name
from under the heavens. I will then make of you
a nation mightier and greater than they.

15 When I had come down again from the blaz-
ing, fiery mountain, with the two tablets of the
covenant in both my hands,* 16 I saw how you
had sinned against the LORD, your God, by mak-
ing for yourselves a molten calf. You had already
turned aside from the way which the LORD had
commanded you.* 17 I took hold of the two tab-
lets and with both hands cast them from me and
broke them before your eyes.* 18 Then, as before,
I lay prostrate before the LORD for forty days and
forty nights; I ate no food, I drank no water, be-
cause of all the sin you had committed in the sight
of the LORD, doing wrong and provoking him.*

DT

†

8:15 *Saraph*: see note on Nm 21:6.
9:4 *Before me*: Hebrew reads "before you."

*

8:15 Dt 32:13; Ex 17:6; Nm 20:8–11; 21:6–9; Ps 114:8; Wis 11:4.
8:17 Dt 9:4–5.
8:19 Dt 4:25–26; 30:18; 2 Kgs 17:7–18.
9:1 Dt 1:28; 4:38.
9:2 Dt 1:28; 2:10–11, 21; Nm 13:22, 28, 33; Jos 11:21–22; 14:12, 15; 15:13–14; 21:11; Jgs 1:20.
9:3 Dt 4:24; 31:3.
9:4 Dt 8:17.
9:5 Dt 1:8.
9:6 Dt 9:13; 10:16; 31:27; Ex 32:9; 33:3; 34:9; Is 48:4; Jer 17:23; 19:15.
9:7 Dt 31:27; Ex 14:10–14; 2 Kgs 21:15; Jer 7:25–26.
9:8–21 Ex 32:1–34:29.
9:8 Ex 32:10.
9:9 Dt 4:13–14; 5:22; 9:11, 18, 25; 10:10; Ex 24:12–18; 34:28.
9:10 Dt 5:22; 10:4; Ex 31:18.
9:12–14 Dt 5:6–10; Ex 32:7–10.
9:15 Ex 32:15.
9:16 Dt 5:6–10; Ex 32:1–6; Ps 106:19–22.
9:17 Ex 32:19.
9:18 Dt 10:10; Ex 32:31; 34:28.

19 For I dreaded the fierce anger of the LORD against
you: his wrath would destroy you.* Yet once again
the LORD listened to me. 20 With Aaron, too, the
LORD was deeply angry, and would have destroyed
him; but I prayed for Aaron also at that time.*
21 Then, taking the calf, the sinful object you had
made, I burnt it and ground it down to powder as
fine as dust, which I threw into the wadi that went
down the mountainside.*

22 At Taberah, at Massah, and at Kibroth-hat-
taavah likewise, you enraged the LORD.* 23 And
when the LORD sent you up from Kadesh-barnea
saying, Go up and take possession of the land I
have given you, you rebelled against this com-
mand of the LORD, your God, and would not
believe him or listen to his voice.* 24 You have
been rebels against the LORD from the day I first
knew you.

25 * Those forty days, then, and forty nights,
I lay prostrate before the LORD, because he had
threatened to destroy you. 26 And I prayed to
the Lord and said: O Lord GOD, do not destroy
your people, the heritage you redeemed in your
greatness and have brought out of Egypt with
your strong hand.* 27 Remember your servants,
Abraham, Isaac, and Jacob. Do not look upon
the stubbornness of this people nor upon their
wickedness and sin,* 28 lest the land from which
you have brought us say, "The LORD was not able
to bring them into the land he promised them,
and out of hatred for them, he brought them out
to let them die in the wilderness."* 29 They are
your people and your heritage, whom you have
brought out by your great power and with your
outstretched arm.*

10 1 * At that time the LORD said to me, Cut
two stone tablets like the first ones* and
come up the mountain to me. Also make an ark
out of wood. 2 I will write upon the tablets the
words that were on the tablets that you broke,
and you shall place them in the ark. 3 So I made
an ark of acacia wood, and cut two stone tablets
like the first ones, and went up the mountain
with the two tablets in my hand.* 4 * The LORD
then wrote on the tablets, as he had written
before, the ten words† that the LORD had spoken
to you on the mountain from the midst of the
fire on the day of the assembly; and the LORD
gave them to me. 5 Then I turned and came down
from the mountain, and placed the tablets in the
ark I had made.* There they have remained, as
the LORD commanded me.

6 * The Israelites set out from Beeroth Bene-
jaakan for Moserah; Aaron died there and was
buried. His son Eleazar succeeded him as priest.*
7 From there they set out for Gudgodah, and
from Gudgodah for Jotbathah, a region where
there is water in the wadies. 8 At that time the
LORD set apart the tribe of Levi to carry the ark
of the covenant of the LORD,* to stand before
the LORD to minister to him, and to bless in his
name, as they have done to this day. 9 For this
reason, Levi has no hereditary portion with his
relatives;* the LORD himself is his portion, as the
LORD, your God, promised him.

10 Meanwhile I stayed on the mountain as I
did before, forty days and forty nights, and once
again the LORD listened to me. The LORD was un-
willing to destroy you. 11 The LORD said to me,
Go now and set out at the head of the people,*
that they may enter in and possess the land that I
swore to their ancestors I would give them.

The Lord's Majesty and Compassion

12 * Now, therefore, Israel, what does the LORD,
your God, ask of you but to fear the LORD, your
God, to follow in all his ways, to love and serve
the LORD, your God, with your whole heart and
with your whole being,* 13 to keep the command-
ments and statutes of the LORD that I am com-
manding you today for your own well-being?*
14 Look, the heavens, even the highest heavens,
belong to the LORD, your God, as well as the earth
and everything on it.* 15 Yet only on your ances-
tors did the LORD set his heart to love them. He
chose you, their descendants, from all the peo-
ples, as it is today.* 16 Circumcise therefore the
foreskins of your hearts,† and be stiff-necked no
longer. 17 For the LORD, your God, is the God of
gods, the Lord of lords, the great God, mighty
and awesome, who has no favorites, accepts no

---

†

10:4 *Ten words*: the ten commandments (cf. 4:13).

10:16 *Circumcise therefore the foreskins of your hearts*: cf. 30:6; Jer 4:4; Rom 2:29. The "uncircumcised heart" (Lv 26:41; Jer 9:25; Ez 44:7, 9) is closed and unreceptive to God, just as "uncircumcised ears" (Jer 6:10) are closed to the word of the Lord, and "uncircumcised lips" (Ex 6:12, 30) are a hindrance to speaking on behalf of the Lord.

---

*

9:19 Dt 10:10; Ex 32:11–14.
9:20 Ex 32:1–6, 21–25, 35.
9:21 Ex 32:20.
9:22 Dt 6:16; Ex 17:1–7; Nm 11:1–34.
9:23 Dt 1:19–33.
9:25–29 Ex 32:11–14.
9:26 Dt 4:20; 7:8.
9:27 Dt 7:8.
9:28 Dt 32:26–27; Nm 14:13–16.
9:29 Dt 4:20; Ex 6:6–7.
10:1–11 Ex 34:1–28.
10:1 Ex 34:1.
10:3 Ex 34:4.
10:4 Dt 4:13; 5:22; Ex 20:1–17; 34:1–4, 27–29.
10:5 Ex 40:20; 1 Kgs 8:9.
10:6–7 Nm 33:31–33.
10:6 Nm 3:1–4, 32; 20:22–29.
10:8 Dt 21:5; 33:8–11; Ex 32:25–29; Nm 3:6–10; 6:22–27; 8:23–26.
10:9 Dt 18:1–8; Nm 18:20.
10:11 Dt 1:6; Ex 32:34; 33:1.
10:12–13 Ps 15; 24:3–5; Mi 6:6–8.
10:12 Dt 6:5, 13; 8:6; 11:13.
10:13 Dt 4:1; 5:10, 29–33; 6:2; 7:9; 11:1, 13, 22.
10:14 1 Kgs 8:27; Neh 9:6; Ps 148:4.
10:15 Dt 7:6–8; Ex 19:5–6.

Cultural Connection

Kwanzaa as a Way of Life

The heart of the Law is love, our love for God and God's love for us. We express that love through the values we live out. Conflicts occur when the way we rank our values conflicts with the way others rank their values. For example, you may place a value on completing all your schoolwork, studying, and excelling in school. Another person sitting near you in class may not place the same high value on school. The two of you may come into conflict because this person disrupts the class and makes it difficult for you to understand what the teacher is explaining.

This is why a universal value system is important. It is why the Book of Deuteronomy has laws on everything from worship to sanitation. These laws gave the Israelites a common value system.

Kwanzaa is the name of a value system accepted by many African peoples. It was developed by Maulana Karenga after studying many different cultures throughout Africa. In 1965, he codified the unifying aspects of each of these cultures into the seven principles of Kwanzaa (also known as the Nguzo Saba). The seven principles are written in Swahili (an African trade and business language) and speak to the holistic development of the individual, family, community, nation, and race. Kwanzaa is celebrated from December 26 to January 1. It is good that more and more African Americans are celebrating it each year, but these principles must be fully put into practice year-round as a way of life.

Kwanzaa is not a religion or a religious holiday, but it can strengthen the faith that you already practice. Look up the Bible passages listed with the following Kwanzaa principles to learn more about each one:

1. *umoja* (unity): Psalm 133, 1 Cor 12:12–2
2. *kujichagulia* (self-determination): Jdt 8:9–36
3. *ujima* (collective work and responsibility): Dt 8:11–18
4. *ujamaa* (cooperative economics): Mt 16:25
5. *nia* (purpose): Rom 8:28
6. *kuumba* (creativity): Mt 25:14–30
7. *imani* (faith): Gal 6:9

▶ **Dt 10:12–22**

bribes,* 18 who executes justice for the orphan and
the widow, and loves the resident alien, giving
them food and clothing.* 19 So you too should
love the resident alien, for that is what you were
in the land of Egypt.* 20 The LORD, your God, shall
you fear, and him shall you serve; to him hold fast
and by his name shall you swear.* 21 He is your
praise; he is your God, who has done for you those
great and awesome things that your own eyes have
seen.* 22 Seventy strong your ancestors went down
to Egypt,* and now the LORD, your God, has made
you as numerous as the stars of heaven.

Recalling the Wonders of the Lord

11 1 Love the LORD, your God, therefore, and
keep his charge, statutes, ordinances, and
commandments always.* 2 Recall today that it
was not your children, who have neither known
nor seen the discipline of the LORD, your God—
his greatness, his strong hand and outstretched
arm;* 3 the signs and deeds he wrought in the
midst of Egypt, on Pharaoh, king of Egypt, and
on all his land;* 4 what he did to the Egyptian
army and to their horses and chariots, engulfing
them in the waters of the Red Sea† as they pur-
sued you,* so that the LORD destroyed them even
to this day; 5 what he did for you in the wilder-
ness until you came to this place; 6 and what he
did to the Reubenites Dathan and Abiram, sons
of Eliab, when the earth opened its mouth and
swallowed them up out of the midst of Israel,
with their families and tents and every living

† **11:4** *The Red Sea*: Hebrew *yam suph*, that is, "sea of reeds" or "reedy sea."

* **10:17** Dt 1:17; 16:19; Ex 15:11; 2 Chr 19:7; Jb 34:19; Ps 47:2; 136:2–3; Dn 2:47; Acts 10:34; Rom 2:11; Gal 2:6; 1 Tm 6:15; Rev 17:14; 19:16. **10:18** Ps 68:5–6; 99:4; 146:7–9. **10:19** Dt 24:17–22; Ex 22:21–24; 23:9; Lv 19:33–34. **10:20** Dt 6:13; Mt 4:10; Lk 4:8. **10:21** Ps 109:1; Jer 17:14. **10:22** Dt 1:10; Gn 46:8–27; Ex 1:5; Acts 7:14. **11:1** Gn 26:5; 1 Kgs 2:3. **11:2** Dt 4:9; 6:20–25. **11:3** Dt 6:22; 7:18–19; 26:8; 29:1–2; 34:11; Ps 78:42–51. **11:4** Ex 14:26–31; 15:1–10; Jos 24:6–7; Ps 78:53; 106:9–11.

thing that belonged to them—* 7 but it was you who saw with your own eyes all these great deeds that the LORD has done.

The Gift of Rain

8 * So keep all the commandments I give you today, that you may be strong enough to enter in and take possession of the land that you are crossing over to possess, 9 and that you may have long life on the land which the LORD swore to your ancestors he would give to them and their descendants, a land flowing with milk and honey. 10 The land you are to enter and possess is not like the land of Egypt from which you have come, where you would sow your seed and then water it by hand,† as in a vegetable garden. 11 * No, the land into which you are crossing to take possession is a land of mountains and valleys that drinks in rain from the heavens, 12 a land which the LORD, your God, looks after; the eyes of the LORD, your God, are upon it continually through the year, from beginning to end.

13 † * If, then, you truly listen to my commandments which I give you today, loving and serving the LORD, your God, with your whole heart and your whole being, 14 I will give the seasonal rain to your land, the early rain† and the late rain, that you may have your grain, wine and oil to gather in; 15 and I will bring forth grass in your fields for your animals. Thus you may eat and be satisfied. 16 * But be careful lest your heart be so lured away that you serve other gods and bow down to them.* 17 For then the anger of the LORD will flare up against you and he will close up the heavens, so that no rain will fall, and the soil will not yield its crops, and you will soon perish from the good land the LORD is giving you.

Need for Fidelity

18 * Therefore, take these words of mine into your heart and soul. Bind them on your arm as a sign, and let them be as a pendant on your forehead. 19 Teach them to your children, speaking of them when you are at home and when you are away, when you lie down and when you get up, 20 and write them on the doorposts of your houses and on your gates, 21 so that, as long as the heavens are above the earth, you and your children may live on in the land which the LORD swore to your ancestors he would give them.

22 * For if you are careful to observe this entire commandment I am giving you, loving the LORD, your God, following his ways exactly, and holding fast to him, 23 the LORD will dispossess all these nations before you, and you will dispossess nations greater and mightier than yourselves. 24 * Every place where you set foot shall be yours: from the wilderness and the Lebanon, from the Euphrates River to the Western Sea,† shall be your territory. 25 None shall stand up against you; the LORD, your God, will spread the fear and dread of you through any land where you set foot, as he promised you.*

Blessing and Curse

26 * See, I set before you this day a blessing and a curse: 27 a blessing for obeying the commandments of the LORD, your God, which I give you today; 28 a curse if you do not obey the commandments of the LORD, your God, but turn aside from the way I command you today, to go after other gods, whom you do not know.* 29 When the LORD, your God, brings you into the land which you are to enter and possess, then on Mount Gerizim you shall pronounce the blessing,* on Mount Ebal, the curse.† 30 (These are beyond the Jordan, on the other side of the western road in the land of the Canaanites who live in the Arabah, opposite Gilgal beside the oak of Moreh.)* 31 Now you are about to cross the Jordan to enter and possess the land which the LORD, your God, is giving you. When, therefore, you take possession of it and settle there, 32 be careful to observe all the statutes and ordinances that I set before you today.

B. The Deuteronomic Code

One Center of Worship

12 1 These are the statutes and ordinances which you must be careful to observe in the land which the LORD, the God of your

†

11:10 *By hand*: lit., "by foot," probably referring to a kind of mechanism for irrigation from the Nile.

11:13–15 Here as elsewhere Moses shifts between speaking of the Lord in the third person and speaking for the Lord in the first person.

11:14 *The early rain*: the rains which begin in October or November and continue intermittently throughout the winter. *The late rain*: the heavy showers of March and April. In Palestine crops are sown in autumn and harvested in spring and summer.

11:24 *The Western Sea*: the Mediterranean.

11:29 For the full ceremony of blessing and curse, see chaps. 27–28. Gerizim and Ebal are mountains in Samaria, separated by a deep ravine.

*

11:6 Nm 16:1–35; Ps 106:16–17.
11:8–9 Dt 5:33; 6:1–3.
11:11–12 Dt 8:7–10.
11:13–15 Dt 7:12–14; 10:12–13; 28:1–14; Lv 26:3–5; Ps 104:14; Jer 5:24.
11:16–17 Dt 4:25–27; 6:14–15; 28:15–68.
11:16 Dt 5:6–10; 7:1–6; 13:2–19; 1 Kgs 8:35–36.
11:18–21 Dt 6:6–9.
11:22–23 Dt 7:1; 9:1–3; 10:12–13.
11:24 Dt 1:7; Ex 23:31; Jos 1:3.
11:25 Dt 2:25; 7:23–24; Ex 23:27.
11:26–28 Dt 28:1–68; 30:1, 15–20; Lv 26:3–45.
11:28 Dt 32:16–18.
11:29 Dt 27:12–13; Jos 8:30–35.
11:30 Gn 12:6; 35:4.

ancestors, has given you to possess, throughout
the time you live on its soil.* 2 * Destroy entirely
all the places where the nations you are to dis-
possess serve their gods, on the high mountains,
on the hills, and under every green tree.* 3 Tear
down their altars, smash their sacred pillars,
burn up their asherahs, and chop down the idols
of their gods, that you may destroy the very name
of them from that place.

4 That is not how you are to act toward the
LORD, your God. 5 Instead,* you shall seek out
the place which the LORD, your God, chooses out
of all your tribes and designates as his dwelling
to put his name there.† * There you shall go,
6 bringing your burnt offerings and sacrifices,
your tithes and personal contributions, your vo-
tive and voluntary offerings, and the firstlings of
your herds and flocks.* 7 There, too, in the pres-
ence of the LORD, your God, you and your fami-
lies shall eat and rejoice in all your undertakings,
in which the LORD, your God, has blessed you.*

8 You shall not do as we are doing here today,
everyone doing what is right in their own sight,*
9 since you have not yet reached your resting
place, the heritage which the LORD, your God,
is giving you. 10 But after you have crossed the
Jordan and dwell in the land which the LORD,
your God, is giving you as a heritage, when he
has given you rest from all your enemies round
about and you live there in security,* 11 † * then
to the place which the LORD, your God, chooses
as the dwelling place for his name you shall bring
all that I command you: your burnt offerings and
sacrifices, your tithes and personal contributions,
and every special offering you have vowed to the
LORD. 12 You shall rejoice in the presence of the
LORD, your God, with your sons and daughters,
your male and female slaves, as well as with the
Levite within your gates, who has no hereditary
portion with you.

13 * Be careful not to sacrifice your burnt of-
ferings in any place you like, 14 but offer them
in the place which the LORD chooses in one of
your tribal territories; there you shall do what I
command you.

Profane and Sacred Slaughter

15 † However, in any of your communities you
may slaughter and eat meat freely, according to
the blessing that the LORD, your God, has given
you; the unclean as well as the clean may eat it,
as they do the gazelle or the deer.* 16 † Only, you
shall not eat of the blood, but must pour it out on
the ground like water.* 17 Moreover, you may not,
in your own communities, partake of your tithe of
grain or wine or oil, of the firstborn of your herd
or flock, of any offering you have vowed, of your
voluntary offerings, or of your personal contribu-
tions. 18 These you must eat in the presence of the
LORD, your God, in the place that the LORD, your
God, chooses, along with your son and daughter,
your male and female slave, and the Levite within
your gates; and there, in the presence of the LORD,
you shall rejoice in all your undertakings. 19 Be
careful, also, that you do not neglect the Levite as
long as you live in your land.*

20 * After the LORD, your God, has enlarged
your territory, as he promised you,* and you
think, "I will eat meat," as it is your desire to eat
meat, you may eat it freely; 21 and if the place
where the LORD, your God, chooses to put his
name is too far, you may slaughter in the manner
I have commanded you any of your herd or flock
that the LORD has given you, and eat it freely in
your own community. 22 You may eat it as you
would the gazelle or the deer: the unclean and
the clean eating it together. 23 * But make sure
that you do not eat of the blood; for blood is life;
you shall not eat that life with the flesh. 24 Do not
eat of the blood, therefore, but pour it out on the

DT

†

12:5 *The place . . . to put his name there*: Moses thus designates Jerusalem (Mt. Zion), in accordance with the Deuteronomic doctrine that the Lord "chooses" Zion, as the place where eventually the Temple will be built, as he chooses the house of David to reign over Israel; see 2 Sm 7; 1 Kgs 8; Ps 132. But the Lord's presence in Jerusalem consists in putting his "name" there (12:11, 21; 14:23–24; 16:2, 6, 11; 26:2; 1 Kgs 8:44, 49; 9:3; 11:36; 14:21; 2 Kgs 17:34; 21:4, 7; 23:27). The Lord himself "cannot be contained" in an earthly dwelling (1 Kgs 8:27), but because he says of the Jerusalem Temple that "my name will be there" (1 Kgs 8:16, 29; 2 Kgs 23:27), he is present. This theology allows God in a way to dwell with Israel and at the same time preserves divine transcendence. See note on 1 Kgs 8:12–13.

12:11 Sacrifice is to be confined to the single place that the Lord has chosen; eventually this was Jerusalem.

12:15 At this point a distinction is being made between cultic sacrifice and slaughter of animals for food. *In any of your communities*: lit., "within your gates."

12:16 The blood was understood to be the source or vehicle of life and so was not to be consumed. Cf. Gn 9:4.

*

12:1 Dt 4:44–45.
12:2–28 Dt 5:7–10; Ex 20:24–26; 2 Kgs 18:3–6, 22; 23:4–9.
12:2–3 Dt 7:5, 24–25; Ex 23:23–24; 34:11–14; Nm 33:51–52; Jgs 17:3–5; 1 Kgs 12:28–30; 14:22–24; 2 Kgs 16:4; 17:7–12; Jer 2:20; 3:6–10; Hos 4:12–13.
12:5–7 Dt 12:11–12; 14:22–26; 15:19–20; 16:2, 6, 10–11, 14–15; 26:2.
12:5 2 Sm 7:13; 1 Kgs 8:16–21, 27–30.
12:6 Dt 14:22–27; 15:19–23; 23:21–23; 26:12–15; Lv 1:3–17; 3:1–17; 6:2–6; 7:29–36; 27:1–8; Nm 15:18–21; 28:2–8; 30:2–15; Am 4:4–5; 5:22.
12:7 Dt 12:12, 18–19; 14:26–27; 15:20; 16:11, 14; 26:11.
12:8 Dt 6:18; 12:28; Jgs 17:6; 21:25.
12:10 Dt 3:18–20; 11:22–25; Jos 23:1; 2 Sm 7:1; 1 Kgs 5:17–18; 8:56.
12:11–12 Dt 12:5–7; 14:22–26; 15:19–20; 16:2, 6, 10–11, 14–15; 26:2.
12:13–14 Jos 22:10–34.
12:15 Dt 12:20–22; 15:22; Lv 7:19–21.
12:16 Dt 12:23–27; 15:23; Gn 9:4; Lv 3:17; 17:10–14; 19:26; 1 Sm 14:31–35.
12:19 Dt 14:27.
12:20–27 Lv 17:3–9.
12:20 Dt 19:8; Gn 28:14; Ex 34:24.
12:23–25 Dt 12:16; 15:23; Gn 9:4; Lv 3:17; 17:10–14; 19:26; 1 Sm 14:31–35.

ground like water. [25] Do not eat of it, that you
and your children after you may prosper for do-
ing what is right in the sight of the LORD. [26] How-
ever, any sacred gifts or votive offerings that you
may have, you shall bring with you to the place
which the LORD chooses, [27] and there you must
sacrifice your burnt offerings, both the flesh and
the blood, on the altar of the LORD, your God;
of your other sacrifices the blood indeed must
be poured out against the altar of the LORD, your
God,* but their flesh you may eat.

[28] Be careful to heed all these words I command
you today, that you and your descendants after
you may forever prosper for doing what is good
and right in the sight of the LORD, your God.*

Warning Against Abominable Practices

[29] * When the LORD, your God, cuts down from
before you the nations you are going in to dis-
possess, and you have dispossessed them and are
settled in their land, [30] be careful that you not be
trapped into following them after they have been
destroyed before you. Do not inquire regarding
their gods, "How did these nations serve their
gods, so I might do the same." [31] You shall not
worship the LORD, your God, that way, because
they offered to their gods every abomination that
the LORD detests, even burning their sons and
daughters to their gods.*

Penalties for Enticing to Idolatry

13 [1] Every word that I command you, you
shall be careful to observe, neither adding
to it nor subtracting from it.

[2] * If there arises in your midst a prophet or a
dreamer† who promises you a sign or wonder,
[3] saying, "Let us go after other gods," whom you
have not known, "and let us serve them," and the
sign or wonder foretold to you comes to pass,
[4] do not listen to the words of that prophet or
that dreamer; for the LORD, your God, is testing
you to know whether you really love the LORD,
your God, with all your heart and soul.* [5] The
LORD, your God, shall you follow, and him shall
you fear; his commandments shall you observe,
and to his voice shall you listen; him you shall
serve, and to him you shall hold fast.* [6] But that
prophet or that dreamer shall be put to death,
because, in order to lead you astray from the way
which the LORD, your God, has commanded you
to take, the prophet or dreamer has spoken apos-
tasy against the LORD, your God, who brought
you out of the land of Egypt and redeemed you
from the house of slavery. Thus shall you purge
the evil from your midst.*

[7] If your brother, your father's child or your
mother's child, your son or daughter, your be-
loved spouse, or your intimate friend entices you
secretly, saying, "Come, let us serve other gods,"
whom you and your ancestors have not known,
[8] any of the gods of the surrounding peoples,
near to you or far away, from one end of the
earth to the other: [9] do not yield or listen to any
such person; show no pity or compassion and do
not shield such a one,* [10] * but kill that person.
Your hand shall be the first raised to put such a
one to death; the hand of all the people shall fol-
low. [11] You shall stone that person to death, for
seeking to lead you astray from the LORD, your
God, who brought you out of the land of Egypt,
out of the house of slavery. [12] And all Israel shall
hear of it and fear, and never again do such evil
as this in your midst.*

[13] If you hear it said concerning one of the cit-
ies which the LORD, your God, gives you to dwell
in, [14] that certain scoundrels have sprung up in
your midst and have led astray the inhabitants
of their city, saying, "Come, let us serve other
gods," whom you have not known, [15] you must
inquire carefully into the matter and investigate
it thoroughly. If you find that it is true and an
established fact that this abomination has been
committed in your midst,* [16] * you shall put the
inhabitants of that city to the sword, placing the
city and all that is in it, even its livestock, un-
der the ban. [17] Having heaped up all its spoils
in the middle of its square, you shall burn the
city with all its spoils as a whole burnt offering
to the LORD, your God. Let it be a heap of ruins
forever, never to be rebuilt. [18] You shall not hold
on to anything that is under the ban; then the
LORD will turn from his burning anger and show
you mercy, and in showing you mercy multiply
you as he swore to your ancestors, [19] because you
have listened to the voice of the LORD, your God,
keeping all his commandments, which I give
you today, doing what is right in the sight of the
LORD, your God.

---

† **13:2, 4, 6** *Dreamer*: a false prophet who pretended to have received revelations from God in a dream; cf. Jer 23:25–32; 27:9; Zec 10:2. But dreams could also be a means of true prophecy (Nm 12:6; Jl 3:1) and of genuine revelations (Gn 20:3, 6; 31:11, 24; 37:5, 9; Mt 1:20; 2:12, 13, 19; etc.).

---

* **12:27** Lv 17:11.
12:28 Dt 4:40; 5:29; 6:2–3, 17–18; 12:25.
12:29–31 Dt 7:1–5, 25; Ex 23:33; 34:12; Jgs 2:2–3.
12:31 Dt 18:10; Lv 18:21; 20:2–5; 2 Kgs 3:27; 16:3; 21:6; 23:10; Jer 7:31; 19:5.
13:2–19 Dt 6:4, 14–15; 17:2–7.
13:4 Dt 8:2, 16.
13:5 Dt 6:4–5; 10:20; 11:22.
13:6 Dt 17:7, 12; 19:19; 21:21; 22:21–22, 24; 24:7; Jer 28:16; 29:32.
13:9 Dt 7:16; 19:13, 21; 25:12.
13:10–11 Dt 17:5–7; 21:21; 22:20–24; Jos 7:25–26; 1 Kgs 21:13–14.
13:12 Dt 17:13; 21:21.
13:15 Dt 17:4; 19:18.
13:16–17 Dt 20:16–18; Jos 6:17, 24; 7:25–26; 8:28.

Improper Mourning Rites

14 1 You are children of the LORD, your God.
You shall not gash yourselves nor shave
the hair above your foreheads for the dead.* 2 For
you are a people holy to the LORD, your God;
the LORD, your God, has chosen you from all the
peoples on the face of the earth to be a people
specially his own.*

Clean and Unclean Animals

3 You shall not eat any abominable thing.*
4 * These are the animals you may eat: the ox,
the sheep, the goat, 5 the deer, the gazelle, the
roebuck, the wild goat, the ibex, the antelope,
and the mountain sheep. 6 Any among the an-
imals that has divided hooves, with the foot
cloven in two, and that chews the cud you may
eat. 7 But you shall not eat any of the following
that chew the cud or have cloven hooves: the
camel, the hare, and the rock badger, which
indeed chew the cud, but do not have divided
hooves; they are unclean for you. 8 And the pig,
which indeed has divided hooves, with cloven
foot, but does not chew the cud, is unclean for
you. Their flesh you shall not eat, and their dead
bodies you shall not touch.
9 These you may eat, of all that live in the wa-
ter: whatever has both fins and scales you may
eat, 10 but all those that lack either fins or scales
you shall not eat; they are unclean for you.
11 You may eat all clean birds. 12 † But you shall
not eat any of the following: the griffon vulture,
the bearded vulture, the black vulture, 13 the
various kites and falcons, 14 all kinds of crows,
15 the eagle owl, the kestrel, the long-eared owl,
all species of hawks, 16 the little owl, the screech
owl, the barn owl, 17 the horned owl, the osprey,
the cormorant, 18 the stork, any kind of heron,
the hoopoe, and the bat. 19 † All winged insects
are also unclean for you and shall not be eaten.
20 Any clean winged creatures you may eat.
21 You shall not eat the carcass of any animal
that has died of itself; but you may give it to a
resident alien within your gates to eat, or you
may sell it to a foreigner. For you are a people
holy to the LORD, your God.*
You shall not boil a young goat in its mother's
milk.†

Tithes

22 Each year you shall tithe all the produce of
your seed that grows in the field;* 23 then in the
place which the LORD, your God, chooses as the
dwelling place of his name* you shall eat in his
presence the tithe of your grain, wine and oil, as
well as the firstlings of your herd and flock, that
you may learn always to fear the LORD, your God.
24 * But if, when the LORD, your God, blesses you,
the journey is too much for you and you are not
able to bring your tithe, because the place which
the LORD, your God, chooses to put his name is
too far for you, 25 you may exchange the tithe for
money, and with the money securely in hand, go
to the place which the LORD, your God, chooses.
26 You may then exchange the money for what-
ever you desire, oxen or sheep, wine or beer, or
anything else you want, and there in the presence
of the LORD, your God, you shall consume it and
rejoice, you and your household together.* 27 But
do not neglect the Levite within your gates, for he
has no hereditary portion with you.*
28 * At the end of every third year you shall
bring out all the tithes of your produce for that
year and deposit them within your own commu-
nities, 29 that the Levite who has no hereditary
portion with you, and also the resident alien,
the orphan and the widow within your gates,
may come and eat and be satisfied; so that the
LORD, your God, may bless you in all that you
undertake.

Debts and the Poor

15 1 At the end of every seven-year period†
you shall have a remission of debts,*
2 and this is the manner of the remission. Cred-
itors shall remit all claims on loans made to a
neighbor, not pressing the neighbor, one who

†

14:12–18 The identification of several of the birds in these verses is uncertain.

14:19–20 Lv 11:20–23 suggests that the unclean winged insects are those that walk on the ground; the clean winged creatures are those that leap on the ground, such as certain species of locusts.

14:21 *Boil a young goat in its mother's milk*: the meaning of this regulation is obscure but it may have a humane concern similar to the prohibitions against slaughtering an animal and its young on the same day (Lv 22:27–28) and capturing a mother bird along with her fledgling or eggs (Dt 22:6–7). See note on Ex 23:19.

15:1 *At the end of every seven-year period*: in every seventh, or sabbatical, year. Cf. 15:9; 31:10; and compare Jer 34:14 with Dt 15:12. *A remission of debts*: it is debated whether a full cancellation of debts is meant, or merely a suspension of payment on them or on their interest, but the former is more likely. Cf. Ex 23:11 where the same Hebrew root is used of a field that is "let lie fallow" in the sabbatical year.

*

14:1 Dt 32:5–6, 18–20; Lv 19:27–28; 21:5; Ps 103:13; Is 1:2, 4; 30:1; Jer 3:14, 19, 22; 16:6; 31:9, 20; 41:4–5; Hos 2:1; 11:1–4.
14:2 Dt 7:6; Ex 19:5–6.
14:3 Acts 10:14.
14:4–20 Lv 11:2–23.
14:21 Ex 22:30; 23:19; 34:26; Lv 17:15; 22:8; Ez 44:31.
14:22 Gn 14:20; 28:22; Lv 27:30–33; Nm 18:21–32; 1 Sm 8:15, 17; 2 Chr 31:2–19; Neh 12:44; Am 4:4.
14:23 Dt 12:5–7, 11–12, 17–18; 15:19–20.
14:24–26 Mk 11:15; Jn 2:13–14.
14:26 Dt 12:7.
14:27 Dt 12:12, 19.
14:28–29 Dt 26:12–15.
15:1 Dt 31:10; Lv 25:1–55; Neh 10:31.

is kin, because the LORD's remission has been
proclaimed. 3 You may press a foreigner, but you
shall remit the claim on what your kin owes to
you.* 4 * However, since the LORD, your God, will
bless you abundantly in the land the LORD, your
God, will give you to possess as a heritage, there
shall be no one of you in need 5 if you but listen
to the voice of the LORD, your God, and care-
fully observe this entire commandment which I
enjoin on you today. 6 Since the LORD, your God,
will bless you as he promised, you will lend to
many nations, and borrow from none;* you will
rule over many nations, and none will rule over
you.

7 * If one of your kindred is in need in any
community in the land which the LORD, your
God, is giving you, you shall not harden your
heart nor close your hand against your kin who
is in need. 8 Instead, you shall freely open your
hand and generously lend what suffices to meet
that need.* 9 Be careful not to entertain the mean
thought, "The seventh year, the year of remis-
sion, is near," so that you would begrudge your
kin who is in need and give nothing, and your
kin would cry to the LORD against you and you
would be held guilty.* 10 When you give, give
generously and not with a stingy heart; for that,
the LORD, your God, will bless you in all your
works and undertakings. 11 The land will never
lack for needy persons; that is why I command
you: "Open your hand freely to your poor and to
your needy kin in your land."*

Hebrew Slaves

12 * If your kin, a Hebrew man or woman, sells
himself or herself to you, he or she is to serve you
for six years, but in the seventh year you shall re-
lease him or her as a free person. 13 * When you
release a male from your service, as a free person,
you shall not send him away empty-handed,
14 but shall weigh him down with gifts from your
flock and threshing floor and wine press; as the
LORD, your God, has blessed you, so you shall
give to him. 15 For remember that you too were
slaves in the land of Egypt, and the LORD, your
God, redeemed you. That is why I am giving you
this command today.* 16 * But if he says to you,
"I do not wish to leave you," because he loves
you and your household, since he is well off with
you, 17 you shall take an awl and put it through
his ear† into the door, and he shall be your slave
forever. Your female slave, also, you shall treat in
the same way. 18 Do not be reluctant when you
let them go free, since the service they have given
you for six years was worth twice a hired laborer's
salary; and the LORD, your God, will bless you in
everything you do.

Firstlings

19 * You shall consecrate to the LORD, your
God, every male firstling born in your herd and
in your flock. You shall not work the firstlings
of your cattle, nor shear the firstlings of your
flock. 20 In the presence of the LORD, your God,
you shall eat them year after year, you and
your household, in the place that the LORD will
choose.* 21 * But if a firstling has any defect,
lameness or blindness, any such serious defect,
you shall not sacrifice it to the LORD, your God,
22 but in your own communities you may eat it,
the unclean and the clean eating it together, as
you would a gazelle or a deer. 23 Only, you must
not eat of its blood; you shall pour it out on the
ground like water.

Feast of the Passover

16 1 Observe the month of Abib† by keeping
the Passover of the LORD, your God,* since
it was in the month of Abib that the LORD, your
God, brought you out of Egypt by night. 2 You
shall offer the Passover sacrifice from your flock
and your herd to the LORD, your God, in the place
the LORD will choose as the dwelling place of his
name.* 3 * You shall not eat leavened bread with
it. For seven days you shall eat with it only un-
leavened bread, the bread of affliction, so that
you may remember as long as you live the day
you left the land of Egypt; for in hurried flight you
left the land of Egypt. 4 No leaven is to be found
with you in all your territory for seven days, and
none of the meat which you sacrificed on the eve-
ning of the first day shall be kept overnight for
the next day.

5 You may not sacrifice the Passover in any of

---

† **15:17** *His ear*: cf. Ex 21:6 and note there.

16:1 *Abib*: "ear of grain, ripe grain," the name of the month in which the barley harvest fell, corresponding to our March and April; at a later period this month received the Babylonian name of "Nisan."

---

* **15:3** Dt 23:20.
15:4–6 Dt 7:12–14; 28:1–14.
15:6 Dt 28:12.
15:7–11 Ex 22:25.
15:8 Dt 24:19; Lv 25:35; Ps 37:21–22; Prv 19:17; Sir 29:1–2; Mt 5:42.
15:9 Dt 24:15; Ex 22:23–24, 27.
15:11 Dt 15:8; Mt 26:11.
15:12–18 Ex 21:2–11; Jer 34:8–22.
15:13–15 Ex 3:21–22; 12:35–36.
15:15 Dt 5:15; 10:19; 16:12; 24:18, 22.
15:16–17 Ex 21:5–6.
15:19 Ex 13:2, 11–16; 22:29–30; 34:19–20; Lv 22:27; 27:26; Nm 18:15–18.
15:20 Dt 12:6–7, 17–18; 14:23.
15:21–23 Dt 12:15–16, 22–24; 17:1; Lv 22:17–25; Mal 1:8.
16:1–8 Ex 12:2–13:10; 23:15; 34:18; Lv 23:5–8; Nm 28:16–25; Jos 5:10–12; 2 Kgs 23:21–23; 2 Chr 30:1–27; 35:1–19; Ez 45:21–24.
16:2 Dt 12:5, 11; 16:6.
16:3–4 Ex 12:34, 39; 13:6–7; 34:18.

the communities which the LORD, your God, gives you; 6 only at the place which the LORD, your God, will choose as the dwelling place of his name, and in the evening at sunset, at the very time when you left Egypt, shall you sacrifice the Passover.* 7 You shall cook and eat it at the place the LORD, your God, will choose; then in the morning you may return to your tents. 8 For six days you shall eat unleavened bread, and on the seventh day there shall be a solemn assembly for the LORD, your God; on that day you shall do no work.*

Feast of Weeks

9 * You shall count off seven weeks; begin to count the seven weeks from the day when the sickle is first put to the standing grain. 10 You shall then keep the feast of Weeks† for the LORD, your God, and the measure of your own voluntary offering which you will give shall be in proportion to the blessing the LORD, your God, has given you. 11 You shall rejoice in the presence of the LORD, your God, together with your son and daughter, your male and female slave, and the Levite within your gates, as well as the resident alien, the orphan, and the widow among you, in the place which the LORD, your God, will choose as the dwelling place of his name.* 12 Remember that you too were slaves in Egypt, so carry out these statutes carefully.

Feast of Booths

13 * You shall celebrate the feast of Booths† for seven days, when you have gathered in the produce from your threshing floor and wine press. 14 You shall rejoice at your feast,* together with your son and daughter, your male and female slave, and also the Levite, the resident alien, the orphan and the widow within your gates. 15 For seven days you shall celebrate this feast for the LORD, your God, in the place which the LORD will choose; since the LORD, your God, has blessed you in all your crops and in all your undertakings, you will be full of joy.

16 Three times a year,* then, all your males shall appear before the LORD, your God, in the place which he will choose: at the feast of Unleavened Bread, at the feast of Weeks, and at the feast of Booths. They shall not appear before the LORD empty-handed, 17 but each with his own gift, in proportion to the blessing which the LORD, your God, has given to you.

Justice

18 * In all the communities which the LORD, your God, is giving you, you shall appoint judges and officials throughout your tribes to administer true justice for the people. 19 You must not distort justice: you shall not show partiality;* you shall not take a bribe, for a bribe blinds the eyes even of the wise and twists the words even of the just. 20 Justice, justice alone shall you pursue, so that you may live and possess the land the LORD, your God, is giving you.

Illicit Worship

21 * You shall not plant an asherah† of any kind of wood next to the altar of the LORD, your God, which you will build;* 22 nor shall you erect a sacred pillar, such as the LORD, your God, hates.

17 1 You shall not sacrifice to the LORD, your God, an ox or a sheep with any serious defect;* that would be an abomination to the LORD, your God.

2 * If there is found in your midst, in any one of the communities which the LORD, your God, gives you, a man or a woman who does evil in the sight of the LORD, your God, and transgresses his covenant,* 3 by going to serve other gods, by bowing down to them, to the sun or the moon or any of the host of heaven, contrary to my command;* 4 and if you are told or hear of it, you must investigate it thoroughly. If the truth of the matter is established that this abomination has been committed in Israel, 5 you shall bring the man or the woman who has done this evil deed out to your gates† and stone the man or the woman to death. 6 Only on the testimony of two or three witnesses shall a person be put

†

16:10 *Feast of Weeks*: a celebration of the grain harvest, later known as "Pentecost"; cf. Acts 2:1.

16:13 *Feast of Booths*: also called Tabernacles; a harvest festival at the end of the agricultural year. In later times, during the seven days of the feast the Israelites camped in booths made of branches erected on the roofs of their houses or in the streets in commemoration of their wanderings in the wilderness, where they dwelt in such temporary shelters.

16:21–22 *Asherah . . . sacred pillar*: see note on 7:5; Ex 34:13.

17:5 *Out to your gates*: outside the gates, so as not to defile the city; cf. Lv 24:14; Nm 15:36; Acts 7:58; Heb 13:12.

*

16:6 Dt 12:5, 11; 16:2.
16:8 Ex 13:6; Lv 23:36; Nm 29:35; Is 1:13; Am 5:21.
16:9–12 Ex 23:16; 34:22; Lv 23:15–21; Nm 28:26–31.
16:11 Dt 12:5–7, 11–12, 18.
16:13–15 Dt 31:10–13; Ex 23:16; 34:22; Lv 23:34–43; Nm 29:12–38; 1 Kgs 8:2, 62–66; Ezr 3:4; Neh 8:14; Ez 45:25.
16:14 Dt 16:11.
16:16 Dt 12:7; 16:11, 14; Ex 23:14–15, 17; 34:23–24; 2 Chr 8:13.
16:18–20 Dt 1:13–17; 17:8–13; 19:17; 21:5; Ex 18:13–26; 2 Chr 19:5–11.
16:19 Dt 1:16–17; 10:17–18; Ex 23:2–3, 6–8; Lv 19:15; Prv 17:23; 18:5; 24:23; Is 1:23; Mi 7:3; Jn 7:24; Jas 2:9.
16:21–17:7 Dt 5:7–10; 6:4–5; 12:29–14:2.
16:21–22 Dt 7:5; Ex 34:13; 1 Kgs 14:15; 2 Kgs 23:6, 15; 2 Chr 33:3.
17:1 Lv 22:20.
17:2–7 Dt 13:2–19.
17:2 Jos 7:11, 15; 23:16; Jgs 2:20; 2 Kgs 18:12; Jer 34:18; Hos 6:7; 8:1.
17:3 Dt 4:19; 2 Kgs 17:16; 21:3; 23:5; Jer 8:2; Ez 8:16.

Did You Know?

The Torah

The Hebrew word *Torah* means "instruction" or "teaching," and only over time has come to mean "the Law." Torah refers most fundamentally to the Law that was recorded as given by God to Moses on Mount Sinai. As the people of Israel lived the Torah, it became equated with their very life and existence. It was the key for their organization as a people and gave consistency to their struggle to live their covenant with God.

Jewish people refer to the first five books of the Bible (the Pentateuch) as the Torah because those books contain the Law and instructions on how to live it. The other books of the Old Testament are also strongly connected to the Torah. The historical books record how the people and their kings kept the Torah or disobeyed it. When they obeyed, they were blessed with happiness, health, and prosperity. When they disobeyed, they were punished with barrenness, destruction, and death. The prophets in the prophetic books call the people to faithfulness to the Law. They condemn idolatry and injustice and call the people to live the spirit of the Torah.

What law are Christians called to live by? For a hint, see the beatitudes (Mt 5:1—7:28), the Letter of Paul to the Galatians, and the Letter of James.

▶ Dt 17:8–11

DT

to death;* no one shall be put to death on the
testimony of only one witness. 7The hands of
the witnesses shall be the first raised to put the
person to death, and afterward the hands of all
the people.* Thus shall you purge the evil from
your midst.

Judges

8 * If there is a case for judgment which proves
too baffling for you to decide, in a matter of
bloodshed or of law or of injury, matters of dis-
pute within your gates, you shall then go up to
the place which the LORD, your God, will choose,
9 to the levitical priests or to the judge who is in
office at that time. They shall investigate the case
and then announce to you the decision.* 10 You
shall act according to the decision they announce
to you in the place which the LORD will choose,
carefully observing everything as they instruct
you. 11 You shall carry out the instruction they
give you and the judgment they pronounce,
without turning aside either to the right or left
from the decision they announce to you. 12 Any-
one who acts presumptuously and does not obey
the priest† who officiates there in the ministry of
the LORD, your God, or the judge, shall die. Thus
shall you purge the evil from Israel. 13 And all the
people, on hearing of it, shall fear, and will never
again act presumptuously.*

The King

14 * When you have come into the land which
the LORD, your God, is giving you, and have
taken possession of it and settled in it, should
you then decide, "I will set a king over me, like
all the surrounding nations,"* 15 you may in-
deed set over you a king whom the LORD, your
God, will choose.* Someone from among your
own kindred you may set over you as king; you
may not set over you a foreigner, who is no kin
of yours. 16 † But he shall not have a great num-
ber of horses; nor shall he make his people go
back again to Egypt to acquire many horses, for
the LORD said to you, Do not go back that way
again.* 17 Neither shall he have a great number
of wives, lest his heart turn away,* nor shall he
accumulate a vast amount of silver and gold.
18 When he is sitting upon his royal throne, he
shall write a copy of this law† upon a scroll from
the one that is in the custody of the levitical

†

17:12 *The priest*: the high priest; *the judge*: a layman. The court system here, involving lay and priestly officials, resembles the one whose establishment is attributed to King Jehoshaphat in 2 Chr 19:8–11 (cf. Ex 18:17–23 and Dt 1:17).

17:16–17 This restriction on royal acquisitions may have in mind the excesses of Solomon's reign mentioned in 1 Kgs 10:1–11:6. *Horses*: chariotry for war. Egypt engaged in horse trading, and the danger envisioned here is that some king might make Israel a vassal of Egypt for military aid.

17:18 *A copy of this law*: the source of the name Deuteronomy, which in Hebrew is literally "double" or "copy"; in the Septuagint translated as *deuteronomion*, literally "a second law." In Jerome's Latin Vulgate as *deuteronium*.

*

17:6 Dt 19:15; Nm 35:30; Jn 8:17; 2 Cor 13:1.
17:7 Dt 13:6, 10.
17:8–9 Ex 18:13–26.
17:9 Dt 21:5; 2 Chr 19:8; Ezr 7:25.
17:13 Dt 13:12.
17:14–20 1 Sm 10–25.
17:14 Dt 26:1; 1 Sm 8:5, 19–20.
17:15 1 Sm 9:16; 10:24; 16:1–13; 1 Kgs 19:15–16; 2 Kgs 9:1–13.
17:16 Dt 28:68; 1 Sm 8:10–12; 1 Kgs 4:26; 10:26–29; Is 2:7.
17:17 1 Kgs 10:10–25; 11:1–8; Neh 13:26; Is 2:7.

priests.* 19 † * It shall remain with him and he
shall read it as long as he lives, so that he may
learn to fear the LORD, his God, and to observe
carefully all the words of this law and these stat-
utes, 20 so that he does not exalt himself over his
kindred or turn aside from this commandment
to the right or to the left, and so that he and his
descendants may reign long in Israel.

Priests

18 1 The levitical priests, the whole tribe of Levi,
shall have no hereditary portion with Israel;
they shall eat the fire offerings of the LORD and the
portions due to him.* 2 They shall have no heri-
tage among their kindred; the LORD himself is their
heritage, as he has told them.* 3 This shall be the
due of the priests from the people: those who are
offering a sacrifice, whether an ox or a sheep, shall
give the priest the shoulder, the jowls and the
stomach. 4 The first fruits of your grain, your wine,
and your oil,* as well as the first shearing of your
flock, you shall also give him. 5 For the LORD, your
God, has chosen him out of all your tribes to be
in attendance to minister in the name of the LORD,
him and his descendants for all time.*

6 When a Levite goes from one of your commu-
nities anywhere in Israel in which he has been re-
siding, to visit, as his heart may desire, the place
which the LORD will choose, 7 and ministers there
in the name of the LORD, his God, like all his fel-
low Levites who stand before the LORD there, 8 he
shall receive the same portions to eat, along with
his stipends and patrimony.†

Prophets

9 When you come into the land which the
LORD, your God, is giving you, you shall not
learn to imitate the abominations of the nations
there.* 10 * Let there not be found among you
anyone who causes their son or daughter to pass
through the fire,† or practices divination, or is
a soothsayer, augur, or sorcerer, 11 or who casts
spells, consults ghosts and spirits, or seeks oracles
from the dead. 12 Anyone who does such things is
an abomination to the LORD, and because of such
abominations the LORD, your God, is dispossess-
ing them before you.* 13 You must be altogether
sincere with the LORD, your God. 14 Although
these nations whom you are about to dispossess
listen to their soothsayers and diviners, the LORD,
your God, will not permit you to do so.

15 A prophet like me† will the LORD, your God,
raise up for you from among your own kindred;
that is the one to whom you shall listen.* 16 This
is exactly what you requested of the LORD, your
God, at Horeb on the day of the assembly, when
you said, "Let me not again hear the voice of the
LORD, my God, nor see this great fire any more,
or I will die."* 17 And the LORD said to me, What
they have said is good. 18 I will raise up for them
a prophet like you from among their kindred,
and will put my words into the mouth of the
prophet; the prophet shall tell them all that I
command.* 19 Anyone who will not listen to my
words which the prophet speaks in my name, I
myself will hold accountable for it.* 20 But if a
prophet presumes to speak a word in my name*
that I have not commanded, or speaks in the
name of other gods, that prophet shall die.

21 Should you say to yourselves, "How can we
recognize that a word is one the LORD has not
spoken?", 22 if a prophet speaks in the name of
the LORD but the word does not come true, it is
a word the LORD did not speak. The prophet has
spoken it presumptuously; do not fear him.

Cities of Refuge

19 1 * When the LORD, your God, cuts down
the nations whose land the LORD, your
God, is giving you, and you have dispossessed
them and settled in their cities and houses,*
2 you shall set apart three cities† in the land the

DT

17:19 The only positive requirement imposed upon the king is strict adherence to the Mosaic or Deuteronomic law. In that respect, the king's primary task was to be a model Israelite.

18:8 *His stipends and patrimony*: meaning of the Hebrew is uncertain.

18:10–11 *Causes their son or daughter to pass through the fire*: to Molech. See note on Lv 18:21. Such human sacrifices are classed here with various occult and magical practices because they were believed to possess powers for averting a calamity; cf. 2 Kgs 3:27. Three other categories of magic are listed here: divination of the future (by a soothsayer or augur); black magic (by a sorcerer or one who casts spells); and necromancy (by one who consults ghosts and spirits, or seeks oracles from the dead to divine the future).

18:15 *A prophet like me*: from the context (opposition to the practices described in vv. 10–11) it seems that Moses is referring in general to all the true prophets who were to succeed him. This passage came to be understood in a quasi-Messianic sense in the New Testament (Mt 17:5; Jn 6:14; 7:40; Acts 3:22; 7:37).

19:2 *Set apart three cities*: the Israelites were to have at least six cities of refuge, three in the land east of the Jordan and three in the land of Canaan west of the Jordan (Nm 35:9–34); but since the three cities east of the Jordan had now been appointed (Dt 4:41–43), refer-

---

17:18 Dt 31:9, 24–26; Jos 8:32.
17:19–20 Dt 5:32–6:3; 2 Sm 7:12–16; 1 Kgs 2:4; Ps 132:11–18.
18:1 Nm 18:8–9, 20–24; Jos 13:14; 18:7; 2 Chr 31:2–19; 1 Cor 9:13.
18:2 Nm 18:20; Jos 13:33.
18:4 Dt 26:1–11; Nm 18:12; 2 Chr 31:5; Neh 13:10–13.
18:5 Dt 10:8; Jer 33:18.
18:9 Dt 12:29–31; Lv 18:24–30.
18:10–11 Dt 12:31; Ex 22:18; Lv 18:21; 19:31; 20:6, 27; 1 Sm 28:7–19; 2 Kgs 17:17; 21:6; 23:10, 24; Is 8:19–20; Ez 21:21.
18:12 Dt 9:4.
18:15 Mt 17:5; Mk 9:7; Lk 9:35; Jn 1:45; 6:14; 7:40; Acts 3:22; 7:37.
18:16 Ex 20:19.
18:18 Ex 4:10–16; Jer 1:9; 15:19; Ez 3:1–4.
18:19 Jer 11:21–23; Am 7:10–17; Acts 3:23.
18:20, 22 Dt 13:2–6; 1 Kgs 22:1–40; Jer 14:13–16; 23:9–40; 28:1–17; Ez 13:1–23.
19:1–13 Dt 4:41–43; Ex 21:12–14; Nm 35:9–34; Jos 20:1–9.
19:1 Dt 6:10–11; 12:29.

LORD, your God, is giving you to possess. [3]You shall measure the distances and divide into three regions the land of which the LORD, your God, is giving you possession, so that every homicide will be able to find a refuge.

[4]This is the case of a homicide who may take refuge there and live: when someone strikes down a neighbor unintentionally and not out of previous hatred. [5]For example, if someone goes with a neighbor to a forest to cut wood, wielding an ax to cut down a tree, and its head flies off the handle and hits the neighbor a mortal blow, such a person may take refuge in one of these cities and live. [6]Should the distance be too great, the avenger of blood† might in hot anger pursue, overtake, and strike the killer dead, even though that one does not deserve the death penalty since there had been no previous hatred; [7]for this reason I command you: Set apart three cities.

[8]* But if the LORD, your God, enlarges your territory, as he swore to your ancestors, and gives you all the land he promised your ancestors he would give, [9]because you carefully observe this whole commandment which I give you today, loving the LORD, your God, and ever walking in his ways, then add three more cities to these three. [10]Thus, in the land which the LORD, your God, is giving you as a heritage, innocent blood will not be shed and you will not become guilty of bloodshed.*

[11]However, if someone, hating a neighbor, lies in wait, attacks, and strikes the neighbor dead, and then flees to one of these cities, [12]the elders of the killer's own city shall send and have the killer taken from there, to be handed over to the avenger of blood and slain. [13]Do not show pity, but purge from Israel the innocent blood, so that it may go well with you.*

DT

Removal of Landmarks

[14]You shall not move your neighbor's boundary markers† erected by your forebears in the heritage that will be allotted to you in the land the LORD, your God, is giving you to possess.*

False Witnesses

[15]* One witness alone shall not stand against someone in regard to any crime or any offense that may have been committed; a charge shall stand only on the testimony of two or three witnesses.*

[16]If a hostile witness rises against someone to accuse that person of wrongdoing, [17]the two parties in the dispute shall appear in the presence of the LORD, in the presence of the priests and judges in office at that time,* [18]* and the judges must investigate it thoroughly. If the witness is a false witness and has falsely accused the other,* [19]you shall do to the false witness just as that false witness planned to do to the other. Thus shall you purge the evil from your midst. [20]The rest shall hear and be afraid, and never again do such an evil thing as this in your midst.* [21]Do not show pity. Life for life,† eye for eye, tooth for tooth, hand for hand, and foot for foot!*

Courage in War

20 [1]When you go out to war against your enemies and you see horses and chariots and an army greater than your own, you shall not be afraid of them, for the LORD, your God, who brought you up from the land of Egypt, will be with you.

[2]When you are drawing near to battle, the priest shall come forward and speak to the army, [3]and say to them, "Hear, O Israel! Today you are drawing near for battle against your enemies. Do not be weakhearted or afraid, alarmed or frightened by them. [4]For it is the LORD, your God, who goes with you to fight for you against your enemies and give you victory."*

[5]Then the officials shall speak to the army:* "Is there anyone who has built a new house and not yet dedicated it? Let him return home, lest he die in battle and another dedicate it. [6]Is there anyone who has planted a vineyard and not yet plucked its fruit? Let him return home, lest he die in battle and another pluck its fruit. [7]Is there anyone who has betrothed a woman and not yet married her? Let him return home, lest he die in battle and another marry her."* [8]The officials shall continue to speak to the army: "Is there anyone who is afraid and weakhearted?* Let him return home, or else he might make the hearts of his fellows melt as his does."

[9]When the officials have finished speaking

---

† ence is made here only to the three west of the Jordan. The execution of this command is narrated in Jos 20.

19:6 *The avenger of blood*: see note on Nm 35:12.

19:14 *Move your neighbor's boundary markers*: a prohibition against furtively extending one's property by moving a neighbor's boundary stone.

19:21 *Life for life . . .*: this phrasing of the *lex talionis* may seem exaggerated, but the law itself is meant to ensure equity and proportional punishment; cf. note on Ex 21:22–25.

*

19:8 Dt 11:22–25; 12:20; Gn 15:18–21; 28:14; Ex 23:31.
19:10 Dt 21:8–9.
19:13 Dt 13:6, 9.
19:14 Dt 27:17; Jb 24:2; Prv 22:28; 23:10; Hos 5:10.
19:15–21 Dt 5:20; Ex 20:16; 23:1.
19:15 Dt 17:6; Nm 35:30; Mt 18:16; Jn 8:17; 2 Cor 13:1.
19:17 Dt 1:17; 17:8–12.
19:18–19 Dn 13:61–62.
19:18 Dt 13:15; 17:4.
19:20 Dt 13:11.
19:21 Ex 21:23–25; Lv 24:19–20; Mt 5:38.
20:4 Dt 1:30; 3:22; Ex 14:14; 15:3; Jos 23:10; Jgs 4:14.
20:5–8 1 Mc 3:56.
20:7 Dt 24:5.
20:8 Jgs 7:3.

to the army, military commanders shall be ap-
pointed over them.

Cities of the Enemy

10 * When you draw near a city to attack it, of-
fer it terms of peace. 11 If it agrees to your terms of
peace and lets you in, all the people to be found
in it shall serve you in forced labor. 12 * But if it
refuses to make peace with you and instead joins
battle with you, lay siege to it, 13 and when the
LORD, your God, delivers it into your power, put
every male in it to the sword; 14 but the women
and children and livestock and anything else in
the city—all its spoil—you may take as plunder
for yourselves, and you may enjoy this spoil of
your enemies, which the LORD, your God, has
given you.
15 † That is how you shall deal with any city
at a considerable distance from you, which does
not belong to these nations here. 16 * But in the
cities of these peoples that the LORD, your God,
is giving you as a heritage, you shall not leave a
single soul alive. 17 You must put them all under
the ban—the Hittites, Amorites, Canaanites, Per-
izzites, Hivites, and Jebusites—just as the LORD,
your God, has commanded you, 18 so that they
do not teach you to do all the abominations that
they do for their gods, and you thus sin against
the LORD, your God.

Trees of a Besieged City

19 * When you are at war with a city and have to
lay siege to it for a long time before you capture
it, you shall not destroy its trees by putting an ax
to them. You may eat of them, but you must not
cut them down. Are the trees of the field human
beings, that they should be included in your
siege? 20 However, those trees which you know
are not fruit trees you may destroy. You may cut
them down to build siegeworks against the city
that is waging war with you, until it falls.

Absolution of Untraced Murder†

21 1 If the corpse of someone who has been
slain is found lying in the open, in the
land the LORD, your God, is giving you to pos-
sess, and it is not known who killed the person,
2 your elders and judges shall go out and mea-
sure the distances to the cities that are in the
neighborhood of the corpse. 3 * When it is estab-
lished which city is nearest the corpse, the elders
of that city shall take a heifer that has never been
put to work or worn a yoke; 4 the elders of that
city shall bring the heifer down to a wadi with an
everflowing stream at a place that has not been
plowed or sown, and shall break the heifer's neck
there in the wadi. 5 The priests, the descendants
of Levi, shall come forward, for the LORD, your
God, has chosen them to minister to him and
to bless in the name of the LORD, and every case
of dispute or assault shall be for them to decide.
6 Then all the elders of that city nearest the corpse
shall wash their hands† over the heifer whose
neck was broken in the wadi, 7 and shall declare,

Live It!

Facing Life's Battles

What are the wars in your life? Where do you experience conflict and lack of peace? We all hope that we will not face war in armed conflict. But in a sense, war is around us in the conflicts of everyday life.

We have fights with family and friends. We battle the pressures of society and our peers. We are at odds with the future. Deuteronomy 20:1 tells us that we are not to fear times of war because our God is with us and will be our strength.

When we face conflict, our faith will be tested, but we must hold strong and true to what God tells us. If we let our heart be filled with God, the wars we face will become opportunities for God's love to triumph.

What conflicts do you encounter these days? Do you sense that God is with you in these conflicts? If so, how? Pray for peace-filled ways to resolve conflict.

▶ Dt 20:1

DT

†

20:15 Deuteronomy makes a distinction between treatment of nations far away and those close at hand whose abhorrent religious practices might, or did, influence Israel's worship. This harsh policy was to make sure the nations nearby did not pass their practices on to Israel (cf. chap. 7).

21:1–9 This law has to do with absolving the community of bloodguilt that accrues to it and to the land when a homicide occurs and the murderer cannot be identified and punished.

21:6 *Wash their hands*: a symbolic gesture in protestation of one's own innocence when human blood is unjustly shed; cf. Mt 27:24.

*

20:10–11 Jos 9:23–27; 11:19; 2 Sm 10:19.
20:12–14 Nm 31:7, 9, 11; Jos 22:8.
20:16–18 Dt 7:1–2; 12:29–31; Jos 10:40; 11:11, 14.
20:19–20 2 Kgs 3:18, 25.
21:3–4 Nm 19:2–3.

"Our hands did not shed this blood,† and our eyes did not see the deed. 8 Absolve, O LORD, your people Israel, whom you have redeemed, and do not let the guilt of shedding innocent blood remain in the midst of your people Israel." Thus they shall be absolved from the guilt of bloodshed, 9 and you shall purge the innocent blood from your midst, and do what is right in the eyes of the LORD.*

Marriage with a Female Captive

10 * When you go out to war against your enemies and the LORD, your God, delivers them into your power, so that you take captives, 11 if you see a beautiful woman among the captives and become so enamored of her that you wish to have her as a wife, 12 and so you take her home to your house, she must shave her head,† cut her nails, 13 lay aside her captive's garb, and stay in your house, mourning her father and mother for a full month. After that, you may come to her, and you shall be her husband and she shall be your wife. 14 If later on you lose your liking for her, you shall give her her freedom, if she wishes it; you must not sell her for money. Do not enslave her, since you have violated her.*

DT

Rights of the Firstborn

15 * If a man has two wives, one loved and the other unloved, and if both the loved and the unloved bear him sons, but the firstborn is the son of the unloved wife: 16 when he comes to bequeath his property to his sons he may not consider as his firstborn the son of the wife he loves, in preference to the son of the wife he does not love, the firstborn. 17 On the contrary, he shall recognize as his firstborn the son of the unloved wife, giving him a double share of whatever he happens to own, since he is the first fruits of his manhood, and to him belong the rights of the firstborn.*

The Stubborn and Rebellious Son

18 * If someone has a stubborn and rebellious son who will not listen to his father or mother, and will not listen to them even though they discipline him,* 19 his father and mother shall take hold of him and bring him out to the elders at the gate† of his home city, 20 where they shall say to the elders of the city, "This son of ours is a stubborn and rebellious fellow who will not listen to us; he is a glutton and a drunkard."* 21 Then all his fellow citizens shall stone him to death. Thus shall you purge the evil from your midst, and all Israel will hear and be afraid.*

Corpse of a Criminal

22 * If a man guilty of a capital offense is put to death and you hang him on a tree,† 23 his corpse shall not remain on the tree overnight.* You must bury it the same day; anyone who is hanged is a curse of God.† You shall not defile the land which the LORD, your God, is giving you as a heritage.

Concern for the Neighbor

22 1 * You shall not see your neighbor's ox or sheep going astray and ignore it; you must bring it back. 2 If this neighbor does not live near you, or you do not know who the owner may be, take it to your own house and keep it with you until your neighbor claims it; then return it. 3 You shall do the same with a donkey; you shall do the same with a garment; and you shall do the same with anything else which your neighbor loses and you happen to find. You may not ignore them.

4 You shall not see your neighbor's donkey or ox fallen on the road and ignore it; you must help in lifting it up.

Various Precepts

5 A woman shall not wear a man's garment, nor shall a man put on a woman's clothing; for anyone who does such things is an abomination to the LORD, your God.*

6 * If, while walking along, you come across a bird's nest with young birds or eggs in it, in any tree or on the ground, and the mother bird is sitting on them, you shall not take away the mother

---

† **21:7** *This blood*: the blood of the slain, or the bloodguilt effected by the killing.

21:12–13 *Shave her head . . .*: these symbolic actions probably signified the transition or change of status of the woman or perhaps the end of her period of mourning for her previous husband or family.

21:19 *The gate*: in the city walls. This open space served as the forum for the administration of justice. Cf. 22:15; 25:7; Ruth 4:1, 2, 11; Is 29:21; Am 5:10, 12, 15.

21:22 *You hang him on a tree*: some understand, "impaled on a stake." In any case the hanging or impaling was not the means used to execute the criminal; he was first put to death by the ordinary means, stoning, and his corpse was then exposed on high as a warning for others. Cf. Jos 8:29; 10:26; 1 Sm 31:10; 2 Sm 21:9.

21:23 Gal 3:13 applies these words to the crucifixion of Jesus, who "redeemed us from the curse of the law, becoming a curse for us."

---

* **21:9** Dt 19:13.
21:10–14 Dt 20:14.
21:14 Dt 15:12–18; 22:13–19, 28–29; 24:1–3; Jer 34:15–16.
21:15–17 Gn 21:9–13; 1 Kgs 1:5–21.
21:17 Gn 49:3–4.
21:18–21 Dt 5:16; 27:16; Ex 20:12; 21:15, 17; Lv 20:9.
21:18 Ps 78:8; Jer 5:23.
21:20 Prv 23:20–21; 28:7; Mt 11:19; Lk 7:34.
21:21 Dt 13:6, 11–12; 22:21, 24; Lv 20:2; 24:14–16.
21:22–23 Jos 8:29; 10:26–27; 1 Sm 31:8–13; 2 Sm 4:12.
21:23 Gal 3:13.
22:1–4 Ex 23:4–5.
22:5 Dt 7:25–26.
22:6–7 Lv 22:28.

bird along with her brood. 7 You must let the
mother go, taking only her brood, in order that
you shall prosper and have a long life.
8 When you build a new house, put a parapet
around the roof, so that you do not bring blood-
guilt upon your house if someone falls off.*
9 †* You shall not sow your vineyard with two
different kinds of seed, or else its produce shall
become forfeit, both the crop you have sown and
the yield of the vineyard. 10 You shall not plow
with an ox and a donkey harnessed together.
11 You shall not wear cloth made from wool and
linen woven together.
12 You shall put tassels on the four corners of
the cloak that you wrap around yourself.*

Marriage Legislation

13 If a man, after marrying a woman and having
relations with her, comes to dislike her,* 14 and
accuses her of misconduct and slanders her by
saying, "I married this woman, but when I ap-
proached her I did not find evidence of her virgin-
ity," 15 the father and mother of the young woman
shall take the evidence of her virginity† and bring
it to the elders at the city gate. 16 There the father
of the young woman shall say to the elders, "I
gave my daughter to this man in marriage, but he
has come to dislike her, 17 and now accuses her
of misconduct, saying: 'I did not find evidence of
your daughter's virginity.' But here is the evidence
of my daughter's virginity!" And they shall spread
out the cloth before the elders of the city. 18 Then
these city elders shall take the man and discipline
him,† 19 and fine him one hundred silver shekels,
which they shall give to the young woman's fa-
ther, because the man slandered a virgin in Israel.
She shall remain his wife, and he may not divorce
her as long as he lives. 20 But if this charge is true,
and evidence of the young woman's virginity is
not found, 21 they shall bring the young woman
to the entrance of her father's house and there the
men of her town shall stone her to death, because
she committed a shameful crime in Israel by pros-
tituting herself in her father's house. Thus shall
you purge the evil from your midst.*
22 If a man is discovered lying with a woman
who is married to another, they both shall die,
the man who was lying with the woman as well
as the woman.* Thus shall you purge the evil
from Israel.
23 If there is a young woman, a virgin who is
betrothed,† and a man comes upon her in the
city and lies with her, 24 you shall bring them
both out to the gate of the city and there stone
them to death: the young woman because she
did not cry out though she was in the city, and
the man because he violated his neighbor's wife.
Thus shall you purge the evil from your midst.
25 But if it is in the open fields that a man comes
upon the betrothed young woman, seizes her
and lies with her, only the man who lay with her
shall die. 26 You shall do nothing to the young
woman, since the young woman is not guilty of
a capital offense. As when a man rises up against
his neighbor and murders him, so in this case:†*
27 it was in the open fields that he came upon her,
and though the betrothed young woman may
have cried out, there was no one to save her.
28 * If a man comes upon a young woman, a
virgin who is not betrothed, seizes her and lies
with her, and they are discovered, 29 the man
who lay with her shall give the young woman's
father fifty silver shekels and she will be his wife,
because he has violated her. He may not divorce
her as long as he lives.

23 1 A man shall not marry his father's wife,†
nor shall he dishonor his father's bed.*

Membership in the Assembly

2 † No one whose testicles have been crushed
or whose penis has been cut off may come into
the assembly of the LORD.* 3 No one born of an
illicit union may come into the assembly of the
LORD, nor any descendant of such even to the
tenth generation may come into the assembly
of the LORD.* 4 * No Ammonite or Moabite may
ever come into the assembly of the LORD, nor
may any of their descendants even to the tenth
generation come into the assembly of the LORD,

†

22:9–11 Some understand these laws as serving to preserve distinctions set by God in the creation. *Become forfeit*: to the sanctuary; lit., "be holy"; cf. Lv 19:19; Jos 6:19.

22:15 *The evidence of her virginity*: the bridal garment or sheet stained with blood from the first nuptial relations.

22:18 *Discipline him*: whip him, as prescribed in 25:1–3.

22:23 *A young woman, a virgin who is betrothed*: a girl who is married but not yet brought to her husband's home and whose marriage is therefore still unconsummated.

22:26 *So in this case*: in the absence of witnesses ("in the open field"), the presumption must be that the woman is the victim, and so guiltless.

23:1 *Father's wife*: stepmother.

23:2 Exclusion of an emasculated male may have had to do with association of emasculation with the practices of other peoples, or it may have been rejection of someone with a significant blemish who was thus not suitable for participation in the sacral assembly.

*

22:8 Dt 19:10.
22:9–11 Lv 19:19.
22:12 Nm 15:38–41; Mt 23:5.
22:13 Dt 24:1.
22:21 Dt 13:6; Gn 34:7; 2 Sm 13:12.
22:22 Dt 5:18; Ex 20:14; Lv 20:10; Ez 16:38–40; Jn 8:3–5.
22:26 Dt 19:4–6.
22:28–29 Dt 22:19; Ex 22:16–17.
23:1 Dt 27:20; Gn 9:20–27; 49:4; Lv 18:6–19; 20:11; Ez 22:10.
23:2 Lv 21:16–24.
23:3 Gn 19:30–38; Lv 18:6–18.
23:4–6 Nm 22:1–24:25; Ru 4:9–17; Ezr 10:10–44; Neh 13:1–3, 23–27.

5 because they would not come to meet you with
food and water on your journey after you left
Egypt, and because they hired Balaam, son of
Beor, from Pethor in Aram Naharaim, to curse
you. 6 The LORD, your God, would not listen to
Balaam but turned his curse into a blessing for
you, because the LORD, your God, loves you.
7 Never seek their welfare or prosperity as long
as you live.* 8 * Do not abhor the Edomite: he
is your brother. Do not abhor the Egyptian: you
were a resident alien in his country. 9 Children
born to them may come into the assembly of the
LORD in the third generation.

Cleanliness in Camp

10 When in camp during an expedition against
your enemies, you shall keep yourselves from
anything bad. 11 * If one of you becomes unclean
because of a nocturnal emission, he shall go out-
side the camp; he shall not come back into the
camp. 12 Toward evening, he shall bathe in water;
then, when the sun has set, he may come back
into the camp. 13 Outside the camp you shall
have a place set aside where you shall go. 14 You
shall keep a trowel in your equipment and, when
you go outside to relieve yourself, you shall dig
a hole with it and then cover up your excrement.
15 Since the LORD, your God, journeys along in
the midst of your camp to deliver you and to give
your enemies over to you, your camp must be
holy, so that he does not see anything indecent
in your midst and turn away from you.*

Various Precepts

16 * You shall not hand over to their master
any slaves who have taken refuge with you from
their master. 17 Let them live among you in any
place they choose, in any one of your communi-
ties† that seems good to them. Do not oppress
them.

18 There shall be no temple prostitute† among
the Israelite women, nor a temple prostitute
among the Israelite men.* 19 You shall not offer
a prostitute's fee or a dog's pay† as any kind of
votive offering in the house of the LORD, your
God; both these things are an abomination to
the LORD, your God.*

20 * You shall not demand interest from your
kindred on a loan of money or of food or of
anything else which is loaned. 21 From a for-
eigner you may demand interest, but you may
not demand interest from your kindred, so that
the LORD, your God, may bless you in all your
undertakings on the land you are to enter and
possess.

22 * When you make a vow to the LORD, your
God, you shall not delay in fulfilling it; for the
LORD, your God, will surely require it of you and
you will be held guilty. 23 Should you refrain
from making a vow, you will not be held guilty.
24 But whatever your tongue utters you must be
careful to do, just as you freely vowed to the
LORD, your God, with your own mouth.

25 When you go through your neighbor's vine-
yard, you may eat as many grapes as you wish,
until you are satisfied, but do not put them in
your basket. 26 When you go through your neigh-
bor's grainfield, you may pluck some of the ears
with your hand, but do not put a sickle to your
neighbor's grain.

Marriage Legislation†

24 1 * When a man, after marrying a woman,
is later displeased with her because he
finds in her something indecent, and he writes
out a bill of divorce and hands it to her, thus
dismissing her from his house, 2 if on leaving his
house she goes and becomes the wife of another
man, 3 and the second husband, too, comes to
dislike her and he writes out a bill of divorce
and hands it to her, thus dismissing her from
his house, or if this second man who has mar-
ried her dies, 4 then her former husband, who
dismissed her, may not again take her as his wife
after she has become defiled. That would be an
abomination before the LORD, and you shall not

†

23:17 *In any one of your communities*: from this it would seem that the slave in question is a fugitive from a foreign country.

23:18–19 *Temple prostitute*: Heb. *qedesha*, lit., "holy one," a title of the goddess of fertility. The role or function of the *qedesha* is debated; some see this as simply a term for a prostitute (Heb. *zona*). Others see it as designating a cultic role but not necessarily one involving sexual activity. The evidence is insufficient to give a final answer.

23:19 *Dog's pay*: "dog" is a derogatory term for a male temple prostitute.

24:1–4 This law is directly concerned only with forbidding a divorced man from remarrying his former wife, and indirectly with checking hasty divorces, by demanding sufficient cause and certain legal formalities. Divorce itself is taken for granted and tolerated as an existing custom whose potential evils this law seeks to lessen. Cf. 22:19, 29; Mal 2:14–16. *Something indecent*: a rather indefinite phrase, meaning perhaps "immodest conduct," but possibly including any kind of objectionable conduct. By New Testament times Jewish opinion differed concerning what was sufficient ground for divorce; cf. Mt 19:3.

23:7 Ezr 9:12.
23:8 Dt 2:2–8; 26:5; Gn 12:10–20; 25:19–26; 36:6–9; 46:5–7; 47:27.
23:11–12 Lv 15:16–17.
23:15 Dt 1:30; 20:4; 31:6, 8; 2 Sm 7:6.
23:16–17 1 Kgs 2:39–40.
23:18 Gn 38:21–22; 1 Kgs 14:24; 15:12; 22:46; 2 Kgs 23:7; Hos 4:14.
23:19 Dt 7:25–26; Is 23:17–18.
23:20–21 Dt 15:1–11; 24:10–13; Ex 22:25; Lv 25:35–38; Ez 18:8, 13, 17; 22:12; Lk 6:34–35.
23:22–24 Gn 28:20–22; Nm 21:2–3; 30:1–15; Jgs 11:30–40; 1 Sm 1:11; Ps 56:12–13; 66:13–15; 132:1–5; Eccl 5:3–5.
24:1–4 Dt 22:13–19, 28–29; Sir 7:26; Jer 3:1; Mt 5:31–32; 19:3–9.

bring such guilt upon the land the LORD, your
God, is giving you as a heritage.*
5 * When a man is newly wed, he shall not go
out on a military expedition, nor shall any duty
be imposed on him. He shall be exempt for one
year for the sake of his family, to bring joy to the
wife he has married.

Pledges and Kidnappings

6 † No one shall take a hand mill or even its
upper stone as a pledge for debt, for that would
be taking as a pledge the debtor's life.
7 If anyone is caught kidnapping a fellow Isra-
elite, enslaving or selling the victim, that kidnap-
per shall be put to death.* Thus shall you purge
the evil from your midst.

Skin Diseases

8 * In an attack of scaly infection† you shall
be careful to observe exactly and to carry out all
the instructions the levitical priests give you, as I
have commanded them: observe them carefully.
9 * Remember what the LORD, your God, did to
Miriam on the journey after you left Egypt.

Loans and Wages

10 When you make a loan of any kind to your
neighbor, you shall not enter the neighbor's
house to receive the pledge, 11 but shall wait out-
side until the person to whom you are making
the loan brings the pledge outside to you. 12 If the
person is poor, you shall not sleep in the pledged
garment, 13 but shall definitely return it at sunset,
so that your neighbor may sleep in the garment*
and bless you. That will be your justice before the
LORD, your God.
14 * You shall not exploit a poor and needy
hired servant, whether one of your own kindred
or one of the resident aliens who live in your
land, within your gates.* 15 On each day you
shall pay the servant's wages before the sun goes
down, since the servant is poor and is counting
on them. Otherwise the servant will cry to the
LORD against you, and you will be held guilty.*

Individual Responsibility

16 Parents shall not be put to death for their
children, nor shall children be put to death for
their parents; only for one's own crime shall a
person be put to death.*

Rights of the Unprotected

17 * You shall not deprive the resident alien or
the orphan of justice, nor take the clothing of
a widow as pledge. 18 For, remember, you were
slaves in Egypt, and the LORD, your God, re-
deemed you from there; that is why I command
you to do this.
19 * When you reap the harvest in your field
and overlook a sheaf in the field, you shall not go
back to get it; let it be for the resident alien, the
orphan, and the widow, so that the LORD, your
God, may bless you in all your undertakings.

Did You Know?

The Poor, the Strangers, the Widows, and the Orphans

One remarkable aspect of Israel's covenant was the command to care for the poor, the "aliens" or strangers, the widows, and the orphans. These four groups were the outsiders in ancient Israel because they fell outside Israel's socioeconomic system. Those who were poor often had no means to sustain themselves. Strangers, or aliens, were not part of Israel's tribal organization. Widows depended on the charity of others. Orphans were destitute because they had no family to help them survive.

God provides a reason why Israel must care for the poor and oppressed. Just as the Israelites were enslaved in Egypt—when they were poor, oppressed, orphans in a foreign land—and God responded to their cry for help, so they must care for the poor, oppressed, forgotten, and marginalized in their midst. Can this be any less true for us today?

▶ Dt 24:10–21

†

24:6 Since the Israelites ground their grain into flour only in sufficient quantity for their current need, to deprive a debtor of his hand mill was equivalent to condemning him to starvation.

24:8 *Scaly infection*: the Hebrew word seems to have to do with one or more skin diseases that produce scales, such as psoriasis. Its precise meaning is uncertain. See note on Lv 13:1–14:57.

*

24:4 Dt 7:25–26.
24:5 Dt 20:7.
24:7 Dt 13:6; Ex 21:16.
24:8 Lv 13:1–14:57.
24:9 Nm 12:10–15.
24:13 Dt 6:25; Ex 22:25–26; Am 2:8.
24:14–15 Lv 19:13; Sir 34:26–27; Jer 22:13.
24:14 Dt 1:16.
24:15 Dt 15:9; Mt 20:1–16.
24:16 Dt 7:10; 2 Kgs 14:6; 2 Chr 25:4; Jer 31:29–30; Ez 18:20.
24:17–18 Dt 10:17–19; 15:15; 24:22; 27:19; Ex 22:21–24; 23:9.
24:19–22 Ex 23:10–11; Lv 19:9–10; 23:22; Ru 2:1–23.

20 When you knock down the fruit of your olive trees, you shall not go over the branches a second time; let what remains be for the resident alien, the orphan, and the widow. 21 When you pick your grapes, you shall not go over the vineyard a second time; let what remains be for the resident alien, the orphan, and the widow. 22 For remember that you were slaves in the land of Egypt; that is why I command you to do this.

Limits on Punishments

25 1 When there is a dispute and the parties draw near for judgment, and a decision is given, declaring one party in the right and the other in the wrong, 2 if the one in the wrong deserves whipping, the judge shall have him lie down and in the presence of the judge receive the number of lashes the crime warrants. 3 Forty lashes† may be given, but no more;* or else, if more lashes are added to these many blows, your brother will be degraded in your sight.

Treatment of Oxen†

4 You shall not muzzle an ox when it treads out grain.*

Levirate Marriage

5 * When brothers live together† and one of them dies without a son, the widow of the deceased shall not marry anyone outside the family; but her husband's brother shall come to her, marrying her and performing the duty of a brother-in-law.* 6 The firstborn son she bears shall continue the name of the deceased brother, that his name may not be blotted out from Israel. 7 But if a man does not want to marry his brother's wife, she shall go up to the elders at the gate and say, "My brother-in-law refuses to perpetuate his brother's name in Israel and does not intend to perform his duty toward me." 8 Thereupon the elders of his city shall summon him and speak to him. If he persists in saying, "I do not want to marry her," 9 † his sister-in-law, in the presence of the elders, shall go up to him and strip his sandal from his foot and spit in his face, declaring, "This is how one should be treated who will not build up his brother's family!" 10 And his name shall be called in Israel, "the house of the man stripped of his sandal."

Various Precepts

11 When two men are fighting and the wife of one intervenes to save her husband from the blows of his opponent, if she stretches out her hand and seizes the latter by his genitals, 12 you shall chop off her hand; show no pity.

13 * You shall not keep two differing weights in your bag, one heavy and the other light; 14 nor shall you keep two different ephahs† in your house, one large and the other small. 15 But use a full and just weight, a full and just ephah, so that you may have a long life on the land the LORD, your God, is giving you. 16 For everyone who does these things, everyone who does what is dishonest, is an abomination to the LORD, your God.*

17 † * Bear in mind what Amalek did to you on the journey after you left Egypt, 18 how he surprised you along the way, weak and weary as you were, and struck down at the rear all those who lagged behind; he did not fear God. 19 Therefore, when the LORD, your God, gives you rest from all your enemies round about in the land which the LORD, your God, is giving you to possess as a heritage, you shall blot out the memory of Amalek from under the heavens. Do not forget!

Thanksgiving for the Harvest

26 1 * When you have come into the land which the LORD, your God, is giving you as a heritage, and have taken possession and settled in it, 2 you shall take some first fruits* of the various products of the soil which you harvest from the land the LORD, your God, is giving you; put them in a basket and go to the place which the LORD, your God, will choose

†

25:3 *Forty lashes*: while the punishment is severe, the law seeks to limit it from being overly harsh and inhumane. Later Jewish practice limited the number to thirty-nine; cf. 2 Cor 11:24.

25:4 This is comparable in spirit to 22:6–7; Israelites are not to be grasping and calculating. St. Paul argues from this verse that laborers have the right to live on the fruits of their labor; cf. 1 Cor 9:9; 1 Tm 5:18.

25:5 *When brothers live together*: when relatives of the same clan, though married, hold their property in common. It was only in this case that the present law was to be observed, since one of its purposes was to keep the property of the deceased within the same clan. Such a marriage of a widow with her brother-in-law is known as a "levirate" marriage from the Latin word *levir*, meaning "a husband's brother."

25:9–10 The penalty decreed for a man who refuses to comply with this law of family loyalty is public disgrace; the widow is to spit in his face. Some commentators connect this symbolic act with the ceremony mentioned in Ru 4:7, 8.

25:14 *Ephahs*: see note on Is 5:10.

25:17–19 This attack on Israel by Amalek is not mentioned elsewhere in the Old Testament, although it probably was connected with the battle mentioned in Ex 17:8. A campaign against Amalek was carried out by Saul; cf. 1 Sm 15.

*

25:3 2 Cor 11:24.
25:4 Prv 12:10; 1 Cor 9:9; 1 Tm 5:18.
25:5–10 Gn 38:1–30; Ru 4:5–10; Lk 20:27–33.
25:5 Mt 22:24; Mk 12:19; Lk 20:28.
25:13–16 Lv 19:35–36; Prv 16:11; 20:23; Ez 45:10; Hos 12:7; Mi 6:11.
25:16 Dt 7:25–26.
25:17–19 Ex 17:8–16; 1 Sm 15:2–33.
26:1–11 Dt 14:22–29; 16:1–17; Ex 22:29; Lv 23:9–21; Nm 28:26–31.
26:2 Dt 12:5, 11; 18:4; Ex 23:19; 34:26; Tb 1:6–7.

DT

as the dwelling place for his name. 3 There you
shall go to the priest in office at that time and
say to him, "Today I acknowledge to the LORD,
my God, that I have indeed come into the land
which the LORD swore to our ancestors to give
us."* 4 The priest shall then take the basket from
your hands and set it in front of the altar of the
LORD, your God. 5 Then you shall declare in the
presence of the LORD, your God, "My father was
a refugee Aramean† who went down to Egypt
with a small household and lived there as a
resident alien.* But there he became a nation
great, strong and numerous. 6 * When the Egyp-
tians maltreated and oppressed us, imposing
harsh servitude upon us, 7 we cried to the LORD,
the God of our ancestors, and the LORD heard
our cry and saw our affliction, our toil and our
oppression. 8 Then the LORD brought us out of
Egypt with a strong hand and outstretched arm,
with terrifying power, with signs and wonders,*
9 and brought us to this place, and gave us this
land, a land flowing with milk and honey.*
10 Now, therefore, I have brought the first fruits
of the products of the soil which you, LORD, have
given me." You shall set them before the LORD,
your God, and you shall bow down before the
LORD, your God. 11 Then you and your house-
hold, together with the Levite and the resident
aliens who live among you, shall celebrate with
all these good things which the LORD, your God,
has given you.*

Declaration Concerning Tithes

12 When you have finished setting aside all the
tithes of your produce in the third year,* the year
of the tithes, and have given them to the Levite,
the resident alien, the orphan and the widow,
that they may eat and be satisfied in your own
communities, 13 you shall declare before the LORD,
your God, "I have purged my house of the sacred
portion and I have given it to the Levite, the resi-
dent alien, the orphan and the widow, just as you
have commanded me. I have not transgressed any
of your commandments, nor forgotten any. 14 † I
have not eaten any of the tithe while in mourn-
ing; I have not brought any of it while unclean; I
have not offered any of it to the dead. I have thus
obeyed the voice of the LORD, my God, and done
just as you have commanded me.* 15 Look down,
then, from heaven, your holy abode, and bless
your people Israel and the fields you have given
us, as you promised on oath to our ancestors, a
land flowing with milk and honey."*

The Covenant

16 * This day the LORD, your God, is command-
ing you to observe these statutes and ordinances.
Be careful, then, to observe them with your
whole heart and with your whole being. 17 To-
day you have accepted the LORD's agreement:
he will be your God, and you will walk in his
ways, observe his statutes, commandments, and
ordinances, and obey his voice. 18 And today the
LORD has accepted your agreement: you will be
a people specially his own, as he promised you,
you will keep all his commandments, 19 and he
will set you high in praise and renown and glory
above all nations he has made, and you will
be a people holy to the LORD, your God, as he
promised.

The Altar on Mount Ebal

27 1 Then Moses, with the elders of Israel,
commanded the people, saying: Keep this
whole commandment which I give you today.
2 On the day you cross the Jordan into the land
which the LORD, your God, is giving you, set up
some large stones and coat them with plaster.
3 Write on them,* at the time you cross, all the
words of this law, so that you may enter the land
which the LORD, your God, is giving you, a land
flowing with milk and honey, just as the LORD,
the God of your ancestors, promised you. 4 When
you cross the Jordan, on Mount Ebal you shall
set up these stones concerning which I command
you today, and coat them with plaster, 5 * and
you shall build there an altar to the LORD, your
God, an altar made of stones that no iron tool
has touched. 6 You shall build this altar of the
LORD, your God, with unhewn stones, and shall
offer on it burnt offerings to the LORD, your God.
7 You shall also offer communion sacrifices† and
eat them there, rejoicing in the presence of the
LORD, your God. 8 On the stones you shall in-
scribe all the words of this law very clearly.
9 Moses, with the levitical priests, then said to

DT

† **26:5** *Aramean*: probably in reference to the origin of the patriarchs from Aram Naharaim (cf. Gn 24:10; 25:20; 28:5; 31:20, 24).

26:14 These are allusions to foreign religious practices. *To the dead*: to feed the spirits of the dead, or perhaps to worship Baal.

27:7 *Communion sacrifices*: The principal feature of this ritual (see Lv 3:1–17) is the sharing of the sacrifice with God, the priest and the person offering the sacrifice, who eat it as a holy thing (cf. Ex 24:5).

* **26:3** Dt 1:8, 20–21.
26:5 Gn 46:5–7, 26–27; Ex 1:7, 9; Acts 7:14–15.
26:6–7 Ex 1:8–22; 2:23–25; 3:7–10; 6:9; Nm 20:15–16; 1 Kgs 12:4.
26:8 Dt 4:34; 6:21–22; Ex 12:51.
26:9 Ex 3:8.
26:11 Dt 12:7, 12.
26:12 Dt 14:28–29.
26:14 Dt 14:1; Lv 11:24–25; 22:3; Jer 16:7.
26:15 1 Kgs 8:39, 43, 49; Ps 102:19.
26:16–19 Dt 7:6; 8:6; 10:12–13; 11:22; 14:2; 27:9; 28:1, 9; 29:12–13; Ex 6:7; 19:5–6; 24:7; Lv 26:12; 2 Sm 7:24; Jer 7:23; 31:33; Ez 11:20; Hos 2:23.
27:3 Jos 8:32.
27:5–7 Ex 20:24–25; Jos 8:30–31.

all Israel: Be silent, Israel, and listen! This day
you have become the people of the LORD, your
God.* [10]You shall obey the voice of the LORD,
your God, and keep his commandments and
statutes which I am giving you today.

Preparation for Blessings and Curses

[11]That same day Moses commanded the peo-
ple, saying: [12]* When you cross the Jordan, these
shall stand on Mount Gerizim to bless the peo-
ple: Simeon, Levi, Judah, Issachar, Joseph and
Benjamin. [13]And these shall stand on Mount
Ebal for the curse: Reuben, Gad, Asher, Zebulun,
Dan and Naphtali.

The Twelve Curses

[14]The Levites shall proclaim in a loud voice
to all the Israelites: [15]† "Cursed be anyone who
makes a carved or molten idol,* an abomination
to the LORD, the work of a craftsman's hands, and
sets it up in secret!" And all the people shall an-
swer, "Amen!"

[16]"Cursed be anyone who dishonors father
or mother!"* And all the people shall answer,
"Amen!"

[17]"Cursed be anyone who moves a neighbor's
boundary markers!"* And all the people shall
answer, "Amen!"

[18]"Cursed be anyone who misleads the blind
on their way!"* And all the people shall answer,
"Amen!"

[19]"Cursed be anyone who deprives the resi-
dent alien, the orphan or the widow of justice!"*
And all the people shall answer, "Amen!"

[20]"Cursed be anyone who has relations with his
father's wife, for he dishonors his father's bed!"*
And all the people shall answer, "Amen!"

[21]"Cursed be anyone who has relations with
any animal!"* And all the people shall answer,
"Amen!"

[22]"Cursed be anyone who has relations with
his sister, whether his father's daughter or his
mother's daughter!"* And all the people shall
answer, "Amen!"

[23]"Cursed be anyone who has relations with
his mother-in-law!"* And all the people shall
answer, "Amen!"

[24]"Cursed be anyone who strikes down a
neighbor in secret!"* And all the people shall
answer, "Amen!"

[25]"Cursed be anyone who accepts payment to
kill an innocent person!"* And all the people
shall answer, "Amen!"

[26]"Cursed be anyone whose actions do not up-
hold the words of this law!"* And all the people
shall answer, "Amen!"

Blessings for Obedience

28 [1]Now,* * if you diligently obey the voice
of the LORD, your God, carefully observ-
ing all his commandments which I give you to-
day, the LORD, your God, will set you high above
all the nations of the earth.* [2]All these blessings
will come upon you and overwhelm you when
you obey the voice of the LORD, your God:

[3] * May you be blessed in the city,
and blessed in the country!
[4] Blessed be the fruit of your womb,
the produce of your soil and the offspring
of your livestock,
the issue of your herds and the young of
your flocks!*
[5] Blessed be your grain basket and your
kneading bowl!
[6] May you be blessed in your coming in,
and blessed in your going out!† *

Victory and Prosperity

[7]The LORD will beat down before you the ene-
mies that rise up against you; they will come out
against you from one direction, and flee before
you in seven.† * [8]The LORD will affirm the bless-
ing upon you, on your barns and on all your
undertakings; he will bless you in the land that
the LORD, your God, is giving you. [9]The LORD
will establish you as a holy people, as he swore
to you,* if you keep the commandments of the

---

† **27:15–26** The ceremony described here reflects the structure of covenant. The people assent to the directives their covenant Lord sets forth; their "Amen" ratifies the proscription of idolatry, injustice, incest, murder, and infidelity in general. Thus the "love" of the Lord which is at the heart of Israel's existence as his covenant people (6:4–5) is spelled out in terms of particular actions. The "Amen" is an acceptance of the curses or sanctions entailed by breaking faith with the Lord. Cf. 30:15–20, a concise statement of covenant theology.

28:6 *In your coming in . . . in your going out*: at the beginning and end of every action, or in all actions in general. The rhetorical figure is called merismus. See also 6:7.

28:7 *From one direction . . . in seven*: in one disciplined body, contrasted with many scattered groups.

27:9 Dt 26:17–19.
27:12–13 Dt 11:26–29; Jos 8:33–35.
27:15 Dt 4:15–20; 5:8–9; Ex 20:4, 23; 34:17; Lv 19:4; 26:1; Ps 115:4–8; Wis 14:8.
27:16 Dt 5:16; 21:18–21; Ex 20:12; 21:17; Lv 20:9.
27:17 Dt 19:14.
27:18 Lv 19:14.
27:19 Dt 24:17–18; Ex 22:21–24; 23:9; Lv 19:33–34.
27:20 Dt 23:1; Lv 18:7–8; 20:11.
27:21 Ex 22:18; Lv 18:23; 20:15–16.
27:22 Lv 18:9; 20:17.
27:23 Lv 18:17; 20:14.
27:24 Dt 5:17; 21:1; Ex 20:13; 21:12; Nm 35:20–21.
27:25 Dt 16:19; Ex 23:7–8.
27:26 Jer 11:3; Gal 3:10.
28:1–68 Lv 26:3–45.
28:1–14 Dt 7:12–16; 11:13–15.
28:1 Dt 26:19; Ps 89:27; Is 55:3–5.
28:3–6 Dt 28:16–19.
28:4 Dt 7:13–14; 30:9; Ex 23:26; Lv 26:9.
28:6 Ps 121:8.
28:7 Dt 9:1–3; Ex 23:27–28; Lv 26:6–8.
28:9 Dt 26:18–19; Ex 19:5–6.

DT

LORD, your God, and walk in his ways. 10 All the
peoples of the earth will see that the name of
the LORD is proclaimed over you,† and they will
be afraid of you.* 11 The LORD will generously
increase the fruit of your womb, the offspring
of your livestock, and the produce of your soil,
upon the land which the LORD swore to your an-
cestors he would give you.* 12 The LORD will open
up for you his rich storehouse, the heavens, to
give your land rain in due season and to bless all
the works of your hands. You will lend to many
nations but borrow from none.* 13 The LORD will
make you the head not the tail, the top not the
bottom, if you obey the commandments of the
LORD, your God, which I am giving you today,
observing them carefully, 14 not turning aside,
either to the right or to the left, from any of the
words which I am giving you today, following
other gods and serving them.*

Curses for Disobedience

15 But if you do not obey the voice of the
LORD, your God,* carefully observing all his
commandments and statutes which I give you
today, all these curses shall come upon you and
overwhelm you:
16 * May you be cursed in the city, and cursed
in the country! 17 Cursed be your grain basket
and your kneading bowl! 18 Cursed be the fruit
of your womb, the produce of your soil and
the offspring of your livestock, the issue of your
herds and the young of your flocks! 19 May you
be cursed in your coming in, and cursed in your
going out!

Sickness and Defeat

20 The LORD will send on you a curse, panic,
and frustration in everything you set your hand
to, until you are speedily destroyed and per-
ish for the evil you have done in forsaking me.
21 * The LORD will make disease cling to you until
he has made an end of you from the land you
are entering to possess. 22 The LORD will strike
you with consumption, fever, and inflamma-
tion, with fiery heat and drought, with blight
and mildew, that will pursue you until you per-
ish. 23 The heavens over your heads will be like
bronze and the earth under your feet like iron.*
24 For rain the LORD will give your land powdery
dust, which will come down upon you from the
heavens until you are destroyed. 25 The LORD will
let you be beaten down before your enemies;
though you advance against them from one di-
rection, you will flee before them in seven,† so
that you will become an object of horror to all
the kingdoms of the earth.* 26 Your corpses will
become food for all the birds of the air and for
the beasts of the field, with no one to frighten
them off.* 27 The LORD will strike you with Egyp-
tian boils* and with tumors, skin diseases and
the itch, from none of which you can be cured.
28 * And the LORD will strike you with madness,
blindness and panic, 29 so that even at midday
you will grope in the dark as though blind, un-
able to find your way.

Despoilment

You will be oppressed and robbed continu-
ally, with no one to come to your aid. 30 Though
you betroth a wife, another will have her.
Though you build a house, you will not live in it.
Though you plant a vineyard, you will not pluck
its fruits.* 31 * Your ox will be slaughtered before
your eyes, but you will not eat its flesh. Your
donkey will be stolen in your presence, but you
will never get it back. Your flocks will be given
to your enemies, with no one to come to your
aid. 32 Your sons and daughters will be given
to another people while you strain your eyes
looking for them every day, having no power to
do anything. 33 A people you do not know will
consume the fruit of your soil and of all your la-
bor, and you will be thoroughly oppressed and
continually crushed, 34 until you are driven mad
by what your eyes must look upon. 35 The LORD
will strike you with malignant boils of which
you cannot be cured, on your knees and legs,
and from the soles of your feet to the crown of
your head.

Exile

36 * The LORD will bring you, and your king
whom you have set over you, to a nation which
you and your ancestors have not known, and
there you will serve other gods, of wood and
stone, 37 and you will be a horror, a byword, a
taunt among all the peoples to which the LORD
will drive you.

† **28:10** *The name of the LORD is proclaimed over you*: an expression signifying ownership and protection. Cf. 2 Sm 12:28; 1 Kgs 8:43; Is 4:1; 63:19; Jer 7:10–11; 14:9; 15:16; 25:29; Am 9:12.

28:25 *From one direction . . . in seven*: see note on v. 7.

* **28:10** Dt 2:25; 11:25; Is 61:9.
28:11 Dt 28:4.
28:12 Dt 15:6.
28:14 Dt 5:32.
28:15 Bar 1:20; Dn 9:11; Mal 2:2.
28:16–19 Dt 28:3–6.
28:21–22 Lv 26:16, 25; Jer 14:12; Am 4:9–10; Hg 2:17.
28:23 Lv 26:19.
28:25 Dt 1:44; 28:7; Lv 26:17, 37.
28:26 Ps 79:2; Jer 7:33; 34:20.
28:27 Dt 7:15; 28:60; Ex 9:8–12.
28:28–29 Is 59:10.
28:30 Dt 20:5–7; Am 5:11.
28:31–34 Jer 5:17; Lam 5:1–18; Am 7:17.
28:36–37 Dt 4:27–28; 1 Kgs 9:6–9; 2 Kgs 25:6–7, 11; 2 Chr 7:19–22; 33:11; 36:6, 20; Jer 16:13; 24:8–9; 25:8–11; Ez 17:12.

DT

Fruitless Labors

38 * Though you take out seed to your field,
you will harvest but little, for the locusts will
devour it. 39 Though you plant and cultivate vine-
yards, you will not drink or store up the wine, for
the worms will eat them. 40 Though you have ol-
ive trees throughout your country, you will have
no oil for ointment, for your olives will drop
off. 41 Though you beget sons and daughters,
they will not remain with you, for they will go
into captivity. 42 Buzzing insects will take posses-
sion of all your trees and the crops of your soil.
43 * The resident aliens among you will rise above
you higher and higher, while you sink lower and
lower. 44 They will lend to you, not you to them.
They will become the head, you the tail.
45 All these curses will come upon you, pur-
suing you and overwhelming you, until you are
destroyed, because you would not obey the voice
of the LORD, your God, by keeping his command-
ments and statutes which he gave you.* 46 They
will be a sign and a wonder† for you and your
descendants for all time. 47 Since you would not
serve the LORD, your God, with heartfelt joy for
abundance of every kind, 48 in hunger and thirst,
in nakedness and utter want, you will serve the
enemies whom the LORD will send against you.
He will put an iron yoke on your neck, until he
destroys you.*

Invasion and Siege

49 * The LORD will raise up against you a nation
from afar, from the end of the earth, that swoops
down like an eagle, a nation whose language
you do not understand, 50 a nation of fierce ap-
pearance, that shows neither respect for the aged
nor mercy for the young. 51 They will consume
the offspring of your livestock and the produce
of your soil, until you are destroyed; they will
leave you no grain or wine or oil, no issue of
herd, no young of flock, until they have brought
about your ruin. 52 They will besiege you in each
of your communities, until the great, fortified
walls, in which you trust, come tumbling down
all over your land. They will besiege you in ev-
ery community throughout the land which the
LORD, your God, has given you, 53 * and because
of the siege and the distress to which your enemy
subjects you, you will eat the fruit of your womb,
the flesh of your own sons and daughters whom
the LORD, your God, has given you. 54 The most
refined and fastidious man among you will be-
grudge his brother and his beloved wife and his
surviving children, 55 any share in the flesh of his
children that he himself is using for food because
nothing else is left him—such the siege and
distress to which your enemy will subject you
in all your communities. 56 The most fastidious
woman among you, who would not venture to
set the sole of her foot on the ground, so refined
and fastidious is she, will begrudge her beloved
husband and her son and daughter 57 the after-
birth that issues from her womb and the infants
she brings forth because she secretly eats them
for want of anything else—such the siege and
distress to which your enemy will subject you in
your communities.

Plagues

58 If you are not careful to observe all the words
of this law which is written in this book, and to
fear this glorious and awesome name, the LORD,
your God,* 59 * the LORD will bring upon you
and your descendants wondrous calamities, se-
vere and constant calamities, and malignant and
constant sicknesses. 60 He will bring back upon
you all the diseases of Egypt† which you dread,
and they will cling to you. 61 Even any sickness
or calamity not written in this book of the law,
that too the LORD will bring upon you until you
are destroyed. 62 You who were numerous as the
stars of the heavens* will be left few in number,
because you would not obey the voice of the
LORD, your God.

Exile

63 * Just as the LORD once took delight in mak-
ing you prosper and grow, so will the LORD now
take delight in ruining and destroying you, and
you will be plucked out of the land you are now
entering to possess. 64 The LORD will scatter you
among all the peoples from one end of the earth
to the other, and there you will serve other gods,
of wood and stone, which you and your ances-
tors have not known. 65 Among these nations
you will find no rest, not even a resting place for
the sole of your foot, for there the LORD will give

---

†

28:46 *A sign and a wonder*: an ominous example, attracting attention; cf. 29:21–28.

28:60 *He will bring back upon you all the diseases of Egypt*: such as the Lord had promised to remove from the people (7:15); cf. v. 27.

*

28:38–42 Dt 28:18; Lv 26:20; Lam 1:5; Mi 6:15; Zep 1:13; Hg 1:6.
28:43–44 Dt 15:6; 28:12–13.
28:45 Dt 28:15.
28:48 Jer 28:14.
28:49–52 Jer 5:15–17; 6:22–26; Bar 4:15–16.
28:53–57 Lv 26:29; 2 Kgs 6:28–29; Jer 19:9; Lam 2:20; 4:10; Bar 2:3.
28:58 Dt 6:13; Jos 24:14.
28:59–61 Dt 7:15; 28:21–22, 27.
28:62 Dt 1:10; 10:22; 26:5; Jer 42:2.
28:63–67 Dt 4:26–28; 30:9; Lv 26:33–39.

you an anguished heart and wearied eyes† and
a trembling spirit. 66 Your life will hang in sus-
pense and you will stand in dread both day and
night, never sure of your life. 67 In the morning
you will say, "Would that it were evening!" and
in the evening you will say, "Would that it were
morning!" because of the dread that your heart
must feel and the sight that your eyes must see.
68 The LORD will send you back in ships to Egypt,
by a route which I told you that you would never
see again;* and there you will offer yourselves for
sale to your enemies as male and female slaves,
but there will be no buyer.

69 These are the words of the covenant which
the LORD commanded Moses to make with the
Israelites in the land of Moab, in addition to the
covenant he made with them at Horeb.

III. Third Address

Past Favors Recalled

29 1 Moses summoned all Israel and said
to them, You have seen with your own
eyes all that the LORD did in the land of Egypt to
Pharaoh and all his servants and to all his land,
2 the great testings your own eyes have seen, and
those great signs and wonders.* 3 But the LORD
has not given you a heart to understand, or eyes
to see, or ears to hear until this day.* 4 * I led you
for forty years in the wilderness. Your clothes did
not fall from you in tatters nor your sandals from
your feet; 5 it was not bread that you ate, nor
wine or beer that you drank—so that you might
know that I, the LORD, am your God. 6 * When
you came to this place, Sihon, king of Heshbon,
and Og, king of Bashan, came out to engage us
in battle, but we defeated them 7 and took their
land, and gave it as a heritage to the Reubenites,
Gadites, and the half-tribe of Manasseh.* 8 Ob-
serve carefully the words of this covenant, there-
fore, in order that you may succeed in whatever
you do.*

All Israel Bound by Covenant

9 You are standing today, all of you, in the
presence of the LORD, your God—your tribal
heads, elders, and officials, all of the men of
Israel, 10 your children, your wives, and the
resident alien who lives in your camp, from
those who cut wood to those who draw water for
you— 11 to enter into the covenant of the LORD,
your God, which the LORD, your God, is making
with you today, with its curse, 12 so that he may
establish you today as his people and he may be
your God, as he promised you and as he swore
to your ancestors, to Abraham, Isaac and Jacob.
13 * But it is not with you alone that I am making
this covenant, with its curse, 14 but with those
who are standing here with us today in the pres-
ence of the LORD, our God, and with those who
are not here with us† today.

Warning Against Idolatry

15 You know that we lived in the land of Egypt
and that we passed through the nations, that you
too passed through 16 and saw the loathsome
things and idols of wood and stone, of gold and
silver, that they possess. 17 There may be among
you a man or woman, or a clan or tribe, whose
heart is now turning away from the LORD, our
God, to go and serve the gods of these nations;
there may be among you a root bearing poison
and wormwood; 18 if any such persons, after
hearing the words of this curse, should congratu-
late themselves, saying in their hearts, "I am safe,
even though I walk in stubbornness of heart,"
thereby sweeping away moist and dry alike,† *
19 the LORD will never consent to pardon them.
Instead, the LORD's burning wrath will flare up
against them; every curse written in this book
will pounce on them, and the LORD will blot
out their names from under the heavens.* 20 The
LORD will single them out from all the tribes of
Israel for doom, in keeping with all the curses of
the covenant written in this book of the law.

Punishment for Idolatry

21 * Future generations, your descendants who
will rise up after you, as well as the foreigners
who will come here from distant lands, when
they see the calamities of this land and the ills
the LORD has inflicted upon it— 22 all its soil
burned out by sulphur and salt, unsown and
unfruitful, without a blade of grass, like the ca-
tastrophe of Sodom and Gomorrah,* Admah
and Zeboiim,† which the LORD overthrew in his

DT

†

28:65 *Wearied eyes*: cf. v. 32.

29:14 *Not here with us*: this includes future generations. This attitude appears also in 5:3.

29:18 *Sweeping away moist and dry alike*: possibly a proverbial expression: because of Israel's infidelity the Lord will punish the just with the wicked (cf. Gn 18:25), rooting out good plants in irrigated soil, together with worthless plants growing in dry ground.

29:22 *Admah and Zeboiim*: neighboring cities of Sodom and Gomorrah in the Jordan Plain and identified in the tradition as destroyed with them. Cf. Hos 11:8; Jer 50:40.

*

28:68 Jer 42–44; Hos 8:13; 9:3, 6; 11:5.
29:1–2 Dt 4:34, 37–38; 6:21–23; 7:19; 26:5–9.
29:3 Is 6:9–10; Jer 5:21; Ez 12:2; Mt 13:14–15; Mk 4:12; Lk 8:10; Jn 12:40; Acts 28:26–27.
29:4–5 Dt 8:2–4.
29:6 Dt 1:4; 2:31–33; 3:1–3; Nm 21:23–24, 33–35.
29:7 Dt 3:16–17; Nm 32:33.
29:8 Jos 1:7–8; 1 Kgs 2:3.
29:13–14 Dt 5:3.
29:18 Jer 7:10.
29:19 Dt 9:14; 25:19.
29:21–27 Dt 4:25–28.
29:22 Gn 19:24–25; Hos 11:8.

Live It!

"Choose life."

This statement is a powerful summons to all of us who are believers. We live in a culture that is constantly filled and refilled with images of violence and death, especially in the media and entertainment. Many people seem to choose options that lead to death rather than life. Temptations to do so are everywhere. Pope John Paul II spoke often of the "culture of death" so prevalent in the world today.

God calls us to choose life—every time. What options before us lead to life rather than death? What choices give life to others?

Life is what we are called to—a full life, lived out in God's presence, a life lived in service to others. Think about the choices you make each day. Your decision to greet someone or smile at someone can make a big difference. That difference can be life giving. Choose life. It is always the right choice!

▶ Dt 30:19

DT

furious wrath— 23 * they and all the nations will
ask, "Why has the LORD dealt thus with this land?
Why this great outburst of wrath?" 24 And they
will say, "Because they abandoned the covenant
of the LORD, the God of their ancestors, which he
had made with them when he brought them out
of the land of Egypt, 25 and they went and served
other gods and bowed down to them, gods
whom they did not know and whom he had not
apportioned to them.* 26 * So the anger of the
LORD flared up against this land and brought on
it every curse written in this book. 27 The LORD
uprooted them from their soil in anger, fury, and
great wrath, and cast them out into another land,
as they are today." 28 The hidden things† belong
to the LORD our God, but the revealed things are
for us and for our children forever, to observe all
the words of this law.

Compassion for the Repentant

30 1 † * When all these things, the blessing
and the curse which I have set before
you, come upon you,* and you take them to
heart in any of the nations where the LORD, your
God, has dispersed you, 2 * and return to the
LORD, your God, obeying his voice, according to
all that I am commanding you today, you and
your children, with your whole heart and your
whole being, 3 the LORD, your God, will restore
your fortunes and will have compassion on you;
he will again gather you from all the peoples
where the LORD, your God, has scattered you.
4 Though you may have been dispersed to the
farthest corner of the heavens, even from there
will the LORD, your God, gather you; even from
there will he bring you back.* 5 The LORD, your
God, will then bring you into the land your
ancestors once possessed, that you may possess
it; and he will make you more prosperous and
numerous than your ancestors.* 6 The LORD, your
God, will circumcise your hearts† and the hearts
of your descendants,* so that you will love the
LORD, your God, with your whole heart and your
whole being, in order that you may live. 7 The
LORD, your God, will put all those curses on your
enemies and the foes who pursued you.* 8 You,
however, shall again obey the voice of the LORD
and observe all his commandments which I am
giving you today. 9 Then the LORD, your God, will
generously increase your undertakings, the fruit
of your womb, the offspring of your livestock,
and the produce of your soil;* for the LORD, your
God, will again take delight in your prosperity,
just as he took delight in your ancestors', 10 be-
cause you will obey the voice of the LORD, your
God, keeping the commandments and statutes
that are written in this book of the law, when you
return to the LORD, your God, with your whole
heart and your whole being.
11 * For this command which I am giving you
today is not too wondrous or remote for you. 12 It
is not in the heavens, that you should say, "Who
will go up to the heavens to get it for us and tell

---

† **29:28** *The hidden things*: probably the events of the future. *The revealed things*: the covenant and its provisions, including the sanctions of blessing and curse. This aphorism may mean: leave "hidden things" to God; what matters is to keep the law.

30:1–5 Text such as this suggests a postexilic perspective; cf. also chaps. 31–32.

30:6 *Circumcise your hearts*: see note on 10:16.

---

* **29:23–24** 1 Kgs 9:8–9; Jer 5:19; 9:12–16; 16:10–13; 22:8–9.
29:25 Dt 4:19; 32:8–9.
29:26–27 Dt 29:20–21; Dn 9:11–14.
30:1–10 Dt 4:29–31; Lv 26:40–45.
30:1 Dt 11:26–28; 27:11–28:69.
30:2–3 Dt 4:29–30; 6:5; 30:10; 1 Kgs 8:47–48; Jer 24:7; 29:14; 33:26; Ez 39:25; Am 9:14; Zep 3:20.
30:4 Neh 1:9; Is 43:5–7; Jer 31:10; 32:37; Ez 36:24; 37:21.
30:5 Jer 23:3.
30:6 Dt 6:5; 10:16; Ez 11:19–20; 36:26–28.
30:7 Dt 7:15.
30:9 Dt 28:4, 11; 30:2.
30:11–14 Dt 6:6; 11:18; Jer 1:9; Bar 3:29–31; Rom 10:6–8.

us of it, that we may do it?" 13 Nor is it across
the sea, that you should say, "Who will cross the
sea to get it for us and tell us of it, that we may
do it?" 14 No, it is something very near to you, in
your mouth† and in your heart, to do it.

The Choice Before Israel

15 See, I have today set before you life and
good, death and evil.* 16 If you obey the com-
mandments of the LORD, your God, which I am
giving you today, loving the LORD, your God, and
walking in his ways, and keeping his command-
ments, statutes and ordinances, you will live
and grow numerous, and the LORD, your God,
will bless you in the land you are entering to
possess.* 17 * If, however, your heart turns away
and you do not obey, but are led astray and bow
down to other gods and serve them, 18 I tell you
today that you will certainly perish; you will not
have a long life on the land which you are cross-
ing the Jordan to enter and
possess. 19 I call heaven and
earth today to witness against
you:* I have set before you
life and death, the blessing
and the curse. Choose life,
then, that you and your de-
scendants may live, 20 by
loving the LORD, your God,
obeying his voice, and hold-
ing fast to him. For that will mean life for you,
a long life for you to live on the land which the
LORD swore to your ancestors, to Abraham, Isaac,
and Jacob, to give to them.*

> **Choose life, then, that you and your descendants may live.**
> (Dt 30:19)

The Lord's Leadership

31 1 When Moses had finished speaking these
words to all Israel, 2 he said to them, I am
now one hundred and twenty years old* and am
no longer able to go out and come in; besides,
the LORD has said to me, Do not cross this Jordan.
3 It is the LORD, your God, who will cross before
you; he will destroy these nations before you,
that you may dispossess them.* (It is Joshua who
will cross before you, as the LORD promised.)
4 * The LORD will deal with them just as he dealt
with Sihon and Og, the kings of the Amorites,
and with their country, when he destroyed them.
5 When, therefore, the LORD delivers them up to
you, you shall deal with them according to the
whole commandment which I have given you.*
6 Be strong and steadfast; have no fear or dread of
them, for it is the LORD, your God, who marches
with you; he will never fail you or forsake you.*

Call of Joshua

7 Then Moses summoned Joshua and in the
presence of all Israel said to him,* "Be strong
and steadfast, for you shall bring this people
into the land which the LORD swore to their an-
cestors he would give them; it is you who will
give them possession of it. 8 It is the LORD who
goes before you; he will be with you and will
never fail you or forsake you. So do not fear or
be dismayed."*

The Reading of the Law

9 * When Moses had written down this law,
he gave it to the levitical priests who carry the
ark of the covenant of the
LORD, and to all the elders of
Israel.* 10 Moses commanded
them, saying, On the feast
of Booths,* at the prescribed
time in the year for remis-
sion† which comes at the end
of every seven-year period,
11 when all Israel goes to ap-
pear before the LORD, your
God, in the place which he will choose, you shall
read this law aloud in the presence of all Israel.
12 Assemble the people—men, women and chil-
dren, as well as the resident aliens who live in
your communities—that they may hear and so
learn to fear the LORD, your God, and to observe
carefully all the words of this law. 13 Their chil-
dren also, who do not know it yet, shall hear and
learn to fear the LORD, your God, as long as you
live on the land which you are about to cross the
Jordan to possess.

Commission to Joshua

14 * The LORD said to Moses, The time is now
approaching for you to die. Summon Joshua,
and present yourselves at the tent of meeting that
I may commission him. So Moses and Joshua
went and presented themselves at the tent of
meeting. 15 And the LORD appeared at the tent in

DT

†

30:14 *In your mouth*: that is, memorized and recited; cf. 6:7; 11:19. *And in your heart*: internalized and appropriated; cf. 6:6; 11:18.
31:10 *The year for remission*: cf. 15:1–3 and note there.

*

30:15 Dt 11:26–28; Jer 21:8.
30:16 Dt 4:1; 8:1; 11:22.
30:17–18 Dt 5:7; 6:4; 8:19–20.
30:19 Dt 4:26; 11:26–28; 28:2, 15; 31:28.
30:20 Dt 1:8; 4:1, 40.
31:2 Dt 1:37; 3:23–28; 4:21–24; 34:7; Gn 6:3; Ex 7:7; Nm 20:12; Acts 7:23, 30.
31:3 Dt 1:30–33; 3:22, 28; 9:3.
31:4 Dt 2:26–3:7; 3:21–22; Nm 21:21–35.
31:5 Dt 7:1–5; 20:16–18.
31:6 Dt 1:29; 20:3–4.
31:7–8 Dt 1:21; 31:23; Jos 1:6–9; 10:25.
31:8 Ex 3:12; Jos 1:5, 17; 3:7; 2 Sm 7:9.
31:9–13 Dt 31:24–27.
31:9 Dt 10:1–5, 8.
31:10–12 Dt 12:5; 15:1–11; 16:13–15; 2 Kgs 23:2; Neh 8:1–8.
31:14–15 Ex 33:7–11; Nm 12:5.

a column of cloud; the column of cloud stood at the entrance of the tent.

A Command to Moses

16 The LORD said to Moses, Soon you will be at rest with your ancestors, and then this people will prostitute themselves† by following the foreign gods among whom they will live in the land they are about to enter.* They will forsake me and break the covenant which I have made with them. 17 * At that time my anger will flare up against them; I will forsake them and hide my face from them; they will become a prey to be devoured, and much evil and distress will befall them. At that time they will indeed say, "Is it not because our God is not in our midst that these evils have befallen us?" 18 Yet I will surely hide my face at that time because of all the evil they have done in turning to other gods. 19 Now, write out this song* for yourselves. Teach it to the Israelites and have them recite it, so that this song may be a witness for me against the Israelites. 20 For when I have brought them into the land flowing with milk and honey which I promised on oath to their ancestors, and they have eaten and are satisfied and have grown fat, if they turn to other gods and serve them, despising me and breaking my covenant, 21 then, when great evil and distress befall them, this song will speak to them as a witness, for it will not be forgotten if their descendants recite it. For I know what they are inclined to do even at the present time, before I have brought them into the land which I promised on oath. 22 So Moses wrote this song that same day, and he taught it to the Israelites.

Commission of Joshua

23 Then he commissioned Joshua, son of Nun, and said to him, Be strong and steadfast, for it is you who will bring the Israelites into the land which I promised them on oath.* I myself will be with you.

The Law Placed in the Ark

24 When Moses had finished writing out on a scroll the words of this law in their entirety, 25 Moses gave the Levites* who carry the ark of the covenant of the LORD this order: 26 Take this book of the law and put it beside the ark of the covenant of the LORD, your God, that there it may be a witness against you.* 27 For I already know how rebellious and stiff-necked you will be. Why, even now, while I am alive among you, you have been rebels against the LORD! How much more, then, after I am dead!* 28 * Assemble all your tribal elders and your officials before me, that I may speak these words for them to hear and so may call heaven and earth to witness against them. 29 * For I know that after my death you are sure to act corruptly and to turn aside from the way along which I commanded you, so that evil will befall you in time to come because you have done what is evil in the LORD's sight, and provoked him by your deeds.

The Song of Moses

30 Then Moses recited the words of this song in their entirety, for the whole assembly of Israel to hear:

32 1† Give ear, O heavens, and let me speak;
let the earth hear the words of my mouth!*
2 May my teaching soak in like the rain,
and my utterance drench like the dew,
Like a downpour upon the grass,
like a shower upon the crops.
3 For I will proclaim the name of the LORD,
praise the greatness of our God!

4 The Rock—how faultless are his deeds,
how right all his ways!
A faithful God, without deceit,
just and upright is he!*

5 Yet his degenerate children have treated him basely,
a twisted and crooked generation!*
6 Is this how you repay the LORD,
so foolish and unwise a people?
Is he not your father who begot you,
the one who made and established you?*

7 Remember the days of old,
consider the years of generations past.

† **31:16** *Prostitute themselves*: lit., "whore after," a play on the phrase "go after," viz. after other gods.

32:1–43 The whole song is a poetic sermon, having for its theme the Lord's benefits to Israel (vv. 1–14) and Israel's ingratitude and idolatry in turning to the gods of the nations; these sins will be punished by the nations themselves (vv. 15–29); in turn, the foolish pride of the nations will be punished, and the Lord's honor will be vindicated (vv. 30–43).

* **31:16** Dt 32:16–17; Ex 34:15–16; Jgs 2:11–23; 8:27, 33; 1 Kgs 11:1–10; 2 Kgs 17:7–41; Jer 11:9–10; Hos 4:12; 9:1.
31:17–18 Dt 1:42; 32:19–25; Nm 14:42.
31:19 Dt 6:6–9; 31:21; 32:1–43.
31:23 Dt 31:7–8; Nm 27:15–23; Jos 1:1–9.
31:24–25 Dt 31:9.
31:26 Dt 10:1–5; Ex 40:20; 1 Kgs 8:9.
31:27 Dt 9:6–7, 22–24.
31:28 Dt 31:12–13, 19–22; 30:19; 32:1–43.
31:29 Jgs 2:11–23.
32:1 Dt 4:26; 30:19; 31:28.
32:4 Dt 7:9; 32:15, 18, 30–31; 2 Sm 22:3; Ps 18:2, 31, 46; 92:15; Is 17:10; Hb 1:12; Rev 15:3.
32:5 Dt 9:12; 14:1; 31:29; Ps 78:8; Is 1:2–4; Lk 9:41.
32:6 Ex 4:22–23; Is 63:16; 64:8; Jer 31:9; Hos 11:1–4.

Cultural Connection

Hispanics Live the History of Salvation

As Moses did, Hispanics express their faith in the Lord of history:

Lord, you who are the Lord of all,
we, the Hispanic people of the United States,
conscious of being a people with its own identity,
born of common roots,
cultural traditions, language, and faith,
and in diversity united,
direct this prayer to you.

Lord and master of history,
we, a people, as we experience the same hungers and hurts,
make a preferential option for the poor,
and we stand in solidarity with this suffering humanity.

From your creative womb, we have been born;
we are your family, your believing people.
In this moment of grace, we feel ourselves called
to a "prophetic mission";
working together and participating in community,
we speak in your name to church and society.

Raised up as a people, intent on being authors
of our own history,
we walk with hope and in a progressive process.
Together we contribute to the coming of
the Kingdom of God here and now,
struggling to establish the new society, with an economy, relationships, and values based on the love and the justice of your Son, Jesus Christ.

We ask this in company with Mary,
the mother of all believers.
Amen.

(Secretariat for Hispanic Affairs, *Prophetic Voices*, p. 23)

Ask your father, he will inform you,
your elders, they will tell you:*
8 When the Most High allotted each nation its heritage,
when he separated out human beings,*
He set up the boundaries of the peoples
after the number of the divine beings;†
9 But the LORD's portion was his people;
his allotted share was Jacob.*

10 He found them in a wilderness,
a wasteland of howling desert.
He shielded them, cared for them,
guarded them as the apple of his eye.*
11 As an eagle incites its nestlings,
hovering over its young,
So he spread his wings, took them,
bore them upon his pinions.*
12 The LORD alone guided them,
no foreign god was with them.*

13 *He had them mount the summits of the land,†
fed them the produce of its fields;
He suckled them with honey from the crags
and olive oil from the flinty rock;
14 Butter from cows and milk from sheep,
with the best of lambs;
Bashan† bulls and goats,
with the cream of finest wheat;
and the foaming blood of grapes you drank.

15 So Jacob ate and was satisfied,
Jeshurun† grew fat and kicked;
you became fat and gross and gorged.

†

32:8 *Divine beings*: lit., "sons of God" (see also v. 43); members of the divine assembly; cf. 1 Kgs 22:19; Jb 1:6; 2:1; 38:7; Ps 82; 89:6–7. The nations are portrayed as having their respective tutelary deities.

32:13 *The land*: Canaan.

32:14 *Bashan*: a fertile grazing land east of the Jordan, famous for its sleek, strong cattle. Cf. Ps 22:13; Ez 39:18; Am 4:1.

32:15 *Jeshurun*: a term for Israel from *yashar*, meaning "upright"; its use here is possibly ironic.

*

32:7 Dt 4:32–34.
32:8 Gn 14:18–22; Nm 24:16; Jb 1:6; 2:1; Ps 29:1; 47:2; 82:6; 83:18; 89:5–7; Is 14:14; Acts 17:26.
32:9 Dt 7:6; Ex 19:5–6; Ps 33:12; Sir 17:17; Jer 10:16; Zec 2:16.
32:10 Dt 1:31; 2:7; 8:15; Ps 17:8; Prv 7:2; Jer 2:2–3, 6; Hos 2:15; 13:5–6; Zec 2:12.
32:11 Ex 19:4.
32:12 Ex 15:13; Is 43:12; Hos 13:4.
32:13–14 Dt 8:7–10; Ps 81:16.

They forsook the God who made them
and scorned the Rock of their salvation.*
16 With strange gods they incited him,
with abominations provoked him to anger.*
17 They sacrificed to demons, to "no-gods,"
to gods they had never known,
Newcomers from afar,
before whom your ancestors had never
trembled.
18 You were unmindful of the Rock that begot
you,
you forgot the God who gave you birth.*

19 The LORD saw and was filled with loathing,
provoked by his sons and daughters.*
20 He said, I will hide my face from them,
and see what becomes of them.
For they are a fickle generation,
children with no loyalty in them!*
21 Since they have incited me with a "no-god,"
and provoked me with their empty idols,
I will incite them with a "no-people";†
with a foolish nation I will provoke them.*
22 For by my wrath a fire is kindled
that has raged to the depths of Sheol,
It has consumed the earth with its yield,
and set on fire the foundations of the
mountains.*
23 I will heap evils upon them
and exhaust all my arrows against them:*
24 Emaciating hunger and consuming fever
and bitter pestilence,
And the teeth of wild beasts I will send
among them,
with the venom of reptiles gliding in the
dust.*
25 Out in the street the sword shall bereave,
and at home the terror
For the young man and the young woman
alike,
the nursing babe as well as the gray beard.*
26 I said: I will make an end of them
and blot out their name from human
memory,
27 Had I not feared the provocation by the enemy,
that their foes might misunderstand,
And say, "Our own hand won the victory;
the LORD had nothing to do with any of it."*
28 For they are a nation devoid of reason,†
having no understanding.
29 If they had insight they would realize this,
they would understand their end:
30 "How could one rout a thousand,
or two put ten thousand to flight,
Unless it was because their Rock sold them,
the LORD delivered them up?"

31 Indeed, their "rock" is not like our Rock;
our enemies are fools.
32 For their vine is from the vine of Sodom,
from the vineyards of Gomorrah.
Their grapes are grapes of poison,
and their clusters are bitter.*
33 Their wine is the venom of serpents,
the cruel poison of vipers.
34 Is not this stored up with me,
sealed up in my storehouses?
35 Vengeance is mine and recompense,
for the time they lose their footing;
Because the day of their disaster is at hand
and their doom is rushing upon them!*

36 Surely, the LORD will do justice for his people;
on his servants he will have pity.
When he sees their strength is gone,
and neither bond nor free† is left,*
37 He will say, Where are their gods,*
the rock in whom they took refuge,
38 Who ate the fat of their sacrifices
and drank the wine of their libations?
Let them rise up now and help you!
Let them be your protection!
39 See now that I, I alone, am he,
and there is no god besides me.
It is I who bring both death and life,
I who inflict wounds and heal them,
and from my hand no one can deliver.*
40 For I raise my hand to the heavens
and will say: As surely as I live forever,
41 When I sharpen my flashing sword,

32:21 *"No-god" . . . "no-people"*: worship of the gods of the nations brings destruction at the hands of a foreign invader. A false god cannot sustain or protect (cf. Jer 14:22); and though the nations seem "foolish" (see their characterization in such passages as Ps 114:1; Is 28:11; 33:19), they will prove to be anything but nonentities when the Lord stirs them up against Israel (Is 9:10–12). For the "no-" or "not-" construction, see Hos 1:6, 9; 2:1, 25.

32:28–35 The reference is to the nations, not to Israel.

32:36 *Neither bond nor free*: an all-inclusive expression; cf. 1 Kgs 14:10; 2 Kgs 9:8.

32:15 Dt 8:12–18; 31:20; 33:5, 26; Neh 9:25; Is 44:2.
32:16–17 Dt 31:16; Ps 78:58; 81:9; 106:34–39.
32:18 Is 49:15; Jer 2:32.
32:19 Dt 4:24.
32:20 Dt 31:17–18; Nm 6:25–26.
32:21 Dt 28:49–50; Jgs 2:14–15; Is 9:11–12; Rom 10:19.
32:22 Dt 4:24; Ps 18:7–8; 50:3; Lam 4:11.
32:23 Dt 32:42; Ps 7:12–13; 18:14; Ez 5:16.
32:24 Dt 28:21–22.
32:25 Lv 26:25; Jer 6:11; Lam 1:20; 2:21; Ez 7:15.
32:27 Dt 9:26–29; Ex 32:11–14; Ps 74:18.
32:32 Dt 29:23.
32:35 Ps 94:1; Is 59:18; 61:2; Hos 9:7.
32:36 2 Mc 7:6; Ps 9:8; 135:14.
32:37–38 Jgs 10:14; 1 Kgs 18:27; Jer 2:28.
32:39 Dt 4:35; 6:4; 1 Sm 2:6–8; Tb 13:2; Jb 5:18; Wis 16:13; Is 30:26; 43:10–13; 44:6; Hos 6:1–2.

and my hand lays hold of judgment,
With vengeance I will repay my foes
and requite those who hate me.*
42 I will make my arrows drunk with blood,
and my sword shall devour flesh—
With the blood of the slain and the captured,
from the long-haired heads of the enemy.

43 Exult with him, you heavens,
bow to him, all you divine beings!
For he will avenge the blood of his servants,
take vengeance on his foes;
He will require those who hate him,
and purge his people's land.*

44 So Moses, together with Hoshea,† son of
Nun, went and spoke all the words of this song
in the hearing of the people.*

Final Appeal

45 When Moses had finished speaking all these
words to all Israel, 46 he said to them,* Take to
heart all the words that I am giving in witness
against you today, words you should command
your children, that they may observe carefully
every word of this law. 47 For this is no trivial
matter for you, but rather your very life; by this
word you will enjoy a long life on the land you
are crossing the Jordan to possess.*

Moses Looks upon Canaan

48 On that very day the LORD said to Moses,
49 Ascend this mountain of the Abarim,† Mount
Nebo in the land of Moab facing Jericho, and
view the land of Canaan, which I am giving to
the Israelites as a possession.* 50 Then you shall
die on the mountain you are about to ascend,
and shall be gathered to your people, just as your
brother Aaron died on Mount Hor† and there
was gathered to his people,* 51 because both of
you broke faith with me among the Israelites at
the waters of Meribath-kadesh in the wilderness
of Zin: you did not manifest my holiness among
the Israelites.†* 52 You may indeed see the land
from a distance, but you shall not enter that land
which I am giving to the Israelites.*

Blessing upon the Tribes†

33 1 This is the blessing with which Moses,
the man of God, blessed the Israelites be-
fore he died.*
2* He said:

The LORD came from Sinai
and dawned on his people from Seir;
he shone forth from Mount Paran.
With him were myriads of holy ones;
at his right hand advanced the gods.†
3 Indeed, lover of the peoples,
all the holy ones are at your side;
They follow at your heels,
carry out your decisions.
4 Moses charged us with the law,
as a possession for the assembly of Jacob.*
5 A king arose† in Jeshurun
when the chiefs of the people assembled,
and the tribes of Israel united.*

6 May Reuben live and not die out,*
but let his numbers be few.

7 Of Judah he said this:

Hear, LORD, the voice of Judah,
and bring him to his people.†
His own hands defend his cause;
be a help against his foes.*

8 Of Levi he said:*

Give to Levi your Thummim,
your Urim† to your faithful one;

DT

†

32:44 *Hoshea*: a variant of "Joshua." Cf. note on Nm 13:16.

32:49 *Abarim*: probably the mountain range to the east of the Dead Sea.

32:50 *Mount Hor*: on the western border of Seir or Edom; cf. Nm 20:23–28; 33:37–38. Dt 10:6 locates elsewhere the place of Aaron's death.

32:51 Cf. note on 3:26.

33:1–29 This poem, called the Blessing of Moses, consists of a series of poetic characterizations of each of the tribes of Israel (vv. 6–25), introduced (vv. 2–3) and concluded (vv. 26–27) by a theophany; vv. 4–5 lead into the blessing proper; and the poem ends with a blessing on Israel as a whole (vv. 28–29). This catalog of the tribal units of the people Israel resembles the Blessing of Jacob (Gn 49) and the Song of Deborah (Jgs 5, especially vv. 14–18); all three poems seem to date from the early premonarchic period.

33:2 *Gods*: the divine beings who constitute the armies of the Lord, the heavenly hosts (Sabaoth); see note on 32:8. These "holy ones" (v. 3) are the retinue of the Lord, the warrior God, in his march from the southern mountains (Sinai, Seir, Paran).

33:5 *A king arose*: it is unclear whether this refers to divine kingship or the beginning of the monarchy in Israel. *Jeshurun*: see note on 32:15.

33:7 *Bring him to his people*: this probably refers to the isolated position of the tribe of Judah (cf. Jgs 1:17–19); according to some commentators the reference is to the divided kingdom.

33:8 *Thummim . . . Urim*: devices priests used for divination (cf. note on Ex 28:30).

*

32:41 Is 1:24; Na 1:2.
32:43 Dt 32:1, 8; Is 49:13.
32:44 Dt 31:14–15, 23.
32:46 Dt 4:9.
32:47 Dt 4:40; 6:1–2.
32:49 Dt 34:1; Nm 27:12.
32:50 Dt 10:6; Nm 20:23–29; 27:13; 33:38–39.
32:51 Ex 17:1–7; Nm 20:1–13; 27:14; Ps 106:32–33.
32:52 Dt 3:27; 34:4.
33:1 Jos 14:6; Ps 90:1.
33:2–3 Ex 15:14–17; 19:18–20; Nm 10:36; Jgs 5:4–5; Ps 68:7–8, 17; 89:7; Hb 3:3–6.
33:4 Dt 4:44; Jn 1:17; 7:19.
33:5 Dt 32:15.
33:6 Gn 49:3–4.
33:7 Gn 49:8–12.
33:8–11 Gn 49:5–7.

Him you tested at Massah,
contended against him at the waters of Meribah.*
9† He said of his father and mother,
"I have no regard for them";
His brothers he would not acknowledge,
and his own children he did not recognize.
For they kept your words,
and your covenant they upheld.*
10 *They teach your ordinances to Jacob,
your law to Israel.
They bring incense to your nostrils,
and burnt offerings to your altar.
11 Bless, LORD, his strength,
be pleased with the work of his hands.
Crush the loins of his adversaries
and of his foes, that they may not rise.

12 Of Benjamin he said:

The beloved of the LORD,
he abides in safety beside him;
He shelters him all day long;
the beloved abides at his breast.†*

13 Of Joseph he said:*

Blessed by the LORD is his land
with the best of heaven above
and of the abyss crouching beneath;
14 With the best of the produce of the sun,
and the choicest yield of the months;
15 With the finest gifts of the ancient mountains
and the best from the everlasting hills;
16 With the best of the earth and its fullness,
and the favor of the one who dwells on Sinai.
Let these come upon the head of Joseph
and upon the brow of the prince among his brothers.*
17 His firstborn bull, majesty is his!
His horns are the horns of a wild ox;
With them he gores the peoples,
attacks the ends of the earth.
These are the myriads of Ephraim,
and these the thousands of Manasseh.

18 Of Zebulun he said:*

Rejoice, Zebulun, in your expeditions,
exult, Issachar, in your tents!
19 They invite peoples to the mountain
where they offer right sacrifices,
Because they suck up the abundance of the seas†
and the hidden treasures of the sand.

20 Of Gad he said:*

Blessed be the one who has made Gad so vast!
He lies there like a lion;
he tears the arm, the head as well.
21 He saw that the best should be his,
for there the commander's portion was assigned;
he came at the head of the people.
He carried out the justice of the LORD
and his ordinances for Israel.*

22 Of Dan he said:

Dan is a lion's cub,*
that springs away from a viper!

23 Of Naphtali he said:

Naphtali, abounding with favor,
filled with the blessing of the LORD,
take possession of the west and south.*

24 Of Asher he said:*

Most blessed† of sons be Asher!
May he be the favorite among his brothers,
and may he dip his foot in oil!
25 May the bolts of your gates be iron and bronze;
may your strength endure through all your days!

26 There is none like the God of Jeshurun,
who rides the heavens in his power,
who rides the clouds in his majesty;*

---

†

33:9 The reference is probably to the Levites' slaughter of other Israelites after the incident of the golden calf; cf. Ex 32:27–29.

33:12 *Abides at his breast*: an image of security under divine protection.

33:19 *The abundance of the seas*: perhaps the wealth that comes from sea trade or from fishing. *The hidden treasures of the sand*: possibly an allusion to the valuable purple dye extracted from certain marine shells found on the coast of northern Palestine.

33:24 *Most blessed*: Hebrew *baruk*; but the name Asher may suggest a play on the Hebrew *'ashre*, "happy"; cf., e.g., v. 29; Ps 1:1. *Oil*: the land of the tribe of Asher was covered with olive groves.

---

*

33:8 Dt 6:16; 9:22; 32:51; Ex 17:1–7; 28:30; Lv 8:8; Nm 20:1–13; 1 Sm 14:41–42.
33:9 Lk 14:26.
33:10–11 Dt 10:8; 17:9–11; 18:1–8; Ex 30:7–8; Lv 10:11; 2 Kgs 17:27–28; Mal 2:4–9.
33:12 Gn 49:27.
33:13–17 Gn 49:22–26.
33:16 Ex 3:1–6; Jgs 5:6.
33:18–19 Gn 49:13–15.
33:20–21 Gn 49:19.
33:21 Nm 32:1–32; Jos 1:12–15; 1 Chr 5:18–22; 12:8–15.
33:22 Gn 49:16–17.
33:23 Gn 49:21; Jos 19:32–39.
33:24–25 Gn 49:20.
33:26 Dt 32:15; Ps 18:10; 68:4, 33; 104:3; Is 19:1.

27 The God of old is a refuge;
a support are the arms of the Everlasting.
He drove the enemy out of your way
and he said, "Destroy!"*
28 Israel abides securely,
Jacob dwells apart,
In a land of grain and wine,
where the heavens drip with dew.*
29 Happy are you, Israel! Who is like you,
a people delivered by the LORD,
Your help and shield,
and the sword of your glory.
Your enemies cringe before you;
you stride upon their backs.*

IV. The Death of Moses

34 1 Then Moses went up from the plains of
Moab to Mount Nebo,* the peak of Pis-
gah which faces Jericho, and the LORD showed
him all the land—Gilead, and as far as Dan, 2 all
Naphtali, the land of Ephraim and Manasseh, all
the land of Judah as far as the Western Sea,* 3 the
Negeb, the plain (the valley of Jericho, the City
of Palms), and as far as Zoar. 4 The LORD then said
to him, This is the land* about which I promised
on oath to Abraham, Isaac, and Jacob, "I will give
it to your descendants." I have let you see it with
your own eyes, but you shall not cross over. 5 So
there, in the land of Moab, Moses, the servant
of the LORD, died* as the LORD had said; 6 and he
was buried in a valley in the land of Moab, op-
posite Beth-peor; to this day no one knows the
place of his burial.* 7 Moses was one hundred
and twenty years old* when he died, yet his eyes
were undimmed and his vigor unabated. 8 The Is-
raelites wept for Moses in the plains of Moab for
thirty days, till they had completed the period of
grief and mourning for Moses.
9 Now Joshua, son of Nun,* was filled with the
spirit of wisdom, since Moses had laid his hands
upon him; and so the Israelites gave him their
obedience, just as the LORD had commanded
Moses.
10 * Since then no prophet has arisen in Israel
like Moses, whom the LORD knew face to face,
11 * in all the signs and wonders the LORD sent
him to perform in the land of Egypt against
Pharaoh and all his servants and against all his
land, 12 and all the great might and the awesome
power that Moses displayed in the sight of all
Israel.

Moses' Death

Why did Moses die on the brink of entering the Promised Land? This question has disturbed many generations of believers. The one who received God's call to lead the Israelites out of slavery, who amazed Pharaoh with wonders and called down plagues on Egypt, who opened the Red Sea and received the tablets of the Law on Mount Sinai—this great leader did not get to enjoy the success of his work! Numbers 20:11–12 points to Moses' lack of trust and God's subsequent punishment as the reason for Moses not entering the Promised Land. Deuteronomy 34:1–6 simply tells us that Moses died on Mount Nebo and that his burial place was forgotten. Moses' death at the end of Deuteronomy leaves the Israelites on the banks of the Jordan River, still waiting for God's promise to be fulfilled.

We also experience times when we don't get to enjoy the success of our work or are waiting for a promise to be fulfilled. For example, you may volunteer for some project and never really see the results of your time and effort. But that's not the point, is it? We don't volunteer so that we can take credit for the result. Rather we do it because it is a good and right thing to do. We are helping build the Reign of God. So it was with Moses. He had done what he was called to do—no more, no less. And as the Israelites stood on the verge of entering the Promised Land, we too stand on the verge of our final destination—eternity with God in heaven.

▶ **Deuteronomy, chapter 34**

*

33:27 Dt 7:1, 17–24.
33:28 Dt 7:12–16; Gn 27:28; Nm 23:9.
33:29 Dt 4:7–8; Gn 15:1; 2 Sm 22:3; Ps 28:7; 119:114.
34:1 Dt 3:27; 32:49.
34:2 Dt 11:24.
34:4 Dt 1:8; 3:27; 32:52; Gn 12:7; 15:18–21.
34:5 Dt 32:50; Ex 14:31; Nm 12:7–8; Jos 1:1–2, 7, 13, 15; 1 Kgs 8:53, 56; Mal 3:22.
34:6 Dt 3:29.
34:7 Dt 31:2.
34:9 Nm 27:18–23; Jos 1:17.
34:10 Dt 5:4; 18:15; Ex 33:11; Nm 12:8; Sir 45:5.
34:11–12 Dt 4:34; Ex 4:21; 7:1, 8–12.

Introduction to the Historical Books

Have you ever noticed that many older people enjoy telling stories about the past? Sometimes it seems that their past experiences are more real to them than present-day events. Those of us who are younger may get tired of hearing about the "good old days." Still, a lot is to be gained from listening carefully to the memories of our elders. The sixteen historical books of the Old Testament, like the voices of respected elders, tell the stories of God at work in ancient Israel. In reading these stories, we can see more clearly how God works in today's world.

In Depth

The historical books recount the period of Israelite history from 1250 to 100 BC. In those books, we read about the following events:

- the Israelites' settlement in the Promised Land and their struggle to protect themselves from their enemies (the Books of Joshua and Judges)
- the rise of a united kingdom under David (1 and 2 Samuel, 1 Kings)
- the division of the kingdom into northern and southern kingdoms, and the various kings and prophets of each, until the fall of Jerusalem in 587 BC (1 and 2 Kings, 1 and 2 Chronicles)
- the return from Exile and the rebuilding of the nation (Ezra and Nehemiah)
- the Jewish resistance to Greek domination in the second century before Christ (1 and 2 Maccabees)

The historical books of the Old Testament are not like the history books we read in school. Those who write history books today generally try to report the facts with little interpretation. "Let the events speak for themselves," they say. However, those who wrote the historical books of the Old Testament had a different purpose: "Let us tell you what the events *mean in the light of our faith in God.*" Thus, the history contained in these books is often called sacred history because it reveals God's message and God's purpose in history.

Scripture scholars find evidence of two general groups shaping the final form of the historical books. The first group is called the Deuteronomic school of writers because it was responsible for the highly influential Book of Deuteronomy. This group also wrote Joshua, Judges, 1 and 2 Samuel, and 1 and 2 Kings. The Deuteronomists were convinced that God rewarded the good and punished the wicked in this world. Thus, you will find in these books a repeated pattern of (1) God's offer of love, (2) the people's faithlessness and sin, (3) God's just punishment, (4) the people's repentance and cry for help, (5) God's forgiveness and mercy, and (6) the people's repeated sin.

The second group (or person), sometimes called the Chronicler, is responsible for 1 and 2 Chronicles, and probably Ezra and Nehemiah. The Chronicler still emphasized that God rewards the faithful and punishes the unfaithful, but the measurement for what is faithful had changed. Instead of emphasizing faithfulness to the Sinai Covenant, the Chronicler emphasized faithfulness to proper worship, particularly worship at the Temple in Jerusalem. The Chronicler wrote after the return of the exiles to the Holy Land to emphasize the importance of worship in the rebuilt second Temple.

Some of the religious truths you will learn from reading these books are as follows:

- God is not removed from the affairs of this world but cares deeply about what is happening in human history.
- People are happier when they follow the Law of God than when they turn away from the Law.
- All human beings, from the beginning of history, are joined in a common struggle to find sense and meaning in the ups and downs of life.

As you read these books, remember that the authors' understanding of God is not the same as Jesus' understanding. Although not denying the truths about God taught by these books, reading them in light of Jesus' teaching in the New Testament provides a fuller understanding of God's unconditional love and unlimited mercy. For Christians, both the Old Testament and the New Testament shed light on each other; both are the true Word of God.

Other Background

- The Book of Ruth was not originally one of the historical books. It was written later than the books it is now sandwiched between.
- The Books of 1 and 2 Chronicles review the same historical period as 1 and 2 Samuel and 1 and 2 Kings.
- The Books of 1 and 2 Maccabees give overlapping accounts of the Jewish resistance to the Seleucid persecution and the rise of the Maccabees (Hasmoneans) to power as their leaders. 1 and 2 Maccabees are inspired books included in all Catholic Bibles. However, they are not included in many Protestant Bibles. See the sidebar, 'The Case of the Missing Books,' near Tobit 1:16 for a fuller explanation of this difference between Catholic and Protestant Bibles.

When you were young, did you ask to hear your favorite story over and over again? Often familiar stories appeal to us because of their simple justice—good triumphs over evil. There is something reassuring in knowing that in the end, good wins out and evil is punished, no matter how many times we hear it. That is the basic message of the Book of Joshua. In the conquest of the Promised Land, the author reminds us that those who follow God are rewarded, and those who do not are punished, pure and simple.

The Book of Joshua

At a Glance

- **I. Conquest of Canaan (1:1—12:24).**
- **II. Division of the Land (13:1—21:45).**
- **III. Return of the Transjordan Tribes and Joshua's Farewell (22:1—24:33).**

Quick Facts

Period Covered: after the desert wandering, from about 1250 to 1200 BC

Inspired Author: unknown, from the Deuteronomic tradition, the book took its present form in the seventh or sixth century BC

Themes: Israel's conquest of the Promised Land, the triumph of good and the punishment of evil

Of Note: The name Jesus is the Greek form of Joshua, which means "God saves."

In Depth

The Book of Joshua is named after the Israelite hero who succeeds Moses and leads the people in their takeover of the Promised Land. At the beginning of the book, Joshua promises the Israelites they will conquer the land of Canaan and make it their own if they are faithful to the Covenant of Moses. They respond with enthusiasm: "As completely as we obeyed Moses, we will obey you" (1:17). The author describes how by remaining true to the Commandments of God, the various Israelite tribes, under Joshua's leadership, take over the land and settle in it with their families and livestock (see map 2, "The Exodus from Egypt").

Today, biblical scholars doubt that the conquest of the Promised Land by the twelve Tribes of Israel was as complete and easy as it is written in Joshua. Archaeologists have found evidence that Canaanites continued to live in the area after the "conquest." The historical memories preserved in the book were reshaped by subsequent storytellers who lived after the Promised Land had been lost, to emphasize an important lesson of faith: God would preserve the Israelites on their land as long as they obeyed the Commandments. The belief in the triumph of good and the punishment of evil is at the heart of the Book of Joshua. Like Judges, 1 and 2 Samuel, and 1 and 2 Kings, the Book of Joshua is written from the same point of view as the Book of Deuteronomy, which insists that God rewards the just and punishes the wicked in this world (see Dt 30:15–20). The Book of Joshua challenges us to remember that God is our surest hope in all the ups and downs of history.

Joshua

3:14

I. Conquest of Canaan

Divine Promise of Assistance

1 [1]After Moses, the servant of the LORD, had
died, the LORD said to Moses' aide Joshua, son
of Nun: [2]† Moses my servant is dead. So now,
you and the whole people with you, prepare to
cross the Jordan to the land that I will give the
Israelites. [3]* Every place where you set foot I have
given you, as I promised Moses. [4]† All the land of
the Hittites, from the wilderness and the Lebanon
east to the great river Euphrates and west to the
Great Sea, will be your territory.* [5]No one can
withstand you as long as you live. As I was with
Moses, I will be with you:* I will not leave you
nor forsake you. [6]Be strong and steadfast, so that
you may give this people possession of the land
I swore to their ancestors that I would give them.
[7]* Only be strong and steadfast, being careful to
observe the entire law which Moses my servant
enjoined on you. Do not swerve from it either
to the right or to the left, that you may succeed
wherever you go. [8]Do not let this book of the
law depart from your lips. Recite it by day and by
night,* that you may carefully observe all that is
written in it; then you will attain your goal; then
you will succeed. [9]I command you: be strong and
steadfast! Do not fear nor be dismayed, for the
LORD, your God, is with you wherever you go.
[10]* So Joshua commanded the officers of the
people: [11]"Go through the camp and command
the people, 'Prepare your provisions, for three
days from now you shall cross the Jordan here,
to march in and possess the land the LORD, your
God, is giving as your possession.' "

The Transjordan Tribes

[12]* Joshua addressed the Reubenites, the Gad-
ites, and the half-tribe of Manasseh: [13]"Remember
what Moses, the servant of the LORD, commanded
you when he said, 'The LORD, your God, is about
to give you rest; he will give you this land.' [14]Your
wives, your children, and your livestock may re-
main in the land Moses gave you here beyond
the Jordan. But all the warriors among you must
cross over armed, ahead of your kindred, and you
must help them [15]until the LORD has settled your
kindred, and they like you possess the land the
LORD, your God, is giving them. Afterward you

†

1:2–9 The beginning of the Book of Joshua strongly emphasizes the credentials of Joshua as Moses' worthy successor (vv. 2, 3, 4, 7; cf. v. 17; 3:7; 4:14; 5:15). The movement Joshua leads, whereby the Israelites take possession of the land of Canaan, is thus made continuous with the exodus from Egypt, even though (except for Joshua and Caleb) the generation that left Egypt under Moses' leadership has died out (5:4, 6), and the people who will make the land of Canaan the land of Israel are a new generation. Thus the book is at pains to establish the continuity between exodus and conquest.

1:4 The frontiers are as follows: in the south the wilderness of Sinai, in the north the Lebanon range, in the east the Euphrates, and in the west the Great Sea, the Mediterranean. These boundaries are ideal rather than actual.

*

1:3–4 Jos 14:9; Gn 15:18; Dt 11:24–25; 34:4.
1:4 Gn 10:19; Nm 13:17, 21–22; 34:3–12.
1:5 Dt 3:21–22; 31:8, 23; Heb 13:5.
1:7–8 Dt 2:27; 5:29; 17:11, 20; 28:14; Ps 1:1–3.
1:8 Ps 1:2.
1:10–11 Dt 20:5–9.
1:12–18 Nm 32; Dt 3:12–20.

Live It!

Be Not Afraid

"Be strong and steadfast! Do not fear nor be dismayed, for the LORD, your God, is with you wherever you go" (Jos 1:9).

Living proof:

Saint Joan of Arc was a humble, uneducated peasant maiden from fifteenth-century France. Inspired by saintly voices, she overcame numerous obstacles to lead the French troops into battle against British invaders.

Saint Thomas More, a distinguished scholar and lawyer, refused to approve King Henry VIII's divorce and remarriage and establishment of the Church of England.

Dorothy Day, twentieth-century American cofounder of the Catholic Worker movement, challenged all Christians to serve poor and homeless people and dedicated her life to nonviolence.

In 1980, Archbishop Oscar Romero of El Salvador was shot while saying Mass, because he dared to speak against the military groups that were terrorizing and killing the poor people of his diocese.

These four people, along with many others, have taken to heart God's words to Joshua. If you are not familiar with their stories, take time to learn more about these Catholic heroes.

▶ Jos 1:5–9

may return and possess your own land, which
Moses, the servant of the LORD, has given you
east of the Jordan."* [16]They answered Joshua,
"We will do all you have commanded us, and we
will go wherever you send us. [17]As completely as
we obeyed Moses, we will obey you. Only, may
the LORD, your God, be with you as God was with
Moses. [18]Anyone who rebels against your orders
and does not obey all your commands shall be
put to death. Only be strong and steadfast."

Spies Saved by Rahab

2 [1]Then Joshua, son of Nun, secretly sent
out two spies from Shittim, saying, "Go,
reconnoiter the land and Jericho." When the two
reached Jericho, they went into the house of a
prostitute named Rahab,* where they lodged.
[2]But a report was brought to the king of Jericho:
"Some men came here last night, Israelites, to spy
out the land." [3]So the king of Jericho sent Rahab
the order, "Bring out the men who have come to
you and entered your house, for they have come
to spy out the entire land." [4]The woman* had
taken the two men and hidden them, so she said,
"True, the men you speak of came to me, but I
did not know where they came from. [5]At dark,
when it was time to close the gate, they left, and
I do not know where they went. You will have to
pursue them quickly to overtake them." [6]Now,
she had led them to the roof, and hidden them
among her stalks of flax spread out† there. [7]But
the pursuers set out along the way to the fords
of the Jordan. As soon as they had left to pursue
them, the gate was shut.
[8]Before the spies lay down, Rahab went up to
them on the roof [9]and said:† "I know that the
LORD has given you the land, that a dread of you
has come upon us, and that all the inhabitants of
the land tremble with fear because of you.* [10]For
we have heard how the LORD dried up the waters
of the Red Sea before you when you came out of
Egypt,* and what you did to Sihon and Og, the
two kings of the Amorites beyond the Jordan,
whom you destroyed under the ban. [11]We heard,
and our hearts melted within us; everyone is utterly dispirited because of you, since the LORD,
your God, is God in heaven above and on earth
below.* [12]* Now then, swear to me by the LORD
that, since I am showing kindness to you, you in
turn will show kindness to my family.* Give me
a reliable sign [13]that you will allow my father
and mother, brothers and sisters, and my whole
family to live, and that you will deliver us from
death." [14]"We pledge our lives for yours," they
answered her. "If you do not betray our mission,

†

2:6 *Stalks of flax spread out*: to dry in the sun, after they had been soaked in water, according to the ancient process of preparing flax for linen-making. In the Near East the flax harvest occurs near the time of the feast of the Passover (4:19; 5:10); cf. Ex 9:31.

2:9–11 Rahab's speech is Deuteronomic in content and style. Through her, the author expresses a theological conviction: the Lord, the God of Israel, is God above all gods; the formation of the people Israel and its success is the Lord's doing; and all the rulers of the neighboring nations do well to panic at what the Lord is doing (cf. 5:1). Rahab the prostitute is pointedly mentioned in the Matthean genealogy of Jesus (Mt 1:5) and in Jas 2:25.

*

1:15 Jos 22:4; Dt 3:20.
2:1 Dt 1:22; Mt 1:5; Jas 2:25.
2:4 Jos 6:17; Heb 11:31.
2:9 Ex 15:15–16; 23:27.
2:10 Jos 4:23; Ex 14:21; Nm 21:23–26, 33–35.
2:11 Jos 5:1; Dt 4:39; Rom 10:9.
2:12–13 Jgs 1:22–26.
2:12 Jos 2:18; 6:23, 25.

Pray It!

A Prayer Against Prejudice

Creator of diverse people, the Israelites united themselves with Rahab, someone outside their group, and trusted her. Lead me to be open to befriending those who are different from me so that I may learn to trust them as well.

Forgive my friends and me for every time we have looked at someone different and considered her or him to be of lesser quality. Forgive us for each time we have talked about certain people as if we were superior. Forgive our cliques that look down on others and won't associate with them. Help us to forgive those who have looked down on us.

Amen.

▶ **Joshua, chapter 2**

we will be faithful in showing kindness to you
when the LORD gives us the land."
15 Then she let them down through the window
with a rope; for she lived in a house built into the
city wall.† 16 "Go up into the hill country," she
said, "that your pursuers may not come upon
you. Hide there for three days, until they return;
then you may go on your way." 17 They answered
her, "We are free of this oath that you made us
take, unless, 18 when we come into the land, you
tie this scarlet cord in the window through which
you are letting us down. Gather your father and
mother, your brothers, and all your family into
your house. 19 Should any of them pass outside
the doors of your house, their blood will be on
their own heads, and we will be guiltless. But
if anyone in your house is harmed, their blood
will be on our heads. 20 If, however, you betray
our mission, we will be free of the oath you have
made us take." 21 "Let it be as you say," she re-
plied, and sent them away. When they were gone,
she tied the scarlet cord in the window.
22 They went up into the hill country, where
they stayed three days until their pursuers, who
had sought them all along the road without
finding them, returned. 23 Then the two came
back down from the hills, crossed the Jordan to
Joshua, son of Nun, and told him all that had
happened to them. 24 They assured Joshua, "The
LORD has given all this land into our power; in-
deed, all the inhabitants of the land tremble with
fear because of us."

Preparations for Crossing the Jordan

3 1 Early the next morning, Joshua and all the Is-
raelites moved from Shittim and came to the
Jordan, where they stayed before crossing over.
2 * Three days later the officers went through
the camp 3 * and issued these commands to the
people: "When you see the ark of the covenant
of the LORD, your God, which the levitical priests
will carry, you must break camp and follow it,
4 that you may know the way to take, for you
have not gone over this road before. But let there
be a space of two thousand cubits between you
and the ark: do not come nearer to it." 5 Joshua
also said to the people, "Sanctify yourselves, for
tomorrow the LORD will perform wonders among
you." 6 And he told the priests, "Take up the ark
of the covenant and cross ahead of the people";
so they took up the ark of the covenant and went
before the people.
7 * Then the LORD said to Joshua: Today I will
begin to exalt you in the sight of all Israel, that
they may know that, as I was with Moses, so I
will be with you.* 8 Now command the priests
carrying the ark of the covenant, "When you
come to the edge of the waters of the Jordan,
there take your stand."
9 So Joshua said to the Israelites, "Come here
and listen to the words of the LORD, your God."
10 He continued: "By this you will know that there
is a living God in your midst: he will certainly
dispossess before you the Canaanites, Hittites,
Hivites, Perizzites, Girgashites, Amorites, and Jeb-
usites.* 11 The ark of the covenant of the Lord of
the whole earth will cross the Jordan before you.
12 Now choose twelve men,* one from each of the
tribes of Israel. 13 When the soles of the feet of the
priests carrying the ark of the LORD, the Lord of
the whole earth, touch the waters of the Jordan, it
will cease to flow; the water flowing down from
upstream will halt in a single heap."†

JOS

† **2:15** *A house built into the city wall*: the city wall formed the back wall of the house; remains of such houses have been found at ancient sites. The upper story of Rahab's house was evidently higher than the city wall. It was through the window of such a house that St. Paul escaped from Damascus; cf. Acts 9:25; 2 Cor 11:33.

3:13 *Heap*: Heb. *néd*, the same word found in Ex 15:8; the narrative echoes the ancient Song of Miriam (Ex 15:1–18), which celebrates the crossing of the Red Sea. Thus the language provides another parallel between Joshua and Moses, conquest and exodus.

* **3:2** Jos 2:1. **3:3** Nm 10:33. **3:7** Jos 1:5; Dt 31:23. **3:7** Jos 1:5; 4:14. **3:10** Ex 33:2; Dt 7:1. **3:12** Jos 4:2, 4.

The Crossing Begun

14 The people set out from their tents to cross the Jordan, with the priests carrying the ark of the covenant ahead of them. 15 When those bearing the ark came to the Jordan and the feet of the priests bearing the ark were immersed in the waters of the Jordan—which overflows all its banks during the entire season of the harvest—† 16 the waters flowing from upstream halted, standing up in a single heap* for a very great distance indeed, from Adam, a city in the direction of Zarethan; those flowing downstream toward the Salt Sea of the Arabah disappeared entirely.† Thus the people crossed over opposite Jericho. 17 The priests carrying the ark of the covenant of the LORD stood on dry ground in the Jordan riverbed* while all Israel crossed on dry ground, until the whole nation had completed the crossing of the Jordan.

Memorial Stones

4 1 After the entire nation had completed the crossing of the Jordan, 2 the LORD said to Joshua: Choose twelve men* from the people, one from each tribe, 3 and command them, "Take up twelve stones from this spot in the Jordan riverbed where the priests have been standing.* Carry them over with you, and place them where you are to stay tonight."

4 Summoning the twelve men he had selected from among the Israelites, one from each tribe, 5 Joshua said to them: "Go to the Jordan riverbed in front of the ark of the LORD, your God; lift to your shoulders one stone apiece, so that they will equal in number the tribes of the Israelites. 6 In the future, these are to be a sign among you. When your children ask you,† 'What do these stones mean to you?'* 7 you shall answer them, 'The waters of the Jordan ceased to flow before the ark of the covenant of the LORD when it crossed the Jordan.'* Thus these stones are to serve as a perpetual memorial to the Israelites." 8 The twelve Israelites did as Joshua had commanded: they took up twelve stones from the Jordan riverbed as the LORD had said to Joshua, one for each of the tribes of the Israelites. They carried them along to the camp site, and there they placed them. 9 Joshua set up the twelve stones that had been in the Jordan riverbed on the spot where the priests stood who were carrying the ark of the covenant. They are there to this day.

10 † The priests carrying the ark stood in the Jordan riverbed until everything had been done that the LORD had commanded Joshua to tell the people, just as Moses had commanded Joshua. The people crossed over quickly, 11 and when all the people had completed the crossing, the ark of the LORD also crossed; and the priests were now in front of them. 12 The Reubenites, Gadites, and half-tribe of Manasseh, armed, marched in the vanguard of the Israelites, as Moses had ordered. 13 About forty thousand troops, equipped for battle, crossed over before the LORD to the plains of Jericho for war.

14 That day the LORD exalted Joshua in the sight of all Israel,* and so during his whole life they feared him as they had feared Moses.

15 Then the LORD said to Joshua: 16 Command the priests carrying the ark of the covenant to come up from the Jordan. 17 Joshua commanded the priests, "Come up from the Jordan," 18 and when the priests carrying the ark of the covenant of the LORD had come up from the Jordan riverbed, as the soles of their feet regained the dry ground, the waters of the Jordan resumed their course and as before overflowed all its banks.

19 The people came up from the Jordan on the tenth day of the first month, and camped in Gilgal on the eastern limits of Jericho.* 20 At Gilgal Joshua set up the twelve stones that had been taken from the Jordan, 21 saying to the Israelites, "In the future, when your children ask their parents, 'What do these stones mean?' 22 you shall inform them, 'Israel crossed the Jordan here on dry ground.' 23 For the LORD, your God, dried up the waters of the Jordan in front of you until you crossed over, just as the LORD, your God, had done at the Red Sea, drying it up in front of us until we crossed over,* 24 in order that all the peoples of the earth may know that the hand of the LORD is mighty, and that you may fear the LORD, your God, forever."*

---

† **3:15** *Season of the harvest*: toward the end of March and the beginning of April, when the barley and other crops that grew during the rainy season of winter were reaped. The crossing took place "on the tenth day of the first month" of the Hebrew year, which began with the first new moon after the spring equinox; cf. 4:19. At this time of the year the Jordan would be swollen as a result of the winter rains and the melting snow of Mount Hermon.

3:16 Some scholars have suggested that this account may reflect an annual ritual reenactment of the event near the sanctuary of Gilgal.

4:6 *When your children ask you*: reminiscent of the question and response at the Passover meal, Ex 12:26–27.

4:10–18 After the digression about the memorial stones, the author resumes the narrative by briefly repeating the story of the crossing, which had already been told in 3:14–17.

---

* **3:16** Ps 114:3.
3:17 Jos 4:7, 22.
4:2 Jos 3:12.
4:3 Jos 3:13; 4:8–9; Dt 27:2.
4:6 Ex 12:26–27; Dt 6:7, 20–25.
4:7 Jos 3:13, 16.
4:14 Jos 3:7.
4:19 Ex 12:2–3.
4:23 Ex 14:21.
4:24 Ex 9:3; 14:31; 16:3.

Rites at Gilgal

5 1 When all the kings of the Amorites to the
west of the Jordan and all the kings of the
Canaanites by the sea heard that the LORD had
dried up the waters of the Jordan before the Isra-
elites until they crossed over, their hearts melted
and they were utterly dispirited because of the
Israelites.
2 * On this occasion the LORD said to Joshua:
Make flint knives and circumcise Israel for the
second time. 3 So Joshua made flint knives and
circumcised the Israelites at Gibeath-haaraloth.†
4 This was the reason for the circumcision: Of all
the people who had come out of Egypt, every
male of military age had died in the wilderness*
during the journey after they came out of Egypt.
5 Though all the men who came out were cir-
cumcised, none of those born in the wilderness
during the journey after the departure from Egypt
were circumcised. 6 Now the Israelites wandered
forty years in the wilderness, until all the warriors
among the people that came forth from Egypt
died off because they had not listened to the voice
of the LORD. For the LORD swore* that he would
not let them see the land he had sworn to their
ancestors to give us, a land flowing with milk and
honey. 7 * It was the children God raised up in
their stead whom Joshua circumcised, for these
were yet with foreskins, not having been circum-
cised on the journey. 8 When the circumcision of
the entire nation was complete, they remained
in camp where they were, until they recovered.
9 Then the LORD said to Joshua: Today I have re-
moved the reproach of Egypt from you.* There-
fore the place is called Gilgal† to the present day.
10 * While the Israelites were encamped at Gil-
gal on the plains of Jericho, they celebrated the
Passover on the evening of the fourteenth day of
the month.† 11 On the day after the Passover they
ate of the produce of the land in the form of un-
leavened cakes and parched grain. On that same
day 12 after they ate of the produce of the land,
the manna ceased. No longer was there manna
for the Israelites, who that year ate of the yield of
the land of Canaan.*

Siege at Jericho

13 † While Joshua was near Jericho, he raised
his eyes and saw one who stood facing him,
drawn sword in hand.* Joshua went up to him
and asked, "Are you one of us or one of our
enemies?" 14 He replied, "Neither. I am the com-
mander† of the army of the LORD: now I have
come." Then Joshua fell down to the ground in
worship, and said to him, "What has my lord
to say to his servant?" 15 The commander of the
army of the LORD replied to Joshua, "Remove
your sandals from your feet, for the place on
which you are standing is holy."* And Joshua
did so.

6 1 Now Jericho was in a state of siege because
of the presence of the Israelites. No one left
or entered. 2 And to Joshua the LORD said: I have
delivered Jericho, its king, and its warriors into
your power. 3 * Have all the soldiers circle the
city, marching once around it. Do this for six
days, 4 with seven priests carrying ram's horns
ahead of the ark. On the seventh day march
around the city seven times, and have the priests
blow the horns. 5 When they give a long blast on
the ram's horns and you hear the sound of the
horn, all the people shall shout aloud. The wall
of the city will collapse, and the people shall at-
tack straight ahead.
6 Summoning the priests, Joshua, son of Nun,
said to them, "Take up the ark of the covenant
with seven of the priests carrying ram's horns in
front of the ark of the LORD." 7 And he ordered the
people, "Proceed and surround the city, with the
picked troops marching ahead of the ark of
the LORD." 8 When Joshua spoke to the people,
the seven priests who carried the ram's horns
before the LORD marched and blew their horns,
and the ark of the covenant of the LORD followed
them. 9 In front of the priests with the horns
marched the picked troops; the rear guard fol-
lowed the ark, and the blowing of horns was kept
up continually as they marched. 10 But Joshua
had commanded the people, "Do not shout or
make any noise or outcry until I tell you, 'Shout!'

†

5:3 *Gibeath-haaraloth*: "Hill of the Foreskins."

5:9 *The place is called Gilgal*: by popular etymology, because of the similarity of sound with the Hebrew word *gallothi*, "I have removed." Gilgal probably means "circle," i.e., the place of the circle of standing stones. Cf. 4:4–8.

5:10 *The month*: the first month of the year, later called Nisan; see note on 3:15. The crossing of the Jordan occurred, therefore, about the same time of the year as did the crossing of the Red Sea; cf. Ex 12–14.

5:13–6:26 The account of the siege of Jericho embraces: (1) the command of the Lord to Joshua (5:13–6:5); (2) Joshua's instructions to the Israelites, with a brief summary of how these orders were carried out (6:6–11); (3) a description of the action on each of the first six days (6:12–14); (4) the events on the seventh day (6:15–26).

5:14 *Commander*: the leader of the heavenly army of the Lord of hosts is either the Lord or an angelic warrior; if the latter, he is a messenger who speaks in the person of the one who sent him. *I have come*: the solemn language of theophany; cf., e.g., Ps 50:3; 96:13.

*

5:2 Gn 17; 34; Ex 4:24–26.
5:4 Nm 14:29; 26:64–65; 1 Cor 10:5.
5:6 Nm 14:33–34; Heb 3:11, 17.
5:7 Gn 17:8–14.
5:9 Jos 4:19; Eph 2:11–22.
5:10 Ex 12:6; Nm 9:3–5.
5:12 Ex 16:35.
5:13 Ex 23:20.
5:15 Ex 3:5; Acts 7:33.
6:3–5 Nm 10:2–9; 2 Sm 6:15–16.

Then you must shout." 11 So he had the ark of the
LORD circle the city, going once around it, after
which they returned to camp for the night.
12 Early the next morning, Joshua had the
priests take up the ark of the LORD. 13 The seven
priests bearing the ram's horns marched in front
of the ark of the LORD, blowing their horns.
Ahead of these marched the picked troops, while
the rear guard followed the ark of the LORD, and
the blowing of horns was kept up continually.
14 On this second day they again marched around
the city once before returning to camp; and for
six days in all they did the same.
15 On the seventh day, beginning at daybreak,
they marched around the city seven times in the
same manner; on that day only did they march
around the city seven times. 16 The seventh time
around, the priests blew the horns and Joshua
said to the people, "Now shout, for the LORD has
given you the city. 17 * The city and everything
in it is under the ban. Only Rahab the prostitute
and all who are in the house with her are to live,
because she hid the messengers we sent. 18 * But
be careful not to covet or take anything that is
under the ban;† otherwise you will bring upon
the camp of Israel this ban and the misery of it.
19 All silver and gold, and the articles of bronze
or iron, are holy to the LORD. They shall be put in
the treasury of the LORD."

The Fall of Jericho

20 As the horns blew, the people began to
shout. When they heard the sound of the horn,
they raised a tremendous shout. The wall col-
lapsed,† and the people attacked the city straight
ahead and took it.* 21 They observed the ban by
putting to the sword all living creatures* in the
city: men and women, young and old, as well as
oxen, sheep and donkeys.
22 * To the two men who had spied out the
land, Joshua said, "Go into the prostitute's house
and bring out the woman with all her family,
as you swore to her you would do." 23 The spies
entered and brought out Rahab, with her fa-
ther, mother, brothers, and all her family; her
entire family they led forth and placed outside
the camp of Israel. 24 The city itself they burned
with all that was in it;* but the silver, gold, and
articles of bronze and iron they placed in the
treasury of the house of the LORD. 25 † Because
Rahab the prostitute had hidden the messengers
whom Joshua had sent to reconnoiter Jericho,
Joshua let her live, along with her father's house
and all her family, who dwell in the midst of Is-
rael to this day.
26 * On that occasion Joshua imposed the
oath: Cursed before the LORD be the man who at-
tempts to rebuild this city, Jericho. At the cost of
his firstborn will he lay its foundation, and at the
cost of his youngest son will he set up its gates.†
27 Thus the LORD was with Joshua so that his
fame spread throughout the land.*

Defeat at Ai

7 1 But the Israelites acted treacherously with
regard to the ban; Achan, son of Carmi, son
of Zabdi, son of Zerah of the tribe of Judah, took
goods that were under the ban,* and the anger of
the LORD flared up against the Israelites.
2 * Joshua next sent men from Jericho to Ai,
which is near Beth-aven and east of Bethel, with
the order, "Go up and reconnoiter the land."
When they had explored Ai, 3 they returned to
Joshua and advised, "Do not send all the peo-
ple up; if only about two or three thousand go
up, they can attack and overcome Ai. You need
not tire all the people: the enemy there are few."
4 About three thousand of the people made the
attack, but they fled before the army at Ai, 5 who
killed some thirty-six of them. They pursued
them from the city gate to the Shebarim, and
defeated them on the descent, so that the confi-
dence of the people melted away like water.
6 Joshua, together with the elders of Israel, tore
their garments and fell face down before the ark
of the LORD until evening; and they threw dust on
their heads. 7 "Alas, Lord GOD," Joshua prayed,
"why did you ever allow this people to cross over
the Jordan, delivering us into the power of the
Amorites, that they might destroy us? Would that
we had been content to dwell on the other side
of the Jordan. 8 Please, Lord, what can I say, now
that Israel has turned its back to its enemies?
9 When the Canaanites and the other inhabitants

JOS

†

6:18 *Under the ban*: doomed to destruction; see notes on Lv 27:28; Nm 18:14; 21:3.

6:20 The blowing of the horns and the shouting, features of the ritual procession with the ark of the covenant (cf. 1 Chr 15:28; 2 Chr 5:11–14), are the people's counterpart of the Lord's theophany; cf. note on Jgs 5:4–5; and Jgs 7:15–22; 2 Chr 13:15. The Lord gives the victory; this is the theological point of the story.

6:25 The genealogy of Jesus in Matthew (1:2–16) presents Rahab the prostitute as the wife of Salmon (1:5) and so the ancestor of David (Ru 4:18–22) and of Jesus.

6:26 *At the cost of his firstborn . . . its gates*: this curse was fulfilled when Hiel rebuilt Jericho as a fortified city during the reign of Ahab, king of Israel; cf. 1 Kgs 16:34.

*

6:17 Jos 2:4; Dt 20:17; Heb 11:31.
6:18 Jos 7:12, 25; Dt 13:18.
6:20 2 Mc 12:15; Heb 11:30.
6:21 Gn 15:16; Dt 7:2.
6:22–23 Jos 2:13–14.
6:24 Jos 8:2.
6:26 Jos 9:23; 1 Kgs 16:34.
6:27 Jos 1:5.
7:1 Jos 6:18; 22:20; 1 Chr 2:7.
7:2 Nm 13:17–20.

of the land hear of it, they will close in around
us and efface our name from the earth. What will
you do for your great name?"*
10 The Lord replied to Joshua: Stand up. Why
are you lying there? 11 * Israel has sinned: they
have transgressed the covenant† which I en-
joined on them. They have taken goods subject
to the ban. They have stolen and lied, placing the
goods in their baggage. 12 If the Israelites cannot
stand up to their enemies, but must turn their
back to them, it is because they are under the
ban. I will not continue to be with you unless
you remove that which is banned from among
you. 13 Get up, sanctify the people.* Tell them,
"Sanctify yourselves before tomorrow, for thus
says the Lord, the God of Israel: That which
is banned is in your midst, Israel. You cannot
stand up to your enemies until you remove it
from among you. 14 In the morning you must
come forward by tribes. The tribe which the Lord
designates shall come forward by clans; the clan
which the Lord designates shall come forward by
families; the family which the Lord designates
shall come forward one by one. 15 Whoever is
designated as having incurred the ban shall be
destroyed by fire, with all that is his, because he
has trangressed the covenant of the Lord and has
committed a shameful crime in Israel."*

Achan's Guilt and Punishment

16 Early the next morning Joshua had Israel
come forward by tribes, and the tribe of Judah
was designated.† 17 Then he had the clans of
Judah come forward, and the clan of Zerah was
designated. He had the clan of Zerah* come for-
ward by families, and Zabdi was designated. 18 Fi-
nally he had that family come forward one by
one, and Achan, son of Carmi, son of Zabdi, son
of Zerah of the tribe of Judah, was designated.
19 Joshua said to Achan, "My son, give glory to
the Lord, the God of Israel, and praise him by
telling me what you have done; do not hide it
from me." 20 Achan answered Joshua, "I have in-
deed sinned against the Lord, the God of Israel.
This is what I have done: 21 Among the spoils, I
saw a beautiful Babylonian mantle, two hundred
shekels of silver, and a bar of gold fifty shekels in
weight; I coveted them and I took them. They are
now hidden in the ground inside my tent, with
the silver underneath." 22 Joshua sent messengers
and they ran to the tent and there they were,
hidden in the tent, with the silver underneath.
23 They took them from the tent, brought them
to Joshua and all the Israelites, and spread them
out before the Lord.
24 Then Joshua and all Israel took Achan, son
of Zerah, with the silver, the mantle, and the bar
of gold, and with his sons and daughters, his
ox, his donkey and his sheep, his tent, and all
his possessions, and led them off to the Valley
of Achor. 25 Joshua said, "What misery have you
caused us? May the Lord bring misery upon you
today!"* And all Israel stoned him to death.
They burnt them with fire and they stoned them.
26 Over Achan they piled a great heap of stones,
which remains to the present day.* Then the
Lord turned from his anger. That is why the place
is called the Valley of Achor† to this day.

Capture of Ai

8 1 * The Lord then said to Joshua: Do not be
afraid or dismayed. Take all the army with
you and prepare to attack Ai.* I have delivered
the king of Ai into your power, with his people,
city, and land. 2 Do to Ai and its king what you
did to Jericho and its king—except that you may
take its spoil and livestock as plunder.* Set an
ambush behind the city. 3 So Joshua and all the
soldiers prepared to attack Ai. Picking out thirty
thousand warriors,† Joshua sent them off by
night 4 with these orders: "See that you ambush
the city from the rear. Do not be very far from
the city. All of you must be ready. 5 The rest of the
people and I will come up to the city, and when
they make a sortie against us as they did the last
time, we will flee from them. 6 They will keep
coming out after us until we have drawn them
away from the city, for they will think, 'They are
fleeing from us as they did the last time.' When
we flee, 7 then you rise from ambush and take
possession of the city, which the Lord, your God,
will deliver into your power. 8 When you have

† **7:11** *Transgressed the covenant*: the Hebrew word translated "transgressed" appears frequently in the first five chapters where it is used to describe how Israel "crossed" the Jordan River. There is a wordplay here to emphasize Israel's responsibility to follow God to the promised land and so to obey and not transgress the divine command.

7:16–18 *Was designated*: probably by means of the Urim and Thummim; cf. 1 Sm 14:38–42. See note on Ex 28:30.

7:26 *Achor*: "misery," or "disaster." The reference is to the saying of Joshua in v. 25, with an allusion also to the similar-sounding name of Achan.

8:3 *Thirty thousand warriors*: this figure of the Hebrew text, which seems extremely high, may be due to a copyist's error; some manuscripts of the Septuagint have "three thousand," which is the number of the whole army in the first, unsuccessful attack (7:4); the variant reading in v. 12 mentions "five thousand." More likely, the word for "thousand" here and in other military contexts may designate a squad or fighting unit, itself composed of significantly fewer warriors.

* **7:9** Nm 14:13–19.
7:11–12 Jos 6:17–19.
7:13 Jos 3:5; Lv 20:7; 1 Sm 16:5.
7:15 Dt 13:15–16.
7:17 Nm 26:20.
7:25 Jos 6:18; 22:20; Dt 13:15–16; 1 Chr 2:7.
7:26 Jos 8:29; Dt 13:18.
8:1–26 Jgs 20:20–38.
8:1 Jos 2:24; Dt 1:21.
8:2 Jos 6:21, 24; Dt 20:14.

Catholic Connection

The Parts of the Mass

Not long after entering the Promised Land, the Israelites followed Moses' command to renew their covenant with God. They prepared the altar, gathered everyone together, brought out the ark of the covenant, read from the Law of Moses, and agreed to renew the covenant. Through these acts, the Israelites reaffirmed their relationship with God and thanked him for all he had done for them.

Just as the altar was a visible sign of God's presence for the Israelites and their need for rededication and renewal as God's people, the altar is a visible sign of Christ's presence for Christians. Catholics gather around the altar to remember and celebrate Jesus' sacrificial death, his Resurrection, and our New Covenant with God. We gather around the altar as the table of the Lord to share a meal. We remember the story of our faith, and we are joined together as a community of faith. These actions form the structure of the Catholic Mass.

The Mass celebrated by most of the world's Catholics, called the Latin rite, is divided into two main parts: the Liturgy of the Word and the Liturgy of the Eucharist.

The Mass begins with the **introductory rites** where those assembled sing, acknowledge Christ's presence, express sorrow for their sins, and pray. Through these rites, all gather together as one in preparation to hear God's word and receive Christ in the Eucharist.

After the opening, the **Liturgy of the Word** begins with readings from the Sacred Scriptures and the assembly singing a Psalm. After the Gospel reading, the priest or deacon gives a homily, which is a short reflection on the readings. Immediately following the homily, the assembly affirms its faith by reciting the Nicene Creed. The Liturgy of the Word concludes with the community offering prayers of intercession.

The **Liturgy of the Eucharist** begins with the preparation of the altar and members of the assembly bringing up the gifts of bread and wine. The priest then prays the Eucharistic prayer, which gives thanks to God and recalls Christ's saving work. Through this prayer, the bread and wine become the Body and Blood of Christ. In response, those assembled agree to unite themselves to Christ's sacrifice in anticipation of the eternal life God promises by saying "Amen." Next everyone prays the Lord's Prayer and offers one another a sign of peace. Then, members receive the Body and Blood of Christ in communion. The Mass ends with the **concluding rites** when the assembly receives a blessing and is sent forth to live what they have celebrated.

▶ **Jos 8:30–35**

Catechism, nos. 1345–1355

JOS

taken the city, set it on fire in obedience to the
LORD's command. These are my orders to you."*
9 Then Joshua sent them away. They went to the
place of ambush, taking up their position to the
west of Ai, toward Bethel. Joshua, however, spent
that night with the army.
10 Early the next morning Joshua mustered the
army and went up to Ai at its head, with the el-
ders of Israel. 11 When all the troops he led were
drawn up in position before the city, they pitched
camp north of Ai, on the other side of the ravine.
12 He took about five thousand warriors and set
them in ambush between Bethel and Ai, west of
the city. 13 Thus the people took up their stations,
with the main body north of the city and the am-
bush west of it, and Joshua waited overnight in
the valley. 14 The king of Ai saw this, and he and
all his army came out very early in the morning
to engage Israel in battle at the place in front
of the Arabah, not knowing that there was an
ambush behind the city. 15 Joshua and the main
body of the Israelites fled toward the wilderness,
pretending defeat, 16 until the last of the soldiers
in the city had been called out to pursue them.
Since they were drawn away from the city, with
everyone pursuing Joshua, 17 not a soldier re-
mained in Ai or Bethel. They abandoned the city,
leaving it open, as they pursued Israel.
18 Then the LORD directed Joshua: Stretch out
the javelin in your hand toward Ai, for I will
deliver it into your power. Joshua stretched out
the javelin in his hand toward the city, 19 and as
soon as he did so, the men in ambush rose from
their post, rushed in, captured the city, and im-
mediately set it on fire. 20 By the time the army
of Ai looked back, the smoke from the city was
going up to the heavens. Escape in any direction
was impossible, because the Israelites retreat-
ing toward the wilderness now turned on their
pursuers; 21 for when Joshua and the main body
of Israelites saw that the city had been taken by
ambush and was going up in smoke, they struck
back at the forces of Ai. 22 Since those in the
city came out to intercept them, Ai's army was
hemmed in by Israelites on both sides, who cut
them down without any fugitives or survivors*
23 except the king, whom they took alive and
brought to Joshua.
24 When Israel finished killing all the inhabi-
tants of Ai in the open, who had pursued them
into the wilderness, and all of them to the last
man fell by the sword, then all Israel returned
and put to the sword those inside the city.
25 There fell that day a total of twelve thousand
men and women, the entire population of Ai.
26 * Joshua kept the javelin in his hand stretched
out until he had carried out the ban on all the in-
habitants of Ai. 27 However, the Israelites took for
themselves as plunder the livestock and the spoil
of that city, according to the command of the
LORD issued to Joshua. 28 Then Joshua destroyed
Ai by fire, reducing it to an everlasting mound of
ruins, as it remains today.* 29 He had the king of
Ai hanged on a tree until evening;* then at sunset
Joshua ordered the body removed from the tree
and cast at the entrance of the city gate, where a
great heap of stones was piled up over it, which
remains to the present day.

Altar on Mount Ebal

30 † * Later, on Mount Ebal, Joshua built to
the LORD, the God of Israel, an altar 31 of unhewn
stones on which no iron tool had been used,*
just as Moses, the servant of the LORD, had com-
manded the Israelites, as recorded in the book
of the law. On this altar they sacrificed burnt
offerings to the LORD and made communion sac-
rifices. 32 There, in the presence of the Israelites,
Joshua inscribed upon the stones a copy of the
law written by Moses. 33 And all Israel, resident
alien and native alike, with their elders, officers,
and judges, stood on either side of the ark facing
the levitical priests who were carrying the ark of
the covenant of the LORD.* Half of them were
facing Mount Gerizim and half Mount Ebal, just
as Moses, the servant of the LORD, had first com-
manded for the blessing of the people of Israel.
34 * Then were read aloud all the words of the
law, the blessings and the curses, exactly as writ-
ten in the book of the law. 35 * Every single word
that Moses had commanded, Joshua read aloud
to the entire assembly, including the women and
children, and the resident aliens among them.

Confederacy Against Israel

9 1 When the news reached all the kings west
of the Jordan, in the mountain regions
and in the Shephelah, and all along the coast
of the Great Sea as far as the Lebanon: Hittites,
Amorites, Canaanites, Perizzites, Hivites, and
Jebusites,* 2 they gathered together to launch a
common attack against Joshua and Israel.

† 8:30–35 These ceremonies were prescribed in Dt 11:29 and 27:2–26.

8:8 Jos 6:24.
8:22 Dt 7:2.
8:26 Ex 17:11–13.
8:28 Dt 13:16.
8:29 Jos 10:26–27; Dt 21:22–23; Jn 19:31.
8:30–35 Dt 27:1–8, 12–13.
8:31 Ex 20:24–25.
8:33 Jos 3:3; Dt 11:27; 31:9, 12.
8:34 Dt 28:2–68; 30:19; 31:11; Neh 8:2–3.
8:35 Dt 31:12.
9:1 Jos 3:10; 5:1; Ex 3:8, 17; 23:23; Dt 1:7.

The Gibeonite Deception

3 On hearing what Joshua had done to Jericho
and Ai, the inhabitants of Gibeon* 4 formed their
own scheme. They chose provisions for a jour-
ney, making use of old sacks for their donkeys,
and old wineskins, torn and mended. 5 They
wore old, patched sandals and shabby garments;
and all the bread they took was dry and crumbly.
6 Thus they journeyed to Joshua in the camp at
Gilgal, where they said to him and to the Isra-
elites, "We have come from a far-off land; now,
make a covenant with us."* 7 But the Israelites re-
plied to the Hivites,† "You may be living in land
that is ours. How, then, can we make a covenant
with you?" 8 But they answered Joshua, "We are
your servants." Then Joshua asked them, "Who
are you? Where do you come from?" 9 They an-
swered him, "Your servants have come from a
far-off land, because of the fame of the LORD,
your God. For we have heard reports of all that
he did in Egypt* 10 and all that he did to the two
kings of the Amorites beyond the Jordan,* Si-
hon, king of Heshbon, and Og, king of Bashan,
who lived in Ashtaroth. 11 So our elders and all
the inhabitants of our land said to us, 'Take
along provisions for the journey and go to meet
them. Say to them: "We are your servants; now
make a covenant with us." ' 12 This bread of ours
was still warm when we brought it from home
as provisions the day we left to come to you,
but now it is dry and crumbly. 13 Here are our
wineskins, which were new when we filled them,
but now they are torn. Look at our garments and
sandals; they are worn out from the very long
journey." 14 Then the Israelite leaders partook of
their provisions, without inquiring of the LORD.*
15 So Joshua made peace with them and made a
covenant to let them live,* which the leaders of
the community sealed with an oath.

Gibeonites Made Vassals

16 Three days after the covenant was made,
the Israelites heard that these people were from
nearby, and would be living in Israel. 17 The
third day on the road, the Israelites came to
their cities of Gibeon, Chephirah, Beeroth, and
Kiriath-jearim, 18 but did not attack them, be-
cause the leaders of the community had sworn
to them by the LORD, the God of Israel. When the
entire community grumbled against the leaders,
19 these all remonstrated with the community,
"We have sworn to them by the LORD, the God
of Israel, and so we cannot harm them. 20 Let us
therefore let them live, and so deal with them
that no wrath fall upon us because of the oath we
have sworn to them."* 21 Thus the leaders said
to them, "Let them live, and become hewers of
wood and drawers of water† for the entire com-
munity." So the community did as the leaders
advised them.*
22 Joshua summoned the Gibeonites and said
to them, "Why did you deceive us and say, 'We
live far off from you'?—You live among us!
23 Now are you accursed: every one of you shall
always be a slave, hewers of wood and draw-
ers of water, for the house of my God." 24 They
answered Joshua, "Your servants were fully in-
formed of how the LORD, your God, commanded
Moses his servant that you be given the entire
land and that all its inhabitants be destroyed
before you. Since, therefore, at your advance,
we were in great fear for our lives, we acted as
we did.* 25 And now that we are in your power,
do with us what is good and right in your eyes."
26 † Joshua did what he had decided: while he
saved them from being killed by the Israelites,
27 on that day he made them, as they still are,
hewers of wood and drawers of water for the
community and for the altar of the LORD, in the
place the LORD would choose.

The Siege of Gibeon

10 1 Now when Adonizedek, king of Jerusa-
lem, heard that Joshua had captured Ai
and put it under the ban, and had done to that
city and its king as he had done to Jericho and
its king,* and that the inhabitants of Gibeon had
made their peace with Israel, remaining among
them, 2 there was great fear abroad, because Gib-
eon was a great city, like one of the royal cities,
greater even than Ai, and all its men were war-
riors. 3 So Adonizedek, king of Jerusalem, sent
to Hoham, king of Hebron, Piram, king of Jar-
muth, Japhia, king of Lachish, and Debir, king of
Eglon, with this message: 4 "Come and help me
attack Gibeon, for it has made peace with Joshua
and the Israelites."* 5 The five Amorite kings, of

†

9:7 *The Hivites*: apparently the Gibeonites belonged to this larger ethnic group (cf. also 11:19), although in 2 Sm 21:2 they are classed as Amorites; both groups are listed among the seven nations of Canaan whom, according to Dt 7:1–2, the Israelites were to dispossess.

9:21 *Hewers of wood and drawers of water*: proverbial terms for those who do menial work; cf. Dt 29:10–11.

9:26–27 Later on, Saul violated the immunity of the Gibeonites, but David vindicated it; cf. 2 Sm 21:1–9.

*

9:3 Jos 6:21, 24.
9:6 Ex 23:32; Dt 7:2.
9:9–10 Jos 2:10–11.
9:10 Nm 21:25, 33–35; Dt 1:4.
9:14 Nm 27:21.
9:15 Jos 11:19; 2 Sm 21:2.
9:20 Jos 22:20.
9:21 Dt 29:11.
9:24 Ex 23:27–28; Dt 7:1–2.
10:1 Jos 6:21, 24; 8:26–29.
10:4 Jos 9:15.

Jerusalem, Hebron, Jarmuth, Lachish, and Eglon,† gathered with all their forces, and marched against Gibeon to make war on it. 6 Thereupon, the Gibeonites sent an appeal to Joshua in his camp at Gilgal: "Do not abandon your servants. Come up here quickly and save us. Help us, because all the Amorite kings of the mountain country have joined together against us."*

Joshua's Victory

7 So Joshua marched up from Gilgal with all his army and all his warriors. 8 The LORD said to Joshua: Do not fear them, for I have delivered them into your power. Not one of them will be able to withstand you. 9 After an all-night march from Gilgal, Joshua made a surprise attack upon them, 10 and the LORD threw them into disorder before Israel. The Israelites inflicted a great slaughter on them at Gibeon and pursued them down the Beth-horon slope, attacking them as far as Azekah and Makkedah.

11 While they fled before Israel along the descent of Beth-horon, the LORD hurled great stones from the heavens† above them all the way to Azekah, killing many.* More died from these hailstones than the Israelites killed with the sword. 12 It was then, when the LORD delivered up the Amorites to the Israelites, that Joshua prayed to the LORD, and said in the presence of Israel:

Sun, stand still at Gibeon,
Moon, in the valley of Aijalon!
13 The sun stood still,
the moon stayed,
while the nation took vengeance on its foes.*

This is recorded† in the Book of Jashar. The sun halted halfway across the heavens; not for an entire day did it press on. 14 Never before or since was there a day like this, when the LORD obeyed the voice of a man; for the LORD fought for Israel. 15 Then Joshua and all Israel returned to the camp at Gilgal.

Execution of Amorite Kings

16 The five kings who had fled hid in the cave at Makkedah. 17 When Joshua was told, "The five kings have been found, hiding in the cave at Makkedah," 18 he said, "Roll large stones to the mouth of the cave and post guards over it. 19 But do not remain there yourselves. Pursue your enemies, and harry them in the rear. Do not allow them to reach their cities, for the LORD, your God, has delivered them into your power."

20 Once Joshua and the Israelites had finally inflicted the last blows in this very great slaughter, and the survivors had escaped from them into the fortified cities, 21 all the army returned to Joshua and the camp at Makkedah in victory; no one uttered a sound against the Israelites. 22 Then Joshua said, "Open the mouth of the cave and bring me those five kings from the cave." 23 They did so; they brought out to him from the cave the five kings, of Jerusalem, Hebron, Jarmuth, Lachish, and Eglon. 24 When they brought the five kings out to Joshua, he summoned all the army of Israel and said to the commanders of the soldiers who had marched with him, "Come forward and put your feet on the necks of these kings." They came forward and put their feet upon their necks. 25 * Then Joshua said to them, "Do not be afraid or dismayed, be firm and steadfast. This is what the LORD will do to all the enemies against whom you fight." 26 * Thereupon Joshua struck and killed the kings, and hanged them on five trees, where they remained hanging until evening. 27 At sunset Joshua commanded that they be taken down from the trees and be thrown into the cave where they had hidden; over the mouth of the cave large stones were placed, which remain until this very day.

Conquest of Southern Canaan

28 * Makkedah, too, Joshua captured and put to the sword at that time. He put the city, its king, and every person in it under the ban, leaving no survivors. Thus he did to the king of Makkedah what he had done to the king of Jericho. 29 Joshua then passed on with all Israel from Makkedah to Libnah, and attacked it, 30 and the LORD delivered it, with its king, into the power of Israel. He put it to the sword with every person there, leaving no survivors. Thus he did to its king what he had done to the king of Jericho. 31 Joshua next passed on with all Israel from Libnah to Lachish, where they set up a camp during the attack. 32 The LORD delivered Lachish into the power of Israel, so that

†

10:5 *Hebron . . . Eglon*: these four cities were to the south and southwest of Jerusalem.

10:11 *Great stones from the heavens*: the hailstones mentioned in the next sentence.

10:13 *This is recorded*: the reference is to the preceding poetic passage. Evidently the *Book of Jashar*, like the *Book of the Wars of the Lord* (Nm 21:14), recounted in epic style the exploits of Israel's early heroes. *The sun halted*: lit., "the sun stood"; this obscure passage may suppose a longer than natural day caused when the sun stopped moving across the sky, or it may refer to the sun stopping its light-giving function, perhaps through an eclipse. In any case it was seen as a sign that God fought Israel's battle (v. 42; cf. Ex 14:14).

*

10:6 Jos 9:6.
10:11 Jb 38:22–23.
10:13 Sir 46:4; Is 28:21.
10:25 Jos 1:9.
10:26–27 Jos 8:29; Dt 21:22–23.
10:28 Jos 6:21.

on the second day Joshua captured it and put it
to the sword with every person in it, just as he
had done to Libnah. 33 At that time Horam, king
of Gezer, came up to help Lachish, but Joshua
defeated him and his people, leaving him no sur-
vivors. 34 From Lachish, Joshua passed on with all
Israel to Eglon; encamping near it, they attacked
it 35 and captured it the same day, putting it to
the sword. On that day he put under the ban ev-
ery person in it, just as he had done at Lachish.
36 From Eglon, Joshua went up with all Israel to
Hebron, which they attacked 37 and captured.
They put it to the sword with its king, all its cities,
and every person there, leaving no survivors, just
as Joshua had done to Eglon. He put it under the
ban and every person in it. 38 Then Joshua and all
Israel turned back to Debir and attacked it, 39 cap-
turing it with its king and all its cities. They put
them to the sword and put under the ban every
person in it, leaving no survivors. Thus he did to
Debir and its king what he had done to Hebron,
as well as to Libnah and its king.

40 * Joshua conquered the entire land; the
mountain regions, the Negeb, the Shephelah,
and the mountain slopes, with all their kings.
He left no survivors, but put under the ban ev-
ery living being, just as the LORD, the God of Is-
rael, had commanded. 41 Joshua conquered them
from Kadesh-barnea to Gaza, and all the land of
Goshen† to Gibeon. 42 All these kings and their
lands Joshua captured all at once, for the LORD,
the God of Israel, fought for Israel. 43 Thereupon
Joshua with all Israel returned to the camp at
Gilgal.

JOS

Northern Confederacy

11 1 When Jabin, king of Hazor,† learned of
this, he sent a message to Jobab, king of
Madon, to the king of Shimron, to the king
of Achshaph, 2 and to the northern kings in the
mountain regions and in the Arabah near Chin-
neroth, in the Shephelah, and in Naphath-dor
to the west.* 3 These were Canaanites to the
east and west, Amorites, Hittites, Perizzites, and
Jebusites in the mountain regions, and Hivites
at the foot of Hermon in the land of Mizpah.*
4 They came out with all their troops, an army
numerous as the sands on the seashore, and with
a multitude of horses and chariots.* 5 All these
kings made a pact and together they marched to
the waters of Merom,† where they encamped to
fight against Israel.

6 The LORD said to Joshua, "Do not fear them,
for by this time tomorrow I will present them
slain to Israel. You must hamstring their horses
and burn their chariots." 7 Joshua with his whole
army came upon them suddenly at the waters of
Merom and fell upon them. 8 The LORD delivered
them into the power of the Israelites, who de-
feated them and pursued them to Greater Sidon,
to Misrephoth-maim,* and eastward to the val-
ley of Mizpeh. They struck them all down, leav-
ing no survivors. 9 Joshua did to them as the LORD
had commanded: he hamstrung their horses and
burned their chariots.

Conquest of Northern Canaan

10 At that time Joshua, turning back, captured
Hazor and struck down its king with the sword;
for Hazor formerly was the chief of all those
kingdoms. 11 He also struck down with the sword
every person there, carrying out the ban, till none
was left alive. Hazor itself he burned. 12 All the
cities of those kings, and the kings themselves,
Joshua captured and put to the sword, carrying
out the ban on them, as Moses, the servant of the
LORD, had commanded.* 13 However, Israel did
not destroy by fire any of the cities built on their
mounds, except Hazor, which Joshua burned.
14 All the spoil and livestock of these cities the Is-
raelites took as plunder; but the people they put
to the sword, until they had destroyed the last
of them, leaving none alive. 15 As the LORD had
commanded his servant Moses, so Moses com-
manded Joshua, and Joshua acted accordingly.*
He left nothing undone that the LORD had com-
manded Moses should be done.

Survey of the Conquest

16 So Joshua took all this land: the mountain
regions, the entire Negeb, all the land of Go-
shen, the Shephelah, the Arabah, as well as the
mountain regions and Shephelah of Israel,*
17 from Mount Halak that rises toward Seir* as
far as Baal-gad in the Lebanon valley at the foot
of Mount Hermon. All their kings he captured
and put to death. 18 Joshua waged war against all
these kings for a long time. 19 With the exception

†

10:41 *Goshen*: a town and its surrounding district at the southern end of the Judean mountains (cf. 11:16; 15:51); not to be confused with the land of Goshen in northeastern Egypt (Gn 45:10).

11:1–3 *Hazor, Madon, Shimron,* and *Chinneroth*: cities and their surrounding districts in eastern Galilee. *Achshaph* and *Naphath-dor*: southwest of Galilee. *The mountain regions*: in central and northern Galilee.

11:5 *The waters of Merom*: of uncertain identification, perhaps Tel Qarnei Hittin, about seven and a half kilometers west of modern Tiberias.

*

10:40 Dt 20:16–17.
11:2 Jos 12:3.
11:3 Jos 3:10.
11:4 Ex 15:1, 21.
11:8 Jos 13:6.
11:12 Dt 7:2; 20:16–17.
11:15 Dt 7:2; 31:7–8.
11:16 Jos 10:41; 12:8.
11:17 Jos 12:7; Dt 7:24.

of the Hivites who lived in Gibeon, no city made
peace with the Israelites; all were taken in bat-
tle.* [20]For it was the LORD's doing to make their
hearts obstinate to meet Israel in battle, that
they might be put under the ban without mercy,
and be destroyed as the LORD had commanded
Moses.*
[21] † At that time Joshua penetrated the moun-
tain regions and exterminated the Anakim in
Hebron,* Debir, Anab, the entire mountain re-
gion of Judah, and the entire mountain region
of Israel. Joshua put them and their cities under
the ban, [22]so that no Anakim were left in the
land of the Israelites. However, some survived in
Gaza, in Gath, and in Ashdod. [23] * Thus Joshua
took the whole land, just as the LORD had said to
Moses. Joshua gave it to Israel as their heritage,
apportioning it among the tribes. And the land
had rest from war.†

Lists of Conquered Kings

12 †[1]These are the kings of the land whom
the Israelites conquered and whose lands
they occupied, east of the Jordan, from the River
Arnon to Mount Hermon, including all the east-
ern section of the Arabah: [2]* First, Sihon, king
of the Amorites, who lived in Heshbon. His do-
main extended from Aroer, which is on the bank
of the Wadi Arnon, to include the wadi itself, and
the land northward through half of Gilead to the
Wadi Jabbok at the border with the Ammonites,
[3]as well as the Arabah from the eastern side of
the Sea of Chinnereth, as far south as the eastern
side of the Salt Sea of the Arabah in the direction
of Beth-jeshimoth,* southward under the slopes
of Pisgah. [4]Secondly, the border of Og, king of
Bashan, a survivor of the Rephaim, who lived
at Ashtaroth and Edrei.* [5]He ruled over Mount
Hermon, Salecah, and all Bashan as far as the
boundary of the Geshurites and Maacathites, and
over half of Gilead as far as the territory of Sihon,
king of Heshbon. [6]It was Moses, the servant of
the LORD, and the Israelites who conquered them;
Moses, the servant of the LORD, gave possession
of their land to the Reubenites, the Gadites, and
the half-tribe of Manasseh.*
[7]This is a list of the kings of the land whom
Joshua and the Israelites conquered west of the
Jordan, from Baal-gad in the Lebanon valley to
Mount Halak which rises toward Seir; Joshua

†

11:21–23 Most of the land assigned to the tribe of Judah was not conquered by it until the early period of the Judges. See note on Jgs 1:1–36.

11:23 *The land had rest from war*: later passages (15:13–17; 17:12–13) show individual tribes still fighting against the remaining Canaanites. This verse forms the conclusion to the first part of the book.

12:1–24 This chapter, inserted between the two principal parts of the book (chaps. 1–11 and 13–21), resembles the lists of conquered cities which are inscribed on monuments of Egyptian and Assyrian rulers. Perhaps this list was copied here from some such public Israelite record.

11:19 Jos 9:3, 7, 15.
11:20 Dt 2:30; 20:16–17.
11:21 Jos 15:13–14; Nm 13:22; Dt 1:28; 9:1–3.
11:23 Jos 14:1–19:51; Nm 34:2–12; Heb 4:8–10.
12:2–5 Nm 21:21–35; Dt 1:4; 2:24–37.
12:3 Jos 13:20.
12:4 Nm 34:11–12.
12:6 Nm 32:33; Dt 3:12–13.

Did You Know?

The Conquest of Canaan

A strong parallel connects the beginning of the story of Joshua—the crossing of the Jordan River, God's direction and protection of the Israelites (symbolized by the ark), and the renewal of the covenant at Mount Ebal—and the events of the Exodus from Egypt. The parallel reinforces how the conquest of Canaan was part of God's continued liberation of the Chosen People and a key moment in the history of Israel.

As the Israelites moved in on the Promised Land, the Canaanites were one of several groups of people that the Israelites had to deal with. Joshua 12:8 also mentions Hittites, Amorites, Perizzites, Hivites, and Jebusites. But the Canaanites seemed to be the dominant inhabitants. They were primarily an agricultural society and believed that their gods, called baals, controlled the rains, the seasons, and the fertility of the soil. For the Israelites, God was revealed as the only God over all creation and history.

The conquest of the Canaanites through violence might make you wonder what the Israelites believed about God. Basically, they believed that the Canaanite baals were an offense against God. Because the Canaanites would not change, the Israelites felt justified in killing them and taking their land (see "Holy War," near Nm 2:1). Later, Christians would not be able to justify such actions because of Jesus' teaching that everyone is loved by God and that we must love even our enemies. But at the time Joshua was written, God and God's plan for humanity had not yet been fully revealed.

▶ **Joshua, chapter 12**

apportioned their land and gave possession of it
to the tribes of Israel; 8 it included the mountain
regions and Shephelah, the Arabah, the slopes,
the wilderness, and the Negeb, belonging to the
Hittites, Amorites, Canaanites, Perizzites, Hi-
vites, and Jebusites: 9 The king of Jericho, one;*
the king of Ai, which is near Bethel, one; 10 the
king of Jerusalem, one; the king of Hebron, one;
11 the king of Jarmuth, one; the king of Lachish,
one;* 12 the king of Eglon, one; the king of Gezer,
one;* 13 the king of Debir, one; the king of Ge-
der, one;* 14 the king of Hormah, one; the king
of Arad, one; 15 the king of Libnah, one; the
king of Adullam, one;* 16 the king of Makke-
dah, one; the king of Bethel, one;* 17 the king of
Tappuah, one; the king of Hepher, one;* 18 the
king of Aphek, one; the king of Lasharon, one;*
19 the king of Madon, one; the king of Hazor,
one;* 20 the king of Shimron, one; the king of
Achshaph, one;* 21 the king of Taanach, one; the
king of Megiddo, one;* 22 the king of Kedesh,
one; the king of Jokneam, at Carmel, one;* 23 the
king of Dor, in Naphath-dor, one; the king of
Goyim at Gilgal, one;* 24 and the king of Tirzah,
one—thirty-one kings in all.

II. Division of the Land

Division of Land Commanded

13 1 When Joshua was old and advanced in
years, the LORD said to him:* Though now
you are old and advanced in years, a very large
part of the land still remains to be possessed.
2 This is the remaining land: all Geshur† and all
the districts of the Philistines 3 (from the stream
adjoining Egypt to the boundary of Ekron in the
north is reckoned Canaanite territory, though
held by the five lords of the Philistines in Gaza,
Ashdod, Ashkelon, Gath, and Ekron); 4 also
where the Avvim are in the south;* all the land
of the Canaanites from Mearah of the Sidonians
to Aphek, and the boundaries of the Amorites;*
5 and the Gebalite territory; and all the Lebanon
on the east, from Baal-gad at the foot of Mount
Hermon to Lebo-hamath. 6 All the inhabitants
of the mountain regions between Lebanon and
Misrephoth-maim, all Sidonians, I will drive
out before the Israelites;* at least include these
areas in the division of the Israelite heritage,
just as I have commanded you. 7 Now, there-
fore, apportion among the nine tribes and the
half-tribe of Manasseh the land which is to be
their heritage.

The Eastern Tribes

8 * Now the other half of the tribe of Manas-
seh, as well as the Reubenites and Gadites, had
taken as their heritage what Moses, the servant
of the LORD, had given them east of the Jordan:
9 from Aroer on the bank of the Wadi Arnon and
the city in the wadi itself, through the tableland
of Medeba and Dibon, 10 with the rest of the cit-
ies of Sihon, king of the Amorites, who reigned
in Heshbon, to the boundary of the Ammonites;
11 also Gilead and the territory of the Geshurites
and Maacathites, all Mount Hermon, and all Ba-
shan as far as Salecah, 12 the entire kingdom in
Bashan of Og, who was king at Ashtaroth and
Edrei (he was a holdover from the remnant of
the Rephaim). These Moses defeated and dispos-
sessed. 13 But the Israelites did not dispossess the
Geshurites and Maacathites, so that Geshur and
Maacath dwell in the midst of Israel to this day.
14 * However, Moses assigned no heritage to the
tribe of Levi; the LORD, the God of Israel, is their
heritage, as the LORD had promised them.

Reuben

15 * This is what Moses gave to the tribe of
the Reubenites by their clans:* 16 Their territory
reached from Aroer, on the bank of the Wadi Ar-
non, and the city in the wadi itself, through the
tableland about Medeba, 17 to include Heshbon
and all its towns on the tableland, Dibon, Ba-
moth-baal, Beth-baal-meon, 18 Jahaz, Kedemoth,
Mephaath, 19 Kiriathaim, Sibmah, Zereth-shahar
on the knoll within the valley, 20 Beth-peor, the
slopes of Pisgah, Beth-jeshimoth, 21 and the other
cities of the tableland and of the whole kingdom
of Sihon. This Amorite king, who reigned in
Heshbon, Moses had defeated, with the princes
of Midian, vassals of Sihon who were settled in
the land: Evi, Rekem, Zur, Hur, and Reba;* 22 Ba-
laam, son of Beor, the diviner, the Israelites killed
with the sword, together with those they struck
down.* 23 The boundary of the Reubenites was
the Jordan. These cities and their villages were
the heritage of the Reubenites by their clans.

†

13:2 *Geshur*: not to be confused with the large Aramean district of the same name in Bashan (vv. 11–13; Dt 3:14); here it is a region to the south of the Philistine country, since vv. 2–5 list the unconquered lands along the coast from south to north; cf. also 1 Sm 27:8.

*

12:9 Jos 6:2; 8:23.
12:10–11 Jos 10:23.
12:12 Jos 10:23, 33.
12:13 Jos 10:38–39; 15:36.
12:15 Jos 10:29–30; 15:35.
12:16 Jos 8:17; 10:28.
12:17 Jos 15:34.
12:18 Jos 15:53.
12:19 Jos 11:1, 10.
12:20 Jos 11:1.
12:21 Jos 17:11.
12:22 Jos 19:37.
12:23 Jos 11:2.
13:1 Jos 23:1.
13:4 Jgs 3:3.
13:4 Jos 1:4.
13:6 Jos 11:8.
13:8 Jos 12:6; Nm 32:33.
13:14 Jos 14:3–4; Nm 18:20–24.
13:15–31 Dt 3:12–17.
13:15–23 Nm 21:25–31; 32:37–38.
13:21 Nm 21:24; 31:8; Dt 3:10.
13:22 Nm 31:8.

Gad

[24] * This is what Moses gave to the tribe of the
Gadites by their clans: [25] Their territory included
Jazer, all the cities of Gilead, and half the land of
the Ammonites as far as Aroer, toward Rabbah
[26] (that is, from Heshbon to Ramath-mizpeh and
Betonim, and from Mahanaim to the boundary
of Lo-debar); [27] and in the Jordan valley: Beth-
haram, Beth-nimrah, Succoth, Zaphon, the other
part of the kingdom of Sihon, king of Heshbon,
with the bank of the Jordan to the southeastern
tip of the Sea of Chinnereth. [28] These cities and
their villages were the heritage of the clans of
the Gadites.

Manasseh

[29] * This is what Moses gave to the half-tribe
of Manasseh; the half-tribe of the Manassites, by
their clans, had [30] territory including Mahanaim,
all of Bashan, the entire kingdom of Og, king
of Bashan, and all the villages of Jair, which are
sixty cities in Bashan. [31] Half of Gilead, with Ash-
taroth and Edrei, royal cities of Og in Bashan, fell
to the descendants of Machir, son of Manasseh,
to half the Machirites, by their clans.

[32] These are the heritages which Moses gave
when he was in the plains of Moab, beyond the
Jordan east of Jericho. [33] But Moses gave no heri-
tage to the tribe of Levi: the LORD, the God of Is-
rael, is their heritage, as he had promised them.*

The Western Tribes

14 [1] These are the portions which the Isra-
elites received as heritage in the land of
Canaan.* Eleazar the priest, Joshua, son of Nun,
and the heads of families in the tribes of the Is-
raelites determined [2] their heritage by lot, as the
LORD had commanded through Moses concern-
ing the remaining nine and a half tribes.* [3] To
two and a half tribes Moses had already given a
heritage beyond the Jordan; to the Levites he had
given no heritage among them:* [4] the descen-
dants of Joseph formed two tribes, Manasseh and
Ephraim. But the Levites were given no share of
the land except cities to live in, with their pasture
lands for the herds and flocks.*

[5] As the LORD had commanded Moses, so the
Israelites did: they apportioned the land.

Caleb's Portion

[6] * When the Judahites approached Joshua in
Gilgal, the Kenizzite Caleb, son of Jephunneh,
said to him: "You know the word the LORD spoke
to Moses, the man of God, concerning you and
concerning me in Kadesh-barnea. [7] * I was forty
years old when Moses, the servant of the LORD,
sent me from Kadesh-barnea to reconnoiter the
land; and I brought back to him a frank report.
[8] * My fellow scouts who went up with me made
the people's confidence melt away, but I was
completely loyal to the LORD, my God. [9] On that
occasion Moses swore this oath, 'The land where
you have set foot shall become your heritage
and that of your descendants forever, because
you have been completely loyal to the LORD, my
God.' [10] Now, as he promised, the LORD has pre-
served me these forty-five years since the LORD
spoke thus to Moses while Israel journeyed in the
wilderness; and now I am eighty-five years old,*
[11] but I am still as strong today as I was the day
Moses sent me forth, with no less vigor whether
it be for war or for any other tasks.† * [12] Now give
me this mountain region which the LORD prom-
ised me that day, as you yourself heard. True,
the Anakim are there, with large fortified cities,
but if the LORD is with me I shall be able to dis-
possess them, as the LORD promised."* [13] Joshua
blessed Caleb, son of Jephunneh, and gave him
Hebron as his heritage.* [14] Therefore Hebron re-
mains the heritage of the Kenizzite Caleb, son of
Jephunneh, to the present day, because he was
completely loyal to the LORD, the God of Israel.
[15] Hebron was formerly called Kiriath-arba, for
Arba, the greatest among the Anakim.* And the
land had rest from war.

Boundaries of Judah

15 [1] The lot for the tribe of Judah by their
clans fell toward the boundary of Edom,
the wilderness of Zin in the Negeb, in the ex-
treme south.* [2] * Their southern boundary ran
from the end of the Salt Sea,† from the tongue of
land that faces the Negeb, [3] and went southward
below the pass of Akrabbim, across through Zin,
up to a point south of Kadesh-barnea, across to
Hezron, and up to Addar; from there, looping
around Karka, [4] it crossed to Azmon and then

JOS

†

14:11 *War . . . other tasks*: lit., "to go forth and to come in," i.e., to conduct military expeditions and to return after victory; cf. 1 Sm 18:16; 2 Sm 5:2.

15:2 *Salt Sea*: the Dead Sea. The "tongue," a prominent feature of the landscape, is a spit of land thrusting into the Dead Sea from its eastern shore; it is now called by its Arabic name, *'el lisân*, "tongue."

*

13:24–28 Nm 32:34–36. **13:29–31** Nm 32:39–42.

13:33 Jos 18:7; Nm 18:20.
14:1 Jos 17:4; 21:1; Nm 27:19–22; 34:17–18.
14:2 Nm 26:55; 33:54; 34:13.
14:3 Jos 13:8, 14, 33.
14:4 Jos 21:3–40; Gn 48:5.
14:6 Nm 14:24, 30; 32:12; Dt 1:36, 38.
14:7 Nm 14:6–9.
14:8 Nm 13:31–33; 14:24; 32:12; Dt 1:36.
14:10 Nm 14:30.
14:11 Sir 46:1–10.
14:12 Jos 11:21–22.
14:13 Jos 10:36–37; 15:13–19; 21:11–12.
14:15 Jgs 1:10.
15:1 Nm 34:3.
15:2–4 Nm 34:3–12.

joined the Wadi of Egypt† before coming out at
the sea. (This is your southern boundary.) 5 The
eastern boundary was the Salt Sea as far as the
mouth of the Jordan.

The northern boundary climbed northward
from the tongue of the sea, toward the mouth of
the Jordan, 6 * up to Beth-hoglah, and ran north
of Beth-arabah, up to Eben-Bohan-ben-Reuben.
7 Thence the boundary climbed to Debir, north
of the Valley of Achor,* in the direction of the
Gilgal that faces the pass of Adummim, on the
south side of the wadi; from there it crossed
to the waters of En-shemesh and emerged at
En-rogel. 8 Climbing again to the Valley of Ben-
hinnom† on the southern flank of the Jebusites
(that is, Jerusalem), the boundary rose to the top
of the mountain at the northern end of the Valley
of Rephaim,* which bounds the Valley of Hin-
nom on the west. 9 From the top of the mountain
it ran to the fountain of waters of Nephtoah,*
extended to the cities of Mount Ephron, and
continued to Baalah, or Kiriath-jearim. 10 From
Baalah the boundary curved westward to Mount
Seir and passed north of the ridge of Mount
Jearim (that is, Chesalon); it descended to Beth-
shemesh, and ran across to Timnah. 11 It then
extended along the northern flank of Ekron, con-
tinued through Shikkeron, and across to Mount
Baalah, from there to include Jabneel, before it
came out at the sea. 12 The western boundary was
the Great Sea† and its coast. This was the com-
plete boundary of the Judahites by their clans.

JOS

Conquest by Caleb

13 * As the LORD had commanded, Joshua gave
Caleb, son of Jephunneh,* a portion among the
Judahites, namely, Kiriath-arba (Arba was the
father of Anak), that is, Hebron. 14 * And Ca-
leb dispossessed from there the three Anakim,
the descendants of Anak: Sheshai, Ahiman, and
Talmai. 15 From there he marched up against the
inhabitants of Debir,* which was formerly called
Kiriath-sepher. 16 Caleb said, "To the man who
attacks Kiriath-sepher and captures it, I will give
my daughter Achsah in marriage." 17 † Othniel
captured it, the son of Caleb's brother Kenaz; so
Caleb gave him his daughter Achsah in marriage.
18 When she came to him, she induced him to ask
her father for some land. Then, as she alighted
from the donkey, Caleb asked her, "What do
you want?" 19 She answered, "Give me a present!
Since you have assigned to me land in the Negeb,
give me also pools of water." So he gave her the
upper and the lower pools.

Cities of Judah†

20 This is the heritage of the tribe of Judahites
by their clans: 21 The cities of the tribe of the
Judahites in the extreme southern district to-
ward Edom were: Kabzeel, Eder, Jagur, 22 Kinah,
Dimonah, Adadah, 23 Kedesh, Hazor, and Ith-
nan; 24 Ziph, Telem, Bealoth, 25 Hazor-hadattah,
and Kerioth-hezron (that is, Hazor); 26 Amam,
Shema, Moladah, 27 Hazar-gaddah, Heshmon,
Beth-pelet, 28 Hazar-shual, Beer-sheba, and Biz-
iothiah; 29 Baalah, Iim, Ezem, 30 Eltolad, Che-
sil, Hormah, 31 Ziklag, Madmannah, Sansannah,
32 Lebaoth, Shilhim, and Ain and Rimmon; a
total of twenty-nine cities with their villages.

33 In the Shephelah: Eshtaol, Zorah, Ashnah,
34 Zanoah, Engannim, Tappuah, Enam, 35 Jar-
muth, Adullam, Socoh, Azekah, 36 Shaaraim,
Adithaim, Gederah, and Gederothaim; fourteen
cities and their villages. 37 Zenan, Hadashah,
Migdal-gad, 38 Dilean, Mizpeh, Joktheel, 39 La-
chish, Bozkath, Eglon, 40 Cabbon, Lahmas, Chit-
lish, 41 Gederoth, Beth-dagon, Naamah, and
Makkedah; sixteen cities and their villages. 42 Lib-
nah, Ether, Ashan, 43 Iphtah, Ashnah, Nezib,
44 Keilah, Achzib, and Mareshah; nine cities and
their villages. 45 Ekron and its towns and villages;
46 from Ekron to the sea, all the towns that lie
alongside Ashdod, and their villages; 47 Ashdod
and its towns and villages; Gaza and its towns
and villages, as far as the Wadi of Egypt and the
coast of the Great Sea.

48 In the mountain regions: Shamir, Jattir, So-
coh, 49 Dannah, Kiriath-sannah (that is, Debir),
50 Anab, Eshtemoh, Anim, 51 Goshen, Holon, and
Giloh; eleven cities and their villages. 52 Arab, Du-
mah, Eshan, 53 Janim, Beth-tappuah, Aphekah,
54 Humtah, Kiriath-arba (that is, Hebron), and
Zior; nine cities and their villages. 55 Maon, Car-
mel, Ziph, Juttah, 56 Jezreel, Jokdeam, Zanoah,

† **15:4** *Wadi of Egypt*: the natural boundary between Gaza and the Sinai Peninsula.

15:8 *The Valley of Ben-hinnom*: the southern limit of Jerusalem. *Ben-hinnom* means "son of Hinnom." The place was also called Valley of Hinnom, in Hebrew *ge-hinnom*, whence the word "Gehenna" is derived.

15:12 *Great Sea*: the Mediterranean.

15:17–19 The story of Othniel is told again in Jgs 1:13–15; cf. also Jgs 3:9–11.

15:20–62 This elaborate list of the cities of Judah was probably taken from a document made originally for administrative purposes; the cities are divided into four provincial districts, some of which have further subdivisions. For similar lists of the cities of Judah, cf. 19:2–7; 1 Chr 4:28–32; Neh 11:25–30. This list has suffered in transmission, so that the totals given in vv. 32 and 36 are not exact; many of the cities cannot be identified.

15:6 Jos 18:18–19, 22.
15:7 Jos 7:26; 18:16–18.
15:8 Jos 18:16.
15:9 Jos 18:15.
15:13–19 Jgs 1:10–15.
15:13 Jos 14:13–15.
15:14 Nm 13:22; Jgs 1:20.
15:15 Jos 10:38.

57 Kain, Gibbeah, and Timnah; ten cities and
their villages. 58 Halhul, Beth-zur, Gedor, 59 Maa-
rath, Beth-anoth, and Eltekon; six cities and their
villages. Tekoa, Ephrathah (that is, Bethlehem),
Peor, Etam, Kulom, Tatam, Zores, Karim, Gallim,
Bether, and Manoko; eleven cities and their vil-
lages. 60 Kiriath-baal (that is, Kiriath-jearim) and
Rabbah; two cities and their villages.*
61 In the wilderness:† Beth-arabah, Middin,
Secacah, 62 Nibshan, Ir-hamelah, and En-gedi;
six cities and their villages. 63 But the Jebusites
who lived in Jerusalem the Judahites could not
dispossess; so the Jebusites dwell in Jerusalem
beside the Judahites to the present day.*

The Joseph Tribes†

16 1 The lot that fell to the Josephites ex-
tended from the Jordan at Jericho to the
waters of Jericho east of the wilderness; then the
boundary went up from Jericho to the heights at
Bethel.† 2 Leaving Bethel for Luz, it crossed the
ridge to the border of the Archites at Ataroth,
3 and descended westward to the border of the
Japhletites, to that of the Lower Beth-horon, and
to Gezer, and from there to the sea.*

Ephraim

4 Within the heritage of Manasseh and Ephraim,
sons of Joseph, 5 the dividing line† for the heri-
tage of the Ephraimites by their clans ran from
east of Ataroth-addar to Upper Beth-horon*
6 and thence to the sea. From Michmethath*
on the north, their boundary curved eastward
around Taanath-shiloh, and continued east of it
to Janoah; 7 from there it descended to Ataroth
and Naarah, and reaching Jericho, it ended at
the Jordan. 8 From Tappuah the boundary ran
westward to the Wadi Kanah and ended at the
sea. This was the heritage of the Ephraimites by
their clans, 9 including the villages that belonged
to each city set aside for the Ephraimites within
the heritage of the Manassites. 10 But they did not
dispossess the Canaanites living in Gezer;* they
live within Ephraim to the present day, though
they have been put to forced labor.

Manasseh

17 1 * Now as for the lot that fell to the tribe
of Manasseh* as the firstborn of Joseph:
since Manasseh's eldest son, Machir, the father
of Gilead, was a warrior, who had already ob-
tained Gilead and Bashan, 2 the allotment was
now made to the rest of the Manassites by their
clans: the descendants of Abiezer, Helek, Asriel,
Shechem, Hepher, and Shemida; these are the
other male children of Manasseh, son of Joseph,
by their clans.
3 * Furthermore, Zelophehad, son of Hepher,
son of Gilead, son of Machir, son of Manasseh,
had no sons, but only daughters, whose names
were Mahlah, Noah, Hoglah, Milcah, and Tir-
zah. 4 These presented themselves to Eleazar the
priest, to Joshua, son of Nun, and to the leaders,
saying, "The LORD commanded Moses to give us
a heritage among our relatives." So in accordance
with the command of the LORD a heritage was
given them among their father's relatives. 5 Thus
ten shares fell to Manasseh apart from the land
of Gilead and Bashan beyond the Jordan,* 6 since
these female descendants of Manasseh received
each a portion among his sons. The land of Gil-
ead fell to the rest of the Manassites.
7 Manasseh bordered on Asher.† From Mich-
methath, near Shechem, another boundary ran
southward to include the inhabitants of En-Tap-
puah, 8 because the district of Tappuah belonged
to Manasseh, although Tappuah itself was an
Ephraimite city on the border of Manasseh. 9 This
same boundary continued down to the Wadi Ka-
nah.* The cities that belonged to Ephraim from
among the cities in Manasseh were those to the
south of that wadi; thus the territory of Manasseh
ran north of the wadi and ended at the sea. 10 The
land on the south belonged to Ephraim and that
on the north to Manasseh; with the sea as their
common boundary, they reached Asher on the
north and Issachar on the east.
11 * Moreover, in Issachar and in Asher Ma-
nasseh was awarded Beth-shean and its towns,
Ibleam and its towns, the inhabitants of Dor and

†

15:61 *In the wilderness*: in the Jordan rift near the Dead Sea.

16:1–17:18 After the boundaries and cities of Judah, the most important tribe, are given, the land of the next most important group, the two Joseph tribes of Ephraim and Manasseh, is described, though it was separated from Judah by the territories of Benjamin (18:11–20) and Dan (19:40–48).

16:1–3 This line formed the southern boundary of Ephraim and the northern boundaries of Benjamin and of Dan.

16:5 *The dividing line*: separating Ephraim from Manasseh. Ephraim's northern border (v. 5) is given in an east-to-west direction; its eastern border (vv. 6–7) in a north-to-south direction.

17:7 *Manasseh bordered on Asher*: only at the extreme north-western section of Manasseh's territory. The boundary given in the following sentences (vv. 7–10) is a more detailed description of the one already mentioned in 16:5–7, as separating Manasseh from Ephraim.

*

15:60 Jos 18:14.
15:63 Jgs 1:21; 2 Sm 5:6.
16:3 Jos 10:10, 33.
16:5 Jos 18:13.
16:6–9 Jos 17:7–9.
16:10 Jgs 1:29.
17:1–3 Nm 26:29–33.
17:1 Gn 41:51; 46:20; 48:18; 50:23; Dt 3:13, 15.
17:3–6 Nm 27:1–7; 36:2.
17:5 Nm 13:30–31.
17:9 Jos 16:8–9.
17:11 1 Chr 7:29.

its towns, the inhabitants of Endor and its towns,
the inhabitants of Taanach and its towns, the in-
habitants of Megiddo and its towns (the third is
Naphath-dor). 12 Since the Manassites were not
able to dispossess these cities, the Canaanites
continued to inhabit this region. 13 When the Is-
raelites grew stronger they put the Canaanites to
forced labor, but they did not dispossess them.

Protest of Joseph Tribes

14 The descendants of Joseph said to Joshua,
"Why have you given us only one lot and one
share as our heritage?* Our people are too
many, because of the extent to which the LORD
has blessed us." 15 Joshua answered them, "If you
are too many, go up to the forest and clear out a
place for yourselves there in the land of the Per-
izzites and Rephaim, since the mountain regions
of Ephraim are so narrow." 16 For the Josephites
said, "Our mountain regions are not enough for
us; on the other hand, the Canaanites living in
the valley region all have iron chariots, in partic-
ular those in Beth-shean and its towns, and those
in the valley of Jezreel." 17 Joshua therefore said
to Ephraim and Manasseh, the house of Joseph,
"You are a numerous people and very strong.
You shall not have merely one share, 18 for the
mountain region which is now forest shall be
yours when you clear it. Its adjacent land shall
also be yours if, despite their strength and iron
chariots, you dispossess the Canaanites."

JOS

18 1 The whole community of the Israelites
assembled at Shiloh, where they set up
the tent of meeting; and the land was subdued
before them.*

The Seven Remaining Portions

2 There remained seven tribes among the Is-
raelites that had not yet received their heritage.
3 Joshua therefore said to the Israelites, "How
much longer will you put off taking steps to pos-
sess the land which the LORD, the God of your
ancestors, has given you? 4 Choose three represen-
tatives from each of your tribes; I will send them
to go throughout the land and describe it for
purposes of acquiring their heritage. When they
return to me 5 you shall divide it into seven parts.
Judah is to retain its territory in the south,* and
the house of Joseph its territory in the north. 6 You
shall bring to me here the description of the land
in seven sections. I will then cast lots for you here
before the LORD, our God. 7 For the Levites have
no share among you,* because the priesthood
of the LORD is their heritage; while Gad, Reuben,
and the half-tribe of Manasseh have already re-
ceived the heritage east of the Jordan which Mo-
ses, the servant of the LORD, gave them."
8 When those who were to describe the land
were ready for their journey, Joshua commanded
them, "Go throughout the land and describe it;
return to me and I will cast lots for you here be-
fore the LORD in Shiloh." 9 So they went through
the land, described its cities in writing in seven
sections, and returned to Joshua in the camp at
Shiloh. 10 Joshua then cast lots for them before
the LORD in Shiloh, and divided up the land for
the Israelites into their separate shares.

Benjamin

11 One lot fell to the tribe of Benjaminites by
their clans. The territory allotted them lay be-
tween the descendants of Judah and those of
Joseph. 12 * Their northern boundary† began at
the Jordan and went over the northern flank of
Jericho, up westward into the mountains, until
it reached the wilderness of Beth-aven. 13 From
there it crossed over to the southern flank of Luz
(that is, Bethel). Then it ran down to Ataroth-
addar, on the mountaintop south of Lower Beth-
horon.* 14 For the western border, the boundary
line swung south from the mountaintop op-
posite Beth-horon until it reached Kiriath-baal
(that is, Kiriath-jearim; this city belonged to the
Judahites). This was the western boundary. 15 The
southern boundary began at the limits of Kiriath-
jearim and projected to the spring at Nephtoah.
16 * It went down to the edge of the mountain
on the north of the Valley of Rephaim, where it
faces the Valley of Ben-hinnom; and continuing
down the Valley of Hinnom along the southern
flank of the Jebusites, reached En-rogel. 17 Inclin-
ing to the north, it extended to En-shemesh, and
thence to Geliloth, opposite the pass of Adum-
mim. Then it dropped to Eben-Bohan-ben-Reu-
ben, 18 across the northern flank of the Arabah
overlook, down into the Arabah. 19 From there
the boundary continued across the northern
flank of Beth-hoglah and extended northward to
the tongue of the Salt Sea, toward the southern
end of the Jordan. This was the southern bound-
ary. 20 The Jordan bounded it on the east. This

† **18:12–20** Benjamin's northern boundary (vv. 12–13) corresponded to part of the southern boundary of Ephraim (16:1–2). Their western border (v. 14) was the eastern border of Dan (cf. 19:40–47). Their southern boundary (vv. 15–19) corresponded to part of the northern boundary of Judah (15:5–9).

* **17:14** Jos 16:4; Gn 48:19–22. **18:1** Jos 11:23; 14:15; 19:51. **18:5** Jos 15:1–17:18. **18:7** Jos 13:8, 33. **18:12–13** Jos 16:1–5. **18:13** Gn 28:19. **18:16–18** Jos 15:6–8.

was how the heritage of the Benjaminites by their
clans was bounded on all sides.
21 Now the cities belonging to the tribe of
the Benjaminites by their clans were: Jericho,
Beth-hoglah, Emek-keziz, 22 Beth-arabah, Zema-
raim, Bethel, 23 Avvim, Parah, Ophra, 24 Chephar-
ammoni, Ophni, and Geba; twelve cities and
their villages. 25 Also Gibeon, Ramah, Beeroth,
26 Mizpeh, Chephirah, Mozah, 27 Rekem, Irpeel,
Taralah, 28 Zela, Haeleph, the Jebusite city (that
is, Jerusalem), Gibeah, and Kiriath; fourteen cit-
ies and their villages. This was the heritage of the
clans of Benjaminites.

Simeon

19 1 The second lot fell to Simeon. The her-
itage of the tribe of Simeonites by their
clans lay within that of the Judahites. 2 * For
their heritage they received Beer-sheba, Shema,
Moladah, 3 Hazar-shual, Balah, Ezem, 4 Eltolad,
Bethul, Hormah, 5 Ziklag, Bethmar-caboth, Ha-
zar-susah, 6 Beth-lebaoth, and Sharuhen; thirteen
cities and their villages. 7 Also Ain, Rimmon,
Ether, and Ashan; four cities and their villages,
8 besides all the villages around these cities as
far as Baalath-beer (that is, Ramoth-negeb). This
was the heritage of the tribe of the Simeonites by
their clans. 9 This heritage of the Simeonites was
within the confines of the Judahites; for since the
portion of the latter was too large for them, the
Simeonites obtained their heritage within it.

Zebulun

10 † The third lot fell to the Zebulunites by
their clans. The boundary of their heritage was
at Sarid. 11 Their boundary went up west and
through Mareal, reaching Dabbesheth and the
wadi that is near Jokneam. 12 From Sarid east-
ward it ran to the district of Chisloth-tabor, on
to Daberath, and up to Japhia. 13 From there it
continued eastward to Gath-hepher and to Eth-
kazin, extended to Rimmon, and turned to Neah.
14 Skirting north of Hannathon, the boundary
ended at the valley of Iphtahel. 15 Thus, with Kat-
tath, Nahalal, Shimron, Idalah, and Bethlehem,
there were twelve cities and their villages. 16 This
was the heritage of the Zebulunites by their
clans, these cities and their villages.

Issachar

17 † The fourth lot fell to Issachar. The territory
of the Issacharites by their clans 18 included Jez-
reel, Chesulloth, Shunem, 19 Hapharaim, Shion,
Anaharath, 20 Rabbith, Kishion, Ebez, 21 Remeth,
En-gannim, En-haddah, and Beth-pazzez. 22 The
boundary reached Tabor, Shahazumah, and
Beth-shemesh, ending at the Jordan: sixteen cit-
ies and their villages. 23 This was the heritage of
the Issacharites by their clans, these cities and
their villages.

Asher

24 † The fifth lot fell to the Asherites by their
clans. 25 Their territory included Helkath, Hali,
Beten, Achshaph, 26 Allammelech, Amad, and
Mishal, and reached Carmel on the west, and
Shihor-libnath. 27 In the other direction, it ran
eastward of Beth-dagon, reached Zebulun and the
valley of Iphtahel; then north of Beth-emek and
Neiel, it extended northward to Cabul, 28 Ebron,
Rehob,* Hammon, and Kanah, near Greater Si-
don. 29 Then the boundary turned back to Ramah
and to the fortress city of Tyre; thence it cut back
to Hosah and ended at the sea. Thus, with Maha-
lab, Achzib, 30 Ummah, Acco, Aphek, and Rehob,
there were twenty-two cities and their villages.
31 This was the heritage of the tribe of the Asher-
ites by their clans, these cities and their villages.

Naphtali

32 † The sixth lot fell to the Naphtalites. 33 Their
boundary extended from Heleph, from the oak
at Zaanannim, including Adami-nekeb and Jab-
neel, to Lakkum, and ended at the Jordan. 34 In
the opposite direction, westerly, it ran through
Aznoth-tabor and from there extended to Huk-
kok; it reached Zebulun on the south, Asher on
the west, and the Jordan on the east. 35 The forti-
fied cities were Ziddim, Zer, Hammath, Rakkath,
Chinnereth, 36 Adamah, Ramah, Hazor, 37 Ke-
desh, Edrei, En-hazor, 38 Yiron, Migdal-el, Ho-
rem, Beth-anath, and Beth-shemesh;* nineteen

†

19:10–16 Zebulun's territory was in the central section of the Jezreel Valley and of southern Galilee; it was bounded on the south by Manasseh, on the southeast by Issachar, on the northeast and north by Naphtali, and on the west by Asher. The site of the later city of Nazareth was within its borders. Bethlehem of Zebulun was, of course, distinct from the city of the same name in Judah. *Twelve cities*: apparently seven of the names are missing from v. 15, unless some of the places mentioned in vv. 12–14 are to be included in the number.

19:17–23 Issachar's land was on the eastern watershed of the Jezreel Valley, but also included the southeastern end of the Galilean mountains. It was surrounded by Manasseh on the south and east, by Naphtali on the north, and by Zebulun on the west. Jezreel (v. 18) dominated the valley to which it gave its name, the later form of which was Esdraelon.

19:24–31 Asher inherited the western slope of the Galilean hills as far as the Mediterranean, with Manasseh to the south, Zebulun and Naphtali to the east, and Phoenicia to the north.

19:32–39 Naphtali received eastern Galilee; Asher was to the west and Zebulun and Issachar were to the south, while the upper Jordan and Mount Hermon formed the eastern border. Part of the tribe of Dan later on occupied the northern extremity of Naphtali's lands, at the sources of the Jordan (v. 47).

*

19:2–8 1 Chr 4:28–33.
19:28–30 Jgs 1:31.
19:38 Jgs 1:33.

cities and their villages. 39This was the heritage of the tribe of the Naphtalites by their clans, these cities and their villages.

Dan

40† The seventh lot fell to the tribe of Danites by their clans. 41Their heritage was the territory of Zorah, Eshtaol, Ir-shemesh, 42Shaalabbin, Aijalon, Ithlah,* 43Elon, Timnah, Ekron, 44Eltekoh, Gibbethon, Baalath, 45Jehud, Bene-berak, Gath-rimmon, 46Me-jarkon, and Rakkon, with the coast at Joppa. 47* But the territory of the Danites was too small for them; so the Danites marched up and attacked Leshem,† which they captured and put to the sword. Once they had taken possession of Leshem, they dwelt there and named it after their ancestor Dan. 48This was the heritage of the tribe of the Danites by their clans, these cities and their villages.

Joshua's City

49When the last of them had received the portions of the land they were to inherit, the Israelites assigned a heritage in their midst to Joshua, son of Nun. 50According to the command of the LORD, they gave him the city he requested, Timnah-serah* in the mountain region of Ephraim. He rebuilt the city and made it his home.

51These are the heritages which Eleazar the priest, Joshua, son of Nun, and the heads of families in the tribes of the Israelites apportioned by lot in the presence of the LORD, at the door of the tent of meeting in Shiloh. Thus they finished dividing the land.

Cities of Refuge

20 1* The LORD said to Joshua:† 2Tell the Israelites: Designate for yourselves the cities of refuge of which I spoke to you through Moses, 3to which anyone guilty of inadvertent and unintentional homicide may flee for asylum from the avenger of blood. 4To one of these cities the killer shall flee, and standing at the entrance of the city gate, shall plead his case in the hearing of the elders of the city, who must receive him and assign him a place in which to live among them. 5Though the avenger of blood pursues him, they shall not deliver up to him the one who killed a neighbor unintentionally, when there had been no hatred previously. 6Once he has stood judgment before the community, he shall live on in that city until the death of the high priest who is in office at the time. Then the killer may return home to the city from where he originally fled.

List of Cities

7So they set apart Kedesh in Galilee in the mountain region of Naphtali, Shechem in the mountain region of Ephraim, and Kiriath-arba (that is, Hebron) in the mountain region of Judah.* 8And beyond the Jordan east of Jericho they designated Bezer in the wilderness on the tableland in the tribe of Reuben, Ramoth in Gilead in the tribe of Gad, and Golan in Bashan in the tribe of Manasseh.* 9These are the designated cities to which any Israelite or alien residing among them who had killed a person unintentionally might flee to escape death at the hand of the avenger of blood, until the killer could appear before the community.

Levitical Cities

21 1The heads of the Levite families† approached Eleazar the priest, Joshua, son of Nun, and the heads of families of the other tribes of the Israelites* 2at Shiloh in the land of Canaan, and said to them, "The LORD commanded, through Moses, that cities be given us to dwell in, with pasture lands for our livestock."* 3Out of their own heritage, according to the command of the LORD, the Israelites gave the Levites the following cities with their pasture lands.

4When the first lot among the Levites fell to the clans of the Kohathites, the descendants of Aaron the priest obtained by lot from the tribes of Judah, Simeon, and Benjamin, thirteen cities. 5From the clans of the tribe of Ephraim, from the tribe of Dan, and from the half-tribe of Manasseh, the rest of the Kohathites obtained by lot ten cities.* 6From the clans of the tribe of Issachar, from the tribe of Asher, from the tribe of Naphtali, and from the half-tribe of Manasseh, the Gershonites obtained by lot thirteen cities. 7From the tribes of Reuben, Gad, and Zebulun, the clans of the Merarites obtained twelve cities. 8These cities with their pasture lands the

---

† **19:40–46** The original territory of Dan was a small enclave between Judah, Benjamin, Ephraim, and the Philistines.

19:47 *Leshem*: called Laish in Jgs 18, where the story of the migration of the Danites is told at greater length.

20:1–9 The laws concerning the cities of refuge are given in Nm 35:9–28; Dt 19:1–13; see notes on Nm 35:16–25; Dt 19:2.

21:1 The order to establish special cities for the Levites is given in Nm 35:1–8. The forty-eight cities listed here were hardly the exclusive possession of the Levites; at least the more important of them, such as Hebron, Shechem, and Ramoth in Gilead, were certainly peopled for the most part by the tribe in whose territory they were situated. But in all these cities the Levites had special property rights which they did not possess in other cities; cf. Lv 25:32–34.

---

* **19:42** Jgs 1:35.
19:47 Jgs 18:27–29.
19:50 Jos 24:30; Jgs 2:9.
20:1–9 Ex 21:12–14; Nm 35:9–15; Dt 4:41–43; 19:1–10.
20:7 Jos 15:13; 19:37; 21:21.
20:8 Jos 21:27, 36.
21:1 Ex 6:16–19; Nm 3:17–20.
21:2–3, 8 Nm 35:1–8.
21:5 Gn 46:11.

Israelites gave by lot to the Levites, as the LORD
had commanded through Moses.

Cities of the Priests

9 * From the tribes of the Judahites and Simeon-
ites they gave the following cities 10 and assigned
them to the descendants of Aaron in the Kohath-
ite clan of the Levites, since the first lot fell to
them: 11 first, Kiriath-arba (Arba was the father of
Anak), that is, Hebron, in the mountain region of
Judah, with the adjacent pasture lands, 12 although
the open country and villages belonging to the
city had been given to Caleb, son of Jephunneh,
as his holding.* 13 Thus to the descendants of
Aaron the priest were given the city of refuge for
homicides at Hebron, with its pasture lands; also,
Libnah with its pasture lands, 14 Jattir with its pas-
ture lands, Eshtemoa with its pasture lands, 15 Ho-
lon with its pasture lands, Debir with its pasture
lands, 16 Ain with its pasture lands, Juttah with its
pasture lands, and Beth-shemesh with its pasture
lands: nine cities from these two tribes. 17 From the
tribe of Benjamin they obtained Gibeon with its
pasture lands, Geba with its pasture lands, 18 An-
athoth* with its pasture lands, and Almon with
its pasture lands: four cities. 19 These cities which
with their pasture lands belonged to the priestly
descendants of Aaron, were thirteen in all.

Cities of the Other Kohathites

20 * The rest of the Kohathite clans among
the Levites obtained by lot, from the tribe of
Ephraim, four cities. 21 They were assigned, with
its pasture lands, the city of refuge for homicides
at Shechem in the mountain region of Ephraim;
also Gezer with its pasture lands, 22 Kibzaim with
its pasture lands, and Beth-horon with its pasture
lands. 23 From the tribe of Dan they obtained
Elteke with its pasture lands, Gibbethon with its
pasture lands, 24 Aijalon with its pasture lands,
and Gath-rimmon with its pasture lands: four cit-
ies. 25 From the half-tribe of Manasseh, Taanach
with its pasture lands, and Gath-rimmon with
its pasture lands: two cities. 26 These cities which
with their pasture lands belonged to the rest of
the Kohathite clans were ten in all.

Cities of the Gershonites

27 * The Gershonite clan of the Levites received
from the half-tribe of Manasseh the city of refuge
for homicides at Golan in Bashan, with its pas-
ture lands; and also Beth-Astharoth with its pas-
ture lands: two cities. 28 From the tribe of Issachar
they obtained Kishion with its pasture lands,
Daberath with its pasture lands, 29 Jarmuth with
its pasture lands, and En-gannim with its pasture
lands: four cities. 30 From the tribe of Asher, Mi-
shal with its pasture lands, Abdon with its pas-
ture lands, 31 Helkath with its pasture lands, and
Rehob with its pasture lands: four cities. 32 From
the tribe of Naphtali, the city of refuge for homi-
cides at Kedesh in Galilee, with its pasture lands;
also Hammath with its pasture lands, and Kartan
with its pasture lands: three cities. 33 The cities
which belonged to the Gershonite clans, with
their pasture lands, were thirteen in all.

Cities of the Merarites

34 * The Merarite clans, the last of the Levites,
received, from the tribe of Zebulun, Jokneam
with its pasture lands, Kartah with its pasture
lands, 35 Dimnah with its pasture lands, and Na-
halal with its pasture lands: four cities. 36 Also,
across the Jordan, from the tribe of Reuben, the
city of refuge for homicides at Bezer with its pas-
ture lands, Jahaz with its pasture lands, 37 Kede-
moth with its pasture lands, and Mephaath with
its pasture lands: four cities. 38 From the tribe of
Gad, the city of refuge for homicides at Ramoth in
Gilead with its pasture lands, Mahanaim with its
pasture lands, 39 Heshbon with its pasture lands,
and Jazer with its pasture lands: four cities in all.
40 The cities allotted to the Merarite clans, the last
of the Levites, were therefore twelve in all.

41 Thus the total number of cities* within the
territory of the Israelites which, with their pas-
ture lands, belonged to the Levites, was forty-
eight. 42 With each and every one of these cities
went the pasture lands round about it.

43 And so the LORD gave Israel the entire land
he had sworn to their ancestors he would give
them.* Once they had taken possession of it, and
dwelt in it, 44 the LORD gave them peace on every
side, just as he had promised their ancestors.
Not one of their enemies could withstand them;
the LORD gave all their enemies into their power.
45 Not a single word of the blessing* that the
LORD had promised to the house of Israel failed;
it all came true.

III. Return of the Transjordan Tribes and Joshua's Farewell

The Eastern Tribes Dismissed

22 1 At that time Joshua summoned the Reu-
benites, the Gadites, and the half-tribe
of Manasseh 2 and said to them:* "You have

21:9–19 1 Chr 6:39–66.
21:12 Jos 14:14; 15:13.
21:18 Jer 1:1.
21:20–26 1 Chr 6:51–55.
21:27–33 1 Chr 6:56–61.
21:34–38 1 Chr 6:62–66.
21:41 Nm 35:7.
21:43 Gn 12:7; 13:15; 15:18; 26:3; 28:4, 13.
21:45 Jos 23:14–15.
22:2–6 Jos 1:12–17; Nm 32:20–32; Dt 3:18–20.

A Prayer for Understanding

When the Israelite tribes located east of the Jordan build a large altar to worship God, the Israelite tribes who settled west of the Jordan become concerned. They think that by building more altars, the tribes to the east are compromising their belief in one God. Some are ready to go to war over this issue. But maintaining unity among the tribes is also important. So, the western tribes wisely send Phinehas and others to insist on the importance of one place of worship. Listening to the eastern tribes, Phinehas understands their good intentions, and war is avoided.

Think about times when you have jumped to conclusions about other people's actions. Then say the following prayer:

God of love and wisdom, a misunderstanding almost led to war among the Israelites. Help me to avoid jumping to conclusions about the actions of others. Help me to listen and understand their intentions, as Phinehas did. And let me be gracious in recognizing when I am wrong. Amen.

▶ Jos 22:13–20

JOS

observed all that Moses, the servant of the LORD,
commanded you, and have listened to my voice
in everything I commanded you. 3 For many
years now, even until today, you have not aban-
doned your allies, but have taken care to observe
the commands of the LORD, your God. 4 Now that
the LORD, your God, has settled your allies as he
promised them, you may return to your tents,
to your own land, which Moses, the servant of
the LORD, gave you, across the Jordan.* 5 But be
very careful to observe the commandment and
the law which Moses, the servant of the LORD,
commanded you: love the LORD, your God,*
follow him in all his ways, keep his command-
ments, hold fast to him, and serve him with your
whole heart and your whole self." 6 Joshua then
blessed them and sent them away, and they went
to their tents.
7 (For, to half of the tribe of Manasseh Moses
had assigned land in Bashan;* and to the other
half Joshua had given a portion along with their
allies west of the Jordan.) When Joshua sent
them away to their tents and blessed them, 8 he
said, "Now that you are returning to your own
tents with great wealth, with abundant live-
stock, with silver, gold, bronze and iron, and
with a very large supply of clothing, divide these
spoils of your enemies with your allies there."*
9 So the Reubenites, the Gadites, and the half-
tribe of Manasseh left the other Israelites at
Shiloh in the land of Canaan and returned to
the land of Gilead, their own land, which they
had received according to the LORD's command
through Moses.*

The Altar Beside the Jordan

10 When the Reubenites, the Gadites, and the
half-tribe of Manasseh came to the region of the
Jordan in the land of Canaan, they built an altar
there at the Jordan, an impressively large altar.
11 The other Israelites heard the report:* "The
Reubenites, the Gadites, and the half-tribe of
Manasseh have built an altar" in the region of
the Jordan facing the land of Canaan,† across
from the Israelites. 12 When the Israelites heard
this, they assembled at Shiloh, as the entire Isra-
elite community to take military action against
them.†

Accusation of the Western Tribes

13 The Israelites sent Phinehas, son of Eleazar
the priest, to the Reubenites, the Gadites, and
the half-tribe of Manasseh in the land of Gilead,*
14 and with him ten leaders, one from each tribe
of Israel, each one the head of an ancestral house
among the clans of Israel. 15 When these came to
the Reubenites, the Gadites, and the half-tribe
of Manasseh in the land of Gilead, they said
to them: 16 "Thus says the whole community of
the LORD: What act of treachery is this you have
committed against the God of Israel? This day

†

22:11 *In the region of the Jordan facing the land of Canaan*: on the eastern side of the Jordan valley. The river itself formed the boundary between these eastern tribes and the rest of the tribes who lived in what was formerly Canaan—though the term "Canaan" could also be used of both sides of the Jordan valley (cf. v. 10). The Transjordan tribes naturally built their altar in their own territory.

22:12 *To take military action against them*: the western Israelites considered this altar, which seemed to violate the customary unity of the sanctuary (cf. Lv 17:1–9; Dt 12:4–14), as constituting rebellion against the Lord and compromising national unity.

*

22:4 Jos 13:8.
22:5 Dt 6:5–6, 17; 10:12; 11:1, 13, 22.
22:7 Jos 17:5.
22:8 Nm 31:27.
22:9 Jos 18:1; Nm 32:1, 26, 29.
22:11 Dt 12:5, 11–14; 13:13–17.
22:13 Ex 6:25; Sir 45:23–24.

you have turned from following the LORD; by building an altar of your own you have rebelled against the LORD this day. 17 Is the iniquity of Peor not enough, by which we made ourselves impure, even to this day, and a plague came upon the community of the LORD?* 18 If today you turn away from following the LORD, and rebel against the LORD, tomorrow he will be angry with the whole community of Israel! 19 If you consider the land you now possess unclean,† cross over to the land the LORD possesses, where the tabernacle of the LORD stands, and share that with us. But do not rebel against the LORD, nor involve us in rebellion, by building an altar of your own in addition to the altar of the LORD, our God. 20 When Achan, son of Zerah,* acted treacherously by violating the ban, was it not upon the entire community of Israel that wrath fell? Though he was but a single man, he did not perish alone† for his guilt!"

Reply of the Eastern Tribes

21 The Reubenites, the Gadites, and the half-tribe of Manasseh replied to the heads of the Israelite clans: 22 "The LORD is the God of gods. The LORD, the God of gods,† knows and Israel shall know. If now we have acted out of rebellion or treachery against the LORD, our God, do not try to save us this day, 23 and if we have built an altar of our own to turn from following the LORD, or to sacrifice burnt offerings, grain offerings, or communion sacrifices upon it, the LORD himself will exact the penalty. 24 We did it rather out of our anxious concern lest in the future your children should say to our children: 'What have you to do with the LORD, the God of Israel? 25 For the LORD has placed the Jordan as a boundary between you and us, you Reubenites and Gadites. You have no share in the LORD.' Thus your children would prevent ours from revering the LORD. 26 So we thought, 'Let us act for ourselves by building this altar of our own'—not for burnt offerings or sacrifice, 27 * but as witness between us and you and our descendants, that we have the right to provide for the service of the LORD in his presence with our burnt offerings, sacrifices, and communion sacrifices. Now in the future your children cannot say to our children, 'You have no share in the LORD.' 28 Our thought was that, if in the future they should speak thus to us or to our descendants, we could answer: 'Look at the copy of the altar of the LORD which our ancestors made, not for burnt offerings or for sacrifices, but to witness† between you and us.' 29 Far be it from us to rebel against the LORD or to turn now from following the LORD by building an altar for burnt offering, grain offering, or sacrifice in addition to the altar of the LORD, our God, which stands before his tabernacle."

30 When Phinehas the priest and the leaders of the community, the heads of the Israelite clans, heard what the Reubenites, the Gadites, and the Manassites had to say, they were satisfied. 31 Phinehas, son of Eleazar the priest, said to the Reubenites, the Gadites, and the Manassites, "Today we know that the LORD is in our midst. Since you have not rebelled against the LORD by this act of treachery, you have delivered the Israelites from the hand of the LORD."

32 Phinehas, son of Eleazar the priest, and the leaders returned from the Reubenites and the Gadites in the land of Gilead to the Israelites in the land of Canaan, and reported the matter to them. 33 The report satisfied the Israelites, who blessed God and decided not to take military action against the Reubenites and Gadites nor to ravage the land where they lived.

34 The Reubenites and the Gadites gave the altar its name† as a witness among them that the LORD is God.

Joshua's Final Plea

23 1 Many years later, after the LORD had given the Israelites rest from all their enemies round about them, and when Joshua was old and advanced in years,* 2 he summoned all Israel, including their elders, leaders, judges, and officers, and said to them: "I am old and advanced in years.* 3 You have seen all that the LORD, your God, has done for you against all these nations; for it has been the LORD, your God, who fought for you. 4 * See, I have apportioned among your tribes as their heritage the nations that survive, as well as those I destroyed, between the Jordan and the Great Sea in the west. 5 The LORD, your God, will drive them out and dispossess them at your

†

22:19 *Unclean*: not sanctified by the tabernacle.

22:20 *Achan . . . did not perish alone*: his guilt caused the failure of the first attack on Ai (7:4–23); this fact is adduced as an argument for the solidarity and mutual responsibility of all the Israelites.

22:22 *The LORD, the God of gods*: the Hebrew, which cannot be adequately rendered in English here, adds to the divine name Yhwh ("the LORD") two synonymous words for "God," *'el* and *'elohim*. The repetition of these three sacred words adds force to the protestations of fidelity and innocence.

22:28 *To witness*: far from being destined to form a rival sanctuary, the copy of the altar is intended by the eastern tribes solely as a means of teaching their children to be faithful to the one true sanctuary beyond the Jordan.

22:34 The name of this altar was the Hebrew word for "witness," *'ed*.

22:17 Nm 25:3–4; Dt 4:3.
22:20 Jos 7:1, 5.
22:27 Ex 27:1–8; Dt 12:5–6, 11–14.
23:1 Jos 13:1.
23:2 Dt 29:10.
23:4 Jos 13:2–7; 14:2; 18:10; Ps 78:55.

Catholic Social Teaching

Living the Covenant Today

Some people think the Israelites were completely homogenous and without differences, but nothing could be further from the truth. Joshua 24:1 tells how Joshua summoned the leaders of the twelve Tribes of Israel to present themselves before God. In this gathering, they embraced their common faith in God and renewed the Covenant of Sinai, setting aside their differences and political struggles.

One of the major themes of Catholic social teaching is the *Call to Family, Community, and Participation*. What this means is that as humans we are not just spiritual but also social beings. How we organize society directly affects the ability of people to grow in community. Marriage and family must be supported as well as participation in all levels of government. We all need to work together for the common good and to ensure that the needs of everyone are met, especially the most vulnerable. The very word *society* implies people coming together to associate on a variety of levels. Socializing, supporting one another, and actively working to make the world a better place are all ways to live out this important teaching.

- What can you do to foster more unity in your family, school, church, and neighborhood?
- How can you get more involved in bringing people together?

Jos 24:1–28
Call to Family, Community, and Participation

approach, so that you will take possession of
their land as the LORD, your God, promised you.
6 Therefore be strong and be careful to observe all
that is written in the book of the law of Moses,
never turning from it right or left,* 7 or mingling
with these nations that survive among you. You
must not invoke their gods by name, or swear
by them, or serve them, or bow down to them,*
8 but you must hold fast to the LORD, your God, as
you have done up to this day. 9 At your approach
the LORD has dispossessed great and strong nations;
not one has withstood you up to this day.
10 One of you puts to flight a thousand, because
it is the LORD, your God, himself who fights for
you,* as he promised you. 11 As for you, take
great care to love the LORD, your God. 12 For if you
ever turn away from him and join with the remnant
of these nations that survive among you,
by intermarrying and intermingling with them,*
13 know for certain that the LORD, your God, will
no longer dispossess these nations at your approach.
Instead they will be a snare and a trap for
you, a scourge for your sides and thorns for your
eyes, until you perish from this good land which
the LORD, your God, has given you.*
14 "Today, as you see, I am going the way of
all the earth.† So now acknowledge with your
whole heart and soul that not one of all the
promises the LORD, your God, made concerning
you has failed. Every one has come true for you;
not one has failed. 15 * But just as every promise
the LORD, your God, made to you has come true
for you, so will he bring upon you every threat,†
even so far as to exterminate you from this good
land which the LORD, your God, has given you.
16 If you transgress the covenant of the LORD, your
God, which he enjoined on you, to go and serve
other gods and bow down to them, the anger of
the LORD will flare up against you and you will
quickly perish from the good land he has given
you."

Covenant Ceremony

24 1 * Joshua gathered together all the tribes
of Israel at Shechem, summoning the
elders, leaders, judges, and officers of Israel.
When they stood in ranks before God, 2 Joshua
addressed all the people: "Thus says the LORD,
the God of Israel: In times past your ancestors,
down to Terah,* father of Abraham and Nahor,

†

23:14 *Going the way of all the earth*: drawing near to death, the inevitable end of all; cf. 1 Kgs 2:1–2.

23:15 *Every threat*: mentioned especially in the list of curses in Dt 28:15–68.

*

23:6 Jos 1:7.
23:7 Ex 20:3–6; Dt 5:7–10; 7:2–11.
23:10 Ex 14:14; Lv 26:8; Dt 3:22.
23:12 Ex 34:16; Dt 7:3.
23:13 Nm 33:55.
23:15 Lv 26:14–39; Dt 28:15–68.
24:1 Ex 19:17.
24:2 Gn 11:26, 31; 31:53.

lived beyond the River† and served other gods.
3 But I brought your father Abraham from the re-
gion beyond the River and led him through the
entire land of Canaan.* I made his descendants
numerous, and gave him Isaac. 4 To Isaac I gave
Jacob and Esau.* To Esau I assigned the moun-
tain region of Seir to possess, while Jacob and his
children went down to Egypt.
5 "Then I sent Moses and Aaron, and struck
Egypt with the plagues and wonders that I
wrought in her midst.* Afterward I led you out.
6 And when I led your ancestors out of Egypt,
you came to the sea, and the Egyptians pursued
your ancestors to the Red Sea with chariots and
charioteers.* 7 When they cried out to the LORD,*
he put darkness between you and the Egyptians,
upon whom he brought the sea so that it covered
them. Your eyes saw what I did to Egypt. After
you dwelt a long time in the wilderness, 8 * I
brought you into the land of the Amorites who
lived east of the Jordan. They fought against you,
but I delivered them into your power. You took
possession of their land, and I destroyed
them at your approach. 9 * Then Ba-
lak, son of Zippor, king of Moab,
prepared to war against Israel.
He summoned Balaam, son of
Beor, to curse you, 10 * but I
would not listen to Balaam. In-
stead, he had to bless you, and
I delivered you from his power.
11 Once you crossed the Jordan*
and came to Jericho, the citizens
of Jericho fought against you, but I
delivered them also into your power.
12 And I sent the hornets† ahead of you
which drove them—the Amorites, Perizzites, Ca-
naanites, Hittites, Girgashites, Hivites, and Jeb-
usites—out of your way; it was not your sword
or your bow.* 13 I gave you a land you did not
till and cities you did not build, to dwell in; you
ate of vineyards and olive groves you did not
plant.*
14 * "Now, therefore, fear the LORD and serve
him completely and sincerely. Cast out the gods
your ancestors served beyond the River and in
Egypt, and serve the LORD. 15 * If it is displeasing
to you to serve the LORD, choose today whom
you will serve, the gods your ancestors served
beyond the River or the gods of the Amorites in
whose country you are dwelling. As for me and
my household, we will serve the LORD."
16 But the people answered, "Far be it from us
to forsake the LORD to serve other gods. 17 For
it was the LORD, our God, who brought us and
our ancestors up out of the land of Egypt, out of
the house of slavery. He performed those great
signs before our very eyes and protected us along
our entire journey and among all the peoples
through whom we passed. 18 At our approach
the LORD drove out all the peoples, including the
Amorites who dwelt in the land. Therefore we
also will serve the LORD, for he is our God."
19 Joshua in turn said to the people, "You may
not be able to serve the LORD, for he is a holy
God; he is a passionate God* who will not for-
give your transgressions or your sins. 20 If you
forsake the LORD and serve strange gods, he will
then do evil to you and destroy you, after having
done you good."
21 But the people answered Joshua, "No!
We will serve the LORD." 22 Joshua
therefore said to the people, "You
are witnesses against yourselves
that you have chosen to serve
the LORD." They replied, "We
are witnesses!" 23 "Now, there-
fore, put away the foreign gods
that are among you and turn
your hearts to the LORD, the
God of Israel." 24 Then the people
promised Joshua, "We will serve
the LORD, our God, and will listen to
his voice."
25 So Joshua made a covenant with the people
that day and made statutes and ordinances for
them at Shechem. 26 Joshua wrote these words in
the book of the law of God. Then he took a large
stone and set it up there under the terebinth that
was in the sanctuary of the LORD.* 27 And Joshua
said to all the people, "This stone shall be our
witness,* for it has heard all the words which
the LORD spoke to us. It shall be a witness against
you, should you wish to deny your God." 28 Then
Joshua dismissed the people, each to their own
heritage.*

Fear the LORD and serve him completely and sincerely.
(Jos 24:14)

†

24:2 *Beyond the River*: east of the Euphrates; cf. Gn 11:28–31.
24:12 *The hornets*: see note on Ex 23:28.

*

24:3 Gn 12:1; Acts 7:2–4.
24:4 Gn 36:8; 46:1, 6; Acts 7:15.
24:5 Ex 3:10; 7:14; 12:30.
24:6 Ex 12:37, 51; 14:9.
24:7 Ex 14:10, 20, 27–28.
24:8 Nm 21:21–35.
24:9 Nm 22:2–5.
24:10 Nm 23:1–24:25.
24:11 Jos 3:14; 6:1.
24:12 Jos 3:10; 11:20; Ex 23:28; Dt 7:20; Ps 44:3.
24:13 Dt 6:10–11.
24:14 Dt 10:12; 1 Sm 7:3; 12:24; Tb 14:9.
24:15 Dt 30:15–19; Jgs 2:11–13.
24:19 Ex 20:5; 23:21; 34:14; Lv 19:2; Dt 5:9.
24:26 Gn 28:18; 31:45; Jgs 9:6.
24:27 Jos 4:1–9; Gn 31:48, 52; Dt 31:19, 21, 26.
24:28 Jgs 2:6.

Death of Joshua

29 * After these events, Joshua, son of Nun,
servant of the Lord, died at the age of a hun-
dred and ten, 30 and they buried him within the
borders of his heritage at Timnath-serah* in the
mountain region of Ephraim north of Mount
Gaash.† 31 Israel served the Lord during the en-
tire lifetime of Joshua, and of those elders who
outlived Joshua and who knew all the work the
Lord had done for Israel. 32 * The bones of Jo-
seph,† which the Israelites had brought up from
Egypt, were buried in Shechem in the plot of
ground Jacob had bought from the sons of Ha-
mor, father of Shechem, for a hundred pieces of
money. This was a heritage of the descendants of
Joseph. 33 When Eleazar, son of Aaron, also died,
he was buried on the hill which had been given
to his son Phinehas* in the mountain region of
Ephraim.

†

24:30 Following this verse the Greek translation of the Bible (the Septuagint) adds: "They laid with him there, in the tomb where they buried him, the flint knives with which he had circumcised the Israelites at Gilgal, when he brought them out of Egypt, as Yhwh commanded them. There they are to this very day."

24:32 Joseph's bones (Gn 50:24–26) and Jacob's purchase of the burial ground (Gn 33:18–20) relate Joshua with Genesis. *A hundred pieces of money*: see note on Gn 33:19.

*

24:29–31 Jgs 2:7–9.
24:30 Jos 19:50.
24:32 Gn 33:19; 50:24; Ex 13:19.
24:33 Jos 22:13.

"Mom and Dad treat me like such a child." "I can't get a job without experience, but how can I get experience if I can't get a job?" The teenage years often feel like an in-between time, when young people pass from being children to becoming adults who must take responsibility for their own lives. This time of transition holds many challenges. In some ways, the Book of Judges is about Israel's "teenage years." It tells about the difficulties faced by God's People in an in-between time: the two hundred years between the conquest of Canaan under Joshua and the establishment of the kingdom of Israel under Saul.

At a Glance

- **I. The Situation in Canaan Following the Israelite Conquest (1:1—3:6).**
- **II. Stories of the Judges (3:7—16:31).**
- **III. Further Stories of the Tribes of Dan and Benjamin (17:1—21:25).**

Quick Facts

Period Covered: from 1220 to 1000 BC

Inspired Author: The book was put into final form by an unknown person from the Deuteronomic school, sometime during the Israelite monarchy.

Themes: God raises up mighty heroes to protect the people. God works even through flawed heroes.

In Depth

In the Book of Judges, the twelve Tribes of Israel face two especially difficult challenges: how to live peacefully with one another and how to withstand the attacks of foreign armies. God answers the Israelites' prayers for help by raising up extraordinary men and women to lead the Tribes. These famous leaders—Gideon, Deborah, Samson, and nine others—are called judges, but they aren't judges in courtrooms wearing black robes. They are local elders and military heroes who are chosen by God's Spirit to lead the Israelites in times of crisis.

The pattern we observe in the Book of Joshua also appears in the Book of Judges: when the people obey God's laws, they thrive; when they are disobedient, they suffer and need to be rescued by a leader raised up by God's Spirit. The stories in Judges probably began as regional tales about local heroes. As they were collected and edited by the author of Judges, they became national stories influenced by the message of Deuteronomy: faithfulness to God is the only road to personal and tribal security.

The Book of Judges reminds us that the challenges of life, especially in the in-between times, are best handled through prayer and reliance on God. We can trust God to lead us through all difficulties, both great and small.

The Book of Judges

Judges

4:4–5

I. The Situation in Canaan Following the Israelite Conquest

Canaanites in Palestine

1 [1] † After the death of Joshua the Israelites con-
sulted the LORD, asking, "Who shall be first
among us to attack the Canaanites and to do bat-
tle with them?" [2] The LORD answered: Judah shall
attack: I have delivered the land into his power.*
[3] Judah then said to his brother Simeon, "Come
up with me into the territory allotted to me, and
let us do battle with the Canaanites. I will likewise
go with you into the territory allotted to you." So
Simeon went with him.*
[4] When Judah attacked, the LORD delivered the
Canaanites and Perizzites into their power, and
they struck down ten thousand of them in Bezek.
[5] * They came upon Adonibezek in Bezek and
fought against him. When they struck down the
Canaanites and Perizzites, [6] Adonibezek fled. They
pursued him, and when they caught him, they
cut off his thumbs and big toes. [7] "Seventy kings,"
said Adonibezek, "used to pick up scraps under
my table with their thumbs and big toes cut off.
As I have done, so has God repaid me." He was
brought to Jerusalem, and he died there. [8] † The Ju-
dahites fought against Jerusalem, captured it, and
put it to the sword, setting the city itself on fire.*
[9] Afterward the Judahites went down to fight
against the Canaanites who lived in the mountain
region, in the Negeb, and in the foothills.* [10] Judah
also marched against the Canaanites who lived
in Hebron, which was formerly called Kiriath-
arba, and defeated Sheshai, Ahiman, and Talmai.*
[11] They marched from there against the inhabitants
of Debir, which was formerly called Kiriath-sepher.
[12] Caleb said, "To the man who attacks Kiriath-se-
pher and captures it, I will give my daughter Ach-
sah in marriage." [13] * Othniel captured it, the son
of Caleb's younger brother Kenaz; so Caleb gave
him his daughter Achsah in marriage. [14] When she
came to him, she induced him to ask her father for
some land. Then, as she alighted from the donkey,
Caleb asked her, "What do you want?" [15] She an-
swered, "Give me a present. Since you have put me
in the land of the Negeb, give me pools of water."
So Caleb gave her what she wanted, both the up-
per and the lower pool.
[16] * The descendants of Hobab the Kenite,

1:1–36 The chapter depicts the Israelite settlement of Canaan as a gradual and incomplete process (cf. Ex 23:29–30; Dt 7:22). This picture contrasts sharply with that found in Joshua, where the conquest is rapid and total. Accordingly, some scholars believe that Jgs 1 derives from an early account, which is less idealized and more realistic than that on which Joshua is based. Others, noting that Judah is presented as the only tribe that was completely successful in driving foreigners from its territory, think that the account was written at a late date and reflects suspicion in Judah about foreign elements in the Israelite populations of outlying areas (cf. 2 Kgs 17:24–33).

1:8 See note on 1:21 below.

1:2 Jgs 20:18.
1:3 Jgs 1:17.
1:5 Jos 10:1.
1:8 Jos 10:1–27; 2 Sm 5:6–9.
1:9 Jos 10:40; 11:16; 12:8.
1:10 Jos 15:13–19; Nm 13:22; Jos 14:15.
1:13 Jgs 3:9.
1:16 Jgs 4:11; Nm 10:29–32.

Moses' father-in-law,† came up with the Judah-
ites from the City of Palms to the wilderness of
Arad, which is in the Negeb, and they settled
among the Amalekites.
17 * Then Judah went
with his brother Simeon, and they defeated the
Canaanites who lived in Zephath. They put the
city under the ban and renamed it Hormah.† *
18 Judah captured Gaza with its territory, Ashke-
lon with its territory, Ekron with its territory, and
Ashdod† with its territory.*
19 The LORD was with
Judah, so they gained possession of the moun-
tain region. But they could not dispossess those
who lived on the plain, because they had iron
chariots.
20 * As Moses had commanded, they
gave Hebron to Caleb, who then drove the three
sons of Anak away from there.
21 † As for the Jebusites dwelling in Jerusalem,
the Benjaminites did not dispossess them, so
that the Jebusites live with the Benjaminites in
Jerusalem to the present day.*
22 The house of Joseph, too, went up against
Bethel, and the LORD was with them.
23 The
house of Joseph reconnoitered Bethel, which
formerly was called Luz.*
24 The scouts saw a
man coming out of the city and said to him,
"Tell us the way into the city, and we will show
you mercy."
25 He showed them the way into
the city, and they put the city to the sword; but
they let the man and his whole clan go free.
26 The man then went to the land of the Hittites,
where he built a city and called it Luz, which is
its name to this day.
27 * Manasseh did not take possession of Beth-
shean with its towns or of Taanach with its
towns. Nor did they dispossess the inhabitants
of Dor and its towns, those of Ibleam and its
towns, or those of Megiddo and its towns. The
Canaanites continued to live in this district.
28 When Israel grew stronger, they conscripted the
Canaanites as laborers, but did not actually drive
them out.
29 * Ephraim did not drive out the Ca-
naanites living in Gezer, and so the Canaanites
lived among them in Gezer.
30 * Nor did Zebulun dispossess the inhab-
itants of Kitron or those of Nahalol; the Ca-
naanites lived among them and became forced
laborers.
31 * Nor did Asher dispossess the inhabitants
of Acco or those of Sidon, or take possession
of Mahaleb, Achzib, Helbah, Aphik, or Rehob.
32 So the Asherites settled among the Canaanite
inhabitants of the land, for they had not dispos-
sessed them.

Pray It!

Water in the Desert

Caleb's daughter, Achsah, asks for *Gulloth-mayim* (Jgs 1:15) as her wedding present. *Gulloth-mayim* means "basins of water," and presumably, she is asking for a place with springs of fresh water. Achsah's new home will be in the desert, and she knows that her family will need water. She's not afraid to ask for what she needs.

Clearly, Achsah's request fits into God's master plan. However, we know that we don't always get what we pray for. When that happens, we need to remind ourselves that God's plan may mean that our prayers are not always answered in a way that we want. That is when we need to trust the wisdom of God in our lives.

In your prayer time, reflect or journal on the following questions:

- Which prayers of yours have not been answered or have been answered differently than you requested?
- Why is "thy will be done" a good way to end your prayer time?

▶ **Jgs 1:14–15**

J G S

† **1:16** *Hobab the Kenite, Moses' father-in-law*: as in 4:11. However, in Nm 10:29 Hobab is identified as Moses' brother-in-law, while Reuel is identified as Moses' father-in-law (see also Ex 2:18). The more common name of Moses' father-in-law is Jethro, also a Midianite (e.g., Ex 3:1). It is impossible to sort out the relationships among these three men in the ancient traditions. *City of Palms*: Jericho (cf. Dt 34:3) or a town in the Negeb.

1:17 *The ban . . . Hormah*: the narrator relates the city-name "Hormah" to "the ban" (Hebrew *herem*), which commanded the Israelites to devote to the Lord—and thus to destroy—whatever was captured within the land (cf. Dt 20:10–18).

1:18 *Gaza . . . Ashkelon . . . Ekron . . . Ashdod*: four of the five major cities of the Philistines (see note on 3:3). Since these cities were on the coastal plain, the statement that Judah captured them is contrary to v. 19, which notes Judah's failure to drive out the inhabitants of the lowlands. In the Septuagint the problem is removed by changing the beginning of this verse to read "Judah did not dispossess . . . ."

1:21 According to Jos 18:16, Jerusalem was assigned to the tribe of Benjamin. According to the notice in 1:8 above, the city was burned by the Judahites, but elsewhere (2 Sm 5:6–9) we learn that it was not actually taken from the Jebusites until David captured it and made it his capital.

* **1:17** Jos 1:3.
1:17 Nm 21:3; Jos 12:14.
1:18 Jos 11:22.
1:20 Jos 14:6–15.
1:21 Jos 15:63; 18:16; 2 Sm 5:6–9.
1:23 Gn 28:19; Jos 18:13.
1:27–28 Jos 17:11–13.
1:29 Jos 16:10.
1:30 Jos 19:10–16.
1:31–32 Jos 19:24–31.

Live It!

Obeying Authority

Think of a time when you disobeyed a parent or teacher. What were the consequences? Disobedience to legitimate authority tends to bring about negative consequences. Just read Judges 2:10–15. The people turned from God, and their separation from God led to defeat at the hands of their enemies.

God places parents, teachers, and other authority figures in our lives to protect and support us. Their love and care are an extension of God's love and care. From their vantage point, they often see a bigger picture than we do. When we disobey their reasonable requests, we build walls between them and us, preventing God's love from reaching us. On the other hand, obedience leads to more trust, responsibility, and freedom. Of course, as Jesus himself showed us, no one is obligated to obey requests or directions that are abusive, demeaning, or immoral.

So, the next time you are having a problem with a person in authority, ask yourself, "Might obedience in this situation somehow bring me closer to God?"

▶ **Jgs 2:10–15**

33 * Nor did Naphtali drive out the inhabitants
of Beth-shemesh or those of Beth-anath. They
settled among the Canaanite inhabitants of the
land and the inhabitants of Beth-shemesh and
Beth-anath became forced laborers for them.
34 The Amorites hemmed in the Danites in
the mountain region, not permitting them to
come down onto the plain. 35 So the Amorites
continued to live in Harheres, Aijalon, and Sha-
albim, but as the power of the house of Joseph
grew, they were conscripted as laborers.
36 The territory of the Amorites extended from
the Akrabbim pass, from Sela and upward.

Infidelities of the Israelites

2 1 A messenger of the LORD went up from
Gilgal to Bochim and said, I brought you
up from Egypt and led you into the land which
I promised on oath to your ancestors. I said, I
will never break my covenant with you, 2 but you
must not make a covenant with the inhabitants
of this land; you must pull down their altars.*
But you did not listen to me. Look what you have
done! 3 For I also said,† I will not clear them out
of your way; they will become traps for you, and
their gods a snare for you.*
4 When the messenger of the LORD had spoken
these things to all the Israelites, the people wept
aloud. 5 They named that place Bochim,† and
they offered sacrifice there to the LORD.
6 * Then Joshua dismissed the people, and the
Israelites went, each to their own heritage, to take
possession of the land. 7 The people served the
LORD during the entire lifetime of Joshua, and of
those elders who outlived Joshua and who had
seen all the great work the LORD had done for
Israel. 8 Joshua, son of Nun, the servant of the
LORD, died at the age of a hundred and ten, 9 and
they buried him within the borders of his heri-
tage at Timnath-heres in the mountain region of
Ephraim north of Mount Gaash.*
10 † When the rest of that generation were also
gathered to their ancestors, and a later generation
arose that did not know the LORD or the work he
had done for Israel, 11 * the Israelites did what
was evil in the sight of the LORD. They served the
Baals,† 12 and abandoned the LORD, the God of
their ancestors, the one who had brought them
out of the land of Egypt. They followed other
gods, the gods of the peoples around them, and
bowed down to them, and provoked the LORD.
13 Because they had abandoned the LORD and
served Baal and the Astartes,† 14 the anger of the
LORD flared up against Israel, and he delivered

†

2:3 *I also said*: the Lord explicitly warned the Israelites of the consequences of disobedience; see Nm 33:55 and especially Jos 23:13.

2:5 *Bochim*: Hebrew for "weepers."

2:10–19 This long thematic passage establishes the cyclical pattern for the stories found in the rest of the book. When the Israelites are secure, they forsake the Lord and worship other gods. In punishment the Lord places them in the power of a foreign oppressor. But when they cry out in distress, the Lord takes pity on them and raises up a judge, who delivers them from the oppressor. The Israelites remain faithful to the Lord during the lifetime of the judge, but when the judge dies they again abandon the Lord, and the cycle begins anew.

2:11 *The Baals*: the title "Baal," meaning "lord" or "master," belonged to a large number of Canaanite, Phoenician, and Syrian deities, including especially the great storm god Hadad Baal, widely revered as lord of the earth. The plural form, which occurs here, was used by the biblical writers to refer to foreign gods in general.

2:13 *The Astartes*: Ashtoreth, or Astarte, was an important Canaanite and Phoenician goddess. The plural form used here probably refers to foreign goddesses in general.

*

1:33 Jos 19:32–39.
2:2 Ex 23:32; 34:12–13; Dt 7:2, 5; 12:2–3.
2:3 Ex 23:33; Dt 7:16; Jos 23:13.
2:6–9 Jos 24:28–31.
2:9 Jos 19:49–50.
2:11–14 Jgs 3:7–8, 12; 4:1–2; 6:1; 10:6–8; 13:1.

them into the power of plunderers who despoiled them. He sold them into the power of the enemies around them, and they were no longer able to withstand their enemies. 15 Whenever they marched out, the hand of the LORD turned against them, as the LORD had said, and as the LORD had sworn to them;* and they were in great distress. 16 But the LORD raised up judges to save them from the power of their plunderers; 17 but they did not listen to their judges either, for they prostituted themselves by following other gods, bowing down to them. They were quick to stray from the way their ancestors had taken, who obeyed the commandments of the LORD; but these did not. 18 When the LORD raised up judges for them, he would be with the judge and save them from the power of their enemies as long as the judge lived. The LORD would change his mind when they groaned in their affliction under their oppressors. 19 But when the judge died, they would again do worse than their ancestors, following other gods, serving and bowing down to them, relinquishing none of their evil practices or stubborn ways.*

20 * The anger of the LORD flared up against Israel, and he said: Because this nation has transgressed my covenant, which I enjoined on their ancestors, and has not listened to me, 21 I for my part will not clear away for them any more of the nations Joshua left when he died. 22 * They will be made to test Israel, to see whether or not they will keep to the way of the LORD and continue in it as their ancestors did. 23 Therefore the LORD allowed these nations to remain instead of expelling them immediately. He had not delivered them into the power of Joshua.

3 1 These are the nations the LORD allowed to remain, so that through them he might test Israel, all those who had not experienced any of the Canaanite wars— 2 to teach warfare to those generations of Israelites who had never experienced it: 3 * the five lords of the Philistines,† and all the Canaanites, the Sidonians, and the Hivites who lived in the mountain region of the Lebanon between Baal-hermon and Lebo-hamath. 4 These served as a test for Israel, to know whether they would obey the commandments the LORD had enjoined on their ancestors through Moses. 5 So the Israelites settled among the Canaanites, Hittites, Amorites, Perizzites, Hivites, and Jebusites.* 6 They took their daughters in marriage, and gave their own daughters to their sons in marriage,* and served their gods.

II. Stories of the Judges

Othniel

7 * Then the Israelites did what was evil in the sight of the LORD; they forgot the LORD, their God, and served the Baals and the Asherahs,† 8 and the anger of the LORD flared up against them. He sold them into the power of Cushan-rishathaim,† king of Aram Naharaim; and the Israelites served Cushan-rishathaim for eight years. 9 But when the Israelites cried out to the LORD,* he raised up a savior for them, to save them. It was Othniel, son of Caleb's younger brother Kenaz.* 10 The spirit of the LORD came upon him,* and he judged Israel. When he marched out to war, the LORD delivered Cushan-rishathaim, king of Aram, into his power, and his hold on Cushan-rishathaim was firm. 11 So the land was at rest for forty years,* until Othniel, son of Kenaz, died.

Ehud

12 Again the Israelites did what was evil in the sight of the LORD, so he strengthened Eglon, king of Moab, against Israel because they did what was evil in the sight of the LORD. 13 Taking the Ammonites and Amalek as allies, he went and defeated Israel, taking possession of the City of Palms. 14 So the Israelites served Eglon, king of Moab, for eighteen years.

15 But when the Israelites cried out to the LORD, he raised up for them a savior, Ehud, son of Gera, a Benjaminite who was left-handed.† The Israelites would send their tribute to Eglon, king of Moab, by him. 16 Ehud made himself a two-edged dagger a foot long, and strapped it under his clothes on his right thigh. 17 He presented the tribute to Eglon, king of Moab; now Eglon was

J G S

---

† **3:3** *The Philistines*: a people of Aegean origin who settled on the coastal plain of southern Canaan in the twelfth century B.C.; from their name derives the geographic designation Palestine. Israel competed for control of the country against a group of their cities: Gaza, Ashkelon, Ashdod, Gath, and Ekron.

3:7 *The Asherahs*: Asherah was an important goddess, whose presence in the cult was represented by a wooden pole, also called an "asherah"; see notes on Ex 34:13 and Dt 7:5. Here the plural is used to refer to goddesses in general.

3:8 *Cushan-rishathaim*: this king is not known from other biblical or extrabiblical sources. His title, "king of Aram Naharaim," indicates that he was a Mesopotamian ruler.

3:15 *Left-handed*: this detail is important because it shows why Ehud is able to conceal a weapon on his right thigh (3:16). There is also a wordplay involved, since "Benjaminite" in Hebrew could also mean "right-handed man."

---

* **2:15** Lv 26:14–39; Dt 28:15–68.
2:19 Jgs 3:12; 4:1; 8:33–34.
2:20–21 Jos 23:13; Jgs 2:2–3.
2:22 Jgs 3:1, 4.
3:3 Jos 13:2–5.
3:5 Ex 3:8, 17; 23:23; 33:2; 34:11; Dt 7:1; 20:17; Jos 3:10; 24:11.
3:6 Ex 34:16; Dt 7:3; Jos 23:12.
3:7–8 Jgs 2:11–14.
3:9 Jgs 3:15; 4:3; 6:6, 7; 10:10; 1 Sm 12:8, 10.
3:9 Jgs 1:13.
3:10 Jgs 6:34; 11:29; 13:25; 14:6, 19; 15:14; 1 Sm 11:6.
3:11 Jgs 3:30; 5:31; 8:28.

Pray It!

Wartime Women

In Judges, chapter 4, Deborah, a judge and prophet, rallies Barak and the Israelites to war, and Jael, another woman (who is not an Israelite), delivers the final blow to the enemy's commander, Sisera. In chapter 5, Deborah leads the victory celebration with an elaborate prayer-song that is probably one of the oldest texts in the Bible (see also Exodus, chapter 15).

In the Bible, women are often innocent victims of war. Usually, they do not do the fighting but are raped, killed, or widowed. Is Jael's violence the answer to this abuse? Is Jael a hero, or is she still a victim of war, forced to make a violent choice in order to survive in a violent world? The writer of the Book of Judges gives no judgment on her actions.

When we are no longer victims but have become people who abuse others, has the situation really improved, or are we just doing to others what we would never want done to us? In light of Jesus' teachings, these are important questions to ask. Let us pray:

God of love, please deliver us from being both victims of violence and agents of violence. Amen.

▶ Judges, chapter 4

JGS

a very fat man. 18 When he had finished present-
ing the tribute, he dismissed the troops who had
carried the tribute. 19 But he himself turned back
at the sculptured stones near Gilgal, and said, "I
have a secret message for you, O king." And the
king said, "Silence!" Then when all his atten-
dants had left his presence, 20 Ehud went in to
him where he sat alone in his cool upper room.
Ehud said, "I have a word from God for you."
So the king rose from his throne. 21 Then Ehud
with his left hand drew the dagger from his right
thigh, and thrust it into Eglon's belly. 22 The hilt
also went in after the blade, and the fat closed
over the blade because he did not withdraw the
dagger from the body.
23 Then Ehud went out onto the porch, shut-
ting the doors of the upper room on Eglon and
locking them. 24 When Ehud had left and the ser-
vants had come, they saw that the doors of the
upper room were locked, and thought, "He must
be easing himself in the cool chamber." 25 They
waited until they were at a loss when he did not
open the doors of the upper room. So they took
the key and opened them, and there was their
lord lying on the floor, dead.
26 During their delay Ehud escaped and, passing
the sculptured stones, took refuge in Seirah. 27 On
his arrival he sounded the horn in the mountain
region of Ephraim, and the Israelites went down
from the mountains with him as their leader.
28 "Follow me," he said to them, "for the LORD has
delivered your enemies the Moabites into your
power."* So they followed him down and seized
the fords of the Jordan against the Moabites, per-
mitting no one to cross. 29 On that occasion they
slew about ten thousand Moabites, all of them
strong warriors. Not one escaped. 30 So Moab was
brought under the power of Israel* at that time;
and the land had rest for eighty years.*

Shamgar

31 After him there was Shamgar,† son of
Anath,* who slew six hundred Philistines with
an oxgoad.* He, too, was a savior for Israel.

Deborah and Barak

4 1* The Israelites again did what was evil in
the sight of the LORD; Ehud was dead. 2 So the
LORD sold them into the power of the Canaanite
king, Jabin, who reigned in Hazor. The general
of his army was Sisera, who lived in Harosheth-
ha-goiim.* 3* But the Israelites cried out to the
LORD; for with his nine hundred iron chariots
Jabin harshly oppressed the Israelites for twenty
years.
4 At that time the prophet Deborah, wife of
Lappidoth, was judging Israel. 5 She used to sit
under Deborah's palm tree, between Ramah and
Bethel in the mountain region of Ephraim, where
the Israelites came up to her for judgment. 6 She
had Barak, son of Abinoam,* summoned from
Kedesh of Naphtali. She said to him, "This is
what the LORD, the God of Israel, commands: Go,
march against Mount Tabor, and take with you

† **3:31** Shamgar is the first of the so-called minor judges; cf. Introduction.

* **3:28** Nm 21:34; Dt 2:24; Jos 2:24; Jgs 4:7, 14; 7:7, 9, 15.
3:30 Jgs 8:28; 11:23; 1 Sm 7:13.
3:30 Jgs 3:11; 5:31; 8:28.
3:31 Jgs 5:6.
3:31 Jgs 15:15; 2 Sm 23:8, 18.
4:1 Jgs 2:19; 3:12; 8:33–34.
4:2 Jos 11:1–15; Ps 83:10; 1 Sm 12:9.
4:3 Jgs 3:9, 15; 6:6, 7; 10:10; 1 Sm 12:8, 10.
4:6 Heb 11:32.

ten thousand men from Naphtali and Zebulun.
7 I will draw Sisera, the general of Jabin's army,
out to you at the Wadi Kishon,* together with
his chariots and troops, and I will deliver them
into your power." 8 But Barak answered her, "If
you come with me, I will go; if you do not come
with me, I will not go." 9 "I will certainly go with
you," she replied, "but you will not gain glory for
the expedition on which you are setting out, for
it is into a woman's power that the LORD is going
to sell Sisera." So Deborah arose and went with
Barak and journeyed with him to Kedesh.
10 Barak summoned Zebulun and Naphtali to
Kedesh, and ten thousand men followed him.*
Deborah also went up with him. 11 † Now Heber
the Kenite had detached himself from Cain, the
descendants of Hobab, Moses' father-in-law,*
and had pitched his tent by the terebinth of Zaa-
nannim, which was near Kedesh.
12 It was reported to Sisera that Barak, son of
Abinoam, had gone up to Mount Tabor. 13 So
Sisera called out all nine hundred of his iron
chariots and all his forces from Harosheth-ha-
goiim to the Wadi Kishon. 14 Deborah then said
to Barak, "Up! This is the day on which the
LORD has delivered Sisera into your power. The
LORD marches before you." So Barak went down
Mount Tabor, followed by his ten thousand
men. 15 And the LORD threw Sisera and all his
chariots and forces into a panic before Barak.*
Sisera himself dismounted from his chariot and
fled on foot, 16 but Barak pursued the chariots
and the army as far as Harosheth-ha-goiim. The
entire army of Sisera fell beneath the sword, not
even one man surviving.
17 Sisera fled on foot to the tent of Jael, wife of
Heber the Kenite, for there was peace between
Jabin, king of Hazor, and the family of Heber
the Kenite. 18 Jael went out to meet Sisera and
said to him, "Turn aside, my lord, turn aside with
me; do not be afraid." So he went into her tent,
and she covered him with a rug. 19 He said to
her, "Please give me a little water to drink. I am
thirsty." So she opened a skin of milk, gave him
a drink, and then covered him.* 20 "Stand at the
entrance of the tent," he said to her. "If anyone
comes and asks, 'Is there someone here?' say,
'No!'" 21 Jael, wife of Heber, got a tent peg and
took a mallet in her hand. When Sisera was in a
deep sleep from exhaustion, she approached him
stealthily and drove the peg through his temple
and down into the ground, and he died.* 22 Then
when Barak came in pursuit of Sisera, Jael went
out to meet him and said to him, "Come, I will
show you the man you are looking for." So he
went in with her, and there lay Sisera dead, with
the tent peg through his temple.
23 Thus on that day God humbled the Ca-
naanite king, Jabin, before the Israelites; 24 their
power weighed ever more heavily on him, until
at length they finished off the Canaanite king,
Jabin.

Live It!

The Battle Within

Although the story of Deborah is inspiring, partly because so few women leaders are portrayed in the Bible, it is also a story of war and violence. The Book of Judges records one battle after another. It is wearying to read of so much fighting and of rejoicing over someone's having a tent peg pounded into his head.

We need to keep our perspective here and understand that the way the Israelites viewed life at that time was simple: If they were victorious, God was with them. If they were defeated, God had been offended and had turned away from them.

What can we learn from this story? It teaches that God never turns away from us. The real victories to celebrate are the personal battles we win each day as we strive to become more faithful to God. Jesus calls us to make peace rather than war. Our greatest enemy is often within, as we strive to be the person God wants us to be, whether our name is Deborah or Joshua, Jennifer or Carlos.

- What battle is going on inside you today? What choice in this battle leads to greater faithfulness to God?

▶ **Judges, chapter 4**

† **4:11** It was characteristic of the Kenites that they encamped alongside or among other nomadic groups, such as the Amalekites (cf. 1:16; 1 Sm 15:6). They are most often mentioned in connection with tribes living in the southern part of Judah, but Heber's group seems to have moved north and pitched its tents in the lower Galilee. *Cain*: in this case a collective term for the Kenites. For Hobab, see 1:16.

4:7 Jgs 5:21; Ps 83:10.
4:10 Jgs 5:18.
4:11 Nm 10:29; Jgs 1:16.
4:15 Ex 14:24; Jos 10:10; 1 Sm 7:10.
4:19 Jgs 5:25.
4:21 Jgs 5:26.

Song of Deborah

5 1* On that day Deborah sang this song—and Barak, son of Abinoam:

2† When uprising broke out in Israel,
when the people rallied for duty—bless the LORD!
3 Hear, O kings! Give ear, O princes!
I will sing, I will sing to the LORD,
I will make music to the LORD, the God of Israel.
4†* LORD, when you went out from Seir,
when you marched from the plains of Edom,
The earth shook, the heavens poured,
the clouds poured rain,
5 The mountains streamed,
before the LORD, the One of Sinai,
before the LORD, the God of Israel.
6 In the days of Shamgar, son of Anath,*
in the days of Jael, caravans ceased:
Those who traveled the roads
now traveled by roundabout paths.*
7 Gone was freedom beyond the walls,
gone indeed from Israel.
When I, Deborah, arose,
when I arose, a mother in Israel.†
8 New gods were their choice;
then war was at the gates.
No shield was to be found, no spear,
among forty thousand in Israel!
9 My heart is with the leaders of Israel,
with the dedicated ones of the people—
bless the LORD;
10 Those who ride on white donkeys,
seated on saddle rugs,
and those who travel the road,
Sing of them
11 to the sounds of musicians at the wells.
There they recount the just deeds of the LORD,
his just deeds bringing freedom to Israel.
12 Awake, awake, Deborah!
Awake, awake, strike up a song!
Arise, Barak!
Take captive your captors, son of Abinoam!
13 Then down went Israel against the mighty,
the army of the LORD went down for him
against the warriors.
14† From Ephraim, their base in the valley;
behind you, Benjamin, among your troops.
From Machir came down commanders,
from Zebulun wielders of the marshal's staff.
15 The princes of Issachar were with Deborah,
Issachar, faithful to Barak;
in the valley they followed at his heels.
Among the clans of Reuben
great were the searchings of heart!
16 Why did you stay beside your hearths
listening to the lowing of the herds?
Among the clans of Reuben
great were the searchings of heart!
17 Gilead stayed beyond the Jordan;
Why did Dan spend his time in ships?
Asher remained along the shore,
he stayed in his havens.
18 Zebulun was a people who defied death,
Naphtali, too, on the open heights!*
19 The kings came and fought;
then they fought, those kings of Canaan,
At Taanach by the waters of Megiddo;
no spoil of silver did they take.
20 From the heavens the stars† fought;
from their courses they fought against Sisera.*
21 The Wadi Kishon swept them away;
the wadi overwhelmed them, the Wadi Kishon.*
Trample down the strong!†
22 Then the hoofs of the horses hammered,
the galloping, galloping of steeds.
23 "Curse Meroz,"† says the messenger of the LORD,
"curse, curse its inhabitants!
For they did not come when the LORD helped,
the help of the LORD against the warriors."
24 Most blessed of women is Jael,*

†

5:2–31 This canticle is an excellent example of early Hebrew poetry, even though some of its verses are now obscure.

5:4–5 The Lord himself marches to war in support of Israel. Storm and earthquake are part of the traditional imagery of theophany; cf. Ex 19:16, 18–20; Dt 33:2–3; Ps 18:7–15; 77:17–20; 144:5–7.

5:7 *A mother in Israel*: the precise meaning of the term "mother" is unclear, except that it seems to indicate Deborah's position of leadership, and so may be a title (cf. 2 Sm 20:19).

5:14–22 The poet praises the tribes that participated in the war against Sisera: Ephraim, Benjamin, Machir (later regarded as a clan of Manasseh), Zebulun, Issachar, and Naphtali, the tribe of Barak (cf. 4:6). By contrast, the tribes of Reuben, Gilead (elsewhere a region occupied by Reubenites and Gadites), Dan, and Asher are chided for their lack of participation. The more distant tribes of Judah and Simeon are not mentioned, and some historians believe they were not part of Israel at this time.

5:20–21 *Stars*: the heavenly host, or angelic army. The roles played by the stars and the flash floods underscore the divine involvement in the battle (cf. 5:4–5).

5:21 *Trample down the strong!*: the meaning of these words is obscure. If this interpretation is correct, Deborah is the one addressed.

5:23 *Meroz*: an unknown locality in which Israelites probably resided, since its inhabitants are cursed for their failure to participate in the battle.

*

5:1 Ex 15:1.
5:4–5 Dt 33:2; Ps 68:8–9; Hb 3:3–15.
5:6 Jgs 3:31.
5:6 Is 33:8.
5:18 Jgs 4:10.
5:20 Jgs 4:15.
5:21 Jgs 4:7, 13; Ps 83:10.
5:24 Jgs 4:17; Jdt 13:18; Lk 1:42.

the wife of Heber the Kenite,
blessed among tent-dwelling women!
25 He asked for water, she gave him milk,
in a princely bowl she brought him curds.*
26 *With her hand she reached for the peg,
with her right hand, the workman's
hammer.
She hammered Sisera, crushed his head;
she smashed, pierced his temple.
27 At her feet he sank down, fell, lay still;
down at her feet he sank and fell;
where he sank down, there he fell, slain.

28† From the window she looked down,
the mother of Sisera peered through the
lattice:
"Why is his chariot so long in coming?
why are the hoofbeats of his chariots
delayed?"
29 The wisest of her princesses answers her;
she even replies to herself,
30 "They must be dividing the spoil they took:
a slave woman or two for each man,
Spoil of dyed cloth for Sisera,
spoil of ornate dyed cloth,
a pair of ornate dyed cloths for my neck in
the spoil."

31 So perish all your enemies, O LORD!*
But may those who love you be like the
sun rising in its might!

And the land was at rest for forty years.*

The Call of Gideon

6 1 The Israelites did what was evil in the sight
of the LORD, who therefore delivered them
into the power of Midian for seven years, 2 so
that Midian held Israel subject. From fear of Mid-
ian the Israelites made dens in the mountains,
the caves, and the strongholds.* 3 For it used to
be that whenever the Israelites had completed
sowing their crops, Midian, Amalek, and the
Kedemites† would come up, 4 encamp against
them, and lay waste the produce of the land
as far as the outskirts of Gaza, leaving no sus-
tenance in Israel, and no sheep, ox, or donkey.
5 For they would come up with their livestock,
and their tents would appear as thick as locusts.
They would be too many to count when they
came into the land to lay it waste. 6 * Israel was
reduced to utter poverty by Midian, and so the
Israelites cried out to the LORD.
7 When Israel cried out to the LORD because of
Midian, 8 * the LORD sent a prophet to the Isra-
elites who said to them: Thus says the LORD, the
God of Israel: I am the one who brought you up
from Egypt; I brought you out of the house of
slavery. 9 I rescued you from the power of Egypt
and all your oppressors. I drove them out before
you and gave you their land. 10 And I said to
you: I, the LORD, am your God; you shall not fear
the gods of the Amorites in whose land you are
dwelling. But you did not listen to me.
11 Then the messenger of the LORD came and
sat under the terebinth in Ophrah that belonged
to Joash the Abiezrite. Joash's son Gideon* was
beating out wheat in the wine press to save it
from the Midianites, 12 and the messenger of
the LORD appeared to him and said: The LORD
is with you, you mighty warrior! 13 "My lord,"
Gideon said to him, "if the LORD is with us, why
has all this happened to us? Where are his won-
drous deeds about which our ancestors told us
when they said, 'Did not the LORD bring us up
from Egypt?' For now the LORD has abandoned
us and has delivered us into the power of Mid-
ian." 14 * The LORD turned to him and said: Go
with the strength you have, and save Israel from
the power of Midian. Is it not I who send you?
15 But he answered him, "Please, my Lord, how
can I save Israel? My family is the poorest in Ma-
nasseh, and I am the most insignificant in my
father's house."* 16 The LORD said to him: I will
be with you,† and you will cut down Midian to
the last man. 17 He answered him, "If you look
on me with favor, give me a sign that you are the
one speaking with me. 18 Please do not depart
from here until I come to you and bring out my
offering and set it before you." He answered: I
will await your return.
19 So Gideon went off and prepared a young
goat and an ephah† of flour in the form of un-
leavened cakes. Putting the meat in a basket and
the broth in a pot, he brought them out to him
under the terebinth and presented them. 20 * The

†

5:28–30 The scene shifts to the household of the slain Canaanite general, where the anxious foreboding of Sisera's mother is countered by the assurances of the noblewomen.

6:3 *Midian, Amalek, and the Kedemites*: three groups of camel nomads, whose raids were a constant threat to settled peoples like the Israelites during the period of the Judges.

6:16 *I will be with you*: narratives telling how the Lord commissions someone for a task depict the person's reactions of reluctance, confusion, or sense of inadequacy, and the Lord's reassurance ("I will be with you"), sometimes accompanied by a sign (cf. Ex 3:12; Jer 1:8). Lk 1:28–37 is modeled on this pattern.

6:19 *Ephah*: see note on Is 5:10.

*

5:25 Jgs 4:19.
5:26–27 Jgs 4:21.
5:31 Ps 83.
5:31 Jgs 3:11, 30; 8:28.
6:2 1 Sm 13:6.
6:6–7 Jgs 3:9, 15; 4:3; 10:10; 1 Sm 12:8, 10.
6:8–10 Jgs 2:1–3; 10:11–14.
6:11 Heb 11:32.
6:14 Ex 3:10–12.
6:15 1 Sm 9:21.
6:20–22 Jgs 13:19–22.

Pray It!

Trusting God

The true test of love is loving without testing. Gideon keeps testing God; he cannot bring himself to believe God's promises. Judges, chapters 6–8, gives a full picture of this hero who never quite understands what loving God is all about. Even after his victory and his words of devotion to God, he makes a gold idol (see Jgs 8:22–28).

Most people are tempted to test God in some way: "God, I'll know you are there for me if I get this job." Fortunately, God is big enough to accept our testing. Just do not expect God to answer every request—at least not exactly the way you would like God to answer it.

How do you test God? Is your prayer more trusting than Gideon's prayer? The next time you feel anxious or afraid, use one of these Scripture passages for your prayer: Psalm 25; Psalm 27; John, chapter 14; 1 John 4:7–21. Challenge yourself to trust God without testing.

▶ Jgs 6:36–40

messenger of God said to him: Take the meat and
unleavened cakes and lay them on this rock; then
pour out the broth. When he had done so, 21 the
messenger of the LORD stretched out the tip of the
staff he held. When he touched the meat and un-
leavened cakes, a fire came up from the rock and
consumed the meat and unleavened cakes. Then
the messenger of the LORD disappeared from
sight. 22 † Gideon, now aware that it had been
the messenger of the LORD, said, "Alas, Lord GOD,
that I have seen the messenger of the LORD face to
face!"* 23 The LORD answered him: You are safe.
Do not fear. You shall not die. 24 So Gideon built
there an altar to the LORD and called it Yahweh-
shalom.† * To this day it is still in Ophrah of the
Abiezrites.
25 That same night the LORD said to him: Take
your father's bull, the bull fattened for seven
years, and pull down your father's altar to Baal.
As for the asherah† beside it, cut it down 26 and
build an altar to the LORD, your God, on top of
this stronghold with the pile of wood. Then take
the fattened bull and offer it as a whole-burnt
sacrifice on the wood from the asherah you have
cut down. 27 So Gideon took ten of his servants
and did as the LORD had commanded him. But
he was too afraid of his family and of the towns-
people to do it by day; he did it at night. 28 Early
the next morning the townspeople found that
the altar of Baal had been dismantled, the ashe-
rah beside it cut down, and the fattened bull
offered on the altar that was built. 29 They asked
one another, "Who did this?" They inquired and
searched until they were told, "Gideon, son of
Joash, did it." 30 So the townspeople said to Jo-
ash, "Bring out your son that he may die, for he
has dismantled the altar of Baal and cut down
the asherah that was beside it." 31 But Joash re-
plied to all who were standing around him, "Is it
for you to take action for Baal, or be his savior?
Anyone who takes action for him shall be put to
death by morning. If he is a god, let him act for
himself,* since his altar has been dismantled!"
32 So on that day Gideon was called Jerubbaal,† *
because of the words, "Let Baal take action
against him, since he dismantled his altar."
33 Then all Midian and Amalek and the Ked-
emites mustered and crossed over into the valley
of Jezreel, where they encamped. 34 And Gideon
was clothed with the spirit of the LORD,† * and he
blew the horn summoning Abiezer to follow him.
35 He sent messengers throughout Manasseh, and
they, too, were summoned to follow him; he also
sent messengers throughout Asher, Zebulun, and
Naphtali, and they advanced to meet the others.
36 Gideon said to God, "If indeed you are going
to save Israel through me, as you have said, 37 I
am putting this woolen fleece on the threshing
floor, and if dew is on the fleece alone, while all
the ground is dry, I shall know that you will save

†

6:22 Ancient Israel thought that seeing God face to face meant mortal danger, as Ex 33:20 indicates and as Gideon's reaction here shows. Compare the reaction of Samson's parents (13:22–23) when they realize they have been conversing with the Lord.

6:24 *Yahweh-shalom*: a reference to the Lord's words, "You are safe" (v. 23), lit., "Peace be to you!"

6:25 *The asherah*: see note on Ex 34:13.

6:32 *Jerubbaal*: similar in sound to the Hebrew words meaning, "Let Baal take action."

6:34 *Clothed with the spirit of the LORD*: narratives about the selection of leaders in early Israel typically attribute their prowess to "the spirit of the Lord," not to their own qualities (cf. v. 15). The Lord's spirit "comes upon" them (3:10; 11:29; 13:25) or "rushes upon" them (14:6, 19; 15:14; 1 Sm 11:6), and they are transformed into effective leaders. Here, Gideon is "clothed" with the Lord's spirit; cf. the clothing or vesture imagery in Is 59:17; 61:10; Ez 16:10–14; Jb 29:14.

*

6:22 Gn 32:31; Dt 5:24–26; Jgs 13:22.
6:24 Gn 33:20; 35:7; Ex 7:15.
6:31 1 Kgs 18:27.
6:32 1 Sm 12:11.
6:34 Jgs 3:10; 11:29; 13:25; 14:6, 19; 15:14; 1 Sm 11:6.

Israel through me, as you have said." 38 That is
what happened. Early the next morning when he
wrung out the fleece, he squeezed enough dew
from it to fill a bowl. 39 Gideon then said to God,
"Do not be angry with me if I speak once more.
Let me make just one more test with the fleece.
Let the fleece alone be dry, but let there be dew
on all the ground." 40 That is what God did that
night: the fleece alone was dry, but there was dew
on all the ground.

Defeat of Midian

7 1 Early the next morning Jerubbaal* (that is,
Gideon) encamped by the spring of Harod
with all his soldiers. The camp of Midian was
north of him, beside the hill of Moreh in the
valley. 2 The LORD said to Gideon: You have too
many soldiers with you for me to deliver Midian
into their power, lest Israel vaunt itself against
me and say, "My own power saved me."† *
3 So announce in the hearing of the soldiers, "If
anyone is afraid or fearful, let him leave!* Let
him depart from Mount Gilead!"† Twenty-two
thousand of the soldiers left, but ten thousand
remained. 4 The LORD said to Gideon: There are
still too many soldiers. Lead them down to the
water and I will test them for you there. If I tell
you that a certain man is to go with you, he
must go with you. But no one is to go if I tell
you he must not. 5 † When Gideon led the sol-
diers down to the water, the LORD said to him:
Everyone who laps up the water as a dog does
with its tongue you shall set aside by himself;
and everyone who kneels down to drink raising
his hand to his mouth you shall set aside by him-
self. 6 Those who lapped up the water with their
tongues numbered three hundred, but all the rest
of the soldiers knelt down to drink the water.
7 The LORD said to Gideon: By means of the three
hundred who lapped up the water I will save you
and deliver Midian into your power. So let all
the other soldiers go home. 8 They took up such
supplies as the soldiers had with them, as well as
their horns, and Gideon sent the rest of the Isra-
elites to their tents, but kept the three hundred
men. Now the camp of Midian was below him
in the valley.

9 That night the LORD said to Gideon: Go, de-
scend on the camp, for I have delivered it into
your power. 10 If you are afraid to attack, go down
to the camp with your aide Purah 11 and listen
to what they are saying. After that you will have
the courage to descend on the camp. So he went
down with his aide Purah to the outposts of the
armed men in the camp. 12 * The Midianites, Am-
alekites, and all the Kedemites were lying in the
valley, thick as locusts. Their camels could not
be counted, for they were as many as the sands
on the seashore. 13 † When Gideon arrived, one
man was telling another about a dream. "I had
a dream," he said, "that a round loaf of barley
bread was rolling into the camp of Midian. It
came to a certain tent and struck it and turned
it upside down, and the tent collapsed." 14 "This
can only be the sword of the Israelite Gideon,
son of Joash," the other replied. "God has deliv-
ered Midian and all the camp into his power."
15 When Gideon heard the account of the dream
and its explanation, he bowed down. Then re-
turning to the camp of Israel, he said, "Arise, for
the LORD has delivered the camp of Midian into
your power."

16 He divided the three hundred men into three
companies, and provided them all with horns
and with empty jars and torches inside the jars.
17 "Watch me and follow my lead," he told them.
"I shall go to the edge of the camp, and as I do,
you must do also. 18 When I and those with me
blow horns, you too must blow horns all around
the camp and cry out, 'For the LORD and for Gid-
eon!' " 19 So Gideon and the hundred men who
were with him came to the edge of the camp at
the beginning of the middle watch,† just after the
posting of the guards. They blew the horns and
broke the jars they were holding. 20 When the
three companies had blown their horns and bro-
ken their jars, they took the torches in their left
hands, and in their right the horns they had been
blowing, and cried out, "A sword for the LORD
and for Gideon!" 21 They all remained standing
in place around the camp, while the whole camp
began to run and shout and flee. 22 When they
blew the three hundred horns, the LORD set the
sword of one against another throughout the

JGS

† **7:2** *My own power saved me*: Deuteronomic theology constantly warns Israel against attributing success to their own efforts; cf. Dt 6:10–12; 8:17.

7:3 *Mount Gilead*: since the well-known highlands of Gilead were east of the Jordan River, some other hill of Gilead must be intended here. Perhaps its name is preserved in Ain Jalud (or Galud), the modern Arabic name of the spring of Harod, where Gideon's army is encamped (v. 1). The narrator plays on the Hebrew word "fearful" (*hared*) and the name of the spring, *harod*.

7:5 The point of this selection process is clear: the battle against the nomadic raiders is going to be won not because of the numerical superiority of the Israelite troops but because of the power of the Lord.

7:13 The dream seems to foretell the victory of the agricultural Israelites (the barley loaf) over the nomadic Midianites (the tent).

7:19 *At the beginning of the middle watch*: at the start of the second of the three watches into which the night was divided. The sentinels were changed at the beginning of a watch, thus making the camp momentarily vulnerable.

* **7:1** Jgs 6:32.
7:2 Dt 8:17; 9:4.
7:3 Dt 20:8.
7:12 Jgs 6:3.

camp, and they fled as far as Beth-shittah in the
direction of Zeredah, near the border of Abel-
meholah at Tabbath.
23 * The Israelites were called to arms from
Naphtali, from Asher, and from all Manasseh,
and they pursued Midian. 24 Gideon also sent
messengers throughout the mountain region
of Ephraim to say, "Go down to intercept Mid-
ian, and seize the water courses against them as
far as Beth-barah, as well as the Jordan." So all
the Ephraimites were called to arms, and they
seized the water courses as far as Beth-barah, and
the Jordan as well. 25 * They captured the two
princes of Midian, Oreb and Zeeb, killing Oreb
at the rock of Oreb and Zeeb at the wine press of
Zeeb. Then they pursued Midian, but they had
the heads of Oreb and Zeeb brought to Gideon
beyond the Jordan.

8 1 * But the Ephraimites said to him, "What
have you done to us, not summoning us
when you went to fight against Midian?" And
they quarreled bitterly with him. 2 But he an-
swered them, "What have I done in comparison
with you? Is not the gleaning of Ephraim better
than the vintage of Abiezer?* 3 It was into your
power God delivered the princes of Midian, Oreb
and Zeeb.* What have I been able to do in com-
parison with you?" When he said this, their anger
against him subsided.
4 When Gideon reached the Jordan and crossed
it, he and his three hundred men were exhausted
and famished. 5 So he said to the people of Suc-
coth, "Will you give my followers some loaves
of bread? They are exhausted, and I am pursuing
Zebah and Zalmunna, kings of Midian." 6 But
the princes of Succoth replied, "Are the hands
of Zebah and Zalmunna already in your posses-
sion, that we should give food to your army?"†
7 Gideon said, "Very well; when the LORD has
delivered Zebah and Zalmunna into my power,
I will thrash your bodies with desert thorns and
briers." 8 He went up from there to Penuel and
made the same request of them, but the people
of Penuel answered him as had the people of
Succoth. 9 So to the people of Penuel, too, he
said, "When I return in peace, I will demolish
this tower."
10 Now Zebah and Zalmunna were in Kar-
kor with their force of about fifteen thousand
men; these were all who were left of the whole
Kedemite army, a hundred and twenty thousand
swordsmen having fallen. 11 Gideon went up by
the route of the tent-dwellers east of Nobah and
Jogbehah, and attacked the force when it felt
secure. 12 Zebah and Zalmunna fled and Gid-
eon pursued them. He captured the two kings
of Midian, Zebah and Zalmunna, terrifying the
entire force.
13 Then Gideon, son of Joash, returned from
battle by the pass of Heres. 14 He captured a
young man of Succoth and questioned him,
and he wrote down for him the seventy-seven
princes and elders of Succoth. 15 So he went to
the princes of Succoth and said, "Here are Zebah
and Zalmunna, with whom you taunted me,
'Are the hands of Zebah and Zalmunna already
in your possession, that we should give food
to your weary men?' " 16 He seized the elders
of the city, and with desert thorns and briers
he thrashed the people of Succoth. 17 He also
demolished the tower of Penuel and killed the
people of the city.
18 Then he said to Zebah and Zalmunna, "What
about the men you killed at Tabor?" "They were
all like you," they replied. "They appeared to be
princes." 19 "They were my brothers, my mother's
sons," he said. "As the LORD lives, if you had
spared their lives, I would not kill you." 20 Then
he said to his firstborn, Jether, "Go, kill them."
But the boy did not draw his sword, for he was
afraid, for he was still a boy. 21 * Zebah and Zal-
munna said, "Come, kill us yourself, for as a
man is, so is his strength." So Gideon stepped
forward and killed Zebah and Zalmunna. He
also took the crescents that were on the necks of
their camels.
22 * The Israelites then said to Gideon, "Rule
over us—you, your son, and your son's son—for
you saved us from the power of Midian." 23 But
Gideon answered them, "I will not rule over you,
nor shall my son rule over you. The LORD must
rule over you."*
24 Gideon went on to say, "Let me make a re-
quest of you. Give me, each of you, a ring from
his spoils." (Since they were Ishmaelites,† the
enemy had gold rings.) 25 "We will certainly give
them," they replied, and they spread out a cloak
into which everyone threw a ring from his spoils.
26 The gold rings he had requested weighed

†

8:6 *Are the hands . . . already in your possession . . . ?*: i.e., can you already boast of victory? The hands of slain enemies were sometimes cut off and counted as trophies.

8:24 *Ishmaelites*: evidently used here as a general term for nomads, whose wealth was in the form of gold and flocks. The genealogies in Genesis place the Midianites as descendants of Abraham and his wife Keturah (Gn 25:1–2), and the Ishmaelites as the descendants of Ishmael, son of Abraham and Hagar, Sarah's Egyptian slave (Gn 25:12–16).

*

7:23 Jgs 6:35.
7:25 Ps 83:12; Is 10:26.
8:1 Jgs 12:1.
8:2 Jgs 6:34.
8:3 Jgs 7:25.
8:21 Ps 83:12.
8:22 1 Sm 8:5; Hos 13:10.
8:23 1 Sm 8:7; 10:19; 12:12.

seventeen hundred gold shekels, apart from the
crescents and pendants, the purple garments
worn by the kings of Midian, and apart from the
trappings that were on the necks of their camels.
27 * Gideon made an ephod out of the gold and
placed it in his city, Ophrah. All Israel prostituted
themselves there, and it became a snare to Gid-
eon and his household.
28 Midian was brought into subjection by the
Israelites; they no longer held their heads high,
and the land had rest for forty years,* during the
lifetime of Gideon.

Gideon's Son Abimelech

29 Then Jerubbaal, son of Joash, went to live
in his house. 30 * Now Gideon had seventy sons,
his own offspring, for he had many wives. 31 His
concubine† who lived in Shechem also bore him
a son, whom he named Abimelech. 32 At a good
old age Gideon, son of Joash, died and was bur-
ied in the tomb of Joash his father in Ophrah of
the Abiezrites. 33 * But after Gideon was dead,
the Israelites again prostituted themselves by fol-
lowing the Baals, making Baal-berith† their god.
34 The Israelites did not remember the LORD, their
God, who had delivered them from the power of
their enemies all around them. 35 Nor were they
loyal to the house of Jerubbaal (Gideon) for all
the good he had done for Israel.

9 1 Abimelech, son of Jerubbaal, went to his
mother's kin in Shechem,* and said to them
and to the whole clan to which his mother's
family belonged, 2 "Put this question to all the
lords of Shechem: 'Which is better for you: that
seventy men, all Jerubbaal's sons, rule over you,
or that one man rule over you?' You must re-
member that I am your own flesh and bone."*
3 When his mother's kin repeated these words
on his behalf to all the lords of Shechem, they
set their hearts on Abimelech, thinking, "He is
our kin." 4 They also gave him seventy pieces of
silver from the temple of Baal-berith, with which
Abimelech hired worthless men and outlaws as
his followers. 5 He then went to his father's house
in Ophrah, and killed his brothers, the seventy
sons of Jerubbaal, on one stone. Only the youn-
gest son of Jerubbaal, Jotham, escaped, for he
was hidden. 6 Then all the lords of Shechem and
all Beth-millo came together and made Abime-
lech king by the terebinth at the memorial pillar
in Shechem.
7 When this was reported to Jotham, he went
and stood at the top of Mount Gerizim and cried
out in a loud voice:

"Hear me, lords of Shechem,
and may God hear you!
8 One day the trees went out
to anoint a king over themselves.
So they said to the olive tree,
'Reign over us.'
9 But the olive tree answered them,
'Must I give up my rich oil,
whereby gods and human beings are
honored,†
and go off to hold sway over the trees?'
10 Then the trees said to the fig tree,
'Come; you reign over us!'
11 But the fig tree answered them,
'Must I give up my sweetness
and my sweet fruit,
and go off to hold sway over the trees?'
12 Then the trees said to the vine,
'Come you, reign over us.'
13 But the vine answered them,
'Must I give up my wine
that cheers gods† and human beings,
and go off to hold sway over the trees?'
14 Then all the trees said to the buckthorn,
'Come; you reign over us!'
15 The buckthorn answered the trees,
'If you are anointing me in good faith,
to make me king over you,
come, and take refuge in my shadow.
But if not, let fire come from the buckthorn
and devour the cedars of Lebanon.'*

16 "Now then, if you have acted in good faith
and integrity in appointing Abimelech your
king, if you have acted with good will toward
Jerubbaal and his house, and if you have treated
him as he deserved— 17 for my father fought for
you at the risk of his life when he delivered you
from the power of Midian, 18 but you have risen
against my father's house today and killed his
seventy sons upon one stone and made Abime-
lech, the son of his maidservant,* king over the

†

8:31 *Concubine*: a wife of secondary rank.

8:33 *Baal-berith*: a divine epithet meaning "lord of the covenant." The same deity is called El-berith, "god of the covenant," in 9:46.

9:9 *Whereby gods and human beings are honored*: olive oil had a variety of cultic uses (e.g., Lv 2:1, 6, 15; 24:2), and it was also used in the consecration of priests and kings for office (e.g., Ex 30:25, 30; 1 Sm 10:1; 16:13).

9:13 *Cheers gods*: wine was part of a number of types of offerings in the Israelite cult (cf. Ex 29:40; Lv 23:13; Nm 15:7, 10), and it was also used widely in the worship of foreign gods (cf. Dt 32:37–38; Is 65:11).

*

8:27 Jgs 17:5; 18:14.
8:28 Jgs 3:11, 30; 5:31.
8:30 Jgs 9:2, 5; 10:4; 12:9, 14.
8:33–34 Jgs 2:19; 3:12; 4:1.
9:1 Jgs 8:31.
9:2 2 Sm 5:1; 19:12, 13.
9:15 2 Kgs 14:9.
9:18 Jgs 8:31.

lords of Shechem, because he is your kin— 19 if,
then, you have acted in good faith and integrity
toward Jerubbaal and his house today, then re-
joice in Abimelech and may he in turn rejoice
in you! 20 But if not, let fire come forth from
Abimelech and devour the lords of Shechem
and Beth-millo, and let fire come forth from the
lords of Shechem and Beth-millo and devour
Abimelech." 21 Then Jotham fled and escaped to
Beer, where he remained for fear of his brother
Abimelech.

22 When Abimelech had ruled Israel for three
years, 23 God put an evil spirit* between Abime-
lech and the lords of Shechem, and the lords of
Shechem broke faith with the house of Abime-
lech. 24 This was to repay the violence done to
the seventy sons of Jerubbaal and to avenge their
blood upon their brother Abimelech, who killed
them, and upon the lords of Shechem, who en-
couraged him to kill his brothers. 25 The lords of
Shechem then set men in ambush for him on the
mountaintops, and they robbed all who passed
them on the road. It was reported to Abimelech.

26 Now Gaal, son of Ebed, and his kin came,
and when they passed through Shechem, the
lords of Shechem put their trust in him. 27 They
went out into the fields, harvested the grapes
from their vineyards, trod them out, and held
a festival. Then they went to the temple of
their god, where they ate and drank and cursed
Abimelech. 28 * Gaal, son of Ebed, said, "Who is
Abimelech? And who is Shechem that we should
serve him? Did not the son of Jerubbaal and
his lieutenant Zebul serve the men of Hamor,
father of Shechem?* So why should we serve
him? 29 Would that these troops were entrusted
to my command! I would depose Abimelech. I
would say to Abimelech, 'Get a larger army and
come out!' "

30 When Zebul, the ruler of the city, heard what
Gaal, son of Ebed, had said, he was angry 31 and
sent messengers to Abimelech in Arumah to say,
"Gaal, son of Ebed, and his kin have come to
Shechem and are stirring up the city against you.
32 So take action tonight, you and the troops who
are with you, and set an ambush in the fields.
33 Promptly at sunrise tomorrow morning, make
a raid on the city. When he and the troops who
are with him come out against you, deal with
him as best you can."

34 During the night Abimelech went into ac-
tion with all his soldiers and set up an ambush
outside of Shechem in four companies. 35 Gaal,
son of Ebed, went out and stood at the entrance
of the city gate. When Abimelech and his soldiers
rose from their place of ambush, 36 Gaal saw the
soldiers and said to Zebul, "There are soldiers
coming down from the mountaintops!" But Ze-
bul answered him, "It is the shadow of the hills
that you see as men." 37 But Gaal went on to say,
"Soldiers are coming down from the region of
Tabbur-haarez, and one company is coming by
way of Elon-meonenim." 38 Zebul said to him,
"Where now is your boast, when you said, 'Who
is Abimelech that we should serve him?' Are
these not the troops for whom you expressed
contempt? Go out now and fight with them."
39 So Gaal went out at the head of the lords of
Shechem to fight against Abimelech; 40 but when
Abimelech went after him, he fled from him.
Many fell slain right up to the entrance of the
gate. 41 Abimelech returned to Arumah, and Ze-
bul drove Gaal and his kin away so that they
could no longer remain at Shechem.

42 The next day, the army marched out into
the field, and it was reported to Abimelech. 43 He
divided the troops he had into three companies,
and set up an ambush in the fields. He watched
until he saw the army leave the city and then
went on the attack against them. 44 Abimelech
and the company with him rushed in and stood
by the entrance of the city gate, while the other
two companies rushed upon all who were in the
field and attacked them. 45 That entire day Abim-
elech fought against the city. He captured it,
killed the people who were in it, and demolished
the city itself, sowing it with salt.† *

46 When they heard of this, all the lords of the
Migdal-shechem went into the crypt of the tem-
ple of El-berith. 47 It was reported to Abimelech
that all the lords of the Migdal-shechem were
gathered together. 48 So he went up Mount Zal-
mon with all his soldiers, took his ax in his hand,
and cut down some brushwood. This he lifted to
his shoulder, then said to the troops with him,
"Hurry! Do just as you have seen me do." 49 So
all the soldiers likewise cut down brushwood
and, following Abimelech, placed it against the
crypt. Then they set the crypt on fire over them,
so that every one of the people of the Migdal-
shechem, about a thousand men and women,
perished.

50 Abimelech proceeded to Thebez, encamped,
and captured it. 51 Now there was a strong tower
in the middle of the city, and all the men and
women and all the lords of the city fled there,

† **9:45** *Sowing it with salt*: a severe measure, since it rendered the soil barren and useless.

* **9:23** 1 Sm 16:14; 18:10; 19:9; 1 Kgs 22:19–23.
9:28 1 Sm 25:10.
9:28 Gn 33:19; 34:2.
9:45 Dt 29:23; Jer 17:6; Ps 107:34.

JGS

shutting themselves in and going up to the roof
of the tower. 52 Abimelech came up to the tower
and fought against it. When he came close to the
entrance of the tower to set it on fire, 53 a cer-
tain woman cast the upper part of a millstone†
down on Abimelech's head, and it fractured his
skull.* 54 He immediately called his armor-bearer
and said to him, "Draw your sword and put
me to death so they will not say about me, 'A
woman killed him.'"* So his attendant ran him
through and he died. 55 When the Israelites saw
that Abimelech was dead, they all left for their
homes.

56 Thus did God repay the evil that Abime-
lech had done to his father in killing his seventy
brothers. 57 God also brought all the wickedness
of the people of Shechem back on their heads,
for the curse of Jotham, son of Jerubbaal, over-
took them.

Tola

10 1 After Abimelech, Tola,† son of Puah, son
of Dodo, a man of Issachar, rose up to
save Israel; he lived in Shamir in the mountain
region of Ephraim. 2 When he had judged Israel
twenty-three years, he died and was buried in
Shamir.

Jair

3 Jair the Gileadite came after him and judged
Israel twenty-two years. 4* He had thirty sons
who rode on thirty donkeys† and possessed
thirty cities in the land of Gilead (these are called
Havvoth-jair to the present day).* 5 Jair died and
was buried in Kamon.

Oppression by the Ammonites

6* The Israelites again did what was evil in the
sight of the LORD, serving the Baals and Ashtarts,
the gods of Aram, the gods of Sidon, the gods of
Moab, the gods of the Ammonites, and the gods
of the Philistines. Since they had abandoned
the LORD and would not serve him, 7 the LORD
became angry with Israel and he sold them into
the power of the Philistines and the Ammonites.
8 For eighteen years they afflicted and oppressed
the Israelites in Bashan, and all the Israelites in
the Amorite land beyond the Jordan in Gilead.
9 The Ammonites also crossed the Jordan to

Pray It!

The Effects of Sin

Once again the Israelites lapse into sin and worship other gods (see Jgs 10:6). Once again they cry out to God to save them (see verse 10). Did they think their sins would have no effect on their lives?

Listen to these words from Pope John Paul II:

> There is no sin, not even the most intimate and secret one, the most strictly individual one, that exclusively concerns the person committing it. With greater or lesser violence, with greater or lesser harm, every sin has repercussions on the . . . whole human family.

Have you done anything today that brought harm to you or others? Have you used your gifts and talents as God intended them to be used? Have you neglected an opportunity to share God's love with another person?

Lord, you know all things. Look on me with love, and hear my prayer. Forgive my sins, and give me strength to turn away from the lure of sin. Help me to be more generous in serving you and my neighbor. Help me to be a true follower of your Son, Jesus. Amen.

▶ Jgs 10:10–16

fight against Judah, Benjamin and the house of
Ephraim, so that Israel was in great distress.
10* Then the Israelites cried out to the LORD,
"We have sinned against you, for we have aban-
doned our God and served the Baals." 11* The
LORD answered the Israelites: Did not the Egyp-
tians, the Amorites,* the Ammonites, the Philis-
tines, 12 the Sidonians, the Amalekites, and the
Midianites* oppress you? Yet when you cried out
to me, and I saved you from their power, 13 you

JGS

---

† **9:53** *The upper part of a millstone*: a common hand mill consisted of a large flat stone base and a smaller upper stone (cf. Dt 24:6) shaped so that it could be held in the hands and rolled or ground against the lower stone. It is an upper stone that the woman hurls over the wall to kill Abimelech.

10:1–5 *Tola . . . Jair*: two more of the so-called "minor judges"; see Introduction.

10:4 *Donkeys*: mounts signifying rank and wealth; cf. 5:10; 12:14.

* **9:53** 2 Sm 11:21.
9:54 1 Sm 31:4; 2 Sm 1:9; 1 Chr 10:4.
10:4 Jgs 8:30; 9:2, 5; 12:9, 14.
10:4 Dt 3:14.
10:6–8 Jgs 2:11–14; 3:7–8, 12; 4:1–2; 6:1; 13:1.
10:10 Jgs 3:9, 15; 4:3; 6:6, 7; 1 Sm 12:8, 10.
10:11–14 Jgs 2:1–3; 6:8–10.
10:11 Nm 21:21–32.
10:12 Jgs 6:1–6.

still abandoned me and served other gods. Therefore I will save you no more.* 14 Go and cry out to the gods you have chosen; let them save you in your time of distress. 15 But the Israelites said to the LORD, "We have sinned. Do to us whatever is good in your sight. Only deliver us this day!" 16 And they cast out the foreign gods from their midst and served the LORD, so that he grieved over the misery of Israel.

17 The Ammonites were called out for war and encamped in Gilead, while the Israelites assembled and encamped at Mizpah. 18 The captains of the army of Gilead said to one another, "The one who begins the war against the Ammonites shall be leader of all the inhabitants of Gilead."*

Jephthah

11 1 Jephthah* the Gileadite was a warrior. He was the son of a prostitute, fathered by Gilead. 2 Gilead's wife had also borne him sons. When they grew up the sons of the wife had driven Jephthah away, saying to him, "You shall inherit nothing in our father's house, for you are the son of another woman." 3 So Jephthah had fled from his brothers and taken up residence in the land of Tob.* Worthless men had joined company with him, and went out with him on raids.*

4 Some time later, the Ammonites went to war with Israel. 5 As soon as the Ammonites were at war with Israel, the elders of Gilead went to bring Jephthah from the land of Tob. 6 "Come," they said to Jephthah, "be our commander so that we can fight the Ammonites." 7 "Are you not the ones who hated me and drove me from my father's house?" Jephthah replied to the elders of Gilead, "Why do you come to me now, when you are in distress?" 8 * The elders of Gilead said to Jephthah, "This is the reason we have come back to you now: if you go with us to fight against the Ammonites, you shall be the leader of all of the inhabitants of Gilead." 9 Jephthah answered the elders of Gilead, "If you bring me back to fight against the Ammonites and the LORD delivers them up to me, I will be your leader." 10 The elders of Gilead said to Jephthah, "The LORD is witness between us that we will do as you say." 11 So Jephthah went with the elders of Gilead, and the army made him their leader and commander. Jephthah gave all his orders in the presence of the LORD in Mizpah.

12 Then he sent messengers to the king of the Ammonites to say, "What do you have against me that you come to fight with me in my land?" 13 The king of the Ammonites answered the messengers of Jephthah, "Israel took away my land from the Arnon to the Jabbok and the Jordan when they came up from Egypt.* Now restore it peaceably."

14 Again Jephthah sent messengers to the king of the Ammonites, 15 saying to him, "This is what Jephthah says: 'Israel did not take the land of Moab or the land of the Ammonites.* 16 For when they came up from Egypt, Israel went through the wilderness to the Red Sea and came to Kadesh. 17 Israel then sent messengers to the king of Edom saying, "Let me pass through your land." But the king of Edom did not give consent.* They also sent to the king of Moab, but he too was unwilling. So Israel remained in Kadesh.* 18 Then they went through the wilderness, and bypassing the land of Edom and the land of Moab, they arrived east of the land of Moab and encamped across the Arnon.* Thus they did not enter the territory of Moab, for the Arnon is the boundary of Moab.* 19 * Then Israel sent messengers to the Amorite king Sihon, who was king of Heshbon. Israel said to him, "Let me pass through your land to my own place." 20 But Sihon refused to let Israel pass through his territory. He gathered all his soldiers, and they encamped at Jahaz and fought Israel. 21 But the LORD, the God of Israel, delivered Sihon and his entire army into the power of Israel, who defeated them and occupied all the land of the Amorites who lived in that region. 22 They occupied all of the Amorite territory from the Arnon to the Jabbok and the wilderness to the Jordan.* 23 Now, then, it was the LORD, the God of Israel, who dispossessed the Amorites for his people, Israel. And you are going to dispossess them? 24 Should you not take possession of that which your god Chemosh† gave you to possess, and should we not take possession of all that the LORD, our God, has dispossessed for us? 25 Now, then, are you any better than Balak, son of Zippor, king of Moab? Did he ever quarrel with Israel or make war against them?* 26 Israel has dwelt in Heshbon and its

JGS

---

† **11:24** *Chemosh*: the god of the Moabites (1 Kgs 11:7; 2 Kgs 23:13) not the Ammonites, whose god was Milcom (1 Kgs 11:5; 2 Kgs 23:13). Much of the disputed land, which lay between the Jabbok and Arnon Rivers, was actually in Moab, and many of the details of this passage (vv. 12–28) seem more applicable to a quarrel with the king of the Moabites than with the king of the Ammonites.

---

* **10:13** Jgs 2:21.
10:18 Jgs 11:5–11.
11:1 Heb 11:32.
11:3 2 Sm 10:6, 8.
11:3 Jgs 9:4; 1 Sm 22:2.
11:8–11 Jgs 10:18.
11:13 Nm 21:24.
11:15 Dt 2:9, 19.
11:17 Nm 21:14–21.
11:17 Dt 1:46.
11:18 Nm 20:21; 21:4, 10–12; Dt 2:8.
11:18 Nm 21:13; 22:36.
11:19–21 Nm 21:21–26; Dt 2:26–36.
11:22 Jgs 11:13.
11:25 Nm 22–24; Jos 24:9–10; Mi 6:5.

Reading & Studying the Bible

What Is the Bible?

The Bible—which is also called the Sacred Scriptures—tells the story of the loving relationship between God and humankind. Through the sacred writings, God reveals to humankind the truth about God and God's will for us. It is a library of books that is divided into two parts: the Old Testament (before Jesus) and the New Testament (after Jesus' birth). Each part consists of a collection of books that are grouped into these sections:

- *The Pentateuch* (five books) tells about God's Chosen People, the Israelites. You'll read about their early stories, their history, and the laws God gave them.
- *The historical books* pick up Israelite history from 1250 BC to 100 BC. You will find accounts of the Israelites' settling the Promised Land, the rise and fall of their kings, their dispersion into exile, and their eventual return to the Promised Land.
- *The biblical novellas* are three books that contain entertaining stories told to instruct and encourage the people of God during critical times. They illustrate truths that transcend history.
- *The wisdom and poetry books* are a collection of hymns, poems, proverbs, and stories. They use imaginative language to make their points.
- *The prophets* are people who speak God's word. In these books, you will find comfort and promise, as well as be challenged to act with justice and mercy.
- *The Gospels* (Good News) focus on the person and teachings of Jesus. *The Acts of the Apostles* shows how the Church was formed and how the first Christians spread the Good News. These books cover the time period from 5 BC to the early AD 60s.
- The *letters,* or *epistles* (written by Paul, his followers, and other disciples), are actual letters that describe the new Christian faith, give advice, and offer words of hope. *Revelation* is a collection of mystical visions written to encourage the early Christians who were being persecuted.

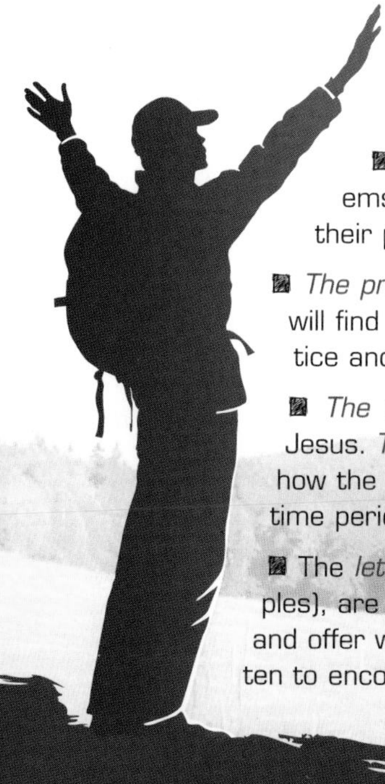

Core Catholic Teachings on Reason and Revelation

The Catholic Church makes frequent appeal to human reason in teaching about the religious truths God has revealed:

- Revelation is God making himself and his divine plan known to the human race through words and deeds in human history.
- The human person must trust that God has revealed to the Church what God wants it to know for its salvation.
- In listening to the message of Creation and to the voice of conscience, every person can come to certainty about the existence of God.
- Through the natural light of human reason, the one true God can be known from his works—that is, from the world and from the human person. This is one reason the Church teaches that salvation is possible for every person, even those who have never heard of Jesus Christ.
- God has revealed God's self in order to restore the communion that human beings were created to have with God, before the relationship was broken by original sin.
- Revelation is communicated in the Bible's stories of how God made God's self known to the Chosen People by acting throughout their history. But when those attempts met with failure, God took a radical step. God sent God's son, Jesus Christ, into the world as the savior. While remaining fully God, Jesus Christ took on a human nature: he is both true God and true man. Thus Jesus Christ is the full and complete Revelation of who God is, and through Christ, God established the covenant with the human race forever. As the Bible tells us, "[Christ] is the image of the invisible God" (Col 1:15).
- Everything needed to be known about God; everything needed to be known for eternal union with God has been revealed in Christ. Nothing more needs to be added or taken away.

Core Catholic Teachings on the Scriptures and Tradition

The Catholic Church teaches:

- Christ promised to send the Holy Spirit to his closest followers, the Apostles, after he physically left them to ascend into heaven: "When he comes, the Spirit of truth, he will guide you to all truth" (Jn 16:13). The Holy Spirit helped the Apostles to remember and understand all that Jesus did and taught. These truths about Jesus and his teachings are therefore called the Apostolic Tradition, or sometimes just the Tradition.
- Under the inspiration of the Holy Spirit, the Apostles handed on everything they knew about Jesus to the first Christians and to the generation of leaders that followed them.
- The Holy Spirit inspired people in the early Church to create written documents explaining what the Apostles had handed down about Jesus.
- The Scriptures and Tradition are two sources of Revelation. They are closely connected and together form a single sacred deposit of truth under the guidance of the Holy Spirit. They can never be in conflict, and each one helps us to understand the other.
- The Church looks to God's Revelation in the Scriptures and Tradition as the only authentic and complete source for knowledge about God and God's will for the whole human race. It is the responsibility of the Church, through her teaching, her worship, and her ministries, to transmit to every new generation all that God has revealed.
- As the successors of the Apostles, it is the particular and exclusive responsibility of the bishops in union with the Pope—the Magisterium—to faithfully teach, interpret, and preserve the Scriptures and Tradition for all believers until Christ returns in glory.

"[Christ] is the image of the invisible God."

— Col 1:15

Overview of Salvation History

Primeval History

The Bible starts with some imaginative stories that tell how God made everything, along with the first humans, Adam and Eve. God's Creation was good, but evil crept into the world. After several generations, God decided to flood the world. But God saved Noah, his family, and specimens of land animals on an ark (boat) in order to give humans a chance to start over.

Patriarchs and Matriarchs (1850–1750 BC)

Abraham and Sarah arrived in Canaan, the land God had promised them. They were old, but God gave them a son, Isaac, who had two sons with his wife Rebecca. The younger was Jacob, whom God named Israel. Israel had twelve sons, but his favorite was Joseph. Joseph's jealous brothers sold him as a slave in Egypt, but God helped him to prosper. When Joseph's brothers visited Egypt, Joseph recognized them and told them to come live with him.

Egypt and Exodus (1750–1290 BC)

Israel's descendants (sometimes called Hebrews, Israelites, the Tribes of Israel, or the Children of Israel) became a small nation. But a new Egyptian dynasty came to power and made the Hebrews slaves. Eventually, God told Moses to bring them out of Egypt. To convince Pharaoh to let his cheap labor go, God sent a series of plagues, including the killing of all firstborn sons. The Hebrews were saved by putting the blood of a lamb over their doors. After the Hebrews left, Pharaoh sent his army to bring them back, trapping them at the Red Sea. God made the waters separate so the Hebrew people could escape; then God made the waters fall back, drowning the pursuing army. The Passover meal celebrates this victory.

Settling the Promised Land (1290–1020 BC)

While the Hebrew people were on their way back to Canaan, God made a covenant (an agreement) with them at Mount Sinai. God gave them laws, including the Ten Commandments. God told them to build a tabernacle (worship tent) and the ark of the Covenant (a box symbolizing God's presence). After a generation, the Hebrew people invaded Canaan under the leadership of Joshua. The land was divided into territories, roughly corresponding to the twelve Tribes of Israel. For over two hundred years, the Hebrews fought for the land; there was no central power, so God would occasionally raise up local leaders called judges.

The Kingdom United (1020–922 BC)

God allowed Samuel, the last of the judges, to make Saul the first king. Samuel poured oil on Saul's head, "anointing" him for leadership. The Hebrew word for an "anointed person" is *messiah* (the Greek word is *christ*). The next king was David, the greatest human king the little nation of Israel would ever have. God promised that David's house would be established forever. Next was David's son Solomon the Wise, who built a great palace and the first Temple in Jerusalem. But during Solomon's son's reign, the kingdom divided into two.

The Kingdom Divided (922–587 BC)

The northern kingdom was called Israel, and it went through several dynasties. The southern kingdom was Judah, and the Davidic dynasty stayed in power. Sadly, most of the kings were not faithful to God. So God would send prophets like Elijah to speak the word of God and call the people to faithfulness. When the northern kingdom fell to Assyria, it ceased to exist. Babylon in turn defeated Assyria and then later crushed Judah; Jerusalem and the Temple were utterly destroyed. Many Jews (inhabitants of Judah) were sent into exile in Babylon.

The Exile and the Return (587–5 BC)

Stories about heroes like Daniel kept the faith alive for Jews who were in exile. When Persia defeated Babylon, they let the Jews return home. By 515 BC, the Temple had been rebuilt. Eventually, the Greeks controlled the region and became brutally disrespectful, so Judas Maccabeus led a successful revolt. For a time, Israel was free, until Rome conquered the region in 63 BC. Weary from dark centuries of domination, the Jews began to hope for a new King, a Messiah (Christ), a Son of David, who would restore glory to Israel. In time millions would recognize a baby lying in a manger as the Christ—a light shining in the darkness.

The Life of Jesus, the Christ (5 BC–AD 30)

The angel Gabriel appeared to Mary, a young virgin, and told her she was going to have a baby—Jesus. The child would be conceived by the Holy Spirit and called the Son of God. Jesus was born in Bethlehem, with only a manger for a bed; we celebrate his birth on Christmas. Wise Men guided by a star brought gifts to Jesus; we celebrate this on Epiphany. Jesus grew up in Nazareth in Galilee.

Meanwhile, John the Baptist was baptizing people in the Jordan River when he recognized Jesus as "the Lamb of God." Jesus began teaching, often using stories called parables; he soon had a large following of disciples. Jesus preached the Gospel—Good News—with words that were both challenging and promising: we are to love God and our neighbor; this is God's greatest commandment. Even though we sin, God loves us—unconditionally—and offers us forgiveness; this is God's promise. Jesus performed many miracles, which were signs of the coming of the Reign of God. Some believed, and their faith was strengthened; others rejected Jesus.

The Death and Resurrection of Jesus, the Christ (AD 30)

Many of the Jewish leaders were upset because Jesus talked like he was above Jewish law, claimed to be the Christ, and even claimed to be God. So the authorities planned to kill him. Shortly before he was arrested, Jesus rode into Jerusalem like a king, while crowds honored him with palm branches (Palm Sunday). Later that week (Holy Thursday), Jesus ate a Passover meal with his disciples; this would be their Last Supper (and the first Eucharist). The next day (Good Friday), Jesus was crucified (brutal execution on a cross) under the authority of the Roman governor Pontius Pilate. Early Sunday morning (Easter), some women came to visit his tomb and were told that Jesus had come back to life; several times after his Resurrection, Jesus appeared to his disciples. Forty days later (Ascension Day), Jesus was lifted up into heaven.

The Early Christian Church (AD 30–70)

Fifty days after Jesus' Resurrection on Pentecost (the name of a Jewish feast day), the Holy Spirit came to the disciples and they started preaching in many languages. Thousands believed! Some refer to it as the birth of the Church. Stephen was the first martyr. Paul saw a vision of Jesus and became the first Christian missionary. Peter also had a startling vision—God told him salvation was for the Jews and the Gentiles (non-Jews). Days of persecution were ahead; Rome became increasingly intolerant and destroyed the Temple in AD 70. But Christianity kept spreading and growing. Jesus' mission of spreading the Good News of salvation continues through the Church today.

Understanding God's Revelation

The Bible was written under the inspiration of the Holy Spirit to reveal the truths about God's saving plan for humanity and for all of creation. But like any work of ancient literature, written thousands of years ago in a culture very different from our own, the Bible must be interpreted to be properly understood. If we do not follow good principles of interpretation when reading the Bible, we can arrive at misleading and even erroneous conclusions about what God is trying to say to us.

One way to describe the Church's teaching is to say that there are "lenses" through which we can look at the Bible's books and stories in order to understand what the human authors were trying to communicate to the people of their time. These lenses can also be called "contexts," because they help us put a particular book or story in its proper context or perspective. These are the lenses or contexts:

Historical Context (Conditions of the Time and Culture)

The human authors of the Bible assumed the readers of their time knew basic facts about their world. Two thousand years later, those facts may not be as apparent to us! But the work of biblical scholars has helped us to be more aware of some of the history behind the Bible's books and stories. And the more you know about biblical history, the better you will understand the meaning of certain words and events.

Literary Context (Literary Genres in Use at the Time)

It is important to remember that the Bible is more like a library than a one-volume history book. The authors of the seventy-three books of the Bible used many different literary styles to get across their ideas. Some books are short hero stories; some are religious history; some are collections of the sayings of prophets, collections of short wise sayings, or letters; and some are written in symbolic language. To properly understand the book, we must first understand what kind of literary style, or genre, the book uses. We do this automatically with writing styles we come across every day. In a news story, we expect facts based on real events; in a fairy tale, we expect to learn some truth, but we know the story itself didn't happen in real life. We must apply the same process to the Bible.

Cultural Context (Modes of Feeling, Speaking, and Narrating Then Current)

Every culture has its own cultural practices and traditions. The impact of culture affects almost every facet of life, such as the way we cut our hair; the way we dress; what we eat; how we relate to family, friends, and strangers; the way we do business; even whether we keep pets and, if we do, what kind. Without an understanding of another culture's traditions, many of that culture's practices may seem strange or even repulsive to us.

Unity of the Whole Scripture (Salvation History) Context

In order to understand what the human authors intended, we must consider the books of the Bible as independent documents. This is done to discover each author's purpose when the book was first written. But the Bible is more than just a collection of independent books that have no relationship to one another. When we put them all together, we can see God's bigger plan emerging—a plan the human authors could not fully see or comprehend until the New Testament was written. This overall plan for the salvation of God's people is often called salvation history.

Our interpretation of the Bible does not end after we consider what the human author's intention was in writing a particular book or passage. Next we must ask, "How does this book or passage fit into salvation history?" Many books and resources are available to help us learn about salvation history; being familiar with it is important if we hope to interpret the Bible correctly.

Living Tradition Context

Not all God's revealed truths are contained within the Bible. An oral tradition preceded the writing of the Gospels. Not everything in the oral tradition was written down in the Gospels (see Jn 21:25) or even fully understood at the time the New Testament was written. But guided by the Holy Spirit, all that God revealed through the life and teaching of Christ has been kept alive in the Church. This revelation is passed on through the Bible and through the living Tradition that has been passed on from the Apostles. Together the Scriptures and Tradition form a single deposit of faith. To understand all that God is revealing in the Bible, we must also consider Sacred Tradition.

Harmony Between Elements of Faith Context

This context, also called "the analogy of faith," means that ultimately there can be no contradiction between the truths God has revealed. The truths God reveals for our salvation are in harmony with one another. When, at times, there appear to be contradictions from the human authors' points of view, there are no contradictions in God's revealed truth.

"The truths God reveals for our salvation are in harmony with one another."

Core Catholic Understandings on Biblical Inspiration and Interpretation

The way Catholics interpret the Bible has sometimes been a source of conflict between Catholics and other Christians.

- All Christians believe that God is the ultimate author of the Bible because the Holy Spirit inspired the human authors in their writing. But some Christians—sometimes called fundamentalists or literalists—believe that every part of the Bible must be absolutely true in every way: historically true, geographically true, and scientifically true. Thus, for example, they believe God created the world in six twenty-four-hour days.
- The Catholic Church teaches that the Holy Spirit inspired the biblical authors to write what God wanted known for salvation. The Holy Spirit did not take over the biblical authors' humanity when they wrote. Thus the authors were subject to natural human limitations, and they also used their human creativity in their writing. To continue the example above, Catholics believe in the religious truth that God created the world and everything in it, without having to believe that the world was literally created in six twenty-four-hour days.
- Catholics understand that the Bible is without error in communicating what God wants known for salvation without having to be historically and scientifically correct in every detail.

Seven Important Questions for Interpreting the Bible

Based on the six contexts the Church uses for interpreting the Bible, here are seven summary questions you can ask when studying any book or story in the Scriptures:

1. What was the historical situation at the time this book was written? How did the human author(s) address this situation?
2. What is this book or passage's literary genre? What are the rules for understanding it?
3. Is there a cultural practice or attitude reflected in this book or passage that we need to understand to appreciate the human author's intention?
4. How does this book or story fit into the overall story of salvation history?
5. How does Sacred Tradition help us to understand this book or story? How does this book or story help us to better understand God's revealed truths in Sacred Tradition?
6. Is the truth I understand from this book or story consistent with the rest of the Scriptures and Tradition?
7. When I look at everything I learned from these six questions, what spiritual truth is God revealing?

villages, Aroer and its villages, and all the cities
on the banks of the Arnon for three hundred
years.* Why did you not recover them during
that time? 27 As for me, I have not sinned against
you, but you wrong me by making war against
me. Let the LORD, who is judge, decide this day
between the Israelites and the Ammonites!' "
28 But the king of the Ammonites paid no heed
to the message Jephthah sent him.

Jephthah's Vow

29 The spirit of the LORD came upon Jephthah.*
He passed through Gilead and Manasseh, and
through Mizpah of Gilead as well, and from Miz-
pah of Gilead he crossed over against the Am-
monites. 30 † Jephthah made a vow to the LORD.*
"If you deliver the Ammonites into my power,"
he said, 31 "whoever comes out of the doors of
my house to meet me when I return from the
Ammonites in peace shall belong to the LORD. I
shall offer him up as a burnt offering."
32 Jephthah then crossed over against the Am-
monites to fight against them, and the LORD
delivered them into his power. 33 He inflicted
a very severe defeat on them from Aroer to the
approach of Minnith—twenty cities in all—and
as far as Abel-keramin. So the Ammonites were
brought into subjection by the Israelites. 34 When
Jephthah returned to his house in Mizpah, it
was his daughter who came out to meet him,
with tambourine-playing and dancing. She was
his only child: he had neither son nor daugh-
ter besides her. 35 When he saw her, he tore his
garments and said, "Ah, my daughter! You have
struck me down and brought calamity upon me.
For I have made a vow† to the LORD and I cannot
take it back."* 36 "Father," she replied, "you have
made a vow to the LORD. Do with me as you have
vowed, because the LORD has taken vengeance
for you against your enemies the Ammonites."
37 Then she said to her father, "Let me have this
favor. Do nothing for two months, that I and my
companions may go wander in the mountains to
weep for my virginity." 38 "Go," he replied, and
sent her away for two months. So she departed
with her companions and wept for her virgin-
ity in the mountains. 39 At the end of the two
months she returned to her father, and he did to
her as he had vowed. She had not had relations
with any man.
It became a custom in Israel 40 for Israelite
women to go yearly to mourn the daughter of
Jephthah the Gileadite for four days of the year.

The Shibboleth Incident

12 1 The men of Ephraim were called out, and
they crossed over to Zaphon. They said
to Jephthah, "Why did you go to fight with the
Ammonites without calling us to go with you?*
We will burn your house on top of you." 2 Jeph-
thah answered them, "My soldiers and I were
engaged in a contest with the Ammonites. They
were pressing us hard, and I cried out to you, but
you did not come to save me from their power.
3 When I saw that you were not coming to save
me, I took my life in my own hand and crossed
over against the Ammonites, and the LORD deliv-
ered them into my power. Why, then, should you
come up against me this day to fight with me?"
4 Then Jephthah gathered together all the men
of Gilead and fought against Ephraim. The men
of Gilead defeated Ephraim, 5 and Gilead seized
the fords of the Jordan against Ephraim. When
any of the fleeing Ephraimites said, "Let me
pass," the men of Gilead would say to him, "Are
you an Ephraimite?" If he answered, "No!" 6 they
would ask him to say "Shibboleth."† If he said
"Sibboleth," not pronouncing it exactly right,
they would seize him and kill him at the fords
of the Jordan. Forty-two thousand Ephraimites
fell at that time.
7 Jephthah judged Israel for six years, and Jeph-
thah the Gileadite died and was buried in his city
in Gilead.*

Ibzan

8 After him Ibzan† of Bethlehem judged Israel.
9 * He had thirty sons and thirty daughters whom
he gave in marriage outside the family, while
bringing in thirty wives for his sons from outside

†

11:30–40 Jephthah's rash vow and its tragic consequences reflect a widespread folklore motif, most familiar in the Greek story of Iphigenia and her father, Agamemnon. The sacrifice of children was strictly forbidden by Mosaic law (Lv 18:21; 20:2–5), and when the biblical writers report its occurrence, they usually condemn it in strong terms (2 Kgs 16:3; 21:6; Jer 7:31; 19:5). In this case, however, the narrator simply records the old story, offering no comment on the acceptability of Jephthah's extreme gesture. The story may have been preserved because it provided an explanation of the custom described in vv. 39–40 according to which Israelite women mourned Jephthah's daughter annually in a four-day ceremony.

11:35 *Made a vow*: lit., "opened my mouth"; so in v. 36.

12:6 *Shibboleth*: Hebrew meaning "ear of grain" or "torrent of water." Though the Ephraimites probably spoke the same dialect of Hebrew as their Gileadite neighbors, there was enough regional variation in their pronunciation of the initial sound of this word to betray them to their enemies.

12:8–15 *Ibzan . . . Elon . . . Abdon*: three more of the so-called "minor judges"; see Introduction.

*

11:26 Nm 21:25; Dt 2:36.
11:29 Jgs 3:10; 6:34; 13:25; 14:6, 19; 15:14; 1 Sm 11:6.
11:30 Gn 28:20–22; 1 Sm 1:11; 2 Sm 15:7–8.
11:35 Nm 30:3; Dt 23:22; Eccl 5:4.
12:1 Jgs 8:1.
12:7 Jgs 10:2, 5; 12:10, 12, 15; 15:20.
12:9 Jgs 8:30; 9:2, 5; 10:4; 12:14.

Introducing...

Samson

The story of Samson in Judges, chapters 13–16, is one of the most well known in the Bible. Most of us know Samson for his great feats of strength, such as killing a lion barehanded and slaying a thousand men with the jawbone of a donkey. But did you also know that Samson's birth was announced by an angel and that the Book of Judges says "the spirit of the LORD rushed upon him" (14:19) more often for Samson than for any other judge? Samson was a Nazirite as well as a judge. Nazirites took vows to abstain from alcohol, avoid contact with dead bodies, and refrain from cutting their hair.

Like many of the other judges, Samson was a flawed hero. He broke all his Nazirite vows, was controlled by lust, and used his great strength for personal revenge. Despite these flaws, God chose to use Samson. Samson paid for his sins, but ultimately, his tragic death brought victory over the Philistines. Once again God's purposes were accomplished, even through a flawed and sinful human being.

the family. He judged Israel for seven years. 10 Ib-
zan died and was buried in Bethlehem.

Elon

11 After him Elon the Zebulunite judged Israel;
he judged Israel for ten years. 12 Elon the Zebu-
lunite died and was buried at Aijalon in the land
of Zebulun.

Abdon

13 After him Abdon, son of Hillel, the Pira-
thonite, judged Israel. 14 * He had forty sons and
thirty grandsons, who rode on seventy donkeys.
He judged Israel for eight years. 15 Abdon, son of
Hillel, the Pirathonite, died and was buried in
Pirathon in the land of Ephraim in the mountain
region of the Amalekites.

The Birth of Samson

13 1 * The Israelites again did what was evil in
the sight of the LORD, who therefore deliv-
ered them into the power of the Philistines for
forty years.
2 There was a certain man from Zorah, of the
clan of the Danites,† whose name was Manoah.
His wife was barren and had borne no children.*
3 * An angel of the LORD appeared to the woman
and said to her: Though you are barren and have
had no children, you will conceive and bear a
son. 4 * Now, then, be careful to drink no wine
or beer and to eat nothing unclean, 5 for you will
conceive and bear a son. No razor shall touch
his head, for the boy is to be a nazirite for God†
from the womb. It is he who will begin to save
Israel from the power of the Philistines.
6 The woman went and told her husband, "A
man of God came to me; he had the appearance
of an angel of God, fearsome indeed. I did not
ask him where he came from, nor did he tell me
his name. 7 But he said to me, 'You will conceive
and bear a son. So drink no wine or beer, and
eat nothing unclean. For the boy shall be a naz-
irite for God from the womb, until the day of
his death.' " 8 Manoah then prayed to the LORD.
"Please, my Lord," he said, "may the man of God
whom you sent return to us to teach us what to
do for the boy who is to be born."
9 God heard the prayer of Manoah, and the
angel of God came again to the woman as she
was sitting in the field; but her husband Manoah
was not with her. 10 The woman ran quickly and
told her husband. "The man who came to me the
other day has appeared to me," she said to him;
11 so Manoah got up and followed his wife. When
he reached the man, he said to him, "Are you the
one who spoke to my wife?" I am, he answered.
12 Then Manoah asked, "Now, when what you
say comes true, what rules must the boy follow?
What must he do?" 13 The angel of the LORD an-
swered Manoah: Your wife must be careful about
all the things of which I spoke to her. 14 She must
not eat anything that comes from the vine, she
must not drink wine or beer, and she must not
eat anything unclean. Let her observe all that I
have commanded her. 15 Then Manoah said to
the angel of the LORD, "Permit us to detain you,
so that we may prepare a young goat for you."

JGS

† **13:2** *The clan of the Danites*: before the migration described in chap. 18 the tribe of Dan occupied a small territory west of Benjamin, adjacent to the Philistine plain; see note on 3:3.

13:5 *A nazirite for God*: according to the rules for nazirites set forth in Nm 6:2–8, Samson's vows would have obliged him to abstain from wine and other products of the vine and to keep his hair uncut. As the story that follows shows, the last requirement proved especially fateful in Samson's life.

12:14 Jgs 9:2, 5; 10:4; 12:9.
13:1 Jgs 2:11–14; 3:7–8, 12; 4:1–2; 6:1; 10:6–8.
13:2 1 Sm 1:2; Lk 1:7.
13:3 1 Sm 1:20; Lk 1:13, 31.
13:4–5 Nm 6:1–5; 1 Sm 1:11; Lk 1:15.

16 But the angel of the LORD answered Manoah:
Though you detained me, I would not eat your
food. But if you want to prepare a burnt offering,
then offer it up to the LORD. For Manoah did not
know that he was the angel of the LORD. 17 † Then
Manoah said to the angel of the LORD, "What is
your name, that we may honor you when your
words come true?" 18 * The angel of the LORD an-
swered him: Why do you ask my name? It is won-
drous. 19 * Then Manoah took a young goat with
a grain offering and offered it on the rock to the
LORD, who works wonders. While Manoah and
his wife were looking on, 20 as the flame rose to
the heavens from the altar, the angel of the LORD
ascended in the flame of the altar. When Manoah
and his wife saw this, they fell on their faces to
the ground; 21 but the angel of the LORD was seen
no more by Manoah and his wife.* Then Ma-
noah, realizing that it was the angel of the LORD,
22 said to his wife, "We will certainly die,† for we
have seen God." 23 But his wife said to him, "If
the LORD had meant to kill us, he would not have
accepted a burnt offering and grain offering from
our hands! Nor would he have let us see all this,
or hear what we have heard."

24 The woman bore a son and named him
Samson, and when the boy grew up the LORD
blessed him. 25 The spirit of the LORD came upon
him for the first time* in Mahaneh-dan, between
Zorah and Eshtaol.

Marriage of Samson

14 1 Samson went down to Timnah where he
saw one of the Philistine women. 2 On his
return he told his father and mother, "I saw in
Timnah a woman, a Philistine. Get her for me as
a wife." 3 * His father and mother said to him, "Is
there no woman among your kinsfolk or among
all your people, that you must go and take a
woman from the uncircumcised Philistines?"
But Samson answered his father, "Get her for
me, for she is the one I want." 4 * Now his father
and mother did not know that this had been
brought about by the LORD, who was seeking an
opportunity against the Philistines;† for at that
time they ruled over Israel.*
5 So Samson went down to Timnah with his
father and mother. When he turned aside to the
vineyards of Timnah, a young lion came roaring
out toward him. 6 * But the spirit of the LORD
rushed upon Samson, and he tore the lion apart
barehanded,* as one tears a young goat. Without
telling his father or mother what he had done,
7 he went down and spoke to the woman. He
liked her. 8 Later, when he came back to marry
her, he turned aside to look at the remains of the
lion, and there was a swarm of bees in the lion's
carcass, and honey. 9 So he scooped the honey
out into his hands and ate it as he went along.
When he came to his father and mother, he gave
them some to eat, but he did not tell them that he
had scooped the honey from the lion's carcass.
10 His father also went down to the woman,
and Samson gave a feast there, since it was cus-
tomary for the young men to do this. 11 Out of
their fear of him, they brought thirty men to be
his companions. 12 Samson said to them, "Let me
propose a riddle to you. If within the seven days
of the feast you solve it for me, I will give you
thirty linen tunics and thirty sets of garments.
13 But if you cannot answer it for me, you must
give me thirty tunics and thirty sets of garments."
"Propose your riddle," they responded, "and we
will listen to it." 14 So he said to them,

"Out of the eater came food,
out of the strong came sweetness."

For three days they were unable to answer the
riddle, 15 and on the fourth day they said to Sam-
son's wife,* "Trick your husband into solving the
riddle for us, or we will burn you and your fam-
ily.* Did you invite us here to reduce us to pov-
erty?" 16 † * So Samson's wife wept at his side and
said, "You just hate me! You do not love me! You
proposed a riddle to my people, but did not tell
me the answer." He said to her, "If I did not tell
even my father or my mother, must I tell you?"

†

13:17–19 Manoah asks for a name so that he will know how to acknowledge the help of the visitor, but the angel will say only that his name is "wondrous," i.e., beyond human comprehension. Manoah's response is to dedicate his offering to "the Lord, who works wonders."

13:22 *We will certainly die*: seeing God face to face was believed to be fatal, as explained in note on 6:22, where Gideon's reaction is similar to that of Manoah here.

14:4 *An opportunity against the Philistines*: although the story of Samson's first love might be taken as an illustration of the danger of foreign marriages, the narrator explains it differently. Samson's infatuation with the Timnite woman was the Lord's way of creating an opportunity to punish the Philistines for their oppression of Israel.

14:16 The story of Samson and the Timnite woman is very similar in its narrative structure to the better-known story of Samson and Delilah (16:1–22). In both, Samson's success in his conflict with the Philistines depends on keeping a secret. In both stories Samson is betrayed by the Philistine woman he loves when she importunes him to reveal the secret to her and then, when he gives in, divulges it to her people.

13:18 Gn 32:30.
13:19–20 Jgs 6:19–21.
13:21–23 Jgs 6:22–23.
13:25 Jgs 3:10; 6:34; 11:29; 14:6, 19; 15:14; 1 Sm 11:6.
14:3 Gn 24:3–4; 26:34–35; 28:1–2, 6–9.
14:4 1 Sm 10:14–16; Lk 2:41–51.
14:4 2 Kgs 5:7.
14:6 Jgs 3:10; 6:34; 11:29; 13:25; 14:19; 15:14; 1 Sm 11:6.
14:6 1 Sm 17:34–36; 2 Sm 23:20.
14:15 Jgs 16:5.
14:15 Jgs 15:6.
14:16 Jgs 16:15.

JGS

17 But she wept beside him during the seven days
the feast lasted, and on the seventh day, he told
her the answer, because she pressed him, and she
explained the riddle to her people.*
18 On the seventh day, before the sun set, the
men of the city said to him,

"What is sweeter than honey,
what is stronger than a lion?"

He replied to them,

"If you had not plowed with my heifer,
you would not have solved my riddle."

19 * The spirit of the LORD rushed upon him,
and he went down to Ashkelon, where he killed
thirty of their men and stripped them; he gave
their garments to those who had answered the
riddle. Then he went off to his own family in
anger, 20 and Samson's wife was married to the
companion who had been his best man.*

Samson Defeats the Philistines

15 1 After some time, in the season of the
wheat harvest, Samson visited his wife,
bringing a young goat. But when he said, "Let me
go into my wife's room," her father would not let
him go in. 2 He said, "I thought you hated her, so
I gave her to your best man. Her younger sister
is better; you may have her instead." 3 Samson
said to him, "This time I am guiltless if I harm
the Philistines." 4 So Samson went and caught
three hundred jackals, and turning them tail to
tail, he took some torches and tied one between
each pair of tails. 5 He then kindled the torches
and set the jackals loose in the standing grain of
the Philistines, thus burning both the shocks and
standing grain, the vineyards and olive groves.
6 * When the Philistines asked, "Who has done
this?" they were told, "Samson, the son-in-law
of the Timnite, because his wife was taken and
given to his best man." So the Philistines went
up and destroyed her and her family by fire.*
7 Samson said to them, "If this is how you act, I
will not stop until I have taken revenge on you."
8 And he struck them hip and thigh—a great
slaughter. Then he went down and stayed in a
cleft of the crag of Etam.
9 The Philistines went up and encamped in
Judah, deploying themselves against Lehi.*
10 When the men of Judah asked, "Why have you
come up against us?" they answered, "To take
Samson prisoner; to do to him as he has done to
us." 11 Three thousand men of Judah went down
to the cleft of the crag of Etam and said to Sam-
son, "Do you not know that the Philistines are
our rulers? Why, then, have you done this to us?"
He answered them, "As they have done to me, so
have I done to them." 12 They said to him, "We
have come down to bind you and deliver you to
the Philistines." Samson said to them, "Swear
to me that you will not attack me yourselves."
13 "No," they replied, "we will only bind you and
hand you over to them. We will certainly not kill
you." So they bound him with two new ropes
and brought him up from the crag. 14 When he
reached Lehi, and the Philistines came shouting
to meet him,* the spirit of the LORD rushed upon
him: the ropes around his arms became like flax
that is consumed by fire, and his bonds melted
away from his hands. 15 Coming upon the fresh
jawbone of an ass, he reached out, grasped it,
and with it killed a thousand men.* 16 Then
Samson said,

"With the jawbone of an ass
I have piled them in a heap;
With the jawbone of an ass
I have slain a thousand men."

17 As he finished speaking he threw the jaw-
bone from him; and so that place was named
Ramath-lehi.† 18 Being very thirsty, he cried to
the LORD and said, "You have put this great vic-
tory into the hand of your servant. Must I now
die of thirst and fall into the hands of the uncir-
cumcised?" 19 Then God split the cavity in Lehi,
and water issued from it, and Samson drank till
his spirit returned and he revived. Hence it is
called En-hakkore† in Lehi to this day.
20 Samson judged Israel for twenty years in the
days of the Philistines.*

16 1 Once Samson went to Gaza, where he saw
a prostitute and visited her. 2 The people
of Gaza were told, "Samson has come here," and
they surrounded him with an ambush at the city
gate all night long. And all the night they waited,
saying, "At morning light we will kill him."

†

15:17 *Ramath-lehi*: "Jawbone Height"; in Hebrew *lehi* means "jawbone."

15:19 *En-hakkore*: understood as "the spring of the crier," an allusion to Samson's cry in v. 18. The story is used to explain the name of a well-known spring in Lehi. The Hebrew also means "Partridge Spring."

*

14:17 Jgs 16:16–18.
14:19 Jgs 3:10; 6:34; 11:29; 13:25; 14:6; 15:14; 1 Sm 11:6.
14:20 Jgs 15:2, 6.
15:6 Jgs 14:20.
15:6 Jgs 14:15.
15:9 2 Sm 23:11–12.
15:14 Jgs 3:10; 6:34; 11:29; 13:25; 14:6, 19; 1 Sm 11:6.
15:15 Jgs 3:31; 2 Sm 23:12.
15:20 Jgs 10:2, 5; 12:7, 10, 12, 15; 16:31.

[3]Samson lay there until midnight. Then he rose
at midnight, seized the doors of the city gate and
the two gateposts, and tore them loose, bar and
all. He hoisted them on his shoulders and carried
them to the top of the ridge opposite Hebron.

Samson and Delilah

[4]After that he fell in love with a woman in
the Wadi Sorek whose name was Delilah. [5] * The
lords of the Philistines came up to her and said,
"Trick him and find out where he gets his great
strength, and how we may overcome and bind
him so as to make him helpless. Then for our
part, we will each give you eleven hundred pieces
of silver."
[6]So Delilah said to Samson, "Tell me where
you get your great strength and how you may
be bound so as to be made helpless." [7]"If they
bind me with seven fresh bowstrings that have
not dried," Samson answered her, "I shall grow
weaker and be like anyone else." [8]So the lords
of the Philistines brought her seven fresh bow-
strings that had not dried, and she bound him
with them. [9]She had men lying in wait in the
room, and she said to him, "The Philistines are
upon you, Samson!" But he snapped the bow-
strings as a thread of tow is snapped by a whiff of
flame; and his strength remained unexplained.
[10]Delilah said to Samson, "You have mocked
me and told me lies. Now tell me how you may
be bound." [11]"If they bind me tight with new
ropes, with which no work has been done," he
answered her, "I shall grow weaker and be like
anyone else." [12]So Delilah took new ropes and
bound him with them. Then she said to him,
"The Philistines are upon you, Samson!" For
there were men lying in wait in the room. But he
snapped the ropes off his arms like thread.
[13]Delilah said to Samson again, "Up to now
you have mocked me and told me lies. Tell me
how you may be bound." He said to her, "If you
weave the seven locks of my hair into the web
and fasten them with the pin, I shall grow weaker
and be like anyone else." [14]So when he went to
bed, Delilah took the seven locks of his hair and
wove them into the web, and fastened them with
the pin. Then she said, "The Philistines are upon
you, Samson!" Awakening from his sleep, he
pulled out both the loom and the web.
[15] * Then she said to him, "How can you say
'I love you' when your heart is not mine? Three
times already you have mocked me, and not told
me where you get your great strength!" [16] * She
pressed him continually and pestered him till he
was deathly weary of it. [17]So he told her all that
was in his heart and said, "No razor has touched

Live It!

Manipulation

You'd think Samson would catch on, wouldn't you? Delilah tries to coax from Samson the secret of his strength. By the third attempt, it seems rather obvious that she wants to betray him to the Philistines. Nonetheless, Samson is finally pestered into revealing his secret, and Delilah uses the information to betray him.

Have you ever been betrayed by a friend? Have you ever trusted someone with a secret only to discover later that your secret is out? It makes it that much harder to trust again, to be open and to share yourself with another. When the person who betrays your confidence is someone you love, the betrayal is even more painful.

We need to do some soul searching here. Ask yourself: Am I the kind of person who can be trusted with someone's secret? Have I ever betrayed a confidence?

It is easier than we like to think to be like Delilah—abusing the trust built up in a relationship and manipulating another person, even someone we care deeply about. We need to resolve to be people of integrity, who would never betray a confidence for personal gain.

▶ **Jgs 16:4–22**

my head, for I have been a nazirite for God from
my mother's womb.* If I am shaved, my strength
will leave me, and I shall grow weaker and be
like anyone else." [18]When Delilah realized that
he had told her all that was in his heart, she
summoned the lords of the Philistines, saying,
"Come up this time, for he has told me all that
is in his heart." So the lords of the Philistines
came to her and brought the money with them.*
[19]She put him to sleep on her lap, and called for
a man who shaved off the seven locks of his hair.
He immediately became helpless, for his strength

* **16:5** Jgs 14:15. **16:15** Jgs 14:16. **16:16–18** Jgs 14:17. **16:17** Jgs 13:5. **16:18** Jgs 16:5.

had left him.† 20 When she said "The Philistines
are upon you, Samson!" he woke from his sleep
and thought, "I will go out as I have done time
and again and shake myself free." He did not
realize that the LORD had left him. 21 But the Phi-
listines seized him and gouged out his eyes. Then
they brought him down to Gaza and bound him
with bronze fetters, and he was put to grinding
grain in the prison. 22 But the hair of his head be-
gan to grow as soon as it was shaved.

The Death of Samson

23 * The lords of the Philistines assembled to of-
fer a great sacrifice to their god Dagon† and to cel-
ebrate. They said, "Our god has delivered Samson
our enemy into our power." 24 When the people
saw him, they praised their god. For they said,

"Our god has delivered into our power
our enemy, the ravager of our land,
the one who has multiplied our slain."

25 When their spirits were high, they said, "Call
Samson that he may amuse us." So they called
Samson from the prison, and he provided amuse-
ment for them. They made him stand between
the columns, 26 and Samson said to the atten-
dant who was holding his hand, "Put me where I
may touch the columns that support the temple,
so that I may lean against them." 27 The temple
was full of men and women: all the lords of the
Philistines were there, and from the roof about
three thousand men and women looked on as
Samson provided amusement. 28 Samson cried
out to the LORD and said, "Lord GOD, remember
me! Strengthen me only this once that I may
avenge myself on the Philistines at one blow for
my two eyes." 29 Samson grasped the two middle
columns on which the temple rested and braced
himself against them, one at his right, the other
at his left. 30 Then saying, "Let me die with the
Philistines!" Samson pushed hard, and the tem-
ple fell upon the lords and all the people who
were in it. Those he killed by his dying were more
than those he had killed during his lifetime.
31 His kinsmen and all his father's house went
down and bore him up for burial in the grave of
Manoah his father between Zorah and Eshtaol.
He had judged Israel for twenty years.*

III. Further Stories of the Tribes of Dan and Benjamin

Micah and the Levite

17 1 There was a man from the mountain re-
gion of Ephraim whose name was Micah.
2 † He said to his mother, "The eleven hundred
pieces of silver that were taken from you, about
which you pronounced a curse and even said it in
my hearing—I have that silver. I took it. So now
I will restore it to you." Then his mother said,
"May my son be blessed by the LORD!" 3 When he
restored the eleven hundred pieces of silver to his
mother, she said, "I consecrate the silver to the
LORD from my own hand on behalf of my son to
make an idol overlaid with silver."† * 4 So when
he restored the silver to his mother, she took two
hundred pieces and gave them to the silversmith,
who made of them an idol overlaid with silver.
So it remained in the house of Micah. 5 The man
Micah had a shrine, and he made an ephod and
teraphim,† * and installed one of his sons, who
became his priest.* 6 † In those days there was
no king in Israel; everyone did what was right in
their own eyes.*
7 There was a young man from Bethlehem of
Judah, from the clan of Judah; he was a Levite
residing there.* 8 The man set out from the city,
Bethlehem of Judah, to take up residence wher-
ever he could find a place. On his journey he
came into the mountain region of Ephraim as
far as the house of Micah. 9 "Where do you come
from?" Micah asked him. He answered him, "I
am a Levite, from Bethlehem in Judah, and I am
on my way to take up residence wherever I can
find a place." 10 "Stay with me," Micah said to
him. "Be father and priest to me,* and I will give
you ten silver pieces a year, a set of garments,
and your living." He pressed the Levite, 11 and
he agreed to stay with the man. The young man

---

†

16:19 See note on 13:5.

16:23 *Dagon*: an ancient Syrian grain deity (cf. Hebrew *dagan*, "grain") whom the Philistines adopted as their national god after their arrival on the coast of Canaan.

17:2 The narrator picks up the story after a number of events, including a theft and a mother's curse, have already taken place.

17:3 *An idol overlaid with silver*: two nouns in Hebrew, one indicating a wooden image and the other denoting an image cast from metal. The probable interpretation is that the woman intends for her silver to be recast as a covering for an image of a god, possibly the Lord. This was forbidden in Mosaic law (cf. Ex 20:4 and Dt 5:8).

17:5 *An ephod and teraphim*: cultic paraphernalia. An ephod was a priestly garment, especially that worn by the high priest (cf. Ex 28 and 39), which contained a pocket for objects used for divination. Teraphim were household idols (Gn 31:19, 34–35; 1 Sm 19:13), which may also have had a divinatory function.

17:6 This refrain, which will be repeated fully or in part three more times (18:1; 19:1; 21:25), calls attention to the disorder and lawlessness that prevailed before the establishment of kingship in Israel. In this case the problem is cultic impropriety, seen not only in the making of an idol but in the establishment of a local temple, complete with an ephod and teraphim.

---

*

16:23 1 Sm 5:2–5.
16:31 Jgs 10:2, 5; 12:7, 10, 12, 15; 15:20.
17:3 Ex 20:4; Lv 19:4; Dt 5:8.
17:5 Jgs 18:14, 18.
17:5 1 Sm 7:1.
17:6 Jgs 18:1; 19:1; 21:25.
17:7 Jgs 19:1.
17:10 Jgs 18:19.

became like one of his own sons. 12 † Micah in-
stalled the Levite, and the young man became his
priest, remaining in the house of Micah. 13 Then
Micah said, "Now I know that the LORD will pros-
per me, since I have the Levite as my priest."

Migration of the Danites

18 1 In those days there was no king in Israel.*
In those days the tribe of the Danites were
in search of a heritage to dwell in, for up to that
time no heritage had been allotted† to them
among the tribes of Israel.*
2 So the Danites sent from their clans five pow-
erful men of Zorah and Eshtaol, to reconnoiter
the land and scout it. "Go, scout the land," they
were told. They went into the mountain region
of Ephraim, and they spent the night there.
3 While they were near the house of Micah,*
they recognized the voice† of the young Levite,*
so they turned aside. They asked him, "Who
brought you here? What are you doing here?
What is your interest here?" 4 "This is what Mi-
cah has done for me," he replied to them. "He
has hired me and I have become his priest."*
5 They said to him, "Consult God, that we may
know whether the journey we are making will
lead to success."* 6 The priest said to them, "Go
in peace! The journey you are making is under
the eye of the LORD."
7 So the five men went on and came to Laish.
They saw the people there living securely after the
manner of the Sidonians, quiet and trusting, with
no lack of any natural resource. They were distant
from the Sidonians and had no dealings with the
Arameans.† 8 When the five returned to their kin
in Zorah and Eshtaol, they were asked, "What do
you have to report?" 9 They replied, "Come, let
us attack them, for we have seen the land and it
is very good. Are you going to hesitate? Do not
be slow to go in and take possession of the land!
10 When you go you will come to a trusting peo-
ple. The land stretches out in both directions,
and God has indeed given it into your power—a
place where no natural resource is lacking."*
11 So six hundred of the clan of the Danites,
men armed with weapons of war, set out from
Zorah and Eshtaol. 12 They marched up into Ju-
dah and encamped near Kiriath-jearim; for this
reason the place is called Mahaneh-dan† to this
day (it lies west of Kiriath-jearim).*
13 From there they passed on into the moun-
tain region of Ephraim and came to the house
of Micah. 14 Then the five men who had gone to
reconnoiter the land spoke up and said to their
kindred, "Do you know that in these houses
there are an ephod, teraphim, and an idol over-
laid with silver?* Now decide what you must
do!" 15 So turning in that direction, they went to
the house of the young Levite at the home of Mi-
cah and greeted him. 16 The six hundred Danites
stationed themselves at the entrance of the gate
armed with weapons of war. 17 The five men who
had gone to reconnoiter the land went up 18 and
entered the house of Micah with the priest stand-
ing there. They took the idol, the ephod, the tera-
phim and the metal image. When the priest said
to them, "What are you doing?" 19 they said to
him, "Be still! Put your hand over your mouth!
Come with us and be our father and priest.* Is it
better for you to be priest for the family of one
man or to be priest for a tribe and a clan in Is-
rael?" 20 The priest, agreeing, took the ephod, the
teraphim, and the idol, and went along with the
troops. 21 As they turned to depart, they placed
their little ones, their livestock, and their goods
at the head of the column.
22 * When the Danites had gone some distance
from the house of Micah, Micah and the men in
the houses nearby mustered and overtook them.
23 They called to the Danites, who turned and
said to Micah, "What do you want that you have
called this muster?" 24 "You have taken my god,
which I made for myself, and you have gone off
with my priest as well," he answered. "What is
left for me? How, then, can you ask me, 'What
do you want?' " 25 The Danites said to him, "Do
not let your voice be heard near us, or aggravated
men will attack you, and you will have forfeited
your life and the lives of your family!" 26 Then
the Danites went on their way, and Micah, seeing

---

†

17:12–13 Previously one of Micah's sons served as priest (v. 5). But Micah's family were probably Ephraimites (cf. v. 1) rather than Levites, and the story reflects a sense that only Levites were to be consecrated as priests; cf. Nm 18:7, where descent from Aaron is further specified as a requirement to be a priest. Thus Micah believes it will be to his advantage to retain the itinerant Levite.

18:1 *No heritage . . . allotted*: according to Jos 19:40–48, the Danites received an allotment in the central part of the country (cf. note on 13:2 above). The point here may be that since they were unable to take full possession of that original allotment, as indicated by the notice in Jgs 1:34, they are now seeking territory elsewhere.

18:3 *Recognized the voice*: this might indicate that the Danite scouts were personally acquainted with the young Levite, but it is more likely to mean that, being originally from Judah, his dialect or accent was noticeably different from others in Micah's household.

18:7 *The Sidonians . . . the Arameans*: the people of Laish were not in regular contact with their neighbors, including the Sidonians or Phoenicians in the coastal district to the west and the Arameans in the regions to the north and east. This isolation is mentioned to underscore the vulnerability of the peaceful and unfortified city.

18:12 *Mahaneh-dan*: Hebrew, "camp of Dan."

---

*

18:1 Jgs 17:6; 19:1; 21:25.
18:1 Jgs 1:34; Jos 19:40–48.
18:3 Jgs 17:1.
18:3 Jgs 17:7–12.
18:4 Jgs 17:10.
18:5 Jgs 1:1; 1 Sm 14:18–19, 36–44; 23:2, 4, 9–12; 30:7–8.
18:10 1 Chr 5:40.
18:12 Jgs 13:25.
18:14 Jgs 17:4–5.
18:19 Jgs 17:10.
18:22–26 Gn 31:22–32:1.

JGS

that they were too strong for him, turned back
and went home.
27 * Having taken what Micah had made and
his priest, they marched against Laish, a quiet
and trusting people; they put them to the sword
and destroyed the city by fire. 28 No one came to
their aid, since the city was far from Sidon and
they had no dealings with the Arameans; the city
was in the valley that belongs to Beth-rehob.
The Danites then rebuilt the city and occupied
it. 29 They named it Dan after their ancestor Dan,
who was born to Israel.* But Laish was the name
of the city formerly. 30 † The Danites set up the
idol for themselves, and Jonathan, son of Ger-
shom, son of Moses,* and his descendants were
priests for the tribe of the Danites until the time
the land went into captivity. 31 They maintained
the idol Micah had made as long as the house of
God was in Shiloh.†

The Levite from Ephraim

19 1 In those days, when there was no king in
Israel,† * there was a Levite residing in re-
mote parts of the mountain region of Ephraim*
who had taken for himself a concubine from
Bethlehem of Judah. 2 But his concubine spurned
him and left him for her father's house in Beth-
lehem of Judah, where she stayed for some four
months. 3 Her husband then set out with his
servant and a pair of donkeys, and went after her
to soothe her and bring her back. He arrived at
her father's house, and when the young woman's
father saw him, he came out joyfully to meet
him. 4 His father-in-law, the young woman's
father, urged him to stay, and so he spent three
days eating and drinking and passing the night
there. 5 On the fourth day they rose early in the
morning and he prepared to go. But the young
woman's father said to his son-in-law, "Fortify
yourself with a little food; you can go later on."
6 So they stayed and the two men ate and drank
together. Then the young woman's father said
to the husband, "Why not decide to spend the
night here and enjoy yourself?" 7 The man made
a move to go, but when his father-in-law pressed
him he went back and spent the night there.
8 On the fifth morning he rose early to depart,
but the young woman's father said, "Fortify
yourself!" He coaxed him, and he tarried until
the afternoon, and the two of them ate. 9 Then
when the husband was ready to go with his con-
cubine and servant, the young woman's father
said to him, "See, the day is wearing on toward
evening. Stay for the night. See, the day is coming
to an end. Spend the night here and enjoy your-
self. Early tomorrow you can start your journey
home." 10 The man, however, refused to stay an-
other night; he and his concubine set out with a
pair of saddled donkeys, and traveled until they
came opposite Jebus, which is Jerusalem. 11 Since
they were near Jebus with the day far gone, the
servant said to his master, "Come, let us turn off
to this city of the Jebusites and spend the night
in it." 12 But his master said to him, "We will not
turn off to a foreigner's city,* where there are no
Israelites. We will go on to Gibeah. 13 Come," he
said to his servant, "let us make for some other
place and spend the night in either Gibeah or
Ramah."* 14 So they continued on their way un-
til the sun set on them when they were opposite
Gibeah of Benjamin.
15 † There they turned off to enter Gibeah for
the night.* The man went in and sat down in
the town square, but no one took them inside to
spend the night. 16 In the evening, however, an
old man came from his work in the field; he was
from the mountain region of Ephraim, though
he was living in Gibeah where the local people
were Benjaminites. 17 * When he noticed the
traveler in the town square, the old man asked,
"Where are you going, and where have you come
from?" 18 He said to him, "We are traveling from
Bethlehem of Judah far up into the mountain
region of Ephraim, where I am from. I have been
to Bethlehem of Judah, and now I am going
home; but no one has taken me into his house.

JGS

†

18:30 Micah's shrine is now reinstalled at Laish-Dan. In the time of the kings of Israel and Judah, Dan was the site of one of the two national sanctuaries of the Northern Kingdom, both of which are strongly condemned by the editors of the Books of Kings, who regarded Jerusalem as the only acceptable place for a temple (1 Kgs 12:26–30). This verse draws a direct connection between Micah's temple and the later royal sanctuary at Dan. Seen in this light the account of the establishment of Micah's shrine, with its idol cast from stolen silver, becomes a highly polemical foundation story for the temple at Dan. *Jonathan, son of Gershom, son of Moses*: Micah's Levite is now identified as the son or descendant of Gershom, Moses' eldest son (Ex 2:22; 18:3). In the traditional Hebrew text an additional letter has been suspended over the name "Moses" to alter it to "Manasseh," thus protecting Moses from association with idol worship. *Captivity*: although Samaria fell in 722/721 B.C., much of the northern part of the country, probably including Dan, had been subjugated about a decade earlier by the Assyrian emperor Tilgath-pileser III.

18:31 *Shiloh*: a major sanctuary which has a role in the final episode of Judges (21:12, 21).

19:1 *No king in Israel*: see note on 17:6. The violent story that follows is offered as another example of the disorder that prevailed before the inauguration of the monarchy.

19:15–21 The narrative casts a very unfavorable light on Gibeah of Benjamin, the town from which Israel's first king would come (cf. 1 Sm 9:1–2). No Benjaminite offers hospitality to the Levite and his travel party, who are obliged to wait at night in the town square until an Ephraimite residing in Gibeah welcomes them into his home.

*

18:27–29 Jos 19:47.
18:29 Gn 30:5–6.
18:30 Ex 2:22; 18:3.
19:1 Jgs 17:6; 18:1; 21:25.
19:1 Jgs 17:7.
19:12 Jgs 1:21; 2 Sm 5:6.
19:13 Jos 18:25.
19:15 Jgs 20:4.
19:17–21 Gn 19:1–3.

19 We have straw and fodder for our donkeys, and
bread and wine for myself and for your maid-
servant and the young man who is with your
servant; there is nothing else we need." 20 "Rest
assured," the old man said to him, "I will provide
for all your needs, but do not spend the night in
the public square." 21 So he led them to his house
and mixed fodder for the donkeys. Then they
washed their feet, and ate and drank.*

The Outrage at Gibeah

22 † * While they were enjoying themselves, the
men of the city, a bunch of scoundrels, surrounded
the house and beat on the door. They said to the
old man who was the owner of the house, "Bring
out the man who has come into your house, so
that we may get intimate with him." 23 The man
who was the owner of the house went out to them
and said, "No, my brothers; do not be so wicked.
This man has come into my house; do not com-
mit this terrible crime. 24 Instead, let me bring out
my virgin daughter and this man's concubine.
Humiliate them, or do whatever you want; but
against him do not commit such a terrible crime."
25 But the men would not listen to him. So the
man seized his concubine and thrust her outside
to them. They raped her and abused her all night
until morning, and let her go as the sun was com-
ing up. 26 At the approach of morning the woman
came and collapsed at the entrance of the house
in which her husband was, and lay there until
morning. 27 When her husband rose in the morn-
ing and opened the door of the house to start out
again on his journey, there was the woman, his
concubine, collapsed at the entrance of the house
with her hands on the threshold. 28 "Come, let us
go," he said to her, but there was no answer. So
the man placed her on a donkey and started out
again for home.
29 † On reaching home, he got a knife and
took hold of the body of his concubine. He cut
her up limb by limb into twelve pieces and sent
them throughout the territory of Israel.* 30 He in-
structed the men whom he sent, "Thus you shall
say to all the men of Israel: 'Has such a thing ever
happened from the day the Israelites came up
from the land of Egypt to this day?† * Take note
of it; form a plan and give orders.' "

Assembly of Israelites

20 1 So all the Israelites came out as one,
from Dan to Beer-sheba† * including the
land of Gilead, and the assembly gathered to the
LORD at Mizpah. 2 The leaders of all the people, all
the staff-bearers of Israel,† presented themselves
in the assembly of the people of God—four hun-
dred thousand foot soldiers who carried swords.
3 Meanwhile, the Benjaminites heard that the Isra-
elites had gone up to Mizpah. The Israelites asked,
"How did this evil thing happen?" 4 and the Levite,
the husband of the murdered woman, testified: "It
was at Gibeah of Benjamin, which my concubine
and I had entered for the night.* 5 * The lords of
Gibeah rose up against me and surrounded me in
the house at night. I was the one they intended to
kill, but they abused my concubine and she died.
6 * So I took my concubine and cut her up and
sent her through every part of the territory of Is-
rael, because of the terrible thing they had done in
Israel. 7 So now, all you Israelites, give your judg-
ment and counsel in this matter."* 8 All the people
rose as one to say, "None of us will leave for our
tents or return to our homes. 9 Now as for Gibeah,
this is what we will do: We will go up against it by
lot, 10 taking from all the tribes of Israel ten men
for every hundred, a hundred for every thousand,
a thousand for every ten thousand, and procuring
supplies for the soldiers who will go to exact from
Gibeah of Benjamin the full measure of the terri-
ble thing it committed in Israel."
11 So all the men of Israel gathered against the
city, united as one. 12 The tribes of Israel sent men
throughout the tribe of Benjamin to say, "What
is this evil that has occurred among you? 13 Now
give up the men, the scoundrels who are in Gib-
eah, that we may put them to death and thus
purge the evil from Israel." But the Benjaminites
refused to listen to their kindred, the Israelites.
14 Instead, the Benjaminites assembled from their
cities at Gibeah, to march out to battle with the Is-
raelites. 15 On that day the Benjaminites mustered
from their cities twenty-six thousand swordsmen,
in addition to the inhabitants of Gibeah, who
mustered seven hundred picked men 16 † who
were left-handed, every one of them able to sling
a stone at a hair without missing. 17 The men of

---

†

19:22–25 This part of the grim story closely parallels that of the assault on Lot's angelic visitors in Gn 19:4–8.

19:29 The Levite's gruesome way of summoning the tribes is a drastic version of that used by Saul in 1 Sm 11:7, where he dismembers a yoke of oxen.

19:30 *Has such a thing ever happened . . . ?*: the outrage became a byword in Israel, so that in the eighth century the prophet Hosea could invoke "the days of Gibeah" (Hos 9:9; cf. 10:9) to signify corruption and wrongdoing.

20:1 *From Dan to Beer-sheba*: the entire country, from north to south. *The land of Gilead*: Israelite territory east of the Jordan.

20:2 *The staff-bearers of Israel*: the tribal leaders.

20:16 The strange notice that the Gibeahite warriors were

---

*

19:21 Gn 18:4; 24:32; 43:24.
19:22–25 Gn 19:4–9.
19:29 1 Sm 11:7.
19:30 Hos 9:9; 10:9.
20:1 1 Sm 3:20; 2 Sm 3:10; 17:11; 24:2, 15; 1 Kgs 5:5.
20:4 Jgs 19:15.
20:5 Jgs 19:22–28.
20:6 Jgs 19:29.
20:7 Jgs 19:30.

Israel, without Benjamin, mustered four hun-
dred thousand swordsmen, all of them warriors.
[18]They went up to Bethel and consulted God.
When the Israelites asked, "Who shall go up first
for us to do battle with the Benjaminites?" the
LORD said: Judah first.† * [19] † The Israelites rose in
the morning and encamped against Gibeah.

War with Benjamin

[20]The men of Israel marched out to do battle
with Benjamin and drew up in battle array against
them at Gibeah. [21]The Benjaminites marched out
of Gibeah that day and felled twenty-two thousand
men of Israel. [22] † But the army of the men of Israel
took courage and again drew up for battle in the
place where they had drawn up on the previous
day. [23]Then the Israelites went up and wept before
the LORD until evening. "Shall I again engage my
brother Benjamin in battle?" they asked the LORD;
and the LORD answered: Attack! [24]When the Israel-
ites drew near to the Benjaminites on the second
day, [25]Benjamin marched out of Gibeah against
them again and felled eighteen thousand Israelites,
all of them swordsmen. [26]So the entire Israelite
army went up and entered Bethel, where they sat
weeping before the LORD. They fasted that day until
evening and presented burnt offerings and com-
munion offerings before the LORD. [27]The Israelites
consulted the LORD (for the ark of the covenant of
the LORD was there in those days, [28]and Phinehas,
son of Eleazar, son of Aaron,† was standing in his
presence in those days), and asked, "Shall I again
go out to battle with my brother Benjamin, or
shall I stop?" The LORD said: Attack! For tomorrow
I will deliver him into your power. [29] † * So Israel
set men in ambush around Gibeah.

[30]When the Israelites went up against the Ben-
jaminites on the third day, they drew up against
Gibeah as on other occasions. [31]When the Benja-
minites marched out to meet the army, they be-
gan, as on other occasions, to strike down some
of the troops along the highways, one of which
goes up to Bethel and one to Gibeah in the open
country; about thirty Israelites were slain. [32]The
Benjaminites thought, "They are routed before
us as previously." The Israelites, however, were
thinking, "We will flee and draw them out from
the city onto the highways." [33]And then all the
men of Israel rose from their places, forming up
at Baal-tamar, and the Israelites in ambush rushed
from their place west of Gibeah [34]and advanced
against Gibeah with ten thousand picked men
from all Israel. The fighting was severe, but no one
knew that a disaster was closing in. [35]The LORD de-
feated Benjamin before Israel; and on that day the
Israelites killed twenty-five thousand one hun-
dred men of Benjamin, all of them swordsmen.

[36]Then the Benjaminites saw that they were
defeated. The men of Israel gave ground to Benja-
min, trusting in the ambush they had set at Gib-
eah. [37]Then the men in ambush, having made a
sudden dash against Gibeah, marched in and put
the whole city to the sword. [38]The arrangement
the men of Israel had with the men in ambush
was that they would send up a smoke signal
from the city, [39]and the men of Israel would
then wheel about in the battle. Benjamin, having
begun by killing off some thirty of the men of Is-
rael, thought, "Surely they are completely routed
before us, as in the earlier fighting." [40]But when
the signal, the column of smoke, began to rise up
from the city, Benjamin looked back and there
was the whole city going up in smoke toward
heaven. [41]Then when the men of Israel wheeled
about, the men of Benjamin were thrown into
confusion, for they realized that disaster was
closing in on them. [42]They retreated before the
men of Israel in the direction of the wilder-
ness, but the fighting kept pace with them, and
those who had been in the city were spreading
destruction in between. [43]They surrounded the
men of Benjamin, pursued them from Nohah
and drove them along to a point east of Gibeah.
[44]Eighteen thousand from Benjamin fell, all of
them warriors. [45]They turned and fled into the
wilderness to the crag of Rimmon. The Israelites
picked off five thousand men on the highways
and kept pace with them as far as Gidom, where
they struck down another two thousand of them.
[46]The total of those from Benjamin who fell that
day was twenty-five thousand swordsmen, all of
them warriors. [47]Six hundred men turned and

left-handed was probably added here under the influence of the Ehud story; cf. 3:15 and the note there.

20:18 *Judah first*: as in 1:2, where the enemy is the Canaanites. This time the attack is against fellow Israelites, an indication of how far things have deteriorated in these days when as yet "there was no king in Israel"; see note on 17:6.

20:19–25 The Israelites are defeated twice by the Benjaminites.

20:22–23 These two verses seem to be transposed. The day of supplication described in v. 23 must have preceded the assembly for battle reported in v. 22.

20:28 *Phinehas, son of Eleazar, son of Aaron*: the main line of the priesthood was traced through a grandson of Aaron by this name; see Ex 6:25 and Nm 25:10–13. Whether the priest identified here is the same man or his lineal descendant, the mention of his name adds authority to the sanctuary at Bethel. The reference to the ark of the covenant in the preceding verse has the same effect.

20:29–46 The Israelites are successful in their third attempt to defeat Benjamin. Leaving an ambush behind, they decoy the enemy troops out of the city by pretending to be routed as on the two previous occasions. The stratagem is strongly reminiscent of that employed in the conquest of Ai (Jos 8). Two accounts of the present battle against Gibeah are preserved, one in 20:29–36a and another in 20:36b–46.

* **20:18** Jgs 1:1–2. **20:29–46** Jos 8:3–24.

fled into the wilderness to the crag of Rimmon,
where they remained for four months.*
48 Then the men of Israel turned back against
the Benjaminites, putting them to the sword—
the inhabitants of the cities, the livestock, and all
they came upon.* Moreover they destroyed by
fire all the cities they came upon.

Ensuring a Future for Benjamin

21 1 † The men of Israel took an oath at Miz-
pah: "None of us will give his daughter
in marriage to anyone from Benjamin." 2 So the
people went to Bethel and remained there before
God until evening, raising their voices in bitter
weeping.* 3 They said, "LORD, God of Israel, why
has this happened in Israel that today one tribe
of Israel should be lacking?" 4 Early the next day
the people built an altar there and offered burnt
offerings and communion offerings. 5 Then the
Israelites asked, "Are there any among all the
tribes of Israel who did not come up to the LORD
for the assembly?" For there was a solemn oath
that anyone who did not go up to the LORD at
Mizpah should be put to death.*
6 The Israelites were disconsolate over their
brother Benjamin and said, "Today one tribe has
been cut off from Israel. 7 What can we do about
wives for the survivors, since we have sworn by
the LORD not to give them any of our daughters in
marriage?" 8 And when they asked, "Is there one
among the tribes of Israel who did not come up to
the LORD in Mizpah?" they found that none of the
men of Jabesh-gilead had come to the encamp-
ment for the assembly. 9 A roll call of the people
was taken, and none of the inhabitants of Jabesh-
gilead* was present. 10 So the assembly sent twelve
thousand warriors there with orders, "Go put the
inhabitants of Jabesh-gilead to the sword. 11 This is
what you are to do: Every male and every woman
who has had relations with a male you shall put
under the ban."† * 12 Finding among the inhabi-
tants of Jabesh-gilead four hundred young virgin
women, who had not had relations with a man,
they brought them to the camp at Shiloh, in the
land of Canaan.* 13 Then the whole assembly sent
word to the Benjaminites at the crag of Rimmon,*
offering them peace. 14 † So Benjamin returned
at that time, and they were given as wives the
women of Jabesh-gilead who had been spared;
but these proved to be not enough for them.
15 The people had regrets about Benjamin be-
cause the LORD had made a breach among the
tribes of Israel.* 16 The elders of the assembly
said, "What shall we do for wives for the survi-
vors? For the women of Benjamin have been an-
nihilated."* 17 They said, "There must be heirs for
the survivors of Benjamin, so that a tribe will not
be wiped out from Israel. 18 Yet we cannot give
them any of our daughters in marriage." For the
Israelites had taken an oath, "Cursed be he who
gives a wife to Benjamin!" 19 Then they thought
of the yearly feast of the LORD at Shiloh,* north
of Bethel, east of the highway that goes up from
Bethel to Shechem, and south of Lebonah. 20 And
they instructed the Benjaminites, "Go and set an
ambush in the vineyards. 21 When you see the
women of Shiloh come out to join in the dances,
come out of the vineyards and catch a wife for
each of you from the women of Shiloh; then go
on to the land of Benjamin. 22 When their fathers
or their brothers come to complain to us, we
shall say to them, 'Release them to us as a kind-
ness, since we did not take a woman for every
man in battle. Nor did you yourselves give your
daughters to them, thus incurring guilt.' "†
23 The Benjaminites did this; they carried off
wives for each of them from the dancers they
had seized, and they went back each to his own
heritage, where they rebuilt the cities and settled
them. 24 At that time the Israelites dispersed from
there for their own tribes and clans; they set out
from there each to his own heritage.
25 † In those days there was no king in Israel;
everyone did what was right in their own sight.*

JGS

†

21:1–7 The victorious Israelites now become concerned about the survival of the tribe they have defeated. Despite the large number of Benjaminites killed in the final battle (20:46) and the general carnage that followed (20:48), there does not seem to be a shortage of men. The problem is rather a shortage of wives for the surviving men, the result of a previously unmentioned vow the Israelites took not to permit their daughters to marry Benjaminites.

21:11 *Under the ban*: see note on 1:17. In this case the sanction is imposed not because of the rules for the conquest of the promised land (cf. Dt 20:10–18) but because of the failure of the men of Jabesh-gilead to honor their oath and report for the assembly.

21:14 Very strong political ties existed between the people of Jabesh-gilead and the Benjaminites, especially those involving Saul, the Benjaminite king of Israel. See 1 Sm 11, where Saul rescues Jabesh from an Ammonite siege, and 1 Sm 31:11–13, where the people of Jabesh exert themselves to ensure that the bodies of Saul and his sons should receive honorable burial.

21:22 *Release them . . . guilt*: this verse is difficult. Evidently the elders intend to make two arguments in support of their request that the men of Shiloh release their claims on the abducted women. The first argument seems to be that an insufficient number of women were taken "in battle"—i.e., the raid on Jabesh-gilead—to provide "a woman for every man"—i.e., a wife for every Benjaminite. The second argument is that since the women have been kidnapped, the men of Shiloh will not be guilty of having violated the oath mentioned above in 21:1, 7, and 18.

21:25 See note on 17:6. This final editorial comment calls attention to the chaos that followed the Benjaminite civil war and the near anarchy that characterized the various efforts to meet the need for wives for the Benjaminites.

*

20:47 Jgs 21:13.
20:48 Dt 13:15–17.
21:2 Jgs 20:26.
21:5 Jgs 20:8–10.
21:9 1 Sm 11:1–11; 31:11–13; 2 Sm 2:4–7; 21:11–14.
21:11 Nm 31:17.
21:12 Jos 21:2; 22:9.
21:13 Jgs 20:47.
21:15 2 Sm 6:8.
21:16 Jgs 20:48.
21:19 1 Sm 1:3, 21.
21:25 Jgs 17:6; 18:1; 19:1.

The Book of Ruth

Tracing one's family tree has become a popular pastime. People comb through courthouse files, study old tombstones in search of names and dates, and write to churches in foreign countries looking for baptismal and marriage records. In learning about our ancestors, we gain a better sense of our place in history and who we should be in light of that history. Ruth is a beautiful story of love and loyalty about one of Israel's ancestors. The story helps God's People understand who they are and how they should live.

At a Glance

I. **Naomi in Moab (chapter 1).**

II. **The Meeting (chapters 2–3).**

III. **Boaz Marries Ruth (chapter 4).**

Quick Facts

Period Covered: sometime from 1200 to 1000 BC

Inspired Author: unknown, probably took its final form in the sixth century BC

Themes: God's plan includes non-Israelites. God works through ordinary people.

In Depth

The Book of Ruth offers a surprising revelation about the family tree of King David: Ruth, King David's great-grandmother, was a foreigner, born and reared in the land of Moab. The Book of Ruth took its final form long after the death of her famous great-grandson, but it seems to preserve an accurate memory: King David was of mixed ancestry. Many Israelites were probably shocked that God worked through a member of an enemy tribe to advance the divine plan.

The Book of Ruth is sandwiched between the Books of Judges and 1 Samuel because its events take place during the time of the judges. It teaches some extremely important lessons:

- Ruth was faithful to Naomi, her mother-in-law, even though she was of a different race and different faith. Ruth challenged the ancient Israelites, who tended to view foreigners with suspicion and to see nothing good in their enemies.
- If God's plan included a Moabite woman among David's ancestors, then God's love and favor must extend beyond the boundaries of Israel. After the Exile, when Jewish marriages to foreigners were outlawed, the little Book of Ruth presented a huge challenge!
- God works through the faithfulness of ordinary people living ordinary lives. No kings, wars, or dramatic miracles appear in the Book of Ruth.

The Book of Ruth is action packed and full of dialogue. Some of the traditions of ancient Israel may seem strange to us today, but we can still gain a deeper understanding of ourselves and our faith by reading the story of King David's great-grandmother.

Ruth

Naomi in Moab

1 [1]Once back in the time of the judges† there
was a famine in the land; so a man from Beth-
lehem of Judah left home with his wife and two
sons to reside on the plateau of Moab. [2]The man
was named Elimelech, his wife Naomi, and his
sons Mahlon and Chilion; they were Ephrathites
from Bethlehem of Judah. Some time after their
arrival on the plateau of Moab, [3]Elimelech, the
husband of Naomi, died, and she was left with
her two sons. [4]They married Moabite women,
one named Orpah, the other Ruth. When they
had lived there about ten years, [5]both Mahlon
and Chilion died also, and the woman was left
with neither her two boys† nor her husband.
[6]She and her daughters-in-law then prepared to
go back from the plateau of Moab because word
had reached her there that the LORD had seen to
his people's needs† and given them food. [7]She
and her two daughters-in-law left the place where
they had been living. On the road back to the land
of Judah, [8]Naomi said to her daughters-in-law,
"Go back, each of you to your mother's house.†
May the LORD show you the same kindness as you
have shown to the deceased and to me. [9]* May
the LORD guide each of you to find a husband and
a home in which you will be at rest." She kissed
them good-bye, but they wept aloud, [10]crying,
"No! We will go back with you, to your people."
[11]Naomi replied, "Go back, my daughters. Why
come with me? Have I other sons in my womb
who could become your husbands?† [12]Go, my
daughters, for I am too old to marry again. Even
if I had any such hope, or if tonight I had a hus-
band and were to bear sons, [13]would you wait for
them and deprive yourselves of husbands until
those sons grew up? No, my daughters, my lot is
too bitter for you, because the LORD has extended
his hand against me." [14]Again they wept aloud;
then Orpah kissed her mother-in-law good-bye,
but Ruth clung to her.
[15]"See now," she said, "your sister-in-law has
gone back to her people and her god. Go back

†

1:1–2 *Back in the time of the judges*: the story looks back three generations before King David (4:17) into the time of the tribal confederation described in the Book of Judges. David's Moabite connections are implied in 1 Sm 22:3–4. *Bethlehem of Judah*: Bethlehem, a town in which part of the Judean clan-division called Ephrathah lived; cf. 1 Chr 2:50–51; 4:4; Mi 5:1. Jos 19:15 mentions a different Bethlehem in the north. *The plateau of Moab*: on the east side of the Jordan valley rift, where the hills facing west get more rain, and where agricultural conditions differ from those in Judah. *Ephrathites*: a reminder of David's origins; cf. Mi 5:1.

1:5 *Boys*: the way the storyteller chooses certain words as guides is shown here; "boy" will not appear again until 4:16.

1:6 *Had seen to his people's needs*: lit., "had visited his people."

1:8 *Mother's house*: the women's part of the home, but also perhaps the proper location for arranging marriage; Sg 3:4; 8:2; Gn 24:28. *Kindness*: Hebrew *hesed*. The powerful relationship term used here will recur in 2:20 and 3:10; kindness operates on both the divine-human and human-human level in Ruth.

1:11 *Other sons . . . husbands*: a reference to a customary practice known from Dt 25:5–10, levirate marriage, which assigns responsibility to the brother-in-law to produce heirs in order to perpetuate the name and hold the patrimonial land of a man who died childless. How far the responsibility extended beyond blood brothers is unclear; cf. Gn 38:8 and the upcoming scene in Ru 4:5–6. Naomi imagines the impossible: were she to have more sons they could take Ruth and Orpah as their wives.

*

1:9 Ru 3:1.

Pray It!

Wherever You Go

Ruth is under no obligation to leave her homeland and go to Israel with her mother-in-law, very likely facing a life of poverty. But her loyalty is rewarded, and she finds new life among God's People.

After reading Ruth's story, reflect on these questions:

- What do you find inspiring in Ruth's story?
- To whom are you faithful?
- What would have to be present in a relationship for you to have the kind of loyalty Ruth showed to Naomi?
- Can you make Ruth's words to Naomi your prayer to God?

Where you lead, I will follow; where you direct me, I will live; your people shall be my family. (Adapted from Ru 1:16)

after your sister-in-law!" 16 † But Ruth said, "Do
not press me to go back and abandon you!

Wherever you go I will go,
  wherever you lodge I will lodge.
Your people shall be my people
  and your God, my God.
17 Where you die I will die,
  and there be buried.

May the LORD do thus to me, and more, if even
death separates me from you!" 18 Naomi then
ceased to urge her, for she saw she was deter-
mined to go with her.

The Return to Bethlehem

19 So they went on together until they reached
Bethlehem. On their arrival there, the whole
town was excited about them, and the women
asked: "Can this be Naomi?" 20 * But she said to
them, "Do not call me Naomi ['Sweet']. Call me
Mara ['Bitter'], for the Almighty has made my life
very bitter. 21 † * I went away full, but the LORD
has brought me back empty. Why should you
call me 'Sweet,' since the LORD has brought me
to trial, and the Almighty has pronounced evil
sentence on me." 22 Thus it was that Naomi came
back with her Moabite daughter-in-law Ruth,
who accompanied her back from the plateau of
Moab. They arrived in Bethlehem at the begin-
ning of the barley harvest.†

The Meeting

2 1 † Naomi had a powerful relative named
Boaz,* through the clan of her husband
Elimelech. 2 † Ruth the Moabite said to Naomi,
"I would like to go and glean grain in the field
of anyone who will allow me." Naomi said to
her, "Go ahead, my daughter." 3 So she went.
The field she entered to glean after the harvesters
happened to be the section belonging to Boaz, of
the clan of Elimelech. 4 † Soon, along came Boaz
from Bethlehem and said to the harvesters, "The
LORD be with you," and they replied, "The LORD
bless you." 5 Boaz asked the young man over-
seeing his harvesters, "Whose young woman is
this?" 6 The young man overseeing the harvesters
answered, "She is the young Moabite who came
back with Naomi from the plateau of Moab.*
7 † She said, 'I would like to gather the gleanings
into sheaves after the harvesters.' Ever since she
came this morning she has remained here until
now, with scarcely a moment's rest."

†

1:16–17 Ruth's adherence to her mother-in-law in 1:14 is now expressed in a profound oath of loyalty, culminating in a formulary found frequently in Samuel and Kings; cf. especially 1 Sm 20:13. *Even death*: burial in Naomi's family tomb means that not even death will separate them.

1:21 Naomi's despair is made clear by her play on the meaning of her name in v. 20 and now by her accusation, like that in many psalms and in Job, that God has acted harshly toward her. The language belongs to the realm of judicial proceedings. By crying out in this way, the faithful Israelite opens the door to change, since the cry assumes that God hears and will do something about such seemingly unjust circumstances.

1:22 Barley and wheat harvests come in succession, from as early as April–May into June–July; Dt 16:9–12 suggests that the grain harvest lasts about seven weeks. The time reference leads effectively to the next episode.

2:1 Kinship ties and responsibilities now become very important. Boaz is introduced as one of a group surrounding Naomi through her husband's kin who are expected to extend care. The particular term used here (*moda'*, "relative") is picked up in 3:2; otherwise, most of the terminology about this responsibility to care will use the vocabulary of redeeming (*go'el*, "redeemer").

2:2 Israelite custom made provision for the poor, the widow, the stranger and the orphan to gather what was left behind by the harvesters, and instructed farmers not to cut to the edges of their fields, for the sake of these marginalized; Lv 19:9–10; 23:22; Dt 24:19–22.

2:4 The story brings Boaz upon the scene quickly, but he moves among his workers with the grace of a man of prominence, greeting them and being received with courtesy. The Hebrew blessing formulas used are frequent in Jewish and Christian liturgies.

2:7 The verse is somewhat garbled, but the points are clear that Ruth has been appropriately deferential in seeking permission to glean, and has worked steadily since arriving. Or perhaps she has waited patiently until Boaz arrives to gain permission.

*

1:20 Ex 15:23.
1:21 Ru 3:17; 1 Kgs 17:20.
2:1 Ru 3:2, 12; Mt 1:5.
2:6 Ru 1:22.

Chapters 2–3

[8]Boaz then spoke to Ruth, "Listen, my daugh-
ter. Do not go to glean in anyone else's field; you
are not to leave here. Stay here with my young
women. [9]Watch to see which field is to be har-
vested, and follow them. Have I not commanded
the young men to do you no harm? When you are
thirsty, go and drink from the vessels the young
people have filled." [10]Casting herself prostrate
upon the ground, she said to him, "Why should
I, a foreigner, be favored with your attention?"
[11] * Boaz answered her: "I have had a complete
account of what you have done for your mother-
in-law after your husband's death; you have left
your father and your mother and the land of
your birth, and have come to a people whom
previously you did not know. [12] * May the LORD
reward what you have done! May you receive
a full reward from the LORD, the God of Israel,
under whose wings you have come for refuge."
[13]She said, "May I prove worthy of your favor,
my lord. You have comforted me. You have spo-
ken to the heart of your servant†—and I am not
even one of your servants!" [14]At mealtime Boaz
said to her, "Come here and have something to
eat; dip your bread in the sauce." Then as she sat
near the harvesters, he handed her some roasted
grain and she ate her fill and had some left over.
[15]As she rose to glean, Boaz instructed his young
people: "Let her glean among the sheaves them-
selves without scolding her, [16]and even drop
some handfuls and leave them for her to glean;
do not rebuke her."

[17]She gleaned in the field until evening, and
when she beat out what she had gleaned it came
to about an ephah† of barley, [18]which she took
into the town and showed to her mother-in-law.
Next she brought out what she had left over from
the meal and gave it to her. [19]So her mother-in-
law said to her, "Where did you glean today?
Where did you go to work? May the one who
took notice of you be blessed!" Then she told her
mother-in-law with whom she had worked. "The
man at whose place I worked today is named
Boaz," she said. [20] * "May he be blessed by the
LORD, who never fails to show kindness to the

Live It!

Stand by Me

Loyalty is one of those old-fashioned words, isn't it? How often do we hear it mentioned these days? And what exactly does it mean? The story of Naomi and Ruth gives us an inspiring example of loyalty. After Ruth's husband dies and her mother-in-law decides to return home to Bethlehem, Naomi tells her two widowed daughters-in-law that they should return to their homes and marry again. But Ruth decides to stay with Naomi, which means leaving her own land of Moab and settling in Judea, a foreign land. Ruth's words to Naomi are a powerful statement of what it means to be loyal: "Wherever you go I will go, wherever you lodge I will lodge, your people shall be my people, and your God my God" (Ru 1:16). In other words, "No matter what, I will stand by you."

We are also called to be loyal—especially to our families and friends. In other words, we are to stand by the people we are close to, especially when they are experiencing hard times. Even when it's tough to do so, we are to remain faithful. Loyalty creates trust and deepens relationships.

- To what or whom are you loyal? When have you experienced disloyalty, especially in a friend? How have you proven your loyalty to others? to God?

▶ **Ru 1:1–18**

† **2:13** *Servant*: only here is the language of servanthood used. Ruth has spoken with very deferential words to Boaz, but then seems to think that she has assumed too much.

2:17 *Ephah*: see note on Is 5:10.

2:11 Ru 1:14–17.
2:12 Ru 3:9; Dt 32:37; Ps 91:4.
2:20 Gn 24:27; Lv 25:25; 27:9–33.

living and to the dead," Naomi exclaimed to her daughter-in-law. She continued, "This man is a near relative of ours, one of our redeemers."† [21] "He even told me," added Ruth the Moabite, "Stay with my young people until they complete my entire harvest." [22] "You would do well, my daughter," Naomi rejoined, "to work with his young women; in someone else's field you might be insulted." [23] So she stayed gleaning with Boaz's young women until the end of the barley and wheat harvests.

Ruth Again Presents Herself

3 When Ruth was back with her mother-in-law, [1] Naomi said to her, "My daughter, should I not be seeking a pleasing home for you?* [2] † Now! Is not Boaz,* whose young women you were working with, a relative of ours? This very night he will be winnowing barley at the threshing floor. [3] Now, go bathe and anoint yourself; then put on your best attire and go down to the threshing floor. Do not make yourself known to the man before he has finished eating and drinking. [4] But when he lies down, take note of the place where he lies; then go uncover a place at his feet† and you lie down. He will then tell you what to do." [5] "I will do whatever you say," Ruth replied. [6] She went down to the threshing floor and did just as her mother-in-law had instructed her.

[7] Boaz ate and drank to his heart's content, and went to lie down at the edge of the pile of grain. She crept up, uncovered a place at his feet, and lay down. [8] Midway through the night, the man gave a start and groped about, only to find a woman lying at his feet. [9] "Who are you?" he asked. She replied, "I am your servant Ruth. Spread the wing of your cloak† over your servant, for you are a redeemer." [10] He said, "May the LORD bless you, my daughter! You have been even more loyal now than before in not going after the young men, whether poor or rich. [11] Now rest assured, my daughter, I will do for you whatever you say; all my townspeople know you to be a worthy woman.† [12] * Now, I am in fact a redeemer, but there is another redeemer closer than I.† [13] Stay where you are for tonight, and tomorrow, if he will act as redeemer for you, good. But if he will not, as the LORD lives, I will do it myself. Lie there until morning."* [14] So she lay at his feet until morning, but rose before anyone could recognize another, for Boaz had said, "Let it not be known that this woman came to the threshing floor." [15] Then he said to her, "Take off the shawl you are wearing; hold it firmly." When she did so, he poured out six measures of barley and helped her lift the bundle; then he himself left for the town.

[16] She, meanwhile, went home to her mother-in-law, who asked, "How did things go, my daughter?" So she told her all the man had done for her, [17] and concluded, "He gave me these six measures of barley and said, 'Do not go back to your mother-in-law empty.'"* [18] Naomi then said, "Wait here, my daughter, until you learn what happens, for the man will not rest, but will settle the matter today."

Boaz Marries Ruth

4 [1] Boaz went to the gate† and took a seat there. Along came the other redeemer* of whom he had spoken. Boaz called to him by name, "Come, sit here." And he did so. [2] Then Boaz picked out ten of the elders† of the town and asked them to sit nearby. When they had done this, [3] he said to the other redeemer: "Naomi, who has come back from the plateau of Moab, is putting up for sale the piece of land that belonged to our kinsman Elimelech. [4] † So I thought I would inform you. Before those here present, including the elders of

---

2:20 For the first time, the story uses the Hebrew word *go'el*, "redeemer," for the responsibilities of the circle of kinship surrounding Naomi and Ruth and their deceased relatives. Involved are the recovery or retention of family land (Lv 25:25; 27:9–33; Jer 32:6–25), release of a relative from voluntary servitude to pay debts (Lv 25:47–55), and "redeeming blood" or vengeance, attested in passages which regulate such vengeance. No explicit connection is made elsewhere in the Bible between marriage responsibilities and redeeming.

3:2 Ruth's determined action to bring relief to Naomi's and her own circumstances now impels Naomi to move, using means available in Israelite custom which no one in the story has up to this point brought into play.

3:4 *Uncover a place at his feet*: Naomi advocates a course of action that will lead Boaz to act. Israelite custom and moral expectations strongly suggest that there is no loss of virtue involved in the scene.

3:9 *Spread the wing of your cloak*: Ez 16:8 makes it clear that this is a request for marriage. Ruth connects it to "redeemer" responsibility. A wordplay on "wing" links what Boaz is asked to do to what he has asked God to do for Ruth in 2:12.

3:11 *Worthy Woman*: the language corresponds to the description of Boaz in 2:1 (lit., "strong and worthy"); the two worthy people are linked in character to one another, as they have already proven to be in their generous behavior toward the ones in need of their care. The townspeople, lit., "all the gate of my people," will ratify this at the gate in the sequel.

3:12 *Another redeemer closer than I*: Boaz knows of a closer relative who would have a prior right to buy the field and marry Ruth.

4:1 The gate of an Israelite town was the place where commercial and other legal matters were dealt with in publicly witnessed fashion.

4:2 *Ten of the elders*: to serve as judges in legal matters as well as witnesses of the settlement of business affairs; cf. Dt 25:7–9.

4:4 Although the laws governing inheritance by Israelite widows are not specified in the Bible, Naomi seems to have the right of disposal of a piece of Elimelech's land. The redemption custom in Lv 25:25 would then guide the procedure.

3:1 Ru 1:9.
3:2 Ru 2:1.
3:12 Ru 4:1.
3:13 Ru 1:16; 4:5.
3:17 Ru 1:21.
4:1 Ru 3:12.

Catholic Social Teaching

Service to the Poor and the Community

The story of Ruth was a challenge to the Israelites' tendency to distrust foreigners. It is also an example of how service to the poor was an integral part of Israel's society. In the story, Boaz, a wealthy and respected person, both provides for the poor and looks beyond the differences of race and faith to marry Ruth. Boaz's goal is to do God's will. His marriage to Ruth ensures that Naomi's land is redeemed and that she will have descendants to claim the land. Ruth's faithfulness and Boaz's integrity serve to gradually restore Naomi's hope in God's care.

In the New Testament, it becomes even clearer that God makes no distinctions between people of different races and cultures. And Jesus teaches that caring for the poor is one of the requirements for being God's People. Catholic social teaching reminds us that we are one human family and challenges us to go beyond national, racial, ethnic, economic, and ideological boundaries in creating one human family.

- How do you treat people of different races, and how much is service to poor people a part of your life?
- Pray that you can follow Ruth and Boaz's example and be an instrument of faith, hope, and justice for people in need.

Ru 4:14–17
Solidarity

my people, purchase the field; act as redeemer.*
But if you do not want to do it, tell me so, that I
may know, for no one has a right of redemption
prior to yours, and mine is next." He answered,
"I will act as redeemer."
5 † Boaz continued, "When you acquire the
field from Naomi, you also acquire responsibil-
ity for Ruth the Moabite,* the widow of the late
heir, to raise up a family for the deceased on his
estate." 6 The redeemer replied, "I cannot exercise
my right of redemption for that would endanger
my own estate. You do it in my place, for I can-
not." 7 * Now it used to be the custom in Israel
that, to make binding a contract of redemption
or exchange, one party would take off a sandal†
and give it to the other. This was the form of
attestation in Israel. 8 So the other redeemer, in
saying to Boaz, "Acquire it for yourself," drew
off his sandal. 9 Boaz then said to the elders and
to all the people, "You are witnesses today that
I have acquired from Naomi all the holdings of
Elimelech, Chilion and Mahlon. 10 I also acquire
Ruth the Moabite, the widow of Mahlon, as my
wife, in order to raise up a family for her late
husband on his estate, so that the name of the
deceased may not perish from his people and his
place. Do you witness this today?" 11 * All those
at the gate, including the elders, said, "We do.
May the LORD make this woman come into your
house like Rachel and Leah, who between them
built up the house of Israel. Prosper in Ephra-
thah! Bestow a name in Bethlehem! 12 With the
offspring the LORD will give you from this young
woman, may your house become like the house
of Perez, whom Tamar bore to Judah."†
13 Boaz took Ruth. When they came together
as husband and wife, the LORD enabled her to
conceive and she bore a son. 14 Then the women
said to Naomi, "Blessed is the LORD who has not
failed to provide you today with a redeemer.
May he become famous in Israel! 15 He will re-
store your life and be the support of your old

4:5–6 Although redemption and levirate practices are not otherwise linked in the Bible, they belong in the same area of need. Boaz claims that buying Elimelech's field obligates the other redeemer to produce an heir for Mahlon, who would then inherit the land. That would jeopardize this redeemer's overall holdings, since he would lose the land he had paid for. He can afford the first step but not the second, and cedes his responsibility to Boaz, who is willing to do both.

4:7 *Take off a sandal*: the legislation in Dt 25:8–10 provides that if a "redeemer" refuses to carry out the obligation of marrying his brother's wife, the woman shall strip off his sandal as a gesture of insult. In later years, when the obligation of carrying out this function of the "redeemer" was no longer keenly felt, the removal of the sandal may have become a formalized way of renouncing the rights/obligations of the "redeemer," as in this text.

4:12 Gn 38 contains a story about Tamar similar to Ruth's in levirate marriage. Judah, under less laudable circumstances, fulfills the same role as Boaz will, and Perez, son of Judah and Tamar, perpetuates the line. Thus two non-Israelite women, Tamar and Ruth, are important links in David's genealogy.

4:4 Lv 25:25.
4:5 Ru 3:13.
4:7 Dt 25:9.
4:11 Gn 29:31–30:24; 35:16–19.

age, for his mother is the daughter-in-law who
loves you. She is worth more to you than seven
sons!" 16 Naomi took the boy, cradled him†
against her breast, and cared for him. 17 The
neighbor women joined the celebration: "A son
has been born to Naomi!"* They named him
Obed. He was the father of Jesse, the father of
David.

18 * These are the descendants of Perez: Perez
was the father of Hezron,* 19 Hezron was the
father of Ram, Ram was the father of Ammina-
dab, 20 * Amminadab was the father of Nahshon,
Nahshon was the father of Salma, 21 Salma was
the father of Boaz, Boaz was the father of Obed,
22 * Obed was the father of Jesse, and Jesse be-
came the father of David.

†

4:16 *Cradled him*: the child belongs to Naomi in the sense that he now becomes the redeemer in the family, as stated in 4:14. This tender act by Naomi is not necessarily adoptive and differs from the relationship in Gn 30:3; cf. Nm 11:12. Naomi now has a "boy" to replace her two lost "boys" in 1:5.

4:17 Lk 1:58.
4:18–22 1 Chr 2:4–15; Mt 1:3–6.
4:18 Gn 46:12; Nm 26:21; 1 Chr 4:1.
4:20 Ex 6:23; Nm 1:7; 2:3; 7:12–17; 10:14.
4:22 1 Sm 16:2–13.

One of the basic ongoing tensions in many countries is the role of government: some believe the government interferes too much in their lives, while others feel the government should do more. Issues like health care and the environment are good examples. The First Book of Samuel reflects a similar tension in Israel as the days of the judges come to an end and the first kings make their appearance. This period of Israelite history is filled with mighty struggles and colorful personalities, including a king who gradually loses his sanity and the shining hero who replaces him.

At a Glance

I. **The Last Judges, Eli and Samuel (1:1—7:17).**

II. **Establishment of the Monarchy (8:1—12:25).**

III. **Saul and David (13:1—31:13).**

Quick Facts

Period Covered: from approximately 1080 to 1040 BC

Inspired Author: unknown, from the Deuteronomic tradition, probably using ancient court records and hero stories

Theme: tension between the need for a king and the people's reliance on God

Of Note: First and Second Samuel, originally one book, were made into two books when they were translated from Hebrew into Greek.

In Depth

This book is named after Samuel, the last of the judges and a reluctant kingmaker. Samuel was a prophet anointed to speak God's word to the nation. God works through the prophet's words to remind the people of Israel to be faithful to the terms of the covenant. The people wanted a king, so Samuel anointed Saul to be the first king to rule the whole nation. God works through the king's laws and regulations to ensure that the people of Israel are faithful to the terms of the covenant. In First Samuel, the rule of the judges gradually gives way to the rule of the kings, with an obvious gain and an obvious loss for the people.

When kings begin to rule Israel in place of judges and prophets, the people gain a more structured way of life and develop a greater national identity. These changes also make them stronger in facing threats from other nations. But at the same time, the people lose a great deal of personal freedom and independence. They are taxed and even forced into labor to support the king's government and building plans. Echoes of the debate between the charismatic style of judges and the structured rule of kings can be found throughout First Samuel (see "Doublets," near 9:1).

Israel's kings were understood as being chosen by God and as being responsible for God's interests. First Samuel clearly emphasizes that the success of kings depends on their obedience to God's Law. First Samuel reminds us that final authority in human affairs rests in no human being but in God alone. Human systems are never perfect; they must constantly be reviewed and renewed.

16:13

1 Samuel

I. The Last Judges, Eli and Samuel

Elkanah and His Family at Shiloh

1 [1]There was a certain man from Ramathaim,
a Zuphite from the hill country of Ephraim.
His name was Elkanah, the son of Jeroham, son
of Elihu, son of Tohu, son of Zuph, an Ephraim-
ite.* [2]He had two wives, one named Hannah, the
other Peninnah; Peninnah had children, but Han-
nah had no children. [3]Each year this man went
up from his city to worship and offer sacrifice to
the LORD of hosts at Shiloh, where the two sons
of Eli, Hophni and Phinehas, were ministering
as priests of the LORD.* [4]When the day came for
Elkanah to offer sacrifice, he used to give por-
tions to his wife Peninnah and to all her sons and
daughters, [5]but he would give a double portion
to Hannah because he loved her, though the LORD
had closed her womb.* [6]Her rival,† to upset her,
would torment her constantly, since the LORD
had closed her womb.* [7]Year after year, when
she went up to the house of the LORD, Peninnah
would provoke her, and Hannah would weep and
refuse to eat.† [8]Elkanah, her husband, would say
to her: "Hannah, why are you weeping? Why are
you not eating? Why are you so miserable? Am I
not better for you than ten sons?"*

Hannah's Prayer

[9]Hannah rose after one such meal at Shiloh,
and presented herself before the LORD; at the time
Eli the priest was sitting on a chair near the door-
post of the LORD's temple. [10]In her bitterness she
prayed to the LORD, weeping freely, [11]and made
this vow: "O LORD of hosts, if you look with pity
on the hardship of your servant, if you remember
me and do not forget me, if you give your hand-
maid a male child, I will give him to the LORD all
the days of his life. No razor shall ever touch his
head."† * [12]As she continued praying before the
LORD, Eli watched her mouth, [13]for Hannah was
praying silently; though her lips were moving, her
voice could not be heard. Eli, thinking she was
drunk, [14]said to her, "How long will you make
a drunken spectacle of yourself? Sober up from
your wine!" [15]"No, my lord!" Hannah answered.
"I am an unhappy woman. I have had neither
wine nor liquor; I was only pouring out my heart
to the LORD. [16]Do not think your servant a worth-
less woman; my prayer has been prompted by my
deep sorrow and misery." [17]Eli said, "Go in peace,

†

1:6 *Her rival*: Hebrew *sara*, "rival wife, co-wife"; in the Talmud, a technical term for a second or co-wife.

1:7 In biblical narrative, the social status gained by producing children, especially males, often set woman against woman; cf. e.g., Gn 16, 21, 30. Peninnah's provocations may be the arrogant boasting mentioned in 2:3.

1:11 *No razor . . .* : the Septuagint adds "he shall drink neither wine nor liquor." This addition is a further suggestion that Samuel is dedicated to God under a nazirite vow (Nm 6:4–5); see note on v. 22.

*

1:1 1 Chr 6:19–20.
1:3 Ex 23:14–17; 34:23; Dt 16:16; Jgs 21:19.
1:5 Dt 21:15–17.
1:6 Gn 16:4–5; 29:31; Jgs 13:2; Lk 1:7.
1:8 Ru 4:15.
1:11 Nm 6:1–5; Jgs 13:2–5; 16:17; Lk 1:15.

and may the God of Israel grant you what you
have requested." 18 She replied, "Let your servant
find favor in your eyes," and left. She went to her
quarters, ate and drank with her husband, and no
longer appeared downhearted. 19 Early the next
morning they worshiped before the LORD, and
then returned to their home in Ramah. When
they returned Elkanah had intercourse with his
wife Hannah, and the LORD remembered her.

Hannah Bears a Son

20 She conceived and, at the end of her preg-
nancy, bore a son whom she named Samuel.†
"Because I asked the LORD for him." 21 The next
time her husband Elkanah was going up with the
rest of his household to offer the customary sacri-
fice to the LORD and to fulfill his vows, 22 Hannah
did not go, explaining to her husband, "Once
the child is weaned, I will take him to appear
before the LORD and leave him there forever."†
23 Her husband Elkanah answered her: "Do what
you think best; wait until you have weaned him.
Only may the LORD fulfill his word!" And so she
remained at home and nursed her son until she
had weaned him.*

Hannah Presents Samuel to the Lord

24 Once he was weaned, she brought him up with
her, along with a three-year-old bull, an ephah† of
flour, and a skin of wine, and presented him at
the house of the LORD in Shiloh. 25 After they had
slaughtered the bull, they brought the child to Eli.
26 Then Hannah spoke up: "Excuse me, my lord!
As you live, my lord, I am the woman who stood
here near you, praying to the LORD. 27 I prayed
for this child, and the LORD granted my request.
28 Now I, in turn, give him to the LORD; as long as
he lives, he shall be dedicated to the LORD." Then
they worshiped there before the LORD.

2 1 And Hannah prayed:†

"My heart exults in the LORD,
my horn is exalted by my God.
I have swallowed up my enemies;
I rejoice in your victory.*
2 There is no Holy One like the LORD;
there is no Rock like our God.*
3 Speak boastfully no longer,
Do not let arrogance issue from your
mouths.†
For an all-knowing God is the LORD,
a God who weighs actions.*
4 "The bows of the mighty are broken,
while the tottering gird on strength.*
5 The well-fed hire themselves out for bread,
while the hungry no longer have to toil.
The barren wife bears seven sons,
while the mother of many languishes.*
6 "The LORD puts to death and gives life,
casts down to Sheol and brings up again.*

Pray It!

Prayers of Strong and Holy Women

Compare Hannah's prayer in 1 Samuel 2:1–10 to Mary's prayer in Luke 1:46–55. Notice the joy, the confident faith in God's way, and the understanding that God will raise up those who are hungry, poor, and in need. Notice also how God will deal with the proud, the powerful, and the rich, especially in Mary's prayer. These holy women identify in their lives and in their prayers the bigger picture of what God is all about.

What strong and holy women in your life keep you in their prayers? Take some time now to pray for each of them.

▶ **1 Sm 2:1–10**

---

† **1:20** *Samuel*: Hannah's explanation associates her son's name with the narrative's wordplay on the Hebrew verbs *s'l* ("ask," vv. 17, 27), *his'il* ("hand over, dedicate," v. 28), *sa'ul* ("dedicated," v. 28), and the noun *se'elah* ("request," vv. 17, 27). The name, however, is related to the Hebrew root *s'l* only through assonance. It means "his name is El/God," not "the one requested of or dedicated (*sa'ul*) to God" (v. 28), which is the meaning of the name Saul. The author may have lifted the *s'l* wordplay from a narrative about Saul to portray Samuel as God's gracious answer to Hannah's request.

1:22 *Leave him there forever*: a Qumran manuscript adds "I will give him as a nazirite forever"; it interprets v. 11 to mean that Hannah dedicates Samuel under a nazirite vow (cf. Nm 6:4–5).

1:24 *Ephah*: see note on Is 5:10.

2:1–10 Hannah appeals to a God who maintains order by keeping human affairs in balance, reversing the fortunes of the arrogant, who, like Peninnah, boast of their good fortune (vv. 1, 3, 9) at the expense of those like Hannah who receive less from the Lord. Hannah's admission places her among the faithful who trust that God will execute justice on their behalf. The reference "his king . . . his anointed" (v. 10) recalls the final sentence of the Book of Judges and introduces the kingship theme that dominates the Books of Samuel.

2:3 *Speak . . . mouths*: addressed to the enemies mentioned in v. 1.

* **1:23** Dt 9:5; 2 Sm 7:25; 1 Kgs 2:4.
2:1 Dt 33:17; 2 Sm 22:3; Ps 18:2; 89:18; Is 61:10; Lk 1:47, 69.
2:2 2 Sm 22:3; Ps 18:2.
2:3 Ps 75:5–6.
2:4 Is 40:29.
2:5 Ru 4:15; Jer 15:9.
2:6 Dt 32:39; Tb 4:19; Jb 5:11; Ps 30:4; Wis 16:13; Lk 1:52.

7 The LORD makes poor and makes rich,
humbles, and also exalts.
8 He raises the needy from the dust;
from the ash heap lifts up the poor,
To seat them with nobles
and make a glorious throne their heritage.

"For the pillars of the earth are the LORD's,
and he has set the world upon them.*
9 He guards the footsteps of his faithful ones,
but the wicked shall perish in the darkness;
for not by strength does one prevail.
10 The LORD's foes shall be shattered;
the Most High in heaven thunders;
the LORD judges the ends of the earth.
May he give strength to his king,
and exalt the horn of his anointed!"*

11 When Elkanah returned home to Ramah, the
child remained in the service of the LORD under
the priest Eli.

Wickedness of Eli's Sons

12 Now the sons of Eli were wicked; they had
respect neither for the LORD 13 nor for the priests'
duties toward the people. When someone offered
a sacrifice, the priest's servant would come with a
three-pronged fork, while the meat was still boil-
ing,* 14 and would thrust it into the basin, kettle,
caldron, or pot. Whatever the fork brought up,
the priest would take for himself. They treated all
the Israelites who came to the sanctuary at Shi-
loh in this way. 15 In fact, even before the fat was
burned, the priest's servant would come and say
to the one offering the sacrifice, "Give me some
meat to roast for the priest. He will not accept
boiled meat from you, only raw meat." 16 And if
this one protested, "Let the fat be burned first,
then take whatever you wish," he would reply,
"No, give it to me now, or else I will take it by
force."* 17 Thus the young men sinned grievously
in the presence of the LORD, treating the offerings
to the LORD with disdain.

The Lord Rewards Hannah

18 Meanwhile the boy Samuel, wearing a linen
ephod,† was serving in the presence of the LORD.
19 His mother used to make a little garment for
him, which she would bring him each time she
went up with her husband to offer the customary
sacrifice. 20 And Eli would bless Elkanah and his
wife, as they were leaving for home. He would
say, "May the LORD repay you with children from
this woman for the gift she has made to the
LORD!" 21 The LORD favored Hannah so that she
conceived and gave birth to three more sons and
two daughters, while young Samuel grew up in
the service of the LORD.*

Eli's Futile Rebuke

22 When Eli was very old, he kept hearing how
his sons were treating all Israel, and that they were
behaving promiscuously† with the women serv-
ing at the entry of the meeting tent. 23 So he said
to them: "Why are you doing such things? I hear
from everyone that your behavior is depraved.
24 Stop this, my sons! The report that I hear the
LORD's people spreading is not good. 25 If someone
sins against another, anyone can intercede for the
sinner with the LORD; but if anyone sins against
the LORD, who can intercede† for the sinner?" But
they disregarded their father's warning, since the
LORD wanted them dead. 26 Meanwhile, young
Samuel was growing in stature and in worth in
the estimation of the LORD and the people.*

The Fate of Eli's House†

27 A man of God came to Eli and said to him:
"Thus says the LORD: I went so far as to reveal
myself to your father's house when they were
in Egypt as slaves to the house of Pharaoh. 28 I
chose them out of all the tribes of Israel to be
my priests, to go up to my altar, to burn incense,
and to wear the ephod† in my presence; and
I assigned all the fire offerings of the Israelites
to your father's house.* 29 Why do you stare

---

†

2:18 *Linen ephod*: not the same as the high priest's ephod (Ex 28:6–14) or the ephod used in divination (v. 28). Samuel wore the same kind of a ceremonial garment as the priests did (1 Sm 22:18). David also wore an ephod when he danced before the ark (2 Sm 6:14).

2:22 *Behaving promiscuously*: this part of the verse, which recalls Ex 38:8, is a gloss; it is lacking in the oldest Greek translation, and in 4QSam[a].

2:25 *Who can intercede*: Eli's sons fail to understand that their crime is directly against God and that God will punish them for it. Their behavior is set in sharp contrast to Samuel's, which meets with God's approval.

2:27–36 These verses describe the punishment of Eli from a point of view contemporary with the reform of Josiah (2 Kgs 23:9; cf. v. 36); they hint at the events recorded in 1 Sm 22:18–23 and 1 Kgs 2:27. The older story of this divine warning occurs in 1 Sm 3:11–14. *A man of God*: often an anonymous figure whose speech foreshadows events in the near future. Cf. 1 Sm 9:6; 1 Kgs 13:1; 2 Kgs 23:16–17.

2:28 *Ephod*: a portable container, presumably of cloth, for the lots used in ritual consultation of God during the days of the Judges (Jgs 17:5; 18:14–15) and into the time of David (1 Sm 14:3; 23:6–9; 30:7–8). Attached to the ephod of the high priest described in Ex 28:6–8 is a "breastpiece of decision" which symbolized, but did not facilitate, such consultation. The Exodus text codifies a later form of the tradition.

*

2:8 Jb 9:6; 38:6; Ps 75:4; 104:5; 113:8; 121:3.
2:10 Ps 98:9.
2:13–15 Ex 29:27–28; Lv 7:29–36; Dt 18:3.
2:16 Lv 3:3–5; Nm 18:17.
2:21 1 Sm 3:19.
2:26 Lk 2:52.
2:28 1 Sm 23:9; 30:7–8; Jgs 17:5.

greedily at my sacrifices and at the offerings that
I have prescribed? Why do you honor your sons
more than you honor me, fattening yourselves
with the choicest part of every offering of my
people Israel? 30 * This, therefore, is the oracle of
the LORD, the God of Israel: I said in the past that
your family and your father's house should min-
ister in my presence forever. But now—oracle of
the LORD: Far be it from me! I will honor those
who honor me, but those who despise me shall
be cursed. 31 Yes, the days are coming when I
will break your strength and the strength of your
father's house, so that no one in your family
lives to old age. 32 You shall witness, like a disap-
pointed rival, all the benefits enjoyed by Israel,
but no member of your household shall ever
grow old. 33 I will leave you one man at my altar
to wear out his eyes and waste his strength, but
the rest of your family shall die by the sword.
34 This is a sign for you—what happens to your
two sons, Hophni and Phinehas. Both of them
will die on the same day.* 35 I will choose a
faithful priest who shall do what I have in heart
and mind. I will establish a lasting house for him
and he shall serve in the presence of my anointed
forever. 36 Then whoever is left of your family will
grovel before him for a piece of silver or a loaf of
bread, saying: Please assign me a priestly func-
tion, that I may have a crust of bread to eat."*

Revelation to Samuel

3 1 During the time young Samuel was minister
to the LORD under Eli, the word of the LORD
was scarce and vision infrequent. 2 † One day Eli
was asleep in his usual place. His eyes had lately
grown so weak that he could not see. 3 The lamp
of God was not yet extinguished,† and Samuel
was sleeping in the temple of the LORD where the
ark of God was.* 4 The LORD called to Samuel,
who answered, "Here I am." 5 He ran to Eli and
said, "Here I am. You called me." "I did not call
you," Eli answered. "Go back to sleep." So he
went back to sleep. 6 Again the LORD called Sam-
uel, who rose and went to Eli. "Here I am," he
said. "You called me." But he answered, "I did
not call you, my son. Go back to sleep."
7 Samuel did not yet recognize the LORD, since
the word of the LORD had not yet been revealed
to him. 8 The LORD called Samuel again, for the
third time. Getting up and going to Eli, he said,

Pray It!

Eli Teaches Samuel How to Pray

Eli taught Samuel to listen to God's voice with a simple sentence: "Speak, LORD, for your servant is listening" (1 Sm 3:9). Let's look at that sentence as a prayer:

"Speak, LORD . . ." This is an invitation. It shows openness and readiness. It shows your recognition of God: You are the Almighty, and I am ready to hear what you have to say.

". . . for your servant . . ." This shows humility. It is a recognition of yourself: I am your servant. It is my desire to do what you want. My life's purpose is to serve you.

". . . is listening." This demonstrates your response: I am not going to ignore you. I am not going to daydream or just pretend to pay attention. I will take in your message, and it will become part of me.

► **1 Sm 3:1–19**

"Here I am. You called me." Then Eli understood
that the LORD was calling the youth. 9 So he said
to Samuel, "Go to sleep, and if you are called, re-
ply, 'Speak, LORD, for your servant is listening.'"
When Samuel went to sleep in his place, 10 the
LORD came and stood there, calling out as be-
fore: Samuel, Samuel! Samuel answered, "Speak,
for your servant is listening." 11 The LORD said to
Samuel: I am about to do something in Israel
that will make the ears of everyone who hears
it ring.* 12 On that day I will carry out against
Eli everything I have said about his house, be-
ginning to end. 13 I announce to him that I am
condemning his house once and for all, because
of this crime: though he knew his sons were
blaspheming God, he did not reprove them.*
14 Therefore, I swear to Eli's house: No sacrifice
or offering will ever expiate its crime.† 15 Sam-
uel then slept until morning, when he got up
early and opened the doors of the temple of the

---

† **3:2–18** The call of Samuel: This section may be divided as follows: 1. the triple summons (vv. 2–9); 2. God's revelation (vv. 10–14); 3. Samuel informs Eli (vv. 15–18).

3:3 *Not yet extinguished*: referring to the nighttime setting of this narrative (cf. Ex 27:20–21) and foreshadowing a permanently extinguished lamp when the ark is captured and Shiloh destroyed.

3:14 Lv 4:3–12 presents another view: the offering of a bull can expiate priestly sin.

---

* **2:30–31** 2 Sm 22:26; 1 Kgs 2:27; Ps 18:25.
2:34 1 Sm 4:11.
2:36 2 Kgs 23:9.
3:3 Ex 27:20–22.
3:11 2 Kgs 21:12.
3:13 1 Sm 2:27–36.

LORD. He was afraid to tell Eli the vision, 16 but
Eli called to him, "Samuel, my son!" He replied,
"Here I am." 17 Then Eli asked, "What did he say
to you? Hide nothing from me! May God do
thus to you, and more,† if you hide from me a
single thing he told you." 18 So Samuel told him
everything, and held nothing back. Eli answered,
"It is the LORD. What is pleasing in the LORD's
sight, the LORD will do."

Samuel Acknowledged as Prophet

19 Samuel grew up, and the LORD was with him,
not permitting any word of his to go unfulfilled.*
20 * Thus all Israel from Dan to Beer-sheba came
to know that Samuel was a trustworthy prophet
of the LORD. 21 The LORD continued to appear at
Shiloh, manifesting himself to Samuel at Shi-
loh through his word. Samuel's word spread
throughout Israel.

Defeat of the Israelites†

4 1 At that time, the Philistines gathered for an
attack on Israel. Israel went out to engage
them in battle and camped at Ebenezer, while
the Philistines camped at Aphek. 2 The Philistines
then drew up in battle formation against Israel.
After a fierce struggle Israel was defeated by the
Philistines, who killed about four thousand men
on the battlefield. 3 When the troops retired to
the camp, the elders of Israel said, "Why has the
LORD permitted us to be defeated today by the
Philistines? Let us fetch the ark of the LORD from
Shiloh that it may go into battle among us and
save us from the grasp of our enemies."*

Loss of the Ark

4 So the people sent to Shiloh and brought
from there the ark of the LORD of hosts, who is
enthroned upon the cherubim.† The two sons of
Eli, Hophni and Phinehas, accompanied the ark
of God.* 5 When the ark of the LORD arrived in the
camp, all Israel shouted so loudly that the earth
shook. 6 The Philistines, hearing the uproar, asked,
"What does this loud shouting in the camp of the
Hebrews mean?" On learning that the ark of the
LORD had come into the camp, 7 the Philistines
were frightened, crying out, "Gods have come to
their camp. Woe to us! This has never happened
before. 8 Woe to us! Who can deliver us from the
power of these mighty gods?† These are the gods
who struck the Egyptians with various plagues in
the desert. 9 Take courage and act like soldiers,
Philistines; otherwise you will become slaves to
the Hebrews, as they were your slaves. Fight like
soldiers!" 10 The Philistines fought and Israel was
defeated; everyone fled to their own tents.† It was
a disastrous defeat; Israel lost thirty thousand foot
soldiers. 11 The ark of God was captured, and Eli's
two sons, Hophni and Phinehas, were dead.*

Death of Eli

12 A Benjaminite fled from the battlefield and
reached Shiloh that same day, with his clothes
torn and his head covered with dirt.* 13 When
he arrived, Eli was sitting in his chair beside the
gate, watching the road, for he was troubled at
heart about the ark of God. The man, however,
went into the city to announce his news; then
the whole city cried out. 14 When Eli heard the
uproar, he wondered why there was such com-
motion. Just then the man rushed up to inform
him. 15 Eli was ninety-eight years old, and his eyes
would not focus. So he could not see. 16 The man
said to Eli: "I have come from the battlefield;
today I fled from there." He asked, "What hap-
pened, my son?" 17 And the messenger answered:
"Israel fled from the Philistines; in fact, the troops
suffered heavy losses. Your two sons, Hophni and
Phinehas, are dead, and the ark of God has been
captured." 18 At this mention of the ark of God,
Eli fell backward from his chair into the gateway;
he died of a broken neck since he was an old man
and heavy. He had judged Israel for forty years.
19 His daughter-in-law, the wife of Phinehas,
was pregnant and about to give birth. When she
heard the news about the capture of the ark of
God and the deaths of her father-in-law and her
husband, she crouched down in labor, and gave
birth. 20 She was about to die when the women
standing around her said to her, "Do not be
afraid, you have given birth to a son." Yet she
neither answered nor paid any attention.* 21 She
named the child Ichabod, saying, "Gone is the
glory from Israel," referring to the capture of the

†

3:17 *May God do thus to you, and more*: an oath formula which strengthens Eli's demand by threatening divine punishment if Samuel does not obey. Cf. 14:44; 20:13; 25:22; 2 Sm 3:9, 35; 19:14.

4:1–7:1 The Ark Narrative: A striking indication that this is an independent narrative is the absence of any mention of Samuel. *The Philistines*: one of the Sea Peoples, of Aegean origin, who occupied the coastal plain of Palestine and threatened the Israelites who settled the inland hills.

4:4 *Enthroned upon the cherubim*: this divine title first occurs in the Old Testament at the sanctuary at Shiloh (cf. 2 Sm 6:2); God is represented seated upon a throne borne through the heavens by cherubim, creatures partly human being, partly beast (cf. Ez 1 and 10).

4:8 *These mighty gods*: the Philistines, who were polytheists, presume that the Israelites also honored several gods.

4:10 *To their own tents*: the defeat is so catastrophic that the soldiers abandon the army for home; cf. 2 Sm 18:17.

*

3:19 1 Sm 2:21.
3:20 Jgs 20:1; 2 Sm 3:10; 17:11; 24:2.
4:3 Nm 10:35; 14:42–44.
4:4 Ex 25:21–22.
4:11 1 Sm 2:34.
4:12 Jos 7:6; 2 Sm 1:2; Jer 7:12.
4:20 1 Sm 14:3; Gn 35:16–20.

1 S M

ark of God and to her father-in-law and her hus-
band. 22 She said, "Gone is the glory from Israel,"
because the ark of God had been captured.*

The Ark in the Temple of Dagon

5 1 † * The Philistines, having captured the ark
of God, transferred it from Ebenezer to
Ashdod.* 2 They then took the ark of God and
brought it into the temple of Dagon, placing it
beside Dagon. 3 When the people of Ashdod rose
early the next morning, Dagon was lying face
down on the ground before the ark of the LORD.
So they picked Dagon up and put him back in
his place. 4 But early the next morning, when
they arose, Dagon lay face down on the ground
before the ark of the LORD, his head and hands
broken off and lying on the threshold, his trunk
alone intact. 5 For this reason, neither the priests
of Dagon nor any others who enter the temple of
Dagon tread on the threshold of Dagon in Ash-
dod to this very day.

The Ark Is Carried About

6 Now the hand of the LORD weighed heavily
on the people of Ashdod, ravaging them and
afflicting the city and its vicinity with tumors.†
* 7 On seeing how matters stood, the people of
Ashdod decided, "The ark of the God of Israel
must not remain with us, for his hand weighs
heavily on us and Dagon our god." 8 So they
summoned all the Philistine leaders and in-
quired of them, "What shall we do with the ark
of the God of Israel?" The people of Gath replied,
"Let them move the ark of the God of Israel to
us." So they moved the ark of the God of Israel
to Gath. 9 But after it had been brought there, the
hand of the LORD was against the city, resulting in
utter turmoil: the LORD afflicted its inhabitants,
young and old, and tumors broke out on them.
10 The ark of God was next sent to Ekron; but as
it entered that city, the people there cried out,
"Why have they brought the ark of the God of
Israel here to kill us and our kindred?" 11 Then
they, too, sent a summons to all the Philistine
leaders and pleaded: "Send away the ark of the
God of Israel. Send it back to its place so it does
not kill us and our kindred." A deadly panic had
seized the whole city, since the hand of God lay
heavy upon it. 12 Those who escaped death were
afflicted with tumors. Thus the outcry from the
city went up to the heavens.

The Ark Is Returned

6 1 The ark of the LORD had been in the land
of the Philistines seven months 2 when they
summoned priests and diviners to ask, "What
shall we do with the ark of the LORD? Tell us what
we should send back with it." 3 They replied: "If
you intend to send back the ark of the God of Is-
rael, you must not send it alone, but must, by all
means, make amends to God through a reparation
offering.† Then you will be healed, and will learn
why God continues to afflict you." 4 When asked
further, "What reparation offering should be
our amends to God?" they replied: "Five golden
tumors and five golden mice to correspond to
the number of Philistine leaders, since the same
plague has struck all of you and your leaders.
5 Therefore, make images of the tumors and of the
mice that are devastating your land and so give
glory to the God of Israel. Perhaps then God will
lift his hand from you, your gods, and your land.
6 Why should you become stubborn, the way the
Egyptians and Pharaoh were stubborn? Was it not
after he had dealt ruthlessly with them that the Is-
raelites were released and departed?* 7 So now set
to work and make a new cart. Then take two milk
cows that have not borne the yoke; hitch them to
the cart, but drive their calves indoors away from
them.† * 8 You shall next take the ark of the LORD
and place it on the cart, putting the golden articles
that you are offering as reparation for your guilt
in a box beside it. Start it on its way, and let it
go. 9 Then watch! If it goes up to Beth-shemesh†
along the route to the LORD's territory, then it was
the LORD who brought this great calamity upon
us; if not, we will know that it was not the LORD's
hand, but a bad turn, that struck us."

The Ark in Beth-shemesh

10 They acted upon this advice. Taking two
milk cows, they hitched them to the cart but
shut up their calves indoors. 11 Then they placed
the ark of the LORD on the cart, along with the

†

5:1–12 The Philistines take the ark to Dagon's temple in Ashdod to confirm their victory. Their action, however, underscores Dagon's impotence and the Lord's power. The narrator relates the transfer of the ark from Ashdod to Gath and then Ekron as the progress of a conquering warrior king through the Philistine cities along the central plain. The Philistines' humiliation recalls the climax of the Samson story (Jgs 16:13–21).

5:6 *Tumors*: the Septuagint adds that mice, suggestive of bubonic plague, infested their fields, thus anticipating the golden mice in 6:4–5. One symptom of bubonic plague is swollen lymph nodes ("tumors").

6:3 *A reparation offering*: an offering to make amends for unwitting transgressions against holy things or property rights; cf. Lv 6:1–3.

6:7 *But drive their calves indoors away from them*: a test to confirm the source of the Philistines' trouble. Left to their instincts, milk cows would remain near their calves rather than head for the road to Beth-shemesh.

6:9 *Beth-shemesh*: a border city (about twenty-four miles west of Jerusalem) between Philistine and Israelite territory.

*

4:22 Ps 78:61.
5:1–5 Jgs 16:23–30; Is 45:5–6, 20–21.
5:1 Jos 13:3.
5:6 Ps 32:4.
6:6 Ex 7:14; 8:15; 9:34.
6:7 Nm 19:2; Dt 21:3; 2 Sm 6:3.

box containing the golden mice and the images
of the tumors. 12 The cows went straight for the
route to Beth-shemesh and continued along this
road, mooing as they went, turning neither right
nor left. The Philistine leaders followed them as
far as the border of Beth-shemesh. 13 The people
of Beth-shemesh were harvesting the wheat in
the valley. They looked up and rejoiced when
they saw the ark. 14 The cart came to the field
of Joshua the Beth-shemite and stopped there.
At a large stone in the field, the wood of the
cart was split up and the cows were offered as a
burnt offering to the LORD.* 15 The Levites, mean-
while, had taken down the ark of God and the
box beside it, with the golden articles, and had
placed them on the great stone. The people of
Beth-shemesh also offered other burnt offerings
and sacrifices to the LORD that day.* 16 After wit-
nessing this, the five Philistine leaders returned
to Ekron the same day.
17 The golden tumors the Philistines sent back
as a reparation offering to the LORD were as fol-
lows: one for Ashdod, one for Gaza, one for Ash-
kelon, one for Gath, and one for Ekron. 18 The
golden mice, however, corresponded to the
number of all the cities of the Philistines belong-
ing to the five leaders, including fortified cities
and open villages.† The large stone on which the
ark of the LORD was placed is still in the field of
Joshua the Beth-shemite at the present time.*

Penalty for Irreverence

19 The descendants of Jeconiah did not join
in the celebration with the inhabitants of Beth-
shemesh when they saw the ark of the LORD, and
seventy of them were struck down. The people
mourned over this great calamity which the LORD
had inflicted upon them. 20 The men of Beth-
shemesh asked, "Who can stand in the presence
of the LORD, this Holy God? To whom can the
ark go so that we are rid of it?" 21 They then sent
messengers to the inhabitants of Kiriath-jearim,
saying, "The Philistines have returned the ark of
the LORD; come down and get it."

7 1 So the inhabitants of Kiriath-jearim came
for the ark of the LORD and brought it into the
house of Abinadab on the hill, appointing his
son Eleazar as guardian of the ark of the LORD.

Samuel the Judge

2 From the day the ark came to rest in Kiriath-
jearim, a long time, twenty years, elapsed, and
the whole house of Israel turned to the LORD.
3 Then Samuel addressed the whole house of Is-
rael: "If you would return to the LORD with your
whole heart, remove your foreign gods and your
Astartes, fix your hearts on the LORD, and serve
him alone, then the LORD will deliver you from
the hand of the Philistines."* 4 So the Israelites
removed their Baals and Astartes,† and served the
LORD alone. 5 Samuel then gave orders, "Gather all
Israel to Mizpah, that I may pray to the LORD for
you."* 6 When they had gathered at Mizpah, they
drew water and poured it out† on the ground
before the LORD, and they fasted that day, saying,
"We have sinned against the LORD." It was at Miz-
pah that Samuel began to judge the Israelites.*

Rout of the Philistines

7 When the Philistines heard that the Israelites
had gathered at Mizpah, their leaders went up
against Israel. Hearing this, the Israelites became
afraid of the Philistines 8 and appealed to Sam-
uel, "Do not stop crying out to the LORD our God
for us, to save us from the hand of the Philis-
tines."* 9 Samuel therefore took an unweaned
lamb and offered it whole as a burnt offering to
the LORD.* He cried out to the LORD for Israel, and
the LORD answered him. 10 While Samuel was sac-
rificing the burnt offering, the Philistines drew
near for battle with Israel. That day, however,
the LORD thundered loudly against the Philis-
tines, and threw them into such confusion that
they were defeated by Israel.* 11 Thereupon the
Israelites rushed out from Mizpah and pursued
the Philistines, striking them down even beyond
Beth-car. 12 Samuel then took a stone and placed
it between Mizpah and Jeshanah; he named it
Ebenezer,† explaining, "As far as this place the
LORD has been our help." 13 Thus were the Philis-
tines subdued, never again to enter the territory
of Israel, for the hand of the LORD was against
them as long as Samuel lived.* 14 The cities from

†

6:18 *Open villages*: the plague devastated both fortified cities and villages, an indication of the Lord's power over the Philistines.

7:4 *Baals and Astartes*: a Deuteronomistic phrase; cf. Jgs 2:13; 10:6; 1 Sm 12:10. Baal and Astarte were Canaanite divinities.

7:6 *Drew water and poured it out*: this ritual act does not appear elsewhere in the Old Testament. Linked with fasting and admission of sin, it seems to function as a purification ritual that washes away the guilt incurred by worshiping the Canaanite Baal and his consort Astarte. Its effectiveness is immediately evident when the Lord thunders a response to Samuel's offering.

7:12 *Ebenezer*: "stone of the helper," i.e., the Lord.

*

6:14 2 Sm 24:21–25.
6:15 Dt 31:25; 1 Chr 15:2.
6:18 1 Sm 7:12; Gn 31:52; Jos 24:27.
7:3 1 Sm 12:10, 20, 24; Jos 24:23; Jgs 6:6–10; 10:10–16.
7:5 1 Sm 10:17; Jgs 20:1.
7:6 Jgs 20:26; Ps 22:14; Lam 2:19.
7:8 Jos 24:7; Jgs 3:9, 15; 6:6; 10:15.
7:9–10 2 Sm 22:14–15; Sir 46:16–18.
7:10 Ex 9:23; 2 Sm 22:14.
7:13 Jgs 3:20; 8:28; 11:33.

Ekron to Gath which the Philistines had taken
from Israel were restored to them. Israel also
freed the territory of these cities from Philistine
domination. There was also peace between Israel
and the Amorites.†
15 Samuel judged Israel as long as he lived.
16 He made a yearly circuit, passing through
Bethel, Gilgal and Mizpah† and judging Israel
at each of these places. 17 Then he used to return
to Ramah, for that was his home. There, too, he
judged Israel and built an altar to the LORD.*

II. Establishment of the Monarchy

Request for a King

8 1 † In his old age Samuel appointed his sons
judges over Israel.* 2 His firstborn was named
Joel, his second son, Abijah; they judged at Beer-
sheba. 3 His sons did not follow his example, but
looked to their own gain, accepting bribes and
perverting justice.* 4 Therefore all the elders of
Israel assembled and went to Samuel at Ramah
5 and said to him, "Now that you are old, and
your sons do not follow your example, appoint a
king over us, like all the nations, to rule us."*
6 Samuel was displeased when they said, "Give
us a king to rule us." But he prayed to the LORD.
7 The LORD said: Listen to whatever the people
say. You are not the one they are rejecting. They
are rejecting me as their king.* 8 They are acting
toward you just as they have acted from the day
I brought them up from Egypt to this very day,
deserting me to serve other gods. 9 Now listen to
them; but at the same time, give them a solemn
warning and inform them of the rights of the
king who will rule them.

The Governance of the King

10 Samuel delivered the message of the LORD
in full to those who were asking him for a king.
11 He told them: "The governance of the king
who will rule you will be as follows: He will take
your sons and assign them to his chariots and
horses, and they will run before his chariot.*
12 He will appoint from among them his com-
manders of thousands and of hundreds. He will
make them do his plowing and harvesting and

Did You Know?

Doublets

Often more than one version of a story is recorded in the Bible. Genesis has two stories of the Creation (see Gn 1:1—2:4, 2:4–25). The First Book of Samuel has two different attitudes toward the request to have a king in Israel. Compare the anti-king passages of 1 Samuel 8:10–22 and 10:17–19 with the pro-king passages of 9:15–16 and chapter 11. Most likely, the difference of opinion comes from different parts of Israel. The Bible sometimes uses two versions of a story, called doublets, to allow consideration of both sides of an issue.

produce his weapons of war and chariotry.* 13 He
will use your daughters as perfumers, cooks, and
bakers. 14 He will take your best fields, vineyards,
and olive groves, and give them to his servants.*
15 He will tithe your crops and grape harvests
to give to his officials† and his servants.* 16 He
will take your male and female slaves, as well as
your best oxen and donkeys, and use them to do
his work. 17 He will also tithe your flocks. As for
you, you will become his slaves.* 18 On that day
you will cry out because of the king whom you
have chosen, but the LORD will not answer you
on that day."

Persistent Demand

19 The people, however, refused to listen to
Samuel's warning and said, "No! There must be
a king over us.* 20 We too must be like all the
nations, with a king to rule us, lead us in war-
fare, and fight our battles." 21 Samuel listened to
all the concerns of the people and then repeated
them to the LORD. 22 The LORD said: Listen to
them! Appoint a king to rule over them. Then
Samuel said to the people of Israel, "Return, each
one of you, to your own city."†

7:14 *The Amorites*: enemies in Transjordan. Israel is now secure, safe from external and internal threat.

7:16 *Bethel, Gilgal and Mizpah*: Bethel and Mizpah are located about five and eight miles north of Jerusalem respectively, in the district around Ramah, Samuel's home. Perhaps Gilgal, which has not been definitively located, was also in this area.

8:1–22 From this chapter on, the editors of 1 Samuel provide two and sometimes three perspectives on the same event: e.g., the selection of Saul as king is recounted in chap. 8; 10:17–24; chap. 12.

8:15 *Officials*: lit., eunuchs. These high-ranking administrators were not necessarily emasculated.

8:22 *To your own city*: Samuel will later reassemble the people at Mizpah (10:17) to acclaim Saul as their king.

7:17 1 Sm 9:12; 14:35.
8:1 1 Chr 6:13.
8:3 1 Sm 2:12–17; Ex 23:8; Dt 16:19; Prv 17:23.
8:5–6 Dt 17:14–15; Hos 13:10; Acts 13:21.
8:7–8 1 Sm 12:1, 12–13; Jgs 8:22–23; 10:13; 1 Kgs 9:9.
8:11 1 Sm 10:25; Dt 17:14–20; 1 Kgs 12.
8:12 2 Sm 15:1; 1 Kgs 1:5.
8:14 Dt 14:22–23.
8:15 1 Sm 22:7; 1 Kgs 21:1–24; Ez 46:18.
8:17 1 Kgs 12:4.
8:19 1 Sm 10:19.

Saul

9 1 There was a powerful man from Benjamin named Kish, who was the son of Abiel, son of Zeror, son of Becorath, son of Aphiah, a Benjaminite.* 2 He had a son named Saul, who was a handsome young man. There was no other Israelite more handsome than Saul; he stood head and shoulders above the people.*

The Lost Donkeys

3 Now the donkeys of Saul's father, Kish, had wandered off. Kish said to his son Saul, "Take one of the servants with you and go out and hunt for the donkeys." 4 So they went through the hill country of Ephraim, and through the land of Shalishah. Not finding them there, they continued through the land of Shaalim without success. They also went through the land of Benjamin, but they failed to find the animals. 5 When they came to the land of Zuph, Saul said to the servant who was with him, "Come, let us turn back, lest my father forget about the donkeys and become anxious about us." 6 The servant replied, "Listen! There is a man of God in this city, a man held in high esteem; everything he says comes true. Let us go there now! Perhaps he can advise us about the journey we have undertaken." 7 * But Saul said to his servant, "If we go, what can we offer the man? The food in our bags has run out; we have no present to give the man of God. What else do we have?" 8 Again the servant answered Saul, "I have a quarter shekel of silver.† If I give that to the man of God, he will advise us about the journey." 9 * (In former times in Israel, anyone who went to consult God used to say, "Come, let us go to the seer." For the one who is now called prophet was formerly called seer.) 10 Saul then said to his servant, "You are right! Come on, let us go!" So they headed toward the city where the man of God lived.

Meeting the Young Women

11 * As they were going up the path to the city, they met some young women coming out to draw water and they asked them, "Is the seer in town?" 12 * The young women answered, "Yes, there—straight ahead. Hurry now; just today he came to the city, because the people have a sacrifice today on the high place.† 13 When you enter the city, you may reach him before he goes up to the high place to eat. The people will not eat until he arrives; only after he blesses the sacrifice will the invited guests eat. Go up immediately, for you should find him right now."

Saul Meets Samuel

14 So they went up to the city. As they entered it—there was Samuel coming toward them on his way to the high place. 15 The day before Saul's arrival, the LORD had revealed to Samuel:* 16 At this time tomorrow I will send you a man from the land of Benjamin whom you are to anoint as ruler of my people Israel. He shall save my people from the hand of the Philistines. I have looked upon my people; their cry has come to me.* 17 When Samuel caught sight of Saul, the LORD assured him: This is the man I told you about; he shall govern my people. 18 Saul met Samuel in the gateway and said, "Please tell me where the seer lives." 19 Samuel answered Saul: "I am the seer. Go up ahead of me to the high place and eat with me today. In the morning, before letting you go, I will tell you everything on your mind. 20 As for your donkeys that were lost three days ago, do not worry about them, for they have been found. Whom should Israel want if not you and your father's family?" 21 Saul replied: "Am I not a Benjaminite, from the smallest of the tribes of Israel,† and is not my clan the least among the clans of the tribe of Benjamin? Why say such things to me?"*

The Meal†

22 Samuel then took Saul and his servant and brought them into the room. He seated them at the head of the guests, of whom there were about thirty. 23 He said to the cook, "Bring the portion I gave you and told you to put aside." 24 So the cook took up the leg and what went with it, and placed it before Saul. Samuel said: "This is a reserved portion that is set before you. Eat, for it was kept for you until this time; I explained that I was inviting some guests." Thus Saul dined with Samuel that day. 25 When they came down from the high place into the city, a mattress was spread for Saul on the roof, 26 and he slept there.

†

9:8 *A quarter shekel of silver*: about a tenth of an ounce of silver.

9:12 *On the high place*: the local sanctuary on the top of a hill, where the sacrifice was offered and the sacrificial meal eaten.

9:21 *Smallest of the tribes of Israel*: Saul's objection is a common element in call narrative, e.g., Ex 3:11; 4:10; Jgs 6:15.

9:22–24 At this ritual meal, Samuel treats the youthful Saul as if he were already king. Saul receives the part of the sacrificed animal reserved for the priest and his family, perhaps the sheep's fat tail. Legal texts (Ex 29:22; Lv 3:9; 7:3–4) require the priest to burn this portion of the sheep on the altar.

*

9:1 1 Sm 14:51; 1 Chr 8:33.
9:2 1 Sm 10:23; 16:12.
9:7–8 Nm 22:7; 1 Kgs 14:3; 2 Kgs 4:42; 5:15; 8:8–9.
9:9 Sir 46:15.
9:11 Gn 24:11–14; Ex 2:16.
9:12 1 Sm 7:17; 16:2, 5; 20:6, 29; Dt 12:13; 1 Kgs 3:2, 4.
9:15 Acts 13:21.
9:16 1 Sm 10:1; Jgs 6:14.
9:21 1 Sm 15:17.

Saul's Anointing

At daybreak Samuel called to Saul on the roof,
"Get up, and I will send you on your way." Saul
got up, and he and Samuel went outside the city
together. 27 As they were approaching the edge of
the town, Samuel said to Saul, "Tell the servant
to go on ahead of us, but you stay here for a mo-
ment, that I may give you a word from God."

10 1 Then, from a flask he had with him,
Samuel poured oil on Saul's head and
kissed him, saying: "The LORD anoints you ruler
over his people Israel. You are the one who will
govern the LORD's people and save them from the
power of their enemies all around them.*

The Signs Foretold

"This will be the sign† for you that the LORD
has anointed you ruler over his heritage: 2 When
you leave me today, you will meet two men near
Rachel's tomb† at Zelzah in the territory of Benja-
min. They will say to you, 'The donkeys you went
to look for have been found. Now your father is
no longer worried about the donkeys, but is anx-
ious about you and says: What shall I do about
my son?'* 3 Farther on, when you arrive at the oak
of Tabor,† three men will meet you as they go up
to God at Bethel; one will be bringing three young
goats, another three loaves of bread, and the third
a skin of wine. 4 They will greet you and offer you
two elevated offerings of bread, which you should
accept from them. 5 * After that you will come to
Gibeath-elohim, where the Philistine garrison†
is located. As you enter that city, you will meet
a band of prophets coming down from the high
place. They will be preceded by lyres, tambou-
rines, flutes, and harps, and will be in prophetic
ecstasy. 6 The spirit of the LORD will rush upon
you, and you will join them in their prophetic
ecstasy and will become a changed man.* 7 When
these signs have come to pass, do whatever lies to
hand, because God is with you. 8 * Now go down
ahead of me to Gilgal, for I shall come down to
you, to offer burnt offerings and to sacrifice com-
munion offerings. Wait seven days until I come to
you; I shall then tell you what you must do."†

The Signs Come to Pass

9 As Saul turned to leave Samuel, God changed
his heart. That very day all these signs came to
pass . . . . 10 † From there they arrived at Gibeah,
where a band of prophets met Saul, and the spirit
of God rushed upon him, so that he joined them
in their prophetic ecstasy.* 11 When all who had
known him previously saw him in a prophetic
state among the prophets, they said to one an-
other, "What has happened to the son of Kish?
Is Saul also among the prophets?"* 12 And some-
one from that district responded, "And who is
their father?" Thus the saying arose, "Is Saul also
among the prophets?" 13 When he came out of
the prophetic ecstasy, he went home.

Silence About the Kingship

14 Saul's uncle asked him and his servant,
"Where have you been?" Saul replied, "Looking
for the donkeys. When we could not find them,
we went to Samuel." 15 Saul's uncle said, "Tell
me, then, what Samuel said to you." 16 Saul said
to his uncle, "He assured us that the donkeys had
been found." But Saul told him nothing about
what Samuel had said about the kingship.

Saul Chosen King

17 Samuel called the people together to the
LORD at Mizpah* 18 and addressed the Israelites:
"Thus says the LORD, the God of Israel: It was I
who brought Israel up from Egypt and delivered
you from the power of the Egyptians and from
the power of all the kingdoms that oppressed
you.* 19 But today you have rejected your God,
who saves you from all your evils and calamities,
by saying, 'No! You must appoint a king over us.'
Now, therefore, take your stand before the LORD
according to your tribes and families."* 20 So
Samuel had all the tribes of Israel come forward,
and the tribe of Benjamin was chosen.† 21 Next

†

10:1 *The sign*: the role of the new ruler is confirmed by specific signs; cf. Ex 7:9.

10:2 Here, as in Jer 31:15, Rachel's tomb is placed at Ramah, north of Jerusalem. Later tradition understood Ephrath (Gn 35:19–20) as Bethlehem and placed the tomb farther south (Mt 2:16–18).

10:3 *Oak of Tabor*: or terebinth. Such a tree often indicates a shrine.

10:5 *The Philistine garrison*: the Hebrew word for "garrison" has been explained alternatively to mean a stele established to mark the Philistine occupation, or an inspector or officer for the collection of taxes. *Prophetic ecstasy*: a condition of religious enthusiasm often induced by communal rituals of music and dancing.

10:8 By inserting this verse, with its seven days, an editor has named in the very context of Saul's anointing the condition which in a later narrative will be the grounds for the rejection of the dynastic character of Saul's kingship (13:8–15).

10:10 An editor has abridged a longer version of this story by omitting mention of the first two signs Samuel has given (vv. 2–4).

10:20 *Was chosen*: probably by casting lots; cf. 14:40–42; Jos 7:14, 17.

*

10:1 1 Sm 9:16–17; 16:13; 24:7; Jgs 9:9; 1 Kgs 1:39; Acts 13:21.
10:2 Jer 31:15; Mk 14:13.
10:5–6 1 Sm 13:3; 16:13; 19:20–21.
10:6 1 Sm 11:6; 16:13; Jgs 14:6, 19; 15:14; 2 Kgs 3:15.
10:8 1 Sm 13:8; Lv 3:1.
10:10 1 Sm 19:20–24; Nm 11:25.
10:11 1 Sm 19:24.
10:17 1 Sm 7:5.
10:18 Ex 20:2; Lv 11:45; 25:38; Nm 15:41; Dt 5:6; Jgs 6:8–9.
10:19 1 Sm 8:19.

he had the tribe of Benjamin come forward by clans, and the clan of Matri was chosen, and finally Saul, son of Kish, was chosen. But when they went to look for him, he was nowhere to be found. 22 * Again they consulted the LORD, "Is there still someone else to come forward?" The LORD answered: He is hiding among the baggage. 23 They ran to bring him from there; when he took his place among the people, he stood head and shoulders above all the people.* 24 Then Samuel addressed all the people, "Do you see the man whom the LORD has chosen? There is no one like him among all the people!" Then all the people shouted out, "Long live the king!"*

25 Samuel next explained to the people the rules of the monarchy,† wrote them in a book, and placed them before the presence of the LORD. Samuel then sent the people back to their own homes.* 26 Saul also went home to Gibeah, accompanied by warriors whose hearts the LORD had touched. 27 But some worthless people said, "How can this fellow save us?" They despised him and brought him no tribute.† *

Defeat of the Ammonites

11 1 † About a month later, Nahash the Ammonite went up and besieged Jabesh-gilead. All the people of Jabesh begged Nahash, "Make a treaty with us, and we will serve you."* 2 But Nahash the Ammonite replied, "This is my condition for making a treaty with you: I will gouge out the right eye of every man,† and thus bring shame on all Israel." 3 The elders of Jabesh said to him: "Give us seven days to send messengers throughout the territory of Israel. If there is no one to save us, we will surrender to you." 4 When the messengers arrived at Gibeah of Saul and reported the news in the people's hearing, they all wept aloud. 5 Just then Saul came in from the field, behind his oxen. "Why are the people weeping?" he asked. They repeated the message of the inhabitants of Jabesh for him. 6 As he listened to this report, the spirit of God rushed upon him and he became very angry.* 7 Taking a yoke of oxen, he cut them into pieces and sent them throughout the territory of Israel† by messengers saying, "If anyone does not come out to follow Saul and Samuel, the same thing will be done to his oxen!" The dread of the LORD came upon the people and they went forth as one.* 8 When Saul reviewed them in Bezek,† there were three hundred thousand Israelites and seventy thousand Judahites.

9 To the messengers who had come he said, "Tell the inhabitants of Jabesh-gilead that tomorrow, when the sun grows hot, they will be saved." The messengers went and reported this to the inhabitants of Jabesh, and they rejoiced. 10 The men of Jabesh said to Nahash, "Tomorrow we will surrender to you, and you may do with us whatever you want." 11 The next day, Saul arranged his troops in three companies and invaded the camp during the dawn watch. They slaughtered Ammonites until the day had gotten hot; by then the survivors were so scattered that no two of them were left together.

Saul Accepted as King

12 † The people then said to Samuel: "Who questioned whether Saul should rule over us? Hand them over and we will put them to death."* 13 But Saul objected, "No one will be put to death this day, for today the LORD has rescued Israel."* 14 Samuel said to the people, "Come, let us go to Gilgal to renew the kingship there." 15 So all the people went to Gilgal, and there they made Saul king in the LORD's presence. They also sacrificed communion offerings there before the LORD, and Saul and all the Israelites rejoiced greatly.

Samuel's Integrity

12 † 1 † Samuel addressed all Israel: "I have granted your request in every respect," he said. "I have set a king over you* 2 and now the king will lead you. As for me, I am old and gray,

---

† **10:25** *Rules of the monarchy*: a charter describing the relationship between the king and the people.

10:27 *Tribute*: a gift to honor a new ruler as a pledge of one's loyalty; see Gn 32:14; Jgs 3:15; 2 Sm 8:2.

11:1 A text from Qumran (1QSam[a]) introduces this chapter with the report that Nahash, king of the Ammonites, had attacked the Gadites and the Reubenites, gouging out their right eyes. Seven thousand of them had fled to Jabesh-gilead. This additional information would explain why Nahash besieged Jabesh-gilead. There is no consensus among scholars whether the Qumran text represents an original reading or a secondary expansion.

11:2 *Right eye of every man*: thus rendering them incapable of military action.

11:7 *Throughout the territory of Israel*: Saul's gesture summons the Israelite confederacy to a coordinated response against Nahash; cf. Jgs 19:29 for a similar action. *Dread of the LORD*: often a panic that immobilizes Israel's enemies; here, however, it has the opposite effect and incites the Israelites to battle.

11:8 *Bezek*: probably modern Khirbet Ibziq, northeast of Shechem, on the west slope of the Jordan valley, opposite Jabesh-gilead.

11:12–14 With the defeat of the Ammonites, Saul demonstrates his ability to command Israel's army and defend the land. At Gilgal, Saul's kingship is ratified; ironically, he loses his kingship at the same place (13:7).

12:1–25 This chapter narrates the transition from the leadership of the judges to the rule of the king. The Deuteronomistic redactor has Samuel contrast the wickedness of Israel's ancestors with the

---

* **10:22** 1 Sm 30:24.
10:23 1 Sm 9:2; 16:7.
10:24 2 Sm 16:16; 1 Kgs 1:25; 2 Kgs 11:12.
10:25 1 Sm 8:11; Dt 17:14–20.
10:27 1 Sm 11:12.
11:1 1 Sm 12:12; 31:11; 2 Sm 10:2.
11:6 1 Sm 16:13; Jgs 14:6, 19; 15:14.
11:7 1 Kgs 11:30; 2 Kgs 13:18.
11:12 1 Sm 10:27.
11:13 2 Sm 19:23.
12:1 1 Sm 8:7, 9, 22.

and my sons are among you. I was your leader from my youth to the present day. 3 Here I stand! Answer me in the presence of the LORD and the LORD's anointed. Whose ox have I taken? Whose donkey have I taken? Whom have I cheated? Whom have I wronged? From whom have I accepted a bribe and shut my eyes because of it? I will make restitution to you."* 4 They replied, "You have neither cheated us, nor oppressed us, nor accepted anything from anyone." 5 So he said to them, "The LORD is witness against you this day, and the LORD's anointed is witness, that you have found nothing in my possession." "The LORD is witness," they said.

Samuel Admonishes the People

6 Samuel continued: "The LORD is witness, who appointed Moses and Aaron and brought your ancestors up from the land of Egypt.* 7 Now take your stand, that I may judge you in the presence of the LORD according to all the gracious acts that the LORD has done for you and your ancestors. 8 When Jacob and his sons went to Egypt and the Egyptians oppressed them, your ancestors cried out to the LORD. The LORD then sent Moses and Aaron to bring them out of Egypt and settled them in this place.* 9 But they forgot the LORD their God; and so the LORD sold them into the power of Sisera, the captain of the army of Hazor, the power of the Philistines, and the power of the king of Moab, who made war against them.* 10 They cried out to the LORD and said, 'We have sinned because we abandoned the LORD and served the Baals and Astartes. Now deliver us from the power of our enemies, and we will serve you.'* 11 The LORD sent Jerubbaal, Barak, Jephthah, and Samuel; he delivered you from the power of your enemies on every side, so that you could live in security.* 12 Yet, when you saw Nahash, king of the Ammonites, advancing against you, you said to me, 'No! A king must rule us,' even though the LORD your God is your king.*

Warnings for People and King

13 "Now here is the king you chose. See! The LORD has given you a king.* 14 If you fear and serve the LORD, if you listen to the voice of the LORD and do not rebel against the LORD's command, if both you and the king, who rules over you, follow the LORD your God—well and good. 15 But if you do not listen to the voice of the LORD and if you rebel against the LORD's command, the hand of the LORD will be against you and your king. 16 Now then, stand ready to witness the great marvel the LORD is about to accomplish before your eyes. 17 Are we not in the harvest time for wheat?† Yet I will call upon the LORD, and he will send thunder and rain. Thus you will see and understand how great an evil it is in the eyes of the LORD that you have asked for a king."* 18 Samuel called upon the LORD, and the LORD sent thunder and rain that day.

Assistance Promised

Then all the people feared the LORD and Samuel. 19 They said to Samuel, "Pray to the LORD your God for us, your servants, that we may not die for having added to all our other sins the evil of asking for a king." 20 "Do not fear," Samuel answered them. "You have indeed committed all this evil! Yet do not turn from the LORD, but serve him with your whole heart. 21 Do not turn aside to gods who are nothing,† who cannot act and deliver. They are nothing.* 22 For the sake of his own great name† the LORD will not abandon his people, since the LORD has decided to make you his people.* 23 As for me, far be it from me to sin against the LORD by ceasing to pray for you and to teach you the good and right way.* 24 But you must fear the LORD and serve him faithfully with all your heart, for you have seen the great things the LORD has done among you. 25 If instead you continue to do evil, both you and your king shall be swept away."

III. Saul and David

13 1 [Saul was . . . years old when he became king and he reigned . . . -two years over Israel.]†

†

Lord's gracious deliverance (vv. 6–12). The people realize that their demand for a king has compounded that wickedness. Now that the Lord has given them a king, Samuel urges the people and their king to serve the Lord wholeheartedly (vv. 13–25).

12:1–5 Samuel's upright leadership is set in sharp contrast to the despotic powers of the king described in chap. 8. By their testimony, the people witness to Samuel's righteousness.

12:17 *Harvest time for wheat*: in May–June. Since this is a period of little or no rainfall in Israel, the people will not mistake the sign for a natural phenomenon.

12:21 *Gods who are nothing*: Hebrew *tohu*, lit., "emptiness," cf. Gn 1:2 (. . . *webohu*); here, idols without power or substance, as in Is 41:29.

12:22 *His own great name*: were the Lord to abandon his people, even if they abandon him, he would diminish his stature or reputation in the divine council or among the nations (e.g., Ez 20:9). Throughout the Old Testament the Lord is encouraged to deliver Israel, despite its evil, "for the sake of his name."

13:1 A formula like that of 2 Sm 5:4 was introduced here at some

*

12:3 Ex 20:17; 23:8; Nm 16:15; Dt 16:19; Sir 46:19.
12:6 Mi 6:4.
12:8 Gn 46:5; Ex 1:11; 2:23–25.
12:9 Jgs 3:12–15; 4:2–3; 10:7; 13:1.
12:10 1 Sm 7:3–4; Jgs 10:10.
12:11 Jgs 6:14, 32; 11:1.
12:12 1 Sm 8:6–7, 19; 11:1–2; Jgs 8:23.
12:13 1 Sm 8:7.
12:17 Ex 9:23, 28–30; 1 Kgs 18:1.
12:21 Dt 32:37–39; Is 41:29; 44:9–10.
12:22 Ex 18:10; Dt 4:34; Jos 7:9; Is 48:9; Jer 14:21; Dn 3:34.
12:23 Ex 32:11.

Saul Offers Sacrifice

2 Saul chose three thousand of Israel, of whom two thousand remained with him in Michmash and in the hill country of Bethel, and one thousand were with Jonathan in Gibeah of Benjamin. He sent the rest of the army back to their tents. 3 Now Jonathan struck the Philistine garrison† in Gibeah, and the Philistines got word of it. Then Saul sounded the horn throughout the land, saying, "Let the Hebrews hear!"* 4 Then all Israel heard the report, "Saul has struck the garrison of the Philistines! Israel has become odious to the Philistines!" Then the army was called up to Saul in Gilgal. 5 The Philistines also assembled for battle against Israel, with thirty thousand chariots,† six thousand horsemen, and foot soldiers as numerous as the sand on the seashore.* They came up and encamped in Michmash, east of Beth-aven.* 6 When the soldiers saw they were in danger because the army was hardpressed, they hid themselves in caves, thickets, rocks, caverns, and cisterns. 7 Other Hebrews crossed the Jordan into the land of Gad and Gilead. Saul, however, held out in Gilgal, all his army trembling in fear behind him.† 8 He waited seven days, until the appointed time Samuel had set, but Samuel did not come, and the army deserted Saul.* 9 He then said, "Bring me the burnt offering and communion offerings!" Then he sacrificed the burnt offering.

King Saul Reproved

10 As he finished sacrificing the burnt offering, there came Samuel! So Saul went out toward him in order to greet him. 11 Samuel asked him, "What have you done?" Saul explained: "When I saw that the army was deserting me and you did not come on the appointed day, and that the Philistines were assembling at Michmash, 12 I said to myself, 'Now the Philistines will come down against me at Gilgal, and I have not yet sought the LORD's blessing.' So I thought I should sacrifice the burnt offering." 13 Samuel replied to Saul: "You have acted foolishly! Had you kept the command the LORD your God gave you, the LORD would now establish your kingship in Israel forever; 14 but now your kingship shall not endure. The LORD has sought out a man after his own heart† to appoint as ruler over his people because you did not observe what the LORD commanded you."*

Philistine Invasion

15 Then Samuel set out from Gilgal and went his own way; but what was left of the army went up after Saul to meet the soldiers, going from Gilgal to Gibeah of Benjamin. Saul then counted the soldiers he had with him, about six hundred.* 16 Saul, his son Jonathan, and the soldiers they had with them were now occupying Geba of Benjamin, and the Philistines were encamped at Michmash. 17 Meanwhile, raiders left the camp of the Philistines in three bands.* One band took the Ophrah road toward the district of Shual; 18 another turned in the direction of Beth-horon; and the third took the road for Geba that overlooks the Valley of the Hyenas toward the desert.

Disarmament of Israel†

19 Not a single smith was to be found anywhere in Israel, for the Philistines had said, "Otherwise the Hebrews will make swords or spears."* 20 All Israel, therefore, had to go down to the Philistines to sharpen their plowshares, mattocks, axes, and sickles. 21 The price for the plowshares and mattocks was two thirds of a shekel, and a third of a shekel for sharpening the axes and for setting the ox-goads. 22 And so on the day of battle neither sword nor spear could be found in the hand of any of the soldiers with Saul or Jonathan. Only Saul and his son Jonathan had them.

Jonathan's Exploit

23 An outpost of the Philistines had pushed forward to the pass of Michmash.*

14 1 One day Jonathan, son of Saul, said to his armor-bearer, "Come, let us go over to the Philistine outpost on the other side." But

---

† time; but the age of Saul when he became king remains a blank, and the two years assigned for his reign in the Masoretic text cannot be correct. Acts 13:21 offers the round number of forty years.

13:3–4 *The Philistine garrison*: see note on 10:5. *Let the Hebrews hear*: a different reading of these verses, based on the Greek, would yield: "And the Philistines heard that the Hebrews (or: the slaves) had revolted. Saul in the meantime sounded the trumpet throughout all the land (v. 4), and all Israel heard that Saul . . . ."

13:5 *Thirty thousand chariots*: some Greek manuscripts read "three thousand chariots."

13:7–15 These verses, like 10:8, anticipate the rejection of Saul; a different occasion and motivation for this are given in chap. 15 and 28:17–18.

13:14 *After his own heart*: i.e., of his choosing, for his purpose. While the verse undoubtedly refers to David, it concerns the Lord's decision to continue the kingship, even though he has rejected Saul, by selecting the heir to Saul's throne.

13:19–22 These details emphasize the Philistines' military power and superior technology, a reminder that an Israelite victory depends on God.

---

* **13:3** 1 Sm 14:1–15; Jgs 3:27; 6:34; 2 Sm 20:1–2.
13:5 Gn 22:17; 41:49; Jgs 7:12.
13:5 1 Sm 14:22.
13:8 1 Sm 10:8.
13:14 1 Sm 15:28; 25:30; 2 Sm 7:15–16; Ps 78:70; Acts 13:22.
13:15 1 Sm 14:2.
13:17 1 Sm 14:15.
13:19 Jgs 5:8.
13:23 1 Sm 14:15.

he did not inform his father—* 2Saul was sit-
ting under the pomegranate tree in Migron on
the outskirts of Gibeah; with him were about six
hundred men. 3Ahijah, son of Ahitub, brother
of Ichabod, the son of Phinehas, son of Eli, the
priest of the LORD at Shiloh, was wearing the
ephod—nor did the soldiers know that Jona-
than had gone.* 4Flanking the ravine through
which Jonathan intended to cross to the Philis-
tine outpost were rocky crags on each side, one
named Bozez and the other Seneh. 5One crag
was to the north, toward Michmash; the other
to the south, toward Geba. 6Jonathan said to
his armor-bearer: "Come, let us go over to that
outpost of the uncircumcised. Perhaps the LORD
will help us, because it is no more difficult for
the LORD to grant victory by means of a few than
it is by means of many."* 7His armor-bearer re-
plied, "Do whatever you think best; I am with
you in whatever you decide." 8Jonathan contin-
ued: "When we cross over to those men, we will
be visible to them. 9If they say to us, 'Stay there
until we can come to you,' we will stop where we
are; we will not go up to them. 10But if they say,
'Come up to us,' we will go up, because the LORD
has delivered them into our hand. That will be
our sign."† * 11When the two of them came into
the view of the Philistine outpost, the Philistines
remarked, "Look, some Hebrews† are coming
out of the holes where they have been hiding."
12The men of the outpost called to Jonathan and
his armor-bearer. "Come up here," they said,
"and we will teach you a lesson." So Jonathan
said to his armor-bearer, "Climb up after me,
for the LORD has delivered them into the hand of
Israel." 13Jonathan clambered up with his armor-
bearer behind him. As the Philistines fell before
Jonathan, his armor-bearer, who followed him,
would finish them off. 14In this first attack Jon-
athan and his armor-bearer killed about twenty
men within half a furlong. 15Then terror spread
through the camp and the countryside; all the
soldiers in the outpost and in the raiding parties
shuddered in terror. The earth shook with an
awesome shuddering.† *

Rout of the Philistines

16Saul's sentinels in Gibeah of Benjamin saw
that the enemy camp had scattered and were
running in all directions. 17Saul said to those
around him, "Count the troops and find out if
any of us are missing." When they had taken the
count, they found Jonathan and his armor-bearer
missing. 18Saul then said to Ahijah, "Bring the
ephod here." (Ahijah was wearing the ephod
before the Israelites at that time.) 19While Saul
was speaking to the priest, the uproar in the Phi-
listine camp kept increasing. So he said to the
priest, "Withdraw your hand." 20And Saul and all
his men rallied and rushed into the fight, where
the Philistines, wholly confused, were thrusting
swords at one another.* 21The Hebrews who
had previously sided with the Philistines and had
gone up with them to their camp turned to join
the Israelites under Saul and Jonathan.* 22Like-
wise, all the Israelites who were hiding in the
hill country of Ephraim, hearing that the Philis-
tines were fleeing, kept after them in the battle.*
23† Thus the LORD saved Israel that day.

Saul's Oath

The battle continued past Beth-aven. 24Even
though the Israelites were exhausted that day,
Saul laid an oath on them, saying, "Cursed be
the one who takes food before evening, before
I am able to avenge myself on my enemies." So
none of the people tasted food. 25Now there was
a honeycomb lying on the ground, 26and when
the soldiers came to the comb the honey was
flowing; yet no one raised a hand from it to his
mouth, because the people feared the oath.

Violation of the Oath

27Jonathan, who had not heard that his fa-
ther had put the people under oath, thrust out
the end of the staff he was holding and dipped
it into the honeycomb. Then he raised it to his
mouth and his eyes brightened. 28At this, one
of the soldiers spoke up: "Your father put the
people under a strict oath, saying, 'Cursed be the
one who takes food today!' As a result the people
are weakened." 29* Jonathan replied: "My father
brings trouble to the land. Look how bright my
eyes are because I had this little taste of honey.
30What is more, if the army had eaten freely of
the enemy's plunder when they came across it to-
day, surely the slaughter of the Philistines would
have been the greater by now!"

†

14:10 *That will be our sign*: Jonathan acknowledges that the battle is in God's hands.

14:11 *Hebrews*: while this term is often used by foreigners of Israelites, in this verse it seems to be a derogatory epithet for soldiers who deserted Saul's army while he was waiting for Samuel to arrive in Gilgal.

14:15 *Awesome shuddering*: lit., "shuddering caused by God"; the panic in the Philistine camp is the work of Israel's warrior God.

14:23 The victory apparently cleared the Philistines off the main ridge of mountains in the territories of Benjamin and Ephraim.

*

14:1 1 Sm 13:3.
14:3 1 Sm 2:28; 4:21; 14:18; 23:9; 30:7.
14:6 1 Sm 17:26, 36, 47; Jgs 14:3; Sir 39:18; 1 Mc 3:19.
14:10 Jos 8:1; 10:8; Jgs 12:3.
14:15 2 Sm 22:8; Jl 2:10–11.
14:20 Jgs 7:22.
14:21 1 Sm 29:4.
14:22 1 Sm 13:6.
14:29 Jos 7:25; 1 Kgs 18:17–18.

Consuming the Blood

31 After the Philistines were routed that day from Michmash to Aijalon, the people were completely exhausted. 32 So the army pounced upon the plunder and took sheep, oxen, and calves, slaughtering them on the ground and eating the meat with the blood in it.* 33 Informed that the army was sinning against the LORD by eating the meat with blood in it, Saul said: "You have broken faith. Roll a large stone here for me." 34 He continued: "Mingle with the people and tell each of them, 'Bring an ox or sheep to me. Slaughter them here and then eat. But you must not sin against the LORD by eating meat with blood in it.' " So that night they all brought whatever oxen they had seized, and they slaughtered them there; 35 and Saul built an altar to the LORD—this was the first time he built an altar to the LORD.*

Jonathan in Danger of Death

36 Then Saul said, "Let us go down in pursuit of the Philistines by night, to plunder them until daybreak and leave no one alive." They replied, "Do what you think best." But the priest said, "Let us consult God." 37 So Saul inquired of God: "Shall I go down in pursuit of the Philistines? Will you deliver them into the hand of Israel?" But he received no answer on this occasion.* 38 "All officers of the army," Saul announced, "come forward. Find out how this sin was committed today. 39 As the LORD lives who has given victory to Israel, even if my son Jonathan has committed it, he shall surely die!" But none of the people answered him. 40 So he said to all Israel, "Stand on one side, and my son Jonathan and I will stand on the other." The people responded, "Do what you think best."* 41 And Saul said to the LORD, the God of Israel: "Why did you not answer your servant this time? If the blame for this resides in me or my son Jonathan, LORD, God of Israel, respond with Urim; but if this guilt is in your people Israel, respond with Thummim."† Jonathan and Saul were designated, and the people went free.* 42 Saul then said, "Cast lots between me and my son Jonathan." And Jonathan was designated. 43 Saul said to Jonathan, "Tell me what you have done." Jonathan replied, "I only tasted a little honey from the end of the staff I was holding. Am I to die for this?" 44 Saul declared, "May God do thus to me, and more, if you do not indeed die, Jonathan!"*

Rescue of Jonathan

45 But the soldiers protested to Saul: "Is Jonathan to die, the man who won this great victory for Israel? This must not be! As the LORD lives, not a single hair of his head shall fall to the ground, for God was with him in what he did today!" Thus the soldiers rescued† Jonathan and he did not die.* 46 After that Saul gave up the pursuit of the Philistines, who returned to their own territory.

Saul's Victories

47 After taking possession of the kingship over Israel, Saul waged war on its enemies all around—Moab, the Ammonites, Edom, the kings of Zobah, and the Philistines. Wherever he turned, he was successful* 48 and fought bravely. He defeated Amalek and delivered Israel from the hand of those who were plundering them.*

Saul's Family

49 The sons of Saul were Jonathan, Ishvi, and Malchishua; the name of his firstborn daughter was Merob; the name of the younger was Michal.* 50 The name of Saul's wife was Ahinoam, daughter of Ahimaaz. The name of his general was Abner, son of Ner, Saul's uncle; 51 Kish, Saul's father, and Ner, Abner's father, were sons of Abiel.*

52 There was heavy fighting with the Philistines during Saul's lifetime. Whenever Saul saw any strong or brave man, he took him into his service.

Disobedience of Saul

15 †1 Samuel said to Saul: "It was I the LORD sent to anoint you king over his people Israel. Now, therefore, listen to the message of the LORD.* 2 Thus says the LORD of hosts: I will punish what Amalek did to the Israelites when he barred their way as they came up from Egypt.* 3 Go, now, attack Amalek, and put under the ban†

14:41 *Urim . . . Thummim*: objects, one representing a positive response and the other a negative response, kept in the front pocket of the priest's ephod, a garment worn as a breastplate, and used to ascertain God's will in certain instances, e.g., whether Saul should help rout the Philistines. Saul consults the priest but is too impatient to finish the consultation and hurries impulsively into battle.

14:45 *Rescued*: the Hebrew word used is that for the "redemption" of the firstborn (Ex 13:13–15).

15:1–35 The rejection of Saul sets the stage for the remainder of 1 Samuel. The audience knows that, in the ensuing struggle between David and Saul, David will triumph as king.

15:3 *Put under the ban*: this terminology mandates that all traces

---

14:32 1 Sm 15:19, 21; Gn 4:9; Lv 3:17; 7:26–27; 17:10–14; Acts 15:20, 29.
14:35 1 Sm 7:17; Jgs 6:24.
14:37 1 Sm 28:6, 15.
14:40 Jos 7:13–15.
14:41 1 Sm 10:20; 28:6; Ex 28:30; Dt 33:8.
14:44 1 Sm 3:17; Ru 1:17.
14:45 2 Sm 14:11; 1 Kgs 1:52.
14:47 2 Sm 1:22; 8:2–5.
14:48 1 Sm 15:7.
14:49 1 Sm 18:20, 25; 31:2; 1 Chr 8:33; 9:39; 10:2.
14:51 1 Sm 9:1.
15:1 Jos 3:9; 2 Kgs 20:16; Is 28:14.
15:2 Ex 17:8–10, 16; Dt 25:17–19.

everything he has. Do not spare him; kill men and
women, children and infants, oxen and sheep,
camels and donkeys."*
4 Saul alerted the army, and at Telaim reviewed
two hundred thousand foot soldiers and ten
thousand men of Judah.† 5 Saul went to the city
of Amalek and set up an ambush in the wadi.
6 * He warned the Kenites: "Leave Amalek, turn
aside and come down so I will not have to de-
stroy you with them, for you were loyal to the
Israelites when they came up from Egypt."† After
the Kenites left, 7 Saul routed Amalek from Hav-
ilah to the approaches of Shur, on the frontier
of Egypt.* 8 He took Agag, king of Amalek, alive,
but the rest of the people he destroyed by the
sword, putting them under the ban. 9 He and his
troops spared Agag and the best of the fat sheep
and oxen, and the lambs. They refused to put
under the ban anything that was worthwhile,
destroying only what was worthless and of no
account.

Samuel Rebukes Saul

10 Then the word of the LORD came to Sam-
uel: 11 I regret having made Saul king, for he has
turned from me and has not kept my command.
At this Samuel grew angry and cried out to the
LORD all night.* 12 Early in the morning he went
to meet Saul, but was informed that Saul had
gone to Carmel, where he set up a monument
in his own honor, and that on his return he had
gone down to Gilgal. 13 When Samuel came to
him, Saul greeted him: "The LORD bless you! I
have kept the command of the LORD." 14 But Sam-
uel asked, "What, then, is this bleating of sheep
that comes to my ears, the lowing of oxen that I
hear?" 15 Saul replied: "They were brought from
Amalek. The people spared the best sheep and
oxen to sacrifice to the LORD, your God; but the
rest we destroyed, putting them under the ban."
16 Samuel said to Saul: "Stop! Let me tell you
what the LORD said to me last night." "Speak!"
he replied. 17 Samuel then said: "Though little
in your own eyes, are you not chief of the tribes
of Israel? The LORD anointed you king of Israel*
18 and sent you on a mission, saying: Go and put
the sinful Amalekites under a ban of destruction.
Fight against them until you have exterminated
them.* 19 Why then have you disobeyed the
LORD? You have pounced on the spoil, thus do-
ing what was evil in the LORD's sight."* 20 Saul
explained to Samuel: "I did indeed obey the LORD
and fulfill the mission on which the LORD sent
me. I have brought back Agag, the king of Ama-
lek, and, carrying out the ban, I have destroyed
the Amalekites. 21 But from the spoil the army
took sheep and oxen, the best of what had been
banned, to sacrifice to the LORD your God in Gil-
gal."* 22 * But Samuel said:

"Does the LORD delight in burnt offerings and
sacrifices
as much as in obedience to the LORD's
command?
Obedience is better than sacrifice,
to listen, better than the fat of rams.†
23 For a sin of divination is rebellion,
and arrogance, the crime of idolatry.

Live It!

Power and Corruption

"Power corrupts." We have often heard that phrase. And in 1 Samuel 15:22–23, we have a vivid example. King Saul once again has decided to take matters in his own hands and goes against the word of the Lord. He seems to assume that his role as king exempts him from obedience to God. But Samuel reminds Saul that he has assumed way too much. No king, no president, no prime minister is above the law, especially when that law comes from God.

- In what ways have you served in a leadership role? How have you been tempted to abuse your privileges?

▶ 1 Sm 15:22–23

---

† of the Amalekites (people, cities, animals, etc.) be exterminated. No plunder could be seized for personal use. In the light of Dt 20:16–18, this injunction would eliminate any tendency toward syncretism. The focus of this chapter is that Saul fails to execute this order.

15:4 The numbers here are not realistic; compare 14:2.

15:6 The Kenites honored the terms of an alliance with Israel.

15:22 Samuel's reprimand echoes that of the prophets. Cultic practice is meaningless, even hypocritical, unless accompanied by an attentiveness to God's will.

*
15:3 1 Sm 27:8; 30:17; Ex 17:16; Nm 24:20; Jos 6:17.
15:6 Nm 24:21.
15:7 1 Sm 27:8.
15:11 1 Sm 15:35; Gn 6:6–7.
15:17 1 Sm 9:21.
15:18 1 Sm 28:18.
15:19 1 Sm 14:32.
15:21 Lv 27:28.
15:22 Prv 21:3; Hos 6:6; Am 5:21–25; Zec 10:2; Mt 9:13; 12:7; Heb 10:9.

Because you have rejected the word of the
LORD,
the LORD in turn has rejected you as
king."*

Rejection of Saul

24 Saul admitted to Samuel: "I have sinned, for I have transgressed the command of the LORD and your instructions. I feared the people and obeyed them.* 25 Now forgive my sin, and return with me, that I may worship the LORD." 26 But Samuel said to Saul, "I will not return with you, because you rejected the word of the LORD and the LORD has rejected you as king of Israel."* 27 As Samuel turned to go, Saul seized a loose end of his garment, and it tore off.* 28 So Samuel said to him: "The LORD has torn the kingdom of Israel from you this day, and has given it to a neighbor of yours, who is better than you.* 29 The Glory of Israel neither deceives nor repents,† for he is not a mortal who repents."* 30 But Saul answered: "I have sinned, yet honor me now before the elders of my people and before Israel. Return with me that I may worship the LORD your God." 31 And so Samuel returned with him, and Saul worshiped the LORD.

God does not see as a mortal, who sees the appearance. The LORD looks into the heart.
(1 Sm 16:7)

Samuel Executes Agag

32 Afterward Samuel commanded, "Bring Agag, king of Amalek, to me." Agag came to him struggling and saying, "So it is bitter death!" 33 And Samuel said,

"As your sword has made women childless,
so shall your mother be childless among
women."

Then he cut Agag to pieces before the LORD in Gilgal.* 34 Samuel departed for Ramah, while Saul went up to his home in Gibeah of Saul. 35 Never again, as long as he lived, did Samuel see Saul. Yet he grieved over Saul, because the LORD repented that he had made him king of Israel.*

Samuel Is Sent to Bethlehem

16 1* The LORD said to Samuel: How long will you grieve for Saul, whom I have rejected as king of Israel? Fill your horn with oil, and be on your way. I am sending you to Jesse of Bethlehem, for from among his sons I have decided on a king.† 2 But Samuel replied: "How can I go? Saul will hear of it and kill me." To this the LORD answered: Take a heifer along and say, "I have come to sacrifice to the LORD." 3 Invite Jesse to the sacrifice, and I myself will tell you what to do; you are to anoint for me the one I point out to you.*

Samuel Anoints David

4 Samuel did as the LORD had commanded him. When he entered Bethlehem, the elders of the city came trembling to meet him and asked, "Is your visit peaceful, O seer?" 5 He replied: "Yes! I have come to sacrifice to the LORD. So purify yourselves and celebrate with me today." He also had Jesse and his sons purify themselves and invited them to the sacrifice.* 6 As they came, he looked at Eliab and thought, "Surely the anointed is here before the LORD." 7 But the LORD said to Samuel: Do not judge from his appearance or from his lofty stature, because I have rejected him. God does not see as a mortal, who sees the appearance. The LORD looks into the heart.* 8* Then Jesse called Abinadab and presented him before Samuel, who said, "The LORD has not chosen him." 9 Next Jesse presented Shammah, but Samuel said, "The LORD has not chosen this one either." 10 In the same way Jesse presented seven sons before Samuel, but Samuel said to Jesse, "The LORD has not chosen any one of these." 11 Then Samuel asked Jesse, "Are these all the sons you have?" Jesse replied, "There is still the youngest, but he is tending the sheep." Samuel said to Jesse, "Send for him; we will not sit down to eat until he arrives here."* 12 Jesse had the young man brought

†

15:29 *Nor repents*: the apparent contradiction between this verse and vv. 11, 35 leads some scholars to consider it a gloss (cf. Nm 23:19). However, this phrase can be understood to underscore the definitive character of Samuel's declaration that Saul has lost the kingship.

16:1 David is anointed two more times after Saul's death (2 Sm 2:4; 5:3). In 17:28, his brother Eliab is not aware of David's selection. These repetitions and inconsistencies reflect the final editor's use of multiple sources.

*

15:23 Dt 18:10.
15:24 1 Sm 26:21.
15:26 1 Kgs 11:11, 30–31.
15:27 1 Sm 24:6; 1 Kgs 11:29–31.
15:28 1 Sm 28:17; 2 Sm 7:15–16.
15:29 Nm 23:19.
15:33 Ex 21:23; Jgs 8:21.
15:35 1 Sm 28:15.
16:1 Ru 4:17–22; 1 Kgs 1:39; 1 Chr 11:3; Is 11:1; Mt 2:6; Lk 2:4.
16:3 1 Sm 9:13, 22, 24.
16:5 1 Sm 9:12–13; 20:26; Ex 19:10; Jb 1:5.
16:7 1 Sm 10:23–24; 1 Kgs 11:4; 1 Chr 28:9; Prv 15:11; Jer 17:10; 20:12; Lk 16:15; Acts 1:24.
16:8–11 1 Sm 17:12–13; 1 Chr 2:13–15.
16:11 1 Sm 17:15, 28, 34; 2 Sm 7:8; Ps 78:70–71.

to them. He was ruddy, a youth with beautiful eyes, and good looking. The LORD said: There—anoint him, for this is the one!* [13]Then Samuel, with the horn of oil in hand, anointed him in the midst of his brothers, and from that day on, the spirit of the LORD rushed upon David. Then Samuel set out for Ramah.*

David Wins Saul's Approval

[14]† * The spirit of the LORD had departed from Saul, and he was tormented by an evil spirit from the LORD. [15]So the servants of Saul said to him: "Look! An evil spirit from God is tormenting you. [16]If your lordship will order it, we, your servants here attending to you, will look for a man skilled in playing the harp. When the evil spirit from God comes upon you, he will play and you will feel better." [17]Saul then told his servants, "Find me a good harpist and bring him to me." [18]* One of the servants spoke up: "I have observed that a son of Jesse of Bethlehem is a skillful harpist. He is also a brave warrior, an able speaker, and a handsome young man. The LORD is certainly with him."

David Made Armor-Bearer

[19]Accordingly, Saul dispatched messengers to ask Jesse to send him his son David, who was with the flock. [20]Then Jesse took five loaves of bread, a skin of wine, and a young goat, and sent them to Saul with his son David.* [21]Thus David came to Saul and entered his service. Saul became very fond of him and made him his armor-bearer.* [22]Saul sent Jesse the message, "Let David stay in my service, for he meets with my approval." [23]Whenever the spirit from God came upon Saul, David would take the harp and play, and Saul would be relieved and feel better, for the evil spirit would leave him.

The Challenge of Goliath

17 [1]The Philistines rallied their forces for battle at Socoh in Judah and camped between Socoh and Azekah at Ephes-dammim. [2]Saul and the Israelites rallied and camped in the valley of the Elah, drawing up their battle line to meet the Philistines. [3]The Philistines were stationed on one hill and the Israelites on an opposite hill, with a valley between them.

16:13

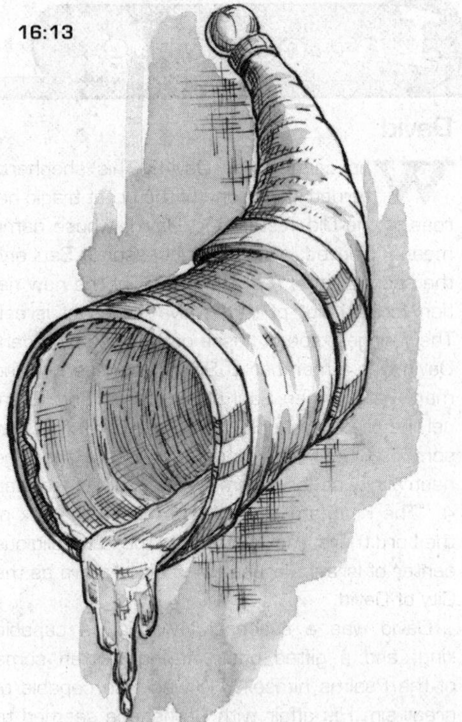

[4]A champion named Goliath of Gath came out from the Philistine camp; he was six cubits and a span† tall. [5]He had a bronze helmet on his head and wore a bronze breastplate of scale armor weighing five thousand shekels, [6]bronze greaves, and had a bronze scimitar slung from his shoulders. [7]The shaft of his javelin was like a weaver's beam, and its iron head weighed six hundred shekels.† His shield-bearer went ahead of him.* [8]He stood and shouted to the ranks of Israel: "Why come out in battle formation? I am a Philistine, and you are Saul's servants. Choose one of your men, and have him come down to me. [9]If he beats me in combat and kills me, we will be your vassals; but if I beat him

† **16:14–23** These verses explain Saul's loss of divine favor and David's rise to power. By approving the young man, Saul identifies David as his legitimate successor. Of the two traditions in the Hebrew text about David's entry into Saul's service, the Greek translation retains only the one found in vv. 14–23; 17:1–11, 32–54. *An evil spirit from the LORD*: Saul's erratic behavior is attributed to a change in the Lord's relationship with him. Cf. Jgs 9:23, where the Lord puts an evil spirit between Abimelech and the citizens of Shechem.

17:4 *Six cubits and a span*: about nine feet nine inches (a cubit equals about eighteen inches; a span equals about eight inches). The Greek text and 4QSam[a] read: "four cubits and a span" (six feet nine inches). The description of the Philistine's might and his powerful weapons contrasts with the picture of the youthful David who trusts in God.

17:7 *Six hundred shekels*: over fifteen pounds.

* **16:12** 1 Sm 9:2.
16:13 1 Sm 10:6; 11:6; Jgs 3:10; 9:9; Sir 46:13.
16:14 1 Sm 18:10–11.
16:18 1 Sm 18:12, 14, 28; 2 Sm 5:10; 17:8; Jn 3:2.
16:20 1 Sm 9:7–8; 10:3–4; 16:1; 17:17–19.
16:21 1 Sm 18:2.
17:7 2 Sm 21:19; 1 Chr 11:23; 20:5.

Introducing...

David

Who cannot love David? This shepherd-turned-king is one of the great tragic heroes of the Old Testament. David, whose name means "beloved," was the successor to Saul and the second king (1000–961 BC) of the new nation formed out of the twelve Tribes of Israel. The youngest son of Jesse of the tribe of Judah, David was a member of Saul's court as a young man. Later, when Saul disappointed God, Samuel the prophet anointed David as Saul's successor. After Saul was killed, David established the neutral city of Jerusalem as his capital (see map 4, "The Kingdom Years"). He moved the ark of the Lord there, making this city the new religious center of Israel. Jerusalem is also known as the City of David.

David was a successful warrior, a capable king, and a gifted poet, having written some of the Psalms himself. He was also capable of great sin. His affair with Bathsheba seemed to lead to a string of violence and betrayal affecting his whole family. One of his sons, Absalom, even inspired a revolt against David. But through it all, David was passionately in love with God. God recognized this and promised David that someone from his house would sit upon the throne in Israel.

When Israel was destroyed and its kings taken prisoners, the people developed a hope that another anointed one, a messiah from the house of David, would rise up and lead Israel in God's ways once again. It is this hope for the Davidic messiah that is fulfilled by Jesus in the New Testament.

and kill him, you shall be our vassals and serve us." 10 The Philistine continued: "I defy the ranks of Israel today. Give me a man and let us fight together." 11 When Saul and all Israel heard this challenge of the Philistine, they were stunned and terrified.

1 SM

† 17:12–31 Here the final editor begins an alternative account of David's encounter with the Philistine hero, which continues in vv. 50–51 and concludes in 17:55–18:5.

David Comes to the Camp†

12 David was the son of an Ephrathite named Jesse from Bethlehem in Judah who had eight sons. In the days of Saul Jesse was old and well on in years.* 13 The three oldest sons of Jesse had followed Saul to war; the names of these three sons who had gone off to war were Eliab the firstborn; Abinadab the second; and Shammah the third. 14 David was the youngest. While the three oldest had joined Saul, 15 David would come and go from Saul's presence to tend his father's sheep at Bethlehem.*

16 Meanwhile the Philistine came forward and took his stand morning and evening for forty days.

17 Now Jesse said to his son David: "Take this ephah of roasted grain and these ten loaves for your brothers, and bring them quickly to your brothers in the camp. 18 Also take these ten cheeses for the field officer. Greet your brothers and bring home some token from them. 19 Saul and your brothers, together with all Israel, are at war with the Philistines in the valley of the Elah." 20 Early the next morning, having left the flock with a shepherd, David packed up and set out, as Jesse had commanded him. He reached the barricade of the camp just as the army, on their way to the battleground, were shouting their battle cry.* 21 The Israelites and the Philistines drew up opposite each other in battle array. 22 David entrusted what he had brought to the keeper of the baggage and hastened to the battle line, where he greeted his brothers.* 23 While he was talking with them, the Philistine champion, by name Goliath of Gath, came up from the ranks of the Philistines and spoke as before, and David listened. 24 When the Israelites saw the man, they all retreated before him, terrified. 25 The Israelites had been saying: "Do you see this man coming up? He comes up to insult Israel. The king will make whoever kills him a very wealthy man. He will give his daughter to him and declare his father's family exempt from taxes in Israel."* 26 David now said to the men standing near him: "How will the man who kills this Philistine and frees Israel from disgrace be rewarded? Who is this uncircumcised Philistine that he should insult the armies of the living God?"* 27 They repeated the same words to him and said, "That is how the man who kills him will be rewarded." 28 When Eliab, his oldest brother, heard him speaking with the men, he

* 17:12 1 Sm 16:1, 10; Ru 1:2.
17:15 1 Sm 16:11; 18:2; 2 Sm 7:8; Ps 78:70–71.
17:20 1 Sm 26:5.
17:22 1 Sm 25:13.
17:25 1 Sm 18:17; Jos 15:16.
17:26 1 Sm 18:25; Dt 5:26; Jgs 15:18; 2 Kgs 19:4; Is 37:4; Jer 10:10.

grew angry with David and said: "Why did you
come down? With whom have you left those
sheep in the wilderness? I know your arrogance
and dishonest heart. You came down to enjoy
the battle!"* 29 David protested, "What have I
done now? I was only talking." 30 He turned from
him to another and asked the same question; and
everyone gave him the same answer as before.
31 The words that David had spoken were over-
heard and reported to Saul, who sent for him.

David Challenges Goliath

32 Then David spoke to Saul: "My lord should
not lose heart. Let your servant go and fight this
Philistine." 33 But Saul answered David, "You
cannot go up against this Philistine and fight
with him, for you are only a youth, while he has
been a warrior from his youth." 34 * Then David
told Saul: "Your servant used to tend his father's
sheep, and whenever a lion or bear came to carry
off a sheep from the flock, 35 I would chase after
it, attack it, and snatch the prey from its mouth.
If it attacked me, I would seize it by the throat,
strike it, and kill it. 36 Your servant has killed both
a lion and a bear. This uncircumcised Philistine
will be as one of them, because he has insulted
the armies of the living God."
37 David continued: "The same LORD who de-
livered me from the claws of the lion and the
bear will deliver me from the hand of this Phi-
listine." Saul answered David, "Go! the LORD will
be with you."*

Preparation for the Encounter

38 Then Saul dressed David in his own tunic,
putting a bronze helmet on his head and arming
him with a coat of mail. 39 David also fastened
Saul's sword over the tunic. He walked with dif-
ficulty, however, since he had never worn armor
before. He said to Saul, "I cannot go in these, be-
cause I am not used to them." So he took them
off. 40 Then, staff in hand, David selected five
smooth stones from the wadi and put them in
the pocket of his shepherd's bag. With his sling
in hand, he approached the Philistine.

David's Victory

41 † With his shield-bearer marching before him,
the Philistine advanced closer and closer to David.
42 When he sized David up and saw that he was
youthful, ruddy, and handsome in appearance, he
began to deride him. 43 He said to David, "Am I a

Live It!

Taking On Goliath

David makes it look so easy. A slingshot, a stone, a skillful aim, and it's all over. Goliath is dead, and the Israelites win the day. It is a story that gives hope to anyone who has ever been bullied or harassed.

A David lives in each of us, and plenty of Goliaths are out there ready to defeat us. The Goliaths we encounter can include peer pressure, an addiction, an abusive situation, or simply self-doubt. We may feel overpowered by these Goliaths, sure that they are too big for us to handle. But they are not! Those of us who believe in God, as David did, know that we are not alone. As followers of Jesus, we rely not on violence but on love and the support of the Christian community to defeat the Goliaths in our lives. We can make David's story our own.

- Identify a Goliath in your life right now, and journal about it. What stepping-stone can you take in defeating it?

▶ **1 Samuel, chapter 17**

dog that you come against me with a staff?" Then
the Philistine cursed David by his gods 44 and said
to him, "Come here to me, and I will feed your
flesh to the birds of the air and the beasts of the
field."* 45 David answered him: "You come against
me with sword and spear and scimitar, but I come
against you in the name of the LORD of hosts, the
God of the armies of Israel whom you have in-
sulted. 46 Today the LORD shall deliver you into my
hand; I will strike you down and cut off your head.
This very day I will feed your dead body and the
dead bodies of the Philistine army to the birds of
the air and the beasts of the field; thus the whole
land shall learn that Israel has a God. 47 All this
multitude, too, shall learn that it is not by sword or
spear that the LORD saves. For the battle belongs to
the LORD, who shall deliver you into our hands."*

† **17:41–47** The two combatants trade theological taunts. God uses the most unlikely opponent to destroy Goliath.

* **17:28** 1 Sm 16:6.
17:34–35 Jgs 14:6; Sir 47:3.
17:37 Prv 28:1.
17:44 Dt 28:26; Ps 79:2–3; Is 18:6; Jer 7:33; 15:3.
17:47 1 Sm 14:6, 10; Ps 33:16.

48 The Philistine then moved to meet David at
close quarters, while David ran quickly toward
the battle line to meet the Philistine. 49 David
put his hand into the bag and took out a stone,
hurled it with the sling, and struck the Philistine
on the forehead. The stone embedded itself in
his brow, and he fell on his face to the ground.
50 Thus David triumphed over the Philistine with
sling and stone; he struck the Philistine dead,
and did it without a sword in his hand.* 51 Then
David ran and stood over him; with the Philis-
tine's own sword which he drew from its sheath
he killed him, and cut off his head.*

Flight of the Philistines

When the Philistines saw that their hero was
dead, they fled. 52 Then the men of Israel and
Judah sprang up with a battle cry and pursued
them to the approaches of Gath and to the gates
of Ekron, and Philistines fell wounded along
the road from Shaaraim as far as Gath and Ek-
ron. 53 When they returned from their pursuit of
the Philistines, the Israelites looted their camp.
54 * David took the head of the Philistine and
brought it to Jerusalem; but he kept Goliath's
armor in his own tent.†

David Presented to Saul

55 As Saul watched David go out to meet the
Philistine, he asked his general Abner, "Abner,
whose son is that young man?" Abner replied,
"On your life, O king, I have no idea."* 56 And
the king said, "Find out whose son the lad is."
57 So when David returned from slaying the Phi-
listine, Abner escorted him into Saul's presence.
David was still holding the Philistine's head.
58 Saul then asked him, "Whose son are you,
young man?" David replied, "I am the son of
your servant Jesse of Bethlehem."

David and Jonathan

18 1 By the time David finished speaking with
Saul, Jonathan's life became bound up
with David's life; he loved him as his very self.*
2 Saul retained David on that day and did not
allow him to return to his father's house.* 3 Jon-
athan and David made a covenant, because Jon-
athan loved him as his very self. 4 Jonathan took
off† the cloak he was wearing and handed it over
to David, along with his military dress, even his
sword, bow, and belt.* 5 David then carried out
successfully every mission on which Saul sent
him. So Saul put him in charge of his soldiers;
this met with the approval of the whole army,
even Saul's officers.

Saul's Jealousy

6 At the approach of Saul and David, on Da-
vid's return after striking down the Philistine,
women came out from all the cities of Israel to
meet Saul the king, singing and dancing, with
tambourines, joyful songs, and stringed instru-
ments.† * 7 The women played and sang:

"Saul has slain his thousands,
David his tens of thousands."*

8 Saul was very angry and resentful of the song,
for he thought: "They give David tens of thou-
sands, but only thousands to me. All that re-
mains for him is the kingship." 9 From that day
on, Saul kept a jealous eye on David.
10 * The next day an evil spirit from God rushed
upon Saul, and he raged in his house. David
was in attendance, playing the harp as at other
times, while Saul was holding his spear. 11 Saul
poised the spear, thinking, "I will nail David to
the wall!" But twice David escaped him. 12 Saul
then began to fear David because the LORD was
with him but had turned away from Saul. 13 Saul
sent him out of his presence and appointed him
a field officer. So David led the people on their
military expeditions 14 and prospered in all his
ways, for the LORD was with him. 15 Seeing how
he prospered, Saul feared David. 16 But all Israel
and Judah loved David, since he led them on
their expeditions.† *

Saul Plots Against David

17 Saul said to David, "Look, I will give you
my older daughter, Merob, in marriage if you
become my warrior and fight the battles of the
LORD." Saul thought, "I will not lay a hand on
him. Let the hand of the Philistines strike him."*
18 But David answered Saul: "Who am I? And
who are my kindred or my father's clan in Israel

†

17:54 Jerusalem was a Jebusite city; it came under Israelite control only at the beginning of David's rule. As a young shepherd, David would not have had a military tent. In 21:10, Goliath's sword is in the Nob temple.

18:4 *Jonathan took off*: with the details in this verse, the narrator identifies David as Jonathan's replacement and Saul's heir to the throne. Cf. 23:17 and Gn 41:39–43.

18:6 *Stringed instruments*: perhaps a lute-like instrument with three strings; the Hebrew word, *shalshim*, perhaps related to the root *shlsh* ("three"), occurs only here in the Old Testament.

18:16 *Led them on their expeditions*: lit., "go out and come in," i.e., through the city gates; an idiom for military victory.

17:50 1 Mc 4:30; Sir 47:4.
17:51 1 Sm 21:10.
17:54 1 Sm 31:9.
17:55 1 Sm 14:50.
18:1 1 Sm 19:1–7; 20:17; 23:16; 2 Sm 1:26; 9:1.
18:2 1 Sm 16:21; 17:15.
18:4 2 Sm 1:22.
18:6 Ex 15:20–21; Jgs 11:34; Jdt 15:12.
18:7 1 Sm 21:12; 29:5; Ps 91:7; Sir 47:6–7.
18:10–11 1 Sm 16:14; 19:9–10; 20:33; 22:6; 26:8.
18:16 2 Sm 5:2.
18:17 1 Sm 14:49; 17:25.

that I should become the king's son-in-law?" 19But when the time came for Saul's daughter Merob to be given to David, she was given as wife to Adriel the Meholathite instead.*

20Now Saul's daughter Michal loved David. When this was reported to Saul, he was pleased.* 21He thought, "I will offer her to him as a trap, so that the hand of the Philistines may strike him." So for the second time Saul said to David, "You shall become my son-in-law today." 22Saul then ordered his servants, "Speak to David privately and say: The king favors you, and all his officers love you. You should become son-in-law to the king." 23But when Saul's servants mentioned this to David, he said: "Is becoming the king's son-in-law a trivial matter in your eyes? I am poor and insignificant." 24When his servants reported David's answer to him, 25Saul commanded them, "Say this to David: The king desires no other price for the bride than the foreskins of one hundred Philistines, that he may thus take vengeance on his enemies." Saul intended to have David fall into the hands of the Philistines.* 26When the servants reported this offer to David, he was pleased with the prospect of becoming the king's son-in-law. Before the year was up, 27David arose and went with his men and slew two hundred Philistines. He brought back their foreskins and counted them out before the king that he might become the king's son-in-law. So Saul gave him his daughter Michal as wife. 28Then Saul realized that the LORD was with David and that his own daughter Michal loved David. 29So Saul feared David all the more and was his enemy ever after.

30The Philistine chiefs continued to make forays, but each time they took the field, David was more successful against them than any of Saul's other officers, and his name was held in great esteem.

Persecution of David

19 1Saul discussed his intention to kill David with his son Jonathan and with all his servants. But Saul's son Jonathan, who was very fond of David,* 2told him: "My father Saul is trying to kill you. Therefore, please be on your guard tomorrow morning; stay out of sight and remain in hiding. 3I, however, will go out and stand beside my father in the countryside where you are, and will speak to him about you. If I learn anything, I will let you know."

4Jonathan then spoke well of David to his father Saul, telling him: "The king should not harm his servant David. He has not harmed you, but has helped you very much by his deeds.† 5When he took his life in his hands and killed the Philistine, and the LORD won a great victory for all Israel, you were glad to see it. Why, then, should you become guilty of shedding innocent blood by killing David without cause?"* 6Saul heeded Jonathan's plea and swore, "As the LORD lives, he shall not be killed." 7So Jonathan summoned David and repeated the whole conversation to him. He then brought David to Saul, and David served him as before.

David Escapes from Saul

8When war broke out again, David went out to fight against the Philistines and inflicted such a great defeat upon them that they fled from him. 9* Then an evil spirit from the LORD came upon Saul as he was sitting in his house with spear in hand while David was playing the harp nearby. 10Saul tried to pin David to the wall with the spear, but David eluded Saul, and the spear struck only the wall, while David got away safely.

11The same night, Saul sent messengers to David's house to guard it, planning to kill him in the morning. David's wife Michal informed him, "Unless you run for your life tonight, tomorrow you will be killed."† 12Then Michal let David down through a window, and he made his escape in safety.* 13Michal took the teraphim† and laid it in the bed, putting a tangle of goat's hair at its head and covering it with a blanket.* 14When Saul sent officers to arrest David, she said, "He is sick." 15Saul, however, sent the officers back to see David and commanded them, "Bring him up to me in his bed, that I may kill him." 16But when the messengers entered, they found the teraphim in the bed, with the tangle of goat's hair at its head. 17Saul asked Michal: "Why did you lie to me like this? You have helped my enemy to get away!" Michal explained to Saul: "He threatened me, saying 'Let me go or I will kill you.' "

David and Saul in Ramah

18When David got safely away, he went to Samuel in Ramah, informing him of all that Saul

†

19:4 Jonathan reminds Saul that David has served him loyally and done nothing to earn a traitor's death. Cf. 24:18–20.

19:11 This story may have originally followed 18:29, placing the episode of David's escape on the night of his marriage with Michal.

19:13 *Teraphim*: a life-sized image of a household god in human form; cf. also note on Gn 31:19. Elsewhere in the Deuteronomistic History, use of teraphim is condemned (15:23; 2 Kgs 23:24).

18:19 1 Sm 21:8; 24:16.
18:20 1 Sm 14:49; 25:44; 26:23; 2 Sm 3:13.
18:25 1 Sm 17:26; Gn 34:12.
19:1 1 Sm 18:1; 20:1–3.
19:5 1 Sm 17:55–56; Dt 19:10; Ps 119:109.
19:9–10 1 Sm 16:14; 18:10–11.
19:12 Jos 2:15; Acts 9:25; 2 Cor 11:33.
19:13 Gn 31:19; Jgs 17:5; 18:14, 18, 20; Ez 21:26.

had done to him. Then he and Samuel went to stay in Naioth.† 19 When Saul was told that David was at Naioth in Ramah, 20 he sent officers to arrest David. But when they saw the band of prophets presided over by Samuel in a prophetic state, the spirit of God came upon them and they too fell into the prophetic ecstasy.* 21 Informed of this, Saul sent other messengers, who also fell into the prophetic ecstasy. For the third time Saul sent messengers, but they too fell into a prophetic ecstasy.

Saul Among the Prophets

22 Finally Saul went to Ramah himself. Arriving at the large cistern in Secu, he asked, "Where are Samuel and David?" Someone answered, "At Naioth in Ramah." 23 As he walked from there to Naioth in Ramah, the spirit of God came upon him also, and he continued on, acting like a prophet until he reached Naioth in Ramah. 24 Then he, too, stripped himself of his garments and remained in a prophetic state in the presence of Samuel;† all that day and night he lay naked. That is why they say, "Is Saul also among the prophets?"*

David Consults with Jonathan

20 1 David fled from Naioth in Ramah, and went to Jonathan. "What have I done?" he asked him. "What crime or what offense does your father hold against me that he seeks my life?"* 2 Jonathan answered him: "Heaven forbid that you should die! My father does nothing, great or small, without telling me. Why, then, should my father conceal this from me? It cannot be true!" 3 But David replied: "Your father is well aware that I am favored with your friendship, so he has decided, 'Jonathan must not know about this or he will be grieved.' Nevertheless, as the LORD lives and as you live, there is only a step between me and death." 4 Jonathan then said to David, "I will do whatever you say." 5 David answered: "Tomorrow is the new moon, when I should in fact dine with the king. Let me go and hide in the open country until evening.* 6 If it turns out that your father misses me, say, 'David urged me to let him go on short notice to his city Bethlehem, because his whole clan is holding its seasonal sacrifice there.'* 7 If he says, 'Very well,' your servant is safe. But if he becomes quite angry, you can be sure he has planned some harm. 8* Do this kindness for your servant because of the LORD's covenant into which you brought us: if I am guilty, kill me yourself! Why should you give me up to your father?" 9 But Jonathan answered: "Not I! If ever I find out that my father is determined to harm you, I will certainly let you know." 10 David then asked Jonathan, "Who will tell me if your father gives you a harsh answer?"

Mutual Agreement

11 Jonathan replied to David, "Come, let us go out into the field." When they were out in the open country together, 12 Jonathan said to David: "As the LORD, the God of Israel, lives, I will sound out my father about this time tomorrow. Whether he is well disposed toward David or not, I will inform you. 13* Should it please my father to bring any harm upon you, may the LORD do thus to Jonathan and more,† if I do not inform you of it and send you on your way in peace. May the LORD be with you even as he was with my father. 14 Only this: if I am still alive, may you show me the kindness of the LORD. But if I die, 15 never cut off your kindness from my house. And when the LORD cuts off all the enemies of David from the face of the land, 16 the name of Jonathan must never be cut off from the family of David, or the LORD will make you answer for it." 17 And in his love for David, Jonathan renewed his oath to him, because he loved him as he loved himself.

18 Jonathan then said to him: "Tomorrow is the new moon; you will be missed, since your place will be vacant. 19 On the third day you will be missed all the more. Go to the spot where you hid on the other occasion and wait near the mound there.* 20 On the third day of the month I will shoot arrows to the side of it, as though aiming at a target. 21 I will then send my attendant to recover the arrows. If in fact I say to him, 'Look, the arrow is this side of you; pick it up,' come, for you are safe. As the LORD lives, there will be nothing to fear. 22 But if I say to the boy, 'Look, the arrow is beyond you,' go, for the LORD sends you away. 23 However, in the matter which you and I have discussed, the LORD shall be between you and me forever." 24 So David hid in the open country.

---

†

19:18 *Naioth*: meaning "the pastures." This place appears only in chaps. 19–20 and is associated with Ramah.

19:24 *In the presence of Samuel*: this verse, which disagrees with 15:35, is further evidence of the diverse origins of these accounts. *"Is Saul also among the prophets?"*: although similar to the story of Saul's prophetic ecstasy in 10:10–13, this account offers a more disparaging portrait of Saul.

20:13 See note on 3:17.

*

19:20 1 Sm 10:5–6, 10; Nm 11:25.
19:24 1 Sm 10:10–12; 2 Sm 6:20.
20:1 1 Sm 19:1–7, 11–17; 21:11; 27:4; Gn 31:36.
20:5 Nm 10:10; 28:11–15; Ezr 3:5; Neh 10:34.
20:6 1 Sm 17:12.
20:8–9 1 Sm 18:3; 23:17–18.
20:13–16 1 Sm 10:7; 17:37; 18:12, 14; 24:22–23; 2 Sm 9:1–13; 21:7.
20:19 1 Sm 19:1–7.

David's Absence

On the day of the new moon, when the king
sat down at the feast to dine, 25 he took his usual
place against the wall. Jonathan sat facing him,
while Abner sat at the king's side. David's place
was vacant. 26 * Saul, however, said nothing that
day, for he thought, "He must have become
unclean by accident."† 27 On the next day, the
second day of the month, David's place was still
vacant. So Saul asked his son Jonathan, "Why
has the son of Jesse not come to table yesterday
or today?" 28 Jonathan explained to Saul: "David
pleaded with me to let him go to Bethlehem.
29 'Please let me go,' he begged, 'for we are having
a clan sacrifice in our city, and my brothers insist
on my presence. Now then, if you think well of
me, give me leave to visit my brothers.' That is
why he has not come to the king's table." 30 But
Saul grew angry with Jonathan and said to him:
"Son of a rebellious woman, do I not know that,
to your own disgrace and to the disgrace of your
mother's nakedness, you are the companion of
Jesse's son? 31 For as long as the son of Jesse lives
upon the earth, you cannot make good your claim
to the kingship!† Now send for him, and bring
him to me, for he must die."* 32 But Jonathan
argued with his father Saul: "Why should he die?
What has he done?" 33 At this Saul brandished his
spear to strike him, and thus Jonathan learned
that his father was determined to kill David.*
34 Jonathan sprang up from the table in a rage
and ate nothing that second day of the month,
because he was grieved on David's account, and
because his father had humiliated him.

Jonathan's Farewell

35 The next morning Jonathan, accompanied
by a young boy, went out into the field for his
appointment with David. 36 There he said to the
boy, "Run and find the arrows." And as the boy
ran, he shot an arrow past him. 37 When the boy
made for the spot where Jonathan had shot the
arrow, Jonathan called after him, "The arrow is
farther on!" 38 Again he called to the boy, "Hurry,
be quick, don't delay!" Jonathan's boy picked
up the arrow and brought it to his master. 39 The
boy suspected nothing; only Jonathan and David
knew what was meant. 40 Then Jonathan gave his
weapons to his boy and said to him, "Go, take
them to the city." 41 When the boy had gone,
David rose from beside the mound and fell on
his face to the ground three times in homage.
They kissed each other and wept aloud together.
42 * At length Jonathan said to David, "Go in
peace, in keeping with what the two of us have
sworn by the name of the LORD: 'The LORD shall
be between you and me, and between your off-
spring and mine forever.' "

21 1 Then David departed on his way, while
Jonathan went back into the city.

Friends Forever

David and Jonathan have one of the most touching stories of friendship in the Bible. In 1 Samuel 18:1–4, Jonathan makes a special covenant with David. In chapter 20, their deep love leads them to risk their lives for each other. Saul, the king and Jonathan's father, is acting like a madman. He is insanely jealous of David and wants him dead.

Yet, Jonathan and David bring God into their relationship. This gives them the wisdom to see what is right and do it. When they have to part (see 20:41–42), they cry and embrace and remind each other of their vows.

Not many teenagers deal with situations as drastic as this, but tension with parents over your choice of friends can be common. Parents may not understand why you like a person they dislike. It can leave you with a sense of being stuck in the middle.

Your response should be like David and Jonathan's, keeping God part of all your relationships. Each friendship then becomes a living prayer, and God will guide you through conflicts and help you make good decisions.

▶ **1 Samuel, chapter 20**

20:26 The meal on the first day of the month would have had religious overtones, and a ritual impurity (Lv 15:16; Dt 23:10–12) would have barred David from sharing in it.

20:31 *Your claim to the kingship*: Saul admits his intention that Jonathan should succeed him and that David is a threat to his lineage (cf. 23:17). However Jonathan has already acknowledged David's kingship (18:3–4) and his own subservient role (20:13–16).

20:26 1 Sm 16:5; Lv 7:20–21; 15:1–3.
20:31 2 Sm 12:5.
20:33 1 Sm 18:11.
20:42 2 Sm 9:1; 21:7.

The Holy Bread

2 David went to Ahimelech, the priest of Nob,
who came trembling to meet him. He asked,
"Why are you alone? Is there no one with
you?"† * 3 David answered the priest: "The king
gave me a commission and told me, 'Do not
let anyone know anything about the business
on which I have sent you or the commission I
have given you.' For that reason I have arranged
a particular meeting place with my men. 4 * Now
what do you have on hand? Give me five loaves,
or whatever you can find." 5 † But the priest re-
plied to David, "I have no ordinary bread on
hand, only holy bread; if the men have abstained
from women, you may eat some of that." 6 Da-
vid answered the priest: "We have indeed stayed
away from women. In the past whenever I went
out on a campaign, all the young men were
consecrated—even for an ordinary campaign.
All the more so are they consecrated with their
weapons today!" 7 So the priest gave him holy
bread, for no other bread was on hand except the
showbread which had been removed from be-
fore the LORD and replaced by fresh bread when
it was taken away.* 8 One of Saul's servants was
there that day, detained before the LORD;† his
name was Doeg the Edomite, the chief of Saul's
shepherds.*

The Sword of Goliath

9 David then asked Ahimelech: "Do you have a
spear or a sword on hand? I brought along neither
my sword nor my weapons, because the king's
business was urgent." 10 The priest replied: "The
sword of Goliath the Philistine, whom you killed
in the Valley of Elah, is here wrapped in a garment
behind an ephod.† If you wish to take it, do so;
there is no sword here except that one." "There is
none like it," David cried, "give it to me!"*

David a Fugitive

11 That same day David fled from Saul, going
to Achish, king of Gath.* 12 But the servants of
Achish said to him, "Is this not David, the king
of the land? Is it not for him that during their
dances they sing out,

'Saul has slain his thousands,
David his tens of thousands'?"*

13 David took note of these remarks and became
very much afraid of Achish, king of Gath.† 14 So,
he feigned insanity in front of them and acted
like a madman in their custody, drumming on
the doors of the gate and drooling onto his
beard. 15 Finally Achish said to his servants: "You
see the man is mad. Why did you bring him to
me? 16 Do I not have enough madmen, that you
bring this one to rant in my presence? Should
this fellow come into my house?"

22 1 David left Gath and escaped to the cave
of Adullam. When his brothers and the
rest of his family heard about it, they came down
to him there.* 2 He was joined by all those in dif-
ficulties or in debt, or embittered,† and became
their leader. About four hundred men were with
him.

3 From there David went to Mizpeh of Moab
and said to the king of Moab, "Let my father and
mother stay with you, until I learn what God will
do for me." 4 He left them with the king of Moab;
they stayed with him as long as David remained
in the stronghold.†

5 But Gad the prophet said to David: "Do not
remain in the stronghold! Leave! Go to the land
of Judah." And so David left and went to the for-
est of Hereth.*

Doeg Betrays Ahimelech

6 Now Saul heard that David and his men
had been located. At the time he was sitting in
Gibeah under a tamarisk tree on the high place,
holding his spear, while all his servants stood by
him.* 7 So he said to them: "Listen, men of Ben-
jamin! Will the son of Jesse give all of you fields
and vineyards? Will he appoint any of you an

†

21:2 Ahimelech realizes that he risks incurring Saul's anger if David has come to Nob as a fugitive.

21:5–6 According to Lv 24:5–9, the showbread consisted of twelve loaves that were replaced each sabbath. Since the old bread was to be consumed by the priests, Ahimelech questions David regarding the ritual purity of his men (see 2 Sm 11:11). David's answer supposes the discipline of a military campaign under the conditions of "holy war" (Dt 23:10–15).

21:8 *Detained before the LORD*: perhaps to fulfill a ritual obligation. David's arrival at Nob seems to coincide with a festival day, since the showbread has recently been replaced with fresh bread. *Shepherds*: i.e., Saul's palace guard. Cf. 22:9–10, where Doeg has easy access to Saul.

21:10 *Ephod*: here an object or image large enough to conceal Goliath's sword. Cf. Gideon's ephod in Jgs 8:27.

21:13 *Gath*: a Philistine city (see note on 5:1–12), the home of Goliath.

22:2 *Embittered*: Hebrew *mar-nephesh*, "bitter of spirit," used of Hannah, deprived of a child, in 1:10, and of David's soldiers, whose women and children the Amalekites had seized (30:6). Cf. also 2 Sm 17:8. David becomes a hero for those who have endured loss or deprivation.

22:4–5 *Stronghold*: seemingly connected with the cave complex in v. 1.

*

21:2 1 Sm 16:4; Is 10:32; Mk 2:26.
21:4 Lv 24:5, 9.
21:7 Lv 24:5–9; Mt 12:3–4; Mk 2:26; Lk 6:3–5.
21:8 1 Sm 22:9.
21:10 1 Sm 17:51, 54.
21:11 1 Sm 27:2; 29:5.
21:12 1 Sm 18:7; 29:5.
22:1 2 Sm 23:13; Ps 63; Mi 1:15.
22:5 2 Sm 24:11–13.
22:6 1 Sm 14:2; Jgs 4:5.

officer over a thousand or a hundred men?* 8 Is that why you have all conspired against me? Why no one told me that my son had made a pact with the son of Jesse? None of you has shown compassion for me by revealing to me that my son has incited my servant to ambush me, as is the case today."* 9 * Then Doeg the Edomite, who was standing with Saul's officers, spoke up: "I saw the son of Jesse come to Ahimelech, son of Ahitub, in Nob. 10 He consulted the LORD for him, furnished him with provisions, and gave him the sword of Goliath the Philistine."

Slaughter of the Priests

11 So the king summoned Ahimelech the priest, son of Ahitub, and all his family, the priests in Nob. They all came to the king. 12 "Listen, son of Ahitub!" Saul declared. "Yes, my lord," he replied. 13 Saul questioned him, "Why have you conspired against me with the son of Jesse by giving him food and a sword and by consulting God for him, that he might rise up against me in ambush, as is the case today?" 14 Ahimelech answered the king: "Who among all your servants is as loyal as David, the king's son-in-law, captain of your bodyguard, and honored in your own house? 15 Is this the first time I have consulted God for him? No indeed! Let not the king accuse his servant or anyone in my family of such a thing. Your servant knows nothing at all, great or small, about the whole matter." 16 But the king said, "You shall certainly die, Ahimelech, with all your family." 17 The king then commanded his guards standing by him: "Turn and kill the priests of the LORD, for they gave David a hand. They knew he was a fugitive and yet failed to inform me." But the king's servants refused to raise a hand to strike the priests of the LORD.*

18 The king therefore commanded Doeg, "You, turn and kill the priests!" So Doeg the Edomite himself turned and killed the priests that day—eighty-five who wore the linen ephod. 19 Saul also put the priestly city of Nob to the sword, including men and women, children and infants, and oxen, donkeys and sheep.

Abiathar Escapes

20 One son of Ahimelech, son of Ahitub, named Abiathar,† escaped and fled to David.* 21 When Abiathar told David that Saul had slain the priests of the LORD, 22 David said to him: "I knew that day, when Doeg the Edomite was there, that he would certainly tell Saul. I am responsible for the slaughter of all your family. 23 Stay with me. Do not be afraid; whoever seeks your life must seek my life also. You are under my protection."†

Keilah Liberated

23 1 David was informed that the Philistines were attacking Keilah and plundering the threshing floors.* 2 So he consulted the LORD, asking, "Shall I go and attack these Philistines?" The LORD answered, Go, attack them, and free Keilah.* 3 But David's men said to him: "Even in Judah we have reason to fear. How much more so if we go to Keilah against the forces of the Philistines!" 4 Again David consulted the LORD, who answered: Go down to Keilah, for I will deliver the Philistines into your power.* 5 So David went with his men to Keilah and fought against the Philistines. He drove off their cattle and inflicted a severe defeat on them, and freed the inhabitants of Keilah.

6 Abiathar, son of Ahimelech, who had fled to David, went down with David to Keilah, taking the ephod with him.*

Flight from Keilah

7 When Saul was told that David had entered Keilah, he thought: "God has put him in my hand, for he has boxed himself in by entering a city with gates and bars." 8 Saul then called all the army to war, in order to go down to Keilah and besiege David and his men. 9 When David found out that Saul was planning to harm him, he said to the priest Abiathar, "Bring the ephod here."* 10 "LORD God of Israel," David prayed, "your servant has heard that Saul plans to come to Keilah, to destroy the city on my account. 11 Will they hand me over? Will Saul come down as your servant has heard? LORD God of Israel, tell your servant." The LORD answered: He will come down. 12 David then asked, "Will the citizens of Keilah deliver me and my men into the hand of Saul?" The LORD answered: They will deliver you. 13 So David and his men, about six hundred in number, left Keilah and wandered from place to

†

22:20 *Abiathar*: the sole survivor of Eli's household (2:27–36). David now has in his service the only priest of the Lord left in the land and exclusive access to the ephod for consulting the Lord (cf. 23:9–13). David later appoints Abiathar co-high priest with Zadok in Jerusalem (2 Sm 20:25), but Solomon exiles Abiathar to Anathoth when the priest does not support his bid for the throne. Cf. 1 Kgs 2:26–27.

22:23 *You are under my protection*: once again a sharp contrast is drawn between Saul, who kills the Lord's priests, and David, who protects the lone survivor.

*

22:7 1 Sm 8:14.
22:8 1 Sm 18:3; 20:8; 23:18.
22:9–10 1 Sm 21:2–10; Ps 52.
22:17 1 Sm 2:31, 33; 21:7.
22:20 1 Sm 23:6; 30:7; 2 Sm 20:25; 1 Kgs 2:26–27.
23:1 Jos 15:44.
23:2 1 Sm 28:6.
23:4 1 Sm 17:47.
23:6 1 Sm 22:20; 30:7.
23:9 1 Sm 2:28.

place. When Saul was informed that David had fled from Keilah, he did not go forth.

David and Jonathan in Horesh

14 David now lived in the strongholds in the wilderness, or in the barren hill country near Ziph. Though Saul sought him continually, the LORD did not deliver David into his hand. 15 While David was in the wilderness of Ziph at Horesh he was afraid that Saul had come out to seek his life. 16 Then Saul's son, Jonathan, came down to David at Horesh and encouraged him in the LORD.* 17 He said to him: "Have no fear, my father Saul shall not lay a hand to you. You shall be king of Israel† and I shall be second to you. Even my father Saul knows this."* 18 The two of them made a covenant before the LORD in Horesh, where David remained, while Jonathan returned to his home.*

Treachery of the Ziphites

19 Some of the Ziphites went up to Saul in Gibeah and said, "David is hiding among us in the strongholds at Horesh on the hill of Hachilah, south of Jeshimon.* 20 Therefore, whenever the king wishes to come down, let him do so. It will be our task to deliver him into the king's hand." 21 Saul replied: "The LORD bless you for your compassion toward me.* 22 Go now and make sure once more! Take note of the place where he sets foot for I am told that he is very cunning. 23 Look around and learn in which of all the various hiding places he is holding out. Then come back to me with reliable information, and I will go with you. If he is in the region, I will track him down out of all the families of Judah." 24 So they went off to Ziph ahead of Saul. At this time David and his men were in the wilderness below Maon, in the Arabah south of the wasteland.*

Escape from Saul

25 When Saul and his men came looking for him, David got word of it and went down to the gorge in the wilderness below Maon. Saul heard of this and pursued David into the wilderness below Maon. 26 As Saul moved along one side of the gorge, David and his men took to the other. David was anxious to escape Saul, while Saul and his men were trying to outflank David and his men in order to capture them. 27 Then a messenger came to Saul, saying, "Come quickly, because the Philistines have invaded the land." 28 Saul interrupted his pursuit of David and went to meet the Philistines. This is how that place came to be called the Rock of Divisions.

David Spares Saul†

24 1 David then went up from there and stayed in the strongholds of Engedi. 2 When Saul returned from the pursuit of the Philistines, he was told that David was in the desert near Engedi. 3 So Saul took three thousand of the best men from all Israel and went in search of David and his men in the direction of the wild goat crags. 4 When he came to the sheepfolds along the way, he found a cave, which he entered to relieve himself. David and his men were occupying the inmost recesses of the cave.*

5 David's servants said to him, "This is the day about which the LORD said to you: I will deliver your enemy into your hand; do with him as you see fit." So David moved up and stealthily cut off an end of Saul's robe. 6 Afterward, however, David regretted that he had cut off an end of Saul's robe.* 7 He said to his men, "The LORD forbid that I should do such a thing to my master, the LORD's anointed, to lay a hand on him, for he is the LORD's anointed."* 8 With these words David restrained his men and would not permit them to attack Saul. Saul then left the cave and went on his way. 9 David also stepped out of the cave, calling to Saul, "My lord the king!" When Saul looked back, David bowed, his face to the ground in homage, 10 and asked Saul: "Why do you listen to those who say, 'David is trying to harm you'? 11 You see for yourself today that the LORD just now delivered you into my hand in the cave. I was told to kill you, but I took pity on you instead. I decided, 'I will not raise a hand against my master, for he is the LORD's anointed.' 12 Look here, my father. See the end of your robe which I hold. I cut off an end of your robe and did not kill you. Now see and be convinced that I plan no harm and no rebellion. I have done you no wrong, though you are hunting me down to take my life.* 13 May the LORD judge between me and you. May the LORD exact justice from you in my case. I shall not lay a hand on you. 14 As the old proverb says, 'From the wicked comes wickedness.' Thus I will not lay a hand on you.

†

23:17 *King of Israel*: to emphasize the inevitability of the Lord's plan, the narrator frames Jonathan's statement with two accounts of David's mercy toward Saul.

24:1 The first of two accounts (see chap. 26) in which David spares Saul's life. The two accounts, which do not make reference to each other, are probably alternative versions of the same story.

*

23:16 1 Sm 18:1.
23:17 1 Sm 20:14–16.
23:18 1 Sm 18:3; 20:8.
23:19 1 Sm 26:1–3; Ps 54.
23:21 2 Sm 2:5.
23:24 1 Sm 25:2.
24:4 Ps 57.
24:6 1 Sm 15:27.
24:7 1 Sm 10:1; 26:9; 31:4; 2 Sm 1:14.
24:12 Rom 12:19.

15 What is the king of Israel attacking? What are
you pursuing? A dead dog! A single flea!* 16 The
LORD will be the judge to decide between us. May
the LORD see this, defend my cause, and give me
justice against you!"*

Saul's Remorse

17 When David finished saying these things to
Saul, Saul answered, "Is that your voice, my son
David?" And he wept freely. 18 Saul then admit-
ted to David: "You are more in the right than I
am. You have treated me graciously, while I have
treated you badly. 19 You have declared this day
how you treated me graciously: the LORD deliv-
ered me into your hand and you did not kill me.
20 For if someone comes upon an enemy, do they
send them graciously on their way? So may the
LORD reward you graciously for what you have
done this day. 21 And now, since I know that you
will certainly become king and that the kingship
over Israel shall come into your possession,*
22 swear to me by the LORD that you will not cut
off my descendants and that you will not blot
out my name from my father's house."* 23 David
gave Saul his oath and Saul returned home, while
David and his men went up to the stronghold.

Death of Samuel

25 1 Samuel died, and all Israel gathered to
mourn him; they buried him at his home
in Ramah.* Then David went down to the wil-
derness of Paran.

Nabal and Abigail

2 There was a man of Maon who had property
in Carmel; he was very wealthy, owning three
thousand sheep and a thousand goats. At the
time, he was present for the shearing of his flock
in Carmel.* 3 The man's name was Nabal and his
wife was Abigail. The woman was intelligent and
attractive, but Nabal, a Calebite, was harsh and
bad-mannered.* 4 While in the wilderness, David
heard that Nabal was shearing his flock, 5 so he
sent ten young men, instructing them: "Go up
to Carmel. Pay Nabal a visit and greet him in
my name. 6 Say to him, 'Peace be with you, my
brother, and with your family, and with all who
belong to you. 7 I have just heard that shearers
are with you. Now, when your shepherds were
with us, we did them no injury, neither did they
miss anything while they were in Carmel. 8 Ask
your servants and they will tell you. Look kindly
on these young men, since we come at a festival
time. Please give your servants and your son Da-
vid† whatever you can.' "

9 When David's young men arrived, they de-
livered the entire message to Nabal in David's
name, and then waited. 10 But Nabal answered
the servants of David: "Who is David? Who is
the son of Jesse? Nowadays there are many ser-
vants who run away from their masters. 11 Must
I take my bread, my wine, my meat that I have
slaughtered for my own shearers, and give them
to men who come from who knows where?"
12 So David's young men retraced their steps and
on their return reported to him all that had been
said. 13 Thereupon David said to his men, "Let
everyone strap on his sword." And everyone did
so, and David put on his own sword. About four

Did You Know?

The Lord's Anointed

Throughout human history, oil has been used as medicine, perfume, and a symbol of blessing. The Israelite kings and prophets were anointed with oil to symbolize the powerful Spirit of God present to them as they fulfilled their important role. Often it was olive oil mixed with a small amount of perfume. Oil plays a symbolic role throughout the Bible and has historically played an important role in the life of the Church. In many Old Testament texts, oil was reserved for priests, kings, and people of high importance. Today, we use oil in most of the sacraments of the Church because we are the "priestly people."

The Hebrew word *mashiah*, translated in 1 Samuel 24:7 as "anointed [one]," is the root of the English word *messiah*. Often applied to kings in the Old Testament, this title was attached in the second century BC to the one "like David" who was expected to come (see Dn 9:25). *Mashiah* translated in Greek is *christos*, which became the title given to Jesus by his followers: Jesus, the Christ; Jesus, the anointed one; Jesus, the Messiah.

† **25:8** *Your son David*: this kinship language may reflect a political or social relationship between Nabal and David. Nabal, however, does not acknowledge it.

* **24:15** 2 Sm 9:8; 16:9.
24:16 1 Sm 18:19, 31; 26:19; Ps 35:1–3; 43:1.
24:21 1 Sm 26:25.
24:22 2 Sm 9:1–3.
25:1 1 Sm 28:3; Sir 46:13–20.
25:2 1 Sm 23:24; Jos 15:55.
25:3 1 Sm 27:3; Dt 1:35–36; Jos 14:6–15; 1 Chr 2:42, 45.

hundred men went up after David, while two
hundred remained with the baggage.
14 Abigail, Nabal's wife, was informed of this
by one of the servants, who said: "From the wil-
derness David sent messengers to greet our mas-
ter, but he screamed at them. 15 Yet these men
were very good to us. We were not harmed, nei-
ther did we miss anything all the while we were
living among them during our stay in the open
country. 16 Day and night they were a wall of pro-
tection for us, the whole time we were pasturing
the sheep near them. 17 Now, see what you can
do, for you must realize that otherwise disaster is
in store for our master and for his whole house.
He is such a scoundrel that no one can talk to
him." 18 Abigail quickly got together two hundred
loaves, two skins of wine, five dressed sheep, five
seahs of roasted grain, a hundred cakes of pressed
raisins, and two hundred cakes of pressed figs,
and loaded them on donkeys. 19 She then said to
her servants, "Go on ahead; I will follow you."
But to her husband Nabal she said nothing.
20 Hidden by the mountain, she came down
riding on a donkey, as David and his men were
coming down from the opposite direction. When
she met them, 21 David had just been saying: "In-
deed, it was in vain that I guarded all this man's
possessions in the wilderness, so that nothing of
his was missing. He has repaid good with evil.
22 May God do thus to David, and more, if by
morning I leave a single male alive among all
those who belong to him."* 23 As soon as Ab-
igail saw David, she dismounted quickly from
the donkey and, falling down, bowed low to the
ground before David in homage.
24 As she fell at his feet she said: "My lord, let
the blame be mine. Please let your maidservant
speak to you; listen to the words of your maidser-
vant.* 25 My lord, do not pay any attention to that
scoundrel Nabal, for he is just like his name. His
name means fool,† and he acts the fool. I, your
maidservant, did not see the young men whom
my lord sent. 26 Now, therefore, my lord, as the
LORD lives, and as you live, the LORD has kept you
from shedding blood and from avenging yourself
by your own hand. May your enemies and those
who seek to harm my lord become as Nabal!† *
27 Accept this gift, then, which your maidservant
has brought for my lord, and let it be given to
the young men who follow my lord. 28 Please
forgive the offense of your maidservant, for the
LORD shall certainly establish a lasting house for
my lord, because my lord fights the battles of the
LORD. Let no evil be found in you your whole
life long.* 29 If any adversary pursues you to seek
your life, may the life of my lord be bound in
the bundle of the living† in the care of the LORD
your God; may God hurl out the lives of your
enemies as from the hollow of a sling.* 30 And
when the LORD fulfills for my lord the promise
of success he has made concerning you, and ap-
points you as ruler over Israel,* 31 you shall not
have any regrets or burdens on your conscience,
my lord, for having shed innocent blood or for
having rescued yourself. When the LORD bestows
good on my lord, remember your maidservant."
32 David said to Abigail: "Blessed is the LORD, the
God of Israel, who sent you to meet me today.
33 Blessed is your good judgment and blessed are
you yourself. Today you have prevented me from
shedding blood and rescuing myself with my
own hand. 34 Otherwise, as the LORD, the God of
Israel, lives, who has kept me from harming you,
if you had not come so promptly to meet me, by
dawn Nabal would not have had so much as one
male left alive." 35 David then took from her what
she had brought him and said to her: "Go to
your home in peace! See, I have listened to your
appeal and have granted your request."

Nabal's Death

36 When Abigail came to Nabal, he was hosting
a banquet in his house like that of a king, and
Nabal was in a festive mood and very drunk. So
she said not a word to him until daybreak the
next morning. 37 But then, when Nabal was so-
ber, his wife told him what had happened. At this
his heart died within him, and he became like a
stone. 38 About ten days later the LORD struck Na-
bal and he died. 39 Hearing that Nabal was dead,
David said: "Blessed be the LORD, who has de-
fended my cause against the insult from Nabal,
and who restrained his servant from doing evil,
but has repaid Nabal for his evil deeds."

David Marries Abigail and Ahinoam

David then sent a proposal of marriage to Ab-
igail.* 40 When David's servants came to Abigail

†

25:25 Hebrew *nabal* means "fool" (cf. Is 32:5–7). Abigail, on the other hand, acts wisely to save herself and her household by offering prudent counsel to the future king of Israel.

25:26 Abigail, encouraging David to trust in God's promise, anticipates that some misfortune will shortly overtake Nabal, as in fact it does (vv. 37–38).

25:29 *The bundle of the living*: the figure is perhaps taken from the practice of tying up valuables in a kerchief or bag for safekeeping. Abigail desires that David enjoy permanent peace and security, but that his enemies be subject to constant agitation and humiliation like a stone whirled about, cast out of the sling, and thereafter disregarded.

*

25:22 1 Kgs 16:11; 21:21; 2 Kgs 9:8.
25:24 2 Sm 14:9.
25:26 Dt 20:4; Jgs 7:2.
25:28 1 Kgs 11:38.
25:29 Ps 69:28.
25:30 1 Sm 13:14; 2 Sm 3:10.
25:39 1 Kgs 2:44.

in Carmel, they said to her, "David has sent us to
make his proposal of marriage to you." 41 Rising
and bowing to the ground, she answered, "Let
your maidservant be the slave who washes the
feet of my lord's servants." 42 She got up immedi-
ately, mounted a donkey, and followed David's
messengers, with her five maids attending her.
She became his wife. 43 * David also married
Ahinoam of Jezreel. Thus both of them were his
wives. 44 But Saul gave David's wife Michal, Saul's
own daughter, to Palti, son of Laish, who was
from Gallim.*

David Spares Saul Again†

26 1 * Men from Ziph came to Saul in Gib-
eah, reporting that David was hiding on
the hill of Hachilah at the edge of Jeshimon. 2 So
Saul went down to the wilderness of Ziph with
three thousand of the best warriors of Israel, to
search for David in the wilderness of Ziph. 3 Saul
camped beside the road on the hill of Hachilah,
at the edge of Jeshimon. David, who was living in
the wilderness, saw that Saul had come into the
wilderness after him 4 and sent out scouts, who
confirmed Saul's arrival. 5 David then went to the
place where Saul was encamped and saw the spot
where Saul and his general, Abner, son of Ner,
had their sleeping quarters. Saul was lying within
the camp, and all his soldiers were bivouacked
around him.* 6 David asked Ahimelech the Hit-
tite, and Abishai, son of Zeruiah and brother of
Joab, "Who will go down into the camp with me
to Saul?" Abishai replied, "I will."* 7 So David
and Abishai reached Saul's soldiers by night, and
there was Saul lying asleep within the camp, his
spear thrust into the ground at his head and Ab-
ner and his troops sleeping around him.

8 Abishai whispered to David: "God has deliv-
ered your enemy into your hand today. Let me
nail him to the ground with one thrust of the
spear; I will not need to strike him twice!"* 9 But
David said to Abishai, "Do not harm him, for
who can lay a hand on the LORD's anointed and
remain innocent? 10 As the LORD lives," David
declared, "only the LORD can strike him: either
when the time comes for him to die, or when he
goes out and perishes in battle.† * 11 But the LORD
forbid that I lay a hand on the LORD's anointed!
Now take the spear at his head and the water jug,
and let us be on our way." 12 So David took the
spear and the water jug from their place at Saul's
head, and they withdrew without anyone seeing
or knowing or awakening. All remained asleep,
because a deep slumber† from the LORD had
fallen upon them.*

David Taunts Abner

13 Crossing over to an opposite slope, David
stood on a distant hilltop. With a great distance
between them 14 David called to the army and
to Abner, son of Ner, "Will you not answer, Ab-
ner?" Then Abner shouted back, "Who is it that
calls me?" 15 David said to Abner: "Are you not a
man? Who in Israel is your equal? Why were you
not guarding your lord the king when one of his
subjects came to assassinate the king, your lord?
16 What you have done is not right. As the LORD
lives, you people deserve death because you have
not guarded your lord, the anointed of the LORD.
Go, look: where are the king's spear and the wa-
ter jug that was at his head?"

Saul Admits His Guilt

17 Saul recognized David's voice and asked,
"Is that your voice, David my son?"† David an-
swered, "Yes, my lord the king." 18 He continued:
"Why does my lord pursue his servant? What
have I done? What evil am I planning? 19 Please,
now, let my lord the king listen to the words of
his servant. If the LORD has incited you against
me, may an offering please the LORD. But if it
is the people who have done so, may they be
cursed before the LORD. They have driven me
away so that today I have no share in the LORD's
heritage,† but am told: 'Go serve other gods!'*
20 Do not let my blood spill on the ground far
from the presence of the LORD. For the king of
Israel has come out to seek a single flea as if
he were hunting partridge† in the mountains."
21 Then Saul said: "I have done wrong. Come
back, David, my son! I will not harm you again,
because you considered my life precious today
even though I have been a fool and have made
a serious mistake." 22 But David answered: "Here

---

†

26:1 The second account of David sparing Saul's life; cf. note on 24:1.

26:10 *Perishes in battle*: David's words foreshadow how Saul will die (31:3–4). They also emphasize that David, unlike Saul, knows his proper place before God. David comes to the kingship innocent of Saul's blood, although the king pursues him like an enemy and David has had two opportunities to kill him.

26:12 *Deep slumber*: as in Gn 2:21; 15:12; Is 29:10. The Lord aids David's foray into Saul's camp and allows David to come and go undetected.

26:17 *David my son*: Saul's reference to David as his son, which appears three times in this chapter (vv. 17, 21, 25), alludes to David's role as his successor.

26:19 *The LORD's heritage*: the land and people of Israel (Dt 32:8–9; Ps 33:12). If driven from the land, David could not take

---

*

25:43 1 Sm 27:3.
25:44 1 Sm 18:20; 27:3; 30:5; 2 Sm 2:2, 13–16; 1 Chr 3:1.
26:1–2 1 Sm 23:19–20; Ps 54.
26:5 1 Sm 17:20.
26:6 2 Sm 3:30; 1 Chr 2:16.
26:8 1 Sm 18:11; 19:10; 20:33.
26:10 Ps 37:13.
26:12 Gn 2:21; 15:12.
26:19 1 Sm 24:16.

is the king's spear. Let an attendant come over to
get it. 23 The LORD repays everyone's righteousness
and faithfulness. Although the LORD delivered
you into my hands today, I could not lay a hand
on the LORD's anointed.* 24 Just as I regarded your
life as precious today, so may the LORD regard my
life as precious and deliver me from all dangers."
25 Then Saul said to David: "Blessed are you, my
son David! You shall certainly succeed in whatever you undertake." David went his way, and
Saul returned to his place.*

David Flees to the Philistines

27 1 David said to himself: "I shall perish
some day at the hand of Saul. I have no
choice but to escape to the land of the Philistines; then Saul will give up his continual search
for me throughout the land of Israel, and I will
be out of his reach." 2 Accordingly, David departed with his six hundred soldiers and went
over to Achish, son of Maoch, king of Gath.*
3 David and his men lived in Gath with Achish;
each one had his family, and David had his two
wives, Ahinoam from Jezreel and Abigail, the
widow of Nabal from Carmel.* 4 When Saul
learned that David had fled to Gath, he no longer
searched for him.

5 David said to Achish: "If I meet with your
approval, let me have a place to live in one of
the country towns. Why should your servant
live with you in the royal city?" 6 That same day
Achish gave him Ziklag, which has, therefore,
belonged to the kings of Judah† up to the present time.* 7 In all, David lived a year and four
months in Philistine territory.*

David Raids Israel's Foes

8 David and his men went out on raids against
the Geshurites, Girzites, and Amalekites—peoples living in the land between Telam, on the
approach to Shur, and the land of Egypt.* 9 In
attacking the land David would not leave a man
or woman alive, but would carry off sheep, oxen,
donkeys, camels, and clothes. Then he would
return to Achish, 10 who would ask, "Against
whom did you raid this time?" David would
reply, "Against the Negeb of Judah,"† or "Against
the Negeb of Jerahmeel," or "Against the Negeb
of the Kenites."* 11 David never left a man or
woman alive to be brought to Gath. He thought,
"They will betray us and say, 'This is what David
did.'" This was his custom as long as he lived
in Philistine territory. 12 Achish trusted David,
thinking, "His people Israel must certainly detest
him. I shall have him as my vassal forever."

28 1 In those days the Philistines mustered
their military forces to fight against Israel. So Achish said to David, "You realize, of
course, that you and your warriors† must march
out for battle with me." 2 David answered Achish,
"Good! Now you shall learn what your servant
can do." Then Achish said to David, "I shall appoint you as my permanent bodyguard."
3 Now, Samuel was dead. All Israel had
mourned him and buried him in his city, Ramah. Meanwhile Saul had driven mediums and
diviners out of the land.*

Saul in Despair

4 The Philistines rallied and, coming to Shunem, they encamped. Saul, too, mustered all
Israel; they camped on Gilboa. 5 When Saul saw
the Philistine camp, he grew afraid and lost heart
completely. 6 He consulted the LORD; but the
LORD gave no answer, neither in dreams nor by
Urim nor through prophets.* 7 Then Saul said
to his servants, "Find me a medium† through
whom I can seek counsel." His servants answered
him, "There is a woman in Endor who is a medium."*

The Medium at Endor

8 So he disguised himself, putting on other
clothes, and set out with two companions. They
came to the woman at night, and Saul said to
her, "Divine for me; conjure up the spirit I tell
you."* 9 But the woman answered him, "You
know what Saul has done, how he expelled the
mediums and diviners from the land. Then why
are you trying to entrap me and get me killed?"
10 But Saul swore to her by the LORD, "As the

---

† part in worship of Israel's God; nonetheless, God has blessed David (cf. v. 25).

26:20 *Partridge*: lit., "the caller." The metaphor is built on clever wordplay: in v. 14, David calls out to the army and Abner asks the caller's identity. David calls out the answer: "the caller" is the object of the king's pursuit.

27:6 Ziklag was a royal city and not part of Israel's tribal land holdings. Jerusalem later enjoyed a similar status (2 Sm 5:7–9).

27:10 *The Negeb of Judah*: David deceives Achish by assuring him that he has attacked Israelite territory.

28:1 *You and your warriors*: David is faced with a potentially dangerous dilemma: either to reveal his continuing loyalty to his own people or to obey Achish and fight against his own people.

28:7 *A medium*: Saul's own prohibition of necromancy and divination (v. 3) was in keeping with the consistent teaching of the Old Testament (cf. Lv 19:31; 20:6, 27; Dt 18:10).

---

* **26:23** 1 Sm 18:20.
26:25 1 Sm 18:14; 24:21.
27:2 1 Sm 21:11–16.
27:3 1 Sm 25:3, 44; 30:3–5; 2 Sm 2:3.
27:6 1 Sm 30:1.
27:7 1 Sm 29:3.
27:8 1 Sm 15:3, 7; Jos 13:2–3.
27:10 1 Sm 30:14, 29; 1 Chr 2:9, 25, 42.
28:3 1 Sm 25:1; Sir 46:20.
28:6 1 Sm 14:37, 41; Ex 28:30; Lv 8:8.
28:7 Lv 19:31; 20:27; Dt 18:10–12; 2 Kgs 21:6; 1 Chr 10:13–14; Acts 16:16.
28:8 1 Sm 15:23; 1 Kgs 14:2.

LORD lives, you shall incur no blame for this."
11 "Whom do you want me to conjure up?" the
woman asked him. "Conjure up Samuel for me,"
he replied.

Samuel Appears

12 When the woman saw Samuel, she shrieked
at the top of her voice and said to Saul, "Why
have you deceived me? You are Saul!" 13 But the
king said to her, "Do not be afraid. What do you
see?" "I see a god rising from the earth," she re-
plied. 14 "What does he look like?" asked Saul.
"An old man is coming up wrapped in a robe,"
she replied. Saul knew that it was Samuel, and so
he bowed his face to the ground in homage.

Saul's Doom

15 † Samuel then said to Saul, "Why do you
disturb me by conjuring me up?" Saul replied: "I
am in great distress, for the Philistines are waging
war against me and God has turned away from
me. Since God no longer answers me through
prophets or in dreams, I have called upon you
to tell me what I should do."* 16 To this Samuel
said: "But why do you ask me, if the LORD has
abandoned you for your neighbor?* 17 The LORD
has done to you what he declared through me:
he has torn the kingdom from your hand and
has given it to your neighbor David.
18 "Because you disobeyed the LORD's directive
and would not carry out his fierce anger against
Amalek, the LORD has done this to you today.*
19 Moreover, the LORD will deliver Israel, and you
as well, into the hands of the Philistines. By to-
morrow you and your sons will be with me, and
the LORD will have delivered the army of Israel
into the hands of the Philistines."*
20 Immediately Saul fell full length on the
ground, in great fear because of Samuel's mes-
sage. He had no strength left, since he had
eaten nothing all that day and night. 21 Then the
woman came to Saul and, seeing that he was
quite terror-stricken, said to him: "Remember,
your maidservant obeyed you: I took my life in
my hands and carried out the request you made
of me. 22 Now you, in turn, please listen to your
maidservant. Let me set out a bit of food for
you to eat, so that you are strong enough to go
on your way." 23 But he refused, saying, "I will
not eat." However, when his servants joined
the woman in urging him, he listened to their
entreaties, got up from the ground, and sat on
a couch. 24 The woman had a stall-fed calf in the
house, which she now quickly slaughtered. Then
taking flour, she kneaded it and baked unleav-
ened bread. 25 She set the meal before Saul and
his servants, and they ate. Then they got up and
left the same night.

David's Aid Rejected

29 1 Now the Philistines had mustered all
their forces in Aphek, and the Israelites
were encamped at the spring in Jezreel.* 2 As the
Philistine lords were marching their units of a
hundred and a thousand, David and his warriors
were marching in the rear guard with Achish.
3 The Philistine commanders asked, "What are
those Hebrews doing here?" Achish answered
them: "Why, that is David, the officer of Saul,
king of Israel. He has been with me for a year or
two, and from the day he came over to me until
now I have never found fault in him."* 4 But the
Philistine commanders were angered at this and
said to him: "Send that man back! Let him return
to the place you picked out for him. He must not
go down into battle with us; during the battle he
might become our enemy. For how else can he
win back his master's favor, if not at the expense
of our soldiers?* 5 Is this not the David for whom
they sing during their dances,

'Saul has slain his thousands,
David his tens of thousands'?"*

6 So Achish summoned David and said to him:
"As the LORD lives, you are honest, and I would
want you with me in all my battles. To this day
I have found nothing wrong with you since you
came to me. But in the view of the chiefs you
are not welcome. 7 Leave peacefully, now, and
do nothing that might displease the Philistine
chiefs." 8 But David said to Achish: "What have I
done? What fault have you found in your servant
from the day I entered your service until today,
that I cannot go to fight against the enemies of
my lord the king?" 9 "I recognize," Achish an-
swered David, "that you are trustworthy, like an
angel of God. But the Philistine commanders are
saying, 'He must not go with us into battle.' 10 So
the first thing tomorrow, you and your lord's
servants who came with you, go to the place I
picked out for you. Do not take to heart their
worthless remarks; for you have been valuable in
my service. But make an early morning start, as

†

28:15–19 The consultation with the medium serves to remind the reader that the Lord's plan for David marches onward; no sorcery can thwart it.

*

28:15 1 Sm 14:37; Sir 46:20.
28:16 1 Sm 15:27–28.
28:18 1 Sm 15:18–19, 26.
28:19 1 Sm 31:2–6; Sir 46:20.
29:1 1 Sm 4:1.
29:3 1 Sm 27:7.
29:4 1 Chr 12:19–20.
29:5 1 Sm 18:6–7; 21:12.

soon as it grows light, and be on your way." 11 So
David and his warriors left early in the morning
to return to the land of the Philistines, and the
Philistines went on up to Jezreel.

Ziklag in Ruins

30 1 Before David and his men reached Zik-
lag on the third day, the Amalekites had
raided the Negeb and Ziklag. They stormed
Ziklag, and set it on fire.* 2 They took captive
the women and all who were in the city, young
and old, killing no one, and they herded them
off when they left. 3 David and his men arrived
at the city to find it burned to the ground and
their wives, sons, and daughters taken captive.
4 Then David and those who were with him wept
aloud until they could weep no more. 5 David's
two wives, Ahinoam of Jezreel and Abigail, the
widow of Nabal from Carmel, had also been
carried off.* 6 Now David found himself in great
danger, for the soldiers spoke of stoning him, so
bitter were they over the fate of their sons and
daughters. David took courage in the LORD his
God 7* and said to Abiathar, the priest, son of
Ahimelech, "Bring me the ephod!" When Abi-
athar brought him the ephod, 8 David inquired
of the LORD, "Shall I pursue these raiders? Can I
overtake them?" The LORD answered him: Go in
pursuit, for you will certainly overtake them and
bring about a rescue.

Raid on the Amalekites

9 So David went off with his six hundred as far
as the Wadi Besor, where those who were to re-
main behind halted. 10 David continued the pur-
suit with four hundred, but two hundred were
too exhausted to cross the Wadi Besor and re-
mained behind. 11 An Egyptian was found in the
open country and brought to David. They gave
him food to eat and water to drink; 12 they also
offered a cake of pressed figs and two cakes of
pressed raisins. When he had eaten, he revived,
for he had not taken food nor drunk water for
three days and three nights. 13 Then David asked
him, "To whom do you belong? Where did you
come from?" "I am an Egyptian, the slave of an
Amalekite," he replied. "My master abandoned
me three days ago because I fell sick. 14 We raided
the Negeb of the Cherethites, the territory of Ju-
dah, and the Negeb of Caleb; and we set Ziklag
on fire."* 15 David then asked him, "Will you
lead me down to these raiders?" He answered,
"Swear to me by God that you will not kill me or
hand me over to my master, and I will lead you
down to the raiders." 16 So he led them down,
and there were the Amalekites lounging all over
the ground, eating, drinking, and celebrating be-
cause of all the rich plunder they had taken from
the land of the Philistines and from the land of
Judah.

The Plunder Recovered

17 From dawn to sundown the next day Da-
vid attacked them, allowing no one to escape
except four hundred young men, who mounted
their camels and fled.* 18 David recovered every-
thing the Amalekites had taken, and he rescued
his two wives. 19 Nothing was missing, small or
great, plunder or sons or daughters, of all that the
Amalekites had taken. David brought back every-
thing. 20 Moreover, David took all the sheep and
oxen, and as they drove these before him, they
shouted, "This is David's plunder!"

Division of the Plunder

21 When David came to the two hundred men
who had been too exhausted to follow him,
whom he had left behind at the Wadi Besor, they
came out to meet David and the men with him.
As David approached, he greeted them. 22 But
all the greedy and worthless among those who
had accompanied David said, "Since they did
not accompany us, we will not give them any-
thing from the plunder, except for each man's
wife and children." 23 But David said: "You must
not do this, my brothers, after what the LORD has
given us. The LORD has protected us and delivered
into our hands the raiders that came against us.*
24 Who could agree with this proposal of yours?
Rather, the share of the one who goes down to
battle shall be the same as that of the one who
remains with the baggage—they share alike."*
25 And from that day forward he made this a law
and a custom in Israel, as it still is today.*

David's Gifts to Judah

26 When David came to Ziklag, he sent part of
the plunder to his friends, the elders of Judah,†
saying, "This is a gift to you from the plunder of
the enemies of the LORD," namely, 27 to those in
Bethel, Ramoth-negeb, Jattir, 28 Aroer, Siphmoth,
Eshtemoa, 29 Racal, Jerahmeelite cities and Kenite

†

30:26 *Elders of Judah*: David consolidates his power in southern Judah in preparation for his anointing at Hebron (2 Sm 5:3).

30:1 1 Sm 15:2; 27:6, 10; 1 Chr 12:21.
30:5 1 Sm 25:42; 27:3; 30:5.
30:7–8 1 Sm 2:28; 23:6; Ex 28:30.
30:14 1 Sm 27:10; Ez 25:16.
30:17 1 Sm 15:3; Jos 6:17; Jgs 7:12.
30:23 Dt 20:4, 14.
30:24 1 Sm 17:22; 25:13.
30:25 Nm 31:27.

cities,* 30 Hormah, Borashan, Athach, 31 Hebron,
and to all the places that David and his men had
frequented.*

Death of Saul and His Sons

31 1 * Now the Philistines went to war against
Israel, and the Israelites fled before them,
and fell, slain on Mount Gilboa. 2 The Philistines
pressed hard after Saul and his sons. When the
Philistines had struck down Jonathan, Abina-
dab, and Malchishua, sons of Saul,* 3 the fury of
the battle converged on Saul. Then the archers
hit him, and he was severely wounded. 4 Saul
said to his armor-bearer, "Draw your sword and
run me through; otherwise these uncircumcised
will come and abuse me." But the armor-bearer,
badly frightened, refused, so Saul took his own
sword and fell upon it.* 5 * When the armor-
bearer saw that Saul was dead, he too fell upon
his sword and died with him. 6 Thus Saul, his
three sons, and his armor-bearer died together
on that same day. 7 When the Israelites on the
slope of the valley and those along the Jordan
saw that the men of Israel had fled and that Saul
and his sons were dead, they abandoned their
cities and fled. Then the Philistines came and
lived in those cities.
8 On the following day, when the Philistines
came to strip the slain, they found Saul and his
three sons fallen on Mount Gilboa. 9 They cut off
Saul's head and stripped him of his armor; these
they sent throughout the land of the Philistines
to bring the good news to the temple of their
idols and to the people.* 10 They put his armor
in the temple of Astarte but impaled his body on
the wall of Beth-shan.

Burial of Saul

11 * When the inhabitants of Jabesh-gilead
heard what the Philistines had done to Saul, 12 all
their warriors set out and traveled through the
night; they removed the bodies of Saul and his
sons from the wall of Beth-shan, and, returning
to Jabesh, burned them.† 13 Then they took their
bones and buried them under the tamarisk tree
in Jabesh, and fasted for seven days.

Live It!

Suicide Is Not an Answer

In 1 Samuel 31:4, Saul commits suicide out of fear of what his enemies would do to him. His death leaves a gap for the Israelites, and David, Saul's enemy, deeply mourns his death in 2 Samuel, chapter 1.

A popular newspaper advice columnist printed a letter from someone who was writing to share a thought on suicide. He had decided that his life was not worth living anymore and planned to kill himself. The moment before he was about to do it, he thought about who would find him, and then he stopped. He realized that he couldn't put someone through the pain and suffering of finding him dead from suicide. Because he thought of another, he no longer looked at his life as hopeless.

No life is worthless! No pain is invincible! No matter how overwhelming your struggles and challenges seem, there are people who can help you, and people who could not bear to lose you. Seek God for help, seek others for help—suicide is never a solution!

For more on suicide, see "Judas's Suicide," near Matthew 27:3–10.

1 Sm 31:1–6

† **31:12** *Burned them*: cremation was not an Israelite custom. The people of Jabesh-gilead repay Saul's victory over the Ammonites on their behalf (chap. 11) by providing burial and funeral rites for him and his sons. Probably the damaged state of the corpus necessitated cremation.

30:29 1 Sm 27:10.
30:31 2 Sm 2:1–4.
31:1–13 2 Sm 1:1–16; 4:4; 1 Chr 10:1–12.
31:2 1 Sm 14:49; 28:19; 1 Chr 10:2–3.
31:4 1 Sm 24:6; Jgs 9:54; 1 Chr 10:4.
31:5 1 Sm 10:1; 26:9; 2 Mc 14:42.
31:9 1 Sm 17:54; 2 Sm 1:20; 2 Mc 15:35.
31:11–13 1 Sm 11:1–11; 2 Sm 2:4–7; 21:12–14.

“**Politician** Guilty of Taking Bribes!” “Military Officer Charged with Sexual Misconduct!” “Pro Athlete Convicted of Using Drugs!” Sometimes it seems as if the news is filled with one scandal after another. “What's happening in the world today?” we may ask in despair. “Are there no honest, decent people left?” After reading Second Samuel, you will realize that scandals involving the rich and powerful are nothing new. But more important, God's will rises above human sin and weakness to accomplish good.

In Depth

The main character in Second Samuel is King David, whom we already met in First Samuel. The youngest of Jesse's sons, David is secretly anointed to succeed King Saul; he kills Goliath, plays music in Saul's court, and is befriended by the king's son Jonathan. At the beginning of Second Samuel, when David takes the throne and quickly extends Israel's boundaries in every direction, everything looks hopeful for the nation.

As Second Samuel continues, however, we discover that this hero is far from perfect: he sleeps with Bathsheba, the wife of one of his soldiers, and then tries to deceive the man when Bathsheba reports that she is pregnant. Later, he has the soldier killed and takes Bathsheba as his own. Soon, several tragedies befall his family, and further bad decisions hurt his reign, leaving us with a mixed picture of the second king of Israel. Was David a great saint or a great sinner?

It was during David's reign that the people's understanding of their covenant relationship with God began to center less on the Exodus experience and more on the ideas of king and kingdom (see 7:1–17). This fact is underlined in a memorable way when David, after completing his own magnificent palace, declares that he will build a house for God. But God does not want a temple; God wishes to maintain a covenantal relationship with the people of Israel through all history: “Your throne shall be firmly established forever” (verse 16).

Although a talented military leader and a powerful ruler, King David shared our broken human nature. The author of Second Samuel reminds us that even the great and the mighty stand in need of God's help and mercy; even they must keep God's covenant. Because of David's reliance on God, he became a symbol of the ideal king and of the future messiah. David's greatness—and our own—comes from a willing reliance on God.

At a Glance

David Mourns Saul's Death (1:1—2:7).

IV. The Reign of David (2:8—20:26).

V. Appendixes (21:1—24:25).

Quick Facts

Period Covered: from 1000 to 961 BC

Inspired Author: same as for First Samuel

Theme: David's rise to power and his fall into sin

Of Note: Samuel does not appear in this book, even though it carries his name.

The Second Book of Samuel

2 Samuel

Report of Saul's Death

1 [1]After the death of Saul, David returned from
his victory over the Amalekites and stayed in
Ziklag two days.* [2]On the third day a man came
from the field of battle, one of Saul's people, with
his garments torn and his head covered with dirt.
Going to David, he fell to the ground in hom-
age. [3]David asked him, "Where have you come
from?" He replied, "From the Israelite camp: I
have escaped." [4]"What happened?" David said.
"Tell me." He answered that the soldiers had fled
the battle and many of them had fallen and were
dead; and that Saul and his son Jonathan were
dead. [5]Then David said to the youth who was
reporting to him, "How do you know that Saul
and his son Jonathan are dead?" [6]* The youth
reporting to him replied: "I happened to find my-
self on Mount Gilboa and saw Saul leaning on his
spear, with chariots and horsemen closing in on
him. [7]He turned around and saw me, and called
me to him. When I said, 'Here I am,' [8]he asked
me, 'Who are you?' and I replied, 'An Amalekite.'
[9]Then he said to me, 'Stand over me, please, and
put me to death, for I am in great suffering, but
still alive.' [10]So I stood over him and put him to
death, for I knew that he could not survive his
wound. I removed the crown from his head and
the armlet from his arm and brought them here
to my lord."
[11]David seized his garments and tore them, and
so did all the men who were with him.* [12]They
mourned and wept and fasted until evening for
Saul and his son Jonathan, and for the people of
the LORD and the house of Israel, because they had
fallen by the sword.* [13]David said to the youth
who had reported to him, "Where are you from?"
He replied, "I am the son of a resident alien, an
Amalekite." [14]David said to him, "How is it that
you were not afraid to put forth your hand to des-
ecrate the LORD's anointed?"* [15]David then called
one of the attendants and said to him, "Come,
strike him down"; so he struck him and he died.
[16]David said to him, "Your blood is on your head,
for you testified against yourself when you said, 'I
put the LORD's anointed to death.' "

Lament for Saul and Jonathan

[17]Then David chanted this lament for Saul and
his son Jonathan [18](he commanded that it be
taught to the Judahites; it is recorded in the Book
of Jashar):*

19 Alas! the glory of Israel,
  slain upon your heights!
How can the warriors have fallen!
20 Do not report it in Gath,
  as good news in Ashkelon's streets,
Lest Philistine women rejoice,
  lest the women of the uncircumcised exult!*
21 O mountains of Gilboa,
  upon you be neither dew nor rain,

* **1:1** 1 Sm 30:17–20; 31:1–13.
1:6–10 2 Sm 4:10; 1 Sm 31:1–4; 1 Chr 10:1–4.
1:11 2 Sm 13:31.
1:12 1 Sm 31:13.
1:14 1 Sm 10:1; 24:7; Ps 105:15.
1:18 Jos 10:13.
1:20 Jgs 16:23; 1 Sm 31:9; Mi 1:10.

Live It!

David the Musician

Most of us know that music can be a powerful force. Most of us listen to music every day. It helps us get through hard times. It is also an essential part of most celebrations. What would a wedding be like without music? What would a party be like without music? No doubt each of us has a favorite song or musician we turn to often, especially when we need a lift. And no doubt God works through music to touch our hearts.

David also knew the power of music. His song of mourning for Saul and Jonathan is an emotional tribute to both men, but especially to his close friend, Jonathan. If you are a musician, you know that God also works through you to touch the hearts of others and speak to them. Let David be your inspiration. He played the lyre (harp), sang, and wrote beautiful songs, which we call psalms. He prayed through music. There is a saying that goes, "Those who sing pray twice." David seemed to live that out in his life.

- What are the songs and music that help you to pray and to recall God's presence? If you are a musician, when have you felt God's presence while making music?

▶ 2 Sm 1:17–27

nor surging from the deeps!†
Defiled there the warriors' shields,
the shield of Saul—no longer anointed
with oil!*
22 From the blood of the slain,
from the bodies of the warriors,
The bow of Jonathan did not turn back,
nor the sword of Saul return unstained.† *
23 Saul and Jonathan, beloved and dear,
separated neither in life nor death,
swifter than eagles, stronger than lions!
24 Women of Israel, weep over Saul,
who clothed you in scarlet and in finery,
covered your clothing with ornaments of
gold.
25 How can the warriors have fallen
in the thick of battle!
Jonathan—slain upon your heights!
26 I grieve for you, Jonathan my brother!
Most dear have you been to me;
More wondrous your love to me
than the love of women.*
27 How can the warriors have fallen,
the weapons of war have perished!

David Is Anointed King

2 [1]After this, David inquired of the LORD,
"Shall I go up into one of the cities of Ju-
dah?" The LORD replied to him: Go up. Then
David asked, "Where shall I go?" He replied: To
Hebron. [2]So David went up there, with his two
wives, Ahinoam of Jezreel and Abigail, the wife
of Nabal of Carmel.* [3]David also brought up his
men with their families, and they dwelt in the
towns of Hebron. [4]Then the men of Judah came
there and anointed David king over the house
of Judah.
A report reached David that the people of
Jabesh-gilead had buried Saul.* [5]So David sent
messengers to the people of Jabesh-gilead and
said to them: "May you be blessed by the LORD
for having done this kindness to your lord Saul
in burying him. [6]And now may the LORD show
you kindness and fidelity. For my part, I will
show generosity to you for having done this. [7]So
take courage and prove yourselves valiant, for
though your lord Saul is dead, the house of Ju-
dah has anointed me king over them."

IV. The Reign of David

Ishbaal King of Israel

[8]Abner, son of Ner, captain of Saul's army,
took Ishbaal,† son of Saul, and brought him over
to Mahanaim,* [9]where he made him king over
Gilead, the Asherites, Jezreel, Ephraim, Benja-
min, and the rest of Israel. [10]Ishbaal, son of Saul,
was forty years old when he became king over
Israel, and he reigned two years; but the house of
Judah followed David. [11]In all, David was king

† **1:21** *Surging from the deeps*: this conjectural reading of the Hebrew yields a parallelism with dew and rain: the mountains where the warriors have fallen in battle are to be desiccated, deprived of water from above (rain, dew) and below (the primordial deeps).

1:22 *Unstained*: lit., "empty." The sword was conceived as a devouring mouth; see, e.g., 2:26.

2:8 *Ishbaal*: here and elsewhere in the Hebrew text, his name appears as "Ishbosheth"; the second part of Ishbaal, *-baal*, refers to the Canaanite god Baal, and is therefore suppressed, replaced by *bosheth*, "shame."

1:21 Gn 27:28.
1:22 1 Sm 14:47.
1:26 1 Sm 18:1–4.
2:2 1 Sm 25:42–43.
2:4 1 Sm 31:11–13.
2:8 1 Sm 14:50.

in Hebron over the house of Judah seven years
and six months.*

Combat near Gibeon

12 Now Abner, son of Ner, and the servants of
Ishbaal, Saul's son, set out from Mahanaim for
Gibeon. 13 Joab, son of Zeruiah, and the servants
of David also set out and encountered them at
the pool of Gibeon. And they sat down, one
group on one side of the pool and the other on
the opposite side. 14 Then Abner said to Joab, "Let
the young men rise and perform for us."† Joab re-
plied, "All right." 15 So they rose and were counted
off: twelve of the Benjaminites of Ishbaal, son of
Saul, and twelve of David's servants. 16 Then each
one grasped his opponent's head and thrust his
sword into his opponent's side, and they all fell
down together.† And so that place was named
the Field of the Sides; it is in Gibeon.

Death of Asahel

17 The battle that day was very fierce, and Ab-
ner and the men of Israel were defeated by Da-
vid's servants. 18 The three sons of Zeruiah were
there—Joab, Abishai, and Asahel.* Asahel, who
was as fleet of foot as a gazelle in the open field,
19 set out after Abner, turning neither right nor left
in his pursuit. 20 Abner turned around and said,
"Is that you, Asahel?" He replied, "Yes." 21 Abner
said to him, "Turn right or left; seize one of the
young men and take what you can strip from
him." But Asahel would not stop pursuing him.
22 Once more Abner said to Asahel: "Stop pursu-
ing me! Why must I strike you to the ground?
How could I show my face to your brother
Joab?"* 23 Still he refused to stop. So Abner struck
him in the abdomen with the heel of his spear,
and the weapon protruded from his back. He fell
there and died on the spot. All who came to the
place where Asahel had fallen and died, halted.
24 But Joab and Abishai continued the pursuit of
Abner. The sun had gone down when they came
to the hill of Ammah which lies east of the valley
toward the wilderness near Geba.

Truce Between Joab and Abner

25 Here the Benjaminites rallied around Abner,
forming a single group, and made a stand on a
hilltop. 26 Then Abner called to Joab and said:
"Must the sword devour forever? Do you not
know that afterward there will be bitterness? How
long before you tell the people to stop pursuing
their brothers?" 27 Joab replied, "As God lives, if
you had not spoken, it would be morning before
the people would be stopped from pursuing their
brothers." 28 Joab then sounded the horn, and
all the people came to a halt, pursuing Israel no
farther and fighting no more. 29 Abner and his
men marched all night long through the Ara-
bah, crossed the Jordan, marched all through the
morning, and came to Mahanaim. 30 Joab, coming
from the pursuit of Abner, assembled all the men.
Nineteen other servants of David were missing,
besides Asahel. 31 But David's servants had struck
down and killed three hundred and sixty men of
Benjamin, followers of Abner. 32 They took up
Asahel and buried him in his father's tomb in
Bethlehem. Joab and his men made an all-night
march, and dawn found them in Hebron.

3 1 There followed a long war between the
house of Saul and the house of David, in
which David grew ever stronger, but the house
of Saul ever weaker.

Sons Born in Hebron

2* Sons were born to David in Hebron: his
firstborn, Amnon, of Ahinoam from Jezreel; 3 the
second, Chileab, of Abigail the wife of Nabal of
Carmel; the third, Absalom, son of Maacah, who
was the daughter of Talmai, king of Geshur;*
4 the fourth, Adonijah, son of Haggith; the fifth,
Shephatiah, son of Abital;* 5 and the sixth, Ith-
ream, by David's wife Eglah. These were born to
David in Hebron.

Ishbaal and Abner Quarrel

6 During the war between the house of Saul
and the house of David, Abner was gaining
power in the house of Saul. 7 Now Saul had had
a concubine, Rizpah, the daughter of Aiah. And
Ishbaal, son of Saul, said to Abner, "Why have
you slept with my father's concubine?"† * 8 En-
raged at the words of Ishbaal, Abner said, "Am
I a dog's head from Judah? As of today, I have
been loyal to the house of Saul your father, to
his brothers and his friends, and I have kept you
out of David's clutches; and today you charge me
with a crime involving a woman! 9 May God do
thus to Abner, and more, if I do not carry out for
David what the LORD swore to him—* 10 that is,
take away the kingdom from the house of Saul

---

†

2:14 *Perform*: lit., "play."

2:16 The nature of this gruesome game is not clear, and the place name is variously given in the older texts.

3:7 Asserting a right to the late king's harem was tantamount to claiming his kingship; cf. 16:21–22; 1 Kgs 2:21–22.

*

2:11 2 Sm 5:5; 1 Kgs 2:11.
2:18 2 Sm 23:24; 1 Chr 2:16; 27:7.
2:22 2 Sm 3:27–28, 30.
3:2–5 1 Chr 3:1–4.
3:3 2 Sm 13:37; 15:8.
3:4 1 Kgs 1:5.
3:7 2 Sm 16:21–22; 21:8–10; 1 Kgs 2:21–22.
3:9 Ru 1:17.

and establish the throne of David over Israel as well as Judah, from Dan to Beer-sheba."* 11 Ishbaal was no longer able to say a word to Abner, he feared him so.

Abner and David Reconciled

12 Then Abner sent messengers to David in Telam, where he was at the moment, to say, "Make a covenant with me, and you have me on your side, to bring all Israel over to you." 13 He replied, "Good, I will make a covenant with you. But one thing I require of you. You must not appear before me unless you bring back Michal, Saul's daughter, when you come to present yourself to me."* 14 At the same time David sent messengers to Ishbaal, son of Saul, to say, "Give me my wife Michal, whom I betrothed by paying a hundred Philistine foreskins." 15 Ishbaal sent for her and took her away from her husband Paltiel, son of Laish,* 16 who followed her weeping as far as Bahurim. But Abner said to him, "Go back!" So he turned back.

17 Abner then had a word with the elders of Israel: "For some time you have been wanting David as your king. 18 Now take action, for the LORD has said of David: By David my servant I will save my people Israel from the power of the Philistines and from the power of all their enemies." 19 Abner also spoke with Benjamin, and then went to speak with David in Hebron concerning all that would be agreeable to Israel and to the whole house of Benjamin. 20 When Abner, accompanied by twenty men, came to David in Hebron, David prepared a feast for Abner and for the men who were with him. 21 Then Abner said to David, "I will now go to assemble all Israel for my lord the king, that they may make a covenant with you; you will then be king over all whom you wish to rule." So David let Abner go on his way in peace.

Death of Abner

22 Just then David's servants and Joab were coming in from an expedition, bringing much plunder with them. Abner, having been dismissed by David, was no longer with him in Hebron but had gone on his way in peace. 23 When Joab and the whole force he had with him arrived, he was informed, "Abner, son of Ner, came to David, and he let him go on his way in peace." 24 So Joab went to the king and said: "What have you done? Abner came to you! Why did you let him get away? 25 Don't you know Abner? He came to trick you, to learn your comings and goings, to learn everything you do." 26 Joab then left David and sent messengers after Abner to bring him back from the cistern of Sirah; but David did not know. 27 When Abner returned to Hebron, Joab took him aside within the city gate to speak with him privately. There he stabbed him in the abdomen, and he died for the blood of Asahel, Joab's brother.* 28 Later David heard of it and said: "Before the LORD, I and my kingdom are forever innocent.* 29 May the blood of Abner, son of Ner, be on the head of Joab and all his family. May Joab's family never be without one suffering from a discharge, or one with a skin disease, or a man who holds the distaff, or one falling by the sword, or one in need of food!"† 30 Joab and Abishai his brother had been lying in wait for Abner because he killed Asahel their brother in battle at Gibeon.

David Mourns Abner

31 Then David said to Joab and to all the people who were with him, "Tear your garments, put on sackcloth, and mourn over Abner." King David himself followed the bier.* 32 When they had buried Abner in Hebron, the king wept aloud at the grave of Abner, and all the people wept. 33 And the king sang this lament over Abner:

> Should Abner have died like a fool?
> 34 Your hands were not bound with chains,
> nor your feet placed in fetters;
> As one falls before the wicked, you fell.

And all the people continued to weep for him. 35 Then they went to console David with food while it was still day. But David swore, "May God do thus to me, and more, if before the sun goes down I eat bread or anything else."* 36 All the people noted this with approval, just as everything the king did met with their approval. 37 So on that day all the people and all Israel came to know that it was not the king's doing that Abner, son of Ner, was put to death. 38 The king then said to his servants: "Do you not know that a prince, a great man, has fallen today in Israel. 39 Although I am the anointed king, I am weak this day, and these men, the sons of Zeruiah, are too ruthless for me. May the LORD repay the evildoer in accordance with his evil deed."*

Death of Ishbaal

4 1 When Ishbaal, son of Saul, heard that Abner was dead in Hebron, he lost his resolve

---

† 3:29 An assortment of imprecations, consisting of physical ailments, weakness, violent death, and poverty.

3:10 2 Sm 5:2; 1 Sm 25:30.
3:13 1 Sm 18:20–27.
3:15 1 Sm 25:44.
3:27 2 Sm 2:17–23; 1 Kgs 2:5, 31–33.
3:28, 30 2 Sm 2:22–23.
3:31 2 Sm 21:10.
3:35 Ru 1:17.
3:39 Ps 28:4; Is 3:11.

and all Israel was alarmed. 2 Ishbaal, son of Saul,
had two company leaders named Baanah and
Rechab, sons of Rimmon the Beerothite, of the
tribe of Benjamin—Beeroth, too, was ascribed
to Benjamin:* 3 the Beerothites fled to Gittaim,
where they have been resident aliens to this
day.* 4 (Jonathan, son of Saul, had a son with
crippled feet. He was five years old when the
news about Saul and Jonathan came from Jez-
reel; his nurse took him and fled, but in their
hasty flight, he fell and became lame. His name
was Meribbaal.)† * 5 The sons of Rimmon the
Beerothite, Rechab and Baanah, came into the
house of Ishbaal during the heat of the day,
while he was lying on his bed in the afternoon.
6 The gatekeeper of the house had dozed off
while sifting wheat, and was asleep. So Rechab
and his brother Baanah slipped past her 7 and en-
tered the house while Ishbaal was lying asleep in
his bedroom. They struck and killed him, and cut
off his head. Then, taking the head, they traveled
on the Arabah road all night long.

The Murder Avenged

8 They brought the head of Ishbaal to David in
Hebron and said to the king: "This is the head
of Ishbaal, son of your enemy Saul, who sought
your life. Thus has the LORD this day avenged my
lord the king on Saul and his posterity." 9 But
David replied to Rechab and his brother Baanah,
sons of Rimmon the Beerothite: "As the LORD
lives, who rescued me from every distress: 10 the
man who reported to me, 'Saul is dead,' and
thought he was bringing good news, that man I
seized and killed in Ziglag: that was the reward
I gave him.* 11 How much more now, when
wicked men have slain an innocent man in bed
at home, must I require his blood from you and
purge you from the land!" 12 So at David's com-
mand, the young men killed them and cut off
their hands and feet, hanging them up near the
pool in Hebron. But he took the head of Ishbaal
and buried it in Abner's grave in Hebron.*

David King of Israel

5 1 * All the tribes of Israel came to David in
Hebron, and they said: "Look! We are your
bone and your flesh. 2 In days past, when Saul
was still our king, you were the one who led
Israel out in all its battles and brought it back.
And the LORD said to you: You shall shepherd
my people Israel; you shall be ruler over Israel."*
3 Then all the elders of Israel came to the king
in Hebron, and at Hebron King David made a
covenant with them in the presence of the LORD;
and they anointed David king over Israel. 4 David
was thirty years old when he became king, and
he reigned forty years: 5 in Hebron he was king
over Judah seven years and six months, and in
Jerusalem he was king thirty-three years over all
Israel and Judah.*

Capture of Zion†

6 * Then the king and his men went to Jeru-
salem against the Jebusites who inhabited the
land. They told David, "You shall not enter here:
the blind and the lame will drive you away!"
which was their way of saying, "David shall not
enter here."* 7 David nevertheless captured the
fortress of Zion, which is the City of David. 8 On
that day David said: "All who wish to strike at
the Jebusites must attack through the water shaft.
The lame and the blind shall be the personal
enemies of David." That is why it is said, "The
blind and the lame shall not enter the palace."*
9 David took up residence in the fortress which
he called the City of David. David built up the
city on all sides, from the Millo toward the cen-
ter.* 10 David became ever more powerful, for the
LORD of hosts was with him.* 11 * Hiram, king
of Tyre, sent envoys to David along with cedar
wood, and carpenters and masons, who built a
house for David.* 12 David now knew† that the
LORD had truly established him as king over Israel
and had exalted his kingdom for the sake of his
people Israel.

†

4:4 *Meribbaal*: Hebrew has *mephiboseth*; see note on 2:8. His name, in fact, is Meribbaal; cf. 1 Chr 8:34; 9:40. He is the subject of chap. 9 below. The text of this verse may owe its present place to the fact that ancient copies of the Books of Samuel tended to confuse his name with that of his uncle Ishbaal, Saul's son and successor, a principal figure in chaps. 2–4.

5:6–12 David's most important military exploit, the taking of Jerusalem, is here presented before his battles with the Philistines, vv. 17–25, which took place earlier. The sense of vv. 6 and 8 is in doubt. Perhaps the Jebusites boasted that Jerusalem was impregnable, using a metaphorical or proverbial expression that claimed the city was defensible even by people not suited for military action. The saying then received a different sense (v. 8), to the effect that "the blind and the lame" were David's enemies. Mt 21:14 and Lk 14:13 seem to play off, and transform, this saying.

5:12 *David now knew*: Hiram's carpenters and masons built David a house of cedar, the very model of a Canaanite king's palace. This house then represented the consolidation of David's royal power, in the Canaanite mode, with Jerusalem as David's personal fiefdom and capital city.

*

4:2 2 Sm 9:3; Jos 9:17–18.
4:3 Jos 18:25.
4:4 2 Sm 9:3; 19:25.
4:10 2 Sm 1:6–10, 14, 16.
4:12 Dt 21:22–23; 1 Sm 31:10.
5:1–5 1 Chr 11:1–3.
5:2 2 Sm 3:10; Dt 17:15; 1 Sm 18:16.
5:5 2 Sm 2:11; 1 Kgs 2:11; 1 Chr 3:4.
5:6–10 1 Chr 11:4–9.
5:6 Jos 15:63; Jgs 1:19, 21; Is 29:3.
5:8 Lv 21:18; Mt 21:14–15.
5:9 1 Kgs 3:1; 9:15; 11:27.
5:10 Ps 78:70–72; 89; 132:13.
5:11–25 1 Chr 14:1–16.
5:11–12 1 Kgs 5:15; 1 Chr 14:1–2.

David's Family in Jerusalem

13 * David took more concubines and wives in Jerusalem after he had come from Hebron, and more sons and daughters were born to him. 14 These are the names of those who were born to him in Jerusalem: Shammua, Shobab, Nathan, Solomon, 15 Ibhar, Elishua, Nepheg, Japhia, 16 Elishama, Beeliada, and Eliphelet.

Rout of the Philistines

17 When the Philistines had heard that David was anointed king over Israel, they marched out in force to come after him. When David heard this, he went down to the refuge.† 18 Meanwhile the Philistines had come and deployed themselves in the valley of Rephaim.† 19 David inquired of the LORD, "Shall I attack the Philistines, and will you deliver them into my power?" The LORD answered David: Attack, for I will surely deliver the Philistines into your power. 20 So David went to Baal-perazim,† and he defeated them there. He said, "The LORD has broken through my enemies before me just as water breaks through a dam." Therefore that place was called Baal-perazim. 21 The Philistines abandoned their gods there, and David and his men carried them away. 22 Once again the Philistines came up and deployed themselves in the valley of Rephaim, 23 and again David inquired of the LORD, who replied: Do not attack the front—circle behind them and come against them near the balsam trees. 24 When you hear the sound of marching† in the tops of the balsam trees, act decisively, for then the LORD has already gone before you to strike the army of the Philistines. 25 David did as the LORD commanded him, and routed the Philistines from Gibeon as far as Gezer.

The Ark Brought to Jerusalem

6 1 * David again assembled all the picked men of Israel, thirty thousand in number. 2 Then David and all the people who were with him set out for Baala of Judah to bring up from there the ark of God, which bears the name "the LORD of hosts enthroned above the cherubim."* 3 They transported the ark of God on a new cart and took it away from the house of Abinadab on the hill. Uzzah and Ahio, sons of Abinadab, were guiding the cart,* 4 with Ahio walking before it, 5 while David and all the house of Israel danced before the LORD with all their might, with singing, and with lyres, harps, tambourines, sistrums, and cymbals.* 6 As they reached the threshing floor of Nodan, Uzzah stretched out his hand to the ark of God and steadied it, for the oxen were tipping it. 7 Then the LORD became angry with Uzzah; God struck him on that spot, and he died there in God's presence. 8 David was angry because the LORD's wrath had broken out against Uzzah. Therefore that place has been called Perez-uzzah† even to this day. 9 David became frightened of the LORD that day, and he said, "How can the ark of the LORD come to me?" 10 So David was unwilling to take the ark of the LORD with him into the City of David. David deposited it instead at the house of Obed-edom the Gittite.

11 The ark of the LORD remained in the house of Obed-edom the Gittite for three months, and the LORD blessed Obed-edom and all his household.* 12 * When it was reported to King David that the LORD had blessed the household of Obed-edom and all that he possessed because of the ark of God, David went to bring up the ark of God from the house of Obed-edom into the City of David with joy.* 13 As soon as the bearers of the ark of the LORD had advanced six steps, he sacrificed an ox and a fatling. 14 Then David came dancing before the LORD with abandon, girt with a linen ephod.† * 15 David and all the house of Israel were bringing up the ark of the LORD with shouts of joy and sound of horn. 16 As the ark of the LORD was entering the City of David, Michal, daughter of Saul, looked down from her window, and when she saw King David jumping and dancing before the LORD, she despised him in her heart. 17 * They brought in the ark of the LORD and set it in its place within the tent which David had pitched for it. Then David sacrificed burnt offerings and communion offerings before the LORD. 18 When David had finished sacrificing burnt offerings and communion offerings, he

---

†

5:17 *Refuge*: probably near Adullam (1 Sm 22:1–5).

5:18–25 The successive defeats of the Philistines in the valley of Rephaim southwest of Jerusalem had the effect of blocking their access to the mountain ridge near Gibeon, and confining them to their holdings on the coast and in the foothills beyond Gezer to the west and south.

5:20 *Baal-perazim*: here the title *ba'al*, "master, lord," refers to the Lord; *perazim* is the plural of *perez*, which means "breaking" or "bursting," as in 6:8.

5:24 *Sound of marching*: the wind in the treetops suggestive of the footsteps of the Lord and the heavenly host.

6:8 *Perez-uzzah*: this Hebrew phrase means "the breaking out against Uzzah"; see note on 5:20.

6:14 *Girt with a linen ephod*: the ephod was some sort of priestly vestment (probably like an apron); cf. Ex 28:4; Jgs 17:5; 1 Sm 2:18, 28; 14:3; 22:18; 23:6. The cultic procession that accompanies the ark to the holy mountain, Zion, is led by King David, dancing ecstatically and wearing a priestly vestment.

---

*

5:13–16 1 Chr 3:5–8; 14:3–7.
6:1–11 1 Chr 13:1–14.
6:2 Ex 25:10; Jos 15:9; 1 Chr 13:6; Ps 132:8–10.
6:3 1 Sm 4:3–4; 6:7–8; 7:1; Dn 3:55.
6:5 Ps 68:24–25; 150:3–5.
6:11 1 Chr 26:4.
6:12–23 1 Chr 15:1–29; Ps 24:7–10.
6:12 1 Kgs 8:1.
6:14 1 Sm 2:18.
6:17–19 Lv 1:1–17; 3:1–17; 1 Chr 16:1–3.

blessed the people in the name of the LORD of hosts, 19 and distributed among all the people, the entire multitude of Israel, to every man and every woman, one loaf of bread, one piece of meat, and one raisin cake. Then all the people returned to their homes.

20 † When David went home to bless his own house,* Michal, the daughter of Saul, came out to meet him and said, "How well the king of Israel has honored himself today, exposing himself to the view of the slave girls of his followers, as a commoner might expose himself!" 21 But David replied to Michal: "I was dancing before the LORD. As the LORD lives, who chose me over your father and all his house when he appointed me ruler over the LORD's people, Israel, not only will I make merry before the LORD,* 22 but I will demean myself even more. I will be lowly in your eyes, but in the eyes of the slave girls you spoke of I will be somebody." 23 Saul's daughter Michal was childless to the day she died.

The Oracle of Nathan

7 1 * After the king had taken up residence in his house, and the LORD had given him rest from his enemies on every side,* 2 the king said to Nathan the prophet, "Here I am living in a house of cedar, but the ark of God dwells in a tent!"* 3 Nathan answered the king, "Whatever is in your heart, go and do, for the LORD is with you."* 4 But that same night the word of the LORD came to Nathan: 5 Go and tell David my servant, Thus says the LORD: Is it you who would build me a house to dwell in?* 6 I have never dwelt in a house from the day I brought Israel up from Egypt to this day, but I have been going about in a tent or a tabernacle. 7 As long as I have wandered about among the Israelites, did I ever say a word to any of the judges whom I commanded to shepherd my people Israel: Why have you not built me a house of cedar?

8 Now then, speak thus to my servant David, Thus says the LORD of hosts:† I took you from the pasture, from following the flock, to become ruler over my people Israel.* 9 I was with you wherever you went, and I cut down all your enemies before you. And I will make your name like that of the greatest on earth.* 10 I will assign a place for my people Israel and I will plant them in it to dwell there; they will never again be disturbed, nor shall the wicked ever again oppress them, as they did at the beginning, 11 and from the day when I appointed judges over my people Israel. I will give you rest from all your enemies. Moreover, the LORD also declares to you that the LORD will make a house for you:* 12 * when your

Live It!

The Dance of Life

It's a sacred celebration! How else could we describe the festivities surrounding the triumphant bringing of the ark of the Lord into Jerusalem? And King David is leading the way, dancing before the Lord "with abandon" (2 Sm 6:14). What a scene that must have been! What a wonderfully uninhibited way for David to express his great joy at escorting the ark into the city he has made his own.

So often we attend religious rituals as mere observers, much like Michal, David's wife, being critical and uninvolved. David shows us the true way to celebrate—with singing and dancing and eating. We need to celebrate together the presence of the Lord in our lives! Here David is our role model. Let us sing the song in our heart and dance to the music God has planted within us.

- How can we do a better job of celebrating the Lord in our lives? Are we observers or participants in the dance of life?

▶ **2 Sm 6:11–19**

† **6:20–23** Michal's reaction to David's dancing comes from her conception of how a king should comport himself. David rejects this understanding, saying he needs no instruction from the house of the failed king, Saul.

7:8–16 The message Nathan delivers to David, called the Dynastic Oracle, is prompted by David's intention to build a house (i.e., a temple) for the Lord, like David's own house (i.e., palace) of cedar. David is told, in effect, not to bother building a house for the Lord; rather, the Lord will make a house for him—a dynasty, the House of David. Not only will he have descendants (v. 12) who will sit upon the throne of Israel (v. 13), their rule will last forever (vv. 13, 16); and even if they transgress the Lord's commands, the line of David will never be removed from kingship as Saul was (cf. 1 Sm 13; 15). The oracle establishes the Davidic king as standing in relationship to the Lord as a son to a father (v. 14; cf. Ps 2:7; 89:27). The Dynastic Oracle, with cognate texts in the Scriptures, is the basis for Jewish expectations of an anointed king (1 Sm 12:3, 5), son of David (Mt 21:9); cf. Acts 2:30; Heb 1:5.

6:20 1 Chr 16:43.
6:21 1 Sm 13:14; 15:28.
7:1–29 1 Chr 17:1–27.
7:1 Dt 12:10; 25:19; 1 Kgs 5:4.
7:2 Ex 39:32.
7:3 Ps 132:1–5.
7:5 1 Kgs 5:3; 8:16, 27; 1 Chr 22:8; 28:3; Is 66:1; Acts 7:48–49.
7:8 1 Sm 16:13; 17:15–20; Ps 78:70–71; Am 7:14–15.
7:9 Ps 89:27.
7:11 2 Sm 23:5; 1 Kgs 2:4–24.
7:12–15 1 Kgs 5:19; 8:19; 1 Chr 22:10; 2 Chr 7:18; Ps 89:4, 26–29, 36–37; Lk 1:32; Heb 1:5.

Pray It!

David Praises God

"Then King David went in and sat before the LORD and said, 'Who am I, Lord GOD, and what is my house, that you should have brought me so far?'" (2 Sm 7:18). When was the last time you brought yourself before God, like King David, simply to offer praise for all God has done for you?

It is easy for us to feel too busy to take time for God. Then we complain and get frustrated because God does not seem to be around to give our lives direction. Taking quiet moments to place ourselves in humility before our God and to praise God for the good we experience is important.

Find a quiet place. Take just fifteen minutes. No radio, no television, no book. Think of all the positive and happy things in your life, and in your own words, say, "Thank you, God, for caring for me and the people I love!"

► 2 Sm 7:18–29

days have been completed and you rest with
your ancestors, I will raise up your offspring after
you, sprung from your loins, and I will establish
his kingdom. 13 He it is† who shall build a house
for my name, and I will establish his royal throne
forever. 14 I will be a father to him, and he shall
be a son to me. If he does wrong, I will reprove
him with a human rod and with human punish-
ments;* 15 but I will not withdraw my favor from
him as I withdrew it from Saul who was before
you.* 16 Your house and your kingdom are firm
forever before me; your throne shall be firmly
established forever.† * 17 In accordance with all
these words and this whole vision Nathan spoke
to David.

David's Thanksgiving

18 Then King David went in and sat in the
LORD's presence and said, "Who am I, Lord GOD,
and what is my house, that you should have
brought me so far?* 19 And yet even this is too
little in your sight, Lord GOD! For you have made
a promise regarding your servant's house reach-
ing into the future, and giving guidance to the
people, Lord GOD! 20 What more can David say to
you? You know† your servant, Lord GOD! 21 For
your servant's sake and as you have had at heart,
you have brought about this whole magnificent
disclosure to your servant. 22 Therefore, great are
you, Lord GOD! There is no one like you, no God
but you, as we have always heard.* 23 What other
nation on earth is there like your people Israel?
What god has ever led a nation, redeeming it
as his people and making a name by great and
awesome deeds, as you drove out the nations
and their gods before your people, whom you re-
deemed for yourself from Egypt?* 24 * You have
established for yourself your people Israel as
your people forever, and you, LORD, have become
their God. 25 Now, LORD God, confirm the prom-
ise that you have spoken concerning your servant
and his house forever. Bring about what you
have promised 26 so that your name may be for-
ever great. People will say: 'The LORD of hosts is
God over Israel,' when the house of your servant
David is established in your presence. 27 Because
you, LORD of hosts, God of Israel, have revealed
to your servant, 'I will build you a house,' your
servant now finds the courage to make this prayer
before you. 28 Since you, Lord GOD, are truly God
and your words are truth and you have made this
generous promise to your servant,* 29 do, then,
bless the house of your servant, that it may be
in your presence forever—since you, Lord GOD,
have promised, and by your blessing the house
of your servant shall be blessed forever."

Summary of David's Wars

8 1 * After this, David defeated the Philistines
and subdued them; and David took . . .†
from the Philistines. 2 He also defeated Moab
and measured them with a line. Making them lie

†

7:13 *He it is*: Solomon, in the event.

7:16 The unconditional promise made here, and reflected in Ps 89:34–35, stands in contrast to the tradition in Ps 132:12, where the continuation of the line of David depends on their fidelity to the Lord; cf. also 1 Kgs 2:4; 6:12; 8:25.

7:20 *Know*: give recognition, choose, single out: cf. Gn 18:19; Ex 33:12; Am 3:2.

8:1 *David took . . .*: the original Hebrew seems irretrievable. The transmitted text gives "the bridle of the cubit"; 1 Chr 18:1 understood "Gath and its towns"; others implausibly read "dominion of the capital city."

*

7:14 Ps 2:7; 89:26; Prv 3:12.
7:15 2 Sm 23:5; 1 Sm 13:14; 15:26, 28; 2 Kgs 19:34; 1 Chr 17:11–14; Ps 89:33–34.
7:16 2 Sm 23:5; Dn 2:44; 1 Mc 2:57; Mk 11:10; Lk 1:32–33; Heb 1:8.
7:18 1 Chr 17:16.
7:22 Ex 15:11; Is 45:5.
7:23 Dt 4:7, 34.
7:24–25 Ex 6:7; Dt 7:6; 26:17; 29:13.
7:28 Nm 23:19; Jn 17:17.
8:1–18 1 Chr 18:1–17.
8:3–8 2 Sm 10:15–19.

down on the ground, he measured two lengths
of line for death, and a full length for life.† Thus
the Moabites became subject to David, paying
tribute. 3 * David then defeated Hadadezer, son
of Rehob, king of Zobah, when he went to re-
establish his dominion at the River.* 4 David
captured from him one thousand seven hundred
horsemen and twenty thousand foot soldiers. Da-
vid hamstrung all the chariot horses, but left one
hundred for his chariots.* 5 The Arameans of Da-
mascus came to help Hadadezer, king of Zobah,
but David also defeated twenty-two thousand of
them in Aram. 6 David then placed garrisons in
the Damascus region of Aram, and the Arameans
became David's subjects, paying tribute. The LORD
brought David victory in all his undertakings.
7 David took the golden shields that were carried
by Hadadezer's attendants and brought them to
Jerusalem. (These Shishak, king of Egypt, took
away when he came to Jerusalem in the days
of Rehoboam, son of Solomon.) 8 From Tebah
and Berothai, cities of Hadadezer, King David
removed a very large quantity of bronze. 9 When
Toi, king of Hamath, heard that David had de-
feated the entire army of Hadadezer, 10 Toi sent
his son Hadoram to wish King David well and to
congratulate him on having waged a victorious
war against Hadadezer; for Hadadezer had been
at war with Toi. Hadoram also brought with him
articles of silver, gold, and bronze. 11 These also
King David consecrated to the LORD along with
the silver and gold that he had taken for this
purpose from all the nations he had subdued:
12 from Edom, Moab, the Ammonites, the Philis-
tines, and Amalek, and from the spoils of Hadad-
ezer, son of Rehob, king of Zobah.

13 On his return,† David made a name for
himself by defeating eighteen thousand Edom-
ites in the Valley of Salt.* 14 He set up garrisons
in Edom, and all the Edomites became David's
subjects. Thus the LORD brought David victory in
all his undertakings.

David's Officials

15 * David was king over all Israel; he dispensed
justice and right to all his people. 16 Joab, son of
Zeruiah, was in command of the army. Jehosha-
phat, son of Ahilud, was chancellor. 17 Zadok, son
of Ahitub, and Ahimelech, son of Abiathar, were
priests.† Shavsha was scribe. 18 Benaiah, son of Je-
hoiada, was in command of the Cherethites and
the Pelethites; and David's sons were priests.*

David and Meribbaal

9 1 David asked, "Is there any survivor of Saul's
house to whom I may show kindness for the
sake of Jonathan?"* 2 Now there was an official
of the house of Saul named Ziba. He was sum-
moned to David, and the king asked him, "Are
you Ziba?" He replied, "Your servant."* 3 Then
the king asked, "Is there any survivor of Saul's
house to whom I may show God's kindness?"
Ziba answered the king, "There is still Jonathan's
son, the one whose feet are crippled."* 4 The king
asked him, "Where is he?" and Ziba answered
the king, "He is in the house of Machir, son of
Ammiel, in Lodebar."* 5 So King David sent for
him and had him brought from the house of
Machir, son of Ammiel, from Lodebar. 6 When
Meribbaal, son of Jonathan, son of Saul, came to
David, he fell face down in homage. David said,
"Meribbaal," and he answered, "Your servant."
7 "Do not be afraid," David said to him, "I will
surely be kind to you for the sake of Jonathan
your father. I will restore to you all the lands of
Saul your grandfather, and you shall eat at my
table always." 8 Bowing low, he answered, "What
am I, your servant, that you should pay attention
to a dead dog like me?"* 9 The king then called
Ziba, Saul's attendant, and said to him: "All that
belonged to Saul and to his entire house, I am
giving to your lord's son. 10 You and your sons
and servants must till the land for him. You
shall bring in the produce, which shall be food
for your lord's household to eat. But Meribbaal,
your lord's son, shall always eat at my table."
Now Ziba had fifteen sons and twenty servants.
11 Ziba answered the king, "Whatever my lord
the king commands his servant, so shall your
servant do." And so Meribbaal ate at David's
table like one of the king's sons.* 12 Meribbaal
had a young son whose name was Mica; and

†

8:2 *Two lengths . . . a full length for life*: usually taken to mean that two-thirds of them were executed; but it could mean that two-thirds were spared, if the line was used full length in their case but doubled on itself to make "two lines" for those to be put to death. Note the contrasting good relations in 1 Sm 22:3–4.

8:13 *On his return*: possibly to Jerusalem, after the revolt of Absalom (chaps. 15–18), which this catalogue of victories would avoid mentioning. 1 Chr 18:12 attributes the defeat of the Edomites to Abishai, while the superscription of Ps 60 attributes it to Joab.

8:17 *Zadok . . . Ahimelech, son of Abiathar, were priests*: the names of Abiathar and Ahimelech are frequently associated with David (1 Sm 22:20; 23:6; 30:7; 2 Sm 15:24, 29, 35; 17:15; 19:12; 20:25), but they show Abiathar acting as priest, not Ahimelech: Abiathar shared the priestly office with Zadok in David's reign and even during Solomon's early years (1 Kgs 2:26; 4:4). Ahimelech was the name of Abiathar's father. This verse and 1 Chr 18:16 may indicate that Abiathar had a son named Ahimelech who also acted

*

8:3 2 Sm 10:6; 1 Kgs 11:23.
8:4 Jos 11:6, 9.
8:13 2 Kgs 14:7.
8:15–18 2 Sm 20:23–26; 1 Kgs 4:1–6; 1 Chr 18:14–17.
8:18 2 Sm 15:18; 20:7, 23; 23:20.
9:1 2 Sm 21:7; 1 Sm 18:1–4; 20:8–10, 15–17, 42.
9:2 2 Sm 16:1–4; 19:27.
9:3 2 Sm 4:4.
9:4 2 Sm 17:27.
9:8 1 Sm 24:15.
9:11 2 Sm 19:29.

all the tenants of Ziba's household worked for Meribbaal.* [13]But Meribbaal lived in Jerusalem, because he always ate at the king's table. He was lame in both feet.*

Campaigns Against Ammon

10 [1]* After this,† the king of the Ammonites died, and Hanun his son succeeded him as king. [2]David said, "I will show kindness to Hanun, the son of Nahash, as his father showed kindness to me." Therefore David sent his servants to Hanun to console him concerning his father. But when David's servants had entered the land of the Ammonites, [3]the Ammonite princes said to their lord Hanun, "Do you think David is doing this—sending you these consolers—to honor your father? Is it not rather to explore the city, to spy on it, and to overthrow it, that David has sent his servants to you?" [4]So Hanun seized David's servants, shaved off half their beards, cut away the lower halves of their garments at the buttocks, and sent them away.* [5]David was told of it and he sent word for them to be intercepted, for the men had been greatly disgraced. "Remain at Jericho," the king told them, "until your beards have grown again; then come back here."

[6]† When the Ammonites realized that they were in bad odor with David, they sent for and hired twenty thousand Aramean foot soldiers from Beth-rehob and Zobah, as well as the king of Maacah with one thousand men, and twelve thousand men from Tob.*

[7]When David heard of this, he sent Joab and his whole army of warriors against them.* [8]The Ammonites marched out and lined up for battle at the entrance of their city gate, while the Arameans of Zobah and Rehob and the men of Tob and Maacah remained apart in the open field. [9]When Joab saw that there was a battle line both in front of and behind him, he chose some of the best fighters of Israel and lined them up against the Arameans; [10]the rest of the army he placed under the command of his brother Abishai and lined up to oppose the Ammonites. [11]And he said, "If the Arameans prove too strong for me, you must come and save me; and if the Ammonites prove too strong for you, I will come to save you. [12]Hold firm and let us show ourselves courageous for the sake of our people and the cities of our God; and may the LORD do what is good in his sight." [13]Joab therefore advanced with his men for battle with the Arameans, but they fled before him. [14]And when the Ammonites saw that the Arameans had fled, they too fled before Abishai, and reentered their city. Joab then ceased his attack on the Ammonites and came to Jerusalem. [15]* Seeing themselves vanquished by Israel, the Arameans held a full muster of troops. [16]Hadadezer sent for and brought Arameans from beyond the River. They came to Helam, with Shobach, the captain of Hadadezer's army, at their head. [17]When this was reported to David, he gathered all Israel together, crossed the Jordan, and went to Helam. The Arameans drew up in formation against David and gave battle. [18]But the Arameans fled before Israel, and David killed seven hundred of their chariot fighters and forty thousand of their foot soldiers. He struck down Shobach, commander of the army, and he died on the field. [19]When Hadadezer's vassal kings saw themselves vanquished by Israel, they made peace with the Israelites and became their subjects. After this, the Arameans were afraid to give further aid to the Ammonites.

David's Sin

11 [1]At the turn of the year,† the time when kings go to war, David sent out Joab along with his officers and all Israel, and they laid waste the Ammonites and besieged Rabbah. David himself remained in Jerusalem.* [2]One evening David rose from his bed and strolled about on the roof of the king's house. From the roof he saw a woman bathing; she was very beautiful. [3]David sent people to inquire about the woman and was told, "She is Bathsheba, daughter of Eliam, and wife of Uriah the Hittite, Joab's armor-bearer."* [4]Then David sent messengers and took her. When she came to him, he took her to bed, at a time when she was just purified after her period; and she returned to her house.* [5]But the woman had become pregnant; she sent a message to inform David, "I am pregnant."

[6]So David sent a message to Joab, "Send me Uriah the Hittite." Joab sent Uriah to David. [7]And when he came, David asked him how Joab was, how the army was, and how the war was

---

† as a priest, like his father and his namesake grandfather, in the last years of David.

10:1 *After this*: early in the reign of David, since Hanun's father Nahash (1 Chr 19:1) had been ruling in Ammon at the beginning of Saul's reign (1 Sm 11) and Solomon was not yet born (2 Sm 11:1; 12:24).

10:6–9 A Hebrew text from Qumran (4QSam[a]) comes closer in these verses to what is given in 1 Chr 19:6–9. The scene of the conflict is more likely the Ammonite capital, Rabbath-Ammon (v. 8; cf. Josephus *Ant.*, vii, 123), than Medeba (1 Chr 19:7).

11:1 *At the turn of the year*: in the spring.

---

* **9:12** 1 Chr 8:34.
9:13 2 Sm 21:7.
10:1–19 1 Chr 19:1–19.
10:4 Is 20:4.
10:6 2 Sm 8:3; 1 Sm 14:47.
10:7 2 Sm 11:1.
10:15–19 2 Sm 8:3–8; 1 Chr 9:16–19.
11:1 2 Sm 10:7; 1 Chr 20:1.
11:3 2 Sm 23:39.
11:4 Lv 15:19.

going, and Uriah answered that all was well.
8 David then said to Uriah, "Go down to your
house and bathe your feet." Uriah left the king's
house, and a portion from the king's table was
sent after him. 9 But Uriah slept at the entrance
of the king's house with the other officers of his
lord, and did not go down to his own house.
10 David was told, "Uriah has not gone down to
his house." So he said to Uriah, "Have you not
come from a journey? Why, then, did you not
go down to your house?" 11 Uriah answered Da-
vid, "The ark and Israel and Judah are staying in
tents, and my lord Joab and my lord's servants
are encamped in the open field. Can I go home
to eat and to drink and to sleep with my wife? As
the LORD lives and as you live, I will do no such
thing."* 12 Then David said to Uriah, "Stay here
today also, and tomorrow I will send you back."
So Uriah stayed in Jerusalem that day. On the fol-
lowing day, 13 David summoned him, and he ate
and drank with David, who got him drunk. But
in the evening he went out to sleep on his bed
among his lord's servants, and did not go down
to his house. 14 The next morning David wrote a
letter to Joab which he sent by Uriah. 15 This is
what he wrote in the letter: "Place Uriah up front,
where the fighting is fierce. Then pull back and
leave him to be struck down dead." 16 So while
Joab was besieging the city, he assigned Uriah
to a place where he knew the defenders were
strong. 17 When the men of the city made a sortie
against Joab, some officers of David's army fell,
and Uriah the Hittite also died.
18 Then Joab sent David a report of all the de-
tails of the battle, 19 instructing the messenger,
"When you have finished giving the king all
the details of the battle, 20 the king may become
angry and say to you: 'Why did you go near the
city to fight? Did you not know that they would
shoot from the wall above? 21 Who killed Abime-
lech, son of Jerubbaal? Was it not a woman who
threw a millstone down on him from the wall
above, so that he died in Thebez? Why did you go
near the wall?' Then you in turn are to say, 'Your
servant Uriah the Hittite is also dead.' "* 22 The
messenger set out, and on his arrival he reported
to David everything Joab had sent him to tell.†
23 He told David: "The men had the advantage
over us and came out into the open against us,
but we pushed them back to the entrance of the
city gate. 24 Then the archers shot at your servants
from the wall above, and some of the king's ser-
vants died; and your servant Uriah the Hittite is
also dead." 25 David said to the messenger: "This
is what you shall say to Joab: 'Do not let this be
a great evil in your sight, for the sword devours
now here and now there. Strengthen your attack
on the city and destroy it.' Encourage him."
26 When the wife of Uriah heard that her hus-
band had died, she mourned her lord. 27 But
once the mourning was over, David sent for her
and brought her into his house. She became his
wife and bore him a son. But in the sight of the
LORD what David had done was evil.

Live It!

Lust and Its Consequences

What the king wants, the king gets. That seems to be the message of 2 Samuel 11:1–5. We are spared many of the details about the encounter between David and Bathsheba, but we do know this: Bathsheba is married to Uriah, so David has coveted another man's wife and committed adultery. When Bathsheba becomes pregnant, David attempts to deceive Uriah into thinking the baby is Uriah's, by bringing him home to have sex with Bathsheba. But Uriah refuses to do so because he and his comrades are in the midst of a war. Finally, David arranges for Uriah to be murdered in battle.

In one brief episode, David has broken four commandments. He has given in to lust, and it has led him into a situation that will affect his family, his kingship, and the whole nation of Israel.

It is so easy to give in to temptation, especially lust, because it can be so alluring, and because we generally fail to think beyond the moment. A dangerous thing.

▶ 2 Sm 11:1–5

† **11:22–24** In these verses the Greek text has David, angry with Joab, repeat exactly the questions Joab had foreseen in vv. 20–21. In v. 24 of our oldest Greek text, the messenger specifies that about eighteen men were killed. The Greek is considerably longer than the transmitted Hebrew text, suggesting that the Hebrew may have lost some sentences.

* **11:11** 1 Sm 4:3–4. **11:21** Jgs 9:50–54.

Live It!

The Power of a Good Story

Stories can be powerful. Jesus knew the power of stories, so he often responded to questions by telling a story.

The prophet Nathan also knew the power of stories. His challenge was to force David to come to grips with what he had done with Bathsheba and Uriah. In Second Samuel, Nathan cleverly creates a story in which David is to assume his familiar role as judge. David hears the case and is furious at the actions of the rich man in it, declaring that he should die for what he has done. Then, with four words, Nathan turns David's world upside down: "You are the man!" (12:7).

What can David say? He just condemned himself, and he knows it. Nathan has cleverly forced him into a moment of truth. You may want to read Psalm 51, which poetically records David's confession.

Yes, a story can be a powerful thing. Just ask Nathan. Or David. Or Jesus.

▶ 2 Sm 12:1–12

Nathan's Parable†

12 1 The LORD sent Nathan to David, and
when he came to him, he said: "Tell me
how you judge this case: In a certain town there
were two men, one rich, the other poor.* 2 The
rich man had flocks and herds in great numbers.
3 But the poor man had nothing at all except one
little ewe lamb that he had bought. He nour-
ished her, and she grew up with him and his
children. Of what little he had she ate; from his
own cup she drank; in his bosom she slept; she
was like a daughter to him. 4 Now, a visitor came
to the rich man, but he spared his own flocks and
herds to prepare a meal for the traveler who had
come to him: he took the poor man's ewe lamb
and prepared it for the one who had come to
him." 5 David grew very angry with that man and
said to Nathan: "As the LORD lives, the man who
has done this deserves death! 6 He shall make
fourfold restitution† for the lamb because he has
done this and was unsparing."* 7 Then Nathan
said to David: "You are the man!

Nathan's Indictment

"Thus says the LORD God of Israel: I anointed
you king over Israel. I delivered you from the
hand of Saul.* 8 I gave you your lord's house and
your lord's wives for your own. I gave you the
house of Israel and of Judah. And if this were
not enough, I could count up for you still more.
9 Why have you despised the LORD and done what
is evil in his sight? You have cut down Uriah the
Hittite with the sword; his wife you took as your
own, and him you killed with the sword of the
Ammonites. 10 Now, therefore, the sword shall
never depart from your house, because you have
despised me and have taken the wife of Uriah the
Hittite to be your wife.* 11 Thus says the LORD: I
will bring evil upon you out of your own house.
I will take your wives before your very eyes, and
will give them to your neighbor: he shall lie with
your wives in broad daylight.† * 12 You have
acted in secret, but I will do this in the presence
of all Israel, in the presence of the sun itself."

David's Repentance

13 Then David said to Nathan, "I have sinned
against the LORD." Nathan answered David: "For
his part, the LORD has removed your sin. You
shall not die,* 14 but since you have utterly
spurned the LORD by this deed, the child born to
you will surely die." 15 Then Nathan returned to
his house.

The LORD struck the child that the wife of
Uriah had borne to David, and it became des-
perately ill. 16 David pleaded with God on behalf
of the child. He kept a total fast, and spent the
night lying on the ground clothed in sackcloth.
17 The elders of his house stood beside him to get

† 12:1–7 David has committed adultery with Bathsheba and arranged the death of her husband. Instead of directly indicting the king for this criminal abuse of his royal authority, the prophet Nathan tells David a story. In the story, a parable of David's own actions, a powerful man takes cruel advantage of his vulnerable neighbor. Hearing the story, David is outraged and denounces the rich man—thus unwittingly pronouncing judgment on himself ("You are the man," v. 7).

12:6 *Fourfold restitution*: David's judgment foreshadows the deaths of four of his own sons: the child born of his adulterous union with Bathsheba (v. 18); Amnon (13:28–29); Absalom (18:15; 19:1); and Adonijah (1 Kgs 2:24–25).

12:11 *In broad daylight*: lit., "before the eyes of the sun"; the phrase echoes "before your very eyes" and anticipates "in the presence of the sun itself" (v. 12). The reference is to Absalom's action in appropriating his father's harem (16:22).

* 12:1 Sir 47:1.
12:6 Ex 21:37; Lk 19:8.
12:7 1 Sm 16:13.
12:10 2 Sm 13:28–29; 18:14.
12:11 2 Sm 16:21–22.
12:13 1 Kgs 21:29; Ps 32:5; 51:4; Sir 47:11.

him to rise from the ground; but he would not,
nor would he take food with them. 18 On the sev-
enth day, the child died. David's servants were
afraid to tell him that the child was dead, for
they said: "When the child was alive, we spoke
to him, but he would not listen to what we said.
How can we tell him the child is dead? He may
do some harm!" 19 But David noticed his ser-
vants whispering among themselves and realized
that the child was dead. He asked his servants,
"Is the child dead?" They said, "Yes." 20 Rising
from the ground, David washed and anointed
himself, and changed his clothes. Then he went
to the house of the LORD and worshiped. He
returned to his own house and asked for food;
they set it before him, and he ate. 21 His servants
said to him: "What is this you are doing? While
the child was living, you fasted and wept and
kept vigil; now that the child is dead, you rise
and take food." 22 He replied: "While the child
was living, I fasted and wept, thinking, 'Who
knows? The LORD may grant me the child's life.'
23 But now he is dead. Why should I fast? Can I
bring him back again? I shall go to him, but he
will not return to me."* 24 Then David consoled
Bathsheba his wife. He went and slept with her;
and she conceived and bore him a son, who was
named Solomon. The LORD loved him 25 and sent
the prophet Nathan to name him Jedidiah,† on
behalf of the LORD.

End of the Ammonite War

26 * Joab fought against Rabbah of the Am-
monites and captured that royal city. 27 He sent
messengers to David to say: "I have fought
against Rabbah and have taken the water-city.
28 Therefore, assemble the rest of the soldiers,
join the siege against the city, and capture it,
lest I be the one to capture the city and mine
be the name people mention, not yours." 29 So
David assembled the rest of the soldiers, went to
Rabbah, fought against it, and captured it. 30 He
took the crown of Milcom from the idol's head,
a talent† of gold in weight, with precious stones;
this crown David wore on his own head. He also
brought out a great amount of spoil from the
city. 31 He deported the people of the city and
set them to work with saws, iron picks, and iron
axes, or put them to work at the brickmold. He
dealt thus with all the cities of the Ammonites.
Then David and his whole army returned to Je-
rusalem.

Live It!

Family Violence

How should we react to the story of the rape of Tamar by her half-brother, Amnon, and the subsequent murder of Amnon by Absalom to avenge his sister's disgrace? This story of lust, cruelty, and revenge has all the makings of a TV movie or a bestselling paperback. So, what is it doing in the Bible?

We have to remind ourselves that these are all David's children. We also have to remind ourselves that after Nathan confronts David about his affair with Bathsheba and his arrangement of Uriah's death, he tells David that "the sword shall never depart from your house" (2 Sm 12:10).

This brutal chain of events unfolds within one family. We are all aware of families in which members do not get along. More serious is the fact that families are often caught up in domestic violence, which can pass from one generation to the next. So how do we stop the "sword of violence" within families?

Each of us needs to make sure we are doing what we can to build bridges in our own families rather than putting up walls. And we need to seek help for individuals who are affected by domestic violence. There are many resources available for people so affected.

- What can you do to help someone affected by family violence? Where can you go for help?

▶ **2 Samuel, chapter 13**

Amnon's Rape of Tamar

13 1 After this, the following occurred. David's
son Absalom had a beautiful sister named
Tamar, and David's son Amnon loved her.* 2 He
was in such anguish over his sister Tamar that
he became sick; she was a virgin, and Amnon
thought it impossible to do anything to her.

† **12:25** *Jedidiah*: the name means "beloved of Yhwh."
12:30 *A talent*: since this would normally be more than seventy-five pounds, the report may have been embellished.

* **12:23** Jb 7:9–10.
12:26–31 1 Chr 20:1–3.
13:1 2 Sm 3:2–3; 1 Chr 3:9.

3 Now Amnon had a friend named Jonadab,
son of David's brother Shimeah, who was very
clever.† * 4 He asked him, "Prince, why are you
so dejected morning after morning? Why not
tell me?" So Amnon said to him, "I am in love
with Tamar, my brother Absalom's sister." 5 Then
Jonadab replied, "Lie down on your bed and pre-
tend to be sick. When your father comes to visit
you, say to him, 'Please let my sister Tamar come
and encourage me to take food. If she prepares
something in my presence, for me to see, I will
eat it from her hand.' " 6 So Amnon lay down and
pretended to be sick. When the king came to visit
him, Amnon said to the king, "Please let my sister
Tamar come and prepare some fried cakes before
my eyes, that I may take food from her hand."
7 David then sent home a message to Tamar,
"Please go to the house of your brother Amnon
and prepare some food for him." 8 Tamar went
to the house of her brother Amnon, who was in
bed. Taking dough and kneading it, she twisted
it into cakes before his eyes and fried the cakes.
9 Then she took the pan and set out the cakes
before him. But Amnon would not eat; he said,
"Have everyone leave me." When they had all
left him, 10 Amnon said to Tamar, "Bring the
food into the bedroom, that I may have it from
your hand." So Tamar picked up the cakes she
had prepared and brought them to her brother
Amnon in the bedroom. 11 But when she brought
them close to him so he could eat, he seized her
and said to her, "Come! Lie with me, my sister!"
12 But she answered him, "No, my brother! Do
not force me! This is not done in Israel. Do not
commit this terrible crime.* 13 Where would I
take my shame? And you would be labeled a fool
in Israel.† So please, speak to the king; he will not
keep me from you."* 14 But he would not listen to
her; he was too strong for her: he forced her down
and raped her. 15 Then Amnon felt intense hatred
for her; the hatred he felt for her far surpassed the
love he had had for her. Amnon said to her, "Get
up, leave." 16 She replied, "No, brother, because
sending me away would be far worse than this
evil thing you have done to me." He would not
listen to her, 17 but called the youth who was his
attendant and said, "Send this girl outside, away
from me, and bar the door after her." 18 Now she
had on a long tunic, for that is how virgin prin-
cesses dressed in olden days. When his attendant
put her out and barred the door after her, 19 Tamar
put ashes on her head and tore the long tunic in
which she was clothed. Then, putting her hands
to her head, she went away crying loudly. 20 Her
brother Absalom said to her: "Has your brother
Amnon been with you? Keep still now, my sister;
he is your brother. Do not take this so to heart."
So Tamar remained, devastated, in the house of
her brother Absalom. 21 King David, when he
heard of the whole affair, became very angry.
He would not, however, antagonize Amnon, his
high-spirited son; he loved him, because he was
his firstborn. 22 And Absalom said nothing, good
or bad, to Amnon; but Absalom hated Amnon for
having humiliated his sister Tamar.

Absalom's Plot

23 Two years went by. It was sheep-shearing
time for Absalom in Baal-hazor near Ephraim,
and Absalom invited all the king's sons. 24 Absa-
lom went to the king and said: "Your servant has
hired the shearers. Please, may the king come
with all his servants to your servant." 25 But the
king said to Absalom, "No, my son, all of us
should not go lest we be a burden to you." And
though Absalom urged him, he would not go
but began to bid him good-bye. 26 Absalom then
said, "If not you, then please let my brother Am-
non come with us." The king asked him, "Why
should he go with you?" 27 But at Absalom's urg-
ing, the king sent Amnon and with him all his
other sons. Absalom prepared a banquet fit for a
king. 28 * But Absalom had instructed his atten-
dants: "Now watch! When Amnon is merry with
wine and I say to you, 'Kill Amnon,' put him to
death. Do not be afraid, for it is I who order you
to do it. Be strong and act like warriors."

Death of Amnon

29 When the attendants did to Amnon as Ab-
salom had commanded, all the king's other sons
rose up, mounted their mules, and fled. 30 While
they were still on the road, a report reached David:
"Absalom has killed all the king's sons and not
one of them is left." 31 The king stood up, tore his
garments, and lay on the ground. All his servants
standing by him also tore their garments.* 32 But
Jonadab, son of David's brother Shimeah, spoke
up: "Let not my lord think that all the young
men, the king's sons, have been killed! Amnon

13:3 *Clever*: lit., "wise." Jonadab's "wisdom" extends only to sly cleverness in getting things done; he devises the plan that will enable Amnon to pursue his infatuation. In the categories of the Old Testament wisdom tradition, Jonadab is a fool.

13:13 *A fool in Israel*: a play on *nebala* (v. 12), "terrible crime," lit., "folly."

13:3 2 Sm 21:21.
13:12 Lv 18:9; 20:17; Dt 22:21; 27:22.
13:13 Gn 34:7–8.
13:28–29 2 Sm 12:10.
13:31 2 Sm 1:11.

alone is dead, for Absalom was set on this ever since Amnon humiliated his sister Tamar. 33 Now let my lord the king not take so to heart that report, 'All the king's sons are dead.' Amnon alone is dead." 34 Meanwhile, Absalom had taken flight. Then the servant on watch looked out and saw a large group coming down the slope from the direction of Bahurim. He came in and reported this to the king: "I saw some men coming down the mountainside from the direction of Bahurim." 35 So Jonadab said to the king: "There! The king's sons have come. It is as your servant said." 36 No sooner had he finished speaking than the king's sons came in, weeping aloud. The king, too, and all his servants wept very bitterly. 37 But Absalom, who had taken flight, went to Talmai, son of Ammihud, king of Geshur,* 38 and stayed in Geshur for three years. 39 All that time the king continued to mourn his son; but his intention of going out against Absalom abated as he was consoled over the death of Amnon.

The Wise Woman of Tekoa

14 1 Now Joab, son of Zeruiah, knew how the king felt toward Absalom. 2 Joab sent to Tekoa and brought from there a wise woman, to whom he said: "Pretend to be in mourning. Put on mourning apparel and do not anoint yourself with oil, that you may appear to be a woman who has long been mourning someone dead. 3 Then go to the king and speak to him in this manner." And Joab told her what to say.

4 So the woman of Tekoa went to the king and fell to the ground in homage, saying, "Help, O king!" 5 * The king said to her, "What do you want?" She replied: "Alas, I am a widow; my husband is dead. 6 Your servant had two sons, who quarreled in the field, with no one to part them, and one of them struck his brother and killed him. 7 Then the whole clan confronted your servant and demanded: 'Give up the one who struck down his brother. We must put him to death for the life of his brother whom he has killed; we must do away with the heir also.' Thus they will quench my remaining hope† and leave my husband neither name nor posterity upon the earth."* 8 The king then said to the woman: "Go home. I will issue a command on your behalf." 9 The woman of Tekoa answered him, "Upon me and my family be the blame, my lord king; the king and his throne are innocent." 10 Then the king said, "If anyone says a word to you, have him brought to me, and he shall not touch you again." 11 But she said, "Please, let the king remember the LORD your God, that the avenger of blood may not go too far in destruction and that my son may not be done away with." He replied, "As the LORD lives, not a hair of your son shall fall to the ground."

12 But the woman continued, "Please let your servant say still another word to my lord the king." He replied, "Speak." 13 So the woman said: "Why, then, do you think the way you do against the people of God? In pronouncing as he has, the king shows himself guilty, in not bringing back his own banished son. 14 We must indeed die; we are then like water that is poured out on the ground and cannot be gathered up. Yet, though God does not bring back to life, he does devise means so as not to banish† anyone from him.* 15 And now, if I have presumed to speak to the king of this matter, it is because the people have given me cause to fear. And so your servant thought: 'Let me speak to the king. Perhaps he will grant the petition of his servant. 16 For the king must surely listen and rescue his servant from the grasp of one who would destroy both me and my son from the heritage of God.' 17 And your servant says, 'Let the word of my lord the king lead to rest;† indeed, my lord the king is like an angel of God, discerning good and evil. The LORD your God be with you.' "*

18 The king answered the woman, "Now do not conceal from me anything I may ask you!" The woman said, "Let my lord the king speak." 19 So the king asked, "Is the hand of Joab with you in all this?" And the woman answered: "As you live, my lord the king, it is just as my lord has said, and not otherwise. It was your servant Joab who instructed me and told your servant all these things she was to say. 20 Your servant Joab did this in order to approach the matter in a roundabout way. But my lord is wise with the wisdom of an angel of God, knowing all things on earth."

Absalom's Return

21 Then the king said to Joab: "I am granting this request. Go and bring back young Absalom." 22 Falling to the ground in homage and blessing the king, Joab said, "This day your servant knows that I am in good favor with you, my lord king,

†

14:7 *Hope*: lit., "glowing coal." The image is similar to that of a lighted lamp, e.g., Ps 132:17, or small hearth fire, to keep alive the ancestral name.

14:14 *Not to banish*: a possible allusion to the religious institution of cities of refuge for involuntary murderers; see Nm 35:9–15.

14:17 *Rest*: cf. Ru 1:9; Ps 95:11; Mi 2:10. The reference here is to a return home for Absalom.

*

13:37 2 Sm 3:3; 15:8.
14:5–7 2 Kgs 6:26–28.
14:7 Nm 35:19.
14:14 Jb 7:9; 14:7–12; Ps 88:4, 10–12.
14:17, 20 1 Sm 29:9.

since the king has granted the request of your
servant." 23 Joab then went off to Geshur and
brought Absalom to Jerusalem. 24 But the king
said, "Let him go off to his own house; he shall
not appear before† me." So Absalom went off to
his house and did not appear before the king.
25 In all Israel there was no man more praised
for his beauty than Absalom, flawless from the
sole of his foot to the crown of his head. 26 When
he shaved his head—as he used to do at the end
of every year, because his hair became too heavy
for him—the hair weighed two hundred shek-
els according to the royal standard. 27 Absalom
had three sons born to him, besides a daughter
named Tamar, who was a beautiful woman.*

Absalom Is Pardoned

28 Absalom lived in Jerusalem for two years
without appearing before the king. 29 Then he
sent a message asking Joab to send him to the
king, but Joab would not come to him. Although
he asked him a second time, Joab would not
come. 30 He therefore instructed his servants:
"You see Joab's field that borders mine, where he
has barley. Go, set it on fire." And so Absalom's
servants set the field on fire.* Joab's farmhands
came to him with torn garments and told him,
"Absalom's servants set your field on fire." 31 Joab
went to Absalom in his house and asked him,
"Why have your servants set my field on fire?"
32 Absalom answered Joab: "I sent you a message:
Come here, that I may send you to the king to
say: 'Why did I come back from Geshur? I would
be better off if I were still there!' Now, let me ap-
pear before the king. If I am guilty, let him put me
to death." 33 Joab went to the king and reported
this. The king then called Absalom; he came to
him and in homage fell on his face to the ground
before the king. Then the king kissed Absalom.

Absalom's Ambition

15 1 After this, Absalom provided himself with
chariots, horses, and a retinue of fifty.*
2 Moreover, Absalom used to rise early and stand
alongside the road leading to the gate. If some-
one had a lawsuit to be decided by the king,
Absalom would call to him and say, "From what
city are you?" And when he replied, "Your ser-
vant is of such and such a tribe of Israel," 3 Ab-
salom would say to him, "Your case is good and
just, but there is no one to hear you in the king's
name." 4 And he would continue: "If only I could
be appointed judge in the land! Then everyone
who has a lawsuit to be decided might come to
me and I would render him justice." 5 Whenever
a man approached him to show homage, he
would extend his hand, hold him, and kiss him.
6 By behaving in this way toward all the Israelites
who came to the king for judgment, Absalom
was stealing the heart of Israel.

Conspiracy in Hebron

7 After a period of four years, Absalom said to
the king: "Please let me go to Hebron and fulfill
a vow I made to the LORD. 8 For while living in
Geshur in Aram, your servant made this vow: 'If
the LORD ever brings me back to Jerusalem, I will
worship him in Hebron.' "* 9 The king said to
him, "Go in peace," and he went off to Hebron.
10 Then Absalom sent agents throughout the
tribes of Israel to say, "When you hear the sound
of the horn, say, 'Absalom is king in Hebron!' "
11 Two hundred men had accompanied Absalom
from Jerusalem. They had been invited and went
in all innocence, knowing nothing. 12 Absalom
also sent to Ahithophel the Gilonite, David's
counselor, an invitation to come from his town,
Giloh, for the sacrifices he was about to offer. So
the conspiracy gained strength, and the people
with Absalom increased in numbers.*

David Flees Jerusalem

13 An informant came to David with the re-
port, "The Israelites have given their hearts to
Absalom,* and they are following him." 14 At
this, David said to all his servants who were with
him in Jerusalem: "Get up, let us flee, or none
of us will escape from Absalom. Leave at once,
or he will quickly overtake us, and then bring
disaster upon us, and put the city to the sword."
15 The king's servants answered him, "Whatever
our lord the king chooses to do, we are your ser-
vants." 16 Then the king set out, accompanied by
his entire household, except for ten concubines
whom he left behind to care for the palace.* 17 As
the king left the city, with all his officers accom-
panying him, they halted opposite the ascent of
the Mount of Olives, at a distance, 18 while the
whole army marched past him.

David and Ittai

As all the Cherethites and Pelethites, and the
six hundred Gittites who had entered his service
from that city, were passing in review before the

---

† **14:24** *Appear before*: lit., "see the face of," a term from court etiquette; so also in vv. 28, 32.

14:27 2 Sm 18:18.
14:30 Jgs 15:4–5.
15:1 1 Sm 8:11; 1 Kgs 1:5.
15:8 2 Sm 3:3; 13:37.
15:12 2 Sm 16:23.
15:13 Ps 3.
15:16 2 Sm 16:21–22; 20:3.

king,* [19]the king said to Ittai the Gittite: "Why
should you also go with us? Go back and stay
with the king, for you are a foreigner and you,
too, are an exile from your own country. [20]You
came only yesterday, and today shall I have you
wander off with us wherever I have to go? Re-
turn and take your brothers with you, and may
the LORD show you kindness and fidelity." [21]But
Ittai answered the king, "As the LORD lives, and
as my lord the king lives, your servant shall be
wherever my lord the king is, whether for death
or for life."* [22]So the king said to Ittai, "Go,
then, march on." And Ittai the Gittite, with all his
men and all the dependents that were with him,
marched on. [23]The whole land wept aloud as the
last of the soldiers went by, and the king crossed
the Wadi Kidron with all the soldiers moving on
ahead of him by way of the ascent of the Mount
of Olives, toward the wilderness.

David and the Priests

[24]Zadok, too, and all the Levites bearing the
ark of the covenant of God set down the ark of
God until the whole army had finished marching
out of the city; and Abiathar came up. [25]Then the
king said to Zadok: "Take the ark of God back
to the city. If I find favor with the LORD, he will
bring me back and permit me to see it and its
lodging place. [26]But if he should say, 'I am not
pleased with you,' I am ready; let him do to me
as he sees fit."* [27]The king also said to Zadok
the priest: "Look, you and Abiathar return to the
city in peace, and both your sons with you, your
own son Ahimaaz, and Abiathar's son Jonathan.
[28]Remember, I shall be waiting at the fords near
the wilderness until a report from you comes to
me." [29]So Zadok and Abiathar took the ark of
God back to Jerusalem and remained there.

[30]As David went up the ascent of the Mount
of Olives, he wept without ceasing. His head was
covered, and he was walking barefoot. All those
who were with him also had their heads covered
and were weeping as they went.* [31]When David
was told, "Ahithophel is among the conspirators
with Absalom," he said, "O LORD, turn the coun-
sel of Ahithophel to folly!"*

David and Hushai

[32]When David reached the top, where God
was worshiped, Hushai the Archite was there to
meet him, with garments torn and dirt upon his
head.* [33]David said to him: "If you come with
me, you will be a burden to me; [34]but if you re-
turn to the city and say to Absalom, 'Let me be
your servant, O king; I was formerly your father's
servant, but now I will be yours,' you will thwart
for me the counsel of Ahithophel.* [35]You will
have the priests Zadok and Abiathar there with
you. If you hear anything from the king's house,
you shall report it to the priests Zadok and Abi-
athar, [36]who have there with them their two
sons, Zadok's son Ahimaaz and Abiathar's son
Jonathan. Through them you shall send on to me
whatever you hear." [37]So David's friend Hushai
went into the city, Jerusalem, as Absalom was
about to enter it.

David and Ziba

16 [1]David went a little beyond the top and
Ziba, the servant of Meribbaal, was there
to meet him with saddled donkeys laden with
two hundred loaves of bread, an ephah of cakes
of pressed raisins, an ephah of summer fruits,
and a skin of wine.* [2]The king said to Ziba,
"What are you doing with all this?" Ziba replied:
"The donkeys are for the king's household to ride
on. The bread and summer fruits are for your
servants to eat, and the wine to drink when they
grow weary in the wilderness." [3]Then the king
said, "And where is your lord's son?" Ziba an-
swered the king, "He is staying in Jerusalem, for
he said, 'Today the house of Israel will restore to
me my father's kingdom.' "* [4]The king therefore
said to Ziba, "So! Everything Meribbaal had is
yours." Then Ziba said: "I pay you homage, my
lord the king. May I find favor with you!"*

David and Shimei

[5]As King David was approaching Bahurim,
there was a man coming out; he was of the same
clan as the house of Saul, and his name was
Shimei, son of Gera. He kept cursing as he came
out,* [6]and throwing stones at David and at all
King David's officers, even though all the sol-
diers, including the royal guard, were on David's
right and on his left. [7]Shimei was saying as he
cursed: "Get out! Get out! You man of blood, you
scoundrel! [8]The LORD has paid you back for all
the blood shed from the family of Saul,† whom
you replaced as king, and the LORD has handed
over the kingdom to your son Absalom. And
now look at you: you suffer ruin because you are

† **16:8** *Blood shed . . . Saul*: probably refers to the episode recounted in 21:1–14.

* **15:18** 2 Sm 8:18. **15:21** Ru 1:16–17. **15:26** 2 Sm 16:10. **15:30** 2 Sm 19:5; Mi 1:8. **15:31** 2 Sm 16:23; 17:14, 23. **15:32** 2 Sm 16:16. **15:34** 2 Sm 16:19. **16:1** 2 Sm 4:4; 9:1–13; 19:18, 25. **16:3** 2 Sm 19:26–27. **16:4** 2 Sm 19:30. **16:5** 2 Sm 3:16; 19:17, 22–23; 1 Kgs 2:8.

2 SM

a man of blood." 9 Abishai, son of Zeruiah, said to the king: "Why should this dead dog curse my lord the king? Let me go over and take off his head."* 10 But the king replied: "What business is it of mine or of yours, sons of Zeruiah, that he curses? Suppose the LORD has told him to curse David; who then will dare to say, 'Why are you doing this?' "* 11 Then David said to Abishai and to all his servants: "If my own son, who came forth from my loins, is seeking my life, how much more might this Benjaminite do so! Let him alone and let him curse, for the LORD has told him to.* 12 Perhaps the LORD will look upon my affliction and repay me with good for the curses he is uttering this day." 13 David and his men continued on the road, while Shimei kept up with them on the hillside, all the while cursing and throwing stones and dirt as he went.* 14 The king and all the soldiers with him arrived at the Jordan tired out, and stopped there to rest.

Absalom's Counselors

15 In the meantime Absalom, with all the Israelites, entered Jerusalem, and Ahithophel was with him. 16 When David's friend Hushai the Archite came to Absalom, he said to him: "Long live the king! Long live the king!"* 17 But Absalom asked Hushai: "Is this your devotion to your friend? Why did you not go with your friend?" 18 Hushai replied to Absalom: "On the contrary, I am his whom the LORD and all this people and all Israel have chosen, and with him I will stay. 19 Furthermore, as I was in attendance upon your father, so will I be before you. Whom should I serve, if not his son?"*

20 Then Absalom said to Ahithophel, "Offer your counsel on what we should do." 21 Ahithophel replied to Absalom: "Go to your father's concubines, whom he left behind to take care of the palace. When all Israel hears how odious you have made yourself to your father, all those on your side will take courage."* 22 So a tent was pitched on the roof for Absalom, and Absalom went to his father's concubines in view of all Israel.*

Counsel of Ahithophel

23 Now the counsel given by Ahithophel at that time was as though one sought the word of God. Such was all the counsel of Ahithophel both to David and to Absalom.*

17 1 Ahithophel went on to say to Absalom: "Let me choose twelve thousand men and be off in pursuit of David tonight. 2 If I come upon him when he is weary and discouraged, I shall cause him panic, and all the people with him will flee, and I shall strike down the king alone. 3 Then I can bring back the rest of the people to you, as a bride returns to her husband. It is the death of only one man you are seeking; then all the people will be at peace." 4 This plan sounded good to Absalom and to all the elders of Israel.

Counsel of Hushai

5 Then Absalom said, "Now call Hushai the Archite also; let us hear what he too has to say." 6 When Hushai came to Absalom, Absalom said to him: "This is Ahithophel's plan. Shall we follow his plan? If not, give your own." 7 Hushai replied to Absalom, "This time Ahithophel has not given good counsel." 8 And he went on to say: "You know that your father and his men are warriors, and that they are as fierce as a bear in the wild robbed of her cubs. Moreover, since your father is a skilled fighter, he will not spend the night with the army.* 9 Even now he lies hidden in one of the caves or in one of his other places. And if some of our soldiers should fall at the first attack, whoever hears of it will say, 'Absalom's followers have been slaughtered.' 10 Then even the brave man with the heart of a lion—his heart will melt. For all Israel knows that your father is a fighter and those who are with him are brave. 11 This is what I counsel: Let all Israel be assembled, from Dan to Beer-sheba, as numerous as the sands by the sea, and you yourself go with them. 12 We can then attack him wherever we find him, settling down upon him as dew alights on the ground. None shall survive—neither he nor any of his followers. 13 And if he retires into a city, all Israel shall bring ropes to that city and we can drag it into the gorge, so that not even a pebble of it can be found." 14 Then Absalom and all the Israelites said, "The counsel of Hushai the Archite is better than the counsel of Ahithophel." For the LORD had commanded that Ahithophel's good counsel should be thwarted, so that he might bring Absalom to ruin.*

David Told of the Plan

15 Then Hushai said to the priests Zadok and Abiathar: "This is the counsel Ahithophel gave Absalom and the elders of Israel, and this is what I counseled. 16 So send a warning to David immediately: 'Do not spend the night at the fords near the wilderness, but cross over without fail. Otherwise the king and all the people with him

* **16:9** 2 Sm 19:22; 1 Sm 24:15; 26:6.
16:10 2 Sm 15:25–26; 19:23.
16:11 2 Sm 12:11.
16:13 2 Sm 19:19–24.
16:16 2 Sm 15:32–37.
16:19 2 Sm 15:34.
16:21 2 Sm 15:16; 20:3.
16:22 2 Sm 12:11–12.
16:23 2 Sm 15:12, 31; 17:23.
17:8 Hos 13:8.
17:14 2 Sm 15:31, 34.

will be destroyed.' " [17] Now Jonathan and Ahim-
aaz were staying at En-rogel. A maidservant was
to come with information for them, and they in
turn were to go and report to King David. They
could not risk being seen entering the city, [18] but
an attendant did see them and informed Absa-
lom. They hurried on their way and reached the
house of a man in Bahurim who had a cistern in
his courtyard. They let themselves down into it,
[19] and the woman took the cover and spread it
over the mouth of the cistern, strewing crushed
grain on the cover so that nothing could be no-
ticed. [20] When Absalom's servants came to the
woman at the house, they asked, "Where are
Ahimaaz and Jonathan?" The woman replied,
"They went by a short while ago toward the
water." They searched, but found no one, and
so returned to Jerusalem. [21] As soon as they left,
Ahimaaz and Jonathan came up out of the cis-
tern and went on to report to King David. They
said to him: "Leave! Cross the water at once, for
Ahithophel has given such and such counsel in
regard to you." [22] So David and all his people
moved on and crossed the Jordan. By daybreak,
there was no one left who had not crossed.

[23] When Ahithophel saw that his counsel was
not acted upon, he saddled his donkey and de-
parted, going to his home in his own city. Then,
having left orders concerning his household, he
hanged himself. And so he died and was buried
in his father's tomb.*

[24] Now David had arrived at Mahanaim while
Absalom crossed the Jordan accompanied by
all the Israelites. [25] Absalom had put Amasa in
command of the army in Joab's place. Amasa
was the son of an Ishmaelite named Ithra, who
had married Abigail, daughter of Jesse and sister
of Joab's mother Zeruiah.* [26] Israel and Absalom
encamped in the land of Gilead.

[27] When David came to Mahanaim, Shobi,
son of Nahash from Rabbah of the Ammonites,
Machir, son of Ammiel from Lodebar, and Bar-
zillai, the Gileadite from Rogelim,* [28] brought
beds and covers, basins and pottery, as well as
wheat, barley, flour, roasted grain, beans, lentils,
[29] honey, and butter and cheese from the flocks
and herds, for David and those who were with
him to eat; for they said, "The people will be
hungry and tired and thirsty in the wilderness."

Preparation for Battle

18 [1] After mustering the troops he had with
him, David placed officers in command of
units of a thousand and units of a hundred. [2] Da-
vid then divided the troops three ways, a third
under Joab, a third under Abishai, son of Zeruiah
and brother of Joab, and a third under Ittai the
Gittite. The king said to the troops, "I intend to
go out with you myself." [3] But they replied: "You
must not come out with us. For if we flee, no one
will care; even if half of us die, no one will care.
But you are worth ten thousand of us. Therefore
it is better that we have you to help us from the
city." [4] The king said to them, "I will do what you
think best." So the king stood by the gate as all
the soldiers marched out in units of a hundred
and a thousand. [5] But the king gave this com-
mand to Joab, Abishai, and Ittai: "Be gentle with
young Absalom for my sake." All the soldiers
heard as the king gave commands to the various
leaders with regard to Absalom.

Defeat of Absalom's Forces

[6] David's army then took the field against Is-
rael, and a battle was fought in the forest near
Mahanaim. [7] The forces of Israel were defeated
by David's servants, and the casualties there that
day were heavy—twenty thousand men. [8] The
battle spread out over that entire region, and the
forest consumed more combatants that day than
did the sword.

Death of Absalom

[9] Absalom unexpectedly came up against Da-
vid's servants. He was mounted on a mule, and,
as the mule passed under the branches of a large
oak tree, his hair caught fast in the tree. He hung
between heaven and earth while the mule under
him kept going. [10] Someone saw this and re-
ported to Joab, "I saw Absalom hanging from an
oak tree." [11] Joab said to the man who told him
this: "If you saw him, why did you not strike him
to the ground on the spot? Then it would have
been my duty to give you fifty pieces of silver and
a belt." [12] But the man replied to Joab: "Even if
I already held a thousand pieces of silver in my
two hands, I would not lay a hand on the king's
son, for in our hearing the king gave you and
Abishai and Ittai a command: 'Protect the youth
Absalom for my sake.' [13] Had I been disloyal and
killed him, it would all have come out before
the king, and you would stand aloof." [14] Joab
replied, "I will not waste time with you in this
way." And taking three pikes in hand, he thrust
for the heart of Absalom. He was still alive in the
tree.* [15] When ten of Joab's young armor-bearers
closed in on Absalom, and killed him with fur-
ther blows, [16] Joab then sounded the horn, and
the soldiers turned back from the pursuit of

17:23 2 Sm 15:31; 16:23.
17:25 2 Sm 19:14; 20:4–13.
17:27 2 Sm 9:4; 19:32; 1 Kgs 2:7; Ezr 2:61.
18:14 2 Sm 12:10; 13:28–29.

Live It!

Surviving Grief

It is a cold winter day when the state trooper comes to the door with the news that James Washington has just lost his son in an automobile accident. James falls to the ground in utter pain. Michael was just sixteen years old. James weeps as the trooper helps him up; the young officer begins to cry as he thinks of his own son, just three years old.

There is no greater loss for parents than the death of a child. In 2 Samuel 19:1, King David is devastated by the death of his son Absalom, despite Absalom's betrayal. There is no easy answer or explanation when someone we love dies. How could God allow this? It is too hard to understand. What helps is to allow ourselves to mourn like David and to place ourselves in God's healing hands.

Life continues. Joab challenges David not to forget the people who have served him faithfully and count on his leadership (see verses 6–8). In our grief, we must not forget the family and friends who grieve with us. We need them, and they need us to heal the pain of loss.

▶ 2 Sm 19:1–9

the Israelites, because Joab called them to halt.
17 They took Absalom and cast him into a deep
pit in the forest, and built up a very large mound
of stones over him. And all the Israelites fled to
their own tents.*
18 During his lifetime Absalom had taken a
pillar and set it up for himself in the King's Valley,
for he said, "I have no son to perpetuate my
name." The pillar which he named for himself is
called Absalom's Monument to the present day.*

David Told of Absalom's Death

19 Then Ahimaaz, son of Zadok, said, "Let
me run to take the good news to the king that
the LORD has set him free from the power of
his enemies." 20 But Joab said to him: "You are
not the man to bring the news today. On some
other day you may take the good news, but today
you would not be bringing good news, for
in fact the king's son is dead." 21 Then Joab said
to a Cushite, "Go, tell the king what you have
seen." The Cushite bowed to Joab and ran off.
22 But Ahimaaz, son of Zadok, said to Joab again,
"Come what may, permit me also to run after the
Cushite." Joab replied: "Why do you want to run,
my son? You will receive no reward." 23 But he
insisted, "Come what may, I want to run." Joab
said to him, "Run." Ahimaaz took the way of the
Jordan plain and outran the Cushite.
24 Now David was sitting between the two
gates, and a lookout mounted to the roof of the
gate above the city wall, where he looked out
and saw a man running all alone. 25 The lookout
shouted to inform the king, who said, "If he is
alone, he has good news to report." As he kept
coming nearer, 26 the lookout spied another runner.
From his place atop the gate he cried out,
"There is another man running by himself." And
the king responded, "He, too, is bringing good
news." 27 Then the lookout said, "I notice that the
first one runs like Ahimaaz, son of Zadok." The
king replied, "He is a good man; he comes with
good news."* 28 Then Ahimaaz called out and
greeted the king. With face to the ground he paid
homage to the king and said, "Blessed be the LORD
your God, who has delivered up the men who
rebelled against my lord the king." 29 But the king
asked, "Is young Absalom safe?" And Ahimaaz replied,
"I saw a great disturbance when the king's
servant Joab sent your servant on, but I do not
know what it was." 30 The king said, "Step aside
and remain in attendance here." So he stepped
aside and remained there. 31 When the Cushite
came in, he said, "Let my lord the king receive the
good news that this day the LORD has freed you
from the power of all who rose up against you."
32 But the king asked the Cushite, "Is young Absalom
all right?" The Cushite replied, "May the enemies
of my lord the king and all who rebel against
you with evil intent be as that young man!"

19 1 The king was shaken, and went up to the
room over the city gate and wept. He said
as he wept, "My son Absalom! My son, my son
Absalom! If only I had died instead of you, Absalom,
my son, my son!"

Joab Reproves David

2 Joab was told, "The king is weeping and
mourning for Absalom," 3 and that day's victory

* 18:17 Jos 7:26; 8:29; 10:27.
18:18 2 Sm 14:27.
18:27 2 Kgs 9:20.

was turned into mourning for the whole army
when they heard, "The king is grieving for his
son." 4 The soldiers stole into the city that day
like men shamed by flight in battle. 5 Meanwhile
the king covered his face and cried out in a loud
voice, "My son Absalom! Absalom! My son, my
son!"* 6 So Joab went to the king's residence and
said: "Though they saved your life and your sons'
and daughters' lives, and the lives of your wives
and your concubines, you have put all your ser-
vants to shame today 7 by loving those who hate
you and hating those who love you. For you have
announced today that officers and servants are
nothing to you. Indeed I am now certain that if
Absalom were alive today and all of us dead, that
would be fine with you. 8 Now then, get up! Go
out and speak kindly to your servants. I swear by
the LORD that if you do not go out, not a single
man will remain with you overnight, and this
will be a far greater disaster for you than any that
has come upon you from your youth until now."
9 So the king got up and sat at the gate. When all
the people were told, "The king is sitting at the
gate," they came into his presence.

The Reconciliation

Now the Israelites had fled to their separate
tents, 10 but throughout the tribes of Israel all the
people were arguing among themselves, saying
to one another: "The king delivered us from the
grasp of our enemies, and it was he who rescued
us from the grasp of the Philistines. Now, he has
fled the country before Absalom, 11 but Absalom,
whom we anointed over us, has died in battle.
Why, then, should you remain silent about re-
storing the king to his palace?" When the talk of
all Israel reached the king, 12 David sent word to
the priests Zadok and Abiathar: "Say to the elders
of Judah: 'Why should you be last to restore the
king to his palace? 13 You are my brothers, you
are my bone and flesh. Why should you be last
to restore the king?' 14 Also say to Amasa: 'Are you
not my bone and flesh? May God do thus to me,
and more, if you do not become commander of
my army permanently in place of Joab.' "* 15 He
won the hearts of the Judahites all together, and
so they sent a message to the king: "Return, with
all your servants."

David and Shimei

16 So the king returned, and when he reached
the Jordan, Judah had come to Gilgal to meet him
and to bring him across the Jordan. 17 Shimei,
son of Gera, the Benjaminite from Bahurim,
hurried down with the Judahites to meet King
David,* 18 accompanied by a thousand men from
Benjamin. Ziba, too, the servant of the house
of Saul, accompanied by his fifteen sons and
twenty servants, hastened to the Jordan before
the king.* 19 * They crossed over the ford to bring
the king's household over and to do whatever
he wished. When Shimei, son of Gera, crossed
the Jordan, he fell down before the king 20 and
said to him: "May my lord not hold me guilty;
do not remember or take to heart the wrong that
your servant did the day my lord the king left
Jerusalem. 21 For your servant knows that I have
done wrong. But I now am the first of the whole
house of Joseph to come down today to meet
my lord the king." 22 But Abishai, son of Zeruiah,
countered: "Shimei must be put to death for this.
He cursed the anointed of the LORD." 23 David
replied: "What has come between you and me,
sons of Zeruiah, that you would become my ad-
versaries this day? Should anyone die today in
Israel? Am I not aware that today I am king over
Israel?"* 24 Then the king said to Shimei, "You
shall not die." And the king gave him his oath.

David and Meribbaal

25 Meribbaal, son of Saul, also went down to
meet the king. He had not cared for his feet nor
trimmed his mustache nor washed his clothes
from the day the king left until he returned
safely. 26 When he came from Jerusalem to meet
the king, the king asked him, "Why did you not
go with me, Meribbaal?"* 27 He replied: "My lord
king, my servant deceived me. For your servant
said to him, 'Saddle the donkey for me, that I
may ride on it and go with the king'; your servant
is lame.* 28 But he slandered your servant before
my lord the king. But my lord the king is like an
angel of God. Do whatever seems good to you.
29 For though my father's entire house deserved
only death from my lord the king, yet you placed
your servant among those who eat at your table.
What right do I still have to make further appeal
to the king?"* 30 But the king said to him: "Why
do you go on talking? I say, 'You and Ziba shall
divide the property.' "* 31 Meribbaal answered
the king, "Indeed let him take it all, now that my
lord the king has returned safely to his house."

David and Barzillai

32 Barzillai the Gileadite also came down from
Rogelim and escorted the king to the Jordan for

19:5 2 Sm 15:30.
19:14 2 Sm 17:25; 20:4.
19:17 2 Sm 16:5–13.
19:18 2 Sm 16:1–4; 19:25–31.
19:19–24 2 Sm 16:13; Ex 22:27; 1 Kgs 2:8–9.
19:23 2 Sm 16:9–10; 1 Sm 11:13; 1 Kgs 2:8–9, 36–46.
19:26 2 Sm 16:3.
19:27 2 Sm 9:2–13.
19:29 2 Sm 9:9–11.
19:30 2 Sm 16:4.

his crossing, taking leave of him at the Jordan.*
33 It was Barzillai, a very old man of eighty, who
had provided for the king during his stay in Ma-
hanaim; he was a very great man. 34 The king said
to Barzillai, "Cross over with me, and I will pro-
vide for your old age as my guest in Jerusalem."
35 But Barzillai answered the king: "How much
longer have I to live, that I should go up to Jeru-
salem with the king? 36 I am now eighty years old.
Can I distinguish between good and evil? Can
your servant taste what he eats and drinks, or still
hear the voices of men and women singers? Why
should your servant be any further burden to my
lord the king? 37 In escorting the king across the
Jordan, your servant is doing little enough! Why
should the king give me this reward? 38 Please let
your servant go back to die in my own city by
the tomb of my father and mother. Here is your
servant Chimham. Let him cross over with my
lord the king. Do for him whatever seems good
to you." 39 Then the king said to him, "Chimham
shall cross over with me, and for him I will do
whatever seems good to you. And anything else
you would like me to do for you, I will do."
40 Then all the people crossed over the Jordan but
the king remained; he kissed Barzillai and bade
him farewell as he returned to his own place.
41 Finally the king crossed over to Gilgal, accom-
panied by Chimham.

Israel and Judah Quarrel

All of the people of Judah and half of the peo-
ple of Israel had escorted the king across. 42 But
then all these Israelites began coming to the king
and saying, "Why did our brothers the Judahites
steal you away and bring the king and his house-
hold across the Jordan, along with all David's
men?" 43 All the Judahites replied to the men of
Israel: "Because the king is our relative. Why are
you angry over this? Have we had anything to
eat at the king's expense? Or have portions from
his table been given to us?" 44 The Israelites an-
swered the Judahites: "We have ten shares in the
king. Also, we are the firstborn† rather than you.
Why do you slight us? Were we not first to speak
of restoring our king?" Then the Judahites in turn
spoke even more fiercely than the Israelites.*

Sheba's Rebellion

20 1 Now a scoundrel named Sheba, the son
of Bichri, a Benjaminite, happened to be
there. He sounded the horn and cried out,

"We have no share in David,
nor any heritage in the son of Jesse.
Everyone to your tents, O Israel!"*

2 So all the Israelites left David to follow Sheba,
son of Bichri. But the Judahites, from the Jor-
dan to Jerusalem, remained loyal to their king.
3 David came to his house in Jerusalem, and
the king took the ten concubies whom he had
left behind to care for the palace and placed
them under guard. He provided for them, but
never again saw them. And so they remained
shut away to the day of their death, lifelong
widows.*

Amasa's Death

4 Then the king said to Amasa: "Summon the
Judahites for me within three days. Then pre-
sent yourself here."* 5 Accordingly Amasa set
out to summon Judah, but delayed beyond the
time set for him. 6 Then David said to Abishai:
"Sheba, son of Bichri, may now do us more
harm than Absalom did. Take your lord's ser-
vants and pursue him, lest he find fortified
cities and take shelter while we look on." 7 So
Joab and the Cherethites and Pelethites and all
the warriors marched out behind Abishai from
Jerusalem to campaign in pursuit of Sheba, son
of Bichri.* 8 † They were at the great stone in
Gibeon when Amasa met them. Now Joab had
a belt over his tunic, from which was slung
a sword in its sheath at his thigh; the sword
would slide out downwards.* 9 Joab asked Am-
asa, "Is everything all right, my brother?" and
with his right hand held Amasa's beard as if
to kiss him. 10 And since Amasa was not on his
guard against the sword in Joab's other hand,
Joab stabbed him in the abdomen with it, so
that his entrails burst forth to the ground, and
he died; there was no second thrust. Then Joab
and Abishai his brother pursued Sheba, son of
Bichri.* 11 One of Joab's attendants stood by
Amasa and said, "Let him who favors Joab and
is for David follow Joab." 12 Amasa lay covered
with blood in the middle of the highroad, and
the man noticed that all the soldiers were stop-
ping. So he rolled Amasa away from the road
to the field and spread a garment over him, be-
cause he saw how all who came upon him were
stopping. 13 When he had been removed from
the road, everyone went on after Joab in pursuit
of Sheba, son of Bichri.

†
19:44 The firstborn had special rights over the other siblings.
20:8 The text of this verse is quite uncertain.

19:32 2 Sm 17:27–29; 1 Kgs 2:7; Ezr 2:61.
19:44 1 Kgs 11:31.
20:1 1 Kgs 12:16.
20:3 2 Sm 15:16; 16:20–22.
20:4 2 Sm 17:25; 19:14.
20:7 2 Sm 8:18.
20:8 2 Sm 2:13.
20:10 1 Kgs 2:5.

Joab Pursues Sheba

14 Sheba had passed through all the tribes of
Israel to Abel Beth-maacah. Then all the Bich-
rites assembled and they too entered the city
after him. 15 So all Joab's troops came and be-
sieged him in Abel Beth-maacah. They built up
a mound against the city, so that it stood against
the rampart, and were battering the wall to knock
it down. 16 Then a wise woman from the city
called out, "Listen, listen! Tell Joab, 'Come here,
so I can speak with you.'" 17 When Joab had
come near her, the woman said, "Are you Joab?"
And he replied, "Yes." She said to him, "Listen to
what your servant has to say." He replied, "I am
listening." 18 Then she went on to say: "There is a
saying from long ago,† 'Let them ask if they will
in Abel or in Dan whether loyalty is finished 19 or
ended in Israel.' You are seeking to batter down
a city that is a mother in Israel. Why do you wish
to swallow up the heritage of the LORD?"* 20 Joab
answered, "Not at all, not at all! I do not wish to
swallow or batter anything. 21 That is not the case
at all. A man from the hill country of Ephraim,
whose name is Sheba, son of Bichri, has rebelled
against King David. Give him up, just him, and
I will withdraw from the city." Then the woman
said to Joab, "His head shall be thrown to you
across the wall." 22 In her wisdom, the woman
went to all the people, and they cut off the head
of Sheba, son of Bichri, and threw it out to Joab.
He then sounded the horn, and they scattered
from the city to their own tents, while Joab re-
turned to Jerusalem to the king.

David's Officials

23 Joab was in command of the whole army of
Israel. Benaiah, son of Jehoiada, was in command
of the Cherethites and Pelethites.* 24 Adoram was
in charge of the forced labor. Jehoshaphat, son of
Ahilud, was the chancellor. 25 Shawsha was the
scribe. Zadok and Abiathar were priests.* 26 Ira
the Jairite was also David's priest.

V. Appendixes

Gibeonite Vengeance

21 1 In David's time there was a famine for
three years, year after year. David sought
the presence of the LORD, who said: There is
bloodguilt on Saul and his family because he put
the Gibeonites to death.* 2 So the king called the
Gibeonites and spoke to them. (Now the Gib-
eonites were not Israelites, but survivors of the
Amorites; and although the Israelites had given
them their oath, Saul had sought to kill them
off in his zeal for the Israelites and for Judah.)*
3 David said to the Gibeonites, "What must I do
for you and how must I make atonement, that
you may bless the heritage of the LORD?" 4 The
Gibeonites answered him, "We have no claim
against Saul and his house for silver or gold,
nor is it our place to put anyone to death in Is-
rael." Then he said, "I will do for you whatever
you propose." 5 They said to the king, "As for
the man who was exterminating us and who
intended to destroy us that we might have no
place in all the territory of Israel, 6 let seven men
from among his descendants be given to us, that
we may execute them before the LORD in Gibeon,
on the LORD's mountain." The king replied, "I
will give them up." 7 The king, however, spared
Meribbaal, son of Jonathan, son of Saul, because
of the LORD's oath that formed a bond between
David and Saul's son Jonathan.* 8 But the king
took Armoni and Meribbaal, the two sons that
Aiah's daughter Rizpah had borne to Saul, and
the five sons of Saul's daughter Merob that she
had borne to Adriel, son of Barzillai the Meho-
lathite,* 9 and delivered them into the power of
the Gibeonites, who then executed them on the
mountain before the LORD. The seven fell at the
one time; they were put to death during the first
days of the harvest—that is, at the beginning of
the barley harvest.

10 Then Rizpah, Aiah's daughter, took sackcloth
and spread it out for herself on the rock from the
beginning of the harvest until rain came down
on them from the heavens, fending off the birds
of the heavens from settling on them by day,
and the wild animals by night.* 11 When David
was informed of what Rizpah, Aiah's daughter,
the concubine of Saul, had done, 12 he went and
obtained the bones of Saul and of his son Jona-
than from the citizens of Jabesh-gilead, who had
stolen them away secretly from the public square
of Beth-shan, where the Philistines had hanged
them at the time they defeated Saul on Gilboa.*
13 When he had brought up from there the bones
of Saul and of his son Jonathan, the bones of
those who had been executed were also gathered
up. 14 Then the bones of Saul and of his son Jon-
athan were buried in the land of Benjamin, at
Zela, in the tomb of his father Kish. After all that

---

† **20:18–19** This proverbial expression is obscure but seems to reflect a tradition that this Danite town was associated with oracles or other sorts of revelation. Cf. Mt 16:13–17; and the intertestamental *Testament of Levi* 2:3.

20:19 Gn 49:16.
20:23 2 Sm 8:16–18; 23:20.
20:25 2 Sm 8:17–18.
21:1 2 Sm 24:13.
21:2 Jos 9:3–27.
21:7 2 Sm 9:13; 1 Sm 18:3; 20:8–10, 15–16, 42.
21:8 2 Sm 3:7.
21:10 2 Sm 3:31; 12:16.
21:12 1 Sm 31:10–13.

Live It!

The Lord Is My Rock

Build on the rock! What exactly does that mean? Have you ever watched a house being built? One of the first things a contractor does is level the ground and put in a foundation. Upon the foundation, the structure begins to grow. A solid foundation will enable that house to stand for many years.

The same goes for our lives, both personally and communally. What is the foundation—the rock—that your life is built on? In 2 Samuel 22:2, King David says to the Lord, "[You are] my rock, my fortress, my deliverer." David built his life on the rock and foundation of the Lord. As a result, he found refuge in times of fear. It was this rock that saved David and the people of Israel from the hands of their enemies. Because of David's reliance on God, his kingdom is seen by later generations of Jews as the ideal kingdom for Israel.

You too can find this same refuge, this same saving grace. Starting today, build your life with the Lord as your foundation (see Mt 7:24–27). The next time you face a battle, be it drugs or envy or anger or lust, stand on the rock!

▶ **2 Sm 22:1–4**

the king commanded had been carried out, God granted relief to the land.*

Exploits in Philistine Wars

15 There was another battle between the Philistines and Israel. David went down with his servants and fought the Philistines, but David
grew tired. 16 Dadu, a descendant of the Rephaim, whose bronze spear weighed three hundred shekels, was about to take him captive. Dadu was girt with a new sword and thought he would kill David,
17 but Abishai, son of Zeruiah, came to help him, and struck and killed the Philistine. Then David's men swore to him, "You must not go out to battle with us again, lest you quench the lamp of Israel."*
18 * After this, there was another battle with the Philistines, in Gob. On that occasion Sibbecai the Hushathite struck down Saph, a descendant of the Rephaim.*
19 * There was another battle with the Philistines, in Gob, and Elhanan, son of Jair from Bethlehem, killed Goliath of Gath, whose spear shaft was like a weaver's beam.
20 There was another battle, at Gath, and there was a giant, who had six fingers on each hand and six toes on each foot—twenty-four in all. He too was descended from the Rephaim.
21 And when he insulted Israel, Jonathan, son of David's brother Shimei, struck him down.*
22 These four were descended from the Rephaim in Gath, and they fell at the hands of David and his servants.

Song of Thanksgiving†

22 1 David proclaimed the words of this song to the LORD when the LORD had rescued him from the grasp of all his enemies and from the grasp of Saul.*
2 He said:*

O LORD, my rock, my fortress, my deliverer,
3 my God, my rock of refuge!
My shield, my saving horn,†
my stronghold, my refuge,
my savior, from violence you keep me safe.*
4 Praised be the LORD, I exclaim!
I have been delivered from my enemies.

5 The breakers of death surged round about me,
the menacing floods† terrified me;
6 The cords of Sheol tightened;
the snares of death lay in wait for me.
7 In my distress I called out: LORD!
I cried out to my God;

† **22:1–51** This psalm of thanksgiving also appears in the Psalter, with a few small variants, as Ps 18. In both places it is attributed to David. Two main sections can be distinguished. In the first part, after an introductory stanza of praise to God (vv. 2–4), the writer describes the peril he was in (vv. 5–7), and then poetically depicts, under the form of a theophany, God's intervention in his behalf (vv. 8–20), concluding with an acknowledgment of God's justice (vv. 21–31). In the second part, God is praised for having prepared the psalmist for war (vv. 32–35), given him victory over his enemies (vv. 36–39), whom he put to flight (vv. 40–43), and bestowed on him dominion over many peoples (vv. 44–46). The entire song ends with an expression of grateful praise (vv. 47–51).

22:3 *My saving horn*: my strong savior. The horn, such as that of an enraged bull, was a symbol of strength; cf. Lk 1:69.

22:5–6 *Breakers . . . floods*: traditional Old Testament imagery for lethal danger, from which the Lord is uniquely able to rescue; cf. Ps 69:2, 15–16; 89:10–11; Jon 2:3–6.

* **21:14** 2 Sm 24:25. **21:17** 1 Kgs 11:36; 15:4; 2 Kgs 8:19. **21:18–22** 1 Chr 20:4–8. **21:18** 2 Sm 23:27. **21:19–20** 1 Sm 17:4, 7. **21:21** 2 Sm 13:3. **22:1** Ps 18:1. **22:2–51** Ps 18:3–51. **22:3** 1 Sm 2:1–2.

From his temple† he heard my voice,
my cry reached his ears.
8 The earth rocked and shook;†
the foundations of the heavens trembled;
they shook as his wrath flared up.
9 Smoke rose in his nostrils,
a devouring fire from his mouth;
it kindled coals into flame.
10 He parted the heavens and came down,
a dark cloud under his feet.*
11 Mounted on a cherub† he flew,
borne along on the wings of the wind.*
12 He made darkness the cover about him,
a mass of water, heavy thunderheads.
13 From the brightness of his presence
coals were kindled to flame.
14 The LORD thundered from heaven;
the Most High made his voice resound.
15 He let fly arrows and scattered them;
lightning, and dispersed them.*
16 Then the bed of the sea appeared;
the world's foundations lay bare,
At the roar of the LORD,
at the storming breath of his nostrils.*
17 He reached down from on high and
seized me,
drew me out of the deep waters.*
18 He rescued me from my mighty enemy,
from foes too powerful for me.
19 They attacked me on a day of distress,
but the LORD came to my support.
20 He set me free in the open;
he rescued me because he loves me.

21 The LORD acknowledged my righteousness;
rewarded my clean hands.
22 For I kept the ways of the LORD;
I was not disloyal to my God.
23 His laws were all before me,
his decrees I did not cast aside.
24 I was honest toward him;
I was on guard against sin.
25 So the LORD rewarded my righteousness,
the cleanness of my hands in his sight.
26 *Toward the faithful you are faithful;†
to the honest you are honest;
27 Toward the sincere you are sincere;
but to the perverse you are devious.
28 Humble people you save,
though on the haughty your eyes look
down.
29 You are my lamp, O LORD!
My God brightens the darkness about me.
30 With you I can rush an armed band,
with my God to help I can leap a wall.
31 God's way is unerring;
the LORD's promise is tried and true;
he is a shield for all who trust in him.*

32 Truly, who is God except the LORD?
Who but our God is the rock?
33 This God who girded me with might,
kept my way unerring,
34 Who made my feet swift as a deer's,
set me safe on the heights,*
35 Who trained my hands for war,
my arms to bend even a bow of bronze.

36 You have given me your protecting shield,
and your help has made me great.
37 You gave me room to stride;
my feet never stumbled.
38 I pursued my enemies and overtook them;
I did not turn back till I destroyed them.
39 I struck them down, and they did not rise;
they fell dead at my feet.
40 You girded me with strength for war;
subdued adversaries at my feet.
41 My foes you put to flight before me;
those who hated me I destroyed.
42 They cried for help, but no one saved them,
cried to the LORD but got no answer.
43 I ground them fine as the dust of the earth;
like mud in the streets I trod them down.
44 You rescued me from the strife of my people;
you made me head over nations.
A people I had not known became my slaves;
45 Foreigners cringed before me;
as soon as they heard of me they obeyed.
46 Their courage failed;
they came trembling from their fortresses.
47 The LORD lives! Blessed be my rock!
Exalted be God, the rock of my salvation.

†

22:7 *His temple*: his heavenly abode.

22:8–10 The Lord's coming is depicted by means of a storm theophany, including earthquake (vv. 8, 16) and thunderstorm (vv. 9–15); cf. Jgs 5:4–5; Ps 29; 97:2–6; Hb 3.

22:11 *Mounted on a cherub*: in the traditional storm theophany, as here, the Lord appears with thunder, lightning, earthquake, rain, darkness, cloud, and wind. Sometimes these are represented as his retinue; sometimes he is said to ride upon the clouds or "the wings of the wind" (Ps 104:3). The parallelism in v. 11 suggests that the winged creatures called cherubim are imagined as bearing the Lord aloft. In the iconography of the ark of the covenant, the Lord was "enthroned upon the cherubim"; cf. Ex 37:7–9; 1 Sm 4:4; 2 Sm 6:2; 2 Kgs 19:15; Ps 80:2; 99:1.

22:26–27 People are treated by God in the same way they treat him and other people.

*

22:10 Ps 144:5.
22:11 Ex 25:18–22.
22:15 Ps 144:6.
22:16 Ex 15:8.
22:17 Ps 144:7.
22:26–27 1 Sm 2:30.
22:31 Prv 30:5.
22:34 Ps 62:3; Hb 3:19.

48 O God who granted me vindication,
subdued peoples under me,
49 and helped me escape from my enemies,
Truly you have exalted me above my
adversaries,
from the violent you have rescued me.
50 Thus I will proclaim you, LORD, among the
nations;
I will sing the praises of your name.*
51 You have given great victories to your king,
and shown kindness to your anointed,
to David and his posterity forever.

The Last Words of David†

23 [1]These are the last words of David:

The oracle of David, son of Jesse;
the oracle of the man God raised up,
Anointed of the God of Jacob,
favorite of the Mighty One of Israel.*
2 The spirit of the LORD spoke through me;
his word was on my tongue.*
3 The God of Israel spoke;
of me the Rock of Israel said,
"One who rules over humankind with justice,
who rules in the fear of God,*
4 Is like the light at sunrise
on a cloudless morning,
making the land's vegetation glisten after
rain."*
5 Is not my house firm before God?
He has made an eternal covenant with me,
set forth in detail and secured.*
Will he not bring to fruition
all my salvation and my every desire?
6 But the wicked are all like thorns to be cast
away;
they cannot be taken up by hand.*
7 One wishing to touch them
must be armed with iron or the shaft of a
spear.
They must be utterly consumed by fire.

David's Warriors

[8]These are the names of David's warriors.† Ishbaal, the son of Hachamoni, chief of the Three. He brandished his spear over eight hundred whom he had slain in a single encounter.* [9]Next to him was Eleazar, the son of Dodo the Ahohite, one of the Three warriors with David at Ephes-dammim, when they insulted the Philistines who had massed there for battle. The Israelites had retreated,* [10]but he stood there and struck down the Philistines until his hand grew tired from clutching the sword. The LORD brought about a great victory on that day; the army turned back to rejoin Eleazar, but only to strip the slain. [11]Next to him was Shammah, son of Agee the Hararite. The Philistines had assembled at Lehi, where there was a plot of land full of lentils. The people were fleeing before the Philistines,* [12]but he took his stand in the middle of the plot, kept it safe, and cut down the Philistines. Thus the LORD brought about a great victory. Such deeds as these the Three warriors performed.

[13]Three of the Thirty chiefs went down to David in the cave of Adullam during the harvest, while a Philistine clan was encamped in the Valley of Rephaim.* [14]David was then in the stronghold, and there was a garrison of Philistines in Bethlehem. [15]Now David had a craving and said, "If only someone would give me a drink of water from the cistern by the gate of Bethlehem!" [16]Thereupon the three warriors broke through the encampment of the Philistines, drew water from the cistern by the gate of Bethlehem, and carried it back to David. But he refused to drink it, and instead poured it out† to the LORD, [17]saying: "The LORD forbid that I do such a thing! Could I drink the blood of these men who went at the risk of their lives?" So he refused to drink it.

[18]Abishai, the brother of Joab, son of Zeruiah, was the chief of the Thirty; he brandished his spear over three hundred whom he had slain. He made a name among the Thirty, [19]but was more famous than any of the Thirty, becoming their leader. However, he did not attain to the Three.

[20]Benaiah, son of Jehoiada, a valiant man of mighty deeds, from Kabzeel, killed the two sons of Ariel of Moab. Also, he went down and killed the lion in the cistern on a snowy day.* [21]He likewise slew an Egyptian, a huge man. The Egyptian carried a spear, but Benaiah came against him with a staff; he wrested the spear from the Egyptian's hand, and killed him with

†

23:1–7 *The last words of David*: the text of this short composition is difficult in places; it views David's career in retrospect.

23:8–39 There are thirty-seven warriors in all named in this list. First there are the Three warriors most noted for single-handed exploits (vv. 8–12). Then comes the story of a daring adventure by three unnamed members of the larger group of the Thirty (vv. 13–17). Next come the commanders of the king's bodyguard, Abishai (vv. 18–19) and Benaiah (vv. 20–23), with whom must be counted Asahel (v. 24) and Joab (vv. 18, 24, 37), and finally the group of the Thirty (vv. 24–39).

23:16 *Poured it out*: as a libation.

*

22:50 Ps 22:23; Rom 15:9.
23:1 1 Kgs 2:1–9; Sir 47:8.
23:2 Is 59:21; Jer 1:9.
23:3 Ps 72:1–4.
23:4 Jgs 5:31; Ps 72:6.
23:5 2 Sm 7:11, 15–16; Ps 89:30; Is 55:3.
23:6 Dt 13:14.
23:8–39 1 Chr 11:11–41; 27:1–15.
23:9 1 Sm 17:1.
23:11 Jgs 15:9.
23:13 1 Sm 22:1; Mi 1:15.
23:20 2 Sm 8:18; 20:23; Jgs 14:6; 1 Kgs 2:29–30.

that spear. 22 Such deeds as these Benaiah, the
son of Jehoiada, performed; and he made a
name among the Thirty warriors 23 but was more
famous than any of the Thirty. However, he did
not attain to the Three. David put him in charge
of his bodyguard.* 24 Asahel,* brother of Joab,
was among the Thirty; Elhanan, son of Dodo,
from Bethlehem; 25 Shammah, from En-harod;
Elika, from En-harod; 26 Helez, from Beth-pelet;
Ira, son of Ikkesh, from Tekoa; 27 Abiezer, from
Anathoth; Sibbecai, from Husha;* 28 Zalmon,
from Ahoh; Maharai, from Netophah; 29 He-
led, son of Baanah, from Netophah; Ittai, son
of Ribai, from Gibeah of Benjamin; 30 Benaiah,
from Pirathon; Hiddai, from the valley of Gaash;
31 Abibaal, from Beth-arabah; Azmaveth, from
Bahurim; 32 Eliahba, from Shaalbon; Jashen the
Gunite; Jonathan, 33 son of Shammah the Hara-
rite; Ahiam, son of Sharar the Hararite; 34 Eliph-
elet, son of Ahasbai, from Beth-maacah; Eliam,
son of Ahithophel, from Gilo; 35 Hezrai, from
Carmel; Paarai the Arbite; 36 Igal, son of Nathan,
from Zobah; Bani the Gadite; 37 Zelek the Am-
monite; Naharai, from Beeroth, the armor-bearer
of Joab, son of Zeruiah; 38 Ira, from Jattir; Gareb,
from Jattir; 39 Uriah the Hittite—thirty-seven in
all.*

David's Census; the Plague

24 1 The LORD's anger against Israel flared
again,* and he incited David against
them: "Go, take a census of Israel and Judah."
2 The king therefore said to Joab and the lead-
ers of the army who were with him, "Tour all
the tribes of Israel from Dan to Beer-sheba and
register the people, that I may know their num-
ber." 3 But Joab replied to the king: "May the
LORD your God increase the number of people a
hundredfold for my lord the king to see it with
his own eyes. But why does it please my lord to
do a thing of this kind?" 4 However, the king's
command prevailed over Joab and the leaders of
the army, so they left the king's presence in or-
der to register the people of Israel. 5 Crossing the
Jordan, they began near Aroer, south of the city
in the wadi, and turned in the direction of Gad
toward Jazer. 6 They continued on to Gilead and
to the district below Mount Hermon. Then they
proceeded to Dan; from there they turned toward
Sidon, 7 going to the fortress of Tyre and to all the
cities of the Hivites and Canaanites, and ending
up in the Negeb of Judah, at Beer-sheba. 8 Thus
they toured the whole land, reaching Jerusalem
again after nine months and twenty days. 9 Joab
then reported the census figures to the king: of
men capable of wielding a sword, there were in
Israel eight hundred thousand, and in Judah five
hundred thousand.
10 Afterward, however, David regretted having
numbered the people. David said to the LORD:
"I have sinned grievously in what I have done.*
Take away, LORD, your servant's guilt, for I have
acted very foolishly."† 11 When David rose in
the morning, the word of the LORD came to the
prophet Gad, David's seer, saying: 12 Go, tell Da-
vid: Thus says the LORD: I am offering you three
options; choose one of them, and I will give you
that. 13 Gad then went to David to inform him.
He asked: "Should three years of famine come
upon your land; or three months of fleeing from
your enemy while he pursues you; or is it to be
three days of plague in your land? Now consider
well: what answer am I to give to him who sent
me?"* 14 David answered Gad: "I am greatly
distressed. But let us fall into the hand of God,
whose mercy is great, rather than into human
hands." 15 Thus David chose the plague. At the
time of the wheat harvest it broke out among the
people. The LORD sent plague over Israel from
morning until the time appointed, and from Dan
to Beer-sheba seventy thousand of the people
died. 16 But when the angel stretched forth his
hand toward Jerusalem to destroy it, the LORD
changed his mind about the calamity, and said
to the angel causing the destruction among the
people: Enough now! Stay your hand.* The an-
gel of the LORD was then standing at the threshing
floor of Araunah the Jebusite.* 17 When David
saw the angel who was striking the people, he
said to the LORD: "It is I who have sinned; it is I,
the shepherd, who have done wrong. But these
sheep, what have they done? Strike me and my
father's family!"

David Offers Sacrifices

18 On the same day Gad went to David and
said to him, "Go and set up an altar to the LORD
on the threshing floor of Araunah the Jebusite."
19 According to Gad's word, David went up as the
LORD had commanded. 20 Now Araunah looked

† **24:10** The narrative supposes that since the people belonged to the Lord rather than to the king, only the Lord should know their exact number. Further, since such an exact numbering of the people would make it possible for the king to exercise centralized power, imposing taxation, conscription, and expropriation upon Israel, the story shares the view of monarchy found in 1 Sm 8:4–18. See also Nm 3:44–51, where census taking requires an apotropaic offering.

* **23:23** 1 Sm 22:14.
23:24 2 Sm 2:18–23.
23:27 2 Sm 21:18.
23:39 2 Sm 11:3.
24:1–25 1 Chr 21:1–27.
24:10 1 Sm 24:6; 1 Chr 21:7–8.
24:13 2 Sm 21:1.
24:16 Gn 6:6; Ex 32:14; 1 Chr 21:15; Jon 3:10.

down and saw the king and his servants coming
toward him while he was threshing wheat. So he
went out and bowed down before the king, his
face to the ground. 21 Then Araunah asked, "Why
does my lord the king come to his servant?"
David replied, "To buy the threshing floor from
you, to build an altar to the LORD, that the plague
may be withdrawn from the people." 22 * But
Araunah said to David: "Let my lord the king
take it and offer up what is good in his sight.
See, here are the oxen for burnt offerings, and
the threshing sledges and the yokes of oxen for
wood. 23 All this does Araunah give to the king."
Araunah then said to the king, "May the LORD
your God accept your offering." 24 The king, how-
ever, replied to Araunah, "No, I will buy it from
you at the proper price, for I cannot sacrifice to
the LORD my God burnt offerings that cost me
nothing." So David bought the threshing floor
and the oxen for fifty silver shekels. 25 Then Da-
vid built an altar to the LORD there, and sacrificed
burnt offerings and communion offerings. The
LORD granted relief to the land, and the plague
was withdrawn from Israel.

* **24:16** Ex 12:23; 2 Kgs 19:35. **24:22–23** 1 Sm 6:14; 1 Kgs 19:21.

The ancient Egyptians had an advanced civilization, yet today the remains of their handiwork lie buried under centuries of sand. The great Roman Empire spanned the Western world at the time of Jesus, yet today, only scattered ruins testify to its existence. The same is true of the glorious but short-lived Israelite kingdom. The Books of First and Second Kings trace its tragic collapse from the glories of Solomon's Temple to the Babylonian Exile.

In Depth

If the kingships of Saul and David could be described as the spring and summer of the Israelite kingdom, the Books of First and Second Kings describe its fall and winter. The beginning of First Kings covers the glorious late summer under King Solomon. Solomon accumulated great riches, constructed a beautiful Temple, and built Jerusalem into a city rivaling any other center of power. But the summer was quickly over at Solomon's death, when the kingdom was split in two (see map 3, "The Kingdom Years"). The northern kingdom, called Israel, and the southern kingdom, called Judah, were ruled by a succession of kings, most of whom proved to be weak and sinful leaders. Their incompetence had disastrous consequences: the two kingdoms fell to foreign powers. Israel fell to the Assyrians in 722 BC, and Judah to the Babylonians in 587 BC.

The sorrow we hear in First and Second Kings is accompanied by a clear explanation: the people have fallen because of their wickedness and the wickedness of their leaders. Not surprisingly, the author of First and Second Kings fashions the history of God's People into a kind of morality tale, emphasizing the importance of faithfulness to the covenant and the law.

Of special interest in these books is the appearance of the classical prophet. Unlike the prophets of other lands, who were mere tools in the ruler's hand, the great prophets of Israel and Judah, like Elijah and Elisha, often directly opposed royal decisions and actions. Their job was not to pamper the ruler's pride but to speak God's word clearly and boldly.

As we read about the terrible crises that the kingdoms of Judah and Israel faced, we can reflect on one of the basic truths of human history: Apart from God, there is no hope. Only one thing remains as history passes: God's promise.

At a Glance

I. **The Reign of Solomon (1 Kgs 1:1—11:43).**
II. **The Reign of Jeroboam (1 Kgs 12:1—14:20).**
III. **Kings of Judah and Israel (1 Kgs 14:21—16:34).**
IV. **The Story of Elijah (1 Kgs 17:1—19:21).**
V. **The Story of Ahab (1 Kgs 20:1—2 Kgs 1:18).**
VI. **Elisha Succeeds Elijah (2 Kgs 2:1–25).**
VII. **Stories of Elisha and Joram (2 Kgs 3:1—9:13).**
VIII. **The End of the Omrid Dynasty (2 Kgs 9:14—11:20).**
IX. **Kings of Judah and Israel (2 Kgs 12:1—17:5).**
X. **The End of Israel (2 Kgs 17:6–41).**
XI. **The End of Judah (2 Kgs 18:1—25:30).**

Quick Facts

Period Covered: from 961 to 587 BC
Inspired Author: unknown, from the Deuteronomic tradition
Theme: the history of Israel's and Judah's kings from Solomon until the fall of Jerusalem

The First and Second Books of Kings

1 Kings

I. The Reign of Solomon†

David's Old Age

1 [1] † When King David was old and advanced in
years, though they covered him with blankets
he could not get warm. [2] His servants therefore
said to him, "Let a young virgin be sought to at-
tend my lord the king,† and to nurse him. If she
sleeps with you, my lord the king will be warm."
[3] So they sought for a beautiful girl throughout
the territory of Israel, and found Abishag the
Shunamite. So they brought her to the king. [4] The
girl was very beautiful indeed, and she nursed the
king and took care of him. But the king did not
have relations with her.

Adonijah's Ambition

[5] Adonijah, son of Haggith, boasted, "I shall
be king!" and he provided himself with chariots,
horses, and a retinue of fifty to go before him.*
[6] Yet his father would never antagonize him by
asking, "Why are you doing this?" Adonijah was
also very handsome, and next in age to Absalom
by the same mother. [7] He consulted with Joab,
son of Zeruiah, and with Abiathar the priest, and
they became Adonijah's supporters. [8] However,
Zadok the priest, Benaiah, son of Jehoiada, Na-
than the prophet, Shimei and Rei, and David's
warriors did not support Adonijah.
[9] Adonijah slaughtered sheep, oxen, and fatlings
at the stone Zoheleth near En-rogel† and invited
all his brothers, the king's sons, and all the royal
officials of Judah; [10] but he did not invite Nathan
the prophet, or Benaiah, or the warriors, or Solo-
mon his brother.

Solomon Proclaimed King

[11] Then Nathan said to Bathsheba, Solomon's
mother: "Have you not heard that Adonijah, son
of Haggith, has become king, and our lord David
does not know? [12] Come now, let me advise you
so that you may save your life and the life of your
son Solomon. [13] Go, visit King David, and say to

1:1–11:43 The story of the reign of Solomon comprises twelve major units, organized concentrically. That is, the first unit (1:1–2:12a) balances the last (11:26–43), the second (2:12b–46) balances the second last (11:14–25), and so forth. (See the structural notes at the beginning of each major unit.) The center of the whole story is a diptych that narrates the construction of the Temple (6:1–7:51) and its dedication (8:1–9:10).

1:1–2:12a The first major unit of the Solomon story concludes the so-called Succession Narrative (2 Sm 9–20; 1 Kgs 1–2). This unit tells how Solomon, a younger son, came to succeed David on the throne of Israel through the intervention of the prophet Nathan. Compare the last unit of the Solomon story, 11:26–43, where the prophet Ahijah begins the process whereby Jeroboam becomes king of the northern tribes after Solomon's death. The story of Solomon's accession is itself concentrically arranged: David's decline, Adonijah's rise, Solomon's supporters, David's decision, Solomon's inauguration, Adonijah's fall, David's death. Chronicles has no developed parallel to this story (see 1 Chr 23:1).

1:2 The fulsome use of royal titles and the elaborate etiquette in the Succession Narrative suggest the raw ambition of the contending parties and the oppressive atmosphere of the court.

1:9 *En-rogel*: the modern Job's Well just southeast of Jerusalem. It marked the ancient boundary between the tribes of Benjamin and Judah (Jos 15:7; 18:16).

1:5 2 Sm 15:1.

him, 'Did you not, my lord king, swear to your
handmaid: Your son Solomon shall be king after
me; it is he who shall sit upon my throne? Why,
then, has Adonijah become king?' 14 And while
you are still there speaking to the king, I will
come in after you and confirm your words."
15 So Bathsheba visited the king in his room.
The king was very old, and Abishag the Shunamite
was caring for the king.† 16 Bathsheba bowed in
homage to the king. The king said to her, "What
do you wish?"† 17 She answered him: "My lord,
you swore to your servant by the LORD, your God,
'Solomon your son will be king after me; it is he
who shall sit upon my throne.' 18 But now Adoni-
jah has become king, and you, my lord king, do
not know it.† 19 He has sacrificed bulls, fatlings,
and sheep in great numbers; he has invited all
the king's sons, Abiathar the priest, and Joab, the
commander of the army, but not your servant
Solomon. 20 † Now, my lord king, all Israel is
looking to you to declare to them who is to sit
upon the throne of my lord the king after him.
21 If this is not done, when my lord the king rests
with his ancestors, I and my son Solomon will be
considered criminals."
22 While she was still speaking to the king, Na-
than the prophet came in. 23 They told the king,
"Nathan the prophet is here." He entered the
king's presence and did him homage, bowing
to the floor. 24 Then Nathan said: "My lord king,
did you say, 'Adonijah shall be king after me and
shall sit upon my throne'? 25 For today he went
down and sacrificed bulls, fatlings, and sheep
in great numbers; he invited all the king's sons,
the commanders of the army, and Abiathar the
priest, and even now they are eating and drink-
ing in his company and saying, 'Long live King
Adonijah!' 26 But me, your servant, he did not
invite; nor Zadok the priest, nor Benaiah, son
of Jehoiada, nor your servant Solomon. 27 If this
was done by order of my lord the king, you did
not tell me, your servant, who is to sit upon the
throne of my lord the king after him."
28 King David answered, "Call Bathsheba here."
When she entered the king's presence and stood
before him, 29 the king swore, "As the LORD lives,
who has redeemed my life from all distress,
30 this very day I will fulfill the oath I swore to
you by the LORD, the God of Israel, 'Your son Sol-
omon shall be king after me and shall sit upon
my throne in my place.' " 31 Bowing to the floor
in homage to the king, Bathsheba said, "May my
lord, King David, live forever!"
32 Then King David said, "Call Zadok the
priest, Nathan the prophet, and Benaiah, son
of Jehoiada." When they had entered the king's
presence, 33 he said to them: "Take with you the
royal officials. Mount my son Solomon upon
my own mule and escort him down to Gihon.
34 There Zadok the priest and Nathan the prophet
shall anoint him king over Israel, and you shall
blow the ram's horn and cry, 'Long live King Sol-
omon!' 35 When you come back up with him, he
is to go in and sit upon my throne. It is he that
shall be king in my place: him I designate ruler of
Israel and of Judah." 36 Benaiah, son of Jehoiada,
answered the king: "So be it! May the LORD, the
God of my lord the king, so decree! 37 As the LORD
has been with my lord the king, so may he be
with Solomon, and make his throne even greater
than that of my lord, King David!"
38 So Zadok the priest, Nathan the prophet,
Benaiah, son of Jehoiada, and the Cherethites
and Pelethites† went down, and mounting Sol-
omon on King David's mule, escorted him to
Gihon. 39 Then Zadok the priest took the horn of
oil from the tent and anointed Solomon. They
blew the ram's horn and all the people shouted,
"Long live King Solomon!" 40 Then all the people
went up after him, playing flutes and rejoicing so
much the earth split with their shouting.

Adonijah Submits to Solomon

41 Adonijah and all the guests who were with
him heard it, just as they ended their banquet.
When Joab heard the sound of the ram's horn, he
asked, "Why this uproar in the city?" 42 As he was
speaking, Jonathan, son of Abiathar the priest,
arrived. Adonijah said, "Come, you are a man of
worth and must bring good news." 43 Jonathan
answered Adonijah, "Hardly!† Our lord, King
David, has made Solomon king. 44 The king sent

†

1:15 Entering the king's chambers, Bathsheba confronts two realities: he is very old; and she herself, the woman for whom David once committed adultery and murder, has been replaced at the king's side and in his bed.

1:16 Throughout 1 Kgs 1 the key question is "Who shall be king (*malak*)?" David's feeble, two-syllable question to Bathsheba is an ironic echo of that key word: "What do you wish?" renders the Heb. *mahlak?*

1:18 Bathsheba uses a clever wordplay to conceal the rivalry between Solomon and Adonijah and imply that the real rivalry is between David and Adonijah. She repeatedly addresses David as "my lord king" (*'adoni hammelek*), but claims that "Adonijah has become king" (*'adoniya malak*). *Know*: the term means both "be aware of" and "recognize, acknowledge, ratify."

1:20 There was no precedent for determining succession to the throne of Israel. Adonijah and his supporters assumed that primogeniture would assure the succession as it did in the monarchies of the surrounding nations. But Bathsheba persuades David that he is free to name anyone he chooses.

1:38 *Cherethites and Pelethites*: mercenaries in David's bodyguard. They became part of his retinue after he defeated the Philistines and established himself in Jerusalem; cf. 2 Sm 8:18; 15:18; 20:23.

1:43 *Hardly*: Jonathan's first word, *'abal*, whose meaning (such as "indeed," "on the contrary") must be discerned from the context,

Introducing...

Solomon

Solomon was one of the sons of David and Bathsheba. He ruled for forty years after King David died, and he was the third and last king to rule over the united kingdom of Israel.

There is an old saying that often our personal strengths are our greatest weaknesses. This is true of Solomon. He was a tremendous organizer, an able ruler, a clever politician, and a great builder—it was during his reign that the first Temple was built in Jerusalem. To fulfill these great accomplishments, however, Solomon taxed his people heavily, married foreign women to seal political alliances with other nations, and used forced labor to complete his building projects. These things offended God and made Solomon unpopular with the people of Israel.

When Solomon died, ten of the original twelve Tribes from the northern part of Israel left the kingdom and set up their own kingdom. Israel never again existed as a united kingdom ruled by an Israelite king. The author of Kings attributes this more to Solomon's acceptance of other gods near the end of his life than to his political mistakes.

with him Zadok the priest, Nathan the prophet,
Benaiah, son of Jehoiada, and the Cherethites
and Pelethites, and they mounted him upon the
king's own mule. 45 Zadok the priest and Nathan
the prophet anointed him king at Gihon, and
they went up from there rejoicing, so that the
city is in an uproar. That is the noise you hear.
46 Moreover, Solomon has taken his seat on the
royal throne, 47 and moreover the king's servants
have come to pay their respects to our lord, King
David, saying, 'May your God make Solomon's
name more famous than your name, his throne
greater than your throne!' And the king in his bed
did homage. 48 This is what the king said: 'Blessed
be the LORD, the God of Israel, who has this day
provided one to sit upon my throne, so that I see
it with my own eyes.' " 49 All the guests of Ado-
nijah got up trembling, and went each their way,
50 but Adonijah, in fear of Solomon, got up and
went to grasp the horns of the altar.†
51 It was reported to Solomon: "Adonijah, in
fear of King Solomon, is clinging to the horns
of the altar and saying, 'Let King Solomon first
swear that he will not kill me, his servant, with
the sword.' " 52 Solomon answered, "If he proves
worthy, not a hair of his shall fall to the ground.
But if evil is found in him, he shall die." 53 King
Solomon sent to have him brought down from
the altar, and he came and paid homage to King
Solomon. Solomon then said to him, "Go to
your house."

David's Last Instructions and Death

2 1 When the time of David's death drew near,
he gave these instructions to Solomon his
son: 2 "I am going the way of all the earth. Be
strong and be a man! 3 * Keep the mandate of the
LORD, your God, walking in his ways and keeping
his statutes, commands, ordinances, and decrees
as they are written in the law of Moses, that you
may succeed in whatever you do, and wherever
you turn, 4 * and that the LORD may fulfill the
word he spoke concerning me: If your sons so
conduct themselves that they walk before me
in faithfulness with their whole heart and soul,
there shall never be wanting someone of your
line on the throne of Israel.
5 † * "You yourself know what Joab, son of
Zeruiah, did to me—what he did to the two com-
manders of Israel's armies, Abner, son of Ner,
and Amasa, son of Jether: he killed them and
brought the blood of war into a time of peace,
and put the blood of war on the belt about his
waist and the sandal on his foot. 6 Act with all
the wisdom you possess; do not let his gray head
go down to Sheol in peace. 7 * But be true to the
sons of Barzillai the Gileadite, and have them
among those who eat at your table. For they were
loyal to me when I was fleeing from your brother

---

† may be ironic. This irony is deepened by an untranslatable wordplay in Hebrew: a very similar word means "to mourn," which is an appropriate comment about the death of Adonijah's hopes for the throne.

1:50 *Horns of the altar*: the protuberances on each of the four corners of the altar (Ex 27:2; 29:12). By grasping the horns of the altar Adonijah is claiming asylum (Ex 21:13–14; 1 Kgs 2:28).

2:5–9 David urges Solomon to purge Joab and Shimei and supplies him with justification for doing so. Joab had killed Abner (2 Sm 3:22–30) and Amasa (2 Sm 20:4–12), thereby bringing blood guilt upon himself and perhaps upon his master David. Shimei had cursed David (2 Sm 16:5–8), though David pledged that Shimei would not be killed for it (2 Sm 19:16–24). David's motives, however, may have been more personal. Joab also killed David's son Absalom and chided David for his untimely public display of grief (2 Sm 18:9–19:8), and David may have felt himself free of the promise he made to Shimei because that promise was coerced by the presence of Shimei's thousand partisans backing him at the time.

2:3 Dt 17:18–19.
2:4 2 Sm 7:11–16; Ps 132:11–12.
2:5 2 Sm 3:22–30; 20:8–10.
2:7 2 Sm 17:27–29; 19:32–41.

Absalom. 8 * You also have with you Shimei, son
of Gera, the Benjaminite of Bahurim, who cursed
me bitterly the day I was going to Mahanaim.
When he came down to meet me at the Jordan, I
swore to him by the LORD: 'I will not kill you by
the sword.' 9 But you must not let him go unpun-
ished. You are wise; you will know what to do to
send his gray head down to Sheol in blood."
10 * David rested with his ancestors and was
buried in the City of David. 11 * David was king
over Israel for forty years: he was king seven years
in Hebron and thirty-three years in Jerusalem.

The Kingdom Made Secure†

12 Then Solomon sat on the throne of David
his father, and his kingship was established.
13 Adonijah, son of Haggith, came to Bath-
sheba, the mother of Solomon. "Do you come
in peace?" she asked. "In peace," he answered,
14 and he added, "I have something to say to
you." She replied, "Speak." 15 So he said: "You
know that the kingship was mine, and all Israel
expected me to be king. But the kingship passed
me by and went to my brother; by the LORD's
will it went to him. 16 But now there is one favor
I would ask of you. Do not refuse me." And she
said, "Speak on." 17 † He said, "Please ask King
Solomon, who will not refuse you, to give me
Abishag the Shunamite to be my wife." 18 Bath-
sheba replied, "Very well, I will speak to the king
for you."
19 Then Bathsheba went to King Solomon to
speak to him for Adonijah, and the king stood
up to meet her and paid her homage. Then he
sat down upon his throne, and a throne was pro-
vided for the king's mother, who sat at his right.
20 She said, "There is one small favor I would ask
of you. Do not refuse me." The king said to her,
"Ask it, my mother, for I will not refuse you."
21 So she said, "Let Abishag the Shunamite be
given to your brother Adonijah to be his wife."
22 King Solomon answered his mother, "And why
do you ask that Abishag the Shunamite be given
to Adonijah? Ask the kingship for him as well,
for he is my older brother! Ask for him, for Abi-
athar the priest, for Joab, son of Zeruiah!" 23 And
King Solomon swore by the LORD: "May God do
thus to me and more, if Adonijah has not spoken
this word at the cost of his life. 24 * And now, as
the LORD lives, who has established me and set
me on the throne of David my father and made
for me a house as he promised, this day shall
Adonijah be put to death." 25 Then King Solo-
mon sent Benaiah, son of Jehoiada, who struck
him dead.
26 * The king said to Abiathar the priest: "Go to
your estate in Anathoth. Though you deserve to
die, I will not put you to death at this time, be-
cause you carried the ark of the Lord GOD before
David my father and shared in all the hardships
my father endured."† 27 * So Solomon dismissed
Abiathar from the office of priest of the LORD,
thus fulfilling the word the LORD had spoken in
Shiloh against the house of Eli.
28 When the news came to Joab, since he had
sided with Adonijah, though not with Absalom,
he fled to the tent of the LORD and clung to the
horns of the altar. 29 King Solomon was told,
"Joab has fled to the tent of the LORD and is by
the altar." He sent Benaiah, son of Jehoiada,
with the order, "Go, strike him down." 30 Bena-
iah went to the tent of the LORD and said to him,
"The king says, 'Come out.' " But he answered,
"No! I will die here." Benaiah reported to the
king, "This is what Joab said to me in reply."
31 The king answered him: "Do as he has said.
Strike him down and bury him, and remove
from me and from my father's house the blood
which Joab shed without provocation. 32 * The
LORD will bring blood upon his own head, be-
cause he struck down two men better and more
just than himself, and slew them with the sword
without my father David's knowledge: Abner,
son of Ner, commander of Israel's army, and Am-
asa, son of Jether, commander of Judah's army.
33 Their blood will be upon the head of Joab and
his descendants. But upon David and his descen-
dants, upon his house and his throne, there shall
be peace forever from the LORD." 34 Benaiah, son
of Jehoiada, went back, struck him down and
killed him; he was buried in his house in the wil-
derness. 35 The king appointed Benaiah, son of
Jehoiada, over the army in his place; Zadok the
priest the king put in place of Abiathar.
36 Then the king summoned Shimei and said
to him: "Build yourself a house in Jerusalem

†

2:12–46 The second major unit of the Solomon story shows how Solomon eliminated people he considered threats to the security of his throne. It is marked by a device called "inclusion," where the text repeats a word, phrase, or idea at the beginning and end of a literary unit (see vv. 12b, 46b). Compare 11:14–25, where Solomon is unable to eliminate other threats to his security.

2:17–25 Abishag had belonged to David's harem (1:3–4), which Solomon inherited. Adonijah's request could imply a challenge to Solomon's accession and so exposes Adonijah to the suspicion of insurrection that will cost him his life; cf. 2 Sm 3:6–11; 16:21–22.

2:26 The narrator indulges in a subtle wordplay: Abiathar's exile to Anathoth (*'anatot*) continues the series of hardships he has endured (*hit'annita*).

*

2:8 2 Sm 16:5–13; 19:17–24.
2:10 Acts 2:29.
2:11 2 Sm 2:1–4; 5:1–5.
2:24 2 Sm 7:11–16.
2:26 1 Sm 22:20–23.
2:27 1 Sm 2:27–33.
2:32 2 Sm 3:22–30; 20:8–10.

Live It!

God, Give Me Wisdom!

Isn't it interesting that of all the things Solomon could have asked God for, he chose wisdom? Actually, he asked for an understanding heart. That really is a wonderful thing to ask God for. And indeed Solomon was noted for his wisdom, far and wide.

We generally associate wisdom with old age. There is some truth in that connection. As we grow through life and gain experience, we tend to grow wiser. That growth is a sign of maturity. We know there are some people who never seem to learn from their mistakes, and we know there are also foolish old people. But generally, as we mature, we become wiser.

- Why not make Solomon's prayer for an understanding heart your own? In what ways have you become more mature?

▶ 1 Kgs 3:4–15

and stay there. Do not go anywhere else. 37 For
the day you leave, and cross the Wadi Kidron,
be certain you shall surely die. Your blood shall
be upon your own head." 38 Shimei answered
the king: "I accept. Your servant will do just as
my lord the king has said." So Shimei stayed in
Jerusalem for a long time. 39 But three years later,
two of Shimei's servants ran away to Achish, son
of Maacah, king of Gath, and Shimei was told,
"Your servants are in Gath." 40 So Shimei rose,
saddled his donkey, and went to Achish in Gath
in search of his servants; and Shimei returned
from Gath with his servants. 41 When Solomon
was told that Shimei had gone from Jerusalem to
Gath, and had returned, 42 the king summoned
Shimei and said to him: "Did I not have you
swear by the LORD and warn you clearly, 'The day
you leave and go anywhere else, be certain you
shall surely die'? And you answered, 'I accept and
obey.'† 43 Why, then, have you not kept the oath
of the LORD and the command that I gave you?"
44 * And the king said to Shimei: "In your heart
you know very well the evil that you did to David
my father. Now the LORD is bringing your own
evil upon your head. 45 But King Solomon shall
be blessed, and David's throne shall be established before the LORD forever." 46 The king then
gave the order to Benaiah, son of Jehoiada, who
went out and struck him dead.

And the royal power was established in Solomon's hand.

Early Promise of Solomon's Reign†

3 1 * Solomon allied himself by marriage with
Pharaoh, king of Egypt. He married the
daughter of Pharaoh and brought her to the City
of David, until he should finish building his own
house, and the house of the LORD, and the wall
around Jerusalem. 2 The people were sacrificing
on the high places, however, for up to that time
no house had been built for the name of the
LORD. 3 Although Solomon loved the LORD, walking in the statutes of David his father, he offered
sacrifice and burned incense on the high places.
4 The king went to Gibeon to sacrifice there,
because that was the great high place. Upon its
altar Solomon sacrificed a thousand burnt offerings. 5 In Gibeon the LORD appeared to Solomon
in a dream at night. God said: Whatever you ask
I shall give you. 6 Solomon answered: "You have
shown great kindness to your servant, David my
father, because he walked before you with fidelity, justice, and an upright heart; and you have
continued this great kindness toward him today,
giving him a son to sit upon his throne. 7 Now,
LORD, my God, you have made me, your servant,
king to succeed David my father; but I am a mere
youth, not knowing at all how to act— 8 I, your
servant, among the people you have chosen, a
people so vast that it cannot be numbered or
counted. 9 Give your servant, therefore, a listening heart to judge your people and to distinguish
between good and evil. For who is able to give
judgment for this vast people of yours?"
10 The Lord was pleased by Solomon's request.
11 So God said to him: Because you asked for
this—you did not ask for a long life for yourself,

† **2:42–44** In his charge against Shimei, Solomon misrepresents the truth in two ways. He did not make Shimei take an oath. And he imposed capital punishment only on crossing the Wadi Kidron, to the east of Jerusalem. This was presumably to prevent Shimei from returning to his home, Bahurim, which lay in that direction; Gath, however, is southwest of Jerusalem. Solomon's next words to Shimei reveal that he is really being punished for cursing David, not for violating Solomon's command.

3:1–15 The third major unit of the Solomon story depicts the bright beginning of his reign. It includes the narrator's remarks about Solomon's marriage and his building projects, and a divine appearance to Solomon. Compare 11:1–13, where the same themes recur, but in negative fashion. The story of the divine appearance is told also in 2 Chr 1:1–13.

* **2:44** 2 Sm 16:5–13; 19:17–24. **3:1** 1 Kgs 7:8; 9:24.

nor for riches, nor for the life of your enemies—but you asked for discernment to know what is right— 12 I now do as you request. I give you a heart so wise and discerning that there has never been anyone like you until now, nor after you will there be anyone to equal you. 13 * In addition, I give you what you have not asked for: I give you such riches and glory that among kings there will be no one like you all your days. 14 And if you walk in my ways, keeping my statutes and commandments, as David your father did, I will give you a long life. 15 Solomon awoke; it was a dream! He went to Jerusalem, stood before the ark of the covenant of the Lord, sacrificed burnt offerings and communion offerings, and gave a feast for all his servants.

Solomon's Listening Heart†

16 Later, two prostitutes came to the king and stood before him. 17 One woman said: "By your leave, my lord, this woman and I live in the same house, and I gave birth in the house while she was present. 18 On the third day after I gave birth, this woman also gave birth. We were alone; no one else was in the house with us; only the two of us were in the house. 19 This woman's son died during the night when she lay on top of him. 20 So in the middle of the night she got up and took my son from my side, as your servant was sleeping. Then she laid him in her bosom and laid her dead son in my bosom. 21 I rose in the morning to nurse my son, and he was dead! But when I examined him in the morning light, I saw it was not the son I had borne." 22 The other woman answered, "No! The living one is my son, the dead one is yours." But the first kept saying, "No! the dead one is your son, the living one is mine!" Thus they argued before the king. 23 Then the king said: "One woman claims, 'This, the living one, is my son, the dead one is yours.' The other answers, 'No! The dead one is your son, the living one is mine.' " 24 The king continued, "Get me a sword." When they brought the sword before the king, 25 he said, "Cut the living child in two, and give half to one woman and half to the other." 26 † The woman whose son was alive, because she was stirred with compassion for her son, said to the king, "Please, my lord, give her the living baby—do not kill it!" But the other said, "It shall be neither mine nor yours. Cut it in two!" 27 The king then answered, "Give her the living baby! Do not kill it! She is the mother." 28 When all Israel heard the judgment the king had given, they were in awe of him, because they saw that the king had in him the wisdom of God for giving right judgment.

Solomon's Riches: Domestic Affairs†

4 1 Solomon was king over all Israel, 2 and these were the officials he had in his service:

Azariah, son of Zadok, the priest;
3 Elihoreph and Ahijah, sons of Shisha, scribes;
Jehoshaphat, son of Ahilud, the chancellor;

Pray It!

A Wise Heart

A famous prayer, often called the "Peace Prayer," by Saint Francis of Assisi (AD 1181–1226), contains the line "Lord, grant that I may not so much seek to be . . . understood, as to understand."

It is almost as if Saint Francis is echoing the prayer of King Solomon, who lived two thousand years before him. The request is the same. Both men ask God to give them the gift of a wise heart—the ability to see things as God sees things.

What a difference wisdom can make in our lives. What a wonderful thing to pray for. What a blessing to increase the amount of wisdom in our world. What inspiring examples we have in the prayers of Solomon a millennium before Jesus, and of Francis a millennium after.

Let us ask God daily for a wise heart.

▶ 1 Kgs 3:9

1 KGS

† **3:16–5:14** The fourth major unit of the Solomon story shows how Solomon used the three gifts that the Lord gave him in 3:12–13: a listening heart (3:16–28), riches (4:1–5:8), universal renown (5:9–14). In each case his gifts benefited the populace, from the lowest classes (3:16–28) to his whole people (4:20; 5:5) to the whole world (5:9–14). Compare 9:26–10:29, where the same three gifts all redound to the benefit of Solomon himself.

3:26–27 The true mother reveals herself by an uncommon and tender word for the child, "baby." With this, and the woman's willingness to give up her child, Solomon realizes that she is the true mother, and quotes her words exactly in rendering his judgment.

4:1–5:8 The sub-unit on Solomon's riches is organized around domestic affairs (4:1–20) and international affairs (5:1–5), with a short appendix on Solomon's horses and chariots (5:6–8). Compare 9:26–10:29, where comparable elements reappear.

* **3:13** Eccl 1:12–13; Wis 7:7–11; Mt 6:29.

Cultural Connection

How Excellent

The First Book of Kings says, "Solomon's wisdom surpassed that of all the peoples of the East and all the wisdom of Egypt" (5:10).

This should be a source of pride for young African Americans. The people of Egypt and of the East are dark-skinned people. Ancient southern Egypt included the country of modern Ethiopia. The people in these countries must have been well known for their wisdom in order for the biblical author to use them in a comparison with Solomon. African Americans can praise God for their African ancestors: the wise, black people from Egypt and the East.

▶ 1 Kgs 5:10

4 Benaiah, son of Jehoiada, in charge of the
army;
Zadok and Abiathar, priests;
5 Azariah, son of Nathan, in charge of the
governors;
Zabud, son of Nathan, priest and companion
to the king;
6 Ahishar, master of the palace; and
Adoniram, son of Abda, in charge of the
forced labor.

7 † Solomon had twelve governors over all
Israel who supplied food for the king and his
household, each having to provide for one
month in the year. 8 Their names were:†

the son of Hur in the hill country of Ephraim;
9 the son of Deker in Makaz, Shaalbim, Beth-
shemesh, and Elon Beth-hanan;
10 the son of Hesed in Arubboth, as well as in
Socoh and the whole region of Hepher;
11 the son of Abinadab, in all Naphath-dor;
he was married to Taphath, Solomon's
daughter;
12 Baana, son of Ahilud, in Taanach and
Megiddo and all Beth-shean near
Zarethan below Jezreel, from Beth-shean
to Abel-meholah to beyond Jokmeam;
13 the son of Geber in Ramoth-gilead, having
charge of the villages of Jair, son of
Manasseh, in Gilead; and of the district
of Argob in Bashan—sixty large walled
cities with gates barred with bronze;
14 Ahinadab, son of Iddo, in Mahanaim;
15 Ahimaaz, in Naphtali; he was married to
Basemath, another daughter of Solomon;
16 Baana, son of Hushai, in Asher and Aloth;
17 Jehoshaphat, son of Paruah, in Issachar;
18 Shimei, son of Ela, in Benjamin;
19 Geber, son of Uri, in the land of Gilead, the
land of Sihon, king of the Amorites, and
of Og, king of Bashan.

There was one governor besides, in the land of
Judah.† 20 * Judah and Israel were as numerous
as the sands by the sea; they ate and drank and
rejoiced.

Solomon's Riches: International Affairs

5 1 † Solomon ruled over all the kingdoms
from the River† to the land of the Philistines,
down to the border of Egypt; they paid Solomon
tribute and served him as long as he lived. 2 † Sol-
omon's provisions for each day were thirty kors
of fine flour, sixty kors of meal, 3 ten fatted oxen,
twenty pasture-fed oxen, and a hundred sheep,

† **4:7–19** The administration of the kingdom thus initiated by Solomon continued in its main features for the duration of the monarchy in Israel and Judah. Note the use of "all Israel" to mean only the northern tribes (see also 5:27). Solomon's exactions did not fall evenly on the whole people, but favored his own southern tribe of Judah. Eventually this inequity would lead to the dissolution of the union of Israel and Judah (12:1–19).

4:8–19 Several of the governors are identified only by their fathers' names.

4:19 *One governor . . . land of Judah*: the royal territory of Judah had its own peculiar administration different from that of the twelve northern districts, each of which had to supply the king and his household with a month's provisions of food each year (v. 7).

5:1–32 This translation follows the numeration of the Hebrew Bible, rather than the Vulgate; in many English translations, 5:1–14 is 4:21–34, and 5:15 is 5:1.

5:1 *The River*: that is, the Euphrates. This claim may be exaggerated, but "from the Euphrates to the border of Egypt" was the traditional description of the extent of the Davidic holdings.

5:2 The list of Solomon's supplies may have originally belonged with the list of governors in 4:7–19, but the author has placed it here to imply that Solomon's vassal kingdoms, not his own citizenry, supplied his vast daily needs. The daily provisions listed could have supported several thousand people. *Kors*: see note on Ez 45:14.

* **4:20** Gn 22:17; 32:13; Dn 3:36; Hos 1:10; Heb 11:12.

not counting harts, gazelles, roebucks, and fatted
fowl. [4]He had dominion over all the land west of
the River, from Tiphsah to Gaza, and all its kings,
and he had peace on all his borders round about.
[5]* Thus Judah and Israel lived in security, every-
one under their own vine and fig tree from Dan
to Beer-sheba, as long as Solomon lived.

Solomon's Riches: Chariots and Horses

[6]* Solomon had forty thousand stalls for
horses for chariots and twelve thousand horse-
men. [7]† The governors, one for each month,
provided food for King Solomon and for all the
guests at King Solomon's table. They left nothing
unprovided. [8]For the chariot horses and draft an-
imals also, each brought his quota of barley and
straw to the required place.

Solomon's Renown

[9]* Moreover, God gave Solomon wisdom,
exceptional understanding, and knowledge, as
vast as the sand on the seashore. [10]Solomon's
wisdom surpassed that of all the peoples of the
East and all the wisdom of Egypt. [11]He was wiser
than anyone else—wiser than Ethan the Ezrahite,
or Heman, Chalcol, and Darda, the musicians—
and his fame spread throughout the neighboring
peoples. [12]Solomon also uttered three thousand
proverbs, and his songs numbered a thousand
and five. [13]He spoke of plants, from the cedar on
Lebanon to the hyssop growing out of the wall,
and he spoke about beasts, birds, reptiles, and
fishes. [14]* People from all nations came to hear
Solomon's wisdom, sent by all the kings of the
earth who had heard of his wisdom.

Preparations for the Temple†

[15]When Hiram, king of Tyre, heard that Sol-
omon had been anointed king in place of his
father, he sent an embassy to him; for Hiram had
always been David's friend.† [16]Solomon sent
back this message to Hiram: [17]* "You know that
David my father, because of the wars that beset
him, could not build a house for the name of the
LORD his God until such time as the LORD should

Chapter 5

put his enemies under the soles of his feet. [18]But
now the LORD, my God, has given me rest on all
sides, without adversary or misfortune. [19]* So I
intend to build a house for the name of the LORD,
my God, as the LORD said to David my father:
Your son whom I will put upon your throne in
your place shall build the house for my name.
[20]Give orders, then, to have cedars from the Leb-
anon cut down for me. My servants shall accom-
pany yours, and I will pay you whatever you say
for your servants' wages. For you know that there
is no one among us who is skilled in cutting
timber like the Sidonians." [21]When Hiram had
heard the words of Solomon, he was overjoyed,
and said, "Blessed be the LORD this day, who has
given David a wise son over this numerous peo-
ple." [22]† Hiram then sent word to Solomon, "I
have heard the proposal you sent me, and I will
provide all the cedars and fir trees you desire.
[23]My servants shall bring them down from the
Lebanon to the sea, and I will arrange them into
rafts in the sea and bring them wherever you say.
There I will break up the rafts, and you shall take
the lumber. You, for your part, shall furnish the
provisions I desire for my household." [24]So Hi-
ram continued to provide Solomon with all the
cedars and fir trees he desired, [25]while Solomon
gave Hiram twenty thousand kors of wheat to

---

†

5:7 This verse suggests that the governors also saw to the provender for Solomon's animals (v. 8).

5:15–32 The fifth major unit of the Solomon story explains the preparations Solomon made for the construction of the Temple. He negotiates with Hiram of Tyre for materiel (5:15–26), and conscripts a labor force for personnel (5:27–32). Compare 9:11–23, which returns to the same two themes after the Temple has been built and dedicated. 2 Chr 2:1–17 presents another version of the same material.

5:15 *David's friend*: the term "to be a friend," lit., "to love," is political, and means that David and Hiram had been allies. The purpose of Hiram's embassy is to determine whether Solomon is willing to continue the alliance. This unspoken agenda lies behind the negotiations about materials for the Temple, as the concluding v. 26 makes clear.

5:22–23 Although his reply is couched in polite, diplomatic language, Hiram renegotiates Solomon's terms in his own favor. No Israelites are to enter Tyrian territory, and Solomon is not to pay the salary of Hiram's laborers but rather to furnish "provisions" for his household—the same language used of the tribute Solomon received from his own vassals in v. 2.

---

*

5:5 Sir 47:13.
5:6 1 Kgs 10:26; Dt 17:16; 2 Chr 1:14; 9:25.
5:9–14 Sir 47:15–17.
5:14 1 Kgs 10:1.
5:17 2 Sm 7:5–7; 1 Chr 22:7–8.
5:19 2 Sm 7:12–13.

provide for his household, and twenty kors† of
hand-pressed oil. Solomon gave Hiram all this
every year. 26 The LORD gave Solomon wisdom
as he promised him. So there was peace be-
tween Hiram and Solomon, and the two of them
made† a covenant.
27 King Solomon raised thirty thousand forced
laborers from all Israel.† 28 He sent them to the
Lebanon for a month in relays of ten thousand,
so that they spent one month in the Lebanon and
two months at home. Adoniram was in charge of
the forced labor. 29 Solomon had seventy thou-
sand carriers and eighty thousand stonecutters in
the mountain, 30 in addition to three thousand
three hundred overseers answerable to Solomon,
who were in charge of the work and directed the
people engaged in the work. 31 By order of the
king, fine, large blocks of stone were quarried
to give the house a foundation of hewn stone.
32 Solomon's and Hiram's builders, along with
others from Gebal,† shaped them, and prepared
the wood and stones for building the house.

Building of the Temple†

6 1 In the four hundred and eightieth year af-
ter the Israelites went forth from the land of
Egypt, in the fourth year of Solomon's reign over
Israel, in the month of Ziv (the second month),
he began to build the house of the LORD.†
2 The house which King Solomon built for
the LORD was sixty cubits long, twenty wide, and
thirty high. 3 The porch in front of the nave of the
house was twenty cubits from side to side along
the width of the house, and ten cubits deep in
front of the house. 4 Windows with closed lattices
were made for the house, 5 and adjoining the wall
of the house he built a substructure around its
walls that enclosed the nave and the inner sanc-
tuary, and he made side chambers all around.
6 The lowest story was five cubits wide, the mid-
dle one six cubits wide, the third seven cubits
wide, because he put recesses along the outside
of the house to avoid fastening anything into the
walls of the house. 7 The house was built of stone
dressed at the quarry, so that no hammer or ax,
no iron tool, was to be heard in the house dur-
ing its construction. 8 The entrance to the middle
story was on the south side of the house; stairs
led up to the middle story and from the middle
story to the third. 9 When he had finished build-
ing the house, it was roofed in with rafters and
boards of cedar. 10 He built the substructure five
cubits high all along the outside of the house, to
which it was joined by cedar beams.
11 The word of the LORD came to Solomon:
12 * As to this house you are building—if you
walk in my statutes, carry out my ordinances,
and observe all my commands, walking in them,
I will fulfill toward you my word which I spoke
to David your father. 13 I will dwell in the midst
of the Israelites and will not forsake my people
Israel.
14 When Solomon finished building the house,
15 its inside walls were lined with cedar paneling:
he covered the interior with wood from floor to
ceiling, and he covered its floor with fir planking.
16 At the rear of the house a space of twenty cubits
was set off by cedar panels from the floor to the
ceiling, enclosing the inner sanctuary, the holy
of holies. 17 The house was forty cubits long, that
is, the nave, the part in front. 18 The cedar in the
interior of the house was carved in the form of
gourds and open flowers; all was of cedar, and
no stone was to be seen.

5:25 *Twenty kors*: this means about two thousand gallons of the finest olive oil available, hand-pressed rather than produced in large olive presses, so that no debris (such as crushed olive pits, powder from the grinding stones) would contaminate the oil. Also see note on 2 Chr 2:9.

5:26 *Made*: lit., "cut." The story of Solomon's arrangements with Hiram is framed by references to political alliance between Israel and Tyre (vv. 15, 26). Since, in Hebrew idiom, Hiram and Solomon "cut" a covenant, this suggests that the agreement they reach for "cutting" wood (which clearly favors Hiram) reflects the terms of the larger treaty.

5:27 *All Israel*: see note on 4:7–19.

5:32 *Gebal*: Byblos.

6:1–7:51 The central units of the Solomon story describe the building of the Temple (6:1–7:51) and its dedication ceremony (8:1–9:10). The account of the construction of the Temple ("the house") is organized to give the reader a guided tour. Approaching from a distance, we see ground plans (6:2–3) and structural work in stone (6:4–8) and wood (6:9–10). After a brief interruption that recounts a divine word to Solomon (6:11–13), we enter the Temple to view the paneling and ornamentation of the nave (6:14–18), the gilded walls and golden entrance of the inner sanctuary or holy of holies (6:19–22), with its priceless interior decoration and furnishings (6:23–28). As we leave, we admire the interior carvings and gilded floor of the inner sanctuary (6:29–30), return to the nave through carved and gilded doors (6:31–32), and exit from the nave through another set of carved and gilded doors (6:33–35) to the courtyard (6:36). Our guide briefly points out the nearby palace complex (7:1–12); then we walk around the courtyard to marvel at Hiram's heroic works in bronze: the two columns (7:15–22), the "sea" (7:23–26), and the ten stands and basins set along either side of the Temple buildings (7:27–39). The account ends with the smaller bronze vessels Hiram made for the Temple services (7:40–47) and the gold vessels that Solomon made (7:48–50). Unfortunately, several factors make it impossible to use the account to produce a satisfactory model of Solomon's Temple. Throughout the account there are numerous technical architectural terms whose meaning is lost to us; and it is moreover likely that the author is describing the Temple as it stood in his own time, centuries after Solomon's day. The Chronicler also describes the construction of the Temple in 2 Chr 3:1–4:22 and its dedication in 2 Chr 5:1–7:22.

6:1 Construction of the Temple is here dated in relation to the traditional date of the exodus from Egypt, rounded off to a conventional twelve generations of forty years each. This chronology means that the Temple was built approximately midway between Israel's two foundational deliverances, the exodus and the return from the Babylonian exile. The schematization of history implied in these figures recommends caution in using them for historical reconstruction.

6:12 2 Sm 7:13–16.

19 In the innermost part of the house† he set
up the inner sanctuary to house the ark of the
LORD's covenant. 20 In front of the inner sanc-
tuary (it was twenty cubits long, twenty wide,
and twenty high, and he covered it with pure
gold), he made an altar of cedar. 21 Solomon
covered the interior of the house with pure gold,
and he drew golden chains across in front of
the inner sanctuary, and covered it with gold.
22 He covered the whole house with gold, until
the whole house was done, and the whole altar
that belonged to the inner sanctuary he covered
with gold. 23 In the inner sanctuary he made two
cherubim, each ten cubits high, made of pine.
24 Each wing of a cherub was five cubits so that
the span from wing tip to wing tip was ten cubits.
25 The second cherub was also ten cubits: the two
cherubim were identical in size and shape; 26 the
first cherub was ten cubits high, and so was the
second. 27 He placed the cherubim in the inmost
part of the house; the wings of the cherubim
were spread wide, so that one wing of the first
touched the side wall and the wing of the second
touched the other wall; the wings pointing to the
middle of the room touched each other. 28 He
overlaid the cherubim with gold.

29 The walls of the house on all sides of both
the inner and the outer rooms had carved fig-
ures of cherubim, palm trees, and open flowers.
30 The floor of the house of both the inner and
the outer rooms was overlaid with gold. 31 At the
entrance of the inner sanctuary, doors of pine
were made; the doorframes had five-sided posts.
32 The two doors were of pine, with carved figures
of cherubim, palm trees, and open flowers. The
doors were overlaid with gold, and the cheru-
bim and the palm trees were also covered with
beaten gold. 33 He did the same at the entrance
to the nave, where the doorposts were of pine
and were four-sided. 34 The two doors were of fir
wood, each door consisting of two panels hinged
together; 35 and he carved cherubim, palm trees,
and open flowers, and plated them with gold.
36 He walled off the inner court with three courses
of hewn stones and one course of cedar beams.

37 The foundations of the LORD's house were
laid in the month of Ziv in the fourth year, 38 and
it was finished, in all particulars, exactly accord-
ing to plan, in the month of Bul, the eighth
month, in the eleventh year. Thus Solomon built
it in seven years.

7 1 † * To finish the building of his own house
Solomon took thirteen years. 2 He built the
House of the Forest of Lebanon one hundred cu-
bits long, fifty wide, and thirty high; it was sup-
ported by four rows of cedar columns, with cedar
beams upon the columns. 3 Moreover, it had a
ceiling of cedar above the rafters resting on the
columns; these rafters numbered forty-five, fif-
teen to a row. 4 There were lattices in three rows,
each row facing the next, 5 and all the openings
and doorposts were squared with lintels, each
facing across from the next. 6 He also made the
Porch of Columns, fifty cubits long and thirty
wide. The porch extended across the front, and
there were columns with a canopy in front of
them. 7 He also made the Porch of the Throne
where he gave judgment—that is, the Porch of
Judgment; it was paneled with cedar from floor
to ceiling beams. 8 * The house in which he lived
was in another court, set in deeper than the Porch
and of the same construction. (Solomon made a
house like this Porch for Pharaoh's daughter,
whom he had married.)† 9 All these buildings
were of fine stones, hewn to size and trimmed
front and back with a saw, from the foundation
to the bonding course and outside as far as the
great court. 10 The foundation was made of fine,
large blocks, some ten cubits and some eight cu-
bits. 11 Above were fine stones hewn to size, and
cedar wood. 12 The great court had three courses
of hewn stones all around and a course of cedar
beams. So also were the inner court of the house
of the LORD and its porch.

13 King Solomon brought Hiram† from Tyre.
14 He was a bronze worker, the son of a widow
from the tribe of Naphtali; his father had been
from Tyre. He was endowed with wisdom, un-
derstanding, and knowledge for doing any work
in bronze. He came to King Solomon and did all
his metal work.

15 † * He fashioned two bronze columns,
each eighteen cubits high and twelve cubits in

†

6:19 *The innermost part of the house*: the inner sanctuary or holy of holies reserved exclusively for the Lord, enthroned upon the cherubim over the ark of the covenant (2 Chr 3:10–13). See note on Ex 25:18–20.

7:1–12 The account of Solomon's building of the Temple (the Lord's "house") is interrupted by an account of his building of the palace (Solomon's "house"), which contained also the main buildings of public administration. The passage is anachronistic, since 6:38–7:1 and 9:10 imply that the palace was not begun until the Temple was completed. By placing the account here, the narrator highlights the fact that Solomon spent almost twice as long on his own "house" as on the Lord's.

7:8 Solomon did not build the house for Pharaoh's daughter until Temple and palace were finished (3:1). By mentioning this marriage, the narrator keeps before the reader a developing theme in the Solomon story: the king's building activities for his foreign wives, which eventually implicate him in idolatry (3:1; 7:8; 9:24; 11:1–8).

7:13 *Hiram*: a craftsman, not the king of Tyre (5:15–26).

7:15 The two bronze columns were called Jachin and Boaz (v. 21; also 2 Chr 3:17); the significance of the names is unclear.

*

7:1 1 Kgs 9:10.
7:8 1 Kgs 3:1; 9:24.
7:15–18 Jer 52:21–23.

circumference. 16 He also made two capitals cast in bronze, to be placed on top of the columns, each of them five cubits high. 17 There were meshes made like netting and braid made like chains for the capitals on top of the columns, seven for each capital. 18 † He also cast pomegranates, two rows around each netting to cover the capital on top of the columns. 19 The capitals on top of the columns (in the porch) were made like lilies, four cubits high. 20 And the capitals on the two columns, both above and adjoining the bulge where it crossed out of the netting, had two hundred pomegranates in rows around each capital. 21 He set up the columns at the temple porch; one he set up to the south, and called it Jachin, and the other to the north, and called it Boaz.† 22 The top of the columns was made like a lily. Thus the work on the columns was completed.

23 Then he made the molten sea;† it was made with a circular rim, and measured ten cubits across, five in height, and thirty in circumference. 24 Under the brim, gourds encircled it for ten cubits around the compass of the sea; the gourds were in two rows and were cast in one mold with the sea. 25 This rested on twelve oxen, three facing north, three facing west, three facing south, and three facing east, with their haunches all toward the center; upon them was set the sea. 26 It was a handbreadth thick, and its brim resembled that of a cup, being lily-shaped. Its capacity was two thousand baths.†

27 He also made ten stands of bronze, each four cubits long, four wide, and three high. 28 When these stands were constructed, panels were set within the framework. 29 On the panels within the frames there were lions, oxen, and cherubim; and on the frames likewise, above and below the lions and oxen, there were wreaths in hammered relief. 30 Each stand had four bronze wheels and bronze axles. The four legs of each stand had cast braces, which were under the basin; they had wreaths on each side. 31 The mouth of the basin was inside, and a cubit above, the crown, whose opening was round, made like a receptacle, a cubit and a half in depth. There was carved work at the opening, on panels that were square, not circular. 32 The four wheels were below the paneling, and the axletrees of the wheels and the stand were of one piece. Each wheel was a cubit and a half high. 33 The wheels were constructed like chariot wheels; their axletrees, rims, spokes, and hubs were all cast. 34 The four braces reached the four corners of each stand, and formed part of the stand. 35 At the top of the stand there was a raised collar half a cubit high, and the handles and panels on top of the stand formed part of it. 36 On the flat ends of the handles and on the panels, wherever there was a bare space, cherubim, lions, and palm trees were carved, as well as wreaths all around. 37 This was how he made the ten stands, all of the same casting, the same size, the same shape. 38 He made ten bronze basins, each four cubits in diameter with a capacity of forty baths, one basin atop each of the ten stands.

39 He placed the stands, five on the south side of the house and five on the north. The sea he placed off to the southeast from the south side of the house.

40 When Hiram had made the pots, shovels, and bowls, he finished all his work for King Solomon in the house of the LORD: 41 two columns; two nodes for the capitals on top of the columns; two pieces of netting covering the two nodes for the capitals on top of the columns; 42 four hundred pomegranates in double rows on both pieces of netting that covered the two nodes of the capitals on top of the columns; 43 ten stands; ten basins on the stands; 44 one sea; twelve oxen supporting the sea; 45 pots, shovels, and bowls. All these articles which Hiram made for King Solomon in the house of the LORD were of burnished bronze. 46 The king had them cast in the neighborhood of the Jordan, between Succoth and Zarethan, in thick clay molds. 47 Solomon did not weigh all the articles because they were so numerous; the weight of the bronze, therefore, was not determined.

48 Solomon made all the articles that were for the house of the LORD: the golden altar; the table on which the showbread lay; 49 the lampstands of pure gold, five to the right and five to the left before the inner sanctuary; their flowers, lamps, and tongs of gold; 50 basins, snuffers, bowls, cups, and firepans of pure gold; hinges of gold for the doors of the innermost part of the house, or holy of holies, and for the doors of the outer room, the nave. 51 * When all the work undertaken by

---

† columns stood to the right and left of the Temple porch, and may have been intended to mark the entrance to the building as the entrance to God's private dwelling. Their extraordinary size and elaborate decoration would have made them the most impressive parts of the Temple visible to the ordinary viewer, who was not permitted into the nave, let alone into the innermost sanctuary. According to Jer 52:21, the columns were hollow, the bronze exterior being "four fingers thick."

7:18–20 The Hebrew text is corrupt in many places here, and alternative readings attested in the ancient versions are secondary attempts to make sense of the text. A clearer description of the columns and their decoration is found in vv. 41–42.

7:21 *Jachin . . . Boaz*: see note on 7:15.

7:23–26 *The molten sea*: this was a large circular tank containing about twelve thousand gallons of water.

7:26 *Baths*: see note on Is 5:10.

---

* **7:51** 2 Sm 8:9–12.

King Solomon in the house of the LORD was com-
pleted,† he brought in the votive offerings of his
father David, and put the silver, gold, and other
articles in the treasuries of the house of the LORD.

Dedication of the Temple†

8 1 Then Solomon assembled the elders of Israel
and all the heads of the tribes, the princes in
the ancestral houses of the Israelites. They came
to King Solomon in Jerusalem, to bring up the
ark of the LORD's covenant from the city of David
(which is Zion). 2 All the people of Israel assem-
bled before King Solomon during the festival in
the month of Ethanim (the seventh month).†
3 When all the elders of Israel had arrived, the
priests took up the ark; 4 and they brought up
the ark of the LORD and the tent of meeting with
all the sacred vessels that were in the tent. The
priests and Levites brought them up. 5 King Sol-
omon and the entire community of Israel, gath-
ered for the occasion before the ark, sacrificed
sheep and oxen too many to number or count.
6 † The priests brought the ark of the covenant of
the LORD to its place, the inner sanctuary of the
house, the holy of holies, beneath the wings of
the cherubim. 7 The cherubim had their wings
spread out over the place of the ark, sheltering
the ark and its poles from above. 8 * The poles
were so long that their ends could be seen from
the holy place in front of the inner sanctuary.
They cannot be seen from outside, but they re-
main there to this day. 9 * There was nothing in
the ark but the two stone tablets which Moses
had put there at Horeb, when the LORD made a
covenant with the Israelites after they went forth
from the land of Egypt. 10 * When the priests left
the holy place, the cloud filled the house of the
LORD 11 so that the priests could no longer min-
ister because of the cloud, since the glory of the
LORD had filled the house of the LORD. 12 † * Then
Solomon said,

"The LORD intends to dwell in the dark cloud;
13 I have indeed built you a princely house,
the base for your enthronement forever."

14 The king turned and blessed the whole as-
sembly of Israel, while the whole assembly of
Israel stood. 15 He said: "Blessed be the LORD, the
God of Israel, who with his own mouth spoke a
promise to David my father and by his hand ful-
filled it, saying: 16 * Since the day I brought my
people Israel out of Egypt, I have not chosen a
city out of any tribe of Israel for the building of a
house, that my name might be there; but I have
chosen David to rule my people Israel. 17 When
David my father wished to build a house for the
name of the LORD, the God of Israel, 18 the LORD
said to him: In wishing to build a house for my
name, you did well. 19 But it is not you who will
build the house, but your son, who comes from
your loins; he shall build the house for my name.
20 Now the LORD has fulfilled the word he spoke:
I have succeeded David my father, and I sit on
the throne of Israel, as the LORD has spoken,
and I have built this house for the name of the
LORD, the God of Israel. 21 I have provided there a
place for the ark in which is the covenant of the
LORD that he made with our ancestors when he
brought them out of the land of Egypt."

Solomon's Prayer

22 Solomon stood before the altar of the LORD
in the presence of the whole assembly of Israel,
and stretching forth his hands toward heaven,
23 he said, "LORD, God of Israel, there is no God
like you in heaven above or on earth below; you
keep covenant and love toward your servants

† **7:51** The account of the Temple's construction has been punctuated by references to "building" (*banah*) or "finishing" (*killah*) it (6:1b, 9a, 14, 38; 7:40). Here, at the end of the account, the narrator uses a different verb for its "completion," *shillem*, which allows him to play on the name of Solomon (*shelomo*).

8:1–66 The account of the Temple's dedication ceremony is organized concentrically: Solomon gathers the assembly (vv. 1–13), blesses it (vv. 14–21), utters a long dedicatory prayer (vv. 22–53), blesses the assembly again (vv. 54–61), and dismisses it (vv. 62–66). To this account is appended an appearance of the Lord to Solomon (9:2–9) that balances the divine word to Solomon in the account of the Temple's construction (6:11–13).

8:2 "The seventh month" ("Ethanim" in the Canaanite calendar) corresponded to late September/early October. The great festival at that time of year is the feast of Booths, or Succoth/Sukkoth (see Lv 23:33–43; Dt 16:13–15). The feast was important enough to warrant holding the dedication ceremony either a month before or eleven months after the Temple was completed in the eighth month (6:38).

8:6–9 The transfer of the ark of the covenant into the newly constructed Temple building, God's act of possession (8:10–13), and Solomon's dedicatory prayer and sacrifices constituted the Temple's solemn dedication and made of it the place of God's presence in the midst of Israel for which David had hoped (2 Sm 6:12–15; 7:1–3). Later God expresses approval of the Temple with an oracle (1 Kgs 9:3–9).

8:12–13 This brief poem is rich in layered meanings. The "dark cloud" in which the Lord intends to dwell refers not only to the cloud that filled the Temple (v. 10) but to the darkness of the windowless holy of holies and to the mystery of the God enthroned invisibly upon the cherubim as well. Solomon calls the Temple he offers God a firm base, using terminology similar to that used for God's firm establishment of Solomon's own kingdom (2:12, 46). Finally, Solomon intends this as a place for God to *yashab*, but the Hebrew word *yashab* can mean "to dwell" or "to sit." In other words, the Temple can be understood both as a place where God resides and as the earthly foundation of God's heavenly throne. The double meaning allows an understanding of the divine presence as both transcendent and graciously immanent. See Solomon's sentiments in 8:27, and the frequent reference in 8:30–52 to God's hearing in heaven prayers that were offered in or toward the Temple.

8:8 Ex 25:13–15.
8:9 Ex 25:16; 34:27–28; Dt 10:5; Heb 9:4.
8:10 Ex 13:21; 40:34–38.
8:12 Ex 20:21; Dt 4:11; 5:22; Ps 97:2.
8:16–19 2 Sm 7:5–8, 12–13.

Pray It!

Holy Places

Solomon knows that the Temple will not hold God. Holy places are not cages to keep God contained. People need holy places more than God does. We gather together in public holy places to experience God's presence as a community. But we can also meet God one-on-one in private holy places, special to us alone.

Try creating a holy space in your bedroom. Clear out a corner, and place there a small table and a chair or rug to sit on. On the table, put your Bible and an object or two to help you focus on God. You might use a candle, a special picture or statue, or something from a retreat or a special place. Try to spend a little time each day in your holy space with God.

▶ 1 Kgs 8:27–30

who walk before you with their whole heart,
24 the covenant that you kept toward your ser-
vant, David my father, what you promised him;
your mouth has spoken and your hand has ful-
filled this very day. 25 * And now, LORD, God of Is-
rael, keep toward your servant, David my father,
what you promised: There shall never be wanting
someone from your line to sit before me on the
throne of Israel, provided that your descendants
keep to their way, walking before me as you have.
26 Now, God of Israel, may the words you spoke
to your servant, David my father, be confirmed.
27 "Is God indeed to dwell on earth? If the
heavens and the highest heavens cannot contain
you, how much less this house which I have
built! 28 Regard kindly the prayer and petition
of your servant, LORD, my God, and listen to the
cry of supplication which I, your servant, utter
before you this day. 29 May your eyes be open
night and day toward this house, the place of
which you said, My name shall be there; listen to
the prayer your servant makes toward this place.
30 Listen to the petition of your servant and of
your people Israel which they offer toward this
place. Listen, from the place of your enthrone-
ment, heaven, listen and forgive.
31 * "If someone sins in some way against
a neighbor and is required to take an oath
sanctioned by a curse, and comes and takes the
oath before your altar in this house, 32 listen in
heaven; act and judge your servants. Condemn
the wicked, requiting their ways; acquit the just,
rewarding their justice.
33 "When your people Israel are defeated by
an enemy because they sinned against you, and
then they return to you, praise your name, pray
to you, and entreat you in this house, 34 listen in
heaven and forgive the sin of your people Israel,
and bring them back to the land you gave their
ancestors.
35 "When the heavens are closed, so that there
is no rain, because they have sinned against you,
but they pray toward this place and praise your
name, and turn from their sin because you have
afflicted them, 36 listen in heaven and forgive the
sin of your servants, your people Israel (for you
teach them the good way in which they should
walk). Give rain to this land of yours which you
have given to your people as their heritage.
37 "If there is famine in the land or pestilence;
or if blight comes, or mildew, or locusts, or
caterpillars; if an enemy of your people presses
upon them in the land and at their gates; what-
ever plague or sickness there may be; 38 whatever
prayer or petition any may make, any of your
people Israel, who know heartfelt remorse and
stretch out their hands toward this house, 39 lis-
ten in heaven, the place of your enthronement;
forgive and take action. Render to each and all ac-
cording to their ways, you who know every heart;
for it is you alone who know the heart of every
human being. 40 So may they revere you as long as
they live on the land you gave our ancestors.
41 "To the foreigners, likewise, who are not of
your people Israel, but who come from a distant
land for the sake of your name 42 (since people
will hear of your great name and your mighty
hand and your outstretched arm), when they
come and pray toward this house, 43 listen in
heaven, the place of your enthronement. Do all
that the foreigner asks of you, that all the peoples
of the earth may know your name, may revere
you as do your people Israel, and may know that
your name has been invoked upon this house
that I have built.
44 "When your people go out to war against
their enemies, by whatever way you send them,
and they pray to the LORD toward the city you
have chosen and the house I have built for your
name, 45 listen in heaven to their prayer and peti-
tion, and uphold their cause.

8:25 1 Kgs 2:4; 9:5; 2 Sm 7:14–16; Jer 33:17. **8:31** Ex 22:6–10.

46 * "When they sin against you (for there is no one who does not sin), and in your anger against them you deliver them to an enemy, so that their captors carry them off to the land of the enemy, far or near, 47 and they have a change of heart in the land of their captivity and they turn and entreat you in the land of their captors and say, 'We have sinned and done wrong; we have been wicked'; 48 if with their whole heart and soul they turn back to you in the land of their enemies who took them captive, and pray to you toward the land you gave their ancestors, the city you have chosen, and the house I have built for your name, 49 listen in heaven, your dwelling place, to their prayer and petition, and uphold their cause. 50 Forgive your people who have sinned against you and all the offenses they have committed against you, and grant them mercy in the sight of their captors, so that these will be merciful to them. 51 For they are your people and your heritage, whom you brought out of Egypt, from the midst of the iron furnace.

52 "Thus may your eyes be open to the petition of your servant and to the petition of your people Israel; thus may you listen to them whenever they call upon you. 53 For you have set them apart from all the peoples of the earth to be your heritage, as you declared through Moses your servant when you brought our ancestors out of Egypt, Lord my GOD."

54 After Solomon finished offering this entire prayer and petition to the LORD, he rose from before the altar of the LORD, where he had been kneeling, hands outstretched toward heaven. 55 He stood and blessed the whole assembly of Israel, saying in a loud voice: 56 "Blessed be the LORD who has given rest to his people Israel, just as he promised. Not a single word has gone unfulfilled of the entire gracious promise he made through Moses his servant. 57 May the LORD, our God, be with us as he was with our ancestors and may he not forsake us nor cast us off. 58 May he draw our hearts to himself, that we may walk in his ways and keep the commands, statutes, and ordinances that he enjoined on our ancestors. 59 May these words of mine, the petition I have offered before the LORD, our God, be present to the LORD our God day and night, that he may uphold the cause of his servant and the cause of his people Israel as each day requires, 60 so that all the peoples of the earth may know that the LORD is God and there is no other. 61 † Your heart must be wholly devoted to the LORD, our God, observing his statutes and keeping his commandments, as on this day."

62 The king and all Israel with him offered sacrifices before the LORD. 63 † Solomon offered as communion offerings to the LORD twenty-two thousand oxen and one hundred twenty thousand sheep. Thus the king and all the Israelites dedicated the house of the LORD. 64 On that day the king consecrated the middle of the court facing the house of the LORD; he offered there the burnt offerings, the grain offerings, and the fat of the communion offerings, because the bronze altar before the LORD was too small to hold the burnt offering, the grain offering, and the fat of the communion offering. 65 On this occasion Solomon and all Israel with him, a great assembly from Lebo-hamath to the Wadi of Egypt, celebrated the festival before the LORD, our God, for seven days. 66 On the eighth day he dismissed the people, who blessed the king and went to their tents, rejoicing and glad of heart because of all the blessings the LORD had given to David his servant and to his people Israel.

Promise and Warning to Solomon

9 1 After Solomon finished building the house of the LORD, the house of the king, and everything else that he wanted to do, 2 * the LORD appeared to Solomon a second time, as he had appeared to him in Gibeon. 3 The LORD said to him: I have heard the prayer of petition which you offered in my presence. I have consecrated this house which you have built and I set my name there forever; my eyes and my heart shall be there always. 4 As for you, if you walk before me as David your father did, wholeheartedly and uprightly, doing all that I have commanded you, keeping my statutes and ordinances, 5 * I will establish your royal throne over Israel forever, as I promised David your father: There shall never be wanting someone from your line on the throne of Israel. 6 But if ever you and your descendants turn from following me, fail to keep my commandments and statutes which I set before you, and proceed to serve other gods and bow down to them, 7 I will cut off Israel from the land I gave them and repudiate the house I have consecrated for my name. Israel shall become a proverb and a byword among all nations, 8 * and this house

---

†

8:61 In urging the people to be "wholly devoted" (*shalem*), Solomon plays on his own name (*shelomo*), as if to imply that he himself exemplifies perfect fidelity to God.

8:63 "Communion offerings" (*shelamim*) is another wordplay on the name of Solomon.

*

8:46 Eccl 7:20; 1 Jn 1:8.
9:2 1 Kgs 3:4–15; 6:11–13; 11:9–13.
9:5 2 Sm 7:16.
9:8 Dt 29:23; Jer 22:8.

shall become a heap of ruins. Every passerby
shall gasp in horror and ask, "Why has the LORD
done such things to this land and to this house?"
9 And the answer will come: "Because they aban-
doned the LORD, their God, who brought their
ancestors out of the land of Egypt, and they em-
braced other gods, bowing down to them and
serving them. That is why the LORD has brought
upon them all this evil."

After Building the Temple†

10 * After the twenty years during which Sol-
omon built the two houses, the house of the
LORD and the house of the king— 11 Hiram, king
of Tyre, supplying Solomon with all the cedar
wood, fir wood, and gold he wished, and King
Solomon giving Hiram in return twenty cities in
the land of Galilee— 12 Hiram left Tyre to see the
cities Solomon had given him, but he was not
satisfied with them. 13 So he said, "What are these
cities you have given me, my brother?"† And he
called them the land of Cabul, as they are called
to this day. 14 Hiram, however, had sent King Sol-
omon one hundred and twenty talents of gold.†
15 This is an account of the conscript labor force
King Solomon raised in order to build the house
of the LORD, his own house, Millo,† the wall of
Jerusalem, Hazor, Megiddo, Gezer 16 (Pharaoh,
king of Egypt, had come up and taken Gezer
and, after destroying it by fire and slaying all
the Canaanites living in the city, had given it as
a farewell gift to his daughter, Solomon's wife;
17 Solomon then rebuilt Gezer), Lower Beth-
horon, 18 Baalath, Tamar in the desert of Judah,
19 all his cities for supplies, cities for chariots and
cities for cavalry, and whatever Solomon desired
to build in Jerusalem, in Lebanon, and in the
entire land under his dominion. 20 All the people
who were left of the Amorites, Hittites, Perizzites,
Hivites, and Jebusites, who were not Israelites—
21 those of their descendants who were left in
the land and whom the Israelites had not been
able to destroy under the ban—these Solomon
conscripted as forced laborers, as they are to this
day. 22 But Solomon made none of the Israelites
forced laborers, for they were his fighting force,
his ministers, commanders, adjutants, chariot
officers, and cavalry. 23 There were five hundred
fifty overseers answerable to Solomon's gover-
nors for the work, directing the people engaged
in the work.
24 * As soon as Pharaoh's daughter went up
from the City of David to her house, which he
had built for her, Solomon built Millo. 25 Three
times a year Solomon used to offer burnt of-
ferings and communion offerings on the altar
which he had built to the LORD, and to burn in-
cense before the LORD.

Thus he completed the temple.†

Solomon's Gifts†

26 King Solomon also built a fleet at Ezion-
geber, which is near Elath on the shore of the
Red Sea in the land of Edom.† 27 To this fleet
Hiram sent his own servants, expert sailors, with
the servants of Solomon. 28 They went to Ophir,
and obtained four hundred and twenty talents of
gold and brought it to King Solomon.

Solomon's Listening Heart: the Queen of Sheba†

10 1 * The queen of Sheba,† having heard a
report of Solomon's fame, came to test
him with subtle questions. 2 She arrived in Jeru-
salem with a very numerous retinue, and with
camels bearing spices, a large amount of gold,
and precious stones. She came to Solomon and
spoke to him about everything that she had on

---

† **9:10–25** This unit of the Solomon story corresponds to 5:15–32. It comprises the same two themes, negotiations with Hiram of Tyre (vv. 10–14) and use of conscripted labor (vv. 15–23); the last two verses mark the end of the account of Solomon's building projects (vv. 24–25). Chronicles has an incomplete parallel in 2 Chr 8:1–13.

9:13 *Brother*: a term for a treaty partner; cf. 20:32–33. *Cabul*: the meaning is uncertain; perhaps "of no value."

9:14 The talent was a measure of weight that varied in the course of ancient Israel's history from forty-five to one hundred thirty pounds. This would mean that, at the least, Hiram sent five thousand pounds of gold to Solomon, and the figure may be as much as three times that amount.

9:15 *Millo*: probably means ground fill, and may refer to an artificial earthwork or platform of stamped ground south of the Temple area. It was begun by David (2 Sm 5:9); cf. 1 Kgs 9:24; 11:27.

9:25 With these words the account of the construction and dedication of the Temple, which began in 6:1, comes to a close. The verb "complete" (*shillem*) is a play on Solomon's name (*shelomo*); see also the note on 7:51.

9:26–10:29 The next major unit of the Solomon story returns to the theme of the three gifts the Lord gave Solomon in 3:12–13: a listening heart (10:1–13), riches (9:26–27; 10:14–22, 26–29), universal renown (10:23–25). In 3:16–5:14, where the same three themes structure the passage, the emphasis was on the benefits these gifts brought to the whole nation; here it is on the luxury they afford to Solomon's own court. The material in 9:26–28; 10:11–12, 22 dealing with Solomon's commercial fleet corresponds to the material on Solomon's international affairs in 5:1–5. Chronicles has a partial parallel to this material in 2 Chr 9:17–28; see also 2 Chr 1:14–17.

9:26 *Ezion-geber . . . Edom*: the first mention of maritime commerce in the Israelite kingdom; Edom was subject after David conquered it; cf. 2 Sm 8:13–14.

10:1–13 The sub-unit on Solomon's wisdom contrasts with 3:16–28. There Solomon's gifts led him to listen to the humblest of his subjects; he accomplished justice and was revered by all his people. Here the emphasis is on his clever speech to a foreign monarch. She is duly impressed by the glory of his court, but it is she, not Solomon, who recalls the monarch's duty of establishing justice (v. 9). The unit is interrupted briefly by a remark about Solomon's maritime commerce (10:11–12).

10:1 *Queen of Sheba*: women rulers among the Arabs are recorded in eighth-century B.C. Assyrian inscriptions. Sheba was for centuries the leading principality in what is now Yemen.

---

* **9:10** 1 Kgs 6:38–7:1.
9:24 1 Kgs 3:1; 7:8.
10:1 Mt 12:42; Lk 11:31.

her mind. [3] King Solomon explained everything
she asked about, and there was nothing so ob-
scure that the king could not explain it to her.
[4] When the queen of Sheba witnessed Solomon's
great wisdom, the house he had built, [5] the food
at his table, the seating of his ministers, the at-
tendance and dress of his waiters, his servers,
and the burnt offerings he offered in the house of
the LORD, it took her breath away. [6] "The report I
heard in my country about your deeds and your
wisdom is true," she told the king. [7] "I did not
believe the report until I came and saw with my
own eyes that not even the half had been told
me. Your wisdom and prosperity surpass the
report I heard. [8] Happy are your servants, happy
these ministers of yours, who stand before you
always and listen to your wisdom. [9] Blessed be
the LORD, your God, who has been pleased to
place you on the throne of Israel. In his endur-
ing love for Israel, the LORD has made you king
to carry out judgment and justice." [10] Then she
gave the king one hundred and twenty gold tal-
ents, a very large quantity of spices, and precious
stones. Never again did anyone bring such an
abundance of spices as the queen of Sheba gave
to King Solomon.

[11] Hiram's fleet, which used to bring gold from
Ophir, also brought from there a very large quan-
tity of almug† wood and precious stones. [12] With
this wood the king made supports for the house
of the LORD and for the house of the king, and
harps and lyres for the singers. Never again was
any such almug wood brought or seen to the
present day.

[13] King Solomon gave the queen of Sheba ev-
erything she desired and asked for, besides what
King Solomon gave her from Solomon's royal
bounty. Then she returned with her servants to
her own country.

Solomon's Riches: Domestic Affairs†

[14] * The gold that came to Solomon in one
year weighed six hundred and sixty-six gold tal-
ents, [15] in addition to what came from the tolls
on travelers, from the traffic of merchants, and
from all the kings of Arabia and the governors of
the country. [16] * King Solomon made two hun-
dred shields of beaten gold (six hundred shekels
of gold went into each shield) [17] and three hun-
dred bucklers of beaten gold (three minas of gold
went into each buckler); and the king put them
in the house of the Forest of Lebanon. [18] The king
made a large ivory throne, and overlaid it with
refined gold. [19] The throne had six steps, a back
with a round top, and an arm on each side of the
seat, with two lions standing next to the arms,
[20] and twelve other lions standing there on the
steps, two to a step, one on either side of each
step. Nothing like this was made in any other
kingdom. [21] All King Solomon's drinking vessels
were gold, and all the utensils in the house of the
Forest of Lebanon were pure gold. There was no
silver, for in Solomon's time silver was reckoned
as nothing. [22] For the king had a fleet of Tarshish
ships† at sea with Hiram's fleet. Once every three
years the fleet of Tarshish ships would come with
a cargo of gold, silver, ivory, apes, and peacocks.

Solomon's Renown

[23] Thus King Solomon surpassed all the kings
of the earth in riches and wisdom. [24] And the
whole world sought audience with Solomon,
to hear the wisdom God had put into his heart.
[25] They all brought their yearly tribute: vessels
of silver and gold, garments, weapons, spices,
horses and mules—what was due each year.

Solomon's Riches: Chariots and Horses

[26] * Solomon amassed chariots and horses;
he had one thousand four hundred chariots
and twelve thousand horses; these he allocated
among the chariot cities and to the king's ser-
vice in Jerusalem. [27] * The king made silver as
common in Jerusalem as stones, and cedars as
numerous as the sycamores of the Shephelah.
[28] Solomon's horses were imported from Egypt
and from Cilicia, where the king's merchants
purchased them. [29] A chariot imported from
Egypt cost six hundred shekels of silver, a horse
one hundred and fifty shekels; they were ex-
ported at these rates to all the Hittite and Ara-
mean kings.

1 KGS

†

10:11–12 *Almug*: the identification of this wood is unknown.

10:14–29 The material on Solomon's riches, like that in 4:1–5:8, is organized around domestic affairs, international affairs, and chariots and horses (see note on 4:1–5:8), but contrasts with that earlier passage. There, Solomon's domestic administration produced prosperity for all Judah and Israel (4:20); here the focus is on the wealth and luxury of Solomon's own palace (10:14–21). There his international hegemony assured peace for all Judah and Israel (5:5); here his maritime ventures simply bring him more and more wealth (9:26–28; 10:11–12, 22). There even his livestock benefited from his prudent administration; here chariotry and horses are just another commodity to be traded (10:26–29).

10:22 *Tarshish ships*: large, strong vessels for long voyages. Tarshish was probably the ancient Tartessus, a Phoenician colony in southern Spain. *Ivory, apes, and peacocks*: the Hebrew words are obscure and the translations conjectural; however, the reference is certainly to exotic luxury items.

*

10:14 Dt 17:17; Sir 47:18.
10:16 1 Kgs 14:26–28; 2 Sm 8:7.
10:26 1 Kgs 5:6; Dt 17:16; 2 Chr 1:14; 9:25.
10:27 Dt 17:17; Sir 47:18.

Pray It!

Solomon's Sin

Sometimes when we think we are strongest, we are actually weakest. Solomon replaces his poverty of spirit with pride (see 1 Kgs 3:4–14). He seems to believe that he is strong enough to go against God's command not to take foreign wives and that he can withstand the influence of their foreign gods. But Solomon falls into the sin of idolatry (worshiping other gods), breaking the covenant.

Have you ever considered doing something you knew was wrong? Did you tell yourself that it wouldn't hurt to do it just this once? Maybe that is what Solomon said when he took his first foreign wife.

In your prayer time, reflect or journal on the following questions:

- Think of a time when you deliberately gave in to temptation. What excuses did you use to do so?
- What takes your attention away from God?
- Have you ever tried asking God to give you strength to avoid doing something wrong?
- Pray Psalm 86:11 to end your prayer.

▶ 1 Kgs 11:1–8

The End of Solomon's Reign†

11 1 * King Solomon loved many foreign
women besides the daughter of Pharaoh—
Moabites, Ammonites, Edomites, Sidonians, Hit-
tites— 2 * from nations of which the LORD had
said to the Israelites: You shall not join with
them and they shall not join with you, lest they
turn your hearts to their gods. But Solomon held
them† close in love. 3 He had as wives seven
hundred princesses and three hundred concu-
bines, and they turned his heart.
4 When Solomon was old his wives had turned
his heart to follow other gods, and his heart was
not entirely with the LORD, his God, as the heart
of David his father had been. 5 Solomon fol-
lowed Astarte, the goddess of the Sidonians, and
Milcom, the abomination of the Ammonites.
6 Solomon did what was evil in the sight of the
LORD, and he did not follow the LORD unreserved-
ly as David his father had done. 7 Solomon then
built a high place to Chemosh, the abomination
of Moab, and to Molech, the abomination of the
Ammonites, on the mountain opposite Jerusa-
lem. 8 He did the same for all his foreign wives
who burned incense and sacrificed to their gods.
9 * The LORD became angry with Solomon, be-
cause his heart turned away from the LORD, the
God of Israel, who had appeared to him twice
10 and commanded him not to do this very thing,
not to follow other gods. But he did not observe
what the LORD commanded. 11 So the LORD said
to Solomon: Since this is what you want, and
you have not kept my covenant and the statutes
which I enjoined on you, I will surely tear the
kingdom away from you and give it to your ser-
vant. 12 * But I will not do this during your life-
time, for the sake of David your father; I will tear
it away from your son's hand. 13 Nor will I tear
away the whole kingdom. I will give your son
one tribe for the sake of David my servant and
for the sake of Jerusalem, which I have chosen.

Threats to Solomon's Kingdom†

14 The LORD then raised up an adversary†
against Solomon: Hadad the Edomite, who was
of the royal line in Edom. 15 * Earlier, when Da-
vid had conquered Edom, Joab, the commander
of the army, while going to bury the slain, killed
every male in Edom. 16 Joab and all Israel re-
mained there six months until they had killed
off every male in Edom. 17 But Hadad, with some
Edomite servants of his father, fled toward Egypt.
Hadad was then a young boy. 18 They left Midian
and came to Paran; they gathered men from Pa-
ran and came to Egypt, to Pharaoh, king of Egypt;
he gave Hadad a house, appointed him rations,

---

† **11:1–13** The next major unit of the Solomon story corresponds to 3:1–15. Like the earlier passage it includes the narrator's remarks about Solomon's foreign wives and his building projects, and a divine word commenting on Solomon's conduct. However, where 3:1–15 is generally positive toward Solomon, the present passage is unrelievedly negative. Chronicles has no parallel to this material.

11:2 *Them*: both the nations and their gods.

11:14–25 This unit of the Solomon story corresponds to 2:12b–46, where Solomon secured his kingdom by eliminating three men he perceived as threats. In this passage, we learn of two foreigners the Lord raised up as "adversaries" to Solomon as early as the beginning of his reign (despite Solomon's complacent claim to Hiram in 5:18 that he had no adversary). In the next section we will learn of a third opponent, Israelite rather than foreign, who turns out to be the "servant of Solomon" announced by the Lord in 11:11. Chronicles has no parallel to this material.

11:14 *Adversary*: Hebrew *śatan*, one who stands in opposition; in this context a political opponent.

---

* **11:1–3** Dt 17:17; Sir 47:19–20. **11:2** Ex 34:16. **11:9** 1 Kgs 3:4–15; 6:11–13; 9:2–9. **11:12–13** 1 Kgs 11:34–36. **11:15** 2 Sm 8:13–14.

and assigned him land. 19 Hadad won great favor
with Pharaoh, so that he gave him in marriage
his sister-in-law, the sister of Queen Tahpenes,
his own wife. 20 Tahpenes' sister bore Hadad a
son, Genubath. Tahpenes weaned him in Phar-
aoh's palace. And Genubath lived in Pharaoh's
house, with Pharaoh's own sons. 21 When Hadad
in Egypt heard that David rested with his ances-
tors and that Joab, the commander of the army,
was dead, he said to Pharaoh, "Give me leave to
return to my own land." 22 Pharaoh said to him,
"What do you lack with me, that you are seek-
ing to return to your own land?" He answered,
"Nothing, but please let me go!"

23 God raised up against Solomon another
adversary, Rezon, the son of Eliada, who had
fled from his lord, Hadadezer, king of Zobah,
24 * when David was slaughtering them. Rezon
gathered men about him and became leader of a
marauding band. They went to Damascus, settled
there, and made him king in Damascus. 25 Rezon
was an adversary of Israel as long as Solomon
lived, in addition to the harm done by Hadad,
and he felt contempt for Israel. He became king
over Aram.

Ahijah Announces Jeroboam's Kingship†

26 Solomon had a servant, Jeroboam, son of
Nebat, an Ephraimite from Zeredah with a
widowed mother named Zeruah. He rebelled
against the king. 27 This is how he came to rebel.
King Solomon was building Millo, closing up
the breach of the City of David, his father. 28 Jer-
oboam was a very able man, and when Solomon
saw that the young man was also a good worker,
he put him in charge of all the carriers con-
scripted from the house of Joseph.

29 At that time Jeroboam left Jerusalem, and
the prophet Ahijah the Shilonite met him on the
road. The prophet was wearing a new cloak,†
and when the two were alone in the open coun-
try, 30 * Ahijah took off his new cloak, tore it into
twelve pieces, 31 * and said to Jeroboam: "Take
ten pieces for yourself. Thus says the LORD, the
God of Israel: I am about to tear the kingdom
out of Solomon's hand and will give you ten of
the tribes. 32 He shall have one tribe for the sake
of my servant David, and for the sake of Jerusa-
lem, the city I have chosen out of all the tribes
of Israel. 33 For they have forsaken me and have
bowed down to Astarte, goddess of the Sidoni-
ans, Chemosh, god of Moab, and Milcom, god
of the Ammonites. They have not walked in my
ways or done what is right in my eyes, according
to my statutes and my ordinances, as David his
father did. 34 Yet I will not take any of the king-
dom from Solomon himself, but will keep him
a prince as long as he lives, for the sake of David
my servant, whom I have chosen, who kept my
commandments and statutes.

35 But I will take the kingdom from his son's
hand and give it to you—that is, the ten tribes.
36 I will give his son one tribe, that David my
servant may always have a holding before me in
Jerusalem, the city I have chosen, to set my name
there. 37 You I will take and you shall reign over
all that you desire and shall become king of Is-
rael. 38 If, then, you heed all that I command you,
walking in my ways, and do what is right in my
eyes by keeping my statutes and my command-
ments like David my servant, I will be with you. I
will build a lasting house for you, just as I did for
David; I will give Israel to you. 39 I will humble
David's line for this, but not forever."

40 When Solomon tried to have Jeroboam
killed, Jeroboam fled to Shishak, king of Egypt.
He remained in Egypt until Solomon's death.

41 The rest of the acts of Solomon, with all that
he did and his wisdom, are recorded in the book
of the acts of Solomon. 42 Solomon was king in
Jerusalem over all Israel for forty years. 43 Solo-
mon rested with his ancestors and was buried in
the City of David, his father, and Rehoboam his
son succeeded him as king.

II. The Reign of Jeroboam†

Political Disunity†

12 1 Rehoboam went to Shechem,† where all
Israel had come to make him king. 2 When

† **11:26–43** The last major unit of the Solomon story tells how the prophet Ahijah announces the divine intention to take the larger part of Solomon's kingdom from his control and give it to Jeroboam, Solomon's servant. This counterbalances the first unit of the story, 1:1–2:12a, where another prophet, Nathan, managed to influence the royal succession and obtain the throne for Solomon. The unit is also the first part of the story of Jeroboam (11:26–14:20). It thus acts as a literary hinge connecting the two stories. Chronicles contains a death notice for Solomon in 2 Chr 9:29–31.

11:29 The narrator uses a powerful wordplay here. In the Hebrew consonantal text, Ahijah's cloak (*slmh*) is indistinguishable from Solomon's name (*slmh*). Since a prophetic gesture such as Ahijah's was understood as effecting the event it announced, Ahijah's tearing of his cloak embodies the divine action that will tear Solomon's kingdom apart (cf. vv. 11–13).

12:1–14:20 Like the story of the reign of Solomon, the story of the reign of Jeroboam is concentrically organized. Ahijah's oracle of promise to Jeroboam (11:26–43) belongs to both stories, ending that of Solomon (see note on 1:1–11:43) and beginning that of Jeroboam; it corresponds to Ahijah's oracle of condemnation in 14:1–20. Within those literary boundaries are accounts of political (12:1–20) and religious (13:11–34) disunity between Israel and Judah. The center of the story is the account of Jeroboam's heterodox cultic innovations (12:26–31).

12:1–20 The first major unit of the Jeroboam story was Ahijah's oracle (11:26–40), followed by the notice of Solomon's death

* **11:24** 2 Sm 8:3–6. **11:30** 1 Sm 15:27–28. **11:31–32** 1 Kgs 12:20.

Did You Know?

The Kingdom of Israel Splits

When the people of Israel first came to settle in Canaan, they organized into twelve Tribes, ruled by chieftains, that supported and protected one another. As Israel grew in size, it was necessary to have one central ruler who would unite the tribes into one nation. Saul was the first king of this united Israel. David followed Saul and expanded the kingdom's territory. David's son Solomon continued ruling over the expanded kingdom and engaged in expensive building projects.

At Solomon's death, many Israelites wanted a less demanding king. They had suffered under the burden of heavy taxes and forced labor. When Solomon's son Rehoboam refused to make any changes (see 1 Kgs 12:11), ten of the northern tribes pulled away and placed their own king, Jeroboam, on the throne. The northern kingdom was called Israel. The southern kingdom, composed of two tribes, was called Judah (see map 4, "The Kingdom Years"). The kingdom was now split in two, and it was never again reunited.

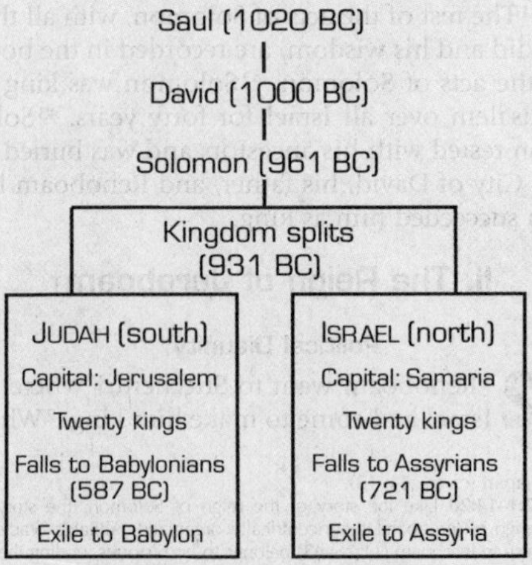

▶ 1 Kgs 12:1–19

Jeroboam, son of Nebat, heard about it, he was
still in Egypt. He had fled from King Solomon
and remained in Egypt, 3 and they sent for him.
Then Jeroboam and the whole assembly of
Israel came and they said to Rehoboam, 4 "Your
father put a heavy yoke on us. If you now lighten
the harsh servitude and the heavy yoke your father imposed on us, we will be your servants."
5 He answered them, "Come back to me in three
days," and the people went away.
6 King Rehoboam asked advice of the elders
who had been in his father Solomon's service
while he was alive, and asked, "How do you advise me to answer this people?" 7 They replied,
"If today you become the servant of this people
and serve them, and give them a favorable answer, they will be your servants forever." 8 But
he ignored the advice the elders had given him,
and asked advice of the young men who had
grown up with him and were in his service. 9 He
said to them, "What answer do you advise that
we should give this people, who have told me,
'Lighten the yoke your father imposed on us'?"
10 The young men who had grown up with him
replied, "This is what you must say to this people
who have told you, 'Your father made our yoke
heavy; you lighten it for us.' You must say, 'My
little finger is thicker than my father's loins. 11 My
father put a heavy yoke on you, but I will make
it heavier. My father beat you with whips, but I
will beat you with scorpions.' " 12 Jeroboam and
the whole people came back to King Rehoboam
on the third day, as the king had instructed them:
"Come back to me in three days." 13 Ignoring the
advice the elders had given him, the king gave
the people a harsh answer. 14 He spoke to them
as the young men had advised: "My father made
your yoke heavy, but I will make it heavier. My
father beat you with whips, but I will beat you
with scorpions." 15 * The king did not listen to
the people, for this turn of events was from the
LORD: he fulfilled the word the LORD had spoken
through Ahijah the Shilonite to Jeroboam, son
of Nebat. 16 * When all Israel saw that the king

† (11:41–43). This is the second major unit. It tells how Jeroboam came to the throne of Israel after the intransigence of Solomon's son Rehoboam provoked the northern tribes to secede from Jerusalem. The political disunity of the two kingdoms fulfills the word spoken by Ahijah. Compare 13:11–32, where Jeroboam's improper cultic innovations produce religious disunity as well. The scene is concentrically arranged: narrative introduction, first interview, first consultation, second consultation, second interview, narrative conclusion. Chronicles has a parallel version of this story in 2 Chr 10:1–19.

12:1 *Shechem*: chief city of the northern tribes, where a covenant had previously been made between the Lord and his people and a stone of witness had been erected in memory of the event (Jos 24:25–27). *All Israel*: see note on 4:7–19.

12:15 1 Kgs 11:26–39. **12:16** 2 Sm 20:1.

did not listen to them, the people answered the king:

"What share have we in David?†
We have no heritage in the son of Jesse.
To your tents, Israel!
Now look to your own house, David."

So Israel went off to their tents. 17 But Rehoboam continued to reign over the Israelites who lived in the cities of Judah.

18 King Rehoboam then sent out Adoram,† who was in charge of the forced labor, but all Israel stoned him to death. King Rehoboam then managed to mount his chariot and flee to Jerusalem. 19 And so Israel has been in rebellion against the house of David to this day. 20 When all Israel heard that Jeroboam had returned, they summoned him to an assembly and made him king over all Israel. None remained loyal to the house of David except the tribe of Judah alone.

Divine Approval†

21 On his arrival in Jerusalem, Rehoboam assembled all the house of Judah and the tribe of Benjamin—one hundred and eighty thousand elite warriors—to wage war against the house of Israel, to restore the kingdom to Rehoboam, son of Solomon. 22 However, the word of God came to Shemaiah, a man of God: 23 Say to Rehoboam, son of Solomon, king of Judah, and to all the house of Judah and to Benjamin, and to the rest of the people: 24 Thus says the LORD: You must not go out to war against your fellow Israelites. Return home, each of you, for it is I who have brought this about. They obeyed the word of the LORD and turned back, according to the word of the LORD.

25 Jeroboam built up Shechem in the hill country of Ephraim and lived there. Then he left it and built up Penuel.

Jeroboam's Cultic Innovations†

26 Jeroboam thought to himself: "Now the kingdom will return to the house of David. 27 If this people go up to offer sacrifices in the house of the LORD in Jerusalem, the hearts of this people will return to their master, Rehoboam, king of Judah, and they will kill me and return to Rehoboam, king of Judah." 28 * The king took counsel, made two calves of gold, and said to the people: "You have been going up to Jerusalem long enough. Here are your gods, O Israel, who brought you up from the land of Egypt." 29 * And he put one in Bethel, the other in Dan.† 30 This led to sin, because the people frequented these calves in Bethel and in Dan. 31 He also built temples on the high places and made priests from among the common people who were not Levites.

Divine Disapproval†

32 Jeroboam established a feast in the eighth month on the fifteenth day of the month like the pilgrimage feast in Judah, and he went up to the altar. He did this in Bethel, sacrificing to the calves he had made. He stationed in Bethel the priests of the high places he had built. 33 Jeroboam went up to the altar he built in Bethel on the fifteenth day of the eighth month, the month he arbitrarily chose. He established a feast for the Israelites, and he went up to the altar to burn incense.

13 1 A man of God came from Judah to Bethel by the word of the LORD, while Jeroboam was standing at the altar to burn incense. 2 * He cried out against the altar by the word of the LORD: "Altar, altar, thus says the LORD: A child shall be born to the house of David, Josiah by

†

12:16 *What share have we in David?*: even in David's time the northern tribes seemed ready to withdraw from the union with Judah (2 Sm 20:1). The unreasonable attitude of Rehoboam toward them intensified the discontent caused by the oppression of Solomon (v. 4) and thus precipitated the political separation of the two kingdoms. In the view of the Deuteronomistic historian (1 Kgs 11:35–36; 12:24), this was by the Lord's decree.

12:18 *Adoram*: the name is a shortened form of "Adoniram" (see 4:6; 5:28). If this is the same Adoram who held the position in David's day (2 Sm 20:24), he would have been a very old man.

12:21–25 The center of this unit is a divine oracle delivered by a man of God of the Southern Kingdom in which the Lord affirms his approval of the secession of the northern tribes. Compare 13:1–10, where another man of God from Judah proclaims the Lord's condemnation of Jeroboam's religious separatism. Chronicles has a very similar version of Shemaiah's oracle in 2 Chr 11:1–4.

12:26–31 At the center of the story of Jeroboam the narrator describes how the king went beyond the political separation of Israel from Judah to create a separatist religious system as well. Jeroboam feared that continued worship in the single Temple in Jerusalem would threaten the political independence of his kingdom. To prevent this he established sanctuaries with non-levitical clergy in his own territory. At two of the sanctuaries he set up golden calves, which the narrator depicts as idols. Thus begins what will later be called "the sin of Jeroboam" (13:34), a theme that will be echoed throughout 1–2 Kings in the condemnations of almost every king of the Northern Kingdom. Historically, Jeroboam's innovations were not as heterodox as our narrative portrays them. Bethel was an ancient and traditional site for worship of the Lord; and the calves were probably intended to be a dais for the deity invisibly enthroned upon them, rather like the cherubim atop the ark of the covenant.

12:29 *Bethel . . . Dan*: at the southern and northern boundaries of the separate kingdom of Israel, where sanctuaries had existed in the past (Gn 12:8; 13:3–4; 28:10–22; 35:1–15; Jgs 18:1–31).

12:32–13:10 This unit of the Jeroboam story corresponds to 12:21–25. Before Jeroboam's cultic innovations, a man of God from Judah proclaimed the Lord's approval of the political separation of the kingdoms. After Jeroboam's cultic innovations, a man of God from Judah proclaims the Lord's disapproval of Israel's religious separatism. The unit begins with a long, detailed introduction about the dedication festival Jeroboam holds at Bethel (12:32–33); then follows the scene of the ceremony disrupted by the oracle of the man of God (13:1–10).

*

12:28 Ex 32:1–10.
12:29 Tb 1:5.
13:2 2 Kgs 23:16.

name, who shall slaughter upon you the priests
of the high places who burn incense upon you,
and they shall burn human bones upon you."
3 * He also gave a sign that same day and said:
"This is the sign that the LORD has spoken: The
altar shall be torn apart and the ashes on it shall
be scattered." 4 When the king heard the word of
the man of God which he was crying out against
the altar in Bethel, Jeroboam stretched forth his
hand from the altar and said, "Seize him!" But
the hand he stretched forth against him with-
ered, so that he could not draw it back. 5 (The
altar was torn apart and the ashes from the altar
were scattered, in accordance with the sign the
man of God gave by the word of the LORD.)
6 Then the king said to the man of God, "En-
treat the LORD, your God, and intercede for me
that my hand may be restored." So the man of
God entreated the LORD, and the king's hand was
restored as it was before. 7 The king told the man
of God, "Come with me to the house for some
refreshment so that I may give you a present."
8 The man of God said to the king, "If you gave me
half your palace, I would not go with you, nor eat
bread or drink water in this place. 9 For I was in-
structed by the word of the LORD: Do not eat bread
or drink water, and do not return by the way you
came." 10 So he departed by another road and did
not go back the way he had come to Bethel.

Prophetic Disunity†

11 There was an old prophet living in Bethel,
whose son came and told him all that the man of
God had done that day in Bethel. When his sons
repeated to their father the words the man of God
had spoken to the king, 12 the father asked them,
"Which way did he go?" So his sons pointed out
to him the road taken by the man of God who
had come from Judah. 13 Then he said to his sons,
"Saddle the donkey for me." When they had sad-
dled it, he mounted 14 and followed the man of
God, whom he found seated under a terebinth.
When he asked him, "Are you the man of God
who came from Judah?" he answered, "Yes."
15 Then he said, "Come home with me and have
some bread." 16 "I cannot return with you or go
with you, and I cannot eat bread or drink water
with you in this place," he answered, 17 "for I was
told by the word of the LORD: You shall not eat
bread or drink water there, and do not go back the
way you came." 18 But he said to him, "I, too, am
a prophet like you, and an angel told me by the
word of the LORD: Bring him back with you to your
house to eat bread and drink water." But he was
lying to him. 19 So he went back with him, and ate
bread and drank water in his house. 20 But while
they were sitting at table, the word of the LORD
came to the prophet who had brought him back,
21 and he cried out to the man of God who had
come from Judah: "Thus says the LORD: Because
you rebelled against the charge of the LORD and
did not keep the command which the LORD, your
God, gave you, 22 but returned and ate bread and
drank water in the place where he told you, Do
not eat bread or drink water, your corpse shall not
be brought to the grave of your ancestors." 23 After
he had eaten bread and drunk, they saddled for
him the donkey that belonged to the prophet who
had brought him back, 24 and he set out. But a lion
met him on the road, and killed him. His body lay
sprawled on the road, and the donkey remained
standing by it, and so did the lion.
25 Some passersby saw the body lying in the
road, with the lion standing beside it, and carried
the news to the city where the old prophet lived.
26 On hearing it, the prophet who had brought
him back from his journey said: "It is the man of
God who rebelled against the charge of the LORD.
The LORD has delivered him to a lion, which
mangled and killed him, according to the word
which the LORD had spoken to him." 27 Then he
said to his sons, "Saddle the donkey for me,"
and they saddled it. 28 He went off and found
the body sprawled on the road with the donkey
and the lion standing beside it. The lion had not
eaten the body nor had it harmed the donkey.
29 The prophet lifted up the body of the man of
God and put it on the donkey, and brought him
back to the city to mourn and to bury him. 30 He
laid the man's body in his own grave, and they
mourned over it: "Alas, my brother!" 31 * After
he had buried him, he said to his sons, "When I
die, bury me in the grave where the man of God
is buried. Lay my bones beside his. 32 * For the
word which he proclaimed by the word of the
LORD against the altar in Bethel and against all
the temples on the high places in the cities of
Samaria shall certainly come to pass."
33 Even after this, Jeroboam did not turn from
his evil way, but again made priests for the high

† **13:11–34** The next major unit illustrates how Jeroboam's cultic innovations begin to alienate prophetic figures of the two kingdoms. Nevertheless, the Lord's word is stronger than any human attempt to thwart it. The two prophets also foreshadow the destinies of their respective kingdoms. Israel's experiment with idolatry can tempt Judah to abandon its faithfulness to the Lord. If Judah succumbs, and no longer speaks the word that can call Israel back to the true God, then the only hope for reuniting the two kingdoms will be when they have both died the death of exile.

* **13:3** 2 Kgs 23:15. **13:31** 2 Kgs 23:17–18. **13:32** 2 Kgs 23:19–20.

places from among the common people. Whoever desired it was installed as a priest of the high places. 34 This is the account of the sin of the house of Jeroboam for which it was to be cut off and destroyed from the face of the earth.

Ahijah Announces Jeroboam's Downfall†

14 1 At that time Abijah, son of Jeroboam, took sick. 2 * So Jeroboam said to his wife, "Go and disguise yourself so that no one will recognize you as Jeroboam's wife. Then go to Shiloh, where you will find Ahijah the prophet. It was he who spoke the word that made me king over this people. 3 Take along ten loaves, some cakes, and a jar of honey, and go to him. He will tell you what will happen to the child." 4 The wife of Jeroboam did so. She left and went to Shiloh and came to the house of Ahijah.

Now Ahijah could not see because age had dimmed his sight. 5 But the LORD said to Ahijah: Jeroboam's wife is coming to consult you about her son, for he is sick. Thus and so you must tell her. When she comes, she will be in disguise. 6 So Ahijah, hearing the sound of her footsteps as she entered the door, said, "Come in, wife of Jeroboam. Why are you in disguise? For my part, I have been commissioned to give you bitter news. 7 Go, tell Jeroboam, 'Thus says the LORD, the God of Israel: I exalted you from among the people and made you ruler of my people Israel. 8 I tore the kingdom away from the house of David and gave it to you. Yet you have not been like my servant David, who kept my commandments and followed me with his whole heart, doing only what is right in my sight. 9 You have done more evil than all who were before you: you have gone and made for yourself other gods and molten images to provoke me; but me you have cast behind your back. 10 * Therefore, I am bringing evil upon the house of Jeroboam:

I will cut off from Jeroboam's line every male
—bond or free—in Israel;
I will burn up what is left of the house of
Jeroboam
as dung is burned, completely.
11 * Anyone of Jeroboam's line who dies in the
city,
dogs will devour;
anyone who dies in the field,
the birds of the sky will devour.

For the LORD has spoken!' 12 As for you, leave, and go home! As you step inside the city, the child will die, 13 and all Israel will mourn him and bury him, for he alone of Jeroboam's line will be laid in the grave, since in him alone of Jeroboam's house has something pleasing to the LORD, the God of Israel, been found. 14 The LORD will raise up for himself a king over Israel who will cut off the house of Jeroboam—today, at this very moment! 15 The LORD will strike Israel like a reed tossed about in the water and will pluck out Israel from this good land which he gave their ancestors, and will scatter them beyond the River,† because they made asherahs for themselves, provoking the LORD. 16 He will give up Israel because of the sins Jeroboam has committed and caused Israel to commit." 17 So Jeroboam's wife left and went back; when she came to Tirzah and crossed the threshold of her house, the child died. 18 He was buried and all Israel mourned him, according to the word of the LORD spoken through his servant Ahijah the prophet.

19 The rest of the acts of Jeroboam, how he fought and how he reigned, these are recorded in the book of the chronicles of the kings of Israel. 20 The length of Jeroboam's reign was twenty-two years. He rested with his ancestors, and Nadab his son succeeded him as king.

III. Kings of Judah and Israel†

Reign of Rehoboam

21 † Rehoboam, son of Solomon, became king in Judah. Rehoboam was forty-one years old when he became king, and he reigned seventeen years in Jerusalem, the city in which, out of all the tribes of Israel, the LORD chose to set his name. His mother's name was Naamah the Ammonite. 22 Judah did evil in the LORD's sight and they angered him even more than their ancestors

† **14:1–20** The last major unit of the Jeroboam story recounts the story of Ahijah of Shiloh's oracle condemning the entire house of Jeroboam; this is followed by a formulaic notice of Jeroboam's death and the succession of his son. Compare the first unit of the Jeroboam story, 11:26–43, which recounted Ahijah's oracle proclaiming Jeroboam's kingship, followed by the formulaic notice of the death of Solomon.

14:15 *The River*: the Euphrates; see note on 5:1.

14:21–16:34 The treatment of the events of Jeroboam's reign shows that the author believes that the political division of the kingdoms embodies the Lord's will, but that their religious separation is undesirable. The Israelites are, in effect, one people of God under two royal administrations. This complex arrangement is reflected in the way 1–2 Kings organizes the history of the divided kingdoms. Each reign is treated as a unity: the kings, whether of Israel or Judah, are legitimate rulers. But the accounts of northern and southern kings are interwoven in the order in which each came to the throne, without regard to which kingdom they ruled: the people of God is one.

14:21 The account of each king's reign follows the same basic pattern: a formulaic introduction, a theological evaluation based on religious fidelity, a brief account of an event from the king's reign, and a formulaic conclusion.

* **14:2** 1 Kgs 11:29–39. **14:10** 1 Kgs 15:29–30. **14:11** 1 Kgs 16:4; 21:22.

had done. 23 They, too, built for themselves high
places, sacred pillars, and asherahs,† upon every
high hill and under every green tree. 24 There
were also pagan priests in the land. Judah imi-
tated all the abominable practices of the nations
whom the LORD had driven out of the Israelites'
way. 25 † In the fifth year of King Rehoboam, Shi-
shak, king of Egypt, attacked Jerusalem. 26 * He
took everything, including the treasures of the
house of the LORD and the treasures of the house
of the king, even the gold shields Solomon had
made. 27 To replace them, King Rehoboam made
bronze shields, which he entrusted to the officers
of the guard on duty at the entrance of the royal
house. 28 Whenever the king visited the house of
the LORD, those on duty would carry the shields,
and then return them to the guardroom.

29 The rest of the acts of Rehoboam, with all
that he did, are recorded in the book of the
chronicles of the kings of Judah. 30 There was war
between Rehoboam and Jeroboam all their days.
31 Rehoboam rested with his ancestors; he was
buried with his ancestors in the City of David.
His mother's name was Naamah the Ammonite.
His son Abijam succeeded him as king.

Reign of Abijam

15 1 In the eighteenth year of King Jeroboam,
son of Nebat, Abijam became king of Ju-
dah; 2 he reigned three years in Jerusalem. His
mother's name was Maacah, daughter of Abish-
alom.

3 He followed all the sins his father had com-
mitted before him, and his heart was not entirely
with the LORD, his God, as was the heart of Da-
vid his father. 4 Yet for David's sake the LORD, his
God, gave him a holding in Jerusalem, raising
up his son after him and permitting Jerusalem
to endure, 5 * because David had done what was
right in the sight of the LORD and did not disobey
any of his commands as long as he lived, except
in the case of Uriah the Hittite.

6 There was war between Rehoboam and Jer-
oboam all their days. 7 The rest of the acts of
Abijam, with all that he did, are recorded in the
book of the chronicles of the kings of Judah.
There was war between Abijam and Jeroboam.
8 Abijam rested with his ancestors; they buried
him in the City of David, and his son Asa suc-
ceeded him as king.

Reign of Asa

9 In the twentieth year of Jeroboam, king of
Israel, Asa, king of Judah, became king; 10 he
reigned forty-one years in Jerusalem. His moth-
er's† name was Maacah, daughter of Abishalom.
11 Asa did what was right in the sight of the LORD
like David his father, 12 banishing the pagan
priests from the land and removing all the idols
his ancestors had made. 13 He also deposed his
grandmother Maacah from her position as queen
mother, because she had made an outrageous
object for Asherah. Asa cut down this object and
burned it in the Wadi Kidron. 14 The high places
did not disappear; yet Asa's heart was entirely
with the LORD as long as he lived. 15 He brought
into the house of the LORD his father's and his
own votive offerings of silver and gold and vari-
ous vessels. 16 There was war between Asa and Ba-
asha, king of Israel, all their days. 17 Baasha, king
of Israel, attacked Judah and fortified Ramah to
blockade Asa, king of Judah. 18 Asa then took all
the silver and gold remaining in the treasuries of
the house of the LORD and the house of the king.
Entrusting them to his ministers, King Asa sent
them to Ben-hadad, son of Tabrimmon, son of
Hezion, king of Aram,† who ruled in Damascus.
He said: 19 "There is a treaty between you and me,
as there was between your father and my father. I
am sending you a present of silver and gold. Go,
break your treaty with Baasha, king of Israel, that
he may withdraw from me." 20 Ben-hadad agreed
with King Asa and sent the leaders of his troops
against the cities of Israel. They attacked Ijon,
Dan, Abel-beth-maacah, and all Chinnereth,
besides all the land of Naphtali. 21 When Baa-
sha heard of it, he left off fortifying Ramah, and
stayed in Tirzah. 22 Then King Asa summoned all
Judah without exception, and they carried away
the stones and beams with which Baasha was
fortifying Ramah. With them King Asa built Geba
of Benjamin and Mizpah. 23 All the rest of the
acts of Asa, with all his valor and all that he did,
and the cities he built, are recorded in the book
of the chronicles of the kings of Judah. But in his
old age, Asa had an infirmity in his feet. 24 Asa

†

14:23 *Asherahs*: see note on Ex 34:13.

14:25–28, 30 The narrator recounts Shishak's campaign here to imply that it was punishment for Judah's evil, and perhaps to cast him as supporting Jeroboam in his constant warfare with Rehoboam. (Shishak was named as Jeroboam's protector and patron in 11:40.) Egyptian records of the campaign list one hundred fifty cities conquered in Israel as well as Judah, but Jerusalem is not one of them. Chronicles has a parallel version of this account in 2 Chr 12:9–11.

15:10 Maacah was in fact Asa's grandmother (see v. 2), but "king's mother" was perhaps a title for the *gebira*, the "Great Lady" or "queen mother" (see, for instance, 2:19). This influential position was usually held by the king's biological mother, but Maacah may have retained it after the early death of her son Abijam.

15:18 *Ben-hadad . . . king of Aram*: Ben-hadad I, third successor of Rezon, who had thrown off the yoke of the Israelites during the reign of Solomon and become king of Aram (11:23–24). Chronicles has a parallel version of this account in 2 Chr 16:1–6. *Who ruled*: lit., "sitting," i.e., enthroned, possibly also meaning "resident" or "residing."

14:26 1 Kgs 10:16–17. **15:5** 2 Sm 11:1–27.

rested with his ancestors; he was buried with his
ancestors in the City of David his father, and his
son Jehoshaphat succeeded him as king.

Reign of Nadab

25 Nadab, son of Jeroboam, became king of Is-
rael in the second year of Asa, king of Judah. For
two years he reigned over Israel.
26 He did what was evil in the LORD's sight,
walking in the way of his father and the sin he
had caused Israel to commit. 27 Baasha, son of
Ahijah, of the house of Issachar, plotted against
him and struck him down at Gibbethon of the
Philistines, which Nadab and all Israel were be-
sieging. 28 Baasha killed him in the third year of
Asa, king of Judah, and succeeded him as king.
29 * Once he was king, he killed the entire house
of Jeroboam, not leaving a single soul but de-
stroying Jeroboam utterly, according to the word
of the LORD spoken through his servant, Ahijah
the Shilonite, 30 because of the sins Jeroboam
committed and caused Israel to commit, by
which he provoked the LORD, the God of Israel,
to anger.
31 The rest of the acts of Nadab, with all that he
did, are recorded in the book of the chronicles of
the kings of Israel. 32 There was war between Asa
and Baasha, king of Israel, all their days.

Reign of Baasha

33 In the third year of Asa, king of Judah, Ba-
asha, son of Ahijah, became king of all Israel in
Tirzah for twenty-four years.
34 He did what was evil in the LORD's sight,
walking in the way of Jeroboam and the sin he
had caused Israel to commit.

16 1 The word of the LORD came to Jehu, son
of Hanani, against Baasha: 2 Inasmuch as I
exalted you from the dust and made you ruler of
my people Israel, but you have walked in the way
of Jeroboam and have caused my people Israel to
sin, provoking me to anger by their sins, 3 * I will
burn up what is left of Baasha and his house; I
will make your house like that of Jeroboam, son
of Nebat:

4 * One of Baasha's line who dies in the city,
dogs will devour;
One who dies in the field,
the birds of the sky will devour.

5 The rest of the acts of Baasha, what he did
and his valor, are recorded in the book of the
chronicles of the kings of Israel. 6 Baasha rested
with his ancestors; he was buried in Tirzah, and
his son Elah succeeded him as king. 7 (Through
the prophet Jehu, son of Hanani, the word of the
LORD came against Baasha and his house, because
of all the evil Baasha did in the sight of the LORD,
provoking him to anger by his deeds so that he
became like the house of Jeroboam, and because
of what he destroyed.)

Reign of Elah

8 In the twenty-sixth year of Asa, king of Judah,
Elah, son of Baasha, became king of Israel in Tir-
zah for two years.
9 His servant Zimri, commander of half his
chariots, plotted against him. As he was in Tir-
zah, drinking to excess in the house of Arza, mas-
ter of his palace in Tirzah, 10 * Zimri entered; he
struck and killed him in the twenty-seventh year
of Asa, king of Judah, and succeeded him as king.
11 Once he was king, seated on the throne, he
killed the whole house of Baasha, not sparing a
single male relative or friend of his. 12 * Zimri de-
stroyed the entire house of Baasha, according to
the word the LORD spoke against Baasha through
Jehu the prophet, 13 because of all the sins which
Baasha and his son Elah committed and caused
Israel to commit, provoking the LORD, the God of
Israel, to anger by their idols.
14 The rest of the acts of Elah, with all that he
did, are recorded in the book of the chronicles of
the kings of Israel.

Reign of Zimri

15 In the twenty-seventh year of Asa, king of
Judah, Zimri became king for seven days in Tir-
zah.
The army was encamped at Gibbethon of
the Philistines 16 when they heard, "Zimri has
formed a conspiracy and has killed the king." So
that day in the camp all Israel made Omri, com-
mander of the army, king of Israel. 17 Omri and
all Israel with him marched up from Gibbethon
and besieged Tirzah. 18 When Zimri saw that the
city was captured, he entered the citadel of the
king's house and burned it down over him. He
died 19 because of the sins he had committed,
doing what was evil in the LORD's sight by walk-
ing in the way of Jeroboam and the sin he had
caused Israel to commit.
20 The rest of the acts of Zimri, with the con-
spiracy he carried out, are recorded in the book
of the chronicles of the kings of Israel.

1 KGS

* **15:29** 1 Kgs 14:10–11.
* **16:3** 1 Kgs 16:11; 21:22.
* **16:4** 1 Kgs 14:11.
* **16:10** 2 Kgs 9:31.
* **16:12** 1 Kgs 16:2–4.

Civil War

21 At that time the people of Israel were divided
in two, half following Tibni, son of Ginath, to
make him king, and half for Omri. 22 The parti-
sans of Omri prevailed over those of Tibni, son
of Ginath. Tibni died and Omri became king.

Reign of Omri

23 In the thirty-first year of Asa, king of Judah,
Omri became king of Israel for twelve years; the
first six of them he reigned in Tirzah.
24 He then bought the mountain of Samaria
from Shemer for two silver talents and built
upon the mountain the city he named Samaria,
after Shemer, the former owner. 25 But Omri did
what was evil in the LORD's sight, more than any
of his predecessors. 26 In every way he imitated
the sinful conduct of Jeroboam, son of Nebat,
and the sin he had caused Israel to commit, thus
provoking the LORD, the God of Israel, to anger
by their idols.
27 The rest of the acts of Omri, what he did and
his valor, are recorded in the book of the chroni-
cles of the kings of Israel. 28 Omri rested with his
ancestors; he was buried in Samaria, and Ahab
his son succeeded him as king.

Reign of Ahab

29 Ahab, son of Omri, became king of Israel in
the thirty-eighth year of Asa, king of Judah. Ahab,
son of Omri, reigned over Israel in Samaria for
twenty-two years.
30 Ahab, son of Omri, did what was evil in the
LORD's sight more than any of his predecessors.
31 It was not enough for him to follow the sins
of Jeroboam, son of Nebat. He even married
Jezebel, daughter of Ethbaal, king of the Sidoni-
ans, and began to serve Baal, and worship him.
32 Ahab set up an altar to Baal in the house of
Baal which he built in Samaria, 33 and also made
an asherah. Ahab did more to provoke the LORD,
the God of Israel, to anger than any of the kings
of Israel before him. 34 * During his reign, Hiel
from Bethel rebuilt Jericho. At the cost of Abi-
ram, his firstborn son, he laid the foundation,
and at the cost of Segub, his youngest son, he set
up the gates, according to the word of the LORD
spoken through Joshua, son of Nun.†

IV. The Story of Elijah†

Elijah Proclaims a Drought†

17 1 Elijah the Tishbite,† * from Tishbe in Gil-
ead, said to Ahab: "As the LORD, the God
of Israel, lives, whom I serve, during these years
there shall be no dew or rain except at my word."
2 The word of the LORD came to Elijah: 3 Leave
here, go east and hide in the Wadi Cherith, east
of the Jordan. 4 You shall drink of the wadi, and
I have commanded ravens to feed you there. 5 So
he left and did as the LORD had commanded. He
left and remained by the Wadi Cherith, east of
the Jordan. 6 * Ravens brought him bread and
meat in the morning, and bread and meat in the
evening, and he drank from the wadi.
7 After some time, however, the wadi ran dry,
because no rain had fallen in the land. 8 * So
the word of the LORD came to him: 9 Arise, go to
Zarephath of Sidon and stay there. I have com-
manded a widow there to feed you. 10 He arose
and went to Zarephath. When he arrived at the
entrance of the city, a widow was there gathering
sticks; he called out to her, "Please bring me a
small cupful of water to drink." 11 She left to get
it, and he called out after her, "Please bring along
a crust of bread." 12 She said, "As the LORD, your
God, lives, I have nothing baked; there is only a
handful of flour in my jar and a little oil in my
jug. Just now I was collecting a few sticks, to go
in and prepare something for myself and my
son; when we have eaten it, we shall die." 13 Eli-
jah said to her, "Do not be afraid. Go and do as
you have said. But first make me a little cake and

† **16:34** See note on Jos 6:26.

17:1–19:21 The central section of 1–2 Kings tells the story of the dynasty of Omri. That dynasty begins and ends in civil war (1 Kgs 16:21–22; 2 Kgs 9–11). Most of the story is set during the reigns of Ahab of Israel (1 Kgs 16:29–22:40) and his son Joram (2 Kgs 3:1–9:26) and focuses particularly on the interaction of the king with various prophets, especially Ahab with Elijah and Joram with Elisha. The story of Ahab itself contains two large complexes, a series of narratives about Elijah (1 Kgs 17:1–19:21) and a series about hostility between Ahab and the prophets (1 Kgs 20:1–22:38).

17:1–24 The story of Elijah is in three parts. The first (chap. 17) describes how Elijah proclaimed a drought on God's authority and how he survived during the drought. The second (chap. 18) describes how he ends the drought by bringing the populace back to exclusive worship of the Lord. The third (chap. 19) describes Elijah's despair at the failure of his prophetic mission and his consequent attempt to resign from the prophetic office.

17:1 This verse introduces the enigmatic figure of Elijah the Tishbite. (The name "Elijah" means "the Lord is my God." The meaning of "Tishbite" is unknown; it may refer to a place or to a social class.) His appearance before Ahab is abrupt and involves several matters that will unify the whole Elijah story. His claim to "serve the Lord" (lit., to "stand before the Lord") points forward to 19:13, where he refuses to do so; the center of narrative tension on this level is the question of the prophet's autonomy in God's service. His proclamation of a drought points forward to 18:41–45 where he announces the drought's end; the center of narrative tension on this level is the struggle between the Lord and the Canaanite fertility god Baal for the loyalties of Israel. His claim that the drought is due to his own word of power ("except at my word") points forward to 17:24 where the widow acknowledges the divine source of the word Elijah speaks; the center of narrative tension on this level is the gradual characterization of the prophet as one who receives a divine word (vv. 2, 8), obeys it (v. 5), conveys an effective divine word of threat (v. 1) or promise (vv. 14, 16), and even speaks an effective human word of entreaty to God (vv. 20, 22).

* **16:34** Jos 6:26. **17:1** Sir 48:1–12; Jas 5:17–18. **17:6** Ex 16:8, 12. **17:8–16** 2 Kgs 4:1–7; Lk 4:25–26.

bring it to me. Afterwards you can prepare some-
thing for yourself and your son. 14 For the LORD,
the God of Israel, says: The jar of flour shall not
go empty, nor the jug of oil run dry, until the day
when the LORD sends rain upon the earth." 15 She
left and did as Elijah had said. She had enough to
eat for a long time—he and she and her house-
hold. 16 The jar of flour did not go empty, nor the
jug of oil run dry, according to the word of the
LORD spoken through Elijah.

17 * Some time later the son of the woman, the
owner of the house, fell sick, and his sickness
grew more severe until he stopped breathing.
18 So she said to Elijah, "Why have you done this
to me, man of God? Have you come to me to call
attention to my guilt and to kill my son?" 19 Eli-
jah said to her, "Give me your son." Taking him
from her lap, he carried him to the upper room
where he was staying, and laid him on his own
bed. 20 He called out to the LORD: "LORD, my God,
will you afflict even the widow with whom I am
staying by killing her son?" 21 Then he stretched
himself out upon the child three times and he
called out to the LORD: "LORD, my God, let the
life breath return to the body of this child."
22 The LORD heard the prayer of Elijah; the life
breath returned to the child's body and he lived.
23 Taking the child, Elijah carried him down into
the house from the upper room and gave him to
his mother. Elijah said, "See! Your son is alive."
24 The woman said to Elijah, "Now indeed I
know that you are a man of God, and it is truly
the word of the LORD that you speak."

Elijah Ends the Drought†

18 1 Long afterward, in the third year, the
word of the LORD came to Elijah: Go, pre-
sent yourself to Ahab, that I may send rain upon
the earth. 2 So Elijah went to present himself to
Ahab.

Now the famine in Samaria was severe, 3 and
Ahab had summoned Obadiah, master of his
palace, who greatly revered the LORD. 4 When Jez-
ebel was slaughtering the prophets of the LORD,
Obadiah took a hundred prophets, hid them
away by fifties in caves, and supplied them with
food and water. 5 Ahab said to Obadiah, "Go
through the land to all sources of water and to all
the wadis. We may find grass and keep the horses
and mules alive, so that we shall not have to
slaughter any of the beasts." 6 Dividing the land
to explore between them, Ahab went one way by
himself, Obadiah another way by himself. 7 As
Obadiah was on his way, Elijah met him. Recog-
nizing him, Obadiah fell prostrate and asked, "Is
it you, my lord Elijah?" 8 He said to him, "Yes. Go
tell your lord, 'Elijah is here!' "† 9 But Obadiah
said, "What sin has your servant committed, that
you are handing me over to Ahab to be killed?
10 As the LORD, your God, lives, there is no nation
or kingdom where my lord has not sent in search
of you. When they replied, 'He is not here,' he
made each kingdom and nation swear they could
not find you. 11 And now you say, 'Go tell your
lord: Elijah is here!' 12 After I leave you, the spirit
of the LORD will carry you to some place I do not
know, and when I go to inform Ahab and he
does not find you, he will kill me—though your
servant has revered the LORD from his youth!
13 Have you not been told, my lord, what I did
when Jezebel was murdering the prophets of the
LORD—that I hid a hundred of the prophets of
the LORD, fifty each in caves, and supplied them
with food and water? 14 And now you say, 'Go tell
your lord: Elijah is here!' He will kill me!" 15 Eli-
jah answered, "As the LORD of hosts lives, whom I
serve, I will present myself to him today."

16 So Obadiah went to meet Ahab and in-
formed him, and Ahab came to meet Elijah.
17 When Ahab saw Elijah, he said to him, "Is it
you, you disturber of Israel?" 18 He answered,
"It is not I who disturb Israel, but you and your
father's house, by forsaking the commands of
the LORD and you by following the Baals. 19 Now
summon all Israel to me on Mount Carmel, as
well as the four hundred and fifty prophets of
Baal and the four hundred prophets of Asherah
who eat at Jezebel's table." 20 So Ahab sum-
moned all the Israelites and had the prophets
gather on Mount Carmel.

21 Elijah approached all the people and said,
"How long will you straddle the issue? If the
LORD is God, follow him; if Baal, follow him."
But the people did not answer him. 22 So Elijah
said to the people, "I am the only remaining
prophet of the LORD, and there are four hundred

† **18:1–45** The story of the conflict with the prophets of Baal (vv. 21–40) is embedded in the story of the drought and its ending (vv. 1–20, 41–45). The connection between the two stories is found in Canaanite theology, in whose pantheon Baal, "the Cloud Rider," the god of rain and storm, was recognized as the one who brings fertility. Worship of many gods was virtually universal in the ancient world; the Israelite requirement of exclusive worship of the Lord (Ex 20:3) was unique. The people of Israel had apparently become comfortable worshiping both Baal and the Lord, perhaps assigning mutually exclusive spheres of influence to each. By claiming authority over the rain (17:1; 18:1), the Lord was challenging Baal's power in Baal's own domain. The entire drought story in chaps. 17–18 implies what becomes explicit in 18:21–40: this is a struggle between the Lord and Baal for the loyalties of the people of Israel.

18:8 *Elijah is here*: the Hebrew *hinneh 'eliyahu* involves a pun. The sentence means both "Elijah is here," informing Ahab that the prophet has been found, and "Behold, Yhwh is my God" (the meaning of the name "Elijah").

17:17–24 2 Kgs 4:18–37; Lk 7:11–16.

Introducing...

Elijah and Elisha

You don't want to mess with Elijah and Elisha. They are take-no-prisoners kinds of prophets. According to First Kings, Elijah has 450 prophets of Baal killed after publicly humiliating them (see 18:40). And when a bunch of boys call Elisha "baldy," they are attacked by bears (see 2 Kgs 2:23–24).

Elijah, whose name means "Yahweh is my God," shows up in the second half of First Kings, reminding the Israelites that God is their God alone and that keeping God's covenant means not worshiping the Canaanite baals (gods). In a dramatic story, he shows the idol-worshiping King Ahab and Queen Jezebel that God is superior to their false gods (see 1 Kgs 18:21–40).

Elijah was recorded as being carried to heaven in a fiery chariot (see 2 Kgs 2:11) as a sign of his greatness, and he was expected to reappear before the "day of the LORD" arrived (see Mal 3:23). By New Testament times, Elijah had come to represent the prophets as Moses had come to represent the Law. Referring to Moses and Elijah was a way of summarizing everything God had revealed before Christ.

Elisha was Elijah's disciple and successor. He plays an important role in the first half of Second Kings. Elisha's name means "God is salvation." He was a man of wisdom and a miracle worker.

These "tough guys" also had tender hearts. Both miraculously multiplied food for widows (see 1 Kgs 17:16, 2 Kgs 4:5), and both brought a dead child back to life (see 1 Kgs 17:22, 2 Kgs 4:34). Elijah and Elisha are revered both for their uncompromising faith and for their compassion for the "little ones."

---

and fifty prophets of Baal. 23 Give us two young
bulls. Let them choose one, cut it into pieces,
and place it on the wood, but start no fire. I shall
prepare the other and place it on the wood, but
shall start no fire. 24 You shall call upon the name
of your gods, and I will call upon the name of the
LORD. The God who answers with fire is God." All
the people answered, "We agree!"
25 Elijah then said to the prophets of Baal,
"Choose one young bull and prepare it first, for
there are more of you. Call upon your gods, but
do not start the fire." 26 Taking the young bull that
was turned over to them, they prepared it and
called upon Baal from morning to noon, saying,
"Baal, answer us!" But there was no sound, and
no one answering. And they hopped around the
altar they had prepared. 27 When it was noon, Eli-
jah taunted them: "Call louder, for he is a god;
he may be busy doing his business, or may be
on a journey. Perhaps he is asleep and must be
awakened." 28 They called out louder and slashed
themselves with swords and spears according to
their ritual until blood gushed over them. 29 Noon
passed and they remained in a prophetic state un-
til the time for offering sacrifice. But there was no
sound, no one answering, no one listening.
30 Then Elijah said to all the people, "Come
here to me." When they drew near to him, he
repaired the altar of the LORD which had been de-
stroyed. 31 He took twelve stones, for the number
of tribes of the sons of Jacob, to whom the LORD
had said: Israel shall be your name. 32 He built
the stones into an altar to the name of the LORD,
and made a trench around the altar large enough
for two measures of grain. 33 When he had ar-
ranged the wood, he cut up the young bull and
laid it on the wood. 34 He said, "Fill four jars with
water and pour it over the burnt offering and over
the wood." "Do it again," he said, and they did it
again. "Do it a third time," he said, and they did
it a third time. 35 The water flowed around the al-
tar; even the trench was filled with the water. 36 At
the time for offering sacrifice, Elijah the prophet
came forward and said, "LORD, God of Abraham,
Isaac, and Israel, let it be known this day that
you are God in Israel and that I am your servant
and have done all these things at your command.
37 * Answer me, LORD! Answer me, that this peo-
ple may know that you, LORD, are God and that
you have turned their hearts back to you." 38 The
LORD's fire came down and devoured the burnt
offering, wood, stones, and dust, and lapped up
the water in the trench. 39 Seeing this, all the peo-
ple fell prostrate and said, "The LORD is God! The
LORD is God!" 40 * Then Elijah said to them, "Seize
the prophets of Baal. Let none of them escape!"
They seized them, and Elijah brought them down
to the Wadi Kishon and there he slaughtered
them. 41 Elijah then said to Ahab, "Go up, eat and
drink, for there is the sound of a heavy rain." 42 So
Ahab went up to eat and drink, while Elijah went
up to the top of Carmel, crouched down to the
earth, and put his head between his knees. 43 He
said to his servant, "Go up and look out to sea."

* **18:37** Ex 32:13. **18:40** Ex 32:26–28.

He went up and looked, but reported, "There is
nothing." Seven times he said, "Go look again!"
44 And the seventh time the youth reported,
"There is a cloud as small as a man's hand rising
from the sea." Elijah said, "Go and say to Ahab,
'Harness up and go down the mountain before
the rain stops you.' " 45 All at once the sky grew
dark with clouds and wind, and a heavy rain fell.
Ahab mounted his chariot and headed for Jez-
reel. 46 But the hand of the LORD was on Elijah. He
girded up his clothing and ran before Ahab as far
as the approaches to Jezreel.

Flight to Horeb†

19 1 Ahab told Jezebel all that Elijah had
done—that he had murdered all the
prophets by the sword. 2 Jezebel then sent a mes-
senger to Elijah and said, "May the gods do thus
to me and more, if by this time tomorrow I have
not done with your life what was done to each
of them." 3 Elijah was afraid and fled for his life,
going to Beer-sheba of Judah. He left his servant
there 4 * and went a day's journey into the wil-
derness, until he came to a solitary broom tree
and sat beneath it. He prayed for death: "Enough,
LORD! Take my life, for I am no better than my an-
cestors." 5 He lay down and fell asleep under the
solitary broom tree, but suddenly a messenger†
touched him and said, "Get up and eat!" 6 He
looked and there at his head was a hearth cake
and a jug of water. After he ate and drank, he
lay down again, 7 but the angel of the LORD came
back a second time, touched him, and said, "Get
up and eat or the journey will be too much for
you!" 8 * He got up, ate, and drank; then strength-
ened by that food, he walked forty days and forty
nights to the mountain of God, Horeb.
9 There he came to a cave, where he took shel-
ter. But the word of the LORD came to him: Why
are you here, Elijah? 10 He answered: "I have been
most zealous for the LORD, the God of hosts, but
the Israelites have forsaken your covenant. They
have destroyed your altars and murdered your
prophets by the sword. I alone remain, and they
seek to take my life." 11 * Then the LORD said: Go
out and stand on the mountain before the LORD;†
the LORD will pass by. There was a strong and vi-
olent wind rending the mountains and crushing
rocks before the LORD—but the LORD was not in
the wind; after the wind, an earthquake—but
the LORD was not in the earthquake; 12 after another
earthquake, fire—but the LORD was not in the
fire; after the fire, a light silent sound.†
13 When he heard this, Elijah hid his face in
his cloak and went out and stood at the entrance

Pray It!

Looking for God

Elijah was told to meet God on the mountain. God's presence could have been in fire, in an earthquake, or in a great wind, but God was in none of these. God was in the tiny whispering sound.

Let's face it. Our lives tend to be pretty noisy and cluttered. How will we ever hear God in that tiny whispering sound? In order to hear God's voice, we need to take time away from the noise and clutter to just be quiet in God's presence. We also know that God often "whispers" to us through our friends, our family, and often through teachers and counselors. Like Elijah we have to be open to God's voice speaking through others as well as through the events in our lives.

God is always with us, in the quiet depths of our heart and in the people and situations God has placed in our lives. We need to be like Elijah—tuning out things that are not God and tuning in to God's presence. Taking quiet time to think and pray is a great start.

► **1 Kgs 19:9–13**

†

19:1–21 The story of Elijah's journey to Mount Horeb begins as a flight from danger, but takes a surprising turn. The prophet makes his solitary way to the mountain where the Lord had appeared to Moses and the Israelites ("Horeb" is an alternate name for "Sinai"). Like Moses on the holy mountain, Elijah experiences a theophany and receives a commission.

19:5–7 Sound asleep, Elijah is startled awake by an unspecified "messenger." Only in v. 7 is the figure identified as a messenger (or "angel") of the Lord.

19:11–13 To "stand before the Lord" is a literal translation of a Hebrew idiom meaning "to serve the Lord"; Elijah has used this idiom twice before to describe himself as the Lord's servant (17:1; 18:15). The Lord's command, then, means that Elijah is to take up once again the prophetic service to which he has been appointed. The Lord's question, "Why are you here?" (v. 9, repeated in v. 13), could imply an accusation that he is abandoning his prophetic office. In v. 15, the Lord tells him to go back.

19:12 Compare these divine manifestations to Elijah with those to Moses on the same mountain (Ex 19:16–19; 33:18–23; 34:5–6; Dt 4:10–15). Though various phenomena, such as wind, storms, earthquakes, fire, accompany the divine presence, they do not constitute the presence itself which, like the "silent sound," is mysterious and ultimately ungraspable. Moses and Elijah, the two figures who experienced God's theophany on this mountain, reappear with Jesus on another mountain at his transfiguration (Mt 17:1–9; Mk 9:2–9; Lk 9:28–36).

*

19:4 Jon 4:6–9.
19:8 Ex 34:28.
19:11–13 Ex 33:18–23; 34:5–6.

of the cave. A voice said to him, Why are you
here, Elijah? 14 * He replied, "I have been most
zealous for the LORD, the God of hosts, but the
Israelites have forsaken your covenant. They have
destroyed your altars and murdered your proph-
ets by the sword. I alone remain, and they seek
to take my life." 15 † * The LORD said to him: Go
back! Take the desert road to Damascus. When
you arrive, you shall anoint Hazael as king of
Aram. 16 * You shall also anoint Jehu, son of
Nimshi, as king of Israel, and Elisha, son of Sha-
phat of Abel-meholah, as prophet to succeed
you. 17 Anyone who escapes the sword of Hazael,
Jehu will kill. Anyone who escapes the sword of
Jehu, Elisha will kill. 18 * But I will spare seven
thousand in Israel—every knee that has not bent
to Baal, every mouth that has not kissed him.

19 † Elijah set out, and came upon Elisha, son
of Shaphat, as he was plowing with twelve yoke
of oxen; he was following the twelfth. Elijah
went over to him and threw his cloak on him.
20 * Elisha left the oxen, ran after Elijah, and said,
"Please, let me kiss my father and mother good-
bye, and I will follow you." Elijah answered, "Go
back! What have I done to you?" 21 Elisha left
him and, taking the yoke of oxen, slaughtered
them; he used the plowing equipment for fuel to
boil their flesh, and gave it to the people to eat.
Then he left and followed Elijah to serve him.

V. The Story of Ahab†

Ahab's Victories over Aram†

20 1 Ben-hadad, king of Aram, gathered all
his forces and, accompanied by thirty-
two kings with horses and chariotry, set out to
besiege and attack Samaria. 2 He sent messengers
to Ahab, king of Israel, within the city, 3 and said
to him, "This is Ben-hadad's message: 'Your silver
and gold are mine, and your wives and your fine
children are mine.' " 4 The king of Israel answered,
"Just as you say, my lord king, I and all I have are
yours." 5 But the messengers came again and said,
"This is Ben-hadad's message: 'I sent you word:
Give me your silver and gold, your wives and
your children. 6 But now I say: At this time to-
morrow I will send my servants to you, and they
shall ransack your house and the houses of your
servants. They shall seize and take away whatever
you consider valuable.' " 7 The king of Israel then
summoned all the elders of the land and said:
"Understand clearly that this man is intent on evil.
When he sent to me for my wives and children,
my silver and my gold, I did not refuse him." 8 All
the elders and all the people said to him, "Do not
listen. Do not give in." 9 Accordingly he directed
the messengers of Ben-hadad, "Say this: 'To my
lord the king: I will do all that you demanded of
your servant the first time. But this I cannot do.' "
The messengers left and reported this. 10 Ben-
hadad then responded, "May the gods do thus to
me and more, if there will remain enough dust in
Samaria to make handfuls for all my followers."
11 The king of Israel replied, "Tell him, 'Let not
one who puts on armor boast like one who takes
it off.' " 12 Ben-hadad was drinking in the pavil-
ions with the kings when he heard this reply. He
commanded his servants, "Get ready!"; and they
got ready to storm the city.

13 Then a prophet came up to Ahab, king of
Israel, and said: "The LORD says, Do you see
all this vast army? Today I am giving it into
your power, that you may know that I am the
LORD." 14 But Ahab asked, "Through whom will
it be given over?" He answered, "The LORD says,
Through the aides of the provincial governors."
Then Ahab asked, "Who is to attack?" He replied,
"You are." 15 So Ahab mustered the aides of the
provincial governors, two hundred thirty-two
of them. Behind them he mustered all the Is-
raelite soldiery, who numbered seven thousand
in all. 16 † They marched out at noon, while
Ben-hadad was drinking heavily in the pavilions
with the thirty-two kings who were his allies.

19:15–17 Elijah himself carried out only the last of the three commissions entrusted to him (vv. 19–21); Elisha performed the first himself (2 Kgs 8:7–19), and the second, the anointing of Jehu, through one of his followers (2 Kgs 9:1–10).

19:19–21 Elijah's act of throwing his mantle over the shoulders of Elisha associates him with Elijah as a servant (v. 21). Elisha will later succeed to Elijah's position and prophetic power (2 Kgs 2:1–15). Elisha's prompt response, destroying his plow and oxen, signifies a radical change from his former manner of living.

20:1–22:54 Although coverage of Ahab's reign began in 16:29, he was only a secondary character in the chapters about Elijah. Now attention focuses on Ahab. Each of these chapters tells a story of the king (20:1–34; 21:1–16; 22:1–4, 29–38), to which is attached a scene of prophetic condemnation (20:30–42; 21:17–29; 22:5–28). As relations between Ahab and the prophets of the Lord deteriorate, the scenes of prophetic condemnation get longer and the condemnations themselves become more pointed. Some historians doubt that the stories of hostility between Israel and Aram (chaps. 20 and 22) originally pertained to the reign of Ahab. If this is correct, their original setting may have been several decades later.

20:1–34 This story recounts two battles through which Ahab won freedom for Israel from vassalage to Ben-hadad of Syria. The story is chiastically arranged: negotiations (vv. 1–12), battle (vv. 13–21), battle (vv. 22–30), negotiations (vv. 31–34). The ensuing prophetic condemnation is surprising, since the portrait of Ahab in vv. 1–34 is apparently quite positive.

20:16–19 The narrator uses a sort of verbal split-screen technique to show us two separate and simultaneous scenes. At the gates of Samaria, the Israelite forces are coming out to battle (v. 16a): first the aides (lit., "young men"; v. 17a), then the whole army (v. 19). Meanwhile in the Aramean camp Ben-hadad is getting drunk (v. 16b), receiving reports (v. 17b) and issuing commands (v. 18).

19:14 Rom 11:3.
19:15 2 Kgs 8:7–15.
19:16 2 Kgs 2:1–15; 9:1–10.
19:18 Rom 11:4.
19:20 Lk 9:61–62.

17 When the aides of the provincial governors marched out first, Ben-hadad received word, "Some men have marched out of Samaria." 18 He answered, "Whether they have come out for peace or for war, take them alive." 19 But when these had come out of the city—the aides of the provincial governors with the army following them— 20 each of them struck down his man. The Arameans fled with Israel pursuing them, while Ben-hadad, king of Aram, escaped on a chariot horse. 21 Then the king of Israel went out and destroyed the horses and chariots. Thus he inflicted a severe defeat on Aram.

22 Then the prophet approached the king of Israel and said to him: "Go, regroup your forces. Understand clearly what you must do, for at the turning of the year† the king of Aram will attack you." 23 Meanwhile the servants of the king of Aram said to him: "Their gods are mountain gods. That is why they defeated us. But if we fight them on level ground, we shall be sure to defeat them. 24 This is what you must do: Take the kings from their posts and put prefects in their places. 25 Raise an army as large as the army you have lost, horse for horse, chariot for chariot. Let us fight them on level ground, and we shall surely defeat them." He took their advice and did this. 26 At the turning of the year, Ben-hadad mustered Aram and went up to Aphek to fight against Israel. 27 The Israelites, too, were mustered and supplied with provisions; then they went out to meet the enemy. The Israelites, encamped opposite, looked like little flocks of goats, while Aram covered the land. 28 A man of God approached and said to the king of Israel: "The LORD says, Because Aram has said the LORD is a god of mountains, not a god of plains, I will give all this vast army into your power that you may know I am the LORD." 29 They were encamped opposite each other for seven days. On the seventh day battle was joined, and the Israelites struck down one hundred thousand foot soldiers of Aram in one day. 30 The survivors fled into the city of Aphek, where the wall collapsed on twenty-seven thousand of them. Ben-hadad, too, fled, and took refuge within the city, in an inner room.

31 His servants said to him: "We have heard that the kings of the house of Israel are merciful kings. Allow us, therefore, to garb ourselves in sackcloth, with cords around our heads, and go out to the king of Israel. Perhaps he will spare your life." 32 Dressed in sackcloth girded at the waist and wearing cords around their heads, they went to the king of Israel and said, "Your servant Ben-hadad says, 'Spare my life!' " He asked, "Is he still alive? He is my brother."† 33 Hearing this as a good omen, the men quickly took him at his word and said, "Ben-hadad is your brother." He answered, "Go and get him." When Ben-hadad came out to him, the king had him mount his chariot. 34 Ben-hadad said to him, "The cities my father took from your father I will restore, and you may set up bazaars for yourself in Damascus, as my father did in Samaria." Ahab replied, "For my part, I will set you free on those terms." So he made a covenant with him and then set him free.

Prophetic Condemnation

35 Acting on the word of the LORD, one of the guild prophets said to his companion, "Strike me." But he refused to strike him. 36 Then he said to him, "Since you did not obey the voice of the LORD, a lion will attack you when you leave me." When he left him, a lion came upon him and attacked him.* 37 Then the prophet met another man and said, "Strike me." The man struck him a blow and wounded him. 38 The prophet went on and waited for the king on the road, disguising himself with a bandage over his eyes. 39 As the king was passing, he called out to the king and said: "Your servant went into the thick of the battle, and suddenly someone turned and brought me a man and said, 'Guard this man. If he is missing, you shall have to pay for his life with your life or pay out a talent of silver.'† 40 But while your servant was occupied here and there, the man disappeared." The king of Israel said to him, "That is your sentence. You have decided it yourself." 41 He quickly removed the bandage from his eyes, and the king of Israel recognized him as one of the prophets. 42 * He said to him: "The LORD says, Because you have set free the man I put under the ban,† your life shall pay for his life, your people for his people." 43 * Disturbed and angry, the king of Israel set off for home and entered Samaria.

20:22 *At the turning of the year*: the idiom may mean "next year about this time" or "at the beginning of the year," i.e., the spring (cf. 2 Sm 11:1).

20:32 *He is my brother*: cf. note on 9:13.

20:39 The "man" is ostensibly a prisoner of war, to be kept or sold as a slave. In the event he escapes, the one charged with guarding him would be obliged either to pay a fine or to take his place as a slave. The fine, however, is exorbitant: a talent of silver is roughly one hundred times the price of an ordinary slave (see Ex 21:32). This is the only clue Ahab will get that he is being set up and that the story is really about himself in his dealings with Ben-hadad. In 2 Sm 14:1–20, the wise woman of Tekoa uses the same technique with King David: she tells a story that elicits a reaction from the king; David is tricked into pronouncing judgment on himself, as the story parallels his own situation. The prophet Nathan (2 Sm 12:1–7) likewise uses a story that leads David to see his sin for what it is.

20:42 *Under the ban*: cf. note on Dt 2:34.

20:36 1 Kgs 13:24. **20:42** 1 Kgs 22:35. **20:43** 1 Kgs 21:4.

Seizure of Naboth's Vineyard†

21 1 Naboth the Jezreelite had a vineyard in
Jezreel next to the palace of Ahab, king of
Samaria. Some time later, 2 Ahab said to Naboth,
"Give me your vineyard to be my vegetable garden, since it is close by, next to my house. I will
give you a better vineyard in exchange, or, if you
prefer, I will give you its value in money." 3 Na-
both said to Ahab, "The LORD forbid that I should
give you my ancestral heritage."† 4 Ahab went
home disturbed and angry at the answer Naboth
the Jezreelite had given him: "I will not give you
my ancestral heritage." Lying down on his bed,
he turned away and would not eat. 5 His wife Jez-
ebel came to him and said to him, "Why are you
so sullen that you will not eat?" 6 He answered
her, "Because I spoke to Naboth the Jezreelite
and said to him, 'Sell me your vineyard, or, if you
prefer, I will give you a vineyard in exchange.'
But he said, 'I will not give you my vineyard.' "
7 Jezebel his wife said to him, "What a king of
Israel you are! Get up! Eat and be cheerful. I will
give you the vineyard of Naboth the Jezreelite."
8 So she wrote letters in Ahab's name and, hav-
ing sealed them with his seal, sent them to the
elders and to the nobles who lived in the same
city with Naboth. 9 This is what she wrote in the
letters: "Proclaim a fast and set Naboth at the
head of the people. 10 Next, set two scoundrels
opposite him to accuse him: 'You have cursed
God and king.' Then take him out and stone him
to death."
11 His fellow citizens—the elders and the no-
bles who dwelt in his city—did as Jezebel had
ordered in the letters she sent them. 12 They pro-
claimed a fast and set Naboth at the head of the
people. 13 Two scoundrels came in and sat oppo-
site Naboth, and the scoundrels accused him in
the presence of the people, "Naboth has cursed
God and king." And they led him out of the city
and stoned him to death. 14 Then they sent word
to Jezebel: "Naboth has been stoned to death."
15 When Jezebel learned that Naboth had been
stoned to death, she said to Ahab, "Go, take pos-
session of the vineyard of Naboth the Jezreelite
which he refused to sell you, because Naboth is
not alive, but dead." 16 When Ahab heard that
Naboth was dead, he started on his way down
to the vineyard of Naboth the Jezreelite, to take
possession of it.

Prophetic Condemnation

17 Then the word of the LORD came to Elijah the
Tishbite: 18 Go down to meet Ahab, king of Israel,
who is in Samaria. He will be in the vineyard of
Naboth, where he has gone to take possession.
19 * Tell him: "Thus says the LORD: After murder-
ing, do you also take possession?" And tell him,
"Thus says the LORD: In the place where the dogs
licked up the blood of Naboth, the dogs shall
lick up your blood, too."
20 † Ahab said to Elijah, "Have you found me
out, my enemy?" He said, "I have found you.
Because you have given yourself up to doing evil
in the LORD's sight, 21 * I am bringing evil upon
you: I will consume you and will cut off every
male belonging to Ahab, whether bond or free,
in Israel. 22 I will make your house like that of Jer-
oboam, son of Nebat, and like the house of Ba-
asha, son of Ahijah, because you have provoked
me by leading Israel into sin."
23 Against Jezebel, too, the LORD declared: The
dogs shall devour Jezebel in the confines of Jez-
reel.

24 Anyone of Ahab's line who dies in the city,
dogs will devour;
Anyone who dies in the field,
the birds of the sky will devour.

25 Indeed, no one gave himself up to the doing
of evil in the sight of the LORD as did Ahab, urged
on by his wife Jezebel. 26 He became completely
abominable by going after idols, just as the Am-
orites had done, whom the LORD drove out of the
Israelites' way.
27 When Ahab heard these words, he tore his
garments and put on sackcloth over his bare
flesh. He fasted, slept in the sackcloth, and went
about subdued. 28 Then the word of the LORD
came to Elijah the Tishbite, 29 * Have you seen
how Ahab has humbled himself before me?
Since he has humbled himself before me, I will
not bring the evil in his time. I will bring the evil
upon his house in his son's time.

---

† **21:1–16** The story tells how Jezebel manipulates important structures of Israelite social order, law, and religious observance to eliminate a faithful Israelite landowner who frustrates Ahab's will.

21:3 *Heritage*: Hebrew *naḥalah*. Naboth is unwilling to sell or exchange his vineyard. According to the Israelite system of land tenure and distribution, land was held in common within a social unit. The ancestral *naḥalah* was not private property, to be alienated at will.

21:20–26 In these verses the narrator uses against the third Israelite dynasty the same condemnation formula that was uttered against the first two dynasties, those of Jeroboam (14:9–11) and Baasha (16:2–4). Part of the formula is put in Elijah's mouth, in an oracle against Ahab and his descendants (vv. 21–22), and part of it in an aside to the reader that extends the condemnation to Ahab's wife, Jezebel, and his whole household (vv. 23–24). The oracle against Jezebel will be fulfilled in 2 Kgs 9:36; the obliteration of the dynasty will be recounted in the bloody stories of 2 Kgs 9–11.

---

* **21:19** 1 Kgs 22:38; 2 Kgs 9:26.
21:21–23 1 Kgs 14:10–11; 15:29; 16:3–4, 11; 2 Kgs 9:8–10, 36.
21:29 2 Kgs 9:25–26.

Ahab's Defeat by Aram†

22 1 Three years passed without war between Aram and Israel. 2 In the third year, however, King Jehoshaphat of Judah came down to the king of Israel. 3 The king of Israel said to his servants, "Do you not know that Ramoth-gilead is ours and we are doing nothing to take it from the king of Aram?" 4 He asked Jehoshaphat, "Will you come with me to fight against Ramoth-gilead?" Jehoshaphat answered the king of Israel, "You and I are as one, and your people and my people, your horses and my horses as well."

Prophetic Condemnation

5 Jehoshaphat also said to the king of Israel, "Seek the word of the LORD at once." 6 The king of Israel assembled the prophets, about four hundred of them, and asked, "Shall I go to fight against Ramoth-gilead or shall I refrain?" They said, "Attack. The Lord will give it into the power of the king."† 7 But Jehoshaphat said, "Is there no other prophet of the LORD here we might consult?" 8 The king of Israel answered, "There is one other man through whom we might consult the LORD; but I hate him because he prophesies not good but evil about me. He is Micaiah, son of Imlah." Jehoshaphat said, "Let not the king say that." 9 So the king of Israel called an official and said to him, "Get Micaiah, son of Imlah, at once."

10 The king of Israel and Jehoshaphat, king of Judah, were seated, each on his throne, clothed in their robes of state in the square at the entrance of the gate of Samaria, and all the prophets were prophesying before them. 11 * Zedekiah, son of Chenaanah, made himself two horns of iron† and said, "The LORD says, With these you shall gore Aram until you have destroyed them." 12 The other prophets prophesied in a similar vein, saying: "Attack Ramoth-gilead and conquer! The LORD will give it into the power of the king."

13 Meanwhile, the messenger who had gone to call Micaiah said to him, "Look now, the prophets are unanimously predicting good for the king. Let your word be the same as any of theirs; speak a good word." 14 Micaiah said, "As the LORD lives, I shall speak whatever the LORD tells me."

15 When he came to the king, the king said to him, "Micaiah, shall we go to fight at Ramoth-gilead, or shall we refrain?" He said, "Attack and conquer! The LORD will give it into the power of the king." 16 But the king answered him, "How many times must I adjure you to tell me nothing but the truth in the name of the LORD?" 17 † So Micaiah said:

"I see all Israel
  scattered on the mountains,
  like sheep without a shepherd,
And the LORD saying,
  These have no master!
  Let each of them go back home in peace."

18 The king of Israel said to Jehoshaphat, "Did I not tell you, he does not prophesy good about me, but only evil?" 19 † Micaiah continued: "Therefore hear the word of the LORD: I saw the LORD seated on his throne, with the whole host of heaven standing to his right and to his left. 20 The LORD asked: Who will deceive Ahab, so that he will go up and fall on Ramoth-gilead?† And one said this, another that, 21 until this spirit came forth and stood before the LORD, saying, 'I will deceive him.' The LORD asked: How? 22 He answered, 'I will go forth and become a lying spirit in the mouths of all his prophets.' The LORD replied: You shall succeed in deceiving him. Go forth and do this. 23 So now, the LORD has put a lying spirit in the mouths of all these prophets of yours; the LORD himself has decreed evil against you."

24 Thereupon Zedekiah, son of Chenaanah, came up and struck Micaiah on the cheek, saying, "Has the spirit of the LORD, then, left me to speak with you?" 25 Micaiah said, "You shall find out on the day you go into an inner room to

†

22:1–40 This chapter presents a contrasting parallel to chap. 20, where Ahab enjoyed victories over Aram's aggression. Here Ahab is the aggressor, but falls in battle against Aram. Like the preceding chapters, it contains a story of Ahab plus an episode of prophetic condemnation. The story ends with the formulaic conclusion to Ahab's reign (vv. 39–40). Chronicles has a parallel version of this account in 2 Chr 18:1–34. After the story of Ahab's death come accounts of the reign of Jehoshaphat (paralleled in 2 Chr 20:31–37) and of the beginning of the reign of Ahaziah.

22:6 Though Ahab is clearly intended to understand the oracle as prophesying his success, the prophets' words are ambiguous. "The lord" (not "the LORD," i.e., the proper name of Israel's God) who will give victory is unidentified, as is the king to whom it will be given.

22:11 The "two" horns probably symbolize the coalition of two kings, Ahab and Jehoshaphat.

22:17 Micaiah's oracle uses the common ancient metaphor of "shepherd" for the king. It means that the Israelite forces will be left leaderless because the king (or perhaps both kings: the word "master" could be singular or plural in Hebrew) will die in battle.

22:19–23 Since Ahab's intention to attack Ramoth-gilead is unshaken, Micaiah reveals God's plan to trick Ahab to his death, and thus virtually dares Ahab to walk into the trap with his eyes open. The work of the "lying spirit" explains the ambiguities of the prophets' original oracle in v. 6. Prophets "stand in the council of the Lord" and are privy to its deliberations; cf. Jer 23:22.

22:20 *Fall on Ramoth-gilead*: lit., "heights of Gilead"; even the Lord's words are double-meaning. God wants Ahab to "fall on" (that is, attack) Ramoth-gilead so that he will "fall on" (that is, die on) Ramoth-gilead.

*

22:11 Dt 33:17.

hide." 26 The king of Israel then said, "Seize Micaiah and take him back to Amon, prefect of the city, and to Joash, the king's son, 27 and say, 'This is the king's order: Put this man in prison and feed him scanty rations of bread and water until I come back in safety.' " 28 * But Micaiah said, "If you return in safety, the LORD has not spoken through me." (He also said, "Hear, O peoples, all of you.")†

Ahab at Ramoth-gilead

29 The king of Israel and Jehoshaphat, king of Judah, went up to Ramoth-gilead, 30 and the king of Israel said to Jehoshaphat, "I will disguise myself and go into battle, but you put on your own robes." So the king of Israel disguised himself and entered the battle. 31 In the meantime the king of Aram had given his thirty-two chariot commanders the order, "Do not fight with anyone, great or small, except the king of Israel alone."

32 When the chariot commanders saw Jehoshaphat, they cried out, "There is the king of Israel!" and wheeled to fight him. But Jehoshaphat cried out, 33 and the chariot commanders, seeing that he was not the king of Israel, turned away from him. 34 But someone drew his bow at random, and hit the king of Israel between the joints of his breastplate. He ordered his charioteer, "Rein about and take me out of the ranks, for I am wounded."

35 * The battle grew fierce during the day, and the king, who was propped up in his chariot facing the Arameans, died in the evening. The blood from his wound flowed to the bottom of the chariot. 36 At sunset a cry went through the army, "Every man to his city, every man to his land!"

37 And so the king died, and came back to Samaria, and they buried him there. 38 * When they washed out the chariot at the pool of Samaria, the dogs licked up his blood and prostitutes bathed there, as the LORD had prophesied.

39 The rest of the acts of Ahab, with all that he did, including the ivory house he built and all the cities he built, are recorded in the book of the chronicles of the kings of Israel. 40 Ahab rested with his ancestors, and his son Ahaziah succeeded him as king.

Reign of Jehoshaphat

41 Jehoshaphat, son of Asa, became king of Judah in the fourth year of Ahab, king of Israel. 42 Jehoshaphat was thirty-five years old when he became king, and he reigned twenty-five years in Jerusalem. His mother's name was Azubah, daughter of Shilhi.

43 He walked in the way of Asa his father unceasingly, doing what was right in the LORD's sight. 44 Nevertheless, the high places did not disappear, and the people still sacrificed on the high places and burned incense there. 45 Jehoshaphat also made peace with the king of Israel.

46 The rest of the acts of Jehoshaphat, with his valor, what he did and how he fought, are recorded in the book of the chronicles of the kings of Judah. 47 He removed from the land the rest of the pagan priests who had remained in the reign of Asa his father. 48 There was no king in Edom, but an appointed regent. 49 Jehoshaphat made Tarshish ships to go to Ophir for gold; but in fact the ships did not go, because they were wrecked at Ezion-geber. 50 That was the time when Ahaziah, son of Ahab, had said to Jehoshaphat, "Let my servants accompany your servants in the ships." But Jehoshaphat would not agree. 51 Jehoshaphat rested with his ancestors; he was buried with his ancestors in the City of David his father, and his son Jehoram succeeded him as king.

Reign of Ahaziah†

52 Ahaziah, son of Ahab, became king over Israel in Samaria in the seventeenth year† of Jehoshaphat, king of Judah; he reigned two years over Israel.

53 He did what was evil in the sight of the LORD, walking in the way of his father, his mother, and Jeroboam, son of Nebat, who caused Israel to sin. 54 He served Baal and worshiped him, thus provoking the LORD, the God of Israel, just as his father had done.

---

†

22:28 The last words of the verse are a scribal gloss attributing to Micaiah, son of Imlah, the opening words of the book of a different Micaiah (Micah), the prophet of Moresheth, the sixth of the twelve minor prophets of the Old Testament canon.

22:52–54 The account of Ahaziah's reign continues in 2 Kings.

22:52 *Seventeenth year*: so the present Hebrew text. This is consistent with the figures in 2 Kgs 3:1, but together those figures conflict with information in 1 Kgs 22:42 and 2 Kgs 1:17. The problem of the chronology of the kings of Israel and Judah has never been convincingly resolved; it is complicated by the fact that the ancient Greek translation sometimes has different lengths of reign and different accession dates. See further note on 2 Kgs 3:1.

---

*

22:28 Mi 1:2.
22:35 1 Kgs 20:42.
22:38 1 Kgs 21:19.

For background on this book, see the introduction to 1 and 2 Kings before 1 Kings.

2 Kings

2:11

Reign of Ahaziah, Continued

1 [1]After Ahab's death, Moab rebelled against
Israel.*
[2]Ahaziah fell through the lattice of his roof
terrace at Samaria and was injured. So he sent
out messengers with the instructions: "Go and
inquire of Baalzebub,† the god of Ekron, whether
I shall recover from this injury."
[3]Meanwhile, the messenger of the LORD said to
Elijah the Tishbite: Go and meet the messengers
of Samaria's king, and tell them: "Is it because
there is no God in Israel that you are going to in-
quire of Baalzebub, the god of Ekron?" [4]For this,
the LORD says: You shall not leave the bed upon
which you lie; instead, you shall die. And Elijah
departed. [5]The messengers then returned to Aha-
ziah, who asked them, "Why have you returned?"
[6]They answered, "A man met us and said to us,
'Go back to the king who sent you and tell him:
The LORD says: Is it because there is no God in Is-
rael that you are sending to inquire of Baalzebub,
the god of Ekron? For this you shall not leave the
bed upon which you lie; instead, you shall die.' "
[7]The king asked them, "What was the man like
who met you and said these things to you?" [8]They
replied, "He wore a hairy garment† with a leather
belt around his waist." "It is Elijah the Tishbite!"
he exclaimed.
[9]Then the king sent a captain with his company
of fifty men after Elijah. The prophet was seated
on a hilltop when he found him. He said, "Man
of God, the king commands you, 'Come down.' "
[10]Elijah answered the captain, "Well, if I am a
man of God, may fire come down from heaven
and consume you and your fifty men." And fire
came down from heaven and consumed him and
his fifty men.* [11]The king sent another captain
with his company of fifty men after Elijah. He
shouted up and said, "Man of God, the king says,
'Come down immediately!' " [12]Elijah answered
them, "If I am a man of God, may fire come
down from heaven and consume you and your
fifty men." And divine fire† came down from
heaven and consumed him and his fifty men.
[13]The king sent a third captain with his company
of fifty men. When the third captain had climbed
the hill, he fell to his knees before Elijah, plead-
ing with him. He said, "Man of God, let my life
and the lives of these fifty men, your servants,
count for something in your sight! [14]Already fire
has come down from heaven, consuming the first

†

1:2 *Baalzebub*: in this form, "Baal of flies." The name in the Hebrew text is a derisive alteration of Baalzebul, "Prince Baal." The best New Testament evidence supports the latter form in Mt 10:25; Lk 11:15.

1:8 *Hairy garment*: a sign of prophetic calling; see Zec 13:4. John the Baptizer wore a similarly distinctive mantle; see Mt 3:4; Mk 1:6.

1:12 *Divine fire*: lit., "fire of God," which in Hebrew sounds quite like "man of God." The play on words is the basis for Elijah's retort. This story was told among the people to enhance the dignity of the prophet and to reflect the power of God whom he served. A similar phrase, "the LORD's fire," described the miraculous divine fire that fell from a cloudless sky to consume Elijah's offering in 1 Kgs 18:38.

*

1:1 2 Kgs 3:4–27. **1:10** Lv 10:1–2; Sir 48:3; Lk 9:51–55.

Live It!

Elijah, Prophet of God in Solidarity with the People

Elijah was a passionate prophet who read the history of the monarchy (Israel's kings) from the perspective of God. He saw division in the people of Israel. On the one hand were the kings, the noblemen, and the leaders of the army; on the other hand were the peasants, the widows, and the persecuted prophets. The covenant had been broken. Elijah denounced the unfaithfulness of Queen Jezebel and Kings Ahab and Ahaziah. They had introduced idolatry in the form of the false god Baal, who favored the powerful and allowed injustices.

Elijah's faithfulness to the covenant and his solidarity with the poor led him to speak against kings and queens, to fight false prophets, and to intervene in national affairs. The powerful rulers wanted to kill him and silence his voice. After his dramatic departure (see 2 Kgs 2:11), the people never forgot him; they always expected his return.

- Who do you see as a contemporary Elijah in our world today? In what ways and in what situations are you called to be a prophet?

▶ 2 Kgs 2:11

two captains with their companies of fifty men.
But now, let my life count for something in your
sight!" [15]Then the messenger of the LORD said
to Elijah: Go down with him; you need not be
afraid of him. So Elijah left and went down with
him to the king. [16]He declared to the king: "Thus
says the LORD: Because you sent messengers to
inquire of Baalzebub, the god of Ekron—do you
think there is no God in Israel to inquire of?—
you shall not leave the bed upon which you lie;
instead you shall die."*

[17]Ahaziah died according to the word of the
LORD spoken by Elijah. Since he had no son, Jo-
ram† succeeded him as king, in the second year
of Joram, son of Jehoshaphat, king of Judah.

[18]The rest of the acts of Ahaziah, which he
did, are recorded in the book of chronicles of the
kings of Israel.

VI. Elisha Succeeds Elijah†

Elijah's Journey

2 [1]When the LORD was about to take Elijah up
to heaven in a whirlwind, he and Elisha were
on their way from Gilgal.†

[2]Elijah said to Elisha, "Stay here, please. The
LORD has sent me on to Bethel." Elisha replied,
"As the LORD lives, and as you yourself live, I will
not leave you." So they went down to Bethel.
[3]The guild prophets who were in Bethel went
out to Elisha and asked him, "Do you know that
today the LORD will take your master from you?"
He replied, "Yes, I know that. Be still."

[4]Elijah said to him, "Elisha, stay here, please.
The LORD has sent me on to Jericho." Elisha re-
plied, "As the LORD lives, and as you yourself live,
I will not leave you." So they came to Jericho.
[5]The guild prophets who were in Jericho ap-
proached Elisha and asked him, "Do you know
that today the LORD will take your master from
you?" He replied, "Yes, I know that. Be still."

[6]Elijah said to him, "Stay here, please. The
LORD has sent me on to the Jordan." Elisha re-
plied, "As the LORD lives, and as you yourself
live, I will not leave you." So the two went on to-
gether. [7]Fifty of the guild prophets followed and
stood facing them at a distance, while the two of
them stood next to the Jordan.

Elisha Succeeds Elijah

[8]Elijah took his mantle, rolled it up and struck
the water: it divided, and the two of them crossed
over on dry ground.*

[9]* When they had crossed over, Elijah said to

† **1:17** *Joram*: in 2 Kings the name "Joram" (*yoram*) and its variant "Jehoram" (*yehoram*) are used interchangeably. To avoid the impression that they are different names and designate different people, both forms are rendered "Joram" in this translation. Confusion arises, however, because the king of Israel whose reign is recounted beginning in 3:1 and the contemporary king of Judah whose reign is recounted beginning in 8:16 share this name. On the relationship of Joram of Israel to Joram of Judah, see note on 3:1.

2:1–25 The story of Elisha's succession to Elijah's prophetic office is oddly set between the death of Ahaziah (1:17) and the accession of his successor (3:1). The effect is to place this scene, which is the central scene in the whole of 1–2 Kings, outside of time. It thereby becomes almost mythic in its import and reminds us that, behind the transitory flow of kings and kingdoms, stand the eternal word of God and the prophets who give it voice. Just as 1–2 Kings pivots on this chapter, so this scene too is concentrically constructed. Together Elijah and Elisha journey to Bethel, thence to Jericho, and thence across the Jordan. There Elijah is taken up in the whirlwind and Elijah's mantle of power comes to Elisha. Now alone, Elisha crosses the Jordan again, returns to Jericho and thence back to Bethel.

2:1 *Gilgal*: there are several places in the Hebrew Bible named Gilgal; the word probably means "circle," viz. of stones. Here the route of the prophets' journey rules out the most famous Gilgal (Jos

* **1:16** Sir 48:6. **2:8** Ex 14:15–22; Jos 3:14–17. **2:9–15** Nm 11:16–17, 24–29.

Elisha, "Request whatever I might do for you,
before I am taken from you." Elisha answered,
"May I receive a double portion of your spirit."†
10 He replied, "You have asked something that is
not easy. Still, if you see me taken up from you,
your wish will be granted; otherwise not." 11 As
they walked on still conversing, a fiery chariot
and fiery horses came between the two of them,
and Elijah went up to heaven in a whirlwind,*
12 and Elisha saw it happen. He cried out, "My
father! my father!† Israel's chariot and steeds!"
Then he saw him no longer.

He gripped his own garment, tore it into two
pieces, 13 and picked up the mantle which had
fallen from Elijah. Then he went back and stood
at the bank of the Jordan. 14 Wielding the mantle
which had fallen from Elijah, he struck the water
and said, "The LORD, the God of Elijah—where is
he now?"† He struck the water: it divided, and
he crossed over.

Elisha's Journey

15 The guild prophets in Jericho, who were on
the other side, saw him and said, "The spirit of
Elijah rests on Elisha." They went to meet him,
bowing to the ground before him.* 16 They said,
"Among your servants are fifty brave men. Let
them go in search of your master. Perhaps the
spirit of the LORD has lifted him up and left him on
some mountain or in some valley." He answered,
"Do not send them."* 17 But they kept urging him,
until he was embarrassed and said, "Send them."
So they sent the fifty men, who searched for three
days without finding him.* 18 When they returned
to Elisha in Jericho, where he was staying, he said
to them, "Did I not tell you not to go?"

19 * The inhabitants of the city complained to
Elisha, "The site of the city is fine indeed, as my
lord can see, but the water is bad and the land
sterile." 20 Elisha said, "Bring me a new bowl and
put salt into it." When they had brought it to
him, 21 he went out to the spring and threw salt
into it, saying, "Thus says the LORD: I have puri-
fied this water. Never again shall death or steril-
ity come from it." 22 And the water has stayed
pure even to this day, according to the word
Elisha had spoken.

23 † From there Elisha went up to Bethel. While
he was on the way, some little boys came out
of the city and jeered at him: "Go away, baldy;
go away, baldy!" 24 The prophet turned and saw
them, and he cursed them in the name of the
LORD. Then two she-bears came out of the woods
and tore forty-two of the children to pieces.

25 From there he went to Mount Carmel, and
returned to Samaria from there.

VII. Stories of Elisha and Joram†

Reign of Joram of Israel

3 1 Joram, son of Ahab, became king over Is-
rael in Samaria in the eighteenth year of Je-
hoshaphat, king of Judah, and he reigned twelve
years.†

2 * He did what was evil in the LORD's sight,
though not like his father and mother. He did
away with the pillar of Baal that his father had
made, 3 but he still held fast unceasingly to the
sins which Jeroboam, son of Nebat, caused Israel
to commit.

War Against Moab: Drought

4 † Now Mesha, king of Moab, who raised
sheep, used to pay the king of Israel as tribute a

† 4–5), the one near Jericho. This Gilgal may have been located in the area of modern Jiljulieh, approximately seven miles north of Bethel, which seems to preserve the ancient name.

2:9 *Double portion of your spirit*: as the firstborn son inherited a double portion of his father's property (Dt 21:17), so Elisha asks to inherit from Elijah his spirit of prophecy in the degree befitting his principal disciple. In Nm 11:17–25, God bestows some of the spirit of Moses on others.

2:12 *My father*: a religious title accorded prophetic leaders; cf. 6:21; 8:9; and 13:14, where King Joash of Israel reacts to Elisha's own impending death with the same words Elisha uses here.

2:14 *The LORD, the God of Elijah—where is he now?*: the words in Hebrew have an incantatory quality, as if Elisha is invoking both the divine name and the name of his departed master in an attempt to duplicate Elijah's miracle.

2:23–24 This story probably was told to warn children of the importance of respect for prophets.

3:1–9:13 After the formulaic introduction to the reign of Joram of Israel, this section falls into two parts. The first contains several stories about the prophet Elisha, both in private and in public life. There are four longer stories, arranged in an ABBA pattern: drought during war with Moab (vv. 4–27), restoration of the Shunammite's son (4:8–37), healing of Naaman (5:1–27), famine during war with Aram (6:24–7:20). The last three of these stories are each preceded and followed by short anecdotal tales about Elisha. The second part of this section turns to the political realm. Elisha carries out the Lord's commissions to Elijah (1 Kgs 19:15–17) to anoint Hazael king of Aram (2 Kgs 8:7–15) and Jehu king of Israel (9:1–13). To prepare for the story of Jehu's insurrection (9:14–11:20), the narrator places between those two narratives notices about the royal succession in Judah (8:16–24, 25–29). The formulaic conclusions to the reigns of Joram of Israel and Ahaziah of Judah (8:25–29) are missing, since the deaths of both will be recounted in the story of Jehu's insurrection.

3:1 The contradiction between 1:17 and v. 1 regarding the year when Joram succeeded Ahaziah of Israel makes any reconstruction of the chronology of Israel's and Judah's kings uncertain. Some scholars think that one or the other notice is simply incorrect. Others propose to explain the discrepancy by a co-regency: Jehoshaphat of Judah would have shared the throne with his son Joram from Jehoshaphat's seventeenth year until he died in the twenty-fifth year of his reign (1 Kgs 22:42; see also 2 Kgs 8:16). The issue is further complicated by the speculation of some historians that "Joram of Israel" ("son" of Ahab of Israel: v. 1) and "Joram of Judah" ("son-in-law" of Ahab of Israel: 8:18) were in fact the same person, in whom the royal houses and separate realms of Israel and Judah were briefly reunited.

3:4 In the period of oral tradition, it seems that stories of kings

* **2:11** Gn 5:24; 1 Mc 2:58; Sir 48:9–12; Acts 1:9. **2:15** 1 Kgs 19:19; Sir 48:12. **2:16** 1 Kgs 18:12. **2:17** 1 Kgs 17:2; 18:10. **2:19–22** 2 Kgs 4:38–41. **3:2** 1 Kgs 16:32.

hundred thousand lambs and the wool of a hun-
dred thousand rams. 5But when Ahab died, the
king of Moab rebelled against the king of Israel.
6King Joram set out from Samaria and mustered
all Israel. 7* Then he sent Jehoshaphat, the king
of Judah, the message: "The king of Moab has
rebelled against me. Will you come with me to
Moab to fight?" He replied, "I will. You and I are
as one, your people and my people, and your
horses and my horses as well." 8He said, "By
what route shall we attack?" and the other said,
"By way of the wilderness of Edom."
9So the king of Israel set out, accompanied by
the king of Judah and the king of Edom. After a
roundabout journey of seven days the water gave
out for the army and for the animals with them.
10The king of Israel exclaimed, "Alas! The LORD
has called three kings together only to deliver
us into the power of Moab." 11But Jehoshaphat
asked, "Is there no prophet of the LORD here
through whom we may inquire of the LORD?"
One of the servants of the king of Israel replied,
"Elisha, son of Shaphat, who poured water on
the hands of Elijah,† is here." 12Jehoshaphat
agreed, "He has the word of the LORD." So the
king of Israel, along with Jehoshaphat and the
king of Edom, went down to Elisha. 13Elisha
asked the king of Israel, "What do you want with
me? Go to the prophets of your father and to the
prophets of your mother." The king of Israel re-
plied, "No, the LORD has called these three kings
together only to deliver us into the power of
Moab." 14Then Elisha said, "As the LORD of hosts
lives, whom I serve, were it not that I respect Je-
hoshaphat, the king of Judah, I should neither
look at you nor notice you at all. 15Now get me a
minstrel." When the minstrel played, the hand of
the LORD came upon Elisha, 16and he announced:
"Thus says the LORD: Provide many catch basins
in this wadi. 17For the LORD says: Though you
will see neither wind nor rain, yet this wadi will
be filled with water for you to drink, and for your
livestock and pack animals. 18And since the LORD
does not consider this enough, he will also de-
liver Moab into your power. 19You shall destroy
every fortified city and every choice city, fell every
fruit tree, stop up all the springs, and ruin every
fertile field with stones."*
20In the morning, at the time of the sacrifice,
water came from the direction of Edom and
filled the land.
21Meanwhile, all Moab had heard that the
kings had come to war against them; troops
from the youngest on up were mobilized and
stationed at the border. 22When they rose early
that morning, the sun was shining across the wa-
ter. The Moabites saw the water as red as blood,
23and said, "This is blood! The kings have fought
among themselves and killed one another.
Quick! To the spoils, Moab!" 24But when they
reached the camp of Israel, the Israelites rose up
and attacked the Moabites, who fled from them.
They ranged through the countryside destroying
Moab— 25leveling the cities, each one casting the
stones onto every fertile field and filling it, stop-
ping up every spring, felling every fruit tree, until
only the stones of Kir-hareseth† remained. Then
the slingers surrounded and attacked it. 26When
he saw that the battle was going against him, the
king of Moab took seven hundred swordsmen to
break through to the king of Edom, but he failed.
27So he took his firstborn, who was to succeed
him as king, and offered him as a burnt offering
upon the wall. The wrath against Israel† was so
great that they gave up the siege and returned to
their own land.*

The Widow's Oil

4 1* A certain woman, the widow of one of
the guild prophets, cried out to Elisha: "My
husband, your servant, is dead. You know that he
revered the LORD, yet now his creditor has come
to take my two children into servitude."† 2Elisha
answered her, "What am I to do for you? Tell me
what you have in the house." She replied, "This
servant of yours has nothing in the house but
a jug of oil." 3He said, "Go out, borrow vessels
from all your neighbors—as many empty vessels
as you can. 4Then come back and close the door
on yourself and your children; pour the oil into
all the vessels, and as each is filled, set it aside."
5So she went out. She closed the door on herself

2 KGS

† were often told without identifying the kings by name. (Vestiges of this anonymity are still visible in 1 Kgs 3:16–28; 20:4–43; 22:1–38; 2 Kgs 6:8–7:20.) Names (such as "Ahab" in 1 Kgs 20:13–14; 22:20) were added later. As a consequence, the historical attachment of such stories to the kings about whom they are told is open to question. (See note on 1 Kgs 20:1–22:54.) The present story about a campaign against Moab by Joram and Jehoshaphat has several striking similarities to the campaign against Ramoth-gilead by Ahab and Jehoshaphat in 1 Kgs 22:1–38. There exists a Moabite inscription that contains Mesha's self-aggrandizing account of his successful rebellion against Israel, but the times and places it mentions are different from those implied in vv. 4–27.

3:11 *Poured water on the hands of Elijah*: possibly a metaphor for "was Elijah's servant." But the phrase occurs nowhere else in the Old Testament and its meaning is not certain.

3:25 *Kir-hareseth*: a major city of Moab, identified with modern Kerak, east of the Dead Sea; cf. Is 16:7, 11; Jer 48:31, 36.

3:27 *The wrath against Israel*: probably the wrath of Chemosh, the Moabite god to whom the child was offered. The Israelites, intimidated by this wrath, retreat.

4:1 *His creditor . . . into servitude*: Israelite law permitted the selling of wife and children into slavery for debt; cf. Ex 21:7; Am 2:6; 8:6; Is 50:1.

3:7–11 1 Kgs 22:3–8. **3:19** Dt 20:19. **3:27** Jgs 11:30–31. **4:1–7** 1 Kgs 17:8–16.

and her children and, as they handed her the vessels, she would pour in oil. 6 When all the vessels were filled, she said to her son, "Bring me another vessel." He answered, "There is none left." And then the oil stopped. 7 She went and told the man of God, who said, "Go sell the oil to pay off your creditor; with what remains, you and your children can live."

Elisha Raises the Shunammite's Son

8 One day Elisha came to Shunem, where there was a woman of influence, who pressed him to dine with her. Afterward, whenever he passed by, he would stop there to dine. 9 So she said to her husband, "I know that he is a holy man of God. Since he visits us often, 10 let us arrange a little room on the roof and furnish it for him with a bed, table, chair, and lamp, so that when he comes to us he can stay there."*

11 One day Elisha arrived and stayed in the room overnight. 12 Then he said to his servant Gehazi, "Call this Shunammite woman." He did so, and when she stood before Elisha, 13 he told Gehazi, "Say to her, 'You have troubled yourself greatly for us; what can we do for you? Can we say a good word for you to the king or to the commander of the army?' " She replied, "I am living among my own people."† 14 Later Elisha asked, "What can we do for her?" Gehazi answered, "She has no son, and her husband is old." 15 Elisha said, "Call her." He did so, and when she stood at the door, 16 Elisha promised, "This time next year you will be cradling a baby son." She said, "My lord, you are a man of God; do not deceive your servant."* 17 Yet the woman conceived, and by the same time the following year she had given birth to a son, as Elisha had promised; 18 and the child grew up healthy.*

One day the boy went out to his father among the reapers. 19 He said to his father, "My head! My head!" And his father said to the servant, "Carry him to his mother." 20 The servant picked him up and carried him to his mother; he sat in her lap until noon, and then died. 21 She went upstairs and laid him on the bed of the man of God. Closing the door on him, she went out 22 and called to her husband, "Let me have one of the servants and a donkey. I must go quickly to the man of God, and I will be back." 23 He asked, "Why are you going to him today? It is neither the new moon nor the sabbath." But she said, "It is all right." 24 When the donkey was saddled, she said to her servant, "Lead on! Do not stop my donkey unless I tell you." 25 She kept going till she reached the man of God on Mount Carmel. When he saw her at a distance, the man of God said to his servant Gehazi: "There is the Shunammite! 26 Hurry to meet her, and ask if everything is all right with her, with her husband, and with the boy." "Everything is all right," she replied. 27 But when she reached the man of God on the mountain, she clasped his feet. Gehazi came near to push her away, but the man of God said: "Let her alone, she is in bitter anguish; the LORD hid it from me and did not let me know." 28 She said, "Did I ask my lord for a son? Did I not say, 'Do not mislead me'?" 29 He said to Gehazi, "Get ready for a journey. Take my staff with you and be off; if you meet anyone, give no greeting,† and if anyone greets you, do not answer. Lay my staff upon the boy." 30 But the boy's mother cried out: "As the LORD lives and as you yourself live, I will not release you." So he started back with her.

31 Meanwhile, Gehazi had gone on ahead and had laid the staff upon the boy, but there was no sound, no response. He returned to meet Elisha and told him, "The boy has not awakened." 32 When Elisha reached the house, he found the boy dead, lying on the bed. 33 He went in, closed the door on them both, and prayed to the LORD. 34 Then he lay upon the child on the bed, placing his mouth upon the child's mouth, his eyes upon the eyes, and his hands upon the hands. As Elisha stretched himself over the child, the boy's flesh became warm.* 35 He arose, paced up and down the room, and then once more stretched himself over him, and the boy sneezed seven times and opened his eyes.* 36 Elisha summoned Gehazi and said, "Call the Shunammite." He called her, and she came to him, and Elisha said to her, "Take your son." 37 She came in and fell at his feet in homage; then she took her son and left.

The Poisoned Stew

38 * When Elisha returned to Gilgal, there was a famine in the land. Once, when the guild prophets were seated before him, he said to his servant, "Put the large pot on, and make some

†

4:13 *I am living among my own people*: the Shunammite woman declines Elisha's offer. Surrounded by the support of her family and her clan, she is secure. Ironically, at some point in the future Elisha's advice will send her to live among foreigners (see 8:1–2).

4:29 *Give no greeting*: a profuse exchange of greetings and compliments would normally surround the chance encounter of acquaintances on the road. This would, however, take time, and Gehazi's mission was urgent. Compare Lk 10:4.

*

4:10 1 Kgs 17:9.
4:16 Gn 18:9–15.
4:18–37 1 Kgs 17:17–24; Lk 7:11–16; Acts 20:10–12.
4:34–37 Sir 48:13.
4:35 Heb 11:35.
4:38–41 2 Kgs 2:19–22.

Live It!

Feed Your Soul

Elisha's miracle in 2 Kings 4:44 fed the body, but it is just as important to feed the appetite of the soul, such as the need for hope, for affirmation, and for being loved. It's easy to go to the nearest fast-food restaurant to satisfy your physical appetite, but when it comes to feeding your soul, where do you go?

God gives us plenty of opportunities to feed our soul. We just need to take advantage of them. Go to church. Participate in your youth program. Start a Bible study. Go on a retreat or to a youth conference. Talk to friends about your faith and theirs. Take a walk and pray. You'll find that feeding your faith can be fun, and it often costs less than a value meal at your local fast-food restaurant.

▶ **2 Kgs 4:42–44**

vegetable stew for the guild prophets." 39 Some-
one went out into the field to gather herbs and
found a wild vine, from which he picked a sack-
ful of poisonous wild gourds. On his return he
cut them up into the pot of vegetable stew with-
out anybody's knowing it. 40 The stew was served,
but when they began to eat it, they cried, "Man
of God, there is death in the pot!" And they
could not eat it. 41 He said, "Bring some meal."
He threw it into the pot and said, "Serve it to the
people to eat." And there was no longer anything
harmful in the pot.

The Barley Loaves

42 * A man came from Baal-shalishah bring-
ing the man of God twenty barley loaves made
from the first fruits, and fresh grain in the ear.
Elisha said, "Give it to the people to eat." 43 But
his servant objected, "How can I set this before a
hundred?" Elisha again said, "Give it to the peo-
ple to eat, for thus says the LORD: You will eat and
have some left over." 44 He set it before them, and
when they had eaten, they had some left over,
according to the word of the LORD.

Elisha Cures Naaman's Leprosy

5 1 Naaman, the army commander of the king
of Aram, was highly esteemed and respected
by his master, for through him the LORD had
brought victory to Aram. But valiant as he was,
the man was a leper.† 2 Now the Arameans had
captured from the land of Israel in a raid a little
girl, who became the servant of Naaman's wife.
3 She said to her mistress, "If only my master
would present himself to the prophet in Sa-
maria! He would cure him of his leprosy."
4 Naaman went and told his master, "This is
what the girl from the land of Israel said." 5 The
king of Aram said, "Go. I will send along a letter
to the king of Israel." So Naaman set out, taking
along ten silver talents, six thousand gold pieces,
and ten festal garments.
6 He brought the king of Israel the letter, which
read: "With this letter I am sending my servant
Naaman to you, that you may cure him of his
leprosy." 7 When he read the letter, the king of
Israel tore his garments and exclaimed: "Am I
a god with power over life and death, that this
man should send someone for me to cure him
of leprosy? Take note! You can see he is only
looking for a quarrel with me!"* 8 When Elisha,
the man of God, heard that the king of Israel
had torn his garments, he sent word to the king:
"Why have you torn your garments? Let him
come to me and find out that there is a prophet
in Israel."
9 Naaman came with his horses and chariot
and stopped at the door of Elisha's house. 10 Eli-
sha sent him the message: "Go and wash seven
times in the Jordan, and your flesh will heal, and
you will be clean."* 11 But Naaman went away an-
gry, saying, "I thought that he would surely come
out to me and stand there to call on the name
of the LORD his God, and would move his hand
over the place, and thus cure the leprous spot.
12 Are not the rivers of Damascus, the Abana and
the Pharpar, better than all the waters of Israel?
Could I not wash in them and be cleansed?"†
With this, he turned about in anger and left.

†

5:1 *Leper*: the terms traditionally translated "leper" and "leprosy" covered a wide variety of skin disorders like psoriasis, eczema, and seborrhea, but probably not Hansen's disease (modern "leprosy"); there is no clear evidence of its existence in biblical times.

5:12 *Wash in them and be cleansed*: typical of the ambiguity in ritual healing or cleanliness. The muddy waters of the Jordan are no match hygienically for the mountain spring waters of Damascus; ritually, it is the other way around.

*

4:42–44 Mt 14:13–21; 15:32–38; Mk 6:34–44; 8:1–9; Lk 9:10–17; Jn 6:1–13.

5:7 1 Sm 2:6; Jn 5:21.

5:10 Jn 9:7.

13 But his servants came up and reasoned with
him: "My father, if the prophet told you to do
something extraordinary, would you not do it?
All the more since he told you, 'Wash, and be
clean'?" 14 So Naaman went down and plunged
into the Jordan seven times, according to the
word of the man of God. His flesh became again
like the flesh of a little child, and he was clean.*
15 He returned with his whole retinue to the
man of God. On his arrival he stood before him
and said, "Now I know that there is no God in
all the earth, except in Israel. Please accept a gift
from your servant."* 16 Elisha replied, "As the
LORD lives whom I serve, I will not take it." And
despite Naaman's urging, he still refused. 17 Naa-
man said: "If you will not accept, please let me,
your servant, have two mule-loads of earth,† for
your servant will no longer make burnt offerings
or sacrifices to any other god except the LORD.
18 But may the LORD forgive your servant this:
when my master enters the temple of Rimmon
to bow down there, as he leans upon my arm, I
too must bow down in the temple of Rimmon.
When I bow down in the temple of Rimmon,
may the LORD please forgive your servant this."
19 Elisha said to him, "Go in peace."†
Naaman had gone some distance 20 when
Gehazi, the servant of Elisha, the man of God,
thought to himself: "My master was too easy on
this Aramean Naaman, not accepting what he
brought. As the LORD lives, I will run after him
and get something out of him." 21 So Gehazi
hurried after Naaman. Seeing that someone was
running after him, Naaman alighted from his
chariot to wait for him. He asked, "Is everything
all right?" 22 Gehazi replied, "Yes, but my master
sent me to say, 'Two young men have just come
to me, guild prophets from the hill country of
Ephraim. Please give them a talent of silver and
two festal garments.'" 23 Naaman said, "I insist!
Take two talents," and he pressed him. He tied
up two silver talents in bags and gave them, with
two festal garments, to two of his servants, who
carried them before Gehazi. 24 When he reached
the hill, Gehazi received these things, appropri-
ated them for his house, and sent the men on
their way.
25 He went in and stood by Elisha his master,
who asked him, "Where have you been, Ge-
hazi?" He answered, "Your servant has not gone
anywhere." 26 But Elisha said to him: "Was I not
present in spirit when someone got down from
his chariot to wait for you? Is this a time to take
money or to take garments, olive orchards or
vineyards, sheep or cattle, male or female ser-
vants? 27 The leprosy of Naaman shall cling to
you and your descendants forever." And Gehazi
went out, a leper with skin like snow.†

The Lost Ax

6 1 The guild prophets once said to Elisha:
"This place where we live with you is too
cramped for us. 2 Let us go to the Jordan, where
by getting one beam apiece we can build our-
selves a place to live." Elisha said, "Go." 3 One
of them requested, "Please agree to accompany
your servants." He replied, "Yes, I will come."
4 So he went with them, and when they ar-
rived at the Jordan they began to cut down trees.
5 While one of them was felling a tree trunk, the
iron ax blade slipped into the water. He cried out,
"Oh, no, master! It was borrowed!" 6 "Where did
it fall?" asked the man of God. When he pointed
out the spot, Elisha cut off a stick, threw it into
the water, and brought the iron to the surface.

Did You Know?

New Testament Parallels

The story in 2 Kgs 4:42–44 reminds us of a famous story about Jesus feeding a crowd of people with a tiny amount of food. This story is famous because it is the only one told six times in the Gospels. Jesus feeds a crowd of five thousand in all four Gospels (see Mt 14:13–21, Mk 6:34–44, Lk 9:10–17, Jn 6:1–14) and a crowd of four thousand in two Gospels (see Mt 15:32–39, Mk 8:1–9).

Several events in the Old Testament have close parallels in the New Testament. For Christians these Old Testament parallels have even richer meaning in the light of Jesus' life and ministry.

▶ **2 Kgs 4:42–44**

2 KGS

†

5:17 *Two mule-loads of earth*: worship of the Lord is associated with the soil of the Holy Land, where he is present.

5:19 *Go in peace*: Elisha understands and approves the situation of Naaman who, though now a worshiper of the God of Israel, is required by his courtly office to assist his master, the king ("leans upon my arm," v. 18), worshiping in the temple of the Canaanite god Baal-Rimmon.

5:27 *With skin like snow*: "snow" is often used to describe the skin conditions covered by the term "leprosy" (Ex 4:6; Nm 12:10; see note on 5:1). It is unclear whether the comparison is with the white color, dry flakes, or moist shine, any of which can occur in the relevant skin diseases.

*

5:14 Lk 4:27. **5:15** Lk 17:17–19.

7 He said, "Pick it up." And the man stretched out
his hand and grasped it.

The Aramean Ambush

8 When the king of Aram was waging war on
Israel, he would make plans with his servants:
"I will bivouac at such and such a place." 9 But
the man of God would send word to the king of
Israel, "Be careful! Do not pass by this place, for
Aram will attack there." 10 So the king of Israel
would send word to the place which the man of
God had indicated, and alert it; then they would
be on guard. This happened several times.
11 Greatly disturbed over this, the king of Aram
called together his officers and asked them, "Will
you not tell me who among us is for the king of
Israel?" 12 "No one, my lord king," answered one
of the officers. "The Israelite prophet Elisha can
tell the king of Israel the very words you speak in
your bedroom." 13 He said, "Go, find out where
he is, so that I may take him captive."
Informed that Elisha was in Dothan, 14 he
sent there a strong force with horses and chari-
ots. They arrived by night and encircled the city.
15 Early the next morning, when the servant of
the man of God arose and went out, he saw the
force with its horses and chariots surrounding
the city. "Alas!" he said to Elisha. "What shall
we do, my lord?" 16 Elisha answered, "Do not be
afraid. Our side outnumbers theirs." 17 Then he
prayed, "O LORD, open his eyes, that he may see."
And the LORD opened the eyes of the servant, and
he saw that the mountainside was filled with fi-
ery chariots and horses around Elisha.*
18 When the Arameans came down to get him,
Elisha prayed to the LORD, "Strike this people
blind, I pray you." And the LORD struck them
blind, according to Elisha's word. 19 Then Elisha
said to them: "This is the wrong road, and this
is the wrong city. Follow me! I will take you to
the man you want." And he led them to Samaria.
20 When they entered Samaria, Elisha prayed, "O
LORD, open their eyes that they may see." The
LORD opened their eyes, and they saw that they
were inside Samaria. 21 When the king of Israel
saw them, he asked, "Shall I kill them, my father?
Shall I kill them?" 22 Elisha replied, "You must
not kill them. Do you slay those whom you have
taken captive with your sword or bow?† Serve
them a meal. Let them eat and drink, and then go
back to their master." 23 The king spread a great
feast for them. When they had eaten and drunk
he sent them away, and they went back to their
master. No more Aramean raiders came into the
land of Israel.

War Against Aram: Famine

24 After this, Ben-hadad, king of Aram, mus-
tered his whole army and laid siege to Samaria.
25 Because of the siege the famine in Samaria was
so severe that a donkey's head sold for eighty
pieces of silver, and a fourth of a kab of "dove
droppings"† for five pieces of silver.
26 * One day, as the king of Israel was walking
on the city wall, a woman cried out to him, "Save
us, my lord king!" 27 He replied, "If the LORD does
not save you, where could I find means to save
you? On the threshing floor? In the wine press?"
28 Then the king asked her, "What is your trou-
ble?" She replied: "This woman said to me, 'Give
up your son that we may eat him today; then to-
morrow we will eat my son.' 29 So we boiled my
son and ate him. The next day I said to her, 'Now
give up your son that we may eat him.' But she
hid her son." 30 When the king heard the woman's
words, he tore his garments. And as he was walk-
ing on the wall, the people saw that he was wear-
ing sackcloth underneath, next to his skin.
31 The king exclaimed, "May God do thus to
me, and more, if the head of Elisha, son of Sha-
phat, stays on him today!"
32 Meanwhile, Elisha was sitting in his house
in conference with the elders. The king had sent
one of his courtiers; but before the messenger
reached him, Elisha said to the elders: "Do you
know that this murderer is sending someone to
cut off my head? When the messenger comes, see
that you close the door and hold it fast against
him. His master's footsteps are echoing behind
him." 33 While Elisha was still speaking, the mes-
senger came down to him and said, "This evil is
from the LORD. Why should I trust in the LORD
any longer?"†

7 1 Elisha replied: "Hear the word of the LORD!
Thus says the LORD: At this time tomorrow a
seah of fine flour will sell for a shekel, and two
seahs of barley for a shekel, in the market† of

6:22 *With your sword or bow*: since the king would not slay prisoners who had surrendered to his power, much less should he slay prisoners captured by God's power. This wartime practice stands in contrast to that of holy war, where prisoners were placed under the ban and so devoted to destruction (see 1 Kgs 20:35–43).

6:25 *"Dove droppings"*: it is unclear whether this phrase is to be read literally (e.g., dung used as fuel) or as the nickname of a type of edible plant, as attested in Arabic. A kab was probably around a quart.

6:33 The messenger speaks in the king's name. Similarly, Elisha's response in the next verse can be spoken of as delivered to the king (7:18).

7:1 *Market*: lit., "gate," the principal place of trading in ancient walled cities in time of peace.

6:17 2 Kgs 2:11; 7:6; Ps 68:18. **6:26–29** Dt 28:53–57.

Samaria." 2 But the adjutant, upon whose arm the king leaned, answered the man of God, "Even if the LORD were to make windows in heaven, how could this happen?" Elisha said, "You shall see it with your own eyes, but you shall not eat of it."

3 At the city gate four lepers were asking one another, "Why should we sit here until we die?* 4 If we decide to go into the city, we shall die there, for there is famine in the city. If we remain here, we shall die too. So come, let us desert to the camp of the Arameans. If they let us live, we live; if they kill us, we die." 5 At twilight they left for the Arameans; but when they reached the edge of the camp, no one was there. 6 * The Lord had caused the army of the Arameans to hear the sound of chariots and horses, the sound of a large army, and they had reasoned among themselves, "The king of Israel has hired the kings of the Hittites and the kings of Egypt to fight us." 7 Then in the twilight they had fled, abandoning their tents, their horses, and their donkeys, the whole camp just as it was, and fleeing for their lives.

8 After the lepers reached the edge of the camp, they went first into one tent, ate and drank, and took silver, gold, and clothing from it, and went out and hid them. Back they came into another tent, took things from it, and again went out and hid them. 9 Then they said to one another: "We are not doing right. This is a day of good news, and we are keeping silent. If we wait until morning breaks, we will be blamed. So come, let us go and inform the palace." 10 They came and summoned the city gatekeepers. They said, "We went to the camp of the Arameans, but no one was there—not a human voice, only the horses and donkeys tethered, and the tents just as they were left." 11 The gatekeepers announced this and it was reported within the palace.

12 Though it was night, the king got up; he said to his servants, "Let me tell you what the Arameans have done to us. Knowing that we are starving, they have left their camp to hide in the field. They are thinking, 'The Israelites will leave the city and we will take them alive and enter it.' " 13 † One of his servants, however, suggested: "Let some of us take five of the horses remaining in the city—they are just like the whole throng of Israel that has reached its limit—and let us send scouts to investigate." 14 They took two chariots, and horses, and the king sent them to reconnoiter the Aramean army with the order, "Go and find out." 15 They followed the Arameans as far as the Jordan, and the whole route was strewn with garments and other objects that the Arameans had thrown away in their haste. The messengers returned and told the king. 16 The people went out and plundered the camp of the Arameans.

Then a seah of fine flour sold for a shekel and two seahs of barley for a shekel, according to the word of the LORD. 17 The king had put in charge of the gate the officer upon whose arm he leaned; but the people trampled him to death at the gate, just as the man of God had predicted when the messenger came down to him. 18 This was in accordance with the word the man of God spoke to the king: "Two seahs of barley will sell for a shekel, and a seah of fine flour for a shekel at this time tomorrow in the market of Samaria." 19 The adjutant had answered the man of God, "Even if the LORD were to make windows in heaven, how could this happen?" And Elisha had replied, "You shall see it with your own eyes, but you shall not eat of it." 20 And that is what happened to him, for the people trampled him to death at the gate.

The Shunammite's Return

8 1 Elisha once said to the woman whose son he had restored to life: "Get ready! Leave with your household and live wherever you can, because the LORD has decreed a seven-year famine which is coming upon the land."* 2 The woman got ready and did as the man of God said, setting out with her household, and living in the land of the Philistines for seven years.

3 At the end of the seven years, the woman returned from the land of the Philistines and went out to the king to appeal for her house and her field. 4 The king was talking with Gehazi, the servant of the man of God: "Tell me all the great things that Elisha has done." 5 Just as he was telling the king how his master had restored a dead person to life, the very woman whose son Elisha had restored to life came to the king appealing for her house and field. Gehazi said, "My lord king, this is the woman, and this is that son of hers whom Elisha restored to life." 6 The king questioned the woman, and she told him her story. With that the king placed an official† at her disposal, saying, "Restore all her property to her, with all that the field produced from the day she left the land until now."

†

7:13 The Hebrew of this verse is difficult and its meaning is uncertain.

8:6 *An official*: lit., "eunuch," and perhaps actually so in this instance.

*

7:3 Lv 13:46. **7:6–7** 2 Kgs 6:17; 2 Sm 5:24. **8:1** 2 Kgs 4:18–37.

Did You Know?

Grading Kings

As you read the remaining chapters of Second Kings, notice that the author gives a kind of report card for each of the rulers of Israel and Judah. Jehoram, for example, receives an F: "He did what was evil in the LORD's sight" (8:18). Josiah receives an A: "He did what was rght in the LORD's sight, walking in the way of David his father, not turning right or left" (22:2). The author, who wrote after the fall of both kingdoms, provides a theological reason for Israel's and Judah's failure. Because most of the rulers continually violated God's law, they were largely responsible for the fall of the kingdoms.

Elisha and Hazael of Aram†

7 * Elisha came to Damascus at a time when
Ben-hadad, king of Aram, lay sick. When he was
told, "The man of God has come here," 8 the king
said to Hazael, "Take a gift with you and go call on
the man of God. Consult the LORD through him,
'Will I recover from this sickness?' "* 9 Hazael went
to visit him, carrying a present, and with forty
camel loads of the best goods of Damascus. On
his arrival, he stood before Elisha and said, "Your
son Ben-hadad, king of Aram, has sent me to you
to ask, 'Will I recover from my sickness?' " 10 Eli-
sha answered, "Go and tell him, 'You will surely
recover.' But the LORD has showed me that he will
surely die." 11 Then he stared him down until he
became ill at ease. The man of God wept, 12 and
Hazael asked, "Why are you weeping, my lord?"
Elisha replied, "Because I know the evil that you
will inflict upon the Israelites. You will burn their
fortresses, you will slay their youth with the sword,
you will dash their little children to pieces, you
will rip open their pregnant women."* 13 Hazael
exclaimed, "How can your servant, a dog† like me,
do anything so important?" Elisha replied, "The
LORD has showed you to me as king over Aram."
14 Hazael left Elisha and returned to his master,
who asked, "What did Elisha tell you?" Hazael re-
plied, "He said, 'You will surely recover.' " 15 The
next day, however, Hazael took a cloth, dipped it
in water, and spread it over the king's face, so that
he died. And Hazael succeeded him as king.

Reign of Joram of Judah

16 † In the fifth year of Joram, son of Ahab,
king of Israel, Joram, son of Jehoshaphat, king
of Judah, became king. 17 He was thirty-two years
old when he became king, and he reigned eight
years in Jerusalem.
18 He walked in the way of the kings of Israel
as the house of Ahab had done, since the daugh-
ter of Ahab was his wife; and he did what was
evil in the LORD's sight. 19 Even so, the LORD was
unwilling to destroy Judah, for the sake of his
servant David. For he had promised David that
he would leave him a holding in the LORD's pres-
ence for all time.* 20 During Joram's reign, Edom
revolted against the rule of Judah and installed a
king of its own. 21 Thereupon Joram with all his
chariots crossed over to Zair. He arose by night
and broke through the Edomites when they had
surrounded him and the commanders of his
chariots. Then his army fled homeward. 22 To this
day Edom has been in revolt against the rule of
Judah. Libnah also revolted at that time.*
23 The rest of the acts of Joram, with all that he
did, are recorded in the book of the chronicles of
the kings of Judah. 24 Joram rested with his an-
cestors; he was buried with his ancestors in the
City of David, and his son Ahaziah succeeded
him as king.

Reign of Ahaziah of Judah†

25 In the twelfth year of Joram, son of Ahab,
king of Israel, Ahaziah, son of Joram, king of
Judah, became king. 26 Ahaziah was twenty-two
years old when he became king, and he reigned
one year in Jerusalem. His mother's name was
Athaliah, daughter of Omri, king of Israel.†
27 He walked in the way of the house of Ahab
and did what was evil in the LORD's sight like the
house of Ahab, since he was related to them by
marriage. 28 He joined Joram, son of Ahab, in
battle against Hazael, king of Aram, at Ramoth-

† **8:7–15** Elisha carries out the commission the Lord gave Elijah in 1 Kgs 19:15. See note on 2 Kgs 3:1–9:13.

8:13 To call oneself a "dog" is to admit one's insignificance (1 Sm 24:15; 2 Sm 9:8); it is not necessarily a term of contempt, as in English. Hazael focuses on the question of his power, making no comment on the atrocities Elisha predicts he will commit.

8:16 On the apparent contradictions among 1:17, 3:1, and this verse, see note on 3:1.

8:25–29 The narrative of Ahaziah's reign, like that of Joram of Israel, lacks the standard formulaic conclusion. The deaths of both kings, and indeed the obliteration of the whole house of Omri, will be recounted in the story of Jehu's insurrection.

8:26 It is unclear whether Athaliah was Omri's daughter (v. 26) or his granddaughter (v. 18). Perhaps "daughter" here is being used loosely for "female descendant."

* **8:7–15** 1 Kgs 19:15.
8:8 1 Kgs 14:1–3.
8:12 2 Kgs 13:3–7.
8:19 2 Sm 7:12–16; 1 Kgs 11:36; 15:4.
8:22 Gn 27:40.

gilead, where the Arameans wounded Joram.*
29 King Joram returned to Jezreel to be healed of
the wounds which the Arameans had inflicted on
him at Ramah in his battle against Hazael, king
of Aram. Then Ahaziah, son of Joram, king of Ju-
dah, went down to Jezreel to visit Joram, son of
Ahab, for he was sick.

Elisha and Jehu of Israel†

9 1 * Elisha the prophet called one of the guild
prophets and said to him: "Get ready for a
journey. Take this flask of oil with you, and go
to Ramoth-gilead. 2 When you get there, look for
Jehu, son of Jehoshaphat, son of Nimshi. Enter
and take him away from his companions and
bring him into an inner chamber. 3 From the
flask you have, pour oil on his head, and say,
'Thus says the LORD: I anoint you king over Israel.'
Then open the door and flee without delay."
4 The aide (the prophet's aide) went to Ra-
moth-gilead. 5 When he arrived, the commanders
of the army were in session. He said, "I have a
message for you, commander." Jehu asked, "For
which one of us?" "For you, commander," he
answered. 6 Jehu got up and went into the house.
Then the prophet's aide poured the oil on his
head and said, "Thus says the LORD, the God of
Israel: I anoint you king over the people of the
LORD, over Israel. 7 † You shall destroy the house
of Ahab your master; thus will I avenge the blood
of my servants the prophets, and the blood of all
the other servants of the LORD shed by Jezebel.
8 * The whole house of Ahab shall perish:

I will cut off from Ahab's line every male,
whether bond or free in Israel.

9 I will make the house of Ahab like that of Jero-
boam, son of Nebat, and like that of Baasha, son
of Ahijah. 10 In the confines of Jezreel, the dogs
shall devour Jezebel so that no one can bury
her." Then he opened the door and fled.
11 When Jehu rejoined his master's servants,
they asked him, "Is all well? Why did that mad-
man come to you?" He replied, "You know that
kind of man and his talk." 12 But they said, "Tell
us another lie!" So he told them, "This is what
the prophet's aide said to me, 'Thus says the
LORD: I anoint you king over Israel.' " 13 At once
each took his garment, spread it under Jehu on
the bare steps, blew the horn, and cried out,
"Jehu is king!"

VIII. The End of the Omrid Dynasty†

Death of Joram of Israel

14 * Jehu, son of Jehoshaphat, son of Nimshi,
formed a conspiracy against Joram. (Joram, with
all Israel, had been besieging Ramoth-gilead
against Hazael, king of Aram, 15 but had returned
to Jezreel to be healed of the wounds the Ara-
means had inflicted on him in the battle against
Hazael, king of Aram.)
Jehu said to them, "If this is what you really
want, see that no one escapes from the city to
report in Jezreel."
16 Then Jehu mounted his chariot and drove to
Jezreel, where Joram lay ill and Ahaziah, king of
Judah, had come to visit him. 17 The watchman
standing on the tower in Jezreel saw the troop of
Jehu coming and reported, "I see chariots." Joram
said, "Get a driver and send him to meet them
and to ask whether all is well." 18 So a horseman
went out to meet him and said, "The king asks,
'Is everything all right?' " Jehu said, "What does
it matter to you how things are? Get behind me."
The watchman reported to the king, "The mes-
senger has reached them, but is not returning."
19 Joram sent a second horseman, who went to
them and said, "The king asks, 'Is everything all
right?' " "What does it matter to you how things
are?" Jehu replied. "Get behind me." 20 The
watchman reported, "He has reached them, but is
not returning. The driving is like that of Jehu, son
of Nimshi; he drives like a madman." 21 * "Hitch
up my chariot," said Joram, and they hitched
up his chariot. Then Joram, king of Israel, and
Ahaziah, king of Judah, set out, each in his own
chariot, to meet Jehu. They reached him near the
plot of ground of Naboth the Jezreelite.
22 When Joram recognized Jehu, he asked, "Is
everything all right, Jehu?" Jehu replied, "How
could everything be all right as long as all the
harlotry and sorcery† of your mother Jezebel

2 KGS

†

9:1–13 Elisha carries out the commission the Lord gave Elijah in 1 Kgs 19:16. See note on 2 Kgs 3:1–9:13.

9:7–10 The author has Elisha's emissary expand considerably the speech Elisha told him to deliver by adding the same type of prophetic indictments and sanctions as were invoked on previous occasions against the dynasties of Jeroboam (1 Kgs 14:10–11), of Baasha (1 Kgs 16:3–4), and of Ahab himself (1 Kgs 21:21–24).

9:14–11:20 Death pervades this section. The dynasty founded by Omri (1 Kgs 16:23) drowns in a bloodbath, taking numberless others along with it. The scenes are in three parallel sets of three: death comes (1) to Joram of Israel, Ahab's son; to Ahaziah of Judah, his son-in-law; and to Jezebel, the Baalist queen mother of Israel; (2) then to seventy descendants of Ahab; to forty-two relatives of Ahaziah of Judah; and to numerous Baal worshipers; (3) finally to Jehu of Israel; to the blood royal of Judah; and to Athaliah, the Baalist queen mother of Judah and last of the Omrids.

9:22 *Harlotry and sorcery*: both terms are metaphors referring to Jezebel's worship of the foreign god Baal.

*

8:28–29 2 Kgs 9:14–15.
9:1–13 1 Kgs 19:16.
9:8–10 1 Kgs 14:10–11; 16:3–4; 21:21–24.
9:14–15 2 Kgs 8:28–29.
9:21–26 1 Kgs 21:1–24.

continues?" 23 Joram reined about and fled, cry-
ing to Ahaziah, "Treason, Ahaziah!" 24 But Jehu
had drawn his bow and he shot Joram between
the shoulders, so that the arrow went through
his heart and he collapsed in his chariot. 25 Then
Jehu said to his adjutant Bidkar, "Take him and
throw him into the plot of ground in the field of
Naboth the Jezreelite. For remember when you
and I were driving teams behind Ahab his father,
the LORD delivered this oracle against him: 26 As
surely as I saw yesterday the blood of Naboth
and the blood of his sons—oracle of the LORD—I
will repay you for it in that very plot of ground—
oracle of the LORD. So now take him and throw
him into this plot of ground, in keeping with the
word of the LORD."

Death of Ahaziah of Judah

27 * Seeing what was happening, Ahaziah, king
of Judah, fled toward Beth-haggan. Jehu pursued
him, shouting, "Him too!" They struck him as he
rode through the pass of Gur near Ibleam, but he
continued his flight as far as Megiddo and died
there. 28 His servants brought him in a chariot to
Jerusalem and they buried him in his grave with
his ancestors in the City of David. 29 In the elev-
enth year of Joram, son of Ahab, Ahaziah became
king over Judah.

Death of Jezebel

30 Jehu came to Jezreel, and when Jezebel
heard of it, she shadowed her eyes, adorned her
hair, and looked down from her window. 31 As
Jehu came through the gate, she cried out, "Is
all well, you Zimri, murderer of your master?"*
32 Jehu looked up to the window and shouted,
"Who is on my side? Who?" At this, two or three
eunuchs looked down toward him. 33 "Throw
her down," he ordered. They threw her down,
and some of her blood spurted against the wall
and against the horses. Jehu trod over her body
34 and, after eating and drinking, he said: "Attend
to that accursed woman and bury her; for she
was the daughter of a king." 35 But when they
went to bury her, they found nothing of her
but the skull, the feet, and the hands. 36 They re-
turned to Jehu, and when they told him, he said,
"This is the word the LORD spoke through his ser-
vant Elijah the Tishbite: In the confines of Jezreel
the dogs shall devour the flesh of Jezebel.* 37 The
corpse of Jezebel shall be like dung in the field
in the confines of Jezreel, so that no one can say:
This was Jezebel."

Death of the Sons of Ahab of Israel

10 1 * Ahab had seventy sons in Samaria. Jehu
wrote letters and sent them to Samaria,
to the elders who were rulers of Jezreel and to
Ahab's guardians. Jehu wrote: 2 "Since your mas-
ter's sons are with you, as well as his chariots,
horses, fortified city, and weaponry, when this
letter reaches you 3 decide which is the best and
the fittest of your master's sons, place him on
his father's throne, and fight for your master's
house." 4 They were overcome with fright and
said, "If the two kings could not withstand him,
how can we?" 5 So the master of the palace and
the chief of the city, along with the elders and
the guardians, sent this message to Jehu: "We are
your servants, and we will do everything you tell
us. We will proclaim no one king; do whatever
you think best." 6 So Jehu wrote them a second
letter: "If you are on my side and will obey me,
bring along the heads of your master's sons† and
come to me in Jezreel at this time tomorrow."
(The seventy princes were in the care of promi-
nent men of the city, who were rearing them.)
7 When the letter arrived, they took the princes
and slew all seventy of them, put their heads
in baskets, and sent them to Jehu in Jezreel. 8 A
messenger came in and told him, "They have
brought the heads of the princes." He said, "Pile
them in two heaps at the gate of the city until
morning."
9 In the morning he came outside, stood there,
and said to all the people: "You are guiltless, for
it was I who conspired against my lord and slew
him. But who killed all these? 10 Know that not
a single word which the LORD has spoken against
the house of Ahab shall fail. The LORD has ac-
complished what he decreed through his servant
Elijah."* 11 (And so Jehu slew all who were left
of the house of Ahab in Jezreel, as well as all
his powerful supporters, intimates, and priests,
leaving him no survivor.)* 12 Then he went back
inside.

Death of the Relatives of Ahaziah of Judah

He set out for Samaria and, at Beth-eked-
haroim on the way, 13 Jehu came across rela-
tives of Ahaziah, king of Judah. "Who are you?"
he asked, and they said, "We are relatives of

---

† **10:6** *Heads of your master's sons*: Jehu's command is cleverly ambiguous. He allows the Samarian leaders to understand "heads" either literally or metaphorically as "most important individuals." Then, when the leaders decapitate Ahab's potential successors, Jehu can claim to be innocent of their blood (v. 9).

* **9:27–28** 2 Chr 22:7–9.
9:31 1 Kgs 16:8–13.
9:36 1 Kgs 21:23.
10:1–11 Jgs 9:5; 1 Kgs 15:29; 16:11–12; 21:8.
10:10 1 Kgs 21:17–29.
10:11 Hos 1:4.

Ahaziah. We are going down to visit the princes
and the family of the queen mother."† 14 "Take
them alive," Jehu ordered. They were taken alive,
forty-two in number, then slain at the pit of
Beth-eked. Not one of them survived.

15 When he set out from there, Jehu met Je-
honadab, son of Rechab, on the road. He greeted
him and asked, "Are you with me wholeheart-
edly, as I am with you?" "Yes," he replied. "If you
are, give me your hand." He gave him his hand,
and he had him mount his chariot,* 16 and said,
"Come with me and see my zeal for the LORD."
And they took him along in his chariot.

Slaughter of the Worshipers of Baal

17 When he arrived in Samaria, Jehu slew all
who were left of Ahab's line in Samaria, doing
away with them completely, according to the
word the LORD spoke to Elijah.

18 Jehu gathered all the people together and
said to them: "Ahab served Baal to some extent,
but Jehu will serve him yet more.* 19 Now sum-
mon for me all Baal's prophets, all his servants,
and all his priests. See that no one is absent, for I
have a great sacrifice for Baal. Whoever is absent
shall not live." This Jehu did as a ruse, so that he
might destroy the servants of Baal.*

20 Jehu said further, "Proclaim a solemn as-
sembly in honor of Baal." They did so, 21 and
Jehu sent word of it throughout all Israel. All the
servants of Baal came; there was no one who did
not come; they came to the temple of Baal, and
it was filled from wall to wall. 22 Then Jehu said
to the custodian of the wardrobe, "Bring out gar-
ments for all the servants of Baal." When he had
brought out the garments for them, 23 Jehu, with
Jehonadab, son of Rechab, entered the temple of
Baal and said to the servants of Baal, "Search and
be sure that there is no one who serves the LORD
here with you, but only servants of Baal." 24 Then
they proceeded to offer sacrifices and burnt of-
ferings. Now Jehu had stationed eighty troops
outside with this warning, "Any of you who lets
someone escape of those whom I shall deliver
into your hands shall pay life for life."

25 As soon as he finished offering the burnt of-
fering, Jehu said to the guards and aides, "Go in
and slay them. Let no one escape." So the guards
and aides put them to the sword and cast them
out. Afterward they went into the inner shrine
of the temple of Baal, 26 and took out the pillars
of the temple of Baal. They burned the shrine,
27 tore down the pillar of Baal, tore down the
temple of Baal, and turned it into a latrine, as it
remains today.

28 Thus Jehu destroyed Baal in Israel.

Death of Jehu of Israel

29 However, Jehu did not desist from the sins
which Jeroboam, son of Nebat, had caused Is-
rael to commit, the golden calves at Bethel and
at Dan.*

30 The LORD said to Jehu: Because you have
done well what is right in my eyes, and have
done to the house of Ahab all that was in my
heart, your sons to the fourth generation shall sit
upon the throne of Israel.* 31 But Jehu was not
careful to walk in the law of the LORD, the God of
Israel, with all his heart, since he did not desist
from the sins which Jeroboam had caused Israel
to commit. 32 * At that time the LORD began to
dismember Israel. Hazael defeated the Israelites
throughout their territory 33 east of the Jordan
(all the land of Gilead, of the Gadites, Reuben-
ites, and Manassites), from Aroer on the wadi
Arnon up through Gilead and Bashan.

34 The rest of the acts of Jehu, with all that he
did and all his valor, are recorded in the book
of the chronicles of the kings of Israel. 35 Jehu
rested with his ancestors and was buried in Sa-
maria, and his son Jehoahaz succeeded him as
king. 36 The length of Jehu's reign over Israel was
twenty-eight years in Samaria.

Death of the Heirs of Ahaziah of Judah

11 1 * When Athaliah, the mother of Ahaziah,
saw that her son was dead, she began to
kill off the whole royal family. 2 But Jehosheba,†
daughter of King Joram and sister of Ahaziah,
took Joash, Ahaziah's son, and spirited him
away, along with his nurse, from the bedroom
where the princes were about to be slain. He was
concealed from Athaliah, and so he did not die.
3 For six years he remained hidden with her in the
house of the LORD, while Athaliah ruled as queen
over the land.

---

† **10:13** Since Athaliah, the queen mother in Judah, was of the Israelite royal house (8:18, 26), both the "princes" (lit., the "king's sons") and the queen mother's "family" (lit., her "sons") would belong to the royal houses of both kingdoms. They may thus be numbered among the seventy "sons of Ahab" killed in vv. 1–7. Because "sons" can refer to more remote offspring, the queen mother's "sons" may include Ahaziah's brothers, sons, nephews, as well as the "relatives" (lit., the "brothers") of Ahaziah who are speaking in this scene.

11:2 According to 2 Chr 22:11, Jehosheba was the wife of Jehoiada, the high priest. If this is historical, it would explain her access to the Temple's residential precincts.

* **10:15** 1 Kgs 20:33; 1 Chr 2:55; Jer 35:1–19.
10:18 1 Kgs 16:30–33.
10:19 1 Kgs 18:19, 40.
10:29 1 Kgs 12:28–30.
10:30 2 Kgs 15:12.
10:32 2 Kgs 8:12; Am 1:3.
11:1–2 Jgs 9:5.

Death of Athaliah

4 But in the seventh year, Jehoiada summoned
the captains of the Carians† and of the guards.
He had them come to him in the house of the
LORD, made a covenant with them, exacted an
oath from them in the house of the LORD, and
then showed them the king's son. 5 He gave them
these orders: "This is what you must do: one
third of you who come on duty on the sabbath
shall guard the king's house; 6 another third shall
be at the gate Sur; and the last third shall be at
the gate behind the guards. You shall guard the
palace on all sides, 7 while the two of your divi-
sions who are going off duty that week shall keep
guard over the house of the LORD for the king.
8 You shall surround the king, each with drawn
weapons, and anyone who tries to approach the
guard detail is to be killed; stay with the king,
wherever he goes."
9 The captains did just as Jehoiada the priest
commanded. Each took his troops, both those
going on duty for the week and those going off
duty that week, and came to Jehoiada the priest.
10 * He gave the captains King David's spear and
quivers, which were in the house of the LORD.
11 And the guards, with drawn weapons, lined up
from the southern to the northern limit of the
enclosure, surrounding the altar and the temple
on the king's behalf. 12 Then Jehoiada brought
out the king's son and put the crown and the
testimony† upon him. They proclaimed him
king and anointed him, clapping their hands and
shouting, "Long live the king!"
13 When Athaliah heard the noise made by the
people, she came before them in the house of
the LORD. 14 When she saw the king standing by
the column,† as was the custom, and the captains
and trumpeters near the king, and all the people
of the land rejoicing and blowing trumpets, Ath-
aliah tore her garments and cried out, "Treason,
treason!" 15 Then Jehoiada the priest instructed
the captains in command of the force: "Escort her
with a guard detail. If anyone follows her, let him
die by the sword." For the priest had said, "She
must not die in the house of the LORD." 16 So they
seized her, and when she reached the Horse Gate
of the king's house, she was put to death.
17 * Then Jehoiada made a covenant between
the LORD and the king and the people,† by which
they would be the LORD's people; and another
between the king and the people. 18 Thereupon
all the people of the land went to the temple
of Baal and demolished it. They shattered its
altars and images completely, and slew Mattan,
the priest of Baal, before the altars. Jehoiada the
priest appointed a detachment for the house of
the LORD, 19 and took the captains, the Carians,
the guards, and all the people of the land, and
they led the king down from the house of the
LORD; they came through the guards' gate to the
king's house, and Joash took his seat on the royal
throne. 20 All the people of the land rejoiced and
the city was quiet, now that Athaliah had been
slain with the sword at the king's house.

IX. Kings of Judah and Israel†

Reign of Joash of Judah

12 1 Joash was seven years old when he be-
came king. 2 In the seventh year of Jehu,
Joash became king, and he reigned forty years in
Jerusalem. His mother's name was Zibiah, from
Beer-sheba.
3 Joash did what was right in the LORD's sight
as long as he lived, because Jehoiada the priest
guided him, 4 though the high places did not dis-
appear; the people continued to sacrifice and to
burn incense on the high places.
5 Joash said to the priests: "All the funds for
sacred purposes that are brought to the house of
the LORD—the census tax, personal redemption
money—and all funds that are freely brought to
the house of the LORD, 6 the priests may take for
themselves, each from his own vendor. However,
they must make whatever repairs on the temple
may prove necessary." 7 Nevertheless, as late as
the twenty-third year of the reign of King Joash,
the priests had not made needed repairs on the
temple. 8 Accordingly, King Joash summoned the
priest Jehoiada and the other priests. He asked,
"Why do you not repair the temple? You must

†

11:4 *Carians*: foreign mercenaries serving as the royal bodyguard. Compare "Cherethites and Pelethites" in 1 Kgs 1:38.

11:12 *Testimony*: that is, the two tablets of the law preserved in the ark in the Temple. Presumably they were placed upon the king during his installation ceremony as a reminder of the law he was to uphold.

11:14 *By the column*: the king's special place in the Temple court; cf. 23:3; 2 Chr 23:13. *People of the land*: in this period, the phrase referred to the important citizenry, whose influence sometimes extended to the selection of royal successors (cf. 2 Kgs 11:14–20; 15:5; 16:15; 21:24; 23:6, 30–35; 24:14; 25:3, 19). In postexilic times, by contrast, the phrase was used of the poor.

11:17 There are two covenants. One is between the Lord as one party and the people, headed by the king, as the other. The second covenant, between king and people, is comparable to that made between David and the elders of Israel at Hebron (2 Sm 5:3).

12:1–17:5 This section recounts briefly the reigns of the last several kings of Israel and the kings of Judah contemporary with them. As always, the accounts of the kings are given in the order in which each came to the throne, without regard to which kingdom they ruled. See note on the similar section that begins in 1 Kgs 14:21.

11:10 2 Sm 8:7. **11:17** 2 Kgs 23:3.

no longer take funds from your vendors, but
you shall turn them over for the repairs.” 9 So
the priests agreed that they would neither take
funds from the people nor make the repairs on
the temple.
10 Jehoiada the priest then took a chest, bored
a hole in its lid, and set it beside the altar, on
the right as one entered the house of the LORD.
The priests who kept the doors would put into
it all the silver that was brought to the house of
the LORD. 11 * When they noticed that there was
a large amount of silver in the chest, the royal
scribe would come up with the high priest, and
they would gather up and weigh all the silver that
was in the house of the LORD. 12 The amount thus
realized they turned over to the workers assigned
to the house of the LORD. They in turn would
pay it to the carpenters and builders working in
the house of the LORD, 13 and to the masons and
stone cutters, and for the purchase of the wood
and hewn stone used in repairing the breaches,
and for any other expenses that were necessary
to repair the house of the LORD. 14 None of the
valuables brought to the house of the LORD were
used there to make silver basins, snuffers, bowls,
trumpets, or any gold or silver article. 15 Instead,
they were given to the workers, and with them
they repaired the house of the LORD. 16 More-
over, no reckoning was asked of those who were
provided with the funds to give to the workers,
because they held positions of trust. 17 The funds
from reparation offerings and from purification
offerings, however, were not brought to the
house of the LORD; they belonged to the priests.
18 Then Hazael, king of Aram, came up and
attacked Gath. When he had taken it, Hazael
resolved to go on to attack Jerusalem. 19 Joash,†
king of Judah, took all the sacred offerings pre-
sented by his forebears, Jehoshaphat, Jehoram,
and Ahaziah, kings of Judah, as well as his own,
and all the gold there was in the treasuries of the
house of the LORD and the king’s house, and sent
them to King Hazael of Aram, who then turned
away from Jerusalem.
20 The rest of the acts of Joash, with all that he
did, are recorded in the book of the chronicles
of the kings of Judah. 21 Certain of his officials†
entered into a conspiracy and struck Joash down
at Beth-millo. 22 Jozacar, son of Shimeath, and
Jehozabad, son of Shomer, were the officials who
struck and killed him. He was buried with his an-
cestors in the City of David, and his son Amaziah
succeeded him as king.

Reign of Jehoahaz of Israel

13 1 In the twenty-third year of Joash, son of
Ahaziah, king of Judah, Jehoahaz, son of
Jehu, became king over Israel in Samaria for sev-
enteen years.
2 He did what was evil in the LORD’s sight: he
did not depart from following the sins that Jer-
oboam, son of Nebat, had caused Israel to com-
mit. 3 The LORD was angry with Israel and for a
long time gave them into the power of Hazael,
king of Aram, and of Ben-hadad, son of Hazael.
4 Then Jehoahaz entreated the LORD, who heard
him, since he saw the oppression to which the
king of Aram had subjected Israel.* 5 So the LORD
gave Israel a savior,† and the Israelites, freed
from the power of Aram, dwelt in their own tents
as formerly. 6 Nevertheless, they did not desist
from the sins the house of Jeroboam had caused
Israel to commit, but persisted in them. The
Asherah† remained even in Samaria.* 7 No army
was left to Jehoahaz, except fifty horses with ten
chariots and ten thousand foot soldiers, since the
king of Aram had destroyed them and trampled
them like dust.
8 The rest of the acts of Jehoahaz, with all that
he did and his valor, are recorded in the book of
the chronicles of the kings of Israel. 9 Jehoahaz
rested with his ancestors; he was buried in Sa-
maria and his son Joash succeeded him as king.

Reign of Joash of Israel

10 In the thirty-seventh year of Joash, king of
Judah, Joash, son of Jehoahaz, became king over
Israel in Samaria sixteen years.
11 He did what was evil in the LORD’s sight; he
did not desist from any of the sins Jeroboam,
son of Nebat, had caused Israel to commit, but
persisted in them.
12 † The rest of the acts of Joash, with all that
he did and his valor, and how he fought with

12:19 *Joash*: in 2 Kings the name “Joash” and its variant “Jehoash” are interchangeable (see note on “Joram” and “Jehoram” at 1:17), whether in reference to the king of Judah (vv. 1–22) or his slightly later contemporary, Joash of Israel (13:10–25). Both forms are rendered “Joash” in this translation.

12:21 *Officials*: lit., “servants.” The Hebrew *ebed* (“servant”) has a wide range of meanings, always including service to another.

13:5 *A savior*: i.e., a military leader (cf. Jgs 3:9, 15). Here the identity of the savior is unclear, but the reappearance of a militant Elisha in this chapter after an absence of several chapters and nearly thirty years suggests the narrator may have had him in mind. Two generations later Joash’s grandson, Jeroboam II, will also “save” Israel (14:27).

13:6 *Asherah*: see note on Ex 34:13.

13:12–13 The conclusion to the reign of Joash is given again in 14:15–16. In both places it disrupts the standard pattern followed in the Books of Kings. The account of Joash’s reign ends in vv. 12–13; this leaves the story of Elisha’s last illness (in which Joash figures prominently) suspended between regnal accounts, much as the story of Elisha’s succession to Elijah’s prophetic office (chap. 2) was

12:11–16 2 Kgs 22:3–7. **13:4** 2 Kgs 14:26–27. **13:6** Ex 34:13; 1 Kgs 16:33.

14:4

Amaziah, king of Judah, are recorded in the book
of the chronicles of the kings of Israel. 13 Joash
rested with his ancestors. Then Jeroboam sat on
his throne. Joash was buried in Samaria with the
kings of Israel.

Elisha's Deathbed Prophecy

14 When Elisha was suffering from the sickness
of which he was to die, Joash, king of Israel,
went down to weep over him. "My father, my
father!"† he exclaimed, "Israel's chariot and
steeds!"* 15 Elisha said to him, "Take bow and
arrows," and he took bow and arrows. 16 † Elisha
said to the king of Israel, "Rest your hand on the
bow," and he rested his hand on it. Elisha placed
his hands over the king's hands 17 and said,
"Open the window toward the east." He opened
it. Elisha said, "Shoot," and he shot. He said,

"An arrow of victory for the LORD!
An arrow of victory over Aram!
You will beat Aram at Aphek and finish him!"

18 Then he said to the king of Israel, "Take the
arrows," which he did. Elisha said to the king
of Israel, "Beat the ground!" He beat the ground
three times and stopped. 19 The man of God be-
came angry with him and said, "You should have
beat five or six times. You would have beaten
Aram and finished him. Now you will beat Aram
only three times."

20 And so Elisha died and was buried.
At that time of year, bands of Moabites used to
raid the land. 21 Once some people were burying
a man, when suddenly they saw such a raiding
band. So they cast the man into the grave of Eli-
sha, and everyone went off. But when the man
came in contact with the bones of Elisha, he
came back to life and got to his feet.*
22 King Hazael of Aram oppressed Israel all the
days of Jehoahaz. 23 But the LORD was gracious
with Israel and looked on them with compassion
because of his covenant with Abraham, Isaac,
and Jacob. He was unwilling to destroy them or
to cast them out from his presence even up to
now. 24 So when King Hazael of Aram died and
his son Ben-hadad succeeded him as king, 25 Jo-
ash, son of Jehoahaz, took back from Ben-hadad,
son of Hazael, the cities Hazael had taken in bat-
tle from Jehoahaz, his father. Three times Joash
beat him, and thus recovered the cities of Israel.

Reign of Amaziah of Judah

14 1 In the second year† of Joash, son of Jeho-
ahaz, king of Israel, Amaziah, son of Joash,
king of Judah, became king. 2 He was twenty-five
years old when he became king, and he reigned
twenty-nine years in Jerusalem. His mother's
name was Jehoaddin, from Jerusalem.
3 He did what was right in the LORD's eyes,
though not like David his father. He did just as his
father Joash had done, 4 though the high places
did not disappear, and the people continued to
sacrifice and to burn incense on the high places.
5 When Amaziah had the kingdom firmly in
hand, he struck down the officials who had
struck down the king, his father. 6 But their chil-
dren he did not put to death, according to what
is written in the book of the law of Moses, which
the LORD commanded: "Parents shall not be put
to death for their children, nor shall children be
put to death for their parents; only for one's own
crimes shall a person be put to death."*
7 Amaziah struck down ten thousand Edomites
in the Salt Valley. He took Sela in battle and re-
named it Joktheel, the name it has to this day.*
8 Then Amaziah sent messengers to Joash, son
of Jehoahaz, son of Jehu, king of Israel, with
this message: "Come, let us meet face to face."

† suspended between the accounts of Ahaziah and Joram. In 14:15–16 the concluding formula for Joash's reign interrupts the account of the reign of Amaziah of Judah (14:1–22), much as Joash himself invaded Amaziah's kingdom (14:11–14).

13:14 *My father, my father*: the way the king addresses the dying Elisha echoes Elisha's address to Elijah in 2:12.

13:16–19 Symbolic acts, like prophetic oracles, were understood to unleash the power they expressed. Similar symbolic acts are seen in Ex 17:8–13; Jos 8:18–20; Ez 4:1–3.

14:1–2 *In the second year . . . twenty-nine years in Jerusalem*: as they stand, the chronological data in the introductions to the reigns of the kings of Judah and Israel are incompatible with one another. The kings of Judah between Athaliah and Ahaz are assigned too many years in all to correspond to the reigns in Israel from Jehu to the fall of Samaria. Various theories have been proposed in an attempt to explain the discrepancy, such as co-regencies, or textual corruption in the process of transmission.

* **13:14** 2 Kgs 2:12. **13:21** Sir 48:14. **14:6** Dt 24:16; Ez 18:20. **14:7** 2 Sm 8:13–14.

[9]Joash, king of Israel, sent this reply to Amaziah,
king of Judah: "A thistle of Lebanon sent word
to a cedar of Lebanon, 'Give your daughter to
my son in marriage,' but an animal of Lebanon
passed by and trampled the thistle underfoot.*
[10]You have indeed struck down Edom, and
your heart is lifted up; enjoy your glory, but stay
home! Why bring misfortune and failure on
yourself and on Judah with you?" [11]But Amaziah
did not listen. So Joash, king of Israel, advanced,
and he and Amaziah, king of Judah, met face
to face at Beth-shemesh of Judah, [12]and Judah
was defeated by Israel, and all fled to their tents.
[13]But Amaziah, king of Judah, son of Joash, son
of Ahaziah, was captured by Joash, king of Israel,
at Beth-shemesh. When they came to Jerusalem
Joash tore down the wall of Jerusalem, from the
Gate of Ephraim to the Corner Gate, four hun-
dred cubits. [14]He took all the gold and silver and
all the vessels found in the house of the LORD and
in the treasuries of the king's house, and hostages
as well. Then he returned to Samaria.

[15]† The rest of the acts of Joash, what he did
and his valor, and how he made war against Am-
aziah, king of Judah, are recorded in the book of
the chronicles of the kings of Israel. [16]Joash rested
with his ancestors; he was buried in Samaria with
the kings of Israel, and his son Jeroboam suc-
ceeded him as king.

[17]† Amaziah, son of Joash, king of Judah, sur-
vived Joash, son of Jehoahaz, king of Israel, by
fifteen years. [18]The rest of the acts of Amaziah
are recorded in the book of the chronicles of the
kings of Judah. [19]When a conspiracy was formed
against him in Jerusalem, he fled to Lachish. But
he was pursued to Lachish and killed there. [20]He
was brought back on horses and was buried in
Jerusalem with his ancestors in the City of David.
[21]Thereupon all the people of Judah† took Aza-
riah, who was only sixteen years old, and made
him king to succeed Amaziah, his father. [22]It was
he who rebuilt Elath and restored it to Judah, af-
ter the king rested with his ancestors.

Reign of Jeroboam II of Israel

[23]In the fifteenth year of Amaziah, son of Joash,
king of Judah, Jeroboam, son of Joash, king of Is-
rael, became king in Samaria for forty-one years.

[24]He did evil in the LORD's sight; he did not
desist from any of the sins that Jeroboam, son
of Nebat, had caused Israel to commit. [25]He
restored the boundaries of Israel from Lebo-
hamath to the sea of the Arabah,† as the LORD,
the God of Israel, had foretold through his ser-
vant, the prophet Jonah, son of Amittai, from
Gath-hepher. [26]For the LORD saw the very bitter
affliction of Israel, where there was neither bond
nor free, no one at all to help Israel. [27]Since the
LORD had not resolved to wipe out the name of
Israel from under the heavens, he saved them
through Jeroboam, son of Joash.

[28]The rest of the acts of Jeroboam, with all that
he did and his valor, how he fought, and how
he regained Damascus and Hamath for Israel,
are recorded in the book of the chronicles of the
kings of Israel. [29]Jeroboam rested with his ances-
tors, the kings of Israel, and his son Zechariah
succeeded him as king.

Reign of Azariah of Judah

15 [1]In the twenty-seventh year† of Jeroboam,
king of Israel, Azariah, son of Amaziah,
king of Judah, became king. [2]He was sixteen
years old when he became king, and he reigned
fifty-two years in Jerusalem. His mother's name
was Jecholiah, from Jerusalem.

[3]He did what was right in the LORD's sight, just
as his father Amaziah had done, [4]though the high
places did not disappear, and the people contin-
ued to sacrifice and to burn incense on the high
places. [5]The LORD afflicted the king, and he was a
leper until the day he died. He lived in a house
apart, while Jotham, the king's son, was master of
the palace and ruled the people of the land.†

[6]The rest of the acts of Azariah, and all that he
did, are recorded in the book of the chronicles of
the kings of Judah. [7]Azariah rested with his ances-
tors, and was buried with them in the City of Da-
vid, and his son Jotham succeeded him as king.

Reign of Zechariah of Israel

[8]In the thirty-eighth year of Azariah, king of
Judah, Zechariah, son of Jeroboam, became king
over Israel in Samaria for six months.

[9]He did what was evil in the LORD's sight, as
his ancestors had done, and did not desist from
the sins that Jeroboam, son of Nebat, had caused
Israel to commit. [10]Shallum, son of Jabesh, plot-
ted against him and struck him down at Ibleam.
He killed him and reigned in his place.

---

†

14:15–16 See note on 13:12–13.

14:17 See note on vv. 1–2.

14:21 *All the people of Judah*: this phrase may refer to the army (compare, for example, "all Israel" in 1 Kgs 16:16–17). If this is its meaning here, then Amaziah's assassination and Azariah's succession are owing to a military coup. *Azariah*: also called Uzziah in many texts.

14:25 *Sea of the Arabah*: the Dead Sea. *Jonah, son of Amittai*: see note on Jon 1:1.

15:1 *Twenty-seventh year*: see note on 14:1–2.

15:5 *People of the land*: see note on 11:14.

---

*

14:9 Jgs 9:8–15.

11 As for the rest of the acts of Zechariah, these
are recorded in the book of the chronicles of the
kings of Israel. 12 This was the word the LORD had
spoken to Jehu: Sons of your line to the fourth
generation shall sit upon the throne of Israel;
and so it was.*

Reign of Shallum of Israel

13 Shallum, son of Jabesh, became king in the
thirty-ninth year of Uzziah, king of Judah; he
reigned one month in Samaria.

14 Menahem, son of Gadi, came up from Tir-
zah to Samaria, and struck down Shallum, son
of Jabesh, in Samaria. He killed him and reigned
in his place.

15 As for the rest of the acts of Shallum, with
the conspiracy he carried out, these are recorded
in the book of the chronicles of the kings of
Israel. 16 At that time, Menahem attacked Tap-
puah, all its inhabitants, and its whole district
as far as Tirzah, because they did not let him in.
He attacked them; he even ripped open all their
pregnant women.

Reign of Menahem of Israel

17 In the thirty-ninth year of Azariah, king of
Judah, Menahem, son of Gadi, became king over
Israel for ten years in Samaria. 18 He did what was
evil in the LORD's sight as long as he lived, not de-
sisting from the sins that Jeroboam, son of Nebat,
had caused Israel to commit. 19 Pul,† king of As-
syria, came against the land. But Menahem gave
Pul a thousand talents of silver to have his help
in holding onto his kingdom. 20 Menahem paid
out silver on behalf of Israel, that is, for all the
people of substance, by giving the king of Assyria
fifty shekels of silver for each one. So the king of
Assyria went home and did not stay in the land.

21 The rest of the acts of Menahem, with all that
he did, are recorded in the book of the chronicles
of the kings of Israel. 22 Menahem rested with his
ancestors, and his son Pekahiah succeeded him
as king.

Reign of Pekahiah of Israel

23 In the fiftieth year of Azariah, king of Judah,
Pekahiah, son of Menahem, became king over
Israel in Samaria for two years.
24 He did what was evil in the LORD's sight, not
desisting from the sins that Jeroboam, son of Ne-
bat, had caused Israel to commit. 25 His adjutant
Pekah, son of Remaliah, conspired against him,
and struck him down at Samaria within the pal-
ace stronghold; he had with him fifty men from
Gilead. He killed him and reigned in his place.
26 As for the rest of the acts of Pekahiah, with all
that he did, these are recorded in the book of the
chronicles of the kings of Israel.

Reign of Pekah of Israel

27 † In the fifty-second year of Azariah, king
of Judah, Pekah, son of Remaliah, became king
over Israel in Samaria for twenty years.
28 He did what was evil in the LORD's sight, not
desisting from the sins that Jeroboam, son of Ne-
bat, had caused Israel to commit. 29 In the days
of Pekah, king of Israel, Tiglath-pileser, king of
Assyria, came and took Ijon, Abel-beth-maacah,
Janoah, Kedesh, Hazor, Gilead, and Galilee—all
the land of Naphtali—deporting the inhabitants
to Assyria. 30 † Hoshea, son of Elah, carried out
a conspiracy against Pekah, son of Remaliah; he
struck and killed him, and succeeded him as king
in the twentieth year of Jotham, son of Uzziah.
31 As for the rest of the acts of Pekah, with all
that he did, these are recorded in the book of the
chronicles of the kings of Israel.

Reign of Jotham of Judah

32 In the second year of Pekah, son of Rema-
liah, king of Israel, Jotham, son of Uzziah, king
of Judah, became king. 33 He was twenty-five
years old when he became king, and he reigned
sixteen years in Jerusalem. His mother's name
was Jerusha, daughter of Zadok.
34 He did what was right in the LORD's sight,
just as his father Uzziah had done, 35 though the
high places did not disappear, and the people
continued to sacrifice and to burn incense on the
high places. It was he who built the Upper Gate†
of the LORD's house.

36 The rest of the acts of Jotham, with what he
did, are recorded in the book of the chronicles
of the kings of Judah. 37 It was at that time that
the LORD began to unleash Rezin, king of Aram,
and Pekah, son of Remaliah, against Judah.*

†

15:19 *Pul*: the Babylonian throne name of the Assyrian Tiglath-pileser III; cf. v. 29.

15:27 The twenty years here ascribed to Pekah are difficult to reconcile with other chronological notices about the kings. One theory would see Pekah and Menahem as rival kings over parts of a divided Israelite territory; this could explain Menahem's concern for Assyrian support (vv. 19–20) and Assyria's attack on Pekah (v. 29). See 16:1 and note on 14:1–2.

15:30 The twenty years here reckoned to Jotham of Judah may include his co-regency with Azariah (v. 5); otherwise they are impossible to reconcile with v. 33, which ascribes him only sixteen years. The verse also appears to contradict 16:1, which has Jotham's son and successor, Ahaz, coming to the throne while Pekah still reigns in Israel, and 17:1, which dates Hoshea's accession to the throne to the twelfth year of Ahaz.

15:35 *The Upper Gate*: also called the Gate of Benjamin; cf. Jer 20:2; Ez 9:2.

*

15:12 2 Kgs 10:30. **15:37** Is 7:1–16.

38 Jotham rested with his ancestors; he was buried
with his ancestors in the City of David his father,
and his son Ahaz succeeded him as king.

Reign of Ahaz of Judah†

16 1 In the seventeenth year of Pekah, son of
Remaliah, Ahaz, son of Jotham, king of
Judah, became king. 2 Ahaz was twenty years old
when he became king, and he reigned sixteen
years in Jerusalem.
He did not do what was right in the sight of
the LORD his God, as David his father had done.
3 He walked in the way of the kings of Israel; he
even immolated his child by fire, in accordance
with the abominable practices of the nations
whom the LORD had dispossessed before the
Israelites.* 4 Further, he sacrificed and burned
incense on the high places, on hills, and under
every green tree.*
5 Then Rezin, king of Aram, and Pekah, son of
Remaliah, king of Israel, came up to Jerusalem
to attack it. Although they besieged Ahaz, they
were unable to do battle. 6 (In those days Rezin,
king of Aram, recovered Elath for Aram, and
drove the Judahites out of it. The Edomites then
entered Elath, which they have occupied until
the present.)
7 Meanwhile, Ahaz sent messengers to Tiglath-
pileser, king of Assyria, with the plea: "I am your
servant and your son. Come up and rescue me
from the power of the king of Aram and the king
of Israel, who are attacking me." 8 Ahaz took the
silver and gold that were in the house of the
LORD and in the treasuries of the king's house
and sent them as a present to the king of Assyria.
9 The king of Assyria listened to him and moved
against Damascus, captured it, deported its in-
habitants to Kir, and put Rezin to death.
10 King Ahaz went to Damascus to meet Tiglath-
pileser, king of Assyria. When he saw the altar in
Damascus, King Ahaz sent to Uriah the priest a
model of the altar and a detailed design of its
construction. 11 Uriah the priest built an altar ac-
cording to the plans which King Ahaz sent him
from Damascus, and had it completed by the
time King Ahaz returned from Damascus. 12 On
his arrival from Damascus, the king inspected
the altar; the king approached the altar, went up
13 and sacrificed his burnt offering and grain of-
fering, pouring out his libation, and sprinkling
the blood of his communion offerings on the al-
tar. 14 The bronze altar that stood before the LORD
he brought from the front of the temple—that
is, from the space between the new altar and the
house of the LORD—and set it on the north side
of his altar. 15 * King Ahaz commanded Uriah
the priest, "Upon the large altar sacrifice the
morning burnt offering and the evening grain
offering, the king's burnt offering and grain of-
fering, and the burnt offering and grain offering
of the people of the land.† Their libations you
must sprinkle on it along with all the blood of
burnt offerings and sacrifices. But the old bronze
altar shall be mine for consultation." 16 Uriah the
priest did just as King Ahaz had commanded.
17 King Ahaz detached the panels from the stands
and removed the basins from them; he also took
down the bronze sea from the bronze oxen that
supported it, and set it on a stone pavement.
18 In deference to the king of Assyria he removed
the sabbath canopy that had been set up in the
house of the LORD and the king's outside en-
trance† to the temple.
19 The rest of the acts of Ahaz, with what he
did, are recorded in the book of the chronicles
of the kings of Judah. 20 Ahaz rested with his an-
cestors; he was buried with his ancestors in the
City of David, and his son Hezekiah succeeded
him as king.

Reign of Hoshea of Israel

17 1 In the twelfth year of Ahaz, king of Judah,
Hoshea, son of Elah, became king in Sa-
maria over Israel for nine years.
2 He did what was evil in the LORD's sight, yet
not to the extent of the kings of Israel before
him. 3 Shalmaneser,† king of Assyria, advanced
against him, and Hoshea became his vassal and
paid him tribute.* 4 But the king of Assyria found
Hoshea guilty of conspiracy for sending messen-
gers to the king of Egypt at Sais, and for failure to
pay the annual tribute to the king of Assyria. So
the king of Assyria arrested and imprisoned him.
5 Then the king of Assyria† occupied the whole

†

16:1–20 Firmly dated events bearing on chaps. 16–20 are: the fall of Damascus (16:9) in 732 B.C., the fall of Samaria (18:9–11) in 722/721 B.C., and Sennacherib's invasion of Judah (18:13) in 701 B.C., which both in Kings and in Is 36:1 occurs in the fourteenth year of Hezekiah. These data make it possible to connect the chronology of Israel and Judah to the larger chronology of ancient Near Eastern history, but they also complicate further the already vexed problem of inconsistencies in the biblical data about accession years and lengths of reign.

16:15 *People of the land*: see note on 11:14. *For consultation*: perhaps the introduction into Judah of the Babylonian practice of reading omens from animal sacrifices; cf. Ez 21:26.

16:18 *Sabbath canopy . . . outside entrance*: the Hebrew is obscure, but as a vassal Ahaz must have had to divest himself of signs of sovereignty.

17:3 *Shalmaneser*: son and successor of the Assyrian king Tiglath-pileser III. *Vassal*: lit., "servant"; cf. 16:7; so also in 24:1.

17:5 *The king of Assyria*: Shalmaneser was succeeded by Sargon II, who usurped the Assyrian throne in 722/721 B.C. In his inscriptions,

*

16:3 Lv 18:21; Dt 18:10.
16:4 Dt 12:2.
16:15 Ex 29:38–41; Nm 28:3–8.
17:3 2 Kgs 18:9.

Did You Know?

The First Captivity

The Second Book of Kings describes two captivities and exiles. The first one is the Assyrian conquest of the northern kingdom, Israel, which occurred in 721 BC (see map 5, "The Assyrian Empire"). According to the author of Second Kings, Israel fell first because its kings and people were even less faithful to God than the kings and people of Judah, the southern kingdom. Notice that the Assyrian conquest is described in the briefest detail (see 17:5–6), but the reasons for it are described in great detail (see verses 7–18).

▶ 2 Kgs 17:5–18

land and attacked Samaria, which he besieged
for three years.

X. The End of Israel†

Israelites Deported

6 In Hoshea's ninth year, the king of Assyria
took Samaria, deported the Israelites to Assyria,
and settled them in Halah, and at the Habor, a
river of Gozan, and in the cities of the Medes.*
7 This came about because the Israelites sinned
against the LORD, their God, who had brought
them up from the land of Egypt, from under the
hand of Pharaoh, king of Egypt. They venerated
other gods, 8 * they followed the rites of the na-
tions whom the LORD had dispossessed before
the Israelites and those that the kings of Israel
had practiced. 9 They adopted unlawful prac-
tices toward the LORD, their God. They built high
places in all their cities, from guard post to garri-
soned town. 10 They set up pillars and asherahs†
for themselves on every high hill and under every
green tree. 11 They burned incense there, on all
the high places, like the nations whom the LORD
had sent into exile at their coming. They did
evil things that provoked the LORD, 12 and served
idols, although the LORD had told them: You
must not do this.
13 * The LORD warned Israel and Judah by ev-
ery prophet and seer: Give up your evil ways
and keep my commandments and statutes, in
accordance with the entire law which I enjoined
on your ancestors and which I sent you by my
servants the prophets. 14 But they did not lis-
ten. They grew as stiff-necked as their ancestors,
who had not believed in the LORD, their God.*
15 They rejected his statutes, the covenant he had
made with their ancestors, and the warnings he
had given them. They followed emptiness and
became empty; they followed the surrounding
nations whom the LORD had commanded them
not to imitate.* 16 They abandoned all the com-
mandments of the LORD, their God: they made
for themselves two molten calves; they made
an asherah; they bowed down to all the host of
heaven; they served Baal.* 17 * They immolated
their sons and daughters by fire. They practiced
augury and divination. They surrendered them-
selves to doing what was evil in the LORD's sight,
and provoked him.
18 * The LORD became enraged, and removed
them from his presence. Only the tribe of Ju-
dah was left. 19 Even the people of Judah did not
keep the commandments of the LORD, their God,
but followed the rites practiced by Israel. 20 So
the LORD rejected the entire people of Israel: he
afflicted them and delivered them over to plun-
derers, finally casting them from his presence.*
21 When he tore Israel away from the house of
David, they made Jeroboam, son of Nebat, king;
but Jeroboam lured the Israelites away from the
LORD, causing them to commit a great sin.* 22 The
Israelites imitated Jeroboam in all the sins he
committed; they would not depart from them.
23 Finally, the LORD removed Israel from his
presence, just as he had declared through all
his servants, the prophets. Thus Israel went into
exile from their native soil to Assyria until this
very day.

† Sargon claims to have captured Samaria during the first year of his reign.

17:6–41 This brief section is the Deuteronomistic historian's theological reflection on the causes and aftermath of Assyria's conquest of the Northern Kingdom. The text contrasts the Israelites, who were deported (v. 6) because they abandoned the worship of the Lord (vv. 7–23), with the foreigners who were brought into the land (v. 24) and undertook, however imperfectly, to worship the Lord alongside their own traditional deities (vv. 25–34a). The last verses recapitulate the apostasy of the Israelites (vv. 34b–40) and the syncretism of the foreigners (v. 41). This is a deliberately disparaging, and not wholly accurate, account of the origin of the Samaritans; it reflects the hostility the Judahites continued to hold toward the inhabitants of the northern territories.

17:10 *Asherahs*: see note on Ex 34:13.

* **17:6** 2 Kgs 18:10–11; Tb 1:2.
17:8–12 Ex 23:24; 34:13; Dt 12:2.
17:13 Jer 25:5.
17:14 Dt 9:13.
17:15 Jer 2:5.
17:16 Ex 34:13; Dt 4:19; 17:2–3; 1 Kgs 12:28; 16:33.
17:17 Lv 18:21; Dt 18:10.
17:18 Sir 48:15.
17:20 Jer 25:9.
17:21 1 Kgs 12:20, 26–33; 13:34.

Foreigners Deported to Israel

24 The king of Assyria brought people from
Babylon, Cuthah, Avva, Hamath, and Sephar-
vaim, and settled them in the cities of Samaria
in place of the Israelites. They took possession
of Samaria and dwelt in its cities. 25 When they
first settled there, they did not venerate the LORD,
so he sent lions among them that killed some of
them. 26 A report reached the king of Assyria: "The
nations you deported and settled in the cities of
Samaria do not know the proper worship of the
god of the land, so he has sent lions among them
that are killing them, since they do not know the
law of the god of the land." 27 The king of Assyria
gave the order, "Send back some of the priests
you deported, to go there and settle, to teach
them the proper worship of the god of the land."
28 So one of the priests who had been deported
from Samaria returned and settled in Bethel, and
began to teach them how to venerate the LORD.

29 Thus each of these nations continued to
make its own gods, setting them up in the
shrines of the high places the Samarians had
made: each nation in the cities in which they
dwelt. 30 The Babylonians made Sukkot-Benot;†
the people of Cuth made Nergal; those from
Hamath made Ashima; 31 those from Avva made
Nibhaz and Tartak; and those from Sepharvaim
immolated their children by fire to their city
gods, King Hadad and King Anu. 32 At the same
time, they were venerating the LORD, appoint-
ing from their own number priests for the high
places to officiate for them in the shrines on the
high places. 33 They were both venerating the
LORD and serving their own gods. They followed
the custom of the nations from among whom
they had been deported.

34 To this very day they continue to act accord-
ing to their former customs, not venerating the
LORD nor observing the statutes and regulations,
the law and commandment, that the LORD en-
joined on the descendants of Jacob, whom he
had named Israel.* 35 When the LORD made a
covenant with them, he commanded them: You
must not venerate other gods, nor bow down
to them, nor serve them, nor offer sacrifice to
them,* 36 but only to the LORD, who brought you
up from the land of Egypt with great power and
outstretched arm. Him shall you venerate, to him
shall you bow down, and to him shall you offer
sacrifice. 37 You must be careful always to observe
the statutes and ordinances, the law and com-
mandment, which he wrote for you; you must
not venerate other gods. 38 The covenant I made
with you, you must not forget; you must not
venerate other gods. 39 You must venerate only
the LORD, your God; it is he who will deliver you
from the power of all your enemies. 40 But they
did not listen; they continued to act according to
their former customs.

41 But these nations were both venerating the
LORD and serving their own idols. Their children
and children's children are still acting like their
ancestors, to this very day.

XI. The End of Judah†

Reign of Hezekiah

18 1 In the third year of Hoshea, son of Elah,
king of Israel, Hezekiah, son of Ahaz, king
of Judah, became king. 2 He was twenty-five
years old when he became king, and he reigned
twenty-nine years in Jerusalem. His mother's
name was Abi, daughter of Zechariah.

3 He did what was right in the LORD's sight, just
as David his father had done. 4 It was he who
removed the high places, shattered the pillars,
cut down the asherah,† and smashed the bronze
serpent Moses had made, because up to that time
the Israelites were burning incense to it. (It was
called Nehushtan.)* 5 He put his trust in the LORD,
the God of Israel; and neither before nor after him
was there anyone like him among all the kings of
Judah. 6 Hezekiah held fast to the LORD and never
turned away from following him, but observed
the commandments the LORD had given Moses.
7 The LORD was with him, and he succeeded in
all he set out to do. He rebelled against the king
of Assyria and did not serve him. 8 It was he who
struck the Philistines as far as Gaza, and all its ter-
ritory from guard post to garrisoned town.

---

† **17:30** *Sukkot-Benot*: several of the divine names in vv. 30–31 are problematic or conjectural. Sukkot-Benot is unknown, but the name may have been corrupted from that of Sarpanitu, the consort of the Babylonian god Marduk.

18:1–25:30 The Books of Kings end, as they began, with the people of the Lord in a single kingdom, Judah, centered on the capital, Jerusalem, and the Solomonic Temple. The reigns of two reformer kings, both praised, are recounted at length: Hezekiah (chaps. 18–20) and Josiah (22:1–23:30). Each is followed by shorter accounts of two kings who are condemned: Manasseh and Amon (chap. 21) and Jehoahaz and Jehoiakim (23:31–24:7). The book ends with the last days of Judah under Jehoiachin and Zedekiah and the beginning of the Babylonian exile.

18:4 *Asherah*: see note on Ex 34:13. *Nehushtan*: the name *nehushtan* contains several wordplays in Hebrew. It recalls the word "serpent" (*nahash*), the word "bronze" (*nehoshet*), and the word "to read omens" (*nihesh*). The sentence is also unclear about who named the bronze serpent "Nehushtan"—whether Moses when he made it, or the people when they venerated it, or Hezekiah when he destroyed it.

---

* **17:34** Gn 32:29; 35:10.
17:35–38 Ex 20:3–6.
18:4 Ex 23:24; 34:13; Nm 21:4–9; Dt 12:2; Wis 16:5–7; Jn 3:14.

9 † In the fourth year of King Hezekiah, which was the seventh year of Hoshea, son of Elah, king of Israel, Shalmaneser, king of Assyria, attacked Samaria and laid siege to it, 10 * and after three years they captured it. In the sixth year of Hezekiah, the ninth year of Hoshea, king of Israel, Samaria was taken. 11 The king of Assyria then deported the Israelites to Assyria and led them off to Halah, and the Habor, a river of Gozan, and the cities of the Medes. 12 This happened because they did not obey the LORD, their God, but violated his covenant; they did not obey nor do all that Moses, the servant of the LORD, commanded.*

Sennacherib and Hezekiah

13 † In the fourteenth year of King Hezekiah, Sennacherib, king of Assyria,† attacked all the fortified cities of Judah and captured them.* 14 Hezekiah, king of Judah, sent this message to the king of Assyria at Lachish: "I have done wrong. Leave me, and whatever you impose on me I will bear." The king of Assyria exacted three hundred talents of silver and thirty talents of gold from Hezekiah, king of Judah. 15 Hezekiah gave him all the funds there were in the house of the LORD and in the treasuries of the king's house. 16 At the same time, Hezekiah removed the nave doors and the uprights of the house of the LORD, which the king of Judah had ordered to be overlaid with gold, and gave them to the king of Assyria.*

17 The king of Assyria sent the general, the lord chamberlain, and the commander† from Lachish with a great army to King Hezekiah at Jerusalem. They went up and came to Jerusalem, to the conduit of the upper pool on the highway of the fuller's field, where they took their stand. 18 They called for the king, but Eliakim, son of Hilkiah, the master of the palace, came out, along with Shebnah the scribe and the chancellor Joah, son of Asaph.*

19 The commander said to them, "Tell Hezekiah, 'Thus says the great king, the king of Assyria: On what do you base this trust of yours? 20 Do you think mere words substitute for strategy and might in war? In whom, then, do you place your trust, that you rebel against me? 21 Do you trust in Egypt, that broken reed of a staff, which pierces the hand of anyone who leans on it? That is what Pharaoh, king of Egypt, is to all who trust in him.* 22 Or do you people say to me, "It is in the LORD our God we trust!"? Is it not he whose high places and altars Hezekiah has removed, commanding Judah and Jerusalem, "Worship before this altar in Jerusalem"?'

23 "Now, make a wager with my lord, the king of Assyria: I will give you two thousand horses if you are able to put riders on them. 24 How then can you turn back even a captain, one of the least servants of my lord, trusting, as you do, in Egypt for chariots and horses? 25 Did I come up to destroy this place without the LORD? The LORD himself said to me: Go up and destroy that land!"

26 Then Eliakim, son of Hilkiah, and Shebnah and Joah said to the commander: "Please speak to your servants in Aramaic; we understand it. Do not speak to us in the language of Judah within earshot of the people who are on the wall." 27 But the commander replied: "Was it to your lord and to you that my lord sent me to speak these words? Was it not rather to those sitting on the wall, who, with you, will have to eat their own excrement and drink their urine?"†

28 Then the commander stepped forward and cried out in a loud voice in the language of Judah, "Listen to the words of the great king, the king of Assyria. 29 Thus says the king: Do not let Hezekiah deceive you, for he cannot rescue you from my hand. 30 And do not let Hezekiah induce you to trust in the LORD, saying, 'The LORD will surely rescue us, and this city will not be handed over to the king of Assyria.' 31 Do not listen to Hezekiah, for thus says the king of Assyria: Make peace with me, and surrender to me! Eat, each of you, from your vine, each from your own fig tree. Drink water, each from your own well, 32 until I arrive and take you to a land like your own, a land of grain and wine, a land of bread and vineyards, a land of rich olives and honey. Live, and do not die! And do not listen to Hezekiah when he would incite you by saying, 'The LORD will rescue us.' 33 Has any of the gods of the nations ever rescued his land from the power

---

† **18:9** The correlations between the reigns of Hezekiah and Hoshea in vv. 9–10 conflict with other biblical data and with the date for the fall of Samaria, 722/721 B.C. (see note on 16:1–20). Since Sennacherib's invasion in the fourteenth year of Hezekiah (v. 13) took place in 701, Hezekiah cannot have been on the throne twenty years earlier. Various solutions have been proposed: scribal errors in writing the numbers; a Hezekian co-regency with his father Ahaz beginning in 729; etc. None of the solutions has won a consensus among historians.

18:13–20:19 This material is found also in Is 36–39, with one long addition (Is 38:9–20) and only a few other changes.

18:13 Sennacherib succeeded Sargon II as king of Assyria. His Judean campaign was waged in 701 B.C. See notes on 16:1–20 and 18:9.

18:17 *General, the lord chamberlain . . . commander*: the text lists three major functionaries by their Assyrian titles, of which only the first, more nearly "lord lieutenant," is military in origin; the commander was technically the king's chief butler.

18:27 *Excrement . . . urine*: the reference is to the famine that results from a prolonged siege (compare 6:24–25; Dt 28:53–57). For public reading, ancient tradition (e.g., the Qere reading of the Masoretic text) softened the terms to "eat their own waste and drink their own bodies' water."

18:10–11 2 Kgs 17:5–6; Tb 1:2.
18:12 2 Kgs 17:6–23; Ex 24:7.
18:13–19:36 Sir 48:18–21.
18:16 1 Kgs 6:31–35.
18:18 Is 22:15–25.
18:21 Is 30:1–7; 31:1–3; Ez 29:6–7.

of the king of Assyria? 34 Where are the gods of
Hamath and Arpad? Where are the gods of Seph-
arvaim, Hena, and Ivvah? Did they indeed rescue
Samaria from my power?† 35 Which of the gods
for all these lands ever rescued his land from my
power? Will the LORD then rescue Jerusalem from
my power?" 36 But the people remained silent
and did not answer at all, for the king's com-
mand was, "Do not answer him."
37 Then the master of the palace, Eliakim, son
of Hilkiah, Shebnah the scribe, and the chancel-
lor Joah, son of Asaph, came to Hezekiah with
their garments torn, and reported to him the
words of the commander.

Hezekiah and Isaiah

19 1 When King Hezekiah heard this, he tore
his garments, covered himself with sack-
cloth, and went into the house of the LORD. 2 He
sent Eliakim, the master of the palace, Shebnah
the scribe, and the elders of the priests, covered
with sackcloth, to tell the prophet Isaiah, son of
Amoz, 3 "Thus says Hezekiah:

A day of distress and rebuke,
  a day of disgrace is this day!
Children are due to come forth,
  but the strength to give birth is lacking.†

4 Perhaps the LORD, your God, will hear all the
words of the commander, whom his lord, the
king of Assyria, sent to taunt the living God,
and will rebuke him for the words which the
LORD, your God, has heard. So lift up a prayer for
the remnant that is here." 5 When the servants
of King Hezekiah had come to Isaiah, 6 he said
to them, "Tell this to your lord: Thus says the
LORD: Do not be frightened by the words you
have heard, by which the deputies of the king of
Assyria have blasphemed me.* 7 I am putting in
him such a spirit that when he hears a report he
will return to his land. I will make him fall by the
sword in his land."
8 When the commander, on his return, heard
that the king of Assyria had withdrawn from La-
chish, he found him besieging Libnah.

Sennacherib, Hezekiah, and Isaiah

9 The king of Assyria heard a report: "Tirhakah,
king of Ethiopia, has come out to fight against
you." Again he sent messengers to Hezekiah
to say: 10 "Thus shall you say to Hezekiah, king
of Judah: Do not let your God in whom you
trust deceive you by saying, 'Jerusalem will not
be handed over to the king of Assyria.' 11 You,
certainly, have heard what the kings of Assyria
have done to all the lands: they put them under
the ban! And are you to be rescued? 12 * Did the
gods of the nations whom my fathers destroyed
deliver them—Gozan, Haran, Rezeph, or the
Edenites in Telassar? 13 Where are the king of Ha-
math, the king of Arpad, or the kings of the cities
Sepharvaim, Hena and Ivvah?"
14 Hezekiah took the letter from the hand of
the messengers and read it; then he went up to
the house of the LORD, and spreading it out be-
fore the LORD, 15 Hezekiah prayed in the LORD's
presence: "LORD, God of Israel, enthroned on the
cherubim! You alone are God over all the king-
doms of the earth. It is you who made the heav-
ens and the earth.* 16 Incline your ear, LORD, and
listen! Open your eyes, LORD, and see! Hear the
words Sennacherib has sent to taunt the living
God. 17 Truly, O LORD, the kings of Assyria have
laid waste the nations and their lands. 18 They
gave their gods to the fire—they were not gods
at all, but the work of human hands—wood and
stone, they destroyed them. 19 Therefore, LORD,
our God, save us from this man's power, that all
the kingdoms of the earth may know that you
alone, LORD, are God."*
20 Then Isaiah, son of Amoz, sent this mes-
sage to Hezekiah: "Thus says the LORD, the God
of Israel, to whom you have prayed concerning
Sennacherib, king of Assyria: I have listened!
21 † This is the word the LORD has spoken con-
cerning him:

She despises you, laughs you to scorn,
  the virgin daughter Zion!
Behind you she wags her head,
  daughter Jerusalem.
22 Whom have you insulted and blasphemed,
  at whom have you raised your voice
And lifted up your eyes on high?
  At the Holy One of Israel!
23 Through the mouths of your messengers
  you insulted the Lord when you said,
'With my many chariots I went up
  to the tops of the peaks,

2 KGS

† **18:34** *Did they indeed . . . power?*: some time after the fall of Samaria in 722/721 B.C., Hamath, Arpad, and other small states in the region formed an anti-Assyrian coalition. If the coalition had succeeded, it could have broken Assyrian control over the whole region, including Samaria, and allowed the kingdom of Israel to free itself. When Assyria crushed the coalition, it also crushed Israel's hopes for liberation.

19:3 See note on Is 37:3.

19:21–31 Verses 21–28 are addressed to Sennacherib, vv. 29–31 to Judah.

* **19:6** Is 10:5–14.
19:12–13 2 Kgs 17:6, 24; 18:34.
19:15 Ex 25:17–22; 1 Kgs 6:23–28; 8:6–7.
19:19 1 Kgs 18:36.

to the recesses of Lebanon,
To cut down its lofty cedars,
its choice cypresses;
I reached to the farthest shelter,
the forest ranges.
24 I myself dug wells
and drank foreign waters,
Drying up all the rivers of Egypt
beneath the soles of my feet.'

25 "Have you not heard?
A long time ago I prepared it,
from days of old I planned it.
Now I have brought it about:
You are here to reduce
fortified cities to heaps of ruins,
26 Their people powerless,
dismayed and distraught.
They are plants of the field,
green growth,
thatch on the rooftops,
Grain scorched by the east wind.
27 I know when you stand or sit,
when you come or go*
and how you rage against me.
28 Because you rage against me,
and your smugness has reached my ears,
I will put my hook in your nose
and my bit in your mouth,
And make you leave by the way you came.

29 "This shall be a sign for you:
This year you shall eat the aftergrowth,
next year, what grows of itself;
But in the third year, sow and reap,
plant vineyards and eat their fruit!
30 The remaining survivors of the house of Judah
shall again strike root below
and bear fruit above.
31 For out of Jerusalem shall come a remnant,
and from Mount Zion, survivors.
The zeal of the LORD of hosts shall do this.

32 "Therefore, thus says the LORD about the
king:

He shall not come as far as this city,
nor shoot there an arrow,
nor confront it with a shield,
Nor cast up a siege-work against it.
33 By the way he came he shall leave,
never coming as far as this city,
oracle of the LORD.
34 I will shield and save this city
for my own sake and the sake of David my
servant."*

35 That night the angel of the LORD went forth
and struck down one hundred and eighty-five
thousand men in the Assyrian camp. Early the
next morning, there they were, dead, all those
corpses!* 36 So Sennacherib, the king of As-
syria, broke camp, departed, returned home, and
stayed in Nineveh.
37 When he was worshiping in the temple of
his god Nisroch, his sons Adrammelech and
Sharezer struck him down with the sword and
fled into the land of Ararat. His son Esarhaddon
reigned in his place.

End of Hezekiah's Reign

20 1* In those days, when Hezekiah was
mortally ill, the prophet Isaiah, son of
Amoz, came and said to him: "Thus says the
LORD: Put your house in order, for you are about
to die; you shall not recover." 2 He turned his
face to the wall and prayed to the LORD: 3 "Ah,
LORD, remember how faithfully and wholeheart-
edly I conducted myself in your presence, doing
what was good in your sight!" And Hezekiah
wept bitterly. 4 Before Isaiah had left the central
courtyard, the word of the LORD came to him:
5 Go back and tell Hezekiah, the leader of my
people: "Thus says the LORD, the God of David
your father:

I have heard your prayer;
I have seen your tears.
Now I am healing you.
On the third day you shall go up
to the house of the LORD.
6 I will add to your life fifteen years.
I will rescue you and this city
from the hand of the king of Assyria;
I will be a shield to this city
for my own sake and the sake of David my
servant."

7 Then Isaiah said, "Bring a poultice of figs and
apply it to the boil for his recovery." 8 Hezekiah
asked Isaiah, "What is the sign that the LORD
will heal me and that I shall go up to the house
of the LORD on the third day?" 9 Isaiah replied,
"This will be the sign for you from the LORD that
he will carry out the word he has spoken: Shall
the shadow go forward or back ten steps?" 10 "It
is easy for the shadow to advance ten steps,"
Hezekiah answered. "Rather, let it go back ten
steps." 11 So Isaiah the prophet invoked the LORD.
He made the shadow go back the ten steps it

19:27 Ps 139:2–3. **19:34** 2 Sm 7:12. **19:35** 1 Mc 7:41; 2 Mc 8:19. **20:1–11** Sir 48:23.

had descended on the staircase to the terrace of
Ahaz.
[12]At that time, Berodach-baladan,† son of
Baladan, king of Babylon, sent letters and gifts
to Hezekiah when he heard that he had been
ill. [13]Hezekiah listened to the envoys and then
showed off his whole treasury: his silver, gold,
spices and perfumed oil, his armory, and every-
thing in his storerooms; there was nothing in his
house or in all his realm that Hezekiah did not
show them. [14]Then Isaiah the prophet came to
King Hezekiah and asked him: "What did these
men say to you? Where did they come from?"
Hezekiah replied, "They came from a distant
land, from Babylon." [15]He asked, "What did they
see in your house?" Hezekiah answered, "They
saw everything in my house. There is nothing
in my storerooms that I did not show them."
[16]Then Isaiah said to Hezekiah: "Hear the word
of the LORD: [17]The time is coming when all that
is in your house, everything that your ancestors
have stored up until this day, shall be carried
off to Babylon; nothing shall be left, says the
LORD. [18]Some of your own descendants, your
offspring, your progeny, shall be taken and made
attendants in the palace of the king of Babylon."
[19]Hezekiah replied to Isaiah, "The word of the
LORD which you have spoken is good." For he
thought, "There will be peace and stability in my
lifetime."
[20]The rest of the acts of Hezekiah, with all
his valor, and how he constructed the pool and
conduit† and brought water into the city, are re-
corded in the book of the chronicles of the kings
of Judah.* [21]Hezekiah rested with his ancestors,
and his son Manasseh succeeded him as king.

Reign of Manasseh

21 [1]Manasseh was twelve years old when
he became king, and he reigned fifty-
five years in Jerusalem. His mother's name was
Hephzibah.
[2]He did what was evil in the LORD's sight, fol-
lowing the abominable practices of the nations
whom the LORD had dispossessed before the
Israelites. [3]He rebuilt the high places which Hez-
ekiah his father had destroyed. He set up altars to
Baal and also made an asherah, as Ahab, king of
Israel, had done. He bowed down to the whole
host of heaven and served them.* [4]He built
altars in the house of the LORD, of which the LORD
had said: In Jerusalem I will set my name. [5]And
he built altars for the whole host of heaven in the
two courts of the house of the LORD. [6]He immo-
lated his child by fire. He practiced soothsaying
and divination, and reintroduced the consulting
of ghosts and spirits.
He did much evil in the LORD's sight and pro-
voked him to anger.* [7]The Asherah idol he had
made, he placed in the LORD's house, of which
the LORD had said to David and to his son Sol-
omon: In this house and in Jerusalem, which I
have chosen out of all the tribes of Israel, I shall
set my name forever.* [8]I will no longer make
Israel step out of the land I gave their ancestors,
provided that they are careful to observe all I
have commanded them and the entire law which
Moses my servant enjoined upon them. [9]But
they did not listen.
Manasseh misled them into doing even greater
evil than the nations the LORD had destroyed at
the coming of the Israelites. [10]Then the LORD
spoke through his servants the prophets: [11]"Be-
cause Manasseh, king of Judah, has practiced
these abominations, and has done greater evil
than all that was done by the Amorites before
him, and has led Judah into sin by his idols,*
[12]therefore, thus says the LORD, the God of Israel:
I am about to bring such evil on Jerusalem and
Judah that, when any hear of it, their ears shall
ring: [13]I will measure Jerusalem with the same
cord as I did Samaria, and with the plummet I
used for the house of Ahab. I will wipe Jerusa-
lem clean as one wipes a dish, wiping it inside
and out.* [14]I will cast off the survivors of my in-
heritance. I will deliver them into enemy hands,
to become prey and booty for all their enemies,
[15]because they have done what is evil in my
sight and provoked me from the day their ances-
tors came forth from Egypt until this very day."
[16]Manasseh shed so much innocent blood that
it filled the length and breadth of Jerusalem, in
addition to the sin he caused Judah to commit by
doing what was evil in the LORD's sight.
[17]The rest of the acts of Manasseh, with all that
he did and the sin he committed, are recorded in
the book of the chronicles of the kings of Judah.
[18]Manasseh rested with his ancestors; he was
buried in his palace garden, the garden of Uzza,
and his son Amon succeeded him as king.

†

20:12 *Berodach-baladan*: this famous king's name is more correctly recorded in Is 39:1 as "Merodach-baladan." The Babylonian form, Marduk-apal-idinna, means "Marduk has granted a son." Historically, any embassy from him to Hezekiah must have been aimed at establishing an anti-Assyrian strategy of cooperation.

20:20 *Pool and conduit*: Hezekiah's tunnel is described in more detail in 2 Chr 32:30.

*

20:20 Sir 48:17.
21:3 2 Kgs 17:16; 1 Kgs 16:31–33.
21:6 Lv 18:21; 19:26; Dt 18:10–14; 1 Sm 28:3.
21:7 2 Sm 7:13; 1 Kgs 8:16; 9:3.
21:11 Jer 15:4.
21:13 Is 34:11; Lam 2:8; Am 7:7–9.

Reign of Amon

19 Amon was twenty-two years old when he
became king, and he reigned two years in Jeru-
salem. His mother's name was Meshullemeth,
daughter of Haruz, from Jotbah.

20 He did what was evil in the LORD's sight, as
his father Manasseh had done. 21 He walked in
all the ways of his father; he served the idols his
father had served, and bowed down to them.
22 He abandoned the LORD, the God of his ances-
tors, and did not walk in the way of the LORD.

23 Officials of Amon plotted against him and
killed the king in his palace, 24 but the people of
the land† then slew all who had plotted against
King Amon, and the people of the land made his
son Josiah king in his stead. 25 The rest of the acts
of Amon, which he did, are recorded in the book
of the chronicles of the kings of Judah. 26 He was
buried in his own grave in the garden of Uzza,
and his son Josiah succeeded him as king.

Reign of Josiah

22 1 Josiah was eight years old when he
became king, and he reigned thirty-one
years in Jerusalem. His mother's name was Jedi-
dah, daughter of Adaiah, from Bozkath.

2 He did what was right in the LORD's sight,
walking in the way of David his father, not turn-
ing right or left.

The Book of the Law

3 * In his eighteenth year, King Josiah sent the
scribe Shaphan,† son of Azaliah, son of Meshul-
lam, to the house of the LORD with these orders:
4 "Go to the high priest Hilkiah and have him
calculate the valuables that have been brought
to the house of the LORD, which the doorkeep-
ers have collected from the people. 5 Then have
him turn them over to the master workers in the
house of the LORD, and have them give them to
the ordinary workers who are in the house of the
LORD to repair its breaches: 6 to the carpenters, the
builders, and the masons, and to purchase wood
and hewn stone. 7 No reckoning shall be asked
of them regarding the funds provided to them,
because they hold positions of trust."

8 The high priest Hilkiah informed the scribe
Shaphan, "I have found the book of the law† in
the temple of the LORD." Hilkiah gave the book to
Shaphan, who read it. 9 Then the scribe Shaphan
went to the king and reported, "Your servants have
smelted down the silver deposited in the temple
and have turned it over to the master workers in
the house of the LORD." 10 The scribe Shaphan also
informed the king, "Hilkiah the priest has given
me a book," and then Shaphan read it in the pres-
ence of the king. 11 When the king heard the words
of the book of the law, he tore his garments.

12 The king then issued this command to Hil-
kiah the priest, Ahikam, son of Shaphan, Achbor,
son of Micaiah, Shaphan the scribe, and Asaiah
the king's servant: 13 "Go, consult the LORD for
me, for the people, and for all Judah, about the
words of this book that has been found, for the
rage of the LORD has been set furiously ablaze
against us, because our ancestors did not obey
the words of this book, nor do what is written
for us." 14 So Hilkiah the priest, Ahikam, Ach-
bor, Shaphan, and Asaiah went to Huldah the
prophet, wife of Shallum, son of Tikvah, son
of Harhas, keeper of the wardrobe; she lived in
Jerusalem, in the Second Quarter. When they
had spoken to her, 15 she said to them, "Thus
says the LORD, the God of Israel: Say to the man
who sent you to me, 16 Thus says the LORD: I am
about to bring evil upon this place and upon its
inhabitants—all the words of the book which
the king of Judah has read. 17 Because they have
abandoned me and have burned incense to other
gods, provoking me by all the works of their
hands, my rage is ablaze against this place and it
cannot be extinguished.

18 "But to the king of Judah who sent you to
consult the LORD, give this response: Thus says
the LORD, the God of Israel: As for the words you
have heard, 19 because you were heartsick and
have humbled yourself before the LORD when
you heard what I have spoken concerning this
place and its inhabitants, that they would be-
come a desolation and a curse; and because you
tore your garments and wept before me, I in turn
have heard, oracle of the LORD. 20 I will therefore
gather you to your ancestors; you shall go to your
grave in peace, and your eyes shall not see all the
evil I am about to bring upon this place." This
they reported to the king.

23 1 The king then had all the elders of Judah
and of Jerusalem summoned before him.

21:24 *People of the land*: see note on 11:14.

22:3 *Shaphan*: head of a prominent family in the reign of Josiah, secretary to the king, bearer and reader of the newly found book of the law (vv. 3–13; 25:22). He and his sons favored the reform of King Josiah and supported the prophet Jeremiah; cf. Jer 26:24; 29:1–3; 36:10–12; 39:14.

22:8 *Book of the law*: probably an early edition of material now found in the Book of Deuteronomy.

22:3–7 2 Kgs 12:11–16.

2The king went up to the house of the LORD with
all the people of Judah and all the inhabitants of
Jerusalem: priests, prophets, and all the people,
great and small. He read aloud to them all the
words of the book of the covenant that had been
found in the house of the LORD.* 3The king stood
by the column and made a covenant in the pres-
ence of the LORD to follow the LORD and to ob-
serve his commandments, statutes, and decrees
with his whole heart and soul, and to re-establish
the words of the covenant written in this book.
And all the people stood by the covenant.

Josiah's Religious Reform

4Then the king commanded the high priest
Hilkiah, his assistant priests, and the doorkeep-
ers to remove from the temple of the LORD all the
objects that had been made for Baal, Asherah,
and the whole host of heaven. These he burned
outside Jerusalem on the slopes of the Kidron;
their ashes were carried to Bethel.* 5He also put
an end to the idolatrous priests whom the kings
of Judah had appointed to burn incense on the
high places in the cities of Judah and in the vi-
cinity of Jerusalem, as well as those who burned
incense to Baal, to the sun, moon, and signs of
the zodiac, and to the whole host of heaven.*
6From the house of the LORD he also removed
the Asherah to the Wadi Kidron, outside Jerusa-
lem; he burned it and beat it to dust, in the Wadi
Kidron, and scattered its dust over the graveyard
of the people of the land.† * 7He tore down the
apartments of the cult prostitutes in the house
of the LORD, where the women wove garments
for the Asherah.* 8He brought in all the priests
from the cities of Judah, and then defiled, from
Geba to Beer-sheba, the high places where they
had offered incense. He also tore down the high
places of the gates, which were at the entrance of
the Gate of Joshua, governor of the city, north
of the city gate. 9(The priests of the high places
could not function at the altar of the LORD in Je-
rusalem; but they, along with their relatives, ate
the unleavened bread.)
10The king also defiled Topheth in the Valley
of Ben-hinnom, so that there would no longer
be any immolation of sons or daughters by fire†
in honor of Molech.* 11He did away with the
horses which the kings of Judah had dedicated to
the sun; these were at the entrance of the house
of the LORD, near the chamber of Nathan-melech
the official, which was in the large building. The
chariots of the sun he destroyed by fire. 12He
also demolished the altars made by the kings of
Judah on the roof (the roof terrace of Ahaz), and
the altars made by Manasseh in the two courts
of the LORD's house. He pulverized them and
threw the dust into the Wadi Kidron.* 13The king
defiled the high places east of Jerusalem, south
of the Mount of the Destroyer,† which Solomon,

Pray It!

Josiah Brings Back the Ways of God

What happened to the covenant? What happened to the Israelites' true traditions and prayer rituals? After worshiping false gods for so long, it seems as if people just forgot about the covenant! Then in 2 Kgs 22:8, Hilkiah discovers an old book, King Josiah reads it, and a religious reform is started. Josiah's reform is an effort to know and obey God's law and to restore worship to the one, true God. The holy days and holy ways of God are back—at least for a while (see also 2 Chronicles, chapters 34–35).

Reading can be powerful. Christians have a tremendous tradition of spiritual writings that inspire and renew faith. Spiritual autobiographies like *The Confessions of Saint Augustine; The Story of a Soul*, by Saint Thérèse of Lisieux; and *The Seven Storey Mountain*, by Thomas Merton, are classics. You might try starting with entertaining fictional books that have a strong spiritual message, like the seven volumes of The Chronicles of Narnia, by C. S. Lewis, or the Joshua books, by Joseph F. Girzone. For other suggestions of spiritual writings you might enjoy, ask a parent, youth minister, teacher, or pastor.

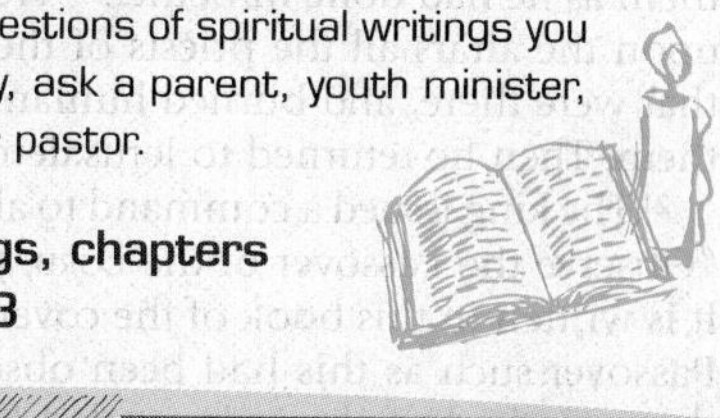

2 Kings, chapters 22–23

2 KGS

† **23:6** *People of the land*: see note on 11:14.
23:10 *Topheth . . . by fire*: Topheth was a cultic site probably in the Hinnom Valley just west of Jerusalem where, apparently, children were immolated to the deity Molech (Hebrew *melek*, "king," deformed in the biblical tradition to "Molech"). The practice was condemned by Deuteronomic law and denounced by Jeremiah (Dt 12:31; Jer 7:29–31). In Jer 19 the deity is identified as the Canaanite god Baal.
23:13 *Mount of the Destroyer*: the name of the mountain in Hebrew is a wordplay. "The Mount of the *mashchit*" means "the Mount

* **23:2** Dt 17:18–19.
23:4 Sir 49:3.
23:5 Dt 4:19; 17:2–7.
23:6 Dt 16:21.
23:7 Dt 23:18–19.
23:10 Lv 18:21; Dt 18:10–12.
23:12 2 Kgs 20:11; 21:5.

king of Israel, had built in honor of Astarte, the Sidonian horror, of Chemosh, the Moabite horror, and of Milcom, the Ammonites' abomination.* 14 He broke to pieces the pillars, cut down the asherahs, and filled the places where they had been with human bones.*

15 Likewise the altar which was at Bethel, the high place built by Jeroboam, son of Nebat, who caused Israel to sin—this same altar and high place he tore down and burned, grinding the high place to powder and burning the asherah.* 16 When Josiah turned and saw the graves there on the mountainside, he ordered the bones taken from the graves and burned on the altar, and thus defiled it, according to the LORD's word proclaimed by the man of God as Jeroboam stood by the altar on the feast day. When the king looked up and saw the grave of the man of God who had proclaimed these words, 17 he asked, "What is that marker I see?" The people of the city replied, "The grave of the man of God who came from Judah and proclaimed the very things you have done to the altar in Bethel." 18 "Let him be," he said, "let no one move his bones." So they left his bones undisturbed together with the bones of the prophet who had come from Samaria.† 19 Josiah also removed all the temples on the high places in the cities of Samaria which the kings of Israel had built, provoking the LORD; he did the very same to them as he had done in Bethel. 20 He slaughtered upon the altars all the priests of the high places that were there, and burned human bones upon them. Then he returned to Jerusalem.

21 The king issued a command to all the people: "Observe the Passover of the LORD, your God, as it is written in this book of the covenant."* 22 No Passover such as this had been observed during the period when the judges ruled Israel, or during the entire period of the kings of Israel and the kings of Judah, 23 until the eighteenth year of King Josiah, when this Passover of the LORD was kept in Jerusalem.

24 Further, Josiah purged the consultation of ghosts and spirits, with the household gods, idols,† and all the other horrors to be seen in the land of Judah and in Jerusalem, so that he might carry out the words of the law that were written in the book that Hilkiah the priest had found in the house of the LORD.*

25 Before him there had been no king who turned to the LORD as he did, with his whole heart, his whole being, and his whole strength, in accord with the entire law of Moses; nor did any king like him arise after him.* 26 Yet the LORD did not turn from his fiercely burning anger against Judah, because of all the provocations that Manasseh had given. 27 The LORD said: Even Judah will I put out of my sight as I did Israel. I will reject this city, Jerusalem, which I chose, and the house of which I said: There shall my name be.

28 The rest of the acts of Josiah, with all that he did, are recorded in the book of the chronicles of the kings of Judah. 29 In his time Pharaoh Neco, king of Egypt, went up toward the Euphrates River against the king of Assyria.† King Josiah set out to meet him, but was slain at Megiddo at the first encounter. 30 His servants brought his body on a chariot from Megiddo to Jerusalem, where they buried him in his own grave. Then the people of the land took Jehoahaz, son of Josiah, anointed him, and proclaimed him king to succeed his father.

Reign of Jehoahaz

31 Jehoahaz was twenty-three years old when he became king, and he reigned three months in Jerusalem. His mother's name was Hamutal, daughter of Jeremiah, from Libnah.*

32 He did what was evil in the LORD's sight, just as his ancestors had done. 33 Pharaoh Neco took him prisoner at Riblah in the land of Hamath, thus ending his reign in Jerusalem. He imposed a fine upon the land of a hundred talents of silver and a talent of gold.† 34 Pharaoh Neco then made Eliakim, son of Josiah, king in place of Josiah his father; he changed his name to Jehoiakim. Jehoahaz he took away with him to Egypt,

---

† of the Destroyer" or perhaps "the Mount of Destruction." The word plays on *mishchah*, "anointment," and on *mashiach*, "anointed one," both of which are references to the ceremony that consecrated the king. The mountain in question was the Mount of Olives, whose trees produced oil for the royal anointing. In the present context, both sides of the wordplay allude to Solomon, the anointed king (*mashiach*), whose building of non-Yahwistic shrines on this very mountain resulted in the destruction (*mashchit*) of the Davidic realm (see 1 Kgs 11:4–13). *Horror . . . abomination*: all three idols are described with pejorative terms.

23:18 *From Samaria*: an anachronistic use of the name of the later capital city for the whole region. The prophet was from Bethel; cf. 1 Kgs 13:11.

23:24 *Household gods, idols*: teraphim. See note on Gn 31:19.

23:29 *Against the king of Assyria*: the narrator depicts Neco's advance as an attack on Assyrian forces. The Babylonian record of the event, however, implies that Neco intended to support the remnant of Assyrian forces against a Babylonian onslaught in order to prop up a buffer state between Egypt and Babylon and assure Egyptian control of the Syro-Palestinian region.

23:33 *A talent of gold*: unless the fine imposed was a mere token, this figure seems too low; cf. 18:14. A number may have dropped from the Hebrew text; various ancient translations read "ten" or "one hundred" here.

---

* **23:13** 1 Kgs 11:4–8. **23:14** Dt 16:21; 1 Kgs 14:23. **23:15–20** 1 Kgs 12:26–13:34. **23:21** Dt 16:1–8. **23:24** 2 Kgs 21:6; Gn 31:19; Dt 18:10–14; Jgs 18:14. **23:25** Dt 6:5; Sir 49:1–3. **23:31** 2 Kgs 24:18.

where he died. 35 Jehoiakim gave the silver and
gold to Pharaoh, but taxed the land to raise the
amount Pharaoh demanded. He exacted the sil-
ver and gold from the people of the land, from
each proportionately, to pay Pharaoh Neco.

Reign of Jehoiakim

36 Jehoiakim was twenty-five years old when he
became king, and he reigned eleven years in Jeru-
salem. His mother's name was Zebidah, daughter
of Pedaiah, from Rumah.
37 He did what was evil in the LORD's sight, just
as his ancestors had done.

24 1 During Jehoiakim's reign Nebuchad-
nezzar, king of Babylon, attacked, and
Jehoiakim became his vassal for three years.
Then Jehoiakim turned and rebelled against him.
2 The LORD loosed against him bands of Chalde-
ans, Arameans, Moabites, and Ammonites; he
unleashed them against Judah to destroy him,
according to the LORD's word spoken through his
servants the prophets. 3 This befell Judah because
the LORD had stated that he would put them out
of his sight for the sins Manasseh had commit-
ted in all that he did, 4 and especially because of
the innocent blood he shed; he filled Jerusalem
with innocent blood, and the LORD would not
forgive.*
5 The rest of the acts of Jehoiakim, with all that
he did, are recorded in the book of the chronicles
of the kings of Judah. 6 Jehoiakim rested with his
ancestors, and his son Jehoiachin succeeded him
as king. 7 The king of Egypt did not again leave
his own land, for the king of Babylon had taken
all that belonged to the king of Egypt from the
wadi of Egypt to the Euphrates River.

Reign of Jehoiachin

8 Jehoiachin was eighteen years old when he
became king, and he reigned three months in
Jerusalem. His mother's name was Nehushta,
daughter of Elnathan, from Jerusalem.
9 He did what was evil in the LORD's sight, just
as his father had done.
10 * At that time officers of Nebuchadnezzar,
king of Babylon, attacked Jerusalem, and the city
came under siege. 11 Nebuchadnezzar, king of
Babylon, himself arrived at the city while his of-
ficers were besieging it. 12 Then Jehoiachin, king
of Judah, together with his mother, his ministers,
officers, and functionaries, surrendered to the
king of Babylon, who, in the eighth year of his
reign,† took him captive. 13 He carried off all the
treasures of the house of the LORD and the trea-
sures of the king's house, and broke up all the
gold utensils that Solomon, king of Israel, had
provided in the house of the LORD, as the LORD
had decreed.* 14 He deported all Jerusalem: all
the officers and warriors of the army, ten thou-
sand in number, and all the artisans and smiths.
Only the lowliest of the people of the land† were
left. 15 He deported Jehoiachin to Babylon, and
the king's mother, his wives, his functionaries,
and the chiefs of the land he led captive from
Jerusalem to Babylon.* 16 All seven thousand
soldiers of the army, and a thousand artisans and
smiths, all of them trained warriors, these too the
king of Babylon brought captive to Babylon. 17 In
place of Jehoiachin the king of Babylon made
Mattaniah, Jehoiachin's uncle, king; he changed
his name to Zedekiah.*

Reign of Zedekiah

18 † Zedekiah was twenty-one years old when
he became king, and he reigned eleven years
in Jerusalem. His mother's name was Hamutal,
daughter of Jeremiah, from Libnah.*
19 He did what was evil in the sight of the LORD,
just as Jehoiakim had done. 20 This befell Jerusa-
lem and Judah because the LORD was so angry
that he cast them out of his sight.
Zedekiah rebelled against the king of Bab-
ylon.

25 1 In the tenth month of the ninth year of
Zedekiah's reign, on the tenth day of the
month, Nebuchadnezzar, king of Babylon, and
his whole army advanced against Jerusalem, en-
camped around it, and built siege walls on every
side. 2 The siege of the city continued until the
eleventh year of Zedekiah. 3 On the ninth day of
the month,† when famine had gripped the city,
and the people of the land had no more food,

†

24:12 *The eighth year of his reign*: that is, of Nebuchadnezzar's reign, not Jehoiachin's. The year was 597 B.C.

24:14 *People of the land*: see note on 11:14.

24:18–25:30 Much of this material closely parallels Jer 52; some of the events are also recounted in Jer 39.

25:3 *Ninth day of the month*: the text does not say which month, but Jer 39:2 and 52:6 set the breaching of the city walls in the fourth month; in later times that was the date of a fast commemorating the event (cf. Zec 8:19). *People of the land*: the influential citizens (see note on 11:14); even they, whose resources went beyond those of the ordinary people, were starving.

*

24:4 2 Kgs 21:16.
24:10–17 Dn 1:1–2.
24:13 2 Kgs 20:17.
24:15 Est A:3; 2:6.
24:17 Jer 37:1.
24:18 2 Kgs 23:31.

2 KGS

Did You Know?

The Fall of Jerusalem

The second conquest and exile described in Second Kings (see "The First Captivity," near 2 Kgs 17:5–18, for the first) involves the southern kingdom, Judah. Judah was conquered by the Babylonians in 587 BC, which is why that event is often referred to as the Babylonian Exile (see map 6, "The Babylonian Empire"). The author of Kings implies that the kingdom of Judah lasted longer than the kingdom of Israel because it had faithful reformer kings like Hezekiah and Josiah. The fall of Judah was particularly devastating because both Jerusalem, David's city, and the Temple, the central place of worship, were destroyed. The whole Book of Lamentations is an expression of the sorrow and grief the people experienced as a result.

▶ 2 Kgs 25:1–21

4 the city walls were breached. That night, all the
soldiers came to the gate between the two walls
near the king's garden (the Chaldeans had the
city surrounded), while the king went toward
the Arabah.† 5 But the Chaldean army pursued
the king and overtook him in the desert near Jer-
icho, abandoned by his whole army. 6 The king
was therefore arrested and brought to Riblah to
the king of Babylon, who pronounced sentence
on him. 7 They slew Zedekiah's sons before his
eyes; then they put out his eyes, bound him with
fetters, and brought him to Babylon.
8 On the seventh day of the fifth month (this
was in the nineteenth year of Nebuchadnezzar,
king of Babylon), Nebuzaradan, captain of the
bodyguard, came to Jerusalem as the agent of
the king of Babylon. 9 He burned the house of the
LORD, the house of the king, and all the houses
of Jerusalem (every noble house); he destroyed
them by fire.* 10 The Chaldean troops who were
with the captain of the guard tore down the walls
that surrounded Jerusalem, 11 and Nebuzaradan,
captain of the guard, led into exile the last of the
army remaining in the city, and those who had
deserted† to the king of Babylon, and the last
of the commoners. 12 But some of the country's
poor the captain of the guard left behind as vine-
dressers and farmers.
13 The bronze columns that belonged to the
house of the LORD, and the stands and the
bronze sea in the house of the LORD, the Chal-
deans broke into pieces; they carried away the
bronze to Babylon.* 14 They took also the pots,
the shovels, the snuffers, the cups and all the
bronze articles used for service.* 15 The fire pans
and the bowls that were of solid gold or silver
the captain of the guard also carried off.* 16 The
two columns, the one bronze sea, and the stands,
which Solomon had made for the house of the
LORD—the weight in bronze of all these articles
was never calculated.* 17 Each of the columns
was eighteen cubits high; a bronze capital three
cubits high surmounted each column, and a net-
ting with pomegranates encircled the capital, all
of bronze; and they were duplicated on the other
column, on the netting.*
18 The captain of the guard also took Seraiah,
the chief priest, Zephaniah, an assistant priest,
and the three doorkeepers. 19 And from the city
he took one officer who was a commander of
soldiers, five courtiers in the personal service of
the king who were still in the city, the scribe in
charge of the army who mustered the people of
the land,† and sixty of the people of the land still
remaining in the city. 20 The captain of the guard,
Nebuzaradan, arrested these and brought them
to the king of Babylon at Riblah, and 21 the king
of Babylon struck them down and put them to
death in Riblah, in the land of Hamath. And thus
Judah went into exile from their native soil.

Governorship of Gedaliah

22 * As for the people whom he had allowed
to remain in the land of Judah, Nebuchadnez-
zar, king of Babylon, appointed Gedaliah, son of
Ahikam, son of Shaphan, over them. 23 Hearing
that the king of Babylon had appointed Gedaliah
over them, all the army commanders and the
troops came to him at Mizpah: Ishmael, son of
Nethaniah, Johanan, son of Kareah, Seraiah, son
of Tanhumeth the Netophathite, and Jaazaniah,

---

† **25:4** The Hebrew text of this verse is missing some words. The present translation is based on a likely reconstruction.

25:11 *Those who had deserted*: perhaps on the advice of Jeremiah; cf. Jer 38:2–3.

25:19 *People of the land*: see note on 11:14.

---

* **25:9** Ps 74:2–7.
25:13 2 Kgs 16:17; 1 Kgs 7:15–39; Jer 27:19–23.
25:14 1 Kgs 7:40–45.
25:15 1 Kgs 7:50.
25:16 1 Kgs 7:47.
25:17 1 Kgs 7:15–20; Jer 52:21–23.
25:22–26 Jer 40:7–41:18.

son of the Maakite, each with his troops. 24 Gedaliah gave the commanders and their troops his oath. He said to them, "Do not be afraid of the Chaldean officials. Remain in the country and serve the king of Babylon, so that all will be well with you."

25 But in the seventh month Ishmael, son of Nethaniah, son of Elishama, of royal descent, came with ten others, attacked Gedaliah and killed him, along with the Judahites and Chaldeans who were in Mizpah with him. 26 Then all the people, great and small, left with the army commanders and went to Egypt for fear of the Chaldeans.

Release of Jehoiachin

27 In the thirty-seventh year of the exile of Jehoiachin, king of Judah, on the twenty-seventh day of the twelfth month, Evil-merodach, king of Babylon, in the inaugural year of his own reign, raised up Jehoiachin, king of Judah, from prison. 28 He spoke kindly to him and gave him a throne higher than that of the other kings who were with him in Babylon. 29 Jehoiachin took off his prison garb; he ate regularly in the king's presence as long as he lived; 30 and for his allowance the king granted him a regular allowance, in fixed daily amounts, for as long as he lived.

The First and Second Books of

Chronicles

Wait! That's not the way I saw it! Doesn't it seem that there is always more than one version of an event? This often happens with accidents. Two individuals can witness the same accident with very different points of view. The First and Second Books of Chronicles provide a second interpretation, or version, of the history of the people of Israel, presenting that history from another point of view. In contrast to the previous account, the account in these books tends to downplay the covenant and emphasizes the importance of institutional ritual and worship of God.

In Depth

The Chronicler is the name given to the unknown author (or authors) of First and Second Chronicles. The Chronicler, writing after the Israelites' return from the Exile in Babylon, has a unique perspective, so unique that he almost never mentions the Sinai Covenant or Moses (central themes throughout other parts of the Old Testament). Because the Israelites still hope to have their own king, the Chronicler emphasizes that fidelity to Temple worship is necessary for God's promises regarding land and kingship to be fulfilled.

The Chronicler uses two types of material—genealogies and legends edited to emphasize the Chronicler's point—to summarize Israel's history from the Creation to around 525 BC. But he focuses primarily on kings David and Solomon. They are praised extensively because of their role in centralizing worship in Jerusalem and building the Temple. Many of the negative stories about David from Second Samuel—such as his affair with Bathsheba—are not even mentioned. The Chronicler wants nothing to tarnish the people's memory of an ideal kingdom that might one day be restored.

Second Chronicles also focuses on the southern kingdom of Judah and ignores the northern kingdom of Israel after Solomon's death. This may well be due to a bias of the priestly class in Jerusalem against the religious practice of the northern tribes. This bias lasted into Jesus' time.

The goal of First and Second Chronicles was to give the Israelites hope for the future after returning from the Exile. The Chronicler reminds them that if they maintain their religious practices and worship of God, they will continue to be God's People.

At a Glance

- **I. Genealogical Tables (1 Chr 1:1—9:34).**
- **II. The History of David (1 Chr 9:35—29:30).**
- **I. The Reign of Solomon (2 Chr 1:1—9:31).**
- **II. The Post-Solomonic Monarchy of Judah (2 Chr 10:1—36:23).**

Quick Facts

Period Covered: Creation to the end of the Babylonian captivity

Inspired Author: a Levite cantor and scribe writing after the return to Jerusalem around 400 BC

Theme: Israel can secure its future by continuing its worship in the pattern established by David by being united as one people worshiping the one true God at the Temple in Jerusalem.

1 Chronicles

Chapter 15

I. Genealogical Tables†

From Adam to Abraham

1 1 Adam, Seth, Enosh,* 2 Kenan, Mahalalel, Ja-
red,* 3 Enoch, Methuselah, Lamech,* 4 Noah,
Shem, Ham, and Japheth.* 5 The sons of Japheth
were Gomer, Magog, Madai, Javan, Tubal, Me-
shech, and Tiras.* 6 The sons of Gomer were
Ashkenaz, Riphath, and Togarmah. 7 The sons of
Javan were Elishah, Tarshish, the Kittim, and the
Rodanim.

8 The sons of Ham were Cush, Mizraim, Put,
and Canaan. 9 The sons of Cush were Seba, Hav-
ilah, Sabta, Raama, and Sabteca. The sons of
Raama were Sheba and Dedan. 10 Cush became
the father of Nimrod, who was the first to be a
warrior on the earth.* 11 * Mizraim became the
father of the Ludim, Anamim, Lehabim, Naph-
tuhim, 12 Pathrusim, Casluhim, and Caphtorim,
from whom the Philistines sprang. 13 Canaan be-
came the father of Sidon, his firstborn, and Heth,
14 and the Jebusites, the Amorites, the Girgashites,
15 the Hivites, the Arkites, the Sinites, 16 the Arvad-
ites, the Zemarites, and the Hamathites.

17 * The sons of Shem were Elam, Asshur,
Arpachshad, Lud, and Aram. The sons of Aram
were Uz, Hul, Gether, and Mash. 18 Arpachshad
became the father of Shelah, and Shelah became
the father of Eber. 19 Two sons were born to Eber;
the first was named Peleg (for in his time the
world was divided),† and his brother was named
Joktan. 20 Joktan became the father of Almodad,
Sheleph, Hazarmaveth, Jerah, 21 Hadoram, Uzal,
Diklah, 22 Ebal, Abimael, Sheba, 23 Ophir, Havi-
lah, and Jobab; all these were the sons of Joktan.

24 * Shem, Arpachshad, Shelah, 25 Eber, Peleg,
Reu, 26 Serug, Nahor, Terah, 27 Abram, that is,
Abraham.*

From Abraham to Jacob

28 The sons of Abraham were Isaac and Ish-
mael.* 29 These were their generations:

Nebaioth, the firstborn of Ishmael, then Kedar,
Adbeel, Mibsam, 30 Mishma, Dumah, Massa, Ha-
dad, Tema, 31 Jetur, Naphish, and Kedemah. These
were the sons of Ishmael.*

32 The sons of Keturah, Abraham's concubine:
she bore Zimran, Jokshan, Medan, Midian, Ish-
bak, and Shuah. The sons of Jokshan were Sheba

†

1:1–9:34 The Chronicler's intention seems to have been to retell, from his particular viewpoint, the story of God's people from creation down to his own day. Since his primary interest was the history of David and the Davidic dynasty of Judah, he hurries through everything that preceded the death of Saul, David's predecessor as king, by the use of genealogical lists. The sources for these genealogies are mostly the books, already largely in their present form in the Chronicler's time, that eventually formed the Hebrew canon. For any given portion of these chapters, see the cross-references to their scriptural sources.

1:19 *Divided*: see note on Gn 10:25.

*

1:1 Gn 5:3, 6, 9.
1:2–4 Gn 5:9–32; 10:2–32.
1:3 Gn 4:24.
1:4 Gn 5:32; 6:10; 9:18.
1:5–7 Gn 10:2–4.
1:10 Gn 10:8.
1:11–16 Gn 10:13–18.
1:17–23 Gn 10:22–29; 11:10–18.
1:24–27 Gn 11:10–26; Lk 3:34–36.
1:27 Gn 17:5; Neh 9:7.
1:28 Gn 16:11, 15; 21:2–3; Gal 4:22–23; Heb 11:11.
1:29–31 Gn 25:13–16.

Did You Know?

Genealogies

Look at all these names! Our present-day interest in family trees obviously has ancient roots. The first nine chapters of First Chronicles consist entirely of family trees—or genealogies—tracing the history of Israel from Adam to Saul. In a culture where not only money and identity but also the offices of priest and king passed from one generation to another, it was essential to be able to trace one's tribal roots.

The many genealogies of the Old Testament answer important questions: How were the various tribes related to one another? Who were a particular tribe's ancestors? What right did a certain group or person have to the office of priest or king? The Chronicler lists the genealogies of David and Levi in considerable detail. The kingship and the priesthood were clearly of special interest to him.

▶ 1 Chronicles, chapters 1–9

and Dedan. 33 The sons of Midian were Ephah,
Epher, Hanoch, Abida, and Eldaah. All these
were the sons of Keturah.*
34 Abraham begot Isaac. The sons of Isaac were
Esau and Israel.*
35 The descendants of Esau were Eliphaz, Reuel,
Jeush, Jalam, and Korah. 36 The descendants of El-
iphaz were Teman, Omar, Zephi, Gatam, Kenaz,
Timna, and Amalek. 37 The descendants of Reuel
were Nahath, Zerah, Shammah, and Mizzah.*
38 The sons of Seir† were Lotan, Shobal, Zib-
eon, Anah, Dishon, Ezer, and Dishan. 39 The sons
of Lotan were Hori and Homam; Timna was the
sister of Lotan. 40 The sons of Shobal were Alian,
Manahath, Ebal, Shephi, and Onam. The sons of
Zibeon were Aiah and Anah. 41 The sons of Anah:
Dishon. The sons of Dishon were Hemdan, Esh-
ban, Ithran, and Cheran. 42 The sons of Ezer were
Bilhan, Zaavan, and Jaakan. The sons of Dishan
were Uz and Aran.*
43 * The kings who reigned in the land of
Edom before the Israelites had kings were the
following: Bela, son of Beor, the name of whose
city was Dinhabah. 44 When Bela died, Jobab, son
of Zerah, from Bozrah, succeeded him as king.*
45 When Jobab died, Husham, from the land of
the Temanites, succeeded him as king.* 46 Hu-
sham died and Hadad, son of Bedad, succeeded
him as king. He overthrew the Midianites on the
Moabite plateau, and the name of his city was
Avith. 47 Hadad died and Samlah of Masrekah
succeeded him as king. 48 Samlah died and Shaul
from Rehoboth on the Euphrates succeeded him
as king. 49 When Shaul died, Baalhanan, son of
Achbor, succeeded him as king. 50 Baalhanan
died and Hadad succeeded him as king. The
name of his city was Pai, and his wife's name
was Mehetabel. She was the daughter of Matred,
who was the daughter of Mezahab. 51 * After Ha-
dad died, there were chiefs in Edom: the chiefs
of Timna, Aliah, Jetheth, 52 Oholibamah, Elah,
Pinon, 53 Kenaz, Teman, Mibzar, 54 Magdiel, and
Iram were the chiefs of Edom.

2 1 These were the sons of Israel: Reuben, Sim-
eon, Levi, Judah, Issachar, Zebulun,* 2 Dan,
Joseph, Benjamin, Naphtali, Gad, and Asher.*

Judah

3 The sons of Judah† were: Er, Onan, and She-
lah; these three Bathshua, a Canaanite woman,
bore to him. But Judah's firstborn, Er, was wicked
in the sight of the Lord, so he took his life.* 4 Ju-
dah's daughter-in-law Tamar bore him Perez and
Zerah, so that he had five sons in all.*
5 The sons of Perez were Hezron and Hamul.*
6 The sons of Zerah were Zimri, Ethan, Heman,
Calcol, and Darda—five in all.* 7 The sons of
Zimri: Carmi. The sons of Carmi: Achar, who
brought trouble upon Israel by violating the ban.*
8 The sons of Ethan: Azariah. 9 The sons born to
Hezron were Jerahmeel, Ram, and Chelubai.† *
10 † Ram became the father of Amminadab,

1:38 *Seir*: another name for Esau (v. 35) or Edom (v. 43).

2:3–4:23 The Chronicler had two reasons for placing his genealogy of the tribe of Judah before those of the other tribes, and for making it longer than all the others: his interest in David, who was of the tribe of Judah; and the prominence of descendants of that tribe among the Jews of the Chronicler's time.

2:9 *Chelubai*: a variant form of the name Caleb (vv. 18, 42), a different person from the Chelub mentioned in 4:11.

2:10–17 These verses list the immediate ancestors of David. A similar list appears in Ru 4:18–22.

1:32–33 Gn 25:1–4.
1:34 Gn 21:2–3; 25:19, 25–26; 32:28–29; Mt 1:2; Lk 3:34.
1:35–37 Gn 36:4–5, 10–13, 15–19.
1:38–42 Gn 36:20–28.
1:43–54 Gn 36:31–43.
1:44 Is 34:6; 63:1; Jer 49:13, 22.
1:45 Gn 36:11; Jb 2:11; Jer 49:7, 20.
1:51–54 Gn 36:40–43.
2:1 Gn 29:32–35; 30:18, 20; 35:23.
2:2 Gn 30:6, 8, 11, 13, 24; 35:18, 24–26.
2:3 1 Chr 4:21; Gn 38:1–5; 46:12.
2:4 Gn 38:7, 13–30; 46:12; Mt 1:3.
2:5 Gn 46:12.
2:6 1 Kgs 5:11.
2:7 Jos 7:1, 18–21, 24–25; 22:20.
2:9 Mt 1:3.

and Amminadab became the father of Nahshon, a prince of the Judahites.* 11 * Nahshon became the father of Salmah. Salmah became the father of Boaz. 12 Boaz became the father of Obed. Obed became the father of Jesse. 13 * Jesse became the father of Eliab, his firstborn, of Abinadab, the second son, Shimea, the third,* 14 Nethanel, the fourth, Raddai, the fifth, 15 Ozem, the sixth, and David, the seventh. 16 Their sisters were Zeruiah and Abigail. Zeruiah had three sons: Abishai, Joab, and Asahel.* 17 Abigail bore Amasa, whose father was Jether the Ishmaelite.*

18 † By his wife Azubah, Caleb, son of Hezron, became the father of a daughter, Jerioth. Her sons were Jesher, Shobab, and Ardon.* 19 When Azubah died, Caleb married Ephrath, who bore him Hur.* 20 Hur became the father of Uri, and Uri became the father of Bezalel.* 21 Then Hezron had relations with the daughter of Machir, the father of Gilead, whom he married when he was sixty years old. She bore him Segub.* 22 Segub became the father of Jair, who possessed twenty-three cities in the land of Gilead.* 23 Geshur and Aram took from them the villages of Jair, that is, Kenath and its towns, sixty cities in all, which had belonged to the sons of Machir, the father of Gilead.* 24 After the death of Hezron, Caleb had relations with Ephrathah, the widow of his father Hezron, and she bore him Ashhur, the father of Tekoa.*

25 The sons of Jerahmeel,† the firstborn of Hezron, were Ram, the firstborn, then Bunah, Oren, and Ozem, his brothers.* 26 Jerahmeel also had another wife, named Atarah, who was the mother of Onam. 27 The sons of Ram, the firstborn of Jerahmeel, were Maaz, Jamin, and Eker. 28 The sons of Onam were Shammai and Jada. The sons of Shammai were Nadab and Abishur. 29 Abishur's wife, who was named Abihail, bore him Ahban and Molid. 30 The sons of Nadab were Seled and Appaim. Seled died childless. 31 The sons of Appaim: Ishi. The sons of Ishi: Sheshan. The sons of Sheshan: Ahlai.* 32 The sons of Jada, the brother of Shammai, were Jether and Jonathan. Jether died childless. 33 The sons of Jonathan were Peleth and Zaza. These were the sons of Jerahmeel. 34 Sheshan had no sons, only daughters; he had an Egyptian slave named Jarha. 35 Sheshan gave his daughter in marriage to his slave Jarha, and she bore him Attai. 36 Attai became the father of Nathan. Nathan became the father of Zabad. 37 Zabad became the father of Ephlal. Ephlal became the father of Obed. 38 Obed became the father of Jehu. Jehu became the father of Azariah. 39 Azariah became the father of Helez. Helez became the father of Eleasah. 40 Eleasah became the father of Sismai. Sismai became the father of Shallum. 41 Shallum became the father of Jekamiah. Jekamiah became the father of Elishama.

42 The sons of Caleb,† the brother of Jerahmeel: Mesha his firstborn, who was the father of Ziph. Then the sons of Mareshah, who was the father of Hebron. 43 The sons of Hebron were Korah, Tappuah, Rekem, and Shema. 44 Shema became the father of Raham, who was the father of Jorkeam. Rekem became the father of Shammai. 45 The son of Shammai: Maon, who was the father of Bethzur. 46 Ephah, Caleb's concubine, bore Haran, Moza, and Gazez. Haran became the father of Gazez. 47 The sons of Jahdai were Regem, Jotham, Geshan, Pelet, Ephah, and Shaaph. 48 Maacah, Caleb's concubine, bore Sheber and Tirhanah. 49 She also bore Shaaph, the father of Madmannah, Sheva, the father of Machbenah, and the father of Gibea. Achsah was Caleb's daughter.*

50 These were sons of Caleb, sons of Hur,† the firstborn of Ephrathah: Shobal, the father of Kiriath-jearim, 51 Salma, the father of Bethlehem, and Hareph, the father of Bethgader. 52 The sons of Shobal, the father of Kiriath-jearim, were Reaiah, half of the Manahathites, 53 and the clans of Kiriath-jearim: the Ithrites, the Puthites, the Shumathites, and the Mishraites. From these the Zorahites and the Eshtaolites derived.* 54 The sons of Salma were Bethlehem, the Netophathites, Atroth-beth-Joab, half of the Manahathites, and the Zorites. 55 The clans of the Sopherim dwelling in Jabez were the Tirathites, the Shimeathites, and the Sucathites. They were the Kenites, who descended from Hammath, the ancestor of the Rechabites.*

---

†

2:18–24 These verses record the descendants of Caleb. In 4:15 as well as frequently in the Pentateuch (see Nm 13:6; 14:6, 30; 26:65; etc.), Caleb is called the son of Jephunneh. Here his father is called Hezron, perhaps because the Calebites were reckoned as part of the clan of the Hezronites.

2:25–41 The Jerahmeelites were a clan living in the Negeb of Judah.

2:42–49 Another list (see vv. 18–24) of the Calebites, a clan inhabiting the south of Judah.

2:50–55 The Hurites were a clan dwelling to the south and west of Jerusalem and related to the Calebites.

*

2:10 Mt 1:4.
2:11–12 Nm 1:7; Mt 1:4–5.
2:13–15 1 Sm 16:6–13; 17:13–14.
2:13 2 Chr 11:18.
2:16 2 Sm 2:18.
2:17 2 Sm 17:25; 19:14; 20:4–13.
2:18 1 Chr 2:24.
2:19 1 Chr 2:24.
2:20 Ex 24:14; 31:2; 35:30; 2 Chr 1:5.
2:21 Nm 26:29; 27:1; 32:39; Jos 13:31; Jgs 5:14.
2:22 Nm 32:41; 1 Kgs 4:13.
2:23 Dt 3:14; Jos 13:30.
2:24 1 Chr 2:19; 2 Sm 14:2; 2 Chr 11:6.
2:25 1 Sm 27:10; 30:29; Jb 32:2.
2:31 1 Chr 4:20.
2:49 Jos 15:16; Jgs 1:12.
2:53 Jgs 18:2.
2:55 Nm 24:21; Jgs 1:16; 4:11; 1 Sm 15:6; Jer 35.

3 1 † * These were the sons of David born to
him in Hebron: the firstborn, Amnon, by
Ahinoam of Jezreel; the second, Daniel,† by
Abigail of Carmel; 2 the third, Absalom, son
of Maacah, who was the daughter of Talmai,
king of Geshur; the fourth, Adonijah, son of
Haggith; 3 the fifth, Shephatiah, by Abital; the
sixth, Ithream, by his wife Eglah. 4 Six in all
were born to him in Hebron, where he reigned
seven years and six months. Then he reigned
thirty-three years in Jerusalem.* 5 * In Jerusalem
the following were born to him: Shimea,† Sho-
bab, Nathan, Solomon—four by Bathsheba, the
daughter of Ammiel;* 6 Ibhar, Elishua, Eliphelet,
7 Nogah, Nepheg, Japhia, 8 Elishama, Eliada, and
Eliphelet—nine. 9 All these were sons of David,
in addition to other sons by concubines; and Ta-
mar was their sister.*

10 † * The son of Solomon was Rehoboam,
whose son was Abijah, whose son was Asa,
whose son was Jehoshaphat,* 11 whose son was
Joram, whose son was Ahaziah, whose son was
Joash,* 12 whose son was Amaziah, whose son
was Azariah, whose son was Jotham,* 13 whose
son was Ahaz, whose son was Hezekiah, whose
son was Manasseh,* 14 whose son was Amon,
whose son was Josiah.* 15 The sons of Josiah
were: the firstborn Johanan; the second, Jehoia-
kim; the third, Zedekiah; the fourth, Shallum.† *
16 The sons of Jehoiakim were: Jeconiah, his son;
Zedekiah, his son.*

17 The sons of Jeconiah† the captive were: She-
altiel,* 18 Malchiram, Pedaiah, Shenazzar,† Jek-
amiah, Hoshama, and Nedabiah. 19 The sons of
Pedaiah were Zerubbabel† and Shimei. The sons
of Zerubbabel were Meshullam and Hananiah;
Shelomith was their sister. 20 The sons of Meshul-
lam were Hashubah, Ohel, Berechiah, Hasadiah,
Jushabhesed—five. 21 The sons of Hananiah
were Pelatiah, Jeshaiah, Rephaiah, Arnan, Oba-
diah, and Shecaniah. 22 The sons of Shecaniah
were Shemaiah, Hattush, Igal, Bariah, Neariah,
Shaphat—six.* 23 The sons of Neariah were Eli-
oenai, Hizkiah, and Azrikam—three. 24 The sons
of Elioenai were Hodaviah, Eliashib, Pelaiah, Ak-
kub, Johanan, Delaiah, and Anani—seven.

4 1 † The sons of Judah were: Perez, Hezron,
Carmi, Hur, and Shobal.* 2 Reaiah, the son
of Shobal, became the father of Jahath, and Ja-
hath became the father of Ahumai and Lahad.
These were the clans of the Zorathites.

3 These were the sons of Hareph, the father
of Etam: Jezreel, Ishma, and Idbash; their sister
was named Hazzelelponi. 4 Penuel was the father
of Gedor, and Ezer the father of Hushah. These
were the sons of Hur, the firstborn of Ephrathah,
the father of Bethlehem.

5 Ashhur, the father of Tekoa, had two wives,
Helah and Naarah.* 6 Naarah bore him Ahuz-
zam, Hepher, the Temenites, and the Ahash-
tarites. These were the sons of Naarah. 7 The sons
of Helah were Zereth, Izhar, Ethnan, and Koz.
8 Koz became the father of Anub and Zobebah,
as well as of the clans of Aharhel, son of Harum.
9 Jabez was the most distinguished of his broth-
ers. His mother had named him Jabez, saying, "I
bore him with pain." 10 Jabez prayed to the God
of Israel: "Oh, that you may truly bless me and
extend my boundaries! May your hand be with
me and make me free of misfortune, without
pain!" And God granted his prayer.

11 Chelub, the brother of Shuhah, became the
father of Mehir, who was the father of Eshton.
12 Eshton became the father of Bethrapha, Pa-
seah, and Tehinnah, the father of the city of Na-
hash. These were the men of Recah.

13 The sons of Kenaz were Othniel and Seraiah.
The sons of Othniel were Hathath and Meono-
thai;* 14 Meonothai became the father of Oph-
rah. Seraiah became the father of Joab, the father
of Geharashim, so called because they were

3:1–9 A list of David's sons.

3:1 *Daniel*: he is called Chileab in 2 Sm 3:3.

3:5 *Shimea*: he bears the name Shammua in 2 Sm 5:14. *Ammiel*: Bathsheba's father is called Eliam in 2 Sm 11:3.

3:10–16 The kings of Judah from Solomon down to the destruction of Jerusalem by the Babylonians.

3:15 *Shallum*: another name for Jehoahaz, Josiah's immediate successor; cf. Jer 22:11.

3:17–24 The descendants of King Jeconiah down to the time of the Chronicler. If twenty-five years are allowed for each generation, the ten generations between Jeconiah and Anani (the last name on the list) would put the birth of the latter at about 405 B.C.—an important item in establishing the approximate date of the Chronicler's work in its final form.

3:18 *Shenazzar*: presumably he is the same as Sheshbazzar (Ezr 1:8, 11; 5:14–16), the prince of Judah who was the first Jewish governor of Judah after the exile. Both forms of the name probably go back to the Babylonian name Sin-ab-ussar, meaning "O [god] Sin, protect [our] father!"

3:19 *Zerubbabel*: here called the son of Pedaiah, though elsewhere (Hg 1:12, 14; 2:2, 23; Ezr 3:2, 8; 5:2; Neh 12:1) his father's name is given as Shealtiel. The latter indication may merely point to the fact that Zerubbabel succeeded Shealtiel as head of the house of David.

4:1–43 Genealogies of the southern tribes, Judah and Simeon.

3:1–4 2 Sm 3:2–5.
3:4 2 Sm 2:11; 5:5.
3:5–8 2 Sm 5:14–16.
3:5 2 Sm 11:3.
3:9 2 Sm 13:1–2.
3:10–17 Mt 1:7–12.
3:10 1 Kgs 11:43; 14:31; 15:1, 8, 24; 2 Chr 9:31; 12:16; 13:23; 17:1.
3:11 1 Kgs 22:51; 2 Chr 21:1; 22:1; 24:1, 27.
3:12 2 Kgs 12:21; 14:21; 15:7; 2 Chr 25:1; 26:1, 23; 27:1.
3:13 2 Kgs 15:38; 16:20; 20:21; 2 Chr 28:1, 27; 32:33.
3:14 2 Kgs 21:18, 26; 2 Chr 33:20, 25.
3:15 2 Kgs 23:34; 24:17; 2 Chr 36:4, 10.
3:16 2 Kgs 24:6, 17; 2 Chr 36:8, 10.
3:17, 19 Ezr 2:2; 3:2, 8; 5:2; Sir 49:11; Hg 1:1, 12, 14; Mt 1:12–13; Lk 3:27.
3:22 Neh 3:29.
4:1 1 Chr 2:4–5, 7, 9, 50; Gn 38:29; 46:12; Mt 1:3.
4:5 1 Chr 2:24.
4:13 Jos 15:17; Jgs 1:13; 3:9, 11.

artisans. 15 The sons of Caleb, son of Jephun-
neh, were Ir, Elah, and Naam. The sons of Elah:
Kenaz.* 16 The sons of Jehallelel were Ziph, Zi-
phah, Tiria, and Asarel. 17 The sons of Ezrah were
Jether, Mered, Epher, and Jalon. Jether became
the father of Miriam, Shammai, and Ishbah, the
father of Eshtemoa.* 18 Mered's Egyptian wife
bore Jered, the father of Gedor, Heber, the father
of Soco, and Jekuthiel, the father of Zanoah.
These were the sons of Bithiah, the daughter of
Pharaoh, whom Mered married. 19 The sons of
his Jewish wife, the sister of Naham, the father
of Keilah, were Shimon the Garmite and Ishi the
Maacathite. 20 The sons of Shimon were Amnon,
Rinnah, Benhanan, and Tilon. The son of Ishi
was Zoheth and the son of Zoheth. . . .

21 The sons of Shelah, son of Judah, were: Er,
the father of Lecah; Laadah, the father of Ma-
reshah; the clans of the linen weavers' guild in
Bethashbea;* 22 Jokim; the people of Cozeba;
and Joash and Saraph, who held property in
Moab, but returned to Bethlehem. (These are
events of old.) 23 They were potters and inhabi-
tants of Netaim and Gederah, where they lived
in the king's service.

Simeon

24 The sons of Simeon were Nemuel, Jamin,
Jachin, Zerah, and Shaul,* 25 whose son was
Shallum, whose son was Mibsam, whose son
was Mishma. 26 The sons of Mishma were his
son Hammuel, whose son was Zaccur, whose
son was Shimei. 27 Shimei had sixteen sons and
six daughters. His brothers, however, did not
have many sons, and as a result all their clans did
not equal the number of the Judahites.

28 They dwelt in Beer-sheba, Moladah, Hazar-
shual, 29 Bilhah, Ezem, Tolad, 30 Bethuel, Hor-
mah, Ziklag, 31 Beth-marcaboth, Hazar-susim,
Bethbiri, and Shaaraim. Until the reign of David,
these were their cities 32 and their villages. Etam,
also, and Ain, Rimmon, Tochen, and Ashan—
five cities,* 33 together with all their outlying
villages as far as Baal. Here is where they dwelt,
and so it was inscribed of them in their family
records.

34 Meshobab, Jamlech, Joshah, son of Amaziah,
35 Joel, Jehu, son of Joshibiah, son of Seraiah,
son of Asiel, 36 Elioenai, Jaakobah, Jeshohaiah,
Asaiah, Adiel, Jesimiel, Benaiah, 37 Ziza, son
of Shiphi, son of Allon, son of Jedaiah, son of
Shimri, son of Shemaiah— 38 these just named
were princes in their clans, and their ancestral
houses spread out to such an extent* 39 that they
went to the approaches of Gedor,† east of the
valley, seeking pasture for their flocks. 40 They
found abundant and good pastures, and the land
was spacious, quiet, and peaceful—for the Ham-
ites dwelt there formerly. 41 They who have just
been listed by name set out during the reign of
Hezekiah, king of Judah, and attacked their tents
and also the Meunites who were there. They put
them under the ban that is still in force to this
day and dwelt in their place because they found
pasture there for their flocks.*

42 Five hundred of them (the Simeonites) went
to Mount Seir, with Pelatiah, Neariah, Rephaiah,
and Uzziel, sons of Ishi, at their head. 43 They
attacked the surviving Amalekites who had es-
caped, and have lived there to the present day.*

Reuben

5 1 † The sons of Reuben, the firstborn of Israel.
(He was indeed the firstborn, but because he
defiled the couch of his father his birthright was
given to the sons of Joseph, son of Israel, so that
he is not listed in the family records according to
his birthright.* 2 Judah, in fact, became powerful
among his brothers, so that the ruler came from
him, though the birthright had been Joseph's.)*
3 The sons of Reuben, the firstborn of Israel, were
Hanoch, Pallu, Hezron, and Carmi.* 4 His son
was Joel, whose son was Shemaiah, whose son
was Gog, whose son was Shimei, 5 whose
son was Micah, whose son was Reaiah, whose
son was Baal, 6 whose son was Beerah, whom
Tilgath-pileser, the king of Assyria, took into
exile; he was a prince of the Reubenites.* 7 His
brothers who belonged to his clans, when they
were listed in the family records according to
their descendants, were: Jeiel, the chief, and
Zechariah, 8 and Bela, son of Azaz, son of Shema,
son of Joel. The Reubenites lived in Aroer and as
far as Nebo and Baal-meon;* 9 toward the east
they dwelt as far as the wilderness which extends
from the Euphrates River, for they had much
livestock in the land of Gilead.* 10 In Saul's time
they waged war with the Hagrites, and when

† **4:39** *Gedor*: the Greek reads Gerar, probably correctly.
5:1–26 Genealogies of the Transjordanian tribes, Reuben, Gad, and the half-tribe of Manasseh.

* **4:15** Nm 13:6; 14:6; 32:12; Jos 14:6, 14.
4:17 1 Sm 30:28.
4:21 1 Chr 2:3; Gn 38:5; 46:12; Nm 26:20.
4:24 Gn 46:10; Ex 6:15; Nm 26:12–13.
4:28–32 Jos 19:2–8.
4:38 Nm 1:2.
4:41 2 Kgs 18:1–2; 2 Chr 29:1.
4:43 Ex 17:8, 14; Dt 25:17–19; 1 Sm 14:48; 15:3, 7–8; 2 Sm 8:12.
5:1 Gn 35:22; 48:5, 15–22; 49:3–4; Dt 33:6.
5:2 1 Chr 28:4; Gn 49:8–12.
5:3 Gn 46:9; Ex 6:14; Nm 26:5–6.
5:6 2 Kgs 15:29.
5:8 Jos 13:9, 16–17; Nm 32:3, 38.
5:9 Jos 22:9.

they had defeated them they dwelt in their tents throughout the region east of Gilead.*

Gad

11 The Gadites lived alongside them in the land of Bashan as far as Salecah.* 12 Joel was chief, Shapham was second in command, and Janai was judge in Bashan.* 13 Their brothers, according to their ancestral houses, were: Michael, Meshullam, Sheba, Jorai, Jacan, Zia, and Eber—seven. 14 These were the sons of Abihail, son of Huri, son of Jaroah, son of Gilead, son of Michael, son of Jeshishai, son of Jahdo, son of Buz. 15 Ahi, son of Abdiel, son of Guni, was the head of their ancestral houses. 16 They dwelt in Gilead, in Bashan and its towns, and in all the pasture lands of Sirion to the borders. 17 All were listed in the family records in the time of Jotham, king of Judah, and of Jeroboam, king of Israel.

18 The Reubenites, Gadites, and the half-tribe of Manasseh were warriors, men who bore shield and sword and who drew the bow, trained in warfare—forty-four thousand seven hundred and sixty men fit for military service. 19 When they waged war against the Hagrites and against Jetur, Naphish, and Nodab,* 20 they received help so that the Hagrites and all who were with them were delivered into their power. For during the battle they cried out to God, and he heard them because they had put their trust in him.* 21 Along with one hundred thousand persons they also captured their livestock: fifty thousand camels, two hundred fifty thousand sheep, and two thousand donkeys. 22 Many were slain and fell; for "From God the victory." They dwelt in their place until the time of the exile.*

The Half-tribe of Manasseh

23 The half-tribe of Manasseh lived in the land of Bashan as far as Baal-hermon, Senir, and Mount Hermon; they were numerous. 24 The following were the heads of their ancestral houses: Epher, Ishi, Eliel, Azriel, Jeremiah, Hodaviah, and Jahdiel—men who were warriors, famous men, and heads over their ancestral houses.

25 However, they acted treacherously toward the God of their ancestors by prostituting themselves to follow the gods of the peoples of the land, whom God had destroyed before them.* 26 Therefore the God of Israel stirred up against them the anger of Pul,† king of Assyria, and the anger of Tilgath-pilneser [*sic*], king of Assyria, who deported the Reubenites, the Gadites, and the half-tribe of Manasseh and brought them to Halah, Habor, and Hara, and to the river Gozan, where they have remained to this day.*

Levi†

27 The sons of Levi were Gershon, Kohath, and Merari.* 28 The sons of Kohath were Amram, Izhar, Hebron, and Uzziel.* 29 The children of Amram were Aaron, Moses, and Miriam. The sons of Aaron were Nadab, Abihu, Eleazar, and Ithamar.* 30 † Eleazar became the father of Phinehas. Phinehas became the father of Abishua. 31 Abishua became the father of Bukki. Bukki became the father of Uzzi. 32 Uzzi became the father of Zerahiah. Zerahiah became the father of Meraioth. 33 Meraioth became the father of Amariah. Amariah became the father of Ahitub. 34 Ahitub became the father of Zadok. Zadok became the father of Ahimaaz. 35 Ahimaaz became the father of Azariah. Azariah became the father of Johanan. 36 Johanan became the father of Azariah, who served as priest in the temple Solomon built in Jerusalem. 37 Azariah became the father of Amariah. Amariah became the father of Ahitub. 38 Ahitub became the father of Zadok. Zadok became the father of Shallum. 39 Shallum became the father of Hilkiah. Hilkiah became the father of Azariah. 40 Azariah became the father of Seraiah. Seraiah became the father of Jehozadak. 41 Jehozadak was one of those who went into the exile which the LORD inflicted on Judah and Jerusalem through Nebuchadnezzar.

6 1 The sons of Levi were Gershon, Kohath, and Merari.* 2 The sons of Gershon were named Libni and Shimei.* 3 The sons of Kohath were Amram, Izhar, Hebron, and Uzziel.* 4 The sons of Merari were Mahli and Mushi.*

These were the clans of Levi, according to their ancestors. 5 Of Gershon: his son Libni, whose son was Jahath, whose son was Zimmah, 6 whose son

---

† **5:26** *Pul*: the Chronicler seems to speak of two different kings here, but Pul was the name which the Assyrian king Tilgath-pileser III (745–727 B.C.) adopted as king of Babylon.

5:27–6:66 The tribe of Levi. The Chronicler's list gives special prominence to Levi's son Kohath, from whom were descended both the Aaronite priests (vv. 28–41) and the leading group of Temple singers (6:18–23).

5:30–41 The line of preexilic high priests. The list seems to become confused in vv. 36–38, which repeat the same names, mostly in inverse order, that occur in vv. 34–36. A similar but shorter list occurs, with variations, in Ezr 7:1–5.

* **5:10** Ps 83:6–7.
5:11 Jos 13:11, 24–28.
5:12 Gn 46:16.
5:19 1 Chr 1:31; 5:10; Gn 25:15; Ps 83:6–7.
5:20 Dt 33:20–21.
5:22 Nm 32:39; Dt 3:8–10; Jgs 3:3.
5:25 Ex 34:14–16; 2 Kgs 17:7.
5:26 2 Kgs 15:9, 29; 17:6.
5:27 1 Chr 6:1; 23:6; Gn 46:11; Ex 6:16; Nm 26:57.
5:28 1 Chr 6:3; Ex 6:18.
5:29 Ex 6:20; Nm 26:59–60.
6:1 1 Chr 5:27; 23:6; Gn 46:11; Ex 6:16; Nm 26:57.
6:2 Ex 6:17.
6:3 Ex 6:18; Nm 3:19; 26:59.
6:4 1 Chr 6:14; Ex 6:19; Nm 3:20; 26:58.

was Joah, whose son was Iddo, whose son was
Zerah, whose son was Jetherai.
7 The sons of Kohath: his son Amminadab,
whose son was Korah, whose son was Assir,
8 whose son was Elkanah, whose son was Ebi-
asaph, whose son was Assir, 9 whose son was
Tahath, whose son was Uriel, whose son was
Uzziah, whose son was Shaul. 10 The sons of El-
kanah were Amasai and Ahimoth, 11 whose son
was Elkanah, whose son was Zophai, whose son
was Nahath, 12 whose son was Eliab, whose
son was Jeroham, whose son was Elkanah, whose
son was Samuel. 13 The sons of Samuel were Joel,
the firstborn, and Abijah, the second.
14 The sons of Merari: Mahli, whose son was
Libni, whose son was Shimei, whose son was Uz-
zah,* 15 whose son was Shimea, whose son was
Haggiah, whose son was Asaiah.
16 The following were established by David for
the service of song† in the LORD's house at the
time when the ark had a resting place. 17 They
served as singers before the tabernacle of the tent
of meeting until Solomon built the house of the
LORD in Jerusalem, and they performed their ser-
vices according to the order prescribed for them.
18 Those who so performed are the following,
together with their sons.
Among the Kohathites: Heman, the chanter,
son of Joel, son of Samuel, 19 son of Elkanah,
son of Jeroham, son of Eliel, son of Toah, 20 son
of Zuph, son of Elkanah, son of Mahath, son of
Amasi, 21 son of Elkanah, son of Joel, son of Az-
ariah, son of Zephaniah, 22 son of Tahath, son of
Assir, son of Ebiasaph, son of Korah,* 23 son of
Izhar, son of Kohath, son of Levi, son of Israel.
24 His brother Asaph stood at his right hand.
Asaph was the son of Berechiah, son of Shimea,
25 son of Michael, son of Baaseiah, son of Malchi-
jah, 26 son of Ethni, son of Zerah, son of Adaiah,
27 son of Ethan, son of Zimmah,* son of Shimei,
28 son of Jahath, son of Gershon, son of Levi.
29 Their brothers, the Merarites, stood at the
left: Ethan, son of Kishi, son of Abdi, son of
Malluch, 30 son of Hashabiah, son of Amaziah,
son of Hilkiah, 31 son of Amzi, son of Bani, son
of Shemer, 32 son of Mahli, son of Mushi, son of
Merari, son of Levi.*
33 Their brother Levites were appointed to all
the other services of the tabernacle of the house
of God.* 34 However, it was Aaron and his sons
who made the sacrifice on the altar for burnt
offerings and on the altar of incense; they alone
had charge of the holy of holies and of making
atonement for Israel, as Moses, the servant of
God, had commanded.*
35 These were the sons of Aaron: his son Ele-
azar, whose son was Phinehas, whose son was
Abishua, 36 whose son was Bukki, whose son
was Uzzi, whose son was Zerahiah, 37 whose son
was Meraioth, whose son was Amariah, whose
son was Ahitub, 38 whose son was Zadok, whose
son was Ahimaaz.
39 † The following were their dwelling places,
by encampments in their territories. To the
sons of Aaron who belonged to the clan of the
Kohathites, since the lot fell to them, 40 was as-
signed Hebron in the land of Judah, with its
adjacent pasture lands. 41 However, the open
country and the villages belonging to the city
had been given to Caleb, the son of Jephunneh.
42 There were assigned to the sons of Aaron: He-
bron a city of refuge, Libnah with its pasture
lands, Jattir with its pasture lands, Eshtemoa
with its pasture lands, 43 Holon with its pasture
lands, Debir with its pasture lands, 44 Ashan with
its pasture lands, Jetta with its pasture lands, and
Beth-shemesh with its pasture lands. 45 Also from
the tribe of Benjamin: Gibeon with its pasture
lands, Geba with its pasture lands, Almon with
its pasture lands, Anathoth with its pasture lands.
In all, they had thirteen cities with their pasture
lands. 49 The Israelites assigned these cities with
their pasture lands to the Levites, 50 designating
them by name and assigning them by lot from
the tribes of the Judahites, Simeonites, and Ben-
jaminites.
46 The other Kohathites obtained ten cities by
lot for their clans from the tribe of Ephraim,
from the tribe of Dan, and from the half-tribe
of Manasseh. 47 The clans of the Gershonites ob-
tained thirteen cities from the tribes of Issachar,
Asher, and Naphtali, and from the half-tribe of
Manasseh in Bashan. 48 The clans of the Merarites
obtained twelve cities by lot from the tribes of
Reuben, Gad, and Zebulun.
51 The clans of the Kohathites obtained cities
by lot from the tribe of Ephraim. 52 They were as-
signed cities of refuge: Shechem in the mountain
region of Ephraim, with its pasture lands, Gezer
with its pasture lands, 53 Kibzaim with its pasture

---

† **6:16–32** The cultic functions performed by the levitical families in the postexilic Temple at the time of the Chronicler are here traced back to David, in a way analogous to that in which all the laws in the Pentateuch are attributed to Moses.

6:39–66 For the rights of the Levites in the cities assigned to them, see note on Jos 21:1.

* **6:14** 1 Chr 6:4; Ex 6:19; Nm 3:20; 26:58.
6:22 Ex 6:24.
6:27 1 Chr 6:2, 5.
6:32 Ex 6:19; Nm 26:58.
6:33 1 Chr 15:17, 19; 16:41–42; 2 Chr 5:12.
6:34 1 Chr 16:39–40.

lands, and Beth-horon with its pasture lands.
54 From the tribe of Dan: Elteke with its pasture
lands, Gibbethon with its pasture lands, Aijalon
with its pasture lands, and Gath-rimmon with its
pasture lands. 55 From the half-tribe of Manasseh:
Taanach with its pasture lands and Ibleam with
its pasture lands. These belonged to the rest of
the Kohathite clan.
56 The clans of the Gershonites received from
the half-tribe of Manasseh: Golan in Bashan with
its pasture lands and Ashtaroth with its pasture
lands. 57 From the tribe of Issachar: Kedesh with
its pasture lands, Daberath with its pasture lands,
58 Ramoth with its pasture lands, and Engannim
with its pasture lands. 59 From the tribe of Asher:
Mashal with its pasture lands, Abdon with its
pasture lands, 60 Hilkath with its pasture lands,
and Rehob with its pasture lands. 61 From the
tribe of Naphtali: Kedesh in Galilee with its pas-
ture lands, Hammon with its pasture lands, and
Kiriathaim with its pasture lands.
62 The rest of the Merarites received from the
tribe of Zebulun: Jokneam with its pasture lands,
Kartah with its pasture lands, Rimmon with its
pasture lands, and Tabor with its pasture lands.
63 Across the Jordan at Jericho (that is, east of the
Jordan) they received from the tribe of Reuben:
Bezer in the desert with its pasture lands, Jahzah
with its pasture lands, 64 Kedemoth with its pas-
ture lands, and Mephaath with its pasture lands.
65 From the tribe of Gad: Ramoth in Gilead with
its pasture lands, Mahanaim with its pasture
lands, 66 Heshbon with its pasture lands, and Ja-
zer with its pasture lands.

Issachar

7 1 † The sons of Issachar were Tola, Puah, Ja-
shub, and Shimron: four.* 2 The sons of Tola
were Uzzi, Rephaiah, Jeriel, Jahmai, Ibsam, and
Shemuel, heads of the ancestral houses of Tola,
mighty warriors in their generations. In the time
of David they numbered twenty-two thousand six
hundred.* 3 The sons of Uzzi: Izarahiah. The sons
of Izarahiah were Michael, Obadiah, Joel, and
Isshiah. All five of these were chiefs. 4 Along with
them, in their generations, according to ancestral
houses, were thirty-six thousand men in organized
military troops, since they had more wives and
children 5 than their fellow tribesmen. In all the
clans of Issachar there was a total of eighty-seven
thousand warriors listed in their family records.

Benjamin

6 The sons of Benjamin were Bela, Becher, and
Jediael—three.* 7 The sons of Bela were Ezbon,
Uzzi, Uzziel, Jerimoth, and Iri—five. They were
heads of their ancestral houses and warriors.
Their family records listed twenty-two thousand
and thirty-four. 8 The sons of Becher were Zemi-
rah, Joash, Eliezer, Elioenai, Omri, Jeremoth,
Abijah, Anathoth, and Alemeth—all these were
sons of Becher.* 9 Their family records listed
twenty thousand two hundred of their kindred
who were heads of their ancestral houses and
warriors. 10 The sons of Jediael: Bilhan. The sons
of Bilhan were Jeush, Benjamin, Ehud, Chenaa-
nah, Zethan, Tarshish, and Ahishahar. 11 All these
were sons of Jediael, heads of ancestral houses
and warriors. They numbered seventeen thou-
sand two hundred men fit for military service
. . .† 12 Shupham and Hupham.*

Dan, Naphtali and Manasseh

The sons of Dan: Hushim. 13 The sons of Naph-
tali were Jahziel, Guni, Jezer, and Shallum. These
were sons of Bilhah.* 14 The sons of Manasseh,
whom his Aramean concubine bore:* she bore
Machir, the father of Gilead.* 15 Machir took a wife
whose name was Maacah; his sister's name was
Molecheth. Manasseh's second son was named
Zelophehad, who had only daughters.* 16 Maacah,
Machir's wife, bore a son whom she named Peresh.
He had a brother named Sheresh, whose sons were
Ulam and Rakem. 17 The sons of Ulam: Bedan.
These were the sons of Gilead, the son of Machir,
the son of Manasseh. 18 His sister Molecheth bore
Ishhod, Abiezer, and Mahlah. 19 The sons of She-
mida were Ahian, Shechem, Likhi, and Aniam.

Ephraim

20 * The sons of Ephraim: Shuthelah, whose son
was Bered, whose son was Tahath, whose son
was Eleadah, whose son was Tahath, 21 whose
son was Zabad. Ephraim's son Shuthelah, and
Ezer and Elead, who were born in the land, were
killed by the inhabitants of Gath because they
had gone down to take away their livestock.
22 Their father Ephraim mourned a long time,
but after his relatives had come and comforted
him, 23 he had relations with his wife, who con-
ceived and bore a son whom he named Beriah,
since evil† had befallen his house.* 24 He had a

---

†

7:1–40 The seven northern tribes.
7:11 The Hebrew text appears to be defective.
7:23 *Beriah . . . evil*: the name sounds like the Hebrew word for "evil," with the preposition *be*.

*

7:1 Gn 46:13.
7:2 Nm 26:23–24; Jgs 10:1.
7:6 Gn 46:21; Nm 26:38.
7:8 Gn 46:21.
7:12 Nm 26:39.
7:12–13 Gn 46:24; Nm 26:48–49.
7:14–19 Nm 26:29–32.
7:14 Nm 26:29; Jos 17:1.
7:15 Nm 26:33; Jos 17:3.
7:20 Nm 26:35.
7:23 1 Chr 8:13.

daughter, Sheerah, who built Lower and Upper Beth-horon and Uzzen-sheerah. 25 Zabad's son was Rephah, whose son was Resheph, whose son was Telah, whose son was Tahan, 26 whose son was Ladan, whose son was Ammihud, whose son was Elishama,* 27 whose son was Nun, whose son was Joshua.

28 Their property and their dwellings were in Bethel and its towns, Naaran to the east, Gezer and its towns to the west, and also Shechem and its towns as far as Ayyah and its towns.* 29 Manasseh, however, had possession of Beth-shean and its towns, Taanach and its towns, Megiddo and its towns, and Dor and its towns. In these dwelt the sons of Joseph, the son of Israel.*

Asher

30 The sons of Asher were Imnah, Ishvah, Ishvi, and Beriah; their sister was Serah.* 31 Beriah's sons were Heber and Malchiel, who was the father of Birzaith. 32 Heber became the father of Japhlet, Shomer, Hotham, and their sister Shua. 33 The sons of Japhlet were Pasach, Bimhal, and Ashvath; these were the sons of Japhlet. 34 The sons of Shomer were Ahi, Rohgah, Jehubbah, and Aram. 35 The sons of his brother Hotham were Zophah, Imna, Shelesh, and Amal. 36 The sons of Zophah were Suah, Harnepher, Shual, Beri, Imrah, 37 Bezer, Hod, Shamma, Shilshah, Ithran, and Beera. 38 The sons of Jether were Jephunneh, Pispa, and Ara. 39 The sons of Ulla were Arah, Hanniel, and Rizia. 40 All these were sons of Asher, heads of ancestral houses, distinguished men, warriors, and chiefs among the princes. Their family records numbered twenty-six thousand men fit for military service.

Benjamin

8 1 † Benjamin became the father of Bela, his firstborn, Ashbel, the second son, Aharah, the third,* 2 Nohah, the fourth, and Rapha, the fifth. 3 The sons of Bela were Addar and Gera, the father of Ehud. 4 The sons of Ehud were Abishua, Naaman, Ahoah,* 5 Gera, Shephuphan, and Huram. 6 These were the sons of Ehud, family heads over those who dwelt in Geba and were deported to Manahath. 7 Also Naaman, Ahijah, and Gera. The last, who led them into exile, became the father of Uzza and Ahihud. 8 Shaharaim became a father on the Moabite plateau after he had put away his wives Hushim and Baara. 9 By his wife Hodesh he begot Jobab, Zibia, Mesha, Malcam, 10 Jeuz, Sachia, and Mirmah. These were his sons, family heads. 11 By Hushim he begot Abitub and Elpaal. 12 The sons of Elpaal were Eber, Misham, Shemed (who built Ono and Lod with its nearby towns),* 13 and Beriah, and Shema. They were family heads of those who dwelt in Aijalon, and they put the inhabitants of Gath to flight. 14 Their relatives were Elpaal, Shashak, and Jeremoth. 15 Zebadiah, Arad, Eder, 16 Michael, Ishpah, and Joha were the sons of Beriah. 17 Zebadiah, Meshullam, Hizki, Heber, 18 Ishmerai, Izliah, and Jobab were the sons of Elpaal. 19 Jakim, Zichri, Zabdi, 20 Elienai, Zillethai, Eliel, 21 Adaiah, Beraiah, and Shimrath were the sons of Shimei. 22 Ishpan, Eber, Eliel, 23 Abdon, Zichri, Hanan, 24 Hananiah, Elam, Anthothijah, 25 Iphdeiah, and Penuel were the sons of Shashak. 26 Shamsherai, Shehariah, Athaliah, 27 Jaareshiah, Elijah, and Zichri were the sons of Jeroham. 28 These were family heads in their generations, chiefs who dwelt in Jerusalem.

29 * In Gibeon dwelt Jeiel, the founder of Gibeon, whose wife's name was Maacah; 30 also his firstborn son, Abdon, and Zur, Kish, Baal, Ner, Nadab, 31 Gedor, Ahio, Zecher, and Mikloth. 32 Mikloth became the father of Shimeah. These, too, dwelt with their relatives in Jerusalem, opposite their fellow tribesmen. 33 * Ner became the father of Kish, and Kish became the father of Saul. Saul became the father of Jonathan, Malchishua, Abinadab, and Eshbaal.* 34 The son of Jonathan was Meribbaal, and Meribbaal became the father of Micah.* 35 The sons of Micah were Pithon, Melech, Tarea, and Ahaz. 36 Ahaz became the father of Jehoaddah, and Jehoaddah became the father of Alemeth, Azmaveth, and Zimri. Zimri became the father of Moza.* 37 Moza became the father of Binea, whose son was Raphah, whose son was Eleasah, whose son was Azel. 38 Azel had six sons, whose names were Azrikam, his firstborn, Ishmael, Sheariah, Azariah, Obadiah, and Hanan; all these were the sons of Azel.* 39 The sons of Eshek, his brother, were Ulam, his firstborn, Jeush, the second son, and Eliphelet, the third. 40 The sons of Ulam were warriors, skilled with the bow, and they had many sons and grandsons: one hundred and fifty. All these were the sons of Benjamin.

† **8:1–40** A second, variant list (cf. 7:6–11) of the Benjaminites, highlighting the family of Saul (vv. 33–40).

7:26 Nm 1:10; 2:18; 7:48; 10:22.
7:28 Gn 12:8; 1 Kgs 9:16.
7:29 Jos 17:11.
7:30 Gn 46:17; Nm 26:44–46.
8:1 1 Chr 7:6; Gn 46:21; Nm 26:38–44.
8:4 Jgs 3:15.
8:12 Neh 11:35.
8:29–32 1 Chr 9:35–38.
8:33–38 1 Chr 9:39–44.
8:33 1 Chr 10:2; 1 Sm 9:1; 14:49, 51; 31:2.
8:34 2 Sm 4:4; 9:6; 10:12.
8:36 1 Chr 9:42.
8:38 1 Chr 9:43.

9 1 Thus all Israel was listed in family lists, and
these are recorded in the book of the kings
of Israel.*
Now Judah had been exiled to Babylon be-
cause of its treachery. 2 † * The first to settle
again in their cities and dwell there were certain
Israelites, the priests, the Levites, and the temple
servants.*

Jerusalemites

3 In Jerusalem lived Judahites and Benjamin-
ites; also Ephraimites and Manassites. 4 Among
the Judahites was Uthai, son of Ammihud, son of
Omri, son of Imri, son of Bani, one of the sons of
Perez, son of Judah. 5 Among the Shelanites were
Asaiah, the firstborn, and his sons. 6 Among the
Zerahites were Jeuel and six hundred and ninety
of their relatives. 7 Among the Benjaminites were
Sallu, son of Meshullam, son of Hodaviah, son
of Hassenuah, 8 as well as Ibneiah, son of Jero-
ham; Elah, son of Uzzi, son of Michri; Meshul-
lam, son of Shephatiah, son of Reuel, son of
Ibnijah. 9 Their kindred of various families were
nine hundred and fifty-six. All those named were
heads of their ancestral houses.
10 Among the priests were Jedaiah; Jehoiarib;
Jachin; 11 Azariah, son of Hilkiah, son of Me-
shullam, son of Zadok, son of Meraioth, son of
Ahitub, the ruler of the house of God; 12 Adaiah,
son of Jeroham, son of Pashhur, son of Malchi-
jah; Maasai, son of Adiel, son of Jahzerah, son of
Meshullam, son of Meshillemith, son of Immer.
13 Their brothers, heads of their ancestral houses,
were one thousand seven hundred and sixty,
valiant in the work of the service of the house
of God.
14 Among the Levites were Shemaiah, son of
Hasshub, son of Azrikam, son of Hashabiah,
one of the sons of Merari; 15 Bakbakkar; Heresh;
Galal; Mattaniah, son of Mica, son of Zichri, a
descendant of Asaph; 16 Obadiah, son of Shema-
iah, son of Galal, a descendant of Jeduthun; and
Berechiah, son of Asa, son of Elkanah, whose
family lived in the villages of the Netophathites.
17 The gatekeepers were Shallum, Akkub, Tal-
mon, Ahiman, and their brothers; Shallum was
the chief. 18 Previously they had stood guard at
the king's gate on the east side; now they be-
came gatekeepers for the encampments of the
Levites. 19 Shallum, son of Kore, son of Ebiasaph,
a descendant of Korah, and his brothers of the
same ancestral house of the Korahites had as
their assigned task the guarding of the threshold
of the tent, just as their fathers had guarded the
entrance to the encampment of the LORD. 20 Phin-
ehas, son of Eleazar, had been their chief in times
past; the LORD was with him.* 21 Zechariah, son
of Meshelemiah, guarded the gate of the tent of
meeting.* 22 In all, those who were chosen for
gatekeepers at the threshold were two hundred
and twelve. They were inscribed in the family re-
cords of their villages. David and Samuel the seer
had established them in their position of trust.
23 Thus they and their sons kept guard over the
gates of the house of the LORD, the house which
was then a tent. 24 The gatekeepers were stationed
at the four sides, to the east, the west, the north,
and the south.* 25 Their brothers who lived in
their own villages took turns in assisting them
for seven-day periods,* 26 while the four chief
gatekeepers were on permanent duty. These were
the Levites who also had charge of the chambers
and treasures of the house of God. 27 They would
spend the night near the house of God, for it was
in their charge and they had the duty of opening
it each morning.
28 Some of them had charge of the vessels used
there, tallying them as they were brought in and
taken out. 29 Others were appointed to take care
of the utensils and all the sacred vessels, as well
as the fine flour, the wine, the oil, the frankin-
cense, and the spices. 30 It was the sons of priests,
however, who mixed the spiced ointments.*
31 * Mattithiah, one of the Levites, the firstborn
of Shallum the Korahite, was entrusted with pre-
paring the cakes. 32 Benaiah the Kohathite, one
of their brothers, was in charge of setting out the
showbread each sabbath.*
33 These were the singers and the gatekeepers,
family heads over the Levites. They stayed in the
chambers when free of duty, for day and night
they had to be ready for service. 34 These were the
levitical family heads by their generations, chiefs
who dwelt in Jerusalem.

II. The History of David

Genealogy of Saul

35 * Jeiel, the founder of Gibeon, dwelt in Gib-
eon; his wife's name was Maacah. 36 His firstborn

† **9:2–34** The inhabitants of Jerusalem after the exile. A similar list, though with many variants in the names, occurs in Neh 11:3–24.

* **9:1** 2 Chr 16:11; 20:34; 25:26; 27:7; 33:18; 36:8.
9:2–34 Neh 11:3–24.
9:2 Ezr 2:70; 7:7; Neh 11:3.
9:20 Ex 6:25; Nm 25:7, 11; Jgs 20:28.
9:21 1 Chr 26:2, 14.
9:24 1 Chr 26:13.
9:25 2 Chr 23:4–5.
9:30 Ex 30:20–33.
9:31–32 1 Chr 23:29; Lv 2:1–15; 6:13–16; 7:11.
9:32 Ex 25:30; Lv 24:5–8.
9:35–44 1 Chr 8:29–38.

son was Abdon; then came Zur, Kish, Baal, Ner,
Nadab, [37] Gedor, Ahio, Zechariah, and Mikloth.
[38] Mikloth became the father of Shimeam. These,
too, with their relatives, dwelt opposite their rel-
atives in Jerusalem. [39] Ner became the father of
Kish, and Kish became the father of Saul. Saul
became the father of Jonathan, Malchishua,
Abinadab, and Eshbaal. [40] The son of Jonathan
was Meribbaal, and Meribbaal became the father
of Micah. [41] The sons of Micah were Pithon, Me-
lech, Tahrea, and Ahaz. [42] Ahaz became the father
of Jehoaddah, and Jehoaddah became the father
of Alemeth, Azmaveth, and Zimri. Zimri became
the father of Moza. [43] Moza became the father of
Binea, whose son was Rephaiah, whose son was
Eleasah, whose son was Azel. [44] Azel had six sons,
whose names were Azrikam, his firstborn, Ish-
mael, Sheariah, Azariah, Obadiah, and Hanan;
these were the sons of Azel.

Death of Saul and His Sons

10 [1] * Now the Philistines went to war against
Israel, and Israel fled before them, and
they fell, slain on Mount Gilboa. [2] The Philistines
pressed hard after Saul and his sons. When the
Philistines had struck down Jonathan, Abinadab,
and Malchishua, sons of Saul, [3] the fury of the
battle converged on Saul. Then the archers hit
him, and he was severely wounded.
[4] Saul said to his armor-bearer, "Draw your
sword and run me through; otherwise these un-
circumcised will come and abuse me." But the
armor-bearer, badly frightened, refused, so Saul
took his own sword and fell upon it. [5] When
the armor-bearer saw that Saul was dead, he too
fell upon his sword and died. [6] Thus Saul, and
his three sons, his whole house, died together.
[7] When all the Israelites in the valley saw that
Saul and his sons had fled and that they had
died, they abandoned their cities and fled. Then
the Philistines came and lived in those cities.
[8] On the following day, when the Philistines
came to strip the slain, they found Saul and his
sons fallen on Mount Gilboa. [9] They stripped
him, and took his head and his armor; these
they sent throughout the land of the Philistines
to bring the good news to their idols and to the
people. [10] They put his armor in the temple of
their gods, but his skull they impaled at the tem-
ple of Dagon.

Burial of Saul

[11] When all the inhabitants of Jabesh-gilead
heard all that the Philistines had done to Saul,
[12] all their warriors set out, recovered the corpses
of Saul and his sons, and brought them to Ja-
besh. They buried their bones under the oak of
Jabesh, and fasted for seven days.*
[13] † Thus Saul died because of his treason
against the LORD in disobeying his word, and also
because he had sought counsel from a ghost,*
[14] rather than from the LORD. Therefore the LORD
took his life, and turned his kingdom over to Da-
vid, the son of Jesse.*

David Is Made King

11 [1] * Then all Israel gathered around David
in Hebron, and they said: "Look! We are
your bone and your flesh. [2] In days past, when
Saul was still the king, it was you who led Is-
rael in all its battles. And now the LORD, your
God, has said to you: You shall shepherd my
people Israel; you shall be ruler over my people
Israel."* [3] Then all the elders of Israel came to
the king at Hebron, and at Hebron David made
a covenant with them in the presence of the
LORD; and they anointed David king over Israel,
in accordance with the word of the LORD given
through Samuel.*

Jerusalem Captured

[4] Then David and all Israel went to Jerusalem,
that is, Jebus, where the inhabitants of the land
were called Jebusites.* [5] The inhabitants of Jebus
said to David, "You shall not enter here." David
nevertheless captured the fortress of Zion, which
is the City of David. [6] David said, "Whoever
strikes the Jebusites first shall be made chief and
captain." Joab, the son of Zeruiah, was the first
to attack; and so he became chief.* [7] David took
up residence in the fortress, which therefore was
called the City of David. [8] He built up the city
on all sides, from the Millo all the way around,
while Joab restored the rest of the city.* [9] David
became ever more powerful, for the LORD of hosts
was with him.

David's Warriors

[10] * These were David's chief warriors who,
together with all Israel, supported him in his

1 CHR

---

† **10:13–14** The Chronicler explains why Saul met his tragic end: he had disobeyed the Lord's command given through the prophet Samuel (1 Sm 15:3–9), and had consulted a necromancer (1 Sm 28:6–19), contrary to the Mosaic law (Dt 18:10–11).

---

* **10:1–12** 1 Sm 31:1–13.
10:12 2 Sm 2:5.
10:13 Dt 18:10–14; 1 Sm 13:13–14; 15:3, 11, 26.
10:14 1 Sm 15:28; 2 Sm 3:9–10.
11:1–9 2 Sm 5:1–10.
11:2 1 Sm 18:5, 13–16, 30; 19:8.
11:3 1 Sm 16:1, 13; 2 Sm 2:4.
11:4 Jos 15:8; Jgs 1:21; 19:10–11.
11:6 2 Sm 8:16.
11:8 1 Kgs 9:15, 24; 11:27; 2 Chr 32:5.
11:10–41 2 Sm 23:8–39.

reign in order to make him king, according to the LORD's word concerning Israel.

11 Here is the list of David's warriors:

Ishbaal, the son of Hachamoni, chief of the Three.† He brandished his spear over three hundred, whom he had slain in a single encounter.

12 Next to him was Eleazar, the son of Dodo the Ahohite, one of the Three warriors.* 13 He was with David at Pas-dammim, where the Philistines had massed for battle. There was a plot of land full of barley. The people were fleeing before the Philistines,* 14 but he took his stand in the middle of the plot, kept it safe, and cut down the Philistines. Thus the LORD brought about a great victory.

15 Three of the Thirty chiefs went down to the rock, to David, who was in the cave of Adullam while the Philistines were encamped in the valley of Rephaim.* 16 David was then in the stronghold, and a Philistine garrison was at Bethlehem. 17 David had a strong craving, and said, "If only someone would give me a drink of water from the cistern by the gate of Bethlehem!" 18 Thereupon the Three broke through the encampment of the Philistines, drew water from the cistern by the gate of Bethlehem, and carried it back to David. But David refused to drink it. Instead, he poured it out† to the LORD, 19 saying, "God forbid that I should do such a thing! Could I drink the blood of these men who risked their lives? For at the risk of their lives they brought it." So he refused to drink it. Such deeds as these the Three warriors performed.

20 * Abishai, the brother of Joab, was the chief of the Thirty;† he brandished his spear over three hundred, whom he had slain. He made a name beside the Three,* 21 but was twice as famous as any of the Thirty, becoming their leader. However, he did not attain to the Three.

22 Benaiah, son of Jehoiada, a valiant man of mighty deeds, from Kabzeel, killed the two sons of Ariel of Moab. Also, he went down and killed the lion in the cistern on a snowy day. 23 He likewise slew the Egyptian, a huge man five cubits tall. The Egyptian carried a spear that was like a weaver's beam, but Benaiah came against him with a staff; he wrested the spear from the Egyptian's hand, and killed him with that spear. 24 Such deeds as these Benaiah, the son of Jehoiada, performed, and he made a name beside the Three warriors, 25 but was more famous than any of the Thirty. However, he did not attain to the Three. David put him in charge of his bodyguard.*

26 Also these warriors: Asahel, the brother of Joab; Elhanan, son of Dodo, from Bethlehem;* 27 Shammoth, from En-harod; Helez, from Beth-pelet; 28 Ira, son of Ikkesh, from Tekoa; Abiezer, from Anathoth; 29 Sibbecai, from Husha; Ilai, from Ahoh;* 30 Maharai, from Netophah; Heled, son of Baanah, from Netophah;* 31 Ithai, son of Ribai, from Gibeah of Benjamin; Benaiah, from Pirathon;* 32 Hurai, from Nahale-gaash; Abiel, from Beth-arabah; 33 Azmaveth, from Bahurim; Eliahba, from Shaalbon; 34 Jashen the Gunite; Jonathan, son of Shagee the Hararite; 35 Ahiam, son of Sachar the Hararite; Elipheleth, son of 36 Ahasbai, from Beth-maacah; Ahijah, from Gilo; 37 Hezro, from Carmel; Naarai, the son of Ezbai; 38 Joel, brother of Nathan, from Rehob, the Gadite; 39 Zelek the Ammonite; Naharai, from Beeroth, the armor-bearer of Joab, son of Zeruiah; 40 Ira, from Jattir; Gareb, from Jattir; 41 Uriah the Hittite; Zabad, son of Ahlai, 42 and, in addition to the Thirty, Adina, son of Shiza, the Reubenite, chief of the tribe of Reuben; 43 Hanan, son of Maacah; Joshaphat the Mithnite; 44 Uzzia, the Ashterathite; Shama and Jeiel, sons of Hotham, from Aroer; 45 Jediael, son of Shimri, and Joha, his brother, the Tizite; 46 Eliel the Mahavite; Jeribai and Joshaviah, sons of Elnaam; Ithmah, from Moab; 47 Eliel, Obed, and Jaasiel the Mezobian.

David's Early Followers

12 1 The following men came to David in Ziklag while he was still under banishment from Saul, son of Kish; they, too, were among the warriors who helped him in his battles.* 2 They were archers who could use either the right or the left hand, both in slinging stones and in shooting arrows with the bow. They were some of Saul's kinsmen, from Benjamin. 3 Ahiezer was their chief, along with Joash, both sons of Shemaah of Gibeah; also Jeziel and Pelet, sons of Azmaveth; Beracah; Jehu, from Anathoth;* 4 Ishmaiah the Gibeonite, a warrior among the Thirty, and over the Thirty; 5 Jeremiah; Jahaziel; Johanan; Jozabad from Gederah; 6 Eluzai; Jerimoth; Bealiah;

11:11 *The Three*: the Chronicler actually names only two of these figures, Ishbaal and Eleazar. According to 2 Sm 23:11, the third member of the Three was Shammah.

11:18 *Poured it out*: as a libation.

11:20 *The Thirty*: they are listed by name in vv. 26–47. The parallel list in 2 Sm 23:8–39 often differs in names and spellings; for the numbers, see note on 2 Sm 23:8–39.

11:12 1 Chr 27:4.
11:13 1 Sm 17:1.
11:15 1 Chr 14:9; 2 Sm 5:18, 22.
11:20–21 2 Sm 23:18–19.
11:20 1 Chr 18:12; 1 Sm 26:6–10; 2 Sm 16:9; 18:2; 21:17.
11:25 2 Sm 8:18; 20:23.
11:26 1 Chr 2:16; 27:7.
11:29 1 Chr 27:11.
11:30 1 Chr 27:13.
11:31 1 Chr 27:14.
12:1 1 Sm 27:1–7.
12:3 1 Chr 27:12.

Shemariah; Shephatiah the Haruphite; 7 Elkanah,
Isshiah, Azarel, Joezer, and Jashobeam, who were
Korahites; 8 Joelah and Zebadiah, sons of Jero-
ham, from Gedor.
9 Some of the Gadites also went over to David
when he was at the stronghold in the wilderness.
They were valiant warriors, experienced soldiers
equipped with shield and spear, fearsome as li-
ons, swift as gazelles on the mountains.* 10 Ezer
was their chief, Obadiah was second, Eliab third,
11 Mishmannah fourth, Jeremiah fifth, 12 Attai
sixth, Eliel seventh, 13 Johanan eighth, Elzabad
ninth, 14 Jeremiah tenth, and Machbannai elev-
enth. 15 These Gadites were army commanders,
the lesser over hundreds and the greater over
thousands. 16 It was they who crossed over the
Jordan in the first month, when it was overflow-
ing both its banks, and chased away all who were
in the valleys to the east and to the west.
17 Some Benjaminites and Judahites also came
to David at the stronghold. 18 David went out to
meet them and addressed them in these words:
"If you come peacefully, to help me, I am of a
mind to have you join me. But if you have come
to betray me to my enemies though my hands
have done no wrong, may the God of our ances-
tors see and punish you."
19 Then a spirit clothed Amasai, the chief of the
Thirty, and he answered David:

"We are yours, O David,
  we are with you, son of Jesse.
Peace, peace to you,
  and peace to him who helps you;
  may your God be your helper!"

So David received them and placed them among
the leaders of his troops.
20 Men from Manasseh also deserted to Da-
vid when he came with the Philistines to battle
against Saul. However, he did not help the Phi-
listines, for their lords took counsel and sent him
home, saying, "At the cost of our heads he will
desert to his master Saul." 21 As he was returning
to Ziklag, therefore, these deserted to him from
Manasseh: Adnah, Jozabad, Jediael, Michael, Joz-
abad, Elihu, and Zillethai, chiefs of thousands
of Manasseh.† 22 They helped David by taking
charge of his troops, for they were all warriors
and became commanders of his army. 23 And
from day to day men kept coming to David's
help until there was a vast encampment, like
God's own encampment.

The Assembly at Hebron

24 This is the muster of the detachments of
armed troops that came to David at Hebron to
bring Saul's kingdom over to him, as the LORD
had ordained. 25 † Judahites bearing shields and
spears: six thousand eight hundred armed troops.
26 Of the Simeonites, warriors fit for battle: seven
thousand one hundred. 27 Of the Levites: four
thousand six hundred, 28 along with Jehoiada,
leader of the line of Aaron, with another three
thousand seven hundred, 29 and Zadok, a young
warrior, with twenty-two princes of his father's
house. 30 Of the Benjaminites, the kinsmen of
Saul: three thousand—until this time, most of
them had kept their allegiance to the house
of Saul. 31 Of the Ephraimites: twenty thousand
eight hundred warriors, men renowned in their
ancestral houses. 32 Of the half-tribe of Manasseh:
eighteen thousand, designated by name to come
and make David king. 33 Of the Issacharites, their
chiefs who were endowed with an understanding
of the times and who knew what Israel had to
do: two hundred chiefs, together with all their
kinsmen under their command. 34 From Zebulun,
men fit for military service, set in battle array with
every kind of weapon for war: fifty thousand men
rallying with a single purpose. 35 From Naphtali:
one thousand captains, and with them, armed
with shield and lance, thirty-seven thousand
men. 36 Of the Danites, set in battle array: twenty-
eight thousand six hundred. 37 From Asher, fit for
military service and set in battle array: forty thou-
sand. 38 From the other side of the Jordan, of the
Reubenites, Gadites, and the half-tribe of Manas-
seh, men equipped with every kind of weapon of
war: one hundred and twenty thousand.
39 All these soldiers, drawn up in battle order,
came to Hebron with the resolute intention of
making David king over all Israel. The rest of
Israel was likewise of one mind to make Da-
vid king. 40 They remained with David for three
days, eating and drinking, for their relatives had
prepared for them. 41 Moreover, their neighbors
from as far as Issachar, Zebulun, and Naphtali
came bringing food on donkeys, camels, mules,
and oxen—provisions in great quantity of meal,
pressed figs, raisins, wine, oil, oxen, and sheep.
For there was rejoicing in Israel.

†

12:21 See note on 27:1–15.

12:25–38 The Chronicler here takes the brief account of David's installation as king in 2 Sm 5:1–3 (= 1 Chr 11:1–3) and expands it in line with his exaltation of David and his dynasty.

*

12:9 Dt 33:20.

Transfer of the Ark

13 1 * After David had taken counsel with his
commanders of thousands and of hun-
dreds, that is, with every leader, 2 he said to the
whole assembly of Israel: "If it seems good to
you, and is so decreed by the LORD our God, let
us send to the rest of our kindred from all the dis-
tricts of Israel, and also the priests and the Levites
from their cities with pasture lands, that they may
join us;* 3 and let us bring the ark of our God here
among us, for in the days of Saul we did not con-
sult it." 4 And the whole assembly agreed to do it,
for it seemed right in the eyes of all the people.
5 Then David assembled all Israel, from Shihor
of Egypt† to Lebo-hamath, to bring the ark of
God from Kiriath-jearim.* 6 David and all Israel
went up to Baalah, that is, to Kiriath-jearim, of
Judah, to bring up from there the ark of God,
which was known by the name "LORD enthroned
upon the cherubim."* 7 They transported the ark
of God on a new cart from the house of Abin-
adab; Uzzah and Ahio were guiding the cart,
8 while David and all Israel danced before God
with all their might, with singing, and with lyres,
harps, tambourines, cymbals, and trumpets.
9 As they reached the threshing floor of Chi-
don,† Uzzah stretched out his hand to steady
the ark, for the oxen were tipping it. 10 Then the
LORD became angry with Uzzah and struck him,
because he had laid his hand on the ark; he died
there in God's presence. 11 David was angry be-
cause the LORD's anger had broken out against
Uzzah. Therefore that place has been called
Perez-uzzah† even to this day.
12 David was afraid of God that day, and he
said, "How can I bring in the ark of God to me?"
13 Therefore he did not take the ark with him
into the City of David, but deposited it instead
at the house of Obed-edom the Gittite. 14 The ark
of God remained in the house of Obed-edom
with his family for three months, and the LORD
blessed Obed-edom's household and all that he
possessed.*

David in Jerusalem

14 1 * Hiram, king of Tyre, sent envoys to Da-
vid along with cedar wood, and masons
and carpenters to build him a house.† * 2 David
now knew† that the LORD had truly established
him as king over Israel, for his kingdom was
greatly exalted for the sake of his people Israel.
3 David took other wives in Jerusalem and be-
came the father of more sons and daughters.
4 These are the names of those who were born
to him in Jerusalem: Shammua, Shobab, Na-
than, Solomon, 5 Ibhar, Elishua, Elpelet, 6 No-
gah, Nepheg, Japhia, 7 Elishama, Beeliada, and
Eliphelet.*

The Philistine Wars

8 When the Philistines had heard that David
was anointed king over all Israel, they marched
out in force looking for him. But when David
heard of this, he went out against them. 9 Mean-
while the Philistines had come and raided the
valley of Rephaim.* 10 David inquired of God,
"Shall I attack the Philistines, and will you de-
liver them into my power?" The LORD answered
him, "Attack, for I have delivered them into your
power." 11 So they attacked, at Baal-perazim, and
David defeated them there. Then David said, "By
my hand God has broken through my enemies
just as water breaks through a dam." Therefore
that place was called Baal-perazim.† 12 The Phi-
listines abandoned their gods there, and David
ordered them to be burnt.*
13 Once again the Philistines raided the valley,
14 and again David inquired of God. But God
answered him: Do not try to pursue them, but
go around them and come against them near
the balsam trees. 15 When you hear the sound of
marching in the tops of the balsam trees, then go
forth to battle, for God has already gone before
you to strike the army of the Philistines. 16 David
did as God commanded him, and they routed
the Philistine army from Gibeon to Gezer.
17 Thus David's fame was spread abroad
through every land, and the LORD put the fear of
him on all the nations.

Preparations for Moving the Ark

15 1 David built houses for himself in the City
of David and prepared a place for the ark
of God, pitching a tent for it there. 2 At that time
he said, "No one may carry the ark of God except

1 CHR

†

13:5 *Shihor of Egypt*: the eastern branch of the Nile delta. *Lebo-hamath*: in southern Syria.

13:9 *Chidon*: in 2 Sm 6:6 the name is Nodan (variant: Nacon).

13:11 *Perez-uzzah*: this Hebrew phrase means "the breaking out against Uzza."

14:1 The Chronicler's account of David's establishment as king and his victories over the Philistines follows 2 Sm 5:11–25, but makes David's rule even more prominent.

14:2 *David now knew*: see note on 2 Sm 5:12.

14:11 See note on 2 Sm 5:20.

*

13:1–14 2 Sm 6:1–11.
13:2 Nm 35:1–8; Jos 14:4; 21:2–42.
13:5 1 Chr 15:3; Jos 13:3, 5; 1 Sm 6:21; 7:1–2; 2 Sm 6:1–11.
13:6 Jos 15:9; 18:14; 1 Sm 4:4; 7:1.
13:14 1 Chr 26:4–5.
14:1–16 2 Sm 5:11–25.
14:1 2 Sm 5:11; 2 Chr 2:4.
14:3–7 1 Chr 3:5–8; 2 Sm 5:13–16.
14:9 1 Chr 11:15.
14:12 Dt 7:5, 25.

the Levites, for the LORD chose them to carry the
ark of the LORD and to minister to him forever."*
3 Then David assembled all Israel to Jerusalem to
bring up the ark of the LORD to its place, which
he had prepared for it.* 4 David also convened
the sons of Aaron and the Levites: 5 of the sons of
Kohath, Uriel, their chief, and one hundred and
twenty of his brothers; 6 of the sons of Merari,
Asaiah, their chief, and two hundred and twenty
of his brothers; 7 of the sons of Gershon, Joel,
their chief, and one hundred and thirty of his
brothers; 8 of the sons of Elizaphan, Shemaiah,
their chief, and two hundred of his brothers; 9 of
the sons of Hebron, Eliel, their chief, and eighty
of his brothers; 10 of the sons of Uzziel, Ammin-
adab, their chief, and one hundred and twelve of
his brothers.
11 David summoned the priests Zadok and
Abiathar, and the Levites Uriel, Asaiah, Joel, She-
maiah, Eliel, and Amminadab,* 12 and said to
them: "You heads of the levitical houses, sanc-
tify yourselves along with your brothers to bring
up the ark of the LORD, the God of Israel, to the
place which I have prepared for it.* 13 Because
you were not with us the first time, the LORD our
God broke out against us, for we did not seek
him aright."* 14 Accordingly, the priests and the
Levites sanctified themselves to bring up the ark
of the LORD, the God of Israel. 15 The Levites car-
ried the ark of God on their shoulders with poles,
as Moses had commanded according to the word
of the LORD.*
16 David commanded the commanders of the
Levites to appoint their brothers as singers and
to play on musical instruments, harps, lyres, and
cymbals, to make a loud sound of rejoicing.*
17 Therefore the Levites appointed Heman, son
of Joel, and, among his brothers, Asaph, son of
Berechiah; and among the sons of Merari, their
brothers, Ethan, son of Kushaiah;* 18 and, to-
gether with these, their brothers of the second
rank: the gatekeepers Zechariah, Uzziel, Shemir-
amoth, Jehiel, Unni, Eliab, Benaiah, Maaseiah,
Mattithiah, Eliphelehu, Mikneiah, Obed-edom,
and Jeiel. 19 The singers, Heman, Asaph, and
Ethan, sounded brass cymbals. 20 Zechariah, Uz-
ziel, Shemiramoth, Jehiel, Unni, Eliab, Maaseiah,
and Benaiah played on harps set to "Alamoth."†
21 But Mattithiah, Eliphelehu, Mikneiah, Obed-
edom, and Jeiel led the song on lyres set to

Chapters 14–15

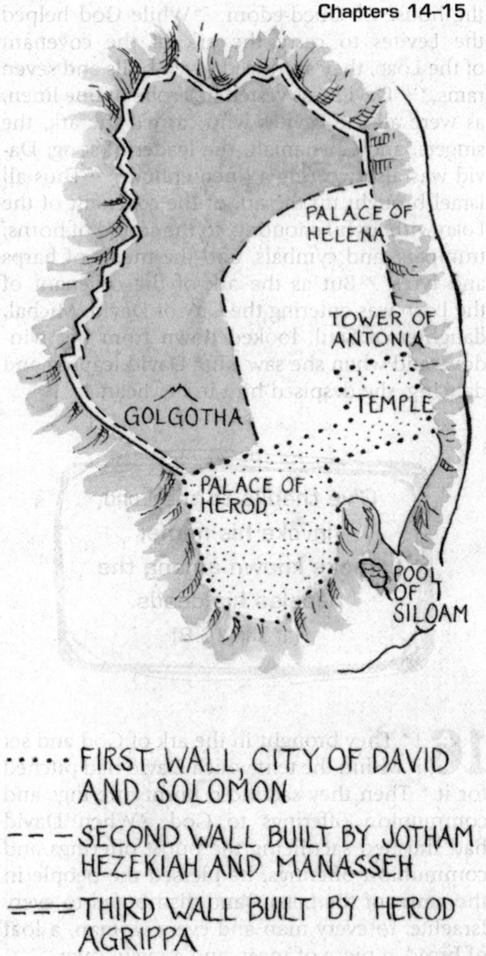

"sheminith." 22 Chenaniah was the chief of the
Levites in the singing; he directed the singing, for
he was skillful.* 23 Berechiah and Elkanah were
gatekeepers before the ark. 24 The priests, Sheb-
aniah, Joshaphat, Nethanel, Amasai, Zechariah,
Benaiah, and Eliezer, sounded the trumpets be-
fore the ark of God.* Obed-edom and Jeiel were
also gatekeepers before the ark.

The Ark Comes to Jerusalem

25 * Thus David, the elders of Israel, and the
commanders of thousands went to bring up the
ark of the covenant of the LORD with joy from

† **15:20–21** *Alamoth . . . sheminith*: musical terms of uncertain meaning. *Alamoth*, lit., "young women," occurs in the superscription to Ps 46. The term *sheminith*, in v. 21, might mean "bass" or "octave"; cf. Ps 6:1; 12:1.

15:2 Nm 1:50; 7:9; Dt 10:8; 31:25; 1 Sm 6:15; Jos 3:8.
15:3 1 Chr 13:5; 2 Sm 6:15, 17.
15:11 1 Chr 16:39; 2 Sm 8:17; 15:29, 35.
15:12 2 Chr 29:5, 15, 34; 30:3, 15, 24.
15:13 1 Chr 13:3.
15:15 Ex 25:10–22; Nm 1:50; 7:9; 2 Chr 35:3.
15:16 1 Chr 13:8; 16:5; 2 Chr 5:12; 29:25; Neh 12:27.
15:17 1 Chr 6:31–47; 25:1–8.
15:22 1 Chr 26:29.
15:24 Nm 10:8; Jos 6:4–8.
15:25–29 2 Sm 6:12–16.

the house of Obed-edom. 26 While God helped
the Levites to carry the ark of the covenant
of the LORD, they sacrificed seven bulls and seven
rams.* 27 David was vested in a robe of fine linen,
as were all the Levites who carried the ark, the
singers, and Chenaniah, the leader of song; Da-
vid was also wearing a linen ephod.* 28 Thus all
Israel brought up the ark of the covenant of the
LORD with joyful shouting, to the sound of horns,
trumpets, and cymbals, and the music of harps
and lyres. 29 But as the ark of the covenant of
the LORD was entering the City of David, Michal,
daughter of Saul, looked down from her win-
dow, and when she saw King David leaping and
dancing, she despised him in her heart.*

> **Give thanks to the LORD,**
> **invoke his name;**
> **make known among the**
> **peoples his deeds.**
> (1 Chr 16:8)

16 1 * They brought in the ark of God and set
it within the tent which David had pitched
for it.* Then they sacrificed burnt offerings and
communion offerings to God. 2 When David
had finished sacrificing the burnt offerings and
communion offerings, he blessed the people in
the name of the LORD, 3 and distributed to every
Israelite, to every man and every woman, a loaf
of bread, a piece of meat, and a raisin cake.

David's Directives for the Levites

4 He then appointed certain Levites to minister
before the ark of the LORD, to celebrate, thank,
and praise the LORD, the God of Israel.* 5 Asaph
was their chief, and second to him were Zech-
ariah, Uzziel, Shemiramoth, Jehiel, Mattithiah,
Eliab, Benaiah, Obed-edom, and Jeiel. These
were to play on harps and lyres, while Asaph was
to sound the cymbals, 6 and the priests Benaiah
and Jahaziel were to be the regular trumpeters
before the ark of the covenant of God.

7 On that same day, David appointed Asaph
and his brothers to sing for the first time these
praises of the LORD:

8† Give thanks to the LORD, invoke his name;*
make known among the peoples his deeds.
9 Sing praise, play music;
proclaim all his wondrous deeds.
10 Glory in his holy name;
rejoice, O hearts that seek the LORD!
11 Rely on the mighty LORD;
constantly seek his face.
12 Recall the wondrous deeds he has done,
his signs, and his words of judgment,
13 You sons of Israel, his servants,
offspring of Jacob, the chosen ones!
14 The LORD is our God;
who rules the whole earth.
15 He remembers forever his covenant
the pact imposed for a thousand
generations—
16 Which was made with Abraham,
confirmed by oath to Isaac,
17 And ratified as binding for Jacob,
an everlasting covenant for Israel:
18 "To you will I give the land of Canaan,
your own allotted heritage."
19 When they were few in number,
a handful, and strangers there,
20 Wandering from nation to nation,
from one kingdom to another,
21 He let no one oppress them;
for their sake he rebuked kings:
22 "Do not touch my anointed,
to my prophets do no harm."
23 *Sing to the LORD, all the earth,
announce his salvation, day after day.
24 Tell his glory among the nations;
among all peoples, his wondrous deeds.
25 For great is the LORD and highly to be praised;
to be feared above all gods.
26 For the gods of the nations all do nothing,
but the LORD made the heavens.
27 Splendor and majesty go before him;
power and rejoicing are in his holy place.
28 Give to the LORD, you families of nations,
give to the LORD glory and might;
29 Give to the LORD the glory due his name!
Bring gifts, and come before him;
bow down to the LORD, splendid in
holiness.
30 Tremble before him, all the earth;
the world will surely stand fast, never to be
moved.
31 Let the heavens be glad and the earth rejoice;

---

† **16:8–36** A hymn composed of parts of several psalms: vv. 8–22 = Ps 105:1–15; vv. 23–33 = Ps 96:1–13; vv. 34–36 = Ps 106:1, 47–48. There are minor textual variants between this hymn and the psalms it is drawn from.

* **15:26** 2 Sm 6:17; 2 Chr 29:21. **15:27** 1 Sm 2:18; 2 Sm 6:14. **15:29** 2 Sm 6:20–23. **16:1–3** 2 Sm 6:17–19. **16:1** 1 Chr 15:1. **16:4** Sir 47:9. **16:8–22** Ps 105:1–15. **16:23–33** Ps 96:1–13.

Catholic Connection

Types of Prayer

Think of all the time you spend during the week e-mailing, texting, or talking on the phone with your friends. What would happen to your friendship if one of you consistently failed to respond to the other? The relationship most likely would not last long. In order to maintain relationships, both parties need to communicate with one another. Our relationship with God also relies on good communication. In 1 Chronicles 16:37–42, we read how King David wanted to help the Israelites stay close to God, so he established regular times and forms of prayer to remind the Israelites of God's presence and their identity as God's people.

Our need to be close to God through prayer is just as important today as it was for King David. For when we pray, we open our heart and enter into conversation with God. You can use the events of your day as a guide to help you open those lines of communication. Here are some suggestions:

- Feeling blessed? Offer prayers of **blessings and adoration** in response to all the ways you have been blessed by God's immeasurable goodness and greatness.
- Have a need? Offer a **prayer of petition** by simply asking God for whatever is needed, acknowledging your dependency on God and trusting in God's goodness.
- Have a friend in need? Offer a **prayer of intercession** asking God for help on his or her behalf.
- Feeling thankful? Offer a **prayer of thanksgiving** for God's mercy and love. Join in the ultimate prayer of thanksgiving by participating in the Church's celebration of the Eucharist.
- Feeling in awe of God? Offer a **prayer of praise** and acknowledge God, not for what God has done for you, but for simply being God.

No matter what form of prayer we use, there are different ways we can express it. We can put the desires of our heart into words, whether spoken aloud or interiorly, in **vocal prayer**. We can reflect on the Scriptures, or other spiritual writings, and listen to what God is saying to us through them in **meditative prayer**. Finally, we can pray deep in our heart by focusing on Jesus in **contemplative prayer,** which enables us to simply be present with Christ whom we love and who loves us.

Setting aside a regular time for prayer each day is essential if you hope to maintain your relationship with God. It will help you remember that God is always present and that you are a disciple of Christ.

1 Chr 16:37–42

Catechism, nos. 2623–2649, 2697–2758

Live It!

Where Do We Place God?

How the world loves boxes and containers and compartments! Remember the old saying, "A place for everything and everything in its place"? There is something comforting in knowing that everything is where it should be.

Don't we often try to put God away in a special place? Isn't it more convenient to think of God as residing "up there" in the tabernacle or sanctuary? Perhaps that is why, in 1 Chronicles 17:4–6, God seems less than enthusiastic about David's desire to build a temple. The danger is clear: identify God with a building, however grand and beautiful, and in people's minds, God *stays* there.

When we enter a chapel or a church, we become reverent, sensing that we are in the presence of God. And, indeed, we are. But we need to remember that we do not leave God behind when we step out of that structure. Simply put, God cannot and will not be confined, despite our best efforts.

Our God walks with us. God's place is everywhere.

- How can you practice living in the constant presence of God?

▶ **1 Chr 17:1–15**

let them say among the nations: The LORD
is king.
32 Let the sea and what fills it resound;
let the plains be joyful and all that is in
them!
33 Then let all the trees of the forest exult
before the LORD, who comes,
who comes to rule the earth.
34 *Give thanks to the LORD, who is good,
whose love endures forever;
35 And say, "Save us, O God, our savior,
gather us and deliver us from among the
nations,
That we may give thanks to your holy name
and glory in praising you."
36 Blessed be the LORD, the God of Israel,
from everlasting to everlasting!
Let all the people say, Amen! Hallelujah.

37 Then David left Asaph and his brothers
there before the ark of the covenant of the LORD
to minister before the ark regularly according to
the daily ritual; 38 he also left there Obed-edom
and sixty-eight of his brothers, including Obed-
edom, son of Jeduthun, and Hosah, to be gate-
keepers.*
39 But the priest Zadok and his priestly broth-
ers he left before the tabernacle of the LORD on
the high place at Gibeon,* 40 to make burnt of-
ferings to the LORD on the altar for burnt offerings
regularly, morning and evening, and to do all
that is written in the law of the LORD which he
commanded Israel.* 41 With them were Heman
and Jeduthun and the others who were chosen
and designated by name to give thanks to the
LORD, "whose love endures forever,"* 42 with
trumpets and cymbals for accompaniment, and
instruments for sacred song. The sons of Jedu-
thun kept the gate.*
43 Then all the people departed, each to their
own homes, and David returned to bless his
household.*

The Oracle of Nathan

17 1 * After David had taken up residence in
his house, he said to Nathan the prophet,
"See, I am living in a house of cedar, but the ark
of the covenant of the LORD is under tentcloth."*
2 Nathan replied to David, "Whatever is in your
heart, go and do, for God is with you."
3 But that same night the word of God came
to Nathan: 4 Go and tell David my servant, Thus
says the LORD: It is not you who are to build the
house for me to dwell in.* 5 For I have never
dwelt in a house, from the day I brought Israel
up, even to this day, but I have been lodging in
tent or tabernacle. 6 As long as I have wandered
about with all Israel, did I ever say a word to any
of the judges of Israel whom I commanded to
shepherd my people, Why have you not built me
a house of cedar? 7 Now then, speak thus to my
servant David, Thus says the LORD of hosts: I took
you from the pasture, from following the flock,
to become ruler over my people Israel.* 8 I was
with you wherever you went, and I cut down all

16:34–36 Ps 106:1, 47–48.
16:38 1 Chr 15:24.
16:39 1 Kgs 3:4.
16:40 Ex 29:38–42; Lv 6:9; Nm 28:3, 6; 2 Chr 13:11.
16:41 2 Chr 5:12; 7:3, 6; 20:21; Ezr 3:11.
16:42 2 Chr 29:27.
16:43 2 Sm 6:19–20.
17:1–27 2 Sm 7:1–29.
17:1 1 Chr 15:1; 2 Sm 5:11.
17:4 1 Chr 28:3; 1 Kgs 8:19.
17:7 1 Sm 16:11.

your enemies before you. I will make your name
like that of the greatest on the earth. 9 I will as-
sign a place for my people Israel and I will plant
them in it to dwell there; they will never again
be disturbed, nor shall the wicked ever again op-
press them, as they did at the beginning, 10 and
during all the time when I appointed judges over
my people Israel. And I will subdue all your en-
emies. Moreover, I declare to you that the LORD
will build you a house: 11 when your days have
been completed and you must join your ances-
tors, I will raise up your offspring after you who
will be one of your own sons, and I will establish
his kingdom.* 12 He it is who shall build me a
house, and I will establish his throne forever.*
13 I will be a father to him, and he shall be a son
to me, and I will not withdraw my favor from
him as I withdrew it from the one who was be-
fore you;* 14 but I will maintain him in my house
and in my kingdom forever, and his throne shall
be firmly established forever.
15 In accordance with all these words and this
whole vision Nathan spoke to David.

David's Thanksgiving

16 Then King David came in and sat in the
LORD's presence, and said: "Who am I, LORD
God, and what is my house, that you should
have brought me so far? 17 And yet, even this
is too little in your sight, O God! For you have
made a promise regarding your servant's house
reaching into the future, and you have looked
on me as henceforth the most notable of men,
LORD God.* 18 What more can David say to you?
You have known† your servant. 19 LORD, for your
servant's sake and in keeping with your purpose,
you have done this great thing. 20 LORD, there is
no one like you, no God but you, just as we have
always heard.*
21 "Is there, like your people Israel, whom you
redeemed from Egypt, another nation on earth
whom a god went to redeem as his people? You
won for yourself a name for great and awesome
deeds by driving out the nations before your
people.* 22 You made your people Israel your
own forever, and you, LORD, became their God.
23 Now, LORD, may the promise that you have
spoken concerning your servant and his house
remain firm forever. Bring about what you have
promised, 24 that your name, LORD of hosts, God
of Israel, may be great and abide forever, while
the house of your servant is established in your
presence.
25 "Because you, my God, have revealed to
your servant that you will build him a house,
your servant dares to pray before you.* 26 Since
you, LORD, are truly God and have made this
generous promise to your servant, 27 do, then,
bless the house of your servant, that it may be in
your presence forever—since it is you, LORD, who
blessed it, it is blessed forever."*

David's Victories

18 1 * After this, David defeated the Philis-
tines and subdued them; and he took Gath
and its towns away from the Philistines. 2 He
also defeated Moab, and the Moabites became
David's subjects, paying tribute.
3 David then defeated Hadadezer, king of Zo-
bah, toward Hamath, who was on his way to set
up his victory stele at the river Euphrates. 4 David
captured from him one thousand chariots, seven
thousand horsemen, and twenty thousand foot
soldiers. David hamstrung all the chariot horses,
but left one hundred for his chariots.* 5 The Ar-
ameans of Damascus came to help Hadadezer,
king of Zobah, but David also defeated twenty-
two thousand of their men in Aram. 6 Then
David set up garrisons in the Damascus region
of Aram, and the Arameans became David's sub-
jects, paying tribute. Thus the LORD made David
victorious in all his campaigns.
7 David took the golden shields that were
carried by Hadadezer's attendants and brought
them to Jerusalem. 8 David likewise took away
from Tibhath and Cun, cities of Hadadezer, large
quantities of bronze; Solomon later used it to
make the bronze sea and the pillars and the ves-
sels of bronze.*
9 When Tou, king of Hamath, heard that David
had defeated the entire army of Hadadezer, king
of Zobah, 10 he sent his son Hadoram to wish
King David well and to congratulate him on hav-
ing waged a victorious war against Hadadezer;
for Hadadezer had been at war with Tou. He also
brought gold, silver and bronze articles of every
sort.* 11 These also King David consecrated to the
LORD along with all the silver and gold that he
had taken from the nations: from Edom, Moab,
the Ammonites, the Philistines, and Amalek.

1 CHR

† **17:18** *Known*: given David recognition, chosen him, singled him out; cf. Gn 18:19; Ex 33:12; Am 3:2.

* **17:11** 2 Sm 7:12–13.
17:12 1 Chr 22:10; 28:6, 10.
17:13 2 Sm 7:14.
17:17 2 Sm 7:19.
17:20 Sir 36:4.
17:21 Dt 4:7; 2 Sm 7:23.
17:25 2 Sm 7:27.
17:27 Nm 22:6.
18:1–13 2 Sm 8:1–14.
18:4 2 Sm 8:14; Jos 11:6, 9.
18:8 2 Sm 8:8; 1 Kgs 7:15, 23, 27.
18:10 2 Sm 8:10.

12 Abishai, the son of Zeruiah, also defeated
eighteen thousand Edomites in the Valley of
Salt.* 13 He set up garrisons in Edom, and all the
Edomites became David's subjects. Thus the LORD
brought David victory in all his undertakings.

David's Officials

14 * David was king over all Israel; he dis-
pensed justice and right to all his people. 15 Joab,
son of Zeruiah, was in command of the army;
Jehoshaphat, son of Ahilud, was chancellor;*
16 Zadok, son of Ahitub, and Ahimelech, son of
Abiathar, were priests;† Shavsha was scribe;*
17 Benaiah, son of Jehoiada, was in command of
the Cherethites and the Pelethites; and David's
sons were the chief assistants to the king.† *

Campaigns Against Ammon

19 1 * Afterward Nahash, king of the Am-
monites, died and his son succeeded him
as king. 2 David said, "I will show kindness to
Hanun, the son of Nahash, for his father showed
kindness to me." Therefore he sent envoys to
console him over his father. But when David's
servants had entered the land of the Ammonites
to console Hanun, 3 the Ammonite princes said
to Hanun, "Do you think David is doing this—
sending you these consolers—to honor your fa-
ther? Have not his servants rather come to you to
explore the land, spying it out for its overthrow?"
4 So Hanun seized David's servants and had them
shaved and their garments cut off halfway at the
hips. Then he sent them away. 5 David was told
about the men, and he sent word for them to be
intercepted, for the men had been greatly dis-
graced. "Remain at Jericho," the king told them,
"until your beards have grown again; then come
back here."

6 When the Ammonites realized that they had
put themselves in bad odor with David, Hanun
and the Ammonites sent a thousand talents of
silver to hire chariots and horsemen from Aram
Naharaim, from Aram-maacah, and from Zobah.
7 They hired thirty-two thousand chariots along
with the king of Maacah and his army, who came
and encamped before Medeba. The Ammonites
also assembled from their cities and came out
for war.
8 When David heard of this, he sent Joab and
his whole army of warriors against them. 9 The
Ammonites marched out and lined up for battle
at the entrance of the city, while the kings who
had come to their help remained apart in the
open field. 10 When Joab saw that there was a
battle line both in front of and behind him, he
chose some of the best fighters among the Isra-
elites and lined them up against the Arameans;
11 the rest of the army, which he placed under
the command of his brother Abishai, then lined
up to oppose the Ammonites. 12 And he said: "If
the Arameans prove too strong for me, you must
come and save me; and if the Ammonites prove
too strong for you, I will save you. 13 Hold firm
and let us show ourselves courageous for the sake
of our people and the cities of our God; and may
the LORD do what is good in his sight." 14 Joab
therefore advanced with his men to engage the
Arameans in battle; but they fled before him.
15 And when the Ammonites saw that the Ara-
means had fled, they too fled before his brother
Abishai, and entered their city. Joab then came
to Jerusalem.

16 Seeing themselves vanquished by Israel, the
Arameans sent messengers to bring out the Ar-
ameans from beyond the Euphrates, with Sho-
phach, the commander of Hadadezer's army, at
their head. 17 When this was reported to David,
he gathered all Israel together, crossed the Jor-
dan, and met them. With the army of David
drawn up to fight the Arameans, they gave bat-
tle. 18 But the Arameans fled before Israel, and
David killed seven thousand of their chariot
fighters and forty thousand of their foot soldiers;
he also put to death Shophach, the commander
of the army. 19 When the vassals of Hadadezer
saw themselves vanquished by Israel, they made
peace with David and became his subjects. After
this, the Arameans refused to come to the aid of
the Ammonites.

20 1 At the turn of the year,† the time when
kings go to war, Joab led the army out
in force, laid waste the land of the Ammonites,
and went on to besiege Rabbah; David himself
remained in Jerusalem. When Joab had attacked
Rabbah and destroyed it, 2 David took the crown

†

18:16 *Zadok . . . and Ahimelech, son of Abiathar, were priests*: emendation—the Masoretic text here reads "Abimelech," not "Ahimelech"; but 2 Sm 8:17, the Chronicler's source, has "Ahimelech." See note there.

18:17 *Chief assistants to the king*: according to 2 Sm 8:18, the Chronicler's source here, David's sons were priests. The Chronicler's modification reflects his conviction that only Aaron's descendants could be priests.

20:1 *At the turn of the year*: thus in 2 Sm 11 begins the story of David's adultery with Bathsheba and his murder of her husband Uriah, but the Chronicler omits it.

*

18:12 2 Sm 8:13; 2 Kgs 14:7.
18:14–17 2 Sm 8:15–18.
18:15 1 Chr 11:6; 2 Sm 8:16; 1 Kgs 4:3.
18:16 1 Chr 24:3, 6, 31; 2 Sm 8:17.
18:17 1 Chr 11:22; 2 Sm 8:18; 1 Kgs 1:38, 44.
19:1–19 2 Sm 10:1–19.

of Milcom from the idol's head. It was found to
weigh a talent of gold, with precious stones on
it; this crown David wore on his own head. He
also brought out a great amount of spoil from
the city. 3 He deported the people of the city
and set them to work with saws, iron picks, and
axes. David dealt thus with all the cities of the
Ammonites. Then David and his whole army re-
turned to Jerusalem.*

Victories over the Philistines

4* Afterward there was another battle with
the Philistines, at Gezer. At that time, Sibbecai
the Hushathite struck down Sippai, one of the
descendants of the Rephaim, and the Philistines
were subdued.*
5 There was another battle with the Philistines,
and Elhanan, the son of Jair, slew Lahmi, the
brother of Goliath† of Gath, whose spear shaft
was like a weaver's beam.*
6 There was another battle, at Gath, and there
was a giant, who had six fingers to each hand and
six toes to each foot; twenty-four in all. He too
was descended from the Rephaim. 7 He defied
Israel, and Jonathan, the son of Shimea, David's
brother, slew him. 8 These were the descendants
of the Rephaim of Gath who died at the hands of
David and his servants.

David's Census; the Plague

21 1* A satan† rose up against Israel, and he
incited David to take a census of Israel.*
2 David therefore said to Joab and to the other
generals of the army, "Go, number the Israelites
from Beer-sheba to Dan, and report back to me
that I may know their number." 3 But Joab re-
plied: "May the LORD increase his people a hun-
dredfold! My lord king, are not all of them my
lord's subjects? Why does my lord seek to do this
thing? Why should he bring guilt upon Israel?"
4 However, the king's command prevailed over
Joab, who departed and traversed all of Israel,
and then returned to Jerusalem. 5 Joab reported
the census figures to David: of men capable of
wielding a sword, there were in all Israel one
million one hundred thousand, and in Judah
four hundred and seventy thousand. 6 Levi and
Benjamin, however, he did not include in the
census, for the king's command was repugnant
to Joab.* 7 This command was evil in the sight
of God, and he struck Israel. 8 Then David said to
God, "I have sinned greatly in doing this thing.
Take away your servant's guilt, for I have acted
very foolishly."
9 Then the LORD spoke to Gad, David's seer,
in these words:* 10 Go, tell David: Thus says the
LORD: I am laying out three options; choose one
of them, and I will inflict it on you. 11 Accord-
ingly, Gad went to David and said to him: "Thus
says the LORD: Decide now— 12 will it be three

Live It!

True Repentance

Think of a time when you said you were sorry, just because you felt you had to. Now think of a time when you were truly sorry for causing harm to another by doing something God had commanded you not to do. There is a big difference between going through the motions of repentance and being truly repentant before another and before God. For example, David sinned by ordering a census to count his people (see 1 Chr 21:2). He accepted a consequence that he hoped would be the easiest (see verse 13). But when he saw the harm he had caused, he became truly repentant and asked God's mercy upon the Israelites (see verse 17).

Repentance requires true sorrow and asking God to change our heart. It leads to an active response to make amends with God and with the Church. Such repentance is called reconciliation, and Catholics celebrate it in the sacrament of Penance and Reconciliation.

► **1 Chr 21:1–17**

† **20:5** *Elhanan . . . slew Lahmi, the brother of Goliath*: with this notice the Chronicler solves the difficulty of the apparent contradiction between 1 Sm 17:49, 51 (David killed Goliath) and 2 Sm 21:19 (Elhanan killed Goliath).

21:1 *A satan*: in the parallel passage (2 Sm 24:1) David is led astray because of the Lord's anger. The Chronicler's modification reflects the changed theological outlook of postexilic Israel, when evil was no longer attributed directly to God. At an earlier period the Hebrew word *satan* ("adversary," or, especially in a court of law, "accuser") designated both human beings (1 Kgs 11:14) and a "son of God" who accused people before God (Jb 1:6–12; 2:1–7; Zec 3:1–2). In later Judaism (cf. Wis 2:24) and in the New Testament, *satan*, or the "devil" (from *diablos*, the Greek translation of the Hebrew word), designates an evil spirit who tempts people to do wrong.

20:2–3 2 Sm 12:30–31.
20:4–8 2 Sm 21:18–22.
20:4 1 Chr 11:29; 27:11.
20:5 1 Chr 11:26; 1 Sm 17:4, 23.
21:1–27 2 Sm 24:1–25.
21:1 Zec 3:1–2.
21:6 1 Chr 27:24; Nm 1:49.
21:9 1 Chr 29:29; 1 Sm 9:9; 2 Chr 29:25.

years of famine; or three months of fleeing your
enemies, with the sword of your foes ever at your
back; or three days of the LORD's own sword, a
plague in the land, with the LORD's destroying
angel in every part of Israel? Now consider: What
answer am I to give him who sent me?" 13 Then
David said to Gad: "I am in serious trouble. But
let me fall into the hand of the LORD, whose
mercy is very great, rather than into hands of
men."
14 Therefore the LORD sent a plague upon Israel,
and seventy thousand Israelites died. 15 God also
sent an angel to Jerusalem to destroy it; but as the
angel was on the point of destroying it, the LORD
saw and changed his mind about the calamity,
and said to the destroying angel, "Enough now!
Stay your hand!"*

Ornan's Threshing Floor

The angel of the LORD was then standing by the
threshing floor of Ornan the Jebusite. 16 When
David raised his eyes, he saw the angel of the
LORD standing between earth and heaven, drawn
sword in hand stretched out against Jerusalem.*
David and the elders, clothed in sackcloth, fell
face down, 17 and David prayed to God: "Was it
not I who ordered the census of the people? I am
the one who sinned, I did this wicked thing. But
these sheep, what have they done? O LORD, my
God, strike me and my father's family, but do not
afflict your people with this plague!"
18 Then the angel of the LORD commanded
Gad to tell David to go up and set up an altar
to the LORD on the threshing floor of Ornan
the Jebusite.* 19 David went up at the word of
Gad, which he spoke in the name of the LORD.
20 Ornan turned around and saw the king; his
four sons who were with him hid themselves,
but Ornan kept on threshing wheat. 21 But as Da-
vid came toward Ornan, he looked up and saw
that it was David, and left the threshing floor
and bowed down before David, his face to the
ground. 22 David said to Ornan: "Sell me the site
of this threshing floor, that I may build on it an
altar to the LORD. Sell it to me at its full price, that
the plague may be withdrawn from the people."
23 But Ornan said to David: "Take it as your own,
and let my lord the king do what is good in his
sight. See, I also give you the oxen for the burnt
offerings, the threshing sledges for the wood, and
the wheat for the grain offering. I give it all to
you." 24 But King David replied to Ornan: "No!
I will buy it from you properly, at its full price.
I will not take what is yours for the LORD, nor
bring burnt offerings that cost me nothing." 25 So
David paid Ornan six hundred shekels of gold†
for the place.

Altar for Burnt Offerings

26 David then built an altar there to the LORD,
and sacrificed burnt offerings and communion
offerings. He called upon the LORD, who an-
swered him by sending down fire from heaven
upon the altar for burnt offerings.* 27 Then the
LORD gave orders to the angel to return his sword
to its sheath.
28 Once David saw that the LORD had answered
him at the threshing floor of Ornan the Jebusite,
he continued to offer sacrifices there. 29 The tab-
ernacle of the LORD, which Moses had made in
the wilderness, and the altar for burnt offerings
were at that time on the high place at Gibeon.*
30 But David could not go into his presence to in-
quire of God, for he was fearful of the sword of
the angel of the LORD.

22 1 Thus David said, "This is the house of
the LORD God, and this is the altar for
burnt offerings for Israel."* 2 † David then or-
dered that the resident aliens in the land of Israel
should be brought together, and he appointed
them stonecutters to hew out stone blocks for
building the house of God.* 3 David also laid up
large stores of iron to make nails for the doors
of the gates, and clamps, together with so much
bronze that it could not be weighed,* 4 and cedar
trees without number. The Sidonians and Tyri-
ans brought great stores of cedar logs to David.*
5 David said: "My son Solomon is young and in-
experienced; but the house that is to be built for
the LORD must be made so magnificent that it will
be renowned and glorious in all lands. Therefore
I will make preparations for it." Thus before his
death David laid up materials in abundance.*

Charge to Solomon

6 Then he summoned his son Solomon and
commanded him to build a house for the LORD,

---

†

21:25 *Six hundred shekels of gold*: according to 2 Sm 24:24, David paid only fifty shekels of silver for Ornan's threshing floor; the Chronicler's higher figure reflects the value the site of the future Temple had in his eyes.

22:2–4 According to 1 Kgs 5:15–32, Solomon himself made the material preparations for building the Temple, even though David had wished to do so (1 Kgs 5:17–19). The Chronicler, however, seeks to enhance David's role in the building of the Temple.

*

21:15 Gn 6:6; Ex 32:14; 2 Sm 24:16; Jon 3:10.
21:16 Jos 5:13.
21:18 2 Chr 3:1.
21:26 Lv 9:24; Jgs 6:21; 1 Kgs 18:38; 2 Chr 7:1; 2 Mc 2:10–12.
21:29 1 Chr 16:39; 1 Kgs 8:4; 2 Chr 1:3.
22:1 1 Chr 21:18, 26, 28; 2 Chr 3:1.
22:2 1 Kgs 5:31–32; 9:20–21; 2 Chr 2:16–17.
22:3 1 Chr 18:8; 1 Kgs 7:47.
22:4 Ezr 3:7; 2 Chr 2:9.
22:5 1 Chr 29:1.

the God of Israel. 7 * David said to Solomon:
"My son, it was my purpose to build a house
myself for the name of the LORD, my God. 8 But
this word of the LORD came to me: You have
shed much blood, and you have waged great
wars. You may not build a house for my name,
because you have shed too much blood upon the
earth in my sight. 9 However, a son will be born
to you. He will be a peaceful man, and I will give
him rest from all his enemies on every side. For
Solomon shall be his name, and in his time I will
bestow peace† and tranquility on Israel.* 10 It is
he who shall build a house for my name; he shall
be a son to me, and I will be a father to him,*
and I will establish the throne of his kingship
over Israel forever.

11 "Now, my son, the LORD be with you, and
may you succeed in building the house of the
LORD your God, as he has said you shall. 12 But
may the LORD give you prudence and discern-
ment when he gives you command over Israel,
so that you keep the law of the LORD, your God.
13 Only then shall you succeed, if you are careful
to observe the statutes and ordinances which the
LORD commanded Moses for Israel. Be strong and
steadfast; do not fear or be dismayed.* 14 See,
with great effort I have laid up for the house of
the LORD a hundred thousand talents of gold,† a
million talents of silver, and bronze and iron in
such great quantities that they cannot be weighed.
I have also laid up wood and stones, to which
you must add.* 15 Moreover, you have available
workers, stonecutters, masons, carpenters, and
experts in every craft, 16 without number, skilled
with gold, silver, bronze, and iron. Set to work,
therefore, and the LORD be with you!"

Charge to the Officials

17 David also commanded all of the officials
of Israel to help his son Solomon: 18 "Is not the
LORD your God with you? Has he not given you
rest on every side? Indeed, he has delivered the
inhabitants of the land into my power, and the
land is subdued before the LORD and his peo-
ple.* 19 Therefore, devote your hearts and souls
to seeking the LORD your God. Proceed to build
the sanctuary of the LORD God, that the ark of
the covenant of the LORD and God's sacred ves-
sels may be brought into the house built for the
name of the LORD."*

The Levitical Divisions

23 1 When David had grown old and was
near the end of his days, he made his son
Solomon king over Israel.* 2 He then gathered
together all the officials of Israel, along with the
priests and the Levites.

3 The Levites thirty years old and above were
counted, and their total number was found to be
thirty-eight thousand.* 4 Of these, twenty-four
thousand were to direct the service of the house
of the LORD, six thousand were to be officials and
judges, 5 four thousand were to be gatekeepers,*
and four thousand were to praise the LORD with
the instruments which [David] had devised for
praise. 6 David apportioned them into divisions
according to the sons of Levi: Gershon, Kohath,
and Merari.*

7 To the Gershonites belonged Ladan and
Shimei. 8 The sons of Ladan: Jehiel the chief,
then Zetham and Joel; three in all.* 9 The sons
of Shimei were Shelomoth, Haziel, and Haran;
three. These were the heads of the families of
Ladan. 10 The sons of Shimei were Jahath, Zizah,
Jeush, and Beriah; these were the sons of Shimei,
four in all. 11 Jahath was the chief and Zizah was
second to him; but Jeush and Beriah had few
sons, and therefore they were classed as a single
family, exercising a single office.

12 The sons of Kohath: Amram, Izhar, Hebron,
and Uzziel; four in all.* 13 The sons of Amram
were Aaron and Moses. Aaron was set apart to
be consecrated as most holy, he and his sons for-
ever, to offer sacrifice before the LORD, to minister
to him, and to bless in his name forever.* 14 As
for Moses, however, the man of God, his sons
were counted as part of the tribe of Levi. 15 The
sons of Moses were Gershom and Eliezer.* 16 The
sons of Gershom: Shubael the chief.* 17 The sons
of Eliezer were Rehabiah the chief—Eliezer had
no other sons, but the sons of Rehabiah were
very numerous. 18 The sons of Izhar: Shelomith

†

22:9 The Hebrew word for peace, *shalom*, is reflected in the name Solomon, in Hebrew, *Shelomo*. The Chronicler draws a contrast here between Solomon, the "peaceful man," and David, who "waged great wars" (v. 8). David was prevented from building the Temple, not only because his time was taken up in waging war (1 Kgs 5:17), but also because he shed much blood (1 Chr 22:8), thereby making himself, in the Chronicler's view, ritually unfit for the task.

22:14 *A hundred thousand talents of gold*: about 3,775 tons of gold. *A million talents of silver*: about 37,750 tons of silver. These highly exaggerated figures are intended to stress the inestimable value of the Temple as the center of Israelite worship. More modest figures are given in 1 Kgs 9:14, 28; 10:10, 14.

*

22:7–10 1 Chr 17:1–14; 28:2–7; 2 Sm 7:1–16; 1 Kgs 5:17–19; 8:17–21.
22:9 2 Sm 12:24.
22:10 Heb 1:5.
22:13 1 Chr 28:7, 20; Dt 31:6, 23; Jos 1:6–7, 9; 1 Kgs 2:2–3.
22:14 1 Chr 29:2–5.
22:18 1 Chr 23:25; Jos 21:44; 23:1; 2 Sm 7:1.
22:19 1 Kgs 8:6, 21; 2 Chr 5:7; 6:11.
23:1 1 Chr 28:5; 1 Kgs 1:30.
23:3 Nm 4:3, 23, 30, 35, 39, 43, 47; 8:23–26; 2 Chr 31:17.
23:5 1 Chr 9:22.
23:6 1 Chr 6:1, 16–30; 26:1–19; Ex 6:16; Nm 3:17; 26:57.
23:8 1 Chr 26:21–22; 29:8.
23:12 1 Chr 26:23; Ex 6:18; Nm 3:19; 26:58–61.
23:13 1 Chr 6:49; Ex 6:20; 28:1; Nm 6:23.
23:15 Ex 2:22; 18:3–4.
23:16 1 Chr 26:24.

the chief. 19 The sons of Hebron: Jeriah, the chief, Amariah, the second, Jahaziel, the third, and Jekameam, the fourth.* 20 The sons of Uzziel: Micah, the chief, and Isshiah, the second.*

21 The sons of Merari: Mahli and Mushi. The sons of Mahli: Eleazar and Kish.* 22 Eleazar died leaving no sons, only daughters; the sons of Kish, their kinsmen, married them.* 23 The sons of Mushi: Mahli, Eder, and Jeremoth; three in all.*

24 These were the sons of Levi according to their ancestral houses, the family heads as they were enrolled one by one according to their names. They performed the work of the service of the house of the LORD beginning at twenty years of age.*

25 David said: "The LORD, the God of Israel, has given rest to his people, and has taken up his dwelling in Jerusalem forever.* 26 Henceforth the Levites need not carry the tabernacle or any of the equipment for its service."* 27 For by David's last words the Levites were enlisted from the time they were twenty years old. 28 Their duty is to assist the sons of Aaron in the service of the house of the LORD, having charge of the courts, the chambers, and the preservation of everything holy: they take part in the service of the house of God. 29 They also have charge of the showbread, of the fine flour for the grain offering, of the wafers of unleavened bread, and of the baking and mixing, and of all measures of quantity and size.* 30 They are to be present every morning to offer thanks and to praise the LORD, and likewise in the evening;* 31 and at every sacrifice of burnt offerings to the LORD on sabbaths, new moons, and feast days, in such numbers as are prescribed, they must always be present before the LORD* 32 and observe what is prescribed for them concerning the tent of meeting, the sanctuary, and the sons of Aaron, their kinsmen, in the service of the house of the LORD.*

The Priestly Divisions

24 1 There were also divisions for the sons of Aaron. The sons of Aaron were Nadab, Abihu, Eleazar, and Ithamar.* 2 Nadab and Abihu died before their father, leaving no sons; therefore only Eleazar and Ithamar served as priests.* 3 David, with Zadok, a descendant of Eleazar, and Ahimelech, a descendant of Ithamar, apportioned them their offices in the priestly service.* 4 But since the sons of Eleazar were found to be more numerous by male heads than those of Ithamar, the former were divided into sixteen groups, and the latter into eight groups, each under its family heads. 5 Their functions were assigned impartially by lot, for there were officers of the holy place, and officers of God, descended both from Eleazar and from Ithamar. 6 The scribe Shemaiah, son of Nethanel, a Levite, recorded them in the presence of the king, and of the officials, of Zadok the priest, and of Ahimelech, son of Abiathar,† and of the heads of the ancestral houses of the priests and of the Levites, listing two successive family groups from Eleazar before each one from Ithamar.*

7 * The first lot fell to Jehoiarib, the second to Jedaiah, 8 the third to Harim, the fourth to Seorim, 9 the fifth to Malchijah, the sixth to Mijamin, 10 the seventh to Hakkoz, the eighth to Abijah,* 11 the ninth to Jeshua, the tenth to Shecaniah, 12 the eleventh to Eliashib, the twelfth to Jakim, 13 the thirteenth to Huppah, the fourteenth to Ishbaal, 14 the fifteenth to Bilgah, the sixteenth to Immer, 15 the seventeenth to Hezir, the eighteenth to Happizzez, 16 the nineteenth to Pethahiah, the twentieth to Jehezkel, 17 the twenty-first to Jachin, the twenty-second to Gamul, 18 the twenty-third to Delaiah, the twenty-fourth to Maaziah. 19 This was the appointed order of their service when they functioned in the house of the LORD according to the precepts given them by Aaron, their father, as the LORD, the God of Israel, had commanded him.*

Other Levites

20 * Of the remaining Levites, there were Shubael, of the sons of Amram, and Jehdeiah, of the sons of Shubael; 21 Isshiah, the chief, of the sons of Rehabiah; 22 Shelomith of the Izharites, and Jahath of the sons of Shelomith. 23 The sons of Hebron were Jeriah, the chief, Amariah, the second, Jahaziel, the third, Jekameam, the fourth. 24 The sons of Uzziel were Micah; Shamir, of the sons of Micah; 25 Isshiah, the brother of Micah; and Zechariah, a descendant of Isshiah. 26 The sons of Merari were Mahli, Mushi, and the sons of his son Uzziah. 27 The sons of Merari through his son Uzziah: Shoham, Zaccur, and Ibri. 28 The

† **24:6** *Ahimelech, son of Abiathar*: see note on 18:16.

* **23:19** 1 Chr 24:23.
23:20 1 Chr 24:24–25.
23:21 1 Chr 6:29; 24:26, 28–29; Ex 6:19; Nm 3:20, 33.
23:22 1 Chr 24:28–29.
23:23 1 Chr 6:47; 24:30.
23:24 2 Chr 31:17; Ezr 3:8.
23:25 1 Chr 22:18; Ps 132:13.
23:26 1 Chr 15:15; 2 Chr 35:3.
23:29 1 Chr 9:29, 31–32; Lv 2:1, 4–5; 24:5–8.
23:30 Nm 28:3–8.
23:31 Nm 28:2–29:39.
23:32 Nm 3:6–9; 18:2–5.
24:1 Ex 6:23; Nm 3:2–4; 26:60.
24:2 Lv 10:1–7, 12; Nm 3:2, 4.
24:3 1 Chr 18:16; 2 Sm 8:17; 2 Chr 8:14.
24:6 1 Chr 18:16; 2 Sm 8:17.
24:7–10 1 Chr 9:10–13; Ezr 2:36–38; Neh 7:39–42; 11:10–14.
24:10 Lk 1:5.
24:19 2 Chr 23:8.
24:20–31 1 Chr 23:7–23.

1 CHR

sons of Mahli were Eleazar, who had no sons,
29 and Jerahmeel, of the sons of Kish. 30 The sons
of Mushi were Mahli, Eder, and Jerimoth.

These were the sons of the Levites according
to their ancestral houses. 31 They too, in the same
manner as their kinsmen, the sons of Aaron, cast
lots in the presence of King David, Zadok, Ahimelech, and the heads of the priestly and levitical
families; the more important family did so in the
same way as the less important one.*

The Singers

25 1 David and the leaders of the liturgy set
apart for the service the sons of Asaph,
Heman, and Jeduthun, who prophesied† to the
accompaniment of lyres and harps and cymbals.*

This is the list of those who performed this
service: 2 Of the sons of Asaph: Zaccur, Joseph,
Nethaniah, and Asharelah, sons of Asaph, under the direction of Asaph, who prophesied
under the guidance of the king. 3 Of Jeduthun,
these sons of Jeduthun: Gedaliah, Zeri, Jeshaiah,
Shimei, Hashabiah, and Mattithiah; six, under the direction of their father Jeduthun, who
prophesied to the accompaniment of a lyre, to
give thanks and praise to the LORD. 4 Of Heman,
these sons of Heman: Bukkiah, Mattaniah, Uzziel, Shubael, and Jerimoth; Hananiah, Hanani,
Eliathah, Giddalti, Romamti-ezer, Joshbekashah,
Mallothi, Hothir, and Mahazioth. 5 All these were
the sons of Heman, the king's seer for divine
matters; to exalt him God gave Heman fourteen
sons and three daughters.* 6 All these, whether of
Asaph, Jeduthun, or Heman, were under their fathers' direction in the singing in the house of the
LORD to the accompaniment of cymbals, harps
and lyres, serving in the house of God, under the
guidance of the king.* 7 Their number, together
with that of their kinsmen who were trained in
singing to the LORD, all of them skilled men, was
two hundred and eighty-eight. 8 They cast lots for
their functions equally, young and old, master
and pupil alike.*

9 The first lot fell to Asaph, to the family of
Joseph; he and his sons and his kinsmen were
twelve. Gedaliah was the second; he and his kinsmen and his sons were twelve. 10 The third was
Zaccur, his sons, and his kinsmen: twelve. 11 The
fourth fell to Izri, his sons, and his kinsmen:
twelve. 12 The fifth was Nethaniah, his sons, and
his kinsmen: twelve. 13 The sixth was Bukkiah,
his sons, and his kinsmen: twelve. 14 The seventh was Jesarelah, his sons, and his kinsmen:
twelve. 15 The eighth was Jeshaiah, his sons, and
his kinsmen: twelve. 16 The ninth was Mattaniah,
his sons, and his kinsmen: twelve. 17 The tenth
was Shimei, his sons, and his kinsmen: twelve.
18 The eleventh was Uzziel, his sons, and his kinsmen: twelve. 19 The twelfth fell to Hashabiah, his
sons, and his kinsmen: twelve. 20 The thirteenth
was Shubael, his sons, and his kinsmen: twelve.
21 The fourteenth was Mattithiah, his sons, and
his kinsmen: twelve. 22 The fifteenth fell to Jeremoth, his sons, and his kinsmen: twelve. 23 The
sixteenth fell to Hananiah, his sons, and his
kinsmen: twelve. 24 The seventeenth fell to Joshbekashah, his sons, and his kinsmen: twelve.
25 The eighteenth fell to Hanani, his sons, and
his kinsmen: twelve. 26 The nineteenth fell to
Mallothi, his sons, and his kinsmen: twelve.
27 The twentieth fell to Eliathah, his sons, and
his kinsmen: twelve. 28 The twenty-first fell to
Hothir, his sons, and his kinsmen: twelve. 29 The
twenty-second fell to Giddalti, his sons, and his
kinsmen: twelve. 30 The twenty-third fell to Mahazioth, his sons, and his kinsmen: twelve. 31 The
twenty-fourth fell to Romamti-ezer, his sons, and
his kinsmen: twelve.

Divisions of Gatekeepers

26 1 * As for the divisions of gatekeepers:
Of the Korahites was Meshelemiah, the
son of Kore, one of the sons of Abiasaph.
2 Meshelemiah's sons: Zechariah, the firstborn,
Jediael, the second son, Zebadiah, the third,
Jathniel, the fourth, 3 Elam, the fifth, Jehohanan,
the sixth, Eliehoenai, the seventh. 4 Obed-edom's
sons: Shemaiah, the firstborn, Jehozabad, a second son, Joah, the third, Sachar, the fourth, Nethanel, the fifth, 5 Ammiel, the sixth, Issachar, the
seventh, Peullethai, the eighth, for God blessed
him. 6 To his son Shemaiah were born sons who
ruled over their family, for they were warriors.
7 The sons of Shemaiah were Othni, Rephael,
Obed, and Elzabad; also his kinsmen who were
men of substance, Elihu and Semachiah. 8 All
these were the sons of Obed-edom, who, together
with their sons and their kinsmen, were men of
substance, fit for the service. Of Obed-edom,

1 CHR

---

† **25:1** This list of twenty-four classes of Temple singers balances the list of the twenty-four classes of priests (24:4–19). The last nine names in v. 4, which seem to form a special group, were perhaps originally fragments or incipits (the opening words) of hymns. With some slight changes in the vocalization, these names would mean: "Have mercy on me, O LORD," "Have mercy on me," "You are my God," "I magnify," "I extol the help of . . . ," "Sitting in adversity," "I have fulfilled," "He made abundant," and "Visions."

---

* **24:31** 1 Chr 25:8; 26:13.
25:1 1 Chr 6:16–32; 15:16–17, 19; 16:37; 2 Chr 5:12; 35:15; Neh 12:27, 45.
25:5 2 Chr 35:15.
25:6 1 Chr 15:16.
25:8 1 Chr 24:31.
26:1 1 Chr 9:19; 2 Chr 8:14; 23:19; 35:15; Neh 12:45.

sixty-two. 9 Of Meshelemiah, eighteen sons and
kinsmen, men of substance.
10 Hosah, a descendant of Merari, had these
sons: Shimri, the chief (for though he was not
the firstborn, his father made him chief),* 11 Hil-
kiah, the second son, Tebaliah, the third, Zech-
ariah, the fourth. All the sons and kinsmen of
Hosah were thirteen.
12 To these divisions of the gatekeepers, by
their chief men, were assigned watches for them
to minister in the house of the LORD, for each
group in the same way. 13 They cast lots for each
gate, small and large families alike. 14 When the
lot was cast for the east side, it fell to Meshele-
miah. Then they cast lots for his son Zechariah,
a prudent counselor, and the north side fell to
his lot.* 15 To Obed-edom fell the south side,
and to his sons the storehouse. 16 To Hosah fell
the west side with the Shallecheth gate at the
ascending highway. For each family, watches
were established. 17 On the east, six watched each
day, on the north, four each day, on the south,
four each day, and at the storehouse they were
two and two; 18 as for the large building† on the
west, there were four at the highway and two at
the large building. 19 These were the classes of the
gatekeepers, sons of Korah and Merari.

Treasurers

20 Their brother Levites had oversight of the
treasuries of the house of God and the treasur-
ies of votive offerings.* 21 Among the sons of
Ladan the Gershonite, the family heads were
sons of Jehiel:* 22 * the sons of Jehiel, Zetham
and his brother Joel, who oversaw the treasures
of the house of the LORD. 23 Of the Amramites,
Izharites, Hebronites, and Uzzielites, 24 Shubael,
son of Gershom, son of Moses, was principal
overseer of the treasures. 25 * His associate was
of the line of Eliezer, whose son was Rehabiah,
whose son was Jeshaiah, whose son was Joram,
whose son was Zichri, whose son was Shelomith.
26 This Shelomith and his kinsmen oversaw all
the treasures of the votive offerings dedicated by
King David, the heads of the families, the com-
manders of thousands and of hundreds, and the
commanders of the army;* 27 what came from
wars and from spoils, they dedicated for the sup-
port of the house of the LORD. 28 Also, whatever
Samuel the seer, Saul, son of Kish, Abner, son
of Ner, Joab, son of Zeruiah, and all others had
consecrated, was under the charge of Shelomith
and his kinsmen.

Magistrates

29 Among the Izharites, Chenaniah and his
sons were in charge of Israel's civil affairs† as
officials and judges.* 30 Among the Hebronites,
Hashabiah* and his kinsmen, one thousand
seven hundred men of substance, had the ad-
ministration of Israel on the western side of the
Jordan for all the work of the LORD and the ser-
vice of the king. 31 Among the Hebronites, Jerijah
was their chief according to their family records.
In the fortieth year of David's reign search was
made, and there were found among them war-
riors at Jazer of Gilead.* 32 His kinsmen were also
men of substance, two thousand seven hundred
heads of families. King David appointed them to
the administration of the Reubenites, the Gad-
ites, and the half-tribe of Manasseh for every-
thing pertaining to God and to the king.

Army Commanders†

27 1 This is the list of the Israelite family
heads, commanders of thousands and of
hundreds, and other officers who served the king
in all that pertained to the divisions, of twenty-
four thousand men each, that came and went
month by month throughout the year.
2 Over the first division for the first month was
Ishbaal, son of Zabdiel, and in his division were
twenty-four thousand men; 3 a descendant of
Perez, he was chief over all the commanders of
the army for the first month. 4 Over the division
of the second month was Eleazar, son of Dodo,
from Ahoh, and in his division were twenty-four
thousand men.* 5 * The third army commander,
for the third month, was Benaiah, son of Jehoi-
ada the chief priest, and in his division were
twenty-four thousand men. 6 This Benaiah was a
warrior among the Thirty and over the Thirty. His
son Ammizabad was over his division. 7 Fourth,
for the fourth month, was Asahel, brother of

---

† **26:18** *The large building*: *parbar*, mentioned also in 2 Kgs 23:11; the meaning of the word is unclear.

26:29 *Civil affairs*: lit., "external work," i.e., conduct of affairs external to the Temple.

27:1–15 This list of army commanders is similar to, but distinct from, the list of David's warriors given in 11:10–47. The schematic enumeration of the soldiers presented here appears artificial and exaggerated (12 x 24,000 = 288,000 men!). However, the Hebrew word (*'eleph*) translated "thousand" might also designate a military unit of much smaller size.

* **26:10** 1 Chr 16:38.
26:14 1 Chr 9:21.
26:20 1 Chr 28:12; 1 Kgs 7:51.
26:21 1 Chr 23:7–8; 29:8.
26:22–24 1 Chr 23:8, 12, 16.
26:25 1 Chr 23:17–18; 24:21.
26:26 2 Sm 8:11.
26:29 1 Chr 23:4.
26:30 1 Chr 27:17; Neh 11:15–16.
26:31 1 Chr 23:19; 29:27; Jos 13:25.
27:4 1 Chr 11:12; 2 Sm 23:9.
27:5–6 1 Chr 11:22–25; 18:17; 2 Sm 23:20–23.

Joab, and after him his son Zebadiah, and in
his division were twenty-four thousand men.*
8 Fifth, for the fifth month, was the command-
er Shamhuth, a descendant of Zerah, and in his
division were twenty-four thousand men. 9 Sixth,
for the sixth month, was Ira, son of Ikkesh, from
Tekoa, and in his division were twenty-four thou-
sand men. 10 Seventh, for the seventh month, was
Hellez, from Beth-pelet, of the Ephraimites, and
in his division were twenty-four thousand men.
11 Eighth, for the eighth month, was Sibbecai
the Hushathite, a descendant of Zerah, and in
his division were twenty-four thousand men.*
12 Ninth, for the ninth month, was Abiezer from
Anathoth, of Benjamin, and in his division were
twenty-four thousand men. 13 Tenth, for the
tenth month, was Maharai from Netophah, a
descendant of Zerah, and in his division were
twenty-four thousand men. 14 Eleventh, for the
eleventh month, was Benaiah the Pirathonite,
of the Ephraimites, and in his division were
twenty-four thousand men. 15 Twelfth, for the
twelfth month, was Heldai the Netophathite, of
the family of Othniel, and in his division were
twenty-four thousand men.

Tribal Leaders

16 Over the tribes of Israel, for the Reubenites
the leader was Eliezer, son of Zichri; for the Sim-
eonites, Shephatiah, son of Maacah; 17 for Levi,
Hashabiah, son of Kemuel; for Aaron, Zadok;
18 for Judah, Eliab,* one of David's brothers;
for Issachar, Omri, son of Michael; 19 for Zeb-
ulun, Ishmaiah, son of Obadiah; for Naphtali,
Jeremoth, son of Azriel; 20 for the Ephraimites,
Hoshea, son of Azaziah; for the half-tribe of Ma-
nasseh, Joel, son of Pedaiah; 21 for the half-tribe
of Manasseh in Gilead, Iddo, son of Zechariah;
for Benjamin, Jaasiel, son of Abner; 22 for Dan,
Azarel, son of Jeroham. These were the com-
manders of the tribes of Israel.
23 David did not count those who were twenty
years of age or younger, for the LORD had prom-
ised to multiply Israel like the stars of the heav-
ens.* 24 Joab, son of Zeruiah, began to take the
census, but he did not complete it, for because
of it wrath fell upon Israel. Therefore the num-
ber was not recorded in the book of chronicles
of King David.*

Overseers

25 Over the treasuries of the king was Azma-
veth,* the son of Adiel. Over the treasuries in the
country, the cities, the villages, and the towers
was Jonathan, son of Uzziah. 26 Over the farm
workers who tilled the soil was Ezri, son of Che-
lub. 27 Over the vineyards was Shimei from Ra-
mah, and over their produce for the wine cellars
was Zabdi the Shiphmite. 28 Over the olive trees
and sycamores of the Shephelah was Baalhanan
the Gederite, and over the stores of oil was Jo-
ash. 29 Over the cattle that grazed in Sharon was
Shitrai the Sharonite, and over the cattle in the
valleys was Shaphat, the son of Adlai; 30 over the
camels was Obil the Ishmaelite; over the donkeys
was Jehdeiah the Meronothite; 31 and over the
flocks was Jaziz the Hagrite. All these were the
overseers of King David's possessions.

David's Court

32 Jonathan, David's uncle and a man of intel-
ligence, was counselor and scribe; he and Jehiel,
the son of Hachmoni, attended the king's sons.
33 Ahithophel was also the king's counselor, and
Hushai the Archite was the king's friend.* 34 After
Ahithophel† came Jehoiada, the son of Benaiah,
and Abiathar. The commander of the king's army
was Joab.

The Assembly at Jerusalem

28 1 David assembled at Jerusalem all the
commanders of Israel, the tribal com-
manders, the commanders of the divisions who
were in the service of the king, the commanders
of thousands and of hundreds, those in com-
mand of all the king's estates and possessions,
and his sons, together with the courtiers, the war-
riors, and every person of substance.* 2* King
David rose to his feet and said: "Hear me, my
kinsmen and my people. It was my purpose to
build a house of repose myself for the ark of the
covenant of the LORD, the footstool for the feet of
our God;† and I was preparing to build it. 3 But
God said to me, You may not build a house for
my name, for you are a man who waged wars
and shed blood. 4 However, the LORD, the God
of Israel, chose me from all my father's family to
be king over Israel forever. For he chose Judah as

†

27:34 *After Ahithophel*: after Ahithophel's suicide (2 Sm 17:23), Jehoiada succeeded him as the king's counselor. *Abiathar*: David's priest, along with Zadok. See note on 18:16.

28:2 *The ark . . . the footstool . . . of our God*: the Lord, who was invisibly enthroned upon the cherubim associated with the ark of the covenant at Shiloh and later in the Jerusalem Temple, had the ark as his footstool; cf. Ps 99:5; 132:7. There was no ark in the postexilic Temple. Cf. note on 2 Chr 5:9.

27:7 2 Sm 2:18; 23:24.
27:11 1 Chr 11:29; 20:4; 2 Sm 21:18.
27:18 1 Chr 2:13.
27:23 Gn 22:17.
27:24 2 Sm 24:10.
27:25 2 Sm 23:31.
27:33 2 Sm 15:12, 32–37; 16:16–19, 23; 17:5–16, 23.
28:1 1 Chr 27:2–22, 25–31; 11:10–47.
28:2–3 1 Chr 17:4; 22:7–10; 2 Sm 7:5; 1 Kgs 5:3; Ps 132:3–7.

leader, then one family of Judah, that of my fa-
ther; and finally, among all the sons of my father,
it pleased him to make me king over all Israel.*
5 And of all my sons—for the LORD has given me
many sons—he has chosen my son Solomon
to sit on the throne of the LORD's kingship over
Israel.* 6 For he said to me: It is your son Solo-
mon who shall build my house and my courts,
for I have chosen him for my son, and I will be
a father to him.* 7 I will establish his kingdom
forever, if he perseveres in carrying out my com-
mandments and ordinances as he does now.
8 Therefore, in the sight of all Israel, the assembly
of the LORD, and in the hearing of our God: keep
and carry out all the commandments of the LORD,
your God, that you may continue to possess this
good land and afterward leave it as an inheri-
tance to your children forever.*
9 "As for you, Solomon, my son, know the
God of your father and serve him with a whole
heart and a willing soul, for the LORD searches all
hearts and understands all the mind's thoughts. If
you search for him, he will be found; but if you
abandon him, he will cast you off forever.* 10 See,
then! The LORD has chosen you to build a house
as his sanctuary. Be strong and set to work."

1 CHR

Temple Plans Given to Solomon

11 Then David gave to his son Solomon the
design of the portico and of the house itself,
with its storerooms, its upper rooms and inner
chambers, and the shrine containing the cover
of the ark.* 12 He provided also the design for
all else that he had in mind by way of courts
for the house of the LORD, with the surrounding
compartments for the treasuries of the house of
God and the treasuries for the votive offerings,
13 as well as for the divisions of the priests and
Levites, for all the work of the service of the
house of the LORD, and for all the liturgical ves-
sels of the house of the LORD. 14 He specified the
weight of gold to be used in the golden vessels
for the various services and the weight of silver
to be used in the silver vessels for the various
services; 15 likewise for the golden menorahs and
their lamps he specified the weight of gold for
each menorah and its lamps, and for the silver
menorahs he specified the weight of silver for
each menorah and its lamps, depending on the
use to which each menorah was to be put.* 16 He
specified the weight of gold for each table that
was to hold the showbread, and the silver for
the silver tables; 17 the pure gold for the forks,
basins, and pitchers; the weight of gold for each
golden bowl and the weight of silver for each
silver bowl; 18 the refined gold, and its weight, to
be used for the altar of incense; and, finally, gold
to fashion the chariot:† the cherubim spreading
their wings and covering the ark of the covenant
of the LORD.* 19 All this he wrote down, by the
hand of the LORD, to make him understand it—
the working out of the whole design.
20 Then David said to his son Solomon: "Be
strong and steadfast, and go to work; do not fear
or be dismayed, for the LORD God, my God, is
with you. He will not fail you or abandon you
before you have completed all the work for the
service of the house of the LORD.* 21 The divisions
of the priests and Levites are ready for all the ser-
vice of the house of God; they will be with you
in all the work with all those who are eager to
show their skill in every kind of craftsmanship.
Also the commanders and all the people will do
everything that you command."*

Offerings for the Temple

29 1 King David then said to the whole as-
sembly: "My son Solomon, whom alone
God has chosen, is still young and inexperienced;
the work, however, is great, for this palace is not
meant for human beings, but for the LORD God.*
2 For this reason I have stored up for the house of
my God, as far as I was able, gold for what will be
made of gold, silver for what will be made of sil-
ver, bronze for what will be made of bronze, iron
for what will be made of iron, wood for what will
be made of wood, onyx stones and settings for
them, carnelian and mosaic stones, every other
kind of precious stone, and great quantities of
marble.* 3 But now, because of the delight I take
in the house of my God, in addition to all that I
stored up for the holy house, I give to the house
of my God my personal fortune in gold and sil-
ver: 4 three thousand talents of Ophir gold, and
seven thousand talents of refined silver, for over-
laying the walls of the rooms,* 5 for the various
utensils to be made of gold and silver, and for
every work that is to be done by artisans. Now,
who else will contribute generously and conse-
crate themselves this day to the LORD?"*

† **28:18** *Chariot*: this reference is probably inspired by the vision account in Ez 1:4–24; 10:1–22.

* **28:4** 1 Chr 17:23; Gn 49:8–12; 1 Sm 16:6–13. **28:5** 1 Chr 3:1–9; 14:3–7; 22:9; 23:1; Wis 9:7. **28:6** 1 Chr 17:11–14; 22:9–10; 2 Sm 7:12–13. **28:8** Dt 4:5. **28:9** 1 Chr 29:17; 2 Chr 15:2; 1 Kgs 8:61. **28:11** Ex 25:9, 40; 26:30. **28:15** Ex 25:31–37. **28:18** Ex 25:18–22; 30:1–10; 1 Kgs 6:23–28. **28:20** 1 Chr 22:13; Jos 1:5. **28:21** Ex 36:1–5. **29:1** 1 Chr 22:5; 28:5. **29:2** 1 Chr 22:14. **29:4** 2 Chr 9:10; 1 Kgs 9:28; 10:11. **29:5** Ex 25:2; 35:5–6.

Cultural Connection

God's Name

As David neared the end of his life and reign, he blessed God's name in the midst of the people. The Israelites, who believed in one God, were surrounded by other cultures who believed in many different gods, both good and evil. The name of the Israelites' one God was sacred and precious to them, and they often associated God's name with power, glory, majesty, and victory over all creation.

In Hmong, the name of God is *Huab Tais Ntuj*, which can be translated as Highest One or Emperor Spirit or Overriding Spirit. The Hmong culture developed as a subculture within the Central Highlands of China. The Hmong believed in different spirits, both good and evil, angelic and demonic. So, in naming God Highest Emperor, overriding all other spirits, they clearly also developed a belief in one God with power over all creation.

▶ 1 Chr 29:10–22

6Then the heads of the families, the tribal
commanders of Israel, the commanders of thou-
sands and of hundreds, and those who had
command of the king's affairs came forward
willingly* 7and contributed for the service of
the house of God five thousand talents and ten
thousand darics of gold, ten thousand talents of
silver, eighteen thousand talents of bronze, and
one hundred thousand talents of iron.* 8Those
who had precious stones gave them into the
keeping of Jehiel the Gershonite for the treasury
of the house of the LORD.* 9The people rejoiced
over these free-will offerings, for they had been
contributed to the LORD wholeheartedly. King
David also rejoiced greatly.*

David's Prayer

10Then David blessed the LORD in the sight of
the whole assembly. David said:

"Blessed are you, LORD,
God of Israel our father,
from eternity to eternity.
11 Yours, LORD, are greatness and might,
majesty, victory, and splendor.
For all in heaven and on earth is yours;
yours, LORD, is kingship;
you are exalted as head over all.
12 Riches and glory are from you,
and you have dominion over all.
In your hand are power and might;
it is yours to give greatness and strength
to all.*
13 Therefore, our God, we give you thanks
and we praise the majesty of your name.

14"But who am I, and who are my people,
that we should have the means to contribute so
freely? For everything is from you, and what we
give is what we have from you. 15For before you
we are strangers and travelers, like all our ances-
tors. Our days on earth are like a shadow, with-
out a future.* 16LORD our God, all this wealth
that we have brought together to build you a
house for your holy name comes from you and
is entirely yours. 17I know, my God, that you
put hearts to the test and that you take pleasure
in integrity. With a whole heart I have willingly
given all these things, and now with joy I have
seen your people here present also giving to you
generously. 18LORD, God of our ancestors Abra-
ham, Isaac, and Israel,* keep such thoughts in
the hearts and minds of your people forever, and
direct their hearts toward you. 19Give to my son
Solomon a wholehearted desire to keep your
commandments, precepts, and statutes, that he
may carry out all these plans and build the palace
for which I have made preparation."
20Then David told the whole assembly, "Now
bless the LORD your God!" And the whole assem-
bly blessed the LORD, the God of their ancestors,
bowing down in homage before the LORD and

29:6 1 Chr 27:1, 25–31; 28:1.
29:7 Ezr 2:69; 8:27; Neh 7:70–71.
29:8 1 Chr 23:8; 26:21.
29:9 2 Kgs 12:4.
29:12 2 Chr 20:6; Wis 6:3.
29:15 Lv 25:23; Wis 2:5; 5:9.
29:18 Ex 3:6, 15; 4:5; 1 Kgs 18:36.

before the king. [21]On the following day they
brought sacrifices and burnt offerings to the
LORD, a thousand bulls, a thousand rams, and
a thousand lambs, together with their libations
and many other sacrifices for all Israel; [22]and on
that day they ate and drank in the LORD's pres-
ence with great rejoicing.

Solomon Anointed

Then for a second time† they proclaimed
David's son Solomon king, and they anointed
him for the LORD as ruler, and Zadok as priest.
[23]Thereafter Solomon sat on the throne of the
LORD as king succeeding his father David; he
prospered, and all Israel obeyed him.* [24]All the
commanders and warriors, and also all the other
sons of King David, swore allegiance to King Sol-
omon. [25]And the LORD exalted Solomon greatly
in the eyes of all Israel, giving him a glorious
reign such as had not been enjoyed by any king
over Israel before him.*

David's Death

[26]Thus David, the son of Jesse, had reigned
over all Israel. [27]He was king over Israel for forty
years: he was king seven years in Hebron and
thirty-three years in Jerusalem.* [28]He died at a
ripe old age, rich in years and wealth and glory,
and his son Solomon succeeded him as king.*
[29]Now the deeds of King David, first and last,
are recorded in the history of Samuel the seer, the
history of Nathan the prophet, and the history
of Gad the seer,* [30]together with the particulars
of his reign and valor, and of the events that af-
fected him and all Israel and all the kingdoms
of the earth.

† **29:22** *For a second time*: the first time is in 23:1 where David appoints Solomon his successor. Now there is a solemn public ratification of that appointment.

* **29:23** 1 Chr 28:5; 2 Chr 9:8; 1 Kgs 2:12.
29:25 2 Chr 1:12; 1 Kgs 3:13.
29:27 2 Sm 5:5; 1 Kgs 2:11.
29:28 1 Chr 23:1.
29:29 1 Chr 21:9; 1 Sm 22:5.

For background on this book, see the introduction to 1 and 2 Chronicles before 1 Chronicles.

2 Chronicles

I. The Reign of Solomon

Solomon at Gibeon

1 1 Solomon, son of David, strengthened his
hold on the kingdom, for the LORD, his God,
was with him, making him ever greater. 2 Sol-
omon summoned all Israel, the commanders
of thousands and of hundreds, the judges, the
princes of all Israel, and the family heads; 3 * and,
accompanied by the whole assembly, Solomon
went to the high place at Gibeon, because the
tent of meeting of God, made in the wilderness
by Moses, the LORD's servant, was there. 4 David
had, however, brought up the ark of God from
Kiriath-jearim to Jerusalem, where he had pro-
vided a place and pitched a tent for it; 5 the bronze
altar made by Bezalel, son of Uri, son of Hur, he
put in front of the tabernacle of the LORD.† There
Solomon and the assembly sought out the LORD,*
6 and Solomon offered sacrifice in the LORD's pres-
ence on the bronze altar at the tent of meeting; he
sacrificed a thousand burnt offerings upon it.

7 That night God appeared to Solomon and said
to him: Whatever you ask, I will give you. 8 Solo-
mon answered God: "You have shown great favor
to David my father, and you have made me king
to succeed him. 9 Now, LORD God, may your word
to David my father be confirmed, for you have
made me king over a people as numerous as the
dust of the earth.* 10 Give me, therefore, wisdom
and knowledge to govern this people, for other-
wise who could rule this vast people of yours?"
11 God then replied to Solomon: Because this
has been your wish—you did not ask for riches,
treasures, and glory, or the life of those who hate
you, or even for a long life for yourself, but you
have asked for wisdom and knowledge in order
to rule my people over whom I have made you
king— 12 wisdom and knowledge are given you. I
will also give you riches, treasures, and glory, such
as kings before you never had, nor will those who
come after you.

Solomon's Wealth

13 Solomon returned to Jerusalem from the high
place at Gibeon, from before the tent of meeting,
and became king over Israel. 14 Solomon amassed
chariots and horses: he had one thousand four
hundred chariots and twelve thousand horses;
these he allocated among the chariot cities and to
the king's service in Jerusalem.* 15 The king made
silver and gold as common in Jerusalem as stones,
and cedars as numerous as the sycamores of the

† **1:5** *The bronze altar . . . the tabernacle of the LORD*: by this notice, the Chronicler justifies Solomon's worship at the high place of Gibeon. He pictures the tabernacle, i.e., the Mosaic meeting tent, and the bronze altar made at Moses' command (Ex 31:1–9) as remaining at Gibeon after David had installed the ark of the covenant in another tent in Jerusalem (1 Chr 15:1, 25; 16:1). Bezalel's altar was made of acacia wood plated with bronze (Ex 27:1–2). Later, Solomon made an all-bronze altar for the Temple in Jerusalem (2 Chr 4:1).

1:3–12 1 Kgs 3:4–15; 1 Chr 21:29.
1:5 Ex 27:1–2; 31:2; 1 Chr 2:20.
1:9 Gn 13:16; 28:14.
1:14 2 Chr 9:25; 1 Kgs 10:26–29.

Did You Know?

Wisdom and the Torah

What a deal for Solomon! God tells him to ask for anything and Solomon will have it (see 2 Chr 1:7). Solomon prays to be wise (see verse 10), which pleases God because it indicates Solomon's desire to rule God's people according to God's will. But what is wisdom? For the Chronicler, wisdom is ultimately living one's life in conformity with God's instruction, or the Torah (see Dt 17:8–11). Wisdom is evident in the person who worships God correctly and lives a moral life in keeping with the law, and in the king who governs justly. To learn more about the Israelites' view of wisdom, take a look at the wisdom books in the next section of the Old Testament. For a New Testament perspective, see Luke 2:41–52 and 1 Corinthians 1:18–31.

▶ 2 Chr 1:7–12

Shephelah.* 16 Solomon's horses were imported
from Egypt and Cilicia,† where the king's agents
purchased them at the prevailing price.* 17 A
chariot imported from Egypt cost six hundred
shekels of silver, a horse one hundred and fifty
shekels; so they were exported to all the Hittite
and Aramean kings.*

Preparations for the Temple

18 Solomon gave orders for the building of a
house for the name of the LORD and also a king's
house for himself.

2 1 Solomon conscripted seventy thousand
men to carry stones and eighty thousand to
cut the stones in the mountains, and over these
he placed three thousand six hundred overseers.*
2 * Moreover, Solomon sent this message to Hu-
ram, king of Tyre: "As you dealt with David my
father, and sent him cedars to build a house for
his dwelling— 3 now I am going to build a house
for the name of the LORD, my God, and to con-
secrate it to him, for the burning of fragrant in-
cense in his presence, for the perpetual display of
the showbread, for burnt offerings morning and
evening, and for the sabbaths, new moons, and
festivals of the LORD, our God: such is Israel's per-
petual obligation.* 4 And the house I am going to
build must be great, for our God is greater than
all other gods. 5 Yet who is really able to build
him a house, since the heavens and even the
highest heavens cannot contain him? And who
am I that I should build him a house,* unless it
be to offer incense in his presence? 6 Now, send
me men skilled at work in gold, silver, bronze,
and iron, in purple, crimson, and violet fabrics,
and who know how to do engraved work, to
join the skilled craftsmen who are with me in
Judah and Jerusalem, whom David my father ap-
pointed. 7 Also send me boards of cedar, cypress
and cabinet wood from Lebanon, for I realize
that your servants know how to cut the wood of
Lebanon. My servants will work with yours 8 in
order to prepare for me a great quantity of wood,
since the house I intend to build must be great
and wonderful. 9 I will furnish as food for your
servants, the woodcutters, twenty thousand kors
of wheat, twenty thousand kors of barley, twenty
thousand baths of wine, and twenty thousand
baths of oil."† *
10 Huram, king of Tyre, wrote an answer which
he sent to Solomon: "Because the LORD loves his
people, he has placed you over them as king."
11 He added: "Blessed be the LORD, the God of
Israel, who made heaven and earth, for hav-
ing given King David a wise son of intelligence
and understanding, who will build a house for
the LORD and also his own royal house.* 12 * I
am now sending you a craftsman of great skill,
Huram-abi, 13 son of a Danite woman† and of
a father from Tyre; he knows how to work with
gold, silver, bronze, and iron, with stone and
wood, with purple, violet, fine linen, and crim-
son, and also how to do all kinds of engraved
work and to devise every type of design that
may be given him and your craftsmen and the

†

1:16–17 *Egypt and Cilicia*: it seems likely that the horses came from Cilicia and the chariots from Egypt. Some scholars find a reference to Musur, a mountain district north of Cilicia, rather than to Egypt (Misrayim) in 1 Kgs 10:28–29, the Chronicler's source for this notice. The Chronicler himself probably understood the source to be speaking of Egypt; cf. 2 Chr 9:28.

2:9 There is probably some exaggeration here. The parallel passage in 1 Kgs 5:25 does not list the barley or the wine, and mentions only twenty kors of olive oil. *Kors*: see note on Ez 45:14; *baths*: see note on Is 5:10. The amount given in Chronicles would be one hundred times as much (20,000 baths equals 2,000 kors).

2:13 *A Danite woman*: in 1 Kgs 7:14 she is called a widow of the tribe of Naphtali. The Danites had settled in the northern section of Naphtali's territory (Jgs 18:27–29). Bezalel, the head artisan in the time of Moses, had as his assistant a member of the tribe of Dan (Ex 31:6).

*

1:15 1 Kgs 10:27.
1:16 1 Kgs 10:28.
1:17 1 Kgs 10:29.
2:1 2 Chr 2:17; 5:29–30.
2:2–9 1 Kgs 5:15–20; 1 Chr 14:1.
2:3 Lv 24:5–8; Nm 28–29.
2:5 2 Chr 6:18.
2:9 1 Kgs 5:25; Ezr 3:7.
2:11 1 Kgs 5:21.
2:12–13 Ex 31:1–5; 1 Kgs 7:13–14.

craftsmen of my lord David your father. 14 * And
now, let my lord send to his servants the wheat,
barley, oil, and wine which he has promised.
15 For our part, we will cut trees on Lebanon, as
many as you need, and send them down to you
in rafts to the port of Joppa, whence you may
take them up to Jerusalem."*

16 * Thereupon Solomon took a census of all
the alien men resident in the land of Israel (fol-
lowing the census David his father had taken of
them); they were found to number one hundred
fifty-three thousand six hundred. 17 Of these he
made seventy thousand carriers and eighty thou-
sand cutters in the mountains, and three thou-
sand six hundred overseers to keep the people
working.*

Building of the Temple

3 1 * Then Solomon began to build the house
of the LORD in Jerusalem on Mount Moriah,†
which had been shown to David his father, in the
place David had prepared, the threshing floor of
Ornan the Jebusite. 2 He began to build in the sec-
ond month of the fourth year of his reign. 3 These
were the specifications laid down by Solomon
for building the house of God: the length was
sixty cubits according to the old measure, and the
width was twenty cubits;* 4 the front porch along
the width of the house was also twenty cubits,
and it was twenty cubits high.† He covered its in-
terior with pure gold.* 5 The nave he overlaid with
cypress wood and overlaid that with fine gold,
embossing on it palms and chains.* 6 He also cov-
ered the house with precious stones for splendor;
the gold was from Parvaim. 7 The house, its beams
and thresholds, as well as its walls and its doors,
he overlaid with gold, and he engraved cherubim
upon the walls. 8 He also made the room of the
holy of holies. Its length corresponded to the
width of the house, twenty cubits, and its width
was also twenty cubits. He overlaid it with fine
gold to the amount of six hundred talents.* 9 The
weight of the nails was fifty gold shekels. The up-
per chambers he likewise overlaid with gold.

10 * For the room of the holy of holies he made
two cherubim of carved workmanship, which
were then covered with gold. 11 The wings of the
cherubim spanned twenty cubits: one wing of
each cherub, five cubits in length, extended to
a wall of the house, while the other wing, also
five cubits in length, touched the correspond-
ing wing of the other cherub. 12 The wing of
the cherub, five cubits, touched the wall of the
house, and the other wing, five cubits, was joined
to the wing of the other cherub. 13 The combined
wingspread of the two cherubim was thus twenty
cubits. They stood upon their own feet, facing
toward the nave. 14 He made the veil† of violet,
purple, crimson, and fine linen, and had cheru-
bim embroidered upon it.*

15 * In front of the house he set two columns
thirty-five cubits high; the capital of each was
five cubits. 16 He devised chains in the form of a
collar with which he encircled the capitals of the
columns, and he made a hundred pomegran-
ates which he set on the chains. 17 He set up the
columns to correspond with the nave, one for
the right side and the other for the left, and he
called the one to the right Jachin and the one to
the left Boaz.

4 1 Then he made a bronze altar twenty cubits
long, twenty cubits wide and ten cubits high.*
2 * He also made the molten sea. It was made with
a circular rim, and measured ten cubits across,
five in height, and thirty in circumference. 3 Un-
der the brim a ring of figures of oxen† encircled it
for ten cubits, all the way around the compass of
the sea; there were two rows of oxen cast in one
mold with the sea. 4 This rested on twelve oxen,
three facing north, three facing west, three facing
south, and three facing east, with their haunches
all toward the center; upon them was set the sea.
5 It was a handbreadth thick, and its brim resem-
bled that of a cup, being lily-shaped. It had a
capacity of three thousand baths.†

6 Then he made ten basins for washing, placing
five of them to the right and five to the left. In these

2 CHR

---

† **3:1** *Mount Moriah*: Gn 22:2 speaks of a "height in the land of Moriah." This is the only place in the Bible where the Temple mount is identified with the site where Abraham was to have sacrificed Isaac.

3:4 *The front porch . . . twenty cubits high*: this figure, not given in 1 Kgs 7, is based on a variant Greek text that may be due to a later revision. The Hebrew text itself has "one hundred and twenty cubits high." The Chronicler nearly doubles the height of the two freestanding columns adjacent to the porch in 2 Chr 3:15 as compared with the source, 1 Kgs 7:15–16.

3:14 *The veil*: this was suspended at the entrance of the holy of holies, in imitation of the veil of the Mosaic meeting tent (Ex 26:31–32). Solomon's Temple had doors at this point, according to 1 Kgs 6:31. Apparently the Temple of the Chronicler's time did have a veil, just as did Herod's Temple (Mt 27:51; Mk 15:38; Lk 23:45).

4:3 *Oxen*: in 1 Kgs 7:24 this double row of ornaments is described as consisting of gourds. The text of Kings available to the Chronicler may have been corrupt at this point since the two words sound similar in Hebrew. In 4:16 the Chronicler speaks of forks while 1 Kgs 7:40 refers to bowls.

4:5 *Three thousand baths*: two thousand baths according to 1 Kgs 7:26; see note on 1 Kgs 7:23–26.

* **2:14–15** 1 Kgs 5:22–26.
2:15 Ezr 3:7.
2:16–17 1 Chr 22:2.
2:17 2 Chr 2:1.
3:1–2 Gn 22:2; 1 Kgs 6:1; 1 Chr 21:22–26; 22:1.
3:3 1 Kgs 6:2.
3:4 1 Kgs 6:3.
3:5 1 Kgs 6:15; Ez 41:1.
3:8 1 Kgs 6:16–17, 20.
3:10–13 1 Kgs 6:23–27.
3:14 Mt 27:51.
3:15–17 1 Kgs 7:15–20; Ez 40:49.
4:1 Ez 43:13–17.
4:2–5 1 Kgs 7:23–26.

Chapter 4

the victims for the burnt offerings were washed;
but the sea was for the priests to wash in.*
7 He made the menorahs of gold, ten of them
as was prescribed, and placed them in the nave,
five to the right and five to the left.* 8 He made
ten tables and had them set in the nave, five to
the right and five to the left; and he made a hun-
dred golden bowls.* 9 He made the court of the
priests and the great courtyard* and the gates of
the courtyard; the gates he covered with bronze.
10 The sea he placed off to the southeast from the
south side of the house.*
11* When Huram had made the pots, shovels,
and bowls, he finished all his work for King Sol-
omon in the house of God: 12 two columns; two
nodes for the capitals on top of the columns;
and two pieces of netting covering the two nodes
for the capitals on top of the columns; 13 four
hundred pomegranates in double rows on both
pieces of netting that covered the two nodes of
the capitals on top of the columns. 14 He made
the stands, and the basins on the stands; 15 one
sea, and the twelve oxen under it; 16 pots, shov-
els, forks, and all the articles Huram-abi made
for King Solomon for the house of the LORD;
they were of burnished bronze. 17 The king had
them cast in the neighborhood of the Jordan, be-
tween Succoth and Zeredah, in thick clay molds.
18 Solomon made all these vessels, so many in
number that the weight of the bronze could not
be determined.
19 Solomon made all the articles that were for
the house of God: the golden altar, the tables on
which the showbread lay, 20 the menorahs and
their lamps of pure gold which were to burn as
prescribed before the inner sanctuary, 21 flowers,
lamps, and gold tongs (this was of purest gold),
22 snuffers, bowls, cups, and firepans of pure
gold. As for the entrance to the house, its inner
doors to the holy of holies, as well as the doors
to the nave of the temple, were of gold.

Dedication of the Temple

5 1* When all the work undertaken by Sol-
omon for the house of the LORD was com-
pleted, he brought in the votive offerings of
David his father, putting the silver, the gold, and
other articles in the treasuries of the house of
God. 2 Then Solomon assembled the elders of Is-
rael and all the heads of the tribes, the princes in
the ancestral houses of the Israelites, to Jerusalem
to bring up the ark of the LORD's covenant from
the City of David, which is Zion. 3 All the people
of Israel assembled before the king during the
festival of the seventh month.† 4* When all the
elders of Israel had arrived, the Levites† took up
the ark; 5 and they brought up the ark and the tent
of meeting with all the sacred vessels that were in
the tent. The levitical priests brought them up.
6 King Solomon and the entire community of
Israel, gathered for the occasion before the ark,
sacrificed sheep and oxen too many to number
or count. 7 The priests brought the ark of the cov-
enant of the LORD to its place: the inner sanctuary
of the house, the holy of holies, beneath the wings
of the cherubim. 8 The cherubim had their wings
spread out over the place of the ark, covering the
ark and its poles from above. 9 The poles were so
long that their ends could be seen from the holy
place in front of the inner sanctuary. (They cannot
be seen from outside, but they remain there to this
day.)† 10 There was nothing in the ark but the two
tablets which Moses had put there at Horeb when

†

5:3 *Festival of the seventh month*: feast of Booths (Tabernacles); cf. notes on 7:9–10; 1 Kgs 8:2.

5:4 *The Levites*: the parallel passage in 1 Kgs 8:3 reads "the priests"; but in 2 Chr 5:5 the Deuteronomic expression "levitical priests" is used, as it is in 23:18; 30:27.

5:9 *They remain there to this day*: the Chronicler must have copied this notice from his source (1 Kgs 8:8), losing sight of the fact that there was no ark in the Temple of his own day. (According to 2 Mc 2:4–8, the ark of Solomon's Temple was concealed by Jeremiah at the time of the Babylonian destruction of Jerusalem.)

*

4:6 1 Kgs 7:38–39; Ez 40:38.
4:7 1 Kgs 7:49.
4:8 1 Kgs 7:50; 1 Chr 28:16.
4:9 1 Kgs 7:12.
4:10 1 Kgs 7:39.
4:11–22 1 Kgs 7:40–51.
5:1–14 1 Kgs 7:51–8:13.
5:4–5 2 Chr 35:3.

the LORD made a covenant with the Israelites after
they went forth from Egypt.
11 When the priests left the holy place (all the
priests who were present had purified themselves
regardless of the rotation of their various divi-
sions), 12 the Levites who were singers, all who
belonged to Asaph, Heman, Jeduthun, and their
sons and brothers, clothed in fine linen, with
cymbals, harps, and lyres, stood east of the al-
tar, and with them a hundred and twenty priests
blowing trumpets.
13 When the trumpeters and singers were heard
as a single voice praising and giving thanks to
the LORD, and when they raised the sound of the
trumpets, cymbals, and other musical instru-
ments to "Praise the LORD, who is so good, whose
love endures forever," the cloud filled the house
of the LORD.* 14 The priests could no longer min-
ister because of the cloud, since the glory of the
LORD had filled the house of God.*

6 1 * Then Solomon said:

"The LORD intends to dwell in the dark cloud;
2 I have built you a princely house,
the base for your enthronement forever."

3 * The king turned and blessed the whole assem-
bly of Israel, while the whole assembly of Israel
stood. 4 He said: "Blessed be the LORD, the God of
Israel, who with his own mouth spoke a promise
to David my father and by his hand fulfilled it,
saying: 5 Since the day I brought my people out
of the land of Egypt, I have not chosen a city out
of any tribe of Israel for the building of a house,
that my name might be there; nor have I chosen
any man to be ruler of my people Israel; 6 but
now I have chosen Jerusalem, that my name may
be there, and I have chosen David† to rule my
people Israel. 7 When David my father wished to
build a house for the name of the LORD, the God
of Israel, 8 the LORD said to him: In wishing to
build a house for my name, you did well. 9 But
it is not you who will build the house, but your
son, who comes from your loins: he shall build
the house for my name.
10 "Now the LORD has fulfilled the word he
spoke. I have succeeded David my father, and I
sit on the throne of Israel, as the LORD has said,
and I have built this house for the name of the
LORD, the God of Israel. 11 I have placed there the
ark, in which is the covenant of the LORD that he
made with the Israelites."

Solomon's Prayer

12 * Then he stood before the altar of the LORD
in the presence of the whole assembly of Israel
and stretched forth his hands. 13 † Solomon had
made a bronze platform five cubits long, five
cubits wide, and three cubits high, which he had
placed in the middle of the courtyard. Having
ascended it, Solomon knelt in the presence of
the whole assembly of Israel and stretched forth
his hands toward heaven. 14 He said: "LORD, God
of Israel, there is no God like you in heaven or
on earth; you keep the covenant and love toward
your servants who walk before you with their
whole heart, 15 the covenant that you kept to-
ward your servant, David my father. That which
you promised him, your mouth has spoken and
your hand has fulfilled this very day. 16 And now,
LORD, God of Israel, keep toward your servant,
David my father, what you promised: There shall
never be wanting someone from your line to sit
before me on the throne of Israel, provided that
your descendants keep to their way, walking by
my law, as you have. 17 Now, LORD, God of Israel,
may the words which you spoke to David your
servant be confirmed.
18 "Is God indeed to dwell with human beings
on earth? If the heavens and the highest heavens
cannot contain you, how much less this house
which I have built! 19 Regard kindly the prayer
and petition of your servant, LORD, my God, and
listen to the cry of supplication which I, your ser-
vant, utter before you. 20 May your eyes be open
day and night toward this house, the place where
you have decreed your name shall be; listen to
the prayer your servant makes toward this place.
21 Listen to the petition of your servant and of
your people Israel which they offer toward this
place. Listen, from the place of your enthrone-
ment, heaven, and listen and forgive.
22 "If someone sins against a neighbor and is
required to take an oath sanctioned by a curse,
and comes and takes the oath before your altar
in this house, 23 listen in heaven: act and judge
your servants. Condemn the wicked, requiting
their ways; acquit the just, rewarding their jus-
tice. 24 When your people Israel are defeated by

† **6:6** *Jerusalem . . . David*: Ps 132:11, 13 puts in parallel the Lord's choice of David and Zion, the royal house of David and the mountain in Jerusalem as the site for the Lord's house.

6:13 This verse has no equivalent in 1 Kgs 8:22–23, the Chronicler's source. Solomon is depicted as praying on "a bronze platform . . . in the middle of the courtyard" because in the time of the Chronicler only priests were permitted to pray before the altar.

5:13 Ps 136; Jer 33:11.
5:14 2 Chr 7:2; 1 Kgs 8:10–11.
6:1–2 1 Kgs 8:12–13.
6:3–11 1 Kgs 8:14–21.
6:12–40 1 Kgs 8:22–53.

an enemy because they have sinned against you,
and then they turn, praise your name, pray to
you, and entreat you in this house, 25 listen from
heaven and forgive the sin of your people Israel,
and bring them back to the land you gave them
and their ancestors. 26 When the heavens are
closed so that there is no rain, because they have
sinned against you, but they pray toward this
place and praise your name, and turn from their
sin because you have afflicted them, 27 listen in
heaven and forgive the sin of your servants, your
people Israel. (For you teach them the good way
in which they should walk.) Give rain upon this
land of yours which you have given to your peo-
ple as their heritage.
28 "If there is famine in the land or pestilence;
or if blight comes, or mildew, or locusts swarm,
or caterpillars; when their enemies besiege them
at any of their gates; whatever plague or sickness
there may be; 29 whatever prayer of petition any
may make, any of your people Israel, who know
affliction and pain and stretch out their hands
toward this house, 30 listen from heaven, the
place of your enthronement, and forgive. Render
to each and all according to their ways, you who
know every heart; for it is you alone who know
the heart of every human being. 31 So may they
revere you and walk in your ways as long as they
live on the land you gave our ancestors.
32 "To the foreigners, likewise, who are not of
your people Israel, but who come from a distant
land for the sake of your great name, your mighty
hand and outstretched arm, and come in prayer
to this house, 33 listen from heaven, the place of
your enthronement. Do all that the foreigner
asks of you, that all the peoples of the earth may
know your name, may revere you as do your
people Israel, and may know that your name has
been invoked upon this house that I have built.
34 "When your people go out to war against
their enemies, by whatever way you send them,
and they pray to you toward the city you have
chosen and the house I have built for your name,
35 listen from heaven to their prayer and petition,
and uphold their cause. 36 When they sin against
you (for there is no one who does not sin), and
in your anger against them you deliver them to
an enemy, so that their captors carry them off
to another land, far or near, 37 and they have a
change of heart in the land of their captivity and
they turn and entreat you in the land of their cap-
tors and say, 'We have sinned and done wrong;
we have been wicked,' 38 if with all their heart
and soul they turn back to you in the land of
those who took them captive, and pray toward
their land which you gave their ancestors, the
city you have chosen, and the house which I have
built for your name, 39 listen from heaven, the
place of your enthronement, to their prayer and
petitions, and uphold their cause. Forgive your
people who have sinned against you. 40 Now, my
God, may your eyes be open and your ears be at-
tentive to the prayer of this place. 41 And now:

"Arise, LORD God, come to your resting place,
you and your majestic ark.
Your priests, LORD God, will be clothed with
salvation,
your faithful ones rejoice in good things.
42 LORD God, do not reject the plea of your
anointed,
remember the devotion of David, your
servant."*

7 1* When Solomon had ended his prayer, fire
came down from heaven and consumed the
burnt offerings and the sacrifices, and the glory
of the LORD filled the house. 2 But the priests
could not enter the house of the LORD, for the
glory of the LORD filled the house of the LORD.*
3 All the Israelites looked on while the fire came
down and the glory of the LORD was upon the
house, and they fell down upon the pavement
with their faces to the earth and worshiped,
praising the LORD, "who is so good, whose love
endures forever." 4 The king and all the people of-
fered sacrifices before the LORD.* 5 King Solomon
offered as sacrifice twenty-two thousand oxen,
and one hundred twenty thousand sheep.*

End of the Dedication

Thus the king and all the people dedicated
the house of God. 6 The priests were standing at
their stations, as were the Levites, with the mu-
sical instruments of the LORD which King David
had made to give thanks to the LORD, "whose
love endures forever," when David offered praise
through them. The priests opposite them blew
the trumpets and all Israel stood.*
7 Then Solomon consecrated the middle of the
court facing the house of the LORD; he offered
there the burnt offerings and the fat of the com-
munion offerings, since the bronze altar which
Solomon had made could not hold the burnt of-
fering, the grain offering, and the fat.*
8 On this occasion Solomon and with him
all Israel, a great assembly from Lebo-hamath

6:41–42 Ps 132:8–10.
7:1–10 Jgs 6:21; 1 Kgs 8:54–66; 1 Chr 21:26; 2 Mc 2:10.
7:2 2 Chr 5:14; Ex 24:16; 1 Kgs 8:10–11.
7:4 2 Chr 5:13; 1 Kgs 8:62; Ps 136:1.
7:5 1 Kgs 8:63.
7:6 Nm 10:8, 10; Ps 136:1.
7:7 1 Kgs 8:64.
7:8 1 Kgs 8:65.

to the Wadi of Egypt, celebrated the festival for seven days.* 9 * On the eighth day they held a solemn assembly, for they had celebrated the dedication of the altar for seven days and the feast† for seven days. 10 On the twenty-third day of the seventh month he dismissed the people to their tents, rejoicing and glad of heart because of all the blessings the LORD had given to David, to Solomon, and to his people Israel. 11 * Solomon finished building the house of the LORD, the house of the king, and everything else he wanted to do in regard to the house of the LORD and his own house.

God's Promise to Solomon

12 The LORD appeared to Solomon during the night and said to him: I have heard your prayer, and I have chosen this place for my house of sacrifice. 13 If I close heaven so that there is no rain, if I command the locust to devour the land, if I send pestilence among my people, 14 if then my people, upon whom my name has been pronounced, humble themselves and pray, and seek my face and turn from their evil ways, I will hear them from heaven and pardon their sins and heal their land. 15 Now, therefore, my eyes shall be open and my ears attentive to the prayer of this place; 16 now I have chosen and consecrated this house that my name may be there forever; my eyes and my heart shall be there always.

17 As for you, if you walk before me as David your father did, doing all that I have commanded you and keeping my statutes and ordinances, 18 I will establish the throne of your kingship as I covenanted with David your father when I said, There shall never be wanting someone from your line as ruler in Israel. 19 But if ever you turn away and forsake my commandments and statutes which I set before you, and proceed to serve other gods, and bow down to them, 20 I will uproot the people from the land I gave and repudiate the house I have consecrated for my name. I will make it a proverb and a byword among all nations. 21 And this house which is so exalted—every passerby shall be horrified and ask: "Why has the LORD done such things to this land and to this house?" 22 And the answer will come: "Because they abandoned the LORD, the God of their ancestors, who brought them out of the land of Egypt, and they embraced other gods, bowing down to them and serving them. That is why he has brought upon them all this evil."

Public Works

8 1 * After the twenty years during which Solomon built the house of the LORD and his own house, 2 he built up the cities which Huram had given him,† and settled Israelites there. 3 Then Solomon went to Hamath of Zoba and conquered it. 4 He built Tadmor† in the wilderness and all the supply cities, which he built in Hamath. 5 * He built Upper Beth-horon and Lower Beth-horon, fortified cities with walls, gates, and bars; 6 also Baalath, all the supply cities belonging to Solomon, and all the cities for the chariots, the cities for horses, and whatever else Solomon desired to build in Jerusalem, in Lebanon, and in the entire land under his dominion. 7 All the people who were left of the Hittites, Amorites, Perizzites, Hivites, and Jebusites who were not Israelites— 8 those of their descendants who were left in the land and whom the Israelites had not destroyed—Solomon conscripted as forced laborers, as they are to this day. 9 But Solomon made none of the Israelites forced laborers for his works, for they were his fighting force, commanders, adjutants, chariot officers, and cavalry. 10 They were also King Solomon's two hundred and fifty overseers who directed the people.

Solomon's Piety

11 Solomon brought the daughter of Pharaoh up from the City of David to the house which he had built for her, for he said, "No wife of mine shall dwell in the house of David, king of Israel, for the places where the ark of the LORD has come are holy."

12 In those times Solomon sacrificed burnt offerings to the LORD upon the altar of the LORD which he had built in front of the porch, 13 as was required to be done day by day according to the command of Moses, especially on the sabbaths, at the new moons, and on the fixed festivals three times a year: on the feast of the

†

7:9–10 *The feast*: Booths, celebrated on the fifteenth day of the seventh month and followed by a solemn octave lasting through the twenty-second day (Lv 23:33–36; Nm 29:12–35); the people are therefore sent home on the twenty-third day of the month (v. 10). The festival (v. 8) marking the dedication of the altar and of the Temple was held during the seven days prior to the feast of Booths, i.e., from the seventh to the fourteenth day of the seventh month. According to 1 Kgs 8:3, 65–66 the dedication of the Temple was celebrated concomitantly with the seven days of the feast of Booths, after which the people were dismissed on the eighth day.

8:2 *The cities which Huram had given him*: according to 1 Kgs 9:10–14, it was Solomon who ceded the cities to the king of Tyre as payment for the timber and gold received from him. Since, however, 1 Kgs 9:12 states that Hiram was not satisfied with the cities, the Chronicler may have inferred that he gave them back to Solomon.

8:4 *Tadmor*: later known as Palmyra, an important caravan city in the Syrian desert. The parallel passage in 1 Kgs 9:18 has "Tamar," in southern Judah; cf. Ez 47:19; 48:28. But Solomon may well have fortified Tadmor against the Arameans.

*

7:9–10 1 Kgs 8:66. **7:11–22** 1 Kgs 9:1–9. **8:1–2** 1 Kgs 9:10–11. **8:5–12** 1 Kgs 9:17–25.

Live It!

Money Talks

"You can't take it with you." How often have we heard this statement? We know it's true. Yet we are so easily impressed with wealth and riches. King Solomon, whose wealth is described in 2 Chronicles 9:13–28, would be right at home in our world, which seems so taken with the rich and the famous.

A common saying of those promoting sustainable living is "Live simply, so others may simply live." This is a powerful summons to us who live in a society obsessed with shopping and buying and always getting the latest and the best. In the meantime, so much of the world has to go without even the basic necessities of life.

- Think about the clothes you have, for instance. Do you wear all of them?
- What do you spend your money on? Are you generous or pretty tight-fisted? What values are expressed in how you spend your money? Is there a way that you can spend your money so the lives of others could improve?
- What is one thing you can do today to live more simply?

► 2 Chr 9:13–28

Unleavened Bread, the feast of Weeks, and the
feast of Booths.*
14 And according to the ordinance of David his
father he appointed the various divisions of the
priests for their service, and the Levites according
to their functions of praise and attendance upon
the priests, as the daily duty required. The gate-
keepers by their divisions stood guard at each gate,
since such was the command of David, the man of
God.* 15 There was no deviation from the king's
command in whatever related to the priests and
Levites or the treasuries. 16 All of Solomon's work
was carried out successfully from the day the foun-
dation of the house of the LORD was laid until its
completion. The house of the LORD was finished.

Glories of the Court

17 In those times Solomon went to Ezion-
geber and to Elath on the seashore of the land
of Edom.* 18 Huram had his servants send him
ships and his own servants, expert seamen; they
went with Solomon's servants to Ophir, and
obtained there four hundred and fifty talents of
gold and brought it to King Solomon.*

The Queen of Sheba

9 1 * The queen of Sheba, having heard a re-
port of Solomon's fame, came to Jerusalem
to test him with subtle questions, accompanied
by a very numerous retinue and by camels bear-
ing spices, a large amount of gold, and precious
stones. She came to Solomon and spoke to him
about everything that she had on her mind.
2 Solomon explained to her everything she asked
about, and there was nothing so obscure that
Solomon could not explain it to her.*
3 * When the queen of Sheba witnessed Solo-
mon's great wisdom, the house he had built, 4 the
food at his table, the seating of his ministers, the
attendance and dress of his waiters, his cupbear-
ers and their dress, and the burnt offerings he
sacrificed in the house of the LORD, it took her
breath away. 5 "The report I heard in my country
about your deeds and your wisdom is true," she
told the king. 6 "I did not believe the report until
I came and saw with my own eyes that not even
the half of your great wisdom had been told me.
You have surpassed the report I heard. 7 Happy
your servants, happy these ministers of yours,
who stand before you always and listen to your
wisdom. 8 Blessed be the LORD, your God, who
was pleased to set you on his throne as king for
the LORD, your God. In the love your God has
for Israel, to establish them forever, he has made
you king over them to carry out judgment and
justice." 9 Then she gave the king one hundred
and twenty gold talents, a very large quantity
of spices, and precious stones. Never again did
anyone bring such an abundance of spices as the
queen of Sheba gave to King Solomon.
10 The servants of Huram and of Solomon who
brought gold from Ophir also brought cabinet
wood and precious stones. 11 With the cabinet
wood the king made stairs for the house of the
LORD and the house of the king, and harps and
lyres for the chanters. The like of these had not
been seen before in the land of Judah.*
12 King Solomon gave the queen of Sheba ev-
erything she desired and asked for, more than
she had brought to the king. Then she returned
with her servants to her own country.*

8:13 Ex 23:14; Nm 28–29; 1 Kgs 9:25.
8:14 1 Chr 23–26; Neh 12:46.
8:17 1 Kgs 9:26.
8:18 1 Kgs 9:27–28.
9:1 1 Kgs 10:1–2.
9:2 1 Kgs 10:3.
9:3–9 1 Kgs 10:4–9.
9:10–11 1 Kgs 10:11–12.
9:12 1 Kgs 10:13.

13 * The gold that came to Solomon in one
year weighed six hundred and sixty-six gold tal-
ents, 14 in addition to what came from the tolls
on travelers and what the merchants brought. All
the kings of Arabia also, and the governors of the
country, brought gold and silver to Solomon.
15 King Solomon made two hundred large
shields of beaten gold (six hundred shekels of
gold went into each shield) 16 and three hundred
bucklers of beaten gold (three hundred shekels
of gold went into each buckler); and the king put
them in the house of the Forest of Lebanon.
17 The king made a large ivory throne, and
overlaid it with fine gold. 18 The throne had six
steps; a footstool of gold was fastened to the
throne, and there was an arm on each side of the
seat, with two lions standing next to the arms,
19 and twelve other lions standing there on the
steps, two to a step. Nothing like this was made
in any other kingdom. 20 All King Solomon's
drinking vessels were gold, and all the utensils
in the house of the Forest of Lebanon were pure
gold. There was no silver, for in Solomon's time
silver was reckoned as nothing. 21 For the king
had ships that went to Tarshish with the servants
of Huram. Once every three years the fleet of
Tarshish ships would come with a cargo of gold,
silver, ivory, apes, and monkeys.

Solomon's Renown

22 Thus King Solomon surpassed all the kings
of the earth in riches and wisdom.
23 All the kings of the earth sought audience
with Solomon, to hear the wisdom God had put
into his heart. 24 They all brought their tribute: ves-
sels of silver and gold, garments, weapons, spices,
horses, and mules—what was due each year.
25 Solomon had four thousand stalls for horses,
chariots, and twelve thousand horses; these he al-
located among the chariot cities and to the king's
service in Jerusalem. 26 He was ruler over all the
kings from the River to the land of the Philistines
and down to the border of Egypt. 27 The king
made silver as common in Jerusalem as stones,
and cedars as numerous as the sycamores of the
Shephelah. 28 † Solomon's horses were imported
from Egypt and from all the lands.

The Death of Solomon

29 * The remainder of the acts of Solomon, first
and last, are recorded in the acts of Nathan the
prophet, in the prophecy of Ahijah the Shilonite,
and in the visions of Iddo the seer concerning
Jeroboam, son of Nebat. 30 Solomon was king in
Jerusalem over all Israel for forty years. 31 Solo-
mon rested with his ancestors and was buried in
the City of David, his father, and Rehoboam his
son succeeded him as king.

II. The Post-Solomonic Monarchy of Judah

Division of the Kingdom

10 1 * Rehoboam went to Shechem, where
all Israel† had come to make him king.
2 When Jeroboam, son of Nebat, heard about
it, he was in Egypt where he had fled from King
Solomon; and he returned from Egypt. 3 They
sent for him; Jeroboam and all Israel came and
said to Rehoboam: 4 "Your father put on us a
heavy yoke. If you now lighten the harsh servi-
tude and the heavy yoke your father imposed
on us, we will be your servants." 5 He answered
them, "Come back to me in three days," and the
people went away.
6 King Rehoboam asked advice of the elders
who had been in his father Solomon's service
while he was still alive, and asked, "How do
you advise me to answer this people?" 7 They
replied, "If you will deal kindly with this peo-
ple and please them, giving them a favorable
reply, they will be your servants forever." 8 But
he ignored the advice the elders had given him
and asked advice of the young men who had
grown up with him and were in his service. 9 He
said to them, "What answer do you advise us to
give this people, who have told me, 'Lighten the
yoke your father imposed on us'?" 10 The young
men who had grown up with him replied: "This
is what you must say to this people who have
told you, 'Your father laid a heavy yoke on us;
lighten it for us.' You must say, 'My little finger
is thicker than my father's loins. 11 My father
put a heavy yoke on you; I will make it heavier.
My father beat you with whips; I will use scor-
pions!'"
12 On the third day, Jeroboam and the whole
people came back to King Rehoboam as the king
had instructed them: "Come back to me in three
days." 13 Ignoring the advice the elders had given
him, King Rehoboam gave the people a harsh
answer. 14 He spoke to them as the young men

2 CHR

9:28 See note on 1:16–17.

10:1 *All Israel*: as in the source (1 Kgs 12:1), this term designates the northern tribes, as distinct from Judah and Benjamin. Elsewhere the Chronicler, writing on his own, speaks comprehensively of "those Israelites who lived in the cities of Judah" (10:17), and "all the Israelites [lit., all Israel] in Judah and Benjamin" (11:3).

9:13–28 1 Kgs 10:14–28.
9:29–31 1 Kgs 11:41–43.
10:1–14 1 Kgs 12:1–14.

had advised: "My father laid a heavy yoke on you; I will make it heavier. My father beat you with whips; I will use scorpions." 15 The king did not listen to the people, for this turn of events was from God: the LORD fulfilled the word he had spoken through Ahijah the Shilonite to Jeroboam, the son of Nebat.*

16 * When all Israel saw that the king did not listen to them, the people answered the king:

"What share have we in David?
We have no heritage in the son of Jesse.
Everyone to your tents, Israel!
Now look to your own house, David!"

So all Israel went off to their tents, 17 but the Israelites who lived in the cities of Judah had Rehoboam as their king. 18 King Rehoboam then sent out Hadoram, who was in charge of the forced labor, but the Israelites stoned him to death. King Rehoboam, however, managed to mount his chariot and flee to Jerusalem. 19 And so Israel has been in rebellion against the house of David to this day.

11 1 * On his arrival in Jerusalem, Rehoboam assembled the house of Judah and Benjamin—one hundred and eighty thousand elite warriors—to wage war against Israel and restore the kingdom to Rehoboam. 2 However, the word of the LORD came to Shemaiah, a man of God: 3 Say to Rehoboam, son of Solomon, king of Judah, and to all the Israelites in Judah and Benjamin: 4 "Thus says the LORD: You must not go out to war against your kinsmen. Return home, each of you, for it is I who have brought this about." They obeyed the word of the LORD and turned back from going against Jeroboam.

Rehoboam's Works†

5 Rehoboam took up residence in Jerusalem and built fortified cities in Judah. 6 He built up Bethlehem, Etam, Tekoa, 7 Beth-zur, Soco, Adullam, 8 Gath, Mareshah, Ziph, 9 Adoraim, Lachish, Azekah, 10 Zorah, Aijalon, and Hebron; these were fortified cities in Judah and Benjamin. 11 Then he strengthened the fortifications and put commanders in them, along with supplies of food, oil, and wine. 12 In every city were shields and spears, and he made them very strong. Thus Judah and Benjamin remained his.

Refugees from the North

13 Now the priests and Levites throughout Israel presented themselves to him from all parts of their land, 14 for the Levites left their assigned pasture lands and their holdings and came to Judah and Jerusalem, because Jeroboam and his sons rejected them as priests of the LORD.* 15 In their place, he himself appointed priests for the high places as well as for the satyrs and calves he had made.* 16 After them, all those, of every tribe of Israel, who set their hearts to seek the LORD, the God of Israel, came to Jerusalem to sacrifice to the LORD, the God of their ancestors. 17 Thus they strengthened the kingdom of Judah and made Rehoboam, son of Solomon, prevail for three years; for they walked in the way of David and Solomon three years.

Rehoboam's Family

18 Rehoboam married Mahalath, daughter of Jerimoth, son of David and of Abihail, daughter of Eliab, son of Jesse. 19 She bore him sons: Jehush, Shemariah, and Zaham. 20 After her, he married Maacah, daughter of Absalom, who bore him Abijah,* Attai, Ziza, and Shelomith. 21 Rehoboam loved Maacah, daughter of Absalom, more than all his other wives and concubines; he had taken eighteen wives and sixty concubines, and he fathered twenty-eight sons and sixty daughters. 22 Rehoboam put Abijah, son of Maacah, first among his brothers, as leader, for he intended to make him king. 23 He acted prudently, distributing his various sons throughout all the districts of Judah and Benjamin, in all the fortified cities; and he gave them generous provisions and sought an abundance of wives for them.

Rehoboam's Apostasy

12 1 Once Rehoboam had established himself as king and was firmly in charge, he abandoned the law of the LORD, and so did all Israel with him.* 2 So in the fifth year of King Rehoboam, Shishak, king of Egypt, attacked Jerusalem, for they had acted treacherously toward the LORD.* 3 He had twelve hundred chariots and sixty thousand horsemen, and there was no counting the army that came with him from Egypt—Libyans, Sukkites,† and Ethiopians. 4 They captured the fortified cities of Judah and came as far as Jerusalem. 5 Then Shemaiah* the

†

11:5–12 These verses have no parallel in 1 Kings; they are apparently based on a separate source.

12:3 *Sukkites*: foreign mercenaries in the Egyptian army.

*

10:15 1 Kgs 11:29–39; 12:15.
10:16–19 1 Kgs 12:16–19.
11:1–4 1 Kgs 12:21–24.
11:14 1 Kgs 12:32.
11:15 Lv 17:7; 1 Kgs 12:32.
11:20 1 Kgs 15:2.
12:1 1 Kgs 11:4; 14:22.
12:2 1 Kgs 14:25.
12:5 2 Chr 11:2.

prophet came to Rehoboam and the command-
ers of Judah who had gathered at Jerusalem be-
cause of Shishak, and said to them: "Thus says
the LORD: You have abandoned me, and so I have
abandoned you to the power of Shishak."
6 Then the commanders of Israel and the king
humbled themselves saying, "The LORD is in the
right." 7 When the LORD saw that they had hum-
bled themselves, the word of the LORD came to
Shemaiah: Because they have humbled them-
selves, I will not destroy them; I will give them
some deliverance, and my wrath shall not be
poured out upon Jerusalem through Shishak.
8 But they shall be his servants. Then they will
know what it is to serve me and what it is to
serve the kingdoms of the earth. 9 * Thereupon
Shishak, king of Egypt, attacked Jerusalem and
took away the treasures of the house of the LORD
and the treasures of the house of the king. He
took everything, including the gold shields that
Solomon had made. 10 To replace them, King
Rehoboam made bronze shields, which he en-
trusted to the officers of the attendants on duty at
the entrance of the king's house. 11 Whenever the
king visited the house of the LORD, the attendants
would carry them, and then return them to the
guardroom. 12 Because he had humbled himself,
the anger of the LORD turned from him so as not
to destroy him completely; in Judah, moreover,
there was some good.
13 King Rehoboam was firmly in power in Je-
rusalem and continued to rule. Rehoboam was
forty-one years old when he became king, and he
reigned seventeen years in Jerusalem, the city in
which, out of all the tribes of Israel, the LORD chose
to set his name. His mother's name was Naamah,
the Ammonite.* 14 He did evil, for he had not set
his heart to seek the LORD. 15 * The acts of Reho-
boam, first and last, are recorded in the history of
Shemaiah the prophet and of Iddo the seer (his
family record). There were wars between Reho-
boam and Jeroboam all their days. 16 Rehoboam
rested with his ancestors; he was buried in the City
of David. His son Abijah† succeeded him as king.

War Between Abijah and Jeroboam

13 1 * In the eighteenth year of King Jero-
boam, Abijah became king of Judah; 2 he
reigned three years in Jerusalem. His mother was
named Micaiah, daughter of Uriel of Gibeah.
There was war between Abijah and Jeroboam.

Live It!

Selling Out

King Rehoboam, son of Solomon, sold out and abandoned the law of the Lord after he thought his rule was secure (see 2 Chr 12:1). The Chronicler tells us that the Lord abandoned Rehoboam to the Egyptians because of this. Fortunately, Rehoboam and his officers repented, and the Lord showed mercy on them.

Popularity has its price. It sometimes can seem so important to hang out with the "right" people, but what do you have to give up to do that? Is it worth the price? What happens to you when you compromise your values to gain the approval of others, or when you see someone you are close to do something just to be accepted?

It is so easy to fall into the trap of "selling out." But what happens to our soul when that happens?

▶ 2 Chr 12:1–12

3 † Abijah joined battle with a force of four
hundred thousand picked warriors, while Jero-
boam lined up against him in battle with eight
hundred thousand picked and valiant warriors.
4 Abijah stood on Mount Zemaraim, which is in
the highlands of Ephraim, and said: "Listen to
me, Jeroboam and all Israel! 5 Do you not know
that the LORD, the God of Israel, has given David
kingship over Israel forever, to him and to his
sons, by a covenant of salt?† 6 Yet Jeroboam, son
of Nebat, the servant of Solomon, son of David,
arose and rebelled against his lord!* 7 Worth-
less men, scoundrels, joined him and overcame
Rehoboam, son of Solomon, when Rehoboam
was young and inexperienced, and no match for
them. 8 But now, do you think you are a match
for the kingdom of the LORD led by the descen-
dants of David, simply because you are a huge

2 CHR

†

12:16 *Abijah*: in 1 Kgs 14:31–15:8 this king is called Abijam.
13:3–21 This passage is a free composition of the Chronicler based on the reference in 1 Kgs 15:6 to the war between Abijam (so in Kings, "Abijah" in Chronicles) and Jeroboam.
13:5 *Covenant of salt*: see note on Nm 18:19.

*

12:9–11 1 Kgs 14:25–28.
12:13 1 Kgs 14:21.
12:15–16 1 Kgs 14:29–31.
13:1–2 1 Kgs 15:1–2.
13:6 1 Kgs 11:26.

multitude and have with you the golden calves
which Jeroboam made you for gods? 9 Have you
not expelled the priests of the LORD, the sons of
Aaron, and the Levites, and made for yourselves
priests like the peoples of other lands? Everyone
who comes to consecrate himself with a young
bull and seven rams becomes a priest of no-gods.
10 But as for us, the LORD is our God, and we have
not abandoned him. The priests ministering to
the LORD are sons of Aaron, and the Levites also
have their offices. 11 They sacrifice burnt offerings
to the LORD and fragrant incense morning after
morning and evening after evening; they set out
the showbread on the pure table, and the lamps
of the golden menorah burn evening after eve-
ning; for we observe our duties to the LORD, our
God, but you have abandoned him. 12 See, God
is with us, at our head, and his priests are here
with trumpets to sound the attack against you.
Israelites, do not fight against the LORD, the God
of your ancestors, for you will not succeed!"
13 But Jeroboam had an ambush go around
them to come at them from the rear; so that
while his army faced Judah, his ambush lay be-
hind them. 14 When Judah turned and saw that
they had to battle on both fronts, they cried out
to the LORD and the priests sounded the trum-
pets. 15 Then the Judahites shouted; and when
they shouted, God struck down Jeroboam and
all Israel before Abijah and Judah. 16 The Israel-
ites fled before Judah, and God delivered them
into their power. 17 Abijah and his people in-
flicted a severe defeat upon them; five hundred
thousand picked men of Israel fell slain. 18 The
Israelites were humbled on that occasion, while
the Judahites were victorious because they relied
on the LORD, the God of their ancestors. 19 Abijah
pursued Jeroboam and seized cities from him:
Bethel and its dependencies, Jeshanah and its
dependencies, and Ephron and its dependencies.
20 Jeroboam did not regain power during Abijah's
time; the LORD struck him down and he died,
21 while Abijah continued to grow stronger. He
married fourteen wives and fathered twenty-two
sons and sixteen daughters.

Death of Abijah

22 * The rest of the acts of Abijah, his deeds
and his words, are recorded in the midrash of the
prophet Iddo. 23 Abijah rested with his ancestors;
they buried him in the City of David and his son
Asa succeeded him as king. During his time, the
land had ten years of peace.

Asa's Initial Reforms

14 1 * Asa did what was good and right in the
sight of the LORD, his God. 2 He removed
the illicit altars and the high places, smashed the
sacred pillars, and cut down the asherahs. 3 He
told Judah to seek the LORD, the God of their
ancestors, and to observe the law and the com-
mandment. 4 He removed the high places and
incense stands from all the cities of Judah, and
under him the kingdom had peace. 5 He built for-
tified cities in Judah, for the land had peace and
no war was waged against him during these years,
because the LORD had given him rest. 6 He said
to Judah: "Let us build these cities and surround
them with walls, towers, gates and bars. The land
is still ours, for we have sought the LORD, our
God; we sought him, and he has given us rest on
every side." So they built and prospered.

The Ethiopian Invasion†

7 Asa had an army of three hundred thousand
shield- and lance-bearers from Judah, and from
Benjamin two hundred and eighty thousand
who carried bucklers and were archers, all of
them valiant warriors. 8 Zerah the Ethiopian ad-
vanced against them with a force of one million
men and three hundred chariots, and he came as
far as Mareshah.* 9 Asa went out to meet him and
they drew up for battle in the valley of Zepha-
thah, near Mareshah. 10 Asa called upon the LORD,
his God: "LORD, there is none like you to help the
powerless against the strong. Help us, LORD, our
God, for we rely on you, and in your name we
have come against this multitude. You are the
LORD, our God; do not let men prevail against
you."* 11 And so the LORD defeated the Ethiopi-
ans before Asa and Judah, and the Ethiopians
fled. 12 Asa and those with him pursued them as
far as Gerar, and the Ethiopians fell until there
were no survivors, for they were crushed before
the LORD and his army, which carried away enor-
mous spoils. 13 Then the Judahites conquered all
the cities around Gerar, for the fear of the LORD
was upon them; they plundered all the cities, for
there was much plunder in them. 14 They also at-
tacked the tents of the cattle-herders and carried
off a great number of sheep and camels. Then
they returned to Jerusalem.

† **14:7–14** This Ethiopian invasion of Judah is not mentioned in 1 Kings. The account is likely a legend intended to show the pious King Asa being rewarded with divine assistance. It could, however, reflect an incursion by nomads from the Negeb in Asa's time.

* **13:22–23** 2 Chr 12:15–16; 1 Kgs 15:7–8.
14:1–2 2 Chr 33:15; Ex 23:24; 34:13; 1 Kgs 15:11–12.
14:8 2 Chr 16:8.
14:10 2 Chr 32:8.

Further Reforms

15 1The spirit of God came upon Azariah, son
of Oded. 2He went forth to meet Asa and
said to him: "Hear me, Asa and all Judah and
Benjamin! The LORD is with you when you are
with him, and if you seek him he will be found;
but if you abandon him, he will abandon you.*
3For a long time Israel was without a true God,
without a priest-teacher, without instruction,
4but when in their distress they turned to the
LORD, the God of Israel, and sought him, he was
found by them.* 5At that time there was no peace
for anyone to go or come; rather, there were many
terrors upon the inhabitants of the lands. 6Nation
crushed nation and city crushed city,* for God
overwhelmed them with every kind of distress.
7But as for you, be strong and do not slack off, for
there shall be a reward for what you do."*
8When Asa heard these words and the proph-
ecy (Oded the prophet), he was encouraged to
remove the detestable idols from the whole land
of Judah and Benjamin and from the cities he
had taken in the highlands of Ephraim, and to
restore the altar of the LORD which was before the
vestibule of the LORD. 9Then he gathered all Judah
and Benjamin, together with those of Ephraim,
Manasseh, and Simeon who were resident with
them; for many had defected to him from Israel
when they saw that the LORD, his God, was with
him. 10They gathered at Jerusalem in the third
month† of the fifteenth year of Asa's reign, 11and
sacrificed to the LORD on that day seven hundred
oxen and seven thousand sheep from the spoils
they had brought. 12*They entered into a cov-
enant to seek the LORD, the God of their ancestors,
with all their heart and soul; 13and everyone who
would not seek the LORD, the God of Israel, was
to be put to death, from least to greatest, man or
woman. 14They swore an oath to the LORD with a
loud voice, with shouting and with trumpets and
horns. 15All Judah rejoiced over the oath, for they
had sworn it with their whole heart and sought
him with complete desire. The LORD was found by
them,* and gave them rest on every side.
16*He also deposed Maacah, the mother† of
King Asa, from her position as queen mother be-
cause she had made an obscene object for Ashe-
rah; Asa cut down this object, smashed it, and
burnt it in the Wadi Kidron. 17The high places
did not disappear from Israel, yet Asa's heart was
undivided as long as he lived. 18He brought into
the house of God his father's and his own votive
offerings: silver, gold, and vessels. 19There was
no war until the thirty-fifth year of Asa's reign.

> **Live It!**
>
> ## Keep On Turning
>
> *Conversion*. This is an important word for Christians. Its Latin root means "to turn around." We turn from sin and toward God, as individuals and as a people. In 2 Chronicles 15:8–15, we read about King Asa and his people hearing the words of the prophet Azariah and then turning away from idols and turning back to God.
>
> Conversion is not a one-time event. It is a process all of us go through again and again as our faith and understanding grow. We are reminded of that especially during the season of Lent. On Ash Wednesday, as individuals and as a community, we hear, "Repent, and believe in the Gospel" (Roman Missal). The Israelites went through the same thing. Again and again, they were called to turn back to God.
>
> If we are committed to following Jesus, conversion is a lifelong process of deepening our faith.
>
> - Where are you most in need of conversion? Where is our nation most in need of conversion?
>
> ▶ 2 Chr 15:8–15
>
> 

Asa's Infidelity

16 1*In the thirty-sixth year of Asa's reign,
Baasha, king of Israel, attacked Judah
and fortified Ramah to block all movement for
Asa, king of Judah. 2Asa then brought out silver
and gold from the treasuries of the house of the

† **15:10–12** With this description of a covenant ceremony in "the third month" of a year beginning in the spring, the Chronicler provides a basis for the later understanding of the ancient Jewish spring feast of Weeks as a commemoration of the covenant on Mount Sinai; see Ex 19:1–3; Lv 23:16 and note on Lv 23:16–21. In the Greek period the feast came to be called Pentecost, from the Greek word for "fifty," i.e., fifty days or seven weeks after Passover. The Chronicler's presentation here has also influenced the celebration of Christian Pentecost as the "birthday of the Church"; cf. Acts 2.

15:16 *Mother*: see note on 1 Kgs 15:10.

15:2 Jer 29:13–14; Hos 3:4–5.
15:4 Dt 4:29–30.
15:6 Is 19:2.
15:7 Is 7:4; Jer 31:16.
15:12–13 Neh 10:29–30.
15:15 Dt 4:29.
15:16–18 1 Kgs 15:13–15.
16:1–6 1 Kgs 15:16–21.

LORD and the house of the king and sent them
to Ben-hadad, king of Aram, who ruled in Da-
mascus. He said: 3 "There is a treaty between you
and me, as there was between your father and
my father. I am sending you silver and gold. Go,
break your treaty with Baasha, king of Israel, that
he may withdraw from me." 4 Ben-hadad agreed
with King Asa and sent the leaders of his troops
against the cities of Israel. They attacked Ijon,
Dan, Abel-maim, besides all the store cities of
Naphtali. 5 When Baasha heard of it, he left off
fortifying Ramah, putting an end to his work.
6 Then King Asa commandeered all Judah and
they carried away the stones and beams with
which Baasha was fortifying Ramah. With them
he fortified Geba and Mizpah.

7 At that time Hanani the seer came to Asa,
king of Judah, and said to him: "Because you
relied on the king of Aram and did not rely on
the LORD, your God, the army of the king of
Aram has escaped† your power. 8 * Were not the
Ethiopians and Libyans a vast army, with great
numbers of chariots and horses? And yet, be-
cause you relied on the LORD, he delivered them
into your power. 9 The eyes of the LORD roam over
the whole earth,* to encourage those who are
devoted to him wholeheartedly. You have acted
foolishly in this matter, for from now on you will
have wars." 10 But Asa became angry with the seer
and imprisoned him in the stocks, so greatly was
he enraged at him over this. Asa also oppressed
some of his people at this time.

11 * Now the acts of Asa, first and last, are re-
corded in the book of the kings of Judah and
Israel. 12 In the thirty-ninth year of his reign, Asa
contracted disease in his feet; it became worse,
but even with this disease he did not seek the
LORD, only physicians. 13 Asa rested with his an-
cestors; he died in the forty-first year of his reign.
14 They buried him in the tomb he had hewn for
himself in the City of David, after laying him on
a couch that was filled with spices and various
kinds of aromatics compounded into an oint-
ment; and they kindled a huge fire for him.

Jehoshaphat's Zeal for the Law

17 1 His son Jehoshaphat succeeded him as
king and strengthened his position against
Israel.* 2 He placed armed forces in all the
fortified cities of Judah, and set garrisons in
the land of Judah and in the cities of Ephraim
which Asa his father had taken. 3 The LORD was
with Jehoshaphat,† for he walked in the earlier
ways of David his father, and did not seek the
Baals. 4 Rather, he sought the God of his father
and walked in his commands, and not the prac-
tices of Israel. 5 Through him, the LORD made the
kingdom secure, and all Judah gave Jehoshaphat
gifts, so that great wealth and glory was his.
6 Thus he was encouraged† to follow the LORD's
ways, and once again he removed the high places
and the asherahs from Judah.*

7 In the third year of his reign he sent his of-
ficials, Ben-hail, Obadiah, Zechariah, Nethanel,
and Micaiah, to teach in the cities of Judah.
8 With them he sent the Levites Shemaiah, Neth-
aniah, Zebadiah, Asahel, Shemiramoth, Jehon-
athan, Adonijah, and Tobijah, together with
Elishama and Jehoram the priests.* 9 They taught
in Judah, having with them the book of the law
of the LORD; they traveled through all the cities of
Judah and taught among the people.*

His Power

10 Now the fear of the LORD was upon all the
kingdoms of the countries surrounding Judah, so
that they did not war against Jehoshaphat. 11 Some
of the Philistines brought Jehoshaphat gifts and a
tribute of silver; the Arabians also brought him a
flock of seven thousand seven hundred rams and
seven thousand seven hundred he-goats.

12 Jehoshaphat grew ever greater. He built
strongholds and store cities in Judah. 13 He car-
ried out many works in the cities of Judah, and
he had soldiers, valiant warriors, in Jerusalem.
14 This was their mustering according to their an-
cestral houses. From Judah, the commanders of
thousands: Adnah the commander, and with him
three hundred thousand valiant warriors. 15 Next
to him, Jehohanan the commander, and with
him two hundred eighty thousand. 16 Next to him,
Amasiah, son of Zichri, who offered himself to the
LORD, and with him two hundred thousand valiant
warriors. 17 From Benjamin: Eliada, a valiant war-
rior, and with him two hundred thousand armed
with bow and buckler. 18 Next to him, Jehozabad,
and with him one hundred and eighty thousand
equipped for war. 19 These attended the king; in

2 CHR

† **16:7** *The king of Aram has escaped*: the Lucianic recension of the Septuagint reads, "the king of Israel escaped." This may well be the original reading, since according to the story Asa hired the king of Aram as an ally against Israel.

17:3 *The LORD was with Jehoshaphat*: along with his successors Hezekiah and Josiah, Jehoshaphat is one of the Chronicler's exemplary kings.

17:6 *Thus he was encouraged*: lit., "his heart was high," a phrase that ordinarily describes arrogance and rebelliousness; in this case, however, it introduces a notice of Jehoshaphat's fidelity to the Lord.

* **16:8** 2 Chr 14:8–14. **16:9** Ps 33:13–15. **16:11–14** 1 Kgs 15:23–24. **17:1** 1 Kgs 15:24. **17:6** 2 Chr 20:33; Ex 34:13. **17:8** 2 Chr 19:8. **17:9** Ezr 7:25.

addition to those whom the king had stationed in
the fortified cities throughout all Judah.

Alliance with Israel

18 1 * Jehoshaphat therefore had wealth and
glory in abundance; but he became related
to Ahab by marriage. 2 After some years he went
down to Ahab at Samaria; Ahab slaughtered nu-
merous sheep and oxen for him and for the peo-
ple with him, and incited him to go up against
Ramoth-gilead. 3 Ahab, king of Israel, asked Je-
hoshaphat, king of Judah, "Will you come with
me to Ramoth-gilead?" He answered, "You and
I are as one, and your people and my people as
well. We will be with you in the battle." 4 Jehosh-
aphat also said to the king of Israel, "Seek the
word of the LORD at once."

Prophets in Conflict

5 The king of Israel assembled the prophets,
four hundred of them, and asked, "Shall we
go to fight against Ramoth-gilead, or shall I re-
frain?" They said, "Attack. God will give it into
the power of the king." 6 But Jehoshaphat said,
"Is there no other prophet of the LORD here we
might consult?" 7 The king of Israel answered,
"There is one other man through whom we may
consult the LORD; but I hate him, because he
prophesies not good but always evil about me.
He is Micaiah, son of Imlah." Jeshoshaphat said,
"Let not the king say that." 8 So the king of Israel
called an official, and said to him, "Get Micaiah,
son of Imlah, at once." 9 The king of Israel and
Jehoshaphat, king of Judah, were seated, each on
his throne, clothed in their robes of state in the
square at the entrance of the gate of Samaria, and
all the prophets were prophesying before them.
10 Zedekiah, son of Chenaanah, made himself
two horns of iron and said: "The LORD says: With
these you shall gore Aram until you have de-
stroyed them." 11 The other prophets prophesied
in the same vein, saying: "Attack Ramoth-gilead,
and conquer! The LORD will give it into the power
of the king." 12 † Meanwhile the messenger who
had gone to call Micaiah said to him: "Look now,
the words of the prophets are as one in speaking
good for the king. Let your word be at one with
theirs; speak a good word." 13 Micaiah said, "As
the LORD lives, I shall speak whatever my God
says."
14 When he came to the king, the king said to
him, "Micah, shall we go to fight at Ramoth-
gilead, or shall I refrain?" He said, "Attack
and conquer! They will be delivered into your
power." 15 But the king answered him, "How
many times must I adjure you to tell me noth-
ing but the truth in the name of the LORD?" 16 So
Micaiah said:

"I see all Israel
 scattered on the mountains,
 like sheep without a shepherd,
And the LORD saying,
 These have no masters!
 Let each of them go back home in peace."

17 The king of Israel said to Jehoshaphat, "Did
I not tell you, he does not prophesy good
about me, but only evil?" 18 Micaiah continued:
"Therefore hear the word of the LORD. I saw
the LORD seated on his throne, with the whole
host of heaven standing to his right and to his
left. 19 The LORD asked: Who will deceive Ahab,
king of Israel, so that he will go up and fall on
Ramoth-gilead? And one said this, another that,
20 until this spirit came forth and stood before
the LORD, saying, 'I will deceive him.' The LORD
asked: How? 21 He answered, 'I will go forth and
become a lying spirit in the mouths of all his
prophets.' The LORD replied: You shall succeed in
deceiving him. Go forth and do this. 22 So now
the LORD has put a lying spirit in the mouths of
these prophets of yours; but the LORD himself has
decreed evil against you."
23 Thereupon Zedekiah, son of Chenaanah,
came up and struck Micaiah on the cheek, say-
ing, "Has the spirit of the LORD, then, passed
from me to speak with you?" 24 Micaiah said,
"You shall find out on the day you go into an
innermost room to hide." 25 The king of Israel
then said: "Seize Micaiah and take him back to
Amon, prefect of the city, and to Joash the king's
son, 26 and say, 'This is the king's order: Put this
man in prison and feed him scanty rations of
bread and water until I come back in safety!' "
27 But Micaiah said, "If ever you return in safety,
the LORD has not spoken through me." (He also
said, "Hear, O peoples, all of you!")†

Ahab's Death

28 The king of Israel and Jehoshaphat, king
of Judah, went up to Ramoth-gilead, 29 and the
king of Israel said to Jehoshaphat, "I will dis-
guise myself and go into battle. But you, put on

†

18:12–22 See note on 1 Kgs 22:19–23.
18:27 *"Hear, O peoples, all of you!"*: this quotation, which also appears in 1 Kgs 22:28, ascribes to the prophet Micaiah ben Imlah the opening words of the book of the prophet Micah of Moresheth (Mi 1:2), who was active a century later.

18:1–34 1 Kgs 22:1–35.

your own robes." So the king of Israel disguised
himself and they entered the battle. 30 In the
meantime, the king of Aram had given his char-
iot commanders the order, "Fight with no one,
great or small, except the king of Israel alone."
31 When the chariot commanders saw Jehosha-
phat, they thought, "There is the king of Israel!"
and wheeled to fight him. But Jehoshaphat cried
out and the LORD helped him; God induced them
to leave him alone. 32 The chariot commanders,
seeing that he was not the king of Israel, turned
away from him. 33 But someone drew his bow at
random and hit the king of Israel between the
joints of his breastplate. He ordered his chari-
oteer, "Rein about and take me out of the ranks,
for I am wounded."* 34 The battle grew fierce
during the day, and the king of Israel braced
himself up in his chariot facing the Arameans un-
til evening. He died as the sun was setting.

Jehoshaphat Rebuked

19 1 Jehoshaphat king of Judah returned in
safety to his house in Jerusalem. 2 Jehu
the seer, son of Hanani,† went out to meet King
Jehoshaphat and said to him: "Should you help
the wicked and love those who hate the LORD?
For this reason, wrath is upon you from the LORD.
3 Yet some good has been found† in you, since
you have removed the asherahs from the land
and have set your heart to seek God."

Judges Appointed

4 Jehoshaphat dwelt in Jerusalem; but he went
out again among the people from Beer-sheba
to the highlands of Ephraim and brought them
back to the LORD, the God of their ancestors. 5 He
appointed judges in the land, in all the fortified
cities of Judah, city by city, 6 and he said to them:
"Take care what you do, for the judgment you
give is not human but divine; for when it comes
to judgment God will be with you.* 7 And now,
let the fear of the LORD be upon you. Act carefully,
for with the LORD, our God, there is no injustice,
no partiality, no bribe-taking."* 8 In Jerusalem
also, Jehoshaphat appointed some Levites and
priests and some of the family heads of Israel for
the LORD's judgment and the disputes of those
who dwell in Jerusalem.* 9 He gave them this
command: "Thus you shall act: in the fear of the
LORD, with fidelity and with an undivided heart.
10 And in every dispute that comes to you from
your kin living in their cities, whether it con-
cerns bloodguilt or questions of law, command,
statutes, or ordinances, warn them lest they incur
guilt before the LORD and his wrath come upon
you and your kin. Do that and you shall not
incur guilt.* 11 See now, Amariah is chief priest
over you for everything that pertains to the LORD,
and Zebadiah, son of Ishmael, is leader of the
house of Judah in all that pertains to the king;
and the Levites will be your officials. Take firm
action, and the LORD will be with the good."

Invasion from Edom

20 1 † After this the Moabites, the Ammon-
ites, and with them some Meunites came
to fight against Jehoshaphat. 2 Jehoshaphat was
told: "A great multitude is coming against you
from across the sea, from Edom; they are al-
ready in Hazazon-tamar" (which is En-gedi).
3 Frightened, Jehoshaphat resolved to consult the
LORD. He proclaimed a fast throughout all Judah.
4 Then Judah gathered to seek the LORD's help;
from every one of the cities of Judah they came
to seek the LORD.*

Jehoshaphat's Prayer

5 Jehoshaphat stood up in the assembly of
Judah and Jerusalem in the house of the LORD
before the new court, 6 and he said: "LORD, God
of our ancestors, are you not God in heaven,
and do you not rule over all the kingdoms of
the nations? In your hand is power and might,
and no one can withstand you.* 7 Was it not
you, our God, who dispossessed the inhabitants
of this land before your people Israel and gave
it forever to the descendants of Abraham, your
friend? 8 They have dwelt in it and they built in
it a sanctuary for your name. They have said:
9 'If evil comes upon us, the sword of judgment,
or pestilence, or famine, we will stand before
this house and before you, for your name is in
this house, and we will cry out to you in our
affliction, and you will hear and save!'* 10 And
now, see the Ammonites, Moabites, and those
of Mount Seir whom you did not allow Israel to

† **19:2** *Jehu the seer, son of Hanani*: probably not the Jehu, son of Hanani, who prophesied against Baasha of Israel almost fifty years earlier (1 Kgs 16:1).

19:3 *Has been found*: theological passive, i.e., God is the implied agent.

20:1–30 This account seems to be a free composition of the Chronicler. However, there could well have been a raid of nomads against Judah in the reign of Jehoshaphat, similar to the one that occurred under Asa (14:8–14). The story may also be connected in some way with the campaign of Israel and Judah against Moab launched through the territory of Edom (2 Kgs 3:4–27).

* **18:33** 2 Chr 35:23; 1 Kgs 22:34.
19:6 Dt 1:16–18; 16:19–20.
19:7 Dt 10:17.
19:8 2 Chr 17:8–9; Dt 17:8–13; Ps 122:3–5.
19:10 Dt 17:8–13.
20:4 Jer 36:6.
20:6 2 Chr 32:7; Dt 4:39.
20:9 2 Chr 6:28–31; 7:13–14; 1 Kgs 8:37–40.

invade when they came from the land of Egypt,
but instead they passed them by and did not de-
stroy them:* [11]See how they are now repaying us
by coming to drive us out of the possession you
have given us. [12]O our God, will you not bring
judgment on them? We are powerless before this
vast multitude that is coming against us. We our-
selves do not know what to do, so our eyes are
turned toward you."

Victory Prophesied

[13]All Judah was standing before the LORD, with
their little ones, their wives, and their children.
[14]And the spirit of the LORD came upon Jahaziel,
son of Zechariah, son of Benaiah, son of Jeiel,
son of Mattaniah, a Levite of the clan of Asaph,
in the midst of the assembly, [15]and he said: "Pay
attention, all of Judah, inhabitants of Jerusalem,
and King Jehoshaphat! The LORD says to you: Do
not fear or be dismayed at the sight of this vast
multitude, for the battle is not yours but God's.
[16]Go down against them tomorrow. You will
see them coming up by the ascent of Ziz, and
you will come upon them at the end of the wadi
which opens on the wilderness of Jeruel. [17]You
will not have to fight in this encounter. Take your
places, stand firm, and see the salvation of the
LORD; he will be with you, Judah and Jerusalem.
Do not fear or be dismayed. Tomorrow go out
to meet them, and the LORD will be with you."*
[18]Then Jehoshaphat knelt down with his face to
the ground, and all Judah and the inhabitants of
Jerusalem fell down before the LORD in worship.
[19]Levites from among the Kohathites and Korah-
ites stood up to sing the praises of the LORD, the
God of Israel, their voices ever louder.

The Invaders Destroyed

[20]Early in the morning they went out to the
wilderness of Tekoa. As they were going out, Je-
hoshaphat halted and said: "Listen to me, Judah
and inhabitants of Jerusalem! Let your faith in
the LORD, your God, be firm, and you will be
firm.* Have faith in his prophets and you will
succeed." [21]† After taking counsel with the peo-
ple, he appointed some to sing to the LORD and
some to praise the holy Splendor as it went forth
at the head of the army. They sang: "Give thanks
to the LORD, whose love endures forever."* [22]At
the moment they began their jubilant praise, the
LORD laid an ambush against the Ammonites,
Moabites, and those of Mount Seir who were
coming against Judah, so that they were defeated.
[23]For the Ammonites and Moabites set upon
the inhabitants of Mount Seir and exterminated
them according to the ban.* And when they had
finished with the inhabitants of Seir, each helped
to destroy the other.

[24]When Judah came to the watchtower of the
wilderness and looked toward the throng, there
were only corpses fallen on the ground, with no
survivors. [25]Jehoshaphat and his people came to
gather the spoils, and they found an abundance
of cattle and personal property, garments and
precious vessels. They took so much that they
were unable to carry it all; it took them three
days to gather the spoils, there was so much of it.
[26]On the fourth day they held an assembly in the
Valley of Berakah†—for there they blessed the
LORD; that is why the place is called the Valley of
Berakah to this day. [27]Then all the men of Judah
and Jerusalem, with Jehoshaphat at their head,
returned to Jerusalem with joy; for the LORD had
given them joy over their enemies. [28]They came
to Jerusalem, with harps, lyres, and trumpets,
to the house of the LORD. [29]And the fear of God
came upon all the kingdoms of the surround-
ing lands when they heard how the LORD had
fought against the enemies of Israel. [30]Thereafter
Jehoshaphat's kingdom had peace, for his God
gave him rest on every side.

Jehoshaphat's Other Deeds

[31]* Thus Jehoshaphat reigned over Judah. He
was thirty-five years old when he became king,
and he reigned twenty-five years in Jerusalem.
His mother's name was Azubah, daughter of
Shilhi. [32]He walked in the way of Asa his father
unceasingly, doing what was right in the LORD's
sight. [33]Nevertheless, the high places did not dis-
appear and the people had not yet set their hearts
on the God of their ancestors.

[34]The rest of the acts of Jehoshaphat, first and
last, are recorded in the chronicle of Jehu, son of
Hanani, which was incorporated into the book
of the kings of Israel. [35]After this, Jehoshaphat

†

20:21 In accordance with Israelite conceptions of Holy War (cf. Ex 14:13–14), this highly stylized narrative presents the Lord as active in battle, while the people have only to sing hymns of praise; the enemy, in panic, fight among themselves to their mutual destruction (v. 23). *Splendor*: the Lord "goes before," i.e., leads, the army of Israel (cf. 2 Sm 5:24) with the heavenly hosts. Israel's God is depicted as present "enthroned upon the cherubim" atop the ark of the covenant. By postexilic times, the ark had disappeared, but the Lord was still present to his people. Here that presence is described as "holy Splendor," a phrase found in Ps 29:2; 96:9. Cf. the cognate image of cloud and fire that led Israel in the wilderness (Ex 13:21–22), or the cloud of the Lord's glory that fills the sanctuary (Ex 40:34; 1 Kgs 8:10–11).

20:26 *Berakah*: the Hebrew word for "blessing."

*

20:10 Dt 2:4–5, 9–10, 18–19.
20:17 Ex 14:13–14; Is 8:10.
20:20 Is 7:9.
20:21 Ps 136:1.
20:23 Jos 6:17.
20:31–34 1 Kgs 22:41–45.

Did You Know?

The Role of the Prophet

The letter from Elijah to King Jehoram discussed in 2 Chronicles 21:12–15 underscores the principal role of the Hebrew prophet: to be God's voice, the one who speaks for God. Although many early figures are called prophets, including Moses and Deborah, the classical prophet—*nabi'* in Hebrew—appeared later in Israelite history. The primary function of the prophet was not to foretell the future but to announce God's judgment, to confront those who violated God's law, and to console those who suffered. In short, the prophets were the conscience of the Israelite nation.

▶ 2 Chr 21:12–15

king of Judah joined with Ahaziah king of Israel—he acted wickedly. 36 * He joined with him in building ships to go to Tarshish; the fleet was built at Ezion-geber. 37 But Eliezer, son of Dodavahu from Mareshah, prophesied against Jehoshaphat. He said: "Because you have joined with Ahaziah, the LORD will shatter your work." And the ships were wrecked and were unable to sail to Tarshish.

21 1 Jehoshaphat rested with his ancestors; he was buried with them in the City of David. Jehoram, his son, succeeded him as king.* 2 He had brothers, Jehoshaphat's sons: Azariah, Jehiel, Zechariah, Azariah, Michael, and Shephatiah; all these were sons of King Jehoshaphat of Judah. 3 Their father gave them many gifts of silver, gold, and precious objects, together with fortified cities in Judah, but the kingship he gave to Jehoram because he was the firstborn.

Jehoram's Evil Deeds

4 When Jehoram had acceded to his father's kingdom and was firmly in power, he killed all his brothers with the sword, and also some of the princes of Israel. 5 * Jehoram was thirty-two years old when he became king, and he reigned eight years in Jerusalem. 6 He walked in the way of the kings of Israel as the house of Ahab had done, since the daughter of Ahab† was his wife; and he did what was evil in the LORD's sight. 7 Even so, the LORD was unwilling to destroy the house of David because of the covenant he had made with David and because of his promise to leave him and his sons a holding for all time.*

8 * During his time Edom revolted against the rule of Judah and installed its own king. 9 Thereupon Jehoram with his officers and all his chariots crossed over. He arose by night and broke through the Edomites when they had surrounded him and the commanders of his chariots. 10 To this day Edom has been in revolt against the rule of Judah. Libnah also revolted at that time against his rule because he had abandoned the LORD, the God of his ancestors. 11 He also set up high places in the mountains of Judah, prostituting the inhabitants of Jerusalem, leading Judah astray.

Jehoram Punished

12 A letter came to him from Elijah† the prophet with this message: "Thus says the LORD, the God of David your father: Because you have not walked in the way of your father Jehoshaphat, nor of Asa, king of Judah, 13 but instead have walked in the way of the kings of Israel, leading Judah and the inhabitants of Jerusalem into prostitution, like the harlotries of the house of Ahab, and because you have killed your brothers of your father's house, who were better than you, 14 the LORD will strike your people, your children, your wives, and all that is yours with a great plague. 15 You shall have severe pains from a disease in your bowels, which will fall out because of the disease, day after day."

16 Then the LORD stirred up against Jehoram the animosity of the Philistines and of the Arabians who were neighbors of the Ethiopians. 17 They came up against Judah, breached it, and carried away all the wealth found in the king's house, along with his sons and his wives. He was left with only one son, Jehoahaz, his youngest. 18 After these events, the LORD afflicted him with a disease of the bowels for which there was no cure. 19 Some time later, after a period of two years had elapsed,

†

21:6 *The daughter of Ahab*: her name was Athaliah. In 22:2 (and its source, 2 Kgs 8:26) she is called the daughter of Ahab's father Omri, but this should probably be understood in the sense of granddaughter.

21:12 *Elijah*: this is the Chronicler's only mention of this prophet of the Northern Kingdom. It is doubtful that Elijah was still living in the reign of Jehoram of Judah; in any case, the attribution of the letter to him has a folkloristic quality.

*

20:36–37 1 Kgs 22:48–49.
21:1 1 Kgs 22:51.
21:5–7 1 Kgs 8:17–19.
21:7 1 Kgs 11:36; 2 Kgs 8:19.
21:8–10 Gn 27:40; 2 Kgs 8:20–22.

his bowels fell out because of the disease and he
died in great pain. His people did not make a fire
for him as they had for his ancestors.* 20 He was
thirty-two years old when he became king, and he
reigned eight years in Jerusalem. He departed un-
loved; and they buried him in the City of David,
though not in the tombs of the kings.*

Ahaziah

22 1 * Then the inhabitants of Jerusalem made
Ahaziah, his youngest son, king to succeed
him, since all the older sons had been killed by the
band that had come into the camp with the Arabi-
ans. Thus Ahaziah, son of Jehoram, reigned as the
king of Judah. 2 Ahaziah was twenty-two years old
when he became king, and he reigned one year
in Jerusalem. His mother's name was Athaliah,
daughter of Omri. 3 He, too, walked in the ways
of the house of Ahab, because his mother was his
counselor in doing evil. 4 To his own destruction,
he did what was evil in the sight of the LORD, like
the house of Ahab, since they were his counselors
after the death of his father.

5 He was also following their counsel when he
joined Jehoram, son of Ahab, king of Israel, in
battle against Hazael, king of Aram, at Ramoth-
gilead, where the Arameans wounded Jehoram.
6 He returned to Jezreel to be healed of the
wounds that had been inflicted on him at Ramah
in his battle against Hazael, king of Aram. Then
Ahaziah, son of Jehoram, king of Judah, went
down to Jezreel to visit Jehoram, son of Ahab,
for he was sick. 7 Now from God came Ahaziah's
downfall, that he should join Jehoram; for after
his arrival he rode out with Jehoram to Jehu,
son of Nimshi, whom the LORD had anointed
to cut down the house of Ahab.* 8 While Jehu
was executing judgment on the house of Ahab,
he also came upon the princes of Judah and the
nephews of Ahaziah who were his attendants,
and he killed them.* 9 Then he looked for Aha-
ziah himself. They caught him hiding in Samaria
and brought him to Jehu, who put him to death.
They buried him, for they said, "He was the
grandson of Jehoshaphat, who sought the LORD
with his whole heart."* Now the house of Aha-
ziah did not retain the power of kingship.†

Usurpation of Athaliah

10 * When Athaliah, the mother of Ahaziah,
saw that her son was dead, she began to kill off
the whole royal family of the house of Judah.
11 But Jehosheba, a daughter of the king, took Jo-
ash, Ahaziah's son, and spirited him away from
among the king's sons who were about to be
slain, and put him and his nurse in a bedroom.
In this way Jehosheba, the daughter of King Jeho-
ram, a sister of Ahaziah and wife of Jehoiada the
priest, concealed the child from Athaliah, so that
she did not put him to death. 12 For six years he
remained hidden with them in the house of God,
while Athaliah ruled as queen over the land.

Athaliah Overthrown

23 1 * In the seventh year, Jehoiada took
courage and brought into covenant with
himself the captains: Azariah, son of Jehoram;
Ishmael, son of Jehohanan; Azariah, son of
Obed; Maaseiah, son of Adaiah; and Elishaphat,
son of Zichri. 2 They journeyed about Judah, gath-
ering the Levites from all the cities of Judah and
also the heads of the Israelite families, and they
came to Jerusalem. 3 The whole assembly made a
covenant with the king in the house of God. Je-
hoiada said to them: "Here is the king's son who
must reign, as the LORD promised concerning the
sons of David. 4 This is what you must do: a third
of your number, both priests and Levites, who
come on duty on the sabbath must guard the
thresholds, 5 another third must be at the king's
house, and the final third at the Foundation
Gate, when all the people will be in the courts
of the LORD's house. 6 Let no one enter the LORD's
house except the priests and those Levites who
are ministering. They may enter because they
are holy; but all the other people must observe
the prescriptions of the LORD. 7 The Levites shall
surround the king on all sides, each with drawn
weapon. Whoever tries to enter the house is to be
killed. Stay with the king wherever he goes."

8 The Levites and all Judah did just as Jehoiada
the priest commanded. Each took his troops,
both those going on duty for the week and
those going off duty that week, since Jehoiada
the priest had not dismissed any of the divi-
sions.* 9 Jehoiada the priest gave to the captains
the spears, shields, and bucklers of King David
which were in the house of God. 10 He stationed
all the people, each with spear in hand, from the
southern to the northern limit of the enclosure,
surrounding the altar and the temple on the
king's behalf. 11 Then they brought out the king's
son and put the crown and the testimony upon
him, and proclaimed him king. Jehoiada and his

† **22:9** This account of the death of Ahaziah of Judah does not agree with that given in 2 Kgs 9:27–28.

* **21:19** 2 Chr 16:14. **21:20** 2 Kgs 8:24. **22:1–6** 2 Kgs 8:24–29. **22:7** 2 Kgs 9:21. **22:8** 2 Kgs 10:12–14. **22:9** 2 Kgs 9:27–28. **22:10–12** 2 Kgs 11:1–3. **23:1–17, 19–21** 2 Kgs 11:4–20. **23:8** 2 Kgs 11:9; 1 Chr 24:19.

2 CHR

sons anointed him, and they cried, "Long live
the king!"
12 When Athaliah heard the noise of the people
running and acclaiming the king, she came be-
fore them in the house of the LORD. 13 When she
saw the king standing by his column† at the en-
trance, the captains and the trumpeters near the
king, and all the people of the land rejoicing and
blowing trumpets, while the singers with their
musical instruments were leading the acclaim,
Athaliah tore her garments, saying, "Treason!
treason!" 14 Then Jehoiada the priest brought out
the captains in command of the force: "Escort
her with a guard detail. If anyone follows her, let
him die by the sword." For the priest had said,
"You must not put her to death in the house of
the LORD." 15 So they seized her, and when she
reached the Horse Gate of the royal palace, they
put her to death.
16 Then Jehoiada made a covenant between
himself and all the people and the king, that
they should be the LORD's people. 17 Thereupon
all the people went to the temple of Baal and de-
molished it. They shattered its altars and images
completely, and killed Mattan, the priest of Baal,
before the altars. 18 Then Jehoiada gave the charge
of the LORD's house into the hands of the levitical
priests, to whom David had assigned turns in the
LORD's house for sacrificing the burnt offerings of
the LORD, as is written in the law of Moses, with
rejoicing and song, as David had provided.*
19 Moreover, he stationed guards at the gates of
the LORD's house so that no one unclean in any
respect might enter. 20 Then he took the captains,
the nobles, the rulers among the people, and
all the people of the land, and led the king out
of the LORD's house; they came within the up-
per gate of the king's house, and seated the king
upon the royal throne. 21 All the people of the
land rejoiced and the city was quiet, now that
Athaliah had been slain with the sword.

The Temple Restored

24 1 * Joash was seven years old when he be-
came king, and he reigned forty years in
Jerusalem. His mother's name was Zibiah, from
Beer-sheba. 2 Joash did what was right in the
LORD's sight as long as Jehoiada the priest lived.
3 Jehoiada provided him with two wives, and he
became the father of sons and daughters.
4 After some time, Joash decided to restore the
house of the LORD. 5 He gathered together the
priests and Levites and said to them: "Go out to
all the cities of Judah and gather money† from
all Israel that you may repair the house of your
God over the years. You must hurry this project."
But the Levites did not. 6 Then the king sum-
moned Jehoiada, who was in charge, and said to
him: "Why have you not required the Levites to
bring in from Judah and Jerusalem the tax levied
by Moses, the servant of the LORD, and by the as-
sembly of Israel, for the tent of the testimony?"*
7 For the wicked Athaliah and her sons had dam-
aged the house of God and had even turned over
to the Baals the holy things of the LORD's house.
8 At the king's command, therefore, they made
a chest, which they put outside the gate of the
LORD's house.* 9 They had it proclaimed through-
out Judah and Jerusalem that the tax which
Moses, the servant of God, had imposed on Is-
rael in the wilderness should be brought to the
LORD.* 10 All the princes and the people rejoiced;
they brought what was asked and cast it into the
chest until it was filled. 11 Whenever the chest
was brought to the royal officials by the Levites
and they noticed that there was a large amount
of money, the royal scribe and an overseer for
the chief priest would come up, empty the chest,
and then take it back and return it to its place.
This they did day after day until they had col-
lected a large sum of money. 12 Then the king
and Jehoiada gave it to the workers in charge of
the labor on the LORD's house, who hired ma-
sons and carpenters to restore the LORD's house,
and also iron- and bronze-smiths to repair it.
13 The workers labored, and the task of restora-
tion progressed under their hands. They restored
the house of God according to its original form,
and reinforced it. 14 After they had finished, they
brought the rest of the money to the king and to
Jehoiada, who had it made into utensils for the
house of the LORD, utensils for the service and
the burnt offerings, and basins and other gold
and silver utensils.† They sacrificed burnt offer-
ings in the LORD's house continually all the days
of Jehoiada. 15 Jehoiada grew old, full of years,

23:13 *By his column*: there was a special place reserved for the king in the eastern gateway of the Temple court where the altar for burnt offerings stood. The king occupied this place on feasts and sabbaths at the time of the prescribed offerings, or when he came to make voluntary offerings of his own; cf. 2 Kgs 11:14 and Ez 46:1–8.

24:5 *Gather money*: according to 2 Kgs 12:5 the people themselves brought the money, consisting at least in part of voluntary contributions, to the Temple. By the time of the Chronicler, a fixed head tax for the upkeep of the Temple had been introduced; see 2 Chr 34:9; Neh 10:32; Ex 30:12–16. This was still in force in New Testament times (Mt 17:24–25).

24:14 See the parallel in 2 Kgs 12:14–15; the passages are difficult to reconcile.

23:18 1 Chr 23:13.
24:1–14 2 Kgs 12:1–13.
24:6 Ex 25:1–9; Neh 10:33.
24:8 2 Chr 34:9.
24:9 Ex 30:13.

and died; he was a hundred and thirty years old.
16 They buried him in the City of David with the
kings, because of the good he had done in Israel,
especially for God and his house.

Joash's Apostasy

17 After the death of Jehoiada, the princes of
Judah came and paid homage to the king; then
the king listened to them. 18 They abandoned the
house of the LORD, the God of their ancestors,
and began to serve the asherahs and the idols;*
and because of this crime of theirs, wrath came
upon Judah and Jerusalem. 19 Although prophets
were sent to them to turn them back to the LORD
and to warn them, the people would not listen.
20 * Then the spirit of God clothed Zechariah,
son of Jehoiada the priest. He took his stand
above the people and said to them: "Thus says
God, Why are you transgressing the LORD's com-
mands, so that you cannot prosper? Because you
have abandoned the LORD, he has abandoned
you." 21 But they conspired against him, and
at the king's command they stoned him in the
court of the house of the LORD. 22 Thus King Jo-
ash was unmindful of the devotion shown him
by Jehoiada, Zechariah's father, and killed the
son. As he was dying, he said, "May the LORD see
and avenge."

Joash Punished

23 At the turn of the year a force of Arameans
came up against Joash. They invaded Judah and
Jerusalem, killed all the princes of the people,
and sent all their spoil to the king of Damascus.*
24 Though the Aramean force was small, the LORD
handed over a very large force into their power,*
because Judah had abandoned the LORD, the God
of their ancestors. So judgment was meted out to
Joash. 25 * After the Arameans had departed from
him, abandoning him to his many injuries, his
servants conspired against him because of the
murder of the son of Jehoiada the priest. They
killed him on his sickbed. He was buried in the
City of David, but not in the tombs of the kings.
26 Those who conspired against him were Za-
bad, son of Shimeath from Ammon, and Jehoz-
abad, son of Shimrith from Moab. 27 An account
of his sons, the great tribute imposed on him,
and his rebuilding of the house of God is written
in the midrash of the book of the kings. His son
Amaziah succeeded him as king.*

Amaziah's Good Start

25 1 * Amaziah was twenty-five years old
when he became king, and he reigned
twenty-nine years in Jerusalem. His mother's
name was Jehoaddan, from Jerusalem. 2 He did
what was right in the LORD's sight, though not
wholeheartedly. 3 When he had the kingdom
firmly in hand, he struck down the officials who
had struck down the king, his father. 4 But their
children he did not put to death, for he acted ac-
cording to what is written in the law, in the Book
of Moses, which the LORD commanded: "Parents
shall not be put to death for their children, nor
shall children be put to death for their parents;
they shall each die for their own sin."*
5 Amaziah gathered Judah and placed them,
out of all Judah and Benjamin according to their
ancestral houses, under leaders of thousands and
of hundreds. When he made a count of those
twenty years old and over, he found that there
were three hundred thousand picked men fit for
war, capable of handling lance and shield. 6 He
also hired a hundred thousand valiant warriors
from Israel for a hundred talents of silver. 7 But
a man of God came to him and said: "O king,
let not the army of Israel go with you, for the
LORD is not with Israel—with any Ephraimite.
8 Instead, go on your own, strongly prepared
for the battle; why should the LORD hinder you
in the face of the enemy: for with God is power
to help or to hinder." 9 Amaziah answered the
man of God, "But what is to be done about the
hundred talents that I paid for the troops of Is-
rael?" The man of God replied, "The LORD can
give you much more than that." 10 Amaziah then
disbanded the troops that had come to him from
Ephraim, and sent them home. But they became
furiously angry with Judah, and returned home
blazing with anger.
11 Amaziah now assumed command of his
army. They proceeded to the Valley of Salt, where
they killed ten thousand men of Seir.* 12 The Ju-
dahites also brought back another ten thousand
alive, led them to the summit of Sela, and then
threw them down from that rock† so that their
bodies split open. 13 Meanwhile, the troops Am-
aziah had dismissed from going into battle with
him raided the cities of Judah from Samaria to
Beth-horon. They struck down three thousand of
the inhabitants and carried off much plunder.

2 CHR

---

† **25:12** *Sela . . . rock*: a pun—the name of the city, Sela, in Hebrew means "rock."

---

* **24:18** Ex 34:13.
24:20 Jgs 6:34.
24:23 2 Kgs 12:17–18.
24:24 Dt 32:30.
24:25–26 2 Kgs 12:21–22.
24:27 2 Kgs 12:19, 22.
25:1–4 2 Kgs 14:1–6.
25:4 Dt 24:16; 2 Kgs 14:5–6; Ez 18:20.
25:11 2 Kgs 14:7.

Amaziah's Apostasy

14 When Amaziah returned from his conquest
of the Edomites he brought back with him the
gods of the people of Seir. He set these up as his
own gods; he bowed down before them and of-
fered sacrifice to them. 15 Then the anger of the
LORD blazed out against Amaziah, and he sent a
prophet to him who said: "Why have you sought
this people's gods that could not deliver their own
people from your power?" 16 While he was still
speaking, however, the king said to him: "Have
you been appointed the king's counselor? Stop!
Why should you have to be killed?" Therefore the
prophet stopped. But he said, "I know that God's
counsel is your destruction, for by doing this you
have refused to listen to my counsel."

Amaziah Punished

17 * Having taken counsel, Amaziah, king of
Judah, sent word to Joash, son of Jehoahaz, son
of Jehu, the king of Israel, saying, "Come, let us
meet face to face." 18 Joash, king of Israel, sent
this reply to Amaziah, king of Judah: "A thistle of
Lebanon sent word to a cedar of Lebanon, 'Give
your daughter to my son in marriage,' but an
animal of Lebanon passed by and trampled the
thistle underfoot.* 19 You are thinking,

'See, I have struck down Edom!'
Your heart is lifted up,
And glories in it. Stay home!
Why bring misfortune and failure
on yourself and on Judah with you?"

20 But Amaziah did not listen; for it was God's
doing that they be handed over because they
sought the gods of Edom.
21 So Joash, king of Israel, advanced, and he
and Amaziah, king of Judah, met face to face
at Beth-shemesh of Judah, 22 and Judah was de-
feated by Israel, and all fled to their tents. 23 But
Amaziah, king of Judah, son of Joash, son of Je-
hoahaz, was captured by Joash, king of Israel, at
Beth-shemesh. Joash brought him to Jerusalem
and tore down the wall of Jerusalem from the
Gate of Ephraim to the Corner Gate, four hun-
dred cubits. 24 He took all the gold and silver and
all the vessels found in the house of God with
Obed-edom,† and in the treasuries of the king's
house, and hostages as well. Then he returned
to Samaria.
25 * Amaziah, son of Joash, king of Judah,
survived Joash, son of Jehoahaz, king of Israel,
by fifteen years. 26 The rest of the acts of Ama-
ziah, first and last, are recorded in the book of
the kings of Judah and Israel. 27 Now from the
time that Amaziah turned away from the LORD, a
conspiracy was formed against him in Jerusalem,
and he fled to Lachish. But he was pursued to
Lachish and killed there. 28 He was brought back
on horses and was buried with his ancestors in
the City of Judah.†

Uzziah's Projects

26 1 * All the people of Judah took Uzziah,
who was only sixteen years old, and
made him king to succeed Amaziah his father.
2 It was he who rebuilt Elath and restored it to
Judah, after the king rested with his ancestors.
3 Uzziah was sixteen years old when he became
king, and he reigned fifty-two years in Jerusalem.
His mother's name was Jecoliah, from Jerusalem.
4 He did what was right in the LORD's sight, just as
his father Amaziah had done.
5 He was prepared to seek God as long as Zech-
ariah† lived,* who taught him to fear God; and as
long as he sought the LORD, God made him pros-
per. 6 He went out and fought the Philistines and
razed the walls of Gath, Jabneh, and Ashdod, and
built cities in the district of Ashdod and in Phi-
listia.* 7 God helped him against the Philistines,
against the Arabians who dwelt in Gurbaal, and
against the Meunites. 8 The Ammonites paid trib-
ute to Uzziah and his fame spread as far as Egypt,
for he grew stronger and stronger. 9 Moreover,
Uzziah built towers in Jerusalem at the Corner
Gate, at the Valley Gate, and at the Angle, and he
fortified them. 10 He built towers in the wilder-
ness and dug numerous cisterns, for he had many
cattle. He had plowmen in the Shephelah and the
plains, farmers and vinedressers in the highlands
and the garden land. He was a lover of the soil.
11 Uzziah also had a standing army of fit sol-
diers divided into bands according to the number
in which they were mustered by Jeiel the scribe
and Maaseiah the recorder, under the command
of Hananiah, one of the king's officials. 12 The
entire number of family heads over these valiant
warriors was two thousand six hundred, 13 and at

†

25:24 *With Obed-edom*: perhaps an Edomite priest (cf. v. 14), or possibly a member of a levitical family of gatekeepers; cf. 1 Chr 15:18; 26:12–15.

25:28 *The City of Judah*: i.e., Jerusalem, the capital of Judah; the parallel passage (2 Kgs 14:20) reads "the City of David."

26:5 *Zechariah*: not otherwise identified, but cf. 29:1.

*

25:17–24 2 Kgs 14:8–14.
25:18 Jgs 9:7–15; 2 Kgs 14:9.
25:25–28 2 Kgs 14:17–20.
26:1–4 2 Kgs 14:21–22; 15:1–3.
26:5 2 Chr 24:2.
26:6 Am 1:8.

their disposal was a mighty army of three hundred seven thousand five hundred fighting men of great valor to help the king against his enemies. 14 Uzziah provided for them—for the entire army—bucklers, lances, helmets, breastplates, bows, and slingstones. 15 He also built machines in Jerusalem, devices designed to stand on the towers and at the angles of the walls to shoot arrows and cast large stones. His name spread far and wide; the help he received was wondrous, so strong did he become.

Pride and Fall

16 But after he had become strong, he became arrogant to his own destruction and acted treacherously with the LORD, his God. He entered the temple of the LORD to make an offering on the altar of incense. 17 But Azariah the priest, and with him eighty other priests of the LORD, courageous men, followed him. 18 They stood up to King Uzziah, saying to him: "It is not for you, Uzziah, to burn incense to the LORD, but for the priests, the sons of Aaron, who have been consecrated for this purpose.* Leave the sanctuary, for you have acted treacherously and no longer have a part in the glory that comes from the LORD God." 19 Uzziah, who was holding a censer for burning the incense, became angry. But at the very moment he showed his anger to the priests, while they were looking at him in the house of the LORD beside the altar of incense, leprosy broke out on his forehead.* 20 Azariah the chief priest and all the other priests examined him, and when they saw that his forehead was leprous, they rushed him out. He let himself be expelled, for the LORD had afflicted him. 21 * King Uzziah remained a leper till the day he died. As a leper he lived in a house apart, for he was excluded from the house of the LORD. Therefore his son Jotham was master of the palace and ruled the people of the land.

22 The rest of the acts of Uzziah, first and last, were written by Isaiah the prophet, son of Amoz. 23 Uzziah rested with his ancestors and was buried with them in the field adjoining the royal cemetery, for they said, "He was a leper." His son Jotham succeeded him as king.

Jotham

27 1 * Jotham was twenty-five years old when he became king, and he reigned sixteen years in Jerusalem. His mother's name was Jerusha, daughter of Zadok. 2 He did what was right in the LORD's sight, just as his father Uzziah had done, though he did not enter the temple of the LORD. The people, however, continued to act corruptly.

3 It was he who built the Upper Gate of the LORD's house and did much construction on the wall of Ophel. 4 Moreover, he built cities in the hill country of Judah, and in the wooded areas he set up fortresses and towers. 5 He fought with the king of the Ammonites and conquered them. That year the Ammonites paid him one hundred talents of silver, together with ten thousand kors of wheat and ten thousand of barley. They brought the same to him also in the second and in the third year. 6 Thus Jotham continued to grow strong because he made sure to walk before the LORD, his God. 7 * The rest of the acts of Jotham, his wars and his activities, are recorded in the book of the kings of Israel and Judah. 8 He was twenty-five years old when he became king, and he reigned sixteen years in Jerusalem. 9 Jotham rested with his ancestors and was buried in the City of David, and his son Ahaz succeeded him as king.

Ahaz's Misdeeds

28 1 * Ahaz was twenty years old when he became king, and he reigned sixteen years in Jerusalem. He did not do what was right in the sight of the LORD as David his father had done. 2 He walked in the ways of the kings of Israel and even made molten idols for the Baals. 3 Moreover, he offered sacrifice in the Valley of Ben-hinnom, and immolated his children by fire in accordance with the abominable practices of the nations whom the LORD had dispossessed before the Israelites.* 4 He sacrificed and burned incense on the high places, on hills, and under every green tree.

Ahaz Punished

5 † Therefore the LORD, his God, delivered him into the power of the king of Aram. The Arameans defeated him and carried away captive a large number of his people, whom they brought to Damascus. He was also delivered into the power of the king of Israel, who defeated him with great slaughter.* 6 For Pekah, son of Remaliah, killed

2 CHR

†

28:5–8, 16–23 The account of Ahaz's reign in 2 Kings refers to hostilities of Syria (Aram) and Israel against Judah, the revolt of the Edomites, submission to Tiglath-pileser, king of Assyria, the stripping of Temple treasures to pay him tribute, and, in deference to him, shaping the cult of the Jerusalem Temple according to patterns seen in Damascus (2 Kgs 16:5–18; cf. Is 7:1–2). The account in Kings relates all this to an attack of Syria and Israel on Judah (735 B.C.), as they attempted to force Judah into an anti-Assyrian coalition; but the Chronicler, who does not mention the attack, depicts these troubles as the result of, or examples of, Ahaz's infidelity.

26:18 Ex 30:7.
26:19 Nm 12:10.
26:21–23 2 Kgs 15:5–7; Lv 13:46; Nm 19:20.
27:1–3 2 Kgs 15:32–35.
27:7–9 2 Kgs 15:36–38.
28:1–4 2 Kgs 16:1–4.
28:3 Lv 18:21; 2 Kgs 16:3.
28:5 2 Kgs 16:5; Is 7:1–9.

Pray It!

Renewing Your Prayer Life

Hezekiah was one of Judah's reformer kings. Before he became king, the people had neglected the Temple in Jerusalem for a long time. At the beginning of Hezekiah's reign, the Temple needed some intense effort to get it back in order.

Sometimes our prayer lives suffer from neglect too. We get busy and do not take enough time to pray, or we forget to pray altogether. When we decide to commit ourselves to regular prayer, it may take some intense effort to get rid of our bad habits.

Imagine your prayer life as being like the Temple. How does it look? Is it in need of a little dusting? full of cobwebs? ready for major renovation? What steps can you take to make sure you do not neglect your prayer life?

It is also easy to fall into a rut when we pray. One way to energize your prayer life is to try different ways to pray. You could begin your prayer with a line from a psalm that you like or by picturing Jesus beside you. Other alternatives would be to start prayer with a song that means a lot to you or to simply place yourself in the Holy Presence of God.

▶ 2 Chr 29:1–11

one hundred and twenty thousand of Judah in a
single day, all of them valiant men, because they
had abandoned the LORD, the God of their ances-
tors. 7 Zichri, an Ephraimite warrior, killed Maa-
seiah, the king's son, and Azrikam, the master of
the palace, and also Elkanah, who was second
to the king. 8 The Israelites took away as captives
two hundred thousand of their kinfolk's wives,
sons, and daughters; they also took from them
much plunder, which they brought to Samaria.

Oded's Prophecy

9 In Samaria there was a prophet of the LORD
by the name of Oded. He went out to meet the
army returning to Samaria and said to them: "It
was because the LORD, the God of your ancestors,
was angry with Judah that he delivered them
into your power. You, however, have killed them
with a fury that has reached up to heaven. 10 And
now you are planning to subjugate the people of
Judah and Jerusalem as your slaves and bond-
women. Are not you yourselves, therefore, guilty
of a crime against the LORD, your God? 11 Now
listen to me: send back the captives you have
carried off from among your kin, for the burning
anger of the LORD is upon you."

12 At this, some of the Ephraimite leaders, Az-
ariah, son of Johanan, Berechiah, son of Meshil-
lemoth, Jehizkiah, son of Shallum, and Amasa,
son of Hadlai, themselves stood up in opposi-
tion to those who had returned from the war.
13 They said to them: "Do not bring the captives
here, for what you are planning will make us
guilty before the LORD and increase our sins and
our guilt. Great is our guilt, and there is burning
anger upon Israel." 14 Therefore the soldiers left
their captives and the plunder before the princes
and the whole assembly. 15 Then the men just
named proceeded to help the captives. All of
them who were naked they clothed from the
spoils; they clothed them, put sandals on their
feet, gave them food and drink, anointed them,
and all who were weak they set on donkeys. They
brought them to Jericho, the City of Palms, to
their kinfolk. Then they returned to Samaria.*

Further Sins of Ahaz

16 At that time King Ahaz sent an appeal for
help to the kings of Assyria.* 17 The Edomites
had returned, attacked Judah, and carried off
captives.* 18 The Philistines too had raided the
cities of the Shephelah and the Negeb of Judah;
they captured Beth-shemesh, Aijalon, Gederoth,
Soco and its dependencies, Timnah and its de-
pendencies, and Gimzo and its dependencies,
and settled there. 19 For the LORD had brought
Judah low because of Ahaz, king of Israel,† who
let Judah go its own way and committed treach-
ery against the LORD. 20 Tiglath-pileser, king of
Assyria, did indeed come to him, but to oppress
him rather than to lend strength.* 21 Though
Ahaz plundered the LORD's house and the houses
of the king and the princes to pay off the king of
Assyria, it was no help to him.*

22 While he was already in distress, the same
King Ahaz increased his treachery to the LORD.

† **28:19** *Ahaz, king of Israel*: in his account of the period of the divided monarchy, the Chronicler regularly uses the term "Israel" as here to designate, not the Northern Kingdom, but the entire people. See note on 10:1.

* **28:15** Lk 10:25–37. **28:16** 2 Kgs 16:7. **28:17** 2 Kgs 16:6. **28:20** 2 Kgs 16:10; Is 7:17–20; 8:5–8. **28:21** 2 Kgs 16:8.

23 He sacrificed to the gods of Damascus who had defeated him, saying, "Since it was the gods of the kings of Aram who helped them, I will sacrifice to them that they may help me also." However, they only furthered his downfall and that of all Israel.* 24 Ahaz gathered up the utensils of God's house and broke them in pieces. He closed the doors of the LORD's house and made altars for himself in every corner of Jerusalem.* 25 In every city throughout Judah he set up high places to offer sacrifice to other gods. Thus he provoked the LORD, the God of his ancestors, to anger.

26 * The rest of his words and his deeds, first and last, are recorded in the book of the kings of Judah and Israel. 27 Ahaz rested with his ancestors and was buried in Jerusalem—in the city, for they did not bring him to the tombs of the kings of Israel. His son Hezekiah succeeded him as king.

Hezekiah's Reforms

29 1 * Hezekiah was twenty-five years old when he became king, and he reigned twenty-nine years in Jerusalem. His mother's name was Abijah, daughter of Zechariah. 2 He did what was right in the LORD's sight, just as David his father had done. 3 In the first month of the first year of his reign, he opened the doors of the LORD's house and repaired them.* 4 He summoned the priests and Levites, gathering them in the open space to the east, 5 and said to them: "Listen to me, you Levites! Sanctify yourselves now and sanctify the house of the LORD, the God of your ancestors, and clean out the filth from the sanctuary. 6 Our ancestors acted treacherously and did what was evil in the eyes of the LORD, our God. They abandoned him, turned away their faces from the LORD's dwelling, and turned their backs on him. 7 They also closed the doors of the vestibule, extinguished the lamps, and failed to burn incense and sacrifice burnt offerings in the sanctuary to the God of Israel.* 8 * Therefore the anger of the LORD has come upon Judah and Jerusalem; he has made them an object of terror, horror, and hissing, as you see with your own eyes. 9 For our ancestors fell by the sword, and our sons, our daughters, and our wives have been taken captive because of this. 10 Now, I intend to make a covenant with the LORD, the God of Israel, that his burning anger may turn away from us. 11 My sons, do not be negligent any longer, for it is you whom the LORD has chosen to stand before him, to minister to him, to be his ministers and to offer incense."

12 Then the Levites arose: Mahath, son of Amasai, and Joel, son of Azariah, of the Kohathites; of the descendants of Merari: Kish, son of Abdi, and Azariah, son of Jehallel; of the Gershonites: Joah, son of Zimmah, and Eden, son of Joah; 13 of the sons of Elizaphan: Shimri and Jeuel; of the sons of Asaph: Zechariah and Mattaniah; 14 of the sons of Heman: Jehuel and Shimei; of the sons of Jeduthun: Shemiah and Uzziel. 15 They gathered their kinfolk together and sanctified themselves; then they came as the king had ordered, in keeping with the words of the LORD, to cleanse the LORD's house.

16 The priests entered the interior of the LORD's house to cleanse it. Whatever they found in the LORD's temple that was unclean they brought out to the court of the LORD's house, where the Levites took it from them and carried it out to the Wadi Kidron. 17 They began the work of consecration on the first day of the first month, and on the eighth day of the month they reached the vestibule of the LORD; they consecrated the LORD's house over an eight-day period, and on the sixteenth day of the first month, they had finished.

18 Then they went inside to King Hezekiah and said: "We have cleansed the entire house of the LORD, the altar for burnt offerings with all its utensils, and the table for the showbread with all its utensils. 19 We have restored and consecrated all the articles which King Ahaz had thrown away during his reign because of his treachery; they are now before the LORD's altar."

The Rite of Expiation

20 Then King Hezekiah hastened to convoke the princes of the city and went up to the LORD's house. 21 Seven bulls, seven rams, seven lambs, and seven he-goats were presented as a purification offering for the kingdom, for the sanctuary, and for Judah. Hezekiah ordered the sons of Aaron, the priests, to offer them on the altar of the LORD. 22 They slaughtered the bulls, and the priests collected the blood and splashed it on the altar. Then they slaughtered the rams and splashed the blood on the altar; then they slaughtered the lambs and splashed the blood on the altar. 23 Then the he-goats for the purification offering were led before the king and the assembly, who laid their hands upon them. 24 The priests then slaughtered them and offered their blood on the altar to atone for the sin of all Israel. For the king had said, "The burnt offering and the purification offering are for all Israel."

25 He stationed the Levites in the LORD's house with cymbals, harps, and lyres, according to

2 CHR

28:23 2 Kgs 16:12–13; Is 10:20.
28:24 2 Chr 29:3; 30:14; 2 Kgs 16:17.
28:26–27 2 Kgs 16:19–20.
29:1–2 2 Kgs 18:2–3.
29:3 2 Chr 28:24.
29:7 2 Kgs 16:15.
29:8–9 Lv 26:32–33; Dt 28:25; Jer 25:18.

the command of David, of Gad the king's seer, and of Nathan the prophet; for this command was from the LORD through his prophets. 26 The Levites were stationed with the instruments of David, and the priests with the trumpets. 27 Then Hezekiah ordered the burnt offering to be sacrificed on the altar. At the very moment the burnt offering began, they also began the song of the LORD, to the accompaniment of the trumpets and the instruments of David, king of Israel. 28 The entire assembly bowed down, and the song was sung and the trumpets sounded until the burnt offering had been completed. 29 Once the burnt offering was completed, the king and all who were with him knelt and worshiped. 30 King Hezekiah and the princes then told the Levites to sing the praises of the LORD in the words of David and of Asaph the seer. They sang praises till their joy was full, then fell down and worshiped.

31 Hezekiah then said: "You have dedicated yourselves to the LORD. Approach, and bring forward the sacrifices and thank offerings for the house of the LORD." Then the assembly brought forward the sacrifices and thank offerings and all their voluntary burnt offerings. 32 The number of burnt offerings that the assembly brought forward was seventy oxen, one hundred rams, and two hundred lambs: all of these as a burnt offering to the LORD. 33 As consecrated gifts there were six hundred oxen and three thousand sheep. 34 Since there were too few priests to skin all the victims for the burnt offerings, their fellow Levites assisted them until the task was completed and the priests had sanctified themselves. The Levites, in fact, were more careful than the priests to sanctify themselves.* 35 The burnt offerings were indeed many, along with the fat of the communion offerings and the libations for the burnt offerings. Thus the service of the house of the LORD was re-established. 36 Hezekiah and all the people rejoiced over what God had re-established for the people, and at how suddenly this had been done.

Invitation to Passover

30 1 Hezekiah sent word to all Israel and Judah, and even wrote letters to Ephraim and Manasseh, saying that they should come to the house of the LORD in Jerusalem to celebrate the Passover to the LORD, the God of Israel.* 2 * The king, his princes, and the entire assembly in Jerusalem had agreed to celebrate the Passover during the second month. 3 They could not celebrate it at the regular time because the priests had not sanctified themselves in sufficient numbers, and the people were not gathered at Jerusalem. 4 This seemed right to the king and the entire assembly, 5 and they issued a decree to be proclaimed throughout all Israel from Beer-sheba to Dan, that everyone should come to celebrate the Passover to the LORD, the God of Israel, in Jerusalem; for not many had kept it in the prescribed manner. 6 By the king's command, the couriers, with the letters written by the king and his princes, went through all Israel and Judah. They said: "Israelites, return to the LORD, the God of Abraham, Isaac, and Israel, that he may return to you, the remnant left from the hands of the Assyrian kings. 7 Do not be like your ancestors and your kin who acted treacherously toward the LORD, the God of their ancestors, so that he handed them over to desolation, as you yourselves now see.* 8 Do not be stiff-necked, as your ancestors were; stretch out your hands to the LORD and come to his sanctuary that he has consecrated forever, and serve the LORD, your God, that he may turn his burning anger from you. 9 If you return to the LORD, your kinfolk and your children will find mercy with their captors and return to this land. The LORD, your God, is gracious and merciful and he will not turn away his face from you if you return to him."*

10 So the couriers passed from city to city in the land of Ephraim and Manasseh and as far as Zebulun, but they were derided and scoffed at. 11 Nevertheless, some from Asher, Manasseh, and Zebulun humbled themselves and came to Jerusalem. 12 In Judah, however, the hand of God brought it about that the people were of one heart to carry out the command of the king and the princes by the word of the LORD. 13 Thus many people gathered in Jerusalem to celebrate the feast of Unleavened Bread in the second month; it was a very great assembly.

Passover Celebrated

14 They proceeded to remove the altars that were in Jerusalem as well as all the altars of incense, and cast them into the Wadi Kidron.* 15 They slaughtered the Passover on the fourteenth day of the second month. The priests and Levites were shamed into sanctifying themselves and brought burnt offerings into the house of the LORD. 16 They stood in the places prescribed for them according to the law of Moses, the man of God. The priests splashed the blood given them by the Levites; 17 for many in the assembly had not sanctified themselves, and the Levites were

29:34 1 Chr 15:12.
30:1 Ex 12:1–28.
30:2–3 Nm 9:6–13.
30:7 Acts 7:51.
30:9 1 Kgs 8:50.
30:14 2 Chr 28:24–25.
30:17 2 Chr 35:6.

in charge of slaughtering the Passover victims for
all who were unclean so as to consecrate them
to the LORD.* 18The greater part of the people, in
fact, chiefly from Ephraim, Manasseh, Issachar,
and Zebulun, had not cleansed themselves. Nev-
ertheless they ate the Passover, contrary to the
prescription; because Hezekiah prayed for them,
saying, "May the good LORD grant pardon to 19all
who have set their heart to seek God, the LORD,
the God of their ancestors, even though they are
not clean as holiness requires." 20The LORD heard
Hezekiah and healed the people.
21Thus the Israelites who were in Jerusalem
celebrated the feast of Unleavened Bread with
great rejoicing for seven days, and the Levites and
the priests sang the praises of the LORD day after
day with all their strength. 22Hezekiah spoke
encouragingly to all the Levites who had shown
themselves well skilled in the service of the LORD.
And when they had completed the seven days
of festival, sacrificing communion offerings and
singing praises to the LORD, the God of their an-
cestors, 23the whole assembly agreed to celebrate
another seven days. So with joy they celebrated
seven days more. 24King Hezekiah of Judah had
contributed a thousand bulls and seven thou-
sand sheep to the assembly, and the princes a
thousand bulls and ten thousand sheep. The
priests sanctified themselves in great numbers,
25and the whole assembly of Judah rejoiced, to-
gether with the priests and Levites and the rest
of the assembly that had come from Israel, as
well as the resident aliens from the land of Is-
rael and those that lived in Judah. 26There was
great rejoicing in Jerusalem, for since the days
of Solomon, son of David, king of Israel, there
had been nothing like it in the city. 27Then the
levitical priests rose and blessed the people; their
voice was heard and their prayer reached heaven,
God's holy dwelling.

Liturgical Reforms

31 1After all this was over, those Israelites
who had been present went forth to the
cities of Judah and smashed the sacred pillars,
cut down the asherahs, and tore down the high
places and altars throughout Judah, Benjamin,
Ephraim, and Manasseh, until they were all de-
stroyed.* Then the Israelites returned to their
cities, each to his own possession.
2Hezekiah re-established the divisions of the
priests and the Levites according to their former
divisions, assigning to each priest and Levite
his proper service, whether in regard to burnt
offerings or communion offerings, thanksgiv-
ing or praise, or ministering in the gates of the
encampment of the LORD. 3From his own wealth
the king allotted a portion for burnt offerings,
those of morning and evening and those on sab-
baths, new moons, and festivals, as is written in
the law of the LORD.* 4He also commanded the
people living in Jerusalem to provide for the sup-
port of the priests and Levites, that they might
firmly adhere to the law of the LORD.
5As soon as the order was promulgated, the
Israelites brought, in great quantities, the best
of their grain, wine, oil, and honey, and all the
produce of the fields; they gave a generous tithe
of everything.* 6Israelites and Judahites living
in other cities of Judah also brought in tithes of
oxen, sheep, and votive offerings consecrated to

Live It!

Giving the Best of the Best

In 2 Chronicles 31:5, we read about how the people "brought, in great quantities, the best of their grain, wine, oil, and honey, and all the produce of the fields." They gave the best of the best, in gratitude for the gifts from God. That is what being generous is all about. True generosity springs from the heart and motivates us to give the best of what we have, not just what we do not want or need anymore.

The word *tithe* appears in this verse. For the Israelites, to tithe meant to give 10 percent of one's earnings as a tax for the upkeep of the Temple. Some Christians continue the spirit of tithing by giving 10 percent of all they earn to their church and other charities. They are offering God their best, the firstfruits of their labor (see Lk 21:1–4 and Acts 4:32–37).

We all need to search our heart and continue this tradition of offering our best back to God—not because it makes us look good and gives us "extra points" with God, but because it comes from our gratitude for the gifts we have received.

▶ **2 Chr 31:2–10**

31:1 2 Chr 34:3–4; 2 Kgs 18:4.
31:3 Nm 28–29; 1 Chr 29:3; Ez 45:17.
31:5 Nm 18:18–24; Dt 14:22–23.

the LORD, their God; these they brought in and heaped up in piles.* [7]It was in the third month that they began to establish these heaps, and they completed them in the seventh month.† [8]When Hezekiah and the princes had come and seen the piles, they blessed the LORD and his people Israel. [9]Then Hezekiah questioned the priests and the Levites concerning the piles, [10]and the priest Azariah, head of the house of Zadok, answered him, "Since they began to bring the offerings to the house of the LORD, we have eaten, been satisfied, and had much left over, for the LORD has blessed his people. This great supply is what was left over."*

[11]Hezekiah then gave orders that chambers be constructed in the house of the LORD. When this had been done, [12]they deposited the offerings, tithes, and votive offerings there for safekeeping. The overseer of these things was Conaniah the Levite, and his brother Shimei was second in command. [13]Jehiel, Azaziah, Nahath, Asahel, Jerimoth, Jozabad, Eliel, Ismachiah, Mahath, and Benaiah were supervisors subject to Conaniah the Levite and his brother Shimei by appointment of King Hezekiah and of Azariah, the prefect of the house of God. [14]Kore, the son of Imnah, a Levite and the keeper of the eastern gate, was in charge of the voluntary offerings made to God; he distributed the offerings made to the LORD and the most holy of the votive offerings. [15]Under him in the priestly cities were Eden, Miniamin, Jeshua, Shemaiah, Amariah, and Shecaniah, who faithfully made the distribution to their brothers, great and small alike, according to their divisions.

[16]There was also a register by ancestral houses of males three years of age† and over, for all priests who were eligible to enter the house of the LORD according to the daily schedule to fulfill their service in the order of their divisions.* [17]The priests were inscribed in their family records according to their ancestral houses, as were the Levites twenty years of age and over according to their various offices and divisions.* [18]A distribution was also made to all who were inscribed in the family records, for their little ones, wives, sons and daughters—thus for the entire assembly, since they were to sanctify themselves by sharing faithfully in the votive offerings. [19]The sons of Aaron, the priests who lived on the lands attached to their cities, had in every city men designated by name to distribute portions to every male of the priests and to every Levite listed in the family records.

[20]Hezekiah did this in all Judah. He did what was good, upright, and faithful before the LORD, his God. [21]Everything that he undertook, for the service of the house of God or for the law and the commandment, was to seek his God. He did this with all his heart, and he prospered.*

Sennacherib's Invasion

32 [1]But after all this and all Hezekiah's fidelity, there came Sennacherib, king of Assyria. He invaded Judah and besieged the fortified cities, intending to breach and take them.* [2]When Hezekiah saw that Sennacherib was coming with the intention of attacking Jerusalem, [3]he took the advice of his princes and warriors to stop the waters of the springs outside the city; they promised their help. [4]* A large force was gathered and stopped all the springs and also the stream running nearby. For they said, "Why should the kings of Assyria come and find an abundance of water?" [5]He then looked to his defenses: he rebuilt the wall where it was broken down, raised towers upon it, and built another wall outside.* He strengthened the Millo of the City of David and made a great number of spears and shields. [6]Then he appointed army commanders over the people. He gathered them together in his presence in the open space at the gate of the city and encouraged them with these words: [7]"Be strong and steadfast; do not be afraid or dismayed because of the king of Assyria and all the horde coming with him, for there is more with us than with him.* [8]He has only an arm of flesh, but we have the LORD, our God, to help us and to fight our battles."* And the people took confidence from the words of Hezekiah, king of Judah.

Threat of Sennacherib

[9]* After this, while Sennacherib, king of Assyria, himself remained at Lachish with all his forces, he sent his officials to Jerusalem with this message for Hezekiah, king of Judah, and all the Judahites who were in Jerusalem: [10]"Thus says Sennacherib, king of Assyria: In what are you trusting, now that you are under siege in Jerusalem? [11]Is not Hezekiah deceiving you, delivering

---

† **31:7** *Third month . . . seventh month*: between the late spring feast of Weeks or Pentecost and the fall feast of Booths or Tabernacles, there is seldom any rain in Palestine; at the end of this dry period the problem of storage (v. 11) would become acute.

31:16 *Three years of age*: this may be a textual error for "thirty years." According to Nm 4:3, 23, 30, men of the priestly clans served from the ages of thirty to fifty.

* **31:6** Neh 12:44–47; 13:10–13.
31:10 Lv 25:19–22.
31:16 1 Chr 23:3–4.
31:17 1 Chr 23:6–24.
31:21 Ps 119:2.
32:1 2 Kgs 18:13.
32:4 Is 22:9, 11.
32:5 Neh 2:17–18.
32:7 2 Chr 14:10; 20:6–12.
32:8 Is 31:3.
32:9–20 2 Kgs 18:17–37; Is 36:1–22.

you over to a death of famine and thirst, by his
claim that 'the LORD, our God, will rescue us from
the grasp of the king of Assyria'? 12 Has not this
same Hezekiah removed the Lord's own high
places and altars and commanded Judah and
Jerusalem, 'You shall bow down before one altar
only, and on it alone you shall offer incense'?
13 Do you not know what my fathers and I have
done to all the peoples of other lands? Were the
gods of the nations in those lands able to rescue
their lands from my hand? 14 Who among all the
gods of those nations which my fathers put under the ban was able to rescue their people from
my hand? Will your god, then, be able to rescue
you from my hand? 15 Let not Hezekiah mislead
you further and deceive you in any such way.
Do not believe him! Since no other god of any
other nation or kingdom has been able to rescue
his people from my hand or the hands of my
fathers, how much the less shall your god rescue
you from my hand!"
16 His officials said still more against the LORD
God and against his servant Hezekiah, 17 for he
had written letters to deride the LORD, the God
of Israel, speaking of him in these terms: "As
the gods of the nations in other lands have not
rescued their people from my hand, neither
shall Hezekiah's god rescue his people from my
hand."* 18 In a loud voice they shouted in the
language of Judah to the people of Jerusalem
who were on the wall, to frighten and terrify
them so that they might capture their city. 19 They
spoke of the God of Israel as though he were one
of the gods of the other peoples of the earth, a
work of human hands. 20 But because of this,
King Hezekiah and Isaiah the prophet, son of
Amoz, prayed and cried out to heaven.*

Sennacherib's Defeat

21 Then the LORD sent an angel, who destroyed
every warrior, leader, and commander in the
camp of the Assyrian king, so that he had to return shamefaced to his own country. And when
he entered the temple of his god, some of his
own offspring struck him down there with the
sword.* 22 Thus the LORD saved Hezekiah and
the inhabitants of Jerusalem from the hand of
Sennacherib, king of Assyria, as from every other
power; he gave them rest on every side. 23 Many
brought gifts for the LORD to Jerusalem and costly
objects for Hezekiah, king of Judah, who thereafter was exalted in the eyes of all the nations.*

Hezekiah's Later Reign

24 In those days Hezekiah became mortally ill.
He prayed to the LORD, who answered him by
giving him a sign.* 25 Hezekiah, however, did not
respond with like generosity, for he had become
arrogant. Therefore wrath descended upon him
and upon Judah and Jerusalem. 26 * But then
Hezekiah humbled himself for his pride—both
he and the inhabitants of Jerusalem; and therefore the wrath of the LORD did not come upon
them during the time of Hezekiah.
27 * Hezekiah possessed very great wealth and
glory. He made treasuries for his silver, gold,
precious stones, spices, jewels, and other precious things of all kinds; 28 also storehouses for
the harvest of grain, for wine and oil, and barns

Live It!

Perseverance

King Hezekiah persevered and prospered. He had many riches and provided for the people in his kingdom. One great accomplishment was a tunnel he had dug under the City of David (see 2 Chr 32:30). The tunnel allowed the springs of Gihon to flow into the city so that the people had easier access to water.

That tunnel, more than seventeen hundred feet long, was carved through stone. Today, it would not take much to complete such a task, but in Hezekiah's time, it was done little by little with simple tools.

Perseverance is a valuable skill that everyone can benefit from, especially when great obstacles stand in the way. People can get discouraged and lose heart when faced with difficult tasks. Those who refuse to be discouraged or to give up can serve as a source of encouragement and vision for others.

- When you've been faced with an obstacle or difficult situation, what or who motivated you to persevere? Have you ever gotten discouraged and given up? Why did you?

▶ **2 Chr 32:27–33**

32:17 2 Kgs 19:9–13; Is 37:9–13.
32:20 2 Kgs 19:14–19; Is 37:14–20.
32:21 2 Kgs 19:35–37; Is 37:36–38.
32:23 2 Chr 17:10–11.
32:24 2 Kgs 20:1–11; Is 38:1–8.
32:26, 31 2 Kgs 20:12–19; Is 39:1–8.
32:27–28 2 Kgs 20:13; Is 39:2.

for the various kinds of cattle and flocks. 29 He built cities for himself, and he acquired sheep and oxen in great numbers, for God gave him very great riches. 30 This same Hezekiah stopped the upper outlet for water from Gihon and redirected it underground westward to the City of David. Hezekiah prospered in all his works.* 31 Nevertheless, in respect to the ambassadors of the Babylonian officials who were sent to him to investigate the sign that had occurred in the land, God abandoned him as a test, to know all that was in his heart.

32 The rest of Hezekiah's acts, including his good deeds, are recorded in the vision of Isaiah the prophet, son of Amoz, and in the book of the kings of Judah and Israel. 33 Hezekiah rested with his ancestors; he was buried at the approach to the tombs† of the descendants of David. All Judah and the inhabitants of Jerusalem paid him honor at his death. His son Manasseh succeeded him as king.

Manasseh's Impiety

33 1 * Manasseh was twelve years old when he became king, and he reigned fifty-five years in Jerusalem. 2 He did what was evil in the LORD's sight, following the abominable practices of the nations whom the LORD dispossessed before the Israelites. 3 He rebuilt the high places which Hezekiah his father had torn down. He set up altars to the Baals, and also made asherahs. He bowed down to the whole host of heaven and served them. 4 He built altars in the house of the LORD, of which the LORD had said: In Jerusalem shall my name be forever; 5 and he built altars to the whole host of heaven in the two courts of the house of the LORD. 6 It was he, too, who immolated his children by fire in the Valley of Ben-hinnom. He practiced soothsaying and divination, and reintroduced the consulting of ghosts and spirits.

He did much evil in the LORD's sight and provoked him to anger. 7 An idol he had made he placed in the house of God, of which God had said to David and to his son Solomon: In this house and in Jerusalem, which I have chosen out of all the tribes of Israel, I shall set my name forever. 8 I will no longer make Israel step out of the land I assigned to your ancestors, provided that they are careful to observe all I commanded them, the entire law, the statutes, and the ordinances given by Moses.

9 Manasseh misled Judah and the inhabitants of Jerusalem into doing even greater evil than the nations the LORD had destroyed at the coming of the Israelites. 10 The LORD spoke to Manasseh and his people, but they paid no attention.

Manasseh's Conversion

11 * Therefore the LORD brought against them the army commanders of the Assyrian king; they captured Manasseh with hooks, shackled him with chains, and transported him to Babylon.† 12 In his distress, he began to appease the LORD, his God. He humbled himself abjectly before the God of his ancestors, 13 and prayed to him.† The LORD let himself be won over: he heard his prayer and restored him to his kingdom in Jerusalem. Then Manasseh knew that the LORD is indeed God.

14 Afterward he built an outer wall for the City of David to the west of Gihon in the valley, extending to the Fish Gate and encircling Ophel; he built it very high. He stationed army officers in all the fortified cities of Judah. 15 He removed the foreign gods and the idol from the LORD's house and all the altars he had built on the mount of the LORD's house and in Jerusalem, and cast them outside the city.* 16 He restored the altar of the LORD, and sacrificed on it communion offerings and thank offerings, and commanded Judah to serve the LORD, the God of Israel. 17 Though the people continued to sacrifice on the high places, they now did so to the LORD, their God.

18 * The rest of the acts of Manasseh, his prayer to his God, and the words of the seers who spoke to him in the name of the LORD, the God of Israel, are written in the chronicles of the kings of Israel. 19 His prayer and how his supplication was heard, all his sins and his treachery, the sites where he built high places and set up asherahs and carved images before he humbled himself, all this is recorded in the chronicles of his seers. 20 Manasseh rested with his ancestors and was buried in his own palace. His son Amon succeeded him as king.

2 CHR

32:33 *The approach to the tombs*: lit., "the ascent of the tombs," perhaps "the upper section of the tombs," i.e., their most prominent and honored place.

33:11 There is no evidence elsewhere for such an imprisonment of King Manasseh in Babylon. According to the Assyrian inscriptions, however, Manasseh did pay tribute to the Assyrian kings Esarhaddon (680–669 B.C.) and Asshurbanipal (668–627 B.C.). He may well then have been obliged to go to Nineveh, Assyria's capital (rather than to Babylon as the Chronicler has it), to take his oath of allegiance as vassal to the king of Assyria.

33:13 *And prayed to him*: these words inspired an unknown writer to compose the apocryphal "Prayer of Manasseh," which since the Council of Trent appears as an appendix to many editions of the Vulgate Bible and is used in the Church's liturgy.

32:30 2 Kgs 20:20–21.
33:1–10 2 Kgs 21:1–9.
33:11 Jb 36:8; Ez 19:9.
33:15 2 Chr 14:2.
33:18, 20 2 Kgs 21:17–18.

Reign of Amon

21 * Amon was twenty-two years old when he
became king, and he reigned two years in Jerusa-
lem. 22 He did what was evil in the LORD's sight,
as his father Manasseh had done. Amon offered
sacrifice to all the idols his father Manasseh had
made, and served them. 23 Moreover, he did not
humble himself before the LORD as his father Ma-
nasseh had humbled himself; on the contrary,
Amon only increased his guilt. 24 His officials
plotted against him and put him to death in his
palace, 25 but the people of the land then slew
all who had plotted against King Amon, and the
people of the land made his son Josiah king in
his stead.

Josiah's Reforms

34 1 * Josiah was eight years old when he
became king, and he reigned thirty-one
years in Jerusalem. 2 He did what was right in
the LORD's sight, walking in the way of David his
father, not turning right or left. 3 * In the eighth
year of his reign, while he was still a youth, he
began to seek after the God of David his father.
Then in his twelfth year† he began to purify Ju-
dah and Jerusalem of the high places, the ashe-
rahs, and the carved and molten images. 4 In his
presence, the altars of the Baals were torn down;
the incense stands erected above them he broke
down; the asherahs and the carved and molten
images he smashed and beat into dust, which he
scattered over the tombs of those who had sac-
rificed to them; 5 and the bones of the priests he
burned upon their altars. Thus he purified Judah
and Jerusalem. 6 He did likewise in the cities of
Manasseh, Ephraim, Simeon, and in the ruined
villages of the surrounding country as far as
Naphtali; 7 he tore down the altars and asherahs,
and the carved images he beat into dust, and
broke down the incense stands throughout the
land of Israel. Then he returned to Jerusalem.

The Temple Restored

8 * In the eighteenth year of his reign, in or-
der to purify the land and the temple, he sent
Shaphan, son of Azaliah, Maaseiah, the ruler of
the city, and Joah, son of Joahaz, the chancellor,
to restore the house of the LORD, his God. 9 They
came to Hilkiah the high priest and turned over
the money brought to the house of God which
the Levites, the guardians of the threshold, had
collected from Manasseh, Ephraim, and all the
remnant of Israel, as well as from all of Judah,
Benjamin, and the inhabitants of Jerusalem.*
10 They turned it over to the master workers in
the house of the LORD, and these in turn used it
to pay the workers in the LORD's house who were
restoring and repairing it. 11 They also gave it to
the carpenters and the masons to buy hewn stone
and timber for the tie beams and rafters of the
buildings which the kings of Judah had allowed
to fall into ruin. 12 The men worked faithfully at
their task; their overseers were Jahath and Oba-
diah, Levites of the line of Merari, and Zechariah
and Meshullam, of the Kohathites, who directed
them. All those Levites who were skillful with
musical instruments 13 were in charge of the men
who carried the burdens, and they directed all the
workers in every kind of labor. Some of the other
Levites were scribes, officials, and gatekeepers.

The Finding of the Law

14 * When they brought out the money that
had been deposited in the house of the LORD, Hil-
kiah the priest found the book of the law of the
LORD given through Moses. 15 He reported this
to Shaphan the scribe, saying, "I have found the
book of the law in the house of the LORD." Hil-
kiah gave the book to Shaphan, 16 who brought
it to the king at the same time that he made his
report to him. He said, "Your servants are do-
ing everything that has been entrusted to them;
17 they have smelted down the silver deposited in
the LORD's house and have turned it over to the
overseers and the workers." 18 Then Shaphan the
scribe also informed the king, "Hilkiah the priest
has given me a book," and then Shaphan read it
in the presence of the king.

19 When the king heard the words of the law,
he tore his garments. 20 The king then issued this
command to Hilkiah, to Ahikam, son of Sha-
phan, to Abdon, son of Michah, to Shaphan the
scribe, and to Asaiah, the king's servant: 21 "Go,
consult the LORD for me and for those who are
left in Israel and Judah, about the words of the
book that has been found, for the anger of the
LORD burns furiously against us, because our an-
cestors did not keep the word of the LORD and
have not done all that is written in this book."

34:3 *In his twelfth year*: ca. 628 B.C., i.e., around the time of the Assyrian emperor Asshurbanipal's death, which enabled Judah to free itself from Assyrian domination. On the basis of 2 Kgs 22:1–23:25 alone, one might suppose that Josiah's reform began only after and as a result of the discovery of the book of the law in the Temple, in the eighteenth year of his reign (622 B.C.). But the Chronicler is no doubt right in placing the beginning of the reform at an earlier period. The repair of the Temple itself, which led to the finding of the book of the law, was likely part of a cultic reform initiated by Josiah.

33:21–25 2 Kgs 21:19–26.
34:1–2 2 Kgs 22:1–2.
34:3–7 2 Chr 14:1–4; 31:1; 2 Kgs 23:4–20.
34:8–13 2 Kgs 22:3–7.
34:9 2 Chr 24:8–9.
34:14–28 2 Kgs 22:8–20.

22 Then Hilkiah and others from the king went to Huldah the prophet, wife of Shallum, son of Tokhath, son of Hasrah, keeper of the wardrobe; she lived in Jerusalem, in the Second Quarter. They spoke to her as they had been instructed, 23 and she said to them: "Thus says the LORD, the God of Israel: Say to the man who sent you to me, 24 Thus says the LORD: I am about to bring evil upon this place and upon its inhabitants, all the curses written in the book that was read before the king of Judah. 25 Because they have abandoned me and have burned incense to other gods, provoking me by all the works of their hands, my anger burns against this place and it cannot be extinguished.

26 "But to the king of Judah who sent you to consult the LORD, give this response: Thus says the LORD, the God of Israel: As for the words you have heard, 27 because you were heartsick and have humbled yourself before God when you heard his words concerning this place and its inhabitants; because you humbled yourself before me, tore your garments, and wept before me, I in turn have heard—oracle of the LORD. 28 I will gather you to your ancestors and you shall go to your grave in peace, and your eyes shall not see all the evil I am about to bring upon this place and upon its inhabitants."

This they reported to the king.

Covenant Renewal

29 * The king then had all the elders of Judah and of Jerusalem summoned before him. 30 The king went up to the house of the LORD with all the people of Judah and the inhabitants of Jerusalem: priests, Levites, and all the people, great and small. He read aloud to them all the words of the book of the covenant that had been found in the house of the LORD. 31 The king stood by the column† and made a covenant in the presence of the LORD to follow the LORD and to observe his commandments, statutes, and decrees with his whole heart and soul, carrying out the words of the covenant written in this book. 32 He thereby committed all who were in Jerusalem and Benjamin, and the inhabitants of Jerusalem acted according to the covenant of God, the God of their ancestors. 33 Josiah removed every abomination from all the territories belonging to the Israelites, and he obliged all who were in Israel to serve the LORD, their God. During his lifetime they did not turn away from following the LORD, the God of their ancestors.*

The Passover

35 1 * Josiah celebrated in Jerusalem a Passover to honor the LORD; the Passover sacrifice was slaughtered on the fourteenth day of the first month.* 2 He reappointed the priests to their duties and confirmed them in the service of the LORD's house. 3 He said to the Levites who were to instruct all Israel, and who were consecrated to the LORD: "Put the holy ark in the house built by Solomon, son of David, king of Israel. It shall no longer be a burden on your shoulders. Serve now the LORD, your God, and his people Israel.* 4 Prepare yourselves by your ancestral houses and your divisions according to the prescriptions of David, king of Israel, and the prescriptions of his son Solomon. 5 Stand in the sanctuary according to the branches of the ancestral houses of your kin, the common people, so that the distribution of the Levites and the families may be the same.* 6 Slaughter the Passover sacrifice, sanctify yourselves, and be at the disposition of your kin, that all may be done according to the word of the LORD given through Moses."*

7 Josiah contributed to the common people a flock of lambs and young goats,* thirty thousand in number, each to serve as a Passover victim for all who were present, and also three thousand oxen; these were from the king's property. 8 His princes also gave a voluntary offering to the people, the priests, and the Levites. Hilkiah, Zechariah, and Jehiel, prefects of the house of God, gave to the priests two thousand six hundred Passover victims along with three hundred oxen.* 9 Conaniah and his brothers Shemaiah, Nethanel, Hashabiah, Jehiel, and Jozabad, the rulers of the Levites, contributed to the Levites five thousand Passover victims, together with five hundred oxen.

10 When the service had been arranged, the priests took their places, as did the Levites in their divisions according to the king's command. 11 The Passover sacrifice was slaughtered, whereupon the priests splashed some of the blood and the Levites proceeded with the skinning. 12 They separated out what was destined for the burnt offering and gave it to various groups of the ancestral houses of the common people to offer to the LORD, as is written in the book of Moses. They did the same with the oxen. 13 They cooked the Passover on the fire as prescribed, and also cooked the sacred portions in pots, caldrons, and pans,

---

† **34:31** *The column*: see note on 23:13.

34:29–31 2 Kgs 23:1–3. **34:33** 2 Kgs 23:4–20.

35:1–19 2 Kgs 23:21–23. **35:1** Ex 12:1–28; 2 Kgs 23:21. **35:3** 2 Chr 5:4; 1 Chr 15:12, 15. **35:5** 1 Chr 24–26. **35:6** 2 Chr 30:17. **35:7** Ex 12:5. **35:8** Nm 7:1–83.

then brought them quickly to all the common people.* 14 Afterward they prepared the Passover for themselves and for the priests. Indeed the priests, the sons of Aaron, were busy sacrificing burnt offerings and the fatty portions until night; therefore the Levites prepared for themselves and for the priests, the sons of Aaron. 15 The singers, the sons of Asaph, were at their posts as commanded by David and by Asaph, Heman, and Jeduthun, the king's seer. The gatekeepers were at every gate; there was no need for them to leave their stations, for their fellow Levites prepared for them. 16 Thus the entire service of the LORD was arranged that day so that the Passover could be celebrated and the burnt offerings sacrificed on the altar of the LORD, as King Josiah had commanded. 17 The Israelites who were present on that occasion kept the Passover and the feast of the Unleavened Bread for seven days. 18 * No such Passover had been observed in Israel since the time of Samuel the prophet; no king of Israel had observed a Passover like that celebrated by Josiah, the priests, and Levites, all of Judah and Israel that were present, and the inhabitants of Jerusalem. 19 It was in the eighteenth year of Josiah's reign that this Passover was observed.

Josiah's End

20 After Josiah had done all this to restore the temple, Neco, king of Egypt, came up to fight at Carchemish on the Euphrates, and Josiah went out to meet him. 21 Neco sent messengers to him, saying: "What quarrel is between us, king of Judah? I have not come against you this day, for my war is with another kingdom, and God has told me to hasten. Do not interfere with God who is with me; let him not destroy you." 22 But Josiah would not withdraw from him, for he was seeking a pretext to fight with him. Therefore he would not listen to the words of Neco that came from the mouth of God, but went out to fight in the plain of Megiddo. 23 Then the archers shot King Josiah, who said to his servants, "Take me away, I am seriously wounded."* 24 His servants took him from his own chariot, placed him in the one he had in reserve, and brought him to Jerusalem, where he died. He was buried in the tombs of his ancestors, and all Judah and Jerusalem mourned him. 25 Jeremiah also composed a lamentation for Josiah, which is recited to this day by all the male and female singers in their lamentations for Josiah. These have been made an ordinance for Israel, and can be found written in the Lamentations.†

26 * The rest of the acts of Josiah, his good deeds in accord with what is written in the law of the LORD, 27 and his words, first and last, are recorded in the book of the kings of Israel and Judah.

Jehoahaz

36 1 * The people of the land took Jehoahaz, son of Josiah, and made him king in Jerusalem to succeed his father. 2 Jehoahaz was twenty-three years old when he became king, and he reigned three months in Jerusalem. 3 The king of Egypt deposed him in Jerusalem and fined the land one hundred talents of silver and a talent of gold. 4 Then the king of Egypt made Eliakim, the brother of Jehoahaz, king over Judah and Jerusalem, changing his name to Jehoiakim. Neco took Jehoahaz his brother away and brought him to Egypt.

Jehoiakim

5 Jehoiakim was twenty-five years old when he became king, and he reigned eleven years in Jerusalem. He did what was evil in the sight of the LORD, his God.* 6 * Nebuchadnezzar, king of Babylon, attacked and bound him in chains to take him to Babylon.† 7 Nebuchadnezzar also carried away to Babylon some of the vessels of the house of the LORD and put them in his palace in Babylon. 8 The rest of the acts of Jehoiakim, the abominable things that he did, and what therefore happened to him, are recorded in the book of the kings of Israel and Judah. His son Jehoiachin succeeded him as king.*

Jehoiachin

9 Jehoiachin was eighteen years old when he became king, and he reigned three months and ten days in Jerusalem. He did what was evil in the LORD's sight.* 10 At the turn of the year, King Nebuchadnezzar sent for him and had him brought to Babylon, along with precious vessels

†

35:25 There is no mention of such a lamentation for Josiah composed by Jeremiah in either 2 Kings or Jeremiah; but see note on Zec 12:11. *Lamentations*: probably a reference to the Book of Lamentations.

36:6 *Nebuchadnezzar . . . bound him in chains to take him to Babylon*: the Chronicler does not state that Jehoiakim was actually taken to Babylon. According to 2 Kgs 24:1–6, Jehoiakim revolted after being Nebuchadnezzar's vassal for three years; he died in Jerusalem before the city surrendered to the Babylonians. Dn 1:1–2, apparently based on 2 Chr 36:6–7, does speak of Jehoiakim's deportation to Babylon.

*

35:13 Ex 12:8–9.
35:18–19 2 Kgs 23:22–23.
35:23 2 Chr 18:33–34.
35:26 2 Kgs 23:28.
36:1–4 2 Kgs 23:30–34; 1 Chr 3:15–16.
36:5 2 Kgs 23:36–37; Jer 22:18–19.
36:6 2 Kgs 24:1–2.
36:8 2 Kgs 24:5.
36:9 2 Kgs 24:8–9.

Live It!

Stiff Neck

It happened so quickly. I was waiting at a stoplight when the car behind me slammed into my car and my neck snapped back. Whiplash! It hurt, but it didn't seem very serious. I was much more upset at the damage that had been done to my car. But by the next morning, I was in agony. I could barely move my head, and my neck was stiff and sore. By the end of the day, my neck was in a brace, and I was taking pain medication.

Now I understand a little better why the Bible so often uses the metaphor of stiff-necked people (see 2 Chr 36:13). To be unable or unwilling to turn their heads deprives people of the ability to look toward God. They just keep looking straight ahead as if it were not possible to look in any other direction. You miss out on a lot if you don't or can't look from side to side, believe me!

- How often have you refused to turn toward God or to gain a new perspective on life?

▶ 2 Chr 36:11–14

from the house of the LORD. He made his brother
Zedekiah† king over Judah and Jerusalem.*

Zedekiah

11 Zedekiah was twenty-one years old when
he became king, and he reigned eleven years in
Jerusalem.* 12 He did what was evil in the sight
of the LORD, his God, and he did not humble
himself before Jeremiah the prophet, who spoke
for the LORD.* 13 He also rebelled against King
Nebuchadnezzar, who had made him swear by
God. He became stiff-necked and hardened his
heart rather than return to the LORD, the God
of Israel.* 14 Likewise all the princes of Judah,
the priests, and the people added treachery to
treachery, practicing all the abominations of the
nations and defiling the LORD's house which he
had consecrated in Jerusalem.

The Fall of Judah

15 Early and often the LORD, the God of their
ancestors, sent his messengers to them, for he
had compassion on his people and his dwelling
place.* 16 But they mocked God's messengers, de-
spised his words, and scoffed at his prophets, un-
til the LORD's anger against his people blazed up
beyond remedy.* 17 Then he brought up against
them the king of the Chaldeans, who killed their
young men with the sword in their own sanctu-
ary, with compassion for neither young men nor
young women, neither the old nor the infirm; all
of them he delivered into his power.* 18 All the
utensils of the house of God, large and small, the
treasures of the LORD's house, and the treasures of
the king and his princes, all these he brought to
Babylon.* 19 They burnt the house of God, tore
down the walls of Jerusalem, burnt down all its
palaces, and destroyed all its precious objects.*
20 Those who escaped the sword he carried cap-
tive to Babylon, where they became servants to
him and his sons until the Persian kingdom
came to power. 21 All this was to fulfill the word
of the LORD spoken by Jeremiah: Until the land
has retrieved its lost sabbaths, during all the time
it lies waste it shall have rest while seventy years
are fulfilled.

Decree of Cyrus

22 † In the first year of Cyrus, king of Persia,
in order to realize the word of the LORD spo-
ken by Jeremiah, the LORD roused the spirit of
Cyrus, King of Persia, to spread this proclama-
tion throughout his kingdom, both by word of
mouth and in writing:* 23 "Thus says Cyrus, king
of Persia: The LORD, the God of heaven, has given
to me all the kingdoms of the earth. He has also
charged me to build him a house in Jerusalem,
which is in Judah. All among you, therefore, who
belong to his people, may their God be with
them; let them go up."

†

36:10 *His brother Zedekiah*: Zedekiah was actually the brother of Jehoiakim and the uncle of Jehoiachin (2 Kgs 24:17; Jer 37:1), though scarcely older than his nephew (2 Kgs 24:8, 18; 2 Chr 36:9, 11).

36:22–23 These verses are identical with those of Ezr 1:1–3a and were to prevent the work from ending on a note of doom.

*

36:10 2 Kgs 24:10–17.
36:11 2 Kgs 24:18–19; Jer 52:1.
36:12 Jer 37:1–2.
36:13 2 Kgs 24:20; Jer 52:4; Ez 17:13–16.
36:15 Jer 7:25; Heb 1:1.
36:16 Mt 23:34–37.
36:17 Lam 1:15; 5:11–14.
36:18 2 Kgs 25:14–15.
36:19 2 Kgs 25:9–10; Lam 2:8.
36:22 Ezr 1:1–4.

The Books of Ezra and Nehemiah

Imagine the worst vacation ever. The car breaks down twice, you are sick almost the whole time, and the weather is awful. You can't wait to get home—but when you walk in the front door, you see that the house is trashed. Now imagine how the Israelites felt. They didn't just have a bad vacation; they spent fifty years as captives in a foreign land. When they finally returned home, they faced the overwhelming task of rebuilding Jerusalem and starting their new life. Fortunately, they had Ezra and Nehemiah to help lead and encourage them.

At a Glance

I. The Return from Exile (Ezr 1:1—6:22).

II. The Work of Ezra (Ezr 7:1—10:44).

I. The Deeds of Nehemiah (Neh 1:1—7:72).

II. Promulgation of the Law (Neh 8:1—10:40).

III. Dedication of the Wall; Other Reforms (Neh 11:1—13:31).

Quick Facts

Period Covered: from the Exiles' return to Jerusalem through Nehemiah's tenure as governor of Judah, from 538 to about 400 BC

Inspired Author: a scribe (the Chronicler) drawing on Ezra's and Nehemiah's memoirs and other sources

Themes: the return of the Israelites from captivity, the rebuilding of Jerusalem and the Temple

In Depth

In 587 BC, the land of Judah and the city of Jerusalem were conquered by the Babylonians, and many Israelites were exiled to Babylon. The Books of Ezra and Nehemiah pick up the story with the return of some Israelites from Babylon to Judah in 538 BC. The two books were originally a single work, perhaps written in their final form by the same person (or persons) who wrote First and Second Chronicles.

Ezra, a descendant of Israelite priests, was born in Babylonian captivity and became a priest. Because priests couldn't exercise their religious functions during the Exile, they dedicated themselves to studying the Scriptures. Eventually, Ezra was sent to Judah by the Persian emperor Artaxerxes to restore Israel's faithfulness to God. Ezra appointed scribes and judges to establish civil and moral order in the new community returned from Exile.

Nehemiah was a Jewish cupbearer for Emperor Artaxerxes (a cupbearer tastes the contents of whatever the emperor drinks to assure it is not poisoned). When Nehemiah heard reports of Jerusalem's poverty and ruin, he persuaded the emperor to appoint him governor of Judah to help rebuild the city. Nehemiah turned out to be a gifted governor. Under Nehemiah's direction, Jerusalem's walls were rebuilt, and economic and social reforms helped restore order and hope to the community.

Ezra and Nehemiah's leadership was extremely important to Israel as the people returned and began the difficult task of rebuilding Jerusalem. The need to save the faith and customs of the Israelites led to a strict observance of the law and the beginnings of modern Judaism.

Ezra

9:3–5

I. The Return from Exile

The Decree of Cyrus

1 1 * In the first year of Cyrus,† king of Persia, in
order to fulfill the word of the LORD spoken by
Jeremiah, the LORD stirred up the spirit of Cyrus
king of Persia to issue a proclamation throughout
his entire kingdom, both by word of mouth and
in writing: 2 "Thus says Cyrus, king of Persia: 'All
the kingdoms of the earth the LORD, the God of
heaven,† has given to me, and he has charged me
to build him a house in Jerusalem, which is in Ju-
dah. 3 Those among you who belong to any part of
his people, may their God be with them! Let them
go up to Jerusalem in Judah to build the house of
the LORD the God of Israel, that is, the God who is
in Jerusalem. 4 Let all those who have survived, in
whatever place they may have lived, be assisted by
the people of that place with silver, gold, goods,
and livestock, together with voluntary offerings
for the house of God in Jerusalem.' "

5 Then the heads of ancestral houses† of Ju-
dah and Benjamin and the priests and Levites—
everyone, that is, whose spirit had been stirred
up by God—prepared to go up to build the house
of the LORD in Jerusalem. 6 * All their neighbors
gave them help in every way, with silver, gold,
goods, livestock, and many precious gifts, be-
sides all their voluntary offerings. 7 * King Cyrus,
too, had the vessels of the house of the LORD
brought forth that Nebuchadnezzar had taken
from Jerusalem and placed in the house of his
god. 8 Cyrus, king of Persia, had them brought
forth by the treasurer Mithredath, who counted
them out to Sheshbazzar, prince of Judah.† 9 This
was the inventory: baskets of goldware, thirty;
baskets of silverware, one thousand and twenty-
nine; 10 golden bowls, thirty; silver bowls, four
hundred and ten; other vessels, one thousand.
11 Total of the gold and silver vessels: five thou-
sand four hundred.† All these Sheshbazzar took
with him when the exiles were brought up from
Babylon to Jerusalem.

†

1:1 *In the first year of Cyrus*: the first regnal year of Cyrus was 539 B.C., but his first year as ruler of Babylon, after the conquest of that city, was 538 B.C., the year in which he issued an edict, replicated on the famous Cyrus cylinder, permitting the repatriation of peoples deported by the Babylonians.

1:2 *The God of heaven*: this title, used as in 7:12, 21, 23, corresponds to a title of the Zoroastrian supreme deity Ahura Mazda, though it is not certain that Cyrus was a Zoroastrian.

1:5 *Heads of ancestral houses*: the ancestral house was the basic organizational unit of the postexilic community, consisting of an extended kinship group claiming descent from a common ancestor. The patriarchs of these units played an important role in civic government.

1:8 *Sheshbazzar, prince of Judah*: often identified with Shenassar, fourth son of Jehoiachin, king of Judah, exiled in 598 B.C. (see 1 Chr 3:17–18), and therefore the uncle of Zerubbabel (Ezr 3:2–4). This identification is uncertain.

1:11 *Five thousand four hundred*: either this figure or the figures given for one or more of the items listed have been corrupted in the transmission of the text.

1:1 Ezr 6:3–5; 2 Chr 36:22–23; Jer 25:11–12; 29:10; Zec 1:12.
1:6 Ex 3:21–22; 11:2; 12:35.
1:7 2 Kgs 25:14–15.

A Census of the Returned Exiles

2 1 † * These are the inhabitants of the prov-
ince who returned from the captivity of the
exiles, whom Nebuchadnezzar, king of Babylon,
had carried away to Babylon, and who came
back to Jerusalem and Judah, to their various
cities 2 (those who returned with Zerubbabel,
Jeshua, Nehemiah, Seraiah, Reelaiah, Mordecai,
Bilshan, Mispar, Bigvai, Rehum, and Baanah):
The census of the people of Israel: 3 descen-
dants of Parosh, two thousand one hundred
and seventy-two; 4 descendants of Shephatiah,
three hundred and seventy-two; 5 descendants of
Arah, seven hundred and seventy-five; 6 descen-
dants of Pahath-moab, who were descendants
of Jeshua and Joab, two thousand eight hundred
and twelve; 7 descendants of Elam, one thou-
sand two hundred and fifty-four; 8 descendants
of Zattu, nine hundred and forty-five; 9 descen-
dants of Zaccai, seven hundred and sixty; 10 de-
scendants of Bani, six hundred and forty-two;
11 descendants of Bebai, six hundred and twenty-
three; 12 descendants of Azgad, one thousand
two hundred and twenty-two; 13 descendants of
Adonikam, six hundred and sixty-six; 14 descen-
dants of Bigvai, two thousand and fifty-six; 15 de-
scendants of Adin, four hundred and fifty-four;
16 descendants of Ater, who were descendants of
Hezekiah, ninety-eight; 17 descendants of Bezai,
three hundred and twenty-three; 18 descendants
of Jorah, one hundred and twelve; 19 descendants
of Hashum, two hundred and twenty-three; 20 de-
scendants of Gibeon, ninety-five; 21 descendants
of Bethlehem, one hundred and twenty-three;
22 people of Netophah, fifty-six; 23 people of An-
athoth, one hundred and twenty-eight; 24 people
of Beth-azmaveth, forty-two; 25 people of Kiriath-
jearim, Chephirah, and Beeroth, seven hundred
and forty-three; 26 people of Ramah and Geba, six
hundred and twenty-one; 27 people of Michmas,
one hundred and twenty-two; 28 people of Bethel
and Ai, two hundred and twenty-three; 29 descen-
dants of Nebo, fifty-two; 30 descendants of Mag-
bish, one hundred and fifty-six; 31 descendants of
the other Elam, one thousand two hundred and
fifty-four; 32 descendants of Harim, three hun-
dred and twenty; 33 descendants of Lod, Hadid,
and Ono, seven hundred and twenty-five; 34 de-
scendants of Jericho, three hundred and forty-
five; 35 descendants of Senaah, three thousand six
hundred and thirty.

Live It!

The Spirit of Giving

Nine eleven. Whenever we hear those two words, we are reminded of a horrible day in the history of the United States. The image of the twin towers of the World Trade Center burning and collapsing will stay with us forever. That event affected all of us, but it especially affected the citizens of New York City. Many stories of heroism surround that awful time. The people of New York City and the entire nation came together to grieve and especially to rebuild. Countless people volunteered untold hours to help with rescue efforts and clean-up. Countless more donated money to the families of those directly affected by the tragedy. Despite the horror of the attack, the aftermath of September 11, 2001, brought millions of people together to help rebuild a broken city. It was perhaps one of our finest hours as a nation.

For the Jews returning to Jerusalem, the task of rebuilding their ruined city must have seemed just as overwhelming, if not more so. (Their whole city was destroyed.) King Cyrus understood this and asked that family, friends, and neighbors help by giving whatever they could to the rebuilding effort.

- Who has been there to help you when you have felt completely overwhelmed? How do you offer help to others in their times of tragedy and crisis?

▶ Ezr 1:6–11

36 The priests: descendants of Jedaiah, of the
house of Jeshua, nine hundred and seventy-three;
37 descendants of Immer, one thousand and fifty-
two; 38 descendants of Pashhur, one thousand
two hundred and forty-seven; 39 descendants of
Harim, one thousand and seventeen.

40 * The Levites: descendants of Jeshua and
Kadmiel, of the descendants of Hodaviah, sev-
enty-four.

† **2:1–67** As it now stands, this list, which also appears at Neh 7:6–72, is an expanded form of lists of Babylonian repatriates from the sixth century B.C. It served to establish membership in the reconstituted Temple community; civic status and perhaps also title to property depended on this membership.

* **2:1** Neh 7:6–72. **2:40** Neh 12:23.

Pray It!

Holy Tears

Ezra 3:12 tells us that many of the older Israelites who remembered the first Temple wept at the grand celebration that marked its rebirth. Were they shedding tears of joy that the Temple was being built again? Or were they shedding tears of sorrow over what they had lost and never regained? Most likely, they were doing both.

Weeping can be a holy and healing part of life. Unfortunately, some people believe that strong men and women never cry. But tears are appropriate on many occasions: the loss of a dear friend or family member, reconciliation with someone after a long separation, and the moment we recognize we have sinned and hurt someone deeply, to name a few. Recall that moving scene in the Gospel where the sinful woman washed Jesus' feet with her tears (see Lk 7:36–50). We should bring our tears to God in prayer. They will turn into holy tears as God's healing love enters our lives.

▶ **Ezr 3:10–13**

41 The singers:† descendants of Asaph, one
hundred and twenty-eight.
42 The gatekeepers:† descendants of Shallum,
descendants of Ater, descendants of Talmon,
descendants of Akkub, descendants of Hatita, de-
scendants of Shobai, one hundred and thirty-nine
in all.
43 The temple servants: descendants of Ziha, de-
scendants of Hasupha, descendants of Tabbaoth,
44 descendants of Keros, descendants of Siaha, de-
scendants of Padon, 45 descendants of Lebanah,
descendants of Hagabah, descendants of Akkub,
46 descendants of Hagab, descendants of Shamlai,
descendants of Hanan, 47 descendants of Giddel,
descendants of Gahar, descendants of Reaiah,
48 descendants of Rezin, descendants of Nekoda,
descendants of Gazzam, 49 descendants of Uzza,
descendants of Paseah, descendants of Besai, 50 de-
scendants of Asnah, descendants of the Meunites,
descendants of the Nephusites, 51 descendants of
Bakbuk, descendants of Hakupha, descendants of
Harhur, 52 descendants of Bazluth, descendants
of Mehida, descendants of Harsha, 53 descendants
of Barkos, descendants of Sisera, descendants of
Temah, 54 descendants of Neziah, descendants of
Hatipha.
55 Descendants of Solomon's servants: descen-
dants of Sotai, descendants of Hassophereth,
descendants of Peruda, 56 descendants of Jaalah,
descendants of Darkon, descendants of Giddel,
57 descendants of Shephatiah, descendants of Hat-
til, descendants of Pochereth-hazzebaim, descen-
dants of Ami. 58 The total of the temple servants
together with the descendants of Solomon's ser-
vants was three hundred and ninety-two.
59 The following who returned from Tel-melah,
Tel-harsha, Cherub, Addan, and Immer were un-
able to prove that their ancestral houses and their
descent were Israelite: 60 descendants of Delaiah,
descendants of Tobiah, descendants of Nekoda,
six hundred and fifty-two. 61 * Also, of the priests:
descendants of Habaiah, descendants of Hakkoz,
descendants of Barzillai (he had married one of
the daughters of Barzillai the Gileadite and was
named after him). 62 These searched their fam-
ily records, but their names could not be found
there, and they were excluded from the priest-
hood. 63 * The governor† ordered them not to
partake of the most holy foods until there should
be a priest to consult the Urim and Thummim.
64 The entire assembly taken together came
to forty-two thousand three hundred and sixty,
65 not counting their male and female servants,
who numbered seven thousand three hundred
and thirty-seven. They also had two hundred
male and female singers. 66 Their horses num-
bered seven hundred and thirty-six, their mules
two hundred and forty-five, 67 their camels four
hundred and thirty-five, their donkeys six thou-
sand seven hundred and twenty.
68 When they arrived at the house of the LORD

†

2:41 *The singers*: the term covers the composition as well as the rendition of liturgical music. Since they are listed as distinct from Levites (2:40), they had not yet attained levitical status, as in Chronicles (e.g., 1 Chr 9:33–34; 23:3–6).

2:42 *The gatekeepers*: their principal task was to protect the ritual purity of the temple area (e.g., 2 Chr 23:19). The author assumes that they were established by David as a distinct levitical category (1 Chr 15:18; 26:1–19).

2:63 *The governor*: the honorific title was also held by Nehemiah (Neh 8:9; 10:2). The identity of the governor is unknown; both Sheshbazzar (Ezr 5:14) and Zerubbabel (Hg 1:1, 14; 2:2, 21) are identified as governors of Judah in the early Persian period. Mal 1:8 refers to an unnamed governor, and the names of other occupants of the office (Yehoezer, Ahzai, Elnathan) occur on seal impressions, though their date is uncertain. *Urim and Thummim*: cf. Ex 28:30.

2:61 2 Sm 17:27; 19:32–33; 1 Kgs 2:7.

2:63 Nm 27:21; Dt 33:8; 1 Sm 14:41–42; 28:6.

in Jerusalem, some of the heads of ancestral
houses made voluntary offerings for the house
of God, to rebuild it in its place. 69 According to
their means they contributed to the treasury for
the temple service: sixty-one thousand drachmas
of gold, five thousand minas of silver, and one
hundred priestly robes. 70 The priests, the Levites,
and some of the people took up residence in
Jerusalem; the singers, the gatekeepers, and the
temple servants settled in their cities. Thus all the
Israelites settled in their cities.

Restoration of Worship

3 1 * Now when the seventh month† came,
after the Israelites had settled in their cities,
the people gathered as one in Jerusalem. 2 Then
Jeshua, son of Jozadak, together with his kinsmen
the priests, and Zerubbabel, son of Shealtiel, to-
gether with his kinsmen, began building the altar
of the God of Israel in order to offer on it the
burnt offerings prescribed in the law of Moses,
the man of God. 3 * They set the altar on its foun-
dations, for they lived in fear of the peoples of the
lands,† and offered burnt offerings to the LORD
on it, both morning and evening. 4 * They also
kept the feast of Booths in the manner prescribed,
and they offered the daily burnt offerings in the
proper number required for each day. 5 Thereafter
they offered regular burnt offerings, the sacrifices
prescribed for the new moons and all the festi-
vals sacred to the LORD, and those which anyone
might bring as a voluntary offering to the LORD.

Laying the Foundations of the Temple

6 From the first day of the seventh month
they reinstituted the burnt offering to the LORD,
though the foundation of the LORD's temple had
not yet been laid. 7 * Then they hired stonecutters
and carpenters, and sent food and drink and oil
to the Sidonians and Tyrians that they might ship
cedar trees from the Lebanon to the port of Joppa,
as Cyrus, king of Persia, had authorized. 8 In the
year after their coming to the house of God in Je-
rusalem, in the second month, Zerubbabel, son
of Shealtiel, and Jeshua, son of Jozadak, together
with the rest of their kinsmen, the priests and
Levites and all who had come from the captivity
to Jerusalem, began by appointing the Levites
twenty years of age and over to supervise the
work on the house of the LORD. 9 Jeshua and his
sons and kinsmen, with Kadmiel and Binnui, son
of Hodaviah, and their sons and their kindred,
the Levites, together undertook to supervise those
who were engaged in the work on the house of
God. 10 * While the builders were laying the
foundation of the LORD's temple, the priests in
their vestments were stationed with trumpets and
the Levites, sons of Asaph, with cymbals to praise
the LORD in the manner laid down by David, king
of Israel. 11 * They alternated in songs of praise
and thanksgiving to the LORD, "for he is good, for
his love for Israel endures forever";† and all the
people raised a great shout of joy, praising the
LORD because the foundation of the LORD's house
had been laid. 12 * Many of the priests, Levites,
and heads of ancestral houses, who were old
enough to have seen the former house, cried out
in sorrow as they watched the foundation of the
present house being laid. Many others, however,
lifted up their voices in shouts of joy. 13 No one
could distinguish the sound of the joyful shout-
ing from the sound of those who were weeping;

Did You Know?

The Second Temple

The first Temple, built during Solomon's reign, was destroyed in 587 BC when the southern kingdom of Judah was conquered by the Babylonians. The Persian king, Cyrus II, conquered Babylon in 539 BC and a year later liberated the Jewish exiles in Babylon. He also decreed that the Temple in Jerusalem be rebuilt (see Ezr 6:3). Between the years 520 and 515, the second Temple was rebuilt in Jerusalem. The second Temple was an essential aspect of the Israelites' rebuilding of their life, culture, and religion after the Babylonian Exile. This Temple, rather than a king, became the central focus of Jewish identity.

†

3:1–2 *The seventh month*: Tishri (September–October), apparently of the first year of the return (538 B.C.), followed by events in the second year (v. 8). In that case it was Sheshbazzar who laid the foundations of the Temple (5:16), and it was in the second year of Darius I (520 B.C.) that Jeshua and Zerubbabel resumed work on the Temple that had been temporarily interrupted (Ezr 4:24–5:1; Hg 1:1; 2:1). The author, or a later editor, has set the construction and dedication of the Temple under Darius I back into the earliest period of the return. Shealtiel was the oldest son of King Jehoiachin (1 Chr 3:17–19); Zerubbabel was therefore Jehoiachin's grandson; see note on Ezr 1:8.

3:3 *Peoples of the lands*: referring either to those who had never left Judah or to neighboring peoples—Edomites, Arabs, inhabitants of Samaria—who opposed those who returned.

3:11 *"For he is good . . . forever"*: a refrain occurring frequently in liturgies of ancient Israel (cf. Ps 136).

*

3:1 Neh 7:7–78.
3:3 Dt 9:25; 1 Kgs 8:64.
3:4 Ex 23:16; Nm 28:3–8; Dt 16:13–15.
3:7 1 Chr 22:4; 2 Chr 2:9.
3:10 Ezr 2:41.
3:11 1 Chr 16:34; 2 Chr 5:13; 7:3; Ps 106:1; 136:1; Jer 33:11.
3:12 Hg 2:3.

for the people raised a mighty clamor which was
heard far away.

Outside Interference

4 1 When the enemies of Judah and Benjamin
heard that the exiles were building a tem-
ple for the LORD, the God of Israel, 2 * they ap-
proached Zerubbabel and the heads of ancestral
houses and said to them, "Let us build with you,
for we seek your God just as you do, and we have
sacrificed to him since the days of Esarhaddon,
king of Assyria,† who brought us here." 3 But
Zerubbabel, Jeshua, and the rest of the heads of
ancestral houses of Israel answered them, "It is
not your responsibility to build with us a house
for our God, but we alone must build it for the
LORD, the God of Israel, as Cyrus king of Persia
has commanded us." 4 Thereupon the local in-
habitants† discouraged the people of Judah and
frightened them off from building. 5 They also
bribed counselors to work against them and to
frustrate their plans during all the years of Cyrus,
king of Persia, and even into the reign of Da-
rius,† king of Persia.

Later Hostility

6 In the reign of Ahasuerus,† at the beginning
of his reign, they prepared a written accusation
against the inhabitants of Judah and Jerusalem.
7 † Again, in the time of Artaxerxes, Tabeel and
the rest of his fellow officials, in concert with
Mithredath, wrote to Artaxerxes, king of Persia.
The document was written in Aramaic and was
accompanied by a translation.
8 † Then Rehum, the governor, and Shimshai,
the scribe, wrote the following letter against Jeru-
salem to King Artaxerxes: 9 "Rehum, the governor,
Shimshai, the scribe, and their fellow officials,
judges, legates, and agents from among the Per-
sians, Urukians, Babylonians, Susians (that is,
Elamites), 10 and the other peoples whom the great
and illustrious Osnappar† transported and settled
in the city of Samaria and elsewhere in the prov-
ince West-of-Euphrates, as follows . . . ." 11 This is
a copy of the letter that they sent to him:
"To King Artaxerxes, your servants, the men of
West-of-Euphrates, as follows: 12 Let it be known
to the king that the Jews who came up from you
to us have arrived at Jerusalem and are now re-
building this rebellious and evil city. They are
completing its walls, and the foundations have
already been laid. 13 Now let it be known to the
king that if this city is rebuilt and its walls com-
pleted, they will no longer pay taxes, tributes,
or tolls; eventually the throne will be harmed.
14 Now, since we eat the salt of the palace† and it
is not fitting for us to look on while the king is
being dishonored, we have sent this message to
inform the king, 15 so that inquiry may be made
in the historical records of your fathers. In the
historical records you will discover and verify
that this is a rebellious city, harmful to kings and
provinces; its people have been acting seditiously
there since ancient times. That is why this city
was destroyed. 16 We therefore inform the king,
that if this city is rebuilt and its walls completed
again, you will thereupon not have a portion in
the province West-of-Euphrates."
17 The king sent this answer: "To Rehum, the
governor, Shimshai, the scribe, and their fel-
low officials living in Samaria and elsewhere in
the province West-of-Euphrates, greetings: 18 The
communication which you sent us has been read
in translation in my presence. 19 When at my
command inquiry was made, it was verified that
from ancient times this city has risen up against
kings and that rebellion and sedition have been
fostered there. 20 Powerful kings once ruled in
Jerusalem who controlled all West-of-Euphrates,
and taxes, tributes, and tolls were paid to them.
21 Give orders, therefore, to stop these men. This
city may not be rebuilt until a further decree has
been issued by me. 22 Take care that you do not
neglect this matter. Why should evil increase to
harm the throne?"
23 * As soon as a copy of King Artaxerxes' let-
ter had been read before Rehum, the governor,
Shimshai, the scribe, and their fellow officials,
they immediately went to the Jews in Jerusalem
and stopped their work by force of arms. 24 As a

†

4:2 *Esarhaddon, king of Assyria*: the enemies represent themselves as descendants of foreigners forcibly resettled in the Samaria region after the incorporation of the Northern Kingdom into the Assyrian empire (722 B.C.; cf. 2 Kgs 17:24). We have no record of a settlement under Esarhaddon (681–669 B.C.); the Aramaic source (Ezr 4:10) refers to a different resettlement under Osnappar/Ashurbanipal (668–627 B.C.).

4:4 *Local inhabitants*: lit., "the people of the land."

4:5 *Darius*: Darius I (522–486 B.C.). The Temple-building narrative continues in v. 24. In between (vv. 6–23) is a series of notices about opposition to the returned exiles voiced at the Persian court in the early fifth century B.C., after the Temple had been built.

4:6 *Ahasuerus*: Xerxes (486–465 B.C.); the early years of his reign were occupied with revolts in several parts of the empire.

4:7 There is a note placed in the original text to indicate a change from Hebrew to Aramaic. The Aramaic section beginning here ends with 6:18; in 7:12–26 a royal letter is cited in Aramaic.

4:8–23 The letter to Artaxerxes I (465–424 B.C.) deals with the building of the fortification walls of Jerusalem, not the building of the Temple. The interruption of the work on the city wall some time before 445 B.C. was the occasion for the arrival of Nehemiah in the province (Neh 1:1–4; 2:1–5).

4:10 *Osnappar*: probably Ashurbanipal; see note on 4:2.

4:14 *Eat the salt of the palace*: the idiom signifies sharing in the benefits of the palace.

*

4:2 Ezr 4:10. **4:23** Neh 1:3.

Cultural Connection

The Rebirth of a Nation

Among the first things oppressive governments often do, historically speaking, is destroy or shut down religious establishments and make religious gatherings illegal. This is what happened to the Israelites taken into exile. But when oppressive governments can no longer hold the people down, when oppressive methods lose their grip, one of the first things the people do is bring back religious establishments and religious gatherings. This is what the Israelites did upon return to their land.

The reopening of the Catholic Cathedral in Moscow, Russia, in December 1999, marked the symbolic end of Roman Catholic religious persecution in Russia. For over eighty years, radical socialist, Marxist, and communist political leaders persecuted almost all religious communities in Russia, especially Roman Catholics. Faith and religion were seen as not just unimportant but as unnecessary and unwanted, to say the least.

Russia now struggles to rise above those years of oppression, and not just the religious oppression but the social and economic oppression as well. Many see the reopening of the Catholic Cathedral as an important step toward rebuilding the wounded country and leading it out of its past misery.

Have you ever felt uncomfortable speaking about your beliefs in a group of people? What kinds of statements did people make that caused you to feel uncomfortable sharing your beliefs? How can you help to eliminate intolerance of this kind?

Ezra, chapter 5

result, work on the house of God in Jerusalem
ceased. This interruption lasted until the second
year of the reign of Darius,† king of Persia.

The Work Resumed Under Darius; Further Problems

5 1 * Then the prophets Haggai and Zechariah,†
son of Iddo, began to prophesy to the Jews in
Judah and Jerusalem in the name of the God of
Israel. 2 Thereupon Zerubbabel, son of Sheal-
tiel, and Jeshua, son of Jozadak, began again to
build the house of God in Jerusalem, with the
prophets of God giving them support. 3 At that
time Tattenai, governor of West-of-Euphrates,
came to them, along with Shethar-bozenai, and
their fellow officials, and asked of them: "Who
issued the decree for you to build this house and
complete this edifice? 4 What are the names of
the men who are building this structure?" 5 But
the eye of their God was upon the elders of the
Jews, and they were not delayed during the time
a report went to Darius and a written order came
back concerning this matter.

6 A copy of the letter which Tattenai, governor
of West-of-Euphrates, along with Shethar-boze-
nai and their fellow officials from West-of-
Euphrates, sent to King Darius; 7 they sent him a
report in which was written the following:
"To King Darius, all good wishes! 8 Let it be
known to the king that we have visited the prov-
ince of Judah and the house of the great God: it is
being rebuilt of cut stone and the walls are being
reinforced with timber; the work is being carried
out diligently, prospering under their hands. 9 We
then questioned the elders, addressing to them
the following words: 'Who issued the decree for
you to build this house and complete this edi-
fice?' 10 We also asked them their names, in order
to give you a list of the men who are their lead-
ers. 11 This was their answer to us: 'We are the ser-
vants of the God of heaven and earth, and we are
rebuilding the house built here many years ago,
which a great king of Israel built and completed.
12 But because our ancestors provoked the wrath
of the God of heaven, he delivered them into the
power of the Chaldean, Nebuchadnezzar, king

† **4:24** *The second year . . . of Darius*: that is, 520 B.C.; it marks the beginning of the successful restoration of the Temple, completed within the five years following (5:1–6:18).

5:1 *The prophets Haggai and Zechariah*: Haggai and Zechariah were active during the early years of Darius I. They document the rebuilding of the Temple and the messianic expectations associated with the Davidic descendant Zerubbabel.

* **5:1** Hg 1:14–2:9; Zec 4:9.

5:8

of Babylon, who destroyed this house and exiled
the people to Babylon. 13 * However, in the first
year of Cyrus, king of Babylon, King Cyrus issued
a decree for the rebuilding of this house of God.
14 Moreover, the gold and silver vessels of the
house of God, which Nebuchadnezzar had taken
from the temple in Jerusalem and carried off to
the temple in Babylon, King Cyrus ordered to be
removed from the temple in Babylon, and they
were given to a certain Sheshbazzar, whom he
named governor. 15 He commanded him: Take
these vessels and deposit them in the temple of
Jerusalem, and let the house of God be rebuilt
on its former site. 16 Then this same Sheshbazzar
came and laid the foundations of the house of
God in Jerusalem. Since that time to the present
the building has been going on, and is not yet
completed.' 17 Now, if it please the king, let a
search be made in the royal archives of Babylon
to discover whether a decree really was issued by
King Cyrus for the rebuilding of this house of
God in Jerusalem. And may the king's decision
in this matter be communicated to us."

The Decree of Darius

6 1 † Thereupon King Darius issued an order
to search the archives in which the treasures
were stored in Babylon. 2 * However, a scroll was
found in Ecbatana, the stronghold in the prov-
ince of Media, containing the following text:
"Memorandum. 3 In the first year of his reign,
King Cyrus issued a decree: With regard to the
house of God in Jerusalem: the house is to be re-
built as a place for offering sacrifices and bringing
burnt offerings. Its height is to be sixty cubits and
its width sixty cubits. 4 It shall have three courses
of cut stone for each one of timber. The costs are
to be borne by the royal house. 5 Also, let the gold
and silver vessels of the house of God which Neb-
uchadnezzar took from the temple of Jerusalem
and brought to Babylon be sent back; let them be
returned to their place in the temple of Jerusalem
and deposited in the house of God."
6 "Now, therefore, Tattenai, governor of West-
of-Euphrates, and Shethar-bozenai, and you,
their fellow officials in West-of-Euphrates, stay
away from there. 7 Let the governor and the el-
ders of the Jews continue the work on that house
of God; they are to rebuild it on its former site.
8 I also issue this decree concerning your dealing
with these elders of the Jews in the rebuilding of
that house of God: Let these men be repaid for
their expenses, in full and without delay from the
royal revenue, deriving from the taxes of West-of-
Euphrates, so that the work not be interrupted.
9 Whatever else is required—young bulls, rams,
and lambs for burnt offerings to the God of
heaven, wheat, salt, wine, and oil, according to
the requirements of the priests who are in Jeru-
salem—let that be delivered to them day by day
without fail, 10 that they may continue to offer
sacrifices of pleasing odor to the God of heaven
and pray for the life of the king and his sons. 11 I
also issue this decree: if any man alters this edict,
a beam is to be taken from his house, and he is
to be lifted up and impaled on it; and his house
is to be reduced to rubble for this offense. 12 And
may the God who causes his name to dwell there
overthrow every king or people who may under-
take to alter this decree or to destroy this house
of God in Jerusalem. I, Darius, have issued this
decree; let it be diligently executed."

The Task Finally Completed

13 Then Tattenai, the governor of West-of-
Euphrates, and Shethar-bozenai, and their fel-
low officials carried out with all diligence the
instructions King Darius had sent them. 14 The
elders of the Jews continued to make progress
in the building, supported by the message of the

† 6:1–2 Babylon was the capital city of the satrapy to which Judah belonged; it was therefore the natural place to look. The decree was discovered eventually, however, in Ecbatana (Hamadan), the former capital of the Medes and summer residence of the Persian kings. Cf. the Hebrew version of the decree (1:2–4).

* 5:13 Ezr 1:1–5. 6:2 Ezr 1:4–11.

prophets, Haggai and Zechariah, son of Iddo. They finished the building according to the command of the God of Israel and the decrees of Cyrus and Darius, and of Artaxerxes, king of Persia. 15 They completed this house on the third day of the month Adar, in the sixth year of the reign of King Darius. 16 The Israelites—priests, Levites, and the other returned exiles—celebrated the dedication of this house of God with joy. 17 For the dedication of this house of God, they offered one hundred bulls, two hundred rams, and four hundred lambs, together with twelve he-goats as a sin offering for all Israel, in keeping with the number of the tribes of Israel. 18 Finally, they set up the priests in their classes and the Levites in their divisions for the service of God in Jerusalem, as is prescribed in the book of Moses.

The Passover

19 * The returned exiles kept the Passover on the fourteenth day of the first month. 20 The Levites, every one of whom had purified himself for the occasion, sacrificed the Passover for all the exiles, for their colleagues the priests, and for themselves. 21 The Israelites who had returned from the exile and all those who had separated themselves from the uncleanness of the Gentiles in the land shared in it, seeking the LORD, the God of Israel. 22 * They joyfully kept the feast of Unleavened Bread for seven days, for the LORD had filled them with joy by making the king of Assyria† favorable to them, so that he gave them help in their work on the house of God, the God of Israel.

II. The Work of Ezra

Ezra, Priest and Scribe

7 1 † * After these events, during the reign of Artaxerxes, king of Persia, Ezra, son of Seraiah, son of Azariah, son of Hilkiah, 2 son of Shallum, son of Zadok, son of Ahitub, 3 son of Amariah, son of Azariah, son of Meraioth, 4 son of Zerahiah, son of Uzzi, son of Bukki, 5 son of Abishua, son of Phinehas, son of Eleazar, son of Aaron, the high priest— 6 * this Ezra came up from Babylon. He was a scribe, well-versed in the law of Moses given by the LORD, the God of Israel. The king granted him all that he requested, because the hand of the LORD, his God, was over him.

7 Some of the Israelites and some priests, Levites, singers, gatekeepers, and temple servants also came up to Jerusalem in the seventh year of King Artaxerxes. 8 Ezra came to Jerusalem in the fifth month of that seventh year of the king. 9 On the first day of the first month he began the journey up from Babylon, and on the first day of the fifth month he arrived at Jerusalem, for the favoring hand of his God was over him. 10 * Ezra had set his heart on the study and practice of the law of the LORD and on teaching statutes and ordinances in Israel.

The Decree of Artaxerxes

11 This is a copy of the rescript which King Artaxerxes gave to Ezra the priest-scribe, the scribe versed in matters concerning the LORD's commandments and statutes for Israel:

12 * "Artaxerxes, king of kings, to Ezra the priest, scribe of the law of the God of heaven, greetings! And now, 13 I have issued this decree, that anyone in my kingdom belonging to the people of Israel, its priests or Levites, who is willing to go up to Jerusalem with you, may go, 14 for you are the one sent by the king and his seven counselors to supervise Judah and Jerusalem with regard to the law of your God which is in your possession, 15 and to bring the silver and gold which the king and his counselors have freely contributed to the God of Israel, whose dwelling is in Jerusalem, 16 as well as all the silver and gold which you may receive throughout the province of Babylon, together with the voluntary offerings the people and priests freely contribute for the house of their God in Jerusalem. 17 Therefore, you must use this money with all diligence to buy bulls, rams, lambs, and the grain offerings and libations proper to these, and offer them on the altar of the house of your God in Jerusalem. 18 You and your kinsmen may do whatever seems best to you with the remainder of the silver and gold, as your God wills. 19 The vessels given to you for the service of the house of your God you are to deposit before the God of Jerusalem. 20 Whatever else you may be required to supply for the needs of the house of your God, you may draw from the royal

† **6:22** *The king of Assyria*: "Assyria" is perhaps used in a broad sense for the Persian empire; or the editor may have in mind the account of Hezekiah's Passover which refers to those who had escaped the hand of the king of Assyria (2 Chr 30:6).

7:1–10 The editor's introduction to Ezra's autobiographical narrative. The context suggests the seventh year of Artaxerxes I, therefore, 458 B.C., as the date of Ezra's arrival in Jerusalem. The arguments often advanced for 398 B.C., the seventh year of Artaxerxes II, or less often for the thirty-seventh year of Artaxerxes I, that is, 428 B.C., are inconclusive. For Ezra's descent from Aaron, the editor has drawn selectively on 1 Chr 5:27–41. Seraiah, the chief priest executed by the Babylonians after the fall of Jerusalem (2 Kgs 25:18–21), cannot be Ezra's father in a literal sense, and Ezra was not himself high priest.

* **6:19** Ex 12:1–20; 2 Chr 30:14–27; 35:1–19.
6:22 2 Chr 30:6.
7:1 1 Chr 5:27–41.
7:6 Ezr 7:28; 8:18; Neh 2:8, 18.
7:10 Ps 119:45.
7:12 Ezr 1:2–4.

treasury. 21 I, Artaxerxes the king, issue this decree
to all the treasurers of West-of-Euphrates: What-
ever Ezra the priest, scribe of the law of the God
of heaven, requests of you, let it be done with all
diligence, 22 within these limits: silver, one hun-
dred talents; wheat, one hundred kors;† wine,
one hundred baths; oil, one hundred baths; salt,
without limit. 23 Let everything that is decreed by
the God of heaven be carried out exactly for the
house of the God of heaven, that wrath may not
come upon the realm of the king and his sons.
24 We also inform you that it is not permitted
to impose taxes, tributes, or tolls on any priest,
Levite, singer, gatekeeper, temple servant, or any
other servant of that house of God.

25 * "As for you, Ezra, in accordance with the
wisdom of your God† which is in your posses-
sion, appoint magistrates and judges to adminis-
ter justice to all the people in West-of-Euphrates,
to all, that is, who know the laws of your God.
Instruct those who do not know these laws. 26 All
who will not obey the law of your God and the
law of the king, let judgment be executed upon
them with all diligence, whether death, or cor-
poral punishment, or confiscation of goods, or
imprisonment."

Ezra Prepares for the Journey

27 Blessed be the LORD, the God of our ances-
tors, who put it into the heart of the king thus
to glorify the house of the LORD in Jerusalem,
28 * and who let me find favor with the king, with
his counselors, and with all the most influential
royal officials. I therefore took courage and, with
the hand of the LORD, my God, over me, I gath-
ered together Israelite leaders to make the return
journey with me.

Ezra's Caravan

8 1 These are the heads of the ancestral houses
and the genealogies of those who returned
with me from Babylon during the reign of King
Artaxerxes:

2 Of the descendants of Phinehas, Gershon;
of the descendants of Ithamar, Daniel; of the
descendants of David, Hattush, 3 son of Sheca-
niah; of the descendants of Parosh, Zechariah,
and with him one hundred and fifty males were
enrolled; 4 of the descendants of Pahath-moab,
Eliehoenai, son of Zerahiah, and with him two
hundred males; 5 of the descendants of Zattu,
Shecaniah, son of Jahaziel, and with him three
hundred males; 6 of the descendants of Adin,
Ebed, son of Jonathan, and with him fifty males;
7 of the descendants of Elam, Jeshaiah, son of
Athaliah, and with him seventy males; 8 of the
descendants of Shephatiah, Zebadiah, son of
Michael, and with him eighty males; 9 of the
descendants of Joab, Obadiah, son of Jehiel,
and with him two hundred and eighteen males;
10 of the descendants of Bani, Shelomoth, son of
Josiphiah, and with him one hundred and sixty
males; 11 of the descendants of Bebai, Zechariah,
son of Bebai, and with him twenty-eight males;
12 of the descendants of Azgad, Johanan, son of
Hakkatan, and with him one hundred and ten
males; 13 of the descendants of Adonikam, youn-
ger sons, whose names were Eliphelet, Jeiel, and
Shemaiah, and with them sixty males; 14 of the
descendants of Bigvai, Uthai, son of Zakkur, and
with him seventy males.

Final Preparations for the Journey

15 I assembled them by the river that flows to-
ward Ahava,† where we camped for three days.
There I perceived that both laymen and priests
were present, but I could not discover a single
Levite. 16 So I sent for discerning leaders, Eliezer,
Ariel, Shemaiah, Jarib, Elnathan, Nathan, Zech-
ariah, and Meshullam, 17 with a command for
Iddo, the leader in the place Casiphia, instruct-
ing them what to say to Iddo and his kinsmen,
and to the temple servants in Casiphia, in order
to procure for us ministers for the house of our
God. 18 * Since the favoring hand of our God was
over us, they sent to us a well-instructed man,
one of the descendants of Mahli, son of Levi,
son of Israel, namely Sherebiah, with his sons
and kinsmen, eighteen men. 19 They also sent us
Hashabiah, and with him Jeshaiah, descendants
of Merari, and their kinsmen and their sons,
twenty men. 20 * Of the temple servants, those
whom David and the princes appointed to serve
the Levites, there were two hundred and twenty.
All these were enrolled by name.

21 Then I proclaimed a fast, there by the river
of Ahava, that we might humble ourselves be-
fore our God to seek from him a safe journey
for ourselves, our children, and all our posses-
sions. 22 * For I was ashamed to ask the king

†

7:22 *Kors*: see note on Ez 45:14; *baths*: see note on Is 5:10.

7:25 *The wisdom of your God*: with reference to the law (cf. Dt 4:6). The law in question was certainly not new, since it was assumed to be known by Jews in Judah and elsewhere. It corresponded to Pentateuchal law, though perhaps this had not yet been given its final form.

8:15 *Ahava*: an unidentified location near Babylon; also the name of the river or canal on which it stood (vv. 21, 31). A location near water was dictated by ritual as well as practical reasons (cf. Ps 137:1; Ez 1:1, 3; 3:15).

*

7:25 Dt 4:6; 2 Chr 17:7–9; Ps 37:30–31; 119:98.
7:28 Ezr 7:6.
8:18 Ezr 7:6.
8:20 Ezr 2:43.
8:22 Neh 2:9.

for troops and horsemen to protect us against
enemies along the way, since we had said to the
king, "The favoring hand of our God is over all
who seek him, but his fierce anger is against all
who forsake him." 23 So we fasted, seeking this
from our God, and it was granted. 24 Next I se-
lected twelve of the priestly leaders along with
Sherebiah, Hashabiah, and ten of their kinsmen,
25 and I weighed out before them the silver and
the gold and the vessels offered for the house of
our God by the king, his counselors, his officials,
and all the Israelites of that region. 26 I weighed
out into their hands these amounts: silver, six
hundred and fifty talents; silver vessels, one
hundred; gold, one hundred talents; 27 twenty
golden bowls valued at a thousand darics; two
vases of excellent polished bronze, as precious
as gold. 28 I addressed them in these words: "You
are consecrated to the LORD, and the vessels are
also consecrated; the silver and the gold are a
voluntary offering to the LORD, the God of your
ancestors. 29 Watch over them carefully until you
weigh them out in Jerusalem in the presence of
the chief priests and Levites and the leaders of
ancestral houses of Israel, in the chambers of the
house of the LORD." 30 The priests and the Levites
then took over the silver, the gold, and the ves-
sels that had been weighed out, to bring them to
Jerusalem, to the house of our God.

Arrival in Jerusalem

31 We set out from the river of Ahava on the
twelfth day of the first month to go to Jerusalem.
The hand of our God remained over us, and he
protected us from enemies and robbers along the
way. 32 We arrived in Jerusalem, where we rested
for three days. 33 On the fourth day, the silver,
the gold, and the vessels were weighed out in the
house of our God and given to the priest Mere-
moth, son of Uriah, with whom was Eleazar, son
of Phinehas; they were assisted by the Levites
Jozabad, son of Jeshua, and Noadiah, son of Bin-
nui. 34 Everything was in order as to number and
weight, and the total weight was registered. At
that same time, 35 those who had returned from
the captivity, the exiles, offered as burnt offerings
to the God of Israel twelve bulls for all Israel,
ninety-six rams, seventy-seven lambs, and twelve
goats as sin offerings: all these as a burnt offering
to the LORD. 36 † Finally, the orders of the king
were presented to the king's satraps and to the
governors in West-of-Euphrates, who gave their
support to the people and to the house of God.

† **8:36** The story of Ezra's mission is apparently continued from this point by Neh 7:72b–8:18, which may be read before Ezr 9:1.

Live It!

Who Belongs, and Who Does Not?

In Ezra, chapters 9–10, Ezra tells the people to reject their foreign wives and children. Nehemiah does the same in Nehemiah 13:23–27. This probably strikes us as harsh, but we can try to understand the Israelites' situation. Only a remnant of the Israelites was left to re-establish Israel's identity. History had taught the Israelites that intermarriage led to a watering down of their faith and of the people's loyalty to their religious practices. Back then, the only way to survive as a people was to separate from outsiders.

This separation led to an even greater animosity between the Jews from Judah and their cousins in faith, the Samaritans. We see some of this prejudice in the Gospels (see Jn 4:1–42 and "Discrimination in Jesus' Time," near Lk 10:25–37). Christians have had similar separations throughout our history. Today, the Church teaches us to be faithful to our beliefs but also to be open to others who believe differently and discover together what we have in common.

- Why is it often so hard for people to be open to those from other faith traditions?

▶ **Ezra, chapters 9–10**

The Crisis of Mixed Marriages

9 1 * When these matters had been concluded,
the leaders approached me with this report:
"Neither the Israelite laymen nor the priests nor
the Levites have kept themselves separate from
the peoples of the lands and their abomina-
tions—Canaanites, Hittites, Perizzites, Jebusites,
Ammonites, Moabites, Egyptians, and Amo-
rites— 2 for they have taken some of their daugh-
ters as wives for themselves and their sons, thus
intermingling the holy seed with the peoples of
the lands. Furthermore, the leaders and rulers
have taken a prominent part in this apostasy!"

9:1 Dt 7:1; Neh 9:2.

Ezra's Reaction

3 * When I had heard this, I tore my cloak
and my mantle, plucked hair from my head and
beard, and sat there devastated. 4 * Around me
gathered all who were in dread of the sentence of
the God of Israel† on the apostasy of the exiles,
while I remained devastated until the evening
sacrifice. 5 Then, at the time of the evening sac-
rifice, I rose in my wretchedness, and with cloak
and mantle torn I fell on my knees, stretching
out my hands to the LORD, my God.

A Penitential Prayer

6 † * I said: "My God, I am too ashamed and
humiliated to raise my face to you, my God, for
our wicked deeds are heaped up above our heads
and our guilt reaches up to heaven. 7 From the
time of our ancestors even to this day our guilt
has been great, and for our wicked deeds we have
been delivered, we and our kings and our priests,
into the hands of the kings of foreign lands, to
the sword, to captivity, to pillage, and to dis-
grace, as is the case today.

8 * "And now, only a short time ago, mercy
came to us from the LORD, our God, who left us
a remnant and gave us a stake in his holy place;
thus our God has brightened our eyes and given
us relief in our slavery. 9 * For slaves we are, but
in our slavery our God has not abandoned us;
rather, he has turned the good will of the kings
of Persia toward us. Thus he has given us new
life to raise again the house of our God and re-
store its ruins, and has granted us a protective
wall in Judah and Jerusalem. 10 But now, our
God, what can we say after all this? For we have
abandoned your commandments, 11 * which you
gave through your servants the prophets: The
land which you are entering to take as your pos-
session is a land unclean with the filth of the
peoples of the lands, with the abominations
with which they have filled it from one end to
the other by their uncleanness. 12 * Do not, then,
give your daughters to their sons in marriage,
and do not take their daughters for your sons.
Never promote their welfare and prosperity; thus
you will grow strong, enjoy the produce of the
land, and leave it as an inheritance to your chil-
dren forever.

13 "After all that has come upon us for our
evil deeds and our great guilt—though you, our
God, have made less of our sinfulness than it
deserved and have allowed us to survive as we
do— 14 shall we again violate your command-
ments by intermarrying with these abominable
peoples? Would you not become so angered with
us as to destroy us without remnant or survivor?
15 LORD, God of Israel, you are just; yet we have
been spared, the remnant we are today. Here we
are before you in our sins. Because of all this, we
can no longer stand in your presence."

Response to the Crisis

10 1 While Ezra prayed and acknowledged
their guilt, weeping and prostrate be-
fore the house of God, a very large assembly
of Israelites gathered about him, men, women,
and children; and the people wept profusely.
2 Then Shecaniah, the son of Jehiel, one of the
descendants of Elam, made this appeal to Ezra:
"We have indeed betrayed our God by taking as
wives foreign women of the peoples of the land.
Yet in spite of this there still remains a hope for
Israel. 3 Let us therefore enter into a covenant
before our God to dismiss all our foreign wives
and the children born of them, in keeping with
what you, my lord, advise, and those who are in
dread of the commandments of our God. Let it
be done according to the law! 4 Rise, then, for
this is your duty! We are with you, so have cour-
age and act!"

5 Ezra stood and demanded an oath from
the leaders of the priests, from the Levites and
from all Israel that they would do as had been
proposed; and they swore it. 6 Then Ezra left his
place before the house of God and entered the
chamber of Johanan, son of Eliashib,† where he
spent the night neither eating food nor drinking
water, for he was in mourning over the apos-
tasy of the exiles. 7 A proclamation was made
throughout Judah and Jerusalem that all the
exiles should gather together in Jerusalem, 8 and
that whoever failed to appear within three days
would, according to the judgment of the leaders

† **9:4** *All who were in dread . . . God of Israel*: lit., "all who trembled"; these people are also mentioned at 10:3, and a similar designation occurs at Is 66:2, 5, a text more or less contemporary with this passage. The allusion may be to a distinct social group of rigorist tendencies who supported Ezra's marriage reform.

9:6–15 The prayer attributed to Ezra is a communal confession of sin, of a kind characteristic of the Second Temple period (cf. Neh 9:6–37; Dn 9:4–19; 1QS 1:4–2:1), but adapted to the present situation.

10:6 *Johanan, son of Eliashib*: if this Eliashib is identical with the high priest of that name during Nehemiah's mission (Neh 3:1), it would be difficult to avoid the conclusion that Ezra followed Nehemiah. But Eliashib is a common name, and, on the hypothesis of Nehemiah's chronological priority, it would be unlikely that Ezra would consort with a family which had "defiled the priesthood" (Neh 13:28–29).

* **9:3** Ps 119:136.
9:4 Ezr 10:3; Is 66:2, 5.
9:6 Neh 9:6–37; Ps 38:4; Dn 9:4–19.
9:8 Is 4:3.
9:9 Ps 106:46.
9:11 Lv 18:24–25; Ez 36:17.
9:12 Dt 7:3.

and elders, suffer the confiscation of all his pos-
sessions, and would be excluded from the assem-
bly of the exiles.
9 All the men of Judah and Benjamin gathered
together in Jerusalem within the three-day pe-
riod: it was in the ninth month,† on the twenti-
eth day of the month. All the people, sitting in
the open place before the house of God, were
trembling both over the matter at hand and be-
cause it was raining. 10 * Then Ezra, the priest,
stood up and said to them: "Your apostasy in
taking foreign women as wives has added to
Israel's guilt. 11 But now, give praise to the LORD,
the God of your ancestors, and do his will: sep-
arate yourselves from the peoples of the land
and from the foreign women." 12 In answer, the
whole assembly cried out with a loud voice: "Yes,
it is our duty to do as you say! 13 But the people
are numerous and it is the rainy season, so that
we cannot remain outside; besides, this is not
a task that can be performed in a single day or
even two, for those of us who have sinned in this
regard are many. 14 Let our leaders represent the
whole assembly; then let all those in our cities
who have taken foreign women for wives appear
at appointed times, accompanied by the elders
and magistrates of each city in question, till we
have turned away from us our God's burning
anger over this affair." 15 Only Jonathan, son of
Asahel, and Jahzeiah, son of Tikvah, were against
this proposal, with Meshullam and Shabbethai
the Levite supporting them.
16 † The exiles did as agreed. Ezra the priest
appointed as his assistants men who were heads
of ancestral houses, one for each ancestral house,
all of them designated by name. They held ses-
sions to examine the matter, beginning with the
first day of the tenth month. 17 By the first day of
the first month they had finished dealing with
all the men who had taken foreign women for
wives.

The List of Transgressors

18 Among the priests, the following were found
to have taken foreign women for wives: Of the
descendants of Jeshua, son of Jozadak, and his
kinsmen: Maaseiah, Eliezer, Jarib, and Geda-
liah. 19 They pledged themselves to dismiss their
wives, and as a guilt offering for their guilt they
gave a ram from the flock. 20 Of the descendants
of Immer: Hanani and Zebadiah; 21 of the de-
scendants of Harim: Maaseiah, Elijah, Shema-
iah, Jehiel, and Uzziah; 22 of the descendants of
Pashhur: Elioenai, Maaseiah, Ishmael, Nethanel,
Jozabad, and Elasah.
23 * Of the Levites: Jozabad, Shimei, Kelaiah
(also called Kelita), Pethahiah, Judah, and Eli-
ezer.
24 Of the singers: Eliashib; of the gatekeepers:
Shallum, Telem, and Uri.
25 Of the people of Israel: Of the descendants
of Parosh: Ramiah, Izziah, Malchijah, Mijamin,
Eleazar, Malchijah, and Benaiah; 26 of the de-
scendants of Elam: Mattaniah, Zechariah, Jehiel,
Abdi, Jeremoth, and Elijah; 27 of the descendants
of Zattu: Elioenai, Eliashib, Mattaniah, Jere-
moth, Zabad, and Aziza; 28 of the descendants of
Bebai: Jehohanan, Hananiah, Zabbai, and Ath-
lai; 29 of the descendants of Bani: Meshullam,
Malluch, Adaiah, Jashub, Sheal, and Jeremoth;
30 of the descendants of Pahath-moab: Adna,
Chelal, Benaiah, Maaseiah, Mattaniah, Bezalel,
Binnui, and Manasseh; 31 of the descendants
of Harim: Eliezer, Isshijah, Malchijah, Shema-
iah, Shimeon, 32 Benjamin, Malluch, Shemariah;
33 of the descendants of Hashum: Mattenai,
Mattattah, Zabad, Eliphelet, Jeremai, Manasseh,
Shimei; 34 of the descendants of Begui: Maa-
dai, Amram, Uel, 35 Benaiah, Bedeiah, Cheluhi,
36 Vaniah, Meremoth, Eliashib, 37 Mattaniah,
Mattenai, and Jaasu; 38 of the descendants of
Binnui: Shimei, 39 Shelemiah, Nathan, and Ada-
iah; 40 of the descendants of Zachai: Shashai,
Sharai, 41 Azarel, Shelemiah, Shemariah, 42 Shal-
lum, Amariah, Joseph; 43 of the descendants of
Nebo: Jeiel, Mattithiah, Zabad, Zebina, Jaddai,
Joel, Benaiah.
44 † All these had taken foreign wives; but they
sent them away, both the women and their chil-
dren.

†

10:9 *The ninth month*: Kislev (November–December), during the first of two rainy seasons in Palestine.

10:16–17 The work of the committee lasted three months, from the first day of the tenth month, Tebeth (December–January), to the first day of the first month, Nisan (March–April), of the following year.

10:44 Some scholars find the continuation of the account of the marriage reform in Neh 9:1–5, though the date given at Neh 9:1 would fit better after Ezr 10:15; cf. Hg 2:10–14. The abrupt conclusion to Ezr 9–10 suggests that the policy of forced separation from foreign wives, not mandated by any law known to us, did not succeed. Assuming the chronological priority of Ezra, marriage outside the community was still prevalent during Nehemiah's administration, and the remarkable demographic expansion of Judaism in the following centuries would be difficult to explain if Ezra's measures had been put into effect.

*

10:10 Neh 9:2. **10:23** Neh 8:7; 10:11.

For background on this book, see the introduction to Ezra and Nehemiah before Ezra.

Nehemiah

I. The Deeds of Nehemiah

Nehemiah Hears Bad News

1 [1] † The words of Nehemiah, son of Hacaliah.
In the month Kislev of the twentieth year, I
was in the citadel of Susa [2] when Hanani, one of
my brothers, came with other men from Judah.
I asked them about the Jews, the remnant pre-
served after the captivity, and about Jerusalem.
[3] They answered me: "The survivors of the cap-
tivity there in the province are in great distress
and under reproach. The wall of Jerusalem has
been breached, its gates gutted by fire." [4] When I
heard this report, I began to weep and continued
mourning for several days, fasting and praying
before the God of heaven.

[5] † * I prayed: "LORD, God of heaven, great and
awesome God, you preserve your covenant of
mercy with those who love you and keep your
commandments. [6] * May your ears be attentive,
and your eyes open, to hear the prayer that I,
your servant, now offer in your presence day and
night for your servants the Israelites, confessing
the sins we have committed against you, I and
my ancestral house included. [7] * We have greatly
offended you, not keeping the commandments,
the statutes, and the ordinances you entrusted to
your servant Moses. [8] * But remember the admo-
nition which you addressed to Moses, your ser-
vant, when you said: If you prove faithless, I will
scatter you among the peoples; [9] but if you return
to me and carefully keep my commandments,
even though your outcasts have been driven to
the farthest corner of the world, I will gather them
from there, and bring them back to the place I
have chosen as the dwelling place for my name.
[10] * They are your servants, your people, whom
you freed by your great might and strong hand.
[11] * LORD, may your ears be attentive to the prayer
of your servant and that of all your servants who
willingly revere your name. Grant success to your
servant this day, and let him find favor with this
man"—for I was cupbearer to the king.†

Appointment by the King

2 [1] In the month Nisan of the twentieth year
of King Artaxerxes, when the wine was in my
charge, I took some and offered it to the king. Be-
cause I had never before been sad in his presence,
[2] the king asked me, "Why do you look sad? If you
are not sick, you must be sad at heart." Though I
was seized with great fear, [3] I answered the king:
"May the king live forever! How could I not look

---

† **1:1** The first mission of Nehemiah, from the twentieth year of Artaxerxes I, lasted from the spring (2:1) of 445 B.C. until 433 B.C. (5:14). It is recounted in 1:1–6:15; 12:27–43; 6:16–7:5; 11:1–21; in terms of chronology, these texts may usefully be read in that order. *Kislev*: the ninth month (November–December). *Susa*: the winter residence of the Persian kings, in southwest Iran.

1:5 Nehemiah's prayer is a communal confession of sin, characteristic of Second Temple piety; cf. Ezr 9:6–15; Neh 9:6–37; Dn 9:4–19.

1:11 *Cupbearer to the king*: an important official in the royal household.

---

* **1:5** Dt 7:9, 12; Dn 9:4. **1:6** 2 Chr 6:40. **1:7** Dn 3:29–30. **1:8** Dt 30:1–5. **1:10** Dt 9:29. **1:11** Ps 118:25.

sad when the city where my ancestors are buried
lies in ruins, and its gates consumed by fire?"
4 The king asked me, "What is it, then, that you
wish?" I prayed to the God of heaven 5 and then
answered the king: "If it please the king, and if
your servant is deserving of your favor, send me
to Judah, to the city where my ancestors are bur-
ied, that I may rebuild it." 6 Then the king, with
the queen seated beside him, asked me, "How
long will your journey take and when will you re-
turn?" My answer was acceptable to the king and
he agreed to let me go; I set a date for my return.
7 I asked the king further: "If it please the king,
let letters be given to me for the governors of
West-of-Euphrates, that they may give me safe-
conduct till I arrive in Judah; 8 * also a letter
for Asaph, the keeper of the royal woods, that
he may give me timber to make beams for the
gates of the temple citadel, for the city wall and
the house that I will occupy." Since I enjoyed
the good favor of my God, the king granted my
requests. 9 * Thus I proceeded to the governors
of West-of-Euphrates and presented the king's
letters to them. The king also sent with me army
officers and cavalry.
10 When Sanballat the Horonite† and Tobiah
the Ammonite official had heard of this, they
were very much displeased that someone had
come to improve the lot of the Israelites.

Circuit of the City

11 * When I arrived in Jerusalem, and had been
there three days, 12 I set out by night with only
a few other men and with no other animals but
my own mount (for I had not told anyone what
my God had inspired me to do for Jerusalem).
13 † I rode out at night by the Valley Gate, passed
by the Dragon Spring, and came to the Dung
Gate, observing how the walls of Jerusalem were
breached and its gates consumed by fire. 14 Then
I passed over to the Fountain Gate and to the
King's Pool. Since there was no room here for my
mount to pass with me astride, 15 I continued on
foot up the wadi by night, inspecting the wall all
the while, until I once more reached the Valley
Gate, by which I went back in. 16 The magistrates
knew nothing of where I had gone or what I was
doing, for as yet I had disclosed nothing to the
Jews, neither to the priests, nor to the nobles, nor

Pray It!

Nehemiah Prepares for Action

Do you ever watch the news and think, Why bother trying to make the world a better place? Christians are called to social action—action for justice, action to make the world a better place. But social sin can scare Christians away from social action. Social sin—such as poverty, racism, violence, materialism, and indifference—seems too big for any individual to do much about. In the overwhelming face of social sin, it is easy to say, "I give up."

But then we have Nehemiah's example. When Nehemiah heard of the results of Israel's collective sin, he could have said, "I give up." Instead, he turned to God in fasting and prayer. In your prayer time, reflect or journal on the following questions:

- What social issue are you most concerned about?
- What can you do to learn more about this issue?
- How can you get more involved in acting on this issue?
- What do you need to bring to God in prayer about this issue?

▶ **Nehemiah, chapter 1**

NEH

2:10 *Sanballat the Horonite*: the governor of the province of Samaria (3:33–34), apparently a native of one of the Beth-horons. A letter from the Jews living at Elephantine in southern Egypt, dated 408–407 B.C., mentions "Delayah and Shelemyah, the sons of Sanballat, the governor of Samaria," and papyri discovered in the Wadi ed-Dâliyeh in the Jordan Valley refer to a Sanballat, governor of Samaria, during the last years of Persian rule. Although his own name was Babylonian—Sin-uballit, i.e., "Sin (the moon god) has given life"—his two sons had names based on the divine name Yhwh. *Tobiah the Ammonite official*: the governor of the province of Ammon in Transjordan. His title, "official," lit., "servant" (in Hebrew, *'ebed*), could also be understood as "slave," and Nehemiah perhaps meant it in this derogatory sense. The Tobiads remained a powerful family even in Maccabean times, and something of their history is known from 2 Maccabees (3:11; 12:17), Josephus (*Ant.* 12:160–236), the Zeno papyri of the third century B.C., and excavation at 'Araq el-'Emir in Jordan. Sanballat and Tobiah, together with Geshem the Arab (Neh 2:19; 6:1–2), who was probably in charge of Edom and the regions to the south and southeast of Judah, opposed the rebuilding of Jerusalem's walls on political grounds; the city was the capital of a rival province.

2:13–15 Nehemiah left Jerusalem by the Valley Gate near the northwestern end of the old City of David and went south down the Tyropoean Valley toward the Dragon Spring (or the En-rogel [Jos 15:7; 18:16; 2 Sm 17:17; 1 Kgs 1:9], now known as Job's Well) at the juncture of the Valley of Hinnom and the Kidron Valley. He then turned north at the Dung Gate (or the Potsherd Gate of Jer 19:2) at the southern end of the city and proceeded up the wadi, that is, the Kidron Valley, passing the Fountain Gate (at the Spring of Gihon) and the King's Pool (unidentified); finally he turned west and then south to his starting point.

2:8 Ezr 7:6.
2:9 Ezr 8:22.
2:11 Ezr 8:32.

to the magistrates, nor to the others who were to
do the work.

Decision to Rebuild the City Wall

17 Afterward I said to them: "You see the trou-
ble we are in: how Jerusalem lies in ruins and
its gates have been gutted by fire. Come, let us
rebuild the wall of Jerusalem, so that we may
no longer be a reproach!" 18 * Then I explained
to them how God had shown his gracious favor
to me, and what the king had said to me. They
replied, "Let us begin building!" And they under-
took the work with vigor.
19 When they heard about this, Sanballat the
Horonite, Tobiah the Ammonite official, and
Geshem the Arab† mocked and ridiculed us.
"What are you doing?" they asked. "Are you re-
belling against the king?" 20 My answer to them
was this: "It is the God of heaven who will grant
us success. We, his servants, shall set about the
rebuilding; but you have neither share nor claim
nor memorial† in Jerusalem."

List of Workers

3 1 † * Eliashib the high priest and his priestly
kinsmen took up the task of rebuilding the
Sheep Gate. They consecrated it and set up its
doors, its bolts, and its bars, then continued
the rebuilding to the Tower of the Hundred,
the Tower of Hananel. 2 At their side the men of
Jericho were rebuilding, and next to them was
Zaccur, son of Imri. 3 * The Fish Gate was rebuilt
by the people of Hassenaah; they timbered it and
set up its doors, its bolts, and its bars. 4 At their
side Meremoth, son of Uriah, son of Hakkoz,
carried out the work of repair; next to him was
Meshullam, son of Berechiah, son of Mesheza-
bel; and next to him was Zadok, son of Baana.
5 Next to him the Tekoites carried out the work
of repair; however, some of their most power-
ful men would not submit to the labor asked by
their masters. 6 The Mishneh Gate† was repaired
by Joiada, son of Paseah; and Meshullam, son of
Besodeiah; they timbered it and set up its doors,
its bolts, and its bars. 7 At their side Melatiah the
Gibeonite did the repairing, together with Jadon
the Meronothite, and the men of Gibeon and of
Mizpah, who were under the jurisdiction of the
governor of West-of-Euphrates. 8 Next to them
the work of repair was carried out by Uzziel,
son of Harhaiah, a member of the goldsmiths'

Did You Know?

Rebuilding Hiroshima and Nagasaki

Nehemiah faced the difficult task of rebuilding a city completely destroyed by war. Unfortunately, this type of destruction has happened too many times in human history. We all remember how the twin towers of the destroyed World Trade Center were virtual cities that were utterly destroyed in a terrorist attack. But the most dramatic destruction of entire cities in modern times was the atomic bombing of Hiroshima and Nagasaki, Japan, on August 6 and August 9, 1945. The bombings flattened those cities and melted and destroyed objects and people within 1.5 miles of its epicenter. The Catholic Church condemns all such indiscriminate destruction—whether by atomic, biological, or chemical weapons.

Although the effects of these bombings were catastrophic, they did not wipe out the human spirit. Since that day, citizens of Hiroshima and Nagasaki have been recovering and rebuilding, first by burying the dead, then by rebuilding homes, stores, churches, and temples. Today, Hiroshima and Nagasaki are thriving cities. The destruction and rebuilding of these cities are probably best summarized in this haiku, written by Yasuhiko Shigemoto, who was a teenager when the bomb hit Hiroshima:

How freely
butterflies are flying about
in the A-bomb Dome!

("My Haiku of Hiroshima")

▶ Neh 2:17–18

NEH

† **2:19** *Geshem the Arab*: see also 6:1–2; in 6:6 the name occurs as Gashmu. He is known from a contemporary inscription as ruler of the Kedarite Arabs, who were threatening Judah from the south and east.

2:20 *Neither share nor claim nor memorial*: although Sanballat and Tobiah worshiped Yhwh, Nehemiah would not let them participate in any of the activities of the religious community in Jerusalem.

3:1–32 The construction work on the gates and walls of the city is described in counterclockwise direction, beginning and ending at the Sheep Gate (to the north of the Temple). The exact locations of many of the topographical points mentioned are uncertain.

3:6 *The Mishneh Gate*: the gate leading into the second, expanded quarter of the city; cf. 2 Kgs 22:14; Zep 1:10.

2:18 Ezr 7:6.
3:1 Jer 31:38.
3:3 Ezr 2:35; Zep 1:10.

guild, and at his side was Hananiah, one of the perfumers' guild. They restored Jerusalem as far as the Broad Wall.† 9 Next to them the work of repair was carried out by Rephaiah, son of Hur, administrator of half the district of Jerusalem, 10 and at his side was Jedaiah, son of Harumaph, who repaired opposite his own house. Next to him Hattush, son of Hashabneiah, carried out the work of repair. 11 The adjoining sector, as far as the Oven Tower, was repaired by Malchijah, son of Harim, and Hasshub, son of Pahath-moab. 12 At their side the work of repair was carried out by Shallum, son of Hallohesh, administrator of half the district of Jerusalem, together with his daughters. 13 The Valley Gate was repaired by Hanun and the inhabitants of Zanoah; they rebuilt it and set up its doors, its bolts, and its bars. They also repaired a thousand cubits of the wall up to the Dung Gate. 14 The Dung Gate was repaired by Malchijah, son of Rechab, administrator of the district of Beth-haccherem; he rebuilt it and set up its doors, its bolts, and its bars. 15 The Fountain Gate was repaired by Shallum, son of Colhozeh, administrator of the district of Mizpah; he rebuilt it, roofed it, and set up its doors, its bolts, and its bars. He also repaired the wall of the Aqueduct Pool near the King's Garden as far as the steps that lead down from the City of David. 16 After him, the work of repair was carried out by Nehemiah, son of Azbuk, administrator of half the district of Beth-zur, to a place opposite the tombs of David, as far as the Artificial Pool and the barracks.

17 After him, these Levites carried out the work of repair: Rehum, son of Bani, and next to him, for his own district, was Hashabiah, administrator of half the district of Keilah. 18 After him, their kinsmen carried out the work of repair: Binnui, son of Henadad, administrator of half the district of Keilah; 19 next to him Ezer, son of Jeshua, administrator of Mizpah, who repaired the adjoining sector, the Corner, opposite the ascent to the arsenal. 20 After him, Baruch, son of Zabbai, repaired the adjoining sector from the Corner to the entrance of the house of Eliashib, the high priest. 21 After him, Meremoth, son of Uriah, son of Hakkoz, repaired the adjoining sector from the entrance of Eliashib's house to its end.

22 After him, the work of repair was carried out by the priests, men of the surrounding country. 23 After them, Benjamin and Hasshub carried out the repair in front of their houses; after them, Azariah, son of Maaseiah, son of Ananiah, made the repairs alongside his house. 24 After him, Binnui, son of Henadad, repaired the adjoining sector from the house of Azariah to the Corner (that is, to the Angle). 25 After him, Palal, son of Uzai, carried out the work of repair opposite the Corner and the tower projecting from the Upper Palace at the quarters of the guard. After him, Pedaiah, son of Parosh, carried out the work of repair 26 to a point opposite the Water Gate on the east, and the projecting tower. 27 After him, the Tekoites repaired the adjoining sector opposite the great projecting tower, to the wall of Ophel.

28 Above the Horse Gate the priests carried out the work of repair, each opposite his own house. 29 * After them Zadok, son of Immer, carried out the repair opposite his house, and after him the repair was carried out by Shemaiah, son of Shecaniah, keeper of the East Gate. 30 After him, Hananiah, son of Shelemiah, and Hanun, the sixth son of Zalaph, repaired the adjoining sector; after them, Meshullam, son of Berechiah, repaired the place opposite his own lodging. 31 After him, Malchijah, a member of the goldsmiths' guild, carried out the work of repair as far as the quarters of the temple servants and the merchants, in front of the Gate of Inspection and as far as the upper chamber of the Angle. 32 Between the upper chamber of the Angle and the Sheep Gate, the goldsmiths and the merchants carried out the work of repair.

Opposition from Judah's Enemies

33 When Sanballat heard that we were rebuilding the wall, he became angry and very much incensed. He ridiculed the Jews, 34 saying in the presence of his associates and the troops of Samaria: "What are these miserable Jews trying to do? Will they complete their restoration in a single day? Will they recover these stones, burnt as they are, from the heaps of dust?" 35 Tobiah the Ammonite was beside him, and he said: "Whatever they are building—if a fox attacks it, it will breach their wall of stones!" 36 Hear, our God, how we were mocked! Turn back their reproach upon their own heads and deliver them up as plunder in a land of captivity! 37 * Do not hide their crime and do not let their sin be blotted out in your sight, for they insulted the builders to their faces! 38 We, however, continued to build the wall, and soon it was completed up to half its height. The people worked enthusiastically.

4

1 When Sanballat, Tobiah, the Arabs, the Ammonites, and the Ashdodites heard that the restoration of the walls of Jerusalem was

† **3:8** *The Broad Wall*: perhaps identical with the wall, seven meters thick, discovered in the Jewish quarter of the Old City.

* **3:29** Ez 40:6. **3:37** Neh 6:14; 13:29; Jer 18:23.

NEH

Live It!

Nehemiah's Strength

Many young people have traumatic experiences, such as the divorce of their parents, domestic and community violence, the death of a parent or sibling, prejudice, and poverty. Some young people come through these experiences as victims, unable to take any control in their lives. Others take the attitude "if you can't beat them, join them," and become cynical, violent, or antisocial. But some rise above their hurt to live happy and healthy lives. What can account for the difference in people's reactions?

Perhaps Nehemiah provides a clue. He was confronted by cynical people (see Neh 3:33–35) and violent people (see 4:1–3). But he trusted in something bigger than himself. "It is the God of heaven who will grant us success" (2:20), he proclaimed to those with negative attitudes.

Prayer and faith in God gave Nehemiah strength to take action in difficult times. They can work for us too. Don't let life's traumas make you powerless. Don't let them make you cynical and part of the problem. Pray and have faith, and you too will have the strength to meet your problems with action.

▶ **Nehemiah, chapter 4**

progressing—for the gaps were beginning to be
closed up—they became extremely angry. 2 They
all plotted together to come and fight against
Jerusalem and to throw us into confusion. 3 We
prayed to our God and posted a watch against
them day and night for fear of what they might
do. 4 Meanwhile the Judahites were saying:

"Slackened is the bearers' strength,
there is no end to the rubbish;
Never will we be able
to rebuild the wall."

5 Our enemies thought, "Before they are aware
of it or see us, we will come into their midst, kill
them, and put an end to the work."
6 When the Jews who lived near them had
come to us from one place after another, and
had told us ten times over that they were about
to attack us, 7 I stationed guards down below, be-
hind the wall, near the exposed points, assigning
them by family groups with their swords, spears,
and bows. 8 I made an inspection, then addressed
these words to the nobles, the magistrates, and
the rest of the people: "Do not fear them! Keep
in mind the LORD, who is great and to be feared,
and fight for your kindred, your sons and daugh-
ters, your wives and your homes." 9 When our
enemies realized that we had been warned and
that God had upset their plan, we all went back,
each to our own task at the wall.
10 * From that time on, however, only half my
work force took a hand in the work, while the
other half, armed with spears, bucklers, bows,
and breastplates, stood guard behind the whole
house of Judah 11 as they rebuilt the wall. The
load carriers, too, were armed; each worked with
one hand and held a weapon with the other.
12 Every builder, while working, had a sword tied
at his side. A trumpeter stood beside me, 13 for I
had said to the nobles, the magistrates, and the
rest of the people: "Our work is scattered and
extensive, and we are widely separated from one
another along the wall; 14 wherever you hear the
trumpet sound, join us there; our God will fight
with us." 15 Thus we went on with the work, half
with spears in hand, from daybreak till the stars
came out.
16 At the same time I told the people to spend
the nights inside Jerusalem, each with an atten-
dant, so that they might serve as a guard by night
and a working force by day. 17 Neither I, nor my
kindred, nor any of my attendants, nor any of the
bodyguard that accompanied me took off our
clothes; everyone kept a weapon at hand.

Social and Economic Problems

5 1 * Then there rose a great outcry of the peo-
ple and their wives against certain of their
Jewish kindred.† 2 Some said: "We are forced
to pawn our sons and daughters in order to get
grain to eat that we may live." 3 Others said: "We
are forced to pawn our fields, our vineyards, and
our houses, that we may have grain during the
famine." 4 Still others said: "To pay the king's tax

† **5:1** *Certain of their Jewish kindred*: probably Jews who had returned from Babylonia who formed the social and economic elite in the province.

* **4:10** Ps 149:6. **5:1** Jer 34:8–22.

Catholic Social Teaching

Hunger Pains

When Nehemiah's people were hungry, he saw the problem right away. The problem was not a lack of food. It was that some people were using their wealth and influence to control who got the food (see Neh 5:7–8). Nehemiah took the radical step of demanding that the powerful and wealthy stop taking advantage of those less well off. He demanded that the wealthy restore the money and property they had taken from others through unjust charging of interest (see verses 10–11).

Experts tell us that much the same is true today. People are starving not because food is scarce but because political and economic conditions prevent them from getting the food. Catholic social teaching asserts that human dignity can be respected and nurtured only if basic rights and responsibilities are met. Those basics include food, shelter, and clothing. Christians have an obligation to make sure people have access to food. Nehemiah acted, and so must we.

What can you do to make sure this is happening?

Nehemiah, chapter 5
Rights and Responsibilities

we have borrowed money on our fields and vine-
yards. 5* And though these are our own kindred,
and our children are as good as theirs, we have
had to reduce our sons and daughters to slav-
ery, and violence has been done to some of our
daughters! Yet we can do nothing about it, for
our fields and vineyards belong to others."
6 I was extremely angry when I heard the rea-
sons for their complaint. 7* After some delib-
eration, I called the nobles and magistrates to
account, saying to them, "You are exacting in-
terest from your own kindred!"† I then rebuked
them severely, 8* saying to them: "As far as we
were able, we bought back our Jewish kindred
who had been sold to Gentiles; you, however, are
selling your own kindred, to have them bought
back by us." They remained silent, for they could
find no answer. 9 I continued: "What you are
doing is not good. Should you not conduct your-
selves out of fear of our God rather than fear of
the reproach of our Gentile enemies? 10 I myself,
my kindred, and my attendants have lent the
people money and grain without charge. Let us
put an end to this usury! 11 Return to them this
very day their fields, vineyards, olive groves, and
houses, together with the interest on the money,
the grain, the wine, and the oil that you have
lent them." 12 They answered: "We will return
everything and exact nothing further from them.
We will do just what you ask." Then I called for
the priests to administer an oath to them that
they would do as they had promised. 13 I shook
out the folds of my garment, saying, "Thus may
God shake from home and fortune every man
who fails to keep this promise, and may he thus
be shaken out and emptied!" And the whole as-
sembly answered, "Amen," and praised the LORD.
Then the people did as they had promised.

Nehemiah's Record

14 Moreover, from the time that King Arta-
xerxes appointed me governor in the land of
Judah, from his twentieth to his thirty-second
year—during these twelve years neither I nor my
kindred lived off the governor's food allowance.
15 The earlier governors,† my predecessors, had
laid a heavy burden on the people, taking from
them each day forty silver shekels for their food;
then, too, their attendants oppressed the people.
But I, because I feared God, did not do this. 16 In
addition, though I had acquired no land of my
own, I did my part in this work on the wall, and
all my attendants were gathered there for the
work. 17 Though I set my table for a hundred and
fifty persons, Jews and magistrates, as well as
the neighboring Gentiles who came to us, 18 and

† **5:7** *You are exacting interest from your own kindred!*: contrary to the Mosaic law (Dt 23:20).

5:15 *The earlier governors*: both Sheshbazzar (Ezr 5:14) and Zerubbabel (Hg 1:1, 14; 2:2, 21) are said to be governors, and Mal 1:8 mentions a governor but does not name him. Other names are known from seal impressions of uncertain date.

* **5:5** Ex 21:7; Lv 25:39. **5:7** Dt 23:20. **5:8** Lv 25:48.

though the daily preparations were made at my expense—one ox, six choice sheep, poultry—besides all kinds of wine in abundance every ten days, despite this I did not claim the governor's allowance, for the labor lay heavy upon this people. 19 Keep in mind, my God, to my credit all that I did for this people.

Plots Against Nehemiah

6 1 When it had been reported to Sanballat, Tobiah, Geshem the Arab, and our other enemies that I had rebuilt the wall and that there was no breach left in it (though up to that time I had not yet set up the doors in the gates), 2 Sanballat and Geshem sent me this message: "Come, let us hold council together at Chephirim in the plain of Ono." They were planning to do me harm. 3 I sent messengers to them with this reply: "I am engaged in a great enterprise and am unable to come down. Why should the work stop, while I leave it to come down to you?" 4 Four times they sent me this same proposal, and each time I gave the same reply. 5 Then, the fifth time, Sanballat sent me the same message by one of his servants, who bore an unsealed letter 6 containing this text: "Among the nations it has been reported—Gashmu† is witness to this—that you and the Jews are planning a rebellion; that for this reason you are rebuilding the wall; and that you are to be their king. 7 Also, that you have set up prophets in Jerusalem to proclaim you king of Judah. Now, since matters like these will reach the ear of the king, come, let us hold council together." 8 I sent him this answer: "Nothing of what you report is happening; rather, it is the invention of your own mind." 9 They were all trying to intimidate us, thinking, "They will be discouraged from continuing with the work, and it will never be completed." But instead, I then redoubled my efforts.

10 I went to the house of Shemaiah, son of Delaiah, son of Mehetabel, who was confined to his house, and he said: "Let us meet in the house of God, inside the temple building; let us lock the doors of the temple. For they are coming to kill you—by night they are coming to kill you." 11 My answer was: "A man like me take flight? Should a man like me enter the temple to save his life? I will not go!" 12 For on consideration, it was plain to me that God had not sent him; rather, because Tobiah and Sanballat had bribed him, he voiced this prophecy concerning me, 13 that I might act on it out of fear and commit this sin. Then they would have had a shameful story with which to discredit me. 14 * Keep in mind Tobiah and Sanballat, my God, because of these things they did; keep in mind as well Noadiah the woman prophet and the other prophets who were trying to intimidate me.

Completion of the Work

15 The wall was finished on the twenty-fifth day of Elul;† the work had taken fifty-two days. 16 * When all our enemies had heard of this, and all the neighboring Gentiles round about had taken note of it, they were very discouraged, for they knew that it was with our God's help that this work had been completed. 17 At that same time, however, many letters were going to Tobiah from the nobles of Judah, and Tobiah's letters were reaching them, 18 for many in Judah were in league with him, since he was the son-in-law of Shecaniah, son of Arah, and his son Jehohanan had married the daughter of Meshullam, son of Berechiah. 19 They would praise his good deeds in my presence and relate to him whatever I said; and Tobiah sent letters trying to intimidate me.

7 1 Now that the wall had been rebuilt, I had the doors set up, and the gatekeepers, the singers, and the Levites were put in charge of them. 2 Over Jerusalem I placed Hanani, my brother, and Hananiah, the commander of the citadel, who was more trustworthy and God-fearing than most. 3 I said to them: "The gates of Jerusalem are not to be opened until the sun is hot, and while the sun is still shining they shall shut and bar the doors. Appoint as sentinels the inhabitants of Jerusalem, some at their watch posts, and others in front of their own houses."

Census of the Province

4 Now, the city was quite wide and spacious, but its population was small, and none of the houses had been rebuilt. 5 When my God had inspired me to gather together the nobles, the magistrates, and the people, and to examine their family records, I came upon the family list of those who had returned in the earliest period. There I found the following written:

6 † * These are the inhabitants of the province

†

6:6 *Gashmu*: elsewhere (vv. 1–2; 2:19) the name is given as Geshem.

6:15 *Elul*: the sixth month (August–September). *Fifty-two days*: according to Josephus (*Ant.* 11:174–183), the rebuilding of the walls of Jerusalem by Nehemiah took two years and four months.

7:6–72 See note on Ezr 2:1–67.

*

6:14 Jer 23:9–40; Zec 13:3.
6:16 Ps 118:22–23; 127:1.
7:6 Ezr 2:1–70.

who returned from the captivity of the exiles
whom Nebuchadnezzar, king of Babylon, had
carried away, and who came back to Jerusalem
and Judah, to their own cities: 7 They returned
with Zerubbabel, Jeshua, Nehemiah, Azariah,
Raamiah, Nahamani, Mordecai, Bilshan, Mispe-
reth, Bigvai, Nehum, and Baanah.

The census of the people of Israel: 8 descen-
dants of Parosh, two thousand one hundred and
seventy-two; 9 descendants of Shephatiah, three
hundred and seventy-two; 10 descendants of Arah,
six hundred and fifty-two; 11 descendants of Pa-
hath-moab who were descendants of Jeshua and
Joab, two thousand eight hundred and eighteen;
12 descendants of Elam, one thousand two hun-
dred and fifty-four; 13 descendants of Zattu, eight
hundred and forty-five; 14 descendants of Zaccai,
seven hundred and sixty; 15 descendants of Bin-
nui, six hundred and forty-eight; 16 descendants
of Bebai, six hundred and twenty-eight; 17 de-
scendants of Azgad, two thousand three hundred
and twenty-two; 18 descendants of Adonikam, six
hundred and sixty-seven; 19 descendants of Bigvai,
two thousand and sixty-seven; 20 descendants of
Adin, six hundred and fifty-five; 21 descendants of
Ater who were descendants of Hezekiah, ninety-
eight; 22 descendants of Hashum, three hundred
and twenty-eight; 23 descendants of Bezai, three
hundred and twenty-four; 24 descendants of Ha-
riph, one hundred and twelve; 25 descendants of
Gibeon, ninety-five; 26 people of Bethlehem and
Netophah, one hundred and eighty-eight; 27 peo-
ple of Anathoth, one hundred and twenty-eight;
28 people of Beth-azmaveth, forty-two; 29 people
of Kiriath-jearim, Chephirah, and Beeroth, seven
hundred and forty-three; 30 people of Ramah and
Geba, six hundred and twenty-one; 31 people of
Michmas, one hundred and twenty-two; 32 peo-
ple of Bethel and Ai, one hundred and twenty-
three; 33 people of Nebo, fifty-two; 34 descendants
of the other Elam, one thousand two hundred
and fifty-four; 35 descendants of Harim, three
hundred and twenty; 36 descendants of Jericho,
three hundred and forty-five; 37 descendants of
Lod, Hadid, and Ono, seven hundred and twen-
ty-one; 38 descendants of Senaah, three thousand
nine hundred and thirty.

39 The priests: descendants of Jedaiah of the
house of Jeshua, nine hundred and seventy-three;
40 descendants of Immer, one thousand and fifty-
two; 41 descendants of Pashhur, one thousand
two hundred and forty-seven; 42 descendants of
Harim, one thousand and seventeen.

43 The Levites: descendants of Jeshua, Kadmiel
of the descendants of Hodeviah, seventy-four.

44 The singers: descendants of Asaph, one hun-
dred and forty-eight.

45 The gatekeepers: descendants of Shallum,
descendants of Ater, descendants of Talmon, de-
scendants of Akkub, descendants of Hatita, descen-
dants of Shobai, one hundred and thirty-eight.

46 The temple servants: descendants of Ziha,
descendants of Hasupha, descendants of Tab-
baoth, 47 descendants of Keros, descendants
of Sia, descendants of Padon, 48 descendants of
Lebana, descendants of Hagaba, descendants of
Shalmai, 49 descendants of Hanan, descendants
of Giddel, descendants of Gahar, 50 descendants
of Reaiah, descendants of Rezin, descendants of
Nekoda, 51 descendants of Gazzam, descendants
of Uzza, descendants of Paseah, 52 descendants
of Besai, descendants of the Meunites, descen-
dants of the Nephusites, 53 descendants of Bak-
buk, descendants of Hakupha, descendants of
Harhur, 54 descendants of Bazlith, descendants of
Mehida, descendants of Harsha, 55 descendants
of Barkos, descendants of Sisera, descendants of
Temah, 56 descendants of Neziah, descendants of
Hatipha.

57 Descendants of Solomon's servants: descen-
dants of Sotai, descendants of Sophereth, de-
scendants of Perida, 58 descendants of Jaala,
descendants of Darkon, descendants of Giddel,
59 descendants of Shephatiah, descendants of
Hattil, descendants of Pochereth-hazzebaim, de-
scendants of Amon. 60 The total of the temple ser-
vants and the descendants of Solomon's servants
was three hundred and ninety-two.

61 The following who returned from Tel-melah,
Tel-harsha, Cherub, Addon, and Immer were un-
able to prove that their ancestral houses and their
descent were Israelite: 62 descendants of Delaiah,
descendants of Tobiah, descendants of Nekoda,
six hundred and forty-two. 63 Also, of the priests:
descendants of Hobaiah, descendants of Hakkoz,
descendants of Barzillai (he had married one of
the daughters of Barzillai the Gileadite and was
named after him). 64 These men searched their
family records, but their names could not be
found written there; hence they were disquali-
fied from the priesthood, 65 and the governor†
ordered them not to partake of the most holy
foods until there should be a priest to consult the
Urim and Thummim.

66 The entire assembly taken together came
to forty-two thousand three hundred and sixty,
67 not counting their male and female servants,
who were seven thousand three hundred and
thirty-seven. They also had two hundred male

NEH

† **7:65, 69** *The governor*: see note on Ezr 2:63.

and female singers. Their horses were seven
hundred and thirty-six, their mules two hundred
and forty-five, 68 their camels four hundred and
thirty-five, their donkeys six thousand seven
hundred and twenty.
69 Certain of the heads of ancestral houses con-
tributed to the temple service. The governor put
into the treasury one thousand drachmas of gold,
fifty basins, thirty vestments for priests, and five
hundred minas of silver. 70 Some of the heads of
ancestral houses contributed to the treasury for
the temple service: twenty thousand drachmas
of gold and two thousand two hundred minas
of silver. 71 The contributions of the rest of the
people amounted to twenty thousand drachmas
of gold, two thousand minas of silver, and sixty-
seven vestments for priests.
72 The priests, the Levites, the gatekeepers, the
singers, the temple servants, and all Israel took
up residence in their cities.

II. Promulgation of the Law

Ezra Reads the Law

8 1 † * Now when the seventh month came, the
whole people gathered as one in the square
in front of the Water Gate, and they called upon
Ezra the scribe to bring forth the book of the law
of Moses which the LORD had commanded for
Israel. 2 * On the first day of the seventh month,
therefore, Ezra the priest brought the law before
the assembly, which consisted of men, women,
and those children old enough to understand.
3 In the square in front of the Water Gate, Ezra
read out of the book from daybreak till midday,
in the presence of the men, the women, and
those children old enough to understand; and
all the people listened attentively to the book
of the law. 4 Ezra the scribe stood on a wooden
platform that had been made for the occasion; at
his right side stood Mattithiah, Shema, Anaiah,
Uriah, Hilkiah, and Maaseiah, and on his left
Pedaiah, Mishael, Malchijah, Hashum, Hash-
baddanah, Zechariah, Meshullam. 5 Ezra opened
the scroll so that all the people might see it, for
he was standing higher than any of the people.
When he opened it, all the people stood. 6 Ezra
blessed the LORD, the great God, and all the peo-
ple, their hands raised high, answered, "Amen,
amen!" Then they knelt down and bowed be-
fore the LORD, their faces to the ground. 7 * The
Levites Jeshua, Bani, Sherebiah, Jamin, Akkub,
Shabbethai, Hodiah, Maaseiah, Kelita, Azariah,
Jozabad, Hanan, and Pelaiah explained the law
to the people, who remained in their places.
8 * Ezra read clearly from the book of the law of
God, interpreting it so that all could understand
what was read. 9 Then Nehemiah, that is, the
governor, and Ezra the priest-scribe, and the Le-
vites who were instructing the people said to all
the people: "Today is holy to the LORD your God.
Do not lament, do not weep!"—for all the peo-
ple were weeping as they heard the words of the
law. 10 * He continued: "Go, eat rich foods and
drink sweet drinks, and allot portions to those
who had nothing prepared; for today is holy to
our LORD. Do not be saddened this day, for re-
joicing in the LORD is your strength!" 11 And the
Levites quieted all the people, saying, "Silence!
Today is holy, do not be saddened." 12 Then all
the people began to eat and drink, to distribute
portions, and to celebrate with great joy, for they
understood the words that had been explained
to them.

The Feast of Booths

13 On the second day, the heads of ancestral
houses of the whole people, and also the priests
and the Levites, gathered around Ezra the scribe
to study the words of the law. 14 * They found
it written in the law commanded by the LORD
through Moses that the Israelites should dwell
in booths during the feast of the seventh month;
15 * and that they should have this proclama-
tion made throughout their cities and in Jeru-
salem: "Go out into the hill country and bring
in branches of olive, oleaster, myrtle, palm,
and other trees in leaf, to make booths, as it is
written." 16 The people went out and brought
in branches with which they made booths for
themselves, on the roof of their houses, in their
courtyards, in the courts of the house of God,
and in the squares of the Water Gate and the
Gate of Ephraim. 17 * So the entire assembly of
the returned exiles made booths and dwelt in
them. Now the Israelites had done nothing of
this sort from the days of Jeshua, son of Nun,
until this occasion; therefore there was very great
joy. 18 Ezra read from the book of the law of God
day after day, from the first day to the last. They
kept the feast for seven days, and the solemn as-
sembly on the eighth day, as was required.

† **8:1–18** Chronologically this belongs after Ezr 8:36. The gloss mentioning Nehemiah in Neh 8:9 was inserted in this Ezra section after the dislocation of several parts of Ezra-Nehemiah had occurred. There is no clear evidence of a simultaneous presence of Nehemiah and Ezra in Jerusalem; Neh 12:26, 36 are also scribal glosses.

8:1 Ezr 3:1.
8:2 Lv 23:23–25; Nm 29:1–6.
8:7 Neh 10:10–13.
8:8 Ezr 7:6.
8:10 Est 9:19.
8:14 Ex 23:14–16; Lv 23:33–36; Nm 29:1–38; Ez 45:25.
8:15 Ps 118:27.
8:17 2 Chr 30:26; 35:18.

NEH

Public Confession of Sin

9 1 † * On the twenty-fourth day of this month,
the Israelites gathered together while fast-
ing and wearing sackcloth, their heads covered
with dust. 2 * Those of Israelite descent separated
themselves from all who were of foreign extrac-
tion, then stood forward and confessed their sins
and the guilty deeds of their ancestors. 3 When
they had taken their places, they read from the
book of the law of the LORD their God, for a
fourth of the day, and during another fourth they
made their confession and bowed down before
the LORD their God. 4 Standing on the platform
of the Levites were Jeshua, Binnui, Kadmiel,
Shebaniah, Bunni, Sherebiah, Bani, and Che-
nani, who cried out to the LORD their God, with a
loud voice. 5 * The Levites Jeshua, Kadmiel, Bani,
Hashabneiah, Sherebiah, Hodiah, Shebaniah,
and Pethahiah said,

Arise, bless the LORD, your God, from eternity to eternity!
(Neh 9:5)

"Arise, bless the LORD, your God,
from eternity to eternity!"
"And may they bless your glorious name,
which is exalted above all blessing and praise."

6 † "You are the LORD, you alone;
You made the heavens,
the highest heavens and all their host,
The earth and all that is upon it,
the seas and all that is in them.
To all of them you give life,
the heavenly hosts bow down before you.

7 *You are the LORD God
who chose Abram,
Who brought him from Ur of the Chaldees,
who named him Abraham.

8 *You found his heart faithful in your sight,
you made the covenant with him
To give the land of the Canaanites,
Hittites, Amorites,
Perizzites, Jebusites, and Girgashites
to him and his descendants.
You fulfilled your promises,
for you are just.

9 *You saw the affliction of our ancestors in Egypt,
you heard their cry by the Red Sea;

10 *You worked signs and wonders against Pharaoh,
against all his servants and the people of his land,
Because you knew of their insolence toward them;
thus you made for yourself a name even to this day.

11 *The sea you divided before them,
on dry ground they passed through the midst of the sea;
Their pursuers you hurled into the depths,
like a stone into the mighty waters.

12 *With a column of cloud you led them by day,
and by night with a column of fire,
To light the way of their journey,
the way in which they must travel.

13 *On Mount Sinai you came down,
you spoke with them from heaven;
You gave them just ordinances, true laws,
good statutes and commandments;

14 *Your holy sabbath you made known to them,
commandments, statutes, and law you prescribed for them,
by the hand of Moses your servant.

15 *Food from heaven you gave them in their hunger,
water from a rock you sent them in their thirst.
You told them to enter and occupy the land
which you had sworn to give them.

16 But they, our ancestors, proved to be insolent;
they were obdurate† and did not obey your commandments.

17 *They refused to obey and no longer remembered
the wonders you had worked for them.
They were obdurate and appointed a leader
in order to return to their slavery in Egypt.
But you are a forgiving God, gracious and merciful,
slow to anger and rich in mercy;
you did not forsake them.

†

9:1–5 The feast of Booths is followed by a penitential liturgy. Since it includes separation from foreigners, some read it as a sequel to Ezr 9–10.

9:6–37 The Septuagint attributes the prayer to Ezra; cf. Ezr 9:6–15.

9:16 *They were obdurate*: lit., "they stiffened their necks."

*

9:1 Dn 9:3. **9:2** Ezr 9:1–2; 10:11. **9:5** Ps 41:14; 106:48; Dn 2:20; 3:52. **9:7** Gn 12:1; 17:5. **9:8** Gn 15:18–19. **9:9** Ex 2:23–24. **9:10** Ex 7–11; 14. **9:11** Ex 15:5, 10. **9:12** Ex 13:21–22. **9:13** Ex 19–24. **9:14** Ex 20:8. **9:15** Ex 16:4; 17:1–2. **9:17** Ex 34:6; Nm 14:1–4; Dt 9:9.

NEH

18 *Though they made for themselves a molten
calf,
and proclaimed, 'Here is your God who
brought you up from Egypt,'
and were guilty of great insults,
19 Yet in your great mercy
you did not forsake them in the desert.
By day the column of cloud did not cease to
lead them on their journey,
by night the column of fire did not cease to
light the way they were to travel.
20 *Your good spirit you bestowed on them,
to give them understanding;
Your manna you did not withhold from their
mouths,
and you gave them water in their thirst.
21 *Forty years in the desert you sustained them:
they did not want;
Their garments did not become worn,
and their feet did not swell.
22 *You gave them kingdoms and peoples,
which you divided among them as border
lands.
They possessed the land of Sihon, king of
Heshbon,
and the land of Og, king of Bashan.
23 *You made their children as numerous as the
stars of the heavens,
and you brought them into the land
which you had commanded their ancestors
to enter and possess.
24 The children went in to possess the land;
you humbled before them the Canaanite
inhabitants
and gave them into their power,
Their kings and the peoples of the land,
to do with them as they wished.
25 *They captured fortified cities and fertile land;
they took possession of houses filled with
all good things,
Cisterns already dug, vineyards, olive groves,
and fruit trees in abundance.
They ate and had their fill,
fattened and feasted on your great
goodness.
26 *But they were contemptuous and rebelled
against you:
they cast your law behind their backs.
They murdered your prophets
who bore witness against them to bring
them back to you:
they were guilty of great insults.
27 *Therefore you gave them into the power of
their enemies,
who oppressed them.
But in the time of their oppression they
would cry out to you,
and you would hear them from heaven,
And according to your great mercy give them
saviors
to deliver them from the power of their
enemies.
28 As soon as they had relief,
they would go back to doing evil in your
sight.
Again you abandoned them to the power of
their enemies,
who crushed them.
Once again they cried out to you, and you
heard them from heaven
and delivered them according to your
mercy, many times over.
29 *You bore witness against them,
to bring them back to your law.
But they were insolent
and would not obey your commandments;
They sinned against your ordinances,
which give life to those who keep them.
They turned stubborn backs, stiffened their
necks,
and would not obey.
30 You were patient with them for many years,
bearing witness against them through your
spirit, by means of your prophets;
Still they would not listen.
Therefore you delivered them into the
power of the peoples of the lands.
31 Yet in your great mercy you did not
completely destroy them
and did not forsake them, for you are a
gracious and merciful God.
32 *Now, our God, great, mighty, and awesome
God,
who preserves the covenant of mercy,
do not discount all the hardship that has
befallen us,
Our kings, our princes, our priests,
our prophets, our ancestors, and your
entire people,
from the time of the kings of Assyria until
this day!
33 *In all that has come upon us you have been
just,
for you kept faith while we have done evil.

9:18 Ex 32:4, 8.
9:20 Dt 2:7.
9:21 Dt 8:4.
9:22 Nm 21:21–35; Dt 1:4; 2:26–3:11.
9:23 Dt 1:10.
9:25 Dt 3:5; 6:10–11; 11:11; 32:15.
9:26 Wis 2:10–20.
9:27 Dn 9:19.
9:29 Lv 18:5; Dt 30:16; 32:47.
9:32 Lam 5.
9:33 Dn 3:27; 9:14.

34 Yes, our kings, our princes, our priests, and
our ancestors
have not kept your law;
They paid no attention to your
commandments
and the warnings which you gave them.
35 While they were still in their kingdom,
in the midst of the many good things that
you had given them
And in the wide, fertile land
that you had spread out before them,
They did not serve you
nor turn away from their evil deeds.
36 Today we are slaves!
As for the land which you gave our
ancestors
That they might eat its fruits and good
things—
see, we have become slaves upon it!
37 Its rich produce goes to the kings
you set over us because of our sins,
Who rule over our bodies and our cattle as
they please.
We are in great distress!"

Signatories to the Pact

10 1 † In view of all this, we are entering into
a firm pact, which we are putting into writ-
ing. On the sealed document appear the names
of our princes, our Levites, and our priests.
2 On the sealed document: the governor Nehe-
miah, son of Hacaliah, and Zedekiah.
3 * Seraiah, Azariah, Jeremiah, 4 Pashhur, Am-
ariah, Malchijah, 5 Hattush, Shebaniah, Mal-
luch, 6 Harim, Meremoth, Obadiah, 7 Daniel,
Ginnethon, Baruch, 8 Meshullam, Abijah, Mija-
min, 9 Maaziah, Bilgai, Shemaiah: these are the
priests.
10 The Levites: Jeshua, son of Azaniah; Bin-
nui, of the descendants of Henadad; Kadmiel;
11 * and their kinsmen Shebaniah, Hodiah, Kel-
ita, Pelaiah, Hanan, 12 Mica, Rehob, Hashabiah,
13 Zaccur, Sherebiah, Shebaniah, 14 Hodiah, Bani,
Beninu.
15 The leaders of the people: Parosh, Pahath-
moab, Elam, Zattu, Bani, 16 Bunni, Azgad, Be-
bai, 17 Adonijah, Bigvai, Adin, 18 Ater, Hezekiah,
Azzur, 19 Hodiah, Hashum, Bezai, 20 Hariph,
Anathoth, Nebai, 21 Magpiash, Meshullam, He-
zir, 22 Meshezabel, Zadok, Jaddua, 23 Pelatiah,
Hanan, Anaiah, 24 Hoshea, Hananiah, Hasshub,
25 Hallhohesh, Pilha, Shobek, 26 Rehum, Hashab-
nah, Maaseiah, 27 Ahiah, Hanan, Anan, 28 Mal-
luch, Harim, Baanah.

Provisions of the Pact

29 The rest of the people, priests, Levites, gate-
keepers, singers, temple servants, and all others
who have separated themselves from the local
inhabitants in favor of the law of God, with their
wives, their sons, their daughters, all who are of
the age of discretion, 30 * join their influential
kindred, and with the sanction of a curse take
this oath to follow the law of God given through
Moses, the servant of God, and to observe care-
fully all the commandments of the LORD, our
Lord, his ordinances and his statutes.
31 * We will not marry our daughters to the
local inhabitants, and we will not accept their
daughters for our sons.
32 * When the local inhabitants bring in mer-
chandise or any kind of grain for sale on the
sabbath day, we will not buy from them on the
sabbath or on any other holy day. In the seventh
year we will forgo the produce, and forgive every
kind of debt.
33 * We impose these commandments on our-
selves: to give a third of a shekel each year for
the service of the house of our God, 34 for the
showbread, the daily grain offering, the daily
burnt offering, for the sabbaths, new moons, and
festivals, for the holy offerings and sin offerings
to make atonement for Israel, for every service of
the house of our God. 35 * We, priests, Levites,
and people, have determined by lot concerning
the procurement of wood: it is to be brought to
the house of our God by each of our ancestral
houses at stated times each year, to be burnt on
the altar of the LORD, our God, as the law pre-
scribes. 36 * We have agreed to bring each year to
the house of the LORD the first fruits of our fields
and of our fruit trees, of every kind; 37 also, as is
prescribed in the law, to bring to the house of
our God, to the priests who serve in the house
of our God, the firstborn of our children and our
animals, including the firstborn of our flocks and
herds. 38 * The first batch of our dough, and our
offerings of the fruit of every tree, of wine and
oil, we will bring to the priests, to the chambers
of the house of our God. The tithe of our fields

† **10:1–39** This section belongs to the Nehemiah narrative rather than to that of Ezra. It is best read after Neh 13:31, since the stipulations of the pact seem to presuppose Nehemiah's measures recorded in Neh 13. *In view of all this*: considering the situation described in Neh 13:4–31.

10:3 Neh 12:1–7, 12–26.
10:11 Ezr 10:23.
10:30 Neh 13:23–27.
10:31 Neh 13:15–22; Dt 7:2–4; Ezr 9:2, 12.
10:32 Neh 5:1–13; 13:15–22; Ex 20:8; Lv 25:2–7.
10:33 Lv 24:5–9; 2 Chr 24:6, 9–10.
10:35 Neh 13:31.
10:36 Ex 13:1, 11–16; Dt 26:1.
10:38 Neh 13:10–14; Nm 18:21–32.

we will bring to the Levites; they, the Levites, shall take the tithe in all the cities of our service. 39 An Aaronite priest shall be with the Levites when they take the tithe, and the Levites shall bring the tithe of the tithes to the house of our God, to the chambers of the treasury. 40 For to these chambers the Israelites and Levites bring the offerings of grain, wine, and oil; there also are housed the vessels of the sanctuary, and the ministering priests, the gatekeepers, and the singers. We will not neglect the house of our God.

III. Dedication of the Wall; Other Reforms

Resettlement of Jerusalem

11 1 † * The administrators took up residence in Jerusalem, and the rest of the people cast lots to bring one man in ten to reside in Jerusalem, the holy city, while the other nine would remain in the other cities. 2 The people blessed all those who willingly agreed to take up residence in Jerusalem.

3 * These are the heads of the province who took up residence in Jerusalem. In the cities of Judah dwelt Israelites, priests, Levites, temple servants, and the descendants of Solomon's servants, each on the property they owned in their own cities.

4 In Jerusalem dwelt both Judahites and Benjaminites. Of the Judahites: Athaiah, son of Uzziah, son of Zechariah, son of Amariah, son of Shephatiah, son of Mehallalel, of the sons of Perez; 5 Maaseiah, son of Baruch, son of Colhozeh, son of Hazaiah, son of Adaiah, son of Joiarib, son of Zechariah, a son of the Shelanites. 6 The total of the descendants of Perez who dwelt in Jerusalem was four hundred and sixty-eight people of substance.

7 These were the Benjaminites: Sallu, son of Meshullam, son of Joed, son of Pedaiah, son of Kolaiah, son of Maaseiah, son of Ithiel, son of Jeshaiah, 8 and his kinsmen, warriors, nine hundred and twenty-eight in number. 9 Joel, son of Zichri, was their commander, and Judah, son of Hassenuah, was second in command of the city.

10 Among the priests were: Jedaiah; Joiarib; Jachin; 11 Seraiah, son of Hilkiah, son of Meshullam, son of Zadok, son of Meraioth, son of Ahitub, the ruler of the house of God, 12 and their kinsmen who carried out the temple service, eight hundred and twenty-two; Adaiah, son of Jeroham, son of Pelaliah, son of Amzi, son of Zechariah, son of Pashhur, son of Malchijah, 13 and his kinsmen, heads of ancestral houses, two hundred and forty-two; and Amasai, son of Azarel, son of Ahzai, son of Meshillemoth, son of Immer, 14 and his kinsmen, warriors, one hundred and twenty-eight. Their commander was Zabdiel, son of Haggadol.

15 Among the Levites were Shemaiah, son of Hasshub, son of Azrikam, son of Hashabiah, son of Bunni; 16 Shabbethai and Jozabad, levitical chiefs who were placed over the external affairs of the house of God; 17 Mattaniah, son of Micah, son of Zabdi, son of Asaph, director of the psalms, who led the thanksgiving at prayer; Bakbukiah, second in rank among his kinsmen; and Abda, son of Shammua, son of Galal, son of Jeduthun. 18 The total of the Levites in the holy city was two hundred and eighty-four.

19 The gatekeepers were Akkub, Talmon, and their kinsmen, who kept watch over the gates; one hundred and seventy-two in number.

20 The rest of Israel, including priests and Levites, were in all the other cities of Judah in their own inheritances.

21 The temple servants lived on Ophel. Ziha and Gishpa were in charge of the temple servants.

22 * The prefect of the Levites in Jerusalem was Uzzi, son of Bani, son of Hashabiah, son of Mattaniah, son of Micah; he was one of the descendants of Asaph, the singers appointed to the service of the house of God— 23 for they had been appointed by royal decree, and there was a fixed schedule for the singers assigning them their daily duties.

24 Pethahiah, son of Meshezabel, a descendant of Zerah, son of Judah, was royal deputy in all affairs that concerned the people.

Other Settlements

25 As concerns their villages with their fields: Judahites lived in Kiriath-arba and its dependencies, in Dibon and its dependencies, in Jekabzeel and its villages, 26 in Jeshua, Moladah, Beth-pelet, 27 in Hazarshual, in Beer-sheba and its dependencies, 28 in Ziklag, in Meconah and its dependencies, 29 in En-rimmon, Zorah, Jarmuth, 30 Zanoah, Adullam, and their villages, Lachish and its fields, Azekah and its dependencies. They were settled from Beer-sheba to Ge-hinnom.

31 Benjaminites were in Geba, Michmash, Aija,

NEH

---

† **11:1–19** This list of the family heads who lived in Jerusalem at the time of Nehemiah is best read after Neh 7:72. It parallels at many points the list of early settlers in 1 Chr 9:2–17.

* **11:1** Neh 7:4.
11:3 1 Chr 9:2–34.
11:22 2 Chr 20:14.

Bethel and its dependencies, 32 Anathoth, Nob, Ananiah, 33 Hazor, Ramah, Gittaim, 34 Hadid, Zeboim, Neballat, 35 Lod, Ono, and the Valley of the Artisans.

36 Some divisions of the Levites from Judah were attached to Benjamin.

Priests and Levites at the Time of Zerubbabel

12 1 * The following are the priests and Levites who returned with Zerubbabel, son of Shealtiel, and Jeshua: Seraiah, Jeremiah, Ezra, 2 Amariah, Malluch, Hattush, 3 Shecaniah, Rehum, Meremoth, 4 Iddo, Ginnethon, Abijah, 5 Mijamin, Maadiah, Bilgah, 6 Shemaiah, and Joiarib, Jedaiah, 7 Sallu, Amok, Hilkiah, Jedaiah. These were the priestly heads and their kinsmen in the days of Jeshua.

8 The Levites were Jeshua, Binnui, Kadmiel, Sherebiah, Judah, Mattaniah, who, together with his kinsmen, was in charge of the thanksgiving hymns, 9 while Bakbukiah and Unno and their kinsmen ministered opposite them by turns.

High Priests

10 † Jeshua became the father of Joiakim, Joiakim the father of Eliashib, and Eliashib the father of Joiada; 11 Joiada the father of Johanan, and Johanan the father of Jaddua.

Priests and Levites Under Joiakim

12 * In the days of Joiakim these were the priestly family heads: for Seraiah, Meraiah; for Jeremiah, Hananiah; 13 for Ezra, Meshullam; for Amariah, Jehohanan; 14 for Malluchi, Jonathan; for Shebaniah, Joseph; 15 for Harim, Adna; for Meremoth, Helkai; 16 for Iddo, Zechariah; for Ginnethon, Meshullam; 17 for Abijah, Zichri; for Miamin, . . . ; for Moadiah, Piltai; 18 for Bilgah, Shammua; for Shemaiah, Jehonathan; 19 and for Joiarib, Mattenai; for Jedaiah, Uzzi; 20 for Sallu, Kallai; for Amok, Eber; 21 for Hilkiah, Hashabiah; for Jedaiah, Nethanel.

22 In the time of Eliashib, Joiada, Johanan, and Jaddua, the heads of ancestral houses of the priests were written down in the Book of Chronicles, up until the reign of Darius the Persian. 23 The sons of Levi: the family heads were written down in the Book of Chronicles, up until the time of Johanan, the son of Eliashib.

24 * The heads of the Levites were Hashabiah, Sherebiah, Jeshua, Binnui, Kadmiel. Their kinsmen who stood opposite them to sing praises and thanksgiving in fulfillment of the command of David, the man of God, one section opposite the other, 25 * were Mattaniah, Bakbukiah, Obadiah.

Meshullam, Talmon, and Akkub were gatekeepers. They guarded the storerooms at the gates.

26 All these lived in the time of Joiakim, son of Jeshua, son of Jozadak (and in the time of Nehemiah the governor and of Ezra the priest-scribe).

Dedication of the Wall

27 † At the dedication of the wall of Jerusalem, the Levites were sought out wherever they lived and were brought to Jerusalem to celebrate a joyful dedication with thanksgiving hymns and the music of cymbals, harps, and lyres. 28 The levitical singers gathered together from the region about Jerusalem, from the villages of the Netophathites, 29 from Beth-gilgal, and from the plains of Geba and Azmaveth (for the singers had built themselves settlements about Jerusalem). 30 The priests and Levites first purified themselves, then they purified the people, the gates, and the wall.

31 I had the administrators of Judah go up on the wall, and I arranged two great choirs. The first of these proceeded to the right, along the top of the wall, in the direction of the Dung Gate, 32 followed by Hoshaiah and half the administrators of Judah, 33 along with Azariah, Ezra, Meshullam, 34 Judah, Benjamin, Shemaiah, and Jeremiah, 35 priests with the trumpets, and also Zechariah, son of Jonathan, son of Shemaiah, son of Mattaniah, son of Micaiah, son of Zaccur, son of Asaph, 36 and his kinsmen Shemaiah, Azarel, Milalai, Gilalai, Maai, Nethanel, Judah, and Hanani, with the musical instruments of David, the man of God. Ezra the scribe was at their head. 37 At the Fountain Gate they went straight up by the steps of the City of David and continued along the top

†

12:10–11 Jeshua was the high priest when Zerubbabel was governor, in the last decades of the sixth century B.C. (Hg 1:1, 12, 14; 2:2, 4). He was the grandfather of Eliashib, the high priest early in Nehemiah's governorship (445–433 B.C.; Neh 3:1, 20, 21) and perhaps later. Eliashib, the grandfather of Johanan, was a grown man, if not yet a high priest, at the time of Ezra, ca. 400 B.C. (Ezr 10:6; and note). According to Josephus (*Ant.* 11:120–183), whose testimony here is doubtful, Jaddua, son of Johanan, died as an old man about the time that Alexander the Great died, 323 B.C. If, as seems probable, this list of the postexilic high priests, at least as far as Johanan, comes from the author himself (cf. Neh 12:23) and not from a later scribe, it is of prime importance for dating the author's work in the first decades of the fourth century B.C.

12:27–43 The dedication of the wall of Jerusalem took place, no doubt, soon after the restoration of the wall and its gates had been completed. This section, therefore, is best read after Neh 6:15.

*

12:1 Neh 12:12–22.
12:12 Neh 10:3–9; 12:1–6.
12:24 Ezr 2:40.
12:25 Neh 11:17.

of the wall above the house of David until they came to the Water Gate on the east.

[38] The second choir proceeded to the left, followed by myself and the other half of the administrators, along the top of the wall past the Oven Tower as far as the Broad Wall, [39] then past the Ephraim Gate to the Mishneh Gate, the Fish Gate, the Tower of Hananel, and the Hundred Tower, as far as the Sheep Gate. They came to a halt at the Prison Gate.

[40] Both choirs took up a position in the house of God; I, too, and half the magistrates with me, [41] together with the priests Eliakim, Maaseiah, Minjamin, Micaiah, Elioenai, Zechariah, Hananiah, with the trumpets, [42] and Maaseiah, Shemaiah, Eleazar, Uzzi, Jehohanan, Malchijah, Elam, and Ezer. The singers were heard under the leadership of Jezrahiah. [43] Great sacrifices were offered on that day, and they rejoiced, for God had given them cause for great rejoicing. The women and the children joined in, and the rejoicing at Jerusalem could be heard from far off.

[44] † * At that time men were appointed over the chambers set aside for stores, offerings, first fruits, and tithes; in them they were to collect from the fields of the various cities the portions legally assigned to the priests and Levites. For Judah rejoiced in its appointed priests and Levites [45] who carried out the ministry of their God and the ministry of purification (as did the singers and the gatekeepers) in accordance with the prescriptions of David and Solomon, his son. [46] * For in the days of David and Asaph, long ago, there were leaders of singers for songs of praise and thanksgiving to God. [47] * All Israel, in the days of Zerubbabel and in the days of Nehemiah, gave the singers and the gatekeepers their portions, according to their daily needs. They made their consecrated offering to the Levites, and the Levites made theirs to the descendants of Aaron.

NEH

13 [1] † * At that time, when the book of Moses was being read in the hearing of the people, it was found written there: "No Ammonite or Moabite may ever be admitted into the assembly of God; [2] * for they did not meet the Israelites with food and water, but they hired Balaam to curse them, though our God turned the curse into a blessing." [3] * When they had heard the law, they separated all those of mixed descent from Israel.

Reform in the Temple

[4] † Before this, the priest Eliashib, who had been placed in charge of the chambers of the house of our God and who was an associate of Tobiah, [5] * had set aside for the latter's use a large chamber in which had previously been stored the grain offerings, incense and vessels, the tithes in grain, wine, and oil allotted to the Levites, singers, and gatekeepers, and the offerings due the priests. [6] During all this time I had not been in Jerusalem, for in the thirty-second year of Artaxerxes,† king of Babylon, I had gone back to the king. After a suitable period of time, however, I asked leave of the king [7] and returned to Jerusalem, where I discovered the evil thing that Eliashib had done for Tobiah, in setting aside for him a chamber in the courts of the house of God. [8] This displeased me very much, so I had all of Tobiah's household goods thrown outside the chamber. [9] Then I gave orders to purify the chambers, and I brought back the vessels of the house of God, the grain offerings, and the incense.

[10] I learned, too, that the portions due the Levites were no longer being given, so that the Levites and the singers who should have been carrying out the services had deserted to their own fields. [11] I reprimanded the magistrates, demanding, "Why is the house of God neglected?" Then I brought the Levites together and had them resume their stations. [12] * All Judah once more brought in the tithes of grain, wine, and oil to the storerooms. [13] In charge of the storerooms I appointed Shelemiah the priest, Zadok the scribe, and Pedaiah, one of the Levites, together with Hanan, son of Zaccur, son of Mattaniah, as their assistant; for they were considered trustworthy. It was their duty to make the distribution to their kinsmen. [14] Remember this to my credit, my God! Do not forget the good deeds I have done for the house of my God and its services!

Sabbath Observance

[15] * In those days I perceived that people in Judah were treading the wine presses on the

†

12:44–47 This account of the provisions made for the Temple services is a composition either of the author or of a later scribe. The gloss mentioning Nehemiah is not in the Septuagint.

13:1–3 These verses serve as an introduction to the reforms Nehemiah instituted during his second mission in Jerusalem (vv. 4–31). The part of the Book of Moses read to the people is freely quoted here from Dt 23:3–6.

13:4–31 This is part of the "Memoirs of Nehemiah"; it is continued in 10:1–40.

13:6 *In the thirty-second year of Artaxerxes*: Artaxerxes I, therefore 433 B.C. *After . . . time*: it is not known when Nehemiah returned to Jerusalem or how long his second period of activity there lasted.

*

12:44 1 Chr 23–26; 2 Chr 8:14.
12:46 2 Chr 29:30; 35:15.
12:47 Neh 10:39; 13:10–11; Nm 18:26.
13:1 Dt 23:3–6.
13:2 Nm 22–24.
13:3 Neh 13:23–28.
13:5 Neh 12:44.
13:12 Neh 10:38–39; 12:44–45, 47; 2 Chr 31:6.
13:15 Neh 10:32; Ex 20:8.

sabbath; that they were bringing in sheaves of
grain, loading them on their donkeys, together
with wine, grapes, figs, and every other kind of
load, and bringing them to Jerusalem on the
sabbath day. I warned them to sell none of
these provisions. 16 In Jerusalem itself the Tyri-
ans residing there were importing fish and every
other kind of merchandise and selling it to the
Judahites on the sabbath. 17 I reprimanded the
nobles of Judah, demanding: "What is this evil
thing you are doing, profaning the sabbath day?
18 Did not your ancestors act in this same way,
with the result that our God has brought all this
evil upon us and upon this city? Would you add
to the wrath against Israel by once more profan-
ing the sabbath?"

19 When the shadows were falling on the gates
of Jerusalem before the sabbath, I ordered the
doors to be closed and prohibited their reopen-
ing until after the sabbath. I posted some of my
own people at the gates so that no load might
enter on the sabbath day. 20 The merchants and
sellers of various kinds of merchandise spent the
night once or twice outside Jerusalem, 21 but then
I warned them: "Why do you spend the night
alongside the wall? If you keep this up, I will beat
you!" From that time on, they did not return on
the sabbath. 22 Then I ordered the Levites to pu-
rify themselves and to watch the gates, so that
the sabbath day might be kept holy. This, too,
remember in my favor, my God, and have mercy
on me in accordance with your great mercy!

Mixed Marriages

23 * Also in those days I saw Jews who had
married women of Ashdod, Ammon, or Moab.
24 Of their children, half spoke the language of
Ashdod,† or of one of the other peoples, and
none of them knew how to speak the language
of Judah. 25 So I reprimanded and cursed them; I
beat some of their men and pulled out their hair;
and I adjured them by God: "You shall not marry
your daughters to their sons nor accept any of
their daughters for your sons or for yourselves!
26 * Did not Solomon, the king of Israel, sin be-
cause of them? Though among the many nations
there was no king like him, and though he was
beloved of his God and God had made him king
over all Israel, yet even he was led into sin by for-
eign women. 27 Must it also be heard of you that
you have done this same terrible evil, betraying
our God by marrying foreign women?"

28 * One of the sons of Joiada, son of Eliashib
the high priest, was the son-in-law of Sanballat
the Horonite! I drove him from my presence.
29 Remember against them, my God, how they
defiled the priesthood and the covenant of the
priesthood and the Levites!

30 So I cleansed them of all foreign contam-
ination. I established the various functions for
the priests and Levites, so that each had an ap-
pointed task. 31 * I also provided for the procure-
ment of wood at stated times and for the first
fruits. Remember this in my favor, my God!

† **13:24** *Language of Ashdod*: more likely an Aramaic rather than a Philistine dialect. *The language of Judah*: probably Hebrew.

* **13:23** Neh 10:31; 13:1–3; Dt 23:3; Ezr 9–10. **13:26** 1 Kgs 11:1–13. **13:28** Neh 2:10; 13:4–5, 7–9. **13:31** Neh 10:35–36.

Introduction to the Biblical Novellas

Can you remember some of your favorite books as a child? Books like *Goodnight Moon*, *Horton Hears a Who*, and *The Giving Tree* entertain us and inspire us with positive messages. We remember them all our lives. The books of Tobit, Judith, and Esther also contain imaginative stories that you will remember long after you finish them. All three have evil villains, wonderful heroes, and happy endings. Let their truths entertain and inspire you to be courageous in following God, even when you are facing what seems like impossible odds.

In Depth

The Bible conveys the Word of God in many literary forms: historical narrative, poetry, prophetic exhortation, wisdom sayings, and novellas (edifying stories). In the Constitution on Divine Revelation from Vatican II (*Dei Verbum*), the council fathers give instruction on how to approach this variety: "Attention must be paid to literary forms, for the fact is that truth is differently presented and expressed in the various types of historical writing, in prophetical and poetical texts, and in other forms of literary expression. Hence the interpreter must look for that meaning which the sacred writer intended to express and did in fact express through the medium of a contemporary literary form" (DV 12).

The Books of Tobit, Judith, and Esther are often grouped together. They are stories told to instruct the people concerning the ways of God, to encourage them in critical times, and to entertain. They are aids to the imagination. While they may contain kernels of historical fact, these stories are told primarily to illustrate truths that transcend history.

The author of the Book of Tobit, writing in the second century B.C., tells a story about the life of a devout family in seventh-century Assyria. He gives the people of his own time an example to follow as they struggle with the tensions of living a faithful Jewish life in the midst of a non-Jewish civilization. Tobit, suffering from the affliction of blindness, perseveres in good works and prayer, as do the other characters in the story. God sends an angel who, while hidden from them, leads them to health and happiness. The conclusion demonstrates that God does answer prayer and that perseverance in good works does not go unrewarded.

The author of the Book of Judith gives many clues that this story is beyond history. All the worst enemies of the people—the Assyrians of the eighth and seventh centuries, the sixth-century Babylonian king Nebuchadnezzar—are rolled into one terror. The hero, Judith, is modeled on the heroes of the Book of Judges, yet her story is also reminiscent of a second-century hero, Judas Maccabeus (1–2 Maccabees). Even the conflation of time indications—the eighteenth year of Nebuchadnezzar (2:1; the year 587 B.C., when he destroyed Jerusalem and took the Jews into exile) with the return from exile and rededication of the Temple (4:3; the events of 538 and 515 respectively)—

suggests God's deliverance from the most terrible circumstances. The story may be set in a time long past, but it is meant to encourage the people of the late second century to trust in God when their way of life is threatened. God can use even the most unlikely means, such as a widow, a biblical figure of powerlessness and vulnerability, to deliver them from their enemies.

The Book of Esther includes several historical elements. The Persian king Xerxes (486–465 B.C.), the city of Susa, a court official named Marduka, are all known from other sources. But further investigation shows this is not meant to be a historical account. There is no record of Xerxes having any other queen than Amestris and no mention of such a massacre during his reign. The book has a different purpose: to suggest a historical basis to the festival of Purim, perhaps originally a Persian feast. Through the story of Esther, Purim becomes a celebration of God's rescue of the people from persecution and certain death.

The message conveyed in these stories is not confined to one geographic place or historical period. It remains a valid expression of God's care for faithful people in every time and place.

Other Background

- Tobit, Judith, and Esther are inspired stories that use history as a backdrop. Their purpose is to inspire fidelity to God's Law in hard times.
- Tobit, Judith, and parts of Esther are not found in every translation of the Old Testament and are not contained in many Protestant Bibles. See "The Case of the Missing Books," near Tobit 1:16.
- Judith, Esther, and the Book of Ruth are the only books of the Bible named after women. All three of these faithful women are models of courage and cleverness in responding to God's call.

There's nothing quite like a good story. Such a story often involves good people struggling, a young hero, and love overcoming challenges. Throw in an undercover angel and a miraculous cure, and these are the elements that make up the Book of Tobit. Part fairy tale, part love story, and part religious adventure, this short story will bring a smile to your face and maybe even a tear to your eye. Enjoy!

At a Glance

I. Tobit's Ordeals (1:3—3:6).

II. Sarah's Plight (3:7–17).

III. Preparation for the Journey (4:1—6:1).

IV. Tobiah's Journey to Media (6:2–18).

V. Marriage and Healing of Sarah (7:1—9:6).

VI. Tobiah's Return Journey to Nineveh and the Healing of Tobit (10:1—11:18).

VII. Raphael Reveals His Identity (12:1–22).

VIII. Tobit's Song of Praise (13:1–18).

IX. Epilogue (14:1–15).

Quick Facts

Setting: Although fictional, the book reflects the historical situation of the Israelites deported from Israel to Nineveh in 721 BC.

Inspired Author: unknown, writing sometime in the second century BC

Theme: In time, God will aid the faithful who suffer. God always rewards the faithful, even if it takes a while.

Of Note: Raphael is one of only three angels named in the Bible; the others are Michael and Gabriel.

In Depth

For the author of the Book of Tobit, understanding God's will was not difficult. The conviction that God rewards good people, especially those who have experienced great suffering, is evident on every page. In the story, the faithful Tobit, who is blinded after doing a good deed, and the virtuous Sarah, who is ridiculed because she has had seven husbands die on their wedding night, pray for death because of their suffering and humiliation. In answer to their prayers, God sends the angel Raphael to lead Tobit's son Tobias on a journey to Sarah's town. The story ends happily—but you will have to read it yourself to find out exactly how.

The Book of Tobit is inspired folklore that teaches a moral lesson. The author was writing at a time when the Jews were governed by oppressive Greek rulers, and the people needed the reassurance of this happy tale. They had not forgotten the fall of Jerusalem or the Exile in Babylon, and Israel's suffering weighed heavily on them. What was the advantage of following God's law if all they had to look forward to was more suffering? (Belief in an afterlife had not yet developed among the Jewish people.) The book assured the faithful that God would eventually reward them: it was just a matter of time.

Although the book's miraculous answers may seem too simple to modern-day readers, its insistence on God's presence in human life and God's concern for those who suffer remains as important as ever. All people—even Christians who believe in life after death—need encouragement to face the challenges of this world with faith and hope.

Tobit

Tobit

1 1 This book tells the story of Tobit,† son of
Tobiel, son of Hananiel, son of Aduel, son
of Gabael, son of Raphael, son of Raguel, of the
family of Asiel and the tribe of Naphtali. 2 During
the days of Shalmaneser,† king of the Assyrians,
he was taken captive from Thisbe, which is south
of Kedesh Naphtali in upper Galilee, above and to
the west of Asher, north of Phogor.*

I. Tobit's Ordeals

His Virtue

3 I, Tobit, have walked all the days of my life on
paths of fidelity and righteousness. I performed
many charitable deeds for my kindred and my
people who had been taken captive with me to
Nineveh, in the land of the Assyrians. 4 When
I lived as a young man in my own country, in
the land of Israel, the entire tribe of my ancestor
Naphtali broke away from the house of David,
my ancestor, and from Jerusalem, the city that
had been singled out of all Israel's tribes that all
Israel might offer sacrifice there. It was the place
where the temple, God's dwelling, had been built
and consecrated for all generations to come.
5 * All my kindred, as well as the house of Naph-
tali, my ancestor, used to offer sacrifice on every
hilltop in Galilee to the calf that Jeroboam, king
of Israel, had made in Dan.†
6 * But I alone used to go often to Jerusalem
for the festivals, as was prescribed for all Israel by
longstanding decree.† Bringing with me the first
fruits of crops, the firstlings of the flock, the tithes
of livestock, and the first shearings of sheep,* I
used to hasten to Jerusalem 7 * and present them
to the priests, Aaron's sons, at the altar. To the
Levites ministering in Jerusalem I used to give the
tithe of grain, wine, olive oil, pomegranates, figs,
and other fruits. Six years in a row, I used to give
a second tithe in money, which each year I would
go to pay in Jerusalem. 8 The third-year tithe I gave
to orphans, widows, and converts who had joined
the Israelites. Every third year I would bring them
this offering, and we ate it in keeping with the

---

†

1:1 *Tobit*: in the Aramaic text the name is given as Tobi, an abbreviated form of Tobiyah (Ezr 2:60) or of Tobiyahu (2 Chr 17:8), a name that means "Yhwh is my welfare." *Tobiel*: "El [God] is my welfare." *Hananiel*: "El [God] has shown mercy." The book abounds in theophoric names.

1:2 *Shalmaneser* (V) (727–722 B.C.): began the siege of Samaria; the inhabitants of the Northern Kingdom were taken into captivity by his successor, Sargon II (722–705); cf. 2 Kgs 17:1–6. *Thisbe* and *Phogor*: unidentified towns of Galilee. *Kedesh Naphtali*: cf. Jos 20:7; 2 Kgs 15:29. *Asher*: probably Hazor (Jos 11:1).

1:5 Jeroboam established sanctuaries in Dan and Bethel so that the people would no longer have to go to Jerusalem for the festivals. The gold statues of calves that he placed in the sanctuaries were considered the throne of Yhwh; but the people may have tended to worship the images themselves. Jeroboam also encouraged high places or hilltop shrines (1 Kgs 12:26–33).

1:6–8 *Longstanding decree*: Dt 12:11, 13–14. Refusing to worship at Jeroboam's shrines, the faithful Tobit continued to bring his offerings to Jerusalem; see 2 Chr 11:16. For the various tithes, cf. Lv 27:30–33; Nm 18:20–32; 2 Chr 31:4–6; Dt 14:22–29; 26:12–13.

*

1:2 2 Kgs 17:3; 18:9–12.
1:5 1 Kgs 12:26–32.
1:6 Ex 23:14–15, 17; 34:23.
1:6 Dt 16:16.
1:7–8 Nm 18:12–13, 24; Dt 14:22–29; 18:4–5.

decree laid down in the Mosaic law concerning it, and according to the commands of Deborah, the mother of my father Tobiel; for my father had died and left me an orphan.

Did You Know?

The Case of the Missing Books

The Book of Tobit is treated differently in some versions of the Bible. Some put it in a section of books separated from the rest of the Old Testament. Some do not include it at all. We can find an explanation to this puzzle if we look back in time.

Sometime in the second or third century BC, Jewish scholars translated the Scriptures from Hebrew and Aramaic into Greek. Many Jews living throughout the Mediterranean world spoke Greek, which had become a common language in that area at the time. For Greek-speaking Jews, this translation, called the Septuagint, was the Bible they used. Because most of the early Christians spoke Greek, including Jews such as Paul, the Septuagint was adopted by the Church as its Bible (Old Testament).

After the destruction of the Jerusalem Temple by the Romans in AD 70, leading rabbis strove to reorganize Jewish worship, which could no longer center on the Temple in Jerusalem. They reviewed the existing editions of the Bible and developed an official list of thirty-nine holy books. They rejected certain books contained in the Greek Septuagint for which there was no existing original Hebrew or Aramaic text, such as Tobit, Judith, First and Second Maccabees, Wisdom, Sirach, Baruch, and additions to the Books of Esther and Daniel.

Many centuries later, the Christian reformer Martin Luther used the Jewish canon of the Old Testament in his translation of the Bible. He placed the additional books in a separate section, entitling them the Apocrypha (from the Greek for "hidden"). The Catholic Church and the Orthodox churches continue to use the fuller Greek canon, preferring the term *deuterocanonical* (from the Greek for "second canon") for the disputed books.

9 When I reached manhood, I married Anna, a
woman of our ancestral family. By her I had a son
whom I named Tobiah. 10 Now, after I had been
deported to the Assyrians and came as a captive
to Nineveh, all my kindred and my people used
to eat the food of the Gentiles,* 11 but I refrained
from eating that Gentile food. 12 Because I was
mindful of God with all my heart, 13 the Most
High granted me favor and status with Shalman-
eser, so that I became purchasing agent for all
his needs.* 14 Until he died, I would go to Me-
dia to buy goods for him there. I also deposited
pouches of silver worth ten talents† in trust with
my kinsman Gabael, son of Gabri, who lived at
Rages, in the land of Media. 15 When Shalmane-
ser died and his son Sennacherib† came to rule
in his stead, the roads to Media became unsafe,
so I could no longer go to Media.

Courage in Burying the Dead

16 In the days of Shalmaneser I had performed
many charitable deeds for my kindred, members
of my people. 17 * I would give my bread to the
hungry and clothing to the naked. If I saw one of
my people who had died and been thrown be-
hind the wall of Nineveh, I used to bury him.†
18 Sennacherib returned from Judea, having fled
during the days of the judgment enacted against
him by the King of Heaven because of the blas-
phemies he had uttered; whomever he killed I
buried. For in his rage he killed many Israelites,
but I used to take their bodies away by stealth
and bury them. So when Sennacherib looked for
them, he could not find them. 19 But a certain
Ninevite went and informed the king about me,
that I was burying them, and I went into hiding.
When I realized that the king knew about me
and that I was being hunted to be put to death, I
became afraid and took flight. 20 All my property
was confiscated; I was left with nothing. All that I
had was taken to the king's palace, except for my
wife Anna and my son Tobiah.†
21 But forty days did not pass before two of
the king's sons assassinated him and fled to

†

1:14 *Silver worth ten talents*: a great sum of money; about ten thousand dollars, at least. *Rages*: modern Rai, about five miles southeast of Tehran. *Media*: the northwestern part of modern Iran.

1:15 *Sennacherib* (705–681 B.C.): the son of Sargon II; neither was descended from Shalmaneser. On such historical inconsistencies, see Introduction; also notes on 5:6; 6:2; 9:2; 14:15.

1:17–18 Tobit risked his own life to bury the dead. Deprivation of burial was viewed with horror by the Jews. Cf. 4:3–4; 6:15; 14:12–13.

1:20 *Tobiah*: the son bears the fuller form of his father's name; see note on 1:1.

1:10 Lv 11; Dt 14:3–21; Acts 15:29; 1 Cor 8:7–13.
1:13 Dn 2:48–49.
1:17 Jb 31:16–20.

the mountains of Ararat. A son of his, Esarhad-
don,† succeeded him as king. He put Ahiqar, my
kinsman Anael's son, in charge of all the credit
accounts of his kingdom, and he took control
over the entire administration.* 22 Then Ahiqar
interceded on my behalf, and I returned to Nin-
eveh. Ahiqar had been chief cupbearer, keeper of
the signet ring, treasury accountant, and credit
accountant under Sennacherib, king of the Assyr-
ians; and Esarhaddon appointed him as Second
to himself. He was, in fact, my nephew, of my
father's house, and of my own family.

2 1 Thus under King Esarhaddon I returned to
my home, and my wife Anna and my son To-
biah were restored to me. Then on our festival of
Pentecost, the holy feast of Weeks,† a fine dinner
was prepared for me, and I reclined to eat.* 2 The
table was set for me, and the dishes placed before
me were many. So I said to my son Tobiah: "Son,
go out and bring in whatever poor person you
find among our kindred exiled here in Nineveh
who may be a sincere worshiper of God to share
this meal with me. Indeed, son, I shall wait for
you to come back."†

3 Tobiah went out to look for some poor per-
son among our kindred, but he came back and
cried, "Father!" I said to him, "Here I am, son."
He answered, "Father, one of our people has been
murdered! He has been thrown out into the mar-
ket place, and there he lies strangled." 4 I sprang to
my feet, leaving the dinner untouched, carried the
dead man from the square, and put him in one
of the rooms until sundown, so that I might bury
him. 5 I returned and washed† and in sorrow ate
my food.* 6 I remembered the oracle pronounced
by the prophet Amos against Bethel:*

"I will turn your feasts into mourning,
and all your songs into dirges."

7 Then I wept. At sunset I went out, dug a grave,
and buried him.

8 My neighbors mocked me, saying: "Does he
have no fear? Once before he was hunted, to be
executed for this sort of deed, and he ran away;
yet here he is again burying the dead!"

Tobit's Blindness

9 That same night I washed and went into my
courtyard, where I lay down to sleep beside the
wall. Because of the heat I left my face uncovered.
10 I did not know that sparrows were perched on
the wall above me; their warm droppings settled
in my eyes, causing white scales† on them. I went
to doctors for a cure, but the more they applied
ointments, the more my vision was obscured by
the white scales, until I was totally blind. For four
years I was unable to see, and all my kindred were
distressed at my condition. Ahiqar, however, took
care of me for two years, until he left for Elam.

11 At that time my wife Anna worked for hire
at weaving cloth, doing the kind of work women
do. 12 When she delivered the material to her
employers, they would pay her a wage. On the
seventh day of the month of Dystrus,† she fin-
ished the woven cloth and delivered it to her
employers. They paid her the full salary and also
gave her a young goat for a meal. 13 On entering
my house, the goat began to bleat. So I called
to my wife and said: "Where did this goat come
from? It was not stolen, was it? Give it back to its
owners; we have no right to eat anything stolen!"
14 * But she said to me, "It was given to me as a
bonus over and above my wages." Yet I would
not believe her and told her to give it back to its
owners. I flushed with anger at her over this. So
she retorted: "Where are your charitable deeds
now? Where are your righteous acts? Look! All
that has happened to you is well known!"†

3 1 Then sad at heart, I groaned and wept
aloud. With sobs I began to pray:†

Tobit's Prayer for Death

2 "You are righteous, Lord,
and all your deeds are just;
All your ways are mercy and fidelity;

1:21 *Esarhaddon*: 681–669 B.C. *Ahiqar*: a hero of ancient folklore, known for his outstanding wisdom. *The Story (or Wisdom) of Ahiqar* was very popular in antiquity and is extant in many different forms: Aramaic, Syriac, Armenian, Arabic (*Arabian Nights*), Greek (*Aesop's Fables*), Slavonic, Ethiopic, and Romanian. The sacred author makes Tobit the uncle of the famous Ahiqar in order to enhance Tobit's own prestige. See note on 14:10.

2:1 *Feast of Weeks*: also called by its Greek name, Pentecost, was celebrated fifty days after the Passover. Cf. Lv 23:15–21; Dt 16:9–12.

2:2 Almsgiving and charity to the poor are important virtues taught by the book (4:7–11, 16–17; 12:8–9; 14:10–11). *A sincere worshiper of God*: lit., "who is mindful of God with the whole heart."

2:5 *Washed*: because of ritual defilement from touching a corpse (Nm 19:11–13).

2:10 *White scales*: or white films. A primitive way of describing an eye ailment that results in blindness. *Elam*: or in Greek, *Elymais*, an ancient district northeast of the head of the Persian Gulf.

2:12 *Seventh day of the month of Dystrus*: late in winter. The Macedonian month Dystros corresponds to the Jewish month of Shebat (January–February). *A meal*: lit., "for the hearth"; the gift had probably been made in view of some springtime festival like the Jewish Purim.

2:14 Anna's sharp rebuke calls to mind the words of Job's wife (Jb 2:9).

3:1 *Pray*: prayer is a significant theme, occurring at six major turning points in the story (3:2–6, 11–15; 8:5–8, 15–17; 11:14–15; 13:1–18).

1:21 2 Kgs 19:37; 2 Chr 32:21; 2 Mc 8:19; Sir 48:21; Is 37:38.
2:1 Lv 23:15–21; Nm 28:26–31; Dt 16:9–12.
2:5 Nm 19:11–22.
2:6 1 Mc 1:39; Am 8:10.
2:14 Jb 2:9.

Pray It!

Praying for Death

Tobit and Sarah are at the end of their rope. They have experienced such suffering and disgrace that life no longer has any meaning for them. They know suicide is wrong, so they each pray that God will send death to end their suffering and humiliation (see Tb 3:6,10).

It is not uncommon for people who are very sick or in great pain or very old to pray for death, like Tobit. Unfortunately, young people who have experienced great loss or trauma often wish for death too, like Sarah. No one can completely explain the mystery of why we—both young and old—suffer. But we know that God is with us through our suffering, and God's grace can help us endure whatever comes our way. At those times, however, it is often hard to see God. That is why we need to be there for one another. We can act as God's hands and presence. Through our loving actions and prayers, we can support one another in our suffering.

What people do you know who are suffering to the point of despair? Take a few moments to remember these people in prayer, and call or write to let them know you are thinking of them.

▶ **Tobit, chapter 3**

you are judge of the world.*
3 And now, Lord, be mindful of me
and look with favor upon me.
Do not punish me for my sins,
or for my inadvertent offenses,
or for those of my ancestors.*

"They sinned against you,
4 and disobeyed your commandments.
So you handed us over to plunder, captivity,
and death,
to become an object lesson, a byword, and
a reproach
in all the nations among whom you
scattered us.*

5 "Yes, your many judgments are right
in dealing with me as my sins,
and those of my ancestors, deserve.
For we have neither kept your
commandments,
nor walked in fidelity before you.

6 "So now, deal with me as you please;
command my life breath to be taken
from me,
that I may depart from the face of the earth
and become dust.
It is better for me to die than to live,†
because I have listened to undeserved
reproaches,
and great is the grief within me.*

"Lord, command that I be released from such
anguish;
let me go to my everlasting abode;
Do not turn your face away from me, Lord.
For it is better for me to die
than to endure so much misery in life,
and to listen to such reproaches!"

II. Sarah's Plight

Sarah Falsely Accused

7 † On that very day, at Ecbatana in Media,
it so happened that Raguel's daughter Sarah
also had to listen to reproaches from one of her
father's maids. 8 For she had been given in mar-
riage to seven husbands, but the wicked demon
Asmodeus† kept killing them off before they
could have intercourse with her, as is prescribed
for wives. The maid said to her: "You are the one
who kills your husbands! Look! You have al-
ready been given in marriage to seven husbands,
but you do not bear the name of a single one
of them. 9 Why do you beat us? Because your

TB

†

3:6 *It is better for me to die than to live*: in his distress Tobit uses the words of the petulant Jonah (Jon 4:3, 8), who wished to die because God did not destroy the hated Ninevites. In similar circumstances, Moses (Nm 11:15), Elijah (1 Kgs 19:4), and Job (Jb 7:15) also prayed for death. *Everlasting abode*: a reference to Sheol, the dismal abode of the dead from which no one returns (Jb 7:9–10; 14:12; Is 26:14). See note on Tb 4:6.

3:7 From here on, the story is told in the third person. Verse 7 relates one of the several marvelous coincidences that the storyteller uses to suggest divine providence; see also vv. 16–17; 4:1; 5:4. *Ecbatana*: Hamadan in modern Iran; this was the capital of ancient Media. *Raguel*: the Greek form of the Hebrew name *Re'u'el*, "friend of God."

3:8 *Asmodeus*: in Persian *aeshma daeva*, "demon of wrath," adopted into Aramaic with the sense of "the Destroyer." It will be subdued (8:3) by Raphael (v. 17), whose name means "God has healed."

3:2 Ps 25:10; 119:137; Dn 3:27.
3:3 Ex 34:7.
3:4 Dt 28:15; Bar 1:16–22; 2:4–5; 3:8; Dn 9:5–6.
3:6 Nm 11:15; 1 Kgs 19:4; Jb 7:15; Jon 4:3, 8.

husbands are dead? Go, join them! May we never
see son or daughter of yours!"
10 That day Sarah was sad at heart. She went in
tears to an upstairs room in her father's house
and wanted to hang herself. But she reconsid-
ered, saying to herself: "No! May people never
reproach my father and say to him, 'You had
only one beloved daughter, but she hanged her-
self because of her misfortune.' And thus would
I bring my father laden with sorrow in his old
age to Hades. It is far better for me not to hang
myself, but to beg the Lord that I might die, and
no longer have to listen to such reproaches in
my lifetime."*
11 At that same time, with hands outstretched
toward the window,† she implored favor:

Sarah's Prayer for Death

"Blessed are you, merciful God!
Blessed be your holy and honorable name
forever!
May all your works forever bless you.*
12 Now to you, Lord, I have turned my face
and have lifted up my eyes.
13 Bid me to depart from the earth,
never again to listen to such reproaches.

14 "You know, Master, that I am clean
of any defilement with a man.
15 I have never sullied my own name
or my father's name in the land of my
captivity.

"I am my father's only daughter,
and he has no other child to be his heir,
Nor does he have a kinsman or close relative
whose wife I should wait to become.
Seven husbands of mine have already died.
Why then should I live any longer?
But if it does not please you, Lord, to take my
life,
look favorably upon me and have pity
on me,
that I may never again listen to such
reproaches!"

An Answer to Prayer

16 At that very time, the prayer of both of
them was heard in the glorious presence of God.
17 * So Raphael was sent to heal them both: to
remove the white scales from Tobit's eyes, so
that he might again see with his own eyes God's
light; and to give Sarah, the daughter of Raguel,
as a wife to Tobiah, the son of Tobit, and to rid
her of the wicked demon Asmodeus. For it fell to
Tobiah's lot† to claim her before any others who
might wish to marry her.
At that very moment Tobit turned from the
courtyard to his house, and Raguel's daughter
Sarah came down from the upstairs room.

III. Preparation for the Journey

A Father's Instruction

4 1 That same day Tobit remembered the
money he had deposited in trust with Gabael
at Rages in Media. 2 He thought to himself, "Now
that I have asked for death, why should I not
call my son Tobiah and let him know about this
money before I die?" 3 So he called his son To-
biah; and when he came, he said to him:† "Son,
when I die, give me a decent burial. Honor your
mother, and do not abandon her as long as she
lives. Do whatever pleases her, and do not grieve
her spirit in any way.* 4 Remember, son, how she
went through many dangers for you while you
were in her womb. When she dies, bury her in
the same grave with me.
5 "Through all your days, son, keep the Lord in
mind, and do not seek to sin or to transgress the
commandments. Perform righteous deeds all the
days of your life, and do not tread the paths of
wickedness. 6 * For those who act with fidelity,
all who practice righteousness, will prosper in
their affairs.†
7 "Give alms from your possessions. Do not
turn your face away from any of the poor, so that
God's face will not be turned away from you.*
8 Give in proportion to what you own. If you
have great wealth, give alms out of your abun-
dance; if you have but little, do not be afraid to

---

† **3:11** *Toward the window*: that is, looking in prayer toward Jerusalem; cf. Dn 6:11. "Blessed are you" and "Blessed be God" are traditional openings of Jewish prayers (Tb 8:5, 15; 11:14; 13:1).

3:17 *It fell to Tobiah's lot*: according to the patriarchal custom of marriage within the family group. Tobiah was Sarah's closest eligible relative (6:12). Cf. 4:12–13; Gn 24:4; 28:2; Ru 3:9–12; 4:1–12.

4:3–19 A collection of maxims that parallel those in the wisdom literature, especially Proverbs and Sirach (see Introduction): duties toward parents (vv. 3–4; cf. also 14:13); perseverance in virtue and avoidance of evil (vv. 5–6, 14b); necessity and value of almsgiving and charity (vv. 7–11, 16–17); marriage within the clan (vv. 12–13a); industry (v. 13b); prompt payment of wages (v. 14a); the golden rule (v. 15a); temperance (v. 15b); docility (v. 18); prayer (v. 19).

4:6 It was commonly thought in the Old Testament that virtue guaranteed earthly prosperity, and sin earthly disaster (Prv 10:2; cf. Dt 28).

---

* **3:10** Tb 6:15; Gn 37:35; 42:38; 44:29, 31.
3:11 1 Kgs 8:44, 48; Ps 28:2; 134:2; Dn 6:11.
3:17 Tb 4:12–13; 6:12–13; Gn 24:3–4.
4:3 Ex 20:12; Prv 23:22; Sir 7:27.
4:6 Tb 13:6; Jn 3:21; Eph 4:15.
4:7–8 Tb 12:8–10; Dt 15:7–8, 11; Prv 19:17; Sir 4:1–6; 14:13; Lk 14:13; 1 Jn 3:17.

TB

Cultural Connection

Give Food to the Hungry

In China, whenever you see a friend, it is customary to ask whether he or she has eaten a meal yet. If your friend responds, "No, I haven't eaten yet," it may mean that his or her last meal was yesterday or even the day before that. Then you invite your friend to your home and share whatever food you have. This custom goes back to the great famine of China (1958–1959), when people were dying of starvation and even eating tree bark.

Tobit gives his son good advice when he instructs him to share his food with the hungry and his clothing with the poor (see Tb 4:16).

Read Matthew 25:31–46 to hear how seriously Jesus wants us to follow this advice.

▶ Tb 4:16

give alms even of that little. [9] You will be storing up a goodly treasure for yourself against the day of adversity.* [10] For almsgiving delivers from death and keeps one from entering into Darkness. [11] Almsgiving is a worthy offering in the sight of the Most High for all who practice it.*

[12] "Be on your guard, son, against every kind of fornication, and above all, marry a woman of your own ancestral family. Do not marry a foreign woman, one who is not of your father's tribe, because we are descendants of the prophets, who were the first to speak the truth. Noah prophesied first, then Abraham, Isaac, and Jacob, our ancestors from the beginning of time. Son, remember that all of them took wives from among their own kindred and were blessed in their children, and that their posterity would inherit the land.* [13] Therefore, son, love your kindred. Do not act arrogantly toward any of them, the sons and daughters of your people, by refusing to take a wife for yourself from among them. For in arrogance there is ruin and great instability. In idleness there is loss and dire poverty, for idleness is the mother of famine.

[14] "Do not keep with you overnight the wages of those who have worked for you, but pay them at once. If you serve God thus, you will receive your reward. Be on your guard, son, in everything you do; be wise in all that you say and discipline yourself in all your conduct.* [15] Do to no one what you yourself hate. Do not drink wine till you become drunk or let drunkenness accompany you on your way.*

[16] * "Give to the hungry some of your food, and to the naked some of your clothing. Whatever you have left over, give away as alms; and do not let your eye begrudge the alms that you give. [17] * Pour out your wine and your bread on the grave of the righteous, but do not share them with sinners.†

[18] "Seek counsel from every wise person, and do not think lightly of any useful advice. [19] * At all times bless the Lord, your God, and ask him that all your paths may be straight and all your endeavors and plans may prosper. For no other nation possesses good counsel, but it is the Lord who gives all good things. Whomever the Lord chooses to raise is raised; and whomever the Lord chooses to cast down is cast down to the recesses of Hades. So now, son, keep in mind these my commandments, and never let them be erased from your heart.

[20] "Now, I must tell you, son, that I have deposited in trust ten talents of silver with Gabael, the son of Gabri, at Rages in Media. [21] Do not fear, son, that we have lived in poverty. You will have great wealth, if you fear God, avoid all sin, and do what is good before the Lord your God."*

The Angel Raphael

5 [1] Then Tobiah replied to his father Tobit: "Everything that you have commanded me, father, I shall do. [2] But how will I be able to get that money from him, since he does not know me, and I do not know him? What sign can I

TB

† **4:17** Tobit counsels his son to give alms in honor of the dead or, more probably, to give the "bread of consolation" to the family of the deceased. Cf. Jer 16:7; Ez 24:17.

4:9 Mt 6:20–21. **4:11** Sir 3:30; 29:12. **4:12** Tb 3:15, 17; 6:12; Gn 11:29, 31; 25:20; 28:1–4; 29:15–30; Ex 34:16; Dt 7:3; Jgs 14:3. **4:14** Lv 19:3; Dt 24:15. **4:15** Mt 7:12; Lk 6:31. **4:16** Dt 15:10; Is 58:7; Mt 25:35–36; 2 Cor 9:7. **4:17** Jer 16:7; Lk 14:13. **4:19** Dt 4:6; Ps 119:10. **4:21** 1 Tm 6:6–10.

give him so that he will recognize and trust me,
and give me the money? I do not even know the
roads to Media, in order to go there." 3Tobit an-
swered his son Tobiah: "He gave me his bond,†
and I gave him mine; I divided his into two parts,
and each of us took one part; I put one part with
the money. It is twenty years since I deposited
that money! So, son, find yourself a trustworthy
person who will make the journey with you, and
we will give him wages when you return; but
bring back that money from Gabael while I am
still alive."
4Tobiah went out to look for someone who
would travel with him to Media, someone who
knew the way. He went out and found the angel
Raphael standing before him (though he did not
know† that this was an angel of God).* 5Tobiah
said to him, "Where do you come from, young
man?" He replied, "I am an Israelite, one of your
kindred. I have come here to work." Tobiah
said to him, "Do you know the way to Media?"
6"Yes," he replied, "I have been there many
times. I know the place well and am acquainted
with all the routes. I have often traveled to Me-
dia; I used to stay with our kinsman Gabael, who
lives at Rages in Media. It is a good two days'
journey from Ecbatana to Rages,† for Rages is
situated in the mountains, but Ecbatana is in the
middle of the plain." 7Tobiah said to him, "Wait
for me, young man, till I go in and tell my father;
for I need you to make the journey with me. I
will pay you your wages."* 8He replied, "Very
well, I will wait; but do not be long."
9Tobiah went in and informed his father To-
bit: "I have found someone of our own Israelite
kindred who will go with me!" Tobit said, "Call
the man in, so that I may find out from what
family and tribe he comes, and whether he is
trustworthy enough to travel with you, son."
10Tobiah went out to summon him, saying,
"Young man, my father is calling for you." When
Raphael entered the house, Tobit greeted him
first. He replied, "Joyful greetings to you!" Tobit
answered, "What joy is left for me? Here I am, a
blind man who cannot see the light of heaven,
but must remain in darkness, like the dead
who no longer see the light! Though alive, I am
among the dead. I can hear people's voices, but
I do not see them." The young man said, "Take
courage! God's healing is near; so take courage!"
Tobit then said: "My son Tobiah wants to go to
Media. Can you go with him to show him the
way? I will pay you your wages, brother." He
answered: "Yes, I will go with him, and I know
all the routes. I have often traveled to Media
and crossed all its plains so I know well the
mountains and all its roads." 11Tobit asked him,
"Brother, tell me, please, from what family and
tribe are you?" 12He replied, "Why? What need
do you have for a tribe? Aren't you looking for a
hired man?" Tobit replied, "I only want to know,
brother, whose son you truly are and what your
name is."*
13He answered, "I am Azariah,† son of the
great Hananiah, one of your own kindred."
14Tobit exclaimed: "Welcome! God save you,
brother! Do not be provoked with me, brother,
for wanting to learn the truth about your family.
It turns out that you are a kinsman, from a noble
and good line! I knew Hananiah and Nathan,
the two sons of the great Shemeliah. They used
to go to Jerusalem with me, where we would
worship together. They were not led astray; your
kindred are good people. You are certainly of
good lineage. So welcome!"
15Then he added: "For each day I will give you
a drachma as wages,† as well as expenses for you
and for my son. So go with my son, and 16I will
even add a bonus to your wages!" The young
man replied: "I will go with him. Do not fear.
In good health we will leave you, and in good
health we will return to you, for the way is safe."
17Tobit said, "Blessing be upon you, brother."
Then he called his son and said to him: "Son,
prepare whatever you need for the journey, and
set out with your kinsman. May God in heaven
protect you on the way and bring you back to me
safe and sound; may his angel accompany you
for your safety, son."
Tobiah left to set out on his journey, and he
kissed his father and mother. Tobit said to him,
"Have a safe journey." 18But his mother began

† 5:3 *Bond*: a document called in Greek *cheirographon*. In the Middle Ages, notably in England, a deed and its duplicate were written on one piece of parchment, with the Latin word *chirographum* inscribed across the top of the sheet or between the two copies of the text. The document was then cut in two in either a straight or a wavy line, the parts being given to the persons concerned. Perhaps this procedure was derived from the present verse of Tobit. Duplicate documents, usually one part open and the other sealed, are well known from the ancient Near East.

5:4 *He did not know*: the theme of an angel in disguise occurs frequently in folklore as well as in the Old Testament (Gn 18; cf. Heb 13:2).

5:6 *It is a good two days' journey from Ecbatana to Rages*: Alexander's army took eleven days in forced marches to cover this distance, about 180 miles. (See notes on 1:15; 3:7 and Introduction.)

5:13–14 Azariah, "Yhwh has helped"; Hananiah, "Yhwh has shown mercy"; Nathan is a shortened form of Nathaniah, "Yhwh has given"; Shemeliah may be a Greek corruption of the Hebrew name, Shemaiah, "Yhwh has heard."

5:15 *A drachma as wages*: the normal wages, about seventeen cents, a day's wage for a laborer.

* **5:4** Heb 13:2. **5:7** Tb 12:2. **5:12** Jgs 13:17–18.

Live It!

Angels Among Us

Many older Catholics were taught as children that they were to leave a bit of space on their chair for their guardian angel. We smile at that story, partly because it was a creative way to make angels real in the lives of children, and partly because it points to a truth about God's presence in our lives.

In the fictional story of Tobit, we meet the angel Raphael. In other parts of the Bible, angels serve primarily as God's messengers. But Raphael is much more than a messenger. He disguises himself as a kindly but unknown relative who guides Tobias to the secrets he needs to know to relieve both Tobit's and Sarah's suffering.

The truth is that many angels are around us. Most of us have heard stories about kind strangers who appear seemingly out of nowhere to help and then disappear. Our seat may not have a lot of room for an angel, but our world certainly does. Angels remind us that God is with us, protecting us and guiding us.

- Have you, or has someone you know, been touched by an angel? In return, look for opportunities to be someone else's "angel."

to weep and she said to Tobit: "Why have you
sent my child away? Is he not the staff of our
hands, as he goes in and out before us? 19 Do not
heap money upon money! Rather relinquish it
in exchange for our child! 20 What the Lord has
given us to live on is certainly enough for us."
21 Tobit reassured her: "Do not worry! Our son
will leave in good health and come back to us
in good health. Your own eyes will see the day
when he returns to you safe and sound. So, do
not worry; do not fear for them, my sister.† 22 For
a good angel† will go with him, his journey will
be successful, and he will return in good health."
1 Then she stopped weeping.

IV. Tobiah's Journey to Media

On the Way to Rages

6 2 When the young man left home, accompa-
nied by the angel, the dog followed Tobiah
out and went along with them. Both journeyed
along, and when the first night came, they
camped beside the Tigris River.† 3 When the
young man went down to wash his feet in the Ti-
gris River, a large fish leaped out of the water and
tried to swallow his foot. He shouted in alarm.
4 But the angel said to the young man, "Grab the
fish and hold on to it!" He seized the fish and
hauled it up on dry land. 5 The angel then told
him: "Slit the fish open and take out its gall,
heart, and liver, and keep them with you; but
throw away the other entrails. Its gall, heart, and
liver are useful for medicine."† 6 After Tobiah had
slit the fish open, he put aside the gall, heart, and
liver. Then he roasted and ate part of the fish; the
rest he salted and kept for the journey.

Raphael's Instructions

Afterward the two of them traveled on together
till they drew near to Media. 7 Then the young
man asked the angel this question: "Brother Az-
ariah, what medicine is in the fish's heart, liver,
and gall?" 8 He answered: "As for the fish's heart
and liver, if you burn them to make smoke in the
presence of a man or a woman who is afflicted
by a demon or evil spirit, any affliction will flee
and never return. 9 As for the gall, if you apply it
to the eyes of one who has white scales, blowing
right into them, sight will be restored."
10 When they had entered Media and were
getting close to Ecbatana, 11 Raphael said to the
young man, "Brother Tobiah!" He answered,
"Here I am!" Raphael continued, "Tonight we
must stay in the house of Raguel, who is a rela-
tive of yours. He has a beautiful daughter named
Sarah, 12 but no other son or daughter apart from
Sarah. Since you are Sarah's closest relative, you
more than any other have the right to marry her.
Moreover, her father's estate is rightfully yours
to inherit. The girl is wise, courageous, and very
beautiful; and her father is a good man who
loves her dearly."* 13 He continued: "You have

†

5:21 *My sister*: "sister" was a term of endearment used in antiquity even for one's wife; similarly "brother" for one's husband. Cf. 7:11, 15; 8:4, 21; 10:6, 13; Sg 4:9–10, 12; 5:1–2.

5:22 *A good angel*: a reference to a guardian angel, though Tobit does not know, of course, that Raphael himself, disguised as Azariah, is the good angel in this case.

6:2 *Tigris River*: this river is actually west of Nineveh, so they would not have come to it on their way to Media. See note on 1:15 and the Introduction.

6:5 *Its gall . . . medicine*: belief in the healing power of these organs was common among the physicians of antiquity.

*

6:12 Tb 4:12–13; Nm 36:8.

the right to marry her. So listen to me, brother. Tonight I will speak to her father about the girl so that we may take her as your bride. When we return from Rages, we will have the wedding feast for her. I know that Raguel cannot keep her from you or promise her to another man; he would incur the death penalty as decreed in the Book of Moses.† For he knows that you, more than anyone else, have the right to marry his daughter. Now listen to me, brother; we will speak about this girl tonight, so that we may arrange her engagement to you. Then when we return from Rages, we will take her and bring her back with us to your house."

14 But Tobiah said to Raphael in reply, "Brother Azariah, I have heard that she has already been given in marriage to seven husbands, and that they have died in the bridal chamber. On the very night they approached her, they would die. I have also heard it said that it was a demon that killed them. 15 So now I too am afraid of this demon, because it is in love with her and does not harm her; but it kills any man who wishes to come close to her. I am my father's only child. If I should die, I would bring the life of my father and mother down to their grave in sorrow over me; they have no other son to bury them!"*

16 Raphael said to him: "Do you not remember your father's commands? He ordered you to marry a woman from your own ancestral family. Now listen to me, brother; do not worry about that demon. Take Sarah. I know that tonight she will be given to you as your wife! 17 When you go into the bridal chamber, take some of the fish's liver and the heart, and place them on the embers intended for incense, and an odor will be given off. 18 As soon as the demon smells the odor, it will flee and never again show itself near her. Then when you are about to have intercourse with her, both of you must first get up to pray.† Beg the Lord of heaven that mercy and protection be granted you. Do not be afraid, for she was set apart for you before the world existed. You will save her, and she will go with you. And I assume that you will have children by her, and they will be like brothers for you. So do not worry."

When Tobiah heard Raphael's words that she was his kinswoman, and of the lineage of his ancestral house, he loved her deeply, and his heart was truly set on her.

V. Marriage and Healing of Sarah

At the House of Raguel

7 1 When they entered Ecbatana, Tobiah said, "Brother Azariah, bring me straight to the house of our kinsman Raguel." So he did, and they came to the house of Raguel, whom they found seated by his courtyard gate. They greeted him first, and he answered, "Many greetings to you, brothers! Welcome! You have come in peace! Now enter in peace!" And he brought them into his house. 2 He said to his wife Edna, "How this young man resembles Tobit, the son of my uncle!" 3 So Edna asked them, saying, "Where are you from, brothers?" They answered, "We are descendants of Naphtali, now captives in Nineveh." 4 She said to them, "Do you know our kinsman Tobit?" They answered her, "Indeed, we do know him!" She asked, "Is he well?" 5 They answered, "Yes, he is alive and well." Then Tobiah said, "He is my father!" 6 Raguel jumped up, kissed him, and broke into tears. 7 Then, finding words, he said, "A blessing upon you, son! You are the son of a good and noble father. What a terrible misfortune that a man so righteous and charitable has been afflicted with blindness!" He embraced his kinsman Tobiah and continued to weep. 8 His wife Edna also wept for Tobit; and their daughter Sarah also began to weep.

Marriage of Tobiah and Sarah

9 Afterward, Raguel slaughtered a ram from the flock and gave them a warm reception. When they had washed, bathed, and reclined to eat and drink, Tobiah said to Raphael, "Brother Azariah, ask Raguel to give me my kinswoman Sarah." 10 Raguel overheard the words; so he said to the young man: "Eat and drink and be merry tonight, for no man has a greater right to marry my daughter Sarah than you, brother. Besides, not even I have the right to give her to anyone but you, because you are my closest relative. However, son, I must frankly tell you the truth. 11 I have given her in marriage to seven husbands who were kinsmen of ours, and all died on the very night they approached her. But now, son, eat and drink. The Lord will look after you both." Tobiah answered, "I will neither eat nor drink anything here until you settle what concerns me."

†

6:13 *Raguel . . . Book of Moses*: Nm 36:6–8 prescribed marriage within the ancestral tribe for daughters who had no brothers who might inherit the ancestral property, but no death penalty is mentioned.

6:18 *Get up to pray*: prayer, combined with ritual action, drives out the demon.

*

6:15 Tb 3:10.

Raguel said to him: "I will do it. She is yours
as decreed by the Book of Moses. It has been
decided in heaven that she be given to you!
Take your kinswoman; from now on you are her
brother, and she is your sister.† She is given to
you today and here ever after. May the Lord of
heaven prosper you both tonight, son, and grant
you mercy and peace." 12 Then Raguel called his
daughter Sarah, and she came to him. He took
her by the hand and gave her to Tobiah with these
words: "Take her according to the law. According
to the decree written in the Book of Moses I give
her to be your wife. Take her and bring her safely
to your father. And may the God of heaven grant
both of you a safe journey in peace!"* 13 He then
called her mother and told her to bring writing
materials. He wrote out a copy of a marriage con-
tract stating that he gave Sarah to Tobiah as his
wife as decreed by the law of Moses. Her mother
brought the material, and he drew up the con-
tract, to which he affixed his seal.*
14 Afterward they began to eat and drink.
15 Later Raguel called his wife Edna and said,
"My sister, prepare the other bedroom and bring
Sarah there." 16 She went, made the bed in the
room, as he had told her, and brought Sarah
there. After she had cried over her, she wiped
away her tears and said, 17 "Take courage, my
daughter! May the Lord of heaven grant you joy
in place of your grief! Courage, my daughter!"
Then she left.

Expulsion of the Demon

8 1 When they had finished eating and drink-
ing, they wanted to retire. So they brought
the young man out and led him to the bedroom.
2 Tobiah, mindful of Raphael's instructions, took
the fish's liver and heart from the bag where he
had them, and put them on the embers intended
for incense.† 3 The odor of the fish repulsed
the demon, and it fled to the upper regions of
Egypt;† Raphael went in pursuit of it and there
bound it hand and foot. Then Raphael returned
immediately.
4 When Sarah's parents left the bedroom and
closed the door behind them, Tobiah rose from
bed and said to his wife, "My sister, come, let
us pray and beg our Lord to grant us mercy and
protection." 5 She got up, and they started to pray
and beg that they might be protected. He began
with these words:

"Blessed are you, O God of our ancestors;
blessed be your name forever and ever!
Let the heavens and all your creation bless
you forever.*
6 You made Adam, and you made his wife Eve
to be his helper and support;
and from these two the human race has
come.
You said, 'It is not good for the man to be
alone;
let us make him a helper like himself.'*
7 Now, not with lust,
but with fidelity I take this kinswoman as
my wife.
Send down your mercy on me and on her,
and grant that we may grow old together.
Bless us with children."

8 They said together, "Amen, amen!" 9 Then they
went to bed for the night.
But Raguel got up and summoned his ser-
vants. They went out with him and dug a grave,
10 for he said, "Perhaps Tobiah will die; then
we would be a laughingstock and an object of
mockery." 11 When they had finished digging
the grave, Raguel went back into the house and
called his wife, 12 saying, "Send one of the maids
in to see whether he is alive. If he has died, let
us bury him without anyone knowing about it."
13 They sent the maid, lit a lamp, and opened
the bedroom door; she went in and found them
sleeping together. 14 The maid came out and told
them that Tobiah was alive, and that nothing was
wrong. 15 Then they praised the God of heaven in
these words:

"Blessed are you, God, with every pure
blessing!
Let all your chosen ones bless you forever!
16 Blessed are you, for you have made me
happy;
what I feared did not happen.
Rather you have dealt with us
according to your abundant mercy.
17 Blessed are you, for you have shown mercy
toward two only children.

†

7:11 *You are her brother, and she is your sister:* the marriage formula is similar to a marriage contract from the fifth century B.C. found at Elephantine in Egypt: "She is my wife and I am her husband from this day forever."

8:2–3 The manner of coping with demonic influences among the ancients seems strange to us. However, the fish here is a folktale element, suggesting the hero's fight with a dragon, and not a recipe for exorcism. It is clear that the author places primary emphasis on the value of prayer to God (6:18; 8:4–8), on the role of the angel as God's agent, and on the pious disposition of Tobiah.

8:3 The desert was considered the dwelling place of demons. Cf. Is 13:21; 34:14; Mt 4:1; 12:43.

*

7:12 Gn 24:50–51.
7:13 Tb 6:12.
8:5 Dn 3:26.
8:6 Gn 2:18–23.

Grant them, Master, mercy and protection,
and bring their lives to fulfillment
with happiness and mercy."

18 Then Raguel told his servants to fill in the grave
before dawn.

Wedding Feast

19 He asked his wife to bake many loaves of
bread; he himself went out to the herd and
brought two steers and four rams, which he or-
dered to be slaughtered. So they began to prepare
the feast. 20 He summoned Tobiah and said to
him, "For fourteen days† you shall not stir from
here, but shall remain here eating and drinking
with me; you shall bring joy to my daughter's af-
flicted spirit. 21 Now take half of what I own here;
go back in good health to your father. The other
half will be yours when I and my wife die. Take
courage, son! I am your father, and Edna is your
mother; we belong to you and to your sister both
now and forever. So take courage, son!"

The Money Recovered

9 1 Then Tobiah called Raphael and said to
him: 2 "Brother Azariah, take along with
you from here four servants and two camels and
travel to Rages.† Go to Gabael's house and give
him this bond. Get the money and then bring
him along with you to the wedding celebration.
3 For you know that my father will be counting
the days. If I should delay even by a single day,
I would cause him intense grief. 4 You have wit-
nessed the oath that Raguel has sworn; I cannot
violate his oath." 5 So Raphael, together with the
four servants and two camels, traveled to Rages
in Media, where they stayed at Gabael's house.
Raphael gave Gabael his bond and told him
about Tobit's son Tobiah, that he had married
and was inviting him to the wedding celebration.
Gabael got up and counted out for him the mon-
eybags with their seals, and they packed them on
the camels.

6 The following morning they both got an
early start and traveled to the wedding celebra-
tion. When they entered Raguel's house, they
found Tobiah reclining at table. He jumped up
and greeted Gabael, who wept and blessed him,
exclaiming: "Good and noble child, son of a
good and noble, righteous and charitable man,
may the Lord bestow a heavenly blessing on you
and on your wife, and on your wife's father and
mother. Blessed be God, because I have seen the
very image of my cousin Tobit!"

VI. Tobiah's Return Journey to Nineveh and the Healing of Tobit

Anxiety of the Parents

10 1 Meanwhile, day by day, Tobit was keep-
ing track of the time Tobiah would need
to go and to return. When the number of days
was reached and his son did not appear, 2 he said,
"Could it be that he has been detained there? Or
perhaps Gabael has died, and there is no one to
give him the money?" 3 And he began to grieve.
4 His wife Anna said, "My son has perished and
is no longer among the living!" And she began
to weep aloud and to wail over her son: 5 "Alas,
child, light of my eyes, that I have let you make
this journey!" 6 But Tobit kept telling her: "Be
still, do not worry, my sister; he is safe! Proba-
bly they have to take care of some unexpected
business there. The man who is traveling with
him is trustworthy and one of our kindred. So
do not grieve over him, my sister. He will be
here soon." 7 But she retorted, "You be still, and
do not try to deceive me! My son has perished!"
She would rush out and keep watch every day
at the road her son had taken. She ate nothing.
After the sun had set, she would go back home
to wail and cry the whole night through, getting
no sleep at all.*

Departure from Ecbatana

Now when the fourteen days of the wedding
celebration, which Raguel had sworn to hold for
his daughter, had come to an end, Tobiah went
to him and said: "Send me off, now, since I know
that my father and mother do not believe they
will ever see me again. So I beg you, father, let
me depart and go back to my own father. I have
already told you how I left him." 8 Raguel said to
Tobiah: "Stay, son, stay with me. I am sending
messengers to your father Tobit, and they will
give him news of you." 9 But Tobiah insisted,
"No, I beg you to send me back to my father."

10 Raguel then promptly handed over to To-
biah his wife Sarah, together with half of all
his property: male and female slaves, oxen and
sheep, donkeys and camels, clothing, money,
and household goods. 11 He saw them safely
off. Embracing Tobiah, he said to him: "Fare-
well, son. Have a safe journey. May the Lord of

TB

† **8:20** *For fourteen days*: because of the happy, and unexpected, turn of events, Raguel doubles the time of the wedding feast. When Tobiah returns home, the usual seven-day feast is held (11:18). Cf. Jgs 14:12.

9:2 *To Rages*: see note on 5:6.

10:7 Gn 45:26.

heaven grant prosperity to you and to your wife
Sarah. And may I see children of yours before I
die!" 12 Then he said to his daughter Sarah, "My
daughter, honor your father-in-law and your
mother-in-law, because from now on they are
as much your parents as the ones who brought
you into the world. Go in peace, daughter; let
me hear a good report about you as long as I
live." Finally he said good-bye to them and let
them go.

Edna also said to Tobiah: "My child and beloved kinsman, may the Lord bring you back safely, and may I live long enough to see children of you and of my daughter Sarah before I die. Before the Lord, I entrust my daughter to your care. Never cause her grief all the days of your life. Go in peace, son. From now on I am your mother, and Sarah is your sister. Together may we all prosper throughout the days of our lives." She kissed them both and saw them safely off.

13 Tobiah left Raguel, full of happiness and joy, and he blessed the Lord of heaven and earth, the King of all, for making his journey so successful. Finally he blessed Raguel and his wife Edna, and added, "I have been commanded by the Lord to honor you all the days of your life!"

Homeward Journey

11 1 As they drew near to Kaserin, which is op-
posite Nineveh, 2 Raphael said: "You know
how we left your father. 3 Let us hurry on ahead
of your wife to prepare the house while they are
still on the way." 4 So both went on ahead to-
gether, and Raphael said to him, "Take the gall
in your hand!" And the dog ran along behind
them.
5 Meanwhile, Anna sat watching the road by
which her son was to come. 6 When she saw him
coming, she called to his father, "Look, your son
is coming, and the man who traveled with him!"
7 Raphael said to Tobiah before he came near
to his father: "I know that his eyes will be
opened. 8 Apply the fish gall to his eyes, and the
medicine will make the white scales shrink and
peel off from his eyes; then your father will have
sight again and will see the light of day."

Sight Restored

9 Then Anna ran up to her son, embraced him,
and said to him, "Now that I have seen you again,
son, I am ready to die!" And she sobbed aloud.*
10 Tobit got up and stumbled out through the
courtyard gate to meet his son. Tobiah went up to
him 11 with the fish gall in his hand and blew into
his eyes. Holding him firmly, he said, "Courage,
father." Then he applied the medicine to his eyes,
and it made them sting. 12, 13 Tobiah used both
hands to peel the white scales from the corners
of his eyes. Tobit saw his son and threw his arms
around him. 14 Weeping, he exclaimed, "I can see
you, son, the light of my eyes!" Then he prayed,

"Blessed be God,
  blessed be his great name,
  and blessed be all his holy angels.
May his great name be with us,
  and blessed be all the angels throughout all
    the ages.
15 God it was who afflicted me,
  and God who has had mercy on me.
  Now I see my son Tobiah!"

Then Tobit went back in, rejoicing and praising
God with full voice. Tobiah related to his father
how his journey had been a success; that he had
brought back the money; and that he had mar-
ried Raguel's daughter Sarah, who was about to
arrive, for she was near the gate of Nineveh.*
16 Rejoicing and blessing God, Tobit went out
to the gate of Nineveh to meet his daughter-in-
law. When the people of Nineveh saw him com-
ing, walking along briskly, with no one leading
him by the hand, they were amazed. 17 Before
them all Tobit proclaimed how God had shown
mercy to him and opened his eyes. When Tobit
came up to Sarah, the wife of his son Tobiah,
he blessed her and said: "Welcome, my daugh-
ter! Blessed be your God for bringing you to
us, daughter! Blessed are your father and your
mother. Blessed be my son Tobiah, and blessed
be you, daughter! Welcome to your home with
blessing and joy. Come in, daughter!" That day
there was joy for all the Jews who lived in Nine-
veh. 18 Ahiqar and his nephew Nadin† were also
on hand to rejoice with Tobit. Tobiah's wedding
feast was celebrated with joy for seven days, and
many gifts were given to him.

VII. Raphael Reveals His Identity

Raphael's Wages†

12 1 When the wedding celebration came to
an end, Tobit called his son Tobiah and
said to him, "Son, see to it that you pay his wages

† **11:18** *Nadin*: see note on 14:10.
12:1–5 Tobit and his son generously agree to give Raphael far more than the wages agreed upon in 5:15–16.

* **11:9** Gn 33:4; 45:14; 46:29–30; Lk 15:20.
11:15 Tb 13:2; Dt 32:39; 1 Sm 2:6.

TB

to the man who made the journey with you and give him a bonus too." [2]Tobiah said: "Father, how much shall I pay him? It would not hurt to give him half the wealth he brought back with me.* [3]He led me back safe and sound, healed my wife, brought the money back with me, and healed you. How much should I pay him?" [4]Tobit answered, "It is only fair, son, that he should receive half of all that he brought back." [5]So Tobiah called Raphael and said, "Take as your wages half of all that you have brought back, and farewell!"

Exhortation†

[6]Raphael called the two of them aside privately and said to them: "Bless God and give him thanks before all the living for the good things he has done for you, by blessing and extolling his name in song. Proclaim before all with due honor the deeds of God, and do not be slack in thanking him.† [7]A king's secret should be kept secret, but one must declare the works of God and give thanks with due honor. Do good, and evil will not overtake you. [8]Prayer with fasting is good. Almsgiving with righteousness is better than wealth with wickedness. It is better to give alms than to store up gold,* [9]for almsgiving saves from death, and purges all sin. Those who give alms will enjoy a full life,* [10]but those who commit sin and do evil are their own worst enemies.

Raphael's Identity

[11]"I shall now tell you the whole truth and conceal nothing at all from you. I have already said to you, 'A king's secret should be kept secret, but one must declare the works of God with due honor.' [12]* Now when you, Tobit, and Sarah prayed, it was I who presented the record of your prayer before the Glory of the Lord; and likewise whenever you used to bury the dead.† [13]When you did not hesitate to get up and leave your dinner in order to go and bury that dead man, [14]I was sent to put you to the test. At the same time, however, God sent me to heal you and your daughter-in-law Sarah. [15]I am Raphael, one of the seven angels who stand and serve before the Glory of the Lord."*

[16]Greatly shaken, the two of them fell prostrate in fear. [17]But Raphael said to them: "Do not fear; peace be with you! Bless God now and forever. [18]As for me, when I was with you, I was not acting out of any favor on my part, but by God's will. So bless God every day; give praise with song. [19]Even though you saw me eat and drink, I did not eat or drink anything; what you were seeing was a vision. [20]So now bless the Lord on earth and give thanks to God. Look, I am ascending to the one who sent me. Write down all that has happened to you."* And he ascended. [21]They stood up but were no longer able to see him. [22]They kept blessing God and singing his praises, and they continued to give thanks for these marvelous works that God had done, because an angel of God appeared to them.

VIII. Tobit's Song of Praise

13 [1]† Then Tobit spoke and composed a song of joyful praise; he said:

Blessed be God who lives forever,
because his kingship lasts for all ages.*
2 For he afflicts and shows mercy,
casts down to the depths of Hades,
brings up from the great abyss.
What is there that can snatch from his hand?*

3 Give thanks to him, you Israelites, in the presence of the nations,
for though he has scattered you among them,
4 even there recount his greatness.
Exalt him before every living being,
because he is your Lord, and he is your God,
our Father and God forever and ever!
5 He will afflict you for your iniquities,
but will have mercy on all of you.
He will gather you from all the nations
among whom you have been scattered.*

6 When you turn back to him with all your heart,

---

† **12:6–10** In the fashion of a wisdom teacher, Raphael gives the two men a short exhortation similar to the one Tobit gave his son in 4:3–19.

12:6–7 The faithful considered the praise of God their most esteemed privilege. Without it, life was meaningless; cf. Is 38:16–20.

12:12 Raphael is one of the seven Angels of the Presence, specially designated intercessors who present prayers to God. Angelology was developing in this period. The names of two other of these seven angels are given in the Bible: Gabriel (Dn 8:16; 9:21; Lk 1:19, 26) and Michael (Dn 10:13, 21; 12:1; Jude 9; Rev 12:7). See 1 Enoch for the names of the rest.

13:1–18 Tobit's hymn of praise is divided into two parts. The first part (vv. 1–8) is a song of praise that echoes themes from the psalms; the second (vv. 9–18) is addressed to Jerusalem in the style of those prophets who spoke of a new and ideal Jerusalem (Is 60; cf. Rev 21). *Joyful praise*: words for joy and gladness occur throughout this prayer (vv. 1, 7, 10, 11, 13, 14, 16, 18).

---

* **12:2** Tb 5:3, 7, 15–16.
12:8 Tb 4:7–11; Sir 29:8–13.
12:9 Dn 4:24.
12:12 Jb 33:23–24; Acts 10:4; Rev 8:3–4.
12:15 Lk 1:19; Rev 8:2.
12:20 Jgs 13:20.
13:1 Tb 3:11; 8:5, 15; 1 Chr 29:10; Dn 3:26.
13:2 Tb 11:15; 13:9; Dt 32:39; 1 Sm 2:6; Wis 16:13.
13:5 Dt 30:3; Neh 1:9.

Pray It!

Hope for the Faithful

When the Jews lived under the influence of Greek culture, there was a great need for hope. The story of Tobit and Tobias, whose names mean "goodness" and "God is good," was written to give hope to those who continue to be faithful to God, even in difficult times.

Tobit is the model of the good Israelite at all times and places. God's saving actions for him and his family symbolize God's actions toward Israel. In this spirit, before his death, Tobit sings a beautiful hymn in thanksgiving for God's goodness and with hope in the triumph of Jerusalem over its oppressors.

- Recognize the goodness of God in your life and the ways in which you fail God.
- Take a moment to pray in Tobit's style. Praise God for the blessings in your life; ask forgiveness for the times you have failed God; give thanks for the times God has answered your prayers in a wiser way than what you had asked for. Pray not only for yourself but for all people, with hope for the triumph of God's love and peace over the self-centeredness, hatred, and violence so common today.

▶ Tobit, chapter 13

and with all your soul do what is right
before him,
Then he will turn to you,
and will hide his face from you no longer.*

Now consider what he has done for you,
and give thanks with full voice.
Bless the Lord of righteousness,
and exalt the King of the ages.

In the land of my captivity I give thanks,
and declare his power and majesty to a
sinful nation.
According to your heart do what is right
before him:
perhaps there will be pardon for you.

7 As for me, I exalt my God,
my soul exalts the King of heaven,
and rejoices all the days of my life.
Let all sing praise to his greatness,
8 let all speak and give thanks in Jerusalem.

9 Jerusalem, holy city,
he will afflict you for the works of your
hands,†
but will again pity the children of the
righteous.*

10 Give thanks to the Lord with righteousness,
and bless the King of the ages,
so that your tabernacle may be rebuilt in
you with joy.
May he gladden within you all who are
captives;
may he cherish within you all who are
distressed
for all generations to come.*

11 A bright light will shine to the limits of the
earth.
Many nations will come to you from afar,
And inhabitants of all the ends of the earth
to your holy name,
Bearing in their hands gifts for the King of
heaven.
Generation after generation will offer joyful
worship in you;
your name will be great forever and ever.*

12 Cursed be all who despise you and revile you;
cursed be all who hate you and speak a
harsh word against you;
cursed be all who destroy you
and pull down your walls,
And all who overthrow your towers
and set fire to your homes.
But blessed forever be all those who respect
you.*

13 Go, then, rejoice and exult over the children
of the righteous,
for they will all be gathered together
and will bless the Lord of the ages.
14 Happy are those who love you,
and happy are those who rejoice in your
peace.
Happy too are all who grieve

† **13:9** *Works of your hands*: idols.

13:6 Dt 30:2.
13:9 Tb 11:15; Mi 7:19; Rev 21.
13:10 Is 44:26, 28; Am 9:11; Zec 1:16.
13:11 Is 2:3–4; 9:1; 49:6; 60:1; Mi 4:2; Zec 8:22.
13:12 Bar 4:31–32.
13:14 Ps 122:6; Is 66:10.

over all your afflictions,
For they will rejoice over you
and behold all your joy forever.*
15 My soul, bless the Lord, the great King;
16 for Jerusalem will be rebuilt as his house
forever.
Happy too will I be if a remnant of my
offspring survives
to see your glory and to give thanks to the
King of heaven!
The gates of Jerusalem will be built with
sapphire and emerald,
and all your walls with precious stones.
The towers of Jerusalem will be built with
gold,
and their battlements with purest gold.*
17 The streets of Jerusalem will be paved
with rubies and stones of Ophir;
18 The gates of Jerusalem will sing hymns of
gladness,
and all its houses will cry out, Hallelujah!
Blessed be the God of Israel for all ages!
For in you the blessed will bless the holy
name forever and ever.

IX. Epilogue

Parting Advice

14 1 So the words of Tobit's hymn of praise
came to an end. Tobit died in peace at
the age of a hundred and twelve and was bur-
ied with honor in Nineveh. 2 He was fifty-eight
years old when he lost his eyesight, and after he
recovered it he lived in prosperity, giving alms;
he continued to fear God and give thanks to the
divine Majesty.
3 As he was dying, he summoned his son To-
biah and Tobiah's seven sons, and commanded
him, "Son, take your children* 4 and flee into
Media, for I believe God's word that Nahum†
spoke against Nineveh. It will all happen and
will overtake Assyria and Nineveh; indeed all
that was said by Israel's prophets whom God sent
will come to pass. Not one of all their words will
remain unfulfilled, but everything will take place
in the time appointed for it. So it will be safer
in Media than in Assyria or Babylon. For I know
and believe that whatever God has said will be
accomplished. It will happen, and not a single
word of the prophecies will fail.
As for our kindred who dwell in the land of
Israel, they will all be scattered and taken into
captivity from the good land. All the land of
Israel will become a wilderness; even Samaria
and Jerusalem will be a wilderness! For a time,
the house of God will be desolate and will be
burned.* 5 But God will again have mercy on
them and bring them back to the land of Israel.
They will build the house again, but it will not
be like the first until the era when the appointed
times will be completed.† Afterward all of them
will return from their captivity, and they will re-
build Jerusalem with due honor. In it the house
of God will also be rebuilt, just as the prophets of
Israel said of it.* 6 * All the nations of the world
will turn and reverence God in truth; all will cast
away their idols, which have deceitfully led them
into error.† 7 They will bless the God of the ages
in righteousness. All the Israelites truly mindful
of God, who are to be saved in those days, will
be gathered together and will come to Jerusalem;
in security will they dwell forever in the land of
Abraham, which will be given to them. Those
who love God sincerely will rejoice, but those
who commit sin and wickedness will disappear
completely from the land.*
8, 9 "Now, my children, I give you this com-
mand: serve God sincerely and do what is pleas-
ing in his sight; you must instruct your children
to do what is right and to give alms, to be mind-
ful of God and at all times to bless his name
sincerely and with all their strength. Now, as for
you, son, leave Nineveh; do not stay here. 10 The
day you bury your mother next to me, do not
even stay overnight within the confines of the
city. For I see that there is much wickedness in it,
and much treachery is practiced in it, and people
are not ashamed. See, my son, all that Nadin†

TB

†

14:4–5 *Nahum*: one of the minor prophets, whose book contains oracles of doom against Nineveh. Here, in keeping with the period in which the story is set, the author makes Tobit speak as if the punishment of Nineveh, the destruction of Jerusalem (587 B.C.), the exile from Judah and the return, would all take place in the future. The technique of using the facts of past history as seemingly future predictions is a frequent device of apocalyptic writers. *The good land*: a favorite name for the promised land. Cf. Dt 1:35; 3:25; 4:21–22.

14:5 *Until the era . . . completed*: a reference to the coming of the day of the Lord, when a new, more perfect temple was to be expected. Cf. Heb 9:1–14.

14:6 Conversion of the nations is also to come with the day of the Lord.

14:10 *Nadin*: in the *Story of Ahiqar*, the hero Ahiqar, chancellor under the Assyrian kings Sennacherib and Esarhaddon, adopts his nephew Nadin and prepares him to become his successor. But Nadin treacherously plots to have his uncle put to death. Ahiqar hides in a friend's house and is finally vindicated when Nadin's scheme is discovered. Thereupon Nadin is thrown into a dungeon where he dies. It was Ahiqar's almsgiving that delivered him from death; see note on 2:2. The Greek and Latin versions of the Book of Tobit read the name as Nadab, but the Aramaic form has the ancient name Nadin, which is also found in the fifth-century B.C. Aramaic *Story of Ahiqar*.

*

13:16 Tb 14:5; Is 54:11–13; 62:2; Rev 21:10–21.
14:3 Gn 47:29–30.
14:4 Na 2:2–3:19.
14:5 Neh 12:27; Jer 31:38.
14:6 Is 60:1–4.
14:7 Is 60:21; Jer 32:37; Ez 34:28; 37:25; 39:26.

did to Ahiqar, the very one who reared him. Was not Ahiqar brought down alive into the earth? Yet God made Nadin's disgraceful crime rebound against him. Ahiqar came out again into the light, but Nadin went into the everlasting darkness, for he had tried to kill Ahiqar. Because Ahiqar had given alms he escaped from the deadly trap Nadin had set for him. But Nadin fell into the deadly trap himself, and it destroyed him.* [11] So, my children, see what almsgiving does, and also what wickedness does—it kills! But now my spirit is about to leave me."

Death of Tobit and Tobiah

They laid him on his bed, and he died; and he was buried with honor. [12] When Tobiah's mother died, he buried her next to his father. He then departed with his wife and children for Media, where he settled in Ecbatana with his father-in-law Raguel.* [13] He took respectful care of his aging father-in-law and mother-in-law; and he buried them at Ecbatana in Media. Then he inherited Raguel's estate as well as that of his father Tobit. [14] He died highly respected at the age of one hundred seventeen. [15] But before he died, he saw and heard of the destruction of Nineveh. He saw the inhabitants of the city being led captive into Media by Cyaxares,† the king of Media. Tobiah blessed God for all that he had done against the Ninevites and Assyrians. Before dying he rejoiced over Nineveh, and he blessed the Lord God forever and ever.

† **14:15** *Cyaxares*: Nabopolassar, king of Babylon, and Cyaxares conquered and destroyed Nineveh in 612 B.C.; see note on 1:15.

* **14:10** Tb 1:21–22. **14:12** Tb 4:4.

The Book of Judith

Do you like to cheer for the underdog? If so, you are like most people. Whether in a court of law, on a football field, or in politics, we get a thrill from seeing the high and mighty toppled by a courageous and determined underdog. This theme is evident in some of the most popular stories of the Old Testament: a group of Hebrew slaves escapes Pharaoh's army, the teenage David topples the giant Goliath, the prophet Daniel escapes injury in the lions' den. Judith's story is another in which the little people—against all odds—somehow come out on top.

At a Glance

I. **Assyrian Threat** (1:1—3:10).

II. **Siege of Bethulia** (4:1—7:32).

III. **Judith, Instrument of the Lord** (8:1—10:10).

IV. **Judith Goes Out to War** (10:11—13:20).

V. **Victory and Thanksgiving** (14:1—16:25).

Quick Facts

Setting: a wisdom story without a clear historical setting

Inspired Author: unknown, writing at the end of the second or the beginning of the first century BC

Themes: a woman of faith and courage, God's saving power

In Depth

As the Book of Judith opens, the mighty Assyrian army is on the march against Jerusalem. To block the advance, the citizens of the small town of Bethulia are asked by the high priest to resist the army's movement. With little hope of success but a great deal of courage, the Bethulians accept the challenge. When they are at the point of surrender, a childless widow named Judith steps forward. Putting all her trust in the "God of the lowly, helper of those of little account, supporter of the weak, protector of those in despair, savior of those without hope" (9:11), she bravely delivers her nation from certain defeat.

The story of Judith must have presented a challenge to the male-dominated world of the Israelites. As a childless widow, Judith would have had little social standing. Yet she succeeds where the king, the priests, and the leaders of the city fail. It is interesting that the name Judith is probably not even a proper name. It simply means "Jewish woman." In a sense, Judith stands for all the Jewish women of the past who have served God through their faith, courage, and decisive action.

Because of its many historical errors, the Book of Judith is clearly a fictional work. With remarkable storytelling flair, the author underlines one of the major elements of Hebrew faith: "O Lord, great are you and glorious, / marvelous in power and unsurpassable" (16:13). This was the kind of faith the underdog People of God needed as they faced the growing might of the Roman Empire.

Judith

9:1

I. Assyrian Threat†

Nebuchadnezzar Against Arphaxad†

1 [1] It was the twelfth year† of the reign of Nebu-
chadnezzar, who ruled over the Assyrians in the
great city of Nineveh. At that time Arphaxad was
ruling over the Medes in Ecbatana.* [2] † Around
Ecbatana he built a wall of hewn stones, three cu-
bits thick and six cubits long. He made the walls
seventy cubits high and fifty cubits wide. [3] At its
gates he raised towers one hundred cubits high
with foundations sixty cubits wide. [4] He made its
gates seventy cubits high and forty cubits wide
to allow passage of his mighty forces, with his
infantry in formation. [5] At that time King Neb-
uchadnezzar waged war against King Arphaxad
in the vast plain that borders Ragau.† [6] Rallying
to him were all who lived in the hill country, all
who lived along the Euphrates, the Tigris, and the
Hydaspes, as well as Arioch, king of the Elamites,
in the plains. Thus many nations joined the ranks
of the Chelodites.† *

[7] Then Nebuchadnezzar, king of the Assyrians,
contacted all the inhabitants of Persia† and all
who lived in the west, the inhabitants of Cilicia
and Damascus, Lebanon and Antilebanon, and all
who lived along the seacoast, [8] the peoples of Car-
mel, Gilead, Upper Galilee, and the vast plain of
Esdraelon, [9] and all in Samaria and its cities, and
west of the Jordan as far as Jerusalem, Bethany,
Chelous, Kadesh,* and the river of Egypt; Tahpan-
hes,* Raamses, all the land of Goshen, [10] Tanis,
Memphis* and beyond, and all the inhabitants of
Egypt as far as the borders of Ethiopia.

[11] But all the inhabitants of the whole land†

1:1–3:10 This section consists of an introduction to Nebuchadnezzar (1:1–16), his commissioning of Holofernes (2:1–13), and a description of the campaigns Holofernes leads against the disobedient vassal nations of the west (2:14–3:10).

1:1–16 Introduction to Nebuchadnezzar and his campaign against Arphaxad. Nebuchadnezzar (605/4–562 B.C.), the most famous Neo-Babylonian king, destroyed Jerusalem in 587 B.C., the eighteenth year of his reign (see Jer 32:1). His depiction here as an Assyrian is an invention of the author, as is the description of Arphaxad, an otherwise unknown king of the Medes, in Ecbatana.

1:1 *Twelfth year*: in the twelfth year of Nebuchadnezzar (593 B.C.) Zedekiah, king of Judah, refused to join a revolt against him (see Jer 27:3; 28:1). *Nineveh*: capital of Assyria, destroyed in 612 B.C.

1:2–4 Since a cubit was the distance from the elbow to the fingertip (approximately eighteen inches), these dimensions are prodigious. The massive wall around Ecbatana is described as 105 feet high and 75 feet thick, with each stone measuring four and a half feet thick and nine feet long. The tower gates are 150 feet high and 60 feet wide. Such unlikely massive structures have never been found at Ecbatana, which lies beneath the modern city of Hamadan, located in the Zagros mountains of northwest Iran. Ecbatana is mentioned in vv. 1, 2, 14 as Arphaxad's headquarters. Tradition claims Esther and Mordecai are buried there.

1:5 Ragau, the place where Arphaxad is slain (v. 15), one of the oldest settlements in Iran, is located on a plain one hundred miles northeast of Ecbatana. In the Book of Tobit it is the home of Gabael (Tb 1:14; 4:1, 20; 5:6; 6:13; 9:2, 5).

1:6 *Chelodites*: Greek *Cheleoud*, probably a corruption of "Chaldeans," i.e., the Neo-Babylonians.

1:7 Mention of Persia suggests a postexilic setting for the book, since this area would have been designated Media before the middle of the fifth century B.C.

1:1 Gn 10:22; Ezr 6:2; Tb 3:7; 5:6; 6:10; 7:1; 14:12–13; 2 Mc 9:3; Jon 1:2; 3:2–3.
1:6 Gn 14:1, 9.
1:9 Nm 34:4; Dt 32:51; Jos 15:23.
1:9 Jer 2:16; 43:7–9; 44:1; 46:14.
1:10 Is 19:13; Jer 2:16; 44:1; 46:14, 19; Ez 30:13, 15; Hos 9:6.

made light of the summons of Nebuchadnezzar, king of the Assyrians, and would not join him in the war. They were not afraid of him, since he was only a single opponent. So they sent back his envoys empty-handed and disgraced.* 12 Then Nebuchadnezzar fell into a violent rage against all the land, and swore by his throne and his kingdom that he would take revenge on all the territories of Cilicia, Damascus, and Syria, and would destroy with his sword all the inhabitants of Moab, Ammon, the whole of Judea, and all those living in Egypt as far as the coasts of the two seas.†

Defeat of Arphaxad

13 In the seventeenth year† he mustered his forces against King Arphaxad and was victorious in his campaign. He routed the whole force of Arphaxad, his entire cavalry, and all his chariots, 14 and took possession of his cities. He pressed on to Ecbatana, took its towers, sacked its marketplaces, and turned its glory into shame. 15 He captured Arphaxad in the mountains of Ragau, ran him through with spears, and utterly destroyed him once and for all. 16 Then he returned to Nineveh with all his consolidated forces, a very great multitude of warriors; and there he and his forces relaxed and feasted for one hundred and twenty days.*

Revenge Planned Against the Western Nations†

2 1 In the eighteenth year,† on the twenty-second day of the first month, there was a discussion in the palace of Nebuchadnezzar, king of the Assyrians, about taking revenge on all the land, as he had threatened.* 2 He summoned all his attendants and officers, laid before them his secret plan, and with his own lips recounted in full detail the wickedness of all the land. 3 They decided to destroy all who had refused to obey the order he had issued.

4 When he had fully recounted his plan, Nebuchadnezzar, king of the Assyrians, summoned Holofernes, the ranking general† of his forces, second only to himself in command, and said to him: 5 "Thus says the great king, the lord of all the earth: Go forth from my presence, take with you men of proven valor, one hundred and twenty thousand infantry and twelve thousand cavalry,* 6 and proceed against all the land of the west, because they disobeyed the order I issued. 7 Tell them to have earth and water† ready, for I will come against them in my wrath; I will cover all the land with the feet of my soldiers, to whom I will deliver them as spoils. 8 Their wounded will fill their ravines and wadies, the swelling river will be choked with their dead; 9 and I will deport them as exiles to the very ends of the earth.

10 "Go before me and take possession of all their territories for me. If they surrender to you, guard them for me until the day of their sentencing. 11 As for those who disobey, show them no mercy, but deliver them up to slaughter and plunder in all the land you occupy.* 12 For as I live,† and by the strength of my kingdom, what I have spoken I will accomplish by my own hand.* 13 Do not disobey a single one of the orders of your lord; fulfill them exactly as I have commanded you, and do it without delay."

Campaigns of Holofernes†

14 So Holofernes left the presence of his lord, and summoned all the commanders, generals, and officers of the Assyrian forces. 15 He mustered one hundred and twenty thousand picked troops, as his lord had commanded, and twelve thousand mounted archers, 16 and drew them up as a vast force organized for battle. 17 He took along a very large number of camels, donkeys, and mules for carrying their supplies; innumerable sheep, cattle, and goats for their food;*

†

1:11 References to "the whole land," "all the land" are used ten times in the first two chapters (vv. 11, 12; 2:1, 2, 5, 6, 7, 9, 10, 19). This signifies all the nations west of Persia as far as Egypt that were subject to Nebuchadnezzar, i.e., the whole earth or world (esp. 2:9). These and similar formulations throughout the book build the case that the "God of heaven" (5:8; 6:19; 11:17) is the true "Master of heaven and earth" (9:12).

1:12 *The two seas*: probably the Mediterranean to the Persian Gulf, though possibly the Red Sea and Mediterranean.

1:13 *Seventeenth year*: 588 B.C. Without help from the vassal nations, Nebuchadnezzar defeats Arphaxad.

2:1–13 Nebuchadnezzar commissions Holofernes to take vengeance on the vassal nations that refused him auxiliary military support (see 1:7–12).

2:1 *Eighteenth year*: 587 B.C. Most of the story is set in the catastrophic year when the historical Nebuchadnezzar, king of Babylon, destroyed Jerusalem.

2:4 *The ranking general*: Holofernes is so identified six times in Judith. See also 4:1; 5:1; 6:1; 10:13; 13:15. Holofernes and Bagoas (12:11) are Persian names; two officers of Artaxerxes III Ochos (358–338 B.C.) were so named.

2:7 *Earth and water*: in the Persian period, offering these to a conqueror was a symbolic gesture signifying humble submission of one asking for a treaty.

2:12 *As I live*: an oath proper to God; see the promissory oath of God the divine warrior in Dt 32:39–42; cf. Is 49:18; Jer 22:24; Ez 5:11. *By my own hand*: in his pride, Nebuchadnezzar claims to do this by his own hand (cf. Is 10:13). In contrast, Judith claims that God will deliver Israel "by my hand" (8:33; 12:4).

2:14–3:10 As Holofernes attacks the western nations, terror sweeps across the empire at large (2:28), then Judea (4:1–2), and finally Bethulia (7:1). In these verses, the line of advance is from Nineveh to Damascus and all who submit are nonetheless devastated and forced to worship Nebuchadnezzar.

*

1:11 2 Sm 17:3; Ez 33:24.
1:16 Est 1:3–4.
2:1 Jer 32:1; 52:29.
2:5 2 Kgs 18:19, 28; 1 Mc 5:13; 10:6.
2:11 Dt 7:2; Jos 11:20; Is 15:13; Is 36:4, 13; Hos 13:18.
2:12 Dt 32:39–41.
2:17 Gn 41:49.

18 abundant provisions for each man, and much
gold and silver from the royal palace.
19 Then he and all his forces set out on their
expedition in advance of King Nebuchadnezzar,
to overrun all the lands of the western region
with their chariots, cavalry, and picked infantry.
20 A huge, irregular force, too many to count, like
locusts, like the dust of the earth, went along
with them.*
21 After a three-day march† from Nineveh, they
reached the plain of Bectileth, and camped oppo-
site Bectileth near the mountains to the north of
Upper Cilicia. 22 From there Holofernes took all
his forces, the infantry, cavalry, and chariots, and
marched into the hill country. 23 He devastated
Put and Lud,† and plundered all the Rassisites
and the Ishmaelites on the border of the wilder-
ness toward the south of the Chelleans.*
24 Then, following the Euphrates, he went
through Mesopotamia, and battered down ev-
ery fortified city along the Wadi Abron, until he
reached the sea. 25 He seized the territory of Ci-
licia, and cut down everyone who resisted him.
Then he proceeded to the southern borders of
Japheth, toward Arabia. 26 He surrounded all the
Midianites, burned their tents, and sacked their
encampments.* 27 Descending to the plain of
Damascus at the time of the wheat harvest, he set
fire to all their fields, destroyed their flocks and
herds, looted their cities, devastated their plains,
and put all their young men to the sword.*
28 * Fear and dread of him fell upon all the
inhabitants of the coastland, upon those in Si-
don and Tyre,* and those who dwelt in Sur and
Ocina, and the inhabitants of Jamnia. Those in
Azotus and Ascalon also feared him greatly.†

Submission of the Vassal Nations

3 1 So they sent messengers to him to sue for
peace in these words: 2 "We, the servants of
Nebuchadnezzar the great king, lie prostrate
before you; do with us as you will. 3 See, our
dwellings and all our land and every wheat field,
our flocks and herds, and all our encampments
are at your disposal; make use of them as you
please. 4 Our cities and their inhabitants are also
at your service; come and deal with them as you
see fit."
5 After the spokesmen had reached Holofernes
and given him this message, 6 he went down
with his forces to the seacoast, stationed garri-
sons in the fortified cities, and took selected men
from them as auxiliaries. 7 The people of these
cities and all the inhabitants of the country-
side received him with garlands and dancing to
the sound of timbrels. 8 But he devastated their
whole territory and cut down their sacred groves,
for he was allowed to destroy all the gods of the
land, so that every nation might worship only
Nebuchadnezzar, and all their tongues and tribes
should invoke him as a god.† * 9 At length Hol-
ofernes reached Esdraelon in the neighborhood
of Dothan,† the approach to the main ridge of
the Judean mountains; 10 he set up his camp be-
tween Geba† and Scythopolis, and stayed there
a whole month to replenish all the supplies of
his forces.

II. Siege of Bethulia†

Israel Prepares for War†

4 1 When the Israelites who lived in Judea
heard of all that Holofernes, the ranking
general of Nebuchadnezzar king of the Assyrians,
had done to the nations, and how he had looted
all their shrines† and utterly destroyed them,
2 they were in very great fear of him, and greatly
alarmed for Jerusalem and the temple of the
Lord, their God. 3 Now, they had only recently
returned from exile, and all the people of Judea

†

2:21 *A three-day march*: no ancient army could have traveled three hundred miles from Nineveh to Cilicia in three days.

2:23 *Put and Lud*: mentioned together in Jer 46:9; Ez 27:10; 30:5. Put is thought to be in Libya in Africa; Lud is usually identified with Lydia in Asia Minor. Rather than indicating definite localities here, Put and Lud add assonance and prophetic overtones to the narrative.

2:28 Symbolic of the completeness of the terror that descended on the area, seven towns are listed: Tyre, Sidon, Sur, Ocina, Jamnia, Ashdod, and Ashkelon.

3:8 *Invoke him as a god*: Holofernes violates Nebuchadnezzar's instructions (see 2:5–13). No Assyrian, Neo-Babylonian, or Persian king is known to have claimed divinity. During Hellenistic times, Ptolemy V (203–181 B.C.) and the Seleucid Antiochus IV made claims to divinity. In Dn 3 and 6, divinity is ascribed to Nebuchadnezzar and Darius, respectively.

3:9 *Dothan*: a town in Ephraimite territory fourteen miles north of Shechem, mentioned elsewhere only twice (Gn 37:17 and 2 Kgs 6:13), but five times in Judith (3:9; 4:6; 7:3, 18; 8:3). Destroyed in 810 B.C. by Aramean invasions, Dothan was deserted until the Hellenistic period when a small settlement was constructed. Because it is mentioned so often, Dothan is sometimes thought to be the author's home.

3:10 *Geba*: location uncertain. Scythopolis, the Greek name for ancient Beth-shean (Jos 17:11), the only city in Judith given its Greek name, strategically guarded the eastern end of the Valley of Jezreel.

4:1–7:32 In this section the focus narrows to Judea and specifically the little town of Bethulia. The scenes alternate between the Assyrian camp (5:1–6:13; 7:1–3, 6–18) and Judea/Bethulia (4:1–15; 6:14–21; 7:4–5, 19–32).

4:1–15 Here the scene shifts to Judea where Israel hears and is greatly terrified about Holofernes' destruction of the neighboring places of worship. At Joakim's instruction they take defensive measures and then pray fervently that God will not allow their sanctuary to be destroyed.

4:1 *Shrines*: the Greek word *hiera* is used only here and may mean holy places or things. By contrast, the sanctuary in Jerusalem

*

2:20 Ex 10:4, 13, 14; Jgs 6:5; 7:12; Ps 105:34; Jl 1:4.
2:23 Gn 2:2; 10:6, 22; Is 66:19; Ez 30:5.
2:26 Gn 37:36; Ex 2:15; Jgs 6–8.
2:27 Gn 34:26; Jos 6:21; 1 Sm 15:8.
2:28 Ex 15:16; Ps 55:6.
2:28 Ez 26:7–14; 29:17–20.
3:8 Ex 34:13; 2 Kgs 18:4; 23:14–15; 2 Chr 14:2; 17:6; 31:1; 34:4.

were just now reunited, and the vessels, the altar,
and the temple had been purified from profana-
tion.† * 4 So they sent word to the whole region
of Samaria, to Kona, Beth-horon, Belmain, and
Jericho, to Choba and Aesora, and to the valley
of Salem.† 5 The people there secured all the high
hilltops, fortified the villages on them, and since
their fields had recently been harvested, stored
up provisions in preparation for war.

6 Joakim, who was high priest† in Jerusalem in
those days, wrote to the inhabitants of Bethulia
and Betomesthaim, which is opposite Esdraelon,
facing the plain near Dothan,* 7 and instructed
them to keep firm hold of the mountain passes,
since these offered access to Judea. It would be
easy to stop those advancing, as the approach
was only wide enough for two at a time.† 8 The
Israelites carried out the orders given them by
Joakim, the high priest, and the senate of the
whole people of Israel, in session in Jerusalem.*

Israel at Prayer

9 All the men of Israel cried to God with great
fervor and humbled themselves. 10 They, along
with their wives, and children, and domestic
animals, every resident alien, hired worker, and
purchased slave, girded themselves with sack-
cloth.† * 11 And all the Israelite men, women, and
children who lived in Jerusalem fell prostrate in
front of the temple† * and sprinkled ashes on
their heads, spreading out their sackcloth be-
fore the Lord.* 12 The altar, too, they draped in
sackcloth;† and with one accord they cried out
fervently to the God of Israel not to allow their
children to be seized, their wives to be taken cap-
tive, the cities of their inheritance to be ruined,
or the sanctuary to be profaned and mocked for
the nations to gloat over.

13 The Lord heard their cry† and saw their
distress. The people continued fasting for many
days throughout Judea and before the sanctu-
ary of the Lord Almighty in Jerusalem.* 14 Also
girded with sackcloth, Joakim, the high priest,
and all the priests in attendance before the Lord,
and those who ministered to the Lord offered the
daily burnt offering, the votive offerings, and the
voluntary offerings of the people.* 15 With ashes
upon their turbans, they cried to the Lord with
all their strength to look with favor on the whole
house of Israel.*

Achior in the Assyrian War Council†

5 1 It was reported to Holofernes, the ranking
general of the Assyrian forces, that the Israel-
ites were ready for battle, had blocked the moun-
tain passes, fortified the high hilltops, and placed
roadblocks in the plains. 2 In great anger he
summoned all the rulers of Moab, the governors
of Ammon, and all the satraps of the coastland*
3 and said to them: "Now tell me, you Canaan-
ites, what sort of people is this that lives in the
hill country? Which cities do they inhabit? How
large is their force? In what does their power and
strength consist? Who has set himself up as their
king and the leader of their army? 4 Why have
they alone of all the inhabitants of the west re-
fused to come out to meet me?"

5 † Then Achior, the leader of all the Ammon-
ites, said to him: "My lord, please listen to a
report from your servant. I will tell you the truth
about this people that lives in the hill country
near here. No lie shall escape your servant's lips.
6 "These people are descendants of the Chal-
deans. 7 They formerly lived in Mesopotamia,
for they did not wish to follow the gods of their
ancestors who were in the land of the Chalde-
ans.* 8 Since they abandoned the way of their
ancestors, and worshiped the God of heaven,†

---

is *naos*, "temple" (v. 2); *oikos*, "house" (v. 3); and *hagia*, lit., "holy things" (v. 12).

4:3 *Returned from exile . . . purified from profanation*: conflated historical references associated with events in 538 B.C. (return from exile) and 515 B.C. (dedication of the Second Temple) or perhaps even 164 B.C. (the rededication of the Second Temple in the Maccabean period).

4:4 Of the eight cities listed, only the locations of Beth-horon, Jericho, and Samaria are known. Salem, mentioned in Gn 17:17, is thought to be an ancient name of Jerusalem.

4:6 *Joakim, who was high priest*: see also vv. 8, 14; 15:8. Joakim exercises religious and military authority comparable to that of Jonathan in Maccabean times (cf. 1 Mc 10:18–21). *Bethulia and Betomesthaim*: unknown locations mentioned only in Judith. Bethulia may mean "House of God" (*byt 'l/yh*) or "House of Ascent" (*byt 'lyh*), perhaps a reference to either Bethel or Shechem.

4:7 *Only wide enough for two at a time*: such a narrow pass near Esdraelon cannot be identified.

4:10 *Sackcloth*: traditional sign of penitence and supplication is here taken to the extreme. Cf. Jon 3:8.

4:11 *Fell prostrate in front of the temple*: for a parallel to this ceremony of entreaty see Jl 1:13, 14; 2:15–17.

4:12 *The altar . . . draped in sackcloth*: attested nowhere else in the Bible.

4:13 *The Lord heard their cry*: this anticipates the role of Judith, the instrument of deliverance (chap. 16), though the people believe God has abandoned them (7:25).

5:1–6:13 The scene shifts to the Assyrian camp below Bethulia where Holofernes talks with Achior and then expels him to the foot of the hill below the little town.

5:5–21 Achior (Heb. "brother of light") traces the covenant of Israel from Abraham to the exile and defends the inviolability of the people because their powerful God will defend them if they do not sin. He later identifies the head Judith displays as that of Holofernes (14:6–10). He may be modeled on the famous sage, Ahiqar (see note on Tb 1:21). Achior is wise, but the wisdom granted Judith by God is more effective than his.

5:8 *God of heaven*: a common expression in Persian times; see also 6:19; 11:17 (cf. 7:28; 9:12; 13:18).

4:3 1 Mc 4:36–61; 2 Mc 10:3–5.
4:6 Dn 13:1, 4, 28, 29, 63.
4:8 2 Mc 11:27.
4:10 Neh 9:1; Est 4:1–4; Jl 1:13, 14; Jon 3:5, 6, 8.
4:11 1 Chr 29:20; 2 Mc 3:15.
4:11 2 Sm 21:10.
4:13 Est 4:16; Jl 2:15.
4:14 Ex 29:38–46; Nm 28:1–8; Ezr 3:4.
4:15 Lv 16:4; Ez 24:23; 44:18; Zec 3:5.
5:2 Dt 2:21; 2 Kgs 24:2.
5:7 Gn 11:31.

the God whom they had come to know, their
ancestors expelled them from the presence of
their gods. So they fled to Mesopotamia and
lived there a long time. 9 Their God told them
to leave the place where they were living and
go to the land of Canaan. Here they settled, and
grew very rich in gold, silver, and a great abun-
dance of livestock.* 10 Later, when famine had
gripped the land of Canaan, they went down into
Egypt. They stayed there as long as they found
sustenance and there they grew into such a great
multitude that the number of their people could
not be counted.* 11 * The king of Egypt, however,
rose up against them, and shrewdly forced them
to labor at brickmaking; they were oppressed
and made into slaves. 12 But they cried to their
God, and he struck the whole land of Egypt with
plagues for which there was no remedy. So the
Egyptians drove them out. 13 Then God dried up
the Red Sea before them* 14 and led them along
the route to Sinai and Kadesh-barnea. They drove
out all the inhabitants of the wilderness 15 and
settled in the land of the Amorites. By their
strength they destroyed all the Heshbonites,*
crossed the Jordan, and took possession of all
the hill country.* 16 They drove out before them
the Canaanites, the Perizzites, the Jebusites, the
Shechemites,† and all the Gergesites,* and they
lived there a long time.

17 * "As long as the Israelites did not sin in the
sight of their God, they prospered, for their God,
who hates wickedness, was with them. 18 † But
when they abandoned the way he had prescribed
for them, they were utterly destroyed by frequent
wars, and finally taken as captives into foreign
lands. The temple of their God was razed to
the ground, and their cities were occupied by
their enemies.* 19 But now they have returned
to their God, and they have come back from the
Diaspora where they were scattered. They have
reclaimed Jerusalem, where their sanctuary is,
and have settled again in the hill country, be-
cause it was unoccupied.

20 * "So now, my master† and lord, if these
people are inadvertently at fault, or if they are
sinning against their God, and if we verify this
offense of theirs, then we will be able to go up
and conquer them. 21 But if they are not a guilty
nation, then let my lord keep his distance; other-
wise their Lord and God will shield them, and we
will be mocked in the eyes of all the earth."

22 Now when Achior had finished saying these
things, all the people standing round about the
tent murmured; and the officers of Holofernes
and all the inhabitants of the seacoast and of
Moab alike said he should be cut to pieces.
23 * "We are not afraid of the Israelites," they
said, "for they are a powerless people, incapa-
ble of a strong defense. 24 Therefore let us attack,
master Holofernes. They will become fodder for
your great army."

6 1 When the noise of the crowd surrounding
the council had subsided, Holofernes, the
ranking general of the Assyrian forces, said to
Achior, in the presence of the whole throng of
foreigners, of the Moabites, and of the Ammonite
mercenaries: 2 "Who are you,† Achior and the mer-
cenaries of Ephraim, to prophesy among us as you
have done today, and to tell us not to fight against
the people of Israel because their God shields
them? Who is God beside Nebuchadnezzar? He
will send his force and destroy them from the
face of the earth. Their God will not save them;*
3 but we, the servants of Nebuchadnezzar, will
strike them down with one blow, for they will be
unable to withstand the force of our cavalry. 4 We
will overwhelm them with it, and their mountains
shall be drunk with their blood, and their plains
filled with their corpses. Not a trace of them shall
survive our attack; they will utterly perish. So says
King Nebuchadnezzar, lord of all the earth. For he
has spoken, and his words will not be in vain. 5 As
for you, Achior, you Ammonite mercenary, for
saying these things in a moment of perversity, you
will not see my face after today, until I have taken
revenge on this people that came out of Egypt.
6 Then at my return, the sword of my army or the
spear of my attendants will pierce your sides, and
you will fall among their wounded. 7 My servants
will now conduct you to the hill country, and
leave you at one of the cities beside the passes.

---

† **5:16** *Shechemites*: perhaps anticipates the allusion in Judith's prayer (9:2) to Simeon's revenge on these people.

5:18–19 Knowledge of the Babylonian exile is presupposed; cf. also 4:3.

5:20 *Master*: the Greek word *despota*, usually applied to God in the Septuagint, is applied to Holofernes five times in the Book of Judith (vv. 20, 24; 7:9, 11; 11:10), and only once to God (9:12).

6:2 *Who are you*: repeated by Judith in 8:12 to the officials of Bethulia and modified in 12:14 in her response to Bagoas' invitation on Holofernes' behalf. The question, "Who is God?" motivates the entire narrative. Holofernes defends Nebuchadnezzar; Judith defends the Lord.

---

* **5:9** Gn 11:31–12:5; 13:2.
5:10 Gn 42:1–5; 46:1–7; Ex 1:7.
5:11–12 Ex 1:10–14; 5:1–21; 7:1–11:10.
5:13 Ex 14:21; Jos 2:10; 4:23; Ps 106:9; Wis 19:7; Heb 11:29.
5:15 Nm 21:25–28, 30, 34; Dt 1:4; 2:24, 26, 30; 3:2, 6; 4:46.
5:15 Jos 3.
5:16 Gn 10:16; 15:20; Dt 7:1; Jos 3:10; 24:12; 1 Chr 1:14.
5:17–18 Dt 28–30; Jgs 2:11–15; Ps 106:40–46.
5:18 2 Kgs 25.
5:20–21 Jdt 8:18–23; 11:10; Tb 3:3.
5:23–24 Jdt 6:2; 9:7–8; 16:2.
6:2 Jdt 3:8; 9:7–8; 1 Kgs 22:15–17; 2 Kgs 18:32–35; Is 36:18–20; Dn 3:14–18.

8 You will not die until you are destroyed together
with them. 9 If you still harbor the hope that they
will not be taken, then there is no need for you to
be downcast.* I have spoken, and not one of my
words will fail to be fulfilled."
10 Then Holofernes ordered the servants who
were standing by in his tent to seize Achior, con-
duct him to Bethulia, and hand him over to the
Israelites. 11 So the servants seized him and took
him out of the camp into the plain. From the
plain they led him up into the hill country until
they reached the springs below Bethulia.
12 When the men of the city saw them, they
seized their weapons and ran out of the city to
the top of the hill, and all the slingers kept them
from coming up by hurling stones at them. 13 So,
taking cover below the hill, they bound Achior
and left him lying at the foot of the hill; then
they returned to their lord.

Achior in Bethulia†

14 The Israelites came down from their city
and found him, untied him, and brought him
into Bethulia. They placed him before the rul-
ers of the city, 15 who in those days were Uz-
ziah,† son of Micah of the tribe of Simeon, and
Chabris, son of Gothoniel, and Charmis, son of
Melchiel.* 16 They then convened all the elders
of the city, and all their young men, as well as
the women, gathered in haste at the place of as-
sembly. They placed Achior in the center of the
people, and Uzziah questioned him about what
had happened. 17 He replied by giving them an
account of what was said in the council of Hol-
ofernes, and of all his own words among the
Assyrian rulers, and of all the boasting threats of
Holofernes against the house of Israel.
18 At this the people fell prostrate and wor-
shiped God,† and they cried out: 19 "Lord, God of
heaven, look at their arrogance! Have mercy on
our people in their abject state, and look with fa-
vor this day on the faces of those who are conse-
crated to you." 20 Then they reassured Achior and
praised him highly. 21 Uzziah brought him from
the place of assembly to his home, where he gave
a banquet for the elders. That whole night they
called upon the God of Israel for help.

The Campaign Against Israel†

7 1 The following day Holofernes ordered his
whole army, and all the troops who had
come to join him, to break camp and move
against Bethulia, seize the passes into the hills,
and make war on the Israelites. 2 That same day
all their fighting men went into action. Their
forces numbered a hundred and seventy thou-
sand infantry and twelve thousand cavalry, not
counting the baggage train or the men who ac-
companied it on foot, a very great army. 3 They
encamped at the spring in the valley near Bethu-
lia, and spread crosswise toward Dothan as far
as Balbaim, and lengthwise from Bethulia to
Cyamon, which faces Esdraelon.
4 When the Israelites saw how many there
were, they were greatly distressed and said to one
another, "Soon they will strip the whole land
bare. Neither the high mountains nor the valleys
nor the hills will bear their weight." 5 Yet they all
seized their weapons, lighted fires on their tow-
ers, and kept watch throughout the night.*

The Siege of Bethulia†

6 On the second day Holofernes led out all his
cavalry in the sight of the Israelites who were in
Bethulia. 7 He reconnoitered the ascents to their
city and located their springs of water; these he
seized, stationing armed detachments around
them, while he himself returned to his troops.
8 All the rulers of the Edomites, all the leaders
of the Moabites, together with the generals of the
coastal region, came to Holofernes and said:*
9 "Master, please listen to what we have to say,
that there may be no losses among your forces.
10 These Israelite troops do not rely on their
spears, but on the height of the mountains where
they dwell, for it is not easy to reach the summit
of their mountains.* 11 Therefore, master, do not
attack them in regular formation, and not a sin-
gle one of your troops will fall. 12 Stay in your
camp, and spare every man of your force. Have
some of your servants keep control of the spring
of water that flows out at the base of the moun-
tain, 13 for that is where the inhabitants of Bethu-
lia get their water. Then thirst will destroy them,

†

6:14–21 The scene shifts back to Bethulia where Achior tells the town leaders and citizens all that Holofernes has planned against them. The people cry out to God for help.

6:15 *Uzziah*: *Ozeias* is the Greek equivalent of the Hebrew *'uzziyyah*, "Yah-is-my-strength." His compromise in 7:30 highlights the irony of his name. *Chabris . . . Charmis*: unknown outside Judith.

6:18 *The people fell prostrate and worshiped God*: here in response to Achior's report, the people properly turn to God in their distress. See 4:12.

7:1–5 The scene returns to the Assyrian camp (vv. 1–3) and then shifts back to Bethulia (vv. 4–5). Holofernes orders war preparations; Israel sees and is greatly terrified.

7:6–32 The scene is set first in the Assyrian camp where Holofernes moves against Bethulia (vv. 6–18), and then in Bethulia where the people cry out to God and, when their courage fails, determine it is time to surrender (vv. 19–32).

*

6:9 Gn 4:5; 40:7.
6:15 Gn 29:33; 34:25, 30; 35:23.
7:5 1 Mc 12:28–29; 2 Mc 10:36.
7:8 Gn 36:1; 1 Mc 5:3.
7:10 1 Kgs 20:23, 28; 2 Kgs 19:23; Ps 95:4; Is 37:24.

and they will surrender their city. Meanwhile, we and our troops will go up to the nearby hilltops and encamp there to guard against anyone's leaving the city. 14They and their wives and children will languish with hunger, and even before the sword strikes them they will be laid low in the streets where they live. 15Thus you will render them dire punishment for their rebellion and their refusal to meet you peacefully."

16Their words pleased Holofernes and all his attendants, and he ordered their proposal to be carried out. 17So the Ammonites moved camp, together with five thousand Assyrians. They encamped in the valley and held the water supply and the springs of the Israelites. 18The Edomites and the Ammonites went up and encamped in the hill country opposite Dothan; and they sent some of their men to the southeast opposite Egrebel, near Chusi, which is on Wadi Mochmur. The rest of the Assyrian army was encamped in the plain, covering all the land. Their tents and equipment were spread out in profusion everywhere, and they formed a vast multitude.

The Distress of the Israelites

19The Israelites cried to the Lord, their God, for they were disheartened, since all their enemies had them surrounded, and there was no way of escaping from them.† 20The whole Assyrian army, infantry, chariots, and cavalry, kept them thus surrounded for thirty-four days.† All the reservoirs of water failed the inhabitants of Bethulia, 21and the cisterns ran dry, so that on no day did they have enough water to drink, for their drinking water was rationed. 22Their children were listless, and the women and youths were fainting from thirst and were collapsing in the streets and gateways of the city, with no strength left in them.

23So all the people, including youths, women, and children, went in a crowd to Uzziah and the rulers of the city. They cried out loudly and said before all the elders: 24"May God judge between you and us! You have done us grave injustice in not making peace with the Assyrians.* 25There is no one to help us now! God has sold us into their hands by laying us prostrate before them in thirst and utter exhaustion.* 26So now, summon them and deliver the whole city as plunder to the troops of Holofernes and to all his forces; 27we would be better off to become their prey. Although we would be made slaves, at least we would live, and not have to see our little ones dying before our eyes, and our wives and children breathing their last.* 28We adjure you by heaven and earth and by our God, the Lord of our ancestors, who is punishing us for our sins and the sins of our ancestors,† that this very day you do as we have proposed."*

29All in the assembly with one accord broke into shrill wailing and cried loudly to the Lord their God. 30But Uzziah said to them, "Courage, my brothers and sisters! Let us endure patiently five days more for the Lord our God to show mercy toward us; for God will not utterly forsake us. 31But if these days pass and help does not come to us, I will do as you say." 32Then he dismissed the people. The men returned to their posts on the walls and towers of the city, the women and children went back to their homes. Throughout the city they were in great misery.

III. Judith, Instrument of the Lord†

Description of Judith

8 1†*Now in those days Judith, daughter of Merari,* son of Ox, son of Joseph, son of Oziel, son of Elkiah, son of Ananias, son of Gideon, son of Raphain, son of Ahitub, son of Elijah, son of Hilkiah, son of Eliab, son of Nathanael, son of Salamiel, son of Sarasadai, son of Simeon, son of Israel, heard of this. 2Her husband, Manasseh,† of her own tribe and clan, had died at the time of the barley harvest. 3While he was supervising those who bound the sheaves in the field, he was overcome by the heat; and he collapsed on his bed and died in Bethulia, his native city. He was buried with his ancestors in the field between Dothan and Balamon. 4*Judith was living as a widow† in her home for

†

7:19 The prayers of the Israelites shift focus from concern for the Temple and Jerusalem (4:12), to concern that God see the arrogance of the enemy and show pity on the covenant people (6:18), to expression of fear and loss of courage regarding their own safety (7:19).

7:20 *Thirty-four days*: the Bethulians lose heart after being without water; Judith will spend four days in the enemy camp (12:10) and the Israelites will plunder the enemy camp for thirty days (15:11).

7:28 In keeping with the deuteronomic theme of retribution, the Bethulians interpret their persecution as punishment for their sins and the sins of their ancestors (see Ex 20:5; 34:7; Ez 18). In 8:18–27, Judith argues that they are being tested.

8:1–10:10 In this section the hero is introduced (8:1–8) and prepares to deliver Israel (8:9–10:10).

8:1 Judith has the longest genealogy accorded any biblical woman, with family ties back to Israel/Jacob.

8:2 *Manasseh*: Judith's marriage was endogamous, within her own tribe. The tribe and clan are identified as hers, though usually it is the husband's tribe and clan that are noted.

8:4 *Widow*: in a reversal of traditional property law, Judith holds title to her husband's estate (see v. 7). However, she will give a part of her inheritance to her late husband's family before her death (16:24); she chooses not to remarry (16:22).

*

7:24 Ex 5:21.
7:25 Est 7:4.
7:27 Ex 14:12; 16:3; 1 Mc 1:62–63.
7:28 Ps 106:6; Lam 5:7.
8:1 Gn 26:34; Jer 36:14, 21, 23.
8:1 Gn 46:11; Ex 6:16; Nm 3:17.
8:4 1 Sm 25:39–42; 2 Sm 11:27; Is 54:4; Lam 1:1; 5:3.

Cultural Connection

The Principle of *Kujichagulia*

That man over there says that women need to be helped into carriages, and lifted over ditches, and to have the best place everywhere. Nobody ever helps me into carriages, or over mud puddles, or gives me any best place! And ain't I a woman? (Sojourner Truth, 1851)

When people who are abused cower quietly in corners, injustice lives on. Bent heads, muffled voices, and terrified spirits invite wrongs to continue.

Judith was a biblical heroine who refused to let her role be determined by others. As a woman and a widow, she had little social standing in ancient Israel. Yet, she did not let this keep her from speaking out and challenging the community leaders to action.

Sojourner Truth was a modern hero who refused to keep quiet despite being mistreated and devalued. Her womanhood was slighted, and her personhood was trampled, yet she traveled America to tell all who would listen about the evils of slavery.

The Kwanzaa principle of *kujichagulia* (see "Kwanzaa as a Way of Life," near Dt 10:12–22), or self-determination, sometimes requires us to stand up and speak out. Silence can be compliance. Thank God for the gift of boldness of speech! It gives us the power to speak the truth even in the most oppressive situations.

Dear God, give me the boldness of Judith and Sojourner Truth to address the wrongs of this world. Amen.

Jdt 8:9–36

three years and four months. 5 She set up a tent
for herself on the roof of her house, put sackcloth
about her waist, and wore widow's clothing.*
6 She fasted all the days of her widowhood, ex-
cept sabbath eves and sabbaths, new moon eves
and new moons, feastdays and holidays of the
house of Israel.* 7 She was beautiful in appear-
ance and very lovely to behold.* Her husband,
Manasseh, had left her gold and silver, male and
female servants, livestock and fields, which she
was maintaining. 8 No one had a bad word to say
about her, for she feared God greatly.

Judith and the Elders†

9 So when Judith heard of the harsh words that
the people, discouraged by their lack of water,
had spoken against their ruler, and of all that
Uzziah had said to them in reply, swearing that
he would hand over the city to the Assyrians at
the end of five days, 10 she sent her maid who
was in charge of all her things† to summon Uz-
ziah, Chabris, and Charmis, the elders of her city.
11 When they came, she said to them: "Listen to
me, you rulers of the people of Bethulia. What
you said to the people today is not right. You
pronounced this oath, made between God and
yourselves, and promised to hand over the city
to our enemies unless within a certain time the
Lord comes to our aid. 12 Who are you to put
God to the test today, setting yourselves in the
place of God in human affairs?† * 13 And now it
is the Lord Almighty you are putting to the test,
but you will never understand anything! 14 You
cannot plumb the depths of the human heart
or grasp the workings of the human mind; how
then can you fathom God, who has made all
these things, or discern his mind, or understand
his plan?*

†

8:9–10:10 This section opens with a repetition of the information that Judith heard about the discouragement of the people and about Uzziah's vow (cf. v. 1). Judith's plan to save Israel then takes shape. In her own home, she meets with the elders of Bethulia (vv. 9–36), prays (9:1–14), prepares herself and the food she will need in the Assyrian camp (10:1–5), goes out to meet the elders again at the gate of Bethulia (10:6–8), and sets out with her maid for the Assyrian camp (10:9–10).

8:10 *Her maid who was in charge of all her things*: cf. Gn 15:2; 24:2; 39:4. Judith's first act in the story is to send this unnamed maid (*habra*, lit., "graceful one" or "favorite slave," v. 33; 10:2, 5, 17; 13:9; 16:23) to summon the town officials (see also other terms for female servants, *paidiske* in 10:10 and *doule* in 12:15; 13:3). Her last act in the story will be to give this woman her freedom (16:23).

8:12 Judith reprimands the leaders for putting God to the test (cf. Dt 6:16). She will argue that the right to test belongs to God (vv. 25–27).

*

8:5 Jos 2:6, 8; Jgs 3:20–25; 1 Sm 9:25–26; 2 Sm 11:2; 16:22; 2 Kgs 4:10; 23:12; Ps 102:8; Acts 10:9.
8:6 Lk 2:37.
8:7 Gn 12:11; 29:17; Est 2:7.
8:12 Dt 6:16; Jb 38:2; 40:2, 7–8; Ps 106:14; Mal 3:15.
8:14 Ps 139:17–18; Wis 9:13; Is 40:13; Rom 11:33–34; 1 Cor 2:11.

"No, my brothers, do not anger the Lord our God. [15] † For if he does not plan to come to our aid within the five days, he has it equally within his power to protect us at such time as he pleases, or to destroy us in the sight of our enemies. [16] Do not impose conditions on the plans of the Lord our God. God is not like a human being to be moved by threats, nor like a mortal to be cajoled.

[17] "So while we wait for the salvation that comes from him, let us call upon him to help us, and he will hear our cry if it pleases him. [18] For there has not risen among us in recent generations, nor does there exist today, any tribe, or clan, or district, or city of ours that worships gods made by hands, as happened in former days.* [19] It was for such conduct that our ancestors were handed over to the sword and to pillage, and fell with great destruction before our enemies.* [20] But since we acknowledge no other god but the Lord, we hope that he will not disdain us or any of our people. [21] If we are taken, then all Judea will fall, our sanctuary will be plundered, and God will demand an account from us for their profanation. [22] For the slaughter of our kindred, for the taking of exiles from the land, and for the devastation of our inheritance, he will hold us responsible among the nations. Wherever we are enslaved, we will be a scandal and a reproach in the eyes of our masters. [23] Our servitude will not work to our advantage, but the Lord our God will turn it to disgrace.

[24] "Therefore, my brothers, let us set an example† for our kindred. Their lives depend on us, and the defense of the sanctuary, the temple, and the altar rests with us. [25] * Besides all this, let us give thanks to the Lord our God for putting us to the test as he did our ancestors.* [26] Recall how he dealt with Abraham, and how he tested Isaac, and all that happened to Jacob in Syrian Mesopotamia while he was tending the flocks of Laban, his mother's brother. [27] He has not tested us with fire, as he did them, to try their hearts, nor is he taking vengeance on us. But the Lord chastises those who are close to him in order to admonish them."

[28] Then Uzziah said to her: "All that you have said you have spoken truthfully, and no one can deny your words. [29] For today is not the first time your wisdom has been evident, but from your earliest days all the people have recognized your understanding, for your heart's disposition is right. [30] The people, however, were so thirsty that they forced us to do for them as we have promised, and to bind ourselves by an oath that we cannot break.† * [31] But now, since you are a devout woman, pray for us that the Lord may send rain to fill up our cisterns. Then we will no longer be fainting from thirst."

[32] Then Judith said to them: "Listen to me! I will perform a deed that will go down from generation to generation among our descendants. [33] Stand at the city gate tonight to let me pass through with my maid; and within the days you have specified before you will surrender the city to our enemies, the Lord will deliver Israel by my hand. [34] You must not inquire into the affair, for I will not tell you what I am doing until it has been accomplished." [35] Uzziah and the rulers said to her, "Go in peace, and may the Lord God go before you to take vengeance upon our enemies!" [36] Then they withdrew from the tent and returned to their posts.

The Prayer of Judith†

9 [1] Judith fell prostrate, put ashes upon her head, and uncovered the sackcloth she was wearing. Just as the evening incense was being offered in the temple of God in Jerusalem, Judith cried loudly to the Lord:* [2] "Lord, God of my father Simeon, into whose hand you put a sword to take revenge upon the foreigners† who had defiled a virgin by violating her, shaming her by uncovering her thighs, and dishonoring her by polluting her womb. You said, 'This shall not be done!' Yet they did it. [3] Therefore

†

8:15–16 God's plans are in opposition to Nebuchadnezzar's plans (2:2, 4). *To protect . . . or to destroy*: Judith defends God's freedom (cf. Jb 1:21; 2:10).

8:24 *Let us set an example*: when Judith says "us," she includes herself. She proposes that she together with Uzziah, Chabris, and Charmis model a faithful response to God's test for the wavering people. "Let us give thanks to the Lord our God for putting us to the test" (v. 25) repeats her intention. "Us" for Uzziah does not include her (see vv. 30, 31).

8:30–31 *An oath that we cannot break*: Uzziah's request that Judith pray for rain underscores his lack of imagination concerning how God's deliverance might come.

9:1–14 Judith prepares to confront the enemy by turning to God, the source of her strength. Her prayer, an individual lament, moves from a remembrance of God's saving deeds of the past to an appeal to God to exercise the same power in the present. Judith contrasts the empty pride of the Assyrians with God's surpassing might, powerful enough to be exercised in unlikely ways, even through the hand of a woman.

9:2 *The foreigners*: Shechem, the Hivite, violated Dinah, Jacob and Leah's daughter (Gn 34:2). *Defiled a virgin by violating her*: meaning of the Greek is unclear; lit., "who loosened the virgin's womb (*metran*) to defilement." Some read "headdress" or "girdle" (*mitran*) instead of "womb" (*metran*).

*

8:18 Jdt 5:20–21; 11:10.
8:19 Ps 78:56–57; 106:13–14; Jer 7:16–20.
8:25 Dt 8:5; Tb 12:14; Ps 94:12; Prv 3:11–12; Wis 3:4–6; Sir 2:1–6; Heb 12:5–6.
8:25 Gn 22:1–19; 32:22–32; Ex 20:20; Dt 8:16.
8:30 Ex 32:22; 1 Sm 15:20–24.
9:1 Ex 30:7–8; 1 Chr 28:18; Ezr 9:5; Ps 141:2; Dn 9:21.

you handed over their rulers to slaughter; and
you handed over to bloodshed the bed in which
they lay deceived, the same bed that had felt the
shame of their own deceiving. You struck down
the slaves together with their masters, and the
masters upon their thrones.† 4 Their wives you
handed over to plunder, and their daughters to
captivity, and all the spoils you divided among
your favored children, who burned with zeal for
you and in their abhorrence of the defilement of
their blood called on you for help. O God, my
God, hear me also, a widow.
5 "It is you who were the author of those events
and of what preceded and followed them. The
present and the future you have also planned.*
Whatever you devise comes into being. 6 The
things you decide come forward and say, 'Here
we are!' All your ways are in readiness, and your
judgment is made with foreknowledge.*
7 "Here are the Assyrians, a vast force, priding
themselves on horse and chariot, boasting of the
power of their infantry, trusting in shield and
spear, bow and sling.* They do not know that
you are the Lord who crushes wars;† 8 Lord is
your name. Shatter their strength in your might,
and crush their force in your wrath.* For they
have resolved to profane your sanctuary, to de-
file the tent where your glorious name resides,
and to break off the horns of your altar with the
sword. 9 † See their pride, and send forth your
fury upon their heads.* Give me, a widow, a
strong hand to execute my plan.* 10 By the deceit
of my lips, strike down slave together with ruler,
and ruler together with attendant. Crush their
arrogance by the hand of a female.*
11 †* "Your strength is not in numbers, nor
does your might depend upon the powerful.*
You are God of the lowly, helper of those of lit-
tle account, supporter of the weak, protector of
those in despair, savior of those without hope.
12 "Please, please, God of my father, God of
the heritage of Israel, Master of heaven and earth,
Creator of the waters, King of all you have cre-
ated, hear my prayer! 13 Let my deceitful words†
* wound and bruise those who have planned
dire things against your covenant, your holy tem-
ple, Mount Zion, and the house your children
possess.* 14 Make every nation and every tribe
know clearly that you are God, the God of all
power and might, and that there is no other who
shields the people of Israel but you alone."

Judith Prepares to Depart

10 1 As soon as Judith had ceased her prayer
to the God of Israel and finished all these
words, 2 she rose from the ground. She called her
maid and they went down into the house, which
she used only on sabbaths and feast days. 3 She
took off the sackcloth she had on, laid aside the
garments of her widowhood, washed her body
with water, and anointed herself with rich oint-
ment. She arranged her hair, put on a diadem,
and dressed in the festive attire she had worn
while her husband, Manasseh, was living.* 4 She
chose sandals for her feet, and put on her an-
klets, bracelets, rings, earrings, and all her other
jewelry.* Thus she made herself very beautiful,
to entice the eyes of all the men who should see
her.†
5 She gave her maid a skin of wine and a jug
of oil. She filled a bag with roasted grain, dried
fig cakes, and pure bread.† * She wrapped all her
dishes and gave them to the maid to carry.*
6 Then they went out to the gate of the city
of Bethulia and found Uzziah and the elders of
the city, Chabris and Charmis, standing there.
7 When they saw Judith transformed in looks
and differently dressed, they were very much as-
tounded at her beauty and said to her, 8 "May the
God of our ancestors grant you favor and make

---

†

9:3 Because Shechem had deceived and violated Dinah, her brothers, Simeon and Levi, tricked Shechem and the men of his city into being circumcised, and then killed them while they were recovering from the circumcision (Gn 34:13–29).

9:7–8 *You are the Lord who crushes wars; Lord is your name*: cf. Ex 15:3, "The Lord is a warrior; Lord is his name" and Jdt 16:2, "The Lord is a God who crushes wars."

9:9–10 In a five-fold petition, Judith asks that God see their pride, send fury on their heads, give her a strong hand, strike down the enemy through her deceit, and crush their pride by the hand of a female (*theleia*, see also 13:15 and 16:5, rather than the more usual *gyne*, *woman*). In an androcentric society, there was no greater dishonor for a male than that he die at the hand of a female (see Jgs 9:53–54). Nine verses emphasize that by her hand God's deliverance is accomplished: 8:33; 9:9, 10; 12:4; 13:4, 14, 15; 15:10; and 16:5.

9:11–12 Ten titles for God are arranged in two groups of five on either side of the repeated Greek particle, *nai nai* ("verily" or "please"). The title "Master of heaven and earth" (v. 12; see notes on 1:11 and 5:20) is unique to Judith in the Septuagint, as are also "God of the heritage of Israel" and "Creator of the waters."

9:13 *Deceitful words*: twice Judith asks God to make her a successful liar in order to preserve her people (vv. 10, 13).

10:4 Judith's beauty overcomes all who meet her (8:7; 10:7, 14, 19, 23; 11:21, 23; 12:13).

10:5 Concern for Israel's dietary laws, reflected in her selection of wine, roasted grain, and bread, emphasizes Judith's religious fidelity (cf. 1 Sm 25:18 and Dn 1:8–16).

---

*

9:5 Is 41:22–23; 42:9; 43:9; 44:7; 46:10.
9:6 Jb 38:35; Is 46:9–13; Bar 3:35.
9:7 Ex 15:1, 21.
9:8 Ex 15:3; Ps 46:9–10; 76:4–5.
9:9 Ex 15:7.
9:9 Ex 3:19–20; 4:2, 4, 6, 7, 17, 20; 5:21; 6:1; 7:4, 5, 15, 17, 19; 8:1, 2, 12, 13; 9:3, 22; 10:12, 21, 22; 12:11; 13:3, 9, 14, 16; 14:16, 21, 26, 27; 15:6, 9, 12, 20; Jgs 5:26.
9:10 Jgs 4:9.
9:11 Ps 33:16–17.
9:11 Ex 15:2; Jgs 7:2; 1 Sm 17:45–47; 2 Chr 16:8–9.
9:13 Jdt 10:4; 11:20, 23; 16:6, 9; Est C:24.
9:13 Dn 11:28.
10:3 Gn 43:24; Lv 8:6; 22:6; Tb 6:3; Ez 16:4, 9.
10:4 Gn 24:47, 53; 35:4; Ex 3:22; 12:35; 32:3; 35:22; Nm 31:50; Is 3:18, 21; Hos 2:15.
10:5 1 Sm 25:18.
10:5 Jdt 12:2; Est C:28.

your design successful, for the glory of the Isra-
elites and the exaltation of Jerusalem." 9 Judith
bowed down to God.

Judith and Her Maid Leave Bethulia

Then she said to them, "Order the gate of the
city opened for me, that I may go to accomplish
the matters we discussed." So they ordered the
young men to open the gate for her, as she had
requested, 10 and they did so. Then Judith and her
maidservant went out. The men of the city kept
her in view as she went down the mountain and
crossed the valley; then they lost sight of her.

IV. Judith Goes out to War†

11 As Judith and her maid walked directly across
the valley, they encountered the Assyrian patrol.
12 The men took her in custody and asked her,
"To what people do you belong? Where do you
come from, and where are you going?"* She re-
plied: "I am a daughter of the Hebrews, and I am
fleeing from them, because they are about to be
delivered up to you as prey. 13 I have come to see
Holofernes, the ranking general of your forces,
to give him a trustworthy report; in his presence
I will show him the way by which he can ascend
and take possession of the whole hill country
without a single one of his men suffering injury
or loss of life."*

14 When the men heard her words and gazed
upon her face, which appeared marvelously
beautiful to them, they said to her, 15 "By hasten-
ing down to see our master, you have saved your
life. Now go to his tent; some of us will accom-
pany you to hand you over to him. 16 When you
stand before him, have no fear in your heart; give
him the report you have given us, and he will
treat you well." 17 So they selected a hundred of
their men as an escort for her and her maid, and
these conducted them to the tent of Holofernes.

18 As the news of her arrival spread among the
tents, a crowd gathered in the camp. They came
and stood around her as she waited outside the
tent of Holofernes, while he was being informed
about her. 19 They marveled at her beauty, regard-
ing the Israelites with wonder because of her,
and they said to one another, "Who can despise
this people who have such women among them?
It is not good to leave one of their men alive, for
if any were to be spared they could beguile the
whole earth."

Judith Meets Holofernes

20 Then the guards of Holofernes and all his at-
tendants came out and ushered her into the tent.
21 Holofernes was reclining on his bed under a
canopy† woven of purple, gold, emeralds, and
other precious stones. 22 When they announced
her to him, he came out to the front part of the
tent, preceded by silver lamps. 23 When Judith
came before Holofernes and his attendants, they
all marveled at the beauty of her face. She fell
prostrate and paid homage to him, but his ser-
vants raised her up.*

11 1 Then Holofernes said to her: "Take cour-
age, woman! Have no fear in your heart! I
have never harmed anyone who chose to serve
Nebuchadnezzar, king of all the earth. 2 As for
your people who live in the hill country, I would
never have raised my spear against them, had
they not insulted me. They have brought this
upon themselves. 3 But now tell me why you
have fled from them and come to us? In any
case, you have come to safety. Take courage!
Your life is spared tonight and for the future.*
4 No one at all will harm you. Rather, you will be
well treated, as are the servants of my lord, King
Nebuchadnezzar."

5 Judith answered him: "Listen to the words
of your servant, and let your maidservant speak
in your presence! I will say nothing false to my
lord† this night. 6 If you follow the words of your
maidservant, God will successfully perform a deed
through you, and my lord will not fail to achieve
his designs.† 7 I swear by the life of Nebuchad-
nezzar, king of all the earth, and by the power of
him who has sent you to guide all living things,
that not only do human beings serve him through
you; but even the wild animals, and the cattle, and
the birds of the air, because of your strength, will
live for Nebuchadnezzar and his whole house.*
8 Indeed, we have heard of your wisdom and clev-
erness.* The whole earth is aware that you above
all others in the kingdom are able, rich in experi-
ence, and distinguished in military strategy.

†

10:11–13:20 In this section Judith and her maid arrive in the Assyrian camp (10:11–19), where Judith meets (10:20–12:9) and triumphs over Holofernes (12:10–13:10a). Then she and her maid return to Bethulia and announce the victory (13:10b–20).

10:21 *Canopy*: netting for protection against insects. A prized possession in this story (cf. 13:15; 16:19).

11:5–6 Here the word "lord" has a double meaning, indicating both Holofernes and God. Much irony is evident in Judith's conversation with Holofernes (e.g., 12:4).

11:6 *Designs*: cf. 10:8; 11:6; 13:5 where this word is used as a synonym for Judith's "affair" (8:34), which she kept secret as she carried out the plan of her God (8:15, 16), unlike her counterpart Nebuchadnezzar, who told all the details of his plan (2:2, 4).

*

10:12 Gn 16:8.
10:13 Jdt 11:5–6.
10:23 Ru 2:10; 1 Sm 25:41; 2 Sm 14:4.
11:3 2 Mc 11:19.
11:7 Jgs 8:19; 1 Sm 14:45; 25:26; 28:10; 2 Sm 11:11; Ez 17:16; Dn 2:38.
11:8 Sir 1:6; 42:18.

9 * "As for Achior's speech in your council, we
have heard it. When the men of Bethulia res-
cued him, he told them all he had said to you.
10 So then, my lord and master, do not disregard
his word, but bear it in mind, for it is true. In-
deed our people are not punished, nor does the
sword prevail against them, except when they
sin against their God.* 11 But now their sin† has
caught up with them, by which they will bring
the wrath of their God upon them when they
do wrong; so that my lord will not be repulsed
and fail, but death will overtake them. 12 Because
their food has given out and all their water is
running low, they have decided to kill their an-
imals, and are determined to consume all the
things which God in his laws has forbidden them
to eat. 13 They have decided that they would use
the first fruits of grain and the tithes of wine and
oil, which they had consecrated and reserved
for the priests who minister in the presence of
our God in Jerusalem—things which the people
should not so much as touch with their hands.*
14 They have sent messengers to Jerusalem to
bring back permission from the senate, for even
there people have done these things.* 15 On the
very day when the response reaches them and
they act upon it, they will be handed over to you
for destruction.

16 "As soon as I, your servant, learned all this,
I fled from them. God has sent me to perform
with you such deeds as will astonish people
throughout the whole earth who hear of them.
17 Your servant is, indeed, a God-fearing woman,
serving the God of heaven night and day. Now
I will remain with you, my lord; but each night
your servant will go out into the valley and pray
to God. He will tell me when they have commit-
ted their offenses. 18 Then I will come and let you
know, so that you may march out with all your
forces, and not one of them will be able to with-
stand you. 19 I will lead you through the heart of
Judea until you come to Jerusalem, and there in
its center I will set up your throne. You will drive
them like sheep that have no shepherd, and not
even a dog will growl at you.* This was told to
me in advance and announced to me, and I have
been sent to tell you."

20 Her words pleased Holofernes and all his
attendants. They marveled at her wisdom and
exclaimed, 21 "No other woman from one end
of the earth to the other looks so beautiful and
speaks so wisely!" 22 Then Holofernes said to
her: "God has done well in sending you ahead
of your people, to bring victory to our hands,
and destruction to those who have despised my
lord. 23 You are not only beautiful in appearance,
but you are also eloquent. If you do as you have
said, your God will be my God;† you will live in
the palace of King Nebuchadnezzar and be re-
nowned throughout the whole earth."

12 1 Then he ordered them to lead her into
the room where his silver dinnerware was
kept, and ordered them to set a table for her
with his own delicacies to eat and his own wine
to drink. 2 But Judith said, "I cannot eat any† of
them, because it would be a scandal.* Besides, I
will have enough with the things I brought with
me." 3 Holofernes asked her, "But if your pro-
visions give out, where can we get more of the
same to provide for you? None of your people
are with us." 4 Judith answered him, "As surely
as you live, my lord, your servant will not use up
her supplies before the Lord accomplishes by my
hand what he has determined."

5 Then the attendants of Holofernes led her to
her tent, where she slept until the middle of the
night. Toward the early morning watch, she rose*
6 and sent this message to Holofernes, "Give or-
ders, my lord, to let your servant go out for
prayer." 7 So Holofernes ordered his guards not
to hinder her. Thus she stayed in the camp three
days. Each night she went out to the valley of
Bethulia, where she bathed herself† at the spring
of the camp.* 8 After bathing, she prayed to the
Lord, the God of Israel, to direct her way for the
triumph of her people. 9 Then she returned puri-
fied to the tent and remained there until her food
was brought to her toward evening.*

Judith at the Banquet of Holofernes

10 On the fourth day Holofernes gave a ban-
quet for his servants alone, to which he did
not invite any of the officers. 11 And he said to
Bagoas, the eunuch in charge of his personal af-
fairs, "Go and persuade the Hebrew woman in

† **11:11** *Sin*: but in 8:18–20 Judith asserts that the people have not committed idolatry in recent generations.

11:23 *Your God will be my God*: in 3:8, Holofernes insisted that Nebuchadnezzar alone is god.

12:2 *Cannot eat any*: the food of Gentiles was avoided by pious Jews (see Dn 1:8, 13, 15; Tb 1:10–11) because it might have been prohibited as unclean (see Lv 11:13–44), sacrificed to idols (see Ex 34:15; Dt 32:37–38), or contaminated with blood (see Lv 7:26–27). In addition, eating together symbolized the sharing of life.

12:7 *Bathed herself*: she bathes to purify herself after contact with the Gentiles. Her nightly departure from the camp provides for her escape (cf. 13:10).

11:9–10 Jdt 5:5.
11:10 Jdt 5:21; 8:18.
11:13 Nm 18:8–9.
11:14 1 Mc 2:31–41.
11:19 Ex 11:7.
12:2 Tb 1:10–11; Est C:28; 1 Mc 1:62–63; 2 Mc 5:27; 6:18–7:2; Dn 1:8.
12:5 Ex 14:24; 1 Sm 11:11.
12:7 Tb 7:9.
12:9 2 Sm 3:35.

Live It!

Dead Drunk!

Getting drunk is a pretty common way for people to have a good time—young and old. It seems like harmless fun, but we all know that it can lead to some dire consequences. It is very easy to be taken advantage of when you are drunk or passed out. Every year we learn of college students who have died from too much alcohol. And drinking and driving can be deadly.

In the Book of Judith, chapter 13, Judith takes advantage of Holofernes' drunkenness to kill him. She gives the term *dead drunk* a whole new meaning. If you do not believe that getting drunk can destroy your life, think again. It doesn't take a widow with a sword to help drunkenness destroy your life.

▶ **Jdt 12:15—13:10**

your care to come and to eat and drink with us.
12 It would bring shame on us to be with such a
woman without enjoying her. If we do not se-
duce her, she will laugh at us."*
13 So Bagoas left the presence of Holofernes,
and came to Judith and said, "So lovely a maid-
servant should not be reluctant to come to my
lord to be honored by him, to enjoy drinking
wine with us, and to act today like one of the
Assyrian women who serve in the palace of Neb-
uchadnezzar." 14 Judith replied, "Who am I to
refuse my lord? Whatever is pleasing to him I will
promptly do. This will be a joy† for me until the
day of my death."
15 So she proceeded to put on her festive gar-
ments and all her finery. Meanwhile her servant
went ahead and spread out on the ground oppo-
site Holofernes the fleece Bagoas had furnished
for her daily use in reclining while eating.*
16 Then Judith came in and reclined. The heart
of Holofernes was in rapture over her and his
passion was aroused. He was burning with the
desire to possess her, for he had been biding his
time to seduce her from the day he saw her.*
17 Holofernes said to her, "Drink and be happy
with us!" 18 Judith replied, "I will gladly drink,
my lord, for today is the greatest day of my whole
life." 19 She then took the things her servant had
prepared and ate and drank in his presence.
20 Holofernes, charmed by her, drank a great
quantity of wine, more than he had ever drunk
on any day since he was born.

Judith Beheads Holofernes

13 1 When it grew late, his servants quickly
withdrew. Bagoas closed the tent from the
outside and dismissed the attendants from their
master's presence. They went off to their beds,
for they were all tired because the banquet had
lasted so long. 2 Judith was left alone in the tent
with Holofernes, who lay sprawled on his bed,
for he was drunk with wine. 3 Judith had ordered
her maidservant to stand outside the bedcham-
ber and to wait, as on the other days, for her to
come out; she had said she would be going out
for her prayer. She had also said this same thing
to Bagoas.
4 When all had departed, and no one, small
or great, was left in the bedchamber, Judith
stood by Holofernes' bed and prayed silently,
"O Lord, God of all might, in this hour look
graciously on the work of my hands for the
exaltation of Jerusalem. 5 Now is the time for
aiding your heritage and for carrying out my
design to shatter the enemies who have risen
against us."* 6 She went to the bedpost near the
head of Holofernes, and taking his sword from
it, 7 she drew close to the bed, grasped the hair
of his head, and said, "Strengthen me this day,
Lord, God of Israel!" 8 Then with all her might
she struck his neck twice and cut off his head.*
9 She rolled his body off the bed and took the
canopy from its posts. Soon afterward, she came
out and handed over the head of Holofernes to
her maid, 10 who put it into her food bag. Then
the two went out together for prayer as they were
accustomed to do.

Judith and Her Maid Return to Bethulia

They passed through the camp, and skirting
that valley, went up the mountain to Bethulia,
and approached its gates. 11 From a distance, Ju-
dith shouted to the guards at the gates: "Open!
Open the gate! God, our God, is with us. Once
more he has shown his strength in Israel and his
power against the enemy, as he has today!"

† 12:14 *Joy*: the irony of this response is obvious; see also the joy of 14:9 and Judith's "new song" in chap. 16.

* **12:12** Dn 13:37, 54, 57–58.
12:15 Tb 9:6; Ez 23:41.
12:16 Dn 13:20, 39.
13:5 Gn 24:45; 1 Sm 1:13.
13:8 Jgs 4:21; 1 Sm 17:51; 31:9.

Judith Displays the Head of Holofernes

12 † When the citizens heard her voice, they
hurried down to their city gate and summoned
the elders of the city. 13 All the people, from the
least to the greatest, hurriedly assembled, for her
return seemed unbelievable. They opened the
gate and welcomed the two women. They made
a fire for light and gathered around the two.
14 Judith urged them with a loud voice: "Praise
God, give praise! Praise God, who has not with-
drawn his mercy from the house of Israel, but
has shattered our enemies by my hand this very
night!" 15 Then she took the head out of the bag,
showed it to them, and said: "Here is the head
of Holofernes, the ranking general of the Assyr-
ian forces, and here is the canopy under which
he lay in his drunkenness. The Lord struck him
down by the hand of a female!† 16 Yet I swear
by the Lord, who has protected me in the way
I have walked, that it was my face that seduced
Holofernes to his ruin, and that he did not defile
me with sin or shame."
17 All the people were greatly astonished. They
bowed down and worshiped God, saying with
one accord, "Blessed are you, our God, who
today have humiliated the enemies of your peo-
ple." 18 Then Uzziah said to her, "Blessed are you,
daughter, by the Most High God, above all the
women on earth; and blessed be the Lord God,
the creator of heaven and earth, who guided your
blow at the head of the leader of our enemies.*
19 Your deed of hope will never be forgotten by
those who recall the might of God.* 20 May God
make this redound to your everlasting honor, re-
warding you with blessings, because you risked
your life when our people were being oppressed,
and you averted our disaster, walking in the
straight path before our God." And all the people
answered, "Amen! Amen!"*

V. Victory and Thanksgiving†

Judith's Plan of Attack

14 1 Then Judith said to them: "Listen to me,†
my brothers and sisters. Take this head
and hang it on the parapet of your wall.* 2 At
daybreak, when the sun rises on the earth, each

Did You Know?

Violence in the Old Testament

Is it hard to believe that God strengthened Judith to cut off Holofernes' head (see Jdt 13:7–8)? or that God was angry at Saul for not destroying Agag and his possessions (see 1 Sm 15:18–19)? or that Jephthah had to sacrifice his daughter because of a vow he had made (see Jgs 11:29–40)? The violence portrayed in the Old Testament is often horrifying, especially when the Old Testament authors view it as part of God's will.

In the ancient world, tribes and nations viewed their gods as the leaders of their armies. The Hebrews were no exception. One of God's oldest titles is "LORD, God of hosts" (Ps 89:9, Is 6:3), the image is of an almighty warrior who fought on Israel's side (see Ex 15:3, 1 Sm 14:23). The enemies of Israel were seen as God's enemies, and their destruction as God's will. The military victories of Joshua, Saul, and David were understood as proof of heaven's blessing on the nation.

Later in history, as the Israelites experienced one agonizing defeat after another and the prophets challenged them to consider God's love for all nations, a new understanding of God's will began to develop in certain Jewish circles. Later prophets spoke of beating "swords into plowshares" (Is 2:4), of making "a covenant of peace" (Ez 37:26), of seeking "to do justice and to love goodness, / and to walk humbly with your God" (Mi 6:8). From their own painful history, the Chosen People started to see that war and violence always meant unspeakable suffering for many, and they began to question whether holy war was part of God's will.

▶ Jdt 13:1–10

†

13:12–20 Elements from chaps. 8–9 are echoed here. The assembly of the people at Judith's return parallels the meeting of the town officials summoned by Judith in 8:10. Uzziah blesses Judith in 8:5 and again in 13:18–20.

13:15 *By the hand of a female*: cf. 16:5 and note on 9:9–10.

14:1–16:25 This section describes Judith's plan to attack the Assyrian camp (14:1–5) and its execution (14:11–15:7). Between the plan and its execution, Achior identifies the head of Holofernes and is converted to Judaism. The book concludes with the victory celebration (15:8–14), hymn of thanksgiving (16:1–20), and a description of Judith's final days (16:21–25). Elements from chaps. 8–9 recur here: Judith, widow of Manasseh (8:2; 16:22), lived alone in Bethulia on her estate (8:4; 16:22), with servants and property (8:7; 16:21). Judith's instructions begin with the words "listen to me" (8:11; 14:1). Her prayer for success (9:1–14) is balanced by a prayer and display of success in 14:14–16.

14:1–5 *Listen to me*: an imperative (used also in 8:11, 32) opens

*

13:18 Jgs 5:24; Lk 1:42.
13:19 Sir 35:9.
13:20 Dt 27:15–26; Ps 41:14; 72:19; 89:53.
14:1 1 Sm 17:54; 31:9–10; 2 Sm 20:21; 2 Kgs 10:7–8; 1 Mc 7:47; 2 Mc 15:30; Mt 14:8.

of you seize your weapons, and let all the able-
bodied men rush out of the city under command
of a captain, as if about to go down into the val-
ley against the Assyrian patrol, but without going
down. 3 The Assyrians will seize their weapons
and hurry to their camp to awaken the generals of
the army. When they run to the tent of Holofer-
nes and do not find him, panic will seize them,
and they will flee before you.* 4 Then you and
all the other inhabitants of the whole territory of
Israel will pursue them and strike them down in
their tracks. 5 But before doing this, summon for
me Achior the Ammonite, that he may see and
recognize the one who despised the house of Is-
rael and sent him here to meet his death."

Achior's Conversion†

6 So they called Achior from the house of
Uzziah. When he came and saw the head of
Holofernes in the hand of one of the men in the
assembly of the people, he collapsed in a faint.
7 Then, after they lifted him up, he threw himself
at the feet of Judith in homage, saying: "Blessed
are you in every tent of Judah! In every nation,
all who hear your name will be struck with ter-
ror.* 8 But now, tell me all that you did during
these days." So Judith told him, in the midst of
the people, all that she had done, from the day
she left until the time she began speaking to
them. 9 When she had finished her account, the
people cheered loudly, so that the city resounded
with shouts of joy. 10 Now Achior, seeing all that
the God of Israel had done, believed firmly in
God. He circumcised the flesh of his foreskin and
he has been united with the house of Israel to the
present day.*

Panic in the Assyrian Camp

11 At daybreak they hung the head of Hol-
ofernes on the wall. Then all the Israelite men
took up their weapons and went out by groups
to the mountain passes.* 12 When the Assyrians
saw them, they notified their commanders, who,
in turn, went to their generals, their division
leaders, and all their other leaders. 13 They came
to the tent of Holofernes and said to the one in
charge of all his things, "Awaken our lord, for
the slaves have dared come down against us in
battle, to their utter destruction." 14 So Bagoas
went in and knocked at the entry of the tent,
presuming that Holofernes was sleeping with
Judith. 15 When no one answered, he parted the
curtains, entered the bedchamber, and found
him thrown on the floor dead, with his head
gone! 16 He cried out loudly, weeping, groaning,
and howling, and tore his garments. 17 Then he
entered the tent where Judith had her quarters;
and, not finding her, he rushed out to the troops
and cried: 18 "The slaves have duped us! One He-
brew woman has brought shame on the house of
King Nebuchadnezzar. Look! Holofernes on the
ground—without a head!"*
19 When the leaders of the Assyrian forces heard
these words, they tore their tunics and were over-
come with great distress. Their loud cries and
shouts were heard throughout the camp.

15 1 On hearing what had happened, those
still in their tents were horrified. 2 Over-
come with fear and dread, no one kept ranks any
longer. They scattered in all directions, and fled
along every path, both through the valley and
in the hill country.* 3 Those who were stationed
in the hill country around Bethulia also took to
flight. Then the Israelites, every warrior among
them, came charging down upon them.
4 Uzziah sent messengers to Betomasthaim, to
Choba and Kona, and to the whole territory of
Israel to report what had happened and to urge
them all to attack the enemy and destroy them.
5 On hearing this, all the Israelites, with one ac-
cord, attacked them and cut them down as far as
Choba. Even those from Jerusalem and the rest
of the hill country took part in this, for they too
had been notified of the happenings in the camp
of their enemy. The Gileadites and the Galileans
struck the enemy's flanks with great slaughter,
even beyond Damascus and its borders. 6 The
remaining people of Bethulia swept down on
the camp of the Assyrians, plundered it, and
acquired great riches. 7 The Israelites, when they
returned from the slaughter, took possession of
what was left. Even the towns and villages in the
hill country and on the plain got an enormous
quantity of spoils, for there was a tremendous
amount of it.

†

Judith's instruction that the people display the head of Holofernes on the parapet and themselves in ranks before the enemy at daybreak. The strategy is to throw the Assyrians into panic and strike them down in their confusion; cf. 15:1–3.

14:6–10 Recognizing the head of Holofernes, Achior faints. Then he throws himself down before Judith, acclaiming her blessed in Judah and every nation. After listening to all she had done, Achior is circumcised and joins the house of Israel. Since this violates the prohibition of Dt 23:4 that no Ammonite or Moabite shall enter the assembly, even to the tenth generation, some suggest that the book was not included in the Hebrew scriptures for this reason. However, see Is 56:3–6.

*

14:3 1 Mc 7:44.
14:7 Jgs 5:24.
14:10 Dt 23:4.
14:11 2 Mc 8:23; 12:20.
14:18 Jgs 9:54.
15:2 Gn 9:2; Dt 11:25; 1 Mc 7:18; Sir 4:17.

Israel Celebrates Judith's Victory

[8]Then the high priest Joakim and the senate
of the Israelites who lived in Jerusalem came to
see for themselves the good things that the Lord
had done for Israel, and to meet and congratu-
late Judith. [9]When they came to her, all with one
accord blessed her, saying:

"You are the glory of Jerusalem!†
You are the great pride of Israel!
You are the great boast of our nation!
10 By your own hand you have done all this.
You have done good things for Israel,
and God is pleased with them.
May the Almighty Lord bless you forever!"

And all the people said, "Amen!"

[11]For thirty days† all the people plundered
the camp, giving Judith the tent of Holofernes,
with all his silver, his beds, his dishes, and all
his furniture. She took them and loaded her
mule, hitched her carts, and loaded these things
on them.

[12]All the women of Israel gathered to see her,
and they blessed her and performed a dance in
her honor.* She took branches in her hands
and distributed them to the women around her,
[13]and she and the other women crowned them-
selves with olive leaves. Then, at the head of all
the people, she led the women in the dance,
while the men of Israel followed, bearing their
weapons, wearing garlands and singing songs
of praise. [14]† Judith led all Israel in this song of
thanksgiving, and the people loudly sang this
hymn of praise:

Pray It!

Judith Leads the Prayer-Song

In the Book of Judith, chapter 16, Judith sings praises to God and leads the people in a holy celebration after victory over the enemy.

Notice the similarity to Miriam's song (see Exodus, chapter 15), Deborah's song (see Judges, chapter 5), and even Tobit's song (see Tobit, chapter 13).

Singing, dancing, and retelling special stories go hand in hand with praising God. Try singing a favorite religious or spiritual song as your prayer today.

▶ **Jdt 16:1–20**

Judith's Hymn of Deliverance

16 [1]And Judith sang:

"Strike up a song to my God with tambourines,*
sing to the Lord with cymbals;
Improvise for him a new song,
exalt and acclaim his name.
2 For the Lord is a God who crushes wars;*
he sets his encampment among his people;
he delivered me from the hands of my pursuers.
3 "The Assyrian came from the mountains of the north,
with myriads of his forces he came;
Their numbers blocked the wadis,
their cavalry covered the hills.
4 He threatened to burn my territory,
put my youths to the sword,
Dash my infants to the ground,
seize my children as plunder.
And carry off my virgins as spoil.
5 "But the Lord Almighty thwarted them,
by the hand of a female!
6 Not by youths was their champion struck down,*
nor did Titans bring him low,
nor did tall giants attack him;*
But Judith, the daughter of Merari,
by the beauty of her face brought him down.
7 She took off her widow's garb
to raise up the afflicted in Israel.

†

15:9 In the Lectionary of the Catholic Church, this passage is one of several choices for feasts of Mary (e.g., the Presentation of Mary). These words of praise are also echoed in antiphons for the Liturgy of the Hours on Marian feasts.

15:11 *Thirty days*: the central actions in each half of the book are accomplished in a total of thirty-four days. Bethulia was without water for thirty-four days (7:20). Judith spent four days in the enemy camp and the Israelites plunder the Assyrian camp for thirty days.

15:14–16:17 Judith's hymn of deliverance is patterned on the Song of Miriam (Ex 15:20–21).

*

15:12 Ex 15:20; Jgs 11:34; 1 Sm 18:6; Jer 31:4.
16:1 Gn 31:27; Ex 15:20; 1 Sm 18:6; 2 Sm 6:5; 1 Chr 13:8; Ps 68:26; 81:3; 149:3; Jer 31:4.
16:2 Ex 15:3; Ps 46:10.
16:6 1 Sm 17:4, 51.
16:6 Gn 6:1–4; Dt 2:10, 21; 2 Sm 21:16–22; 1 Chr 20:4–8.

She anointed her face with fragrant oil;
8 fixed her hair with a diadem,
and put on a linen robe to beguile him.
9 Her sandals ravished his eyes,*
her beauty captivated his mind,
the sword cut through his neck!*

10 "The Persians trembled at her boldness,
the Medes were daunted at her daring.
11 When my lowly ones shouted,
and my weak ones cried out,
The enemy was terrified,
screamed and took to flight.
12 Sons of maidservants pierced them through;
wounded them like deserters' children.
They perished before the ranks of my Lord.

13 "I will sing a new song to my God.*
O Lord, great are you and glorious,
marvelous in power and unsurpassable.
14 Let your every creature serve you;
for you spoke, and they were made.
You sent forth your spirit, and it created them;*
no one can resist your voice.*
15 For the mountains to their bases
are tossed with the waters;
the rocks, like wax, melt before your
glance.*

"But to those who fear you,
you will show mercy.
16 Though the sweet fragrance of every sacrifice
is a trifle,
and the fat of all burnt offerings but little
in your sight,
one who fears the Lord is forever great.

17 "Woe to the nations that rise against my
people!
the Lord Almighty will requite them;
in the day of judgment he will punish
them:
He will send fire and worms into their
flesh,*
and they will weep and suffer forever."

18 When they arrived at Jerusalem, they wor-
shiped God. As soon as the people were purified,
they offered their burnt offerings, voluntary of-
ferings, and donations.* 19 Judith dedicated to
God all the things of Holofernes that the people
had given her, putting under the ban the canopy
that she herself had taken from his bedcham-
ber.* 20 For three months the people continued
their celebration in Jerusalem before the sanctu-
ary, and Judith remained with them.

The Renown and Death of Judith

21 When those days were over, all of them
returned to their inheritance. Judith went back
to Bethulia and remained on her estate. For the
rest of her life she was renowned throughout the
land. 22 Many wished to marry her, but she gave
herself to no man all the days of her life from
the time her husband, Manasseh, died and was
gathered to his people. 23 Her fame continued to
increase, and she lived in the house of her hus-
band, reaching the advanced age of one hundred
and five.† * She set her maid free. And when she
died in Bethulia, they buried her in the cave of
her husband, Manasseh;* 24 and the house of Is-
rael mourned her for seven days.† * Before she
died, she distributed her property to the relatives
of her husband, Manasseh, and to her own rel-
atives.*

25 * During the lifetime of Judith and for a
long time after her death, no one ever again
spread terror† among the Israelites.

---

†

16:23 *One hundred and five*: long life was a sign of blessing (see Jb 42:16; Prv 16:31; 20:29). The fact that the Maccabean period was one hundred and five years long (168–63 B.C.) may account for assigning this age to Judith.

16:24 *Seven days*: the customary period for mourning the dead (1 Sm 31:13).

16:25 *Spread terror*: Judith is compared to the heroes of the Book of Judges (cf. Jgs 3:11, 30).

*

16:9 Sg 7:2; Ez 16:10.
16:9 Jgs 5:26.
16:13 Ps 33:3; 40:4; 96:1; 98:1; 144:9; 149:1; Is 42:10.
16:14 Gn 1; Ps 104:30; 148:5.
16:14 Est C:3–4; Ps 33:9; Is 55:11.
16:15 Ps 97:5; Mi 1:4; Na 1:5.
16:17 Sir 7:17; Is 66:24; Mk 9:48.
16:18 Nm 19:11–22; 31:19.
16:19 Lv 7:16.
16:23 Jb 42:16; Prv 16:31; 20:29; Sir 18:9; Lk 2:36.
16:23 Gn 23:19; 25:9; 49:29–32; 50:13.
16:24 Gn 50:3; 1 Sm 31:13; 1 Chr 10:12; Sir 22:12.
16:24 Nm 27:6–11.
16:25 Jgs 3:11, 30; 5:31; 8:28.

Most of us cannot understand what would possess a group of people to plot the complete destruction of another group of people. Yet, in our own time, ethnic groups have been targeted for extinction through wars, concentration camps, and death squads. The Book of Esther is the story of a genocidal plot against a Jewish population and how Mordecai and his courageous cousin Esther prevented the plot from being carried out.

At a Glance

I. Prologue (A:1–17).

II. Esther Becomes Queen (1:1—2:23).

III. Haman's Plot Against the Jews (3:1–13; B:1–7; 3:14–15).

IV. Esther and Mordecai Plead for Help (4:1–16; C:1—D:16; 5:1–5).

V. Haman's Downfall (5:6—8:2).

VI. The Jewish Victory and the Feast of Purim (8:3–12; E:1–24; 8:13—9:23).

VII. Epilogue: The Rise of Mordecai (9:24—10:3; F:1–11).

Quick Facts

Setting: Persia after the Babylonian Exile

Inspired Authors: *Hebrew version.* unknown, probably written in the third or second century BC
Greek version. unknown, written between 116 to 48 BC.

Themes: God's love for the little ones, the origin of the feast of Purim

Of Note: Catholic Bibles include the Greek version of Esther, inserted as additions A to F.

In Depth

In the five centuries before Jesus, many of the Jewish people who were uprooted from their homeland had to be on the lookout for their safety. Several of the late Old Testament books—Sirach, Tobit, and Daniel—reflect the challenges these emigrant Jews had to face. The story of Queen Esther belongs to this group. Like Joseph in Egypt, Esther rose to a position of power in a foreign government. When a plot was hatched to destroy the Jews, she used her influence with the king of Persia to save her people. Each year, Esther's victory is celebrated in the Jewish feast of Purim (see 9:18–32)—the feast of little people who have triumphed over larger forces.

Like the Book of Daniel, the Book of Esther has come down to us in two versions: the Hebrew and the Greek. The difference in style between these two versions is obvious:

- The shorter Hebrew text is clearly not a historical document and does not even mention God's name. The Greek text, a later reworking of the Hebrew, adds sections to bring out the religious dimension of the story and to make the book appear more historical.
- The Hebrew version emphasizes the human actors; the Greek version, the divine Actor. The two versions stress different aspects of the same truth: God is the Savior of the Chosen People (Greek) but works through human beings to achieve that goal (Hebrew).

Despite the confusing numbering, the book reads as a unified story; it's full of action and has a happy ending. What is more, it challenges us to recognize in our hatred of others the seeds of unthinkable destruction.

Esther

I. Prologue

Dream of Mordecai

A 1 In the second year of the reign of Ahasuerus
the great, on the first day of Nisan, Morde-
cai, son of Jair, son of Shimei, son of Kish, of the
tribe of Benjamin, had a dream.† * 2 † He was a
Jew residing in the city of Susa, a prominent man
who served at the king's court, 3 and one of the
captives whom Nebuchadnezzar, king of Bab-
ylon, had taken from Jerusalem with Jeconiah,
king of Judah.*
4 * This was his dream.† There was noise and
tumult, thunder and earthquake—confusion
upon the earth. 5 Two great dragons advanced,
both poised for combat. They uttered a mighty
cry, 6 and at their cry every nation prepared for
war, to fight against the nation of the just. 7 It was
a dark and gloomy day. Tribulation and distress,
evil and great confusion, lay upon the earth. 8 The
whole nation of the just was shaken with fear at
the evils to come upon them, and they expected
to perish. 9 * Then they cried out to God, and
from their crying there arose, as though from a
tiny spring, a mighty river, a flood of water. 10 The
light of the sun broke forth; the lowly were ex-
alted and they devoured the boastful.
11 Having seen this dream and what God in-
tended to do, Mordecai awoke. He kept it in
mind, and tried in every way, until night, to un-
derstand its meaning.

Mordecai Thwarts an Assassination†

12 * Mordecai lodged in the courtyard with Big-
than and Teresh, two eunuchs of the king who
guarded the courtyard. 13 He overheard them plot-
ting, investigated their plans, and discovered that
they were preparing to assassinate King Ahasuerus.
So he informed the king about them. 14 The king
had the two eunuchs questioned and, upon their
confession, put to death. 15 Then the king had these
things recorded; Mordecai, too, put them into writ-
ing. 16 The king also appointed Mordecai to serve at
the court, and rewarded him for his actions.*
17 Haman, however, son of Hammedatha, a

†

A:1 The genealogy of Mordecai is designed to reflect opposition to Israel's enemy Haman, an Agagite (v. 17). In 1 Sm 15:1–9, Saul (whose father's name was Kish, of the tribe of Benjamin) conquered Agag the Amalekite.

A:2–3 Repeats information from 2:5–6, on which see note, but states that Mordecai is already a court official. In the Hebrew text, Mordecai is not given this rank until 7:10–8:2.

A:4 An interpretation of the dream that relates its features to the plot of the book is given in F:1–6.

A:12–17 Retells the story in 2:21–23, but with several differences. Addition A has Mordecai inform the king directly, whereas in 2:22 Mordecai informs the king through Esther after she has become queen. A:16 has Mordecai rewarded immediately after his service, whereas the Hebrew text defers the reward of Mordecai to 6:3–13. In A:17, the failure of the eunuchs' plot becomes Haman's reason for seeking the destruction of Mordecai and his people, something which the Hebrew text attributes to Mordecai's refusal to bow to Haman (see note on 3:2).

*

A:1 Est 2:5.
A:3 Est 2:6; 2 Kgs 24:15; 2 Chr 36:9–10; Jer 22:24–30; 24:1; 29:1–2.
A:4–10 Est F:2, 4–6.
A:9–10 Est F:3.
A:12–15 Est 2:21–23; 6:1–3.
A:16 Est 6:3.

Bougean,† who was held in high honor by the
king, sought to harm Mordecai and his people
because of the two eunuchs of the king.*

II. Esther Becomes Queen

The Banquet of Ahasuerus

1 1 † During the reign of Ahasuerus—the same
Ahasuerus who ruled over a hundred and
twenty-seven provinces from India to Ethiopia—
2 while he was occupying the royal throne in
the royal precinct of Susa,† 3 in the third year of
his reign, he gave a feast for all his officials and
ministers: the Persian and Median army officers,
the nobles, and the governors of the provinces.*
4 For as many as a hundred and eighty days, he
displayed the glorious riches of his kingdom and
the resplendent wealth of his royal estate.

5 At the end of this time the king gave a feast
of seven days in the garden court of the royal
palace for all the people, great and small, who
were in the royal precinct of Susa. 6 There were
white cotton draperies and violet hangings, held
by cords of fine crimson linen from silver rings
on marble pillars. Gold and silver couches were
on a mosaic pavement, which was of porphyry,
marble, mother-of-pearl, and colored stones.
7 Drinks were served in a variety of golden cups,
and the royal wine flowed freely, as befitted the
king's liberality. 8 By ordinance of the king the
drinking was unstinted, for he had instructed all
the stewards of his household to comply with the
good pleasure of everyone. 9 Queen Vashti also
gave a feast for the women in the royal palace of
King Ahasuerus.

Refusal of Vashti

10 On the seventh day, when the king was merry
with wine, he instructed Mehuman, Biztha, Har-
bona, Bigtha, Abagtha, Zethar, and Carkas, the
seven eunuchs who attended King Ahasuerus,*
11 to bring Queen Vashti into his presence wear-
ing the royal crown, that he might display her
beauty to the populace and the officials, for she
was lovely to behold. 12 But Queen Vashti re-
fused to come at the royal order issued through
the eunuchs. At this the king's wrath flared up,
and he burned with fury. 13 He conferred with
the sages who understood the times, because the
king's business was conducted in general consul-
tation with lawyers and jurists. 14 He summoned
Carshena, Shethar, Admatha, Tarshish, Meres,
Marsena, and Memucan, the seven Persian and
Median officials who were in the king's personal
service and held first rank in the realm,* 15 and
asked them, "What is to be done by law with
Queen Vashti for disobeying the order of King
Ahasuerus issued through the eunuchs?"

16 In the presence of the king and of the offi-
cials, Memucan answered: "Queen Vashti has not
wronged the king alone, but all the officials and
the populace throughout the provinces of King
Ahasuerus. 17 For the queen's conduct will become
known to all the women, and they will look with
disdain upon their husbands when it is reported,
'King Ahasuerus commanded that Queen Vashti
be ushered into his presence, but she would not
come.' 18 This very day the Persian and Median
noblewomen who hear of the queen's conduct
will recount it to all the royal officials, and dis-
dain and rancor will abound. 19 If it please the
king, let an irrevocable royal decree† be issued by
him and inscribed among the laws of the Persians
and Medes, forbidding Vashti to come into the
presence of King Ahasuerus and authorizing the
king to give her royal dignity to one more worthy
than she.* 20 Thus, when the decree that the king
will issue is published throughout his realm, vast
as it is, all wives will honor their husbands, from
the greatest to the least."

21 This proposal pleased the king and the offi-
cials, and the king acted on the advice of Memu-
can. 22 He sent letters to all the royal provinces,
to each province in its own script and to each
people in its own language, to the effect that ev-
ery man should be lord in his own home.

The Search for a New Queen

2 1 After this, when King Ahasuerus' wrath had
cooled, he thought over what Vashti had done
and what had been decreed against her. 2 Then the
king's personal attendants suggested: "Let beauti-
ful young virgins be sought for the king. 3 Let the
king appoint emissaries in all the provinces of his

†

A:17 *A Bougean*: the origin of this term is unknown; it may represent a garbled attempt to render the Hebrew "Agagite" (3:1). In the Greek additions Haman not only knows the plot to assassinate the king, but is apparently a co-conspirator.

1:1 The Hebrew text opens with a portrait of the power and luxury of the Persian king Ahasuerus (Xerxes I, whose empire consisted of only about thirty provinces).

1:2 Susa was the winter capital of the Persian empire. The "royal precinct" (sometimes translated "stronghold" or "citadel") was a well-fortified section of the city that included the king's residence. The Book of Esther depicts other citizens living in this section as well.

1:19 *An irrevocable royal decree*: the first of several in the book. In a satiric portrayal, even a minor domestic disagreement is resolved through a sweeping international edict. The irrevocable nature of the decree is intended to increase its force, but creates problems if the king needs to adapt to new information or conditions. See note on 8:8.

*

A:17 Est 3:1–15; B:1–7; E:13.
1:3 Jdt 1:16.
1:10 Dn 5:1.
1:14 1 Chr 12:32; Ezr 7:14.
1:19 Est 8:5, 8; Dn 6:8–9.

EST

Did You Know?

Diaspora Jews

The fictional story of Esther implies that Mordecai and Esther were members of the Diaspora. The Greek word *diaspora* means "scattered abroad." It refers to the Jews who lived outside of Palestine. When the Babylonians destroyed Jerusalem (587 BC), many of the Jews who were forced to leave the land of Israel decided to settle in various Greco-Roman cities and not return home. They maintained their Jewish identity by adapting the language and customs of their new home into their Jewish traditions. The Diaspora Jews were responsible for the translation of the Hebrew Bible into Greek, a translation called the Septuagint.

realm to gather all beautiful young virgins into the
harem in the royal precinct of Susa. Under the
care of the royal eunuch Hegai, guardian of
the women, let cosmetics be given them. 4 Then
the young woman who pleases the king shall
reign in place of Vashti." This suggestion pleased
the king, and he acted accordingly.
5 There was in the royal precinct of Susa a certain Jew named Mordecai,† son of Jair, son of
Shimei, son of Kish, a Benjaminite, 6 who had
been exiled from Jerusalem with the captives
taken with Jeconiah, king of Judah, whom Nebuchadnezzar, king of Babylon, had deported.*
7 He became foster father to his cousin Hadassah, that is, Esther,† when she lost both father
and mother. The young woman was beautifully
formed and lovely to behold. On the death of
her father and mother, Mordecai adopted her as
his own daughter.*
8 When the king's order and decree had been
proclaimed and many young women brought
together to the royal precinct of Susa under the
care of Hegai, Esther also was brought in to the
royal palace under the care of Hegai, guardian
of the women. 9 The young woman pleased him
and won his favor. So he promptly furnished her
with cosmetics and provisions. Then choosing
seven maids for her from the royal palace, he
transferred both her and her maids to the best
place in the harem. 10 Esther did not reveal her
nationality or family, for Mordecai had commanded her not to do so.
11 Day by day Mordecai would walk about in
front of the court of the harem to learn how Esther was faring and what was to become of her.
12 After the twelve months' preparation decreed
for the women, each one went in turn to visit
King Ahasuerus. During this period of beautifying treatment, six months were spent with oil of
myrrh, and the other six months with perfumes
and cosmetics. 13 Then, when each one was to visit
the king, she was allowed to take with her from
the harem to the royal palace whatever she chose.
14 She would go in the evening and return in the
morning to a second harem under the care of the
royal eunuch Shaashgaz, guardian of the concubines. She could not return to the king unless he
was pleased with her and had her summoned by
name.* 15 As for Esther, daughter of Abihail and
adopted daughter of his nephew Mordecai, when
her turn came to visit the king, she did not ask
for anything but what the royal eunuch Hegai,
guardian of the women, suggested. And she won
the admiration of all who saw her.

Ahasuerus Chooses Esther

16 Esther was led to King Ahasuerus in his palace in the tenth month, Tebeth, in the seventh
year of his reign. 17 The king loved Esther more
than all other women, and of all the virgins she
won his favor and good will. So he placed the
royal crown on her head and made her queen
in place of Vashti. 18 Then the king gave a great
feast in honor of Esther to all his officials and
servants, granting a holiday to the provinces and
bestowing gifts with royal generosity.

Mordecai Thwarts an Assassination†

19 * As was said, from the time the virgins had
been brought together, and while Mordecai was
passing his time at the king's gate, 20 Esther had
not revealed her family or nationality, because
Mordecai had told her not to; and Esther continued to follow Mordecai's instructions, just as

†

2:5 *Mordecai*: a Babylonian name, deriving from the god Marduk. Like Esther, Mordecai may have had a Jewish name as well, although in his case we do not know what it is. The chronology of the book makes him well over one hundred years old, since he was deported with Jehoiachin about 598 B.C.; cf. A:1.

2:7 *Esther*: a Babylonian name, deriving from the goddess Ishtar. She is given a Hebrew name as well, "Hadassah," which means "myrtle."

2:19–23 This story is retold and placed at the beginning of the book in Greek addition A:12–17, with significant differences (see note). The Greek also has a translation of the account in 2:19–23 at this point in the narrative.

*

2:6 Est A:3; 2 Kgs 24:15; 2 Chr 36:9–10; Jer 22:24–30; 24:1; 29:1–2.
2:7 Est 2:15.
2:14 Est 2:19–20; 4:11, 16.
2:19–20 Est 2:14.

EST

Catholic Social Teaching

Body Count

G*enocide.* Such a frightening word. The complete destruction of a people. This is what King Ahasuerus plots in the Book of Esther: to destroy all the Jews in his kingdom. Fortunately, he does not succeed.

In our time, we know only too well that the past two centuries have been marked by many attempts to exterminate whole groups of people. The most systematic and ambitious of these attempts was that of Adolf Hitler and the Third Reich. Six million Jews were put to death in Nazi concentration camps, along with four million other "undesirables." Every decade seems to bring new stories of genocide and "ethnic cleansing" somewhere on our planet.

Catholic social teaching calls us to solidarity. That means we cannot avoid the fact that as followers of Christ, we are brothers and sisters with everyone in the world. We are one human family, despite our cultural and ethnic differences. And we must strive to promote peace in a world that often seems dedicated to violence. We need to work for justice, which will lead to a lasting peace. We must always think globally, for we are part of a very large family!

What can you do to promote solidarity in your school, parish, or community?

▶ **Est 3:1–7**
Solidarity

she had when she was being brought up by him. 21 * During the time that Mordecai spent at the king's gate, Bigthan and Teresh, two of the royal eunuchs who guarded the entrance, became angry and plotted to assassinate King Ahasuerus. 22 When the plot became known to Mordecai, he told Queen Esther, who in turn informed the king in Mordecai's name. 23 The matter was investigated and verified, and both of them were impaled on stakes.† This was written in the annals in the king's presence.

III. Haman's Plot Against the Jews

Mordecai Refuses to Honor Haman

3 1 After these events King Ahasuerus promoted Haman, son of Hammedatha the Agagite, to high rank, seating him above all his fellow officials.* 2 All the king's servants who were at the royal gate would kneel and bow down to Haman, for that is what the king had ordered in his regard.* Mordecai, however, would not kneel and bow down.† 3 The king's servants who were at the royal gate said to Mordecai, "Why do you disobey the king's order?"* 4 When they had reminded him day after day and he would not listen to them, they informed Haman, to see whether Mordecai's explanation would prevail, since he had told them that he was a Jew.

Haman's Reprisal

5 When Haman observed that Mordecai would not kneel and bow down to him, he was filled with anger. 6 But he thought it was beneath him to attack only Mordecai. Since they had told Haman of Mordecai's nationality, he sought to destroy all the Jews, Mordecai's people, throughout the realm of King Ahasuerus. 7 In the first month, Nisan, in the twelfth year of King Ahasuerus, the *pur*, or lot,† was cast in Haman's presence to determine the day and the month for the destruction of Mordecai's people on a single day, and the lot fell on the thirteenth day of the twelfth month, Adar.*

Decree Against the Jews

8 Then Haman said to King Ahasuerus: "Dispersed among the nations throughout the provinces of your kingdom, there is a certain people

†

2:23 *Impaled on stakes*: a method of execution used by the Persians, known from ancient records and reliefs.

3:2 We are not told the reasons for Mordecai's refusal to bow. It may be the result of a form of Jewish piety that refuses to offer such homage to any mortal; see also Greek addition C:5–7.

3:7 *The pur, or lot*: the Hebrew text preserves the Akkadian word *pur* because its plural, *purim*, became the name of the feast of Purim commemorating the deliverance of the Jews; cf. 9:24, 26. The lot functions as a kind of horoscope to determine the most favorable day for the pogrom.

*

2:21–23 Est A:12–15; 6:1–3.
3:1 Est B:3; 5:11; E:11.
3:2 Est C:5; 5:9, 13; 6:10, 12.
3:3 Est 4:16.
3:7 Est 9:24–32; F:10.

living apart. Their laws differ from those of every other people and they do not obey the laws of the king; so it is not proper for the king to tolerate them.* 9 If it please the king, let a decree be issued to destroy them; and I will deliver to the procurators ten thousand silver talents for deposit in the royal treasury."* 10 The king took the signet ring† from his hand and gave it to Haman, son of Hammedatha the Agagite, the enemy of the Jews.* 11 The king said to Haman, "The silver is yours, as well as the people, to do with as you please."†

12 So the royal scribes were summoned on the thirteenth day of the first month, and they wrote, at the dictation of Haman, an order to the royal satraps, the governors of every province, and the officials of every people, to each province in its own script and to each people in its own language. It was written in the name of King Ahasuerus and sealed with the royal signet ring. 13 Letters were sent by couriers to all the royal provinces, to destroy, kill and annihilate all the Jews, young and old, including women and children in one day, the thirteenth day of the twelfth month, Adar, and to seize their goods as spoil.*

B 1 This is a copy of the letter:

"The great King Ahasuerus writes to the satraps of the hundred and twenty-seven provinces from India to Ethiopia, and the governors subordinate to them, as follows: 2 When I came to rule many peoples and to hold sway over the whole world, not being carried away by a sense of my own authority but always acting fairly and with mildness, I determined to provide for my subjects a life of lasting tranquility; and, by making my kingdom civilized and safe for travel to its farthest borders, to restore the peace desired by all people.* 3 When I consulted my counselors as to how this might be accomplished, Haman, who excels among us in discretion, who is outstanding for constant good will and steadfast loyalty, and who has gained a place in the kingdom second only to me,* 4 brought it to our attention that, mixed among all the nations throughout the world, there is one people of ill will, which by its laws is opposed to every other people and continually disregards the decrees of kings, so that the unity of empire blamelessly designed by us cannot be established.*

5 "Having noted, therefore, that this nation, and it alone, is continually at variance with all people, lives by divergent and alien laws, is inimical to our government, and does all the harm it can to undermine the stability of the kingdom, 6 we hereby decree that all those who are indicated to you in the letters of Haman, who is in charge of the administration and is a second father to us, shall, together with their wives and children, be utterly destroyed by the swords of their enemies, without any pity or mercy, on the fourteenth day† of the twelfth month, Adar, of the current year;* 7 so that when these people, whose present ill will is of long standing, have gone down into Hades by a violent death on a single day, they may leave our government completely stable and undisturbed for the future."

(3) 14 A copy of the decree to be promulgated as law in every province was published to all the peoples, that they might be prepared for that day. 15 The couriers set out in haste at the king's command; meanwhile, the decree was promulgated in the royal precinct of Susa. The king and Haman then sat down to drink, but the city of Susa was thrown into confusion.

IV. Esther and Mordecai Plead for Help

Mordecai Exhorts Esther

4 1 When Mordecai learned all that was happening, he tore his garments, put on sackcloth and ashes, and went through the city crying out loudly and bitterly,* 2 till he came before the royal gate, which no one clothed in sackcloth might enter. 3 Likewise in each of the provinces, wherever the king's decree and law reached, the Jews went into deep mourning, with fasting, weeping, and lament; most of them lay on sackcloth and ashes.

4 Esther's maids and eunuchs came and told her. Overwhelmed with anguish, the queen sent garments for Mordecai to put on, so that he might take off his sackcloth; but he refused. 5 Esther then summoned Hathach, one of the king's eunuchs whom he had placed at her service, and

---

†

3:10 *Signet ring*: a ring containing a seal that was impressed on documents to authenticate them. With this ring, Haman can issue decrees in the king's name.

3:11 Although Ahasuerus seems to refuse the bribe, this is probably a polite way of accepting it that makes him appear munificent (compare Gn 23:11–15, where Ephron tells Abraham that he "gives" him the field and, after a few more pleasantries, sets a very high price for it). Both 4:7 and 7:4 seem to assume Ahasuerus has accepted the money.

B:6 *Fourteenth day*: only the Greek text here names the fourteenth of Adar as the day set aside for the destruction of the Jews. The Hebrew text consistently gives the date as the thirteenth of Adar (e.g., 3:13) as does Greek addition E:20; see note on 9:17–19.

*

3:8 Est 3:13; B:4; E:24; Wis 2:14–15; Dn 3:8–12.
3:9 Est 7:4.
3:10 Gn 41:42.
3:13 Est B:6; 7:4.
B:2 Est E:8–9.
B:3 Est 3:1; 5:11; E:11.
B:4 Est 3:8; E:24.
B:6 Est 3:13; 7:4; E:11.
4:1 Jdt 4:12.

commanded him to find out what this action of
Mordecai meant and the reason for it. 6 So Ha-
thach went out to Mordecai in the public square in
front of the royal gate, 7 and Mordecai recounted
all that had happened to him, as well as the exact
amount of silver Haman had promised to pay to
the royal treasury for the slaughter of the Jews.
8 He also gave him a copy of the written decree for
their destruction that had been promulgated in
Susa, to show and explain to Esther. Hathach was
to instruct her to go to the king and to plead and
intercede with him on behalf of her people.†
9 Hathach returned to Esther and told her what
Mordecai had said. 10 Then Esther replied to Ha-
thach and gave him this message for Mordecai:
11 "All the servants of the king and the people of
his provinces know that any man or woman who
goes to the king in the inner court without being
summoned is subject to the same law—death.
Only if the king extends the golden scepter will
such a person live. Now as for me, I have not
been summoned to the king for thirty days."*
12 When Esther's words were reported to Mor-
decai, 13 he had this reply brought to her: "Do not
imagine that you are safe in the king's palace, you
alone of all the Jews. 14 Even if you now remain
silent, relief and deliverance will come to the Jews
from another source;† but you and your father's
house will perish. Who knows—perhaps it was
for a time like this that you became queen?"
15 Esther sent back to Mordecai the response:
16 "Go and assemble all the Jews who are in Susa;
fast on my behalf, all of you, not eating or drink-
ing night or day for three days. I and my maids
will also fast in the same way. Thus prepared, I
will go to the king, contrary to the law. If I per-
ish, I perish!"* 17 Mordecai went away and did
exactly as Esther had commanded.

Prayer of Mordecai

C 1 Recalling all that the Lord had done, Mor-
decai prayed to the Lord 2 and said: "Lord,
Lord, King and Ruler of all, everything is in your
power, and there is no one to oppose you when it
is your will to save Israel. 3 You made heaven and
earth and every wonderful thing under heaven.
4 You are Lord of all, and there is no one who can
resist you, the Lord. 5 * You know all things. You
know, Lord, that it was not out of insolence or ar-
rogance or desire for glory that I acted thus in not
bowing down to the arrogant Haman. 6 I would
have gladly kissed the soles of his feet for the

Did You Know?

The Silent Women of the Bible

"Mordecai went away and did exactly as Esther had commanded him" (Est C:1). What a surprise: to hear of a man in the ancient world taking orders from a woman! As a fictional character, Esther, like Judith, has an exceptional role in the Old Testament. However, many women who appear in stories that have an historical core are not even named: Jephthah's daughter and Samson's mother, for instance. Even the Hebrew women whose names have become famous—Sarah, Rebekah, Rachel, Miriam, Bathsheba—played second fiddle to their more famous husbands. They depended on indirect influence or trickery to get what they wanted.

In the biblical world, a woman was defined by her relationships with men. Before marriage she belonged to her father's household and had no status outside of it. Once married, a woman left her father's family and joined the family of her husband. If her husband died, she remained in the new family, rearing children for her deceased spouse or, if childless, marrying a brother-in-law. Although many women undoubtedly lived happily under this system, many others just as surely suffered abuse or felt oppressed. The stories of Lot's daughters (see Gn 19:8) and the woman of Gibeah (see Jgs 19:24–30) testify to this horrifying truth.

A system of scriptural interpretation that was developed during recent decades attempts to give voice to the many silent, forgotten, abused women of the Bible. More and more biblical scholars reread the familiar stories, searching for quiet messages that have long been overlooked. All of us—males and females alike—can benefit from this effort to listen to the voices of these women who have been silenced for so many centuries.

▶ **Est 4:15—C:1**

4:8 The Greek text adds the following to Mordecai's message to Esther: "Remember the days of your lowly estate, when you were brought up in my charge; for Haman, who is second to the king, has asked for our death. Invoke the Lord and speak to the king for us: save us from death."

4:14 *From another source*: probably Mordecai refers to divine aid; the Greek additions (C) are explicit about this.

4:11 Est 2:14; 4:12; D:12.
4:16 Est C:12–13.
C:5–7 Est 3:2; 5:9.

salvation of Israel. 7 But I acted as I did so as not
to place the honor of a mortal above that of God.
I will not bow down to anyone but you, my Lord.
It is not out of arrogance that I am acting thus.
8 And now, Lord God, King, God of Abraham,
spare your people, for our enemies regard us with
deadly envy and are bent upon destroying the in-
heritance that was yours from the beginning. 9 Do
not spurn your portion, which you redeemed
for yourself out of the land of Egypt. 10 Hear my
prayer; have pity on your inheritance and turn
our mourning into feasting, that we may live to
sing praise to your name, Lord. Do not silence the
mouths of those who praise you."

11 All Israel, too, cried out with all their strength,
for death was staring them in the face.

Prayer of Esther

12 * Queen Esther, seized with mortal anguish,
fled to the Lord for refuge. 13 Taking off her splen-
did garments, she put on garments of distress and
mourning. In place of her precious ointments
she covered her head with dung and ashes. She
afflicted her body severely and in place of her fes-
tive adornments, her tangled hair covered her.

14 Then she prayed to the Lord, the God of Is-
rael, saying: "My Lord, you alone are our King.
Help me, who am alone and have no help but
you, 15 for I am taking my life in my hand.*
16 From birth, I have heard among my people that
you, Lord, chose Israel from among all nations,
and our ancestors from among all their forebears,
as a lasting inheritance, and that you fulfilled
all your promises to them.* 17 But now we have
sinned in your sight, and you have delivered us
into the hands of our enemies, 18 because we
worshiped their gods. You are just, O Lord. 19 But
now they are not satisfied with our bitter servi-
tude, but have sworn an oath to their idols 20 to
do away with the decree you have pronounced,
to destroy your inheritance, to close the mouths
of those who praise you, to extinguish the glory
of your house and your altar, 21 to open the
mouths of the nations to acclaim their worthless
gods, and to extol a mortal king forever.

22 "Lord, do not relinquish your scepter to
those who are nothing. Do not let our foes gloat
over our ruin, but turn their own counsel against
them and make an example of the one who be-
gan this against us. 23 Be mindful of us, Lord.
Make yourself known in the time of our distress
and give me courage, King of gods and Ruler
of every power. 24 Put in my mouth persuasive
words in the presence of the lion, and turn his
heart to hatred for our enemy, so that he and his
co-conspirators may perish. 25 Save us by your
power, and help me, who am alone and have no
one but you, Lord.

26 "You know all things. You know that I hate
the pomp of the lawless, and abhor the bed of
the uncircumcised or of any foreigner. 27 You
know that I am under constraint, that I abhor
the sign of grandeur that rests on my head when
I appear in public. I abhor it like a polluted rag,
and do not wear it in private. 28 I, your servant,
have never eaten at the table of Haman, nor have
I graced the banquet of the king or drunk the
wine of libations.† 29 From the day I was brought
here till now, your servant has had no joy except
in you, Lord, God of Abraham. 30 O God, whose
power is over all, hear the voice of those in de-
spair. Save us from the power of the wicked, and
deliver me from my fear."

Esther Goes to Ahasuerus†

D 1 On the third day, ending her prayers, she
took off her prayer garments and arrayed
herself in her splendid attire. 2 In making her ap-
pearance, after invoking the all-seeing God and
savior, she took with her two maids; 3 on the one
she leaned gently for support, 4 while the other
followed her, bearing her train. 5 She glowed
with perfect beauty and her face was as joyous
as it was lovely, though her heart was pounding
with fear. 6 She passed through all the portals till
she stood before the king, who was seated on his
royal throne, clothed in full robes of state, and
covered with gold and precious stones, so that he
inspired great awe. 7 As he looked up in extreme
anger, his features fiery and majestic, the queen
staggered, turned pale and fainted, collapsing
against the maid in front of her. 8 But God
changed the king's anger to gentleness. In great
anxiety he sprang from his throne, held her in his
arms until she recovered, and comforted her with
reassuring words. 9 "What is it, Esther?" he said
to her. "I am your brother.† Take courage! 10 You
shall not die; this order of ours applies only to
our subjects. 11 Come near!" 12 Raising the golden
scepter, he touched her neck with it, embraced
her, and said, "Speak to me."*

13 She replied: "I saw you, my lord, as an angel

† **C:28** *Wine of libations*: offered in sacrifice to the gods.

D:1–16 Addition D expands on and replaces 5:1–2 of the Hebrew text.

D:9 *Brother*: along with "sister," a common term of affection between lovers or husband and wife. See, e.g., Sg 4:9–12; 8:1; Tb 5:22; 7:11.

* **C:12–13** Est 4:16. **C:15** Est 4:16. **C:16** Dt 4:20; 7:6; 9:29; 14:2; 26:18; 32:9. **D:12** Est 4:11.

of God, and my heart was shaken by fear of
your majesty. 14 For you are awesome, my lord,
though your countenance is full of mercy." 15 As
she said this, she fainted. 16 The king was shaken
and all his attendants tried to revive her.

5 1 † [Now on the third day, Esther put on her
royal garments and stood in the inner court-
yard, looking toward the royal palace, while the
king was seated on his royal throne in the audi-
ence chamber, facing the palace doorway. 2 When
he saw Queen Esther standing in the courtyard,
she won his favor and he extended toward her
the golden scepter he held. She came up to him,
and touched the top of the scepter.]
3 Then the king said to her, "What is it, Queen
Esther? What is your request? Even if it is half of
my kingdom, it shall be granted you."* 4 Esther
replied, "If it please your majesty, come today
with Haman to a banquet I have prepared." 5 The
king ordered, "Have Haman make haste to fulfill
the wish of Esther."

V. Haman's Downfall

First Banquet of Esther

So the king went with Haman to the banquet
Esther had prepared. 6 During the drinking of the
wine, the king said to Esther, "Whatever you ask
for shall be granted, and whatever request you
make shall be honored, even if it is for half my
kingdom."* 7 Esther replied: "This is my petition
and request: 8 if I have found favor with the king
and if it pleases your majesty to grant my peti-
tion and honor my request, let the king come
with Haman tomorrow to a banquet I will pre-
pare; and tomorrow I will do as the king asks."

Haman's Plot Against Mordecai

9 That day Haman left happy and in good spir-
its. But when he saw that Mordecai at the royal
gate did not rise, and showed no fear of him,
he was filled with anger toward him.* 10 Haman
restrained himself, however, and went home,
where he summoned his friends and his wife Ze-
resh. 11 He recounted the greatness of his riches,
the large number of his sons, and how the king
had promoted him and placed him above the
officials and royal servants.* 12 "Moreover," Ha-
man added, "Queen Esther invited no one but
me to come with the king to the banquet she pre-
pared; again tomorrow I am to be her guest with
the king. 13 Yet none of this satisfies me as long as
I continue to see the Jew Mordecai sitting at the
royal gate."* 14 His wife Zeresh and all his friends
said to him, "Have a stake set up, fifty cubits in
height, and in the morning ask the king to have
Mordecai impaled on it. Then go to the banquet
with the king in good spirits." This suggestion
pleased Haman, and he had the stake erected.*

Mordecai's Reward from the King

6 1 That night the king, unable to sleep, asked
that the chronicle of notable events be brought
in. While this was being read to him, 2 the passage
occurred in which Mordecai reported Bigthan and
Teresh, two of the royal eunuchs who guarded the
entrance, for seeking to assassinate King Ahasue-
rus.* 3 The king asked, "What was done to honor
and exalt Mordecai for this?" The king's atten-
dants replied, "Nothing was done for him."*
4 † "Who is in the court?" the king asked.
Now Haman had entered the outer court of the
king's palace to suggest to the king that Mordecai
should be impaled on the stake he had raised
for him.* 5 The king's attendants answered him,
"Haman is waiting in the court." The king said,
"Let him come in." 6 When Haman entered, the
king said to him, "What should be done for the
man whom the king wishes to reward?" Now Ha-
man thought to himself, "Whom would the king
wish to honor more than me?" 7 So he replied to
the king: "For the man whom the king wishes to
honor 8 there should be brought the royal robe
the king wore and the horse the king rode with
the royal crest placed on its head. 9 The robe
and the horse should be given to one of the no-
blest of the king's officials, who must clothe the
man the king wishes to reward, have him ride on
the horse in the public square of the city, and cry
out before him, 'This is what is done for the man
whom the king wishes to honor!' "* 10 Then the
king said to Haman: "Hurry! Take the robe and
horse as you have proposed, and do this for the
Jew Mordecai, who is sitting at the royal gate. Do
not omit anything you proposed."* 11 So Haman
took the robe and horse, clothed Mordecai, had
him ride in the public square of the city, and
cried out before him, "This is what is done for
the man whom the king wishes to honor!"

---

†

5:1–2 The Hebrew text translated here is a short form of the account which is in Greek addition D.

6:4–13 Haman's presumption that the king wants to honor him creates the irony that Haman himself prescribes and fulfills the elaborate terms of Mordecai's reward. This comic reversal mirrors the fatal reversal to come: Haman and those who hate the Jews find that their plot to destroy them recoils on their own head.

*

5:3 Est 5:6; 7:2; 9:12.
5:6 Est 5:3.
5:9 Est 3:2–3; C:5–7; 6:10, 12.
5:11 Est 3:1; B:3; E:11; 9:6–10.
5:13 Est 3:2–3; 6:10, 12.
5:14 Est 6:4; 7:9–10.
6:2 Est A:12–14; 2:21–23.
6:3 Est A:16.
6:4 Est 5:14; 7:9–10.
6:9 Gn 41:42–43; 1 Kgs 1:33; Dn 5:29.
6:10 Est 2:21; 3:2–3; 5:9, 13.

12 Mordecai then returned to the royal gate, while
Haman hurried home grieving, with his head cov-
ered.* 13 When he told his wife Zeresh and all his
friends everything that had happened to him, his
advisers and his wife Zeresh said to him, "If Mor-
decai, before whom you are beginning to fall, is of
Jewish ancestry, you will not prevail against him,
but will surely be defeated by him."

Esther's Second Banquet

14 While they were speaking with him, the
king's eunuchs arrived and hurried Haman off to
the banquet Esther had prepared.

7 1 So the king and Haman went to the banquet
with Queen Esther. 2 Again, on this second
day, as they were drinking wine, the king said to
Esther, "Whatever you ask, Queen Esther, shall
be granted you. Whatever request you make,
even for half the kingdom, shall be honored."*
3 Queen Esther replied: "If I have found favor
with you, O king, and if it pleases your majesty,
I ask that my life be spared, and I beg that you
spare the lives of my people. 4 For we have been
sold, I and my people, to be destroyed, killed,
and annihilated. If we were only to be sold into
slavery I would remain silent, for then our dis-
tress would not have been worth troubling the
king."* 5 King Ahasuerus said to Queen Esther,
"Who and where is the man who has dared to do
this?"* 6 Esther replied, "The enemy oppressing
us is this wicked Haman." At this, Haman was
seized with dread of the king and queen.
7 The king left the banquet in anger and went
into the garden of the palace, but Haman stayed
to beg Queen Esther for his life, since he saw
that the king had decided on his doom. 8 When
the king returned from the palace garden to the
banquet hall, Haman had thrown himself on
the couch on which Esther was reclining; and the
king exclaimed, "Will he also violate the queen
while she is with me in my own house!" Scarcely
had the king spoken when the face of Haman
was covered over.

Punishment of Haman

9 * Harbona, one of the eunuchs who attended
the king, said, "At the house of Haman stands
a stake fifty cubits high. Haman made it for
Mordecai, who gave the report that benefited the
king." The king answered, "Impale him on it."
10 So they impaled Haman on the stake he had
set up for Mordecai, and the anger of the king
abated.

8 1 That day King Ahasuerus gave the house of
Haman, enemy of the Jews, to Queen Esther;
and Mordecai was admitted to the king's pres-
ence, for Esther had revealed his relationship to
her.* 2 The king removed his signet ring that he
had taken away from Haman, and gave it to Mor-
decai; and Esther put Mordecai in charge of the
house of Haman.*

VI. The Jewish Victory and the Feast of Purim

The Second Royal Decree

3 Esther again spoke to the king. She fell at
his feet and tearfully implored him to revoke
the harm done by Haman the Agagite and the
plan he had devised against the Jews. 4 The king
stretched forth the golden scepter to Esther. So
she rose and, standing before him, 5 said: "If it
seems good to the king and if I have found favor
with him, if the thing seems right to the king
and I am pleasing in his eyes, let a document
be issued to revoke the letters that the schemer
Haman, son of Hammedatha the Agagite, wrote
for the destruction of the Jews in all the royal
provinces.* 6 For how can I witness the evil that
is to befall my people, and how can I behold the
destruction of my kindred?"
7 King Ahasuerus then said to Queen Esther and
to the Jew Mordecai: "Now that I have given Es-
ther the house of Haman, and they have impaled
him on the stake because he was going to attack
the Jews, 8 * you in turn may write in the king's
name what you see fit concerning the Jews and
seal the letter with the royal signet ring." For a
decree written in the name of the king and sealed
with the royal signet ring cannot be revoked.†
9 At that time, on the twenty-third day of the
third month, Sivan, the royal scribes were sum-
moned. Exactly as Mordecai dictated, they wrote
to the Jews and to the satraps, governors, and
officials of the hundred and twenty-seven prov-
inces from India to Ethiopia: to each province

---

† **8:8** *A decree written . . . cannot be revoked*: the king cannot directly grant Esther's request (v. 5) to revoke the previous decree against the Jews because of the irrevocable character of the laws of the Medes and Persians (see 1:19 and note). He can, however, empower Esther to issue another decree in his name to counteract the earlier one. The second decree authorizes the Jews to defend themselves against those who would kill them, which is what they do in 9:2. This is why the outcome of the two decrees is that the attackers are killed instead of the Jews, rather than a simple cancellation of all hostilities.

---

* **6:12** Est 2:21; 3:2–3; 5:9, 13. **7:2** Est 5:3. **7:4** Est 3:13; B:6. **7:5** Est 3:8–9. **7:9–10** Est 5:14; 6:4. **8:1** Est 9:1; Prv 11:8; 26:27; Mt 7:2. **8:2** Prv 13:22; Dn 2:48–49. **8:5** Est 1:19. **8:8** Est 1:19.

in its own script and to each people in its own
language, and to the Jews in their own script and
language. 10 These letters, which he wrote in the
name of King Ahasuerus and sealed with the
royal signet ring, he sent by mounted couriers
riding thoroughbred royal steeds. 11 * In these
letters the king authorized the Jews in each and
every city to gather and defend their lives, to de-
stroy, kill, and annihilate every armed group of
any nation or province that might attack them,
along with their wives and children, and to seize
their goods as spoil 12 on a single day throughout
the provinces of King Ahasuerus, the thirteenth
day of the twelfth month, Adar.

E 1 The following is a copy of the letter:
"The great King Ahasuerus to the governors
of the provinces in the hundred and twenty-sev-
en satrapies from India to Ethiopia, and to those
who are loyal to our government: Greetings!
2 "Many have become more ambitious the
more they were showered with honors through
the bountiful generosity of their patrons. 3 Not
only do they seek to do harm to our subjects
but, incapable of dealing with such greatness,
they even begin plotting against their own bene-
factors. 4 Not only do they drive out gratitude
from among humankind but, with the arrogant
boastfulness of those to whom goodness has no
meaning, they suppose they will escape the stern
judgment of the all-seeing God.
5 "Often, too, the fair speech of friends en-
trusted with the administration of affairs has
induced many placed in authority to become
accomplices in the shedding of innocent blood,
and has involved them in irreparable calamities
6 by deceiving with malicious slander the sincere
good will of rulers. 7 This can be verified in the
ancient stories that have been handed down to
us, but more fully when you consider the wicked
deeds perpetrated in your midst by the pestilen-
tial influence of those undeserving of authority.
8 * We must provide for the future, so as to ren-
der the kingdom undisturbed and peaceful for
all people, 9 taking advantage of changing condi-
tions and always deciding matters coming to our
attention with equitable treatment.
10 "For instance, Haman, son of Hammeda-
tha, a Macedonian,† certainly not of Persian
blood, and very different from us in generosity,
was hospitably received by us. 11 He benefited
so much from the good will we have toward
all peoples that he was proclaimed 'our father,'
before whom everyone was to bow down; and
he attained a position second only to the royal
throne.* 12 But, unable to control his arrogance,
he strove to deprive us of kingdom and of life,
13 and by weaving intricate webs of deceit he
demanded the destruction of Mordecai, our
savior and constant benefactor, and of Esther,
our blameless royal consort, together with their
whole nation.* 14 For by such measures he hoped
to catch us defenseless and to transfer the rule of
the Persians to the Macedonians. 15 But we find
that the Jews, who were doomed to extinction by
this archcriminal, are not evildoers, but rather
are governed by very just laws 16 and are the chil-
dren of the Most High, the living God of majesty,
who has maintained the kingdom in a flourish-
ing condition for us and for our forebears.
17 "You will do well, then, to ignore the letter
sent by Haman, son of Hammedatha, 18 for he
who composed it has been impaled, together
with his entire household, before the gates of
Susa. Thus swiftly has God, who governs all,
brought just punishment upon him.*
19 "You shall exhibit a copy of this letter pub-
licly in every place to certify that the Jews may
follow their own laws 20 and that you may help
them on the day set for their ruin, the thirteenth
day of the twelfth month, Adar, to defend them-
selves against those who attack them. 21 For God,
the ruler of all, has turned that day from one of
destruction of the chosen people into one of joy
for them. 22 Therefore, you too must celebrate this
memorable day among your designated feasts
with all rejoicing, 23 so that both now and in the
future it may be a celebration of deliverance for
us and for Persians of good will, but for those
who plot against us a reminder of destruction.
24 "Every city and province without exception
that does not observe this decree shall be ruth-
lessly destroyed with fire and sword, so that it will
be left not merely untrodden by people, but even
shunned by wild beasts and birds forever."*

(8) 13 A copy of the letter to be promul-
gated as law in each and every prov-
ince was published among all the peoples, so
that the Jews might be prepared on that day to

† **E:10** *Macedonian*: throughout the book Haman is identified with terms of contempt—in the Hebrew text as an Agagite (3:1, 10; 8:3, 5; 9:24; cf. note on A:17), thus making him a descendant of Agag, king of the Amalekites, a group hated by the Israelites; in the Greek additions Haman is identified as a Macedonian, reflecting the enmity between the Persians and the Macedonians after Macedonia's conquest of Persia in the fourth century B.C.

* **8:11–12** Est 9:1–4. **E:8–9** Est B:2. **E:11** Est B:3, 6. **E:13** Est A:17. **E:18** Est 7:10; 9:14. **E:24** Est 3:8–9; B:4.

Did You Know?

Purim

The feast of Purim ("lots" in Hebrew) is a minor festival in the Jewish calendar. Purim is celebrated in late winter and is marked by the retelling of the legendary victory of Queen Esther and Mordecai, the exchange of gifts, and the sharing of meals.

▶ Est 9:20–32

avenge themselves on their enemies. 14 Couriers
mounted on royal steeds sped forth in haste at
the king's order, and the decree was promulgated
in the royal precinct of Susa.
15 Mordecai left the king's presence clothed in
a royal robe of violet and of white cotton, with a
large crown of gold and a mantle of fine crimson
linen. The city of Susa shouted with joy,* 16 and
for the Jews there was splendor and gladness, joy
and triumph. 17 In each and every province and
in each and every city, wherever the king's order
arrived, there was merriment and joy, banquet-
ing and feasting for the Jews. And many of the
peoples of the land identified themselves as Jews,
for fear of the Jews fell upon them.*

The Massacre Reversed

9 1 * When the day arrived on which the order
decreed by the king was to be carried out,
the thirteenth day of the twelfth month, Adar,
on which the enemies of the Jews had expected
to overpower them, the situation was reversed:
the Jews overpowered those who hated them.
2 The Jews mustered in their cities throughout the
provinces of King Ahasuerus to attack those who
sought to do them harm, and no one could with-
stand them, for fear of them fell upon all the peo-
ples. 3 Moreover, all the officials of the provinces,
the satraps, governors, and royal procurators sup-
ported the Jews out of fear of Mordecai; 4 for Mor-
decai was powerful in the royal palace, and the
report was spreading through all the provinces
that he was continually growing in power.
5 The Jews struck down all their enemies with
the sword, killing and destroying them; they
did to those who hated them as they pleased.*
6 * In the royal precinct of Susa, the Jews killed
and destroyed five hundred people. 7 They also
killed Parshandatha, Dalphon, Aspatha, 8 Pora-
tha, Adalia, Aridatha, 9 Parmashta, Arisai, Aridai,
and Vaizatha, 10 * the ten sons of Haman, son of
Hammedatha, the foe of the Jews. However, they
did not engage in plundering.
11 On the same day, when the number of those
killed in the royal precinct of Susa was reported to
the king, 12 he said to Queen Esther: "In the royal
precinct of Susa the Jews have killed and destroyed
five hundred people, as well as the ten sons of Ha-
man. What must they have done in the other royal
provinces! You shall again be granted whatever
you ask, and whatever you request shall be hon-
ored." 13 So Esther said, "If it pleases your majesty,
let the Jews in Susa be permitted again tomorrow
to act according to today's decree, and let the ten
sons of Haman be impaled on stakes." 14 The king
then gave an order that this be done, and the
decree was published in Susa. So the ten sons of
Haman were impaled,* 15 and the Jews in Susa
mustered again on the fourteenth of the month
of Adar and killed three hundred people in Susa.
However, they did not engage in plundering.*
16 The other Jews, who dwelt in the royal prov-
inces, also mustered and defended themselves, and
obtained rest from their enemies. They killed sev-
enty-five thousand of those who hated them, but
they did not engage in plunder.* 17 This happened
on the thirteenth day of the month of Adar.

The Feast of Purim†

On the fourteenth of the month they rested,
and made it a day of feasting and rejoicing.
18 The Jews in Susa, however, mustered on the
thirteenth and fourteenth of the month. But on
the fifteenth they rested, and made it a day of joy-
ful banqueting. 19 That is why the rural Jews, who
dwell in villages, celebrate the fourteenth of the
month of Adar as a day of joyful banqueting, a
holiday on which they send food to one another.
20 Mordecai recorded these events and sent
letters to all the Jews, both near and far, in all
the provinces of King Ahasuerus. 21 † He ordered
them to celebrate every year both the fourteenth
and the fifteenth of the month of Adar 22 as the
days on which the Jews obtained rest from their
enemies and as the month which was turned for
them from sorrow into joy, from mourning into

† **9:17–19** According to Esther, Jewish feasting on the day after the defeat of their enemies establishes the date of the holiday. Since in Susa the fighting lasts for two days, the Jews of that community initially celebrate Purim a day later than Jews elsewhere.

8:15 Dn 5:7.
8:17 Est 9:27.
9:1–2 Est 8:11–12.
9:5 Jdt 15:6.
9:6–10 Est 5:11; B:3; E:11.
9:10 Est 9:15; Jdt 15:7, 11.
9:14 Est 7:10; E:18.
9:15 Est 9:10.
9:16 Jdt 15:6.

celebration. They were to observe these days with
joyful banqueting, sending food to one another
and gifts to the poor. 23 † The Jews adopted as
a custom what they had begun doing and what
Mordecai had written to them.*

VII. Epilogue: The Rise of Mordecai

Summary of the Story

24 * Haman, son of Hammedatha the Agagite,
the foe of all the Jews, had planned to destroy
them and had cast the *pur*, or lot, for the time of
their defeat and destruction. 25 Yet, when the plot
became known to the king, the king ordered in
writing that the wicked plan Haman had devised
against the Jews should instead be turned against
Haman and that he and his sons should be im-
paled on stakes.* 26 And so these days have been
named Purim after the word *pur*.

Thus, because of all that was contained in this
letter, and because of what they had witnessed
and experienced in this event, 27 the Jews estab-
lished and adopted as a custom for themselves,
their descendants, and all who should join them,
the perpetual obligation of celebrating these two
days every year in the manner prescribed by this
letter, and at the time appointed.* 28 These days
were to be commemorated and kept in every
generation, by every clan, in every province, and
in every city. These days of Purim were never to
be neglected among the Jews, nor forgotten by
their descendants.

Esther and Mordecai Act in Concert†

29 Queen Esther, daughter of Abihail, and Mor-
decai the Jew, wrote to confirm with full authority
this second letter about Purim, 30 and Mordecai sent
documents concerning peace and security to all the
Jews in the hundred and twenty-seven provinces
of Ahasuerus' kingdom.* 31 Thus were established,
for their appointed time, these days of Purim
which Mordecai the Jew and Queen Esther had
designated for the Jews, just as they had previously
enjoined upon themselves and upon their descen-
dants the duty of fasting and supplication. 32 The
command of Esther confirmed these prescriptions
for Purim and was recorded in the book.

The Rise of Mordecai Completed

10 1 King Ahasuerus levied a tax on the land
and on the islands of the sea. 2 All the acts
of his power and valor, as well as a detailed ac-
count of the greatness of Mordecai, whom the
king promoted, are recorded in the chronicles of
the kings of Media and Persia. 3 The Jew Morde-
cai was next in rank to King Ahasuerus, in high
standing among the Jews, popular with many of
his kindred, seeking the good of his people and
speaking out on behalf of the welfare of all its
descendants.*

Mordecai's Dream Fulfilled

F 1 * Then Mordecai said: "This is the work of
God. 2 I recall the dream I had about these very
things, and not a single detail has been left unful-
filled— 3 the tiny spring that grew into a river, and
there was light, and sun, and many waters. The
river is Esther, whom the king married and made
queen. 4 The two dragons are myself and Haman.
5 The nations are those who assembled to destroy
the name of the Jews, 6 but my people is Israel,
who cried to God and was saved.

"The Lord saved his people and delivered us
from all these evils. God worked signs and great
wonders, such as have not occurred among the na-
tions. 7 For this purpose he arranged two lots:† one
for the people of God, the second for all the other
nations. 8 These two lots were fulfilled in the hour,
the time, and the day of judgment before God and
among all the nations. 9 God remembered his peo-
ple and rendered justice to his inheritance.

10 * "Gathering together with joy and happi-
ness before God, they shall celebrate these days
on the fourteenth and fifteenth of the month
Adar throughout all future generations of his
people Israel."

Colophon†

11 In the fourth year of the reign of Ptolemy
and Cleopatra, Dositheus, who said he was a
priest and Levite, and his son Ptolemy brought
the present letter of Purim, saying that it was gen-
uine and that Lysimachus, son of Ptolemy, of the
community of Jerusalem, had translated it.

†

9:21 Mordecai creates a compromise among the Jews by making Purim a two-day festival.

9:23 According to the story, the two-day celebration has its roots in popular observance, which Mordecai's leadership reinforces and regularizes.

9:29–32 In attempting to give the impression of concerted action between Esther and Mordecai, the Hebrew text here presents several unresolved difficulties. Verse 29 makes Mordecai and Esther joint authors of a letter that is ascribed in v. 32 to Esther alone. Verse 31 makes Mordecai and Esther joint authors of a letter that is ascribed in vv. 20–22 to Mordecai alone. Finally, it is difficult to see the purpose of confirming a second letter in the second letter itself.

F:7 *Two lots*: this passage of the Greek text gives an additional interpretation of the feast. The two lots are drawn by God to determine, respectively, the destiny of Israel and that of the nations; contrast with 3:7 of the Hebrew text.

F:11 Several "Ptolemies" (Greek kings reigning in Egypt) had wives named Cleopatra. This postscript dates the Greek version somewhere between 116 B.C. and 48 B.C.

*

9:23 Est 9:29.
9:24–26 Est 3:7; F:10.
9:25 Est 6:5–13.
9:27 Est 8:12, 17.
9:30 Est 9:23–26.
10:3 2 Mc 15:14.
F:1–6 Est A:4–10.
F:10 Est 3:7; 9:17–18, 21, 24–28.

The First Book of **Maccabees**

Have you ever listened as two fighting siblings tell their parents about a conflict? Usually, each child blames the other one and protests his or her complete innocence. Sometimes you have to wonder if they are even talking about the same fight. In a similar way, the author of First Maccabees, reporting on the Jewish resistance to the persecution of their pagan rulers, tells one version of the story. This book defends the violent resistance of one family, while Second Maccabees has a broader perspective in telling of other forms of Jewish resistance.

At a Glance

I. **Crisis and Response (1:1—2:70).**

II. **Leadership of Judas Maccabeus (3:1—9:22).**

III. **Leadership of Jonathan (9:23—12:53).**

IV. **Leadership of Simon (13:1—16:24).**

Quick Facts

Period Covered: from 175 to 134 BC

Inspired Author: unknown, writing around 100 BC

Theme: God brings Israel to freedom through the family of Mattathias.

Of Note: First Maccabees is not found in some Protestant Bibles (see "The Case of the Missing Books," near Tb 1:16).

In Depth

The writer of First Maccabees has a clear purpose in mind: to defend the family of Mattathias, whose sons—the Maccabees—held positions of authority in the Jewish community. The most famous of them, Judas Maccabeus, led the Jews in a successful revolt (167–164 BC) against the Greek persecution—an incredible feat given the military might of the Greeks. After Judas's death, his brothers and nephews held positions of power, and Israel remained free from foreign domination for the next hundred years.

For traditional Jews, the power of the Maccabees posed a problem: because Mattathias's bloodline could be traced to neither King David nor Aaron the priest, by what right had his descendants assumed kingly and priestly authority? Against such criticism, the author of First Maccabees tries to prove that God's plan was accomplished through Mattathias's family.

The interpretation of Jewish history contained in First Maccabees invites us to believe in God's choice of Mattathias's sons as saviors of the nation. Even more important, it invites us to believe in the utter reliability of God: "And so, consider this from generation to generation, / that none who hope in Heaven shall fail in strength" (2:61).

1 Maccabees

I. Crisis and Response

From Alexander to Antiochus

1 [1] * After Alexander the Macedonian, Philip's
son, who came from the land of Kittim,† had
defeated Darius, king of the Persians and Medes,
he became king in his place, having first ruled in
Greece. [2] He fought many battles, captured for-
tresses, and put the kings of the earth to death.
[3] He advanced to the ends of the earth, gathering
plunder from many nations; the earth fell silent
before him, and his heart became proud and ar-
rogant. [4] He collected a very strong army and won
dominion over provinces, nations, and rulers,
and they paid him tribute.

[5] But after all this he took to his bed, realizing
that he was going to die. [6] So he summoned his
noblest officers, who had been brought up with
him from his youth, and divided his kingdom
among them while he was still alive. [7] Alexander
had reigned twelve years† when he died.

[8] So his officers took over his kingdom, each in
his own territory, [9] and after his death they all put
on diadems,† and so did their sons after them for
many years, multiplying evils on the earth.

[10] There sprang from these a sinful offshoot,
Antiochus Epiphanes, son of King Antiochus,
once a hostage at Rome. He became king in the
one hundred and thirty-seventh year† of the king-
dom of the Greeks.

Lawless Jews

[11] * In those days there appeared in Israel trans-
gressors of the law who seduced many, saying:
"Let us go and make a covenant with the Gentiles
all around us; since we separated from them,
many evils have come upon us." [12] The proposal
was agreeable; [13] some from among the people
promptly went to the king, and he authorized
them to introduce the ordinances of the Gentiles.
[14] Thereupon they built a gymnasium† in Jeru-
salem according to the Gentile custom. [15] They
disguised their circumcision and abandoned the

†

1:1 *Land of Kittim*: Greece. The name referred originally to inhabitants of Kiti, capital of the isle of Cyprus, then to any Cypriots (Is 23:1; Jer 2:10), later to Greeks in general, and finally even to Romans. See note on Dn 11:30. *Darius*: Darius III, Codoman (336–331 B.C.).

1:7 *Twelve years*: 336–323 B.C. The division of the empire was not fully settled until 305 B.C.

1:9 *Diadems*: decorated bands of white cloth worn around the head, symbolizing kingship. The Ptolemies, based in Egypt, controlled Judea until 198 B.C., when they were replaced by the Seleucids, based in Syria.

1:10 *The one hundred and thirty-seventh year*: Antiochus IV seized the throne in September, 175 B.C. Dates are given in this book according to the beginning of the Seleucid era, which however was reckoned in two different ways. Antiochians considered this date to be October, 312 B.C. (Syrian calendar), while Babylonians and Jewish priests accepted April, 311 B.C. as the commencement of the era (Temple calendar). The author of 1 Maccabees dates political events by the Syrian calendar but religious events by the Temple calendar. Accordingly, the civil New Year occurred variously in September or October, the religious New Year in March or April.

1:14 *Gymnasium*: symbol and center of Greek athletic and intellectual life, it was the chief instrument of Hellenistic culture. Jewish youth were attracted by sports and encouraged to join youth clubs. They received training in military skills and in the duties of citizens. Many were won over to paganism, and some even sought surgical correction of their circumcision (since physical exercise was carried out in nudity).

1:1–10 Dn 8:20–22; 11:3–4, 21. **1:11–15** 2 Mc 4:12–17.

holy covenant; they allied themselves with the
Gentiles and sold themselves to wrongdoing.

Antiochus in Egypt

16 * When his kingdom seemed secure, An-
tiochus undertook to become king of the land
of Egypt and to rule over both kingdoms. 17 He
invaded Egypt with a strong force, with char-
iots, elephants† and cavalry, and with a large
fleet, 18 to make war on Ptolemy,† king of Egypt.
Ptolemy was frightened at his presence and fled,
and many were wounded and fell dead. 19 The
fortified cities in the land of Egypt were captured,
and Antiochus plundered the land of Egypt.

Robbery of the Temple

20 * After Antiochus had defeated Egypt in the
one hundred and forty-third year,† he returned and
went up against Israel and against Jerusalem with a
strong force. 21 He insolently entered the sanctuary†
and took away the golden altar, the lampstand for
the light with all its utensils, 22 the offering table,
the cups and bowls, the golden censers, and the
curtain. The cornices and the golden ornament
on the facade of the temple—he stripped it all off.
23 And he took away the silver and gold and the pre-
cious vessels; he also took all the hidden treasures
he could find. 24 Taking all this, he went back to his
own country. He shed much blood and spoke with
great arrogance.

25 And there was great mourning throughout all
  Israel,
26 and the rulers and the elders groaned.
Young women and men languished,
  and the beauty of the women faded.
27 Every bridegroom took up lamentation,
  while the bride sitting in her chamber
  mourned,
28 And the land quaked on account of its
  inhabitants,
  and all the house of Jacob was clothed with
  shame.

Attack and Occupation

29 * Two years later, the king sent the Mysian
commander† to the cities of Judah, and he came
to Jerusalem with a strong force. 30 He spoke to
them deceitfully in peaceful terms, and they be-
lieved him. Then he attacked the city suddenly,
in a great onslaught, and destroyed many of
the people in Israel. 31 He plundered the city
and set fire to it, demolished its houses and its
surrounding walls. 32 And they took captive the
women and children, and seized the animals.
33 Then they built up the City of David with a
high, strong wall and strong towers, and it be-
came their citadel.† 34 There they installed a sin-
ful race, transgressors of the law, who fortified
themselves inside it. 35 They stored up weapons
and provisions, depositing there the plunder
they had collected from Jerusalem, and they be-
came a great snare.

36 The citadel became an ambush against the
  sanctuary,
  and a wicked adversary to Israel at all
  times.
37 They shed innocent blood around the
  sanctuary;
  they defiled the sanctuary.
38 Because of them the inhabitants of Jerusalem
  fled away,
  she became the abode of strangers.
She became a stranger to her own offspring,
  and her children forsook her.
39 * Her sanctuary became desolate as a
  wilderness;
  her feasts were turned into mourning,
Her sabbaths to shame,
  her honor to contempt.
40 As her glory had been, so great was her
  dishonor:
  her exaltation was turned into mourning.

Religious Persecution

41 * Then the king wrote to his whole kingdom
that all should be one people, 42 and abandon
their particular customs. All the Gentiles con-
formed to the command of the king, 43 and many
Israelites delighted in his religion; they sacrificed
to idols and profaned the sabbath.
44 The king sent letters by messenger to Jerusa-
lem and to the cities of Judah, ordering them to

1:17 *Elephants*: an important part of Seleucid armament (cf. 6:34–37).

1:18 Ptolemy VI Philometer, a nephew of Antiochus.

1:20 *Defeated Egypt in the one hundred and forty-third year*: 169 B.C. No mention is made in 1 Maccabees of the second expedition to Egypt a year later, described in 2 Mc 5:1, 11; Dn 11:25, 29 records both.

1:21 *Entered the sanctuary*: to pay his soldiers, Antiochus seized the sacred vessels and the money deposited at the Temple (see 2 Mc 3:10–11).

1:29 *Mysian commander*: in 2 Mc 5:24 he is identified as "Apollonius, commander of the Mysians" (mercenaries from Asia Minor). The Greek text of 1 Mc 1:29 ("chief collector of tribute") reflects a misreading of the Hebrew original.

1:33 *Citadel*: literally, *akra* means fortress. This was a garrison for foreign troops and renegade Jews that was established near the Temple area and fell to Simon only in 141 B.C. (13:49–50).

1:16–19 2 Mc 5:1–10; Dn 11:25–30.
1:20–24 2 Mc 5:11–21.
1:29–40 2 Mc 5:24–26.
1:39–40 Am 8:10; Tb 2:6.
1:41–64 2 Mc 6:1–11.

follow customs foreign to their land; 45 to prohibit burnt offerings, sacrifices, and libations in the sanctuary, to profane the sabbaths and feast days, 46 to desecrate the sanctuary and the sacred ministers, 47 to build pagan altars and temples and shrines, to sacrifice swine and unclean animals, 48 to leave their sons uncircumcised, and to defile themselves with every kind of impurity and abomination; 49 so that they might forget the law and change all its ordinances. 50 Whoever refused to act according to the command of the king was to be put to death.*

51 In words such as these he wrote to his whole kingdom. He appointed inspectors over all the people, and he ordered the cities of Judah to offer sacrifices, each city in turn. 52 Many of the people, those who abandoned the law, joined them and committed evil in the land. 53 They drove Israel into hiding, wherever places of refuge could be found.

54 On the fifteenth day of the month Kislev, in the year one hundred and forty-five,† the king erected the desolating abomination upon the altar of burnt offerings, and in the surrounding cities of Judah they built pagan altars.* 55 They also burned incense at the doors of houses and in the streets. 56 Any scrolls of the law† that they found they tore up and burned. 57 Whoever was found with a scroll of the covenant, and whoever observed the law, was condemned to death by royal decree. 58 So they used their power against Israel, against those who were caught, each month, in the cities. 59 On the twenty-fifth day of each month they sacrificed on the pagan altar that was over the altar of burnt offerings. 60 In keeping with the decree, they put to death women who had their children circumcised, 61 and they hung their babies from their necks; their families also and those who had circumcised them were killed.

62 But many in Israel were determined and resolved in their hearts not to eat anything unclean; 63 they preferred to die rather than to be defiled with food or to profane the holy covenant; and they did die. 64 And very great wrath came upon Israel.

Mattathias and His Sons

2 1 In those days Mattathias, son of John, son of Simeon, a priest of the family of Joarib,* left Jerusalem and settled in Modein.† 2 He had five sons: John, who was called Gaddi; 3 Simon, who was called Thassi; 4 Judas, who was called Maccabeus; 5 Eleazar, who was called Avaran; and Jonathan, who was called Apphus. 6 When he saw the sacrileges that were being committed in Judah and in Jerusalem, 7 he said:

"Woe is me! Why was I born
to see the ruin of my people,
the ruin of the holy city—
To dwell there
as it was given into the hands of enemies,
the sanctuary into the hands of strangers?
8 Her temple has become like a man disgraced,
9 her glorious vessels carried off as spoils,
Her infants murdered in her streets,
her youths by the sword of the enemy.*
10 What nation has not taken its share of her realm,
and laid its hand on her spoils?
11 All her adornment has been taken away.
Once free, she has become a slave.
12 We see our sanctuary laid waste,
our beauty, our glory.
The Gentiles have defiled them!
13 Why are we still alive?"

14 Then Mattathias and his sons tore their garments, put on sackcloth, and mourned bitterly.

Pagan Worship Refused and Resisted

15 The officers of the king in charge of enforcing the apostasy came to the city of Modein to make them sacrifice. 16 Many of Israel joined them, but Mattathias and his sons drew together. 17 Then the officers of the king addressed Mattathias: "You are a leader, an honorable and great man in this city, supported by sons and kindred. 18 Come now, be the first to obey the king's command, as all the Gentiles and Judeans and those who are left in Jerusalem have done. Then you and your sons shall be numbered among the King's Friends,† and you and your sons shall be honored with silver and gold and many gifts."

19 But Mattathias answered in a loud voice: "Although all the Gentiles in the king's realm obey him, so that they forsake the religion of their ancestors and consent to the king's orders, 20 yet

†

1:54 *Fifteenth day of the month Kislev, in the year one hundred and forty-five*: December 6, 167 B.C. *Desolating abomination*: in the original Hebrew, a contemptuous pun on the title "Lord of heaven" given to the god to whom an image or perhaps an altar was erected upon the altar of burnt offerings in the Temple of Jerusalem; cf. Dn 9:27; 11:31.

1:56 *Scrolls of the law*: one or more of the first five books of the Old Testament, the traditional law of Israel.

2:1 *Modein*: a village about twenty miles northwest of Jerusalem, the family's ancestral home (see 2:70; 9:19).

2:18 *The King's Friends*: a regular order of nobility at Hellenistic courts (see 10:65; 11:27).

*

1:50 1 Mc 2:29–38; 2 Mc 6:18–7:42.
1:54 Dn 9:27; 11:31; Mk 13:14.
2:1 1 Chr 9:10; 24:7.
2:9 Lam 2:11, 21.

Live It!

Religious Persecution

The Jews were facing a societal attack on their faith. But Mattathias and his sons chose to fight the official and cultural pressure to turn away from their faith.

- Are there times when you feel persecuted because of your belief in God?
- In what subtle ways does contemporary society ridicule people with religious beliefs?
- If you were to be judged or questioned because of your religion, how would you respond?

▶ 1 Mc 2:19–22

I and my sons and my kindred will keep to the
covenant of our ancestors. 21 Heaven forbid that
we should forsake the law and the command-
ments. 22 We will not obey the words of the king
by departing from our religion in the slightest
degree."

23 As he finished saying these words, a certain
Jew came forward in the sight of all to offer sac-
rifice on the altar in Modein according to the
king's order. 24 When Mattathias saw him, he was
filled with zeal; his heart was moved and his just
fury was aroused; he sprang forward and killed
him upon the altar. 25 At the same time, he also
killed the messenger of the king who was forcing
them to sacrifice, and he tore down the altar.
26 Thus he showed his zeal for the law, just as
Phinehas did with Zimri, son of Salu.*

27 Then Mattathias cried out in the city, "Let
everyone who is zealous for the law and who
stands by the covenant follow me!" 28 Then he
and his sons fled to the mountains, leaving be-
hind in the city all their possessions.*

29 At that time many who sought righteousness
and justice went out into the wilderness† to set-
tle there, 30 they and their children, their wives
and their animals, because misfortunes pressed
so hard on them. 31 It was reported to the officers
and soldiers of the king who were in the City of
David, in Jerusalem, that those who had flouted
the king's order had gone out to secret refuges in
the wilderness. 32 * Many hurried out after them,
and having caught up with them, camped oppo-
site and prepared to attack them on the sabbath.
33 The pursuers said to them, "Enough of this!
Come out and obey the king's command, and
you will live." 34 But they replied, "We will not
come out, nor will we obey the king's command
to profane the sabbath." 35 Then the enemy at-
tacked them at once. 36 But they did not retaliate;
they neither threw stones, nor blocked up their
secret refuges. 37 They said, "Let us all die in in-
nocence; heaven and earth are our witnesses that
you destroy us unjustly." 38 So the officers and
soldiers attacked them on the sabbath, and they
died with their wives, their children and their an-
imals, to the number of a thousand persons.

39 When Mattathias and his friends heard of it,
they mourned deeply for them. 40 They said to
one another, "If we all do as our kindred have
done, and do not fight against the Gentiles for
our lives and our laws, they will soon destroy us
from the earth." 41 So on that day they came to
this decision: "Let us fight against anyone who
attacks us on the sabbath, so that we may not all
die as our kindred died in their secret refuges."

42 Then they were joined by a group of Haside-
ans,† mighty warriors of Israel, all of them
devoted to the law. 43 And all those who were
fleeing from the persecutions joined them and
supported them. 44 They gathered an army and
struck down sinners in their wrath and the law-
less in their anger, and the survivors fled to the
Gentiles for safety. 45 Mattathias and his friends
went about and tore down the pagan altars;
46 they also forcibly circumcised any uncircum-
cised boys whom they found in the territory of
Israel. 47 They put to flight the arrogant, and the
work prospered in their hands. 48 They saved
the law from the hands of the Gentiles and of
the kings and did not let the sinner triumph.

Farewell of Mattathias

49 When the time came for Mattathias to die,
he said to his sons: "Arrogance and scorn have
now grown strong; it is a time of disaster and vi-
olent wrath. 50 Therefore, my children, be zealous

†

2:29 *The wilderness*: the sparsely inhabited mountain country southward from Jerusalem and west of the Dead Sea, in the region where the Dead Sea Scrolls were found.

2:42 *Hasideans*: in Hebrew *hasidim*, "pious ones," a militant religious group devoted to the strict observance of the law. They first supported the Maccabean movement, but subsequently opposed it, regarding it as too political (see 7:12–18).

*

2:26 Nm 25:6–15; Ps 106:28–31; Sir 45:23–24; 1 Mc 2:54.

2:28 2 Mc 5:27.

2:32–38 2 Mc 6:11.

for the law and give your lives for the covenant of our ancestors.

51 "Remember the deeds that our ancestors did
in their times,
and you shall win great honor and an
everlasting name.
52 Was not Abraham found faithful in trial,
and it was credited to him as
righteousness?*
53 Joseph, when in distress, kept the
commandment,
and he became master of Egypt.*
54 Phinehas our ancestor, for his burning zeal,
received the covenant of an everlasting
priesthood.*
55 Joshua, for executing his commission,
became a judge in Israel.*
56 Caleb, for bearing witness before the
assembly,
received an inheritance in the land.*
57 David, for his loyalty,
received as a heritage a throne of eternal
kingship.*
58 Elijah, for his burning zeal for the law,
was taken up to heaven.*
59 Hananiah, Azariah and Mishael, for their
faith,
were saved from the fire.*
60 Daniel, for his innocence,
was delivered from the mouths of lions.*
61 And so, consider this from generation to
generation,
that none who hope in Heaven shall fail in
strength.
62 Do not fear the words of sinners,
for their glory ends in corruption and
worms.*
63 Today exalted, tomorrow not to be found,
they have returned to dust,
their schemes have perished.
64 Children! be courageous and strong in
keeping the law,
for by it you shall be honored.

65 "Here is your brother Simeon who I know is a wise counselor; listen to him always, and he will be a father to you. 66 And Judas Maccabeus, a mighty warrior from his youth, shall be the leader of your army and wage the war against the nations. 67 Gather about you all who observe the law, and avenge your people. 68 Pay back the Gentiles what they deserve, and observe the precepts of the law."

69 Then he blessed them, and he was gathered to his ancestors. 70 He died in the year one hundred and forty-six,† and was buried in the tombs of his ancestors in Modein, and all Israel mourned him greatly.

II. Leadership of Judas Maccabeus

Judas and His Early Victories

3 1 Then his son Judas, who was called Maccabeus, took his place. 2 All his brothers and all who had joined his father supported him, and they gladly carried on Israel's war.

3 He spread abroad the glory of his people,
and put on his breastplate like a giant.
He armed himself with weapons of war;
he fought battles and protected the camp
with his sword.
4 In his deeds he was like a lion,
like a young lion roaring for prey.
5 He pursued the lawless, hunting them out,
and those who troubled his people he
destroyed by fire.
6 The lawless were cowed by fear of him,
and all evildoers were dismayed.
By his hand deliverance was happily achieved,
7 and he afflicted many kings.
He gave joy to Jacob by his deeds,
and his memory is blessed forever.
8 He went about the cities of Judah
destroying the renegades there.
He turned away wrath from Israel,
9 was renowned to the ends of the earth;
and gathered together those who were
perishing.

10 Then Apollonius† gathered together the Gentiles, along with a large army from Samaria, to fight against Israel. 11 When Judas learned of it, he went out to meet him and struck and killed him. Many fell wounded, and the rest fled. 12 They took their spoils, and Judas took the sword of Apollonius and fought with it the rest of his life.

13 But Seron, commander of the Syrian army, heard that Judas had mustered an assembly of faithful men ready for war. 14 So he said, "I

† **2:70** *In the year one hundred and forty-six*: 166 B.C.
3:10 *Apollonius*: the Mysian commander mentioned in 1 Mc 1:29; 2 Mc 5:24.

* **2:52** Gn 15:6; 22:1–18.
2:53 Gn 39:7–10; 41:39–43.
2:54 Nm 25:6–15.
2:55 Jos 1, 2, 5.
2:56 Nm 13:30; 14:6–9, 24; Jos 14:14.
2:57 2 Sm 2:4; 7:16.
2:58 1 Kgs 19:10, 14; 2 Kgs 2:11.
2:59 Dn 3:26.
2:60 Dn 6:23.
2:62 2 Mc 9:5–10, 28.

will make a name for myself and win honor in the kingdom. I will wage war against Judas and his followers, who have despised the king's command." 15 And again a large company of renegades advanced with him to help him take revenge on the Israelites.

16 When he reached the ascent of Beth-horon,† Judas went out to meet him with a few men. 17 But when they saw the army coming against them, they said to Judas: "How can we, few as we are, fight such a strong host as this? Besides, we are weak since we have not eaten today." 18 But Judas said: "Many are easily hemmed in by a few; in the sight of Heaven there is no difference between deliverance by many or by few; 19 for victory in war does not depend upon the size of the army, but on strength that comes from Heaven.* 20 With great presumption and lawlessness they come against us to destroy us and our wives and children and to despoil us; 21 but we are fighting for our lives and our laws. 22 He† will crush them before us; so do not fear them." 23 When he finished speaking, he rushed suddenly upon Seron and his army, who were crushed before him. 24 He pursued Seron down the descent of Beth-horon into the plain. About eight hundred† of their men fell, and the rest fled to the land of the Philistines. 25 Then Judas and his brothers began to be feared, and dread fell upon the Gentiles about them. 26 His fame reached the king, and the Gentiles talked about the battles of Judas.

The King's Strategy

27 When King Antiochus heard these reports, he was filled with rage; so he ordered that all the forces of his kingdom be gathered, a very strong army. 28 He opened his treasury, gave his soldiers a year's pay, and commanded them to be prepared for anything. 29 But then he saw that this exhausted the money in his treasury; moreover the tribute from the province was small because of the dissension and distress he had brought upon the land by abolishing the laws which had been in effect from of old. 30 He feared that, as had happened once or twice, he would not have enough for his expenses and for the gifts that he was accustomed to give with a lavish hand—more so than all previous kings. 31 Greatly perplexed, he decided to go to Persia and levy tribute on those provinces, and so raise a large sum of money.

32 He left Lysias, a noble of royal descent, in charge of the king's affairs from the Euphrates River to the frontier of Egypt, 33 and commissioned him to take care of his son Antiochus until his return. 34 He entrusted to him half of his forces, and the elephants, and gave him instructions concerning everything he wanted done. As for the inhabitants of Judea and Jerusalem, 35 Lysias was to send an army against them to crush and destroy the power of Israel and the remnant of Jerusalem and efface their memory from the place. 36 He was to settle foreigners in all their territory and distribute their land by lot. 37 † The king took the remaining half of the army and set out from Antioch, his capital, in the year one hundred and forty-seven; he crossed the Euphrates River and went through the provinces beyond.

Preparations for Battle

38 * Lysias chose Ptolemy, son of Dorymenes, and Nicanor† and Gorgias, powerful men among the King's Friends, 39 and with them he sent forty thousand foot soldiers and seven thousand cavalry to invade and ravage the land of Judah according to the king's orders. 40 Setting out with their whole force, they came and pitched their camp near Emmaus† in the plain. 41 When the merchants of the region heard of their prowess, they came to the camp, bringing a huge sum of silver and gold, along with fetters, to buy the Israelites as slaves. A force from Edom and from Philistia joined with them.

42 Judas and his brothers saw that evils had multiplied and that armies were encamped within their territory. They learned of the orders which the king had given to destroy and utterly wipe out the people. 43 So they said to one another, "Let us raise our people from their ruin and fight for them and for our sanctuary!"

44 The assembly gathered together to prepare for battle and to pray and ask for mercy and compassion.

†

3:16 *Beth-horon*: the famous pass leading up from the coastal plain to the Judean hill country. Here Joshua won an important battle (Jos 10:10–11), and in A.D. 66 a Roman force under Cestius was trapped and massacred.

3:22 *He*: out of reverence for God, the author of 1 Maccabees prefers to use the pronoun and other expressions, such as "Heaven," instead of the divine name. Cf. v. 50.

3:24 *About eight hundred*: the figures given in this book for strength of armies and number of casualties are not always to be taken literally. In accordance with biblical usage, they indicate rather the importance of the battle described or the greatness of the victory.

3:37 This expedition, in the spring of 165 B.C., resulted in failure; cf. chap. 6.

3:38 *Nicanor*: perhaps the leader of another attack against the Jews four years later; he was finally killed by Judas; cf. 7:26–46.

3:40 *Emmaus*: probably not the village mentioned in Lk 24:13 but a settlement about twenty miles west of Jerusalem at the edge of the hill country.

*

3:19 1 Sm 14:6. **3:38–60** 2 Mc 8:9–23.

45 Jerusalem was uninhabited, like a wilderness;
not one of her children came in or went
out.
The sanctuary was trampled on,
and foreigners were in the citadel;
it was a habitation for Gentiles.
Joy had disappeared from Jacob,
and the flute and the harp were silent.

46 †Thus they assembled and went to Mizpah
near Jerusalem, because formerly at Mizpah there
was a place of prayer for Israel.* 47 That day they
fasted and wore sackcloth; they sprinkled ashes
on their heads and tore their garments. 48 They
unrolled the scroll of the law, to learn about the
things for which the Gentiles consulted the im-
ages of their idols.† 49 They brought with them
the priestly garments, the first fruits, and the
tithes; and they brought forward the nazirites† *
who had completed the time of their vows.
50 And they cried aloud to Heaven: "What shall
we do with these, and where shall we take them?
51 For your sanctuary has been trampled on and
profaned, and your priests are in mourning and
humbled. 52 Now the Gentiles are gathered to-
gether against us to destroy us. You know what
they plot against us. 53 How shall we be able to
resist them unless you help us?" 54 Then they
blew the trumpets and cried out loudly.
55 After this Judas appointed officers for the
people, over thousands, over hundreds, over fif-
ties, and over tens. 56 He proclaimed that those
who were building houses, or were just married,
or were planting vineyards, and those who were
afraid, could each return home, according to
the law.* 57 Then the army moved off, and they
camped to the south of Emmaus. 58 Judas said:
"Arm yourselves and be brave; in the morning
be ready to fight these Gentiles who have assem-
bled against us to destroy us and our sanctuary.
59 It is better for us to die in battle than to witness
the evils befalling our nation and our sanctuary.
60 Whatever is willed in heaven will be done."

Victory over Gorgias

4 1 Now Gorgias took five thousand infantry
and a thousand picked cavalry, and this de-
tachment set out at night 2 in order to fall upon
the camp of the Jews in a surprise attack. Some
from the citadel were his guides. 3 Judas heard of
it and himself set out with his soldiers to attack
the king's army at Emmaus 4 while these forces
were still scattered away from the camp. 5 During
the night Gorgias came into the camp of Judas,
and found no one there; so he sought them in the
mountains, saying, "They are fleeing from us."
6 But at daybreak Judas appeared in the plain
with three thousand men; furthermore they
lacked the helmets and swords they wanted.
7 They saw the army of the Gentiles,† strong,
breastplated, and flanked with cavalry, and made
up of experienced soldiers. 8 * Judas said to the
men with him: "Do not fear their numbers or
dread their attack. 9 Remember how our ances-
tors were saved in the Red Sea, when Pharaoh
pursued them with an army.* 10 So now let us
cry to Heaven in the hope that he will favor us,
remember the covenant with our ancestors, and
destroy this army before us today. 11 All the Gen-
tiles shall know that there is One who redeems
and delivers Israel."
12 When the foreigners looked up and saw
them marching toward them, 13 they came out
of their camp for battle. The men with Judas
blew the trumpet, and 14 joined the battle. They
crushed the Gentiles, who fled toward the plain.
15 Their whole rear guard fell by the sword, and
they were pursued as far as Gazara† and the
plains of Idumaea, to Azotus and Jamnia. About
three thousand of their men fell.
16 When Judas and the army returned from
the pursuit, 17 he said to the people: "Do not be
greedy for plunder; for there is a fight ahead of
us, 18 and Gorgias and his army are near us on
the mountain. But now stand firm against our
enemies and fight them. Afterward you can freely
take the plunder."
19 As Judas was finishing this speech, a detach-
ment† appeared, looking down from the moun-
tain. 20 They saw that their army had been put to
flight and their camp was burning. The smoke
they saw revealed what had happened. 21 When
they realized this, they completely lost heart;
and when they also saw the army of Judas in the
plain ready to attack, 22 they all fled to the land
of the foreigners.†

†

3:46 *Mizpah . . . a place of prayer for Israel*: a holy place of great antiquity eight miles north and slightly west of Jerusalem. It was here that Samuel began to judge the Israelites (1 Sm 7:5–11; 10:17).

3:48 *To learn . . . idols*: favorable omens for the coming battle. A contrast is intended between the idol worship of the pagans and the consultation of the word of God by the Jews; cf. 2 Mc 8:23.

3:49 *Nazirites*: see note on Nm 6:2–21.

4:7 *Army of the Gentiles*: the main force; cf. 3:39–40; 4:1–2.

4:15 *Gazara*: Gezer of the Hebrew Bible, five miles northwest of Emmaus; *Azotus*, Hebrew Ashdod, lay to the southwest; *and Jamnia*, Hebrew Jabneel (Jos 15:11) or Jabneh (2 Chr 26:6), to the west of Gazara.

4:19 *A detachment*: i.e., Gorgias' force; cf. vv. 1–5.

4:22 *The land of the foreigners*: i.e., territory controlled by the

*

3:46 Jgs 20:1; 1 Sm 7:5–9; 10:17.
3:49 Nm 6:1–21.
3:56 Dt 20:5–8.
4:8–11 Dt 20:3–4; Jgs 7:2–3.
4:9 Ex 14:21–31.

23 Then Judas went back to plunder the camp, and they took much gold and silver, cloth dyed blue and marine purple, and great treasure. 24 As they returned, they were singing hymns and glorifying Heaven, "who is good, whose mercy endures forever."* 25 Thus Israel experienced a great deliverance that day.

Victory over Lysias

26 * But those of the foreigners who had escaped went and told Lysias all that had occurred. 27 When he heard it he was disturbed and discouraged, because things had not turned out in Israel as he intended and as the king had ordered.

28 So the following year he gathered together sixty thousand picked men and five thousand cavalry, to fight them. 29 They came into Idumea and camped at Beth-zur,† and Judas met them with ten thousand men. 30 Seeing that the army was strong, he prayed thus:

"Blessed are you, Savior of Israel, who crushed the attack of the mighty one by the hand of your servant David and delivered the foreign camp into the hand of Jonathan, the son of Saul, and his armor-bearer.* 31 Give this army into the hands of your people Israel; make them ashamed of their troops and their cavalry. 32 Strike them with cowardice, weaken the boldness of their strength, and let them tremble at their own destruction. 33 Strike them down by the sword of those who love you, that all who know your name may sing your praise."

34 Then they engaged in battle, and about five thousand of Lysias' army fell in hand-to-hand fighting. 35 † When Lysias saw the tide of the battle turning, and the increased boldness of Judas, whose men were ready either to live or to die nobly, he withdrew to Antioch and began to recruit mercenaries so as to return to Judea with greater numbers.*

Purification and Rededication of the Temple

36 * Then Judas and his brothers said, "Now that our enemies have been crushed, let us go up to purify the sanctuary† and rededicate it." 37 So the whole army assembled, and went up to Mount Zion. 38 They found the sanctuary desolate, the altar desecrated, the gates burnt, weeds growing in the courts as in a thicket or on some mountain, and the priests' chambers demolished.* 39 Then they tore their garments and made great lamentation; they sprinkled their heads with ashes 40 and prostrated themselves. And when the signal was given with trumpets, they cried out to Heaven.

41 Judas appointed men to attack those in the citadel, while he purified the sanctuary. 42 He chose blameless priests, devoted to the law; 43 these purified the sanctuary and carried away the stones of the defilement to an unclean place. 44 They deliberated what ought to be done with the altar for burnt offerings that had been desecrated.* 45 They decided it best to tear it down, lest it be a lasting shame to them that the Gentiles had defiled it; so they tore down the altar. 46 They stored the stones in a suitable place on the temple mount, until the coming of a prophet who could determine what to do with them.* 47 Then they took uncut stones, according to the law, and built a new altar like the former one.* 48 They also repaired the sanctuary and the interior of the temple and consecrated the courts. 49 They made new sacred vessels and brought the lampstand, the altar of incense, and the table into the temple.* 50 Then they burned incense on the altar and lighted the lamps on the lampstand, and these illuminated the temple. 51 They also put loaves on the table and hung up the curtains. Thus they finished all the work they had undertaken.

52 They rose early on the morning of the twenty-fifth day of the ninth month, that is, the month of Kislev, in the year one hundred and forty-eight,† 53 and offered sacrifice according to the law on the new altar for burnt offerings that they had made.* 54 On the anniversary of the day on which the Gentiles had desecrated it, on that very day it was rededicated with songs, harps, lyres, and cymbals. 55 All the people prostrated themselves and adored and praised Heaven, who had given them success.

56 For eight days they celebrated the dedication of the altar and joyfully offered burnt offerings and sacrifices of deliverance and praise. 57 They ornamented the facade of the temple with gold

---

† Syrians. The Greek term used here is the same as that used throughout 1–2 Samuel in Greek for Philistine territory and intends to compare Maccabean victories to those of Saul and David.

4:29 *Beth-zur*: an important frontier city (between Judea and Idumea) in the mountain area, fifteen miles south of Jerusalem.

4:35 According to 2 Mc 11:13–15, peace negotiations followed between Lysias and Judas.

4:36 *The sanctuary*: the whole Temple area with its walls, courts and outbuildings, to be distinguished from the Temple proper, the oblong edifice with porch, main room and inner shrine.

4:52 *Twenty-fifth day of the ninth month . . . in the year one hundred and forty-eight*: December 14, 164 B.C.

4:24 Ps 118:1–4, 29; 136.
4:26–35 2 Mc 11:1–15.
4:30 1 Sm 17:48–58.
4:35 1 Mc 6:28–31.
4:36–61 2 Mc 10:1–8.
4:38 Ps 74:2–7.
4:44 1 Kgs 8:64.
4:46 1 Mc 14:41; Dt 18:15.
4:47 Ex 20:25.
4:49 Ex 25:23–39; 30:1–6.
4:53 Ex 30:10; Ez 43:18–27.

crowns and shields; they repaired the gates and the priests' chambers and furnished them with doors. 58 There was great joy among the people now that the disgrace brought by the Gentiles was removed. 59 Then Judas and his brothers and the entire assembly of Israel decreed that every year for eight days, from the twenty-fifth day of the month Kislev,* the days of the dedication† of the altar should be observed with joy and gladness on the anniversary.

60 At that time they built high walls and strong towers around Mount Zion, to prevent the Gentiles from coming and trampling it as they had done before. 61 Judas also placed a garrison there to protect it, and likewise fortified Beth-zur, that the people might have a stronghold facing Idumea.

Victories over Hostile Neighbors†

5 1 * When the nations round about heard that the altar had been rebuilt and the sanctuary restored as before, they were enraged. 2 So they decided to destroy the descendants of Jacob who were among them, and they began to kill and eradicate the people. 3 * Then Judas attacked the Edomites† at Akrabattene in Idumea, because they were blockading Israel; he dealt them a heavy blow, humbled and despoiled them. 4 He also remembered the malice of the Baeanites,† who had become a snare and a stumbling block to the people by ambushing them along the roads. 5 He forced them to take refuge in towers, which he besieged; he put them under the ban and burned down their towers along with all who were in them. 6 † * Then he crossed over to the Ammonites, where he found a strong army and a large body of people with Timothy as their leader. 7 He fought many battles with them, routed them, and struck them down. 8 After seizing Jazer and its villages, he returned to Judea.

Liberation of Jews in Galilee and Gilead

9 The Gentiles in Gilead assembled to destroy the Israelites who were in their territory; these then fled to the stronghold of Dathema.† 10 They sent a letter to Judas and his brothers saying: "The Gentiles around us have assembled against us to destroy us, 11 and they are preparing to come and seize this stronghold to which we have fled. Timothy is the leader of their army. 12 Come at once to rescue us from them, for many of us have fallen. 13 All our kindred who were in the territory of the Tobiads† have been killed; the Gentiles have captured their wives, their children and their goods, and they have slain there about a thousand men."*

14 While they were reading this letter, suddenly other messengers, with garments torn, arrived from Galilee to deliver a similar message: 15 that "the inhabitants of Ptolemais,† Tyre, and Sidon, and the whole of Gentile Galilee have joined forces to destroy us." 16 When Judas and the people heard this, a great assembly convened to consider what they should do for their kindred who were in distress and being attacked by enemies.

17 Judas said to his brother Simon: "Choose men for yourself, and go, rescue your kindred in Galilee; my brother Jonathan and I will go to Gilead."

18 He left Joseph, son of Zechariah, and

Did You Know?

Hanukkah

Hanukkah, or the feast of Dedication, is a joyful eight-day celebration in the month of Chislev (December). On each night of the festival, a candle is lit in joyful remembrance of the Maccabees' rededication of the Temple in Jerusalem after it was robbed and desecrated by Antiochus IV Epiphanes (see 1 Mc 4:56). Even more deeply, the candlelight symbolizes the gratitude of the Jewish people for the survival, often against great odds, of their age-old faith.

1 Mc 4:52–59

1 MC

† **4:59** *Days of the dedication*: institution of the feast of Hanukkah, also called the feast of Dedication (Jn 10:22). Josephus calls it the feast of Lights (*Ant.* 12:325).

5:1 The events of this chapter occurred within the year 163 B.C.

5:3 *Edomites*: lit., "sons of Esau"; here a pejorative term for the Idumeans. Cf. also 5:65. *Akrabattene*: either a district southwest of the Dead Sea or on the eastern border of Judea and Samaria.

5:4 *Baeanites*: 2 Mc 10:15–23 calls them simply Idumeans.

5:6–8 This summary anticipates the order of events and would fit better between vv. 36 and 37. It corresponds to 2 Mc 12:17–23. The action was probably a reprisal for the massacre referred to in 1 Mc 5:13. Timothy may have been a local ruler, or the Seleucid governor of Transjordan. *Jazer*: a town on the road from the Jordan to Amman.

5:9 *Dathema*: the exact location is uncertain; it was east of the Jordan (in Gilead) and a night's journey from Bozrah (v. 29).

5:13 *Tobiads*: a prominent Jewish family that settled east of the Jordan.

5:15 *Ptolemais*: Hebrew Acco (Jgs 1:31), modern Acre, on the coast north of Haifa.

* **4:59** Jn 10:22.
5:1–2 1 Mc 13:6.
5:3–5 2 Mc 10:15–23.
5:6–7 2 Mc 8:30–33.
5:13 2 Mc 12:17.

Azariah, leader of the people, with the rest of
the army in Judea to guard it. 19 He commanded
them, "Take charge of these people, but do not
join battle against the Gentiles until we return."
20 Three thousand men were allotted to Simon
to go into Galilee, and eight thousand men to
Judas, for Gilead.

21 Simon went into Galilee and fought many
battles with the Gentiles. They were crushed
before him, 22 and he pursued them to the very
gate of Ptolemais. About three thousand of the
Gentiles fell, and he gathered their spoils. 23 He
took with him the Jews who were in Galilee and
in Arbatta,† with their wives and children and all
that they had, and brought them to Judea with
great rejoicing.

24 * Judas Maccabeus and his brother Jonathan
crossed the Jordan and marched for three days
through the wilderness. 25 There they met some
Nabateans,† who received them peaceably and
told them all that had happened to their kindred
in Gilead: 26 "Many of them are shut up in Boz-
rah, in Bosor near Alema, in Chaspho, Maked,
and Carnaim"—all of these are large, fortified
cities— 27 "and some are shut up in other cities
of Gilead. Tomorrow their enemies plan to attack
the strongholds and to seize and destroy all these
people in one day."

28 Thereupon Judas suddenly changed direc-
tion with his army, marched across the wilder-
ness to Bozrah, and captured the city. He put
every male to the sword, took all their spoils,
and set fire to the city. 29 † He led his army from
that place by night, and they marched toward the
stronghold. 30 When morning came, they looked
ahead and saw a countless multitude, with lad-
ders and machines for capturing the stronghold,
beginning to attack. 31 When Judas perceived
that the struggle had begun and that the noise of
the battle was resounding to heaven with trum-
pet blasts and loud shouting, 32 he said to the
men of his army, "Fight for our kindred today."
33 He came up behind them with three columns
blowing their trumpets and crying out in prayer.
34 When the army of Timothy realized that it was
Maccabeus, they fled before him, and he inflicted
on them a great defeat. About eight thousand of
their men fell that day.

35 Then he turned toward Alema† and attacked
and captured it; he killed every male, took spoils,
and burned it down. 36 From there he moved on
and took Chaspho, Maked, Bosor, and the other
cities of Gilead.

37 * After these events Timothy assembled an-
other army and camped opposite Raphon, on
the other side of the wadi. 38 Judas sent men
to spy on the camp, and they reported to him:
"All the Gentiles around us have rallied to him,
making a very large force; 39 they have also hired
Arabians to help them, and have camped beyond
the wadi, ready to attack you." So Judas went for-
ward to meet them.

40 As Judas and his army were approaching the
flowing wadi, Timothy said to the officers of his
army: "If he crosses over to us first, we shall not
be able to resist him; he will certainly defeat us.*
41 But if he is hesitant and camps on the other
side of the river, we will cross over to him and
defeat him." 42 But when Judas reached the flow-
ing wadi, he stationed the officers of the people
beside it and gave them this order: "Do not al-
low anyone to encamp; all must go into battle."
43 He was the first to cross to the attack, with all
the people behind him, and all the Gentiles were
crushed before them. They threw away their arms
and fled to the temple enclosure at Carnaim.
44 But Judas' troops captured the city and burnt
the temple enclosure with all who were in it. So
Carnaim was subdued, and Judas met with no
more resistance.

Return to Jerusalem

45 * Then Judas assembled all the Israelites,
great and small, who were in Gilead, with their
wives and children and their goods, a very large
company, to go into the land of Judah. 46 When
they reached Ephron,† a large and strongly forti-
fied city along the way, they found it impossible
to go around it on either the right or the left; they
would have to march right through it.* 47 But the
people in the city shut them out and blocked up
the gates with stones. 48 Then Judas sent them
this peaceful message: "Let us cross your territory
in order to reach our own; no one will harm you;
we will only march through." But they would not
open to him. 49 So Judas ordered a proclamation
to be made in the camp that everyone should
take up positions where they were. 50 When the

†

5:23 *Arbatta*: (or, Narbatta), probably south of Mount Carmel.

5:25 *Nabateans*: an Arab people who acquired wealth and power as caravan merchants in the final two centuries B.C. They established Petra as their capital and for a time controlled all of Transjordan, even as far as Damascus. It was from a Nabatean governor of Damascus that Paul escaped (2 Cor 11:32–33).

5:29 Cf. v. 9.

5:35 *Alema*: see v. 26; other manuscripts read Maapha, which may be Mizpah of Gilead (Jgs 11:29).

5:46 *Ephron*: a city in Transjordan opposite Beth-shan (v. 52), about nine miles east of the Jordan River. Situated on a height, it dominated the valleys of the two tributaries of the Jordan.

5:24–36 2 Mc 12:10–16. **5:37–44** 2 Mc 12:17–25. **5:40** 1 Sm 14:9–10. **5:45–54** 2 Mc 12:26–31. **5:46** Nm 20:17–21; 21:21–25.

men of the army took up their positions, he
assaulted the city all that day and night, and it
was delivered into his hand. 51 He put every male
to the sword, leveled the city, took spoils and
passed through it over the slain.
52 Then they crossed the Jordan to the great
plain in front of Beth-shan; 53 and Judas kept
gathering the stragglers and encouraging the peo-
ple the whole way, until he reached the land of
Judah. 54 They ascended Mount Zion in joy and
gladness and sacrificed burnt offerings, because
not one of them had fallen; they had returned
in safety.

Joseph and Azariah Defeated

55 In those days when Judas and Jonathan were
in the land of Gilead, and Simon his brother was
in Galilee opposite Ptolemais, 56 Joseph, son of
Zechariah, and Azariah, the leaders of the army,
heard about the brave deeds and the fighting that
they were doing. 57 They said, "Let us also make
a name for ourselves by going out and fighting
against the Gentiles around us." 58 They gave or-
ders to those of their army who were with them,
and marched against Jamnia.† 59 But Gorgias
and his men came out of the city to meet them
in battle. 60 Joseph and Azariah were routed and
were pursued to the frontiers of Judea, and about
two thousand Israelites fell that day. 61 It was a
great setback for the people, because they had
not obeyed Judas and his brothers, thinking that
they would do brave deeds. 62 But they were not
of the family through whom Israel's deliverance
was given.

Victories at Hebron and Azotus

63 The valiant Judas and his brothers were
greatly honored in all Israel and among all the
Gentiles, wherever their name was heard; 64 and
people gathered about them and praised them.
65 * Then Judas and his brothers went out and
attacked the Edomites in the land toward the
south; he took Hebron and its villages, and he
destroyed its strongholds and burned the towers
around it. 66 He then set out for the land of the
foreigners and passed through Marisa. 67 On that
day some priests fell in battle who had gone out
rashly to fight in their desire to do brave deeds.
68 Judas then turned toward Azotus in the land
of the foreigners. He destroyed their altars and
burned the carved images of their gods; and after
plundering their cities he returned to the land
of Judah.

6 1 * As King Antiochus passed through the
eastern provinces, he heard that in Persia
there was a city, Elam,† famous for its wealth
in silver and gold, 2 and that its temple was very
rich, containing gold helmets, breastplates, and
weapons left there by the first king of the Greeks,
Alexander, son of Philip, king of Macedon. 3 He
went therefore and tried to capture and loot the
city. But he could not do so, because his plan
became known to the people of the city 4 who
rose up in battle against him. So he fled and in
great dismay withdrew from there to return to
Babylon.
5 While he was in Persia, a messenger brought
him news that the armies that had gone into the
land of Judah had been routed; 6 that Lysias had
gone at first with a strong army and been driven
back; that the people of Judah had grown strong
by reason of the arms, wealth, and abundant
spoils taken from the armies they had cut down;
7 that they had pulled down the abomination
which he had built upon the altar in Jerusalem;
and that they had surrounded with high walls
both the sanctuary, as it had been before, and his
city of Beth-zur.*
8 When the king heard this news, he was as-
tonished and very much shaken. Sick with grief
because his designs had failed, he took to his
bed. 9 There he remained many days, assailed
by waves of grief, for he thought he was going
to die. 10 So he called in all his Friends and said
to them: "Sleep has departed from my eyes, and
my heart sinks from anxiety. 11 I said to myself:
'Into what tribulation have I come, and in what
floods of sorrow am I now! Yet I was kindly and
beloved in my rule.' 12 But I now recall the evils I
did in Jerusalem, when I carried away all the ves-
sels of silver and gold that were in it, and for no
cause gave orders that the inhabitants of Judah
be destroyed. 13 I know that this is why these evils
have overtaken me; and now I am dying, in bitter
grief, in a foreign land."
14 Then he summoned Philip, one of his
Friends, and put him in charge of his whole
kingdom. 15 He gave him his diadem, his robe,
and his signet ring, so that he might guide the

1 MC

†

5:58 *Jamnia*: Yavneh (see 10:69), the capital of the province of Azotus (Ashdod).

6:1 *Elam*: in fact, the mountainous region north of the Persian Gulf, rather than a city. The city may have been Persepolis. This section continues the story from 3:37 and pertains to events preceding those in 4:37–39.

*

5:65–68 2 Mc 12:36–46.
6:1–13 2 Mc 1:13–17; 9:1–29; Dn 11:40–45.
6:7 1 Mc 1:54; 4:41–61.

1
MC

Did You Know?

A Just War

Have you ever believed in something so strongly that you could justify a war to protect it? The Maccabees did, and they led a violent resistance against terrible religious persecution.

The Catholic Church teaches that "all citizens and all governments are obliged to work for the avoidance of war" (*Catechism*, no. 2308). But it also teaches that there can be occasions for legitimate defense by military force (no. 2309), or what is sometimes called a just war. The criteria for a just war are as follows:

- All other means to avoid war must be exhausted.
- The damage done by the aggressor must be grave and certain.
- There must be serious prospects of success.
- The use of arms must not produce evils that are greater than the evil to be eliminated.

No one should be required to participate in any war that does not meet all these criteria.

War is not the answer; peace is. But at times in history, some Christians have felt that the only response to a grave injustice was violent resistance. However, no Christian is obligated to fight in a war if doing so goes against his or her conscience—although he or she may be required to serve the community in some other way—and nonviolent resistance is always an option (see "Nonviolent Resistance," near 2 Mc 7:1).

king's son Antiochus and bring him up to be
king. 16 So King Antiochus died there in the one
hundred and forty-ninth year.† 17 When Lysias
learned that the king was dead, he set up the
king's son Antiochus,† whom he had reared as
a child, to be king in his place; and he gave him
the title Eupator.*

Siege of the Citadel

18 Those in the citadel were hemming Israel in
around the sanctuary, continually trying to harm
them and to strengthen the Gentiles.* 19 And so
Judas planned to destroy them, and assembled
the people to besiege them. 20 So in the one
hundred and fiftieth year† they assembled and
besieged the citadel, for which purpose he constructed platforms and siege engines. 21 But some
of the besieged escaped, and some renegade
Israelites joined them. 22 They went to the king
and said: "How long will you fail to do justice
and to avenge our kindred? 23 We agreed to serve
your father and to follow his orders and obey
his edicts. 24 And for this our own people have
become our enemies; they have put to death as
many of us as they could find and have seized
our inheritances. 25 They have acted aggressively
not only against us, but throughout their whole
territory. 26 Look! Today they have besieged the
citadel in Jerusalem in order to capture it, and
they have fortified the sanctuary and Beth-zur.
27 Unless you act quickly to prevent them, they
will do even worse things than these, and you
will not be able to stop them."

28 * When the king heard this he was enraged,
and he called together all his Friends, the officers
of his army, and the commanders of the cavalry.
29 Mercenary forces also came to him from other
kingdoms and from the islands of the seas. 30 His
army numbered a hundred thousand footsoldiers, twenty thousand cavalry, and thirty-two
elephants trained for war. 31 They passed through
Idumea and camped before Beth-zur. For many
days they attacked it; they constructed siege engines, but the besieged made a sortie and burned
these, and they fought bravely.

Battle of Beth-zechariah

32 Then Judas marched away from the citadel
and moved his camp to Beth-zechariah,† opposite the king's camp. 33 The king, rising before
dawn, moved his force hastily along the road
to Beth-zechariah; and the troops prepared for
battle and sounded the trumpet. 34 They made
the elephants drunk on the juice of grapes and
mulberries to get them ready to fight. 35 The
beasts were distributed along the phalanxes, each

†

6:16 *The one hundred and forty-ninth year*: September 22, 164, to October 9, 163 B.C. A Babylonian list of the Seleucid kings indicates that Antiochus died in November or early December of 164, about the same time as the rededication of the Temple.

6:17 *The king's son Antiochus*: Antiochus V Eupator ("of a good father"), then about nine years old. He was in Antioch, still in the charge of Lysias, who proceeded to govern and wage wars in his name. Both were put to death two years later, when Demetrius, brother of Antiochus IV, arrived to claim the kingship; cf. 7:1–3.

6:20 *The one hundred and fiftieth year*: October, 163, to September, 162 B.C.

6:32 *Beth-zechariah*: south of Jerusalem, and six miles north of Beth-zur.

6:17 2 Mc 10:10–11.
6:18 1 Mc 1:33–36.
6:28–54 2 Mc 13:1–26.

elephant having assigned to it a thousand men in coats of mail, with bronze helmets on their heads, and five hundred picked cavalry. 36 These accompanied the beast wherever it was; wherever it moved, they moved too and never left it. 37 Each elephant was outfitted with a strong wooden tower, fastened to it by a harness; each tower held three soldiers who fought from it, besides the Indian driver. 38 The remaining cavalry were stationed on one or the other of the two flanks of the army, to harass the enemy and to be protected by the phalanxes. 39 When the sun shone on the gold and bronze shields, the mountains gleamed with their brightness and blazed like flaming torches. 40 Part of the king's army spread out along the heights, while some were on low ground, and they marched forward steadily in good order. 41 All who heard the noise of their numbers, the tramp of their marching, and the clanging of the arms, trembled; for the army was very great and strong.

42 Judas with his army advanced to fight, and six hundred men of the king's army fell. 43 Eleazar, called Avaran, saw one of the beasts covered with royal armor and bigger than any of the others, and so he thought the king was on it.* 44 He gave up his life to save his people and win an everlasting name for himself. 45 He dashed courageously up to it in the middle of the phalanx, killing men right and left, so that they parted before him. 46 He ran under the elephant, stabbed it and killed it. The beast fell to the ground on top of him, and he died there. 47 But when Judas' troops saw the strength of the royal army and the ardor of its forces, they retreated from them.

The Siege of Jerusalem

48 Some of the king's army went up to Jerusalem to attack them, and the king established camps in Judea and at Mount Zion. 49 He made peace with the people of Beth-zur, and they evacuated the city, because they had no food there to enable them to withstand a siege, for that was a sabbath year in the land.† * 50 The king took Beth-zur and stationed a garrison there to hold it. 51 For many days he besieged the sanctuary, setting up platforms and siege engines, fire-throwers, catapults and mechanical bows for shooting arrows and projectiles. 52 The defenders countered by setting up siege engines of their own, and kept up the fight a long time. 53 But there were no provisions in the storerooms, because it was the seventh year, and the reserves had been eaten up by those who had been rescued from the Gentiles and brought to Judea. 54 Few men remained in the sanctuary because the famine was too much for them; the rest scattered, each to his own home.

Peace Treaty

55 * Lysias heard that Philip, whom King Antiochus, before his death, had appointed to train his son Antiochus to be king, 56 had returned from Persia and Media with the army that accompanied the king, and that he was seeking to take over the government. 57 So he hastily decided to withdraw. He said to the king, the leaders of the army, and the soldiers: "We are growing weaker every day, our provisions are scanty, the place we are besieging is strong, and it is our duty to take care of the affairs of the kingdom.* 58 Therefore let us now come to terms with these people and make peace with them and all their nation. 59 Let us grant them freedom to live according to their own laws as formerly; it was on account of their laws, which we abolished, that they became enraged and did all these things."

60 The proposal pleased the king and the leaders; he sent peace terms to the Jews, and they accepted. 61 So the king and the leaders swore an oath to them, and on these terms the Jews evacuated the fortification. 62 But when the king entered Mount Zion and saw how the place was fortified, he broke the oath he had sworn and gave orders to tear down the encircling wall. 63 Then he departed in haste and returned to Antioch, where he found Philip in control of the city. He fought against him and took the city by force.

Expedition of Bacchides and Alcimus

7 1 * In the one hundred and fifty-first year,† Demetrius, son of Seleucus, set out from Rome, arrived with a few men at a coastal city, and began to rule there. 2 As he was entering the royal palace of his ancestors, the soldiers seized Antiochus and Lysias to bring them to him. 3 When he was informed of this, he said, "Do not show me their faces." 4 So the soldiers killed them, and Demetrius assumed the royal throne.

5 Then all the lawless men and renegades of

---

† **6:49** *A sabbath year in the land*: when sowing and reaping were prohibited (Ex 23:10–11; Lv 25:2–7). The year without a harvest (autumn of 164 to autumn of 163) was followed by a food shortage.

7:1–3 *The one hundred and fifty-first year*: the spring of 161 B.C. Demetrius, son of Seleucus, was the lawful heir to the kingdom; but when only nine years old, he was taken as a hostage to Rome in place of his uncle, who ruled as Antiochus IV Epiphanes. At the age of twenty-five Demetrius fled secretly from Rome and, with the support of the Syrians, overcame his rival Antiochus V and put him to death. *The royal palace*: at Antioch.

---

* **6:43** 2 Mc 13:15. **6:49** Lv 25:1–7. **6:55–63** 2 Mc 13:23–26. **6:57** 2 Mc 11:13–15. **7:1–7** 2 Mc 14:1–11.

Israel came to him. They were led by Alcimus,†
who desired to be high priest. 6 They made this
accusation to the king against the people: "Judas
and his brothers have destroyed all your friends
and have driven us out of our land. 7 So now,
send a man whom you trust to go and see all the
destruction Judas has wrought on us and on the
king's territory, and let him punish them and all
their supporters."

8 So the king chose Bacchides, one of the
King's Friends, who ruled the province of West-
of-Euphrates, a great man in the kingdom, and
faithful to the king. 9 He sent him and the ren-
egade Alcimus, to whom he granted the high
priesthood, with orders to take revenge on the
Israelites. 10 They set out and, on arriving in the
land of Judah with a great army, sent messengers
who spoke deceitfully to Judas and his brothers
in peaceful terms. 11 But these paid no attention
to their words, seeing that they had come with a
great army.

12 A group of scribes, however, gathered about
Alcimus and Bacchides to ask for a just agree-
ment. 13 * The Hasideans were the first among
the Israelites to seek peace with them, 14 for they
said, "A priest of the line of Aaron has come with
the army, and he will not do us any wrong." 15 He
spoke with them peacefully and swore to them,
"We will not seek to injure you or your friends."
16 So they trusted him. But he arrested sixty of
them and killed them in one day, according to
the words that he wrote:†

17 "The flesh of your faithful,
and their blood they have spilled all
around about Jerusalem,
and no one was left to bury them."*

18 Then fear and dread of them came upon all the
people, who said: "There is no truth or justice
among them; they violated the agreement and
the oath that they swore."

19 Bacchides withdrew from Jerusalem and
camped in Beth-zaith.† He had many of the men
who deserted to him arrested and some of the
people. He killed them and threw them into a
great cistern. 20 He handed the province over to
Alcimus, leaving troops to help him, while he
himself returned to the king.

21 Alcimus struggled to maintain his high
priesthood, 22 and all those who were troubling
the people gathered about him. They took pos-
session of the land of Judah and caused great
distress in Israel. 23 When Judas saw all the evils
that Alcimus and those with him were bringing
upon the Israelites, even more than the Gentiles
had, 24 he went about all the borders of Judea
and took revenge on the men who had deserted,
preventing them from going out into the coun-
try. 25 But when Alcimus saw that Judas and his
followers were gaining strength and realized that
he could not resist them, he returned to the king
and accused them of grave crimes.

Defeat of Nicanor

26 * Then the king sent Nicanor, one of his
honored officers, who was a bitter enemy of Is-
rael, with orders to destroy the people. 27 Nicanor
came to Jerusalem with a large force and deceit-
fully sent to Judas† and his brothers this peace-
able message: 28 "Let there be no fight between
me and you. I will come with a few men to meet
you face to face in peace."

29 So he came to Judas, and they greeted one
another peaceably. But Judas' enemies were pre-
pared to seize him. 30 When he became aware
that Nicanor had come to him with deceit in
mind, Judas was afraid of him and would not
meet him again.* 31 When Nicanor saw that his
plan had been discovered, he went out to fight
Judas near Capharsalama.† 32 About five hun-
dred men of Nicanor's army fell; the rest fled to
the City of David.†

33 * After this, Nicanor went up to Mount Zion.
Some of the priests from the sanctuary and some
of the elders of the people came out to greet him
peaceably and to show him the burnt offering
that was being sacrificed for the king. 34 But he
mocked and ridiculed them, defiled them,† and
spoke arrogantly. 35 In a rage he swore: "If Judas
and his army are not delivered to me at once,
when I return victorious I will burn this temple

7:5–6 *Alcimus*: a Jew hostile to the Maccabees, who became high priest after the death of Menelaus (2 Mc 14:3). He received confirmation in his office from the new king Demetrius (1 Mc 7:9), and brought malicious charges against Judas and his brothers and the people (1 Mc 7:6).

7:16 *The words that he wrote*: based on Ps 79:2–3. But who is "he"—David, Alcimus, Judas, or someone else?

7:19 *Beth-zaith*: about three miles north of Beth-zur and twelve miles south of Jerusalem.

7:27 *Nicanor . . . deceitfully sent to Judas*: a more favorable picture of Nicanor, as an honest man who became a personal friend of Judas, is given in 2 Mc 14:17–25. Their friendship was broken by the intrigues of Alcimus (2 Mc 14:26–30).

7:31 *Capharsalama*: a village north of Jerusalem whose precise location is disputed.

7:32 *City of David*: the citadel occupied by the Seleucid garrison in Jerusalem.

7:34 *Defiled them*: spitting on the priests caused them to become legally defiled.

* **7:13–14** 1 Mc 2:42. **7:17** Ps 79:2–3. **7:26–27** 1 Mc 3:38; 2 Mc 8:9; 14:12–13. **7:30** 2 Mc 14:30. **7:33–38** 2 Mc 14:31–36.

down." He went away in great anger. 36 * The
priests, however, went in and stood before the al-
tar and the sanctuary. They wept and said: 37 "You
have chosen this house to bear your name, to be
a house of prayer and supplication for your peo-
ple. 38 Take revenge on this man and his army,
and let them fall by the sword. Remember their
blasphemies, and do not let them continue."
39 Nicanor left Jerusalem and camped at Beth-
horon, where the Syrian army joined him. 40 But
Judas camped in Adasa† with three thousand
men. Here Judas uttered this prayer: 41 * "When
they who were sent by the king† blasphemed,
your angel went out and killed a hundred and
eighty-five thousand of them.* 42 In the same
way, crush this army before us today, and let the
rest know that Nicanor spoke wickedly against
your sanctuary; judge him according to his wick-
edness."
43 The armies met in battle on the thirteenth
day of the month Adar. Nicanor's army was
crushed, and he himself was the first to fall in the
battle.* 44 When his army saw that Nicanor had
fallen, they threw down their weapons and fled.
45 The Jews pursued them a day's journey from
Adasa to near Gazara, blowing the trumpets be-
hind them as signals. 46 From all the surrounding
villages of Judea people came out and outflanked
them. They turned them back, and all the ene-
mies fell by the sword; not a single one escaped.
47 Then the Jews collected the spoils and the
plunder; they cut off Nicanor's head and his
right arm, which he had lifted up so arrogantly.
These they brought and displayed in the sight
of Jerusalem. 48 The people rejoiced greatly, and
observed that day as a day of much joy. 49 They
decreed that it should be observed every year on
the thirteenth of Adar.† 50 And so for a few days†
the land of Judah was at rest.

Eulogy of the Romans

8 1 † Judas had heard of the reputation of the
Romans. They were valiant fighters and acted
amiably to all who took their side. They estab-
lished a friendly alliance with all who applied
to them. 2 He was also told of their battles and
the brave deeds that they performed against the
Gauls,† conquering them and forcing them to
pay tribute; 3 and what they did in Spain to get
possession of the silver and gold mines there.
4 By planning and persistence they subjugated
the whole region, although it was very remote
from their own. They also subjugated the kings
who had come against them from the far cor-
ners of the earth until they crushed them and
inflicted on them severe defeat. The rest paid
tribute to them every year. 5 Philip† and Perseus,
king of the Macedonians, and the others who
opposed them in battle they overwhelmed and
subjugated. 6 Antiochus† the Great, king of Asia,
who fought against them with a hundred and
twenty elephants and with cavalry and chariots
and a very great army, was defeated by them.
7 They took him alive and obliged him and the
kings who succeeded him to pay a heavy tribute,
to give hostages and to cede 8 Lycia, Mysia, and
Lydia† from among their best provinces. The Ro-
mans took these from him and gave them to King
Eumenes. 9 † When the Greeks planned to come
and destroy them, 10 the Romans discovered it,
and sent against the Greeks a single general who
made war on them. Many were wounded and

†

7:40 *Adasa*: a village between Jerusalem and Beth-horon.

7:41 *They who were sent by the king*: 2 Kgs 18:19–25, 29–35; 19:10–13 recount in detail the boastful threats made by Sennacherib, the Assyrian king, through his emissaries. *Your angel*: a reference to 2 Kgs 19:35, which describes the fate of the Assyrian army which besieged Jerusalem in the days of Hezekiah, king of Judah.

7:49 *The thirteenth of Adar*: March 27, 160 B.C. This day in the Jewish calendar was called the "Day of Nicanor" (2 Mc 15:36), but it was not long celebrated by the Jews.

7:50 *For a few days*: about one month following the death of Nicanor. After that began the attack of Bacchides resulting in the death of Judas (9:1–18).

8:1 This chapter contains the account of the embassy which Judas sent to Rome, probably before the death of Nicanor, to conclude a treaty of alliance between Rome and the Jewish nation. Without precise chronology, the pertinent data are gathered into a unified theme.

The image of the Roman Republic greatly impressed the smaller Eastern peoples seeking support against their overlords (vv. 1–16), because of Roman success in war (vv. 2–11) and effective aid to their allies (vv. 12–13). Numerous interventions by Rome in the politics of the Near East bear witness to its power and prestige in the second century B.C. See 1:10; 7:2; 12:3; 15:15–24; 2 Mc 11:34. With the increased Roman control of Palestine after 63 B.C., the Republic and later the Empire became heartily detested. The eulogy of Rome in this chapter is one of the reasons why 1 Maccabees was not preserved by the Palestinian Jews of the century that followed.

8:2 *Gauls*: probably the Celts of northern Italy and southern France, subdued by the Romans in 222 B.C., and again in 200–191 B.C.; but also those in Asia Minor (the Galatians), whom the Romans defeated in 189 B.C.

8:5 *Philip*: Philip V of Macedonia, defeated by a Graeco-Roman alliance at Cynoscephalae in 197 B.C. Perseus, his son, was defeated at Pydna in 168 B.C., and died a prisoner. With this, the kingdom of Macedonia came to an end.

8:6 *Antiochus*: Antiochus III, greatest of the Seleucid kings. He was defeated at Magnesia in 190 B.C. By the Treaty of Apamea in 189 B.C., he was obliged to pay Rome a crushing indemnity of 15,000 talents. The weakening of Antiochene power and the growing military and economic influence of Rome may have led Antiochus IV to adopt the policy of political, religious, and cultural unification of Syria and Palestine.

8:8 *Lycia, Mysia, and Lydia*: regions in western Asia Minor. "Lycia" and "Mysia" are restored here by conjectural emendation; the Greek text has "India, Media," most likely through scribal error. *Eumenes*: Eumenes II (197–158 B.C.), king of Pergamum, an ally of Rome who benefited greatly from Antiochus' losses.

8:9–10 The revolt of the Achaean League, inserted here, occurred in 146 B.C., after Judas' time. It was crushed by the Roman consul Lucius Mummius and marked the end of Greek independence.

*

7:36–38 1 Kgs 8:29–30, 33–34, 43.
7:41 2 Kgs 19:35–36; Is 37:36–37.
7:41–42 2 Mc 8:19; 15:22–24.
7:43 2 Mc 15:25–36.

fell, and the Romans took their wives and children captive. They plundered them, took possession of their land, tore down their strongholds and reduced them to slavery even to this day. 11 All the other kingdoms and islands that had ever opposed them they destroyed and enslaved; with their friends, however, and those who relied on them, they maintained friendship. 12 They subjugated kings both near and far, and all who heard of their fame were afraid of them. 13 Those whom they wish to help and to make kings, they make kings; and those whom they wish, they depose; and they were greatly exalted. 14 Yet with all this, none of them put on a diadem or wore purple as a display of grandeur. 15 But they made for themselves a senate chamber, and every day three hundred and twenty men took counsel, deliberating on all that concerned the people and their well-being. 16 They entrust their government to one man† every year, to rule over their entire land, and they all obey that one, and there is no envy or jealousy among them.

Treaty with the Romans

17 So Judas chose Eupolemus, son of John, son of Accos, and Jason, son of Eleazar, and sent them to Rome to establish friendship and alliance with them.* 18 He did this to lift the yoke from Israel, for it was obvious that the kingdom of the Greeks was subjecting them to slavery. 19 After making a very long journey to Rome, the envoys entered the senate chamber and spoke as follows: 20 "Judas, called Maccabeus, and his brothers, with the Jewish people, have sent us to you to establish alliance and peace with you, and to be enrolled among your allies and friends." 21 The proposal pleased the Romans, 22 and this is a copy of the reply they inscribed on bronze tablets and sent to Jerusalem,† to remain there with the Jews as a record of peace and alliance:*

23 "May it be well with the Romans and the Jewish nation at sea and on land forever; may sword and enemy be far from them. 24 But if war is first made on Rome, or any of its allies in any of their dominions, 25 the Jewish nation will fight along with them wholeheartedly, as the occasion shall demand; 26 and to those who wage war they shall not give or provide grain, weapons, money, or ships, as seems best to Rome. They shall fulfill their obligations without receiving any recompense. 27 In the same way, if war is made first on the Jewish nation, the Romans will fight along with them willingly, as the occasion shall demand, 28 and to those who attack them there shall not be given grain, weapons, money, or ships, as seems best to Rome. They shall fulfill their obligations without deception. 29 On these terms the Romans have made an agreement with the Jewish people. 30 But if both parties hereafter agree to add or take away anything, they shall do as they choose, and whatever they shall add or take away shall be valid.

31 "Moreover, concerning the wrongs that King Demetrius is doing to them, we have written to him thus: 'Why have you made your yoke heavy upon our friends and allies the Jews? 32 If they petition against you again, we will enforce justice and make war on you by sea and land.' "

Death of Judas

9 1 When Demetrius heard that Nicanor and his army had fallen in battle, he again sent Bacchides and Alcimus into the land of Judah, along with the right wing of his army. 2 They took the road to Galilee, and camping opposite the ascent at Arbela, they captured it† and killed many people. 3 In the first month of the one hundred and fifty-second year,† they encamped against Jerusalem. 4 Then they set out for Berea with twenty thousand men and two thousand cavalry. 5 Judas, with three thousand picked men, had camped at Elasa. 6 When they saw the great number of the troops, they were very much afraid, and many slipped away from the camp, until only eight hundred of them remained.

7 When Judas saw that his army was melting away just as the battle was imminent, he was brokenhearted, because he had no time to gather them together. 8 In spite of his discouragement he said to those who remained: "Let us go forward to meet our enemies; perhaps we can put up a good fight against them." 9 They tried to dissuade him, saying: "We certainly cannot. Let us save our own lives now, and come back with

†

8:16 *They entrust their government to one man*: actually the Roman Republic had two consuls chosen yearly as joint heads of the government.

8:22 *The reply . . . on bronze tablets and sent to Jerusalem*: the decree of the Senate would be inscribed on bronze and kept in the Roman Capitol, with only a copy in letter form sent to Jerusalem.

9:2 *They took the road . . . Arbela, they captured it*: this passage is restored, in part, by conjectural emendation. The present Greek text could be translated, "They took the road to Gilgal, and camping opposite Mesaloth at Arbela, they captured it." But Arbela (modern Khirbet Irbid) was in Galilee, on a high hill overlooking the western shore of the Sea of Galilee. Gilgal, on the contrary, was in the Jordan valley near Jericho. "Mesaloth" is probably a corrupt form of a Hebrew word meaning "steps, ascent." It is possible, however, that all these terms referred to places in the Judean hills.

9:3 *The first month of the one hundred and fifty-second year*: April/May 160 B.C., by the Temple calendar.

8:17 1 Mc 12:1–4; 15:15–22. **8:22** 1 Mc 14:17–18.

our kindred, and then fight against them. Now
we are too few." 10 But Judas said: "Far be it from
me to do such a thing as to flee from them! If our
time has come, let us die bravely for our kindred
and not leave a stain upon our honor!"
11 Then the army of Bacchides moved out of
camp and took its position for combat. The cav-
alry were divided into two squadrons, and the
slingers and the archers came on ahead of the
army, and in the front line were all the best war-
riors. Bacchides was on the right wing. 12 Flanked
by the two squadrons, the phalanx attacked as
they blew their trumpets. Those who were on
Judas' side also blew their trumpets. 13 The earth
shook with the noise of the armies, and the bat-
tle raged from morning until evening.
14 When Judas saw that Bacchides was on the
right, with the main force of his army, all the
most stouthearted rallied to him, 15 and the right
wing was crushed; Judas pursued them as far as
the mountain slopes.† 16 But when those on the
left wing saw that the right wing was crushed,
they closed in behind Judas and those with him.
17 The battle became intense, and many on both
sides fell wounded. 18 Then Judas fell, and the
rest fled.
19 Jonathan and Simon took their brother
Judas and buried him in the tomb of their an-
cestors at Modein. 20 All Israel wept for him with
great lamentation. They mourned for him many
days, and they said, 21 "How the mighty one has
fallen, the savior of Israel!"* 22 The other acts of
Judas, his battles, the brave deeds he performed,
and his greatness have not been recorded; but
they were very many.

III. Leadership of Jonathan

Jonathan Succeeds Judas

23 After the death of Judas, the lawless raised
their heads in every part of Israel, and all kinds
of evildoers appeared. 24 In those days there was
a very great famine, and the country deserted to
them. 25 Bacchides chose renegades and made
them masters of the country. 26 These sought
out and hunted down the friends of Judas and
brought them to Bacchides, who punished and
derided them. 27 There was great tribulation in
Israel, the like of which had not been since the
time prophets ceased to appear among them.
28 Then all the friends of Judas came together
and said to Jonathan: 29 "Ever since your brother
Judas died, there has been no one like him to
lead us against our enemies, both Bacchides and
those of our nation who are hostile to us. 30 Now
therefore we have chosen you today to be our
ruler and leader in his place, to fight our battle."
31 From that moment Jonathan accepted the lead-
ership, and took the place of Judas his brother.

Bacchides Pursues Jonathan

32 When Bacchides learned of it, he sought to
kill him. 33 But Jonathan and his brother Simon
and all who were with him discovered this, and

Live It!

What Makes a Hero?

History is full of heroes, those bigger-than-life men and women like Judas Maccabeus who have made a difference because of their courageous acts and their willingness to take risks that frighten other people. What makes someone a hero? Is each of us capable of heroism?

Someone we have grown up with, who now seems ordinary, could one day be a hero. None of us knows when we could be called on to do something heroic. We need an openness to God's call and a willingness to take a risk—to let go of our fears and to reach deep within ourselves for courage and strength. You may amaze yourself at what you can accomplish in extraordinary situations. The stuff of heroes, of great and brave persons such as Judas Maccabeus, is already within us. We need only to believe in ourselves and believe that God is with us.

You may not end up in a history book or be memorialized in a statue, but you can make a difference in the lives of one or perhaps many people. What really counts is to be a hero in the eyes of God.

► 1 Mc 9:19–22

† 9:15 *As far as the mountain slopes*: conjectural emendation. The Greek text has "as far as Mount Azotus"; this is most unlikely. Apparently the Greek translator mistook the Hebrew word *ashdot*, "slopes," for *ashdod*, "Azotus."

9:21 2 Sm 1:19, 25, 27; Jgs 3:9.

they fled to the wilderness of Tekoa† and camped
by the waters of the pool of Asphar. [34] †
35 Jonathan sent his brother† as leader of the
convoy to implore his friends, the Nabateans,
to let them deposit with them their great quan-
tity of baggage.* 36 But the tribe of Jambri from
Medaba† made a raid and seized and carried off
John and everything he had.
37 After this, word was brought to Jonathan
and his brother Simon: "The tribe of Jambri are
celebrating a great wedding, and with a large
escort they are bringing the bride, the daugh-
ter of one of the great princes of Canaan, from
Nadabath." 38 Remembering the blood of John
their brother, they went up and hid themselves
under cover of the mountain. 39 As they watched
there appeared a noisy throng with much bag-
gage; then the bridegroom and his friends and
kinsmen had come out to meet them with tam-
bourines and musicians with their instruments.
40 Jonathan and his party rose up against them
from their ambush and killed them. Many fell
wounded; the rest fled toward the mountain; all
their spoils were taken. 41 Thus the wedding was
turned into mourning, and the sound of their
music into lamentation. 42 Having taken their
revenge for the blood of their brother, they re-
turned to the marshes of the Jordan.
43 When Bacchides heard of it, he came on the
sabbath to the banks of the Jordan with a large
force. 44 Then Jonathan said to his companions,
"Let us rise up now and fight for our lives, for
today is not like yesterday and the day before.
45 The battle is before us, behind us are the wa-
ters of the Jordan, on either side of us, marsh
and thickets; there is no way of escape.† 46 Cry
out now to Heaven so that you may be delivered
from the hand of our enemies." 47 When they
joined battle, Jonathan raised his hand to strike
Bacchides, but Bacchides backed away from him.
48 Jonathan and those with him jumped into the
Jordan and swam across to the other side, but the
enemy did not pursue them across the Jordan.
49 About a thousand men on Bacchides' side fell
that day.
50 On returning to Jerusalem, Bacchides built
strongholds in Judea: the Jericho fortress, as
well as Emmaus, Beth-horon, Bethel, Timnath,
Pharathon, and Tephon, with high walls and
gates and bars.† 51 In each he put a garrison to
harass Israel. 52 He fortified the city of Beth-zur,
Gazara and the citadel, and put troops in them
and stores of provisions. 53 He took as hostages
the sons of the leading people of the country
and put them in custody in the citadel at Jeru-
salem.*
54 In the one hundred and fifty-third year, in
the second month,† Alcimus ordered the wall of
the inner court of the sanctuary to be torn down,
thus destroying the work of the prophets. But he
only began to tear it down. 55 Just at that time
Alcimus was stricken, and his work was inter-
rupted; his mouth was closed and he was para-
lyzed, so that he could no longer utter a word or
give orders concerning his household. 56 Alcimus
died in great agony at that time. 57 Seeing that Al-
cimus was dead, Bacchides returned to the king,
and the land of Judah was at rest for two years.
58 Then all the lawless took counsel and said:
"Jonathan and those with him are living in peace
and security. Now then, let us have Bacchides re-
turn, and he will capture all of them in a single
night." 59 So they went and took counsel with
him. 60 When Bacchides was setting out with a
large force, he sent letters secretly to all his allies
in Judea, telling them to seize Jonathan and his
companions. They were not able to do this, how-
ever, because their plan became known. 61 In fact,
Jonathan's men seized about fifty of the men of
the country who were leaders in the conspiracy
and put them to death.
62 Then Jonathan and those with him, along
with Simon, withdrew to Bethbasi† in the wil-
derness; he rebuilt its ruins and fortified it.
63 When Bacchides learned of this, he gathered
together his whole force and sent word to those
who were in Judea. 64 He came and camped be-
fore Bethbasi, and constructing siege engines, he
fought against it for many days.
65 Leaving his brother Simon in the city, Jon-
athan, accompanied by a small group of men,
went out into the countryside. 66 He struck down
Odomera and his kindred and the tribe of
Phasiron in their encampment; these men had
begun to attack and they were going up with
their forces. 67 Simon and those with him then

†

9:33 *Tekoa*: home of the prophet Amos in the wild country above the Dead Sea, southeast of Jerusalem.

9:34 Omitted, it is a dittography of v. 43.

9:35 *Jonathan sent his brother*: this was John who was called Gaddi (2:2; cf. 9:36, 38).

9:36 *Medaba*: northeast of the Dead Sea.

9:45 Jonathan's force may have been trapped in one of the many oxbows of the lower Jordan. Bacchides had crossed and caught them still on the east bank.

9:50 These sites constitute a ring on the edges of the province of Judea.

9:54 *In the one hundred and fifty-third year, in the second month*: May, 159 B.C. *The work of the prophets*: probably Haggai and Zechariah, who were instrumental in building the Second Temple after the Babylonian exile; cf. Hg 1:12–14; Zec 4:8–10; Ezr 5:1–2.

9:62 *Bethbasi*: two miles east of Bethlehem and six miles north of Tekoa.

*

9:35 1 Mc 5:25. **9:53** 1 Mc 10:9.

sallied forth from the city and set fire to the siege
engines. 68 They fought against Bacchides, and he
was crushed. They caused him great distress, be-
cause the enterprise he had planned was in vain.
69 He was enraged with the lawless men who had
advised him to invade the province. He killed
many of them and resolved to return to his own
country.
70 Jonathan learned of this and sent ambassa-
dors to agree on peace with him and to obtain
the release of the prisoners. 71 He agreed to do
as Jonathan asked. He swore an oath to him that
he would never try to do him any harm for the
rest of his life; 72 and he released to him the pris-
oners he had previously taken from the land of
Judah. Thereupon he returned to his own land
and never came into their territory again. 73 Then
the sword ceased from Israel. Jonathan settled in
Michmash;† he began to judge the people and he
eliminated the renegades from Israel.

Jonathan Becomes High Priest

10 1 In the one hundred and sixtieth year,†
Alexander Epiphanes, son of Antiochus,
came up and took Ptolemais. They accepted him
as king and he began to reign there. 2 When King
Demetrius heard of it, he mustered a very large
army and marched out to engage him in battle.
3 Demetrius sent a letter to Jonathan written in
peaceful terms, to exalt him; 4 for he said: "Let
us be the first to make peace with him, before he
makes peace with Alexander against us, 5 since he
will remember all the wrongs we have done to
him, his brothers, and his nation."
6 So Demetrius authorized him to gather an
army and procure arms as his ally; and he or-
dered that the hostages in the citadel be released
to him. 7 Accordingly Jonathan went to Jerusalem
and read the letter to all the people and to those
who were in the citadel. 8 They were struck with
fear when they heard that the king had given him
authority to gather an army. 9 Those in the citadel
released the hostages to Jonathan, and he gave
them back to their parents.* 10 Thereafter Jona-
than dwelt in Jerusalem, and began to build and
restore the city. 11 He ordered those doing the
work to build the walls and to encircle Mount
Zion with square stones for its fortification, and
they did so. 12 The foreigners in the strongholds
that Bacchides had built took flight; 13 all of them
left their places and returned to their own lands.
14 Only in Beth-zur did some remain of those
who had abandoned the law and the command-
ments, for it was a place of refuge.
15 King Alexander heard of the promises that
Demetrius had made to Jonathan; he was also
told of the battles and brave deeds of Jonathan
and his brothers and of the troubles that they had
endured. 16 He said, "Shall we ever find another
man like him? Let us now make him our friend
and ally." 17 So he sent Jonathan a letter written
in these terms: 18 "King Alexander sends greetings
to his brother Jonathan. 19 We have heard of you,
that you are a mighty warrior and worthy to be
our friend. 20 We have therefore appointed you
today to be high priest of your nation; you are to
be called the King's Friend, and you are to look
after our interests and preserve friendship with
us." He also sent him a purple robe and a crown
of gold.* 21 Jonathan put on the sacred vestments
in the seventh month of the one hundred and
sixtieth year at the feast of Booths,† and he gath-
ered an army and procured many weapons.

A Letter from Demetrius to Jonathan

22 When Demetrius heard of these things, he
was distressed and said: 23 "Why have we al-
lowed Alexander to get ahead of us by gaining
the friendship of the Jews and thus strengthen-
ing himself? 24 I too will write them encouraging
words and offer honors and gifts, so that they
may support me." 25 So he sent them this mes-
sage: "King Demetrius sends greetings to the
Jewish nation. 26 We have heard how you have
kept the treaty with us and continued in our
friendship and not gone over to our enemies,
and we are glad. 27 Continue, therefore, to keep
faith with us, and we will reward you with favors
in return for what you do in our behalf. 28 We
will grant you many exemptions and will bestow
gifts on you.
29 * "I now free you and exempt all the Jews
from the tribute, the salt tax, and the crown lev-
ies. 30 Instead of collecting the third of the grain

†

9:73 *Michmash*, southeast of Bethel, famous for the exploits of Jonathan, son of Saul; see 1 Sm 14. It was Jonathan's base from 157 to 152 B.C. *Began to judge*: exercise the governing authority as in the Book of Judges. With Jerusalem and the garrison towns (v. 50) firmly in Seleucid hands, Jonathan's freedom of action was greatly restricted.

10:1 *The one hundred and sixtieth year*: 152 B.C. *Alexander . . . Antiochus*: Alexander Balas claimed to be a son of Antiochus IV. He had the backing of the Romans, who had never forgiven Demetrius for becoming king without their permission. The latter meanwhile had become unpopular with his own people as well as with the Jews.

10:21 *Jonathan . . . feast of Booths*: Jonathan began to discharge the office of high priest in October 152 B.C. For seven years after the death of Alcimus there had been no high priest in Jerusalem. It was taken for granted that the king, though a Gentile, had the power to appoint one (2 Mc 4:7, 23–24). The Maccabees, though a priestly family (1 Mc 2:1), were not of the line of Zadok, and some in Israel (perhaps the Qumran community) regarded Jonathan's tenure as a usurpation.

10:9 1 Mc 9:53.
10:20 1 Mc 2:18.
10:29–30 1 Mc 11:28, 34.

and the half of the fruit of the trees that should be my share, I renounce the right from this day forward. Neither now nor in the future will I collect them from the land of Judah or from the three districts annexed from Samaria.† 31 Let Jerusalem and her territory, her tithes and her tolls, be sacred and free from tax. 32 I also yield my authority over the citadel in Jerusalem, and I transfer it to the high priest, that he may put in it such men as he shall choose to guard it. 33 Every Jew who has been carried into captivity from the land of Judah into any part of my kingdom I set at liberty without ransom; and let all their taxes, even those on their cattle, be canceled.

34 Let all feast days, sabbaths, new moon festivals, appointed days, and the three days that precede each feast day, and the three days that follow, be days of immunity and exemption for all Jews in my kingdom. 35 No one will have authority to exact payment from them or to harass any of them in any matter.

36 "Let thirty thousand Jews be enrolled in the king's army and allowances be given them, as is due to all the king's soldiers. 37 Let some of them be stationed in the king's principal strongholds, and of these let some be given positions of trust in the affairs of the kingdom. Let their superiors and their rulers be chosen from among them, and let them follow their own laws, as the king has commanded in the land of Judah.

38 "Let the three districts that have been added to Judea from the province of Samaria be annexed to Judea so that they may be under one rule and obey no other authority than the high priest. 39 Ptolemais and its confines I give as a present to the sanctuary in Jerusalem for the necessary expenses of the sanctuary. 40 I make a yearly personal grant of fifteen thousand silver shekels out of the royal revenues, taken from appropriate places. 41 All the additional funds that the officials did not hand over as they had done in the first years shall henceforth be handed over for the services of the temple. 42 Moreover, the dues of five thousand silver shekels that used to be taken from the revenue of the sanctuary every year shall be canceled, since these funds belong to the priests who perform the services. 43 All who take refuge in the temple of Jerusalem or in any of its precincts, because of money they owe the king, or because of any other debt, shall be released, together with all the goods they possess in my kingdom. 44 The cost of rebuilding and restoring the structures of the sanctuary shall be covered out of the royal revenue. 45 Likewise the cost of building the walls of Jerusalem and fortifying it all around, and of building walls in Judea, shall be donated from the royal revenue."

46 When Jonathan and the people heard these words, they neither believed nor accepted them, for they remembered the great evil that Demetrius had done in Israel, and the great tribulation he had brought upon them. 47 They therefore decided in favor of Alexander, for he had been the first to address them peaceably, and they remained his allies for the rest of his life.

48 Then King Alexander gathered together a large army and encamped opposite Demetrius. 49 The two kings joined battle, and when the army of Demetrius fled, Alexander pursued him, and overpowered his soldiers. 50 He pressed the battle hard until sunset, and Demetrius fell that day.

Treaty of Ptolemy and Alexander

51 Alexander sent ambassadors to Ptolemy, king of Egypt, with this message: 52 "Now that I have returned to my realm, taken my seat on the throne of my ancestors, and established my rule by crushing Demetrius and gaining control of my country— 53 for I engaged him in battle, he and his army were crushed by us, and we assumed his royal throne— 54 let us now establish friendship with each other. Give me now your daughter for my wife; and as your son-in-law, I will give to you and to her gifts worthy of you."

55 King Ptolemy answered in these words: "Happy the day on which you returned to the land of your ancestors and took your seat on their royal throne! 56 I will do for you what you have written; but meet me in Ptolemais, so that we may see each other, and I will become your father-in-law as you have proposed."

57 So Ptolemy with his daughter Cleopatra† set out from Egypt and came to Ptolemais in the one hundred and sixty-second year. 58 There King Alexander met him, and Ptolemy gave him his daughter Cleopatra in marriage. Their wedding was celebrated at Ptolemais with great splendor according to the custom of kings.

59 King Alexander also wrote to Jonathan to come and meet him. 60 So he went with pomp to Ptolemais, where he met the two kings and gave them and their friends silver and gold and many

---

† **10:30** *The three districts annexed from Samaria*: mentioned by name in 11:34. The present Greek text, by a scribal error, has added "and Galilee" after "Samaria."

10:57 *Cleopatra*: Cleopatra Thea, then about fifteen years old. She later married Demetrius II, and later still, his brother Antiochus VII. Ptolemais (Acco) on the coast of Palestine was a neutral site. *The one hundred and sixty-second year*: 151/150 B.C.

gifts and thus won their favor.* 61 Some villain-
ous men of Israel, transgressors of the law, united
against him to accuse him, but the king paid no
heed to them. 62 The king ordered Jonathan to
be divested of his garments and to be clothed
in royal purple; and so it was done. 63 The king
also had him seated at his side. He said to his
magistrates: "Go with him to the center of the
city and make a proclamation that no one is to
bring charges against him on any grounds or be
troublesome to him for any reason." 64 * When
his accusers saw the honor paid to him according
to the king's proclamation, and him clothed in
purple, they all fled. 65 And so the king honored
him, enrolling him among his Chief Friends, and
he made him governor and chief of the province.
66 So Jonathan returned in peace and happiness
to Jerusalem.

Jonathan Defeats Apollonius

67 In the one hundred and sixty-fifth year,†
Demetrius, son of Demetrius, came from Crete
to the land of his ancestors. 68 When King Alex-
ander heard of it he was greatly troubled, and
returned to Antioch. 69 Demetrius set Apollonius
over Coelesyria.† Having gathered a large army,
Apollonius encamped at Jamnia. From there he
sent this message to Jonathan the high priest:

70 "You are the only one who resists us. I am
laughed at and put to shame on your account.
Why are you exercising authority against us in
the mountains? 71 If you have confidence in
your forces, come down now to us in the plain,
and let us test each other's strength there; for
the forces of the cities are on my side. 72 Inquire
and find out who I am and who the others are
who are helping me. People are saying that you
cannot make a stand against us because your
ancestors were twice put to flight† in their own
land. 73 Now you too will be unable to withstand
our cavalry and such a force as this in the plain,
where there is not a stone or a pebble or a place
to flee."

74 When Jonathan heard the message of Apol-
lonius, he was provoked. Choosing ten thousand
men, he set out from Jerusalem, and Simon his
brother joined him to help him. 75 He encamped
near Joppa, but the people of the city shut him
out because Apollonius had a garrison in Joppa.
When they attacked it, 76 the people of the city
became afraid and opened the gates, and so Jon-
athan took possession of Joppa.†

77 When Apollonius heard of it, he drew up
three thousand cavalry and a large force of in-
fantry. He marched toward Azotus as though he
were going on through, but at the same time he
was advancing into the plain, because he had
such a large number of cavalry to rely on. 78 Jona-
than pursued him toward Azotus, and the armies
engaged in battle. 79 Apollonius, however, had
left a thousand cavalry in hiding behind them.
80 Jonathan discovered that there was an ambush
behind him; his army was surrounded. From
morning until evening they showered his troops
with arrows. 81 But his troops held their ground,
as Jonathan had commanded, while the enemy's
horses became tired out.

82 Then Simon brought forward his force, and
engaged the phalanx in battle. Since the cavalry
were exhausted, the phalanx was crushed by him
and fled, 83 while the cavalry too were scattered
over the plain. They fled to Azotus and entered
Beth-dagon, the temple of their idol, to save
themselves. 84 But Jonathan burned and plun-
dered Azotus with its neighboring towns, and
destroyed by fire both the temple of Dagon and
those who had taken refuge in it.* 85 Those who
fell by the sword, together with those who were
burned alive, came to about eight thousand.

86 Then Jonathan left there and encamped at
Askalon, and the people of that city came out
to meet him with great pomp. 87 Jonathan and
those with him then returned to Jerusalem, with
much spoil. 88 When King Alexander heard of
these events, he accorded new honors to Jona-
than. 89 He sent him a gold buckle, such as is usu-
ally given to King's Kinsmen;† he also gave him
Ekron and all its territory as a possession.

Alliance of Ptolemy and Demetrius II

11 1 Then the king of Egypt gathered forces
as numerous as the sands of the seashore,
and many ships; and he sought by deceit to take
Alexander's kingdom and add it to his own. 2 He
set out for Syria with peaceful words, and the
people in the cities opened their gates to wel-
come him, as King Alexander had ordered them
to do, since Ptolemy was his father-in-law. 3 But
when Ptolemy entered the cities, he stationed a
garrison of troops in each one.

†

10:67 *The one hundred and sixty-fifth year*: 147 B.C. *Demetrius*: Demetrius II Nicator.

10:69 *Coelesyria*: originally the region between the Lebanon and anti-Lebanon mountains, it came later to refer to Palestine also. *Jamnia*: on the coast, also known as Yavneh (5:58).

10:72 *Twice put to flight*: the reference is unclear.

10:76 *Joppa*: about forty miles northwest of Jerusalem. For the first time the Maccabees took possession of a seaport, though nominally it was on behalf of King Alexander.

10:89 *Kinsmen*: a rank higher than Chief Friends.

*

10:60 1 Mc 2:18.

10:64–65 1 Mc 2:18; 11:27.

10:84 1 Mc 11:4; 1 Sm 5:2–5.

[4]As they neared Azotus, they showed him the temple of Dagon destroyed by fire, Azotus and its suburbs demolished, corpses lying about, and the charred bodies of those burned in the war, for they had heaped them up along his route.* [5]They told the king what Jonathan had done in order to denigrate him; but the king said nothing. [6]Jonathan met the king with pomp at Joppa, and they greeted each other and spent the night there. [7]Jonathan accompanied the king as far as the river called Eleutherus† and then returned to Jerusalem.

[8]And so King Ptolemy took possession of the cities along the seacoast as far as Seleucia by the sea,† plotting evil schemes against Alexander all the while. [9]He sent ambassadors to King Demetrius, saying: "Come, let us make a covenant with each other; I will give you my daughter whom Alexander has married, and you shall reign over your father's kingdom. [10]I regret that I gave him my daughter, for he has sought to kill me."† [11]He was criticizing Alexander, however, because he coveted his kingdom. [12]After taking his daughter away, Ptolemy gave her to Demetrius and broke with Alexander; the enmity between them was now evident. [13]Then Ptolemy entered Antioch and assumed the crown† of Asia; thus he set upon his head two crowns, that of Egypt and that of Asia.

[14]Now King Alexander was in Cilicia at that time, because the people of that region had revolted. [15]When Alexander heard the news, he came against Ptolemy in battle. Ptolemy marched out and met him with a strong force and routed him. [16]When Alexander fled to Arabia to seek protection, King Ptolemy was triumphant. [17]Zabdiel the Arabian cut off Alexander's head and sent it to Ptolemy. [18]But three days later King Ptolemy himself died, and his troops in the strongholds were killed by the inhabitants of the strongholds. [19]Thus Demetrius became king in the one hundred and sixty-seventh year.†

Alliance of Jonathan and Demetrius II

[20]In those days Jonathan gathered together the people of Judea to attack the citadel in Jerusalem, and they set up many siege engines against it. [21]But some transgressors of the law, enemies of their own nation, went to the king and informed him that Jonathan was besieging the citadel. [22]When Demetrius heard this, he was enraged; and as soon as he heard it, he set out and came to Ptolemais. He wrote to Jonathan to discontinue the siege and to meet him for a conference at Ptolemais as soon as possible.

[23]On hearing this, Jonathan ordered the siege to continue. He selected some elders and priests of Israel and put himself at risk. [24]Taking with him silver, gold and apparel, and many other presents, he went to the king at Ptolemais, and found favor with him. [25]Although certain renegades of his own nation kept on bringing charges against him, [26]the king treated him just as his predecessors had done and exalted him in the presence of all his Friends. [27]He confirmed him in the high priesthood and in the other honors he had previously held, and had him enrolled among his Chief Friends.

[28]Jonathan asked the king to exempt Judea and the three districts of Samaria from tribute, promising him in return three hundred talents.* [29]The king agreed and wrote a letter to Jonathan about all these matters as follows:

[30]* "King Demetrius sends greetings to his brother† Jonathan and to the Jewish nation. [31]We are sending you, for your information, a copy of the letter that we wrote to Lasthenes† our Kinsman concerning you. [32]'King Demetrius sends greetings to his father Lasthenes. [33]Upon the Jewish nation, who are our friends and observe their obligations to us, we have decided to bestow benefits because of the good will they show us. [34]* Therefore we confirm their possession, not only of the territory of Judea, but also of the three districts of Aphairema,† Lydda, and Ramathaim. These districts, together with all their dependencies, are hereby transferred from Samaria to Judea for those who offer sacrifices in Jerusalem in lieu of the royal taxes the king used to receive yearly from the produce of earth and trees. [35]From payment of the other things

11:7 *Eleutherus*: two hundred miles north of Joppa, in the second century B.C. the northern limit of Coelesyria.

11:8 *Seleucia by the sea*: at the mouth of the Orontes, the port city of Antioch.

11:10 *I regret . . . to kill me*: according to Josephus, Ammonius, a friend of Alexander, had tried to assassinate Ptolemy, and the latter claimed that Alexander was the instigator, thus calumniating him to gain his kingdom (v. 11).

11:13 *Crown*: lit., diadem.

11:19 *The one hundred and sixty-seventh year*: 146/145 B.C. The two deaths (vv. 17–18) occurred in the summer of 145 B.C.

11:30 *Brother*: this term and "father" in v. 32 are honorific expressions used of the Kinsmen.

11:31 *Lasthenes*: leader of the mercenary troops who had come with Demetrius from Crete. He was now the young king's chief minister and was apparently responsible for the disastrous policy (v. 38) of disbanding the national army.

11:34 *Aphairema*: the Ophrah of Jos 18:23; 1 Sm 13:17; the Ephron of 2 Chr 13:19; and the Ephraim of Jn 11:54—modern et-Taiyibeh, five miles northeast of Bethel. *Lydda*: the Lod of the postexilic Jews (Ezr 2:33; Neh 11:35) and the hometown of Aeneas, who was cured by Peter (Acts 9:32–34). It is ten miles southeast of Joppa. *Ramathaim*: the Ramathaim-zophim of 1 Sm 1:1, and the Arimathea of Mt 27:57, modern Rentis, nine miles northeast of Lydda.

11:4 1 Mc 10:84.
11:28 1 Mc 10:29; 11:34–35.
11:30–37 1 Mc 10:25–45.
11:34–35 1 Mc 10:29; 11:28.

that would henceforth be due to us, namely, the tithes and taxes, as well as the salt tax, and the crown tax—from all these we grant them release. 36 Henceforth and forever not one of these provisions shall ever be revoked. 37 See to it, therefore, that a copy of these instructions be made and given to Jonathan. Let it be displayed on the holy mountain in a conspicuous place.' "

The Intrigue of Trypho

38 When King Demetrius saw that the land was peaceful under his rule and that he had no opposition, he dismissed his entire army, each to his own home, except the foreign troops which he had hired from the islands of the nations. So all the soldiers who had served under his predecessors became hostile to him. 39 When a certain Trypho, who had previously supported Alexander, saw that all the troops were grumbling against Demetrius, he went to Imalkue the Arabian, who was raising Alexander's young son Antiochus.* 40 Trypho kept urging Imalkue to hand over the boy to him, so that he might succeed his father as king. He told him of all that Demetrius had done and of the hostility his soldiers had for him; and he remained there for many days.

Jonathan Aids Demetrius II

41 Meanwhile Jonathan sent the request to King Demetrius to withdraw the troops in the citadel from Jerusalem and from the other strongholds, for they were constantly waging war on Israel. 42 Demetrius, in turn, sent this word to Jonathan: "I will do not only this for you and your nation, but I will greatly honor you and your nation when I find the opportunity. 43 Now, therefore, you will do well to send men to fight for me, because all my troops have revolted." 44 So Jonathan sent three thousand good fighting men to him at Antioch. When they came to the king, he was delighted over their arrival. 45 The populace, one hundred and twenty thousand strong, massed in the center of the city in an attempt to kill the king. 46 So the king took refuge in the palace, while the populace gained control of the main streets of the city and prepared for battle. 47 Then the king called the Jewish force to his aid. They all rallied around him and spread out through the city. On that day they killed about a hundred thousand in the city. 48 At the same time, they set the city on fire and took much spoil. Thus they saved the king. 49 When the populace saw that the Jewish force controlled the city, they lost courage and cried out to the king in supplication, 50 "Extend the hand of friendship to us, and make the Jews stop attacking us and the city." 51 So they threw down their weapons and made peace. The Jews thus gained honor in the eyes of the king and all his subjects, and they became renowned throughout his kingdom. Finally they returned to Jerusalem with much plunder.

52 But when King Demetrius was sure of his royal throne, and the land was peaceful under his rule, 53 he broke all his promises and became estranged from Jonathan. Instead of repaying Jonathan for all the favors he had received from him, he caused him much distress.

Alliance of Jonathan and Antiochus VI

54 After this, Trypho returned and brought with him the young boy Antiochus, who became king and put on the diadem.* 55 All the soldiers whom Demetrius had discharged rallied around Antiochus and fought against Demetrius, who was routed and fled. 56 Trypho captured the elephants and occupied Antioch. 57 Then young Antiochus wrote to Jonathan: "I confirm you in the high priesthood and appoint you ruler over the four districts, and to be one of the King's Friends." 58 He also sent him gold dishes and a table service, gave him the right to drink from gold cups, to dress in royal purple, and to wear a gold buckle.* 59 Likewise, he made Jonathan's brother Simon governor of the region from the Ladder of Tyre† to the borders of Egypt.

Campaigns of Jonathan and Simon

60 Jonathan set out and traveled through the province of West-of-Euphrates† and its cities, and all the forces of Syria espoused his cause as allies. When he arrived at Askalon, the citizens welcomed him with pomp. 61 But when he set out for Gaza, the people of Gaza shut him out. So he besieged it, and burned and plundered its suburbs. 62 Then the people of Gaza appealed to Jonathan, and he granted them terms of peace. He took the sons of their leaders as hostages and sent them to Jerusalem. He then traveled on through the province as far as Damascus.

63 Jonathan heard that the generals of Demetrius had come with a strong force to Kadesh in

1 MC

†

11:59 *Ladder of Tyre*: modern Ras en-Naqurah, where the mountains reach the sea, so that the coastal road must ascend in a series of steps. Thus the Maccabees controlled the coastal area from Syria to Egypt.

11:60 *The province of West-of-Euphrates*: refers here to the territory of Palestine and Coelesyria, but not Upper Syria; cf. 7:8.

*

11:39 1 Mc 12:39.
11:54 1 Mc 11:39; 12:39.
11:58 1 Mc 2:18.

Galilee, intending to remove him from office.
64 So he went to meet them, leaving his brother
Simon in the province. 65 * Simon encamped
against Beth-zur, attacked it for many days, and
shut in the inhabitants. 66 They appealed to him,
and he granted them terms of peace. He expelled
them from the city, took possession of it, and put
a garrison there.
67 Meanwhile, Jonathan and his army pitched
their camp near the waters of Gennesaret, and
at daybreak they went to the plain of Hazor.†
68 There the army of the foreigners met him on
the plain. Having first detached an ambush in the
mountains, this army mounted a frontal attack.
69 Then those in ambush rose out of their places
and joined in the battle. 70 All of Jonathan's men
fled; no one stayed except the army commanders
Mattathias, son of Absalom, and Judas, son of
Chalphi. 71 Jonathan tore his clothes, threw dust
on his head, and prayed. 72 Then he went back
to the battle and routed them, and they fled.
73 Those of his men who were running away saw
it and returned to him; and with him they pur-
sued the enemy as far as their camp in Kadesh,
and there they encamped. 74 About three thou-
sand of the foreign troops fell on that day. Then
Jonathan returned to Jerusalem.

Alliances with Rome and Sparta

12 1 When Jonathan saw that the time was
right, he chose men and sent them to
Rome to confirm and renew the friendship with
the Romans.* 2 He also sent letters to the Spar-
tans and other places to the same effect.
3 After reaching Rome, the men entered the
senate chamber and said, "The high priest Jona-
than and the Jewish people have sent us to renew
the friendship and alliance of earlier times with
them." 4 The Romans gave them letters addressed
to authorities in various places, with the request
to provide them with safe conduct to the land
of Judah.
5 This is a copy of the letter that Jonathan wrote
to the Spartans: 6 "Jonathan the high priest, the
senate of the nation, the priests, and the rest of
the Jewish people send greetings to their brothers
the Spartans. 7 Long ago a letter was sent† to the
high priest Onias from Arius, who then reigned
over you, stating that you are our brothers, as
the attached copy shows.* 8 Onias welcomed the
envoy with honor and received the letter, which
spoke clearly of alliance and friendship. 9 Though
we have no need of these things, since we have
for our encouragement the holy books that are
in our possession,† * 10 we have ventured to send
word to you for the renewal of brotherhood and
friendship, lest we become strangers to you; a
long time has passed since you sent your mes-
sage to us. 11 We, on our part, have unceasingly
remembered you in the sacrifices and prayers
that we offer on our feasts and other appropriate
days, as it is right and proper to remember broth-
ers. 12 We likewise rejoice in your renown. 13 But
many tribulations and many wars have beset us,
and the kings around us have attacked us. 14 We
did not wish to be troublesome to you and to
the rest of our allies and friends in these wars.
15 For we have the help of Heaven for our sup-
port, and we have been saved from our enemies,
and our enemies have been humbled. 16 So we
have chosen Numenius, son of Antiochus, and
Antipater, son of Jason, and we have sent them
to the Romans to renew with them the friendship
and alliance of earlier times.* 17 We have also or-
dered them to come to you and greet you, and to
deliver to you our letter concerning the renewal
of our brotherhood. 18 Therefore kindly send us
an answer on this matter."
19 This is a copy of the letter that they sent to
Onias: 20 * "Arius, king of the Spartans, sends
greetings to Onias the high priest. 21 A document
has been found stating that the Spartans and the
Jews are brothers and that they are of the family
of Abraham. 22 Now that we have learned this,
kindly write to us about your welfare. 23 We, for
our part, declare to you that your animals and
your possessions are ours, and ours are yours.
We have, therefore, given orders that you should
be told of this."

More Campaigns of Jonathan and Simon

24 Then Jonathan heard that the officers of
Demetrius had returned to attack him with a
stronger army than before. 25 So he set out from
Jerusalem and met them in the territory of Ha-
math,† giving them no opportunity to enter
his province. 26 The spies he had sent into their
camp came back and reported to him that the

†

11:67 *Plain of Hazor*: the site of the ancient Canaanite city (Jos 11:10), ten miles north of the Lake of Gennesaret.

12:7 *Long ago a letter was sent*: i.e., a century and a half before. *Onias*: Onias I, high priest from 323 to 300 or 290 B.C. *Arius*: Arius I, king from 309 to 265 B.C.

12:9 *The holy books . . . in our possession*: a reference to "the law, the prophets and other books," as mentioned in the Prologue to Sirach.

12:25 *Territory of Hamath*: the Seleucid territory of Upper Syria northeast of Coelesyria and separated from it by the Eleutherus River. The latter territory was under the command of Jonathan (11:59–60).

11:65–66 1 Mc 9:52; 10:14.
12:1 1 Mc 8:17.
12:7 1 Mc 12:20–23.
12:9 2 Mc 2:14.
12:16 1 Mc 14:22; 15:15.
12:20–23 1 Mc 12:7.

enemy were preparing to attack them that night.
27 Therefore, when the sun set, Jonathan ordered
his men to keep watch, with their weapons at
the ready for battle, throughout the night; and
he set outposts around the camp. 28 When the
enemy heard that Jonathan and his men were
ready for battle, their hearts sank with fear and
dread. They lighted fires in their camp and then
withdrew. 29 But because Jonathan and his men
were watching the campfires burning, they did
not know until the morning what had happened.
30 Then Jonathan pursued them, but he could
not overtake them, for they had crossed the river
Eleutherus. 31 So Jonathan turned aside against
the Arabians who are called Zabadeans, and he
struck them down and plundered them. 32 Then
he broke camp, marched on toward Damascus
and traveled through the whole region.
33 Simon also set out and traveled as far as
Askalon and its neighboring strongholds. He
then turned to Joppa and took it by surprise,
34 for he heard that its people intended to hand
over the stronghold to the supporters of Demetrius. He left a garrison there to guard it.
35 When Jonathan returned, he assembled the
elders of the people, and with them he made
plans for building strongholds in Judea, 36 for
making the walls of Jerusalem still higher, and
for erecting a high barrier between the citadel
and the city, to separate it from the city and isolate it, so that its garrison could neither buy nor
sell. 37 The people therefore gathered together
to build up the city, for part of the wall of the
eastern valley had collapsed. And Jonathan repaired the quarter called Chaphenatha. 38 Simon
likewise built up Adida in the Shephelah, and
fortified it by installing gates and bars.

Capture of Jonathan

39 Then Trypho sought to become king of Asia,
assume the diadem, and do violence to King
Antiochus.* 40 But he was afraid that Jonathan
would not permit him, but would fight against
him. Looking for a way to seize and kill him,
he set out and came to Beth-shan. 41 Jonathan
marched out to meet him with forty thousand
picked fighting men and came to Beth-shan.
42 But when Trypho saw that Jonathan had arrived with a large army he was afraid to do him
violence. 43 Instead, he received him with honor,
introduced him to all his friends, and gave him
presents. He also ordered his friends and soldiers
to obey him as they would himself. 44 Then he
said to Jonathan: "Why have you put all these
people to so much trouble when we are not at
war? 45 Now pick out a few men to stay with you,
send the rest to their homes, and then come with
me to Ptolemais. I will hand it over to you together with other strongholds and the remaining
troops, as well as all the officials; then I will turn
back and go home. That is why I came here."
46 Jonathan trusted him and did as he said.
He dismissed his troops, and they returned to
the land of Judah. 47 But he kept with him three
thousand men, of whom he left two thousand in
Galilee while one thousand accompanied him.
48 Then as soon as Jonathan entered Ptolemais,
the people of Ptolemais closed the gates and
seized him; all who had entered with him, they
killed with the sword.*
49 Then Trypho sent soldiers and cavalry to
Galilee and the Great Plain† to destroy all
Jonathan's men. 50 These, upon learning that
Jonathan had been captured and killed along
with his companions, encouraged one another
and went out in close formation, ready to fight.
51 As their pursuers saw that they were ready to
fight for their lives, they turned back. 52 Thus
all Jonathan's men came safely into the land of
Judah. They mourned Jonathan and those who
were with him. They were in great fear, and all
Israel fell into deep mourning. 53 All the nations
round about sought to crush them. They said,
"Now that they have no leader or helper, let us
make war on them and wipe out their memory
from the earth."*

IV. Leadership of Simon

Simon as Leader

13 1 When Simon heard that Trypho was gathering a large army to invade and ravage the
land of Judah, 2 and saw that the people were
trembling with terror, he went up to Jerusalem.
There he assembled the people 3 and exhorted
them in these words: "You know what I, my
brothers, and my father's house have done for
the laws and the sanctuary; what battles and
hardships we have seen. 4 For the sake of this, for
the sake of Israel, all my brothers have perished,
and I alone am left. 5 Far be it from me, then, to
save my own life in any time of distress, for I am
not better than my brothers. 6 But I will avenge
my nation and the sanctuary, as well as your
wives and children, for out of hatred all the Gentiles have united to crush us."*

† **12:49** *The Great Plain*: of Beth-shan (v. 41), where Jonathan's disbanded troops remained.

* **12:39** 1 Mc 11:39–40, 54–55.
12:48 1 Mc 5:15, 22, 55.
12:53 1 Mc 5:2; 13:6.
13:6 1 Mc 5:2; 12:53.

7 As the people heard these words, their spirit
was rekindled. 8 They shouted in reply: "You are
our leader in place of your brothers Judas and
Jonathan. 9 Fight our battles, and we will do ev-
erything that you tell us." 10 So Simon mustered
all the men able to fight, and hastening to com-
plete the walls of Jerusalem, fortified it on every
side. 11 He sent Jonathan, son of Absalom, to
Joppa with a strong force; Jonathan drove out the
occupants and remained there.

Trypho's Deceit

12 Then Trypho moved from Ptolemais with a
large army to invade the land of Judah, bring-
ing Jonathan with him as a prisoner. 13 Simon
encamped at Adida, facing the plain. 14 When
Trypho learned that Simon had succeeded his
brother Jonathan, and that he intended to fight
him, he sent ambassadors to him with this mes-
sage: 15 "It was on account of the money your
brother Jonathan owed the royal treasury in
connection with the offices that he held, that
we have detained him. 16 Now send a hundred
talents of silver, and two of his sons as hostages
to guarantee that when he is set free he will not
revolt against us, and we will release him."

17 Simon knew that they were speaking deceit-
fully to him. Nevertheless, for fear of provoking
much hostility among the people, he sent for the
money and the boys, 18 lest the people say "Jon-
athan perished because I would not send Trypho
the money and the boys." 19 So he sent the boys
and the hundred talents; but Trypho broke his
promise and would not release Jonathan.

20 † Next Trypho moved to invade and ravage
the country. His troops went around by the road
that leads to Adora, but Simon and his army
moved along opposite him everywhere he went.
21 The people in the citadel kept sending emissar-
ies to Trypho, pressing him to come to them by
way of the wilderness, and to send them provi-
sions. 22 Although Trypho got all his cavalry ready
to go, there was a very heavy snowfall that night,
and he could not go on account of the snow. So
he left for Gilead. 23 When he was approaching
Baskama,† he had Jonathan killed and buried him
there. 24 Then Trypho returned to his own land.

Jonathan's Tomb

25 Simon sent for the remains of his brother
Jonathan, and buried him in Modein, the city
of his ancestors. 26 All Israel bewailed him with
solemn lamentation, mourning over him for
many days. 27 Then Simon erected over the
tomb of his father and his brothers a monu-
ment of stones, polished front and back, and
raised high enough to be seen at a distance.
28 He set up seven pyramids facing one another
for his father and his mother and his four
brothers.* 29 For the pyramids he devised a
setting of massive columns, which he adorned
with suits of armor as a perpetual memorial,
and next to the armor carved ships, which
could be seen by all who sailed the sea. 30 This
tomb which he built at Modein is there to the
present day.

Alliance of Simon and Demetrius II

31 Trypho dealt treacherously with the young
King Antiochus. He killed him 32 and became
king in his place, putting on the crown of Asia.
Thus he brought much evil on the land.* 33 Si-
mon, for his part, built up the strongholds of Ju-
dea, fortifying them all around with high towers,
thick walls, and gates with bars, and he stored
up provisions in the strongholds. 34 Simon also
chose men and sent them to King Demetrius to
obtain for the land an exemption from taxation,
since Trypho did nothing but plunder. 35 King
Demetrius replied favorably and sent him the
following letter:

36 "King Demetrius sends greetings to Simon,
high priest and friend of kings, and to the elders
and the Jewish people. 37 We have received the
gold crown and the palm branch that you sent.
We are ready to make a lasting peace with you
and to write to our officials to grant you exemp-
tion. 38 Whatever decrees we have made in your
regard remain in force, and the strongholds that
you have built you may keep. 39 We pardon any
oversights and offenses committed up to now, as
well as the crown tax that you owe. Any other tax
that used to be collected in Jerusalem shall no
longer be collected there. 40 Any of you qualified
for enrollment in our service may be enrolled.
Let there be peace between us."

41 Thus in the one hundred and seventieth
year,† the yoke of the Gentiles was removed
from Israel, 42 and the people began to write in
their records and contracts, "In the first year of
Simon, great high priest, governor, and leader
of the Jews."

---

† **13:20–21** The invaders made a wide flanking movement to invade Judea from the south (see 4:29; 6:31). Adora was a few miles southwest of Beth-zur. They would avoid Beth-zur itself and other strongholds of the Maccabees by following the way of the wilderness.

13:23 *Baskama*: perhaps northeast of the Sea of Galilee.

13:41 *The one hundred and seventieth year*: March, 142, to April, 141 B.C., by the Temple calendar.

* **13:28** 2 Sm 18:18. **13:32** 1 Mc 8:6.

Simon Captures Gazara

43 * In those days Simon besieged Gazara†
and surrounded it with troops. He made a siege
machine, brought it up against the city, and at-
tacked and captured one of the towers. 44 Those
in the siege machine leaped down into the city
and a great tumult arose there. 45 Those in the
city, together with their wives and children, went
up on the wall, with their garments rent, and
cried out in loud voices, begging Simon to grant
them terms of peace. 46 They said, "Treat us not
according to our evil deeds but according to your
mercy." 47 So Simon came to terms with them
and did not attack them. He expelled them from
the city, however, and he purified the houses in
which there were idols. Then he entered the city
with hymns and songs of praise. 48 After remov-
ing from it everything that was impure, he settled
there people who observed the law. He improved
its fortifications and built himself a residence.

Simon Captures the Citadel

49 The people in the citadel in Jerusalem were
prevented from going out into the country and
back to buy or sell; they suffered greatly from
hunger, and many of them died of starvation.
50 They finally cried out to Simon, and he gave
them terms of peace. He expelled them from
the citadel and cleansed it of impurities. 51 On
the twenty-third day of the second month,†
in the one hundred and seventy-first year, the
Jews entered the citadel with shouts of praise, the
waving of palm branches, the playing of harps
and cymbals and lyres, and the singing of hymns
and canticles, because a great enemy of Israel had
been crushed.* 52 Simon decreed that this day
should be celebrated every year with rejoicing. He
also strengthened the fortifications of the temple
mount alongside the citadel, and he and his peo-
ple dwelt there. 53 Seeing that his son John† was
now a grown man, Simon made him commander
of all his soldiers, and he dwelt in Gazara.

Capture of Demetrius II

14 1 In the one hundred and seventy-second
year,† King Demetrius assembled his army
and marched into Media to obtain help so that
he could fight Trypho. 2 When Arsaces,† king
of Persia and Media, heard that Demetrius had
entered his territory, he sent one of his generals
to take him alive. 3 The general went forth and
attacked the army of Demetrius; he captured
him and brought him to Arsaces, who put him
under guard.

Praise of Simon

4 The land was at rest all the days of Simon,
who sought the good of his nation.
His rule delighted his people
and his glory all his days.*
5 As his crowning glory he took Joppa for a port
and made it a gateway to the isles of the
sea.*
6 He enlarged the borders of his nation
and gained control of the country.
7 He took many prisoners of war
and made himself master of Gazara, Beth-
zur, and the citadel.
He cleansed the citadel of its impurities;
there was no one to withstand him.
8 The people cultivated their land in peace;
the land yielded its produce,
the trees of the field their fruit.*
9 Old men sat in the squares,
all talking about the good times,
while the young men put on the glorious
raiment of war.*
10 He supplied the cities with food
and equipped them with means of defense,
till his glorious name reached the ends of
the earth.
11 He brought peace to the land,
and Israel was filled with great joy.*
12 Every one sat under his vine and fig tree,
with no one to disturb them.*
13 No attacker was left in the land;
the kings in those days were crushed.
14 He strengthened all the lowly among his
people
and was zealous for the law;
he destroyed the lawless and the wicked.
15 The sanctuary he made splendid
and multiplied its furnishings.

Alliance with Rome and Sparta

16 When people in Rome and even in Sparta
heard that Jonathan had died, they were deeply

† **13:43** *Gazara*: ancient Gezer, a key position in the Shephelah, fortified by Bacchides in 160 B.C.; cf. 9:52.

13:51 *The twenty-third day of the second month*: June 3, 141 B.C.

13:53 *John*: John Hyrcanus, who was to succeed his father as ruler and high priest; cf. 16:23–24.

14:1 *The one hundred and seventy-second year*: 141/140 B.C. The expedition began most probably in the spring of 140.

14:2 *Arsaces*: Arsaces VI, also called Mithridates I, the Parthian king (171–138 B.C.). Parthians had overrun Persia and now held Babylonia, both of which had hitherto belonged to the Seleucid empire. The Greeks and Macedonians in these countries had appealed to Demetrius for help.

* **13:43–48** 2 Mc 10:32–38.
13:51 1 Mc 1:36.
14:4 1 Mc 3:3–9.
14:5 1 Mc 12:33; 13:11.
14:8 Lv 26:3–4; Zec 8:12.
14:9 Zec 8:4–5.
14:11 Lv 26:6.
14:12 Mi 4:4; Zec 3:10.

grieved.† 17 But when they heard that his brother Simon had become high priest in his place and was master of the territory and its cities, 18 they sent him inscribed tablets of bronze to renew with him the friendship and alliance that they had established with his brothers Judas and Jonathan.* 19 These were read before the assembly in Jerusalem.

20 This is a copy of the letter that the Spartans sent: "The rulers and the city of the Spartans send greetings to Simon the high priest, the elders, the priests, and the rest of the Jewish people, our brothers. 21 The ambassadors sent to our people have informed us of your glory and renown, and we rejoiced at their coming. 22 In accordance with what they said we have recorded the following in the public decrees: Numenius, son of Antiochus, and Antipater, son of Jason, ambassadors of the Jews, have come to us to renew their friendship with us.* 23 The people have resolved to receive these men with honor, and to deposit a copy of their words in the public archives, so that the people of Sparta may have a record of them. A copy of this decree has been made for Simon the high priest."

24 After this, Simon sent Numenius to Rome with a large gold shield weighing a thousand minas, to confirm the alliance with the Romans.

Official Honors for Simon

25 When the people heard of these things, they said, "How shall we thank Simon and his sons? 26 He and his brothers and his father's house have stood firm and repulsed Israel's enemies, and so have established its freedom." So they made an inscription on bronze tablets, which they affixed to pillars on Mount Zion.

27 The following is a copy of the inscription: "On the eighteenth day of Elul,† in the one hundred and seventy-second year, that is, the third year under Simon the great high priest in Asaramel, 28 in a great assembly of priests, people, rulers of the nation, and elders of the region, the following proclamation was made to us:

29 " 'Since there have often been wars in our country, Simon, son of the priest Mattathias, descendant of Joarib, and his brothers have put themselves in danger and resisted the enemies of their nation, so that their sanctuary and law might be maintained, and they have thus brought great glory to their nation. 30 Jonathan rallied the nation, became their high priest, and was gathered to his people. 31 When their enemies sought to invade and ravage their country and to violate their sanctuary, 32 Simon rose up and fought for his nation, spending large sums of his own money to equip his nation's forces and give them their pay. 33 He fortified the cities of Judea, especially the border city of Beth-zur, formerly the site of the enemy's weaponry, and he stationed there a garrison of Jewish soldiers. 34 He also fortified Joppa by the sea and Gazara on the border of Azotus, a place previously occupied by the enemy; these cities he settled with Jews and furnished them with all that was necessary for their restoration. 35 When the people saw Simon's fidelity and the glory he planned to bring to his nation, they made him their leader and high priest because of all he had accomplished and the justice and fidelity he had shown his nation. In every way he sought to exalt his people.

36 " 'In his time and under his guidance they succeeded in driving the Gentiles out of their country and those in the City of David in Jerusalem, who had built for themselves a citadel from which they used to sally forth to defile the environs of the sanctuary and inflict grave injury on its purity. 37 In this citadel he stationed Jewish soldiers, and he strengthened its fortifications for the security of the land and the city, while he also built up the wall of Jerusalem to a greater height. 38 Consequently, King Demetrius confirmed him in the high priesthood, 39 made him one of his Friends, and conferred great honor on him.* 40 This was because he had heard that the Romans had addressed the Jews as friends, allies, and brothers, that they had received Simon's envoys with honor, 41 and that the Jewish people and their priests had decided the following: Simon shall be their leader and high priest forever until a trustworthy prophet arises.* 42 He shall act as governor over them, and shall have charge of the sanctuary, to make regulations concerning its functions and concerning the country, its weapons and strongholds. 43 He shall be obeyed by all. All contracts in the country shall be written in his name, and he shall be clothed in purple and gold.* 44 It shall not be lawful for any of the people or priests to nullify any of these decisions, or to contradict the orders given by him, or to convene an assembly in the country

---

† **14:16** The embassy to Rome and Sparta was sent soon after Simon's accession to power, and the replies were received before Demetrius' expedition (vv. 1–3), probably in 142 B.C.

14:27 *Eighteenth day of Elul*: September 13, 140 B.C. *Asaramel*: perhaps a Hebrew name meaning "court of the people of God."

---

* **14:18** 1 Mc 8:22.
14:22 1 Mc 12:16; 15:15.
14:39 1 Mc 2:18.
14:41 1 Mc 4:46; 9:27.
14:43 1 Mc 10:20, 89.

Praying with the Bible

"My dear young friends, I urge you to become familiar with the Bible, and to have it at hand so that it can be your compass pointing out the road to follow."

(Message of the Holy Father Benedict XVI to the Youth of the World on the Occasion of the 21st World Youth Day)

The Bible is one of the greatest sources of inspiration we can tap into. When we pray with the Bible, God can deeply touch and change our lives. The more we are willing to pray with the Scriptures, the more we can enter into the profound mystery of God's relationship with all of humanity. God's word is the compass that leads us more deeply into the immense heart of God. This is why the Church proclaims the Scriptures every time we worship together and why all are encouraged to use the Bible in our private prayer.

The pages of this insert teach specific techniques for praying with the Bible. Look these over and think about which suggestions might work for you.

By praying with the Scriptures, we discover that God's story is our story. God's life is intimately connected with our lives. The unfinished part of the story is our response to God's love for us. Each of us has a part in the great story of God's salvation of all humanity.

Tips for Praying with the Bible

For our spiritual journey, our earthly pilgrimage, God has provided us with a guide who knows of the human experience from the inside out. God the Father has given us Jesus the Son as the Way, the way to the New Jerusalem—one of the biblical descriptions of heaven.

Jesus shows us the importance of prayer for our journey. Through prayer Jesus clearly understood the will of his Father. Through prayer Jesus gained and maintained his burning desire to do the will of God. We know from the Gospels that the Hebrew Scriptures were an important part of Jesus' prayer life. The Bible was a compass that helped point Jesus to his Father. God wishes the Bible to be the same for us. So here are some tips for using the Bible in your prayer:

Tip 1: Be Creative in Making Time for Prayer

Your life is busy. Sometimes finding even fifteen minutes for prayer seems impossible, but it can be done. Allow your daily routine to call you to prayer. Mark a favorite psalm in your Bible and pray it when you get up in the morning. When you head off for school, say a short verse like "Prosper the work of our hands" (Ps 90:17, see "Memorizing Bible Passages" section). Before going to bed, spend a few minutes using lectio divina (see next section) to listen to God before going to sleep.

Tip 2: Engage Your Imagination

When praying with the Bible, use your imagination to let the Bible stories come alive in a personal way. Put yourself in the Bible story, and ask, "What do I see? What do I smell? What do I hear?" Pretend you are one of the people in the story, and ask, "How do I feel about what is happening or what is being said?"

Tip 3: Listen

Saint Ambrose once said, "We speak to [God] when we pray; we listen to him when we read the [Scriptures]." Prayer is a dialogue with God, and Scripture is one of the primary ways God speaks to us. So when you read the Bible, it is always a good idea to take a quiet moment to "listen." What might God be saying to you through these sacred words?

"What might God be saying to YOU through these sacred words?"

Lectio Divina

Lectio divina is a very ancient art for praying with the Bible. It is a prayer technique for reading the Bible slowly and contemplatively, allowing God's word to shed insights on your life. It cultivates the ability to listen deeply, to hear the word of God with the ear of your heart. Lectio divina was practiced in the early Christian monasteries of the third and fourth centuries. In the sixth century, it was written into the Rule of Saint Benedict as a requirement for the spiritual life of monks.

The Movements of Lectio Divina

In traditional lectio divina, there are five movements. These movements lead you from hearing the word of God to applying God's word to your everyday life.

Step 1: Lectio (lex–ee–oh). This step is the reading of and listening to the word of God. This is a reverential listening, listening in a spirit of silence and awe because it is the sacred word of God. In this step, listen for a word or phrase from the Scripture passage that is God's word for you today.

Step 2: Meditatio (med–it–tots–ee–oh). This step is meditation on the Scripture passage. Allow the word of God to interact with your thoughts, your hopes, your memories, and your desires. Allow the Scriptures to touch you and affect you at your deepest level of being.

Step 3: Oratio (or–ot–see–oh). This step is responding to God with conscious prayer. It is both a dialogue with God and an offering of a part of yourself to God. In this prayer, open your real self to be touched and changed by the word of God.

Step 4: Contemplatio (con–tem–plot–see–oh). This step is contemplation. In silence, rest in the unconditional love of God.

Step 5: Actio (ax–ee–oh) (also known as operatio). In this step, ask yourself:

- What does the word of God invite me to do?
- What does this passage of Scripture call me to do or undo, or to be?

How to Pray Using Lectio Divina

The following steps are a guide to praying with the Bible using lectio divina. You can use this method with any passage of Scripture, but it works best when the passage isn't too long. For example, you can use lectio divina with the next Sunday's Gospel reading.

Step 1: Lectio

Read the Scripture passage. Try reading it out loud. Try reading it several times. Let the words sink in deeply. Open your mind and heart to the meaning of the words.

Step 2: Meditatio

Reflect on the Scripture passage. Ask yourself questions such as the following:

- What does this passage say to me?
- Who am I in this passage?
- What do I see? What do I hear?
- What do I think?
- Which character do I most relate to?
- What do I most need to learn from this?

Try taking notes on your answers to the questions. Try journaling about the insights you gain through reflection.

Step 3: Oratio

Pray with the passage of Scripture you are reflecting on. What does the word invite you to pray about? Let the following questions guide you:

- What do I want to communicate to God?
- What am I longing for in my relationship with God?
- What do I desire in my prayer life?
- What secrets of my heart are ready to be expressed? Is there joy? grief? fear? gratitude?

Express your inner thoughts to God in prayer.

Step 4: Contemplatio

Simply let yourself rest in the presence of God. Let go of all distracting thoughts. Settle into the tenderness of God's love.

Step 5: Actio

Answer the following questions with utter honesty:

- How is God challenging me?
- Is there a good thing God is calling me to do?
- Is there a harmful thing God wants me to stop doing?
- What is the next step I need to take?

Decide on a course of action (large or small). Commit to following through with your plan.

Memorizing Bible Passages

Saint Augustine provides us with an image for short, effective prayers that are based on Scripture. He describes the prayers of monks in Egyptian monasteries of the third century AD. The monks' prayers were short and to the point, and the monks continuously repeated them, as if trying to bombard God with prayer. We too can pray this way by memorizing short passages of Scripture and repeating them regularly.

To do this, find short passages of Scripture that you can memorize and pray when situations in your life call them forth. In other words, let your daily life trigger your prayer. Here are some examples of this kind of prayer:

- "My Lord and my God" (Jn 20:28) could be a prayer whenever you walk by a cross or crucifix.
- "May the favor of the Lord our God be ours. / Prosper the work of our hands" (Ps 90:17) could be a prayer before a test.
- "Father, into your hands I commend my spirit" (Lk 23:46) could be a prayer before you go to sleep.
- "How great are your works, LORD!" (Ps 92:6) could be a prayer whenever you are outdoors with God's creation.
- "A clean heart create for me, God" (Ps 51:12) could be a morning prayer as you set out on a new day.

You can create your own daily Scripture prayers. As you read and reflect on the Scriptures, write down short phrases that appeal to you. Then ask yourself, "What things in my everyday life do these phrases connect with?" Then when you experience these things, they will trigger your memory and you can pray the Scripture phrase.

A rich source for such prayers is the Book of Psalms. Each week at Mass, a psalm is used as a response between the first and second readings. Listen carefully to the refrain and create a short prayer out of it. Think of how this prayer connects to ordinary tasks in your life. Then each time one of these tasks occurs, say your psalm prayer.

"A clean heart create for me, God"

— Ps 51:12

Praying with the Psalms

The Psalms are Israel's religious poetry and song. They express the people's very real and concrete experiences of God. The Psalms are filled with the same wide range of feelings and moods that we experience in our lives today. The people who wrote the Psalms poured out their hearts to God in words of joy and sorrow, regret and celebration, earnest pleading and praise. These are the prayers of people who struggled to live righteous lives.

There are many different kinds of psalms. There are psalms of lament, which express the anguish and sorrow experienced in illness, death, and personal loss. There are psalms of thanksgiving and rejoicing, which recognize God's hand when the people are rescued from evil or wickedness. There are psalms of praise to a majestic God, witnessed in all of creation.

The Book of Psalms serves as a common book of prayer for Jews and Christians. As Catholics we use psalms at Mass, the Liturgy of the Hours, and many other times when we gather for prayer. Because they address feelings and experiences common to all, they speak to us today just as strongly as they did to the people who first used them thousands of years ago.

Saint Athanasius advised us to hear the Psalms as being addressed to us, as believers in the present. So read Psalms slowly and reverently, savoring each word as if God is saying it for the first time. You will gain deeper insights if you read the Psalms in this way.

When you read the Psalms, look for their rhythm and repetition. Just as modern music and poetry use rhythm and repetition to emphasize certain things, so the Psalms use rhythm and repetition to emphasize their authors' keen insights into our relationship with God. Perhaps you will share the experience of Saint Ambrose, who once said, "When I am reading divine Scripture God walks again in the earthly Paradise."

"When I am reading divine Scripture God walks again in the earthly Paradise."

Psalm Theme Index

The Psalms are a wonderful place to turn when you are seeking ways to express your feelings in prayer. This index covers a range of emotions and moods to help you pray the Psalms in all of life's situations.

Ambiguity: Psalm 97:7–12

Anger: Psalms 9:1–6, 25:19–22, 35:1–10, 37:8–17

Anxiety: Psalms 69:1–8, 88:1–7, 94:16–23, 102:3–11

Betrayal: Psalms 41:4–13, 55:13–23

Bullying: Psalm 70

Compassion of God: Psalms 102:12–17, 113, 145:13–21, 146:5–10

Confession of sin: Psalms 38:12–22, 51:3–6, 119:65–72, 143:1–6

Death: Psalms 6:1–10; 18:1–6; 39:1–6; 49:10–20; 88:13–18; 102:23–28; 116:1–4,12–19; 118:10–17

Despair: Psalms 6:1–5; 22:1–5,14–21; 38:1–11; 40:11–17; 55:1–11; 119:25-32; 130:1–4

Envy: Psalm 73:1–3

Face of God: Psalms 27:7–14, 80:1–7, 119:129–136

Faith: Psalms 25:1–5, 116:1–10, 146:1–7

Fear of God: Psalm 76:7–12

Folly: Psalms 14, 53:1–3, 94:11

Forgiveness: Psalms 25:1–18, 32:1–5, 51:7–9, 85:1–3, 103:6–13

Generosity: Psalm 112:6–10

Gossip: Psalms 7:6–17, 50:16–23, 141:1–4

Guilt: Psalms 4:1–3, 25:11–18, 51:1–2, 79:8–10

Holiness: Psalm 77:11–15; 93; 99:1–5

Hope: Psalms 9:13–20, 33:14–22, 39:7–8, 43:1–5, 62:1–8, 65:1–8, 71:3-14, 91:1–12, 119:41–45, 146:1–7

Hypocrisy: Psalm 36:1–6

Joy: Psalms 16:1–11, 35:27–28, 43:1–5, 67:1–7, 71:20–24, 98:1–9, 126:1–6, 149:1–5

Judgment: Psalms 50:1–6, 73:1–20, 111:6–10

Justice: Psalms 9:7–10, 18:31–42, 33:1–5, 37:18–28

Law: Psalms 19:7–10, 37:28–34, 119:89–96

Light: Psalms 36:7–12, 43, 119:105

Love: Psalms 17:6–9, 18:1–3, 25:6–10, 26:1–3, 36:5–10, 63:1–4, 98:1–6, 108:1–7, 136:1–26

Nationalism and religion: Psalms 72:1–11, 132:11–18

Poverty: Psalms 9:11–20, 22:21–26, 34:1–10, 72:12–14, 107:39–43, 146:5–10, 147:1–6

(Psalm Theme Index continued)

Pride: Psalms 20:6–9; 52; 94:1–11; 119:97–104,161–168

Resurrection: Psalms 16:9–11, 27:13–14, 88:8–12

Righteousness: Psalms 5:8–12, 7:6–17, 11:1–5, 15, 31:1–8, 119:137–144

Self-pity: Psalms 69:22–29, 119:25–32

Sickness: Psalms 6:6–10, 38:1–11, 39:7–11, 107:17–22

Sin: Psalms 32:1–5, 38:12–22, 51:1–6, 85:1–3, 130:1–8

Steadfast love of God: Psalms 17:1–7, 86:14–17, 103:14–22, 117, 136:23–26

Success: Psalm 18:43–50

Thanksgiving: Psalms 30:4–12, 75:1–3, 92:1–9, 100:1–5, 107:1–9, 118:19–29, 147:1–11

Truth: Psalms 43, 86:8–13

Values: Psalms 85:10–13, 101

Waiting: Psalms 13, 37:28–34, 39:7–10, 119:122–128, 130:5–8

Wisdom of God: Psalms 51:6, 104:24

“God’s word is the compass that leads us more deeply into the immense heart of God.”

without his consent, to be clothed in purple or
wear a gold buckle. 45 Whoever acts otherwise or
violates any of these prescriptions shall be liable
to punishment.

46 " 'Thus all the people approved of grant-
ing Simon the right to act in accord with these
decisions, 47 and Simon accepted and agreed to
be high priest, governor, and ethnarch† of the
Jewish people and priests, and to have authority
over all.' "

48 It was decreed that this inscription should
be engraved on bronze tablets, to be set up in a
conspicuous place in the precincts of the sanctu-
ary, 49 and that copies of it should be deposited
in the treasury, where they would be available to
Simon and his sons.

Letter of Antiochus VII

15 1 Antiochus,† son of King Demetrius, sent
a letter from the islands of the sea to Si-
mon, the priest and ethnarch of the Jews, and to
all the nation, 2 which read as follows:

"King Antiochus sends greetings to Simon,
the high priest and ethnarch, and to the Jewish
nation. 3 Whereas certain villains have gained
control of the kingdom of our ancestors, I intend
to reclaim it, that I may restore it to its former
state. I have recruited a large number of merce-
nary troops and equipped warships. 4 I intend to
make a landing in the country so that I may take
revenge on those who have ruined our country
and laid waste many cities in my kingdom.

5 "Now, therefore, I confirm to you all the tax
exemptions that the kings before me granted you
and whatever other privileges they conceded to
you. 6 I authorize you to coin your own money,
as legal tender in your country. 7 Jerusalem and
its sanctuary shall be free. All the weapons you
have prepared and all the strongholds you have
built and now occupy shall remain in your pos-
session. 8 All debts, present or future, due to the
royal treasury shall be canceled for you, now and
for all time. 9 When we establish our kingdom,
we will greatly honor you and your nation and
the temple, so that your glory will be manifest in
all the earth."

10 In the one hundred and seventy-fourth year†
Antiochus invaded the land of his ancestors, and
all the troops rallied to him, so that few were left
with Trypho. 11 Pursued by Antiochus, Trypho
fled to Dor, by the sea,† 12 realizing what trou-
bles had come upon him now that his soldiers
had deserted him. 13 Antiochus encamped before
Dor with a hundred and twenty thousand infan-
try and eight thousand cavalry. 14 While he sur-
rounded the city, his ships closed from the sea,
so that he pressed it hard by land and sea and let
no one go in or out.

Roman Alliance Renewed

15 Meanwhile, Numenius and his companions
came from Rome with letters containing this
message to various kings and countries:* 16 "Lu-
cius,† Consul of the Romans, sends greetings to
King Ptolemy. 17 Ambassadors of the Jews, our
friends and allies, have come to us to renew their
earlier friendship and alliance. They had been
sent by Simon the high priest and the Jewish
people, 18 and they brought with them a gold
shield of a thousand minas.* 19 Therefore we
have decided to write to various kings and coun-
tries, that they are not to venture to harm them,
or wage war against them or their cities or their
country, and are not to assist those who fight
against them. 20 We have also decided to accept
the shield from them. 21 If, then, any troublemak-
ers from their country take refuge with you, hand
them over to Simon the high priest, so that he
may punish them according to their law."

22 The consul sent identical letters to Kings
Demetrius, Attalus,† Ariarthes and Arsaces; 23 to
all the countries—Sampsames, the Spartans, De-
los, Myndos, Sicyon, Caria, Samos, Pamphylia,
Lycia, Halicarnassus, Rhodes, Phaselis, Cos, Side,
Aradus, Gortyna, Cnidus, Cyprus, and Cyrene.
24 A copy of the letter was also sent to Simon the
high priest.

Hostility from Antiochus VII

25 When King Antiochus encamped before
Dor, he assaulted it continuously both with
troops and with the siege engines he had made.
He blockaded Trypho by preventing anyone
from going in or out. 26 Simon sent to Antiochus'
support two thousand elite troops, together with
silver and gold and much equipment. 27 But he

14:47 *Ethnarch*: a subordinate ruler over an ethnic group whose office needed confirmation by a higher authority within the empire.

15:1 *Antiochus*: Antiochus VII Sidetes, son of Demetrius I, and younger brother of Demetrius II (now a prisoner of the Parthians). At the age of twenty he set out from the island of Rhodes to take his brother's place and drive out the usurper Trypho.

15:10 *The one hundred and seventy-fourth year*: 138 B.C.

15:11 *Dor, by the sea*: a fortress on the Palestinian coast, fifteen miles south of Carmel.

15:16 *Lucius*: perhaps Lucius Caecilius Metellus, consul in 142 B.C., or Lucius Calpurnicus Piso, consul in 140–139 B.C. This document pertains to Simon's first years as leader.

15:22 *Attalus*: Attalus II of Pergamum, reigned 159–138 B.C. *Ariarthes*: Ariarthes V of Cappadocia, reigned 162–130 B.C. *Arsaces*: see note on 14:2.

15:15 1 Mc 8:17; 12:16; 14:22, 24. **15:18** 1 Mc 14:24.

refused to accept the aid; in fact, he broke all the
agreements he had previously made with Simon
and became hostile toward him.*
28 He sent Athenobius, one of his Friends, to
confer with Simon and say: "You are occupying
Joppa and Gazara and the citadel of Jerusalem;
these are cities of my kingdom. 29 You have laid
waste their territories, done great harm to the
land, and taken possession of many districts
in my kingdom. 30 Now, therefore, give up the
cities you have seized and the tribute money of
the districts you control outside the territory of
Judea; 31 or instead, pay me five hundred talents
of silver for the devastation you have caused and
five hundred talents more for the tribute money
of the cities. If you do not do this, we will come
and make war on you."
32 So Athenobius, the king's Friend, came to
Jerusalem and on seeing the splendor of Simon's
court, the gold and silver plate on the sideboard,
and his rich display, he was amazed. When he
gave him the king's message, 33 Simon said to
him in reply: "It is not foreign land we have
taken nor have we seized the property of others,
but only our ancestral heritage which for a time
had been unjustly held by our enemies. 34 Now
that we have the opportunity, we are holding on
to the heritage of our ancestors. 35 As for Joppa
and Gazara, which you demand, those cities
were doing great harm to our people and our
country. For these we will give you a hundred
talents." Athenobius made no reply, 36 but re-
turned to the king in anger. When he told him of
Simon's words, of his splendor, and of all he had
seen, the king fell into a violent rage.

Victory over Cendebeus

37 Trypho had boarded a ship and escaped to
Orthosia.† 38 Then the king appointed Cende-
beus commander-in-chief of the seacoast, and
gave him infantry and cavalry forces. 39 He or-
dered him to encamp against Judea and to for-
tify Kedron† and strengthen its gates, so that he
could wage war on the people. Meanwhile the
king went in pursuit of Trypho. 40 When Cen-
debeus came to Jamnia, he began to harass the
people and to make incursions into Judea, where
he took people captive and massacred them.
41 As the king ordered, he fortified Kedron and
stationed cavalry and infantry there, so that they
could go out and patrol the roads of Judea.

16 1 John then went up from Gazara and told
his father Simon what Cendebeus was do-
ing.* 2 Simon called his two oldest sons, Judas
and John, and said to them: "I and my brothers
and my father's house have fought the wars of Is-
rael from our youth until today, and many times
we succeeded in saving Israel. 3 I have now grown
old, but you, by the mercy of Heaven, have come
to maturity. Take my place and my brother's, and
go out and fight for our nation; and may the help
of Heaven be with you!"
4 John then mustered in the land twenty thou-
sand warriors and cavalry. Setting out against
Cendebeus, they spent the night at Modein,
5 rose early, and marched into the plain. There,
facing them, was an immense army of foot sol-
diers and cavalry, and between the two armies
was a wadi. 6 John and his people took their po-
sition against the enemy. Seeing that his people
were afraid to cross the wadi, John crossed first.
When his men saw this, they crossed over after
him.* 7 Then he divided his infantry and put
his cavalry in the center, for the enemy's cavalry
were very numerous. 8 They blew the trumpets,
and Cendebeus and his army were routed; many
of them fell wounded, and the rest fled toward
the stronghold. 9 It was then that John's brother
Judas fell wounded; but John pursued them until
Cendebeus reached Kedron, which he had for-
tified. 10 Some took refuge in the towers on the
plain of Azotus, but John set fire to these, and
about two thousand of the enemy perished. He
then returned to Judea in peace.*

Murder of Simon and His Sons

11 Ptolemy, son of Abubus, had been ap-
pointed governor of the plain of Jericho, and he
had much silver and gold, 12 being the son-in-
law of the high priest. 13 But his heart became
proud and he was determined to get control of
the country. So he made treacherous plans to do
away with Simon and his sons. 14 As Simon was
inspecting the cities of the country and provid-
ing for their needs, he and his sons Mattathias
and Judas went down to Jericho in the one hun-
dred and seventy-seventh year, in the eleventh
month† (that is, the month Shebat). 15 The son
of Abubus gave them a deceitful welcome in the
little stronghold called Dok† which he had built.
He served them a sumptuous banquet, but he
had his men hidden there. 16 Then, when Simon

†

15:37 *Orthosia*: a port between Tripoli and the Eleutherus River.

15:39 *Kedron*: a few miles southeast of Jamnia and facing the fortress of Gazara held by John Hyrcanus (13:53; 16:1).

16:14 *In the one hundred and seventy-seventh year, in the eleventh month*: January–February, 134 B.C., by the Temple calendar.

16:15 *Dok*: a fortress built on a cliff three miles northwest of Jericho, near modern Ain Duq.

*

15:27 1 Mc 15:5–9. **16:1** 1 Mc 13:53. **16:6** 1 Mc 5:40–43. **16:10** 1 Mc 10:84.

and his sons were drunk, Ptolemy and his men
sprang up, weapons in hand, rushed upon Si-
mon in the banquet hall, and killed him, his two
sons, and some of his servants. 17 By this vicious
act of treachery he repaid good with evil.
18 Then Ptolemy wrote a report and sent it
to the king, asking him to send troops to help
him and to turn over to him their country and
its cities. 19 He sent other men to Gazara to do
away with John. To the army officers he sent
letters inviting them to come to him so that he
might present them with silver, gold, and gifts.
20 He also sent others to seize Jerusalem and the
temple mount. 21 But someone ran ahead and
brought word to John at Gazara that his father
and his brothers had perished, and "Ptolemy
has sent men to kill you also." 22 On hearing
this, John was utterly astounded. When the men
came to kill him, he seized them and put them to
death, for he knew that they sought to kill him.
23 † Now the rest of the acts of John, his wars
and the brave deeds he performed, his rebuilding
of the walls, and all his achievements—* 24 these
are recorded in the chronicle of his high priest-
hood, from the time that he succeeded his father
as high priest.

1 MC

† **16:23–24** John Hyrcanus was ruler and high priest from 134 B.C. till his death in 104 B.C. These verses suggest that the book was written, or at least completed, only after he died.

* **16:23** 1 Mc 9:22.

The Second Book of

Maccabees

When you are suffering, what is your first response? To escape? to look for relief? to cry out in pain? These are normal and healthy responses: no well-adjusted person chooses to suffer willingly. Sometimes, though, people inflict unspeakable suffering on one another, especially through violence such as rape and torture. What meaning could there be in such suffering? In response, Second Maccabees insists that God will vindicate all those who suffer innocently at the hands of the unjust.

At a Glance

I. **Letters to the Jews in Egypt (1:1—2:18).**

II. **Compiler's Preface (2:19–32).**

III. **Heliodorus' Attempt To Profane the Temple (3:1–40).**

IV. **Profanation and Persecution (4:1—7:42).**

V. **Victories of Judas and Purification of the Temple (8:1—10:9).**

VI. **Renewed Persecution (10:10—15:36).**

VII. **Epilogue (15:37–39).**

Quick Facts

Period Covered: from 180 to 161 BC

Inspired Author: someone around 100 BC, summarizing a lost work by Jason of Cyrene

Themes: differing responses to persecution, the just and suffering, the glorification of God's holy martyrs

Of Note: Second Maccabees is not found in every version of the Old Testament (see "The Case of the Missing Books," near Tb 1:16).

In Depth

In 167 BC, the Jewish people faced a new persecution under the Seleucid (Greek) king Antiochus IV Epiphanes. In an effort to unify the many different peoples under his rule, Antiochus imposed his own language, customs, and religion on all of them, including the Jews. Second Maccabees covers some of the same history as First Maccabees but with different purposes: to show the variety of ways the Jews resisted persecution and to give hope to persecuted Jews in the author's time.

The Book of Job had already struggled with the mystery of human suffering and concluded that only God could understand it. Not content with this answer, the author of Second Maccabees presses forward with new insights:

- In the famous story of the martyrdom of a Jewish mother and her seven sons (see 7:1–42), Second Maccabees talks about the resurrection of the dead.
- In chapter 12, the value of praying for the dead is commended.
- In chapter 15, the book speaks confidently of the prayers of the saints in Heaven for those on earth.

Second Maccabees is less concerned with the facts of history than with the meaning of history. It insists that whenever God's faithful people suffer, they can be assured of receiving justice—if not in this life, then in the resurrection. The book shows how the Jewish faith continued to develop as it faced the sometimes painful events of history.

2 Maccabees

I. Letters to the Jews in Egypt

Letter 1: 124 B.C.

1 [1]The Jews in Jerusalem and in the land of Ju-
dea send greetings to their kindred, the Jews in
Egypt, and wish them true peace! [2]May God do
good to you and remember his covenant with his
faithful servants, Abraham, Isaac and Jacob, [3]give
to all of you a heart to worship him and to do
his will wholeheartedly and with a willing spirit,
[4]open your heart to his law and commandments
and grant you peace, [5]hear your prayers, and be
reconciled to you, and never forsake you in time of
adversity. [6]Even now we are praying for you here.
[7]In the reign of Demetrius,† the one hundred
and sixty-ninth year, we Jews wrote to you during
the height of the distress that overtook us in those
years after Jason and his followers revolted against
the holy land and the kingdom,* [8]set fire to the
gatehouse and shed innocent blood. But we prayed
to the Lord, and our prayer was heard;† we offered
sacrifices and fine flour; we lighted the lamps and
set out the loaves of bread.* [9]We are now remind-
ing you to celebrate the feast of Booths in the
month of Kislev.† [10]Dated in the one hundred and
eighty-eighth year.†

Letter 2: 164 B.C.

The people of Jerusalem and Judea, the sen-
ate, and Judas send greetings and good wishes to
Aristobulus, teacher of King Ptolemy and member
of the family of the anointed priests, and to the
Jews in Egypt. [11]Since we have been saved by God
from grave dangers, we give him great thanks as
befits those who fought against the king;† [12]* for it
was God who drove out those who fought against
the holy city. [13]When their leader arrived in Per-
sia with his seemingly irresistible army, they were
cut to pieces in the temple of the goddess Nanea†
through a deceitful stratagem employed by Nanea's
priests. [14]† On the pretext of marrying the goddess,

†

1:7 *Demetrius*: Demetrius II, king of Syria (145–139, 129–125 B.C.). *The one hundred and sixty-ninth year*: i.e., of the Seleucid era, 143 B.C. Regarding the dates in 1 and 2 Maccabees, see note on 1 Mc 1:10. On the troubles caused by Jason and his revolt against the kingdom, i.e., the rule of the legitimate high priest, see 2 Mc 4:7–22.

1:8 *Our prayer was heard*: in the victory of the Maccabees.

1:9 *Feast of Booths in the month of Kislev*: really the feast of the Dedication of the Temple, Hanukkah (2 Mc 10:1–8), celebrated on the twenty-fifth of Kislev (Nov.–Dec.). Its solemnity resembles that of the actual feast of Booths (Lv 23:33–43), celebrated on the fifteenth of Tishri (Sept.–Oct.); cf. 2 Mc 1:18.

1:10 *The one hundred and eighty-eighth year*: 124 B.C. The date pertains to the preceding, not the following letter. *Senate*: the council of Jewish elders of Jerusalem; cf. 1 Mc 12:6. *King Ptolemy*: Ptolemy VI Philometor, ruler of Egypt from 180 to 145 B.C.; he is mentioned also in 1 Mc 1:18; 10:51–59.

1:11–12 *The king*: Antiochus IV of Syria, the bitter persecutor of the Jews, who, as leader of the Syrian army that invaded Persia, perished there in 164 B.C.

1:13 *Nanea*: an oriental goddess comparable to Artemis of the Greeks.

1:14–17 Differing accounts of the death of Antiochus IV are found in 2 Mc 9:1–29 and in 1 Mc 6:1–16 (see also Dn 11:40–45). The writer of this letter had probably heard a distorted rumor of the king's death. This and other indications suggest that the letter was written very soon after Antiochus IV died, perhaps in 164 B.C.

*

1:7 2 Mc 4:7–20.
1:8 1 Mc 4:50–51.
1:12–17 2 Mc 9:1–29; 1 Mc 6:1–13; Dn 11:40–45.

Antiochus with his Friends had come to the place to get its great treasures as a dowry. 15 When the priests of Nanea's temple had displayed the treasures and Antiochus with a few attendants had come inside the wall of the temple precincts, the priests locked the temple as soon as he entered. 16 Then they opened a hidden trapdoor in the ceiling, and hurling stones at the leader and his companions, struck them down. They dismembered the bodies, cut off their heads and tossed them to the people outside. 17 Forever blessed be our God, who has thus punished the impious!

18 † Since we shall be celebrating the purification of the temple on the twenty-fifth day of the month Kislev,* we thought it right to inform you, that you too may celebrate the feast of Booths and of the fire that appeared when Nehemiah, the rebuilder of the temple† and the altar, offered sacrifices. 19 For when our ancestors were being led into captivity in Persia,† devout priests at the time took some of the fire from the altar and hid it secretly in the hollow of a dry cistern, making sure that the place would be unknown to anyone. 20 Many years later, when it so pleased God, Nehemiah, commissioned by the king of Persia, sent the descendants of the priests who had hidden the fire to look for it. 21 When they informed us that they could not find any fire, but only a thick liquid, he ordered them to scoop some out and bring it. After the material for the sacrifices had been prepared, Nehemiah ordered the priests to sprinkle the wood and what lay on it with the liquid. 22 This was done, and when at length the sun, which had been clouded over, began to shine, a great fire blazed up, so that everyone marveled. 23 While the sacrifice was being burned, the priests recited a prayer, and all present joined in with them. Jonathan led and the rest responded with Nehemiah.

24 The prayer was as follows: "Lord, Lord God, creator of all things, awesome and strong, just and merciful, the only king and benefactor, 25 who alone are gracious, just, almighty, and eternal, Israel's savior from all evil, who chose our ancestors and sanctified them: 26 accept this sacrifice on behalf of all your people Israel and guard and sanctify your portion. 27 Gather together our scattered people, free those who are slaves among the Gentiles, look kindly on those who are despised and detested, and let the Gentiles know that you are our God. 28 Punish those who lord it over us and in their arrogance oppress us. 29 Plant your people in your holy place, as Moses said."*

30 Then the priests sang hymns. 31 After the sacrifice was consumed, Nehemiah ordered the rest of the liquid to be poured upon large stones. 32 As soon as this was done, a flame blazed up, but its light was lost in the brilliance coming from the altar. 33 When the event became known and the king of the Persians was told that, in the very place where the exiled priests had hidden the fire, a liquid was found with which Nehemiah and his people had burned the sacrifices, 34 the king, after verifying the fact, fenced the place off and declared it sacred. 35 To those whom the king favored, he distributed many benefits he received. 36 Nehemiah and his companions called the liquid nephthar, meaning purification, but most people named it naphtha.† *

2 1 In the records it will be found that Jeremiah the prophet ordered the deportees to take some of the fire with them as indicated, 2 and that the prophet, in giving them the law, directed the deportees not to forget the commandments of the Lord or be led astray in their thoughts, when seeing the gold and silver idols and their adornments.* 3 With other similar words he exhorted them that the law should not depart from their hearts.

4 † The same document also tells how the prophet, in virtue of an oracle, ordered that the tent and the ark should accompany him, and how he went to the very mountain that Moses climbed to behold God's inheritance.* 5 When Jeremiah arrived there, he found a chamber in a cave in which he put the tent, the ark, and the altar of incense; then he sealed the entrance. 6 Some of those who followed him came up intending to mark the path, but they could not find it. 7 When Jeremiah heard of this, he reproved them: "The place is to remain unknown until God gathers his people together again and shows them mercy. 8 Then the Lord will disclose these things, and the glory of

---

†

1:18–36 This legendary account of Nehemiah's miraculous fire is incorporated in the letter because of its connection with the Temple and its rededication. *Booths*: see note on v. 9.

1:18 *Nehemiah, the rebuilder of the temple*: he rebuilt the walls of Jerusalem, but the Temple had been rebuilt by Zerubbabel almost a century before.

1:19 *Persia*: actually Babylonia, which later became part of the Persian empire.

1:36 By a play on words, the Greek term *naphtha* (petroleum) is assimilated to some Semitic word, perhaps *nephthar*, meaning "loosened."

2:4–5 This legendary account is given for the purpose of explaining why the postexilic Temple was the legitimate place of worship even without these sacred objects. *The very mountain*: Nebo; cf. Dt 32:49; 34:1.

*

1:18 2 Mc 6:7; 10:5; 1 Mc 1:59; 4:59.
1:29 2 Mc 2:18; Ex 15:17; Dt 30:3–5.
1:36 2 Mc 2:18; 10:3; 14:36.
2:2 Bar 6:1–72.
2:4 Dt 32:49; 34:1; Rev 11:19.

the Lord and the cloud will be seen, just as they
appeared in the time of Moses and of Solomon
when he prayed that the place† might be greatly
sanctified."*
[9]It is also related how Solomon in his wisdom
offered a sacrifice for the dedication and the com-
pletion of the temple. [10]Just as Moses prayed to
the Lord and fire descended from the sky and
consumed the sacrifices, so also Solomon prayed
and fire came down and consumed the burnt of-
ferings.* [11]† Moses had said, "Because it had not
been eaten, the purification offering was con-
sumed."* [12]Solomon also celebrated the feast in
the same way for eight days.
[13]These same things are also told in the records
and in Nehemiah's memoirs,† as well as how he
founded a library and collected the books about
the kings and the prophets, the books of David,
and the royal letters about votive offerings. [14]In
like manner Judas also collected for us all the
books that had been scattered because of the war,
and we now have them in our possession.* [15]If
you need them, send messengers to get them for
you.
[16]As we are about to celebrate the purification,
we are writing: you should celebrate the feast days.
[17]It is God who has saved all his people and has
restored to all of them their inheritance, the king-
dom, the priesthood, and the sacred rites, [18]as he
promised through the law. For we hope in God,
that he will soon have mercy on us and gather us
together from everywhere under the heavens to
his holy place, for he has rescued us from great
perils and has purified the place.*

II. Compiler's Preface

[19]This is the story of Judas Maccabeus and his
brothers, of the purification of the great temple,
the dedication of the altar, [20]the campaigns against
Antiochus Epiphanes and his son Eupator,† [21]and
of the heavenly manifestations accorded to the
heroes who fought bravely for the Jewish people.
Few as they were, they plundered the whole land,
put to flight the barbarian hordes, [22]regained pos-
session of the temple renowned throughout the
world, and liberated the city. They re-established
the laws that were in danger of being abolished,
while the Lord favored them with every kindness.
[23]All this, detailed by Jason of Cyrene in five vol-
umes, we will try to condense into a single book.
[24]For in view of the flood of data, and the dif-
ficulties encountered, given such abundant ma-
terial, by those who wish to plunge into accounts
of the history, [25]we have aimed to please those
who prefer simply to read, to make it easy for the
studious who wish to commit things to memory,
and to be helpful to all. [26]For us who have under-
taken the labor of making this digest, the task, far
from being easy, is one of sweat and of sleepless
nights. [27]Just so, the preparation of a festive ban-
quet is no light matter for one who seeks to give
enjoyment to others. Similarly, to win the grat-
itude of many we will gladly endure this labor,
[28]leaving the responsibility for exact details to the
historian, and confining our efforts to presenting
only a summary outline. [29]As the architect of a
new house must pay attention to the whole struc-
ture, while the one who undertakes the decora-
tion and the frescoes has to be concerned only
with what is needed for ornamentation, so I think
it is with us.* [30]To enter into questions and ex-
amine them from all sides and to be busy about
details is the task of the historian; [31]but one who
is making an adaptation should be allowed to
aim at brevity of expression and to forgo com-
plete treatment of the matter. [32]Here, then, let us
begin our account without adding to what has
already been said; it would be silly to lengthen
the preface to the history and then cut short the
history itself.

III. Heliodorus' Attempt to Profane the Temple†

Heliodorus' Arrival in Jerusalem

3 [1]While the holy city lived in perfect peace and
the laws were strictly observed because of the
piety of the high priest Onias† and his hatred of
evil,* [2]the kings themselves honored the place
and glorified the temple with the most magnifi-
cent gifts. [3]Thus Seleucus,† king of Asia, defrayed
from his own revenues all the expenses necessary
for the liturgy of sacrifice.
[4]But a certain Simon, of the priestly clan of

†

2:8 *The place*: the Temple of Jerusalem.

2:11 The statement attributed here to Moses seems to be based on Lv 10:16–20.

2:13 *Nehemiah's memoirs*: a lost apocryphal work, or perhaps Neh 1–7, 11–13.

2:20 For the account of the campaigns against Antiochus IV Epiphanes, see 4:7–10:9; and for the account of those against his son Antiochus V Eupator, see 10:10–13:26.

3:1–40 This legendary episode about Heliodorus is recounted here for the purpose of stressing the inviolability of the Temple of Jerusalem; its later profanation was interpreted as owing to the sins of the people; cf. 5:17–18.

3:1 *Onias*: Onias III was high priest from 196 to 175 B.C. and died in 171 B.C. He was the son of Simon, whose praises are sung in Sir 50:1–21.

3:3 *Seleucus*: Seleucus IV Philopator, who reigned from 187 to 175 B.C.

*

2:8 Ex 40:34–35; 1 Kgs 8:11.
2:10 Lv 9:23–24; 2 Chr 7:1.
2:11 Lv 10:16–20.
2:14 1 Mc 1:57.
2:18 Dt 30:3–5.
2:29 2 Mc 15:38–39.
3:1 2 Mc 5:19–20; 15:12.

Bilgah,† who had been appointed superintendent of the temple, had a quarrel with the high priest about the administration of the city market.* 5 Since he could not prevail against Onias, he went to Apollonius of Tarsus, who at that time was governor of Coelesyria and Phoenicia, 6 and reported to him that the treasury in Jerusalem was full of such untold riches that the sum total of the assets was past counting and that since they did not belong to the account of the sacrifices, it would be possible for them to fall under the authority of the king.

7 When Apollonius had an audience with the king, he informed him about the riches that had been reported to him. The king chose his chief minister Heliodorus and sent him with instructions to seize those riches. 8 So Heliodorus immediately set out on his journey, ostensibly to visit the cities of Coelesyria and Phoenicia, but in reality to carry out the king's purpose.

9 When he arrived in Jerusalem and had been graciously received by the high priest of the city, he told him about the information that had been given, and explained the reason for his presence, and he inquired if these things were really true. 10 The high priest explained that there were deposits for widows and orphans,* 11 and some was the property of Hyrcanus, son of Tobias,† a man who occupied a very high position. Contrary to the misrepresentations of the impious Simon, the total amounted only to four hundred talents of silver and two hundred of gold. 12 It was utterly unthinkable to defraud those who had placed their trust in the sanctity of the place and in the sacred inviolability of a temple venerated all over the world.

Heliodorus' Plan To Rob the Temple

13 But Heliodorus, because of the orders he had from the king, said that in any case this money must be confiscated for the royal treasury. 14 So on the day he had set he went in to take an inventory of the funds. There was no little anguish throughout the city. 15 Priests prostrated themselves before the altar in their priestly robes, and called toward heaven for the one who had given the law about deposits to keep the deposits safe for those who had made them.* 16 Whoever saw the appearance of the high priest was pierced to the heart, for the changed complexion of his face revealed his mental anguish. 17 The terror and bodily trembling that had come over the man clearly showed those who saw him the pain that lodged in his heart. 18 People rushed out of their houses and crowded together making common supplication, because the place was in danger of being profaned. 19 Women, girded with sackcloth below their breasts, filled the streets. Young women secluded indoors all ran, some to the gates, some to the walls, others peered through the windows— 20 all of them with hands raised toward heaven, making supplication. 21 It was pitiful to see the populace prostrate everywhere and the high priest full of dread and anguish. 22 While they were imploring the almighty Lord to keep the deposits safe and secure for those who had placed them in trust, 23 Heliodorus went on with his plan.

God Protects the Temple

24 But just as Heliodorus was arriving at the treasury with his bodyguards, the Lord of spirits and all authority produced an apparition so great that those who had been bold enough to accompany Heliodorus were panic-stricken at God's power and fainted away in terror. 25 There appeared to them a richly caparisoned horse, mounted by a fearsome rider. Charging furiously, the horse attacked Heliodorus with its front hooves. The rider was seen wearing golden armor. 26 Then two other young men, remarkably strong, strikingly handsome, and splendidly attired, appeared before him. Standing on each side of him, they flogged him unceasingly, inflicting innumerable blows. 27 Suddenly he fell to the ground, enveloped in great darkness. His men picked him up and laid him on a stretcher. 28 They carried away helpless the man who a moment before had entered that treasury under arms with a great retinue and his whole bodyguard. They clearly recognized the sovereign power of God.

The Restoration and Testimony of Heliodorus

29 As Heliodorus lay speechless because of God's action and deprived of any hope of recovery, 30 the people praised the Lord who had marvelously glorified his own place; and the temple, charged so shortly before with fear and commotion, was filled with joy and gladness, now that the almighty Lord had appeared. 31 Quickly some of the companions of Heliodorus begged Onias to call upon the Most High to spare the life of one who was about to breathe his last. 32 The high priest, suspecting that

---

†

3:4 *Bilgah*: a priestly family mentioned in 1 Chr 24:14; Neh 12:5, 18.

3:11 *Hyrcanus, son of Tobias*: a member of the Tobiad family of Transjordan (Neh 2:10; 6:17–19; 13:4–8). Hyrcanus' father was Joseph, whose mother was the sister of the high priest Onias II.

*

3:4 2 Mc 4:23. **3:10** Dt 14:29; 26:12. **3:15** Ex 22:6–14.

the king might think that Heliodorus had suffered some foul play at the hands of the Jews, offered a sacrifice for the man's recovery. [33] While the high priest was offering the sacrifice of atonement, the same young men dressed in the same clothing again appeared and stood before Heliodorus. "Be very grateful to the high priest Onias," they told him. "It is for his sake that the Lord has spared your life. [34] Since you have been scourged by Heaven, proclaim to all God's great power." When they had said this, they disappeared.

[35] After Heliodorus had offered a sacrifice to the Lord and made most solemn vows to the one who had spared his life, he bade Onias farewell, and returned with his soldiers to the king. [36] Before all he gave witness to the deeds of the most high God that he had seen with his own eyes. [37] When the king asked Heliodorus what sort of person would be suitable to be sent to Jerusalem next, he answered: [38] "If you have an enemy or one who is plotting against the government, send him there, and you will get him back with a flogging, if indeed he survives at all; for there is certainly some divine power about the place. [39] The one whose dwelling is in heaven watches over that place and protects it, and strikes down and destroys those who come to harm it." [40] This was how the matter concerning Heliodorus and the preservation of the treasury turned out.

IV. Profanation and Persecution

Simon Accuses Onias

4 [1] The Simon mentioned above as the informer about the funds against his own country slandered Onias as the one who incited Heliodorus and instigated the whole miserable affair. [2] He dared to brand as a schemer against the government the man who was the benefactor of the city, the protector of his compatriots, and a zealous defender of the laws. [3] When Simon's hostility reached such a pitch that murders were being committed by one of his henchmen, [4] Onias saw that the opposition was serious and that Apollonius, son of Menestheus, the governor of Coelesyria and Phoenicia, was abetting Simon's wickedness. [5] So he had recourse to the king, not as an accuser of his compatriots, but as one looking to the general and particular good of all the people. [6] He saw that without royal attention it would be impossible to have a peaceful government, and that Simon would not desist from his folly.

Pray It!

Arrogance

Arrogance seems to run in the family of Simon. First, Simon seeks to embarrass the high priest, Onias, because of a minor disagreement (see 2 Mc 3:1–14). When that fails, he falsely accuses Onias of a crime (see 4:1–6). Several years later, Simon's brother bribes his way into power (see verses 23–29).

We have all encountered arrogant people who think they can do no wrong, and when they do err, cover it up by attacking others. Many of us are intimidated by such people and resent that we feel talked down to or easily dismissed as unimportant. So, how should we respond to arrogant people? The most obvious solution is to ignore them. If that is not possible, then we need to react to them calmly and confidently. Finally, we should keep them in our prayers. Their arrogance can be masking an insecurity or a hurt that needs God's healing touch.

In your prayer time, reflect or journal on the following questions:

- Who intimidates you by her or his arrogant behavior?
- How could you respond in a loving and just way?
- What do you need to bring to God in prayer?

▶ 2 Mc 3:1—4:29

Jason as High Priest

[7] But Seleucus died,† and when Antiochus surnamed Epiphanes succeeded him on the throne, Onias' brother Jason obtained the high priesthood by corrupt means:* [8] in an interview, he promised the king three hundred and sixty talents of silver, as well as eighty talents from another source of income. [9] Besides this he would undertake to pay a

2 MC

† **4:7** *Seleucus died*: he was murdered by Heliodorus. Antiochus Epiphanes was his younger brother. Onias' brother showed his enthusiasm for the Greek way of life (v. 10) by changing his Hebrew name Joshua, or Jesus, to the Greek name Jason.

* **4:7** 2 Mc 1:7; 1 Mc 1:10.

hundred and fifty more, if he was given authority to establish a gymnasium and a youth center† for it and to enroll Jerusalemites as citizens of Antioch.

[10]When Jason received the king's approval and came into office, he immediately initiated his compatriots into the Greek way of life. [11]He set aside the royal concessions granted to the Jews through the mediation of John, father of Eupolemus† (that Eupolemus who would later go on an embassy to the Romans to establish friendship and alliance with them); he set aside the lawful practices and introduced customs contrary to the law.* [12]* With perverse delight he established a gymnasium† at the very foot of the citadel, where he induced the noblest young men to wear the Greek hat. [13]The craze for Hellenism and the adoption of foreign customs reached such a pitch, through the outrageous wickedness of Jason, the renegade and would-be high priest, [14]that the priests no longer cared about the service of the altar. Disdaining the temple and neglecting the sacrifices, they hastened, at the signal for the games, to take part in the unlawful exercises at the arena. [15]What their ancestors had regarded as honors they despised; what the Greeks esteemed as glory they prized highly. [16]For this reason they found themselves in serious trouble: the very people whose manner of life they emulated, and whom they desired to imitate in everything, became their enemies and oppressors. [17]It is no light matter to flout the laws of God, as subsequent events will show.

[18]When the quinquennial games were held at Tyre in the presence of the king, [19]the vile Jason sent representatives of the Antiochians of Jerusalem, to bring three hundred silver drachmas for the sacrifice to Hercules. But the bearers themselves decided that the money should not be spent on a sacrifice, as that was not right, but should be used for some other purpose. [20]So the contribution meant for the sacrifice to Hercules by the sender, was in fact applied to the construction of triremes† by those who brought it.

[21]When Apollonius, son of Menestheus, was sent to Egypt for the coronation of King Philometor,† Antiochus learned from him that the king was opposed to his policies. He took measures for his own security; so after going to Joppa, he proceeded to Jerusalem. [22]There he was received with great pomp by Jason and the people of the city, who escorted him with torchlights and acclamations; following this, he led his army into Phoenicia.

Menelaus as High Priest

[23]Three years later Jason sent Menelaus,† brother of the aforementioned Simon, to deliver the money to the king, and to complete negotiations on urgent matters. [24]But after his introduction to the king, he flattered him with such an air of authority that he secured the high priesthood for himself, outbidding Jason by three hundred talents of silver. [25]He returned with the royal commission, but with nothing that made him worthy of the high priesthood; he had the temper of a cruel tyrant and the rage of a wild beast. [26]So Jason, who had cheated his own brother and now saw himself cheated by another man, was driven out as a fugitive to the country of the Ammonites. [27]But Menelaus, who obtained the office, paid nothing of the money he had promised to the king, [28]in spite of the demand of Sostratus, the commandant of the citadel, whose duty it was to collect the taxes. For this reason, both were summoned before the king. [29]Menelaus left his brother Lysimachus as his deputy in the high priesthood, while Sostratus left Crates, commander of the Cypriots.*

Murder of Onias

[30]While these things were taking place, the people of Tarsus and Mallus† rose in revolt, because their cities had been given as a gift to Antiochis, the king's concubine. [31]So the king hastened off to settle the affair, leaving Andronicus, one of his nobles, as his deputy. [32]Menelaus, for his part, thinking this a good opportunity, stole some gold vessels from the temple and presented them to Andronicus; he had already sold other vessels in Tyre and in the neighboring cities. [33]When Onias had clear evidence, he accused Menelaus publicly, after withdrawing to the inviolable sanctuary at

†

4:9 *Youth center*: an educational institution in which young men were trained both in Greek intellectual culture and in physical fitness. *Citizens of Antioch*: honorary citizens of Antioch, a Hellenistic city of the Seleucid Kingdom that had a corporation of such Antiochians, who enjoyed certain political and commercial privileges.

4:11 *Eupolemus*: one of the two envoys sent to Rome by Judas Maccabeus (1 Mc 8:17).

4:12 Since the *gymnasium*, where the youth exercised naked (Greek *gymnos*), lay in the Tyropoeon Valley to the east of the citadel, it was directly next to the Temple on its eastern side. *The Greek hat*: a wide-brimmed hat, traditional headgear of Hermes, the patron god of athletic contests; it formed part of the distinctive costume of the members of the "youth center."

4:20 *Triremes*: war vessels with three banks of oars.

4:21 *Philometor*: Ptolemy VI, king of Egypt, ca. 172 to ca. 145 B.C.

4:23 *Menelaus*: Jewish high priest from ca. 172 to his execution in 162 B.C. (13:3–8).

4:30 *Mallus*: a city of Cilicia (v. 36) in southeastern Asia Minor, about thirty miles east of Tarsus.

*

4:11 1 Mc 8:17.
4:12–17 1 Mc 1:11–15.
4:29 2 Mc 4:39–42.

Daphne, near Antioch. 34 Thereupon Menelaus approached Andronicus privately and urged him to seize Onias. So Andronicus went to Onias, treacherously reassuring him by offering his right hand in oath, and persuaded him, in spite of his suspicions, to leave the sanctuary. Then, with no regard for justice, he immediately put him to death.

35 As a result, not only the Jews, but many people of other nations as well, were indignant and angry over the unjust murder of the man. 36 When the king returned from the region of Cilicia, the Jews of the city,† together with the Greeks who detested the crime, went to see him about the murder of Onias. 37 Antiochus was deeply grieved and full of pity; he wept as he recalled the prudence and noble conduct of the deceased. 38 Inflamed with anger, he immediately stripped Andronicus of his purple robe, tore off his garments, and had him led through the whole city to the very place where he had committed the outrage against Onias; and there he put the murderer to death. Thus the Lord rendered him the punishment he deserved.

More Outrages

39 Many acts of sacrilege had been committed by Lysimachus in the city† with the connivance of Menelaus. When word spread, the people assembled in protest against Lysimachus, because a large number of gold vessels had been stolen. 40 As the crowds, now thoroughly enraged, began to riot, Lysimachus launched an unjustified attack against them with about three thousand armed men under the leadership of a certain Auranus, a man as advanced in folly as he was in years. 41 Seeing Lysimachus' attack, people picked up stones, pieces of wood or handfuls of the ashes lying there and threw them in wild confusion at Lysimachus and his men. 42 As a result, they wounded many of them and even killed a few, while they put all to flight. The temple robber himself they killed near the treasury.

43 Charges about this affair were brought against Menelaus. 44 When the king came to Tyre, three men sent by the senate pleaded the case before him. 45 But Menelaus, seeing himself on the losing side, promised Ptolemy, son of Dorymenes, a substantial sum of money if he would win the king over.* 46 So Ptolemy took the king aside into a colonnade, as if to get some fresh air, and persuaded him to change his mind. 47 Menelaus, who was the cause of all the trouble, the king acquitted of the charges, while he condemned to death those poor men who would have been declared innocent even if they had pleaded their case before Scythians. 48 Thus, those who had prosecuted the case on behalf of the city, the people, and the sacred vessels, quickly suffered unjust punishment. 49 For this reason, even Tyrians, detesting the crime, provided sumptuously for their burial. 50 But Menelaus, thanks to the greed of those in power, remained in office, where he grew in wickedness, scheming greatly against his fellow citizens.

Jason's Revolt

5 1 About this time Antiochus sent his second expedition† into Egypt.* 2 * It then happened that all over the city, for nearly forty days, there appeared horsemen, clothed in garments of a golden weave, charging in midair—companies fully armed with lances and drawn swords; 3 squadrons of cavalry in battle array, charges and countercharges on this side and that, with brandished shields and bristling spears, flights of arrows and flashes of gold ornaments, together with armor of every sort. 4 Therefore all prayed that this vision might be a good omen.

5 But when a false rumor circulated that Antiochus was dead, Jason† gathered at least a thousand men and suddenly attacked the city. As the defenders on the walls were forced back and the city was finally being taken, Menelaus took refuge in the citadel. 6 For his part, Jason continued the merciless slaughter of his fellow citizens, not realizing that triumph over one's own kindred is the greatest calamity; he thought he was winning a victory over his enemies, not over his own people. 7 Even so, he did not gain control of the government, but in the end received only disgrace for his treachery, and once again took refuge in the country of the Ammonites. 8 At length he met a miserable end. Called to account before Aretas,† ruler of the Arabians, he fled from city to city, hunted by all, hated as an apostate from the laws, abhorred as the executioner of his country and

†

4:36 *The city*: Antioch. But some understand the Greek to mean "each city."

4:39 *The city*: Jerusalem. Menelaus was still in Syria.

5:1 *Second expedition*: the first invasion of Egypt by Antiochus IV in 169 B.C. (1 Mc 1:16–20) is not mentioned in 2 Maccabees, unless the coming of the Syrian army to Palestine (2 Mc 4:21–22) is regarded as the first invasion. The author of 2 Maccabees apparently combines the first pillage of Jerusalem in 169 B.C. after Antiochus' first invasion of Egypt (1 Mc 1:20–28; cf. 2 Mc 5:5–7) with the second pillage of the city two years later (167 B.C.), following the king's second invasion of Egypt in 168 B.C. (1 Mc 1:29–35; cf. 2 Mc 5:24–26).

5:5 *Jason*: brother of Onias III, claimant of the high priesthood (4:7–10). Later he was supplanted by Menelaus, who drove him into Transjordan (4:26).

5:8 *Aretas*: King Aretas I of the Nabateans; cf. 1 Mc 5:25.

*

4:45 2 Mc 8:8; 1 Mc 3:38.
5:1–10 1 Mc 1:16–19; Dn 11:25–30.
5:2–3 2 Mc 3:24–26; 10:29–30; 11:8.

his compatriots. Driven into Egypt, 9 he set out
by sea for the Lacedaemonians, among whom he
hoped to find protection because of his relations
with them. He who had exiled so many from their
country perished in exile; 10 and he who had cast
out so many to lie unburied went unmourned and
without a funeral of any kind, nor any place in the
tomb of his ancestors.

Revenge by Antiochus

11 * When these happenings were reported to
the king, he thought that Judea was in revolt. Rag-
ing like a wild animal, he set out from Egypt and
took Jerusalem by storm. 12 He ordered his soldiers
to cut down without mercy those whom they met
and to slay those who took refuge in their houses.
13 There was a massacre of young and old, a kill-
ing of women and children, a slaughter of young
women and infants. 14 In the space of three days,
eighty thousand were lost, forty thousand meeting
a violent death, and the same number being sold
into slavery.

15 Not satisfied with this, the king dared to en-
ter the holiest temple in the world; Menelaus, that
traitor both to the laws and to his country, served
as guide. 16 He laid his impure hands on the sa-
cred vessels and swept up with profane hands the
votive offerings made by other kings for the ad-
vancement, the glory, and the honor of the place.
17 Antiochus became puffed up in spirit, not real-
izing that it was because of the sins of the city's
inhabitants that the Sovereign Lord was angry for
a little while: hence the disregard of the place.*
18 If they had not become entangled in so many
sins, this man, like that Heliodorus sent by King
Seleucus to inspect the treasury, would have been
flogged and turned back from his presumptuous
act as soon as he approached. 19 The Lord, how-
ever, had not chosen the nation for the sake of
the place, but the place for the sake of the nation.
20 Therefore, the place itself, having shared in the
nation's misfortunes, afterward participated in
their good fortune; and what the Almighty had
forsaken in wrath was restored in all its glory, once
the great Sovereign Lord became reconciled.

21 * Antiochus carried off eighteen hundred
talents from the temple and hurried back to Anti-
och, thinking in his arrogance that he could make
the land navigable and the sea passable on foot,
so carried away was he with pride. 22 He left gov-
ernors to harass the nation: at Jerusalem, Philip,
a Phrygian by birth,† and in character more bar-
barous than the man who appointed him;* 23 at
Mount Gerizim,† Andronicus; and besides these,
Menelaus, who lorded it over his fellow citizens
more than the others. Out of hatred for the Jew-
ish citizens, 24 * the king sent Apollonius,† com-
mander of the Mysians, at the head of an army of
twenty-two thousand, with orders to kill all the
grown men and sell the women and children into
slavery. 25 When this man arrived in Jerusalem, he
pretended to be peacefully disposed and waited
until the holy day of the sabbath; then, finding
the Jews refraining from work, he ordered his men
to parade fully armed. 26 All those who came out
to watch, he massacred, and running through the
city with armed men, he cut down a large number
of people.

27 But Judas Maccabeus and about nine others
withdrew to the wilderness to avoid sharing in de-
filement; there he and his companions lived like
the animals in the hills, eating what grew wild.*

Abolition of Judaism

6 1 * Not long after this the king sent an Athe-
nian senator† to force the Jews to abandon
the laws of their ancestors and live no longer by
the laws of God, 2 also to profane the temple in
Jerusalem and dedicate it to Olympian Zeus,† and
the one on Mount Gerizim to Zeus the Host to
Strangers, as the local inhabitants were wont to
be.* 3 This was a harsh and utterly intolerable evil.
4 The Gentiles filled the temple with debauchery
and revelry; they amused themselves with pros-
titutes and had intercourse with women even in
the sacred courts. They also brought forbidden
things into the temple,* 5 so that the altar was
covered with abominable offerings prohibited by
the laws.

6 No one could keep the sabbath or celebrate
the traditional feasts, nor even admit to being a
Jew. 7 Moreover, at the monthly celebration of the

---

† **5:22** *Philip, a Phrygian by birth*: the Philip of 2 Mc 6:11 and 8:8, but probably not the same as Philip the regent of 2 Mc 9:29 and 1 Mc 6:14.

5:23 *Mount Gerizim*: the sacred mountain of the Samaritans at Shechem; cf. 2 Mc 6:2.

5:24 *Apollonius*: the Mysian commander of 1 Mc 1:29; mentioned also in 2 Mc 3:5; 4:4.

6:1 *Athenian senator*: or, Geron the Athenian, since *geron* can also be a proper name.

6:2 *Olympian Zeus*: equated with the Syrian Baal Shamen ("the lord of the heavens"), a term which the Jews mockingly rendered as *shiqqus shomem*, "desolating abomination" (Dn 9:27; 11:31; 12:11; 1 Mc 1:54).

5:11–21 1 Mc 1:20–24.
5:17 2 Mc 6:12–16; 7:16–19, 32–38.
5:21 1 Mc 1:23–24.
5:22 2 Mc 6:11; 8:8.
5:24–26 1 Mc 1:29–40.
5:27 2 Mc 8:1; 1 Mc 2:28.
6:1 1 Mc 1:41–63.
6:2 1 Mc 1:46, 54; Dn 9:27; 11:31; 12:11.
6:4 Ez 23:36–49; Dn 11:31; Am 2:7.

king's birthday the Jews, from bitter necessity, had
to partake of the sacrifices, and when the festival of
Dionysus† was celebrated, they were compelled to
march in his procession, wearing wreaths of ivy.*
8 Following upon a vote of the citizens of Ptole-
mais, a decree was issued ordering the neighboring
Greek cities to adopt the same measures, obliging
the Jews to partake of the sacrifices 9 and putting to
death those who would not consent to adopt the
customs of the Greeks. It was obvious, therefore,
that disaster had come upon them. 10 Thus, two
women who were arrested for having circumcised
their children were publicly paraded about the
city with their babies hanging at their breasts and
then thrown down from the top of the city wall.*
11 Others, who had assembled in nearby caves to
observe the seventh day in secret, were betrayed
to Philip and all burned to death. In their respect
for the holiness of that day, they refrained from
defending themselves.*

God's Purpose

12 * Now I urge those who read this book not
to be disheartened by these misfortunes, but to
consider that these punishments were meant not
for the ruin but for the correction of our nation.
13 It is, in fact, a sign of great kindness to punish
the impious promptly instead of letting them go
for long. 14 * Thus, in dealing with other nations,
the Sovereign Lord patiently waits until they reach
the full measure of their sins before punishing
them; but with us he has decided to deal differ-
ently, 15 in order that he may not have to punish
us later, when our sins have reached their fullness.
16 Therefore he never withdraws his mercy from
us. Although he disciplines us with misfortunes,
he does not abandon his own people. 17 Let these
words suffice for recalling this truth. Without fur-
ther ado we must go on with our story.

Martyrdom of Eleazar

18 † Eleazar, one of the foremost scribes, a man
advanced in age and of noble appearance, was be-
ing forced to open his mouth to eat pork.* 19 But
preferring a glorious death to a life of defilement,
he went forward of his own accord to the instru-
ment of torture, 20 spitting out the meat as they
should do who have the courage to reject food un-
lawful to taste even for love of life.

Live It!

Teaching by Example

Second Maccabees tells the story of Eleazar, a dignified, elderly scribe who has followed God his whole life. Rather than compromise his principles, Eleazar courageously accepts death by torture. He knows his example will influence younger people (see 6:28). His example gives others courage (see verse 31).

Young people watch and learn. An old television commercial shows a father and son driving along in a car. The son has a toy steering wheel in front of him and imitates his father's driving. When the father turns the wheel, so does the son. When the father switches the turn signal, so does the son. Then the father pulls a cigarette from a pack. He lights it and begins smoking. The next scene shows the son going for the pack of cigarettes.

The next time you find yourself struggling to make the right choice, think about the example you might be giving to someone younger than you.

▶ **2 Mc 6:18–31**

21 Those in charge of that unlawful sacrifice took
the man aside, because of their long acquaintance
with him, and privately urged him to bring his
own provisions that he could legitimately eat,
and only to pretend to eat the sacrificial meat pre-
scribed by the king. 22 Thus he would escape death,
and be treated kindly because of his old friendship
with them. 23 But he made up his mind in a no-
ble manner, worthy of his years, the dignity of his
advanced age, the merited distinction of his gray
hair, and of the admirable life he had lived from
childhood. Above all loyal to the holy laws given
by God, he swiftly declared, "Send me to Hades!"

† **6:7** *Dionysus*: also called Bacchus, the god of the grape harvest and of wine; ivy was one of his symbols.

6:18–7:42 The stories of Eleazar and of the mother and her seven sons, among the earliest models of "martyrology," were understandably popular. Written to encourage God's people in times of persecution, they add gruesome details to the record of tortures, and place long speeches in the mouths of the martyrs.

6:7 1 Mc 1:58–59.
6:10 1 Mc 1:60–61.
6:11 1 Mc 2:32–38.
6:12–16 2 Mc 5:17; 7:16–19, 32–38.
6:14 Wis 11:9–10; 12:2, 22.
6:18 Lv 11:6–8.

Did You Know?

Nonviolent Resistance

The article "A Just War," near 1 Maccabees 6:32, discusses just war as a response to the Seleucid persecution of the Jews. Second Maccabees, chapters 6–7, hints at another response—nonviolent resistance. Despite being ordered to forsake their faith and to adopt Greek customs, Jews resisted. We read of women continuing to have their baby boys circumcised (see 6:10), of secret gatherings to celebrate the Sabbath (see 6:11), and of martyrs refusing to eat unlawful meat (see 6:19, 7:1). Although the stories focus on the violent responses and tortures inflicted by the Greeks, they indicate that at least part of the population neither gave up its religious practices nor took up arms in violent conflict.

Christians have continued to develop the concept of nonviolent resistance—sometimes called pacifism. Nonviolent resistance is rooted in Jesus' teachings to turn the other cheek (see Mt 5:39) and "love your enemies" (5:44). Nonviolent resistance is not passive. It confronts evil and refuses to cooperate with it without resorting to violence. Those who practice nonviolent resistance accept the suffering that results because they know God can bring good out of the suffering of the just. The Catholic Church teaches that nonviolent resistance gives witness to God's redeeming love and that no person who objects to committing violence should be forced into military service.

Christian nonviolence is a challenge for everyone. How do you practice it in your relationships with others? In what situations, if any, do you think it is necessary to respond with violence? In what situations would you refuse to participate in military service?

24 "At our age it would be unbecoming to make
such a pretense; many of the young would think
the ninety-year-old Eleazar had gone over to an
alien religion. 25 If I dissemble to gain a brief mo-
ment of life, they would be led astray by me, while
I would bring defilement and dishonor on my old
age. 26 Even if, for the time being, I avoid human
punishment, I shall never, whether alive or dead,
escape the hand of the Almighty. 27 Therefore, by
bravely giving up life now, I will prove myself wor-
thy of my old age, 28 and I will leave to the young a
noble example of how to die willingly and nobly
for the revered and holy laws."

He spoke thus, and went immediately to the in-
strument of torture. 29 Those who shortly before
had been kindly disposed, now became hostile
toward him because what he had said seemed to
them utter madness.* 30 When he was about to die
under the blows, he groaned, saying: "The Lord in
his holy knowledge knows full well that, although
I could have escaped death, I am not only endur-
ing terrible pain in my body from this scourging,
but also suffering it with joy in my soul because
of my devotion to him." 31 This is how he died,
leaving in his death a model of nobility and an
unforgettable example of virtue not only for the
young but for the whole nation.

Martyrdom of a Mother and Her Seven Sons

7 1 It also happened that seven brothers with
their mother were arrested and tortured with
whips and scourges by the king to force them to
eat pork in violation of God's law.* 2 One of the
brothers, speaking for the others, said: "What do
you expect to learn by questioning us? We are
ready to die rather than transgress the laws of our
ancestors."

3 At that the king, in a fury, gave orders to have
pans and caldrons heated. 4 These were quickly
heated, and he gave the order to cut out the tongue
of the one who had spoken for the others, to scalp
him and cut off his hands and feet, while the rest
of his brothers and his mother looked on. 5 When
he was completely maimed but still breathing, the
king ordered them to carry him to the fire and fry
him. As a cloud of smoke spread from the pan,
the brothers and their mother encouraged one an-
other to die nobly, with these words: 6 "The Lord
God is looking on and truly has compassion on
us, as Moses declared in his song, when he openly
bore witness, saying, 'And God will have compas-
sion on his servants.' "*

7 After the first brother had died in this manner,
they brought the second to be made sport of. Af-
ter tearing off the skin and hair of his head, they
asked him, "Will you eat the pork rather than have
your body tortured limb by limb?" 8 Answering in
the language of his ancestors, he said, "Never!" So
he in turn suffered the same tortures as the first.

6:29 Wis 3:1–4; 5:4. **7:6** Dt 32:36–38.
7:1 Jer 15:9.

Cultural Connection

I Will Sacrifice Myself

If I were a bird
and able to fly afar,
I would like to be a white dove
to guide the people to freedom.
If I were the cloud in the sky,
I would shelter and bring rains
to the rice field.
If I were a grain of sand
I would throw myself down
to make a path for the people.
I will sacrifice my life
for the suffering people.
I would sacrifice myself
no matter how many times
I would have to die.

("For the People," by Nid, Thailand,
in *Your Will Be Done*)

This song was written by a twenty-two-year-old Thai student. He was later shot and killed by police officers at a demonstration against the return of a corrupt leader. His love for Thailand echoes the love of the mother and her seven sons for God and their Jewish faith in chapter 7 of Second Maccabees.

2 Maccabees, chapter 7

9 With his last breath he said: "You accursed fiend,
you are depriving us of this present life, but the
King of the universe will raise us up† to live again
forever, because we are dying for his laws."*
10 After him the third suffered their cruel sport.
He put forth his tongue at once when told to do
so, and bravely stretched out his hands, 11 as he
spoke these noble words: "It was from Heaven that
I received these; for the sake of his laws I disregard
them; from him I hope to receive them again."
12 Even the king and his attendants marveled at
the young man's spirit, because he regarded his
sufferings as nothing.
13 After he had died, they tortured and maltreat-
ed the fourth brother in the same way. 14 When he
was near death, he said, "It is my choice to die at
the hands of mortals with the hope that God will
restore me to life; but for you, there will be no res-
urrection to life."
15 They next brought forward the fifth brother
and maltreated him. 16 Looking at the king, he
said:* "Mortal though you are, you have power
over human beings, so you do what you please.
But do not think that our nation is forsaken by
God. 17 Only wait, and you will see how his great
power will torment you and your descendants."
18 After him they brought the sixth brother.
When he was about to die, he said: "Have no vain
illusions. We suffer these things on our own ac-
count, because we have sinned against our God;
that is why such shocking things have happened.
19 Do not think, then, that you will go unpunished
for having dared to fight against God."
20 Most admirable and worthy of everlasting re-
membrance was the mother who, seeing her seven
sons perish in a single day, bore it courageously
because of her hope in the Lord. 21 Filled with a
noble spirit that stirred her womanly reason with
manly emotion, she exhorted each of them in
the language of their ancestors with these words:
22 * "I do not know how you came to be in my
womb; it was not I who gave you breath and life,
nor was it I who arranged the elements you are
made of. 23 Therefore, since it is the Creator of the
universe who shaped the beginning of human-
kind and brought about the origin of everything,
he, in his mercy, will give you back both breath
and life, because you now disregard yourselves for
the sake of his law."
24 Antiochus, suspecting insult in her words,
thought he was being ridiculed. As the youngest
brother was still alive, the king appealed to him,
not with mere words, but with promises on oath,
to make him rich and happy if he would abandon

† 7:9 *The King of the universe will raise us up*: here, and in vv. 11, 14, 23, 29, 36, belief in the future resurrection of the body, at least for the just, is clearly stated; cf. also 12:44; 14:46; Dn 12:2.

* 7:9 2 Mc 12:44; 14:46; Dn 12:1–3.
7:16–19 2 Mc 5:17; 6:12–16; 7:32.
7:22–23 2 Mc 7:11, 28; Jb 1:10–12; Ps 139:13–16; Eccl 11:5.

his ancestral customs: he would make him his
Friend and entrust him with high office. 25 When
the youth paid no attention to him at all, the king
appealed to the mother, urging her to advise her
boy to save his life. 26 After he had urged her for a
long time, she agreed to persuade her son. 27 She
leaned over close to him and, in derision of the
cruel tyrant, said in their native language: "Son,
have pity on me, who carried you in my womb for
nine months, nursed you for three years, brought
you up, educated and supported you to your pres-
ent age. 28 I beg you, child, to look at the heavens
and the earth and see all that is in them; then you
will know that God did not make them out of ex-
isting things.† In the same way humankind came
into existence. 29 Do not be afraid of this execu-
tioner, but be worthy of your brothers and accept
death, so that in the time of mercy I may receive
you again with your brothers."

30 She had scarcely finished speaking when the
youth said: "What is the delay? I will not obey the
king's command. I obey the command of the law
given to our ancestors through Moses. 31 But you,
who have contrived every kind of evil for the He-
brews, will not escape the hands of God. 32 We, in-
deed, are suffering because of our sins.* 33 Though
for a little while our living Lord has been angry,
correcting and chastising us, he will again be rec-
onciled with his servants. 34 But you, wretch, most
vile of mortals, do not, in your insolence, buoy
yourself up with unfounded hopes, as you raise
your hand against the children of heaven. 35 You
have not yet escaped the judgment of the almighty
and all-seeing God. 36 Our brothers, after enduring
brief pain, have drunk of never-failing life, under
God's covenant. But you, by the judgment of God,
shall receive just punishments for your arrogance.
37 Like my brothers, I offer up my body and my
life for our ancestral laws, imploring God to show
mercy soon to our nation, and by afflictions and
blows to make you confess that he alone is God.
38 Through me and my brothers, may there be an
end to the wrath of the Almighty that has justly
fallen on our whole nation."

39 At that, the king became enraged and treated
him even worse than the others, since he bitterly
resented the boy's contempt. 40 Thus he too died
undefiled, putting all his trust in the Lord. 41 Last
of all, after her sons, the mother was put to death.
42 Enough has been said about the sacrificial meals
and the excessive cruelties.

2
MC

V. Victories of Judas and Purification of the Temple

Resistance from Judas Maccabeus

8 1 * Judas Maccabeus and his companions en-
tered the villages secretly, summoned their
kindred, and enlisted others who had remained
faithful to Judaism. Thus they assembled about
six thousand men. 2 They implored the Lord to
look kindly upon this people, who were being op-
pressed by all; to have pity on the sanctuary, which
was profaned by renegades; 3 to have mercy on the
city, which was being destroyed and was about to
be leveled to the ground; to listen to the blood
that cried out to him; 4 to remember the criminal
slaughter of innocent children and the blasphe-
mies uttered against his name; and to manifest his
hatred of evil.

5 * Once Maccabeus got his men organized, the
Gentiles could not withstand him, for the Lord's
wrath had now changed to mercy. 6 Coming by
surprise upon towns and villages, he set them on
fire. He captured strategic positions, and put to
flight not a few of the enemy. 7 He preferred the
nights as being especially favorable for such at-
tacks. Soon talk of his valor spread everywhere.

First Victory over Nicanor†

8 When Philip saw that Judas was gaining
ground little by little and that his successful ad-
vances were becoming more frequent, he wrote
to Ptolemy, governor of Coelesyria and Phoe-
nicia, to come to the aid of the king's interests.*
9 * Ptolemy promptly selected Nicanor, son of Pa-
troclus, one of the Chief Friends, and sent him at
the head of at least twenty thousand armed men
of various nations to wipe out the entire Jewish
nation. With him he associated Gorgias, a general,
experienced in the art of war.* 10 Nicanor planned
to raise the two thousand talents of tribute owed
by the king to the Romans† by selling captured
Jews into slavery. 11 So he immediately sent word
to the coastal cities, inviting them to buy Jewish
slaves and promising to deliver ninety slaves for
a talent†—little anticipating the punishment that
was to fall upon him from the Almighty.

†

7:28 *God did not make them out of existing things*: that is, all things were made solely by God's omnipotent will and creative word; cf. Heb 11:3. This statement has often been taken as a basis for "creation out of nothing" (Latin *creatio ex nihilo*).

8:8–29, 34–35 This account of the campaign of Nicanor and Gorgias against Judas is paralleled, with certain differences, in 1 Mc 3:38–4:24.

8:10 *Tribute owed by the king to the Romans*: the payment imposed on Antiochus III in 188 B.C. by the treaty of Apamea.

8:11 *Ninety slaves for a talent*: a low price for so many slaves, thus expressing the opponents' contempt for the Jews.

*

7:32 2 Mc 5:17; 6:12–16; 7:16–19.
8:1–7 2 Mc 5:27; 1 Mc 3:10–26.
8:5–7 1 Mc 3:3–9.
8:8 2 Mc 4:45; 1 Mc 3:38.
8:9–23 1 Mc 3:38–59.
8:9 1 Mc 7:26.

12 When Judas learned of Nicanor's advance and informed his companions about the approach of the army, 13 those who were fearful and those who lacked faith in God's justice deserted and got away. 14 But the others sold everything they had left, and at the same time entreated the Lord to deliver those whom the ungodly Nicanor had sold before even capturing them. 15 They entreated the Lord to do this, if not for their sake, at least for the sake of the covenants made with their ancestors, and because they themselves invoked his holy and glorious name. 16 Maccabeus assembled his forces, six thousand strong, and exhorted them not to be panic-stricken before the enemy, nor to fear the very large number of Gentiles unjustly attacking them, but to fight nobly. 17 They were to keep before their eyes the lawless outrage perpetrated by the Gentiles against the holy place and the affliction of the humiliated city, as well as the subversion of their ancestral way of life. 18 He said, "They trust in weapons and acts of daring, but we trust in almighty God, who can by a mere nod destroy not only those who attack us but even the whole world." 19 He went on to tell them of the times when help had been given their ancestors: both the time of Sennacherib, when a hundred and eighty-five thousand of his men perished,* 20 and the time of the battle in Babylonia against the Galatians,† when only eight thousand Jews fought along with four thousand Macedonians; yet when the Macedonians were hard pressed, the eight thousand, by the help they received from Heaven, destroyed one hundred and twenty thousand and took a great quantity of spoils. 21 * With these words he encouraged them and made them ready to die for their laws and their country.

Then Judas divided his army into four, 22 placing his brothers, Simon, Joseph,† and Jonathan, each over a division, assigning them fifteen hundred men apiece.* 23 There was also Eleazar.† After reading to them from the holy book and giving them the watchword, "The help of God," Judas himself took charge of the first division and joined in battle with Nicanor.* 24 With the Almighty as their ally, they killed more than nine thousand of the enemy, wounded and disabled the greater part of Nicanor's army, and put all of them to flight. 25 They also seized the money of those who had come to buy them as slaves. When they had pursued the enemy for some time, they were obliged to return by reason of the late hour. 26 It was the day before the sabbath, and for that reason they could not continue the pursuit. 27 They collected the enemy's weapons and stripped them of their spoils, and then observed the sabbath with fervent praise and thanks to the Lord who kept them safe for that day on which he allotted them the beginning of his mercy. 28 After the sabbath, they gave a share of the spoils to those who were tortured and to widows and orphans; the rest they divided among themselves and their children.* 29 When this was done, they made supplication in common, imploring the merciful Lord to be completely reconciled with his servants.

Other Victories

30 They also challenged the forces of Timothy and Bacchides, killed more than twenty thousand of them, and captured some very high fortresses. They divided the considerable plunder, allotting half to themselves and the rest to victims of torture, orphans, widows, and the aged. 31 They collected the enemies' weapons and carefully stored them in strategic places; the rest of the spoils they carried to Jerusalem. 32 They also killed the commander of Timothy's forces, a most wicked man, who had done great harm to the Jews. 33 While celebrating the victory in their ancestral city, they burned both those who had set fire to the sacred gates and Callisthenes, who had taken refuge in a little house; so he received the reward his wicked deeds deserved.

34 * The thrice-accursed Nicanor, who had brought the thousand slave dealers to buy the Jews, 35 after being humbled through the Lord's help by those whom he had thought of no account, laid aside his fine clothes and fled alone across country like a runaway slave, until he reached Antioch. He was eminently successful in destroying his own army. 36 So he who had promised to provide tribute for the Romans by the capture of the people of Jerusalem proclaimed that the Jews had a champion, and that because they followed the laws laid down by him, they were unharmed.

†

8:20 *Galatians*: a mercenary force, defeated by Jews and Macedonians in Babylon. Nothing else is known about this battle.

8:22 *Joseph*: called John in 1 Mc 2:2; 9:36, 38. This paragraph interrupts the story of Nicanor's defeat, which is resumed in v. 34. The purpose of the author apparently is to group together the defeats suffered by the Syrians on various occasions. Battles against Timothy are recounted in 1 Mc 5:37–44 and 2 Mc 12:10–25; against Bacchides, in 1 Mc 7:8–20.

8:23 *Eleazar*: this parenthetical reference notes the existence of a fifth brother; cf. 1 Mc 2:5.

8:19 2 Mc 15:22; 2 Kgs 19:35–36; 1 Mc 7:41–42; Is 37:36–37.
8:21–29 1 Mc 4:1–25.
8:22 1 Mc 2:2–5; 5:18, 55–62.
8:23 1 Mc 3:48.
8:28 Nm 31:25–47; Dt 26:12–13; 1 Sm 30:21–25.
8:34–35 2 Mc 8:23–24; 1 Mc 7:26.

Punishment and Death of Antiochus IV†

9 1* About that time Antiochus retreated in disgrace from the region of Persia. 2 He had entered the city called Persepolis and attempted to rob the temples and gain control of the city. Thereupon the people had swift recourse to arms, and Antiochus' forces were routed, so that in the end Antiochus was put to flight by the people of that region and forced to beat a shameful retreat. 3 On his arrival in Ecbatana, he learned what had happened to Nicanor and to Timothy's forces. 4 Overcome with anger, he planned to make the Jews suffer for the injury done by those who had put him to flight. Therefore he ordered his charioteer to drive without stopping until he finished the journey. Yet the condemnation of Heaven rode with him, because he said in his arrogance, "I will make Jerusalem the common graveyard of Jews as soon as I arrive there."

5 So the all-seeing Lord, the God of Israel, struck him down with an incurable and invisible blow; for scarcely had he uttered those words when he was seized with excruciating pains in his bowels and sharp internal torment,* 6 a fit punishment for him who had tortured the bowels of others with many barbarous torments. 7 Far from giving up his insolence, he was all the more filled with arrogance. Breathing fire in his rage against the Jews, he gave orders to drive even faster. As a result he hurtled from the speeding chariot, and every part of his body was racked by the violent fall. 8 Thus he who previously, in his superhuman presumption, thought he could command the waves of the sea, and imagined he could weigh the mountaintops in his scales, was now thrown to the ground and had to be carried on a litter, clearly manifesting to all the power of God.* 9 The body of this impious man swarmed with worms, and while he was still alive in hideous torments, his flesh rotted off, so that the entire army was sickened by the stench of his corruption.* 10 Shortly before, he had thought that he could reach the stars of heaven, and now, no one could endure to transport the man because of this intolerable stench.

11 At last, broken in spirit, he began to give up his excessive arrogance, and to gain some understanding, under the scourge of God, for he was racked with pain unceasingly. 12 When he could no longer bear his own stench, he said, "It is right to be subject to God, and not to think one's mortal self equal to God."* 13 Then this vile man vowed to him who would never again show him mercy, the Sovereign Lord, 14 that the holy city, toward which he had been hurrying with the intention of leveling it to the ground and making it a common graveyard, he would now set free; 15 that the Jews, whom he had judged not even worthy of burial, but fit only to be thrown out with their children to be eaten by vultures and wild animals—all of them he would make equal to the Athenians; 16 that he would adorn with the finest offerings the holy temple which he had previously despoiled, restore all the sacred vessels many times over, and provide from his own revenues the expenses required for the sacrifices. 17 Besides all this, he would become a Jew himself and visit every inhabited place to proclaim there the power of God. 18 But since his sufferings were not lessened, for God's just judgment had come upon him, he lost hope for himself and wrote the following letter to the Jews in the form of a supplication. It read thus:

19 † "To the worthy Jewish citizens, Antiochus, king and general, sends hearty greetings and best wishes for their health and prosperity. 20 If you and your children are well and your affairs are going as you wish, I thank God very much, for my hopes are in heaven. 21 Now that I am ill, I recall with affection your esteem and goodwill. On returning from the regions of Persia, I fell victim to a troublesome illness; so I thought it necessary to form plans for the general security of all. 22 I do not despair about my health, since I have much hope of recovering from my illness. 23 Nevertheless, I know that my father, whenever he went on campaigns in the hinterland, would name his successor, 24 so that, if anything unexpected happened or any unwelcome news came, the people throughout the realm would know to whom the government had been entrusted, and so not be disturbed. 25 I am also bearing in mind that the neighboring rulers,

†

9:1–29 In order to keep together the various accounts of God's punishment of the persecutors of his people, the author places here the stories of Antiochus' illness and death (in actuality the king died about the same time as the purification of the Temple, i.e., 164 B.C.; cf. 1 Mc 4:36–59; 6:1–16; 2 Mc 10:1–8); of Judas' campaigns in Idumea and Transjordan; cf. 1 Mc 5:1–51; 2 Mc 10:14–38; and of the first expedition of Lysias (1 Mc 4:26–35; 2 Mc 11:1–15).

9:19–27 Despite the statement in v. 18 this letter is not really a supplication. It is rather a notification to all the king's subjects of the appointment of his son as his successor and a request that they be loyal to the new king. Apparently the same letter, which has every appearance of being authentic, was sent to the various peoples throughout the kingdom, with only a few words of address changed for each group.

*

9:1–29 2 Mc 1:12–17; 1 Mc 6:1–13; Dn 11:40–45.
9:5 Acts 12:20–23.
9:8 Jb 38:8–11; Ps 65:6–7; Is 40:12.
9:9 Jdt 16:17; Sir 7:17; Is 14:11; 66:24; Acts 12:23.
9:12 Dn 4:31–34.

especially those on the borders of our kingdom,
are on the watch for opportunities and waiting to
see what will happen. I have therefore appointed
as king my son Antiochus, whom I have often be-
fore entrusted and commended to most of you,
when I made hurried visits to the outlying prov-
inces. I have written to him what is written here.
[26]Therefore I beg and entreat each of you to re-
member the general and individual benefits you
have received, and to continue to show goodwill
toward me and my son. [27]I am confident that, fol-
lowing my policy, he will treat you with equity
and kindness in his relations with you."
[28]So this murderer and blasphemer, after ex-
treme sufferings, such as he had inflicted on oth-
ers, died a miserable death in the mountains of a
foreign land. [29]His foster brother† Philip brought
the body home; but fearing Antiochus' son, he
later withdrew into Egypt, to Ptolemy Philome-
tor.*

Purification of the Temple

10 [1]* When Maccabeus and his companions,
under the Lord's leadership, had recovered
the temple and the city, [2]they destroyed the al-
tars erected by the foreigners in the marketplace
and the sacred shrines. [3]After purifying the tem-
ple, they made another altar. Then, with fire struck
from flint, they offered sacrifice for the first time
in two years,† burned incense, and lighted lamps.
They also set out the showbread. [4]When they had
done this, they prostrated themselves and begged
the Lord that they might never again fall into
such misfortunes, and that if they should sin at
any time, he might chastise them with modera-
tion and not hand them over to blasphemous and
barbarous Gentiles. [5]On the anniversary of the
day on which the temple had been profaned by
the foreigners, that is, the twenty-fifth of the same
month Kislev, the purification of the temple took
place. [6]The Jews celebrated joyfully for eight days
as on the feast of Booths, remembering how, a lit-
tle while before, they had spent the feast of Booths
living like wild animals in the mountains and in
caves. [7]Carrying rods entwined with leaves,†
beautiful branches and palms, they sang hymns
of grateful praise to him who had successfully
brought about the purification of his own place.
[8]By public decree and vote they prescribed that

Chapter 10

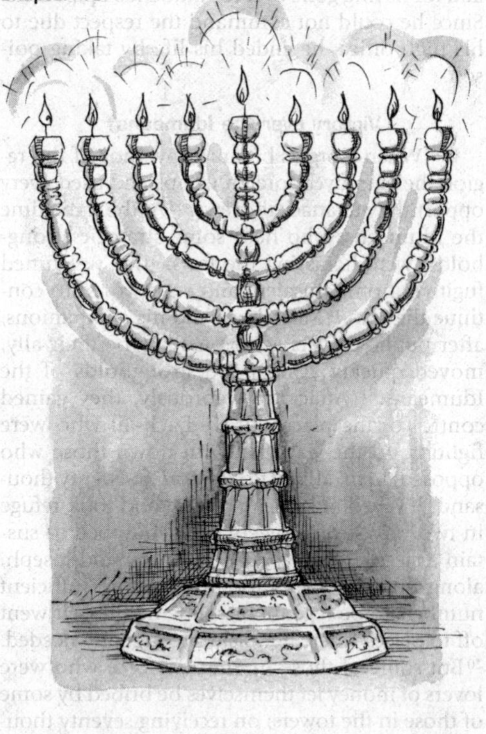

the whole Jewish nation should celebrate these
days every year. [9]Such was the end of Antiochus
surnamed Epiphanes.

VI. Renewed Persecution

Accession of Antiochus V

[10]Now we shall relate what happened under
Antiochus Eupator, the son of that godless man,
and shall give a summary of the chief evils caused
by the wars. [11]When Eupator succeeded to the
kingdom, he put a certain Lysias in charge of the
government as commander-in-chief of Coelesyria
and Phoenicia. [12]Ptolemy, called Macron,† had
taken the lead in treating the Jews fairly because
of the previous injustice that had been done them,
and he endeavored to have peaceful relations with
them. [13]As a result, he was accused before Eupator
by the King's Friends. In fact, on all sides he heard
himself called a traitor for having abandoned Cy-
prus, which Philometor had entrusted to him,

2 MC

†

9:29 *Foster brother*: an honorary title conferred by the king on prominent courtiers, whether or not they had been raised with him. Philip tried to seize control of Antioch from the young Antiochus V (1 Mc 6:55–56, 63) and fled to Egypt when he failed.

10:3 *Two years*: three years according to 1 Mc 1:54 and 4:52.

10:7 *Rods entwined with leaves*: the wreathed wands (*thyrsoi*) carried in processions honoring Dionysus (6:7) were apparently not regarded as distinctively pagan.

10:12 *Ptolemy, called Macron*: son of Dorymenes (4:45); he supported Antiochus IV in 168 B.C. during his invasion of Cyprus.

*

9:29 1 Mc 6:55–56, 63. **10:1–8** 1 Mc 4:36–61.

and for having gone over to Antiochus Epiphanes.
Since he could not command the respect due to
his high office, he ended his life by taking poi-
son.

Victory over the Idumeans†

14 * When Gorgias became governor of the re-
gion, he employed foreign troops and used every
opportunity to attack the Jews. 15 At the same time
the Idumeans, who held some strategic strong-
holds, were harassing the Jews; they welcomed
fugitives from Jerusalem and endeavored to con-
tinue the war. 16 Maccabeus and his companions,
after public prayers asking God to be their ally,
moved quickly against the strongholds of the
Idumeans. 17 Attacking vigorously, they gained
control of the places, drove back all who were
fighting on the walls, and cut down those who
opposed them, killing no fewer than twenty thou-
sand. 18 When at least nine thousand took refuge
in two very strong towers, well equipped to sus-
tain a siege, 19 Maccabeus left Simon and Joseph,
along with Zacchaeus and his forces, in sufficient
numbers to besiege them, while he himself went
off to places where he was more urgently needed.
20 But some of those in Simon's force who were
lovers of money let themselves be bribed by some
of those in the towers; on receiving seventy thou-
sand drachmas, they allowed a number of them
to escape. 21 When Maccabeus was told what had
happened, he assembled the rulers of the people
and accused those men of having sold their kin-
dred for money by setting their enemies free to
fight against them. 22 So he put them to death as
traitors, and without delay captured the two tow-
ers. 23 As he was successful at arms in all his under-
takings, he destroyed more than twenty thousand
in the two strongholds.

Victory over Timothy

24 Timothy, who had previously been defeated
by the Jews,† gathered a tremendous force of for-
eign troops and collected a large number of cav-
alry from Asia; then he appeared in Judea, ready to
conquer it by force. 25 At his approach, Maccabeus
and his companions made supplication to God,
sprinkling earth upon their heads and girding their
loins in sackcloth. 26 Lying prostrate at the foot of
the altar, they begged him to be gracious to them,
and to be an enemy to their enemies, and a foe to
their foes, as the law declares.* 27 After the prayer,
they took up their weapons and advanced a con-
siderable distance from the city, halting when
they were close to the enemy. 28 As soon as dawn
broke,† the armies joined battle, the one having as
pledge of success and victory not only their valor
but also their reliance on the Lord, and the other
taking fury as their leader in the fight.
29 * In the midst of the fierce battle, there ap-
peared to the enemy five majestic men from the
heavens riding on golden-bridled horses, lead-
ing the Jews. 30 They surrounded Maccabeus,
and shielding him with their own armor, kept
him from being wounded. They shot arrows and
hurled thunderbolts at the enemy, who were be-
wildered and blinded, routed in utter confusion.
31 Twenty thousand five hundred of their foot sol-
diers and six hundred cavalry were slain.
32 Timothy, however, fled to a well-fortified
stronghold called Gazara, where Chaereas was
in command.* 33 For four days Maccabeus and
his forces eagerly besieged the fortress. 34 Those
inside, relying on the strength of the place, kept
repeating outrageous blasphemies and uttering
abominable words. 35 When the fifth day dawned,
twenty young men in the army of Maccabeus, an-
gered over such blasphemies, bravely stormed the
wall and with savage fury cut down everyone they
encountered. 36 Similarly, others climbed up and
swung around on the defenders; they put the tow-
ers to the torch, spread the fire and burned the
blasphemers alive. Still others broke down the
gates and let in the rest of the troops, who took
possession of the city. 37 Timothy had hidden in
a cistern, but they killed† him, along with his
brother Chaereas, and Apollophanes. 38 On com-
pleting these exploits, they blessed, with hymns of
grateful praise, the Lord who shows great kindness
to Israel and grants them victory.

Defeat of Lysias†

11 1 * Very soon afterward, Lysias, guardian and
kinsman of the king and head of the gov-
ernment, being greatly displeased at what had

† **10:14–23** Probably the same campaign of Judas against the Idumeans that is mentioned in 1 Mc 5:1–3.

10:24 *Timothy, who had previously been defeated by the Jews*: as recounted in 8:30–33.

10:28 *As soon as dawn broke*: the same battle at dawn as in 1 Mc 5:30–34.

10:37 *Timothy . . . they killed*: apparently Timothy is still alive in 12:2, 18–25. Perhaps there was more than one Timothy. Or the present passage is not in chronological order. Gazara, v. 32 (Gezer), was not captured by the Jews until much later (cf. 1 Mc 9:50–52; 13:53). See 1 Mc 5:8 for the capture of Jazer.

11:1–12 The defeat of Lysias at Beth-zur probably occurred before the purification of the Temple; cf. 1 Mc 4:26–35.

* **10:14** 1 Mc 5:3–5.
10:26 Ex 23:22.
10:29–30 2 Mc 3:24–26; 5:2–3; 11:8.
10:32 1 Mc 13:43–48.
11:1–15 1 Mc 4:26–35.

happened, 2 mustered about eighty thousand infantry and all his cavalry and marched against the Jews. His plan was to make their city a Greek settlement; 3 to levy tribute on the temple, as he did on the shrines of the other nations; and to put the high priesthood up for sale every year.* 4 He did not take God's power into account at all, but felt exultant confidence in his myriads of foot soldiers, his thousands of cavalry, and his eighty elephants.* 5 So he invaded Judea, and when he reached Beth-zur, a fortified place about five stadia† from Jerusalem, launched a strong attack against it.

6 When Maccabeus and his companions learned that Lysias was besieging the strongholds, they and all the people begged the Lord with lamentations and tears to send a good angel to save Israel.* 7 Maccabeus himself was the first to take up arms, and he exhorted the others to join him in risking their lives to help their kindred. Then they resolutely set out together. 8 Suddenly, while they were still near Jerusalem, a horseman appeared at their head, clothed in white garments and brandishing gold weapons.* 9 Then all of them together thanked the merciful God, and their hearts were filled with such courage that they were ready to assault not only human beings but even the most savage beasts, or even walls of iron. 10 Now that the Lord had shown mercy toward them, they advanced in battle order with the aid of their heavenly ally. 11 Hurling themselves upon the enemy like lions, they laid low eleven thousand foot soldiers and sixteen hundred cavalry, and put all the rest to flight. 12 Most of those who survived were wounded and disarmed, while Lysias himself escaped only by shameful flight.

Peace Negotiations

13 * But Lysias was not a stupid man. He reflected on the defeat he had suffered, and came to realize that the Hebrews were invincible because the mighty God was their ally. He therefore sent a message 14 persuading them to settle everything on just terms, and promising to persuade the king also, and to induce him to become their friend. 15 Maccabeus, solicitous for the common good, agreed to all that Lysias proposed; and the king granted on behalf of the Jews all the written requests of Maccabeus to Lysias.

16 These are the terms of the letter which Lysias wrote to the Jews: "Lysias sends greetings to the Jewish people. 17 John and Absalom, your envoys, have presented your signed communication and asked about the matters contained in it. 18 Whatever had to be referred to the king I called to his attention, and the things that were acceptable he has granted. 19 If you maintain your loyalty to the government, I will endeavor to further your interests in the future. 20 On the details of these matters I have authorized my representatives, as well as your envoys, to confer with you. 21 Farewell." The one hundred and forty-eighth year,† the twenty-fourth of Dioscorinthius.

22 The king's letter read thus: "King Antiochus sends greetings to his brother Lysias. 23 Now that our father has taken his place among the gods, we wish the subjects of our kingdom to be undisturbed in conducting their own affairs. 24 We have heard that the Jews do not agree with our father's change to Greek customs but prefer their own way of life. They are petitioning us to let them retain their own customs. 25 Since we desire that this people too should be undisturbed, our decision is that their temple be restored to them and that they live in keeping with the customs of their ancestors. 26 Accordingly, please send them messengers to give them our assurances of friendship, so that, when they learn of our decision, they may have nothing to worry about but may contentedly go about their own business."

27 The king's letter to the people was as follows: "King Antiochus sends greetings to the Jewish senate and to the rest of the Jews. 28 If you are well, it is what we desire. We too are in good health. 29 Menelaus has told us of your wish to return home and attend to your own affairs. 30 Therefore, those who return by the thirtieth of Xanthicus will have our assurance of full permission 31 to observe their dietary and other laws, just as before, and none of the Jews shall be molested in any way for faults committed through ignorance. 32 I have also sent Menelaus to reassure you. 33 Farewell." In the one hundred and forty-eighth year, the fifteenth of Xanthicus.†

34 The Romans also sent them a letter as follows: "Quintus Memmius and Titus Manius, legates of the Romans, send greetings to the Jewish people. 35 What Lysias, kinsman of the king, has granted

---

† **11:5** *Five stadia*: one stadium is equal to about six hundred six feet. The actual distance to Beth-zur is about twenty miles.

11:21 *The one hundred and forty-eighth year*: 164 B.C. The reading of the name of the month and its position in the calendar are uncertain. The most likely chronological sequence of the four letters is vv. 16–21; vv. 34–38; vv. 27–33; vv. 22–26.

11:33 The date, which is the same as the date of the Romans' letter (v. 38), cannot be correct. The king's letter must be connected with the peace treaty of the one hundred forty-ninth year of the Seleucid era, i.e., 163 B.C. Perhaps the mention of the month of Xanthicus in the body of the letter (v. 30) caused the date of the Romans' letter to be transferred to this one.

---

* **11:3** 2 Mc 4:7–8, 23–24. **11:4** 1 Mc 3:34. **11:6** Ex 23:20. **11:8** 2 Mc 3:24–26; 5:2–3; 10:29–30. **11:13–33** 1 Mc 6:57–61.

you, we also approve. 36 But for the matters that he decided should be submitted to the king, send someone to us immediately with your decisions so that we may present them to your advantage, for we are on our way to Antioch. 37 Make haste, then, to send us those who can inform us of your preference. 38 Farewell." In the one hundred and forty-eighth year, the fifteenth of Xanthicus.†

Incidents at Joppa and Jamnia

12 1 After these agreements were made, Lysias returned to the king, and the Jews went about their farming. 2 But some of the local governors, Timothy and Apollonius, son of Gennaeus,† as also Hieronymus and Demophon, to say nothing of Nicanor, the commander of the Cyprians, would not allow them to live in peace and quiet.

3 Some people of Joppa also committed this outrage: they invited the Jews who lived among them, together with their wives and children, to embark on boats which they had provided. There was no hint of enmity toward them. 4 This was done by public vote of the city. When the Jews, wishing to live on friendly terms and not suspecting anything, accepted the invitation, the people of Joppa took them out to sea and drowned at least two hundred of them.

5 As soon as Judas heard of the barbarous deed perpetrated against his compatriots, he summoned his men; 6 and after calling upon God, the just judge, he marched against the murderers of his kindred. In a night attack he set the harbor on fire, burned the boats, and put to the sword those who had taken refuge there. 7 Because the gates of the town were shut, he withdrew, intending to come back later and wipe out the entire population of Joppa.

8 On hearing that the people of Jamnia planned in the same way to wipe out the Jews who lived among them, 9 he attacked the Jamnians by night, setting fire to the harbor and the fleet, so that the glow of the flames was visible as far as Jerusalem, thirty miles away.

More Victories by Judas

10 * When the Jews had gone about a mile from there† in the march against Timothy, they were attacked by Arabians numbering at least five thousand foot soldiers and five hundred cavalry. 11 After a hard fight, Judas and his companions, with God's help, were victorious. The defeated nomads begged Judas to give pledges of friendship, and they promised to supply the Jews with livestock and to be of service to them in any other way. 12 Realizing that they could indeed be useful in many respects, Judas agreed to make peace with them. After the pledges of friendship had been exchanged, the Arabians withdrew to their tents.

13 He also attacked a certain city called Caspin, fortified with earthworks and walls and inhabited by a mixed population of Gentiles. 14 Relying on the strength of their walls and their supply of provisions, the besieged treated Judas and his men with contempt, insulting them and even uttering blasphemies and profanity. 15 But Judas and his men invoked the aid of the great Sovereign of the world, who, in the days of Joshua, overthrew Jericho without battering rams or siege engines; then they furiously stormed the walls.* 16 Capturing the city by the will of God, they inflicted such indescribable slaughter on it that the adjacent pool, which was about a quarter of a mile wide, seemed to be filled with the blood that flowed into it.

17 * When they had gone on some ninety miles, they reached Charax, where there were certain Jews known as Toubians.† * 18 But they did not find Timothy in that region, for he had already departed from there without having done anything except to leave behind in one place a very strong garrison. 19 But Dositheus and Sosipater, two of Maccabeus' captains, marched out and destroyed the force of more than ten thousand men that Timothy had left in the stronghold. 20 Meanwhile, Maccabeus divided his army into cohorts, with a commander over each cohort, and went in pursuit of Timothy, who had a force of a hundred and twenty thousand foot soldiers and twenty-five hundred cavalry. 21 When Timothy learned of the approach of Judas, he sent on ahead of him the women and children, as well as the baggage, to a place called Karnion, which was hard to besiege and even hard to reach because of the difficult terrain of that region. 22 But when Judas' first cohort appeared, the enemy was overwhelmed with fear and terror at the manifestation of the all-seeing One. Scattering in every direction, they rushed away in such headlong flight that in many cases they wounded one another, pierced by the points

†

11:38 The date is March 12, 164 B.C.

12:2 *Apollonius, son of Gennaeus*: not the Apollonius who was the son of Menestheus (4:21). *Nicanor*: probably distinct from the Nicanor of 14:2.

12:10 *From there*: not from Jamnia (vv. 8–9) or Joppa (vv. 3–7), but from a place in Transjordan; vv. 10–26 parallel the account given in 1 Mc 5:9–13, 24–54 of Judas' campaign in northern Transjordan.

12:17 *Certain Jews known as Toubians*: because they lived "in the land of Tob" (1 Mc 5:13).

*

12:10–16 1 Mc 5:24–36. **12:15** Jos 6:1–21. **12:17–26** 1 Mc 5:37–44. **12:17** 1 Mc 5:13.

of their own swords. 23 Judas pressed the pursuit vigorously, putting the sinners to the sword and destroying as many as thirty thousand men.

24 Timothy himself fell into the hands of those under Dositheus and Sosipater; but with great cunning, he begged them to spare his life and let him go, because he had in his power the parents and relatives of many of them, and would show them no consideration. 25 When he had fully confirmed his solemn pledge to restore them unharmed, they let him go for the sake of saving their relatives.

26 * Judas then marched to Karnion and the shrine of Atargatis,† where he killed twenty-five thousand people. 27 After the defeat and destruction of these, he moved his army to Ephron, a fortified city inhabited by Lysias and people of many nationalities. Robust young men took up their posts in defense of the walls, from which they fought valiantly; inside were large supplies of war machines and missiles. 28 But the Jews, invoking the Sovereign who powerfully shatters the might of enemies, got possession of the city and slaughtered twenty-five thousand of the people in it.

29 Then they set out from there and hastened on to Scythopolis,† seventy-five miles from Jerusalem. 30 But when the Jews who lived there testified to the goodwill shown by the Scythopolitans and to their kind treatment even in times of adversity, 31 Judas and his men thanked them and exhorted them to be well disposed to their nation in the future also. Finally they arrived in Jerusalem, shortly before the feast of Weeks.

32 After this feast, also called Pentecost, they lost no time in marching against Gorgias, governor of Idumea, 33 who opposed them with three thousand foot soldiers and four hundred cavalry. 34 In the ensuing battle, a few of the Jews were slain. 35 A man called Dositheus, a powerful horseman and one of Bacenor's men,† caught hold of Gorgias, grasped his military cloak and dragged him along by brute strength, intending to capture the vile wretch alive, when a Thracian horseman attacked Dositheus and cut off his arm at the shoulder. Then Gorgias fled to Marisa.

36 After Esdris and his men had been fighting for a long time and were weary, Judas called upon the Lord to show himself their ally and leader in the battle. 37 Then, raising a battle cry in his ancestral language, and with hymns, he charged Gorgias' men when they were not expecting it and put them to flight.

Expiation for the Dead

38 Judas rallied his army and went to the city of Adullam. As the seventh day was approaching, they purified themselves according to custom and kept the sabbath there. 39 On the following day, since the task had now become urgent, Judas and his companions went to gather up the bodies of the fallen and bury them with their kindred in their ancestral tombs. 40 But under the tunic of each of the dead they found amulets sacred to the idols of Jamnia, which the law forbids the Jews to wear. So it was clear to all that this was why these men had fallen.* 41 They all therefore praised the ways of the Lord, the just judge who brings to light the things that are hidden. 42 † Turning to supplication, they prayed that the sinful deed might be fully blotted out. The noble Judas exhorted the people to keep themselves free from sin, for they had seen with their own eyes what had happened because of the sin of those who had fallen.* 43 He then took up a collection among all his soldiers, amounting to two thousand silver drachmas, which he sent to Jerusalem to provide for an expiatory sacrifice. In doing this he acted in a very excellent and noble way, inasmuch as he had the resurrection in mind; 44 for if he were not expecting the fallen to rise again, it would have been superfluous and foolish to pray for the dead. 45 But if he did this with a view to the splendid reward that awaits those who had gone to rest in godliness, it was a holy and pious thought. 46 Thus he made atonement for the dead that they might be absolved from their sin.

Death of Menelaus

13 1 * In the one hundred and forty-ninth year,† Judas and his men learned that Antiochus Eupator was invading Judea with a large force, 2 and that with him was Lysias, his guardian, who was in charge of the government. They led†

†

12:26 *Atargatis*: a Syrian goddess, represented by the body of a fish, who in Hellenistic times was identified with Astarte and Artemis.

12:29 *Scythopolis*: the Greek name of the city of Beth-shan; cf. 1 Mc 5:52.

12:35 *One of Bacenor's men*: certain ancient witnesses to the text have "one of the Toubians"; cf. v. 17.

12:42–45 This is the earliest statement of the doctrine that prayers (v. 42) and sacrifices (v. 43) for the dead are efficacious. Judas probably intended his purification offering to ward off punishment from the living. The author, however, uses the story to demonstrate belief in the resurrection of the just (7:9, 14, 23, 36), and in the possibility of expiation for the sins of otherwise good people who have died. This belief is similar to, but not quite the same as, the Catholic doctrine of purgatory.

13:1 *In the one hundred and forty-ninth year*: 163/162 B.C.

13:2 *They led*: the Greek means literally "each (of them) led," but it is unlikely that the author meant the already immense numbers to be doubled; the numbers are similar to those in 1 Mc 6:30.

*

12:26–31 1 Mc 5:45–54. **12:40** Dt 7:25–26. **12:42** Jos 7:1–26. **13:1–26** 1 Mc 6:28–54.

Catholic Connection

Final Judgment

When a loved one dies, we often turn our attention to life after death and our deepest hopes. Take for example the passage about Judas Maccabeus and his fallen warriors. During battle the warriors had broken the First Commandment by wearing charms that contained symbols worshiping a false god. While burying the dead, Judas discovers their sin and immediately calls for his followers to pray for the fallen. Judas's call to pray for the dead is born out of hope in God's mercy, hope in the ability to influence God's mercy on behalf of those who have died, and a belief that there is something more after death.

The hopes and beliefs shown by Judas Maccabeus are still embraced by the Catholic Church today. The Church believes there is something more after death—much more! The Church teaches that when we die, our souls will receive what is called a "particular judgment," where Christ will judge our soul and determine whether we enter heaven or hell. Heaven is eternal happiness, where we know God face to face and live in perfect peace with God and one another. Hell is total separation from God, resulting from one's own choice to reject God's love and mercy. There also are those who die in God's friendship but who still need to be purified of their sins and, therefore, are unable to enter heaven. According to Church teaching, these individuals undergo a purification called Purgatory. The Church calls us to pray for those who have died and may need to be purified of their sins, just as Judas prayed for his fallen comrades, so that they too will enjoy eternal salvation.

At the end of time, there will be a Final Judgment. This judgment will be preceded by the resurrection of the body, where the graves will open and every soul will be united with her or his body. At this judgment, everyone will stand before Christ and receive her or his final reward or punishment, heaven or hell. Then those who are found worthy of the eternal reward will live forever in perfect peace, happiness, and love in God's everlasting Kingdom.

2 Mc 12:38–45

Catechism, nos. 1020–1060

2 MC

a Greek army of one hundred and ten thousand
foot soldiers, fifty-three hundred cavalry, twenty-
two elephants, and three hundred chariots armed
with scythes.
3 Menelaus also joined them, and with great
duplicity kept urging Antiochus on, not for the
welfare of his country, but in the hope of being es-
tablished in office. 4 But the King of kings* aroused
the anger of Antiochus against the scoundrel.
When the king was shown by Lysias that Menelaus
was to blame for all the trouble, he ordered him
to be taken to Beroea† and executed there in the
customary local method. 5 There is at that place a
tower seventy-five feet high, full of ashes,† with
a circular rim sloping down steeply on all sides
toward the ashes. 6 Anyone guilty of sacrilege or
notorious for certain other crimes is brought up
there and then hurled down to destruction. 7 In
such a manner was Menelaus, that transgressor of
the law, fated to die, deprived even of burial. 8 It
was altogether just that he who had committed so
many sins against the altar with its pure fire and
ashes, in ashes should meet his death.

Battle near Modein

9 The king was advancing, his mind full of savage
plans for inflicting on the Jews things worse than
those they suffered in his father's time. 10 When
Judas learned of this, he urged the people to call
upon the Lord day and night, now more than
ever, to help them when they were about to be
deprived of their law, their country, and their holy
temple; 11 and not to allow this people, which had
just begun to revive, to be subjected again to blas-
phemous Gentiles. 12 When they had all joined in
doing this, and had implored the merciful Lord
continuously with weeping and fasting and pros-
trations for three days, Judas encouraged them
and told them to stand ready.
13 After a private meeting with the elders, he de-
cided that, before the king's army could invade
Judea and take possession of the city, the Jews
should march out and settle the matter with God's
help. 14 Leaving the outcome to the Creator of the
world, and exhorting his followers to fight nobly
to death for the laws, the temple, the city, the
country, and the government, he encamped near
Modein. 15 Giving his troops the battle cry "God's
Victory," he made a night attack on the king's pa-
vilion with a picked force of the bravest young
men and killed about two thousand in the camp.
He also stabbed the lead elephant and its rider.*
16 Finally they withdrew in triumph,† having filled
the camp with terror and confusion. 17 Day was
just breaking when this was accomplished with
the help and protection of the Lord.

Treaty with Antiochus V

18 * The king, having had a taste of the Jews'
boldness, tried to take their positions by a strata-
gem. 19 So he marched against Beth-zur, a strong
fortress of the Jews; but he was driven back,
checked, and defeated. 20 Judas sent supplies to the
men inside, 21 but Rhodocus, of the Jewish army,
betrayed military secrets† to the enemy. He was
found out, arrested, and imprisoned. 22 The king
made a second attempt by negotiating with the
people of Beth-zur. After giving them his pledge
and receiving theirs, he withdrew 23 and attacked
Judas' men. But he was defeated. Next he heard
that Philip, who was left in charge of the govern-
ment in Antioch, had rebelled. Dismayed, he ne-
gotiated with the Jews, submitted to their terms,
and swore to observe all their rights. Having come
to this agreement, he offered a sacrifice, and hon-
ored the sanctuary and the place with a generous
donation. 24 He received Maccabeus, and left Heg-
emonides as governor of the territory from Ptol-
emais to the region of the Gerrhenes.† 25 When he
came to Ptolemais, the people of Ptolemais were
angered by the peace treaty; in fact they were so in-
dignant that they wanted to annul its provisions.
26 But Lysias took the platform, defended the
treaty as well as he could and won them over by
persuasion. After calming them and gaining their
goodwill, he returned to Antioch. That is the story
of the king's attack and withdrawal.

14 1 * Three years later,† Judas and his com-
panions learned that Demetrius, son of
Seleucus, had sailed into the port of Tripolis with
a powerful army and a fleet, 2 and that he had oc-
cupied the country, after doing away with Anti-
ochus and his guardian Lysias.
3 A certain Alcimus, a former high priest,† who
had willfully incurred defilement before the time

†

13:4 *Beroea*: the Greek name of Aleppo in Syria.

13:5 *Ashes*: probably smoldering ashes; the tower resembles the ancient Persian fire towers.

13:16 *They withdrew in triumph*: according to 1 Mc 6:47 they fled.

13:21 *Military secrets*: probably about the lack of provisions in the besieged city; cf. 1 Mc 6:49.

13:24 *Gerrhenes*: probably the inhabitants of Gerar, southeast of Gaza.

14:1 *Three years later*: actually, Demetrius (I Soter), son of Seleucus (IV), landed at Tripolis in the year 151 of the Seleucid era (1 Mc 14:4), i.e., 162/161 B.C.; cf. 1 Mc 7:1–7.

14:3 *Alcimus, a former high priest*: he was apparently appointed high priest by Antiochus V after Menelaus was executed, and then deposed for collaborating with the Seleucids.

*

13:4 1 Tm 6:15; Rev 17:14; 19:16.
13:15 1 Mc 6:43–46.
13:18–23 1 Mc 6:48–53.
14:1–11 1 Mc 7:1–7.

of the revolt, realized that there was no way for him to be safe and regain access to the holy altar. 4 So he went to King Demetrius around the one hundred and fifty-first year and presented him with a gold crown and a palm branch, as well as some of the customary olive branches from the temple. On that day he kept quiet.* 5 But he found an opportunity to further his mad scheme when he was invited to the council by Demetrius and questioned about the dispositions and intentions of the Jews. He replied: 6 "Those Jews called Hasideans, led by Judas Maccabeus,† are warmongers, who stir up sedition and keep the kingdom from enjoying peace.* 7 For this reason, now that I am deprived of my ancestral dignity, that is to say, the high priesthood, I have come here, 8 first, out of my genuine concern for the king's interests, and second, out of consideration for my own compatriots, since our entire nation is suffering no little affliction from the rash conduct of the people just mentioned. 9 When you have informed yourself in detail on these matters, O king, provide for our country and its hard-pressed people with the same gracious consideration that you show toward all. 10 As long as Judas is around, it is impossible for the government to enjoy peace." 11 When he had said this, the other Friends who were hostile to Judas quickly added fuel to Demetrius' indignation.

Dealings with Nicanor

12 * The king immediately chose Nicanor, who had been in command of the elephants, and appointed him governor of Judea. He sent him off 13 with orders to put Judas to death, to disperse his followers, and to set up Alcimus as high priest of the great temple. 14 The Gentiles from Judea, who had fled before Judas, flocked to Nicanor, thinking that the misfortunes and calamities of the Jews would mean prosperity for themselves.

15 * When the Jews heard of Nicanor's coming, and that the Gentiles were rallying to him, they sprinkled themselves with earth and prayed to him who established his people forever, and who always comes to the aid of his heritage by manifesting himself. 16 At their leader's command, they set out at once from there and came upon the enemy at the village of Adasa. 17 Judas' brother Simon had engaged Nicanor, but he suffered a slight setback because of the sudden appearance of the enemy.

18 However, when Nicanor heard of the valor of Judas and his companions, and the great courage with which they fought for their country, he shrank from deciding the issue by bloodshed. 19 So he sent Posidonius, Theodotus and Mattathias to exchange pledges of friendship. 20 After a long discussion of the terms, each leader communicated them to his troops; and when general agreement was expressed, they assented to the treaty. 21 A day was set on which the leaders would meet by themselves. From each side a chariot came forward, and thrones were set in place. 22 Judas had posted armed men in readiness at strategic points for fear that the enemy might suddenly commit some treachery. But the conference was held in the proper way.

23 Nicanor stayed on in Jerusalem, where he did nothing out of place. He disbanded the throngs of people who gathered around him; 24 and he always kept Judas in his company, for he felt affection† for the man. 25 He urged him to marry and have children; so Judas married and settled into an ordinary life.

Nicanor's Threat Against Judas

26 When Alcimus saw their mutual goodwill, he took the treaty that had been made, went to Demetrius, and said that Nicanor was plotting against the government, for he had appointed Judas, that conspirator against the kingdom, as his successor. 27 Stirred up by the villain's slander, the king became enraged. He wrote to Nicanor, stating that he was displeased with the treaty, and ordering him to send Maccabeus at once as a prisoner to Antioch. 28 When this message reached Nicanor he was dismayed and troubled at the thought of annulling his agreement with a man who had done no wrong. 29 However, there was no way of opposing the king, so he watched for an opportunity to carry out this order by a stratagem. 30 But Maccabeus, noticing that Nicanor was more harsh in his dealings with him, and acting with unaccustomed rudeness when they met, concluded that this harshness was not a good sign. So he gathered together not a few of his men, and went into hiding from Nicanor.

31 * When Nicanor realized that he had been

†

14:6 *Hasideans, led by Judas Maccabeus*: according to 1 Mc 2:42 and 7:12–17, the Hasideans were a party separate from the Maccabees.

14:24 *Affection*: compare 1 Mc 7:26–32, where there is no hint of this cordial relationship between Nicanor and Judas.

14:37–46 The story of Razis belongs to the "martyrology" class of literature; it is similar to the stories in 6:18–7:42.

*

14:4 1 Mc 7:5–7, 25.
14:6 1 Mc 2:42; 7:12–17.
14:12–13 2 Mc 8:9; 1 Mc 3:38; 7:26–27.
14:15–19 1 Mc 7:26–32.
14:31–36 1 Mc 7:30–38.

cleverly outwitted by the man, he went to the great
and holy temple, at a time when the priests were
offering the customary sacrifices, and ordered
them to surrender Judas. 32 As they declared un-
der oath that they did not know where the man
they sought was, 33 he stretched out his right arm
toward the temple and swore this oath: "If you
do not hand Judas over to me as prisoner, I will
level this shrine of God to the ground; I will tear
down the altar, and erect here a splendid temple
to Dionysus."
34 With these words he went away. The priests
stretched out their hands toward heaven, calling
upon the unfailing defender of our nation in these
words: 35 "Lord of all, though you are in need of
nothing, you were pleased to have a temple for
your dwelling place among us. 36 Therefore, Holy
One, Lord of all holiness, preserve forever unde-
filed this house, which has been so recently pu-
rified."*

Martyrdom of Razis†

37 A certain Razis, one of the elders of Jerusalem,
was denounced to Nicanor as a patriot. A man
highly regarded, he was called a father of the Jews
because of his goodwill toward them. 38 In the
days before the revolt, he had been convicted of
being a Jew, and had risked body and soul in his
ardent zeal for Judaism. 39 Nicanor, to show his
disdain for the Jews, sent more than five hundred
soldiers to arrest him. 40 He thought that by arrest-
ing that man he would deal the Jews a hard blow.
41 But when the troops, on the point of cap-
turing the tower, were forcing the outer gate and
calling for fire to set the door ablaze, Razis, now
caught on all sides, turned his sword against him-
self, 42 preferring to die nobly† rather than fall into
the hands of vile men and suffer outrages unwor-
thy of his noble birth. 43 In the excitement of the
struggle he failed to strike exactly. So while the
troops rushed in through the doors, he gallantly
ran up to the top of the wall and courageously
threw himself down into the crowd. 44 But as they
quickly drew back and left an opening, he fell
into the middle of the empty space. 45 Still breath-
ing, and inflamed with anger, he got up and ran
through the crowd, with blood gushing from his
frightful wounds. Then, standing on a steep rock,
46 as he lost the last of his blood, he tore out his
entrails and flung them with both hands into the
crowd, calling upon the Lord of life and of spirit to
give these back to him again. Such was the man-
ner of his death.*

Nicanor's Arrogance

15 1 When Nicanor learned that Judas and his
companions were in the territory of Sa-
maria, he decided he could attack them in com-
plete safety on the day of rest. 2 The Jews who were
forced to accompany him pleaded, "Do not mas-
sacre them so savagely and barbarously, but show
respect for the day which the All-seeing has exalted
with holiness above all other days." 3 At this the
thrice-accursed wretch asked if there was a ruler in
heaven who prescribed the keeping of the sabbath
day.* 4 They replied, "It is the living Lord, the ruler
in heaven, who commands the observance of the
sabbath day." 5 Then he said, "I, the ruler on earth,
command you to take up arms and carry out the
king's business." Nevertheless he did not succeed
in carrying out his cruel plan.
6 In his utter boastfulness and arrogance Nica-
nor had determined to erect a public victory mon-
ument† over Judas and his companions. 7 But
Maccabeus remained confident, fully convinced
that he would receive help from the Lord. 8 He
urged his men not to fear the attack of the Gen-
tiles, but mindful of the help they had received
in the past from Heaven, to expect now the vic-
tory that would be given them by the Almighty.
9 By encouraging them with words from the law
and the prophets,† and by reminding them of
the battles they had already won, he filled them
with fresh enthusiasm. 10 Having stirred up their
courage, he gave his orders and pointed out at the
same time the perfidy of the Gentiles and their vi-
olation of oaths. 11 When he had armed each of
them, not so much with the security of shield and
spear as with the encouragement of noble words,
he cheered them all by relating a dream, a kind of
waking vision, worthy of belief.
12 What he saw was this: Onias, the former high
priest,† a noble and good man, modest in bear-
ing, gentle in manner, distinguished in speech,
and trained from childhood in all that belongs
to excellence, was praying with outstretched arms
for the whole Jewish community.* 13 Then in the
same way another man appeared, distinguished by

†

14:42 *Die nobly*: Razis's willingness to die nobly rather than to fall into enemy hands had a precedent in Saul (1 Sm 31:4). Razis took his life because he was convinced that God would restore his body in the resurrection of the dead (see 7:11, 22–23; 14:46).

15:6 *Public victory monument*: a heap of stones covered with the arms and armor of the fallen enemy.

15:9 *The law and the prophets*: the first of the three parts of the Hebrew Scriptures, called the sacred books (1 Mc 12:9; 2 Mc 2:14).

15:12 *Onias, the former high priest*: Onias III (3:1–40). Evidently the author believed that departed just persons were in some way alive even before their resurrection.

*

14:36 2 Mc 15:34.
14:46 2 Mc 7:9–11.
15:3 1 Mc 7:34.
15:12 2 Mc 3:1–40.

Introducing...

Jewish Sects

In the last two centuries before Christ, a diversity of ways of being Jewish emerged. Different groups arose emphasizing different ways of remaining faithful to their Jewish heritage. These groups, or factions, within a religion are sometimes called sects. Primarily three sects emerged within Judaism.

Pharisees. The Pharisees were descendants of the Hasidim, Jews devoted to a strict observance of the law who opposed King Antiochus IV Epiphanes' attempts to destroy the Jewish religion. *Pharisee* means "separated" and probably reflects the Pharisees' rigorous observance of the law. They were often greatly respected. In the New Testament, Jesus argues with some Pharisees but is also a guest of others. Saint Paul was a Pharisee. Not surprisingly, some of the Pharisees' teachings were similar to those of the early Christians.

Sadducees. The Sadducees were a conservative Jewish sect that emerged in the first century BC and lasted only to around AD 70. The Sadducees were wealthy and politically influential landowners, and some of them had important roles in the Temple. They emphasized the necessity of worshiping at the Temple in Jerusalem. Unlike the Pharisees, they did not believe in the resurrection of the body.

Essenes. The Essenes, like the Pharisees, seem to have descended from the Hasidim. They existed in the first century BC and disappeared after AD 70. *Essene* can mean "healer" or "pious." The Essenes did not believe in the necessity of Temple sacrifice and often lived together in isolated communities where they practiced a simple lifestyle. Some of them were connected with the desert monastery at Qumran and were responsible for writing the Dead Sea Scrolls. John the Baptist's preaching and some of Jesus' teaching in the Gospels closely reflected the writings and teachings of the Essenes.

his white hair and dignity, and with an air of wondrous and majestic authority. 14 Onias then said of him, "This is a man† who loves his fellow Jews and fervently prays for the people and the holy city—the prophet of God, Jeremiah." 15 Stretching out his right hand, Jeremiah presented a gold sword to Judas. As he gave it to him he said, 16 "Accept this holy sword as a gift from God; with it you shall shatter your adversaries."

17 Encouraged by Judas' words, so noble and capable of instilling valor and stirring young hearts to courage, they determined not merely to march, but to charge gallantly and decide the issue by hand-to-hand combat with the utmost courage, since city, sanctuary and temple were in danger. 18 They were not so much concerned about wives and children, or family and relations; their first and foremost fear was for the consecrated sanctuary.* 19 Those who were left in the city suffered no less an agony, anxious as they were about the battle in the open country. 20 Everyone now awaited the decisive moment. The enemy were already drawing near with their troops drawn up in battle line, their beasts placed in strategic positions, and their cavalry stationed on the flanks.

Defeat of Nicanor

21 Maccabeus, surveying the hosts before him, the variety of weaponry, and the fierceness of their beasts, stretched out his hands toward heaven and called upon the Lord who works wonders; for he knew that it is not weapons but the Lord's decision that brings victory to those who deserve it. 22 Calling upon God, he spoke in this manner: "You, master, sent your angel in the days of King Hezekiah of Judea, and he slew a hundred and eighty-five thousand men of Sennacherib's camp.* 23 And now, Sovereign of the heavens, send a good angel to spread fear and trembling ahead of us. 24 By the might of your arm may those be struck down who have blasphemously come against your holy people!" With these words he ended his prayer.

25 * Nicanor and his troops advanced to the sound of trumpets and battle songs. 26 But Judas and his troops met the enemy with supplication and prayers. 27 Fighting with their hands and praying to God with their hearts, they laid low at least thirty-five thousand, and rejoiced greatly over this

† **15:14** *A man*: regarded by the postexilic Jews as one of the greatest figures in their history; cf. 2:1; Mt 16:14. *Who . . . prays for the people*: Jeremiah's prayer in heaven has been taken in the Roman Catholic tradition as a biblical witness to the intercession of the saints.

* **15:18** 1 Mc 4:36.
15:22–23 2 Mc 8:19; 2 Kgs 19:35–36; 1 Mc 7:41–42; Is 37:36–37.
15:25–36 1 Mc 7:43.

manifestation of God's power. [28]When the battle
was over and they were joyfully departing, they
discovered Nicanor fallen there in all his armor;
[29]so they raised tumultuous shouts in their ances-
tral language in praise of the divine Sovereign.
[30]Then Judas, that man who was ever in body
and soul the chief defender of his fellow citizens,
and had maintained from youth his affection for
his compatriots, ordered Nicanor's head and right
arm up to the shoulder to be cut off and taken
to Jerusalem. [31]When he arrived there, he assem-
bled his compatriots, stationed the priests before
the altar, and sent for those in the citadel.† [32]He
showed them the vile Nicanor's head and the
wretched blasphemer's arm that had been boast-
fully stretched out against the holy dwelling of the
Almighty. [33]He cut out the tongue of the godless
Nicanor, saying he would feed it piecemeal to
the birds and would hang up the other wages of
his folly opposite the temple. [34]At this, everyone
looked toward heaven and praised the Lord who
manifests himself: "Blessed be the one who has
preserved undefiled his own place!" [35]Judas hung
Nicanor's head and arm on the wall of the citadel,
a clear and evident sign to all of the Lord's help.*
[36]By public vote it was unanimously decreed never
to let this day pass unobserved, but to celebrate
the thirteenth day of the twelfth month, called
Adar in Aramaic, the eve of Mordecai's Day.† *

VII. Epilogue

Compiler's Apology

[37]Since Nicanor's doings ended in this way,
with the city remaining in the possession of the
Hebrews from that time on, I will bring my story
to an end here too. [38]* If it is well written and to
the point, that is what I wanted; if it is poorly done
and mediocre, that is the best I could do. [39]Just
as it is unpleasant to drink wine by itself or just
water, whereas wine mixed with water makes a
delightful and pleasing drink, so a skillfully com-
posed story delights the ears of those who read the
work. Let this, then, be the end.

†

15:31 *Those in the citadel*: presumably Jewish soldiers; actually, the citadel was still in the possession of the Syrians (1 Mc 13:50).

15:36 *Mordecai's Day*: the feast of Purim, celebrated on the fourteenth and fifteenth days of Adar (Est 3:7; 9:20–23; F:10).

*

15:35 1 Sm 31:9–10.

15:36 1 Mc 7:49.

15:38–39 2 Mc 2:19–32.

Introduction to the Wisdom and Poetry Books

The LORD is my shepherd; there is nothing I lack.

(Ps 23:1)

A mild answer turns back wrath,
but a harsh word stirs up anger.

(Prv 15:1)

There is an appointed time for everything, and a time for every affair under the heavens.

(Eccl 3:1)

The books these words are taken from, the wisdom and poetry books of the Old Testament, are among the most quoted books of the Bible. The distilled wisdom they contain and the beauty of the language they use have universal appeal. Across cultures and across time, these books touch thoughtful minds and inquiring hearts.

In Depth

This section of the Bible contains a variety of books. The Book of Psalms consists of religious hymns, many written for use in Jewish worship. The Song of Songs is a love poem. The Book of Job is a debate on why innocent people suffer. The Book of Wisdom, Proverbs, and Ben Sira give advice on moral and virtuous living. And Ecclesiastes is a sort of journal on the purpose of human life. The most obvious common element among these books is the use of poetic language to convey their message. These are not the only books of the Old Testament that use poetry, but they make such extensive application of it that a little background on the nature of Hebrew poetry is helpful for reading them.

The most important feature of Hebrew poetry is parallelism. Parallelism involves the repetition of words or ideas in successive lines of a verse. Sometimes, the second line contrasts with the first:

Because the LORD knows the way of the just,
but the way of the wicked leads to ruin.

(Ps 1:6)

Other times, the second line completes the thought of the first:

The LORD looks down from heaven
upon the children of men,
To see if even one is wise,
if even one seeks God.

(14:2)

Still other times, the second line seems to restate the first line more forcefully:

For I know my transgressions;
my sin is always before me.

(51:5)

In its many forms, parallelism—not a rhythmic pattern or rhyming words—is the organizing principle of Hebrew poetry.

Hebrew poetry also uses symbolic language that is characteristic of poetry in any language. This includes metaphors ("My God, my rock of refuge" [18:3]) and similes ("As the deer longs for streams of water, / so my soul longs for you, O God" [42:2]). To appreciate the beauty of Old Testament poetry and feel its impact, one must be willing to wrestle with symbolic ways of interpreting words and phrases.

Whereas the other books of the Old Testament emphasize ancient Israel's distinctive religious values, the wisdom and poetry books focus on its unique view of wisdom. Wisdom literature is something the ancient Israelites shared with neighboring cultures. The Egyptians, Sumerians, and Babylonians all had literature that offered practical, time-tested advice for people seeking trustworthy guidance. For the Israelites, however, true wisdom was more than mere common sense: it was a gift from God given to those who sought it. Some passages of the wisdom literature even describe wisdom personified as divine, beautiful, eternal, holy, and with feminine characteristics (see Wis 7:22—8:8 and Ben Sira, chapter 1).

In general, the wisdom writings have these characteristics:

- few references to the law or the covenant
- a minimal interest in Israel's history
- a search for harmony and the meaning of life
- a willingness to explore the difficult mysteries of life, such as suffering and death
- a commitment to discovering the moral lessons of everyday experiences
- a fundamental belief that good and wise living is rewarded, whereas evil and foolish ways lead to ruin

The poetry and wisdom books of the Old Testament had an enormous influence on the writers of the New Testament and continue to be popular. Their poetic structure, which often makes them difficult to comprehend, also gives them a richness and depth that centuries of reading and rereading have not exhausted. Each time you read from these books, you will discover new treasures to enrich your life.

Other Background

- The Book of Psalms is quoted more often in the New Testament than is any other Old Testament book. Also, it is used extensively in the Church's liturgy.
- Job and Ecclesiastes posed serious challenges to the traditional understanding of Israelite faith. For help in understanding why, see the introductions to these books.
- Solomon's reputation for wisdom was so great that he was indicated as the author of four books actually written by others: Proverbs, Ecclesiastes, Song of Songs, and Wisdom.
- The Book of Wisdom and Ben Sira are not found in all translations of the Old Testament (see "The Case of the Missing Books," near Tb 1:16).

Suffering is an abundant reality in our world. You've seen the images—a mother holding her poor, dead child, against the background of a country ravaged by drought; the innocent victims of war and violence; the devastation resulting from natural disasters like hurricanes and earthquakes. Or perhaps you have watched someone close to you suffer from a debilitating illness, or the grief that comes with losing a loved one. Inevitably, the questions arise: Why do innocent people suffer? How can God allow this to happen? These are the basic questions struggled with in the Book of Job.

In Depth

At the time Job was written, most Israelites believed that if they obeyed God's Commandments, God would bless them and protect them in this life. The Israelites also believed that if people were suffering or poor, God was punishing them for some sin they or their parents had committed, even if they did not know what that sin was. The Israelites' thinking was extremely logical—because God is all-powerful and completely just, God will not allow people or communities to suffer unless they have sinned in some way.

The Book of Job challenges that way of thinking. Job is a good man who has received great wealth and a wonderful family from God. In fact, Job's final defense in chapter 31 is one of the finest summaries of the Old Testament vision of a righteous person. The Book of Job begins with God's allowing Job's wealth and children and health to be taken from him. Three friends come to mourn with Job. In a series of lengthy debates, they point out that his misfortunes must be the result of some sin or wrong he has committed. Job maintains his innocence, sometimes forcefully, and demands another explanation from God. Finally, God appears to Job and overwhelms him with questions about the nature of the universe. Job realizes that God is beyond human knowledge and that some mysteries—including suffering—can never be completely understood; they can only be accepted.

The Book of Job does not give the final answer about why bad things happen to good people. But it does make it clear that good people do suffer and that their suffering is not a punishment sent by God. And Job is a reminder to the Israelites and to us that God's purposes are too far beyond human understanding for anyone to claim to know everything there is to know about God.

At a Glance

- **I. Prologue (1:1—2:13).**
- **II. First Cycle of Speeches (3:1—14:22).**
- **III. Second Cycle of Speeches (15:1—21:34).**
- **IV. Third Cycle of Speeches (22:1—27:21).**
- **V. The Poem on Wisdom (28:1–28).**
- **VI. Job's Final Summary of His Cause (29:1—31:37).**
- **VII. Elihu's Speeches (32:1—37:24).**
- **VIII. The Lord and Job Meet (38:1—42:6).**
- **IX. Epilogue (42:7–17).**

Quick Facts

Inspired Author: unknown, written during the sixth or fifth centuries BC

Theme: Why do good people suffer? God's power, presence, and wisdom are beyond human understanding.

Of Note: Job is a story within a story: chapters 1–2 and 42:7–17 constitute a folktale; set within that tale, in 3:1—42:6, is a poetic debate about the cause of suffering.

Job

38:1

I. Prologue

Job's Piety

1 1 In the land of Uz† there was a blameless and
upright man named Job,* who feared God and
avoided evil. 2 Seven sons and three daughters
were born to him; 3 and he had seven thousand
sheep, three thousand camels, five hundred yoke
of oxen, five hundred she-donkeys, and a very
large household, so that he was greater than any-
one in the East.† 4 His sons used to take turns giv-
ing feasts, sending invitations to their three sisters
to eat and drink with them. 5 And when each feast
had run its course, Job would send for them and
sanctify them, rising early and offering sacrifices
for every one of them. For Job said, "It may be
that my children have sinned and cursed† God in
their hearts." Job did this habitually.

The Interview Between the Lord and the Satan

6 * One day, when the sons of God† came to
present themselves before the LORD, the satan also
came among them.* 7 The LORD said to the satan,
"Where have you been?" Then the satan answered
the LORD and said,* "Roaming the earth and
patrolling it." 8 The LORD said to the satan, "Have
you noticed my servant Job? There is no one on
earth like him, blameless and upright, fearing God
and avoiding evil." 9 The satan answered the LORD
and said, "Is it for nothing that Job is God-fearing?
10 Have you not surrounded him and his family
and all that he has with your protection? You have
blessed the work of his hands, and his livestock
are spread over the land. 11 * But now put forth
your hand and touch all that he has, and surely he
will curse you to your face." 12 The LORD said to the
satan, "Very well, all that he has is in your power;
only do not lay a hand on him." So the satan went
forth from the presence of the LORD.

The First Trial

13 One day, while his sons and daughters were
eating and drinking wine in the house of their el-
dest brother, 14 a messenger came to Job and said,
"The oxen were plowing and the donkeys grazing
beside them, 15 and the Sabeans† carried them off
in a raid. They put the servants to the sword, and
I alone have escaped to tell you." 16 He was still
speaking when another came and said, "God's
fire has fallen from heaven and struck the sheep
and the servants and consumed them; I alone

†

1:1 *Uz*: somewhere in Edom or Arabia; see Lam 4:21. *Job*: the name probably means "Where is the (divine) father?" In Hebrew it is almost a homonym with the word for "enemy" (see note on 13:24; cf. 33:10).

1:3 *The East*: that is, east of Palestine.

1:5 *Cursed*: lit., "blessed." So also in v. 11; 2:5, 9.

1:6 *Sons of God*: members of the divine council; see Gn 6:1–4; Dt 32:8; Ps 82:1. *The satan*: lit., "adversary" (as in 1 Kgs 11:14). Here a member of the heavenly court, "the accuser" (Zec 3:1). In later biblical traditions this character will be developed as the devil (Gk. *diabolos*, "adversary").

1:15 *Sabeans*: from southern Arabia.

*

1:1 Jb 2:3.
1:6–8 Jb 2:1–3.
1:6 Gn 6:2, 4; Zec 3:1; Lk 22:31; Rev 12:9.
1:7 1 Pt 5:8.
1:11 Jb 2:5.

have escaped to tell you." 17 He was still speaking
when another came and said, "The Chaldeans†
formed three columns, seized the camels, carried
them off, and put the servants to the sword; I
alone have escaped to tell you." 18 He was still
speaking when another came and said, "Your
sons and daughters were eating and drinking
wine in the house of their eldest brother, 19 and
suddenly a great wind came from across the des-
ert and smashed the four corners of the house. It
fell upon the young people and they are dead; I
alone have escaped to tell you."

Job's Reaction

20 Then Job arose and tore his cloak and cut off
his hair. He fell to the ground and worshiped.
21 He said,

"Naked I came forth from my mother's
womb,*

† **1:17** *Chaldeans*: from southern Mesopotamia; in the mid-first millennium B.C., synonymous with "Babylonians."

* **1:21** Eccl 5:14; 1 Tm 6:7.

Introducing...

Satan

Does the word *Satan* conjure for you an image of a demon with horns and a tail, torturing people in the fires of hell? or perhaps an evil presence wandering the world looking for souls to corrupt? Does it surprise you that Job 1:6 and Zechariah 3:1 present Satan as actually working for God? In fact, the word *Satan* is more of a job description than a name; it means "adversary." In the Old Testament, Satan is depicted as a member of God's court whose responsibility it is to accuse or test humans before God. (Although, contrary to popular belief, the snake in the Garden of Eden is never identified as Satan in Genesis. This is a later biblical teaching; see Wis 2:24; Rev 12:9; 20:2).

It is only much later that Satan is seen as the enemy of God and the controller of the forces of evil. The notion of Satan as an evildoer seems to have been borrowed from a similar figure in Persian religion and developed in Israel as time passed. By the New Testament period, Satan is identified as a powerful agent of evil fighting against God (see 1 Thes 2:18), is instrumental in Jesus' death (see Lk 22:3), tempts people to sin (see 1 Cor 7:5), and is called the devil (see Rv 12:9). The good news is that in the death and Resurrection of Jesus, God overcomes the evil associated with Satan, both now and forever.

▶ Jb 1:6—2:10

Live It!

In Good Times and Bad

Have you ever felt so angry at the loss of something that you cursed and swore at God? Have you ever felt like just giving up on God because of your loss? In Job 1:13–19, a man named Job experiences an unimaginable loss. His children, his home, and his property are all destroyed at the same time. Job responds with great anger and great pain, but instead of cursing or blaming God, he blesses (praises) God (see verse 21).

Job never loses his faith in God, even when he loses so much else. Through most of the rest of this book, he struggles to understand why this has happened to him. Job is an important model for us. When faced with great suffering, he does not lose his belief in the goodness of God, nor does he let his friends talk him into false confessions of sinfulness. Like Job, we must not fall into the trap of thinking that when bad things happen, God is punishing us.

Furthermore, when we try to explain suffering by saying things like, "God has a reason for everything," we risk making God out to be detached and uncaring, someone who wills evil into the world and upon his people. This is not the God of our faith. Instead of trying to explain suffering, we must reach out to God, the good and compassionate healer who offers us comfort in our times of distress.

▶ Jb 1:13–21

and naked shall I go back there.†
The LORD gave and the LORD has taken away;
blessed be the name of the LORD!"

22 In all this Job did not sin,* nor did he charge
God with wrong.

The Second Interview

2 1 One day, when the sons of God* came to
present themselves before the LORD, the sa-
tan also came with them. 2 The LORD said to the
satan, "Where have you been?" Then the satan
answered the LORD and said, "Roaming the earth
and patrolling it." 3 The LORD said to the satan,
"Have you noticed my servant Job? There is no
one on earth like him, blameless and upright,
fearing God and avoiding evil.* He still holds
fast to his innocence although you incited me
against him to ruin him for nothing." 4 The satan
answered the LORD and said, "Skin for skin!† All
that a man has he will give for his life. 5 * But
put forth your hand and touch his bone and his
flesh. Then surely he will curse you to your face."
6 And the LORD said to the satan, "He is in your
power; only spare his life."

The Second Trial

7 So the satan went forth from the presence of
the LORD and struck Job with severe boils from
the soles of his feet to the crown of his head.

Job's Reaction

8 He took a potsherd to scrape himself, as he
sat among the ashes. 9 Then his wife said to him,*
"Are you still holding to your innocence? Curse
God and die!"† 10 But he said to her, "You speak
as foolish women do. We accept good things
from God; should we not accept evil?" Through
all this, Job did not sin in what he said.*

Job's Three Friends

11 Now when three of Job's friends heard of all
the misfortune that had come upon him, they set
out each one from his own place: Eliphaz from
Teman,† Bildad from Shuh, and Zophar from
Naamath. They met and journeyed together to
give him sympathy and comfort. 12 But when, at a
distance, they lifted up their eyes and did not rec-
ognize him, they began to weep aloud; they tore
their cloaks and threw dust into the air over their
heads. 13 Then they sat down upon the ground
with him seven days and seven nights, but none
of them spoke a word to him; for they saw how
great was his suffering.

Live It!

Being There

What is the best way to respond to the suffering of another? Many of us shy away from funerals and hospitals because we just don't know what to say or how to act.

In Job 2:11–13, Job was visited by three friends. They did not recognize him at first because of his great suffering; then they cried. And then something remarkable happened: "They sat down upon the ground with him seven days and seven nights, but none of them spoke a word to him; for they saw how great was his suffering" (verse 13).

We must give Job's friends credit for being there, for spending time with him, and for letting him know they cared, especially when they first arrived. That is all we have to do for a friend who is hurting—offer a hug and a simple "I'm sorry," and then just stay around. Though this sounds easy, it can be very hard; we can feel so helpless. We need to keep in mind that what matters most is that we are there. That is what will be remembered.

If you know people are suffering or grieving, don't avoid them. Go up to them, let them know how you feel, and just be there for them. That is all. And that is a lot.

▶ **Jb 2:11–13**

II. First Cycle of Speeches

Job's Complaint

3 1 After this, Job opened his mouth and cursed
his day.† 2 Job spoke out and said:

1:21 *Go back there*: to the earth; cf. Gn 2:7; see note on Sir 40:1.

2:4 *Skin for skin*: a proverbial expression derived perhaps from bartering; the precise meaning is unclear.

2:9 *Curse God and die*: the presupposition is that such blasphemy would be met with immediate death.

2:11 *Teman*: in Edom (see Gn 36:9–11). The Temanites (Jer 49:7; cf. Ob 8) enjoyed a reputation for wisdom. *Shuh* and *Naamath*: locations unknown.

3:1 *His day*: that is, the day of his birth.

1:22 Jb 2:10; Jas 5:11.
2:1 Jb 1:6.
2:3 Jb 1:1.
2:5 Jb 1:11.
2:9 Jb 19:17.
2:10 Jb 1:22; Sir 2:4.

3 Perish the day on which I was born,*
the night when they said, "The child is a boy!"
4 May that day be darkness:
may God† above not care for it,
may light not shine upon it!
5 May darkness and gloom claim it,
clouds settle upon it,
blackness of day† affright it!
6 May obscurity seize that night;
may it not be counted among the days of the year,
nor enter into the number of the months!
7 May that night be barren;
let no joyful outcry greet it!
8 Let them curse it who curse the Sea,
those skilled at disturbing Leviathan!†
9 May the stars of its twilight be darkened;
may it look for daylight, but have none,
nor gaze on the eyes of the dawn,
10 Because it did not keep shut the doors of the womb
to shield my eyes from trouble!
11 Why did I not die at birth,*
come forth from the womb and expire?
12 Why did knees receive me,
or breasts nurse me?
13 For then I should have lain down and been tranquil;
had I slept, I should then have been at rest
14 With kings and counselors of the earth
who rebuilt what were ruins
15 Or with princes who had gold
and filled their houses with silver.
16 Or why was I not buried away like a stillborn child,
like babies that have never seen the light?
17 There† the wicked cease from troubling,
there the weary are at rest.
18 The captives are at ease together,
and hear no overseer's voice.
19 Small and great are there;
the servant is free from the master.
20 Why is light given to the toilers,
life to the bitter in spirit?
21 They wait for death and it does not come;
they search for it more than for hidden treasures.
22 They rejoice in it exultingly,
and are glad when they find the grave:
23 A man whose path is hidden from him,
one whom God has hemmed in!†
24 For to me sighing comes more readily than food;
my groans well forth like water.
25 For what I feared overtakes me;
what I dreaded comes upon me.
26 I have no peace nor ease;
I have no rest, for trouble has come!

Eliphaz's First Speech

4 1 Then Eliphaz the Temanite answered and said:

2 If someone attempts a word with you, would you mind?
How can anyone refrain from speaking?
3 Look, you have instructed many,
and made firm their feeble hands.
4 Your words have upheld the stumbler;
you have strengthened faltering knees.
5 But now that it comes to you, you are impatient;
when it touches you, you are dismayed.
6 Is not your piety a source of confidence,
and your integrity of life your hope?
7 Reflect now, what innocent person perishes?*
Where are the upright destroyed?
8 As I see it, those who plow mischief
and sow trouble will reap them.
9 By the breath of God they perish,*
and by the blast of his wrath they are consumed.
10 Though the lion† roars, though the king of beasts cries out,
yet the teeth of the young lions are broken;
11 The old lion perishes for lack of prey,
and the cubs of the lioness are scattered.
12 A word was stealthily brought to me,†
my ear caught a whisper of it.
13 In my thoughts during visions of the night,*
when deep sleep falls on mortals,
14 Fear came upon me, and shuddering,
that terrified me to the bone.
15 Then a spirit passed before me,
and the hair of my body stood on end.

†

3:4 *God*: in Heb. *'Eloah*, another name for the divinity, used frequently in Job.

3:5 *Blackness of day*: that is, an eclipse.

3:8 *Leviathan*: a mythological sea monster symbolizing primeval chaos. It is parallel to Sea, which was the opponent of Baal in the Ugaritic legends. Cf. 9:13; 26:13; 40:25–41:26; Ps 74:13–14; 104:26; Is 27:1.

3:17 *There*: in death.

3:23 *Hemmed in*: contrast the same verb as used in 1:10.

4:10 *The lion*: used figuratively here for the violent, rapacious sinner who cannot prevail against God.

4:12–21 A dramatic presentation of the idea of human nothingness in contrast to God's greatness (v. 17). The message of the "private revelation" that stirs Eliphaz so deeply is in reality expressed countless times in the Bible. The statements of the friends are often "truths" that are insensitive or irrelevant to Job's questioning.

*

3:3 Jer 20:14.
3:11 Jb 10:18–19.
4:7 Ps 37:25.
4:9 Ps 18:16; Is 11:4; 2 Thes 2:8.
4:13 Jb 33:15.

16 It paused, but its likeness I could not recognize;
a figure was before my eyes,
in silence I heard a voice:*
17 "Can anyone be more in the right than God?*
Can mortals be more blameless than their Maker?
18 Look, he puts no trust in his servants,*
and even with his messengers he finds fault.
19 How much more with those who dwell in houses of clay,
whose foundation is in the dust,
who are crushed more easily than a moth!
20 Morning or evening they may be shattered;
unnoticed, they perish forever.
21 The pegs of their tent are plucked up;
they die without knowing wisdom."

5 1 Call now! Will anyone respond to you?
To which of the holy ones† will you turn?
2 Surely impatience kills the fool
and indignation slays the simpleton.
3 I have seen a fool spreading his roots,*
but I cursed his household suddenly:
4 May his children be far from safety;
may they be crushed at the gate† without a rescuer.
5 What they have reaped may the hungry eat up,
or God take away by blight,
or the thirsty swallow their substance.
6 For not from dust does mischief come,
nor from the soil does trouble sprout.
7 Human beings beget mischief
as sparks† fly upward.
8 In your place, I would appeal to God,
and to God I would state my plea.
9† He does things great and unsearchable,
things marvelous and innumerable.
10 He gives rain upon the earth
and sends water upon the fields;
11 * He sets up the lowly on high,
and those who mourn are raised to safety.
12 He frustrates the plans of the cunning,
so that their hands achieve no success;
13 He catches the wise in their own ruses,*
and the designs of the crafty are routed.
14 They meet with darkness in the daytime,
at noonday they grope as though it were night.
15 But he saves the poor from the sword of their mouth,†
from the hand of the mighty.
16 Thus the needy have hope,
and iniquity closes its mouth.
17 Happy the one whom God reproves!
The Almighty's† discipline do not reject.
18 For he wounds, but he binds up;*
he strikes, but his hands give healing.
19 Out of six troubles he will deliver you,
and at the seventh† no evil shall touch you.
20 In famine he will deliver you from death,
and in war from the power of the sword;
21 From the scourge of the tongue you shall be hidden,
and you shall not fear approaching ruin.
22 At ruin and want you shall laugh;
the beasts of the earth, do not fear.
23 With the stones of the field shall your covenant be,
and the wild beasts shall be at peace with you.
24 And you shall know that your tent is secure;
taking stock of your household, you shall miss nothing.
25 You shall know that your descendants are many,
and your offspring like the grass of the earth.
26 You shall approach the grave in full vigor,
as a shock of grain comes in at its season.
27 See, this we have searched out; so it is!
This we have heard, and you should know.

Job's First Reply

6 1 Then Job answered and said:

2 Ah, could my anguish but be measured
and my calamity laid with it in the scales,
3 They would now outweigh the sands of the sea!
Because of this I speak without restraint.
4 For the arrows of the Almighty are in me,*
and my spirit drinks in their poison;
the terrors of God are arrayed against me.
5 Does the wild donkey bray when it has grass?†
Does the ox low over its fodder?
6 Can anything insipid be eaten without salt?
Is there flavor in the white of an egg?

5:1 *Holy ones*: members of the heavenly court; cf. 1:6 and note. They were viewed as heavenly intercessors.
5:4 *At the gate*: of the city, where justice was administered.
5:7 *Sparks*: in Hebrew, "sons of resheph," which the ancient versions took as the name of a bird. Resheph was an underworld deity of plague, but the word also means "flames" in Sg 8:6.
5:9 Perhaps to be omitted here; it is a duplicate of 9:10.
5:15 *From the sword of their mouth*: the Hebrew is obscure.
5:17 *Almighty*: standard translation of Heb. *Shaddai*.
5:19 *Six . . . the seventh*: proverbial expression for any large number; cf. Prv 24:16; Lk 17:4.
6:5–6 Job would not complain if his life were as pleasant to him as fodder to a hungry animal; but his life is as disagreeable as insipid food. *White of an egg*: thus the obscure Hebrew has been understood in Jewish tradition; some render it "mallow juice."

4:16 1 Kgs 19:12.
4:17 Jb 9:2; 15:14–16; 25:4; Ps 130:3; 143:2.
4:18 Jb 15:15; 2 Pt 2:4; Jude 6.
5:3 Ps 37:35–36.
5:11 1 Sm 2:7–8; Ps 113:7; Lk 1:52.
5:13 1 Cor 3:19.
5:18 Hos 6:1–2.
6:4 Ps 88:17.

Pray It!

Suffering

Job's words in Job, chapter 7, are almost a prayer describing his suffering and asking, Why me? Job isn't worried about being polite; he says it like it is. What can you learn from Job about prayer during suffering?

First, you need to be honest with God and yourself. If you are hurt or in pain, don't play games with God. Tell God what you are feeling, in your own words. Write it down in a journal if you want to. And be honest. Because if you aren't honest with God, you probably aren't being honest with yourself.

Second, let all your feelings out, just like Job did—including your anger. God is big enough to handle it. When you suppress your negative feelings, they may come out in unhealthy ways. So, let God help you deal with them.

Finally, let your prayer lead you to take some action. Job debated with his friends. That's probably how people did counseling back then! Your prayer to God for help might lead you to a counselor, a minister, or a support group. God works in many ways.

▶ **Job, chapter 7**

7 I refuse to touch them;
they are like loathsome food to me.
8 Oh, that I might have my request,
and that God would grant what I long for:
9 Even that God would decide to crush me,
that he would put forth his hand and cut me off!
10 Then I should still have consolation
and could exult through unremitting pain,
because I have not transgressed the commands of the Holy One.
11 What strength have I that I should endure,
and what is my limit that I should be patient?
12 Have I the strength of stones,
or is my flesh of bronze?
13 Have I no helper,*
and has my good sense deserted me?
14 A friend owes kindness to one in despair,
though he has forsaken the fear of the Almighty.
15 My companions are undependable as a wadi,
as watercourses that run dry in the wadies;
16 Though they may be black with ice,
and with snow heaped upon them,
17 Yet once they flow, they cease to be;
in the heat, they disappear from their place.
18 Caravans wander from their routes;
they go into the wasteland and perish.
19 The caravans of Tema† search,
the companies of Sheba have hopes;
20 They are disappointed, though they were confident;
they come there and are frustrated.
21 It is thus that you have now become for me;†
you see a terrifying thing and are afraid.
22 Have I said, "Give me something,
make a bribe on my behalf from your possessions"?
23 Or "Deliver me from the hand of the enemy,
redeem me from oppressors"?
24 Teach me, and I will be silent;
make me understand how I have erred.
25 How painful honest words can be;
yet how unconvincing is your argument!
26 Do you consider your words as proof,
but the sayings of a desperate man as wind?
27 You would even cast lots for the orphan,
and would barter over your friend!
28 Come, now, give me your attention;
surely I will not lie to your face.
29 Think it over; let there be no injustice.
Think it over; I still am right.
30 Is there insincerity on my tongue,
or cannot my taste discern falsehood?

7

1* Is not life on earth a drudgery,†
its days like those of a hireling?
2 Like a slave who longs for the shade,
a hireling who waits for wages,
3 So I have been assigned months of futility,

† 6:19 *Tema*: in northwest Arabia. *Sheba*: home of the Sabeans; see note on 1:15.

6:21 It is only at this point that the previous lines (vv. 1–20) are clearly directed to the three friends. The style of replying in these chapters (3–31) is often indirect. Job and the friends become mouthpieces through which the author presents current views on divine retribution in dramatic fashion. In chap. 7, Job will not even speak directly to the friends.

7:1 *Drudgery*: taken by some to refer to military service; cf. also 14:14.

* 6:13 Jb 19:14–15. 7:1 Jb 14:14.

and troubled nights have been counted off
for me.
4 When I lie down I say, "When shall I arise?"
then the night drags on;
I am filled with restlessness until the
dawn.
5 My flesh is clothed with worms and scabs;*
my skin cracks and festers;
6 My days are swifter than a weaver's shuttle;
they come to an end without hope.
7 Remember that my life is like the wind;*
my eye will not see happiness again.
8 The eye that now sees me shall no more
behold me;
when your eye is on me, I shall be gone.
9 As a cloud dissolves and vanishes,*
so whoever goes down to Sheol shall not
come up.
10 They shall not return home again;
their place shall know them no more.
11 My own utterance I will not restrain;
I will speak in the anguish of my spirit;
I will complain in the bitterness of my
soul.
12† Am I the Sea, or the dragon,
that you place a watch over me?†
13 When I say, "My bed shall comfort me,
my couch shall ease my complaint,"
14 Then you frighten me with dreams
and terrify me with visions,
15 So that I should prefer strangulation
and death rather than my existence.†
16 I waste away: I will not live forever;*
let me alone, for my days are but a breath.
17† What are human beings, that you make much
of them,
or pay them any heed?
18 You observe them every morning*
and try them at every moment!
19 How long before you look away from me,
and let me alone till I swallow my spit?
20 If I sin, what do I do to you,
O watcher of mortals?
Why have you made me your target?
Why should I be a burden for you?
21 Why do you not pardon my offense,
or take away my guilt?
For soon I shall lie down in the dust;
and should you seek me I shall be gone.

Bildad's First Speech

8 [1] Bildad the Shuhite answered and said:
2 How long will you utter such things?
The words from your mouth are a mighty
wind!
3 Does God pervert judgment,*
does the Almighty pervert justice?
4 If your children have sinned against him
and he has left them in the grip of their
guilt,
5 Still, if you yourself have recourse to God
and make supplication to the Almighty,
6 Should you be blameless and upright,
surely now he will rouse himself for you
and restore your rightful home.
7 Though your beginning was small,
your future will flourish indeed.
8 Inquire of the former generations,
pay attention to the experience of their
ancestors—*
9 As we are but of yesterday and have no
knowledge,
because our days on earth are but a
shadow—*
10 Will they not teach you and tell you
and utter their words of understanding?
11† Can the papyrus grow up without mire?
Can the reed grass flourish without water?
12 While it is yet green and uncut,
it withers quicker than any grass.
13 So is the end of everyone who forgets God,
and so shall the hope of the godless perish.
14 His confidence is but a gossamer thread,
his trust is a spider's house.
15 He shall lean upon his house, but it shall not
stand;
he shall cling to it, but it shall not endure.
16 He thrives in full sun,
and over his garden his shoots go forth;
17 About a heap of stones his roots are entwined;
among the rocks he takes hold.
18 Yet if one tears him from his place,
it will disown him: "I have never seen you!"
19 There he lies rotting beside the road,
and out of the soil another sprouts.
20 Behold, God will not cast away the upright;
neither will he take the hand of the wicked.

†

7:12–21 Job now speaks not to his friends (who never speak to God), but to God. He does this frequently; cf. 9:28; 10:2–22; 13:20–28; 14:13–22.

7:12 An allusion to the personification of primeval chaos as a monstrous ocean vanquished by God; see note on 3:8.

7:15 *Existence*: lit., bones; the Hebrew is unclear.

7:17–18 An ironic allusion to Ps 8:5.

8:11–13 As marsh plants need water, so human beings need God. These verses may be a quotation from the teaching of the ancestors; cf. v. 10.

*

7:5 Jb 2:7–8.
7:7 Ps 144:4.
7:9–10 Jb 10:21; 14:10–12; 2 Sm 12:23; 14:14; Wis 2:1.
7:16 Jb 14:1–2, 5.
7:18 Ps 17:3.
8:3 Jb 34:10–12.
8:8 Dt 4:32; 32:7.
8:9 Jb 14:2; Ps 102:12; 109:23; 144:4; Wis 2:5.

21 Once more will he fill your mouth with
laughter
and your lips with rejoicing.
22 Those who hate you shall be clothed with
shame,
and the tent of the wicked shall be no
more.

Job's Second Reply

9 [1]Then Job answered and said:
2 I know well that it is so;
but how can anyone be in the right before
God?
3 Should one wish to contend with him,†
he could not answer him once in a
thousand times.
4 God is wise in heart and mighty in strength;
who has withstood him and remained
whole?
5 He removes the mountains before they
know it;
he overturns them in his anger.
6 He shakes the earth out of its place,*
and the pillars beneath it tremble.
7 He commands the sun, and it does not rise;
he seals up the stars.
8 He alone stretches out the heavens*
and treads upon the back of the sea.
9 He made the Bear and Orion,
the Pleiades and the constellations of the
south;
10 He does things great and unsearchable,
things marvelous and innumerable.
11 Should he come near me, I do not see him;
should he pass by, I am not aware of him;
12 Should he seize me forcibly, who can resist?
Who can say to him, "What are you doing?"
13 He is God and he does not relent;
the helpers of Rahab† bow beneath him.
14 How then could I give him any answer,
or choose out arguments against him!
15 Even though I were right, I could not answer,*
but should rather beg for what was due me.
16 If I appealed to him and he answered me,
I could not believe that he would listen
to me;
17 With a storm he might overwhelm me,
and multiply my wounds for nothing;
18 He would not allow me to draw breath,
but might fill me with bitter griefs.
19 If it be a question of strength, he is mighty;
or of judgment, who will call him to
account?
20 Though I were right, my own mouth might
condemn me;*
were I innocent, it might put me in the
wrong.
21 I am innocent, but I cannot know it;
I despise my life.
22 It is all one! therefore I say:
Both the innocent and the wicked he
destroys.*
23 When the scourge slays suddenly,
he scoffs at the despair of the innocent.
24 The earth is given into the hands of the
wicked;
he covers the faces of its judges.
If it is not he, who then is it?
25 My days are swifter than a runner,
they flee away; they see no happiness;*
26 They shoot by like skiffs of reed,
like an eagle swooping upon its prey.
27 If I say: I will forget my complaining,
I will lay aside my sadness and be of good
cheer,
28 Then I am in dread of all my pains;
I know that you† will not hold me innocent.
29 It is I who will be accounted guilty;
why then should I strive in vain?
30 If I should wash myself with soap
and cleanse my hands with lye,
31 Yet you would plunge me in the ditch,
so that my garments would abhor me.
32 For he is not a man like myself, that I should
answer him,
that we should come together in judgment.
33 Would that there were an arbiter between us,
who could lay his hand upon us both
34 and withdraw his rod from me,
So that his terrors did not frighten me;
35 that I might speak without being afraid of
him.
Since this is not the case with me,
10:1† I loathe my life.*

10 I will give myself up to complaint;
I will speak from the bitterness of my soul.
2 I will say to God: Do not put me in the
wrong!

---

† **9:3** Job begins to explore the possibility of challenging God in a lawsuit, a theme that will recur (10:2), but he knows the odds are against him (vv. 12–20).

9:13 *Rahab*: another name for the primeval sea-monster; see notes on 3:8 and Ps 89:11; cf. Jb 7:12; 26:12.

9:28–31 *You*: refers to God.

10:1 *I loathe my life*: these words complete the thought of 9:35.

---

* **9:6** Jb 26:11.
9:8 Ps 104:2; Is 40:22.
9:15 Jb 10:15.
9:20 Jb 15:6.
9:22 Eccl 9:2.
9:25 Jb 7:6.
10:1 Jb 9:21.

Let me know why you oppose me.
3† Is it a pleasure for you to oppress,
to spurn the work of your hands,
and shine on the plan of the wicked?
4 Have you eyes of flesh?
Do you see as mortals see?
5 Are your days like the days of a mortal,*
and are your years like a human lifetime,
6 That you seek for guilt in me
and search after my sins,
7 Even though you know that I am not wicked,*
and that none can deliver me out of your hand?
8 Your hands have formed me and fashioned me;
will you then turn and destroy me?
9 Oh, remember that you fashioned me from clay!*
Will you then bring me down to dust again?
10 Did you not pour me out like milk,
and thicken me like cheese?
11 With skin and flesh you clothed me,
with bones and sinews knit me together.
12 Life and love you granted me,
and your providence has preserved my spirit.
13 Yet these things you have hidden in your heart;
I know they are your purpose:
14 If I should sin, you would keep a watch on me,
and from my guilt you would not absolve me.
15 If I should be wicked, alas for me!
even if righteous, I dare not hold up my head,
sated with shame, drenched in affliction!
16 Should it lift up, you hunt me like a lion:
repeatedly you show your wondrous power against me,
17 You renew your attack† upon me
and multiply your harassment of me;
in waves your troops come against me.
18 Why then did you bring me forth from the womb?*
I should have died and no eye have seen me.
19 I should be as though I had never lived;
I should have been taken from the womb to the grave.
20 Are not my days few? Stop!
Let me alone, that I may recover a little
21 Before I go whence I shall not return,*
to the land of darkness and of gloom,
22 The dark, disordered land
where darkness is the only light.

Zophar's First Speech

11 [1]And Zophar the Naamathite answered and said:

2 Should not many words be answered,
or must the garrulous man necessarily be right?
3 Shall your babblings keep others silent,
and shall you deride and no one give rebuke?
4 Shall you say: "My teaching is pure,
and I am clean in your sight"?
5 But oh, that God would speak,†
and open his lips against you,
6 And tell you the secrets of wisdom,
for good sense has two sides;
So you might learn that God
overlooks some of your sinfulness.
7 Can you find out the depths of God?*
or find out the perfection of the Almighty?
8 It is higher than the heavens; what can you do?
It is deeper than Sheol; what can you know?
9 It is longer than the earth in measure,
and broader than the sea.
10 If he should seize and imprison
or call to judgment, who then could turn him back?
11 For he knows the worthless
and sees iniquity; will he then ignore it?
12 An empty head will gain understanding,
when a colt of a wild jackass* is born human.†
13 If you set your heart aright
and stretch out your hands toward him,
14 If iniquity is in your hand, remove it,
and do not let injustice dwell in your tent,
15 Surely then you may lift up your face in innocence;
you may stand firm and unafraid.
16 For then you shall forget your misery,
like water that has ebbed away you shall regard it.
17 Then your life shall be brighter than the noonday;

†

10:3–12 These lines are a delicate mixture of sarcasm and prayer; Job "reminds" God, challenging the divine providence. Note the piteous tone of the final request in vv. 20–22.

10:17 *Attack*: or "witnesses," continuing the metaphor of lawsuit used in these chapters.

11:5 This is another of many ironies (e.g., cf. 11:16–19) that occur throughout the book. Zophar does not know that God will speak (chaps. 38–42), but contrary to what he thinks.

11:12 *A colt . . . is born human*: the Hebrew is obscure. As translated, it seems to be a proverb referring to an impossible event.

*

10:5 Jb 36:26.
10:7 Jb 2:3, 9; Dt 32:39; Wis 16:15.
10:9 Jb 4:19; 33:6; Gn 2:7; 3:19; Ps 146:4.
10:18 Jb 3:3, 11.
10:21 Jb 7:9–10; 16:22.
11:7 Rom 11:33.
11:12 Jb 39:5–8.

its gloom shall become like the morning,
18 And you shall be secure, because there is hope;
you shall look round you and lie down in safety;*
19 you shall lie down and no one will disturb you.
Many shall entreat your favor,
20 but the wicked, looking on, shall be consumed with envy.
Escape shall be cut off from them,
their only hope their last breath.

Job's Third Reply

12 1 † Then Job answered and said:

2 No doubt you are the people
with whom wisdom shall die!
3 But I have intelligence as well as you;*
I do not fall short of you;
for who does not know such things as these?
4 I have become the sport of my neighbors:†
"The one whom God answers when he calls upon him,
The just, the perfect man," is a laughingstock;*
5 The undisturbed esteem my downfall a disgrace
such as awaits unsteady feet;
6 Yet the tents of robbers are prosperous,
and those who provoke God are secure,
whom God has in his power.†
7 But now ask the beasts to teach you,
the birds of the air to tell you;
8 Or speak to the earth to instruct you,
and the fish of the sea to inform you.
9 Which of all these does not know
that the hand of God has done this?
10 In his hand is the soul of every living thing,*
and the life breath of all mortal flesh.
11 Does not the ear judge words
as the mouth tastes food?*
12 So with old age is wisdom,*
and with length of days understanding.
13 With him are wisdom and might;
his are counsel and understanding.
14 If he knocks a thing down, there is no rebuilding;*
if he imprisons, there is no release.
15 He holds back the waters and there is drought;*
he sends them forth and they overwhelm the land.
16 With him are strength and prudence;
the misled and the misleaders are his.
17 He sends counselors away barefoot,
makes fools of judges.
18 He loosens the belt of kings,
ties a waistcloth on their loins.†
19 He sends priests away barefoot,
leads the powerful astray.
20 He silences the trusted adviser,
takes discretion from the elders.
21 He pours shame on nobles,*
the waistband of the strong he loosens.
22 He uncovers deep things from the darkness,
brings the gloom into the light.
23 He makes nations great and destroys them,
spreads peoples abroad and abandons them.
24 He takes understanding from the leaders of the land,
makes them wander in a pathless desert.
25 They grope in the darkness without light;
he makes them wander like drunkards.

13 1 All this my eye has seen;
my ear has heard and perceived it.
2 What you know, I also know;*
I do not fall short of you.
3 But I would speak with the Almighty;*
I want to argue with God.
4 But you gloss over falsehoods,
you are worthless physicians, every one of you!
5 Oh, that you would be altogether silent;
that for you would be wisdom!
6 Hear now my argument
and listen to the accusations from my lips.
7 Is it for God that you speak falsehood?
Is it for him that you utter deceit?
8 Is it for him that you show partiality?
Do you make accusations on behalf of God?
9 Will it be well when he shall search you out?
Can you deceive him as you do a mere human being?
10 He will openly rebuke you
if in secret you show partiality.
11 Surely his majesty will frighten you

†

12:1 Job begins his third and longest speech to the friends with sarcasm, and eventually he accuses them of falsehood (13:4–11). The dialogue between them becomes increasingly sharp. With the appeal to learning from beasts and birds (12:7), Job launches into what seems to be a bitter parody of the power of God.

12:4–5 The Hebrew is somewhat obscure, but the general sense is that the wicked mock the pious when the latter appear to be abandoned by God; cf. Ps 22:7–9; Mt 27:39–43.

12:6 *Whom God has in his power*: the Hebrew is obscure. The line may be a scribal error; some of the phrases occur in vv. 9, 10.

12:18 He reduces kings to the condition of slaves, who wear only a cloth wrapped about the waist.

*

11:18 Lv 26:6; Ps 4:9.
12:3 Jb 13:2; 15:9.
12:4 Jb 21:3; 30:1.
12:10 Acts 17:28.
12:11 Jb 34:3.
12:12 Jb 32:7.
12:14 Jer 1:10; Rev 3:7.
12:15 Gn 7:11–24.
12:21 Ps 107:40.
13:2 Jb 12:3; 15:9.
13:3 Jb 23:4.

and dread of him fall upon you.
12 Your reminders are ashy maxims,
your fabrications mounds of clay.
13 Be silent! Let me alone that I may speak,
no matter what happens to me.
14 I will carry my flesh between my teeth,
and take my life in my hand.†
15 Slay me though he might,* I will wait for him;†
I will defend my conduct before him.
16 This shall be my salvation:
no impious man can come into his presence.
17 Pay close attention to my speech,
give my statement a hearing.
18 Behold, I have prepared my case,*
I know that I am in the right.
19 If anyone can make a case against me,
then I shall be silent and expire.
20 Two things only do not use against me,†
then from your presence I need not hide:
21 Withdraw your hand far from me,
do not let the terror of you frighten me.
22 Then call me, and I will respond;
or let me speak first, and answer me.
23 What are my faults and my sins?
My misdeed, my sin make known to me!
24 Why do you hide your face
and consider me your enemy?† *
25 Will you harass a wind-driven leaf
or pursue a withered straw?
26 For you draw up bitter indictments against me,
and punish in me the faults of my youth.
27 You put my feet in the stocks;
you watch all my paths
and trace out all my footsteps,
28 Though I wear out like a leather bottle,
like a garment the moth has consumed.

14 1 Man born of woman
is short-lived and full of trouble,† *
2 Like a flower that springs up and fades,*
swift as a shadow that does not abide.
3 Upon such a one will you set your eyes,
bringing me into judgment before you?
4 Can anyone make the unclean clean?*
No one can.
5 Since his days are determined—
you know the number of his months;
you have fixed the limit which he cannot pass—
6 Look away from him and let him be,
while, like a hireling, he completes his day.
7 For a tree there is hope;
if it is cut down, it will sprout again,
its tender shoots will not cease.
8 Even though its root grow old in the earth
and its stump die in the dust,
9 Yet at the first whiff of water it sprouts
and puts forth branches like a young plant.
10 But when a man dies, all vigor leaves him;*
when a mortal expires, where then is he?
11 As when the waters of a lake fail,
or a stream shrivels and dries up,
12 So mortals lie down, never to rise.
Until the heavens are no more, they shall not awake,
nor be roused out of their sleep.*
13 Oh, that you would hide me in Sheol,
shelter me till your wrath is past,
fix a time to remember me!
14 If a man were to die, and live again,
all the days of my drudgery I would wait*
for my relief to come.
15 You would call, and I would answer you;
you would long for the work of your hands.
16 Surely then you would count my steps,*
and not keep watch for sin in me.
17 My misdeeds would be sealed up in a pouch,†
and you would cover over my guilt.
18 Mountains fall and crumble,
rocks move from their place,
19 And water wears away stone,
and floods wash away the soil of the land—
so you destroy the hope of mortals!
20 You prevail once for all against them and they pass on;
you dismiss them with changed appearance.
21 If their children are honored, they are not aware of it;
or if disgraced, they do not know about them.

†

13:14 The second half of the verse is a common biblical expression for risking one's life; cf. Jgs 12:3; 1 Sm 19:5; 28:21; Ps 119:109; the first half of the verse must have a similar meaning. Job is so confident of his innocence that he is willing to risk his life by going to judgment with God.

13:15 Many translations adopt the Ketib reading, "I have no hope."

13:20 In 13:20–14:22, Job directs his address to God; cf. 7:8–21; 9:28–10:22. His three friends never do this.

13:24 The Hebrew word for "enemy" (*'oyeb*) is very close to the Hebrew form of Job's name (*'iyyob*). The play on the word implies that God has confused the two.

14:1 The sorrowful lament of Job is that God should relent in view of the limited life of human beings. When compared to plant life, which dies but can revive, the death of human beings is final. Job's wild and "unthinkable" wish in vv. 13–17 is a bold stroke of imagination and desire: if only in Sheol he were protected till God would remember him! Were he to live again (v. 14), things would be different, but alas, God destroys "the hope of mortals" (v. 19).

14:17 *Sealed up in a pouch*: hidden away and forgotten.

*

13:15 Jb 27:5.
13:18 Jb 33:9.
13:24 Jb 19:11; 33:10.
14:1 Jb 10:20; 15:14; Ps 39:5–6; 89:46; Wis 2:1.
14:2 Jb 8:9; Ps 90:6; 102:12; 103:15; 109:23; 144:4; Is 40:6–7; Jas 1:10.
14:4 Ps 51:4, 7.
14:10 Jb 20:7.
14:12 Jb 7:10.
14:14 Jb 7:1.
14:16 Jb 31:4; 34:21.

22 Only for themselves, their pain;
only for themselves, their mourning.

III. Second Cycle of Speeches

Second Speech of Eliphaz

15 1 † Then Eliphaz the Temanite answered and said:

2 Does a wise man answer with windy opinions,
or puff himself up with the east wind?
3 Does he argue in speech that does not avail,
and in words that are to no profit?
4 You in fact do away with piety,
you lessen devotion toward God,
5 Because your wickedness instructs your mouth,
and you choose to speak like the crafty.
6 Your own mouth condemns you, not I;*
your own lips refute you.
7 Were you the first to be born?
Were you brought forth before the hills?
8 Do you listen in on God's council*
and restrict wisdom to yourself?
9 What do you know that we do not know,*
or understand that we do not?
10 There are gray-haired old men among us,
more advanced in years than your father.
11 Are the consolations of God not enough for you,
and speech that deals gently with you?
12 Why does your heart carry you away,
and why do your eyes flash,
13 So that you turn your anger against God
and let such words escape your mouth!
14 How can any mortal be blameless,*
anyone born of woman be righteous?*
15 If in his holy ones God places no confidence,*
and if the heavens are not without blame in his sight,
16 How much less so is the abominable and corrupt:
people who drink in iniquity like water!
17 I will show you, if you listen to me;
what I have seen I will tell—
18 What the wise relate
and have not contradicted since the days of their ancestors,
19 To whom alone the land was given,
when no foreigner moved among them:
20 The wicked is in torment all his days,
and limited years are in store for the ruthless;
21 The sound of terrors is in his ears;
when all is prosperous, a spoiler comes upon him.
22 He despairs of escaping the darkness,
and looks ever for the sword;
23 A wanderer, food for vultures,
he knows destruction is imminent.
24 A day of darkness fills him with dread;
distress and anguish overpower him,
like a king expecting an attack.
25 Because he has stretched out his hand against God
and arrogantly challenged the Almighty,
26 Rushing defiantly against him,
with the stout bosses of his shields.
27 Although he has covered his face with his crassness,
padded his loins with blubber,
28 He shall dwell in ruined cities,
in houses that are deserted,
crumbling into rubble.
29 He shall not be rich, his possessions shall not endure;
his property shall not spread over the land.
30 A flame shall sear his early growth,
and with the wind his blossoms shall disappear.
31 Let him not trust in his height, misled,
even though his height be like the palm tree.†
32 He shall wither before his time,
his branches no longer green.
33 He shall be like a vine that sheds its grapes unripened,
like an olive tree casting off its blossom.
34 For the breed of the impious shall be sterile,*
and fire shall consume the tents of extortioners.
35 They conceive malice, bring forth deceit,*
give birth to fraud.†

Job's Fourth Reply

16 1 Then Job answered and said:

2 I have heard this sort of thing many times.*
Troublesome comforters, all of you!

†

15:1 The tone of Eliphaz's speech is now much rougher. In vv. 7–9 he ridicules Job's knowledge with a sarcastic question about whether he was a member of the divine council before creation and thus had unique wisdom (according to Prv 8:22–31, only Woman Wisdom existed before creation). Verses 20–35 are a typical description of the fate of the wicked.

15:31 The translation is uncertain.

15:35 The plans of the wicked yield nothing but futile results. Cf. Ps 7:15; Is 59:4.

*

15:6 Jb 9:20.
15:8 Jb 11:7; Wis 9:13; Jer 23:18; Rom 11:34; 1 Cor 2:11, 16.
15:9 Jb 12:3; 13:2.
15:14–16 Jb 25:4–6.
15:14 Jb 14:4.
15:15 Jb 4:18–19.
15:34 Wis 3:11, 18.
15:35 Ps 7:15; Is 59:4.
16:2 Jb 12:3.

3 Is there no end to windy words?
What sickness makes you rattle on?
4 I also could talk as you do,
were you in my place.
I could declaim over you,
or wag my head at you;
5 I could strengthen you with talk,
with mere chatter give relief.
6 If I speak, my pain is not relieved;
if I stop speaking, nothing changes.
7 But now he has exhausted me;
you have stunned all my companions.
8 You† have shriveled me up; it is a witness,
my gauntness rises up to testify against me;
9 His wrath tears and assails me,
he gnashes his teeth against me;
My enemy looks daggers at me.
10 They gape at me with their mouths;
They strike me on the cheek with insults;
they are all enlisted against me.
11 God has given me over to the impious;
into the hands of the wicked he has cast me.
12 I was in peace, but he dislodged me,
seized me by the neck, dashed me to pieces.
He has set me up for a target;
13 his arrows strike me from all directions.
He pierces my sides without mercy,
pours out my gall upon the ground.
14 He pierces me, thrust upon thrust,
rushes at me like a warrior.
15 I have sewn sackcloth on my skin,
laid my horn low in the dust.
16 My face is inflamed with weeping,
darkness covers my eyes,
17 Although my hands are free from violence,
and my prayer sincere.
18 O earth, do not cover my blood,
nor let my outcry come to rest!†
19 Even now my witness† is in heaven,
my advocate is on high.
20 My friends it is who wrong me;
before God my eyes shed tears,
21 That justice may be done for a mortal with
God:
as for a man with his neighbor.
22 For my years are numbered,
and I go the road of no return.

17 1 My spirit is broken, my days finished,
my burial at hand.
2 Surely mockers surround me,
at their provocation, my eyes grow dim.
3 Put up a pledge for me with you:†
who is there to give surety for me?
4 You darken their minds to knowledge;
therefore you will not exalt them.
5 For a share of property he informs on friends,
while the eyes of his children grow dim.
6 I am made a byword of the people;*
I am one at whom people spit.
7 My eyes are blind with anguish,
and my whole frame is like a shadow.
8 The upright are astonished at this,
the innocent aroused against the wicked.
9 The righteous holds to his way,
the one with clean hands increases in
strength.
10 But turn now, and come on again;
I do not find a wise man among you!
11 My days pass by, my plans are at an end,
the yearning of my heart.
12 They would change the night into day;
where there is darkness they talk of
approaching light.
13† If my only hope is dwelling in Sheol,
and spreading my couch in darkness,
14 If I am to say to the pit, "You are my father,"
and to the worm "my mother," "my sister,"
15 Where then is my hope,
my happiness, who can see it?
16 Will they descend with me into Sheol?
Shall we go down together into the dust?

Bildad's Second Speech

18 1 Then Bildad the Shuhite answered and said:

2 When will you put an end to words?
Reflect, and then we can have discussion.
3 Why are we accounted like beasts,
equal to them in your sight?
4 You who tear yourself in your anger—
shall the earth be neglected on your account
or the rock be moved out of its place?
5 Truly, the light of the wicked is extinguished;
the flame of his fire casts no light.
6 In his tent light is darkness;
the lamp above him goes out.*
7 His vigorous steps are hemmed in,
his own counsel casts him down.

† **16:8** *You*: God. Job then describes in vv. 9–17 the savage treatment that he has received from God.

16:18 As the exposed blood of those who were unjustly slain cries to heaven for vengeance (Gn 4:10; Ez 24:6–9), so Job's sufferings demand redress.

16:19 *Witness*: refers perhaps to God (is Job appealing to God against God?), or to a mediator (cf. 9:33), or to a personification of Job's prayer.

17:3 Addressed to God; v. 10 to Job's friends.

17:13–16 Job elaborates another of the vivid descriptions of "life" in Sheol; cf. 3:13–23; 10:21–22.

17:6 Jb 30:9.

18:6 Jb 21:17; Prv 13:9; 24:20.

8 A net catches him by the feet,
he wanders into a pitfall.
9 A trap seizes him by the heel,
a snare lays hold of him.
10 A noose is hidden for him on the ground,
a netting for him on the path.
11 On every side terrors frighten him;*
they harry him at each step.
12 His strength is famished,
disaster is ready at his side,
13 His skin is eaten to the limbs,
the firstborn of Death† eats his limbs.
14 He is plucked from the security of his tent;
and marched off to the king of terrors.†
15 Fire lodges in his tent,
over his abode brimstone is scattered.
16 Below, his roots dry up,
and above, his branches wither.
17 His memory perishes from the earth,*
and he has no name in the countryside.
18 He is driven from light into darkness,
and banished from the world.
19 He has neither offshoot nor offspring among his people,
no survivor where once he dwelt.
20 Those who come after shall be appalled at his fate;
those who went before are seized with horror.
21 So is it then with the dwelling of the impious;
such is the place of the one who does not know God!

Job's Fifth Reply

19 1 † Then Job answered and said:

2 How long will you afflict my spirit,
grind me down with words?
3 These ten times you have humiliated me,
have assailed me without shame!
4 Even if it were true that I am at fault,
my fault would remain with me;
5 If truly you exalt yourselves at my expense,
and use my shame as an argument against me,
6 Know then that it is God who has dealt unfairly with me,
and compassed me round with his net.
7 If I cry out "Violence!" I am not answered.*
I shout for help, but there is no justice.
8 He has barred my way and I cannot pass;
veiled my path in darkness;
9 He has stripped me of my glory,
taken the diadem from my brow.
10 He breaks me down on every side, and I am gone;
he has uprooted my hope like a tree.
11 He has kindled his wrath against me;
he counts me one of his enemies.*
12 His troops advance as one;
they build up their road to attack me,
encamp around my tent.
13 My family has withdrawn from me,*
my friends are wholly estranged.
14 My relatives and companions neglect me,
my guests have forgotten me.
15 Even my maidservants consider me a stranger;
I am a foreigner in their sight.
16 I call my servant, but he gives no answer,
though I plead aloud with him.
17 My breath is abhorrent to my wife;*
I am loathsome to my very children.
18 Even young children despise me;
when I appear, they speak against me.
19 All my intimate friends hold me in horror;
those whom I loved have turned against me!*
20 My bones cling to my skin,
and I have escaped by the skin of my teeth.†
21 Pity me, pity me, you my friends,
for the hand of God has struck me!
22 Why do you pursue me like God,
and prey insatiably upon me?
23 Oh, would that my words were written down!*
Would that they were inscribed in a record:†
24 That with an iron chisel and with lead
they were cut in the rock forever!
25 As for me, I know that my vindicator lives,†
and that he will at last stand forth upon the dust.*
26 This will happen when my skin has been stripped off,
and from my flesh I will see God:

†

18:13 *Firstborn of Death*: that is, disease, plague.

18:14 *The king of terrors*: of Sheol, of Death (cf. the "terrors" in v. 11). However, the Hebrew of this verse is obscure.

19:1 Job continues railing against his friends (vv. 2–5), and describing God's savage attack in words reminiscent of 16:9–17.

19:20 *Skin of my teeth*: although the metaphor is not clear, this has become a proverbial expression for a narrow escape. It does not fit Job's situation here.

19:23–24 What Job is about to say is so important that he wants it recorded in a permanent manner.

19:25–27 The meaning of this passage is obscure because the original text has been poorly preserved and the ancient versions do not agree among themselves. Job asserts three times that he shall see a future vindicator (Hebrew *goel*), but he leaves the time and manner of this vindication undefined. The Vulgate translation has Job indicating a belief in resurrection after death, but the Hebrew and the other ancient versions are less specific.

*

18:11 Jb 15:20–24; 27:20.
18:17 Ps 34:17; Prv 2:22; 10:7.
19:7 Jb 30:20.
19:11 Jb 13:24; 33:10.
19:13 Jb 6:13.
19:17 Jb 2:9.
19:19 Sir 6:8.

27 I will see for myself,
my own eyes, not another's, will behold him:
my inmost being is consumed with longing.
28 But you who say, "How shall we persecute him,
seeing that the root of the matter is found in him?"
29 Be afraid of the sword for yourselves,
for your anger is a crime deserving the sword;
that you may know that there is a judgment.

Zophar's Second Speech

20 1 Then Zophar the Naamathite answered and said:

2 So now my thoughts provide an answer for me,
because of the feelings within me.
3 A rebuke that puts me to shame I hear,
and from my understanding a spirit gives me a reply.
4 Do you not know this: from of old,
since human beings were placed upon the earth,
5 The triumph of the wicked is short
and the joy of the impious but for a moment?*
6 Though his pride mount up to the heavens
and his head reach to the clouds,
7 Yet he perishes forever like the dung he uses for fuel,
and onlookers say, "Where is he?"*
8 Like a dream he takes flight and cannot be found;
he fades away like a vision of the night.
9 The eye which saw him does so no more;
nor shall his dwelling again behold him.
10 His sons will restore to the poor,
and his hands will yield up his riches.*
11 Though his bones are full of youthful vigor,
it shall lie with him in the dust.
12 Though wickedness is sweet in his mouth,
and he hides it under his tongue,
13 Though he retains it and will not let it go
but keeps it still within his mouth,
14 Yet in his stomach the food shall turn;
it shall be venom of asps inside him.
15 The riches he swallowed he shall vomit up;
God shall make his belly disgorge them.
16 The poison of asps he shall drink in;
the viper's fangs shall slay him.
17 He shall see no streams of oil,†
no torrents of honey or milk.
18 He shall give back his gains, never used;
like his profit from trade, never enjoyed.
19 Because he has oppressed and neglected the poor,
and stolen a house he did not build;
20 For he has known no quiet in his greed,
in his treasure he cannot save himself.*
21 None of his survivors will consume it,
therefore his prosperity shall not endure.
22 * When he has more than enough, distress shall be his,
every sort of trouble shall come upon him.
23 When he has filled his belly,
God shall send against him the fury of his wrath
and rain down his missiles upon him.
24 Should he escape an iron weapon,
a bronze bow shall pierce him through;
25 The dart shall come out of his back,
a shining point out of his gall-bladder:
terrors fall upon him.
26 Complete darkness is in store for his treasured ones;
a fire unfanned shall consume him;*
any survivor in his tent shall be destroyed.
27 The heavens shall reveal his guilt,
and the earth rise up against him.
28 The flood shall sweep away his house,
torrents in the day of God's anger.
29 This is the portion of the wicked,
the heritage appointed him by God.† *

Job's Sixth Reply

21 1 Then Job answered and said:

2 At least listen to my words,*
and let that be the consolation you offer.
3 Bear with me while I speak;
and after I have spoken, you can mock!
4 Is my complaint toward any human being?
Why should I not be impatient?
5 Look at me and be appalled,
put your hands over your mouths.
6 When I think of it, I am dismayed,
and shuddering seizes my flesh.

---

† **20:17** *Oil*: olive oil, one of the main agricultural products of ancient Palestine, a land proverbially rich in honey and milk; see Ex 3:8; etc.

20:29 Zophar ends his lecture in the style of Bildad (cf. 18:19) with a summary appraisal of what he has been saying about the fate of the wicked.

* **19:23** Jb 31:35.
19:25–26 Phil 3:20; Ti 2:13.
20:5 Jb 21:13; Ps 37:35–36.
20:7 Jb 14:10; Ps 37:10, 36.
20:10 Jb 27:14.
20:20 Eccl 5:9; Lk 12:20.
20:22 Jb 15:20–35.
20:26 Dt 32:22.
20:29 Jb 27:13.
21:2 Jb 13:17.

7† Why do the wicked keep on living,
grow old, become mighty in power?*
8 Their progeny is secure in their sight;
their offspring are before their eyes.
9 Their homes are safe, without fear,
and the rod of God is not upon them.
10 Their bulls breed without fail;
their cows calve and do not miscarry.
11 They let their young run free like sheep,
their children skip about.
12 They sing along with drum and lyre,
and make merry to the sound of the pipe.
13 They live out their days in prosperity,
and tranquilly go down to Sheol.*
14 Yet they say to God, "Depart from us,*
for we have no desire to know your ways!
15 What is the Almighty that we should serve
him?
And what do we gain by praying to him?"*
16 Their happiness is not in their own hands.
The designs of the wicked are far from me!*
17 How often is the lamp of the wicked put out?
How often does destruction come upon
them,
the portion God allots in his anger?
18 Let them be like straw before the wind,
like chaff the storm carries away!
19 "God is storing up the man's misery for his
children"?—
let him requite the man himself so that he
knows it!
20 Let his own eyes behold his calamity,
and the wrath of the Almighty let him
drink!
21 For what interest has he in his family after
him,
when the number of his months is finished?
22 Can anyone teach God knowledge,
seeing that he judges those on high?†
23 One dies in his full vigor,
wholly at ease and content;
24 His figure is full and nourished,
his bones are moist with marrow.
25 Another dies with a bitter spirit,
never having tasted happiness.
26 Alike they lie down in the dust,
and worms cover them both.
27 See, I know your thoughts,
and the arguments you plot against me.
28 For you say, "Where is the house of the great,
and where the dwelling place of the wicked?"
29 Have you not asked the wayfarers
and do you not acknowledge the witness
they give?
30 On the day of calamity the evil man is spared,
on the day that wrath is released.
31 Who will charge him to his face about his
conduct,
and for what he has done who will repay
him?
32 He is carried to the grave
and at his tomb they keep watch.
33 Sweet to him are the clods of the valley.
All humankind will follow after him,
and countless others before him.
34 How empty the consolation you offer me!
Your arguments remain a fraud.

IV. Third Cycle of Speeches†

Eliphaz's Third Speech

22 1 Then Eliphaz the Temanite answered
and said:

2 Can a man be profitable to God?*
Can a wise man be profitable to him?
3 Does it please the Almighty that you are just?*
Does he gain if your ways are perfect?†
4 Is it because of your piety that he reproves
you—
that he enters into judgment with you?
5 Is not your wickedness great,
your iniquity endless?
6 You keep your relatives' goods in pledge
unjustly,†
leave them stripped naked of their
clothing.*
7 To the thirsty you give no water to drink,
and from the hungry you withhold bread;
8 As if the land belonged to the powerful,
and only the privileged could dwell in it!
9 You sent widows away empty-handed,
and the resources of orphans are
destroyed.*

†

21:7 In vv. 7–29 Job launches into a realistic description of the fate of the wicked, contrary to the claims made by the friends.

21:22 *Those on high*: the heavenly beings; cf. 1:6; Ps 82:1–8.

22:1–27:23 The traditional three cycles of speeches breaks down in chaps. 22–27, because Zophar does not appear. This may be interpreted as a sign that the three friends see no point in further dialogue, or that Job's replies have reduced them to silence, or that there has been a mistake in the transmission of the text (hence various transferrals of verses have been proposed to include Zophar, but without any textual evidence).

22:3 Another irony: God will "gain," because he will have been proved right in his claim to the satan that Job is "perfect."

22:6–9 This criticism of Job by Eliphaz is untrue (cf. 31:19), but he is driven to it by his belief that God always acts justly, even when he causes someone to suffer; suffering is due to wrongdoing (cf. v. 29).

21:7 Jb 12:6; Ps 37:35; 73:3; Eccl 8:14; Jer 12:1–2; Mal 3:14–15.
21:13 Jb 34:20.
21:14 Jb 22:17.
21:15 Mal 3:14.
21:16 Jb 22:18.
22:2 Jb 9:2.
22:3 Jb 35:7.
22:6 Jb 24:3; Dt 24:6, 17; Ez 18:12, 16.

10 Therefore snares are round about you,*
sudden terror makes you panic,
11 Or darkness—you cannot see!
A deluge of waters covers you.
12 Does not God, in the heights of the heavens,*
behold the top of the stars, high though
they are?
13 Yet you say, "What does God know?*
Can he judge through the thick darkness?
14 Clouds hide him so that he cannot see
as he walks around the circuit of the
heavens!"
15 Do you indeed keep to the ancient way
trodden by the worthless?
16 They were snatched before their time;
their foundations a river swept away.
17 They said to God, "Let us alone!"
and, "What can the Almighty do to us?"
18 Yet he had filled their houses with good things.
The designs of the wicked are far from
me!† *
19 The just look on and are glad,
and the innocent deride them:† *
20 "Truly our enemies are destroyed,
and what was left to them, fire has
consumed!"
21 Settle with him and have peace.
That way good shall come to you:
22 Receive instruction from his mouth,
and place his words in your heart.
23 If you return to the Almighty, you will be
restored;
if you put iniquity far from your tent,
24 And treat raw gold as dust,
the fine gold of Ophir† as pebbles in the
wadi,
25 Then the Almighty himself shall be your gold
and your sparkling silver.
26 For then you shall delight in the Almighty,
you shall lift up your face toward God.
27 Entreat him and he will hear you,*
and your vows you shall fulfill.
28 What you decide shall succeed for you,
and upon your ways light shall shine.
29 For when they are brought low, you will say,
"It is pride!"
But downcast eyes he saves.*
30 He will deliver whoever is innocent;
you shall be delivered if your hands are
clean.*

Job's Seventh Reply

23 [1]Then Job answered and said:
2 Today especially my complaint is bitter,
his hand is heavy upon me in my
groanings.
3 Would that I knew how to find him,
that I might come to his dwelling!
4 I would set out my case before him,
fill my mouth with arguments;
5 I would learn the words he would answer me,
understand what he would say to me.
6 Would he contend against me with his great
power?
No, he himself would heed me!
7 There an upright man might argue with him,
and I would once and for all be delivered
from my judge.
8 But if I go east, he is not there;†
or west, I cannot perceive him;
9 The north enfolds him, and I cannot catch
sight of him;
The south hides him, and I cannot see him.
10 Yet he knows my way;
if he tested me, I should come forth like
gold.*
11 My foot has always walked in his steps;
I have kept his way and not turned aside.
12 From the commands of his lips I have not
departed;
the words of his mouth I have treasured in
my heart.
13 But once he decides, who can contradict him?
What he desires, that he does.*
14 For he will carry out what is appointed for me,
and many such things he has in store.
15 Therefore I am terrified before him;
when I take thought, I dread him.
16 For it is God who has made my heart faint,
the Almighty who has terrified me.
17 Yes, would that I had vanished in darkness,
hidden by the thick gloom before me.

24 [1] Why are times not set by the Almighty,
and why do his friends not see his days?†

22:18 The second part of the verse repeats 21:16.
22:19 *Them*: the wicked. Eliphaz obviously thinks that the just can be pleased by God's punishment of the wicked. Such pleasure at the downfall of the wicked is expressed elsewhere, e.g., Ps 58:11; 63:12.
22:24 *Ophir*: see note on Ps 45:10.
23:8 Job's confident desire to confront God (vv. 2–7, contrary to his fears in 9:14–20 and 13:21–27) gives way to his dark night: God's absence (vv. 8–9), which also terrifies (vv. 13–17).
24:1 After his failure to find God, Job takes up the question: Why does God not favor his friends by the speedy punishment of his enemies?

22:9 Jb 29:12–13; Dt 24:17; 27:19.
22:10 Jb 18:8–10.
22:12 Jb 11:8.
22:13–14 Ps 10:11; 73:11; 94:7; Is 29:15; Ez 8:12; 9:9.
22:18 Jb 21:16.
22:19 Ps 107:42.
22:27 Jb 33:26.
22:29 Ps 138:6; Prv 29:23; Mt 23:12; Lk 1:52; Jas 4:10; 1 Pt 5:5.
22:30 Jb 17:9; Ps 18:21, 25; 24:4.
23:10 Ps 66:10; Prv 17:3; Mal 3:3; 1 Pt 1:7.
23:13 Jb 42:2; Ps 115:3; 135:6.

Did You Know?

A Long Debate

Why are Job's friends so insistent that sin and suffering are connected? Why do they go on, chapter after chapter, telling Job that his suffering is a punishment for his sins? The author of the Book of Job uses the debate of Job and his friends to contrast two positions. The position of Job's friends is that God rewards people who are good and punishes those who are wicked: if Job is suffering terribly, then Job must have sinned terribly. Job's repeated denial of sin reveals the second position, which is that sometimes innocent people suffer. This second position is harder to argue because it leaves a huge question: Why?

Because Job has too much integrity to repent for sins he never committed (see Jb 27:1–6), he keeps searching for another answer. Finally, Job makes an oath of innocence. Such an oath has God as its witness, and if it is false, it requires that God strike down the person who made it. But God appears to Job in an awesome show of power (see chapters 38–41) and reminds Job that human intelligence is too limited to comprehend the deeper mysteries of creation. God alone knows why innocent people suffer; Job must trust God's plan.

Read chapters 20–24 to get a sense of the long debate in Job about human suffering. This debate reflects the long history of the Israelites wrestling with this complex question.

2 People remove landmarks;
they steal herds and pasture them.
3 The donkeys of orphans they drive away;
they take the widow's ox for a pledge.
4 They force the needy off the road;
all the poor of the land are driven into hiding.
5 Like wild donkeys in the wilderness,
they go forth to their task of seeking prey;
the steppe provides food for their young;
6 They harvest fodder in the field,
and glean in the vineyard of the wicked.
7 They pass the night naked, without clothing;
they have no covering against the cold;
8 They are drenched with rain from the mountains,
and for want of shelter they cling to the rock.
9 Orphans are snatched from the breast,
infants of the needy are taken in pledge.†
10 They go about naked, without clothing,
and famished, they carry the sheaves.†
11 Between the rows they press out the oil;
they tread the wine presses, yet are thirsty.
12 In the city the dying groan,
and the souls of the wounded cry out.
Yet God does not treat it as a disgrace!
13 They are rebels against the light:*
they do not recognize its ways;
they do not stay in its paths.
14 When there is no light the murderer rises,
to kill the poor and needy;
in the night he acts like a thief.
15 The eye of the adulterer watches for the twilight;*
he says, "No eye will see me."
He puts a mask over his face;
16 in the dark he breaks into houses;
By day they shut themselves in;
they do not know the light.
17 Indeed, for all of them morning is deep darkness;
then they recognize the terrors of deep darkness.
18 He is swift on the surface of the water:†
their portion in the land is accursed,
they do not turn aside by way of the vineyards.
19 Drought and heat snatch away the snow waters,
Sheol, those who have sinned.
20 May the womb forget him,
may the worm find him sweet,
may he no longer be remembered;
And may wickedness be broken like a tree.
21 May his companion be barren, unable to give birth,
may his widow not prosper!
22 He† sustains the mighty by his strength,

† **24:9** This verse continues the description of the plight of the poor in vv. 2–4, and may belong there.

24:10 This verse is a variant of v. 7, and may be an erroneous scribal repetition.

24:18–24 These verses are inconsistent with Job's views elsewhere. Moreover, they are in general poorly preserved, and in some cases obscure.

24:22 *He*: God.

* **24:13** Jn 3:19–20. **24:15** Prv 7:9–10.

to him who rises without assurance of his life
23 he gives safety and support,
and his eyes are on their ways.
24 They are exalted for a while, and then are no more;
laid low, like everyone else they are gathered up;
like ears of grain they shrivel.
25 If this be not so, who can make me a liar,
and reduce my words to nothing?

Bildad's Third Speech

25 1 † Then Bildad the Shuhite answered and said:
2 Dominion and dread are his
who brings about harmony in his heavens.
3 Is there any numbering of his troops?†
Yet on which of them does his light not rise?
4 How can anyone be in the right against God,*
or how can any born of woman be innocent?
5 Even the moon is not bright
and the stars are not clean in his eyes.
6 How much less a human being, who is but a worm,
a mortal, who is only a maggot?*

Job's Reply

26 1 Then Job answered and said:†
2 What help you give to the powerless,
what strength to the feeble arm!
3 How you give counsel to one without wisdom;
how profuse is the advice you offer!
4 With whose help have you uttered those words,
whose breath comes forth from you?*
5 The shades† beneath writhe in terror,*
the waters, and their inhabitants.
6 Naked before him is Sheol,†
and Abaddon has no covering.*
7 He stretches out Zaphon† over the void,
and suspends the earth over nothing at all;
8 He binds up the waters in his clouds,
yet the cloud is not split by their weight;
9 He holds back the appearance of the full moon
by spreading his clouds before it.
10 He has marked out a circle† on the surface of the deep*
as the boundary of light and darkness.
11 The pillars of the heavens tremble
and are stunned at his thunderous rebuke;*
12 By his power he stilled Sea,
by his skill he crushed Rahab;†
13 By his wind the heavens were made clear,
his hand pierced the fleeing serpent.† *
14 Lo, these are but the outlines of his ways,
and what a whisper of a word we hear of him:
Who can comprehend the thunder of his power?

Job's Reply

27 1 Job took up his theme again and said:
2 As God lives,† who takes away my right,*
the Almighty, who has made my life bitter,
3 So long as I still have life breath in me,
the breath of God in my nostrils,
4 My lips shall not speak falsehood,
nor my tongue utter deceit!
5 Far be it from me to account you right;
till I die I will not renounce my innocence.*
6 My justice I maintain and I will not relinquish it;
my heart does not reproach me for any of my days.
7† Let my enemy be as the wicked
and my adversary as the unjust!
8 For what hope has the impious when he is cut off,
when God requires his life?
9 Will God then listen to his cry

†

25:1 At this point any structure in the dialogues disappears. Bildad's speech is very short, and there follow two speeches attributed to Job, with significantly different introductions in 27:1 and 29:1, and with no intervening third speech of Zophar.

25:3 *His troops*: the heavenly host, or army, the stars (cf. Jgs 5:20), later understood as angels.

26:1–14 Perhaps to be read as Job's reply to Bildad's short speech.

26:5 *Shades*: the dead in Sheol, the nether world; cf. Ps 88:11; Is 26:14.

26:6 *Sheol*: cf. note on Ps 6:6. *Abaddon*: Hebrew for "(place of) destruction," a synonym for nether world; cf. Jb 28:22; Rev 9:11.

26:7 *Zaphon*: lit., "the north," used here as a synonym for the firmament, the heavens; cf. Is 14:13.

26:10 *Circle*: the horizon of the ocean which serves as the boundary for the activity of light and darkness; cf. Prv 8:27.

26:12 *Rahab*: another name for the primeval sea-monster; see notes on Jb 3:8 and Ps 89:11; cf. also Jb 7:12; 9:13.

26:13 *The fleeing serpent*: the same term occurs in Is 27:1 in apposition to Leviathan; see note on Jb 3:8.

27:2–6 *As God lives . . . far be it*: Job affirms two oaths about his innocence by the very God whom he has accused of violating his right. Such is the paradoxical situation of a tortured person who cannot give the lie to his personal justice, but also refuses to renounce God. He dares God to be "just" as he, Job, understands this.

27:7–23 These verses are inconsistent with Job's views elsewhere, and may be part of a missing speech of Zophar; cf. notes on 24:18–24 and 25:1. Or possibly they are an ironic description of the fate of the three friends.

*

25:4 Jb 4:17; 9:2; 35:2.
25:6 Jb 4:19; 15:16.
26:4 Gn 2:7.
26:5 Prv 9:18.
26:6 Ps 139:7–12.
26:10 Jb 38:8–11; Prv 8:29.
26:11 Jb 9:6; Ps 18:16; 104:7.
26:13 Is 27:1.
27:2 Jb 34:5.
27:5 Jb 2:3, 9; 13:15; 33:9.

when distress comes upon him,
10 If he delights in the Almighty
and calls upon God constantly?
11 I will teach you what is in God's hand,
and the way of the Almighty I will not
conceal.
12 Look, you yourselves have all seen it;
why do you spend yourselves in empty
words!
13 This is the portion of the wicked with God,
the heritage oppressors receive from the
Almighty:*
14 Though his children be many, the sword
awaits them.
His descendants shall want for bread.
15 His survivors shall be buried in death;
their widows shall not weep.
16 Though he heap up silver like dust
and store away mounds of clothing,
17 What he has stored the righteous shall wear,
and the innocent shall divide the silver.
18 He builds his house as of cobwebs,
or like a booth put up by a watchman.
19 He lies down a rich man, one last time;
he opens his eyes—nothing is there.*
20 Terrors flood over him like water,
at night the tempest carries him off.
21 The east wind seizes him and he is gone;
it sweeps him from his place;
22 It hurls itself at him without pity,
as he tries to flee from its power.
23 It claps its hands at him,
and whistles at him from its place.

V. The Poem on Wisdom

Where Is Wisdom to be Found?

28 1 There is indeed a mine for silver,†
and a place for refining gold.
2 Iron is taken from the earth,
and copper smelted out of stone.
3† He sets a boundary for the darkness;
the farthest confines he explores.
4 He breaks open a shaft far from habitation,
unknown to human feet;
suspended, far from people, they sway.
5 The earth, though out of it comes forth bread,
is in fiery upheaval underneath.
6 Its stones are the source of lapis lazuli,
and there is gold in its dust.
7 The path no bird of prey knows,
nor has the hawk's eye seen it.
8 The proud beasts have not trodden it,
nor has the lion gone that way.
9 He sets his hand to the flinty rock,
and overturns the mountains at their root.
10 He splits channels in the rocks;
his eyes behold all that is precious.
11 He dams up the sources of the streams,
and brings hidden things to light.
12 As for wisdom—where can she be found?
Where is the place of understanding?*
13 Mortals do not know her path,
nor is she to be found in the land of the
living.
14 The Deep says, "She is not in me";
and the Sea says, "She is not with me."
15 Solid gold cannot purchase her,
nor can her price be paid with silver.*
16 She cannot be bought with gold of Ophir,†
with precious onyx or lapis lazuli,
17 Gold or crystal cannot equal her,
nor can golden vessels be exchanged for her.
18 Neither coral nor crystal should be thought of;
the value of wisdom surpasses pearls.
19 Ethiopian topaz does not equal her,
nor can she be weighed out for pure gold.
20 As for wisdom, where does she come from?
Where is the place of understanding?
21 She is hidden from the eyes of every living
thing;
even from the birds of the air she is
concealed.
22 Abaddon† and Death say,
"Only by rumor have we heard of her."
23† But God understands the way to her;*
it is he who knows her place.*
24 For he beholds the ends of the earth
and sees all that is under the heavens.
25 When he weighed out the wind,
and measured out the waters;
26 When he made a rule for the rain

†

28:1–28 This chapter contains a beautifully vivid description of that Wisdom which is beyond the attainment of creatures and known only to God. The pronouns referring to Wisdom may be translated as either feminine or neuter; in view of Wisdom's role as God's companion and partner in creation (see Prv 8:22–30; Sir 24:1–21; Wis 9:9; Bar 3:9–4:4), the feminine is used here. There is no consensus about the authorship of this poem; it may originally have been an independent composition incorporated into the Book of Job.

28:3–4 The subject of the verbs in these verses has no clear antecedent; the context of vv. 2–6 suggests miners. The Hebrew of v. 4 is especially difficult. The general sense of vv. 1–11 is that one can find minerals in the earth; in contrast, where is Wisdom to be found (vv. 12, 20)?

28:16 *Ophir*: cf. note on Ps 45:10.

28:22 *Abaddon*: cf. note on Jb 26:6.

28:23–27 In reply to the question of vv. 12, 20, these verses indicate that the creator (vv. 24–26) knows the "place" of wisdom and even "established" her, but the specifics are not given. For further development of this theme, cf. Sir 1:1–10 and Bar 3:9–4:4.

*

27:13 Jb 20:4–29.
27:19 Ps 49:18; 76:6.
28:12 Eccl 7:24–25; Bar 3:14–15, 29–33.
28:15 Prv 3:14; 8:10–11, 19; 16:16; Wis 7:7–11.
28:23–27 Prv 8:22–31.
28:23 Prv 2:6; Sir 1:1; Jas 1:5.
28:26 Jb 38:25; Prv 3:20.

and a path for the thunderbolts,*
27 Then he saw wisdom and appraised her,
established her, and searched her out.
28† And to mortals he said:
See: the fear of the Lord is wisdom;
and avoiding evil is understanding.*

VI. Job's Final Summary of His Cause

29 1† Job took up his theme again and said:

2 Oh, that I were as in the months past,
as in the days when God watched over me:*
3 While he kept his lamp shining above my head,
and by his light I walked through darkness;
4 As I was in my flourishing days,
when God sheltered my tent;
5 When the Almighty was still with me,
and my children were round about me;
6 When my footsteps were bathed in cream,
and the rock flowed with streams of oil.†
7 Whenever I went out to the gate of the city
and took my seat in the square,
8 The young men saw me and withdrew,
and the elders rose up and stood;
9 Officials refrained from speaking
and covered their mouths with their hands;*
10 The voice of the princes was silenced,
and their tongues stuck to the roofs of their mouths.
11 The ear that heard blessed me;
the eye that saw acclaimed me.
12 For I rescued the poor who cried out for help,
the orphans, and the unassisted;
13 The blessing of those in extremity came upon me,
and the heart of the widow I made joyful.
14 I wore my righteousness like a garment;
justice was my robe and my turban.
15 I was eyes to the blind,
and feet to the lame was I.
16 I was a father to the poor;
the complaint of the stranger I pursued,
17 And I broke the jaws of the wicked man;
from his teeth I forced the prey.
18 I said: "In my own nest I shall grow old;
I shall multiply years like the phoenix.†
19 My root is spread out to the waters;
the dew rests by night on my branches.
20 My glory is fresh within me,
and my bow is renewed in my hand!"
21 For me they listened and waited;
they were silent for my counsel.
22 Once I spoke, they said no more,
but received my pronouncement drop by drop.
23 They waited for me as for the rain;
they drank in my words like the spring rains.
24 When I smiled on them they could not believe it;
they would not let the light of my face be dimmed.
25 I decided their course and sat at their head,
I lived like a king among the troops,
like one who comforts mourners.

30 1 But now they hold me in derision
who are younger than I,*
Whose fathers I should have disdained
to rank with the dogs of my flock.
2 Such strength as they had meant nothing to me;
their vigor had perished.
3 In want and emaciating hunger*
they fled to the parched lands:
to the desolate wasteland by night.
4 They plucked saltwort† and shrubs;
the roots of the broom plant were their food.
5 They were banished from the community,
with an outcry like that against a thief—
6 To dwell on the slopes of the wadies,
in caves of sand and stone;
7 Among the bushes they brayed;
under the nettles they huddled together.
8 Irresponsible, of no account,
they were driven out of the land.
9 Yet now they sing of me in mockery;
I have become a byword among them.*
10 They abhor me, they stand aloof,
they do not hesitate to spit in my face!

J B

†

28:28 This verse may be a later addition expressing a commonplace of the wisdom tradition; see cross-references. The addition seems to tie the poem in with the description of Job as fearing God and avoiding evil (1:1, 8; 2:3).

29:1 This chapter begins Job's soliloquy, which will end in 31:40. He describes in florid and exaggerated terms his former lifestyle with all its blessings, a deliberate contrast to his current plight, which will be further described in chap. 30.

29:6 Hyperbole to express abundance; see note on 20:17.

29:18 *Phoenix*: a legendary bird which, after several centuries of life, consumed itself in fire, then rose from its ashes in youthful freshness.

30:4 *Saltwort*: found in salt marshes and very sour to the taste; eaten by the extremely poor as a cooked vegetable. *Broom plant*: the juniper or brushwood; cf. Ps 120:4; a figure of bitterness and poverty, because of its bitter-tasting roots which are practically inedible.

*

28:28 Ps 111:10; Prv 1:7; 9:10; Sir 1:13–21.
29:2 Jb 1:10.
29:9 Wis 8:10–12.
30:1 Jb 12:4; 19:18.
30:3–8 Jb 24:5–6.
30:9 Jb 17:6.

Live It!

Hey, God! Did You Hear Me?

How do we know that God hears and answers our prayers? The books of Job and the Psalms describe many instances of both cries for help and God's responses to those cries. In our day-to-day reality, however, we can't always tell when God is answering our prayers. It isn't like we walk by trees that burn and speak to us, or hear whispers in the wind that call our name, or see and hear angels who give us God's answer. But God does hear and answer our prayers. One way to determine how God is answering our prayers is through discernment.

In the discernment process, an adult mentor or spiritual director can help you try to figure out what God is saying to you. If you don't already know of someone who can help you in this way (like a priest, religion teacher, campus or youth minister, or parent), you can ask at your parish or school for help in finding an adult mentor.

Even after engaging in the discernment process, the answers still aren't going to appear to most of us in dramatic and miraculous ways. In order to discover how God is speaking to us, we must simply pay attention to the common, ordinary experiences and relationships of our everyday lives—experiences and relationships in which God is abundantly present, helping us to understand more about ourselves and our place in this world.

▶ Jb 30:20

11† Because he has loosened my bowstring and
afflicted me,
they have thrown off restraint in my
presence.
12 On my right the young rabble rise up;
they trip my feet,
they build their approaches for my ruin.
13 They tear up my path,
they promote my ruin,
no helper is there against them.
14 As through a wide breach they advance;
amid the uproar they come on in waves;
15 terrors roll over me.
My dignity is driven off like the wind,
and my well-being vanishes like a cloud.
16 And now my life ebbs away from me,
days of affliction have taken hold of me.
17† At night he pierces my bones,
my sinews have no rest.
18 With great difficulty I change my clothes,
the collar of my tunic fits around my waist.
19 He has cast me into the mire;
I have become like dust and ashes.
20 I cry to you, but you do not answer me;*
I stand, but you take no notice.
21 You have turned into my tormentor,
and with your strong hand you attack me.
22 You raise me up and drive me before the wind;
I am tossed about by the tempest.
23 Indeed I know that you will return me to
death
to the house destined for everyone alive.*
24 Yet should not a hand be held out
to help a wretched person in distress?
25 Did I not weep for the hardships of others;
was not my soul grieved for the poor?*
26 Yet when I looked for good, evil came;
when I expected light, darkness came.
27 My inward parts seethe and will not be stilled;
days of affliction have overtaken me.
28 I go about in gloom, without the sun;
I rise in the assembly and cry for help.
29 I have become a brother to jackals,
a companion to ostriches.
30 My blackened skin falls away from me;
my very frame is scorched by the heat.
31 My lyre is tuned to mourning,
and my reed pipe to sounds of weeping.

31

1 I made a covenant with my eyes
not to gaze upon a virgin.
2 What portion comes from God above,
what heritage from the Almighty on high?
3 Is it not calamity for the unrighteous,
and woe for evildoers?
4 Does he not see my ways,
and number all my steps?*
5 If I have walked in falsehood†
and my foot has hastened to deceit,

---

† 30:11 God is the subject of the verbs. *Loosened my bowstring*: i.e., disarmed and disabled me.

30:17–23 Job here refers to God's harsh treatment of him. Cf. 16:9–17; 19:6–12.

31:5–34 In a series of purificatory oaths, Job protests his innocence.

* 30:20 Jb 19:7.
30:23 Heb 9:27.
30:25 Jb 29:12–16.
31:4 Jb 14:16; 34:21; Ps 139:3; Prv 5:21.

6 Let God weigh me in the scales of justice;
thus will he know my innocence!*
7 If my steps have turned out of the way,
and my heart has followed my eyes,
or any stain clings to my hands,
8 Then may I sow, but another eat,
and may my produce be rooted up!
9 If my heart has been enticed toward a woman,
and I have lain in wait at my neighbor's door;
10 Then may my wife grind for another,
and may others kneel over her!
11 For that would be heinous,
a crime to be condemned,*
12 A fire that would consume down to Abaddon†
till it uprooted all my crops.*
13 Had I refused justice to my manservant
or to my maidservant, when they had a complaint against me,
14 What then should I do when God rises up?
What could I answer when he demands an account?
15 Did not he who made me in the belly make him?
Did not the same One fashion us in the womb?
16 If I have denied anything that the poor desired,*
or allowed the eyes of the widow to languish
17 While I ate my portion alone,
with no share in it for the fatherless,
18 Though like a father he† has reared me from my youth,
guiding me even from my mother's womb—
19 If I have seen a wanderer without clothing,
or a poor man without covering,
20 Whose limbs have not blessed me
when warmed with the fleece of my sheep;
21 If I have raised my hand against the innocent
because I saw that I had supporters at the gate—†
22 Then may my arm fall from the shoulder,
my forearm be broken at the elbow!
23 For I dread calamity from God,
and his majesty will overpower me.
24 Had I put my trust in gold
or called fine gold my security;
25 Or had I rejoiced that my wealth was great,
or that my hand had acquired abundance—
26 Had I looked upon the light† as it shone,*
or the moon in the splendor of its progress,
27 And had my heart been secretly enticed
to blow them a kiss with my hand,
28 This too would be a crime for condemnation,
for I should have denied God above.*
29 Had I rejoiced at the destruction of my enemy
or exulted when evil came upon him,*
30 Even though I had not allowed my mouth to sin
by invoking a curse against his life—
31 Had not the men of my tent exclaimed,
"Who has not been filled with his meat!"†
32 No stranger lodged in the street,
for I opened my door to wayfarers—
33† Had I, all too human, hidden my sins
and buried my guilt in my bosom
34 Because I feared the great multitude
and the scorn of the clans terrified me—
then I should have remained silent, and not come out of doors!
35† Oh, that I had one to hear my case:
here is my signature:† let the Almighty answer me!
Let my accuser write out his indictment!*
36 Surely, I should wear it on my shoulder†
or put it on me like a diadem;
37 Of all my steps I should give him an account;
like a prince† I should present myself before him.
38 If my land has cried out against me
till its furrows wept together;
39 If I have eaten its strength without payment
and grieved the hearts of its tenants;
40 Then let the thorns grow instead of wheat
and stinkweed instead of barley!

The words of Job are ended.

†

31:12 *Abaddon*: see note on 26:6.

31:18 *He*: presumably God.

31:21 *Gate*: cf. notes on 5:4; Ru 4:1.

31:26–28 *Light*: of the sun. Job never sinned by worshiping the sun or the moon. *Blow them a kiss*: an act of idolatrous worship.

31:31 The members of his extended family will testify to his hospitality.

31:33–34 Job's present protest is made, not in spite of hidden sins which he had been unwilling to disclose, but out of genuine innocence. *All too human*: can also be translated "like Adam."

31:35–37 This concluding bravado fits better after v. 40a.

31:35 *My signature*: lit., *"tau,"* the last letter of the Hebrew alphabet, shaped like a cross. Job issues a subpoena to God, and challenges him to follow proper legal procedure as well.

31:36 *On my shoulder*: i.e., boldly, proudly.

31:37 *Like a prince*: not as a frightened criminal.

*

31:6 Jb 23:10.
31:11 Ex 20:14; Lv 20:10; Dt 22:22.
31:12 Sir 9:8–9.
31:16–23 Jb 29:12–16.
31:26–27 Dt 4:19.
31:28 Dt 17:2–7.
31:29 Prv 24:17.
31:35 Jb 19:23; 23:3–7.

VII. Elihu's Speeches

32 1 Then the three men ceased to answer
Job, because in his own eyes he was in
the right.* 2 * But the anger of Elihu,† son of
Barachel the Buzite, of the clan of Ram, was
kindled. He was angry with Job for considering
himself rather than God to be in the right. 3 * He
was angry also with the three friends because
they had not found a good answer and had not
condemned Job. 4 But since these men were older
than he, Elihu bided his time before addressing
Job. 5 When, however, Elihu saw that there was
no reply in the mouths of the three men, his
wrath was inflamed. 6 So Elihu, son of Barachel
the Buzite, answered and said:

> **But there is a spirit in human beings, the breath of the Almighty, that gives them understanding.**
> (Jb 32:8)

I am young and you are very old;
therefore I held back and was afraid
to declare to you my knowledge.
7 I thought, days should speak,
and many years teach wisdom!*
8 But there is a spirit in human beings,*
the breath of the Almighty, that gives them understanding.
9 It is not those of many days who are wise,
nor the aged who understand the right.
10 Therefore I say, listen to me;
I also will declare my knowledge!
11 Behold, I have waited for your words,
have given ear to your arguments,
as you searched out what to say.
12 Yes, I followed you attentively:
And look, none of you has convicted Job,
not one could refute his statements.
13 So do not say, "We have met wisdom;†
God can vanquish him but no mortal!"
14 For had he addressed his words to me,
I would not then have answered him with your words.
15 They are dismayed, they make no more reply;
words fail them.
16 Must I wait? Now that they speak no more,
and have ceased to make reply,
17 I too will speak my part;
I also will declare my knowledge!
18 For I am full of words;
the spirit within me compels me.
19 My belly is like unopened wine,
like wineskins ready to burst.
20 Let me speak and obtain relief;
let me open my lips, and reply.
21 I would not be partial to anyone,
nor give flattering titles to any.
22 For I know nothing of flattery;
if I did, my Maker would soon take me away.

33 1 Therefore, O Job, hear my discourse;
listen to all my words.
2 Behold, now I open my mouth;
my tongue and voice form words.
3 I will state directly what is in my mind,
my lips shall speak knowledge clearly;
4 For the spirit of God made me,
the breath of the Almighty keeps me alive.*
5 If you are able, refute me;
draw up your arguments and take your stand.
6 Look, I am like you before God,
I too was pinched from clay.† *
7 Therefore fear of me should not dismay you,
nor should I weigh heavily upon you.
8 But you have said in my hearing,
as I listened to the sound of your words:
9 "I am clean, without transgression;
I am innocent, there is no guilt in me.*
10 Yet he invents pretexts against me
and counts me as an enemy.† *
11 He puts my feet in the stocks,
watches all my paths!"*

---

† **32:2** *Elihu* means "My God is he." This speaker was from Buz, which, according to Jer 25:23, was near Tema and Dedan. A young man, he impetuously and impatiently upbraids Job for his boldness toward God, and the three friends for not successfully answering Job. He undertakes to defend God's absolute justice and to explain more clearly why there is suffering. While fundamentally his position is the same as that of the three friends, he locates the place of suffering in the divine plan. Because Elihu's four speeches (32:6–33:33; 34:2–37; 35:2–16; 36:2–37:24) repeat the substance of the earlier arguments of the three friends and also anticipate the content of the divine speeches (chaps. 39–41), many scholars consider them a later addition to the book.

32:13 *Met wisdom*: in Job's arguments.

33:6 *Pinched from clay*: a reference to the tradition that human beings were made from clay; cf. Gn 2:7; Jb 10:9; Is 64:7.

33:10 *Enemy*: see note on 1:1; cf. 13:24.

32:1 Jb 33:9.
32:2 Jb 13:18; 27:6; 34:5; 35:2.
32:3 Jb 22:5.
32:7 Jb 12:12.
32:8 Jb 33:4.
33:4 Jb 32:8.
33:6 Jb 31:15.
33:9 Jb 10:7; 13:18; 27:5–6; 29:14; 32:1; 34:5.
33:10 Jb 13:24; 19:11.
33:11 Jb 13:27; 31:4.

12 In this you are not just, let me tell you;
for God is greater than mortals.
13 Why, then, do you make complaint against him
that he gives no reply to their words?*
14 For God does speak, once,
even twice, though you do not see it:†
15 In a dream, in a vision of the night,
when deep sleep falls upon mortals
as they slumber in their beds.
16 It is then he opens their ears
and with a warning, terrifies them,
17 By turning mortals from acting
and keeping pride away from a man,
18 He holds his soul from the pit,
his life from passing to the grave.
19 Or he is chastened on a bed of pain,
suffering continually in his bones,
20 So that to his appetite food is repulsive,
his throat rejects the choicest nourishment.*
21 His flesh is wasted, it cannot be seen;
bones, once invisible, appear;
22 His soul draws near to the pit,
his life to the place of the dead.
23 If then there be a divine messenger,†
a mediator, one out of a thousand,
to show him what is right,
24 He will take pity on him and say,
"Deliver him from going down to the pit;
I have found him a ransom."
25 Then his flesh shall become soft as a boy's;
he shall be again as in the days of his youth.
26 He shall pray and God will favor him;
he shall see God's face with rejoicing;*
for he restores a person's righteousness.
27 He shall sing before all and say,
"I sinned and did wrong,
yet I was not punished accordingly.
28 He delivered me from passing to the pit,
and my life sees light."
29 See, all these things God does,
two, even three times, for a man,
30 Bringing back his soul from the pit
to the light, in the light of the living.
31 Be attentive, Job, listen to me!
Be silent and I will speak.
32 If you have anything to say, then answer me.
Speak out! I should like to see you justified.
33 If not, then you listen to me;
be silent, and I will teach you wisdom.

34

1 Then Elihu answered and said:†
2 Hear my discourse, you that are wise;
you that have knowledge, listen to me!
3 For the ear tests words,
as the palate tastes food.*
4 Let us choose what is right;
let us determine among ourselves what is good.
5 For Job has said, "I am innocent,
but God has taken away what is my right.*
6 I declare the judgment on me to be a lie;
my arrow-wound is incurable, sinless though I am."*
7 What man is like Job?
He drinks in blasphemies like water,
8 Keeps company with evildoers
and goes along with the wicked,
9 When he says, "There is no profit
in pleasing God."*
10 Therefore, you that have understanding, hear me:
far be it from God to do wickedness;
far from the Almighty to do wrong!*
11 Rather, he requites mortals for their conduct,
and brings home to them their way of life.*
12 Surely, God cannot act wickedly,
the Almighty cannot pervert justice.*
13 Who gave him charge over the earth,
or who set all the world in its place?*
14 If he were to set his mind to it,
gather to himself his spirit and breath,
15 All flesh would perish together,
and mortals return to dust.*
16 Now you†—understand, hear this!
Listen to the words I speak!
17 Can an enemy of justice be in control,
will you condemn the supreme Just One,
18 Who says to a king, "You are worthless!"
and to nobles, "You are wicked!"
19 Who neither favors the person of princes,
nor respects the rich more than the poor?
For they are all the work of his hands;*

J B

† **33:14** Elihu asserts that God speaks through warning in dream and also through pain. However, his presupposition is that the restored person admits sinfulness (v. 27). This of course is not relevant to Job's situation.
33:23 *Divine messenger*: or "angel," one of the thousands who serve as mediators.
34:1 Elihu replies, although no one else has spoken. This connective phrase (see also 35:1 and 36:1) may indicate that these speeches of Elihu are a secondary addition to the book (see note on 32:2).
34:16 *Now you*: Elihu turns to Job and addresses him directly.

* **33:13** Jb 31:35.
33:20 Jb 6:7.
33:26 Jb 22:26–29.
34:3 Jb 12:11.
34:5 Jb 33:9–10.
34:6 Jb 9:20.
34:9 Jb 9:22–23, 30–31; 21:15; 35:3.
34:10 Jb 36:23.
34:11 Ps 62:13; Prv 24:12; Mt 16:27; Rom 2:6; 2 Cor 5:10; Rev 22:12.
34:12 Jb 8:3.
34:13 Jb 38:4–7.
34:15 Jb 10:9.
34:19 Dt 10:17; 2 Chr 19:7; Wis 6:7; Acts 10:34; Rom 2:11; Eph 6:9; Col 3:25; 1 Pt 1:17.

20 in a moment they die, even at midnight.*
People are shaken, and pass away,
the powerful are removed without lifting a hand;
21 For his eyes are upon our ways,
and all our steps he sees.
22 There is no darkness so dense
that evildoers can hide in it.
23 For no one has God set a time
to come before him in judgment.
24 Without inquiry he shatters the mighty,*
and appoints others in their place,
25 Thus he discerns their works;
overnight they are crushed.
26† Where the wicked are, he strikes them,
in a place where all can see,
27 Because they turned away from him
and did not understand his ways at all:
28 And made the cry of the poor reach him,
so that he heard the cry of the afflicted.
29 If he is silent, who then can condemn?
If he hides his face, who then can behold him,
whether nation or individual?
30 Let an impious man not rule,
nor those who ensnare their people.
31 Should anyone say to God,
"I accept my punishment; I will offend no more;
32 What I cannot see, teach me:
if I have done wrong, I will do so no more,"
33 Would you then say that God must punish,
when you are disdainful?
It is you who must choose, not I;
speak, therefore, what you know.
34 Those who understand will say to me,
all the wise who hear my views:
35 "Job speaks without knowledge,
his words make no sense.*
36 Let Job be tested to the limit,
since his answers are those of the impious;
37 For he is adding rebellion to his sin
by brushing off our arguments
and addressing many words to God."

35 1 † Then Elihu answered and said:
2 Do you think it right to say,
"I am in the right, not God"?*
3 When you ask what it profits you,
"What advantage do I have from not sinning?"*
4 I have words for a reply to you†
and your friends as well.
5 Look up to the skies and see;
behold the heavens high above you.
6 If you sin, what do you do to God?
Even if your offenses are many, how do you affect him?
7 If you are righteous, what do you give him,
or what does he receive from your hand?*
8 Your wickedness affects only someone like yourself,
and your justice, only a fellow human being.
9 In great oppression people cry out;
they call for help because of the power of the great,
10 No one says, "Where is God, my Maker,
who gives songs in the night,
11 Teaches us more than the beasts of the earth,
and makes us wiser than the birds of the heavens?"
12 Though thus they cry out, he does not answer
because of the pride of the wicked.
13 But it is idle to say God does not hear
or that the Almighty does not take notice.
14 Even though you say, "You take no notice of it,"†
the case is before him; with trembling wait upon him.
15 But now that you have done otherwise, God's anger punishes,
nor does he show much concern over a life.
16 Yet Job to no purpose opens his mouth,
multiplying words without knowledge.*

36 1 Elihu continued and said:
2 Wait a little and I will instruct you,
for there are still words to be said for God.
3 I will assemble arguments from afar,
and for my maker I will establish what is right.
4 For indeed, my words are not a lie;
one perfect in knowledge is before you.
5 Look, God is great, not disdainful;
his strength of purpose is great.
He does not preserve the life of the wicked.
6 He establishes the right of the poor;*

† **34:26, 29–30** The extant Hebrew text of these verses is obscure.
35:1 See note on 34:1.
35:4 *A reply to you:* Elihu refers to Job's statement that the innocent suffer as much as the wicked, and especially to Eliphaz's words in 22:2–3.
35:14–15 The text here is uncertain. It seems to indicate that Job should have realized God's indifference is only apparent, and that, because he has not done so, God will punish him.

* **34:20** Jb 21:13.
34:24 Ps 2:9.
34:35 Jb 35:16; 38:2; 42:3.
35:2 Jb 32:2.
35:3 Jb 34:9.
35:7 Jb 22:3; 41:2; Lk 17:10; Rom 11:35.
35:16 Jb 34:35; 38:2; 42:3.
36:6 Ps 72:4, 12–13.

he does not divert his eyes from the just
7 But he seats them upon thrones
with kings, exalted forever.*
8 If they are bound with fetters,
held fast by bonds of affliction,
9 He lets them know what they have done,
and how arrogant are their sins.
10 He opens their ears to correction
and tells them to turn back from evil.
11 If they listen and serve him,
they spend their days in prosperity,
their years in happiness.
12 But if they do not listen, they pass to the grave,
they perish for lack of knowledge.
13 The impious in heart lay up anger;
they do not cry for help when he binds them;
14 They will die young—
their life† among the reprobate.
15 But he saves the afflicted through their affliction,
and opens their ears through oppression.
16† He entices you from distress,
to a broad place without constraint;
what rests on your table is rich food.
17 Though you are full of the judgment of the wicked,
judgment and justice will be maintained.
18 Let not anger at abundance entice you,
nor great bribery lead you astray.
19 Will your wealth equip you against distress,
or all your exertions of strength?
20 Do not long for the night,
when peoples vanish in their place.
21 Be careful; do not turn to evil;
for this you have preferred to affliction.
22† Look, God is exalted in his power.
What teacher is there like him?
23 Who prescribes for him his way?
Who says, "You have done wrong"?*
24 Remember, you should extol his work,
which people have praised in song.
25 All humankind beholds it;
everyone views it from afar.
26 See, God is great beyond our knowledge,
the number of his years past searching out.
27 He holds in check the waterdrops
that filter in rain from his flood,
28 Till the clouds flow with them
and they rain down on all humankind.
29† Can anyone understand the spreading clouds,
the thunderings from his tent?
30 Look, he spreads his light over it,
it covers the roots of the sea.
31 For by these he judges the nations,
and gives food in abundance.
32 In his hands he holds the lightning,
and he commands it to strike the mark.
33 His thunder announces him
and incites the fury of the storm.

37 1 At this my heart trembles
and leaps out of its place.
2 Listen to his angry voice†
and the rumble that comes forth from his mouth!
3 Everywhere under the heavens he sends it,
with his light, to the ends of the earth.
4 Again his voice roars,
his majestic voice thunders;
he does not restrain them when his voice is heard.
5 God thunders forth marvels with his voice;
he does great things beyond our knowing.
6 He says to the snow, "Fall to the earth";
likewise to his heavy, drenching rain.
7 He shuts up all humankind indoors,
so that all people may know his work.
8 The wild beasts take to cover
and remain quiet in their dens.
9 Out of its chamber the tempest comes forth;
from the north winds, the cold.
10 With his breath God brings the frost,
and the broad waters congeal.*
11 The clouds too are laden with moisture,
the storm-cloud scatters its light.
12† He it is who changes their rounds, according to his plans,
to do all that he commands them
across the inhabited world.
13 Whether for punishment or mercy,
he makes it happen.
14 Listen to this, Job!
Stand and consider the marvels of God!
15 Do you know how God lays his command upon them,
and makes the light shine forth from his clouds?
16 Do you know how the clouds are banked,

JB

36:14 *Life*: a miserable life before death or a shadowy existence in Sheol. *Reprobate*: cf. Dt 23:18–19.

36:16–20 The Hebrew text here is obscure. Although each verse makes some sense, they do not constitute a logical sequence.

36:22–25 These verses serve as an introduction to the hymn about the divine marvels, 36:26–37:24, which in some respects anticipates the tone and content of the Lord's speeches in chaps. 38–41.

36:29–31 The translation of these verses is uncertain.

37:2 *Voice*: the thunder.

37:12–13 The translation of these verses is uncertain.

36:7 Ps 113:7–8.
36:23 Jb 34:10; Is 40:13.
37:10 Ps 147:17.

the marvels of him who is perfect in
knowledge?
17 You, who swelter in your clothes
when calm lies over the land from the
south,
18 Can you with him spread out the firmament
of the skies,
hard as a molten mirror?†
19 Teach us then what we shall say to him;
we cannot, for the darkness, make our plea.
20 Will he be told about it when I speak?
Can anyone talk when he is being
destroyed?
21 Rather, it is as the light that cannot be seen
while it is obscured by the clouds,
till the wind comes by and sweeps them
away.†
22 From Zaphon† the golden splendor comes,
surrounding God's awesome majesty!
23 The Almighty! We cannot find him,
preeminent in power and judgment,
abundant in justice, who never oppresses.
24 Therefore people fear him;
none can see him, however wise their
hearts.†

JB

VIII. The Lord and Job Meet

38 1 Then the LORD† answered Job out of the
storm and said:

2 Who is this who darkens counsel
with words of ignorance?
3 Gird up your loins† now, like a man;
I will question you, and you tell me the
answers!*
4 Where were you when I founded the earth?
Tell me, if you have understanding.
5 Who determined its size? Surely you know?
Who stretched out the measuring line
for it?
6 Into what were its pedestals sunk,
and who laid its cornerstone,
7 While the morning stars sang together
and all the sons of God† shouted for joy?
8 Who shut within doors the sea,
when it burst forth from the womb,*
9 When I made the clouds its garment
and thick darkness its swaddling bands?
10 When I set limits for it
and fastened the bar of its door,
11 And said: Thus far shall you come but no
farther,
and here shall your proud waves stop?
12 Have you ever in your lifetime commanded
the morning
and shown the dawn its place
13 For taking hold of the ends of the earth,
till the wicked are shaken from it?
14 The earth is changed as clay by the seal,
and dyed like a garment;
15 But from the wicked their light is withheld,
and the arm of pride is shattered.
16 Have you entered into the sources of the sea,
or walked about on the bottom of the
deep?
17 Have the gates of death been shown to you,
or have you seen the gates of darkness?
18 Have you comprehended the breadth of the
earth?
Tell me, if you know it all.
19 What is the way to the dwelling of light,
and darkness—where is its place?
20 That you may take it to its territory
and know the paths to its home?
21 You know, because you were born then,
and the number of your days is great!†
22 Have you entered the storehouses of the
snow,
and seen the storehouses of the hail
23 Which I have reserved for times of distress,
for a day of war and battle?*
24 What is the way to the parting of the winds,
where the east wind spreads over the earth?
25 Who has laid out a channel for the downpour
and a path for the thunderstorm
26 To bring rain to uninhabited land,
the unpeopled wilderness;
27 To drench the desolate wasteland
till the desert blooms with verdure?
28 Has the rain a father?
Who has begotten the drops of dew?
29 Out of whose womb comes the ice,

†

37:18 *The firmament . . . mirror*: the ancients thought of the sky as a ceiling above which were the "upper waters" (cf. Gn 1:6–7; 7:11); when this ceiling became as hard as metal, the usual rain failed to fall on the earth (cf. Lv 26:19; Dt 28:23).

37:21 Elihu argues that even though God seems not to know our circumstances, he does know them, just as surely as the sun shines behind the clouds.

37:22 *Zaphon*: the mythical mountain of the gods; cf. note on 26:7.

37:24 The concluding remark of Elihu is ironic in view of the appearance of the Lord in the next chapter and Job's claim in 42:5.

38:1 Now the Lord enters the debate and addresses two discourses (chaps. 38–39 and 40–41) to Job, speaking of divine wisdom and power. Such things are altogether beyond the capacity of Job. *Out of the storm*: frequently the background of the appearances of the Lord in the Old Testament; cf. Ps 18; 50; Na 1:3; Hb 3:2–15.

38:3 *Gird up your loins*: prepare for combat—figuratively, be ready to defend yourself in debate.

38:7 *Sons of God*: see note on 1:6.

38:21 Ironic, but not a harsh rebuke.

*

38:3 Jb 40:2.
38:8 Gn 1:9.
38:23 Jos 10:11; Sir 46:5.

and who gives the hoarfrost its birth in the
skies,
30 When the waters lie covered as though with
stone
that holds captive the surface of the deep?
31 Have you tied cords to the Pleiades,†
or loosened the bonds of Orion?
32 Can you bring forth the Mazzaroth in their
season,
or guide the Bear with her children?
33 Do you know the ordinances of the heavens;
can you put into effect their plan on the
earth?
34 Can you raise your voice to the clouds,
for them to cover you with a deluge of
waters?
35 Can you send forth the lightnings on their
way,
so that they say to you, "Here we are"?
36 Who gives wisdom to the ibis,
and gives the rooster† understanding?
37 Who counts the clouds with wisdom?
Who tilts the water jars of heaven
38 So that the dust of earth is fused into a mass
and its clods stick together?
39 Do you hunt the prey for the lion
or appease the hunger of young lions,
40 While they crouch in their dens,
or lie in ambush in the thicket?
41 Who provides nourishment for the raven
when its young cry out to God,*
wandering about without food?

39

1 Do you know when mountain goats are
born,
or watch for the birth pangs of deer,
2 Number the months that they must fulfill,
or know when they give birth,
3 When they crouch down and drop their
young,
when they deliver their progeny?
4 Their offspring thrive and grow in the open,
they leave and do not return.
5 Who has given the wild donkey his freedom,
and who has loosed the wild ass from
bonds?
6 I have made the wilderness his home
and the salt flats his dwelling.
7 He scoffs at the uproar of the city,
hears no shouts of a driver.

Did You Know?

Heaven and Earth

The questions God asks Job about the formation of the cosmos (see Jb 38:4–38) give us a clue about how the ancient Israelites thought the universe was put together. They believed God had created it in three levels: the heavens, which were contained in a giant vault above the earth; the earth itself, which was a disk that rested on the waters of the abyss; and the abyss, which was the underworld. Over time the heavens and the earth developed symbolic meanings. The heavens became known as the place where God dwells and the earth as the place that humans inhabit. Even later, the abyss became known as the place of the dead.

▶ Jb 38:4–38

8 He ranges the mountains for pasture,
and seeks out every patch of green.
9 Will the wild ox consent to serve you,
or pass the nights at your manger?
10 Will you bind the wild ox with a rope in the
furrow,
and will he plow the valleys after you?
11 Will you depend on him for his great strength
and leave to him the fruits of your toil?
12 Can you rely on him to bring in your grain
and gather in the yield of your threshing
floor?
13 The wings of the ostrich† flap away;
her plumage is lacking in feathers.
14 When she abandons her eggs on the ground†
and lets them warm in the sand,
15 She forgets that a foot may crush them,
that the wild beasts may trample them;
16 She cruelly disowns her young
and her labor is useless; she has no fear.
17 For God has withheld wisdom from her
and given her no share in understanding.
18 Yet when she spreads her wings high,
she laughs at a horse and rider.

†

38:31–32 *Pleiades . . . Orion . . . Bear*: cf. 9:9. *Mazzaroth*: it is uncertain what astronomical group is meant by this Hebrew word; perhaps a southern constellation.

38:36 *Ibis . . . rooster*: the translation is uncertain.

39:13 The wings of the ostrich cannot raise her from the ground, but they help her to run swiftly.

39:14–16 People thought that, because the ostrich laid her eggs on the sand, she was thereby cruelly abandoning them; cf. Lam 4:3.

*

38:41 Ps 147:9.

Pray It!

Too Big to Understand

When God asks Job a series of questions about creation and good and evil, he's trying to make one simple point: You can never understand me. I am too big. You are too small.

The author of Job seems to be saying to readers, If you think you've got God all figured out—like Job's friends thought they had, or like even Job wanted to have—you're wrong. The author is reminding readers that God is a mystery—powerful and awesome beyond our imagination and control.

In your prayer time, reflect or journal on the following questions:

- In what ways has God been too big for you to understand?
- Do you expect God to provide you with happiness? peace? friends?
- What happens if God doesn't meet your expectations in the way you want them to be met?
- Can you let go of your expectations and trust in God's love? Why or why not?

▶ **Job, chapters 38–41**

19 Do you give the horse his strength,†
and clothe his neck with a mane?
20 Do you make him quiver like a locust,
while his thunderous snorting spreads terror?
21 He paws the valley, he rejoices in his strength,
and charges into battle.
22 He laughs at fear and cannot be terrified;
he does not retreat from the sword.
23 Around him rattles the quiver,
flashes the spear and the javelin.
24 Frenzied and trembling he devours the ground;
he does not hold back at the sound of the trumpet;
25 at the trumpet's call he cries, "Aha!"
Even from afar he scents the battle,
the roar of the officers and the shouting.
26 Is it by your understanding that the hawk soars,
that he spreads his wings toward the south?
27 Does the eagle fly up at your command
to build his nest up high?
28 On a cliff he dwells and spends the night,
on the spur of cliff or fortress.
29 From there he watches for his food;
his eyes behold it afar off.
30 His young ones greedily drink blood;
where the slain are, there is he.*

40 1 The LORD then answered Job and said:

2 Will one who argues with the Almighty be corrected?
Let him who would instruct God give answer!*

3 Then Job answered the LORD and said:

4† Look, I am of little account; what can I answer you?
I put my hand over my mouth.
5 I have spoken once, I will not reply;
twice, but I will do so no more.

6 Then the LORD answered Job out of the storm and said:

7 Gird up your loins now, like a man.
I will question you, and you tell me the answers!
8† Would you refuse to acknowledge my right?
Would you condemn me that you may be justified?
9 Have you an arm like that of God,
or can you thunder with a voice like his?
10 Adorn yourself with grandeur and majesty,
and clothe yourself with glory and splendor.
11 Let loose the fury of your wrath;
look at everyone who is proud and bring them down.
12 Look at everyone who is proud, and humble them.
Tear down the wicked in their place,
13 bury them in the dust together;

†

39:19–25 A classic description of a war horse.

40:4–5 Job's first reaction is humble, but also seemingly cautious.

40:8–14 The issue is joined in these verses, and the Lord seems to challenge Job to play God and to bring down the proud and wicked.

39:30 Mt 24:28; Lk 17:37. **40:2** Jb 38:3.

in the hidden world imprison them.
14 Then will I too praise you,
for your own right hand can save you.
15 Look at Behemoth,† whom I made along with you,
who feeds on grass like an ox.
16 See the strength in his loins,
the power in the sinews of his belly.
17 He carries his tail like a cedar;
the sinews of his thighs are like cables.
18 His bones are like tubes of bronze;
his limbs are like iron rods.
19 He is the first of God's ways,
only his maker can approach him with a sword.
20 For the mountains bring him produce,
and all wild animals make sport there.
21 Under lotus trees he lies,
in coverts of the reedy swamp.
22 The lotus trees cover him with their shade;
all about him are the poplars in the wadi.
23 If the river grows violent, he is not disturbed;
he is tranquil though the Jordan surges about his mouth.
24 Who can capture him by his eyes,
or pierce his nose† with a trap?
25 Can you lead Leviathan† about with a hook,
or tie down his tongue with a rope?
26 Can you put a ring into his nose,
or pierce through his cheek with a gaff?
27 Will he then plead with you, time after time,
or address you with tender words?
28 Will he make a covenant with you
that you may have him as a slave forever?
29 Can you play with him, as with a bird?
Can you tie him up for your little girls?
30 Will the traders bargain for him?
Will the merchants† divide him up?
31 Can you fill his hide with barbs,
or his head with fish spears?
32 Once you but lay a hand upon him,
no need to recall any other conflict!

41 1 Whoever might vainly hope to do so
need only see him to be overthrown.
2 No one is fierce enough to arouse him;
who then dares stand before me?
3 Whoever has assailed me, I will pay back—
Everything under the heavens is mine.
4 I need hardly mention his limbs,

Live It!

Why?

So, that's it? God just shows up, overwhelms Job with a bunch of questions he can't answer, and then gives Job back double everything he lost? God doesn't even answer Job's question about why he had to suffer!

And what about *our* questions? Why do innocent children die? Why is someone we love taken from us? Why do people die from hunger in a world that has so much? Why did that plane crash? Why did our friend die?

Why was Job satisfied with God's response? Perhaps Job's mind and heart struggled with God's answer, and his heart won. Maybe his heart told him to trust in God's love even when his mind couldn't understand the mystery of his suffering.

With Job the Israelite people began to see the suffering of innocent people as mystery and not as punishment. In the New Testament, this suffering would continue to be seen as mystery but also as something more. The death of Jesus—the ultimate innocent suffering person—and his Resurrection led to the understanding that God ultimately brings good out of the suffering of faithful people (see Jn 12:24–25 and the introduction to First Peter).

Thankfully, the story of our faith does not end with Jesus' suffering on the cross, but with the glory of Jesus' Resurrection. For Christians, death, sin, and suffering hold no power if we believe in the truth of the Resurrection. We may not be able to explain why bad things happen, but we are empowered by a faith that shows us that suffering and evil never have the final word.

▶ Jb 38:1—42:6

† **40:15** *Behemoth*: a primeval monster of chaos; identified by some scholars as the hippopotamus, on which the description of Behemoth is partially based. The point of the Behemoth-Leviathan passages is that only the Lord, not Job, can control the cosmic evil which these forces symbolize.

40:24 *Eyes . . . nose*: the only exposed parts of the submerged beast.

40:25 *Leviathan*: although identified by some scholars as the crocodile, it is more likely another chaos monster; see note on 3:8.

40:30 *Merchants*: lit., "Canaanites," whose reputation for trading was so widespread that their name came to be used for merchants; cf. Prv 31:24.

his strength, and the fitness of his
equipment.
5 Who can strip off his outer garment,
or penetrate his double armor?
6 Who can force open the doors of his face,
close to his terrible teeth?
7 Rows of scales are on his back,
tightly sealed together;
8 They are fitted so close to each other
that no air can come between them;
9 So joined to one another
that they hold fast and cannot be parted.
10 When he sneezes, light flashes forth;
his eyes are like the eyelids of the dawn.
11 Out of his mouth go forth torches;
sparks of fire leap forth.
12 From his nostrils comes smoke
as from a seething pot or bowl.
13 His breath sets coals afire;
a flame comes from his mouth.
14 Strength abides in his neck,
and power leaps before him.
15 The folds of his flesh stick together,
it is cast over him and immovable.
16 His heart is cast as hard as stone;
cast as the lower millstone.
17 When he rises up, the gods are afraid;
when he crashes down, they fall back.
18 Should a sword reach him, it will not avail;
nor will spear, dart, or javelin.
19 He regards iron as chaff,
and bronze as rotten wood.
20 No arrow will put him to flight;
slingstones used against him are but straw.
21 Clubs he regards as straw;
he laughs at the crash of the spear.
22 Under him are sharp pottery fragments,
spreading a threshing sledge upon the mire.
23 He makes the depths boil like a pot;
he makes the sea like a perfume bottle.
24 Behind him he leaves a shining path;
you would think the deep had white hair.
25 Upon the earth there is none like him,
he was made fearless.
26 He looks over all who are haughty,
he is king over all proud beasts.

42 1 Then Job answered the LORD and said:
2 I know that you can do all things,†
and that no purpose of yours can be
hindered.
3 "Who is this who obscures counsel with
ignorance?"
I have spoken but did not understand;
things too marvelous for me, which I did
not know.*
4 "Listen, and I will speak;
I will question you, and you tell me the
answers."
5 By hearsay I had heard of you,
but now my eye has seen you.†
6 Therefore I disown what I have said,
and repent in dust and ashes.†

IX. Epilogue

Job's Restoration

7 And after the LORD had spoken these words to
Job, the LORD said to Eliphaz the Temanite, "My
anger blazes against you and your two friends!†
You have not spoken rightly concerning me, as
has my servant Job. 8 So now take seven bulls and
seven rams, and go to my servant Job, and sac-
rifice a burnt offering for yourselves, and let my
servant Job pray for you.† To him I will show fa-
vor, and not punish your folly, for you have not
spoken rightly concerning me, as has my servant
Job." 9 Then Eliphaz the Temanite, and Bildad
the Shuhite, and Zophar the Naamathite, went
and did as the LORD had commanded them. The
LORD showed favor to Job.
10 The LORD also restored the prosperity of Job,
after he had prayed for his friends; the LORD even
gave to Job twice† as much as he had before.
11 Then all his brothers and sisters came to him,
and all his former acquaintances, and they dined
with him in his house. They consoled and com-
forted him for all the evil the LORD had brought
upon him, and each one gave him a piece of
money† and a gold ring.
12 * Thus the LORD blessed the later days of Job
more than his earlier ones. Now he had fourteen

42:2–4 In his final speech, Job quotes God's own words (see 38:2–3; 40:7).

42:5 In 19:25–27 Job had affirmed a hope to "see" (three times) his vindicator. Now he has seen the Lord about whom he had heard so much.

42:6 A difficult verse. Some doubt, in view of God's commendation in v. 7, that Job does in fact express repentance, and alternative translations are often given. Along with v. 5, it describes a change in Job, which the encounter with the Lord has brought about. *Dust and ashes*: an ambiguous phrase. It can refer to the human condition (cf. Gn 18:27; Jb 30:19) or to Job's ash heap (2:8).

42:7 The three friends of Job (Elihu is ignored in the epilogue) are criticized by the Lord because they had "not spoken rightly" (vv. 7–8).

42:8 An ironic touch: Job becomes the intercessor for his friends.

42:10 *Twice*: this is the fine for damage inflicted upon another; cf. Ex 22:3. The Lord pays up!

42:11 *A piece of money*: lit., *qesitah*, value unknown; also used in Gn 33:19; Jos 24:32. *Gold ring*: for the nose or ear.

42:3 Jb 34:35; 35:16; 38:2; Ps 131:1; Prv 30:18. **42:12** Jb 1:3.

thousand sheep, six thousand camels, a thou-
sand yoke of oxen, and a thousand she-donkeys.
13 He also had seven sons and three daughters:
14 the first daughter he called Jemimah, the sec-
ond Keziah, and the third Keren-happuch.† 15 In
all the land no other women were as beautiful as
the daughters of Job; and their father gave them
an inheritance† among their brothers.

16 After this, Job lived a hundred and forty
years; and he saw his children, his grandchildren,
and even his great-grandchildren.* 17 Then Job
died, old and full of years.

†

42:14 Job's daughters had names symbolic of their charms: *Jemimah*, dove; *Keziah*, precious perfume (cf. Ps 45:9); *Keren-happuch*, cosmetic jar—more precisely, a container for a black powder used like modern mascara.

42:15 Ordinarily daughters did not inherit property unless there were no sons; cf. Nm 27:1–11.

*

42:16 Jb 5:25–26.

The Book of

Psalms

Rock! Pop! Salsa! Rhythm and blues! Hip-hop! Rap! Jazz! Country! Alternative! We each have our own favorite music that somehow resonates with our being, and maybe even expresses our attitude and philosophy toward life. So much so that we often refer to it as *our* music, even though it was written by someone else. In the same way, we can say that the Psalms are Israel's music. They are the hymns or songs that Israel used in its Temple worship. They give voice to the souls of the Israelites and tell about the ups and downs of the Israelites' relationship with God.

At a Glance

Psalms is divided into five books without any particular organizing theme:

I. **First Book (Psalms 1–41).**
II. **Second Book (Psalms 42–72).**
III. **Third Book (Psalms 73–89).**
IV. **Fourth Book (Psalms 90–106).**
V. **Fifth Book (Psalms 107–150).**

Quick Facts

Inspired Authors: many, sometimes called psalmists
Themes: a variety
Of Note: The psalms are used by Catholic Christians regularly at Mass and in the Church's official prayer, the Liturgy of the Hours.

In Depth

The Hebrew version of Psalms is titled *Tehillim*, or Praises, because its hymns praise God. The Greek translation calls them *Psalmoi*, or Psalms, which means "religious songs performed to music." The 150 Psalms can be grouped into one or more of five general categories:

- The *hymns of praise and thanksgiving* sing of God's majesty, power, and wisdom (for example, Psalms 8, 24, 47, 93, 95–99, 113–118, 136, and 150).
- The *hymns of lament or petition* include both individual and communal cries to God for help in some need (for example, Psalms 38, 51, 55, 58, 59, 74, 78, 105, and 106).
- The *hymns of wisdom* sing of Israel's insights into how to live according to God's law and what brings true happiness (for example, Psalms 1, 34, 37, 49, 73, 112, and 128).
- The *liturgical or worship psalms* are used for entrance hymns at liturgies or during worship services at the Temple (for example, Psalms 15, 24, and 134).
- The *historical psalms* sing of the great wonders God has worked throughout the history of Israel (for example, Psalms 78, 105, 106, 135, and 136).

Because of King David's reputation for writing and performing music, he is named as the author of many of the Psalms. Actually, though, many of them were written long after his death. It is more accurate to understand the Psalms as a collection of songs that reflect different times and experiences throughout Israel's existence. Just as your favorite music might tell others what you value as a person, the Psalms tell us about Israel and its wondrous relationship with God.

Psalms

Psalm 150

First Book—Psalms 1–41

PSALM 1†

True Happiness in God's Law

I

1 Blessed is the man who does not walk
in the counsel of the wicked,
Nor stand in the way† of sinners,
nor sit in company with scoffers.*
2 Rather, the law of the LORD† is his joy;
and on his law he meditates day and night.*
3 He is like a tree*
planted near streams of water,
that yields its fruit in season;
Its leaves never wither;
whatever he does prospers.

II

4 But not so are the wicked,† not so!
They are like chaff driven by the wind.*
5 Therefore the wicked will not arise at the
judgment,
nor will sinners in the assembly of the
just.
6 Because the LORD knows the way of the just,*
but the way of the wicked leads to ruin.

PSALM 2†

A Psalm for a Royal Coronation

1 Why do the nations protest
and the peoples conspire in vain?*
2 Kings on earth rise up
and princes plot together
against the LORD and against his anointed
one:†*
3 "Let us break their shackles
and cast off their chains from us!"*
4 The one enthroned in heaven laughs;
the Lord derides them,*

† **Psalm 1** A preface to the whole Book of Psalms, contrasting with striking similes the destiny of the good and the wicked. The Psalm views life as activity, as choosing either the good or the bad. Each "way" brings its inevitable consequences. The wise through their good actions will experience rootedness and life, and the wicked, rootlessness and death.

1:1 *The way*: a common biblical term for manner of living or moral conduct (Ps 32:8; 101:2, 6; Prv 2:20; 1 Kgs 8:36).

1:2 *The law of the LORD*: either the Torah, the first five books of the Bible, or, more probably, divine teaching or instruction.

1:4 *The wicked*: those who by their actions distance themselves from God's life-giving presence.

Psalm 2 A royal Psalm. To rebellious kings (Ps 2:1–3) God responds vigorously (Ps 2:4–6). A speaker proclaims the divine decree (in the legal adoption language of the day), making the Israelite king the earthly representative of God (Ps 2:7–9) and warning kings to obey (Ps 2:10–11). The Psalm has a messianic meaning for the Church; the New Testament understands it of Christ (Acts 4:25–27; 13:33; Heb 1:5).

2:2 *Anointed*: in Hebrew *mashiah*, "anointed"; in Greek *christos*, whence English Messiah and Christ. In Israel kings (Jgs 9:8; 1 Sm 9:16; 16:12–13) and high priests (Lv 8:12; Nm 3:3) received the power of their office through anointing.

* **1:1** Ps 26:4–5; 40:5.
1:2 Jos 1:8; Ps 119; Sir 39:1.
1:3 Ps 52:10; 92:13–15; Jer 17:8.
1:4 Ps 35:5; 83:14–16; Jb 21:18.
1:6 Ps 37:18.
2:1 Rev 11:18.
2:2 Ps 83:6.
2:3 Ps 149:8.
2:4 Ps 37:13; 59:9; Wis 4:18.

Did You Know?

Understanding the Psalms

"Praise God!" "Why am I suffering?" "Save us from oppression and injustice." "God, give me rest." These phrases illustrate types of prayer: praise, lament, and petition. The Book of Psalms includes these and many other kinds of prayer, made by individuals, small groups, or the whole Jewish nation. Yet, throughout the Psalms, there is one constant: human experience is viewed through the eyes of faith. For example, Psalm 3 reflects the human experience of being attacked by others (see verses 1–2).The writer of this psalm, rather than losing all hope, calls God to the rescue (see verse 7). In a similar way, all the Psalms teach us that every human experience can also be a faith experience.

PS

5 Then he speaks to them in his anger,
in his wrath he terrifies them:
6 "I myself have installed my king
on Zion, my holy mountain."
7 I will proclaim the decree of the LORD,
he said to me, "You are my son;
today I have begotten you.*
8 Ask it of me,
and I will give you the nations as your
inheritance,
and, as your possession, the ends of the
earth.
9 With an iron rod you will shepherd them,
like a potter's vessel you will shatter
them."*
10 And now, kings, give heed;
take warning, judges on earth.
11 Serve the LORD with fear;
exult with trembling,
Accept correction
lest he become angry and you perish along
the way
when his anger suddenly blazes up.*
Blessed are all who take refuge in him!

PSALM 3†

Threatened but Trusting

1 A psalm of David, when he fled from his
son Absalom.†*

I

2 How many are my foes, LORD!
How many rise against me!
3† How many say of me,
"There is no salvation for him in God."*
Selah
4 But you, LORD, are a shield around me;
my glory, you keep my head high.*

II

5 With my own voice I will call out to the LORD,
and he will answer me from his holy
mountain. *Selah*
6 I lie down and I fall asleep,
[and] I will wake up, for the LORD sustains
me.*
7 I do not fear, then, thousands of people
arrayed against me on every side.

III

8 Arise, LORD! Save me, my God!
For you strike the cheekbone of all my foes;
you break the teeth of the wicked.*
9 Salvation is from the LORD!
May your blessing be upon your people!*
Selah

PSALM 4†

Trust in God

1 For the leader;† with stringed instruments.
A psalm of David.

I

2 Answer me when I call, my saving God.
When troubles hem me in, set me free;
take pity on me, hear my prayer.*

†

Psalm 3 An individual lament complaining of enemies who deny that God will come to the rescue (Ps 3:2–3). Despite such taunts the psalmist hopes for God's protection even in sleep (Ps 3:4–7). The Psalm prays for an end to the enemies' power to speak maliciously (Ps 3:8) and closes peacefully with an expression of trust (Ps 3:9).

3:1 The superscription, added later, relates the Psalm to an incident in the life of David.

3:3, 3:5, 3:9 *Selah*: the term is generally considered a direction to the cantor or musicians but its exact meaning is not known. It occurs 71 times in 39 Psalms.

Psalm 4 An individual lament emphasizing trust in God. The petition is based upon the psalmist's vivid experience of God as savior (Ps 4:2). That experience of God is the basis for the warning to the wicked: revere God who intervenes on the side of the faithful (Ps 4:3–6). The faithful psalmist exemplifies the blessings given to the just (Ps 4:7–8).

4:1 *For the leader*: many Psalm headings contain this rubric. Its exact meaning is unknown but may signify that such Psalms once stood together in a collection of "the choirmaster," cf. 1 Chr 15:21.

*

2:7 Ps 89:27; 110:2–3; Is 49:1.
2:9 Rev 2:27; 12:5; 19:15.
2:11 Ps 34:9; 146:5; Prv 16:20.
3:1 2 Sm 15:13ff.
3:3 Ps 71:11.
3:4 Ps 7:11; 18:3; 62:7–8; Dt 33:29; Is 60:19.
3:6 Ps 4:9; Prv 3:24.
3:8 Ps 58:7.
3:9 Ps 28:9; Jon 2:10.
4:2 Ps 118:5.

II

3 How long, O people, will you be hard of heart?
Why do you love what is worthless, chase after lies?†* *Selah*
4 Know that the LORD works wonders for his faithful one;
the LORD hears when I call out to him.
5 Tremble† and sin no more;
weep bitterly† within your hearts,
wail upon your beds,*
6 Offer fitting sacrifices
and trust in the LORD.*

III

7 Many say, "May we see better times!
LORD, show us the light of your face!"* *Selah*
8 But you have given my heart more joy
than they have when grain and wine abound.
9*† In peace I will lie down and fall asleep,
for you alone, LORD, make me secure.

PSALM 5†

Prayer for Divine Help

1 For the leader; with wind instruments. A psalm of David.

I

2 Give ear to my words, O LORD;
understand my sighing.*
3 Attend to the sound of my cry,
my king and my God!
For to you I will pray, LORD;
4 in the morning you will hear my voice;
in the morning I will plead before you and wait.*

II

5 You are not a god who delights in evil;
no wicked person finds refuge with you;
6 the arrogant cannot stand before your eyes.
You hate all who do evil;
7 you destroy those who speak falsely.*
A bloody and fraudulent man
the LORD abhors.

III

8 But I, through the abundance of your mercy,†
will enter into your house.
I will bow down toward your holy sanctuary
out of fear of you.*
9 LORD, guide me in your justice because of my foes;
make straight your way before me.*

IV

10 For there is no sincerity in their mouth;
their heart is corrupt.
Their throat† is an open grave;*
on their tongue are subtle lies.
11 Declare them guilty, God;
make them fall by their own devices.*
Drive them out for their many sins;
for they have rebelled against you.

V

12 Then all who trust in you will be glad
and forever shout for joy.*
You will protect them and those will rejoice in you
who love your name.
13 For you, LORD, bless the just one;
you surround him with favor like a shield.

PSALM 6†

Prayer in Distress

1 For the leader; with stringed instruments, "upon the eighth."†
A psalm of David.

I

2 Do not reprove me in your anger, LORD,
nor punish me in your wrath.*
3 Have pity on me, LORD, for I am weak;

†

4:3 *Love what is worthless . . . lies*: these expressions probably refer to false gods worshiped by those the psalmist is addressing.

4:5 *Tremble*: be moved deeply with fear for failing to worship the true God. The Greek translation understood the emotion to be anger, and it is so cited in Eph 4:26. *Weep bitterly . . . wail*: weeping within one's heart and wailing upon one's bed denote sincere repentance because these actions are not done in public or with the community but in the privacy of one's heart and one's home. The same idiom is found in Hos 7:14.

4:9 *In peace I will . . . fall asleep*: the last verse repeats two themes in the Psalm. One is the security of one who trusts in the true God; the other is the interior peace of those who sincerely repent ("on [their] beds"), whose sleep is not disturbed by a guilty conscience.

Psalm 5 A lament contrasting the security of the house of God (Ps 5:8–9, 12–13) with the danger of the company of evildoers (Ps 5:5–7, 10–11). The psalmist therefore prays that God will hear (Ps 5:2–4) and grant the protection and joy of the Temple.

5:8 *Mercy*: used to translate the Hebrew word, *hesed*. This term speaks to a relationship between persons. It is manifested in concrete actions to persons with some need or desire. The one who offers *hesed* has the ability to respond to that need of the other person. Other possible ways to translate *hesed* include "steadfast love" and "loving kindness."

5:10 *Their throat*: their speech brings harm to their hearers (cf. Jer 5:16). The verse mentions four parts of the body, each a source of evil to the innocent.

Psalm 6 The first of the seven Penitential Psalms (Ps 6, 32, 38, 51, 102, 130, 143), a designation dating from the seventh century A.D. for Psalms suitable to express repentance. The psalmist does not, as in many laments, claim to be innocent but appeals to God's mercy (Ps 6:5). Sin here, as often in the Bible, is both the sinful act and its

*

4:3 Ps 62:4.
4:5 Eph 4:26.
4:6 Ps 51:19.
4:7 Ps 31:17; 44:4; 67:1; 80:4; Jb 13:24; Nm 6:25; Dn 9:17.
4:9 Ps 3:6.
5:2 Ps 86:6; 130:1–2.
5:4 Wis 16:28.
5:7 Ps 101:7; Wis 14:9; Heb 1:13.
5:8 Ps 138:2; Jon 2:5.
5:9 Ps 23:3; Prv 4:11; Is 26:7.
5:10 Rom 3:13.
5:11 Ps 141:10.
5:12 Ps 64:11.
6:2 Ps 38:2.

PS

Live It!

Our Cross to Bear

In Psalm 6, the psalmist is praying for deliverance from physical and mental suffering. Christians often refer to the suffering or sacrifice that comes as part of life as their cross to bear, because they see it as connected to Jesus' own suffering on the cross. Indeed, we all have crosses to bear. Some crosses are heavier than others, and like the psalmist, we ask God to deliver us from them. But unlike the psalmist, Christians also pray that God will transform their suffering and use it in some way for the good of others.

- What are some of the crosses you have had to bear? How were you saved from your suffering? How has someone else's suffering or sacrifice helped or inspired you?

▶ Psalm 6

heal me, LORD, for my bones are
shuddering.*
4 My soul too is shuddering greatly—
and you, LORD, how long . . . ?†*
5 Turn back, LORD, rescue my soul;
save me because of your mercy.
6 For in death there is no remembrance of you.
Who praises you in Sheol?†*

II

7 I am wearied with sighing;
all night long I drench my bed with tears;
I soak my couch with weeping.
8 My eyes are dimmed with sorrow,
worn out because of all my foes.*

III

9 Away from me, all who do evil!*
The LORD has heard the sound of my
weeping.
10 The LORD has heard my plea;
the LORD will receive my prayer.
11 My foes will all be disgraced and will shudder
greatly;
they will turn back in sudden disgrace.*

PSALM 7†

God the Vindicator

1 A plaintive song of David, which he sang to the LORD concerning Cush, the Benjaminite.

I

2 LORD my God, in you I trusted;
save me; rescue me from all who
pursue me,*
3 Lest someone maul me like a lion,
tear my soul apart with no one to
deliver.

II

4 LORD my God, if I have done this,†
if there is guilt on my hands,
5 If I have maltreated someone treating me
equitably—
or even despoiled my oppressor without
cause—
6 Then let my enemy pursue and overtake my
soul,
trample my life to the ground,
and lay my honor in the dust.* *Selah*

III

7 Rise up, LORD, in your anger;
be aroused against the outrages of my
oppressors.*
Stir up the justice, my God, you have
commanded.
8 Have the assembly of the peoples gather
about you;
and return on high above them,
9 the LORD will pass judgment on the
peoples.
Judge me, LORD, according to my
righteousness,

---

injurious consequences; here it is physical sickness (Ps 6:3–4, 7–8) and the attacks of enemies (Ps 6:8, 9, 11). The psalmist prays that the effects of personal and social sin be taken away.

6:1 *Upon the eighth*: apparently a musical notation, now lost.

6:4 *How long?*: elliptical for "How long will it be before you answer my prayer?" cf. Ps 13:2–3.

6:6 A motive for God to preserve the psalmist from death: in the shadowy world of the dead no one offers you praise. Sheol is the biblical term for the underworld where the insubstantial souls of dead human beings dwelt. It was similar to the Hades of Greek and Latin literature. In the second century B.C., biblical books begin to speak positively of life with God after death (Dn 12:1–3; Wis 3).

Psalm 7 An individual lament. The psalmist flees to God's presence in the sanctuary for justice and protection (Ps 7:2–3) and takes an oath that only the innocent can swear (Ps 7:4–6). The innocent psalmist can thus hope for the just God's protection (Ps 7:7–14) and be confident that the actions of the wicked will come back upon their own heads (Ps 7:15–17). The justice of God leads the psalmist to praise (Ps 7:18).

7:4 *Have done this*: in the accusation the enemies have made against the psalmist.

6:3 Jer 17:14–15.
6:4 Ps 13:2–3; 74:10; 89:47.
6:6 Ps 30:10; 88:11; 115:17; Is 38:18.
6:8 Ps 31:10; 38:11; 40:13.
6:9 Ps 119:115; Mt 7:23; Lk 13:27.
6:11 Ps 35:4, 26; 40:15; 71:13.
7:2 Ps 6:5; 22:21.
7:6 Ps 143:3.
7:7 Ps 9:4; 19:20.

and my integrity.
10 Let the malice of the wicked end.
Uphold the just one,
O just God,*
who tries hearts and minds.

IV

11 God is a shield above me
saving the upright of heart.*
12 God is a just judge, powerful and
patient,†
not exercising anger every day.
13 If one does not repent,
God sharpens his sword,
strings and readies the bow,*
14 Prepares his deadly shafts,
makes arrows blazing thunderbolts.*

V

15 Consider how one conceives iniquity;
is pregnant with mischief,
and gives birth to deception.*
16 He digs a hole and bores it deep,
but he falls into the pit he has made.*
17 His malice turns back upon his head;
his violence falls on his own skull.

VI

18 I will thank the LORD in accordance with his
justice;
I will sing the name of the LORD Most
High.*

PSALM 8†

Divine Majesty and Human Dignity

1 For the leader; "upon the *gittith*."†
A psalm of David.

2 O LORD, our Lord,
how awesome is your name through all the
earth!

I will sing of your majesty above the heavens
3 with the mouths of babes* and infants.†
You have established a bulwark† against your
foes,
to silence enemy and avenger.†
4 When I see your heavens, the work of your
fingers,
the moon and stars that you set in place—
5† What is man that you are mindful of him,*
and a son of man that you care for him?*
6 Yet you have made him little less than a god,†
crowned him with glory and honor.
7 You have given him rule over the works of
your hands,*
put all things at his feet:
8 All sheep and oxen,
even the beasts of the field,
9 The birds of the air, the fish of the sea,
and whatever swims the paths of the seas.

†

7:12 *Powerful and patient*: the inclusion of these words is drawn from the Septuagint tradition concerning this verse.

Psalm 8 While marvelling at the limitless grandeur of God (Ps 8:2–3), the psalmist is struck first by the smallness of human beings in creation (Ps 8:4–5), and then by the royal dignity and power that God has graciously bestowed upon them (Ps 8:6–9).

8:1 *Upon the gittith*: probably the title of the melody to which the Psalm was to be sung or a musical instrument.

8:3 *With the mouths of babes and infants*: the psalmist realizes that his attempts to praise such an awesome God are hopelessly inadequate and amount to little more than the sounds made by infants. *Established a bulwark*: an allusion to lost myth telling how God built a fortress for himself in the heavens in primordial times in his battle with the powers of chaos. This "bulwark" is the firmament. *Enemy and avenger*: probably cosmic enemies. The primeval powers of watery chaos are often personified in poetic texts (Ps 74:13–14; 89:11; Jb 9:13; 26:12–13; Is 51:9).

8:5 *Man . . . a son of man*: the emphasis is on the fragility and mortality of human beings to whom God has given great dignity.

8:6 *Little less than a god*: Hebrew *'elohim*, the ordinary word for "God" or "the gods" or members of the heavenly court. The Greek version translated *'elohim* by "angel, messenger"; several ancient and modern versions so translate. The meaning seems to be that God created human beings almost at the level of the beings in the heavenly world. Heb 2:9, translating "for a little while," finds the eminent fulfillment of this verse in Jesus Christ, who was humbled before being glorified, cf. also 1 Cor 15:27 where St. Paul applies to Christ the closing words of Ps 8:7.

*

7:10 Ps 17:3; 26:2; 35:24; 43:1; 139:23; Jer 17:10; 20:12.
7:11 Ps 3:4.
7:13 Ps 11:2.
7:14 Is 50:11.
7:15 Jb 15:35; Is 59:4.
7:16 Ps 9:16; 35:8; 57:7; Prv 26:27; Eccl 10:8; Sir 27:26.
7:18 Ps 18:50; 30:5; 135:3; 146:2.
8:3 Mt 21:16; Wis 10:21.
8:5 Ps 144:3; Jb 7:17.
8:5 Heb 2:6ff.
8:7ff Gn 1:26, 28; Wis 9:2; 1 Cor 15:27.

Live It!

Write Your Own Psalm

As you may know, there are many types of psalms (see the introduction to the Book of Psalms). You may also know that more than one person wrote the Psalms. Even today there are psalmists, people who write songs or poems similar in tone and style to the psalms in the Bible. Would you like to write your own psalm? Try it in your journal:

- Choose the type of psalm you want to write.
- Use poetic language and symbolism.
- Illustrate your psalm.
- Set it to music (like the original ones).
- Or, choose an existing Psalm and rewrite it to reflect a current issue.

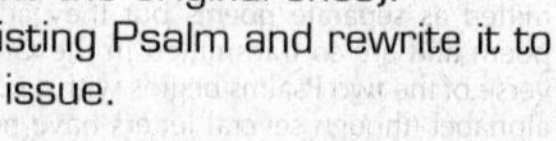

PS

10 O LORD, our Lord,
how awesome is your name through all the earth!

PSALM 9†

Thanksgiving for Victory and Prayer for Justice

1 For the leader; according to *Muth Labben*.†
A psalm of David.

I

2 I will praise you, LORD, with all my heart;
I will declare all your wondrous deeds.
3 I will delight and rejoice in you;
I will sing hymns to your name, Most High.
4 When my enemies turn back,
they stumble and perish before you.

II

5 For you upheld my right and my cause,
seated on your throne, judging justly.
6 You rebuked the nations, you destroyed the wicked;
their name you blotted out for all time.*
7 The enemies have been ruined forever;
you destroyed their cities;
their memory has perished.

III

8 The LORD rules forever,
has set up his throne for judgment.
9 It is he who judges the world with justice,*
who judges the peoples with fairness.
10 The LORD is a stronghold for the oppressed,
a stronghold in times of trouble.*
11 Those who know your name trust in you;
you never forsake those who seek you, LORD.

IV

12 Sing hymns to the LORD enthroned on Zion;
proclaim his deeds among the nations!
13 For the avenger of bloodshed remembers,
does not forget the cry of the afflicted.*

V

14 Be gracious to me, LORD;
see how my foes afflict me!
You alone can raise me from the gates of death.*
15 Then I will declare all your praises,
sing joyously of your salvation
in the gates of daughter Zion.†

VI

16 The nations fall into the pit they dig;
in the snare they hide, their own foot is caught.
17† The LORD is revealed in making judgments:
by the deeds they do the wicked are trapped.* *Higgaion. Selah*†

VII

18 To Sheol the wicked will depart,
all the nations that forget God.
19 For the needy will never be forgotten,
nor will the hope of the afflicted ever fade.*
20 Arise, LORD, let no mortal prevail;
let the nations be judged in your presence.
21 Strike them with terror, LORD;
show the nations they are only human.
Selah

PSALM 10

I

1 Why, LORD, do you stand afar
and pay no heed in times of trouble?
2 Arrogant scoundrels pursue the poor;
they trap them by their cunning schemes.*

II

3 The wicked even boast of their greed;
these robbers curse and scorn the LORD.*
4 In their insolence the wicked boast:
"God does not care; there is no God."*
5 Yet their affairs always succeed;
they ignore your judgment on high;
they sneer at all who oppose them.
6 They say in their hearts, "We will never fall;
never will we see misfortune."
7 Their mouths are full of oaths, violence, and lies;
discord and evil are under their tongues.*
8 They wait in ambush near towns;
their eyes watch for the helpless
to murder the innocent in secret.*
9 They lurk in ambush like lions in a thicket,
hide there to trap the poor,
snare them and close the net.*

---

†

Psalms 9–10 Ps 9 and Ps 10 in the Hebrew text have been transmitted as separate poems but they actually form a single acrostic poem and are so transmitted in the Greek and Latin tradition. Each verse of the two Psalms begins with a successive letter of the Hebrew alphabet (though several letters have no corresponding stanza). The Psalm states loosely connected themes: the rescue of the helpless poor from their enemies, God's worldwide judgment and rule over the nations, the psalmist's own concern for rescue (Ps 9:14–15).

9:1 *Muth Labben*: probably the melodic accompaniment of the Psalm, now lost.

9:15 *Daughter Zion*: an ancient Near Eastern city could sometimes be personified as a woman or a queen, the spouse of the god of the city.

9:17 *The LORD is revealed in making judgments*: God has so made the universe that the wicked are punished by the very actions they perform. *Selah*: see note on Ps 3:3.

---

*

9:6 Jb 18:17.
9:9 Ps 96:10; 98:9.
9:10 Ps 37:39; Is 25:4.
9:13 Jb 16:18.
9:14 Wis 16:13.
9:17 Ps 35:8; Sir 27:26.
9:19 Prv 23:18.
10:2 Is 32:7.
10:3 Ps 36:2.
10:4 Ps 14:1; Jb 22:13; Is 29:15; Jer 5:12; Zep 1:12.
10:7 Is 32:7; Rom 3:14.
10:8 Ps 11:2; Jb 24:14.
10:9 Ps 17:12; Prv 1:11; Jer 5:26.

PS

10 The helpless are crushed, laid low;
they fall into the power of the wicked,
11 Who say in their hearts, "God has forgotten,
shows no concern, never bothers to look."*

III

12 Rise up, LORD! God, lift up your hand!
Do not forget the poor!
13 Why should the wicked scorn God,
say in their hearts, "God does not care"?
14 But you do see;
you take note of misery and sorrow;*
you take the matter in hand.
To you the helpless can entrust their cause;
you are the defender of orphans.*
15 Break the arm of the wicked and depraved;
make them account for their crimes;
let none of them survive.

IV

16 The LORD is king forever;*
the nations have vanished from his land.
17 You listen, LORD, to the needs of the poor;
you strengthen their heart and incline your ear.
18 You win justice for the orphaned and oppressed;*
no one on earth will cause terror again.

PSALM 11†

Confidence in the Presence of God

1 For the leader. Of David.

I

In the LORD I take refuge;
how can you say to me,
"Flee like a bird to the mountains!*
2 See how the wicked string their bows,
fit their arrows to the string
to shoot from the shadows at the upright of heart.*
3† If foundations are destroyed,
what can the just one do?"

II

4 The LORD is in his holy temple;
the LORD's throne is in heaven.*
God's eyes keep careful watch;
they test the children of Adam.
5 The LORD tests the righteous and the wicked,
hates those who love violence,
6 And rains upon the wicked
fiery coals and brimstone,
a scorching wind their allotted cup.†*
7 The LORD is just and loves just deeds;
the upright will see his face.

PSALM 12†

Prayer Against Evil Tongues

1 For the leader; "upon the eighth."
A psalm of David.

I

2 Help, LORD, for no one loyal remains;
the faithful have vanished from the children of men.*
3 They tell lies to one another,
speak with deceiving lips and a double heart.*

II

4 May the LORD cut off all deceiving lips,
and every boastful tongue,
5 Those who say, "By our tongues we prevail;
when our lips speak, who can lord it over us?"*

III

6 "Because they rob the weak, and the needy groan,
I will now arise," says the LORD;
"I will grant safety to whoever longs for it."*

IV

7 The promises of the LORD are sure,
silver refined in a crucible,†
silver purified seven times.*
8 You, O LORD, protect us always;
preserve us from this generation.
9 On every side the wicked roam;
the shameless are extolled by the children of men.

† **Psalm 11** A song of trust. Though friends counsel flight to the mountain country (a traditional hideout) to escape trouble (Ps 11:1–3), the innocent psalmist reaffirms confidence in God, who protects those who seek asylum in the Temple (Ps 11:4–7).

11:3 *Foundations*: usually understood of public order, cf. Ps 82:5.

11:6 *Their allotted cup*: the cup that God gives people to drink is a common figure for their destiny, cf. Ps 16:5; 75:9; Mt 20:22; 26:39; Rev 14:10.

Psalm 12 A lament. The psalmist, thrown into a world where lying and violent people persecute the just (Ps 12:2–3), prays that the wicked be punished (Ps 12:4–5). The prayer is not simply for vengeance but arises from a desire to see God's justice appear on earth. Ps 12:6 preserves the word of assurance spoken by the priest to the lamenter; it is not usually transmitted in such Psalms. In Ps 12:7–8 the psalmist affirms the intention to live by the word of assurance.

12:7 *A crucible*: lit., "in a crucible in the ground." The crucible was placed in the ground for support.

* **10:11** Ps 44:25; 64:6; 73:11; 94:7; Ez 9:9.
10:14 Ps 31:8; 56:9; 2 Kgs 20:5; Is 25:8; Rev 7:17.
10:14 Ex 22:21–22.
10:16 Ps 145:13; Jer 10:10.
10:18 Dt 10:18.
11:1 Ps 55:7; 91:4.
11:2 Ps 7:13; 37:14; 57:5; 64:4.
11:4 Ps 14:2; 102:20; Hb 2:20; Dt 26:15; Is 66:1; Mt 5:34.
11:6 Ps 120:4; 140:11; Prv 16:27; Ez 38:22; Rev 8:5; 20:10.
12:2 Ps 14:3; 116:11; Is 59:15; Mi 7:2.
12:3 Ps 28:3; 55:22; Is 59:3–4; Jer 9:7.
12:5 Sir 5:3.
12:6 Is 33:10.
12:7 Ps 18:31; 19:8; Prv 30:5.

Live It!

Believing

Although it was written thousands of years ago, Psalm 14 could have been written about today's world. The earth is still filled with those who freely say there is no God. Our faith may tell us that such beliefs are foolish, but all people have the freedom to believe as they choose. One cannot be forced to believe in God.

How do we get through to those who refuse to believe? Perhaps the most powerful way we can show others that God exists is through our own actions. God's presence in our world is most clearly revealed when we love one another. We must also trust that God is already at work in the lives of those who do not believe, and hope that one day their eyes will be opened to the presence of God in their lives.

▶ Psalm 14

PSALM 13†

Prayer for Help

[1] For the leader. A psalm of David.

I

2 How long, LORD? Will you utterly forget me?
How long will you hide your face from me?*
3 How long must I carry sorrow in my soul,
grief in my heart day after day?
How long will my enemy triumph over me?

II

4 Look upon me, answer me, LORD, my God!
Give light to my eyes lest I sleep in death,
5 Lest my enemy say, "I have prevailed,"
lest my foes rejoice at my downfall.*

III

6 But I trust in your mercy.
Grant my heart joy in your salvation,
I will sing to the LORD,
for he has dealt bountifully with me!*

PSALM 14†

A Lament over Widespread Corruption

[1] For the leader. Of David.

I

The fool says in his heart,
"There is no God."
Their deeds are loathsome and corrupt;
not one does what is good.*
2 The LORD looks down from heaven
upon the children of men,*
To see if even one is wise,
if even one seeks God.*
3 All have gone astray;
all alike are perverse.
Not one does what is good,
not even one.*

II

4 Will these evildoers never learn?
They devour my people as they devour bread;*
they do not call upon the LORD.*
5 They have good reason, then, to fear;
God is with the company of the just.
6 They would crush the hopes of the poor,
but the poor have the LORD as their refuge.

III

7 *Oh, that from Zion might come
the salvation of Israel!
Jacob would rejoice, and Israel be glad
when the LORD restores his people!†

PSALM 15†

The Righteous Israelite

[1] *A psalm of David.

I

LORD, who may abide in your tent?†
Who may dwell on your holy mountain?†

---

† **Psalm 13** A typical lament, in which the psalmist feels forgotten by God (Ps 13:2–3)—note the force of the repetition of "How long." The references to enemies may suggest some have wished evil on the psalmist. The heartfelt prayer (Ps 13:4–5) passes on a statement of trust (Ps 13:6a), intended to reinforce the prayer, and a vow to thank God when deliverance has come (Ps 13:6b).

Psalm 14 The lament (duplicated in Ps 53) depicts the world as consisting of two types of people: "the fool" (equals the wicked, Ps 14:1–3) and "the company of the just" (Ps 14:4–6; also called "my people," and "the poor"). The wicked persecute the just, but the Psalm expresses the hope that God will punish the wicked and reward the good.

14:7 *Jacob . . . Israel . . . his people*: the righteous poor are identified with God's people.

Psalm 15 The Psalm records a liturgical scrutiny at the entrance to the Temple court (cf. Ps 24:3–6; Is 33:14b–16). The Israelite wishing to be admitted had to ask the Temple official what conduct was

---

* **13:2** Ps 6:4; 44:25; 77:8; 79:5; 89:47; 94:3; Lam 5:20.
13:5 Ps 38:17.
13:6 Ps 116:7.
14:1 Ps 10:4; 36:2; Is 32:6; Jer 5:12.
14:2–3 Rom 3:11–12.
14:2 Ps 11:4; 102:20.
14:3 Ps 12:1.
14:4 Ps 27:2; Is 9:11.
14:4 Ps 79:6.
14:7 Ps 85:2.
15:1 Is 56:7.

Cultural Connection

Living in Your Tent, on Your Holy Hill

Native Americans can appreciate the imagery of Psalm 15. Both tents and hills have a sacred meaning for them. The Lakota have the phrase *mit-a-ku-ye O-ya-sin*, which means "all my relatives." This phrase is often used at the end of a prayer, much like "amen." It expresses the deep belief that all human beings are our brothers and sisters, and we all belong in the Holy Tent of the Great Spirit. All creatures—the two-legged and the four-legged, those that crawl and those that fly—are our relatives. In fact, we are related to all of creation—the sea, the rocks, the caves, the sky, the trees, the holy hills. Native Americans understand human beings as connected to all creation, and they believe that any harm we do to creation we do to ourselves.

▶ **Psalm 15**

II

2 Whoever walks without blame,*
doing what is right,
speaking truth from the heart;
3 Who does not slander with his tongue,
does no harm to a friend,
never defames a neighbor;
4 Who disdains the wicked,
but honors those who fear the LORD;
Who keeps an oath despite the cost,
5 lends no money at interest,†
accepts no bribe against the innocent.*

III

Whoever acts like this
shall never be shaken.

PSALM 16†

God the Supreme Good

1 *A *miktam*† of David.

I

Keep me safe, O God;
in you I take refuge.
2 I say to the LORD,
you are my Lord,
you are my only good.
3 As for the holy ones who are in the land,
they are noble,
in whom is all my delight.
4† They multiply their sorrows
who court other gods.
Blood libations to them I will not pour out,
nor will I take their names upon my lips.
5 LORD, my allotted portion and my cup,
you have made my destiny secure.*
6† Pleasant places were measured out for me;
fair to me indeed is my inheritance.

II

7 I bless the LORD who counsels me;
even at night my heart exhorts me.
8 I keep the LORD always before me;
with him at my right hand, I shall never be
shaken.*
9 Therefore my heart is glad, my soul rejoices;
my body also dwells secure,
10 For you will not abandon my soul to Sheol,
nor let your devout one see the pit.†*

† appropriate to God's precincts. Note the emphasis on virtues relating to one's neighbor.

15:1 *Your tent*: the Temple could be referred to as "tent" (Ps 61:5; Is 33:20), a reference to the tent of the wilderness period and the tent of David (2 Sm 6:17; 7:2), predecessors of the Temple. *Holy mountain*: a venerable designation of the divine abode (Ps 2:6; 3:5; 43:3; 48:2, etc.).

15:5 *Lends no money at interest*: lending money in the Old Testament was often seen as assistance to the poor in their distress, not as an investment; making money off the poor by charging interest was thus forbidden (Ex 22:24; Lv 25:36–37; Dt 23:20).

Psalm 16 In the first section, the psalmist rejects the futile worship of false gods (Ps 16:2–5), preferring Israel's God (Ps 16:1), the giver of the land (Ps 16:6). The second section reflects on the wise and life-giving presence of God (Ps 16:7–11).

16:1 *Miktam*: a term occurring six times in Psalm superscriptions, always with "David." Its meaning is unknown.

16:4 *Take their names*: to use the gods' names in oaths and hence to affirm them as one's own gods.

16:6 *Pleasant places were measured out for me*: the psalmist is pleased with the plot of land measured out to the family, which was to be passed on to succeeding generations ("my inheritance").

16:10 *Nor let your devout one see the pit*: Hebrew *shahath* means here the pit, a synonym for Sheol, the underworld. The

* **15:2** Ps 119:1.
15:5 Ex 22:24; 23:8.
16:1 Ps 25:20.
16:5 Ps 23:5; 73:26; Nm 18:20; Lam 3:24.
16:8 Ps 73:23; 121:5, 8–12; Acts 2:25–28.
16:10 Ps 28:1; 30:4; 49:16; 86:13; Jon 2:7; Acts 13:35.

11 You will show me the path to life,
abounding joy in your presence,
the delights at your right hand forever.

PSALM 17†

Prayer for Rescue from Persecutors

1 A prayer of David.

I

Hear, LORD, my plea for justice;
pay heed to my cry;
Listen to my prayer
from lips without guile.
2 From you let my vindication come;
your eyes see what is right.
3 You have tested my heart,
searched it in the night.*
You have tried me by fire,
but find no malice in me.
My mouth has not transgressed
4 as others often do.
As your lips have instructed me,
I have kept from the way of the lawless.
5 My steps have kept to your paths;
my feet have not faltered.*

II

6 I call upon you; answer me, O God.
Turn your ear to me; hear my speech.
7 Show your wonderful mercy,
you who deliver with your right arm
those who seek refuge from their foes.
8† Keep me as the apple of your eye;
hide me in the shadow of your wings
9 from the wicked who despoil me.*

III

My ravenous enemies press upon me;*
10† they close their hearts,
they fill their mouths with proud roaring.
11 Their steps even now encircle me;
they watch closely, keeping low to the
ground,
12 Like lions eager for prey,
like a young lion lurking in ambush.
13 Rise, O LORD, confront and cast them down;
rescue my soul from the wicked.
14 Slay them with your sword;
with your hand, LORD, slay them;
snatch them from the world in their prime.
Their bellies are being filled with your friends;
their children are satisfied too,
for they share what is left with their young.
15 I am just—let me see your face;
when I awake, let me be filled with your
presence.*

PSALM 18†

A King's Thanksgiving for Victory

1 For the leader. Of David, the servant of the LORD,
who sang to the LORD the words of this song
after the LORD had rescued him from the clutches
of all his enemies and from the hand of Saul.
2 He said:*

I

I love you, LORD, my strength,
3 LORD, my rock, my fortress, my deliverer,
My God, my rock of refuge,
my shield, my saving horn,† my
stronghold!*
4 Praised be the LORD, I exclaim!
I have been delivered from my enemies.

II

5 The cords of death encompassed me;
the torrents of destruction terrified me.
6 The cords† of Sheol encircled me;
the snares of death lay in wait for me.*
7 In my distress I called out: LORD!
I cried out to my God.*
From his temple he heard my voice;
my cry to him reached his ears.
8† The earth rocked and shook;
the foundations of the mountains trembled;

---

† Greek translation derives the word here and elsewhere from the verb *shahath*, "to be corrupt." On the basis of the Greek, Acts 2:25–32; 13:35–37 apply the verse to Christ's resurrection, "Nor will you suffer your holy one to see corruption."

Psalm 17 A lament of an individual unjustly attacked. Confident of being found innocent, the psalmist cries out for God's just judgment (Ps 17:1–5) and requests divine help against enemies (Ps 17:6–9a). Those ravenous lions (Ps 17:9b–12) should be punished (Ps 17:13–14). The Psalm ends with a serene statement of praise (Ps 17:15). The Hebrew text of Ps 17:3–4, 14 is uncertain.

17:8 *Apple of your eye . . . shadow of your wings*: images of God's special care, cf. Dt 32:10; Prv 7:2; Is 49:2.

17:10–12, 14 An extended metaphor: the enemies are lions.

Psalm 18 A royal thanksgiving for a military victory, duplicated in 2 Sm 22. Thanksgiving Psalms are in essence reports of divine rescue. The Psalm has two parallel reports of rescue, the first told from a heavenly perspective (Ps 18:5–20), and the second from an earthly perspective (Ps 18:36–46). The first report adapts old mythic language of a cosmic battle between sea and rainstorm in order to depict God's rescue of the Israelite king from his enemies. Each report has a short hymnic introduction (Ps 18:2–4, 32–36) and conclusion (Ps 18:21–31, 47–50).

18:3 *My saving horn*: my strong savior. The horn referred to is the weapon of a bull and the symbol of fertility, cf. 1 Sm 2:10; Ps 132:17; Lk 1:69.

18:6 *Cords*: hunting imagery, the cords of a snare.

18:8–16 God appears in the storm, which in Palestine comes

---

* **17:3** Ps 26:2; 139:23.
17:5 Ps 18:36; Jb 23:11–12.
17:9–12 Ps 10:9; 22:14, 22; 35:17; 58:7; Jb 4:10–11.
17:9 Ps 36:8; 57:2; 61:5; 63:8; 91:4; Dt 32:10; Ru 2:12; Zec 2:12; Mt 23:37.
17:15 Ps 4:7; 31:17; 67:2; 80:4; Nm 6:25; Dn 9:17.
18:2–51 2 Sm 22:2–51.
18:3 Ps 3:4; 31:3–4; 42:10; Gn 49:24; Dt 32:4.
18:6 Ps 88:8; 93:3–4; 116:3–4.
18:7 Jon 2:3.

they shook as his wrath flared up.*
9 Smoke rose from his nostrils,
a devouring fire from his mouth;
it kindled coals into flame.
10 He parted the heavens and came down,
a dark cloud under his feet.*
11 Mounted on a cherub† he flew,
borne along on the wings of the wind.
12 He made darkness his cloak around him;
his canopy, water-darkened stormclouds.
13 From the gleam before him, his clouds passed,
hail and coals of fire.*
14 The LORD thundered from heaven;
the Most High made his voice resound.*
15 He let fly his arrows† and scattered them;
shot his lightning bolts and dispersed them.*
16 Then the bed of the sea appeared;
the world's foundations lay bare,*
At your rebuke, O LORD,
at the storming breath of your nostrils.
17 He reached down from on high and seized me;
drew me out of the deep waters.*
18 He rescued me from my mighty enemy,
from foes too powerful for me.
19 They attacked me on my day of distress,
but the LORD was my support.
20 He set me free in the open;
he rescued me because he loves me.

III

21 The LORD acknowledged my righteousness,
rewarded my clean hands.*
22 For I kept the ways of the LORD;
I was not disloyal to my God.
23 For his laws were all before me,
his decrees I did not cast aside.
24 I was honest toward him;
I was on guard against sin.
25 So the LORD rewarded my righteousness,
the cleanness of my hands in his sight.
26 Toward the faithful you are faithful;
to the honest man you are honest;*
27 Toward the pure, you are pure;
but to the perverse you are devious.
28 For humble people you save;
haughty eyes you bring low.*
29 For you, LORD, give light to my lamp;
my God brightens my darkness.*
30 With you I can rush an armed band,
with my God to help I can leap a wall.
31 God's way is unerring;
the LORD's promise is refined;
he is a shield for all who take refuge in him.*

IV

32 Truly, who is God except the LORD?
Who but our God is the rock?*
33 This God who girded me with might,
kept my way unerring,
34 Who made my feet like a deer's,
and set me on the heights,*
35 Who trained my hands for war,
my arms to string a bow of bronze.†*

V

36 You have given me your saving shield;
your right hand has upheld me;
your favor made me great.
37 You made room for my steps beneath me;
my ankles never twisted.*
38 I pursued my enemies and overtook them;
I did not turn back till I destroyed them.
39 I decimated them; they could not rise;
they fell at my feet.
40 You girded me with valor for war,
subjugated my opponents beneath me.
41 You made my foes expose their necks to me;
those who hated me I silenced.
42 They cried for help, but no one saved them;
cried to the LORD but received no answer.
43 I ground them to dust before the wind;
I left them like mud in the streets.
44 You rescued me from the strife of peoples;
you made me head over nations.
A people I had not known served me;
45 as soon as they heard of me they obeyed.
Foreigners submitted before me;
46 foreigners cringed;
they came cowering from their dungeons.*

VI

47 The LORD lives! Blessed be my rock!*
Exalted be God, my savior!

† from the west. The introduction to the theophany (Ps 18:8–9) is probably a description of a violent, hot, and dry east-wind storm. In the fall transition period from the rainless summer to the rainy winter such storms regularly precede the rains, cf. Ex 14:21–22.

18:11 *Cherub*: a winged creature, derived from myth, in the service of the deity (Gn 3:24; Ex 25:18–20; 37:6–9). Cherubim were the throne bearers of the deity (Ps 80:2; 99:1; 1 Kgs 6:23–28; 8:6–8).

18:15 *Arrows*: lightning.

18:35 *Bow of bronze*: hyperbole for a bow difficult to bend and therefore capable of propelling an arrow with great force.

* **18:8** Ps 97:3–4; 99:1; Jgs 5:4–5; Is 64:1; Heb 3:9–11.
18:10 Ps 104:3; 144:5; Is 63:19.
18:13 Ex 13:21; 19:16.
18:14 Ps 29; 77:19; Ex 19:19; Jb 37:3–4.
18:15 Ps 144:6; Wis 5:21.
18:16 Ps 77:17; Zec 9:14.
18:17 Ps 144:7.
18:21 Ps 26; 1 Sm 26:23.
18:26 Ps 125:4.
18:28 Jb 22:29; Prv 3:34.
18:29 Ps 27:1; 36:10; 43:3; 119:105; Jb 29:3; Mi 7:8.
18:31 Ps 12:6; 77:13; Prv 30:5.
18:32 Is 44:8; 45:21.
18:34 Heb 3:19.
18:35 Ps 144:1.
18:37 Ps 17:5.
18:46 Mi 7:17.
18:47 Ps 144:1.

Pray It!

"The Heavens Declare the Glory of God"

Does that opening line of Psalm 19 sound familiar? Perhaps you've seen it on a poster or sung it at Mass. The sky constantly tells us how glorious and magnificent God is!

Have you ever watched the awesome show of a thunder and lightning storm? been delighted by a rainbow? marveled at the power behind a tornado or a hurricane? been tickled by a gentle spring breeze? caught snowflakes on your tongue? had leaves dance around you in a brisk autumn wind? lost yourself looking up into a star-filled night? felt breathless watching a magnificent sunset?

As amazing as the sky is, it only hints at how amazing God is! And in the second half of Psalm 19, the psalmist reminds us that God's law is equally wonderful. Read Psalm 19 as your own prayer of praise to God for the many ways God communicates to us.

▶ Psalm 19

PS

48 O God who granted me vengeance,
made peoples subject to me,*
49 and saved me from my enemies,
Truly you have elevated me above my opponents,
from a man of lawlessness you have rescued me.
50 Thus I will praise you, LORD, among the nations;
I will sing praises to your name.*
51 You have given great victories to your king,
and shown mercy to his anointed,
to David and his posterity forever.*

PSALM 19†

God's Glory in the Heavens and in the Law

1 For the leader. A psalm of David.

I

2 The heavens declare the glory of God;
the firmament proclaims the works of his hands.*
3 Day unto day pours forth speech;
night unto night whispers knowledge.
4† There is no speech, no words;
their voice is not heard;
5 A report goes forth through all the earth,
their messages, to the ends of the world.
He has pitched in them a tent for the sun;†
6 it comes forth like a bridegroom from his canopy,
and like a hero joyfully runs its course.
7 From one end of the heavens it comes forth;
its course runs through to the other;
nothing escapes its heat.

II

8 The law of the LORD is perfect,
refreshing the soul.
The decree of the LORD is trustworthy,
giving wisdom to the simple.*
9 The precepts of the LORD are right,
rejoicing the heart.
The command of the LORD is clear,
enlightening the eye.
10 The fear of the LORD is pure,
enduring forever.
The statutes of the LORD are true,
all of them just;
11 More desirable than gold,
than a hoard of purest gold,
Sweeter also than honey
or drippings from the comb.*
12 By them your servant is warned;†
obeying them brings much reward.

III

13 Who can detect trespasses?
Cleanse me from my inadvertent sins.
14 Also from arrogant ones restrain your servant;
let them never control me.
Then shall I be blameless,
innocent of grave sin.
15 Let the words of my mouth be acceptable,

---

† **Psalm 19** The heavenly elements of the world, now beautifully arranged, bespeak the power and wisdom of their creator (Ps 19:2–7). The creator's wisdom is available to human beings in the law (Ps 19:8–11), toward which the psalmist prays to be open (Ps 19:12–14). The themes of light and speech unify the poem.

19:4 *No speech, no words*: the regular functioning of the heavens and the alternation of day and night inform human beings without words of the creator's power and wisdom.

19:5 *The sun*: in other religious literature the sun is a judge and lawgiver since it sees all in its daily course; Ps 19:5b–7 form a transition to the law in Ps 19:8–11. The six synonyms for God's revelation (Ps 19:8–11) are applied to the sun in comparable literature.

19:12 *Warned*: the Hebrew verb means both to shine and to warn, cf. Dn 12:3.

---

* **18:48** Ps 144:2. **18:50** Ps 7:18; 30:5; 57:9; 135:3; 146:2; Rom 15:9. **18:51** Ps 89:28–37; 144:10; 1 Sm 2:10. **19:2** Ps 8:1; 50:6; 97:6. **19:8** Ps 12:7; 119. **19:11** Sir 24:19.

the thoughts of my heart before you,
LORD, my rock and my redeemer.

PSALM 20†

Prayer for the King in Time of War

1 For the leader. A psalm of David.

I

2 The LORD answer you in time of distress;
the name of the God of Jacob defend you!
3 May he send you help from the sanctuary,
from Zion be your support.*
4 May he remember† your every offering,
graciously accept your burnt offering, *Selah*
5 Grant what is in your heart,
fulfill your every plan.
6 May we shout for joy at your victory,†
raise the banners in the name of our God.
The LORD grant your every petition!

II

7 Now I know the LORD gives victory
to his anointed.*
He will answer him from the holy heavens
with a strong arm that brings victory.
8 Some rely on chariots, others on horses,
but we on the name of the LORD our God.*
9 They collapse and fall,
but we stand strong and firm.*
10 LORD, grant victory to the king;
answer when we call upon you.

PSALM 21†

Thanksgiving and Assurances for the King

1 For the leader. A psalm of David.

I

2 LORD, the king finds joy in your power;*
in your victory how greatly he rejoices!
3 You have granted him his heart's desire;
you did not refuse the request of his lips.
Selah
4 For you welcomed him with goodly blessings;
you placed on his head a crown of pure gold.
5 He asked life of you;
you gave it to him,
length of days forever.*
6 Great is his glory in your victory;
majesty and splendor you confer upon him.
7 You make him the pattern of blessings forever,
you gladden him with the joy of your face.
8 For the king trusts in the LORD,
stands firm through the mercy of the Most
High.

II

9 Your hand will find all your enemies;
your right hand will find your foes!
10 At the time of your coming
you will make them a fiery furnace.
Then the LORD in his anger will consume them,
devour them with fire.
11 Even their descendants you will wipe out
from the earth,
their offspring from the human race.
12 Though they intend evil against you,
devising plots, they will not succeed,
13 For you will put them to flight;
you will aim at their faces with your bow.

III

14 Arise, LORD, in your power!*
We will sing and chant the praise of your
might.

PSALM 22†

The Prayer of an Innocent Person

1 For the leader; according to "The deer of the
dawn."† A psalm of David.

I

2 My God, my God, why have you
abandoned me?
Why so far from my call for help,
from my cries of anguish?*
3 My God, I call by day, but you do not answer;

---

† **Psalm 20** The people pray for the king before battle. The people ask for divine help (Ps 20:2–6) and express confidence that such help will be given (Ps 20:7–10). A solemn assurance of divine help may well have been given between the two sections in the liturgy, something like the promises of Ps 12:6; 21:9–13. The final verse (Ps 20:10) echoes the opening verse.

20:4 *Remember*: God's remembering implies readiness to act, cf. Gn 8:1; Ex 2:24.

20:6 *Victory*: the Hebrew root is often translated "salvation," "to save," but in military contexts it can have the specific meaning of "victory."

Psalm 21 The first part of this royal Psalm is a thanksgiving (Ps 21:2–8), and the second is a promise that the king will triumph over his enemies (Ps 21:9–13). The king's confident prayer (Ps 21:3–5) and trust in God (Ps 21:8) enable him to receive the divine gifts of vitality, peace, and military success. Ps 21:14 reprises Ps 21:2. When kings ceased in Israel after the sixth century B.C., the Psalm was sung of a future Davidic king.

Psalm 22 A lament unusual in structure and in intensity of feeling. The psalmist's present distress is contrasted with God's past mercy in Ps 22:2–12. In Ps 22:13–22 enemies surround the psalmist. The last third is an invitation to praise God (Ps 22:23–27), becoming a universal chorus of praise (Ps 22:28–31). The Psalm is important in the New Testament. Its opening words occur on the lips of the crucified Jesus (Mk 15:34; Mt 27:46), and several other verses are quoted, or at least alluded to, in the accounts of Jesus' passion (Mt 27:35, 43; Jn 19:24).

---

* **20:3** Ps 128:5; 134:3.
20:7 Ps 18:51; 144:10; 1 Sm 2:10.
20:8 Ps 147:10–11; 2 Chr 14:10; Prv 21:31; 1 Sm 17:45; Is 31:1; 36:9.
20:9 Is 40:30.
21:2 Ps 63:12.
21:5 1 Kgs 3:14.
21:14 Nm 10:35.
22:2 Is 49:14; 54:7; Mt 27:46; Mk 15:34.

PS

by night, but I have no relief.*
4 Yet you are enthroned as the Holy One;
you are the glory of Israel.*
5 In you our fathers trusted;
they trusted and you rescued them.
6 To you they cried out and they escaped;
in you they trusted and were not
disappointed.*
7† But I am a worm, not a man,
scorned by men, despised by the people.*
8 All who see me mock me;
they curl their lips and jeer;
they shake their heads at me:*
9 "He relied on the LORD—let him deliver him;
if he loves him, let him rescue him."*
10 For you drew me forth from the womb,
made me safe at my mother's breasts.
11 Upon you I was thrust from the womb;
since my mother bore me you are my God.*
12 Do not stay far from me,
for trouble is near,
and there is no one to help.*

II

13 Many bulls† surround me;
fierce bulls of Bashan† encircle me.
14 They open their mouths against me,
lions that rend and roar.*
15 Like water my life drains away;
all my bones are disjointed.
My heart has become like wax,
it melts away within me.
16 As dry as a potsherd is my throat;
my tongue cleaves to my palate;
you lay me in the dust of death.†
17 Dogs surround me;
a pack of evildoers closes in on me.
They have pierced my hands and my feet
18 I can count all my bones.*
They stare at me and gloat;
19 they divide my garments among them;
for my clothing they cast lots.*
20 But you, LORD, do not stay far off;
my strength, come quickly to help me.
21 Deliver my soul from the sword,
my life from the grip of the dog.
22 Save me from the lion's mouth,
my poor life from the horns of wild bulls.*

III

23 Then I will proclaim your name to my
brethren;
in the assembly I will praise you:†*
24 "You who fear the LORD, give praise!
All descendants of Jacob, give honor;
show reverence, all descendants of Israel!
25 For he has not spurned or disdained
the misery of this poor wretch,
Did not turn away† from me,
but heard me when I cried out.
26 I will offer praise in the great assembly;
my vows I will fulfill before those who fear
him.
27 The poor† will eat their fill;
those who seek the LORD will offer praise.
May your hearts enjoy life forever!"*

IV

28 All the ends of the earth
will remember and turn to the LORD;
All the families of nations
will bow low before him.*
29 For kingship belongs to the LORD,
the ruler over the nations.*
30† All who sleep in the earth
will bow low before God;
All who have gone down into the dust
will kneel in homage.
31 And I will live for the LORD;
my descendants will serve you.
32 The generation to come will be told of the
Lord,
that they may proclaim to a people yet
unborn
the deliverance you have brought.*

†

22:1 *The deer of the dawn*: apparently the title of the melody.
22:7 *I am a worm, not a man*: the psalmist's sense of isolation and dehumanization, an important motif of Ps 22, is vividly portrayed here.
22:13–14 *Bulls*: the enemies of the psalmist are also portrayed in less-than-human form, as wild animals (cf. Ps 22:17, 21–22). *Bashan*: a grazing land northeast of the Sea of Galilee, famed for its cattle, cf. Dt 32:14; Ez 39:18; Am 4:1.
22:16 *The dust of death*: the netherworld, the domain of the dead.
22:23 *In the assembly I will praise you*: the person who offered a thanksgiving sacrifice in the Temple recounted to the other worshipers the favor received from God and invited them to share in the sacrificial banquet. The final section (Ps 22:24–32) may be a summary or a citation of the psalmist's poem of praise.
22:25 *Turn away*: lit., "hides his face from me," an important metaphor for God withdrawing from someone, e.g., Mi 3:4; Is 8:17; Ps 27:9; 69:18; 88:15.
22:27 *The poor*: originally the poor, who were dependent on God; the term (*'anawim*) came to include the religious sense of "humble, pious, devout."
22:30 Hebrew unclear. The translation assumes that all on earth (Ps 22:27–28) and under the earth (Ps 22:29) will worship God.

*

22:3 Sir 2:10.
22:4 Is 6:3.
22:6 Ps 25:3; Is 49:23; Dn 3:40.
22:7 Is 53:3.
22:8 Ps 109:25; Mt 27:39; Mk 15:29; Lk 23:35.
22:9 Ps 71:11; Wis 2:18–20; Mt 27:43.
22:11 Ps 71:6; Is 44:2; 46:3.
22:12 Ps 35:22; 38:22; 71:12.
22:14 Ps 17:12; Jb 4:10; 1 Pt 5:8.
22:18 Ps 109:24.
22:19 Mt 27:35; Mk 15:24; Lk 23:34; Jn 19:24.
22:22 Ps 7:2–3; 17:12; 35:17; 57:5; 58:7; 2 Tm 4:17.
22:23 Ps 26:12; 35:18; 40:10; 109:30; 149:1; 2 Sm 22:50; Heb 2:12.
22:27 Ps 23:5; 69:33.
22:28 Ps 86:9; Tb 13:11; Is 45:22; 52:10; Zec 14:16.
22:29 Ps 103:19; Ob 21; Zec 14:9.
22:32 Ps 48:14–15; 71:18; 78:6; 102:19; Is 53:10.

Cultural Connection

The Good Shepherd Looks After Us

The famous Psalm 23 offers two images of God: the Good Shepherd and a generous host. Both images speak of God's closeness and gentle care for us. In the New Testament, Jesus appears as the Good Shepherd who gives his life for the life of his sheep (see Jn 10:1–29). He also appears several times as a host, particularly in the stories about the multiplication of the loaves and the Last Supper.

Similar images repeat time and again in Hispanic homes. The following traditional sayings are just some examples of the caring and generous attitudes among Hispanic families: My home is your home *(Mi casa es su casa)*; God help you! What can I do for you? *(¡Dios te ampare! ¿Cómo puedo ayudarte?)*; Where two eat, three eat; where six eat, seven eat *(Donde comen dos comen tres; donde comen seis comen siete)*; Welcome! We just add water to the beans *(¡Bienvenidos! Le echamos más agua a los frijoles)*; and Stay with us! From wall to wall, all is mattress *(¡Quédense con nosotros! De pared a pared todo es colchón!)*.

As a Christian, you should pray Psalm 23, feeling the closeness of Jesus, the Good Shepherd, and asking his help to be a good shepherd for people in need:

- Pray the psalm slowly, letting God fill you with peace and security.
- Pray the psalm again, this time thinking of friends who might be feeling like sheep without a shepherd. How can you lead them to Jesus? How can you care more for them?

▶ **Psalm 23**

PSALM 23†

The Lord, Shepherd and Host

1 A psalm of David.

I

The Lord is my shepherd;†
there is nothing I lack.*
2 In green pastures he makes me lie down;
to still waters he leads me;
3 *he restores my soul.
He guides me along right paths†
for the sake of his name.
4 Even though I walk through the valley of the shadow of death,*
I will fear no evil, for you are with me;
your rod and your staff comfort me.

II

5† You set a table before me
in front of my enemies;†
You anoint my head with oil;†*
my cup overflows.*
6 Indeed, goodness and mercy† will pursue me
all the days of my life;
I will dwell in the house of the Lord*
for endless days.

PSALM 24†

The Glory of God in Procession to Zion

1 A psalm of David.

I

The earth is the Lord's and all it holds,*
the world and those who dwell in it.
2 For he founded it on the seas,
established it over the rivers.*

II

3 Who may go up the mountain of the Lord?*
Who can stand in his holy place?

---

† **Psalm 23** God's loving care for the psalmist is portrayed under the figures of a shepherd for the flock (Ps 23:1–4) and a host's generosity toward a guest (Ps 23:5–6). The imagery of both sections is drawn from traditions of the exodus (Is 40:11; 49:10; Jer 31:10).

23:1 *My shepherd*: God as good shepherd is common in both the Old Testament and the New Testament (Ez 34:11–16; Jn 10:11–18).

23:3 *Right paths*: connotes "right way" and "way of righteousness."

23:5 *You set a table before me*: this expression occurs in an exodus context in Ps 78:19. *In front of my enemies*: my enemies see that I am God's friend and guest. *Oil*: a perfumed ointment made from olive oil, used especially at banquets (Ps 104:15; Mt 26:7; Lk 7:37, 46; Jn 12:2).

23:6 *Goodness and mercy*: the blessings of God's covenant with Israel.

Psalm 24 The Psalm apparently accompanied a ceremony of the entry of God (invisibly enthroned upon the ark), followed by the people, into the Temple. The Temple commemorated the creation of the world (Ps 24:1–2). The people had to affirm their fidelity before being admitted into the sanctuary (Ps 24:3–6; cf. Ps 15). A choir identifies the approaching God and invites the very Temple gates to bow down in obeisance (Ps 24:7–10).

23:1 Ps 80:2; 95:7; 100:3; Dt 2:7.
23:3 Prv 4:11.
23:4 Jb 10:21–22; Is 50:10.
23:5 Ps 92:11.
23:5 Ps 16:5.
23:6 Ps 27:4.
24:1 Ps 50:12; 89:12; Dt 10:14; 1 Cor 10:26.
24:2 Ps 136:6; Is 42:5.
24:3 Ps 15:1.

Did You Know?

Temple Worship

When Israel was ruled by kings (1000–587 BC), worship in the Temple at Jerusalem was an important part of the people's religious life. Many of the psalms, like Psalm 24, refer to going up to the Temple (the "holy place" in verse 3). Although the first Temple was destroyed in 587 BC, it was later rebuilt. Temple worship started again and continued into Jesus' time. This is what the priests did during some of the Temple ceremonies:

Daily Temple worship
- every morning, presented a burnt offering (a year-old male lamb), grain, drink, and an incense offering
- every evening, presented a second burnt offering and a cereal offering

Sabbath (weekly) Temple worship
- gave two additional burnt offerings
- replaced the twelve loaves of bread, called the bread of Presence (see 1 Kgs 7:48, Mt 12:4, Heb 9:2), recalling the manna with which God fed Israel in the desert
- made an incense offering

Monthly and festival Temple worship
- blew the trumpet
- presented additional burnt offerings and a sin offering (a male goat)
- on the Day of Atonement, laid their hands on a living goat while confessing the people's sins and then sent the goat away into the wilderness

4† "The clean of hand and pure of heart,
who has not given his soul to useless things,
what is vain.
5 He will receive blessings from the LORD,
and justice from his saving God.
6 Such is the generation that seeks him,
that seeks the face of the God of Jacob."
Selah

III

7 Lift up your heads, O gates;†
be lifted, you ancient portals,
that the king of glory may enter.*
8 Who is this king of glory?
The LORD, strong and mighty,
the LORD, mighty in war.
9 Lift up your heads, O gates;
rise up, you ancient portals,
that the king of glory may enter.
10 Who is this king of glory?
The LORD of hosts, he is the king of glory.
Selah

PSALM 25†

Confident Prayer for Forgiveness and Guidance

1 Of David.

I

To you, O LORD, I lift up my soul,
2 *my God, in you I trust;
do not let me be disgraced;*
do not let my enemies gloat over me.
3 No one is disgraced who waits for you,*
but only those who are treacherous without cause.
4 Make known to me your ways, LORD;
teach me your paths.*
5 Guide me by your fidelity and teach me,
for you are God my savior,
for you I wait all the day long.
6 Remember your compassion and your mercy,
O LORD,
for they are ages old.*
7 Remember no more the sins of my youth;*
remember me according to your mercy,
because of your goodness, LORD.

II

8 Good and upright is the LORD,
therefore he shows sinners the way,
9 He guides the humble in righteousness,
and teaches the humble his way.
10 All the paths of the LORD are mercy and truth

†

24:4–5 Lit., "the one whose hands are clean." The singular is used for the entire class of worshipers.

24:7, 9 *Lift up your heads, O gates . . . you ancient portals*: the literal meaning would involve disassembly of the gates, since the portcullis (a gate that moves up and down) was unknown in the ancient world. Extra-biblical parallels might also suggest a full personification of the circle of gate towers: they are like a council of elders, bowed down and anxious, awaiting the return of the army and the great warrior gone to battle.

Psalm 25 A lament. Each verse begins with a successive letter of the Hebrew alphabet. Such acrostic Psalms are often a series of statements only loosely connected. The psalmist mixes ardent pleas (Ps 25:1–2, 16–22) with expressions of confidence in God who forgives and guides.

*

24:7 Ps 118:19–20.
25:2 Ps 86:4; 143:8.
25:2 Ps 71:1.
25:3 Ps 22:6; Is 49:23; Dn 3:40.
25:4 Ps 27:11; 86:11; 119:12, 35; 143:8, 10.
25:6 Sir 51:8.
25:7 Jb 13:26; Is 64:8.

toward those who honor his covenant and
decrees.
11 For the sake of your name, LORD,
pardon my guilt, though it is great.
12 Who is the one who fears the LORD?
God shows him the way he should
choose.*
13 He will abide in prosperity,
and his descendants will inherit the land.*
14 The counsel of the LORD belongs to those who
fear him;
and his covenant instructs them.
15 My eyes are ever upon the LORD,
who frees my feet from the snare.*

III

16 Look upon me, have pity on me,
for I am alone and afflicted.*
17 Relieve the troubles of my heart;
bring me out of my distress.
18 Look upon my affliction and suffering;
take away all my sins.
19 See how many are my enemies,
see how fiercely they hate me.
20 Preserve my soul and rescue me;
do not let me be disgraced, for in you I
seek refuge.
21 Let integrity and uprightness preserve me;
I wait for you, O LORD.
22† Redeem Israel, O God,
from all its distress!

PSALM 26†

Prayer of Innocence

1 Of David.

I

Judge me, LORD!
For I have walked in my integrity.*
In the LORD I trust;
I do not falter.
2 Examine me, Lord, and test me;
search my heart and mind.*
3 Your mercy is before my eyes;
I walk guided by your faithfulness.*

II

4 I do not sit with worthless men,
nor with hypocrites do I mingle.
5 I hate an evil assembly;
with the wicked I do not sit.
6 I will wash my hands† in innocence*
so that I may process around your altar,
Lord,
7 To hear the sound of thanksgiving,
and recount all your wondrous deeds.
8 Lord, I love the refuge of your house,
the site of the dwelling-place of your
glory.*

†

25:22 A final verse beginning with the Hebrew letter *pe* is added to the normal 22-letter alphabet. Thus the letters *aleph, lamed,* and *pe* open the first, middle (Ps 25:11), and last lines of the Psalm. Together, they spell *aleph*, the first letter of the alphabet, from a Hebrew root that means "to learn."

Psalm 26 Like a priest washing before approaching the altar (Ex 30:17–21), the psalmist seeks God's protection upon entering the Temple. Ps 26:1–3, matched by Ps 26:11–12, remind God of past integrity while asking for purification; Ps 26:4–5, matched by Ps 26:9–10, pray for inclusion among the just; Ps 26:6–8, the center of the poem, express the joy in God at the heart of all ritual.

26:6 *I will wash my hands*: the washing of hands was a liturgical act (Ex 30:19, 21; 40:31–32), symbolic of inner as well as outer cleanness, cf. Is 1:16.

*

25:12 Prv 19:23.
25:13 Ps 37:9, 29.
25:15 Ps 123:1, 2; 141:8.
25:16 Ps 86:16; 119:132.
26:1 Ps 7:9.
26:2 Ps 17:3; 139:23.
26:3 Ps 86:11.
26:6 Ps 73:13.
26:8 Ps 29:9; 63:3; Ex 24:16; 25:8.

Pray It!

Integrity and Values

People with integrity have a fundamental set of core values—values that have been instilled in them by parents, teachers, mentors, and role models. When they act, they consistently make sure all their actions and decisions accurately reflect these core principles. There is no disconnect between what they say they believe and what they actually do.

It is impossible for us to have integrity if we follow one set of values in one situation and another set of values in a different situation. The integrity of the writer of Psalm 26 comes from following God in everything (see Ps 26:1). The psalmist even wants to be tested by God (see verse 2) to be sure of complete faithfulness! To have the kind of integrity that the psalmist writes about, we have to let God be the only ruler of our lives. Being able to do that takes a lifetime of growth and conversion.

- What values are you committed to consistently?
- Can you think of times when your actions did not reflect your values or beliefs?

Pray that God will give you strength to do what is right, even when it is most difficult.

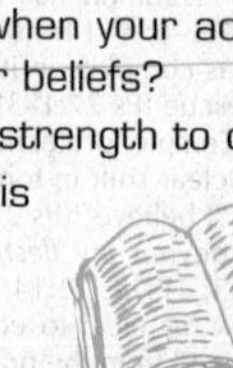

▶ Psalm 26

PS

III

9 Do not take me away with sinners,
nor my life with the men of blood,*
10 In whose hands there is a plot,
their right hands full of bribery.
11 But I walk in my integrity;*
redeem me, be gracious to me!*
12 My foot stands on level ground;†
in assemblies I will bless the LORD.*

PSALM 27†

Trust in God

1 *Of David.

A

I

The LORD is my light and my salvation;
whom should I fear?
The LORD is my life's refuge;
of whom should I be afraid?
2 When evildoers come at me
to devour my flesh,†*
These my enemies and foes
themselves stumble and fall.
3 Though an army encamp against me,
my heart does not fear;
Though war be waged against me,
even then do I trust.

II

4 One thing I ask of the LORD;
this I seek:
To dwell in the LORD's house
all the days of my life,
To gaze on the LORD's beauty,
to visit his temple.*
5 For God will hide me in his shelter
in time of trouble,*
He will conceal me in the cover of his tent;
and set me high upon a rock.
6 Even now my head is held high
above my enemies on every side!
I will offer in his tent
sacrifices with shouts of joy;
I will sing and chant praise to the LORD.

B

I

7 Hear my voice, LORD, when I call;
have mercy on me and answer me.
8 "Come," says my heart, "seek his face";†
your face, LORD, do I seek!*
9 Do not hide your face from me;
do not repel your servant in anger.
You are my salvation; do not cast me off;
do not forsake me, God my savior!
10 Even if my father and mother forsake me,
the LORD will take me in.*

II

11 LORD, show me your way;
lead me on a level path
because of my enemies.*
12 Do not abandon me to the desire of my foes;
malicious and lying witnesses have risen
against me.
13 I believe I shall see the LORD's goodness
in the land of the living.†*
14 Wait for the LORD, take courage;
be stouthearted, wait for the LORD!

PSALM 28†

Petition and Thanksgiving

1 Of David.

I

To you, LORD, I call;
my Rock, do not be deaf to me,*
Do not be silent toward me,
so that I join those who go down to the
pit.*
2 Hear the sound of my pleading when I cry to
you for help
when I lift up my hands toward your holy
place.†*
3 Do not drag me off with the wicked,
with those who do wrong,*

† **26:12** *On level ground*: in safety, where there is no danger of tripping and falling. *In assemblies*: at the Temple. Having walked around the altar, the symbol of God's presence, the psalmist blesses God.

Psalm 27 Tradition has handed down the two sections of the Psalm (Ps 27:1–6; 7–14) as one Psalm, though each part could be understood as complete in itself. Asserting boundless hope that God will bring rescue (Ps 27:1–3), the psalmist longs for the presence of God in the Temple, protection from all enemies (Ps 27:4–6). In part B there is a clear shift in tone (Ps 27:7–12); the climax of the poem comes with "I believe" (Ps 27:13), echoing "I trust" (Ps 27:3).

27:2 *To devour my flesh*: the psalmist's enemies are rapacious beasts (Ps 7:3; 17:12; 22:14, 17).

27:8 *Seek his face*: to commune with God in the Temple. The idiom is derived from the practice of journeying to sacred places, cf. Hos 5:15; 2 Sm 21:1; Ps 24:6.

27:13 *In the land of the living*: or "in the land of life," an epithet of the Jerusalem Temple (Ps 52:7; 116:9; Is 38:11), where the faithful had access to the life-giving presence of God.

Psalm 28 A lament asking that the psalmist, who has taken refuge in the Temple (Ps 28:2), not be punished with the wicked, who are headed inevitably toward destruction (Ps 28:1, 3–5). The statement of praise is exceptionally lengthy and vigorous (Ps 28:6–7). The Psalm ends with a prayer (Ps 28:8–9).

28:2 *Your holy place*: the innermost part of the Temple, the holy of holies, containing the ark, cf. 1 Kgs 6:16, 19–23; 8:6–8.

* **26:9** Ps 28:3.
26:11 Ps 101:6.
26:11 Ps 25:16.
26:12 Ps 22:23; 35:18; 149:1.
27:1 Ps 18:29; 36:10; 43:3; Is 10:17; Mi 7:8.
27:2 Ps 14:4.
27:4 Ps 23:6; 61:5.
27:5 Ps 31:21.
27:8 Ps 24:6; Hos 5:15.
27:10 Is 49:15.
27:11 Ps 25:4; 86:11.
27:13 Ps 116:9; Is 38:11.
28:1 Ps 18:2.
28:1 Ps 30:4; 88:5; 143:7; Prv 1:12.
28:2 Ps 134:2.
28:3 Ps 26:9.

Who speak peace to their neighbors
though evil is in their hearts.*
4 Repay them for their deeds,
for the evil that they do.
For the work of their hands repay them;
give them what they deserve.*
5 Because they do not understand the LORD's works,
the work of his hands,*
He will tear them down,
never to rebuild them.

II

6† Blessed be the LORD,
who has heard the sound of my pleading.
7 The LORD is my strength and my shield,
in whom my heart trusts.
I am helped, so my heart rejoices;
with my song I praise him.

III

8† LORD, you are a strength for your people,
the saving refuge of your anointed.
9 Save your people, bless your inheritance;
pasture and carry them forever!

PSALM 29†

The Lord of Majesty Acclaimed as King of the World

1 A psalm of David.

I

Give to the LORD, you sons of God,†
give to the LORD glory and might;
2 Give to the LORD the glory due his name.
Bow down before the LORD's holy splendor!*

II

3 The voice of the LORD† is over the waters;
the God of glory thunders,
the LORD, over the mighty waters.
4 The voice of the LORD is power;
the voice of the LORD is splendor.*
5 The voice of the LORD cracks the cedars;
the LORD splinters the cedars of Lebanon,
6 Makes Lebanon leap like a calf,
and Sirion† like a young bull.
7 The voice of the LORD strikes with fiery flame;
8 the voice of the LORD shakes the desert;
the LORD shakes the desert of Kadesh.
9† The voice of the LORD makes the deer dance
and strips the forests bare.
All in his Temple say, "Glory!"

III

10 The LORD sits enthroned above the flood!†*
The LORD reigns as king forever!
11 May the LORD give might to his people;†
may the LORD bless his people with peace!*

†

28:6 The psalmist shifts to fervent thanksgiving, probably responding to a priestly or prophetic oracle in Ps 28:5cd (not usually transmitted) assuring the worshiper that the prayer has been heard.

28:8 *Your people . . . your anointed*: salvation is more than individual, affecting all the people and their God-given leader.

Psalm 29 The hymn invites the members of the heavenly court to acknowledge God's supremacy by ascribing glory and might to God alone (Ps 29:1–2a, 9b). Divine glory and might are dramatically visible in the storm (Ps 29:3–9a). The storm apparently comes from the Mediterranean onto the coast of Syria-Palestine and then moves inland. In Ps 29:10 the divine beings acclaim God's eternal kingship. The Psalm concludes with a prayer that God will impart the power just displayed to the Israelite king and through the king to Israel.

29:1 *Sons of God*: members of the heavenly court who served Israel's God in a variety of capacities.

29:3 *The voice of the LORD*: the sevenfold repetition of the phrase imitates the sound of crashing thunder and may allude to God's primordial slaying of Leviathan, the seven-headed sea monster of Canaanite mythology.

29:6 *Sirion*: the Phoenician name for Mount Hermon, cf. Dt 3:9.

29:9b–10 Having witnessed God's supreme power (Ps 29:3–9a), the gods acknowledge the glory that befits the king of the divine and human world.

29:10 *The flood*: God defeated the primordial waters and made them part of the universe, cf. Ps 89:10–13; 93:3–4.

29:11 *His people*: God's people, Israel.

*

28:3 Ps 12:2; 55:22; 62:5; Prv 26:24–28.
28:4 2 Sm 3:39.
28:5 Is 5:12.
29:2 Ps 68:35; 96:7–9.
29:4 Ps 46:7; 77:18–19; Jb 37:4; Is 30:30.
29:10 Bar 3:3.
29:11 Ps 68:36.

The Eye of the Storm

Thunderstorms can be frightening. They often come up quickly and without warning. The winds and lightning that accompany them can be destructive. Children and animals (okay, lots of adults too) are often afraid at the sheer force of it all.

It would be difficult to read Psalm 29 aloud and not be expressive. Statements like "the God of glory thunders" (verse 3), "the voice of the LORD cracks the cedars" (verse 5), and "strikes with fiery flame" (verse 7) evoke a divine splendor that we do not often hear about. The psalmist speaks with admiration about the power and majesty of God.

When have you experienced the awesome power of God?

▶ **Psalm 29**

PS

Cultural Connection

Courage

Psalm 31 ends "Be strong and take heart, / all who hope in the Lord" (verse 25). Courage is an important value for many Native American peoples. For the Lakota tribe, it is one of four primary values. The Lakota word for courage is *woo-hit-i-ka*.

Leaders particularly have to be brave. It takes courage to make unpopular decisions and to go against peer pressure. It takes courage to do the right thing when the wrong thing might be easier or more enjoyable. It takes courage to protect others and to care for their needs. Because these kinds of actions take courage, practicing them will earn you honor.

What is the most courageous thing you have done for the sake of someone else?

To explore the other primary Lakota virtues, see the "Cultural Connections" articles for Psalms 73, 89, and 112.

▶ Psalm 31

PSALM 30†

Thanksgiving for Deliverance

1 A psalm. A song for the dedication of the Temple.† Of David.

I

2 I praise you, Lord, for you raised me up
and did not let my enemies rejoice over me.
3 O Lord, my God,
I cried out to you for help and you healed† me.
4 Lord, you brought my soul up from Sheol;
you let me live, from going down to the pit.†*

II

5 Sing praise to the Lord, you faithful;
give thanks to his holy memory.
6 For his anger lasts but a moment;
his favor a lifetime.
At dusk weeping comes for the night;
but at dawn there is rejoicing.

III

7 Complacent,† I once said,
"I shall never be shaken."
8 Lord, you showed me favor,
established for me mountains of virtue.
But when you hid your face
I was struck with terror.*
9 To you, Lord, I cried out;
with the Lord I pleaded for mercy:
10† "What gain is there from my lifeblood,
from my going down to the grave?
Does dust give you thanks
or declare your faithfulness?
11 Hear, O Lord, have mercy on me;
Lord, be my helper."

IV

12 You changed my mourning into dancing;
you took off my sackcloth
and clothed me with gladness.*
13 So that my glory may praise you
and not be silent.
O Lord, my God,
forever will I give you thanks.

PSALM 31†

Prayer in Distress and Thanksgiving for Escape

1 For the leader. A psalm of David.

2 In you, Lord, I take refuge;*
let me never be put to shame.
In your righteousness deliver me;

Psalm 30 An individual thanksgiving in four parts: praise and thanks for deliverance and restoration (Ps 30:2–4); an invitation to others to join in (Ps 30:5–6); a flashback to the time before deliverance (Ps 30:7–11); a return to praise and thanks (Ps 30:12). Two sets of images recur: 1) going down, death, silence; 2) coming up, life, praising. God has delivered the psalmist from one state to the other.

30:1 *For the dedication of the Temple*: a later adaptation of the Psalm to celebrate the purification of the Temple in 164 B.C. during the Maccabean Revolt.

30:3 *Healed*: for God as healer, see also Ps 103:3; 107:20; Hos 6:1; 7:1; 11:3; 14:5.

30:4 *Sheol . . . pit*: the shadowy underworld residence of the spirits of the dead, here a metaphor for near-death.

30:7 *Complacent*: untroubled existence is often seen as a source of temptation to forget God, cf. Dt 8:10–18; Hos 13:6; Prv 30:9.

30:10 In the stillness of Sheol no one gives you praise; let me live and be among your worshipers, cf. Ps 6:6; 88:11–13; 115:17; Is 38:18.

Psalm 31 A lament (Ps 31:2–19) with a strong emphasis on trust (Ps 31:4, 6, 15–16), ending with an anticipatory thanksgiving (Ps

---

30:4 Ps 28:1; Jon 2:7.
30:8 Ps 104:29.
30:12 Is 61:3; Jer 31:13.
31:2–4 Ps 71:1–3.

3 incline your ear to me;
make haste to rescue me!
Be my rock of refuge,
a stronghold to save me.
4 For you are my rock and my fortress;*
for your name's sake lead me and guide me.
5 Free me from the net they have set for me,
for you are my refuge.
6† Into your hands I commend my spirit;*
you will redeem me, LORD, God of truth.
7 You hate those who serve worthless idols,
but I trust in the LORD.
8 I will rejoice and be glad in your mercy,
once you have seen my misery,
[and] gotten to know the distress of my soul.*
9 You will not abandon me into enemy hands,
but will set my feet in a free and open space.

II

10 Be gracious to me, LORD, for I am in distress;
affliction is wearing down my eyes,
my throat and my insides.
11 My life is worn out by sorrow,
and my years by sighing.
My strength fails in my affliction;
my bones are wearing down.*
12 To all my foes I am a thing of scorn,
and especially to my neighbors
a horror to my friends.
When they see me in public,
they quickly shy away.*
13 I am forgotten, out of mind like the dead;
I am like a worn-out tool.†
14 I hear the whispers of the crowd;
terrors are all around me.†
They conspire together against me;
they plot to take my life.
15 But I trust in you, LORD;
I say, "You are my God."*
16 My destiny is in your hands;
rescue me from my enemies,
from the hands of my pursuers.
17 Let your face shine on your servant;*
save me in your mercy.
18 Do not let me be put to shame,
for I have called to you, LORD.
Put the wicked to shame;
reduce them to silence in Sheol.
19 Strike dumb their lying lips,
which speak arrogantly against the righteous
in contempt and scorn.*

III

20 How great is your goodness, Lord,
stored up for those who fear you.
You display it for those who trust you,
in the sight of the children of Adam.
21 You hide them in the shelter of your presence,
safe from scheming enemies.
You conceal them in your tent,
away from the strife of tongues.*
22 Blessed be the LORD,
marvelously he showed to me
his mercy in a fortified city.
23 Though I had said in my alarm,
"I am cut off from your eyes."*
Yet you heard my voice, my cry for mercy,
when I pleaded with you for help.
24 Love the LORD, all you who are faithful to him.
The LORD protects the loyal,
but repays the arrogant in full.
25 Be strong and take heart,
all who hope in the LORD.

PSALM 32†

Remission of Sin

1 *Of David. A *maskil.*

I

Blessed is the one whose fault is removed,
whose sin is forgiven.
2 Blessed is the man to whom the LORD imputes no guilt,
in whose spirit is no deceit.

II

3 Because I kept silent,† my bones wasted away;
I groaned all day long.*
4 For day and night your hand was heavy
upon me;

† 31:20–24). As is usual in laments, the affliction is couched in general terms. The psalmist feels overwhelmed by evil people but trusts in the "God of truth" (Ps 31:6).

31:6 *Into your hands I commend my spirit*: in Lk 23:46 Jesus breathes his last with this Psalm verse. Stephen in Acts 7:59 alludes to these words as he is attacked by enemies. The verse is used as an antiphon in the Divine Office at Compline, the last prayer of the day.

31:13 *Like a worn-out tool*: a common comparison for something ruined and useless, cf. Is 30:14; Jer 19:11; 22:28.

31:14 *Terrors are all around me*: a cry used in inescapable danger, cf. Jer 6:25; 20:10; 46:5; 49:29.

Psalm 32 An individual thanksgiving and the second of the seven Penitential Psalms (cf. Ps 6). The opening declaration—the forgiven are blessed (Ps 32:1–2)—arises from the psalmist's own experience. At one time the psalmist was stubborn and closed, a victim of sin's power (Ps 32:3–4), and then became open to the forgiving God (Ps 32:5–7). Sin here, as often in the Bible, is not only the personal act of rebellion against God but also the consequences of that act—frustration and waning of vitality. Having been rescued, the psalmist can teach others the joys of justice and the folly of sin (Ps 32:8–11).

32:3 *I kept silent*: did not confess the sin before God.

* **31:4** Ps 18:2.
31:6 Lk 23:46; Acts 7:59.
31:8 Ps 10:14.
31:11 Ps 32:3; 38:10–11.
31:12 Jb 19:13–19.
31:15 Ps 140:7; Is 25:1.
31:17 Ps 67:1; Nm 6:24.
31:19 Ps 12:4.
31:21 Ps 27:5.
31:23 Jon 2:5.
32:1 Is 1:18; Ps 65:3; Rom 4:7–8.
32:3 Ps 31:11.

my strength withered as in dry summer
heat. *Selah*
5 Then I declared my sin to you;
my guilt I did not hide.*
I said, "I confess my transgression to the
Lord,"
and you took away the guilt of my sin. *Selah*
6 Therefore every loyal person should pray to
you
in time of distress.
Though flood waters† threaten,
they will never reach him.*
7 You are my shelter; you guard me from
distress;
with joyful shouts of deliverance you
surround me. *Selah*

III

8 I will instruct you and show you the way you
should walk,
give you counsel with my eye upon you.
9 Do not be like a horse or mule, without
understanding;
with bit and bridle their temper is curbed,
else they will not come to you.

IV

10 Many are the sorrows of the wicked one,
but mercy surrounds the one who trusts in
the Lord.
11 Be glad in the Lord and rejoice, you righteous;
exult, all you upright of heart.*

PS

PSALM 33†

Praise of God's Power and Providence

I

1 Rejoice, you righteous, in the Lord;
praise from the upright is fitting.*
2 Give thanks to the Lord on the harp;
on the ten-stringed lyre offer praise.*
3 Sing to him a new song;
skillfully play with joyful chant.
4 For the Lord's word is upright;
all his works are trustworthy.
5 He loves justice and right.
The earth is full of the mercy of the Lord.*

II

6 By the Lord's word the heavens were made;
by the breath of his mouth all their
host.†*
7† He gathered the waters of the sea as a
mound;
he sets the deep into storage vaults.*

III

8 Let all the earth fear the Lord;
let all who dwell in the world show him
reverence.
9 For he spoke, and it came to be,
commanded, and it stood in place.*
10 The Lord foils the plan of nations,
frustrates the designs of peoples.
11 But the plan of the Lord stands forever,
the designs of his heart through all
generations.*
12 Blessed is the nation whose God is the Lord,
the people chosen as his inheritance.*

IV

13 From heaven the Lord looks down
and observes the children of Adam,*
14 From his dwelling place he surveys
all who dwell on earth.
15 The One who fashioned together their
hearts
is the One who knows all their works.

V

16 A king is not saved by a great army,
nor a warrior delivered by great strength.
17 Useless is the horse for safety;
despite its great strength, it cannot be
saved.
18 Behold, the eye of the Lord is upon those
who fear him,
upon those who count on his mercy,
19 To deliver their soul from death,
and to keep them alive through famine.

VI

20 Our soul waits for the Lord,
he is our help and shield.*
21 For in him our hearts rejoice;
in his holy name we trust.
22 May your mercy, Lord, be upon us;
as we put our hope in you.

---

† **32:6** *Flood waters*: the untamed waters surrounding the earth, a metaphor for danger.

Psalm 33 A hymn in which the just are invited (Ps 33:1–3) to praise God, who by a mere word (Ps 33:4–5) created the three-tiered universe of the heavens, the cosmic waters, and the earth (Ps 33:6–9). Human words, in contrast, effect nothing (Ps 33:10–11). The greatness of human beings consists in God's choosing them as a special people and their faithful response (Ps 33:12–22).

33:6 *All their host*: the stars of the sky are commonly viewed as a vast army, e.g., Neh 9:6; Is 40:26; 45:12; Jer 33:22.

33:7 *The waters . . . as a mound*: ancients sometimes attributed the power keeping the seas from overwhelming land to a primordial victory of the storm-god over personified Sea.

---

* **32:5** Ps 38:19; 51:5.
32:6 Ps 18:5.
32:11 Ps 33:1.
33:1 Ps 32:11; 147:1.
33:2 Ps 92:4; 144:9.
33:5 Ps 119:64.
33:6 Gn 2:1.
33:7 Ps 78:13; Gn 1:9–10; Ex 15:8; Jos 3:16.
33:9 Ps 148:5; Gn 1:3f; Jdt 16:14.
33:11 Prv 19:21; Is 40:8.
33:12 Ps 144:15; Ex 19:6; Dt 7:6.
33:13 Jb 34:21; Sir 15:19; Jer 16:17; 32:19.
33:20 Ps 115:9.

PSALM 34†

Thanksgiving to God Who Delivers the Just

1 Of David, when he feigned madness before Abimelech,† who drove him out and he went away.

I

2 I will bless the LORD at all times;
his praise shall be always in my mouth.*
3 My soul will glory in the LORD;
let the poor hear and be glad.
4 Magnify the LORD with me;
and let us exalt his name together.

II

5 I sought the LORD, and he answered me,
delivered me from all my fears.
6 Look to him and be radiant,
and your faces may not blush for shame.
7 This poor one cried out and the LORD heard,
and from all his distress he saved him.
8 The angel of the LORD encamps
around those who fear him, and he saves them.*
9 Taste and see that the LORD is good;
blessed is the stalwart one who takes refuge in him.*
10 Fear the LORD, you his holy ones;
nothing is lacking to those who fear him.*
11 The rich grow poor and go hungry,
but those who seek the LORD lack no good thing.

III

12 Come, children,† listen to me;*
I will teach you fear of the LORD.
13 Who is the man who delights in life,*
who loves to see the good days?
14 Keep your tongue from evil,
your lips from speaking lies.
15 Turn from evil and do good;*
seek peace and pursue it.
16 The eyes of the LORD are directed toward the righteous*
and his ears toward their cry.
17 The LORD's face is against evildoers
to wipe out their memory from the earth.
18 The righteous cry out, the LORD hears
and he rescues them from all their afflictions.
19 The LORD is close to the brokenhearted,
saves those whose spirit is crushed.
20 Many are the troubles of the righteous,
but the LORD delivers him from them all.
21 He watches over all his bones;
not one of them shall be broken.*
22 Evil will slay the wicked;
those who hate the righteous are condemned.
23 The LORD is the redeemer of the souls of his servants;
and none are condemned who take refuge in him.

PSALM 35†

Prayer for Help Against Unjust Enemies

1 Of David.

I

†Oppose, O LORD, those who oppose me;
war upon those who make war upon me.
2 Take up the shield and buckler;
rise up in my defense.
3 Brandish lance and battle-ax
against my pursuers.
Say to my soul,
"I am your salvation."
4 Let those who seek my life
be put to shame and disgrace.
Let those who plot evil against me*
be turned back and confounded.
5 Make them like chaff before the wind,*
with the angel of the LORD driving them on.
6 Make their way slippery and dark,
with the angel of the LORD pursuing them.

II

7 Without cause they set their snare for me;
without cause they dug a pit for me.
8 Let ruin overtake them unawares;
let the snare they have set catch them;
let them fall into the pit they have dug.*

† **Psalm 34** A thanksgiving in acrostic form, each line beginning with a successive letter of the Hebrew alphabet. In this Psalm one letter is missing and two are in reverse order. The psalmist, fresh from the experience of being rescued (Ps 34:5, 7), can teach the "poor," those who are defenseless, to trust in God alone (Ps 34:4, 12). God will make them powerful (Ps 34:5–11) and give them protection (Ps 34:12–22).

34:1 *Abimelech*: a scribal error for Achish. In 1 Sm 21:13–16, David feigned madness before Achish, not Abimelech.

34:12 *Children*: the customary term for students in wisdom literature.

Psalm 35 A lament of a person betrayed by friends. The psalmist prays that the evildoers be publicly exposed as unjust (Ps 35:1–8), and gives thanks in anticipation of vindication (Ps 35:9–10). Old friends are the enemies (Ps 35:11–16). May their punishment come quickly (Ps 35:17–21)! The last part (Ps 35:22–26) echoes the opening in praying for the destruction of the psalmist's persecutors. The Psalm may appear vindictive, but one must keep in mind that the psalmist is praying for public redress now of a public injustice. There is at this time no belief in an afterlife in which justice will be redressed.

35:1–6 The mixture of judicial, martial, and hunting images shows that the language is figurative. The actual injustice is false ac-

* **34:2** Ps 145:2.
34:8 Ex 14:19.
34:9 Ps 2:12.
34:10 Prv 3:7.
34:12 Prv 1:8; 4:1.
34:13–17 1 Pt 3:10–12.
34:15 Ps 37:27.
34:16 Ps 33:18.
34:21 Jn 19:36.
35:4 Ps 40:15; 71:13.
35:5 Ps 1:4; 83:14; Jb 21:18.
35:8 Ps 7:16; 9:16; 57:7; Prv 26:27; Eccl 10:8; Sir 27:26.

9 Then I will rejoice in the Lord,
exult in God's salvation.
10 My very bones shall say,
"O Lord, who is like you,*
Who rescue the afflicted from the powerful,
the afflicted and needy from the despoiler?"

III

11 Malicious witnesses rise up,
accuse me of things I do not know.
12 They repay me evil for good;
my soul is desolate.*
13† Yet I, when they were ill, put on sackcloth,
afflicted myself with fasting,
sobbed my prayers upon my bosom.
14 I went about in grief as for my brother,
bent in mourning as for my mother.
15 Yet when I stumbled they gathered with glee,
gathered against me and I did not know it.
They slandered me without ceasing;
16 without respect they mocked me,
gnashed their teeth against me.

IV

17 O Lord, how long will you look on?
Restore my soul from their destruction,
my very life from lions!*
18 Then I will thank you in the great assembly;
I will praise you before the mighty throng.*
19 Do not let lying foes rejoice over me,
my undeserved enemies wink knowingly.*
20 They speak no words of peace,
but against the quiet in the land
they fashion deceitful speech.*
21 They open wide their mouths against me.
They say, "Aha! Good!
Our eyes have seen it!"*
22 You see this, Lord; do not be silent;*
Lord, do not withdraw from me.
23 Awake, be vigilant in my defense,
in my cause, my God and my Lord.
24 Defend me because you are just, Lord;
my God, do not let them rejoice over me.
25 Do not let them say in their hearts,
"Aha! Our soul!"†
Do not let them say,
"We have devoured that one!"
26 Put to shame and confound
all who relish my misfortune.
Clothe with shame and disgrace
those who lord it over me.
27 But let those who favor my just cause
shout for joy and be glad.
May they ever say, "Exalted be the Lord
who delights in the peace of his loyal
servant."
28 Then my tongue shall recount your justice,
declare your praise, all the day long.*

PSALM 36†

Human Wickedness and Divine Providence

1 For the leader. Of David, the servant of the Lord.

I

2 Sin directs the heart of the wicked man;
his eyes are closed to the fear of God.*
3 For he lives with the delusion:
his guilt will not be known and hated.†
4 Empty and false are the words of his mouth;
he has ceased to be wise and do good.
5 On his bed he hatches plots;
he sets out on a wicked way;
he does not reject evil.*

II

6† Lord, your mercy reaches to heaven;
your fidelity, to the clouds.*
7 Your justice is like the highest mountains;
your judgments, like the mighty deep;
human being and beast you sustain, Lord.
8 How precious is your mercy, O God!
The children of Adam take refuge in the
shadow of your wings.†*
9 They feast on the rich food of your house;
from your delightful stream* you give them
drink.
10 For with you is the fountain of life,*
and in your light we see light.*
11 Show mercy on those who know you,
your just defense to the upright of heart.
12 Do not let the foot of the proud overtake me,
nor the hand of the wicked disturb me.

† cusation of serious crimes (Ps 35:11, 15, 20–21). The psalmist seeks lost honor through a trial before God.

35:13, 15–17 The Hebrew is obscure.

35:25 *Aha! Our soul!*: an ancient idiomatic expression meaning that we have attained what we wanted.

Psalm 36 A Psalm with elements of wisdom (Ps 36:2–5), the hymn (Ps 36:6–10), and the lament (Ps 36:11–13). The rule of sin over the wicked (Ps 36:2–5) is contrasted with the rule of divine love and mercy over God's friends (Ps 36:6–10). The Psalm ends with a prayer that God's guidance never cease (Ps 36:11–12).

36:3 *Hated*: punished by God.

36:6–7 God actively controls the entire world.

36:8 *The shadow of your wings*: metaphor for divine protection. It probably refers to the winged cherubim in the holy of holies in the Temple, cf. 1 Kgs 6:23–28, 32; 2 Chr 3:10–13; Ez 1:4–9.

* **35:10** Ps 86:8; 89:7, 9; Ex 15:11. **35:12** Ps 27:12; 38:20–21; 109:5; Jer 18:20. **35:17** Ps 17:12; 22:22; 58:7. **35:18** Ps 22:23; 26:12; 35:18; 40:10; 149:1. **35:19** Ps 38:17. **35:20** Ps 120:6–7. **35:21** Ps 40:16; Lam 2:16. **35:22** Ps 22:12; 38:21; 109:1. **35:28** Ps 71:15–16. **36:2** Rom 3:18. **36:5** Mi 2:1. **36:6** Ps 57:11; 71:19. **36:8** Ps 17:8. **36:9** Gn 2:8, 10. **36:10** Is 55:1; Jn 4:14. **36:10** Ps 80:4, 8, 20.

13 There make the evildoers fall;
thrust them down, unable to rise.

PSALM 37†

The Fate of Sinners and the Reward of the Just

1 Of David.

ALEPH

Do not be provoked by evildoers;
do not envy those who do wrong.*
2 Like grass they wither quickly;
like green plants they wilt away.*

BETH

3 Trust in the LORD and do good
that you may dwell in the land† and live secure.*
4 Find your delight in the LORD
who will give you your heart's desire.*

GIMEL

5 Commit your way to the LORD;
trust in him and he will act*
6 And make your righteousness shine like the dawn,
your justice like noonday.*

DALETH

7 Be still before the LORD;
wait for him.
Do not be provoked by the prosperous,
nor by malicious schemers.

HE

8 Refrain from anger; abandon wrath;
do not be provoked; it brings only harm.
9 Those who do evil will be cut off,
but those who wait for the LORD will inherit the earth.*

WAW

10 Wait a little, and the wicked will be no more;
look for them and they will not be there.
11 But the poor will inherit the earth,*
will delight in great prosperity.

ZAYIN

12 The wicked plot against the righteous
and gnash their teeth at them;
13 But my Lord laughs at them,*
because he sees that their day is coming.

HETH

14 The wicked unsheath their swords;
they string their bows
To fell the poor and oppressed,
to slaughter those whose way is upright.*
15 Their swords will pierce their own hearts;
their bows will be broken.

TETH

16 Better the meagerness of the righteous one
than the plenty of the wicked.*
17 The arms of the wicked will be broken,
while the LORD will sustain the righteous.

YODH

18 The LORD knows the days of the blameless;
their heritage lasts forever.
19 They will not be ashamed when times are bad;
in days of famine they will be satisfied.

KAPH

20 The wicked perish,
enemies of the LORD;
They shall be consumed like fattened lambs;
like smoke they disappear.*

LAMEDH

21 The wicked one borrows but does not repay;
the righteous one is generous and gives.
22 For those blessed by the Lord will inherit the earth,
but those accursed will be cut off.

MEM

23 The valiant one whose steps are guided by the LORD,
who will delight in his way,*

† **Psalm 37** The Psalm responds to the problem of evil, which the Old Testament often expresses as a question: why do the wicked prosper and the good suffer? The Psalm answers that the situation is only temporary. God will reverse things, rewarding the good and punishing the wicked here on earth. The perspective is concrete and earthbound: people's very actions place them among the ranks of the good or wicked. Each group or "way" has its own inherent dynamism—eventual frustration for the wicked, eventual reward for the just. The Psalm is an acrostic, i.e., each section begins with a successive letter of the Hebrew alphabet. Each section has its own imagery and logic.

37:3 *The land*: the promised land, Israel, which became for later interpreters a type or figure of heaven, cf. Heb 11:9–10, 13–16. The New Testament Beatitudes (Mt 5:3–12; Lk 6:20–26) have been influenced by the Psalm, especially their total reversal of the present and their interpretation of the happy future as possession of the land.

37:1 Prv 3:31; 23:17; 24:1, 19.
37:2 Ps 90:5–6; 102:12; 103:15–16; Jb 14:2; Is 40:7.
37:3 Ps 128:2.
37:4 Prv 10:24.
37:5 Ps 55:23; Prv 3:5; 16:3.
37:6 Wis 5:6; Is 58:10.
37:9 Ps 25:13; Prv 2:21; Is 57:13.
37:11 Mt 5:4.
37:13 Ps 2:4; 59:9; Wis 4:18.
37:14 Ps 11:2; 57:5; 64:4.
37:16 Prv 15:16; 16:8.
37:20 Wis 5:14.
37:23 Prv 20:24.

24 May stumble, but he will never fall,
for the LORD holds his hand.

NUN

25 Neither in my youth, nor now in old age
have I seen the righteous one abandoned*
or his offspring begging for bread.
26 All day long he is gracious and lends,
and his offspring become a blessing.

SAMEKH

27 Turn from evil and do good,
that you may be settled forever.*
28 For the LORD loves justice
and does not abandon the faithful.

AYIN

When the unjust are destroyed,
and the offspring of the wicked cut off,
29 The righteous will inherit the earth
and dwell in it forever.*

PE

30 The mouth of the righteous utters
wisdom;*
his tongue speaks what is right.
31 God's teaching is in his heart;*
his steps do not falter.

SADHE

32 The wicked spies on the righteous
and seeks to kill him.
33 But the LORD does not abandon him in his
power,
nor let him be condemned when tried.

QOPH

34 Wait eagerly for the LORD,
and keep his way;*
He will raise you up to inherit the earth;
you will see when the wicked are cut off.

RESH

35 I have seen a ruthless scoundrel,
spreading out like a green cedar.*
36 When I passed by again, he was gone;
though I searched, he could not be
found.

SHIN

37 Observe the person of integrity and mark the
upright;
Because there is a future for a man of peace.*
38 Sinners will be destroyed together;
the future of the wicked will be cut off.

TAW

39 The salvation of the righteous is from the
LORD,
their refuge in a time of distress.*
40 The LORD helps and rescues them,
rescues and saves them from the wicked,
because they take refuge in him.

PSALM 38†

Prayer of an Afflicted Sinner

1 A psalm of David. For remembrance.

I

2 LORD, do not punish me in your anger;
in your wrath do not chastise me!*
3 Your arrows have sunk deep in me;*
your hand has come down upon me.
4 There is no wholesomeness in my flesh
because of your anger;
there is no health in my bones because of
my sin.*
5 My iniquities overwhelm me,
a burden too heavy for me.*

II

6 Foul and festering are my sores
because of my folly.
7 I am stooped and deeply bowed;*
every day I go about mourning.
8 My loins burn with fever;
there is no wholesomeness in my flesh.
9 I am numb and utterly crushed;
I wail with anguish of heart.*
10 My Lord, my deepest yearning is before you;
my groaning is not hidden from you.
11 My heart shudders, my strength forsakes me;
the very light of my eyes has failed.*
12 Friends and companions shun my disease;
my neighbors stand far off.
13 Those who seek my life lay snares for me;

---

† **Psalm 38** In this lament, one of the Penitential Psalms (cf. Ps 6), the psalmist acknowledges the sin that has brought physical and mental sickness and social ostracism. There is no one to turn to for help; only God can undo the past and restore the psalmist.

Psalm 39 The lament of a mortally ill person who at first had resolved to remain silently submissive (Ps 39:2–4). But the grief was too much and now the psalmist laments the brevity and vanity of life (Ps 39:5–7), yet remaining hopeful (Ps 39:8–10). The psalmist continues to express both acceptance of the illness and hope for healing in Ps 39:11–13.

* **37:25** Jb 4:7; Sir 2:10.
37:27 Ps 34:14–15; Am 5:14.
37:29 Ps 25:13; Prv 2:21; Is 57:13.
37:30 Prv 10:31.
37:31 Ps 40:9; Dt 6:6; Is 51:7; Jer 31:33.
37:34 Ps 31:24.
37:35 Ps 92:8–9; Is 2:13; Ez 31:10–11.
37:37 Prv 23:18; 24:14.
37:39 Ps 9:10; Is 25:4.
38:2 Ps 6:2.
38:3 Jb 6:4; Lam 3:12; Ps 31:11; 64:7.
38:4 Is 1:5–6.
38:5 Ps 40:13; Ezr 9:6.
38:7 Ps 35:14.
38:9 Ps 102:4–6.
38:11 Ps 6:8; 31:10.

they seek my misfortune, they speak of ruin;
they plot treachery every day.

III

14 But I am like the deaf, hearing nothing,
like the mute, I do not open my mouth,
15 I am even like someone who does not hear,
who has no answer ready.
16 LORD, it is for you that I wait;
O Lord, my God, you respond.*
17 For I have said that they would gloat over me,
exult over me if I stumble.

IV

18 I am very near to falling;
my wounds are with me always.
19 I acknowledge my guilt
and grieve over my sin.*
20 My enemies live and grow strong,
those who hate me grow numerous fraudulently,
21 Repaying me evil for good,
accusing me for pursuing good.*
22 Do not forsake me, O LORD;
my God, be not far from me!*
23 Come quickly to help me,*
my Lord and my salvation!

PSALM 39†

The Vanity of Life

1 For the leader, for Jeduthun.* A psalm of David.

I

2 I said, "I will watch my ways,
lest I sin with my tongue;
I will keep a muzzle on my mouth."
3 Mute and silent before the wicked,
I refrain from good things.
But my sorrow increases;
4 my heart smolders within me.*
In my sighing a fire blazes up,
and I break into speech:

II

5 LORD, let me know my end, the number of my days,
that I may learn how frail I am.
6 To be sure, you establish the expanse of my days;
indeed, my life is as nothing before you.
Every man is but a breath.* *Selah*

III

7 Man goes about as a mere phantom;
they hurry about, although in vain;
he heaps up stores without knowing for whom.
8 And now, LORD, for what do I wait?
You are my only hope.
9 From all my sins deliver me;
let me not be the taunt of fools.
10 I am silent and do not open my mouth
because you are the one who did this.
11 Take your plague away from me;
I am ravaged by the touch of your hand.
12 You chastise man with rebukes for sin;
like a moth you consume his treasures.
Every man is but a breath. *Selah*
13 Listen to my prayer, LORD, hear my cry;
do not be deaf to my weeping!
For I am with you like a foreigner,
a refugee, like my ancestors.*
14 Turn your gaze from me, that I may smile
before I depart to be no more.

PSALM 40†

Gratitude and Prayer for Help

1 For the leader. A psalm of David.

A

2 Surely, I wait for the LORD;
who bends down to me and hears my cry,*
3 Draws me up from the pit of destruction,
out of the muddy clay,*
Sets my feet upon rock,
steadies my steps,
4 And puts a new song† in my mouth,*
a hymn to our God.
Many shall look on in fear
and they shall trust in the LORD.
5 Blessed the man who sets
his security in the LORD,
who turns not to the arrogant
or to those who stray after falsehood.*
6 You, yes you, O LORD, my God,

---

† **Psalm 40** A thanksgiving (Ps 40:2–13) has been combined with a lament (Ps 40:14–17) that appears also in Ps 70. The psalmist describes the rescue in spatial terms—being raised up from the swampy underworld to firm earth where one can praise God (Ps 40:2–4). All who trust God will experience like protection (Ps 40:5–6)! The Psalm stipulates the precise mode of thanksgiving: not animal sacrifice but open and enthusiastic proclamation of the salvation just experienced (Ps 40:7–11). A prayer for protection concludes (Ps 40:12–17).

40:4 *A new song*: a song in response to the new action of God (cf. Ps 33:3; 96:1; 144:9; 149:1; Is 42:10). Giving thanks is not purely a human response but is itself a divine gift.

* **38:16** Ps 13:4. **38:19** Ps 32:5; 51:5. **38:21** Ps 109:5. **38:22** Ps 22:2, 12, 20; 35:22. **38:23** Ps 40:14. **39:1** 1 Chr 16:41; Ps 62:1; 77:1. **39:4** Jer 20:9. **39:6** Ps 62:10; 90:9–10; 144:4; Jb 7:6, 16; 14:1, 5; Eccl 6:12; Wis 2:5. **39:13** Ps 119:19; Gn 23:4; Heb 11:13; 1 Pt 2:11. **40:2** Lam 3:25. **40:3** Ps 28:1; 30:4; 69:3, 15–16; 88:5; Prv 1:12; Jon 2:7. **40:4** Ps 33:3. **40:5** Ps 1:1; Prv 16:20; Jer 17:7.

have done many wondrous deeds!
And in your plans for us
there is none to equal you.*
Should I wish to declare or tell them,
too many are they to recount.*
7† Sacrifice and offering you do not want;*
you opened my ears.
Holocaust and sin-offering you do not request;
8 so I said, "See; I come
with an inscribed scroll written upon me.
9 I delight to do your will, my God;
your law is in my inner being!"*
10 When I sing of your righteousness
in a great assembly,
See, I do not restrain my lips;
as you, LORD, know.*
11 I do not conceal your righteousness
within my heart;
I speak of your loyalty and your salvation.
I do not hide your mercy or faithfulness
from a great assembly.
12 LORD, may you not withhold
your compassion from me;
May your mercy and your faithfulness
continually protect me.*

B

13 But evils surround me
until they cannot be counted.
My sins overtake me,
so that I can no longer see.
They are more numerous than the hairs of my head;
my courage fails me.*
14 LORD, graciously rescue me!*
Come quickly to help me, LORD!
15 May those who seek to destroy my life
be shamed and confounded.
Turn back in disgrace
those who desire my ruin.*
16 Let those who say to me "Aha!"*
Be made desolate on account of their shame.
17 While those who seek you
rejoice and be glad in you.
May those who long for your salvation
always say, "The LORD is great."*
18 Though I am afflicted and poor,
my Lord keeps me in mind.
You are my help and deliverer;
my God, do not delay!

PSALM 41†

Thanksgiving After Sickness

[1] For the leader. A psalm of David.

I

2 Blessed the one concerned for the poor;†
on a day of misfortune, the LORD delivers him.*
3 The LORD keeps and preserves him,
makes him blessed in the land,
and does not betray him to his enemies.
4 The LORD sustains him on his sickbed,
you turn down his bedding whenever he is ill.†

II

5 Even I have said, "LORD, take note of me;
heal me, although I have sinned against you.
6 My enemies say bad things against me:
'When will he die and his name be forgotten?'
7 When someone comes to visit me, he speaks
without sincerity.
His heart stores up malice;
when he leaves, he gossips.*
8 All those who hate me whisper together
against me;
they imagine the worst about me:
9 'He has had ruin poured over him;
that one lying down will never rise again.'
10† Even my trusted friend,
who ate my bread,
has raised his heel against me.*

III

11 "But you, LORD, take note of me to raise me up
that I may repay them."†

---

† **40:7–9.** Obedience is better than sacrifice (cf. 1 Sm 15:22; Is 1:10–20; Hos 6:6; Am 5:22–25; Mi 6:6–8; Acts 7:42–43 [quoting Am 5:25–26]). Heb 10:5–9 quotes the somewhat different Greek version and interprets it as Christ's self-oblation.

Psalm 41 A thanksgiving for rescue from illness (Ps 41:4, 5, 9). Many people, even friends, have interpreted the illness as a divine punishment for sin and have ostracized the psalmist (Ps 41:5–11). The healing shows the return of God's favor and rebukes the psalmist's detractors (Ps 41:12–13).

41:2 *Blessed the one concerned for the poor*: cf. Ps 32:1–2; 34:9; 40:5; 65:5. The psalmist's statement about God's love of the poor is based on the experience of being rescued (Ps 41:1–3).

41:4 *You turn down his bedding whenever he is ill*: the Hebrew is obscure. It suggests ongoing attentive care of the one who is sick.

41:10 *Even my trusted friend . . . has raised his heel against me*: Jn 13:18 cites this verse to characterize Judas as a false friend. *Raised his heel against me*: an interpretation of the unclear Hebrew, "made great the heel against me."

41:11 *That I may repay them*: the healing itself is an act of judgment through which God decides for the psalmist and against the false friends. The prayer is not necessarily for strength to punish enemies.

---

* **40:6** Ps 35:10.
40:6 Ps 71:15; 139:17–18.
40:7–9 Heb 10:5–7; Ps 51:18–19; Am 5:22; Hos 6:6; Is 1:11–15.
40:9 Ps 37:31.
40:10 Ps 22:23; 26:12; 35:18; 149:1.
40:12 Ps 89:34.
40:13 Ps 38:5, 11; Ezr 9:6.
40:14–18 Ps 70:2–6; 71:12.
40:15 Ps 35:4, 26.
40:16 Ps 35:21, 25.
40:17 Ps 35:27.
41:2 Tb 4:7–11.
41:7 Ps 31:12; 38:12–13; 88:8; Jb 19:13–19; Jer 20:10.
41:10 Ps 55:14–15; Jn 13:18.

Psalm 42:2

12 By this I will know you are pleased with me,
that my enemy no longer shouts in
triumph over me.
13 In my integrity may you support me
and let me stand in your presence forever.
14† Blessed be the LORD, the God of Israel,
from all eternity and forever.
Amen. Amen.*

Second Book—Psalms 42–72

PSALM 42†

Longing for God's Presence in the Temple

1 For the leader. A *maskil* of the Korahites.†

I

2 As the deer longs for streams of water,*
so my soul longs for you, O God.
3 My soul thirsts for God, the living God.
When can I enter and see the face of
God?†*
4 My tears have been my bread day and night,*
as they ask me every day, "Where is your
God?"*
5 Those times I recall
as I pour out my soul,*

Pray It!

Randy's First Day of School

Randy and his family have just moved to a new town. Randy is hopeful about this move because he didn't like his old neighborhood and school. There he was often made fun of for his size. So he figures this will be a new start for him, and just maybe the kids here will give him a chance.

Randy is nervous but can't wait to meet some new people. As the principal walks him down to his new homeroom, he has hopeful visions of how great it will be. When they walk into the classroom, all that changes. As the principal introduces him, someone yells from the back of the room, "Hey, hey, hey, it's Fat Albert!" Everyone laughs. Randy smiles, only to hide the pain and anger he feels inside.

Have you ever experienced painful moments like the one Randy went through? Psalm 42 is a good prayer to turn to during moments like these. Verse 6 says, "Wait for God, for I shall again praise him, / my savior and my God." If you follow this advice, the situation may not change, but your heart may find peace rather than anger.

▶ Psalm 42

When I would cross over to the shrine of the
Mighty One,†
to the house of God,
Amid loud cries of thanksgiving,
with the multitude keeping festival.*
6 Why are you downcast, my soul;
why do you groan within me?
Wait for God, for I shall again praise him,
my savior and my God.

†

41:14 The doxology, not part of the Psalm, marks the end of the first of the five books of the Psalter, cf. Ps 72:18–20; 89:53; 106:48.

Psalms 42–43 Ps 42–43 form a single lament of three sections, each section ending in an identical refrain (Ps 42:6, 12; 43:5). The psalmist is far from Jerusalem, and longs for the divine presence that Israel experienced in the Temple liturgy. Despite sadness, the psalmist hopes once again to join the worshiping crowds.

42:1 *The Korahites*: a major guild of Temple singers (2 Chr 20:19) whose name appears in the superscriptions of Ps 42; 44–49; 84–85; 87–88.

42:3 *See the face of God*: "face" designates a personal presence (Gn 33:10; Ex 10:28–29; 2 Sm 17:11). The expressions "see God/God's face" occur elsewhere (Ps 11:7; 17:15; cf. Ex 24:10; 33:7–11; Jb 33:26) for the presence of God in the Temple.

42:5 *The shrine of the Mighty One*: this reading follows the tradition of the Septuagint and the Vulgate.

*

41:14 Neh 9:5.
42:2–3 Ps 63:2; 84:3; 143:6; Is 26:9.
42:3 Ps 27:4.
42:4 Ps 80:6; 102:10.
42:4 Ps 79:10; Jl 2:17.
42:5 Lam 3:20.
42:5 Ps 122:5.

II

7 My soul is downcast within me;
therefore I remember you
From the land of the Jordan† and Hermon,
from Mount Mizar,*
8† Deep calls to deep
in the roar of your torrents,
and all your waves and breakers
sweep over me.*
9 By day may the LORD send his mercy,
and by night may his righteousness be
with me!
I will pray† to the God of my life,
10 I will say to God, my rock:
"Why do you forget me?*
Why must I go about mourning
with the enemy oppressing me?"
11 It shatters my bones, when my adversaries
reproach me,
when they say to me every day: "Where is
your God?"
12 Why are you downcast, my soul,
why do you groan within me?
Wait for God, for I shall again praise him,
my savior and my God.

PSALM 43

1 Grant me justice, O God;
defend me from a faithless people;
from the deceitful and unjust rescue me.*
2 You, O God, are my strength.
Why then do you spurn me?
Why must I go about mourning,
with the enemy oppressing me?
3 *Send your light and your fidelity,†
that they may be my guide;*
Let them bring me to your holy mountain,
to the place of your dwelling,
4 That I may come to the altar of God,
to God, my joy, my delight.
Then I will praise you with the harp,
O God, my God.
5 Why are you downcast, my soul?
Why do you groan within me?
Wait for God, for I shall again praise him,
my savior and my God.

PSALM 44†

God's Past Favor and Israel's Present Need

1 For the leader. A *maskil* of the Korahites.

I

2 O God, we have heard with our own ears;
our ancestors have told us*
The deeds you did in their days,
with your own hand in days of old:
3 You rooted out nations to plant them,*
crushed peoples and expelled them.
4 Not with their own swords did they conquer
the land,*
nor did their own arms bring victory;
It was your right hand, your own arm,
the light of your face for you favored them.*
5 You are my king and my God,*
who bestows victories on Jacob.
6 Through you we batter our foes;
through your name we trample our adversaries.
7 Not in my bow do I trust,
nor does my sword bring me victory.
8 You have brought us victory over our enemies,
shamed those who hate us.
9 In God we have boasted all the day long;
your name we will praise forever.
Selah

II

10 *But now you have rejected and disgraced us;
you do not march out with our armies.*
11 You make us retreat† before the foe;
those who hate us plunder us at will.*
12 You hand us over like sheep to be slaughtered,
scatter us among the nations.*
13 You sell your people for nothing;
you make no profit from their sale.*

---

† **42:7** *From the land of the Jordan*: the sources of the Jordan are in the foothills of Mount Hermon in present-day southern Lebanon. Mount Mizar is presumed to be a mountain in the same range.

42:8 *Deep calls to deep*: to the psalmist, the waters arising in the north are overwhelming and far from God's presence, like the waters of chaos (Ps 18:5; 69:2–3, 15; Jon 2:3–6).

42:9–10 *I will pray . . . I will say*: in the midst of his depression the psalmist turns to prayer. Despite his situation he trusts the Lord to deliver him from his sorrow so that he may enter the Temple precincts and praise him once again (Ps 43:3–4, 5b).

43:3 *Your light and your fidelity*: a pair of divine attributes personified as guides for the pilgrimage. As in Ps 42:9 the psalmist prays that these divine attributes lead him back to Jerusalem and ultimately to God's presence in the Temple.

Psalm 44 In this lament the community reminds God of past favors which it has always acknowledged (Ps 44:2–9). But now God has abandoned Israel to defeat and humiliation (Ps 44:10–17), though the people are not conscious of any sin against the covenant (Ps 44:18–23). They struggle with being God's special people amid divine silence; yet they continue to pray (Ps 44:24–26).

44:11 *You make us retreat*: the corollary of Ps 44:3. Defeat, like victory, is God's doing; neither Israel nor its enemies can claim credit (Ps 44:23).

---

* **42:7** Ps 43:3.
42:8 Ps 18:5; 32:6; 69:2; 88:8; Jon 2:4.
42:10 Ps 18:2; 31:3–4.
43:1 Ps 119:154.
43:3 Ps 18:29; 27:1; 36:10; Mi 7:8.
43:3 Ps 122:1.
44:2 Ps 78:3.
44:3 Ps 78:55; 80:9f.
44:4 Dt 8:17f; Jos 24:12.
44:4 Ps 4:7; 31:17; 67:2; 80:4; Nm 6:25; Dn 9:17.
44:5 Ps 145:1.
44:10–27 Ps 89:39–52.
44:10 Ps 60:12.
44:11 Lv 26:17; Dt 28:25.
44:12 Lv 26:33; Dt 28:64.
44:13 Dt 32:30; Is 52:3.

14 You make us the reproach of our neighbors,*
the mockery and scorn of those around us.
15 You make us a byword among the nations;
the peoples shake their heads at us.
16 All day long my disgrace is before me;
shame has covered my face
17 At the sound of those who taunt and revile,
at the sight of the enemy and avenger.

III

18 All this has come upon us,
though we have not forgotten you,
nor been disloyal to your covenant.
19† Our hearts have not turned back,
nor have our steps strayed from your path.
20 Yet you have left us crushed,
desolate in a place of jackals;†*
you have covered us with a shadow of death.
21 If we had forgotten the name of our God,
stretched out our hands to another god,
22 Would not God have discovered this,
God who knows the secrets of the heart?
23 For you we are slain all the day long,
considered only as sheep to be slaughtered.*

IV

24 Awake! Why do you sleep, O Lord?
Rise up! Do not reject us forever!*
25 Why do you hide your face;*
why forget our pain and misery?
26 For our soul has been humiliated in the dust;*
our belly is pressed to the earth.
27 Rise up, help us!
Redeem us in your mercy.

PSALM 45†

Song for a Royal Wedding

1 For the leader; according to "Lilies." A *maskil* of the Korahites. A love song.

I

2 My heart is stirred by a noble theme,
as I sing my ode to the king.
My tongue is the pen of a nimble scribe.

II

3 You are the most handsome of men;
fair speech has graced your lips,
for God has blessed you forever.*
4 Gird your sword upon your hip, mighty warrior!
In splendor and majesty ride on triumphant!*
5 In the cause of truth, meekness, and justice
may your right hand show your wondrous deeds.
6 Your arrows are sharp;
peoples will cower at your feet;
the king's enemies will lose heart.
7 Your throne, O God,† stands forever;*
your royal scepter is a scepter for justice.
8 You love justice and hate wrongdoing;
therefore God, your God, has anointed you
with the oil of gladness above your fellow kings.
9 With myrrh, aloes, and cassia
your robes are fragrant.
From ivory-paneled palaces†
stringed instruments bring you joy.
10 Daughters of kings are your lovely wives;
a princess arrayed in Ophir's gold†
comes to stand at your right hand.

III

11 Listen, my daughter, and understand;
pay me careful heed.
Forget your people and your father's house,†
12 that the king might desire your beauty.
He is your lord;
13 *honor him, daughter of Tyre.
Then the richest of the people
will seek your favor with gifts.
14 All glorious is the king's daughter as she enters,*
her raiment threaded with gold;
15 In embroidered apparel she is led to the king.
The maids of her train are presented to the king.
16 They are led in with glad and joyous acclaim;
they enter the palace of the king.

---

† **44:19** *Our hearts have not turned back*: Israel's defeat was not caused by its lack of fidelity.

44:20 *A place of jackals*: following Israel's defeat and exile (Ps 44:11–12), the land lies desolate, inhabited only by jackals, cf. Is 13:22; Jer 9:10; 10:22. Others take *tannim* as "sea monster" (cf. Ez 29:3; 32:2) and render: "you crushed us as you did the sea monster."

Psalm 45 A song for the Davidic king's marriage to a foreign princess from Tyre in Phoenicia. The court poet sings (Ps 45:2, 18) of God's choice of the king (Ps 45:3, 8), of his role in establishing divine rule (Ps 45:4–8), and of his splendor as he waits for his bride (Ps 45:9–10). The woman is to forget her own house when she becomes wife to the king (Ps 45:11–13). Her majestic beauty today is a sign of the future prosperity of the royal house (Ps 45:14–17). The Psalm was retained in the collection when there was no reigning king, and came to be applied to the king who was to come, the messiah.

45:7 *O God*: the king, in courtly language, is called "god," i.e., more than human, representing God to the people. Heb 1:8–9 applies Ps 45:7–8 to Christ.

45:9 *Ivory-paneled palaces*: lit., "palaces of ivory." Ivory paneling and furniture decoration have been found in Samaria and other ancient Near Eastern cities, cf. Am 3:15.

45:10 *Ophir's gold*: uncertain location, possibly a region on the coast of southern Arabia or eastern Africa, famous for its gold, cf. 1 Kgs 9:28; 10:11; Jb 22:24.

45:11 *Forget your people and your father's house*: the bride should no longer consider herself a daughter of her father's house, but the wife of the king—the queen.

---

* **44:14–17** Ps 79:4; 80:7; 123:3–4; Jb 12:4; Dn 9:16. **44:20** Jer 9:10. **44:23** Rom 8:36. **44:24** Ps 10:1; 74:1; 77:8; 79:5; 83:2. **44:25** Ps 10:11; 89:47; Jb 13:24. **44:26** Ps 119:25. **45:3** Sg 5:10–16. **45:4** Ps 21:5. **45:7–8** Heb 1:8–9. **45:13** Ps 72:10–11; Is 60:5f. **45:14–16** Ez 16:10–13.

IV

17 The throne of your fathers your sons will have;
you shall make them princes through all the land.*
18 I will make your name renowned through all generations;
thus nations shall praise you forever.*

PSALM 46†

God, the Protector of Zion

1 For the leader. A song of the Korahites. According to *alamoth*.†

I

2 God is our refuge and our strength,
an ever-present help in distress.*
3† Thus we do not fear, though earth be shaken
and mountains quake to the depths of the sea,
4 Though its waters rage and foam
and mountains totter at its surging.* *Selah*

II

5† Streams of the river gladden the city of God,
the holy dwelling of the Most High.*
6 God is in its midst; it shall not be shaken;
God will help it at break of day.*
7 Though nations rage and kingdoms totter,
he utters his voice and the earth melts.*
8† The LORD of hosts is with us;
our stronghold is the God of Jacob. *Selah*

III

9 Come and see the works of the LORD,
who has done fearsome deeds on earth;*
10 Who stops wars to the ends of the earth,
breaks the bow, splinters the spear,
and burns the shields with fire;*
11 *"Be still and know that I am God!
I am exalted among the nations,
exalted on the earth."
12 The LORD of hosts is with us;
our stronghold is the God of Jacob. *Selah*

PSALM 47†

The Ruler of All the Nations

1 For the leader. A psalm of the Korahites.

I

2 All you peoples, clap your hands;
shout to God with joyful cries.*
3 For the LORD, the Most High, is to be feared,
the great king over all the earth,*
4 Who made people subject to us,
nations under our feet,*
5† Who chose our heritage for us,
the glory of Jacob, whom he loves.* *Selah*

II

6† God has gone up with a shout;
the LORD, amid trumpet blasts.*
7 Sing praise to God, sing praise;
sing praise to our king, sing praise.

III

8 For God is king over all the earth;*
sing hymns of praise.
9 God rules over the nations;
God sits upon his holy throne.
10 The princes of the peoples assemble
with the people of the God of Abraham.
For the shields of the earth belong to God,
highly exalted.*

PSALM 48†

The Splendor of the Invincible City

1 A psalm of the Korahites.† A song.

I

2 Great is the LORD and highly praised
in the city of our God:*

†

Psalm 46 A song of confidence in God's protection of Zion with close parallels to Ps 48. The dominant note in Ps 46 is sounded by the refrain, The LORD of hosts is with us (Ps 46:8, 12). The first strophe (Ps 46:2–4) sings of the security of God's presence even in utter chaos; the second (Ps 46:5–8), of divine protection of the city from its enemies; the third (Ps 46:9–11), of God's imposition of imperial peace.

46:1 *Alamoth*: the melody of the Psalm, now lost.

46:3–4 Figurative ancient Near Eastern language to describe social and political upheavals.

46:5 Jerusalem is not situated on a river. This description derives from mythological descriptions of the divine abode and symbolizes the divine presence as the source of all life (cf. Is 33:21; Ez 47:1–12; Jl 4:18; Zec 14:8; Rev 22:1–2).

46:8 The first line of the refrain is similar in structure and meaning to Isaiah's name for the royal child, Emmanuel, With us is God (Is 7:14; 8:8, 10).

Psalm 47 A hymn calling on the nations to acknowledge the universal rule of Israel's God (Ps 47:2–5) who is enthroned as king over Israel and the nations (Ps 47:6–9).

47:5 *Our heritage . . . the glory*: the land of Israel (cf. Is 58:14), which God has given Israel in an act of sovereignty.

47:6 *God has gone up*: Christian liturgical tradition has applied the verse to the Ascension of Christ.

Psalm 48 A Zion hymn, praising the holy city as the invincible dwelling place of God. Unconquerable, it is an apt symbol of God who has defeated all enemies. After seven epithets describing the city (Ps 48:2–3), the Psalm describes the victory by the Divine Warrior over hostile kings (Ps 48:4–8). The second half proclaims the dominion of the God of Zion over all the earth (Ps 48:9–12) and invites

*

45:17 Gn 17:6.
45:18 Is 60:15.
46:2 Ps 48:4; Is 33:2.
46:4 Ps 93:3–4; Jb 9:5–6; Is 24:18–20; 54:10.
46:5 Ps 48:2–3; 76:3.
46:6 Is 7:14.
46:7 Ps 2:1–5; 48:5–8; 76:7–9; Is 17:12–14.
46:9 Ps 48:9–10.
46:10 Ps 76:4.
46:11 Ps 48:11.
47:2 Ps 89:16; Zep 3:14.
47:3 Ps 95:3; Ex 15:18; Is 24:23; 52:7.
47:4 Ps 2:8.
47:5 Is 58:14.
47:6 Ps 24:8, 10; 68:18–19; 98:6.
47:8–9 Ps 72:11; 93:1; 96:10; 97:1; 99:1; Jer 10:7.
47:10 Ps 89:19; Ex 3:6; Is 2:2–4.
48:2 Ps 96:4; 145:3.

PS

His holy mountain,
3 fairest of heights,
the joy of all the earth,*
Mount Zion, the heights of Zaphon,†*
the city of the great king.

II

4 God is in its citadel,
renowned as a stronghold.
5 See! The kings assembled,
together they advanced.
6† When they looked they were astounded;
terrified, they were put to flight!*
7 Trembling seized them there,
anguish, like a woman's labor,*
8 As when the east wind wrecks
the ships of Tarshish!†

III

9† What we had heard we have now seen
in the city of the LORD of hosts,
In the city of our God,
which God establishes forever. *Selah*
10 We ponder, O God, your mercy
within your temple
11 Like your name, O God,
so is your praise to the ends of the earth.*
Your right hand is fully victorious.
12 Mount Zion is glad!
The daughters of Judah rejoice
because of your judgments!*

IV

13 Go about Zion, walk all around it,
note the number of its towers.
14 Consider the ramparts, examine its citadels,
that you may tell future generations:*
15 That this is God,
our God for ever and ever.†
He will lead us until death.

PSALM 49†

Confidence in God Rather than in Riches

1 For the leader. A psalm of the Korahites.†
2 Hear this, all you peoples!
Give ear, all who inhabit the world,
3 You of lowly birth or high estate,
rich and poor together.
4 My mouth shall speak words of wisdom,
my heart shall offer insights.*
5 I will turn my ear to a riddle,†
expound my question on a lyre.

I

6 Why should I fear in evil days,
with the iniquity of my assailants
surrounding me,
7 Of those who trust in their wealth
and boast of their abundant riches?*
8† No man can ransom even a brother,
or pay to God his own ransom.*
9 The redemption of his soul is costly;
and he will pass away forever.
10 Will he live on forever, then,
and never see the Pit of Corruption?
11 Indeed, he will see that the wise die,
and the fool will perish together with the
senseless,*
and they leave their wealth to others.*
12 Their tombs are their homes forever,
their dwellings through all generations,
"They named countries after themselves"
13 —but man does not abide in splendor.
He is like the beasts—they perish.*

II

14 This is the way of those who trust in themselves,
and the end of those who take pleasure in
their own mouth. *Selah*

† pilgrims to announce that God is eternally invincible like Zion itself (Ps 48:13–14).

48:1 *Korahites*: see note on Ps 42:1.

48:3 *The heights of Zaphon*: the mountain abode of the Canaanite storm-god Baal in comparable texts. To speak of Zion as if it were Zaphon was to claim for Israel's God what Canaanites claimed for Baal. Though topographically speaking Zion is only a hill, viewed religiously it towers over other mountains as the home of the supreme God (cf. Ps 68:16–17).

48:6 *When they looked*: the kings are stunned by the sight of Zion, touched by divine splendor. The language is that of holy war, in which the enemy panics and flees at the sight of divine glory.

48:8 *The ships of Tarshish*: large ships, named after the distant land or port of Tarshish, probably ancient Tartessus in southern Spain, although other identifications have been proposed, cf. Is 2:16; 60:9; Jon 1:3.

48:9 *What we had heard we have now seen*: the glorious things that new pilgrims had heard about the holy city—its beauty and awesomeness—they now see with their own eyes. The seeing here contrasts with the seeing of the hostile kings in Ps 48:6.

48:15 *Our God for ever and ever*: Israel's God is like Zion in being eternal and invincible. The holy city is therefore a kind of "sacrament" of God.

Psalm 49 The Psalm affirms confidence in God (cf. Ps 23; 27:1–6; 62) in the face of the apparent good fortune of the unjust rich, cf. Ps 37; 73. Reliance on wealth is misplaced (Ps 49:8–10) for it is of no avail in the face of death (Ps 49:18–20). After inviting all to listen to this axiom of faith (Ps 49:2–5), the psalmist depicts the self-delusion of the ungodly (Ps 49:6–13), whose destiny is to die like ignorant beasts (Ps 49:13, 18; cf. Prv 7:21–23). Their wealth should occasion no alarm, for they will come to nought, whereas God will save the just (Ps 49:14–20).

49:1 *Korahites*: see note on Ps 42:1.

49:5 *Riddle*: the psalmist's personal solution to the perennial biblical problem of the prosperity of the wicked. *Question*: parallel in meaning to problem; in wisdom literature it means the mysterious way of how the world works.

49:8 *No man can ransom even a brother*: an axiom. For the practice of redemption, cf. Jb 6:21–23. A play on the first Hebrew word of Ps 49:8, 16 relates the two verses.

* **48:3** Ps 50:2; Lam 2:15.
48:3 Is 14:13.
48:6 Jgs 5:19.
48:7 Ex 15:14; Jer 4:31.
48:11 Mal 1:11.
48:12 Ps 97:8.
48:14 Ps 22:31–32; 71:18.
49:4 Ps 78:2; Mt 13:35.
49:7 Jb 31:24.
49:8 Prv 10:15; 11:4; Ez 7:19; Mt 16:26.
49:11 Eccl 2:16.
49:11 Ps 39:7; Sir 11:18–19.
49:13 Eccl 3:18–21.

15 Like a herd of sheep they will be put into Sheol,
and Death will shepherd them.
Straight to the grave they descend,
where their form will waste away,
Sheol will be their palace.
16 But God will redeem my life,
will take me† from the hand of Sheol.*
Selah
17 Do not fear when a man becomes rich,
when the wealth of his house grows great.
18 At his death he will not take along anything,
his glory will not go down after him.*
19 During his life his soul uttered blessings;
"They will praise you, for you do well for yourself."
20 But he will join the company of his fathers,
never again to see the light.*
21 In his prime, man does not understand.
He is like the beasts—they perish.

PSALM 50†

The Acceptable Sacrifice

1 A psalm of Asaph.

I

The God of gods, the LORD,
has spoken and summoned the earth
from the rising of the sun to its setting.*
2 From Zion, the perfection of beauty,
God shines forth.*
3 Our God comes and will not be silent!
Devouring fire precedes him,
it rages strongly around him.*
4 He calls to the heavens above
and to the earth to judge his people:
5 "Gather my loyal ones to me,
those who made a covenant with me by sacrifice."
6 The heavens proclaim his righteousness,
for God himself is the judge.* *Selah*

II

7 "Listen, my people, I will speak;
Israel, I will testify against you;
God, your God, am I.
8 Not for your sacrifices do I rebuke you,
your burnt offerings are always before me.
9 I will not take a bullock from your house,
or he-goats from your folds.*
10 For every animal of the forest is mine,
beasts by the thousands on my mountains.
11 I know every bird in the heights;
whatever moves in the wild is mine.
12 Were I hungry, I would not tell you,
for mine is the world and all that fills it.*
13 Do I eat the flesh of bulls
or drink the blood of he-goats?
14 Offer praise as your sacrifice to God;*
fulfill your vows to the Most High.
15 Then call on me on the day of distress;*
I will rescue you, and you shall honor me."

III

16 But to the wicked God says:
"Why do you recite my commandments
and profess my covenant with your mouth?
17 You hate discipline;
you cast my words behind you!
18 If you see a thief, you run with him;
with adulterers you throw in your lot.
19 You give your mouth free rein for evil;
you yoke your tongue to deceit.
20 You sit and speak against your brother,
slandering your mother's son.
21 When you do these things should I be silent?
Do you think that I am like you?
I accuse you, I lay out the matter before your eyes.

IV

22 "Now understand this, you who forget God,
lest I start ripping apart and there be no rescuer.
23 Those who offer praise as a sacrifice honor me;
I will let him whose way is steadfast
look upon the salvation of God."*

PSALM 51†

The Miserere: Prayer of Repentance

1 For the leader. A psalm of David, 2 when Nathan the prophet came to him after he had gone in to Bathsheba.*

I

3 Have mercy on me, God, in accord with your merciful love;

---

† **49:16** *Will take me*: the same Hebrew verb is used of God "taking up" a favored servant: Enoch in Gn 5:24; Elijah in 2 Kgs 2:11–12; the righteous person in Ps 73:24. The verse apparently states the hope that God will rescue the faithful psalmist in the same manner.

Psalm 50 A covenant lawsuit stating that the sacrifice God really wants is the sacrifice of praise accompanied by genuine obedience (cf. Mi 6:1–8). It begins with a theophany and the summoning of the court (Ps 50:1–6). Then in direct address God explains what is required of the faithful (Ps 50:7–15), rebukes the hypocritical worshiper (Ps 50:16–21), and concludes with a threat and a promise (Ps 50:22–23; cf. Is 1:19–20).

Psalm 51 A lament, the most famous of the seven Penitential

---

* **49:16** Ps 16:10; 86:13; 103:4; 116:8.
49:18 Sir 11:18–19; Eccl 5:15; 1 Tm 6:7.
49:20 Jb 10:21–22.
50:1 Dt 10:17; Jos 22:22.
50:2 Ps 48:2.
50:3 Ps 97:3; Dn 7:10.
50:6 Ps 19:2; 97:6.
50:9 Ps 69:32; Am 5:21–22.
50:12 Ps 24:1; 89:12; Dt 10:14; 1 Cor 10:26.
50:14 Heb 13:15.
50:15 Ps 77:3.
50:23 Ps 91:16.
51:2 2 Sm 12.

in your abundant compassion blot out my
transgressions.
4 Thoroughly wash away my guilt;
and from my sin cleanse me.
5 For I know my transgressions;
my sin is always before me.*
6 Against you, you alone have I sinned;
I have done what is evil in your eyes
So that you are just in your word,
and without reproach in your judgment.*
7 Behold, I was born in guilt,
in sin my mother conceived me.†*
8 Behold, you desire true sincerity;
and secretly you teach me wisdom.
9 Cleanse me with hyssop,† that I may be pure;
wash me, and I will be whiter than snow.*
10 You will let me hear gladness and joy;
the bones you have crushed will rejoice.

II

11 Turn away your face from my sins;
blot out all my iniquities.
12 A clean heart create for me, God;
renew within me a steadfast spirit.*
13 Do not drive me from before your face,
nor take from me your holy spirit.*
14 Restore to me the gladness of your salvation;
uphold me with a willing spirit.
15 I will teach the wicked your ways,
that sinners may return to you.
16 Rescue me from violent bloodshed, God, my
saving God,
and my tongue will sing joyfully of your
justice.*
17 Lord, you will open my lips;
and my mouth will proclaim your praise.
18 For you do not desire sacrifice† or I would
give it;
a burnt offering you would not accept.*
19 My sacrifice, O God, is a contrite spirit;
a contrite, humbled heart, O God, you will
not scorn.

Live It!

A Fresh Start

Psalm 51 is a beautiful prayer of sorrow and remorse. It is attributed to King David, who would have written it seeking forgiveness and a fresh start after committing adultery with Bathsheba. Take a few minutes to read this psalm prayerfully and reflect on the marvelous way it asks for God's help in starting over.

In our time too, people can fall into a sinful pattern of having sex outside of marriage. Many people experience a deep regret and sadness in losing their virginity in a short-term and uncommitted relationship. Thinking they can never regain their moral virtue, they then pursue one loveless relationship after another. The promise of Psalm 51 is that they can start fresh at any point in this cycle! Some people call this new beginning a secondary virginity—not, of course, a physical virginity, but a virginity of the heart and soul. It means a commitment not to have sex again, except with the person they marry.

So whenever you are feeling the weight of sin, whether it is premarital sex or some other sin, pray Psalm 51. Let it mark your commitment to start fresh with God's help. Ask God to show you what situations to avoid and what people you need to ask to support you. Remember, God is always ready to forgive you, and all of heaven rejoices each time you make a fresh start!

▶ **Psalm 51**

Psalms, prays for the removal of the personal and social disorders that sin has brought. The poem has two parts of approximately equal length: Ps 51:3–10 and Ps 51:11–19, and a conclusion in Ps 51:20–21. The two parts interlock by repetition of "blot out" in the first verse of each section (Ps 51:3, 11), of "wash (away)" just after the first verse of each section (Ps 51:4) and just before the last verse (Ps 51:9) of the first section, and of "heart," "God," and "spirit" in Ps 51:12, 19. The first part (Ps 51:3–10) asks deliverance from sin, not just a past act but its emotional, physical, and social consequences. The second part (Ps 51:11–19) seeks something more profound than wiping the slate clean: nearness to God, living by the spirit of God (Ps 51:12–13), like the relation between God and people described in Jer 31:33–34. Nearness to God brings joy and the authority to teach sinners (Ps 51:15–16). Such proclamation is better than offering sacrifice (Ps 51:17–19). The last two verses express the hope that God's good will toward those who are cleansed and contrite will prompt him to look favorably on the acts of worship offered in the Jerusalem Temple (Ps 51:19 [20–21]).

51:7 *In sin my mother conceived me*: lit., "In iniquity was I conceived," an instance of hyperbole: at no time was the psalmist ever without sin, cf. Ps 88:15, "I am mortally afflicted since youth," i.e., I have always been afflicted. The verse does not imply that the sexual act of conception is sinful.

51:9 *Hyssop*: a small bush whose many woody twigs make a natural sprinkler. It was prescribed in the Mosaic law as an instrument for sprinkling sacrificial blood or lustral water for cleansing, cf. Ex 12:22; Lv 14:4; Nm 19:18.

51:18 *For you do not desire sacrifice*: the mere offering of the ritual sacrifice apart from good dispositions is not acceptable to God, cf. Ps 50.

51:5 Ps 32:5; 38:19; Is 59:12.
51:6 Rom 3:4.
51:7 Jb 14:4.
51:9 Jb 9:30; Is 1:18; Ez 36:25.
51:12 Ez 11:19.
51:13 Wis 1:5; 9:17; Is 63:11; Hg 2:5; Rom 8:9.
51:16 Ps 30:10.
51:18 Ps 40:7; 50:8; Am 5:21–22; Hos 6:6; Is 1:11–15; Heb 10:5–7.

III

20† Treat Zion kindly according to your good will;
build up the walls of Jerusalem.*
21 Then you will desire the sacrifices of the just,
burnt offering and whole offerings;
then they will offer up young bulls on your altar.

PSALM 52†

The Deceitful Tongue

1 For the leader. A *maskil* of David, 2 when Doeg the Edomite entered and reported to Saul, saying to him: "David has entered the house of Ahimelech."*

I

3 Why do you glory in what is evil, you who are mighty by the mercy of God?
All day long
4 you are thinking up intrigues;
your tongue is like a sharpened razor,
you worker of deceit.*
5 You love evil more than good,
lying rather than saying what is right.*
Selah
6 You love all the words that create confusion,
you deceitful tongue.*

II

7 God too will strike you down forever,
he will lay hold of you and pluck you from your tent,
uproot you from the land of the living.*
Selah
8 The righteous will see and they will fear;
but they will laugh at him:*
9 "Behold the man! He did not take God as his refuge,
but he trusted in the abundance of his wealth,
and grew powerful through his wickedness."*

III

10 But I, like an olive tree† flourishing in the house of God,*
I trust in God's mercy forever and ever.
11 I will thank you forever
for what you have done.
I will put my hope in your name—for it is good,*
—in the presence of those devoted to you.

PSALM 53†

A Lament over Widespread Corruption

1 For the leader; according to *Mahalath*.
A *maskil* of David.

I

2 The fool says in his heart,*
"There is no God."*
They act corruptly and practice injustice;
there is none that does good.
3 God looks out from the heavens
upon the children of Adam,*
To see if there is a discerning person*
who is seeking God.
4 All have gone astray;
each one is altogether perverse.
There is not one who does what is good,
not even one.*

II

5 *Do they not know better, those who do evil,
who feed upon my people as they feed upon bread?*
Have they not called upon God?
6 They are going to fear his name with great fear,
though they had not feared it before.
For God will scatter the bones
of those encamped against you.
They will surely be put to shame,
for God has rejected them.

III

7 Who will bring forth from Zion
the salvation of Israel?
When God reverses the captivity of his people
Jacob will rejoice and Israel will be glad.*

---

† **51:20–21** Most scholars think that these verses were added to the Psalm some time after the destruction of the Temple in 587 B.C. The verses assume that the rebuilt Temple will be an ideal site for national reconciliation.

Psalm 52 A condemnation of the powerful and arrogant (Ps 52:3–6), who bring down upon themselves God's judgment (Ps 52:7). The just, those who trust in God alone, are gladdened and strengthened by the downfall of their traditional enemies (Ps 52:8–9).

52:10 *Like an olive tree*: the righteous will flourish in the house of God like a well-watered olive tree, cf. Ps 92:14; 128:3.

Psalm 53 A lament of an individual, duplicated in Ps 14, except that "God" is used for "the LORD," and Ps 53:6 is different, cf. Ps 14.

51:20 Jer 31:4; Ez 36:33.
52:2 1 Sm 21:8; 22:6ff.
52:4 Ps 12:3; 59:8; 120:2–3; Sir 51:3.
52:5 Jer 4:22; Jn 3:19–20.
52:6 Jer 9:4.
52:7 Ps 27:13; 28:5; 56:14; Jb 18:14; Prv 2:22; Is 38:11.
52:8 Ps 44:14; 64:9.
52:9 Jb 31:24; Prv 11:28.
52:10 Ps 1:3; 92:12–14; Jer 11:16; 17:8.
52:11 Ps 22:23; 26:12; 35:18; 149:1.
53:2–6a Ps 14:1–5a.
53:2 Ps 10:4; 36:2; Is 32:6; Jer 5:12.
53:2b–3 Rom 3:11–12.
53:3 Ps 11:4; 102:20.
53:4 Ps 12:2.
53:5 Ps 79:6.
53:5 Ps 27:2; Is 9:11.
53:7 Ps 85:2.

PSALM 54†

Confident Prayer in Great Peril

[1] For the leader. On stringed instruments. A *maskil*
of David, [2] when the Ziphites came and said to
Saul, "David is hiding among us."*

I

3 O God, by your name† save me.
By your strength defend my cause.
4 O God, hear my prayer.
Listen to the words of my mouth.
5 Strangers have risen against me;
the ruthless seek my life;
they do not keep God before them.*
Selah

II

6 God is present as my helper;*
the Lord sustains my life.
7 Turn back the evil upon my foes;
in your faithfulness, destroy them.*
8 Then I will offer you generous sacrifice
and give thanks to your name, LORD, for it
is good.
9 Because it has rescued me from every trouble,
and my eyes look down on my foes.*

PSALM 55†

A Lament over Betrayal

[1] For the leader. On stringed instruments.
A *maskil* of David.

I

2 Listen, God, to my prayer;*
do not hide from my pleading;
3 hear me and give answer.
I rock with grief; I groan
4 at the uproar of the enemy,
the clamor of the wicked.
They heap trouble upon me,
savagely accuse me.
5 My heart pounds within me;
death's terrors fall upon me.
6 Fear and trembling overwhelm me;
shuddering sweeps over me.
7 I say, "If only I had wings like a dove
that I might fly away and find rest.*

Pray It!

Betrayed!

Maybe you don't have enemies quite as bad as the enemies described in Psalm 55, but you may be able to sympathize with the psalmist when he writes this: "He stretched out his hands at his friends / and broke his covenant" (verse 21).

When you feel betrayed by others like the psalmist does—maybe betrayed by a friend who didn't keep a promise or by a parent who seemed to treat you unfairly or by anyone else for whatever reason—call on God, and say a prayer like this:

I trust you, God; I want to believe you are with me. When others choose to abandon or betray me, help me to know you are here and that I am never alone. May I always honor my covenant with you. Amen.

▶ Psalm 55

8 Far away I would flee;
I would stay in the desert.* [9] I would soon
find a shelter *Selah*
from the raging wind and storm."

II

10 Lord, check and confuse their tongues.
For I see violence and strife in the city
11 making rounds on its walls day and night.
Within are mischief and trouble;
12 treachery is in its midst;
oppression and fraud never leave its streets.*
13 For it is not an enemy that reviled me—
that I could bear—
Not a foe who viewed me with contempt,
from that I could hide.
14 But it was you, my other self,

†

Psalm 54 A lament in which the person under attack calls directly upon God for help (Ps 54:3–5). Refusing to despair, the psalmist hopes in God, who is active in history and just (Ps 54:6–7). The Psalm ends with a serene promise to return thanks (Ps 54:8–9).

54:3 *By your name*: one is present in one's name, hence God as revealed to human beings.

Psalm 55 The psalmist, betrayed by intimate friends (Ps 55:14–15, 20–21), prays that God punish those oath breakers and thus be acknowledged as the protector of the wronged. The sufferings of the psalmist include both ostracism (Ps 55:4) and mental turmoil (Ps 55:5–6), culminating in the wish to flee society (Ps 55:7–9). The wish for a sudden death for one's enemies (Ps 55:16) occurs elsewhere in the Psalms; an example of such a death is the earth opening under the wicked Dathan and Abiram (Nm 16:31–32). The psalmist, confident of vindication, exhorts others to a like trust in the God of justice (Ps 55:23). The Psalm is not so much for personal vengeance as for a public vindication of God's righteousness now. There was no belief in an afterlife where such vindication could take place.

*

54:2 1 Sm 23:19; 26:1.
54:5 Ps 86:14.
54:6 Ps 118:7.
54:7 Ps 143:12.
54:9 Ps 59:11; 91:8; 92:12.
55:2–3 Ps 5:2–3; 86:6; 130:1–2; Lam 3:56; Jon 2:3.
55:7 Ps 11:1.
55:8 Jer 9:1; Rev 12:6.
55:12 Jer 5:1; 6:6; Ez 22:2; Heb 1:3; Zep 3:1.

PS

my comrade and friend,*
15 You, whose company I enjoyed,
at whose side I walked
in the house of God.

III

16 Let death take them;
let them go down alive to Sheol,*
for evil is in their homes and bellies.
17 But I will call upon God,
and the LORD will save me.
18 At dusk, dawn, and noon
I will grieve and complain,
and my prayer will be heard.*
19 He will redeem my soul in peace
from those who war against me,
though there are many who oppose me.
20 God, who sits enthroned forever,*
will hear me and afflict them. *Selah*
For they will not mend their ways;
they have no fear of God.
21 He stretched out his hand at his friends
and broke his covenant.
22 Softer than butter is his speech,
but war is in his heart.
Smoother than oil are his words,
but they are unsheathed swords.*
23 Cast your care upon the LORD,
who will give you support.
He will never allow
the righteous to stumble.*
24 But you, God, will bring them down
to the pit of destruction.*
These bloodthirsty liars
will not live half their days,
but I put my trust in you.*

PSALM 56†

Trust in God

1 For the director. According to *Yonath elem rehoqim*.† A *miktam* of David, when the Philistines seized him at Gath.*

I

2 Have mercy on me, God,
for I am treated harshly;
attackers press me all the day.
3 My foes treat me harshly all the day;
yes, many are my attackers.
O Most High, 4 when I am afraid,
in you I place my trust.
5 I praise the word of God;
I trust in God, I do not fear.*
What can mere flesh do to me?*

II

6 All the day they foil my plans;
their every thought is of evil against me.
7 They hide together in ambush;
they watch my every step;
they lie in wait for my life.*
8 They are evil; watch them, God!
Cast the nations down in your anger!
9 My wanderings you have noted;
are my tears not stored in your flask,†
recorded in your book?*
10 My foes turn back when I call on you.
This I know: God is on my side.
11 I praise the word of God,
I praise the word of the LORD.
12 In God I trust, I do not fear.
What can man do to me?

III

13 I have made vows to you, God;
with offerings I will fulfill them,*
14 For you have snatched me from death,
kept my feet from stumbling,
That I may walk before God
in the light of the living.

PSALM 57†

Confident Prayer for Deliverance

1 For the director. Do not destroy.† A *miktam* of David, when he fled from Saul into a cave.*

I

2 Have mercy on me, God,
have mercy on me.
In you I seek refuge.
In the shadow of your wings† I seek refuge
till harm pass by.*
3 I call to God Most High,

---

† **Psalm 56** Beset physically (Ps 56:2–3) and psychologically (Ps 56:6–7), the psalmist maintains a firm confidence in God (Ps 56:5, 9–10). Nothing will prevent the psalmist from keeping the vow to give thanks for God's gift of life (Ps 56:13). A refrain (Ps 56:5, 11–12) divides the Psalm in two equal parts.

56:1 *Yonath elem rehoqim*: Hebrew words probably designating the melody to which the Psalm was to be sung.

56:9 *Are my tears not stored in your flask*: a unique saying in the Old Testament. The context suggests that the tears are saved because they are precious; God puts a high value on each of the psalmist's troubles.

Psalm 57 Each of the two equal strophes contains a prayer for rescue from enemies, accompanied by joyful trust in God (Ps 57:2–5, 7–11). The refrain prays that God be manifested as saving (Ps 57:6, 12). Ps 108 is nearly identical to part of this Psalm (cf. Ps 57:8–11, Ps 108:2–6).

---

* **55:14** Ps 41:10; Jer 9:3; Mt 26:21–24 par.
55:16 Ps 49:15; Nm 16:33; Prv 1:2; Is 5:14.
55:18 Dn 6:11.
55:20 Ps 29:10; 93:2; Bar 3:3.
55:22 Ps 12:3; 28:3; 57:5; 62:5; 64:4; Prv 26:24–28; Jer 9:7.
55:23 Ps 37:5; Prv 3:5; 16:3; 1 Pt 5:7.
55:24 Ps 28:1; 30:4; 40:3; 88:5; 143:7; Prv 1:12; Jon 2:7.
55:24 Ps 25:2; 56:4; 130:5.
56:1 1 Sm 21:10.
56:5 Ps 130:5.
56:5 Ps 118:6; Heb 13:6.
56:7 Ps 140:5–6.
56:9 Ps 10:14; 2 Kgs 20:5; Is 25:8; Rev 7:17.
56:13 Nm 30:3.
57:1 1 Sm 22:1.
57:2 Ps 17:8; 36:8.

to God who provides for me.
4 May God send help from heaven to save me,
shame those who trample upon me.
May God send fidelity and mercy. *Selah*
5 I must lie down in the midst of lions
hungry for human prey.*
Their teeth are spears and arrows;
their tongue, a sharpened sword.*
6 Be exalted over the heavens, God;
may your glory appear above all the earth.*

II

7 They have set a trap for my feet;
my soul is bowed down;
They have dug a pit before me.
May they fall into it themselves!* *Selah*
8 My heart is steadfast, God,
my heart is steadfast.
I will sing and chant praise.*
9 Awake, my soul;
awake, lyre and harp!
I will wake the dawn.†*
10 I will praise you among the peoples, Lord;
I will chant your praise among the nations.*
11 For your mercy towers to the heavens;
your faithfulness reaches to the skies.*
12 Exalt yourself over the heavens, God;
may your glory appear above all the earth.

PSALM 58†

The Dethroning of Unjust Rulers

1 For the leader. Do not destroy.†
A *miktam* of David.

I

2 Do you indeed pronounce justice, O gods;†
do you judge fairly you children of Adam?*
3 No, you freely engage in crime;
your hands dispense violence to the earth.

II

4 The wicked have been corrupt since birth;
liars from the womb, they have gone astray.
5† Their venom is like the venom of a snake,
like that of a serpent stopping its ears,*
6 So as not to hear the voice of the charmer
or the enchanter with cunning spells.

III

7 O God, smash the teeth in their mouths;
break the fangs of these lions, LORD!*
8 Make them vanish like water flowing away;*
trodden down, let them wither like grass.*
9 Let them dissolve like a snail that oozes away,†
like an untimely birth that never sees the sun.*
10 Suddenly, like brambles or thistles,
have the whirlwind snatch them away.*
11 Then the just shall rejoice to see the vengeance
and bathe their feet in the blood of the wicked.*
12 Then people will say:
"Truly there is a reward for the just;
there is a God who is judge on earth!"

PSALM 59†

Complaint Against Bloodthirsty Enemies

1 For the director. Do not destroy.† A *miktam*
of David, when Saul sent people to watch his
house and kill him.*

I

2 Rescue me from my enemies, my God;
lift me out of reach of my foes.
3 Deliver me from evildoers;
from the bloodthirsty save me.
4 They have set an ambush for my life;
the powerful conspire against me.
For no offense or misdeed of mine, LORD,

---

† **57:1** *Do not destroy*: probably the title of the melody to which the Psalm was to be sung.

57:2 *The shadow of your wings*: probably refers to the wings of the cherubim (powerful winged animals) whose wings spread over the ark in the inner chamber of the Temple (1 Kgs 6:23–28).

57:9 *I will wake the dawn*: by a bold figure the psalmist imagines the sound of music and singing will waken a new day.

Psalm 58 A lament expressing trust in God's power to dethrone all powers obstructing divine rule of the world. First condemned are "the gods," the powers that were popularly imagined to control human destinies (Ps 58:2–3), then "the wicked," the human instruments of these forces (Ps 58:4–6). The psalmist prays God to prevent them from harming the just (Ps 58:7–10). The manifestation of justice will gladden the just; they will see that their God is with them (Ps 58:11). The Psalm is less concerned with personal vengeance than with public vindication of God's justice now.

58:1 *Do not destroy*: probably the title of the melody to which the Psalm was to be sung.

58:2 *Gods*: the Bible sometimes understands pagan gods to be lesser divine beings who are assigned by Israel's God to rule the foreign nations. Here they are accused of injustice, permitting the human judges under their patronage to abuse the righteous, cf. Ps 82.

58:5–6 The image is that of a poisonous snake that is controlled by the voice or piping of its trainer.

58:9 *A snail that oozes away*: empty shells suggested to ancients that snails melted away as they left a slimy trail.

Psalm 59 A lament in two parts (Ps 59:2–9, 11b–17), each ending in a refrain (Ps 59:10, 18). Both parts alternate prayer for vindication (Ps 59:2–3, 4b–5, 11b–14) with vivid depictions of the psalmist's enemies (Ps 59:4–5a, 7–8, 15–16). The near curse in Ps 59:12–13 is not a crude desire for revenge but a wish that God's just rule over human affairs be recognized now.

59:1 *Do not destroy*: probably the title of the melody to which the Psalm was to be sung.

---

* **57:5** Ps 17:11–12; 22:22; 58:7.
57:5 Ps 11:2; 64:4.
57:6 Ps 72:19; Nm 14:21.
57:7 Ps 7:15; 9:16–17; 140:5–6.
57:8 Ps 108:2.
57:9 Jb 38:12.
57:10 Ps 9:12; 18:50.
57:11 Ps 36:6; 71:19.
58:2 Ps 82:2; Dt 16:19.
58:5 Ps 64:4; 140:3; Rom 3:13.
58:7 Ps 3:7.
58:8 Wis 16:29.
58:8 Ps 37:2.
58:9 Jb 3:16.
58:10 Jb 21:18; Hos 13:3; Na 1:10.
58:11 Ps 68:24; Is 63:1–6.
59:1 1 Sm 19:11.

Live It!

The Agony of Defeat

The person who has never lost something or someone important to him or her does not exist. Nor does the athletic team that has never experienced the awful feeling that comes with losing. As a matter of fact, losing is what often inspires athletic teams to get stronger or faster or score more points.

The psalmist who sang Psalm 60 knew how it felt to lose. Although this psalm was written after defeat in battle, its spirit has echoed through the ages by athletic teams and all others who have been defeated in some way. The next time you experience loss, read verses 1–7, and think about how the psalmist calls on God as a helper. Strengthened and inspired by God, there is much that can be gained from defeat.

▶ Ps 60:1–7

5 for no fault they hurry to take up arms.
Come near and see my plight!
6 You, LORD God of hosts, are the God of Israel!
Awake! Punish all the nations.
Have no mercy on these worthless traitors. *Selah*
7 Each evening they return,
growling like dogs, prowling the city.*
8 Their mouths pour out insult;
sharp words are on their lips.
They say: "Who is there to hear?"†
9 But you, LORD, laugh at them;
you deride all the nations.*
10 My strength, for you I watch;
you, God, are my fortress,
11 my loving God.

II

May God go before me,
and show me my fallen foes.
12 Slay them, God,
lest they deceive my people.
Shake them by your power;
Lord, our shield, bring them down.
13 For the sinful words of their mouths and lips
let them be caught in their pride.
For the lies they have told under oath*
14 destroy them in anger,
destroy till they are no more.
Then people will know God rules over Jacob,
yes, even to the ends of the earth.* *Selah*
15 Each evening they return,
growling like dogs, prowling the city.
16 They roam about as scavengers;
if they are not filled, they howl.

III

17 But I shall sing of your strength,
extol your mercy at dawn,
For you are my fortress,
my refuge in time of trouble.
18 My strength, your praise I will sing;
you, God, are my fortress, my loving God.

PSALM 60†

Lament After Defeat in Battle

1 For the leader; according to "The Lily of. . . ."
A *miktam* of David (for teaching), 2 when he fought against Aram-Naharaim and Aram-Zobah; and Joab, coming back, killed twelve thousand Edomites in the Valley of Salt.*

I

3 O God, you rejected us, broke our defenses;
you were angry but now revive us.
4 You rocked the earth, split it open;*
repair the cracks for it totters.
5 You made your people go through hardship,
made us stagger from the wine you gave us.*
6 Raise up a banner for those who revere you,
a refuge for them out of bow shot. *Selah*
7† Help with your right hand and answer us
that your loved ones may escape.

II

8† In the sanctuary God promised:
"I will exult, will apportion Shechem;
the valley of Succoth† I will measure out.
9 Gilead is mine, mine is Manasseh;

---

† **59:8** *Who is there to hear?*: a sample of the enemies' godless reflection. The answer is that God hears their blasphemies.

Psalm 60 The community complains that God has let the enemy win the battle (Ps 60:3–5) and asks for an assurance of victory (Ps 60:6–7). In the oracle God affirms ownership of the land; the invasion of other nations is not permanent and will be reversed ultimately (Ps 60:8–10). With renewed confidence, the community resolves to fight again (Ps 60:11). The opening lament is picked up again (Ps 60:12), but this time with new awareness of God's power and human limitation.

60:7–12 These verses occur again as the second half of Ps 108.

60:8 *I will . . . apportion . . . measure out*: God lays claim to these places. *The valley of Succoth*: probably the lower stretch of the Jabbok valley.

---

* **59:7** Ps 55:11.
59:9 Ps 2:4; 37:13; Wis 4:18.
59:13 Prv 12:13; 18:7.
59:14 Ps 83:18–19; Ez 5:13.
60:2 2 Sm 8:2, 3, 13; 1 Chr 18:2, 3, 12.
60:4 Ps 75:4; Is 24:19.
60:5 Ps 75:9; Is 51:17, 21–22; Jer 25:15.

Ephraim is the helmet for my head,
Judah, my own scepter.†
10† Moab is my washbowl;
upon Edom I cast my sandal.†*
I will triumph over Philistia."

III

11 Who will bring me to the fortified city?†
Who will lead me into Edom?
12 Was it not you who rejected us, God?
Do you no longer march with our armies?*
13 Give us aid against the foe;
worthless is human help.
14 We will triumph with the help of God,
who will trample down our foes.

PSALM 61†

Prayer of the King in Time of Danger

1 For the leader; with stringed instruments. Of David.

I

2 Hear my cry, O God,
listen to my prayer!
3 From the ends of the earth† I call;
my heart grows faint.
Raise me up, set me on a rock,
4 for you are my refuge,
a tower of strength against the foe.*
5 Let me dwell in your tent forever,
take refuge in the shelter of your wings.*
Selah

II

6 For you, O God, have heard my vows,
you have granted me the heritage of those who revere your name.
7 Add days to the life of the king;
may his years be as from generation to generation;*
8 *May he reign before God forever;
send your love and fidelity† to preserve him—*
9 I will duly sing to your name forever,
fulfill my vows day after day.

Pray It!

Decide!

Whom are you going to trust? Where will you find your power? in the right people? in the right clothes? in money? in the right job? or can you trust God to be your rock and your salvation (see Ps 62:3)? Will you let God be your refuge (see 61:4, 62:8) in times of hardship? Why is it so hard sometimes to let your soul wait for God in silence (see 62:2)?

God, I am weak. Help me every day to put my trust in you. Help me to believe that you and I can do anything together.

▶ **Psalm 62**

PSALM 62†

Trust in God Alone

1 For the leader; *'al Jeduthun.*† A psalm of David.

I

2 My soul rests in God alone,*
from whom comes my salvation.
3 God alone is my rock and salvation,
my fortress; I shall never fall.
4 How long will you set yourself against a man?
You shall all be destroyed,
Like a sagging wall
or a tumbled down fence!
5 Even highly placed people
plot to overthrow him.
They delight in lies;
they bless with their mouths,
but inwardly they curse.* *Selah*

†

60:9 *Judah, my own scepter*: an allusion to the Testament of Jacob, Gn 49:10.

60:10 *Moab is my washbowl*: Moab borders the Dead Sea, hence a metaphor for the country. *Upon Edom I cast my sandal*: an ancient legal gesture of taking possession of land.

60:11 *The fortified city*: perhaps Bozrah, the fortified capital of Edom, cf. Is 34:6; 63:1; Am 1:12.

Psalm 61 A lament of the king who feels himself at the brink of death (Ps 61:3) and cries out for the strong and saving presence of God (Ps 61:3b–5). The king cites the prayer being made for him (Ps 61:7–8), and promises to give thanks to God.

61:3 *Ends of the earth*: "earth" being taken in its occasional meaning "the underworld," cf. Jon 2:3.

61:8 *Send your love and fidelity*: as in Ps 43:3 the psalmist asks God to send these two divine attributes like angels to protect the king.

Psalm 62 A song of trust displaying serenity from experiencing God's power (the refrains of Ps 62:2–3 and Ps 62:6–7) and anger toward unjust enemies (Ps 62:4–5). From the experience of being rescued, the psalmist can teach others to trust in God (Ps 62:9–12).

62:1 *'Al Jeduthun*: apparently the Hebrew name for the melody.

*

60:10 Ru 4:7–8.
60:12 Ps 44:10.
61:4 Ps 46:2.
61:5 Ps 17:8; 36:8; 57:2.
61:7 Ps 21:5.
61:8 Ps 72:5; 89:5, 30, 37.
61:8 Ps 85:11; 89:15, 25; Prv 20:28.
62:2–3, 6–7 Ps 18:3; 31:3–4; 42:10; 118:8; 146:3.
62:5 Ps 12:3; 28:3; 55:22; Prv 26:24–25.

II

6 My soul, be at rest in God alone,
from whom comes my hope.
7 God alone is my rock and my salvation,
my fortress; I shall not fall.
8 My deliverance and honor are with God,*
my strong rock;
my refuge is with God.
9 Trust God at all times, my people!
Pour out your hearts to God our refuge!
Selah

III

10 Mortals are a mere breath,
the sons of man but an illusion;*
On a balance they rise;†
together they weigh nothing.
11 Do not trust in extortion;
in plunder put no empty hope.
On wealth that increases,
do not set your heart.*
12† One thing God has said;
two things I have heard:*
Strength belongs to God;
13 so too, my Lord, does mercy,
For you repay each man
according to his deeds.*

PSALM 63†

Ardent Longing for God

1 A psalm of David, when he was
in the wilderness of Judah.*

I

2 O God, you are my God—
it is you I seek!
For you my body yearns;
for you my soul thirsts,
In a land parched, lifeless,
and without water.*
3 I look to you in the sanctuary
to see your power and glory.
4 For your love is better than life;†
my lips shall ever praise you!

II

5 I will bless you as long as I live;
I will lift up my hands, calling on your
name.
6 My soul shall be sated as with choice food,
with joyous lips my mouth shall praise you!
7 I think of you upon my bed,
I remember you through the watches of the
night
8 You indeed are my savior,
and in the shadow of your wings I shout
for joy.*
9 My soul clings fast to you;
your right hand upholds me.

III

10 But those who seek my life will come to ruin;
they shall go down to the depths of the
netherworld!
11 Those who would hand over my life to the
sword shall
become the prey of jackals!
12 But the king shall rejoice in God;
all who swear by the Lord† shall exult,
but the mouths of liars will be shut!*

PSALM 64†

Treacherous Conspirators Punished by God

1 For the leader. A psalm of David.

I

2 O God, hear my anguished voice;
from a dreadful foe protect my life.
3 Hide me from the malicious crowd,
the mob of evildoers.
4 They sharpen their tongues like swords,
bend their bows of poison words.*
5 They shoot at the innocent from ambush,
they shoot him in a moment and do not
fear.
6 They resolve on their wicked plan;
they conspire to set snares;
they say: "Who will see us?"
7 They devise wicked schemes,

†

62:10 *On a balance they rise*: precious objects were weighed by balancing two pans suspended from a beam. The lighter pan rises.

62:12 *One thing . . . two things*: parallelism of numbers for the sake of variation, a common device in Semitic poetry. One should not literally add up the numbers, cf. Am 1:3; Prv 6:16–19; 30:15, 18, 21.

Psalm 63 A Psalm expressing the intimate relationship between God and the worshiper. Separated from God (Ps 63:2), the psalmist longs for the divine life given in the Temple (Ps 63:3–6), which is based on a close relationship with God (Ps 63:7–9). May all my enemies be destroyed and God's true worshipers continue in giving praise (Ps 63:10–11)!

63:4 *For your love is better than life*: only here in the Old Testament is anything prized above life—in this case God's love.

63:12 *All who swear by the Lord*: to swear by a particular god meant that one was a worshiper of that god (Is 45:23; 48:1; Zep 1:5).

Psalm 64 A lament of a person overwhelmed by the malice of the wicked who are depicted in the Psalms as the enemies of the righteous (Ps 64:2–7). When people see God bringing upon the wicked the evil they intended against others, they will know who is the true ruler of the world (Ps 64:8–10). The final verse is a vow of praise (Ps 64:11).

*

62:8 Ps 3:3; Is 26:4; 60:19.
62:10 Ps 39:6–7; 144:4; Jb 7:16; Wis 2:5.
62:11 Jb 31:25; Eccl 5:9; Jer 17:11; Mt 6:19–21, 24.
62:12 Jb 40:5.
62:13 Ps 28:4; 31:24; 2 Sm 3:39; Jb 34:11; Jer 17:10; Mt 16:27; Rom 2:6; 2 Tm 4:14.
63:1 1 Sm 24.
63:2 Ps 42:2; 143:6; Is 26:9.
63:8 Ps 17:8; 36:8.
63:12 Ps 107:42.
64:4 Ps 11:2; 37:14; 55:22; 57:5.

PS

conceal the schemes they devise;
the designs of their hearts are hidden.*

II

8 God shoots an arrow at them;
in a moment they are struck down.*
9 They are brought down by their own tongues;
all who see them flee.*
10 Every person fears and proclaims God's actions,
they ponder his deeds.
11 The righteous rejoices and takes refuge in the LORD;
all the upright give praise.*

PSALM 65†

Thanksgiving for God's Blessings

1 For the leader. A psalm of David. A song.

I

2 To you we owe our hymn of praise,
O God on Zion;
To you our vows† must be fulfilled,
3† you who hear our prayers.
To you all flesh must come*
4 with its burden of wicked deeds.
We are overcome by our sins;
only you can pardon them.*
5 Blessed the one whom you will choose and bring
to dwell in your courts.
May we be filled with the good things of your house,
your holy temple!

II

6 You answer us with awesome deeds† of justice,
O God our savior,
The hope of all the ends of the earth
and of those far off across the sea.*
7 You are robed in power,
you set up the mountains by your might.
8 You still the roaring of the seas,*
the roaring of their waves,
the tumult of the peoples.*
9 Distant peoples stand in awe of your marvels;
the places of morning and evening you make resound with joy.
10† You visit the earth and water it,
make it abundantly fertile.*
God's stream† is filled with water;
you supply their grain.
Thus do you prepare it:
11 you drench its plowed furrows,
and level its ridges.
With showers you keep it soft,
blessing its young sprouts.
12 You adorn the year with your bounty;
your paths† drip with fruitful rain.
13 The meadows of the wilderness also drip;
the hills are robed with joy.
14 The pastures are clothed with flocks,
the valleys blanketed with grain;
they cheer and sing for joy.*

PSALM 66†

Praise of God, Israel's Deliverer

1 For the leader. A song; a psalm.

I

2 Shout joyfully to God, all the earth;
sing of his glorious name;
give him glorious praise.*
3 Say to God: "How awesome your deeds!
Before your great strength your enemies cringe.
4 All the earth falls in worship before you;*
they sing of you, sing of your name!" *Selah*

II

5† Come and see the works of God,
awesome in deeds before the children of Adam.

---

† **Psalm 65** The community, aware of its unworthiness (Ps 65:3–4), gives thanks for divine bounty (Ps 65:5), a bounty resulting from God's creation victory (Ps 65:6–9). At God's touch the earth comes alive with vegetation and flocks (Ps 65:10–13).

65:2 *Vows*: the Israelites were accustomed to promising sacrifices in the Temple if their prayers were heard.

65:3 *To you all flesh must come*: all must have recourse to God's mercy.

65:6 *Awesome deeds*: the acts of creating—installing mountains, taming seas, restraining nations (Ps 65:7–8)—that are visible worldwide (Ps 65:6, 9).

65:10–14 Apparently a description of the agricultural year, beginning with the first fall rains that soften the hard sun-baked soil (Ps 65:9–10).

65:10 *God's stream*: the fertile waters of the earth derive from God's fertile waters in the heavenly world.

65:12 *Paths*: probably the tracks of God's storm chariot dropping rain upon earth.

Psalm 66 In the first part (Ps 66:1–12), the community praises God for powerful acts for Israel, both in the past (the exodus from Egypt and the entry into the land [Ps 66:6]) and in the present (deliverance from a recent but unspecified calamity [Ps 66:8–12]). In the second part (Ps 66:13–20), an individual from the rescued community fulfills a vow to offer a sacrifice of thanksgiving. As often in thanksgivings, the rescued person steps forward to teach the community what God has done (Ps 66:16–20).

66:5–6 cf. the events described in Ex 14:1–15, 21; Jos 3:11–4:24 and Ps 114.

---

* **64:7** Ps 140:3; Prv 6:14. **64:8** Ps 7:13–14; 38:3; Dt 32:42. **64:9** Ps 5:11; 44:14; 52:6. **64:11** Ps 36:8; 57:2. **65:3** Is 66:23. **65:4** Ps 32:1–2; 78:38; Is 1:18. **65:6** Is 66:19. **65:8** Ps 89:10; 107:29; Jb 38:11; Mt 8:26. **65:8** Is 17:12. **65:10** Lv 26:4; Is 30:23, 25; Jl 2:22–23. **65:14** Is 44:23. **66:2** Ps 65:14; Is 44:23. **66:3–4** Ps 18:45; Mi 7:17.

6 He changed the sea to dry land;
through the river they passed on foot.*
There we rejoiced in him,
7 who rules by his might forever,
His eyes are fixed upon the nations.
Let no rebel rise to challenge! *Selah*
8 Bless our God, you peoples;
loudly sound his praise,
9 Who has kept us alive
and not allowed our feet to slip.*
10 You tested us, O God,
tried us as silver tried by fire.*
11 You led us into a snare;
you bound us at the waist as captives.
12† You let captors set foot on our neck;
we went through fire and water;
then you led us out to freedom.*

III

13 I will bring burnt offerings† to your house;
to you I will fulfill my vows,
14 Which my lips pronounced
and my mouth spoke in my distress.
15 Burnt offerings of fatlings I will offer you
and sacrificial smoke of rams;
I will sacrifice oxen and goats. *Selah*
16 Come and hear, all you who fear God,
while I recount what has been done for me.
17 I called to him with my mouth;
praise was upon my tongue.
18 Had I cherished evil in my heart,
the Lord would not have heard.
19 But God did hear
and listened to my voice in prayer.
20 Blessed be God, who did not reject my prayer
and refuse his mercy.

PSALM 67†

Harvest Thanks and Petition

1 For the leader; with stringed instruments.
A psalm; a song.

I

2 May God be gracious to us† and bless us;
may his face shine upon us.* *Selah*
3 So shall your way be known upon the earth,
your victory among all the nations.*
4 May the peoples praise you, God;
may all the peoples praise you!

II

5 May the nations be glad and rejoice;
for you judge the peoples with fairness,
you guide the nations upon the earth.* *Selah*
6 May the peoples praise you, God;
may all the peoples praise you!

III

7 The earth has yielded its harvest;
God, our God, blesses us.*
8 May God bless us still;
that the ends of the earth may revere him.

PSALM 68†

The Exodus and Conquest, Pledge of Future Help

1 For the leader. A psalm of David; a song.

I

2† May God arise;
may his enemies be scattered;
may those who hate him flee before him.*
3 As the smoke is dispersed, disperse them;
as wax is melted by fire,
so may the wicked perish before God.*
4 Then the just will be glad;
they will rejoice before God;
they will celebrate with great joy.

II

5 Sing to God, praise his name;
exalt the rider of the clouds.†
Rejoice before him
whose name is the LORD.*
6 Father of the fatherless, defender of widows*—
God in his holy abode,
7 God gives a home to the forsaken,
who leads prisoners out to prosperity,
while rebels live in the desert.†

---

† **66:12** *You let captors set foot on our neck*: lit., "you let men mount our heads." Conquerors placed their feet on the neck of their enemies as a sign of complete defeat, cf. Jos 10:24. A ceremonial footstool of the Egyptian king Tutankhamen portrays bound and prostrate bodies of enemies ready for the king's feet on their heads, and one of Tutankhamen's ceremonial chariots depicts the king as a sphinx standing with paw atop the neck of an enemy.

66:13 *Burnt offerings*: cf. Lv 1:3–13; 6:1–4; 22:17–20.

Psalm 67 A petition for a bountiful harvest (Ps 67:7), made in the awareness that Israel's prosperity will persuade the nations to worship its God.

67:2 *May God be gracious to us*: the people's petition echoes the blessing pronounced upon them by the priests, cf. Nm 6:22–27.

Psalm 68 The Psalm is extremely difficult because the Hebrew text is badly preserved and the ceremony that it describes is uncertain. The translation assumes the Psalm accompanied the early autumn Feast of Tabernacles (Sukkoth), which included a procession of the tribes (Ps 68:25–28). Israel was being oppressed by a foreign

---

* **66:6** Ps 74:15; 114:3; Ex 14:21f; Jos 3:14ff; Is 44:27; 50:2.
66:9 Ps 91:12; 121:3; 1 Sm 2:9; Prv 3:23.
66:10 Is 48:10.
66:12 Is 43:2.
67:2 Ps 4:7; 31:17; 44:4; 80:4; Dn 9:17.
67:3 Jer 33:9.
67:5 Ps 98:9.
67:7 Ps 85:13; Lv 26:4; Ez 34:27; Hos 2:23–24.
68:2 Nm 10:35.
68:3 Ps 97:5; Jdt 16:15; Wis 5:14; Mi 1:4.
68:5 Ps 18:10; 104:3; Dt 33:26; Is 19:1.
68:6–7 Ps 103:6; 146:7, 9; Ex 22:20–22; Bar 6:37.

Cultural Connection

Black People Praise the Lord

Psalm 68 commands us to sing praises to the Lord. We are told to praise the Lord because God is the "Father of the fatherless, defender of widows" (verse 6), "gives a home to the forsaken" and "leads prisoners out to prosperity" (verse 7), daily "carries us" (verse 20), and "will crush the heads of the enemy" (verse 22).

Near the end of all this praise, the psalmist says, "Let bronze be brought from Egypt, / Ethiopia hurry its hands to God" (verse 32). The psalmist's call to Egypt and Ethiopia is significant for African Americans because the Egyptians and the Ethiopians were North African black people.

Nevertheless, the message of Psalm 68 is for all people, whether they are black, brown, red, yellow, or white. All people ought to submit to the Lord, all people ought to praise the Lord, and all people ought to render their whole self and their whole substance to the Lord. It matters not who we are or where we come from; the Lord is God and worthy of all praise!

▶ Psalm 68

III

8 God, when you went forth before your
people,*
when you marched through the desert, *Selah*
9 The earth quaked, the heavens poured,
before God, the One of Sinai,
before God, the God of Israel.
10 You poured abundant rains, God,
your inheritance was weak and you
repaired it.
11 Your creatures dwelt in it;
you will establish it in your goodness for
the poor, O God.

IV

12 The Lord announced:
"Those bringing news are a great Army.
13 The kings of the armies are in desperate
flight.*
Every household will share the spoil,
14 though you lie down among the sheepfolds,*
you shall be covered with silver as the
wings of a dove,
her feathers bright as fine gold."
15 When the Almighty routs the kings there,
it will be as when snow fell on Zalmon.†

V

16 You mountain of God, mountain of Bashan,
you rugged mountain, mountain of
Bashan,
17 You rugged mountains, why look with envy
at the mountain† where God has chosen to
dwell,
where the LORD resides forever?*
18 God's chariots were myriad, thousands upon
thousands;
from Sinai the Lord entered the holy place.
19 You went up to its lofty height;
you took captives, received slaves as
tribute,*
even rebels, for the LORD God to dwell.

---

† power, perhaps Egypt (Ps 68:31–32)—unless Egypt stands for any oppressor. The Psalm may have been composed from segments of ancient poems, which would explain why the transitions are implied rather than explicitly stated. At any rate, Ps 68:2 is based on Nm 10:35–36, and Ps 68:8–9 are derived from Jgs 5:4–5. The argument develops in nine stanzas (each of three to five poetic lines): 1. confidence that God will destroy Israel's enemies (Ps 68:2–4); 2. call to praise God as savior (Ps 68:5–7); 3. God's initial rescue of Israel from Egypt (Ps 68:8), the Sinai encounter (Ps 68:9), and the settlement in Canaan (Ps 68:10–11); 4. the defeat of the Canaanite kings (Ps 68:12–15); 5. the taking of Jerusalem, where Israel's God will rule the world (Ps 68:16–19); 6. praise for God's past help and for the future interventions that will be modeled on the ancient exodus-conquest (Ps 68:20–24); 7. procession at the Feast of Tabernacles (Ps 68:25–28); 8. prayer that the defeated enemies bring tribute to the Temple (Ps 68:29–32); 9. invitation for all kingdoms to praise Israel's God (Ps 68:33–35).

68:2 The opening line alluding to Nm 10:35 makes clear that God's assistance in the period of the exodus and conquest is the model and assurance of all future divine help.

68:5 *Exalt the rider of the clouds*: God's intervention is in the imagery of Canaanite myth in which the storm-god mounted the storm clouds to ride to battle. Such theophanies occur throughout the Psalm: Ps 68:2–3, 8–10, 12–15, 18–19, 22–24, 29–32, 34–35. See Dt 33:26; Ps 18:8–16; Is 19:1.

68:7 *While rebels live in the desert*: rebels must live in the arid desert, whereas God's people will live in the well-watered land (Ps 68:8–11).

68:15 *Zalmon*: generally taken as the name of a mountain where snow is visible in winter, perhaps to be located in the Golan Heights or in the mountains of Bashan or Hauran east of the Sea of Galilee.

68:17 *The mountain*: Mount Zion, the site of the Temple.

68:8–9 Ps 44:10; 114:4, 7; Jgs 5:4–5; Heb 12:26.
68:13 Jgs 5:19, 22.
68:14 Jgs 5:16.
68:17 Ps 132:13–14; Ez 43:7.
68:19 Ps 47:8; Eph 4:8–10.

VI

20 Blessed be the Lord day by day,
God, our salvation, who carries us.* *Selah*
21 Our God is a God who saves;
escape from death is the LORD God's.
22 God will crush the heads of his enemies,
the hairy scalp of the one who walks in sin.*
23 The Lord has said:
"Even from Bashan I will fetch them,
fetch them even from the depths of the sea.†
24 You will wash your feet in your enemy's blood;
the tongues of your dogs will lap it up."*

VII

25† Your procession comes into view, O God,
your procession into the holy place, my
God and king.
26 The singers go first, the harpists follow;
in their midst girls sound the timbrels.*
27 In your choirs, bless God;
LORD, Israel's fountain.
28 In the lead is Benjamin, few in number;
there the princes of Judah, a large throng,
the princes of Zebulun, the princes of
Naphtali, too.*

VIII

29 Summon again, O God, your power,
the divine power you once showed for us,
30 From your temple on behalf of Jerusalem,
that kings may bring you tribute.
31 Roar at the wild beast of the reeds,†
the herd of mighty bulls, the calves of the
peoples;
trampling those who lust after silver
scatter the peoples that delight in war.
32 Let bronze be brought from Egypt,*
Ethiopia hurry its hands to God.*

IX

33 You kingdoms of the earth, sing to God;*
chant the praises of the Lord, *Selah*
34 Who rides the heights of the ancient heavens,
Who sends forth his voice as a mighty voice?
35 Confess the power of God,
whose majesty protects Israel,
whose power is in the sky.
36 Awesome is God in his holy place,
the God of Israel,
who gives power and strength to his
people.*
Blessed be God!

PSALM 69†

A Cry of Anguish in Great Distress

1 For the leader; according to "Lilies."† Of David.

I

2 Save me, God,
for the waters† have reached my neck.*
3 I have sunk into the mire of the deep,
where there is no foothold.
I have gone down to the watery depths;
the flood overwhelms me.*
4 I am weary with crying out;
my throat is parched.
My eyes fail,
from looking for my God.*
5 More numerous than the hairs of my head
are those who hate me without cause.*
Those who would destroy me are mighty,
my enemies without reason.
Must I now restore
what I did not steal?†

II

6 God, you know my folly;
my faults are not hidden from you.
7 Let those who wait in hope for you, LORD of
hosts,
not be shamed because of me.
Let those who seek you, God of Israel,*
not be disgraced because of me.
8 For it is on your account I bear insult,
that disgrace covers my face.*
9 I have become an outcast to my kindred,
a stranger to my mother's children.*

†

68:23 *Even from Bashan . . . from the depths of the sea*: the heights and the depths, the farthest places where enemies might flee.

68:25–28 *Your procession*: the procession renews God's original taking up of residence on Zion, described in Ps 68:16–19.

68:31 *The wild beast of the reeds*: probably the Nile crocodile, a symbol for Egypt; see Ps 68:32 and Ez 29:2–5.

Psalm 69 A lament complaining of suffering in language both metaphorical (Ps 69:2–3, 15–16, the waters of chaos) and literal (Ps 69:4, 5, 9, 11–13, exhaustion, alienation from family and community, false accusation). In the second part the psalmist prays with special emphasis that the enemies be punished for all to see (Ps 69:23–29). Despite the pain, the psalmist does not lose hope that all be set right, and promises public praise (Ps 69:30–36). The Psalm, which depicts the suffering of the innocent just person vividly, is cited often by the New Testament especially in the passion accounts, e.g., Ps 69:5 in Jn 15:25; Ps 69:22 in Mk 15:23, 36 and parallels and in Jn 19:29. The Psalm prays not so much for personal vengeance as for public vindication of God's justice. There was, at this time, no belief in an afterlife where such vindication could take place. Redress had to take place now, in the sight of all.

69:1 *"Lilies"*: apparently the name of the melody.

69:2 *Waters*: the waters of chaos from which God created the world are a common metaphor for extreme distress, cf. Ps 18:5; 42:8; 88:8; Jon 2:3–6.

69:5 *What I did not steal*: the psalmist, falsely accused of theft, is being forced to make restitution.

*

68:20 Ps 34:2; 145:2; Is 46:3–4; 63:9.
68:22 Dt 32:42.
68:24 Ps 58:11; 1 Kgs 21:19; 22:38; Is 63:1–6.
68:26 Ps 81:2–3; 87:7; 149:3; 150:3–5; 2 Sm 6:5.
68:28 Is 8:23.
68:32 Ez 29:2ff.
68:32 Is 18:7; 45:14.
68:33 Ps 138:4.
68:36 Ps 28:8; 29:11.
69:2 Ps 18:5; 93:3–4; Jb 22:11.
69:3 Ps 40:2; 124:4–5.
69:4 Ps 25:15; 119:82; 123:2; 141:8; Is 38:14.
69:5 Ps 40:13; Lam 3:52; Jn 15:25.
69:7 Ps 40:17.
69:8 Jer 15:15.
69:9 Jb 19:13–15.

10 Because zeal for your house has consumed
me,†
I am scorned by those who scorn you.†*
11 When I humbled my spirit with fasting,*
this led only to scorn.
12 When I clothed myself in sackcloth;
I became a byword for them.
13 Those who sit in the gate gossip about me;
drunkards make me the butt of songs.

III

14 But I will pray to you, LORD,
at a favorable time.
God, in your abundant kindness, answer me
with your sure deliverance.*
15 Rescue me from the mire,*
and do not let me sink.
Rescue me from those who hate me
and from the watery depths.
16 Do not let the flood waters overwhelm me,
nor the deep swallow me,
nor the pit close its mouth over me.
17 Answer me, LORD, in your generous love;
in your great mercy turn to me.
18 Do not hide your face from your servant;
hasten to answer me, for I am in distress.*
19 Come and redeem my life;
because of my enemies ransom me.
20 You know my reproach, my shame, my
disgrace;
before you stand all my foes.
21 Insult has broken my heart, and I despair;
I looked for compassion, but there was
none,*
for comforters, but found none.
22 Instead they gave me poison for my food;
and for my thirst they gave me vinegar.*

IV

23 May their own table be a snare for them,
and their communion offerings a trap.*
24 Make their eyes so dim they cannot see;
keep their backs ever feeble.
25 Pour out your wrath upon them;
let the fury of your anger overtake them.
26 Make their camp desolate,
with none to dwell in their tents.*
27 For they pursued the one you struck,
added to the pain of the one you
wounded.
28 Heap punishment upon their punishment;
let them gain from you no vindication.
29 May they be blotted from the book of life;
not registered among the just!*

V

30 But here I am miserable and in pain;
let your saving help protect me, God,
31† That I may praise God's name in song
and glorify it with thanksgiving.
32 That will please the LORD more than oxen,
more than bulls with horns and hooves:*
33 "See, you lowly ones, and be glad;
you who seek God, take heart!*
34 For the LORD hears the poor,
and does not spurn those in bondage.
35 Let the heaven and the earth praise him,
the seas and whatever moves in them!"

VI

36 For God will rescue Zion,
and rebuild the cities of Judah.*
They will dwell there and possess it;
37 the descendants of God's servants will
inherit it;
those who love God's name will dwell in it.*

PSALM 70†

Prayer for Divine Help

1 For the leader; of David. For remembrance.
2 Graciously rescue me, God!*
Come quickly to help me, LORD!*
3 Let those who seek my life
be confused and put to shame.*
Let those who desire my ruin
turn back in disgrace.
4 Let those who say "Aha!"*
turn back in their shame.
5 But may all who seek you
rejoice and be glad in you,
Those who long for your help
always say, "God be glorified!"*
6 I am miserable and poor.
God, come to me quickly!

PS

---

† **69:10** *Zeal for your house has consumed me*: the psalmist's commitment to God's cause brings only opposition, cf. Jn 2:17. *I am scorned by those who scorn you*: Rom 15:3 uses the verse as an example of Jesus' unselfishness.

69:31 *That I may praise God's name in song*: the actual song is cited in Ps 69:33–35, the word "praise" in Ps 69:35 referring back to "praise" in Ps 69:31.

Psalm 70 A lament of a poor and afflicted person (Ps 70:6) who has no resource except God, and who cries out to be saved from the enemy. The Psalm is almost identical to Ps 40:14–17.

---

* **69:10** Ps 119:139; Jn 2:17; Rom 15:3.
69:11–13 Ps 109:24–25; Jb 30:9; Lam 3:14.
69:14 Is 49:8.
69:15–16 Ps 28:1; 30:4; 32:6; 40:3; 88:5; Prv 1:12.
69:18 Ps 102:3; 143:7.
69:21 Lam 1:2.
69:22 Lam 3:15; Mt 27:34, 48; Mk 15:23.
69:23 Rom 11:9–10.
69:26 Acts 1:20.
69:29 Ps 139:16; Ex 32:32; Is 4:3; Dn 12:1; Mal 3:16; Rev 3:5.
69:32 Ps 40:7; 50:8–9, 14; 51:18; Is 1:11–15; Hos 6:6; Am 5:21–22; Heb 10:5–8.
69:33 Ps 22:27; 35:27; 70:5.
69:36 Is 44:26; Ez 36:10.
69:37 Ps 102:29; Is 65:9.
70:2–6 Ps 40:14–18.
70:2 Ps 71:12.
70:3 Ps 35:4, 26.
70:4 Ps 35:21, 25.
70:5 Ps 35:27.

You are my help and deliverer.
LORD, do not delay!

PSALM 71†

Prayer in Time of Old Age

I

1 In you, LORD, I take refuge;*
let me never be put to shame.*
2 In your justice rescue and deliver me;
listen to me and save me!
3 Be my rock of refuge,
my stronghold to give me safety;
for you are my rock and fortress.*
4 My God, rescue me from the hand of the wicked,
from the clutches of the evil and violent.*
5 You are my hope, Lord;
my trust, GOD, from my youth.
6 On you I have depended since birth;
from my mother's womb you are my strength;*
my hope in you never wavers.
7† I have become a portent to many,
but you are my strong refuge!
8 My mouth shall be filled with your praise,
shall sing your glory every day.

II

9 Do not cast me aside in my old age;
as my strength fails, do not forsake me.
10 For my enemies speak against me;
they watch and plot against me.*
11 They say, "God has abandoned him.
Pursue, and seize him!
No one will come to the rescue!"
12 God, be not far from me;
my God, hasten to help me.*
13 Bring to a shameful end
those who attack me;
Cover with contempt and scorn
those who seek my ruin.*
14 I will always hope in you
and add to all your praise.
15 My mouth shall proclaim your just deeds,
day after day your acts of deliverance,
though I cannot number them all.*
16 I will speak of the mighty works of the Lord;
O GOD, I will tell of your singular justice.

III

17 God, you have taught me from my youth;
to this day I proclaim your wondrous deeds.
18 Now that I am old and gray,*
do not forsake me, God,
That I may proclaim your might
to all generations yet to come,*
Your power 19 and justice, God,
to the highest heaven.
You have done great things;*
O God, who is your equal?*
20 Whatever bitter afflictions you sent me,
you would turn and revive me.
From the watery depths of the earth
once more raise me up.
21 Restore my honor;
turn and comfort me,
22 That I may praise you with the lyre
for your faithfulness, my God,
And sing to you with the harp,
O Holy One of Israel!
23 My lips will shout for joy as I sing your praise;
my soul, too, which you have redeemed.
24 Yes, my tongue shall recount
your justice day by day.
For those who sought my ruin
have been shamed and disgraced.

PSALM 72†

A Prayer for the King

1 Of Solomon.

I

2 O God, give your judgment to the king;
your justice to the king's son;†*
That he may govern your people with justice,
your oppressed with right judgment,*
3 That the mountains may yield their bounty
for the people,
and the hills great abundance,*
4 That he may defend the oppressed among the people,

†

Psalm 71 A lament of an old person (Ps 71:9, 18) whose afflictions are interpreted by enemies as a divine judgment (Ps 71:11). The first part of the Psalm pleads for help (Ps 71:1–4) on the basis of a hope learned from a lifetime's experience of God; the second part describes the menace (Ps 71:9–13) yet remains buoyant (Ps 71:14–16); the third develops the theme of hope and praise.

71:7 *A portent to many*: the afflictions of the sufferer are taken as a manifestation of God's anger, cf. Dt 28:46; Ps 31:12.

Psalm 72 A royal Psalm in which the Israelite king, as the representative of God, is the instrument of divine justice (Ps 72:1–4, 12–14) and blessing (Ps 72:5–7, 15–17) for the whole world. The king is human, giving only what he has received from God. Hence intercession must be made for him. The extravagant language is typical of oriental royal courts.

72:2 *The king . . . the king's son*: the crown prince is the king's son; the prayer envisages the dynasty.

*

71:1–3 Ps 31:2–4.
71:1 Ps 25:2.
71:3 Ps 18:3.
71:4 Ps 140:2.
71:6 Ps 22:11.
71:10 Ps 3:2; 22:8.
71:12 Ps 22:20.
71:13 Ps 35:4; 40:15; 70:3.
71:15 Ps 35:28.
71:18 Is 46:3–4.
71:18 Ps 22:31–32; 48:14–15; 145:4.
71:19 Ps 72:18.
71:19 Ps 86:8.
72:2 Ps 99:4; Jer 23:5.
72:2 Prv 31:8–9.
72:3 Is 52:7; 55:12.

Cultural Connection

Open Up Your Treasure

African Americans and other ethnic groups have often been relegated to the background and their contributions ignored. But as Ecclesiastes 3:1 says, "There is an appointed time for everything, / and a time for every affair under the heavens." And from Psalm 72, we see there is a timing for God's call to us.

Psalm 72:10 says the kings of Sheba and Seba shall come to pay tribute to the King of Israel. Seba was an ancient kingdom, located near Ethiopia, that included black-skinned people.

In Matthew's story of Jesus' birth, God sends a message in the heavens to inform the dark-skinned wise men from the East when it is time to come and open up their treasures to the King.

God is sending a star to us now. God is talking loudly to us. "Get yourself ready, and be prepared to bring your gifts to me," God says. God has opened the door for us to come, but we must be willing to fall down and worship God and open up our treasures. If we do that, we too will be wise people who acknowledge the One who is born King. Are you ready to acknowledge our real King?

▶ Ps 72:10–11

save the children of the poor and crush the
oppressor.

II

5 May they fear you with the sun,
and before the moon, through all generations.*
6 May he be like rain coming down upon the fields,
like showers watering the earth,*
7 That abundance may flourish in his days,
great bounty, till the moon be no more.

III

8† May he rule from sea to sea,
from the river to the ends of the earth.*
9 May his foes kneel before him,
his enemies lick the dust.*
10 May the kings of Tarshish and the islands†
bring tribute,
the kings of Sheba and Seba offer gifts.*
11 May all kings bow before him,
all nations serve him.*
12 For he rescues the poor when they cry out,
the oppressed who have no one to help.
13 He shows pity to the needy and the poor*
and saves the lives of the poor.
14 From extortion and violence he redeems them,
for precious is their blood† in his sight.

IV

15 Long may he live, receiving gold from Sheba,
prayed for without cease, blessed day by day.
16† May wheat abound in the land,
flourish even on the mountain heights.
May his fruit be like that of Lebanon,
and flourish in the city like the grasses of the land.*
17 May his name be forever;
as long as the sun, may his name endure.*
May the tribes of the earth give blessings with his name;†
may all the nations regard him as favored.*
18† Blessed be the LORD God, the God of Israel,
who alone does wonderful deeds.*

†

72:8 *From sea to sea . . . the ends of the earth*: the boundaries of the civilized world known at the time: from the Mediterranean Sea (the western sea) to the Persian Gulf (the eastern sea), and from the Euphrates (the river) to the islands and lands of southwestern Europe, "the ends of the earth." The words may also have a mythic nuance—the earth surrounded by cosmic waters, hence everywhere.

72:10 *Tarshish and the islands*: the far west (Ps 48:6); Arabia and Seba: the far south (1 Kgs 10:1).

72:14 *Their blood*: cf. Ps 116:15.

72:16 The translation of the difficult Hebrew is tentative.

72:17 *May the tribes of the earth give blessings with his name*: an echo of the promise to the ancestors (Gn 12:3; 26:4; 28:14), suggesting that the monarchy in Israel fulfilled the promise to Abraham, Isaac, and Jacob.

72:18–19 A doxology marking the end of Book II of the Psalter.

*

72:5 Ps 89:37–38; Jer 31:35.
72:6 Dt 32:2; Is 45:8; Hos 6:3.
72:8 Dt 11:24; Zec 9:10.
72:9 Is 49:23; Mi 7:17.
72:10 Ps 68:30; Is 60:5–6; 1 Kgs 10:1ff.
72:11 Ps 47:8.
72:13 Prv 31:9.
72:16 Is 27:6; Hos 14:6–8; Am 9:13.
72:17 Ps 21:7.
72:17 Gn 12:3; 22:18; 26:4; Zec 8:13.
72:18 Ps 41:14; 89:53; 106:48; 136:4.

Cultural Connection

Wisdom

Psalm 73 explores the common wisdom question of why the wicked prosper (verse 3). The psalmist finally sees clearly that the wicked eventually fall to ruin (verse 17). The gift of wisdom is also an important value for many Native American peoples. For the Lakota tribe, it is one of four primary values. The Lakota word for wisdom is *wok-sa-pe.*

Wisdom is the ability to see clearly and not be taken in by illusions or outer appearances. The wise person knows that what is inside someone is more important than what is outside. The wise person also knows that we are nothing without the power of *Wakan-Tanka*, the Great Spirit. Because the sun helps us see things the way they really are, many Native Americans face the rising sun each day to pray to God for wisdom.

To explore the other primary Lakota virtues, see the "Cultural Connections" articles for Psalms 31, 89, and 112.

▶ **Psalm 73**

19 Blessed be his glorious name forever;
may he fill all the earth with his glory.*
Amen and amen.

20 The end of the psalms of David, son of Jesse.

Third Book—Psalms 73–89

PSALM 73†

The Trial of the Just

1 A psalm of Asaph.

How good God is to the upright,
to those who are pure of heart!

I

2 But, as for me, my feet had almost stumbled;
my steps had nearly slipped,
3 Because I was envious of the arrogant
when I saw the prosperity of the wicked.*
4 For they suffer no pain;
their bodies are healthy and sleek.
5 They are free of the burdens of life;
they are not afflicted like others.
6 Thus pride adorns them as a necklace;
violence clothes them as a robe.
7 Out of such blindness comes sin;
evil thoughts flood their hearts.*
8 They scoff and spout their malice;
from on high they utter threats.*
9† They set their mouths against the heavens,
their tongues roam the earth.
10† So my people turn to them
and drink deeply of their words.
11 They say, "Does God really know?"
"Does the Most High have any knowledge?"*
12 Such, then, are the wicked,
always carefree, increasing their wealth.

II

13 Is it in vain that I have kept my heart pure,
washed my hands in innocence?*
14 For I am afflicted day after day,
chastised every morning.
15 Had I thought, "I will speak as they do,"
I would have betrayed this generation of your children.
16 Though I tried to understand all this,
it was too difficult for me,
17 Till I entered the sanctuary of God
and came to understand their end.†

---

† **Psalm 73** The opening verse of this probing poem (cf. Ps 37; 49) is actually the psalmist's hard-won conclusion from personal experience: God is just and good! The psalmist describes near loss of faith (Ps 73:2–3), occasioned by observing the wicked who blasphemed God with seeming impunity (Ps 73:4–12). Feeling abandoned despite personal righteousness, the psalmist could not bear the injustice until an experience of God's nearness in the Temple made clear how deluded the wicked were. Their sudden destruction shows their impermanence (Ps 73:13–20). The just can thus be confident, for, as the psalmist now knows, their security is from God (Ps 73:1, 23–28).

73:9 *They set their mouths against the heavens*: in an image probably derived from mythic stories of half-divine giants, the monstrous speech of the wicked is likened to enormous jaws gaping wide, devouring everything in sight.

73:10 The Hebrew is obscure.

73:17 *And came to understand their end*: the psalmist receives a double revelation in the Temple: 1) the end of the wicked comes unexpectedly (Ps 73:18–20); 2) God is with me.

---

* **72:19** Ps 57:5; Nm 14:21.
73:3 Ps 37:1; Jb 21:13.
73:7 Jb 15:27.
73:8 Ps 17:10.
73:11 Ps 10:11; Jb 22:13.
73:13 Ps 26:6; Mal 3:14.

III

18 You set them, indeed, on a slippery road;
you hurl them down to ruin.
19 How suddenly they are devastated;
utterly undone by disaster!
20 They are like a dream after waking, Lord,
dismissed like shadows when you arise.*

IV

21 Since my heart was embittered
and my soul deeply wounded,
22 I was stupid and could not understand;
I was like a brute beast in your presence.
23 Yet I am always with you;
you take hold of my right hand.*
24 With your counsel you guide me,
and at the end receive me with honor.†
25 Whom else have I in the heavens?
None beside you delights me on earth.
26 Though my flesh and my heart fail,
God is the rock of my heart, my portion forever.
27 But those who are far from you perish;
you destroy those unfaithful to you.
28 As for me, to be near God is my good,
to make the Lord God my refuge.
I shall declare all your works
in the gates of daughter Zion.†

PSALM 74†

Prayer at the Destruction of the Temple

1 A *maskil* of Asaph.

I

Why, God, have you cast us off forever?†*
Why does your anger burn against the sheep of your pasture?*
2 Remember your people, whom you acquired of old,
the tribe you redeemed as your own heritage,
Mount Zion where you dwell.*
3 Direct your steps toward the utter destruction,
everything the enemy laid waste in the sanctuary.
4 Your foes roared triumphantly in the place of your assembly;
they set up their own tokens of victory.
5 They hacked away like a forester gathering boughs,
swinging his ax in a thicket of trees.
6 They smashed all its engraved work,
struck it with ax and pick.
7 They set your sanctuary on fire,
profaned your name's abode by razing it to the ground.*
8 They said in their hearts, "We will destroy them all!
Burn all the assembly-places of God in the land!"
9† Even so we have seen no signs for us,
there is no prophet any more,*
no one among us who knows for how long.
10 How long, O God, will the enemy jeer?*
Will the enemy revile your name forever?
11 Why draw back your hand,
why hold back your right hand within your bosom?†

II

12† Yet you, God, are my king from of old,
winning victories throughout the earth.
13 You stirred up the sea by your might;*
you smashed the heads of the dragons on the waters.*
14 You crushed the heads of Leviathan,*
gave him as food to the sharks.
15 You opened up springs and torrents,
brought dry land out of the primeval waters.†

†

73:24 *And at the end receive me with honor*: a perhaps deliberately enigmatic verse. It is understood by some commentators as reception into heavenly glory, hence the traditional translation, "receive me into glory." The Hebrew verb can indeed refer to mysterious divine elevation of a righteous person into God's domain: Enoch in Gn 5:24; Elijah in 2 Kgs 2:11–12; the righteous psalmist in Ps 49:16. Personal resurrection in the Old Testament, however, is clearly attested only in the second century B.C. The verse is perhaps best left unspecified as a reference to God's nearness and protection.

73:28 *In the gates of daughter Zion*: this reading follows the tradition of the Septuagint and Vulgate.

Psalm 74 A communal lament sung when the enemy invaded the Temple; it would be especially appropriate at the destruction of Jerusalem in 587 B.C. Israel's God is urged to look upon the ruined sanctuary and remember the congregation who worshiped there (Ps 74:1–11). People and sanctuary are bound together; an attack on Zion is an attack on Israel. In the second half of the poem, the community brings before God the story of their origins—their creation (Ps 74:12–17)—in order to move God to reenact that deed of creation now. Will God allow a lesser power to destroy the divine project (Ps 74:18–23)?

74:1 *Forever*: the word implies that the disaster is already of long duration, cf. Ps 74:9 and note.

74:9 *Even so we have seen no signs . . .* : ancients often asked prophets to say for how long a divine punishment was to last, cf. 2 Sm 24:13. Here no prophet has arisen to indicate the duration.

74:11 *Why hold back . . . within your bosom*: i.e., idle beneath your cloak.

74:12–17 Comparable Canaanite literature describes the storm-god's victory over all-encompassing Sea and its allies (dragons and Leviathan) and the subsequent peaceful arrangement of the universe, sometimes through the placement of paired cosmic elements (day and night, sun and moon), cf. Ps 89:12–13. The Psalm apparently equates the enemies attacking the Temple with the destructive cosmic forces already tamed by God. Why then are those forces now raging untamed against your own people?

74:15 *Waters*: lit., "rivers" (cf. Ps 24:7; Isa 50:2) upon which, or from which, in primordial times the earth is created.

*

73:20 Jb 20:8.
73:23 Ps 121:5.
74:1 Ps 10:1; 44:24; 77:8.
74:1 Ps 80:5.
74:2 Ps 68:17; 132:13; Ex 15:17; Jer 10:16; 51:19.
74:7 Ps 79:1; Is 64:10.
74:9 Lam 2:9.
74:10 Ps 89:47.
74:13 Ps 89:10.
74:13 Is 51:9–10.
74:14 Jb 3:8; 40:25; Is 27:1.

16 Yours the day and yours the night too;
you set the moon and sun in place.
17 You fixed all the limits of the earth;
summer and winter you made.*
18 Remember how the enemy has jeered, LORD,
how a foolish people has reviled your name.
19 Do not surrender to wild animals those who
praise you;
do not forget forever the life of your afflicted.
20 Look to your covenant,
for the recesses of the land
are full of the haunts of violence.
21 Let not the oppressed turn back in shame;
may the poor and needy praise your name.
22 Arise, God, defend your cause;
remember the constant jeering of the fools.
23 Do not forget the clamor of your foes,
the unceasing uproar of your enemies.

PSALM 75†

God the Judge of the World

1 For the leader. Do not destroy!
A psalm of Asaph; a song.

I

2 We thank you, God, we give thanks;
we call upon your name,
we declare your wonderful deeds.
[You said:]†
3 "I will choose the time;
I will judge fairly.
4 Though the earth and all its inhabitants quake,
I make steady its pillars."* *Selah*

II

5 So I say to the boastful: "Do not boast!"*
to the wicked: "Do not raise your horns!†
6 Do not raise your horns against heaven!
Do not speak with a stiff neck!"*
7 For judgment comes not from east or from
west,
not from the wilderness or the mountains,*
8 But from God who decides,
who brings some low and raises others
high.*
9 Yes, a cup† is in the LORD's hand,
foaming wine, fully spiced.†
When God pours it out,
they will drain it even to the dregs;
all the wicked of the earth will drink.*
10 But I will rejoice forever;
I will sing praise to the God of Jacob,
11 *[Who has said:]
"I will cut off all the horns of the wicked,
but the horns of the righteous will be
exalted."

PSALM 76†

God Defends Zion

1 For the leader; a psalm with stringed
instruments. A song of Asaph.

I

2 Renowned in Judah is God,*
whose name is great in Israel.
3 On Salem† is God's tent, his shelter on Zion.
4 There the flashing arrows were shattered,
shield, sword, and weapons of war.* *Selah*

II

5 Terrible and awesome are you,
stronger than the ancient mountains.†
6 Despoiled are the stouthearted;
they sank into sleep;
the hands of all the men of valor have
failed.*
7 At your roar, O God of Jacob,
chariot and steed lay still.
8 You, terrible are you;
who can stand before you and your great
anger?*
9 From the heavens you pronounced sentence;
the earth was terrified and reduced to
silence,
10 When you arose, O God, for judgment
to save the afflicted of the land. *Selah*

†

Psalm 75 The psalmist gives thanks and rejoices (Ps 75:2, 10) for the direct intervention of God, which is promised in two oracles (Ps 75:3–4, 11). Expecting that divine intervention, the psalmist warns evildoers to repent (Ps 75:5–9).

75:2 *You said*: supplied for clarity here and in Ps 75:11. The translation assumes in both places that the psalmist is citing an oracle of God.

75:5 *Do not raise your horns!*: the horn is the symbol of strength; to raise one's horn is to exalt one's own power as Ps 75:5 explains.

75:9 *A cup*: "the cup of God's wrath" is the punishment inflicted on the wicked, cf. Is 51:17; Jer 25:15–29; 49:12; Eze 23:31–33. *Spiced*: lit., "a mixed drink"; spices or drugs were added to wine, [illegible] Prv 9:2, 5.

76 A song glorifying Zion, the mountain of Jerusalem [illegible] destroyed Israel's enemies. Zion is thus the appropriate [illegible]rate the victory (Ps 76:3–4), a victory described in paral[illegible] (Ps 76:5–7, 8–11). Israel is invited to worship its powerful patron deity (Ps 76:12).

76:3 *Salem*: an ancient name for Jerusalem, used here perhaps on account of its allusion to the Hebrew word for peace, *shalom*, cf. Gn 14:18; Heb 7:1–3.

76:5 *Ancient mountains*: conjectural translation of a difficult Hebrew phrase on the basis of Gn 49:26. The mountains are part of the structure of the universe (Ps 89:12–13).

*

74:16–17 Gn 1.
75:4 Ps 46:3; 60:4; 93:1; 96:10; 104:5; 1 Sm 2:8; Is 24:19.
75:5 1 Sm 2:3; Zec 2:1–4.
75:6 Jb 15:25.
75:7 Mt 24:23–27.
75:8 Jb 5:11; 1 Sm 2:7.
75:9 Ps 60:5; Jb 21:20; Is 51:17, 21–22; Jer 25:15ff; Hab 2:16.
75:11 Ps 92:11.
76:2 Heb 3:2.
76:4 Ps 46:10; 122:6–9.
76:6 2 Kgs 19:35; Jer 51:39; Na 3:18.
76:8 Dt 7:21; 1 Sm 6:20; Na 1:6; Mal 3:2.

11 Surely the wrath of man will give you thanks;
the remnant of your furor will keep your feast.

III

12 Make and keep vows to the LORD your God.*
May all around him bring gifts to the one to be feared,
13 Who checks the spirit of princes,
who is fearful to the kings of earth.

PSALM 77†

Confidence in God During National Distress

1 For the leader; According to *Jeduthun*.
A psalm of Asaph.

I

2 I cry aloud to God,
I cry to God to hear me.
3 On the day of my distress I seek the Lord;
by night my hands are stretched out unceasingly;*
I refuse to be consoled.
4 When I think of God, I groan;
as I meditate, my spirit grows faint.* *Selah*
5 You have kept me from closing my eyes in sleep;
I am troubled and cannot speak.
6 I consider the days of old;
the years long past 7 I remember.*
At night I ponder in my heart;
and as I meditate, my spirit probes:
8 "Will the Lord reject us forever,*
never again show favor?
9 Has God's mercy ceased forever?
The promise to go unfulfilled for future ages?
10 Has God forgotten how to show mercy,
in anger withheld his compassion?" *Selah*
11† I conclude: "My sorrow is this,
the right hand of the Most High has abandoned us."*

II

12† I will recall the deeds of the LORD;
yes, recall your wonders of old.*
13 I will ponder all your works;
on your exploits I will meditate.
14 Your way, God, is holy;
what god is as great as our God?*
15 You are the God who does wonders;
among the peoples you have revealed your might.*
16 With your mighty arm you redeemed your people,
the children of Jacob and Joseph.* *Selah*

Live It!

The Big Picture

Perspective is a valuable thing. It is easy for us to get caught up in the moment, overwhelmed by the urgency of school assignments, sports, and time with family and friends. As difficult as it is, we need to step back for a moment or two and try to grasp the big picture.

When we look back at our lives and see where we have come from, the path often makes sense. The twists and turns that were so frustrating and confusing can now be recognized as temporary diversions on our journey. Everything we experienced—the good and the bad—contains lessons for us. The question is, How good a student are we?

The key to wisdom is reflection. Psalm 77 keeps saying this in different ways: "I ponder" (verse 7), "I consider" (verse 6), and "I will remember" (verse 12). How do you take the time to recall where you have been and to meditate on where you hope to go? Do you learn from the great teacher, life experience? Do you see the whole forest or only the trees right in front of you?

If you don't already spend some time at the end of each day reflecting on the events of that day, begin doing so. Keep a journal on how you felt or what you learned. Over time you will see the big picture emerge and even have a greater sense of God's presence in your life.

▶ **Psalm 77**

† **Psalm 77** A community lament in which the speaker ("I") describes the anguish of Israel at God's silence when its very existence is at stake (Ps 77:2–11). In response the speaker recites the story of how God brought the people into existence (Ps 77:12–20). The question is thus posed to God: Will you allow the people you created to be destroyed?

77:11 *I conclude*: lit., "I said." The psalmist, after pondering the present distress and God's promises to Israel, has decided that God has forgotten the people.

77:12 *I will recall*: the verb sometimes means to make present the great deeds of Israel's past by reciting them, cf. Ps 78:42; 105:5; 106:7.

* **76:12** Nm 30:3.
77:3 Ps 50:15; 88:2.
77:4 Jon 2:8.
77:7 Ps 143:5; Dt 32:7.
77:8–10 Ps 13:2; 44:24; 74:1; 80:5; 89:47; Lam 3:31.
77:11 Ps 17:7; 18:36; Ex 15:6, 12.
77:12 Ps 143:5.
77:14 Ps 18:31; Ex 15:11.
77:15 Ps 86:10; 89:6.
77:16 Gn 46:26–27; Neh 1:10.

17 The waters saw you, God;
the waters saw you and lashed about,
even the deeps of the sea† trembled.*
18 The clouds poured down their rains;
the thunderheads rumbled;
your arrows flashed back and forth.*
19 The thunder of your chariot wheels resounded;
your lightning lit up the world;
the earth trembled and quaked.*
20 Through the sea was your way;
your path, through the mighty waters,
though your footsteps were unseen.*
21 You led your people like a flock
by the hand of Moses and Aaron.*

PSALM 78†

A New Beginning in Zion and David

1 A *maskil* of Asaph.

I

Attend, my people, to my teaching;
listen to the words of my mouth.
2 I will open my mouth in a parable,†
unfold the puzzling events of the past.*
3 What we have heard and know;
things our ancestors have recounted to us.*
4 We do not keep them from our children;
we recount them to the next generation,
The praiseworthy deeds of the LORD and his strength,
the wonders that he performed.*
5 God made a decree in Jacob,
established a law in Israel:*
Which he commanded our ancestors,
they were to teach their children;
6 That the next generation might come to know,
children yet to be born.*
In turn they were to recount them to their children,
7 that they too might put their confidence in God,
And not forget God's deeds,
but keep his commandments.
8 They were not to be like their ancestors,
a rebellious and defiant generation,*
A generation whose heart was not constant,*
and whose spirit was not faithful to God.
9 The ranks of Ephraimite archers,†
retreated on the day of battle.
10 They did not keep God's covenant;
they refused to walk according to his law.
11 They forgot his deeds,
the wonders that he had shown them.

II

A

12 In the sight of their ancestors God did wonders,
in the land of Egypt, the plain of Zoan.†*
13 He split the sea and led them across,*
making the waters stand like walls.*
14 He led them with a cloud by day,
all night with the light of fire.*
15 He split rocks in the desert,
gave water to drink, abundant as the deeps of the sea.*
16 He made streams flow from crags,
caused rivers of water to flow down.

B

17 But they went on sinning against him,
rebelling against the Most High in the desert.*
18 They tested God in their hearts,
demanding the food they craved.*
19 They spoke against God, and said,
"Can God spread a table in the wilderness?*

---

† **77:17** *The deeps of the sea*: Heb. *tehom*; the same word is used in Gn 1:2, where it alludes to the primeval seas which in ancient Semitic cosmography are tamed by God in creation, cf. Ps 74:12–17; 89:12–13 and notes.

Psalm 78 A recital of history to show that past generations did not respond to God's gracious deeds and were punished by God making the gift into a punishment. Will Israel fail to appreciate God's act—the choosing of Zion and of David? The tripartite introduction invites Israel to learn the lessons hidden in its traditions (Ps 78:1–4, 5–7, 8–11); each section ends with the mention of God's acts. There are two distinct narratives of approximately equal length: the wilderness events (Ps 78:12–39) and the movement from Egypt to Canaan (Ps 78:40–72). The structure of both is parallel: gracious act (Ps 78:12–16, 40–55), rebellion (Ps 78:17–20, 56–58), divine punishment (Ps 78:21–31, 59–64), God's readiness to forgive and begin anew (Ps 78:32–39, 65–72). While the Psalm has been thought to reflect the reunification program of either King Hezekiah (late eighth century) or King Josiah (late seventh century) in that the Northern Kingdom (Ephraim, Joseph) is especially invited to accept Zion and the Davidic king, a postexilic setting is also possible. Notable is the inclusion of the David-Zion tradition into the history of Israel recounted in the sources of the Pentateuch.

78:2 *Parable*: Hebrew *mashal* literally refers to some sort of relationship of comparison and can signify a story whose didactic potential becomes clear in the telling, as here in the retrospective examination of the history of Israel. Mt 13:35 cites the verse to explain Jesus' use of parables.

78:9 *Ephraimite archers*: Ephraim was the most important tribe of the Northern Kingdom. Its military defeat (here unspecified) demonstrates its infidelity to God, who otherwise would have protected it.

78:12, 43 *Zoan*: a city on the arm of the Nile, a former capital of Egypt.

---

* **77:17** Ps 18:16; 114:3; Na 1:4.
77:18 Ps 18:14–15; 29; 144:6; Jb 37:3–4; Wis 5:21; Hab 3:10–11; Zec 9:14.
77:19 Ps 18:8; 97:4; 99:1; Ex 19:16; Jgs 5:4–5.
77:20 Neh 9:11; Wis 14:3; Is 51:10; Hab 3:15.
77:21 Ps 78:52; Is 63:11–14; Hos 12:14; Mi 6:4.
78:2 Ps 49:5; Mt 13:35.
78:3 Ps 44:2.
78:4 Ex 10:2; Dt 4:9; Jb 8:8.
78:5 Ps 147:19; Dt 33:4.
78:6 Ps 22:31–32; Dt 4:9; 6:7.
78:8 Dt 31:27; 32:5.
78:8 Ps 95:10.
78:12 Ps 106:7.
78:13–14 Ps 136:13; Ex 14–15.
78:13 Ex 14:22; 15:8.
78:14 Ps 105:39; Ex 13:21; Wis 18:3.
78:15 Ps 105:41; 114:8; Ex 17:1–7; Nm 20:2–13; Dt 8:15; Wis 11:4; Is 48:21.
78:17 Dt 9:7; Ez 20:13.
78:18 Ps 106:14; Ex 16:2–36.
78:19 Ps 23:5.

20 True, when he struck the rock,
water gushed forth,
the wadies flooded.
But can he also give bread,
or provide meat to his people?"

C

21 The LORD heard and grew angry;*
fire blazed up against Jacob;
anger flared up against Israel.
22 For they did not believe in God,
did not trust in his saving power.
23† So he commanded the clouds above;
and opened the doors of heaven.
24 God rained manna upon them for food;
grain from heaven he gave them.*
25 Man ate the bread of the angels;†
food he sent in abundance.
26 He stirred up the east wind in the skies;
by his might God brought on the south wind.
27 He rained meat upon them like dust,
winged fowl like the sands of the sea,
28 They fell down in the midst of their camp,
all round their dwellings.
29 They ate and were well filled;
he gave them what they had craved.
30 But while they still wanted more,
and the food was still in their mouths,
31 God's anger flared up against them,
and he made a slaughter of their strongest,
laying low the youth of Israel.*
32 In spite of all this they went on sinning,
they did not believe in his wonders.

D

33 God ended their days abruptly,
their years in sudden death.
34 When he slew them, they began to seek him;
they again looked for God.*
35 They remembered† that God was their rock,
God Most High, their redeemer.
36 But they deceived him with their mouths,
lied to him with their tongues.
37 Their hearts were not constant toward him;
they were not faithful to his covenant.*
38† But God being compassionate forgave their sin;
he did not utterly destroy them.
Time and again he turned back his anger,
unwilling to unleash all his rage.*
39 He remembered that they were flesh,
a breath that passes on and does not return.

III

A

40 How often they rebelled against God in the wilderness,
grieved him in the wasteland.
41 Again and again they tested God,
provoked the Holy One of Israel.
42 They did not remember his power,
the day he redeemed them from the foe,*
43† When he performed his signs in Egypt,
his wonders in the plain of Zoan.*
44 God turned their rivers to blood;
their streams they could not drink.
45 He sent swarms of insects that devoured them,*
frogs that destroyed them.
46 He gave their harvest to the caterpillar,
the fruits of their labor to the locust.
47 He killed their vines with hail,*
their sycamores with frost.
48 He exposed their cattle to plague,
their flocks to pestilence.*
49 He let loose against them the heat of his anger,
wrath, fury, and distress,
a band of deadly messengers.
50 He cleared a path for his anger;
he did not spare them from death,
but delivered their animals to the plague.
51 He struck all the firstborn of Egypt,*
the first fruits of their vigor in the tents of Ham.
52 Then God led forth his people like sheep,
guided them like a flock through the wilderness.*
53 He led them on secure and unafraid,
while the sea enveloped their enemies.*
54 And he brought them to his holy mountain,
the hill his right hand had won.*
55 He drove out the nations before them,

†

78:23–31 On the manna and the quail, see Ex 16 and Nm 11. Unlike Ex 16, here both manna and quail are instruments of punishment, showing that a divine gift can become deadly because of Israel's apostasy.

78:25 *Bread of the angels*: the translation "angels" comports with the supernatural origin of the manna, though the Hebrew *lechem 'abbirim* is more literally translated as "bread of the strong ones" or "bread of the mighty." In the context of the manna event, this phrase cannot possibly mean the Israelites or any human being.

78:35 *Remembered*: invoked God publicly in worship. Their words were insincere (Ps 78:36).

78:38 God is always ready to forgive and begin anew, as in choosing Zion and David (Ps 78:65–72).

78:43–55 Ex 7–12 records ten plagues. Here there are six divine attacks upon Egypt; the seventh climactic act is God's bringing Israel to the holy land.

*

78:21f Nm 11; Dt 32:22.
78:24 Ps 105:40; Ex 16:4, 14; Dt 8:3; Wis 16:20; Jn 6:31.
78:31 Nm 14:29.
78:34 Dt 32:15, 18; Is 26:16.
78:37 Ps 95:10; Is 29:13.
78:38 Ps 85:4; Ex 32:14; Is 48:9; Ez 20:22.
78:42 Ps 106:21.
78:43f Ps 105:27–36; 135:9; Ex 7:14–11:10; 12:29–36; Wis 16–18.
78:45 Ex 8:17.
78:47 Wis 16:16.
78:48 Ex 9:3.
78:51 Ps 105:36; 136:10; Ex 12:29.
78:52 Ps 77:21.
78:53 Ex 14:26–28.
78:54 Ex 15:17.

allotted them as their inherited portion,
and settled in their tents the tribes of Israel.

B

56 But they tested and rebelled against God Most High,
his decrees they did not observe.
57 They turned disloyal, faithless like their ancestors;
they proved false like a slack bow.
58 They enraged him with their high places,
and with their idols provoked him† to jealous anger.*

C

59 God heard and grew angry;
he rejected Israel completely.
60 He forsook the shrine at Shiloh,†*
the tent he set up among human beings.
61 He gave up his might into captivity,
his glorious ark into the hands of the foe.*
62 God delivered his people to the sword;
he was enraged against his heritage.
63 Fire consumed their young men;
their young women heard no wedding songs.*
64 Their priests fell by the sword;
their widows made no lamentation.

D

65 Then the Lord awoke as from sleep,
like a warrior shouting from the effects of wine.
66 He put his foes to flight;
everlasting shame he dealt them.
67 He rejected the tent of Joseph,
chose not the tribe of Ephraim.
68† God chose the tribe of Judah,
Mount Zion which he loved.*
69 He built his shrine like the heavens,
like the earth which he founded forever.
70 He chose David his servant,
took him from the sheepfolds.*
71 From tending ewes God brought him,
to shepherd Jacob, his people,
Israel, his heritage.*
72 He shepherded them with a pure heart;
with skilled hands he guided them.

PSALM 79†

A Prayer for Jerusalem

1 A psalm of Asaph.

I

O God, the nations have invaded your inheritance;
they have defiled your holy temple;
they have laid Jerusalem in ruins.*
2 They have left the corpses of your servants
as food for the birds of the sky,
the flesh of those devoted to you for the beasts of the earth.*
3 They have poured out their blood like water
all around Jerusalem,
and no one is left to do the burying.*
4 We have become the reproach of our neighbors,
the scorn and derision of those around us.*

II

5 How long, LORD? Will you be angry forever?
Will your jealous anger keep burning like fire?*
6 Pour out your wrath on nations that do not recognize you,
on kingdoms that do not call on your name,*
7 For they have devoured Jacob,
laid waste his dwelling place.
8 Do not remember against us the iniquities of our forefathers;
let your compassion move quickly ahead of us,
for we have been brought very low.*

III

9 Help us, God our savior,
on account of the glory of your name.
Deliver us, pardon our sins
for your name's sake.*
10 Why should the nations say,
"Where is their God?"*
Before our eyes make known to the nations
that you avenge the blood of your servants
which has been poured out.*

78:58 *Provoked him*: lit., "made him jealous."

78:60 *Shiloh*: an important shrine in the north prior to Jerusalem. Despite its holy status, it was destroyed (Ps 78:60–64; cf. Jer 7:12, 14).

78:68, 70 God's ultimate offer of mercy to the sinful, helpless people is Zion and the Davidic king.

Psalm 79 A communal lament complaining that the nations have defiled the Temple and murdered the holy people, leaving their corpses unburied (Ps 79:1–4). The occasion is probably the destruction of Jerusalem by the Babylonian army in 587 B.C. The people ask how long the withdrawal of divine favor will last (Ps 79:5), pray for action now (Ps 79:6–7), and admit that their own sins have brought about the catastrophe (Ps 79:8–9). They seek to persuade God to act for reasons of honor: the nations who do not call upon the Name are running amok (Ps 79:6); the divine honor is compromised (Ps 79:1, 10, 12); God's own servants suffer (Ps 79:2–4, 11).

78:58 Dt 32:16, 21.
78:60 Jos 18:1; 1 Sm 1:3; Jer 7:12; 26:6.
78:61 1 Sm 4:11, 22.
78:63 Dt 32:25; Jer 7:34.
78:68 Ps 48:2; 50:2; Lam 2:15.
78:70 Ps 89:21; Ez 34:23; 37:24; 2 Chr 6:6.
78:71 1 Sm 16:11–13; 2 Sm 7:8.
79:1 2 Kgs 25:9–10; Lam 1:10.
79:2 Jer 7:33.
79:3 1 Mc 7:17; Jer 14:16.
79:4 Ps 44:14; 80:7; 123:3–4; Jb 12:4; Dn 9:16; Zep 2:8.
79:5 Ps 13:2; 44:24; 89:47; Dt 4:24.
79:6 Ps 14:4; Jer 10:25.
79:8 Ps 142:7.
79:9 Ez 20:44; 36:22.
79:10 Ps 42:4; 115:2; Jl 2:17.
79:10 Jl 4:21.

IV

11 Let the groaning of the imprisoned come in
before you;
in accord with the greatness of your arm
preserve those doomed to die.*
12 Turn back sevenfold into the bosom of our
neighbors
the insult with which they insulted you,
Lord.*
13 Then we, your people, the sheep of your
pasture,
will give thanks to you forever;
from generation to generation
we will recount your praise.

PSALM 80†

Prayer to Restore God's Vineyard

1 For the leader; according to "Lilies." *Eduth.*†
A psalm of Asaph.

I

2 O Shepherd of Israel, lend an ear,
you who guide Joseph like a flock!
Seated upon the cherubim, shine forth*
3 upon Ephraim, Benjamin, and Manasseh.
Stir up your power, and come to save us.
4 *O God, restore us;
light up your face and we shall be saved.

II

5 LORD of hosts,
how long will you smolder in anger
while your people pray?*
6 You have fed them the bread of tears,
made them drink tears in great
measure.†*
7 You have left us to be fought over by our
neighbors;
our enemies deride us.*
8 O God of hosts, restore us;
light up your face and we shall be saved.

III

9 You brought a vine† out of Egypt;
you drove out nations and planted it.
10 You cleared out what was before it;
it took deep root and filled the land.
11 The mountains were covered by its shadow,
the cedars of God by its branches.
12 It sent out its boughs as far as the sea,†
its shoots as far as the river.†
13 Why have you broken down its walls,
so that all who pass along the way pluck its
fruit?*
14 The boar from the forest strips the vine;
the beast of the field feeds upon it.*
15 Turn back again, God of hosts;
look down from heaven and see;
Visit this vine,
16 the stock your right hand has planted,
and the son† whom you made strong for
yourself.
17 Those who would burn or cut it down—
may they perish at your rebuke.
18 May your hand be with the man on your
right,†
with the son of man whom you made
strong for yourself.
19 Then we will not withdraw from you;
revive us, and we will call on your name.
20 LORD God of hosts, restore us;
light up your face and we shall be saved.

PSALM 81†

An Admonition to Fidelity

1 For the leader; "upon the *gittith*."† Of Asaph.

I

2 Sing joyfully to God our strength;*
raise loud shouts to the God of Jacob!
3 Take up a melody, sound the timbrel,
the pleasant lyre with a harp.

†

Psalm 80 A community lament in time of military defeat. Using the familiar image of Israel as a vineyard, the people complain that God has broken down the wall protecting the once splendid vine brought from Egypt (Ps 80:9–14). They pray that God will again turn to them and use the Davidic king to lead them to victory (Ps 80:15–19).

80:1 *Lilies . . . . Eduth*: the first term is probably the title of the melody to which the Psalm was to be sung; the second is unexplained.

80:6 Both the Septuagint and the Vulgate translate this verse in the first person, i.e., "You have fed us the bread of tears."

80:9 *A vine*: a frequent metaphor for Israel, cf. Is 5:1–7; 27:2–5; Jer 2:21; Hos 10:1; Mt 21:33.

80:12 *The sea*: the Mediterranean. *The river*: the Euphrates, cf. Gn 15:18; 1 Kgs 5:1. The terms may also have a mythic nuance—the seas that surround the earth; sea and river are sometimes paralleled in poetry.

80:16 The Vulgate and Septuagint use "son of man."

80:18 *The man on your right*: the Davidic king who will lead the army in battle.

Psalm 81 At a pilgrimage feast, probably harvest in the fall, the people assemble in the Temple in accord with the Sinai ordinances (Ps 81:2–6). They hear a divine word (mediated by a Temple speaker) telling how God rescued them from slavery in Egypt (Ps 81:7–9), gave them the fundamental commandment of fidelity (Ps 81:9–11), which would bring punishment if they refused to obey (Ps 81:12–13). But if Israel repents, God will be with them once again, bestowing protection and fertility (Ps 81:14–16).

81:1 *Upon the gittith*: probably the title of the melody to which the Psalm was to be sung or a musical instrument.

*

79:11 Ps 102:21.
79:12 Ps 89:51–52.
80:2 Ps 23:1–3; 95:7; 100:3; Gn 48:15; Ex 25:22; 1 Sm 4:4; 2 Sm 6:2; Mi 7:14.
80:4, 8, 20 Ps 4:7; 31:17; 67:2; 85:5; Nm 6:25; Dn 9:17.
80:5 Ps 13:2; 44:24; 74:1; 79:5; 89:47; Dt 4:24.
80:6 Ps 42:4; 102:10.
80:7 Ps 44:14; 79:4; 123:3–4; Jb 12:4; Dn 9:16; Zep 2:8.
80:13 Ps 89:41.
80:14 Hos 2:14.
81:2 Ps 43:4; 68:26; 149:3; 150:3–4; Jdt 16:1.

4† Blow the shofar at the new moon,
at the full moon, on our solemn feast.*
5 For this is a law for Israel,
an edict of the God of Jacob,*
6 He made it a decree for Joseph
when he came out of the land of Egypt.

II

7† I heard a tongue I did not know:
"I removed his shoulder from the burden;†
his hands moved away from the basket.†*
8 In distress you called and I rescued you;
I answered you in secret with thunder;
At the waters of Meribah† I tested you:*
9 'Listen, my people, I will testify
against you *Selah*
If only you will listen to me, Israel!*
10 There shall be no foreign god among you;†*
you shall not bow down to an alien god.
11 'I am the LORD your God,
who brought you up from the land of Egypt.
Open wide your mouth that I may fill it.'
12 But my people did not listen to my words;
Israel would not submit to me.
13 So I thrust them away to the hardness of their
heart;
'Let them walk in their own machinations.'*
14 O that my people would listen to me,
that Israel would walk in my ways,*
15 In a moment I would humble their foes,
and turn back my hand against their
oppressors.*
16 Those who hate the LORD will try flattering
him,
but their fate is fixed forever.
17 But Israel I will feed with the finest wheat,
I will satisfy them with honey from the
rock."*

PSALM 82†

The Downfall of Unjust Gods

1 A psalm of Asaph.

I

God takes a stand in the divine council,
gives judgment in the midst of the gods.*
2 "How long will you judge unjustly
and favor the cause of the wicked?* *Selah*
3 "Defend the lowly and fatherless;
render justice to the afflicted and needy.
4 Rescue the lowly and poor;
deliver them from the hand of the
wicked."*

II

5† The gods neither know nor understand,
wandering about in darkness,
and all the world's foundations shake.
6 I declare: "Gods though you be,†*
offspring of the Most High all of you,
7 Yet like any mortal you shall die;
like any prince you shall fall."
8 Arise, O God, judge the earth,†
for yours are all the nations.

PSALM 83†

Prayer Against a Hostile Alliance

1 A song; a psalm of Asaph.

I

2 God, do not be silent;
God, do not be deaf or remain unmoved!*
3 See how your enemies rage;
your foes proudly raise their heads.
4 They conspire against your people,
plot against those you protect.*

81:4 *New moon . . . full moon*: the pilgrimage feast of harvest began with a great assembly (Lv 23:24; Nm 29:1), used the new moon as a sign (Nm 29:6), and included trumpets (Lv 23:24).

81:7 *I heard a tongue I did not know*: a Temple official speaks the word of God (Ps 81:5b–16), which is authoritative and unlike merely human words (cf. Nm 24:4, 16).

81:7 *I removed his shoulder from the burden*: A reference to the liberation of Israel from slavery in Egypt. *The basket*: for carrying clay to make bricks, cf. Ex 1:14.

81:8 *Meribah*: place of rebellion in the wilderness; cf. Ex 17:7; Nm 20:13.

81:10 *There shall be no foreign god among you*: as in Ps 50 and 95, Israel is challenged to obey the first commandment of fidelity to God after the proclamation of the exodus.

Psalm 82 As in Ps 58, the pagan gods are seen as subordinate divine beings to whom Israel's God had delegated oversight of the foreign countries in the beginning (Dt 32:8–9). Now God arises in the heavenly assembly (Ps 82:1) to rebuke the unjust "gods" (Ps 82:2–4), who are stripped of divine status and reduced in rank to mortals (Ps 82:5–7). They are accused of misruling the earth by not upholding the poor. A short prayer for universal justice concludes the Psalm (Ps 82:8).

82:5 The gods are blind and unable to declare what is right. Their misrule shakes earth's foundations (cf. Ps 11:3; 75:4), which God made firm in creation (Ps 96:10).

82:6 *I declare: "Gods though you be"*: in Jn 10:34 Jesus uses the verse to prove that those to whom the word of God is addressed can fittingly be called "gods."

82:8 *Judge the earth*: according to Dt 32:8–9, Israel's God had originally assigned jurisdiction over the foreign nations to the subordinate deities, keeping Israel as a personal possession. Now God will directly take over the rulership of the whole world.

Psalm 83 The community lament complains to God of the nations' attempts to wipe out the name of Israel (Ps 83:1–8). The psalmist sees all Israel's enemies throughout its history united in a conspiracy (Ps 83:2–8). May God destroy the current crop of enemies as the enemies of old were destroyed (Ps 83:9–12), and may they be pursued until they acknowledge the name of Israel's God (Ps 83:13–18).

81:4 Lv 23:24; Nm 29:1.
81:5 Ex 23:14ff.
81:7 Ex 1:14; 6:6.
81:8 Ps 95:8; Ex 2:23ff; 17:7; 19:16; Nm 20:13; 27:14.
81:9 Ex 1:14; 6:6.
81:10–11 Ex 20:2–6; Dt 5:6–10.
81:13 Jer 3:17; 7:24.
81:14 Is 48:18.
81:15 Lv 26:7–8.
81:17 Ps 147:14; Dt 32:13–14.
82:1 Is 3:13–14.
82:2 Ps 58:2.
82:4 Dt 1:17.
82:6 2 Pt 1:4.
83:2 Ps 10:1; 44:24; 109:1.
83:4 Jer 11:9.

PS

Catholic Social Teaching

AIDS—a Matter of Compassion

After a local man died of complications due to the AIDS virus, a newspaper carried an article about his life. The writer said: "His worst fears were not realized. His church did not reject him in the end. It surrounded him with love." What an awesome example of love and justice. His parish did not condemn him; it showed compassion for his life.

Even though our faith calls us to show compassion towards those who suffer, we are sometimes tempted to blame those who are suffering for the situation they are in and excuse ourselves from any need to help. We say that people who are poor are too lazy to work, that those who are hungry should get a job, that people dying of AIDS deserve it because of their choices. These attitudes portray a cold justice without mercy. They are not from the mind of God. For God mercy and justice go hand in hand.

Psalm 82 is a plea for God's justice, a cry to "render justice to the afflicted and needy" (verse 3). Catholic social teaching echoes this theme, reminding us that every person's life has a God-given sense of dignity that must always be upheld. This is especially true regarding the weak, needy, orphaned, and destitute. We must never condemn or judge those in dire situations, even if they have made seemingly poor life decisions. Instead, our words and actions must be directed towards lifting up the lowly, surrounding them, as the man's local church did, with great love in their time of need.

▶ **Psalm 82**

Life and Dignity of the Human Person

5 They say, "Come, let us wipe them out as a nation;
let Israel's name be remembered no more!"
6 They scheme with one mind,
they have entered into a covenant against you:*
7† The tents of Edom and the Ishmaelites,
of Moab and the Hagrites,*
8 Gebal, Ammon, and Amalek,*
Philistia and the inhabitants of Tyre.*
9 Assyria, too, in league with them,
backs the descendants of Lot. *Selah*

II

10† Deal with them as with Midian;
as with Sisera and Jabin at the wadi Kishon,*
11 Those destroyed at Endor,
who became dung for the ground.*
12 Make their nobles like Oreb and Zeeb,
all their princes like Zebah and Zalmunna,
13 Who made a plan together,
"Let us take for ourselves the pastures of God."
14 My God, make them like tumbleweed,
into chaff flying before the wind.*
15 As a fire raging through a forest,
a flame setting mountains ablaze,*
16 Pursue them with your tempest;
terrify them with your storm-wind.
17 Cover their faces with shame,
till they seek your name,† LORD.
18 Let them be ashamed and terrified forever;
let them perish in disgrace.
19 Let them know that your name is LORD,
you alone are the Most High over all the earth.*

†

83:7–9 Apart from the Assyrians, all the nations listed here were neighbors of Israel. The Hagrites are a tribe of the desert regions east of Ammon and Moab (1 Chr 5:10, 19–22). Gebal is the Phoenician city of Byblos or perhaps a mountain region south of the Dead Sea. The descendants of Lot are Moab and Edom (Gn 19:36–38 and Dt 2:9). These nations were never united against Israel in the same period; the Psalm has lumped them all together.

83:10–13 For the historical events, see Jgs 4–8.

83:17 *Seek your name*: a variant of the more typical phrase "to seek the face of God" (Ps 24:6; 27:8; 105:4). Seeking the face of God refers to the worshiper having recourse to a temple or sanctuary where in non-Jewish contexts a statue embodies the physical presence of the Deity. In Israel's aniconic tradition no visible image or statue can represent God. This understanding is conveyed here concretely by use of the term "your name" rather than the more typical "your face."

*

83:6 Ps 2:2.
83:7 Nm 20:23; 1 Chr 5:10, 19.
83:8 Ex 17:8.
83:8 Jos 13:2.
83:10 Ex 2:15; Is 9:3; 10:26.
83:11 Jer 8:2.
83:14 Ps 1:4; 35:5; 58:10; Is 5:24; 10:17; 17:13; 29:5; Ez 21:3.
83:15 Ps 50:3.
83:19 Ps 97:9; Dt 4:39; Dn 3:45.

PSALM 84†

Prayer of a Pilgrim to Jerusalem

[1] For the leader; "upon the *gittith*."
A psalm of the Korahites.

I

2 How lovely your dwelling,
O LORD of hosts!*
3 My soul yearns and pines
for the courts of the LORD.*
My heart and flesh cry out
for the living God.
4† As the sparrow finds a home
and the swallow a nest to settle her young,
My home is by your altars,
LORD of hosts, my king and my God!*
5 Blessed are those who dwell in your house!
They never cease to praise you. *Selah*

II

6 Blessed the man who finds refuge in you,
in their hearts are pilgrim roads.
7 As they pass through the Baca valley,†
they find spring water to drink.
The early rain covers it with blessings.
8 They will go from strength to strength†
and see the God of gods on Zion.

III

9 LORD God of hosts, hear my prayer;
listen, God of Jacob. *Selah*
10† O God, watch over our shield;
look upon the face of your anointed.*

IV

11 Better one day in your courts
than a thousand elsewhere.
Better the threshold of the house of my God
than a home in the tents of the wicked.
12 For a sun and shield is the LORD God,
bestowing all grace and glory.
The LORD withholds no good thing
from those who walk without reproach.
13 O LORD of hosts,
blessed the man who trusts in you!

PSALM 85†

Prayer for Divine Favor

[1] For the leader. A psalm of the Korahites.

I

2 You once favored, LORD, your land,
restored the captives of Jacob.*
3 You forgave the guilt of your people,
pardoned all their sins. *Selah*
4 You withdrew all your wrath,
turned back from your burning anger.*

II

5 Restore us, God of our salvation;
let go of your displeasure with us.*
6 Will you be angry with us forever,
prolong your anger for all generations?*
7 Certainly you will again restore our life,
that your people may rejoice in you.
8 Show us, LORD, your mercy;
grant us your salvation.

III

9† I will listen for what God, the LORD, has to say;
surely he will speak of peace
To his people and to his faithful.
May they not turn to foolishness!
10 Near indeed is his salvation for those who
fear him;
glory will dwell in our land.
11† Love and truth will meet;
justice and peace will kiss.*
12 Truth will spring from the earth;
justice will look down from heaven.*
13 Yes, the LORD will grant his bounty;
our land will yield its produce.*
14 Justice will march before him,
and make a way for his footsteps.

PSALM 86†

Prayer in Time of Distress

[1] A prayer of David.

I

Incline your ear, LORD, and answer me,
for I am poor and oppressed.

---

† **Psalm 84** Israelites celebrated three pilgrimage feasts in Jerusalem annually. The Psalm expresses the sentiments of the pilgrims eager to enjoy the divine presence.

84:4 The desire of a restless bird for a secure home is an image of the desire of a pilgrim for the secure house of God, cf. Ps 42:2–3, where the image for the desire of the pilgrim is the thirst of the deer for water.

84:7 *Baca valley*: Hebrew obscure; probably a valley on the way to Jerusalem.

84:8 *Strength to strength*: pass through outer and inner wall.

84:10 *Our shield . . . your anointed*: the king had a role in the liturgical celebration. For the king as shield, cf. Ps 89:19.

Psalm 85 A national lament reminding God of past favors and forgiveness (Ps 85:2–4) and begging for forgiveness and grace now (Ps 85:5–8). A speaker represents the people who wait humbly with open hearts (Ps 85:9–10): God will be active on their behalf (Ps 85:11–13). The situation suggests the conditions of Judea during the early postexilic period, the fifth century B.C.; the thoughts are similar to those of postexilic prophets (Hg 1:5–11; 2:6–9).

85:9 The prophet listens to God's revelation, cf. Heb 2:1.

85:11–13 Divine activity is personified as pairs of virtues.

Psalm 86 An individual lament. The psalmist, "poor and op-

---

* **84:2** Ps 43:3–4; 122:1.
84:3 Ps 42:2–3; 63:2–3; 143:6; Is 26:9.
84:4 Ps 5:3.
84:10 Ps 89:19.
85:2 Ps 14:7; 126:4.
85:4 Ps 78:38; Ex 32:14; Is 48:9.
85:5 Ps 80:4.
85:6 Ps 79:5; 89:47.
85:11 Ps 89:15; 97:2.
85:12 Is 45:8.
85:13 Ps 67:7; Lv 26:4; Ez 34:27; Hos 2:23–24; Zec 8:12.

2 Preserve my life, for I am devoted;
save your servant who trusts in you.
You are my God; 3 be gracious to me,
Lord;
to you I call all the day.
4 Gladden the soul of your servant;
to you, Lord, I lift up my soul.*
5 Lord, you are good and forgiving,
most merciful to all who call on you.*
6 LORD, hear my prayer;
listen to my cry for help.*
7 On the day of my distress I call to you,
for you will answer me.

II

8 None among the gods can equal you,
O Lord;
nor can their deeds compare to yours.*
9 All the nations you have made shall come
to bow before you, Lord,
and give honor to your name.*
10 For you are great and do wondrous deeds;
and you alone are God.

III

11 Teach me, LORD, your way
that I may walk in your truth,*
single-hearted and revering your name.
12 I will praise you with all my heart,
glorify your name forever, Lord my God.
13 Your mercy to me is great;
you have rescued me from the depths of
Sheol.*
14 O God, the arrogant have risen against me;
a ruthless band has sought my life;
to you they pay no heed.
15 But you, Lord, are a compassionate and
gracious God,
slow to anger, abounding in mercy and
truth.*
16 Turn to me, be gracious to me;
give your strength to your servant;
save the son of your handmaid.*
17 Give me a sign of your favor:
make my enemies see, to their
confusion,
that you, LORD, help and comfort me.

PSALM 87†

Zion the True Birthplace

1 *A psalm of the Korahites. A song.

I

His foundation is on holy mountains,
2 The LORD loves the gates† of Zion
more than any dwelling in Jacob.
3 Glorious things are said of you,
O city of God! *Selah*

II

4 Rahab and Babylon I count
among those who know me.
See, Philistia and Tyre, with Ethiopia,
"This one was born there."
5† And of Zion it will be said:
"Each one was born in it."*
The Most High will establish it;*
6 the LORD notes in the register of the
peoples:
"This one was born there."* *Selah*
7 So singers and dancers:
"All my springs are in you."*

PSALM 88†

A Despairing Lament

1 A song; a psalm of the Korahites.
For the leader; according to *Mahalath*.
For singing; a *maskil* of Heman
the Ezrahite.

I

2 LORD, the God of my salvation, I call out by
day;
at night I cry aloud in your presence.*
3 Let my prayer come before you;
incline your ear to my cry.*
4† For my soul is filled with troubles;*
my life draws near to Sheol.
5 I am reckoned with those who go down to
the pit;
I am like a warrior without strength.
6 My couch is among the dead,
like the slain who lie in the grave.

pressed" (Ps 86:1), "devoted" (Ps 86:2), "your servant" (Ps 86:2, 4, 16), "rescued . . . from the depths of Sheol" (Ps 86:13), attacked by the ruthless (Ps 86:14), desires only God's protection (Ps 86:1–7, 11–17).

Psalm 87 A song of Zion, like Ps 46; 48; 76; 132.

87:2 *The gates*: the city itself, a common Hebrew idiom.

87:5–6 The bond between the exile and the holy city was so strong as to override the exile's citizenship of lesser cities.

Psalm 88 A lament in which the psalmist prays for rescue from the alienation of approaching death. Each of the three stanzas begins with a call to God (Ps 88:2, 10, 14) and complains of the death that separates one from God. The tone is persistently grim.

88:4–8 In imagination the psalmist already experiences the alienation of Sheol.

86:4 Ps 25:1; 143:8.
86:5 Jl 2:13.
86:6 Ps 5:2; 130:1–2.
86:8 Ps 35:10; 89:9; Ex 15:11; Dt 3:24; Jer 10:6.
86:9 Ps 22:28; Zec 14:16; Rev 15:4.
86:11 Ps 25:4; 26:3; 27:11; 119:12, 35; 143:8, 10.
86:13 Ps 30:4; 40:3; Jon 2:7.
86:15 Ps 103:8; 130:7; 145:8; Ex 34:6.
86:16 Ps 25:16; 116:16; Wis 9:5.
87:1–2 Ps 76:2–3; 78:68–69.
87:5 Gal 4:26.
87:5 Ps 48:9.
87:6 Is 4:3.
87:7 Ps 68:26; 149:3.
88:2 Ps 77:3.
88:3 Ps 119:170.
88:4–7 Ps 28:1; 30:4; 40:3; 86:13; 143:7; Nm 16:33; Jb 17:1; Jon 2:7.

You remember them no more;
they are cut off from your influence.
7 You plunge me into the bottom of the pit,
into the darkness of the abyss.
8 Your wrath lies heavy upon me;
all your waves crash over me.* *Selah*

II

9 Because of you my acquaintances shun me;
you make me loathsome to them;*
Caged in, I cannot escape;
10 my eyes grow dim from trouble.

All day I call on you, LORD;
I stretch out my hands to you.
11† Do you work wonders for the dead?
Do the shades arise and praise you?* *Selah*

III

12 Is your mercy proclaimed in the grave,
your faithfulness among those who have perished?†
13 Are your marvels declared in the darkness,
your righteous deeds in the land of oblivion?

IV

14 But I cry out to you, LORD;
in the morning my prayer comes before you.
15 Why do you reject my soul, LORD,
and hide your face from me?
16 I have been mortally afflicted since youth;
I have borne your terrors and I am made numb.
17 Your wrath has swept over me;
your terrors have destroyed me.*
18 All day they surge round like a flood;
from every side they encircle me.
19 Because of you friend and neighbor shun me;*
my only friend is darkness.

PSALM 89†

A Lament over God's Promise to David

1 A *maskil* of Ethan the Ezrahite.

A

I

2 I will sing of your mercy forever, LORD*
proclaim your faithfulness through all ages.
3† For I said, "My mercy is established forever;
my faithfulness will stand as long as the heavens.
4 I have made a covenant with my chosen one;
I have sworn to David my servant:
5 I will make your dynasty stand forever
and establish your throne through all ages."* *Selah*

II

6 The heavens praise your marvels, LORD,
your loyalty in the assembly of the holy ones.*
7 Who in the skies ranks with the LORD?
Who is like the LORD among the sons of the gods?†*
8 A God dreaded in the council of the holy ones,
greater and more awesome than all those around him!
9 LORD, God of hosts, who is like you?
Mighty LORD, your faithfulness surrounds you.
10 You rule the raging sea;*
you still its swelling waves.
11 You crush Rahab† with a mortal blow;
with your strong arm you scatter your foes.
12 Yours are the heavens, yours the earth;
you founded the world and everything in it.*
13† Zaphon and Amanus you created;
Tabor and Hermon rejoice in your name.
14 You have a mighty arm.
Your hand is strong; your right hand is ever exalted.
15 Justice and judgment are the foundation of your throne;

88:11–13 The psalmist seeks to persuade God to act out of concern for divine honor: the shades give you no worship, so keep me alive to offer you praise.

88:12 *Perished*: lit., "Abaddon," the deepest part of Sheol.

Psalm 89 The community laments the defeat of the Davidic king, to whom God promised kingship as enduring as the heavens (Ps 89:2–5). The Psalm narrates how God became king of the divine beings (Ps 89:6–9) and how the Davidic king became king of earthly kings (Ps 89:20–38). Since the defeat of the king calls into question God's promise, the community ardently prays God to be faithful to the original promise to David (Ps 89:39–52).

89:3–5 David's dynasty is to be as long-lasting as the heavens, a statement reinforced by using the same verbs (establish, stand) both of the divine love and loyalty and of the Davidic dynasty and throne, cf. Ps 89:29–30.

89:7 *The sons of the gods*: "the holy ones" and "courtiers" of Ps 89:6, 8. These heavenly spirits are members of God's court.

89:11 *Rahab*: a mythological sea monster whose name is used in the Bible mainly as a personification of primeval chaos, cf. Jb 9:13; 26:12; Ps 74:13–14; Is 51:9.

89:13 *Zaphon and Amanus*: two sacred mountains in northern Syria which came to designate the directions of north and south. *Tabor*: a high hill in the valley of Jezreel in northern Israel. *Hermon*: a mountain in Lebanon, forming the southern spur of the Anti-Lebanon range.

88:8 Ps 18:5; 32:6; 42:8; 69:2; Jon 2:4.
88:9 Ps 38:12; 79:4; 80:7; 123:3–4; 142:8; Jb 12:4; 19:13; Lam 3:7; Dn 9:16.
88:11 Ps 6:6; 30:10; 38:18; 115:17.
88:17 Jb 6:4; 20:25.
88:19 Jb 19:13.
89:2 Is 63:7.
89:5 Ps 61:7–8; 132:11; 2 Sm 7:8–16.
89:6 Ps 29:1; 82:1; Jb 1:6; 5:1.
89:7–9 Ps 35:10; 86:8; 113:5; Ex 15:11; Jer 10:6.
89:10–11 Ps 65:8; 74:13–15; 107:29; Jb 7:12; Is 51:9–10.
89:12 Ps 24:1–2; 50:12; Dt 10:14; 1 Cor 10:26.

Cultural Connection

Respect

Respect is an important value for many Native American peoples. For the Lakota tribe, it is one of four primary values. The Lakota word for respect is *wo-wac-in-tan-ka*.

Psalm 89:6–9 speaks to the Lakota people of the power and the awesomeness of the Great Spirit. We owe reverence and respect not only to our God but also to all our God has created—the earth, the animals, and one another. The young respect the elders because the elders are people of history and experience. The old respect the young because they are the future of the world. When everyone lives in respect, the earth is at peace.

To explore the other primary Lakota virtues, see the "Cultural Connections" articles for Psalms 31, 73, and 112.

▶ Psalm 89

mercy and faithfulness march before you.*
16 Blessed the people who know the war cry,
who walk in the radiance of your face, LORD.
17 In your name they sing joyfully all the day;
they rejoice in your righteousness.*
18 You are their majestic strength;
by your favor our horn† is exalted.*
19 Truly the LORD is our shield,
the Holy One of Israel, our king!*

III

20 Then you spoke in vision;*
to your faithful ones you said:
"I have set a leader over the warriors;
I have raised up a chosen one from the people.
21 I have chosen David, my servant;
with my holy oil I have anointed him.
22 My hand will be with him;*
my arm will make him strong.
23 No enemy shall outwit him,
nor shall the wicked defeat him.
24 I will crush his foes before him,
strike down those who hate him.
25 My faithfulness and mercy will be with him;
through my name his horn will be exalted.
26† I will set his hand upon the sea,
his right hand upon the rivers.
27 He shall cry to me, 'You are my father,*
my God, the Rock of my salvation!'
28 I myself make him the firstborn,
Most High† over the kings of the earth.
29 Forever I will maintain my mercy for him;*
my covenant with him stands firm.
30 I will establish his dynasty forever,
his throne as the days of the heavens.
31 If his descendants forsake my teaching,*
do not follow my decrees,
32 If they fail to observe my statutes,
do not keep my commandments,
33 I will punish their crime with a rod
and their guilt with blows.
34 But I will not take my mercy from him,
nor will I betray my bond of faithfulness.*
35 I will not violate my covenant;
the promise of my lips I will not alter.*
36 By my holiness I swore once for all:*
I will never be false to David.
37† His dynasty will continue forever,*
his throne, like the sun before me.
38 Like the moon it will stand eternal,
forever firm like the sky!" *Selah*

B

IV

39 But now you have rejected and spurned,*
been enraged at your anointed.

89:18, 25 *Horn*: a concrete noun for an abstract quality; horn is a symbol of strength.

89:26 *The sea . . . the rivers*: geographically the limits of the Davidic empire (the Mediterranean and the Euphrates); mythologically, the traditional forces of chaos. See note on Ps 89:11.

89:28 *Most High*: a divine title, which is here extended to David as God's own king, cf. Ps 2:7–9; Is 9:5. As God rules over the members of the heavenly council (Ps 89:6–9), so David, God's surrogate, rules over earthly kings.

89:37–38 *Like the sun before me . . . like the sky*: as enduring as the heavenly lights, cf. Ps 89:2–5 and Ps 72:5, 17.

89:15 Ps 85:11–12; 97:2.
89:17 Ps 47:2; Zep 3:14.
89:18 Ps 112:9; 148:14.
89:19 Ps 47:9; 96:10; 97:1; 99:1; Is 6:3.
89:20–21 Ps 78:70; 132:11–12; 2 Sm 7:4, 8–16; 1 Chr 17:3, 7–14; Is 42:1; Acts 13:22.
89:22–25 1 Sm 2:9–10.
89:27–28 Ps 2:7; 110:2–3; 2 Sm 7:9, 14; Col 1:15, 18; Rev 1:5.
89:29–30 Ps 18:51; 61:8; 144:10; 2 Sm 7:11; Is 55:3.
89:31–33 Lv 26:14–33.
89:34 Ps 40:12; Sir 47:22.
89:35 Jer 33:20–21.
89:36 Am 4:2.
89:37–38 Ps 61:8; 72:5; Sir 43:6.
89:39–47 Ps 44:10–25.

40 You renounced the covenant with your servant,
defiled his crown in the dust.
41 You broke down all city walls,*
left his strongholds in ruins.
42 All who pass through seize plunder;
his neighbors deride him.
43 You have exalted the right hand of his foes,
have gladdened all his enemies.*
44 You turned back his sharp sword,
did not support him in battle.
45 You brought to an end his splendor,
hurled his throne to the ground.
46 You cut short the days of his youth,
covered him with shame. *Selah*

V

47 How long, LORD? Will you hide forever?
Must your wrath smolder like fire?*
48 Remember how brief life is,
how frail the sons of man you have created!*
49 What is man, that he should live and not see death?
Who can deliver his soul from the power of Sheol?* *Selah*

VI

50 Where are your former mercies, Lord,
that you swore to David in your faithfulness?
51 Remember, Lord, the insults to your servants,
how I have borne in my bosom the slander of the nations.*
52 Your enemies, LORD, insult;
they insult each step of your anointed.
53† Blessed be the LORD forever! Amen and amen!*

Fourth Book—Psalms 90–106

PSALM 90†

God's Eternity and Human Frailty

1 A prayer of Moses, the man of God.

I

Lord, you have been our refuge
through all generations.
2 Before the mountains were born,
the earth and the world brought forth,
from eternity to eternity you are God.*
3 You turn humanity back into dust,†
saying, "Return, you children of Adam!"*
4 A thousand years in your eyes
are merely a day gone by,*
Before a watch passes in the night,
5† you wash them away;*
They sleep,
and in the morning they sprout again like an herb.
6 In the morning it blooms only to pass away;
in the evening it is wilted and withered.†*

II

7 Truly we are consumed by your anger,
filled with terror by your wrath.
8 You have kept our faults before you,
our hidden sins in the light of your face.*
9 Our life ebbs away under your wrath;*
our years end like a sigh.
10 Seventy is the sum of our years,
or eighty, if we are strong;
Most of them are toil and sorrow;
they pass quickly, and we are gone.
11 Who comprehends the strength of your anger?
Your wrath matches the fear it inspires.
12 Teach us to count our days aright,
that we may gain wisdom of heart.

III

13 Relent, O LORD! How long?
Have pity on your servants!
14 Fill us at daybreak with your mercy,*
that all our days we may sing for joy.
15 Make us glad as many days as you humbled us,
for as many years as we have seen trouble.*
16 Show your deeds to your servants,
your glory to their children.
17 May the favor of the Lord our God be ours.*
Prosper the work of our hands!
Prosper the work of our hands!

---

† **89:53** The doxology at the end of the third book of the Psalms; it is not part of Ps 89.

Psalm 90 A communal lament that describes only in general terms the cause of the community's distress. After confidently invoking God (Ps 90:1), the Psalm turns to a complaint contrasting God's eternity with the brevity of human life (Ps 90:2–6) and sees in human suffering the punishment for sin (Ps 90:7–12). The Psalm concludes with a plea for God's intervention (Ps 90:13–17).

90:3 *Dust*: one word of God is enough to return mortals to the dust from which they were created. Human beings were created from earth in Gn 2:7; 3:19.

90:5 *You wash them away*: the Hebrew of Ps 90:4–5 is unclear.

90:6 *It is wilted and withered*: the transitory nature of the grass under the scorching sun was proverbial, cf. Ps 129:6; Is 40:6–8.

* **89:41–42** Ps 80:13–14. **89:43** Lam 1:5. **89:47** Ps 13:2; 44:25; 74:10; 79:5; Dt 4:24. **89:48** Ps 39:5–6; 62:10; 90:9–10; 144:4; Jb 7:6, 16; 14:1, 5; Eccl 6:12; Wis 2:5. **89:49** Ps 90:3. **89:51** Ps 79:12. **89:53** Ps 41:14; 72:18; 106:48. **90:2** Ps 48:15; 55:20; 93:2; 102:13; Heb 1:12. **90:3** Ps 103:14; 104:29; 146:4; Gn 3:19; 1 Mc 2:63; Jb 34:14–15; Eccl 3:20; 12:7; Sir 40:11. **90:4** 2 Pt 3:8. **90:5** Ps 89:48. **90:6** Ps 37:2; 102:11; 103:15–16; Jb 14:1–2; Is 40:6–8. **90:8** Ps 109:14–15; Hos 7:2. **90:9–10** Ps 39:5–7; 62:10; 102:24–25; 144:4; Gn 6:3; Jb 7:6, 16; 14:5; Prv 10:27; Eccl 6:12; Wis 2:5; Sir 18:8; Is 65:20. **90:14** Ps 17:15. **90:15** Nm 14:34; Jer 31:13. **90:17** Ps 33:22.

PSALM 91†

Security Under God's Protection

I

1 You who dwell in the shelter of the Most High,†
who abide in the shade of the Almighty,†
2 Say to the LORD, "My refuge and fortress,
my God in whom I trust."*
3 He will rescue you from the fowler's snare,
from the destroying plague,
4 He will shelter you with his pinions,
and under his wings you may take refuge;*
his faithfulness is a protecting shield.
5 You shall not fear the terror of the night
nor the arrow that flies by day,*
6 Nor the pestilence that roams in darkness,
nor the plague that ravages at noon.*
7 Though a thousand fall at your side,
ten thousand at your right hand,
near you it shall not come.
8 You need simply watch;
the punishment of the wicked you will see.*
9 Because you have the LORD for your refuge
and have made the Most High your stronghold,
10 No evil shall befall you,
no affliction come near your tent.*
11† For he commands his angels with regard to you,*
to guard you wherever you go.*
12 With their hands they shall support you,
lest you strike your foot against a stone.*
13 You can tread upon the asp and the viper,
trample the lion and the dragon.*

II

14 Because he clings to me I will deliver him;
because he knows my name I will set him on high.*
15 He will call upon me and I will answer;*
I will be with him in distress;*
I will deliver him and give him honor.
16 With length of days I will satisfy him,
and fill him with my saving power.*

Pray It!

Have You Sung This Before?

Psalm 91 might sound familiar! Have you ever sung "On Eagle's Wings" or "Blest Be the Lord"? Both are based on this psalm. Both express confidence that God will protect us, no matter what. This idea was sung long before Jesus lived, and we still sing it today.

And He will raise you up on eagle's wings,
bear you on the breath of dawn,
make you to shine like the sun,
and hold you in the palm of His hand.
(Jan Michael Joncas, "On Eagle's Wings")

Blest be the Lord; blest be the Lord,
the God of mercy, the God who saves.
I shall not fear the dark of night,
nor the arrow that flies by day.
(Dan Schutte, "Blest Be the Lord")

▶ **Psalm 91**

PSALM 92†

A Hymn of Thanksgiving for God's Fidelity

1 A psalm. A sabbath song.

I

2 It is good to give thanks to the LORD,
to sing praise to your name, Most High,*
3 To proclaim your love at daybreak,
your faithfulness in the night,
4 With the ten-stringed harp,
with melody upon the lyre.*
5 For you make me jubilant, LORD, by your deeds;
at the works of your hands I shout for joy.

II

6 How great are your works, LORD!*
How profound your designs!

†

Psalm 91 A prayer of someone who has taken refuge in the Lord, possibly within the Temple (Ps 91:1–2). The psalmist is confident that God's presence will protect the people in every dangerous situation (Ps 91:3–13). The final verses are an oracle of salvation promising salvation to those who trust in God (Ps 91:14–16).

91:1 *The shelter of the Most High*: basically "hiding place" but in the Psalms a designation for the protected Temple precincts, cf. Ps 27:5; 31:21; 61:5. *The shade of the Almighty*: lit., "the shadow of the wings of the Almighty," cf. Ps 17:8; 36:8; 57:2; 63:8. Ps 91:4 makes clear that the shadow is an image of the safety afforded by the outstretched wings of the cherubim in the holy of holies.

91:11–12 The words are cited in Lk 4:10–11; Mt 4:6, as Satan tempts Jesus in the desert.

Psalm 92 A hymn of praise and thanks for God's faithful deeds (Ps 92:2–5). The wicked, deluded by their prosperity (Ps 92:6–9), are punished (Ps 92:10), whereas the psalmist has already experienced God's protection (Ps 92:11–15).

*

91:2 Ps 18:3; 31:3–4; 42:10; 142:6; 2 Sm 22:3.
91:4 Ps 17:8; 36:8; 57:2; 63:8; Dt 32:11; Ru 2:12; Mt 23:37.
91:5 Prv 3:25; Sg 3:8.
91:6 Dt 32:24.
91:8 Ps 92:12.
91:10 Prv 12:21; Dt 7:15.
91:11–12 Mt 4:6; Lk 4:10f.
91:11 Heb 1:14.
91:12 Ps 121:3; Prv 3:23.
91:13 Is 11:8; Lk 10:19.
91:14 Ps 9:11; 119:132.
91:15 Jer 33:3; Zec 13:9.
91:15 Is 43:2.
91:16 Prv 3:2.
92:2 Ps 33:1; 147:1.
92:4 Ps 33:2; 144:9.
92:6–7 Ps 131:1; 139:6, 17; Wis 13:1; 17:1.

7 A senseless person cannot know this;
a fool cannot comprehend.
8 Though the wicked flourish like grass*
and all sinners thrive,
They are destined for eternal destruction;
9 but you, LORD, are forever on high.
10 Indeed your enemies, LORD,
indeed your enemies shall perish;
all sinners shall be scattered.*

III

11 You have given me the strength of a wild ox;*
you have poured rich oil upon me.*
12 My eyes look with glee on my wicked enemies;
my ears shall hear what happens to my
wicked foes.*
13 The just shall flourish like the palm tree,
shall grow like a cedar of Lebanon.*
14† Planted in the house of the LORD,
they shall flourish in the courts of our God.
15 They shall bear fruit even in old age,
they will stay fresh and green,
16 To proclaim: "The LORD is just;
my rock, in whom there is no wrong."*

PSALM 93†

God Is a Mighty King

1 The LORD is king,† robed with majesty;
the LORD is robed, girded with might.*
The world will surely stand in place,
never to be moved.*
2 Your throne stands firm from of old;
you are from everlasting.*
3† The flood has raised up, LORD;
the flood has raised up its roar;
the flood has raised its pounding waves.
4 More powerful than the roar of many waters,
more powerful than the breakers of the sea,
powerful in the heavens is the LORD.
5 Your decrees are firmly established;
holiness befits your house, LORD,
for all the length of days.

PSALM 94†

A Prayer for Deliverance from the Wicked

I

1 LORD, avenging God,
avenging God, shine forth!*
2 Rise up, O judge of the earth;
give the proud what they deserve!*

II

3 How long, LORD, shall the wicked,
how long shall the wicked glory?*
4 How long will they mouth haughty speeches,
go on boasting, all these evildoers?*
5 They crush your people, LORD,
torment your very own.
6 They kill the widow and alien;
the orphan they murder.*
7 They say, "The LORD does not see;
the God of Jacob takes no notice."*

III

8 Understand, you stupid people!
You fools, when will you be wise?*
9 Does the one who shaped the ear not hear?
The one who formed the eye not see?*
10 Does the one who guides nations not rebuke?
The one who teaches man not have
knowledge?
11 The LORD knows the plans of man;
they are like a fleeting breath.*

IV

12 Blessed the one whom you guide, LORD,*
whom you teach by your instruction,
13 To give rest from evil days,
while a pit is being dug for the wicked.
14 For the LORD will not forsake his people,
nor abandon his inheritance.*
15 Judgment shall again be just,
and all the upright of heart will follow it.

V

16 Who will rise up for me against the wicked?
Who will stand up for me against evildoers?
17 If the LORD were not my help,
I would long have been silent in the grave.*

†

92:14 *Planted*: the just are likened to trees growing in the sacred precincts of the Temple, which is often seen as the source of life and fertility because of God's presence, cf. Ps 36:9, 10; Ez 47:1–12.

Psalm 93 A hymn celebrating the kingship of God, who created the world (Ps 93:1–2) by defeating the sea (Ps 93:3–4). In the ancient myth that is alluded to here, Sea completely covered the land, making it impossible for the human community to live. Sea, or Flood, roars in anger against God, who is personified in the storm. God's utterances or decrees are given authority by the victory over Sea (Ps 93:5).

93:1 *The LORD is king*: lit., "the LORD reigns." This Psalm, and Ps 47; 96–99, are sometimes called enthronement Psalms. They may have been used in a special liturgy during which God's ascent to the throne was ritually reenacted. They have also been interpreted eschatologically, pointing to the coming of God as king at the end-time.

93:3 *The flood*: the primordial sea was tamed by God in the act of creation. It is a figure of chaos and rebellion, cf. Ps 46:4.

Psalm 94 A lament of an individual who is threatened by wicked people. The danger affects the whole community. Calling upon God as judge (Ps 94:1–2), the Psalm complains about oppression of the holy community by people within (Ps 94:3–7). Bold declarations of faith fol-

*

92:8 Ps 37:35.
92:10 Ps 68:1–2; 125:5.
92:11 Ps 75:11; Dt 33:17.
92:11 Ps 23:5.
92:12 Ps 91:8.
92:13 Ps 1:3; 52:10; Jer 17:8.
92:16 Dt 32:4.
93:1 Ps 47:8; 96:10; 97:1; 99:1.
93:1 Ps 75:2–3; 104:5.
93:2 Ps 55:20; 90:2; 102:13; Heb 1:12.
94:1 Na 1:2.
94:2 Jer 51:56; Lam 3:64.
94:3 Ps 13:2; 75:5; Jer 12:1.
94:4 Ps 73; Mal 2:17; 3:14.
94:6 Ex 22:21–22; Dt 24:17–22.
94:7 Ps 10:11; 64:6; 73:11; Jb 22:13–14; Ez 9:9.
94:8 Prv 1:22; 8:5.
94:9 Ex 4:11; Prv 20:12.
94:11 Ps 33:15; 1 Cor 3:20.
94:12 Ps 119:71; Jb 5:17.
94:14 1 Sm 12:22; Sir 47:22.
94:17 Ps 6:6; 115:17.

18 When I say, "My foot is slipping,"
your mercy, LORD, holds me up.*
19 When cares increase within me,
your comfort gives me joy.

VI

20 Can unjust judges be your allies,
those who create burdens by decree,
21 Those who conspire against the just
and condemn the innocent to death?
22 No, the LORD is my secure height,
my God, my rock of refuge,
23 *Who will turn back their evil upon them*
and destroy them for their wickedness.
Surely the LORD our God will destroy them!

PSALM 95†

A Call to Praise and Obedience

I

1 Come, let us sing joyfully to the LORD;
cry out to the rock of our salvation.*
2 Let us come before him with a song of praise,
joyfully sing out our psalms.
3 For the LORD is the great God,
the great king over all gods,*
4 Whose hand holds the depths of the earth;
who owns the tops of the mountains.
5 The sea and dry land belong to God,
who made them, formed them by hand.*

II

6 Enter, let us bow down in worship;
let us kneel before the LORD who made us.
7 For he is our God,
we are the people he shepherds,
the sheep in his hands.*

III

Oh, that today you would hear his voice:*
8 Do not harden your hearts as at Meribah,
as on the day of Massah in the desert.†
9 There your ancestors tested me;
they tried me though they had seen my works.*
10 Forty years I loathed that generation;
I said: "This people's heart goes astray;
they do not know my ways."*
11 Therefore I swore in my anger:
"They shall never enter my rest."†

> **Sing to the LORD a new song;**
> **sing to the LORD,**
> **all the earth.**
> **Sing to the LORD,**
> **bless his name;**
> **proclaim his salvation**
> **day after day.**
> (Ps 96:1–2)

PSALM 96†

God of the Universe

I

1 Sing to the LORD a new song;*
sing to the LORD, all the earth.
2 Sing to the LORD, bless his name;
proclaim his salvation day after day.
3 Tell his glory among the nations;
among all peoples, his marvelous deeds.*

II

4† For great is the LORD and highly to be praised,
to be feared above all gods.*
5 For the gods of the nations are idols,
but the LORD made the heavens.*
6 Splendor and power go before him;
power and grandeur are in his holy place.

III

7 Give to the LORD, you families of nations,
give to the LORD glory and might;
8 give to the LORD the glory due his name!*
Bring gifts and enter his courts;
9 bow down to the LORD, splendid in holiness.

† low: denunciation of evildoers (Ps 94:8–11) and assurance to the just (Ps 94:12–15). The Psalm continues with further lament (Ps 94:16–19) and ends with strong confidence in God's response (Ps 94:20–23).

Psalm 95 Twice the Psalm calls the people to praise and worship God (Ps 95:1–2, 6), the king of all creatures (Ps 95:3–5) and shepherd of the flock (Ps 95:7a, 7b). The last strophe warns the people to be more faithful than were their ancestors in the journey to the promised land (Ps 95:7c–11). This invitation to praise God regularly opens the Church's official prayer, the Liturgy of the Hours.

95:8 *Meribah*: lit., "contention"; the place where the Israelites quarreled with God. *Massah*: "testing," the place where they put God to the trial, cf. Ex 17:7; Nm 20:13.

95:11 *My rest*: the promised land as in Dt 12:9. Heb 4 applies the verse to the eternal rest of heaven.

Psalm 96 A hymn inviting all humanity to praise the glories of Israel's God (Ps 96:1–3), who is the sole God (Ps 96:4–6). To the just ruler of all belongs worship (Ps 96:7–10); even inanimate creation is to offer praise (Ps 96:11–13). This Psalm has numerous verbal and thematic contacts with Is 40–55, as does Ps 98. Another version of the Psalm is 1 Chr 16:23–33.

96:4 For references to other gods, see comments on Ps 58 and 82.

* **94:18** Ps 145:14.
94:23 Ps 7:16; 9:16; 35:8; 57:7; Prv 26:27; Eccl 10:8; Sir 27:26.
94:23 Ps 107:42.
95:1 Dt 32:15.
95:3 Ps 47:2; 135:5.
95:5 Ps 24:1–2.
95:7–11 Ps 81:8; 106:32; Heb 3:7–11, 15; 4:3, 5, 7.
95:7 Ps 23:1–3; 100:3; Mi 7:14.
95:9 Nm 14:22; 20:2–13; Dt 6:16; 33:8.
95:10 Ps 78:8; Nm 14:34; Dt 32:5.
96:1 Ps 98:1; Is 42:10.
96:3 Ps 98:4; 105:1.
96:4 Ps 48:2; 95:3; 145:3.
96:5 Ps 97:7; 115:4–8; Is 40:17; 1 Cor 8:4.
96:8 Ps 29:2.

Cultural Connection

Lebanese Catholics

Catholics are a celebratory people. By holding feasts, we celebrate our great God and the wondrous ways God has shown love for us. We also hold feasts in remembrance of the saints who have gone before us. The saints are shining examples of individuals leading lives in unity with the will of God.

In some parts of the Middle East, like Lebanon, Catholic feast days are extravagant events. Each town has a patron saint, and on the eve of his or her feast day, nearly everyone in the community comes to the church. The townspeople pray, eat, and dance in the church all night long, and some even sleep there. Feast days in Lebanon are celebrations that include great processions, festive liturgies, and the participation of the whole community.

In parts of the United States where there are congregations of Middle Eastern Catholics, similar events take place. Some occur on a large scale with overnight festivities, and some occur on a smaller scale, but all have common characteristics: great processions, festive liturgies, good food, and the participation of the whole parish community.

Consider trying to get your youth group or campus ministry team to begin a similar tradition on the feast day of your parish or school.

▶ Psalm 96

Tremble before him, all the earth;
10 *declare among the nations: The LORD is king.
The world will surely stand fast, never to be shaken.
He rules the peoples with fairness.

IV

11 Let the heavens be glad and the earth rejoice;
let the sea and what fills it resound;*
12 let the plains be joyful and all that is in them.
Then let all the trees of the forest rejoice
13 before the LORD who comes,
who comes to govern the earth,*
To govern the world with justice
and the peoples with faithfulness.

PSALM 97†

The Divine Ruler of All

I

1 The LORD is king; let the earth rejoice;
let the many islands be glad.*
2 Cloud and darkness surround him;
justice and right are the foundation of his throne.*
3 Fire goes before him,
consuming his foes on every side.
4 His lightning illumines the world;
the earth sees and trembles.*
5 The mountains melt like wax before the LORD,
before the Lord of all the earth.*
6 The heavens proclaim his justice;
all peoples see his glory.*

II

7 All who serve idols are put to shame,
who glory in worthless things;
all gods† bow down before him.*
8 Zion hears and is glad,
and the daughters of Judah rejoice
because of your judgments, O LORD.*
9 For you, LORD, are the Most High over all the earth,*
exalted far above all gods.
10 You who love the LORD, hate evil,
he protects the souls of the faithful,*

† **Psalm 97** The hymn begins with God appearing in a storm, a traditional picture of some ancient Near Eastern gods (Ps 97:1–6); cf. Ps 18:8–16; Mi 1:3–4; Heb 3:3–15. Israel rejoices in the overthrowing of idol worshipers and their gods (Ps 97:7–9) and the rewarding of the faithful righteous (Ps 97:10–12).

97:7 *All gods*: divine beings thoroughly subordinate to Israel's God. The Greek translates "angels," an interpretation adopted by Heb 1:6.

96:10 Ps 75:4; 93:1.
96:11 Ps 98:7.
96:13 Ps 98:9.
97:1 Ps 75:4; 93:1; 96:10.
97:2 Ps 85:11; 89:15; Ex 19:6; Dt 4:11; 5:22; 1 Kgs 8:12.
97:4 Ps 18:8; 50:3; 77:18; 99:1; Jgs 5:4–5.
97:5 Jdt 16:15; Mi 1:4.
97:6 Ps 50:6.
97:7 Ps 96:5.
97:8 Ps 48:12.
97:9 Ps 83:19.
97:10 Ps 121:7.

rescues them from the hand of the
wicked.
11 Light dawns for the just,
and gladness for the honest of heart.*
12 Rejoice in the LORD, you just,
and give thanks at the remembrance of
his holiness.*

PSALM 98†

The Coming of God

[1] A psalm.

I

Sing a new song to the LORD,
for he has done marvelous deeds.*
His right hand and holy arm
have won the victory.†*
2 The LORD has made his victory known;
has revealed his triumph in the sight of
the nations,
3 He has remembered his mercy and
faithfulness
toward the house of Israel.
All the ends of the earth have seen
the victory of our God.

II

4 Shout with joy to the LORD, all the earth;
break into song; sing praise.
5 Sing praise to the LORD with the lyre,
with the lyre and melodious song.
6 With trumpets and the sound of the horn
shout with joy to the King, the LORD.*

III

7 Let the sea and what fills it resound,*
the world and those who dwell there.
8 Let the rivers clap their hands,
the mountains shout with them for
joy,*
9 *Before the LORD who comes,
who comes to govern the earth,*
To govern the world with justice
and the peoples with fairness.

PSALM 99†

The Holy King

I

1 The LORD is king, the peoples tremble;
he is enthroned on the cherubim,† the
earth quakes.*
2 Great is the LORD in Zion,
exalted above all the peoples.
3 Let them praise your great and awesome name:
Holy is he!*

II

4 O mighty king, lover of justice,
you have established fairness;
you have created just rule in Jacob.*
5 Exalt the LORD, our God;
bow down before his footstool;†*
holy is he!

III

6 Moses and Aaron were among his priests,
Samuel among those who called on his
name;
they called on the LORD, and he answered
them.*
7 From the pillar of cloud he spoke to them;
they kept his decrees, the law he had given
them.*
8 O LORD, our God, you answered them;
you were a forgiving God to them,
though you punished their offenses.*
9 Exalt the LORD, our God;
bow down before his holy mountain;
holy is the LORD, our God.

PSALM 100†

Processional Hymn

[1] A psalm of thanksgiving.

Shout joyfully to the LORD, all you lands;
2 serve the LORD with gladness;
come before him with joyful song.

---

† **Psalm 98** A hymn, similar to Ps 96, extolling God for Israel's victory (Ps 98:1–3). All nations (Ps 98:4–6) and even inanimate nature (Ps 98:7–8) are summoned to welcome God's coming to rule over the world (Ps 98:9).

98:1 *Marvelous deeds . . . victory*: the conquest of all threats to the peaceful existence of Israel, depicted in the Psalms variously as a cosmic force such as sea, or nations bent on Israel's destruction, or evildoers seemingly triumphant. *His right hand and holy arm*: God is pictured as a powerful warrior.

Psalm 99 A hymn to God as the king whose grandeur is most clearly seen on Mount Zion (Ps 99:2) and in the laws given to Israel (Ps 99:4). Israel is special because of God's word of justice, which was mediated by the revered speakers, Moses, Aaron, and Samuel (Ps 99:6–8). The poem is structured by the threefold statement that God is holy (Ps 99:3, 5, 9) and by the twice-repeated command to praise (Ps 99:5, 9).

99:1 *Enthroned on the cherubim*: cherubim were composite beings with animal and human features, common in ancient Near Eastern art. Two cherubim were placed on the ark (or box) of the covenant in the holy of holies. Upon them God was believed to dwell invisibly, cf. Ex 25:20–22; 1 Sm 4:4; 2 Sm 6:2; Ps 80:2.

99:5 *Footstool*: a reference to the ark, cf. 1 Chr 28:2; Ps 132:7.

Psalm 100 A hymn inviting the people to enter the Temple courts with thank offerings for the God who created them.

97:11 Ps 112:4.
97:12 Ps 30:5.
98:1 Ps 96:1; Is 42:10.
98:1 Is 59:16; 63:5.
98:6 Ps 47:6–7.
98:7 Ps 96:11.
98:8 Is 44:23; 55:12.
98:9 Ps 96:13.
98:9 Ps 67:5.
99:1 Ps 18:8–11; 80:2; 93:1; Ex 25:22; 1 Sm 4:4; 2 Sm 6:2.
99:3 Is 6:3.
99:4 Ps 72:1; Jer 23:5.
99:5 Ps 132:7.
99:6 Jer 15:1.
99:7 Ex 33:9; Nm 12:5.
99:8 Ex 32:11; Nm 20:12.

3† Know that the Lord is God,
he made us, we belong to him,
we are his people, the flock he shepherds.*
4 Enter his gates with thanksgiving,
his courts with praise.
Give thanks to him, bless his name;*
5 good indeed is the Lord,
His mercy endures forever,
his faithfulness lasts through every generation.

PSALM 101†

Norm of Life for Rulers

1 A psalm of David.

I

I sing of mercy and justice;
to you, Lord, I sing praise.
2 I study the way of integrity;*
when will you come to me?
I act with integrity of heart
within my household.†*
3 I do not allow into my presence anything base.
I hate wrongdoing;
I will have no part of it.*
4 May the devious heart keep far from me;
the wicked I will not acknowledge.
5 Whoever slanders a neighbor in secret
I will reduce to silence.*
Haughty eyes and arrogant hearts*
I cannot endure.

II

6 I look to the faithful of the land†
to sit at my side.
Whoever follows the way of integrity*
is the one to enter my service.
7 No one who practices deceit
can remain within my house.
No one who speaks falsely
can last in my presence.*
8† Morning after morning I clear all the wicked from the land,
to rid the city of the Lord of all doers of evil.

PSALM 102†

Prayer in Time of Distress

1 The prayer of one afflicted and wasting away whose anguish is poured out before the Lord.

I

2 Lord, hear my prayer;
let my cry come to you.
3 Do not hide your face from me
in the day of my distress.*
Turn your ear to me;
when I call, answer me quickly.
4 For my days vanish like smoke;*
my bones burn away as in a furnace.
5 My heart is withered, dried up like grass,
too wasted to eat my food.
6 From my loud groaning
I become just skin and bones.
7 I am like a desert owl,
like an owl among the ruins.
8 I lie awake and moan,
like a lone sparrow on the roof.
9 All day long my enemies taunt me;
in their rage, they make my name a curse.†
10 I eat ashes like bread,
mingle my drink with tears.*
11 Because of your furious wrath,
you lifted me up just to cast me down.
12 *My days are like a lengthening shadow;*
I wither like the grass.

II

13 But you, Lord, are enthroned forever;
your renown is for all generations.*
14 You will again show mercy to Zion;
now is the time for pity;
the appointed time has come.

†

100:3 Although the people call on all the nations of the world to join in their hymn, they are conscious of being the chosen people of God.

Psalm 101 The king, grateful at being God's chosen (Ps 101:1), promises to be a ruler after God's own heart (Ps 101:2–3), allowing into the royal service only the God-fearing (Ps 101:3–8).

101:2 *Within my household*: the king promises to make his own household, i.e., the royal court, a model for Israel, banning all officials who abuse their power.

101:6 *I look to the faithful of the land*: the king seeks companions only among those faithful to God.

101:8 *Morning after morning*: the morning is the normal time for the administration of justice (2 Sm 15:2; Jer 21:12) and for the arrival of divine aid (Ps 59:17; 143:8; Is 33:2). *I clear all the wicked from the land*: the king, as God's servant, is responsible for seeing that divine justice is carried out.

Psalm 102 A lament, one of the Penitential Psalms. The psalmist, experiencing psychological and bodily disintegration (Ps 102:4–12), cries out to God (Ps 102:1–3). In the Temple precincts where God has promised to be present, the psalmist recalls God's venerable promises to save the poor (Ps 102:13–23). The final part (Ps 102:24–28) restates the original complaint and prayer, and emphasizes God's eternity.

102:9 *They make my name a curse*: enemies use the psalmist's name in phrases such as, "May you be as wretched as this person!"

*

100:3 Ps 23:1; 95:7; Mi 7:14; Is 64:7.
100:4–5 Ps 106:1; 107:1; 118:1; 136:1; 138:8; Jer 33:11.
101:2 Ps 26:11; Is 33:15.
101:2 1 Kgs 9:4.
101:3 Prv 11:20.
101:5 Prv 17:20; 30:10.
101:5 Prv 21:4.
101:6 Ps 26:11; Prv 20:7.
101:7 Ps 5:5; Prv 25:5.
102:3 Ps 69:18; 143:7.
102:4–6 Ps 38:7–9.
102:10 Ps 42:4; 80:6.
102:12 Ps 109:23; 144:4; Jb 8:9; 14:2; Eccl 6:12; Wis 2:5.
102:12 Ps 90:5–6.
102:13 Ps 55:20; 90:2; 93:2; 135:13; 145:13; Lam 5:19; Heb 1:12.

15 Its stones are dear to your servants;
its dust moves them to pity.
16 The nations shall fear your name, LORD,
all the kings of the earth, your glory,*
17 Once the LORD has rebuilt Zion
and appeared in glory,
18 Heeding the plea of the lowly,
not scorning their prayer.
19 Let this be written for the next generation,
for a people not yet born,
that they may praise the LORD:*
20† "The LORD looked down from the holy heights,
viewed the earth from heaven,*
21 To attend to the groaning of the prisoners,
to release those doomed to die."*
22 Then the LORD's name will be declared on Zion,
his praise in Jerusalem,
23 When peoples and kingdoms gather
to serve the LORD.*

III

24 He has shattered my strength in mid-course,
has cut short my days.
25 I plead, O my God,
do not take me in the midst of my days.†*
Your years last through all generations.
26 Of old you laid the earth's foundations;*
the heavens are the work of your hands.
27 They perish, but you remain;
they all wear out like a garment;
Like clothing you change them and they are changed,
28 but you are the same, your years have no end.
29 May the children of your servants live on;
may their descendants live in your presence.*

PSALM 103†

Praise of Divine Goodness

1 Of David.

I

Bless the LORD, my soul;
all my being, bless his holy name!
2 Bless the LORD, my soul;
and do not forget all his gifts,
3 Who pardons all your sins,
and heals all your ills,
4 Who redeems your life from the pit,*
and crowns you with mercy and compassion,
5 Who fills your days with good things,
so your youth is renewed like the eagle's.†

II

6 The LORD does righteous deeds,
brings justice to all the oppressed.*
7 He made known his ways to Moses,
to the Israelites his deeds.

Live It!

Letting Go of Anger

Psalm 103 is a beautiful prayer praising God's love and compassion. Verse 9 reminds us that God will not stay angry forever. What better lesson could we learn from our God? Anger is a natural human emotion—but in imitation of God, we should not hold on to it. When we let go of our anger, we build better relationships, because hidden anger puts other people on the defensive and destroys trust.

How do you let go of anger? Here are some suggestions:

- Express your feelings in a letter or a journal.
- Tell the person you are angry with how you feel and that you would like to reconcile.
- Go for a fast walk or run, or use another form of exercise to "vent" your anger.
- Relax with some quiet, reflective music.
- Try to identify why you feel angry. Often anger is a symptom of another feeling, such as hurt, disappointment, or even tiredness.
- Express your anger in prayer to God, and ask for help in forgiveness.

God's way and God's goodness can be yours if you desire them. Make an effort; God does!

► Psalm 103

†

102:20–23 Both Ps 102:20–21 and Ps 102:22–23 depend on Ps 102:19.

102:25 *In the midst of my days*: when the normal span of life is but half completed, cf. Is 38:10; Jer 17:11.

Psalm 103 The speaker in this hymn begins by praising God for personal benefits (Ps 103:1–5), then moves on to God's mercy toward all the people (Ps 103:6–18). Even sin cannot destroy that mercy (Ps 103:11–13), for the eternal God is well aware of the people's human fragility (Ps 103:14–18). The psalmist invites the heavenly beings to join in praise (Ps 103:19–22).

103:5 *Your youth is renewed like the eagle's*: because of the eagle's long life it was a symbol of perennial youth and vigor, cf. Is 40:31.

*

102:16 Is 59:19; 66:18.
102:19 Ps 22:31–32.
102:20 Ps 11:4; 14:2.
102:21 Ps 79:11.
102:23 Is 60:3–4; Zec 2:15; 8:22.
102:25 Ps 39:5; 90:10; Jb 14:5.
102:26–28 Heb 1:10–12.
102:29 Ps 69:36–37.
103:4 Ps 28:1; 30:4; 40:3; 69:16; 88:5; 143:7; Prv 1:12; Jon 2:7.
103:6 Ps 146:6–7.

8 Merciful and gracious is the LORD,
slow to anger, abounding in mercy.*
9 He will not always accuse,
and nurses no lasting anger;
10 He has not dealt with us as our sins merit,
nor requited us as our wrongs deserve.

III

11 For as the heavens tower over the earth,
so his mercy towers over those who fear
him.*
12 As far as the east is from the west,
so far has he removed our sins from us.
13 As a father has compassion on his children,
so the LORD has compassion on those who
fear him.
14 For he knows how we are formed,
remembers that we are dust.*
15 As for man, his days are like the grass;
he blossoms like a flower in the field.*
16 A wind sweeps over it and it is gone;
its place knows it no more.
17 But the LORD's mercy is from age to age,
toward those who fear him.
His salvation is for the children's children
18 of those who keep his covenant,
and remember to carry out his precepts.

IV

19 The LORD has set his throne in heaven;
his dominion extends over all.
20 Bless the LORD, all you his angels,*
mighty in strength, acting at his behest,
obedient to his command.
21 Bless the LORD, all you his hosts,
his ministers who carry out his will.
22 Bless the LORD, all his creatures,
everywhere in his domain.
Bless the LORD, my soul!

PSALM 104†

Praise of God the Creator

I

1 Bless the LORD, my soul!
LORD, my God, you are great indeed!
You are clothed with majesty and splendor,
2 robed in light as with a cloak.
You spread out the heavens like a tent;*
3 setting the beams of your chambers upon
the waters.†
You make the clouds your chariot;
traveling on the wings of the wind.
4 You make the winds your messengers;
flaming fire, your ministers.*

II

5† You fixed the earth on its foundation,
so it can never be shaken.
6 The deeps covered it like a garment;
above the mountains stood the waters.
7 At your rebuke they took flight;
at the sound of your thunder they fled.*
8 They rushed up the mountains, down the
valleys
to the place you had fixed for them.
9 You set a limit they cannot pass;
never again will they cover the earth.*

III

10 You made springs flow in wadies
that wind among the mountains.
11 They give drink to every beast of the field;*
here wild asses quench their thirst.
12 Beside them the birds of heaven nest;
among the branches they sing.
13 You water the mountains from your
chambers;
from the fruit of your labor the earth
abounds.
14 You make the grass grow for the cattle
and plants for people's work
to bring forth food from the earth,
15 wine to gladden their hearts,
oil to make their faces shine,
and bread to sustain the human heart.
16† The trees of the LORD drink their fill,
the cedars of Lebanon, which you planted.
17 There the birds build their nests;
the stork in the junipers, its home.*
18 The high mountains are for wild goats;
the rocky cliffs, a refuge for badgers.

IV

19 You made the moon to mark the seasons,*
the sun that knows the hour of its setting.

† **Psalm 104** A hymn praising God who easily and skillfully made rampaging waters and primordial night into a world vibrant with life. The psalmist describes God's splendor in the heavens (Ps 104:1–4), how the chaotic waters were tamed to fertilize and feed the world (Ps 104:5–18), and how primordial night was made into a gentle time of refreshment (Ps 104:19–23). The picture is like Gn 1:1–2: a dark and watery chaos is made dry and lighted so that creatures might live. The psalmist reacts to the beauty of creation with awe (Ps 104:24–34). May sin not deface God's work (Ps 104:35)!

104:3 *Your chambers upon the waters*: God's heavenly dwelling above the upper waters of the sky, cf. Gn 1:6–7; Ps 29:10.

104:5–9 God places the gigantic disk of the earth securely on its foundation and then, as a warrior, chases away the enveloping waters and confines them under, above, and around the earth.

104:16–18 Even the exotic flora and fauna of the high mountains of the Lebanon range receive adequate water.

* **103:8** Ps 86:15; 145:8; Ex 34:6–7; Nm 14:18; Jer 3:12; Jl 2:13; Jon 4:2.
103:11 Is 55:9.
103:14 Ps 90:3.
103:15 Ps 37:2; 90:5–6; Is 40:7.
103:20 Ps 148:2; Dn 3:58.
104:2 Prv 8:27–28; Jb 9:8; Is 40:22; Gn 1:6–7; Am 9:6.
104:4 Heb 1:7.
104:7 Ps 29:3.
104:9 Jer 5:22; Gn 9:11–15.
104:11–14 Ps 147:8–9.
104:17 Ez 31:6.
104:19 Sir 43:6.

Catholic Social Teaching

The Urgent Need to Care for Our Planet

Psalm 104 describes the beauty of creation as God is shown actively involved in the unfolding of the natural world. The writer describes the intimate and dependent relationship all living things have with their creator. We are called to revere God's creation and to care for it in a way that reflects God's boundless and ongoing care.

The Church's social teaching underscores the urgency of caring for creation. In a statement on global warming, the United States bishops speak about the threat of climate change and its implications for the most vulnerable of our world. They urge us to recognize the interdependence that exists between all creation and that any action we take must consider the common good. The destruction of a rain forest in one part of the world or a country that uses a disproportionate amount of the earth's resources in another part of the world can have significant impact on the entire planet. Often it is those with the least amount of power to affect political policies who suffer the most; and things will continue to worsen if steps are not taken to reverse this trend.

Caring for creation must be directed by God's plan and not by our own self-interests. When we contribute to the destruction of our environment, we dishonor God and all creation. Let us reflect on how our individual actions impact the global community and pray for the wisdom to understand our role in restoring order to the natural world, because our very survival depends upon it.

- How does my use of energy affect the environment and others? What can I do to reduce my energy use?
- How dependent am I upon having material things? What are some ways I can live more simply so others can simply live?

▶ **Psalm 104**
Care for God's Creation

20 You bring darkness and night falls,
then all the animals of the forest wander about.
21 Young lions roar for prey;
they seek their food from God.*
22 When the sun rises, they steal away
and settle down in their dens.
23 People go out to their work,
to their labor till evening falls.

V

24 How varied are your works, LORD!
In wisdom you have made them all;
the earth is full of your creatures.*
25 There is the sea, great and wide!
It teems with countless beings,
living things both large and small.*
26 There ships ply their course
and Leviathan,† whom you formed to play with.*

VI

27 All of these look to you
to give them food in due time.*
28 When you give it to them, they gather;
when you open your hand, they are well filled.
29† When you hide your face, they panic.
Take away their breath, they perish
and return to the dust.*
30 Send forth your spirit, they are created
and you renew the face of the earth.

VII

31 May the glory of the LORD endure forever;
may the LORD be glad in his works!
32 Who looks at the earth and it trembles,
touches the mountains and they smoke!*
33 I will sing to the LORD all my life;
I will sing praise to my God while I live.*
34 May my meditation be pleasing to him;

† **104:26** *Leviathan*: a sea monster symbolizing primeval chaos, cf. Ps 74:14; Is 27:1; Jb 40:25. God does not destroy chaos but makes it part of the created order.

104:29–30 On one level, the spirit (or wind) of God is the fall and winter rains that provide food for all creatures. On another, it is the breath (or spirit) of God that makes beings live.

* **104:21** Jb 38:39.
104:24 Ps 92:6; Sir 39:16.
104:25 Sir 43:26.
104:26 Jb 3:8; 40:25, 29.
104:27 Ps 136:25; 145:15–16.
104:29 Ps 90:3; Jb 34:14–15; Eccl 3:20.
104:32 Ps 144:5.
104:33 Ps 146:2.

I will rejoice in the LORD.
35 May sinners vanish from the earth,
and the wicked be no more.
Bless the LORD, my soul! Hallelujah!†

PSALM 105†

God's Fidelity to the Promise

I

1 Give thanks to the LORD, invoke his name;*
make known among the peoples his deeds!*
2 Sing praise to him, play music;
proclaim all his wondrous deeds!
3 Glory in his holy name;
let hearts that seek the LORD rejoice!
4 Seek out the LORD and his might;
constantly seek his face.*
5 Recall the wondrous deeds he has done,
his wonders and words of judgment,
6 You descendants of Abraham his servant,
offspring of Jacob the chosen one!

II

7 He the LORD, is our God
whose judgments reach through all the
earth.
8 He remembers forever his covenant,
the word he commanded for a thousand
generations,
9 Which he made with Abraham,
and swore to Isaac,*
10 And ratified in a statute for Jacob,
an everlasting covenant for Israel:
11 "To you I give the land of Canaan,
your own allotted inheritance."*

III

12 When they were few in number,*
a handful, and strangers there,
13 Wandering from nation to nation,
from one kingdom to another people,
14 He let no one oppress them;
for their sake he rebuked kings:†
15† "Do not touch my anointed ones,
to my prophets do no harm."

IV

16 Then he called down a famine on the land,
destroyed the grain that sustained them.†*
17 He had sent a man ahead of them,
Joseph, sold as a slave.*
18 They shackled his feet with chains;
collared his neck in iron,*
19 Till his prediction came to pass,
and the word of the LORD proved him true.*
20 The king sent and released him;
the ruler of peoples set him free.*
21 He made him lord over his household,
ruler over all his possessions,*
22 To instruct his princes as he desired,
to teach his elders wisdom.

V

23 Then Israel entered Egypt;*
Jacob sojourned in the land of Ham.†
24 God greatly increased his people,
made them more numerous than their foes.*
25 He turned their hearts to hate his people,
to treat his servants deceitfully.*
26 He sent his servant Moses,
and Aaron whom he had chosen.*
27† They worked his signs in Egypt*
and wonders in the land of Ham.
28 He sent darkness and it grew dark,
but they rebelled against his word.
29 He turned their waters into blood
and killed their fish.
30 Their land swarmed with frogs,
even the chambers of their kings.
31 He spoke and there came swarms of flies,
gnats through all their country.
32 For rain he gave them hail,
flashes of lightning throughout their land.
33 He struck down their vines and fig trees,
shattered the trees of their country.
34 He spoke and the locusts came,
grasshoppers without number.*
35 They devoured every plant in the land;
they devoured the crops of their fields.
36 He struck down every firstborn in the land,
the first fruits of all their vigor.

---

†

104:35 *Hallelujah*: a frequent word in the last third of the Psalter. The word combines the plural imperative of praise (*hallelu*) with an abbreviated form of the divine name Yah(weh).

Psalm 105 A hymn to God who promised the land of Canaan to the holy people, cf. Ps 78; 106; 136. Israel is invited to praise and seek the presence of God (Ps 105:1–6), who is faithful to the promise of land to the ancestors (Ps 105:7–11). In every phase of the national story—the ancestors in the land of Canaan (Ps 105:12–15), Joseph in Egypt (Ps 105:16–22), Israel in Egypt (Ps 105:23–38), Israel in the desert on the way to Canaan (Ps 105:39–45)—God remained faithful, reiterating the promise of the land to successive servants.

105:14 *Kings*: Pharaoh and Abimelech of Gerar, cf. Gn 12:17; 20:6–7.

105:15 *My anointed ones . . . my prophets*: the patriarchs Abraham, Isaac, and Jacob, who were "anointed" in the sense of being consecrated and recipients of God's revelation.

105:16 *The grain that sustained them*: lit., every "staff of bread."

105:23, 27 *The land of Ham*: a synonym for Egypt, cf. Gn 10:6.

105:27–38 This Psalm and Ps 78:43–51 have an account of the plagues differing in number or in order from Ex 7:14–12:30. Several versions of the exodus story were current.

---

*

105:1–15 1 Chr 16:8–22.
105:1 Ps 18:50; 96:3; 145:5; Is 12:4–5.
105:4 Ps 24:6; 27:8.
105:9 Gn 15:1ff; 26:3.
105:11 Gn 12:7; 15:18.
105:12–13 Dt 4:27; 26:5.
105:16 Gn 41:54, 57.
105:17 Gn 37:28, 36; 45:5.
105:18 Gn 39:20.
105:19 Gn 40–41.
105:20 Gn 41:14.
105:21 Gn 41:41–44.
105:23 Gn 46:1–47:12; Acts 7:15.
105:24 Ex 1:7; Acts 7:17.
105:25 Ex 1:8–14.
105:26 Ex 3:10; 4:27.
105:27–36 Ps 78:43–51; Ex 7–12.
105:34 Jl 1:4.

37 He brought his people out,
laden with silver and gold;*
no one among the tribes stumbled.
38 Egypt rejoiced when they left,
for fear had seized them.

VI

39 He spread a cloud out as a cover,
and made a fire to light up the night.*
40 They asked and he brought them quail;
with bread from heaven he filled them.*
41 He split the rock and water gushed forth;
it flowed through the desert like a river.*
42 For he remembered his sacred promise
to Abraham his servant.
43 He brought his people out with joy,
his chosen ones with shouts of triumph.
44 He gave them the lands of the nations,
they took possession of the wealth of the peoples,*
45 That they might keep his statutes
and observe his teachings.*
Hallelujah!

PSALM 106†

Israel's Confession of Sin

1 Hallelujah!

A

Give thanks to the LORD, who is good,
whose mercy endures forever.*
2 Who can recount the mighty deeds of the LORD,
proclaim in full God's praise?
3 Blessed those who do what is right,
whose deeds are always just.*
4 Remember me, LORD, as you favor your people;
come to me with your saving help,*
5 That I may see the prosperity of your chosen ones,
rejoice in the joy of your people,
and glory with your heritage.

B

6 We have sinned like our ancestors;*
we have done wrong and are guilty.

I

7 Our ancestors in Egypt
did not attend to your wonders.
They did not remember your manifold mercy;
they defied the Most High at the Red Sea.
8 Yet he saved them for his name's sake
to make his power known.*
9 He roared at the Red Sea and it dried up.
He led them through the deep as through a desert.*
10 He rescued them from hostile hands,
freed them from the power of the enemy.
11 The waters covered their oppressors;
not one of them survived.
12 Then they believed his words
and sang his praise.*

II

13 But they soon forgot all he had done;
they had no patience for his plan.
14 In the desert they gave in to their cravings,
tempted God in the wasteland.*
15 So he gave them what they asked
and sent a wasting disease against them.*

III

16 In the camp they challenged Moses*
and Aaron, the holy one of the LORD.
17 The earth opened and swallowed Dathan,
it closed on the followers of Abiram.
18 Against their company the fire blazed;
flames consumed the wicked.

IV

19 At Horeb they fashioned a calf,*
worshiped a metal statue.
20 They exchanged their glory†
for the image of a grass-eating bull.
21 They forgot the God who had saved them,
who had done great deeds in Egypt,*
22 Amazing deeds in the land of Ham,
fearsome deeds at the Red Sea.

PS

---

† **Psalm 106** Israel is invited to praise the God whose mercy has always tempered judgment of Israel (Ps 106:1–3). The speaker, on behalf of all, seeks solidarity with the people, who can always count on God's fidelity despite their sin (Ps 106:4–5). Confident of God's mercy, the speaker invites national repentance (Ps 106:6) by reciting from Israel's history eight instances of sin, judgment, and forgiveness. The sins are the rebellion at the Red Sea (Ps 106:6–12; see Ex 14–15), the craving for meat in the desert (Ps 106:13–15; see Nm 11), the challenge to Moses' authority (Ps 106:16–18; see Nm 16), the golden calf episode (Ps 106:19–23; see Ex 32–34), the refusal to take Canaan by the southern route (Ps 106:24–27; see Nm 13–14 and Dt 1–2), the rebellion at Baal-Peor (Ps 106:28–31; see Nm 25:1–10), the anger of Moses (Ps 106:32–33; see Nm 20:1–13), and mingling with the nations (Ps 106:34–47). The last, as suggested by its length and generalized language, may be the sin that invites the repentance of the present generation. The text gives the site of each sin: Egypt (Ps 106:7), the desert (Ps 106:14), the camp (Ps 106:16), Horeb (Ps 106:19), in their tents (Ps 106:25), Baal-Peor (Ps 106:28), the waters of Meribah (Ps 106:32), Canaan (Ps 106:38).

106:20 *Their glory*: meant as a reference to God.

---

* **105:37** Ex 12:33–36.
105:39 Ps 78:14; Ex 13:21–22; Wis 18:3.
105:40 Ps 78:24–28; Ex 16:13–15; Nm 11:31ff; Wis 16:20.
105:41 Ps 78:15–16; Ex 17:1–7; Nm 20:11.
105:44 Dt 4:37–40.
105:45 Dt 6:20–25; 7:8–11.
106:1 Ps 100:5; 107:1; 1 Chr 16:34; Jer 33:11; Dn 3:89.
106:3 Is 56:1–2.
106:4 Ps 25:7; Neh 5:19.
106:6–7 Ps 78:11–17; Ex 14:11; Lv 26:40; 1 Kgs 8:47; Bar 2:12; Dn 9:5.
106:8 Ez 36:20–22.
106:9 Ex 14:21–31; Is 50:2; 63:11–14; Na 1:4.
106:12 Ex 15:1–21.
106:14 Ps 78:18; Ex 15:24; 16:3; Nm 11:1–6.
106:15 Ps 78:26–31; Nm 11:33.
106:16–18 Nm 16; Dt 11:6; Is 26:11.
106:19–20 Ex 32; Dt 9:8–21; Jer 2:11; Acts 7:41; Rom 1:23.
106:21 Ps 78:42–58; Dt 32:18; Jer 2:32.

23 He would have decreed their destruction,
had not Moses, his chosen one,
Withstood him in the breach†
to turn back his destroying anger.*

V

24 Next they despised the beautiful land;*
they did not believe the promise.
25 In their tents they complained;
they did not heed the voice of the LORD.
26 So with raised hand he swore
he would destroy them in the desert,
27 And scatter their descendants among the nations,
disperse them in foreign lands.

VI

28 They joined in the rites of Baal of Peor,*
ate food sacrificed to the dead.
29 They provoked him by their actions,
and a plague broke out among them.
30 Then Phinehas rose to intervene,
and the plague was brought to a halt.
31 This was counted for him as a righteous deed
for all generations to come.

VII

32 At the waters of Meribah they angered God,*
and Moses suffered because of them.†
33 They so embittered his spirit
that rash words crossed his lips.

VIII

34 They did not destroy the peoples
as the LORD had commanded them,*
35 But mingled with the nations
and imitated their ways.*
36 They served their idols
and were ensnared by them.*
37 They sacrificed to demons†
their own sons and daughters,
38 Shedding innocent blood,
the blood of their own sons and daughters,
Whom they sacrificed to the idols of Canaan,
desecrating the land with bloodshed.
39 They defiled themselves by their actions,
became adulterers by their conduct.
40 So the LORD grew angry with his people,
abhorred his own heritage.
41 He handed them over to the nations,
and their adversaries ruled over them.*
42 Their enemies oppressed them,
kept them under subjection.
43 Many times did he rescue them,
but they kept rebelling and scheming
and were brought low by their own guilt.*
44 Still God had regard for their affliction
when he heard their wailing.
45 For their sake he remembered his covenant
and relented in his abundant mercy,*
46 Winning for them compassion
from all who held them captive.

C

47 Save us, LORD, our God;
gather us from among the nations
That we may give thanks to your holy name
and glory in praising you.*
48† Blessed be the LORD, the God of Israel,
from everlasting to everlasting!
Let all the people say, Amen!*
Hallelujah!

Fifth Book—Psalms 107–150

PSALM 107†

God the Savior of Those in Distress

I

1 "Give thanks to the LORD for he is good,
his mercy endures forever!"*
2 Let that be the prayer of the LORD's redeemed,
those redeemed from the hand of the foe,*
3 Those gathered from foreign lands,
from east and west, from north and south.*

I

4 Some had lost their way in a barren desert;
found no path toward a city to live in.
5 They were hungry and thirsty;

---

† **106:23** *Withstood him in the breach*: the image is that of Moses standing in a narrow break made in the wall to keep anyone from entering.

106:32 *Moses suffered because of them*: Moses was not allowed to enter the promised land because of his rash words (Nm 20:12). According to Dt 1:37, Moses was not allowed to cross because of the people's sin, not his own.

106:37 *Demons*: Hebrew *shedim* occurs in parallelism with "gods" in an important inscription from Transjordan and hence can also be translated "the gods."

106:48 A doxology ending Book IV of the Psalter. It is not part of the Psalm.

Psalm 107 A hymn inviting those who have been rescued by God to give praise (Ps 107:1–3). Four archetypal divine rescues are described, each ending in thanksgiving: from the sterile desert (Ps 107:4–9), from imprisonment in gloom (Ps 107:10–16), from mortal illness (Ps 107:17–22), and from the angry sea (Ps 107:23–32). The number four connotes totality, all the possible varieties of rescue. The same saving activity of God is shown in Israel's history (Ps 107:33–41); whenever the people were endangered God rescued them. The last verses invite people to ponder the persistent saving acts of God (Ps 107:42–43).

---

* **106:23** Ex 32:11; Dt 9:25; Ez 22:30.
106:24–27 Lv 26:33; Nm 14; Dt 1:25–36; Ez 20:15, 23.
106:28–31 Nm 25; Dt 26:14; Sir 45:23–24.
106:32–33 Ps 95:8–9; Ex 17:1–7; Nm 20:2–13; Dt 6:16; 33:8.
106:34 Dt 7:1; Jgs 2:1–5.
106:35 Lv 18:3; Jgs 1:27–35; 3:5.
106:36–38 Lv 18:21; Nm 35:33; Dt 32:17; Jgs 2:11–13, 17, 19; 2 Kgs 16:3; Bar 4:7; 1 Cor 10:20.
106:41 Jgs 2:14–23.
106:43 Is 63:7–9.
106:45 Lv 26:42.
106:47 1 Chr 16:35.
106:48 Ps 41:14; 72:18; 89:53; 1 Chr 16:36; Neh 9:5.
107:1 Ps 100:4–5; 106:1; Jer 33:11.
107:2 Is 63:12.
107:3 Is 43:5–6; 49:12; Zec 8:7.

Cultural Connection

Thankfulness

It's good and natural for people to express thankfulness for their blessings. Psalm 107 is an extended thanksgiving for God's love and saving power. Indonesians have a custom for offering thanks on certain special occasions, such as after a new house is built, during the seventh month of pregnancy, and thirty-five days after the birth of a child.

During a thanksgiving for a new house, the family gathers in the house and offers prayers for the people who will live, eat, work, and die there. Similar prayers are said for a mother during pregnancy and for a child after birth—in thanksgiving for their health, well-being, and happiness. After the prayers, those who are gathered share a simple traditional meal of rice, vegetables, fish or chicken, and fruit.

▶ Psalm 107

their life was ebbing away.*
6 In their distress they cried to the LORD,
who rescued them in their peril,
7 *Guided them by a direct path
so they reached a city to live in.*
8 Let them thank the LORD for his mercy,
such wondrous deeds for the children of Adam.
9 For he satisfied the thirsty,
filled the hungry with good things.*

II

10 Some lived in darkness and gloom,
imprisoned in misery and chains.
11 Because they rebelled against God's word,
and scorned the counsel of the Most High,*
12 He humbled their hearts through hardship;
they stumbled with no one to help.*
13 In their distress they cried to the LORD,
who saved them in their peril;
14 He brought them forth from darkness and the shadow of death
and broke their chains asunder.*
15 Let them thank the LORD for his mercy,
such wondrous deeds for the children of Adam.
16 For he broke down the gates of bronze
and snapped the bars of iron.

III

17 Some fell sick from their wicked ways,
afflicted because of their sins.
18 They loathed all manner of food;*
they were at the gates of death.
19 In their distress they cried to the LORD,
who saved them in their peril,
20 Sent forth his word to heal them,*
and snatched them from the grave.
21 Let them thank the LORD for his mercy,
such wondrous deeds for the children of Adam.
22 Let them offer a sacrifice in thanks,
recount his works with shouts of joy.

IV

23 Some went off to sea in ships,
plied their trade on the deep waters.*
24 They saw the works of the LORD,
the wonders of God in the deep.
25 He commanded and roused a storm wind;
it tossed the waves on high.*
26 They rose up to the heavens, sank to the depths;
their hearts trembled at the danger.
27 They reeled, staggered like drunkards;
their skill was of no avail.*
28 In their distress they cried to the LORD,
who brought them out of their peril;
29 He hushed the storm to silence,
the waves of the sea were stilled.*
30 They rejoiced that the sea grew calm,
that God brought them to the harbor they longed for.
31 Let them thank the LORD for his mercy,
such wondrous deeds for the children of Adam.
32 Let them extol him in the assembly of the people,
and praise him in the council of the elders.

107:5 Dt 8:15; 32:10; Is 49:10.
107:7 Is 35:8; 40:3; 43:19.
107:7 Dt 6:10.
107:9 Lk 1:53.
107:11 Is 42:7, 22; Jb 36:8–9; Prv 1:25.
107:12 Ps 106:43.
107:14 Is 42:7; 49:9; 51:14.
107:18 Jb 6:6–7; 33:20.
107:20 Ps 147:15; Wis 16:12; Is 55:11; Mt 8:8.
107:23 Sir 43:25.
107:25 Jon 1:4.
107:27 Is 29:9.
107:29 Ps 65:8; 89:10; Mt 8:26 par.

V

33† God changed rivers into desert,
springs of water into thirsty ground,*
34 Fruitful land into a salty waste,
because of the wickedness of its people.*
35 He changed the desert into pools of water,
arid land into springs of water,*
36 And settled the hungry there;
they built a city to live in.*
37 They sowed fields and planted vineyards,
brought in an abundant harvest.*
38 *God blessed them, and they increased greatly,
and their livestock did not decrease.*
39 But he poured out contempt on princes,
made them wander trackless wastes,
40 Where they were diminished and brought low
through misery and cruel oppression.
41 While he released the poor man from affliction,
and increased their families like flocks.*
42 The upright saw this and rejoiced;*
all wickedness shut its mouth.
43 Whoever is wise will take note of these things,*
and ponder the merciful deeds of the LORD.

PSALM 108†

Prayer for Victory

1 A song; a psalm of David.

I

2 My heart is steadfast, God;*
my heart is steadfast.
Let me sing and chant praise.
3 Awake, lyre and harp!
I will wake the dawn.*
4 I will praise you among the peoples, LORD;
I will chant your praise among the nations.*
5 For your mercy is greater than the heavens;
your faithfulness, to the skies.*

II

6 Appear on high over the heavens, God;
your glory above all the earth.
7 Help with your right hand and answer us
that your loved ones may escape.

8 God speaks in his holiness:†*
"I will exult, I will apportion Shechem;
the valley of Succoth I will measure out.
9 Gilead is mine, mine is Manasseh;
Ephraim is the helmet for my head,
Judah, my scepter.
10 Moab is my washbowl;
upon Edom I cast my sandal;*
I will shout in triumph over Philistia."

11 Who will bring me to the fortified city?
Who will lead me into Edom?
12 Was it not you who rejected us, God?
Do you no longer march with our armies?*
13 Give us aid against the foe;
worthless is human help.
14 We will triumph with the help of God,
who will trample down our foes.

PSALM 109†

Prayer of a Person Falsely Accused

1 For the leader. A psalm of David.

I

2 O God, whom I praise, do not be silent,*
for wicked and treacherous mouths
attack me.
They speak against me with lying tongues;
3 with hateful words they surround me,
attacking me without cause.
4 In return for my love they slander me,
even though I prayed for them.
5 They repay me evil for good,
hatred for my love.*

II

6 Appoint an evil one over him,
an accuser† to stand at his right hand,
7 That he may be judged and found guilty,

†

107:33–41 God destroyed Sodom and Gomorrah in Gn 18–19, which the Psalm sees as the destruction of the wicked inhabitants of Canaan to prepare the way for Israel (Ps 107:33–34). God then led Israel through the desert to give them a fertile land (Ps 107:35–38) and protected them from every danger (Ps 107:39–41).

Psalm 108 A prayer compiled from two other Psalms: Ps 108:2–6 are virtually the same as Ps 57:8–12; Ps 108:7–14 are the same as Ps 60:7–14. An old promise of salvation (Ps 108:8–10) is combined with a confident assurance (Ps 108:2–6, 13) and petition (Ps 108:7, 12–13).

108:8 *Holiness*: may also be translated as "sanctuary" or as referring to God's heavenly abode.

Psalm 109 A lament notable for the length and vehemence of its prayer against evildoers (Ps 109:6–20); the cry to God (Ps 109:1) and the complaint (Ps 109:22–25) are brief in comparison. The psalmist is apparently the victim of a slander campaign, potentially devastating in a society where reputation and honor are paramount. In the emotional perspective of the Psalm, there are only two types of people: the wicked and their poor victims. The psalmist is a poor victim (Ps 109:22, 31) and by that fact a friend of God and enemy of the wicked. The psalmist seeks vindication not on the basis of personal virtue but because of God's promise to protect the poor.

109:6 *An accuser*: Hebrew *satan*, a word occurring in Job 1–2 and Zec 3:1–2. In the latter passage Satan stands at the right hand of the high priest to bring false accusations against him before God. Here the accuser is human.

*

107:33 Is 35:7; 42:15; 50:2.
107:34 Gn 19:23–28; Dt 29:22; Sir 39:23.
107:35 Ps 114:8; Is 41:8.
107:36 Ez 36:35.
107:37 Is 65:21; Jer 31:5.
107:38 Jb 12:23–25.
107:38 Dt 7:13–14.
107:41 Ps 113:7.
107:42 Ps 58:11; 63:12.
107:43 Hos 14:10.
108:2–6 Ps 57:8–12.
108:3 Jb 38:12.
108:4 Ps 9:12; 18:50; 148:13.
108:5 Ps 36:6; 71:19.
108:8–14 Ps 60:8–14.
108:10 Ru 4:7–8.
108:12 Ps 44:10.
109:2 Ps 35:22; 83:1.
109:5 Ps 35:12; 38:21; Prv 17:13; Jer 18:20.

that his plea may be in vain.
8 May his days be few;
may another take his office.*
9 May his children be fatherless,
his wife, a widow.*
10 May his children wander and beg,
driven from their hovels.
11 May the usurer snare all he owns,
strangers plunder all he earns.
12 May no one treat him with mercy
or pity his fatherless children.
13 May his posterity be destroyed,*
their name rooted out in the next generation.
14 May his fathers' guilt be mentioned to the LORD;
his mother's sin not rooted out.*
15 May their guilt be always before the LORD,*
till their memory is banished from the earth,*
16 For he did not remember to show mercy,
but hounded the wretched poor
and brought death to the brokenhearted.
17 He loved cursing; may it come upon him;
he hated blessing; may none come to him.
18 May cursing clothe him like a robe;
may it enter his belly like water,
his bones like oil.
19 May it be near as the clothes he wears,
as the belt always around him.

20† May this be the reward for my accusers from the LORD,
for those speaking evil against me.

III

21 But you, LORD, are my Lord,
deal kindly with me for your name's sake;
in your great mercy rescue me.
22 For I am poor and needy;
my heart is pierced within me.
23 Like a lengthening shadow I am gone,
I am shaken off like the locust.
24 My knees totter from fasting;*
my flesh has wasted away.
25 I have become a mockery to them;
when they see me, they shake their heads.
26 Help me, LORD, my God;
save me in your mercy.
27 Make them know this is your hand,
that you, LORD, have done this.
28 Though they curse, may you bless;
arise, shame them, that your servant may rejoice.
29 Clothe my accusers with disgrace;
make them wear their shame like a mantle.
30 I will give fervent thanks to the LORD;
before a crowd I will praise him.*
31 For he stands at the right hand of the poor
to save him from those who pass judgment on him.

PSALM 110†

God Appoints the King both King and Priest

1 A psalm of David.

The LORD says to my lord:†
"Sit at my right hand,
while I make your enemies your footstool."†*
2 The scepter of your might:
the LORD extends your strong scepter from Zion.
Have dominion over your enemies!
3 Yours is princely power from the day of your birth.
In holy splendor before the daystar,
like dew I begot you.*
4 The LORD has sworn and will not waver:
"You are a priest forever in the manner of Melchizedek."†*
5 At your right hand is the Lord,
who crushes kings on the day of his wrath,*
6 Who judges nations, heaps up corpses,
crushes heads across the wide earth,
7† Who drinks from the brook by the wayside
and thus holds high his head.*

PS

†

109:20 *May this be the reward . . . from the LORD*: the psalmist prays that God ratify the curses of Ps 109:6–19 and bring them upon the wicked.

Psalm 110 A royal Psalm in which a court singer recites three oracles in which God assures the king that his enemies are conquered (Ps 110:1–2), makes the king "son" in traditional adoption language (Ps 110:3), gives priestly status to the king and promises to be with him in future military ventures (Ps 110:4–7).

110:1 *The LORD says to my lord*: a polite form of address of an inferior to a superior, cf. 1 Sm 25:25; 2 Sm 1:10. The court singer refers to the king. Jesus in the synoptic gospels (Mt 22:41–46 and parallels) takes the psalmist to be David and hence "my lord" refers to the messiah, who must be someone greater than David. *Your footstool*: in ancient times victorious kings put their feet on the prostrate bodies of their enemies.

110:4 *Melchizedek*: Melchizedek was the ancient king of Salem (Jerusalem) who blessed Abraham (Gn 14:18–20); like other kings of the time he performed priestly functions. Heb 7 sees in Melchizedek a type of Christ.

110:7 *Who drinks from the brook by the wayside*: the meaning is uncertain. Some see an allusion to a rite of royal consecration at the Gihon spring (cf. 1 Kgs 1:33, 38). Others find here an image of the divine warrior (or king) pursuing enemies so relentlessly that he does not stop long enough to eat and drink.

*

109:8 Acts 1:20.
109:9 Ex 22:23; Jer 18:21.
109:13 Ps 21:11; Prv 10:7.
109:14 Ex 20:5.
109:15 Ps 90:8.
109:15 Ps 34:16.
109:24–25 Ps 69:11–13.
109:30 Ps 111:1.
110:1 Mt 22:44; Acts 2:34–35; 1 Cor 15:25; Heb 1:13; 8:1; 10:12–13; 1 Pt 3:22.
110:3 Ps 2:7; 89:27; Is 49:1.
110:4 Ps 89:35; 132:11; Gn 14:18; Heb 5:6; 7:21.
110:5 Ps 2:9; Rev 2:27; 12:5; 19:15.
110:7 Ps 3:4.

Cultural Connection

Generosity

"It is good for the man gracious in lending, / who conducts his affairs with justice" (Ps 112:5). Generosity is an important value for many Native American peoples. For the Lakota tribe, it is one of four primary values. The Lakota word for generosity is *wa-can-tog-na-ka.*

In this Native American culture, it is a great insult to be called selfish, and a high compliment to be called generous. You are not able to raise your social status by showing off the things that you own. You can do it only by giving things away. In fact, there is a special ceremony called the *otuhan,* or the "giveaway," in which people give away many of their possessions to honor one another. For example, young people may have a giveaway when they graduate from high school, as a way of honoring all who have helped them along the way.

To explore the other primary Lakota virtues, see the "Cultural Connections" articles for Psalms 31, 73, and 89.

▶ Psalm 112

PSALM 111†

Praise of God for Goodness to Israel

1 Hallelujah!

I will praise the LORD with all my heart*
in the assembled congregation of the upright.†
2 Great are the works of the LORD,
studied by all who delight in them.
3 Majestic and glorious is his work,
his righteousness endures forever.
4 He won renown for his wondrous deeds;
gracious and merciful is the LORD.*
5 He gives food to those who fear him,†
he remembers his covenant forever.
6 He showed his powerful deeds to his people,
giving them the inheritance of the nations.
7 The works of his hands are true and just,
reliable all his decrees,
8 Established forever and ever,
to be observed with truth and equity.
9 He sent release to his people,
decreed his covenant forever;
holy and fearsome is his name.
10† The fear of the LORD is the beginning of wisdom;*
prudent are all who practice it.
His praise endures forever.

PSALM 112†

The Blessings of the Just

1 Hallelujah!

Blessed the man who fears the LORD,
who greatly delights in his commands.*
2 His descendants shall be mighty in the land,
a generation of the upright will be blessed.
3 Wealth and riches shall be in his house;
his righteousness† shall endure forever.
4 Light shines through the darkness for the upright;*
gracious, compassionate, and righteous.
5 It is good for the man gracious in lending,
who conducts his affairs with justice.
6 For he shall never be shaken;

†

Psalm 111 A Temple singer (Ps 111:1) tells how God is revealed in Israel's history (Ps 111:2–10). The deeds reveal God's very self, powerful, merciful, faithful. The poem is an acrostic, each verse beginning with a successive letter of the Hebrew alphabet.

111:1 *In the assembled congregation of the upright*: in the Temple, cf. Ps 149:1.

111:5 *Food to those who fear him*: probably a reference to the manna in the desert, which elsewhere is seen as a type of the Eucharist, cf. Jn 6:31–33, 49–51.

111:10 *The fear of the LORD*: reverence for God.

Psalm 112 An acrostic poem detailing the blessings received by those who remain close to God by obedience to the commandments. Among their blessings are children (Ps 112:2), wealth that enables them to be magnanimous (Ps 112:3, 5, 9), and virtue by which they encourage others (Ps 112:4). The just person is an affront to the wicked, whose hopes remain unfulfilled (Ps 112:10). The logic resembles Ps 1; 111.

112:3 *Righteousness*: in the Second Temple period the word acquired the nuance of liberality and almsgiving, cf. Sir 3:30; 7:10; Mt 6:1–4.

*

111:1 Ps 138:1.
111:4 Ps 103:8; 112:4.
111:10 Prv 1:7; 9:10; Sir 1:16.
112:1 Ps 1:1–2; 119:1–2; 128:1.
112:4 Ps 37:6; 97:11; Prv 13:9; Is 58:10.

the righteous shall be remembered
forever.*
7 He shall not fear an ill report;
his heart is steadfast, trusting the LORD.
8 His heart is tranquil, without fear,
till at last he looks down on his foes.
9 Lavishly he gives to the poor;
his righteousness shall endure forever;*
his horn† shall be exalted in honor.
10 The wicked sees and is angry;
gnashes his teeth and wastes away;
the desire of the wicked come to
nothing.

PSALM 113†

Praise of God's Care for the Poor

1 Hallelujah!

I

Praise, you servants of the LORD,
praise the name of the LORD.*
2 Blessed be the name of the LORD
both now and forever.
3 From the rising of the sun to its setting*
let the name of the LORD be praised.

II

4 High above all nations is the LORD;
above the heavens his glory.*
5 Who is like the LORD our God,
enthroned on high,
6 *looking down on heaven and earth?
7 He raises the needy from the dust,
lifts the poor from the ash heap,*
8 Seats them with princes,
the princes of the people,
9 Gives the childless wife a home,
the joyful mother of children.*
Hallelujah!

PSALM 114†

The Lord's Wonders at the Exodus

1 When Israel came forth from Egypt,
the house of Jacob from an alien people,
2 Judah became God's sanctuary,
Israel, God's domain.*
3† The sea saw and fled;
the Jordan turned back.*
4 The mountains skipped like rams;
the hills, like lambs.*
5 Why was it, sea, that you fled?
Jordan, that you turned back?
6 Mountains, that you skipped like rams?
You hills, like lambs?
7 Tremble, earth, before the Lord,*
before the God of Jacob,
8† Who turned the rock into pools of water,
flint into a flowing spring.*

PSALM 115†

The Greatness of the True God

I

1 Not to us, LORD, not to us
but to your name give glory
because of your mercy and faithfulness.*
2 Why should the nations say,
"Where is their God?"†*
3 Our God is in heaven
and does whatever he wills.*

II

4 Their idols are silver and gold,*
the work of human hands.*
5 They have mouths but do not speak,
eyes but do not see.
6 They have ears but do not hear,
noses but do not smell.

---

†

112:9 *His horn*: the symbol for vitality and honor.

Psalm 113 A hymn exhorting the congregation to praise God's name, i.e., the way in which God is present in the world; the name is mentioned three times in Ps 113:1–3. The divine name is especially honored in the Temple (Ps 113:1) but its recognition is not limited by time (Ps 113:2) and space (Ps 113:3), for God is everywhere active (Ps 113:4–5) especially in rescuing the lowly faithful (Ps 113:7–9).

Psalm 114 A hymn celebrating Israel's escape from Egypt, journey through the wilderness, and entry into the promised land, and the miracles of nature that bore witness to God's presence in their midst. In the perspective of the Psalm, the people proceed directly from Egypt into the promised land (Ps 114:1–2). Sea and Jordan, which stood like soldiers barring the people from their land, flee before the mighty God as the earth recoils from the battle (Ps 114:3–4). The poet taunts the natural elements as one taunts defeated enemies (Ps 114:5–6).

114:3–4 Pairs of cosmic elements such as sea and rivers, mountains and hills, are sometimes mentioned in creation accounts. Personified here as warriors, the pairs tremble in fear before the Divine Warrior. The quaking also recalls the divine appearance in the storm at Sinai (Ex 19:16–19) and elsewhere (Jgs 5:4–5; Ps 18:7–15).

114:8 The miracles of giving drink to the people in the arid desert, cf. Ex 17:1–7; Is 41:17–18.

Psalm 115 A response to the enemy taunt, "Where is your God?" This hymn to the glory of Israel's God (Ps 115:1–3) ridicules the lifeless idols of the nations (Ps 115:4–8), expresses in a litany the trust of the various classes of the people in God (Ps 115:9–11), invokes God's blessing on them as they invoke the divine name (Ps 115:12–15), and concludes as it began with praise of God. Ps 135:15–18 similarly mocks the Gentile gods and has a similar litany and hymn (Ps 135:19–21).

115:2 *Where is their God?*: implies that God cannot help them.

---

*

112:6 Prv 10:7; Wis 8:13.
112:9 Prv 22:9; 2 Cor 9:9.
113:1 Ps 135:1.
113:3 Mal 1:11.
113:4 Ps 148:13.
113:6 Ps 89:7–9.
113:7 Ps 107:41; 1 Sm 2:7–8.
113:9 1 Sm 2:5; Is 54:1.
114:2 Ex 19:6.
114:3 Ps 66:6; 74:15; Ex 14:21f; Jos 3:14ff.
114:4 Ps 29:6; Wis 19:9.
114:7 Ps 68:9.
114:8 Ex 17:6; Nm 20:11.
115:1 Ez 36:22–23.
115:2 Ps 79:10.
115:3 Ps 135:6.
115:4–10 Ps 135:15–19; Wis 15:15–16; Is 44:9f; Jer 10:1–5.
115:4 Is 40:19.

PS

Live It!

What Lasts?

Will a car last forever? a house? the sun? Does anything other than God truly have no end? No matter how much you look, you won't find such a thing. So, why do we spend much of our time with what won't last, rather than what *will* last?

Psalm 115 proclaims the greatness of God and the foolishness of idols. In the end, the things that matter most won't be how many awards you were given, how much money you made, or how many possessions you had, but rather how much you loved others, how much you served, and how much you loved God!

Find a mission trip, outreach, or a way in which you can serve others.

▶ **Psalm 115**

7 They have hands but do not feel,
feet but do not walk;
they produce no sound from their throats.
8 Their makers will be like them,
and anyone who trusts in them.

III

9† The house of Israel trusts in the LORD,*
who is their help and shield.*
10 The house of Aaron trusts in the LORD,
who is their help and shield.
11 Those who fear the LORD trust in the LORD,
who is their help and shield.
12 The LORD remembers us and will bless us,
will bless the house of Israel,
will bless the house of Aaron,
13 Will bless those who fear the LORD,
small and great alike.
14 May the LORD increase your number,
yours and your descendants.
15 May you be blessed by the LORD,
maker of heaven and earth.
16† The heavens belong to the LORD,
but he has given the earth to the children of Adam.*
17† The dead do not praise the LORD,
not all those go down into silence.*
18 It is we who bless the LORD,
both now and forever.
Hallelujah!

PSALM 116†

Thanksgiving to God Who Saves from Death

I

1 I love the LORD, who listened
to my voice in supplication,
2 Who turned an ear to me
on the day I called.
3 I was caught by the cords of death;†*
the snares of Sheol had seized me;
I felt agony and dread.
4 Then I called on the name of the LORD,
"O LORD, save my life!"

II

5 Gracious is the LORD and righteous;
yes, our God is merciful.*
6 The LORD protects the simple;
I was helpless, but he saved me.
7 Return, my soul, to your rest;
the LORD has been very good to you.*
8 For my soul has been freed from death,
my eyes from tears, my feet from stumbling.*
9 I shall walk before the LORD
in the land of the living.†*

III

10† I kept faith, even when I said,
"I am greatly afflicted!"*

† **115:9–11** *The house of Israel . . . the house of Aaron . . . those who fear the LORD*: the laity of Israelite birth, the priests, and the converts to Judaism, cf. Ps 118:2–4; 135:19–21. In the New Testament likewise "those who fear the Lord" means converts to Judaism (cf. Acts 10:2, 22, 35; 13:16, 26).

115:16 *The heavens*: the Septuagint reads here "the heaven of heavens" or "the highest heavens," i.e., above the firmament. See note on Ps 148:4.

115:17 See note on Ps 6:5.

Psalm 116 A thanksgiving in which the psalmist responds to divine rescue from mortal danger (Ps 116:3–4) and from near despair (Ps 116:10–11) with vows and Temple sacrifices (Ps 116:13–14, 17–19). The Greek and Latin versions divide the Psalm into two parts: Ps 116:1–9 and Ps 116:10–19, corresponding to its two major divisions.

116:3 *The cords of death*: death is personified here; it attempts to capture the psalmist with snares and nets, cf. Ps 18:6.

116:9 *The land of the living*: the phrase elsewhere is an epithet of the Jerusalem Temple (cf. Ps 27:13; 52:5; Is 38:11). Hence the psalmist probably refers to being present to God in the Temple.

116:10 *I kept faith, even when I said*: even in the days of despair, the psalmist did not lose all hope.

* **115:9** Ps 118:2–4.
115:9 Ps 33:20.
115:16 Gn 1:28.
115:17 Ps 6:6; 88:11ff; Sir 17:22f; Is 38:18.
116:3 Ps 18:5; Jon 2:3.
116:5 Ex 34:6.
116:7 Ps 13:6.
116:8 Ps 56:14; Is 25:8; Rev 21:4.
116:9 Ps 27:13; 56:14; Is 38:11.
116:10 2 Cor 4:13.

11 I said in my alarm,
"All men are liars!"*
12 How can I repay the LORD
for all the great good done for me?
13 I will raise the cup of salvation†
and call on the name of the LORD.
14 I will pay my vows to the LORD
in the presence of all his people.
15† Dear in the eyes of the LORD
is the death of his devoted.*
16 LORD, I am your servant,
your servant, the child of your
maidservant;*
you have loosed my bonds.
17 I will offer a sacrifice of praise
and call on the name of the LORD.*
18 I will pay my vows to the LORD*
in the presence of all his people,
19 In the courts of the house of the LORD,
in your midst, O Jerusalem.
Hallelujah!

PSALM 117†

The Nations Called To Praise

1 Praise the LORD, all you nations!
Extol him, all you peoples!*
2 His mercy for us is strong;
the faithfulness of the LORD is forever.
Hallelujah!

PSALM 118†

Hymn of Thanksgiving

I

1 Give thanks to the LORD, for he is good,*
his mercy endures forever.
2 Let Israel say:
his mercy endures forever.
3 Let the house of Aaron say,
his mercy endures forever.
4 Let those who fear the LORD say,*
his mercy endures forever.

Live It!

Gratitude

Thank God! Have you ever uttered these words in response to something finally going your way? or perhaps in response to a personal situation that turned out just as you had hoped it would? Psalm 116 is all about this feeling—a feeling of true gratitude towards God for making our lives better.

In our prayers, we may get so caught up in asking God for help that we forget to thank God for the various ways he has already blessed our lives. Psalm 116 reminds us to be grateful at all times, thanking and praising God for the many gifts we have received, especially those we have asked for so diligently.

▶ **Psalm 116**

II

5 In danger I called on the LORD;
the LORD answered me and set me free.
6 The LORD is with me; I am not afraid;
what can mortals do against me?*
7 The LORD is with me as my helper;
I shall look in triumph on my foes.
8 Better to take refuge in the LORD*
than to put one's trust in mortals.
9 Better to take refuge in the LORD
than to put one's trust in princes.

III

10 All the nations surrounded me;
in the LORD's name I cut them off.
11 They surrounded me on every side;
in the LORD's name I cut them off.
12 They surrounded me like bees;*
they burned up like fire among thorns;

†

116:13 *The cup of salvation*: probably the libation of wine poured out in gratitude for rescue, cf. Ex 25:29; Nm 15:5, 7, 10.

116:15 *Dear in the eyes of the LORD*: the meaning is that the death of God's faithful is grievous to God, not that God is pleased with the death, cf. Ps 72:14. In Wis 3:5–6, God accepts the death of the righteous as a sacrificial burnt offering.

Psalm 117 This shortest of hymns calls on the nations to acknowledge God's supremacy. The supremacy of Israel's God has been demonstrated to them by the people's secure existence, which is owed entirely to God's gracious fidelity.

Psalm 118 A thanksgiving liturgy accompanying a procession of the king and the people into the Temple precincts. After an invocation in the form of a litany (Ps 118:1–4), the psalmist (very likely speaking in the name of the community) describes how the people confidently implored God's help (Ps 118:5–9) when hostile peoples threatened its life (Ps 118:10–14); vividly God's rescue is recounted (Ps 118:15–18). Then follows a possible dialogue at the Temple gates between the priests and the psalmist as the latter enters to offer the thanksgiving sacrifice (Ps 118:19–25). Finally, the priests impart their blessing (Ps 118:26–27), and the psalmist sings in gratitude (Ps 118:28–29).

*

116:11 Ps 12:2.
116:15 Ps 72:14; Is 43:4.
116:16 Ps 86:16; 143:12; Wis 9:5.
116:17 Lv 7:12ff.
116:18 Jon 2:10.
117:1 Rom 15:11.
118:1 Ps 100:5; 136:1f.
118:4 Ps 115:9–11.
118:6 Ps 27:1; Heb 13:6.
118:8f Ps 146:3.
118:12 Dt 1:44.

PS

in the LORD's name I cut them off.
13 I was hard pressed and falling,
but the LORD came to my help.*
14 The LORD, my strength and might,
has become my savior.*

IV

15 The joyful shout of deliverance
is heard in the tents of the righteous:
"The LORD's right hand works valiantly;
16 the LORD's right hand is raised;
the LORD's right hand works valiantly."
17 I shall not die but live
and declare the deeds of the LORD.
18 The LORD chastised me harshly,
but did not hand me over to death.

V

19 Open the gates of righteousness;
I will enter and thank the LORD.*
20 This is the LORD's own gate,
through it the righteous enter.
21 I thank you for you answered me;
you have been my savior.
22† The stone the builders rejected
has become the cornerstone.*
23 By the LORD has this been done;
it is wonderful in our eyes.
24 This is the day the LORD has made;
let us rejoice in it and be glad.
25 LORD, grant salvation!†
LORD, grant good fortune!

VI

26 Blessed is he
who comes in the name of the LORD.*
We bless you from the house of the LORD.
27 The LORD is God and has enlightened us.
Join in procession with leafy branches
up to the horns of the altar.

VII

28 You are my God, I give you thanks;
my God, I offer you praise.
29 Give thanks to the LORD, for he is good,
his mercy endures forever.

PSALM 119†

A Prayer to God, the Lawgiver

ALEPH

1 Blessed those whose way is blameless,
who walk by the law of the LORD.*
2 Blessed those who keep his testimonies,
who seek him with all their heart.*
3 They do no wrong;
they walk in his ways.
4 You have given them the command
to observe your precepts with care.
5 May my ways be firm
in the observance of your statutes!
6 Then I will not be ashamed
to ponder all your commandments.
7 I will praise you with sincere heart
as I study your righteous judgments.
8 I will observe your statutes;
do not leave me all alone.

BETH

9 How can the young keep his way without fault?
Only by observing your words.
10 With all my heart I seek you;
do not let me stray from your commandments.
11 In my heart I treasure your promise,
that I may not sin against you.
12 Blessed are you, O LORD;
teach me your statutes.*
13 With my lips I recite
all the judgments you have spoken.
14 I find joy in the way of your testimonies
more than in all riches.
15 I will ponder your precepts
and consider your paths.
16 In your statutes I take delight;
I will never forget your word.

†

118:22 *The stone the builders rejected*: a proverb: what is insignificant to human beings has become great through divine election. The "stone" may originally have meant the foundation stone or capstone of the Temple. The New Testament interpreted the verse as referring to the death and resurrection of Christ (Mt 21:42; Acts 4:11; cf. Is 28:16 and Rom 9:33; 1 Pt 2:7).

118:25 *Grant salvation*: the Hebrew for this cry has come into English as "Hosanna." This cry and the words in Ps 118:26 were used in the gospels to welcome Jesus entering the Temple on Palm Sunday (Mk 11:9–10).

Psalm 119 This Psalm, the longest by far in the Psalter, praises God for giving such splendid laws and instruction for people to live by. The author glorifies and thanks God for the Torah, prays for protection from sinners enraged by others' fidelity to the law, laments the cost of obedience, delights in the law's consolations, begs for wisdom to understand the precepts, and asks for the rewards of keeping them. Several expected elements do not appear in the Psalm: Mount Sinai with its story of God's revelation and gift to Israel of instruction and commandments, the Temple and other institutions related to revelation and laws (frequent in other Psalms). The Psalm is fascinated with God's word directing and guiding human life. The poem is an acrostic; its twenty-two stanzas (of eight verses each) are in the order of the Hebrew alphabet. Each of the eight verses within a stanza begins with the same letter. Each verse contains one word for "instruction." The translation here given attempts to translate each Hebrew word for "instruction" with the same English word. There are, however, nine words for "instruction," not eight, so the principle of a different word for "instruction" in each verse cannot be maintained with perfect consistency. The nine words for "instruction" in the translation are: law, statute, commandment, precept, testimony, word, judgment, way, and promise.

*

118:13 Ps 129:1–2.
118:14 Ex 15:2; Is 12:2.
118:19 Is 26:2.
118:22 Mt 21:42; Lk 20:17; Acts 4:11; Rom 9:33; 1 Pt 2:7.
118:26 Mt 21:9; 23:39.
119:1 Ps 1:1–2; 15:2; 112:1.
119:2 Dt 4:29.
119:12 Ps 25:4; 27:11; 86:11; 143:8, 10.

GIMEL

17 Be kind to your servant that I may live,
that I may keep your word.
18 Open my eyes to see clearly
the wonders of your law.
19 I am a sojourner in the land;†*
do not hide your commandments from me.
20 At all times my soul is stirred
with longing for your judgments.
21 With a curse you rebuke the proud
who stray from your commandments.
22 Free me from disgrace and contempt,
for I keep your testimonies.
23 Though princes meet and talk against me,
your servant meditates on your statutes.
24 Your testimonies are my delight;
they are my counselors.

DALETH

25 My soul clings to the dust;*
give me life in accord with your word.
26 I disclosed my ways and you answered me;
teach me your statutes.
27 Make me understand the way of your
precepts;
I will ponder your wondrous deeds.
28 My soul is depressed;
lift me up acccording to your word.
29 Lead me from the way of deceit;
favor me with your law.
30 The way of loyalty I have chosen;
I have kept your judgments.
31 I cling to your testimonies, LORD;
do not let me come to shame.
32 I will run the way of your commandments,
for you will broaden my heart.

HE

33 LORD, teach me the way of your statutes;
I shall keep them with care.*
34 Give me understanding to keep your law,
to observe it with all my heart.
35 Lead me in the path of your commandments,*
for that is my delight.
36 Direct my heart toward your testimonies
and away from gain.
37 Avert my eyes from what is worthless;
by your way give me life.
38 For your servant, fulfill your promise
made to those who fear you.
39 Turn away from me the taunts I dread,

Pray It!

The Longest Psalm

Psalm 119 is the longest psalm. Also, it has an interesting structure that you cannot appreciate in the English translation: it consists of twenty-two sections, and all the lines of a particular section begin with the same letter of the Hebrew alphabet. All the lines of the first section begin with *Aleph*, the Hebrew equivalent of the letter *A*. All the lines of the second section begin with *Beth*, the Hebrew equivalent of the letter *B*. And so on through the whole Hebrew alphabet!

This type of structure is called an acrostic. An acrostic is a poem in which the beginning letters of each line form a word or a phrase or a logical sequence. You may have written a poem like this in grade school using the word *mother* or *father*.

Write your own acrostic prayer, beginning the lines of the prayer with the letters of your name or of the name of someone or something you would like to pray for.

▶ **Psalm 119**

for your judgments are good.
40 See how I long for your precepts;
in your righteousness give me life.

WAW

41 Let your mercy come to me, LORD,
salvation in accord with your promise.
42 Let me answer my taunters with a word,
for I trust in your word.
43 Do not take the word of truth from my
mouth,
for in your judgments is my hope.
44 I will keep your law always,
for all time and forever.
45 I will walk freely in an open space
because I cherish your precepts.
46 I will speak openly of your testimonies
without fear even before kings.
47 I delight in your commandments,

† **119:19** *A sojourner in the land*: like someone without the legal protection of a native inhabitant, the psalmist has a special need for the guidance of God's teaching.

119:19 Ps 39:13.
119:25 Ps 44:26.
119:33 Ps 19:12.
119:35 Ps 25:4; 27:11; 86:11; 143:8, 10.

PS

which I dearly love.
48† I lift up my hands to your commandments;
I study your statutes, which I love.

ZAYIN

49 Remember your word to your servant
by which you give me hope.
50 This is my comfort in affliction,
your promise that gives me life.
51 Though the arrogant utterly scorn me,
I do not turn from your law.
52 When I recite your judgments of old
I am comforted, LORD.
53 Rage seizes me because of the wicked;
they forsake your law.
54 Your statutes become my songs
wherever I make my home.
55 Even at night I remember your name
in observance of your law, LORD.
56 This is my good fortune,
for I have kept your precepts.

HETH

57 My portion is the LORD;
I promise to observe your words.
58 I entreat you with all my heart:
have mercy on me in accord with your
promise.
59 I have examined my ways
and turned my steps to your testimonies.
60 I am prompt, I do not hesitate
in observing your commandments.
61 Though the snares of the wicked surround me,
your law I do not forget.
62 At midnight I rise to praise you
because of your righteous judgments.
63 I am the friend of all who fear you,
of all who observe your precepts.
64 The earth, LORD, is filled with your mercy;*
teach me your statutes.

TETH

65 You have treated your servant well,
according to your word, O LORD.
66 Teach me wisdom and knowledge,
for in your commandments I trust.
67 Before I was afflicted I went astray,
but now I hold to your promise.
68 You are good and do what is good;
teach me your statutes.
69 The arrogant smear me with lies,
but I keep your precepts with all my heart.
70 Their hearts are gross and fat;*
as for me, your law is my delight.
71 It was good for me to be afflicted,
in order to learn your statutes.
72 The law of your mouth is more precious to me
than heaps of silver and gold.

YODH

73 Your hands made me and fashioned me;
give me understanding to learn your
commandments.
74 Those who fear you rejoice to see me,
because I hope in your word.
75 I know, LORD, that your judgments are
righteous;
though you afflict me, you are faithful.
76 May your mercy comfort me
in accord with your promise to your
servant.
77 Show me compassion that I may live,
for your law is my delight.
78 Shame the proud for leading me astray with
falsehood,
that I may study your testimonies.
79 Let those who fear you turn to me,
those who acknowledge your testimonies.
80 May I be wholehearted toward your statutes,
that I may not be put to shame.

KAPH

81 My soul longs for your salvation;
I put my hope in your word.*
82 My eyes long to see your promise.*
When will you comfort me?
83 I am like a wineskin shriveled by smoke,*
but I have not forgotten your statutes.
84 How long can your servant survive?
When will your judgment doom my foes?
85 The arrogant have dug pits for me;
defying your law.
86 All your commandments are steadfast.
Help me! I am pursued without cause.
87 They have almost put an end to me on earth,
but I do not forsake your precepts.
88 In your mercy give me life,
to observe the testimonies of your mouth.

LAMEDH

89† Your word, LORD, stands forever;*
it is firm as the heavens.

†

119:48 *I lift up my hands to your commandments*: to lift up the hands was an ancient gesture of reverence to God. Here the picture is applied to God's law.

119:89–91 God's word creates the world, which manifests that word by its permanence and reliability.

*

119:64 Ps 33:5.
119:70 Ps 17:10; 73:7; Jb 15:27.
119:81 Ps 130:6.
119:82 Ps 25:15; 123:1–2; 141:8.

PS

90 Through all generations your truth endures;
fixed to stand firm like the earth.
91 By your judgments they stand firm to this day,
for all things are your servants.
92 Had your law not been my delight,
I would have perished in my affliction.
93 I will never forget your precepts;
through them you give me life.
94 I am yours; save me,
for I cherish your precepts.
95 The wicked hope to destroy me,
but I seek to understand your testimonies.
96 I have seen the limits of all perfection,
but your commandment is without bounds.

MEM

97 How I love your law, Lord!†
I study it all day long.
98 Your commandment makes me wiser than my foes,
as it is forever with me.
99 I have more insight than all my teachers,
because I ponder your testimonies.
100 I have more understanding than my elders,
because I keep your precepts.*
101 I keep my steps from every evil path,
that I may observe your word.
102 From your judgments I do not turn,
for you have instructed me.
103 How sweet to my tongue is your promise,
sweeter than honey to my mouth!*
104 Through your precepts I gain understanding;
therefore I hate all false ways.

NUN

105 Your word is a lamp for my feet,
a light for my path.*
106 I make a solemn vow
to observe your righteous judgments.
107 I am very much afflicted, LORD;
give me life in accord with your word.
108 Accept my freely offered praise;*
LORD, teach me your judgments.
109 My life is always at risk,
but I do not forget your law.
110 The wicked have set snares for me,
but from your precepts I do not stray.
111 Your testimonies are my heritage forever;
they are the joy of my heart.
112 My heart is set on fulfilling your statutes;
they are my reward forever.

Pray It!

Connected to God

God's word can indeed light our way as we journey through life. Traditionally, we have heard or read God's word at worship or in the Bible. However, today with the remarkable advances in communication technology, God's word and spiritual messages can be sent through the Internet. There are countless Web sites devoted to spirituality, faith, and religion. Online prayers and meditations are available daily.

As followers of Christ, we are told to be bearers of the Good News. Now more than ever, that Good News can be shared through technology. Like anything else, Internet access can lead us to sites that are destructive to our faith, but we have the option to choose sites that will enhance our faith and actually draw us closer to God. The worldwide availability of the Internet can also connect people across the globe in prayer and inspiration. It is hard for us to imagine a world without books, and yet in biblical times, they did not exist. It is perhaps equally hard for us to imagine our lives without the ability to access information quickly and to be so connected with so many.

The challenge is how to make sure technology truly can serve to light our way to God. How can we better use this powerful force to share both prayer and blessings with others and also to deepen our understanding of the mysteries of our faith?

▶ Ps 119:105

SAMEKH

113 I hate every hypocrite;
your law I love.
114 You are my refuge and shield;
in your word I hope.
115 Depart from me, you wicked,*

† **119:97** *Lord*: the inclusion of "Lord" follows the tradition of the Septuagint and the Vulgate.

* **119:83** Jb 30:30. **119:89** Is 40:8. **119:100** Jb 32:6; Wis 4:8–9. **119:103** Ps 19:11. **119:105** Ps 18:29; Prv 6:23. **119:108** Ps 50:14, 23; Heb 13:15. **119:115** Ps 6:9; 139:19; Jb 21:14.

that I may keep the commandments of my
God.
116 Sustain me by your promise that I may live;
do not disappoint me in my hope.
117 Strengthen me that I may be safe,
ever to contemplate your statutes.
118 You reject all who stray from your statutes,
for vain is their deceit.
119 Like dross you regard all the wicked on earth;
therefore I love your testimonies.
120 My flesh shudders with dread of you;
I fear your judgments.

AYIN

121 I have fulfilled your righteous judgment;
do not abandon me to my oppressors.
122 Guarantee your servant's welfare;
do not let the arrogant oppress me.
123 My eyes long to see your salvation
and the promise of your righteousness.
124 Act with mercy toward your servant;
teach me your statutes.
125 I am your servant; give me discernment
that I may know your testimonies.
126 It is time for the LORD to act;
they have disobeyed your law.
127 Truly I love your commandments
more than gold, more than the finest gold.
128 Thus, I follow all your precepts;
every wrong way I hate.

PE

129 Wonderful are your testimonies;
therefore I keep them.
130 The revelation of your words sheds light,
gives understanding to the simple.
131 I sigh with open mouth,
yearning for your commandments.
132 Turn to me and be gracious,*
according to your judgment for those who
love your name.
133 Steady my feet in accord with your promise;
do not let iniquity lead me.
134 Free me from human oppression,
that I may observe your precepts.
135 Let your face shine upon your servant;
teach me your statutes.
136 My eyes shed streams of tears
because your law is not observed.

SADHE

137 You are righteous, LORD,
and just are your judgments.*
138 You have given your testimonies in
righteousness
and in surpassing faithfulness.
139 I am consumed with rage,
because my foes forget your words.
140 Your servant loves your promise;
it has been proved by fire.
141 Though belittled and despised,
I do not forget your precepts.
142 Your justice is forever right,
your law true.
143 Though distress and anguish come upon me,
your commandments are my delight.
144 Your testimonies are forever righteous;
give me understanding that I may live.

QOPH

145 I call with all my heart, O LORD;
answer me that I may keep your statutes.
146 I call to you to save me
that I may observe your testimonies.
147 I rise before dawn and cry out;
I put my hope in your words.
148 My eyes greet the night watches
as I meditate on your promise.*
149 Hear my voice in your mercy, O LORD;
by your judgment give me life.
150 Malicious persecutors draw near me;
they are far from your law.
151 You are near, O LORD;
reliable are all your commandments.
152 Long have I known from your testimonies
that you have established them forever.

RESH

153 Look at my affliction and rescue me,
for I have not forgotten your law.
154 Take up my cause and redeem me;*
for the sake of your promise give me life.
155 Salvation is far from sinners
because they do not cherish your statutes.
156 Your compassion is great, O LORD;
in accord with your judgments, give me life.
157 Though my persecutors and foes are many,
I do not turn from your testimonies.
158 I view the faithless with loathing*
because they do not heed your promise.
159 See how I love your precepts, LORD;
in your mercy give me life.
160 Your every word is enduring;
all your righteous judgments are forever.

SHIN

161 Princes persecute me without reason,
but my heart reveres only your word.
162 I rejoice at your promise,
as one who has found rich spoil.
163 Falsehood I hate and abhor;

119:132 Ps 25:16; 86:16.
119:137 Tb 3:2.
119:148 Ps 63:7; 77:7.
119:154 Ps 43:1.
119:158 Ps 139:22.

your law I love.
164 Seven times a day I praise you
because your judgments are righteous.
165 Lovers of your law have much peace;*
for them there is no stumbling block.
166 I look for your salvation, LORD,
and I fulfill your commandments.
167 I observe your testimonies;
I love them very much.
168 I observe your precepts and testimonies;
all my ways are before you.

TAW

169 Let my cry come before you, LORD;*
in keeping with your word, give me
understanding.
170 Let my prayer come before you;
rescue me according to your promise.
171 May my lips pour forth your praise,
because you teach me your statutes.
172 May my tongue sing of your promise,
for all your commandments are righteous.
173 Keep your hand ready to help me,
for I have chosen your precepts.
174 I long for your salvation, LORD;
your law is my delight.
175 Let my soul live to praise you;
may your judgments give me help.
176 I have wandered like a lost sheep;
seek out your servant,
for I do not forget your commandments.*

PSALM 120†

Prayer of a Returned Exile

1 A song of ascents.†

The LORD answered me
when I called in my distress:*
2 LORD, deliver my soul from lying lips,
from a treacherous tongue.*

3 What will he inflict on you,
O treacherous tongue,
and what more besides?†
4 A warrior's arrows
sharpened with coals of brush wood!†*

5† Alas, I am a foreigner in Meshech,
I live among the tents of Kedar!
6 Too long do I live
among those who hate peace.
7 When I speak of peace,
they are for war.*

PSALM 121†

The Lord My Guardian

1 A song of ascents.

I raise my eyes toward the mountains.†
From whence shall come my help?*
2 My help comes from the LORD,
the maker of heaven and earth.*

3 He will not allow your foot to slip;*
or your guardian to sleep.
4 Behold, the guardian of Israel
never slumbers nor sleeps.
5† The LORD is your guardian;
the LORD is your shade
at your right hand.*
6 By day the sun will not strike you,
nor the moon by night.*
7 The LORD will guard you from all evil;
he will guard your soul.*
8 The LORD will guard your coming and going
both now and forever.*

† **Psalm 120** A thanksgiving, reporting divine rescue (Ps 120:1) yet with fervent prayer for further protection against lying attackers (Ps 120:2–4). The psalmist is acutely conscious of living away from God's own land where divine peace prevails (Ps 120:5–7).

120:1 *A song of ascents*: Ps 120–134 all begin with this superscription. Most probably these fifteen Psalms once formed a collection of Psalms sung when pilgrims went to Jerusalem, since one "ascended" to Jerusalem (1 Kgs 12:28; Ps 24:3; 122:4; Lk 2:42) or to the house of God or to an altar (1 Kgs 12:33; 2 Kgs 23:2; Ps 24:3). Less probable is the explanation that these Psalms were sung by the exiles when they "ascended" to Jerusalem from Babylonia (cf. Ezr 7:9). The idea, found in the Mishnah, that the fifteen steps on which the Levites sang corresponded to these fifteen Psalms (Middot 2:5) must underlie the Vulgate translation *canticum graduum*, "song of the steps" or "gradual song."

120:3 *More besides*: a common curse formula in Hebrew was "May the Lord do such and such evils to you [the evils being specified], and add still more to them," cf. 1 Sm 3:17; 14:44; 25:22. Here the psalmist is at a loss for a suitable malediction.

120:4 *Coals of brush wood*: coals made from the stalk of the broom plant burn with intense heat. The psalmist thinks of lighted coals cast at his enemies.

120:5 Meshech was in the far north (Gn 10:2) and Kedar was a tribe of the north Arabian desert (Gn 25:13). The psalmist may be thinking generally of all aliens living among inhospitable peoples.

Psalm 121 A blessing given to someone embarking on a dangerous journey whether a soldier going on a campaign or a pilgrim returning home from the Temple. People look anxiously at the wooded hills. Will God protect them on their journey (Ps 121:1)? The speaker declares that God is not confined to a place or a time (Ps 121:2), that every step is guarded (Ps 121:3–4); night and day (Ps 121:5–6) God watches over their every movement (Ps 121:7–8).

121:1 *The mountains*: possibly Mount Zion, the site of the Temple

119:165 Ps 72:7.
119:169 Ps 88:3.
119:176 Is 53:6; Jer 50:6; Lk 15:1–7.
120:1 Jon 2:3.
120:2 Ps 12:3–5; Sir 51:3.
120:4 Ps 11:6; 140:11; Prv 16:27.
120:7 Ps 35:20; 140:3–4.
121:1 Jer 3:23.
121:2 Ps 124:8; 146:6.
121:3 Ps 66:9; 91:12; 1 Sm 2:9; Prv 3:23.
121:5 Ps 16:8; 73:23.
121:6 Wis 18:3; Is 25:4; 49:10.
121:7 Ps 97:10.
121:8 Dt 28:6.

Live It!

The Lord Was on Our Side

You often hear a team or group that has just played well or completed a great task say, "God was with us." The writer of Psalm 124 expresses the same sentiment in verses 1–2. What a gift it is to recognize God's help in our lives. It is God who carries us when we are down, who rescues us when we are in trouble, and who gives us the talent we have. If we reach out in relationship to God and do the things necessary to grow in that relationship, God will most assuredly be with us.

If you have ever been afraid or felt lost, read Psalm 124 and be assured that others have felt the same way. Whether you are unsure about school, a job, a relationship, or your future, just remember, "Our help is in the name of the LORD, / the maker of heaven and earth" (verse 8).

▶ Psalm 124

PSALM 122†

A Pilgrim's Prayer for Jerusalem

1 A song of ascents. Of David.

I

I rejoiced when they said to me,
"Let us go to the house of the LORD."*
2 And now our feet are standing
within your gates, Jerusalem.
3 Jerusalem, built as a city,
walled round about.†*
4 There the tribes go up,
the tribes of the LORD,
As it was decreed for Israel,
to give thanks to the name of the LORD.*
5 There are the thrones of justice,
the thrones of the house of David.

II

6 For the peace of Jerusalem pray:
"May those who love you prosper!
7 May peace be within your ramparts,
prosperity within your towers."*
8 For the sake of my brothers and friends
I say,
"Peace be with you."*
9 For the sake of the house of the LORD, our God,
I pray for your good.

PSALM 123†

Reliance on the Lord

1 A song of ascents.

To you I raise my eyes,
to you enthroned in heaven.*
2 Yes, like the eyes of servants
on the hand of their masters,
Like the eyes of a maid
on the hand of her mistress,
So our eyes are on the LORD our God,
till we are shown favor.
3 Show us favor, LORD, show us favor,
for we have our fill of contempt.*
4 Our souls are more than sated
with mockery from the insolent,
with contempt from the arrogant.

PSALM 124†

God, the Rescuer of the People

1 A song of ascents. Of David.

Had not the LORD been with us,
let Israel say,*

---

and hence of safety, but more probably mountains as a place of dangers, causing anxiety to the psalmist.

121:5–6 The image of shade, a symbol of protection, is apt: God as shade protects from the harmful effects that ancients believed were caused by the sun and moon.

Psalm 122 A song of Zion, sung by pilgrims obeying the law to visit Jerusalem three times on a journey. The singer anticipates joining the procession into the city (Ps 122:1–3). Jerusalem is a place of encounter, where the people praise God (Ps 122:4) and hear the divine justice mediated by the king (Ps 122:5). The very buildings bespeak God's power (cf. Ps 48:13–15). May the grace of this place transform the people's lives (Ps 122:6–9)!

122:3 *Walled round about*: lit., "which is joined to it," probably referring both to the density of the buildings and to the dense population.

Psalm 123 A lament that begins as a prayer of an individual (Ps 123:1), who expresses by a touching comparison exemplary confidence in God (Ps 123:2). The Psalm ends in prayer that God relieve the people's humiliation at the hands of the arrogant (Ps 123:3–4).

Psalm 124 A thanksgiving which teaches that Israel's very existence is owed to God who rescues them. In the first part Israel's enemies are compared to the mythic sea dragon (Ps 124:2b–3a; cf. Jer 51:34) and Flood (Ps 124:3b–5; cf. Is 51:9–10). The Psalm heightens the malice of human enemies by linking them to the primordial enemies of God's creation. Israel is a bird freed from the trapper's snare (Ps 124:6–8)—freed originally from Pharaoh and now from the current danger.

122:1 Ps 43:3–4; 84:2–5.
122:3 Ps 48:13–14.
122:4 Dt 16:16.
122:7 Ps 128:5.
122:8 Jn 20:19ff.
123:1 Ps 25:15; 119:82; 141:8.
123:3 Ps 44:13–14; Jb 12:4.
124:1 Ps 129:1.

2 Had not the LORD been with us,
when people rose against us,
3 Then they would have swallowed us alive,*
for their fury blazed against us.
4 Then the waters would have engulfed us,
the torrent overwhelmed us;*
5 then seething water would have
drowned us.
6 Blessed is the LORD, who did not leave us
to be torn by their teeth.
7 We escaped with our lives like a bird
from the fowler's snare;
the snare was broken,
and we escaped.
8† Our help is in the name of the LORD,
the maker of heaven and earth.*

PSALM 125†

Israel's Protector

[1] A song of ascents.

Those trusting in the LORD are like Mount
Zion,
unshakable, forever enduring.*
2 As mountains surround Jerusalem,
the LORD surrounds his people
both now and forever.*

3 The scepter of the wicked will not prevail
in the land allotted to the just,†
Lest the just themselves
turn their hands to evil.

4 Do good, LORD, to the good,
to those who are upright of heart.*
5 But those who turn aside to crooked
ways
may the LORD send down with the
evildoers.*
Peace upon Israel!*

PSALM 126†

The Reversal of Zion's Fortunes

[1] A song of ascents.

I

When the LORD restored the captives of Zion,*
we thought we were dreaming.
2 Then our mouths were filled with laughter;
our tongues sang for joy.*
Then it was said among the nations,
"The LORD had done great things for them."
3 The LORD has done great things for us;
Oh, how happy we were!
4 Restore our captives, LORD,
like the dry stream beds of the Negeb.†

II

5 Those who sow in tears
will reap with cries of joy.*
6 Those who go forth weeping,
carrying sacks of seed,
Will return with cries of joy,
carrying their bundled sheaves.

PSALM 127†

The Need of God's Blessing

[1] A song of ascents. Of Solomon.

I

Unless the LORD build the house,
they labor in vain who build.
Unless the LORD guard the city,
in vain does the guard keep watch.
2 It is vain for you to rise early
and put off your rest at night,
To eat bread earned by hard toil—
all this God gives to his beloved in sleep.*

II

3 Certainly sons are a gift from the LORD,
the fruit of the womb, a reward.*
4 Like arrows in the hand of a warrior
are the sons born in one's youth.

PS

---

† **124:8** *Our help is in the name*: for the idiom, see Ex 18:4.

Psalm 125 In response to exilic anxieties about the ancient promises of restoration, the Psalm expresses confidence that God will surround the people as the mountains surround Zion (Ps 125:1–2). The just will not be contaminated by the wicked (Ps 125:3). May God judge between the two groups (Ps 125:4–5).

125:3 *The land allotted to the just*: lit., "the lot of the righteous." The promised land was divided among the tribes of Israel by lot (Nm 26:55; Jos 18). The righteous are the members of the people who are obedient to God. If the domination of the wicked were to continue in the land, even the just would be infected by their evil attitudes.

Psalm 126 A lament probably sung shortly after Israel's return from exile. The people rejoice that they are in Zion (Ps 126:1–3) but mere presence in the holy city is not enough; they must pray for the prosperity and the fertility of the land (Ps 126:4). The last verses are probably an oracle of promise: the painful work of sowing will be crowned with life (Ps 126:5–6).

126:4 *Like the dry stream beds of the Negeb*: the psalmist prays for rain in such abundance that the dry riverbeds will run.

Psalm 127 The Psalm puts together two proverbs (Ps 127:1–2, 3–5) on God establishing "houses" or families. The prosperity of human groups is not the work of human beings but the gift of God.

---

* **124:3** Prv 1:12.
124:4 Ps 18:5; 69:2.
124:8 Ps 121:2; 146:6.
125:1 Prv 10:25.
125:2 Dt 32:11.
125:4 Ps 18:25ff.
125:5 Prv 3:32.
125:5 Ps 128:6.
126:1 Ps 14:7.
126:2 Jb 8:21.
126:5 Bar 4:23; Is 65:19.
127:2 Eccl 2:24.
127:3 Ps 115:14; 128:3; Dt 28:11; Prv 17:6.

5 Blessed is the man who has filled his quiver
with them.
He will never be shamed
for he will destroy his foes at the gate.†

PSALM 128†

The Blessed Home of the Just

[1] A song of ascents.

I

Blessed are all who fear the LORD,
and who walk in his ways.*
2 What your hands provide you will enjoy;
you will be blessed and prosper:*
3 Your wife will be like a fruitful vine
within your home,
Your children like young olive plants
around your table.*
4 Just so will the man be blessed
who fears the LORD.

II

5 May the LORD bless you from Zion;
may you see Jerusalem's prosperity
all the days of your life,*
6 and live to see your children's
children.*
Peace upon Israel!*

PSALM 129†

Against Israel's Enemies

[1] A song of ascents.

I

Viciously have they attacked me from my
youth,
let Israel say now.*
2 Viciously have they attacked me from my
youth,*
yet they have not prevailed against me.
3 Upon my back the plowers plowed,
as they traced their long furrows.*
4 But the just LORD cut me free
from the ropes of the wicked.†

II

5 May they recoil in disgrace,
all who hate Zion.
6 May they be like grass on the rooftops†
withered in early growth,*
7 Never to fill the reaper's hands,
nor the arms of the binders of sheaves,
8 And with none passing by to call out:
"The blessing of the LORD be upon you!†
We bless you in the name of the LORD!"*

PSALM 130†

Prayer for Pardon and Mercy

[1] A song of ascents.

I

Out of the depths† I call to you, LORD;
2 Lord, hear my cry!
May your ears be attentive
to my cry for mercy.*
3 If you, LORD, keep account of sins,
Lord, who can stand?*
4 But with you is forgiveness
and so you are revered.†

II

5 I wait for the LORD,
my soul waits
and I hope for his word.*
6 My soul looks for the Lord
more than sentinels for daybreak.*
More than sentinels for daybreak,
7 let Israel hope in the LORD,
For with the LORD is mercy,
with him is plenteous redemption,*
8 And he will redeem Israel
from all its sins.*

†

127:5 *At the gate*: the reference is not to enemies besieging the walls of a city but to adversaries in litigation. Law courts functioned in the open area near the main city gate. The more adult sons a man had, the more forceful he would appear in disputes, cf. Prv 31:23.

Psalm 128 A statement that the ever-reliable God will bless the reverent (Ps 128:1). God's blessing is concrete: satisfaction and prosperity, a fertile spouse and abundant children (Ps 128:2–4). The perspective is that of the adult male, ordinarily the ruler and representative of the household to the community. The last verses extend the blessing to all the people for generations to come (Ps 128:5–6).

Psalm 129 A Psalm giving thanks for God's many rescues of Israel over the long course of their history (Ps 129:1–4); the people pray that their oppressors never know the joy of harvest (Ps 129:5–8).

129:4 *The ropes of the wicked*: usually understood as the rope for yoking animals to the plow. If it is severed, the plowing (cf. Ps 129:3) comes to a halt.

129:6 *Like grass on the rooftops*: after the spring rains, grass would sprout from the coat of mud with which the flat roofs of simple houses were covered, but when the dry summer began there was no moisture in the thin roof-covering to sustain the grass.

129:8 *The blessing of the LORD be upon you*: harvesters greeted one another with such blessings, cf. Ru 2:4.

Psalm 130 This lament, a Penitential Psalm, is the *De profundis* used in liturgical prayers for the faithful departed. In deep sorrow the psalmist cries to God (Ps 130:1–2), asking for mercy (Ps 130:3–4). The psalmist's trust (Ps 130:5–6) becomes a model for the people (Ps 130:7–8).

130:1 *The depths*: Sheol here is a metaphor of total misery. Deep anguish makes the psalmist feel "like those descending to the pit" (Ps 143:7).

130:4 *And so you are revered*: the experience of God's mercy leads one to a greater sense of God.

128:1 Ps 112:1.
128:2 Ps 112:3.
128:3 Ps 144:12; Jb 29:5.
128:5 Ps 20:3; 134:3.
128:6 Jb 42:16; Prv 17:6.
128:6 Ps 125:5.
129:1 Ps 124:1.
129:2 Ps 118:13.
129:3 Is 51:23.
129:6 Is 37:27.
129:8 Ps 118:26.
130:2 Ps 5:2–3; 55:2–3; 86:6; Lam 3:55–56; Jon 2:3.
130:3 Na 1:6.
130:5 Ps 119:81.
130:6 Is 21:11; 26:9.
130:7 Ps 86:15; 100:5; 103:8.
130:8 Ps 25:22; Mt 1:21.

Catholic Connection

Prayer

What do you do when you are sad and overwhelmed by sin? You might begin by crying out to God in prayer! That's just what the psalmist did when faced with the weight of personal sins and the sins of the Israelites. The cry to God for help arose from the very depths of the psalmist's own heart and confidently proclaimed trust in God's mercy and faithfulness. Through this passage, the psalmist gives us insight into the nature of prayer.

Prayer is a turning away from sin toward God. We enter into prayer through faith and the grace of the Holy Spirit, who fills our hearts with hope in God's merciful love. When we pray, we respond to God's ceaseless offer of love and friendship by focusing our heart and mind on God and entering into dialogue with God. This dialogue takes place in the "depths" of our heart where we encounter God and discover our own true self. It serves as a way to develop a loving and personal relationship with God. In order to foster a life of prayer, we must, like the disciples, ask Jesus to teach us how to pray, call on the guidance of the Holy Spirit, and make prayer an integral part of our daily routine. (See "The Lord's Prayer," near Lk 11:1–4, for more on how Jesus teaches us to pray.)

There are many ways we can encounter God in prayer. One way is to pray with the Sacred Scriptures, which open our heart to hear and respond to the living word of God. This type of prayer is often called *lectio divina.* Another way is through the liturgy of the Church, particularly the Mass, where our prayers are united in a special way with Christ and the community. We can also meet God in prayer by recognizing God's presence in each moment of our day. (See "Types of Prayer," near 1 Chr 16:37–42, to learn about additional forms of prayer.)

Praying is not always easy. Sometimes distractions in our lives make it difficult to focus on God. Yet, that is when we need to offer up any distractions to God in prayer so that God may purify our hearts and help us to focus on God's will for us. Other times, we may feel God is not there or that our prayers are not being answered. It is at those times that we are called to simply trust in God's faithfulness, recognizing that God is always present and wants what is best for us.

Ps 130:1–8

Catechism, nos. 2558–2567, 2650–2662

Pray It!

Hold Me, Nurturing God

Psalm 131 is a humble prayer of childlike trust. It gives the wonderful image of God holding us like a child in a mother's lap. Like a mother, God hugs us close and keeps us safe and warm and protected. We don't need to solve problems or be concerned about our performance. We are loved just because we are us. God created us; God loves us and cradles us.

Do you remember sitting quietly in your mother's or grandmother's lap when you were a small child? If so, do you recall her telling you stories or singing you lullabies? How is God's love like that? In your prayer time, imagine being held by God, as a child is held by a mother. You might be surprised at how safe and secure you feel!

▶ Psalm 131

PSALM 131†

Humble Trust in God

1 A song of ascents. Of David.

Lord, my heart is not proud;
nor are my eyes haughty.
I do not busy myself with great matters,
with things too sublime for me.*
2 Rather, I have stilled my soul,
Like a weaned child to its mother,
weaned is my soul.*
3 Israel, hope in the Lord,
now and forever.

PSALM 132†

The Covenant Between David and God

1 A song of ascents.

I

Remember, O Lord, for David
all his hardships;
2 How he swore an oath to the Lord,
vowed to the Mighty One of Jacob:†
3 "I will not enter the house where I live,*
nor lie on the couch where I sleep;
4 I will give my eyes no sleep,
my eyelids no rest,
5 Till I find a place for the Lord,
a dwelling for the Mighty One of Jacob."
6 "We have heard of it in Ephrathah;†
we have found it in the fields of Jaar.†
7 Let us enter his dwelling;
let us worship at his footstool."*
8 "Arise, Lord, come to your resting place,*
you and your mighty ark.
9 Your priests will be clothed with justice;
your devout will shout for joy."
10 For the sake of David your servant,
do not reject your anointed.

II

11 The Lord swore an oath to David in truth,
he will never turn back from it:*
"Your own offspring* I will set upon your
throne.
12 If your sons observe my covenant,
and my decrees I shall teach them,
Their sons, in turn,
shall sit forever on your throne."
13 Yes, the Lord has chosen Zion,
desired it for a dwelling:
14 "This is my resting place forever;
here I will dwell, for I desire it.
15 I will bless Zion with provisions;
its poor I will fill with bread.
16 I will clothe its priests with salvation;
its devout shall shout for joy.*
17 There I will make a horn sprout for David;†*
I will set a lamp for my anointed.

†

Psalm 131 A song of trust, in which the psalmist gives up self-sufficiency (Ps 131:1), like a babe enjoying the comfort of its mother's lap (Ps 131:2), thus providing a model for Israel's faith (Ps 131:3).

Psalm 132 A song for a liturgical ceremony in which the ark, the throne of Israel's God, was carried in procession to the Temple. The singer asks that David's care for the proper housing of the ark be regarded with favor (Ps 132:1–5), and tells how it was brought to Jerusalem (Ps 132:6–10). There follows God's promise of favor to the Davidic dynasty (Ps 132:11–12) and to Zion (Ps 132:13–17). The transfer of the ark to the tent in Jerusalem is described in 2 Sm 6.

132:2, 132:5 *Mighty One of Jacob*: one of the titles of Israel's God, cf. Gn 49:24; Is 49:26; 60:16.

132:6 *Ephrathah*: the homeland of David, cf. Ru 4:11. *The fields of Jaar*: poetic for Kiriath-jearim, a town west of Jerusalem, where the ark remained for several generations, cf. 1 Sm 7:1–2; 2 Sm 6:2; 1 Chr 13:5–6.

132:17 *A horn sprout for David*: the image of the horn, a symbol of strength, is combined with that of a "sprout," a term used for the Davidic descendant (cf. Jer 23:5; 33:15; Zec 3:8; 6:12). Early Christians referred the latter designation to Christ as son of David (Lk 1:69).

*

131:1 Ps 139:6.
131:2 Is 66:12–13.
132:3 2 Sm 7; 1 Chr 28:2.
132:7 Ps 99:5.
132:8–10 Ps 2:2; 89:21; 95:11; Nm 10:35; 2 Chr 6:41–42; Sir 24:7.
132:11–14 Ps 68:17; 1 Kgs 8:13; Sir 24:7.
132:11 Ps 110:4; 2 Sm 7:12.
132:16 2 Chr 6:41; Is 61:10.
132:17 Is 11:1; Jer 33:15; Ez 29:21; Zec 3:8; Lk 1:69.

18 His foes I will clothe with shame,
but on him his crown shall shine."

PSALM 133†

A Vision of a Blessed Community

1 A song of ascents. Of David.

How good and how pleasant it is,
when brothers† dwell together as one!
2 Like fine oil on the head,†*
running down upon the beard,
Upon the beard of Aaron,
upon the collar of his robe.
3 Like dew† of Hermon† coming down
upon the mountains of Zion.*
There the LORD has decreed a blessing,
life for evermore!*

PSALM 134†

Exhortation to the Night Watch to Bless God

1 A song of ascents.

O come, bless the LORD,
all you servants of the LORD†
You who stand in the house of the LORD
throughout the nights.*
2 Lift up your hands toward the sanctuary,*
and bless the LORD.
3 May the LORD bless you from Zion,
the Maker of heaven and earth.*

PSALM 135†

Praise of God, the Ruler and Benefactor of Israel

1 Hallelujah!

I

Praise the name of the LORD!
Praise, you servants of the LORD,*

Did You Know?

Jerusalem, Zion, City of David

Jerusalem, Zion, City of David—you have probably noticed that these three names keep popping up throughout the Psalms. They all refer to the heart of Israel, the city of Jerusalem. When David became king of the united Tribes of Israel, he needed a neutral place between the northern and southern tribes. He conquered Jerusalem and elevated it as the political and religious center—thus, Jerusalem was also known as the City of David. Mount Zion, located within Jerusalem, was the site of the Temple—the sacred place where God dwelt. So, Zion became another way to refer to Jerusalem.

At that time, the Israelites felt that Jerusalem was invincible because it was God's dwelling place. But eventually, Jerusalem and the Temple were destroyed. Afterward, a hope arose that one day, a messiah from David's line would renew Jerusalem and true worship of God on Zion. The New Testament portrays Jesus as the fulfillment of this hope.

▶ Psalm 132

2 Who stand in the house of the LORD,
in the courts of the house of our God!*
3 Praise the LORD, for the LORD is good!
Sing to his name, for it brings joy!
4† For the LORD has chosen Jacob for himself,
Israel as his treasured possession.*

II

5 For I know that the LORD is great,
that our Lord is greater than all gods.*

PS

---

† **Psalm 133** A benediction over a peaceful community, most probably the people Israel, but appropriate too for Israelite families (Ps 133:1). The history of Israel, whether of its ancestors in the Book of Genesis or of later periods, was a history of distinct groups struggling to live in unity. Here that unity is declared blessed, like the holy oils upon the priest Aaron or the dew of the rainless summer that waters the crops (Ps 133:2–3).

133:1 *Brothers*: in biblical Hebrew this word includes both the male and female members of a group united by blood relationships or by shared experiences and values. In this Psalm, the term could be applied most appropriately to the people of Israel, those privileged by God to be his chosen children.

133:2 *Oil on the head*: oil was used at the consecration of the high priest (Ex 30:22–33).

133:3 *Dew*: dew was an important source of moisture in the dry climate (Gn 27:28; Hos 14:6). *Hermon*: the majestic snow-capped mountain visible in the north of Palestine.

Psalm 134 A brief liturgy exhorting all those who serve in the Jerusalem Temple during the night (cf. Is 30:29) to praise God with words and gestures. Although he is the Creator of the whole universe, God's blessings emanate in a unique way from Zion, the city of Jerusalem.

134:1 *Servants of the LORD*: priests and Levites, cf. Dt 10:8; Ps 113:1; 135:1; Dn 3:85.

Psalm 135 The hymn begins and ends with an invitation to praise God (Ps 135:1–3, 19–20) for the great act of choosing Israel (Ps 135:4). The story of Israel's emergence as a people is told in Ps 135:5–14; God created and redeemed the people, easily conquering

---

* **133:2** Ex 30:25, 30.
133:3 Hos 14:6.
133:3 Dt 28:8; 30:20.
134:1 Ps 135:1–2; 1 Chr 9:33.
134:2 Ps 28:2; 141:2.
134:3 Ps 20:3; 128:5; Nm 6:24.
135:1 Ps 113:1.
135:2 Ps 134:1.
135:4 Ps 33:12; 144:15; Ex 19:6; Dt 7:6.
135:5 Ps 95:3; Ex 18:11.

6 Whatever the LORD desires
he does in heaven and on earth,
in the seas and all the depths.*
7 It is he who raises storm clouds from the end
of the earth,
makes lightning for the rain,
and brings forth wind from his
storehouse.*

III

8 He struck down Egypt's firstborn,*
of human being and beast alike,
9 And sent signs and wonders against you,
Egypt,
against Pharaoh and all his servants.
10 It is he who struck down many nations,*
and slew mighty kings—
11 Sihon, king of the Amorites,
and Og, king of Bashan,
all the kings of Canaan—
12 And made their land a heritage,
a heritage for Israel his people.
13 O LORD, your name is forever,
your renown, from generation to
generation!*
14 For the LORD defends his people,
shows mercy to his servants.*

IV

15 The idols of the nations are silver and
gold,*
the work of human hands.
16 They have mouths but do not speak;
they have eyes but do not see;
17 They have ears but do not hear;
nor is there breath in their mouths.
18 Their makers will become like them,
and anyone who trusts in them.

V

19 House of Israel, bless the LORD!*
House of Aaron, bless the LORD!
20 House of Levi, bless the LORD!
You who fear the LORD, bless the LORD!
21 Blessed be the LORD from Zion,
who dwells in Jerusalem!
Hallelujah!

PSALM 136†

Hymn of Thanksgiving for God's Everlasting Mercy

I

1 Praise the LORD, for he is good;*
for his mercy endures forever;
2 Praise the God of gods;
for his mercy endures forever;
3 Praise the Lord of lords;
for his mercy endures forever;

II

4 Who alone has done great wonders,*
for his mercy endures forever;
5 Who skillfully made the heavens,*
for his mercy endures forever;
6 Who spread the earth upon the waters,*
for his mercy endures forever;
7 Who made the great lights,
for his mercy endures forever;
8 The sun to rule the day,
for his mercy endures forever;
9 The moon and stars to rule the night,*
for his mercy endures forever;

III

10 Who struck down the firstborn of Egypt,*
for his mercy endures forever;
11 And led Israel from their midst,
for his mercy endures forever;
12 With mighty hand and outstretched arm,*
for his mercy endures forever;
13 Who split in two the Red Sea,
for his mercy endures forever;
14 And led Israel through its midst,
for his mercy endures forever;
15 But swept Pharaoh and his army into the Red
Sea,*
for his mercy endures forever;
16 Who led the people through the desert,*
for his mercy endures forever;

IV

17 Who struck down great kings,*
for his mercy endures forever;
18 Slew powerful kings,
for his mercy endures forever;

† all opposition. God's defeat of hostile powers means that the powers themselves and their images are useless (Ps 135:15–18). The last three verses appear also in Ps 115:4–8.

135:4 Though all nations are God's, Israel has a special status as God's "treasured" people: Ex 19:5; Dt 7:6; 14:2; 26:18; Mal 3:17.

Psalm 136 The hymn praises Israel's God ("the God of gods," Ps 136:2), who has created the world in which Israel lives. The refrain occurring after every line suggests that a speaker and chorus sang the Psalm in antiphonal fashion. A single act of God is described in Ps 136:4–25. God arranges the heavens and the earth as the environment for human community, and then creates the community by freeing them and giving them land. In the final section (Ps 136:23–25) God, who created the people and gave them land, continues to protect and nurture them.

136:22 *A heritage for Israel*: the land was given to Israel by God to be handed on to future generations.

* **135:6** Ps 115:3.
135:7 Ps 148:8; Jer 10:13; 51:16; Jb 37:9.
135:8–9 Ps 78:51; 105:27, 36; 136:10; Ex 12:29.
135:10–12 Ps 136:17–22; Nm 21:21–35; Dt 2:24–3:17.
135:13 Ps 102:13; Ex 3:15.
135:14 Dt 32:36.
135:15–18 Ps 115:4–6, 8.
135:19–20 Ps 118:2–4.
136:1 Ps 100:5; 118:1.
136:4 Ps 72:18.
136:5 Gn 1:9–19.
136:6 Ps 24:2.
136:9 Jer 31:35.
136:10 Ex 12:29, 51; 14:22, 27; 15:22; Ps 78:51–52; 135:8.
136:12 Dt 4:34.
136:15 Ex 14:21f.
136:16 Dt 8:2, 15.
136:17–22 Ps 135:10–12.

PS

19 Sihon, king of the Amorites,
for his mercy endures forever;
20 Og, king of Bashan,
for his mercy endures forever;
21 And made their lands a heritage,
for his mercy endures forever;
22† A heritage for Israel, his servant,
for his mercy endures forever.

V

23 The Lord remembered us in our low estate,
for his mercy endures forever;
24 Freed us from our foes,
for his mercy endures forever;
25 And gives bread to all flesh,
for his mercy endures forever.

VI

26 Praise the God of heaven,
for his mercy endures forever.

PSALM 137†

Sorrow and Hope in Exile

I

1 By the rivers of Babylon
there we sat weeping
when we remembered Zion.*
2 On the poplars in its midst
we hung up our harps.*
3 For there our captors asked us
for the words of a song;
Our tormentors, for joy:
"Sing for us a song of Zion!"
4 But how could we sing a song of the LORD
in a foreign land?

II

5 If I forget you, Jerusalem,
may my right hand forget.*
6 May my tongue stick to my palate
if I do not remember you,
If I do not exalt Jerusalem
beyond all my delights.

III

7 Remember, LORD, against Edom
that day at Jerusalem.
They said: "Level it, level it
down to its foundations!"*
8 Desolate Daughter Babylon, you shall be
destroyed,
blessed the one who pays you back
what you have done us!*
9† Blessed the one who seizes your children
and smashes them against the rock.*

PSALM 138†

Hymn of a Grateful Heart

1 Of David.

I

I thank you, Lord, with all my heart;*
in the presence of the angels† to you I sing.
2 I bow low toward your holy temple;
I praise your name for your mercy and
faithfulness.
For you have exalted over all
your name and your promise.
3 On the day I cried out, you answered;
you strengthened my spirit.

II

4 All the kings of earth will praise you, LORD,
when they hear the words of your mouth.
5 They will sing of the ways of the LORD:
"How great is the glory of the LORD!"
6 The LORD is on high, but cares for the lowly*
and knows the proud from afar.
7 Though I walk in the midst of dangers,
you guard my life when my enemies rage.
You stretch out your hand;
your right hand saves me.
8 The LORD is with me to the end.
LORD, your mercy endures forever.
Never forsake the work of your hands!

PSALM 139†

The All-knowing and Ever-present God

1 For the leader. A psalm of David.

I

LORD, you have probed me, you know me:
2 you know when I sit and stand;†*

† **Psalm 137** A singer refuses to sing the people's sacred songs in an alien land despite demands from Babylonian captors (Ps 137:1–4). The singer swears an oath by what is most dear to a musician—hands and tongue—to exalt Jerusalem always (Ps 137:5–6). The Psalm ends with a prayer that the old enemies of Jerusalem, Edom and Babylon, be destroyed (Ps 137:7–9).

137:9 *Blessed the one who seizes your children and smashes them against the rock*: the children represent the future generations, and so must be destroyed if the enemy is truly to be eradicated.

Psalm 138 A thanksgiving to God, who came to the rescue of the psalmist. Divine rescue was not the result of the psalmist's virtues but of God's loving fidelity (Ps 138:1–3). The act is not a private transaction but a public act that stirs the surrounding nations to praise God's greatness and care for the people (Ps 138:4–6). The psalmi[st], having experienced salvation, trusts that God will always be ther[e in] moments of danger (Ps 138:7–8).

138:1 *In the presence of the angels*: heavenly beings wh[o are] completely subordinate to Israel's God. The earthly Templ[e repre]sents the heavenly palace of God.

Psalm 139 A hymnic meditation on God's omnipre[sence and] omniscience. The psalmist is keenly aware of God's

* **137:1** Ez 3:15; Lam 3:48.
137:2 Is 24:8; Lam 5:14.
137:5 Jer 51:50.
137:7 Jer 49:7; Lam 4:21–22; Ez 25:12–14.
137:8 Is 47:1-
137:9 Hos 1-:3.
138:1 Ps 9
138:6 Lk
139:2 2

Live It!

The Sacredness of Life

"You formed my inmost being; / you knit me in my mother's womb" (Ps 139:13).

Psalm 139 speaks poetically of God's intimate care for each of us, long before we were even formed. It is perhaps the most powerful argument against abortion in the entire Bible. Who can deny that God gave us life long before we actually saw the light of day? How can we deny that every unborn child is fashioned by the hand of God?

It is easy to get caught up in arguments about individual rights and scientific terminology. But this is not about science or government or even when life begins. It is about poetry and love and the faith God has knit together within each of us in our mother's womb. God has great plans for each of us, whether we have been born, are in the womb, or have not yet even been thought of. God knows and loves us, and has through all eternity.

▶ Psalm 139

you understand my thoughts from afar.
3 You sift through my travels and my rest;
with all my ways you are familiar.
4 Even before a word is on my tongue,
LORD, you know it all.
5 Behind and before you encircle me
and rest your hand upon me.
Such knowledge is too wonderful for me,
far too lofty for me to reach.*

Vhere can I go from your spirit?
From your presence, where can I flee?
8 If I ascend to the heavens, you are there;
if I lie down in Sheol, there you are.*
9 If I take the wings of dawn†
and dwell beyond the sea,†
10 Even there your hand guides me,
your right hand holds me fast.
11 If I say, "Surely darkness shall hide me,
and night shall be my light"†—
12 Darkness is not dark for you,
and night shines as the day.
Darkness and light are but one.*

II

13 You formed my inmost being;
you knit me in my mother's womb.*
14 I praise you, because I am wonderfully made;
wonderful are your works!
My very self you know.
15 My bones are not hidden from you,
When I was being made in secret,
fashioned in the depths of the earth.†
16 Your eyes saw me unformed;
in your book all are written down;*
my days were shaped, before one came
to be.

III

17 How precious to me are your designs,
O God;
how vast the sum of them!
18 Were I to count them, they would outnumber
the sands;
when I complete them, still you are with
me.*
19 When you would destroy the wicked, O God,
the bloodthirsty depart from me!*
20 Your foes who conspire a plot against you
are exalted in vain.

IV

21 Do I not hate, LORD, those who hate you?
Those who rise against you, do I not
loathe?*
22 With fierce hatred I hate them,
enemies I count as my own.

23 Probe me, God, know my heart;
try me, know my thoughts.*
24 See if there is a wicked path in me;
lead me along an ancient path.†

---

is'–6), of God's presence in every part of the universe
prand of God's control over the psalmist's very self (Ps
13ning up Ps 139:1–16, 17–18 express wonder. There
139ostile to God's rule—wicked people. The psalmist
Beyond from their company (Ps 139:19–24).
iterranean.*nd stand*: in all my physical movement.
139:11 *gs of dawn*: go to the extremities of the east.
others. ost bounds of the west; the sea is the Med-
my light: night to me is what day is to

139:15 *The depths of the earth*: figurative language for the womb, stressing the hidden and mysterious operations that occur there.

139:24 *Lead me along an ancient path*: the manner of living of our ancestors, who were faithful to God's will, cf. Jer 6:16.

139:6 Ps 131:1.
139:8 Jb 23:8–9; Jer 23:23–24.
139:12 Jb 12:22.
139:13 Wis 7:1; Eccl 11:5; Jb 1:21.
139:16 Mal 3:16.
139:18 Jb 11:7.
139:19 Jb 21:14.
139:21 Ps 119:158.
139:23 Ps 17:3; 26:2.

Cultural Connection

Celtic Traditions

Many people of the British Isles, especially the Irish, have for hundreds of years celebrated their Celtic traditions. Over the years, their Celtic traditions have become fused with their expressions of their Catholic faith. One of the central Celtic Christian themes is the presence and protection of God. Like the psalmist who wrote Psalm 139, the author of "Saint Patrick's Breastplate" illustrates how the Celts call God into their life and world:

Christ be with me, Christ within me
  Christ behind me, Christ before me,
Christ beside me, Christ to win me,
  Christ to comfort and restore me,
Christ beneath me, Christ above me,
  Christ in quiet, Christ in danger,
Christ in the hearts of all that love me,
  Christ in mouth of friend or stranger.

The next time you want to pray for the presence of God, try praying in the Celtic tradition so beautifully expressed in "Saint Patrick's Breastplate."

▶ Psalm 139

PSALM 140†

Prayer for Deliverance from the Wicked

1 For the leader. A psalm of David.

I

2 Deliver me, LORD, from the wicked;
preserve me from the violent,*
3 From those who plan evil in their hearts,
who stir up conflicts every day,
4† Who sharpen their tongue like a serpent,
venom of asps upon their lips.* *Selah*

II

5 Keep me, LORD, from the clutches of the wicked;
preserve me from the violent,
who plot to trip me up.*
6† The arrogant have set a trap for me;
they have spread out ropes for a net,
laid snares for me by the wayside. *Selah*
7 I say to the LORD: You are my God;*
listen, LORD, to the words of my pleas.
8 LORD, my master, my strong deliverer,
you cover my head on the day of armed conflict.
9 LORD, do not grant the desires of the wicked one;
do not let his plot succeed. *Selah*

III

10 Those who surround me raise their heads;
may the mischief they threaten overwhelm them.
11 Drop burning coals upon them;*
cast them into the watery pit never more to rise.
12 Slanderers will not survive on earth;
evil will hunt down the man of violence to overthrow him.
13 For I know the LORD will take up the cause of the needy,
justice for the poor.
14 Then the righteous will give thanks to your name;
the upright will dwell in your presence.*

† **Psalm 140** A lament seeking rescue from violent and treacherous foes (Ps 140:2–6). The psalmist remains trusting (Ps 140:7–8), vigorously praying that the plans of the wicked recoil upon themselves (Ps 140:9–12). A serene statement of praise ends the Psalm (Ps 140:13). The psalmist is content to be known as one of "the needy," "the poor," "the just," "the upright" (Ps 140:13), a class of people expecting divine protection.

140:4 Similar metaphors for a wicked tongue are used in Ps 52:2; 55:20; 58:3.

140:6 *Have set a trap . . . have spread out ropes for a net*: the same figure, of hunters setting traps, occurs in Ps 9:16; 31:5; 35:7; 64:6, cf. Mt 22:15; Lk 11:54.

* **140:2** Ps 71:4.
140:4 Ps 64:4; Rom 3:13.
140:5 Jer 18:22; Ps 56:7; 57:7.
140:7 Ps 31:15.
140:11 Ps 11:6; 120:4; Gn 19:24.
140:14 Ps 11:7; 16:11; 17:15.

Live It!

God Cares for Those Who Suffer Persecution

Many of us like to think that persecution rarely occurs. Unfortunately, this is not true. All too frequently, people are persecuted because of their color, their ethnic origin, their political beliefs, or even their faith. Harassment can be as subtle as a rude comment or a patronizing attitude, or as aggressive as a beating or killing. Young people know the feeling of persecution. They may experience it because of their origin, the way they look or talk, or what they believe.

Psalm 140 is one of several psalms (see also Psalms 35, 86) and prayers seeking God's help in times of persecution. These typically have two parts. The first part asks for God's protection against persecutors, and the second part praises God's love, justice, and mercy. This illustrates the continual tension for all believers: feeling the need for God's action while at the same time being certain that God cares for them in the midst of their persecution.

For Christians, Jesus is the perfect model of the persecuted person. He was persecuted without reason (see Lk 23:4), and he felt God's absence (see Mk 15:34), but he still put his entire faith and trust in God's will (see Mt 26:39). Following Jesus' example, Christians throughout history have bravely endured persecution, and even death, for their faith.

- Have you or your family experienced some kind of persecution? If so, how and why? If you have ever participated in some kind of persecution of someone else, pray for forgiveness, and if possible make amends.
- Thank God for the blessings you have, and ask God for the strength to endure whatever persecutions come your way. Pray for those who are suffering persecution, regardless of the motive.

▶ Psalm 140

PSALM 141†

Prayer for Deliverance from the Wicked

1 A psalm of David.

LORD, I call to you; hasten to me;
listen to my plea when I call.
2 Let my prayer be incense† before you;
my uplifted hands† an evening offering.*
3 Set a guard, LORD, before my mouth,
keep watch over the door of my lips.*
4 Do not let my heart incline to evil,
to perform deeds in wickedness.
On the delicacies of evildoers
let me not feast.
5† Let a righteous person strike me; it is mercy if
he reproves me.
Do not withhold oil from my head*
while my prayer opposes their evil deeds.
6 May their leaders be cast over the cliff,
so that they hear that my speeches are
pleasing.
7 Like the plowing and breaking up of the
earth,
our bones are strewn at the mouth of
Sheol.
8 For my eyes are upon you, O LORD, my Lord;*
in you I take refuge; do not take away my
soul.
9 Guard me from the trap they have set for me,
from the snares of evildoers.*
10 Let the wicked fall into their own nets,
while only I pass over them safely.

PSALM 142†

A Prayer in Time of Trouble

1 A *maskil* of David, when he was in the cave.†
A prayer.

2 With my own voice I cry to the LORD;
with my own voice I beseech the LORD.

Psalm 141 A lament of an individual (Ps 141:1–2) who is keenly aware that only the righteous can worship God properly and who therefore prays to be protected from the doomed wicked (Ps 141:3–10).

141:2 *Incense*: lit., "smoke," i.e., the fragrant fumes arising from the altar at the burning of sacrificial animals or of aromatic spices; also used in Rev 5:8 as a symbol of prayer. *My uplifted hands*: the gesture of supplication, cf. Ps 28:2; 63:5; 88:10; 119:48; 134:2; 143:6.

141:5–7 The Hebrew text is obscure.

Psalm 142 In this lament imploring God for help (Ps 142:2–4), the psalmist tells how enemies have set a trap (Ps 142:4–5), and prays for rescue (Ps 142:6–8). The speaker feels utterly alone (Ps 142:5), exhausted (Ps 142:7), and may even be imprisoned (Ps 142:7).

141:2 Ps 134:2; Ex 30:8.
141:3 Sir 22:27.
141:5 Prv 9:8; 25:12.
141:8 Ps 25:15; 123:1–2.
141:9 Ps 142:4.

3 Before him I pour out my complaint,
tell of my distress in front of him.
4 When my spirit is faint within me,*
you know my path.*
As I go along this path,
they have hidden a trap for me.*
5 I look to my right hand to see*
that there is no one willing to
acknowledge me.
My escape has perished;
no one cares for me.
6 I cry out to you, LORD,
I say, You are my refuge,*
my portion in the land of the living.*
7 Listen to my cry for help,
for I am brought very low.*
Rescue me from my pursuers,
for they are too strong for me.
8 Lead my soul from prison,
that I may give thanks to your name.
Then the righteous shall gather around me†
because you have been good to me.

PSALM 143†

A Prayer in Distress

1 A psalm of David.

LORD, hear my prayer;
in your faithfulness listen to my pleading;
answer me in your righteousness.
2 Do not enter into judgment with your servant;
before you no one can be just.*
3 The enemy has pursued my soul;
he has crushed my life to the ground.*
He has made me dwell in darkness
like those long dead.*
4 My spirit is faint within me;
my heart despairs.*
5 I remember the days of old;
I ponder all your deeds;
the works of your hands I recall.*
6 I stretch out my hands toward you,
my soul to you like a parched land.* *Selah*
7 Hasten to answer me, LORD;
for my spirit fails me.
Do not hide your face from me,
lest I become like those descending to the
pit.*
8 In the morning let me hear of your mercy,
for in you I trust.
Show me the path I should walk,
for I entrust my life to you.*
9 Rescue me, LORD, from my foes,
for I seek refuge in you.
10 Teach me to do your will,
for you are my God.
May your kind spirit guide me
on ground that is level.
11 For your name's sake, LORD, give me life;
in your righteousness lead my soul out of
distress.
12 In your mercy put an end to my foes;
all those who are oppressing my soul,
for I am your servant.*

PSALM 144†

A Prayer for Victory and Prosperity

1 Of David.

I

†Blessed be the LORD, my rock,
who trains my hands for battle,
my fingers for war;
2 My safeguard and my fortress,
my stronghold, my deliverer,
My shield, in whom I take refuge,
who subdues peoples under me.

---

† Prison is possibly a metaphor for general distress. The last two verses are the vow of praise, made after receiving an assurance of divine help (Ps 142:7).

142:1 *In the cave*: cf. 1 Sm 22:1; 24:1–3; Ps 57:1.

142:8 *Then the righteous shall gather around me*: in the Temple, when the psalmist offers a thanksgiving sacrifice.

Psalm 143 One of the Church's seven Penitential Psalms, this lament is a prayer to be freed from death-dealing enemies. The psalmist addresses God, aware that there is no equality between God and human beings; salvation is a gift (Ps 143:1–2). Victimized by evil people (Ps 143:3–4), the psalmist recites ("remembers") God's past actions on behalf of the innocent (Ps 143:5–6). The Psalm continues with fervent prayer (Ps 143:7–9) and a strong desire for guidance and protection (Ps 143:10–12).

Psalm 144 The Psalm may reflect a ceremony in which the king, as leader of the army, asked God's help (Ps 144:1–8). In Ps 144:9 the poem shifts abruptly from pleading to thanksgiving, and (except for Ps 144:11) shifts again to prayer for the people. The first section (Ps 144:1–2) is a prayer of thanks for victory; the second (Ps 144:3–7a), a humble acknowledgment of human nothingness and a supplication that God show forth saving power; the third (Ps 144:9–11), a promise of future thanksgiving; the fourth (Ps 144:12–15), a wish for prosperity and peace. A prayer for deliverance from treacherous foes serves as a refrain after the second and third sections (Ps 144:7b–8, 11). Except for its final section, the Psalm is made up almost entirely of verses from other Psalms.

144:1–2 Composed of phrases from Ps 18:3, 35, 47–48.

---

*
142:4 Ps 143:4.
142:4 Ps 139:24.
142:4 Ps 141:9.
142:5 Ps 16:8; 73:23; 121:5.
142:6 Ps 91:2, 9.
142:6 Ps 16:5; 27:13; 116:9; Is 38:11.
142:7 Ps 79:8.
143:2 Eccl 7:20; Jb 4:17; Rom 3:20.
143:3 Ps 7:6.
143:3 Lam 3:6.
143:4 Ps 142:4; Jb 17:1.
143:5 Ps 77:6, 12.
143:6 Ps 42:2; 63:2.
143:7 Ps 28:1; 30:4; 88:5; Prv 1:12.
143:8 Ps 25:4; 27:11; 86:11; 119:12, 35.
143:12 Ps 116:16.

PS

Pray It!

A Prayer for the Young

We praise you, God, for all our nation's blessings!
We thank you for our young people, our sons and daughters who come forward to serve the people of God.
We ask you to make them strong, to call them into a trusting relationship with you, and to help them live faithful lives and to be leaders and examples for others.
Happy the people whose God is the Lord!

▶ Psalm 144

II

3† Lord, what is man that you take notice of him;
the son of man, that you think of him?*
4† Man is but a breath,
his days are like a passing shadow.*
5† Lord, incline your heavens and come down;
touch the mountains and make them smoke.*
6 Flash forth lightning and scatter my foes;
shoot your arrows and rout them.
7 Reach out your hand from on high;
deliver me from the many waters;
rescue me from the hands of foreign foes.
8 Their mouths speak untruth;
their right hands are raised in lying oaths.†
9 O God, a new song I will sing to you;
on a ten-stringed lyre I will play for you.*
10 You give victory to kings;
you delivered David your servant.*
From the menacing sword [11] deliver me;
rescue me from the hands of foreign foes.
Their mouths speak untruth;
their right hands are raised in lying oaths.

III

12 May our sons be like plants*
well nurtured from their youth,
Our daughters, like carved columns,
shapely as those of the temple.
13 May our barns be full
with every kind of store.
May our sheep increase by thousands,
by tens of thousands in our fields;
may our oxen be well fattened.
14 May there be no breach in the walls,
no exile, no outcry in our streets.*
15 Blessed the people so fortunate;
blessed the people whose God is the Lord.*

PSALM 145†

The Greatness and Goodness of God

[1] Praise. Of David.

I will extol you, my God and king;
I will bless your name forever and ever.
2 Every day I will bless you;
I will praise your name forever and ever.*
3 Great is the Lord and worthy of much praise,*
whose grandeur is beyond understanding.
4 One generation praises your deeds to the next
and proclaims your mighty works.*
5 They speak of the splendor of your majestic glory,
tell of your wonderful deeds.*
6 They speak of the power of your awesome acts
and recount your great deeds.*
7 They celebrate your abounding goodness
and joyfully sing of your justice.
8 The Lord is gracious and merciful,
slow to anger and abounding in mercy.*
9 The Lord is good to all,
compassionate toward all your works.*
10 All your works give you thanks, Lord
and your faithful bless you.*
11 They speak of the glory of your reign
and tell of your mighty works,

† **144:3** Similar to Ps 8:4.
144:4 Composed of phrases from Ps 39:6; 102:12.
144:5–7 Adapted in large part from Ps 18:10, 15, 17; 104:32.
144:8b, 11b *Their right hands are raised in lying oaths*: the psalmist's enemies give false testimony.
Psalm 145 A hymn in acrostic form; every verse begins with a successive letter of the Hebrew alphabet. Acrostic poems usually do not develop ideas but consist rather of loosely connected statements. The singer invites all to praise God (Ps 145:1–3, 21). The "works of God" make God present and invite human praise (Ps 145:4–7); they climax in a confession (Ps 145:8–9). God's mighty acts show forth divine kingship (Ps 145:10–20), a major theme in the literature of early Judaism and in Christianity.

* **144:3** Jb 7:17.
144:4 Ps 62:10; 90:9–10; Jb 7:16; Eccl 6:12; Wis 2:5.
144:5 Is 63:19.
144:9 Ps 33:2–3.
144:10 Ps 18:51.
144:12 Ps 128:3.
144:14 Is 65:19.
144:15 Ps 33:12.
145:2 Ps 34:2.
145:3 Ps 48:2; 95:3; 96:4; Jb 36:26.
145:4 Ps 22:31–32; 48:14–15; 71:18; 78:4; Ex 10:2; Dt 4:9.
145:5 Ps 96:3; 105:2.
145:6 Ps 66:3.
145:8 Ps 86:5, 15; 103:8; Ex 34:6; Sir 2:11.
145:9 Ps 103:13; Wis 11:24.
145:10 Dn 3:57.

12 Making known to the sons of men your
mighty acts,
the majestic glory of your rule.
13 Your reign is a reign for all ages,
your dominion for all generations.*
The LORD is trustworthy in all his words,
and loving in all his works.
14 The LORD supports all who are falling
and raises up all who are bowed down.*
15 The eyes of all look hopefully to you;
you give them their food in due season.*
16 You open wide your hand
and satisfy the desire of every living thing.
17 The LORD is just in all his ways,
merciful in all his works.*
18 The LORD is near to all who call upon him,
to all who call upon him in truth.*
19 He fulfills the desire of those who fear him;
he hears their cry and saves them.*
20 The LORD watches over all who love him,
but all the wicked he destroys.*
21 My mouth will speak the praises of the LORD;
all flesh will bless his holy name forever
and ever.

PSALM 146†

Trust in God the Creator and Redeemer

1 Hallelujah!

2 Praise the LORD, my soul;
I will praise the LORD all my life,
sing praise to my God while I live.*

I

3 Put no trust in princes,
in children of Adam powerless to save.*
4 Who breathing his last, returns to the earth;
that day all his planning comes to nothing.*

II

5 Blessed the one whose help is the God of
Jacob,
whose hope is in the LORD, his God,
6 The maker of heaven and earth,
the seas and all that is in them,*
Who keeps faith forever,
7 secures justice for the oppressed,*
who gives bread to the hungry.
The LORD sets prisoners free;*
8 the LORD gives sight to the blind.
The LORD raises up those who are bowed
down;*
the LORD loves the righteous.
9 The LORD protects the resident alien,
comes to the aid of the orphan and the
widow,*
but thwarts the way of the wicked.
10 The LORD shall reign forever,
your God, Zion, through all generations!*
Hallelujah!

PSALM 147†

God's Word Restores Jerusalem

1 Hallelujah!

I

How good to sing praise to our God;
how pleasant to give fitting praise.*
2 The LORD rebuilds Jerusalem,
and gathers the dispersed of Israel,*
3 Healing the brokenhearted,
and binding up their wounds.*
4 He numbers the stars,
and gives to all of them their names.*
5 Great is our Lord, vast in power,
with wisdom beyond measure.*
6 The LORD gives aid to the poor,
but casts the wicked to the ground.*

II

7 Sing to the LORD with thanksgiving;
with the lyre make music to our God,*
8† Who covers the heavens with clouds,
provides rain for the earth,
makes grass sprout on the mountains,*
9 Who gives animals their food
and young ravens what they cry for.*
10† He takes no delight in the strength of horses,

PS

†

Psalm 146 A hymn of someone who has learned there is no other source of strength except the merciful God. Only God, not mortal human beings (Ps 146:3–4), can help vulnerable and oppressed people (Ps 146:5–9). The first of the five hymns that conclude the Psalter.

Psalm 147 The hymn is divided into three sections by the calls to praise in Ps 147:1, 7, 12. The first section praises the powerful creator who restores exiled Judah (Ps 147:1–6); the second section, the creator who provides food to animals and human beings; the third and climactic section exhorts the holy city to recognize it has been re-created and made the place of disclosure for God's word, a word as life-giving as water.

147:8–9 God clothes the fields and feeds the birds, cf. Mt 6:26, 30.

147:10–11 Acknowledging one's dependence upon God rather than claiming self-sufficiency pleases God, cf. Ps 20:8; 33:16–19.

*

145:13 Ps 10:16; 102:13; 146:10; Lam 5:19; Dn 3:33; Rev 11:15.
145:14 Ps 94:18; 146:8.
145:15 Ps 136:25; 104:27–28; Mt 6:25–26.
145:17 Dt 32:4.
145:18 Dt 4:7; Is 55:6; 58:9.
145:19 Ps 34:18.
145:20 Jgs 5:31.
146:2 Ps 103:1; 104:33.
146:3 Ps 118:8–9.
146:4 Ps 90:3; 104:29; 1 Mc 2:63; Jb 34:14–15; Eccl 3:20; 12:7; Sir 40:11; Is 2:22.
146:6 Ps 121:2; 124:8; Ex 20:11; Acts 14:15; Rev 14:7.
146:7 Ps 103:6.
146:7 Ps 68:7; Is 49:9; 61:1.
146:8 Ps 145:14.
146:9 Ps 68:6; Dt 10:18.
146:10 Ps 145:13; Lam 5:19.
147:1 Ps 33:1; 92:2.
147:2 Is 11:12; 56:8; Jer 31:10.
147:3 Jb 5:18; Is 30:26; 61:1; Jer 33:6.
147:4 Is 40:26.
147:5 Jdt 16:13; Jer 51:15.
147:6 Ps 146:9; 1 Sm 2:7–8.
147:7 Ps 71:22.
147:8 Ps 104:13f; Jb 5:10; Jer 14:22; Jl 2:23.
147:9 Jb 38:41; Mt 6:26.

Catholic Social Teaching

Care for God's Creation

Psalm 148 calls on all of creation to praise God. As one of the seven themes of Catholic social teaching, caring for God's creation is one way we can respond to God and the needs of others. Working to keep water clean for safe drinking and for the protection of sea life, educating ourselves and others about the effects of pollution on animal habitats and nesting sites, protecting endangered species, and reducing carbon emissions are some of the ways we can fulfill our call to care for God's creation.

Psalm 148 asks us to complete a cycle—God creates, and we are called to be "co-creators" with God, continuing the work of creation by acting as caretakers for the goods of the earth. Our work as co-creators is often referred to as stewardship. Stewardship is centered around the notion that we are on this earth for a short time only and thus we have a moral responsibility to take care of the earth for future generations. Indeed, God demands that we be good stewards of all that he has blessed us with, so that all people can share in the overwhelming goodness of God's creation.

How can you be a better steward of God's creation?

▶ Psalm 148
Care for God's Creation

no pleasure in the runner's stride.*
11 Rather the LORD takes pleasure in those who fear him,
those who put their hope in his mercy.

III

12 Glorify the LORD, Jerusalem;
Zion, offer praise to your God,
13 For he has strengthened the bars of your gates,
blessed your children within you.*
14 He brings peace to your borders,
and satisfies you with finest wheat.*
15† He sends his command to earth;
his word runs swiftly!*
16 Thus he makes the snow like wool,
and spreads the frost like ash;*
17 He disperses hail like crumbs.
Who can withstand his cold?
18 Yet when again he issues his command, it melts them;
he raises his winds and the waters flow.
19 He proclaims his word to Jacob,
his statutes and laws to Israel.*
20 He has not done this for any other nation;
of such laws they know nothing.
Hallelujah!

PSALM 148†

All Creation Summoned To Praise

1 Hallelujah!

I

Praise the LORD from the heavens;
praise him in the heights.
2 Praise him, all you his angels;
give praise, all you his hosts.*
3 Praise him, sun and moon;
praise him, all shining stars.
4 Praise him, highest heavens,†
you waters above the heavens.
5 Let them all praise the LORD's name;
for he commanded and they were created,*
6 Assigned them their station forever,
set an order that will never change.

†

147:15–19 God speaks through the thunder of nature and the word of revealed law, cf. Is 55:10–11. The weather phenomena are well known in Jerusalem: a blizzard of snow and hail followed by a thunderstorm that melts the ice.

Psalm 148 A hymn inviting the beings of heaven (Ps 148:1–6) and of earth (Ps 148:7–14) to praise God. The hymn does not distinguish between inanimate and animate (and rational) nature.

148:4 *Highest heavens*: lit., "the heavens of the heavens," i.e., the space above the firmament, where the "upper waters" are stored, cf. Gn 1:6–7; Dt 10:14; 1 Kgs 8:27; Ps 104:3, 13.

147:10 Ps 20:8; 33:16–18.
147:13 Ps 48:14.
147:14 Ps 81:17.
147:15 Ps 33:9.
147:16 Jb 6:16; 37:10; 38:22.
147:19 Ps 78:5; Bar 3:37; Dt 4:7–8.
148:2 Ps 103:20f; Dn 3:58–63.
148:5 Ps 33:9; Gn 1:3f; Jdt 16:14.

II

7 Praise the LORD from the earth,
you sea monsters and all the deeps of the sea;*
8 Lightning and hail, snow and thick clouds,
storm wind that fulfills his command;
9 Mountains and all hills,
fruit trees and all cedars;*
10 Animals wild and tame,
creatures that crawl and birds that fly;*
11 Kings of the earth and all peoples,
princes and all who govern on earth;
12 Young men and women too,
old and young alike.
13 Let them all praise the LORD's name,
for his name alone is exalted,
His majesty above earth and heaven.*
14† He has lifted high the horn of his people;
to the praise of all his faithful,
the Israelites, the people near to him.
Hallelujah!

PSALM 149†

Praise God with Song and Sword

1 Hallelujah!

Sing to the LORD a new song,
his praise in the assembly of the faithful.*
2 Let Israel be glad in its maker,
the people of Zion rejoice in their king.
3 Let them praise his name in dance,
make music with tambourine and lyre.†*
4 For the LORD takes delight in his people,
honors the poor with victory.
5 Let the faithful rejoice in their glory,
cry out for joy on their couches,†
6 With the praise of God in their mouths,
and a two-edged sword in their hands,*
7 To bring retribution on the nations,
punishment on the peoples,*
8 To bind their kings in shackles,
their nobles in chains of iron,
9 To execute the judgments decreed for them—
such is the glory† of all God's faithful.
Hallelujah!

PSALM 150†

Final Doxology

1 Hallelujah!

Praise God in his holy sanctuary;†*
give praise in the mighty dome of heaven.

Pray It!

Psalm 150, Part 2

Praise God with clarinet and saxophone;
praise God with flute and oboe!
Praise God with French horn and tuba;
praise God with marimba and xylophone!
Praise God with guitar and fiddle;
praise God with banjo and ukulele!
Praise God with bagpipe and accordion;
praise God with piano and calliope!
Praise God with steel drum and harmonica;
praise God with bongo and maracas!
Praise God with soaring classical music;
praise God with mellow blues and tango!
Praise God with reggae and rap;
praise God with jazz and rock!
Praise God with square dancing and line dancing;
praise God with polka and waltz!
Let everyone who has breath and hands and feet and voices—
sopranos, altos, tenors, and basses—
praise the Lord!

▶ Psalm 150

---

†

148:14 *Has lifted high the horn of his people*: the horn symbolizes strength, the concrete noun for the abstract. Of all peoples, God has chosen Israel to return praise and thanks in a special way.

Psalm 149 A hymn inviting the people of Israel to celebrate their God in song and festive dance (Ps 149:1–3, 5) because God has chosen them and given them victory (Ps 149:4). The exodus and conquest are the defining acts of Israel; the people must be ready to do again those acts in the future at the divine command (Ps 149:6–9).

149:3 *Make music with tambourine and lyre*: the verse recalls the great exodus hymn of Ex 15:20.

149:5 *On their couches*: the people reclined to banquet.

149:9 *The glory*: what brings honor to the people is their readiness to carry out the divine will, here conceived as punishing injustice done by the nations.

Psalm 150 The Psalm is a closing doxology both for the fifth book of the Psalms (Ps 107–149) and for the Psalter as a whole. Temple musicians and dancers are called to lead all beings on earth and in heaven in praise of God. The Psalm proclaims to whom praise shall be given, and where (Ps 150:1); what praise shall be given, and why (Ps 150:2); how praise shall be given (Ps 150:3–5), and by whom (Ps 150:6).

150:1 *His holy sanctuary*: God's Temple on earth. *The mighty*

---

*

148:7 Ps 135:6; Gn 1:21.
148:9 Is 44:23.
148:10 Ps 30:5; Gn 1:21, 24f; Dt 4:7.
148:13 Ps 30:5; Dt 4:7.
149:1 Ps 22:23; 26:12; 35:18; 40:10; Jdt 16:1.
149:3 Ps 68:26; 81:2–3; 87:7; 150:3–4.
149:6 Neh 4:10–12; 2 Mc 15:27.
149:7 Wis 3:8.
150:1 Dn 3:53.

2 Give praise for his mighty deeds,*
praise him for his great majesty.
3 Give praise with blasts upon the horn,*
praise him with harp and lyre.
4 Give praise with tambourines and dance,
praise him with strings and pipes.*
5 Give praise with crashing cymbals,
praise him with sounding cymbals.
6 Let everything that has breath
give praise to the LORD!*
Hallelujah!

† *dome of heaven*: lit., "[God's] strong vault"; heaven is here imagined as a giant plate separating the inhabited world from the waters of the heavens.

* **150:2** Dt 3:24. **150:3ff** Ps 81:3–4; 149:3; 2 Sm 6:5; 1 Chr 13:8; 16:5, 42; 2 Chr 5:12–13; 7:6. **150:4** Ps 68:26; Ex 15:20. **150:6** Rev 5:13.

When we pick up the daily newspaper, many of us turn first to the advice columns. "My mom just doesn't understand me," we read. "Why won't she let me make my own decisions?" Or "I think my boyfriend is cheating on me. Should I show him the door?" Or "All my friends take drugs. How do I resist the pressure?" The Book of Proverbs is the advice column of the Old Testament. It covers everything from raising children to choosing friends.

The Book of Proverbs

At a Glance

I. Title and Introduction (1:1–7).

II. Instructions of Parents and of Woman Wisdom (1:8—9:18).

III. First Solomonic Collection of Sayings (10:1—22:16).

IV. Sayings of the Wise (22:17—24:22).

V. Further Sayings of the Wise (24:23–34).

VI. Second Solomonic Collection, Collected under King Hezekiah (25:1—29:27).

VII. Sayings of Agur and Others (30:1–33).

VIII. Sayings of King Lemuel (31:1–9).

IX. Poem on the Woman of Worth (31:10–31).

Quick Facts

Inspired Authors: King Solomon is introduced as the author, probably because of his legendary wisdom. However, the actual authors are unknown, writing from the reign of King Solomon (970–931 BC) to sometime after the Babylonian Exile (587–538 BC).

Of Note: The book is made up of several collections of proverbs.

In Depth

Proverbs teaches that the wise person listens to the "voices" of history: experience, intelligence, and common sense. The ancient Israelites had a long tradition of reflecting on the challenges of life. Over the centuries, a whole body of writings developed to record their reflections. These writings gave advice on common problems and questions people faced, and directions for wise living.

Proverbs is the best-known example of this type of literature in the Old Testament. It contains two basic kinds of writings: longer instructions addressed to young people and short sayings addressed to all. With advice on matters ranging from laziness (see 6:6–11), cheating (see 11:1), pride (see 16:18), and the training of children (see 22:6), to laughter (see 14:13), eyewinks (see 16:30), visiting neighbors (see 25:17), and being a good wife (see 31:10–31), Proverbs is a treasure chest of advice from the ancient world. Although some of the sayings may seem outdated or funny to us today, the overall lesson is something Jesus insists on in the Gospels: Faith is not just a matter of right believing; it is also a matter of right living.

The poetic devices used in Proverbs—found in most wisdom literature—reveal another basic insight of our ancestors in faith: How something is said is as important as what is said. In addition, parallelism makes the generally short sayings in this book easy to memorize. We would do well to consult Proverbs regularly for good advice, and to remember what we read. To all who care to hear, this book tells of the rewards of virtue and the dangers of vice.

Proverbs

3:13

I. Title and Introduction

Purpose of the Proverbs of Solomon†

1 1 The proverbs† of Solomon,* the son of David,
king of Israel:
2 That people may know wisdom and discipline,†
may understand intelligent sayings;
3 May receive instruction in wise conduct,
in what is right, just and fair;
4 That resourcefulness may be imparted to the
naive,†
knowledge and discretion to the young.
5 The wise by hearing them will advance in
learning,
the intelligent will gain sound guidance,
6 To comprehend proverb and byword,
the words of the wise and their riddles.
7 Fear of the LORD† is the beginning of
knowledge;*
fools despise wisdom and discipline.

II. Instructions of Parents and of Woman Wisdom

The Path of the Wicked: Greed and Violence†

8 Hear, my son, your father's instruction,
and reject not your mother's teaching;
9 A graceful diadem will they be for your head;
a pendant for your neck.
10 My son, should sinners entice you,
11 do not go if they say, "Come along with us!
Let us lie in wait for blood,
unprovoked, let us trap the innocent;
12 Let us swallow them alive, like Sheol,
whole, like those who go down to the pit!
13 All kinds of precious wealth shall we gain,
we shall fill our houses with booty;
14 Cast in your lot with us,
we shall all have one purse!"
15 My son, do not walk in the way with them,
hold back your foot from their path!

†

1:1–7 The prologue explains the purpose of the book. The book has a sapiential, ethical, and religious dimension: to bring the inexperienced to knowledge and right conduct, to increase the facility of those already wise for interpreting proverbs, parables and riddles, and to encourage the fulfillment of one's duties to God.

1:1 *Proverbs*: the Hebrew word *mashal* is broader than English "proverb," embracing the instructions of chaps. 1–9 and the sayings, observations, and comparisons of chaps. 10–31.

1:2 *Discipline*: education or formation which dispels ignorance and corrects vice. Note the reprise of v. 2a in v. 7b.

1:4 *Naive*: immature, inexperienced, sometimes the young, hence easily influenced for good or evil.

1:7 *Fear of the LORD*: primarily a disposition rather than the emotion of fear; reverential awe and respect toward God combined with obedience to God's will.

1:8–19 A parental warning to a young person leaving home, for them to avoid the company of the greedy and violent. Two ways lie before the hearer, a way that leads to death and a way that leads to life. The trap which the wicked set for the innocent (v. 11) in the end takes away the lives of the wicked themselves (v. 19). This theme will recur especially in chaps. 1–9. A second theme introduced here is that of founding (or managing) a household and choosing a spouse. A third theme is the human obstacles to attaining wisdom. Here (and in 2:12–15 and 4:10–19), the obstacle is men (always in the plural); in 2:16–19; 5:1–6; 6:20–35; chap. 7; 9:13–18, the obstacle to the quest is the "foreign" woman (always in the singular).

1:1 Prv 10:1; 25:1; 1 Kgs 4:32.

1:7 Prv 9:10; Jb 28:28; Ps 111:10; Sir 1:16.

16 [For their feet run to evil,
they hasten to shed blood.*]
17 In vain a net is spread†
right under the eyes of any bird—
18 They lie in wait for their own blood,
they set a trap for their own lives.
19 This is the way of everyone greedy for loot:
it takes away their lives.

Wisdom in Person Gives a Warning†

20 Wisdom cries aloud in the street,
in the open squares she raises her voice;*
21 Down the crowded ways she calls out,
at the city gates she utters her words:
22† "How long, you naive ones, will you love
naivete,
23 How long will you turn away at my reproof?
[The arrogant delight in their arrogance,
and fools hate knowledge.]
Lo! I will pour out to you my spirit,
I will acquaint you with my words:
24 'Because I called and you refused,
extended my hand and no one took notice;*
25 Because you disdained all my counsel,
and my reproof you ignored—
26 I, in my turn, will laugh at your doom;
will mock when terror overtakes you;
27 When terror comes upon you like a storm,
and your doom approaches like a
whirlwind;
when distress and anguish befall you.'
28 Then they will call me, but I will not answer;
they will seek me, but will not find me,
29 Because they hated knowledge,
and the fear of the LORD they did not
choose.
30 They ignored my counsel,
they spurned all my reproof;
31 Well, then, they shall eat the fruit† of their
own way,
and with their own devices be glutted.

Live It!

Media Literacy

Our society today has a powerful, persuasive tool: the media. We are influenced in many ways by what we read, watch, and hear in the many forms of modern media.

We might buy things because something we read says it's the best. We might look the other way when someone is being robbed because we see so much violence at the movies that it doesn't seem to bother us. We might dance to the beat of a song and not even realize that the words are suggesting an immoral behavior.

Certainly not all the messages in the media are bad. But to resist the influence of the media's negative messages, we must educate ourselves to watch for them. In Proverbs 1:10, 15, we read "My son, should sinners entice you, . . . do not walk in the way with them." Take time to really think about a message in the media before you choose to follow it. Verse 7 says it best: Only a fool despises wisdom!

Prv 1:10

32 For the straying of the naive kills them,
the smugness of fools destroys them.
33 But whoever obeys me dwells in security,
in peace, without fear of harm."*

The Blessings of Wisdom†

2 1 My son, if you receive my words
and treasure my commands,

† **1:17** A difficult verse. The most probable interpretation is that no fowler lifts up the net so the bird can see it. The verse might be paraphrased: God does not let those who walk on evil paths see the net that will entrap them. The passive construction ("a net is spread") is sometimes used to express divine activity. Verse 16 is a later attempt to add clarity. It is a quotation from Is 59:7 and is not in the best Greek manuscripts.

1:20–33 Wisdom is personified as in chaps. 8 and 9:1–6. With divine authority she proclaims the moral order, threatening to leave to their own devices those who disregard her invitation. All three speeches of Woman Wisdom have common features: a setting in city streets; an audience of simple or naive people; a competing appeal (chap. 7 is the competing appeal for chap. 8); an invitation to a relationship that brings long life, riches, repute.

The structure of the speeches is: A: setting (vv. 20–21); B: Wisdom's withdrawal, rebuke and announcement (vv. 22–23); reason and rejection I (vv. 24–27); reason and rejection II (vv. 28–31); summary (v. 32); C: the effects of Wisdom's presence (v. 33). Wisdom's opening speech is an extended threat ending with a brief invitation (v. 33). Her second speech is an extended invitation ending with a brief threat (8:36). The surprisingly abrupt and harsh tone of her speech is perhaps to be explained as a response to the arrogant words of the men in the previous scene (1:8–19).

1:22–23 There is textual confusion. Verse 22bc (in the third person) is an addition, interrupting vv. 22a and 23a (in the second person). The addition has been put in brackets, to separate it from the original poem. The original verses do not ask for a change of heart but begin to detail the consequences of disobedience to Wisdom.

1:31 *Eat the fruit*: sinners are punished by the consequences of their sins. Wisdom's voice echoes that of the parents in vv. 8–19. The parents mediate wisdom in vv. 8–19, but here Wisdom herself speaks.

2:1–22 Chapter 2 is a single poem, an acrostic of twenty-two lines, the number of consonants in the Hebrew alphabet. In vv. 1–11, the letter *aleph*, the first letter of the alphabet, predominates, and in vv. 12–22, the letter *lamed*, the first letter of the second half of the alphabet. A single structure runs through the whole: if (*aleph*)

1:16 Is 59:7.
1:20 Prv 8:1–3; 9:3.
1:24 Is 65:2, 12; 66:4; Jer 7:13.
1:33 Prv 8:33–34.

Catholic Connection

Sources of Moral Truth

We often hear people say that morality is all relative, that it is solely up to each individual to determine what is right and what is wrong. But the Scriptures teach that there is a moral law with moral truths that never change and we must seek to know them. To guide us, Proverbs speaks of one's need to wholeheartedly seek "wisdom," "understanding," and "intelligence." One must "raise your voice," "search her out," and treat this knowledge as a highly treasured prize.

The Catholic Church teaches that there are different expressions of the moral law that each one of us is called to seek wholeheartedly. Together these sources provide us the understanding and insight we need to obey God and work toward the common good.

One expression of the moral law is the natural law. The natural law is the God-given ability to use reason to tell right from wrong. This ability can be found in all people throughout history, regardless of their religion, and leads us to do good and avoid evil. It sounds simple, but sometimes we forget that we each must use reason when confronted with a moral dilemma.

Another expression of the moral law is from the Old Testament. In the Old Testament, we find the "Old Law," which is the law given to Moses and summed up in the Ten Commandments. This law provides us with moral truths regarding ways we are to love God and our neighbor. Knowing and applying the Ten Commandments is essential to making a moral decision.

A third expression is the "New Law" or "Law of the Gospel" given to us by Jesus. The New Law together with the Old Law are essential parts of the moral law that God has revealed to the world. The New Law fulfills and gives us a deeper understanding of the Old Law; it not only shows us how to love God and others, but also, through the power of the Holy Spirit, gives us the grace and strength necessary to follow the law. The Holy Spirit also empowers the Church to serve as a guide to moral truth and to instruct the faithful about faith and morals without error.

Through much prayer and study, we all can wholeheartedly seek moral truth as Proverbs calls us to do. How is God calling you to grow in wisdom, understanding, and insight into moral truth?

Prv 2:1–22

Catechism, nos. 1949–1986

2 Turning your ear to wisdom,†
inclining your heart to understanding;
3 Yes, if you call for intelligence,
and to understanding raise your voice;
4 If you seek her like silver,
and like hidden treasures search her out,
5 Then will you understand the fear of the LORD;
the knowledge of God you will find;
6 For the LORD gives wisdom,
from his mouth come knowledge and
understanding;*
7 He has success in store for the upright,
is the shield of those who walk honestly,
8 Guarding the paths of justice,
protecting the way of his faithful ones,
9 Then you will understand what is right and just,
what is fair, every good path;
10 For wisdom will enter your heart,
knowledge will be at home in your soul,
11 Discretion will watch over you,
understanding will guard you;
12† Saving you from the way of the wicked,
from those whose speech is perverse.
13 From those who have left the straight paths
to walk in the ways of darkness,
14 Who delight in doing evil
and celebrate perversity;
15 Whose ways are crooked,
whose paths are devious;
16† Saving you from a stranger,
from a foreign woman with her smooth
words,*
17 One who forsakes the companion of her youth
and forgets the covenant of her God;
18 For her path sinks down to death,
and her footsteps lead to the shades.† *
19 None who enter there come back,
or gain the paths of life.
20 Thus you may walk in the way of the good,
and keep to the paths of the just.
21† For the upright will dwell in the land,*
people of integrity will remain in it;
22 But the wicked will be cut off from the land,
the faithless will be rooted out of it.

Confidence in God Leads to Prosperity†

3 1 My son, do not forget† my teaching,
take to heart my commands;
2 For many days, and years of life,*
and peace, will they bring you.
3 Do not let love and fidelity forsake you;
bind them around your neck;
write them on the tablet of your heart.
4 Then will you win favor and esteem
before God and human beings.
5 Trust in the LORD with all your heart,
on your own intelligence do not rely;
6 In all your ways be mindful of him,
and he will make straight your paths.
7 Do not be wise in your own eyes,*
fear the LORD and turn away from evil;
8 This will mean health for your flesh
and vigor for your bones.
9 Honor the LORD with your wealth,
with first fruits of all your produce;*
10 Then will your barns be filled with plenty,
with new wine your vats will overflow.
11 The discipline of the LORD, my son, do not
spurn;*
do not disdain his reproof;
12† For whom the LORD loves he reproves,
as a father, the son he favors.*

---

you search . . . then (*aleph*) the Lord/Wisdom will grant . . . saving (*lamed*) you from the wicked man/woman . . . thus (*lamed*) you can walk in the safe way. . . .

2:2–3 *Wisdom . . . understanding . . . intelligence*: various names or aspects of the same gift.

2:12–15 As in 1:8–19, there is an obstacle to the quest for wisdom—deceitful and violent men. Cf. also 4:10–19. They offer a way of life that is opposed to the way of wisdom.

2:16–19 A second obstacle and counter-figure to Wisdom, personified as an attractive woman, is the "stranger," or "foreigner," from outside the territory or kinship group, hence inappropriate as a marriage partner. In Proverbs she comes to be identified with Woman Folly, whose deceitful words promise life but lead to death. Woman Folly appears also in chap. 5, 6:20–35, chap. 7 and 9:13–18. *Covenant*: refers to the vow uttered with divine sanction at the woman's previous marriage, as the parallel verse suggests. She is already married and relations with her would be adulterous.

2:18 *Shades*: the inhabitants of Sheol.

2:21–22 Verses 21–22 echo the ending of Wisdom's speech in 1:32–33, in which refusing Wisdom's invitation meant death and obedience to her meant life. The same set of ideas is found in Ps 37 (especially vv. 3, 9, 11, 22, 29, 34, and 38): to live on (or inherit) the land and to be uprooted from the land are expressions of divine recompense.

3:1–12 The instruction consists of a series of six four-line exhortations in which the second line of each exhortation mentions a reward or benefit. In the first five exhortations, the teacher promises a reward: long life, a good name, divine protection, health, abundant crops. The last exhortation, vv. 11–12, departs from the command-reward scheme, implying that being a disciple of the Lord does not guarantee unalloyed bliss: one must allow God freedom to "reprove" or educate. The process of education is like that described in chap. 2: the father first invites his son (or disciple) to memorize his teaching (v. 1), then to enter upon a relationship of trust with him (v. 3), and finally to place his trust in God, who takes up the parental task of education (v. 5). Education begun by the parent is brought to full completion by God.

3:1 *Do not forget*: this word and several others in the section such as "teaching," "commands," "years of life," and the custom of affixing written teaching to one's body, occur also in Deuteronomy. This vocabulary suggests that Proverbs and Deuteronomy had a common origin in the scribal class of Jerusalem. This section (and vv. 21–34) subtly elaborates Dt 6:5–9, "You shall love the LORD with all your heart (v. 5) . . . Take to heart these words (v. 1) . . . Recite them when you are at home and when you are away (v. 23) . . . when you lie down (v. 24) . . . Bind them (v. 3) on your arm as a sign and let them be a pendant on your forehead" (v. 21).

3:12 One might be tempted to judge the quality of one's relationship to God by one's prosperity. It is an inadequate criterion, for God

---

2:6 Jb 32:8; Wis 7:25; Sir 1:1; Jas 1:5.
2:16 Prv 5:3, 20; 6:24; 7:5; 22:14.
2:18 Prv 5:5; 7:27.
2:21 Prv 10:7, 30; Jb 18:17; Ps 21:9–13; 37:22, 28.
3:2 Prv 4:10; 9:11; 10:27.
3:7 Rom 11:25; 12:16.
3:9 Ex 34:26; Lv 27:30; Dt 26:2; Sir 7:31; 35:7.
3:11 Heb 12:5–6.
3:12 Jdt 8:27; Rev 3:19.

Pray It!

Your Future

Read Proverbs 3:5–8 and think about your plans for the future. How does God play a part in them? Do they include discernment of (prayerful listening to) God's plans for you? Here are some clues for discerning where God is calling you:

- Pray about your future, and ask for God's direction.
- Look at your talents and interests. These are gifts from God to be used for the good of others as well as yourself.
- Imagine yourself doing whatever you are considering. What feelings surface? Peace and joy are usually signs of God's presence. Excessive anxiety, fear, and shame are usually signs of God's absence.
- Talk with a trusted adult about your options. If this person is wise, she or he will not give you a direct answer but will help you sort out where God is leading.

▶ **Prv 3:5–8**

The Benefits of Finding Wisdom†

13 Happy the one who finds wisdom,
the one who gains understanding!*
14 Her profit is better than profit in silver,
and better than gold is her revenue;
15 She is more precious than corals,
and no treasure of yours can compare with her.*
16 Long life is in her right hand,
in her left are riches and honor;
17 Her ways are pleasant ways,
and all her paths are peace;
18 She is a tree of life† to those who grasp her,
and those who hold her fast are happy.*
19 The LORD by wisdom founded the earth,
established the heavens by understanding;
20 By his knowledge the depths† are split,
and the clouds drop down dew.

Justice Toward One's Neighbor Brings Blessing†

21 My son, do not let these slip from your sight:
hold to deliberation and planning;
22 So will they be life to your soul,†
and an adornment for your neck.
23 Then you may go your way securely;
your foot will never stumble;
24 When you lie down, you will not be afraid,
when you rest, your sleep will be sweet.
25 Do not be afraid of sudden terror,
of the ruin of the wicked when it comes;
26 For the LORD will be your confidence,
and will keep your foot from the snare.
27 Do not withhold any goods from the owner
when it is in your power to act.
28 Say not to your neighbor, "Go, come back tomorrow,
and I will give it to you," when all the while you have it.
29 Do not plot evil against your neighbors,
when they live at peace with you.

---

† as a teacher might go counter to student expectations. The discipline of God can involve suffering.

3:13–20 An encomium of Wisdom through the listing of her benefits to the human race and the depiction of her role in creation. Wisdom, or understanding, is more valuable than silver and gold. Its fruit is long life, riches, honor and happiness (vv. 13–18). Even the creation of the universe and its adornment (Gn 1) were not done without wisdom (vv. 19–20). The praise of Wisdom foreshadows the praise of a noble wife in the final poem (31:10–31), even to the singling out of the hands extended in a helpful way toward human beings.

3:18 *A tree of life*: in the Old Testament this phrase occurs only in Proverbs (11:30; 13:12; 15:4) and Genesis (2:9; 3:22, 24). The origins of the concept are obscure; there is no explicit mention of it in ancient Near Eastern literature, though on ancient seals trees are sometimes identified as trees of life. When the man and the woman were expelled from the garden, the tree of life was put off limits to them, lest they "eat of it and live forever" (Gn 3:22). The quest for wisdom gives access to the previously sequestered tree of life. The tree of life is mentioned also in the apocryphal work 1 Enoch 25:4–5. Rev 2 and 22 mention the tree of life as a source of eternal life.

3:20 *Depths*: for the Hebrews, the depths enclosed the great subterranean waters; the rain and dew descended from the waters above the firmament; cf. Gn 1:6–10; Jb 26:8, 12; Ps 18:15; 24:2. The cosmogony provides the reason why Wisdom offers such benefits to human beings: the world was created in wisdom so that all who live in accord with wisdom live in tune with the universe.

3:21–35 As in other instructions, the father in vv. 21–26 urges the son to seek wisdom, which in this case means practicing the virtues of "deliberation and planning," a specification of wisdom. Practicing these virtues brings protection from violence (vv. 22–26) and friendship with God (vv. 32–35). The language is like Ps 91.

Verses 27–35 are arranged according to a clear order. Serving God requires serving one's neighbor through kindness (vv. 27–28), maintaining peace with the good (vv. 29–31), having no envy of the wicked (v. 31), because the Lord's friendship and kindness are with the just, not with the wicked. Matching the six exhortations of vv. 1–12, vv. 27–34 contain six prohibitions. The righteous/wicked contrast is progressively developed: in contrast to the wicked, the righteous are in God's inner circle, their houses are blessed, they deal with a merciful God, and obtain honor.

3:22 *Your soul*: Heb. *nephesh* means "throat, esophagus; life; soul." The meanings are connected. The throat area is the moist, breathing center of the body, which stands for life and for self. The figure of speech is called metonymy, in which one word is substituted for another on the basis of a causal relation, e.g., eye for sight, arm for power, or, as here, "throat area" for life. Proverbs sometimes plays on this concrete meaning of life (e.g., 21:23).

---

* **3:13** Prv 8:34–35. **3:15** Prv 8:11, 19; Wis 7:8–11. **3:18** Prv 4:13; 8:35; 11:30; Gn 2:9; 3:22.

30 Do not contend with someone without cause,
with one who has done you no harm.
31 Do not envy the violent
and choose none of their ways:*
32 To the LORD the devious are an abomination,
but the upright are close to him.
33 The curse of the LORD is on the house of the wicked,
but the dwelling of the just he blesses;
34 Those who scoff, he scoffs at,*
but the lowly he favors.
35 The wise will possess glory,
but fools will bear shame.

The Teacher as Model Disciple†

4 1 Hear, O children, a father's instruction,
be attentive, that you may gain understanding!
2 Yes, excellent advice I give you;
my teaching do not forsake.
3 When I was my father's child,
tender, the darling of my mother,
4 He taught me and said to me:
"Let your heart hold fast my words:*
keep my commands, and live!
5 Get wisdom,† get understanding!
Do not forget or turn aside from the words of my mouth.
6 Do not forsake her, and she will preserve you;
love her, and she will safeguard you;
7 The beginning of wisdom is: get wisdom;
whatever else you get, get understanding.
8 Extol her, and she will exalt you;
she will bring you honors if you embrace her;
9 She will put on your head a graceful diadem;
a glorious crown will she bestow on you."

The Two Ways†

10 Hear, my son, and receive my words,
and the years of your life shall be many.*

True Security

We often hear, "When the going gets tough, the tough get going." But how do we know how to get going? Where do we get going to? Our faith gives us good advice and wise counsel (see Prv 3:21). Prayer keeps us close to God (see verse 26). And knowing we have made the right decision is true security.

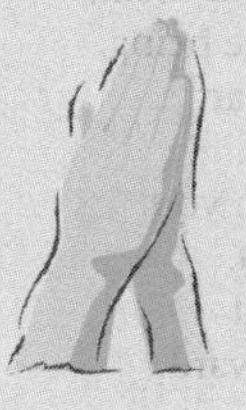

When the going gets tough, first the tough get faithful and prayerful and thoughtful. Then they get going.

▶ Prv 3:21–26

11 On the way of wisdom I direct you,
I lead you on straight paths.
12 When you walk, your step will not be impeded,
and should you run, you will not stumble.
13 Hold fast to instruction, never let it go;
keep it, for it is your life.
14† The path of the wicked do not enter,
nor walk in the way of the evil;
15 Shun it, do not cross it,
turn aside from it, pass on.
16 For they cannot rest unless they have done evil;
if they do not trip anyone they lose sleep.
17 For they eat the bread of wickedness
and drink the wine of violence.
18 But the path of the just is like shining light,
that grows in brilliance till perfect day.†

†

4:1–9 The teacher draws a parallel between his teaching the disciples now and his father's teaching him in his youth (vv. 3–4): what my father taught me about wisdom is what I am teaching you. The poem implies that the teacher has acquired wisdom and has in fact been protected and honored as his father promised long ago. Thus the teacher has the authority of someone who has been under wisdom's sway since earliest youth.

There are two sections, a call for attention and introduction of the speaker (vv. 1–3) and the father's quoting of his own father's teaching (vv. 4–9). Beginning with v. 5, the father's words are no longer quoted, wisdom herself becoming the active agent; she becomes the subject, not the object, of the verbs. Three Hebrew verbs are repeated in the two parts, "to forsake" in vv. 2 and 6, "to keep/guard" in vv. 4 and 6, and "to give/bestow" in vv. 2 and 9. Each verb in its first appearance has the father's words as its object; in its second appearance each verb has wisdom as its subject or object. The teaching process is like that in 2:1–22 and 3:1–12: heeding the words of one's parent puts one in touch with wisdom, who completes the process and bestows her gifts.

4:5, 7 *Get wisdom*: the same Hebrew word "to get" can mean to acquire merchandise and to acquire a wife (18:22; 31:10); both meanings are in keeping with Proverbs' metaphors of acquiring wisdom over gold and silver and of acquiring wisdom as a personified woman, a wife.

4:10–19 A central metaphor of the poem is "the way." The way of wisdom leads directly to life (vv. 10–13); it is a light that grows brighter (v. 18). The wise are bound to shun (vv. 14–17) the dark and violent path of the wicked (v. 19). Singleness of purpose and right conduct proceed from the heart of the wise as from the source of life (vv. 23–26), saving them from destruction on evil paths (4:27; 5:21–23). As in 1:8–19 and 2:12–15, the obstacles to the quest are men and their way. Elsewhere in chaps. 1–9, the obstacle is the foreign woman (2:16–19; chap. 5; 6:20–35; chap. 7; 9:13–18).

4:14–15 One is always free to choose. The righteous may choose to leave their path to walk on the wicked path and the wicked may choose the righteous path.

4:18 *Till perfect day*: lit., "till the day is established"; this may refer to full daylight or to noonday.

*

3:31 Prv 23:17; 24:1, 19; Ps 37:1.
3:34 Prv 1:26.
4:4 Dt 6:1–6.
4:10 Prv 3:2.

19 The way of the wicked is like darkness;
they do not know on what they stumble.

With Your Whole Being Heed My Words and Live†

20 My son, to my words be attentive,
to my sayings incline your ear;
21 Let them not slip from your sight,
keep them within your heart;
22 For they are life to those who find them,*
bringing health to one's whole being.
23 With all vigilance guard your heart,
for in it are the sources of life.
24† Dishonest mouth put away from you,
deceitful lips put far from you.
25 Let your eyes look straight ahead
and your gaze be focused forward.
26 Survey the path for your feet,
and all your ways will be sure.
27 Turn neither to right nor to left,
keep your foot far from evil.

Warning Against Adultery†

5 1 My son, to my wisdom be attentive,
to understanding incline your ear,
2 That you may act discreetly,
and your lips guard what you know.
3 Indeed, the lips of the stranger drip honey,†
and her mouth is smoother than oil;*
4 But in the end she is as bitter as wormwood,
as sharp as a two-edged sword.
5 Her feet go down to death,
her steps reach Sheol;*
6 Her paths ramble, you know not where,
lest you see before you the road to life.
7 So now, children, listen to me,
do not stray from the words of my mouth.
8 Keep your way far from her,*
do not go near the door of her house,
9 Lest you give your honor† to others,*
and your years to a merciless one;
10 Lest outsiders take their fill of your wealth,
and your hard-won earnings go to another's house;
11 And you groan in the end,
when your flesh and your body are consumed;
12 And you say, "Oh, why did I hate instruction,
and my heart spurn reproof!
13 Why did I not listen to the voice of my teachers,
incline my ear to my instructors!
14 I am all but ruined,
in the midst of the public assembly!"
15 Drink water† from your own cistern,
running water from your own well.
16 Should your water sources be dispersed abroad,
streams of water in the streets?
17 Let them be yours alone,
not shared with outsiders;
18 Let your fountain be blessed and have joy of the wife of your youth,
19 your lovely hind, your graceful doe.†
Of whose love you will ever have your fill,
and by her ardor always be intoxicated.
20 Why then, my son, should you be intoxicated with a stranger,
and embrace another woman?
21 Indeed, the ways of each person are plain to the LORD's sight;
all their paths he surveys;*
22 By their own iniquities the wicked will be caught,
in the meshes of their own sin they will be held fast;
23 They will die from lack of discipline,
lost because of their great folly.

†

4:20–27 Acquiring wisdom brings life and health. The learning process involves two stages: (1) hearing the teacher's words and treasuring them in the heart; (2) speaking and acting in accord with the wisdom that one has stored in one's heart. Seven organs of the body are mentioned: ear, eyes, heart, mouth, lips, eyelids ("gaze," v. 25), feet. Each of the organs is to be strained to its limit as the disciple puts wisdom into practice. The physical organ stands for the faculty, e.g., the eye for sight, the foot for movement. The figure of speech is called metonymy; one word is substituted for another on the basis of a causal relation.

4:24–27 In vv. 20–21 the faculties of hearing (ear) and seeing (eye) take in the teaching and the heart stores and ponders it, so in the second half of the poem, vv. 24–27, the faculties of speech, sight, and walking enable the disciple to put the teaching into practice.

5:1–23 This is the first of three poems on the forbidden woman, the "stranger" outside the social boundaries (cf. 2:16–19); the other two are 6:20–35 and chap. 7. Understanding and discretion are necessary to avoid adultery, which leads astray and begets bitterness, bloodshed, and death (vv. 1–6). It destroys honor, wastes the years of life, despoils hard-earned wealth, and brings remorse in the end (vv. 7–14). Conjugal fidelity and love bring happiness and security (vv. 15–20). Cf. 6:20–7:27. The structure of the poem consists of a two-line introduction; part one consists of three stanzas of four lines each warning of the forbidden woman's effect on her lovers (vv. 3–14); part two consists of a stanza of twelve lines exhorting the disciple to marital fidelity (vv. 15–20); and a final stanza of six lines on the perils of the woman (vv. 21–23).

5:3 A metaphorical level is established in the opening description of the forbidden woman: her lips drip honey and her feet lead to death. By her lies, she leads people away from the wisdom that gives life.

5:9 *Honor*: the words "life" and "wealth" have also been read in this place. *A merciless one*: the offended husband; cf. 6:34–35.

5:15–16 *Water*: water may have an erotic meaning as in Sg 4:15, "[You are] a garden fountain, a well of living water." Eating and drinking can be metaphors expressing the mutuality of love. The wife is the opposite of the adulterous woman; she is not an outsider, not unfeeling, not a destroyer of her husband's self and goods. The best defense against adultery is appreciating and loving one's spouse. The best defense against folly is to appreciate and love wisdom.

5:19 *Lovely hind . . . graceful doe*: ancient Near Eastern symbols of feminine beauty and charm; cf. Sg 2:7, 9, 17.

*

4:22 Prv 8:35.
5:3 Prv 7:5.
5:5 Prv 2:18; 7:27.
5:8 Prv 7:25.
5:9 Sir 9:6.

PRV

Miscellaneous Proverbs†

Against Going Surety for One's Neighbor

6 1† My son, if you have become surety to your
neighbor,*
given your hand in pledge to another,
2 You have been snared by the utterance of
your lips,
caught by the words of your mouth;
3 So do this, my son, to free yourself,
since you have fallen into your neighbor's
power:
Go, hurry, rouse your neighbor!
4 Give no sleep to your eyes,
nor slumber to your eyelids;
5 Free yourself like a gazelle from the hunter,
or like a bird from the hand of the fowler.

The Ant and the Sluggard at Harvest

6† Go to the ant,* O sluggard,
study her ways and learn wisdom;
7 For though she has no chief,
no commander or ruler,
8 She procures her food in the summer,
stores up her provisions in the harvest.
9 How long, O sluggard, will you lie there?
when will you rise from your sleep?
10 A little sleep, a little slumber,
a little folding of the arms to rest—†
11 Then poverty will come upon you like a robber,
and want like a brigand.

The Scoundrel

12† Scoundrels, villains, are they
who deal in crooked talk.
13 Shifty of eye,
feet ever moving,
pointing with fingers,
14 They have perversity in their hearts,
always plotting evil,
sowing discord.
15 Therefore their doom comes suddenly;
in an instant they are crushed beyond cure.

Live It!

All the Days of My Life

The phrase "all the days of my life" has been repeated by countless couples on their wedding day, and for some of those couples, it is prophetic. The husband and wife will be together till death separates them, and then they will be reunited in heaven. Though we live in a society where divorce is frequent, many couples make it through all the trials and difficulties and are together to celebrate their twenty-fifth and fiftieth anniversaries.

The writer of Proverbs 5:15–23 is warning men, in particular, against adultery, which remains, even today, a primary reason marriages break up. But one does not have to be a man, or even married, to be challenged by the words of this proverb. We are all called to exhibit the virtue of chastity—sexual self-control—in our relationships. This means we must never abuse the gift of sexuality by using it for self-serving purposes or immediate gratification, remembering that "each man's ways are plain to the LORD's sight" (verse 21).

► **Prv 5:15–23**

PRV

†

6:1–19 Four independent pieces akin to those in 30:1–5, 6–11, 12–15, and 16–19. Some judge the verses to be an ancient addition, but the fact that the pieces differ from the other material in chaps. 1–9 is not a strong argument against their originality. Ancient anthologies did not always have the symmetry of modern collections. An editor may have placed the four pieces in the midst of the three poems on the forbidden woman to shed light on some of their themes. Verses 1–5 warn against getting trapped by one's words to another person (the Hebrew word for "another" is the same used for the forbidden woman); vv. 6–11 proposes the ant as a model of forethought and diligence; vv. 12–15 describes the reprobate who bears some similarity to the seductive woman, especially as portrayed in chap. 7; vv. 16–19 depicts the typical enemy of God, underscoring the person's destructive words.

6:1–5 Unlike other instructions that begin with "my son," this instruction does not urge the hearer to store up the father's words as a means to wisdom, but only to avoid one practice—going surety for one's neighbor. The warning is intensified by repetition of "neighbor" and "free yourself," the mention of bodily organs, and the imagery of hunting. *Given your hand in pledge*: lit., "struck your hands"; this was probably the legal method for closing a contract. To become surety meant intervening in favor of the insolvent debtor and assuming responsibility for the payment of the debt, either by obtaining it from the debtor or substituting oneself. Proverbs is strongly opposed to the practice (11:15; 17:18; 20:16; 22:26–27; 27:13) apparently because of the danger it poses to the freedom of the one providing surety.

6:6–11 The sluggard or lazybones is a type in Proverbs, like the righteous and the wicked. Sometimes the opposite type to the sluggard is the diligent person. Other extended passages on the sluggard are 24:30–34 and 26:13–16. The malice of the type is not low physical energy but the refusal to act. To describe human types, Proverbs often uses comparisons from the animal world, e.g., 27:8 (bird); 28:1, 15 (lion); 30:18–19 (eagle, snake); 30:24–28 (ant, badger, locust, lizard).

6:10 This verse may be regarded as the sluggard's reply or as a continuation of the remonstrance.

6:12–15 Proverbs uses types to make the point that certain ways of acting have inherent consequences. The typifying intensifies the

*

5:21 Jb 14:16; 31:4; 34:21.
6:1 Prv 11:15; 22:26; Sir 8:13; 29:19.
6:6 Prv 30:25.

Live It!

Leaders with Character

Look at the list of the things the Lord hates in Proverbs 6:17–19. It looks like a popular description of a corrupt politician or businessperson! Now take the list and put it in the positive: humble eyes, a truthful tongue, hands that protect the innocent, a heart that plans good, feet that hurry to help, a truthful witness, and someone who brings harmony to families. That's the kind of leader everyone wants! Perhaps you know of a leader in your school, family, church, or local community who exhibits many of these positive qualities. These sorts of leaders have a unique ability to inspire others to follow, providing great insight and direction when one is faced with difficult situations or decisions.

The author of Proverbs is constantly reminding us to be of good character. When you are called to be a leader—and we all will be at some time in our lives—keep the advice of Proverbs in mind. Be a leader of character and integrity by doing the things the Lord loves, not the things the Lord hates.

▶ Prv 6:16–19

What the Lord Rejects

16 There are six things the LORD hates,
yes, seven† are an abomination to him;
17† Haughty eyes, a lying tongue,
hands that shed innocent blood,
18 A heart that plots wicked schemes,
feet that are quick to run to evil,
19 The false witness who utters lies,
and the one who sows discord among kindred.

Warning Against Adultery†

20 Observe, my son, your father's command,
and do not reject your mother's teaching;
21 Keep them fastened over your heart always,
tie them around your neck.
22 When you lie down they† will watch over you,
when you wake, they will share your concerns;
wherever you turn, they will guide you.
23 For the command is a lamp, and the teaching a light,
and a way to life are the reproofs that discipline,
24 Keeping you from another's wife,
from the smooth tongue of the foreign woman.*
25 Do not lust in your heart after her beauty,
do not let her captivate you with her glance!*
26 For the price of a harlot
may be scarcely a loaf of bread,
But a married woman
is a trap for your precious life.
27† Can a man take embers into his bosom,
and his garments not be burned?
28 Or can a man walk on live coals,
and his feet not be scorched?
29 So with him who sleeps with another's wife—
none who touches her shall go unpunished.*
30 Thieves are not despised
if out of hunger they steal to satisfy their appetite.

† picture. All the physical organs—mouth, eyes, feet, fingers—are at the service of evil. Cf. Rom 6:12–13: "Therefore, sin must not reign over your mortal bodies so that you obey their desires. And do not present the parts of your bodies to sin as weapons for wickedness, but present yourselves to God as raised from the dead to life and the parts of your bodies to God as weapons of righteousness."

6:16 *Six . . . seven*: this literary pattern (n, n + 1) occurs frequently; cf., e.g., Am 1–2; Prv 30:18–19.

6:17–19 The seven vices, symbolized for the most part by bodily organs, are pride, lying, murder, intrigue, readiness to do evil, false witness, and the stirring up of discord.

6:20–35 The second of three instructions on adultery (5:1–23; 6:20–35; and chap. 7). The instructions assume that wisdom will protect one from adultery and its consequences: loss of property and danger to one's person. In this poem, the father and the mother urge their son to keep their teaching constantly before his eyes. The teaching will light his way and make it a path to life (v. 23). The teaching will preserve him from the adulterous woman who is far more dangerous than a prostitute. Prostitutes may cost one money, but having an affair with someone else's wife puts one in grave danger. The poem bluntly urges self-interest as a motive to refrain from adultery. The poem has three parts. I (vv. 20–24, ten lines), in which v. 23 repeats "command" and "teaching" of v. 20 and "keeping" in v. 24 completes the fixed pair initiated by "observe" in v. 20; II (vv. 25–29, ten lines) is a self-contained argument comparing the costs of a liaison with a prostitute and a married woman; III (vv. 30–35, twelve lines) draws conclusions from the comparison of adultery with theft: the latter involves property only but adultery destroys one's name and very self. The best protection against such a woman is heeding parental instruction, which is to be kept vividly before one's eyes like a written tablet.

6:22 *They*: Heb. has "she." If this verse is not out of place, then the antecedent of "she" is command (v. 20), or perhaps wisdom.

6:27–29 There is a play on three words of similar sound, *'îsh*, "man," *'ishshâ*, "woman," and *'ésh*, "fire, embers." The question, "Can a man (*'îsh*) take embers (*'ésh*) into his bosom / and his garments not be burned?", has a double meaning. "Into his bosom"

* **6:24** Prv 2:16; 7:5. Sir 9:8; 25:20; Mt 5:28.
6:25 Ex 20:17; Dt 5:21; **6:29** Sir 9:9.

31 Yet if caught they must pay back sevenfold,
yield up all the wealth of their house.
32 But those who commit adultery have no sense;
those who do it destroy themselves.
33† They will be beaten and disgraced,
and their shame will not be wiped away;
34 For passion enrages the husband,
he will have no pity on the day of vengeance;
35 He will not consider any restitution,
nor be satisfied by your many bribes.

The Seduction†

7 1 † My son, keep my words,
and treasure my commands.
2 Keep my commands and live,†
and my teaching as the apple of your eye;
3 Bind them on your fingers,
write them on the tablet of your heart.*
4 Say to Wisdom, "You are my sister!"†
Call Understanding, "Friend!"
5 That they may keep you from a stranger,
from the foreign woman with her smooth words.*
6 For at the window of my house,
through my lattice I looked out†
7 And I saw among the naive,
I observed among the young men,
a youth with no sense,
8 Crossing the street near the corner,
then walking toward her house,
9 In the twilight, at dusk of day,
in the very dark of night.
10 Then the woman comes to meet him,
dressed like a harlot, with secret designs.
11 She is raucous and unruly,
her feet cannot stay at home;
12 Now she is in the streets, now in the open squares,
lurking in ambush at every corner.
13 Then she grabs him, kisses him,
and with an impudent look says to him:
14 "I owed peace offerings,
and today I have fulfilled my vows;
15 So I came out to meet you,
to look for you, and I have found you!
16 With coverlets I have spread my couch,
with brocaded cloths of Egyptian linen;
17 I have sprinkled my bed† with myrrh,
with aloes, and with cinnamon.
18 Come, let us drink our fill of love,
until morning, let us feast on love!
19 For my husband is not at home,†
he has gone on a long journey;
20 A bag of money he took with him,
he will not return home till the full moon."
21 She wins him over by repeated urging,
with her smooth lips she leads him astray.† *
22 He follows her impulsively,
like an ox that goes to slaughter;
Like a stag that bounds toward the net,
23 till an arrow pierces its liver;
Like a bird that rushes into a snare,
unaware that his life is at stake.

---

† has an erotic meaning as in the phrase "wife of one's bosom" (Dt 13:6; 28:54; Sir 9:1). Hence one will destroy one's garments, which symbolize one's public position, by taking fire/another's wife into one's bosom.

6:33–35 The nature of the husband's vengeance is disputed, some believing it is simply a physical beating whereas others hold it is public and involves the death penalty because Lv 20:20 and Dt 22:22 demand the death penalty.

7:1–27 The third and climactic instruction on adultery and seduction is an example story, of the same type as the example story in 24:30–34. By its negative portrayal of the deceitful woman, who speaks in the night to a lone youth, it serves as a foil to trustworthy Wisdom in chap. 8, who speaks in broad daylight to all who pass in the street.

As in 6:20–24, the father warns his son to keep his teaching to protect him from the dangerous forbidden woman. The father's language in 7:4 ("Say to Wisdom, 'You are my sister,' and call Understanding 'Friend' ") sets this admonition apart, however; it is the language of courtship and love. If the son makes Woman Wisdom his companion and lover, she will protect him from the other woman. As in chap. 5, loving the right woman protects the man from the wrong woman.

As motivation, the father in vv. 6–23 tells his son of an incident he once observed while looking out his window—a young man went to the bed of an adulterous woman and wound up dead. As in chap. 5, the realistic details—the purposeful woman, the silent youth, the vow, the perfumed bed—have a metaphorical level. Ultimately the story is about two different kinds of love.

7:1–3 Verses 1–3 are artistically constructed. "Keep" in v. 1a recurs in v. 2a; "commands" in v. 1b recurs in v. 2a; the imperative verb "live" occurs in the very center of the three lines; v. 3, on preserving the teaching upon one's very person, matches vv. 1–2, on preserving the teaching internally by memorizing it.

7:2 *Live*: here as elsewhere (Gn 20:7; 42:18; 2 Kgs 18:32; Jer 27:12, 17; Ez 18:32), the imperative ("Live!") is uttered against the danger of death, e.g., "Do such and such and you will live (=survive the danger); why should you die?"

7:4 *You are my sister*: "sister" and "brother" are examples of love language in the ancient Near East, occurring in Egyptian love poetry and Mesopotamian marriage songs. In Sg 4:9, 10, 12; 5:1, the man calls the woman, "my sister, my bride." Intimate friendship with Woman Wisdom saves one from false and dangerous relationships.

7:6–7 *I looked out . . . I saw . . .* : the perspective is unusual. The narrator looks through a window upon the drama in the street.

7:17 *Bed*: a bed can designate a place of burial in Is 57:2; Ez 32:25; 2 Chr 16:14. *Myrrh . . . aloes*: the spices could be used for funerals as for weddings (Jn 19:39). It is possible that the language is ambivalent, speaking of death as it seems to speak of life. As the woman offers the youth a nuptial feast, she is in reality describing his funerary feast.

7:19–20 *For my husband is not at home*: the woman is calculating. She knows exactly how long her husband will be gone.

7:21 The verbs "to win over" (lit., "to lead astray") and "to lead off" can be used of leading animals such as a donkey (Nm 22:23) or sheep (Jer 23:2 and 50:17). The animal imagery continues as the youth is compared to an ox, a fallow deer, and a bird in the moment they are slaughtered. None of the animals are aware of their impending death.

7:3 Dt 6:8.
7:5 Prv 2:16; 6:24.
7:21 Prv 5:3; 6:24.

Introducing...

Lady Wisdom

As you read the description of wisdom in Proverbs 8:1—9:11, you might get the impression that you are reading about a goddess. But that's not the case. The wisdom writers borrowed from neighboring cultures the idea of describing wisdom as a beautiful and eternal aspect of God. They exquisitely embodied the idea of wisdom in the figure of Lady Wisdom. Lady Wisdom comes from God. She was present at the Creation of the world, and she has a special understanding of the world and its workings. For the wisdom writers, Lady Wisdom was an aspect of God that wise people would want to pursue because she reveals the right ways to live and behave.

▶ Prv 8:1—9:11

24 So now, children, listen to me,†
be attentive to the words of my mouth!
25 Do not let your heart turn to her ways,
do not go astray in her paths;
26 For many are those she has struck down dead,
numerous, those she has slain.
27 Her house is a highway to Sheol,
leading down into the chambers of death.*

The Discourse of Wisdom†

8 1 Does not Wisdom call,
and Understanding raise her voice?*
2 On the top of the heights along the road,
at the crossroads she takes her stand;
3 By the gates at the approaches of the city,
in the entryways she cries aloud:
4 "To you, O people, I call;
my appeal is to you mortals.
5 You naive ones, gain prudence,
you fools,† gain sense.
6 Listen! for noble things I speak;
my lips proclaim honest words.
7† Indeed, my mouth utters truth,
and my lips abhor wickedness.
8 All the words of my mouth are sincere,
none of them wily or crooked;
9 All of them are straightforward to the intelligent,
and right to those who attain knowledge.
10 Take my instruction instead of silver,
and knowledge rather than choice gold.
11 [For Wisdom is better than corals,
and no treasures can compare with her.*]
12 I, Wisdom, dwell with prudence,
and useful knowledge I have.
13 [The fear of the LORD is hatred of evil;]
Pride, arrogance, the evil way,
and the perverse mouth I hate.*
14 Mine are counsel and advice;
Mine is strength; I am understanding.†
15 By me kings reign,
and rulers enact justice;
16 By me princes govern,
and nobles, all the judges of the earth.
17 Those who love me I also love,
and those who seek me find me.
18 With me are riches and honor,*
wealth that endures, and righteousness.
19 My fruit is better than gold, even pure gold,
and my yield than choice silver.*
20 On the way of righteousness I walk,
along the paths of justice,

† **7:24–27** The father addresses "children," a larger audience than his own son; the story is typical, intended for others as an example. The story is a foil to the speech of the other woman in chap. 8.

8:1–36 Chapter 8 is Wisdom's longest speech in the book. Wisdom is here personified as in 1:20–33. She exalts her grandeur and origin, and invites all (vv. 1–11) to be attentive to her salutary influence in human society (vv. 12–21), for she was privileged to be present at the creation of the world (vv. 22–31). Finally, she promises life and the favor of God to those who are devoted to her, death to those who reject her.

The poem has four sections, each (except the fourth) with two parts of five lines each:

I. A. vv. 1–5	B. vv. 6–10
II. A. vv. 12–16	B. vv. 17–21
III. A. vv. 22–26	B. vv. 27–31
IV. vv. 32–36	

Within chaps. 1–9, chap. 8 is the companion piece to Wisdom's first speech in 1:20–33. There she spoke harshly, giving a promise only in the last line; here she speaks invitingly, giving a threat only in the last line.

Chapter 8 is the best-known chapter in Proverbs and has profoundly influenced Jewish and Christian thought. The most explicit and lengthy biblical comment is in Sir 24; it too has thirty-five lines in seven five-line stanzas and develops the theme of Wisdom's intimacy with God and desire to be with human beings. The Gospel of John portrays Jesus in the language of wisdom in Proverbs: Jesus, like Wisdom, calls out to people to listen to him, promises to tell them the truth, seeks disciples, invites them to a banquet, and gives them life. Writers in the patristic period used the language of pre-existent wisdom to express the idea of the pre-existent Word with God.

8:5 *Naive ones . . . fools*: see note on 1:4.

8:7–8 The truth and sincerity of wisdom are absolute because they are of divine origin. They can neither deceive nor tolerate deception. The intelligent understand and accept this. "Straight" and "crooked" in Hebrew and English are metaphors for true, trustworthy and false, deceitful.

8:14 What is here predicated of Wisdom is elsewhere attributed to God (Jb 12:13–16).

7:27 Prv 2:18–19; 5:5.
8:1 Prv 1:20–21; 9:3.
8:11 Prv 3:15; Wis 7:8.
8:13 Prv 6:16–17; 16:5.
8:18 Prv 3:16.
8:19 Prv 3:14.

21 Granting wealth to those who love me,
and filling their treasuries.

22† "The LORD begot me, the beginning of his works,
the forerunner of his deeds of long ago;*
23 From of old I was formed,†
at the first, before the earth.*
24† When there were no deeps I was brought forth,
when there were no fountains or springs of water;
25 Before the mountains were settled into place,
before the hills, I was brought forth;
26 When the earth and the fields were not yet made,
nor the first clods of the world.
27 When he established the heavens, there was I,*
when he marked out the vault over the face of the deep;
28 When he made firm the skies above,
when he fixed fast the springs of the deep;
29 When he set for the sea its limit,
so that the waters should not transgress his command;
When he fixed the foundations of earth,
30 then was I beside him as artisan;†*
I was his delight day by day,
playing before him all the while,
31 Playing over the whole of his earth,
having my delight with human beings.
32† Now, children, listen to me;
happy are they who keep my ways.
33 Listen to instruction and grow wise,
do not reject it!
34 Happy the one who listens to me,
attending daily at my gates,
keeping watch at my doorposts;

Pray It!

The Gifts of Wisdom

To gain wisdom, you have to hunger for it, really want it, and actively seek it out. You will not find it by yourself: wisdom is found where other people are—"by the gates" where people meet (Prv 8:3).

Wisdom's gifts described in Proverbs, chapter 8, include prudence, insight, truth, knowledge, instruction or understanding, strength, and justice. Which of these gifts do you have? Which would you like to develop? Who could help you? Write a prayer to the Holy Spirit, asking for the strength and courage to seek out these gifts.

▶ **Prv 8:1–21**

35 For whoever finds me finds life,*
and wins favor from the LORD;
36 But those who pass me by do violence to themselves;
all who hate me love death."

The Two Women Invite Passersby to Their Banquets†

Woman Wisdom Issues Her Invitation

9 [1] Wisdom has built her house,†
she has set up her seven columns;

PRV

†

8:22–31 Wisdom is of divine origin. She is represented as existing before all things (vv. 22–26), when God planned and created the universe, adorning it with beauty and variety, and establishing its wonderful order (vv. 27–30). The purpose of the two cosmogonies (vv. 22–26 and 27–31) is to ground Wisdom's claims. The first cosmogony emphasizes that she was born before all else (and so deserving of honor) and the second underscores that she was with the Lord during the creation of the universe. The pre-existence of Woman Wisdom with God is developed in Sir 24 and in New Testament hymns to Christ, especially in Jn 1 and Col 1:15–20.

8:23 *Formed*: since the other verbs of the origin of Wisdom in these verses describe birth, it is likely that the somewhat uncertain verb is to be understood of birth as in Ps 139:13.

8:24–26 Perhaps the formless mass from which God created the heavens and the earth; cf. Gn 1:1–2; 2:4–6.

8:30 *Artisan*: the translation of the Hebrew word *'āmôn* has been controverted since antiquity. There have been three main opinions: (1) artisan; (2) trustworthy (friend); (3) ward, nursling. The most likely explanation is that *'āmôn* is artisan, related to Akkadian *ummânu*, legendary sages and heroes who brought divine gifts and culture to the human race. *I was his delight*: the chiastic or ABBA structure of vv. 30–31 unifies the four lines and underscores the analogy between Woman Wisdom's intimate relation to the Lord and her intimate relation to human beings, i.e., "delight" + "playing" parallels "playing" + "delight." She is God's friend and intimate and invites human beings to a similar relationship to God through her.

8:32–36 The final appeal of Woman Wisdom to her disciples is similar to the appeal of the father in 7:24–27.

9:1–6, 13–18 Wisdom and folly are represented as women, each inviting people to her banquet. Wisdom's banquet symbolizes joy and closeness to God. Unstable and senseless Folly furnishes stolen bread and water of deceit and vice that bring death to her guests. The opposition between wisdom and folly was stated at the beginning of chaps. 1–9 (folly in 1:8–19 and wisdom in 1:20–33) and is maintained throughout, down to this last chapter.

In comparable literature, gods might celebrate their sovereign by building a palace and inviting the other gods to come to a banquet and celebrate with them. Presumably, Woman Wisdom is celebrating her grandeur (just described in chap. 8); her grand house is a symbol of her status as the Lord's friend. In order to enter the sacred building and take part in the banquet ("eat of my food"), guests must leave aside their old ways ("forsake foolishness").

Verses 7–12 are unrelated to the two invitations to the banquet. They appear to be based on chap. 1, especially on 1:1–7, 22. The Greek version has added a number of verses after v. 12 and v. 18. In the confusion, 9:11 seems to have been displaced from its original position after 9:6. It has been restored to its original place in the text.

9:1 *House*: house has a symbolic meaning. Woman Wisdom

*

8:22 Wis 9:9; Sir 1:1; 24:9.
8:23 Sir 1:4.
8:27 Prv 3:19; Sir 24:4–5.
8:30 Wis 9:9.
8:35 Prv 3:13–18; 4:22.

2 She has prepared her meat, mixed her wine,
yes, she has spread her table.
3 She has sent out her maidservants; she calls†
from the heights out over the city:*
4 "Let whoever is naive turn in here;
to any who lack sense I say,
5 Come, eat of my food,
and drink of the wine I have mixed!
6 Forsake foolishness that you may live;†
advance in the way of understanding."

"The beginning of wisdom is fear of the LORD, and knowledge of the Holy One is understanding."
(Prv 9:10)

Miscellaneous Aphorisms

7 Whoever corrects the arrogant earns insults;
and whoever reproves the wicked incurs
opprobrium.
8 Do not reprove the arrogant, lest they hate you;
reprove the wise, and they will love you.*
9 Instruct the wise, and they become still wiser;
teach the just, and they advance in
learning.
10 The beginning of wisdom is fear of the LORD,
and knowledge of the Holy One is
understanding.*
11 For by me your days will be multiplied
and the years of your life increased.*
12 If you are wise, wisdom is to your advantage;
if you are arrogant, you alone shall bear it.

Woman Folly Issues Her Invitation

13† Woman Folly is raucous,*
utterly foolish; she knows nothing.
14 She sits at the door of her house
upon a seat on the city heights,
15 Calling to passersby
as they go on their way straight ahead:
16 "Let those who are naive turn in here,
to those who lack sense I say,
17 Stolen water is sweet,
and bread taken secretly is pleasing!"†
18 Little do they know that the shades are there,
that her guests are in the depths of Sheol!†

III. First Solomonic Collection of Sayings†

10 1 The Proverbs of Solomon:
A wise son gives his father joy,
but a foolish son is a grief to his mother.† *
2 Ill-gotten treasures profit nothing,
but justice saves from death.† *
3 The LORD does not let the just go hungry,
but the craving of the wicked he thwarts.†
4 The slack hand impoverishes,
but the busy hand brings riches.*
5 A son who gathers in summer is a credit;
a son who slumbers during harvest, a
disgrace.

†

encourages marital fidelity (2:16–19; 5; 6:20–35; 7), which builds up a household (cf. chap. 5). Some scholars propose that an actual seven-pillared house is referred to, but so far none have been unearthed by archaeologists. Seven may simply connote completeness—a great house.

Some scholars see a connection between the woman's house here and the woman's house in the final poem (31:10–31). In chap. 9, she invites the young man to enter her house and feast, i.e., to marry her. Chapter 31 shows what happens to the man who marries her; he has a house and enjoys "life" understood as consisting of a suitable wife, children, wealth, and honor.

9:3 *She calls*: i.e., invites; this is done indirectly through her maidservants, but the text could also mean that Wisdom herself publicly proclaims her invitation.

9:6 *That you may live*: life in Proverbs is this-worldly, consisting in fearing God or doing one's duty toward God, enjoying health and long life, possessing wealth, good reputation, and a family. Such a life cannot be attained without God's help. Hence Wisdom speaks not of life simply but of life with her; the guest is to live in Wisdom's house.

9:13–18 Woman Folly is the mirror image of Woman Wisdom. Both make identical invitations but only one of the offers is trustworthy. Their hearers must discern which is the true offer. She is depicted with traits of the adulterous woman in 2:16–19; chap. 5; 6:20–35; chap. 7. Woman Folly is restless (cf. 7:11), her path leads to the underworld (2:18; 5:5; 7:27), and she is ignorant (5:6). In this final scene, she appears in single combat with her great nemesis, Woman Wisdom. Though the invitations of the two women appear at first hearing to be the same, they differ profoundly. Wisdom demands that her guests reject their ignorance, whereas Woman Folly trades on their ignorance.

9:17 "Stolen water" seems to refer to adultery, for "water" in 5:15–17 refers to the wife's sexuality; "stolen" refers to stealing the sexuality belonging to another's household. "Secret" evokes the furtive meeting of the wife and the youth in chap. 7.

9:18 The banquet chamber of Folly is a tomb from which no one who enters it is released; cf. 7:27. *Shades*: the Rephaim, the inhabitants of the underworld.

10:1–22:16 The Proverbs of Solomon are a collection of three hundred and seventy-five proverbs on a wide variety of subjects. No overall arrangement is discernible, but there are many clusters of sayings related by vocabulary and theme. One thread running through the whole is the relationship of the "son," the disciple, to the parents, and its effect upon the house(hold). In chaps. 10–14 almost all the proverbs are antithetical; "the righteous" and "the wicked" (ethical), "the wise" and "the foolish" (sapiential), and "the devout, the pious" and "the irreverent" (religious). Chapters 15–22 have fewer sharp antitheses. The sayings are generally witty, often indirect, and are rich in irony and paradox.

10:1 The opening saying ties the whole collection to the first section, for "son," "father," and "mother" evoke the opening line of the first instruction, "Hear, my son, your father's instruction, and reject not your mother's teaching." The son is the subject of parental

*

9:3 Prv 8:1–2.
9:8 Sir 10:27.
9:10 Prv 1:7; Jb 28:28; Ps 111:10; Sir 1:16.
9:11 Prv 3:2; 16:4, 10; 10:27.
9:13–18 Prv 7:7–27.
10:1 Prv 1:1; 15:20; 17:25; 19:13; 25:1; 29:15.
10:2 Prv 11:4, 6.
10:4 Prv 6:11; 12:24; 13:4; 20:13; 28:19.

6 Blessings are for the head of the just;
but the mouth of the wicked conceals violence.†
7 The memory of the just serves as blessing,
but the name of the wicked will rot.†
8 A wise heart accepts commands,
but a babbling fool will be overthrown.†
9 Whoever walks honestly walks securely,
but one whose ways are crooked will fare badly.
10 One who winks at a fault causes trouble,
but one who frankly reproves promotes peace.
11 The mouth of the just is a fountain of life,
but the mouth of the wicked conceals violence.
12 Hatred stirs up disputes,
* but love covers all offenses.†
13 On the lips of the intelligent is found wisdom,
but a rod for the back of one without sense.†
14 The wise store up knowledge,
but the mouth of a fool is imminent ruin.
15 The wealth of the rich is their strong city;
the ruin of the poor is their poverty.†
16 The labor of the just leads to life,
the gains of the wicked, to futility.†*
17 Whoever follows instruction is in the path to life,
but whoever disregards reproof goes astray.*
18 Whoever conceals hatred has lying lips,
and whoever spreads slander is a fool.
19 Where words are many, sin is not wanting;
but those who restrain their lips do well.*
20 Choice silver is the tongue of the just;
the heart of the wicked is of little worth.
21 The lips of the just nourish many,
but fools die for want of sense.†

Did You Know?

Live Justly

In Proverbs, chapter 10, we are given a list of the benefits of being a just person. In this chapter, a just person is one who is fair, right, moral, honest, and truthful. We read that a just person not only receives blessings, life, wisdom, and joy; he or she, by acting justly, also fulfills God's will.

Throughout the New Testament, Jesus tells his followers that his way is the just way. The parables of the good Samaritan (see Lk 10:29–37) and the unforgiving servant (see Mt 18:21–35) are reminders of this. Living as a just person may not be easy, but it is what Christ asks of his followers.

▶ **Proverbs, chapter 10**

22 It is the LORD's blessing that brings wealth,*
and no effort can substitute for it.†
23 Crime is the entertainment of the fool;
but wisdom is for the person of understanding.
24 What the wicked fear will befall them,
but the desire of the just will be granted.
25 When the tempest passes, the wicked are no more;
but the just are established forever.
26 As vinegar to the teeth, and smoke to the eyes,

† exhortation throughout chaps. 1–9. This is the first of many sayings on domestic happiness or unhappiness, between parents and children (e.g., 15:20; 17:21) and between husband and wife (e.g., 12:4; 14:1). Founding or maintaining a household is an important metaphor in the book.

Adult children represented the family (headed by the oldest married male) to the outside world. Foolishness, i.e., malicious ignorance, brought dishonor to the parents and the family.

10:2 *Death*: untimely, premature, or sorrowful. The word "death" can have other overtones (see Wis 1:15).

10:3 The last of the three introductory sayings in the collection, which emphasize, respectively, the sapiential (v. 1), ethical (v. 2), and religious (v. 3) dimensions of wisdom. In this saying, God will not allow the appetite of the righteous to go unfulfilled. The appetite of hunger is singled out; it stands for all the appetites.

10:6 This saying, like several others in the chapter, plays on the different senses of the verb "to cover." As in English, "to cover" can mean to fill (as in Is 60:2) and to conceal (as in Jb 16:18). Colon B can be read either "violence *fills* the mouth (= head) of the wicked" or "the mouth of the wicked *conceals* violence." The ambiguity is intentional; the proverb is meant to be read both ways.

10:7 The name of the righteous continues to be used after their death in blessings such as "May you be as blessed as Abraham," but the wicked, being enemies of God, do not live on in anyone's memory. Their names rot with their bodies.

10:8 The wise take in instruction from their teachers but those who expel or pour out folly through their words will themselves be expelled.

10:12 *Love covers all offenses*: a favorite maxim in the New Testament; cf. 1 Cor 13:7; Jas 5:20; 1 Pt 4:8. Cf. also Prv 17:9.

10:13 An unusual juxtaposition of "lips" and "back." Those who have no wisdom on their lips (words) are fated to feel a punishing rod on their back.

10:15 An observation rather than a moral evaluation of wealth and poverty; but cf. 18:10–11.

10:16 Wages are a metaphor for reward and punishment. The Hebrew word does not mean "sin" here but falling short, a meaning that is frequent in Proverbs. Cf. Rom 6:1: "But what profit did you get then from the things of which you are now ashamed? For the end of those things is death."

10:21 The wise by their words maintain others in life whereas the foolish cannot keep themselves from sin that leads to premature death.

10:22 Human industry is futile without divine approval; cf. Ps 127:1–2; Mt 6:25–34.

10:12 1 Cor 13:4–7; 1 Pt 4:8.
10:16 Prv 11:18–19.
10:17 Prv 15:10.
10:19 Prv 17:27; Sir 20:17; Jas 1:19.
10:22 Sir 11:22.

Live It!

Nothing But the Truth

Do you swear to tell the truth, the whole truth, and nothing but the truth, so help you God? We have all heard these words. They are asked of every witness about to testify in a courtroom. In addition to responding positively to this crucial question, witnesses are called to place a hand on the Bible. All of this is to try to ensure that they will be honest. But despite this oath, some witnesses lie. We call that crime perjury, and it carries a severe penalty because someone's innocence or guilt may be hanging on the sworn testimony.

Proverbs 10:18 tells us, "Whoever conceals hatred has lying lips." Just as dishonesty is an act of hatred, so is honesty an act of love. Ultimately, our lies end up hurting others and damaging our integrity. Whether in the courtroom or in everyday life, we must always strive to tell "the truth, the whole truth, and nothing but the truth."

▶ Prv 10:18–21

PRV

are sluggards to those who send them.
27 Fear of the LORD prolongs life,
but the years of the wicked are cut short.*
28 The hope of the just brings joy,
but the expectation of the wicked perishes.†
29 The LORD is a stronghold to those who walk honestly,
downfall for evildoers.
30 The just will never be disturbed,
but the wicked will not abide in the land.
31 The mouth of the just yields wisdom,
but the perverse tongue will be cut off.
32 The lips of the just know favor,
but the mouth of the wicked, perversion.†

11 1 False scales are an abomination to the LORD,
but an honest weight, his delight.† *
2 When pride comes, disgrace comes;
but with the humble is wisdom.†
3 The honesty of the upright guides them;
the faithless are ruined by their duplicity.
4 Wealth is useless on a day of wrath,† *
but justice saves from death.
5 The justice of the honest makes their way straight,
but by their wickedness the wicked fall.† *
6 The justice of the upright saves them,
but the faithless are caught in their own intrigue.
7 When a person dies, hope is destroyed;*
expectation pinned on wealth is destroyed.†
8 The just are rescued from a tight spot,
but the wicked fall into it instead.
9 By a word the impious ruin their neighbors,*
but through their knowledge the just are rescued.†
10 When the just prosper, the city rejoices;*
when the wicked perish, there is jubilation.
11 Through the blessing of the upright the city is exalted,
but through the mouth of the wicked it is overthrown.
12 Whoever reviles a neighbor lacks sense,
but the intelligent keep silent.
13 One who slanders reveals secrets,*
but a trustworthy person keeps a confidence.
14 For lack of guidance a people falls;
security lies in many counselors.*

†

10:28 The thought is elliptical. Joy comes from fulfillment of one's plans, which the righteous can count on. The opposite of joy thus is not sadness but unfulfillment ("perishes").

10:32 The word used for "favor" is favor shown by an authority (God or the king), not favor shown by a peer. A righteous person's words create a climate of favor and acceptance, whereas crooked words will not gain acceptance. In Hebrew as in English, straight and crooked are metaphors for good and wicked.

11:1 The word pair "abomination" and "delight" (= acceptable) to God is common in Proverbs. Originally the language of ritual, the words came to be applied to whatever pleases or displeases God (cf. also 11:20). False weights were a constant problem even though weights were standardized. Cf. 20:23; Hos 12:8; Am 8:5.

11:2 Disgrace is the very opposite of what the proud so ardently want. Those who do not demand their due receive wisdom.

11:4 Cf. note on 10:2. A day of wrath is an unforeseen disaster (even death). Only one's relationship to God, which makes one righteous, is of any help on such a day.

11:5 In Hebrew as in English, "way" means the course of one's life; similarly, "straight" and "crooked" are metaphors for morally straightforward and for bad, deviant, perverted.

11:7 An ancient scribe added "wicked" to person in colon A, for the statement that hope ends at death seemed to deny life after death. The saying, however, is not concerned with life after death but with the fact that in the face of death all hopes based on one's own resources are vain. The aphorism is the climax of the preceding six verses; human resources cannot overcome mortality (cf. Ps 49:13).

11:9 What the wicked express harms others; what the righteous leave unsaid protects. Verses 9–14 are related in theme: the effect of good and bad people, especially their words, on their community.

*

10:27 Prv 3:2; 4:10; 9:11; 14:27.
11:1 Prv 16:11; 20:10; Lv 19:35–36.
11:4 Prv 10:2.
11:5 Prv 28:18.
11:7 Prv 10:28; Wis 3:18.
11:9 Prv 29:5.
11:10 Prv 28:12; 29:2.
11:13 Prv 20:19.

15 Harm will come to anyone going surety for
another,*
but whoever hates giving pledges is secure.†
16 A gracious woman gains esteem,
and ruthless men gain wealth.†
17 Kindly people benefit themselves,
but the merciless harm themselves.
18 The wicked make empty profits,
but those who sow justice have a sure
reward.*
19 Justice leads toward life,
but pursuit of evil, toward death.
20 The crooked in heart are an abomination to
the LORD,
but those who walk blamelessly are his
delight.†
21 Be assured, the wicked shall not go
unpunished,
but the offspring of the just shall escape.
22 Like a golden ring in a swine's snout
is a beautiful woman without judgment.†
23 The desire of the just ends only in good;
the expectation of the wicked is wrath.
24 One person is lavish yet grows still richer;
another is too sparing, yet is the poorer.†
25 Whoever confers benefits will be amply
enriched,
and whoever refreshes others will be
refreshed.
26 Whoever hoards grain, the people curse,
but blessings are on the head of one who
distributes it!
27 Those who seek the good seek favor,
but those who pursue evil will have evil
come upon them.†
28 Those who trust in their riches will fall,
but like green leaves the just will flourish.*
29 Those who trouble their household inherit
the wind,
and fools become slaves to the wise of heart.

Pray It!

Gossip

Oh, God, forgive me!
I gossiped about someone's family today.
I don't even know if what I said was true.
But it made me feel important to tell it to my friends.
Help me keep my mouth shut!
When someone tells me a secret, seal it into my heart,
and keep it away from my lips!
Gossip can seem like fun, but it hurts people.
I can't stop thinking about how the target of my gossip would feel
if she or he knew what I said about the family.
Oh, God, teach me to be trustworthy!
Amen.

▶ Prv 11:13

30 The fruit of justice is a tree of life,
and one who takes lives is a sage.†
31 If the just are recompensed on the earth,
how much more the wicked and the
sinner!†*

12 1 Whoever loves discipline loves knowledge,
but whoever hates reproof is stupid.†*
2 A good person wins favor from the LORD,
but the schemer he condemns.†
3 No one is made secure by wickedness,

† **11:15** Proverbs is opposed to providing surety for another's loan (see note on 6:1–5) and expresses this view throughout the book.

11:16 Wealth and esteem are good things in Proverbs, but the means for acquiring them are flawed. As precious gifts, they must be granted, not taken. The esteem of others that depends on beauty is as fleeting as beauty itself (cf. 31:30) and the wealth acquired by aggressive behavior lasts only as long as one has physical strength.

11:20 The terminology of ritual (acceptable and unacceptable sacrifice, "abomination" and "delight") is applied to human conduct as in v. 1. The whole of human life is under divine scrutiny, not just ritual.

11:22 Ear and nose rings were common jewelry for women. A humorous saying on the priority of wisdom over beauty in choosing a wife.

11:24 A paradox: spending leads to more wealth.

11:27 The saying is about seeking one thing and finding another. Striving for good leads to acceptance by God; seeking evil means only that trouble will come. The same Hebrew word means evil and trouble.

11:30 Most translations emend Hebrew "wise person" in colon B on the basis of the Greek and Syriac translations to "violence" (similar in spelling), because the verb "to take a life" is a Hebrew idiom for "to kill" (as also in English). The emendation is unnecessary, however, for the saying deliberately plays on the odd meaning: the one who takes lives is not the violent but the wise person, for the wise have a profound influence upon life. There is a similar wordplay in 29:10.

11:31 The saying is not about life after death; "on the earth" means life in the present world. The meaning is that divine judgment is exercised on all human action, even the best. The thought should strike terror into the hearts of habitual wrongdoers.

12:1 Discipline in Proverbs is both doctrine and training. The path to wisdom includes obedience to teachers and parents, acceptance of the community's traditions.

12:2 The antithesis is between the good person who, by reason of that goodness, already has divine acceptance, and the wicked person who, despite great effort, gains only condemnation.

* **11:14** Prv 15:22; 20:18; 24:6.
11:15 Prv 6:1–2.
11:18 Prv 10:16.
11:28 Ps 52:9–10.
11:31 1 Pt 4:18.
12:1 Prv 15:5, 10; Sir 21:6.

but the root of the just will never be
disturbed.†
4 A woman of worth is the crown of her
husband,*
but a disgraceful one is like rot in his
bones.†
5 The plans of the just are right;
the designs of the wicked are deceit.†
6 The words of the wicked are a deadly ambush,
but the speech of the upright saves them.†
7 Overthrow the wicked and they are no more,
but the house of the just stands firm.
8 For their good sense people are praised,
but the perverse of heart are despised.†
9 Better to be slighted and have a servant
than put on airs and lack bread.*
10 The just take care of their livestock,
but the compassion of the wicked is cruel.†
11 Those who till their own land have food in
plenty,
but those who engage in idle pursuits lack
sense.†*
12 A wicked person desires the catch of evil
people,
but the root of the righteous will bear fruit.†
13 By the sin of their lips the wicked are ensnared,
but the just escape from a tight spot.
14 From the fruit of their mouths people have
their fill of good,*
and the works of their hands come back
upon them.†
15 The way of fools is right in their own eyes,
but those who listen to advice are the wise.
16 Fools immediately show their anger,
but the shrewd conceal contempt.
17 Whoever speaks honestly testifies truly,
but the deceitful make lying witnesses.†*
18 The babble of some people is like sword
thrusts,
but the tongue of the wise is healing.
19 Truthful lips endure forever,
the lying tongue, for only a moment.†
20 Deceit is in the heart of those who plot evil,
but those who counsel peace have joy.
21 No harm befalls the just,
but the wicked are overwhelmed with
misfortune.
22 Lying lips are an abomination to the LORD,*
but those who are truthful, his delight.
23 The shrewd conceal knowledge,
but the hearts of fools proclaim folly.†
24 The diligent hand will govern,
but sloth makes for forced labor.*
25 Worry weighs down the heart,
but a kind word gives it joy.*
26 The just act as guides to their neighbors,
but the way of the wicked leads them astray.
27 Sloth does not catch its prey,
but the wealth of the diligent is splendid.
28 In the path of justice is life,
but the way of abomination leads to death.

13 1 A wise son loves correction,
but the scoffer heeds no rebuke.†
2 From the fruit of the mouth one enjoys good
things,*
but from the throat of the treacherous
comes violence.†
3 Those who guard their mouths preserve
themselves;†

P R V

† **12:3** Human beings are described as "made secure" in Jb 21:8; Ps 101:7; 102:29. "Root" in the context means enduring to succeeding generations, as in Mal 3:19 and Jb 8:17.

12:4 In Proverbs a crown is the result and sign of wise conduct. A good wife is a public sign of the husband's shrewd judgment and divine blessing (crown), whereas a bad wife brings him inner pain (rot in the bones).

12:5 The opposite of "just" is not injustice but "deceit." The wicked will be deceived in their plans in the sense that their planning will not succeed.

12:6 Words are a favorite theme of Proverbs. The words of the wicked effect harm to others whereas the words of the righteous protect themselves.

12:8 The heart, the seat of intelligence, will eventually be revealed in the actions that people do, either for praise or for blame.

12:10 The righteous are sympathetically aware of the needs of their livestock and prosper from their herd's good health. The wicked will pay the price for their self-centeredness and cruelty.

12:11 The second line clarifies the first: idleness will give one plenty of nothing. "Lacking sense" is a common phrase for fools.

12:12 A difficult, possibly corrupt saying, but there is no good alternative to the Hebrew text. The wicked desire what the malevolent have captured or killed, but their actions will go for naught because they invite punishment. The righteous, on the other hand, will bear fruit.

12:14 The saying contrasts words and deeds. "Fruit" here is not what one normally eats, as in 1:31; 8:19; 31:16, 31, but the consequences of one's actions. In the second line the things that issue from one's hands (one's deeds) come back to one in recompense or punishment. Prv 13:2a and 18:20 are variants. Cf. Mt 7:17; Gal 6:8.

12:17 What is the rule of thumb for judging legal testimony? Look to the ordinary conduct and daily speech of a witness.

12:19 The saying has a double meaning: lies are quickly found out whereas truthful statements endure; truth-tellers, being favored by God, live long lives, whereas liars invite punishment.

12:23 "Knowledge" here is "what one knows, has in one's heart," not knowledge in general. Fools reveal all they have stored in their heart and it naturally turns out to be folly. Revealing and concealing are constant themes in Proverbs.

13:1 Another in the series on the household, this one on the relation of parents and children. See under 10:1. The scoffer in Proverbs condemns discipline and thus can never become wise. Wise adult children advertise to the community what they received from their parents, for children become wise through a dialectical process involving the parents. A foolish adult child witnesses to foolish parents.

13:2 One's mouth normally eats food from outside, but in the moral life, things are reversed: one eats from the fruit of one's mouth, i.e., one experiences the consequences of one's own actions. Since the mouth of the treacherous is filled with violence, one must assume that they will some day endure violence.

13:3 *Preserve themselves*: in Hebrew, literally to preserve the throat area, the moist breathing center of one's body, thus "life,"

* **12:4** Prv 31:10; Sir 21:1, 16.
12:9 Sir 10:26.
12:11 Prv 28:19; Sir 20:27.
12:14 Prv 13:2; 18:20.
12:17 Prv 14:5.
12:22 Prv 6:17.
12:24 Prv 10:4; 13:4.
12:25 Prv 15:13; 17:22.
13:2 Prv 12:14; 18:20.
13:3 Prv 18:7; 21:23.

those who open wide their lips bring ruin.*
4 The appetite of the sluggard craves but has
nothing,
but the appetite of the diligent is amply
satisfied.
5 The just hate deceitful words,
but the wicked are odious and disgraceful.
6 Justice guards one who walks honestly,
but sin leads the wicked astray.*
7 One acts rich but has nothing;
another acts poor but has great wealth.†
8 People's riches serve as ransom for their lives,
but the poor do not even hear a threat.†
9 The light of the just gives joy,
but the lamp† of the wicked goes out.*
10 The stupid sow discord by their insolence,
but wisdom is with those who take counsel.
11 Wealth won quickly dwindles away,
but gathered little by little, it grows.*
12 Hope deferred makes the heart sick,
but a wish fulfilled is a tree of life.†
13 Whoever despises the word must pay for it,†
but whoever reveres the command will be
rewarded.
14 The teaching of the wise is a fountain of life,
turning one from the snares of death.
15 Good sense brings favor,
but the way of the faithless is their ruin.†
16 The shrewd always act prudently
but the foolish parade folly.†
17 A wicked messenger brings on disaster,
but a trustworthy envoy is a healing remedy.
18 Poverty and shame befall those who let go of
discipline,
but those who hold on to reproof receive
honor.†
19 Desire fulfilled delights the soul,
but turning from evil is an abomination to
fools.
20 Walk with the wise and you become wise,
but the companion of fools fares badly.*
21 Misfortune pursues sinners,
but the just shall be recompensed with good.
22 The good leave an inheritance to their
children's children,
but the wealth of the sinner is stored up for
the just.

Live It!

Break the Cycle of Hopelessness

The story is all too frequent in many urban areas today. . . . A young man joins a gang, thinking that he has finally found a place to belong and that his new "family" will do anything for him. The gang offers many things he doesn't find at home or in school. He spends a great deal of time with his new friends, and before long, they encourage him to do things he doesn't feel comfortable doing. His fellow gang members are able to sell what he has stolen, the money is good, and the gang enjoys freely spending it. The young man, however, ends up in prison, serving time for armed robbery.

Proverbs 13:11 tells us that quick wealth doesn't last. Verse 20 goes further, saying that the companion of fools will not do well in life. For many youth in detention centers or prisons, this story sounds familiar. This proverb offers wisdom that they and many others—maybe we too—need to hear.

In the absence of caring adults, healthy role models, and detention center ministers, the cycle of hopelessness is free to continue and often results in stories like this one. Find out how your parish or youth group can help at-risk youth, young people in prison, or anyone suffering from a lack of real hope. Help them break the cycle of hopelessness.

▶ **Prv 13:11–20**

† "soul," or "self." There is wordplay: if you guard your mouth (= words) you guard your "soul." Fools, on the other hand, do not guard but open their lips and disaster strikes. A near duplicate is 21:23.

13:7 Appearances can be deceiving; possessions do not always reveal the true state of a person.

13:8 Related to v. 7. Possessions enable the wealthy to pay ransom but the poor are "protected" by lack of possessions: they never hear the threat of the pursuer. Cf. the use of the word "threat" in Is 30:17.

13:9 *Light. . . lamp*: symbols of life and prosperity; cf. 4:18–19.

13:12 "Tree of life" occurs in Gn 2–3, Prv 3:18; 11:30; 13:12; 15:4, and Rev 2:7; 22:2, 14, 19. It provides food and healing.

13:13 *Must pay for it*: lit., "is pledge to it," i.e., just as one who has pledged or provided surety for another's loan is obligated to that pledge, so one is not free of a command until one performs it.

13:15 As the behavior of the wise wins them favor that increases their prosperity, like Abigail with David in 1 Sm 25, so the way (= conduct) of the faithless ruins their lives.

13:16 Like 12:23 and 15:2, 3, the saying is about revealing and concealing. The wise reveal their wisdom in their actions whereas fools "parade," spread out their folly for all to see. The verb is used of vendors spreading their wares and of birds spreading their wings.

13:18 The saying plays on letting go and holding on. Wisdom consists in not rejecting discipline and being open to the comments of others, even if they are reproving comments.

13:6 Prv 11:3, 5–6.
13:9 Prv 24:20.
13:11 Prv 28:20, 22.
13:20 Sir 6:34; 8:8, 17.

23 The tillage of the poor yields abundant food,
but possessions are swept away for lack of justice.†
24 Whoever spares the rod hates the child,
but whoever loves will apply discipline.*
25 When the just eat, their hunger is appeased;
but the belly of the wicked suffers want.

14 [1] Wisdom builds her house,
but Folly tears hers down with her own hands.†
2 Those who walk uprightly fear the LORD,
but those who are devious in their ways spurn him.
3 In the mouth of the fool is a rod for pride,
but the lips of the wise preserve them.
4 Where there are no oxen, the crib is clean;
but abundant crops come through the strength of the bull.†
5 A trustworthy witness does not lie,
but one who spouts lies makes a lying witness.† *
6 The scoffer seeks wisdom in vain,
but knowledge is easy for the intelligent.
7 Go from the face of the fool;
you get no knowledge from such lips.
8 The wisdom of the shrewd enlightens their way,
but the folly of fools is deceit.†
9 The wicked scorn a guilt offering,
but the upright find acceptance.
10 The heart knows its own bitterness,
and its joy no stranger shares.†
11 The house of the wicked will be destroyed,
but the tent of the upright will flourish.† *
12 Sometimes a way seems right,
but the end of it leads to death!*
13 Even in laughter the heart may be sad,
and the end of joy may be sorrow.
14 From their own ways turncoats are sated,
from their own actions, the loyal.
15 The naive believe everything,
but the shrewd watch their steps.†
16 The wise person is cautious and turns from evil;
the fool is reckless and gets embroiled.
17 The quick-tempered make fools of themselves,
and schemers are hated.
18 The simple have folly as an adornment,
but the shrewd wear knowledge as a crown.†
19 The malicious bow down before the good,
and the wicked, at the gates of the just.
20 Even by their neighbors the poor are despised,
but a rich person's friends are many.*
21 Whoever despises the hungry comes up short,
but happy the one who is kind to the poor!†
22 Do not those who plan evil go astray?
But those who plan good win steadfast loyalty.
23 In all labor there is profit,
but mere talk tends only to loss.
24 The crown of the wise is wealth;
the diadem of fools is folly.
25 The truthful witness saves lives,
but whoever utters lies is a betrayer.
26 The fear of the LORD is a strong defense,
a refuge even for one's children.
27 The fear of the LORD is a fountain of life,
turning one from the snares of death.
28 A multitude of subjects is the glory of the king;
but if his people are few, a prince is ruined.
29 Long-suffering results in great wisdom;
a short temper raises folly high.† *
30 A tranquil mind gives life to the body,
but jealousy rots the bones.
31 Those who oppress the poor revile their Maker,
but those who are kind to the needy honor him.*
32 The wicked are overthrown by their wickedness,
but the just find a refuge in their integrity.
33 Wisdom can remain silent in the discerning heart,

†

13:23 An observation on the poor. The lands of the poor are as fertile as anyone's, for nature does not discriminate against them. Their problem is lack of justice, which puts their harvest at risk from unscrupulous human beings.

14:1 The relationship between Wisdom, personified as a woman, and building a house is a constant theme. As elsewhere, the book here warns against the wrong woman and praises the right woman.

14:4 If one has no animals, one does not have the burden of keeping the crib full, but without them one will have no crops to fill the barn. Colon B reverses the sense of colon A and also reverses the consonants of *bar* ("clean") to *rab* ("abundant").

14:5 On discerning the truthfulness of witnesses; see 12:17.

14:8 Wisdom enables the shrewd to know their path is right but folly leads fools on the wrong path ("deceit"), which calls down retribution.

14:10 The heart in Proverbs is where a person's sense impressions are stored and reflected upon. It is thus one's most personal and individual part. One's sorrows and joys (= the full range of emotions) cannot be shared fully with another. Verse 13 expresses the same individuality of the human person.

14:11 The traditional fixed pair "house" and "tent" is used to express the paradox that a house can be less secure than a tent if there is no justice.

14:15 The naive gullibly rely on others' words whereas the shrewd watch their own steps.

14:18 The inner quality of a person, simple or wise, will eventually be revealed.

14:21 The paradox is that anyone who spurns the hungry will lack something, but anyone who shows mercy (presumably by giving to the poor) will gain prosperity.

14:29 A series of puns on short and long; lit., "long of nostrils (idiom for "patient"), large in wisdom, / short in breath (idiom for "impatient"), makes folly tall."

*

13:24 Prv 19:18; 22:15; 23:13–14; 29:15; Sir 30:1, 8–13.
14:5 Prv 12:17.
14:11 Prv 3:33; 12:7; 15:25.
14:12 Prv 16:25.
14:20 Prv 19:4, 7; Sir 6:8, 12.
14:29 Prv 16:32; 19:11; Jas 1:19.
14:31 Prv 17:5.

PRV

but among fools she must make herself
known.† *
34 Justice exalts a nation,
but sin is a people's disgrace.†
35 The king favors the skillful servant,
but the shameless one incurs his wrath.

15 1† A mild answer turns back wrath,*
but a harsh word stirs up anger.†
2 The tongue of the wise pours out knowledge,
but the mouth of fools spews folly.
3 The eyes of the LORD are in every place,
keeping watch on the evil and the good.
4 A soothing tongue is a tree of life,
but a perverse one breaks the spirit.
5 The fool spurns a father's instruction,
but whoever heeds reproof is prudent.† *
6 In the house of the just there are ample
resources,
but the harvest of the wicked is in peril.
7 The lips of the wise spread knowledge,
but the heart of fools is not steadfast.†
8 The sacrifice of the wicked is an abomination
to the LORD,*
but the prayer of the upright is his delight.
9 The way of the wicked is an abomination to
the LORD,
but he loves one who pursues justice.*
10 Discipline seems bad to those going astray;
one who hates reproof will die.†
11 Sheol and Abaddon† lie open before the
LORD;
how much more the hearts of mortals!
12 Scoffers do not love reproof;
to the wise they will not go.
13 A glad heart lights up the face,
but an anguished heart breaks the spirit.*
14 The discerning heart seeks knowledge,
but the mouth of fools feeds on folly.†
15 All the days of the poor are evil,
but a good heart is a continual feast.†
16† Better a little with fear of the LORD
than a great fortune with anxiety.
17 Better a dish of herbs where love is
than a fatted ox and hatred with it.
18 The ill-tempered stir up strife,*
but the patient settle disputes.
19 The way of the sluggard is like a thorn hedge,
but the path of the diligent is a highway.
20 A wise son gives his father joy,
but a fool despises his mother.*
21 Folly is joy† to the senseless,
but the person of understanding goes the
straight way.
22 Plans fail when there is no counsel,
but they succeed when advisers are
many.† *
23 One has joy from an apt response;
a word in season, how good it is!† *
24 The path of life leads upward for the prudent,
turning them from Sheol below.†
25 The LORD pulls down the house of the proud,
but preserves intact the widow's landmark.
26 The schemes of the wicked are an
abomination to the LORD,*
but gracious words are pure.†
27 The greedy tear down their own house,
but those who hate bribes will live.†
28 The heart of the just ponders a response,
but the mouth of the wicked spews evil.

†

14:33 Wisdom can remain silent in a wise person as a welcome friend. But it must speak out among fools, for the dissonance is so strong.

14:34 The rare noun "disgrace" occurs elsewhere only in Lv 20:17. In measuring the greatness of a nation, one is tempted to consider territory, wealth, history, but the most important criterion is its relationship to God ("justice").

15:1–7 These verses form a section beginning and ending with the topic of words.

15:1 Paradoxically, where words are concerned soft is powerful and hard is ineffective.

15:5 One becomes wise by keeping and foolish by rejecting. One must accept the tradition of the community.

15:7 "Lips" and "heart" are a fixed pair, in Proverbs signifying, respectively, expression and source. The wise disseminate what they have in their heart, but the wicked are unsound even in the source of their words, their hearts.

15:10 Discipline, always a good thing in Proverbs, seems bad to those deliberately wandering from justice.

15:11 *Sheol and Abaddon*: terms for the abode of the dead, signifying the profound obscurity which is open nevertheless to the sight and power of God; cf. 27:20.

15:14 The contrasts include heart (organ of reflection) and mouth (organ of expression), and the wise and fools. One type feeds its mind with wisdom and the other feeds its face with folly.

15:15 Good heart does not refer to good intentions but to an instructed mind. Wisdom makes poverty not only bearable but even joyful like the joy of feast days.

15:16–17 The sages favor wealth over poverty—but not at any price; cf. Ps 37:16.

15:21 The word "joy" occurs in the first line of vv. 20, 21, and 23. The state of folly is joy to a fool but the wise person is totally absorbed in keeping on the right or straight road.

15:22 Failure to consult makes it likely a plan will not succeed. The point is nicely made by contrasting the singular number in the first line ("no counsel") with the plural number in the second line ("many advisors").

15:23 Conversation is the art of saying the right thing at the right time. It gives pleasure to speaker and hearer alike.

15:24 Death is personified as Sheol, the underworld. "Up" and "down" in Hebrew as in English are metaphors for success and failure (see Dt 28:43). One who stays on the path of life need not fear the punishment that stalks sinners.

15:26 "Pure" here means acceptable. The language of ritual (acceptable or pure) is applied to ordinary human actions. "Gracious words" are words that bring peace to the neighbor.

15:27 The same lesson as the opening scene of Proverbs (1:8–19): one cannot build a house by unjust gain. Injustice will come back upon a house so built.

*

14:33 Prv 1:22; 8:1.
15:1 Prv 25:15; Sir 6:5.
15:5 Prv 12:1; 13:18.
15:8 Prv 21:27; Eccl 4:17; Is 1:11–15.
15:9 Prv 11:20; 21:21.
15:13 Prv 12:25; 17:22; Sir 30:22.
15:18 Prv 6:21; 29:22; Sir 28:11.
15:20 Prv 10:1; 29:3.
15:22 Prv 11:14.
15:23 Prv 25:11; Sir 20:6.
15:26 Prv 6:18.

Pray It!

Offering Your Day to God

Follow the advice of Proverbs 16:3 by starting each day with a prayer like this one:

Dearest Lord, today I offer you all my thoughts, deeds, and words. Let everything I do reflect your love and goodness. Amen.

▶ Prv 16:3

29 The LORD is far from the wicked,
but hears the prayer of the just.
30 A cheerful glance brings joy to the heart;
good news invigorates the bones.
31 The ear that listens to salutary reproof*
is at home among the wise.†
32 Those who disregard discipline hate
themselves,
but those who heed reproof acquire
understanding.
33 The fear of the LORD is training for wisdom,
and humility goes before honors.*

16 1 Plans are made in human hearts,
but from the LORD comes the tongue's
response.†
2 All one's ways are pure† in one's own eyes,
but the measurer of motives is the LORD.*
3 Entrust your works to the LORD,
and your plans will succeed.
4 The LORD has made everything for a purpose,
even the wicked for the evil day.†
5 Every proud heart† is an abomination to the
LORD;*
be assured that none will go unpunished.
6 By steadfast loyalty guilt is expiated,
and by the fear of the LORD evil is avoided.†
7 When the LORD is pleased with someone's ways,
he makes even enemies be at peace with
them.
8 Better a little with justice,
than a large income with injustice.
9 The human heart plans the way,
but the LORD directs the steps.†*
10 An oracle is upon the king's lips,
no judgment of his mouth is false.†
11 Balance and scales belong to the LORD;
every weight in the sack is his concern.*
12 Wrongdoing is an abomination to kings,
for by justice the throne endures.*
13 The king takes delight in honest lips,
and whoever speaks what is right he loves.*
14 The king's wrath is a messenger of death,*
but a wise person can pacify it.
15 A king's smile means life,
and his favor is like a rain cloud in spring.†
16 How much better to get wisdom than gold!
To get understanding is preferable to silver.†*
17 The path of the upright leads away from
misfortune;
those who attend to their way guard their
lives.†
18 Pride goes before disaster,
and a haughty spirit before a fall.
19 It is better to be humble with the poor
than to share plunder with the proud.*
20 Whoever ponders a matter will be successful;
happy the one who trusts in the LORD!
21 The wise of heart is esteemed for discernment,
and pleasing speech gains a reputation for
learning.
22 Good sense is a fountain of life to those who
have it,

†

15:31 To become wise, one must hear and integrate perspectives contrary to one's own, which means accepting "reproof." Wisdom does not isolate one but places one in the company of the wise.

16:1 Words, like actions, often produce results different from those which were planned, and this comes under the agency of God.

16:2 "Pure" in a moral sense for human action is found only in Job and Proverbs. As in v. 1, the contrast is between human intent and divine assessment.

16:4 Even the wicked do not lie outside God's plan.

16:5 *Proud heart*: lit., "high of heart." To forget one is a fallible human being is so basic an error that one cannot escape exposure and punishment.

16:6 As v. 5 used the language of worship to express what is acceptable or not to God, so this saying uses similar language to declare that lovingly loyal conduct undoes the effects of sin.

16:9 As in vv. 1–3, the antithesis is between human plans and divine disposal. The saying uses the familiar metaphor of path for the course of life.

16:10 Six sayings on the king and his divine authority begin here, following the series of sayings about the Lord's governance in 15:33–16:9, in which "LORD" was mentioned nine times.

16:15 The last of six sayings about the king. In the previous verse, royal wrath means death; in this verse royal favor means life. It is significant that royal favor is compared to something not under human control—the clouds preceding the spring rains.

16:16 The point of comparison is the superiority of the pursuit of wisdom and gold, not the relative merits of wealth and wisdom.

16:17 In the metaphor of the two ways, the way of the righteous is protected and the way of the wicked is unprotected. Since the path of the righteous leads therefore away from trouble, one's task is to stay on it, to "attend to" it.

*

15:31 Prv 25:12.
15:33 Prv 1:7; 19:12; Sir 1:24.
16:2 Prv 21:2.
16:5 Prv 6:16–17; 8:13.
16:9 Prv 19:21; 20:24; Jer 10:23.
16:11 Prv 11:1.
16:12 Prv 25:5.
16:13 Prv 14:35; 22:11.
16:14 Prv 19:12; 20:2.
16:16 Prv 8:10–11.
16:19 Prv 11:2.

but folly is the training of fools.
23 The heart of the wise makes for eloquent
speech,
and increases the learning on their lips.
24 Pleasing words are a honeycomb,
sweet to the taste and invigorating to the
bones.
25 Sometimes a way seems right,
but the end of it leads to death! *
26 The appetite of workers works for them,
for their mouths urge them on.† *
27 Scoundrels are a furnace of evil,
and their lips are like a scorching fire.
28 Perverse speech sows discord,
and talebearing separates bosom friends. *
29 The violent deceive their neighbors,
and lead them into a way that is not good.
30 Whoever winks an eye plans perversity;
whoever purses the lips does evil.†
31 Gray hair is a crown of glory; *
it is gained by a life that is just.
32 The patient are better than warriors,
and those who rule their temper, better
than the conqueror of a city. *
33 Into the bag the lot is cast,
but from the LORD comes every decision.†

17 1 Better a dry crust with quiet
than a house full of feasting with strife.†
2 A wise servant will rule over an unworthy son,
and will share the inheritance of the
children.†
3 The crucible for silver, and the furnace for gold,
but the tester of hearts is the LORD.
4 The evildoer gives heed to wicked lips,
the liar, to a mischievous tongue.
5 Whoever mocks the poor reviles their Maker;
whoever rejoices in their misfortune will
not go unpunished. *
6 Children's children are the crown of the elderly,
and the glory of children is their parentage.
7 Fine words ill fit a fool;
how much more lying lips, a noble!
8 A bribe seems a charm to its user;
at every turn it brings success.†
9 Whoever overlooks an offense fosters
friendship,
but whoever gossips about it separates
friends.†
10 A single reprimand does more for a discerning
person
than a hundred lashes for a fool.†
11 The wicked pursue only rebellion,
and a merciless messenger is sent against
them.†
12 Face a bear robbed of her cubs,
but never fools in their folly!†
13 If you return evil for good,
evil will not depart from your house.† *
14 The start of strife is like the opening of a dam;
check a quarrel before it bursts forth!
15 Whoever acquits the wicked, * whoever
condemns the just—
both are an abomination to the LORD.
16 Of what use is money in the hands of fools
when they have no heart to acquire
wisdom?†
17 A friend is a friend at all times,
and a brother is born for the time of
adversity. *
18 Those without sense give their hands in
pledge,
becoming surety for their neighbors. *
19 Those who love an offense love a fight; *
those who build their gate high† court
disaster.
20 The perverse in heart come to no good,
and the double-tongued fall into trouble.†

---

†

16:26 The adage puzzled ancient and modern commentators. The meaning seems to state the paradox that a person does not toil to feed the gullet but that the gullet itself "toils" in the sense that it forces the person to work. As often in Proverbs, the sense organ stands for the faculty by metonymy. Cf. Eccl 6:7.

16:30 A restless or twitching eye or lip betrays the condition of the heart (cf. 6:13).

16:33 Dice were given meanings of "yes" or "no" and then cast for their answer. What came out was the decision. Here the saying interprets the sequence of actions: a human being puts the dice in the bag but what emerges from the bag is the Lord's decision.

17:1 A "better than" saying, stating the circumstances when a dry crust is better than a banquet. Peace and fellowship give joy to a meal, not the richness of the food. For a similar thought, see 15:16 and 16:8.

17:2 Ability is esteemed more highly than ties of blood.

17:8 An observation on the effect of the bribe upon the bribe-giver: it gives an intoxicating feeling of power ("seems"). In v. 23 the evil effects of a bribe are noted.

17:9 A paradox. One finds (love, friend) by concealing (an offense), one loses (a friend) by revealing (a secret). In 10:12 love also covers over a multitude of offenses.

17:10 A wonderful comment on the openness and sensitivity of the wise and the foolish. One type learns from a single word and for the other one hundred blows are not enough.

17:11 The irony is that such people will meet up with what they so energetically pursue—in the form of an unrelenting emissary sent to them.

17:12 Humorous hyperbole. An outraged dangerous beast poses less danger than a fool.

17:13 The paradox is that to pay out evil for good means that the evil will never leave one's own house.

17:16 The exhortation to acquire or purchase wisdom is common in Proverbs. Fools misunderstand the metaphor, assuming they can buy it with money. Their very misunderstanding shows they have no "heart" = mind, understanding. Money in the hand is no good without such a "heart" to store it in.

17:19 *Build their gate high*: a symbol of arrogance.

17:20 The saying employs the familiar metaphors of walking =

---

*

16:25 Prv 14:12.
16:26 Prv 10:4.
16:28 Prv 6:14, 19; 17:9; 26:22; Sir 28:15.
16:31 Prv 20:29.
16:32 Prv 14:29.
17:5 Prv 14:31.
17:13 Mt 5:39; Rom 12:17; 1 Thes 5:15; 1 Pt 3:9.
17:15 Prv 24:24; Is 5:23.
17:17 Prv 18:24.
17:18 Prv 6:1–2; 11:15.
17:19 Prv 15:18.

Live It!

Be Proactive

"The start of strife is like the opening of a dam; / therefore, check a quarrel before it bursts forth!" (Prv 17:14). Have you ever noticed how people quickly congregate when a fight breaks out, especially at school? Many of the spectators seem to be in entertainment mode and are generally on one side or the other. Others want the fight to stop but lack the courage or confidence to break it up. Typically, everyone ends up waiting until someone in authority comes along to intervene or until one of the contenders is hurt and the fight stops.

A fight can begin so quickly—a word, a taunting phrase, a sudden turn and a punch. Some of us have a shorter fuse than others, a temper that flares easily, or an ego that won't allow us to walk away when provoked. To paraphrase the image used in Proverbs 17:14, once the water breaks through the dam, it is very hard to stop. If this sounds like you, then it's important to figure out ways to better control your responses and reactions. If we are always quick to react when provoked, then situations will soon escalate beyond our control. If we are proactive, however, and take time to think and reflect before making decisions, then we are much more likely to respond in ways that reflect the positive values that are at our core.

- How do you react when you see an argument or a fight? Are you reluctant to get involved?
- If you have a quick temper, what can you do to control it? How can you be more proactive?

▶ **Prv 17:14**

PRV

21 Whoever conceives a fool has grief;
the father of a numskull has no joy.
22 A joyful heart is the health of the body,
but a depressed spirit dries up the bones.*
23 A guilty person takes out a bribe from the pocket,
thus perverting the course of justice.†
24 On the countenance of a discerning person is wisdom,*
but the eyes of a fool are on the ends of the earth.†
25 A foolish son is vexation to his father,
and bitter sorrow to her who bore him.*
26 It is wrong to fine an innocent person,
but beyond reason to scourge nobles.
27 Those who spare their words are truly knowledgeable,
and those who are discreet are intelligent.*
28 Even fools, keeping silent, are considered wise;
if they keep their lips closed, intelligent.†

18 1 One who is alienated seeks a pretext,
with all persistence picks a quarrel.
2 Fools take no delight in understanding,
but only in displaying what they think.†
3 With wickedness comes contempt,
and with disgrace, scorn.
4 The words of one's mouth are deep waters,
the spring of wisdom, a running brook.† *
5 It is not good to favor the guilty,
nor to reject the claim of the just.*
6 The lips of fools walk into a fight,
and their mouths are asking for a beating.†
7 The mouths of fools are their ruin;
their lips are a deadly snare.*
8 The words of a talebearer are like dainty morsels:
they sink into one's inmost being.*
9 Those slack in their work
are kin to the destroyer.
10† The name of the LORD is a strong tower;
the just run to it and are safe.
11 The wealth of the rich is their strong city;*
they fancy it a high wall.
12 Before disaster the heart is haughty,*

---

† conducting oneself ("fall into trouble"), and of straight and crooked = right and wrong ("perverse," "double-tongued").

17:23 A sharp look at the sly withdrawing of a bribe from the pocket and a blunt judgment on its significance.

17:24 Wisdom is visible on the countenance (i.e., mouth, lips, tongue) of the wise person; its ultimate source is the heart. Fools have no such source of wisdom within them, a point that is nicely made by referring to the eye of the fool, roving over the landscape.

17:28 Related to v. 27. Words provide a glimpse into the heart. In the unlikely event that fools, who usually pour out words (15:2), were to say nothing, people would not be able to see their folly and would presume them intelligent. Alas, the saying is contrary to fact.

18:2 One grows in wisdom by listening to others, but fools take delight in expounding the contents of their minds.

18:4 Words express a person's thoughts ("deep waters"), which in turn become accessible to others. Cf. 20:5a.

18:6 The bold personification of lips and mouth is similar to Ps 73:9, "They set their mouths against the heavens, their tongues roam the earth." Careless words can lead one into serious trouble.

18:10–11 Contrast this judgment with the observation in 10:15.

17:22 Prv 12:25; 15:13.
17:24 Eccl 8:1.
17:25 Prv 10:1; 29:15.
17:27 Prv 10:19; Sir 1:21; Jas 1:19.
18:4 Prv 20:5; Jn 7:38.
18:5 Prv 24:23; 28:21.
18:7 Prv 10:14; 12:13; 13:3; Eccl 10:12.
18:8 Prv 26:22.
18:11 Prv 10:15.
18:12 Prv 11:2; 16:18; Sir 10:15.

but before honor is humility.
13 Whoever answers before listening,*
theirs is folly and shame.†
14 One's spirit supports one when ill,
but a broken spirit who can bear?†
15 The heart of the intelligent acquires knowledge,
and the ear of the wise seeks knowledge.†
16 Gifts clear the way for people,
winning access to the great.*
17 Those who plead the case first seem to be in the right;
then the opponent comes and cross-examines them.†
18 The lot puts an end to disputes,
and decides a controversy between the mighty.†
19 A brother offended is more unyielding than a stronghold;
such strife is more daunting than castle gates.†
20 With the fruit of one's mouth one's belly is filled,
with the produce of one's lips one is sated.† *
21 Death and life are in the power of the tongue;*
those who choose one shall eat its fruit.†
22 To find a wife is to find happiness,
a favor granted by the LORD.*
23 The poor implore,
but the rich answer harshly.
24 There are friends who bring ruin,
but there are true friends more loyal than a brother.*

19 1 Better to be poor and walk in integrity
than rich and crooked in one's ways.*
2 Desire without knowledge is not good;
and whoever acts hastily, blunders.†
3 Their own folly leads people astray;
in their hearts they rage against the LORD.†
4 Wealth adds many friends,
but the poor are left friendless.*
5 The false witness will not go unpunished,
and whoever utters lies will not escape.† *
6 Many curry favor with a noble;
everybody is a friend of a gift giver.
7 All the kin of the poor despise them;
how much more do their friends shun them!†
8 Those who gain sense truly love themselves;
those who preserve understanding will find success.†
9 The false witness will not go unpunished,
and whoever utters lies will perish.
10 Luxury is not befitting a fool;
much less should a slave rule over princes.
11 It is good sense to be slow to anger,
and an honor to overlook an offense.†
12 The king's wrath is like the roar of a lion,
but his favor, like dew on the grass.† *
13 The foolish son is ruin to his father,*
and a quarrelsome wife is water constantly dripping.†
14 Home and possessions are an inheritance from parents,
but a prudent wife is from the LORD.*
15 Laziness brings on deep sleep,
and the sluggard goes hungry.*
16 Those who keep commands keep their lives,

PRV

†

18:13 To speak without first listening is characteristic of a fool; cf. 10:14; Sir 11:8.

18:14 The paradox is that something as slight as a column of air offers protection against the encroachment of death. If it is stilled, nothing, no matter how powerful, can substitute for it.

18:15 "Knowledge" here refers to what one knows, not knowledge in itself. The mind acquires and stores it, the ear strains toward it.

18:17 A persuasive speech in court can easily make one forget there is another side to the question. When the other party speaks, people realize they made a premature judgment. The experience at court is a lesson for daily life: there are two sides to every question.

18:18 See note on 16:33.

18:19 The Greek version, followed by several ancient versions, has the opposite meaning: "A brother helped by a brother is like a strong and lofty city; it is strong like a well-founded palace." The Greek is secondary as is shown by the need to supply the phrase "by a brother"; further, the parallelism is inadequate. The Hebrew is to be preferred.

18:20 Fruit from the earth is our ordinary sustenance, but "the fruit of one's lips," i.e., our words, also affect our well-being. If our words and our deeds are right, then we are blessed, our "belly is filled."

18:21 This enigmatic saying has provoked many interpretations, e.g., judicious speech brings a reward; those who love the tongue in the sense of rattling on must face the consequences of their loquacity. This translation interprets the verb "love" in colon B in its occasional sense of "choose" (e.g., 12:1; 20:13; Dt 4:37) and interprets its pronominal object as referring to both death and life in colon A. Death and life are set before every person (cf. Dt 30:15–20) and we have the power to choose either one by the quality of our deeds. Words (= "the tongue") are regarded here as the defining actions of human beings.

19:2 When not guided by wisdom, appetite—or desire—is not good. "Running feet" (so the Hebrew) miss the mark, i.e., do not reach their destination.

19:3 One's own folly destroys one's life. It is an indication of that folly that one blames God rather than oneself.

19:5 The punishment fits the crime: those who abuse the legal system will be punished by the same system. They will not be acquitted.

19:7 Closely related to vv. 4 and 6. An observation, not without sympathy, on the social isolation of poor people.

19:8 Wisdom benefits the one who practices it.

19:11 The paradox is that one obtains one thing by giving up another.

19:12 An observation on the exercise of royal power. Both images suggest royal attitudes are beyond human control. Colon A is a variant of 20:2a and colon B of 16:15b.

19:13 One of many sayings about domestic happiness. The perspective is male; the two greatest pains to a father is a malicious son and an unsuitable wife. The immediately following saying is on the noble wife, perhaps to make a positive statement about women.

*

18:13 Sir 11:8.
18:16 Prv 21:14.
18:20 Prv 12:14; 13:2.
18:21 Sir 37:18.
18:22 Prv 12:4; 19:14; Sir 7:26.
18:24 Prv 17:17.
19:1 Prv 28:6.
19:4 Prv 14:20; Sir 13:20–23.
19:5 Dt 19:16–20; Dn 13:61.
19:12 Prv 20:2.
19:13 Prv 10:1; 17:25.
19:14 Prv 18:22.
19:15 Prv 6:9–10.

Pray It!

Fear of the Lord

The phrase "fear of the LORD" is used fourteen times in Proverbs (see, for example, 19:23). You might ask why the author of Proverbs keeps telling us to be afraid of God. But in the Bible, fear of the Lord has less to do with terror and fright than with awe, reverence, and respect. It's a reminder that God is far from ordinary. To fear the Lord is to take God very seriously.

Take some time to reflect or journal on this question: What does it mean to fear the Lord? Describe a time when you were awed by something about God. Explain how you give God respect.

▶ Prv 19:23

but those who despise these ways will die.*

17 Whoever cares for the poor lends to the LORD,*
who will pay back the sum in full.
18 Discipline your son, for there is hope;
but do not be intent on his death.† *
19 A wrathful person bears the penalty;
after one rescue, you will have it to do again.
20 Listen to counsel and receive instruction,
that you may eventually become wise.
21 Many are the plans of the human heart,
but it is the decision of the LORD that endures.*
22 What is desired of a person is fidelity;
rather be poor than a liar.†
23 The fear of the LORD leads to life;
one eats and sleeps free from any harm.
24 The sluggard buries a hand in the dish;
not even lifting it to the mouth.*
25 Beat a scoffer and the naive learn a lesson;
rebuke the intelligent and they gain knowledge.*
26 Whoever mistreats a father or drives away a mother,
is a shameless and disgraceful child.† *
27 My son, stop attending to correction;
start straying from words of knowledge.†
28 An unprincipled witness scoffs at justice,
and the mouth of the wicked pours out iniquity.
29 Rods are prepared for scoffers,
and blows for the backs of fools.*

20

1 Wine is arrogant, strong drink is riotous;
none who are intoxicated by them are wise.† *
2 The terror of a king is like the roar of a lion;*
those who incur his anger forfeit their lives.
3 A person gains honor by avoiding strife,
while every fool starts a quarrel.†
4 In seedtime sluggards do not plow;
when they look for the harvest, it is not there.
5 The intention of the human heart is deep water,
but the intelligent draw it forth.† *
6 Many say, "My loyal friend,"
but who can find someone worthy of trust?
7 The just walk in integrity;
happy are their children after them!
8 A king seated on the throne of judgment
dispels all evil with his glance.†
9 Who can say, "I have made my heart clean,*
I am cleansed of my sin"?†
10 Varying weights, varying measures,
are both an abomination to the LORD.*
11 In their actions even children can playact
though their deeds be blameless and right.†

---

† **19:18** The pain of disciplining the young cannot be compared with the danger no discipline may bring. The chief reason for disciplining the young is their capacity to change; excluded thereby are revenge and punishment.

19:22 The proverb has been read in two ways: (1) "Desire (greed) is a shame to a person," which assumes the rare Hebrew word for "shame" is being used; (2) "What is desired in a person is fidelity." The second interpretation is preferable. The context may be the court: better to forego money (a bribe) than perjure oneself.

19:26 Children who disgrace the family equivalently plunder their father's wealth and expel their mother from the home.

19:27 The meaning was disputed even in antiquity. The interpretation that most respects the syntax is to take it as ironic advice as in 22:6: to stop (listening) is to go (wandering).

20:1 The cause stands for its effect (wine, drunken behavior). In Proverbs wine is a sign of prosperity and a symbol of feasting (3:10; 4:17; 9:2, 5) but also a potential threat to wisdom as in 20:1; 21:17; 23:29–35.

20:3 The honor that one might seek to gain from fighting comes of itself to the person who refrains from fighting.

20:5 The heart is where human plans are made and stored; they remain "deep water" until words reveal them to others. The wise know how to draw up those waters, i.e., express them. Cf. 18:4.

20:8 The royal throne is established in justice and the king is the agent of that justice.

20:9 A claim to sinlessness can be merely self-deception; see 16:2; cf. also 15:11.

20:11 The verb in colon A can mean either "to make oneself known" or "to play another person" (as in Gn 42:7 and 1 Kgs 14:5,

---

* **19:16** Prv 13:13; 16:17.
19:17 Prv 14:21; 22:9; 28:27.
19:18 Prv 13:24; 23:13–14.
19:21 Prv 16:9.
19:24 Prv 26:15.
19:25 Prv 17:10; 21:11.
19:26 Sir 3:16.
19:29 Prv 26:3.
20:1 Prv 23:29–35.
20:2 Prv 19:12.
20:5 Prv 18:4.
20:9 1 Kgs 8:46; 2 Chr 6:36; Eccl 7:20; 1 Jn 1:8.
20:10 Prv 11:1; 20:23.

12 The ear that hears, the eye that sees—
the LORD has made them both.†
13 Do not love sleep lest you be reduced to poverty;
keep your eyes open, have your fill of food.
14 "Bad, bad!" says the buyer,
then goes away only to boast.†
15 One can put on gold and abundant jewels,
but wise lips are the most precious ornament.†
16 Take the garment of the one who became surety for a stranger;*
if for foreigners, exact the pledge!†
17 Bread earned by deceit is sweet,
but afterward the mouth is filled with gravel.
18 Plans made with advice succeed;
with wise direction wage your war.
19 A slanderer reveals secrets;
so have nothing to do with a babbler!
20 Those who curse father or mother—
their lamp will go out† in the dead of night.*
21 Possessions greedily guarded at the outset
will not be blessed in the end.†
22 Do not say, "I will repay evil!"
Wait for the LORD, who will help you.† *
23 Varying weights are an abomination to the LORD,
and false scales are not good.*
24 Our steps are from the LORD;*
how, then, can mortals understand their way?†
25 It is a trap to pledge rashly a sacred gift,
and after a vow, then to reflect.†
26 A wise king winnows the wicked,
and threshes them under the cartwheel.†
27 A lamp from the LORD is human life-breath;
it searches through the inmost being.†
28 His steadfast loyalty safeguards the king,
and he upholds his throne by justice.*
29 The glory of the young is their strength,
and the dignity of the old is gray hair.*
30 Evil is cleansed away by bloody lashes,
and a scourging to the inmost being.

21 1 A king's heart is channeled water in the hand of the LORD;
God directs it where he pleases.†
2 All your ways may be straight in your own eyes,
but it is the LORD who weighs hearts.*
3 To do what is right and just*
is more acceptable to the LORD than sacrifice.†
4 Haughty eyes and a proud heart—
the lamp of the wicked will fail.†
5 The plans of the diligent end in profit,
but those of the hasty end in loss.†
6 Trying to get rich by lying
is chasing a bubble over deadly snares.
7 The violence of the wicked will sweep them away,
because they refuse to do what is right.
8 One's path may be winding and unfamiliar,
but one's conduct is blameless and right.†
9 It is better to dwell in a corner of the housetop
than in a mansion with a quarrelsome woman.† *

---

6). The second meaning makes a better parallel to colon B. The meaning is that if a child can playact, an adult can do so even more. Actions do not always reveal character.

20:12 Human judgments are not ultimate; the Lord expects proper use of these faculties.

20:14 Bartering invites playacting and masking one's true intent. The truth of words depends on their context.

20:15 Wisdom is said to be preferable to gold in 3:14; 8:10, 19; 16:16. Colon B suggests that the gold and jewelry here are ornaments for the face (cf. Gn 24:53; Ex 3:22; Is 61:10). Wise lips are the most beautiful adornment, for they display the wisdom of the heart.

20:16 The text is not clear. See 27:13. Caution in becoming surety is always advised (cf. 6:1–3), and it is especially advisable with strangers.

20:20 *Their lamp will go out*: misfortune, even death, awaits them; cf. 13:9; Ex 21:17.

20:21 By definition, an inheritance is not gained by one's own efforts but is received as a gift. If, when one first receives the inheritance, one drives everyone away, one treats it as if one acquired it by one's own efforts. In an agricultural society, an inheritance would often be a field that would require God's blessing to be fertile.

20:22 Appointing oneself an agent of divine retribution is dangerous. Better to wait for God to effect justice. Cf. 24:17–18.

20:24 An indication of the Lord's inscrutable providence; cf. Jer 10:23; see Prv 21:2; cf. also 14:12.

20:25 This verse cautions against making vows without proper reflection; cf. Dt 23:22–25; Eccl 5:4–5.

20:26 The king is responsible for effecting justice. Judgment is portrayed in agricultural imagery—exposing grain to a current of air so that the chaff is blown away, and passing a wheel over the cereal to break the husk. Winnowing as image for judgment is found throughout the Bible.

20:27 A parallel is drawn between the life-breath that is God's gift (Jb 32:8; 33:2) coursing through the human body (Is 2:22) and the lamp of God, which can be a symbol of divine scrutiny. In Zep 1:12, God declares, "And in that day I will search through Jerusalem with lamps."

21:1 "Channeled water" in Is 32:2 and Prv 5:16 is water that fertilizes arid land. It takes great skill to direct water, whether it be water to fertilize fields or cosmic floods harnessed at creation, for water is powerful and seems to have a mind of its own. It also requires great skill to direct the heart of a king, for it is inscrutable and beyond ordinary human control.

21:3 External rites or sacrifices do not please God unless accompanied by internal worship and right moral conduct; cf. 15:8; 21:27; Is 1:11–15; Am 5:22; Mal 1:12.

21:4 Heart and eyes depict, respectively, the inner and the outer person. "Haughty eyes" peering out from a "proud heart" show a thoroughly arrogant person. How can such a person flourish! Their lamp, which signifies life, will go out.

21:5 The antitheses are diligent and impetuous. The metaphor characterizing each type is taken from the world of commerce. Planning is important; bustle leads to waste.

21:8 One cannot always read others' hearts from their behavior. Unconventional conduct need not indicate evil motives.

21:9 In Proverbs, two great obstacles to a happy household are foolish children and quarrelsome spouses. The nagging wife is also

---

20:16 Prv 27:13.
20:20 Prv 30:11, 17; Ex 21:17; Lv 20:9; Mt 15:4.
20:22 Prv 24:29; Sir 28:1; Mt 5:39; Rom 12:17, 19; 1 Thes 5:15; 1 Pt 3:9.
20:23 Prv 11:1; 20:10.
20:24 Prv 16:9.
20:28 Prv 16:12.
20:29 Prv 16:31.
21:2 Prv 16:2.
21:3 1 Sm 15:22; Hos 6:6.
21:9 Prv 21:19; 25:24; 27:15; Sir 25:23.

10 The soul of the wicked desires evil;
their neighbor finds no pity in their eyes.
11 When scoffers are punished the naive become wise;
when the wise succeed, they gain knowledge.*
12 The Righteous One appraises the house of the wicked,
bringing down the wicked to ruin.†
13 Those who shut their ears to the cry of the poor
will themselves call out and not be answered.
14 A secret gift allays anger,
and a present concealed, violent wrath.†
15 When justice is done it is a joy for the just,
downfall for evildoers.† *
16 Whoever strays from the way of good sense
will abide in the assembly of the shades.†
17 The lover of pleasure will suffer want;
the lover of wine and perfume will never be rich.
18 The wicked serve as ransom for the just,
and the faithless for the upright.† *
19 It is better to dwell in a wilderness
than with a quarrelsome wife and trouble.
20 Precious treasure and oil are in the house of the wise,
but the fool consumes them.
21 Whoever pursues justice and kindness
will find life and honor.†
22 The wise person storms the city of the mighty,
and overthrows the stronghold in which they trust.
23 Those who guard mouth and tongue
guard themselves† from trouble.*
24 Proud, boastful—scoffer is the name:
those who act with overbearing pride.
25 The desire of sluggards will slay them,
for their hands refuse to work.†
26 Some are consumed with avarice all the day,
but the just give unsparingly.
27 The sacrifice of the wicked is an abomination,
the more so when they offer it with bad intent.*
28 The false witness will perish,*
but one who listens will give lasting testimony.
29 The face of the wicked hardens,
but the upright maintains a straight course.†
30 No wisdom, no understanding,
no counsel prevail against the LORD.
31 The horse is equipped for the day of battle,
but victory is the LORD's.

22

1 A good name is more desirable than great riches,
and high esteem, than gold and silver.† *
2 Rich and poor have a common bond:
the LORD is the maker of them all.*
3 The astute see an evil and hide,
while the naive continue on and pay the penalty.† *
4 The result of humility and fear of the LORD
is riches, honor and life.†
5 Thorns and snares are on the path of the crooked;
those who would safeguard their lives will avoid them.
6 Train the young in the way they should go;
even when old, they will not swerve from it.†

† mentioned in 19:13 and 27:15; 25:24 is a duplicate.

21:12 It is difficult to ascertain the subject of the saying. Some hold it is the Lord, the "Righteous One," who is normally the executor of justice in Proverbs. Others believe it is the just person who is the agent of divine justice. "Righteous One" is a title for God in Is 24:16. The best argument for making God the subject of the verb is that elsewhere in Proverbs righteous human beings never do anything to the wicked; only God does.

21:14 Proverbs offers several remedies for anger—a soft word (15:1), patience, and a bribe. The last remedy implies a certain disdain for the disordered passion of anger, for it can be so easily assuaged by a discreetly offered "gift."

21:15 The second line is a duplicate of 10:29b.

21:16 *Assembly of the shades*: those who dwell in Sheol.

21:18 In this bold paradox, the ransom that protects the righteous is the wicked person who attracts, like a lightning rod, the divine wrath that might have been directed at the righteous.

21:21 The paradox is that one comes upon something other than what one pursued. The way to (long and healthy) life and honor is the vigorous pursuit of virtue.

21:23 *Themselves*: see note on 13:3. To guard your "self" (lit., "throat," the moist and breathing center of the body, by metonymy, "life"), you must guard your tongue. Speech in Proverbs is the quintessential human activity and often has a meaning broader than speech alone; it can stand for all human activity. Acting rightly is the best way to protect yourself from evil.

21:25 Desire, or appetite, is the impulse toward food and drink (see Ps 42:3) which spurs animals and human beings into action. But sluggards cannot lift hand to mouth; they bury their hand in the dish (19:24), and so their appetite is thwarted.

21:29 The wicked cannot deter the righteous from walking the straight path, i.e., from practicing virtue.

22:1 "Good name" (Heb. *shem*) and "high esteem" (Heb. *chen*) are declared to be of more value than great riches. Human beings belong to a community and without the acceptance of that community, which is built on esteem and trust, human life is grievously damaged. Riches are less essential to the human spirit.

22:3 The wise see dangers before they are engulfed by them whereas fools, through dullness or boldness, march right on.

22:4 Humiliation can be an occasion for knowing one's place in God's world. Such knowledge is part of fear (or revering) of the Lord. Revering the Lord brings the blessings of wealth, honor, and long life. The saying is perhaps meant to counter the view that humiliation is an unmixed evil; something good can come of it.

22:6 One of the few exhortations in the collection (cf. 14:7; 16:3; 19:18, 20). "Way" in the first colon has been taken in two different senses: (1) the morally right way, "according to the way one ought to go"; (2) personal aptitude, i.e., the manner of life for which one is destined, as "the way of Egypt" (Is 10:24). Neither interpretation, however, accounts for the pronoun in the Hebrew phrase, lit., "his

* **21:11** Prv 19:25.
21:15 Prv 10:29.
21:18 Prv 11:8.
21:23 Prv 13:3.
21:27 Prv 15:8; Sir 34:21–23.
21:28 Prv 19:5, 9.
22:1 Eccl 7:1.
22:2 Prv 29:13.
22:3 Prv 27:12.

7 The rich rule over the poor,
and the borrower is the slave of the lender.†
8 Those who sow iniquity reap calamity,*
and the rod used in anger will fail.†
9 The generous will be blessed,
for they share their food with the poor.
10 Expel the arrogant and discord goes too;
strife and insult cease.
11 The LORD loves the pure of heart;*
the person of winning speech has a king for
a friend.
12 The eyes of the LORD watch over the
knowledgeable,
but he defeats the projects of the faithless.
13 The sluggard says, "A lion is outside;*
I might be slain in the street."†
14 The mouth of the foreign woman is a deep pit;*
whoever incurs the LORD's anger will fall
into it.
15 Folly is bound to the heart of a youth,
but the rod of discipline will drive it out.†
16 Oppressing the poor for enrichment,
giving to the rich: both are sheer loss.†

IV. Sayings of the Wise†

17 The Words of the Wise:†
Incline your ear, and hear my words,*
and let your mind attend to my teaching;
18 For it will be well if you hold them within
you,
if they all are ready on your lips.
19 That your trust may be in the LORD,
I make them known to you today—yes, to
you.
20 Have I not written for you thirty sayings,
containing counsels and knowledge,
21 To teach you truly
how to give a dependable report to one
who sends you?
22 Do not rob the poor because they are poor,
nor crush the needy at the gate;†
23 For the LORD will defend their cause,*
and will plunder those who plunder them.
24 Do not be friendly with hotheads,
nor associate with the wrathful,
25 Lest you learn their ways,
and become ensnared.
26 Do not be one of those who give their hand
in pledge,
those who become surety for debts;*
27 For if you are unable to pay,
your bed will be taken from under you.†
28 Do not remove the ancient landmark†
that your ancestors set up.*

† own way." The most natural solution is to take the whole as ironic advice (like 19:27): yes, go ahead and let the young do exactly what they want; they will become self-willed adults.

22:7 An observation on money and power. One who borrows becomes poor in the sense of indebted, a slave to the lender.

22:8 Agricultural metaphors express the failure of malicious actions. In the first line, bad actions are seeds yielding trouble. In the second line, "the rod" is a flail used to beat grains as in Is 28:27.

22:13 To avoid the effort required for action, the sluggard exaggerates the difficulties that must be overcome.

22:15 Folly is attached to children as the husk is attached to the grain. "Rod" here, as in v. 8, seems to be the flail. Discipline is the process of winnowing away the folly.

22:16 A difficult saying. One possibility is to take it as a seemingly neutral observation on the plight of the poor: taking money from the poor is relatively easy for the powerful but it is dangerous as the poor have the Lord as their defender (24:22–23), who will punish their oppressors. Giving to the rich, perhaps to win their favor by presents and bribes, is equally a waste of money, for the rich will always do what they please in any case.

22:17–24:22 This collection consists of an introduction (22:17–21) urging openness and stating the purpose of the Words and diverse admonitions, aphorisms, and counsels. It is written with faith in the Lord, shrewdness, and a satirical eye. The first part seems aimed at young people intent on a career (22:22–23:11); the second is taken up with the concerns of youth (23:12–35); the third part is interested in the ultimate fate of the good and the wicked (24:1–22). The whole can be described as a guidebook of professional ethics. The aim is to inculcate trust in the Lord and to help readers avoid trouble and advance their careers by living according to wisdom. Its outlook is very practical: avoid bad companions because in time you will take on some of their qualities; do not post bond for others because you yourself will be encumbered; do not promote yourself too aggressively because such promotion is self-defeating; do not abuse sex or alcohol because they will harm you; do not emulate your peers if they are wicked (23:14; 24:1, 19) because such people have no future. Rather, trust the vocation of a sage (22:29–23:9).

The Egyptian *Instructions of Amenemope* (written ca. 1100 B.C.) was discovered in 1923. Scholars immediately recognized it as a source of Prv 22:17–23:11. The Egyptian work has thirty chapters (cf. Prv 22:20); its preface resembled Prv 22:17–21; its first two admonitions matched the first two in Proverbs (Prv 22:22–25). There are many other resemblances as well, some of which are pointed out in the notes. The instruction of a father to his son (or an administrator to his successor) was a well-known genre in Egypt; seventeen works are extant, spanning the period from 2500 B.C. to the first century A.D. The instructions aimed to help a young person live a happy and prosperous life and avoid mistakes that cause difficulties. They make concrete and pragmatic suggestions rather than hold up abstract ideals. Pragmatic though they were, the instructions were religious; they assumed that the gods implanted an order in the world (Egyptian *maat*), which is found both in nature and in the human world. *Amenemope* represents a stage in the development of the Egyptian genre, displaying a new inwardness and quest for serenity while still assuming that the practice of virtue brings worldly success. Proverbs borrows from the Egyptian work with great freedom: it does not, for example, import as such the Egyptian concept of order; it engages the reader with its characteristic wit, irony, and paradox (e.g., 22:26–27; 23:1–3).

22:17–23:35 The maxims warn against: robbing the poor and defenseless (22:22–23), anger (22:24–25), giving surety for debts (22:26–27), advancing oneself by socializing with rulers (23:1–2), anxiety for riches (23:4–5), forcing oneself on a grudging host (23:6–8), intemperance in food and drink (23:19–21, 29–35), and adultery (23:26–28). They exhort to: careful workmanship (22:29), respect for the rights of orphans (23:10–11), correction of the young (23:13–14), filial piety (23:15–16, 22–25), and fear of the Lord (23:17–18).

22:22 *At the gate*: of the city, where justice was administered and public affairs discussed; cf. Ru 4:1. Cf. also Ps 69:13; 127:5; Prv 24:7; 31:23, 31. The Lord will personally avenge those who have no one to defend them.

22:27 Providing surety for a debtor puts one in danger of having the very basics of one's life suddenly seized.

22:28 *Landmark*: marks the boundary of property. To remove it is the equivalent of stealing land. A similar warning is contained in 23:10.

* **22:8** Jb 4:8; Sir 7:3; Hos 8:7.
22:11 Mt 5:8.
22:13 Prv 26:13.
22:14 Prv 23:27.
22:17 Prv 5:1.
22:23 Prv 23:11.
22:26 Prv 6:1–2; 11:15; 17:18.
22:28 Prv 23:10; Dt 19:14; 27:17.

29 Do you see those skilled at their work?
They will stand in the presence of kings,
but not in the presence of the obscure.

23

1 † When you sit down to dine with a ruler,
mark well the one who is before you;
2 Stick the knife in your gullet†
if you have a ravenous appetite.
3 Do not desire his delicacies;
it is food that deceives.
4 Do not wear yourself out to gain wealth,
cease to be worried about it;
5 When your glance flits to it, it is gone!
For assuredly it grows wings,
like the eagle that flies toward heaven.†
6† Do not take food with unwilling hosts,
and do not desire their delicacies;
7 For like something stuck in the throat is that food.
"Eat and drink," they say to you,
but their hearts are not with you;
8 The little you have eaten you will vomit up,
and you will have wasted your agreeable words.
9 Do not speak in the hearing of fools;
they will despise the wisdom of your words.*
10 Do not remove the ancient landmark,*
nor invade the fields of the fatherless;†
11 For their redeemer is strong;
he will defend their cause against you.*
12 Apply your heart to instruction,
and your ear to words of knowledge.
13† Do not withhold discipline from youths;
if you beat them with the rod, they will not die.*
14 Beat them with the rod,*
and you will save them from Sheol.
15 My son, if your heart is wise,
my heart also will rejoice;
16 And my inmost being will exult,
when your lips speak what is right.
17 Do not let your heart envy sinners,*
but only those who always fear the Lord;†
18 For you will surely have a future,
and your hope will not be cut off.*
19 Hear, my son, and be wise,
and guide your heart in the right way.
20 Do not join with wine bibbers,
nor with those who glut themselves on meat.
21 For drunkards and gluttons come to poverty,
and lazing about clothes one in rags.
22† Listen to your father who begot you,
do not despise your mother when she is old.
23 Buy truth and do not sell:
wisdom, instruction, understanding!
24 The father of a just person will exult greatly;
whoever begets a wise son will rejoice in him.*
25 Let your father and mother rejoice;
let her who bore you exult.
26† My son, give me your heart,
and let your eyes keep to my ways,
27 For the harlot is a deep pit,
and the foreign woman a narrow well;
28 Yes, she lies in wait like a robber,*
and increases the number of the faithless.
29† Who scream? Who shout?
Who have strife? Who have anxiety?
Who have wounds for nothing?

†

23:1–9 Four admonitions for someone aspiring to be a sage: be careful about advancing your career by socializing with the great (vv. 1–3); avoid greed (vv. 4–5); do not force yourself on an unwilling host (vv. 6–8); do not waste your wisdom on those who cannot profit from it (v. 9).

23:2 *Stick the knife in your gullet*: a metaphor for self-restraint. The usual translation, "Put a knife to your throat," is misleading, for in English it is a death threat. The exhortation is humorously exaggerated: stick the table-knife in your own gullet rather than take too much food. It assumes that the young courtier is unused to opulent banquets and will be tempted to overindulgence.

23:5 The frustration of covetous intent and elusiveness of wealth are portrayed by the sudden flight of an eagle. *Amenemope*, chap. 7, has a similar statement: "Do not set your heart on wealth. There is no ignoring Fate and Destiny; / Do not let your heart go straying." Proverbs imagines covetous intent as a flight of the eyes, whereas *Amenemope* imagines it as a straying of the heart.

23:6–8 Some humorous advice on not trading on the courtesy of unwilling hosts who, for convention's sake, use the language of welcome. *Amenemope*, chap. 11, gives similar advice: "Do not intrude on a man in his house, / Enter when you have been called; / He may say 'Welcome' with his mouth, / Yet deride you in his thoughts." "Unwilling," lit., "evil of eye," is usually translated "stingy," but the context suggests unwilling. In v. 8, the unwanted guest vomits up the food, thus destroying the desired good impression. Proverbs regards the uninvited banqueters as thieves who will suffer the consequences of their theft. *Amenemope*, chap. 11, is relevant: "Do not covet a poor man's goods, . . . A poor man's goods are a block in the throat, / It makes the gullet vomit."

23:10 In Israel ownership of property and other legal rights were vested mainly in the father as head of the family; thus the widow and fatherless child were vulnerable, left prey to those who would exploit them.

23:13–14 The young will not die from instructional blows but from their absence, for (premature) death results from uncorrected folly. The sardonic humor means the exhortation is not to be taken literally, as an argument for corporal punishment. The next verses (vv. 15–16) are exceedingly tender toward the young.

23:17 Those whom one admires or associates with exercise enormous influence. Do not join the wicked, who are a doomed group. The warning is repeated in 24:1–2, 19–20.

23:22–23 Father and mother are associated with truth and wisdom. One should no more rid oneself of truth and wisdom than rid oneself of one's parents, who are their source.

23:26–28 The exhortation is a condensed version of chap. 7 with its emotional appeal to "my son" to avoid the forbidden woman (7:1–5), her traps (7:21–23), and her intent to add the youth to her list of victims (7:24–27). As in 23:15, 19, 22, a trustful and affectionate relationship between student and teacher is the basis of teaching. The danger of the woman is expressed in imagery that has sexual overtones (cf. 22:14).

23:29–35 A vivid description of the evil effects, physical and psy-

23:9 Prv 9:7.
23:10 Prv 22:28.
23:11 Prv 22:23.
23:13 Prv 13:24; 19:18; Sir 30:1.
23:14 Prv 29:15, 17.
23:17 Prv 3:31; 24:1, 19.
23:18 Prv 24:14.
23:24 Prv 10:1.
23:28 Prv 7:10–27.

Cultural Connection

Wisdom and the Elders

"By wisdom a house is built . . . / by knowledge its rooms are filled" (Prv 24:3–4). Becoming wise is like building and furnishing a house. It doesn't happen all at once; it takes time, experience, and work. Native American cultures understand this. Wisdom is an important value for them.

In many Native American cultures, the elders have the highest place of honor because of their wisdom. Native Americans understand that it takes an entire life to grow wise. The elders have lived through much, and their advice is always worth seeking. They are relied on to settle disagreements because they have learned to judge people by their heart and their integrity, not by their money or possessions. The others in the tribe know that by listening to the elders, they too, over time, will grow wise.

Prv 24:3–4

Who have bleary eyes?
30 Whoever linger long over wine,
whoever go around quaffing wine.*
31 Do not look on the wine when it is red,
when it sparkles in the cup.
It goes down smoothly,
32 but in the end it bites like a serpent,
and stings like an adder.
33 Your eyes behold strange sights,
and your heart utters incoherent things;
34 You are like one sleeping on the high seas,
sprawled at the top of the mast.
35 "They struck me, but it did not pain me;
they beat me, but I did not feel it.
When can I get up,
when can I go out and get more?"†

24 1 † Do not envy the wicked,
nor desire to be with them;*
2 For their hearts plot violence,
and their lips speak of foul play.
3 By wisdom a house is built,
by understanding it is established;
4 And by knowledge its rooms are filled
with every precious and pleasing
possession.
5 The wise are more powerful than the strong,
and the learned, than the mighty,*
6 For by strategy war is waged,
and victory depends on many counselors.*
7† Wise words are beyond fools' reach,*
in the assembly they do not open their
mouth;
8 As they calculate how to do evil,
people brand them troublemakers.
9 The scheme of a fool gains no acceptance,
the scoffer is an abomination to the
community.
10† Did you fail in a day of adversity,
did your strength fall short?
11 Did you fail to rescue those who were being
dragged off to death,†
those tottering, those near death,
12 because you said, "We didn't know
about it"?
Surely, the Searcher of hearts knows
and will repay all according to their deeds.*
13† If you eat honey, my son, because it is good,

† chological, of drunkenness. The emphasis is on the unwise behavior, the folly, caused by alcohol. Cf. 20:1.

23:35 Drunkards become insensible to bodily and moral harm. Their one desire is to indulge again.

24:1–22 A new section (24:1–14)—on the fates of the wicked and foolish—begins with a warning not to take the foolish as role models. The same admonition is repeated in 23:17–18 and 24:19–20. In 24:1, the verb means "to be jealous, zealous; to emulate." The motive stated in the other passages—the wicked have no future—is indirectly stated here.

24:7–9 The verses are unclear; most scholars take them as two or even three single sayings, but, taken singly, the verses are banal. They are best taken as a single statement. Just as vv. 3–6 described the advantages of wisdom, so vv. 7–9 describe the disadvantages of its opposite, folly: it alienates one from the community (v. 7), for fools become notorious (v. 8), dooming their plans and ostracizing themselves.

24:10–12 Excuses for not coming to the aid of one's neighbor in serious trouble do not suffice before God, who sees through self-serving excuses.

24:11 *Rescue . . . death*: perhaps refers to the legal rescue of those unjustly condemned to death.

24:13–14 God's word is sometimes said to be sweeter than honey, e.g., Ps 119:101–103. Cf. also Ps 19:11; Prv 16:24; Ez 3:3; Sir 24:19–22.

* **23:30** Prv 20:1; Sir 19:2; Hos 4:11.
24:1 Prv 3:31; 23:17; Ps 37:1.
24:5 Prv 21:22.
24:6 Prv 20:18.
24:7 Sir 6:21.
24:12 Ps 62:13; Sir 16:12; Mt 16:27; Rom 2:6.

PRV

if pure honey is sweet to your taste,
14 Such, you must know, is wisdom to your soul.
If you find it, you will have a future,
and your hope will not be cut off.*
15† Do not lie in wait at the abode of the just,
do not ravage their dwelling places;
16 Though the just fall seven times, they rise again,
but the wicked stumble from only one mishap.
17† Do not rejoice when your enemies fall,
and when they stumble, do not let your heart exult,
18 Lest the LORD see it, be displeased with you,
and withdraw his wrath from your enemies.
19 Do not be provoked at evildoers,
do not envy the wicked;
20 For the evil have no future,
the lamp of the wicked will be put out.*
21 My son, fear the LORD and the king;
have nothing to do with those who hate them;
22 For disaster will issue suddenly,
and calamity from them both, who knows when?

V. Further Sayings of the Wise†

23 These also are Words of the Wise:
To show partiality in judgment is not good.*
24 Whoever says to the guilty party, "You are innocent,"
will be cursed by nations, scorned by peoples;
25 But those who render just verdicts will fare well,
and on them will come the blessing of prosperity.
26 An honest reply—
a kiss on the lips.†
27 Complete your outdoor tasks,
and arrange your work in the field;
afterward you can build your house.†
28 Do not testify falsely against your neighbor*
and so deceive with your lips.
29 Do not say, "As they did to me, so will I do to them;*
I will repay them according to their deeds."†
30† I passed by the field of a sluggard,
by the vineyard of one with no sense;
31 It was all overgrown with thistles;
its surface was covered with nettles,
and its stone wall broken down.
32 As I gazed at it, I reflected;
I saw and learned a lesson:
33 A little sleep, a little slumber,*
a little folding of the arms to rest—
34 Then poverty will come upon you like a robber,
and want like a brigand.

VI. Second Solomonic Collection, Collected under King Hezekiah†

25 [1]These also are proverbs of Solomon.* The servants of Hezekiah,† king of Judah, transmitted them.

2† It is the glory of God to conceal a matter,
and the glory of kings to fathom a matter.†

†

24:15–16 The just will overcome every misfortune that oppresses them. *Seven times* is an indefinite number.

24:17–18 The admonition is linked to the previous by the words "fall" and "stumble." Premature public celebration of the downfall of enemies equivalently preempts the retribution that belongs to God.

24:23–34 A little collection between the thirty sayings of 22:17–24:22 and the Hezekiah collection in chaps. 25–29. Its title (v. 23) suggests that editors took it as an appendix. At this point, the Greek edition of Proverbs begins to arrange the later sections of the book in a different order than the Hebrew edition.

An editor has arranged originally separate sayings into two parallel groups.

	I.	II.
Conduct in court:	Judges (vv. 24–25)	Witnesses (v. 28)
Speaking, thinking:	Good speech (v. 26)	Bad speech (v. 29)
Wisdom in work:	Positive (v. 27)	Negative (vv. 30–34)

24:26 The kiss is a gesture of respect and affection. The greatest sign of affection and respect for another is to tell that person the truth.

24:27 *House*: can refer to both the building and the family (cf. 2 Sm 7). In the context established by the placement noted above under 24:23, the saying means that neglect of one's field is a sign that one is not building the house properly. In an agricultural society especially, the concept of household includes fields for animals and crops. On the metaphorical level, one must lay a careful preparation before embarking on a great project. This verse is sometimes interpreted as advocating careful and practical preparation for marriage.

24:29 Retribution is a long and complex process that belongs to the Lord, not to individuals. Cf. vv. 12d, 17–18.

24:30–34 Neglect of one's fields through laziness ruins all plans to build a house (v. 27). This vignette is a teaching story, like those in 7:1–27; Ps 37:35–36.

25:1–29:27 Chaps. 25–29 make up the fifth collection in the book, and the third longest. King Hezekiah reigned in Judah in 715–687 B.C. According to 2 Kgs 18–20 and 2 Chr 29–32, he initiated political and religious reforms after the destruction of the Northern Kingdom in 722 B.C. Such reforms probably included copying and editing sacred literature such as Proverbs. Prv 25:1 is an important piece of evidence about the composition of the book, suggesting this collection was added to an already-existing collection also attributed to Solomon. The older collection is probably 10:1–22:16 (or part of it). By the end of the eighth century B.C., therefore, there existed in Israel two large collections of aphorisms.

Chap. 25 has two general themes: (1) social hierarchy, rank, or position; (2) social conflict and its resolution.

25:1 *The servants of Hezekiah*: presumably scribes at the court of Hezekiah. *Transmitted*: lit., "to move, transfer from," hence "to collect," and perhaps also to arrange and compose.

25:2–7 The topic is the king—who he is (vv. 2–3) and how one is to behave in his presence (vv. 4–7).

25:2 God and king were closely related in the ancient world and in the Bible. The king had a special responsibility for divine justice. Hence, God would give him special wisdom to search it out.

24:14 Prv 23:18.
24:20 Prv 13:9.
24:23 Prv 18:5; 28:21; Lv 19:15; Dt 1:17; 16:19.
24:28 Prv 19:5; 25:18.
24:29 Prv 20:22.
24:33 Prv 6:10–11.
25:1 Prv 1:1.

3 Like the heavens in height, and the earth in depth,
the heart of kings is unfathomable.
4† Remove the dross from silver,
and it comes forth perfectly purified;
5 Remove the wicked from the presence of the king,
and his throne is made firm through justice.
6† Claim no honor in the king's presence,
nor occupy the place of superiors;
7 For it is better to be told, "Come up closer!"
than to be humbled before the prince.*
8 What your eyes have seen
do not bring forth too quickly against an opponent;
For what will you do later on
when your neighbor puts you to shame?
9† Argue your own case with your neighbor,
but the secrets of others do not disclose;
10 Lest, hearing it, they reproach you,
and your ill repute never ceases.
11 Golden apples in silver settings
are words spoken at the proper time.
12 A golden earring or a necklace of fine gold—
one who gives wise reproof to a listening ear.
13 Like the coolness of snow in the heat of the harvest
are faithful messengers for those who send them,
lifting the spirits of their masters.
14 Clouds and wind but no rain—
the one who boasts of a gift not given.
15 By patience is a ruler persuaded,*
and a soft tongue can break a bone.
16† If you find honey, eat only what you need,
lest you have your fill and vomit it up.
17 Let your foot be seldom in your neighbors' house,
lest they have their fill of you—and hate you.
18 A club, sword, or sharp arrow—
the one who bears false witness against a neighbor.*
19 A bad tooth or an unsteady foot—
a trust betrayed in time of trouble.†
20 Like the removal of clothes on a cold day, or vinegar on soda,
is the one who sings to a troubled heart.
21† If your enemies are hungry, give them food to eat,
if thirsty, give something to drink;*
22 For live coals you will heap on their heads,
and the LORD will vindicate you.
23 The north wind brings rain,
and a backbiting tongue, angry looks.
24 It is better to dwell in a corner of the housetop
than in a mansion with a quarrelsome wife.† *
25 Cool water to one faint from thirst
is good news from a far country.
26 A trampled fountain or a polluted spring—†
a just person fallen before the wicked.
27 To eat too much honey is not good;
nor to seek honor after honor.†
28 A city breached and left defenseless
are those who do not control their temper.

26

†1 Like snow in summer, like rain in harvest,
honor for a fool is out of place.†
2 Like the sparrow in its flitting, like the swallow in its flight,
a curse uncalled-for never lands.†

†

25:4–5 Wisdom involves virtue as well as knowledge. As in Ps 101 the king cannot tolerate any wickedness in the royal service.

25:6–7 An admonition with a practical motive for putting the teaching into practice. Pragmatic shrewdness suggests that we not promote ourselves but let others do it for us. See Lk 14:7–11.

25:9–10 Another admonition on the use of law courts to settle personal disputes. Speak privately with your opponent lest others' personal business become public and they resent you.

25:16–17 The two admonitions are complementary, expressing nicely the need to restrain the inclination for delightful things, whether for honey or friendship.

25:19 "A time of trouble" defeats all plans (cf. 10:2; 11:4). At such times human resources alone are like a tooth that falls out as one bites or a foot that goes suddenly lame.

25:21–22 A memorable statement of humanity and moderation; such sentiments could be occasionally found even outside the Bible, e.g., "It is better to bless someone than to do harm to one who has insulted you" (Egyptian *Papyrus Insinger*). Cf. Ex 23:4 and Lv 19:17–18. Human beings should not take it upon themselves to exact vengeance, leaving it rather in God's hands. This saying has in view an enemy's vulnerability in time of need, in this case extreme hunger and thirst; such a need should not be an occasion for revenge. The motive for restraining oneself is to allow God's justice to take its own course, as in 20:22 and 24:17–19. *Live coals*: either remorse and embarrassment for the harm done, or increased punishment for refusing reconciliation. Cf. Mt 5:44. Rom 12:20 cites the Greek version and interprets it, "Do not be overcome by evil but overcome evil with good."

25:24 A humorous saying about domestic unhappiness: better to live alone outdoors than indoors with an angry spouse. Prv 21:9 is identical and 21:19 is similar in thought.

25:26 "Spring" is a common metaphor for source. The righteous should be a source of life for others. When they fail, it is as if a spring became foul and its water undrinkable. It is not clear whether the righteous person yielded to a scoundrel out of cowardice or was simply defeated by evil. The latter seems more likely, for other proverbs say the just person will never "fall" (lit., "be moved," 10:30; 12:3). The fall, even temporary, of a righteous person is a loss of life for others.

25:27 *Nor . . . honor*: the text is uncertain.

26:1–28 Concrete images describe the vices of fools (vv. 1–12), of sluggards (vv. 13–16), of meddlers (vv. 17–19), of talebearers (vv. 20–22), and of flatterers (vv. 23–28).

26:1 There is no fit ("out of place") between weather and agricultural season.

26:2 The point is the similarity of actions: a hovering bird that never lands, a groundless curse that never "lands." It hangs in the air posing no threat to anyone.

*

25:7 Lk 14:8–10.
25:15 Prv 15:1, 4.
25:18 Ex 20:16.
25:21 Rom 12:20.
25:24 Prv 21:9.

3 The whip for the horse, the bridle for the ass,
and the rod for the back of fools.*
4† Do not answer fools according to their folly,
lest you too become like them.
5 Answer fools according to their folly,
lest they become wise in their own eyes.
6 Those who send messages by a fool
cut off their feet; they drink down violence.
7† A proverb in the mouth of a fool
hangs limp, like crippled legs.
8 Giving honor to a fool
is like entangling a stone in the sling.
9 A thorn stuck in the hand of a drunkard
is a proverb in the mouth of fools.
10 An archer wounding all who pass by
is anyone who hires a drunken fool.
11 As dogs return to their vomit,
so fools repeat their folly.*
12 You see those who are wise in their own eyes?
There is more hope for fools than for them.
13† The sluggard says, "There is a lion in the street,
a lion in the middle of the square!"*
14 The door turns on its hinges
and sluggards, on their beds.
15 The sluggard buries a hand in the dish,
too weary to lift it to the mouth.*
16 In their own eyes sluggards are wiser
than seven who answer with good judgment.
17 Whoever meddles in the quarrel of another
is one who grabs a passing dog by the ears.
18 Like a crazed archer
scattering firebrands and deadly arrows,
19 Such are those who deceive their neighbor,
and then say, "I was only joking."
20† Without wood the fire dies out;
without a talebearer strife subsides.
21 Charcoal for coals, wood for fire—
such are the quarrelsome, enkindling strife.*
22 The words of a talebearer are like dainty morsels:
they sink into one's inmost being.†*
23 Like a glazed finish on earthenware
are smooth lips and a wicked heart.†
24 With their lips enemies pretend,
but inwardly they maintain deceit;
25 When they speak graciously, do not trust them,*
for seven abominations† are in their hearts.
26 Hatred can be concealed by pretense,
but malice will be revealed in the assembly.†
27 Whoever digs a pit falls into it;
and a stone comes back upon the one who rolls it.*
28 The lying tongue is its owner's enemy,
and the flattering mouth works ruin.

"Do not boast about tomorrow, for you do not know what any day may bring forth."
(Prv 27:1)

27

1 Do not boast about tomorrow,
for you do not know what any day may bring forth.
2 Let another praise you, not your own mouth;
a stranger, not your own lips.
3 Stone is heavy, and sand a burden,
but a fool's provocation is heavier than both.*
4 Anger is cruel, and wrath overwhelming,
but before jealousy who can stand?†
5† Better is an open rebuke
than a love that remains hidden.
6 Trustworthy are the blows of a friend,
dangerous, the kisses of an enemy.†

†

26:4–5 There is no contradiction between these two proverbs. In their answers, the wise must protect their own interests against fools. Or perhaps the juxtaposition of the two proverbs suggests that no single proverb can resolve every problem in life.

26:7–9 Fools either abuse or are unable to use whatever knowledge they have. *A thorn*: a proverb is "words spoken at the proper time" (25:11). Fools have no sense of the right time; their statements are like thorns that fasten on clothing randomly.

26:13–16 Each verse mentions the sluggard, whom Proverbs regards with derision. The criticism is not against low energy but failure to act and take responsibility. Proverbs' ideal is the active person who uses heart, lips, hands, feet to keep to the good path. The verses are examples of the sardonic humor of the book.

26:20–22 The three proverbs have a common theme—the destructive power of slanderous words. Certain words are repeated: wood and fire, talebearer.

26:22 Malicious gossip is compared to delicious food that is swallowed and lodges in the deepest recesses of one's body. Negative comments are seldom forgotten. Prv 18:8 is a duplicate.

26:23 Heart = what is within, and lips (words) = what is expressed, are compared to an earthenware jar covered with glaze.

26:25 *Seven abominations*: many evil intentions.

26:26 Hate may be concealed for a time, but it will eventually issue in a deed and become known in the public assembly. There is a play on words: the consonants of the word "hatred" (*ś'n*) are literally concealed in the word "pretense" (*mś'n*).

27:4 Anger generally subsides with time but jealousy coolly calculates and plots revenge.

27:5–6 Verses 5 and 6 are concerned with true friendship. "Better than" sayings often declare one thing superior to another in view of some value, e.g., 15:17, vegetables are better than meat in view of a milieu of love. In v. 5, a rebuke is better than an act of affection in view of discipline that imparts wisdom.

27:6 The present translation is conjectural. The meaning seems to be that a friend's rebuke can be life-giving and an enemy's kiss can be deadly (like the kiss of Judas in Mt 26:48).

*

26:3 Prv 19:29; Sir 33:25.
26:11 2 Pt 2:22.
26:13 Prv 22:13.
26:15 Prv 19:24.
26:21 Prv 15:18; 29:22.
26:22 Prv 18:8.
26:25 Sir 12:10; 27:33.
26:27 Eccl 10:8; Sir 27:25–26.
27:3 Sir 22:14–15.

7 One who is full spurns honey;
but to the hungry, any bitter thing is sweet.
8 Like a bird far from the nest
so is anyone far from home.†
9 Perfume and incense bring joy to the heart,
but by grief the soul is torn asunder.
10 Do not give up your own friend and your father's friend;
do not resort to the house of your kindred when trouble strikes.
Better a neighbor near than kin far away.†
11 Be wise, my son, and bring joy to my heart,
so that I can answer whoever taunts me.†
12 The astute see an evil and hide;
the naive continue on and pay the penalty.*
13 Take the garment of the one who became surety for a stranger;*
if for a foreign woman, exact the pledge!†
14 Those who greet their neighbor with a loud voice† in the early morning,
a curse can be laid to their charge.
15 For a persistent leak on a rainy day
the match is a quarrelsome wife;*
16 Whoever would hide her hides a stormwind
and cannot tell north from south.
17 Iron is sharpened by iron;
one person sharpens another.†
18 Those who tend a fig tree eat its fruit;
so those attentive to their master will be honored.
19 As face mirrors face in water,
so the heart reflects the person.
20 Sheol and Abaddon can never be satisfied;*
so the eyes of mortals can never be satisfied.†
21 The crucible for silver, the furnace for gold,
so you must assay the praise you receive.
22 Though you pound fools with a pestle,
their folly never leaves them.
23† Take good care of your flocks,
give careful attention to your herds;
24 For wealth does not last forever,
nor even a crown from age to age.
25 When the grass comes up and the new growth appears,
and the mountain greens are gathered in,
26 The lambs will provide you with clothing,
and the goats, the price of a field,
27 And there will be ample goat's milk for your food,
food for your house, sustenance for your maidens.

28

1 The wicked flee though none pursue;
but the just, like a lion, are confident.
2 If a land is rebellious, its princes will be many;
but with an intelligent and wise ruler there is stability.†
3 One who is poor and extorts from the lowly
is a devastating rain that leaves no food.†
4 Those who abandon instruction† praise the wicked,
but those who keep instruction oppose them.
5 The evil understand nothing of justice,†
but those who seek the LORD understand everything.
6 Better to be poor and walk in integrity
than rich and crooked in one's ways.*
7 Whoever heeds instruction is a wise son,
but whoever joins with wastrels disgraces his father.
8 Whoever amasses wealth by interest and overcharge†

†

27:8 The bird symbolizes vulnerability as it flees before danger as in Is 10:14; 16:2; and Ps 11:1. For the importance of place in human life, see Jb 20:8–9. People are defined by their place, but, tragically, war, poverty, or illness can force them from it.

27:10 The adage is about the difference between friends and kin in a crisis. Two admonitions are grounded in one maxim (colon C). The same Hebrew word means both "one who is near" and "friend." The whole proverb urges the reader to cultivate old family friends and neighbors and not to rely exclusively on kin in times of trouble, for kin may not be there for us.

27:11 A father's command to a son to be wise, another way of saying that sons or daughters bring joy or shame to their parents.

27:13 See note on 20:16.

27:14 One interpretation takes the proverb as humorous and the other takes it as serious: (1) an overly loud and ill-timed greeting (lit., "blessing") invites the response of a curse rather than a "blessing" (greeting); (2) the loud voice suggests hypocrisy in the greeting.

27:17 Iron sharpens the "face" (*panim* = surface, edge) of iron, and a human being sharpens the "face" (*panim* = face, words) of another. Human beings learn from each other and grow in wisdom by conversing.

27:20 Sheol, the underworld abode of the dead, is personified as a force that is never satisfied and always desires more. Cf. Is 5:14 and Hos 13:14. The saying is applicable to modern consumerism.

27:23–27 A little treatise on farming in the form of admonitions. It proposes the advantages of field and flock over other forms of wealth. Herds are the most productive wealth, for their value does not diminish; they are a source of money, clothing, and food. The thought is conservative and traditional but the development is vivid and concrete.

28:2 The first line expresses the paradox that rebellion, far from doing away with rulers, actually multiplies them. The second line is corrupt.

28:3 The reference may be to tax farmers who collected taxes and took a commission. The collectors' lack of wealth was the cause of their oppression of poor farmers. They are like a rain too violent to allow crops to grow.

28:4 *Instruction*: *torah*; the word is used both for the teaching of the wise and the law of Moses.

28:5 *Understanding nothing of justice* plays on the twofold sense of justice as righteousness and as punishment that comes on the wicked. On the other hand, *those who seek the LORD understand everything*, i.e., that the Lord punishes the wicked and rewards the righteous (themselves).

28:8 Interest and overcharge were strictly forbidden in the old law among Israelites because it was presumed that the borrower was in distress; cf. Ex 22:25; Lv 25:35–37; Dt 23:20; Ps 15:5; Ez 18:8. Divine providence will take the offender's wealth; cf. Eccl 2:26.

*

27:12 Prv 22:3.
27:13 Prv 20:16.
27:15 Prv 21:9; 25:24.
27:20 Prv 30:16; Eccl 4:8.
28:6 Prv 19:1.

Pray It!

Integrity

A person with integrity does the right thing, even if it doesn't lead to fame or riches. A person with integrity won't lie, steal, or cheat; won't gossip, betray, or insult—not even when everyone else seems to be doing it. A person with integrity is trustworthy, dependable, and reliable. Such a person admits making mistakes and apologizes. Such a person forgives freely and doesn't hold grudges.

Lord, I'm far from perfect. But with every word I speak, every action I take, every choice I make, may I become more aware of how I am growing into a person of integrity.

Prv 28:6

gathers it for the one who is kind to the
poor.
9 Those who turn their ears from hearing
instruction,*
even their prayer is an abomination.
10 Those who mislead the upright into an
evil way
will themselves fall into their own pit,
but the blameless will attain prosperity.
11 The rich are wise in their own eyes,
but the poor who are intelligent see
through them.
12 When the just triumph, there is great glory;
but when the wicked prevail, people hide.†
13 Those who conceal their sins do not prosper,
but those who confess and forsake them
obtain mercy.†
14 Happy those who always fear;†
but those who harden their hearts fall into
evil.
15 A roaring lion or a ravenous bear
is a wicked ruler over a poor people.
16 The less prudent the rulers, the more
oppressive their deeds.
Those who hate ill-gotten gain prolong
their days.
17 Though a person burdened with blood guilt is
in flight even to the grave,
let no one offer support.
18 Whoever walks blamelessly is safe,
but one whose ways are crooked falls into a
pit.
19 Those who cultivate their land will have
plenty of food,
but those who engage in idle pursuits will
have plenty of want.*
20 The trustworthy will be richly blessed;
but whoever hastens to be rich will not go
unpunished.*
21 To show partiality is never good:*
for even a morsel of bread one may do
wrong.†
22 Misers hurry toward wealth,
not knowing that want is coming toward
them.†
23 Whoever rebukes another wins more favor
than one who flatters with the tongue.
24 Whoever defrauds father or mother and says,
"It is no sin,"*
is a partner to a brigand.
25 The greedy person stirs up strife,
but the one who trusts in the LORD will
prosper.
26 Those who trust in themselves are fools,
but those who walk in wisdom are safe.
27 Those who give to the poor have no lack,*
but those who avert their eyes, many curses.
28 When the wicked prevail, people hide;
but at their fall the just abound.*

29 1 Those stiff-necked in the face of reproof
in an instant will be shattered beyond
cure.†

†

28:12 People react in opposite ways to the triumph of good and evil. To the triumph of good, they react by public display, public celebration, and to the triumph of evil, by hiding.

28:13 Concealing the faults of another is a good thing in Proverbs (17:9), but concealing one's own sins is not. Ps 32:1–5 expresses the anguish caused by concealing one's sins rather than bringing them to light so they can be healed by God.

28:14 *Fear* is a different verb than in the phrase "to fear (or revere) the Lord." In its only other biblical occurrence (Is 51:13), the verb means to dread an oppressor. The saying states a paradox: those who fear in the sense of being cautious are declared happy, whereas those who are fearless will fall into traps they did not "fear." In short, there is good fear and bad fear.

28:21 Cf. 24:23. Verse 21b warns that even in a light matter one must remain impartial.

28:22 "Bad of eye" is the Hebrew idiom for miserly. Misers fail to see that poverty is hurrying toward them because of their wrong attitude toward wealth. Because misers are "bad of eye," they do not see the danger.

29:1 The idiom "to stiffen one's neck" occurs in a context of not heeding a message in Dt 10:16 and 2 Kgs 17:14. To stiffen one's neck in this sense risks having it broken, as in 1 Sm 4:18.

*

28:9 Prv 15:8; 21:27.
28:19 Prv 12:11.
28:20 Prv 13:11.
28:21 Prv 24:23.
28:24 Mk 7:11–13.
28:27 Prv 19:17; Sir 4:3–8.
28:28 Prv 28:12.

2 When the just flourish, the people rejoice;
but when the wicked rule, the people groan.† *
3 Whoever loves wisdom gives joy to his father,
but whoever consorts with harlots
squanders his wealth.
4 By justice a king builds up the land;
but one who raises taxes tears it down.†
5 Those who speak flattery to their neighbor
cast a net at their feet.†
6 The sin of the wicked is a trap,
but the just run along joyfully.*
7 The just care for the cause of the poor;
the wicked do not understand such care.†
8 Scoffers enflame the city,
but the wise calm the fury.*
9 If a wise person disputes with a fool,
there is railing and ridicule but no resolution.
10 The bloodthirsty hate the blameless,
but the upright seek his life.†
11 Fools give vent to all their anger;
but the wise, biding their time, control it.*
12 If rulers listen to lying words,
their servants all become wicked.
13 The poor and the oppressor meet:*
the LORD gives light to the eyes of both.
14 If a king is honestly for the rights of the poor,
his throne stands firm forever.*
15 The rod of correction gives wisdom,
but uncontrolled youths disgrace their
mothers.*
16 When the wicked increase, crime increases;
but the just will behold their downfall.†
17 Discipline your children, and they will bring
you comfort,
and give delight to your soul.
18 Without a vision the people lose restraint;
but happy is the one who follows
instruction.†
19 Not by words alone can servants be trained;*
for they understand but do not respond.†
20 Do you see someone hasty in speech?*
There is more hope for a fool!
21 If servants are pampered from childhood
they will turn out to be stubborn.
22 The ill-tempered stir up strife,
and the hotheaded cause many sins.*
23 Haughtiness brings humiliation,
but the humble of spirit acquire honor.† *
24 Partners of a thief hate themselves;†
they hear the imprecation but do not testify.
25 Fear of others becomes a snare,
but the one who trusts in the LORD is safe.
26 Many curry favor with a ruler,
but it is from the LORD that one receives
justice.
27 An abomination to the just, the evildoer;
an abomination to the wicked, one whose
way is straight.

VII. Sayings of Agur and Others

30 1 † The words of Agur, son of Jakeh the Massaite:

The pronouncement of mortal man: "I am
weary, O God;
I am weary, O God, and I am exhausted.
2 I am more brute than human being,
without even human intelligence;
3† Neither have I learned wisdom,

†

29:2 Popular response to a just or unjust ruler is expressed in sound—shouts of joy or groans of anguish. "Rejoice" can mean to express one's joy, i.e., joyous shouts.

29:4 In Hebrew as in English high and low are metaphors for prosperity and depression. A king who is just "causes the land to stand up," i.e., to be prosperous, and one who makes taxes high brings a country low.

29:5 When one addresses deceptive words to someone's face, one equivalently throws a net at their feet to snare them.

29:7 As in 12:10 (on care for animals), the righteous care for those who are without a voice and often treated like animals. Colon B has a double meaning: the wicked have no such knowledge (care for the poor) and they have no knowledge (wisdom), for they are fools.

29:10 An enigmatic saying in that "seek one's life" is a common idiom for killing. The saying probably plays on the idiom, interpreting "to seek the life of another" not as killing but as caring for another (as in 11:30).

29:16 When the wicked grow numerous they sow the seeds of their own destruction, for there is a corresponding increase in offenses calling down divine retribution.

29:18 This much-cited proverb has been interpreted in several different ways. "Vision" and "instruction" mean authoritative guidance for the community. People are demoralized without credible leadership, but any individual heeding traditional instruction can still find happiness. As in 15:15 wisdom enables an individual to surmount days of trouble.

29:19 The give and take of reproving is not possible for servants or slaves. Ancient custom dictated silent acquiescence for them. There is no open and free dialogue, which is part of ancient discipline.

29:23 One's prideful height brings one down and one's lowly state brings glory.

29:24 *Hate themselves*: because they not only incur guilt as accomplices but, by their silence, bring down on themselves the curse invoked on the unknown guilty partner. Such a case is envisioned in Lv 5:1. After a theft, a public proclamation was made, enforced by a curse. No one in a town or city could avoid hearing it. The curse hung over the accomplice. By doing nothing, neither directly stealing nor confessing, accomplices put themselves in serious danger.

30:1–6 Scholars are divided on the original literary unit. Is it vv. 1–3, 1–4, 1–5, or 1–6? The unit is probably vv. 1–6, for a single contrast dominates: human fragility (and ignorance) and divine power (and knowledge). A similar contrast is found in Jb 28; Ps 73; Is 49:1–4. The language of self-abasement is hyperbolic; cf. 2 Sm 9:8; Ps 73:21–22; Jb 25:4–6. *Agur*: an unknown person. *Massaite*: from Massa in northern Arabia, elsewhere referred to as an encampment of the Ishmaelites (Gn 25:14). But Heb. *massa* may not be intended as a place name; it might signify "an oracle," "a prophecy," as in Is 15:1; 17:1; etc.

30:3–4 Agur denies he has secret heavenly knowledge. The pur-

*

29:2 Prv 11:10; 28:12, 28.
29:6 Prv 12:13.
29:8 Prv 11:11.
29:11 Prv 12:16; 25:28; Sir 21:26.
29:13 Prv 22:2.
29:14 Prv 16:12; 20:28; 25:5.
29:15 Prv 13:24; 22:15; 23:13–14; Sir 22:6; 30:1.
29:19 Sir 33:25–30.
29:20 Sir 9:18; Prv 26:12.
29:22 Prv 15:18; 22:24.
29:23 Prv 11:2; 16:18; 18:12.

Live It!

Birds of Prey

The eye that mocks a father,
or scorns the homage due a mother,
Will be plucked out by brook ravens;
devoured by a brood of vultures.
(Prv 30:17)

If this passage reflected reality, most of us would already have been eaten by those birds of prey hovering overhead. For who among us has not at one time mocked our parents, if not to their face, then perhaps to our friends? And is there anyone who has not disobeyed a parent?

We live in a time when families have many different forms. You might live with biological parents, stepparents, adopted parents, or foster parents. Whatever kind and number of parents you have, they need your respect, despite their weaknesses and flaws (although you must not accept verbal, physical, sexual, or other abuse).

The vast majority of us are loved by our parents. In most cases, they are trying their hardest to do what is best for us, even though it doesn't always seem that way. If we can accept this, it might be easier to forgive them their faults and overlook some of the things they do that irritate us.

Let's keep the birds of prey far away!

- What can you do to let your parents know you love them?
- What can you do today to show them more respect?

Prv 30:17

PRV

nor have I the knowledge of the Holy One.
4 Who has gone up to heaven and come down again—
who has cupped the wind in the hollow of the hand?
Who has bound up the waters in a cloak—
who has established all the ends of the earth?
What is that person's name, or the name of his son?"†

5† Every word of God is tested;*
he is a shield to those who take refuge in him.
6 Add nothing to his words,*
lest he reprimand you, and you be proved a liar.

7† Two things I ask of you,
do not deny them to me before I die:
8 Put falsehood and lying far from me,
give me neither poverty nor riches;
provide me only with the food I need;
9 Lest, being full, I deny you,
saying, "Who is the LORD?"
Or, being in want, I steal,
and profane the name of my God.
10 Do not criticize servants to their master,
lest they curse you, and you have to pay the penalty.
11† There are some who curse their fathers,
and do not bless their mothers.*
12 There are some pure in their own eyes,
yet not cleansed of their filth.
13 There are some—how haughty their eyes!
how overbearing their glance!
14 There are some—their teeth are swords,
their teeth are knives,
Devouring the needy from the earth,
and the poor from the human race.
15† The leech has two daughters:
"Give," and "Give."
Three things never get their fill,
four never say, "Enough!"
16 Sheol, a barren womb,*
land that never gets its fill of water,
and fire, which never says, "Enough!"
17 The eye that mocks a father,
or scorns the homage due a mother,
Will be plucked out by brook ravens;

---

pose of the denial is to underline that God directly gives wisdom to those whose conduct pleases him.

30:4 The Hebrew text has the phrase "do you know?" at the end of v. 4, which is supported by the versions. The phrase, however, does not appear in the important Greek manuscripts Vaticanus and Sinaiticus and spoils the sense, for Agur, not God, is the questioner. The phrase seems to be an addition to the Hebrew text, borrowed from Job 38:5, where it also follows a cosmic question.

30:5–6 Verse 5, like the confession of the king in Ps 18:31 (and its parallel, 2 Sm 22:31), expresses total confidence in the one who rescues from death. Agur has refused a word from any other except God and makes an act of trust in God.

30:7–9 A prayer against lying words and for sufficiency of goods, lest reaction to riches or destitution lead to offenses against God.

30:11–14 Perverted people are here classified as unfilial (v. 11), self-righteous (v. 12), proud (v. 13) and rapacious (v. 14).

30:15–16 Here begins a series of numerical sayings; the pattern is n, n + 1. The slight variation in number (two and three, three and four) is an example of parallelism applied to numbers. The poetic

---

30:5 Ps 12:7; 18:31.
30:6 Dt 4:2; 13:1.
30:11 Prv 20:20.
30:16 Prv 27:20.

devoured by a brood of vultures.
18† Three things are too wonderful for me,
yes, four I cannot understand:
19 The way of an eagle in the sky,
the way of a serpent upon a rock,
The way of a ship on the high seas,
and the way of a man with a woman.
20 This is the way of an adulterous woman:
she eats, wipes her mouth,
and says, "I have done no wrong."†
21† Under three things the earth trembles,
yes, under four it cannot bear up:
22 Under a slave who becomes king,
and a fool who is glutted with food;*
23 Under an unloved woman who is wed,
and a maidservant who displaces her mistress.
24† Four things are among the smallest on the earth,
and yet are exceedingly wise:
25 Ants—a species not strong,
yet they store up their food in the summer;
26 Badgers—a species not mighty,
yet they make their home in the crags;
27 Locusts—they have no king,
yet they march forth in formation;
28 Lizards—you can catch them with your hands,
yet they find their way into kings' palaces.
29† Three things are stately in their stride,
yes, four are stately in their carriage:
30 The lion, mightiest of beasts,
retreats before nothing;
31 The strutting cock, and the he-goat,
and the king at the head of his people.
32† If you have foolishly been proud
or presumptuous—put your hand on your mouth;
33 For as the churning of milk produces curds,
and the pressing of the nose produces blood,
the churning of anger produces strife.

VIII. Sayings of King Lemuel†

31 1 The words of Lemuel, king of Massa,† the instruction his mother taught him:

2 What are you doing, my son!†
what are you doing, son of my womb;
what are you doing, son of my vows!
3 Do not give your vigor to women,
or your strength† to those who ruin kings.
4 It is not for kings, Lemuel,
not for kings to drink wine;
strong drink is not for princes,
5 Lest in drinking they forget what has been decreed,
and violate the rights of any who are in need.
6 Give strong drink to anyone who is perishing,
and wine to the embittered;
7 When they drink, they will forget their misery,
and think no more of their troubles.
8 Open your mouth in behalf of the mute,
and for the rights of the destitute;
9 Open your mouth, judge justly,
defend the needy and the poor!

IX. Poem on the Woman of Worth†

10 Who can find† a woman of worth?*
Far beyond jewels is her value.

† technique is attested even outside the Bible. *Two daughters: "Give," and "Give"*: the text is obscure; as the leech (a bloodsucking worm) is insatiable in its desire for blood (v. 15), so are the nether world for victims, the barren womb for offspring, the earth for water, and fire for fuel (v. 16). *Sheol*: here not so much the place of the dead as a force (death) that eventually draws all the living into it; cf. 27:20; Is 5:14; Hb 2:5. *Land . . . fire*: land (especially the dry land of Palestine) always absorbs more water; fire always requires more fuel.

30:18–19 The soaring flight of the eagle, the mysterious movement upon a rock of the serpent which has no feet, the path of the ship through the trackless deep, and the marvelous attraction between the sexes; there is a mysterious way common to them all.

30:20 This verse portrays the indifference of an adulterous woman who casually dismisses her guilt because it cannot be traced.

30:21–23 Shaking heavens are part of general cosmic upheaval in Is 14:16; Jl 2:10; Am 8:8; Jb 9:6. Disturbances in nature mirror the disturbance of unworthy people attaining what they do not deserve. *Glutted with food*: someone unworthy ends up with the fulfillment that befits a wise person. *Unloved woman*: an older woman who, contrary to expectation, finds a husband.

30:24–28 The creatures may be small, but they are wise in knowing how to govern themselves—the definition of wisdom. *Badgers*: the rock badger is able to live on rocky heights that provide security from its enemies. *Locusts*: though vulnerable individually their huge swarms are impossible to deflect.

30:29–31 Four beings with an imperiousness visible in their walk. Only the lion is described in detail; the reader is expected to transpose its qualities to the others.

30:32–33 The same Hebrew verb, "to churn, shake," is applied to milk, the nose (sometimes a symbol of anger), and wrath. In each case something is eventually produced by the constant agitation. The wise make peace and avoid strife, for strife eventually harms those who provoke it.

31:1–9 Though mothers are sources of wisdom in Proverbs (1:8; 6:20), the mother of Lemuel is special in being queen mother, which was an important position in the palace. Queen mothers played an important role in ancient palace life because of their longevity, knowledge of palace politics, and loyalty to their sons; they were in a good position to offer him sound counsel. The language of the poem contains Aramaisms, a sign of its non-Israelite origin.

The first section, vv. 3–5, warns against abuse of sex and alcohol (wine, strong drink) lest the king *forget* the *poor*. The second section, vv. 6–9, urges the use of alcohol (strong drink, wine) so that the downtrodden *poor* can *forget* their poverty. The real subject of the poem is justice for the poor.

31:1 *Massa*: see note on 30:1–6.

31:2 *My son*: in the Septuagint, "my son, my firstborn."

31:3 The Hebrew word here translated "strength" normally means "ways," but the context and a cognate language support "authority" or "strength" here.

31:10–31 An acrostic poem of twenty-two lines; each line begins with a successive letter of the Hebrew alphabet. As with many other acrostic poems in the Bible, the unity of the poem is largely extrinsic, coming not from the narrative logic but from the familiar sequence of letters. The topic is the ideal woman described through her activity

*

30:22 Prv 19:10; Eccl 10:6–7.
31:10 Prv 12:4; Sir 26:1–4, 13–18.

Did You Know?

A Woman's Place

You've probably noticed that women had a much different role in biblical times than they do now. Then it was common, and expected, for women to be in the home—either their father's or their husband's—doing household chores.

Today, the Catholic Church teaches that women and men share equality and that both deserve respect and mutual appreciation. It is not appropriate or just, therefore, to say that a woman's place is in the home. Women now choose where they spend their time!

Thousands of women today hold leadership positions at parish, diocesan, archdiocesan, and national levels. The Church celebrates the inclusion of women in leadership positions and continues to strive for and support a more even distribution of men and women in these positions. If you are a young woman or young man interested in working for the Church, ask for more information at your parish or school.

▶ Prv 31:10–31

11 Her husband trusts her judgment;
he does not lack income.
12 She brings him profit, not loss,†
all the days of her life.
13 She seeks out wool and flax
and weaves with skillful hands.
14 Like a merchant fleet,†
she secures her provisions from afar.
15 She rises while it is still night,
and distributes food to her household,
a portion to her maidservants.
16 She picks out a field and acquires it;
from her earnings she plants a vineyard.
17 She girds herself with strength;
she exerts her arms with vigor.†
18 She enjoys the profit from her dealings;
her lamp is never extinguished at night.†
19 She puts her hands to the distaff,
and her fingers ply the spindle.†
20 She reaches out her hands to the poor,
and extends her arms to the needy.
21 She is not concerned for her household when
it snows—
all her charges are doubly clothed.
22 She makes her own coverlets;
fine linen and purple are her clothing.
23 Her husband is prominent at the city gates
as he sits with the elders of the land.†
24 She makes garments and sells them,
and stocks the merchants with belts.
25 She is clothed with strength and dignity,
and laughs at the days to come.†
26 She opens her mouth in wisdom;
kindly instruction is on her tongue.
27 She watches over† the affairs of her
household,
and does not eat the bread of idleness.
28 Her children rise up and call her blessed;
her husband, too, praises her:
29 "Many are the women of proven worth,
but you have excelled them all."
30 Charm is deceptive and beauty fleeting;
the woman who fears the LORD is to be
praised.†
31 Acclaim her for the work of her hands,
and let her deeds praise her at the city
gates.

---

as a wife. Some have suggested that the traditional hymn extolling the great deeds of a warrior has been transposed to extol a heroic wife; the focus is on her exploits. She runs a household distinguished by abundant food and clothing for all within, by its trade (import of raw materials and export of finished products), and by the renown of its head, her husband, in the community. At v. 28, the voice is no longer that of the narrator but of her children and husband as they praise her. The purpose of the poem has been interpreted variously: an encomium to offset the sometimes negative portrayal of women in the book, or, more symbolically (and more likely), a portrait of a household ruled by Woman Wisdom and a disciple of Woman Wisdom, i.e., he now has a worthy wife and children, a great household, renown in the community.

31:10 *Who can find . . . ?*: in 20:6 and Eccl 8:1 the question implies that finding such a person is well-nigh impossible.

31:12 *Profit, not loss*: a commercial metaphor.

31:14 *Like a merchant fleet*: she has her eye on the far horizon, like the ship of a merchant ready to bring supplies into her larder. It is the only simile ("like") in the poem.

31:17 The metaphor of clothing oneself is used to show the woman's readiness. One can gird on weapons of war and might and splendor (Ps 69:7; Is 52:9).

31:18 *Her lamp is never extinguished at night*: indicates abundance of productive work and its accompanying prosperity; cf. 20:20; Jb 18:6.

31:19 The wife weaves linen cloth from flax and wool from fleece, which she cultivated according to v. 13. *Distaff*: staff for holding the flax, tow, or wool, which in spinning was drawn out and twisted into yarn or thread by the spindle or round stick.

31:23 The husband is mentioned for the first time since vv. 10–12 but as "her husband." He will not be mentioned again until v. 28, where he praises her.

31:25 *Laughs at the days to come*: anticipates the future with joy, free of anxiety.

31:27 *Watches over*: Hebrew *ṣopiyyâ*, perhaps a pun on the Greek *sophia* (= wisdom). *Bread of idleness*: she does not eat from the table of others but from her own labors.

31:30 The true charm of this woman is her religious spirit, for she fears the Lord; cf. note on 1:7.

"**Nothing** is new under the sun." "For in much wisdom there is much sorrow, and whoever increases knowledge increases grief." "You know not what misfortune may come upon the earth." If you were to see these comments on the Internet, what would you think? That you had just found the Web site of the National Association of Pessimists? Would you be surprised to learn that all these lines come from the Bible? The author of Ecclesiastes, who was called Qoheleth (Eccl 1:1), wrote all of them. Yet, the book is hardly a defense of pessimism. The Teacher was pointing out to the Israelites the need for a new understanding of God and life.

In Depth

After a long life of careful observation, the author of Ecclesiastes was disturbed by many things:

- that wise people perished just like fools (see 2:12–17)
- that those who worked hard for a living had to leave their possessions behind in death (see 5:12–16)
- that sometimes bad people lived longer than good people (see 7:15)
- that the most deserving did not always get what they had earned (see 9:11–12)

At a Glance

Introduction (1:1–11).

I. Qoheleth's Investigation of Life (1:12—6:9).

II. Qoheleth's Conclusions (6:10—12:14).

A. No One Can Find Out the Best Way of Acting (7:1—8:17).

B. No One Knows the Future (9:1—12:14).

Quick Facts

Inspired Author: the Teacher, writing in the fourth or third century BC

Themes: Life is not always fair. There are no easy answers. Only in faith in God is true wisdom found.

Of Note: The Book of Ecclesiastes is often attributed to King Solomon, although he did not write it.

Observing these puzzling things, the Teacher asked the obvious question: "Why should we work so hard to be wise and good?" For centuries, believers had struggled to be honest, law-abiding people in the hope of being rewarded by God. And what had they gotten? Sickness, suffering, and death—like everyone else! "Something's wrong!" the Teacher insisted. "Something's terribly wrong!"

After raising the question, the author of Ecclesiastes did not provide an answer—nor is a convincing one to be found in the writings of others in the Old Testament. However, later generations of Jews, pondering the possibility of life after death—a concept that developed late in Jewish religion—began to see things in a different light. Does God possibly reward the faithful in a life beyond the grave? For Christians, the New Testament answers that question with a resounding yes.

The Book of Ecclesiastes stands as a reminder to believers that all things change, even our understanding of God. The Teacher was not a pessimist, but a realist with a mission—to stretch the traditional understanding of faith in order to embrace the difficult questions of life.

The Book of **Ecclesiastes**

Ecclesiastes

9:7

1 1 The words of David's son, Qoheleth, king in
Jerusalem:† *

2 Vanity of vanities,† says Qoheleth,
vanity of vanities! All things are vanity!*

Vanity of Human Toil

3 What profit have we from all the toil
which we toil at under the sun?† *
4 One generation departs and another
generation comes,
but the world forever stays.
5 The sun rises and the sun sets;
then it presses on to the place where it
rises.
6 Shifting south, then north,
back and forth shifts the wind, constantly
shifting its course.
7 All rivers flow to the sea,
yet never does the sea become full.
To the place where they flow,
the rivers continue to flow.
8 All things are wearisome,†
too wearisome for words.
The eye is not satisfied by seeing
nor has the ear enough of hearing.*

9 What has been, that will be; what has been
done, that will be done. Nothing is new under
the sun!* 10 Even the thing of which we say, "See,
this is new!" has already existed in the ages that
preceded us.* 11 There is no remembrance of past
generations;* nor will future generations be re-
membered by those who come after them.†

I. Qoheleth's Investigation of Life

Twofold Introduction

12 I, Qoheleth, was king over Israel in Jerusalem,
13 and I applied my mind to search and investigate
in wisdom all things that are done under the sun.*

A bad business God has given
to human beings to be busied with.

14 I have seen all things that are done under the
sun, and behold, all is vanity and a chase after
wind.† *

†

1:1 *David's son . . . king in Jerusalem*: the intent of the author is to identify himself with Solomon. This is a literary device, by which the author hopes to commend his work to the public under the name of Israel's most famous sage (see 1 Kgs 5:9–14).

1:2 *Vanity of vanities*: a Hebrew superlative expressing the supreme degree of futility and emptiness.

1:3 *Under the sun*: used throughout this book to signify "on the earth."

1:8 *All things are wearisome*: or, "All speech is wearisome."

1:11 Movement in nature and human activity appears to result in change and progress. The author argues that this change and progress are an illusion: "Nothing is new under the sun."

1:14 *A chase after wind*: an image of futile activity, like an attempt to corral the winds; cf. Hos 12:2. The ancient versions understood "affliction, dissipation of the spirit." This phrase concludes sections of the text as far as 6:9.

1:1 Eccl 1:12; 12:9–10.
1:2 Eccl 12:8.
1:3 Eccl 2:11, 22; 3:9; 5:15.
1:8 Eccl 4:8; 5:9–11.
1:9 Eccl 3:15; 6:10.
1:10 Eccl 3:15.
1:11 Eccl 2:16.
1:13 Eccl 8:9.
1:14 Eccl 2:11, 17.

15 What is crooked cannot be made straight,
and you cannot count what is not there.†

16* Though I said to myself, "See, I have
greatly increased my wisdom beyond all who
were before me in Jerusalem, and my mind has
broad experience of wisdom and knowledge,"
17 yet when I applied my mind to know wisdom
and knowledge, madness and folly, I learned that
this also is a chase after wind.*

18 For in much wisdom there is much sorrow;
whoever increases knowledge increases
grief.†

Study of Pleasure-seeking

2 1 I said in my heart,† "Come, now, let me
try you with pleasure and the enjoyment of
good things." See, this too was vanity. 2 Of laugh-
ter I said: "Mad!" and of mirth: "What good does
this do?" 3 Guided by wisdom,† I probed with
my mind how to beguile my senses with wine
and take up folly, until I should understand what
is good for human beings to do under the heav-
ens during the limited days of their lives.
4 I undertook great works; I built myself houses
and planted vineyards; 5 I made gardens and
parks, and in them set out fruit trees of all sorts.
6 And I constructed for myself reservoirs to water
a flourishing woodland. 7 I acquired male and fe-
male slaves, and had slaves who were born in my
house. I also owned vast herds of cattle and flocks
of sheep, more than all who had been before me
in Jerusalem. 8 I amassed for myself silver and
gold, and the treasures of kings and provinces. I
provided for myself male and female singers and
delights of men, many women.† 9 I accumulated
much more than all others before me in Jerusa-
lem; my wisdom, too, stayed with me. 10 Nothing
that my eyes desired did I deny them, nor did I
deprive myself of any joy; rather, my heart rejoiced
in the fruit of all my toil. This was my share for all
my toil. 11* But when I turned to all the works that
my hands had wrought, and to the fruit of the toil
for which I had toiled so much, see! all was vanity
and a chase after wind. There is no profit under
the sun. 12 What about one who succeeds a king?
He can do only what has already been done.†

Live It!

New and Improved!

NEW! IMPROVED! These two words are basic to many ad campaigns. No matter how good a product is, sooner or later, it will be "new and improved." The reason is simple: the advertisers want us to think the product is even better.

The writer of Ecclesiastes would not be very impressed with the claims of advertisers today. The author sounds skeptical in 1:9: "Nothing is new under the sun." The Teacher is not going to be taken in by claims that something is new and improved. This person has seen it all before.

Advertising can get us thinking that our lives aren't good enough, that we have to have more things and new things in order to be happy. In fact, we need to have a little bit of the attitude of the Teacher if we want to find contentment. Throughout the Book of Ecclesiastes, this writer invites us to enjoy what we have now.

- Have you ever gotten something because of its advertising, only to be disappointed afterward?
- Are you content and happy with the things you have—home, food, clothes, and so on?

Eccl 1:1–11

ECCL

1:15 *You cannot count what is not there*: perhaps originally a commercial metaphor alluding to loss or deficit in the accounts ledger.

1:18 *Sorrow . . . grief*: these terms refer not just to a store of knowledge or to psychological or emotional pain. Corporal punishment, sometimes quite harsh, was also employed frequently by parents and teachers.

2:1–11 The author here assumes the role of Solomon who, as king, would have had the wealth and resources at his disposal to acquire wisdom and engage in pleasurable pursuits. Verses 4–8 in particular, with their description of abundant wealth and physical gratifications, parallel the descriptions in 1 Kgs 4–11 of the extravagances of Solomon's reign.

2:3 *Guided by wisdom*: using all the means money can buy, the author sets out on a deliberate search to discover if pleasure constitutes true happiness.

2:8 *Many women*: the final phrase of this verse is difficult to translate. One word, *shiddah*, which appears here in both singular and plural, is found nowhere else in the Hebrew Bible. A suggested meaning is "woman" or "concubine," as it is interpreted here: "many women." The rest of the section (2:1–12) seems to be a description of Solomon's kingdom, and the "many women" would represent his huge harem (1 Kgs 11:1–3). In rabbinic Hebrew the word comes to mean "chest" or "coffer."

2:12 *What . . . been done*: the verse is difficult and elliptical. The words "He can do only" have been added for clarity. The two halves of the verse have been reversed. The author argues that it is useless to repeat the royal experiment described in vv. 1–11. The results would only be the same.

1:16 Eccl 2:9.
1:17 Eccl 1:3; 8:16.
2:11 Eccl 1:3, 17; Sir 44:9.

Pray It!

The Balance of Life

God of all seasons,
Help me to remember the sun when rain is falling.
Help me to remember the rain when the sun is shining.
Teach me to respect the seniors when I am a sophomore.
Teach me to respect the sophomores when I am a senior.
When I win on the field, let me remember the times I lost.
When I lose on the field, let me remember the times I won.
Guide me to appreciate studying when I'm taking a hard test.
Guide me to appreciate hard tests when I'm studying.
During times with friends, remind me of times alone.
During times alone, remind me of times with friends.
Help me to live all moments and remember there is a balance to life.
Amen.

▶ Eccl 3:1–8

Study of Wisdom and Folly

I went on to the consideration of wisdom, mad-
ness and folly. 13 And I saw that wisdom has as
much profit over folly as light has over darkness.

14 Wise people have eyes in their heads,
but fools walk in darkness.

Yet I knew that the same lot befalls both.† *

15 So I said in my heart, if the fool's lot is to be-
fall me also, why should I be wise? Where is the
profit? And in my heart I decided that this too is
vanity. 16 * The wise person will have no more
abiding remembrance than the fool; for in days
to come both will have been forgotten. How is it
that the wise person dies† like the fool! 17 There-
fore I detested life, since for me the work that is
done under the sun is bad; for all is vanity and a
chase after wind.

Study of the Fruits of Toil
To Others the Profits

18 And I detested all the fruits of my toil un-
der the sun, because I must leave them to the
one who is to come after me. 19 And who knows
whether that one will be wise or a fool? Yet that
one will take control of all the fruits of my toil
and wisdom under the sun. This also is vanity.
20 So my heart turned to despair over all the fruits
of my toil under the sun. 21 For here is one who
has toiled with wisdom and knowledge and skill,
and that one's legacy must be left to another
who has not toiled for it. This also is vanity and
a great evil. 22 * For what profit comes to mortals
from all the toil and anxiety of heart with which
they toil under the sun? 23 Every day sorrow and
grief are their occupation; even at night their
hearts are not at rest. This also is vanity.
24 † * There is nothing better for mortals than
to eat and drink and provide themselves with
good things from their toil. Even this, I saw, is
from the hand of God. 25 For who can eat or
drink apart from God? 26 † * For to the one who
pleases God, he gives wisdom and knowledge
and joy; but to the one who displeases, God
gives the task of gathering possessions for the
one who pleases God. This also is vanity and a
chase after wind.

No One Can Determine the Right Time To Act

3 1 † There is an appointed time for everything,
and a time for every affair under the heavens.
2 A time to give birth, and a time to die;
a time to plant, and a time to uproot the plant.

† **2:14** *Yet I knew . . . befalls both*: the author quotes a traditional saying upholding the advantages of wisdom, but then qualifies it. Nothing, not even wisdom itself, can give someone absolute control over their destiny and therefore guarantee any advantage.

2:16 *The wise person dies*: death, until now only alluded to (vv. 14–15), takes center stage and will constantly appear in the author's reflections through the remainder of the book.

2:24–26 The author is not advocating unrestrained indulgence. Rather he counsels acceptance of the good things God chooses to give. This is the first of seven similar conclusions that Qoheleth provides; see 3:12–13, 22; 5:17–18; 8:15; 9:7–9; 11:9.

2:26 According to 7:15 and 9:1–3, God does not make an objective, evidential, moral distinction between saint and sinner. God "gives" as God pleases.

3:1–8 The fourteen pairs of opposites describe various human activities. The poem affirms that God has determined the appropriate moment or "time" for each. Human beings cannot know that moment; further, the wider course of events and purposes fixed by

2:14 Eccl 9:2–3.
2:16 Eccl 1:11; Wis 2:4.
2:22 Eccl 1:3.
2:24 Eccl 3:12–13, 22; 5:17–19; 8:15.
2:26 Eccl 7:26; Prv 13:22.

ECCL

Cultural Connection

A Time for Connections

The *Tao te Ching* (pronounced "Dow deh JING") is the ancient Chinese Book of the Way. This piece of Chinese wisdom literature was written by Lao-tzu, who probably lived about 500 BC, close to the time of the author of Ecclesiastes. See how similar the following passage from the *Tao te Ching* is to Ecclesiastes 3:1–8:

> There is a time for being ahead,
> a time for being behind;
> a time for being in motion,
> a time for being at rest;
> a time for being vigorous,
> a time for being exhausted;
> a time for being safe,
> a time for being in danger.
> (Stephen Mitchell, translator, *Tao te Ching*, no. 29)

▶ Eccl 3:1–8

3 A time to kill, and a time to heal;
a time to tear down, and a time to build.
4 A time to weep, and a time to laugh;
a time to mourn, and a time to dance.
5 A time to scatter stones, and a time to gather them;
a time to embrace, and a time to be far from embraces.
6 A time to seek, and a time to lose;
a time to keep, and a time to cast away.
7 A time to rend, and a time to sew;
a time to be silent, and a time to speak.
8 A time to love, and a time to hate;
a time of war, and a time of peace.

9 * What profit have workers from their toil?
10 I have seen the business that God has given to
mortals to be busied about. 11 * God has made
everything appropriate to its time, but has put
the timeless† into their hearts so they cannot find
out, from beginning to end, the work which God
has done. 12 * I recognized that there is nothing
better than to rejoice and to do well during life.
13 Moreover, that all can eat and drink and enjoy
the good of all their toil—this is a gift of God. 14 I
recognized that whatever God does will endure
forever; there is no adding to it, or taking from
it. Thus has God done that he may be revered.
15 † * What now is has already been; what is to be,
already is: God retrieves what has gone by.

The Problem of Retribution

16 * And still under the sun in the judgment
place I saw wickedness, and wickedness also in
the seat of justice. 17 * I said in my heart, both
the just and the wicked God will judge, since a
time is set for every affair and for every work.†
18 I said in my heart: As for human beings, it is
God's way of testing them and of showing that
they are in themselves like beasts. 19 For the lot
of mortals and the lot of beasts is the same lot:
The one dies as well as the other. Both have the
same life breath. Human beings have no advantage over beasts, but all is vanity. 20 * Both go to
the same place; both were made from the dust,
and to the dust they both return. 21 Who knows†
if the life breath of mortals goes upward and the
life breath of beasts goes earthward? 22 * And I
saw that there is nothing better for mortals than
to rejoice in their work; for this is their lot. Who
will let them see what is to come after them?*

Vanity of Toil

4 1 Again I saw all the oppressions that take place under the sun: the tears of the victims with none to comfort† them! From the hand

† God are beyond them as well.

3:11 *The timeless*: others translate "eternity," "the world," or "darkness." The author credits God with keeping human beings ignorant about God's "work"—present and future.

3:15 The verse is difficult. Literally it reads "and God seeks out what was pursued." It appears to be a variation of the theme in 1:9, "There is nothing new under the sun."

3:17 *A time is set . . . work*: another possible reading would see this verse referring to a judgment in or after death: "a time for every affair and for every work *there*" (that is, in death or in Sheol).

3:21 *Who knows*: the author presumes a negative answer: "No one knows." In place of speculation on impossible questions, the author counsels enjoyment of what is possible (cf. v. 22; but see also 2:10–11).

4:1 *Oppressions . . . victims . . . none to comfort*: the author obviously feels deeply about the plight of the oppressed, but he seems to feel powerless to do anything. The repetition of "none to comfort" is purposeful, and emphatic.

* **3:9** Eccl 1:3.
3:11 Eccl 8:17; 11:5.
3:12 Eccl 2:24.
3:15 Eccl 1:9.
3:16 Eccl 4:1.
3:17 Eccl 8:6a; 11:9; 12:14.
3:20 Eccl 12:7; Gn 3:19; Sir 17:2.
3:22 Eccl 3:12–13; 5:17–18.
3:22 Eccl 8:7; 10:14.

Live It!

How Much Is Enough?

How much wealth does one need? In surveys, most young people reply they want just enough money to be happy. It's an interesting answer because they are implying they don't want to be greedy, but it takes money to be happy!

According to the Teacher, in Ecclesiastes 5:9, those who love money will always want more. What is God trying to tell us here? Maybe that real happiness is not found in material wealth. The more we want, the less satisfied we are. Money can be an evil when it is all we want and think about.

For a week, try to do things with your family and friends that do not cost anything. Play board games, go for walks or hikes, even volunteer some time at a community organization. Consider taking the money you save and donating it to a worthy cause.

▶ **Eccl 5:9**

of their oppressors comes violence, and there is
none to comfort them!* 2 And those now dead,
I declared more fortunate in death than are the
living to be still alive.* 3 And better off than both
is the yet unborn, who has not seen the wicked
work that is done under the sun. 4 Then I saw
that all toil and skillful work is the rivalry of one
person with another. This also is vanity and a
chase after wind.

5 "Fools fold their arms
and consume their own flesh"—†
6 Better is one handful with tranquility
than two with toil and a chase after wind!

Companions and Successors

7 Again I saw this vanity under the sun: 8 those
all alone with no companion, with neither child
nor sibling—with no end to all their toil, and no
satisfaction from riches. For whom do I toil and
deprive myself of good things? This also is vanity
and a bad business. 9 Two are better than one:
They get a good wage for their toil. 10 If the one
falls, the other will help the fallen one. But woe
to the solitary person! If that one should fall,
there is no other to help. 11 So also, if two sleep
together, they keep each other warm. How can
one alone keep warm? 12 Where one alone may
be overcome, two together can resist. A three-ply
cord† is not easily broken.

13 † Better is a poor but wise youth than an
old but foolish king who no longer knows cau-
tion; 14 for from a prison house he came forth to
reign; despite his kingship he was born poor. 15 I
saw all the living, those who move about under
the sun, with the second youth who will succeed
him.† 16 There is no end to all this people, to all
who were before them; yet the later generations
will not have joy in him. This also is vanity and
a chase after wind.

Vanity of Many Words

17 * Guard your step when you go to the house
of God.† Draw near for obedience, rather than
for the fools' offering of sacrifice; for they know
not how to keep from doing evil.

5 1 † Be not hasty in your utterance and let not
your heart be quick to utter a promise in
God's presence. God is in heaven and you are on
earth; therefore let your words be few.*

2 As dreams come along with many cares,
so a fool's voice along with a multitude of
words.

3 * When you make a vow to God, delay not
its fulfillment. For God has no pleasure in fools;
fulfill what you have vowed. 4 It is better not to
make a vow than make it and not fulfill it. 5 Let

†

4:5 *Consume their own flesh*: an enigmatic statement. In the context of vv. 4 and 6 it seems to warn that those who refuse to work for the necessities of life will suffer hunger and impair their bodily health. But the verse could also be intended for the industrious: Even the lazy may manage to have "their own flesh," that is, have sufficient food to eat.

4:12 *A three-ply cord*: an ancient proverb known centuries before biblical times. The progression ("two together . . . three-ply") seems to imply, "If two are good, three are even better."

4:13–16 This passage deals with kingship and succession, but is obscure.

4:15 The king is no sooner dead than the people transfer their allegiance to his successor.

4:17 *The house of God*: the Temple in Jerusalem. *Obedience . . . sacrifice*: the Temple was the place not only for sacrifice but also for instruction in the Law. Sacrifice without obedience was unacceptable; cf. 1 Sm 15:22; Hos 6:6.

5:1–6 Further counsels on prudence and circumspection in fulfilling one's religious obligations. It is not the multitude of words but one's sincerity that counts in the acknowledgment of God's sovereignty (v. 1), especially through obedience (4:17) and reverence (v. 6).

*

4:1 Eccl 3:16; 5:7; 9:4–5.
4:2 Eccl 6:3–5.
4:17 1 Sm 15:22; Ps 40:7–9; Prv 15:8; 21:3; Hos 6:6.
5:1 Ps 115:3, 16; Mt 6:7; Jas 1:19.
5:3 Nm 30:3; Dt 23:22–24; Prv 20:25; Sir 18:22–23.

not your utterances make you guilty, and say not
before his representative, "It was a mistake." Why
should God be angered by your words and de-
stroy the works of your hands? 6 * Despite many
dreams, futilities, and a multitude of words, fear
God!

Gain and Loss of Goods

7 * If you see oppression of the poor, and vio-
lation of rights and justice in the realm, do not
be astonished by the fact, for the high official has
another higher than he watching him and above
these are others higher still—. 8 But profitable for
a land in such circumstances is a king concerned
about cultivation.†

9 * The covetous are never satisfied with money,
nor lovers of wealth with their gain; so this too
is vanity. 10 Where there are great riches, there are
also many to devour them. Of what use are they
to the owner except as a feast for the eyes alone?
11 Sleep is sweet to the laborer, whether there is
little or much to eat; but the abundance of the
rich allows them no sleep.

12 This is a grievous evil which I have seen
under the sun: riches hoarded by their owners
to their own hurt. 13 Should the riches be lost
through some misfortune, they may have off-
spring when they have no means. 14 * As they
came forth from their mother's womb, so again
shall they return, naked as they came, having
nothing from their toil to bring with them.
15 This too is a grievous evil, that they go just as
they came. What then does it profit them to toil
for the wind? 16 All their days they eat in gloom
with great vexation, sickness and resentment.

17 * Here is what I see as good: It is appropriate
to eat and drink and prosper from all the toil one
toils at under the sun during the limited days of
life God gives us; for this is our lot. 18 Those to
whom God gives riches and property, and grants
power to partake of them, so that they receive
their lot and find joy in the fruits of their toil: This
is a gift from God. 19 For they will hardly dwell on
the shortness of life, because God lets them busy
themselves with the joy of their heart.†

Limited Worth of Enjoyment

6 1 There is another evil I have seen under the
sun, and it weighs heavily upon humankind:
2 * There is one to whom God gives riches and
property and honor, and who lacks nothing the
heart could desire; yet God does not grant the
power to partake of them, but a stranger devours
them. This is vanity and a dire plague. 3 Should
one have a hundred children and live many
years, no matter to what great age, still if one has
not the full benefit of those goods, I proclaim
that the child born dead, even if left unburied, is
more fortunate.† 4 * Though it came in vain and
goes into darkness and its name is enveloped
in darkness, 5 though it has not seen the sun or
known anything, yet the dead child has more
peace. 6 Should such a one live twice a thousand
years and not enjoy those goods, do not both go
to the same place?†

7 All human toil is for the mouth,† yet the
appetite is never satisfied. 8 What profit have
the wise compared to fools, or what profit have
the lowly in knowing how to conduct themselves
in life? 9 "What the eyes see is better than what
the desires wander after."† This also is vanity and
a chase after wind.

II. Qoheleth's Conclusions

10 Whatever is, was long ago given its name, and
human nature is known; mortals cannot contend
in judgment with One who is stronger.† 11 For the
more words, the more vanity; what profit is there
for anyone? 12 * For who knows what is good for
mortals in life, the limited days of their vain life,
spent like a shadow? Because who can tell them
what will come afterward under the sun?*

A. No One Can Find Out the Best Way of Acting

Critique of Sages on the Day of Adversity

7 1 A good name is better than good ointment,†
and the day of death than the day of birth.*
2 It is better to go to the house of mourning

5:8 *A king concerned about cultivation*: the Hebrew text is ambiguous and obscure. The author does not criticize the oppression he describes in v. 7. Now perhaps he expresses the hope that the king would use his power to upbuild agriculture in order to alleviate the hunger and suffering of the poor and oppressed.

5:19 The joys of life, though temporary and never assured, keep one from dwelling on the ills which afflict humanity.

6:3 Even a large family and exceptionally long life cannot compensate for the absence of good things and the joy which they bring.

6:6 *Same place*: the grave; cf. 3:20; 12:7.

6:7 *The mouth*: symbolic of human desires.

6:9 Compare the English proverb, "A bird in the hand is worth two in the bush." However, it could also mean, "The seeing of the eyes is better than the wandering of the desire," with the emphasis on the actions of seeing and desiring. Seeing is a way of possessing whereas desire, by definition, can remain frustrated and unfulfilled.

6:10–11 *One who is stronger* is, of course, God. *The more vanity*: contending with God is futile.

7:1 *Ointment*: a good name can be affirmed only with death, when one is normally anointed. The author dialogues in this section (vv. 1–14) with traditional wisdom, alternately affirming or countering its assertions. The real value of traditional wisdom lies in its ability to provoke one to thought and reflection, and not to absolve one from such activity.

5:6 Eccl 3:14.
5:7 Eccl 3:16; 4:1.
5:9 Eccl 4:8; Prv 28:22.
5:14 Jb 1:21; 1 Tm 6:7.
5:17 Eccl 2:24.
6:2 Eccl 2:18–19.
6:4 Eccl 4:2–3; Jb 3:11, 16.
6:12 Jb 8:9; 14:2; Ps 102:12.
6:12 Eccl 3:22; 8:7.
7:1 Eccl 4:2; Prv 22:1.

ECCL

than to the house of feasting,
For that is the end of every mortal,
and the living should take it to heart.*
3 Sorrow is better than laughter;
when the face is sad, the heart grows wise.
4 The heart of the wise is in the house of
mourning,
but the heart of fools is in the house of
merriment.
5 It is better to listen to the rebuke of the wise
than to listen to the song of fools;
6 For as the crackling of thorns under a pot,
so is the fool's laughter.
This also is vanity.
7 Extortion can make a fool out of the wise,
and a bribe corrupts the heart.
8 Better is the end of a thing than its beginning;
better is a patient spirit than a lofty one.
9 Do not let anger upset your spirit,
for anger lodges in the bosom of a fool.

10 Do not say: How is it that former times were
better than these? For it is not out of wisdom that
you ask about this.

11 Wisdom is as good as an inheritance
and profitable to those who see the sun.

12 † For the protection of wisdom is as the protec-
tion of money; and knowledge is profitable be-
cause wisdom gives life to those who possess it.
13 Consider the work of God. Who can make
straight what God has made crooked?* 14 On a
good day enjoy good things, and on an evil day
consider: Both the one and the other God has
made, so that no one may find the least fault
with him.

Critique of Sages on Justice and Wickedness

15 † I have seen all manner of things in my vain
days: the just perishing in their justice, and the
wicked living long in their wickedness. 16 "Be not
just to excess, and be not overwise. Why work
your own ruin? 17 Be not wicked to excess, and
be not foolish. Why should you die before your
time?" 18 It is good to hold to this rule, and not
to let that one go; but the one who fears God will
succeed with both.
19 Wisdom is a better defense for the wise than
ten princes in the city, 20 * yet there is no one on
earth so just as to do good and never sin. 21 Do not
give your heart to every word that is spoken; you
may hear your servant cursing you, 22 for your heart
knows that you have many times cursed others.
23 All these things I probed in wisdom. I said,
"I will acquire wisdom"; but it was far beyond
me. 24 What exists is far-reaching; it is deep, very
deep:† Who can find it out? 25 † * I turned my
heart toward knowledge; I sought and pursued
wisdom and its design, and I recognized that
wickedness is foolishness and folly is madness.

Critique of Advice on Women

26 * More bitter than death I find the woman†
who is a hunter's trap, whose heart is a snare,
whose hands are prison bonds. The one who
pleases God will be delivered from her, but the
one who displeases will be entrapped by her.
27 See, this have I found, says Qoheleth, adding
one to one to find the sum. 28 What my soul still
seeks and has yet to find is this: "One man out
of a thousand have I found, but a woman among
them all I have not found." 29 But this alone I
have found: God made humankind honest, but
they have pursued many designs.

Critique of Advice To Heed Authority

8 1† Who is like the wise person,
and who knows the explanation of things?
Wisdom illumines the face
and transforms a grim countenance.

2 Observe the command of the king, in view
of your oath to God. 3 Be not hasty to withdraw
from the king; do not persist in an unpleasant
situation, for he does whatever he pleases. 4 His
word is sovereign, and who can say to him,
"What are you doing?"
5 † * "Whoever observes a command knows
no harm, and the wise heart knows times and

7:12 St. Jerome's translation of v. 12b gives an edge to wisdom over money: "But learning and wisdom excel in this, that they bestow life on the one who possesses them."

7:15–24 The author continues both to affirm and to counter traditional wisdom. He affirms a certain validity to wisdom, but challenges complacency and mindless optimism. His sense of life's uncertainty and insecurity finds expression, for example, in the irony evident when v. 16 is read in the light of vv. 20–24: How can one be "excessively" just or wise, when justice and wisdom may be out of reach to begin with? The only sure thing is to "fear God" (v. 18).

7:24 *Far-reaching . . . deep*: the spatial metaphor here emphasizes wisdom's inaccessibility, a frequent theme in wisdom literature; cf. Jb 28; Prv 30:1–4; Sir 24:28–29; Bar 3:14–23.

7:25–29 The emphasis is on the devious designs of human beings in general, reflecting the viewpoint of Genesis.

7:26 *More bitter than death . . . the woman*: warnings against the scheming, adulterous woman are common in ancient wisdom (e.g., Prv 2:16–19, etc.).

8:1–4 The author continues to quote traditional wisdom but then to counter and qualify it. He concedes wisdom's advantages (v. 1), but then describes the subservience and sometimes demeaning demands required of the sage in the court of the king (vv. 2–4).

8:5–9 The wise exhibit keen insight about human nature and the course of events (vv. 5–6a). Yet their knowledge and wisdom

---

7:2 Eccl 12:1.
7:13 Eccl 1:15.
7:20 Jb 9:2; 1 Kgs 8:46; Rom 3:23.
7:25 Eccl 1:17.
7:26 Prv 5:4.

judgments." 6 * Yes, there is a time and a judgment for everything. But it is a great evil for mortals 7 * that they are ignorant of what is to come; for who will make known to them how it will be? 8 No one is master of the breath of life so as to retain it, and none has mastery of the day of death. There is no exemption in wartime, nor does wickedness deliver those who practice it. 9 All these things I saw and I applied my heart to every work that is done under the sun, while one person tyrannizes over another for harm.

The Problem of Retribution

10 Meanwhile I saw the wicked buried. They would come and go from the holy place. But those were forgotten in the city who had acted justly. This also is vanity.† 11 Because the sentence against an evil deed is not promptly executed, the human heart is filled with the desire to commit evil— 12 † because the sinner does evil a hundred times and survives. Though indeed I know that it shall be well with those who fear God, for their reverence toward him; 13 and that it shall not be well with the wicked, who shall not prolong their shadowy days, for their lack of reverence toward God.

14 This is a vanity that occurs on earth: There are those who are just but are treated as though they had done evil, and those who are wicked but are treated as though they had done justly. This, too, I say is vanity. 15 * Therefore I praised joy, because there is nothing better for mortals under the sun than to eat and to drink and to be joyful; this will accompany them in their toil through the limited days of life God gives them under the sun.

16 I applied my heart to know wisdom and to see the business that is done on earth, though neither by day nor by night do one's eyes see sleep, 17 * and I saw all the work of God: No mortal can find out the work that is done under the sun. However much mortals may toil in searching, no one finds it out; and even if the wise claim to know, they are unable to find it out.

B. No One Knows the Future

9 1 All this I have kept in my heart and all this I examined: The just, the wise, and their deeds are in the hand of God. Love from hatred† mortals cannot tell; both are before them. 2 * Everything is the same for everybody: the same lot for the just and the wicked, for the good, for the clean and the unclean, for the one who offers sacrifice and the one who does not. As it is for the good, so it is for the sinner; as it is for the one who takes an oath, so it is for the one who fears an oath. 3 Among all the things that are done under the sun, this is the worst, that there is one lot for all. Hence the hearts of human beings are filled with evil, and madness is in their hearts during life; and afterward—to the dead!

4 For whoever is chosen among all the living has hope: "A live dog† is better off than a dead lion." 5 * For the living know that they are to die, but the dead no longer know anything. There is no further recompense for them, because all memory of them is lost. 6 For them, love and hatred and rivalry have long since perished. Never again will they have part in anything that is done under the sun.

Did You Know?

Imagine There Is No Heaven

Some people assume that the ancient Israelites believed in an afterlife as we do today. However, Ecclesiastes speaks of the end of earthly life without any hint of eternal life: "The dead no longer know anything. There is no further recompense for them, because all memory of them is lost" (9:5). The book reflects the author's belief that all life ends with death. It was not until the last two centuries before Jesus that the idea of life after death began to take root among the Jewish people.

▶ Eccl 9:5

ECCL

† confront certain limits, such as the mystery of evil and the time and inevitability of death (vv. 6b–9).

8:10 This difficult verse seems to contrast the wicked, who die enjoying a good reputation as pious individuals, and the just, who are quietly forgotten.

8:12–17 The author admits that traditional wisdom affirms the long life and success of the just and the short unhappy life of the wicked (vv. 12b–13). But he points out clear exceptions: the wicked who live long, and the just who suffer for no apparent reason (v. 14). His puzzlement and frustration prompt a twofold response: acceptance of whatever joy God chooses to give each day, and honest acknowledgment that no one can discover "the work of God" (cf. 3:11; 7:13; 11:5).

9:1–3 *Love from hatred . . . everything is the same*: God seems to bestow divine favor or disfavor (love or hatred) indiscriminately on the just and wicked alike. More ominously, the arbitrariness and inevitability of death and adversity confront every human being, whether good or bad.

9:4–6 *A live dog . . . no further recompense*: human reason and experience persuaded Qoheleth that death with its finality and annihilating power cruelly negates the supreme value—life, and with it, all possibilities (cf. v. 10). Faith in eternal life has its foundation only in hope and trust in God's promise and in God's love.

8:5 Prv 19:16.
8:6 Eccl 3:17; 9:12.
8:7 Eccl 3:22; 6:12; 10:14.
8:15 Eccl 2:24; 3:22; 5:17–18; 9:7.
8:17 Eccl 3:11.
9:2 Eccl 2:14; 3:15.
9:5 Eccl 1:11; 2:16.

7 * Go, eat your bread† with joy and drink
your wine with a merry heart, because it is now
that God favors your works. 8 At all times let
your garments be white, and spare not the per-
fume for your head. 9 Enjoy life with the wife
you love, all the days of the vain life granted you
under the sun. This is your lot in life, for the toil
of your labors under the sun. 10 Anything you
can turn your hand to, do with what power you
have; for there will be no work, no planning,
no knowledge, no wisdom in Sheol where you
are going.

The Time of Misfortune Is Not Known

11 Again I saw under the sun that the race is not
won by the swift, nor the battle by the valiant,
nor a livelihood by the wise, nor riches by the
shrewd, nor favor by the experts; for a time of
misfortune comes to all alike. 12 Human beings
no more know their own time than fish taken
in the fatal net or birds trapped in the snare; like
these, mortals are caught when an evil time sud-
denly falls upon them.

The Uncertain Future and the Sages

13 On the other hand I saw this wise deed
under the sun, which I thought magnificent.
14 Against a small city with few inhabitants ad-
vanced a mighty king, who surrounded it and
threw up great siegeworks about it. 15 But in the
city lived a man who, though poor, was wise,
and he delivered it through his wisdom. Yet no
one remembered this poor man. 16 * Though I
had said, "Wisdom is better than force," yet the
wisdom of the poor man is despised and his
words go unheeded.

17 The quiet words of the wise are better heeded
than the shout of a ruler of fools.
18 Wisdom is better than weapons of war,
but one bungler destroys much good.

10

1 Dead flies corrupt and spoil the
perfumer's oil;
more weighty than wisdom or wealth is a
little folly!†
2 The wise heart turns to the right;
the foolish heart to the left.†

3 Even when walking in the street the fool,
lacking understanding, calls everyone a fool.†
4 Should the anger of a ruler burst upon you,
do not yield your place; for calmness† abates
great offenses.
5 I have seen under the sun another evil, like a
mistake that proceeds from a tyrant: 6 a fool put
in high position, while the great and the rich sit
in lowly places. 7 I have seen slaves on horseback,
while princes† went on foot like slaves.

8 Whoever digs a pit may fall into it,*
and whoever breaks through a wall, a snake
may bite.
9 Whoever quarries stones may be hurt by them,
and whoever chops wood† is in danger
from it.

10 If the ax becomes dull, and the blade is not
sharpened, then effort must be increased. But the
advantage of wisdom is success.

11 If the snake bites before it is charmed,
then there is no advantage in a charmer.†
12 Words from the mouth of the wise win favor,
but the lips of fools consume them.
13 * The beginning of their words is folly,
and the end of their talk is utter madness;
14 yet fools multiply words.
No one knows what is to come,
for who can tell anyone what will be?*
15 The toil of fools wearies them,
so they do not know even the way to town.

No One Knows What Evil Will Come

16 Woe to you, O land, whose king is a youth,†
and whose princes feast in the morning!
17 Happy are you, O land, whose king is of
noble birth,

---

†

9:7–10 *Go, eat your bread . . . enjoy life*: the author confesses his inability to imprison God in a fixed and predictable way of acting. Thus he ponders a practical and pragmatic solution: Seize whatever opportunity one has to find joy, if God grants it.

10:1 *Dead flies . . . a little folly*: wisdom is vulnerable to even the smallest amount of folly. The collection of proverbs and sayings in chaps. 10 and 11 demonstrates the author's sharp insight and strengthens his credentials as a sage. It thus adds weight to his critique of the wisdom tradition's tendencies to self-assurance and naive optimism.

10:2 *Right . . . left*: the right hand is identified with power, moral goodness, favor; the left hand with ineptness and bad luck.

10:3 *Calls everyone a fool*: or, "tells everyone that he (himself) is a fool."

10:4 *Calmness*: a frequent motif of wisdom; silence and reserve characterize the wise, while boisterousness and impetuosity identify the fool.

10:6–7 *A fool . . . the rich . . . slaves . . . princes*: another wisdom motif: astonishment at the reversal of the usual order in the world and in human affairs.

10:8–9 *A pit . . . a wall . . . stones . . . wood*: popular sayings reflecting the need for caution and alertness against the unexpected. Snakes could find a home in the stone walls of ancient Palestine; cf. Am 5:19.

10:10–11 *Ax . . . success . . . snake . . . charmer*: possession of the proper skill (a form of "wisdom") can ensure success, as in the case of a sharpened ax; but one must use it before it is too late (v. 11). Cf. Sir 12:13.

10:16 *A youth*: thus too young and inexperienced to govern effectively. *Feast in the morning*: either concluding a whole night of revelry or beginning a new round of merrymaking.

---

*

9:7 Eccl 2:24; 8:15; 11:9.
9:16 Prv 24:5.
10:8 Prv 26:27; Ps 7:16; Sir 27:29.
10:13 Eccl 5:2; 6:11.
10:14 Eccl 3:22; 6:12; 10:14.

and whose princes dine at the right time—
for vigor† and not in drinking bouts.
18 Because of laziness, the rafters sag;
when hands are slack, the house leaks.
19 A feast is made for merriment
and wine gives joy to the living,
but money answers† for everything.
20 Even in your thoughts do not curse the king,
nor in the privacy of your bedroom curse
the rich;
For the birds of the air may carry your voice,
a winged creature† may tell what you say.

11 1† Send forth your bread upon the face of the
waters;
after a long time you may find it again.
2 Make seven, or even eight portions;
you know not what misfortune may come
upon the earth.

No One Knows What Good Will Come

3† When the clouds are full,
they pour out rain upon the earth.
Whether a tree falls to the south or to the
north,
wherever it falls, there shall it lie.
4 One who pays heed to the wind will never sow,
and one who watches the clouds will never
reap.
5 Just as you do not know how the life breath
enters the human frame in the mother's
womb,
So you do not know the work of God,
who is working in everything.*
6 In the morning sow your seed,
and at evening do not let your hand be idle:
For you do not know which of the two will be
successful,
or whether both alike will turn out well.

Poem on Youth and Old Age

7 † Light is sweet! and it is pleasant for the eyes
to see the sun. 8 However many years mortals
may live, let them, as they enjoy them all, re-
member that the days of darkness will be many.
All that is to come is vanity.

Live It!

Carpe Diem—"Seize the Day"!

"Youth is wasted on the young." Perhaps you have heard that statement uttered by not-so-young adults struggling with growing older. There is some truth in it: many young people do not reflect on life and do not pause to appreciate being young.

The Teacher says some beautiful and profound things about youthfulness. He advises young people to "follow the ways of your heart" (Eccl 11:9) and to "banish misery from your heart" (verse 10). Someone like the Teacher might say today: "Follow your heart, and do not spend so much time worrying. It is a blessing to be young, to have so much energy and so many dreams. There are many pressures and stresses on young people today, but do not let them dominate your life. Enjoy this special time of growth and discovery."

It is good to be young. Seize the day!

▶ Eccl 11:7–10

9 Rejoice, O youth, while you are young
and let your heart be glad in the days of
your youth.
Follow the ways of your heart,
the vision of your eyes;
Yet understand regarding all this
that God will bring you to judgment.
10 Banish misery from your heart
and remove pain from your body,
for youth and black hair are fleeting.†

12 1† Remember your Creator in the days of
your youth,
before the evil days come
And the years approach of which you will say,

10:17 *For vigor*: or, "with self-control, restraint."

10:19 *Money answers*: a stark reminder that such a life requires money. It could also be an affirmation of the power of wealth: "Money conquers all."

10:20 *Birds of the air . . . winged creature*: a common motif in ancient literature, and a vivid reminder of the need for caution in dealing with the rich and powerful.

11:1–2 These two sayings can be understood against a commercial background. They acknowledge the uncertainty and risk such activity involves. At the same time they encourage action and a spirit of adventure. The first (v. 1) speaks of trade and overseas investment: Export your grain ("bread") to foreign markets and you may be surprised at the substantial profits. The second (v. 2) encourages diversification of investment (seven, or even eight shipments of grain) to insure against heavy losses.

11:3–6 Verses 3, 4, and 6 expand on the theme of uncertainty and human inability to assess accurately every situation. Verse 4, however, comments on the disadvantages of too much caution: Only those willing to risk will enjoy success. But only the Creator knows the mystery of the "work of God" (v. 5).

11:7–10 The concluding part of the book opens with a final bittersweet homage to life and an enthusiastic encouragement to rejoice in its gifts while they are within grasp.

11:10 *Fleeting*: lit., "vanity."

12:1–7 The homage to life of 11:7–10 is deliberately balanced

11:5 Eccl 3:11; 7:13; 8:17.

ECCL

Live It!

Remember the Elderly

Ecclesiastes 12:1–8 is a bittersweet poem about the difficulties of the aging process. To understand it, you need to be aware of the metaphors used, like these:

- Guards of the house = arms and hands
- Strong men = legs
- Women who grind = teeth
- Windows = eyes
- Doors = ears or lips
- Silver cord, golden bowl = life itself

Aging is a natural part of life, but it is a struggle for many people. No one enjoys its accompanying loss of mobility, loss of strength, and problems with seeing and hearing. The struggle is even greater if one is alone. If you have aging grandparents, family friends, or neighbors, keep in mind how much they need to be noticed by you. Stay in touch with them so you can learn from their wisdom and so they can be strengthened by your youth!

▶ **Eccl 12:1–8**

"I have no pleasure in them";
2 Before the sun is darkened,
and the light, and the moon, and the stars,
and the clouds return after the rain;
3† When the guardians of the house tremble,
and the strong men are bent;
When the women who grind are idle because they are few,
and those who look through the windows grow blind;
4 When the doors to the street are shut,
and the sound of the mill is low;
When one rises at the call of a bird,
and all the daughters of song are quiet;
5 When one is afraid of heights,
and perils in the street;
When the almond tree blooms,
and the locust grows sluggish
and the caper berry is without effect,
Because mortals go to their lasting home,
and mourners go about the streets;
6† Before the silver cord is snapped
and the golden bowl is broken,
And the pitcher is shattered at the spring,
and the pulley is broken at the well,
7 And the dust returns to the earth as it once was,
and the life breath returns to God who gave it.† *
8 Vanity of vanities, says Qoheleth,
all things are vanity!*

Epilogue

9 † Besides being wise, Qoheleth taught the people knowledge, and weighed, scrutinized and arranged many proverbs. 10 Qoheleth sought to find appropriate sayings, and to write down true sayings with precision. 11 The sayings of the wise are like goads; like fixed spikes are the collected sayings given by one shepherd.† 12 * As to more than these,† my son, beware. Of the making of many books there is no end, and in much study there is weariness for the flesh.

13 † * The last word, when all is heard: Fear God and keep his commandments, for this concerns all humankind; 14 * because God will bring to judgment every work, with all its hidden qualities, whether good or bad.

---

† by the sombre yet shimmering radiance of this poem on old age and death. The poem's enigmatic imagery has often been interpreted allegorically, especially in vv. 3–5. Above all it seeks to evoke an atmosphere as well as an attitude toward death and old age.

12:3–5 An allegorical reading of these verses sees references to the human body—"guardians": the arms; "strong men": the legs; "women who grind": the teeth; "those who look": the eyes; "the doors": the lips; "daughters of song": the voice; "the almond tree blooms": resembling the white hair of old age; "the locust . . . sluggish": the stiffness in movement of the aged; "the caper berry": a stimulant for appetite.

12:6 The golden bowl suspended by the silver cord is a symbol of life; the snapping of the cord and the breaking of the bowl, a symbol of death. *The pitcher . . . the pulley*: another pair of metaphors for life and its ending.

12:7 Death is portrayed in terms of the description of creation in Gn 2:7; the body corrupts in the grave, and the life breath (lit., "spirit"), or gift of life, returns to God who had breathed upon what he had formed.

12:9 A disciple briefly describes and praises the master's skill and reputation as a sage.

12:11 *One shepherd*: perhaps referring to the book's author, who gathers or "shepherds" together its contents. God could also be "the one shepherd," the ultimate depository and source of true wisdom.

12:12 *As to more than these*: the words seem to refer to the writings of Ecclesiastes and other sages. They are adequate and sufficient; any more involves exhaustive labor.

12:13–14 These words reaffirm traditional wisdom doctrine such as fear of God and faithful obedience, perhaps lest some of the more extreme statements of the author be misunderstood. Although the epilogue has been interpreted as a criticism of the book's author, it is really a summary that betrays the unruffled spirit of later sages, who were not shocked by Qoheleth's statements. They honored him as a *hakam* or sage (v. 9), even as they preserved his statements about the futility of life (v. 8), and the mystery of divine judgment (8:17; 11:5).

*
12:7 Eccl 3:20–21; Jb 34:14–15.
12:8 Eccl 1:2.
12:12 Eccl 1:18.
12:13 Eccl 5:6.
12:14 Eccl 11:9.

The Song of Songs

Sex sells. When we see an ad with a beautiful woman slipping out of a sports car or a bare-chested man grabbing an ice-cold soda, we sit up and take notice. Advertisers love to take advantage of our fascination with sex. Once they have our attention, they can sell us something we might not even be interested in! The Song of Solomon—a collection of ancient love poems—reminds us that this powerful force is ultimately a gift from God.

In Depth

From an advertiser's point of view, the Song of Songs is a well-kept secret. How many people are aware of its explicit sexual images? Consider these verses:

- "Let him kiss me with the kisses of his mouth!" (1:2).
- "Your lips drip honey, my bride, / honey and milk are under your tongue" (4:11).
- "Let your breasts be like clusters of the vine / and the fragrance of your breath like apples" (7:9).

Some people find some of the images in this book so surprising that they wonder why the Song of Songs is found in the Bible at all.

Scholars believe that the naming of King Solomon in the Song's first verse is the main reason that this book was preserved and eventually included with the Jewish holy books. Although written long after Solomon's death, this book—like Proverbs and Ecclesiastes—was attributed to him to give it authority.

Through the centuries, some people have not been able to accept the Song of Songs as simply love poetry and have hunted for a deeper meaning. One of the most complex books of the Old Testament, it can be interpreted from many perspectives, i.e., allegorical, cultic, dramatic, and literal. Many people believe that the lover and the beloved in this book stand for Israel and God, or for Jesus and the church. Modern-day scholars, however, begin their interpretation of the Song of Songs at the literal level, that is, as a collection of love poems. The book's inclusion among the other holy books, they insist, is an affirmation of the goodness of human sexuality: human love is holy because it is a gift from God. Catholic scholars generally interpret this book as allegorical of God and Israel, but do not eliminate the possibility of interpreting it literally as an inspired portrayal of human love. The passion and beauty of human sexual attraction is a reflection of the passion and beauty of God's love for us!

At a Glance

I. The Song of Songs by Solomon

Quick Facts

Inspired Author: unknown, probably writing after the Jews' return from the Babylonian Exile in 538 BC

Theme: poetry that expresses the goodness and passion of human love and God's love for his people

Of Note: In other translations, this book is called the Song of Solomon or the Canticle of Canticles.

Song of Songs

1 [1]The Song of Songs,† which is Solomon's.

The Woman Speaks of Her Lover

2†*W Let him kiss me with kisses of his mouth,
for your love is better than wine,†
3 better than the fragrance of your perfumes.†
Your name is a flowing perfume—
therefore young women love you.
4 * Draw me after you! Let us run!†
The king has brought me to his bed chambers.
Let us exult and rejoice in you;
let us celebrate your love: it is beyond wine!
Rightly do they love you!

Love's Boast

5 W I am black and beautiful,
Daughters of Jerusalem†—
Like the tents of Qedar,
like the curtains of Solomon.
6 Do not stare at me because I am so black,†
because the sun has burned me.
The sons of my mother were angry with me;
they charged me with the care of the vineyards:
my own vineyard I did not take care of.

Love's Inquiry

7 W Tell me, you whom my soul loves,
where you shepherd,† where you give rest at midday.
Why should I be like one wandering
after the flocks of your companions?
8 M If you do not know,
most beautiful among women,
Follow the tracks of the flock

1:1 *Song of Songs*: in Hebrew and Aramaic the idiom "the X of Xs" denotes the superlative (e.g., "king of kings" = "the highest king"; cf. Dt 10:17; Eccl 1:2; 12:8; Ezr 7:12; Dn 2:37). The ascription of authorship to Solomon is traditional. The heading may also mean "for Solomon" or "about Solomon."

1:2–8:14 This translation augments the canonical text of the Song with the letters *W, M,* and *D*, placed in the margin, to indicate which of the characters in the Song is speaking: the woman, the man, or the "Daughters of Jerusalem." This interpretive gloss follows an early Christian scribal practice, attested in some Septuagint manuscripts from the first half of the first millennium A.D.

1:2–7 The woman and her female chorus address the man, here viewed as king and shepherd (both are familiar metaphors for God; cf. Ps 23:1; Is 40:11; Jn 10:1–16). There is a wordplay between "kiss" (Hebrew *nashaq*) and "drink" (*shaqah*), anticipating 8:1–2. The change from third person ("let him kiss . . .") to second person (" . . . for your love . . .") is not uncommon in the Song and elsewhere (1:4; 2:4; etc.; Ps 23:1–3, 4–5, 6; etc.) and reflects the woman's move from interior monologue to direct address to her partner.

1:3 *Your perfumes*: *shemen* (perfume) is a play on *shem* (name).

1:4 Another change, but from second to third person (cf. 1:2). The "king" metaphor recurs in 1:12; 3:5–11; 7:6. *Let us exult*: perhaps she is addressing young women, calling on them to join in the praise of her lover.

1:5 *Daughters of Jerusalem*: the woman contrasts herself with the elite city women, who act as her female "chorus" (5:9; 6:1). *Qedar*: a Syrian desert region whose name suggests darkness; tents were often made of black goat hair. *Curtains*: tent coverings, or tapestries. *Solomon*: it could also be read Salma, a region close to Qedar.

1:6 *So black*: tanned from working outdoors in her brothers' vineyards, unlike the city women she addresses. *My own vineyard*: perhaps the woman herself; see 8:8–10 for her relationship to her brothers.

1:7 *Shepherd*: a common metaphor for kings. Here and elsewhere in the Song (3:1; 5:8; 6:1), the woman expresses her desire to be in the company of her lover. The search for the lover and her failure to find him create a degree of tension. Only at the end (8:5–14) do the lovers finally possess each other.

1:2–3 Sg 4:10. **1:4** Sg 4:10.

Cultural Connection

Black and Beautiful

I am black and beautiful,
Daughters of Jerusalem—
Like the tents of Qedar,
like the curtains of Solomon.
(Song 1:5)

Who is speaking to us in this Scripture text? Who is so boldly and confidently proclaiming to us that she is black and beautiful? Some traditions say this is the bride of Solomon, the son of David and the third king of Israel.

Many of the people in the Old Testament world were black Africans or Afro-Asiatics (Asians of black African heritage). They had various shades of dark skin. In Song of Songs 1:5, the bride describes herself as black like the tents of Qedar; in 5:10, she describes her lover as ruddy (reddish) in color.

Some African Americans are ruddy; others are darker. Together, all African Americans are a rainbow of blackness. Whatever shade they are, it is good. And if you are one of them, you are black and beautiful!

▶ **Song 1:5**

and pasture your lambs†
near the shepherds' tents.

Love's Vision

9 M To a mare among Pharaoh's chariotry†
I compare you, my friend:
10 Your cheeks lovely in pendants,
your neck in jewels.
11 We will make pendants of gold for you,
and ornaments of silver.

How Near Is Love!

12 W While the king was upon his couch,
my spikenard† gave forth its fragrance.
13 My lover† is to me a sachet of myrrh;
between my breasts he lies.
14 My lover is to me a cluster of henna†
from the vineyards of En-gedi.
15 M * How beautiful you are, my friend,
how beautiful! your eyes are doves!†
16 W How beautiful you are, my lover—
handsome indeed!
Verdant indeed is our couch;†
17 the beams of our house are cedars,
our rafters, cypresses.

2 1 W I am a flower of Sharon,†
a lily of the valleys.
2 M Like a lily among thorns,
so is my friend among women.
3 W Like an apple tree among the trees of the woods,
so is my lover among men.
In his shadow† I delight to sit,
and his fruit is sweet to my taste.
4 * He brought me to the banquet hall†
and his glance at me signaled love.
5 * Strengthen me with raisin cakes,†
refresh me with apples,
for I am sick with love.
6 * His left hand is under my head

† **1:8** *Pasture your lambs*: both the woman and the man act as shepherds in the Song.

1:9–11 The man compares the woman's beauty to the rich adornment of the royal chariot of Pharaoh. *My friend*: a special feminine form of the word "friend," appearing only in the Song (1:15; 2:2, 10, 13; 4:1, 7; 5:2; 6:4) and used to express endearment and equality in love. Cf. Hos 3:1 for the use of the masculine form of the term in a context with sexual overtones.

1:12 *Spikenard*: a precious perfumed ointment from India; in 4:13–14, a metaphor for the woman herself.

1:13 *My lover*: the woman's favorite term for her partner (used 27 times). *Myrrh*: an aromatic resin of balsam or roses used in cosmetics, incense, and medicines.

1:14 *Henna*: a plant which bears white scented flowers, used in cosmetics and medicines. *En-gedi*: a Judean desert oasis overlooking the Dead Sea.

1:15 *Doves*: doves are pictured in the ancient world as messengers of love.

1:16–17 Continuing the royal metaphor, the meeting place of the lovers, a shepherd's hut of green branches, becomes a palace with beams of cedar and rafters of cypress when adorned with their love.

2:1 *Flower of Sharon*: probably the narcissus, which grows in the fertile Plain of Sharon lying between Mount Carmel and Jaffa on the Mediterranean coast. *Lily*: the lotus plant.

2:3 *Shadow*: suggestive of protection (cf. Jgs 9:15; Ez 17:23; Ps 17:8; 121:5) and, here, of the woman's joy in the presence of her lover.

2:4–6 *The banquet hall*: the sweet things of the table, the embrace of the woman and man, express the richness of their affection and the intimacy of their love.

2:5 *Raisin cakes*: perhaps pastries used in the worship of the fertility goddess (cf. Hos 3:1; Jer 7:18; 44:19). *Apples*: this is the common translation of a fruit that cannot be identified (cf. 2:3; 8:5); it appears frequently in Sumerian love poetry associated with the worship of the goddess Inanna. *Sick*: love-sickness is a popular motif in ancient love poetry.

* **1:15** Sg 4:1, 7. **2:4** Sg 1:4. **2:5** Sg 5:8. **2:6** Sg 8:3.

Cultural Connection

Romantic Love

God loves us passionately and seeks us with the enthusiasm of a lover who memorizes every detail and cherishes every moment (see Song 1:9–17). Romantic, playful love was created by God for us to enjoy. The way we express such love can bring joy and delight; it also can devastate and destroy if it is abused and not respected. Be careful with love. God gave us our sexuality as a gift, not as a weapon.

Hear the tender respect of this love poem from the Cherokee tradition:

You are part of me now
 You touched me.
With your kindness and love
 So enchanted.
Your soft lips are kind.
 Your eyes glow with life.
I'm glad you touched me.
 You're part of me now.
(Lloyd Carl Owle, "You Are Part of Me")

▶ Song 1:9–17

and his right arm embraces me.
7 * I adjure you, Daughters of Jerusalem,†
by the gazelles and the does of the field,
Do not awaken, or stir up love
until it is ready.

Her Lover's Visit Remembered

8 W The sound of my lover! here he comes†
springing across the mountains,
leaping across the hills.
9 My lover is like a gazelle†
or a young stag.
See! He is standing behind our wall,
gazing through the windows,
peering through the lattices.
10 My lover speaks and says to me,
M "Arise, my friend, my beautiful one,
and come!
11 For see, the winter is past,
the rains are over and gone.
12 The flowers appear on the earth,
the time of pruning the vines has come,
and the song of the turtledove is heard in
our land.
13 The fig tree puts forth its figs,
and the vines, in bloom, give forth fragrance.
Arise, my friend, my beautiful one,
and come!
14 My dove in the clefts of the rock,†
in the secret recesses of the cliff,
Let me see your face,
let me hear your voice,
For your voice is sweet,
and your face is lovely."
15 W Catch us the foxes,† the little foxes
that damage the vineyards; for our
vineyards are in bloom!
16 * My lover belongs to me and I to him;
he feeds among the lilies.
17 * Until the day grows cool† and the shadows
flee,
roam, my lover,
Like a gazelle or a young stag
upon the rugged mountains.

Loss and Discovery

3 1 W * On my bed at night I sought him†
whom my soul loves—
I sought him but I did not find him.
2 "Let me rise then and go about the city,†
through the streets and squares;
Let me seek him whom my soul loves."

†

2:7 Cf. 3:5; 5:8; 8:4. *By the gazelles and the does*: perhaps a mitigated invocation of the divinity based on the assonance in Hebrew of the names of these animals with terms for God.

2:8–13 In this sudden change of scene, the woman describes a rendezvous and pictures her lover hastening toward her dwelling until his voice is heard calling her to him.

2:9 *Gazelle*: a frequent motif in ancient poems from Mesopotamia.

2:14 The woman is addressed as though she were a dove in a mountain cleft out of sight and reach.

2:15 A snatch of song in answer to the request of 2:14; cf. 8:13–14. *Foxes*: they threaten to disturb the security of vineyards. The vineyards are women sought after by young lovers, i.e., foxes.

2:17 *Grows cool*: in the evening when the sun is going down. Cf. Gn 3:8. *Rugged*: Hebrew obscure; some interpret it as a geographical name; others, in the sense of spices (cf. 8:14); still others, of sacrifice (Gn 15:10); the image probably refers here to the woman herself.

3:1–5 See the parallel in 5:2–8.

3:2 The motif of seeking/finding here and elsewhere is used by later Christian and Jewish mystics to speak of the soul's search for the divine.

*

2:7 Sg 3:5; 8:4. **2:16** Sg 6:3; 7:10. **2:17** Sg 4:6; 8:14. **3:1–5** Sg 5:2–8.

I sought him but I did not find him.
3 The watchmen found me,
as they made their rounds in the city:
"Him whom my soul loves—have you seen him?"
4 * Hardly had I left them
when I found him whom my soul loves.†
I held him and would not let him go
until I had brought him to my mother's house,
to the chamber of her who conceived me.
5 * I adjure you, Daughters of Jerusalem,
by the gazelles and the does of the field,
Do not awaken or stir up love
until it is ready.

Solomon's Wedding Procession

6 D * Who is this coming up from the desert,†
like columns of smoke

† **3:4** *Whom my soul loves*: the fourfold repetition of this phrase in vv. 1–4 highlights the depth of the woman's emotion and desire. *Mother's house*: cf. 8:2; a place of safety and intimacy, one which implicitly signifies approval of the lovers' relationship.

3:6–11 This may be an independent poem. In context it portrays the lover as King Solomon, escorted by sixty armed men, coming in royal procession to meet a bride.

* **3:4** Sg 8:2.
3:5 Sg 2:7; 8:4.
3:6 Sg 6:10; 8:5.

Live It!

The Illusion of Pornography

Everywhere you look, it seems, you can find ads for phone sex, pornographic magazines and videos, and Internet porn sites. People are lured into the immoral world of false love through an industry that preys on those who are weak and lost, those unfortunate souls searching for love in all the wrong places.

One interpretation proposes that the Song of Solomon is about passion and sexual longing between a bride and a bridegroom. Their love is committed: "My lover belongs to me and I to him" (Song 2:16). Their love is at once both urgent ("Draw me after you! Let us run!" [1:4]) and patient ("Do not awaken, or stir up love / until it is ready" [2:7]). This is not the kind of love offered to us in pornography, which has nothing at all to do with real love.

If you find yourself drawn to pornography, ask yourself: Is this God's purpose for human sexuality? Is this enriching to human love, or degrading? Pray for the strength to avoid the temptation and illusion of pornography. Find an adult or someone you can trust to talk to if this is a problem for you.

▶ Song 2:1–17

Live It!

Sexuality and Dialogue

A number of the love songs included in the Song of Solomon are addressed to the bridegroom and the beloved. It is as if a romantic dialogue has been recorded as lovers express the depth of feeling and desire they have for each other.

Dialogue is an essential aspect in any relationship. Open and honest communication provides the basis for maintaining and deepening the bonds of respect, friendship, and love.

Here is a time-honored test for any deep relationship: Is it possible for the two of you to speak honestly with each other about anything—especially problems and difficulties? Are you willing and able to discuss all dimensions of your love—including sexual feelings and desires?

Young couples often avoid such sensitive conversations. They fall victim to embarrassment and confusion and often leave important things unsaid. Such failure to communicate can result in hurt feelings, misunderstandings, and even behaviors that can lead to manipulation, selfishness, and sin.

Don't be afraid to discuss sexual issues. Always be ready to examine the nature of your relationships, especially when the power and passion of sexuality are present. True sexual love is rooted in dialogue, honest communication, and commitment. It finds its fullest expression in the context of marriage.

▶ Song of Songs, chapters 2–7

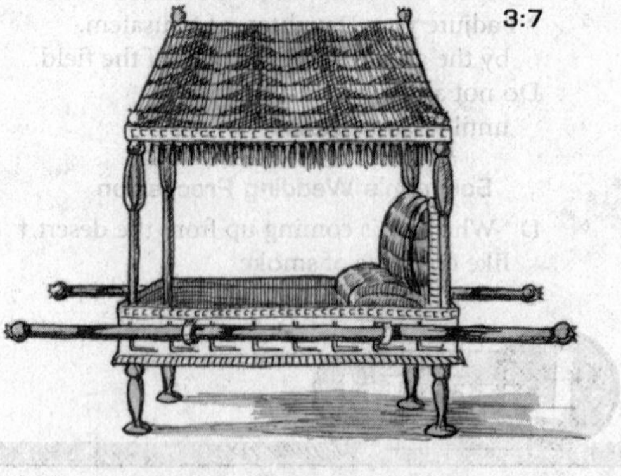

3:7

Perfumed with myrrh and frankincense,
with all kinds of exotic powders?
7 See! it is the litter of Solomon;
sixty valiant men surround it,
of the valiant men of Israel:
8 All of them expert with the sword,
skilled in battle,
Each with his sword at his side
against the terrors† of the night.
9 King Solomon made himself an enclosed litter
of wood from Lebanon.
10 He made its columns of silver,
its roof of gold,
Its seat of purple cloth,
its interior lovingly fitted.†
Daughters of Jerusalem, 11 go out
and look upon King Solomon
In the crown with which his mother has
crowned him
on the day of his marriage,
on the day of the joy of his heart.

The Beauty of the Woman

4 1 M *,* How beautiful you are, my friend,
how beautiful you are!
Your eyes are doves
behind your veil.
Your hair is like a flock of goats
streaming down Mount Gilead.†
2 Your teeth† are like a flock of ewes to be shorn,
that come up from the washing,
All of them big with twins,
none of them barren.
3 Like a scarlet strand, your lips,
and your mouth—lovely!
Like pomegranate† halves, your cheeks
behind your veil.
4 * Like a tower of David, your neck,
built in courses,
A thousand shields hanging upon it,
all the armor of warriors.†
5 * Your breasts are like two fawns,
twins of a gazelle
feeding among the lilies.
6 * Until the day grows cool
and the shadows flee,
I shall go to the mountain of myrrh,
to the hill of frankincense.†
7 You are beautiful in every way, my friend,
there is no flaw in you!†
8 With me from Lebanon, my bride!
With me from Lebanon, come!
Descend from the peak of Amana,
from the peak of Senir and Hermon,†
From the lairs of lions,
from the leopards' heights.

"You have ravished my heart, my sister, my bride; you have ravished my heart with one glance of your eyes."
(Song 4:9)

9 * You have ravished my heart, my sister,† my
bride;
you have ravished my heart with one
glance of your eyes,
with one bead of your necklace.
10 * How beautiful is your love,
my sister, my bride,

3:8 *Terrors*: cf. Ps 91:5; perhaps bandits lying in wait, unidentified dangers lurking in darkness.

3:10 *Lovingly fitted*: translation uncertain. The phrase "Daughters of Jerusalem" is read here with the following verse.

4:1 This section (vv. 1–7) begins a *wasf*, a traditional poetic form describing the physical attributes of one's partner in terms of the natural world (cf. 5:10–16; 6:5b–7; 7:1–7). *Veil*: women of the region customarily veiled their faces for some occasions (cf. 4:3; 6:7; Gn 24:65–67; 38:14–19).

4:2 *Teeth*: praised for whiteness and evenness.

4:3 *Pomegranate*: a fruit with a firm skin and deep red color. The woman's cheek (or perhaps her brow) is compared, in roundness and tint, to a half-pomegranate.

4:4 The ornaments about her neck are compared to the trophies and armaments on the city walls. Cf. 1 Kgs 10:10; 14:26–28; Ez 27:10.

4:6 *Mountain of myrrh . . . hill of frankincense*: spoken figuratively of the woman; cf. 8:14.

4:7 Cf. the description of the church in Eph 5:27.

4:8 *Amana . . . Senir and Hermon*: these rugged heights symbolize obstacles that would separate the lovers; cf. 2:14.

4:9 *Sister*: a term of endearment; brother-sister language forms part of the conventional language of love used in this canticle, the Book of Tobit, and elsewhere in poetry from Egypt, Mesopotamia, and Syro-Palestine.

4:1–3 Sg 6:5–7.
4:1 Sg 1:15.
4:4 Sg 7:5.
4:5 Sg 7:4.
4:6 Sg 2:17.
4:9 Sg 6:5.
4:10 Sg 1:2–3.

How much better is your love than wine,
  and the fragrance of your perfumes than
    any spice!
11 Your lips drip honey,† my bride,
  honey and milk are under your tongue;
And the fragrance of your garments
  is like the fragrance of Lebanon.

The Lover's Garden

12 M * A garden enclosed, my sister, my bride,
  a garden enclosed, a fountain sealed!†
13 Your branches are a grove of pomegranates,
  with fruits of choicest yield:
Henna with spikenard,
14 spikenard and saffron,
Sweet cane and cinnamon,
  with all kinds of frankincense;
Myrrh and aloes,
  with all the finest spices;†
15 A garden fountain, a well of living water,
  streams flowing from Lebanon.
16 Awake,† north wind!
  Come, south wind!
Blow upon my garden
  that its perfumes may spread abroad.
W Let my lover come to his garden
  and eat its fruits of choicest yield.

5 1 M * I have come to my garden, my sister, my
    bride;
  I gather my myrrh with my spices,
I eat my honeycomb with my honey,
  I drink my wine with my milk.
D? Eat, friends; drink!
  Drink deeply, lovers!†

A Fruitless Search

2 W * I was sleeping, but my heart was awake.†
  The sound of my lover knocking!
"Open to me, my sister, my friend,
  my dove, my perfect one!
For my head is wet with dew,
  my hair, with the moisture of the night."
3 I have taken off my robe,†
  am I then to put it on?
I have bathed my feet,
  am I then to soil them?
4 My lover put his hand in through the opening:
  my innermost being† trembled because of
    him.
5 I rose to open for my lover,
  my hands dripping myrrh:
My fingers, flowing myrrh
  upon the handles of the lock.
6 I opened for my lover—
  but my lover had turned and gone!
  At his leaving, my soul sank.
I sought him, but I did not find him;
  I called out after him, but he did not
    answer me.†
7 The watchmen† found me,
  as they made their rounds in the city;
They beat me, they wounded me,
  they tore off my mantle,
  the watchmen of the walls.
8 * I adjure you, Daughters of Jerusalem,
  if you find my lover
What shall you tell him?
  that I am sick with love.

The Lost Lover Described

9 D How does your lover differ from any other
    lover,
  most beautiful among women?
How does your lover differ from any other,
  that you adjure us so?
10 W My lover is radiant and ruddy;†
  outstanding among thousands.
11 His head is gold, pure gold,
  his hair like palm fronds,
  as black as a raven.
12 His eyes are like doves
  beside streams of water,
Bathing in milk,
  sitting† by brimming pools.
13 His cheeks are like beds of spices

4:11 *Honey*: sweet words (cf. Prv 5:3) or perhaps kisses (1:2–3). *Honey and milk*: familiar descriptions for the fertile promised land (Ex 3:8, 17; Lv 20:24; Nm 13:27; Dt 6:3).

4:12 *Garden enclosed . . . fountain sealed*: reserved for the lover alone. Cf. Prv 5:15–19 for similar images used to describe fruitful, committed relationship.

4:14 These plants are all known for their sweet fragrance.

4:16 *Awake*: the same verb is used of love in 3:5. The woman may be the speaker of 16a, as it is she who issues the invitation of 16b. *His garden*: the woman herself.

5:1 *Eat . . . lovers*: the translation and meaning are uncertain.

5:2–8 An experience of anticipation and loss similar to that in 3:1–5. The lover's abrupt appearance resembles that in 2:8–9.

5:3 *Robe*: knee-length undergarment worn by men and women. *Am I then . . . ?*: the woman's refusal is a form of gentle teasing; that she does not really reject her lover is shown by her actions in vv. 5–6. See 1:7–8; 2:14–15, for other teasing interchanges.

5:4 *My innermost being*: lit., "innards." In Gn 25:23, Is 49:1; Ps 71:6, the word appears to carry the meaning of "womb."

5:6 The motif of the locked-out lover is common in classical Greek and Latin poetry.

5:7 *The watchmen*: they do not know the reason for the woman's appearance in the city streets; cf. 3:2–4.

5:10–11 In answer to the question of 5:9 the woman sings her lover's praises (vv. 10–16). *Ruddy*: also used of David (1 Sm 16:12; 17:42). *Gold*: indicates how precious the lover is. *Palm fronds*: his thick, luxuriant growth of hair.

5:12 *Sitting . . .* : the translation of this line is uncertain; it may continue the metaphor of the lover's eyes, or refer to another part of his anatomy (e.g., teeth) which has been omitted from the text.

4:12 Sg 6:2, 11. **5:2** Sg 3:1–2.
5:1 Sg 6:2. **5:8** Sg 2:7; 8:4.

Did You Know?

Sex in the Old Testament

Through its surprisingly graphic sexual content (see, for example, 7:1–10), the Song of Songs has surprised many generations of readers. It reminds us that one of the richest images of the Old Testament is a sexual one: God as the faithful lover of Israel. In Exodus 20:5, we hear of God's jealous love of the Chosen People. By the time of the early prophets, the image of God as lover was fully developed: "On that day—oracle of the LORD, / You shall call me 'My husband'" (Hos 2:18).

Because of ancient Israel's conviction that human love reflects divine love—and vice versa—there was a high regard for human sexuality. This regard was reflected in Israel's sexual morality. Free-for-all sex stood in clear contradiction to the holiness of God, whose faithful love was the model for all human love. The Ten Commandments prohibit not only having sex with someone else's spouse but also desiring someone else's spouse.

Despite these high standards, some Bible stories do not comment on the morality of behavior that would be unacceptable in Christian morality. They make no comment on the many patriarchs and kings who have more than one wife, and take for granted an inferior status of women in marriage. Because moral insights have developed over the centuries, we must remember to read biblical passages in light of the *whole* Bible and the Christian tradition. In the Old Testament, we find the seeds of Christian sexual morality, not its full flower.

yielding aromatic scents;
his lips are lilies
that drip flowing myrrh.

14 His arms are rods of gold
adorned with gems;
His loins, a work of ivory
covered with sapphires.
15 His legs, pillars of alabaster,
resting on golden pedestals.
His appearance, like the Lebanon,
imposing as the cedars.
16 His mouth is sweetness itself;
he is delightful in every way.
Such is my lover, and such my friend,
Daughters of Jerusalem!

The Lost Lover Found

6 1 D Where has your lover gone,
most beautiful among women?
Where has your lover withdrawn
that we may seek him with you?†
2 W * My lover has come down to his garden,†
to the beds of spices,
To feed in the gardens
and to gather lilies.
3 * I belong to my lover, and my lover belongs
to me;
he feeds among the lilies.

The Beauty of the Woman

4 M Beautiful as Tirzah are you, my friend;†
fair as Jerusalem,
fearsome as celestial visions!
5 * Turn your eyes away from me,
for they stir me up.
Your hair is like a flock of goats
streaming down from Gilead.
6 * Your teeth are like a flock of ewes
that come up from the washing,
All of them big with twins,
none of them barren.
7 Like pomegranate halves,
your cheeks behind your veil.
8 Sixty are the queens, eighty the concubines,
and young women without number—
9 One alone† is my dove, my perfect one,
her mother's special one,
favorite of the one who bore her.
Daughters see her and call her happy,
queens and concubines, and they praise her:

†

6:1 The Daughters of Jerusalem are won by this description of the lover and offer their aid in seeking him (cf. 5:6, 9).

6:2–3 The woman implies here that she had never really lost her lover, for he has come down to his garden (cf. 2:16; 4:5). *Feed . . . lilies*: the imagery here evokes both a shepherd pasturing his flocks and erotic play between the lovers (2:16; 4:5, 12, 16).

6:4–9 The man again celebrates the woman's beauty. *Tirzah*: probably meaning "pleasant"; it was the early capital of the Northern Kingdom of Israel (1 Kgs 16). *Celestial visions*: the meaning is uncertain. Military images may be implied here, i.e., the "heavenly hosts" who fight along with God on Israel's behalf (cf. Jgs 5:20), or perhaps a reference to the awesome goddesses of the region who combined aspects of both fertility and war.

6:9 *One alone*: the incomparability of the woman is a favorite motif in love poetry.

6:10 *"Who . . . "*: the speakers may be the women of vv. 8–9. *Moon . . . sun*: lit., "the white" and "the hot," respectively (cf. Is 24:23; 30:26). *Fearsome*: see note on 6:4–9.

*

6:2 Sg 4:12; 5:1.
6:3 Sg 2:16; 7:11.
6:5 Sg 4:9.
6:6–7 Sg 4:1–3.
6:10 Sg 3:6; 8:5.

10 * "Who† is this that comes forth like the
dawn,
beautiful as the white moon, pure as the
blazing sun,
fearsome as celestial visions?"

Love's Meeting

11 W * To the walnut grove† I went down,
to see the young growth of the valley;
To see if the vines were in bloom,
if the pomegranates had blossomed.
12 Before I knew it, my desire had made me
the blessed one of the prince's people.†

The Beauty of the Beloved

7 1 D? Turn, turn, O Shulammite!†
turn, turn that we may gaze upon you!
W How can you gaze upon the Shulammite
as at the dance of the two camps?
2 M How beautiful are your feet in sandals,†
O noble daughter!
Your curving thighs like jewels,
the product of skilled hands.
3 Your valley,† a round bowl
that should never lack mixed wine.
Your belly, a mound of wheat,
encircled with lilies.
4 * Your breasts are like two fawns,
twins of a gazelle.
5 * Your neck like a tower of ivory;
your eyes, pools in Heshbon
by the gate of Bath-rabbim.
Your nose like the tower of Lebanon
that looks toward Damascus.†
6 Your head rises upon you like Carmel;†
your hair is like purple;
a king is caught in its locks.

Love's Desires

7 How beautiful you are, how fair,
my love, daughter of delights!

Pray It!

The Song of Songs

If you looked at human love as a reflection of divine love, then parts of this love poem, called the Song of Songs, could be understood as prayer. Try reading parts of it as your words to God, and other parts as God's words to you. Look at these sections:

- 2:3–6. a prayer describing your passion for God
- 5:6–8. a prayer to God when God seems absent
- 8:6–7. God's words of love to you

The words may seem strange in this context, but if we are passionate about pursuing a human relationship, why can't we be passionate about pursuing our relationship with God? Some of the greatest saints expressed their love of God as a passionate, romantic love. You can do the same in your prayer with God!

8 Your very form resembles a date-palm,†
and your breasts, clusters.
9 I thought, "Let me climb the date-palm!
Let me take hold of its branches!
Let your breasts be like clusters of the vine
and the fragrance of your breath like apples,
10 And your mouth like the best wine—
W that flows down smoothly for my lover,
gliding† over my lips and teeth.
11 * I belong to my lover,†
his yearning is for me.

†

6:11 *Walnut grove*: also a site of activity in a wedding hymn of the Syrian moon goddess Nikkal (cf. the woman compared to the moon in v. 10).

6:12 The text is obscure in Hebrew and in the ancient versions. The Vulgate reads: "I did not know; my soul disturbed me because of the chariots of Aminadab." Based on a parallel in Jgs 5:24, "chariots" is here emended to "blessed one."

7:1 *Shulammite*: the woman is so designated because she is considered to be from Shulam (or Shunem) in the plain of Esdraelon (cf. 1 Kgs 1:3), or because the name may mean "the peaceful one," and thus recall the name of Solomon. *Turn*: she is asked to face the speaker(s). *How . . .* : she refuses to be regarded as a spectacle ("the dance of the two camps" is unknown). Some interpret the episode as an invitation to her to dance.

7:2–6 Another description of the woman's charms. *Sandals*: the woman's sandaled foot was apparently considered quite seductive (Jdt 16:9). *Noble*: a possible connection to the enigmatic "prince" of 6:12. *Curving . . . jewels*: the meaning of these Hebrew words is not certain. Wine and wheat suggest fertility.

7:3 *Valley*: lit., navel; a discreet allusion to her sex.

7:5 The comparison emphasizes the stateliness of her neck, and the clarity of her eyes. *Bath-rabbim*: a proper name which occurs only here; there was a city of Rabbah northeast of Heshbon in Transjordan. Cf. Jer 49:3.

7:6 *Carmel*: a prominent set of cliffs overlooking the Mediterranean.

7:8–9 *Date-palm*: a figure of stateliness. The lover is eager to enjoy the possession of his beloved.

7:10 *Gliding*: the beloved interrupts her partner's compliment by referring to the intoxication of their union. The translation rests on an emendation of the enigmatic "the lips of the sleepers."

7:11–14 The woman's answer assures him of her love, and invites him to return with her to the rural delights associated with their love (cf. also 6:11–12). *Yearning*: used only here and in Gn 3:16; 4:7. The dependency and subordination of woman to man presented as a consequence of sin in the Genesis story is here transcended in the mutuality of true love.

*

6:11 Sg 4:12–5:1; 7:13. **7:4** Sg 4:5. **7:5** Sg 4:4. **7:11** Sg 2:16; 6:3.

12 Come, my lover! Let us go out to the fields,
let us pass the night among the henna.
13 * Let us go early to the vineyards, and see
if the vines are in bloom,
If the buds have opened,
if the pomegranates have blossomed;
There will I give you my love.
14 The mandrakes† give forth fragrance,
and over our doors are all choice fruits;
Fruits both fresh and dried, my lover,
have I kept in store for you.

8 1 Would that you were a brother to me,
nursed at my mother's breasts!
If I met you out of doors, I would kiss you
and none would despise me.
2 * I would lead you, bring you to my mother's
house,
where you would teach me,
Where I would give you to drink
spiced wine, my pomegranate† juice.
3 * His left hand is under my head,
and his right arm embraces me.
4 * I adjure you, Daughters of Jerusalem,
do not awaken or stir up love
until it is ready!

The Return from the Desert

5 D? * Who is this coming up from the desert,
leaning upon her lover?
W Beneath the apple tree I awakened you;†
there your mother conceived you;
there she who bore you conceived.

True Love

6 Set me as a seal† upon your heart,
as a seal upon your arm;
For Love is strong as Death,
longing is fierce as Sheol.
Its arrows are arrows of fire,
flames of the divine.
7 * Deep waters† cannot quench love,
nor rivers sweep it away.
Were one to offer all the wealth of his house
for love,
he would be utterly despised.

An Answer to the Brothers

8 W "We have a little sister;†
she has no breasts as yet.
What shall we do for our sister
on the day she is spoken for?
9 If she is a wall,
we will build upon her a silver turret;
But if she is a door,
we will board her up with cedar planks."
10 I am a wall,†
and my breasts are like towers.
I became in his eyes
as one who brings peace.

A Boast

11 M? Solomon had a vineyard at
Baal-hamon;†
he gave over the vineyard to caretakers.
For its fruit one would have to pay
a thousand silver pieces.
12 My vineyard is at my own disposal;
the thousand pieces are for you, Solomon,
and two hundred for the caretakers of its
fruit.

The Lovers' Yearnings

13 M You who dwell in the gardens,†
my companions are listening for your
voice—
let me hear it!
14 W * Swiftly, my lover,
be like a gazelle or a young stag
upon the mountains of spices.

---

†

7:14 *Mandrakes*: herbs believed to have power to arouse love and promote fertility; cf. Gn 30:14–16.

8:2 *Wine . . . pomegranate*: sexual connotations are implied, since the root "drink" (*shaqah*) is a wordplay on "kiss" (*nashaq*) in v. 1; cf. 1:2.

8:5 *Awakened you*: the speakers in this verse are difficult to identify. Someone (the poet? Daughters?) hails the couple in v. 5a. According to the Masoretic vocalization, the woman is the speaker in v. 5b.

8:6 *Seal*: this could be worn bound to the arm, as here, or suspended at the neck, or as a ring (Jer 22:24). It was used for identification and signatures. *Strong . . . fierce*: in human experience, Death and Sheol are inevitable, unrelenting; in the end they always triumph. Love, which is just as certain of its victory, matches its strength against the natural enemies of life; waters cannot extinguish it nor floods carry it away. It is more priceless than all riches. *Flames of the divine*: the Hebrew is difficult: the short form (-Yah) of the divine name Yhwh found here may associate love with the Lord, or it may be acting as a superlative—i.e., god-sized flames.

8:7 *Deep waters*: often used to designate chaos (Ps 93:4; 144:7; Is 17:12–13; Hb 3:15). The fires of love cannot be extinguished, even by waters of chaos. *Wealth*: love cannot be bought.

8:8–9 The woman quotes the course of action her elder brothers had decided on. While she is yet immature, they will shelter her in view of eventual marriage. *Wall . . . door*: if she is virtuous, she will be honored; if she is not, she will be kept under strict vigilance. *Silver turret*: a precious ornament.

8:10 In reply to the officious and meddling attitude of the brothers, she answers with their terms: she is mature ("wall," "towers"). *Brings peace*: or, "finds peace."

8:11–12 These enigmatic verses have been variously interpreted, depending on who is taken to be the speaker. In v. 11, if the woman, she boasts that she is a vineyard of great value. If the man, he boasts over his possession of her.

8:13–14 As in 2:14, her lover asks for a word or a song and she replies in words similar to those found in 2:17.

7:13 Sg 6:11.
8:2 Sg 3:4.
8:3 Sg 2:6.
8:4 Sg 2:7; 3:5.
8:5 Sg 3:6; 6:10.
8:7 Prv 6:31.
8:14 Sg 2:9, 17; 4:6.

The Book of Wisdom

Do you know what life was like for your great-grandparents? Were they, or other members of your family, immigrants to the United States? How much of their history do you know? Time and distance have a way of fading the memories that keep our roots alive. The same was true for the ancient Jewish people after they had settled in different countries. The Book of Wisdom was written to remind them of their roots and the wisdom of their traditions.

At a Glance

I. The Reward of Righteousness (1:1—6:21).

II. Praise of Wisdom by Solomon (6:22—11:1).

III. Special Providence of God during the Exodus (11:2–16; 12:23–27; 15:18—19:22) with digressions on God's mercy (11:17—12:22) and on the folly and shame of idolatry (13:1—15:17).

Quick Facts

Inspired Author: unknown, writing around 50 BC, making this the latest of all Old Testament books

Theme: the reward of the righteous, the praise of wisdom, the importance of trust in God

Of Note: The book is not found in every version of the Old Testament (see "The Case of the Missing Books," near Tb 1:16).

In Depth

The Jewish people living in Alexandria, Egypt, in the first century BC had long forgotten the difficult transition their ancestors had experienced in moving from Judea. In fact, they had come to feel so much at home in Alexandria that certain leaders began to fear that the Jewish faith and way of life might be lost (see "Diaspora Jews," near Est 2:5). One of those leaders wrote the Book of Wisdom to encourage the "displaced" Jews to remain faithful to their heritage. Although incorporating new ideas into traditional arguments, the author insists that true wisdom is, in fact, very old. Its course can be traced "from the very beginning" (Wis 6:22).

The Book of Wisdom grapples with another problem—good versus evil—in a refreshing way. The author is convinced that there will be a final judgment, in which good people will confront their oppressors "with great assurance," and their oppressors will "be shaken with dreadful fear" (5:1–2). What is more, the just will "live forever" (5:15), whereas the evil will "be utterly laid waste" (4:19). Like Second Maccabees, the Book of Wisdom sees life after death as the answer to the troubling question, Why do innocent people suffer although God is good and just?

The Book of Wisdom claims King Solomon as its honorary author, even though it was written long after his death. In this quiet way, it reminds the Jewish faithful that they must never forget their roots in their ancient faith, even though they feel at home in their new land. The book shows how people of faith take the best of their history and tradition to find new answers in new situations.

Wisdom

I. The Reward of Righteousness†

Exhortation to Righteousness, the Key to Life

1 [1] Love righteousness,† you who judge the earth;*
think of the LORD in goodness,
and seek him in integrity of heart;*
2 Because he is found by those who do not test him,
and manifests himself to those who do not disbelieve him.*
3 For perverse counsels separate people from God,
and his power, put to the proof, rebukes the foolhardy;*
4† Because into a soul that plots evil wisdom does not enter,
nor does she dwell in a body under debt of sin.*
5 For the holy spirit of discipline† flees deceit
and withdraws from senseless counsels
and is rebuked when unrighteousness occurs.*
6 For wisdom is a kindly spirit,
yet she does not acquit blasphemous lips;
Because God is the witness of the inmost self*
and the sure observer of the heart
and the listener to the tongue.*
7 For the spirit of the LORD fills the world,*
is all-embracing, and knows whatever is said.
8 Therefore those who utter wicked things will not go unnoticed,
nor will chastising condemnation pass them by.*
9 For the devices of the wicked shall be scrutinized,
and the sound of their words shall reach the LORD,
for the chastisement of their transgressions;
10 Because a jealous ear hearkens to everything,*
and discordant grumblings are not secret.
11 Therefore guard against profitless grumbling,
and from calumny† withhold your tongues;
For a stealthy utterance will not go unpunished,
and a lying mouth destroys the soul.

† **1:1–6:21** The reward is the gift of immortality, to the righteous (1:15; 3:1–3), but not to the wicked (5:1–13). Contrasts between these two groups dominate chaps. 1–5. The philosophy of the wicked and their persecution of the righteous are dramatically presented in 1:16–2:24. New light is shed on the suffering of the righteous (3:1–9), childlessness (3:13–15), and premature death (4:7–16)—in contrast to the fate of the wicked (3:10–12, 16–19; 4:3–6, 17–20).

1:1 *Righteousness*: not merely the cardinal virtue of justice (cf. 8:7), but the universal moral quality which is the application of wisdom to moral conduct. *You who judge*: "judges" and "kings" (cf. 6:1) are addressed in accordance with the literary customs of the times and with the putative Solomonic authorship, but the real audience is the Jewish community.

1:4 In these verses personified Wisdom is identified with the spirit of the Lord; so also in 9:17.

1:5 *Discipline*: here and elsewhere, another name for Wisdom.

1:11 *Calumny*: speech against God and divine providence is meant.

1:1 1 Chr 29:17; Ps 2:10; Is 26:9.
1:1–2 Sir 1:25.
1:2 1 Chr 28:9.
1:3 Is 59:2.
1:4 Sir 15:7–8; Rom 7:14.
1:5 Is 63:10.
1:6 Jer 17:10.
1:6–7 Jer 23:24–25.
1:7 Wis 12:1.
1:8 Prv 19:5.
1:10–11 Nm 14:27–28.

12 Do not court death† by your erring way of life,
nor draw to yourselves destruction by the works of your hands.
13 Because God did not make death,*
nor does he rejoice in the destruction of the living.
14 For he fashioned all things that they might have being,
and the creatures of the world are wholesome;
There is not a destructive drug among them
nor any domain of Hades† on earth,
15 For righteousness is undying.† *

The Wicked Reject Immortality and Righteousness Alike

16 It was the wicked who with hands and words invited death,
considered it a friend, and pined for it,
and made a covenant with it,
Because they deserve to be allied with it.*

2 1 For, not thinking rightly, they said among themselves:†
"Brief and troubled is our lifetime;*
there is no remedy for our dying,
nor is anyone known to have come back from Hades.
2 For by mere chance were we born,
and hereafter we shall be as though we had not been;
Because the breath in our nostrils is smoke,
and reason a spark from the beating of our hearts,
3 And when this is quenched, our body will be ashes
and our spirit will be poured abroad like empty air.*
4 Even our name will be forgotten in time,
and no one will recall our deeds.
So our life will pass away like the traces of a cloud,
and will be dispersed like a mist
Pursued by the sun's rays
and overpowered by its heat.
5 For our lifetime is the passing of a shadow;
and our dying cannot be deferred

Pray It!

God Knows Our Heart

God, you know my heart (see Wis 1:6) *even better than I do. This could scare me, or it could give me peace—the peace of knowing that despite my weakness and sin, you still love me. I choose to feel peace! And knowing that you see into my heart and still love me, I choose to do good. Give me the courage to do the right thing. Help me never to say a word to injure another person. Give me too the wisdom of loving justice, so that my heart might be a reflection of your own. Amen.*

▶ **Wis 1:6–15**

because it is fixed with a seal; and no one returns.*
6 Come, therefore, let us enjoy the good things that are here,
and make use of creation with youthful zest.*
7 Let us have our fill of costly wine and perfumes,
and let no springtime blossom pass us by;
8 let us crown ourselves with rosebuds before they wither.
9 Let no meadow be free from our wantonness;
everywhere let us leave tokens of our merriment,
for this is our portion, and this our lot.*
10 Let us oppress the righteous poor;
let us neither spare the widow
nor revere the aged for hair grown white with time.*
11 But let our strength be our norm of righteousness;
for weakness proves itself useless.

12† Let us lie in wait for the righteous one,
because he is annoying to us;

†

1:12 *Death*: as will become clear, the author is not speaking of physical death but of spiritual death, the eternal separation from God.

1:14 *Hades*: the Greek term for the Hebrew Sheol, the dwelling place of the dead.

1:15 *Undying*: immortality is not seen as an innate quality of the soul but as a gift of God to the righteous.

2:1–20 In this speech the wicked deny survival after death and indeed invite death by their evil deeds.

2:12–5:23 From 2:12 to 5:23 the author draws heavily on Is 52–62, setting forth his teaching in a series of characters or types taken from Isaiah and embellished with additional details from other

*

1:13–14 Ez 18:32; 33:11; 2 Pt 3:9.
1:15 Is 51:6–8.
1:16 Is 28:15.
2:1 Jb 14:1; 7:9.
2:3 Jb 7:9; Jas 4:14.
2:5 Ps 144:4.
2:6 Is 22:13; 1 Cor 15:32.
2:9 Jer 13:25.
2:10 Ex 22:21–23; Lv 19:32.

he opposes our actions,
Reproaches us for transgressions of the law†
and charges us with violations of our training.*
13 He professes to have knowledge of God
and styles himself a child of the LORD.*
14 To us he is the censure of our thoughts;
merely to see him is a hardship for us,*
15 Because his life is not like that of others,
and different are his ways.
16 He judges us debased;
he holds aloof from our paths as from things impure.
He calls blest the destiny of the righteous
and boasts that God is his Father.*

17 Let us see whether his words be true;
let us find out what will happen to him in the end.*
18 For if the righteous one is the son of God,
God will help him
and deliver him from the hand of his foes.*
19 With violence and torture let us put him to the test
that we may have proof of his gentleness
and try his patience.
20 Let us condemn him to a shameful death;
for according to his own words, God will take care of him."*

21 These were their thoughts, but they erred;
for their wickedness blinded them,*
22† And they did not know the hidden counsels of God;
neither did they count on a recompense for holiness
nor discern the innocent souls' reward.*
23 For God formed us to be imperishable;
the image of his own nature he made us.*
24 But by the envy† of the devil, death entered the world,
and they who are allied with him experience it.*

The Hidden Counsels of God†

A. On Suffering†

3 1 The souls of the righteous are in the hand of God,*
and no torment shall touch them.

"The souls of the righteous are in the hand of God, and no torment shall touch them."
(Wis 3:1)

2 They seemed, in the view of the foolish, to be dead;
and their passing away was thought an affliction
3 and their going forth from us, utter destruction.
But they are in peace.*
4 For if to others, indeed, they seem punished,
yet is their hope full of immortality;
5 Chastised a little, they shall be greatly blessed,
because God tried them
and found them worthy of himself.*
6 As gold in the furnace, he proved them,
and as sacrificial offerings† he took them to himself.*
7 In the time of their judgment† they shall shine
and dart about as sparks through stubble;*
8 They shall judge nations and rule over peoples,
and the LORD shall be their King forever.*
9 Those who trust in him shall understand truth,
and the faithful shall abide with him in love:

† texts. The description of the "righteous one" in 2:12–20 seems to undergird the New Testament passion narrative.

2:12 *Law*: the law of Moses; "training" has the same meaning.

2:22 This verse announces the subject of the next section.

2:24 *Envy*: perhaps because Adam was in the image of God or because Adam had control over all creation. *Devil*: the first biblical text to equate the serpent of Gn 3 with the devil.

3:1–4:19 The central section of chaps. 1–6. The author begins by stating that immortality is the reward of the righteous, and then in the light of that belief comments on three points of the traditional discussion of the problem of retribution (suffering, childlessness, early death) each of which was often seen as a divine punishment.

3:1–12 The author affirms that, for the righteous, sufferings are not punishments but purification and opportunities to show fidelity, whereas for the wicked suffering is truly a punishment.

3:6 *Offerings*: the image is that of the burnt offering, in which the victim is completely consumed by fire.

3:7 *Judgment*: the Greek *episkopé* is God's loving judgment of those who have been faithful to him; the same word is used in 14:11 for the punishment of the wicked at God's judgment. Cf. also v. 13.

* **2:12** Hos 8:1.
2:13 Mt 27:43; Jn 8:55; 10:36–39.
2:14 Mt 9:4.
2:16 Jer 6:30.
2:17 Gn 37:20.
2:18 Ps 22:9; Is 42:1; Mt 27:43; Jn 5:18.
2:20 Jas 5:6.
2:21 Rom 1:21.
2:22 Ps 18:24–25; Prv 11:18; Mt 11:25.
2:23 Gn 1:26–27; Is 54:16 LXX.
2:24 Gn 3:1–24; Rom 5:12.
3:1 Jb 12:10.
3:3 Is 57:2.
3:5 Tb 12:13; 2 Cor 4:17; 1 Pt 1:6–7.
3:6 Ps 51:19; Prv 17:3; Sir 2:5; Is 48:10.
3:7 Dn 12:3; Ob 18; Mal 3:3; Mt 13:43.
3:8 Wis 8:14; Prv 8:16; Dn 7:22; 1 Cor 6:2; Rev 20:4.

Because grace and mercy are with his holy
ones,*
and his care is with the elect.
10 But the wicked shall receive a punishment to
match their thoughts,†
since they neglected righteousness and
forsook the LORD.
11 For those who despise wisdom and
instruction are doomed.*
Vain is their hope, fruitless their labors,
and worthless their works.*
12 Their wives are foolish and their children
wicked,
accursed their brood.*

B. On Childlessness†

13 Yes, blessed is she who, childless and undefiled,
never knew transgression of the marriage
bed;
for she shall bear fruit at the judgment of
souls.†
14 So also the eunuch whose hand wrought no
misdeed,
who held no wicked thoughts against the
LORD—
For he shall be given fidelity's choice reward†
and a more gratifying heritage in the LORD's
temple.*
15 For the fruit of noble struggles is a glorious one;
and unfailing is the root of understanding.†*
16 But the children of adulterers† will remain
without issue,
and the progeny of an unlawful bed will
disappear.*
17 For should they attain long life, they will be
held in no esteem,
and dishonored will their old age be in the
end;
18 Should they die abruptly, they will have no
hope
nor comfort in the day of scrutiny;
19 for dire is the end of the wicked generation.*

4 1 Better is childlessness with virtue;
for immortal is the memory of virtue,
acknowledged both by God and human
beings.*
2 When it is present people imitate it,
and they long for it when it is gone;
Forever it marches crowned in triumph,
victorious in unsullied deeds of valor.
3 But the numerous progeny of the wicked shall
be of no avail;
their spurious offshoots shall not strike
deep root
nor take firm hold.*
4 For even though their branches flourish for a
time,
they are unsteady and shall be rocked by
the wind
and, by the violence of the winds,
uprooted;*
5 Their twigs shall be broken off untimely,
their fruit useless, unripe for eating,
fit for nothing.
6 For children born of lawless unions
give evidence of the wickedness of their
parents, when they are examined.

C. On Early Death†

7 But the righteous one, though he die early,
shall be at rest.*
8 For the age that is honorable comes not with
the passing of time,*
nor can it be measured in terms of years.
9 Rather, understanding passes for gray hair,
and an unsullied life is the attainment of
old age.
10† The one who pleased God was loved,*
living among sinners, was transported—
11 Snatched away, lest wickedness pervert his
mind
or deceit beguile his soul;*
12 For the witchery of paltry things obscures
what is right
and the whirl of desire transforms the
innocent mind.*
13 Having become perfect in a short while,
he reached the fullness of a long career;
14 for his soul was pleasing to the LORD,

---

† **3:10** *To match their thoughts*: a fate as empty as that which they describe in 2:1–5.

3:13–4:6 The true fruit of life is not children but virtue which leads to immortality. The many children of the wicked will be a disappointing fruit.

3:13 See vv. 7–9.

3:14 *Fidelity's choice reward*: cf. Is 56:1–8. *More gratifying*: better than sons and daughters; cf. Is 56:5.

3:15 *Root of understanding*: the root that is understanding (wisdom).

3:16 *Adulterers*: understood here as a type of sinners in general; cf. Is 57:3–5.

4:7–19 Early death is not a punishment for the righteous because genuine old age is the attainment of perfection and early death is a preservation from corruption. The old age and death of the wicked, however, will not be honorable.

4:10–11 There are allusions here to Enoch (Gn 5:21–24), who was young by patriarchal standards, and to Lot (Gn 19:10–11; 2 Pt 2:7–8). Cf. also Is 57:1–2.

---

* **3:9** Wis 4:15; Jb 10:12; Jn 15:10.
3:11 Prv 1:7.
3:11–12 Sir 41:8.
3:12 Dt 28:18.
3:14 Is 56:2–5.
3:15 Sir 1:18.
3:16 2 Sm 12:14.
3:19 Ps 34:22.
4:1 Prv 3:3–4; Sir 16:1–3.
4:3 Sir 23:25.
4:4 Sir 40:15; Is 40:24.
4:7 Wis 3:3.
4:8 Jb 12:12; 32:9; Sir 25:4–6.
4:10 Gn 5:24; Sir 44:16; Heb 11:5.
4:11 Is 57:1–2.
4:12 Wis 2:21; Dn 13:9.

therefore he sped him out of the midst of
wickedness.*
But the people saw and did not understand,
nor did they take that consideration into
account.†
16 Yes, the righteous one who has died will
condemn
the sinful who live;
And youth, swiftly completed, will condemn
the many years of the unrighteous who
have grown old.*
17 For they will see the death of the wise one
and will not understand what the LORD
intended,
or why he kept him safe.
18 They will see, and hold him in contempt;
but the LORD will laugh them to scorn.*
19 And they shall afterward become dishonored
corpses*
and an unceasing mockery among the dead.
For he shall strike them down speechless and
prostrate*
and rock them to their foundations;
They shall be utterly laid waste
and shall be in grief
and their memory shall perish.

The Judgment of the Wicked

20 Fearful shall they come, at the counting up of
their sins,
and their lawless deeds shall convict them
to their face.

5 1† Then shall the righteous one with great
assurance confront*
his oppressors who set at nought his
labors.*
2 Seeing this, the wicked shall be shaken with
dreadful fear,
and be amazed at the unexpected salvation.
3 They shall say among themselves, rueful
and groaning through anguish of spirit:
"This is the one whom once we held as a
laughingstock
and as a type for mockery,
4 fools that we were!
His life we accounted madness,
and death dishonored.
5 See how he is accounted among the heavenly
beings;†
how his lot is with the holy ones!*
6 We, then, have strayed from the way of truth,*
and the light of righteousness did not shine
for us,
and the sun did not rise for us.*
7 We were entangled in the thorns of mischief
and of ruin;
we journeyed through trackless deserts,
but the way of the LORD we never knew.
8 What did our pride avail us?
What have wealth and its boastfulness
afforded us?*
9 All of them passed like a shadow
and like a fleeting rumor;*
10 Like a ship traversing the heaving water:
when it has passed, no trace can be found,
no path of its keel in the waves.
11 Or like a bird flying through the air;
no evidence of its course is to be found—
But the fluid air, lashed by the beating of
pinions,
and cleft by the rushing force
Of speeding wings, is traversed;
and afterward no mark of passage can be
found in it.
12 Or as, when an arrow has been shot at a mark,
the parted air straightway flows together
again
so that none discerns the way it went—
13 Even so, once born, we abruptly came to
nought
and held no sign of virtue to display,
but were consumed in our wickedness."*
14† Yes, the hope of the wicked is like chaff borne
by the wind,
and like fine, storm-driven snow;
Like smoke scattered by the wind,
and like the passing memory of the nomad
camping for a single day.*
15 But the righteous live forever,
and in the LORD is their recompense,
and the thought of them is with the Most
High.*

---

† **4:14** Verse 15 is omitted because it repeats the last two lines of 3:9.

5:1–13 In contrast to their speech in chap. 2 the wicked now regret their assessment of life and righteousness.

5:5 *Heavenly beings*: lit., "sons of God." These are the holy ones, members of the heavenly court, among whom the righteous are to be found. A bodily resurrection does not seem to be envisioned.

5:14–23 A picture of the reward of the righteous which develops into an apocalyptic description of the divine warrior's destruction of evil. The author utilizes Is 59–62.

* **4:14** Gn 19:22, 29; 2 Pt 2:7.
4:16 Mt 12:41–42.
4:18 Ps 37:13.
4:19 Neh 1:10 LXX; Ps 18:8; Is 14:19; Jer 23:39–40.
4:19 2 Mc 3:29.
5:1–2 2 Thes 1:6–7.
5:1 Col 2:15.
5:5 Acts 26:18; Col 1:12.
5:6 Prv 4:18–19; Jn 12:35.
5:6–7 Prv 22:5; Is 59:6–14.
5:8 Ps 49:7; Prv 10:2.
5:9–12 1 Chr 20:15; Jb 9:25–26 LXX; Ps 144:4.
5:13 Ez 33:10.
5:14 Jb 21:18; Ps 1:4; 37:20; Is 17:13.
5:15 Is 62:11; Ez 18:9.

16 Therefore shall they receive the splendid crown,
the beautiful diadem, from the hand of the LORD,
For he will shelter them with his right hand,
and protect them with his arm.*
17 He shall take his zeal for armor*
and arm creation to requite the enemy,
18 Shall put on righteousness for a breastplate,
wear sure judgment for a helmet,
19 Shall take invincible holiness for a shield,*
20 and sharpen his sudden anger for a sword.
The universe will war with him against the foolhardy;
21 Well-aimed bolts of lightning will go forth
and from the clouds will leap to the mark
as from a well-drawn bow;*
22 and as from a sling, wrathful hailstones
shall be hurled.
The waters of the sea will be enraged
and flooding rivers will overwhelm them;*
23 A mighty wind will confront them
and winnow them like a tempest;
Thus lawlessness will lay waste the whole earth
and evildoing overturn the thrones of the mighty.*

Exhortation to Seek Wisdom†

6 1 Hear, therefore, kings, and understand;*
learn, you magistrates† of the earth's expanse!
2 Give ear, you who have power over multitudes
and lord it over throngs of peoples!
3 Because authority was given you by the Lord
and sovereignty by the Most High,
who shall probe your works and scrutinize your counsels!*
4 Because, though you were ministers of his kingdom, you did not judge rightly,
and did not keep the law,†
nor walk according to the will of God,
5 Terribly and swiftly he shall come against you,
because severe judgment awaits the exalted—
6 For the lowly may be pardoned out of mercy*
but the mighty shall be mightily put to the test.
7 For the Ruler of all shows no partiality,
nor does he fear greatness,*
Because he himself made the great as well as the small,
and provides for all alike;
8 but for those in power a rigorous scrutiny impends.

9 To you, therefore, O princes, are my words addressed*
that you may learn wisdom and that you may not fall away.
10 For those who keep the holy precepts
hallowed will be found holy,
and those learned in them will have ready a response.†
11 Desire therefore my words;
long for them and you will be instructed.

12 Resplendent and unfading is Wisdom,
and she is readily perceived by those who love her,
and found by those who seek her.*
13 She hastens to make herself known to those who desire her;*
14 one who watches for her at dawn will not be disappointed,
for she will be found sitting at the gate.
15 For setting your heart on her is the perfection of prudence,
and whoever keeps vigil for her is quickly free from care;
16 Because she makes her rounds, seeking those worthy of her,
and graciously appears to them on the way,
and goes to meet them with full attention.*

17† For the first step toward Wisdom is an earnest desire for discipline;*
18 then, care for discipline is love of her;
love means the keeping of her laws;
To observe her laws is the basis for incorruptibility;
19 and incorruptibility makes one close to God;
20 thus the desire for Wisdom leads to a kingdom.

6:1–21 The first part of the book closes with an exhortation comparable to 1:1–15, and it leads into "Solomon's" personal comments on wisdom in chaps. 7–9.

6:1 *Kings . . . magistrates*: note the inclusion with v. 21 ("kings"). The address to earthly powers is in accord with the opening (1:1), but the true audience remains the Jewish community.

6:4 *Law*: that of Moses; cf. 2:12; 6:10.

6:10 *Response*: a suitable plea before the great Judge. Cf. Prv 22:21; Jb 31:14; Hb 2:1; Sir 8:9.

6:17–20 This type of reasoning approximates the rhetorical sorites, a series of statements in which the predicate of each becomes the subject of the next. Cf. Rom 5:3–5.

5:16 Ex 33:22; Is 62:3; 2 Tm 4:8; 1 Pt 5:4.
5:17 Is 59:17.
5:19–20 Dt 32:40–43.
5:21 Hb 3:9–11.
5:22 Dt 11:4.
5:23 Wis 11:20; Sir 10:13–14.
6:1–2 Wis 1:1; Ps 2:10; Sir 33:19; Mi 3:1, 9.
6:3 2 Chr 36:23; Prv 8:15–16; Jn 19:11; Rom 13:1.
6:6–7 Lk 12:48.
6:7 Dt 1:17; Prv 22:2.
6:9–11 Dt 4:10; Ps 2:12; Sir 32:14; 1 Jn 3:7.
6:12 Wis 7:10; Prv 8:17; Jer 29:13.
6:13–16 Prv 8:3, 17, 34.
6:16 Prv 8:20–21; Sir 15:1–5.
6:17–21 Ps 2:10–12; Prv 4:4–9; 7:1–4; 8:15–16; Dn 7:27; Jn 14:15, 21; 1 Jn 5:3.

Cultural Connection

The Source of Wisdom

Solomon valued wisdom above riches, authority, health, and beauty (see Wis 7:7–10). Native American spirituality values wisdom in a similar way. The elders are seen as the people's connection to history and experience; they are a source of wisdom and sound advice. In fact, all of God's creation is seen as a potential source of wisdom. Notice how this is reflected in the following prayer from the Sioux tradition:

Oh Great Spirit, whose voice I
hear in the winds
And whose breath gives life
to everyone,
Hear me.
I come to you as one of your
many children;
I am weak . . . I am small
. . . I need your wisdom
and your strength.
Let me walk in beauty,
and make my eyes ever
behold the red and purple
sunsets.
Make my hands respect the
things you have made, and
make my ears sharp so I
may hear your voice.
Make me wise, so that I may
understand what you have
taught my people and
The lessons you have hidden
in each leaf and each rock.
I ask for wisdom and
strength,
Not to be superior to my
brothers, but to be able to
fight my greatest enemy,
myself.
Make me ever ready to come
before you with clean
hands and a straight eye,
So as life fades away as a
fading sunset,
My spirit may come to you
without shame.
(Author unknown, "Sioux Prayer")

▶ Wis 7:7–14

21 If, then, you find pleasure in throne and
scepter, you princes of peoples,
honor Wisdom, that you may reign as kings
forever.

II. Praise of Wisdom by Solomon†

Introduction

22 Now what wisdom is, and how she came to
be I shall proclaim;
and I shall conceal no secrets from you,
But from the very beginning I shall search out
and bring to light knowledge of her;
I shall not diverge from the truth.*
23 Neither shall I admit consuming jealousy to
my company,
because that can have no fellowship with
Wisdom.*
24 A multitude of the wise is the safety of the
world,
and a prudent king, the stability of the
people;*
25 so take instruction from my words, to your
profit.

Solomon Is Like All Others

7 1 I too am a mortal, the same as all the rest,*
and a descendant of the first one formed of
earth.†
And in my mother's womb I was molded into
flesh
2 in a ten-month period†—body and blood,
from the seed of a man, and the pleasure
that accompanies marriage.
3 And I too, when born, inhaled the common
air,
and fell upon the kindred earth;
wailing, I uttered that first sound common
to all.
4 In swaddling clothes and with constant care I
was nurtured.
5 For no king has any different origin or birth;
6 one is the entry into life for all,
and in one same way they leave it.*

† **6:22–9:18** In these verses the author identifies with Solomon (without mentioning that name anywhere), and praises the beauty of Wisdom, describing how he sought her out. Thus the readers of the book can find a model in their search for Wisdom.

7:1 *First one formed of earth*: Adam. The author omits throughout the book the proper names of the characters in sacred history of whom he speaks; see especially chap. 10.

7:2 *In a ten-month period*: ten lunar months.

6:22 Tb 12:7, 11; Mt 13:11; Jn 15:15.
6:23 Wis 7:13; Jas 3:14–15.
6:24 Prv 11:14; 24:6; 29:4; Sir 10:1–5.
7:1–2 Wis 10:1; Gn 2:7; Jb 10:9–12; 33:6; 1 Cor 15:47–49.
7:6 Jb 1:21; Lk 2:12; 1 Tm 6:7–8.

Pray It!

How Do You Image God?

Old Testament writers sometimes used attributes of God, such as spirit, word, and justice, as titles for God. Wisdom is another of these titles. Each title gives us some insight into God's nature, although not one of them, or even all of them together, can give us the whole picture. The author of the Book of Wisdom of Solomon describes God's wisdom as a woman, which gives us insight into God's feminine dimension.

Read the qualities of wisdom given in Wisdom 7:22—8:1. This passage summarizes the author's understanding of God's nature. It was probably familiar to New Testament authors. Aspects of it show up in the Letter to the Hebrews (1:1–4) and in the Gospel of John (1:1–14).

Explore your images of God. Choose an attribute of God that is significant for you. It might be love, faithfulness, truth, or some other quality. Write a poem, like the one in Wisdom of Solomon 8:2–8, that describes this quality as a person.

▶ **Wis 7:22—8:8**

Solomon Prayed and Wisdom and Riches Came to Him

7 Therefore I prayed, and prudence was given me;
I pleaded and the spirit of Wisdom came to me.*
8 I preferred her to scepter and throne,*
And deemed riches nothing in comparison with her,
9 nor did I liken any priceless gem to her;
Because all gold, in view of her, is a bit of sand,
and before her, silver is to be accounted mire.
10 Beyond health and beauty I loved her,
And I chose to have her rather than the light,
because her radiance never ceases.*
11 Yet all good things together came to me with her,*
and countless riches at her hands;
12 I rejoiced in them all, because Wisdom is their leader,
though I had not known that she is their mother.† *

Solomon Prays for Help to Speak Worthily of Wisdom

13 Sincerely I learned about her, and ungrudgingly do I share—
her riches I do not hide away;*
14 For she is an unfailing treasure;
those who gain this treasure win the friendship of God,
being commended by the gifts that come from her discipline.†
15 Now God grant I speak suitably
and value these endowments at their worth:
For he is the guide of Wisdom
and the director of the wise.
16 For both we and our words are in his hand,
as well as all prudence and knowledge of crafts.*
17† For he gave me sound knowledge of what exists,
that I might know the structure of the universe and the force of its elements,
18 The beginning and the end and the midpoint of times,
the changes in the sun's course and the variations of the seasons,
19 Cycles of years, positions of stars,
20 natures of living things, tempers of beasts,
Powers of the winds and thoughts of human beings,
uses of plants and virtues of roots—
21 Whatever is hidden or plain I learned,
22 for Wisdom, the artisan of all, taught me.*

Nature and Incomparable Dignity of Wisdom

†For in her is a spirit
intelligent, holy, unique,
Manifold, subtle, agile,

7:12 *Mother*: lit., "she who begets." Although Wisdom herself is begotten of God (Prv 8:22–24), she is here the one who brings into being.

7:14 *Discipline*: cf. note on 1:5.

7:17–22a Wisdom teaches not only righteousness and friendship with God but also sound knowledge of the world, the universe, plants, animals and human beings. See also 1 Kgs 5:9–14; these specialties reflect Hellenistic culture.

7:22b–23 The twenty-one (7 × 3) attributes of the spirit in Wisdom reflect the influence of contemporary philosophy, especially the Stoa, but the personification rests also on Prv 8:22–31 and Sir 24.

7:7 1 Kgs 3:5–15; Prv 2:3–11.
7:8–9 Wis 8:5; 1 Kgs 10:21; Jb 28:15–19; Prv 3:14–16; 8:10, 18–19.
7:10 Prv 6:23.
7:11 Prv 8:21.
7:12 Prv 8:14–15.
7:13 Wis 6:23.
7:16 Wis 3:1.
7:22 Wis 14:2; Prv 8:30.

Catholic Connection

The Cardinal Virtues

The Scriptures refer to seeking wisdom and learning from her. In return, wisdom teaches us virtues—the cardinal virtues of prudence, justice, fortitude, and temperance. Simply put: "Nothing in life is more useful than these" (Wis 8:7).

Prudence. Of the four virtues, prudence sets the course for all other virtues. Prudence enables one to look at a situation and determine the right thing to do and how to go about doing it. It points our conscience in the right direction and helps us to accurately apply moral principles to any situation.

Justice. Justice is ultimately about relationships, our relationship with God, with one another, and with the world around us. This virtue helps us recognize and acknowledge God's limitless power and love. It also helps us treat one another and all of God's creation with love and respect.

Fortitude. Doing the right thing can be scary; fortitude helps us overcome that fear. This virtue helps us withstand persecution, even to the point of sacrificing our own lives for what is right. It also strengthens us when we resolve to avoid temptation and sin.

Temperance. Self-control or temperance helps us keep our lives in proper balance. Our natural attraction to pleasures, whether physical or material, can overwhelm us and lead us astray. This virtue helps us master our desires and keep the attractions within proper limits.

Because virtues are attitudes or habits that guide our heart and mind, we must consciously work to develop them. So take time to learn about your faith, read the Scriptures, and purposely do things that build up these habits. However, if you fail, do not be discouraged; keep trying. And most important, seek God's grace in all that you do.

Try focusing on one cardinal virtue each week during your prayer time and daily activities. At the end of four weeks, look back and see how you have grown in virtue and closeness to God!

Wis 8:7

Catechism, nos. 1803–1811

clear, unstained, certain,
Never harmful, loving the good, keen,*
23 unhampered, beneficent, kindly,
Firm, secure, tranquil,
all-powerful, all-seeing,
And pervading all spirits,
though they be intelligent, pure and very subtle.
24 For Wisdom is mobile beyond all motion,
and she penetrates and pervades all things
by reason of her purity.*
25† For she is a breath of the might of God
and a pure emanation of the glory of the Almighty;
therefore nothing defiled can enter into her.
26 For she is the reflection of eternal light,
the spotless mirror of the power of God,
the image of his goodness.*
27 Although she is one, she can do all things,
and she renews everything while herself perduring;
Passing into holy souls from age to age,
she produces friends of God and prophets.*
28 For God loves nothing so much as the one
who dwells with Wisdom.
29 For she is fairer than the sun*
and surpasses every constellation of the stars.
Compared to light, she is found more radiant;
30 though night supplants light,
wickedness does not prevail over Wisdom.

8 1 Indeed, she spans the world from end to end mightily
and governs all things well.*

Wisdom, the Source of Blessings

2 Her I loved and sought after from my youth;
I sought to take her for my bride†
and was enamored of her beauty.*
3 She adds to nobility the splendor of companionship with God;
even the Ruler of all loved her.
4 For she leads into the understanding of God,
and chooses his works.*
5 If riches are desirable in life,
what is richer than Wisdom, who produces all things?*
6 And if prudence is at work,*
who in the world is a better artisan than she?
7 Or if one loves righteousness,
whose works are virtues,
She teaches moderation and prudence,
righteousness and fortitude,†
and nothing in life is more useful than these.
8 Or again, if one yearns for wide experience,
she knows the things of old, and infers the things to come.
She understands the turns of phrases and the solutions of riddles;
signs and wonders she knows in advance
and the outcome of times and ages.*

Wisdom as Solomon's Counselor and Comfort

9 So I determined to take her to live with me,
knowing that she would be my counselor
while all was well,
and my comfort in care and grief.
10 Because of her I have glory among the multitudes,*
and esteem from the elders, though I am but a youth.
11 I shall become keen in judgment,
and shall be a marvel before rulers.
12 They will wait while I am silent and listen
when I speak;
and when I shall speak the more,
they will put their hands upon their mouths.†
13 Because of her I shall have immortality
and leave to those after me an everlasting memory.*
14 I shall govern peoples, and nations will be my subjects—*
15 tyrannical princes, hearing of me, will be afraid;
in the assembly I shall appear noble, and in war courageous.
16 Entering my house, I shall take my repose beside her;
For association with her involves no bitterness
and living with her no grief,
but rather joy and gladness.*

---

† **7:25–26** Five strong metaphors underline the origins and closeness of Wisdom with God. See the use of this language in Heb 1:3; Col 1:15.

8:2 *I loved . . . my bride*: the erotic quality in the pursuit of and living with Woman Wisdom, who is the Lord's consort (9:4) and loved by him, continues throughout this chapter (vv. 16, 18). It is reflected already in Prv 4:5–9; 7:4–5. See also Sir 15:2–5; 51:13–21.

8:7 *Moderation . . . fortitude*: known also as the cardinal virtues, and recognized in Greek philosophy (Plato).

8:12 *Hands upon their mouths*: a sign of respect for unanswerable wisdom; cf. Jb 40:4.

* **7:22–23** Heb 4:12–13; Jas 3:17. **7:24** Wis 8:1. **7:26** 2 Cor 4:4; Col 1:15; Heb 1:3. **7:27** Ex 33:11; Jb 42:2; Ps 104:29; Jl 3:1. **7:29–30** Sg 6:3, 9. **8:1** Wis 7:24; 15:1. **8:2** Prv 5:13–18; 8:17. **8:4** Prv 8:27–31. **8:5** Prv 8:18–19. **8:6–7** Prv 8:14–15. **8:8** Prv 1:6; Sir 39:1–3; 42:19–20; Dn 2:21. **8:10–12** 1 Kgs 3:28; Jb 29:8–10, 21–22. **8:13** Sir 15:6; 41:12–13; Is 56:5. **8:14** Wis 3:8; Ps 18:48; 47:4. **8:16** Prv 29:6; Sir 15:6; Bar 3:38.

Wisdom is a Gift of God

17 Reflecting on these things,
and considering in my heart
That immortality lies in kinship with
Wisdom,*
18 great delight in love of her,
and unfailing riches in the works of her
hands;
And that in associating with her there is
prudence,
and fair renown in sharing her discourses,
I went about seeking to take her for my
own.
19† Now, I was a well-favored child,
and I came by a noble nature;
20 or rather, being noble, I attained an
unblemished body.
21 And knowing that I could not otherwise
possess her unless God gave it—
and this, too, was prudence, to know
whose gift she is—
I went to the LORD and besought him,*
and said with all my heart:

Solomon's Prayer†

9 1† God of my ancestors, Lord of mercy,*
you who have made all things by your
word*
2 And in your wisdom have established
humankind
to rule the creatures produced by you,*
3 And to govern the world in holiness and
righteousness,
and to render judgment in integrity of
heart:*
4 Give me Wisdom, the consort at your throne,
and do not reject me from among your
children;*
5 For I am your servant, the child of your
maidservant,
a man weak and short-lived
and lacking in comprehension of judgment
and of laws.*
6 Indeed, though one be perfect among mortals,
if Wisdom, who comes from you, be
lacking,
that one will count for nothing.*
7 You have chosen me king over your people
and magistrate over your sons and
daughters.*
8 You have bid me build a temple on your holy
mountain
and an altar in the city that is your dwelling
place,
a copy of the holy tabernacle which you
had established from of old.*
9 Now with you is Wisdom, who knows your
works
and was present when you made the world;
Who understands what is pleasing in your
eyes
and what is conformable with your
commands.*
10 Send her forth from your holy heavens
and from your glorious throne dispatch her
That she may be with me and work with me,
that I may know what is pleasing to you.*
11 For she knows and understands all things,
and will guide me prudently in my affairs
and safeguard me by her glory;*
12 Thus my deeds will be acceptable,
and I will judge your people justly
and be worthy of my father's throne.*

13 For who knows God's counsel,
or who can conceive what the Lord intends?*
14 For the deliberations of mortals are timid,
and uncertain our plans.
15† For the corruptible body burdens the soul
and the earthly tent weighs down the mind
with its many concerns.*
16 Scarcely can we guess the things on earth,
and only with difficulty grasp what is at
hand;
but things in heaven, who can search them
out?*

---

† **8:19–20** Here the author mentions first bodily, then spiritual, excellence. To make it plain that the latter is the governing factor in the harmonious development of the human person, he then reverses the order. The Platonic doctrine of the pre-existence of the soul is often read into these lines, but such an anthropology does not seem to be the intent of the author (cf. 7:1–6). Verse 20 appears to rule out any misunderstanding of v. 19. Verse 21 emphasizes that he did not bring talent to his "birth"; his wisdom is the gift of God.

9:1–18 The author presents his version of Solomon's prayer (1 Kgs 3:6–9; 2 Chr 1:8–10).

9:1–2 The author identifies Wisdom with the word of God just as he again identifies Wisdom with the spirit of God in v. 17. All three are alternate ways of expressing God's activity in relationship with the world and its inhabitants.

9:15–17 Although the expressions in v. 15 draw on the language of Plato concerning the human condition, the conclusion is very biblical: God remains a mystery (Jb 38–39; Eccl 8:17; Is 40:12–14; Rom 11:33–34). The plight of humankind is clearly one of ignorance, unless the "holy spirit" is sent from God.

---

* **8:17** Prv 3:18.
8:21 1 Kgs 3:9; 1 Kgs 5:9; Prv 2:6; Jas 1:5.
9:1–2 Ps 86:15.
9:1 Gn 1; Ps 33:6; Prv 3:19; Jer 10:12; Jn 1:3, 10.
9:2 Ps 8:7–9; Sir 17:3–4.
9:3 1 Kgs 3:6; 9:4–5; Ps 9:8–9.
9:4 2 Chr 1:10.
9:5 1 Kgs 3:7; Ps 116:16.
9:6 Wis 3:17; 1 Kgs 11:4; 1 Cor 3:18–21.
9:7 1 Chr 28:5.
9:8 Ex 25:8–9; 2 Sm 7:13; 1 Chr 28:5; 2 Chr 6:1–2; 7:7; Tb 1:4; Ps 15:1; 48:2–3.
9:9 Dt 6:17–18; Prv 8:22–31; Jn 1:1–3, 10.
9:10 Wis 18:15; Mt 5:34; Jn 3:17; 20:21.
9:11 Wis 8:8.
9:12 1 Kgs 3:6–9.
9:13 Is 40:13; Bar 3:31.
9:15 Jb 4:19.
9:16 Sir 1:3; Jn 3:12.

17 Or who can know your counsel, unless you
give Wisdom
and send your holy spirit from on high?*
18† Thus were the paths of those on earth made
straight,
and people learned what pleases you,
and were saved by Wisdom.*

Wisdom Preserves Her Followers

10 †1 She preserved the first-formed father† of
the world*
when he alone had been created;*
And she raised him up from his fall,
2 and gave him power to rule all things.*
3 But when an unrighteous man† withdrew
from her in his anger,
he perished through his fratricidal wrath.*
4 When on his account the earth was flooded,
Wisdom again saved it,
piloting the righteous man† on frailest
wood.*

5 She, when the nations were sunk in universal
wickedness,
knew the righteous man,† kept him
blameless before God,
and preserved him resolute against pity for
his child.*

6 She rescued a righteous man† from among the
wicked who were being destroyed,*
when he fled as fire descended upon the
Pentapolis—
7 Where as a testimony to its wickedness,
even yet there remain a smoking desert,
Plants bearing fruit that never ripens,
and the tomb of a disbelieving soul,† a
standing pillar of salt.*
8 For those who forsook Wisdom
not only were deprived of knowledge of the
good,
But also left the world a memorial of their folly,
so that they could not even be hidden in
their fall.

9 But Wisdom rescued from tribulations those
who served her.*

10 She, when a righteous man† fled from his
brother's anger,*
guided him in right ways,
Showed him the kingdom of God
and gave him knowledge of holy things;
She prospered him in his labors
and made abundant the fruit of his works,
11 Stood by him against the greed of his
defrauders,
and enriched him;*
12 She preserved him from foes,
and secured him against ambush,
And she gave him the prize for his hard struggle
that he might know that devotion to God†
is mightier than all else.*

13 She did not abandon a righteous man† when
he was sold,*
but rescued him from sin.*
14 She went down with him into the dungeon,
and did not desert him in his bonds,
Until she brought him the scepter of royalty
and authority over his oppressors,
Proved false those who had defamed him,
and gave him eternal glory.

15 The holy people and their blameless
descendants—it was she
who rescued them from the nation that
oppressed them.*
16 She entered the soul of the Lord's servant,†
and withstood fearsome kings with signs
and wonders;*
17 she gave the holy ones the reward of their
labors,*
Conducted them by a wondrous road,
became a shelter for them by day
a starry flame by night.
18 She took them across the Red Sea
and brought them through the deep waters.
19 Their enemies she overwhelmed,

†

9:18 An announcement of the next section.

10:1–21 This chapter prepares for the following section (Wis 11:2–19:22) on the history of Israel in the exodus, by reviewing the dealings of Wisdom with the patriarchs. It has a parallel in Sir 44–50; cf. also Wis 18:9.

10:1–2 Adam.

10:3 Cain.

10:4 Noah.

10:5 Abraham.

10:6 Lot. *Pentapolis*: the five cities, including Sodom; cf. Gn 14:2.

10:7 *Disbelieving soul*: Lot's wife; cf. Gn 19:26.

10:10–12 Jacob.

10:12 *Devotion to God*: in the Greek this signifies "piety" or "religion," and is the equivalent of the Hebrew "fear of the Lord"; cf. Prv 1:7.

10:13–14 Joseph.

10:16 Moses.

*

9:17 Jn 14:26.
9:18 Wis 10:9; Prv 28:26.
10:1–16 Heb 11:17–27.
10:1 Wis 7:1.
10:2 Gn 1:28.
10:3 Gn 4:1–16.
10:4 Wis 14:5–6; Gn 6:5–9.
10:5 Gn 22:7–10.
10:6 Gn 18:22–33; 19:15–25; 2 Pt 2:6–7.
10:7 Gn 19:26; Lk 17:32.
10:9 Wis 16:8.
10:10 Gn 27:43–45; 28:12–15.
10:11 Gn 30:29–30; 31:5–12.
10:12 Gn 32:24–29; 1 Tm 4:8.
10:13–14 Gn 37–45.
10:13 Gn 39:7–10.
10:15 Ex 3:9; 14:30; 19:6.
10:16 Wis 1:4; 7:27; Ex 4:10; Ps 76:13.
10:17–19 Wis 14:3; 19:7; Ex 13:21–22; Ex 14–15; Ps 77:20–21; 78:13, 53; Is 4:5–6.

Catholic Social Teaching

Workers' Rights

"Wisdom rescued from tribulations those who served her" (Wis 10:9). In this passage from the Wisdom of Solomon, workers are rewarded for their labor and taken care of during times of strife. If only this were true for all workers throughout the world! Unfortunately, the reality for many workers is that their labor, which is often performed under unjust conditions, comes with little reward. When unexpected difficulties arise in the workplace due to injury or illness, many workers, instead of being rescued from their troubles, simply lose their jobs, with no safety net to fall back upon.

Catholic social teaching reminds us that there are numerous basic rights that all workers deserve. Included among these are just wages, safe working conditions, reasonable hours, equal pay for equal work, adequate benefits, and the right to unionize. Workers should also be able to maintain their job status when medical or personal difficulties make continuing work temporarily impossible. They should not have to worry about losing their jobs because they get sick or injured, or become pregnant. And yet, this is the reality that many workers—particularly low-wage workers—face in our world, as some employers find it easier to replace workers than to show compassion toward them. In these cases, the dignity of the human person and the dignity of work are both diminished.

In turn, workers also have responsibilities to their employers—namely, to faithfully carry out the work they are entrusted with providing, while treating their employers with the same sort of dignity and respect that they want to be treated with.

- In what ways can you uphold the dignity of work by being a responsible worker?
- How can you advocate for those who are being treated unfairly or discriminated against in the workplace?

Wis 10:9–14
The Dignity of Work and the Rights of Workers

and churned them up† from the bottom of
the depths.
20 Therefore the righteous despoiled the wicked;
and they sang of your holy name, Lord,
and praised in unison your conquering
hand,*
21 Because Wisdom opened the mouths of the
mute,
and gave ready speech to infants.*

11 [1] She prospered their affairs through the holy
prophet.*

III. Special Providence of God During the Exodus†

Introduction

2 They journeyed through the uninhabited desert,
and in lonely places they pitched their tents;*
3 they withstood enemies and warded off
their foes.*
4 When they thirsted, they called upon you,
and water was given them from the sheer
rock,
a quenching of their thirst from the hard
stone.
5 For by the things through which their foes
were punished
they in their need were benefited.*

First Example: Water Punishes the Egyptians and Benefits the Israelites

6 Instead of a river's† perennial source,
troubled with impure blood*
7 as a rebuke to the decree for the slaying of
infants,
You gave them abundant water beyond their
hope,

10:19 *Churned them up*: casting their bodies on the shore.

11:2–19:22 Few verses in chaps. 11–19 can be fully understood without consulting the passages in the Pentateuch which are indicated in the cross-references. The theme of this part of the book is expressed in v. 5 and is illustrated in the following chapters by five examples drawn from Exodus events.

11:6–8 *River*: the Nile; the contrast is between the first plague of

10:20 Ex 12:35–36; 15:1–21.
10:21 Ex 4:10–15; Ps 8:3; Mt 11:25.
11:1 Dt 2:7; Hos 12:14.
11:2–5 Ex 17:2–6; Nm 20:1–13; Ps 63:2; 107:4–7; Jer 2:6.
11:3 Ex 17:8–16; Nm 21:1–3, 21–35; 31:1–12; Ps 118:10–12.
11:5 Wis 16:1–2.
11:6–8 Wis 18:5; Ex 1:22; 7:17–24.

Cultural Connection

Words from a Father to His Son

The following translation of a text originally written in Nahuatl is the wisdom of a native father in sixteenth-century Mexico. This spirit of wisdom still exists in many Mexican families.

My son, . . . my precious feather, you have come to life, been born, been blessed to come into the world in the land of our Lord. The One for whom we live forged your life, gave you shape. We, your mother and father, have watched over you; your aunts and uncles, all your family, have watched over you, have cried for you, have suffered for you that you might be born. (P. 49)

Love and serve others in holiness; respect and obey your mother and father, and do their hearts' desire. Your gift of service, obedience, and respect will be the recompense they deserve. (P. 53)

Push away from you all that is not good: that which is wrong, all the things that dishonor you. . . . Do no damage to the community, or the peace. Because if you do bad things, you will not come away unscathed: you must eventually suffer for such actions. (P. 79)

With these words, I encourage and strengthen you; through them, I console you. Throw away nothing I have told you, nothing you have heard. May all this be your inspiration, helping you always to remember the Lord, our God. (P. 86)

(Miguel Léon-Portilla and Librado Silva Galeana, *Huehuehtlahtolli*, as translated by Richard Wood)

8 after you had shown by the thirst they experienced
how you punished their adversaries.
9 For when they had been tried, though only mildly chastised,*
they recognized how the wicked, condemned in anger, were being tormented.
10 You tested your own people, admonishing them as a father;
but as a stern king you probed and condemned the wicked.
11 Those near and far were equally afflicted:*
12 for a twofold grief† took hold of them*
and a groaning at the remembrance of the ones who had departed.
13 For when they heard that the cause of their own torments
was a benefit to these others, they recognized the Lord.
14 For though they had mocked and rejected him who had been cast out and abandoned long ago,
in the final outcome, they marveled at him,
since their thirst proved unlike that of the righteous.*

Second Example: Animals Punish the Egyptians and Benefit the Israelites

15 In return for their senseless, wicked thoughts,
which misled them into worshiping dumb† serpents and worthless insects,
You sent upon them swarms of dumb creatures for vengeance;*
16 that they might recognize that one is punished by the very things through which one sins.*

Digression on God's Mercy

17 For not without means was your almighty hand,*
that had fashioned the universe from formless matter,†
to send upon them many bears or fierce lions,
18 Or newly created, wrathful, unknown beasts
breathing forth fiery breath,
Or pouring out roaring smoke,

† Egypt (Ex 7:17–24) and the water drawn from the rock in Horeb (Ex 17:5–7; Nm 20:8–11).

11:12 *Twofold grief*: the double distress described in vv. 13–14.

11:15 *Dumb*: that is, irrational.

11:17 *Formless matter*: a Greek philosophical concept is used to interpret the chaos of Gn 1:2.

* **11:9–11** Wis 3:5; 16:3–4; Dt 8:2–5; 2 Mc 6:12–16; Ps 6:2; Prv 3:12. **11:11** Ps 6:2. **11:12–13** Wis 16:8; Ex 14:4, 18. **11:14** Ex 2:3. **11:15** Wis 12:23–24; 15:18–16:1; Ex 7:26–8:11. **11:16** Wis 12:23, 27; Ex 10:16; Prv 1:31–32; 26:27. **11:17–19** Wis 12:8–9; 16:1, 5; Gn 1:1–2; Dt 32:24; 2 Kgs 17:25–26; Hos 13:4–8.

Did You Know?

The Exodus Pattern

The Exodus refers to all the events surrounding God's leading the formerly enslaved Israelites out of Egypt as recorded in the books of Exodus, Leviticus, Numbers, and Deuteronomy. Because the Exodus was an important experience in the Israelites' religious history, later biblical writers began to see in it a pattern in which God rescued the just and punished the wicked.

The author of the Wisdom of Solomon applies the Exodus pattern to explain how the righteous will be rewarded and sinners will be punished in the author's time. Throughout chapters 11–19, the writer refers to the journey through the desert, the Egyptians, the plagues, the manna in the desert, the pillars of fire, and the Red Sea. The author even takes the liberty of adding details that were not recorded in the original books! In doing so, the writer reminds the people of that time that the pattern of the Exodus is being repeated in their lives now, so they should not lose hope that God will be with them always.

▶ Wis 11:1—19:22

or flashing terrible sparks from their eyes.
19 Not only could these attack and completely destroy them;
even their frightful appearance itself could slay.
20 Even without these, they could have been killed at a single blast,
pursued by justice
and winnowed by your mighty spirit.
But you have disposed all things by measure and number and weight.*
21 For great strength is always present with you;
who can resist the might of your arm?*
22 Indeed, before you the whole universe is like a grain from a balance,†
or a drop of morning dew come down upon the earth.*
23† But you have mercy on all, because you can do all things;
and you overlook sins for the sake of repentance.*
24 For you love all things that are
and loathe nothing that you have made;
for you would not fashion what you hate.*
25 How could a thing remain, unless you willed it;
or be preserved, had it not been called forth by you?*
26 But you spare all things, because they are yours,
O Ruler and Lover of souls,*
12:1 for your imperishable spirit is in all things!*

12

2 Therefore you rebuke offenders little by little,
warn them, and remind them of the sins they are committing,
that they may abandon their wickedness and believe in you, Lord!

3 For truly, the ancient inhabitants of your holy land,*
4 whom you hated for deeds most odious—
works of sorcery and impious sacrifices;
5 These merciless murderers of children,
devourers of human flesh,†
and initiates engaged in a blood ritual,
6 and parents who took with their own hands defenseless lives,*
You willed to destroy by the hands of our ancestors,
7 that the land that is dearest of all to you
might receive a worthy colony of God's servants.*
8 But even these you spared, since they were but mortals
and sent wasps as forerunners of your army
that they might exterminate them by degrees.*
9 Not that you were without power to have the wicked vanquished in battle by the righteous,

---

11:22 *Grain from a balance*: a tiny particle used for weighing on sensitive scales.

11:23 The combination of divine mercy and power is an unusual paradox, but cf. 12:15–18; Ps 62:12–13; Sir 2:18. The main emphasis is on a creating that is motivated by love; the divine "imperishable spirit" (either Wisdom as in 1:4, 7, or perhaps the breath of life as in Gn 2:7) is in everything (12:1).

12:5 The horrible crimes here attributed to the Canaanites (cf. also 14:23) were not unheard of in the ancient world.

11:20 Jb 4:9.
11:21 Wis 12:12; 2 Chr 20:6.
11:22 Hos 13:3.
11:23 Wis 12:10; Dt 9:27; Acts 17:30; Rom 2:4; 11:32; 2 Pt 3:9.
11:24 Ps 145:9.
11:25 Is 41:4.
11:26 Wis 12:16; Is 63:9.
12:1 Wis 1:7.
12:3–6 Wis 14:23; Dt 18:9–12; Ps 5:6; 106:28, 34–39; Jer 19:4–5; Ez 16:3, 20–21, 36.
12:6 Nm 33:52.
12:7 Dt 11:12.
12:8 Ex 23:28–30; Dt 7:17–24.

Cultural Connection

Words from a Mother to Her Daughter

The following translation of a text originally written in Nahuatl is the wisdom of a native mother in sixteenth-century Mexico. This spirit of wisdom still exists in many Mexican families.

> Now, my daughter, my turtledove, little woman: you have life, you are born. You have entered the world, emerged from my womb, nourished at my breast. Our Lord forged your life, shaped you, made you within me. . . . Our Lord makes each of us earn our reputation, our honor, our warmth, our passion, our sweetness, our savor. . . .
>
> Sing well, speak well, converse deeply, respond to all, pray deeply; words are not to be bought and sold. Never allow the world to make you stupid, or silly. . . . In this way, you will live among the people, and you will be worthy of all you need . . . you will please our Lord and be worthy of our Lord's kindness and mercy. (Pp. 91–92)
>
> Be not a friend to liars, to thieves, to evil women, to meddlers, to those who are lazy.
>
> And if you have belongings or property, do not waste them; do not display them when you go out to the market. . . . Then you will leave what is yours to your children and grandchildren after you.
>
> If you live in this way, as I have taught you, then in truth, you will live well among your own people, favored by all. (Pp. 95–97)

(Miguel Léon-Portilla and Librado Silva Galeana, *Huehuehtlahtolli*, as translated by Richard Wood)

or wiped out at once by terrible beasts or
by one decisive word;*
10 But condemning them by degrees, you gave
them space for repentance.
You were not unaware that their origins were
wicked
and their malice ingrained,*
And that their dispositions would never
change;
11 for they were a people accursed from the
beginning.
Neither out of fear for anyone
did you grant release from their sins.*
12 For who can say to you, "What have you done?"
or who can oppose your decree?
Or when peoples perish, who can challenge
you, their maker;
or who can come into your presence to
vindicate the unrighteous?*
13 For neither is there any god besides you who
have the care of all,
that you need show you have not unjustly
condemned;*
14 Nor can any king or prince confront you on
behalf of those you have punished.*
15 But as you are righteous, you govern all things
righteously;
you regard it as unworthy of your power
to punish one who has incurred no blame.*
16 For your might is the source of righteousness;
your mastery over all things makes you
lenient to all.*
17 For you show your might when the perfection
of your power is disbelieved;
and in those who know you, you rebuke
insolence.†*
18 But though you are master of might, you
judge with clemency,
and with much lenience you govern us;
for power, whenever you will, attends you.

19 You taught your people, by these deeds,*
that those who are righteous must be kind;
And you gave your children reason to hope
that you would allow them to repent for
their sins.
20 For these were enemies of your servants,
doomed to death;
yet, while you punished them with such
solicitude and indulgence,

† 12:17 The brunt of divine anger and justice is borne by those who know God but defy divine authority and might. Cf. 1:2; 15:2, but also 12:27; 18:13.

* **12:9** Wis 11:18; 18:15; Nm 16:21. **12:10** Wis 11:23; Ps 55:20; Sir 16:9. **12:11** Gn 9:25. **12:12** 2 Sm 16:10; Eccl 8:4; Sir 46:19; Is 45:9; Dn 4:32; Rom 9:19–21. **12:13** Wis 6:7; Dt 3:24; 32:39; Is 44:6, 8. **12:14** Jer 49:19; 50:44. **12:15** Gn 18:23–32; Dt 32:4. **12:16** Wis 2:11; 11:26; Ps 103:19. **12:17** Wis 15:2–3; Ex 9:16. **12:19–20** Wis 11:23; Sir 17:24.

granting time and opportunity to abandon
wickedness,
21 With what exactitude you judged your
children,
to whose ancestors you gave the sworn
covenants of goodly promises! *
22 Therefore to give us a lesson you punish our
enemies with measured deliberation
so that we may think earnestly of your
goodness when we judge,
and, when being judged, we may look for
mercy.

Second Example Resumed

23 Hence those unrighteous who lived a life of
folly,
you tormented through their own
abominations.*
24 For they went far astray in the paths of error,
taking for gods the worthless and
disgusting among beasts,
being deceived like senseless infants.*
25 Therefore as though upon unreasoning
children,
you sent your judgment on them as a
mockery;*
26 But they who took no heed of a punishment
which was but child's play
were to experience a condemnation worthy
of God.
27 For by the things through which they suffered
distress,
being tortured by the very things they
deemed gods,
They saw and recognized the true God whom
formerly they had refused to know;
with this, their final condemnation† came
upon them.*

Digression on False Worship

A. Nature Worship†

13 1 Foolish by nature were all who were in
ignorance of God,
and who from the good things seen did not
succeed in knowing the one who is,†
and from studying the works did not
discern the artisan;*
2 Instead either fire, or wind, or the swift air,
or the circuit of the stars, or the mighty
water,
or the luminaries of heaven, the governors†
of the world, they considered gods.*
3 Now if out of joy in their beauty they thought
them gods,
let them know how far more excellent is
the Lord than these;
for the original source of beauty fashioned
them.*
4 Or if they were struck by their might and
energy,
let them realize from these things how
much more powerful is the one who
made them.*
5 For from the greatness and the beauty of
created things
their original author, by analogy, is seen.
6 But yet, for these the blame is less;†
For they have gone astray perhaps,
though they seek God and wish to find him.
7 For they search busily among his works,
but are distracted by what they see, because
the things seen are fair.
8 But again, not even these are pardonable.
9 For if they so far succeeded in knowledge
that they could speculate about the world,
how did they not more quickly find its
Lord?

B. Idolatry†

10 But wretched are they, and in dead things are
their hopes,
who termed gods things made by human
hands:
Gold and silver, the product of art, and
images of beasts,
or useless stone, the work of an ancient
hand.*

12:27 *Condemnation*: the death of Egyptian firstborn and the destruction of their army in the sea.

13:1–9 The author holds a relatively benign view of the efforts of the philosophers to come to know God from various natural phenomena. This is not a question of proving the existence of God in scholastic style. The author thinks that the beauty and might of the world should have pointed by analogy (v. 5) to the Maker. Instead, those "in ignorance of God" remained fixed on the elements (v. 2, three named, along with the stars). His Greek counterparts are not totally blameless; they should have gone further and acknowledged the creator of nature's wonders (vv. 4–5). Cf. Rom 1:18–23; Acts 17:27–28.

13:1 *One who is*: this follows the Greek translation of the sacred name for God in Hebrew; cf. Ex 3:14.

13:2 *Governors*: the sun and moon (cf. Gn 1:16).

13:6 *The blame is less*: the greater blame is incurred by those mentioned in v. 10; 15:14–16.

13:10–19 The second digression is an example of the polemic against idolatry (cf. Is 44:9–20; Jer 10:3–9; Ps 135:15–18). Whether the idols be of wood or clay, they were made by human beings and have become the source of evil.

12:21 Wis 18:22; Gn 50:24; Dt 7:6–14; Ps 105:8–11.
12:23 Wis 11:16; 16:1.
12:24 Dt 11:28; Jer 5:28; Rom 1:23.
12:25 Jer 4:22.
12:27 Wis 16:16; Ex 14:4, 28.
13:1 Acts 14:17; Eph 4:17–19.
13:2 Gn 1:14–19; Dt 4:19; Jb 31:26–28.
13:3 Ps 8:4.
13:4 Jer 10:2; Bar 6:39.
13:10 Wis 3:11; 15:5, 17; Dt 4:25–28; 7:25; 27:15; Ps 115:4; Hos 14:4; Acts 17:29.

The Carpenter and Wooden Idols

11 A carpenter may cut down a suitable tree*
and skillfully scrape off all its bark,
And deftly plying his art
produce something fit for daily use,*
12 And use the scraps from his handiwork
in preparing his food, and have his fill;
13 Then the good-for-nothing refuse from these
remnants,
crooked wood grown full of knots,
he takes and carves to occupy his spare
time.*
This wood he models with mindless skill,
and patterns it on the image of a human
being
14 or makes it resemble some worthless beast.
When he has daubed it with red and
crimsoned its surface with red stain,
and daubed over every blemish in it,*
15 He makes a fitting shrine for it
and puts it on the wall, fastening it with a
nail.*
16 Thus he provides for it lest it fall down,
knowing that it cannot help itself;
for, truly, it is an image and needs help.*
17 But when he prays about his goods or
marriage or children,*
he is not ashamed to address the thing
without a soul.
For vigor he invokes the powerless;
18 for life he entreats the dead;
For aid he beseeches the wholly incompetent;
for travel, something that cannot even walk;
19 For profit in business and success with his
hands
he asks power of a thing with hands utterly
powerless.

14 1 Again, one preparing for a voyage and
about to traverse the wild waves
cries out to wood more unsound than the
boat that bears him.*
2 For the urge for profits devised this latter,
and Wisdom the artisan produced it.

3† But your providence, O Father! guides it,
for you have furnished even in the sea a
road,
and through the waves a steady path,*
4 Showing that you can save from any danger,

Live It!

God Is My Copilot

Have you ever seen the bumper sticker that says, "God is my copilot"? This seems to be the message in Wisdom of Solomon 14:3. The author seems to be saying, "Don't put your trust in a little idol made of wood; it is the one true God who helps you, who guides you, who sets your course!"

Your life has many challenges. One way to face those challenges is to take God along on the journey. When you feel like you can't go on, call on God. When you fail and stumble, call on God. When you succeed, call on God and celebrate. God is here to be your copilot, to help you navigate through life—so call on God, talk to God. God will answer!

▶ **Wis 14:1–7**

so that even one without skill may embark.*
5 But you will that the products of your
Wisdom be not idle;
therefore people trust their lives even to
most frail wood,
and were safe crossing the waves on a raft.*
6 For of old, when the proud giants were being
destroyed,
the hope of the universe, who took refuge
on a raft,†
left to the world a future for the human
family, under the guidance of your
hand.

7 For blest is the wood through which
righteousness comes about;
8 but the handmade idol is accursed, and its
maker as well:
he for having produced it, and the
corruptible thing, because it was
termed a god.*
9 Equally odious to God are the evildoer and
the evil deed;

† **14:3–6** The wooden ship mentioned in vv. 1–2 prompts a short meditation on the providence of God, who in fact has watched over boats in their dangerous courses. The wood as described in v. 7 became a favorite patristic type for the wood of the cross.
14:6 Noah.

* **13:11–19** Is 44:9–20.
13:11 Wis 15:7; Bar 6:58.
13:13 Dt 4:16.
13:14 Jer 10:9.
13:15 Is 40:20; 41:7; 44:13.
13:16 1 Sm 5:3–5; Bar 6:57.
13:17–19 Wis 15:15.
14:1 Is 46:7.
14:3 Ps 107:23–30; Is 43:16.
14:4 Wis 16:8.
14:5 Wis 10:4.
14:8 Rom 1:23.

10 and the thing made will be punished with
its maker.
11 Therefore upon even the idols of the nations
shall a judgment come,
since they became abominable among
God's works,
Snares for human souls
and a trap for the feet of the senseless.*

The Origin and Evils of Idolatry

12 For the source of wantonness is the devising
of idols;
and their invention, a corruption of life.*
13 For in the beginning they were not,
nor can they ever continue;*
14 for from human emptiness they came into
the world,
and therefore a sudden end is devised for
them.
15† For a father, afflicted with untimely
mourning,
made an image of the child so quickly
taken from him,
And now honored as a god what once was
dead
and handed down to his household
mysteries and sacrifices.
16 Then, in the course of time, the impious
practice gained strength and was
observed as law,
and graven things were worshiped by royal
decrees.*
17 People who lived so far away that they could
not honor him in his presence
copied the appearance of the distant king
And made a public image of him they wished
to honor,
out of zeal to flatter the absent one as
though present.
18 And to promote this observance among those
to whom it was strange,
the artisan's ambition provided a stimulus.
19 For he, perhaps in his determination to please
the ruler,
labored over the likeness† to the best of his
skill;*
20 And the masses, drawn by the charm of the
workmanship,
soon took as an object of worship the one
who shortly before was honored as a
human being.*
21 And this became a snare for the world,
that people enslaved to either grief or
tyranny
conferred the incommunicable Name on
stones and wood.
22 Then it was not enough for them to err in
their knowledge of God;*
but even though they live in a great war
resulting from ignorance,
they call such evils peace.*
23 For while they practice either child sacrifices
or occult mysteries,
or frenzied carousing in exotic rites,*
24 They no longer respect either lives or purity of
marriage;
but they either waylay and kill each other,
or aggrieve each other by adultery.
25 And all is confusion—blood and murder,
theft and guile,*
corruption, faithlessness, turmoil, perjury,
26 Disturbance of good people, neglect of
gratitude,
besmirching of souls, unnatural lust,
disorder in marriage, adultery and
shamelessness.
27 For the worship of infamous idols
is the reason and source and extreme of all
evil.*
28 For they either go mad with enjoyment, or
prophesy lies,
or live lawlessly or lightly perjure
themselves.*
29 For as their trust is in lifeless idols,
they expect no harm when they have sworn
falsely.
30 But on both counts justice shall overtake
them:
because they thought perversely of God by
devoting themselves to idols,*
and because they deliberately swore false
oaths, despising piety.†
31 For it is not the might of those by whom they
swear,
but the just retribution of sinners,

14:15–21 The author develops two examples of idolatry: cult of the dead, and cult of the king.

14:19 *Likeness*: he made this more flattering than the reality.

14:30 *Piety*: the sanctity of oaths.

14:11 Wis 3:7; Nm 33:4; Jos 23:13; Ps 115:4; Jer 6:15; 10:15; 46:25; Hos 9:15.
14:12 Rom 1:23–32.
14:13 Is 2:18.
14:16 1 Mc 1:47–50; Dn 3:4–7.
14:19 Is 44:12–13 LXX.
14:20 Wis 15:4.
14:22–31 Jer 2:20; 3:1–25; Hos 4:1–2, 9–19; Rom 1:26–31; Gal 5:19–21; 1 Tm 1:9–10.
14:22 Jer 6:14; Ez 13:10.
14:23 Wis 12:4–5; 14:15; Is 57:5.
14:25–26 Jer 7:8–9; 22:17.
14:27 Ex 23:13.
14:28 Jer 5:31; 29:26.
14:30 Wis 1:1, 8; 11:20; Jer 5:2, 7.

that ever follows upon the transgression of
the wicked.†

15 [1]† But you, our God, are good and true,
slow to anger, and governing all with
mercy.*
2 For even if we sin, we are yours, and know
your might;
but we will not sin, knowing that we
belong to you.*
3 For to know you well is complete
righteousness,
and to know your might is the root of
immortality.*
4 For the evil creation of human fancy did not
deceive us,
nor the fruitless labor of painters,*
A form smeared with varied colors,
5 the sight of which arouses yearning in a
fool,
till he longs for the inanimate form of a
dead image.
6 Lovers of evil things, and worthy of such hopes
are they who make them and long for them
and worship them.*

The Potter's Clay Idols

7 For the potter, laboriously working the soft
earth,
molds for our service each single article:
He fashions out of the same clay
both the vessels that serve for clean
purposes
and their opposites, all alike;
As to what shall be the use of each vessel of
either class
the worker in clay is the judge.*
8† With misspent toil he molds a meaningless
god from the selfsame clay,
though he himself shortly before was made
from the earth,
And is soon to go whence he was taken,
when the life that was lent him is
demanded back.*
9 But his concern is not that he is to die
nor that his span of life is brief;
Rather, he vies with goldsmiths and
silversmiths
and emulates molders of bronze,
and takes pride in fashioning counterfeits.*
10 Ashes his heart is!† more worthless than earth
is his hope,*
more ignoble than clay his life;
11 Because he knew not the one who fashioned
him,
and breathed into him a quickening soul,
and infused a vital spirit.*
12 Instead, he esteemed our life a mere game,
and our span of life a holiday for gain;
"For one must," says he, "make a profit in
every way, be it even from evil."*
13 For more than anyone else he knows that he
is sinning,
when out of earthen stuff he creates fragile
vessels and idols alike.

14 But most stupid of all and worse than
senseless in mind,
are the enemies of your people who
enslaved them.*
15 For they esteemed all the idols of the nations
as gods,
which cannot use their eyes to see,
nor nostrils to breathe the air,
Nor ears to hear,
nor fingers on their hands for feeling;
even their feet are useless to walk with.*
16 For it was a mere human being who made
them;*
one living on borrowed breath who
fashioned them.
For no one is able to fashion a god like himself;
17 he is mortal, and what he makes with
lawless hands is dead.
For he is better than the things he worships;
he at least lives, but never his idols.

Second Example Resumed

18† Besides, they worship the most loathsome
beasts—*
as regards stupidity, these are worse than
the rest,†

†

14:31 Perjury is a form of deceit which calls for punishment even though it be practiced in the name of a lifeless idol.

15:1–3 As often before (11:26; 12:2; 14:3–6), the author addresses God directly, so that chaps. 11–19 can be conceived as a more or less continuous prayer (cf. 11:7 and 19:22). This is the living God who is in stark contrast to the deadness of the idols that have been discussed. The merciful God (cf. Ex 34:6) is the source of immortality (1:15) for the community.

15:8–9 The author matches the irony of his words about the carpenter in 13:15–19 with this description of the potter's vain work.

15:10 *Ashes his heart is!*: the words of this cry are taken from Is 44:20 (the Septuagint).

15:18–19 The author here returns (11:15; 12:23–27) to the main theme of chaps. 11–19, which was interrupted by the digression of 13:1–15:17.

15:18 *Worse than the rest*: this may mean that the creatures

15:1 Ex 34:6–7; Ps 86:5, 15; 145:8, 9, 14.
15:2 Jb 10:14–15 LXX.
15:3 Wis 3:15; Jn 17:3.
15:4 Wis 13:14.
15:6 Ps 115:8.
15:7 Wis 13:11; Jer 18:3–4; Rom 9:21; 2 Tm 2:20–21.
15:8 Gn 3:19; Eccl 12:7.
15:9 Bar 6:46.
15:10 Jb 13:12 LXX.
15:11 Gn 2:7; Zec 12:1.
15:12 Jas 4:13–14.
15:14 Ex 1:13.
15:15 Wis 14:11; Dt 4:28; Ps 115:4–7; 135:15–18.
15:16–17 Wis 13:10.
15:18 Wis 11:15; 12:24.

19 For beasts are neither good-looking nor
desirable;
they have escaped both the approval of
God and his blessing.*

16 1 Therefore they† were fittingly punished by
similar creatures,
and were tormented by a swarm of
insects.*
2 Instead of this punishment, you benefited
your people
with a novel dish, the delight they craved,
by providing quail for their food,*
3 So that those others, when they desired food,
should lose their appetite even for
necessities,
since the creatures sent to plague them
were so loathsome,
While these, after a brief period of privation,
partook of a novel dish.*
4 For inexorable want had to come upon those
oppressors;
but these needed only to be shown how
their enemies were being tormented.*
5 For when the dire venom of beasts came
upon them*
and they were dying from the bite of
crooked serpents,
your anger endured not to the end.
6 But as a warning, for a short time they were
terrorized,
though they had a sign† of salvation, to
remind them of the precept of your law.
7 For the one who turned toward it was saved,
not by what was seen,
but by you, the savior of all.
8 By this also you convinced our foes
that you are the one who delivers from all
evil.*
9 For the bites of locusts and of flies slew them,
and no remedy was found to save their lives
because they deserved to be punished by
such means;*
10 But not even the fangs of poisonous reptiles
overcame your children,
for your mercy came forth and healed
them.*
11 For as a reminder of your injunctions, they
were stung,
and swiftly they were saved,
Lest they should fall into deep forgetfulness
and become unresponsive to your
beneficence.*
12 For indeed, neither herb nor application
cured them,
but your all-healing word, O LORD!*
13† For you have dominion over life and death;*
you lead down to the gates of Hades and
lead back.
14 Human beings, however, may kill another
with malice,
but they cannot bring back the departed
spirit,
or release the soul that death has confined.
15 Your hand no one can escape.

Third Example: A Rain of Manna for Israel Instead of the Plague of Storms

16 For the wicked who refused to know you
were punished by the might of your arm,
Were pursued by unusual rains and hailstorms
and unremitting downpours,
and were consumed by fire.*
17 For against all expectation, in water which
quenches everything,
the fire grew more active;
For the universe fights on behalf of the
righteous.*
18 Then the flame was tempered*
so that the beasts that were sent upon the
wicked might not be burnt up,
but that these might see and know that they
were struck by the judgment of God;
19 And again, even in the water, fire blazed
beyond its strength
so as to consume the produce of the wicked
land.
20 Instead of this, you nourished your people
with food of angels†
and furnished them bread from heaven,
ready to hand, untoiled-for,

---

† worshiped by the Egyptians (e.g., crocodiles, serpents, scarabs, etc.) were less intelligent than the general run of beasts.

16:1 *They*: the Egyptian idolaters, who are punished according to the principle laid down in 11:5, 15–16.

16:6 *Sign*: the brazen serpent, as related in Numbers 21, but the author deliberately avoids any misunderstanding by addressing the Lord as responsible for the healing, since he is "the savior of all" (v. 7; see also vv. 12 and 26 for the role of the "word" of God).

16:13–14 The author recognizes the power of the Lord over life and death, as expressed in 1 Sm 2:6; Tb 13:2. The traditional imagery of Sheol (gates and confinement) colors the passage.

16:20 *Food of angels*: the famous phrase (cf. the hymn "Panis

* **15:19** Gn 1:25; 3:14. **16:1** Wis 11:15–16; 12:23, 27; Ex 7:27; 8:12, 17. **16:2** Wis 11:13; 19:11–12; Ex 16:13; Nm 11:31–32; Ps 105:40. **16:3** Wis 11:15; Ex 8:10; 16:3. **16:4** Wis 11:8–9. **16:5–6** Nm 21:4–9; Dt 32:24; Jer 8:17 LXX. **16:8** Gn 48:16; 2 Mc 1:24–25. **16:9** Ex 8:16–28; 10:4–19; Ps 78:45–46; 105:31, 34; Rev 9:1–11. **16:10** Dt 32:33. **16:11** Ps 78:11. **16:12** Ex 15:26. **16:13–15** Dt 32:39; 1 Sm 2:6; Tb 13:2; 2 Mc 6:26; 7:23; Ps 78:34, 39; Eccl 8:8; Dn 5:19. **16:16** Wis 11:21; 12:27; Ex 5:2; 9:29–34. **16:17** Wis 10:20; 19:20; Ex 9:23–28; 2 Mc 8:36; 14:34. **16:18–19** Wis 19:20–21.

Living Biblical Principles

> "Today too there is a need for disciples of Christ who give unstintingly of their time and energy to serve the Gospel. There is a need for young people who will allow God's love to burn within them and who will respond generously to his urgent call, just as many young blesseds and saints did in the past and also in more recent times."
>
> **Pope Benedict XVI, Message for WYD, 2008**

How does one follow the road of discipleship today? What special principles and values must a follower of Jesus Christ take on in order to have God's love burn within them so brightly that others will actually see the light? The best answer of course is found in the Scriptures, mainly in the Gospels, specifically through the words and deeds of Jesus himself. This is where the saints of yesterday and today began and it's where all young disciples should also start. And while there are many admirable qualities, principles, and attributes that can be gleaned from the Gospels, here are six that will serve as a solid foundation for would-be followers of Jesus to begin to build their lives around:

- **See God in Everything**
- **Trust in God Always**
- **Stand Up for the Poor and Vulnerable**
- **Be Courageous**
- **Serve Humbly**
- **Share the Faith**

See God in Everything

Catholics are a sacramental people. We believe that God's real presence is all around us, not only in the seven Sacraments we celebrate as a Church, but within the events and people we encounter each day. We are asked to see the world through the eyes of grace, which means that we are baptized to be witnesses to the fact that God's loving and abiding presence saturates all of life with both meaning and mystery. This is one reason that Catholics hold a special and sacred respect for all of life, from conception to natural death, including the sacredness of the environment that we live in. In short, life is all about God and God is all about life!

"Let Us Remember that We Are in the Holy Presence of God"

"Let us remember that we are in the holy presence of God" was the announcement that came every half hour at the schools where teachers trained by John Baptiste de LaSalle (1651–1719) taught, known today as the Christian Brothers. John Baptiste's view of life was that God is everywhere and in all people, and that our response to that God-given life is our prayer back to God, especially when we are teaching or helping the less fortunate. As both a teacher and educator, he made sure that all children were given the gift of education whether or not they could afford it, which was unheard of at the time. He saw education as the way to touch the hearts of young people with the gift of faith which is why he is the patron saint of teachers.

> "I am the Alpha and the Omega,
> the first and the last,
> the beginning and the end."
>
> — Rev 22:13

Trust in God Always

To place your trust in someone you know and can see is one thing, but to trust in what is unseen? How risky! Yet, this is what disciples of Jesus Christ are asked to do—to follow their leader, who himself placed his life and trust into the unseen hands of God. And we all know how that story turned out! Placing our trust in God is vital for a strong and vibrant faith, but having that level of trust does not mean we let God do it all. We still need to live out our faith in the world—approaching darkness, despair, and uncertainty with Christian hope—knowing that when all is said and done, God will be our rock and refuge.

We Have Only Today. Let Us Begin.

Blessed Mother Teresa of Calcutta is well known throughout the world as a modern-day disciple who took up the challenge to serve the poorest of the poor; first in the terrible slums of Calcutta, India, and then worldwide through her religious order, the Sisters of Charity. Mother Teresa's total trust in God allowed her to have both the strength and conviction to continue her mission of service despite doubts, setbacks, and few resources. God provided, time and again, through unexpected donations and/or through an increase in volunteers or fresh supplies, helping her to continue her service of care and compassion. She knew that trusting God and living out her faith were one and the same: "Yesterday is gone. Tomorrow has not yet come. We have only today. Let us begin." (Mother Teresa)

"My deliverance and honor are with God,
my strong rock;
my refuge is with God.
Trust God at all times, my people!
Pour out your hearts to God
our refuge!"

— Ps 62:8–9

Stand Up for the Poor and Vulnerable

Who are the poor and vulnerable? They are all around us, not just the poverty-stricken or worn-torn faces staring back at us from the flat-screen TV. They are the marginalized, those who live on the edge of society—including the homeless, the poor, the ill, and the isolated. They include the outcast, the weak, those who are put down, and those forced to the lower rungs of the social ladder. They are the vulnerable, the ones we are taught to hurry past and look away from. But in the dictionary of discipleship "they" also are our brothers and sisters, our family, and we are required by faith to reach out to them—not with a meaningless hand out, but with a comforting and empowering hand up so they can live a life marked by respect, dignity, and hope.

Climbing Down the Ladder of Success

Elizabeth Ann Seton (1774–1821) began life in luxury and wealth, and then gained more wealth through marriage. But the money and status did not fulfill her. After her husband's death, Elizabeth was drawn to the Catholic Church, especially the Eucharist, and converted to Catholicism, which caused Elizabeth's society friends and family to turn their backs on her. In order to support herself and her family, Elizabeth opened up a school for boys. Eventually, this led to the establishment of the Sisters of Charity of Saint Joseph whose mission was to educate children, especially poor girls who did not have schools to attend. Elizabeth is the patron saint of Catholic schools and the first American-born saint.

"I say to you, whatever you did for one of these least brothers of mine you did for me."

— Mt 25:40

Be Courageous

Young people are often excellent risk takers, and taking risks requires courage. Though some of these risky actions are seen in a negative light, there are other risks that often serve to bring light to others. Befriending an isolated student, speaking out against unjust practices, confronting discrimination, or standing up to those who abuse the environment are not always the easiest things for someone to do. Yet, young people are often found leading the way. Catholic tradition celebrates risk takers—people who have given up their comfort, their lifestyle, and sometimes their very lives to proclaim their faith. These courageous risk takers are called saints, and their lives challenge and inspire others to live out that same courageous faith.

The Seven-Million-Dollar Decision

When Katharine Drexel (1858–1955), the daughter of a wealthy Philadelphia banker, decided to heed Pope Leo XIII's challenge to become a missionary to the Native Americans and African Americans in 1889, the newspaper headlines declared that she "[Gave] Up Seven Million!" The headline illustrates just how much Katharine was willing to risk to answer that challenge. Katharine's risky and courageous decision helped to provide education, needed services, and ultimately dignity to people experiencing the most discrimination in America. Katharine helped to create over a hundred schools and missions to serve these disadvantaged groups, and her courageous and loving vision of service continues to this day through the Sisters of the Blessed Sacrament, the religious order she founded.

"Stand firm in the faith,
be courageous, be strong.
Your every act should be done with love."

— 1 Cor 16:13–14

Serve Humbly

Think of the most faith-filled person you know. Chances are, she or he is one of the most humble individuals you can name. It's no mistake that humility and faith go hand in hand. Humble people proclaim through their actions and words, "It's not about me!" Indeed, living our faith as disciples of Jesus Christ requires that we place God first, so that our deeds point to God and not to ourselves. Living our faith humbly does not mean we must be quiet about what we believe; it simply means that we let the light of God's love and grace shine through us to others, choosing to be a window to God's presence, not a wall to oneself.

Falling into Grace

Imagine the person from school who was voted "Most Popular" or "Most Likely to Party" shaving his or her head and wearing simple used clothing while wandering the streets and hanging out with the outcasts, the sick, and the isolated. Many people would be saddened and shocked by such a loss of power, influence, wealth, and fame—a societal "fall from grace." But to Francis of Assisi, this was a fall into grace. Francis literally turned his back on the sought-after life he had known in order to fully embrace the message of the gospel. His turn toward humility proved to be an attractive beacon of light, and others sought him out, wanting to know for themselves the inner light and faith that reflected from within him.

"If I, therefore, the master and teacher, have washed your feet, you ought to wash one another's feet. I have given you a model to follow, so that as I have done for you, you should also do."
— Jn 13:14–15

Share the Faith

It is one thing to know the faith, another to live the faith, and yet another to share the faith. Disciples of Jesus Christ are called to do all three. A faith that is alive, that echoes the reason for its being, is one that is meant to be passed along so others may be transformed by the God who is at the center of it all. But a faith that is challenging and demands much is not a faith that is easily shared. Today, people want a nice, convenient faith, something that allows them to live their lives undisturbed and unencumbered. So to share this total, radical, and world-changing faith that Jesus lived, died, and rose for is not the easiest of assignments; it is one that requires much resolve, integrity, and commitment.

Spreading the Good News

Blessed Junipero Serra (1713–1784) was a Franciscan priest who was a creative and convincing evangelizer. Junipero shared his faith so effectively through both word and deed that he baptized nearly six thousand people whose hearts were touched by his message. Many of these he met while establishing missions throughout Mexico and California as he promoted the gospel message as well as the dignity of the people he came to serve. Today, the Serra Club, a Catholic organization dedicated to promoting vocations to the priesthood, bears his name.

"Proclaim the word, be persistent whether it is convenient or inconvenient; convince, reprimand, encourage through all patience and teaching. For the time will come when people will not tolerate sound doctine but, following their own desires and insatiable curiosity, will accumulate teachers and will stop listening to the truth and will be diverted to myths. But you, be self-possessed in all circumstances; put up with hardship; perform the work of an evangelist; fulfill your ministry."

— 2 Tm 4:2–5

Seven Significant Themes of Catholic Social Teaching

Living out the six biblical principles requires that we do so while respecting the dignity and worth of all people. The Catholic faith has much to say about being people of justice and peace. Here are seven significant themes that summarize much of Catholic social teaching, which is rooted in the Scriptures and Tradition and should be woven into the biblical principles that every disciple lives by:

- **Life and Dignity of the Human Person**
  At the root of justice is the belief in the dignity and worth of all people. Every person, every life, is precious. People are more important than things. (See articles on pages 30, 765, 1306, 1426.)

- **Call to Family, Community, and Participation**
  The family is sacred and must be supported and strengthened. Much of this strength comes from being an active part of one's community where we can work together for the common good and well-being of all, especially those who are poor and vulnerable. (See articles on pages 302, 1462, 1531, 1691.)

- **Rights and Responsibilities**
  Each person has a responsibility to help protect for all people the basic rights required for human decency, including the right to life. (See articles on pages 551, 988, 1248, 1361.)

- **Option for the Poor and Vulnerable**
  The Gospel call of Jesus Christ challenges us to place the needs of the poor and vulnerable first, even above our own comforts and wants. (See articles on pages 126, 1232, 1311, 1750.)

- **The Dignity of Work and the Rights of Workers**
  Every person has a right to work and earn a living. By honoring fair wages, we assist people in being active participants in God's ongoing work of creation through honest and meaningful employment. (See articles on pages 101, 888, 1347, 1387.)

- **Solidarity**
  As members of a global family, we are all connected by an intricate web of life, whatever our national, racial, ethnic, economic, and ideological differences. This interconnectedness requires us to live together, united as brothers and sisters, in relationships that are marked by peace, love, and reconciliation instead of war, hatred, and mistrust. (See articles on pages 337, 603, 1442, 1661.)

- **Care for God's Creation**
  Care for the earth is a requirement of our faith. We are called to live our faith in relationship with all of God's creation, protecting both people and planet. (See articles on pages 23, 779, 810, 1236.)

endowed with all delights and conforming
to every taste.*
21 For this substance of yours revealed your
sweetness toward your children,
and serving the desire of the one who
received it,
was changed to whatever flavor each one
wished.*
22 Yet snow and ice† withstood fire and were
not melted,
so that they might know that their enemies'
fruits
Were consumed by a fire that blazed in the hail
and flashed lightning in the rain.*
23 But this fire, again, in order that the righteous
might be nourished,
forgot even its proper strength;*
24 For your creation, serving you, its maker,
grows tense for punishment against the
wicked,
but is relaxed in benefit for those who trust
in you.*
25 Therefore at that very time, transformed in all
sorts of ways,
it was serving your all-nourishing bounty
according to what they needed and desired;
26 That your children whom you loved might
learn, O LORD,
that it is not the various kinds of fruits that
nourish,
but your word that preserves those who
believe you!*
27 For what was not destroyed by fire,
melted when merely warmed by a
momentary sunbeam;*
28 To make known that one must give you
thanks before sunrise,
and turn to you at daybreak.*
29 For the hope of the ungrateful melts like a
wintry frost
and runs off like useless water.*

Fourth Example: Darkness Afflicts the Egyptians, While the Israelites Have Light†

17 1 For great are your judgments, and hard to
describe;
therefore the unruly souls went astray.*

Live It!

Wisdom Speaks

My name is Wisdom. In Greek, I am called Sophia. The Bible speaks of me as an aspect, or image, of God. I am sought after by many. I reveal myself to few. I appear many times in the Scriptures, yet I am elusive. What is it about me that is so attractive, so appealing? Solomon prayed for understanding, and I came to him. Indeed, wisdom is often associated with his name.

Those who seek me must desire deep in their heart to know me. That desire is the first step to finding me. The next is patience. Nothing of true and lasting importance comes quickly. I am not "fast food." In fact, you must experience a deep hunger before you can taste me. Quiet time is essential. You must be willing to simply be present, with no agenda. Imagine a "resplendent and unfading" flame (Wis 6:12). Let that be your focus.

Soon, I will come to you. I will seek you out. I will meet you in your thoughts, and we will become friends. We will dance together, you and I. You will be changed, transformed. You will grow deeper, quieter, and peace will begin to fill your soul.

My name is Wisdom. I want to be your friend. I wait for you.

2 For when the lawless thought to enslave the
holy nation,
they themselves lay shackled with darkness,
fettered by the long night,
confined beneath their own roofs as exiles
from the eternal providence.*
3 For they, who supposed their secret sins were
hid*

Angelicus") is taken from Ps 78:24 as rendered by the Septuagint. The "bread from heaven" (cf. Ex 16:4; Ps 105:40) with its marvelous "sweetness" becomes a type of the "bread come down from heaven" in Jn 6:32–51, and plays a large role in later Christian devotion.

16:22 *Snow and ice*: the manna; cf. v. 27; 19:21.

17:1–18:4 The description of the darkness of the ninth plague is a very creative development of Ex 10:21–29. It betrays a wide knowledge of contemporary thought. For the first and only time in the Septuagint the Greek word for "conscience" occurs, in 17:11. There is no Hebrew word that is equivalent; the idea is expressed indirectly. The horrendous darkness is illumined by "fires" (v. 6), i.e., lightnings that only contributed to the terror.

16:20 Ex 16:4; Nm 11:8; Ps 78:24–25; Jn 6:31.
16:21 Ps 34:9.
16:22 Ex 9:25–31; 10:12; Ps 148:8.
16:23 Wis 19:21.
16:24 Wis 5:17, 20; 19:6; Sir 39:25–27.
16:26 Dt 8:3; Mt 4:4.
16:27 Ex 16:21.
16:28 Ps 57:9–10; 92:3.
16:29 Wis 5:14; 2 Sm 14:14.
17:1 Ex 6:6 LXX.
17:2 Wis 18:4; Ex 1:13–14; 9:6; 10:21–23.
17:3–4 Wis 1:7–8; 10:8; 18:17.

under the dark veil of oblivion,
Were scattered in fearful trembling,
terrified by apparitions.
4 For not even their inner chambers kept them unafraid,
for crashing sounds on all sides terrified them,
and mute phantoms with somber looks appeared.
5 No fire had force enough to give light,
nor did the flaming brilliance of the stars
succeed in lighting up that gloomy night.*
6 But only intermittent, fearful fires
flashed through upon them;
And in their terror they thought beholding these was worse
than the times when that sight was no longer to be seen.*
7 And mockeries of their magic art† failed,
and there was a humiliating refutation of their vaunted shrewdness.*
8 For they who undertook to banish fears and terrors from the sick soul
themselves sickened with ridiculous fear.
9 For even though no monstrous thing frightened them,
they shook at the passing of insects and the hissing of reptiles,*
10 And perished trembling,
reluctant to face even the air that they could nowhere escape.
11 For wickedness, of its nature cowardly,
testifies in its own condemnation,
and because of a distressed conscience,
always magnifies misfortunes.*
12 For fear is nought but the surrender of the helps that come from reason;
13 and the more one's expectation is of itself uncertain,
the more one makes of not knowing the cause that brings on torment.
14 So they, during that night, powerless though it was,
since it had come upon them from the recesses of a powerless† Hades,
while all sleeping the same sleep,
15 Were partly smitten by fearsome apparitions
and partly stricken by their souls' surrender;
for fear overwhelmed them, sudden and unexpected.*
16 Thus, then, whoever was there fell
into that prison without bars and was kept confined.*
17 For whether one was a farmer, or a shepherd,
or a worker at tasks in the wasteland,
Taken unawares, each served out the inescapable sentence;
18 for all were bound by the one bond of darkness.*
And were it only the whistling wind,
or the melodious song of birds in the spreading branches,
Or the steady sound of rushing water,
19 or the rude crash of overthrown rocks,
Or the unseen gallop of bounding animals,
or the roaring cry of the fiercest beasts,
Or an echo resounding from the hollow of the hills—
these sounds, inspiring terror, paralyzed them.
20 For the whole world shone with brilliant light*
and continued its works without interruption;
21 But over them alone was spread oppressive night,
an image of the darkness† that was about to come upon them.
Yet they were more a burden to themselves than was the darkness.

18

1 But your holy ones had very great light;
And those others, who heard their voices but did not see their forms,
counted them blest for not having suffered;
2 And because they who formerly had been wronged did not harm them, they thanked them,
and because of the difference between them,† pleaded with them.
3 Instead of this, you furnished the flaming pillar,
a guide on the unknown way,
and the mild sun for an honorable migration.*
4† For they deserved to be deprived of light and imprisoned by darkness,

17:7 *Magic art*: the Egyptian magicians who were successful at first (Ex 7:11, 22) and then failed (Ex 8:14; 9:11) are now powerless against the darkness and the phantoms and are totally discredited.

17:14 *Powerless*: Hades (or Sheol), i.e., the nether world, is often portrayed in the Old Testament as a hostile power, since all must die (Ps 49:8–13), but it has no power against God.

17:21 *Darkness*: of Hades or Sheol; see note on 16:13–14.

18:2 *The difference between them*: God's distinctive manner of treating the Israelites and the Egyptians according to their respective deeds. *Pleaded*: perhaps, for their departure.

18:4 The discussion of physical light climaxes with a reference to the "imperishable light" of the torah.

17:5 Wis 10:17; Jer 23:24 LXX.
17:6 Ex 9:23–24.
17:7 Wis 12:25–26; Ex 7:11–12, 22; 8:3; 9:11; 10:2.
17:9 Wis 16:1; Jer 26:22 LXX.
17:11 Wis 4:6; 10:7; Rom 2:15.
17:15 Ex 11:9–10.
17:16 Wis 18:4; Ex 10:23.
17:18–19 Lv 26:36.
17:20–21 Ex 10:23; Is 9:1; 60:1–3; 2 Pt 2:17.
18:3 Ex 13:21.

they had kept your children confined,
through whom the imperishable light of
the law was to be given to the
world.*

Fifth Example: Death of the Egyptian Firstborn; the Israelites Are Spared

5 When they determined to put to death the
infants of the holy ones,
and when a single boy† had been cast forth
and then saved,
As a reproof you carried off a multitude of
their children
and made them perish all at once in the
mighty water.*
6 That night was known beforehand to our
ancestors,
so that, with sure knowledge of the oaths
in which they put their faith, they
might have courage.*
7 The expectation of your people
was the salvation of the righteous and the
destruction of their foes.*
8 For by the same means with which you
punished our adversaries,
you glorified us whom you had
summoned.*
9 For in secret the holy children of the good
were offering sacrifice
and carried out with one mind the divine
institution,†
So that your holy ones should share alike the
same blessings and dangers,
once they had sung the ancestral hymns of
praise.*
10 But the discordant cry of their enemies
echoed back,
and the piteous wail of mourning for
children was borne to them.*
11 And the slave was smitten with the same
retribution as the master;
even the commoner suffered the same as
the king.*
12 And all alike by one common form of death
had countless dead;
For the living were not even sufficient for the
burial,
since at a single instant their most valued
offspring had been destroyed.*
13 For though they disbelieved at every turn on
account of sorceries,
at the destruction of the firstborn they
acknowledged that this people† was
God's son.*
14† For when peaceful stillness encompassed
everything
and the night in its swift course was half
spent,
15 Your all-powerful word from heaven's royal
throne
leapt into the doomed land,*
16 a fierce warrior bearing the sharp sword of
your inexorable decree,
And alighted, and filled every place with
death,
and touched heaven, while standing upon
the earth.*
17 Then, at once, visions in horrible dreams
perturbed them*
and unexpected fears assailed them;
18 And cast half-dead, one here, another there,
they revealed why they were dying.
19 For the dreams that disturbed them had
proclaimed this beforehand,
lest they perish unaware of why they
endured such evil.

20 The trial of death touched even the righteous,
and in the desert a plague struck the
multitude;
Yet not for long did the anger last.*
21 For the blameless man† hastened to be their
champion,
bearing the weapon of his special office,
prayer and the propitiation of incense;
He withstood the wrath and put a stop to the
calamity,
showing that he was your servant.
22 He overcame the bitterness
not by bodily strength, not by force of
arms;
But by word he overcame the smiter,†
recalling the sworn covenants with their
ancestors.*

†

18:5 *Single boy*: Moses.
18:9 *Divine institution*: the Passover. *Ancestral hymns of praise*: possibly the Hallel psalms, the psalms sung at the end of the Passover meal; cf. Mt 26:30; Mk 14:26.
18:13 *People*: the Israelites (cf. Ex 4:22).
18:14–16 These verses attribute to the personified "word" the actions of the Lord mentioned in Ex 12:13–17 (note the role of the "destroyer" in Ex 12:23 and compare Wis 18:22, 25).
18:21 *Blameless man*: Aaron, acting according to his office of high priest and intercessor (cf. Nm 17:9–15; Ex 28:15–21, 31–38).
18:22 *Smiter*: the destroying angel; cf. v. 25.

*

18:4 Wis 17:2; Ps 119:105; Is 2:3, 5.
18:5 Wis 11:7, 14; Ex 1:16, 22; 2:3, 6–10; 15:10; Neh 9:11.
18:6 Wis 12:21; Ex 6:8; 13:5.
18:7 Ex 14:13.
18:8 Wis 19:22; Ex 3:18; Is 43:3–4.
18:9 Ex 12:21–28; Sir 44–50.
18:10 Ex 12:30; Jer 9:17, 19.
18:11 Ex 11:5; 12:29.
18:12 Nm 33:4.
18:13 Wis 17:7; Ex 4:22–23; 12:12, 29; 13:2, 13, 15.
18:15 Wis 9:10; Ex 15:3.
18:16 1 Chr 21:16; Heb 4:12; Rev 1:16.
18:17–19 Wis 17:3–4.
18:20 Wis 16:5; Nm 17:9–15.
18:22 Wis 12:21; Ex 32:12–13; Ps 20:8.

Live It!

Supernatural Resources

The Book of Wisdom of Solomon ends with an inspiring statement of faith: "For every way, Lord! you magnified and glorified your people; / unfailing, you stood by them in every time and circumstance" (19:22).

Could you say these words? Do you have the kind of faith that is able to see the hand of God at work through everything that happens?

So many times, we pray for God's help, especially if we are struggling or someone we love is suffering. Later, when that particular crisis is over, we quickly forget how God helped us through. The Bible's message is that God is at work through all the times in our lives, even in ways we do not realize at the moment. The Church's word for God's help is *grace*. Unlike most of our natural resources, the supernatural resource of grace is never in danger of being used up. In fact, the more we use it, the more of it there is!

Find a way of keeping track of how God has helped you through life. Perhaps you can maintain a journal of the difficult times you've made it through and the people who have supported you. You might be surprised by this record of how God's grace has been active!

▶ Wis 19:22

23 For when corpses had already fallen one on
another in heaps,
he stood in the midst and checked the anger,
and cut off its way to the living.*
24 For on his full-length robe was the whole
world,
and ancestral glories were carved on the
four rows of stones,
and your grandeur† was on the crown
upon his head.*
25 To these the destroyer yielded, these he
feared;
for this sole trial of anger sufficed.*

19 [1] But merciless wrath assailed the wicked
until the end,
for God knew beforehand what they were
yet to do:*
2 That though they themselves had agreed to
the departure
and had anxiously sent them on their way,
they would regret it and pursue them.*
3 For while they were still engaged in funeral
rites
and mourning at the burials of the dead,
They adopted another senseless plan:
those whom they had driven out with
entreaties
they now pursued as fugitives.*
4 For a compulsion appropriate to this ending
drew them on,
and made them forget what had befallen
them,
That they might complete the torments of
their punishment,
5 and your people might experience a
glorious† journey
while those others met an extraordinary
death.

6† For all creation, in its several kinds, was being
made over anew,
serving your commands, that your children
might be preserved unharmed.*
7 The cloud overshadowed their camp;
and out of what had been water, dry land
was seen emerging:
Out of the Red Sea an unimpeded road,
and a grassy plain out of the mighty
flood.*
8 Over this crossed the whole nation sheltered
by your hand,
and they beheld stupendous wonders.
9 For they ranged about like horses,
and leapt like lambs,
praising you, Lord, their deliverer.*
10 For they were still mindful of what had
happened in their sojourn:
how instead of the young of animals the
land brought forth gnats,

†

18:24 *Glories . . . grandeur*: the name of God and the names of the tribes were inscribed on the high priest's apparel.

19:5 *Glorious*: more precisely, "wondrous," but the word reflects "glorified" in 18:8 and 19:22.

19:6 The cooperation of creation in Israel's deliverance (vv. 7–12) under the direction of the Lord is a favorite theme; cf. 16:24–25.

*

18:23 Nm 14:29–30.
18:24 Ex 28:15–21, 31–38; Sir 45:8–12; 50:11.
18:25 1 Chr 21:15.
19:1 Ex 14:4.
19:2 Ex 12:33; 14:5, 8.
19:3 Wis 18:10, 12; Ex 12:30–36.
19:6 Wis 5:17; 16:24.
19:7 Ex 14:21–29.
19:9 Wis 10:20; 16:8; Ex 15:1–18; Ps 114:4–6.

and instead of fishes the river swarmed
with countless frogs.*
11 And later they saw also a new kind of bird*
when, prompted by desire, they asked for
pleasant foods;
12 For to appease them quail came to them from
the sea.
13 And the punishments came upon the sinners
not without forewarnings from the violence
of the thunderbolts.

For they justly suffered for their own
misdeeds,
since they treated their guests with the
more grievous† hatred.*
14 For those others† did not receive unfamiliar
visitors,*
but these were enslaving beneficent guests.
15 And not that only; but what punishment was
to be theirs†
since they received strangers unwillingly!
16 Yet these,† after welcoming them with
festivities,
oppressed with awful toils
those who had shared with them the same
rights.*
17 And they were struck with blindness,†
as those others had been at the doors of the
righteous man—
When, surrounded by yawning darkness,
each sought the entrance of his own
door.*

18 For the elements, in ever-changing harmony,
like strings of the harp, produce new
melody,
while the flow of music steadily persists.
And this can be perceived exactly from a
review of what took place.
19 For land creatures were changed into water
creatures,
and those that swam went over on land.
20 Fire in water maintained its own strength,*
and water forgot its quenching nature;
21 Flames, by contrast, neither consumed the
flesh
of the perishable animals that went about
in them,
nor melted the icelike, quick-melting kind
of ambrosial food.
22 For every way, LORD! you magnified and
glorified your people;
unfailing, you stood by them in every time
and circumstance.*

†

19:13 *More grievous*: than that of the people of Sodom (Gn 19) with whom the Egyptians are compared.

19:14 *Others*: the people of Sodom refused to receive strangers. *Beneficent*: because of the services rendered by Joseph.

19:15 *Theirs*: the people of Sodom.

19:16 *These*: the Egyptians.

19:17 *Blindness*: the plague of darkness. *Righteous man*: Lot (Gn 19:11).

*

19:10 Ex 7:27–8:3; 8:12–15; Ps 105:30–31.
19:11–12 Wis 16:2; Ps 78:18.
19:13 2 Mc 7:18, 32.
19:14–15 Gn 15:13; Ex 2:22.
19:16 Gn 45:17–20; 47:4–6; Ex 1:11.
19:17 Wis 17:2; Gn 19:11.
19:20–21 Wis 16:17–19, 22–23, 27.
19:22 Wis 18:8; Lv 26:44; Ps 126:3.

The Wisdom of Ben Sira (Ecclesiasticus)

Imagine that many years ago, your grandfather—a learned and wise man—wrote a book summarizing all his wisdom. Recently, you read the book and discovered it has answers to many of the problems you and your friends are struggling with. But the book is written in your grandfather's native language, which your friends don't understand. So, what do you do? You translate the book! This is exactly what the grandson of Jesus Ben Sira did. He translated into Greek the book his grandfather had written in Hebrew.

In Depth

The Wisdom of Ben Sira is unique in the Old Testament because it clearly identifies its author: Jesus Ben Sira, a wise teacher who lived early in the second century BC. Living in Jerusalem during a time of great change, he saw many of his people—especially those who were rich—deserting traditional Jewish beliefs in favor of more fashionable ideas coming from Greece. A book underlining the superiority of Jewish wisdom was needed, Ben Sira thought. So, he collected his class notes into a single volume and offered it to those who desired to learn the ways of living well. Though full of many different kinds of writing—sayings, hymns, prayers, and lists—the book is unified in its overall conviction: "All wisdom is from the Lord / and remains with him forever" (1:1).

At a Glance

I. Praise of Wisdom (chapters 1–43).

II. Praise of Israel's Great Ancestors (44:1—50:24).

III. Epilogue and Canticles (50:25—51:30).

Quick Facts

Inspired Author: Jesus Ben Sira, writing around 175 BC
Theme: the superiority of Jewish wisdom over Greek wisdom
Of Note: The Wisdom of Ben Sira is not found in every version of the Old Testament (see "The Case of the Missing Books," near Tb 1:16).

The Wisdom of Ben Sira holds fast to the long-standing belief that in this life, good is rewarded and evil is punished. Unlike Second Maccabees and Daniel—also written in the second century BC—Ben Sira never mentions the possibility of life after death. But like other wisdom books, it celebrates the glories of wisdom (see chapter 1) and recalls the heroes of Jewish faith (see chapters 44–50). Its view of women is harsher than that of most of the Old Testament, though. In interpreting The Wisdom of Ben Sira, you must take special care not to conclude that women are the source of most of men's troubles!

Sometimes called Ecclesiasticus or Sirach (which is the short form for "son of Sirach"), the Wisdom of Ben Sira was well known among the ancient Jews. It was popular in the early Christian church as well. Its influence can be found in the New Testament, especially in the Letter of James. Long after his death, Ben Sira continues to share the wisdom of the past and offers us trustworthy guidance for the present.

Ben Sira

Foreword

[1]Inasmuch as many and great truths have been given to us through the Law, the prophets, and the authors who followed them,† for which the instruction and wisdom of Israel merit praise, it is the duty of those who read the scriptures not only to become knowledgeable themselves but also to use their love of learning in speech and in writing to help others less familiar. So my grandfather Jesus, who had long devoted himself to the study of the law, the prophets, and the rest of the books of our ancestors, and had acquired great familiarity with them, was moved to write something himself regarding instruction and wisdom. He did this so that those who love learning might, by accepting what he had written, make even greater progress in living according to the Law.

You are invited therefore to read it with good will and attention, with indulgence for any failure on our part, despite earnest efforts, in the interpretation of particular passages. For words spoken originally in Hebrew do not have the same effect when they are translated into another language. That is true not only of this book but of the Law itself, the prophecies, and the rest of the books, which differ no little when they are read in the original.

I arrived in Egypt in the thirty-eighth year of the reign of King Euergetes, and while there, I had access to no little learning. I therefore considered it my duty to devote some diligence and industry to the translation of this book. During this time I applied my skill for many sleepless hours to complete the book and publish it for those living abroad who wish to acquire learning and are disposed to live their lives according to the Law.

† **Foreword** *The Law, the prophets, and the authors who followed them*: an indication of the eventual tripartite division of the Hebrew Scriptures: Law (*torah*), Prophets (*nebi'im*), and Writings (*ketubim*), shortened in the acronym Tanak. *Thirty-eighth . . . Euergetes*: 132 B.C. The reference is to Ptolemy VII, Physkon Euergetes II (170–163; 145–117 B.C.).

The Wisdom of Ben Sira

God's Gift of Wisdom†

1
1 All wisdom† is from the Lord
and remains with him forever.*
2 The sands of the sea, the drops of rain,
the days of eternity—who can count them?
3 Heaven's height, earth's extent,
the abyss and wisdom—who can explore them?

† **1:1–10** This brief poem serves as an introduction to the book. The Lord is the source and preserver of all wisdom, which he pours out upon all. See Jb 28:20–28; Prv 2:6; 8:22–31; Wis 7:25–27.

1:1 *Wisdom*: throughout the book Ben Sira describes in great detail just what wisdom is: sometimes divine (1:6, 8), sometimes a synonym for God's law (24:22–23). Ben Sira makes clear that all wisdom comes from God.

* **1:1** 1 Kgs 3:9.

4 Before all other things wisdom was created;
and prudent understanding, from eternity.‡

6 The root of wisdom—to whom has it been revealed?
Her subtleties—who knows them?‡ *
8† There is but one, wise and truly awesome,
seated upon his throne—the Lord.
9 It is he who created her,
saw her and measured her,*
Poured her forth upon all his works,
10 upon every living thing according to his bounty,
lavished her upon those who love him.

Fear of the Lord Is Wisdom†

11 The fear of the Lord† is glory and exultation,
gladness and a festive crown.
12 The fear of the Lord rejoices the heart,
giving gladness, joy, and long life.‡
13 Those who fear the Lord will be happy at the end,
even on the day of death they will be blessed.

14 The beginning of wisdom is to fear the Lord;
she is created with the faithful in the womb.*
15 With the godly she was created from of old,
and with their descendants she will keep faith.

16 The fullness of wisdom is to fear the Lord;
she inebriates them with her fruits.*
17 Their entire house she fills with choice foods,
their granaries with her produce.

18 The crown of wisdom is the fear of the Lord,
flowering with peace and perfect health.‡
19 Knowledge and full understanding she rains down;
she heightens the glory of those who possess her.
20 The root of wisdom is to fear the Lord;
her branches are long life.
21 The fear of the Lord drives away sins;
where it abides it turns back all anger.

22 Unjust anger can never be justified;
anger pulls a person to utter ruin.
23† Until the right time, the patient remain calm,
then cheerfulness comes back to them.
24 Until the right time they hold back their words;
then the lips of many will tell of their good sense.

25 Among wisdom's treasures is the model for knowledge;
but godliness is an abomination to the sinner.
26 If you desire wisdom, keep the commandments,
and the Lord will bestow her upon you;
27 For the fear of the Lord is wisdom and discipline;
faithfulness and humility are his delight.

28 Do not disobey the fear of the Lord,†
do not approach it with duplicity of heart.*
29 Do not be a hypocrite before others;
over your lips keep watch.
30 Do not exalt yourself lest you fall
and bring dishonor upon yourself;

For then the Lord will reveal your secrets
and cast you down in the midst of the assembly.
Because you did not approach the fear of the Lord,
and your heart was full of deceit.

Trust in God

2 1 My child, when you come to serve the Lord,†
prepare yourself for trials.*
2 Be sincere of heart and steadfast,

---

‡1:4 Other ancient texts read as v. 5:
The wellspring of wisdom is the word of God in the heights,
and its runlets are the ageless commandments.

‡1:6 Other ancient texts read as v. 7:
An understanding of wisdom—to whom has this been disclosed;
her resourcefulness, who has known?

1:8–10 In contrast to Jb 28, wisdom is not only with God, but given to all, especially Israel; see Bar 3:9; 4:4.

1:11–30 This is one of several poems of 22 bicola, or poetic lines, corresponding to the number of letters in the Hebrew alphabet. Ben Sira uses the expression "fear of the Lord" twelve times and the noun "wisdom" seven times to emphasize the connection between the two ideas. He describes the blessings that come to those who fear the Lord, i.e., those who practice true religion by loving and serving God and keeping the Law (2:7–10, 15–17; 4:11–16; see Dt 6:1–5, 24). Such blessings recur throughout the book.

1:11 *Fear of the Lord*: Ben Sira identifies wisdom with the fear of the Lord (vv. 26–27).

‡1:12 Other ancient texts read as v. 12cd:
Fear of the Lord is the Lord's gift;
also for love he makes firm paths.

‡1:18 Other ancient texts read as v. 18cd:
Both are gifts of God toward peace;
splendor opens out for those who love him.

1:23–24 Ben Sira pays close attention to *kaîros*, the right time, occurring some sixty times in his book.

1:28–30 Attempting to serve the Lord with duplicity of heart is hypocrisy and self-exaltation, deserving of public disgrace.

2:1–11 Serving the Lord is not without its trials (v. 1); but no matter what happens, the genuine believer will remain sincere, stead-

---

1:6 Bar 3:15; Jb 28:10, 20.
1:9 Jb 28:27.
1:14 Jb 28:28; Ps 111:10; Prv 1:7; 9:10.
1:16 Eccl 12:13.
1:28 Jas 1:8; 2:8.
2:1 2 Tm 3:10–12.

and do not be impetuous in time of adversity.
3 Cling to him, do not leave him,
that you may prosper in your last days.

4 Accept whatever happens to you;
in periods of humiliation be patient.
5 For in fire gold is tested,
and the chosen, in the crucible of humiliation.*
6 Trust in God, and he will help you;
make your ways straight and hope in him.

7 You that fear the Lord, wait for his mercy,
do not stray lest you fall.
8 You that fear the Lord, trust in him,
and your reward will not be lost.
9 You that fear the LORD, hope for good things,
for lasting joy and mercy.

10 Consider the generations long past and see:
has anyone trusted in the Lord and been disappointed?
Has anyone persevered in his fear and been forsaken?
has anyone called upon him and been ignored?*
11 For the Lord is compassionate and merciful;
forgives sins and saves in time of trouble.

12 Woe to timid hearts and drooping hands,†
to the sinner who walks a double path!
13 Woe to the faint of heart! For they do not trust,
and therefore have no shelter!
14 Woe to you that have lost hope!
what will you do at the Lord's visitation?

15 Those who fear the Lord do not disobey his words;
those who love him keep his ways.*
16 Those who fear the Lord seek to please him;
those who love him are filled with his law.
17 Those who fear the Lord prepare their hearts
and humble themselves before him.

18 Let us fall into the hands of the Lord
and not into the hands of mortals,
For equal to his majesty is his mercy;
and equal to his name are his works.*

Responsibilities to Parents†

3 1 Children, listen to me, your father;
act accordingly, that you may be safe.
2 For the Lord sets a father in honor over his children
and confirms a mother's authority over her sons.
3 Those who honor their father atone for sins;
4 they store up riches who respect their mother.
5 Those who honor their father will have joy in their own children,
and when they pray they are heard.
6 Those who respect their father will live a long life;
those who obey the Lord honor their mother.

7 Those who fear the Lord honor their father,
and serve their parents as masters.
8 In word and deed honor your father,
that all blessings may come to you.*
9 A father's blessing gives a person firm roots,
but a mother's curse uproots the growing plant.*
10 Do not glory in your father's disgrace,
for that is no glory to you!
11 A father's glory is glory also for oneself;
they multiply sin who demean their mother.*

12 My son, be steadfast in honoring your father;
do not grieve him as long as he lives.*
13 Even if his mind fails, be considerate of him;
do not revile him because you are in your prime.
14 Kindness to a father will not be forgotten;
it will serve as a sin offering—it will take lasting root.
15 In time of trouble it will be recalled to your advantage,
like warmth upon frost it will melt away your sins.
16 Those who neglect their father are like blasphemers;

---

† fast, and faithful (vv. 2–3). Misfortune and humiliation are means of purification to prove one's worth (vv. 4–5). Ben Sira believed that patience and unwavering trust in God are ultimately rewarded with the benefits of God's mercy and of lasting joy (vv. 6–11).

2:12–18 A stern warning to those who compromise their faith in time of affliction; they fail in courage and trust and therefore have no security (vv. 12–14). But those who fear the Lord through obedience, reverence, love, and humility find his "mercy equal to his majesty" (vv. 15–18).

3:1–16 Besides the virtues that must characterize our conduct toward God, special duties are enjoined, such as honor and respect toward parents, with corresponding blessings (vv. 1–9). By showing such respect especially to old and infirm parents (vv. 10–13), the sins of children are pardoned (vv. 14–15). Failure to honor father and mother is blasphemy and merits a curse from God (v. 16). Cf. Ex 20:12; Eph 6:2–3.

---

* **2:5** Prv 17:3; Wis 3:6; Is 48:10; 1 Pt 1:7. **2:10** Ps 31:2; 145:18–20. **2:15** Jn 14:23. **2:18** Sir 17:29. **3:8** Ex 20:12; Dt 5:16; Mt 15:4; 19:19; Mk 7:10; 10:19; Lk 18:20; Eph 6:2–3. **3:9** Gn 27:27–29; 49:2–27. **3:11** Prv 17:6. **3:12** Prv 23:22.

S I R

Cultural Connection

Honoring Our Parents in God's Way

You hear Ben Sira 3:1–7 every year on Holy Family Sunday, the weekend after Christmas. This reading calls us to honor our parents, because this is the way God established children's responsibilities toward parents. To honor our parents is to respect them (see verse 6), to be kind to them (see verse 14), to not dishonor them in order to feel superior (see verse 10), and to take care of them and be considerate of them as they age (see verses 12–13). According to Ben Sira, God assures many blessings to those who honor their parents, including safety, happiness, forgiveness of sins, the hearing of their prayers, and a long life.

Hispanics have a long tradition of being parented not only by birth parents but by the extended family, including grandparents, godparents, aunts, and uncles. Today, many young people are also parented by foster parents, stepparents, and adoptive parents.

- Take a moment to think of the adults who have parented you. In what specific ways do you honor and show your love to them? In what ways might you have failed to do so?
- Thank God, our heavenly parent, for the love and sacrifices of all the people who have parented you. Ask God to give you love, understanding, strength, and patience to honor them in word and deed.

▶ Sir 3:1–16

those who provoke their mother are
accursed by their Creator.*

Humility†

17 My son, conduct your affairs with humility,
and you will be loved more than a giver of
gifts.
18 Humble yourself the more, the greater you are,
and you will find mercy in the sight of
God.‡ *
20 For great is the power of the Lord;
by the humble he is glorified.
21 What is too sublime for you, do not seek;
do not reach into things that are hidden
from you.*
22 What is committed to you, pay heed to;
what is hidden is not your concern.
23 In matters that are beyond you do not meddle,
when you have been shown more than you
can understand.
24 Indeed, many are the conceits of human
beings;
evil imaginations lead them astray.

Docility†

25 Without the pupil of the eye, light is missing;
without knowledge, wisdom is missing.
26 A stubborn heart will fare badly in the end;
those who love danger will perish in it.
27 A stubborn heart will have many a hurt;
adding sin to sin is madness.
28 When the proud are afflicted, there is no cure;
for they are offshoots of an evil plant.*
29 The mind of the wise appreciates proverbs,
and the ear that listens to wisdom rejoices.

Alms for the Poor

30 As water quenches a flaming fire,
so almsgiving atones for sins.*
31 The kindness people have done crosses their
paths later on;
should they stumble, they will find support.

4 [1]My child, do not mock the life of the poor;
do not keep needy eyes† waiting.*
2 Do not grieve the hungry,

† **3:17–24** Humility gives you a true estimate of yourself (vv. 17–20; cf. 10:28), so that you will do what should be done, and avoid what is beyond your understanding and strength (vv. 21–23). Intellectual pride, however, leads you astray (v. 24). Ben Sira is perhaps warning his students against the perils of Greek philosophy.

‡**3:18** Other ancient texts read as v. 19:
Many are lofty and famous,
but to the humble he reveals his plan.

3:25–29 The antidote for stubbornness is to be found in the search for knowledge and wisdom.

4:1 *Needy eyes*: when the poor look for help; cf. 18:18.

* **3:16** Prv 19:26; 30:11, 14, 17. **3:18** Mt 23:12; Lk 1:52; 14:11; 18:14. **3:21** Ps 131:1. **3:28** Dt 32:32; Wis 12:10. **3:30** Sir 7:32–36; 29:8–13; Dt 15:7–11; Tb 12:9; Dn 4:24. **4:1** Tb 4:7–11.

Cultural Connection

Celebrating Families

Ben Sira holds family relationships in high esteem. In chapter 3, he emphasizes the importance of honor and respect among family members. Many cultures have special days honoring parents and children. In the United States, we celebrate Mother's Day, Father's Day, and Grandparent's Day.

Japan also has special days honoring family members. Girls' Festival *(Hinamatsuri)* is celebrated on March 3 with doll displays and peach blossoms. Boys' Festival *(Kodomo No Hi)* is celebrated on May 5 with streamers. Respect for the Aged Day *(Keiro No Hi)* is celebrated on September 15. On January 15, the Coming of Age Festival *(Seigin No Hi)* takes place. This day celebrates all young people who have turned twenty during the previous year—the age when young adults are permitted to vote, drink, and smoke.

If you have Japanese friends or acquaintances, consider marking these holidays on your calendar and sending a card or note with a prayer on the appropriate day.

▶ Sir 3:1–16

nor anger the needy.
3 Do not aggravate a heart already angry,
nor delay giving to the needy.
4 A beggar's request do not reject;
do not turn your face away from the poor.
5 From the needy do not turn your eyes;
do not give them reason to curse you.
6 If in their pain they cry out bitterly,
their Rock will hear the sound of their cry.

Social Conduct

7 Endear yourself to the assembly;
before the city's ruler bow your head.
8 Give a hearing to the poor,
and return their greeting with deference;
9 Deliver the oppressed from their oppressors;*
right judgment should not be repugnant to you.
10 Be like a father to orphans,
and take the place of a husband to widows.
Then God will call you his child,
and he will be merciful to you and deliver you from the pit.

The Rewards of Wisdom†

11 Wisdom teaches her children
and admonishes all who can understand her.
12 Those who love her love life;
those who seek her out win the LORD's favor.
13 Those who hold her fast will attain glory,
and they shall abide in the blessing of the LORD.
14 Those who serve her serve the Holy One;
those who love her the Lord loves.*
15 "Whoever obeys me will judge nations;
whoever listens to me will dwell in my inmost chambers.
16 If they remain faithful, they will possess me;
their descendants too will inherit me.
17 "I will walk with them in disguise,
and at first I will test them with trials.
Fear and dread I will bring upon them
and I will discipline them with my constraints.
When their hearts are fully with me,
18 then I will set them again on the straight path
and reveal my secrets to them.
19 But if they turn away from me, I will abandon them
and deliver them over to robbers."

† **4:11–19** The Hebrew text in vv. 15–19 presents wisdom speaking in the first person, as in chap. 24. The precious fruits of wisdom—life, favor, glory, blessings, God's love—arouse desire for her (vv. 11–14). Her disciples are like ministers (v. 14) and judges (v. 15), whose descendants have her for their heritage (v. 16). They enjoy happiness and learn her secrets after surviving her tests (vv. 17–18). Those who fail her are abandoned to destruction (v. 19).

4:9 Jb 29:12, 17. **4:14** Wis 7:28.

SIR

Sincerity and Justice†

20 My son, watch for the right time; fear what is evil;
do not bring shame upon yourself.
21 There is a shame heavy with guilt,
and a shame that brings glory and respect.
22 Show no favoritism to your own discredit;
let no one intimidate you to your own downfall.
23 Do not refrain from speaking at the proper time,
and do not hide your wisdom;
24 For wisdom becomes known through speech,
and knowledge through the tongue's response.
25 Never speak against the truth,
but of your own ignorance be ashamed.
26 Do not be ashamed to acknowledge your sins,
and do not struggle against a rushing stream.
27 Do not abase yourself before a fool;
do not refuse to do so before rulers.
28 Even to the death, fight for what is right,
and the LORD will do battle for you.
29 Do not be haughty in your speech,
or lazy and slack in your deeds.
30 Do not be like a lion at home,
or sly and suspicious with your servants.
31 Do not let your hand be open to receive,
but clenched when it is time to give.

Against Presumption†

5 1 Do not rely on your wealth,
or say, "I have the power."*
2 Do not rely on your strength
in following the desires of your heart.
3 Do not say, "Who can prevail against me?"
for the LORD will exact punishment.
4 Do not say, "I have sinned, yet what has happened to me?"
for the LORD is slow to anger!
5 Do not be so confident of forgiveness
that you add sin upon sin.
6 Do not say, "His mercy is great;
my many sins he will forgive."
For mercy and anger alike are with him;
his wrath comes to rest on the wicked.
7 Do not delay turning back to the LORD,
do not put it off day after day.
For suddenly his wrath will come forth;
at the time of vengeance, you will perish.
8 Do not rely on deceitful wealth,
for it will be no help on the day of wrath.*

Use and Abuse of the Tongue†

9 Do not winnow in every wind,
nor walk in every path.†
10 Be steadfast regarding your knowledge,
and let your speech be consistent.
11 Be swift to hear,
but slow to answer.*
12 If you can, answer your neighbor;
if not, place your hand over your mouth!
13 Honor and dishonor through speaking!
The tongue can be your downfall.
14 Do not be called double-tongued;
and with your tongue do not slander a neighbor.
For shame has been created for the thief,
and sore disgrace for the double-tongued.
15 In little or in much, do not act corruptly;
6 1 Do not be a foe instead of a friend.
A bad name, disgrace, and dishonor you will inherit.
Thus the wicked, the double-tongued!†

Unruly Passions

2 Do not fall into the grip of your passion,*
lest like fire it consume your strength.
3 It will eat your leaves and destroy your fruits,
and you will be left like a dry tree.
4 For fierce passion destroys its owner
and makes him the sport of his enemies.

True Friendship†

5 Pleasant speech multiplies friends,
and gracious lips, friendly greetings.
6 Let those who are friendly to you be many,
but one in a thousand your confidant.

†

4:20–31 The student of wisdom is warned about interior trials of discipline and external dangers to sincerity and justice, namely evil, human respect (vv. 20–22), compromise of liberty in speech and action (vv. 23–25), false shame (v. 26). The student must fight for the truth (vv. 25, 28), avoiding cynicism and laziness (v. 29), and inconsistency (v. 30).

5:1–8 The vices of the rich are pride and independence (vv. 1–2), presumption (v. 3), false security (vv. 4–6), and impenitence (v. 7), which cannot escape the divine wrath (vv. 7–8). Cf. Prv 18:23; 19:1; 28:6.

5:9–6:1 Proper use of the tongue requires constancy in speech (v. 10), prudence (vv. 11–12), good judgment (v. 13), charity (5:15; 6:1); detraction, calumny (v. 14), and double-talk bring shame and disgrace (5:14; 6:1).

5:9 The metaphors indicate careless behavior.

6:1 *Thus . . . double-tongued!*: people will say this against those disgraced by lying and double-talk.

6:5–17 One of several poems Ben Sira wrote on friendship; see also 9:10–16; 12:8–18; 13:1–23; 19:13–17; 22:19–26; 27:16–21. True friends are discerned not by prosperity (v. 11), but through the trials of adversity: distress, quarrels (v. 9), sorrow (v. 10) and misfortune (v. 12). Such friends are rare, a gift from God (vv. 14–17).

*

5:1 Sir 11:24; Prv 27:1; Lk 12:19; 1 Tm 6:17.
5:8 Prv 10:2; 11:4, 28; Ps 52:9.
5:11 Prv 29:20; Eccl 5:1; Jas 1:19.
6:2–3 Sir 9:8; 23:16; 25:21; 41:20, 22; Jb 31:12.

7 When you gain friends, gain them through
testing,*
and do not be quick to trust them.
8 For there are friends when it suits them,
but they will not be around in time of
trouble.
9 Another is a friend who turns into an enemy,
and tells of the quarrel to your disgrace.
10 Others are friends, table companions,
but they cannot be found in time of
affliction.
11 When things go well, they are your other self,
and lord it over your servants.
12 If disaster comes upon you, they turn
against you
and hide themselves.
13 Stay away from your enemies,
and be on guard with your friends.
14 Faithful friends are a sturdy shelter;
whoever finds one finds a treasure.
15 Faithful friends are beyond price,
no amount can balance their worth.
16 Faithful friends are life-saving medicine;
those who fear God will find them.
17 Those who fear the Lord enjoy stable friendship,
for as they are, so will their neighbors be.

Blessings of Wisdom†

18 My child, from your youth choose discipline;
and when you have gray hair you will find
wisdom.
19 As though plowing and sowing, draw close to
her;
then wait for her bountiful crops.
For in cultivating her you will work but little,
and soon you will eat her fruit.

20 She is rough ground to the fool!
The stupid cannot abide her.
21 She will be like a burdensome stone to them,
and they will not delay in casting her aside.
22 For discipline† is like her name,
she is not accessible to many.

23 Listen, my child, and take my advice;
do not refuse my counsel.
24 Put your feet into her fetters,
and your neck under her yoke.
25 Bend your shoulders and carry her
and do not be irked at her bonds.

Pray It!

Friends

God of friendship,
Thank you for my friends, especially for those who give me wise advice.
Thank you for my closest friends whom I see every day, who motivate me to grow and serve.
Thank you for all the good friends whom I used to see more often but don't see as much anymore.
Lord, continue to give me good friends throughout my life, and help me be a better friend to all. Amen.

▶ **Sir 6:5–17**

26 With all your soul draw close to her;
and with all your strength keep her ways.
27 Inquire and search, seek and find;
when you get hold of her, do not let
her go.
28 Thus at last you will find rest in her,
and she will become your joy.

29 Her fetters will be a place of strength;
her snare, a robe of spun gold.
30 Her yoke will be a gold ornament;*
her bonds, a purple cord.
31 You will wear her as a robe of glory,
and bear her as a splendid crown.

32 If you wish, my son, you can be wise;
if you apply yourself, you can be shrewd.
33 If you are willing to listen, you can learn;
if you pay attention, you can be instructed.

34 Stand in the company of the elders;
stay close to whoever is wise.
35 Be eager to hear every discourse;
let no insightful saying escape you.*
36 If you see the intelligent, seek them out;
let your feet wear away their doorsteps!

† **6:18–37** The various figures in each of the eight stanzas urge the search for wisdom through patience (vv. 18–19), persistence (vv. 20–22), docility and perseverance (vv. 23–28). Wisdom bestows rich rewards (vv. 29–31) on those who apply themselves and learn from the wise (vv. 32–36). Although one must strive for wisdom, it is God who grants it (v. 37). Cf. 4:11–19.

6:22 *Discipline*: *musar* (in the sense of wisdom) is a perfect homonym for *musar*, "removed, withdrawn"; thus the path of discipline is not accessible to many.

* **6:7–9** Sir 12:8–9; 37:1–5; Prv 19:4. **6:30** Is 62:3. **6:35** Sir 8:8–9.

37 Reflect on the law of the Most High,
and let his commandments be your constant study.
Then he will enlighten your mind,
and make you wise as you desire.*

Conduct Toward God and Neighbor†

7 1 Do no evil, and evil will not overtake you;†
2 avoid wickedness, and it will turn away from you.
3 Do not sow in the furrows of injustice,
lest you harvest it sevenfold.*
4 Do not seek from God authority
or from the king a place of honor.
5 Do not parade your righteousness before the LORD,
and before the king do not flaunt your wisdom.*
6 Do not seek to become a judge
if you do not have the strength to root out crime,
Lest you show fear in the presence of the prominent
and mar your integrity.
7 Do not be guilty of any evil before the city court
or disgrace yourself before the assembly.
8 Do not plot to repeat a sin;
even for one, you will not go unpunished.
9 Do not say, "He will appreciate my many gifts;
the Most High God will accept my offerings."*
10 Do not be impatient in prayer
or neglect almsgiving.
11 Do not ridicule the embittered;
Remember: there is One who exalts and humbles.†
12 Do not plot mischief against your relative
or against your friend and companion.
13 Refuse to tell lie after lie,
for it never results in good.
14 Do not babble in the assembly of the elders
or repeat the words of your prayer.† *
15 Do not hate hard work;
work was assigned by God.*
16 Do not esteem yourself more than your compatriots;
remember, his wrath will not delay.
17 More and more, humble your pride;
what awaits mortals is worms.† *

Duties of Family Life, Religion and Charity†

18 Do not barter a friend for money,
or a true brother for the gold of Ophir.†
19 Do not reject a sensible wife;
a gracious wife is more precious than pearls.
20 Do not mistreat a servant who works faithfully,
or laborers who devote themselves to their task.*
21 Love wise servants as yourself;
do not refuse them freedom.†
22 Do you have livestock? Look after them;
if they are dependable, keep them.
23 Do you have sons? Correct them
and cure their stubbornness† in their early youth.*
24 Do you have daughters? Keep them chaste,
and do not be indulgent to them.*
25 Give your daughter in marriage, and a worry comes to an end;
but give her to a sensible man.
26 Do you have a wife? Do not mistreat her,
but do not trust the wife you hate.

27 With your whole heart honor your father;
your mother's birth pangs do not forget.*
28 Remember, of these parents you were born;
what can you give them for all they gave you?

29 With all your soul fear God
and revere his priests.
30 With all your strength love your Maker
and do not neglect his ministers.

---

†

7:1–17 In the conduct of social relations wisdom forbids evil and injustice (vv. 1–3), pride (vv. 5, 15–17), ambition and partiality (vv. 4, 6), public disorder (v. 7), presumption and impatience toward God (vv. 9–10), ridicule (v. 11), mischief and deceit toward one's neighbor (vv. 8, 12–13). See the several wisdom poems in Prv 1–9.

7:1 There is a play on "evil" which means both moral wrong and material calamity.

7:11 *One who exalts and humbles*: God; cf. 1 Sm 2:7; Ps 75:8; Lk 1:52.

7:14 *Repeat . . . prayer*: brevity of speech is a wisdom ideal; toward superiors and God it is a sign of respect; cf. Eccl 5:1; Mt 6:7.

7:17 *Worms*: i.e., corruption; the Septuagint adds "fire."

7:18–36 Respect and appreciation, justice and kindness should characterize relations toward members of the household (vv. 18–28), God and the priests (vv. 29–31), the poor and afflicted, the living and the dead (vv. 32–35).

7:18 *Ophir*: the port, at present unidentified, to which the ships of Solomon sailed and from which they brought back gold and silver; cf. note on Ps 45:10.

7:21 After six years of service a Hebrew slave was entitled to freedom; cf. Ex 21:2; Dt 15:12–15.

7:23 *Cure their stubbornness*: keep them from rebellious pride; so with the Greek. Cf. 30:1–13. The Hebrew text, probably not original here, reads: "Choose wives for them while they are young."

---

*

6:37 Ps 1:2.
7:3 Jb 4:8; Prv 22:8; Hos 8:7.
7:5 Jb 9:2; Ps 143:2; Prv 25:6; 1 Cor 4:4.
7:9 Sir 34:21–24; 35:14–15.
7:14 Sir 32:7–10; Mt 6:7.
7:15 Gn 2:15; 3:17.
7:17 Sir 10:11; Jb 17:14; Is 66:24.
7:20 Lv 19:13; Dt 24:14–15; Jas 5:4.
7:23 Sir 30:1–13; Prv 13:24; 19:18; 23:13–14; 29:15, 17.
7:24 Sir 42:9–12.
7:27 Sir 3:1–16; Ex 20:12; Dt 5:16; Tb 4:3–4; Prv 23:22.

31 Honor God and respect the priest;
give him his portion as you have been commanded:*
First fruits and contributions,
his portion of victims and holy offerings.†

32 To the poor also extend your hand,
that your blessing may be complete.
33 Give your gift to all the living,
and do not withhold your kindness from the dead.†
34 Do not avoid those who weep,
but mourn with those who mourn.*
35 Do not hesitate to visit the sick,
because for such things you will be loved.*

36 In whatever you do, remember your last days,
and you will never sin.†

Prudence in Dealing with Others†

8 [1] Do not contend with the mighty,
lest you fall into their power.
2 Do not quarrel with the rich,
lest they pay out the price of your downfall.
For gold has unsettled many,
and wealth perverts the character of princes.*

3 Do not quarrel with loud-mouths,
or heap wood upon their fire.† *
4 Do not associate with the senseless,
lest your ancestors be insulted.
5 Do not reproach one who turns away from sin;*
remember, we all are guilty.†
6 Do not insult one who is old,
for some of us will also grow old.
7 Do not rejoice when someone dies;
remember, we are all to be gathered in.

8 Do not neglect the discourse of the wise,*
but busy yourself with their proverbs;
For in this way you will acquire the training
to stand in the presence of princes.
9 Do not reject the tradition of the elders
which they have heard from their ancestors;
For from it you will learn
how to answer when the need arises.

10 Do not kindle the coals of sinners,
lest you be burned in their flaming fire.
11 Do not give ground before scoundrels;
it will set them in ambush against you.†
12 Do not lend to one more powerful than yourself;
or if you lend, count it as lost.*
13 Do not give collateral beyond your means;
consider any collateral a debt you must pay.

14 Do not go to court against a judge,
for the case will be settled in his favor.
15 Do not travel with the ruthless
lest they weigh you down with calamity;
For they will only go their own way,
and through their folly you will also perish.
16 Do not defy the quick-tempered,
or ride with them through the desert.
For bloodshed is nothing to them;
when there is no one to help, they will destroy you.

17 Do not take counsel with simpletons,
for they cannot keep a confidence.
18 Before a stranger do nothing that should be kept secret,
for you do not know what it will produce later on.† *
19 Open your heart to no one,
do not banish your happiness.

Advice Concerning Women†

9 [1] Do not be jealous of the wife of your bosom,
lest you teach her to do evil against you.†
2 Do not give a woman power over you
to trample on your dignity.*
3 Do not go near a strange woman,

---

† **7:31** *First fruits . . . holy offerings*: cf. Ex 29:27; Lv 7:31–34; Nm 18:8–20; Dt 18:1–5.

7:33 This seems to refer to the observances ordained toward the dead, that is, proper mourning and burial. Cf. 2 Sm 21:12–14; Tb 1:17–18; 12:12.

7:36 *Never sin*: because the last days of the sinner, it was presumed, would be troubled.

8:1–19 The prudent will be circumspect, avoiding conflict with the powerful, the rich and insolent, the impious, the irascible, and judges (vv. 1–3, 10–12, 14, 16). They will not associate with the undisciplined (v. 4) or the ruthless (v. 15), with fools or strangers (vv. 17–19), but with the wise and the elders of the people (vv. 8–9). Caution is a recurring theme in Ben Sira.

8:3 One should avoid increasing the ire of those who are hotheaded; cf. vv. 10, 16.

8:5 *We all are guilty*: cf. 1 Kgs 8:46; 2 Chr 6:36; Jb 25:4; Eccl 7:20; Rom 3:9–10; 5:12; 1 Jn 1:8.

8:11 Giving in to the wicked only encourages them to take advantage.

8:18 To keep a secret, or a confidence, is a major concern of Ben Sira; cf. 1:30; 22:22; 27:16–21; 37:10; 42:1.

9:1–9 Ben Sira writes about women only from the androcentric viewpoint of his culture. Cf. 25:13–26:27.

9:1 Jealousy may lead to suspicion and may prompt a wife to those actions her husband fears.

---

* **7:31** Lv 7:31; Nm 18:18.
7:34 Rom 12:15.
7:35 Mt 25:36.
8:2 Sir 31:5–6; Dt 16:19.
8:3 Prv 26:20–21.
8:5 1 Kgs 8:46; 1 Jn 1:8.
8:8–9 Sir 6:34–36.
8:12 Sir 29:4–7; Prv 17:18.
8:18 Prv 25:9–10.
9:2 Sir 25:21.

Live It!

Friends, Old and New

Out there, somewhere, is a special person you have not yet met, someone who will eventually become a key person in your life. In fact, a lot of such people are out there, somewhere—including future classmates, coworkers, roommates, and friends. The challenge is in finding the particular people who will become close to you and share with you the experiences of your life.

Ben Sira reminds us in Ben Sira 9:10 that in the excitement that accompanies making new friends, we should not forget the pleasure and comfort that an old friend brings us. A friend we have known for a long time is someone to trust, someone who knows and accepts us, in spite of our shortcomings. And when the circumstances of life cause separation from old friends, there is value in reconnecting occasionally, to share where life has taken us or even to seek direction and support if life has become confusing or hard. We need to treasure our tried-and-true friendships, as well as welcome new ones.

Spend some time reflecting on your friends, old and new, and their value in your life.

▶ Sir 9:10

lest you fall into her snares.
4 Do not dally with a singer,
lest you be captivated by her charms.
5 Do not entertain any thoughts about a virgin,
lest you be enmeshed in damages for her.†
6 Do not give yourself to a prostitute
lest you lose your inheritance.*
7 Do not look around the streets of the city
or wander through its squares.
8 Avert your eyes from a shapely woman;
do not gaze upon beauty that is not yours;
Through woman's beauty many have been
ruined,
for love of it burns like fire.*
9 Never recline at table with a married woman,
or drink intoxicants with her,
Lest your heart be drawn to her
and you go down in blood† to the grave.

Choice of Friends†

10 Do not abandon old friends;
new ones cannot equal them.
A new friend is like new wine—
when it has aged, you drink it with pleasure.
11 Do not envy the wicked
for you do not know when their day will
come.
12 Do not delight in the pleasures of the ungodly;
remember, they will not die unpunished.

13 Keep away from those who have power to kill,
and you will not be filled with the dread of
death.
But if you come near them, do not offend
them,
lest they take away your life.
Know that you are stepping among snares
and walking over a net.

14 As best you can, answer your neighbor,
and associate with the wise.
15 With the learned exchange ideas;
and let all your conversation be about the
law of the Most High.
16 Take the righteous for your table companions;
and let your glory be in the fear of God.

Concerning Rulers†

17 Work by skilled hands will earn praise;
but the people's leader is proved wise by
his words.
18 Loud mouths are feared in their city,
and whoever is reckless in speech is hated.

10 [1]A wise magistrate gives stability to his
people,
and government by the intelligent is well
ordered.*
2 As the people's judge, so the officials;*
as the head of a city, so the inhabitants.

† **9:5** Cf. Ex 22:15–16; Dt 22:28–29; Jb 31:1. Cf. note on Ex 22:16.

9:9 *In blood*: perhaps refers to blood revenge; cf. Lv 20:10.

9:10–16 The second of Ben Sira's poems on friendship; cf. note on 6:5–17. In choosing friends, adherence to the law of the Lord should serve as a guide (v. 15). Associate with true friends (v. 10), with the righteous and the learned (vv. 14–16); avoid the company of the mighty and of sinners (vv. 11–13). Cf. 8:1–19.

9:17–10:5 Public office as conducted justly or unjustly benefits or destroys the people, according to the axiom, "as the prince, so the people." God, however, has sovereignty over both.

* **9:6** Prv 5:1–14; 6:24; 29:3.
9:8 Sir 25:20; 41:21; Prv 6:25–29.
10:1 Prv 29:4; Wis 6:24.
10:2–3 Ez 16:44; Prv 29:12.

3 A reckless king destroys his people,
but a city grows through the intelligence of its princes.*
4 Sovereignty over the earth is in the hand of God,
who appoints the right person for the right time.
5 Sovereignty over everyone is in the hand of God,
who imparts his majesty to the ruler.

The Sin of Pride

6 No matter what the wrong, never harm your neighbor
or go the way of arrogance.*
7 Odious to the Lord and to mortals is pride,
and for both oppression is a crime.
8 Sovereignty is transferred from one people to another
because of the lawlessness of the proud.
9 Why are dust and ashes proud?†
Even during life the body decays.
10 A slight illness—the doctor jests;
a king today—tomorrow he is dead.
11 When a people die,
they inherit corruption and worms, gnats and maggots.*

12 The beginning of pride is stubbornness
in withdrawing the heart from one's Maker.
13 For sin is a reservoir of insolence,
a source which runs over with vice;
Because of it God sends unheard-of afflictions
and strikes people with utter ruin.*
14 God overturns the thrones of the proud
and enthrones the lowly in their place.
15 God plucks up the roots of the proud,
and plants the lowly in their place.
16 The Lord lays waste the lands of the nations,
and destroys them to the very foundations of the earth.
17 He removes them from the earth, destroying them,
erasing their memory from the world.
18 Insolence does not befit mortals,
nor impudent anger those born of women.

True Glory†

19 Whose offspring can be honorable? Human offspring.
Those who fear the LORD are honorable offspring.
Whose offspring can be disgraceful? Human offspring.
Those who transgress the commandment are disgraceful offspring.
20 Among relatives their leader is honored;
but whoever fears God is honored among God's people.‡
22 Resident alien, stranger, foreigner, pauper—
their glory is the fear of the LORD.
23 It is not right to despise anyone wise but poor,
nor proper to honor the lawless.*
24 The prince, the ruler, the judge are in honor;
but none is greater than the one who fears God.
25 When the free serve a wise slave,
the wise will not complain.*
26 Do not flaunt your wisdom in managing your affairs,
or boast in your time of need.
27 Better the worker who has goods in plenty
than the boaster who has no food.*

28 My son, with humility have self-esteem;
and give yourself the esteem you deserve.
29 Who will acquit those who condemn themselves?
Who will honor those who disgrace themselves?

30 The poor are honored for their wisdom;
the rich are honored for their wealth.
31 Honored in poverty, how much more so in wealth!
Disgraced in wealth, in poverty how much the more!

11 [1]The wisdom of the poor lifts their head high
and sets them among princes.
2 Do not praise anyone for good looks;
or despise anyone because of appearance.

3 The bee is least among winged creatures,
but it reaps the choicest of harvests.
4 Do not mock the one who wears only a loin-cloth,
or scoff at a person's bitter day.

† **10:9–10** The general implication is that a slight illness today may be followed by death tomorrow. The uncertainty of life leaves no room for pride.

10:19–11:6 Genuine honor comes not from one's place in society but from fear of the Lord and a true estimate of oneself. The Lord exalts the lowly and oppressed; transgressors of the commandment merit dishonor and disgrace.

‡**10:20** Other ancient texts read as v. 21:
The beginning of acceptance is the fear of the Lord;
the beginning of rejection, effrontery and pride.

* **10:3** Prv 29:4–8.
10:6 Lv 19:18.
10:11 Sir 7:17; Jb 17:14; Is 66:24.
10:13 Prv 11:2; 16:18; 18:12.
10:23 Jas 2:1–4.
10:25 Prv 17:2.
10:27 Prv 12:9.

For strange are the deeds of the LORD,
hidden from mortals his work.†
5 Many are the oppressed who rise to the
throne;
some that none would consider wear a
crown.†
6 Many are the exalted who fall into utter
disgrace,
many the honored who are given into the
power of the few.

Moderation and Patience†

7 Before investigating, do not find fault;
examine first, then criticize.
8 Before listening, do not say a word,
interrupt no one in the midst of speaking.*
9 Do not dispute about what is not your
concern;
in the quarrels of the arrogant do not take
part.

10 My son, why increase your anxiety,
since whoever is greedy for wealth will not
be blameless?
Even if you chase after it, you will never
overtake it;
and by fleeing you will not escape.
11 One may work and struggle and drive,
and fall short all the same.*
12 Others go their way broken-down drifters,
with little strength and great misery—
Yet the eye of the LORD looks favorably upon
them,
shaking them free of the stinking mire.
13 He lifts up their heads and exalts them
to the amazement of the many.

14† Good and evil, life and death,*
poverty and riches—all are from the LORD.‡
17 The Lord's gift remains with the devout;
his favor brings lasting success.
18 Some become rich through a miser's life,
and this is their allotted reward:
19 When they say: "I have found rest,*
now I will feast on my goods,"
They do not know how long it will be
till they die and leave them to others.†
20 My child, stand by your agreement and attend
to it,
grow old while doing your work.
21 Do not marvel at the works of a sinner,
but trust in the LORD and wait for his light;
For it is easy in the eyes of the LORD
suddenly, in an instant, to make the poor
rich.
22 God's blessing is the lot of the righteous,
and in due time their hope bears fruit.
23 Do not say: "What do I need?
What further benefits can be mine?"
24 Do not say: "I am self-sufficient.
What harm can come to me now?"
25 The day of prosperity makes one forget
adversity;
the day of adversity makes one forget
prosperity.*

26 For it is easy for the Lord on the day of death†
to repay mortals according to their conduct.
27 A time of affliction brings forgetfulness of
past delights;
at the end of life one's deeds are revealed.
28 Call none happy before death,
for how they end, they are known.

Care in Choosing Friends

29 Not everyone should be brought into your
house,
for many are the snares of the crafty.
30 Like a decoy partridge in a cage, so is the
heart of the proud,
and like a spy they will pick out the weak
spots.
31 For they lie in wait to turn good into evil,
and to praiseworthy deeds they attach
blame.
32 One spark kindles many coals;
a sinner lies in wait for blood.
33 Beware of scoundrels, for they breed only evil,
and they may give you a lasting stain.
34 Admit strangers into your home, and they will
stir up trouble
and make you a stranger to your own
family.

---

† **11:4** The implication is similar to Eccl 7:13; 8:17: the mysterious work of God.

11:5 Cf. 1 Sm 2:8; Ps 75:8; 105:17–22; Lk 1:52.

11:7–28 Discretion should regulate conduct toward others (vv. 7–9); as regards personal interests, one should avoid solicitude for the passing external benefits of life and property (vv. 10–14, 18–19, 21, 23–25) and cultivate the lasting inward gifts of wisdom, virtue (vv. 20, 22), and patience (vv. 25–28).

11:14 In mysterious ways God ultimately governs the lives of men and women.

‡**11:14** Other ancient texts read as vv. 15–16:

15 Wisdom and understanding and knowledge of the Law,
love and virtuous paths, are from the Lord.
16 Error and darkness were formed with sinners from their birth,
and evil grows old with those who exult in evil.

11:19 Cf. the parable of the rich man, Lk 12:16–21.

11:26–28 Ben Sira thought that divine retribution took place only in the present life, and even at the end of life; cf. 9:12; 14:16–17.

---

* **11:8** Prv 18:13. **11:11** Ps 127:2; Eccl 4:8. **11:14** Jb 1:21; 2:10. **11:19** Eccl 4:8; 6:2; Lk 12:19. **11:25** Sir 18:24–25.

12 [1]If you do good, know for whom you are doing it,†
and your kindness will have its effect.
2 Do good to the righteous and reward will be yours,
if not from them, from the LORD.*
3 No good comes to those who give comfort to the wicked,
nor is it an act of mercy that they do.
4 Give to the good but refuse the sinner;
5 refresh the downtrodden but give nothing to the proud.
No arms for combat should you give them,
lest they use these against you;
Twofold evil you will obtain for every good deed you do for them.
6 For God also hates sinners,
and takes vengeance on evildoers.†
8 In prosperity we cannot know our friends;†
in adversity an enemy will not remain concealed.*
9 When one is successful even an enemy is friendly;
but in adversity even a friend disappears.*
10 Never trust your enemies,
for their wickedness is like corrosion in bronze.
11 Even though they act deferentially and peaceably toward you,
take care to be on your guard against them.*
Treat them as those who reveal secrets,†
and be certain that in the end there will still be envy.
12 Do not let them stand near you,
lest they push you aside and take your place.
Do not let them sit at your right hand,
or they will demand your seat,
And in the end you will appreciate my advice,
when you groan with regret, as I warned.

13 Who pities a snake charmer when he is bitten,†
or anyone who goes near a wild beast?
14 So it is with the companion of the proud,
who is involved in their sins:
15 While you stand firm, they make no move;
but if you slip, they cannot hold back.
16 With their lips enemies speak sweetly,
but in their heart they scheme to plunge you into the abyss.
Though enemies have tears in their eyes,
given the chance, they will never have enough of your blood.*
17 If evil comes upon you, you will find them at hand;
pretending to help, they will trip you up,
18 Then they will shake their heads and clap their hands
and hiss repeatedly, and show their true faces.

Caution Regarding Associates†

13 [1] Touch pitch and you blacken your hand;
associate with scoundrels and you learn their ways.
2 Do not lift a weight too heavy for you,
or associate with anyone wealthier than you.
How can the clay pot go with the metal cauldron?
When they knock together, the pot will be smashed:
3 The rich do wrong and boast of it,
while the poor are wronged and beg forgiveness.
4 As long as the rich can use you they will enslave you,
but when you are down and out they will abandon you.
5 As long as you have anything they will live with you,
but they will drain you dry without remorse.
6 When they need you they will deceive you
and smile at you and raise your hopes;
they will speak kindly to you and say,
"What do you need?"
7 They will embarrass you at their dinner parties,
and finally laugh at you.
Afterwards, when they see you, they will pass you by,
and shake their heads at you.
8 Be on guard: do not act too boldly;
do not be like those who lack sense.

9 When the influential draw near, keep your distance;
then they will urge you all the more.

12:1 The import of this verse is brought out in vv. 4–5.
12:6 Verse 7 is a variant of verse 4 and is omitted.
12:8–18 Adversity distinguishes friends from enemies; to trust the latter or permit them intimacy is to invite disaster. Cf. note on 6:5–17.
12:11 Ben Sira has harsh words for those who reveal secrets; see also 8:18; 27:16–21; 42:1; Prv 11:13; 20:19.
12:13 For v. 13a, see especially Eccl 10:11.

13:1–14:2 By means of various images, most of them unfavorable to the rich, Ben Sira indicates the practical impossibility of genuine and sincere companionship between the poor and the rich. He lays down a principle of associating with equals (13:6–19).

12:2 Dt 14:29.
12:8 Prv 17:17.
12:9 Prv 19:4–7.
12:11 Prv 26:24–26.
12:16 Jer 9:7.

10 Do not draw too close, lest you be rebuffed,
but do not keep too far away lest you be
regarded as an enemy.
11 Do not venture to be free with them,
do not trust their many words;
For by prolonged talk they will test you,
and though smiling they will probe you.
12 Mercilessly they will make you a
laughingstock,
and will not refrain from injury or chains.
13 Be on your guard and take care
never to accompany lawless people.‡

15 Every living thing loves its own kind,
and we all love someone like ourselves.
16 Every living being keeps close to its own kind;
and people associate with their own kind.
17 Is a wolf ever allied with a lamb?
So the sinner with the righteous.*
18 Can there be peace between the hyena and
the dog?
Or peace between the rich and the poor?†
19 Wild donkeys of the desert are lion's prey;
likewise the poor are feeding grounds for
the rich.
20 Humility is an abomination to the proud;
and the poor are an abomination to the
rich.
21 When the rich stumble they are supported by
friends;
when the poor trip they are pushed down
by friends.
22 When the rich speak they have many
supporters;
though what they say is repugnant, it wins
approval.
When the poor speak people say, "Come,
come, speak up!"
though they are talking sense, they get no
hearing.
23 When the rich speak all are silent,
their wisdom people extol to the clouds.
When the poor speak people say: "Who is
that?"
If they stumble, people knock them down.*
24 Wealth is good where there is no sin;†
but poverty is evil by the standards of the
proud.
25 The heart changes one's face,
either for good or for evil.*
26 The sign of a good heart is a radiant face;
withdrawn and perplexed is the toiling
schemer.

14 1† Happy those whose mouth causes them
no grief,
those who are not stung by remorse for sin.*
2 Happy are those whose conscience does not
reproach them,
those who have not lost hope.

The Use of Wealth

3 Wealth is not appropriate for the mean-spirited;†
to misers, what use is gold?
4 What they deny themselves they collect for
someone else,
and strangers will live sumptuously on
their possessions.*
5 To whom will they be generous that are stingy
with themselves
and do not enjoy what is their own?
6 None are worse than those who are stingy
with themselves;
they punish their own avarice.
7 If ever they do good, it is by mistake;
in the end they reveal their meanness.
8 Misers are evil people,
they turn away and disregard others.
9 The greedy see their share as not enough;
greedy injustice dries up the soul.
10 The eye of the miserly is rapacious for food,
but there is none of it on their own table.

11† My son, if you have the means, treat yourself
well,
and enjoy life as best you can.*
12 Remember that death does not delay,
and you have not been told the grave's
appointed time.
13 Before you die, be good to your friends;

‡**13:13** Other ancient texts read as v. 14:
If you hear these things in your sleep, wake up!
With your whole life, love the Lord
and call on him for your salvation.

13:18 The hostility between the dogs which guard the flocks (Jb 30:1) and the rapacious hyenas (Jer 12:9) is proverbial in Palestine.

13:24 Ben Sira allows that the rich can be virtuous—but with difficulty; cf. 31:1–11.

14:1–2 A clear conscience, the result of honoring personal commitments and responsibilities, brings contentment and peace.

14:3–10 Ben Sira offers a case study about the miserable life of the "small-hearted" (Heb. *leb qaṭan*) to verify vv. 1–2. They are evil because they do not use their wealth properly to benefit themselves or others. While they are never satisfied that they have enough, they ignore their own needs and hospitality itself, feeding on the generosity of others, in order to protect their own resources. Ironically, after their death, strangers, with no obligation to keep their memory alive, enjoy their wealth.

14:11–19 Three realities govern Ben Sira's attitude toward a proper use of wealth: the inevitability and uncertainty of death, the ephemeral nature of human accomplishments, the lack of reward or punishment after death. He advises generous enjoyment of God's gift of wealth before death.

13:17 2 Cor 6:14–17.
13:21–23 Prv 14:20; 19:4, 7.
13:25 Prv 15:13.
14:1 Sir 5:13–14; 19:16; 25:8; Jas 1:26; 3:2.
14:4 Eccl 2:18–19; 6:2.
14:11–12 Eccl 5:17–19.

give them a share in what you possess.*
14 Do not deprive yourself of good things now
or let a choice portion escape you.
15 Will you not leave your riches to others,
and your earnings to be divided by lot?
16 Give and take, treat yourself well,
for in Sheol there are no joys to seek.
17 All flesh grows old like a garment;
the age-old law is: everyone must die.*
18 As with the leaves growing on a luxuriant tree—
one falls off and another sprouts—
So with the generations of flesh and blood:
one dies and another flourishes.*
19 All human deeds surely perish;
the works they do follow after them.

The Search for Wisdom and Her Blessings†

20 Happy those who meditate on Wisdom,
and fix their gaze on knowledge;*
21 Who ponder her ways in their heart,
and understand her paths;
22 Who pursue her like a scout,
and watch at her entry way;
23 Who peep through her windows,
and listen at her doors;
24 Who encamp near her house
and fasten their tent pegs next to her walls;
25 Who pitch their tent beside her,
and dwell in a good place;†
26† Who build their nest in her leaves,
and lodge in her branches;
27 Who take refuge from the heat in her shade
and dwell in her home.

15 [1]Whoever fears the LORD will do this;
whoever is practiced in the Law will come
to Wisdom.
2 She will meet him like a mother;
like a young bride she will receive him,
3† She will feed him with the bread of learning,
and give him the water of understanding to
drink.*
4 He will lean upon her and not fall;
he will trust in her and not be put to shame.
5 She will exalt him above his neighbors,
and in the assembly she will make him
eloquent.

Pray It!

Taking Responsibility

"It isn't my fault; she made me do it." "He started it!" "They pressured me into doing it!" We have lots of ways of blaming others when bad things happen. Ben Sira 15:11 tells of one way people in Ben Sira's time tried to put the blame on someone else: "It was God's doing." Evidently, some people blamed God when they fell into sin. Ben Sira tells us it isn't God's will when bad things happen as a result of human choice (see verses 14–17)—which is why we need to stop the blame game and take responsibility for our own actions.

In your prayer, take some time to reflect or journal on the following questions:

- Do you tend to blame others when bad things happen?
- Have there been hurtful situations in which you would not accept your part of the responsibility? If so, describe one and explain how you could have owned up to your responsibility.

▶ **Sir 15:11–20**

6 Joy and gladness he will find,
and an everlasting name he will inherit.*
7 The worthless will not attain her,
and the haughty will not behold her.
8 She is far from the impious;
liars never think of her.
9† Praise is unseemly on the lips of sinners,
for it has not been allotted to them by God.
10 But praise is uttered by the mouth of the wise,
and its rightful owner teaches it.

Free Will†

11 Do not say: "It was God's doing that I fell
away,"

†

14:20–15:10 This poem charts the growing intimacy between those seeking Wisdom and Wisdom herself. They move from static reflection to playful pursuit, from camping outside the walls of her house to nesting inside her leafy shade. Ben Sira portrays Wisdom as both mother and bride, a feminine figure who is the fullness of womanhood according to his androcentric society.

14:25 *In a good place*: i.e., where Wisdom dwells.

14:26–27 The shift in imagery creates a more intimate relationship. Those seeking Wisdom dwell within her as a bird nests within a leafy tree.

15:3–6 In this role reversal Woman Wisdom teaches, nourishes, supports, and protects the vulnerable man. For similar imagery cf. Prv 8:4–21, 34–35; 9:1–5; 31:10–31.

15:9–10 There is an intimate association between wisdom and praise of the Lord.

15:11–20 Here Ben Sira links freedom of the will with human responsibility. God, who sees everything, is neither the cause nor the

*

14:13 Prv 3:27–28; Tb 4:7.
14:17 Ps 103:14–16; Jb 14:1–2; Is 40:6; Jas 1:10; 1 Pt 1:24.
14:18 Eccl 1:4.
14:20 Ps 1:2.
15:3 Jn 4:10; 6:31–33.
15:6 Sir 6:28–33.

for what he hates he does not do.
12 Do not say: "He himself has led me astray,"
for he has no need of the wicked.*
13 Abominable wickedness the LORD hates
and he does not let it happen to those who
fear him.

14 God in the beginning created human beings
and made them subject to their own free
choice.*
15 If you choose, you can keep the commandments;
loyalty is doing the will of God.
16 Set before you are fire and water;
to whatever you choose, stretch out your
hand.
17 Before everyone are life and death,
whichever they choose will be given them.*

18 Immense is the wisdom of the LORD;
mighty in power, he sees all things.
19 The eyes of God behold his works,
and he understands every human deed.*
20 He never commands anyone to sin,
nor shows leniency toward deceivers.†

God's Punishment of Sinners†

16 1 Do not yearn for worthless children,
or rejoice in wicked offspring.
2 Even if they be many, do not rejoice in them
if they do not have fear of the LORD.
3 Do not count on long life for them,*
or have any hope for their future.
For one can be better than a thousand;
rather die childless than have impious
children!
4 Through one wise person a city can be peopled;
but through a clan of rebels it becomes
desolate.

5 Many such things my eye has seen,
and even more than these my ear has heard.
6 Against a sinful band fire is kindled,*
upon a godless people wrath blazes.†
7 He did not forgive the princes of old†
who rebelled long ago in their might.*
8 He did not spare the neighbors of Lot,†*
abominable in their pride.
9 He did not spare the doomed people,†
dispossessed because of their sin;
10 Nor the six hundred thousand foot soldiers,†*
sent to their graves for the arrogance of
their hearts.
11 Had there been but one stiff-necked† person,
it would be a wonder had he gone
unpunished.
For mercy and anger alike are with him;
he remits and forgives, but also pours out
wrath.
12 Great as his mercy is his punishment;
he judges people, each according to their
deeds.
13 Criminals do not escape with their plunder;
the hope of the righteous, God never leaves
unfulfilled.
14 Whoever does good has a reward;
each receives according to their deeds.‡
17 Do not say: "I am hidden from God;
and on high who remembers me?
Among so many people I am unknown;
what am I in the world of spirits?
18 Look, the heavens and the highest heavens,
the abyss and the earth tremble at his
visitation.
19 The roots of the mountains and the earth's
foundations—
at his mere glance they quiver and quake.
20 Of me, therefore, he will take no notice;
with my ways who will be concerned?
21 If I sin, no eye will see me;
if all in secret I act deceitfully, who is to
know?*
22 Who tells him about just deeds?

---

† occasion of sin. We have the power to choose our behavior and we are responsible for both the good and the evil we do (vv. 15–17).

15:20 *Deceivers*: those who hold the Lord responsible for their sins.

16:1–23 One child who does God's will is a greater blessing than many sinful offspring (vv. 1–4), for history and experience show that God punishes sin (vv. 5–10). God judges everyone according to their deeds (vv. 11–14); no one can hide from God or escape retribution at his hand (vv. 17–23).

16:6 For Korah and his band (v. 6a), see 45:18–19; Nm 16:1–35; Ps 106:18; for the disgruntled Israelites (v. 6b), Ps 78:21–22.

16:7 *The princes of old*: e.g., the mighty destroyed in the flood (Gn 6:1–4; Wis 14:6; Bar 3:26–28), as well as the king of Babylon (Is 14:4–21) and Nebuchadnezzar (Dn 4:7–30).

16:8 *Neighbors of Lot*: the people of Sodom and Gomorrah, condemned elsewhere for their sexual violence (Gn 19:24–25) and failure at hospitality (Ez 16:49–50).

16:9 *Doomed people*: the Canaanite tribes whose aberrant religious practices, at least in Israelite opinion, caused their downfall: Ex 23:23–24, 27–33; 33:2; 34:11–16; Dt 7:1–2; Wis 12:3–7.

16:10 *Six hundred thousand foot soldiers*: the number given for those rescued by Moses, who murmured against the Lord in the wilderness and died there: 46:1, 7–8; Nm 11:20; 14:1–12, 22–24, 29, 36–38; 26:65; Dt 1:35–38.

16:11 *Stiff-necked*: sinful Israelites; cf. Ex 32:9; 33:3, 5. Not even one Israelite would have gone unpunished for insolence or pride.

‡**16:14** Other ancient texts read as vv. 15–16:
15 The LORD hardened the heart of Pharaoh so that he did not
recognize him
whose acts were manifest under the heavens;

---

* **15:12** Jas 1:13.
15:14 Gn 1:27.
15:17 Dt 30:15–20.
15:19 Ps 33:18; 34:16; Heb 4:13.
16:3–4 Wis 4:1–2.
16:6 Sir 21:9.
16:7 Gn 6:4; Wis 14:6; Bar 3:26–28.
16:8 Gn 19:24–25.
16:10 Nm 14:29.
16:21 Sir 23:18–20.

What can I expect for doing my duty?"
23 Such the thoughts of the senseless;
only the foolish entertain them.

Divine Wisdom Seen in Creation†

24 Listen to me, my son, and take my advice,
and apply your mind to my words,
25 While I pour out my spirit by measure
and impart knowledge with care.
26 When at the first God created his works
and, as he made them, assigned their tasks,*
27 He arranged for all time what they were to do,
their domains from generation to generation.
They were not to go hungry or grow weary,
or ever cease from their tasks.
28 Never does a single one crowd its neighbor,
or do any ever disobey his word.
29 Then the Lord looked upon the earth,
and filled it with his blessings.*
30 Its surface he covered with every kind of living
creature
which must return into it again.

Creation of Human Beings

17 1 The Lord created human beings from the
earth,
and makes them return to earth again.*
2 A limited number of days he gave them,*
but granted them authority over everything
on earth.
3 He endowed them with strength like his own,
and made them in his image.
4 He put fear of them in all flesh,
and gave them dominion over beasts and
birds.‡
6 Discernment, tongues, and eyes,
ears, and a mind for thinking he gave them.
7 With knowledge and understanding he filled
them;
good and evil he showed them.
8 He put fear of him into their hearts
to show them the grandeur of his works,
9 That they might describe the wonders of his
deeds
10 and praise his holy name.
11 He set before them knowledge,
and allotted to them the law of life.
12 An everlasting covenant he made with them,
and his commandments† he revealed to
them.
13 His majestic glory their eyes beheld,
his glorious voice their ears heard.
14 He said to them, "Avoid all evil";
to each of them he gave precepts about
their neighbor.
15 Their ways are ever known to him,
they cannot be hidden from his eyes.‡
17 Over every nation he appointed a ruler,†
but Israel is the Lord's own portion.‡ *
19 All their works are clear as the sun to him,
and his eyes are ever upon their ways.
20 Their iniquities cannot be hidden from him;
all their sins are before the Lord.‡
22 Human goodness is like a signet ring with God,
and virtue he keeps like the apple of his eye.
23 Later he will rise up and repay them,
requiting each one as they deserve.*

Appeal for a Return to God†

24 But to the penitent he provides a way back
and encourages those who are losing hope!
25 Turn back to the Lord and give up your sins,
pray before him and make your offenses few.
26 Turn again to the Most High and away from
iniquity,
and hate intensely what he loathes.
27† Who in Sheol can glorify the Most High*
in place of the living who offer their praise?

---

† [16] His mercy was seen by all his creatures,
and his light and his darkness he apportioned to humankind.

16:24–17:23 In harmony with Gn 1–2, the author describes God's wisdom in creating the universe and everything in it (vv. 24–30), endowing human beings with a moral nature, with wisdom, knowledge, and freedom of will (cf. 15:14) according to his own image (17:1–3, 7). Now they can govern the earth (vv. 3–4), praise God's name (vv. 9–10), obey his law (vv. 11–14), and render to him an account of their deeds (v. 23). Cf. Ps 19; 104.

‡17:4 Other ancient texts read as v. 5:
They received the use of the Lord's five faculties;
of mind, the sixth, he granted them a share,
as also of speech, the seventh, the interpreter of his actions.

17:12 *An everlasting covenant . . . his commandments*: God made several covenants, e.g., Gn 9:8–17; 15:17–21; 17:1–22, entered into with humankind, especially on Mount Sinai, where the people saw God's glory and heard his voice (v. 13; cf. Ex 19:16–24:18).

‡17:15 Other ancient texts read as v. 16:
Their ways are directed toward evils from their youth,
and they are unable to make their hearts flesh rather than stone.

17:17 *Ruler*: this may refer to civil officials or to heavenly beings placed over nations as guardians; see note on Dt 32:8, and the cross-references.

‡17:17 Other ancient texts read as v. 18:
Israel, as his firstborn, he cares for with chastisement;
the light of his love he shares with him without neglect.

‡17:20 Other ancient texts read as v. 21:
But the Lord, being good and knowing how they are formed,
neither neglected them nor ceased to spare them.

17:24–32 Ben Sira opens this poem with a prophetic summons to repent, urging sinners to give up their sins and to pray for forgiveness (vv. 24–26, 29). Ben Sira reflects the belief of his day that there was no life after death (vv. 27–28, 30; see note on 11:26–28). Cf. Ez 18:23, 30–32; 33:11–16. See note on Ps 6:6.

17:27–28 True life consists in praise of God; this is not possible in Sheol.

---

* **16:26** Gn 1:3–30.
16:29 Gn 1:11–31.
17:1 Gn 2:7; 3:19.
17:2–4 Gn 1:26–28; Ps 8:4–9.
17:17 Ex 19:5; Dt 4:19–20; 32:8–9; Dn 10:13–21; 12:1.
17:23 Ps 7:17; Jl 4:4, 7; Jer 23:19; Ez 22:31.
17:27–28 Ps 6:6; 88:4–7; 115:17; Is 38:18.

28 The dead can no more give praise than those
who have never lived;
they who are alive and well glorify the
Lord.
29 How great is the mercy of the Lord,
and his forgiveness for those who return to
him!
30 For not everything is within human reach,
since human beings are not immortal.
31 Is anything brighter than the sun? Yet it can
be eclipsed.
How worthless† then the thoughts of flesh
and blood!
32 God holds accountable the hosts of highest
heaven,
while all mortals are dust and ashes.

The Divine Power and Mercy†

18 1 He who lives forever created the whole
universe;
2 the Lord alone is just.‡
4 To whom has he given power to describe his
works,
and who can search out his mighty deeds?
5 Who can measure his majestic power,
or fully recount his mercies?
6 No one can lessen, increase,
or fathom the wonders of the Lord.
7 When mortals finish, they are only beginning,
and when they stop they are still bewildered.
8 What are mortals? What are they worth?
What is good in them, and what is evil?
9 The number of their days seems great
if it reaches a hundred years.*
10 Like a drop of water from the sea and a grain
of sand,
so are these few years among the days of
eternity.
11 That is why the Lord is patient with them
and pours out his mercy on them.
12 He sees and understands that their death is
wretched,
and so he forgives them all the more.
13 Their compassion is for their neighbor,
but the Lord's compassion reaches all flesh,
Reproving, admonishing, teaching,
and turning them back, as a shepherd his
flock.*
14 He has compassion on those who accept his
discipline,
who are eager for his precepts.

The Need for Prudence

15 My child, add no reproach to your charity,†
or spoil any gift by harsh words.
16 Does not the dew give relief from the
scorching heat?
So a word can be better than a gift.
17 Indeed does not a word count more than a
good gift?
But both are offered by a kind person.
18 The fool is ungracious and abusive,
and a grudging gift makes the eyes
smart.*

19 Before you speak, learn;
before you get sick, prepare the cure.
20 Before you are judged, examine yourself,
and at the time of scrutiny you will have
forgiveness.
21 Before you fall ill, humble yourself;
and when you have sinned, show
repentance.†
Do not delay forsaking your sins;
do not neglect to do so until you are in
distress.

22 Let nothing prevent the prompt payment of
your vows;
do not wait until death to fulfill them.*
23 Before making a vow prepare yourself;
do not be like one who puts the Lord to
the test.
24 Think of wrath on the day of death,
the time of vengeance when he will hide
his face.*
25 Think of the time of hunger in the time of
plenty,
poverty and need in the day of wealth.*
26 Between morning and evening there is a
change of time;
before the Lord all things are fleeting.

---

† **17:31** *Worthless*: cf. Gn 6:5. Though moral fault is not excluded, the thought here is the inability to understand the designs of God. Cf. Wis 9:14–18.

18:1–14 Not only are God's justice and power beyond human understanding (vv. 1–7), his mercy also is boundless and surpasses all human compassion (vv. 8–14); he pities human frailty and mortality.

‡**18:2** Other ancient texts read as v. 3:
He controls the world within the span of his hand,
and everything obeys his will;
For he in his might is the King of all,
separating what is holy among them from what is profane.

18:15–27 The practice of charity, especially almsgiving, is an art which avoids every offense to another (vv. 15–18). Prudence directs the changing circumstances of daily life in view of the time of scrutiny (i.e., the day of reckoning, or death, v. 24).

18:21 Sickness was often viewed as a punishment for sin; hence, the need for repentance. Cf. 38:9–10; Jb 15:20–24.

---

* **18:9** Ps 90:10.
18:13 Ps 23:1–4; Is 40:11; 49:9–10; Jn 10:11–16; Heb 13:20–21; Rev 7:17.
18:18 Sir 20:14–15.
18:22 Nm 30:3; Dt 23:22; Ps 50:14; Prv 20:25; Eccl 5:4.
18:24 Sir 7:16.
18:25 Sir 11:25–27.

27 The wise are discreet in all things;
where sin is rife they keep themselves from wrongdoing.
28 Every wise person teaches wisdom,†
and those who know her declare her praise;
29 Those skilled in words become wise themselves,
and pour forth apt proverbs.

Self-Control†

30 Do not let your passions be your guide,*
but keep your desires in check.
31 If you allow yourself to satisfy your passions,
they will make you the laughingstock of your enemies.
32 Take no pleasure in too much luxury
which brings on poverty redoubled.
33 Do not become a glutton and a drunkard
with nothing in your purse.

19 [1]Whoever does this grows no richer;
those who waste the little they have will be stripped bare.
2 Wine and women make the heart lustful,
and the companion of prostitutes becomes reckless.*
3 Rottenness and worms will possess him,
and the reckless will be snatched away.*
4 Whoever trusts others too quickly has a shallow mind,
and those who sin wrong themselves.

The Proper Use of Speech†

5 Whoever gloats over evil will be destroyed,
6 and whoever repeats gossip has no sense.
7 Never repeat gossip,
and no one will reproach you.*
8 Tell nothing to friend or foe;
and unless it be a sin for you, do not reveal a thing.*
9 For someone may have heard you and watched you,
and in time come to hate you.
10 Let anything you hear die with you;
never fear, it will not make you burst!
11 Having heard something, the fool goes into labor,
like a woman giving birth to a child.
12 Like an arrow stuck in a fool's thigh,
so is gossip in the belly of a fool.
13 Admonish your friend—he may not have done it;
and if he did, that he may not do it again.*
14 Admonish your neighbor—he may not have said it;
and if he did, that he may not say it again.
15 Admonish your friend—often it may be slander;
do not believe every story.
16 Then, too, a person can slip and not mean it;
who has not sinned with his tongue?*
17 Admonish your neighbor before you break with him;

Live It!

Don't Get Burned

It is easy to give in to temptation. Every day, we face decisions that can hurt our relationship with God. Ben Sira soundly advises us not to give in to our base desires (Sir 18:30). These are attitudes and practices that include laziness, drunkenness, and lust, which might bring some immediate pleasure but also lead to long-term problems. Self-control is the strength to resist the lusts that lead to lifelong problems.

An old saying—If you play with matches, you might get burned—is often used by people recovering from addictions. It reminds them that risky behaviors often end up hurting them. It helps them stay focused on their long-term goal of leading a healthy and happy life. If they follow Ben Sira's advice—practice self-control—they won't end up getting burned!

- What base desires tempt you the most?
- What do you need to do to avoid getting burned by them?

▶ **Sir 18:30—19:3**

† **18:28–29** A general statement on the teaching of wisdom, serving either as a conclusion to the preceding section or as an introduction to the following one.

18:30–19:4 Inordinate gratification of the senses makes people unreasonable, slaves of passion, the laughingstock of their enemies, and it leads to an untimely death.

19:5–17 An excellent commentary on bearing false witness (Ex 20:16; Dt 5:20). Ben Sira speaks harshly about calumny, rash judgment, and detraction (vv. 5–7), and urges discreet silence (vv. 8–12). Justice requires that an accused neighbor be given a hearing, and charity urges fraternal correction; both together fulfill the law of the Most High (vv. 13–17); cf. Mt 7:1–2; 18:15–16.

* **18:30** Rom 6:12; 13:14; 2 Tm 2:22; Jas 1:14–15.
19:2 Prv 20:1; 23:20–28.
19:3 Gal 6:8.
19:7 Prv 25:10.
19:8 Sir 8:18–19.
19:13 Lv 19:17; Mt 18:15; Lk 17:3.
19:16 Sir 14:1; Jas 3:2.

Pray It!

Examine Your Conscience

An examination of conscience is a moral inventory of one's life. When we examine our conscience, we can recognize those we have hurt, make amends where possible, and turn our lives around before a pattern of sin becomes a major obstacle in our relationships with God and with others. We can also recognize the positive moral choices we have made. Chapters 19–22 of Ben Sira list some of the sins from Ben Sira's time. Use them as a guide for making your own examination of conscience, as follows:

- Have you gossiped (see 19:5–12)?
- Have you offended others with your language (see 20:18–19)?
- Have you lied (see 20:24–26)?
- Have you stolen from others (see 21:8)?
- Have you been lazy in your use of time (see 22:1–2)?
- Have you disobeyed your parents (see 22:3–5)?

When you have finished this examination, read 22:27—23:6 as your own prayer for God's help against sinning.

▶ Sir 19:5—23:6

and give due place to the Law of the Most
High.‡ *

How to Recognize True Wisdom†

20 All wisdom is fear of the LORD;
and in all wisdom, the observance of the
Law.‡ *
22 The knowledge of wickedness is not wisdom,
nor is there prudence in the counsel of
sinners.
23 There is a shrewdness that is detestable,
while the fool may be free from sin.
24 Better are the God-fearing who have little
understanding
than those of great intelligence who violate
the Law.
25 There is a shrewdness keen but dishonest,
and there are those who are duplicitous to
win a judgment.
26 There is the villain bowed in grief,
but full of deceit within.
27 He hides his face and pretends not to hear,
but when not observed, he will take
advantage of you:
28 Even if his lack of strength keeps him from
sinning,
when he finds the right time he will do
harm.
29 People are known by their appearance;
the sensible are recognized as such when
first met.
30 One's attire, hearty laughter, and gait
proclaim him for what he is.

Conduct of the Wise and the Foolish

20 [1] There is an admonition that is
untimely,†
but the silent person is the wise one.
2 It is much better to admonish than to lose
one's temper;
3 one who admits a fault will be kept from
disgrace.
4 Like a eunuch lusting to violate a young
woman
is the one who does right under
compulsion.†
5 One is silent and is thought wise;
another, for being talkative, is disliked.
6 One is silent, having nothing to say;
another is silent, biding his time.*
7 The wise remain silent till the right time
comes,
but a boasting fool misses the proper time.
8 Whoever talks too much is detested;
whoever pretends to authority is hated.

‡19:17 Other ancient texts read as vv. 18–19:
[18] Fear of the Lord is the beginning of acceptance;
and wisdom from him obtains love.
[19] Knowledge of the Lord's commandments is life-giving
instruction;
those who do what pleases him will harvest the fruit of the
tree of immortality.

19:20–30 True wisdom is contrasted with a dishonest shrewdness.

‡19:20 Other ancient texts read as v. 21:
The slave who says to his master, "What pleases you I will
not do"—
even if he does it later, provokes the one who feeds him.

20:1–8 The wise know the proper times for speech and silence, that is, the occasions when the most benefit can be gained from them. On the ambiguity of silences, see Prv 17:27–28.

20:4 Force can prevent an external act of sin or compel a good deed, but it does not eliminate the internal sin or desire of wrongdoing.

19:17 Lv 19:17.
19:20 Sir 1:1, 12, 14; Jb 28:28; Ps 111:10; Prv 1:7; 9:10.
20:5–6 Prv 17:27–28.

9 There is the misfortune that brings success;†
and there is the gain that turns into loss.
10 There is the gift that profits you nothing,
and there is the gift that must be paid back double.
11 There is the loss for the sake of glory,
and there is the one who rises above humble circumstances.
12 There is one who buys much for little,
but pays for it seven times over.
13 The wise make themselves beloved by a few words,
but the courtesies of fools are wasted.
14 A gift from a fool will do you no good,
for in his eyes this one gift is equal to many.
15 He gives little, criticizes often,
and opens his mouth like a town crier.
He lends today and asks for it tomorrow;
such a person is hateful.
16 A fool says, "I have no friends
nor thanks for my generosity."
Those who eat his bread have a mocking tongue.
17 How many will ridicule him, and how often!

18 A slip on the floor is better than a slip of the tongue;†
in like manner the downfall of the wicked comes quickly.
19 A coarse person, an untimely story;
the ignorant are always ready to offer it.
20 A proverb spoken by a fool is unwelcome,
for he does not tell it at the proper time.

21 There is a person whose poverty prevents him from sinning,
but when he takes his rest he has no regrets.
22 There is a person who is destroyed through shame,
and ruined by foolish posturing.
23 There is one who promises a friend out of shame,
and so makes an enemy needlessly.

24 A lie is a foul blot in a person,
yet it is always on the lips of the ignorant.
25 A thief is better than an inveterate liar,
yet both will suffer ruin.
26 A liar's way leads to dishonor,
and his shame remains ever with him.

27 The wise gain promotion with few words,†
the prudent please the great.
28 Those who work the land have abundant crops,
and those who please the great are pardoned their faults.
29 Favors and gifts blind the eyes;
like a muzzle over the mouth they silence reproofs.*
30 Hidden wisdom and unseen treasure—
what value has either?
31 Better are those who hide their folly
than those who hide their wisdom.‡

Dangers from Sin†

21 1 My child, if you have sinned, do so no more,
and for your past sins pray to be forgiven.
2 Flee from sin as from a serpent
that will bite you if you go near it;
Its teeth, lion's teeth,
destroying human lives.
3 All lawlessness is like a two-edged sword;
when it cuts, there is no healing.*
4 Panic and pride wipe out wealth;
so too the house of the proud is uprooted.
5 Prayer from the lips of the poor is heard at once,
and justice is quickly granted them.
6 Whoever hates correction walks the sinner's path,*
but whoever fears the Lord repents in his heart.
7 Glib speakers are widely known,
but when they slip the sensible perceive it.
8 Those who build their houses with someone else's money
are like those who collect stones for their funeral mounds.
9 A band of criminals is like a bundle of tow;
they will end in a flaming fire.*
10 The path of sinners is smooth stones,
but its end is the pit of Sheol.†

---

† **20:9–17** In a series of paradoxes the author indicates how much true and lasting values differ from apparent ones.

20:18–26 The ill-timed speech brings disaster (vv. 18–20); human respect may lead to rash promises and enmity (vv. 22–23); lies bring dishonor and lasting disgrace (vv. 24–26).

20:27–31 Through prudent speech the wise gain honor and esteem among the great (vv. 27–28). They must beware, however, of accepting bribes, lest they share in evil through silence when they should reprove (vv. 29–31).

‡20:31 Other ancient texts read as v. 32:
It is better to await the inevitable while serving the Lord
than to be the ungoverned helmsman for the careening of one's life.

21:1–10 Under various figures, the consequences of sin are described as destructive of wealth, and even of life, deserving of death (vv. 2–4, 6a, 8–10). Fear of the Lord motivates repentance (vv. 5, 6b).

21:10 *The path of sinners . . . Sheol*: Ben Sira refers to the death that awaits unrepentant sinners; see notes on 11:26–28; 17:24–32.

20:29 Ex 23:8; Dt 16:19. **21:3** Prv 5:4. **21:6** Prv 12:1. **21:9** Sir 16:6; Ps 21:10.

SIR

The Wise and Foolish: A Contrast†

11 Those who keep the Law control their thoughts;
perfect fear of the Lord is wisdom.
12 One who is not clever can never be taught,
but there is a cleverness filled with bitterness.

13 The knowledge of the wise wells up like a flood,
and their counsel like a living spring.*
14 A fool's mind is like a broken jar:
it cannot hold any knowledge at all.

15 When the intelligent hear a wise saying,
they praise it and add to it.
The wanton hear it with distaste
and cast it behind their back.

16 A fool's chatter is like a load on a journey,
but delight is to be found on the lips of the intelligent.
17 The views of the prudent are sought in an assembly,
and their words are taken to heart.

18 Like a house in ruins is wisdom to a fool;
to the stupid, knowledge is incomprehensible chatter.
19 To the senseless, education is fetters on the feet,
like manacles on the right hand.
20 Fools raise their voice in laughter,
but the prudent at most smile quietly.*
21 Like a gold ornament is education to the wise,
like a bracelet on the right arm.

22 A fool steps boldly into a house,
while the well-bred are slow to make an entrance.*
23 A boor peeps through the doorway of a house,
but the educated stay outside.
24 It is rude for one to listen at a door;
the discreet person would be overwhelmed by the disgrace.

25 The lips of the arrogant talk of what is not their concern,
but the discreet carefully weigh their words.
26 The mind of fools is in their mouths,
but the mouth of the wise is in their mind.†
27 When the godless curse their adversary,†
they really curse themselves.
28 Slanderers sully themselves,
and are hated by their neighbors.

On Laziness and Foolishness

22 1† The sluggard is like a filthy stone;†
everyone hisses at his disgrace.
2 The sluggard is like a lump of dung;
whoever touches it shakes it off the hands.

3 An undisciplined child is a disgrace to its father;
if it be a daughter, she brings him to poverty.*
4 A thoughtful daughter obtains a husband of her own;
a shameless one is her father's grief.
5 A hussy shames her father and her husband;
she is despised by both.

6 Like music at the time of mourning is ill-timed talk,†
but lashes and discipline are at all times wisdom.‡
9 Teaching a fool is like gluing a broken pot,*
or rousing another from deep sleep.
10 Whoever talks with a fool talks to someone asleep;
when it is over, he says, "What was that?"

11 Weep over the dead, for their light has gone out;
weep over the fool, for sense has left him.
Weep but less bitterly over the dead, for they are at rest;
worse than death is the life of a fool.
12 Mourning for the dead, seven days—*
but for the wicked fool, a whole lifetime.

---

† **21:11–28** The mind of the wise is a fountain of knowledge (vv. 13, 15); their will is trained to keep the Law (v. 11); their words are gracious, valued, carefully weighed, sincere (vv. 16–17, 25–26); their conduct is respectful, cultured and restrained (vv. 20, 22–24). The mind of the foolish is devoid of knowledge and impenetrable to it (vv. 12, 14, 18–19); their will rejects it (v. 15); their talk is burdensome (v. 16), their laughter unrestrained (v. 20), their conversation shallow and meddlesome (vv. 25–26); their conduct is bold and rude (vv. 22–24); their abuse of others redounds on themselves (vv. 27–28).

21:26 A clever play on words.

21:27 *Curse their adversary*: the curse of the godless often recoils on their own head; cf. Gn 27:29; Nm 24:9.

22:1–15 To Ben Sira, a lazy person and an unruly child are a cause of shame and disgrace; everyone wishes to be rid of them (vv. 1–5). Speaking with a wicked fool is as senseless as talking with someone who is asleep or dead (v. 10). The fool is an intolerable burden that merits a lifetime of mourning (v. 12). Seven days was the usual mourning period. Cf. Gn 50:10; Jdt 16:24.

22:1 *Stone*: used then and even today for wiping oneself after a bowel movement.

22:6 As a joyful song is out of place among mourners so a rebuke may be insufficient when corporal punishment is called for.

‡**22:6** Other ancient texts read as vv. 7–8:
7 Children whose upbringing leads to a wholesome life
veil over the lowly origins of their parents.
8 Children whose pride is in scornful misconduct
besmirch the nobility of their own family.

---

* **21:13** Prv 13:14; 16:22; 18:4. **21:20** Eccl 7:6. **21:22** Prv 25:17. **22:3** Prv 10:1; 17:21, 25; 19:13. **22:9–12** Prv 23:9. **22:12** Gn 50:10; Jdt 16:24.

13 Do not talk much with the stupid,
or visit the unintelligent.
Beware of them lest you have trouble
and be spattered when they shake
themselves off.
Avoid them and you will find rest
and not be wearied by their lack of sense.
14 What is heavier than lead?
What is its name but "Fool"?
15 Sand, salt, and an iron weight
are easier to bear than the stupid person.*

16 A wooden beam firmly bonded into a building†
is not loosened by an earthquake;
So the mind firmly resolved after careful
deliberation
will not be afraid at any time.
17 The mind solidly backed by intelligent thought
is like a stucco decoration on a smooth wall.
18 Small stones lying on an open height
will not remain when the wind blows;
So a timid mind based on foolish plans
cannot stand up to fear of any kind.

The Preservation of Friendship†

19 Whoever jabs the eye brings tears;
whoever pierces the heart bares its feelings.
20 Whoever throws a stone at birds drives them
away;
whoever insults a friend breaks up the
friendship.
21 Should you draw a sword against a friend,
do not despair, for it can be undone.
22 Should you open your mouth against a friend,
do not worry, for you can be reconciled.
But a contemptuous insult, a confidence
broken,
or a treacherous attack will drive any friend
away.

23 Win your neighbor's trust while he is poor,
so that you may rejoice with him in his
prosperity.
In time of trouble remain true to him,
so that you may share in his inheritance
when it comes.

24 The billowing smoke of a furnace precedes
the fire,
so insults precede bloodshed.
25 I am not ashamed to shelter a friend,
and I will not hide from him.
26 But if harm should come to me because of him,
all who hear of it will beware of him.

Prayer†

27 Who will set a guard over my mouth,
an effective seal on my lips,
That I may not fail through them,
and my tongue may not destroy me?*

23 1 Lord, Father and Master of my life,†
do not abandon me to their designs,
do not let me fall because of them!

2 Who will apply the lash to my thoughts,
and to my mind the rod of discipline,
That my failings may not be spared
or the sins of my heart overlooked?
3 Otherwise my failings may increase,
and my sins be multiplied;
And I fall before my adversaries,
and my enemy rejoice over me?
4 Lord, Father and God of my life,
do not give me haughty eyes;
5 remove evil desire from my heart.
6 Let neither gluttony nor lust overcome me;
do not give me up to shameless desires.*

Proper Use of the Tongue†

7 Listen, my children, to instruction concerning
the mouth,
for whoever keeps it will not be ensnared.
8 Through the lips the sinner is caught;
by them the reviler and the arrogant are
tripped up.
9 Do not accustom your mouth to oaths,
or habitually utter the Holy Name.*
10 Just as a servant constantly under scrutiny
will not be without bruises,
So one who swears continually by the Holy
Name
will never remain free from sin.

†

22:16–18 A prudent mind firmly resolved is undisturbed by violent and conflicting thoughts, whereas a foolish person is tossed about by the winds of fear, like small stones whipped about by high winds.

22:19–26 Disputes and violence weaken friendship, and disloyalty and abuse of confidence destroy it utterly (vv. 19–22, 24, 26); but kindness to a poor person in time of poverty and adversity builds up friendship and merits a share in his prosperity and inheritance (vv. 23, 25).

22:27–23:6 Ben Sira implores the divine assistance to preserve him through stern discipline from sins of the tongue (22:27; 23:1), from ignorance of mind and weakness of will (vv. 2–3), and from inclinations of the senses and the flesh, lest he fall into the hands of his enemies or become a prey of shameful desires (vv. 4–6).

23:1–6 *Lord, Father and Master of my life*: these words express the tender personal relationship Ben Sira experiences with God, and introduce his prayer for divine assistance and providence in avoiding sins of pride and lust.

23:7–15 A warning against sins of the tongue through misuse of the sacred Name, against thoughtless swearing (vv. 7–11), blasphemy (v. 12), coarse talk (vv. 13–14), and abusive language (v. 15).

*

22:15 Prv 27:3.
22:27 Ps 141:3.
23:6 Rom 13:13.
23:9 Ex 20:7; Lv 19:12; 24:16; Dt 5:11; Mt 5:33–37; Jas 5:12.

Catholic Connection

Sin and Moral Decision Making

Have you ever intentionally said or done something mean and later wished you could take it back? In the Wisdom of Ben Sira (Ecclesiasticus), Ben Sira offers a wonderful and rather dramatic prayer for help to avoid sinning. Ben Sira uses words like *guard* and *discipline* to describe how diligently his thoughts and words should be monitored. The strong language helps emphasize the importance of avoiding sin and the need to be vigilant in the process.

We too must be vigilant and seek God's help in avoiding sin, for sin is an offense against God that breaks God's law of love. The Church teaches that sin occurs when one goes against the truth and right reason, and one's conscience. It is when a person consciously chooses through thoughts, words, or deeds not to love God, neighbor, or self. Sin harms not only a person's relationship with God but also his or her relationships with other people and one's self.

One way to avoid sin is to always try to make good moral decisions. Whenever we are faced with a decision, we must ask ourselves three questions: First, is the act I am considering doing morally good, like loving my neighbor, or morally evil, like murder? Second, what are my intentions for doing this act? For example, am I helping my neighbor out of love or in the hopes of getting something in return? Third, what are the circumstances surrounding the action? The circumstances cannot change an evil act into a good act, but they may diminish your level of responsibility for committing the act. For example, if you are acting out of fear for your own life when you harm someone else, although the act is still morally evil, your personal responsibility may be diminished. Together all three questions help us determine the moral quality of our actions by examining what we are doing, why we are doing it, and the circumstances surrounding the act.

The Church does make distinctions between two types of sin based on the gravity of the act committed. Some sins, called mortal sins, are so serious they break our relationship with God entirely. These sins are committed when a person goes against his or her conscience and willfully commits a seriously immoral act, like murder. Venial sins entail a less serious immoral act, or a lack of full knowledge or willingness, and only weaken our relationship with God. And rest assured, no matter what, we can always seek God's forgiveness and restore our relationship with him through the sacrament of Penance and Reconciliation.

Sir 22:27—23:6

Catechism, nos. 1749–1761, 1846–1864

11 Those who swear many oaths heap up offenses;
and the scourge will never be far from their houses.
If they swear in error, guilt is incurred;
if they neglect their obligation, the sin is doubly great.*
If they swear without reason they cannot be declared innocent,
for their households will be filled with calamities.

12 There are words comparable to death;
may they never be heard in the inheritance of Jacob.
To the devout all such words are foreign;
they do not wallow in sin.
13 Do not accustom your mouth to coarse talk,
for it involves sinful speech.
14 Keep your father and mother in mind
when you sit among the mighty,*
Lest you forget yourself in their presence
and disgrace your upbringing.
Then you will wish you had never been born
and will curse the day of your birth.
15 Those accustomed to using abusive language
will never acquire discipline as long as they live.

Sins of the Flesh†

16 Two types of people multiply sins,
and a third† draws down wrath:
Burning passion is like a blazing fire,
not to be quenched till it burns itself out;
One unchaste with his kindred
never stops until fire breaks forth.
17 To the unchaste all bread is sweet;
he is never through till he dies.*

18 The man who dishonors his marriage bed
says to himself, "Who can see me?
Darkness surrounds me, walls hide me,
no one sees me. Who can stop me from sinning?"*
He is not mindful of the Most High,
19 fearing only human eyes.
He does not realize that the eyes of the Lord,
ten thousand times brighter than the sun,
Observe every step taken
and peer into hidden corners.
20 The one who knows all things before they exist
still knows them all after they are made.
21 Such a man will be denounced in the streets of the city;*
and where he least suspects it, he will be apprehended.

22 So it is with the woman unfaithful to her husband,
who offers him an heir by another man.
23 First of all, she has disobeyed the law of the Most High;
second, she has wronged her husband;

Live It!

Four-Letter Words

Four-letter words. You've heard them plenty. You have undoubtedly used them yourself. They roll off the tongue so easily. They get attention. They help you fit in with some groups of people.

You might wonder, So, what's the problem with foul language? Why does Ben Sira call it "sinful speech" (Sir 23:13)? Well, part of the problem is that using it easily becomes a habit. You become less aware of when you are using it. You can get yourself into trouble. Ben Sira warns that you may "forget yourself . . . and disgrace your upbringing" (verse 14).

Maybe the worst part of the problem is that frequent use of foul language shows a lack of respect and reverence for others and certainly for God's name. Ben Sira reminds us, "To the devout all such words are foreign" (verse 12).

Certainly, in a language with over 600,000 words, there are more creative ways to express emotion or frustration than relying on those all-too-familiar four-letter words. If you've developed the habit of using them, ask God and your friends to help you stop.

▶ Sir 23:12–15

---

† **23:16–27** Ben Sira treats sexual sins and their consequences. Lust destroys its victims (vv. 16–17, 22–26). A false sense of security aggravates the adulterer's inevitable fate (vv. 18–21).

23:16 *Two types . . . a third*: a numerical proverb, as in 25:1–2, 7–11; 26:5–6, 28; 50:25–26; Prv 6:16–19; 30:15b–16, 18–19, 21–23, 29–31. Ben Sira condemns three kinds of sexual sin: incest (v. 16), fornication (v. 17), and adultery (vv. 18–26).

23:11 Lv 5:4–10.
23:14 Sir 7:27; Ex 20:12; Dt 5:16.
23:17 Prv 9:17.
23:18–19 Jb 24:15; Prv 15:3, 11; 17:3; 24:12; Is 29:15; Ez 8:12.
23:21–22 Lv 18:20; 20:10; Dt 22:21–22.

SIR

Third, through her wanton adultery
she has brought forth children by another man.
24 Such a woman will be dragged before the assembly,†
and her punishment will extend to her children.
25 Her children will not take root;
her branches will not bring forth fruit.
26 She will leave behind an accursed memory;
her disgrace will never be blotted out.

27 Thus all who dwell on the earth shall know,
all who remain in the world shall understand,
That nothing is better than the fear of the Lord,
nothing sweeter than obeying the commandments of the Lord.* ‡

Praise of Wisdom

24 1 Wisdom sings her own praises,†
among her own people she proclaims her glory.
2 In the assembly of the Most High she opens her mouth,
in the presence of his host she tells of her glory:

3 "From the mouth of the Most High I came forth,*
and covered the earth like a mist.
4 In the heights of heaven I dwelt,
and my throne was in a pillar of cloud.
5 The vault of heaven I compassed alone,
and walked through the deep abyss.
6 Over waves of the sea, over all the land,
over every people and nation I held sway.
7 Among all these I sought a resting place.
In whose inheritance should I abide?

8 "Then the Creator of all gave me his command,
and my Creator chose the spot for my tent.
He said, 'In Jacob make your dwelling,
in Israel your inheritance.'
9 Before all ages, from the beginning, he created me,
and through all ages I shall not cease to be.
10 In the holy tent I ministered before him,
and so I was established in Zion.
11 In the city he loves as he loves me, he gave me rest;
in Jerusalem, my domain.
12 I struck root among the glorious people,
in the portion of the Lord, his heritage.

13 "Like a cedar in Lebanon I grew tall,
like a cypress on Mount Hermon;
14 I grew tall like a palm tree in Engedi,
like rosebushes in Jericho;
Like a fair olive tree in the field,
like a plane tree beside water I grew tall.
15 Like cinnamon and fragrant cane,
like precious myrrh I gave forth perfume;
Like galbanum and onycha and mastic,*
like the odor of incense in the holy tent.†

16 "I spread out my branches like a terebinth,
my branches so glorious and so graceful.
17 I bud forth delights like a vine;
my blossoms are glorious and rich fruit.‡
19 Come to me, all who desire me,
and be filled with my fruits.†
20 You will remember me as sweeter than honey,
better to have than the honeycomb.
21 Those who eat of me will hunger still,†
those who drink of me will thirst for more.*
22 Whoever obeys me will not be put to shame,
and those who serve me will never go astray."

23 All this is the book of the covenant of the Most High God,*
the Law which Moses commanded us†
as a heritage for the community of Jacob.‡
25 It overflows, like the Pishon, with wisdom,*
and like the Tigris at the time of first fruits.

†

23:24–25 The judgment of the assembly determined the illegitimacy of children born of adultery or incest and excluded them from the "community of the Lord" (Dt 23:3). Cf. Wis 3:16–19; 4:3–6.

‡23:27 Other ancient texts read as v. 28:
It is a great glory to follow after God,
and for you to be received by him is length of days.

24:1–29 Wisdom speaks in the first person, describing her origin, her dwelling place in Israel, and the reward she gives her followers. As in Proverbs 8, Wisdom is personified as coming from God, yet distinct from him. This description is reflected in the Johannine *logos*, or Word (Jn 1:1–14). It is used extensively in the Roman liturgy.

24:15 These substances, associated with worship, are mentioned in Ex 30:23–28, 34–35 as the ingredients of the anointing oil and the sacred incense. Israel was a priestly nation (Ex 19:6; Is 61:6).

‡24:17 Other ancient texts read as v. 18:
I am the mother of fair love, of reverence,
of knowledge, and of holy hope;
To all my children I give
to be everlasting: to those named by Him.

24:19 Mt 11:28–30 contains a similar invitation.

24:21 The paradox of wisdom is that, far from being satiated, those who partake of her will always desire more.

24:23 Ben Sira now identifies Wisdom and the law of Moses; see also Bar 4:1.

‡24:23 Other ancient texts read as v. 24:
Do not grow weary of striving with the Lord's help,
but cling to him that he may reinforce you.
The Lord Almighty alone is God,
and apart from him there is no savior.

*

23:27 Sir 1:11–30; Prv 3:1–2.
24:3–6 Sir 1:1–4; Prv 2:6; 8:22–36; Wis 7:24–25.
24:15 Ex 30:23–28, 34–35.
24:21 Is 55:1; Jn 4:10–14; 6:35.
24:23 Ex 24:7.
24:23–27 Gn 2:11–14.

26 It runs over, like the Euphrates, with understanding,
and like the Jordan at harvest time.
27 It floods like the Nile with instruction,
like the Gihon† at vintage time.
28 The first human being never finished comprehending wisdom,
nor will the last succeed in fathoming her.
29 For deeper than the sea are her thoughts,
and her counsels, than the great abyss.

30 Now I, like a stream from a river,†
and like water channeling into a garden—
31 I said, "I will water my plants,
I will drench my flower beds."
Then suddenly this stream of mine became a river,
and this river of mine became a sea.
32 Again I will make my teachings shine forth like the dawn;
I will spread their brightness afar off.
33 Again I will pour out instruction like prophecy
and bestow it on generations yet to come.

Those Who Are Worthy of Praise

25 1† With three things I am delighted,
for they are pleasing to the Lord and to human beings:
Harmony among relatives, friendship among neighbors,
and a wife and a husband living happily together.
2 Three kinds of people I hate,
and I loathe their manner of life:
A proud pauper, a rich liar,
and a lecherous old fool.

3 In your youth you did not gather.
How will you find anything in your old age?
4 How appropriate is sound judgment in the gray-haired,
and good counsel in the elderly!
5 How appropriate is wisdom in the aged,
understanding and counsel in the venerable!
6 The crown of the elderly, wide experience;
their glory, the fear of the Lord.
7 There are nine who come to mind as blessed,
a tenth whom my tongue proclaims:†
The man who finds joy in his children,
and the one who lives to see the downfall of his enemies.
8 Happy the man who lives with a sensible woman,
and the one who does not plow with an ox and a donkey combined.†
Happy the one who does not sin with the tongue,
who does not serve an inferior.
9 Happy the one who finds a friend,
who speaks to attentive ears.
10 How great is the one who finds wisdom,
but none is greater than the one who fears the Lord.
11 Fear of the Lord surpasses all else.
To whom can we compare the one who has it?‡

Wicked and Virtuous Women†

13 Any wound, but not a wound of the heart!
Any wickedness, but not the wickedness of a woman!
14 Any suffering, but not suffering from one's foes!
Any vengeance, but not the vengeance of one's enemies!
15 There is no poison worse than that of a serpent,
no venom greater than that of a woman.
16 I would rather live with a dragon or a lion
than live with a wicked woman.*
17 A woman's wicked disposition changes her appearance,
and makes her face as dark as a bear.
18 When her husband sits among his neighbors,
a bitter sigh escapes him unawares.
19 There is hardly an evil like that in a woman;
may she fall to the lot of the sinner!
20 Like a sandy hill to aged feet

†

24:27 *Gihon*: understood by some to have been a name for the Nile; cf. Gn 2:13.

24:30–33 Ben Sira again speaks about himself. He had at first drawn a small portion of the water of wisdom for his own private benefit, but finding it so useful, he soon began to let others share in this boon by teaching them the lessons of wisdom. Like the words of the prophets, Ben Sira's instruction is valuable for all generations (v. 33). The comparison to prophecy is bold and unique.

25:1–2 A numerical saying in threes.

25:7–11 A numerical proverb (9 + 1), in which the tenth element, "the one who fears the Lord," is the most important.

25:8 *An ox and a donkey combined*: the reference is to a man married to two incompatible women (cf. 37:11a); the imagery derives from Dt 22:10.

‡25:11 Other ancient texts read as v. 12:
Fear of the Lord is the beginning of loving him,
and fidelity is the beginning of clinging to him.

25:13–26 The harsh statements Ben Sira makes about women reflect the kind of instruction young Jewish males were exposed to in the early second century B.C. His patriarchal perspective is as unfair as it is one-sided.

*

25:16 Prv 21:9, 19; 25:24; 27:15.

is a garrulous wife to a quiet husband.
21 Do not be enticed by a woman's beauty,
or be greedy for her wealth.
22 Harsh is the slavery and great the shame
when a wife supports her husband.

23 Depressed mind, gloomy face,
and a wounded heart—a wicked woman.
Drooping hands and quaking knees,
any wife who does not make her husband happy.
24 With a woman sin had a beginning,
and because of her we all die.†
25 Allow water no outlet,
and no boldness of speech to a wicked woman.
26 If she does not go along as you direct,
cut her away from you.

26

1 Happy the husband of a good wife;†
the number of his days will be doubled.*
2 A loyal wife brings joy to her husband,
and he will finish his years in peace.
3 A good wife is a generous gift
bestowed upon him who fears the Lord.*
4 Whether rich or poor, his heart is content,
a smile ever on his face.

5 There are three things I dread,
and a fourth which terrifies me:
Public slander, the gathering of a mob,
and false accusation—all harder to bear than death.
6 A wife jealous of another wife is heartache and mourning;†
everyone feels the lash of her tongue.

7 A wicked wife is a chafing yoke;
taking hold of her is like grasping a scorpion.
8 A drunken wife arouses great anger,
for she does not hide her shame.
9 By her haughty stare and her eyelids
an unchaste wife can be recognized.

10 Keep a strict watch over an unruly wife,
lest, finding an opportunity, she use it;*
11 Watch out for her impudent eye,
and do not be surprised if she betrays you:
12 As a thirsty traveler opens his mouth
and drinks from any water nearby,
So she sits down before every tent peg
and opens her quiver for every arrow.

13 A gracious wife delights her husband;
her thoughtfulness puts flesh on his bones.
14 A silent wife is a gift from the Lord;
nothing is worth more than her self-discipline.
15 A modest wife is a supreme blessing;
no scales can weigh the worth of her chastity.
16 The sun rising in the Lord's heavens—
the beauty of a good wife in her well-ordered home.
17 The light which shines above the holy lampstand—†
a beautiful face on a stately figure.
18 Golden columns on silver bases—
so her shapely legs and steady feet.‡

Dangers to Integrity and Friendship

28† Two things bring grief to my heart,
and a third arouses my anger:
The wealthy reduced to want,
the intelligent held in contempt,
And those who pass from righteousness to sin—
the Lord prepares them for the sword.*

---

† **25:24** Ben Sira refers to the story of the first sin in Gn 3:1–6. Cf. 2 Cor 11:3 and 1 Tm 2:14. St. Paul, however, singles out Adam; cf. Rom 5:12–19; 1 Cor 15:22.

26:1–4, 13–18 A good wife is as a gift from God, bringing joy and peace, happiness and contentment to her husband (vv. 1–4) through her thoughtfulness, reserve, modesty and chastity, beauty, grace, and virtue (vv. 13–18).

26:6–12 A repetition of the thought expressed in 25:13–26.

26:17–18 The lampstand and the columns were located in the holy place of the ancient tabernacle (Ex 25:31–40; 26:32).

‡**26:18** Other ancient texts read as vv. 19–27:
19 My child, keep intact the bloom of your youth,
and do not give your strength to strangers.
20 Seek out a fertile field from all the land,
and sow it with your own seed, confident in your fine stock.
21 So shall your offspring prosper,
and grow great, confident in their good descent.
22 A woman for hire is regarded as spittle,
but a married woman is a deadly snare for her lovers.
23 A godless wife will be given to the lawless man as his portion,
but a godly wife will be given to the man who fears the Lord.
24 A shameless woman wears out reproach,
but a virtuous daughter will be modest even before her husband.
25 A headstrong wife is regarded as a bitch,
but the one with a sense of shame fears the Lord.
26 The wife who honors her husband will seem wise to everyone,
but if she dishonors him in her pride, she will be known to everyone as ungodly.
Happy is the husband of a good wife,
for the number of his years will be doubled.
27 A loud-mouthed and garrulous wife will be regarded
as a trumpet sounding the charge,
And every person who lives like this
will spend his life in the anarchy of war.

26:28–27:15 From proper conduct in family life, Ben Sira proceeds to social morality, warning especially against injustice in business (26:29–27:3), and perversity of speech in daily life (27:4–7). The pursuit of justice in these matters is all the more meritorious as it is difficult (27:8–10). The discourses of the godly are marked with wisdom, but the conversations of the wicked with offense, swearing, cursing, quarrels, and even bloodshed (27:11–15).

---

* **26:1** Sir 25:8; Prv 18:22. **26:3** Sir 36:27–29. **26:10** Sir 42:11. **26:28** Ez 18:24–29.

29 A merchant can hardly keep from wrongdoing,
nor can a shopkeeper stay free from sin;

27 1 For the sake of profit many sin,
and the struggle for wealth blinds the eyes.*
2 A stake will be driven between fitted stones—
sin will be wedged in between buying and selling.
3 Unless one holds fast to the fear of the Lord,
with sudden swiftness will one's house be thrown down.
4 When a sieve is shaken, the husks appear;
so do people's faults when they speak.†
5 The furnace tests the potter's vessels;
the test of a person is in conversation.*
6 The fruit of a tree shows the care it has had;
so speech discloses the bent of a person's heart.*
7 Praise no one before he speaks,
for it is then that people are tested.
8 If you strive after justice, you will attain it,
and wear it like a splendid robe.
9 Birds nest with their own kind,
and honesty comes to those who work at it.
10 A lion lies in wait for prey,
so does sin for evildoers.

11 The conversation of the godly is always wisdom,
but the fool changes like the moon.
12 Limit the time you spend among the stupid,
but frequent the company of the thoughtful.
13 The conversation of fools is offensive,
and their laughter is wanton sin.
14 Their oath-filled talk makes the hair stand on end,
and their brawls make one stop the ears.
15 The wrangling of the proud ends in bloodshed,
and their cursing is painful to hear.*

16 Whoever betrays a secret destroys confidence,†
and will never find a congenial friend.*
17 Cherish your friend, keep faith with him;
but if you betray his secrets, do not go after him;
18 For as one might kill another,
you have killed your neighbor's friendship.
19 Like a bird released from your hand,
you have let your friend go and cannot recapture him.
20 Do not go after him, for he is far away,
and has escaped like a gazelle from a snare.
21 For a wound can be bandaged, and an insult forgiven,
but whoever betrays secrets does hopeless damage.*

Malice, Anger and Vengeance

22 Whoever has shifty eyes plots mischief
and those who know him will keep their distance;
23 In your presence he uses honeyed talk,
and admires your words,
But later he changes his tone
and twists the words to your ruin.*
24 I have hated many things but not as much as him,
and the Lord hates him as well.*
25 A stone falls back on the head of the one who throws it high,*
and a treacherous blow causes many wounds.
26 Whoever digs a pit falls into it,
and whoever lays a snare is caught in it.†
27 The evil anyone does will recoil on him
without knowing how it came upon him.

28 Mockery and abuse will befall the arrogant,
and vengeance lies in wait for them like a lion.
29 Those who rejoice in the downfall of the godly will be caught in a snare,
and pain will consume them before they die.
30 Wrath and anger, these also are abominations,
yet a sinner holds on to them.

28 1 The vengeful will face the Lord's vengeance;
indeed he remembers their sins in detail.*

---

† **27:4–7, 11–15** The importance of effective speech is a favorite wisdom topic; e.g., cf. 20:1–8, 18–20; 22:27–23:15.

27:16–28:11 Betrayal of confidence through indiscretion destroys friendship and does irreparable harm (27:16–21); cf. 22:22. False friendship based on hypocrisy and deceit is hateful to Ben Sira and, he adds, to God as well (27:22–24); it soon becomes a victim of its own treachery (27:25–27). The same fate awaits the malicious and vengeful (27:28–28:1). They can obtain mercy and forgiveness only by first forgiving their neighbor, being mindful of death and of the commandments of the Most High (28:2–7). And they must avoid quarrels and strife (28:8–11).

27:26 This expresses a popular idea of act and consequence; an evil (or good) deed is repaid by an evil (or good) result. The frequent metaphor is the digging of a hole for another to fall into; cf. Prv 26:27; Ps 7:14; 9:16; Eccl 10:8.

---

* **27:1** Sir 7:18; 31:5–6; Prv 30:7–9.
27:5 1 Pt 1:7.
27:6 Mt 7:20.
27:15 Sir 23:8–15.
27:16 Prv 11:13; 20:19.
27:21 Sir 22:20.
27:23 Prv 26:24–28.
27:24 Prv 6:16–19.
27:25–27 Ps 7:16–17; Prv 26:27; Eccl 10:8.
28:1 Dt 32:35; Rom 12:19.

Live It!

Just Walk Away

"Hey, did you hear the latest about Valerie?"

"No, what?"

"Well, last Friday night, she and Maria were at Jason's party, and . . ."

"Wait a minute, here comes Maria. Tell me later."

"Cursed be gossips and the double-tongued, / for they destroy the peace of many" (Sir 28:13).

"Guess what I heard!"

"What?"

"Well, Teresa, who is usually so stuck-up—"

"I know. I can't stand her. She thinks she's so cool."

"Well, anyway, she went to this party and . . ."

"Whoever heed it will find no rest, / nor will they dwell in peace" (verse 16).

"I can't believe what I just heard!"

"What? Tell me!"

"I heard that Juan and Sunyub went out last night, got totally trashed, and spent the night together."

"Are you kidding? Sunyub, little miss honor student? And Juan, athlete of the year? Are you sure?"

"I know. I can't believe it either, but I heard it from two different people. . . ."

"Many have fallen by the edge of the sword, / but not as many as by the tongue" (verse 18).

"If you blow upon a spark, it turns into flame, / if you spit on it, it dies out; / yet both you do with your mouth!" (verse 12).

The next time you hear a piece of gossip or a rumor, don't blow on it—spit on it and walk away. Someone's reputation is at stake. One of these times, it could be yours. Check out the third chapter of James in the New Testament for another version of the hazards of gossip and slander.

▶ Sir 28:12–18

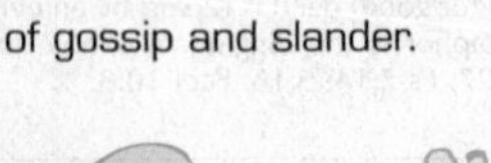

2 Forgive your neighbor the wrong done to you;
then when you pray, your own sins will be forgiven.*
3 Does anyone nourish anger against another
and expect healing from the LORD?*
4 Can one refuse mercy to a sinner like oneself,
yet seek pardon for one's own sins?
5 If a mere mortal cherishes wrath,
who will forgive his sins?
6 Remember your last days and set enmity aside;
remember death and decay, and cease from sin!*
7 Remember the commandments and do not be angry with your neighbor;
remember the covenant of the Most High, and overlook faults.

8 Avoid strife and your sins will be fewer,
for the hot-tempered kindle strife;
9 The sinner disrupts friendships
and sows discord among those who are at peace.*
10 The more the wood, the greater the fire,*
the more the cruelty, the fiercer the strife;
The greater the strength, the sterner the anger,
the greater the wealth, the greater the wrath.
11 Pitch and resin make fire flare up,
and a hasty quarrel provokes bloodshed.

The Evil Tongue†

12 If you blow on a spark, it turns into flame,
if you spit on it, it dies out;
yet both you do with your mouth!
13 Cursed be gossips and the double-tongued,
for they destroy the peace of many.*
14 A meddlesome tongue subverts many,
and makes them refugees among peoples.
It destroys strong cities,
and overthrows the houses of the great.
15 A meddlesome tongue drives virtuous women from their homes,
and robs them of the fruit of their toil.
16 Whoever heed it will find no rest,
nor will they dwell in peace.

† **28:12–26** Further treatment of sins of the tongue and the havoc that results; cf. 5:9–6:1; 19:5–17; 20:18–26; 23:7–15. Gossips and the double-tongued destroy domestic peace (vv. 12–16). The whip, the sword, chains, even Sheol, are not so cruel as the suffering inflicted by an evil tongue (vv. 17–21). Not the godly but those who forsake the Lord are victims of their evil tongues (vv. 22–23). Therefore, guard your mouth and tongue as you would guard treasure against an enemy (vv. 24–26).

* **28:2** Mt 6:14.
28:3 Mt 18:23–35.
28:6 Sir 7:36; 38:20.
28:9 Prv 15:18.
28:10–11 Prv 26:20–21.
28:13 Sir 5:13–6:1.

17 A blow from a whip raises a welt,
but a blow from the tongue will break bones.
18 Many have fallen by the edge of the sword,
but not as many as by the tongue.*
19 Happy the one who is sheltered from it,
and has not endured its wrath;
Who has not borne its yoke
nor been bound with its chains.
20 For its yoke is a yoke of iron,
and its chains are chains of bronze;
21 The death it inflicts is an evil death,
even Sheol is preferable to it.
22 It will have no power over the godly,
nor will they be burned in its flame.
23 But those who forsake the Lord will fall victim to it,
as it burns among them unquenchably;
It will hurl itself against them like a lion,
and like a leopard, it will tear them to pieces.
24 As you fence in your property with thorns,
so make a door and a bolt for your mouth.*
25 As you lock up your silver and gold,
so make balances and scales for your words.
26 Take care not to slip by your tongue
and fall victim to one lying in ambush.

Loans, Alms and Surety†

29 1 The merciful lend to their neighbor,
by holding out a helping hand, they keep the commandments.*
2 Lend to your neighbor in his time of need,
and pay back your neighbor in time.*
3 Keep your promise and be honest with him,
and at all times you will find what you need.
4 Many borrowers ask for a loan
and cause trouble for those who help them.
5 Till he gets a loan, he kisses the lender's hand
and speaks softly of his creditor's money,
But at time of payment, delays,
makes excuses, and finds fault with the timing.
6 If he can pay, the lender will recover barely half,
and will consider that a windfall.
If he cannot pay, the lender is cheated of his money
and acquires an enemy at no extra charge;
With curses and insults the borrower will repay,
and instead of honor will repay with abuse.
7 Many refuse to lend, not out of meanness,
but from fear of being cheated needlessly.
8 But with those in humble circumstances be patient;
do not keep them waiting for your alms.
9 Because of the commandment, help the poor,
and in their need, do not send them away empty-handed.*
10 Lose your money for relative or friend;
do not hide it under a stone to rot.
11 Dispose of your treasure according to the commandments of the Most High,
and that will profit you more than the gold.*
12† Store up almsgiving in your treasury,
and it will save you from every evil.
13 Better than a mighty shield and a sturdy spear
it will fight for you against the enemy.

14† A good person will be surety for a neighbor,
but whoever has lost a sense of shame will fail him.*
15 Do not forget the kindness of your backer,
for he has given his very life for you.
16 A sinner will turn the favor of a pledge into misfortune,
17 and the ungrateful will abandon his rescuer.
18 Going surety has ruined many who were prosperous
and tossed them about like waves of the sea;*
It has exiled the prominent
and sent them wandering through foreign lands.
19 The sinner will come to grief through surety,
and whoever undertakes too much will fall into lawsuits.
20 Help your neighbor according to your means,
but take care lest you fall yourself.

† **29:1–20** Some practical maxims concerning the use of wealth. Give to the poor (vv. 8–9), lend to a needy neighbor, but repay when a loan falls due lest the lender's burden be increased (vv. 1–5) and his kindness abused (vv. 6–7); through charity build up defense against evil (vv. 10–13). Help your neighbor according to your means, but take care not to fall (v. 20), for the shameless play false and bring their protectors and themselves to misfortune and ruin (vv. 14–19).

29:12–13 In Ben Sira's day, almsgiving and righteousness were practically identified.

29:14–17 Ben Sira is more lenient on going surety than earlier sages; cf. Prv 6:1–5.

* **28:18** Jas 3:5–12.
28:24 Sir 22:27; Ps 141:3.
29:1 Dt 15:8; Ps 112:5; Prv 19:17.
29:2 Ex 22:24–26; Lv 25:36; Mt 5:42.
29:9 Sir 4:1–6; Lv 19:9–10; 23:22.
29:11 Sir 17:22–23; Tb 4:7–11.
29:14 Sir 8:13.
29:18 Prv 6:1–2; 11:15.

Frugality and Its Rewards†

21 Life's prime needs are water, bread, and
clothing,
and also a house for decent privacy.*
22 Better is the life of the poor under the shadow
of their own roof
than sumptuous banquets among
strangers.*
23 Whether little or much, be content with what
you have:
then you will hear no reproach as a parasite.
24 It is a miserable life to go from house to house,
for where you are a guest you dare not
open your mouth.
25 You will entertain and provide drink without
being thanked;
besides, you will hear these bitter words:
26 "Come here, you parasite, set the table,
let me eat the food you have there!
27 Go away, you parasite, for one more worthy;
for my relative's visit I need the room!"
28 Painful things to a sensitive person
are rebuke as a parasite and insults from
creditors.

The Training of Children†

30 1 Whoever loves a son will chastise him
often,
that he may be his joy when he grows up.*
2 Whoever disciplines a son will benefit from
him,
and boast of him among acquaintances.
3 Whoever educates a son will make his enemy
jealous,
and rejoice in him among his friends.
4 At the father's death, he will seem not dead,
for he leaves after him one like himself,
5 Whom he looked upon through life with joy,
and in death, without regret.
6 Against his enemies he has left an avenger,
and one to repay his friends with kindness.

7 Whoever spoils a son will have wounds to
bandage,
and will suffer heartache at every cry.
8 An untamed horse turns out stubborn;
and a son left to himself grows up unruly.
9 Pamper a child and he will be a terror for you,
indulge him, and he will bring you grief.
10 Do not laugh with him lest you share sorrow
with him,
and in the end you will gnash your teeth.
11 Do not give him his own way in his youth,
and do not ignore his follies.
12 Bow down his head in his youth,
beat his sides while he is still young,
Lest he become stubborn and disobey you,
and leave you disconsolate.*
13 Discipline your son and make heavy his yoke,
lest you be offended by his shamelessness.

Health and Cheerfulness†

14 Better the poor in vigorous health
than the rich with bodily ills.
15 I would rather have bodily health than any
gold,
and contentment of spirit than pearls.
16 No riches are greater than a healthy body;
and no happiness than a joyful heart.
17 Better is death than a wretched life,*
everlasting sleep than constant illness.
18 Good things set before one who cannot eat
are like food offerings placed before a
tomb.† *
19 What good is an offering to an idol
that can neither eat nor smell?
So it is with the one being punished by the
Lord,
20 who groans at what his eyes behold.
21 Do not give in to sadness,
or torment yourself deliberately.*
22 Gladness of heart is the very life of a person,
and cheerfulness prolongs his days.
23 Distract yourself and renew your courage,
drive resentment far away from you;
For grief has killed many,*
and nothing is to be gained from
resentment.

†

29:21–28 Those who provide their own basic needs of food, clothing and dwelling, and are content with what they have, preserve their freedom and self-respect (vv. 21–23). But if they live as guests, even among the rich, they expose themselves to insult and rebuke (vv. 24–28).

30:1–13 Sound discipline (which would include physical beating) and careful education of children correct self-indulgence and stubbornness, prevent remorse and humiliation, and bring to parents lasting joy and delight, prestige among friends, jealousy of enemies, perpetuation and vindication of themselves through their offspring (vv. 1–6). Lack of discipline and overindulgence of children bring sorrow and disappointment, terror and grief (vv. 7–13).

30:14–25 Health of mind and body and joy of heart Ben Sira judges to be more precious than wealth (vv. 14–16), whereas bitterness, constant illness, and affliction are more difficult to bear than death (vv. 17–20). Sadness, resentment, anxiety, envy, and anger shorten days; they should be dispelled by cheerfulness and gladness of heart, which help to prolong one's days (vv. 21–25).

30:18 The saying ridicules the practice of putting food and drink on the tombs of the dead.

*

29:21 Sir 39:26.
29:22 Sir 40:29.
30:1 Prv 13:24; 19:18; 22:15; 23:13; 29:15; Heb 12:7.
30:12 Sir 7:23; Prv 23:14.
30:17 Sir 41:2.
30:18 Tb 4:17.
30:21 Prv 12:25; 15:13; 17:22.
30:23 Sir 38:18–19.

24 Envy and anger shorten one's days,
and anxiety brings on premature old age.
25 Those who are cheerful and merry at table
benefit from their food.† *

The Proper Attitude Toward Riches†

31 1 Wakefulness over wealth wastes away the
flesh,
and anxiety over it drives away sleep.
2 Wakeful anxiety banishes slumber;
more than a serious illness it disturbs
repose.
3 The rich labor to pile up wealth,
and if they rest, it is to enjoy pleasure;
4 The poor labor for a meager living,
and if they ever rest, they become needy.
5 The lover of gold will not be free from sin;
whoever pursues money will be led astray
by it.
6 Many have come to ruin for the sake of gold,
yet destruction lay before their very eyes;*
7 It is a stumbling block for fools;
any simpleton will be ensnared by it.
8 Happy the rich person found without fault,
who does not turn aside after wealth.*
9 Who is he, that we may praise him?
For he has done wonders among his
people.
10 Who has been tested by gold and been found
perfect?
Let it be for him his glory;
Who could have sinned but did not,
and could have done evil but did not?
11 So his good fortune is secure,
and the assembly will recount his praises.*

Table Etiquette†

12 Are you seated at the table of the great?
Bring to it no greedy gullet,
Nor say, "How much food there is here!"
13 Remember that the greedy eye is evil.
What has been created more greedy than the
eye?
Therefore, it weeps for any cause.*
15 Recognize that your neighbor feels as you do,
and keep in mind everything you dislike.
14 Toward what he looks at, do not put out a
hand;
nor reach for the same dish when he does.
16 Eat, like anyone else, what is set before you,
but do not eat greedily, lest you be
despised.
17 Be the first to stop, as befits good manners;
and do not gorge yourself, lest you give
offense.*
18 If there are many with you at table,
do not be the first to stretch out your hand.
19 Does not a little suffice for a well-bred person?
When he lies down, he does not wheeze.*
20 Moderate eating ensures sound slumber
and a clear mind on rising the next day.
The distress of sleeplessness and of nausea
and colic are with the glutton!
21 Should you have eaten too much,
get up to vomit† and you will have relief.
22 Listen to me, my child, and do not scorn me;
later you will find my advice good.
In whatever you do, be moderate,
and no sickness will befall you.
23 People bless one who is generous with food,
and this testimony to his goodness is
lasting.*
24 The city complains about one who is stingy
with food,
and this testimony to his stinginess is
lasting.
25 Let not wine be the proof of your strength,
for wine has been the ruin of many.
26 As the furnace tests the work of the smith,
so does wine the hearts of the insolent.
27 Wine is very life to anyone,
if taken in moderation.
Does anyone really live who lacks the wine
which from the beginning was created for
joy?*
28 Joy of heart, good cheer, and delight
is wine enough, drunk at the proper time.
29 Headache, bitterness, and disgrace
is wine drunk amid anger and strife.
30 Wine in excess is a snare for the fool;

†

30:25(27) Because of the dislocation of the Greek text, the numbering of this verse follows Ziegler's edition. There are no verses 25–26.

31:1–11 Solicitude for acquiring wealth and anxiety over preserving it disturb repose and easily lead to sin and ruin (vv. 1–7). Cf. Mt 6:25–34. The rich who have not sinned or been seduced by wealth are worthy of highest praise (vv. 8–11).

31:12–32:13 Whoever observes etiquette at table avoids greed and selfishness (31:12–13), is considerate of a neighbor's likes and dislikes and is generous toward him (31:15, 14, 23, 24), observes proper manners (31:16–18), is moderate in eating and drinking (31:19–20, 25–30). A good host is solicitous for the guests (32:1–2), provides conversation and diversion (32:3–6), is modest in speech (32:7, 8, 10), is respectful of elders (32:9), polite in comportment and grateful to God for his favors (32:11–13).

31:21 *Get up to vomit*: the practice of induced vomiting, well-known among Romans, and less well-known among the Jews, seems to be referred to here.

*

30:25 Prv 15:15.
31:6 Sir 8:2.
31:8 Sir 5:1, 8.
31:11 Prv 29:14.
31:13 Prv 23:1–2.
31:17 Sir 37:27–31.
31:19 Eccl 5:11.
31:23 Prv 22:9.
31:27 Ps 104:15; 1 Tm 5:23.

SIR

Live It!

A Tragic Tale

"Wine in excess is a snare for the fool; / it lessens strength and multiplies wounds" (Sir 31:30).

This is the true story of a young man we'll call Kevin. Kevin had a drinking problem. It all began when he had his first beer at age thirteen. It tasted horrible, but all his friends told him to keep drinking, and he would grow to love the feeling it gave him. He did keep drinking, and the alcohol made him feel more outgoing and more funny. This didn't seem all that bad.

Unfortunately, Kevin became an alcoholic. Weekend drinking turned into weekday drinking, and before long, he was drinking on his way to school. Kevin drank so much that he blacked out almost every other day.

One day, Kevin had drunk nearly a fifth of vodka. He was at home and was supposed to be watching his six-year-old sister, Veronica. Kevin got angry at her and slammed her across the side of the head. She fell to the ground and lay there without moving. Kevin tried calling 911 but couldn't see the numbers well enough to dial.

Veronica died as a result of Kevin's blow. Now Kevin has to live with the horror of killing his own sister. He wishes he could tell every thirteen-year-old in the world not to try that first beer.

▶ Sir 31:25–31

it lessens strength and multiplies wounds.
31 Do not wrangle with your neighbor when wine is served,
nor despise him while he is having a good time;
Say no harsh words to him
nor distress him by making demands.

32 [1]If you are chosen to preside at a dinner,
do not be puffed up,
but with the guests be as one of them;
Take care of them first and then sit down;
2 see to their needs, and then take your place,
To share in their joy
and receive a wreath for a job well done.
3 You who are older, it is your right to speak,
but temper your knowledge and do not interrupt the singing.
4 Where there is entertainment, do not pour out discourse,
and do not display your wisdom at the wrong time.
5 Like a seal of carnelian in a setting of gold:
a concert of music at a banquet of wine.
6 A seal of emerald in a work of gold:
the melody of music with delicious wine.
7 Speak, young man, only when necessary,*
when they have asked you more than once.
8 Be brief, say much in few words;
be knowledgeable and yet quiet.
9 When among elders do not be forward,
and with officials do not be too insistent.
10 The lightning that flashes before a hailstorm:
the esteem that shines on modesty.
11 Leave in good time and do not be the last;
go home quickly without delay.
12 There enjoy doing as you wish,
but do not sin through words of pride.
13 Above all, bless your Maker,
who showers his favors upon you.

The Providence of God

14 Whoever seeks God must accept discipline;†
and whoever resorts to him obtains an answer.*
15 Whoever seeks the law will master it,
but the hypocrite will be ensnared by it.*
16 Whoever fears the LORD will understand what is right,
and out of obscurity he will draw forth a course of action.*
17 The lawless turn aside warnings
and distort the law to suit their purpose.*
18 The sensible will not neglect direction;
the proud and insolent are deterred by no fear.
19 Do nothing without deliberation;
then once you have acted, have no regrets.*
20 Do not go on a way set with snares,
and do not stumble on the same thing twice.

† **32:14–33:4** God is shown to reveal himself through the discipline of his law, a clear and safe plan of life for the pious. Direction and deliberation are aids in following it (32:14–16, 18–24; 33:1, 3–4). Sinners and hypocrites, hating the law or distorting it, fail in wisdom and are devoid of security (32:15b, 17, 18b; 33:2).

* **32:7–10** Sir 7:14. **32:14** Sir 4:13. **32:15** Sir 2:16. **32:16** Ps 37:6. **32:17** Sir 21:6; Prv 12:1. **32:19** Sir 37:16; Tb 4:18.

21 Do not trust the road, because of bandits;
22 be careful on your paths.
23 Whatever you do, be on your guard,
for whoever does so keeps the commandments.
24 Whoever keeps the law preserves himself;
and whoever trusts in the LORD shall not be put to shame.

33 [1]No evil can harm the one who fears the LORD;
through trials, again and again he is rescued.*
2 Whoever hates the law is without wisdom,
and is tossed about like a boat in a storm.
3 The prudent trust in the word of the LORD,
and the law is dependable for them as a divine oracle.†
4 Prepare your words and then you will be listened to;
draw upon your training, and give your answer.
5 Like the wheel of a cart is the mind of a fool,
and his thoughts like a turning axle.
6 A mocking friend is like a stallion
that neighs, no matter who the rider may be.

7† Why is one day more important than another,
when the same sun lights up every day of the year?
8 By the LORD's knowledge they are kept distinct;
and he designates the seasons and feasts.*
9 Some he exalts and sanctifies,
and others he lists as ordinary days.*
10 Likewise, all people are of clay,
and from earth humankind was formed;*
11 In the fullness of his knowledge the Lord distinguished them,
and he designated their different ways.
12 Some he blessed and exalted,
and some he sanctified and drew to himself.
Others he cursed and brought low,
and expelled them from their place.
13 Like clay in the hands of a potter,
to be molded according to his pleasure,
So are people in the hands of their Maker,
to be dealt with as he decides.*
14 As evil contrasts with good, and death with life,
so are sinners in contrast with the godly.*
15 See now all the works of the Most High:
they come in pairs, one the opposite of the other.

16 Now I am the last to keep vigil,†
like a gleaner following the grape-pickers;
17 Since by the Lord's blessing I have made progress
till like a grape-picker I have filled my wine press,
18 Consider that not for myself only have I labored,
but for all who seek instruction.

Property and Servants†

19 Listen to me, leaders of the people;
rulers of the congregation, pay heed!*
20a Let neither son nor wife, neither brother nor friend,
have power over you as long as you live.
21 While breath of life is still in you,
let no one take your place.
20b Do not give your wealth to another,
lest you must plead for support yourself.
22 Far better that your children plead with you
than that you should look for a handout from them.
23 Keep control over all your affairs;
bring no stain on your honor.
24 When your few days reach their limit,
at the time of death distribute your inheritance.

25 Fodder and whip and loads for a donkey;
food, correction and work for a slave.
26 Make a slave work, and he will look for rest;
let his hands be idle and he will seek to be free.*

†

33:3 *Oracle*: as the answer given through the Urim and Thummim to the high priest is true, so the law proves itself true to those who obey it. Cf. Ex 28:30; Nm 27:21.

33:7–15 An important doctrine of Ben Sira is his view of the polarities in creation and history; cf. v. 15; 42:24. Contrasts observable in the physical universe as well as in the moral order serve the purposes of divine wisdom (vv. 5–9). All creatures are like clay in the hands of their Maker—the fool and the wise, the sinner and the just (vv. 10–15). This does not imply that some are created to be sinners: God is not the author of wickedness. Divine determinism and human freedom are a mysterious mix.

33:16–18 Ben Sira refers to himself as the most recent of the biblical writers who have endeavored to present true wisdom to their readers.

33:19–33 Public officials should reject every influence that would restrict their freedom in the management of their affairs. They must make their own household subservient to them rather than be subservient to it (vv. 19–24). Slaves are to be given food and work and correction but never to be treated unjustly (vv. 25–30). Great care should be taken of good slaves (vv. 31–33).

33:1 Ps 91:10–13; Mt 4:6; Lk 4:10–11.
33:8 Gn 1:14.
33:9 Ex 20:11; Dt 5:13–14.
33:10 Gn 2:7.
33:13 Wis 15:7; Jer 18:1–6; Rom 9:20–21.
33:14 Sir 42:25.
33:19 Wis 6:1–2.
33:26 Prv 29:19.

SIR

27 The yoke and harness will bow the neck;
and for a wicked slave, punishment in the stocks.
28 Force him to work that he be not idle,
29 for idleness teaches much mischief.
30 Put him to work, as is fitting for him;
and if he does not obey, load him with chains.
But never lord it over any human being,
and do nothing unjust.
31 If you have but one slave, treat him like yourself,
for you have acquired him with your life's blood;
If you have but one slave, deal with him as a brother,
for you need him as you need your life.*
32 If you mistreat him and he runs away,
33 in what direction will you look for him?

Trust in the Lord and Not in Dreams†

34 1 Empty and false are the hopes of the senseless,
and dreams give wings to fools.
2 Like one grasping at shadows or chasing the wind,
so anyone who believes in dreams.
3 What is seen in dreams is a reflection,
the likeness of a face looking at itself.
4 How can the unclean produce what is clean?
How can the false produce what is true?*
5 Divination, omens, and dreams are unreal;
what you already expect, the mind fantasizes.
6 Unless they are specially sent by the Most High,
do not fix your heart on them.
7 For dreams have led many astray,
and those who put their hope in them have perished.
8 Without such deceptions the Law will be fulfilled,
and in the mouth of the faithful is complete wisdom.

9 A much-traveled person knows many things;
and one with much experience speaks sense.
10 An inexperienced person knows little,
11 whereas with travel one adds to resourcefulness.
12 I have seen much in my travels,
and learned more than I could ever say.
13 Often I was in danger of death,
but by these experiences I was saved.
14 Living is the spirit of those who fear the Lord,
15 for their hope is in their savior.
16 Whoever fear the Lord are afraid of nothing
and are never discouraged, for he is their hope.*
17 Happy the soul that fears the Lord!
18 In whom does he trust, and who is his support?
19 The eyes of the Lord are upon those who love him;
he is their mighty shield and strong support,
A shelter from the heat, a shade from the noonday sun,
a guard against stumbling, a help against falling.*
20 He lifts up spirits, brings a sparkle to the eyes,
gives health and life and blessing.

True Worship of God†

21 Ill-gotten goods offered in sacrifice are tainted.
22 Presents from the lawless do not win God's favor.*
23 The Most High is not pleased with the gifts of the godless,
nor for their many sacrifices does he forgive their sins.
24 One who slays a son in his father's presence—
whoever offers sacrifice from the holdings of the poor.
25 The bread of charity is life itself for the needy;*
whoever withholds it is a murderer.
26 To take away a neighbor's living is to commit murder;
27 to deny a laborer wages is to shed blood.

28 If one builds up and another tears down,
what do they gain but trouble?
29 If one prays and another curses,
whose voice will God hear?

† **34:1–20** Confidence placed in dreams, divinations, and omens is false because these are devoid of reality (vv. 1–8). True confidence is founded on knowledge and experience (vv. 9–13), and above all on the fear of the Lord, with its accompanying blessings of divine assistance and protection (vv. 14–20).

34:21–31 To be acts of true religion, sacrifice and penance must be accompanied by the proper moral dispositions. To offer to God goods taken from the poor (vv. 21–27), or to practice penance without interior reform, is a mockery, worthless in the sight of God (vv. 28–31). Cf. Mt 15:4–7; Mk 7:9–13.

* **33:31** Sir 7:20–21.
34:4 Jb 14:4.
34:16 Ps 23:4; 112:7–8; Prv 3:23–24; 28:1.
34:19 Ps 33:18–19; 34:16.
34:22 Sir 35:14–15; Prv 21:27.
34:25–27 Lv 19:13; Dt 24:14–15; Tb 4:14.

30 If one again touches a corpse after bathing,
what does he gain by the purification?*
31 So one who fasts for sins,
but goes and commits them again:
Who will hear his prayer,
what is gained by mortification?

35 †[1]To keep the law is to make many
offerings;*
2 whoever observes the commandments
sacrifices a peace offering.
3 By works of charity one offers fine flour,†
4 and one who gives alms presents a sacrifice
of praise.
5 To refrain from evil pleases the Lord,
and to avoid injustice is atonement.

6 Do not appear before the Lord empty-handed,
7 for all that you offer is in fulfillment of the
precepts.*
8 The offering of the just enriches the altar:
a sweet odor before the Most High.
9 The sacrifice of the just is accepted,
never to be forgotten.

"Give to the Most High as he has given to you, generously, according to your means."
(Sir 35:12)

10 With a generous spirit pay homage to the
Lord,
and do not spare your freewill gifts.*
11 With each contribution show a cheerful
countenance,
and pay your tithes in a spirit of joy.*
12 Give to the Most High as he has given to you,
generously, according to your means.
13 For he is a God who always repays
and will give back to you sevenfold.*
14 But offer no bribes; these he does not accept!
15 Do not trust in sacrifice of the fruits of
extortion,*
For he is a God of justice,
who shows no partiality.*
16 He shows no partiality to the weak
but hears the grievance of the oppressed.†
17 He does not forsake the cry of the orphan,*
nor the widow when she pours out her
complaint.
18 Do not the tears that stream down her cheek
19 cry out against the one that causes them to
fall?
20 Those who serve God to please him are
accepted;
their petition reaches the clouds.
21 The prayer of the lowly pierces the clouds;
it does not rest till it reaches its goal;
Nor will it withdraw till the Most High
responds,
22 judges justly and affirms the right.*

God indeed will not delay,
and like a warrior, will not be still*
Till he breaks the backs of the merciless
23 and wreaks vengeance upon the nations;
Till he destroys the scepter of the proud,
and cuts off the staff of the wicked;
24 Till he requites everyone according to their
deeds,
and repays them according to their
thoughts;
25 Till he defends the cause of his people,
and makes them glad by his salvation.
26 Welcome is his mercy in time of distress
as rain clouds in time of drought.

A Prayer for God's People†

36 [1] Come to our aid, O God of the universe,
[2] and put all the nations in dread of you!
3 Raise your hand against the foreign people,
that they may see your mighty deeds.
4 As you have used us to show them your
holiness,†
so now use them to show us your glory.

---

† **35:1–26** Keeping the commandments of the law and avoiding injustice constitute sacrifice pleasing and acceptable to God (vv. 1–5). Offerings also should be made to him, cheerfully and generously; these he repays sevenfold (vv. 6–13). Extortion from widows and orphans is injustice, and God will hear their cries (vv. 14–22a). Punishing the proud and the merciless and coming to the aid of the distressed, he requites everyone according to their deeds (vv. 22b–26).

35:3 *Fine flour*, together with oil and frankincense, was a prescribed offering to God; cf. Lv 2:1–3.

35:16 Cf. Lv 19:15; Dt 1:17. The divine impartiality is paradoxical, for it is tilted toward the poor.

36:1–22 A prayer that God hasten the day for the gathering of the tribes of Israel, and Zion once more be filled with the divine glory. All the earth will then know that the Lord is the eternal God.

36:4 *Show . . . holiness*: this cultic language is used to indicate God's liberation of his people; cf. Ez 20:41; 28:25.

---

* **34:30** Nm 19:11–12; Prv 26:11; 2 Pt 2:22.
35:1–5 1 Sm 15:22; Ps 51:18–19; Is 1:11–18; Hos 6:6; Am 5:21–24.
35:7 Ex 23:15; 34:20; Dt 16:16.
35:10 Sir 7:31.
35:11 Dt 14:22; 2 Cor 9:7.
35:13 Prv 19:17; Mt 25:34–40.
35:15 Sir 34:21–23; Prv 15:8; 21:27.
35:15 Dt 10:17; 2 Chr 19:7; Jb 34:19; Wis 6:7; Acts 10:34; Rom 2:11; Gal 2:6; 1 Pt 1:17.
35:17–19 Ex 22:22.
35:22 Lk 18:7.
35:22 Is 42:13–16; 2 Pt 3:9.

5 Thus they will know, as we know,
that there is no God but you.
6 Give new signs and work new wonders;
7 show forth the splendor of your right hand
and arm.
8 Rouse your anger, pour out wrath;
9 humble the enemy, scatter the foe.*
10 Hasten the ending, appoint the time,
and let people proclaim your mighty deeds.
11 Let raging fire consume the fugitive,
and your people's oppressors meet
destruction.
12 Crush the heads of the hostile rulers
who say, "There is no one besides me."
13 Gather all the tribes of Jacob,†
16 that they may inherit the land as in days of
old.
17 Show mercy to the people called by your
name:
Israel, whom you named your firstborn.*
18 Take pity on your holy city:
Jerusalem, your dwelling place.*
19 Fill Zion with your majesty,
your temple with your glory.
20 Give evidence of your deeds of old;
fulfill the prophecies spoken in your name.
21 Reward those who have hoped in you,
and let your prophets be proved true.
22 Hear the prayer of your servants,
according to your good will toward your
people.
Thus all the ends of the earth will know
that you are the eternal God.

Choice of Associates†

23 The throat can swallow any food,
yet some foods are more agreeable than
others.
24 The palate tests delicacies put forward as
gifts,
so does a keen mind test deceitful tidbits.
25 One with a tortuous heart brings about grief,
but an experienced person can turn the
tables on him.
26 A woman will accept any man as husband,
but one woman will be preferable to
another.
27 A woman's beauty makes her husband's face
light up,
for it surpasses all else that delights the eye.*
28 And if, besides, her speech is soothing,
her husband's lot is beyond that of mortal
men.
29 A wife is her husband's richest treasure,
a help like himself and a staunch support.*
30 A vineyard with no hedge will be overrun;
and a man with no wife becomes a
homeless wanderer.
31 Who will trust an armed band
that shifts from city to city?
Or a man who has no nest,
who lodges wherever night overtakes him?*

37

1 Every friend declares friendship,
but there are friends who are friends in
name only.*
2 Is it not a sorrow unto death
when your other self becomes your enemy?
3 "Alas, my companion! Why were you created
to fill the earth with deceit?"
4 A harmful friend will look to your table,
but in time of trouble he stands aloof.
5 A good friend will fight with you against the
foe,
and against your enemies he will hold up
your shield.
6 Do not forget your comrade during the battle,
and do not neglect him when you
distribute your spoils.
7 Every counselor points out a way,
but some counsel ways of their own.
8 Watch out when one offers advice;
find out first of all what he wants.
For he also may be thinking of himself—
Why should the opportunity fall to him?
9 He may tell you how good your way will be,
and then stand by to see you impoverished.
10 Seek no advice from your father-in-law,
and from one who is envious of you, keep
your intentions hidden.

---

† **36:13** This verse marks the end of a major dislocation in the Greek text of Sirach (which is followed here) at the head of chap. 33. The verse numbers 1–13 come from the placement of these verses in Greek. Verse 13 here is the first half of a bicolon, the matching half of which is numbered in the Greek 36:16b. Thus although the numbering for vv. 14–15 is not used, none of the text is missing.

36:23–37:15 In the choice of wife, friend, or associate, experience is a discerner of character (36:23–26). Beauty and soothing speech make a woman desirable as wife (36:27–28). The good wife becomes her husband's richest treasure, his help in establishing his household (36:29–31). Good friends fight for comrades and share the spoils with them (37:5–6); false friends deceive and abandon in time of need (37:1–4). A true counselor and associate should be sought among those who keep the commandments, not among those who break them and seek their own advantage (37:7–12). In all things one should pray to God for light and follow conscience (37:13–15).

---

* **36:9** Ps 79:6; Jer 10:25.
36:17 Ex 4:22.
36:18 2 Chr 6:41; Ps 132:8, 14; Is 2:1–3; Mi 4:1–3.
36:26–28 Sir 26:13–18; Prv 12:4; 18:22; 19:14.
36:29 Gn 2:18.
36:31 Prv 27:8.
37:1 Sir 6:7–17.

11 Seek no advice from a woman about her rival,
from a coward about war,
from a merchant about business,
from a buyer about value,
from a miser about generosity,
from a cruel person about well-being,
from a worthless worker about his work,
from a seasonal laborer about the harvest,
from an idle slave about a great task—
pay no attention to any advice they give.

12 Instead, associate with a religious person,
who you know keeps the commandments;
Who is like-minded with yourself
and will grieve for you if you fall.
13 Then, too, heed your own heart's counsel;
for there is nothing you can depend on
more.
14 The heart can reveal your situation
better than seven sentinels on a tower.
15 Then with all this, pray to God
to make your steps firm in the true path.

Wisdom and Temperance

16 A word is the source of every deed;†
a thought, of every act.*
17 The root of all conduct is the heart;
18 four branches it shoots forth:
Good and evil, death and life,
and their absolute mistress is the tongue.*
19 One may be wise and benefit many,
yet appear foolish to himself.
20 One may be wise, but if his words are
rejected,
he will be deprived of all enjoyment.†
22 When one is wise to his own advantage,
the fruits of knowledge are seen in his own
person.
23 When one is wise to the advantage of people,
the fruits of knowledge are lasting.*
24 One wise for himself has full enjoyment,
and all who see him praise him.
25 The days of one's life are numbered,
but the life of Israel, days without
number.
26 One wise among the people wins a heritage
of glory,
and his name lives on and on.*

Pray It!

Healthcare Providers

When was the last time you went to the doctor? How often do you take medicine? Have you ever spent a night in a hospital? It's humbling to realize that the basic health care we take for granted is not available to millions of people in this country and throughout the world.

God gives the skill to heal to doctors, nurses, dentists, pharmacists, therapists, and medical technicians of every kind (see Sir 38:2). Their jobs often demand huge amounts of time and energy. Take a moment to remember in prayer the healthcare providers you know personally, and ask yourself if you have a vocation in the medical profession.

▶ **Sir 38:1–15**

27 My son, while you are well, govern your
appetite,†
and see that you do not allow it what is
bad for you.
28 For not everything is good for everyone,
nor is everything suited to every taste.*
29 Do not go to excess with any enjoyment,*
neither become a glutton for choice foods;
30 For sickness comes with overeating,
and gluttony brings on nausea.
31 Through lack of self-control many have died,
but the abstemious one prolongs life.

Sickness and Death

38 [1] Make friends with the doctor, for he is
essential to you;†
God has also established him in his
profession.
2 From God the doctor has wisdom,
and from the king he receives sustenance.

---

† **37:16–26** Thoughts determine action. Wisdom is the source of good and life; folly, of evil and death (vv. 16–18). If the fruits of a person's wisdom benefit himself, he may be praised in his own lifetime; if they benefit others, the praise endures after him, in their lives (vv. 19–26).

37:20 Verse 21 appears only in Greek, but not in the Hebrew, which is the basis for the translation here.

37:27–31 Temperance and self-control should govern appetite for food, which is intended not to destroy but to preserve life.

38:1–15 The profession of medicine comes from God, who makes the earth yield healing herbs and gives the physician knowledge of their power (vv. 1–8). In illness the sick should cleanse their soul from sin and petition God for help through an offering of sacrifice; the physician, too, does well to invoke God that he may understand the illness and apply the proper remedy (vv. 9–14). The sinner, in contrast, defies both his Maker and the doctor (v. 15).

* **37:16** Sir 32:19. **37:18** Prv 18:21. **37:23** Sir 39:10–11. **37:26** Sir 39:9; 44:13–16. **37:28** 1 Cor 6:12; 10:23. **37:29–31** Sir 31:13, 16–21.

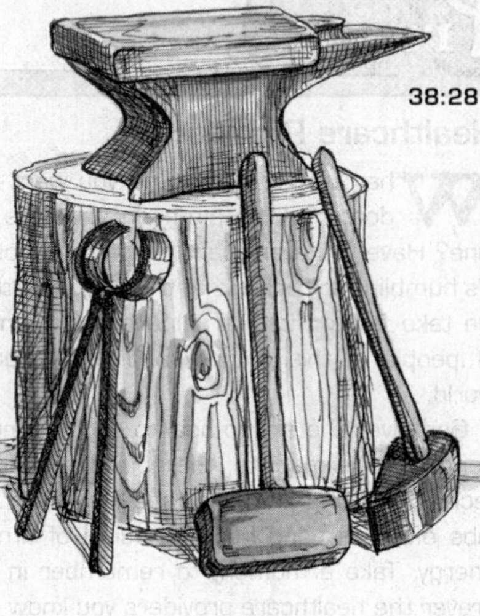

38:28

3 Knowledge makes the doctor distinguished,
and gives access to those in authority.
4 God makes the earth yield healing herbs
which the prudent should not neglect;
5 Was not the water sweetened by a twig,
so that all might learn his power?*
6 He endows people with knowledge,
to glory in his mighty works,
7 Through which the doctor eases pain,
8 and the druggist prepares his medicines.
Thus God's work continues without cease
in its efficacy on the surface of the earth.

9 My son, when you are ill, do not delay,
but pray to God, for it is he who heals.*
10 Flee wickedness and purify your hands;
cleanse your heart of every sin.
11 Offer your sweet-smelling oblation and
memorial,
a generous offering according to your
means.*
12 Then give the doctor his place
lest he leave; you need him too,
13 For there are times when recovery is in his
hands.
14 He too prays to God
That his diagnosis may be correct
and his treatment bring about a cure.
15 Whoever is a sinner before his Maker
will be defiant toward the doctor.

16 My son, shed tears for one who is dead†
with wailing and bitter lament;
As is only proper, prepare the body,
and do not absent yourself from the burial.
17 Weeping bitterly, mourning fully,
pay your tribute of sorrow, as deserved:
A day or two, to prevent gossip;
then compose yourself after your grief.
18 For grief can bring on death,
and heartache can sap one's strength.*
19 When a person is carried away, sorrow is over;
and the life of the poor one is grievous to
the heart.
20 Do not turn your thoughts to him again;
cease to recall him; think rather of the
end.*
21 Do not recall him, for there is no hope of his
return;
you do him no good, and you harm
yourself.*
22 Remember that his fate will also be yours;
for him it was yesterday, for you today.*
23 With the dead at rest, let memory cease;
be consoled, once the spirit has gone.

Vocations of the Skilled Worker and the Scribe†

24 The scribe's wisdom increases wisdom;
whoever is free from toil can become wise.
25 How can one become learned who guides the
plow,
and thrills in wielding the goad like a
lance,
Who guides the ox and urges on the bullock,
and whose every concern is for cattle?
26 His concern is to plow furrows,
and he is careful to fatten the livestock.
27 So with every engraver and designer
who, laboring night and day,
Fashions carved seals,
and whose concern is to vary the pattern.
His determination is to produce a lifelike
impression,
and he is careful to finish the work.

†

38:16–23 A period of mourning for the deceased and care for their burial are proper (vv. 16–17). But grief should not be excessive, for it cannot help the dead, who will not return, and may do harm to the living. The mourner should be realistic (vv. 18–23).

38:24–39:11 Ben Sira has a balanced view of the various vocations of skilled laborers—the farmer, engraver, smith and potter—but the profession of scribe is more excellent (38:24–34). He studies and meditates on the law of the Most High, seeks him in prayer of thanksgiving, petition and repentance for sin (39:1, 5, 7), explores the wisdom of the past and present, travels abroad to observe the conduct of many peoples, and attends rulers and great men. Through the spirit of understanding granted by God, he will show forth his wisdom to the glory of God's law, gaining renown for generations to come (39:2–4, 6–11).

*

38:5 Ex 15:25.
38:9 Is 38:1–3.
38:11 Lv 2:1–3.
38:18 Prv 12:25; 15:13; 17:22.
38:20 Sir 7:36; 18:24; 30:21.
38:21 2 Sm 12:23; Wis 2:1.
38:22 Jas 4:13–15.

28 So too the smith sitting by the anvil,
intent on the iron he forges.
The flame from the fire sears his flesh,
yet he toils away in the furnace heat.
The clang of the hammer deafens his ears;
his eyes are on the object he is shaping.
His determination is to finish the work,
and he is careful to perfect it in detail.

29 So also the potter sitting at his labor,
revolving the wheel with his feet.
He is always concerned for his products,
and turns them out in quantity.
30 With his hands he molds the clay,
and with his feet softens it.
His determination is to complete the glazing,
and he is careful to fire the kiln.

31 All these are skilled with their hands,
each one an expert at his own work;
32 Without them no city could be lived in,
and wherever they stay, they do not go
hungry.
But they are not sought out for the council of
the people,
33 nor are they prominent in the assembly.
They do not sit on the judge's bench,
nor can they understand law and justice.
They cannot expound discipline or judgment,
nor are they found among the rulers.
34 Yet they maintain the fabric of the world,
and their concern is for exercise of their
skill.

39 How different the person who devotes
himself
to the study of the law of the Most High!
1 He explores the wisdom of all the ancients
and is occupied with the prophecies;
2 He preserves the discourses of the famous,
and goes to the heart of involved sayings;
3 He seeks out the hidden meaning of proverbs,
and is busied with the enigmas found in
parables.

4 He is in attendance on the great,
and appears before rulers.
He travels among the peoples of foreign lands
to test what is good and evil among people.
5 His care is to rise early
to seek the Lord his Maker,
to petition the Most High,
To open his mouth in prayer,
to ask pardon for his sins.

6 If it pleases the Lord Almighty,
he will be filled with the spirit of
understanding;
He will pour forth his words of wisdom
and in prayer give praise to the Lord.
7 He will direct his knowledge and his counsel,
as he meditates upon God's mysteries.
8 He will show the wisdom of what he has
learned
and glory in the Law of the Lord's
covenant.

9 Many will praise his understanding;
his name can never be blotted out;
Unfading will be his memory,
through all generations his name will live;*
10 Peoples will speak of his wisdom,
and the assembly will declare his praise.
11 While he lives he is one out of a thousand,
and when he dies he leaves a good name.

Praise of God the Creator†

12 Once more I will set forth my theme
to shine like the moon in its fullness!
13 Listen to me, my faithful children: open up
your petals,
like roses planted near running waters;
14 Send up the sweet odor of incense,
break forth in blossoms like the lily.
Raise your voices in a chorus of praise;
bless the Lord for all his works!
15 Proclaim the greatness of his name,
loudly sing his praises,
With music on the harp and all stringed
instruments;
sing out with joy as you proclaim:

16 The works of God are all of them good;
he supplies for every need in its own time.*
17 At his word the waters become still as in a
flask;
he had but to speak and the reservoirs were
made.*
18 He has but to command and his will is done;
nothing can limit his saving action.

† **39:12–35** Ben Sira invites his disciples to join him in joyfully proclaiming his favorite theme: The works of God are all good; God supplies for every need in its own time (vv. 12–16, 32–35). The sage describes God's omniscience, supreme power and wisdom, whereby all created things, good in themselves, are ever present to him, obey him, and fulfill their intended purpose (vv. 17–21), bringing blessing to the virtuous, but evil and punishment to the wicked who misuse them (vv. 22–31). Cf. similar hymns of praise, 36:1–22; 42:15–43:33.

* **39:9** Sir 37:26; 44:14. **39:16** Sir 39:33; Gn 1:29–31; Eccl 3:11. **39:17** Gn 1:6–10; Ex 14:21–22; Jos 3:15–16.

SIR

19 The works of all humankind are present to him;
nothing is hidden from his eyes.*
20 His gaze spans all the ages:
is there any limit to his saving action?
To him, nothing is small or insignificant,
and nothing too wonderful or hard for him.
21 No cause then to say: "What is the purpose of this?"
Everything is chosen to satisfy a need.
22 His blessing overflows like the Nile;
like the Euphrates it enriches the surface of the earth.
23 Even so, his wrath dispossesses the nations
and turns fertile land into a salt marsh.*
24 For the virtuous his paths are level,
to the haughty they are clogged with stones.
25 Good things for the good he provided from the beginning,
but for the wicked good things and bad.
26 Chief of all needs for human life
are water and fire, iron and salt,
The heart of the wheat, milk and honey,
the blood of the grape, and oil, and clothing.*
27 For the good all these are good,
but for the wicked they turn out evil.

28 There are stormwinds created to punish;
in their fury they can dislodge mountains.
In a time of destruction they hurl their force
and calm the anger of their Maker.
29 Fire and hail, famine and disease:
these too were created for punishment.
30 Ravenous beasts, scorpions, vipers,
and the avenging sword to exterminate the wicked:
All these were created to meet a need,
and are kept in his storehouse for the proper time.
31 When he commands them, they rejoice,
in their assigned tasks they do not disobey his command.

32 That is why from the first I took my stand,
and wrote down as my theme:
33 The works of God are all of them good;
he supplies for every need in its own time.*
34 There is no cause then to say: "This is not as good as that";
for each shows its worth at the proper time.
35 So now with full heart and voice proclaim
and bless his name!

Joys and Miseries of Life

40 1 A great anxiety has God allotted,†
and a heavy yoke, to the children of Adam,*
From the day they leave their mother's womb
until the day they return to the mother of all the living.†
2 Troubled thoughts and fear of heart are theirs
and anxious foreboding until death.
3 Whether one sits on a lofty throne
or grovels in dust and ashes,
4 Whether one wears a splendid crown
or is clothed in the coarsest of garments—
5 There is wrath and envy, trouble and dread,
terror of death, fury and strife.
Even when one lies on his bed to rest,
his cares disturb his sleep at night.
6 So short is his rest it seems like none,
till in his dreams he struggles as he did by day,
Troubled by the visions of his mind,
like a fugitive fleeing from the pursuer.
7 As he reaches safety, he wakes up,
astonished that there was nothing to fear.
8 To all flesh, human being and beast,
but for sinners seven times more,
9 Come plague and bloodshed, fiery heat and drought,
plunder and ruin, famine and death.*
10 For the wicked evil was created,
and because of them destruction hastens.

11 All that is of earth returns to earth,
and what is from above returns above.†
12 All that comes from bribes or injustice will be wiped out,
but loyalty remains forever.
13 Wealth from injustice is like a flooding wadi,
like a mighty stream with lightning and thunder,

---

† **40:1–17** The former idyllic description of the universe is contrasted with the picture of the evils afflicting humanity. Every person, high or low, is burdened from birth to death with fears, anxieties, and troubles, by day and often by night, the time appointed for rest (vv. 1–7). For sinners, the suffering is much greater (vv. 8–10). What they gained by violence and injustice is quickly destroyed; but righteousness will prevail (vv. 14–17).

40:1 *Mother of all the living*: the earth from which human beings were taken. Cf. Gn 2:7; 3:19–20; Jb 1:21; Ps 139:15.

40:11 *All that is of earth . . . returns above*: a reference to bodily mortality and to the divine origin of life. Cf. 41:10; Gn 2:7; 3:19; Jb 34:14–15; Ps 104:29–30; 146:4; Eccl 12:7. The Greek and the Latin render the second half of the verse: "all waters shall return to the sea."

---

* **39:19** Sir 15:18–19; 42:18–20. **39:23** Gn 13:10; 19:24–28; Dt 29:22; Jos 1:2–6; Ps 107:34; Wis 10:7. **39:26** Sir 29:21. **39:33** Sir 39:16; Gn 1:29–31; Eccl 3:11. **40:1** Gn 3:17–19; Jb 7:1; 14:1–2; Eccl 2:23. **40:9** Sir 39:28–31.

14 Which, in its rising, rolls along the stones,
but suddenly, once and for all, comes to an end.*
15 The offshoot of violence will not flourish,
for the root of the godless is on sheer rock.
16 They are like reeds on riverbanks,
withered before all other plants;
17 But goodness, like eternity, will never be cut off,
and righteousness endures forever.

18 Wealth or wages can make life sweet,†
but better than either, finding a treasure.
19 A child or a city will preserve one's name,
but better than either, finding wisdom.
Cattle and orchards make a person flourish;
but better than either, a devoted wife.*
20 Wine and strong drink delight the soul,
but better than either, love of friends.*
21 Flute and harp offer sweet melody,
but better than either, a pure tongue.
22 Grace and beauty delight the eye,
but better than either, the produce of the field.
23 A friend and a neighbor are timely guides,
but better than either, a sensible wife.
24 Relatives and helpers for times of stress;
but better than either, charity that rescues.
25 Gold and silver make one's way secure,
but better than either, sound judgment.
26 Wealth and vigor make the heart exult,
but better than either, fear of God.
In the fear of the Lord there is no want;
whoever has it need seek no other support.
27 The fear of God is a paradise of blessings;
its canopy is over all that is glorious.*

28 My son, do not live the life of a beggar;†
better to die than to beg.
29 When one has to look to a stranger's table,
life is not worth living.
The delicacies offered bring revulsion of spirit,
and to the intelligent, inward torture.*
30 In the mouth of the shameless begging is sweet,
but within him it burns like fire.

41 [1]O death! How bitter is the thought of you†
for the one at peace in his home,
For the one who is serene and always successful,
who can still enjoy life's pleasures.
2 O death! How welcome is your sentence
to the weak, failing in strength,
Stumbling and tripping on everything,
with sight gone and hope lost.*
3 Do not fear death's decree for you;
remember, it embraces those before you and those to come.*
4 This decree for all flesh is from God;
why then should you reject a law of the Most High?
Whether one has lived a thousand years, a hundred, or ten,
in Sheol there are no arguments about life.

5 The children of sinners are a reprobate line,*
and witless offspring are in the homes of the wicked.
6 The inheritance of children of sinners will perish,
and on their offspring will be perpetual disgrace.
7 Children curse their wicked father,
for they suffer disgrace because of him.
8 Woe to you, O wicked people,
who forsake the Law of the Most High.
9 If you have children, calamity will be theirs;
and if you beget them, it will be only for groaning.
When you stumble, there is lasting joy;
and when you die, you become a curse.
10 All that is nought returns to nought,
so too the godless—from void to void.*

11 The human body is a fleeting thing,
but a virtuous name will never be annihilated.*
12 Have respect for your name, for it will stand by you
more than thousands of precious treasures.*
13 The good things of life last a number of days,
but a good name, for days without number.

†

40:18–27 Of the many treasures making life sweet, such as children, friends, music, vigor, the best are called true married love, wisdom, and above all, fear of God; cf. 25:6–11.

40:28–30 Among the Jews, begging was considered degrading to human dignity; it was agreeable only to the shameless, who had lost their sense of honor. Cf. 29:22–23.

41:1–13 Whether death seems bitter to one who enjoys peace, success, and pleasure, or welcome to one who is weak and in despair, it comes to all and must be accepted as the will of God (vv. 1–4). The human body passes away (v. 11). Sinners as well as their offspring pass away as if they had never been (vv. 5–10). Only the good name of the virtuous endures (vv. 11–13).

*

40:14 Sir 23:25–26; Wis 4:3–6.
40:19 Prv 18:22; 19:14.
40:20 Ps 104:15.
40:27 Is 4:5–6.
40:29 Sir 29:24.
41:2 Sir 30:17.
41:3 Sir 38:20–22.
41:5–10 Sir 3:9–11; Wis 3:16–19.
41:10 Sir 40:11; Wis 4:19.
41:11 Prv 10:7.
41:12 Prv 22:1; Eccl 7:1.

SIR

Live It!

Shame on You!

"You ought to be ashamed of yourself!" How many times do we hear that while growing up? Or the simpler, more direct version: "Shame on you!" We've probably heard these and similar expressions often, but what exactly is the point of shame?

Although it is true that sometimes false shaming can be harmful to our growth and development, there are other times when we really should be ashamed of ourselves. We did something that we should not have done. Perhaps we hurt another person or broke a promise or brought dishonor to our family. These are all valid reasons for feeling ashamed, and it is often someone else who brings us to this realization. Upon realizing our mistakes, though, we should never let this sense of shame, or guilt, weigh us down. Rather, we must learn from our missteps, develop a more informed conscience, and make better decisions when faced with similar situations in the future.

Ben Sira knew human nature well and gave advice about true and false shame. Think about times when you have felt ashamed of something. What caused you to feel ashamed? What role does your conscience play in feeling a sense of shame? What do you do with that sense of shame? Think about the role shame plays in the story of Adam and Eve (see Genesis, chapters 2–3) and the story of David and Bathsheba (see 2 Samuel, chapters 11–12).

▶ Sir 41:14—42:8

True and False Shame†

14b Hidden wisdom and concealed treasure,
of what value is either?
15 Better is the person who hides his folly
than the one who hides his wisdom.
14a My children, listen to instruction about
shame;
16a judge of disgrace according to my rules,
16b Not every kind of shame is shameful,
nor is every kind of disgrace to be
recognized.
17 Before father and mother be ashamed of
immorality,
before prince and ruler, of falsehood;
18 Before master and mistress, of deceit;
before the public assembly, of crime;
Before associate and friend, of disloyalty,
19 and in the place where you settle, of theft.
Be ashamed of breaking an oath or a
covenant,
and of stretching your elbow at dinner;
Of refusing to give when asked,
21 of rebuffing your own relatives;
Of defrauding another of his appointed share,
20a of failing to return a greeting;
21c Of gazing at a man's wife,
20b of entertaining thoughts about another
woman;*
22 Of trifling with a servant girl you have,
of violating her bed;
Of using harsh words with friends,
of following up your gifts with insults;*

42 [1]Of repeating what you hear,
of betraying any secret.*
Be ashamed of the right things,
and you will find favor in the sight of all.

But of these things do not be ashamed,
lest you sin to save face:*
2 Of the Law of the Most High and his precepts,
or of justice that acquits the ungodly;
3 Of sharing the expenses of a business or a
journey,
of dividing an inheritance or property;
4 Of accuracy of scales and balances,
of tested measures and weights;*
Of acquiring much or little,
5 of bargaining in dealing with a merchant;
Of constant training of children,
of beating the sides of a wicked servant;*
6 Of a seal to keep a foolish wife at home,
of a key where there are many hands;
7 Of numbering every deposit,
of recording all that is taken in and given
out;
8 Of chastisement for the silly and the foolish,

† **41:14–42:8** Ben Sira illustrates the subject of true and false shame with numerous and detailed examples of wrongdoing (41:14–22) and virtue (42:1–8), following the norm of the commandments.

* **41:20** Sir 9:8; Mt 5:28. **41:22** Sir 18:15; 20:14. **42:1** Sir 27:16. **42:1** Prv 24:23; Jas 2:1. **42:4** Lv 19:35; Prv 11:1; 16:11; 20:10. **42:5** Sir 30:1–13; 33:25–33.

for the aged and infirm answering for
wanton conduct.
Thus you will be truly refined
and recognized by all as discreet.

A Father's Care for His Daughter†

9 A daughter is a treasure that keeps her father
wakeful,
and worry over her drives away sleep:*
Lest in her youth she remain unmarried,
or when she is married, lest she be
childless;
10 While unmarried, lest she be defiled,
or in her husband's house, lest she prove
unfaithful;
Lest she become pregnant in her father's
house,
or be sterile in that of her husband.
11 My son, keep a close watch on your daughter,
lest she make you a laughingstock for your
enemies,
A byword in the city and the assembly of the
people,
an object of derision in public gatherings.*
See that there is no lattice in her room,
or spot that overlooks the approaches to
the house.*
12 Do not let her reveal her beauty to any male,*
or spend her time with married women;
13 For just as moths come from garments,
so a woman's wickedness comes from a
woman.
14 Better a man's harshness than a woman's
indulgence,
a frightened daughter than any disgrace.

The Works of God in Nature†

15 Now will I recall God's works;
what I have seen, I will describe.
By the LORD's word his works were brought
into being;
he accepts the one who does his will.*
16 As the shining sun is clear to all,
so the glory of the LORD fills all his works;
17 Yet even God's holy ones must fail
in recounting the wonders of the LORD,
Though God has given his hosts the strength
to stand firm before his glory.

Live It!

The Sexism of Ben Sira

Let's just get this right out in the open: Ben Sira was sexist by today's standards. As you read Ben Sira 42:9–14, you probably think it's a curse to have a daughter! Verse 14 says, "Better a man's harshness than a woman's indulgence, / and a frightened daughter than any disgrace." Wow, with an attitude like that, Ben Sira wouldn't be welcomed by many modern people.

Once again, we have to remember that the Bible was written by human beings and reflects their cultural standards. Ben Sira's attitude was commonly accepted in his culture. But the cultural standards in the Bible don't always reflect God's truth. That's why we need the help of the larger Church community to properly interpret the Bible. Today, the Church teaches that women and men are to be treated with equal dignity and respect. Let's work together to continue making that vision a reality.

▶ **Sir 42:9–14**

18 He searches out the abyss and penetrates the
heart;
their secrets he understands.
For the Most High possesses all knowledge,
and sees from of old the things that are to
come.
19 He makes known the past and the future,
and reveals the deepest secrets.
20 He lacks no understanding;
no single thing escapes him.*
21 He regulates the mighty deeds of his wisdom;
he is from all eternity one and the same,
With nothing added, nothing taken away;
no need of a counselor for him!*
22 How beautiful are all his works,

† **42:9–14** Ben Sira considers a daughter to be a source of anxiety to her father, lest she fail to marry, or be defiled, or lest, marrying, she be childless, prove unfaithful, or find herself sterile (vv. 9–10). He is advised to keep a close watch on her and on her companions, lest he suffer on her account among the people (vv. 11–12). The exhortations, which take into account only a father's concern, are quite unflattering to young women. The concluding statements (vv. 13–14) show the limitations of Ben Sira's perspective in the male-oriented society of his day.

42:15–43:33 These verses comprise another hymn; cf. 16:24–18:14. In them Ben Sira contemplates God's power, beauty, and goodness as manifested in the mighty work of creating and preserving the universe (42:15–17, 22–25; 43:1–26), his omniscience (42:18–20), perfect wisdom and eternity (42:21). The conclusion is a fervent hymn of praise (43:27–31).

42:9 Sir 7:24–25.
42:11 Dt 22:20–21.
42:12–13 Sir 9:1–9.
42:15 Ps 77:12–13.
42:20 Sir 39:19; Wis 1:6–9.
42:21 Wis 9:13; Is 40:13; Rom 11:34; 1 Cor 2:11.

delightful to gaze upon and a joy to behold!
23 Everything lives and abides forever;
and to meet each need all things are preserved.
24 All of them differ, one from another,
yet none of them has he made in vain;
25 For each in turn, as it comes, is good;
can one ever see enough of their splendor?*

43

1 The beauty of the celestial height and the pure firmament,*
heaven itself manifests its glory.
2 The sun at its rising shines at its fullest,
a wonderful instrument, the work of the Most High!
3 At noon it scorches the earth,
and who can bear its fiery heat?
4 Like a blazing furnace of solid metal,
the sun's rays set the mountains aflame;
Its fiery tongue consumes the world;
the eyes are burned by its fire.
5 Great indeed is the LORD who made it,
at whose orders it urges on its steeds.
6 It is the moon that marks the changing seasons,
governing the times, their lasting sign.*
7 By it we know the sacred seasons and pilgrimage feasts,
a light which wanes in its course:
8 The new moon like its name† renews itself;
how wondrous it is when it changes:
A military signal for the waterskins on high,
it paves the firmament with its brilliance,
9 The beauty of the heavens and the glory of the stars,
a shining ornament in the heights of God.*
10 By the LORD's command the moon keeps its appointed place,
and does not fade as the stars keep watch.
11 Behold the rainbow! Then bless its Maker,
for majestic indeed is its splendor;*
12 It spans the heavens with its glory,
the hand of God has stretched it out in power.
13 His rebuke marks out the path for the hail,
and makes the flashes of his judgment shine forth.
14 For his own purposes he opens the storehouse
and makes the rain clouds fly like vultures.
15 His might gives the clouds their strength,
and breaks off the hailstones.
16 The thunder of his voice makes the earth writhe;
by his power he shakes the mountains.
17 A word from him drives on the south wind,
whirlwind, hurricane, and stormwind.
He makes the snow fly like birds;
it settles down like swarms of locusts.
18 Its shining whiteness blinds the eyes,
the mind marvels at its steady fall.
19 He scatters frost like salt;
it shines like blossoms on the thornbush.
20 He sends cold northern blasts
that harden the ponds like solid ground,
Spreads a crust over every body of water,
and clothes each pool with a coat of armor.
21 When mountain growth is scorched by heat,
and flowering plains as by fire,
22 The dripping clouds restore them all,
and the scattered dew enriches the parched land.
23 His is the plan that calms the deep,
and plants the islands in the sea.
24 Those who go down to the sea recount its extent,
and when we hear them we are thunderstruck;*
25 In it are his creatures, stupendous, amazing,
all kinds of life, and the monsters of the deep.
26 For him each messenger succeeds,
and at his bidding accomplishes his will.*
27 More than this we need not add;
let the last word be, he is the all!†
28 Let us praise him the more, since we cannot fathom him,
for greater is he than all his works;
29 Awesome indeed is the LORD,
and wonderful his power.
30 Lift up your voices to glorify the LORD
as much as you can, for there is still more.
Extol him with renewed strength,
do not grow weary, for you cannot fathom him.
31 For who has seen him and can describe him?
Who can praise him as he is?*
32 Beyond these, many things lie hidden;
only a few of his works have I seen.
33 It is the LORD who has made all things;
to those who fear him he gives wisdom.*

†

43:8 *Like its name*: there is a play in the Hebrew text on the words for moon and renewal. *Waterskins*: clouds as source of rain.

43:27 *The all*: the perfections reflected in creation are found in a transcendent way in God, who alone is their source.

*

42:25 Sir 33:15.
43:1–12 Ps 19:2–5.
43:6 Lv 23:5; Nm 28:11–14; Ps 81:4–6.
43:9 Ps 8:4.
43:11 Gn 9:13.
43:24–25 Ps 104:25–26.
43:26 Ps 33:6.
43:31 Ps 106:2.
43:33 Sir 1:10.

Praise of Israel's Great Ancestors†

44 [1] I will now praise the godly,
our ancestors, in their own time,†
2 The abounding glory of the Most High's portion,
his own part, since the days of old.*
3 Subduers of the land in kingly fashion,
renowned for their might,
Counselors in their prudence,
seers of all things in prophecy,*
4 Resolute princes of the flock,
lawgivers and their rules,
Sages skilled in composition,
authors of sharp proverbs,
5 Composers of melodious psalms,
writers of lyric poems;
6 Stalwart, solidly established,
at peace in their own estates—
7 All these were glorious in their time,
illustrious in their day.
8 Some of them left behind a name
so that people recount their praises.
9 Of others no memory remains,
for when they perished, they perished,
As if they had never lived,
they and their children after them.
10 Yet these also were godly;
their virtues have not been forgotten.
11 Their wealth remains in their families,
their heritage with their descendants.
12 Through God's covenant their family endures,
and their offspring for their sake.
13 And for all time their progeny will endure,
their glory will never be blotted out;
14 Their bodies are buried in peace,
but their name lives on and on.*
15 At gatherings their wisdom is retold,
and the assembly proclaims their praises.

The Early Ancestors

16 [ENOCH† walked with the LORD and was taken,*
that succeeding generations might learn by his example.]
17 NOAH, found just and perfect,
renewed the race in the time of devastation.*

Live It!

Heroes

Who are your heroes? Maybe they include a teacher, a coach, a friend, or a parent. What sets them apart and makes them people you look up to? Their accomplishments? a cause they represent? or a personal trait that only someone who knows them personally would be aware of?

The kind of people we look to as heroes says a lot about us. If our heroes are kind and generous, then maybe we value kindness and generosity. If our heroes are wealthy, perhaps we desire wealth.

Read the last section of Ben Sira, starting with chapter 44, which honors many Old Testament heroes. Ben Sira considered them heroes because their hearts were fixed on the Lord (see 49:3). What an awesome way to describe heroes!

- Whom do you know who has his or her heart fixed on the Lord?
- What does your choice of heroes say about your dreams and values?

Ben Sira, chapters 44–49

Because of his worth there were survivors,
and with a sign to him the deluge ended.
18 A lasting covenant was made with him,
that never again would all flesh be destroyed.
19 ABRAHAM, father of many peoples,
kept his glory without stain:*

---

† **44:1–50:24** As in the previous section God's glory shone forth in the works of nature, so in these chapters it is revealed through the history of God's people as seen in the lives of their ancestors, prophets, priests, and rulers. The example of these great people, whose virtues are recalled here, constitutes a high point of Ben Sira's teaching.

44:1–15 The reader is here introduced to those people of Israel, later mentioned by name, who through various achievements and beneficial social activities have acquired great renown (vv. 1–8, 14–15); and also to those who, though forgotten, endure through the fruit of their virtues and through their families because of God's covenant with them (vv. 9–15).

44:16 *Enoch*: because of his friendship with God and his unusual disappearance from the earth, this prophet's renown was great among the chosen people, particularly in the two centuries just before the coming of Christ; cf. Gn 5:21–24; Heb 11:5. The present verse is an expansion of the original text; cf. 49:14.

---

* **44:2** Dt 32:8–9. **44:3** Sir 39:1. **44:14** Wis 3:2–3. **44:16** Sir 49:14; Gn 5:18–24; Heb 11:5. **44:17** Gn 6:8–9:29; Heb 11:7. **44:19** Gn 12:1–25:10; Rom 4:3; Gal 3:6; Heb 11:8–19; Jas 2:23.

20 He observed the Most High's command,
and entered into a covenant with him;
In his own flesh he incised the ordinance,†
and when tested was found loyal.*
21 For this reason, God promised him with an oath
to bless the nations through his descendants,
To make him numerous as grains of dust,
and to exalt his posterity like the stars,
Giving them an inheritance from sea to sea,
and from the River† to the ends of the earth.

22 For Isaac, too, he renewed the same promise
because of Abraham, his father.
The covenant with all his forebears was confirmed,
23 and the blessing rested upon the head of Israel.*
God acknowledged him as the firstborn,
and gave him his inheritance.
He fixed the boundaries for his tribes
and their division into twelve.

Praise of Moses, Aaron, and Phinehas

45 1 From him came the man†
who would win the favor of all the living:*
Dear to God and human beings,
Moses, whose memory is a blessing.
2 God made him like the angels in honor,
and strengthened him with fearful powers.*
3 At his words God performed signs
and sustained him in the king's presence.
He gave him the commandments for his people,
and revealed to him his glory.*
4 Because of his trustworthiness and meekness
God selected him from all flesh;*
5 He let him hear his voice,
and led him into the cloud,
Where he handed over the commandments,
the law of life and understanding,†
That he might teach his precepts to Jacob,
his judgments and decrees to Israel.

6 He also raised up, like Moses in holiness,†
his brother Aaron, of the tribe of Levi.*
7 He made his office perpetual
and bestowed on him priesthood for his people;
He established him in honor
and crowned him with lofty majesty.
8 He clothed him in splendid garments,
and adorned him with glorious vestments:
Breeches, tunic, and robe
9 with pomegranates at the hem
And a rustle of bells round about,
whose pleasing sound at each step
Would make him heard within the sanctuary,
a reminder for the people;
10 The sacred vestments of gold, violet,
and crimson, worked with embroidery;
The breastpiece for decision, the ephod and cincture
11 with scarlet yarn, the work of the weaver;
Precious stones with seal engravings
in golden settings, the work of the jeweler,
To commemorate in incised letters
each of the tribes of Israel;
12 On his turban a diadem of gold,
its plate engraved with the sacred inscription—
Majestic, glorious, renowned for splendor,
a delight to the eyes, supremely beautiful.
13 Before him, no one had been adorned with these,
nor may they ever be worn by any other
Except his sons and them alone,
generation after generation, for all time.
14 His grain offering is wholly burnt
as an established offering twice each day;
15 For Moses ordained him
and anointed him with the holy oil,
In a lasting covenant with him and his family,
as permanent as the heavens,
That he should serve God in the priesthood
and bless the people in his name.
16 He chose him from all the living
to sacrifice burnt offerings and choice portions,

44:20 *In his own flesh . . . ordinance*: the covenant of circumcision; cf. Gn 17:10–14. *And when tested . . . loyal*: Abraham's willingness to sacrifice his son Isaac at the Lord's command; cf. Gn 22:1–12.

44:21 *The River*: the Euphrates; cf. Gn 2:14.

44:23(end)–45:5 Moses manifested God's power through marvels (vv. 1–3), God's authority through the commandments and the Law (v. 5), and God's mercy through the intimacy granted him by the Lord for his own faithfulness and meekness (v. 4).

45:5 On God's intimacy with Moses, see Ex 33:11; Nm 12:8; Dt 34:10.

45:6–25 Ben Sira here expresses his reverence and esteem for the priesthood of the old covenant. He recalls God's choice of Aaron and his sons for this sublime office (vv. 6–7), and describes in detail the beauty of the high priest's vestments (vv. 8–13). He relates the ordination of Aaron at the hands of Moses (v. 15), and describes the priestly functions, namely, offering sacrifice to God (v. 16), and blessing (v. 15), teaching, governing, and judging the people (v. 17); the inheritance of the high priest (vv. 20–22); the punishment of those who were jealous of Aaron (vv. 18–19); and the confirmation of the covenant of the priesthood with Aaron's descendants through Phinehas (vv. 23–25).

44:20 Gn 17:10–14; 22:1–12.
44:22–23 Gn 26:3–5, 24; 27:28–29; 28:13–15.
45:1 Ex 2:2; 11:3; 33:11; Nm 12:7.
45:2–5 Ex 7–Dt 34.
45:3 Ex 7:1–7; 20:2–17; Dt 5:6–21.
45:4 Nm 12:3, 7.
45:6–22 Ex 28–29; Wis 18:24.

To burn incense, sweet odor as a memorial,
and to atone for the people of Israel.
17 He gave to him the laws,
and authority to prescribe and to judge:
To teach precepts to the people,
and judgments to the Israelites.
18 Strangers rose in anger against him,
grew jealous of him in the desert—
The followers of Dathan and Abiram,
and the band of Korah in their defiance.*
19 When the LORD saw this he became angry,
and destroyed them in his burning wrath.
He brought against them a marvel,
and consumed them in flaming fire.
20 Then he increased the glory of Aaron*
and bestowed upon him his inheritance:
The sacred offerings he allotted to him,
with the showbread† as his portion;
21 The oblations of the LORD are his food,
a gift to him and his descendants.
22 But he holds no land among the people
nor shares with them their heritage;
For the LORD himself is his portion and inheritance
among the Israelites.

23 PHINEHAS too, the son of Eleazar,
was the courageous third of his line
When, zealous for the God of all,
he met the crisis of his people*
And, at the prompting of his noble heart,
atoned for the children of Israel.
24 Therefore, on him also God conferred the right,
in a covenant of friendship, to provide for the sanctuary,
So that he and his descendants
should possess the high priesthood forever.
25 For even his covenant with David,
the son of Jesse of the tribe of Judah,
Was an individual heritage through one son alone;*
but the heritage of Aaron is for all his descendants.

So now bless† the LORD
who has crowned you with glory!
26 May he grant you wisdom of heart
to govern his people in justice,
Lest the benefits you confer should be forgotten,
or your authority, throughout all time.

Joshua, Caleb, the Judges, and Samuel

46 1 Valiant warrior was JOSHUA,† son of Nun,
aide to Moses in the prophetic office,
Formed to be, as his name implies,
the great savior of God's chosen ones,
To punish the enemy
and to give to Israel their heritage.*
2 What glory was his when he raised his hand,
to brandish his sword against the city!*
3 Who could withstand him
when he fought the battles of the LORD?†
4 Was it not by that same hand the sun stopped,
so that one day became two?*
5 He called upon the Most High God
when his enemies beset him on all sides,
And God Most High answered him
with hailstones of tremendous power,
6 That rained down upon the hostile army
till on the slope he destroyed the foe;
That all the doomed nations might know
the LORD was watching over his people's battles.
He was indeed a devoted follower of God
7 and showed himself loyal in Moses' lifetime.
He and CALEB,† son of Jephunneh,
when they opposed the rebel assembly,
Averted God's anger from the people
and suppressed the wicked complaint.*
8 Because of this, these two alone were spared
from the six hundred thousand infantry,
To lead the people into their heritage,
the land flowing with milk and honey.*
9 The strength God gave to Caleb
remained with him even in old age
Till he won his way onto the summits of the land;
his family too received a heritage,*
10 That all the offspring of Jacob might know
how good it is to be a devoted follower of the LORD.

† **45:20** *Showbread*: cf. note on Ex 25:29–30.

45:25–26 *So now bless*: Ben Sira addresses the whole line of high priests, especially Simon II; cf. 50:1.

46:1–6 *Joshua*: whose name means "the Lord is savior" (v. 1), was the instrument through which God delivered his people in marvelous ways (vv. 2–6) by destroying their enemies, whose land he gave to the Israelites as a heritage (v. 1).

46:3 *The battles of the Lord*: cf. Jos 6–11.

46:7–10 *Caleb*: with Joshua he advised Moses to enter Canaan, despite the counsel of their companion scouts and the rebellion of the people. He led the next generation of Israelites into the promised land. He received a portion of land which he himself had conquered; cf. Jos 15:13–14.

* **45:18** Nm 16:1–35.
45:20–21 Nm 18:11–24; Dt 10:9.
45:23 Nm 25:7–13; 1 Mc 2:26, 54; Ps 106:30–31.
45:25 2 Sm 7:12–16.
46:1 Ex 17:9; Nm 27:18–23; Dt 34:9; Jos 1:1–9.
46:2 Jos 8:18–19.
46:4 Jos 10:12–13.
46:7 Nm 13:30; 14:1–3.
46:8 Nm 14:22–38.
46:9 Jos 14:6–13; 15:13.

11 The JUDGES,† each one of them,
whose hearts were not deceived,
Who did not abandon God—
may their memory be ever blessed!*
12 May their bones flourish with new life where they lie,
and their names receive fresh luster in their children!
13 Beloved of his people, dear to his Maker,
pledged in a vow from his mother's womb,
As one consecrated to the LORD in the prophetic office,
was SAMUEL, the judge who offered sacrifice.
At God's word he established the kingdom
and anointed princes to rule the people.*
14 By the law of the LORD he judged the congregation,
and visited the encampments of Jacob.
15 As a trustworthy prophet he was sought out
and his words proved him to be a true seer.
16 He, too, called upon the mighty Lord
when his enemies pressed him on every side,
and offered up a suckling lamb.*
17 Then the LORD thundered from heaven,
and the tremendous roar of his voice was heard.*
18 He brought low the rulers of the enemy
and destroyed all the lords of the Philistines.
19 When Samuel neared the end of life,
he testified before the LORD and his anointed prince,
"No bribe or secret gift have I taken from anyone!"
and no one could accuse him.*
20 Even after death his guidance was sought;
he made known to the king his fate.
From the grave he spoke in prophecy
to put an end to wickedness.*

Nathan, David, and Solomon

47 1 After him came NATHAN†
who served in David's presence.*
2 Like the choice fat of sacred offerings,
so was DAVID in Israel.*
3 He played with lions as though they were young goats,
and with bears, like lambs of the flock.*
4 As a youth he struck down the giant
and wiped out the people's disgrace;
His hand let fly the slingstone
that shattered the pride of Goliath.*
5 For he had called upon the Most High God,
who gave strength to his right arm
To defeat the skilled warrior
and establish the might of his people.
6 Therefore the women sang his praises
and honored him for "the tens of thousands."
When he received the royal crown, he battled*
7 and subdued the enemy on every side.
He campaigned against the hostile Philistines
and shattered their power till our own day.*
8 With his every deed he offered thanks
to God Most High, in words of praise.
With his whole heart he loved his Maker
9 and daily had his praises sung;
10 He added beauty to the feasts
and solemnized the seasons of each year
9b With string music before the altar,
providing sweet melody for the psalms*
10b So that when the Holy Name was praised,
before daybreak the sanctuary would resound.
11 The LORD forgave him his sins
and exalted his strength forever;
He conferred on him the rights of royalty
and established his throne in Israel.*
12 Because of his merits he had as successor†
a wise son, who lived in security:*
13 SOLOMON reigned during an era of peace,
for God brought rest to all his borders.
He built a house to the name of God,
and established a lasting sanctuary.*
14 How wise you were when you were young,
overflowing with instruction, like the Nile in flood!*
15 Your understanding covered the whole earth,
and, like a sea, filled it with knowledge.
16 Your fame reached distant coasts,
and you were beloved for your peaceful reign.

---

† **46:11–20** Of the judges praised and blessed for their fidelity to God in opposing idolatry, Samuel was the greatest (vv. 11–13, 19). He was judge, prophet, and priest. Through his sacrificial offering he obtained victory over the Philistines. He established the kingdom, anointed kings (vv. 13–18), and even after his death foretold the king's fate (v. 20).

47:1–11 An idealized portrait of David; cf. 1 Chronicles.

47:12–24 The standard view of Solomon is echoed by Ben Sira, but he affirms the divine promise (v. 22) to David's line.

* **46:11** Jgs 1:1–16:31. **46:13** 1 Sm 1:10–20; 8:4–10:1; 16:12–13. **46:16** 1 Sm 7:9. **46:17** 1 Sm 7:10–13. **46:19** 1 Sm 12:3. **46:20** 1 Sm 28:14–19. **47:1** 2 Sm 7:2–17. **47:2** 1 Sm 16:11–13. **47:3** 1 Sm 17:34–36. **47:4** 1 Sm 17:49. **47:6** 1 Sm 18:7. **47:7** 2 Sm 5:6–25. **47:9** 1 Chr 16:4–37; 23:5; 25:1–7. **47:11** 2 Sm 12:13; 7:12–16. **47:12** 1 Kgs 2:12. **47:13** 1 Kgs 5:1, 5; 6:2–38. **47:14–18** 1 Kgs 5:9–14; 10:14–29.

17 With song and proverb and riddle,
and with your answers, you astounded the nations.
18 You were called by that glorious name
which was conferred upon Israel.†
Gold you gathered like so much iron;
you heaped up silver as though it were lead.
19 But you abandoned yourself to women
and gave them dominion over your body.*
20 You brought a stain upon your glory,
shame upon your marriage bed,
Wrath upon your descendants,
and groaning upon your deathbed.
21 Thus two governments came into being,
when in Ephraim kingship was usurped.*
22 But God does not withdraw his mercy,
nor permit even one of his promises to fail.
He does not uproot the posterity of the chosen,
nor destroy the offspring of his friends.
So he gave to Jacob a remnant,
to David a root from his own family.*

Rehoboam and Jeroboam

23 Solomon finally slept with his ancestors,
and left behind him one of his sons,
Broad† in folly, narrow in sense,
whose policy made the people rebel.
Then arose the one who should not be remembered,
the sinner who led Israel into sin,*
Who brought ruin to Ephraim
24 and caused them to be exiled from their land.

Elijah and Elisha

25 Their sinfulness grew more and more,
and they gave themselves to every evil†

48 1Until like fire a prophet appeared,
his words a flaming furnace.*
2 The staff of life, their bread, he shattered,
and in his zeal he made them few in number.
3 By God's word he shut up the heavens
and three times brought down fire.*
4 How awesome are you, ELIJAH!
Whose glory is equal to yours?
5 You brought a dead body back to life
from Sheol, by the will of the LORD.*
6 You sent kings down to destruction,
and nobles, from their beds of sickness.*
7 You heard threats at Sinai,
at Horeb avenging judgments.*
8 You anointed the agent of these punishments,
the prophet to succeed in your place.*
9 You were taken aloft in a whirlwind,
in a chariot with fiery horses.*
10 You are destined, it is written, in time to come
to put an end to wrath before the day of the LORD,
To turn back the hearts of parents toward their children,
and to re-establish the tribes of Israel.*
11 Blessed is the one who shall have seen you
before he dies!†

12 When Elijah was enveloped in the whirlwind,
ELISHA was filled with his spirit;†
He worked twice as many marvels,*
and every utterance of his mouth was wonderful.
During his lifetime he feared no one,
nor was anyone able to intimidate his will.
13 Nothing was beyond his power;*
and from where he lay buried, his body prophesied.†
14 In life he performed wonders,
and after death, marvelous deeds.
15 Despite all this the people did not repent,
nor did they give up their sins,
Until they were uprooted from their land
and scattered all over the earth.

†

47:18 Cf. 2 Sm 12:25, where Solomon is called Jedidiah, "beloved of the Lord." A similar term is used of Israel in Jer 11:15.

47:23 *Broad*: the name Rehoboam means "the people is broad, or expansive," that is, widespread. *The sinner*: Jeroboam; cf. 1 Kgs 12:1, 20, 26–32.

47:25–48:11 The prophetic ministry of Elijah amid widespread idolatry is here described as a judgment by fire (48:1). Through his preaching, marvels, and acts of vengeance against God's enemies, he succeeded for a time in restoring faith in and worship of the Lord (vv. 2–8). His mysterious departure from this life gave rise to the belief that he did not die but would return before the day of the Lord. Cf. Mal 3:23–24; Mt 17:9–13.

48:11 Verse 11b is not extant in the Hebrew; it is represented in the Greek tradition by "for we too shall certainly live." But this can hardly be the original reading.

48:12–16 Elisha continued Elijah's work (vv. 12–14), but the obstinacy of the people eventually brought on the destruction of the kingdom of Israel and the dispersion of its subjects. Judah, however, survived under the rule of Davidic kings, both good and bad (vv. 15–16).

48:13 The reference in v. 13b seems to be to 2 Kgs 13:21 where it is related that a dead man, thrown into Elisha's grave, came back to life.

*

47:19 1 Kgs 11:1–10.
47:21 1 Kgs 12:1–25.
47:22 2 Sm 7:15; Ps 89:34–38.
47:23 1 Kgs 11:43; 12:13, 21; 13:34; 2 Kgs 17:6–22.
48:1 1 Kgs 17:1.
48:3 2 Kgs 1:9–14.
48:5 1 Kgs 17:17–23.
48:6 1 Kgs 21:19; 2 Kgs 1:17.
48:7 1 Kgs 19:8–15.
48:8 1 Kgs 19:16–17.
48:9 2 Kgs 2:11.
48:10 Mal 3:23–24; Mt 17:10.
48:12 2 Kgs 2:9–12.
48:13–14 2 Kgs 13:21.

Judah

But Judah remained, a tiny people,
with its ruler from the house of David.*
16 Some of them did what was right,
but others were extremely sinful.

Hezekiah and Isaiah†

17 HEZEKIAH fortified his city
and had water brought into it;*
With bronze tools he cut through the rocks
and dammed up a mountain site for water.†
18 During his reign Sennacherib led an invasion
and sent his adjutant;
He shook his fist at Zion
and blasphemed God in his pride.*
19 The people's hearts melted within them,
and they were in anguish like that of childbirth.
20 But they called upon the Most High God
and lifted up their hands to him;
He heard the prayer they uttered,
and saved them through ISAIAH.*
21 God struck the camp of the Assyrians
and routed them with a plague.*
22 For Hezekiah did what was right
and held fast to the paths of David,
As ordered by the illustrious prophet
Isaiah, who saw truth in visions.
23 In his lifetime he turned back the sun
and prolonged the life of the king.*
24 By his powerful spirit he looked into the future*
and consoled the mourners of Zion;
25 He foretold what would happen till the end of time,
hidden things yet to be fulfilled.

Josiah and the Prophets†

49 1 The name JOSIAH is like blended incense,
made lasting by a skilled perfumer.*
Precious is his memory, like honey to the taste,
like music at a banquet.
2 For he grieved over our betrayals,
and destroyed the abominable idols.
3 He kept his heart fixed on God,
and in times of lawlessness practiced virtue.
4 Except for David, Hezekiah, and Josiah,
they all were wicked;
They abandoned the Law of the Most High,
these kings of Judah, right to the very end.
5 So he gave over their power to others,
their glory to a foreign nation
6 Who burned the holy city
and left its streets desolate,
7 As foretold by JEREMIAH.* They mistreated him
who even in the womb had been made a prophet,
To root out, pull down, and destroy,
and then to build and to plant.*
8 EZEKIEL beheld a vision
and described the different creatures of the chariot;*
9 He also referred to JOB,
who always persevered in the right path.*
10 Then, too, the TWELVE PROPHETS—
may their bones flourish with new life where they lie!—
They gave new strength to Jacob
and saved him with steadfast hope.

The Heroes After the Exile

11 How to extol ZERUBBABEL?†
He was like a signet ring on the right hand,*
12 And JESHUA, Jozadak's son?
In their time they rebuilt the altar
And erected the holy temple,
destined for everlasting glory.
13 Exalted be the memory of NEHEMIAH!
He rebuilt our ruined walls,
Restored our shattered defenses,
and set up gates and bars.*

The Earliest Patriarchs

14 Few on earth have been created like ENOCH;†
he also was taken up bodily.*

---

† **48:17–25** The fidelity of King Hezekiah (vv. 17, 22), the zeal of the prophet Isaiah, and the prayer of the people (v. 20) were effective. The Assyrian oppressors under Sennacherib withdrew (vv. 18–19, 21). The king's life was prolonged. The people were consoled by Isaiah's words about the future (vv. 23–25); the "consolations" refer to Is 40–66.

48:17 The reference is to the famous Siloam tunnel in present-day Jerusalem.

49:1–10 Ben Sira's praise of King Josiah (vv. 1–3) and of the prophets Jeremiah and Ezekiel and the minor prophets (vv. 7–10) derives from their spirit of fidelity to the Lord and his Law (vv. 4–6, 10).

49:11–13 The rebuilding of the Temple and the repair of the walls of the Holy City led to a restoration of religious worship and civil authority.

49:14–16 The patriarchs here mentioned were glorious because of their spirit of religion, i.e., their profound reverence for God and obedience to him. *The splendor of Adam*: suggests his direct origin from God (Gn 1:26–27; 2:7).

---

* **48:15** 2 Kgs 15:29; 18:11–12.
48:17 2 Kgs 20:20; 2 Chr 32:30.
48:18 2 Kgs 18:13–37; Is 36:1–22.
48:20 2 Kgs 19:20.
48:21 2 Kgs 19:35; Is 37:36.
48:23 2 Kgs 20:11; Is 38:8.
48:24–25 2 Kgs 20:17; Is 40:1–11; 42:9; 46:10; 48:6; 61:2–3.
49:1–2 2 Kgs 22:1–2, 10–13, 19; 23:4–15, 19–20, 24; 2 Chr 34:1–7.
49:7 2 Kgs 25:9; 2 Chr 36:19.
49:7 Jer 1:5, 10.
49:8 Ez 1:4–21.
49:9 Ez 14:14, 20.
49:11–12 Ezr 3:2; Hg 1:12; Zec 3:1.
49:13 Neh 1:1–3:32.
49:14 Sir 44:16; Gn 5:18–24.

15 Was ever a man born like JOSEPH?
Even his dead body was provided for.*
16 Glorious, too, were SHEM and SETH and ENOSH;
but beyond that of any living being was the splendor of ADAM.*

Simeon, Son of Jochanan

50 1 Greatest of his family, the glory of his people,
was SIMEON the priest, son of Jochanan,†
In whose time the house of God was renovated,
in whose days the temple was reinforced.
2 In his time also the retaining wall was built
with powerful turrets for the temple precincts.
3 In his time the reservoir was dug,
a pool as vast as the sea.
4 He protected the people against brigands
and strengthened the city against the enemy.
5 How splendid he was as he looked out from the tent,
as he came from behind the veil!
6 Like a star shining among the clouds,
like the full moon at the festal season;
7 Like sun shining upon the temple of the King,
like a rainbow appearing in the cloudy sky;
8 Like blossoms on the branches in springtime,
like a lily by running waters;
Like a green shoot on Lebanon in summer,
9 like the fire of incense at sacrifice;
Like a vessel of hammered gold,
studded with all kinds of precious stones;
10 Like a luxuriant olive tree heavy with fruit,
a plant with branches abounding in oil;
11 Wearing his glorious robes,
and vested in sublime magnificence,*
As he ascended the glorious altar
and lent majesty to the court of the sanctuary.
12 When he received the portions from the priests
while he stood before the sacrificial wood,
His sons stood round him like a garland,
like young cedars on Lebanon;
And like poplars by the brook they surrounded him,
13 all the sons of Aaron in their glory,
With the offerings to the LORD in their hands,
in the presence of the whole assembly of Israel.
14 Once he had completed the service at the altar
and arranged the sacrificial hearth for the Most High,
15 And had stretched forth his hand for the cup,
to offer blood of the grape,
And poured it out at the foot of the altar,
a sweet-smelling odor to God the Most High,*
16 Then the sons of Aaron would sound a blast,
the priests, on their trumpets of beaten metal;
A blast to resound mightily
as a reminder before the Most High.*
17 All the people with one accord
would fall with face to the ground
In adoration before the Most High,
before the Holy One of Israel.

18 Then hymns would re-echo,
and over the throng sweet strains of praise resound.
19 All the people of the land would shout for joy,
praying to the Merciful One,
As the high priest completed the service at the altar
by presenting to God the fitting sacrifice.
20 Then coming down he would raise his hands
over all the congregation of Israel;
The blessing of the LORD would be upon his lips,
the name of the LORD would be his glory.*
21 The people would again fall down
to receive the blessing of the Most High.

22 And now, bless the God of all,†
who has done wonders on earth;
Who fosters growth from the womb,
fashioning it according to his will!
23 May he grant you a wise heart
and abide with you in peace;
24 May his goodness toward Simeon last forever;
may he fulfill for him the covenant with Phinehas
So that it may not be abrogated for him
or his descendants while the heavens last.

† **50:1–21** *Son of Jochanan*: Simeon II, in whose time as high priest (219–196 B.C.) great works were accomplished for the benefit of public worship and welfare (vv. 1–4). Ben Sira, a contemporary, describes detailed liturgical action, perhaps pertaining to the Day of Atonement (Yom Kippur, cf. Lv 16).

50:22–24 Ben Sira urges the reader to praise and bless God for his wondrous works and then invokes a blessing on all that they may enjoy peace and gladness of heart and the abiding goodness of the Most High.

49:15 Gn 37; 39–50; Ex 13:19; Jos 24:32.
49:16 Gn 1:26–30; 2:7; 4:25–26.
50:11 Sir 45:8–13; Ex 28:2–43; 39:1–31.
50:15 Nm 15:5; 28:7.
50:16 Nm 10:10.
50:20 Nm 6:23–27.

Epilogue

25 My whole being loathes two nations,
the third is not even a people:†
26 The inhabitants of Seir† and Philistia,
and the foolish people who dwell in
Shechem.*

27 Wise instruction, appropriate proverbs,†
I have written in this book—
I, Yeshua Ben Eleazar Ben Sira—
as they poured forth from my heart's
understanding.
28 Happy those who meditate upon these things;
wise those who take them to heart!
29 If they put them into practice, they can cope
with anything,
for the fear of the LORD is their lamp.

A Prayer of Thanksgiving

51 1 I give you thanks, LORD and King,†
I praise you, God my savior!
I declare your name, refuge of my life,*
2 because you have ransomed my life from
death;
You held back my body from the pit,
and delivered my foot from the power of
Sheol.*

You have preserved me from the scourge of
the slanderous tongue,
and from the lips of those who went over
to falsehood.
You were with me against those who rise up
against me;
3 You have rescued me according to your
abundant mercy*
From the snare of those who look for my
downfall,
and from the power of those who seek my
life.

From many dangers you have saved me,
4 from flames that beset me on every
side,*
From the midst of fire till there was not a
whiff of it,†
5 from the deep belly of Sheol,
From deceiving lips and painters of lies,
6 from the arrows of a treacherous tongue.

I was at the point of death,
my life was nearing the depths of Sheol;*
7 I turned every way, but there was no one to
help;
I looked for support but there was none.*
8 Then I remembered the mercies of the LORD,
his acts of kindness through ages past;
For he saves those who take refuge in him,
and rescues them from every evil.

9 So I raised my voice from the grave;
from the gates of Sheol I cried for help.
10 I called out: LORD, you are my Father,
my champion, my savior!
Do not abandon me in time of trouble,
in the midst of storms and dangers.*
11 I will always praise your name
and remember you in prayer!

Then the LORD heard my voice,
and listened to my appeal.
12 He saved me from every evil
and preserved me in time of trouble.

---

†

50:25 *Not even a people*: the Samaritans.

50:26 *Seir*: Mount Seir in the territory of the Edomites. *Shechem*: a city in Samaria.

50:27 This colophon may have been the original ending of the book. It is unusual for a biblical writer to append his name.

51:1–30 This chapter contains two appendixes: a prayer (vv. 1–12) and an autobiographical poem praising wisdom (vv. 13–30).

51:4 So complete is the deliverance from fire that even the smell of smoke cannot be detected. Cf. Dn 3:27.

51:12 After this verse the Hebrew text gives the litany of praise contained below. It is similar to Ps 136. Though not found in any versions, and therefore of doubtful authenticity, the litany seems from internal evidence to go back to the time of Ben Sira.

Give praise to the LORD, for he is good, for God's love endures forever;
Give praise to the God of glory, for God's love endures forever;
Give praise to the Guardian of Israel, for God's love endures forever;
Give praise to the creator of all things, for God's love endures forever;
Give praise to the redeemer of Israel, for God's love endures forever;
Give praise to God who gathers the dispersed of Israel, for God's love endures forever;
Give praise to God who builds the city and sanctuary, for God's love endures forever;
Give praise to God who makes a horn sprout forth for the house of David, for God's love endures forever;
Give praise to God who has chosen the sons of Zadok as priests, for God's love endures forever;
Give praise to the Shield of Abraham, for God's love endures forever;
Give praise to the Rock of Isaac, for God's love endures forever;
Give praise to the Mighty One of Jacob, for God's love endures forever;
Give praise to God who has chosen Zion, for God's love endures forever;
Give praise to the King, the king of kings, for God's love endures forever.
He has lifted up the horn of his people! Let this be his praise from all the faithful,
From Israel, the people near to him. Hallelujah! (Cf. Ps 148:14.)

---

*

50:26 2 Kgs 17:24; Jn 4:9.
51:1 Ps 138:1.
51:2 Ps 91:3.
51:3 Ps 56:10–12; 124:2.
51:4 Ps 66:12.
51:6 Ps 88:4; 94:17.
51:7 Ps 22:12; 142:5.
51:10 Ps 89:27; 95:1.

For this reason I thank and praise him;
I bless the name of the LORD.†

Ben Sira's Pursuit of Wisdom

13† When I was young and innocent,
I sought wisdom.*
14 She came to me in her beauty,
and until the end I will cultivate her.

15 As the blossoms yielded to ripening grapes,
the heart's joy,
My feet kept to the level path
because from earliest youth I was familiar with her.

16 In the short time I paid heed,
I met with great instruction.
17 Since in this way I have profited,
I will give my Teacher grateful praise.

18 I resolved to tread her paths;
I have been jealous for the good and will not turn back.
19 I burned with desire for her,
never relenting.
I became preoccupied with her,
never weary of extolling her.

I spread out my hands to the heavens
and I came to know her secrets.
20 For her I purified my hands;
in cleanness I attained to her.

At first acquaintance with her, I gained understanding
such that I will never forsake her.*
21 My whole being was stirred to seek her;
therefore I have made her my prize possession.
22 The LORD has rewarded me with lips,
with a tongue for praising him.

23 Come aside to me, you untutored,
and take up lodging in the house of instruction;† *
24 How long will you deprive yourself of wisdom's food,
how long endure such bitter thirst?
25 I open my mouth and speak of her:
gain wisdom for yourselves at no cost.*

26 Take her yoke upon your neck;
that your mind may receive her teaching.
For she is close to those who seek her,
and the one who is in earnest finds her.*

27 See for yourselves! I have labored only a little,
but have found much.
28 Acquire but a little instruction,
and you will win silver and gold through her.

29 May your soul rejoice in God's mercy;
do not be ashamed to give him praise.
30 Work at your tasks in due season,
and in his own time God will give you your reward.*

†

51:13–30 A Hebrew manuscript from Qumran demonstrates the acrostic style of vv. 13–20. This is an elegant twenty-three-line alphabetic acrostic hymn that describes Ben Sira's relationship to wisdom: (a) his approach to wisdom through prayer, persistent study, and instruction (vv. 13–17); (b) his purification from sin, his enlightenment, and ardent desire to possess wisdom (vv. 18–22). Ben Sira concludes with an urgent invitation to his students to receive instruction in wisdom from him, and to live by it, because wisdom gives herself to those who seek her (vv. 23–26); and for their labor, God will reward them in his own time (vv. 27–30). Cf. Mt 11:28; Eccl 12:14.

51:23 *House of instruction*: this may be a metaphor for Ben Sira's teaching.

*

51:13 Sir 34:9–13; Prv 8:17.
51:20 Prv 4:6.
51:23 Prv 8:5.
51:25 Sir 6:19; Is 55:1–3.
51:26 Sir 6:26–28.
51:30 Sir 2:8; Jb 34:11; Jn 9:4.

Introduction to the Prophets

Have you ever met someone who inspired you to make some needed changes in your life and gave you hope for the future? Someone who was unafraid to speak the truth or to challenge you to live a more just life? If so, you've encountered a modern-day prophet—a person who names what God wants to say to us. In this section of books, you will meet the prophets of the Bible—unique and courageous people who did these things for ancient Israel.

In Depth

What is a prophet? First and foremost, a prophet is a person—or sometimes a group—who speaks for God. The prophet's words spoken in God's name—usually called prophecies or oracles—are God's words. Some people think prophets can predict the future, but this is not their role in the Bible. The biblical prophets were called by God during times of crisis to offer God's People challenge or comfort, depending on their circumstances. So, to properly understand biblical prophecies, we must try to understand the historical situation God was addressing through the prophets.

Through the prophets' inspired messages, God reminded the Israelites of the covenant God had made with them (see "Introduction to the Pentateuch"). If the people or their leaders were not keeping their side of the covenant, the prophets challenged them to do so. If the people were in despair that God was not keeping God's side of the covenant, the prophets promised that God would. Here are some common covenant themes the prophets emphasized:

- *Warnings against idolatry.* The Israelites were constantly tempted to worship the gods of other nations and cultures. The prophets had to keep reminding the kings and people of the first law of the Ten Commandments: "I am the LORD your God, who brought you out of the land of Egypt, out of the house of slavery. You shall not have other gods beside me" (Ex 20:2–3).

- *Warnings to act justly and to treat the poor fairly.* In their greed and struggle for power, the wealthy and the ruling class often cheated and oppressed other people. Operating as Israel's conscience, the prophets were unanimous in challenging Israel to act justly and to care for the poor and marginalized. This did not always make the prophets popular with the kings and the ruling class—they were often ridiculed and even threatened with violence.

- *Attempts to deepen the understanding of God's love and mercy.* Some Israelites felt God would not forgive them after Israel (the northern kingdom) and Judah (the southern kingdom) were conquered by foreign nations. The prophets assured them they would receive God's forgiveness if they turned to God and kept the covenant. In addition, some of the prophets began to teach that God was Lord over—and cared for—all nations, not just Israel.

■ *Promises of hope for the future.* During these troubled and often violent times, it must have seemed to many Israelites that their world was coming to an end. The prophets responded to the people's despair with hope-filled promises that ultimately God's love and justice would prevail. These hopeful prophecies took different forms: the coming of the Ideal Ruler, the restoration of Jerusalem and the Temple, a time of judgment when good is rewarded and evil punished, and so on.

The stories of the earliest prophets—Samuel, Nathan, Elijah, and Elisha—are in the Bible's historical Books of First and Second Samuel and First and Second Kings. God's revelation through the later prophets is recorded in the books of this section of the Bible. The introduction to each book in this section gives background about the historical situation the prophet faced. The timeline in the back of this Bible identifies the time period for each prophet.

As you read these books, keep this in mind: the role of prophets has not died, only changed. In every age, there are people who challenge us to be faithful to God and remind us about God's faithful love for us. In fact, Christians believe that through their Baptism, God calls them to be priest, prophet, and king. You can fulfill your prophetic calling by challenging others to live justly and reminding them of God's love. It's exciting and humbling to be called into such a proud tradition.

Other Background

- Isaiah, Jeremiah, and Ezekiel are sometimes called the major prophets because their books are long and because of the role they played in Israelite history.
- Hosea, Amos, Jeremiah, First Isaiah, Obadiah, Micah, Nahum, Habakkuk, and Zephaniah prophesied before the Babylonian Exile.
- Ezekiel, Second Isaiah, and Lamentations are set during the Exile.
- Joel, Haggai, Zechariah, Malachi, Third Isaiah, and Baruch prophesied after the Exile.
- Jonah wasn't a historical prophet, but a fictional, reluctant prophet.
- Seven of the prophets talk about "the day of the LORD"—a final time of God's judgment when evil will be punished.

Once in a while, Hollywood releases a new movie that is a remake of an older film. The new movie has a new director and new actors and actresses. It keeps the same basic plot as the original but is adapted to appeal to a modern audience. This is what happened with the prophet Isaiah. The original Isaiah was such a hit that, years after he died, a second and even a third person or group adapted his ideas to their situation. The stories of the original Isaiah and his two "remakes" were collected into the single Book of Isaiah we have today.

The Book of

Isaiah

In Depth

Prophets from three different periods in Israel's history contributed to the Book of Isaiah. Chapters 1–39 reflect the prophecies of the original Isaiah, called First Isaiah. His career began with his call in the Temple during the reign of Uzziah around 742 BC (see the timeline at the back of this Bible). First Isaiah advised the kings of Judah about the dangers of alliances with foreign nations and cautioned them to trust only in God. He cried out against the social injustices of the rich ruling class against the poor and taught that God had a plan in which all, rich and poor, powerful and oppressed, would have a part. First Isaiah is responsible for the messianic prophecies, which tell of the coming of a perfect king.

Years later, when Israel was exiled in Babylon (587–538 BC), another prophet, Second Isaiah, reworked First Isaiah's prophecies to address his own people (see chapters 40–55). Second Isaiah's people were struggling to understand why God allowed them to be captives in a strange land. The prophet comforted them with a hopeful message: They had been taken captive so that they would turn away from their sinful practices; now that they had learned their lesson, God would return them to rebuild Israel. Contained in this prophet's writings are the famous servant songs (see "The Servant Songs," near 42:1–7).

After the Israelites returned from exile and resettled in Judah (537–500 BC), they once again fell into patterns of social injustice and religious apathy. Third Isaiah responded by demanding that they practice justice toward one another, and even toward the Gentiles, non-Jews (see chapters 56–66). Realizing that Israel would never be a perfect community, he spoke of "new heavens / and a new earth" (65:17), where people would live according to God's plan.

At a Glance

I. Isaiah 1–39.
A. Indictment of Israel and Judah (1:1—5:30).
B. The Book of Emmanuel (6:1—12:6).
C. Oracles against the Foreign Nations (13:1—23:18).
D. Apocalypse of Isaiah (24:1—27:13).
E. The Lord Alone, Israel's and Judah's Salvation (28:1—33:24).
F. The Lord, Zion's Avenger (34:1—35:10).
G. Historical Appendix (36:1—39:8).
II. Isaiah 40–55.
A. The Lord's Glory in Israel's Liberation (40:1—48:22).
B. Expiation of Sin, Spiritual Liberation of Israel (49:1—55:13).
III. Isaiah 56–66.

Quick Facts

Period Covered: from 742 to 500 BC

Inspired Authors: the three Isaiahs or their followers

Themes: faithfulness to God, justice for the poor, hope for the future, messianic prophecies, God as lord over all nations

Isaiah

Chapter 6

I. Isaiah 1—39

A. Indictment of Israel and Judah

1 [1] † The vision which Isaiah, son of Amoz, saw concerning Judah and Jerusalem in the days of Uzziah, Jotham, Ahaz and Hezekiah, kings of Judah.

Accusation and Appeal

2† Hear, O heavens, and listen, O earth,
for the LORD speaks:
Sons have I raised and reared,
but they have rebelled against me! *
3 An ox knows its owner,
and an ass, † its master's manger;
But Israel does not know,
my people has not understood. *
4 Ah! † Sinful nation, people laden with wickedness,
evil offspring, corrupt children!
They have forsaken the LORD,
spurned the Holy One of Israel,
apostatized, *
5 Why† would you yet be struck,
that you continue to rebel?
The whole head is sick,
the whole heart faint.
6 From the sole of the foot to the head
there is no sound spot in it;
Just bruise and welt and oozing wound,
not drained, or bandaged,
or eased with salve.
7 Your country is waste,
your cities burnt with fire;
Your land—before your eyes
strangers devour it,
a waste, like the devastation of Sodom. † *
8 And daughter Zion† is left
like a hut in a vineyard,

1:1 The title, or inscription, of the book is an editorial addition to identify the prophet and the circumstances of his ministry. *Isaiah*: meaning "the salvation of the Lord," or "the Lord is salvation." *Amoz*: not Amos the prophet. *Judah*: the Southern Kingdom of the tribes of Judah and Benjamin. *Uzziah*: also called Azariah; cf. 2 Kgs 15:1; 2 Chr 26:1.

1:2–31 This chapter is widely considered to be a collection of oracles from various periods in Isaiah's ministry, chosen by the editor as a compendium of his most characteristic teachings.

1:3 *Ox . . . ass*: Isaiah uses animals proverbial for their stupidity and stubbornness to underline Israel's failure to respond to God. *Israel*: a term Isaiah (and other prophets) frequently applies to Judah, especially after the fall of the Northern Kingdom (which Isaiah normally calls Ephraim, as in 7:2, 9, 17; 9:8), but sometimes applies to the entire chosen people, as in 8:14.

1:4 *Ah*: see note on 5:8–24. *Holy One of Israel*: a title used frequently in the Book of Isaiah, rarely elsewhere in the Old Testament (see 5:19, 24; 10:20; 12:6; 17:7; 29:19; 30:11, 12, 15; 31:1; 37:23; 41:14, 16, 20; 43:3, 14; 45:11; 47:4; 48:17; 49:7; 54:5; 55:5; 60:9, 14).

1:5–6 The Hebrew expression translated "Why?" may also be translated "Where?" The ambiguity is probably intentional: "Why, O Israel, would you still be beaten, and where on your bruised body do you want the next blow?" The bruised body is a metaphor for the historical disaster that has overtaken Israel (see v. 7) because of its sins.

1:7 *Sodom*: Sodom and Gomorrah (see vv. 9–10; cf. Gn 19) were proverbial as wicked cities completely overthrown and destroyed by God. Judah, more fortunate, survives at least as a remnant. The devastation of the land and the isolation of Jerusalem suggest the time of Sennacherib's invasion of 701.

1:8 *Daughter Zion*: Jerusalem, as isolated as a little hut erected in a field for the shelter of watchmen and laborers.

1:2 Dt 32:1, 5–6, 18.
1:3 Jer 8:7; Lk 2:12.
1:4 Is 5:24; Dt 32:15.
1:7 Is 13:19; Dt 29:22; Jer 49:18; 50:40; Am 4:11.

Live It!

God Wants Justice, Not Empty Rites

First Isaiah denounces the hypocrisy of practicing empty religious rituals that are not grounded in justice, sincerity, and good deeds. Speaking for God, he calls the people to do good, seek justice, rescue the oppressed, and defend the orphans and the widows.

How can we do this today? By volunteering our time to serve those in need; by speaking out against those who persecute, demean, or ridicule; by educating ourselves about the plight of those who suffer; and by praying vigilantly for the impoverished, oppressed, orphaned, and widowed in our world.

- How do you actively seek justice and take care of people in need?
- In your prayer, ask God's forgiveness for when you have not responded to God's call to practice justice or help people in need.

Is 1:10–20

Like a shed in a melon patch,
like a city blockaded.
9 If the LORD of hosts† had not
left us a small remnant,
We would have become as Sodom,
would have resembled Gomorrah.*

10† Hear the word of the LORD,
princes of Sodom!
Listen to the instruction of our God,
people of Gomorrah!
11 What do I care for the multitude of your
sacrifices?
says the LORD.
I have had enough of whole-burnt rams
and fat of fatlings;
In the blood of calves, lambs, and goats
I find no pleasure.*
12 When you come to appear before me,
who asks these things of you?
13 Trample my courts no more!
To bring offerings is useless;
incense is an abomination to me.
New moon and sabbath, calling assemblies—
festive convocations with wickedness—
these I cannot bear.*
14 Your new moons and festivals I detest;*
they weigh me down, I tire of the load.
15 When you spread out your hands,
I will close my eyes to you;
Though you pray the more,
I will not listen.
Your hands are full of blood!†*
16 Wash yourselves clean!
Put away your misdeeds from before my eyes;
cease doing evil;
17 learn to do good.
Make justice your aim: redress the wronged,
hear the orphan's plea, defend the widow.*

18 Come now, let us set things right,†
says the LORD:
Though your sins be like scarlet,
they may become white as snow;
Though they be red like crimson,
they may become white as wool.*
19 If you are willing, and obey,
you shall eat the good things of the land;
20 But if you refuse and resist,
you shall be eaten by the sword:
for the mouth of the LORD has spoken!

The Purification of Jerusalem

21 How she has become a prostitute,
the faithful city,† so upright!

†

1:9 *LORD of hosts*: God, who is the Creator and Ruler of the armies of Israel, the angels, stars, etc.

1:10–17 A powerful indictment of the religious hypocrisy of rulers and others who neglect just judgment and oppress the weaker members, yet believe they can please God with sacrifices and other external forms of worship. The long list of observances suggests the Lord's tedium with such attempts. *Sodom . . . Gomorrah*: the names are picked up from v. 9, but now to emphasize their wickedness rather than the good fortune of escaping total destruction.

1:15–16 *Hands . . . blood*: oppression of the poor is likened to violence that bloodies the hands, which explains why the hands spread out in prayer (v. 15) are not regarded by the Lord. This climax of the accusations is followed by positive admonitions for reversing the evil situation.

1:18–20 *Let us set things right*: the Hebrew word refers to the arbitration of legal disputes (Jb 23:7). God offers to settle his case with Israel on the basis of the change of behavior demanded above. For Israel it is a life or death choice; life in conformity with God's will or death for continued disobedience.

1:21–28 *Faithful city*: the phrase, found in v. 21 and v. 28, forms an *inclusio* which marks off the passage and also suggests three chronological periods: the city's former ideal state, its present wicked condition (described in vv. 21b–23), and the future ideal conditions intended by God. This will be brought about by a purging judgment

*

1:9 Rom 9:29.
1:11 Ps 50:8–13; Sir 34:23; Mi 6:7.
1:13 Prv 15:8; Jer 6:20.
1:14 Am 5:21–24.
1:15 Prv 1:28; Sir 34:25–31.
1:17 Ex 23:6; Dt 24:17; Sir 4:9–10; Jer 22:3; Ez 22:7; Am 5:14–15; Zec 7:9–10.
1:18 Ps 51:9.

Justice used to lodge within her,
but now, murderers.*
22 Your silver is turned to dross,
your wine is mixed with water.
23 Your princes are rebels
and comrades of thieves;
Each one of them loves a bribe
and looks for gifts.
The fatherless they do not defend,
the widow's plea does not reach them.*
24 Now, therefore, says the Lord,
the LORD of hosts, the Mighty One of Israel:
Ah! I will take vengeance on my foes
and fully repay my enemies!*
25 I will turn my hand against you,
and refine your dross in the furnace,
removing all your alloy.
26 I will restore your judges† as at first,
and your counselors as in the beginning;
After that you shall be called
city of justice, faithful city.*
27† Zion shall be redeemed by justice,
and her repentant ones by righteousness.
28 Rebels and sinners together shall be crushed,
those who desert the LORD shall be
consumed.

Judgment on the Sacred Groves

29† You shall be ashamed of the terebinths which
you desired,
and blush on account of the gardens which
you chose.
30 You shall become like a terebinth whose
leaves wither,
like a garden that has no water.
31 The strong tree shall turn to tinder,
and the one who tends it shall become a
spark;
Both of them shall burn together,
and there shall be none to quench them.

2 1 † This is what Isaiah, son of Amoz, saw concerning Judah and Jerusalem.

Pray It!

From Violence to Love

We hear Isaiah 2:1–5 every three years in church on the first Sunday of Advent. Its "swords into plowshares" theme is all about moving from violence to nonviolence and ultimately to love in our responses to conflict (see also Jl 3:10 and Mi 4:3).

But what exactly is a plowshare? A plowshare is a tool that helps a farmer harvest the fields. The message is that instead of tools of violence (swords), a world of peace needs only tools to feed and nourish its people (plowshares). God's Reign is present when swords are turned into plowshares.

Our society often glorifies violence, weapons, battle, and war. Take a few minutes to pray, reflect, or journal on the following questions:

- Why does our society glorify violence?
- As a member of society, do you support violence or nonviolence? How?
- What nonviolent actions can you take when you find yourself in conflict situations? (For example, walking away from the situation, remaining calm, and counting to ten before responding.)
- How can we be people of love in a world that is all too often hateful?

Is 2:1–5

Zion, the Royal City of God

2† In days to come,
The mountain of the LORD's house

directed primarily against the leaders ("judges . . . counselors").

1:26 *Judges*: the reference must be to royal judges appointed by David and his successors, not to the tribal judges of the Book of Judges, since the "beginning" of Jerusalem as an Israelite city dates only to the time of David. The Davidic era is idealized here; obtaining justice in the historical Jerusalem of David's time was more problematic (see 2 Sm 15:1–6).

1:27–28 These verses expand the oracle that originally ended at v. 26. The expansion correctly interprets the preceding text as proclaiming a purifying judgment on Zion in which the righteous are saved while the wicked perish. The meaning of "by justice" and "by righteousness" is ambiguous. Do these terms refer to God's judgment or to the justice and righteousness of Zion's surviving inhabitants? Is 33:14–16 suggests the latter interpretation.

1:29–31 These verses were secondarily inserted here on the catchword principle; like v. 28 they pronounce judgment on certain parties "together" (v. 31). The terebinths and gardens refer to the sacred groves or asherahs that functioned as idolatrous cultic symbols at the popular shrines or high places (1 Kgs 14:23; 2 Kgs 17:10). Hezekiah cut down these groves during his reform (2 Kgs 18:4); they were a religious issue during Isaiah's ministry (cf. Is 17:7–11). Isaiah threatens those who cultivate these symbols with the same fate that befalls trees when deprived of water.

2:1 This editorial heading probably introduced the collection of chaps. 2–12, to which chap. 1 with its introduction was added later (see note on 1:2–31).

2:2–22 These verses contain two very important oracles, one on the pilgrimage of nations to Mount Zion (vv. 2–4—completed with an invitation to the "house of Jacob," v. 5), the other on the day of the Lord (see note on Am 5:18), which was probably composed from at least two earlier pieces. Whereas vv. 6–8 indict Judah for trust in superstitious

1:21 Jer 3:8; Hos 2:7.
1:23 Ex 23:8; Dt 16:19.
1:24 Dt 32:41.
1:26 Jer 33:7–11; Zec 8:8.

shall be established as the highest mountain
and raised above the hills.
All nations shall stream toward it.*
3 Many peoples shall come and say:
"Come, let us go up to the LORD's mountain,
to the house of the God of Jacob,
That he may instruct us in his ways,
and we may walk in his paths."*
For from Zion shall go forth instruction,
and the word of the LORD from Jerusalem.
4† He shall judge between the nations,
and set terms for many peoples.
They shall beat their swords into plowshares
and their spears into pruning hooks;*
One nation shall not raise the sword against
another,
nor shall they train for war again.*
5† House of Jacob, come,
let us walk in the light of the LORD!

The Lord's Day of Judgment on Pride

6 You have abandoned your people,
the house of Jacob!
Because they are filled with diviners,
and soothsayers, like the Philistines;
with foreigners they clasp hands.*
7 Their land is full of silver and gold,
there is no end to their treasures;
Their land is full of horses,
there is no end to their chariots.
8 Their land is full of idols;
they bow down to the works of their hands,
what their fingers have made.*
9 So all shall be abased,
each one brought low.†
Do not pardon them!
10 Get behind the rocks,
hide in the dust,
From the terror of the LORD
and the splendor of his majesty!
11 The eyes of human pride shall be lowered,
the arrogance of mortals shall be abased,
and the LORD alone will be exalted, on that
day.†
12 For the LORD of hosts will have his day
against all that is proud and arrogant,
against all that is high, and it will be
brought low;
13 Yes, against all the cedars of Lebanon†
and against all the oaks of Bashan,
14 Against all the lofty mountains
and all the high hills,
15 Against every lofty tower
and every fortified wall,
16 Against all the ships of Tarshish
and all stately vessels.
17 Then human pride shall be abased,
the arrogance of mortals brought low,
And the LORD alone will be exalted on that day.
18 The idols will vanish completely.
19 People will go into caves in the rocks
and into holes in the earth,
At the terror of the LORD
and the splendor of his majesty,
as he rises to overawe the earth.
20 On that day people shall throw to moles and
bats
their idols of silver and their idols of gold
which they made for themselves to worship.
21 And they shall go into caverns in the rocks
and into crevices in the cliffs,
At the terror of the LORD
and the splendor of his majesty,
as he rises to overawe the earth.
22† As for you, stop worrying about mortals,
in whose nostrils is but a breath;
for of what worth are they?

Judgment on Jerusalem and Judah

3 1† The Lord, the LORD of hosts,
will take away from Jerusalem and from
Judah

---

† practices and human resources rather than in the Lord, the following verses are directed against humankind in general and emphasize the effect of the "day of the Lord," the humbling of human pride. This may be taken as a precondition for the glorious vision of vv. 2–4. This vision of Zion's glorious future, which is also found in a slightly variant form in Mi 4:1–4, is rooted in the early Zion tradition, cultivated in the royal cult in Jerusalem. It celebrated God's choice of Jerusalem as the divine dwelling place, along with God's choice of the Davidic dynasty (Ps 68:16–17; 78:67–72; 132:13–18). *Highest mountain*: the Zion tradition followed earlier mythological conceptions that associate the abode of deities with very high mountains (Ps 48:2–3). The lifting of Mount Zion is a metaphor for universal recognition of the Lord's authority.

2:4 Once the nations acknowledge God as sovereign, they go up to Jerusalem to settle their disputes, rather than having recourse to war.

2:5 This verse is added as a conclusion to vv. 2–4; cf. Mi 4:4–5, where a quite different conclusion is provided for the parallel version of this oracle.

2:9 Bowing down to idols will not bring deliverance to Israel, but rather total abasement. *Do not pardon them*: this line is so abrupt that it is almost certainly an intrusion in the text.

2:11 *That day*: i.e., the day of the Lord; cf. note on Am 5:18.

2:13 *Lebanon*: Mount Lebanon in Syria, famed for its cedars. *Bashan*: the fertile uplands east of the Sea of Galilee.

2:22 The meaning of this verse, certainly a later addition, is not clear. It is not addressed to God but to a plural subject.

3:1–12 These verses suggest deportation, with resulting social upheaval, and thus may date to sometime after Ahaz submitted as vassal to Assyria. The deportation practiced by Assyria, as later by Babylon, exiled the leading elements of society, such as those named in vv. 2–3; cf. 2 Kgs 24:12, 14–16 for a similar list of those exiled by the Babylonians. Denuding society of its leaders opens the way to near anarchy and a situation in which leadership is seized by or thrust upon those unqualified for it (vv. 5–7). The situation has been provoked by sinfully inept leadership (vv. 4, 8–9, 12). Some suggest

---

* **2:2–4** Mi 4:1–4.
2:3 Is 56:7; 2 Kgs 17:26–28; Jer 31:6–14; Zec 8:20–23.
2:4 Jl 4:10.
2:4 Is 9:7; 11:4; Ps 46:10; Zec 9:10.
2:6 Is 10:32.
2:8 Is 17:7–8; 31:1–3.

Support and staff—
all support of bread,
all support of water:*
2 Hero and warrior,
judge and prophet, diviner and elder,
3 The captain of fifty and the nobleman,
counselor, skilled magician, and expert
charmer.
4 I will place boys as their princes;
the fickle will govern them,*
5 And the people will oppress one another,
yes, each one the neighbor.
The child will be insolent toward the elder,
and the base toward the honorable.*
6 When anyone seizes a brother
in their father's house, saying,
"You have clothes! Be our ruler,
and take in hand this ruin!"—
7 He will cry out in that day:
"I cannot be a healer,*
when there is neither bread nor clothing in
my own house!
You will not make me a ruler of the
people!"
8 Jerusalem has stumbled, Judah has fallen;
for their speech and deeds affront the
LORD,
a provocation in the sight of his majesty.
9 Their very look bears witness against them;*
they boast of their sin like Sodom,*
They do not hide it.
Woe to them!
They deal out evil to themselves.
10 Happy the just, for it will go well with them,
the fruit of their works they will eat.
11 Woe to the wicked! It will go ill with them,
with the work of their hands they will be
repaid.
12 My people—infants oppress them,
women rule over them!
My people, your leaders deceive you,*
they confuse the paths you should follow.

13† The LORD rises to accuse,
stands to try his people.
14 The Lord enters into judgment
with the people's elders and princes:
You, you who have devoured the vineyard;
the loot wrested from the poor is in your
houses.
15 What do you mean by crushing my people,
and grinding down the faces of the poor?
says the Lord, the GOD of hosts.

The Haughty Women of Zion†

16 The LORD said:*
Because the daughters of Zion are
haughty,
and walk with necks outstretched,
Ogling and mincing as they go,
their anklets tinkling with every step,
17 The Lord shall cover the scalps of Zion's
daughters with scabs,
and the LORD shall lay bare their heads.† *

18 † On that day the LORD will do away with the
finery of the anklets, sunbursts, and crescents;
19 the pendants, bracelets, and veils; 20 the head-
dresses, bangles, cinctures, perfume boxes, and
amulets; 21 the signet rings, and the nose rings;
22 the court dresses, wraps, cloaks, and purses;
23 the lace gowns, linen tunics, turbans, and
shawls.

24 Instead of perfume there will be stench,
instead of a girdle, a rope,
And instead of elaborate coiffure, baldness;
instead of a rich gown, a sackcloth skirt.
Then, instead of beauty, shame.
25 Your men will fall by the sword,
and your champions,† in war;*
26 Her gates will lament and mourn,
as the city sits desolate on the ground.*

4 1 Seven women will take hold of one man†
on that day, saying:
"We will eat our own food
and wear our own clothing;
Only let your name be given us,
put an end to our disgrace!"

† that vv. 4 and 12 refer to Ahaz, who may have come to the throne at an early age. Verses 10–11 form a wisdom couplet that was inserted later.

3:13–15 The princes and the elders, here accused of despoiling the poor, are the very ones who should be their defenders. *Loot*: by the Hebrew term (*gazela*) Isaiah conveys the idea of violent seizure, though 10:1–4 suggests the poor could be plundered by legal means.

3:16–4:1 Here and again in 32:9–14 Isaiah condemns the women of the ruling class for their part in Jerusalem's plight.

3:17 A shaven head is a mark of social disgrace; cf. Nm 5:18.

3:18–23 The long list of women's apparel in these verses suggests luxury and vanity; it contains a number of rare words, and the precise meaning of many of the terms is uncertain.

3:25 *Your men . . . your champions*: the second person feminine singular pronoun here shows that the prophet has shifted his attention from the women of Zion to the personified city of Zion.

4:1 *Seven women . . . one man*: deportation (cf. note on 3:1–12) would result in a disproportion of the sexes and leave the female population without enough male partners. The women are willing to marry, not for support, but to avoid disgrace.

* **3:1** Lv 26:26; Ez 4:16.
3:4 Eccl 10:16.
3:5 Mi 7:5–6.
3:7 Is 1:6.
3:9 Jer 3:3.
3:9 Is 1:10.
3:12 Mi 3:5.
3:16 Is 32:9–14; Ez 16:50; Am 4:1–3.
3:17 Jer 13:26; Ez 16:37.
3:25 Hos 14:1.
3:26 Is 47:1; Lam 2:10.

Introducing...

First Isaiah

The name Isaiah means "God is salvation" in Hebrew, and First Isaiah's preaching certainly reflects that message. Born in Jerusalem, he prophesied there during the reigns of Kings Uzziah, Jotham, Ahaz, and Hezekiah, between 742 and 701 BC (see 2 Kings, chapters 15–20, and 2 Chronicles, chapters 26–32). He was married to a prophetess, and they had two sons whose names played a symbolic role in his prophecy: Shear-jashub, meaning "a remnant shall remain," and Maher-shalal-hash-baz, meaning "the spoil speeds, the prey hastes." In his preaching, he emphasized the role of Jerusalem (Zion) as God's dwelling place and home to King David's dynasty. For this reason, he is also called Isaiah of Jerusalem.

First Isaiah had ready access to Judah's kings and was probably a member of an aristocratic family. His education shows in his use of language—he is responsible for some of the loftiest and most beautiful poetry in the Old Testament.

Jerusalem Purified

2† On that day,
The branch† of the LORD will be beauty and glory,
and the fruit of the land will be honor and splendor
for the survivors of Israel.
3 Everyone who remains in Zion,
everyone left in Jerusalem
Will be called holy:
everyone inscribed for life† in Jerusalem.*
4 When the Lord washes away
the filth of the daughters of Zion,
And purges Jerusalem's blood from her midst
with a blast of judgment, a searing blast,*
5 Then will the LORD create,
over the whole site of Mount Zion
and over her place of assembly,
A smoking cloud by day
and a light of flaming fire by night.*
6 For over all, his glory will be shelter and protection:
shade from the parching heat of day,
refuge and cover from storm and rain.*

The Song of the Vineyard†

5 1 Now let me sing of my friend,
my beloved's song about his vineyard.
My friend had a vineyard
on a fertile hillside;
2 He spaded it, cleared it of stones,
and planted the choicest vines;
Within it he built a watchtower,
and hewed out a wine press.
Then he waited for the crop of grapes,
but it yielded rotten grapes.*
3 Now, inhabitants of Jerusalem, people of Judah,
judge between me and my vineyard:
4 What more could be done for my vineyard
that I did not do?*
Why, when I waited for the crop of grapes,
did it yield rotten grapes?
5 Now, I will let you know
what I am going to do to my vineyard:
Take away its hedge, give it to grazing,
break through its wall, let it be trampled!†
6 Yes, I will make it a ruin:
it shall not be pruned or hoed,
but will be overgrown with thorns and briers;
I will command the clouds
not to rain upon it.
7 The vineyard of the LORD of hosts is the house of Israel,
the people of Judah, his cherished plant;
He waited for judgment, but see, bloodshed!
for justice, but hark, the outcry!†

---

† **4:2–6** Usually judged a later addition to the oracles of Isaiah. It relieves the threatening tone of the surrounding chaps. 3 and 5.

4:2 *Branch*: the term (Heb. *semah*) that is sometimes used of the ideal Davidic king of the future (cf. Jer 23:5; 33:15; Zec 3:8; 6:12). However, the parallel "fruit of the land" does not favor that usage here.

4:3 *Inscribed for life*: in God's list of the elect; cf. Ex 32:32.

5:1–7 *Vineyard*: although the term is sometimes used in an erotic context (Sg 1:6; 8:12), "vineyard" or "vine" is used more frequently as a metaphor for God's people (27:2; Ps 80:9, 14, 15; Jer 2:21; 12:10; Ez 17:7; Hos 10:1; Na 2:2). The terms translated "friend" (*yadid*) and "beloved" (*dod*) suggest the Lord's favor (Dt 33:12; 2 Sm 12:25; Ps 127:2) and familial background rather than introducing the piece as a "love song," as is sometimes suggested. The prophet disguises the real theme (the people's infidelity) so that the hearers will participate in the unfavorable judgment called for (vv. 3–4). Cf. the reversal of this parable in 27:2–6.

5:5–6 *Trampled . . . thorns and briers*: this judgment is echoed in the description of the devastated land in 7:23–25.

5:7 *Judgment . . . bloodshed . . . justice . . . outcry*: in Hebrew there is an impressive play on words: *mishpat* parallels *mispah*, *sedaqah* parallels *se'aqah*. See also the threefold "waited for" in vv. 2, 4, 7.

---

* **4:3** Is 6:13; Ob 17; Mal 3:16.
4:4 Is 1:21–28.
4:5 Ex 13:21.
4:6 Is 32:1–2.
5:2 Dt 32:32.
5:4 Mi 6:3–5.

Oracles of Reproach†

8† Ah! Those who join house to house,
who connect field with field,
Until no space remains, and you alone dwell
in the midst of the land!*
9 In my hearing the LORD of hosts has sworn:*
Many houses shall be in ruins,
houses large and fine, with nobody living
there.*
10 Ten acres of vineyard
shall yield but one bath,†
And a homer of seed
shall yield but an ephah.
11† Ah! Those who rise early in the morning
in pursuit of strong drink,
lingering late
inflamed by wine,
12 Banqueting on wine with harp and lyre,
timbrel and flute,*
But the deed of the LORD they do not regard,
the work of his hands they do not see!*
13 Therefore my people go into exile
for lack of understanding,*
Its nobles starving,
its masses parched with thirst.
14 Therefore Sheol enlarges its throat
and opens its mouth beyond measure;*
Down into it go nobility and masses,
tumult and revelry.
15 All shall be abased, each one brought low,
and the eyes of the haughty lowered,*
16 But the LORD of hosts shall be exalted by
judgment,
by justice the Holy God shown holy.*
17 Lambs shall graze as at pasture,
young goats shall eat in the ruins of the rich.
18 Ah! Those who tug at guilt with cords of
perversity,
and at sin as if with cart ropes!
19† Who say, "Let him make haste,
let him speed his work, that we may see it;
On with the plan of the Holy One of Israel!
let it come to pass, that we may know it!"*
20 Ah! Those who call evil good, and good evil,
who change darkness to light, and light
into darkness,
who change bitter to sweet, and sweet into
bitter!*
21 Ah! Those who are wise in their own eyes,
prudent in their own view!*
22 Ah! Those who are champions at drinking
wine,
masters at mixing drink!
23 Those who acquit the guilty for bribes,
and deprive the innocent of justice!*
24 Therefore, as the tongue of fire licks up stubble,
as dry grass shrivels in the flame,
Their root shall rot
and their blossom scatter like dust;
For they have rejected the instruction of the
LORD of hosts,
and scorned the word of the Holy One of
Israel.
25† Therefore the wrath of the LORD blazes against
his people,
he stretches out his hand to strike them;
The mountains quake,*
their corpses shall be like refuse in the
streets.
For all this, his wrath is not turned back,
his hand is still outstretched.

Invasion†

26 He will raise a signal to a far-off nation,
and whistle for it from the ends of the
earth.*
Then speedily and promptly they will
come.
27 None among them is weary, none stumbles,
none will slumber, none will sleep.
None with waist belt loose,
none with sandal thong broken.

†

5:8–24 These verses contain a series of short oracles introduced by the Hebrew particle *hoy* ("Ah!"), an emphatic exclamation, sometimes translated "Woe!"

5:8–10 An oracle against land-grabbers (v. 8); they will be impoverished instead of enriched (vv. 9–10).

5:10 *Ten acres*: a field with ten times the surface area a yoke of oxen could plow in one day. *Bath*: a liquid measure equal to about twelve gallons. *Homer*: a dry measure equal to what a donkey can carry, calculated to be about ten bushels. *Ephah*: a dry measure of about one bushel. So small a harvest is the fruit of the land-grabbers' greed.

5:11–13 An oracle against debauchery and indifference. *Strong drink*: the Hebrew word *shekar* means either beer or a type of wine, perhaps date wine, not distilled liquor.

5:19 An indication that some, presumably of the ruling class, scoff at Isaiah's teaching on the Lord's "plan" and "work" (cf. v. 12; 14:26–27; 28:9–14; 30:10–11).

5:25–30 These verses do not suit their present context. Apparently v. 25 was originally the conclusion of the poem of 9:7–20 directed against the Northern Kingdom; cf. the refrain that occurs here and in 9:11, 16, and 20. Verses 26–30 look to an invasion by Assyria and might originally have come immediately after the poem of 9:1–20 plus 5:25. The insertion of chaps. 6–8 may have occasioned the dislocation, as well as that of 10:1–4a, which may have originally belonged with the "reproach" oracles of 5:8–23.

5:26–30 This oracle threatens a future judgment, an invasion of the Assyrian army, God's instrument for punishing Judah (10:5, 15).

*

5:8 Mi 2:1–3.
5:9 Is 22:14.
5:9 Is 6:12.
5:12 Is 5:22; Am 6:1–7.
5:12 Is 5:19; 10:12; 14:24–27; 19:12, 17; 23:9; 28:21; 30:1.
5:13 Hos 4:6.
5:14 Hb 2:5.
5:15 Is 2:9, 11, 17.
5:16 Is 1:27.
5:19 Jer 17:15; 2 Pt 3:3–4.
5:20 Is 32:4–5.
5:21 Prv 3:7; 26:12; Rom 11:25; 12:16.
5:23 Ex 23:8; Prv 17:15.
5:25 Am 1:1; Zec 14:5; cf. Is 9:18a.
5:26 Is 7:18; 11:12; Jer 4:6; 50:2.

Live It!

Here I Am, Lord!

Phrases from the sixth chapter of Isaiah may be familiar from the song "Here I Am, Lord." This chapter tells of First Isaiah's call, which follows a biblical pattern:

1. *The person has some experience of God.* Isaiah has a dramatic vision of God in the Temple.
2. *God gives the person a mission.* God sends Isaiah to speak to the people.
3. *The person may deny being worthy.* Isaiah knows he has unclean (or sinful) lips.
4. *God addresses the denial and reassures the person.* God purifies Isaiah with fire and words of forgiveness.

You can see the same pattern for Moses' call in Exodus 3:1–12, Samuel's call in 1 Samuel 3:1–14, Jeremiah's call in Jeremiah 1:4–10, and Mary's call in Luke 1:26–38.

Christians are called by God to participate in Jesus' saving mission. They believe everyone needs to discover the way God wants them to live out that call.

- Do you believe that God has a mission for your life?
- How can you use your talents to create a more loving and just world?

▶ **Is 6:1–13**

28 Their arrows are sharp,
and all their bows are bent,
The hooves of their horses like flint,
and their chariot wheels like the whirlwind.
29 They roar like the lion,
like young lions, they roar;
They growl and seize the prey,
they carry it off and none can rescue.
30 They will growl over it, on that day,
like the growling of the sea,
Look to the land—
darkness closing in,
the light dark with clouds!*

B. The Book of Emmanuel

The Sending of Isaiah

6 [1]In the year King Uzziah died,† I saw the
Lord seated on a high and lofty throne,*
with the train of his garment filling the temple.
[2]Seraphim† were stationed above; each of them
had six wings: with two they covered their faces,
with two they covered their feet, and with two
they hovered.* [3]One cried out to the other:

"Holy, holy, holy† is the LORD of hosts!
All the earth is filled with his glory!"

[4]At the sound of that cry, the frame of the door
shook and the house was filled with smoke.† *
[5]Then I said, "Woe is me, I am doomed!†
For I am a man of unclean lips, living among a
people of unclean lips,* and my eyes have seen
the King, the LORD of hosts!" [6]Then one of the
seraphim flew to me, holding an ember which he
had taken with tongs from the altar.
[7]He touched my mouth with it. "See," he said,
"now that this has touched your lips,† your wick-
edness is removed, your sin purged."*
[8]Then I heard the voice of the Lord saying,
"Whom shall I send? Who will go for us?" "Here
I am," I said; "send me!" [9]† And he replied: Go
and say to this people:

†

6:1 *In the year King Uzziah died*: probably 742 B.C., although the chronology of this period is disputed. *A high and lofty throne*: within the holy of holies of the Jerusalem Temple stood two cherubim, or winged sphinxes, whose outstretched wings served as the divine throne (1 Kgs 6:23–28; Ez 1:4–28; 10:1, 20). The ark of the covenant was God's footstool (Ps 132:7–8; 1 Chr 28:2), placed under the cherubim (1 Kgs 8:6–7). *Temple*: the holy place, just in front of the holy of holies.

6:2 *Seraphim*: the plural of *saraph* ("to burn"), a term used to designate the "fiery" serpents of the wilderness (Nm 21:8; Dt 8:15), and to refer to "winged" serpents (Is 14:29; 30:6). Here, however, it is used adjectivally of the cherubim, who are not serpent-like, as seen in the fact that they have faces and sexual parts ("feet"). See the adaptation of these figures by Ezekiel (Ez 1:10–12; 10:4–15).

6:3 *Holy, holy, holy*: these words have been used in Christian liturgy from the earliest times.

6:4 *Smoke*: reminiscent of the clouds which indicated God's presence at Mount Sinai (Ex 19:16–19; Dt 4:11) and which filled the tabernacle (Ex 40:34–38) and the Temple (1 Kgs 8:10–11) at their dedication.

6:5 *Doomed*: there are two roots from which the verb here could be derived; one means "to perish, be doomed," the other "to become silent," and given Isaiah's delight in puns and double entendre, he probably intended to sound both notes. "I am doomed!" is suggested by the popular belief that to see God would lead to one's death; cf. Gn 32:31; Ex 33:20; Jgs 13:22. "I am struck silent!" is suggested by the emphasis on the lips in vv. 5–6, and such silence is attested elsewhere as the appropriate response to the vision of the Lord in the Temple (Hb 2:20).

6:7 *Touched your lips*: Isaiah is thus symbolically purified of sin in preparation for his mission as God's prophet.

6:9–10 Isaiah's words give evidence that he attempted in every

*

5:30 Is 8:22.
6:1 1 Kgs 22:19–23; Jn 12:41.
6:2 Rev 4:8.
6:4 Rev 15:8.
6:5 Is 29:13; Mt 15:1–11; Mk 7:1–13; Col 2:20–23.
6:7 Jer 1:9; Dn 10:16.

Listen carefully, but do not understand!
Look intently, but do not perceive! *
10 Make the heart of this people sluggish,
dull their ears and close their eyes;
Lest they see with their eyes, and hear with their ears,
and their heart understand,
and they turn and be healed. *

11 "How long, O Lord?" I asked. And he replied:

†Until the cities are desolate,
without inhabitants,
Houses, without people,
and the land is a desolate waste.
12 Until the LORD sends the people far away,
and great is the desolation in the midst of the land.
13 If there remain a tenth part in it,
then this in turn shall be laid waste;
As with a terebinth or an oak
whose trunk remains when its leaves have fallen. † *
Holy offspring is the trunk.

The Syro-Ephraimite War†

Crisis in Judah

7 1 In the days of Ahaz, † king of Judah, son of Jo-
tham, son of Uzziah, Rezin, king of Aram, and
Pekah, king of Israel, son of Remaliah, went up to
attack Jerusalem, but they were not able to con-
quer it. * 2 When word came to the house of David
that Aram had allied itself with Ephraim, the heart
of the king and heart of the people trembled, as
the trees of the forest tremble in the wind.

3 Then the LORD said to Isaiah: Go out to meet
Ahaz, you and your son Shear-jashub, † at the
end of the conduit of the upper pool, on the
highway to the fuller's field, 4 and say to him:
Take care you remain calm and do not fear; do
not let your courage fail before these two stumps
of smoldering brands, * the blazing anger of Re-
zin and the Arameans and of the son of Rema-
liah— 5 because Aram, with Ephraim and the son
of Remaliah, has planned† evil against you. They
say, 6 "Let us go up against Judah, tear it apart,
make it our own by force, and appoint the son
of Tabeel† king there."

7 Thus says the Lord GOD:
It shall not stand, it shall not be! *
8† The head of Aram is Damascus,
and the head of Damascus is Rezin;
9 The head of Ephraim is Samaria,
and the head of Samaria is the son of Remaliah.
Within sixty-five years,
Ephraim shall be crushed, no longer a nation.
Unless your faith is firm,
you shall not be firm! *

Emmanuel

10 Again the LORD spoke to Ahaz: 11 Ask for a
sign from the LORD, your God; let it be deep as
Sheol, or high as the sky! † 12 But Ahaz answered,
"I will not ask! I will not tempt the LORD!" †
13 Then he said: Listen, house of David! Is it not
enough that you weary human beings? Must
you also weary my God? 14 Therefore the Lord
himself will give you a sign; † the young woman,

† way, through admonition, threat, and promise, to bring the people to conversion (cf. 1:18–20), so it is unlikely that this charge to "harden" is to be understood as Isaiah's task; more probably it reflects the refusal of the people, more particularly the leaders, who were supposed to "see," "hear," and "understand," a refusal which would then lead to a disastrous outcome (vv. 11–12).

6:11–12 The desolation described would be the result of the sort of deportation practiced by the Assyrians and later by the Babylonians. Isaiah seems to expect this as an eventual consequence of Judah's submission as vassal to the Assyrians; cf. 3:1–3; 5:13.

6:13 *When its leaves have fallen*: the meaning of the Hebrew is uncertain, and the text may be corrupt. *Holy offspring*: part of the phrase is missing from the Septuagint and may be a later addition; it provides a basis for hope for the future.

7:1–8:18 These verses (often termed Isaiah's "Memoirs") contain a series of oracles and narratives (some in first person), all closely related to the Syro-Ephraimite war of 735–732 B.C. Several passages feature three children whose symbolic names refer to the Lord's purposes: Shear-jashub (7:3), Emmanuel (7:10–17; 8:8–10), and Maher-shalal-hash-baz (8:1–4). Judah and its Davidic dynasty should trust God's promises and not fear the combined armies of Israel and Syria; within a very short time these two enemy states will be destroyed, and David's dynasty will continue.

7:1 *Days of Ahaz*: who ruled from 735 to 715 B.C. This attack against Jerusalem by the kings of Aram (Syria) and Israel in 735 B.C. was occasioned by the refusal of Ahaz to enter with them into an anti-Assyrian alliance; cf. 2 Kgs 16.

7:3 *Shear-jashub*: this name means "a remnant will return" (cf. 10:20–22).

7:5 *Planned*: the plans of those who plot against Ahaz shall not be accomplished (v. 7). What the Lord plans will unfailingly come to pass, whereas human plans contrary to those of the Lord are doomed to frustration; cf. 8:10; 14:24–27; 19:11–14; 29:15; 30:1. See further the note on 14:24–27.

7:6 *Son of Tabeel*: a puppet of Jerusalem's enemies. His appointment would interrupt the lawful succession from David.

7:8–9 God had chosen and made a commitment to David's dynasty and his capital city Jerusalem, not to Rezin and his capital Damascus, nor to the son of Remaliah and his capital Samaria (2 Sm 7:12–16; Ps 2:6; 78:68–72; 132:11–18). *Within sixty-five years . . . nation*: this text occurs at the end of v. 8 in the Hebrew. Ahaz would not have been reassured by so distant a promise; the phrase is probably a later addition.

7:11 *Deep . . . sky*: an extraordinary or miraculous sign that would prove God's firm will to save the royal house of David from its oppressors.

7:12 *Tempt the LORD*: Ahaz prefers to depend upon the might of Assyria rather than the might of God.

7:14 Isaiah's sign seeks to reassure Ahaz that he need not fear the invading armies of Syria and Israel in the light of God's promise

* **6:9** Mt 13:10–17; Mk 4:10–12; Lk 8:9–10; Acts 28:25–28. **6:10** Jer 5:21; Jn 12:40. **6:13** Is 10:22. **7:1** 2 Kgs 16:5; 2 Chr 28:5–15. **7:4** Is 8:12; 30:15. **7:7** Is 8:10; Ps 33:10. **7:9** 2 Chr 20:20.

Cultural Connection

God-with-Us!

Many Bibles refer to Isaiah, chapters 7–12, as the Book of Immanuel. In these chapters, First Isaiah announces that Israel's salvation will come from a child from the family of Jesse, the father of King David. This child will be named Immanuel (also spelled Emmanuel), which means "God-with-us." With this message, Isaiah emphasizes that God is with the little ones who trust in God's saving power.

Biblical scholars agree that the child Isaiah is referring to is the son of King Ahaz—the future king Hezekiah. But the Gospel writers later see in this passage a reference to Jesus (see Mt 1:23), the Son of God, who is truly Immanuel, God-with-us.

For Hispanic people, Immanuel is a constant reality. Hispanics give witness of the nearness of God in daily affairs through the following expressions, which you may hear more than a dozen times a day in their communities: "God help you" (*Dios te ayude*), "Go with God" (*Ve con Dios*), "If God wants it" (*Si Dios quiere*), "With God's permission" (*Si Dios lo permite*), "Through the power of God" (*Dios mediante*), "Thanks to God" (*Gracias a Dios*), "For the love of God" (*Por el amor de Dios*), "God give you a good day" (*Buen día te dé Dios*), and "God bless you" (*Dios te bendiga*).

- If you come from a family or community tradition where these faith expressions are common, feel the presence of God each time they are voiced, and use them boldly yourself.
- Think about what happened to you today. How many of these expressions could you have applied to different situations and felt God-with-you? Choose the expression that best fits the yearnings of your heart at this time, and pray with it, repeating it several times.

▶ Isaiah, chapters 7–12

pregnant and about to bear a son, shall name
him Emmanuel. 15 Curds and honey† he will eat
so that he may learn to reject evil and choose
good; 16 for before the child learns to reject evil
and choose good, the land of those two kings
whom you dread shall be deserted.

17 The LORD shall bring upon you and your
people and your father's house such days as have
not come since Ephraim seceded† from Judah
(the king of Assyria). 18 On that day

The LORD shall whistle
for the fly in the farthest streams of Egypt,
and for the bee in the land of Assyria.*
19 All of them shall come and settle
in the steep ravines and in the rocky clefts,
on all thornbushes and in all pastures.

20 † On that day the Lord shall shave with the
razor hired from across the River (the king of As-
syria) the head, and the hair of the feet; it shall
also shave off the beard.*

21 On that day a man shall keep alive a young
cow or a couple of sheep, 22 and from their abun-
dant yield of milk he shall eat curds; curds and
honey shall be the food of all who are left in the
land. 23 † On that day every place where there
were a thousand vines worth a thousand pieces
of silver shall become briers and thorns. 24 One
shall have to go there with bow and arrows, for

† to David (2 Sm 7:12–16). The oracle follows a traditional announcement formula by which the birth and sometimes naming of a child is promised to particular individuals (Gn 16:11; Jgs 13:3). *The young woman*: Hebrew *'almah* designates a young woman of marriageable age without specific reference to virginity. The Septuagint translated the Hebrew term as *parthenos*, which normally does mean virgin, and this translation underlies Mt 1:23. *Emmanuel*: the name means "with us is God." Since for the Christian the incarnation is the ultimate expression of God's willingness to "be with us," it is understandable that this text was interpreted to refer to the birth of Christ.

7:15–16 *Curds and honey*: the only diet available to those who are left after the devastation of the land; cf. vv. 21–25.

7:17 *Such days as have not come since Ephraim seceded*: the days of the kingdom prior to the secession of Ephraim and the other northern tribes (1 Kgs 12). *The king of Assyria*: the final comment appears to be a later editorial gloss indicating days worse than any since the secession.

7:20 God will use the Assyrians from across the River (the Euphrates) as his instrument ("razor") to inflict disgrace and suffering upon his people. Ahaz paid tribute to the Assyrian king Tiglath-pileser III, who decimated Syria and Israel in his campaigns of 734–732 B.C. (cf. 2 Kgs 16:7–9). *The feet*: euphemism for sexual parts; cf. Is 6:2.

7:23–25 Cf. note on 5:5–6.

* **7:18** Is 5:26. **7:20** Is 3:24; 2 Sm 10:4–6; Ez 5:1.

Catholic Connection

Mary

Have you ever wondered what Mary, the mother of Jesus, was like as a young girl? Do you think Mary realized when she heard the reading from Isaiah 7:14 that the prophecy would be fulfilled through her? Imagine what it would be like to discover that you are destined to play such an important role in the salvation of the world!

We know little of Mary's childhood, but the Gospel writers give us insight into how Mary, through faith and the Holy Spirit, helped fulfill Isaiah's prophecy by becoming the Mother of God. Out of faith, Mary, while still a young virgin, willingly responded yes to the angel Gabriel when told that through the power of the Holy Spirit she would give birth to God's only son, Jesus (see Lk 1:26–38). Mary had to have faith that God's Spirit was at work in Jesus' life as he grew from a child into a man (see Lk 2:41–52). It was Mary's faith in God's plan and the power of the Holy Spirit that prompted her to encourage Jesus to begin his public ministry at the wedding at Cana (see Jn 2:1–12) and sustained her as she stood at the foot of the cross during her own son's Crucifixion (see Jn 19:17–30). After Jesus' Resurrection, it was faith in Christ's promises that motivated Mary to stay with the disciples and pray for the coming of the Holy Spirit who would guide them and give them the courage to spread the Gospel message (see Acts 1:12–14).

The Church recognizes Mary as not only the Mother of God but also the Mother of the Church because of the role she has had and continues to have in bringing others to salvation in Christ. Mary is the first to receive what has been promised to all of us—freedom from sin and everlasting life. According to Church teaching, Mary was free from all sin, including original sin, from the moment of her conception. This belief, called the Immaculate Conception, is rooted in the angel Gabriel's words to Mary, which describe her as "favored" or "full of grace." Because Mary was without original sin, which leads to death, the Church also teaches that Mary was taken, body and soul, into heaven without suffering death. This belief is called the Assumption.

Mary's willingness to say yes to God's plan and allow God's Spirit to work in her life has made her a model of faith for all believers. Her rescue from sin and death foreshadows God's promise to those who remain faithful. Ask Mary to pray that God's Spirit will fill your life, so that you too will have the faith needed to say yes to God's plan and bring his message of salvation to the world.

▶ **Is 7:14**

Catechism, nos. 484–511, 721–726, 963–975

all the country shall be briers and thorns.* 25 But
as for all the hills which were hoed with a mat-
tock, for fear of briers and thorns you will not
go there; they shall become a place for cattle to
roam and sheep to trample.*

A Son of Isaiah

8 1 The LORD said to me: Take a large tablet, and
inscribe on it with an ordinary stylus,† "be-
longing to Maher-shalal-hash-baz,"* 2 and call
reliable witnesses† for me, Uriah the priest, and
Zechariah, son of Jeberechiah.
3 Then I went to the prophetess and she con-
ceived and bore a son. The LORD said to me:
Name him Maher-shalal-hash-baz, 4 for before
the child learns to say, "My father, my mother,"
the wealth of Damascus and the spoils of Sa-
maria shall be carried off by the king of Assyria.

The Choice: The Lord or Assyria

5 Again the LORD spoke to me:

6 Because this people† has rejected
the waters of Shiloah that flow gently,
And melts with fear at the display of Rezin
and Remaliah's son,
7 Therefore the Lord is bringing up against them
the waters of the River, great and mighty,
the king of Assyria and all his glory.
It shall rise above all its channels,
and overflow all its banks.
8 It shall roll on into Judah,
it shall rage and pass on—
up to the neck it shall reach.*
But his outspread wings will fill
the width of your land, Emmanuel!
9 Band together, O peoples, but be shattered!
Give ear, all you distant lands!
Arm yourselves, but be shattered! Arm
yourselves, but be shattered!
10 Form a plan, it shall be thwarted;
make a resolve, it shall not be carried out,
for "With us is God!"† *

Disciples of Isaiah

11 For thus said the LORD—his hand strong
upon me—warning me not to walk in the way
of this people:

12† Do not call conspiracy what this people calls
conspiracy,
nor fear what they fear, nor feel dread.
13 But conspire with the LORD of hosts;
he shall be your fear, he shall be your dread.*
14 He shall be a snare,
a stone for injury,
A rock for stumbling
to both the houses of Israel,
A trap and a snare
to those who dwell in Jerusalem;*
15 And many among them shall stumble;
fallen and broken;
snared and captured.*

16 Bind up my testimony, seal the instruction
with my disciples.† 17 I will trust in the LORD, who
is hiding his face from the house of Jacob; yes, I
will wait for him. 18 Here am I and the children
whom the LORD has given me: we are signs† and
portents in Israel from the LORD of hosts, who
dwells on Mount Zion.*
19 And when they say to you, "Inquire of ghosts
and soothsayers who chirp and mutter;† * should
not a people inquire of their gods, consulting the
dead on behalf of the living, 20 for instruction and
testimony?" Surely, those who speak like this are
the ones for whom there is no dawn.†

21 He will pass through it hard-pressed and hungry,
and when hungry, shall become enraged,

---

†

8:1 *Ordinary stylus*: lit., "stylus of men." *Maher-shalal-hash-baz*: a symbolic name to be given to another son of Isaiah (v. 3); it means "quick spoils; speedy plunder," and describes what the Assyrians will do to Syria and Israel.

8:2 *Reliable witnesses*: who would testify that Isaiah had indeed prophesied the future destruction. *Uriah the priest*: cf. 2 Kgs 16:10.

8:6–8 *This people*: Judah. *Waters of Shiloah*: the stream that flows from the Gihon spring into the pool of Shiloah in Jerusalem and provides a sure supply in time of siege; here it symbolizes the divine protection which Judah has rejected by seeking Assyrian support, symbolized by "the River" (i.e., the Euphrates). Ultimately Assyrian power will devastate Judah. *His outspread wings*: the Lord's wings, a recurring symbol for divine protection (Ps 17:8; 36:8; 57:2; 61:5; 91:4; Ru 2:12). Some understand the image to refer to the sides of the flooding river, but this use of the Hebrew word for "wings" is unparalleled elsewhere in classical Hebrew.

8:10 The plan of Israel's enemies will be thwarted because, as the name "Emmanuel" signifies, "with us is God."

8:12–14 Because Isaiah and his followers resisted the official policy of seeking help from Assyria they were labeled "conspirators"; Isaiah uses the term to express what is really the case, cooperating with the Lord.

8:16 *Bind . . . seal . . . with my disciples*: because the prophet's message was not well received at the time, he wanted to preserve it until the future had vindicated him as God's true prophet (cf. 30:8–9).

8:18 *Signs*: in the meantime, while awaiting the vindication of his message, Isaiah and his children with their symbolic names stood as a reminder of God's message to Israel.

8:19 *Chirp and mutter*: a mocking reference to necromancers.

8:20 *Surely . . . no dawn*: reliance on necromancy brings futility.

8:22 *Oppressive gloom . . . without light*: the meaning of the Hebrew here is quite uncertain.

---

*

7:24 Is 32:13.
7:25 Is 5:5; 32:14.
8:1 Is 10:6.
8:8 Is 30:28.
8:10 Is 7:7; 17:12–14.
8:13 Is 29:23; 1 Pt 3:14–15.
8:14 Lk 2:34; Rom 9:32–33; 1 Pt 2:7–8.
8:15 Mt 21:44.
8:18 Is 2:2–5; 4:5; 11:9; 14:32; 28:16; 31:9; 33:5.
8:19 Is 29:4.

and curse king and gods.
He will look upward,
22 and will gaze at the earth,
But will see only distress and darkness,
oppressive gloom,
murky, without light.†

The Promise of Salvation Under a New Davidic King†

23 There is no gloom where there had been distress. Where once he degraded the land of Zebulun and the land of Naphtali, now he has glorified the way of the Sea, the land across the Jordan, Galilee of the Nations.†

9 1 The people who walked in darkness
have seen a great light;
Upon those who lived in a land of gloom
a light has shone.*
2 You have brought them abundant joy
and great rejoicing;
They rejoice before you as people rejoice at harvest,
as they exult when dividing the spoils.
3 For the yoke that burdened them,
the pole on their shoulder,
The rod of their taskmaster,
you have smashed, as on the day of Midian.†*
4 For every boot that tramped in battle,
every cloak rolled in blood,
will be burned as fuel for fire.*
5 For a child† is born to us, a son is given to us;
upon his shoulder dominion rests.
They name him Wonder-Counselor, God-Hero,*
Father-Forever, Prince of Peace.
6 His dominion is vast
and forever peaceful,
Upon David's throne, and over his kingdom,
which he confirms and sustains
By judgment and justice,
both now and forever.*
The zeal of the LORD of hosts will do this!

Pray It!

Christmas Light

Isaiah 9:1–6 describes Immanuel as a wise, brave, courageous, virtuous, and righteous king. Here, First Isaiah may be referring to King Hezekiah, the reformer king of Judah (see 2 Chronicles, chapters 29–33). However, after Hezekiah's death, the passage came to be understood as predicting the coming of a future savior or messiah. That's why the passage is called a messianic prophecy.

Christians see in these words a perfect description of Jesus. In fact, Catholics read these verses at Christmas during midnight Mass. On one of the longest nights of the year, they imagine Jesus' presence in the world as a light dispelling the darkness of sin.

This is the opening prayer for the Christmas Mass at midnight:

O God, who have made this most sacred night
radiant with the splendor of the true light,
grant, we pray, that we, who have known
the mysteries of his light on earth,
may also delight in his gladness in heaven.
Who lives and reigns with you in the
unity of the Holy Spirit,
one God, for ever and ever.
(Roman Missal)

▶ **Is 9:1–6**

Judgment on the Northern Kingdom†

7 The Lord has sent a word against Jacob,
and it falls upon Israel;

† **8:23–9:6** The meaning of 8:23 is somewhat uncertain, for example, whether the expressions translated "once" and "now" refer to times or to individuals, and also whether the verbs speak of degrading and glorifying the territories. If this traditional translation is correct, the passage would seem to promise the former Northern Kingdom of Israel deliverance from the Assyrians and might relate to Hezekiah's program of trying to reincorporate the northern territories into the kingdom of Judah and thus restore the boundaries of the country as it was under David.

8:23 The territories mentioned in this verse are those which the Assyrian king Tiglath-pileser III took from Israel and incorporated into the Assyrian provincial system as a result of the Syro-Ephraimite War of 735–732 B.C. (2 Kgs 15:29). *Zebulun . . . Naphtali*: regions of the former Northern Kingdom of Israel. *The way of the Sea*: the area along the Mediterranean coast south of Mount Carmel which became the Assyrian province of Dor. *Land across the Jordan*: the province of Gilead east of the Jordan. *Galilee of the Nations*: the territory north of Mount Carmel which was incorporated in the Assyrian province of Megiddo. Galilee apparently had a large non-Israelite population. Mt 4:15–16 cites this verse in the context of the beginning of Jesus' public mission in Galilee.

9:3 *Day of Midian*: when God used the judge Gideon to deliver these northern territories from Midianite oppression (Jgs 6–7).

9:5 *A child*: perhaps to be identified with the Emmanuel of 7:14 and 8:8; cf. 11:1–2, 9. This verse may reflect a coronation rather than a birth. *Upon his shoulder*: the reference may be to a particular act in the ritual in which a symbol of the king's authority was placed on his shoulder (cf. 2 Kgs 11:12; Is 22:22).

9:7–20 + 5:25–30 These verses describe a series of judgments God sent against the Northern Kingdom of Israel because of its sins. Despite

* **9:1** Mt 4:15–16. **9:3** Is 10:26; Jgs 7:22–25. **9:4** Ps 46:10. **9:5** Is 10:21. **9:6** Jer 23:5; Lk 1:32–33.

8 And all the people know it—
Ephraim and those who dwell in Samaria—
those who say in arrogance and pride of heart,
9 "Bricks have fallen,
but we will rebuild with cut stone;
Sycamores have been felled,
but we will replace them with cedars."*
10 So the LORD raises up their foes against them
and stirs up their enemies to action—
11 Aram† from the east and the Philistines from the west—
they devour Israel with open mouth.
For all this, his wrath is not turned back,
and his hand is still outstretched!
12 The people do not turn back to the one who struck them,
nor do they seek the LORD of hosts.
13 So the LORD cuts off from Israel head and tail,
palm branch and reed in one day.*
14 (The elder and the noble are the head,
the prophet who teaches falsehood is the tail.)*
15 Those who lead this people lead them astray,
and those who are led are swallowed up.*
16 That is why the Lord does not spare their young men,
and their orphans and widows he does not pity;
For they are totally impious and wicked,
and every mouth speaks folly.
For all this, his wrath is not turned back,
his hand is still outstretched!
17 For wickedness burns like fire,
devouring brier and thorn;
It kindles the forest thickets,
which go up in columns of smoke.*
18 At the wrath of the LORD of hosts the land quakes,
and the people are like fuel for fire;
no one spares his brother.*
19 They hack on the right, but remain hungry;
they devour on the left, but are not filled.
Each devours the flesh of the neighbor;
20 Manasseh devours Ephraim,† and Ephraim Manasseh,
together they turn on Judah.
For all this, his wrath is not turned back,
his hand is still outstretched!

Perversion of Justice

10 1† Ah! Those who enact unjust statutes,
who write oppressive decrees,*
2 Depriving the needy of judgment,
robbing my people's poor of justice,
Making widows their plunder,
and orphans their prey!*
3 What will you do on the day of punishment,
when the storm comes from afar?
To whom will you flee for help?
Where will you leave your wealth,
4 Lest it sink beneath the captive
or fall beneath the slain?
For all this, his wrath is not turned back,
his hand is still outstretched!†

Judgment on Assyria

5† Ah! Assyria, the rod of my wrath,
the staff I wield in anger.*
6 Against an impious nation† I send him,
and against a people under my wrath I order him
To seize plunder, carry off loot,
and to trample them like the mud of the street.
7 But this is not what he intends,
nor does he have this in mind;
Rather, it is in his heart to destroy,
to make an end of not a few nations.
8 For he says, "Are not my commanders all kings?"
9† "Is not Calno like Carchemish,
Or Hamath like Arpad,
or Samaria like Damascus?

---

† the judgments, however, Israel continued to rebel, and God's anger remained unabated, as the recurring refrain emphasizes (9:11, 16, 20). The refrain ties Is 9:7–20 together as a unit, but 9:20 is far too abrupt to be the original conclusion to the oracle. With its series of past judgments and repeated refrain, the oracle resembles Am 4:6–12; by analogy with that model one expects a conclusion in which the prophet turns from the narration of past judgments to the announcement of a future judgment. Is 5:25–30 fits the pattern found in 9:7–20 and provides a suitable and possibly original conclusion for the whole oracle.

9:11 *Aram*: the Syrian kingdom, with its capital at Damascus.

9:20 *Manasseh . . . Ephraim*: two of the leading tribes of the Northern Kingdom. The reference is to the civil wars that marked the final decades of the Northern Kingdom (2 Kgs 15:10, 14–16, 25; cf. Hos 7:3–7).

10:1–4 This is another *hoy*-oracle; cf. note on 5:8–24. It may originally have been part of the collection at 5:8–24.

10:4 *For all this . . . outstretched!*: this refrain appears to be out of place here; cf. 9:11, 16, 20.

10:5–34 These verses contain a series of oracles directed against Assyria. Verses 5–15 portray Assyria as simply the rod God uses to punish Israel, though Assyria does not realize this. The original conclusion to this unit may be the judgment found in vv. 24–27a, which continues the imagery and motifs found in vv. 5–15. Verses 16–23, because of the quite different imagery and motifs, may originally have been an insertion directed against Aram and Israel at the time of the Syro-Ephraimite War.

10:6 *Impious nation*: Judah. It was God's intention to use Assyria merely to punish, not to destroy, the nation.

10:9–10 The cities mentioned were all cities captured, some more than once, by the Assyrians in the eighth century B.C. Verse 9 suggests a certain historical order in the fall of these cities, and v. 10 suggests that all of them had fallen before Samaria (cf. Am 6:2). That

---

* **9:9** Mal 1:4.
9:13 Is 19:15; Dt 28:13, 44.
9:14 Is 28:7.
9:15 Is 3:12.
9:17 Is 5:24; 33:11–12.
9:18 Is 3:5.
10:1 Jer 8:8.
10:2 Is 1:23; 3:14–15.
10:5 Jer 51:20–23.

10 Just as my hand reached out to idolatrous
kingdoms
that had more images than Jerusalem and
Samaria—
11 Just as I treated Samaria and her idols,
shall I not do to Jerusalem and her graven
images?"

12 But when the LORD has brought to an end all
his work on Mount Zion and in Jerusalem,

I will punish the utterance
of the king of Assyria's proud heart,
and the boastfulness of his haughty eyes.
13 For he says:
"By my own power I have done it,
and by my wisdom, for I am shrewd.
I have moved the boundaries of peoples,
their treasures I have pillaged,
and, like a mighty one, I have brought
down the enthroned.
14 My hand has seized, like a nest,
the wealth of nations.
As one takes eggs left alone,
so I took in all the earth;
No one fluttered a wing,
or opened a mouth, or chirped!"
15 Will the ax boast against the one who hews
with it?
Will the saw exalt itself above the one who
wields it?
As if a rod could sway the one who lifts it,
or a staff could lift the one who is not
wood!
16 Therefore the Lord, the LORD of hosts,
will send leanness among his fat ones,†
And under his glory there will be a kindling
like the kindling of fire.*
17 The Light of Israel will become a fire,
the Holy One, a flame,
That burns and consumes its briers
and its thorns in a single day.*
18 And the glory of its forests and orchards
will be consumed, soul and body,
and it will be like a sick man who wastes
away.
19 And the remnant of the trees in his forest
will be so few,
that any child can record them.
20 On that day
The remnant of Israel,
the survivors of the house of Jacob,
will no more lean upon the one who struck
them;
But they will lean upon the LORD,
the Holy One of Israel, in truth.
21 A remnant will return,† the remnant of Jacob,
to the mighty God.
22 Though your people, O Israel,
were like the sand of the sea,*
Only a remnant of them will return;
their destruction is decreed,
as overflowing justice demands.*

23 For the Lord, the GOD of hosts, is about to carry
out the destruction decreed in the midst of the
whole land.*
24 † Therefore thus says the Lord, the GOD of
hosts: My people, who dwell in Zion, do not fear
the Assyrian, though he strikes you with a rod,
and raises his staff against you as did the Egyp-
tians. 25 For just a brief moment more, and my
wrath shall be over, and my anger shall be set
for their destruction. 26 Then the LORD of hosts
will raise against them a scourge such as struck
Midian at the rock of Oreb;* and he will raise
his staff over the sea as he did in Egypt.* 27 On
that day,

His burden shall be taken from your
shoulder,
and his yoke shattered from your neck.*

The March of an Enemy Army†

He has come up from Rimmon,
28 he has reached Aiath, passed through
Migron,
at Michmash he has stored his supplies.
29 He has crossed the ravine,
at Geba he has camped for the night.
Ramah trembles,
Gibeah of Saul has fled.

† implies that one should think primarily of events during the reign of Tiglath-pileser III (745–727).

10:16 *His fat ones*: the strong men of the enemy army.

10:21 *A remnant will return*: in Hebrew, *shear-jashub*, an allusion to the name of Isaiah's son, Shear-jashub; cf. 7:3.

10:24 This verse with its reference to Assyria's rod may introduce the original conclusion to vv. 5–15.

10:27b–32 A poetic description of the march of an enemy army from the north, advancing south to the very gates of Jerusalem, where the enemy waves his hand in a gesture of derision against the city. Though Sennacherib's troops took a different route, advancing down the coast and then approaching Jerusalem from the southeast, the arrogant attitude toward God's chosen city was the same. *Aiath*: the Ai of Jos 7:22–8:29. *Migron*: modern Makrun north of Michmash. *The ravine*: the deep valley between Michmash and Geba (cf. 1 Sm 14:1–5). *Ramah . . . Gibeah . . . Bath-Gallim . . . Laishah . . . Anathoth . . . Madmenah . . . Gebim*: cities north of Jerusalem threatened by the sudden appearance of this enemy army. *Nob*: probably to be identified with the present Mount Scopus from where one has a clear view of Jerusalem.

* **10:16** Is 17:4.
10:17 Is 9:17–18; 30:27–33; 31:9; 33:14.
10:22 Hos 2:1; Rom 9:27–28.
10:22 Is 28:16–18.
10:23 Is 28:22.
10:26 Is 9:3; Jgs 7:25.
10:26 Ex 14:16.
10:27 Is 9:3.

Live It!

Lions and Lambs

There are so many troubled spots in the world. It seems that almost every week, violence and ethnic clashes occur somewhere. How easily we forget that we are all members of the human family.

Yet, we are drawn to the image of the peaceable kingdom in Isaiah 11:6–9. To imagine natural predators such as wolves and lions living together in harmony with lambs and calves, their natural prey, gives us an insight into the Reign of God. Harmony. Peace. Gentleness. No wonder this scene has been the inspiration for numerous artists.

It is a vision we must all aim for, while also doing our best to resist all the things that pull us apart as a human family. We are all in this together. We need to work to make the peaceable Reign of God a reality. It is God's work we do.

It is inspiring that First Isaiah also uses the image of youth to express his vision of peace. What can you as a young person do to help bring about the peaceable kingdom?

▶ Is 11:6–9

30 Cry and shriek, Bath-Gallim!
Hearken, Laishah! Answer her, Anathoth!
31 Madmenah is in flight,
the inhabitants of Gebim seek refuge.
32 Even today he will halt at Nob,
he will shake his fist at the mount of daughter Zion,
the hill of Jerusalem!

33† Now the Lord, the LORD of hosts,
is about to lop off the boughs with terrible violence;
The tall of stature shall be felled,
and the lofty ones shall be brought low;
34 He shall hack down the forest thickets with an ax,
and Lebanon in its splendor shall fall.

The Ideal Davidic King†

11 †1 But a shoot shall sprout from the stump† of Jesse,
and from his roots a bud shall blossom.*
2† The spirit of the LORD shall rest upon him:*
a spirit of wisdom and of understanding,
A spirit of counsel and of strength,
a spirit of knowledge and of fear of the LORD,
3 and his delight shall be the fear of the LORD.
Not by appearance shall he judge,
nor by hearsay shall he decide,
4 But he shall judge the poor with justice,
and decide fairly for the land's afflicted.*
He shall strike the ruthless with the rod of his mouth,
and with the breath of his lips he shall slay the wicked.*
5 Justice shall be the band around his waist,
and faithfulness a belt upon his hips.*
6† Then the wolf shall be a guest of the lamb,
and the leopard shall lie down with the young goat;
The calf and the young lion shall browse together,
with a little child to guide them.*
7 The cow and the bear shall graze,
together their young shall lie down;
the lion shall eat hay like the ox.*
8 The baby shall play by the viper's den,
and the child lay his hand on the adder's lair.
9 They shall not harm or destroy on all my holy mountain;

†

10:33–34 Just when the enemy is about to capture Jerusalem, God intervenes and destroys the hostile army. Cf. 29:1–8; 31:4–9.

11:1–16 Isaiah 11 contains a prophecy of the rise of a new Davidic king who will embody the ancient ideal of Davidic kingship (vv. 1–9), an elaboration of that prophecy in a further description of that king's rule (v. 10), and a prophecy of God's deliverance of the chosen people from exile and cessation of enmities (vv. 11–16).

11:1–9 (10) Here Isaiah looks forward to a new Davidide who will realize the ancient ideals (see Ps 72). The oracle does not seem to have a particular historical person in mind.

11:1 *Shoot . . . stump*: the imagery suggests the bankruptcy of the monarchy as embodied in the historical kings, along with the need for a new beginning, to spring from the very origin from which David and his dynasty arose. *Jesse*: David's father (cf. 1 Sm 16:1–13).

11:2–3 The source of the traditional names of the gifts of the Holy Spirit. The Septuagint and the Vulgate read "piety" for "fear of the Lord" in its first occurrence, thus listing seven gifts.

11:6–9 This picture of the idyllic harmony of paradise is a dramatic symbol of universal peace and justice under the rule of the new Davidic king. The peace and harmony even among carnivores and their natural prey in this description suggest a paradisiac aspect of the reign of the new king.

11:1 Is 4:2; 53:2; Jer 23:5–6; 33:14–16; Zec 3:8; 6:12; Rev 22:16.
11:2 Is 42:1; 1 Sm 16:13; Mt 3:16; Mk 1:10; Jn 1:32.
11:4 Ps 72:2, 4; 98:9.
11:4 2 Thes 2:8; Rev 2:16.
11:5 Eph 6:14.
11:6 Hos 2:20.
11:7 Is 65:25.

Catholic Connection

The Gifts of the Holy Spirit

Have you ever wanted to make the world a better place but did not know where to begin? Isaiah, too, wanted to see the world become a better place. Isaiah prophesied about a world marked by justice and peace and led by the ideal king. This ideal king would embody the following gifts, known as the gifts of the Holy Spirit: wisdom, understanding, counsel, fortitude, knowledge, piety, and fear of the Lord.

Nearly eight hundred years later, Isaiah's ideal king arrived; he was Jesus of Nazareth, the Son of God. Jesus' life, death, and Resurrection reveal that Jesus truly is the ideal king. The Church teaches that the gifts of the Holy Spirit prophesied by Isaiah are fully present in Jesus Christ.

The same gifts embodied in Christ are handed on to Jesus' followers through the grace of Baptism and increased through the sacrament of Confirmation. The gifts shape our heart and character so that we may humbly and willingly follow the guidance offered by the Holy Spirit and by doing so begin to make the world a better place.

Here are some suggestions for using the gifts of the Holy Spirit in your daily life:

- Pray for **wisdom** when life gets complicated and you have lost sight of the big picture.
- Pray for **understanding** when you have a problem and need to figure out what is at the heart of it.
- Pray for **counsel (right judgment)** when a friend asks you for advice.
- Pray for **fortitude (courage)** when you know the right thing to do but are afraid to do it.
- Pray for **knowledge** when you need to separate the truth from lies.
- Pray for **piety** when you are struggling to trust God.
- Pray for **fear of the Lord (awe in God's presence)** every day so that you may know in your heart how very awesome God is.

If each one of us works to develop the gifts of the Holy Spirit in our own lives, then truly we will all be working together to make the world a better place!

Is 11:1–2
Catechism, nos. 1830–1832

Live It!

In God We Trust

In God we trust. Every piece of U.S. currency bears this statement, yet many of us never notice it. First Isaiah proclaims this same message: "God indeed is my salvation; / I am confident and unafraid. / For the LORD is my strength and my might, / and he has been my salvation" (Is 12:2).

How often does fear keep us from trusting? How often does it keep us from being and doing what God is calling us to be and do? We need to reach out to God and to others in our lives and trust that God is with us. Jesus came to tell us that love is more powerful than fear, and his life and death testified to his deep trust in his Father. Many times, he told his disciples, "Do not be afraid."

Let us truly live the words "In God we trust."

► Is 12:1–6

for the earth shall be filled with knowledge
of the LORD,
as water covers the sea.

Restoration†

10 On that day,
The root of Jesse,
set up as a signal for the peoples—
Him the nations will seek out;
his dwelling shall be glorious.*
11 On that day,
The Lord shall again take it in hand
to reclaim the remnant of his people
that is left from Assyria and Egypt,
Pathros, Ethiopia, and Elam,
Shinar, Hamath, and the isles of the sea.*
12 He shall raise a signal to the nations*
and gather the outcasts of Israel;
The dispersed of Judah he shall assemble
from the four corners of the earth.
13 The envy of Ephraim shall pass away,
and those hostile to Judah shall be cut off;
Ephraim shall not envy Judah,
and Judah shall not be hostile to Ephraim;
14 But they shall swoop down on the foothills
of the Philistines to the west,
together they shall plunder the people of
the east;†
Edom and Moab shall be their possessions,
and the Ammonites their subjects.
15 The LORD shall dry up the tongue† of the Sea
of Egypt,
and wave his hand over the Euphrates with
his fierce wind,
And divide it into seven streamlets,
so that it can be crossed in sandals.*
16 There shall be a highway for the remnant of
his people
that is left from Assyria,
As there was for Israel
when it came up from the land of Egypt.*

Song of Thanksgiving†

12 1 On that day, you will say:
I give you thanks, O LORD;
though you have been angry with me,
your anger has abated, and you have
consoled me.
2 God indeed is my salvation;
I am confident and unafraid.
For the LORD is my strength and my might,
and he has been my salvation.*
3 With joy you will draw water
from the fountains of salvation,*
4 And you will say on that day:
give thanks to the LORD, acclaim his name;
Among the nations make known his deeds,
proclaim how exalted is his name.*
5 Sing praise to the LORD for he has done
glorious things;
let this be known throughout all the earth.*
6 Shout with exultation, City of Zion,
for great in your midst
is the Holy One of Israel!*

†

11:10–16 This passage, with its reference to God's people in widely scattered lands, is probably from a much later period. God will restore them to their own land. The reconciliation of Ephraim (i.e., the Northern Kingdom) and Judah reverses what Isaiah saw as a disastrous event of the past (cf. 7:17). God's action is likened to a new exodus, analogous to the time God first acquired Israel in bringing them out of the land of Egypt. *Pathros*: upper Egypt. *Elam*: east of Babylonia. *Shinar*: Babylonia. *Hamath*: on the Orontes River in Syria. *Isles*: or coastlands, in the Mediterranean.

11:14 *People of the east*: tribes in the Arabian Desert (cf. Jgs 6:3, 33; 7:12).

11:15 *Tongue*: perhaps to be identified with the Gulf of Suez.

12:1–6 Israel's thanksgiving to the Lord, expressed in language like that of the Psalms.

*

11:10 Is 2:2–4; Rom 15:12.
11:11 Ex 3:20; Jer 23:7–8; 31:1–22; Zec 10:10.
11:12 Is 18:3.
11:15 Zec 10:11; Rev 16:12.
11:16 Is 51:10; Ex 14:29.
12:2 Ex 15:2; Ps 118:14.
12:3 Jgs 5:11; Jer 2:13; Jn 4:10, 14.
12:4 Ps 105:1; 148:13.
12:5 Is 11:9; Ex 15:1.
12:6 Is 52:8–9; 54:1; Zep 3:14–15.

C. Oracles Against the Foreign Nations†

Babylon†

13 1 An oracle† concerning Babylon; a vision of Isaiah, son of Amoz.

2 Upon the bare mountains set up a signal;
cry out to them,†
Beckon for them to enter
the gates of the nobles.*
3 I have commanded my consecrated ones,†
I have summoned my warriors,
eager and bold to carry out my anger.*
4 Listen! the rumble on the mountains:
that of an immense throng!
Listen! the noise of kingdoms, nations
assembled!
The LORD of hosts is mustering
an army for battle.*
5 They come from a far-off country,
and from the end of the heavens,
The LORD and the instruments of his wrath,
to destroy all the land.
6 Howl, for the day of the LORD† is near;
as destruction from the Almighty it comes.*
7 Therefore all hands fall helpless,*
every human heart melts,
8 and they are terrified,
Pangs and sorrows take hold of them,
like a woman in labor they writhe;
They look aghast at each other,
their faces aflame.*
9 Indeed, the day of the LORD comes,
cruel, with wrath and burning anger;
To lay waste the land
and destroy the sinners within it!*
10 The stars of the heavens and their constellations
will send forth no light;
The sun will be dark at its rising,
and the moon will not give its light.*

Did You Know?

Oracles

In the ancient world, an oracle was understood as a communication of the gods. By means of oracles, First Isaiah presents God's judgment on Israel's enemies, including Egypt, Babylon, Assyria, Philistia, Moab, and Edom (see Isaiah, chapters 13–23). When we read these oracles today, we can understand their angry and vengeful spirit if we recall the terrible suffering that these nations inflicted on Israel. Still, we should also keep in mind the New Testament commandment to avoid revenge in all its forms (see Mt 5:38–48). Jesus calls us to be peacemakers in spite of our suffering.

▶ **Isaiah, chapters 13–23**

11 Thus I will punish the world for its evil
and the wicked for their guilt.
I will put an end to the pride of the arrogant,
the insolence of tyrants I will humble.*
12 I will make mortals more rare than pure gold,
human beings, than the gold of Ophir.†*
13 For this I will make the heavens tremble
and the earth shall be shaken from its place,
At the wrath of the LORD of hosts
on the day of his burning anger.*
14 Like a hunted gazelle,
or a flock that no one gathers,
They shall turn each to their own people
and flee each to their own land.*
15 Everyone who is taken shall be run through;
and everyone who is caught shall fall by
the sword.

†

13:1–23:18 These chapters, which probably existed at one time as an independent collection, consist primarily of oracles from various sources against foreign nations. While some of the material is Isaianic, in many cases it has been reworked by later editors or writers.

13:1–22 Although attributed to Isaiah (v. 1), this oracle does not reflect conditions of Isaiah's time. Babylon did not achieve imperial status until a century later, after its victory over Assyria in 609 B.C. The mention of the Medes (v. 17) rather than Persia suggests a date prior to 550 B.C., when the Median empire of Astyages fell to Cyrus the Persian. Tension is created in that the attackers are not named until v. 17 and the foe to be attacked until v. 19.

13:1 *Oracle*: Heb. *massa'*; used eight more times in this collection.

13:2 *To them*: the Medes (v. 17), who are being summoned to destroy Babylon. *Gates of the nobles*: the reference is apparently to the gates of Babylon and involves a wordplay on the city name (Babylon = *bab ilani*, "gate of the gods").

13:3 *Consecrated ones*: in the sense that they will wage a "holy war" and carry out God's plan.

13:6–8 *Day of the LORD*: described often in prophetic writings, it generally signified the coming of the Lord in power and majesty to destroy his enemies. The figures used convey the idea of horror and destruction (Am 5:18–20). *The Almighty*: Heb. *shaddai*; there is a play on words between destruction (*shod*) and Shaddai, a title for God traditionally rendered as "the Almighty" (cf. Gn 17:1; Ex 6:3).

13:12 *Ophir*: cf. note on Ps 45:10.

*

13:2 Is 5:26; Jer 50:2.
13:3 Jl 4:9.
13:4 Jer 50:9.
13:6 Is 2:12–21; Jer 46:10; Am 5:18–20; Jl 1:15; Zep 1:7; Rev 6:17.
13:7 Jer 6:24; Ez 7:17.
13:8 Is 21:3; Ps 48:7; Mi 4:9.
13:9 Jer 4:7; 18:16; Mal 3:19.
13:10 Is 24:23; Jer 4:23; Zep 1:15; Mt 24:29.
13:11 Is 2:17; Jer 50:32.
13:12 1 Kgs 9:28; Jb 22:24.
13:13 Hg 2:6; Lam 1:12.
13:14 1 Kgs 22:17; Jer 50:16; 51:9.

16 Their infants shall be dashed to pieces in their
sight;
their houses shall be plundered
and their wives ravished.*
17 I am stirring up against them the Medes,
who think nothing of silver
and take no delight in gold.*
18 With their bows they shall shatter the young
men,
And the fruit of the womb they shall not
spare,
nor shall their eye take pity on children.
19 And Babylon, the jewel of kingdoms,
the glory and pride of the Chaldeans,
Shall become like Sodom and Gomorrah,
overthrown by God.*
20 It shall never be inhabited,
nor dwelt in, from age to age;
Arabians shall not pitch their tents there,
nor shepherds rest their flocks there.*
21 But desert demons shall rest there
and owls shall fill the houses;
There ostriches shall dwell,
and satyrs† shall dance.*
22 Wild dogs shall dwell in its castles,
and jackals in its luxurious palaces.
Its time is near at hand
and its days shall not be prolonged.*

Restoration of Israel

14 [1] But the LORD will take pity on Jacob and
again choose Israel, and will settle them
on their own land; foreigners will join them and
attach themselves to the house of Jacob.* [2] The
nations will take them and bring them to their
place, and the house of Israel will possess them†
as male and female slaves on the Lord's land;
they will take captive their captors and rule over
their oppressors.*

Downfall of the King of Babylon

[3] On the day when the LORD gives you rest from
your sorrow and turmoil, from the hard service
with which you served,* [4] you will take up this
taunt-song† against the king of Babylon:*

How the oppressor has come to an end!
how the turmoil has ended!
5 The LORD has broken the rod of the wicked,
the staff of the tyrants*
6 That struck the peoples in wrath
with relentless blows;
That ruled the nations in anger,
with boundless persecution.*
7 The whole earth rests peacefully,
song breaks forth;
8 The very cypresses rejoice over you,
the cedars of Lebanon:
"Now that you are laid to rest,
no one comes to cut us down."*
9 Below, Sheol is all astir
preparing for your coming;
Awakening the shades to greet you,
all the leaders of the earth;
Making all the kings of the nations
rise from their thrones.
10 All of them speak out
and say to you,
"You too have become weak like us,
you are just like us!
11 Down to Sheol your pomp is brought,
the sound of your harps.
Maggots are the couch beneath you,
worms your blanket."*
12 How you have fallen from the heavens,
O Morning Star,† son of the dawn!
How you have been cut down to the earth,
you who conquered nations!*
13 In your heart you said:
"I will scale the heavens;
Above the stars of God†
I will set up my throne;
I will take my seat on the Mount of Assembly,
on the heights of Zaphon.*
14 I will ascend above the tops of the clouds;
I will be like the Most High!"*

---

†

13:21 *Satyrs*: in the popular mind, demons of goatlike form dwelling in ruins, symbols of immorality; cf. Lv 17:7; Is 34:14.

14:2 *Possess them*: Israel will make slaves of the nations who escort it back to its land.

14:4–21 This taunt-song, a satirical funeral lament, is a beautiful example of classical Hebrew poetry. According to the prose introduction and the prosaic conclusion (vv. 22–23), it is directed against the king of Babylon, though Babylon is mentioned nowhere in the song itself. If the reference to Babylon is accurate, the piece was composed long after the time of Isaiah, for Babylon was not a threat to Judah in the eighth century. Some have argued that Isaiah wrote it at the death of an Assyrian king and the references to Babylon were made by a later editor, but this is far from certain.

14:12 *Morning Star*: term addressed to the king of Babylon. The Vulgate translates as "Lucifer," a name applied by the church Fathers to Satan. *Son of the dawn*: Heb., *ben shahar*, may reflect the name of a pagan deity.

14:13–15 *God*: not Elohim, the common word for God, but El, the name of the head of the pantheon in Canaanite mythology, a god who was early identified with the Lord in Israelite thought. *Mount of Assembly*: mountain where the council of the gods met, according to Canaanite mythology. *Zaphon*: the sacred mountain of

---

*

13:16 2 Kgs 8:12; Ps 137:9; Na 3:10.
13:17 Is 21:2; Jer 51:11, 28.
13:19 Dt 29:22; Is 1:7; Jer 49:18; 50:40; Am 4:11.
13:20 Jer 51:62.
13:21 Is 34:13–14; 35:7.
13:22 Ez 32:23.
14:1 Is 56:3; 60:4; Ps 102:14; Jer 24:6; Zec 1:17.
14:2 Is 49:22–23; 60:14; 66:20.
14:3 Ex 33:14; Jos 1:13; Jer 30:10.
14:4 Hb 2:6.
14:5 Is 10:24–27.
14:6 Is 10:5–7.
14:8 Is 37:24; 44:23; 55:12; Ez 31:16.
14:11 Sir 10:11.
14:12 Jb 14:10.
14:13 Jer 51:53; Am 9:2.
14:14 Ez 28:2; Zep 2:15; 2 Thes 2:4.

15 No! Down to Sheol you will be brought
to the depths of the pit!*
16 When they see you they will stare,
pondering over you:
"Is this the man who made the earth tremble,
who shook kingdoms?
17 Who made the world a wilderness,
razed its cities,
and gave captives no release?"
18 All the kings of the nations lie in glory,
each in his own tomb;*
19 But you are cast forth without burial,
like loathsome carrion,
Covered with the slain, with those struck by
the sword,
a trampled corpse,
Going down to the very stones of the pit.*
20 You will never be together with them in the
grave,
For you have ruined your land,
you have slain your people!
Let him never be named,
that offshoot of evil!
21 Make ready to slaughter his sons
for the guilt of their fathers;*
Lest they rise and possess the earth,
and fill the breadth of the world with
cities.†

22 I will rise up against them, says the LORD of
hosts, and cut off from Babylon name and rem-
nant, progeny and offspring, says the LORD.* 23 I
will make it a haunt of hoot owls and a marsh-
land; I will sweep it with the broom of destruc-
tion, oracle of the LORD of hosts.

God's Plan for Assyria†

24 The LORD of hosts has sworn:
As I have resolved,
so shall it be;
As I have planned,
so shall it stand:
25 To break the Assyrian in my land
and trample him on my mountains;
Then his yoke shall be removed from
them,
and his burden from their shoulder.*
26 This is the plan proposed for the whole
earth,
and this the hand outstretched over all the
nations.†
27 The LORD of hosts has planned;
who can thwart him?
His hand is stretched out;
who can turn it back?*

Philistia†

28 In the year that King Ahaz died,† there came
this oracle:

29† Do not rejoice, Philistia, not one of you,
that the rod which struck you is broken;
For out of the serpent's root shall come an
adder,
its offspring shall be a flying saraph.
30 In my pastures the poor shall graze,
and the needy lie down in safety;
But I will kill your root with famine
that shall slay even your remnant.
31 Howl, O gate; cry out, O city!
Philistia, all of you melts away!
For there comes a smoke from the north,†
without a straggler in its ranks.
32 What will one answer the messengers of the
nations?†
"The LORD has established Zion,
and in her the afflicted of his people find
refuge."

---

† Baal, originally the Jebel el-Aqra north of Ugarit, but other mountains have been identified with it, including Mount Zion in Jerusalem (Ps 48:3). The attempt to usurp the place of God (v. 14), coupled with the dramatic reversal ("above the stars of God" to "the depths of the pit") occasioned the interpretation that saw here the rebellion and fall of Satan.

14:21 *Cities*: if the text is correct, it presumably refers to cities as expressions of human pride, authority, and oppression (cf. Gn 11:1–9; Na 3:1–4).

14:24–27 The motif of God's plan or work is a recurring thread running through Isaiah's oracles. The plans of Judah's enemies will not come to pass (7:5–7; 8:9–10; 10:7), but God's plan for his work of disciplining his own people (5:12, 19; 28:21), and then for punishing the foreign agents God used to administer that discipline (10:12) will come to pass.

14:26 *Hand outstretched over all the nations*: as it was once outstretched over Israel (9:11, 16, 20; 5:25).

14:28–31 This oracle seems to reflect the political situation soon after the death of Ahaz in 715 B.C., when Ashdod and the other Philistine cities were trying to create a united front to rebel against Assyria. Ahaz had refused to join the rebels in 735 B.C. and remained loyal to Assyria during the rest of his reign, but the Philistines may have had higher hopes for his son Hezekiah. Judah, however, did not join in Ashdod's disastrous revolt in 713–711 B.C. (cf. 20:1).

14:28 *The year that King Ahaz died*: 715 B.C.

14:29 The occasion for this oracle is usually taken to be the death of an Assyrian king; the Philistines were vassals of Assyria, whereas no victories of Ahaz over the Philistines are recorded. The chronological notice (*in the year that King Ahaz died*) may be incorrect, for no Assyrian king died around 715, the date usually assigned for the death of Ahaz. *Flying saraph*: a winged cobra, often portrayed in Egyptian art and on Israelite seals. The Hebrew *saraph* means "to burn" and perhaps is applied to the cobra because of the burning sensation of its bite.

14:31 *Smoke from the north*: the dust raised from the approach of the Assyrian army.

14:32 *Messengers of the nations*: envoys from Philistia, and from Egypt and Ethiopia, the real powers behind the Philistine revolt (20:1–6; cf. 18:1–2).

---

* **14:15** Ez 28:8–9; 32:23; Mt 11:23; Acts 12:23.
14:18 Jb 3:14–15.
14:19 Is 66:24.
14:21 Ex 20:5; Mt 23:35.
14:22 Jer 51:62; Jb 18:19.
14:25 Is 9:3; 10:27a.
14:27 Is 23:8–9; Jb 40:8; Jer 4:28.

Moab†

15 1 Oracle on Moab:
Laid waste in a night,
Ar of Moab is destroyed;
Laid waste in a night,
Kir of Moab is destroyed.
2 Daughter Dibon has gone up
to the high places to weep;
Over Nebo and over Medeba
Moab is wailing.
Every head is shaved,
every beard sheared off.†*
3 In the streets they wear sackcloth,
and on the rooftops;
In the squares
everyone wails, streaming with tears.*
4 Heshbon and Elealeh cry out,
they are heard as far as Jahaz.
At this the loins of Moab tremble,
his soul quivers within him;*
5 My heart cries out for Moab,
his fugitives reach Zoar,
Eglath-shelishiyah:
The ascent of Luhith
they ascend weeping;
On the way to Horonaim
they utter rending cries;*
6 The waters of Nimrim
have become a waste,
The grass is withered,
new growth is gone,
nothing is green.
7 So now whatever they have acquired or
stored away
they carry across the Wadi of the Poplars.
8 The cry has gone round
the territory of Moab;
As far as Eglaim his wailing,
even at Beer-elim his wailing.
9† The waters of Dimon are filled with blood,
but I will bring still more upon Dimon:
Lions for those who are fleeing from
Moab
and for those who remain in the land!

16 1 Send them forth,† hugging the earth like
reptiles,
from Sela across the desert,
to the mount of daughter Zion.
2 Like flushed birds,
like scattered nestlings,
Are the daughters of Moab
at the fords of the Arnon.†*
3† Offer counsel, take their part;
at high noon make your shade like the night;
Hide the outcasts,
do not betray the fugitives.
4 Let the outcasts of Moab live with you,
be their shelter from the destroyer.
When there is an end to the oppressor,
when destruction has ceased,
and the marauders have vanished from the
land,
5 A throne shall be set up in mercy,
and on it shall sit in fidelity,
in David's tent,
A judge upholding right,
prompt to do justice.*
6 We have heard of the pride of Moab,
how very proud he is,
Of his haughtiness, pride, and arrogance
that his empty words do not match.*
7† Therefore let Moab wail,
let everyone wail for Moab;
For the raisin cakes† of Kir-hareseth
let them sigh, stricken with grief.
8 The terraced slopes of Heshbon languish,
the vines of Sibmah,
Whose clusters once overpowered
the lords of nations,
Reaching as far as Jazer
winding through the wilderness,†
Whose branches spread forth,
crossing over the sea.
9 Therefore I weep with Jazer
for the vines of Sibmah;
I drench you with my tears,
Heshbon and Elealeh;
For on your summer fruits and harvests
the battle cry† has fallen.*

† **15:1–16:14** Both the historical situation reflected in this oracle against Moab and the date of composition are uncertain. Variants of the same poem are found in Jer 48, and there are connections with Nm 21:27–30 as well.

15:2 *Shaved . . . sheared off*: traditional signs of grief.

15:9 There is a play on words between "Dimon" and *dam*, the Hebrew word for blood.

16:1 *Send them forth*: the Hebrew text is disturbed; it could also be understood to refer to tribute (a lamb) sent from Moab to Zion, presumably to encourage the king to receive the Moabite refugees.

16:2 *The Arnon*: principal river of Moab.

16:3–5 Directed to Jerusalem, which should receive the suffering Moabites with mercy, as befits the city of David's family, who were partly descended from Ruth the Moabite; and cf. 1 Sm 22:3–4. This would be a gracious act on Judah's part, since its relations with Moab were strained at best.

16:7–14 Moab had been prosperous; now it has become a desert.

16:7 *Raisin cakes*: masses of dried compressed grapes used as food (cf. 2 Sm 6:19; 1 Chr 16:3; Sg 2:5), and also in the worship of other gods (Hos 3:1).

16:8 *Wilderness*: i.e., eastward. *Sea*: i.e., westward.

16:9–10 *Battle cry . . . shout of joy*: the same Hebrew word

* **15:2** Jer 48:37; Ez 7:18; Am 8:10.
15:3 Is 22:12; Jer 48:38.
15:4 Jer 48:34.
15:5 Jer 48:5, 34.
16:2 Nm 21:13.
16:5 Is 9:6; 11:3–4; 32:1; Jer 23:5; Ps 89:14; Prv 20:28.
16:6 Jer 48:29–30.
16:9 Is 15:5; Jer 48:32.

10 From the orchards are taken away
joy and gladness,
In the vineyards there is no singing,
no shout of joy;
In the wine presses no one treads grapes,
the vintage shout is stilled.*
11 Therefore for Moab
my heart moans like a lyre,
my inmost being for Kir-hareseth.*
12† When Moab wears himself out on the high
places,
and enters his sanctuary to pray,
it shall avail him nothing.*

13 † That is the word the LORD spoke against
Moab in times past. 14 But now the LORD speaks:
In three years, like the years of a hired laborer,
the glory of Moab shall be empty despite all its
great multitude; and the remnant shall be very
small and weak.*

Damascus

17 1 Oracle on Damascus:†
See, Damascus shall cease to be a city
and become a pile of ruins;*
2 Her cities shall be forever abandoned,
for flocks to lie in undisturbed.
3 The fortress shall vanish from Ephraim†
and dominion from Damascus;
The remnant of Aram shall become like the
glory
of the Israelites—
oracle of the LORD of hosts.
4 On that day
The glory of Jacob shall fade,
and his full body shall grow thin.*
5 Like the reaper's mere armful of stalks,
when he gathers the standing grain;
Or as when one gleans the ears
in the Valley of Rephaim.†
6† Only gleanings shall be left in it,
as when an olive tree has been beaten—
Two or three olives at the very top,
four or five on its most fruitful branches—
oracle of the LORD, the God of Israel.*
7 On that day people shall turn to their maker,
their eyes shall look to the Holy One of
Israel.*
8 They shall not turn to the altars, the work of
their hands,
nor shall they look to what their fingers
have made:
the asherahs† or the incense stands.
9 On that day his strong cities shall be
like those abandoned by the Hivites and
Amorites
When faced with the Israelites;
and there shall be desolation.*
10 Truly, you have forgotten the God who saves
you,
the Rock, your refuge, you have not
remembered.*
Therefore, though you plant plants for the
Pleasant One,†
and set out cuttings for a foreign one,*
11 Though you make them grow the day you
plant them
and make them blossom the morning you
set them out,
The harvest shall disappear on a day of
sickness
and incurable pain.
12 Ah! the roaring of many peoples—†
a roar like the roar of the seas!
The thundering of nations—
thunder like the thundering of mighty
waters!*
13† But God shall rebuke them,
and they shall flee far away,
Driven like chaff on the mountains before a
wind,
like tumbleweed before a storm.*

† (*hedad*), which normally refers to the joyful shout of those treading the grapes (cf. Jer 25:30), here is used both for the triumphant shout of the enemy (v. 9) and for the vintagers' shout, which has ceased.

16:12 In vain do the Moabites appeal to their god Chemosh.

16:13–14 A prose application of the preceding poetic oracle against Moab (15:1–16:12); cf. Jer 4:8. *Like the years of a hired laborer*: the fixed period of time for which the hired laborer contracted his services; cf. Is 21:16.

17:1 *Damascus*: capital of Aram or Syria, conquered by Tiglath-pileser III at the end of the Syro-Ephraimite War in 732 B.C.

17:3 *Ephraim*: Israel, leagued with Aram against Judah in the Syro-Ephraimite War. Assyria ravaged and captured most of Israelite territory in 734–733 B.C. *Like the glory of the Israelites*: the remnant of Aram will be no more impressive than the pitiful remnant of the Northern Kingdom.

17:5 *Valley of Rephaim*: a fertile plain just to the southwest of Jerusalem (cf. Jos 15:8; 2 Sm 5:18). Since it was near a large population center, the fields there would be thoroughly gleaned by the poor after the harvest, leaving very few ears of grain.

17:6 Olives not easily picked by hand were knocked from the tree by means of a long stick; cf. 24:13.

17:8 *Asherahs*: see note on Ex 34:13. *Incense stands*: small altars on which incense was burned; cf. Is 27:9; Lv 26:30.

17:10 *The Pleasant One*: an epithet for a foreign god of fertility, probably Adonis, in whose honor saplings were planted.

17:12 *Many peoples*: the hordes that accompanied the invading Assyrians, whom God repels just as he vanquished the primeval waters of chaos; see notes on Jb 3:8; 7:12; Ps 89:11.

17:13–14 The passage seems to evoke the motif of invincibility, part of the early Zion tradition that Jerusalem could not be conquered because God protected it (Ps 48:1–8).

16:10 Is 24:8.
16:11 Is 15:5; Jer 48:36.
16:12 Jer 48:13.
16:14 Dt 15:18.
17:1 2 Kgs 16:9; Jer 49:23; Am 1:3; Zec 9:1.
17:4 Is 10:16.
17:6 Is 24:13.
17:7 Is 5:12.
17:9 Is 27:10.
17:10 Ps 106:13, 21; Jer 2:32; Hos 8:14.
17:10 Is 1:29–31.
17:12 Ps 46:3–7; 93:3–4.
17:13 Ps 76:7; 83:14.

14 At evening, there is terror,
but before morning, they are gone!
Such is the portion of those who despoil us,
the lot of those who plunder us.*

Ethiopia

18 1 Ah! Land of buzzing insects,†
beyond the rivers of Ethiopia,*
2 Sending ambassadors by sea,
in papyrus boats on the waters!
Go, swift messengers,
to a nation tall and bronzed,
To a people dreaded near and far,
a nation strong and conquering,
whose land is washed by rivers.*
3† All you who inhabit the world,
who dwell on earth,
When the signal is raised on the mountain,
look!
When the trumpet blows, listen!
4 For thus says the LORD to me:
I will be quiet, looking on from where I
dwell,*
Like the shimmering heat in sunshine,
like a cloud of dew at harvest time.
5 Before the vintage, when the flowering has
ended,
and the blooms are succeeded by ripening
grapes,
Then comes the cutting of branches with
pruning hooks,
and the discarding of the lopped-off
shoots.
6 They shall all be left to the mountain
vultures
and to the beasts of the earth;
The vultures shall summer on them,
all the beasts of the earth shall winter on
them.

7 Then will gifts be brought to the LORD of
hosts—to the place of the name of the LORD
of hosts, Mount Zion—from a people tall and
bronzed, from a people dreaded near and far,
a nation strong and conquering, whose land is
washed by rivers.*

Egypt

19 1 Oracle on Egypt:
See, the LORD is riding on a swift cloud
on his way to Egypt;
The idols of Egypt tremble before him,
the hearts of the Egyptians melt within
them.*
2 I will stir up Egypt against Egypt:
brother will war against brother,
Neighbor against neighbor,
city against city, kingdom against kingdom.
3 The courage of the Egyptians shall ebb away
within them,
and I will bring their counsel to nought;
They shall consult idols and charmers, ghosts
and clairvoyants.*
4 I will deliver Egypt
into the power of a cruel master,
A harsh king† who shall rule over them—
oracle of the Lord, the LORD of hosts.*
5 The waters shall be drained from the sea,
the river shall parch and dry up;*
6 Its streams shall become foul,
and the canals of Egypt shall dwindle and
parch.*
Reeds and rushes shall wither away,
7 and bulrushes on the bank of the Nile;*
All the sown land along the Nile
shall dry up and blow away, and be no
more.
8 The fishermen shall mourn and lament,
all who cast hook in the Nile;
Those who spread their nets in the water
shall pine away.
9 The linen-workers shall be disappointed,
the combers and weavers shall turn pale;*
10 The spinners shall be crushed,
all the hired laborers shall be despondent.
11 Utter fools are the princes of Zoan!†
the wisest of Pharaoh's advisers give stupid
counsel.
How can you say to Pharaoh,
"I am a descendant of wise men, of ancient
kings"?
12 Where then are your wise men?

---

†

18:1–2 *Land of buzzing insects*: the region of the Upper Nile where these multiplied with great rapidity. *Ethiopia*: in Hebrew, *Kush*. The center of this ancient kingdom corresponds geographically to the modern Sudan, Roman Nubia. *Papyrus boats*: light and serviceable vessels made of bundles of papyrus stalks and sealed with pitch. Egypt, ruled by a dynasty from Ethiopia, had invited Judah to join a coalition against Assyria, but Isaiah told the ambassadors to return to their own people.

18:3–6 A more general address but probably relating to the same topic. The Lord will not act at once, but later there will be a "harvest" of terrible destruction, probably directed against Assyria (cf. 14:24–27).

19:4 *Cruel master . . . harsh king*: possibly the Nubian (Ethiopian) Shabaka who gained control of all of Egypt around 712 B.C.

19:11, 13 *Zoan*, later known as Tanis, and *Memphis* (Hebrew *Noph*) were key cities in the Nile Delta.

---

*

17:14 Is 29:8.
18:1 Zep 3:10.
18:2 Is 18:7.
18:4 Is 8:18; 18:7; 2 Chr 6:30; Ps 33:14.
18:7 Is 45:14; Ps 68:30; Zep 3:10; Mal 1:11.
19:1 Is 13:7.
19:3 Is 8:19; 44:25; Lv 19:31.
19:4 Ez 29:19; 30:10.
19:5 Jer 51:36; Ez 30:12; 32:2.
19:6 2 Kgs 19:24.
19:7 Jb 8:11.
19:9 Ez 27:7.

Let them tell you and make known
What the LORD of hosts has planned
against Egypt.*
13 The princes of Zoan have become fools,
the princes of Memphis have been
deceived.
The chiefs of its tribes
have led Egypt astray.*
14 The LORD has prepared among them
a spirit of dizziness,
And they have made Egypt stagger in whatever
she does,
as a drunkard staggers in his vomit.*
15 Egypt shall accomplish nothing—
neither head nor tail, palm branch nor
reed,† shall accomplish anything.

16 On that day the Egyptians shall be like women, trembling with fear, because of the LORD of hosts shaking his fist at them.* 17 And the land of Judah shall be a terror to the Egyptians. Every time they think of Judah, they shall stand in dread because of the plan the LORD of hosts has in mind for them.

18 On that day there shall be five cities† in the land of Egypt that speak the language of Canaan and swear by the LORD of hosts; one shall be called "City of the Sun."

19 On that day there shall be an altar to the LORD at the center of Egypt, and a sacred pillar to the LORD near its boundary. 20 This will be a sign and witness to the LORD of hosts in the land of Egypt, so that when they cry out to the LORD because of their oppressors, he will send them a savior to defend and deliver them.* 21 The LORD shall make himself known to Egypt, and the Egyptians shall know the LORD in that day; they shall offer sacrifices and oblations, make vows to the LORD and fulfill them.* 22 Although the LORD shall smite Egypt severely, he shall heal them; they shall turn to the LORD and he shall be moved by their entreaty and heal them.*

23 On that day there shall be a highway from Egypt to Assyria; the Assyrians shall enter Egypt, and the Egyptians enter Assyria, and the Egyptians shall worship with the Assyrians.

24 On that day Israel shall be a third party with Egypt and Assyria, a blessing in the midst of the earth,* 25 when the LORD of hosts gives this blessing: "Blessed be my people Egypt, and the work of my hands Assyria, and my heritage, Israel."

Isaiah's Warning Against Trust in Egypt and Ethiopia

20 1 In the year the general sent by Sargon, king of Assyria, came to Ashdod,† fought against it, and captured it— 2 † at that time the LORD had spoken through Isaiah, the son of Amoz: Go and take off the sackcloth from your waist, and remove the sandals from your feet. This he did, walking naked and barefoot.* 3 Then the LORD said: Just as my servant Isaiah has gone naked and barefoot for three years as a sign and portent against Egypt and Ethiopia,* 4 so shall the king of Assyria lead away captives from Egypt, and exiles from Ethiopia, young and old, naked and barefoot, with buttocks uncovered, the shame of Egypt.* 5 They shall be dismayed and ashamed because of Ethiopia, their hope, and because of Egypt, their boast.* 6 The inhabitants of this coastland shall say on that day, "See what has happened to those we hoped in, to whom we fled for help and deliverance from the king of Assyria! What escape is there for us now?"*

Fall of Babylon†

21 1 Oracle on the wastelands by the sea:†
Like whirlwinds sweeping through the Negeb,
it comes from the desert,
from the fearful land.*
2 A harsh vision has been announced to me:
"The traitor betrays,
the despoiler spoils.*
Go up, O Elam; besiege, O Media;†

19:15 *Head . . . reed*: the leaders and the people; cf. 9:13–14.

19:18 *Five cities*: colonies of Jews living together and speaking their native language; cf. Jer 43. *City of the Sun*: the meaning is uncertain, but the reference seems to be to the city known later as Heliopolis.

20:1 *Ashdod*: a city of Philistia. In 713 B.C., Azuri, the king of Ashdod was deposed by Sargon for plotting rebellion, but the citizens of Ashdod rejected the ruler installed by the Assyrian king and followed a certain Yamani, who in 712 B.C., with the protection of Egypt, attempted to draw Edom, Moab, and Judah into a coalition against Assyria. In 711 B.C., Sargon's general marched against Ashdod, and Yamani fled to Ethiopia. Ashdod was captured, and a short time later Ethiopia handed Yamani over to the Assyrians for punishment.

20:2–6 Isaiah's nakedness is a symbolic act to convey the message that Assyria would lead the Egyptians and Ethiopians away as captives. The Judeans and their allies would then realize the folly of having trusted in them. The purpose of the oracle was to dissuade Hezekiah, the Judean king, from being drawn into Ashdod's anti-Assyrian coalition (14:28–32).

21:1–10 This oracle against Babylon is probably to be dated to the period just before the fall of Babylon to the Persians in 539 B.C. (v. 9).

21:1 *Wastelands by the sea*: Babylonia. *Negeb*: the wilderness south of Judah.

21:2 *Elam . . . Media*: nations which, under the leadership of Cyrus, captured Babylon in 539 B.C. *End to all its groaning*: those who were captive of Babylon will be freed.

19:12 Is 14:26; 41:22–23.
19:13 Jer 2:16; Hos 9:6.
19:14 Is 28:7; Jer 48:26.
19:16 Na 3:13.
19:20 Ex 2:23; Jgs 2:18.
19:21 Zec 14:16, 18.
19:22 Hos 6:1.
19:24 Gn 12:2; Zec 8:13.
20:2 1 Sm 19:24.
20:3 Is 8:18.
20:4 2 Sm 10:4.
20:5 Is 30:3, 5.
20:6 Is 31:3; 36:6.
21:1 Is 30:6; Dt 1:19; Jer 2:6.
21:2 Is 24:16; 33:1.

put an end to all its groaning!"*
3 Therefore my loins are filled with anguish,
pangs have seized me like those of a woman in labor;
I am too bewildered to hear,
too dismayed to look.*
4 My mind reels,
shuddering assails me;
The twilight I yearned for
he has turned into dread.*
5 They set the table,
spread out the rugs;
they eat, they drink.† *
Rise up, O princes,
oil the shield!
6 For thus my Lord said to me:
Go, station a watchman,
let him tell what he sees.
7 If he sees a chariot,
a pair of horses,
Someone riding a donkey,
someone riding a camel,
Then let him pay heed,
very close heed.
8 Then the watchman cried,
"On the watchtower, my Lord,
I stand constantly by day;
And I stay at my post
through all the watches of the night.*
9 Here he comes—
a single chariot,
a pair of horses—
He calls out and says,
'Fallen, fallen is Babylon!
All the images of her gods
are smashed to the ground!' "*
10 To you, who have been threshed,
beaten on my threshing floor,
What I have heard
from the LORD of hosts,
The God of Israel,
I have announced to you.*

Dumah

11 Oracle on Dumah:†
They call to me from Seir,
"Watchman, how much longer the night?
Watchman, how much longer the night?"
12 The watchman replies,
"Morning has come, and again night.
If you will ask, ask; come back again."

In the Steppe

13 Oracle: in the steppe:†
In the thicket in the steppe you will spend the night,
caravans of Dedanites.
14 Meet the thirsty, bring them water,
inhabitants of the land of Tema,
greet the fugitives with bread.*
15 For they have fled from the sword,
from the drawn sword;
From the taut bow,
from the thick of battle.

16 For thus the Lord has said to me: In another
year, like the years of a hired laborer,† all the
glory of Kedar shall come to an end. 17 Few of Ke-
dar's stalwart archers shall remain, for the LORD,
the God of Israel, has spoken.

The Valley of Vision

22 1 Oracle on the Valley of Vision:† *
What is the matter with you now, that you have gone up,
all of you, to the housetops,
2† You who were full of noise,
tumultuous city,
exultant town?*
Your slain are not slain with the sword,

†

21:5 Babylon is destroyed while its leaders are feasting; cf. Dn 5. *Oil the shield*: shields were oiled and greased so as to divert blows more easily; cf. 2 Sm 1:21.

21:11–12 *Dumah*: an oasis in north Arabia (cf. Gn 25:14 and 1 Chr 1:30), may be identified with the north Arabian Adummatu mentioned in Assyrian records of Sennacherib's campaign against north Arabia. *Seir*: a site in Edom. The Edomites ask the prophet how much longer they must suffer ("the night" of suffering); he answers ambiguously: "Liberation ("morning") and further suffering ("night")," but perhaps they will later receive a more encouraging answer ("ask; come back again").

21:13–14 *In the steppe*: the north Arabian steppe where the oases referred to were located. *Dedanites*: a north Arabian tribe associated with the oasis of Tema; cf. Gn 10:7; 25:3; Jer 25:23.

21:16 *Year . . . of a hired laborer*: see note on 16:13–14. *Kedar*: a nomadic tribe in Arabia; cf. 42:11; 60:7; Ps 120:5.

22:1–14 The title "oracle on the valley of vision," like the other oracle headings in chaps. 13–23, was supplied by an editor and is taken from v. 5. In all probability it relates to the events of 701, the lifting of Sennacherib's siege of Jerusalem. The death of the Assyrian king Sargon II in 705 occasioned the revolt of many of the vassal nations subject to Assyria, a revolt in which Hezekiah joined, over Isaiah's bitter opposition. The biblical and other data concerning the outcome of this adventure are conflicting and confusing. While 2 Kgs 19 (Is 37) tells of a miraculous deliverance of the city after the siege had been renewed, Assyrian documents and 2 Kgs 18:13–16 report that Sennacherib, Sargon II's successor, devastated Judah (the destruction of 46 cities is mentioned in Assyrian records); Hezekiah had to surrender and paid Sennacherib a heavy indemnity, taken from the Temple treasury and adornments. The inhabitants of Jerusalem apparently took the lifting of the siege as occasion for great rejoicing, a response that Isaiah condemns. They should be mourning the dead and learning that their confidence in allies rather than in the Lord leads to disaster.

22:2–3 The retreat of Judah's soldiers is a further reason that rejoicing is not in order.

*

21:2 Is 13:17; Jer 49:34.
21:3 Is 16:11; Ps 38:8.
21:4 Dt 28:67.
21:5 Dn 5:5.
21:8 Hb 2:1.
21:9 Is 46:1; Jer 50:2; 51:8; Rev 14:8; 18:2.
21:10 Is 51:23; Jer 51:33; Mi 4:13; Hb 3:12.
21:14 Jb 6:19.
22:1 Is 21:2.
22:2 Is 32:13.

nor killed in battle.
3 All your leaders fled away together,
they were captured without use of bow;
All who were found were captured together,
though they had fled afar off.
4 That is why I say: Turn away from me,
let me weep bitterly;
Do not try to comfort me
for the ruin of the daughter of my people.*
5 It is a day of panic, rout and confusion,
from the Lord, the GOD of hosts, in the
Valley of Vision†
Walls crash;
a cry for help to the mountains.
6 Elam takes up the quiver,
Aram mounts the horses
and Kir† uncovers the shields.
7 Your choice valleys are filled with chariots,
horses are posted at the gates—
8 and shelter over Judah is removed.†

On that day you looked to the weapons in the
House of the Forest; 9 † you saw that the breaches
in the City of David were many; you collected
the water of the lower pool. 10 You numbered
the houses of Jerusalem, tearing some down to
strengthen the wall; 11 you made a reservoir be-
tween the two walls for the water of the old pool.
But you did not look to the city's Maker, nor con-
sider the one who fashioned it long ago.

12 On that day the Lord,
the GOD of hosts, called
For weeping and mourning,
for shaving the head and wearing sackcloth.
13 But look! instead, there was celebration and
joy,
slaughtering cattle and butchering sheep,
Eating meat and drinking wine:
"Eat and drink, for tomorrow we die!"*

14 This message was revealed in my hearing from the LORD of hosts:

This iniquity will not be forgiven you until
you die,
says the Lord, the GOD of hosts.

Shebna and Eliakim

15 Thus says the Lord, the GOD of hosts:
Up, go to that official,
Shebna,† master of the palace,
16† "What have you here? Whom have you here,
that you have hewn for yourself a tomb here,
Hewing a tomb on high,
carving a resting place in the rock?"
17 The LORD shall hurl you down headlong,
mortal man!
He shall grip you firmly,
18 And roll you up and toss you like a ball
into a broad land.
There you will die, there with the chariots you
glory in,
you disgrace to your master's house!
19 I will thrust you from your office
and pull you down from your station.
20 On that day I will summon my servant
Eliakim,† son of Hilkiah;*
21 I will clothe him with your robe,
gird him with your sash,
confer on him your authority.
He shall be a father to the inhabitants of
Jerusalem,
and to the house of Judah.*
22 I will place the key† of the House of David on
his shoulder;
what he opens, no one will shut,
what he shuts, no one will open.*
23 I will fix him as a peg in a firm place,
a seat of honor for his ancestral house;
24 On him shall hang all the glory of his
ancestral house:†
descendants and offspring,
all the little dishes, from bowls to jugs.

25 On that day, says the LORD of hosts, the peg fixed in a firm place shall give way, break off and

† **22:5** *Valley of Vision*: frequently identified as the Hinnom Valley, west of Jerusalem.

22:6 *Elam . . . Kir*: the Assyrian forces presumably included auxiliary troops from various places.

22:8 *Shelter over Judah is removed*: the reference is obscure; it has been suggested that Judah's protection was Jerusalem itself, and with the fall of the city the country was exposed. *House of the Forest*: an armory built by Solomon; its columns of wood suggested the trees of a forest; cf. 1 Kgs 7:2; 10:17.

22:9–11 Frenetic efforts made to fortify the city before the impending siege; cf. 2 Kgs 20:20; 2 Chr 32:3–4, 30. Some suggest that the description of these preparations comes from the time of Nebuchadnezzar's assault on Jerusalem in 588. *You did not look to the city's Maker*: Isaiah here makes the crucial point. Jerusalem's safety lay not in military forces nor in alliances with other nations nor in playing power politics but in the Lord, here presented as the creator and founder of the city. Isaiah may be alluding to the belief that the city was inviolable.

22:15 *Shebna*: by the time of the siege of Jerusalem in 36:3, Shebna, the scribe, no longer held the office of master of the palace.

22:16 What is probably Shebna's inscribed tomb has been discovered in the village of Silwan on the eastern slope of Jerusalem.

22:20 *Eliakim*: by the time of the events described in 36:3, Eliakim had replaced Shebna as master of the palace.

22:22 *Key*: symbol of authority; cf. Mt 16:19; Rev 3:7.

22:24–25 Apparently Eliakim proved to be a disappointment, so an oracle of judgment was added to the originally positive oracle to Eliakim.

22:4 Jer 6:26; 9:1; 14:17.
22:13 Is 56:12; Wis 2:6; 1 Cor 15:32.
22:20 2 Kgs 18:18, 37.
22:21 Jb 29:16.
22:22 Rev 3:7.

Catholic Social Teaching

Faith and Politics

Every group we belong to has a leader. Some leaders are committed to serving others; other leaders are corrupt. Like First Isaiah, we have a right to demand integrity from our leaders as well as a responsibility to practice it ourselves.

In Isaiah 22:15–25, the prophet denounces the steward Shebna for his self-seeking ways. Evidently, Shebna is using his position of leadership to prepare an expensive tomb for himself (see verse 16) and to acquire ornate chariots (see verse 18). Isaiah prefers Eliakim to take over his position. The prophet's interest in local politics points out a biblical truth: Our faith applies to our daily lives, including our political choices.

When choosing our school, community, and government leaders, we must seek out people who are committed to protecting basic human rights and enhancing the dignity of the human person. They must be people of integrity—people whose actions and decisions accurately reflect their core values and beliefs. Good leaders are also willing to speak up for the voiceless and advocate for those who are suffering, ensuring that every human being has the opportunity to live life abundantly.

Catholic social teaching reminds us that even if we are not in a position of leadership, as citizens of society, we too have been entrusted with the task of promoting the common good and protecting human dignity.

- What can you do to learn more about the social issues that impact the dignity of people in our world today?
- How can you use your time and talents to provide direct service to those in need?

Is 22:15–25

Rights and Responsibilities

fall, and the weight that hung on it shall be done away with; for the LORD has spoken.

Tyre and Sidon

23 1† Oracle on Tyre:
Wail, ships of Tarshish,
for your port is destroyed;
From the land of the Kittim†
the news reaches them.*
2 Silence! you who dwell on the coast,
you merchants of Sidon,
Whose messengers crossed the sea
3 over the deep waters,
Whose revenue was the grain of Shihor,† the harvest of the Nile,
you who were the merchant among the nations.*
4 Be ashamed, Sidon, fortress on the sea,
for the sea† has spoken,
"I have not been in labor, nor given birth,
nor raised young men,
nor reared young women."
5 When the report reaches Egypt
they shall be in anguish at the report about Tyre.
6 Pass over to Tarshish,†
wail, you who dwell on the coast!
7 Is this your exultant city,
whose origin is from old,
Whose feet have taken her
to dwell in distant lands?
8 Who has planned such a thing
against Tyre, the bestower of crowns,
Whose merchants are princes,
whose traders are the earth's honored men?
9 The LORD of hosts has planned it,

†

23:1–17 This oracle, a satire directed against the Phoenician cities of Tyre and Sidon, is perhaps to be situated at the time of Sennacherib's campaign against the Phoenican cities in 701 B.C, following his subjugation of their Babylonian allies in 703 B.C.

23:1 *Kittim*: Cyprus. The Hebrew word is derived from the term for the well-known city of Cyprus, Kition. In later centuries the term Kittim is used for the Greeks, the Romans, and other distant peoples.

23:3 *Shihor*: a synonym for the Nile.

23:4 *The sea*: here personified, it brings to distant coasts the news that Sidon must disown her children; her people are dispersed.

23:6–7 *Tarshish*: perhaps Tartessus in Spain. *Distant lands*: the reference is to the far-flung colonies established by the Phoenicians throughout the Mediterranean, including North Africa, Spain, and Sardinia. Oceangoing vessels were therefore called Tarshish ships.

23:1 Jer 25:22; Ez 26; Am 1:9; Zec 9:2, 4.
23:3 Ez 27:3.
23:9 Is 14:24–27; 22:11; Ez 28:7.

to disgrace the height of all beauty,
to degrade all the honored of the earth.*
10 Cross to your own land,
ship of Tarshish;
the harbor is no more.
11 His hand he stretches out over the sea,
he shakes kingdoms;
The LORD commanded the destruction
of Canaan's strongholds:† *
12 Crushed, you shall exult no more,
virgin daughter Sidon.
Arise, pass over to the Kittim,
even there you shall find no rest.*
13† Look at the land of the Chaldeans,
the people that has ceased to be.
Assyria founded it for ships,
raised its towers,
Only to tear down its palaces,
and turn it into a ruin.*
14 Lament, ships of Tarshish,
for your stronghold is destroyed.

15 On that day, Tyre shall be forgotten for sev-
enty years,† the lifetime of one king. At the end
of seventy years, the song about the prostitute
will be Tyre's song:

16 Take a harp, go about the city,
forgotten prostitute;
Pluck the strings skillfully, sing many songs,
that you may be remembered.

17 At the end of the seventy years the LORD shall
visit Tyre. She shall return to her hire and serve
as prostitute† with all the world's kingdoms on
the face of the earth.* 18 But her merchandise and
her hire shall be sacred to the LORD. It shall not
be stored up or laid away; instead, her merchan-
dise shall belong to those who dwell before the
LORD, to eat their fill and clothe themselves in
choice attire.

D. Apocalypse of Isaiah†

Judgment upon the World and the Lord's Enthronement on Mount Zion†

24 1 See! The LORD is about to empty the earth
and lay it waste;
he will twist its surface,
and scatter its inhabitants:*
2 People and priest shall fare alike:
servant and master,
Maid and mistress,
buyer and seller,
Lender and borrower,
creditor and debtor.*
3 The earth shall be utterly laid waste, utterly
stripped,
for the LORD has decreed this word.
4 The earth mourns and fades,
the world languishes and fades;
both heaven and earth languish.*
5 The earth is polluted because of its inhabitants,
for they have transgressed laws, violated
statutes,
broken the ancient covenant.† *
6 Therefore a curse devours the earth,
and its inhabitants pay for their guilt;
Therefore they who dwell on earth have
dwindled,
and only a few are left.*
7 The new wine mourns, the vine languishes,
all the merry-hearted groan.*
8 Stilled are the cheerful timbrels,
ended the shouts of the jubilant,
stilled the cheerful harp.*
9 They no longer drink wine and sing;
strong brew is bitter to those who drink it.*
10 Broken down is the city of chaos,†
every house is shut against entry.*
11 In the streets they cry out for lack of wine;
all joy has grown dim,

†

23:11 *Canaan's strongholds*: the fortresses of Phoenicia.

23:13 The reference here seems to be to Assyria's subjugation of Babylon in 703 B.C., which left the coastal cities of Phoenicia as well as Judah open to Sennacherib's invasion in 701 B.C. *Founded it . . . its palaces . . . turn it*: the city of Babylon.

23:15 *Seventy years*: a conventional expression for a long period of time; cf. Jer 25:11 and 29:10.

23:17–18 *Her hire . . . prostitute*: the international trade engaged in by Tyre will become a source of wealth to God's people (cf. 45:14; 60:4–14; Zec 14:14).

24:1–27:13 Although it has become traditional to call these chapters "Apocalypse of Isaiah," and although they do contain some apocalyptic traits, many others are lacking, so that the title is imprecise as a designation. These chapters are not a unified composition and their growth into their present form was a long, complicated process. They echo many themes from chaps. 13–23, "Oracles Against the Foreign Nations," as well as from earlier parts of Isaiah (e.g., the reversal of the "vineyard song," 5:1–7, in 27:2–5). Of particular interest is an unnamed city (24:10–13; 25:2; 26:5–6; 27:10–11), a wicked city, doomed to destruction; to the extent that it is identifiable, it may be Babylon, but more generally it symbolizes all forces hostile to God. And it stands in contrast to another city, also unnamed but no doubt to be identified with Jerusalem (26:1–2).

24:1–23 The world is about to be shaken by a devastating judgment that will overthrow both the human and divine enemies of the Lord, who will then reign in glory over his people on Mount Zion.

24:5 *Ancient covenant*: God's commandments to all humankind (cf. Gn 9:4–6).

24:10 *City of chaos*: a godless city which appears several times in chaps. 24–27; see note on 24:1–27:13.

*

23:11 Is 14:27; Ps 65:8.
23:12 Ez 28:21–22.
23:13 Is 13:21; 34:14; Jer 50:39.
23:17 Rev 17:5; 18:3, 11, 13.
24:1 Is 13:9; Na 2:3, 11.
24:2 Hos 4:9.
24:4 Is 33:9.
24:5 Nm 35:33; Hos 4:2–3.
24:6 Lv 26:15–16.
24:7 Jl 1:10–12.
24:8 Jer 7:34; Hos 2:13.
24:9 Am 6:5–7.
24:10 Is 25:2.

cheer is exiled from the land.*
12 In the city nothing remains but desolation,
gates battered into ruins.
13 For thus it shall be in the midst of the earth,
among the peoples,
As when an olive tree has been beaten,
as with a gleaning when the vintage is done.*
14 These† shall lift up their voice,
they shall sing for joy in the majesty of the
LORD,
they shall shout from the western sea:
15 "Therefore, in the east
give glory to the LORD!
In the coastlands of the sea,
to the name of the LORD, the God of Israel!"*
16 From the end of the earth we hear songs:
"Splendor to the Just One!"
But I said, "I am wasted, wasted away.
Woe is me! The traitors betray;
with treachery have the traitors betrayed!*
17 Terror, pit, and trap
for you, inhabitant of the earth!*
18 One who flees at the sound of terror
will fall into the pit;
One who climbs out of the pit
will be caught in the trap.
For the windows on high are open
and the foundations of the earth shake.*
19 The earth will burst asunder,
the earth will be shaken apart,
the earth will be convulsed.
20 The earth will reel like a drunkard,
sway like a hut;
Its rebellion will weigh it down;
it will fall, never to rise again."*
21 On that day the LORD will punish
the host of the heavens† in the heavens,
and the kings of the earth on the earth.
22 They will be gathered together
like prisoners into a pit;
They will be shut up in a dungeon,
and after many days they will be punished.*
23 Then the moon will blush
and the sun be ashamed,*
For the LORD of hosts will reign
on Mount Zion and in Jerusalem,
glorious in the sight of the elders.† *

Praise for God's Deliverance and the Celebration in Zion†

25 1 O LORD, you are my God,
I extol you, I praise your name;
For you have carried out your wonderful
plans of old,
faithful and true.*
2 For you have made the city a heap,
the fortified city a ruin,
The castle of the insolent, a city no more,
not ever to be rebuilt.*
3 Therefore a strong people will honor you,
ruthless nations will fear you.
4 For you have been a refuge to the poor,
a refuge to the needy in their distress;
Shelter from the rain,
shade from the heat.*
When the blast of the ruthless was like a
winter rain,
5 the roar of strangers like heat in the desert,
You subdued the heat with the shade of a
cloud,
the rain of the tyrants was vanquished.
6 On this mountain† the LORD of hosts
will provide for all peoples
A feast of rich food and choice wines,
juicy, rich food and pure, choice wines.
7 On this mountain he will destroy
the veil that veils all peoples,
The web that is woven over all nations.
8 He will destroy death forever.
The Lord GOD will wipe away
the tears from all faces;
The reproach of his people he will remove
from the whole earth; for the LORD has
spoken.*
9 On that day it will be said:
"Indeed, this is our God; we looked to him,
and he saved us!
This is the LORD to whom we looked;
let us rejoice and be glad that he has
saved us!"*

Judgment on Moab†

10 For the hand of the LORD will rest on this
mountain,

---

† **24:14** *These*: the saved.
24:21 *Host of the heavens*: the stars, which were often regarded as gods; cf. Dt 4:19; Jer 8:2.
24:23 *The elders*: the tradition in Ex 24:9–11 suggests that this refers to the people of God who are to share in the banquet on Mount Zion (Is 25:6–8).
25:1–9 These verses praise God for carrying out his plan to destroy the enemy and to save the poor of his people in Zion (14:32), and they announce the victory banquet to be celebrated in the Lord's city.
25:6 *This mountain*: i.e., Jerusalem's mountain, Zion.
25:10–12 *Moab*: one of Israel's bitterest enemies.

24:11 Jer 48:33; Lam 5:14–15.
24:13 Is 17:6; Mi 7:1.
24:15 Is 42:10, 12; Zep 2:11.
24:16 Is 21:2; 33:1.
24:17 Jer 48:43.
24:18 Gn 7:11; Am 5:19.
24:20 Am 5:2.
24:22 2 Pt 2:4; Jude 6.
24:23 Is 13:10; Jl 3:3–4; 4:15.
24:23 Is 4:5; 60:1–3; Ex 24:9–11; Mi 4:7; Rev 19:4–6.
25:1 Is 12:1, 4; 22:11; 28:29; 37:26.
25:2 Is 17:1; Jer 51:37.
25:4 Is 14:32; 32:2; Na 1:7.
25:8 Is 60:1, 3; 1 Cor 15:53–55; Rev 7:17; 21:4.
25:9 Is 30:18–19.

but Moab will be trodden down
as straw is trodden down in the mire.*
11 He will spread out his hands in its midst,
as a swimmer spreads out his hands to swim;
His pride will be brought low
despite his strokes.*
12 The high-walled fortress he will raze,
bringing it low, leveling it to the ground, to the very dust.*

Judah's Praise and Prayer for Deliverance†

26 1 On that day this song shall be sung in the land of Judah:

"A strong city† have we;
he sets up victory as our walls and ramparts.*
2 Open up the gates
that a righteous nation may enter,
one that keeps faith.*
3 With firm purpose you maintain peace;
in peace, because of our trust in you."*
4 Trust in the LORD forever!
For the LORD is an eternal Rock.*
5 He humbles those who dwell on high,
the lofty city he brings down,
Brings it down to the ground,
levels it to the dust.*
6 The feet of the needy trample on it—
the feet of the poor.
7 The way of the just is smooth;
the path of the just you make level.*
8 The course of your judgments, LORD, we await;
your name and your memory are the desire of our souls.
9 My soul yearns for you at night,
yes, my spirit within me seeks you at dawn;
When your judgment comes upon the earth,
the world's inhabitants learn justice.*
10 The wicked, when spared, do not learn justice;
in an upright land they act perversely,
and do not see the majesty of the LORD.*
11 LORD, your hand is raised high,
but they do not perceive it;
Let them be put to shame when they see your zeal for your people:
let the fire prepared for your enemies
consume them.*
12 LORD, you will decree peace for us,
for you have accomplished all we have done.*
13 LORD, our God, lords other than you have ruled us;
only because of you can we call upon your name.
14 Dead they are, they cannot live,
shades that cannot rise;
Indeed, you have punished and destroyed them,
and wiped out all memory of them.
15 You have increased the nation, LORD,
you have increased the nation, have added to your glory,
you have extended far all the boundaries of the land.*
16 LORD, oppressed by your punishment,
we cried out in anguish under your discipline.*
17 As a woman about to give birth
writhes and cries out in pain,
so were we before you, LORD.*
18 We conceived and writhed in pain,
giving birth only to wind;
Salvation we have not achieved for the earth,
no inhabitants for the world were born.*
19† But your dead shall live, their corpses shall rise!
Awake and sing, you who lie in the dust!
For your dew is a dew of light,
and you cause the land of shades to give birth.*

The Lord's Response†

20 Go, my people, enter your chambers,
and close the doors behind you;
Hide yourselves for a brief moment,
until the wrath is past.*
21 See, the LORD goes forth from his place,
to punish the wickedness of the earth's inhabitants;
The earth will reveal the blood shed upon it,
and no longer conceal the slain.*

†

26:1–19 This text is a mixture of praise for the salvation that will take place, a confession of Judah's inability to achieve deliverance on its own, and earnest prayer that God may quickly bring about the longed-for salvation.

26:1 *Strong city*: Jerusalem, the antithesis of the "city of chaos" (24:10); see note on 24:1–27:13.

26:19 This verse refers not to resurrection of the dead, but to the restoration of the people; cf. Ez 37. The population of Judah was radically reduced by the slaughter and deportations that the historical disasters of the late eighth and seventh centuries B.C. brought upon the country. In this context, a major concern for the future was for an increase in the population, a rebirth of the nation's life.

26:20–21 The time of wrath for Judah would soon be over, and the just punishment of its enemies would begin (cf. Hb 2:1–3).

*

25:10 Zep 2:9–10.
25:11 Is 16:6–7, 14.
25:12 Is 26:5.
26:1 Is 60:18.
26:2 Ps 118:19–20.
26:3 Is 32:17–18; Ps 112:7.
26:4 Is 17:10; 30:29; Ps 62:8.
26:5 Is 25:11–12; 32:19.
26:7 Ps 23:3–4; Prv 11:3, 5.
26:9 Ps 63:2.
26:10 Is 5:12; Eccl 8:11.
26:11 Is 9:6; 30:27; 37:32.
26:12 Jer 29:11; Phil 2:13.
26:15 Is 54:2–3.
26:16 Hos 5:15.
26:17 Mi 4:10.
26:18 Is 37:3.
26:19 Ez 37:5–14; Dn 12:2; Hos 6:2.
26:20 Is 10:25.
26:21 Gn 4:10; Jb 16:18; Ps 106:38; Mi 1:3.

The Judgment and Deliverance of Israel

27 1 On that day,
The LORD will punish with his sword
that is cruel, great, and strong,
Leviathan the fleeing serpent,
Leviathan the coiled serpent;
he will slay the dragon† in the sea.*

2† On that day—
The pleasant vineyard, sing about it!*
3 I, the LORD, am its keeper,
I water it every moment;
Lest anyone harm it,
night and day I guard it.*
4 I am not angry.
But if I were to find briers and thorns,
In battle I would march against it;
I would burn it all.*
5 But if it holds fast to my refuge,
it shall have peace with me;*
it shall have peace with me.

6 In days to come Jacob shall take root,
Israel shall sprout and blossom,
covering all the world with fruit.*
7† Was he smitten as his smiter was smitten?
Was he slain as his slayer was slain?
8 Driving out and expelling, he struggled
against it,
carrying it off with his cruel wind on a day
of storm.*
9 This, then, shall be the expiation of Jacob's
guilt,
this the result of removing his sin:
He shall pulverize all the stones of the altars
like pieces of chalk;
no asherahs or incense altars shall stand.
10 For the fortified city shall be desolate,
an abandoned pasture, a forsaken
wilderness;
There calves shall graze, there they shall lie
down,
and consume its branches.
11 When its boughs wither, they shall be broken
off;
and women shall come to kindle fires with
them.
For this is not an understanding people;
therefore their maker shall not spare them;
their creator shall not be gracious to them.*
12 On that day,
The LORD shall beat out grain
from the channel of the Euphrates to the
Wadi of Egypt,
and you shall be gleaned† one by one,
children of Israel.
13 On that day,†
A great trumpet shall blow,
and the lost in the land of Assyria
and the outcasts in the land of Egypt
Shall come and worship the LORD
on the holy mountain, in Jerusalem.*

E. The Lord Alone, Israel's and Judah's Salvation

The Fate of Samaria†

28 1 Ah! majestic garland
of the drunkards of Ephraim,†
Fading blooms of his glorious beauty,
at the head of the fertile valley,
upon those stupefied with wine.*
2 See, the LORD has a strong one, a mighty one,†
who, like an onslaught of hail, a destructive
storm,
Like a flood of water, great and overflowing,
levels to the ground with violence;*
3 With feet that will trample
the majestic garland of the drunkards of
Ephraim.
4 The fading blooms of his glorious beauty

---

†

27:1 *Leviathan . . . dragon*: the description of Leviathan is almost identical to a passage from a much earlier Ugaritic text. The sea dragon became a symbol of the forces of evil which God vanquishes even as he overcame primeval chaos; cf. notes on 30:7; 51:9–10; Jb 3:8; 7:12; no power can challenge God. Leviathan is even spoken of playfully in Ps 104:26.

27:2–5 This passage mitigates the harsh words on Israel as the Lord's vineyard in 5:1–7; here is given the rain there withheld, though Israel's welfare is still made dependent on fidelity.

27:7–9 Israel was not treated as sternly as were its enemies whom God used to punish it. God did, however, drive Israel from its land, and if it wants to make peace with God, it must change its former cultic practices, destroying its altars and sacred groves (cf. 17:7–11).

27:12 *Gleaned*: God will harvest his people who have been scattered from Assyria to Egypt. Note the same language of gleaning to describe the remnant of the Northern Kingdom in 17:5–6.

27:13 The remnant of Israel will return to Jerusalem for worship; cf. 11:10–16.

28:1–6 These verses once constituted an independent oracle against the Northern Kingdom, probably originally spoken during the time between its overthrow by Assyria in 732 and its destruction in 722/721. Isaiah has reused them as an introduction to his oracle against Judah (vv. 7–22), because the leaders of Judah were guilty of the same excesses that had once marked Ephraim's leadership.

28:1 *Ephraim*: the Northern Kingdom. Its capital, Samaria, was built upon a hill, suggestive of a majestic garland adorning a human head. The characterization of the leadership of Ephraim as drunken underscores its inattention to justice and good government (cf. 5:11–13; Am 6:1–6).

28:2 *A strong one, a mighty one*: Assyria (cf. 8:7–8).

---

*

27:1 Jb 40:25–32; Ps 74:12–14; Ez 32:2.
27:2 Is 5:1; Am 5:11.
27:3 Is 5:2–7.
27:4 Is 10:17.
27:5 Jb 22:21.
27:6 Is 37:31–32; Hos 14:5–6.
27:8 Jer 18:17.
27:11 Is 1:3; 5:13; Jer 4:22.
27:13 Is 11:11–16.
28:1 Hos 7:5; Am 6:1–6.
28:2 Is 25:4–5; 28:17–18; 30:30.

at the head of the fertile valley
Will be like an early fig before summer:
whoever sees it,
swallows it as soon as it is in hand.*
5 On that day the LORD of hosts
will be a glorious crown
And a brilliant diadem
for the remnant of his people,
6 A spirit of judgment
for the one who sits in judgment,
And strength for those
who turn back the battle at the gate.

Against Judah

7 But these also stagger from wine
and stumble from strong drink:
Priest and prophet stagger from strong drink,
overpowered by wine;
They are confused by strong drink,
they stagger in their visions,
they totter when giving judgment.*
8 Yes, all the tables
are covered with vomit,
with filth, and no place left clean.
9† "To whom would he impart knowledge?
To whom would he convey the message?
To those just weaned from milk,
those weaned from the breast?
10 For he says,
'Command on command, command on
command,
rule on rule, rule on rule,
here a little, there a little!' "
11† Yes, with stammering lips and in a strange
language
he will speak to this people,*
12 to whom he said:
"This is the resting place,
give rest to the weary;
And this is the place of repose"—
but they refused to hear.*
13 So for them the word of the LORD shall be:
"Command on command, command on
command,
Rule on rule, rule on rule,
here a little, there a little!"
So that when they walk, they shall stumble
backward,
broken, ensnared, and captured.*
14 Therefore, hear the word of the LORD, you
scoffers,
who rule† this people in Jerusalem:*
15 You have declared, "We have made a
covenant with death,
with Sheol† we have made a pact;
When the raging flood passes through,
it will not reach us;
For we have made lies our refuge,
and in falsehood we have found a hiding
place,"—*
16 Therefore, thus says the Lord GOD:
See, I am laying a stone in Zion,†
a stone that has been tested,
A precious cornerstone as a sure foundation;
whoever puts faith in it will not waver.*
17 I will make judgment a measuring line,
and justice a level.—†
Hail shall sweep away the refuge of lies,
and waters shall flood the hiding place.
18 Your covenant with death shall be canceled
and your pact with Sheol shall not stand.
When the raging flood passes through,
you shall be beaten down by it.*
19 Whenever it passes, it shall seize you;
morning after morning it shall pass,
by day and by night.
Sheer terror
to impart the message!
20 For the bed shall be too short to stretch out in,
and the cover too narrow to wrap in.
21 For the LORD shall rise up as on Mount Perazim,
bestir himself as in the Valley of Gibeon,†

†

28:9–10 The words of those who ridicule Isaiah. The Hebrew of v. 10, by its very sound, conveys the idea of mocking imitation of what the prophet says, as though he spoke like a stammering child: "sau lasau, sau lasau, kau lakau, kau lakau, ze'er sham, ze'er sham." But in v. 13 God repeats these words in deadly earnest, putting them in the mouth of the victorious Assyrian army.

28:11 God will answer the mockers and defend Isaiah. *Strange language*: spoken by the invading army.

28:14 *Who rule*: there is a play on words; the same expression could also mean, "Proverb makers," that is, scoffers of this people.

28:15, 18 *A covenant with death, with Sheol*: an alliance with foreign powers, such as Egypt and Babylon. *Have made lies . . . a hiding place*: this confidence in human aid will prove to be false and deceitful, incapable of averting the dreaded disaster. *Raging flood*: the Assyrian invasion; cf. 8:7–8.

28:16 *A stone in Zion*: the true and sure foundation of salvation, i.e., the presence of God, who had chosen and founded Zion as his city (Ps 78:68–69; Is 14:32) and had chosen the Davidic dynasty to rule over his people (Ps 78:70–72; Is 9:1–6; 11:1–10). *Cornerstone*: the assurance of salvation, rejected by the people of Judah in the prophet's time, is picked up in Ps 118:22 and later applied to Christ; cf. Mt 21:42; Lk 20:17; Acts 4:11; Rom 9:33; 1 Pt 2:7. Chapters 28–31 alternate between threats of the danger of rebelling against Assyria (with implied trust in Egypt) with assurances of the power and protection of the Lord.

28:17 *Line . . . level*: instruments used in constructing a building, to keep it true. They are used metaphorically here to refer to the qualities that Zion, the city of God, must manifest, judgment and justice, not bloodshed (Mi 3:10), nor deceit and violence, which would result in a bulging unstable wall doomed to destruction (Is 30:12–14). Cf. 1 Cor 3:10–17.

28:21 *Mount Perazim . . . Valley of Gibeon*: where David defeated the Philistines; cf. 2 Sm 5:20, 25; 1 Chr 14:11, 16. God's new work

*

28:4 Is 17:6; Na 3:12.
28:7 Is 5:11–12; Mi 2:11.
28:11 Jer 5:15; 1 Cor 14:21; Dt 28:49; Bar 4:15.
28:12 Is 30:9.
28:13 Is 8:15.
28:14 Is 3:1–4; 5:18–21.
28:15 Wis 1:16; Jer 5:12.
28:16 Ps 118:22; Mt 21:42; Acts 4:11; Rom 9:33; 1 Pt 2:6.
28:18 Is 28:2–3.

To carry out his work—strange his work!
to perform his deed—alien his deed!
22 Now, cease scoffing,
lest your bonds be tightened,
For I have heard a decree of destruction
from the Lord, the GOD of hosts,
for the whole land.*

The Parable of the Farmer

23† Give ear and hear my voice,
pay attention and hear my word:
24 Is the plowman forever plowing in order to sow,
always loosening and harrowing the field?
25 When he has leveled the surface,
does he not scatter caraway and sow cumin,†
Put in wheat and barley,
with spelt as its border?
26 His God has taught him this rule,
he has instructed him.
27 For caraway is not threshed with a sledge,
nor does a cartwheel roll over cumin.
But caraway is beaten out with a staff,
and cumin with a rod.
28 Grain is crushed for bread, but not forever;
though he thresh it thoroughly,
and drive his cartwheel and horses over it,
he does not pulverize it.
29 This too comes from the LORD of hosts;
wonderful is his counsel and great his wisdom.*

Judgment and Deliverance of Jerusalem

29 1 Ah! Ariel, Ariel,†
city where David encamped!
Let year follow year,
and feast follow feast,*
2 But I will bring distress upon Ariel,
and there will be mourning and moaning.
You shall be to me like Ariel:*
3 I will encamp like David against you;
I will circle you with outposts
and set up siege works against you.*
4 You shall speak from beneath the earth,
and from the dust below, your words shall come.
Your voice shall be that of a ghost from the earth,
and your words shall whisper from the dust.*
5 The horde of your arrogant shall be like fine dust,
a horde of tyrants like flying chaff.*
Then suddenly, in an instant,
6 you shall be visited by the LORD of hosts,
With thunder, earthquake, and great noise,
whirlwind, storm, and the flame of consuming fire.*
7† Then like a dream,
a vision of the night,
Shall be the horde of all the nations
who make war against Ariel:
All the outposts, the siege works against it,
all who distress it.
8 As when a hungry man dreams he is eating
and awakens with an empty stomach,
Or when a thirsty man dreams he is drinking
and awakens faint, his throat parched,
So shall the horde of all the nations be,
who make war against Mount Zion.

Blindness and Perversity

9† Stupefy yourselves and stay stupid;
blind yourselves and stay blind!
You who are drunk, but not from wine,
who stagger, but not from strong drink!*
10 For the LORD has poured out on you
a spirit of deep sleep.
He has shut your eyes (the prophets)
and covered your heads (the seers).† *

11 For you the vision of all this has become like
the words of a sealed scroll. When it is handed
to one who can read, with the request, "Read
this," the reply is, "I cannot, because it is sealed."
12 When the scroll is handed to one who cannot
read, with the request, "Read this," the reply is,
"I cannot read."

---

will be strange, because instead of fighting for Judah as the Lord did in David's time, God will now fight against Jerusalem (see 29:1–4).

28:23–29 The practical variation of the farmer's work reflects the way God deals with his people, wisely adapted to circumstances; he does not altogether crush them in their weakness.

28:25 *Caraway . . . cumin*: herbs used in seasoning food. *Spelt*: a variety of wheat.

29:1–2 *Ariel*: a poetic name for Jerusalem. It has been variously interpreted to mean "lion of God," "altar hearth of God" (Ez 43:15–16), "city of God," or "foundation of God." In v. 2 the term refers to "altar hearth," i.e., a place of burning for its people (cf. 30:33; 31:9). God will attack Jerusalem, as David did long ago.

29:7–8 Just when the attackers think their capture of Jerusalem is certain, the Lord will snatch victory from their hands and save the city. The sudden shift from the Lord's attack on the city to its deliverance by him is surprising and unexplained; it may reflect the account related in 37:36.

29:9–16 Despite their show of piety, Judah's leaders refused to accept the prophet's words of assurance. They rejected prophetic advice (cf. 30:10–11), did not consult the prophetic oracle in forming their political plans (30:1–2; 31:1), and tried to hide their plans even from God's prophet (v. 15), who, they thought, simply did not understand military and political reality.

29:10 *Prophets . . . seers*: interpretive glosses.

28:22 Is 5:18–19; 10:23.
28:29 Rom 11:33.
29:1 2 Sm 5:6–9.
29:2 Is 33:7.
29:3 2 Kgs 25:1; Ez 4:2.
29:4 Is 8:19; 1 Sm 28:14.
29:5 Is 17:13; Ps 18:43; Jb 21:18.
29:6 Is 30:27, 30.
29:9 Is 19:14; 28:7–8.
29:10 Is 6:10; Rom 11:8.

13 The Lord said:
Since this people draws near with words only
and honors me with their lips alone,
though their hearts are far from me,
And fear of me has become
mere precept of human teaching,*
14 Therefore I will again deal with this people
in surprising and wondrous fashion:
The wisdom of the wise shall perish,
the prudence of the prudent shall vanish.*
15 Ah! You who would hide a plan
too deep for the LORD!
Who work in the dark, saying,
"Who sees us, who knows us?"*
16 Your perversity is as though the potter
were taken to be the clay:
As though what is made should say of its
maker,
"He did not make me!"
Or the vessel should say of the potter,
"He does not understand."*

Redemption†

17 Surely, in a very little while,
Lebanon shall be changed into an orchard,
and the orchard be considered a forest!*
18 On that day the deaf shall hear
the words of a scroll;
And out of gloom and darkness,
the eyes of the blind shall see.*
19 The lowly shall again find joy in the LORD,
the poorest rejoice in the Holy One of Israel.*
20 For the tyrant shall be no more,
the scoffer shall cease to be;
All who are ready for evil shall be cut off,*
21 those who condemn with a mere word,
Who ensnare the defender at the gate,
and leave the just with an empty claim.*
22 Therefore thus says the LORD,
the God of the house of Jacob,
who redeemed Abraham:†
No longer shall Jacob be ashamed,
no longer shall his face grow pale.*
23 For when his children see
the work of my hands in his midst,
They shall sanctify my name;
they shall sanctify the Holy One of Jacob,
be in awe of the God of Israel.*
24 Those who err in spirit shall acquire
understanding,
those who find fault shall receive instruction.

Oracle on the Futility of an Alliance with Egypt†

30 1 Ah! Rebellious children,
oracle of the LORD,
Who carry out a plan that is not mine,
who make an alliance† I did not inspire,
thus adding sin upon sin;*

Pray It!

Preference for the Poor

Isaiah 29:17–21 proclaims that God's power will transform society: the deaf will hear, the blind will see, the lowly will know joy and the poor will rejoice. First Isaiah's words are reflected in Jesus' words in the Beatitudes (see Lk 6:20–26). Both Jesus and Isaiah say that in God's Reign, the rights and needs of the lowliest and the weakest come first (see Isaiah, chapters 58, 61).

The Catholic Church refers to this principle as preferential love for the poor. People who are poor and helpless have a right to a just society where they get what they need to live with dignity and where they have a voice in the structures that govern their lives. One can tell how near a society is to the Reign of God by seeing how it treats the most vulnerable members of the human family. Those who are poor should never be ignored when others have the resources to share.

Write your own prayer describing God's vision for those who are poor. Use Isaiah's words and the Beatitudes for ideas. Share your prayer with your family or youth group.

▶ Is 29:17–21

† **29:17–24** The prophet presents the positive aspects of God's plan in terms of a series of reversals: an end to pride, ignorance, and injustice. Cf. 32:3–5.

29:22 *Who redeemed Abraham*: perhaps by revealing himself and delivering Abraham from idolatrous worship; cf. Gn 12:1–3; 17:1; Jos 24:2–3.

30:1–17 Several independent oracles against making an alliance with Egypt have been strung together in this chapter: vv. 1–5, vv. 6–7, and vv. 8–17. That these were originally separate oracles is indicated by the fact that the oracle in vv. 6–7 is still introduced by its own heading: Oracle on the Beasts of the Negeb.

30:1 *Make an alliance*: lit., "pour out a libation," namely, as part of the ritual of treaty making.

* **29:13** Ez 33:31; Mt 15:8–9; Mk 7:6–7.
29:14 Jer 49:7; 1 Cor 1:19.
29:15 Is 30:1–2; 31:1; Ez 8:12; Jn 3:19–20.
29:16 Is 45:9; Jer 18:6; Rom 9:20.
29:17 Is 32:15.
29:18 Is 35:5; 42:6–7.
29:19 Is 61:1–2.
29:20 Is 28:22.
29:21 Is 5:23; 10:1–2; Am 5:10, 12.
29:22 Is 45:17.
29:23 Is 8:12–13.
30:1 Is 1:4; 5:21; 28:15; 29:15.

2 They go down to Egypt,
without asking my counsel,†
To seek strength in Pharaoh's protection
and take refuge in Egypt's shadow.*
3 Pharaoh's protection shall become your shame,
refuge in Egypt's shadow your disgrace.*
4 When his princes are at Zoan
and his messengers reach Hanes,*
5 All shall be ashamed
of a people that gain them nothing,
Neither help nor benefit,
but only shame and reproach.*
6 Oracle on the Beasts of the Negeb.
Through the distressed and troubled land†
of the lioness and roaring lion,
of the viper and flying saraph,
They carry their riches on the backs of donkeys
and their treasures on the humps of camels
To a people good for nothing,
7 to Egypt whose help is futile and vain.
Therefore I call her
"Rahab† Sit-still."
8† Now come, write it on a tablet they can keep,
inscribe it on a scroll;
That in time to come it may be
an eternal witness.*
9 For this is a rebellious people,
deceitful children,
Children who refuse
to listen to the instruction of the LORD;*
10 Who say to the seers, "Do not see";
to the prophets,† "Do not prophesy truth for us;
speak smooth things to us, see visions that deceive!*
11 Turn aside from the way! Get out of the path!
Let us hear no more
of the Holy One of Israel!"*
12 Therefore, thus says the Holy One of Israel:
Because you reject this word,
And put your trust in oppression and deceit,
and depend on them,*
13 This iniquity of yours shall be
like a descending rift
Bulging out in a high wall
whose crash comes suddenly, in an instant,*
14 Crashing like a potter's jar
smashed beyond rescue,
And among its fragments cannot be found
a sherd to scoop fire from the hearth
or dip water from the cistern.*
15 For thus said the Lord GOD,
the Holy One of Israel:
By waiting and by calm you shall be saved,
in quiet and in trust shall be your strength.
But this you did not will.*
16 "No," you said,
"Upon horses we will flee."
Very well, you shall flee!
"Upon swift steeds we will ride."
Very well, swift shall be your pursuers!*
17 A thousand shall tremble at the threat of one—
if five threaten, you shall flee.
You will then be left like a flagstaff on a mountaintop,
like a flag on a hill.*

Zion's Future Deliverance

18 Truly, the LORD is waiting to be gracious to you,
truly, he shall rise to show you mercy;
For the LORD is a God of justice:
happy are all who wait for him!*
19 Yes, people of Zion, dwelling in Jerusalem,
you shall no longer weep;
He will be most gracious to you when you cry out;
as soon as he hears he will answer you.*
20 The Lord will give you bread in adversity
and water in affliction.
No longer will your Teacher† hide himself,
but with your own eyes you shall see your Teacher,*
21 And your ears shall hear a word behind you:

†

30:2 *Without asking my counsel*: it was a practice to consult God through the prophets or through the priestly oracle before making a major political decision (1 Sm 23:1–12; 1 Kgs 22:5), but Judah's leadership, in its concern for security, was apparently trying to keep its plan for a treaty with Egypt secret even from the prophets, thus implicitly from God (29:15).

30:6 *Distressed . . . land*: the wilderness between Judah and Egypt, through which Judahite messengers had to pass, carrying their tribute to Egypt to buy assistance in the struggle against Assyria. *Flying saraph*: see notes on 6:2; 14:29.

30:7 Here as elsewhere (cf. Ps 87:4) Egypt is compared to Rahab, the raging, destructive sea monster (cf. Is 51:9; Jb 26:12; Ps 89:11); yet Egypt, when asked for aid by Judah, becomes silent and "sits still."

30:8 Isaiah will write down his condemnation of the foolish policy pursued so that the truth of his warning of its dire consequences (vv. 12–17) may afterward be recognized.

30:10 *Seers . . . prophets*: the two terms are synonyms for prophetic figures such as Isaiah (1:1; 2:1; 6:1, 5). There is wordplay between the nouns and their cognate verbs, both of which mean "to see." The authorities are depicted as forbidding prophets to contradict their secret political and military policies.

30:20 *Teacher*: God, who in the past made the people blind and deaf through the prophetic message (6:9–10) and who in his anger

*

30:2 Is 31:1; 36:6.
30:3 Is 20:5; Jer 2:36–37.
30:4 Is 19:11.
30:5 Is 36:6.
30:8 Is 8:1, 16; Jer 36:2; Hb 2:2.
30:9 Is 1:4; 28:12; Jer 7:28.
30:10 Is 29:10; Jer 5:31; 11:21; Am 2:12.
30:11 Jb 21:14–15.
30:12 Is 28:15; Ps 62:11.
30:13 Is 28:17; Ez 13:14.
30:14 Jer 19:11.
30:15 Is 7:4; 8:6; 28:12.
30:16 Is 31:3.
30:17 Is 11:10; Dt 32:30.
30:18 Ex 34:6; Ps 34:9; Jer 17:7.
30:19 Is 25:8; 58:9; 65:24.
30:20 Is 6:9–10; 8:17; 29:18.

"This is the way; walk in it,"
when you would turn to the right or the left.
22 You shall defile your silver-plated idols
and your gold-covered images;
You shall throw them away like filthy rags,
you shall say, "Get out!"*
23 He will give rain for the seed
you sow in the ground,
And the bread that the soil produces
will be rich and abundant.
On that day your cattle will graze
in broad meadows;*
24 The oxen and the donkeys that till the ground
will eat silage tossed to them
with shovel and pitchfork.
25 Upon every high mountain and lofty hill
there will be streams of running water.
On the day of the great slaughter,
when the towers fall,
26 The light of the moon will be like the light of the sun,
and the light of the sun will be seven times greater,
like the light of seven days,
On the day the LORD binds up the wounds of his people
and heals the bruises left by his blows.*

Divine Judgment on Assyria†

27 See, the name of the LORD is coming from afar,
burning with anger, heavy with threat,
His lips filled with fury,
tongue like a consuming fire,*
28 Breath like an overflowing torrent
that reaches up to the neck!
He will winnow the nations with a destructive winnowing
and bridle the jaws of the peoples to send them astray.*
29 For you, there will be singing
as on a night when a feast is observed,
And joy of heart
as when one marches along with a flute
Going to the mountain of the LORD,
to the Rock of Israel.
30 The LORD will make his glorious voice heard,
and reveal his arm coming down
In raging fury and flame of consuming fire,
in tempest, and rainstorm, and hail.*
31 For at the voice of the LORD, Assyria will be shattered,
as he strikes with the rod;
32 And every sweep of the rod of his punishment,
which the LORD will bring down on him,
Will be accompanied by timbrels and lyres,
while he wages war against him.*
33 For his tophet† has long been ready,
truly it is prepared for the king;
His firepit made both deep and wide,
with fire and firewood in abundance,
And the breath of the LORD, like a stream of sulfur,
setting it afire.*

Against the Egyptian Alliance

31 1 Ah! Those who go down to Egypt for help,
who rely on horses;
Who put their trust in chariots because of their number,
and in horsemen because of their combined power,
But look not to the Holy One of Israel
nor seek the LORD!†*
2 Yet he too is wise and will bring disaster;
he will not turn from his threats.
He will rise up against the house of the wicked
and against those who help evildoers.*
3 The Egyptians are human beings, not God,
their horses flesh, not spirit;
When the LORD stretches forth his hand,
the helper shall stumble, the one helped shall fall,
and both of them shall perish together.*
4 For thus says the LORD to me:
As a lion or its young
growling over the prey,
With a band of shepherds
assembled against it,
Is neither dismayed by their shouts
nor cowed by their noise,
So shall the LORD of hosts come down
to wage war upon Mount Zion, upon its height.*

---

† hid his face from the house of Jacob (8:17), shall in the future help them to understand his teaching clearly (cf. Jer 31:34).

30:27–33 God's punishment of Assyria. *The name of the LORD*: here, God himself; cf. Ps 20:2.

30:33 *Tophet*: a site, near Jerusalem, where children were sacrificed by fire to Molech (2 Kgs 23:10), and where, probably, Ahaz sacrificed his son (2 Kgs 16:3). Here, Isaiah speaks of "his tophet," the site prepared for burning up the king of Assyria. *King*: there seems to be a play on words between the Heb. word for king (*melek*) and the name Molech. This defeat of Assyria becomes the occasion for Israel's festal rejoicing (v. 32).

31:1 *Seek the LORD*: a technical expression for seeking a prophetic or priestly oracle, similar to the expression "asking my counsel" in 30:2. The prophet complains that Judah has decided on its policy of alliance with Egypt without first consulting the Lord.

---

* **30:22** Is 2:20; 27:9; 31:7. **30:23** Lv 26:3–5. **30:26** Is 1:6; Jer 30:17; Hos 6:1. **30:27** Is 10:17; 29:6. **30:28** Is 8:7–8; 37:29. **30:30** Is 10:17; 28:2; 29:6. **30:32** Is 10:24–26; 14:24–27. **30:33** Gn 19:24; Ez 38:22. **31:1** Is 5:12, 24; 18:2; 22:11; 29:15; 30:2; 36:6. **31:2** Is 28:21. **31:3** Ps 146:3–5. **31:4** Hos 5:14; Am 1:2; 3:8, 12.

5 Like hovering birds, so the LORD of hosts
shall shield Jerusalem,
To shield and deliver,
to spare and rescue.*

6 Return, O Israelites, to him whom you have
utterly deserted.* 7 On that day each one of you
shall reject his idols of silver and gold, which
your hands have made.*

8 Assyria shall fall by a sword, not wielded by
human being,
no mortal sword shall devour him;
He shall flee before the sword,
and his young men shall be impressed as
laborers.*
9 He shall rush past his crag† in panic,
and his princes desert the standard in
terror,
Says the LORD who has a fire in Zion
and a furnace in Jerusalem.*

The Kingdom of Justice

32 1 See, a king will reign justly
and princes will rule rightly.*
2 Each of them will be like a shelter from the
wind,
a refuge from the rain.
They will be like streams of water in a dry
country,
like the shade of a great rock in a parched
land.*
3 The eyes of those who see will not be closed;
the ears of those who hear will be
attentive.*
4 The hasty of heart shall take thought to know,
and tongues of stutterers shall speak readily
and clearly.
5 No more will the fool be called noble,
nor the deceiver be considered honorable.*
6 For the fool speaks folly,
his heart plans evil:
Godless actions,
perverse speech against the LORD,
Letting the hungry go empty
and the thirsty without drink.*
7 The deceits of the deceiver are evil,
he plans devious schemes:
To ruin the poor with lies,
and the needy when they plead their case.*
8 But the noble plan noble deeds,
and in noble deeds they persist.

The Women of Jerusalem

9 You women so complacent, rise up and hear
my voice,
daughters so confident, give heed to my
words.*
10 In a little more than a year
your confidence will be shaken;
For the vintage will fail,
no fruit harvest will come in.*
11 Tremble, you who are so complacent!
Shudder, you who are so confident!
Strip yourselves bare,
with only a loincloth for cover.*
12 Beat your breasts
for the pleasant fields,
for the fruitful vine;*
13 For the soil of my people,
overgrown with thorns and briers;
For all the joyful houses,
the exultant city.*
14 The castle† will be forsaken,
the noisy city deserted;
Citadel and tower will become wasteland
forever,
the joy of wild donkeys, the pasture of
flocks;*
15† Until the spirit from on high
is poured out on us.
And the wilderness becomes a garden land
and the garden land seems as common as
forest.*
16 Then judgment will dwell in the wilderness
and justice abide in the garden land.
17 The work of justice will be peace;
the effect of justice, calm and security
forever.*
18 My people will live in peaceful country,
in secure dwellings and quiet resting
places.*
19 And the forest will come down completely,
the city will be utterly laid low.†*

†

31:9 *Crag*: the king as the rallying point of the princes. *Panic*: terror is an element of Israel's holy war tradition, in which defeat of the enemy is accomplished by the Lord rather than by human means (cf. v. 8).

32:14 *The castle*: the fortified royal palace in Jerusalem. *Citadel*: Ophel, the fortified hill, with its stronghold called "the great projecting tower" (Neh 3:27).

32:15–18, 20 Extraordinary peace and prosperity will come to Israel under just rulers.

32:19 Probably from a different context, perhaps after v. 14a.

*

31:5 Is 37:35; Dt 32:11; Ps 91:4.
31:6 Is 1:2–4; Jer 3:12.
31:7 Is 2:20; 30:22.
31:8 Is 27:1; 34:5–6; 37:36.
31:9 Is 30:17, 33.
32:1 Is 9:6; 11:4; 16:5; Ps 72:1–4; Jer 23:5–6.
32:2 Is 4:6; 16:4; 25:4.
32:3 Is 6:10; 29:18; 35:5.
32:5 Is 5:20.
32:6 Prv 15:2.
32:7 Is 29:20–21; Mi 2:1.
32:9 Is 3:16–24; Am 6:1.
32:10 Zep 1:13.
32:11 Is 20:2; Jer 4:8; Mi 1:8.
32:12 Is 16:9.
32:13 Is 5:6; 7:23–25; 22:2; 34:13.
32:14 Is 7:25; 24:10–11.
32:15 Is 44:3; Ps 104:30; Ez 37:9–10; Jl 3:1–2.
32:17 Is 9:6; 30:15; 33:15–16; Ps 72:2–3, 7; Jas 3:18.
32:18 Jer 23:6; Mi 4:4.
32:19 Is 10:33–34; 26:5.

20 Happy are you who sow beside every stream,
and let the ox and the donkey go freely! *

Overthrow of Assyria†

33 1 Ah! You destroyer never destroyed,
betrayer never betrayed!
When you have finished destroying, you will
be destroyed;
when you have stopped betraying, you will
be betrayed. *
2 LORD, be gracious to us; for you we wait.
Be our strength every morning,
our salvation in time of trouble! *
3 At the roaring sound, peoples flee;
when you rise in your majesty, nations are
scattered. *
4 Spoil is gathered up as caterpillars gather,
an onrush like the rush of locusts. *
5 The LORD is exalted, enthroned on high;
he fills Zion with right and justice. *
6 That which makes her seasons certain,
her wealth, salvation, wisdom, and
knowledge,
is the fear of the LORD, her treasure. *
7 See, the men of Ariel cry out in the streets,
the messengers of Shalem† weep bitterly.
8 The highways are desolate,
travelers have quit the paths,
Covenants are broken, witnesses spurned;
yet no one gives it a thought. *
9 The country languishes in mourning,
Lebanon withers with shame;
Sharon† is like the Arabah,
Bashan and Carmel are stripped bare. *
10 Now I will rise up, says the LORD,
now exalt myself,
now lift myself up. *
11 You conceive dry grass, bring forth stubble;
my spirit shall consume you like fire.
12 The peoples shall be burned to lime,
thorns cut down to burn in fire. *
13 Hear, you who are far off, what I have done;
you who are near, acknowledge my might.
14 In Zion sinners are in dread,
trembling grips the impious:
"Who of us can live with consuming fire?
who of us can live with everlasting flames?" *

Live It!

Shalom

In Israel, people greet one another by saying "Shalom." In the Bible, *shalom* means "peace" in its fullest sense (see Is 32:16–20). Shalom is not just the absence of war and violence but also the presence of justice, righteousness, happiness, and fullness of life. What better way to greet your neighbors or friends than to wish them shalom.

In your own life, seek peace. Begin each day by praying for peace of mind and heart, and to act with justice in all that you do. The very prayer you speak will become the way you live. Peace can become a reality only when we become a shalom people. It begins with us. Pray for shalom today.

▶ **Is 32:16–20**

15 Whoever walks righteously and speaks
honestly,
who spurns what is gained by oppression,
Who waves off contact with a bribe,
who stops his ears so as not to hear of
bloodshed,
who closes his eyes so as not to look on
evil— *
16 That one shall dwell on the heights,
with fortresses of rock for stronghold,
food and drink in steady supply.
17 Your eyes will see a king† in his splendor,
they will look upon a vast land. *
18 Your mind will dwell on the terror:
"Where is the one who counted, where the
one who weighed?
Where the one who counted the towers?" *
19 You shall no longer see a defiant people,

†

33:1–24 After an introductory address to Assyria (v. 1), there follows a prayer on behalf of Jerusalem which recalls what God had done in the past (vv. 2–6) and a description of the present situation (vv. 7–9). In response, the Lord announces a judgment on Assyria (vv. 10–12) that will lead to the purification of Jerusalem's inhabitants (vv. 13–16). The text ends with an idealized portrait of the redeemed Jerusalem of the future (vv. 17–24).

33:7 *Ariel . . . Shalem*: Jerusalem; cf. 29:1; Gn 14:18; Ps 76:3. There is a play on words between "Shalem," the city name, and *shalom*, Heb. for "peace."

33:9 *Sharon*: the fertile plain near the Mediterranean.

33:17 *King*: either the ideal Davidic king or God; cf. v. 22.

*

32:20 Is 7:25; 30:18, 23.
33:1 Is 10:12; 16:4; 21:2; 24:16.
33:2 Is 25:9; 30:18–19.
33:3 Is 17:13; Nm 10:35; Ps 68:2.
33:4 Is 9:2; 33:23.
33:5 Is 1:26–27; 2:11, 17; 32:1; 33:16.
33:6 Is 11:2; 13:22; 60:22.
33:8 Is 24:5; Jgs 5:6.
33:9 Na 1:4.
33:10 Ps 12:6; Zep 3:8.
33:12 Is 10:17.
33:14 Is 30:27, 30, 32; 31:9.
33:15 Ps 15:2–6; 24:4–5.
33:17 Is 26:15.
33:18 Ps 48:13–14.

a people of speech too obscure to
comprehend,
stammering in a tongue not understood.*
20 Look to Zion, the city of our festivals;
your eyes shall see Jerusalem
as a quiet abode, a tent not to be struck,
Whose pegs will never be pulled up,
nor any of its ropes severed.*
21 Indeed the LORD in majesty will be there for us
a place of rivers and wide streams
on which no galley may go,
where no majestic ship† may pass.*
22 For the LORD is our judge,
the LORD is our lawgiver,
the LORD is our king;
he it is who will save us.
23 The rigging hangs slack;
it cannot hold the mast in place,
nor keep the sail spread out.
Then the blind will divide great spoils
and the lame will carry off the loot.*
24 No one who dwells there will say, "I am sick";
the people who live there will be forgiven
their guilt.*

F. The Lord, Zion's Avenger†

Judgment upon Edom

34 1 Come near, nations, and listen;
be attentive, you peoples!
Let the earth and what fills it listen,
the world and all it produces.*
2 The LORD is angry with all the nations,
enraged against all their host;
He has placed them under the ban,
given them up to slaughter.*
3 Their slain shall be cast out,
their corpses shall send up a stench;
the mountains shall run with their blood,*
4 All the host of heaven shall rot;
the heavens shall be rolled up like a scroll.
All their host shall wither away,
as the leaf wilts on the vine,
or as the fig withers on the tree.*
5 When my sword has drunk its fill in the
heavens,
it shall come down upon Edom for
judgment,
upon a people under my ban.*
6 The LORD has a sword sated with blood,
greasy with fat,
With the blood of lambs and goats,
with the fat of rams' kidneys;
For the LORD has a sacrifice in Bozrah,
a great slaughter in the land of Edom.*
7 Wild oxen shall be struck down with fatlings,
and bullocks with bulls;
Their land shall be soaked with blood,
and their soil greasy with fat.
8† For the LORD has a day of vengeance,
a year of requital for the cause of Zion.*
9 Edom's streams shall be changed into pitch,
its soil into sulfur,
and its land shall become burning pitch;
10 Night and day it shall not be quenched,
its smoke shall rise forever.
From generation to generation it shall lie
waste,
never again shall anyone pass through it.*
11 But the desert owl and hoot owl shall
possess it,
the screech owl and raven shall dwell in it.
The LORD will stretch over it the measuring
line of chaos,
the plumb line of confusion.† *
12 Its nobles shall be no more,
nor shall kings be proclaimed there;
all its princes are gone.*
13 Its castles shall be overgrown with thorns,
its fortresses with thistles and briers.
It shall become an abode for jackals,
a haunt for ostriches.*
14 Wildcats shall meet with desert beasts,
satyrs† shall call to one another;
There shall the lilith repose,
and find for herself a place to rest.

†

33:21–23 *Galley . . . majestic ship*: of a foreign oppressor. Though the broad streams of the future Jerusalem will make it accessible by boat, no foreign invader will succeed in a naval attack on the city, for the Lord will protect it, the enemy fleet will be disabled, and even the weakest inhabitants will gather much plunder from the defeated enemy.

34:1–35:10 These two chapters form a small collection which looks forward to the vindication of Zion, first by defeat of its enemies (chap. 34), then by its restoration (chap. 35). They are generally judged to be later than the time of Isaiah (eighth century), perhaps during the Babylonian exile or thereafter; they are strongly influenced by Deutero-Isaiah (sixth century). In places they reflect themes from other parts of the Isaian collection.

34:8–17 The extreme hostility against Edom in this passage is reflected in a number of other prophetic texts from the seventh and sixth centuries B.C. (cf. e.g., 63:1–6; Jer 49:7–22; Ez 25:12–14). The animus was probably prompted by Edomite infiltration of the southern territories of Judah, especially after the Babylonian conquest of Judah.

34:11 *Chaos . . . confusion*: *tohu . . . bohu* in Hebrew, the terms used to describe the primeval chaos in Gn 1:2.

34:14 *Satyrs*: see note on 13:21. *The lilith*: a female demon thought to roam about the desert.

*

33:19 Is 28:11.
33:20 Is 32:18; Ps 46:6; 122:1–4.
33:21 Ez 47:1–12; Ps 46:5; 48:7.
33:23 2 Sm 8:6–7.
33:24 Mi 7:18–19.
34:1 Mi 1:2.
34:2 Is 24:21.
34:3 Ez 32:4, 6.
34:4 Is 13:10; 24:23; Ez 32:7; Jl 3:3–4; Mt 24:29; 2 Pt 3:10; Rev 6:12–14.
34:5 Jer 46:10.
34:6 Is 63:1; Lv 3:4; 2 Sm 1:22; Jer 49:12–13; Zep 1:7.
34:8 Is 13:9; 63:4.
34:10 Mal 1:4; Rev 14:11; 18:18.
34:11 Is 14:23; 28:17; 2 Kgs 21:13; Zep 2:14.
34:12 Ob 18.
34:13 Is 13:21; Hos 9:6.

15 There the hoot owl shall nest and lay eggs,
hatch them out and gather them in her shadow;
There shall the kites assemble,
each with its mate.
16 Search through the book of the LORD† and read:
not one of these shall be lacking,
For the mouth of the LORD has ordered it,
and his spirit gathers them there.
17 It is he who casts the lot for them;
his hand measures off† their portions;
They shall possess it forever,
and dwell in it from generation to generation.*

Israel's Deliverance†

35 1 The wilderness and the parched land will exult;
the Arabah will rejoice and bloom;*
2 Like the crocus it shall bloom abundantly,
and rejoice with joyful song.
The glory of Lebanon will be given to it,
the splendor of Carmel and Sharon;
They will see the glory of the LORD,
the splendor of our God.*
3 Strengthen hands that are feeble,
make firm knees that are weak,*
4 Say to the fearful of heart:
Be strong, do not fear!
Here is your God,
he comes with vindication;
With divine recompense
he comes to save you.*
5 Then the eyes of the blind shall see,
and the ears of the deaf be opened;*
6 Then the lame shall leap like a stag,
and the mute tongue sing for joy.
For waters will burst forth in the wilderness,
and streams in the Arabah.*
7 The burning sands will become pools,
and the thirsty ground, springs of water;
The abode where jackals crouch
will be a marsh for the reed and papyrus.
8 A highway will be there,
called the holy way;
No one unclean may pass over it,
but it will be for his people;
no traveler, not even fools, shall go astray on it.*
9 No lion shall be there,
nor any beast of prey approach,
nor be found.
But there the redeemed shall walk,*
10 And the ransomed of the LORD shall return,
and enter Zion singing,
crowned with everlasting joy;
They meet with joy and gladness,
sorrow and mourning flee away.*

G. Historical Appendix†

Invasion of Sennacherib

36 1 In the fourteenth year of King Hezekiah,
Sennacherib, king of Assyria, went up
against all the fortified cities of Judah and cap-
tured them.† * 2 From Lachish the king of Assyria
sent his commander with a great army to King
Hezekiah in Jerusalem. When he stopped at the
conduit of the upper pool, on the highway of the
fuller's field, 3 there came out to him the mas-
ter of the palace, Eliakim, son of Hilkiah, and
Shebna the scribe, and the chancellor, Joah, son
of Asaph. 4 The commander said to them, "Tell
Hezekiah: Thus says the great king, the king of
Assyria: On what do you base this trust of yours?
5 Do you think mere words substitute for strategy
and might in war? In whom, then, do you place
your trust, that you rebel against me? 6 Do you
trust in Egypt, that broken reed of a staff which
pierces the hand of anyone who leans on it? That
is what Pharaoh, king of Egypt, is to all who
trust in him.* 7 Or do you say to me: It is in the
LORD, our God, we trust? Is it not he whose high
places and altars Hezekiah has removed,† com-
manding Judah and Jerusalem, 'Worship before
this altar'?*

†

34:16 *Book of the LORD*: a list of God's creatures; cf. Ex 32:32–33; Ps 69:29, "the book of the living"; Ps 139:16, "your book."

34:17 *Casts the lot . . . measures off*: an ironic reference to how land might be distributed to new possessors (cf. Jos 14–21; Mi 2:5).

35:1–10 This chapter contains a number of themes similar to those in Deutero-Isaiah (chaps. 40–55), for example, the blossoming of the wilderness (vv. 1–2; cf. 41:18–19), which is now well-irrigated (v. 7; cf. 43:19–20); sight to the blind (vv. 5–6; cf. 42:7, 16); a highway in the wilderness (v. 8; cf. 41:3); and the return of the redeemed/ransomed to Zion (vv. 9–10; cf. 51:11). Nevertheless, it forms a unit with chap. 34 (see note on 34:1–35:10) and reflects, along with that chapter, themes found in chaps. 1–33.

36:1–39:8 Except for 38:9–20 (Hezekiah's prayer of thanksgiving), this historical appendix describing the siege, etc., is paralleled in 2 Kgs 18:13–20:19, which, however, has certain details proper to itself. The events are also reflected in the cuneiform inscriptions of Sennacherib.

36:1 The occasion for this Assyrian attack was Hezekiah's attempt to reject Judah's status as vassal to Assyria, relying on help from Egypt, a course of action condemned by Isaiah (see notes on 28:15, 18; 28:16; 29:7–8; 30:1–17; etc.). 2 Kgs 19:14–16 reports that Hezekiah surrendered to the Assyrians and paid the tribute imposed on him—a report omitted in the Isaiah text.

36:7 The Assyrians assert that Hezekiah's removal of the high

*

34:17 Jos 18:10; Ps 78:55.
35:1 Is 41:18–19; 55:12–13.
35:2 Is 40:5; 60:13.
35:3 Is 40:29–30; Jb 4:3–4; Heb 12:12.
35:4 Is 41:10; Zec 8:13.
35:5 Is 29:18; 32:3.
35:6 Is 32:3–4; 41:18; 43:19–20; 44:3; Mt 11:5.
35:8 Is 11:16; 43:19; 49:11.
35:9 Is 62:10; Lv 26:6.
35:10 Is 51:11.
36:1 2 Kgs 18:13; 2 Chr 32:1.
36:6 Is 30:2–3, 7.
36:7 2 Kgs 18:4.

Catholic Connection

The Liturgical Year

What is your favorite time of year? Perhaps you like the warmth of summer or the changing leaves of fall. Each season brings its own unique joys. The Church year, called the liturgical year, has seasons too, and each one brings its own joys and message. For example, Isaiah's prophecy in Isaiah 35:1–10 is shared with the Church when it is read at Mass during the Advent Season, as God's people joyfully prepare to celebrate the Messiah's birth and his glorious return.

The Advent Season is the first of six time periods that make up the liturgical year. The others are Christmas, Lent, the Easter Triduum, Easter, and Ordinary Time. Each period focuses on some aspect of Christ's saving work; this is done most particularly in the readings and prayers that are shared during Mass. The Sunday readings follow a three-year cycle (A, B, and C). Each Sunday's readings contain a reading from the Old Testament, one of the Epistles (Letters), and one of the four Gospels (Matthew, Mark, Luke, or John).

The liturgical year begins with the four Sundays prior to Christmas. This season is called **Advent** and is marked by God's people preparing for the celebration of Christ's birth as well as his Second Coming.

The **Christmas Season** begins with the celebration of Jesus' birth on Christmas and continues through the Feast of the Baptism of the Lord. During this time, we celebrate the birth of the Messiah as well as special feasts honoring the Holy Family and Mary.

The forty days of **Lent** begin on Ash Wednesday and continue through to Holy Thursday. This season is marked by repentance and preparations for the celebration of Easter.

The **Easter Triduum** begins on Holy Thursday and ends with Easter Sunday. These three days are the high point during the liturgical year when we focus on Jesus' Passion, death, and Resurrection.

The **Easter Season** spans fifty days from Easter to Pentecost. During this season, we celebrate Christ's Resurrection, the descent of the Holy Spirit, and the birth of the Church.

The remaining weeks during the year that do not fall into one of the other seasons fall into **Ordinary Time**. During Ordinary Time, the Church focuses on living the Gospel message.

Is 35:1–10

Catechism, nos. 1163–1173

8 "Now, make a wager with my lord, the king
of Assyria: I will give you two thousand horses,
if you are able to put riders on them. 9 How then
can you turn back even a captain, one of the least
servants of my lord, trusting, as you do, in Egypt
for chariots and horses? 10 Did I come up to de-
stroy this land without the LORD? The LORD him-
self said to me, Go up and destroy that land!"*
11 Then Eliakim and Shebna and Joah said to
the commander, "Please speak to your servants
in Aramaic; we understand it. Do not speak to
us in the language of Judah within earshot of the
people who are on the wall."†
12 But the commander replied, "Was it to your
lord and to you that my lord sent me to speak
these words? Was it not rather to those sitting
on the wall, who, with you, will have to eat their
own excrement and drink their own urine?"
13 Then the commander stepped forward and
cried out in a loud voice in the language of Ju-
dah, "Listen to the words of the great king, the
king of Assyria. 14 Thus says the king: Do not let
Hezekiah deceive you, for he cannot rescue you.
15 And do not let Hezekiah induce you to trust in
the LORD, saying, 'The LORD will surely rescue us,
and this city will not be handed over to the king
of Assyria.' 16 Do not listen to Hezekiah, for thus
says the king of Assyria:

Make peace with me
  and surrender to me!
Eat, each of you, from your vine,
  each from your own fig tree.
Drink water, each from your own well,*
17 until I arrive and take you
  to a land like your own,
A land of grain and wine,
  a land of bread and vineyards.

18 Do not let Hezekiah seduce you by saying, 'The
LORD will rescue us.' Has any of the gods of the
nations rescued his land from the power of the
king of Assyria?* 19 Where are the gods of Ha-
math and Arpad? Where are the gods of Sephar-
vaim? Where are the gods of Samaria? Have they
saved Samaria from my power?* 20 Who among
all the gods of these lands ever rescued their land
from my power, that the LORD should save Je-
rusalem from my power?" 21 But they remained
silent and did not answer at all, for the king's
command was, "Do not answer him."
22 Then the master of the palace, Eliakim, son
of Hilkiah, Shebna the scribe, and the chancellor
Joah, son of Asaph, came to Hezekiah with their
garments torn, and reported to him the words of
the commander.

37 1 † When King Hezekiah heard this, he
tore his garments, covered himself with
sackcloth, and went into the house of the LORD.
2 He sent Eliakim, the master of the palace, and
Shebna the scribe, and the elders of the priests,
covered with sackcloth, to tell the prophet Isaiah,
son of Amoz,

3 "Thus says Hezekiah:
A day of distress and rebuke,
  a day of disgrace is this day!
Children are due to come forth,
  but the strength to give birth is lacking.† *

4 Perhaps the LORD, your God, will hear the words
of the commander, whom his lord, the king of
Assyria, sent to taunt the living God, and will
rebuke him for the words which the LORD, your
God, has heard. So lift up a prayer for the rem-
nant that is here."
5 When the servants of King Hezekiah had come
to Isaiah, 6 he said to them: "Tell this to your lord:
Thus says the LORD: Do not be frightened by the
words you have heard, by which the deputies of
the king of Assyria have blasphemed me.*

7 I am putting in him such a spirit
  that when he hears a report
  he will return to his land.
  I will make him fall by the sword in his
    land."

8 When the commander, on his return, heard
that the king of Assyria had withdrawn from La-
chish, he found him besieging Libnah. 9 The king
of Assyria heard a report: "Tirhakah,† king of Ethi-
opia, has come out to fight against you." Again he

† places and altars (unofficial sanctuaries) was taken by the Lord as an insult. They declare to Jerusalem's emissaries that the city therefore no longer has a right to the Lord's protection and that they are the ones who truly carry out his will (cf. v. 10).

36:11 The emissaries of King Hezekiah ask that the conversation be carried on in Aramaic, not in Hebrew, for they fear the effect of the Assyrian claims upon the morale of the people.

37:1–35 There appear to be parallel accounts of Hezekiah's appeal and the response received (vv. 1–7 and vv. 14–35): in each, Hezekiah goes to the Temple, refers to the Assyrian boasts (found in 36:15–20; 37:10–14), and receives a favorable response from Isaiah.

37:3 A proverbial expression. In the Bible the pangs of childbirth often typify extreme anguish; cf. 13:8; Jer 6:24; Mi 4:9–10. In this instance there is reference to the desperate situation of Hezekiah from which he would scarcely be able to free himself.

37:9 *Tirhakah*: may have been general of the Egyptian army in 701 B.C.; later he became Pharaoh, one of the Ethiopian dynasty of Egyptian kings (ca. 690–664 B.C.). Many consider that this account

* **36:10** Is 10:5–6. **36:16** 1 Kgs 5:5; Zec 3:10. **36:18** Is 37:11. **36:19** Is 10:9; 37:13. **37:3** Is 26:18. **37:6** Is 7:4; 10:24.

sent messengers to Hezekiah to say: 10 "Thus shall
you say to Hezekiah, king of Judah: Do not let
your God in whom you trust deceive you by say-
ing, 'Jerusalem will not be handed over to the king
of Assyria.'* 11 You, certainly, have heard what the
kings of Assyria have done to all the lands: they
put them under the ban! And are you to be de-
livered? 12 Did the gods of the nations whom my
fathers destroyed deliver them—Gozan, Haran,
Rezeph, and the Edenites in Telassar? 13 Where are
the king of Hamath, the king of Arpad, or a king
of the cities Sepharvaim, Hena or Ivvah?"

14 Hezekiah took the letter from the hand of
the messengers and read it; then he went up to
the house of the LORD, and spreading it out be-
fore the LORD, 15 Hezekiah prayed to the LORD:

16 "LORD of hosts, God of Israel,
enthroned on the cherubim!
You alone are God
over all the kingdoms of the earth.
It is you who made
the heavens and the earth.†
17 Incline your ear, LORD, and listen!
open your eyes, LORD, and see!
Hear all the words Sennacherib has sent
to taunt the living God.
18 Truly, O LORD,
the kings of Assyria have laid waste
the nations and their lands.
19 They gave their gods to the fire
—they were not gods at all,
but the work of human hands—
Wood and stone, they destroyed them.*
20 Therefore, LORD, our God,
save us from this man's power,
That all the kingdoms of the earth may know
that you alone, LORD, are God."

21 † Then Isaiah, son of Amoz, sent this mes-
sage to Hezekiah: "Thus says the LORD, the God
of Israel, to whom you have prayed concerning
Sennacherib, king of Assyria: I have listened!
22 This is the word the LORD has spoken concern-
ing him:*

She despises you, laughs you to scorn,
the virgin daughter Zion;
Behind you she wags her head,
daughter Jerusalem.
23 Whom have you insulted and blasphemed,
at whom have you raised your voice
And lifted up your eyes on high?
At the Holy One of Israel!*
24 Through the mouths of your messengers
you have insulted the Lord when you said:
'With my many chariots I went up
to the tops of the peaks,
to the recesses of Lebanon,
To cut down its lofty cedars,
its choice cypresses;
I reached the farthest shelter,
the forest ranges.
25 I myself dug wells
and drank foreign water;
Drying up all the rivers of Egypt
beneath the soles of my feet.'
26 Have you not heard?
A long time ago I prepared it,
from days of old I planned it,
Now I have brought it about:
You are here to reduce
fortified cities to heaps of ruins,*
27 Their people powerless,
dismayed and distraught,
They are plants of the field,
green growth,
thatch on the rooftops,
Grain scorched by the east wind.
28 I know when you stand or sit,
when you come or go,
and how you rage against me.
29 Because you rage against me
and your smugness has reached my ears,
I will put my hook in your nose
and my bit in your mouth,
And make you leave by the way you came.*
30 This shall be a sign† for you:
This year you shall eat the aftergrowth,
next year, what grows of itself;
But in the third year, sow and reap,
plant vineyards and eat their fruit!
31 The remaining survivors of the house of Judah
shall again strike root below
and bear fruit above.*
32 For out of Jerusalem shall come a remnant,

† in Isaiah combines features of two originally distinct sieges of Jerusalem by Sennacherib.

37:16 In contrast to the empty boasting of the Assyrians, Hezekiah proclaims the Lord as "God over all the kingdoms of the earth."

37:21–37 The reversal of Isaiah's attitude toward Hezekiah's revolt (see note on 36:1) and a wonderful deliverance after Hezekiah had already submitted and paid tribute raise questions difficult to answer. See note on 22:1–14. Some have postulated that chaps. 36–37 combine accounts of two different Assyrian invasions.

37:30 *A sign*: sets a time limit. After two years the normal conditions of life will be resumed. See the similar use of time limits as signs in 7:15–16; 8:4; 16:14; and 21:16. *You*: Hezekiah.

* **37:10** Is 36:14.
37:19 Jer 16:20.
37:22 2 Kgs 19:21.
37:23 Is 10:12.
37:26 Is 10:6, 15.
37:29 Is 30:28.
37:31 Is 27:6.

and from Mount Zion, survivors.
The zeal of the LORD of hosts shall do this.*

33Therefore, thus says the LORD about the king
of Assyria:

He shall not come as far as this city,
nor shoot there an arrow,
nor confront it with a shield,
Nor cast up a siege-work against it.
34 By the way he came he shall leave,
never coming as far as this city,
oracle of the LORD.
35 I will shield and save this city
for my own sake and the sake of David my
servant."*

36Then the angel of the LORD went forth and
struck down one hundred and eighty-five thou-
sand in the Assyrian camp. Early the next morn-
ing, there they were, all those corpses, dead!†*
37So Sennacherib, the king of Assyria, broke
camp, departed, returned home, and stayed in
Nineveh.
38When he was worshiping in the temple of
his god Nisroch, his sons Adrammelech and
Sharezer struck him down with the sword and
fled into the land of Ararat.† His son Esarhaddon
reigned in his place.

Sickness and Recovery of Hezekiah

38 1† In those days,† when Hezekiah was
mortally ill, the prophet Isaiah, son of
Amoz, came and said to him: "Thus says the
LORD: Put your house in order, for you are about
to die; you shall not recover."* 2Hezekiah turned
his face to the wall and prayed to the LORD:
3"Ah, LORD, remember how faithfully and
wholeheartedly I conducted myself in your pres-
ence, doing what was good in your sight!" And
Hezekiah wept bitterly.*
4Then the word of the LORD came to Isaiah:
5Go, tell Hezekiah:† Thus says the LORD, the God
of your father David: I have heard your prayer; I
have seen your tears. Now I will add fifteen years
to your life. 6I will rescue you and this city from
the hand of the king of Assyria; I will be a shield
to this city.*
7This will be the sign for you from the LORD
that the LORD will carry out the word he has spo-
ken: 8See, I will make the shadow cast by the sun
on the stairway to the terrace of Ahaz† go back
the ten steps it has advanced. So the sun came
back the ten steps it had advanced.*

Hezekiah's Hymn of Thanksgiving

9The song of Hezekiah, king of Judah, after
he had been sick and had recovered from his
illness:

10 In the noontime of life† I said,
I must depart!
To the gates of Sheol I have been consigned
for the rest of my years.*
11 I said, I shall see the LORD† no more
in the land of the living.
Nor look on any mortals
among those who dwell in the world.
12 My dwelling, like a shepherd's tent,
is struck down and borne away from me;
You have folded up my life, like a weaver
who severs me from the last thread.†*
From morning to night you make an end
of me;
13 I cry out even until the dawn.
Like a lion he breaks all my bones;
from morning to night you make an end
of me.*
14 Like a swallow I chirp;
I moan like a dove.
My eyes grow weary looking heavenward:
Lord, I am overwhelmed; go security for me!
15† What am I to say or tell him?
He is the one who has done it!
All my sleep has fled,
because of the bitterness of my soul.

†

37:36 The destruction of Sennacherib's army is also recorded by Herodotus, a Greek historian of the fifth century B.C. It was possibly owing to a plague, which the author interprets as God's activity.

37:38 The violent death of Sennacherib (681 B.C.) is also mentioned in non-biblical sources. It occurred twenty years after his invasion of Judah. *Ararat*: the land of Urartu in the mountains north of Assyria.

38:1–39:8 The events of this section—sickness and recovery of Hezekiah, embassy of Merodach-baladan—anticipate the rise of Babylon (chaps. 40–66). They occurred prior to the events of 36:1–37:38, which point back to Assyria (1:1–35:10).

38:1 *In those days*: before the siege of Jerusalem in 701 B.C.

38:5 Since Hezekiah died in 687 B.C., his sickness may have occurred in 702 B.C., that is, fifteen years before.

38:8 *Stairway to the terrace of Ahaz*: this interpretation is based on a reading of the Hebrew text revised according to the Dead Sea Scroll of Isaiah; cf. 2 Kgs 23:12. Many translate the phrase as "steps of Ahaz" and understand this as referring to a sundial.

38:10 *In the noontime of life*: long before the end of a full span of life; cf. Ps 55:24; 102:25.

38:11 *See the LORD*: go to the Temple and take part in its service.

38:12 These two metaphors emphasize the suddenness and finality of death.

38:15–16 The Hebrew text is very problematic and its meaning uncertain.

*

37:32 Is 9:6.
37:35 Is 31:5; 1 Kgs 15:4.
37:36 Is 10:12; 17:14.
38:1 2 Kgs 20:1.
38:3 2 Kgs 18:5–6.
38:6 Is 37:35.
38:8 2 Kgs 20:9–11.
38:10 Jb 17:11–13; Ps 102:25.
38:12 Jb 7:6.
38:13 Jb 23:14.

Pray It!

The Hope of Second Isaiah

Second Isaiah prophesies to the Israelites living in exile in Babylon with words full of love and hope: "Comfort, give comfort to my people, / says your God" (Is 40:1). Isaiah promises these Israelites a new liberation and the eventual restoration of Jerusalem and the Temple (see 44:26–28).

The author of the Gospel of Luke uses Isaiah 40:3–5 to describe the ministry of John the Baptist in announcing Jesus' arrival (see Lk 3:4–6). This writer wants to make it clear that Isaiah's promises are answered by the coming of Jesus.

In your prayer, reflect or journal on the following questions:

- Is there hope for our society?
- What are some things that you are hopeful for?
- Imagine God is speaking words of hope to you. What is God saying?

▶ **Is 40:1–5**

16 Those live whom the LORD protects;
yours is the life of my spirit.
You have given me health and restored my life!
17 Peace in place of bitterness!
You have preserved my life
from the pit of destruction;
Behind your back
you cast all my sins.†
18† For it is not Sheol that gives you thanks,
nor death that praises you;
Neither do those who go down into the pit
await your kindness.*
19 The living, the living give you thanks,
as I do today.
Parents declare to their children,
O God, your faithfulness.
20 The LORD is there to save us.
We shall play our music
In the house of the LORD
all the days of our life.

21 † Then Isaiah said, "Bring a poultice of figs and
apply it to the boil for his recovery." 22 Hezekiah
asked, "What is the sign that I shall go up to the
house of the LORD?"

Embassy from Merodach-baladan

39 1 At that time Merodach-baladan,† son of
Baladan, king of Babylon, sent letters and
gifts to Hezekiah, when he heard that he had
been sick and had recovered.* 2 Hezekiah was
pleased at their coming, and then showed the
messengers his treasury, the silver and gold, the
spices and perfumed oil, his whole armory, and
everything in his storerooms; there was nothing
in his house or in all his realm that Hezekiah did
not show them.*
3 Then Isaiah the prophet came to King Hez-
ekiah and asked him, "What did these men say
to you? Where did they come from?" Hezekiah
replied, "They came to me from a distant land,
from Babylon." 4 He asked, "What did they see
in your house?" Hezekiah answered, "They saw
everything in my house. There is nothing in my
storerooms that I did not show them." 5 Then Isa-
iah said to Hezekiah, "Hear the word of the LORD
of hosts: 6 The time is coming when all that is in
your house, everything that your ancestors have
stored up until this day, shall be carried off to
Babylon;† nothing shall be left, says the LORD.*
7 Some of your own descendants, your progeny,
shall be taken and made attendants in the palace
of the king of Babylon."* 8 Hezekiah replied to
Isaiah, "The word of the LORD which you have
spoken is good."† For he thought, "There will be
peace and stability in my lifetime."

†

38:17 *Behind your back you cast all my sins*: figurative language to express the divine forgiveness of sins, as if God no longer saw or cared about them.

38:18–19 See note on Ps 6:6.

38:21–22 These verses are clearly out of place. Logically they should come after v. 6, as they do in the parallel account in 2 Kgs 20, but the two accounts are not identical, and it appears that the version in Isaiah is abbreviated from that in Kings. If that is so, Is 38:21–22 would be a secondary addition from Kings, inserted by a later reader who thought the account incomplete.

39:1 *Merodach-baladan*: twice king of Babylon, probably from 721 to 710 B.C., and again for nine months, in 704–703. This visit of his messengers, certainly before 701, was in reality a political one. Babylon hoped to lead an anti-Assyrian confederation composed of neighboring states and wanted Judah to join.

39:6 Because Judah preferred to follow a pro-Babylonian policy, instead of trusting in the Lord, it would later be exiled to Babylon.

39:8 Hezekiah was relieved that the disaster would not occur in his lifetime.

38:18 Ps 6:6; 88:11–13. **39:1** 2 Kgs 20:12. **39:2** 2 Chr 32:25–31. **39:6** 2 Kgs 24:13; 25:13–17. **39:7** Dn 1:3–19.

II. Isaiah 40—55†

A. The Lord's Glory in Israel's Liberation

Promise of Salvation

40 1† Comfort, give comfort to my people,
says your God.
2 Speak to the heart of Jerusalem, and proclaim to her
that her service† has ended,
that her guilt is expiated,
That she has received from the hand of the Lord
double for all her sins.*

"In the wilderness prepare the way of the Lord! Make straight in the wasteland a highway for our God!"
(Isa 40:3)

3 A voice proclaims:†
In the wilderness prepare the way of the Lord!
Make straight in the wasteland a highway for our God!*
4 Every valley shall be lifted up,
every mountain and hill made low;
The rugged land shall be a plain,
the rough country, a broad valley.
5 Then the glory of the Lord shall be revealed,
and all flesh shall see it together;
for the mouth of the Lord has spoken.

6 A voice says, "Proclaim!"
I answer, "What shall I proclaim?"
"All flesh is grass,
and all their loyalty like the flower of the field.*
7 The grass withers, the flower wilts,
when the breath of the Lord blows upon it."
"Yes, the people is grass!
8 The grass withers, the flower wilts,
but the word of our God stands forever."

9 Go up onto a high mountain,
Zion, herald of good news!†
Cry out at the top of your voice,
Jerusalem, herald of good news!
Cry out, do not fear!
Say to the cities of Judah:
Here is your God!
10 Here comes with power
the Lord God,
who rules by his strong arm;
Here is his reward with him,
his recompense before him.
11 Like a shepherd he feeds his flock;
in his arms he gathers the lambs,
Carrying them in his bosom,
leading the ewes with care.*

Power of God and the Vanity of Idols

12 Who has measured with his palm the waters,
marked off the heavens with a span,
held in his fingers the dust of the earth,
weighed the mountains in scales
and the hills in a balance?†

†

40:1–55:13 Chapters 40–55 are usually designated Second Isaiah (or Deutero-Isaiah) and are believed to have been written by an anonymous prophet toward the end of the Babylonian exile. Isaiah, who is named frequently in chaps. 1–39, does not appear here; the Assyrians, the great threat during the eighth century, hardly appear; the Judeans are in Babylon, having been taken there by the victorious Babylonians; Cyrus, the Persian king, is named; he will defeat Babylon and release the captives. Second Isaiah, who sees this not as a happy circumstance but as part of God's age-old plan, exhorts the Judeans to resist the temptations of Babylonian religion and stirs up hopes of an imminent return to Judah, where the Lord will again be acknowledged as King (52:7). Because the prophet proclaimed the triumph of Persia over Babylon, his message would have been considered seditious, and it is very likely for this reason that the collection would have circulated anonymously. At some point it was appended to Is 1–39 and consequently was long considered the work of Isaiah of Jerusalem of the eighth century. But the fact that it is addressed to Judean exiles in Babylon indicates a sixth-century date. Nevertheless, this eloquent prophet in many ways works within the tradition of Isaiah and develops themes found in the earlier chapters, such as the holiness of the Lord (cf. note on 1:4) and his lordship of history. Second Isaiah also develops other Old Testament themes, such as the Lord as Israel's redeemer or deliverer (cf. Ex 3:8; 6:6; 15:13; 18:8).

40:1 The "voices" of vv. 3, 6 are members of the heavenly court addressing the prophet; then v. 1 can be understood as the Lord addressing them. It is also possible to translate, with the Vulgate, "Comfort, give comfort, O my people" (i.e., the exiles are called to comfort Jerusalem). The juxtaposition of "my people" and "your God" recalls the covenant formulary.

40:2 *Service*: servitude (cf. Jb 7:1) and exile.

40:3–5 A description of the return of the exiles from Babylon to Jerusalem (Zion). The language used here figuratively describes the way the exiles will take. The Lord leads them, so their way lies straight across the wilderness rather than along the well-watered routes usually followed from Mesopotamia to Israel. Mt 3:3 and gospel parallels adapt these verses to the witness of John the Baptizer to Jesus.

40:9 *Herald of good news*: i.e., of the imminent restoration of the people to their land. This theme of the proclamation of the good news occurs elsewhere in Second Isaiah; cf. also 41:27; 52:7.

40:12 The implicit answer is "the hand of the Lord" (v. 2). *Waters . . . heavens . . . earth*: together form the universe; cf. Gn 1:1–2. *Span*: the distance between the extended little finger and the thumb. *Fingers*: lit., "three fingers" (i.e., thumb, index, and middle).

*

40:2 Is 50:21.
40:3 Mt 3:3; Mk 1:3; Lk 2:27; Jn 1:23.
40:6 Jb 8:12; 14:2; Ps 37:2; Sir 14:18; Jas 1:10; 1 Pt 1:24.
40:11 Is 49:9–10; 63:11; Ez 34:23; 37:24; Jn 10:11.

13 Who has directed the spirit of the LORD,
or instructed him as his counselor?*
14 Whom did he consult to gain knowledge?
Who taught him the path of judgment,
or showed him the way of understanding?

Live It!

Between a Rock and a Soft Place

Joe. Is God a rock or a pillow?

Valerie. A rock, I guess. God is strong and reliable. When I think of a rock, I think of something I can brace myself against when things are changing all around me.

Joe. For me, God is a pillow. God is someone I can come home to and be comfortable with. I can sit back and relax, leaning against God and feeling at ease.

Valerie. But a pillow is so ordinary and doesn't have any character. A rock is distinctive and doesn't change.

Joe. But a rock is so hard and unyielding. What kind of compassion can you get from a rock?

Valerie. What kind of strength can you draw from a pillow?

Joe. The strength that comes from relaxing and resting and being comforted. The strength that comes from being energized to go forward again.

Valerie. I'm sorry, but a pillow seems too soft to be like God.

Joe. And a rock seems much too hard.

Valerie. Isn't God both a pillow and a rock? In chapter 40 of Isaiah, it seems that the pillow image wins out. The picture of a comforting God gathering the lambs conveys a softness that is sometimes hard to find in the Old Testament.

Joe. That's true. There are times when we need a pillow to get comfortable. It is good to know that God is there waiting for us, helping us to feel at home.

Valerie. And it is also good to know that God the rock is there for the times when we need something to hold on to (see Ps 18:2).

► Is 40:1–11

15 See, the nations count as a drop in the bucket,
as a wisp of cloud on the scales;
the coastlands weigh no more than a
speck.†
16 Lebanon would not suffice for fuel,†
nor its animals be enough for burnt
offerings.
17 Before him all the nations are as nought,
as nothing and void he counts them.

18 To whom can you liken God?*
With what likeness can you confront him?
19 An idol? An artisan casts it,
the smith plates it with gold,
fits it with silver chains.† *
20 Is mulberry wood the offering?
A skilled artisan picks out
a wood that will not rot,
Seeks to set up for himself
an idol that will not totter.*

21 Do you not know? Have you not heard?
Was it not told you from the beginning?
Have you not understood from the
founding of the earth?
22 The one who is enthroned above the vault of
the earth,
its inhabitants like grasshoppers,
Who stretches out the heavens like a veil
and spreads them out like a tent to
dwell in,*
23 Who brings princes to nought
and makes the rulers of the earth as
nothing.
24 Scarcely are they planted, scarcely sown,
scarcely their stem rooted in the earth,
When he breathes upon them and they
wither,
and the stormwind carries them away like
straw.

25 To whom can you liken me as an equal?
says the Holy One.
26 Lift up your eyes on high
and see who created† these:
He leads out their army and numbers them,

---

† **40:15** *Drop . . . wisp of cloud . . . a speck*: the smallest constituent parts of the cosmic waters, heavens, and earth mentioned in v. 12.

40:16 *Lebanon . . . fuel*: the famed cedars would not be enough to keep the fires of sacrifice burning.

40:19 *Chains*: needed to hold the idol steady when carried in processions; cf. v. 20; Jer 10:4.

40:26 *Created*: see note on Gn 1:1–2:3. *By name*: for he is their Creator.

40:13 Wis 9:13; Rom 11:34; 1 Cor 2:16; Jb 38:1–11.
40:18–19 Acts 17:29.
40:19 Ps 115:4–7; Jer 10:4.
40:20 Is 44:13.
40:22 Ps 104:2.

Cultural Connection

The Tent and the Circle

Isaiah 40:22–23 has significance in Native American spirituality for several reasons. First, the vault (see verse 22), often depicted in the shape of a circle, is a symbol of unity and healing. In silhouette, the sun, the moon, and the earth are all circles. The poles of a teepee are arranged in a circle, and the teepees of a village are placed in a circle. The people of a nation are called the hoop or the circle, and sit in a circle for the sweat lodge ceremony (see "You Will Be Cleansed," near Ez 36:25–26) and to smoke from the sacred pipe.

Second, the tent (see verse 22) is a symbol of home and family for a people that traditionally dwelled in tents.

Third, the Great Spirit is well described as the one who "sits enthroned above the vault" (verse 22).

Last, the insight that God, the Great Spirit, cares very little about the status of princes and rulers (see verse 23) is powerful to a people that is oppressed, treated violently, scattered, and despised in its homeland. Native Americans have been subjected to such treatment by the explorers, then the colonists, then the pioneers, and now many citizens of the United States.

- Pray for the circle of humanity—that we learn to celebrate the diversity of our cultures and cease oppression of any form.

▶ **Is 40:22–23**

calling them all by name.
By his great might and the strength of his
power
not one of them is missing!*
27 Why, O Jacob, do you say,†
and declare, O Israel,
"My way is hidden from the LORD,
and my right is disregarded by my God"?
28 Do you not know?
Have you not heard?
The LORD is God from of old,
creator of the ends of the earth.
He does not faint or grow weary,
and his knowledge is beyond scrutiny.
29 He gives power to the faint,
abundant strength to the weak.
30 Though young men faint and grow weary,
and youths stagger and fall,
31 They that hope in the LORD will renew their
strength,
they will soar on eagles' wings;
They will run and not grow weary,
walk and not grow faint.

The Liberator of Israel

41 1 Keep silence before me, O coastlands;†
let the nations renew their strength.
Let them draw near and speak;
let us come together for judgment.
2 Who has stirred up from the East the
champion of justice,
and summoned him to be his attendant?
To him he delivers nations
and subdues kings;
With his sword he reduces them to dust,
with his bow, to driven straw.
3 He pursues them, passing on without loss,
by a path his feet scarcely touch.
4 Who has performed these deeds?
Who has called forth the generations from
the beginning?*
I, the LORD, am the first,
and at the last† I am he.
5 The coastlands see, and fear;
the ends of the earth tremble:
they approach, they come on.

† **40:27–28** The exiles, here called Jacob-Israel (Gn 32:29), must not give way to discouragement: their Lord is the eternal God.

41:1–4 Earlier prophets had spoken of the Assyrians and Babylonians as the Lord's instruments for the punishment of Israel's sins; here the Lord is described as raising up and giving victory to a foreign ruler in order to deliver Israel from the Babylonian exile. The ruler is Cyrus (44:28; 45:1), king of Anshan in Persia, a vassal of the Babylonians. He rebelled against the Babylonian overlords in 556 B.C., and after a series of victories, entered Babylon as victor in 539; the following year he issued a decree which allowed the Jewish captives to return to their homeland (2 Chr 36:22–23; Ezr 1:1–4). For Second Isaiah, the meteoric success of Cyrus was the work of the Lord to accomplish the deliverance promised by earlier prophets.

41:4 *The first . . . the last*: God as the beginning and end encompasses all reality. The same designation is used in 44:6 and 48:12.

* **40:26** Ps 147:4–5. **41:4** Is 44:7; 46:10.

Pray It!

The Servant's Mission

Read Isaiah 42:1–7 and then reflect or journal on the following questions:

- What is the servant's mission from God?
- How does Jesus fulfill this mission (compare Is 42:6–7 with Lk 4:18–19)?
- How do you participate in this mission?

▶ **Is 42:1–7**

6 Each one helps his neighbor,
one says to the other, "Courage!"
7 The woodworker encourages the goldsmith,
the one who beats with the hammer, him who strikes on the anvil,
Saying of the soldering, "It is good!"
then fastening it with nails so it will not totter.

8 But you, Israel, my servant,*
Jacob, whom I have chosen,
offspring of Abraham my friend—
9 You whom I have taken from the ends of the earth
and summoned from its far-off places,
To whom I have said, You are my servant;
I chose you, I have not rejected you—
10 Do not fear: I am with you;
do not be anxious: I am your God.
I will strengthen you, I will help you,
I will uphold you with my victorious right hand.

11 Yes, all shall be put to shame and disgrace
who vent their anger against you;
Those shall be as nothing and perish
who offer resistance.
12 You shall seek but not find
those who strive against you;
They shall be as nothing at all
who do battle with you.
13 For I am the LORD, your God,
who grasp your right hand;
It is I who say to you, Do not fear,
I will help you.
14 Do not fear, you worm Jacob,
you maggot Israel;
I will help you—oracle of the LORD;
the Holy One of Israel is your redeemer.†
15 I will make of you a threshing sledge,
sharp, new, full of teeth,
To thresh the mountains and crush them,
to make the hills like chaff.
16 When you winnow them, the wind shall carry them off,
the storm shall scatter them.
But you shall rejoice in the LORD;
in the Holy One of Israel you shall glory.

17 The afflicted and the needy seek water in vain,
their tongues are parched with thirst.
I, the LORD, will answer them;
I, the God of Israel, will not forsake them.
18 I will open up rivers on the bare heights,
and fountains in the broad valleys;
I will turn the wilderness into a marshland,
and the dry ground into springs of water.
19 In the wilderness I will plant the cedar,
acacia, myrtle, and olive;
In the wasteland I will set the cypress,
together with the plane tree and the pine,
20 That all may see and know,
observe and understand,
That the hand of the LORD has done this,
the Holy One of Israel has created it.

21 Present your case, says the LORD;†
bring forward your arguments, says the King of Jacob.
22 Let them draw near and foretell to us
what it is that shall happen!
What are the things of long ago?
Tell us, that we may reflect on them
and know their outcome;
Or declare to us the things to come,†
23 tell what is to be in the future,

†

41:14 *Redeemer*: in Hebrew, *go'el*, one who frees others from slavery and avenges their sufferings; cf. Lv 25:48; Dt 19:6, 12. Cf. note on Ru 2:20.

41:21–29 This indictment of Babylonian gods is patterned on a legal trial, in which they are challenged to prove power over events of history and so justify their status as gods (vv. 21–24). Israel's God, on the other hand, has foretold and now brings to pass Israel's deliverance (vv. 25–27). The accused are unable to respond (vv. 28–29). By such polemics (see also 43:12) the prophet declares that all gods other than the Lord are nonexistent; this implicit claim of monotheism later becomes explicit (see 43:10–11; 45:5–7, 14, 18, 21–22; 46:9; and note on 44:6).

41:22 *Things of long ago . . . things to come*: there are no predictions attributed to idols that have since been fulfilled. Second Isaiah makes frequent reference to "things of long ago," sometimes in conjunction with "things to come" or "new things" in connection with the Lord's

*

41:8–9 Is 44:1–2, 21; 45:4.

that we may know that you are gods!
Do something, good or evil,
that will put us in awe and in fear.
24 Why, you are nothing
and your work is nought;
to choose you is an abomination!

25 I have stirred up one from the north, and he comes;
from the east I summon him† by name;
He shall trample the rulers down like mud,
like a potter treading clay.
26 Who announced this from the beginning, that we might know;
beforehand, that we might say, "True"?
Not one of you foretold it, not one spoke;
not one heard you say,
27 "The first news for Zion: here they come,"
or, "I will give Jerusalem a herald of good news."
28 When I look, there is not one,
not one of them to give counsel,
to make an answer when I question them.
29 Ah, all of them are nothing,
their works are nought,
their idols, empty wind!

The Servant of the Lord

42 1 Here is my servant† whom I uphold,
my chosen one with whom I am pleased.
Upon him I have put my spirit;
he shall bring forth justice to the nations.*
2 He will not cry out, nor shout,
nor make his voice heard in the street.
3 A bruised reed† he will not break,
and a dimly burning wick he will not quench.
He will faithfully bring forth justice.
4 He will not grow dim or be bruised
until he establishes justice on the earth;
the coastlands† will wait for his teaching.

5 Thus says God, the LORD,
who created the heavens and stretched them out,
who spread out the earth and its produce,
Who gives breath to its people
and spirit to those who walk on it:
6 I, the LORD, have called you for justice,

Did You Know?

The Servant Songs

Second Isaiah's four songs of the servant (see Is 42:1–7, 49:1–6, 50:4–9, 52:13—53:12) have had an important place in Christian theology and worship. They portray the qualities of the ideal servant leader. Through these songs, the prophet speaks of hope: the faithful Israelites, though in exile, are still God's servants (see 42:1), chosen from the womb (see 49:1). Through their courageous suffering (see 50:7–8), Israel will be restored to bring salvation to all nations (see 53:5).

It is not surprising that the early Christians saw in the servant songs a remarkable similarity to Jesus' words and actions. The fourth song in particular—which talks of a suffering servant—helped the followers of Jesus understand his suffering and humiliating death on the cross. Because of this, these passages have become part of the Catholic Church's formal worship during Holy Week (the week before Easter): Isaiah 42:1–7 on Monday, 49:1–6 on Tuesday, 50:4–9 on Wednesday, and 52:13—53:12 on Friday.

▶ **Is 42:1–7**

I have grasped you by the hand;
I formed you, and set you
as a covenant for the people,
a light for the nations,*
7 To open the eyes of the blind,
to bring out prisoners from confinement,
and from the dungeon, those who live in darkness.
8 I am the LORD, LORD is my name;
my glory I give to no other,
nor my praise to idols.
9 See, the earlier things have come to pass,
new ones I now declare;

†

activity (cf. 42:9; 43:9, 18; 46:9–10; 48:3–8); both the old things (e.g., creation, exodus) and the new things (release from exile) God brings to pass (cf. 51:9–11), which is why he can declare them beforehand.

41:25 *I summon him*: Cyrus.

42:1–4 *Servant*: three other passages have been popularly called "servant of the Lord" poems: 49:1–7; 50:4–11; 52:13–53:12. Whether the servant is an individual or a collectivity is not clear (e.g., contrast 49:3 with 49:5). More important is the description of the mission of the servant. In the early Church and throughout Christian tradition, these poems have been applied to Christ; cf. Mt 12:18–21.

42:3 *Bruised reed . . .* : images to express the gentle manner of the servant's mission.

42:4 *Coastlands*: for Israel, the world to the west: the islands and coastal nations of the Mediterranean.

42:1 Is 45:6; 49:6. **42:6** Is 45:13.

Pray It!

Be Not Afraid

The words of Isaiah 43:1–5 might sound familiar to you. Most of the song "Be Not Afraid" is based on these verses.

God calls us to be disciples and leaders. God calls us from within our faith community to serve others. How easy is it for you to go forth and do God's work? How easy is it to be not afraid?

Be not afraid.
I go before you always.
Come follow me,
and I will give you rest.
(From Bob Dufford,
"Be Not Afraid")

▶ Is 43:1–5

Before they spring forth
I announce them to you.

The Lord's Purpose for Israel

10 Sing to the LORD a new song,
his praise from the ends of the earth:
Let the sea and what fills it resound,
the coastlands, and those who dwell in them.
11 Let the wilderness and its cities cry out,
the villages where Kedar† dwells;
Let the inhabitants of Sela exult,
and shout from the top of the mountains.
12 Let them give glory to the LORD,
and utter his praise in the coastlands.

13 The LORD goes forth like a warrior,
like a man of war he stirs up his fury;
He shouts out his battle cry,
against his enemies he shows his might:*
14 For a long time I have kept silent,
I have said nothing, holding myself back;
Now I cry out like a woman in labor,
gasping and panting.
15† I will lay waste mountains and hills,
all their undergrowth I will dry up;
I will turn the rivers into marshes,
and the marshes I will dry up.*
16 I will lead the blind on a way they do not know;
by paths they do not know I will guide them.
I will turn darkness into light before them,
and make crooked ways straight.
These are my promises:
I made them, I will not forsake them.*

17 They shall be turned back in utter shame
who trust in idols;
Who say to molten images,
"You are our gods."
18 You deaf ones, listen,†
you blind ones, look and see!
19 Who is blind but my servant,
or deaf like the messenger I send?
Who is blind like the one I restore,
blind like the servant of the LORD?
20 You see many things but do not observe;
ears open, but do not hear.
21 It was the LORD's will for the sake of his justice
to make his teaching great and glorious.

22 This is a people† plundered and despoiled,
all of them trapped in holes,
hidden away in prisons.
They are taken as plunder, with no one to rescue them,
as spoil, with no one to say, "Give back!"
23 Who among you will give ear to this,
listen and pay attention from now on?
24 Who was it that gave Jacob to be despoiled,
Israel to the plunderers?†
Was it not the LORD, against whom we have sinned?
In his ways they refused to walk,
his teaching they would not heed.
25 So he poured out wrath upon them,
his anger, and the fury of battle;
It blazed all around them, yet they did not realize,
it burned them, but they did not take it to heart.

Promises of Redemption and Restoration

43 1 But now, thus says the LORD,
who created you, Jacob, and formed you, Israel:
Do not fear, for I have redeemed you;

†

42:11 *Kedar*: cf. note on 21:16. *Sela*: Petra, the capital of Edom.

42:15–16 Active once more, God will remove the obstacles that hinder the exiles' return, and will lead them by new roads to Jerusalem; cf. 40:3–4.

42:18–20 The Lord rebukes his people for their failures, but their role and their mission endure: they remain his servant, his messenger to the nations.

42:22 *A people*: Israel in exile.

42:24 *Plunderers*: the Assyrians and Babylonians. *We . . . they*: the switch from first- to third-person speech, though puzzling, does not obscure the fact that "the people" is meant.

42:13 Ex 14:3.
42:15 Ex 9:25; 10:15; 14:21; Ps 105:33–35.
42:16 Ex 13:21.

I have called you by name: you are mine.
2 When you pass through waters, I will be with you;
through rivers, you shall not be swept away.
When you walk through fire, you shall not be burned,
nor will flames consume you.
3 For I, the LORD, am your God,
the Holy One of Israel, your savior.
I give Egypt as ransom for you,
Ethiopia and Seba† in exchange for you.
4 Because you are precious in my eyes
and honored, and I love you,
I give people in return for you
and nations in exchange for your life.*
5 Fear not, for I am with you;
from the east I will bring back your offspring,
from the west I will gather you.
6 I will say to the north: Give them up!
and to the south: Do not hold them!
Bring back my sons from afar,
and my daughters from the ends of the earth:*
7 All who are called by my name
I created for my glory;
I formed them, made them.
8 Lead out the people, blind though they have eyes,
deaf though they have ears.

9 Let all the nations gather together,
let the peoples assemble!
Who among them could have declared this,
or announced to us the earlier things?†
Let them produce witnesses to prove themselves right,
that one may hear and say, "It is true!"
10 You are my witnesses†—oracle of the LORD—
my servant whom I have chosen
To know and believe in me
and understand that I am he.
Before me no god was formed,
and after me there shall be none.
11 I, I am the LORD;
there is no savior but me.
12 It is I who declared, who saved,
who announced, not some strange god among you;
You are my witnesses—oracle of the LORD.
I am God,
13 yes, from eternity I am he;
There is none who can deliver from my hand:
I act and who can cancel it?*

14 Thus says the LORD, your redeemer,†
the Holy One of Israel:
For your sake I send to Babylon;
I will bring down all her defenses,
and the Chaldeans shall cry out in lamentation.
15 I am the LORD, your Holy One,
the creator of Israel, your King.
16 Thus says the LORD,
who opens a way in the sea,
a path in the mighty waters,*
17 Who leads out chariots and horsemen,
a powerful army,
Till they lie prostrate together, never to rise,
snuffed out, quenched like a wick.*
18 Remember not† the events of the past,
the things of long ago consider not;
19 See, I am doing something new!
Now it springs forth, do you not perceive it?
In the wilderness I make a way,
in the wasteland, rivers.
20 Wild beasts honor me,
jackals and ostriches,
For I put water in the wilderness
and rivers in the wasteland
for my chosen people to drink,
21 The people whom I formed for myself,
that they might recount my praise.

22 Yet you did not call upon me, Jacob,†
for you grew weary of me, Israel.

†

43:3–4 *Egypt . . . Ethiopia and Seba*: countries which God permitted the Persians to conquer in return for having given Israel its freedom.

43:9 *Who among them . . . ?*: God, and only God, can foretell the future because it is he who brings it to pass. The argument from prediction is an important theme in Second Isaiah and occurs also in 41:22; 43:10; 44:7–8, 26.

43:10 *You are my witnesses*: Israel's role as chosen people now takes a new turn as they are given the active role of bearing witness before humankind to the Lord's role in history by proclaiming events beforehand and bringing them to pass; see also 44:8. The false gods, on the other hand, cannot produce such witnesses (v. 9; cf. 44:9). *I am he*: this formula of self-identification, repeated in vv. 13 and 25, is used here to support the assertion that the Lord alone is God; see also 41:4; 46:4; 48:12; 51:12; 52:6. This expression in part may be behind the self-identification formula used by Jesus in John's gospel (cf. Jn 8:58). *Before . . . after*: another example of the same assertion, that the Lord alone is God; see also note on 44:6.

43:14–17 The destruction of Babylon is described in language that recalls the drowning of the Egyptian army in the Red Sea (Ex 14–15).

43:18 *Remember not*: God's new act of delivering Israel from the Babylonian captivity is presented as so great a marvel as to eclipse even the memory of the exodus from Egypt. This comparison of the return from Babylon to the exodus from Egypt recurs throughout Second Isaiah (cf. 41:17–20; 43:18–21; 48:20–21; 49:8–13; 51:9–11).

43:22–28 The reason for the liberation of the Israelites is not their constancy but rather God's faithfulness to his promise (cf. 40:6–8).

*

43:4 Dt 4:37; Hos 11:1.
43:6 Is 49:22; Ez 16:20.
43:13 Is 41:4.
43:16 Is 51:10–11; Ex 14:21.
43:17 Ex 15:4.

23 You did not bring me sheep for your burnt offerings,
nor honor me with your sacrifices.
I did not exact from you the service of offerings,
nor weary you for frankincense.*
24 You did not buy me sweet cane,†
nor did you fill me with the fat of your sacrifices;
Instead, you burdened me with your sins,
wearied me with your crimes.
25 It is I, I, who wipe out,
for my own sake, your offenses;
your sins I remember no more.
26 Would you have me remember, have us come to trial?
Speak up, prove your innocence!
27 Your first father† sinned;
your spokesmen rebelled against me
28 Till I repudiated the holy princes,
put Jacob under the ban,
exposed Israel to scorn.

44 1 Hear then, Jacob, my servant,
Israel, whom I have chosen.
2 Thus says the LORD who made you,
your help, who formed you from the womb:
Do not fear, Jacob, my servant,
Jeshurun,† whom I have chosen.
3 I will pour out water upon the thirsty ground,
streams upon the dry land;
I will pour out my spirit upon your offspring,
my blessing upon your descendants.
4 They shall spring forth amid grass
like poplars beside flowing waters.*
5 One shall say, "I am the LORD's,"
another shall be named after Jacob,
And this one shall write on his hand,† "The LORD's,"
and receive the name Israel.*

The True God and False Gods

6† Thus says the LORD, Israel's king,
its redeemer, the LORD of hosts:
I am the first, I am the last;
there is no God but me.† *
7 Who is like me? Let him stand up and declare,
make it evident, and confront me with it.
Who of old announced future events?
Let them foretell to us the things to come.
8 Do not fear or be troubled.
Did I not announce it to you long ago?
I declared it, and you are my witnesses.
Is there any God but me?
There is no other Rock,† I know of none!*

9† Those who fashion idols are all nothing;
their precious works are of no avail.
They are their witnesses:†
they see nothing, know nothing,
and so they are put to shame.*
10 Who would fashion a god or cast an idol,
that is of no use?
11 Look, all its company will be shamed;
they are artisans, mere human beings!
They all assemble and stand there,
only to cower in shame.
12 The ironsmith fashions a likeness,
he works it over the coals,
Shaping it with hammers,
working it with his strong arm.
With hunger his strength wanes,
without water, he grows faint.*
13 The woodworker stretches a line,
and marks out a shape with a stylus.
He shapes it with scraping tools,
with a compass measures it off,
Making it the copy of a man,†
human display, enthroned in a shrine.
14 He goes out to cut down cedars,
takes a holm tree or an oak.
He picks out for himself trees of the forest,
plants a fir, and the rain makes it grow.
15 It is used for fuel:
with some of the wood he warms himself,
makes a fire and bakes bread.
Yet he makes a god and worships it,
turns it into an idol and adores it!
16 Half of it he burns in the fire,
on its embers he roasts meat;
he eats the roast and is full.

†

43:24 *Sweet cane*: a fragrant substance used in making incense and the sacred anointing oil; cf. Ex 30:23; Jer 6:20.

43:27 *First father*: Jacob. *Spokesmen*: leaders, priests, prophets.

44:2 *Jeshurun*: see note on Dt 32:15; cf. also Dt 33:5, 26.

44:5 *Write on his hand*: an allusion to the Babylonian custom of tattooing the owner's name on the hand of his slave.

44:6–8 Prediction and fulfillment are here seen as the hallmarks of true divinity. See note on 43:9.

44:6 *No god but me*: with Second Isaiah, Israel's faith is declared to be explicitly monotheistic. However implicit it may have been, earlier formulas did not exclude the existence of other gods, not even that of the first commandment: "You shall not have other gods besides me" (Ex 20:3). Cf. also note on 41:21–29.

44:8 *Rock*: place of refuge, a title here used of God; cf., e.g., Dt 32:4, 18; 1 Sm 2:2; Ps 18:3.

44:9–20 A satire on the makers and worshipers of idols.

44:9 *Their witnesses*: Israel has been called to bear witness to the awesome power of God (cf. 43:10, 12; 44:8), but idol makers cannot testify in support of their creations, for idols cannot act (Dt 4:28; Ps 135:15–18).

44:13 *Copy of a man*: in the biblical view human beings are made in the image of God; here gods are made in the image of human beings.

*

43:23 Jer 6:20.
44:4 Is 54:1–3.
44:5 Is 43:7; 45:14.
44:6 Is 41:4; 43:15; 45:21; 48:3, 12; 51:15; 54:5.
44:8 Is 43:10, 12; Dt 32:4.
44:9 Is 48:5, 7.
44:12 Wis 13:11–16.

He warms himself and says, "Ah!
I am warm! I see the flames!"
17 The rest of it he makes into a god,
an image to worship and adore.
He prays to it and says,
"Help me! You are my god!"
18 They do not know, do not understand;
their eyes are too clouded to see,
their minds, to perceive.
19 He does not think clearly;
he lacks the wit and knowledge to say,
"Half the wood I burned in the fire,
on its embers I baked bread,
I roasted meat and ate.
Shall I turn the rest into an abomination?
Shall I worship a block of wood?"
20 He is chasing ashes!†
A deluded mind has led him astray;
He cannot save himself,
does not say, "This thing in my right
hand—is it not a fraud?"

21 Remember these things, Jacob,
Israel, for you are my servant!
I formed you, a servant to me;
Israel, you shall never be forgotten by me:
22 I have brushed away your offenses like a cloud,
your sins like a mist;
return to me, for I have redeemed you.

23 Raise a glad cry, you heavens—the LORD has
acted!
Shout, you depths of the earth.
Break forth, mountains, into song,
forest, with all your trees.
For the LORD has redeemed Jacob,
shows his glory through Israel.

Cyrus, Anointed of the Lord, Agent of Israel's Liberation

24 Thus says the LORD, your redeemer,
who formed you from the womb:
I am the LORD, who made all things,
who alone stretched out the heavens,
I spread out the earth by myself.*
25 I bring to nought the omens of babblers,
make fools of diviners,
Turn back the wise
and make their knowledge foolish.
26 I confirm the words of my servant,
carry out the plan my messengers
announce.
I say to Jerusalem, Be inhabited!
To the cities of Judah, Be rebuilt!
I will raise up their ruins.
27 I say to the deep, Be dry!
I will dry up your rivers.*
28 I say of Cyrus,† My shepherd!
He carries out my every wish,
Saying of Jerusalem, "Let it be rebuilt,"
and of the temple, "Lay its foundations."*

45 1 Thus says the LORD to his anointed,†
Cyrus,
whose right hand I grasp,
Subduing nations before him,
stripping kings of their strength,
Opening doors before him,
leaving the gates unbarred:
2 I will go before you
and level the mountains;
Bronze doors† I will shatter,
iron bars I will snap.*
3 I will give you treasures of darkness,
riches hidden away,
That you may know I am the LORD,
the God of Israel, who calls you by name.

4 For the sake of Jacob, my servant,
of Israel my chosen one,
I have called you by name,
giving you a title, though you do not
know me.*
5 I am the LORD, there is no other,
there is no God besides me.
It is I who arm you, though you do not
know me,
6 so that all may know, from the rising of the
sun
to its setting, that there is none besides me.†
I am the LORD, there is no other.
7 I form the light, and create the darkness,
I make weal and create woe;†
I, the LORD, do all these things.
8 Let justice descend, you heavens, like dew
from above,
like gentle rain let the clouds drop it down.
Let the earth open and salvation bud forth;

---

† **44:20** *Chasing ashes*: an exercise in futility.
44:28 *Cyrus*: king of Persia (559–529 B.C.); cf. note on 41:1–4.
45:1 *Anointed*: in Hebrew, *mashiah*, from which the word "Messiah" is derived; from its Greek translation, *Christos*, we have the title "Christ." Applied to kings, "anointed" originally referred only to those of Israel, but it is here given to Cyrus because he is the agent of the Lord.
45:2 *Bronze doors*: those defending the city gates of Babylon.
45:6 The nations will come to know that Israel's God is the only God; cf. also vv. 20–25.
45:7 *Create woe*: God created and controls all aspects of creation (light and darkness, order and chaos).

44:24 Is 40:22; Jb 9:8.
44:27 Is 42:15; 51:10.
44:28 Jer 3:15; Ez 34:23.
45:2 Ps 107:16.
45:4 Is 40:26; 44:5.

let righteousness spring up with them!†
I, the LORD, have created this.*
9 Woe to anyone who contends with their Maker;*
a potsherd among potsherds of the earth!†
Shall the clay say to the potter, "What are you doing?"
or, "What you are making has no handles"?
10 Woe to anyone who asks a father, "What are you begetting?"
or a woman, "What are you giving birth to?"
11 Thus says the LORD,
the Holy One of Israel, his maker:
Do you question me about my children,
tell me how to treat the work of my hands?
12 It was I who made the earth
and created the people upon it;
It was my hands that stretched out the heavens;
I gave the order to all their host.
13 It was I who stirred him† up for justice;
all his ways I make level.
He shall rebuild my city
and let my exiles go free
Without price or payment,
says the LORD of hosts.

14 Thus says the LORD:
The earnings of Egypt, the gain of Ethiopia,
and the Sabeans,† tall of stature,
Shall come over to you and belong to you;
they shall follow you, coming in chains.
Before you they shall bow down,
saying in prayer:
"With you alone is God; and there is none other,
no other god!*
15 Truly with you God is hidden,†
the God of Israel, the savior!*
16 They are put to shame and disgrace, all of them;
they go in disgrace who carve images.
17 Israel has been saved by the LORD,
saved forever!
You shall never be put to shame or disgrace
in any future age."
18 For thus says the LORD,
The creator of the heavens,
who is God,
The designer and maker of the earth
who established it,
Not as an empty waste† did he create it,
but designing it to be lived in:
I am the LORD, and there is no other.
19 I have not spoken in secret
from some place in the land of darkness,
I have not said to the descendants of Jacob,
"Look for me in an empty waste."
I, the LORD, promise justice,
I declare what is right.

20 Come and assemble, gather together,
you fugitives from among the nations!
They are without knowledge who bear wooden idols†
and pray to gods that cannot save.
21 Come close and declare;
let them take counsel together:
Who announced this from the beginning,
declared it from of old?
Was it not I, the LORD,
besides whom there is no other God?
There is no just and saving God but me.

22 Turn to me and be safe,
all you ends of the earth,
for I am God; there is no other!
23 By myself I swear,
uttering my just decree,
a word that will not return:
To me every knee shall bend;
by me every tongue shall swear,*
24 Saying, "Only in the LORD
are just deeds and power.
Before him in shame shall come
all who vent their anger against him.
25 In the LORD all the descendants of Israel
shall have vindication and glory."

†

45:8 The Vulgate rendering gave a messianic sense to this verse, using "just one" and "savior" in place of "justice" and "salvation," phraseology taken over in the Advent liturgy, e.g., the "Rorate coeli."

45:9 No one may challenge God's freedom of action, exemplified here by the selection of Cyrus as his anointed.

45:13 *Him*: Cyrus, called by God for the deliverance and restoration of Israel. *Justice*: the Hebrew word (*sedeq*) has multiple connotations; here it relates to the saving victory that the Lord will give to Cyrus for the deliverance of his people Israel. This word and others from the same root frequently have this connotation in Second Isaiah, occurring as a parallel term with "deliverance," "salvation," etc. Cf. its use in 41:10 (rendered "victorious") and 51:5 (rendered "victory").

45:14 *Egypt . . . Ethiopia . . . Sabeans*: the Egyptians and their allies who, when conquered by Cyrus, are seen as acknowledging the God of Israel; cf. 43:3.

45:15 *God is hidden*: i.e., the one known only to Israel, who cannot be represented by wooden or molten images. The concept of the "Deus absconditus," "the hidden God," becomes an important theme in later theology.

45:18 *Empty waste*: an allusion to Gn 1:2, where the earth is waste and void; the same Hebrew word, *tohu*, is used in both passages. Here it points to devastated Judah and Jerusalem, where God wishes to resettle the returning exiles.

45:20 *Who bear wooden idols*: in their religious processions. Such gods have feet but cannot walk; cf. Ps 115:7; Bar 6:25.

*

45:8 Ps 72:6; 85:11.
45:9 Jer 18:6; Rom 9:20.
45:14 Is 43:3.
45:15 Is 55:8; Prv 25:2.
45:23 Rom 14:11; Phil 2:10.

The Gods of Babylon

46 1 Bel bows down, Nebo† stoops,
their idols set upon beasts and cattle;
They must be borne upon shoulders,
a load for weary animals.
2 They stoop and bow down together;
unable to deliver those who bear them,
they too go into captivity.

3 Hear me, O house of Jacob,
all the remnant of the house of Israel,
My burden from the womb,
whom I have carried since birth.*
4 Even to your old age I am he,
even when your hair is gray I will carry you;
I have done this, and I will lift you up,
I will carry you to safety.

5 To whom would you liken me as an equal,
compare me, as though we were alike?
6 There are those who pour out gold from a purse
and weigh out silver on the scales;
They hire a goldsmith to make it into a god
before which they bow down in worship.
7 They lift it to their shoulders to carry;
when they set it down, it stays,
and does not move from the place.
They cry out to it, but it cannot answer;
it delivers no one from distress.

8 Remember this and be firm,
take it to heart, you rebels;
9 remember the former things, those long ago:
I am God, there is no other;
I am God, there is none like me.
10 At the beginning I declare the outcome;
from of old, things not yet done.
I say that my plan shall stand,
I accomplish my every desire.
11 I summon from the east a bird of prey,†
from a distant land, one to carry out my plan.
Yes, I have spoken, I will accomplish it;
I have planned it, and I will do it.
12 Listen to me, you fainthearted,
far from the victory of justice:
13 I am bringing on that victory, it is not far off,
my salvation shall not tarry;
I will put salvation within Zion,
give to Israel my glory.

The Fall of Babylon†

47 1 Come down, sit in the dust,
virgin daughter Babylon;
Sit on the ground, dethroned,
daughter of the Chaldeans.
No longer shall you be called
dainty and delicate.*
2 Take the millstone and grind flour,
remove your veil;
Strip off your skirt, bare your legs,
cross through the streams.
3 Your nakedness shall be uncovered,
and your shame be seen;
I will take vengeance,
I will yield to no entreaty,
says 4 our redeemer,
Whose name is the LORD of hosts,
the Holy One of Israel.

5 Go into darkness and sit in silence,
daughter of the Chaldeans,
No longer shall you be called
sovereign mistress of kingdoms.
6 Angry at my people,
I profaned my heritage
And gave them into your power;
but you showed them no mercy;
Upon the aged
you laid a very heavy yoke.
7 You said, "I shall remain always,
a sovereign mistress forever!"
You did not take these things to heart,
but disregarded their outcome.*
8 Now hear this, voluptuous one,
enthroned securely,
Saying in your heart,
"I, and no one else!†
I shall never be a widow,
bereft of my children"—*
9 Both these things shall come to you
suddenly, in a single day:
Complete bereavement and widowhood
shall come upon you
Despite your many sorceries
and the full power of your spells;†
10 Secure in your wickedness,

---

† **46:1–4** *Bel . . . Nebo*: gods of Babylon; their complete helplessness is here contrasted with God's omnipotence; whereas they must be carried about, the Lord carries Israel as a parent does a child.

46:11 *From the east a bird of prey*: Cyrus; cf. 41:2–4.

47:1–15 A taunt-song, mocking Babylon, once queen of the nations, now a mere slave.

47:8, 10 *I, and no one else*: Babylon is mockingly presented as making the same claim as the Lord (cf. 45:6, 14, 22; 46:9), a claim that events will soon prove to be false and foolish (v. 11).

47:9–13, 15 Babylon was known for its sorcery and astrology.

* **46:3** Is 44:2.
47:1 Dt 28:56.
47:7 Is 14:13–14.
47:8 Zep 2:15; Rev 18:7.

you said, "No one sees me."
Your wisdom and your knowledge
led you astray,
And you said in your heart,
"I, and no one else!"
11 But upon you shall come an evil
you will not be able to charm away;
Upon you shall fall a disaster
you cannot ward off.
Upon you shall suddenly come
a ruin you cannot imagine.
12 Keep on with your spells
and your many sorceries,
at which you toiled from your youth.
Perhaps you can prevail,
perhaps you can strike terror!
13 You wore yourself out with so many
consultations!
Let the astrologers stand forth to save you,
The stargazers who forecast at each new moon
what would happen to you.
14 See, they are like stubble,
fire consumes them;
They cannot deliver themselves
from the spreading flames.
This is no warming ember,
no fire to sit before!
15 Thus do your wizards serve you
with whom you have toiled from your youth;
They wander their separate ways,
with none to save you.

Exhortations to the Exiles

48
1 Hear this, house of Jacob
called by the name Israel,
sprung from the stock of Judah,
You who swear by the name of the LORD
and invoke the God of Israel
without sincerity, without justice,
2 Though you are named after the holy city
and rely on the God of Israel,
whose name is the LORD of hosts.
3 Things of the past I declared long ago,
they went forth from my mouth, I
announced them;
then suddenly I took action and they came
to be.
4 Because I know that you are stubborn
and that your neck is an iron sinew
and your forehead bronze,
5 I declared them to you of old;
before they took place I informed you,
That you might not say, "My idol did them,
my statue, my molten image commanded
them."
6 Now that you have heard, look at all this;
must you not admit it?*
From now on I announce new things to you,
hidden events you never knew.
7 Now, not from of old, they are created,
before today you did not hear of them,
so that you cannot claim, "I have known
them."
8 You never heard, you never knew,
they never reached your ears beforehand.
Yes, I know you are utterly treacherous,
a rebel you were named from the womb.*
9 For the sake of my name I restrain my anger,
for the sake of my renown I hold it back
from you,
lest I destroy you.
10 See, I refined you, but not like silver;
I tested you in the furnace of affliction.*
11 For my sake, for my own sake, I do this;
why should my name be profaned?
My glory I will not give to another.
12 Listen to me, Jacob,
Israel, whom I called!
I, it is I who am the first,
and am I the last.*
13 Yes, my hand laid the foundations of the earth;
my right hand spread out the heavens.
When I summon them,
they stand forth at once.*
14 All of you assemble and listen:
Who among you declared these things?
The one the LORD loves† shall do his will
against Babylon and the offspring of
Chaldea.
15 I myself have spoken, I have summoned him,
I have brought him, and his way succeeds!
16 Come near to me and hear this!
From the beginning I did not speak in secret;
At the time it happens, I am there:
"Now the Lord GOD has sent me, and his
spirit."†
17 Thus says the LORD, your redeemer,
the Holy One of Israel:
I am the LORD, your God,
teaching you how to prevail,

†

48:14 *The one the LORD loves*: the reference is no doubt to Cyrus, who does the Lord's will by overcoming Babylon and releasing Israel from captivity.

48:16 *"Now the Lord . . . spirit"*: said by Cyrus; cf. v. 14.

48:6 Is 42:9.
48:8 Is 43:22–24.
48:10 Is 1:25; Jer 6:29–30; Zec 13:9; Mal 3:2.
48:12 Is 41:4; 44:6; 48:12; Rev 1:8, 17.
48:13 Is 40:22, 26; 45:12, 18.

leading you on the way you should go.
18 If only you would attend to my
commandments,
your peace would be like a river,
your vindication like the waves of the sea,
19 Your descendants like the sand,
the offspring of your loins like its grains,
Their name never cut off
or blotted out from my presence.
20 Go forth from Babylon, flee from Chaldea!
With shouts of joy declare this, announce it;
Make it known to the ends of the earth,
Say: "The LORD has redeemed his servant
Jacob.
21 They did not thirst
when he led them through dry lands;
Water from the rock he set flowing for them;
he cleft the rock, and waters welled forth."*

22 There is no peace† for the wicked,
says the LORD.

B. Expiation of Sin, Spiritual Liberation of Israel

The Servant of the Lord†

49 1 Hear me, coastlands,
listen, distant peoples.*
Before birth the LORD called me,
from my mother's womb he gave me my
name.†
2 He made my mouth like a sharp-edged sword,
concealed me, shielded by his hand.
He made me a sharpened arrow,
in his quiver he hid me.
3 He said to me, You are my servant,
in you, Israel,† I show my glory.
4 Though I thought I had toiled in vain,
for nothing and for naught spent my
strength,
Yet my right is with the LORD,
my recompense is with my God.*
5 For now the LORD has spoken
who formed me as his servant from the
womb,
That Jacob may be brought back to him

Pray It!

The Servant's Success

Isaiah 49:1–6 is the second of the four servant songs (see "The Servant Songs," near Is 42:1–7). In this passage, the servant expresses a feeling of failure (see 49:4). But God responds that the servant will be a success, a "light to the nations" (verse 6). In your prayer, reflect or journal on a time when you felt you failed, but something good happened anyway. How do you now see God's hand at work in the situation?

▶ **Is 49:1–6**

and Israel gathered to him;
I am honored in the sight of the LORD,
and my God is now my strength!
6 It is too little, he says, for you to be my
servant,
to raise up the tribes of Jacob,
and restore the survivors of Israel;*
I will make you a light to the nations,
that my salvation may reach to the ends of
the earth.†
7 Thus says the LORD,
the redeemer, the Holy One of Israel,
To the one despised, abhorred by the nations,
the slave of rulers:
When kings see you, they shall stand up,
and princes shall bow down
Because of the LORD who is faithful,
the Holy One of Israel who has chosen you.*

The Liberation and Restoration of Zion

8 Thus says the LORD:
In a time of favor I answer you,†
on the day of salvation I help you;
I form you and set you
as a covenant for the people,

†

48:22 *No peace*: while the good news proclaimed by the prophet is directed to the people as a whole, "peace," which can represent the fullness of God's blessings and which would here include deliverance from exile, is not extended to all regardless of disposition.

49:1–7 The second of the four "servant of the Lord" oracles (cf. note on 42:1–4).

49:1 *Gave me my name*: designated me for a special task or mission (cf. Jer 1:5).

49:3 *Israel*: the servant is identified with the people of Israel as their ideal representative; however, vv. 5–6 seem to distinguish the servant from Israel.

49:6 The servant's vocation extends beyond the restoration of Israel in order to bring the knowledge of Israel's God to the rest of the earth; cf. Lk 2:32.

49:8 *You*: the individual is not named; perhaps Cyrus or the prophet.

*

48:21 Ex 17:6; Nm 20:11.
49:1 Is 41:9; 43:1; 44:2, 24; 46:3.
49:4 Is 40:27.
49:6 Is 42:1–6; 44:5; 45:14; Lk 2:32; Acts 13:46–47.
49:7 Is 49:23; 55:5.

Live It!

I Will Never Forget You, My People

In chapter 49, Isaiah introduces us to one of the feminine images of God—God as mother. Although we most often use masculine words to describe God, it's easy to imagine God as a loving mother—forgiving us when we make mistakes, embracing us when we need comfort, nurturing us through difficult times, and acting gently toward us at all times. The Hebrew root of the word *compassion* actually means "womb." Thus, a God of compassion and love, a God who will never forget the suffering of God's people, is by definition a God of the womb, a God of motherly tenderness.

Picture the mother figures in your life: perhaps your birth mother, grandmother, adoptive mother, stepmother, or godmother. How do you see God's love reflected in her love?

▶ Is 49:13–16

To restore the land
and allot the devastated heritages,*
9 To say to the prisoners: Come out!
To those in darkness: Show yourselves!
Along the roadways they shall find pasture,
on every barren height shall their
pastures be.*
10 They shall not hunger or thirst;
nor shall scorching wind or sun strike them;
For he who pities them leads them
and guides them beside springs of water.*
11 I will turn all my mountains into roadway,
and make my highways level.*
12 See, these shall come from afar:
some from the north and the west,
others from the land of Syene.†

13 Sing out, heavens, and rejoice, earth,
break forth into song, you mountains,
For the LORD comforts his people
and shows mercy to his afflicted.
14 But Zion said, "The LORD has forsaken me;
my Lord has forgotten me."*
15 Can a mother forget her infant,
be without tenderness for the child of her
womb?
Even should she forget,
I will never forget you.*
16 See, upon the palms of my hands I have
engraved you;†
your walls are ever before me.
17 Your children hasten—
your levelers, your destroyers
go forth from you;
18 Look about and see,
they are all gathering and coming to you.
As I live—oracle of the LORD—
you shall don them as jewels,
bedeck yourself like a bride.

19 Though you were waste and desolate,
a land of ruins,
Now you shall be too narrow for your
inhabitants,
while those who swallowed you up will be
far away.
20 The children of whom you were bereft
shall yet say in your hearing,
"This place is too narrow for me,
make room for me to live in."
21 You shall ask yourself:
"Who has borne me these,
when I was bereft and barren?
Exiled and repudiated,
who has reared them?
I was left all alone;
where then do these come from?"*
22 Thus says the Lord GOD:
See, I will lift up my hand to the nations,
and to the peoples raise my signal;
They shall bring your sons in their arms,
your daughters shall be carried on their
shoulders.*
23 Kings shall be your guardians,
their princesses your nursemaids;
Face to the ground, they shall bow down
before you
and lick the dust at your feet.
Then you shall know that I am the LORD,
none who hope in me shall be ashamed.
24 Can plunder be taken from a warrior,
or captives rescued from a tyrant?
25 Thus says the LORD:

†

49:12 *Syene*: now called Aswan, at the first cataract of the Nile in southern Egypt.

49:16 *Upon the palms . . . you*: for continual remembrance; cf. Ex 13:9, 16; Dt 6:6–9.

*

49:8 2 Cor 6:2.
49:9 Is 42:7, 18–20.
49:10 Is 51:14; Rev 7:16.
49:11 Is 40:3–4.
49:14 Is 40:27.
49:15 Is 43:4; 44:21; 46:3–4.
49:21 Is 54:1–3.
49:22 Is 5:26; 13:2.

Yes, captives can be taken from a warrior,
and plunder rescued from a tyrant;
Those who oppose you I will oppose,
and your sons I will save.
26 I will make your oppressors eat their own flesh,
and they shall be drunk with their own blood
as though with new wine.
All flesh shall know
that I, the LORD, am your savior,
your redeemer, the Mighty One of Jacob.*

Salvation Through the Lord's Servant

50 1 Thus says the LORD:
Where is the bill of divorce
with which I dismissed your mother?†
Or to which of my creditors
have I sold you?
It was for your sins you were sold,
for your rebellions your mother was dismissed.*

2 Why was no one there when I came?
Why did no one answer when I called?†
Is my hand too short to ransom?
Have I not the strength to deliver?
See, with my rebuke I dry up the sea,
I turn rivers into wilderness;
Their fish rot for lack of water,
and die of thirst.*
3 I clothe the heavens in black,
and make sackcloth their covering.

4† The Lord GOD has given me
a well-trained tongue,
That I might know how to answer the weary
a word that will waken them.
Morning after morning
he wakens my ear to hear as disciples do;
5 The Lord GOD opened my ear;
I did not refuse,
did not turn away.†
6 I gave my back to those who beat me,
my cheeks to those who tore out my beard;†
My face I did not hide
from insults and spitting.*

Pray It!

The Servant's Strength

Isaiah 50:4–9 is the third of the four servant songs (see "The Servant Songs," near Is 42:1–7). Read the song twice. The first time, think of how it reflects Jesus' relationship with his heavenly Father. The second time, meditate on the verses that inspire you and give you strength to be a prophet to other young people.

▶ **Is 50:4–9**

7 The Lord GOD is my help,
therefore I am not disgraced;
Therefore I have set my face like flint,
knowing that I shall not be put to shame.*
8 He who declares my innocence is near.
Who will oppose me?
Let us appear together.
Who will dispute my right?
Let them confront me.
9 See, the Lord GOD is my help;
who will declare me guilty?
See, they will all wear out like a garment,
consumed by moths.*
10 Who among you fears the LORD,†
heeds his servant's voice?
Whoever walk in darkness,
without any light,
Yet trust in the name of the LORD
and rely upon their God!*
11 All you who kindle flames
and set flares alight,
Walk by the light of your own fire
and by the flares you have burnt!
This is your fate from my hand:
you shall lie down in a place of torment.

†

50:1 Responding to the people's complaint of utter abandonment by God, the prophet asserts that their sins were responsible for their banishment. Since there was no bill of divorce, the bond between the Lord and his people still exists and he has the power to deliver them (v. 2).

50:2 Israel's faith in God is weak; the people do not answer God's call, nor believe promises of deliverance.

50:4–11 The third of the four "servant of the Lord" oracles (cf. note on 42:1–4); in vv. 4–9 the servant speaks; in vv. 10–11 God addresses the people directly.

50:5 The servant, like a well-trained disciple, does not refuse the divine vocation.

50:6 He willingly submits to insults and beatings. *Tore out my beard*: a grave and painful insult.

50:10–11 The Lord offers a choice to those who walk in darkness: either trust in the true light (v. 10), or walk in their false light and suffer the consequences.

*

49:26 Is 19:2; Ez 38:21; Zec 14:13.
50:1 Is 54:6–8; Dt 24:1–4; Mt 19:3; Mk 10:2–4.
50:2 Ex 7:18; Ps 105:29.
50:6 2 Sm 10:4–6; Mt 26:67; 27:30.
50:7 Ez 3:9.
50:9 Is 51:6–8; Ps 102:27.
50:10 Is 43:1–2; 44:1–2.

Exhortation To Trust in the Lord

51 1 Listen to me, you who pursue justice,
who seek the LORD;
Look to the rock from which you were hewn,
to the quarry† from which you were taken;*
2 Look to Abraham, your father,
and to Sarah, who gave you birth;
Though he was but one when I called him,
I blessed him and made him many.*
3 Yes, the LORD shall comfort Zion,
shall comfort all her ruins;
Her wilderness he shall make like Eden,
her wasteland like the garden of the LORD;
Joy and gladness shall be found in her,
thanksgiving and the sound of song.

4 Be attentive to me, my people;†
my nation, give ear to me.
For teaching shall go forth from me,
and my judgment, as light to the peoples.*
5 I will make my victory come swiftly;
my salvation shall go forth
and my arm shall judge the nations;
In me the coastlands shall hope,
and my arm they shall await.

6 Raise your eyes to the heavens,
look at the earth below;
Though the heavens vanish like smoke,
the earth wear out like a garment
and its inhabitants die like flies,
My salvation shall remain forever
and my victory shall always be firm.†
7 Hear me, you who know justice,
you people who have my teaching at heart:
Do not fear the reproach of others;
remain firm at their revilings.
8 They shall be like a garment eaten by moths,
like wool consumed by grubs;
But my victory shall remain forever,
my salvation, for all generations.*

9 Awake, awake, put on strength,
arm of the LORD!
Awake as in the days of old,
in ages long ago!
Was it not you who crushed Rahab,†
you who pierced the dragon?*
10 Was it not you who dried up the sea,
the waters of the great deep,†
You who made the depths of the sea into a way
for the redeemed to pass through?
11 Those whom the LORD has ransomed will return
and enter Zion singing,
crowned with everlasting joy;
They will meet with joy and gladness,
sorrow and mourning will flee.

12 I, it is I who comfort you.
Can you then fear mortals who die,
human beings who are just grass,
13 And forget the LORD, your maker,
who stretched out the heavens
and laid the foundations of earth?
All the day you are in constant dread
of the fury of the oppressor
When he prepares himself to destroy;
but where is the oppressor's fury?

14 The captives shall soon be released;
they shall not die and go down into the pit,
nor shall they want for bread.
15 For I am the LORD, your God,
who stirs up the sea so that its waves roar;
the LORD of hosts by name.*
16 I have put my words into your mouth,
I covered you, shielded by my hand,
Stretching out the heavens,
laying the foundations of the earth,
saying to Zion: You are my people.

The Cup of the Lord

17 Wake up, wake up!
Arise, Jerusalem,
You who drank at the LORD's hand
the cup of his wrath;
Who drained to the dregs
the bowl of staggering!*
18 She has no one to guide her
of all the children she bore;
She has no one to take her by the hand,
of all the children she reared!—
19 Your misfortunes are double;
who is there to grieve with you?
Desolation and destruction, famine and sword!
Who is there to comfort you?

†

51:1 *Rock . . . quarry*: your glorious ancestry.
51:4–5 The conversion of the nations.
51:6 While the heavens and the earth appear eternal and changeless, they are not so firm and lasting as God's saving will for Israel.
51:9 *Rahab*: see note on 30:7. *The dragon*: see notes on 27:1; Ps 74:12–17.
51:10 *Great deep*: a reference to the primeval chaos (cf. Gn 1:2; 7:11; 49:25; Jb 28:14; Ps 36:7; Jon 2:4).

*

51:1 Rom 9:30–31.
51:2 Ez 33:24; Gn 12:2–4; 22:17.
51:4 Is 2:3.
51:8 Is 50:9.
51:9 Ex 15:16; Jb 9:13; 26:12; Ps 74:13; 89:11.
51:15 Jer 31:35.
51:17 Jer 25:15–17; Ez 23:32–34.

20 Your children lie helpless
at every street corner
like antelopes in a net.
They are filled with the wrath of the LORD,
the rebuke of your God.
21 But now, hear this, afflicted one,
drunk, but not with wine,*
22 Thus says the LORD, your Master,
your God, who defends his people:
See, I am taking from your hand
the cup of staggering;
The bowl of my wrath
you shall no longer drink.
23 I will put it into the hands of your tormentors,
those who said to you,
"Bow down, that we may walk over you."
So you offered your back like the ground,
like the street for them to walk on.

Let Zion Rejoice

52 1 Awake, awake!
Put on your strength, Zion;
Put on your glorious garments,
Jerusalem, holy city.
Never again shall the uncircumcised
or the unclean enter you.
2 Arise, shake off the dust,
sit enthroned, Jerusalem;
Loose the bonds from your neck,
captive daughter Zion!
3 For thus says the LORD:
For nothing you were sold,
without money you shall be redeemed.
4 For thus says the Lord GOD:
To Egypt long ago my people went down,
to sojourn there;
Assyria, too, oppressed them for nought.
5 But now, what am I to do here?
—oracle of the LORD.
My people have been taken away for nothing;
their rulers mock, oracle of the LORD;
constantly, every day, my name is reviled.
6 Therefore my people shall know my name
on that day, that it is I who speaks: Here
I am!
7 How beautiful upon the mountains†
are the feet of the one bringing good news,
Announcing peace, bearing good news,
announcing salvation, saying to Zion,
"Your God is King!"*
8 Listen! Your sentinels raise a cry,
together they shout for joy,
For they see directly, before their eyes,
the LORD's return to Zion.*
9 Break out together in song,
O ruins of Jerusalem!
For the LORD has comforted his people,
has redeemed Jerusalem.
10 The LORD has bared his holy arm
in the sight of all the nations;
All the ends of the earth can see
the salvation of our God.
11 Depart, depart, go out from there,
touch nothing unclean!
Out from there!† Purify yourselves,
you who carry the vessels of the LORD.
12 But not in hurried flight will you go out,
nor leave in headlong haste,
For the LORD goes before you,
and your rear guard is the God of Israel.*

Suffering and Triumph of the Servant of the Lord†

13 See, my servant shall prosper,
he shall be raised high and greatly exalted.
14 Even as many were amazed at him—
so marred were his features,
beyond that of mortals
his appearance, beyond that of human
beings—*
15 So shall he startle many nations,
kings shall stand speechless;
For those who have not been told shall see,
those who have not heard shall ponder it.*

†

52:7–10 God leads the people back from Babylon to Zion, from whose ruined walls sentinels greet the returning exiles.

52:11 *From there*: from Babylon. *Vessels of the LORD*: taken to Babylon by Nebuchadnezzar, now carried back by the exiles returning in procession to Zion; cf. Ezr 1:7.

52:13–53:12 The last of the "servant of the Lord" oracles (see note on 42:1–4). Taken together, these oracles depict a figure of one called by God for a vocation to Israel and the nations (42:4; 49:5–6); the servant's exaltation both opens and closes the passage (52:13; 53:12). The servant responded in fidelity but has suffered opposition (50:4–6). In this fourth oracle the servant is characterized as "a man of suffering" (53:3) and appears to be unjustly put to death (53:8–9). Those who have witnessed his career somehow recognize that he is innocent, has undergone suffering for their sins (53:4–6), and his death is referred to as a reparation offering (see note on 53:10–11). The servant is described in ways that identify him with Israel (which is frequently referred to as "servant" in the context of Second Isaiah—e.g., 41:8, 9; 44:2, 21; 43:4) and is designated as "Israel" in 49:3; yet Israel outside the "servant of the Lord" oracles is not presented as sinless, but rather in exile because of sin (40:2; 42:21–25) and even as servant as deaf and blind (42:18–19). The servant is thus both identified with Israel and distinguished from it. As with the previous servant poems, this chapter helped the followers of Jesus to interpret his suffering, death, and resurrection; see especially the passion narratives.

*

51:21 Is 29:9.
52:7 Is 40:9; Rom 10:15.
52:8 Is 62:6.
52:12 Ex 12:11.
52:14 Ps 69:8.
52:15 Mi 7:16.

53 1 Who would believe what we have heard?†
To whom has the arm of the LORD been revealed?*
2 He grew up like a sapling before him,*
like a shoot from the parched earth;
He had no majestic bearing to catch our eye,
no beauty to draw us to him.
3 He was spurned and avoided by men,
a man of suffering, knowing pain,
Like one from whom you turn your face,
spurned, and we held him in no esteem.*

4 Yet it was our pain that he bore,
our sufferings he endured.
We thought of him as stricken,
struck down by God† and afflicted,*
5 But he was pierced for our sins,
crushed for our iniquity.
He bore the punishment that makes us whole,
by his wounds we were healed.*
6 We had all gone astray like sheep,
all following our own way;
But the LORD laid upon him†
the guilt of us all.*

7 Though harshly treated, he submitted
and did not open his mouth;
Like a lamb led to slaughter
or a sheep silent before shearers,
he did not open his mouth.*
8 Seized and condemned, he was taken away.
Who would have thought any more of his destiny?
For he was cut off from the land of the living,
struck for the sins of his people.
9 He was given a grave among the wicked,
a burial place with evildoers,
Though he had done no wrong,
nor was deceit found in his mouth.*
10 But it was the LORD's will to crush him with pain.
By making his life as a reparation offering,†
he shall see his offspring, shall lengthen his days,
and the LORD's will shall be accomplished through him.
11 Because of his anguish he shall see the light;
because of his knowledge he shall be content;
My servant, the just one, shall justify the many,
their iniquity he shall bear.
12 Therefore I will give him his portion among the many,
and he shall divide the spoils with the mighty,
Because he surrendered himself to death,
was counted among the transgressors,
Bore the sins of many,
and interceded for the transgressors.*

The New Zion

54 1 Raise a glad cry, you barren one† who never bore a child,
break forth in jubilant song, you who have never been in labor,
For more numerous are the children of the deserted wife
than the children of her who has a husband,
says the LORD.*
2 Enlarge the space for your tent,
spread out your tent cloths unsparingly;
lengthen your ropes and make firm your pegs.*
3 For you shall spread abroad to the right and left;
your descendants shall dispossess the nations
and shall people the deserted cities.†

4† Do not fear, you shall not be put to shame;
do not be discouraged, you shall not be disgraced.

53:1–10 *What we have heard*: this fourth servant oracle is introduced by words of the Lord (52:13–15) but is now continued by speakers who are not identified, perhaps those referred to in 52:15, perhaps Israel (cf. "struck for the sins of his people"—v. 8). The Lord is again the speaker in vv. 11–13.

53:4 *Struck down by God*: the Bible often sees suffering as a punishment for sin (e.g., Ps 6:2; 32:1–5), yet sin sometimes appears to go unpunished and the innocent often suffer (cf. Ps 73; the Book of Job). In the case of the servant, the onlookers initially judge him guilty because of his suffering but, in some way not explained, they come to understand that his sufferings are for the sins of others. One notes the element of surprise, for such vicarious suffering, in the form described here, is without parallel in the Old Testament.

53:6 *The LORD laid upon him*: the servant's suffering is no accidental or casual matter, but part of God's plan; see also v. 10. The bystanders' speculation of v. 4 is verified, but not in the sense intended by them.

53:10–11 *Reparation offering*: the Hebrew term *'asham* is used of a particular kind of sacrifice, one that is intended as compensation for that which is due because of guilt. See Lv 5:14–26 and note. *Justify*: the verb means "to be acquitted," "declared innocent," but since the servant bears "their iniquity," an effective rather than simply legal action is suggested.

54:1 Jerusalem, pictured as a wife who had been barren and deserted, now suddenly finds herself with innumerable children (the returning exiles); cf. Gal 4:27 for an application to a new context.

54:3 Those who had taken advantage of the exile to encroach on Jerusalem's territory will be driven out, and the returning exiles will repopulate the cities of Judah.

54:4–8 As with some other Old Testament themes, Second Isaiah uses that of Israel as the Lord's bride in a new manner. Whereas Hosea and Jeremiah had depicted Israel as the Lord's spouse to emphasize both Israel's infidelity and the Lord's continued love (Hos 1–3;

53:1 Is 52:10; Jn 12:38; Rom 10:16.
53:2 Is 11:1.
53:3 Jb 19:18; Ps 31:11–13; Mk 9:11.
53:4 Jer 10:19; Mt 8:17.
53:5 1 Cor 15:3; 1 Pt 2:24.
53:6 Lv 16:21–22.
53:7 Mt 26:63; Acts 8:32.
53:9 1 Pt 2:22–23; 1 Jn 3:5.
53:12 Mk 15:28; Lk 22:37.
54:1 Gal 4:27.
54:2 Is 49:20.

For the shame of your youth you shall forget,
the reproach of your widowhood no longer remember.
5 For your husband is your Maker;
the LORD of hosts is his name,
Your redeemer,† the Holy One of Israel,
called God of all the earth.

6 The LORD calls you back,
like a wife forsaken and grieved in spirit,
A wife married in youth and then cast off,
says your God.*
7 For a brief moment I abandoned you,
but with great tenderness I will take you back.
8 In an outburst of wrath, for a moment
I hid my face from you;
But with enduring love I take pity on you,
says the LORD, your redeemer.

9 This is for me like the days of Noah:
As I swore then that the waters of Noah
should never again flood the earth,
So I have sworn now not to be angry with you,
or to rebuke you.*
10 Though the mountains fall away
and the hills be shaken,
My love shall never fall away from you
nor my covenant of peace† be shaken,
says the LORD, who has mercy on you.*

11 O afflicted one,† storm-battered and unconsoled,
I lay your pavements in carnelians,
your foundations in sapphires;*
12 I will make your battlements of rubies,
your gates of jewels,
and all your walls of precious stones.
13 All your children shall be taught by the LORD;
great shall be the peace of your children.
14 In justice shall you be established,
far from oppression, you shall not fear,
from destruction, it cannot come near.
15 If there be an attack, it is not my doing;
whoever attacks shall fall before you.
16 See, I have created the smith
who blows on the burning coals
and forges weapons as his work;
It is I also who have created
the destroyer to work havoc.
17 Every weapon fashioned against you shall fail;
every tongue that brings you to trial
you shall prove false.

This is the lot of the servants of the LORD,
their vindication from me—oracle of the LORD.

An Invitation to Grace

55 1 All you who are thirsty,†
come to the water!
You who have no money,
come, buy grain and eat;
Come, buy grain without money,
wine and milk without cost!*
2 Why spend your money for what is not bread;
your wages for what does not satisfy?
Only listen to me, and you shall eat well,
you shall delight in rich fare.
3 Pay attention and come to me;
listen, that you may have life.
I will make with you an everlasting covenant,
the steadfast loyalty promised to David.*
4 As I made him a witness to peoples,
a leader and commander of peoples,
5 So shall you summon a nation you knew not,
and a nation† that knew you not shall run to you,
Because of the LORD, your God,
the Holy One of Israel, who has glorified you.*

6† Seek the LORD while he may be found,
call upon him while he is near.
7 Let the wicked forsake their way,
and sinners their thoughts;
Let them turn to the LORD to find mercy;
to our God, who is generous in forgiving.
8 For my thoughts are not your thoughts,
nor are your ways my ways—oracle of the LORD.

†

Jer 2:2; 3:1–15) and Ezekiel to accuse Israel unsparingly (Ez 16; 23), Second Isaiah speaks only of the love with which the Lord restores the people, speaking tender words with no hint of reproach.

54:5 *Redeemer*: cf. note on 41:14.

54:10 *Covenant of peace*: this whole section, vv. 9–17, is given to various assurances of God's love for Israel and of safety from various possible threats; the phrase sums up both the positive aspects of *shalom*, which implies a fullness of blessing, and protection from all that might harm. Cf. also 55:3; Nm 25:12; Ez 34:25; 37:26; Mal 2:5.

54:11 *Afflicted one*: Jerusalem.

55:1–3 The prophet invites all to return, under the figure of a banquet; cf. the covenant banquet in Ex 24:9–11 and wisdom's banquet in Prv 9:1–6. The Lord's covenant with David (2 Sm 7) is now to be extended beyond his dynasty.

55:5 The "nation" is Persia under Cyrus, but the perspective is worldwide.

55:6–9 The invitation to seek the Lord is motivated by the mercy of a God whose "ways" are completely mysterious.

*

54:6 Mal 2:14–15.
54:9 Gn 9:15.
54:10 Ps 46:3; 76:5.
54:11 Rev 21:18–21.
55:1 Jn 4:10–15; 6:35; 7:37–39; Rev 21:6; 22:17.
55:3 2 Sm 7:12–16.
55:5 Acts 13:34.

Live It!

The Optimism of Third Isaiah

The last eleven chapters of Isaiah contain the messages of several prophets known collectively as Third Isaiah. The common element of these prophecies is optimism. They proclaim the hopeful message that God's Covenant will be extended to all nations and that Jerusalem will become God's holy city, the throne of the Eternal King.

Third Isaiah, in contrast to many of the other biblical prophets, proclaims joy as a sign of God's presence. Joy is absent in the lives of many people today, as it was in the time of Isaiah. Let us remember all the wonderful things God has done for us, and we too will find cause for rejoicing!

- When have you experienced true joy in your life?
- Where have you seen the presence of God in your life? in our world?
- How can you help others to experience joy?

▶ Is 56:1—66:24

9 For as the heavens are higher than the earth,
so are my ways higher than your ways,
my thoughts higher than your thoughts.

10† Yet just as from the heavens
the rain and snow come down
And do not return there
till they have watered the earth,
making it fertile and fruitful,
Giving seed to the one who sows
and bread to the one who eats,
11 So shall my word be
that goes forth from my mouth;
It shall not return to me empty,
but shall do what pleases me,
achieving the end for which I sent it.

12 Yes, in joy you shall go forth,
in peace you shall be brought home;
Mountains and hills shall break out in song
before you,
all trees of the field shall clap their hands.
13 In place of the thornbush, the cypress shall
grow,
instead of nettles,† the myrtle.
This shall be to the LORD's renown,
as an everlasting sign that shall not fail.

III. Isaiah 56—66

Salvation for the Just†

56 1† Thus says the LORD:
Observe what is right, do what is just,
for my salvation is about to come,
my justice, about to be revealed.*
2 Happy is the one who does this,
whoever holds fast to it:
Keeping the sabbath without profaning it,
keeping one's hand from doing any evil.*

Obligations and Promises To Share in the Covenant

3† The foreigner joined to the LORD should not
say,
"The LORD will surely exclude me from his
people";
Nor should the eunuch say,
"See, I am a dry tree."*
4 For thus says the LORD:
To the eunuchs who keep my sabbaths,
who choose what pleases me,
and who hold fast to my covenant,*
5 I will give them, in my house

55:10–11 The efficacy of the word of God recalls 40:5, 8.

55:13 *Thornbush . . . nettles*: suggestive of the desert and therefore symbolic of suffering and hardship; *cypress . . . myrtle*: suggestive of fertile land and therefore symbolic of joy and strength. *To the LORD's renown*: lit., "to the name of the Lord."

56:1–8 This poem inaugurates the final section of the Book of Isaiah, often referred to as Third or Trito-Isaiah. While Second or Deutero-Isaiah (Is 40–55) gave numerous references to the hopes of the community of Israel during the Babylonian exile (ca. 587–538 B.C.), Third Isaiah witnesses to the struggles and hoped-for blessings of the postexilic community now back in the homeland of Israel. In this opening poem, the references to "keeping the sabbath" (vv. 2, 4, 6), "holding fast to the covenant" (vv. 4, 6) and "God's holy mountain" as a house of prayer (v. 7), all tell of the postexilic community that was establishing itself again in the land according to the pattern of God's word given through the prophet. The poem can be classified as a "prophetic exhortation" in which the prophet gives instruction for those who wish to live according to God's word and covenant. What is important to note are the conditions placed upon the people of God; while Is 40–55 show an unconditional promise of redemption, these final chapters delineate clear expectations for receiving God's salvific promises. Both the expectations and the great promises of God will unfold in the succeeding chapters of Third Isaiah.

56:1 This opening verse echoes themes that are well known throughout the Book of Isaiah: justice and right judgment (1:27; 5:7, 16; 9:6; 16:5; 26:9; 28:17; 32:1, 16; 33:5; 42:1, 4, 6; 45:8, 13, 19), salvation and deliverance (12:3; 26:18; 33:2; 45:8, 21; 46:13; 51:5, 6, 8). These themes will be developed also throughout Third Isaiah.

56:3 Eunuchs had originally been excluded from the community of the Lord; cf. Dt 23:2; Neh 13:1–3; Wis 3:14.

56:1 Is 59:9, 14, 19–20.
56:2 Is 1:13; 58:13–14; Ex 23:12.
56:3 Dt 23:3–5; Neh 13:1–3.
56:4 Wis 3:14.

and within my walls, a monument and a
name†
Better than sons and daughters;
an eternal name, which shall not be cut off,
will I give them.
6 And foreigners who join themselves to the
LORD,
to minister to him,
To love the name of the LORD,
to become his servants—
All who keep the sabbath without
profaning it
and hold fast to my covenant,
7† Them I will bring to my holy mountain
and make them joyful in my house of
prayer;
Their burnt offerings and their sacrifices
will be acceptable on my altar,
For my house shall be called
a house of prayer for all peoples.*
8† Oracle of the Lord GOD,
who gathers the dispersed of Israel—
Others will I gather to them
besides those already gathered.*

Unworthy Shepherds†

9 All you beasts of the field,†
come to devour,
all you beasts in the forest!*
10† All the sentinels of Israel are blind,
they are without knowledge;
They are all mute dogs,
unable to bark;
Dreaming, reclining,
loving their sleep.
11 Yes, the dogs have a ravenous appetite;
they never know satiety,
Shepherds who have no understanding;
all have turned their own way,
each one covetous for gain:
12 "Come, let me bring wine;
let us fill ourselves with strong drink,
And tomorrow will be like today,
or even greater."*

57 1 The just have perished,
but no one takes it to heart;
The steadfast are swept away,
while no one understands.
Yet the just are taken away from the presence
of evil,
2† and enter into peace;
They rest upon their couches,
the sincere, who walk in integrity.*

An Idolatrous People†

3 But you, draw near,
you children of a sorceress,
offspring of an adulterer and a prostitute!†
4 Against whom do you make sport,
against whom do you open wide your
mouth,
and stick out your tongue?
Are you not rebellious children,
deceitful offspring—
5 You who burn with lust among the oaks,
under every green tree;
You who immolate children in the wadies,
among the clefts of the rocks?† *
6 Among the smooth stones† of the wadi is
your portion,
they, they are your allotment;

†

56:5 *A monument and a name*: literally in Hebrew, "a hand and a name"; a memorial inscription to prevent oblivion for one who had no children; cf. 2 Sm 18:18; Neh 7:5; 13:14.

56:7 This verse continues the theme of universalism found in Is 49:6. As Israel was to be "a light to the nations" so that God's "salvation may reach to the ends of the earth," so now does that come to pass as foreigners, faithful to the divine commands, are brought to the Temple by God and joined to the covenant community of Israel.

56:8 For the gathering of the dispersed people of Israel, cf. Jer 23:3; 31:8–9; Ez 11:17. Here the Lord not only gathers the displaced of Israel, but also unites other peoples to them. Cf. Is 60:3–10; 66:18–21.

56:9–57:21 This section is made up of two pronouncements of judgment (56:9–57:2; 57:3–13) and an oracle of salvation (57:14–21), each of which ends with a reversal of imagery and language. While there are harsh indictments against the corrupt leaders of Israel (56:9–12), a promise of peace is offered to those who are just (57:1–2). Then the judgment and its subsequent punishment for idolaters (57:3–13a) change to an announcement of reward for those who place their trust in God (57:13c). And the promises of salvation (57:14–19) then shift to a word of warning to the wicked (57:20–21).

56:9 *Beasts of the field*: foreign nations, which are invited to come and ravage Israel.

56:10–11 These shepherds of Israel are without "knowledge," a theme developed earlier in the Isaian corpus; cf. 1:3; 6:9–10. Ezekiel 34 has similar condemnatory words against the unfaithful shepherds of Israel.

57:2 Despite their sad fate, the just will ultimately attain peace (most likely in this world); cf. v. 13.

57:3–13 In this courtroom imagery, the idolaters are summoned before the judge (v. 3), their crimes are graphically described (vv. 4–11), their guilt is established, and condemnation is carried out (vv. 12–13b). In contrast to this, v. 13c describes the inheritance of God's land and holy mountain given to those who place their confidence in God instead of in idols.

57:3 Language of sexual infidelity is often used in a figurative way to describe idolatry. Cf. Ez 16:15–22; Hos 2:4–7; Col 3:5.

57:5 Child sacrifice is also attested in 2 Kgs 23:10; Jer 7:31; Ez 16:20; 20:28, 31; 23:37–39.

57:6 *Smooth stones*: the Hebrew word for this expression has the same consonants as the word for "portion"; instead of making the Lord their portion (cf. Ps 16:5), the people adored slabs of stone which they took from the streambeds in valleys and set up as idols; cf. Jer 3:9. Therefore, it is implied, they will be swept away as by a sudden torrent of waters carrying them down the rocky-bottomed gorge to destruction and death without burial.

*

56:7 1 Kgs 8:29–30, 41; Mt 21:13.
56:8 Ps 147:2.
56:9 Jer 12:9–10; Ez 34:5.
56:12 Is 22:13; 28:7; Wis 2:7.
57:2 Wis 3:1–3.
57:5 Dt 12:2; 2 Kgs 17:10; Jer 7:31; 19:5; Ez 20:28, 31.

Indeed, you poured out a drink offering to them,
and brought up grain offerings.
With these things, should I be appeased?
7 Upon a towering and lofty mountain
you set up your bed,
and there you went up to offer sacrifice.*
8 Behind the door and the doorpost
you set up your symbol.
Yes, deserting me, you carried up your bedding;
and spread it wide.
You entered an agreement with them,
you loved their couch, you gazed upon
nakedness.†
9 You approached the king† with oil,
and multiplied your perfumes;
You sent your ambassadors far away,
down even to deepest Sheol.
10 Though worn out with the length of your
journey,
you never said, "It is hopeless";
You found your strength revived,
and so you did not weaken.
11 Whom did you dread and fear,
that you told lies,
And me you did not remember
nor take to heart?
Am I to keep silent and conceal,
while you show no fear of me?
12 I will proclaim your justice†
and your works;
but they shall not help you.
13† When you cry out,
let your collection of idols save you.
All these the wind shall carry off,
a mere breath shall bear them away;
But whoever takes refuge in me shall inherit
the land,
and possess my holy mountain.

The Way to Peace for God's People

14 And I say:
Build up, build up, prepare the way,
remove every obstacle from my people's
way.† *
15† For thus says the high and lofty One,
the One who dwells forever, whose name is
holy:
I dwell in a high and holy place,
but also with the contrite and lowly of spirit,
To revive the spirit of the lowly,
to revive the heart of the crushed.
16 For I will not accuse forever,
nor always be angry;
For without me their spirit fails,
the life breath that I have given.*
17 Because of their wicked avarice I grew angry;
I struck them, hiding myself from them in
wrath.
But they turned back, following the way
of their own heart.*
18 I saw their ways,
but I will heal them.
I will lead them and restore full comfort to
them
and to those who mourn for them,*
19 creating words of comfort.†
Peace! Peace to those who are far and near,
says the LORD; and I will heal them.
20 But the wicked are like the tossing sea
which cannot be still,
Its waters cast up mire and mud.*
21 There is no peace for the wicked!
says my God.*

Reasons for Judgment†

58 1 Cry out full-throated and unsparingly,
lift up your voice like a trumpet blast;
Proclaim to my people their transgression,
to the house of Jacob their sins.*
2 They seek me day after day,
and desire to know my ways,
Like a nation that has done what is just
and not abandoned the judgment of their
God;

---

† **57:8** *Nakedness*: literally in Hebrew, "hand." In this context, it may euphemistically refer to a phallus.

57:9 *The king*: in Hebrew, the word for king is *melek*, similar in sound to the Canaanite god Molech, to whom children were offered as a sacrifice in pagan ritual. The expression "your ambassadors" could be a figurative expression for the children whose death served as an offering to this deity.

57:12 *Justice*: here used sarcastically. The activity described in these verses is far from the justice which God demands of those who are aligned with the covenant (cf. 56:1, 4, 6). In the larger context of Third Isaiah and the whole of the Isaian tradition, justice is a key theological motif. The justice to which God calls Israel will eventually come to its fulfillment in an act of divine intervention (cf. 60:21; 61:3c). Until then, the people of God must strive to live in the ways of justice and right judgment (56:1).

57:13 In v. 6, the smooth stones of the valley are the portion which the unfaithful will receive as their due reward (cf. note on v. 6); while in v. 13c, an inheritance of the land and possession of God's holy mountain will be the portion of the upright.

57:14 *The way . . . my people's way*: the language and imagery are reminiscent of 40:1–2, but in this context, when the people have already returned, the physical road through the desert is replaced by the spiritual way that leads to redemption.

57:15 The God of Israel is presented in both a transcendent and an immanent manner. God's holiness is the transcendent quality; the immanence is shown in the choice of dwelling among the downtrodden and humble.

57:19 *Creating words of comfort*: lit., "fruit of the lips," perhaps referring to praise and thanksgiving for the divine healing; cf. Hos 14:3.

58:1–5 The prophet is commanded to condemn the formalism of the people, specifically their hypocritical fasting.

---

* **57:7** Jer 2:20; Ez 6:13; Hos 4:13. **57:14** Is 40:3–4. **57:16** Gn 2:7. **57:17** Is 56:11. **57:18** Is 61:2. **57:20** Jon 2:3–7. **57:21** Is 48:22. **58:1** Lv 25:9.

Cultural Connection

"If You Want Peace, Work for Justice"

"If you want peace, work for justice" is a famous quote of Pope Paul VI. We hear a similar message in Isaiah 56:1, and 58:6–14 gives us clear examples of works that create justice and peace.

At the core of justice is the understanding that life—all life—is precious. All people are to be honored, protected, and celebrated. Ensuring that this happens is our responsibility, even when it seems to be a burden. The following prayer by a worker of Peace Market in Korea reflects this passion:

Make us keep the sputtering lantern burning
and not to break a wounded reed.
Make us understand
the secret of eternal life
from the pulse of blood in our veins
and realise the worth of a life
from the movement of a warm heart.
Make us not discriminate
the rich and the poor,
the high and the low,
the learned and the ignorant
those we know well and those we do not know.
Oh!
A human life can't be exchanged for the whole world
this supreme task of keeping the lives
of the sons and daughters of God.
Let us realise how lovely it is
to feel the burdens of responsibility.
("Our Prayer," *Your Will Be Done*)

▶ **Is 58:6–14**

They ask of me just judgments,
they desire to draw near to God.
3 "Why do we fast, but you do not see it?
afflict ourselves, but you take no note?"
See, on your fast day you carry out your own pursuits,
and drive all your laborers.*
4 See, you fast only to quarrel and fight
and to strike with a wicked fist!
Do not fast as you do today
to make your voice heard on high!
5 Is this the manner of fasting I would choose,
a day to afflict oneself?
To bow one's head like a reed,
and lie upon sackcloth and ashes?
Is this what you call a fast,
a day acceptable to the LORD?*

Authentic Fasting That Leads to Blessing†

6 Is this not, rather, the fast that I choose:
releasing those bound unjustly,
untying the thongs of the yoke;
Setting free the oppressed,
breaking off every yoke?*
7 Is it not sharing your bread with the hungry,
bringing the afflicted and the homeless into your house;
Clothing the naked when you see them,
and not turning your back on your own flesh?*
8 Then your light shall break forth like the dawn,
and your wound shall quickly be healed;
Your vindication shall go before you,
and the glory of the LORD shall be your rear guard.
9 Then you shall call, and the LORD will answer,
you shall cry for help, and he will say:
"Here I am!"
If you remove the yoke from among you,
the accusing finger, and malicious speech;*
10 If you lavish your food on the hungry
and satisfy the afflicted;
Then your light shall rise in the darkness,
and your gloom shall become like midday;
11 Then the LORD will guide you always
and satisfy your thirst in parched places,
will give strength to your bones
And you shall be like a watered garden,

† **58:6–12** Fasting is not genuine without reforming one's way of life. A true social morality will ensure prosperity.

* **58:3** 1 Sm 7:6; 1 Kgs 21:12; 1 Mc 3:47; Jl 1:1–2:17. **58:5** Zec 7:5. **58:6** Is 35:5–6. **58:7** Ez 18:7, 16; Mt 25:35. **58:9** Am 5:7.

Catholic Connection

The Corporal and Spiritual Works of Mercy

Have you ever done something just to get others to notice you? The Israelites were apparently performing pious acts to get God's attention and complained when God did not notice when they fasted or humbled themselves. In response, God points out that when they fast, they do it for self-serving reasons and commit numerous sins in the process. God then explains what true fasting, or worship, looks like. True worship involves not serving yourself, but serving others. Only then will one's prayers and deeds be answered and blessed by God.

The acts of serving others mentioned in Isaiah form the basis for what the Church calls the corporal and spiritual works of mercy. These works of mercy are founded on God's call for justice and self sacrifice. They are best exemplified in Jesus' command to love one's neighbor and most vividly portrayed in his description of the Final Judgment (see Mt 25:31–46).

The corporal works of mercy focus on addressing the physical needs of others. The word *corporal* actually comes from the Latin word *corpus*, which means *body*. These works include helping the injured, freeing the oppressed, feeding the hungry, clothing the naked, and giving shelter to the homeless. Through all of these acts, we honor God by showing respect for every human being that God created.

The spiritual works of mercy focus on addressing the spiritual needs of others. These works include teaching others about the faith, giving advice, forgiving others, and comforting those who are mourning. Through all these acts, we honor God by being an example of God's love to someone else during an important time in her or his life.

The corporal and spiritual works of mercy will not only help others, but they can also build us up as individuals. Try reading this passage from Isaiah every morning for a week and look for ways that you can live out various works of mercy each day. By focusing on the needs of others, we can learn about Christ's sacrificial love and also find notice and favor with God.

▶ **Is 58:1–9**

Catechism, nos. 2443–2449

like a flowing spring whose waters never
fail.*
12 Your people shall rebuild the ancient ruins;
the foundations from ages past you shall
raise up;
"Repairer of the breach," they shall call you,
"Restorer of ruined dwellings."*

Authentic Sabbath Observance That Leads to Blessing†

13 If you refrain from trampling the sabbath,
from following your own pursuits on my
holy day;
If you call the sabbath a delight,
the LORD's holy day glorious;
If you glorify it by not following your ways,
seeking your own interests, or pursuing
your own affairs—
14 Then you shall delight in the LORD,
and I will make you ride upon the heights
of the earth;
I will nourish you with the heritage of Jacob,
your father,
for the mouth of the LORD has spoken.*

Salvation Delayed

59 1† No, the hand of the LORD is not too
short to save,
nor his ear too dull to hear.*
2 Rather, it is your crimes
that separate you from your God,
It is your sins that make him hide his face
so that he does not hear you.
3 For your hands are defiled with blood,
and your fingers with crime;
Your lips speak falsehood,
and your tongue utters deceit.*
4 No one brings suit justly,
no one pleads truthfully;
They trust an empty plea and tell lies;
they conceive mischief and bring forth
malice.
5† They hatch adders' eggs,
and weave spiders' webs:
Whoever eats the eggs will die,
if one of them is crushed, it will hatch a
viper;*
6 Their webs cannot serve as clothing,
nor can they cover themselves with their
works.
Their works are evil works,
and deeds of violence are in their hands.
7 Their feet run to evil,
and they hasten to shed innocent blood;
Their thoughts are thoughts of wickedness,
violence and destruction are on their
highways.*
8 The way of peace they know not,
and there is no justice on their paths;
Their roads they have made crooked,
no one who walks in them knows peace.

Acknowledgment of Transgressions

9† That is why judgment is far from us
and justice does not reach us.
We look for light, but there is darkness;
for brightness, and we walk in gloom!*
10 Like those who are blind we grope along the
wall,
like people without eyes we feel our way.
We stumble at midday as if at twilight,
among the vigorous, we are like the dead.
11 Like bears we all growl,
like doves we moan without ceasing.
We cry out for justice, but it is not there;
for salvation, but it is far from us.*
12 For our transgressions before you are many,
our sins bear witness against us.
Our transgressions are present to us,
and our crimes we acknowledge:
13 Transgressing, and denying the LORD,
turning back from following our God,
Planning fraud and treachery,
uttering lying words conceived in the heart.
14 Judgment is turned away,
and justice stands far off;
For truth stumbles in the public square,
and uprightness cannot enter.*
15 Fidelity is lacking,
and whoever turns from evil is despoiled.

Divine Intervention

The LORD saw this, and was aggrieved
that there was no justice.

†

58:13–14 Sabbath observance becomes a cornerstone of postexilic piety; cf. 56:2, 4, 6.

59:1–20 This poem brings together a lament of the postexilic community and a harsh word of judgment from the prophet. After the opening rhetorical question, each of the stanzas begins with a reference to the justice and right judgment which are lacking among the people (vv. 4, 9, 14). Toward the end of the poem, God is depicted as a Divine Warrior (vv. 16–20) who is the only one who can intervene in order to bring redemption. This same Divine Warrior imagery is repeated in a similar fashion in 63:1–6.

59:5–6 The eggs signify evil works, doing positive harm; the webs are devices that serve no useful purpose.

59:9–15 The turning point in the poem comes when the people acknowledge their transgressions and describe the horror of their present state. Light is a metaphor for salvation (cf. 9:1; 42:16; 60:1–3, 19–20) and darkness represents sin and disaster.

58:11 Is 51:3; Ps 24.
58:12 Is 61:4.
58:14 Hb 3:19.
59:1 Is 50:2; Nm 11:23.
59:3 Is 1:15.
59:5 Jb 20:12–16.
59:7 Prv 1:15, 19; 2:8–9, 12–13, 15, 18–19; Rom 3:15.
59:9 Am 5:18–19.
59:11 Is 38:14.
59:14 Jb 28:28.

16 He saw that there was no one,
was appalled that there was none to
intervene;
Then his own arm brought about the victory,
and his justice sustained him.
17 He put on justice as his breastplate,
victory as a helmet on his head;
He clothed himself with garments of
vengeance,
wrapped himself in a mantle of zeal.*
18 According to their deeds he repays his
enemies
and requites his foes with wrath;
to the coastlands he renders recompense.
19 Those in the west shall fear the name of the
LORD,
and those in the east, his glory,
Coming like a pent-up stream
driven on by the breath of the LORD.
20 Then for Zion shall come a redeemer,
to those in Jacob who turn from
transgression—oracle of the LORD.*
21† This is my covenant with them,
which I myself have made, says the LORD:
My spirit which is upon you
and my words that I have put in your
mouth
Shall not depart from your mouth,
nor from the mouths of your children
Nor the mouths of your children's children
from this time forth and forever, says the
LORD.*

The Dawning of Divine Glory for Zion

60 1† Arise! Shine, for your light has come,
the glory of the LORD has dawned upon
you.*
2 Though darkness covers the earth,
and thick clouds, the peoples,
Upon you the LORD will dawn,
and over you his glory will be seen.
3 Nations shall walk by your light,
kings by the radiance of your dawning.*

The Nations Come to Zion

4 Raise your eyes and look about;
they all gather and come to you—
Your sons from afar,
your daughters in the arms of their nurses.*
5 Then you shall see and be radiant,
your heart shall throb and overflow.
For the riches of the sea shall be poured out
before you,
the wealth of nations shall come to you.
6 Caravans of camels shall cover you,
dromedaries of Midian and Ephah;
All from Sheba shall come
bearing gold and frankincense,
and heralding the praises of the LORD.
7 All the flocks of Kedar shall be gathered for
you,
the rams of Nebaioth shall serve your needs;
They will be acceptable offerings on my altar,
and I will glorify my glorious house.
8 Who are these that fly along like a cloud,
like doves to their cotes?
9 The vessels of the coastlands are gathering,
with the ships of Tarshish in the lead,
To bring your children from afar,
their silver and gold with them—
For the name of the LORD, your God,
for the Holy One of Israel who has glorified
you.

Honor and Service for Zion†

10 Foreigners shall rebuild your walls,
their kings shall minister to you;
Though in my wrath I struck you,
yet in my good will I have shown you
mercy.*
11 Your gates shall stand open constantly;
day and night they shall not be closed
So that they may bring you the wealth of
nations,
with their kings in the vanguard.*
12 For the nation or kingdom that will not serve
you shall perish;
such nations shall be utterly destroyed!*
13 The glory of Lebanon shall come to you—
the juniper, the fir, and the cypress all
together—
To bring beauty to my sanctuary,
and glory to the place where I stand.*
14 The children of your oppressors shall come,
bowing before you;
All those who despised you,

†

59:21 This verse makes the transition from chaps. 56–59 to chaps. 60–62. Oracles of judgment yield to oracles about God's redemptive action.

60:1–9 The light the prophet proclaims to Zion symbolizes the blessing to come to her: the glory of the Lord, the return of her children, the wealth of nations who themselves will walk by her light. The passage is famous from its use in the Latin liturgy for the feast of Epiphany.

60:10–18 The glorious promises for the future continue: the wealth of the nations (vv. 5, 10), tribute from kings, glorification of the Temple, peace and justice (cf. Ps 85:11).

59:17 Wis 5:17–20; Eph 6:14–16; 1 Thes 5:8.
59:20 Is 35:4; Rom 11:26–27.
59:21 Is 1:27.
60:1 Is 40:5; 49:14–26; 51:17–23.
60:3 Is 42:6; 45:14; 49:6.
60:4 Is 49:18.
60:10 Is 54:11–12.
60:11 Rev 21:25.
60:12 Is 61:2.
60:13 Is 35:2; 66:1.

shall bow low at your feet.
They shall call you "City of the LORD,"
"Zion of the Holy One of Israel."
15 No longer forsaken and hated,
with no one passing through,
Now I will make you the pride of the ages,
a joy from generation to generation.
16 You shall suck the milk of nations,
and be nursed at royal breasts;
And you shall know that I, the LORD, am your savior,
your redeemer, the Mighty One of Jacob.
17 Instead of bronze I will bring gold,
instead of iron I will bring silver;
Instead of wood, bronze;
instead of stones, iron.
I will appoint peace your governor,
and justice your ruler.*
18 No longer shall violence be heard of in your land,
or plunder and ruin within your borders.
You shall call your walls "Salvation"
and your gates "Praise."

Eternal Light for Zion

19† No longer shall the sun
be your light by day,
Nor shall the brightness of the moon
give you light by night;
Rather, the LORD will be your light forever,
your God will be your glory.*
20 No longer will your sun set,
or your moon wane;
For the LORD will be your light forever,
and the days of your grieving will be over.
21 Your people will all be just;
for all time they will possess the land;
They are the shoot that I planted,
the work of my hands, that I might be glorified.*
22 The least one shall become a clan,
the smallest, a mighty nation;
I, the LORD, will swiftly accomplish
these things when the time comes.*

The Anointed Bearer of Glad Tidings

61 1† The spirit of the Lord GOD is upon me,
because the LORD has anointed me;
He has sent me to bring good news to the afflicted,
to bind up the brokenhearted,
To proclaim liberty to the captives,
release to the prisoners,*
2 To announce a year of favor from the LORD
and a day of vindication by our God;
To comfort all who mourn;*
3 to place on those who mourn in Zion
a diadem instead of ashes,
To give them oil of gladness instead of mourning,
a glorious mantle instead of a faint spirit.

Restoration and Blessing

They will be called oaks of justice,
the planting of the LORD to show his glory.
4 They shall rebuild the ancient ruins,
the former wastes they shall raise up
And restore the desolate cities,
devastations of generation upon generation.*
5 Strangers shall stand ready to pasture your flocks,
foreigners shall be your farmers and vinedressers.
6† You yourselves shall be called "Priests of the LORD,"
"Ministers of our God" you shall be called.
You shall eat the wealth of the nations
and in their riches you will boast.*
7 Because their shame was twofold†
and disgrace was proclaimed their portion,
They will possess twofold in their own land;
everlasting joy shall be theirs.*

God's Word of Promise

8 For I, the LORD, love justice,
I hate robbery and wrongdoing;
I will faithfully give them their recompense,
an everlasting covenant I will make with them.*
9 Their offspring shall be renowned among the nations,
and their descendants in the midst of the peoples;
All who see them shall acknowledge them:
"They are offspring the LORD has blessed."

†

60:19–20 The theme of light is taken up again, but in an apocalyptic vein: the Lord's radiant presence replaces physical light.

61:1–2 The prophet proclaims that he has been anointed by the Lord to bring good news (cf. 40:9) to the afflicted and to comfort Zion. The background to the "year of favor" is the jubilee year of release from debts (Lv 25:10–11; Is 49:8).

61:6 The bestowal of a new name suggests a new identity and mission. The whole people will be priests (cf. Ex 19:6), even ministering to nations who will serve God's people.

61:7 *Twofold*: Israel was punished double for infidelity (40:2); the blessings of its restoration will also be double.

*

60:17 Ps 85:11.
60:19 Is 2:5; Rev 21:23; 22:5.
60:21 Is 57:13c.
60:22 Gn 12:2; 17:6.
61:1 Is 40:9; 42:1; 48:16; 52:7; 58:7; Lk 4:18–19.
61:2 Mt 5:4.
61:4 Is 58:12.
61:6 Ex 19:6; 1 Pt 2:9.
61:7 Is 40:2.
61:8 Is 55:3; 54:9–10; 59:21.

Did You Know?

Bride and Bridegroom

In ancient Israel, the bride and bridegroom gradually became a metaphor, or symbol, for the relationship between Israel and God as pictured in Isaiah 61:10 and 62:5. In these passages, Israel is the bride, and God is the faithful bridegroom, who loves her, lavishes her with blessings, and continues to be faithful to her. When Israel strays from the covenant or goes after foreign gods, she is compared to an unfaithful lover, even a prostitute who pursues other partners (for a graphic example, see Ez 16:1–43). The prophet Hosea even marries a prostitute as a living example of God's faithfulness (see Hos 1:2)! The wonder of God's love is that through all of Israel's infidelity (and ours), God always remains willing to take her (and us) back.

▶ Is 61:10

Thanksgiving for God's Deliverance

10† I will rejoice heartily in the LORD,
my being exults in my God;
For he has clothed me with garments of salvation,
and wrapped me in a robe of justice,
Like a bridegroom adorned with a diadem,
as a bride adorns herself with her jewels.*
11 As the earth brings forth its shoots,
and a garden makes its seeds spring up,
So will the Lord GOD make justice spring up,
and praise before all the nations.

A New Name for Zion

62 1† For Zion's sake I will not be silent,
for Jerusalem's sake I will not keep still,
Until her vindication shines forth like the dawn
and her salvation like a burning torch.*
2 Nations shall behold your vindication,
and all kings your glory;
You shall be called by a new name
bestowed by the mouth of the LORD.*
3 You shall be a glorious crown in the hand of the LORD,
a royal diadem in the hand of your God.
4 No more shall you be called "Forsaken,"
nor your land called "Desolate,"
But you shall be called "My Delight is in her,"
and your land "Espoused."
For the LORD delights in you,
and your land shall be espoused.*
5 For as a young man marries a virgin,
your Builder shall marry you;
And as a bridegroom rejoices in his bride
so shall your God rejoice in you.
6 Upon your walls, Jerusalem,
I have stationed sentinels;
By day and by night,
they shall never be silent.
You who are to remind the LORD,
take no rest,
7 And give him no rest,
until he re-establishes Jerusalem
And makes it the praise of the earth.

The Blessings of Salvation for God's People

8† The LORD has sworn by his right hand
and by his mighty arm:
No more will I give your grain
as food to your enemies;
Nor shall foreigners drink the wine,
for which you toiled.*
9 But those who harvest shall eat,
and praise the LORD;
Those who gather shall drink
in my holy courts.*
10† Pass through, pass through the gates,
prepare a way for the people;*
Build up, build up the highway, clear it of stones,
raise up a standard over the nations.
11 The LORD has proclaimed
to the ends of the earth:
Say to daughter Zion,
"See, your savior comes!
See, his reward is with him,
his recompense before him."*

†

61:10–11 The new life of the restored Zion is expressed in nuptial (cf. also 62:5) and agricultural (cf. v. 3; 60:21) imagery.

62:1–12 As in chap. 60, the prophet addresses Zion, announcing the reversal of her fortune. Several motifs reappear: light and glory (60:1–3, 19–20), tribute of nations (60:11), and especially the marriage (61:10; cf. also 54:5–8).

62:8–9 Peace and prosperity are indicated by the absence of invaders who would live off the land.

62:10–11 The gates of Babylon are to be opened for the exiles to return, led by the Lord, as in 40:3–5, 10.

61:10 1 Sm 2:1; Ps 138:1–2.
62:1 Is 42:14; 64:22.
62:2 Rev 2:17; 3:12.
62:4 Is 49:15–16; 54:7–8.
62:8 Is 52:10.
62:9 Dt 12:17–18; 14:23.
62:10 Is 58:14.
62:11 Is 40:10.

12 They shall be called "The Holy People,"
"The Redeemed of the LORD."
And you shall be called "Cared For,"
"A City Not Forsaken."*

The Divine Warrior†

63 1 Who is this that comes from Edom,
in crimsoned garments, from Bozrah?
Who is this, glorious in his apparel,
striding in the greatness of his strength?
"It is I, I who announce vindication,
mighty to save."*
2 Why is your apparel red,
and your garments like one who treads the wine press?*
3 "The wine press I have trodden alone,
and from the peoples no one was with me.
I trod them in my anger,
and trampled them down in my wrath;
Their blood spurted on my garments,
all my apparel I stained.
4 For a day of vindication was in my heart,
my year for redeeming had come.*
5 I looked about, but there was no one to help,
I was appalled that there was no one to lend support;
So my own arm brought me victory
and my own wrath lent me support.*
6 I trampled down the peoples in my anger,
I made them drunk in my wrath,
and I poured out their blood upon the ground."

Prayer for the Return of God's Favor

7† The loving deeds of the LORD I will recall,
the glorious acts of the LORD,
Because of all the LORD has done for us,
the immense goodness to the house of Israel,
Which he has granted according to his mercy
and his many loving deeds.*
8 He said: "They are indeed my people,
children who are not disloyal."
So he became their savior
9 in their every affliction.
It was not an envoy or a messenger,
but his presence that saved them.
Because of his love and pity
the LORD redeemed them,
Lifting them up and carrying them
all the days of old.*
10 But they rebelled
and grieved his holy spirit;
So he turned to become their enemy,
and warred against them.*

11 Then they remembered the days of old, of Moses, his servant:

Where is the one who brought up out of the sea
the shepherd of his flock?
Where is the one who placed in their midst
his holy spirit,*
12 Who guided Moses by the hand,
with his glorious arm?
Where is the one who divided the waters before them—
winning for himself an everlasting renown—
13 Who guided them through the depths,
like horses in open country?
14 As cattle going down into the valley,
they did not stumble.
The spirit of the LORD guided them.
Thus you led your people,
to make for yourself a glorious name.
15 Look down from heaven and regard us
from your holy and glorious palace!
Where is your zealous care and your might,
your surge of pity?*
Your mercy hold not back!
16 For you are our father.
Were Abraham not to know us,
nor Israel to acknowledge us,
You, LORD, are our father,
our redeemer you are named from of old.
17 Why do you make us wander, LORD, from your ways,
and harden our hearts so that we do not fear you?†
Return for the sake of your servants,
the tribes of your heritage.
18 Why have the wicked invaded your holy place,

---

† **63:1–6** Two questions are raised at the approach of a majestic figure coming from Edom. It is the Lord, his garments red with the blood from the judgment battle. Edom (its capital Bozrah) plundered Judah after the fall of Jerusalem; cf. 34:5–17. *Wine press:* here a symbol of a bloody judgment; cf. Lam 1:15; Jl 4:13.

63:7–64:11 This lament of the exilic community recalls God's protection, and especially the memories of the exodus (vv. 7–14), before begging the Lord to come once more to their aid (63:15–64:3), as they confess their sins (64:4–11). The prayer is marked by God's "holy spirit" (63:10–11, 14) and fatherhood (63:8, 9, 16; 64:7).

63:17 The hardening of the heart (Ex 4:21; 7:3) serves to explain Israel's sins—a motif to induce the Lord to relent.

---

* **62:12** Is 62:4.
63:1 Is 34:6; 49:19.
63:2 Rev 19:13.
63:4 Is 34:8; 61:2.
63:5 Is 59:16.
63:7 Is 26:15.
63:9 Dt 4:37–40.
63:10 Dt 32:15; Ps 51:12.
63:11 Heb 13:20.
63:15 Dt 26:15; Bar 2:16.

why have our enemies trampled your
sanctuary?
19† Too long have we been like those you do not
rule,

Pray It!

The Master Potter

Have you ever seen a potter at work? Perhaps you have even made pottery yourself. Pottery making is still practiced today much as it was at the time of Third Isaiah: The potter takes a lump of moist clay and begins to shape it by hand, with an image in mind of what the finished product will look like. The artisan then puts the piece of clay on a potter's wheel and spins the wheel, continuing to form the pot with his or her hands. Because it is designed by hand, rather than mass-produced by machine, each work of the potter is original; there is no other just like it.

The image of God as a potter and each of us as a clay pot reminds us of the second Creation story, where God scoops up clay from the earth and forms the first human being and breathes life into the being (see Gn 2:7). It also reminds us of the description in Psalm 139 of our being knit together in our mother's womb.

The idea of God's hands shaping us like clay is intimate and comforting. No one but the potter knows how much time and love went into the fashioning of a particular pot. The potter gives each pot its own special design and markings. The potter also knows its flaws. The potter and the pot share a bond that seems much like the one between each of us and God. Isaiah 64:7 indeed gives us a vivid and beautiful image for God's relationship with each of us (see also Jer 18:1–6).

In your prayer, reflect or journal on the following questions:

- How has God molded you as a unique person?
- What are your special features and markings (gifts), and what are your flaws (weaknesses)?
- How is God still molding you?

▶ **Is 64:7**

on whom your name is not invoked.
Oh, that you would rend the heavens and
come down,
with the mountains quaking before you,*

64 1 As when brushwood is set ablaze,
or fire makes the water boil!
Then your name would be made known to
your enemies
and the nations would tremble before you,
2 While you worked awesome deeds we could
not hope for,†
3 such as had not been heard of from of old.
No ear has ever heard, no eye ever seen,
any God but you
working such deeds for those who wait for
him.*
4 Would that you might meet us doing right,
that we might be mindful of you in our
ways!
Indeed, you are angry; we have sinned,
we have acted wickedly.
5 We have all become like something unclean,
all our just deeds are like polluted rags;
We have all withered like leaves,
and our crimes carry us away like the wind.*
6 There are none who call upon your name,
none who rouse themselves to take hold of
you;
For you have hidden your face from us
and have delivered us up to our crimes.

A Final Plea

7† Yet, LORD, you are our father;
we are the clay and you our potter:
we are all the work of your hand.
8 Do not be so very angry, LORD,
do not remember our crimes forever;
look upon us, who are all your people!
9 Your holy cities have become a wilderness;
Zion has become wilderness, Jerusalem
desolation!*
10 Our holy and glorious house
in which our ancestors praised you
Has been burned with fire;
all that was dear to us is laid waste.
11 Can you hold back, LORD, after all this?

†

63:19–64:3 A new theophany, like Sinai of old, is invoked so that Israel's enemies will be humbled by God's intervention.

64:2 The translation here omits some words repeated in the Hebrew from 63:19 ("would that you would come down, with the mountains trembling before you").

64:7–11 The motifs of father (63:16) and creator (clay and potter, 29:16; 45:9) are adduced to move the Lord to action in view of the damage done to his "holy cities" and "glorious house."

63:19 Ps 144:5; Mk 1:10.
64:3 1 Cor 2:9.
64:5 Is 1:30; 34:4.
64:9 Ps 79:1; Lam 1.

Can you remain silent, and afflict us so
severely?

65

1† I was ready to respond to those who
did not ask,
to be found by those who did not seek me.
I said: Here I am! Here I am!
To a nation that did not invoke my name.*
2 I have stretched out my hands all day
to a rebellious people,
Who walk in a way that is not good,
following their own designs;*
3 A people who provoke me
continually to my face,
Offering sacrifices in gardens
and burning incense on bricks,
4 Sitting in tombs
and spending the night in caves,
Eating the flesh of pigs,
with broth of unclean meat in their dishes;
5 Crying out, "Hold back,
do not come near me, lest I render you
holy!"†
These things are smoke in my nostrils,
a fire that burns all the day.
6 See, it stands written before me;
I will not remain quiet until I have repaid
in full
7 Your crimes and the crimes of your ancestors
as well,
says the LORD.
Since they burned incense on the mountains,
and insulted me on the hills,
I will at once pour out in full measure
their recompense into their laps.

Fate of the Just and Unjust in Israel

8† Thus says the LORD:
As when the juice is pressed from a cluster,
and someone says, "Do not destroy it,
for there is still good in it,"
So will I do for the sake of my servants:
I will not destroy them all.
9 From Jacob I will bring forth offspring,
from Judah, those who are to possess my
mountains;
My chosen ones shall possess the land,
my servants shall dwell there.
10 Sharon shall become a pasture for the flocks,
the Valley of Achor a resting place for the
cattle,
for my people who have sought me.*
11 But you who forsake the LORD,
who forget my holy mountain,
Who spread a table for Fortune
and fill cups of mixed wine for Destiny,†
12 You I will destine for the sword;
you shall all bow down for slaughter;
Because I called and you did not answer,
I spoke and you did not listen,
But did what is evil in my sight
and things I do not delight in, you chose,*
13 therefore thus says the Lord GOD:
My servants shall eat,
but you shall go hungry;
My servants shall drink,
but you shall be thirsty;
My servants shall rejoice,
but you shall be put to shame;
14 My servants shall shout
for joy of heart,
But you shall cry out for grief of heart,
and howl for anguish of spirit.
15 You will leave your name for a curse to my
chosen ones
when the Lord GOD slays you,
and calls his servants by another name.
16 Whoever invokes a blessing in the land
shall bless by the God of truth;†
Whoever takes an oath in the land
shall swear by the God of truth;
For the hardships of the past shall be
forgotten
and hidden from my eyes.

A World Renewed

17† See, I am creating new heavens
and a new earth;
The former things shall not be remembered
nor come to mind.*
18 Instead, shout for joy and be glad forever
in what I am creating.
Indeed, I am creating Jerusalem to be a joy
and its people to be a delight;

†

65:1–7 These verses serve as a response to the preceding questions about God's inaction (64:6, 11). It is not God who has been absent, but the people who have walked away from God by idolatrous acts and rituals (vv. 3–4). That is the reason for their punishment (vv. 6–7).

65:5 *Render you holy*: unclean food is what these people claim has made them sacred! The prophet ridicules them. Sacredness was understood as something communicable (cf. Ex 19:9–15).

65:8 This verse reflects the remnant theology found elsewhere in the Book of Isaiah: 1:8–9; 4:3; 6:11–13; etc.

65:11–12 *Destiny*: the play on words is found in the Hebrew, in which "destiny" and "destine" are *menî* and *manîthî*.

65:16 *God of truth*: lit., "God of Amen," i.e., the one who keeps his word.

65:17–18 The new creation (cf. 66:22) is described with apocalyptic exuberance: long life, material prosperity, and so forth. As the former events in 43:18 are to be forgotten, so also the new creation wipes out memory of the first creation.

*

65:1 Rom 10:20.
65:2 Rom 10:21.
65:10 Hos 2:17.
65:12 Is 66:4; Prv 1:24; Jer 7:13.
65:17 Is 66:22; Rev 21:1.

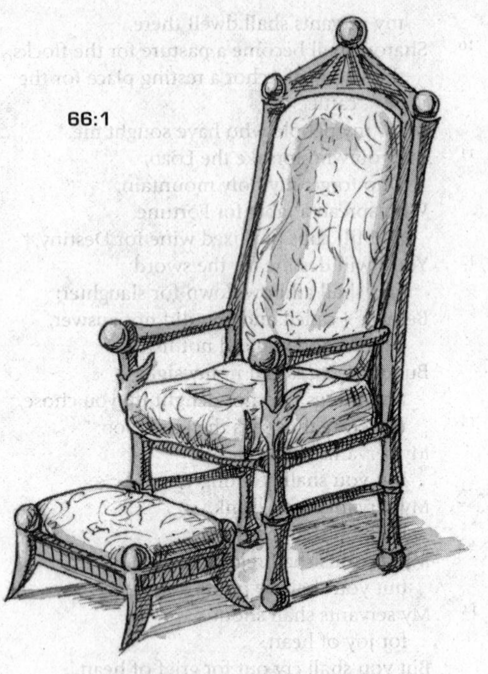

66:1

19 I will rejoice in Jerusalem
and exult in my people.
No longer shall the sound of weeping be
heard there,
or the sound of crying;
20 No longer shall there be in it
an infant who lives but a few days,
nor anyone who does not live a full lifetime;
One who dies at a hundred years shall be
considered a youth,
and one who falls short of a hundred shall
be thought accursed.*
21 They shall build houses and live in them,
they shall plant vineyards and eat their
fruit;
22 They shall not build and others live there;
they shall not plant and others eat.
As the years of a tree, so the years of my
people;
and my chosen ones shall long enjoy
the work of their hands.
23 They shall not toil in vain,
nor beget children for sudden destruction;
For they shall be a people blessed by the LORD
and their descendants with them.
24 Before they call, I will answer;
while they are yet speaking, I will hear.
25† The wolf and the lamb shall pasture together,
and the lion shall eat hay like the ox—
but the serpent's food shall be dust.*
None shall harm or destroy
on all my holy mountain, says the LORD.

True and False Worship

66 1† Thus says the LORD:
The heavens are my throne,
the earth, my footstool.
What house can you build for me?
Where is the place of my rest?*
2 My hand made all these things
when all of them came to be—oracle of the
LORD.
This is the one whom I approve:
the afflicted one, crushed in spirit,
who trembles at my word.*
3† The one slaughtering an ox, striking a man,
sacrificing a lamb, breaking a dog's neck,
Making an offering of pig's blood,
burning incense, honoring an idol—
These have chosen their own ways,
and taken pleasure in their own
abominations.*
4 I in turn will choose affliction for them
and bring upon them what they fear.
Because when I called, no one answered,
when I spoke, no one listened.
Because they did what was evil in my sight,
and things I do not delight in they chose,*
5 Hear the word of the LORD,
you who tremble at his word!
Your kin who hate you
and cast you out because of my name say,
"May the LORD show his glory,
that we may see your joy";
but they shall be put to shame.
6 A voice roaring from the city,
a voice from the temple;
The voice of the LORD
rendering recompense to his enemies!*

Blessings of Prosperity and Consolation

7† Before she is in labor,
she gives birth;*

---

† **65:25** The imagery reflects the ideal era described in 11:6–9; see note there.

66:1–2 The Lord rejects the abuses associated with Temple worship in order to emphasize his concern for the sincere worshiper.

66:3–6 The sacrificial abuses listed will only merit punishment. The true worshipers, the downtrodden, are those who "tremble" (vv. 2, 5) at God's word. Although they are ridiculed by those who reject them (v. 5), the latter will be afflicted with divine punishment; their "choice" will be met by the Lord's choice (v. 4).

66:7–9 The renewal of Zion is pictured in terms of a miraculous, instantaneous birth, facilitated by God's intervention.

---

* **65:20** Dt 4:40.
65:25 Is 11:6–9.
66:1 2 Sm 7:4–7; 1 Kgs 8:27; Acts 7:49; 17:24.
66:2 Ps 24:1–2.
66:3 Lv 11:7.
66:4 Is 65:12; Prv 1:24; Jer 7:13.
66:6 Jl 4:16; Am 1:2.
66:7–9 Is 49:18–21; 54:1.

Before her pangs come upon her,
she delivers a male child.
8 Who ever heard of such a thing,
or who ever saw the like?
Can a land be brought forth in one day,
or a nation be born in a single moment?
Yet Zion was scarcely in labor
when she bore her children.
9 Shall I bring a mother to the point of birth,
and yet not let her child be born? says the Lord.
Or shall I who bring to birth
yet close her womb? says your God.
10† Rejoice with Jerusalem and be glad because of her,
all you who love her;
Rejoice with her in her joy,
all you who mourn over her—*
11 So that you may nurse and be satisfied
from her consoling breast;
That you may drink with delight
at her abundant breasts!
12 For thus says the Lord:
I will spread prosperity over her like a river,
like an overflowing torrent,
the wealth of nations.
You shall nurse, carried in her arms,
cradled upon her knees;
13 As a mother comforts her child,
so I will comfort you;
in Jerusalem you shall find your comfort.*
14 You will see and your heart shall exult,
and your bodies shall flourish like the grass;
The Lord's power shall be revealed to his servants,
but to his enemies, his wrath.
15 For see, the Lord will come in fire,
his chariots like the stormwind;
To wreak his anger in burning rage
and his rebuke in fiery flames.
16 For with fire the Lord shall enter into judgment,
and, with his sword, against all flesh;
Those slain by the Lord shall be many.*

17 † Those who sanctify and purify themselves
to go into the gardens, following one who stands
within, eating pig's flesh, abominable things,
and mice, shall all together come to an end, with
their deeds and purposes—oracle of the Lord.

IS

God Gathers the Nations

18 † I am coming to gather all nations and
tongues; they shall come and see my glory.* 19 I
will place a sign among them; from them I will
send survivors to the nations: to Tarshish, Put
and Lud, Mosoch, Tubal and Javan, to the dis-
tant coastlands which have never heard of my
fame, or seen my glory; and they shall proclaim
my glory among the nations. 20 They shall bring
all your kin from all the nations as an offering
to the Lord, on horses and in chariots, in carts,
upon mules and dromedaries, to Jerusalem, my
holy mountain, says the Lord, just as the Israel-
ites bring their grain offering in a clean vessel to
the house of the Lord. 21 Some of these I will take
as priests and Levites, says the Lord.

22 Just as the new heavens and the new earth
which I am making
Shall endure before me—oracle of the Lord—
so shall your descendants and your name endure.*
23 From new moon to new moon,
and from sabbath to sabbath,
All flesh shall come to worship
before me, says the Lord.*
24† They shall go out and see the corpses*
of the people who rebelled against me;
For their worm shall not die,
their fire shall not be extinguished;
and they shall be an abhorrence to all flesh.

†

66:10–16 The poet addresses the children born of Jerusalem, their mother. In v. 13 the metaphor switches to the Lord as mother (cf. 49:15), comforting her charges but destroying the enemies.

66:17 This verse seems to have some connection with 65:2–3.

66:18–21 God summons the neighboring nations to Zion and from among them will send some to far distant lands to proclaim the divine glory. *All your kin*: Jews in exile. The "gathering of the people and the nations" is an eschatological motif common in the prophetic tradition; cf. 56:8.

66:24 God's enemies lie dead outside the walls of the New Jerusalem; just as in the past, corpses, filth and refuse lay in the Valley of Hinnom (Gehenna) outside the city; cf. 34:1–4; 2 Kgs 23:10.

66:10 Tb 13:14.
66:13 Is 40:1; 49:13.
66:16 Lv 11:29.
66:18 Is 56:1, 8; 59:20.
66:22 Is 65:17; Rev 21:1.
66:23 Is 1:13.
66:24 Is 1:27–28; Mk 9:45.

The Book of **Jeremiah**

Imagine you're watching a movie. One of the leading characters imposes severe hardships on others and then goes off to dine in luxury. Immediately, you know the character is a villain. Another leading character calls for others to endure sacrifice and lives under the same conditions as they do. You know this is a hero, because heroes practice what they preach. Jeremiah the prophet was such a hero; he not only preached a hard message but accepted the trials that came with it.

In Depth

At the beginning of Jeremiah's prophetic ministry, King Josiah ruled the southern kingdom of Judah (see 2 Chronicles, chapters 34–35). He was a good king who expanded Judah's territory and started a religious reform. Jeremiah approved of Josiah and Josiah's reforms, but he was afraid they were too little, too late. Chapters 2–5 of his book contain his prophecies during Josiah's rule. In them, he speaks out against Israel's sin and corruption but hopes things will improve if the people turn to God (see 4:1–2). Unfortunately, King Josiah was suddenly killed in battle, and things went from bad to worse.

Kings Jehoiakim and Zedekiah were the main rulers who followed Josiah, and they were Josiah's complete opposite (see 2 Chr 36:5–14). Both were ruthless, power hungry, and corrupt. During Jehoiakim's reign, Jeremiah had to go into hiding out of fear for his life. Chapters 7–20 of Jeremiah's book contain his prophecies during this time, when his preaching against the sins of Israel became stronger. Chapters 21–29 and 34–45 record his life and preaching during Zedekiah's reign—the last few years before the Babylonian Exile. While Zedekiah ruled, Jeremiah was imprisoned, beaten, and thrown into a well to die.

Jeremiah survived his experience in the well to see Jerusalem and the Temple destroyed by the Babylonians. To give the people hope that God was still on their side, he prophesied the destruction of all Israel's enemies, especially Babylon (see chapters 46–51).

Ultimately, Jeremiah realized that even a new king like David would not be enough to correct what was wrong. The people were unable to fulfill God's commandments because they had hearts of stone. In chapters 30–33, the Book of Consolation, Jeremiah said the Lord would make a new covenant with Israel in the future, and this time, the law would be written on the people's hearts (see 31:31–34).

At a Glance

- **I. Oracles in the Days of Josiah (1:1—6:30).**
- **II. Oracles Primarily from the Days of Jehoiakim (7:1—20:18).**
- **III. Oracles in the Last Years of Jerusalem (21:1—25:38).**
- **IV. The Temple Sermon (26:1–24; cf. 7:1–15).**
- **V. Controversies with the False Prophets (27:1—29:32).**
- **VI. Oracles of the Restoration of Israel and Judah (30:1—35:19).**
- **VII. Jeremiah and the Fall of Jerusalem (36:1—45:5).**
- **VIII. Oracles Against the Nations (46:1—51:64).**
- **IX. Historical Appendix (52:1–34).**

Quick Facts

Period Covered: from 626 to 583 BC

Inspired Authors: Jeremiah and his disciples, including Baruch

Themes: Israel's need for repentance, Jeremiah's struggles, the New Covenant

18:1–6

Jeremiah

I. Oracles in the Days of Josiah

1 1 The words of Jeremiah, son of Hilkiah, one
of the priests from Anathoth,† in the land of
Benjamin. 2 The word of the LORD came to him in
the days of Josiah, son of Amon, king of Judah, in
the thirteenth year of his reign,* 3 and again in the
days of Jehoiakim, son of Josiah, king of Judah,
until the end of the eleventh year of Zedekiah,
son of Josiah, king of Judah—down to the exile
of Jerusalem, in the fifth month.*

Call of Jeremiah

4 The word of the LORD came to me:
5 Before I formed you in the womb I knew you,
before you were born I dedicated you,
a prophet to the nations I appointed you.†*
6 "Ah, Lord GOD!" I said,
"I do not know how to speak. I am too young!"†
7 But the LORD answered me,
Do not say, "I am too young."
To whomever I send you, you shall go;
whatever I command you, you shall speak.
8 Do not be afraid of them,
for I am with you to deliver you—oracle of the LORD.

9 Then the LORD extended his hand and touched
my mouth, saying to me,

See, I place my words in your mouth!*
10 Today I appoint you
over nations and over kingdoms,
To uproot and to tear down,
to destroy and to demolish,
to build and to plant.

11 The word of the LORD came to me: What do
you see, Jeremiah? "I see a branch of the almond
tree,"† I replied. 12 Then the LORD said to me: You
have seen well, for I am watching over my word
to carry it out. 13* A second time the word of the
LORD came to me: What do you see? I replied, "I
see a boiling kettle whose mouth is tipped away
from the north."†
14 The LORD said to me, And from the north evil
will pour out over all who dwell in the land.*

†

1:1 *Anathoth*: a village about three miles northeast of Jerusalem, to which Solomon had exiled Abiathar the priest (1 Kgs 2:26–27); it is likely that Jeremiah belonged to that priestly family.

1:5 Jeremiah was destined to become a prophet before his birth; cf. Is 49:1, 5; Lk 1:15; Gal 1:15–16. *I knew you*: I loved you and chose you. *I dedicated you*: I set you apart to be a prophet. *The nations*: the neighbors of Judah, along with Assyria, Babylonia, and Egypt.

1:6 *I am too young*: like Moses (Ex 3:11, 13; 4:10), Jeremiah at first resists God's call. This narrative is perhaps patterned after the story of Moses' call in order to identify Jeremiah as the prophet "like me" in Dt 18:15.

1:11 There is wordplay between the Hebrew noun *shaqed*, "almond tree," and the Hebrew verb *shoqed*, "watcher/watching." Because the almond tree begins to bloom in late winter in Palestine, it is called "the watcher" for the coming of spring. God is also "watcher," observing the fulfillment of the prophetic word.

1:13 *Kettle . . . the north*: symbol of an invasion from the north; cf. vv. 14–15.

*

1:2 Jer 25:3.
1:3 Jer 25:1.
1:5 Jer 49:1; Gal 1:15–16.
1:9 Dt 18:18; Is 6:7.
1:13 Ez 11:3, 7; 24:3.
1:14 Jer 4:6; 6:1.

Live It!

You Are Not Too Young!

Jeremiah was a young man when God tapped him on the shoulder. In response to God, Jeremiah said, "I do not know how to speak; I am too young" (verse 6). But God gave Jeremiah the words and the ability to become a hero.

When you need to do something difficult for the good of others, remember God's response to Jeremiah: "Do not say, 'I am too young'" (verse 7). God wants you to know that you too are capable of bringing about positive change in the world. God knows what you are able to do and say and be. Listen to God.

▶ Jer 1:4–10

15 Look, I am summoning
all the kingdoms of the north—oracle of
the LORD—
Each king shall come and set up his throne
in the gateways of Jerusalem,
Against all its surrounding walls
and against all the cities of Judah.*
16 I will pronounce my sentence against them
for all their wickedness in forsaking me,
In burning incense to other gods,
in bowing down to the works of their
hands.*
17 But you, prepare yourself;
stand up and tell them
all that I command you.
Do not be terrified on account of them,
or I will terrify you before them;
18 For I am the one who today
makes you a fortified city,
A pillar of iron, a wall of bronze,
against the whole land:
Against Judah's kings and princes,
its priests and the people of the land.*
19 They will fight against you, but not prevail
over you,
for I am with you to deliver you—oracle of
the LORD.

Infidelity of Israel†

2 [1]The word of the LORD came to me: [2]Go, cry
out this message for Jerusalem to hear!

I remember the devotion† of your youth,
how you loved me as a bride,
Following me in the wilderness,
in a land unsown.*
3 Israel was dedicated to the LORD,
the first fruits† of his harvest;
All who ate of it were held guilty,
evil befell them—oracle of the LORD.*
4 Listen to the word of the LORD, house of
Jacob!
All you clans of the house of Israel,
5 thus says the LORD:
What fault did your ancestors find in me
that they withdrew from me,
Went after emptiness,
and became empty themselves?*
6 They did not ask, "Where is the LORD
who brought us up from the land of
Egypt,
Who led us through the wilderness,
through a land of wastes and ravines,
A land of drought and darkness,
a land which no one crosses,
where no one dwells?"*
7 I brought you into the garden land
to eat its fine fruits,
But you entered and defiled my land,
you turned my heritage into an
abomination.*
8 The priests did not ask,
"Where is the LORD?"
The experts in the law† did not know me:
the shepherds rebelled against me.
The prophets prophesied by Baal,
and went after useless idols.*
9 Therefore I will again accuse you—oracle of
the LORD—
even your children's children I will accuse.*
10 Cross to the coast of Cyprus and see,

---

† **2:1–3:5** These chapters may contain some of Jeremiah's early preaching. He portrays Israel as the wife of the Lord, faithful only in the beginning, when she walked behind him (2:2–3, 5; 3:1). Consistent with the marriage metaphor, he describes her present unfaithfulness as adultery (2:20; 3:2–3); now she walks behind the Baals.

2:2 *Devotion*: Heb. *hesed*; Israel's gratitude, fidelity, and love for God.

2:3 *First fruits*: the first yield of a harvest offered as a sign of dependence on and gratitude toward the Lord of the land, thus divine property. Israel, then, is a gift made to God, set apart for his use; cf. Ex 23:19.

2:8 *Experts in the law*: the priests. *The shepherds*: the kings and nobles.

---

* **1:15** Jer 6:22.
1:16 Is 2:8.
1:18 Jer 6:27; 15:20; Ez 3:8.
2:2 Dt 2:7; 32:9–12; Mi 6:4.
2:3 Jer 12:14; Ex 4:22; Dt 7:6; 14:2.
2:5 2 Kgs 17:15; Is 5:4; Mi 6:3.
2:6 Ex 20:2–3; Dt 8:14; Is 63:11–14.
2:7 Lv 18:24–25; Dt 8:7–10; 32:13–14.
2:8 Jer 8:8–9; 23:1, 13.
2:9 Ex 20:5.

send to Kedar† and carefully inquire:
Where has anything like this been done?
11 Does any other nation change its gods?—
even though they are not gods at all!
But my people have changed their glory
for useless things.*
12 Be horrified at this, heavens;
shudder, be appalled—oracle of the LORD.
13 Two evils my people have done:
they have forsaken me, the source of living waters;
They have dug themselves cisterns,
broken cisterns that cannot hold water.*
14 Is Israel a slave, a house-born servant?†
Why then has he become plunder?
15 Against him lions roar,
they raise their voices.
They have turned his land into a waste;
his cities are charred ruins, without an inhabitant.*
16 Yes, the people of Memphis† and Tahpanhes
shave the crown of your head.
17 Has not forsaking the LORD, your God,
done this to you?*
18 And now, why go to Egypt,†
to drink the waters of the Nile?
Why go to Assyria,
to drink the waters of the River?
19 Your own wickedness chastises you,
your own infidelities punish you.
Know then, and see, how evil and bitter
is your forsaking the LORD, your God,
And your showing no fear of me,
oracle of the Lord, the GOD of hosts.*
20 Long ago you broke your yoke,*
you tore off your bonds.
You said, "I will not serve."
On every high hill, under every green tree,
you sprawled and served as a prostitute.†
21 But I had planted you as a choice vine,
all pedigreed stock;
How could you turn out so obnoxious to me,
a spurious vine?*
22 Even if you scour it with lye,
and use much soap,
The stain of your guilt is still before me,
oracle of the Lord GOD.*

Introducing...

Jeremiah

Have you ever felt ridiculed for defending your values or doing a good deed? If so, then you can probably relate to Jeremiah, who once told God:

> You seduced me, LORD, and I let myself be seduced;
> . . . .
> All day long I am an object of laughter;
> everyone mocks me.
> (Jer 20:7)

Jeremiah knew what it was like to be rejected for delivering God's message.

Jeremiah was born in 645 BC of a priestly family from a northern Israelite tribe. He was very young when he began his prophetic career. Like Isaiah, Jeremiah was a prophet for all seasons. He was both optimistic (see chapter 31) and condemning (see 22:18–23). He was courageous (see chapter 37), enduring beatings, imprisonment, and even being thrown into a well to die (see 38:1–6) for the sake of delivering God's message. He loved his people so much that he was sometimes called the weeping prophet because of his bitter tears for them and their fast-approaching doom (see 9:1; 13:7).

The Book of Jeremiah gives us a fascinating inside look at the prophet's relationship with God. Several passages, called the Confessions of Jeremiah, are personal accounts of his struggles with God (see 12:1–6, 15:10–21, 17:12–18, 18:18–23, 20:7–18). If you take the time to read these passages, you may find that your own doubts and struggles aren't all that different.

23 How can you say, "I am not defiled,
I have not pursued the Baals"?
Consider your conduct in the Valley,†

† **2:10** *Kedar*: a nomadic tribe in north Arabia. Cyprus and Kedar represent west and east.

2:14 *House-born servant*: one born in the master's house, in contrast to a slave acquired by purchase or as a captive; cf. Lv 22:11.

2:16 *Memphis*: the capital of Lower Egypt. *Tahpanhes*: a frontier city of Egypt, east of the Delta. *Shave the crown of your head*: an image for Egypt plundering Judah; perhaps a reference to the capture of King Jehoahaz in 609 B.C. (2 Kgs 23:34).

2:18 Egypt and Assyria were the competing foreign powers favored by rival parties within Judah. The desire for such foreign alliances is a further desertion of the Lord, the source of living waters (v. 13), in favor of the above-named powers, symbolized by the waters of the Nile and the Euphrates rivers.

2:20 *Served as a prostitute*: idolatry (because Israel is the "bride" of God); cf. vv. 2–3.

2:23 *The Valley*: probably Ben-hinnom, south of Jerusalem, site

* **2:11** Jer 16:20; Ps 106:20.
2:13 Jer 17:13; Ps 36:9; Is 1:4.
2:15 Jer 9:11.
2:17 Jer 4:18; 30:15.
2:19 Prv 5:22; Hos 5:5.
2:20 Jer 3:6, 13; Jgs 10:6.
2:21 Ex 15:17; Ps 80:9; Is 5:4.
2:22 Jb 9:30.

recall what you have done:
A skittish young camel,
running back and forth,
24 a wild donkey bred in the wilderness,
Sniffing the wind in her desire—
who can restrain her lust?
None seeking her need tire themselves;
in her time they will find her.
25 Stop wearing out your feet
and parching your throat!
But you say, "No use! No!
How I love these strangers,
after them I must go."*
26 As the thief is shamed when caught,
so shall the house of Israel be shamed:
They, their kings, their princes,
their priests and their prophets;*
27 They say to a piece of wood, "You are my
father,"
and to a stone, "You gave me birth."
They turn their backs to me, not their faces;
yet in their time of trouble they cry out,
"Rise up and save us!"
28 Where are the gods you made for yourselves?
Let them rise up!
Will they save you in your time of trouble?
For as numerous as your cities
are your gods, O Judah!
And as many as the streets of Jerusalem
are the altars you have set up for Baal.*
29 Why are you arguing with me?
You have all rebelled against me—oracle of
the LORD.
30 In vain I struck your children;
correction they did not take.
Your sword devoured your prophets
like a ravening lion.*
31 You people of this generation,
consider the word of the Lord:
Have I become a wilderness to Israel,
a land of gloom?
Why then do my people say, "We have
moved on,
we will not come to you any more"?
32 Does a young woman forget her jewelry,
a bride her sash?
Yet my people have forgotten me
days without number.*
33 How well you pick your way
when seeking love!
In your wickedness,
you have gone by ways unclean!
34 On your clothing is
the life-blood of the innocent,
you did not find them committing burglary;
35 Nonetheless you say, "I am innocent;
at least, his anger is turned away from me."
Listen! I will judge you
on that word of yours, "I have not sinned."
36 How frivolous you have become
in changing your course!
By Egypt you will be shamed,
just as you were shamed by Assyria.*
37 From there too you will go out,
your hands upon your head;
For the LORD has rejected those in whom you
trust,
with them you will have no success.*

3 1 If a man divorces his wife*
and she leaves him
and then becomes the wife of another,
Can she return to the first?†
Would not this land be wholly defiled?
But you have played the prostitute with many
lovers,
and yet you would return to me!—oracle of
the LORD.
2 Raise your eyes to the heights, and look,
where have men not lain with you?
Along the roadways you waited for them
like an Arabian† in the wilderness.
You defiled the land
by your wicked prostitution.*
3 Therefore the showers were withheld,
the spring rain did not fall.
But because you have a prostitute's brow,
you refused to be ashamed.*
4 Even now do you not call me, "My father,
you are the bridegroom of my youth?
5 Will he keep his wrath forever,
will he hold his grudge to the end?"
This is what you say; yet you do
all the evil you can.

Judah and Israel

6 The LORD said to me in the days of King Jo-
siah: Do you see what rebellious Israel has done?

---

† of the sanctuary of Topheth, where children were sacrificed to Molech; cf. 7:31.

3:1 *Can she return to the first?*: i.e., her first husband. Here the Hebrew is emended in light of the Septuagint and Dt 24:1–4, which forbids a man to take back a woman once he has divorced her. The prophet uses this analogy to illustrate the presumption of Judah, the unfaithful wife, who assumes she can easily return to the Lord after worshiping other gods.

3:2 *An Arabian*: here depicted as a marauder lying in wait for caravans.

---

* **2:25** Jer 18:12.
2:26 Jer 48:27; Rom 6:21.
2:28 Jer 11:13; Dt 32:38; Jgs 10:14.
2:30 Jer 5:3; Neh 9:26.
2:32 Jer 13:25; Dt 32:18.
2:36 2 Chr 28:16–21.
2:37 2 Sm 13:19.
3:1 Dt 24:1–4.
3:2 Ex 16:24–25.
3:3 Jer 6:15; 8:12.

Cultural Connection

Hispanics Assume Their Mission as Prophets

Jeremiah and many of the other Old Testament prophets call for solidarity with the poor and oppressed. During the Third Encuentro Nacional Hispano de Pastoral, in 1985, Hispanics assumed their mission as prophets in contemporary society. They expressed their solidarity with the social groups in need of liberation and their desire to live and promote justice. The following statements are from the Encuentro:

- We, as Hispanic people, make a preferential option for and in solidarity with the poor and marginalized.
- We, as Hispanic people, make a preferential option for Hispanic youth so that they will participate at all levels of pastoral ministry.
- We, as Hispanic people, want to follow the line of a Church that promotes and exemplifies justice.
- We, as Hispanic people, wish to follow an approach of valuing and promoting women, recognizing their equality and dignity and their role in the Church, the family, and society.

(Secretariat for Hispanic Affairs, *Prophetic Voices*, p. 6)

She has gone up every high mountain, and under
every green tree she has played the prostitute.*
7 And I thought: After she has done all this, she
will return to me. But she did not return. Then,
even though that traitor her sister Judah, saw
8 that, in response to all the adulteries rebel Israel
had committed, I sent her away and gave her a
bill of divorce, nevertheless Judah, the traitor,
her sister, was not frightened; she too went off
and played the prostitute.* 9 With her casual
prostitution, she polluted the land, committing
adultery with stone and wood.* 10 In spite of all
this, Judah, the traitor, her sister, did not return
to me wholeheartedly, but insincerely—oracle
of the LORD.

Restoration of Israel

11 Then the LORD said to me: Rebel Israel is
more just than traitor Judah.* 12 Go, proclaim
these words toward the north, and say:

Return, rebel Israel—oracle of the LORD—
I will not remain angry with you;
For I am merciful, oracle of the LORD,
I will not keep my anger forever.*
13 Only admit your guilt:
how you have rebelled against the LORD,
your God,
How you ran here and there to strangers
under every green tree
and would not listen to my voice—oracle
of the LORD.*
14 Return, rebellious children—oracle of the
LORD—†
for I am your master;
I will take you, one from a city, two from a
clan,
and bring you to Zion.*
15 I will appoint for you shepherds after my own
heart,
who will shepherd you wisely and
prudently.*
16 When you increase in number and are fruitful
in the land—
oracle of the LORD—
They will in those days no longer say,
"The ark of the covenant of the LORD!"
They will no longer think of it, or remember it,
or miss it, or make another one.

17 At that time they will call Jerusalem "the
LORD's throne." All nations will gather together
there to honor the name of the LORD at Jerusa-
lem, and they will no longer stubbornly follow
their wicked heart.* 18 In those days the house
of Judah will walk alongside the house of Israel;

† **3:14–18** A remnant of Israel (v. 14) will reunite with Judah (v. 18). The former Israelite community, represented by the ark of the covenant, will be replaced by a universal alliance, symbolized by Jerusalem, the Lord's throne, to which all nations will be gathered (v. 17).

* **3:6** Jer 2:20; Dt 12:2. **3:8** 2 Kgs 17:6, 18–23; Ez 23:11. **3:9** Jer 2:27. **3:11** Ez 16:51; 23:11. **3:12** Dt 4:29–31. **3:13** Jer 2:20, 25; Lv 26:40. **3:14** Jer 23:3; Is 10:21–22. **3:15** Ez 34:23; Jn 21:15. **3:17** Is 2:2.

together they will come from the land of the north to the land which I gave your ancestors as a heritage.*

Conditions for Forgiveness

19 I thought:
How I would like to make you my children!
So I gave you a pleasant land,
the most beautiful heritage among the nations!
You would call me, "My Father," I thought,
and you would never turn away from me.*
20 But like a woman faithless to her lover,
thus have you been faithless to me,
house of Israel—oracle of the LORD.*
21 A cry is heard on the heights!
the plaintive weeping of Israel's children,
Because they have perverted their way,
they have forgotten the LORD, their God.
22 Return, rebellious children!
I will heal your rebellions.
"Here we are! We belong to you,
for you are the LORD, our God.*
23 Deceptive indeed are the hills,
the mountains, clamorous;
Only in the LORD our God
is Israel's salvation.*
24 The shameful thing† has devoured
our ancestors' worth from our youth,
Their sheep and cattle,
their sons and daughters.
25 Let us lie down in our shame,
let our disgrace cover us,
for we have sinned against the LORD, our God,
We and our ancestors, from our youth to this day;
we did not listen to the voice of the LORD, our God."*

4 1 If you return, Israel—oracle of the LORD—
return to me.
If you put your detestable things out of my sight,
and do not stray,*
2 And swear, "As the LORD lives,"†
in truth, in judgment, and in justice,
Then the nations shall bless themselves in him
and in him glory.*

3 For to the people of Judah and Jerusalem, thus says the LORD:

Till your untilled ground,
and do not sow among thorns.*
4 Be circumcised for the LORD,†
remove the foreskins of your hearts,
people of Judah and inhabitants of Jerusalem;
Or else my anger will break out like fire,
and burn so that no one can quench it,
because of your evil deeds.*

The Invasion from the North

5 Proclaim it in Judah,
in Jerusalem announce it;
Blow the trumpet throughout the land,
call out, "Fill the ranks!"
Say, "Assemble, let us march
to the fortified cities."
6 Raise the signal—to Zion!
Seek refuge! Don't stand there!
Disaster I bring from the north,
and great destruction.
7 Up comes the lion from its lair,
the destroyer of nations has set out,
has left its place,
To turn your land into a desolation,
your cities into an uninhabited waste.*
8 So put on sackcloth,
mourn and wail:
"The blazing anger of the LORD
has not turned away from us."*
9 In that day—oracle of the LORD—
The king will lose heart, and the princes;
the priests will be horrified,
and the prophets stunned.
10 "Ah! Lord GOD," they will say,
"You really did deceive† us
When you said: You shall have peace,
while the sword was at our very throats."*
11 At that time it will be said
to this people and to Jerusalem,
A scorching wind from the bare heights comes

†

3:24 *The shameful thing*: Heb. *bosheth* ("shame"), a term often substituted for the name of Baal, a Canaanite god worshiped at local shrines.

4:2 *As the LORD lives*: this oath, made sincerely, implies Israel's return and loyal adherence to God. Thus the ancient promises are fulfilled; cf. Gn 12:3; 18:18; 22:18; 26:4; Ps 72:17.

4:4 The external rite of circumcision accomplishes nothing unless it is accompanied by the removal of blindness and obstinacy of heart. Jeremiah's view is reflected in Rom 2:25, 29; 1 Cor 7:19; Gal 5:6; 6:13, 15.

4:10 *You really did deceive*: Jeremiah complains that the Lord misled the people by fostering their complacency, leaving them unprepared and unrepentant as judgment approaches.

*

3:18 Jer 30:3; 31:8.
3:19 Jer 31:9, 20; Is 63:16.
3:20 Jer 5:11.
3:22 Hos 3:5.
3:23 Jer 14:8.
3:25 Jer 16:11–12; 22:21.
4:1 Jer 25:5.
4:2 Jer 12:16; Dt 10:20; Is 65:16.
4:3 Hos 10:12; Mt 13:7, 22.
4:4 Jer 9:24.
4:7 Jer 2:15; 5:6.
4:8 Jer 6:26; Is 5:25.
4:10 Jer 6:14.

through the wilderness toward my
daughter, the people.†
Not to winnow, not to cleanse,
12 a strong wind from there comes at my
bidding.
Now I too pronounce
sentence upon them.*
13 See! like storm clouds he advances,
like a whirlwind, his chariots;
Swifter than eagles, his horses:
"Woe to us! we are ruined."
14 Cleanse your heart of evil, Jerusalem,
that you may be saved.
How long will you entertain
wicked schemes?
15 A voice proclaims it from Dan,
announces wickedness from Mount
Ephraim:
16 "Make this known to the nations,
announce it against Jerusalem:
Besiegers are coming from the distant land,
shouting their war cry against the cities of
Judah."*
17 Like watchers in the fields they surround her,
for she has rebelled against me—oracle of
the LORD.*
18 Your conduct, your deeds, have done this to
you;
how bitter is this evil of yours,
how it reaches to your very heart!*
19 My body! my body! how I writhe!†
The walls of my heart!
My heart beats wildly,
I cannot be still;
For I myself have heard the blast of the horn,
the battle cry.
20 Ruin upon ruin is reported;
the whole land is laid waste.
In an instant my tents are ravaged;
in a flash, my shelters.*
21 How long must I see the signal,
hear the blast of the horn!
22 My people are fools,
they do not know me;
They are senseless children,
without understanding;
They are wise at evil,
but they do not know how to do good.*
23 I looked at the earth—it was waste and void;
at the heavens—their light had gone out!*
24 I looked at the mountains—they were quaking!
All the hills were crumbling!
25 I looked—there was no one;
even the birds of the air had flown away!
26 I looked—the garden land was a wilderness,
with all its cities destroyed
before the LORD, before his blazing anger.*
27 For thus says the LORD:
The whole earth shall be waste,
but I will not wholly destroy it.*
28 Because of this the earth shall mourn,
the heavens above shall darken;
I have spoken, I will not change my mind,
I have decided, I will not turn back.*
29 At the shout of rider and archer
each city takes to flight;
They shrink into the thickets,
they scale the rocks:
All the cities are abandoned,
no one lives in them.
30 You now who are doomed, what are you doing
dressing in purple,
bedecking yourself with gold,
Enlarging your eyes with kohl?
You beautify yourself in vain!
Your lovers reject you,
they seek your life.
31 Yes, I hear the cry, like that of a woman in
labor,
like the anguish of a mother bearing her
first child—
The cry of daughter Zion gasping,
as she stretches out her hands:
"Ah, woe is me! I sink exhausted
before my killers!"*

Universal Corruption

5 1 Roam the streets of Jerusalem,
look about and observe,
Search through her squares,
to find even one
Who acts justly
and seeks honesty,
and I will pardon her!
2 They say, "As the LORD lives,"
but in fact they swear falsely.
3 LORD, do your eyes not search for honesty?
You struck them, but they did not flinch;
you laid them low, but they refused
correction;

† **4:11** *My daughter, the people*: the covenant people personified as a young woman. Ezekiel 16 presents Israel and Judah as female infants whom the Lord adopts and then abandons and punishes because they desire other lords.

4:19–21 Probably the prophet's own anguish at the coming destruction of Judah.

* **4:12** Jer 1:16.
4:16 Jer 5:15.
4:17 Jer 6:3.
4:18 Jer 2:17, 19.
4:20 Jer 10:20.
4:22 Dt 32:5–6, 28.
4:23 Is 24:1, 3.
4:26 Lv 26:31.
4:27 Jer 5:18.
4:28 Is 24:4.
4:31 Jer 6:24.

They set their faces harder than stone,
and refused to return.*
4 I thought: These are only the lowly,
they behave foolishly;
For they do not know the way of the LORD,
the justice of their God.*
5 Let me go to the leaders
and speak with them;
For they must know the way of the LORD,
the justice of their God.
But, one and all, they have broken the yoke,
torn off the harness.*
6 Therefore, lions from the forest slay them,
wolves of the desert ravage them,
Leopards keep watch round their cities:
all who come out are torn to pieces,
For their crimes are many,
their rebellions numerous.
7 Why should I pardon you?
Your children have forsaken me,
they swear by gods that are no gods.
I fed them, but they commit adultery;
to the prostitute's house they throng.
8 They are lustful stallions,
each neighs after the other's wife.*
9 Should I not punish them for this?—oracle of
the LORD;
on a nation like this should I not take
vengeance?
10 Climb her terraces, and ravage them,
destroy them completely.
Tear away her tendrils,
they do not belong to the LORD.*
11 For they have openly rebelled against me,
both the house of Israel and the house of
Judah—
oracle of the LORD.*
12 They denied the LORD,†
saying, "He is nothing,
No evil shall come to us,
neither sword nor famine shall we see.*
13 The prophets are wind,
and the word is not with them.
Let it be done to them!"
14 Therefore, thus says the LORD, the God of
hosts,
because you have said this—
See! I make my words
a fire in your mouth,
And this people the wood
that it shall devour!—
15 Beware! I will bring against you
a nation from far away,
O House of Israel—oracle of the LORD;
A long-lived nation, an ancient nation,
a people whose language you do not know,
whose speech you cannot understand.*
16 Their quivers are like open graves;
all of them are warriors.
17 They will devour your harvest and your bread,
devour your sons and your daughters,
Devour your sheep and cattle,
devour your vines and fig trees;
With their swords they will beat down
the fortified cities in which you trust.*

18 Yet even in those days—oracle of the LORD—
I will not completely destroy you.* 19 And when
they ask, "Why has the LORD our God done all
these things to us?" say to them, "As you have
abandoned me to serve foreign gods in your own
land, so shall you serve foreigners in a land not
your own."

20 Announce this to the house of Jacob,
proclaim it in Judah:
21 Pay attention to this,
you foolish and senseless people,
Who have eyes and do not see,
who have ears and do not hear.*
22 Should you not fear me—oracle of the LORD—
should you not tremble before me?
I made the sandy shore the sea's limit,
which by eternal decree it may not
overstep.
Toss though it may, it is to no avail;
though its billows roar, they cannot
overstep.*
23 But this people's heart is stubborn and
rebellious;
they turn and go away,
24 And do not say in their hearts,
"Let us fear the LORD, our God,
Who gives us rain
early and late,† in its time;
Who watches for us
over the appointed weeks of harvest."*
25 Your crimes have prevented these things,
your sins have turned these blessings away
from you.*

† 5:12 *They denied the LORD*: the people act as though God does not matter and will not interfere.

5:24 *Rain early and late*: autumn and spring rains respectively. *Appointed weeks of harvest*: the seven weeks between the Passover (Dt 16:9–10) and the feast of Weeks (Pentecost), when it did not ordinarily rain.

5:3 Jer 2:30.
5:4 Jer 8:7.
5:5 Jer 6:13.
5:8 Jer 13:27.
5:10 Jer 2:21.
5:11 Jer 3:20.
5:12 Jer 14:13; Is 28:15.
5:15 Dt 28:49.
5:17 Dt 28:31.
5:18 Jer 4:27.
5:21 Is 6:9.
5:22 Jb 38:10–11.
5:24 Gn 8:22; Dt 11:14.
5:25 Jer 2:17, 19.

26 For criminals lurk among my people;
like fowlers they set traps,
but it is human beings they catch.*
27 Their houses are as full of treachery
as a bird-cage is of birds;
Therefore they grow powerful and rich,
28 fat and sleek.
They pass over wicked deeds;
justice they do not defend
By advancing the claim of the orphan
or judging the cause of the poor.*
29 Shall I not punish these things?—oracle of the LORD;
on a nation such as this shall I not take vengeance?
30 Something shocking and horrible
has happened in the land:
31 The prophets prophesy falsely,
and the priests teach on their own authority;
Yet my people like it this way;
what will you do when the end comes?*

The Enemy at the Gates

6 1 Seek refuge, Benjaminites,
from the midst of Jerusalem!
Blow the trumpet in Tekoa,
raise a signal over Beth-haccherem;
For disaster threatens from the north,
and mighty destruction.*
2 Lovely and delicate
daughter Zion, you are ruined!
3 Against her, shepherds come with their flocks;†
all around, they pitch their tents against her;
each one grazes his portion.*
4 "Prepare for war against her,
Up! let us rush upon her at midday!"
"Woe to us! the day is waning,
evening shadows lengthen!"
5 "Up! let us rush upon her by night,
destroy her palaces!"*
6 For thus says the LORD of hosts:
Hew down her trees,
throw up a siege mound against Jerusalem.
Woe to the city marked for punishment;
there is nothing but oppression within her!*
7 As a well keeps its waters fresh,
so she keeps fresh her wickedness.
Violence and destruction resound in her;
ever before me are wounds and blows.*
8 Be warned, Jerusalem,
or I will be estranged from you,
And I will turn you into a wilderness,
a land where no one dwells.
9 Thus says the LORD of hosts:
Glean, glean like a vine
the remnant of Israel;
Pass your hand, like a vintager,
repeatedly over the tendrils.
10 To whom shall I speak?
whom shall I warn, and be heard?
See! their ears are uncircumcised,
they cannot pay attention;
See, the word of the LORD has become for them
an object of scorn, for which they have no taste.*
11 But the wrath of the LORD brims up within me,
I am weary of holding it in.
I will pour it out upon the child in the street,
upon the young men gathered together.
Yes, husband and wife will be taken,
elder with ancient.*
12 Their houses will fall to others,
their fields and their wives as well;
For I will stretch forth my hand
against those who dwell in the land—
oracle of the LORD.*
13 Small and great alike, all are greedy for gain;
prophet and priest, all practice fraud.*
14 They have treated lightly
the injury to my people:
"Peace, peace!" they say,
though there is no peace.*
15 They have acted shamefully, committing abominations,
yet they are not at all ashamed,
they do not know how to blush.
Therefore they will fall among the fallen;
in the time of their punishment they shall stumble,
says the LORD.*
16 Thus says the LORD:
Stand by the earliest roads,
ask the pathways of old,†
"Which is the way to good?" and walk it;
thus you will find rest for yourselves.
But they said, "We will not walk it."*
17 I raised up watchmen† for them:
"Pay attention to the sound of the trumpet!"
But they said, "We will not pay attention!"
18 Therefore hear, O nations,

†

6:3 *Shepherds come with their flocks*: foreign invaders with their armies.

6:16 *Pathways of old*: history and the lessons to be learned from it.

6:17 *Watchmen*: the prophets who, like Jeremiah, had upheld God's moral law.

*

5:26 Prv 1:11.
5:28 Jer 12:1; Is 1:23.
5:31 Jer 14:14; Mi 2:11.
6:1 Jer 1:14–15.
6:3 Jer 4:17.
6:5 2 Chr 36:19.
6:6 Jer 32:24; Zep 3:1–4.
6:7 Is 57:20.
6:10 Jer 7:26; 20:8.
6:11 Ez 9:6.
6:12 Jer 8:10; Dt 28:30–32.
6:13 Jer 8:10; 23:11.
6:14 Jer 8:11.
6:15 Jer 3:3; 8:12.
6:16 Jer 7:23–24; 18:15.

and know, O earth,
what I will do with them:
19 See, I bring evil upon this people,
the fruit of their own schemes,
Because they did not pay attention to my words,
because they rejected my law.*
20 Of what use to me is incense that comes from Sheba,
or sweet cane from far-off lands?
Your burnt offerings find no favor with me,
your sacrifices do not please me.*
21 Therefore, thus says the LORD:
See, I will place before this people
obstacles to trip them up;
Parents and children alike,
neighbors and friends shall perish.*
22 Thus says the LORD:
See, a people comes from the land of the north,
a great nation, rising from the very ends of the earth.*
23 Bow and javelin they wield;
cruel and pitiless are they.
They sound like the roaring sea
as they ride forth on horses,
Each in his place for battle
against you, daughter Zion.
24 We hear news of them;
our hands hang helpless,
Anguish takes hold of us,
pangs like a woman in childbirth.*
25 Do not go out into the field,
do not step into the street,
For the enemy has a sword;
terror on every side!
26 Daughter of my people, dress in sackcloth,
roll in the ashes.
Mourn as for an only child
with bitter wailing:
"How suddenly the destroyer
comes upon us!"*
27† A tester for my people I have appointed you,
to search and test their way.*
28 Arch-rebels are they all,
dealers in slander,
bronze and iron, all of them,
destroyers they are.
29 The bellows are scorched,
the lead is consumed by the fire;
In vain has the refiner refined,
the wicked are not drawn off.
30 "Silver rejected" they shall be called,
for the LORD has rejected them.

II. Oracles Primarily from the Days of Jehoiakim

The Temple Sermon†

7 1 The word came to Jeremiah from the LORD:
2 Stand at the gate of the house of the LORD
and proclaim this message there: Hear the word
of the LORD, all you of Judah who enter these
gates to worship the LORD! 3 Thus says the LORD
of hosts, the God of Israel: Reform your ways and
your deeds so that I may dwell with you in this
place.* 4 Do not put your trust in these deceptive
words: "The temple of the LORD! The temple of
the LORD! The temple of the LORD!"* 5 Only if you
thoroughly reform your ways and your deeds; if
each of you deals justly with your neighbor; 6 if
you no longer oppress the alien,† the orphan,
and the widow; if you no longer shed innocent
blood in this place or follow after other gods to
your own harm,* 7 only then will I let you con-
tinue to dwell in this place, in the land I gave
your ancestors long ago and forever.*
8 But look at you! You put your trust in de-
ceptive words to your own loss! 9 Do you think
you can steal and murder, commit adultery and
perjury, sacrifice to Baal, follow other gods that
you do not know,* 10 and then come and stand
in my presence in this house, which bears my
name, and say: "We are safe! We can commit all
these abominations again!"?* 11 Has this house
which bears my name become in your eyes a den
of thieves? I have seen it for myself!—oracle of
the LORD.* 12 Go to my place at Shiloh,† where
I made my name dwell in the beginning. See
what I did to it because of the wickedness of my
people Israel.* 13 And now, because you have
committed all these deeds—oracle of the LORD—
because you did not listen, though I spoke to
you untiringly, and because you did not answer,
though I called you, 14 I will do to this house,
which bears my name, in which you trust, and to

---

† **6:27–30** God appoints Jeremiah to be a "tester" of his people. The passage uses the metaphor of the refining of silver: the silver was extracted from lead ore, but the process in ancient times was inexact, so that sometimes all that was left was a scummy mess, to be thrown out.

7:1–15 The Temple of the Lord will not guarantee safety against enemy invasion or any other misfortune.

7:6 *The alien*: specially protected within Israelite society; cf. Ex 22:20; Nm 9:14; 15:14; Dt 5:14; 28:43.

7:12 *Shiloh*: an important sanctuary where the ark of the covenant was kept, according to the Books of Joshua, Judges, and 1 Samuel. In response to the corrupt behavior of the priests serving there, God allows the Philistines to destroy Shiloh and take the ark of the covenant. Cf. 1 Sm 1:9; 4:3–4; Ps 78:60, 68–69.

---

* **6:19** Prv 1:31.
6:20 Is 1:11; 43:24.
6:21 Is 8:14–15.
6:22 Jer 1:15; 5:15.
6:24 Jer 4:31.
6:26 Jer 25:34; Am 8:10.
6:27 Jer 1:18.
7:3 Jer 18:11; 26:13.
7:4 Mi 3:11.
7:6 Ex 22:21–24.
7:7 Dt 4:40.
7:9 Jer 44:17.
7:10 Jer 32:34.
7:11 Mt 21:13.
7:12 Jos 18:1.

the place which I gave you and your ancestors,
exactly what I did to Shiloh.* 15 I will cast you
out of my sight, as I cast away all your kindred,
all the offspring of Ephraim.*

Abuses in Worship

16 You, now, must not intercede for this peo-
ple! Do not raise a cry or prayer in their behalf!*
Do not press me, for I will not listen to you!
17 Do you not see what they are doing in the cities
of Judah, in the streets of Jerusalem? 18 The chil-
dren gather wood, their fathers light the fire, and
the women knead dough to make cakes for the
Queen of Heaven,† while libations are poured
out to other gods—all to offend me!* 19 Are
they really offending me—oracle of the LORD—
or rather themselves, to their own disgrace?*
20 Therefore, thus says the Lord GOD: my anger
and my wrath will pour out upon this place,
upon human being and beast, upon the trees of
the field and the fruits of the earth; it will burn
and not be quenched.*
21 Thus says the LORD of hosts, the God of Is-
rael: Heap your burnt offerings upon your sac-
rifices; eat up the meat! 22 In speaking to your
ancestors on the day I brought them out of the
land of Egypt, I gave them no command† con-
cerning burnt offering or sacrifice. 23 This rather
is what I commanded them: Listen to my voice;
then I will be your God and you shall be my peo-
ple. Walk exactly in the way I command you, so
that you may prosper.*
24 But they did not listen to me, nor did they
pay attention. They walked in the stubbornness
of their evil hearts and turned their backs, not
their faces, to me.* 25 From the day that your
ancestors left the land of Egypt even to this day,
I kept on sending all my servants the prophets
to you.* 26 Yet they have not listened to me nor
have they paid attention; they have stiffened
their necks and done worse than their ances-
tors.* 27 When you speak all these words to them,
they will not listen to you either. When you call
to them, they will not answer you. 28 Say to them:
This is the nation which does not listen to the
voice of the LORD, its God, or take correction.
Faithfulness has disappeared; the word itself is
banished from their speech.

Did You Know?

The Prophet and the Temple

In ancient Israel, the Temple was considered the dwelling place of God. Most Israelites felt that as long as the Temple stood, God was keeping the covenant promise to stay with Israel. They believed this because Jerusalem and Judea had been spared when the northern kingdom fell to Assyria (721 BC). The Israelites failed to remember that God's covenant with them was a mutual one—that they in turn had to keep their commitment to worship God alone.

Speaking for God at the gates of the Temple, Jeremiah told the people the Temple would be destroyed if Israel continued to disobey the commandments of the covenant (see how the sins he accused them of in Jeremiah 7:8–9 reflect the Ten Commandments). The destruction of the Temple would be a visible sign that the covenant had been broken—not by God, but by the people.

The Temple was destroyed, and then rebuilt. Centuries later, Jesus preached to a new generation who thought the Temple was a guarantee of God's presence and favor. He predicted the Temple would be destroyed again (see Mt 24:1–2).

▶ **Jer 7:1–14**

29 * Cut off your hair† and throw it away!
on the heights raise a lament;
The LORD has indeed rejected and cast off
the generation that draws down his wrath.

30 The people of Judah have done what is evil
in my eyes—oracle of the LORD. They have set
up their detestable things in the house which
bears my name, thereby defiling it.* 31 In the
Valley of Ben-hinnom† they go on building the
high places of Topheth to sacrifice their sons

† **7:18** *Queen of Heaven*: probably Astarte, goddess of fertility (cf. 1 Sm 31:10; 1 Kgs 11:5), worshiped particularly by women (cf. Jer 44:15–19). Such worship was evidently reinforced during the reign of King Manasseh (2 Kgs 21:3–7) and was revived after Josiah's death.

7:22 *I gave them no command*: right conduct rather than formal ritual was God's will concerning his people (v. 23).

7:29 *Hair*: the unshorn hair of the nazirite, regarded as sacred because of a vow, temporary or permanent, to abstain from cutting or shaving the hair; nazirites also avoided contact with a corpse and with all products of the vine; cf. Nm 6:4–8. The cutting of this hair was a sign of extreme mourning.

7:31 *Valley of Ben-hinnom*: this valley was probably south of Jerusalem. *Topheth*: perhaps, "fire pit."

* **7:14** Jer 26:9.
7:15 1 Kgs 9:7; 2 Kgs 17:23.
7:16 Jer 11:14; 14:11.
7:18 Jer 44:17, 19.
7:19 Jb 35:6.
7:20 Jer 36:29; 2 Kgs 22:17.
7:23 Jer 11:4; Lv 26:3, 12.
7:24 Jer 17:23.
7:25 2 Chr 36:15–16; Bar 1:19.
7:26 Jer 19:15; 2 Chr 30:8.
7:29 Jer 9:17–21.
7:30 Jer 32:34.

and daughters by fire, something I never com-
manded or considered. 32 Be assured! Days are
coming—oracle of the LORD—when they will no
longer say "Topheth" or "Valley of Ben-hinnom"
but "Valley of Slaughter." For want of space, To-
pheth will become burial ground.* 33 The corpses
of this people will be food for the birds of the
sky and beasts of the earth, which no one will
drive away.* 34 I will silence the cry of joy, the
cry of gladness, the voice of the bridegroom and
the voice of the bride, in the cities of Judah and
in the streets of Jerusalem; for the land will be
turned to rubble.*

8 1 At that time—oracle of the LORD—the bones
of the kings and princes of Judah, the bones
of the priests and the prophets, and the bones of
the inhabitants of Jerusalem will be brought out
of their graves* 2 and spread out before the sun,
the moon, and the whole host of heaven,† which
they loved and served, which they followed, con-
sulted, and worshiped. They will not be gathered
up for burial, but will lie like dung upon the
ground.* 3 Death will be preferred to life by all
the survivors of this wicked people who remain
in any of the places to which I banish them—
oracle of the LORD of hosts.

Israel's Conduct Incomprehensible

4 Tell them: Thus says the LORD:
When someone falls, do they not rise again?
if they turn away, do they not turn back?
5 Why then do these people resist
with persistent rebellion?
Why do they cling to deception,
refuse to turn back?*
6 I have listened closely:
they speak what is not true;
No one regrets wickedness,
saying, "What have I done?"
Everyone keeps on running their course,
like a horse dashing into battle.*
7 Even the stork in the sky
knows its seasons;
Turtledove, swift, and thrush
observe the time of their return,
But my people do not know
the order of the LORD.*
8 How can you say, "We are wise,*
we have the law of the LORD"?
See, that has been changed into falsehood
by the lying pen of the scribes!†
9 The wise are put to shame,
terrified, and trapped;
Since they have rejected the word of the LORD,
what sort of wisdom do they have?*

Shameless in Their Crimes

10 Therefore, I will give their wives to other men,
their fields to new owners.
Small and great alike, all are greedy for gain,
prophet and priest, all practice fraud.*
11 They have treated lightly
the injury to the daughter of my people:†
"Peace, peace!" they say,
though there is no peace.*
12 They have acted shamefully; they have done
abominable things,
yet they are not at all ashamed,
they do not know how to blush.
Hence they shall be among those who fall;
in their time of punishment they shall
stumble,
says the LORD.*

Threats of Punishment

13 I will gather them all in—oracle of the LORD:
no grapes on the vine,
No figs on the fig trees,
foliage withered!
Whatever I have given them is gone.
14 Why do we remain here?
Let us assemble and flee to the fortified
cities,
where we will meet our doom;
For the LORD our God has doomed us,
he has given us poisoned water to drink,
because we have sinned against the LORD.*
15 We wait for peace to no avail;
for a time of healing, but terror comes
instead.*
16 From Dan is heard
the snorting of horses;
The neighing of stallions
shakes the whole land.
They come to devour the land and everything
in it,
the city and its inhabitants.
17 Yes, I will send against you
poisonous snakes.

---

† **8:2** *Host of heaven*: the stars, worshiped by other nations and even by the inhabitants of Jerusalem, particularly during the reigns of Manasseh and Amon.

8:8 *Lying pen of the scribes*: because the teachings and interpretations of the scribes ran counter to the word of the Lord.

8:11 *Daughter of my people*: see note on 4:11.

* **7:32** Jer 19:6; 32:35.
7:33 Jer 16:4; 34:20.
7:34 Jer 16:9.
8:1 Bar 2:24.
8:2 Dt 4:19.
8:5 Jer 5:3; 7:24, 26.
8:6 Jb 34:31–32.
8:7 Is 1:3.
8:8 Mal 2:8; Rom 2:17–23.
8:9 1 Cor 3:20.
8:10 Jer 6:13; Dt 28:30.
8:11 Jer 6:14.
8:12 Jer 6:15.
8:14 Jer 9:14; 23:15.
8:15 Jer 14:19.

Against them no charm will work
when they bite you—oracle of the LORD.*

The Prophet's Grief over the People's Suffering

18 My joy is gone,
grief is upon me,
my heart is sick.
19 Listen! the cry of the daughter of my people,
far and wide in the land!
"Is the LORD no longer in Zion,
is her King no longer in her midst?"
Why do they provoke me with their idols,
with their foreign nonentities?*
20 "The harvest is over, the summer ended,
but we have not yet been saved!"
21 I am broken by the injury of the daughter of my people.
I am in mourning; horror has seized me.*
22 Is there no balm in Gilead,†
no healer there?
Why does new flesh not grow
over the wound of the daughter of my people?*
23 Oh, that my head were a spring of water,
my eyes a fountain of tears,
That I might weep day and night
over the slain from the daughter of my people!

The Corruption of the People

9 1 Oh, that I had in the wilderness
a travelers' lodging!
That I might leave my people
and depart from them.
They are all adulterers,
a band of traitors.
2 They ready their tongues like a drawn bow;
with lying, and not with truth,
they are powerful in the land.
They go from evil to evil,
and me they do not know—oracle of the LORD.
3 Be on your guard, everyone against his neighbor;
put no trust in any brother.
Every brother imitates Jacob, the supplanter,†
every neighbor is guilty of slander.
4 Each one deceives the other,
no one speaks the truth.
They have accustomed their tongues to lying,
they are perverse and cannot repent.*
5 Violence upon violence,
deceit upon deceit:
They refuse to know me—
oracle of the LORD.
6 Therefore, thus says the LORD of hosts:
I will refine them and test them;
how else should I deal with the daughter of my people?
7 A murderous arrow is their tongue,
their mouths utter deceit;
They speak peaceably with their neighbors,
but in their hearts they lay an ambush!*
8 Should I not punish them for these deeds—
oracle of the LORD;
on a nation such as this should I not take vengeance?*

Dirge over the Ravaged Land

9 Over the mountains I shall break out in cries of lamentation,
over the pastures in the wilderness, in a dirge:
They are scorched, and no one crosses them,
no sound of lowing cattle;
Birds of the air as well as beasts,
all have fled and are gone.*
10 I will turn Jerusalem into a heap of ruins,
a haunt of jackals;
The cities of Judah I will make a waste,
where no one dwells.*

11 Who is wise enough to understand this? To whom has the mouth of the LORD spoken? Let him declare it!

Why is the land ravaged,
scorched like a wilderness no one crosses?*

12 The LORD said: Because they have abandoned my law, which I set before them, and did not listen to me or follow it, 13 but followed instead their stubborn hearts and the Baals, as their ancestors had taught them,* 14 therefore, thus says the LORD of hosts, the God of Israel: See now, I will give this people wormwood to eat and poisoned water to drink.* 15 I will scatter them among nations whom neither they nor their ancestors have known; I will send the sword to pursue them until I have completely destroyed them.*

† **8:22** *Gilead*: a region southeast of the Sea of Galilee noted for its healing balm.
9:3 *Jacob, the supplanter*: in Hebrew, a play on words. In the popular etymology given in Gn 25:26, the name Jacob means "he supplants," for he deprived his brother Esau of his birthright (cf. Gn 25:33).

* **8:17** Dt 32:24.
8:19 Dt 32:21; Mi 4:9.
8:21 Jer 14:17.
8:22 Jer 46:11.
9:4 Jer 12:6.
9:7 Ps 28:3; 62:4.
9:8 Jer 5:9, 29.
9:9 Jer 4:25; 12:4.
9:10 Is 13:22.
9:11 Ps 107:43; Hos 14:10.
9:13 Jer 7:24; 19:4–5.
9:14 Jer 23:15.
9:15 Lv 26:33; Dt 28:36, 64.

16 Thus says the LORD of hosts:
Inquire, and call the wailing women to come;
summon the most skilled of them.
17 Let them come quickly
and raise for us a dirge,
That our eyes may run with tears,
our pupils flow with water.*
18 The sound of the dirge is heard from Zion:
We are ruined and greatly ashamed;
We have left the land,
given up our dwellings!
19 Hear, you women, the word of the LORD,
let your ears receive the word of his mouth.
Teach your daughters a dirge,
and each other a lament:
20 Death has come up through our windows,
has entered our citadels,
To cut down children in the street,
young people in the squares.*
21 Corpses shall fall
like dung in the open field,
Like sheaves behind the harvester,
with no one to gather them.

True Glory

22 Thus says the LORD:
Let not the wise boast of his wisdom,
nor the strong boast of his strength,
nor the rich man boast of his riches;
23 But rather, let those who boast, boast of this,
that in their prudence they know me,*
Know that I, the LORD, act with fidelity,
justice, and integrity on earth.
How I take delight in these—oracle of the LORD.

False Circumcision

24 See, days are coming—oracle of the LORD—
when I will demand an account of all those cir-
cumcised in the foreskin:* 25 Egypt and Judah,
Edom and the Ammonites, Moab, and those who
live in the wilderness and shave their temples.†
For all the nations are uncircumcised, even the
whole house of Israel is uncircumcised at heart.

The Folly of Idolatry

10 1 Hear the word the LORD speaks to you,
house of Israel. 2 Thus says the LORD:

Do not learn the ways of the nations,
and have no fear of the signs in the heavens,†
even though the nations fear them.*
3 For the carvings of the nations are nonentities,
wood cut from the forest,
Fashioned by artisans with the adze,*
4 adorned with silver and gold.
With nails and hammers they are fastened,
so they do not fall.*
5 Like a scarecrow in a cucumber field are they,
they cannot speak;
They must be carried about,
for they cannot walk.
Do not fear them, they can do no harm,
neither can they do good.*
6 No one is like you, LORD,
you are great,
great and mighty is your name.*
7 Who would not fear you,
King of the nations,
for it is your due!
Among all the wisest of the nations,
and in all their domains,
there is none like you.*
8 One and all they are stupid and senseless,
the instruction from nonentities—only
wood!
9 Silver plates brought from Tarshish,
and gold from Ophir,
The work of the artisan
and the handiwork of the smelter,
Clothed with violet and purple—
all of them the work of skilled workers.
10 The LORD is truly God,
he is the living God, the eternal King,
Before whose anger the earth quakes,
whose wrath the nations cannot endure.*

11 Thus shall you say of them: The gods that
did not make heaven and earth—let these perish
from earth and from beneath heaven!†*

12 The one who made the earth by his power,
established the world by his wisdom,
and by his skill stretched out the heavens.*
13 When he thunders, the waters in the heavens
roar,
and he brings up clouds from the end of
the earth,
Makes lightning flash in the rain,
and brings forth the wind from his
storehouses.

---

† **9:25** *Shave their temples*: some Arabian tribes practiced this custom. None of the nations who practice circumcision understand the meaning of their action, not even Israel; no one conforms to life under the covenant.

10:2 *Signs in the heavens*: phenomena in the sky, such as eclipses or comets, used to predict disasters.

10:11 This verse is in Aramaic.

* **9:17** Jer 14:17.
9:20 Jer 14:16.
9:23 Prv 21:30.
9:24 Jer 4:4.
10:2 Bar 6:6.
10:3 Wis 13:11; Is 44:9.
10:4 Is 40:19; 41:7.
10:5 Ps 115:4–8; Bar 6:15.
10:6 Ps 86:8–10.
10:7 Jer 5:22; Ps 47:2, 8.
10:10 Ps 10:16.
10:11 Ps 96:5.
10:12 Ps 104:5.

14 Everyone is too stupid to know;
every artisan is put to shame by his idol:
He has molded a fraud,
without breath of life.*
15 They are nothing, objects of ridicule;
they will perish in their time of punishment.
16 Jacob's portion is nothing like them:
for he is the maker of everything!
Israel is his very own tribe,
LORD of hosts is his name.*

Abandonment of Judah

17 Gather up your bundle from the land,
City living under siege!
18 For thus says the LORD:
Now, at this time
I will sling away the inhabitants of the land;
I will hem them in,
that they may be taken.
19 Woe is me! I am undone,
my wound is beyond healing.
Yet I had thought:
if I make light of my sickness, I can bear it.
20 My tent is ruined,
all its cords are severed.
My children have left me, they are no more:
no one to pitch my tent,
no one to raise its curtains.*
21 How stupid are the shepherds!
The LORD they have not sought;
For this reason they have failed,
and all their flocks scattered.*
22 Listen! a rumor! here it comes,
a great commotion from the land of the north:
To make the cities of Judah a desolation,
the haunt of jackals.

Prayer of Jeremiah

23 I know, LORD,
that no one chooses their way,
Nor determines their course
nor directs their own step.
24 Correct me, LORD, but with equity,
not in anger, lest you diminish me.
25 Pour out your wrath on the nations that do not know you,
on the tribes that do not call your name;
For they have utterly devoured Jacob,
and laid waste his home.*

Plea for Fidelity to the Covenant

11 1The word that came to Jeremiah from the
LORD: 2Speak to the people of Judah and the
inhabitants of Jerusalem, 3and say to them: Thus
says the LORD, the God of Israel: Cursed be anyone
who does not observe the words of this cov-
enant,* 4which I commanded your ancestors the
day I brought them up out of the land of Egypt,
that iron furnace, saying: Listen to my voice and
do all that I command you. Then you shall be
my people, and I will be your God.* 5Thus I will
fulfill the oath I swore to your ancestors, to give
them a land flowing with milk and honey, the
one you have today. "Amen, LORD," I answered.
6Then the LORD said to me: Proclaim all these
words in the cities of Judah and in the streets
of Jerusalem: Hear the words of this covenant
and obey them. 7I warned your ancestors un-
ceasingly from the day I brought them up out
of the land of Egypt even to this day: obey my
voice. 8But they did not listen or obey. They each
walked in the stubbornness of their evil hearts,
till I brought upon them all the threats of this
covenant which they had failed to observe as I
commanded them.*
9A conspiracy has been found, the LORD said
to me, among the people of Judah and the in-
habitants of Jerusalem: 10They have returned to
the crimes of their ancestors who refused to obey
my words. They also have followed and served
other gods; the house of Israel and the house
of Judah have broken the covenant I made with
their ancestors.* 11Therefore, thus says the LORD:
See, I am bringing upon them a disaster they
cannot escape. Though they cry out to me, I will
not listen to them.* 12Then the cities of Judah
and the inhabitants of Jerusalem will go and cry
out to the gods to whom they have been offering
incense. But these gods will give them no help
whatever in the time of their disaster.*

13 For as many as your cities
are your gods, O Judah!
As many as the streets of Jerusalem
are the altars for sacrifice to Baal.*

14Now, you must not intercede for this people;
do not raise on their behalf a cry or prayer! I will
not listen when they call to me in the time of
their disaster.*

Sacrifices of No Avail

15 What right has my beloved in my house,
while she devises her plots?
Can vows and sacred meat turn away
your disaster from you?

10:14 Rom 1:22–23.
10:16 Ps 33:12; Jer 31:35.
10:20 Jer 4:20.
10:21 Jer 23:1; Ez 34:5–6.
10:25 Ps 79:6–7.
11:3 Dt 27:26.
11:4 Dt 4:20; 1 Kgs 8:51.
11:8 2 Kgs 17:14.
11:10 Dt 31:16; Ez 20:21–30.
11:11 Jer 14:12; Mi 3:4.
11:12 Dt 32:37–38.
11:13 Jer 2:28; Hos 10:1.
11:14 Jer 7:16; 14:11.

Did You Know?

The Confessions of Jeremiah

Jeremiah 12:1–6 is the first of five passages that are sometimes called the Confessions of Jeremiah (see 12:1–6, 15:10–21, 17:12–18, 18:18–23, 20:7–18). In the confessions, Jeremiah speaks to God in a very personal, very direct way. He complains to God about the people's stubbornness, he complains about his treatment, and he accuses God of deceiving him. Some scholars believe the confessions are a private journal kept by Jeremiah that he never intended to be made public.

In 12:1–4, Jeremiah asks God why God lets evil people prosper—why doesn't God just slaughter them like sheep? God's reply in verses 5–6 is that things are going to get worse before they get better and that even Jeremiah's own family will turn against him. God never answers Jeremiah directly in any of the confessions—although in 15:19–21, God does promise to support Jeremiah.

If this famous prophet shared his anger, doubts, and fears with God honestly, so can we. Jeremiah's confessions are a good reminder that God wants to share everything with us—not just our happy thoughts.

▶ Jer 12:1–6

JER

Will you still be jubilant
16 when you hear the great tumult?
The LORD has named you
"a spreading olive tree, a pleasure to
behold";
Now he sets fire to it,
its branches burn.

[17]The LORD of hosts who planted you has decreed disaster for you because of the evil done by the house of Israel and by the house of Judah, who provoked me by sacrificing to Baal.*

The Plot Against Jeremiah

[18]I knew it because the LORD informed me: at that time you showed me their doings.

[19]Yet I was like a trusting lamb led to slaughter, not knowing that they were hatching plots against me: "Let us destroy the tree in its vigor; let us cut him off from the land of the living, so that his name will no longer be remembered."*

20 But, you, LORD of hosts, just Judge,
searcher of mind and heart,
Let me witness the vengeance you take on
them,
for to you I have entrusted my cause!*

[21]Therefore, thus says the LORD concerning the men of Anathoth who seek your life and say, "Do not prophesy in the name of the LORD; otherwise you shall die by our hand."* [22]Therefore, thus says the LORD of hosts: I am going to punish them. The young men shall die by the sword; their sons and daughters shall die by famine.* [23]None shall be spared among them, for I will bring disaster upon the men of Anathoth, the year of their punishment.*

12 [1] You would be in the right, O LORD,
if I should dispute with you;
even so, I must lay out the case against you.
Why does the way of the wicked prosper,
why do all the treacherous live in
contentment?*
2 You planted them; they have taken root,
they flourish and bear fruit as well.
You are upon their lips,
but far from their thoughts.*
3 LORD, you know me, you see me,
you have found that my heart is with you.*
Pick them out like sheep for the butcher,
set them apart for the day of slaughter.†
4 How long must the land mourn,
the grass of the whole countryside wither?
Because of the wickedness of those who dwell
in it
beasts and birds disappear,
for they say, "God does not care about our
future."
5 If running against men has wearied you,
how will you race against horses?

---

† **12:3** Jeremiah calls the Lord to account for allowing the wicked to flourish while he himself is persecuted for his fidelity to the Lord's mission; cf. 20:12. See Jesus' judgment, Mk 9:42. The metaphors indicate that Jeremiah has even greater trials ahead of him.

11:17 Is 5:2.
11:19 Jer 18:18; 20:10; Wis 2:20.
11:20 Jer 15:15.
11:21 Am 7:13, 16.
11:22 Jer 18:21–22.
11:23 Jer 23:12.
12:1 Jb 21:7; Mal 3:15.
12:2 Is 29:13.
12:3 Jer 17:18; Jb 23:10.

And if you are safe only on a level stretch,
what will you do in the jungle of the Jordan?

6 Your kindred and your father's house, even they
betray you; they have recruited a force against
you. Do not believe them, even when they speak
fair words to you.*

The Lord's Complaint

7 I have abandoned my house,
cast off my heritage;
The beloved of my soul I have delivered
into the hand of her foes.*
8 My heritage has become for me
like a lion in the thicket;
She has raised her voice against me,
therefore she has incurred my hatred.*
9 My heritage is a prey for hyenas,
is surrounded by vultures;
Come, gather together, all you wild animals,
come and eat!*
10 Many shepherds have ravaged my vineyard,
have trampled down my heritage;
My delightful portion they have turned
into a desert waste.*
11 They have made it a mournful waste,
desolate before me,
Desolate, the whole land,
because no one takes it to heart.
12 Upon every height in the wilderness
marauders have appeared.
The LORD has a sword that consumes
the land from end to end:
no peace for any living thing.*
13 They have sown wheat and reaped thorns,
they have tired themselves out for no purpose;
They are shamed by their harvest,
the burning anger of the LORD.

Judah's Neighbors

14 Thus says the LORD, against all my evil neigh-
bors† who plunder the heritage I gave my people
Israel as their own: See, I will uproot them from
their land; the house of Judah I will uproot in
their midst.*
15 But after uprooting them, I will have com-
passion on them again and bring them back,
each to their heritage, each to their land.* 16 And
if they truly learn my people's custom of swear-
ing by my name, "As the LORD lives," just as they
taught my people to swear by Baal, then they
shall be built up in the midst of my people.*
17 But if they do not obey, I will uproot and de-
stroy that nation entirely—oracle of the LORD.*

Judah's Corruption†

13 1 The LORD said to me: Go buy yourself
a linen loincloth; wear it on your loins,
but do not put it in water. 2 I bought the loin-
cloth, as the LORD commanded, and put it on.
3 A second time the word of the LORD came to
me thus: 4 Take the loincloth which you bought
and are wearing, and go at once to the Perath;
hide it there in a cleft of the rock. 5 Obedient to
the LORD's command, I went to the Perath and
buried the loincloth. 6 After a long time, the LORD
said to me: Go now to the Perath and fetch the
loincloth which I told you to hide there. 7 So I
went to the Perath, looked for the loincloth and
took it from the place I had hidden it. But it was
rotted, good for nothing! 8 Then the word came
to me from the LORD: 9 Thus says the LORD: So
also I will allow the pride of Judah to rot, the
great pride of Jerusalem.* 10 This wicked people
who refuse to obey my words, who walk in the
stubbornness of their hearts and follow other
gods, serving and worshiping them, will be like
this loincloth, good for nothing.* 11 For, as the
loincloth clings to a man's loins, so I made the
whole house of Israel and the whole house of
Judah cling to me—oracle of the LORD—to be my
people, my fame, my praise, my glory. But they
did not listen.*

The Broken Wineflask

12 Now speak to them this word: Thus says the
LORD, the God of Israel: Every wineflask should
be filled with wine. If they reply, "Do we not
know that every wineflask should be filled with
wine?" 13 say to them: Thus says the LORD: Be-
ware! I am making all the inhabitants of this
land drunk, the kings who sit on David's throne,
the priests and prophets, and all the inhabitants
of Jerusalem.* 14 I will smash them against each
other, parents and children together—oracle of
the LORD—showing no compassion, I will neither
spare nor pity, but I will destroy them.*

12:14 *My evil neighbors*: nations surrounding Israel, the land belonging to the Lord; cf. Is 8:8.

13:1–11 In this symbolic action, Jeremiah probably went to the village and spring of Parah, two and a half miles northeast of Anathoth, whose name closely resembled the Hebrew name of the river Euphrates (*Perath*), in order to dramatize the religious corruption of Judah at the hands of the Babylonians.

12:6 Jer 9:4.
12:7 Ps 78:62; Lam 2:1–2.
12:8 Ps 106:40.
12:9 2 Kgs 24:2; Is 56:9.
12:10 Jer 6:3; Is 63:18.
12:12 Is 42:25; 57:21.
12:14 2 Kgs 24:2.
12:15 Am 9:14.
12:16 Dt 6:13.
12:17 Is 60:12.
13:9 Prv 16:18.
13:10 Jer 2:20; 7:24; 16:11.
13:11 Ex 19:5; Dt 26:18–19.
13:13 Jer 25:15–18; Is 51:17.
13:14 Jer 19:10–11.

A Last Warning

15 Listen and give ear, do not be arrogant,
for the LORD speaks.
16 Give glory to the LORD, your God,
before he brings darkness;
Before your feet stumble
on mountains at twilight;
Before the light you look for turns to darkness,
changes into black clouds.*
17 If you do not listen to this in your pride,
I will weep many tears in secret;
My eyes will run with tears
for the LORD's flock, led away to exile.*

Exile

18 Say to the king and to the queen mother:
come down from your throne;
From your heads
your splendid crowns will fall.*
19 The cities of the Negeb are besieged,
with no one to relieve them;
Judah is taken into exile—all of it—
in total exile.

Jerusalem's Disgrace

20 Lift up your eyes and see
those coming in from the north.
Where is the flock entrusted to you,
your splendid sheep?*
21 What will you say when rulers are appointed
over you,
those you taught to be allies?
Will not pains seize you
like those of a woman giving birth?*
22 If you say to yourself:
"Why have these things happened to me?"
For your great guilt your skirts are stripped
away
and you are violated.*
23 Can Ethiopians change their skin,
leopards their spots?
As easily would you be able to do good,
accustomed to evil as you are.*
24 I will scatter them like chaff that flies
on the desert wind.*
25 This is your lot, the portion I have measured
out to you—
oracle of the LORD.
Because you have forgotten me,
and trusted in deception,† *
26 I now will strip away your skirts,
so that your shame is visible.*
27 Your adulteries, your neighings,
your shameless prostitutions:
On the hills, in the fields
I see your detestable crimes.
Woe to you, Jerusalem! How long will it be
before you are clean?*

The Great Drought

14 1 The word of the LORD that came to Jeremiah concerning the drought:*
2 Judah mourns,
her gates are lifeless;
They are bowed to the ground,
and the outcry of Jerusalem goes up.*
3 The nobles send their servants for water,
but when they come to the cisterns
They find no water
and return with empty jars.*
Confounded, despairing, they cover their
heads
4 because of the ruined soil;
Because there is no rain in the land
the farmers are confounded, they cover
their heads.*
5 Even the doe in the field deserts her young
because there is no grass.
6 The wild donkeys stand on the bare heights,
gasping for breath like jackals;
Their eyes grow dim;
there is no grass.
7 Even though our crimes bear witness
against us,
act, LORD, for your name's sake—
Even though our rebellions are many,
and we have sinned against you.*
8 Hope of Israel, LORD,
our savior in time of need!
Why should you be a stranger in the land,
like a traveler stopping only for a night?
9 Why are you like someone bewildered,
a champion who cannot save?
You are in our midst, LORD,
your name we bear:
do not forsake us!*
10 Thus says the LORD about this people:
They so love to wander
that they cannot restrain their feet.
The LORD takes no pleasure in them;

---

† **13:25** Heb. *sheqer*: lit., "deception," often used to designate an idol.

---

* **13:16** Prv 4:18–19; Is 5:30; Am 8:9.
13:17 Jer 14:17; Ps 119:136.
13:18 Jer 22:26; 2 Kgs 24:12, 15.
13:20 Jer 6:22–23.
13:21 2 Kgs 16:7.
13:22 Is 47:2–3.
13:23 Ps 55:20.
13:24 Ps 1:4; 83:14.
13:25 Jb 20:29.
13:26 Ez 16:32.
13:27 Jer 2:20.
14:1 Lv 26:19–20.
14:2 Is 3:26.
14:3 Am 4:8.
14:4 Dt 28:23.
14:7 Dn 9:4–14.
14:9 Is 59:1–2; 63:19.

now he remembers their guilt,
and will punish their sins.*

11 Then the LORD said to me: Do not intercede
for the well-being of this people.* 12 If they fast, I
will not listen to their supplication. If they sacri-
fice burnt offerings or grain offerings, I will take
no pleasure in them. Rather, I will destroy them
with the sword, famine, and plague.*
13 "Ah! Lord GOD," I replied, "it is the prophets
who say to them, 'You shall not see the sword;
famine shall not befall you. Indeed, I will give
you lasting peace in this place.' "*
14 These prophets utter lies in my name, the
LORD said to me: I did not send them; I gave them
no command, nor did I speak to them. They
prophesy to you lying visions, foolish divination,
deceptions from their own imagination.* 15 There-
fore, thus says the LORD: Concerning the prophets
who prophesy in my name, though I did not send
them, and who say, "Sword and famine shall not
befall this land": by sword and famine shall these
prophets meet their end.* 16 The people to whom
they prophesy shall be thrown out into the streets
of Jerusalem because of famine and the sword.
No one shall bury them, their wives, their sons, or
their daughters, for I will pour out upon them their
own wickedness.* 17 Speak to them this word:

Let my eyes stream with tears
night and day, without rest,
Over the great destruction which overwhelms
the virgin daughter of my people,
over her incurable wound.*
18 If I walk out into the field,
look! those slain by the sword;
If I enter the city,
look! victims of famine.
Both prophet and priest ply their trade
in a land they do not know.
19 Have you really cast Judah off?
Is Zion loathsome to you?
Why have you struck us a blow
that cannot be healed?
We wait for peace, to no avail;
for a time of healing, but terror comes
instead.*
20 We recognize our wickedness, LORD,
the guilt of our ancestors:
we have sinned against you.*
21 Do not reject us, for your name's sake,
do not disgrace your glorious throne.
Remember! Do not break your covenant
with us.*
22 Among the idols of the nations are there any
that give rain?

Pray It!

The Empty Promises of False Prophets

In Jeremiah 14:13–16, Jeremiah attacks prophets who preach what the people want to hear. The people want peace and plenty, so that is what the false prophets preach. They offer false and dangerous security.

People deceive themselves when they listen to only what they want to hear. Sometimes, God tells us things that are hard to hear or asks us to do things that are hard to do.

In your prayer, reflect or journal on the following questions:

- When have you tried to ignore God's message for you?
- When have you heard and responded to God even if God's message was difficult?
- What are the hardest things for you to hear or do?

▶ **Jer 14:13–16**

Or can the mere heavens send showers?
Is it not you, LORD,
our God, to whom we look?
You alone do all these things.*

15 1 The LORD said to me: Even if Moses and
Samuel stood before me, my heart would
not turn toward this people. Send them away
from me and let them go.* 2 If they ask you,
"Where should we go?" tell them, Thus says the
LORD: Whoever is marked for death, to death;
whoever is marked for the sword, to the sword;
whoever is marked for famine, to famine; who-
ever is marked for captivity, to captivity.* 3 Four
kinds of scourge I have decreed against them—
oracle of the LORD—the sword to kill them; dogs
to drag them off; the birds of the sky and the
beasts of the earth to devour and destroy them.*
4 And I will make them an object of horror to all

*
14:10 Jer 2:25.
14:11 Jer 11:14; Ex 32:10.
14:12 Jer 6:20; Is 1:11, 13.
14:13 Jer 4:10; 5:12.
14:14 Jer 5:31; 23:16.
14:15 Jer 5:12–13.
14:16 Jer 7:33; 19:7.
14:17 Jer 9:17.
14:19 Jer 8:15; 2 Chr 36:16.
14:20 Ps 106:6; Dn 9:5, 8.
14:21 Jer 14:7; Lv 26:44; Ps 25:11.
14:22 Jer 5:24; Zec 10:1.
15:1 Ps 99:6; Ez 14:14, 16.
15:2 Jer 14:12; Ez 5:12.
15:3 Ez 14:21.

the kingdoms of the earth because of what Manasseh, son of Hezekiah, king of Judah, did in Jerusalem.*

Scene of Tragedy

5 Who will pity you, Jerusalem,
who will grieve for you?
Who will stop to ask
about your welfare?*
6 It is you who have disowned me—oracle of
the LORD—
turned your back upon me;
I stretched out my hand to destroy you,
because I was weary of relenting.*
7 I winnowed them with a winnowing fork
at the gates of the land;
I have bereaved, destroyed my people;
they have not turned from their evil ways.*
8 Their widows were more numerous before me
than the sands of the sea.
I brought against the mother of youths
the destroyer at midday;
Suddenly I struck her
with anguish and terror.
9 The mother of seven faints away,
breathing out her life;
Her sun sets in full day,
she is ashamed, abashed.
Their survivors I will give to the sword
in the presence of their enemies—oracle of
the LORD.*

Jeremiah's Complaint

10 Woe to me, my mother, that you gave me
birth!
a man of strife and contention to all the
land!
I neither borrow nor lend,
yet everyone curses me.*
11 Tell me, LORD, have I not served you for their
good?
Have I not interceded with you
in time of misfortune and anguish?*
12 Can one break iron,
iron from the north, and bronze?
13† Your wealth and your treasures
I give as plunder, demanding no payment,
because of all your sins, throughout all
your territory.
14 And I shall enslave you to your enemies
in a land you do not know,
For fire has broken out from my anger,
it is kindled against you.
15 You know, LORD:
Remember me and take care of me,
avenge me on my persecutors.
Because you are slow to anger, do not
banish me;
know that for you I have borne insult.*
16 When I found your words, I devoured them;
your words were my joy, the happiness of
my heart,
Because I bear your name,
LORD, God of hosts.
17 I did not sit celebrating
in the circle of merrymakers;
Under the weight of your hand I sat alone
because you filled me with rage.*
18 Why is my pain continuous,
my wound incurable, refusing to be healed?
To me you are like a deceptive brook,
waters that cannot be relied on!*
19 Thus the LORD answered me:
If you come back and I take you back,
in my presence you shall stand;
If you utter what is precious and not what is
worthless,
you shall be my mouth.
Then they will be the ones who turn to you,
not you who turn to them.
20 And I will make you toward this people
a fortified wall of bronze.
Though they fight against you,
they shall not prevail,
For I am with you,
to save and rescue you—oracle of the LORD.*
21 I will rescue you from the hand of the wicked,
and ransom you from the power of the
violent.

Jeremiah's Life a Warning

16 [1]This word came to me from the LORD:
[2]Do not take a wife and do not have sons
and daughters in this place, [3]for thus says the
LORD concerning the sons and daughters born in
this place, the mothers who give them birth, the
fathers who beget them in this land: [4]Of deadly
disease they shall die. Unlamented and unburied they will lie like dung on the ground. Sword
and famine will make an end of them, and their

† **15:13–14** Though the wording of these verses is close to that in 17:3–4, the present passage is evidently God's word to Jeremiah, whereas 17:3–4 is evidently a word of judgment on Judah. It is noteworthy that the references to "you" in the present passage are singular, until a shift to plural in "against you" in the last line; this "you" is then doubtless a reference to both the prophet and his enemies.

* **15:4** Jer 24:9; 2 Kgs 21:11–16; 23:26; 24:3–4.
15:5 Is 51:19.
15:6 Am 7:8.
15:7 Is 41:16.
15:9 1 Sm 2:5.
15:10 Jer 20:14.
15:11 Jer 39:11–14.
15:15 Jer 11:20; 12:3; Ps 69:8.
15:17 Ps 25:4.
15:18 Jer 14:19; 30:15.
15:20 Jer 1:18; 6:27.

corpses will become food for the birds of the sky
and the beasts of the earth.*
5 Thus says the LORD: Do not go into a house
of mourning; do not go there to lament or grieve
for them. For I have withdrawn my peace from
this people—oracle of the LORD—my love and
my compassion.* 6 They shall die, the great and
the lowly, in this land, unburied and unlament-
ed.† No one will gash themselves or shave their
heads for them.* 7 They will not break bread with
the bereaved to offer consolation for the dead;
they will not give them the cup of consolation to
drink over the death of father or mother.*
8 Do not enter a house of feasting to sit eating
and drinking with them. 9 For thus says the LORD
of hosts, the God of Israel: Before your eyes and
in your lifetime, I will silence in this place the
song of joy and the song of gladness, the song of
the bridegroom and the song of the bride.*
10 When you proclaim all these words to this
people and they ask you: "Why has the LORD pro-
nounced all this great disaster against us? What is
our crime? What sin have we committed against
the LORD, our God?"—* 11 * you shall answer
them: It is because your ancestors have forsaken
me—oracle of the LORD—and followed other
gods that they served and worshiped; but me they
have forsaken, and my law they did not keep.
12 And you have done worse than your ancestors.
Here you are, every one of you, walking in the
stubbornness of your evil heart instead of listen-
ing to me.* 13 I will throw you out of this land
into a land that neither you nor your ancestors
have known; there you can serve other gods day
and night because I will not show you mercy.

Return from Exile

14 Therefore, days are coming—oracle of the
LORD—when it will no longer be said, "As the
LORD lives, who brought the Israelites out of
Egypt";* 15 but rather, "As the LORD lives, who
brought the Israelites out of the land of the north
and out of all the countries to which he had ban-
ished them." I will bring them back to the land I
gave their ancestors.*

Double Punishment

16 Look!—oracle of the LORD—I will send
many fishermen to catch them. After that, I will
send many hunters to hunt them out from every
mountain and hill and rocky crevice.* 17 For my
eyes are upon all their ways; they are not hidden
from me, nor does their guilt escape my sight.*
18 I will at once repay them double for their crime
and their sin because they profaned my land
with the corpses of their detestable idols, and
filled my heritage with their abominations.*

Conversion of the Nations

19 LORD, my strength, my fortress,
my refuge in the day of distress!
To you nations will come
from the ends of the earth, and say,
"Our ancestors inherited mere frauds,
empty, worthless."*
20 Can human beings make for themselves gods?
But these are not gods at all!*
21 Therefore, I will indeed give them knowledge;
this time I will make them acknowledge
My strength and my power:
they shall know that my name is LORD.*

The Sin of Judah and Its Punishment

17 1 The sin of Judah is written
with an iron stylus,
Engraved with a diamond point
upon the tablets of their hearts,*

And the horns of their altars, 2 when their chil-
dren remember their altars and their asherahs,
beside the green trees, on the high hills, 3 the
peaks in the country.

Your wealth and all your treasures
I give as plunder,
As payment for all your sins
throughout your territory,
4 You will relinquish your hold on your heritage
which I have given you.
I will enslave you to your enemies
in a land you do not know:
For a fire has broken out from my anger,
burning forever.*

True Wisdom

5 Thus says the LORD:
Cursed is the man who trusts in human beings,
who makes flesh his strength,
whose heart turns away from the LORD.*
6 He is like a barren bush in the wasteland

† **16:6–7** These verses refer to popular mourning practices in the land; cf. Dt 14:1–2.

* **16:4** Jer 7:33; 22:18.
16:5 Ez 24:16–17.
16:6 Lv 19:28; Dt 14:1.
16:7 Ez 24:17.
16:9 Jer 7:34; 25:10.
16:10 Jer 2:35; 5:19; 13:22.
16:11 Jer 22:9; Dt 29:25.
16:12 Jer 7:24–26.
16:14 Jer 23:7–8.
16:15 Jer 24:6.
16:16 2 Kgs 24:2; Lam 4:19.
16:17 Jer 32:19; Jb 34:21.
16:18 Is 40:2.
16:19 Jer 2:11; Is 2:2–3.
16:20 Jer 2:11; Gal 4:8.
16:21 Am 5:8.
17:1 Jb 19:24.
17:4 Jer 5:19; Dt 32:22.
17:5 Ps 146:2–3.

Cultural Connection

Children and Green Trees

The land is very important in Native American spirituality; trees, grass, and flowers are treated with respect, love, and awe, similar to that afforded people, because all are connected. It is the greatest wish of the elders that the children learn this lesson and carry it on to their own children. Native Americans would view the loss and destruction of the land described in Jeremiah 17:1–3 as a horrible punishment. See how their value for the land is reflected in this prayer from the Mohawk tradition:

Oh Great Spirit, Creator of all things;
Human Beings, trees, grass, berries.
Help us, be kind to us.
Let us be happy on earth.
Let us lead our children
To a good life and old age.
These our people; give them good minds
To love one another.
Oh Great Spirit,
Be kind to us.
Give these people the favour
To see green trees,
Green grass, flowers, and berries
This next spring;
So we all meet again.
Oh Great Spirit,
We ask of you.

(Author unknown, "Mohawk Indian Prayer")

Jer 17:1–3

that enjoys no change of season,
But stands in lava beds in the wilderness,
a land, salty and uninhabited.
7 Blessed are those who trust in the LORD;
the LORD will be their trust.*
8 They are like a tree planted beside the waters
that stretches out its roots to the stream:
It does not fear heat when it comes,
its leaves stay green;
In the year of drought it shows no distress,
but still produces fruit.*
9 More tortuous than anything is the human heart,
beyond remedy; who can understand it?
10 I, the LORD, explore the mind
and test the heart,
Giving to all according to their ways,
according to the fruit of their deeds.*
11 A partridge that broods but does not hatch
are those who acquire wealth unjustly:
In midlife it will desert them;
in the end they are only fools.*

The Source of Life

12 A throne of glory, exalted from the beginning,
such is our holy place.*
13 O Hope of Israel, LORD!
all who forsake you shall be put to shame;
The rebels shall be enrolled in the netherworld;
they have forsaken the LORD, source of living waters.*

Prayer for Vengeance

14 Heal me, LORD, that I may be healed;
save me, that I may be saved,
for you are my praise.
15 See how they say to me,
"Where is the word of the LORD?
Let it come to pass!"*
16 Yet I did not press you to send disaster;
the day without remedy I have not desired.
You know what passed my lips;
it is present before you.
17 Do not become a terror to me,
you are my refuge in the day of disaster.*
18 Let my persecutors be confounded—not me!
let them be terrified—not me!
Bring upon them the day of disaster,
crush them with double destruction.*

Observance of the Sabbath

19 Thus said the LORD to me: Go, stand at the
Gate of Benjamin,† where the kings of Judah
enter and leave, and at the other gates of Jeru-
salem.* 20 There say to them: Hear the word of
the LORD, you kings of Judah, and all Judah,

† **17:19** *The Gate of Benjamin*: this gate, probably part of the Temple area, is otherwise unknown.

17:7 Ps 1:3. **17:8** Is 58:11. **17:10** Jer 32:19; 1 Sm 16:7; Eccl 12:14. **17:11** Prv 13:11; Lk 12:20. **17:12** Jer 14:21. **17:13** Jer 2:13. **17:15** Is 5:19; 2 Pt 3:4. **17:17** Jer 16:19. **17:18** Jer 15:15; 18:20–23; Ps 35:5–6. **17:19** Jer 7:2.

and all you inhabitants of Jerusalem who enter
these gates! 21 Thus says the LORD: As you love
your lives, take care not to carry burdens on the
sabbath, to bring them in through the gates of
Jerusalem.* 22 Bring no burden from your homes
on the sabbath. Do no work whatever, but keep
holy the sabbath day, as I commanded your an-
cestors,* 23 though they did not listen or give ear,
but stiffened their necks so they could not hear or
take correction.* 24 If you truly obey me—oracle
of the LORD—and carry no burden through the
gates of this city on the sabbath, keeping the sab-
bath day holy and abstaining from all work on
it,* 25 then, through the gates of this city, kings
who sit upon the throne of David will continue
to enter, riding in their chariots or upon their
horses, along with their princes, and the people
of Judah, and the inhabitants of Jerusalem. This
city will remain inhabited forever.* 26 To it peo-
ple will come from the cities of Judah and the
neighborhood of Jerusalem, from the land of
Benjamin and from the Shephelah, from the hill
country and the Negeb, to bring burnt offerings
and sacrifices, grain offerings, incense, and thank
offerings to the house of the LORD.* 27 But if you
do not obey me and keep holy the sabbath day,
if you carry burdens and come through the gates
of Jerusalem on the sabbath, I will set fire to its
gates—a fire never to be extinguished—and it
will consume the palaces of Jerusalem.*

The Potter's Vessel†

18 1 This word came to Jeremiah from the
LORD: 2 Arise and go down to the potter's
house; there you will hear my word. 3 I went
down to the potter's house and there he was,
working at the wheel. 4 Whenever the vessel
of clay he was making turned out badly in his
hand, he tried again, making another vessel of
whatever sort he pleased.* 5 Then the word of the
LORD came to me: 6 Can I not do to you, house
of Israel, as this potter has done?—oracle of the
LORD. Indeed, like clay in the hand of the potter,
so are you in my hand, house of Israel.* 7 * At
one moment I may decree concerning a nation
or kingdom that I will uproot and tear down and
destroy it; 8 but if that nation against whom I
have decreed turns from its evil, then I will have
a change of heart regarding the evil which I have
decreed.* 9 At another moment, I may decree
concerning a nation or kingdom that I will build
up and plant it; 10 but if that nation does what is
evil in my eyes, refusing to obey my voice, then
I will have a change of heart regarding the good
with which I planned to bless it.*

11 And now, tell this to the people of Judah
and the inhabitants of Jerusalem: Thus says the
LORD: Look, I am fashioning evil against you and
making a plan. Return, all of you, from your evil
way; reform your ways and your deeds.* 12 But
they will say, "No use! We will follow our own
devices; each one of us will behave according to
the stubbornness of our evil hearts!"*

Unnatural Apostasy

13 Therefore thus says the LORD:
Ask among the nations—
who has ever heard the like?
Truly horrible things
virgin Israel has done!*
14 Does the snow of Lebanon†
desert the rocky heights?
Do the gushing waters dry up
that flow fresh down the mountains?
15 Yet my people have forgotten me:
they offer incense in vain.
They stumble off their paths,
the ways of old,
Traveling on bypaths,
not the beaten track.*
16 Their land shall be made a waste,
an object of endless hissing:†
All passersby will be horrified,
shaking their heads.*
17 Like the east wind, I will scatter them
before their enemies;
I will show them my back, not my face,
in their day of disaster.*

Another Prayer for Vengeance

18 "Come," they said, "let us devise a plot
against Jeremiah, for instruction will not perish
from the priests, nor counsel from the wise, nor
the word from the prophets. Come, let us destroy

†

18:1–12 The lesson of the potter is that God has the power to destroy or restore, changing his plans accordingly as these nations disobey him or fulfill his will. Cf. Jon 3:10.

18:14 *Lebanon*: here apparently including Mount Hermon, whose snow-capped peak can be seen from parts of Palestine all year round. The prophet contrasts the certainties of nature with Israel's unnatural desertion of the Lord for idols (v. 15).

18:16 *Hissing*: in some ancient Near Eastern cultures hissing was not only a sign of derision but a magical means of keeping demons away; people hissed in order to ward off danger, like whistling in a cemetery.

*

17:21 Neh 13:15–19.
17:22 Ex 20:8; 23:12.
17:23 Jer 5:3; 7:24.
17:24 Is 58:14.
17:25 Jer 22:4.
17:26 Jer 32:44.
17:27 Ez 22:8.
18:4 Rom 9:20–21.
18:6 Wis 15:7; Is 45:9.
18:7 Jer 1:10.
18:8 Jer 26:3; Is 55:7; Ez 18:21, 27; Jon 3:10.
18:10 Nm 14:22–23.
18:11 Jer 7:3; 25:5; 35:15.
18:12 Jer 2:25; 7:24.
18:13 Jer 2:10–11; 5:30.
18:15 Jer 2:13, 32.
18:16 Jer 19:8; Lv 26:32; 1 Kgs 9:8.
18:17 Prv 1:24–31.

him by his own tongue. Let us pay careful atten-
tion to his every word."*

19 Pay attention to me, O LORD,
and listen to what my adversaries say.
20 Must good be repaid with evil
that they should dig a pit to take my life?
Remember that I stood before you
to speak on their behalf,
to turn your wrath away from them.*
21 So now, give their children† to famine,*
deliver them to the power of the sword.
Let their wives be childless and widows;
let their husbands die of pestilence,
their youths be struck down by the sword
in battle.
22 May cries be heard from their homes,
when suddenly you send plunderers against
them.
For they have dug a pit to capture me,
they have hidden snares for my feet;
23 But you, LORD, know
all their planning for my death.
Do not forgive their crime,
and their sin do not blot out from your sight!
Let them stumble before you,
in the time of your anger act against them.*

Symbol of the Potter's Flask

19 1 Thus said the LORD: Go, buy a potter's
earthenware flask. Take along some of the
elders of the people and some of the priests, 2 and
go out toward the Valley of Ben-hinnom, at the
entrance of the Potsherd Gate;† there proclaim
the words which I will speak to you: 3 You shall
say, Listen to the word of the LORD, kings of Judah
and inhabitants of Jerusalem: Thus says the LORD
of hosts, the God of Israel: I am going to bring
such evil upon this place that the ears of all who
hear of it will ring. 4 All because they have forsaken
me and profaned this place by burning incense to
other gods which neither they nor their ancestors
knew; and because the kings of Judah have filled
this place with innocent blood,* 5 building high
places for Baal to burn their children in fire as
offerings to Baal—something I never considered
or said or commanded.* 6 † Therefore, days are
coming—oracle of the LORD—when this place
will no longer be called Topheth, or the Valley of
Ben-hinnom, but rather, the Valley of Slaughter.*
7 In this place I will foil the plan of Judah and
Jerusalem; I will make them fall by the sword be-
fore their enemies, at the hand of those who seek
their lives. Their corpses I will give as food to the
birds of the sky and the beasts of the earth.* 8 I
will make this city a waste and an object of hiss-
ing. Because of all its wounds, every passerby will
be horrified and hiss. 9 I will have them eat the
flesh of their sons and daughters; they shall eat
one another's flesh during the harsh siege under
which their enemies and those who seek their
lives will confine them.*
10 And you shall break the flask in the sight of
the men who went with you, 11 and say to them:
Thus says the LORD of hosts: Thus will I smash
this people and this city, as one smashes a clay
pot so that it cannot be repaired. And Topheth
shall be its burial place, for there will be no other
place for burial.* 12 Thus I will do to this place
and to its inhabitants—oracle of the LORD; I will
make this city like Topheth.* 13 And the houses
of Jerusalem and the houses of the kings of Judah
shall be defiled like the place of Topheth, all the
houses upon whose roofs they burnt incense to
the whole host of heaven and poured out liba-
tions to other gods.*
14 When Jeremiah returned from Topheth, where
the LORD had sent him to prophesy, he stood in the
court of the house of the LORD and said to all the
people:* 15 Thus says the LORD of hosts, the God of
Israel: I will bring upon this city all the evil I have
spoken against it, because they have become stub-
born and have not obeyed my words.*

20 1 Now the priest Pashhur,* son of Immer,
chief officer in the house of the LORD,†
heard Jeremiah prophesying these things. 2 So he
struck the prophet and put him in the stocks at
the upper Gate of Benjamin in the house of the
LORD.* 3 The next morning, after Pashhur had
released Jeremiah from the stocks, the prophet
said to him:* "Instead of Pashhur, the LORD

18:21 *Give their children*: often an extended family is meant, to be rewarded or punished as a unit.

19:2 *Potsherd Gate*: perhaps in the south wall of Jerusalem, through which potsherds and other refuse were thrown into the Valley of Ben-hinnom.

19:6 Cf. note on 7:31.

20:1 *Chief officer in the house of the LORD*: head of the Temple police; cf. 29:26. By entering the Temple court (19:14), Jeremiah had put himself under Pashhur's jurisdiction.

20:3 *Terror on every side*: the name indicates the siege that will beset Jerusalem.

20:4 *Babylon*: mentioned here for the first time in Jeremiah as the land of exile. The prophecy dates from after 605 B.C., when Nebuchadnezzar defeated Egypt and made the Babylonian (Chaldean) empire dominant in Syria and Palestine.

18:18 Jer 11:19; Ps 35:15–16.
18:20 Ps 35:12.
18:21 Ps 109:9–10.
18:23 Neh 4:5; Ps 35:4; 37:32–33.
19:4 Jer 1:16; 2 Kgs 21:16; 24:4.
19:5 Jer 7:31–32; 32:35.
19:6 Jer 7:32.
19:7 Jer 7:33.
19:9 Lv 26:29.
19:11 Jer 7:32.
19:12 2 Kgs 23:10.
19:13 Jer 32:29.
19:14 Jer 26:2.
19:15 Jer 7:26; Prv 29:1.
20:1 Jer 21:1.
20:2 Jer 29:26.
20:3 Jer 6:25.

names you 'Terror on every side.'† 4 For thus says
the LORD: Indeed, I will hand you over to terror,
you and all your friends. Your own eyes shall see
them fall by the sword of their enemies. All Judah
I will hand over to the power of the king of Bab-
ylon,† who shall take them captive to Babylon or
strike them down with the sword. 5 All the wealth
of this city, all its resources and its valuables, all
the treasures of the kings of Judah, I will hand
over to their enemies, who will plunder it and
carry it away to Babylon.* 6 You, Pashhur, and
all the members of your household shall go into
exile. To Babylon you shall go; there you shall die
and be buried, you and all your friends, because
you have prophesied lies to them."*

Jeremiah's Interior Crisis

7 You seduced me,† LORD, and I let myself be
seduced;
you were too strong for me, and you
prevailed.
All day long I am an object of laughter;
everyone mocks me.
8 Whenever I speak, I must cry out,
violence and outrage I proclaim;
The word of the LORD has brought me
reproach and derision all day long.
9 I say I will not mention him,
I will no longer speak in his name.
But then it is as if fire is burning in my heart,
imprisoned in my bones;
I grow weary holding back,
I cannot!*
10 Yes, I hear the whisperings of many:
"Terror on every side!
Denounce! let us denounce him!"
All those who were my friends
are on the watch for any misstep of mine.
"Perhaps he can be tricked; then we will
prevail,
and take our revenge on him."*
11 But the LORD is with me, like a mighty
champion:
my persecutors will stumble, they will not
prevail.
In their failure they will be put to utter shame,
to lasting, unforgettable confusion.*
12 LORD of hosts, you test the just,
you see mind and heart,
Let me see the vengeance you take on them,
for to you I have entrusted my cause.*
13 Sing to the LORD,
praise the LORD,
For he has rescued the life of the poor
from the power of the evildoers!*
14 Cursed be the day†
on which I was born!
May the day my mother gave me birth
never be blessed!*
15 Cursed be the one who brought the news
to my father,
"A child, a son, has been born to you!"
filling him with great joy.
16 Let that man be like the cities
which the LORD relentlessly overthrew;
Let him hear war cries in the morning,
battle alarms at noonday,*
17 because he did not kill me in the womb!
Then my mother would have been my grave,
her womb confining me forever.*
18 Why did I come forth from the womb,
to see sorrow and pain,
to end my days in shame?*

III. Oracles in the Last Years of Jerusalem

Fate of Zedekiah and Jerusalem

21 1 The word which came to Jeremiah from
the LORD when King Zedekiah† sent Pash-
hur, son of Malchiah, and the priest Zephaniah,
son of Maaseiah, to him with this request: 2 In-
quire for us of the LORD, because Nebuchadnez-
zar, king of Babylon, is attacking us. Perhaps the
LORD will act for us in accord with his wonderful
works by making him withdraw from us. 3 But
Jeremiah answered them: This is what you shall
report to Zedekiah: 4 Thus says the LORD, the God
of Israel: I will turn against you the weapons
with which you are fighting the king of Babylon
and the Chaldeans who besiege you outside the
walls. These weapons I will pile up in the midst
of this city,* 5 and I myself will fight against you
with outstretched hand and mighty arm, in anger,
wrath, and great rage!* 6 I will strike down the

JER

† **20:7** *You seduced me*: Jeremiah accuses the Lord of having deceived him; cf. 15:18.

20:14–18 Deception, sorrow and terror have brought the prophet to the point of despair; nevertheless he maintains confidence in God (vv. 11–13); cf. Jb 3:3–12.

21:1 *Zedekiah*: brother of Jehoiakim, appointed king by Nebuchadnezzar after he had carried Jehoiachin away to captivity (2 Kgs 24:17). *Pashhur*: different from the one in 20:1–3 but also one of Jeremiah's enemies; cf. 38:1, 4.

* **20:5** 2 Kgs 20:17; 24:12–16.
20:6 Jer 14:13–14; 28:15.
20:9 Jer 6:11; Jb 32:18.
20:10 Jb 19:19; Ps 31:13; Lk 20:20.
20:11 Jer 1:8; 15:20.
20:12 Jer 11:20.
20:13 Ps 35:9–10; 109:30–31.
20:14 Jer 15:10; Jb 3:1–10; 10:18.
20:16 Gn 19:25; Is 13:19.
20:17 Jb 3:10–11; 10:19.
20:18 Jb 14:1.
21:4 Jer 37:8–10.
21:5 Is 63:10; Lam 2:4–5.

inhabitants of this city, human being and beast;
they shall die in a great pestilence.* 7 After that—
oracle of the LORD—I will hand over Zedekiah,
king of Judah, and his ministers and the people in
this city who survive pestilence, sword, and fam-
ine, to Nebuchadnezzar, king of Babylon, to their
enemies and those who seek their lives. He shall
strike them down with the edge of the sword,
without quarter, without mercy or compassion.*
8 And to this people you shall say: Thus says the
LORD: See, I am giving you a choice between the
way to life and the way to death.* 9 Whoever re-
mains in this city shall die by the sword or famine
or pestilence. But whoever leaves and surrenders
to the Chaldeans who are besieging you shall
live and escape with his life. 10 I have set my face
against this city, for evil and not for good—oracle
of the LORD. It shall be given into the power of the
king of Babylon who shall set it on fire.†

Oracles Regarding the Kings†

11 To the royal house of Judah:
Hear the word of the LORD,
12 house of David!
Thus says the LORD:
Each morning dispense justice,
rescue the oppressed from the hand of the oppressor,
Or my fury will break out like fire
and burn with no one to quench it
because of your evil deeds.*
13 Beware! I am against you, Ruler of the Valley,
Rock of the Plain†—oracle of the LORD.
You say, "Who will attack us,
who can storm our defenses?"
14 I will punish you—oracle of the LORD—
as your deeds deserve!
I will kindle a fire in its forest†
that shall devour all its surroundings.*

22 1 Thus says the LORD: Go down to the pal-
ace of the king of Judah and there deliver
this word: 2 You shall say: Listen to the word of
the LORD, king of Judah, who sit on the throne
of David, you, your ministers, and your people
who enter by these gates!* 3 Thus says the LORD:
Do what is right and just. Rescue the victims
from the hand of their oppressors. Do not wrong
or oppress the resident alien, the orphan, or the
widow, and do not shed innocent blood in this
place.* 4 If you carry out these commands, kings
who succeed to the throne of David will con-
tinue to enter the gates of this house, riding in
chariots or mounted on horses, with their min-
isters, and their people. 5 But if you do not obey
these commands, I swear by myself—oracle of
the LORD: this house shall become rubble. 6 For
thus says the LORD concerning the house of the
king of Judah:

Though you be to me like Gilead,
like the peak of Lebanon,
I swear I shall turn you into a waste,
with cities uninhabited.
7 Against you I will send destroyers,
each with their tools:
They shall cut down your choice cedars,
and cast them into the fire.*

8 Many nations will pass by this city and ask
one another: "Why has the LORD done this to so
great a city?"* 9 And they will be told: "Because
they have deserted their covenant with the LORD,
their God, by worshiping and serving other
gods."*

Jehoahaz

10 Do not weep for him who is dead,†
nor mourn for him!
Weep rather for him who is going away;
never again to see
the land of his birth.*

11 Thus says the LORD concerning Shallum,† son
of Josiah, king of Judah, his father's successor,
who left this place: He shall never return, 12 but
in the place where they exiled him, there he shall
die; he shall never see this land again.

† **21:10** Jeremiah consistently pointed out the uselessness of resistance to Babylon, since the Lord had delivered Judah to Nebuchadnezzar (27:6). Because of this the prophet was denounced and imprisoned as a traitor (37:13–14).

21:11–23:8 This section contains an editor's collection of Jeremiah's oracles against the kings of Judah. They are placed in the chronological order of the kings, and are prefaced by oracles against the kings of Judah in general (21:11–22:9).

21:13 *Ruler of the Valley, Rock of the Plain*: Mount Zion, surrounded by valleys, was regarded by the royal house as impregnable. Despite this natural fortification, God derides it as no more than a rock rising from the plain, useless against the attack of his fury.

21:14 *Its forest*: probably the royal palace, built of cedar wood; cf. 22:14; in 1 Kgs 7:2 the palace is called "the house of the forest of Lebanon."

22:10 *Him who is dead*: Josiah. His successor, Jehoahaz, was deported by Pharaoh Neco to Egypt, where he died (2 Kgs 23:33–34).

22:11 *Shallum*: i.e., Jehoahaz; cf. 1 Chr 3:15. This may have been his name at birth, in which case Jehoahaz would have been his throne name.

21:6 Jer 16:4.
21:7 Jer 24:8–10; Dt 28:49–50.
21:8 Jer 21:9; Dt 30:15, 19.
21:12 Jer 4:4; 22:3; Zec 7:9.
21:14 2 Kgs 25:9; 2 Chr 36:19.
22:2 Jer 17:20.
22:3 Jer 21:12; Ex 22:21–24; Dt 24:17.
22:7 Jer 21:14.
22:8 Dt 29:24–27.
22:9 Jer 19:4; 40:2–3.
22:10 2 Chr 35:23–25.

Jehoiakim

13 Woe to him who builds his house on
wrongdoing,
his roof-chambers on injustice;
Who works his neighbors without pay,†
and gives them no wages.*
14 Who says, "I will build myself a spacious
house,
with airy rooms,"
Who cuts out windows for it,
panels it with cedar,
and paints it with vermilion.
15 Must you prove your rank among kings†
by competing with them in cedar?
Did not your father eat and drink,
And act justly and righteously?
Then he prospered.*
16 Because he dispensed justice to the weak and
the poor,
he prospered.
Is this not to know me?—
oracle of the LORD.*
17 But your eyes and heart are set on nothing
except your own gain,
On shedding innocent blood
and practicing oppression and extortion.*

18 Therefore, thus says the LORD concerning Jehoiakim, son of Josiah, king of Judah:

They shall not lament him,
"Alas! my brother"; "Alas! sister."†
They shall not lament him,
"Alas, Lord! alas, Majesty!"*
19 The burial of a donkey† he shall be given,
dragged forth and cast out
beyond the gates of Jerusalem.*

Jeconiah

20 Climb Lebanon and cry out,†
in Bashan lift up your voice;
Cry out from Abarim,
for all your lovers are crushed.*
21 I spoke to you when you were secure,
but you answered, "I will not listen."
This has been your way from your youth,
not to listen to my voice.
22 The wind shall shepherd all your shepherds,
your lovers shall go into exile.
Surely then you shall be ashamed and
confounded
because of all your wickedness.

Pray It!

Admit It!

Jeremiah's words against King Jehoiakim in Jeremiah 22:21–23 are harsh. Jehoiakim is guilty of some serious sin and is leading the nation to destruction. But he doesn't want to hear about it. In fact, when Jehoiakim is presented with a scroll of Jeremiah's prophecies, he burns it (see 36:23)!

Forgiving God,
Help us to hear the prophets in today's world
who call us to own our sin.
The prophets who call us to end
discrimination,
who call us to care for the needy,
who call us to care for the earth,
who call us to end violence,
who call us to healthy relationships,
who call us to be people of integrity,
avoiding sin in all its forms.
May we be humble enough to admit our
faults
and courageous enough to do
something about
them.

▶ **Jer 22:18–23**

† **22:13** *Without pay*: either by forced labor in public works, or by defrauding the workers. Despite the impoverishment caused in Judah by the payment of foreign tribute, Jehoiakim embarked on a building program in Jerusalem (v. 14); cedar was an expensive building material which had to be imported. Social injustice is the cause of much of the prophetic condemnation of the kings (v. 17).

22:15–16 The rule of Josiah, Jehoiakim's father, shows that authentic kingship is rooted in knowledge of the Lord and creates a society in which the most disadvantaged can expect and receive justice.

22:18 *"Alas! my brother"; "Alas! sister"*: customary cries of mourning.

22:19 *The burial of a donkey*: no burial at all, except to be cast outside the city as refuse. This prophecy describes the popular feeling toward Jehoiakim rather than the actual circumstances of his burial. According to 2 Kgs 24:5 he was buried with his ancestors in Jerusalem.

22:20–23 The prophet first bids Jerusalem to scale Lebanon, Bashan, and Abarim, i.e., the highest surrounding mountains to the north, northeast, and southeast, and gaze on the ruin of its lovers, i.e., the false leaders of Judah, called its shepherds (v. 22); cf. 2:8. Jerusalem still stands (v. 23), apparently as secure as the heights of Lebanon, but destruction is to follow (cf. v. 6).

* **22:13** Lv 19:13; Dt 24:14; Hb 2:9, 12.
22:15 2 Sm 5:11; 7:2; 2 Kgs 23:25.
22:16 Prv 31:9.
22:17 Ez 22:13, 27.
22:18 Jer 16:4–7; 1 Kgs 13:30.
22:19 Jer 36:30.
22:20 Jer 30:14–15; Dt 32:49.

23 You who dwell on Lebanon,
who nest in the cedars,
How you shall groan when pains come upon
you,
like the pangs of a woman in childbirth!

24 As I live—oracle of the LORD—even if you,
Coniah,† son of Jehoiakim, king of Judah, were
a signet ring* on my right hand, I would snatch
you off. 25 I will hand you over to those who
seek your life, to those you dread: Nebuchad-
nezzar, king of Babylon, and the Chaldeans.* 26 I
will cast you out, you and the mother who bore
you,† into a land different from the land of your
birth; and there you will die;* 27 Neither shall re-
turn to the land for which they yearn.*

28 Is this man Coniah a thing despised, to be
broken,
a vessel that no one wants?
Why are he and his offspring cast out?
why thrown into a land they do not know?
29 O land, land, land,
hear the word of the LORD—
30 Thus says the LORD:
* Write this man down as childless,†
a man who will never prosper in his life!
Nor shall any of his descendants prosper,
to sit upon the throne of David,
to rule again over Judah.

A Just Shepherd†

23 1 * Woe to the shepherds who destroy and
scatter the flock of my pasture—oracle of
the LORD. 2 Therefore, thus says the LORD, the God
of Israel, against the shepherds who shepherd
my people: You have scattered my sheep and
driven them away. You have not cared for them,
but I will take care to punish your evil deeds.* 3 I
myself will gather the remnant of my flock from
all the lands to which I have banished them and
bring them back to their folds; there they shall be
fruitful and multiply.* 4 I will raise up shepherds
for them who will shepherd them so that they
need no longer fear or be terrified; none shall be
missing—oracle of the LORD.*

5 See, days are coming—oracle of the LORD—
when I will raise up a righteous branch for
David;
As king he shall reign and govern wisely,
he shall do what is just and right in the
land.*
6 In his days Judah shall be saved,
Israel shall dwell in security.
This is the name to be given him:
"The LORD our justice."*

7 * Therefore, the days are coming—oracle of
the LORD—when they shall no longer say, "As the
LORD lives, who brought the Israelites out of the
land of Egypt"; 8 but rather, "As the LORD lives,
who brought the descendants of the house of
Israel up from the land of the north"—and from
all the lands to which I banished them; they shall
again live on their own soil.

The False Prophets†

9 Concerning the prophets:
My heart is broken within me,
all my bones tremble;
I am like a drunk,
like one overcome by wine,
Because of the LORD,
because of his holy words.
10 The land is filled with adulterers;
because of the curse the land mourns,
the pastures of the wilderness are withered.*
Theirs is an evil course,
theirs is unjust power.
11 Both prophet and priest are godless!
In my very house I find their wickedness—

---

† **22:24** *Coniah*: a shortened form of Jeconiah, the name Jeremiah gives King Jehoiachin (cf. 24:1). *A signet ring*: the seal used by kings and other powerful figures—a symbol of their power and status—mounted in a ring worn constantly on the hand. The Lord says that even were Jehoiachin such a precious possession, he would reject him. Hg 2:23 uses the same imagery to signal the restoration of Zerubbabel. The words in Jer 22:24–30 date from the short three-month reign of Jehoiachin, before he was deported by Nebuchadnezzar.

22:26 *You and the mother who bore you*: the queen mother held a special position in the monarchy of Judah, and in the Books of Kings she is invariably mentioned by name along with the king (1 Kgs 15:2; 2 Kgs 18:2). Jehoiachin did indeed die in Babylon.

22:30 *Childless*: Jehoiachin is considered childless because none of his seven sons became king. His grandson Zerubbabel presided for a time over the Judahite community after the return from exile, but not as king. According to Ezekiel, whose oracles are dated by Jehoiachin's fictitious regnal years, the people expected Jehoiachin to return. Jeremiah's prophecy dispels this hope, despite the words of Hananiah (28:4).

23:1–8 With the false rulers (shepherds) who have governed his people the Lord contrasts himself, the true shepherd, who will in the times of restoration appoint worthy rulers (vv. 1–4). He will provide a new king from David's line who will rule justly, fulfilling royal ideals (vv. 5, 6). "The Lord our justice" is an ironic wordplay on the name of the weak King Zedekiah ("The Lord is justice"). Unlike Zedekiah, the future king will be true to the name he bears. Verses 7–8 may have been added during the exile.

23:9–40 After the collection of oracles against the kings, the editor of the book placed this collection of oracles against the false prophets. With them are associated the priests, for both have betrayed their trust as instructors in the ways of the Lord; cf. 2:8; 4:9; 6:13–14.

---

* **22:24** Hg 2:23.
22:25 Jer 21:7; 34:20.
22:26 2 Kgs 24:15.
22:27 Jer 44:14.
22:30 Jer 36:30; 1 Chr 3:16–17; Mt 1:12.
23:1 Jer 22:22.
23:2 Ez 34:4–10; Zec 11:16–17.
23:3 Jer 29:14; 32:37.
23:4 Jer 3:15; Ez 34:11–12.
23:5 Jer 33:14–16; Is 4:2; 9:5–6; 11:1–5.
23:6 Dn 9:24.
23:7–8 Jer 16:14–15.
23:10 Jer 4:22; 5:7–8; 9:2, 10.

oracle of the LORD.*
12 Hence their way shall become for them
slippery ground.
Into the darkness they shall be driven,
and fall headlong;
For I will bring disaster upon them,
the year of their punishment—oracle of the
LORD.*
13 Among Samaria's prophets
I saw something unseemly:
They prophesied by Baal
and led my people Israel astray.*
14 But among Jerusalem's prophets
I saw something more shocking:
Adultery, walking in deception,†
strengthening the power of the wicked,
so that no one turns from evil;
To me they are all like Sodom,
its inhabitants like Gomorrah.*

15 Therefore, thus says the LORD of hosts against
the prophets:

Look, I will give them wormwood to eat,
and poisoned water to drink;
For from Jerusalem's prophets
ungodliness has gone forth into the whole
land.*
16 Thus says the LORD of hosts:
Do not listen to the words of your prophets,
who fill you with emptiness;
They speak visions from their own fancy,
not from the mouth of the LORD.*
17 They say to those who despise the word of the
LORD,†
"Peace shall be yours";
And to everyone who walks in hardness of
heart,
"No evil shall overtake you."*
18 Now, who has stood in the council of the
LORD,
to see him and to hear his word?
Who has heeded his word so as to
announce it?*
19 See, the storm of the LORD!
His wrath breaks forth
In a whirling storm
that bursts upon the heads of the wicked.*
20 The anger of the LORD shall not abate
until he has carried out completely
the decisions of his heart.
In days to come
you will understand fully.
21 I did not send these prophets,
yet they ran;
I did not speak to them,
yet they prophesied.*
22 Had they stood in my council,
they would have proclaimed my words to
my people,
They would have brought them back from
their evil ways
and from their wicked deeds.
23 Am I a God near at hand only—oracle of the
LORD—*
and not a God far off?†
24 Can anyone hide in secret
without my seeing them?—oracle of the
LORD.
Do I not fill
heaven and earth?—oracle of the LORD.

25 I have heard the prophets who prophesy lies
in my name say, "I had a dream! I had a dream!"
26 How long? Will the hearts of the prophets who
prophesy lies and their own deceitful fancies ever
turn back? 27 By the dreams they tell each other,
they plan to make my people forget my name,
just as their ancestors forgot my name for Baal.*
28 Let the prophets who have dreams tell their
dreams; let those who have my word speak my
word truthfully!

What has straw to do with wheat?†
—oracle of the LORD.*
29 Is not my word like fire—oracle of the LORD—
like a hammer shattering rock?

30 Therefore I am against the prophets—oracle
of the LORD—those who steal my words from
each other.* 31 Yes, I am against the prophets—
oracle of the LORD—those who compose their
own speeches and call them oracles. 32 Yes, I am
against the prophets who tell lying dreams—
oracle of the LORD—those who lead my people
astray by recounting their reckless lies. It was not

†

23:14 Cf. note on 13:25.

23:17–20 Not only are the false prophets personally immoral, but they encourage immorality by prophesying good for evildoers. The true prophet, on the other hand, sees the inevitable consequences of evil behavior.

23:23–24 *Near at hand only . . . far off*: a divine claim that no one can hide from God and that God is aware of all that happens.

23:28–29 *Straw . . . wheat*: a contrast between false and true prophecy. True prophecy is also like fire (cf. 5:14; 20:9), producing violent results (v. 29); Jeremiah's own life is a testimony of this.

*

23:11 Jer 6:13.
23:12 Ps 35:6.
23:13 1 Kgs 18:19.
23:14 Jer 29:21–23; Is 1:9–10.
23:15 Jer 8:14; 9:14.
23:16 Jer 14:14.
23:17 Jer 5:12; Ez 13:10; Mi 3:11; Zec 10:2.
23:18 Jb 15:8; Is 40:13; 1 Cor 2:16.
23:19 Jer 30:23.
23:21 Jer 29:9.
23:23 Jer 16:17; Ps 139:8.
23:27 Jgs 3:7; 8:33.
23:28 Nm 12:6.
23:30 Dt 18:20.

Did You Know?

Fig Trees

The fig tree was widely cultivated in the ancient Near East. Its sweet fruit was a delight to taste, and its broad leaves offered welcome shade from the scorching summer sun. In Jeremiah 24:5–7, ripe figs are presented as an image of the faithful exiles in Babylon. In 1 Kings 5:5, fig leaves symbolize protection and safety. Jesus tells a parable about a fig tree in Luke 13:6–9. Think about it the next time you eat a Fig Newton!

▶ **Jeremiah, chapter 24**

I who sent them or commanded them; they do
this people no good at all—oracle of the LORD.*
33 † And when this people or a prophet or a
priest asks you, "What is the burden of the LORD?"
you shall answer, "You are the burden, and I cast
you off"—oracle of the LORD. 34 If a prophet or a
priest or anyone else mentions "the burden of the
LORD," I will punish that man and his household.
35 Thus you shall ask, when speaking to one an-
other, "What answer did the LORD give?" or "What
did the LORD say?" 36 But "the burden of the LORD"
you shall mention no more. For each of you,
your own word becomes the burden so that you
pervert the words of the living God, the LORD of
hosts, our God. 37 Thus shall you ask the prophet,
"What answer did the LORD give?" or "What did
the LORD say?" 38 But if you ask about "the burden
of the LORD," then thus says the LORD: Because you
use this phrase, "the burden of the LORD," though
I forbade you to use it, 39 therefore I will lift you
on high and cast you from my presence, you and
the city which I gave to you and your ancestors.
40 And I will bring upon you eternal reproach,
eternal shame, never to be forgotten.*

The Two Baskets of Figs†

24 1 The LORD showed me two baskets of figs
placed before the temple of the LORD.*
This was after Nebuchadnezzar, king of Babylon,
had exiled from Jerusalem Jeconiah,† son of Je-
hoiakim, king of Judah, and the princes of Judah,
the artisans and smiths, and brought them to
Babylon. 2 One basket contained excellent figs,
those that ripen early. But the other basket con-
tained very bad figs, so bad they could not be
eaten. 3 Then the LORD said to me: What do you
see, Jeremiah?* "Figs," I replied; "the good ones
are very good, but the bad ones very bad, so bad
they cannot be eaten." 4 Thereupon this word of
the LORD came to me: 5 Thus says the LORD, the
God of Israel: Like these good figs, I will also re-
gard with favor Judah's exiles whom I sent away
from this place into the land of the Chaldeans.*
6 I will look after them for good and bring them
back to this land, to build them up, not tear
them down; to plant them, not uproot them.* 7 I
will give them a heart to know me, that I am the
LORD. They shall be my people and I will be their
God, for they shall return to me with their whole
heart.* 8 But like the figs that are bad, so bad they
cannot be eaten—yes, thus says the LORD—even
so will I treat Zedekiah, king of Judah, and his
princes, the remnant of Jerusalem remaining in
this land and those who have settled in the land
of Egypt.* 9 I will make them an object of horror
to all the kingdoms of the earth, a reproach and
a byword, a taunt and a curse, in all the places
to which I will drive them.* 10 I will send upon
them sword, famine, and pestilence, until they
have disappeared from the land which I gave
them and their ancestors.*

Seventy Years of Exile

25 1 The word that came to Jeremiah con-
cerning all the people of Judah, in the
fourth year of Jehoiakim,† son of Josiah, king
of Judah (the first year of Nebuchadnezzar, king
of Babylon).* 2 This word the prophet Jeremiah
spoke to all the people of Judah and all the in-
habitants of Jerusalem: 3 Since the thirteenth

† **23:33–40** A wordplay on *massa'*, which means both "oracle" (usually of woe) and "burden." In vv. 34–40 the word *massa'* itself is forbidden to the people under the meaning of a divine oracle.

24:1–10 For Jeremiah, as for Ezekiel, no good could be expected from the people who had been left in Judah under Zedekiah or who had fled into Egypt; a future might be expected only for those who would pass through the purifying experience of the exile to form the new Israel.

24:1 *Jeconiah*: alternative form of Jehoiachin (cf. note on 22:24).

25:1–14 *The fourth year of Jehoiakim*: 605 B.C. Officially, the first year of Nebuchadnezzar began the following year; but as early as his victory over Egypt at Carchemish in 605, Nebuchadnezzar wielded dominant power in the Near East. Jeremiah saw in him the fulfillment of his prophecy of the enemy to come from the north (cf. 1:13; 6:22–24). In vv. 11–12 the prophecy of the seventy years' exile occurs for the first time; cf. 29:10. This number signifies that the present generation must die out; cf. forty in the exodus tradition (Nm 14:20–23).

* **23:32** Jer 28:15–17.
23:40 Jer 20:11.
24:1 Am 8:1–2.
24:3 Jer 1:11.
24:5 Jer 29:11; Lv 26:44–45.
24:6 Jer 12:15; Am 9:15.
24:7 Jer 30:22; 31:1; 32:37; Bar 2:31.
24:8 Jer 29:18.
24:9 Jer 15:4; Dt 28:37.
24:10 Jer 14:12.
25:1 Jer 36:1.

year of Josiah, son of Amon, king of Judah, to
this day—that is, twenty-three years—the word
of the LORD has come to me and I spoke to you
untiringly, but you would not listen.* 4 The LORD
kept sending you all his servants the prophets,*
but you refused to listen or pay attention 5 to this
message: Turn back, each of you, from your evil
way and from your evil deeds; then you shall
remain in the land which the LORD gave you and
your ancestors, from of old and forever. 6 Do
not follow other gods to serve and bow down to
them; do not provoke me with the works of your
hands, or I will bring evil upon you.* 7 But you
would not listen to me—oracle of the LORD—
and so you provoked me with the works of your
hands to your own harm.* 8 Hence, thus says the
LORD of hosts: Since you would not listen to my
words, 9 I am about to send for and fetch all the
tribes from the north—oracle of the LORD—and I
will send for Nebuchadnezzar, king of Babylon,
my servant; I will bring them against this land, its
inhabitants, and all these neighboring nations. I
will doom them, making them an object of hor-
ror, of hissing, of everlasting reproach.* 10 Among
them I will put to an end the song of joy and the
song of gladness, the voice of the bridegroom
and the voice of the bride, the sound of the mill-
stone and the light of the lamp. 11 This whole
land shall be a ruin and a waste. Seventy years
these nations shall serve the king of Babylon;*
12 but when the seventy years have elapsed, I will
punish the king of Babylon and that nation and
the land of the Chaldeans for their guilt—oracle
of the LORD. Their land I will turn into everlasting
waste.* 13 Against that land I will fulfill all the
words I have spoken against it, all that is written
in this book, which Jeremiah prophesied against
all the nations. 14 They also shall serve many na-
tions and great kings, and thus I will repay them
according to their own deeds and according to
the works of their hands.*

The Cup of Judgment on the Nations

15 † For thus said the LORD, the God of Israel,
to me: Take this cup of the wine of wrath† from
my hand and have all the nations to whom I will
send you drink it.* 16 They shall drink, and retch,
and go mad, because of the sword I will send
among them.* 17 I took the cup from the hand
of the LORD and gave it as drink to all the nations
to whom the LORD sent me: 18 to Jerusalem, the
cities of Judah, its kings and princes, to make
them a ruin and a waste, an object of hissing and
cursing, as they are today; 19 to Pharaoh, king
of Egypt, and his servants, princes, all his peo-
ple 20 and those of mixed ancestry; all the kings
of the land of Uz;† all the kings of the land of
the Philistines: Ashkelon, Gaza, Ekron, and the
remnant of Ashdod; 21 Edom, Moab, and the Am-
monites; 22 all the kings of Tyre, of Sidon, and of
the shores beyond the sea;† 23 Dedan and Tema
and Buz,† all the desert dwellers who shave their
temples; 24 all the kings of Arabia; 25 all the kings
of Zimri, of Elam, of the Medes; 26 all the kings
of the north, near and far, one after the other; all
the kingdoms upon the face of the earth and after
them the king of Sheshach† shall drink.

27 Tell them: Thus says the LORD of hosts, the
God of Israel: Drink! Get drunk and vomit! Fall,
never to rise, before the sword that I will send
among you!* 28 If they refuse to take the cup
from your hand and drink, say to them: Thus
says the LORD of hosts: You must drink!* 29 Now
that I am inflicting evil on this city, called by my
name, how can you possibly escape? You shall
not escape! I am calling down the sword upon all
the inhabitants of the earth—oracle of the LORD
of hosts. 30 As for you, prophesy against them all
these words and say to them:

The LORD roars from on high,
  from his holy dwelling he raises his voice;
Mightily he roars over his sheepfold,
  a shout like that of vintagers echoes*
  over all the inhabitants of the earth.
31 The uproar spreads
  to the end of the earth;
For the LORD has an indictment against the
    nations,
  he enters into judgment against all flesh:
The wicked shall be given to the sword—
  oracle of the LORD.
32 Thus says the LORD of hosts:
Look! disaster stalks

†

25:15–17 Jeremiah is a prophet to the nations (cf. 1:5) as well as to his own people. All the nations mentioned here appear again in the more extensive collection of Jeremiah's oracles against the nations in chaps. 46–51.

25:15 *Cup . . . wrath*: a metaphor for destruction that occurs often in the Old Testament (cf. Ps 11:6; 75:9; Hb 2:15–16; Ez 23:31–33, etc.).

25:20 *Uz*: the homeland of legendary Job, in Edomite or Arabian territory.

25:22 *The shores beyond the sea*: Phoenician commercial colonies located throughout the Mediterranean world.

25:23 *Dedan and Tema and Buz*: North Arabian tribes.

25:26 *Sheshach*: a contrived word from the Hebrew letters of Babylon.

*

25:3 Jer 1:2.
25:4 2 Chr 36:15.
25:6 Jer 7:6–7.
25:7 Jer 7:17–19.
25:9 Jer 1:15; 43:10.
25:11 Lv 26:32–35.
25:12 Is 13:20–22.
25:14 Jer 27:7; 50:9, 41–42; 51:6, 24.
25:15 Rev 14:10.
25:16 Jer 51:7.
25:27 Ob 16.
25:28 Jer 49:12.
25:30 Jer 51:14.

nation after nation;
A violent storm surges
from the recesses of the earth.

33 On that day, those whom the LORD has slain
will be strewn from one end of the earth to the
other. They will not be mourned, they will not
be gathered, they will not be buried; they shall
lie like dung upon the ground.*

34 Howl, you shepherds, and wail!
roll on the ground, leaders of the flock!
The time for your slaughter has come;
like choice rams you shall fall.
35 There is no flight for the shepherds,
no escape for the leaders of the flock.*
36 Listen! Wailing from the shepherds,
howling from the leaders of the flock!
For the LORD lays waste their grazing place;
37 desolate are the peaceful pastures,
from the burning wrath of the LORD.
38 Like a lion he leaves his lair,
and their land is made desolate
By the sweeping sword,
and the burning wrath of the LORD.*

IV. The Temple Sermon

Jeremiah Threatened with Death

26 1 In the beginning of the reign† of Jehoi-
akim, son of Josiah, king of Judah, this
word came from the LORD: 2 Thus says the LORD:
Stand in the court of the house of the LORD and
speak to the inhabitants of all the cities of Judah
who come to worship in the house of the LORD;
whatever I command you, tell them, and hold
nothing back.* 3 Perhaps they will listen and
turn, all of them from their evil way, so that I
may repent of the evil I plan to inflict upon them
for their evil deeds.* 4 Say to them: Thus says the
LORD: If you do not obey me, by walking accord-
ing to the law I set before you 5 and listening to
the words of my servants the prophets, whom I
kept sending you, even though you do not listen
to them,* 6 I will treat this house like Shiloh,
and make this city a curse for all the nations of
the earth.*

7 Now the priests, the prophets, and all the
people heard Jeremiah speaking these words in
the house of the LORD. 8 When Jeremiah finished
speaking all that the LORD commanded him to
speak to all the people, then the priests, the
prophets, and all the people laid hold of him,
crying, "You must die! 9 Why do you prophesy in
the name of the LORD: 'This house shall become
like Shiloh,' and 'This city shall be desolate, with-
out inhabitant'?" And all the people crowded
around Jeremiah in the house of the LORD.

10 When the princes of Judah heard about
these things, they came up from the house of
the king to the house of the LORD and convened
at the New Gate of the house of the LORD. 11 The
priests and prophets said to the princes and to all
the people, "Sentence this man to death! He has
prophesied against this city! You heard it with
your own ears."* 12 Jeremiah said to the princes
and all the people: "It was the LORD who sent me
to prophesy against this house and city every-
thing you have heard. 13 Now, therefore, reform
your ways and your deeds; listen to the voice of
the LORD your God, so that the LORD will have a
change of heart regarding the evil he has spoken
against you.* 14 As for me, I am in your hands;
do with me what is good and right in your eyes.
15 But you should certainly know that by put-
ting me to death, you bring innocent blood on
yourselves, on this city and its inhabitants. For
in truth it was the LORD who sent me to you, to
speak all these words for you to hear."

16 Then the princes and all the people said to
the priests and the prophets, "This man does not
deserve a death sentence; it is in the name of the
LORD, our God, that he speaks to us." 17 At this,
some of the elders of the land arose and said
to the whole assembly of the people, 18 "Micah
of Moresheth† used to prophesy in the days of
Hezekiah, king of Judah, and he said to all the
people of Judah: Thus says the LORD of hosts:

Zion shall be plowed as a field,
Jerusalem, a heap of ruins,
and the temple mount,
a forest ridge.*

19 Did Hezekiah, king of Judah, and all Judah
condemn him to death? Did he not fear the LORD
and entreat the favor of the LORD, so that the LORD
had a change of heart regarding the evil he had
spoken against them? We, however, are about to
do great evil against ourselves."*

†

26:1 *The beginning of the reign*: a technical expression for the time between a king's accession to the throne and the beginning of his first official (calendar) year as king. Jehoiakim's first regnal year was 608 B.C.

26:18 *Micah of Moresheth*: the prophet Micah, who appears among the canonical minor prophets (cf. Mi 1:1).

*

25:33 Jer 8:2; 16:4, 6.
25:35 Jer 32:4.
25:38 Jer 4:7.
26:2 Jer 7:2.
26:3 Jer 18:3.
26:5 Jer 25:4.
26:6 Jer 7:12, 14.
26:11 Jer 38:4.
26:13 Jer 7:3.
26:18 Mi 1:1; 3:12.
26:19 2 Chr 32:26.

The Fate of Uriah

20 There was another man who used to proph-
esy in the name of the LORD, Uriah, son of
Shemaiah, from Kiriath-jearim; he prophesied
against this city and this land the same message
as Jeremiah. 21 When King Jehoiakim and all his
officers and princes heard his words, the king
sought to have him killed. But Uriah heard of it
and fled in fear to Egypt. 22 Then King Jehoiakim
sent Elnathan, son of Achbor, and others with
him into Egypt, 23 and they brought Uriah out of
Egypt and took him to Jehoiakim the king, who
struck him down with the sword and threw his
corpse into the common burial ground. 24 But
the hand of Ahikam, son of Shaphan,† protected
Jeremiah, so they did not hand him over to the
people to be put to death.

V. Controversies with the False Prophets†

Serve Babylon or Perish

27 1 In the beginning of the reign of Zede-
kiah,† son of Josiah, king of Judah, this
word came to Jeremiah from the LORD: 2 The LORD
said to me: Make for yourself thongs and yoke
bars and put them on your shoulders. 3 Send
them to the kings of Edom, Moab, the Ammon-
ites, Tyre, and Sidon, through the ambassadors
who have come to Jerusalem to Zedekiah, king
of Judah,† 4 and command them to tell their
lords: Thus says the LORD of hosts, the God of
Israel, Thus shall you say to your lords: 5 It was I
who made the earth, human being and beast on
the face of the earth, by my great power, with my
outstretched arm; and I can give them to whom-
ever I think fit.* 6 Now I have given all these
lands into the hand of Nebuchadnezzar, king
of Babylon, my servant; even the wild animals I
have given him to serve him.* 7 All nations shall
serve him and his son and his grandson, until the
time comes for him and his land; then many na-
tions and great kings will enslave him.* 8 Mean-
while, the nation or the kingdom that will not
serve him, Nebuchadnezzar, king of Babylon, or
bend its neck under the yoke of the king of Bab-

27:8

ylon, I will punish that nation with sword, fam-
ine, and pestilence—oracle of the LORD—until I
finish them by his hand.*
9 You, however, must not listen to your proph-
ets,† to your diviners and dreamers, to your
soothsayers and sorcerers, who say to you, "Do
not serve the king of Babylon."* 10 For they
prophesy lies to you, so as to drive you far from
your land, making me banish you so that you
perish.* 11 The people that bends the neck to the
yoke of the king of Babylon to serve him, I will
leave in peace on its own land—oracle of the
LORD—to cultivate it and dwell on it.*
12 To Zedekiah, king of Judah, I spoke the same
words: Bend your necks to the yoke of the king of
Babylon; serve him and his people, so that you
may live.* 13 Why should you and your people die
by sword, famine, and pestilence, in accordance
with the word the LORD has spoken to the nation
that will not serve the king of Babylon?* 14 Do not
listen to the words of the prophets who say to you,
"Do not serve the king of Babylon." They prophesy
lies to you!* 15 I did not send them—oracle of the
LORD—but they prophesy falsely in my name. As a
result I must banish you, and you will perish, you
and the prophets who are prophesying to you.*

†

26:24 *Ahikam, son of Shaphan*: one of Josiah's officials (2 Kgs 22:12) and Jeremiah's friend. He was the father of Gedaliah, who was governor of Judah after Zedekiah's deportation (cf. Jer 39:14; 40:5–7).

27:1–29:32 A special collection of Jeremiah's prophecies dealing with false prophets. Stylistic peculiarities evident in the Hebrew suggest that these three chapters once existed as an independent work.

27:1 *Zedekiah*: The Hebrew text actually has "Jehoiakim," but the content of the chapter indicates that Zedekiah is intended.

27:3 The time is the fourth year of Zedekiah, 594 B.C., the occasion of a delegation from the neighboring states, doubtless for the purpose of laying plans against Nebuchadnezzar.

27:9 *Your prophets*: seers and diviners served non-Israelite kings just as the professional prophets served the kings of Judah.

*

27:5 Jer 32:17.
27:6 Jer 25:9; 43:10; Ez 30:21, 25.
27:7 Jer 25:11; 2 Chr 36:20.
27:8 Jer 25:9; Bar 2:22.
27:9 Jer 29:8.
27:10 Jer 14:13–16.
27:11 Bar 2:21.
27:12 Jer 38:17.
27:13 Jer 24:8–10.
27:14 Jer 14:14; 23:21.
27:15 Jer 20:6.

16 * To the priests and to all the people I said: Thus says the LORD: Do not listen to the words of your prophets who prophesy to you: "The vessels of the house of the LORD will soon be brought back from Babylon," for they prophesy lies to you. 17 Do not listen to them! Serve the king of Babylon that you may live. Why should this city become rubble? 18 If they were prophets, if the word of the LORD were with them, then they would intercede with the LORD of hosts, that the vessels remaining in the house of the LORD and in the house of the king of Judah and in Jerusalem should not also go to Babylon. 19 For thus says the LORD of hosts concerning the pillars, the sea, the stands, and the rest of the vessels remaining in this city, 20 which Nebuchadnezzar, king of Babylon, did not take when he exiled Jeconiah, son of Jehoiakim, king of Judah, from Jerusalem to Babylon, along with all the nobles of Judah and Jerusalem— 21 thus says the LORD of hosts, the God of Israel, concerning the vessels remaining in the house of the LORD, in the house of the king of Judah, and in Jerusalem:* 22 To Babylon they shall go, and there they shall remain, until the day I look for them—oracle of the LORD; then I will bring them back and restore them to this place.

The Two Yokes

28 1 That same year, in the beginning of the reign of Zedekiah, king of Judah, in the fifth month of the fourth year, Hananiah the prophet, son of Azzur, from Gibeon, said to me in the house of the LORD in the sight of the priests and all the people: 2 "Thus says the LORD of hosts, the God of Israel: I have broken the yoke of the king of Babylon. 3 Within two years I will restore to this place all the vessels of the house of the LORD which Nebuchadnezzar, king of Babylon, took from this place and carried away to Babylon. 4 And Jeconiah, son of Jehoiakim, king of Judah, and all the exiles of Judah who went to Babylon, I will bring back to this place—oracle of the LORD—for I will break the yoke of the king of Babylon."

5 Jeremiah the prophet answered the prophet Hananiah in the sight of the priests and all the people standing in the house of the LORD, 6 and said: Amen! thus may the LORD do! May the LORD fulfill your words that you have prophesied, by bringing back the vessels of the house of the LORD and all the exiles from Babylon to this place! 7 But now, listen to the word I am about to speak in your hearing and the hearing of all the people. 8 In the past, the prophets who came before you and me prophesied war, disaster, and pestilence against many lands and mighty kingdoms. 9 But the prophet who prophesies peace is recognized as the prophet whom the LORD has truly sent only when his word comes to pass.*

10 Thereupon Hananiah the prophet took the yoke bar from the neck of Jeremiah the prophet and broke it. 11 He said in the sight of all the people: "Thus says the LORD: Like this, within two years I will break the yoke of Nebuchadnezzar, king of Babylon, from the neck of all the nations." At that, the prophet Jeremiah went on his way.

12 After Hananiah the prophet had broken the yoke bar off the neck of the prophet Jeremiah, the word of the LORD came to Jeremiah: 13 Go tell Hananiah this: Thus says the LORD: By breaking a wooden yoke bar, you make an iron yoke! 14 For thus says the LORD of hosts, the God of Israel: A yoke of iron I have placed on the necks of all these nations serving Nebuchadnezzar, king of Babylon, and they shall serve him; even the wild animals I have given him.* 15 And Jeremiah the prophet said to Hananiah the prophet: Listen to this, Hananiah! The LORD has not sent you, and you have led this people to rely on deception. 16 For this, says the LORD, I am sending you from the face of the earth; this very year you shall die, because you have preached rebellion against the LORD.* 17 Hananiah the prophet died in that year, in the seventh month.

Letter to the Exiles in Babylon

29 1 These are the words of the scroll which Jeremiah the prophet sent from Jerusalem to the remaining elders among the exiles, to the priests, the prophets, and all the people whom Nebuchadnezzar exiled from Jerusalem to Babylon. 2 This was after King Jeconiah and the queen mother, the court officials, the princes of Judah and Jerusalem, the artisans and smiths had left Jerusalem.* 3 Delivered in Babylon by Elasah,† son of Shaphan, and by Gemariah, son of Hilkiah, whom Zedekiah, king of Judah, sent to the king of Babylon, the letter read:

4 Thus says the LORD of hosts, the God of Israel, to all the exiles whom I exiled from Jerusalem to Babylon: 5 Build houses and live in them; plant gardens and eat their fruits. 6 Take wives and

---

† **29:3** *Elasah*: probably the brother of Ahikam (cf. 26:24). *Gemariah*: probably the son of the high priest Hilkiah; cf. 2 Kgs 22:4. Zedekiah had dispatched these men to Nebuchadnezzar for some other purpose, possibly the payment of tribute, but Jeremiah took advantage of their mission to send his letter with them.

* **27:16** Jer 28:3; 2 Chr 36:7, 10, 18.
27:21–22 2 Kgs 25:13–17; 2 Chr 36:18, 22.
28:9 Dt 18:22.
28:14 Jer 27:6–7; Dt 28:48.
28:16 Dt 13:6.
29:2 2 Kgs 24:15.

have sons and daughters; find wives for your sons and give your daughters to husbands, so that they may bear sons and daughters. Increase there; do not decrease. 7 Seek the welfare of the city to which I have exiled you; pray for it to the LORD, for upon its welfare your own depends.* 8 For thus says the LORD of hosts, the God of Israel: Do not be deceived by the prophets and diviners who are among you; do not listen to those among you who dream dreams,* 9 for they prophesy lies to you in my name; I did not send them—oracle of the LORD.*

10 For thus says the LORD: Only after seventy years have elapsed for Babylon will I deal with you and fulfill for you my promise to bring you back to this place.* 11 For I know well the plans I have in mind for you—oracle of the LORD—plans for your welfare and not for woe, so as to give you a future of hope. 12 When you call me, and come and pray to me, I will listen to you.* 13 When you look for me, you will find me. Yes, when you seek me with all your heart, 14 I will let you find me—oracle of the LORD—and I will change your lot; I will gather you together from all the nations and all the places to which I have banished you—oracle of the LORD—and bring you back to the place from which I have exiled you.* 15 As for your saying, "The LORD has raised up for us prophets here in Babylon"—

16 Thus says the LORD concerning the king sitting on David's throne and all the people living in this city, your kinsmen who did not go with you into exile; 17 thus says the LORD of hosts: I am sending against them sword, famine, and pestilence. I will make them like rotten figs, so spoiled that they cannot be eaten. 18 I will pursue them with sword, famine, and pestilence, and make them an object of horror to all the kingdoms of the earth, a curse, a desolation, a hissing, and a reproach to all the nations among which I have banished them,* 19 because they did not listen to my words—oracle of the LORD—even though I kept sending them my servants the prophets, but they would not listen to them—oracle of the LORD.*

20 As for you, listen to the word of the LORD, all you exiles whom I sent away from Jerusalem to Babylon. 21 This is what the LORD of hosts, the God of Israel, says about Ahab, son of Kolaiah, and Zedekiah, son of Maaseiah, who prophesy lies to you in my name: I am handing them over to Nebuchadnezzar, king of Babylon, who will kill them before your eyes.* 22 And because of them this curse will be used by all the exiles of Judah in Babylon: "May the LORD make you like Zedekiah and Ahab, whom the king of Babylon roasted in fire," 23 because they have committed an outrage in Israel, committing adultery with their neighbors' wives, and alleging in my name things I did not command. I know, I am witness—oracle of the LORD.*

The False Prophet Shemaiah

24 To Shemaiah, the Nehelamite, say: 25 Thus says the LORD of hosts, the God of Israel: Because you sent documents in your own name to all the people in Jerusalem, to Zephaniah, the priest, son of Maaseiah, and to all the priests saying: 26 † "It is the LORD who has appointed you priest in place of the priest Jehoiada, to provide officers for the house of the LORD, that you may confine in stocks or pillory any madman who poses as a prophet. 27 Why, then, have you not rebuked Jeremiah of Anathoth who poses as a prophet among you? 28 For he sent this message to us in Babylon: It will be a long time; build houses to live in; plant gardens and eat their fruit. . . ."

29 When the priest Zephaniah read this letter to Jeremiah the prophet, 30 the word of the LORD came to Jeremiah: 31 Send to all the exiles: Thus says the LORD concerning Shemaiah, the Nehelamite: Because Shemaiah prophesies to you, although I did not send him, and has led you to rely on a lie, 32 therefore thus says the LORD, I will punish Shemaiah, the Nehelamite, and his descendants. None of them shall dwell among this people to see the good I will do for this people—oracle of the LORD—because he preached rebellion against the LORD.

VI. Oracles of the Restoration of Israel and Judah

The Restoration†

30 1 This word came to Jeremiah from the LORD: 2 Thus says the LORD, the God of Israel: Write down on a scroll all the words I

---

†

29:26–29 Jeremiah's message to Shemaiah is not completely preserved in the current Hebrew text, hence the incomplete sentence in vv. 25–28.

30:1–31:40 These two chapters contain salvation oracles that originally expressed the double expectation that the Lord would return the exiled survivors of the Northern Kingdom of Israel and reunite Israel and Judah as one kingdom under a just Davidic king. They were probably composed early in Josiah's reign (the reference of v. 9), when he took advantage of Assyria's internal disintegration and asserted control over northern Israel (cf. 2 Kgs 23:15–17). With the destruction of Jerusalem, the oracles were re-worked to include Judah and their fulfillment along with the renewal of the Davidic dynasty became associated with the eschatological "day of the Lord."

---

*

29:7 1 Tm 2:1–2.
29:8 Jer 27:9, 14.
29:9 Jer 5:31.
29:10 Jer 25:11; 2 Chr 36:21–22; Ezr 1:1; Dn 9:2; Zec 1:12; 7:5.
29:12 Jer 33:3.
29:14 Jer 23:3, 8.
29:18 Jer 15:4; 24:9; 34:17–18.
29:19 Jer 25:4.
29:21 Jer 14:14.
29:23 Jer 23:14.

have spoken to you.* 3 For indeed, the days are
coming—oracle of the LORD—when I will restore
the fortunes of my people Israel and Judah—
oracle of the LORD. I will bring them back to the
land which I gave to their ancestors, and they
shall take possession of it.*
4 These are the words the LORD spoke to Israel
and to Judah: 5 Thus says the LORD:

We hear a cry of fear:
terror, not peace.
6 Inquire and see:
does a male give birth?
Why, then, do I see all these men,
their hands on their loins
Like women in labor,
all their faces drained of color?*
7 Ah! How mighty is that day—
there is none like it!
A time of distress for Jacob,
though he shall be saved from it.*

8 On that day—oracle of the LORD of hosts—I
will break his yoke off your neck and snap your
bonds. Strangers shall no longer enslave them;*
9 instead, they shall serve the LORD, their God,
and David, their king,† whom I will raise up for
them.*

10 But you, my servant Jacob, do not fear!—
oracle of the LORD—
do not be dismayed, Israel!
For I will soon deliver you from places far
away,
your offspring from the land of their exile;
Jacob shall again find rest,
secure, with none to frighten him,*
11 for I am with you—oracle of the LORD—to
save you.
I will bring to an end all the nations
among whom I have scattered you;
but you I will not bring to an end.
I will chastise you as you deserve,
I will not let you go unpunished.*
12 For thus says the LORD:
Incurable is your wound,
grievous your injury;*
13 There is none to plead your case,
no remedy for your running sore,
no healing for you.
14 All your lovers have forgotten you,
they do not seek you out.
I struck you as an enemy would strike,
punishing you cruelly.*
15 Why cry out over your wound?
There is no relief for your pain.
Because of your great guilt,
your numerous sins,
I have done this to you.*
16 Yet all who devour you shall be devoured,
all your enemies shall go into exile.
All who plunder you shall become plunder,
all who pillage you I will hand over to be
pillaged.*
17 For I will restore your health;
I will heal your injuries—oracle of the LORD.
"The outcast" they have called you,
"whom no one looks for."*
18 Thus says the LORD:
See! I will restore the fortunes of Jacob's tents,
on his dwellings I will have compassion;
A city shall be rebuilt upon its own ruins,
a citadel restored where it should be.*
19 From them will come praise,
the sound of people rejoicing.
I will increase them, they will not decrease,
I will glorify them, they will not be
insignificant.*
20 His children shall be as of old,
his assembly shall stand firm in my
presence,
I will punish all his oppressors.*
21 His leader† shall be one of his own,
and his ruler shall emerge from his ranks.
He shall approach me when I summon him;
Why else would he dare
approach me?—oracle of the LORD.
22 You shall be my people,
and I will be your God.*
23 Look! The storm of the LORD!
His wrath breaks out
In a whirling storm
that bursts upon the heads of the wicked.*
24 The anger of the LORD will not abate

† **30:9** *David, their king*: a descendant of David ("his leader" in v. 21) who, like his ancestor, would rule a unified kingdom and "walk in the ways of the Lord," as the Deuteronomistic historians claimed David did. Other prophets also refer to this idealized ruler as "David"; cf. Ez 34:23–24; 37:24–25; Hos 3:5.

30:21 *His leader*: cf. v. 9. *Approach me*: i.e., in the sanctuary of the Temple for worship. This new David is given a priestly function to perform on behalf of the assembly. To approach God on one's own brings death; cf. Lv 16:1–2.

* **30:2** Jer 36:2; Hb 2:2; Rev 1:11.
30:3 Jer 29:14; 31:8, 10, 23; 32:37, 44; Ez 39:25; Am 9:14.
30:6 Jer 6:24; 50:43.
30:7 Am 5:18; Zep 1:14–15.
30:8 Is 14:5–6; Ez 34:27.
30:9 Ez 34:23; 37:24; Hos 3:5; Lk 1:69.
30:10 Jer 46:27; Is 43:5.
30:11 Jer 46:28; Ez 11:16–17; Am 9:8–9.
30:12 Jer 10:19; 14:17; 15:18.
30:14 Jer 22:22; Lam 1:19.
30:15 Jer 15:18.
30:16 Jer 2:3.
30:17 Jer 33:6.
30:18 Jer 33:7, 11; Ezr 6:3–15; Ez 36:10.
30:19 Is 35:10; 51:11.
30:20 Is 49:26.
30:22 Jer 24:7; 31:1, 33; 32:38; Lv 26:12; Ez 11:20; 36:28.
30:23 Jer 23:19.
30:24 Jer 23:20.

until he has carried out completely
the decisions of his heart.
In days to come
you will fully understand it.*

Good News of the Return

31 1 At that time—oracle of the LORD—
I will be the God of all the families of Israel,
and they shall be my people.*
2† Thus says the LORD:
The people who escaped the sword
find favor in the wilderness.
As Israel comes forward to receive rest,
3 from afar the LORD appears:
With age-old love I have loved you;
so I have kept my mercy toward you.*
4 Again I will build you, and you shall stay built,
virgin Israel;
Carrying your festive tambourines,
you shall go forth dancing with
merrymakers.
5 You shall again plant vineyards
on the mountains of Samaria;
those who plant them shall enjoy their
fruits.*
6 Yes, a day will come when the watchmen
call out on Mount Ephraim:
"Come, let us go up to Zion,
to the LORD, our God."*

The Road of Return

7 For thus says the LORD:
Shout with joy for Jacob,
exult at the head of the nations;
proclaim your praise and say:
The LORD has saved his people,
the remnant of Israel.*
8 Look! I will bring them back
from the land of the north;
I will gather them from the ends of the earth,
the blind and the lame in their midst,
Pregnant women, together with those in
labor—
an immense throng—they shall return.*
9 With weeping they shall come,
but with compassion I will guide them;
I will lead them to streams of water,
on a level road, without stumbling.
For I am a father to Israel,
Ephraim is my firstborn.*
10 Hear the word of the LORD, you nations,
proclaim it on distant coasts, and say:
The One who scattered Israel, now gathers
them;
he guards them as a shepherd his flock.
11 The LORD shall ransom Jacob,
he shall redeem him from a hand too
strong for him.*
12 Shouting, they shall mount the heights of
Zion,
they shall come streaming to the LORD's
blessings:
The grain, the wine, and the oil,
flocks of sheep and cattle;
They themselves shall be like watered gardens,
never again neglected.*
13 Then young women shall make merry and
dance,
young men and old as well.
I will turn their mourning into joy,
I will show them compassion and have
them rejoice after their sorrows.
14 I will lavish choice portions on the priests,
and my people shall be filled with my
blessings—
oracle of the LORD.

End of Rachel's Mourning

15 Thus says the LORD:
In Ramah† is heard the sound of sobbing,
bitter weeping!
Rachel mourns for her children,
she refuses to be consoled
for her children—they are no more!*
16 Thus says the LORD:
Cease your cries of weeping,
hold back your tears!
There is compensation for your labor—
oracle of the LORD—
they shall return from the enemy's land.
17 There is hope for your future—oracle of the
LORD—
your children shall return to their own
territory.*
18 Indeed, I heard Ephraim rocking in grief:
You chastised me, and I was chastised;

JER

†

31:2–3 Jeremiah describes the exiles of the Northern Kingdom on their way home from the nations where the Assyrians had resettled them (722/721 B.C.). The favor they discover in the wilderness is the appearance of the Lord (v. 3) coming to guide them to Jerusalem. Implicit in these verses is the presentation of the people's return from captivity as a second exodus, a unifying theme in Second Isaiah (chaps. 40–55).

31:15 *Ramah*: a village about five miles north of Jerusalem, where one tradition locates Rachel's tomb (1 Sm 10:2). The wife of Jacob/Israel, Rachel is the matriarchal ancestor of Ephraim, chief among the northern tribes. She personified Israel as a mother whose grief for her lost children is especially poignant because she had to wait a long time to bear them. Mt 2:18 applies this verse to Herod's slaughter of the innocents.

*

31:1 Jer 30:22.
31:3 Dt 7:8; 10:15; Is 43:4; 63:9; Hos 11:1, 4.
31:5 Dt 28:30; Is 65:21; Am 9:14.
31:6 Is 2:3; 27:13; Mi 4:2.
31:7 Is 12:6.
31:8 Jer 3:18; 23:3, 8; Is 35:5–6.
31:9 Ex 4:22.
31:11 Is 44:23; 48:20.
31:12 Is 58:11.
31:15 Mt 2:18.
31:17 Jer 29:10–14.

Pray It!

Rachel Weeps

Rachel was the "mother of Israel," the favored wife of Jacob (see Gn 29:28–30)—the patriarch whose twelve sons formed the twelve Tribes of Israel. In Jeremiah 31:15–17, she is symbolically weeping over the death and captivity of her children—the Israelites—after the Babylonian invasion.

Rachel's weeping has become an image of trauma and unrelenting grief over violence, death, and slaughter, especially when children are involved. For example, Matthew 2:16–18 quotes Jeremiah 31:15–17 in a story about the massacre of infants in Bethlehem. Project Rachel is an organized ministry for women who have had abortions. And Rachel Weeps is a Holocaust exhibition recalling the murder of millions of Jewish men, women, and children.

Jeremiah goes on in verses 16–17 with words of hope. God promises that the scattered children will be brought back. We can trust that God is with the victims of senseless violence and those who grieve for them. Let us pray for Rachel's grief to end.

Jer 31:15–17

I was like an untamed calf.
Bring me back, let me come back,
for you are the LORD, my God.*
19 For after I turned away, I repented;
after I came to myself, I struck my thigh;†
I was ashamed, even humiliated,
because I bore the disgrace of my youth.*
20 Is Ephraim not my favored son,
the child in whom I delight?
Even though I threaten him,
I must still remember him!
My heart stirs for him,
I must show him compassion!—oracle of
the LORD.*

Summons To Return Home

21 Set up road markers,
put up signposts;
Turn your attention to the highway,
the road you walked.
Turn back, virgin Israel,
turn back to these your cities.
22 How long will you continue to hesitate,
rebellious daughter?
The LORD has created a new thing upon the
earth:
woman encompasses man.†

23 Thus says the LORD of hosts, the God of Is-
rael: When I restore their fortunes in the land of
Judah and in its cities, they shall again use this
greeting: "May the LORD bless you, Tent of Justice,
Holy Mountain!"* 24 Judah and all its cities, the
farmers and those who lead the flock shall dwell
there together. 25 For I will slake the thirst of the
faint; the appetite of all the weary I will satisfy.
26 At this I awoke and opened my eyes; my sleep
was satisfying.†
27 See, days are coming—oracle of the LORD—
when I will sow the house of Israel and the house
of Judah with the seed of human beings and
the seed of animals. 28 As I once watched over
them to uproot and tear down, to demolish, to
destroy, and to harm, so I will watch over them
to build and to plant—oracle of the LORD.* 29 In
those days they shall no longer say,

"The parents ate unripe grapes,*
and the children's teeth are set on edge,"†
30 but all shall die because of their own iniquity:
the teeth of anyone who eats unripe grapes shall
be set on edge.

The New Covenant†

31 See, days are coming—oracle of the LORD—
when I will make a new covenant with the house

†

31:19 *Struck my thigh*: a gesture signifying grief and dread (cf. Ez 21:17).

31:22 No satisfactory explanation has been given for this text. Jerome, for example, saw the image as a reference to the infant Jesus enclosed in Mary's womb. Since Jeremiah often uses marital imagery in his description of a restored Israel, the phrase may refer to a wedding custom, perhaps women circling the groom in a dance. It may also be a metaphor describing the security of a new Israel, a security so complete that it defies the imagination and must be expressed as hyperbolic role reversal: any danger will be so insignificant that women can protect their men.

31:26 *I awoke . . . satisfying*: an intrusive comment.

31:29 *"The parents . . . on edge"*: Jeremiah's opponents use this proverb to complain that they are being punished for sins of their ancestors. Jeremiah, however, insists that the Lord knows the depth of their wickedness and holds them accountable for their actions.

31:31–34 The new covenant is an occasional prophetic theme, beginning with Hosea. According to Jeremiah, (a) it lasts forever; (b)

31:18 Lv 26:40–42.
31:19 Dt 30:1–3.
31:20 Hos 11:8.
31:23 Jer 30:3; Ps 122:8.
31:28 Jer 1:10; 18:7.
31:29 Dt 24:16; Ez 18:2.

of Israel and the house of Judah.* 32 It will not
be like the covenant I made with their ancestors
the day I took them by the hand to lead them out
of the land of Egypt. They broke my covenant,
though I was their master—oracle of the LORD.*
33 But this is the covenant I will make with the
house of Israel after those days—oracle of the
LORD. I will place my law within them, and write
it upon their hearts; I will be their God, and they
shall be my people.* 34 They will no longer teach
their friends and relatives, "Know the LORD!"
Everyone, from least to greatest, shall know
me—oracle of the LORD—for I will forgive their
iniquity and no longer remember their sin.*

Certainty of God's Promise

35 Thus says the LORD,
Who gives the sun to light the day,
moon and stars to light the night;
Who stirs up the sea so that its waves roar,
whose name is LORD of hosts:*
36 If ever this fixed order gives way
before me—oracle of the LORD—
Then would the offspring of Israel cease
as a people before me forever.*
37 Thus says the LORD:
If the heavens on high could be measured,
or the foundations below the earth be
explored,
Then would I reject all the offspring of Israel
because of all they have done—oracle of
the LORD.

Jerusalem Rebuilt†

38 See, days are coming—oracle of the LORD—
when the city shall be rebuilt as the LORD's,*
from the Tower of Hananel to the Corner Gate.
39 A measuring line shall be stretched from there
straight to the hill Gareb and then turn to Goah.
40 The whole valley of corpses and ashes, all the
terraced slopes toward the Wadi Kidron, as far
as the corner of the Horse Gate at the east, shall
be holy to the LORD. Never again shall the city be
uprooted or demolished.

Live It!

The Heart of the Matter

The Ten Commandments. The stone tablets on which they were written are the most famous stone tablets in the world, and yet no one knows where they are. The ark of the Covenant, in which they were once kept, was taken during a raid on the Temple (see Jer 52:17–23). What a find they would be today! Imagine all the people flocking to see the original Ten Commandments.

But perhaps their absence makes Jeremiah's beautiful words about the New Covenant in Jeremiah 31:31–34 even more fitting. What was etched in stone on those tablets needs to be etched in our heart. We keep in our heart what is most valuable to us. If we keep God's law there, we have no need for it to be written in stone.

When you look into your heart, what do you find written there?

► **Jer 31:31–34**

Pledge of Restoration†

32 1 The word came to Jeremiah from the
LORD in the tenth year of Zedekiah,† king
of Judah, the eighteenth year of Nebuchadnezzar.
2 At that time the army of the king of Babylon
was besieging Jerusalem, while Jeremiah the
prophet was confined to the court of the guard,
in the house of the king of Judah.* 3 Zedekiah,
king of Judah, had confined him there, saying:
"How dare you prophesy: Thus says the LORD: I
am handing this city over to the king of Babylon

its law (*torah*) is written in human hearts; (c) it gives everyone true knowledge of God, making additional instruction (*torah*) unnecessary. The Dead Sea Scroll community claimed they were partners in a "new covenant." The New Testament presents the death and resurrection of Jesus of Nazareth as inaugurating a new covenant open to anyone who professes faith in Jesus the Christ. Cf. Lk 22:20; 1 Cor 11:25; Heb 8:8–12. *Know the LORD*: cf. note on 22:15–16.

31:38–40 The landmarks in these verses outline the borders of Jerusalem during the time of Nehemiah: the Tower of Hananel (Neh 3:1; 12:39) in the northeast and the Corner Gate (2 Kgs 14:13) in the northwest; Goah in the southeast and Gareb Hill in the southwest; the Valley of Ben-hinnom ("the Valley of corpses and ashes"), which met the Wadi Kidron in the southeast, and the Horse Gate in the eastern wall at the southeast corner of the Temple area.

32:1–44 This chapter recounts a prophecy "in action." At the Lord's command, Jeremiah fulfills his family duty to purchase the land of his cousin, carrying out all the legal details, even putting the deed away for safekeeping against the day he will have to produce it to verify his ownership of the land. The Lord defines the meaning of this symbolic action: In the future, Judah will be restored and daily life will return to normal.

32:1 *The tenth year of Zedekiah*: 588 B.C. *The eighteenth year of Nebuchadnezzar*: dating his reign from his victory at Carchemish; see note on 25:1–14.

31:31 Jer 32:40; Heb 9:15.
31:32 Ex 24:7–8; Dt 5:2.
31:33 Jer 32:40; Ez 37:26; Heb 10:16.
31:34 Is 54:13.
31:35 Gn 1:14–18.
31:36 Jer 33:20–21.
31:38 Neh 12:38; Zec 14:10–11.
32:2 Jer 33:1; 37:20; 38:6; 39:14.

that he may capture it.* 4 Zedekiah, king of Judah, shall not escape the hands of the Chaldeans: he shall indeed be handed over to the king of Babylon. He shall speak with him face to face and see him eye to eye.* 5 He shall take Zedekiah to Babylon. There he shall remain, until I attend to him—oracle of the LORD. If you fight against the Chaldeans, you cannot win!"*

6 † Jeremiah said, This word came to me from the LORD: 7 Hanamel, son of your uncle Shallum, will come to you with the offer:* "Purchase my field in Anathoth, since you, as nearest relative, have the first right of purchase."† 8 And, just as the LORD had said, my cousin Hanamel came to me in the court of the guard and said, "Please purchase my field in Anathoth, in the territory of Benjamin; as nearest relative, you have the first right of possession—purchase it for yourself." Then I knew this was the word of the LORD. 9 So I bought the field in Anathoth from my cousin Hanamel, weighing out for him the silver, seventeen shekels of silver.

10 When I had written and sealed the deed, called witnesses and weighed out the silver on the scales, 11 I accepted the deed of purchase, both the sealed copy, containing title and conditions, and the open copy.† 12 I gave this deed of purchase to Baruch, son of Neriah, son of Mahseiah, in the presence of my cousin Hanamel and the witnesses who had signed the deed of purchase and before all the Judahites sitting around in the court of the guard.*

13 In their presence I gave Baruch this charge: 14 Thus says the LORD of hosts, the God of Israel: Take these deeds of purchase, both the sealed and the open deeds, and put them in an earthenware jar,† so they can last a long time. 15 For thus says the LORD of hosts, the God of Israel: They shall again purchase houses and fields and vineyards in this land.

16 After I had given the deed of purchase to Baruch, son of Neriah, I prayed to the LORD: 17 Ah, my Lord GOD! You made the heavens and the earth with your great power and your outstretched arm; nothing is too difficult for you.* 18 You continue your kindness through a thousand generations; but you repay the ancestors' guilt upon their children who follow them. Great and mighty God, whose name is LORD of hosts,* 19 great in counsel, mighty in deed, whose eyes are fixed on all the ways of mortals, giving to all according to their ways, according to the fruit of their deeds:* 20 you performed signs and wonders in the land of Egypt and to this day, in Israel and among all peoples, you have made a name for yourself as on this day.* 21 You brought your people Israel out of the land of Egypt with signs and wonders, with a strong hand and an outstretched arm, and great terror. 22 And you gave them this land, as you had sworn to their ancestors to give them, a land flowing with milk and honey.* 23 They went in and took possession of it, but they did not listen to your voice. They did not live by your law; they did not do anything you commanded them to do. Then you made all this evil fall upon them.* 24 See, the siegeworks have arrived at this city to capture it; the city is handed over to the Chaldeans who are attacking it, with sword, starvation, and disease. What you threatened has happened—you can see it for yourself.* 25 Yet you told me, my Lord GOD: Purchase the field with silver and summon witnesses, when the city has already been handed over to the Chaldeans!

26 Then this word of the LORD came to Jeremiah: 27 I am the LORD, the God of all the living! Is anything too difficult for me? 28 Therefore the LORD says: I am handing over this city to the Chaldeans and to Nebuchadnezzar, king of Babylon, and he shall capture it. 29 The Chaldeans who are attacking this city shall go in and set the city on fire, burning it and the houses, on whose roofs incense was burned to Baal and libations were poured out to other gods in order to provoke me.* 30 From their youth the Israelites and the Judahites have been doing only what is evil in my eyes; the Israelites have been provoking me with the works of their hands—oracle of the LORD.* 31 This city has so stirred my anger and wrath, from the day it was built to this day, that I must put it out of my sight, 32 for all the evil the Israelites and Judahites have done to provoke

†

32:6–9 Jeremiah's imprisonment by the weak-willed Zedekiah was a technical custody that did not deprive him of all freedom of action.

32:7 *The first right of purchase*: the obligation of the closest relative to redeem the property of a family member in economic distress so that the ancestral land remains within the family (Lv 25:25–28); see note on Ru 2:20.

32:11 *The sealed copy . . . and the open copy*: the legal deed of sale was written on a scroll, which was then rolled up and sealed; a second scroll containing a copy of the legal deed was then rolled around it and left unsealed so the contents of the legal deed would be accessible without destroying the original seal.

32:14 *In an earthenware jar*: to protect the scroll from drying out and disintegrating. Some of the Dead Sea Scrolls were found in such jars.

*

32:3 Jer 26:9; 34:2; 37:6–10.
32:4 Jer 34:3; 38:18, 23; 39:4–7.
32:5 Jer 39:7; 52:11.
32:7 Lv 25:24–34; Ru 4:4.
32:12 Jer 36:4.
32:17 2 Kgs 19:15; Jb 42:2.
32:18 Ex 20:5–6; 34:6; Dt 5:9.
32:19 Jb 34:21; Ps 33:13–15.
32:20 Ex 6:6; Dt 4:34; Ps 135:9.
32:22 Jer 11:5; Gn 15:18; 17:8; 26:3.
32:23 Jer 7:24–26; Dn 9:10–14.
32:24 Jer 21:5; 33:4.
32:29 Jer 21:10; 37:8–10.
32:30 Jer 3:25; 44:8.

me—they, their kings, their princes, their priests,
and their prophets, the people of Judah and the
inhabitants of Jerusalem.* 33 They turned their
backs to me, not their faces; though I taught
them persistently, they would not listen or accept
correction.* 34 Instead they set up their abomina-
tions in the house which bears my name in order
to defile it.* 35 They built high places to Baal in
the Valley of Ben-hinnom to sacrifice their sons
and daughters to Molech;† I never commanded
them to do this, nor did it even enter my mind
that they would practice this abomination, so as
to bring sin upon Judah.*

36 Now, therefore, thus says the LORD, the God
of Israel, concerning this city, which you say is be-
ing handed over to the king of Babylon by means
of the sword, starvation, and disease: 37 See, I
am gathering them from all the lands to which
I drove them in my rising fury and great anger; I
will bring them back to this place and settle them
here in safety.* 38 They shall be my people, and I
will be their God.* 39 I will give them one heart
and one way, that they may fear me always, for
their own good and the good of their children
after them. 40 With them I will make an everlast-
ing covenant, never to cease doing good to them;
I will put fear of me in their hearts so that they
never turn away from me.* 41 I will take delight
in doing good to them: I will plant them firmly
in this land, with all my heart and soul.*

42 For thus says the LORD: Just as I have brought
upon this people all this great evil, so I will
bring upon them all the good I have promised
them.* 43 Fields shall be purchased in this land,
about which you say, "It is a wasteland, without
human beings or animals, handed over to the
Chaldeans."* 44 They will purchase fields with
silver, write up deeds, seal them, and have them
witnessed in the land of Benjamin, in the neigh-
borhood of Jerusalem, in the cities of Judah and
of the hill country, in the cities of the Shephelah
and the Negeb, when I restore their fortunes—
oracle of the LORD.*

Restoration of Jerusalem

33 1 The word of the LORD came to Jeremiah
a second time while he was still confined
in the court of the guard: 2 Thus says the LORD
who made the earth, giving it shape and stability,
LORD is his name: 3 Call to me, and I will answer
you; I will tell you great things beyond the reach
of your knowledge.* 4 Thus says the LORD, the
God of Israel, concerning the houses of this city
and the houses of the kings of Judah, which are
being torn down because of the siegeworks and
the sword:* 5 men come to battle the Chaldeans,
and to fill these houses with the corpses of those
whom I have struck down in my raging anger,
when I hid my face from this city because of all
their wickedness.*

6 Look! I am bringing the city recovery and
healing; I will heal them and reveal to them an
abundance of lasting peace.* 7 I will restore the
fortunes of Judah and Israel, and rebuild them as
they were in the beginning.* 8 I will purify them of
all the guilt they incurred by sinning against me; I
will forgive all their offenses by which they sinned
and rebelled against me.* 9 Then this city shall
become joy for me, a name of praise and pride,
before all the nations of the earth, as they hear of
all the good I am doing for them. They shall fear
and tremble because of all the prosperity I give it.

10 Thus says the LORD: In this place, about
which you say: "It is a waste without people or
animals!" and in the cities of Judah, in the streets
of Jerusalem now deserted, without people, with-
out inhabitant, without animal, there shall yet be
heard* 11 the song of joy, the song of gladness,
the song of the bridegroom, the song of the bride,
the song of those bringing thank offerings to the
house of the LORD: "Give thanks to the LORD of
hosts, for the LORD is good; God's love endures
forever." For I will restore the fortunes of this land
as they were in the beginning, says the LORD.*

12 Thus says the LORD of hosts: In this place,
now a waste, without people or animals, and in
all its cities there shall again be sheepfolds for
the shepherds to rest their flocks. 13 In the cities
of the hill country, of the Shephelah and the
Negeb, in the land of Benjamin and the neigh-
borhood of Jerusalem, and in the cities of Judah,
flocks will again pass under the hands of the one
who counts them, says the LORD.

14 † The days are coming—oracle of the LORD—
when I will fulfill the promise I made to the
house of Israel and the house of Judah. 15 In

JER

†

32:35 *Molech*: a god to whom human sacrifice was offered in the Valley of Ben-hinnom. Here, as in 19:5, he is called "Baal"; see note on Lv 18:21.

33:14–26 This is the longest continuous passage in the Hebrew text of Jeremiah that is missing from the Greek text of Jeremiah. It is probably the work of a postexilic writer who applied parts of Jeremiah's prophecies to new situations. The hope for an eternal Davidic dynasty (vv. 14–17; cf. 2 Sm 7:11–16) and for a perpetual priesthood and sacrificial system (v. 18) was not realized after the exile. On the canonical authority of the Septuagint, see note on Dn 13:1–14:42.

*

32:32 Jer 2:26; Is 3:8.
32:33 Jer 7:24.
32:34 Jer 7:30; 2 Kgs 21:4–5.
32:35 Jer 7:31; 19:5; Ps 106:37–38.
32:37 Jer 23:3; 29:14; Is 11:12; Ez 11:17.
32:38 Jer 24:7; 31:33.
32:40 Jer 31:31–33.
32:41 Dt 30:9.
32:42 Jer 33:10–14; Zec 8:13.
32:43 Jer 33:10.
32:44 Jer 17:26; 33:7.
33:3 Is 48:6.
33:4 Jer 32:24.
33:5 Jer 21:4–6.
33:6 Is 57:18.
33:7 Jer 30:3; 32:44.
33:8 Ez 36:25.
33:10 Jer 32:43.
33:11 1 Chr 16:34; Ezr 3:11; Ps 136:1.

those days, at that time, I will make a just shoot spring up for David; he shall do what is right and just in the land.* 16 In those days Judah shall be saved and Jerusalem shall dwell safely; this is the name they shall call her: "The LORD our justice." 17 For thus says the LORD: David shall never lack a successor on the throne of the house of Israel,* 18 nor shall the priests of Levi ever be lacking before me, to sacrifice burnt offerings, to burn cereal offerings, and to make sacrifices.*

19 This word of the LORD also came to Jeremiah: 20 Thus says the LORD: If you can break my covenant with day* and my covenant with night so that day and night no longer appear in their proper time, 21 only then can my covenant with my servant David be broken, so that he will not have a descendant to act as king upon his throne, and my covenant with the priests of Levi who minister to me. 22 Just as the host of heaven cannot be numbered and the sands of the sea cannot be counted, so I will multiply the descendants of David my servant and the Levites who minister to me.

23 This word of the LORD came to Jeremiah: 24 Have you not noticed what these people are saying: "The LORD has rejected the two tribes he had chosen"? They hold my people in contempt as if it were no longer a nation in their eyes.* 25 * Thus says the LORD: If I have no covenant with day and night, if I did not establish statutes for heaven and earth, 26 then I will also reject the descendants of Jacob and of David my servant, no longer selecting from his descendants rulers for the offspring of Abraham, Isaac, and Jacob. Yes, I will restore their fortunes and show them mercy.

Fate of Zedekiah

34 1 The word which came to Jeremiah from the LORD while Nebuchadnezzar, king of Babylon, and all his army and all the earth's kingdoms under his rule, and all the peoples were attacking Jerusalem and all her cities:* 2 Thus says the LORD, the God of Israel: Go to Zedekiah, king of Judah, and tell him: Thus says the LORD: I am handing this city over to the king of Babylon; he will burn it with fire.* 3 You yourself shall not escape his hand; rather you will be captured and fall into his hand. You shall see the king of Babylon eye to eye and speak to him face to face. Then you shall go to Babylon.*

4 Just hear the word of the LORD, Zedekiah, king of Judah! Then, says the LORD concerning you, you shall not die by the sword. 5 You shall die in peace, and they will burn spices for you as they did for your ancestors, the earlier kings who preceded you, and they shall make lament over you, "Alas, Lord." I myself make this promise—oracle of the LORD.

6 Jeremiah the prophet told all these things to Zedekiah, king of Judah, in Jerusalem, 7 while the army of the king of Babylon was attacking Jerusalem and the remaining cities of Judah, Lachish, and Azekah.† Only these fortified cities were left standing out of all the cities of Judah!

The Pact Broken†

8 This is the word that came to Jeremiah from the LORD after King Zedekiah had made a covenant with all the people in Jerusalem to proclaim freedom: 9 Everyone must free their Hebrew slaves, male and female, so that no one should hold another Judahite in servitude.* 10 All the princes and the people who entered this covenant agreed to set free their slaves, their male and female servants, so that they should no longer be in servitude. But even though they agreed and freed them, 11 afterward they took back their male and female servants whom they had set free and again forced them into servitude.

12 Then this word of the LORD came to Jeremiah: 13 Thus says the LORD, the God of Israel: I myself made a covenant with your ancestors the day I brought them out of the land of Egypt, out of the house of slavery: 14 Every seventh year each of you must set free all Hebrews who have sold themselves to you; six years they shall serve you, but then you shall let them go free. Your ancestors, however, did not listen to me or obey me. 15 As for you, today you repented and did what is right in my eyes by proclaiming freedom for your neighbor and making a covenant before me in the house which bears my name. 16 But then you again profaned my name by taking back

---

34:7 *Lachish, and Azekah*: fortress towns southwest of Jerusalem which Nebuchadnezzar besieged to prevent any help coming to Jerusalem from Egypt. At Lachish, archaeologists found several letters written on ostraca (pottery fragments) dated to 598 or 588 B.C., which mention both Lachish and Azekah.

34:8–22 During the siege of Jerusalem, its citizens made a covenant at Zedekiah's instigation to free Judahites they held in servitude, thus providing additional defenders for the city, leaving slave owners with fewer mouths to feed, and making reparation for past violations of the law, which dictated that Hebrew slaves should serve no longer than six years (Dt 15:12–15). But when the siege was temporarily lifted, when the assistance promised by Pharaoh Hophra arrived (cf. Jer 37:5), the inhabitants of Jerusalem broke the covenant and once more pressed their fellow citizens into slavery (v. 11).

33:15 Jer 23:5; Ps 72:1–4, 12–14; Is 11:1.
33:17 2 Sm 7:16; 1 Kgs 2:4; Ps 89:4–5, 29, 36–37.
33:18 Ez 44:15–16.
33:20–21 Jer 31:36–37; Ps 89:37–38.
33:24 Rom 11:1–2.
33:25–26 Jer 31:36–37; 32:44.
34:1 Jer 52:4; 2 Kgs 25:1.
34:2 Jer 21:10; 32:3, 28.
34:3 Jer 32:4; 52:11.
34:9 Ex 21:2–4; Lv 25:39, 46; Dt 15:12–15.

your male and female slaves whom you had just
set free for life; you forced them to become your
slaves again.* 17 Therefore, thus says the LORD:
You for your part did not obey me by proclaim-
ing freedom for your families and neighbors. So
I now proclaim freedom for you—oracle of the
LORD—for the sword, starvation, and disease.
I will make you an object of horror to all the
kingdoms of the earth. 18 † Those who violated
my covenant and did not observe the terms of
the covenant they made in my presence—I will
make them like the calf which they cut in two so
they could pass between its parts— 19 the princes
of Judah and of Jerusalem, the court officials, the
priests, and all the people of the land, who passed
between the parts of the calf. 20 These I will hand
over to their enemies, to those who seek their
lives: their corpses shall become food for the
birds of the air and the beasts of the field.*
21 Zedekiah, king of Judah, and his princes, I
will hand also over to their enemies, to those
who seek their lives, to the army of the king of
Babylon which is now withdrawing from you.*
22 I am giving the command—oracle of the
LORD—to bring them back to this city. They shall
attack and capture it, and burn it with fire; the
cities of Judah I will turn into a waste, where no
one dwells.*

The Faithful Rechabites

35 1 The word that came to Jeremiah from
the LORD in the days of Jehoiakim,† son
of Josiah, king of Judah: 2 Go to the house† of
the Rechabites, speak to them, and bring them
to the house of the LORD, to one of the rooms
there, and give them wine to drink. 3 So I took
Jaazaniah, son of Jeremiah, son of Habazziniah,
his brothers and all his sons—the whole house
of the Rechabites— 4 and I brought them to the
house of the LORD, to the room of the sons of Ha-
nan,† son of Igdaliah, the man of God, next to
the room of the princes above the room of Maa-
seiah, son of Shallum, the guard at the entrance.
5 I set before the Rechabites bowls full of wine,
and cups, and said to them, "Drink some wine."
6 "We do not drink wine," they said to me; "Jon-
adab,† Rechab's son, our father, commanded us,
'Neither you nor your children shall ever drink
wine.* 7 Build no house and sow no seed; do
not plant vineyards or own any. You must dwell
in tents all your lives, so that you may live long
on the land where you live as resident aliens.'
8 We have obeyed Jonadab, Rechab's son, our
father, in everything that he commanded us: not
drinking wine as long as we live—neither we nor
our wives nor our sons nor our daughters; 9 not
building houses to live in; not owning vineyards
or fields or crops. 10 We live in tents, doing ev-
erything our father Jonadab commanded us.
11 But when Nebuchadnezzar, king of Babylon,
invaded this land, we said, 'Come, let us go into
Jerusalem to escape the army of the Chaldeans
and the army of the Arameans.'† That is why we
are now living in Jerusalem."*
12 Then the word of the LORD came to Jeremiah:
13 Thus says the LORD of hosts, the God of Israel:
Go, say to the people of Judah and to the inhab-
itants of Jerusalem: Will you not take correction
and obey my words?—oracle of the LORD.* 14 The
words of Jonadab, Rechab's son, by which he
commanded his children not to drink wine, have
been upheld: to this day they have not drunk
wine; they obeyed their ancestor's command. I,
however, have spoken to you time and again.
But you did not obey me!* 15 Time and again I
sent you all my servants the prophets, saying:
Turn away, each of you, from your evil way and
reform your actions! Do not follow other gods
to serve them that you may remain in the land
which I gave you and your ancestors. But you did
not pay attention. You did not obey me.* 16 Yes,
the children of Jonadab, Rechab's son, upheld
the command which their father laid on them.
But this people has not obeyed me! 17 Now,
therefore, says the LORD God of hosts, the God of
Israel: I will soon bring upon Judah and all the

† **34:18–19** Both the Old Testament (Gn 15:10–17) and the eighth century B.C. Sefire inscription indicate that sometimes contracting parties ratified an agreement by walking between dismembered animals, invoking upon themselves the animals' fate if they failed to keep their word. *The covenant*: that mentioned in vv. 10, 15.

35:1 *In the days of Jehoiakim*: probably in 599 or 598 B.C. (cf. 2 Kgs 24:1–2).

35:2 *House*: both members of the family of Rechab (cf. v. 3) and the place where they live; cf. note on v. 11. *The Rechabites*: traditionalists who rejected the settled agricultural and urban cultures to which other Israelites had assimilated, maintaining their loyalty to the Lord by perpetuating the semi-nomadic life of their distant ancestors (cf. 2 Kgs 10:15–17). Jeremiah contrasts their adherence to their vows with the Judahites' disregard for divine commands.

35:4 *The sons of Hanan*: probably disciples of Hanan. *Man of God*: occurring only here in Jeremiah, the title frequently is applied to prophets: e.g., Samuel (1 Sm 9:6–10), Elijah (2 Kgs 1:9–13), Elisha (2 Kgs 4–13). Whatever the function of the sons of Hanan, they encourage Jeremiah by lending him their room. *Maaseiah*: perhaps the father of the priest Zephaniah (29:25; 37:3). *Guard at the entrance*: an important priestly responsibility (cf. 52:24).

35:6 *Jonadab*: another spelling of Jehonadab, a contemporary of King Jehu; cf. 2 Kgs 10:15–17.

35:11 *The army of the Arameans*: Nebuchadnezzar enlisted the help of Judah's neighbors in his assault on Jerusalem. *Living in Jerusalem*: the current military threat and the prospect of being killed or captured as plunder drove the Rechabites into the city and away from their tents.

* **34:16** Lv 19:12.
34:20 Jer 7:33; 16:4; 19:7.
34:21 Jer 37:5, 11.
34:22 Jer 37:8; 52:7–13; 2 Chr 36:17, 19.
35:6 Jgs 4:17, 24; 1 Sm 15:6; 2 Kgs 10:15–17.
35:11 2 Kgs 24:1–2.
35:13 Jer 32:33.
35:14 Jer 7:13; 25:3; 2 Chr 36:15–16.
35:15 Jer 25:4–5, 7.

inhabitants of Jerusalem every evil with which I threatened them because I spoke but they did not obey, I called but they did not answer.*

18 But to the house of the Rechabites Jeremiah said: Thus says the LORD of hosts, the God of Israel: Since you have obeyed the command of Jonadab, your father, kept all his commands and done everything he commanded you, 19 therefore, thus says the LORD of hosts, the God of Israel: Never shall there fail to be a descendant of Jonadab, Rechab's son, standing in my presence.

VII. Jeremiah and the Fall of Jerusalem

Baruch, the Scribe of Jeremiah

36 1 In the fourth year of Jehoiakim, son of Josiah, king of Judah, this word came to Jeremiah from the LORD: 2 Take a scroll and write on it all the words I have spoken to you about Israel, Judah, and all the nations, from the day I first spoke to you, from the days of Josiah, until today. 3 Perhaps, if the house of Judah hears all the evil I have in mind to do to them, so that all of them turn from their evil way, then I can forgive their wickedness and their sin.* 4 So Jeremiah called Baruch, son of Neriah, and he wrote down on a scroll what Jeremiah said, all the words which the LORD had spoken to him. 5 Then Jeremiah commanded Baruch: "I cannot enter the house of the LORD; I am barred† from it. 6 So you yourself must go. On a fast day in the hearing of the people in the LORD's house, read the words of the LORD from the scroll you wrote at my dictation; read them also to all the people of Judah who come up from their cities. 7 Perhaps they will present their supplication before the LORD and will all turn back from their evil way; for great is the anger and wrath with which the LORD has threatened this people."*

8 Baruch, son of Neriah, did everything Jeremiah the prophet commanded; from the scroll he read the LORD's words in the LORD's house. 9 In the ninth month, in the fifth year of Jehoiakim, son of Josiah, king of Judah, all the people of Jerusalem and all those who came from Judah's cities to Jerusalem proclaimed a fast before the LORD. 10 So Baruch read the words of Jeremiah from the scroll in the room of Gemariah,† son of the scribe Shaphan, in the upper court of the LORD's house, at the entrance of the New Temple Gate, in the hearing of all the people.

11 Now Micaiah, son of Gemariah, son of Shaphan, heard all the words of the LORD read from the scroll. 12 So he went down to the house of the king, into the scribe's chamber,† where the princes were meeting in session: Elishama, the scribe; Delaiah, son of Shemaiah; Elnathan, son of Achbor; Gemariah, son of Shaphan; Zedekiah, son of Hananiah; and the other princes. 13 Micaiah reported to them all that he had heard Baruch read from his scroll in the hearing of the people. 14 The princes immediately sent Jehudi, son of Nethaniah, son of Shelemiah, son of Cushi, to Baruch with the order: "The scroll you read in the hearing of the people—bring it with you and come." Scroll in hand, Baruch, son of Neriah, went to them. 15 "Sit down," they said to him, "and read it in our hearing." Baruch read it in their hearing, 16 and when they had heard all its words, they turned to each other in alarm and said to Baruch, "We have to tell the king all these things." 17 Then they asked Baruch: "Tell us, please, how did you come to write down all these words? Was it at his dictation?" 18 "Yes, he would dictate all these words to me," Baruch answered them, "while I wrote them down with ink in the scroll." 19 The princes said to Baruch, "Go into hiding, you and Jeremiah; do not let anyone know where you are."

20 They went in to the king, into the courtyard; they had deposited the scroll in the room of Elishama the scribe. When they told the king everything that had happened, 21 the king sent Jehudi to get the scroll. Jehudi brought it from the room of Elishama the scribe, and read it to the king and to all the princes who were attending the king. 22 Now the king was sitting in his winter house, since it was the ninth month, and a fire was burning in the brazier before him. 23 Each time Jehudi finished reading three or four columns, he would cut off the piece with a scribe's knife† and throw it into the fire in the brazier, until the entire scroll was consumed in the fire in the brazier. 24 As they were listening to all these words the king and all his officials did not become alarmed, nor did they tear their garments. 25 And though Elnathan, Delaiah, and Gemariah urged the king not to burn the scroll, he would not listen to them. 26 He commanded Jerahmeel, a royal prince, and Seraiah, son of Azriel, and Shelemiah, son of Abdeel,

---

36:5 *I am barred*: Jeremiah could have been forbidden to enter the Temple for any number of reasons: e.g., his inflammatory preaching (the Temple sermon, 7:1–15; the broken pot); the hostility of Temple guards; the restrictions of arrest.

36:10 *Gemariah*: member of a family friendly to Jeremiah with rights to a room in the gateway fortress overlooking the court of the Temple. His father Shaphan had been Josiah's secretary of state (2 Kgs 22:3). From a window in this room Baruch read Jeremiah's scroll to the people.

36:12 *The scribe's chamber*: the office of the royal secretary.

36:23 *A scribe's knife*: used to sharpen reed pens.

35:17 Jer 11:8–9. **36:3** Jer 26:3; Is 55:6–7. **36:7** 2 Kgs 22:13.

to arrest Baruch, the scribe, and Jeremiah the
prophet. But the LORD had hidden them away.
27 The word of the LORD came to Jeremiah,
after the king burned the scroll and the words
Jeremiah had dictated to Baruch: 28 Take another
scroll, and write on it all the words in the first
scroll, which Jehoiakim, king of Judah, burned.
29 And against Jehoiakim, king of Judah, say this:
Thus says the LORD: You are the one who burned
that scroll, saying, "Why did you write on it:
Babylon's king shall surely come and ravage this
land, emptying it of every living thing"? 30 The
LORD now says of Jehoiakim, king of Judah:* No
descendant of his shall sit on David's throne; his
corpse shall be thrown out, exposed to heat by
day, frost by night.† 31 I will punish him and his
descendants and his officials for their wicked-
ness; upon them, the inhabitants of Jerusalem,
and the people of Judah I will bring all the evil
threats to which they did not listen.
32 Then Jeremiah took another scroll and gave
it to his scribe, Baruch, son of Neriah, who wrote
on it at Jeremiah's dictation all the words con-
tained in the scroll which Jehoiakim, king of Ju-
dah, had burned in the fire, adding many words
like them.

Jeremiah in the Dungeon

37 1 Zedekiah, son of Josiah, became king,
succeeding Coniah, son of Jehoiakim;
Nebuchadnezzar, king of Babylon, appointed
him king over the land of Judah.* 2 Neither he,
nor his officials, nor the people of the land would
listen to the words which the LORD spoke through
Jeremiah the prophet. 3 Yet King Zedekiah sent
Jehucal, son of Shelemiah, and Zephaniah, son
of Maaseiah the priest, to Jeremiah the prophet
with this request: "Please appeal to the LORD, our
God, for us."* 4 At this time Jeremiah still came
and went freely among the people; he had not yet
been put into prison.† 5 Meanwhile, Pharaoh's
army† had set out from Egypt, and when the
Chaldeans who were besieging Jerusalem heard
this report, they withdrew from the city.*
6 Then the word of the LORD came to Jeremiah
the prophet: 7 Thus says the LORD, the God of
Israel: Thus you must say to the king of Judah
who sent you to consult me: Listen! Pharaoh's
army, which has set out to help you, will return
to Egypt, its own land.* 8 The Chaldeans shall
return and attack this city; they shall capture it
and destroy it by fire.*
9 Thus says the LORD: Do not deceive your-
selves, saying: "The Chaldeans are surely leaving
us forever." They are not! 10 Even if you could
defeat the whole Chaldean army that is now at-
tacking you, and only the wounded remained,
each in his tent, these would rise up and destroy
the city with fire.*
11 Now when the Chaldean army withdrew
from Jerusalem because of the army of Pharaoh,*

Pray It!

Facing Fear

You can bet Jeremiah felt fear at times. For example, in Jeremiah 37:17, King Zedekiah asks the prophet if he has had any word from God. Jeremiah has just been beaten and imprisoned (see verse 15). Surely, he has some fear for what will happen to him if he delivers a message that angers the king. But Jeremiah courageously tells Zedekiah that he, Zedekiah, will be handed over to the king of Babylon (see verse 17).

Throughout our lives, when trying to do God's will, we will face situations that cause us to fear for our safety, for our reputation, or even that our friends will abandon us. This isn't the same fear we feel when watching a horror film or riding a roller coaster. It is an anxiety that can cause us to shut down and quit trying. We need to offer up that fear to God and ask the Lord to calm our heart.

Quiet your mind and pray:

Lord, give me the courage I need to be faithful to you. Let my love for you and for other people be so great that my fears will never be able to keep me from doing what is right. Amen!

▶ Jer 37:11–21

36:30 Jehoiakim's son Jehoiachin was named king, but reigned only three months; he was better known for his long exile in Babylon. *His corpse shall be thrown out*: just as Jehoiakim had thrown pieces of the scroll into the fire (cf. 22:19).

37:4 *Put into prison*: as described in 32:1–3. Chronologically, the present episode follows 34:1–7.

37:5 *Pharaoh's army*: the force sent by Pharaoh Hophra; when they arrived, the Chaldeans temporarily lifted the siege against Jerusalem (cf. 34:21).

36:30 Jer 22:19.
37:1 Jer 52:1; 2 Kgs 24:17; 2 Chr 36:10.
37:3 Jer 21:1.
37:5 Ez 17:15; 29:6–7.
37:7 Ez 17:17.
37:8 Jer 34:22.
37:10 Jer 21:4.
37:11 Zec 14:10.

Pray It!

Prayer from the Cistern (Well)

Savior God, like Jeremiah, I often find myself at the bottom. Sometimes, I just fall there; other times, I am thrown there. It's cold, dark, and lonely there.

Bless me with friends, like Ebed-melech, who will care for me and lift me up when I am down or in trouble. And make me the kind of friend who is loyal enough to advocate for those in need and willing to do what is necessary to lift others up.

Amen.

▶ **Jer 38:1–13**

12 Jeremiah set out from Jerusalem to go to the ter-
ritory of Benjamin, to receive his share of property
among the people. 13 But at the Gate of Benjamin,
the captain of the guard, by the name of Irijah,
son of Shelemiah, son of Hananiah, arrested
Jeremiah the prophet, saying, "You are deserting
to the Chaldeans!" 14 "That is a lie!" Jeremiah an-
swered, "I am not deserting to the Chaldeans."
Without listening to him, Irijah kept Jeremiah in
custody and brought him to the princes.
15 The princes were enraged at Jeremiah and
had Jeremiah beaten and imprisoned in the
house of Jonathan the scribe, for they were using
it as a jail.* 16 And so Jeremiah went into a room
in the dungeon, where he remained many days.
17 Then King Zedekiah had him brought to
his palace, and he asked him secretly, "Is there
any word from the LORD?" "There is!" Jeremiah
answered: "You shall be handed over to the
king of Babylon."* 18 Jeremiah then asked King
Zedekiah: "How have I wronged you or your
officials or this people, that you should put me
in prison?* 19 Where are your own prophets who
prophesied for you, saying: 'The King of Babylon
will not attack you or this land'? 20 Please hear
me, my lord king! Grant my petition: do not
send me back into the house of Jonathan the
scribe, or I shall die there."
21 So King Zedekiah ordered that Jeremiah be
confined in the court of the guard and given a
ration of bread every day from the bakers' street
until all the bread in the city was eaten up. Thus
Jeremiah remained in the court of the guard.*

Jeremiah in the Muddy Cistern

38 1 Shephatiah, son of Mattan, Gedaliah, son
of Pashhur, Jucal, son of Shelemiah, and
Pashhur, son of Malchiah, heard the words Jere-
miah was speaking to all the people:† 2 Thus says
the LORD: Those who remain in this city shall die
by means of the sword, starvation, and disease;
but those who go out to the Chaldeans shall live.
Their lives shall be spared them as spoils of war
that they may live.* 3 Thus says the LORD: This city
shall certainly be handed over to the army of the
king of Babylon; he shall capture it.
4 Then the princes said to the king, "This man
ought to be put to death. He is weakening the
resolve† of the soldiers left in this city and of
all the people, by saying such things to them;
he is not seeking the welfare of our people, but
their ruin."* 5 King Zedekiah answered: "He is in
your hands," for the king could do nothing with
them. 6 And so they took Jeremiah and threw
him into the cistern of Prince Malchiah, in the
court of the guard, letting him down by rope.
There was no water in the cistern, only mud, and
Jeremiah sank down into the mud.*
7 Now Ebed-melech, an Ethiopian, a court of-
ficial in the king's house, heard that they had put
Jeremiah in the cistern. The king happened to
be sitting at the Gate of Benjamin, 8 and Ebed-
melech went there from the house of the king
and said to him, 9 "My lord king, these men have
done wrong in all their treatment of Jeremiah the
prophet, throwing him into the cistern. He will
starve to death on the spot, for there is no more
bread in the city."* 10 Then the king ordered
Ebed-melech the Ethiopian: "Take three men
with you, and get Jeremiah the prophet out of the
cistern before he dies." 11 Ebed-melech took the
men with him, and went first to the linen closet
in the house of the king. He took some old, tat-
tered rags and lowered them by rope to Jeremiah
in the cistern. 12 Then he said to Jeremiah, "Put

†

38:1 Jeremiah enjoyed sufficient liberty in the court of the guard (37:21) to speak to the people; cf. 32:6–9. *Gedaliah, son of Pashhur*: the latter is possibly the Pashhur of 20:1. *Pashhur, son of Malchiah*: mentioned in 21:1.

38:4 *He is weakening the resolve*: lit., "he weakens the hands." One of the Lachish ostraca (cf. note on 34:7) makes the same claim against the princes in Jerusalem.

*

37:15 Jer 38:6–13.
37:17 Jer 21:7; 32:3; 34:21.
37:18 Jer 26:19.
37:21 Jer 32:2; 38:28.
38:2 Jer 21:9–10; 39:18; 45:5.
38:4 Jer 26:11.
38:6 Jer 37:14–15.
38:9 Jer 52:6.

these old, tattered rags between your armpits and
the ropes." Jeremiah did so, 13 and they pulled
him up by rope out of the cistern. But Jeremiah
remained in the court of the guard.
14 King Zedekiah summoned Jeremiah the
prophet to meet him at the third entrance of the
house of the LORD. "I have a question to ask you,"
the king said to Jeremiah. "Do not hide anything
from me."* 15 Jeremiah answered Zedekiah: "If I
tell you anything, will you not have me put to
death? If I counsel you, you will not listen to
me!"* 16 But King Zedekiah swore to Jeremiah
secretly: "As the LORD lives who gave us our lives,
I will not kill you, nor will I hand you over to
those men who seek your life."
17 Jeremiah then said to Zedekiah: "Thus says
the LORD God of hosts, the God of Israel: If you
will only surrender to the princes of Babylon's
king, you shall save your life; this city shall not
be destroyed by fire, and you and your house-
hold shall live.* 18 But if you do not surrender
to the princes of Babylon's king, this city shall
fall into the hand of the Chaldeans, who shall
destroy it by fire, and you shall not escape their
hand."*
19 King Zedekiah said to Jeremiah, "I am afraid
of the Judahites who have deserted to the Chal-
deans; I could be handed over to them, and they
will mistreat me."* 20 "You will not be handed
over to them," Jeremiah answered. "I beg you!
Please listen to the voice of the LORD regarding
what I tell you so that it may go well with you
and your life be spared.* 21 But if you refuse to
surrender, this is what the LORD has shown: 22 I
see all the women who remain in the house of
Judah's king being brought out to the princes of
Babylon's king, and they are crying:

'They betrayed you, outdid you,
your good friends!
Now that your feet are sunk in mud,
they slink away.'*

23 All your wives and children shall be brought
out to the Chaldeans, and you shall not escape
their hands; you shall be handed over to the
king of Babylon, and this city shall be destroyed
by fire."*
24 Then Zedekiah said to Jeremiah, "Let no one
know about this conversation, or you shall die.
25 If the princes should hear I spoke with you and
if they should come and ask you, 'Tell us what
you said to the king; do not hide it from us, or
we will kill you,' or, 'What did the king say to
you?' 26 then give them this answer: 'I petitioned
the king not to send me back to Jonathan's house
lest I die there.' " 27 When all the princes came to
Jeremiah and questioned him, he answered them
with the very words the king had commanded.
They said no more to him, for nothing had been
overheard of the conversation. 28 Thus Jeremiah
stayed in the court of the guard until the day Je-
rusalem was taken.*

The Capture of Jerusalem

39 When Jerusalem was taken, 1 in the ninth
year of Zedekiah,* king of Judah, in the
tenth month,† Nebuchadnezzar, king of Bab-
ylon, and all his army marched against Jerusa-
lem and placed it under siege. 2 In the eleventh
year of Zedekiah, on the ninth day of the fourth
month,† the city wall was breached. 3 All the
princes of the king of Babylon came and took
their seats at the middle gate: Nergal-sharezer of
Simmagir, a chief officer; Nebushazban, a high
dignitary; and all the rest of the princes of the
king of Babylon.† 4 When Zedekiah, king of Ju-
dah, and all his warriors saw this, they fled, leav-
ing the city at night by way of the king's garden,†
through a gate between the two walls. He went in
the direction of the Arabah,* 5 but the Chaldean
army pursued them; they caught up with Zede-
kiah in the wilderness near Jericho and took him
prisoner. They brought him to Nebuchadnezzar,
king of Babylon, in Riblah,† in the land of Ha-
math, and he pronounced sentence upon him.*
6 The king of Babylon executed the sons of Zed-
ekiah at Riblah before his very eyes; the king of
Babylon also executed all the nobles of Judah.*
7 He then blinded Zedekiah and bound him in
chains to bring him to Babylon.*
8 The Chaldeans set fire to the king's house

JER

†

39:1 *In the ninth year . . . in the tenth month*: the month Tebet (mid-December to mid-January) of the year 589/588 B.C., according to the Babylonian calendar, whose New Year began in March/April.

39:2 *In the eleventh year . . . the ninth day of the fourth month*: in July, 587 B.C.

39:3 The Babylonian officers act as a military tribunal or government, headed by Nergal-sharezer, Nebuchadnezzar's son and successor.

39:4 *By way of the king's garden*: along the southeast side of the city; the royal garden was in the Kidron Valley. *A gate between the two walls*: the southernmost city gate, at the end of the Tyropoeon Valley. *The Arabah*: the southern Jordan Valley. Zedekiah was perhaps trying to escape across the Jordan when he was captured near Jericho.

39:5 *Riblah*: Nebuchadnezzar's headquarters north of Damascus; Pharaoh Neco had once used the town as a military post (2 Kgs 23:33).

*

38:14 Jer 37:16.
38:15 Lk 22:67–68.
38:17 Jer 27:12–13; 2 Kgs 24:12.
38:18 Jer 32:4.
38:19 1 Sm 31:4.
38:20 2 Chr 20:20.
38:22 Jb 6:15; 19:13–14, 19.
38:23 Jer 41:10.
38:28 Jer 39:14.
39:1–2 Jer 52:4–16; 2 Kgs 25:1–12; Ez 24:1.
39:4 Jer 52:7.
39:5 Jer 32:4–5; 38:18.
39:6 Jer 34:21.
39:7 Jer 32:4–5; Ez 12:13.

Cultural Connection

Risky Business

Ebed-melech is a biblical character we do not hear too much about. But he played a significant role in Jeremiah's life, and he has special meaning for African Americans because he was black. The Bible refers to him as the Ethiopian.

Ebed-melech is important because he was available to God and he was willing to risk his neck. Although Ebed-melech had the king's permission to rescue Jeremiah, he would have lost his life if his plan to do so had been discovered by the king's generals and counselors (see Jer 38:7–13). Ebed-melech shows us that being a servant of God is risky business. We cannot do God's will without taking risks. There is just no such thing as playing it safe and doing what God wants us to do.

Ebed-melech is also important because he was willing to help his "brother." Jeremiah was a Jew, and Ebed-melech was an Ethiopian, but still they were brothers in the Lord. Ebed-melech knew that he had to act when he saw his brother in trouble. When destruction finally came upon Jerusalem, God rewarded Ebed-melech by keeping him safe (see 39:18) because he had trusted in God enough to help his brother Jeremiah.

Lord, grant me a large portion of trust in you, that I might step out at your bidding and not be afraid of the outcome. Amen.

Jer 39:15–18

and the houses of the people and tore down the walls of Jerusalem.* 9 Nebuzaradan, captain of the bodyguard, deported to Babylon the rest of the people left in the city, those who had deserted to him, and the rest of the workers.* 10 But Nebuzaradan, captain of the bodyguard, left in the land of Judah some of the poor who had nothing and at the same time gave them vineyards and farms.*

Jeremiah Released to Gedaliah's Custody

11 Concerning Jeremiah, Nebuchadnezzar, king of Babylon, gave these orders through Nebuzaradan, captain of the bodyguard: 12 "Take him and look after him; do not let anything happen to him. Whatever he may ask, you must do for him."* 13 Thereupon Nebuzaradan, captain of the bodyguard, and Nebushazban, a high dignitary, and Nergal-sharezer, a chief officer, and all the nobles of the king of Babylon, 14 had Jeremiah taken out of the courtyard of the guard and entrusted to Gedaliah, son of Ahikam, son of Shaphan, to bring him home. And so he remained among the people.*

A Word of Comfort for Ebed-melech

15 While Jeremiah was still imprisoned in the court of the guard, the word of the LORD came to him: 16 Go, tell this to Ebed-melech the Ethiopian: Thus says the LORD of hosts, the God of Israel: See, I am now carrying out my words against this city, for evil and not for good; this will happen in your presence on that day.* 17 But on that day I will deliver you—oracle of the LORD; you shall not be handed over to the men you dread. 18 I will make certain that you escape and do not fall by the sword. Your life will be your spoils of war because you trusted in me—oracle of the LORD.*

Jeremiah Still in Judah

40 1 The word† which came to Jeremiah from the LORD, after Nebuzaradan, captain of the bodyguard, had released him in Ramah, where he found him a prisoner in chains among the captives of Jerusalem and Judah being exiled to Babylon.* 2 The captain of the bodyguard took charge of Jeremiah and said to him, "The LORD,

† 40:1 *The word*: this "word" does not actually appear until 42:7.

* **39:8** Jer 21:10; 34:2; 52:13.
39:9 2 Kgs 25:11.
39:10 2 Kgs 25:12, 22.
39:12 Jer 40:4.
39:14 Jer 26:24; 38:28.
39:16 Jer 21:10; Dn 9:12.
39:18 Jer 45:5; Ps 25:3; 37:40.
40:1 Jer 39:14.

your God, decreed ruin for this place. 3 Now he
has made it happen, accomplishing what he
decreed; because you sinned against the LORD
and did not listen to his voice, this decree has
been realized against you. 4 Now, I release you
today from the chains upon your hands; if you
want to come with me to Babylon, then come: I
will look out for you. But if you do not want to
come to Babylon, very well. See, the whole land
lies before you; go wherever you think good and
proper.* 5 Or go to Gedaliah, son of Ahikam, son
of Shaphan, whom the king of Babylon has set
over the cities of Judah. Stay with him among the
people. Or go wherever you want!" The captain
of the bodyguard gave him food and gifts and let
him go.* 6 So Jeremiah went to Gedaliah, son of
Ahikam, in Mizpah,† and dwelt with him among
the people left in the land.*

7 When the military leaders still in the field
with their soldiers heard that the king of Babylon
had set Gedaliah, son of Ahikam, over the land
and had put him in charge of men, women, and
children, from the poor of the land who had not
been deported to Babylon, 8 they and their sol-
diers came to Gedaliah in Mizpah: Ishmael, son
of Nethaniah; Johanan, son of Kareah; Seraiah,
son of Tanhumeth; the sons of Ephai of Neto-
phah; and Jezaniah of Beth-maacah. 9 Gedaliah,
son of Ahikam, son of Shaphan, swore an oath
to them and their men: "Do not be afraid to
serve the Chaldeans. Stay in the land and serve
the king of Babylon, so that everything may go
well with you.* 10 As for me, I will remain in Miz-
pah, as your representative before the Chaldeans
when they come to us. You, for your part, harvest
the wine, the fruit, and the oil, store them in jars,
and remain in the cities you occupied." 11 Then
all the Judahites in Moab, in Ammon, in Edom,
and those in all other lands heard that the king
of Babylon had left a remnant in Judah and had
set over them Gedaliah, son of Ahikam, son of
Shaphan. 12 They all returned to the land of Ju-
dah from the places to which they had scattered.
They went to Gedaliah at Mizpah and had a rich
harvest of wine and fruit.

Assassination of Gedaliah

13 Now Johanan, son of Kareah, and all the
military leaders in the field came to Gedaliah
in Mizpah 14 and said to him, "Surely you are
aware that Baalis, the Ammonite king,† has sent
Ishmael, son of Nethaniah, to assassinate you?"*
But Gedaliah, son of Ahikam, would not believe
them. 15 Then Johanan, son of Kareah, said se-
cretly to Gedaliah in Mizpah: "Please let me go
and kill Ishmael, son of Nethaniah; no one will
know it. What if he assassinates you? All the Ju-
dahites who have now rallied behind you would
scatter and the remnant of Judah would perish."
16 Gedaliah, son of Ahikam, answered Johanan,
son of Kareah, "You must not do that. What you
are saying about Ishmael is a lie!"

41 1 In the seventh month, Ishmael, son of
Nethaniah, son of Elishama, of royal de-
scent, one of the king's nobles, came with ten
men to Gedaliah, son of Ahikam, at Mizpah.*
While they were together at table in Mizpah,
2 Ishmael, son of Nethaniah, and the ten with
him, stood up and struck down Gedaliah, son
of Ahikam, son of Shaphan, with swords. They
killed him, since the king of Babylon had set him
over the land; 3 Ishmael also killed all the Judah-
ites of military age who were with Gedaliah and
the Chaldean soldiers stationed there.

4 The day after the murder of Gedaliah, before
anyone learned about it, 5 eighty men, in ragged
clothes, with beards shaved off and gashes on
their bodies, came from Shechem, Shiloh, and
Samaria, bringing grain offerings and incense
for the house of the LORD. 6 Weeping as he went,
Ishmael son of Nethaniah, set out from Mizpah
to meet them. "Come to Gedaliah, son of Ahi-
kam," he said as he met them. 7 Once they were
inside the city, Ishmael, son of Nethaniah, and
his men slaughtered them and threw them into
the cistern. 8 Ten of them said to Ishmael: "Do
not kill us! We have stores of wheat and barley,
oil and honey hidden in the field." So he spared
them and did not kill them as he had killed their
companions. 9 The cistern into which Ishmael
threw all the bodies of the men he had killed was
the large one King Asa made to defend himself
against Baasha, king of Israel; Ishmael, son of
Nethaniah, filled this cistern with the slain.*

10 Ishmael led away the rest of the people left
in Mizpah, including the princesses,† whom
Nebuzaradan, captain of the bodyguard, had

JER

†

40:6 While Jerusalem had suffered a great deal of damage, the Babylonian leaders' selection of Mizpah as their local headquarters was probably as much a symbolic statement as it was a utilitarian move: Jerusalem and its political and religious worldview had given way to disorder and no longer existed as a symbol of order.

40:14 In an attempt, perhaps, to weaken Babylon's hold on the area and to add Judah to the Ammonite kingdom, Baalis supported Ishmael's claim to the throne of David (cf. 41:1 for Ishmael's genealogy).

41:10 *The princesses*: the women of Judah's royal house.

*

40:4 Jer 39:12.
40:5 Jer 39:14; 2 Kgs 25:22.
40:6 Jer 39:14.
40:9 Jer 27:12–13; 2 Kgs 25:24.
40:14 Jer 41:1–3, 10.
41:1 Jer 40:14–16; 2 Kgs 25:25.
41:9 1 Kgs 15:16; 2 Chr 16:6.

consigned to Gedaliah, son of Ahikam. With
these captives, Ishmael, son of Nethaniah, set out
to cross over to the Ammonites.

Flight to Egypt

11 But when Johanan, son of Kareah, and the
other army leaders with him heard about the
crimes Ishmael, son of Nethaniah, had com-
mitted, 12 they took all their men and set out to
attack Ishmael, son of Nethaniah. They overtook
him at the great pool in Gibeon.† 13 At the sight
of Johanan, son of Kareah, and the other army
leaders, the people with Ishmael rejoiced; 14 all
of those whom Ishmael had taken captive from
Mizpah went back to Johanan, son of Kareah.
15 But Ishmael, son of Nethaniah, escaped from
Johanan with eight men and fled to the Ammon-
ites. 16 Then Johanan, son of Kareah, and all the
military leaders took charge of all the rest of the
people whom Ishmael, son of Nethaniah, had
taken away from Mizpah after he killed Geda-
liah, son of Ahikam—the soldiers, the women
with children, and court officials, whom he
brought back from Gibeon. 17 They set out and
stopped at Geruth Chimham near Bethlehem,
intending to go into Egypt. 18 They were afraid of
the Chaldeans, because Ishmael, son of Netha-
niah, had slain Gedaliah, son of Ahikam, whom
the king of Babylon had set over the land.

42 1 Then all the military leaders, including
Johanan, son of Kareah, Azariah, son of
Hoshaiah, and all the people, from the least to
the greatest, 2 approached Jeremiah the prophet
and said, "Please grant our petition; pray for us to
the LORD, your God, for all this remnant. As you
see, only a few of us remain, but once we were
many. 3 May the LORD, your God, show us the way
we should take and what we should do." 4 "Very
well!" Jeremiah the prophet answered them: "I
will pray to the LORD, your God, as you desire;
whatever the LORD answers, I will tell you; I will
withhold nothing from you."* 5 And they said to
Jeremiah, "May the LORD be a true and faithful
witness against us if we do not follow all the in-
structions the LORD, your God, sends us through
you.* 6 Whether we like it or not, we will obey the
command of the LORD, our God, to whom we are
sending you, so that it may go well with us for
obeying the command of the LORD, our God."*
7 Ten days passed before the word of the LORD
came to Jeremiah. 8 Then he called Johanan, son
of Kareah, his army leaders, and all the people,
from the least to the greatest, 9 and said to them:
Thus says the LORD, the God of Israel, to whom
you sent me to offer your petition: 10 If indeed
you will remain in this land, I will build you
up, and not tear you down; I will plant you, not
uproot you; for I repent of the evil I have done
you.* 11 Do not fear the king of Babylon, as you
do now. Do not fear him—oracle of the LORD—
for I am with you to save you, to rescue you from
his power.* 12 I will take pity on you, so that he
will have pity on you and let you return to your
land.* 13 But if you keep saying, "We will not stay
in this land," thus disobeying the voice of the
LORD, your God, 14 and saying, "No, we will go to
the land of Egypt, where we will not see war, nor
hear the trumpet alarm, nor hunger for bread.
There we will live!"* 15 then listen to the word of
the LORD, remnant of Judah: Thus says the LORD
of hosts, the God of Israel: If you are set on going
to Egypt and settling down there once you arrive,
16 the sword you fear shall overtake you in the
land of Egypt; the hunger you dread shall pur-
sue you to Egypt and there you shall die.* 17 All
those determined to go to Egypt to live shall
die by the sword, famine, and disease: not one
shall survive or escape the evil that I am bringing
upon them.* 18 For thus says the LORD of hosts,
the God of Israel: Just as my furious wrath was
poured out upon the inhabitants of Jerusalem, so
shall my anger be poured out on you when you
reach Egypt. You shall become a malediction and
a horror, a curse and a reproach, and you shall
never see this place again.*

19 The LORD has spoken to you, remnant of
Judah. Do not go to Egypt! Mark well that I am
warning you this day. 20 At the cost of your lives
you have been deceitful, for you yourselves sent
me to the LORD, your God, saying, "Pray for us to
the LORD, our God; whatever the LORD, our God,
shall say, tell us and we will do it." 21 Today I have
told you, but you have not listened to the voice of
the LORD your God, in anything that he has sent
me to tell you.* 22 Have no doubt about this: you
shall die by the sword, famine, and disease in the
place where you want to go and live.*

43 1 When Jeremiah finished telling the peo-
ple all the words the LORD, their God, sent
to them, 2 Azariah, son of Hoshaiah, Johanan,

---

† **41:12** *Gibeon*: modern El-Jib; northwest of Jerusalem. A huge pit carved into limestone provided water in time of siege, here called the great pool, lit., "many waters"; cf. 2 Sm 2:12–14.

* **42:4** 1 Sm 3:18.
42:5 Jgs 11:10.
42:6 Jer 7:23; Dt 5:33; 6:3.
42:10 Jer 31:28; 32:41.
42:11 Jer 30:10–11.
42:12 Ps 106:45–46; Prv 16:7.
42:14 Dt 28:68.
42:16 Jer 44:13–14, 27.
42:17 Jer 29:17–18; 44:14, 28.
42:18 Jer 44:12.
42:21 Zec 7:11–12.
42:22 Jer 44:12; Hos 9:6.

son of Kareah, and all the others had the insolence to say to Jeremiah: "You lie; the LORD, our God, did not send you to tell us, 'Do not to go to Egypt to live there.' 3 Baruch, son of Neriah, is inciting you against us, to hand us over to the Chaldeans to be killed or exiled to Babylon."*

4 So Johanan, son of Kareah, and the rest of the leaders and the people did not listen to the voice of the LORD to stay in the land of Judah.* 5 Instead, Johanan, son of Kareah, and the military leaders took along all the remnant of Judah who had been dispersed among the nations and then had returned to dwell in the land of Judah: 6 men, women, and children, the princesses and everyone whom Nebuzaradan, captain of the bodyguard, had consigned to Gedaliah, son of Ahikam, son of Shaphan; also Jeremiah, the prophet, and Baruch, son of Neriah.* 7 They went to Egypt—they did not listen to the voice of the LORD—and came to Tahpanhes.*

Jeremiah in Egypt

8 The word of the LORD came to Jeremiah in Tahpanhes: 9 Take some large stones in your hand and set them in mortar in the terrace at the entrance to the house of Pharaoh in Tahpanhes, while the Judahites watch. 10 Then say to them: Thus says the LORD of hosts, the God of Israel: I will send for my servant Nebuchadnezzar, king of Babylon. He will place his throne upon these stones which I, Jeremiah, have set up, and stretch his canopy above them.* 11 He shall come and strike the land of Egypt: with death, those marked for death; with exile, those marked for exile; with the sword, those marked for the sword.* 12 He shall set fire to the temples of Egypt's gods, burn the gods and carry them off. He shall pick the land of Egypt clean, as a shepherd picks lice off his cloak, and then depart victorious.* 13 He shall smash the obelisks at the Temple of the Sun in the land of Egypt and destroy with fire the temples of the Egyptian gods.

44

1 The word that came to Jeremiah for all the Judahites who were living in Egypt, those living in Migdol, Tahpanhes, and Memphis, and in Upper Egypt: 2 † Thus says the LORD of hosts, the God of Israel: You yourselves have seen all the evil I brought upon Jerusalem and the other cities of Judah. Today they lie in ruins uninhabited,* 3 because of the evil they did to provoke me, going after other gods, offering incense and serving other gods they did not know, neither they, nor you, nor your ancestors.* 4 Though I repeatedly sent you all my servants the prophets, saying: "You must not commit this abominable deed I hate," 5 they did not listen or incline their ears in order to turn from their evil, no longer offering incense to other gods.* 6 Therefore the fury of my anger poured forth and kindled fire in the cities of Judah and the streets of Jerusalem, to turn them into the ruined wasteland they are today.

7 Now thus says the LORD God of hosts, the God of Israel: Why inflict so great an evil upon yourselves, cutting off from Judah man and woman, child and infant, not leaving yourselves even a remnant? 8 Why do you provoke me with the works of your hands, offering sacrifice to other gods here in the land of Egypt where you have come to live? Will you cut yourselves off and become a curse, a reproach among all the nations of the earth?* 9 Have you forgotten the evil of your ancestors, the evil of the kings of Judah, the evil of their wives, and your own evil and the evil of your wives—all that they did in the land of Judah and in the streets of Jerusalem?* 10 To this day they have not been crushed down, nor have they shown fear. They have not followed my law and my statutes that I set before you and your ancestors.*

11 Therefore, thus says the LORD of hosts, the God of Israel: I have set my face against you for evil, to cut off all Judah. 12 I will take away the remnant of Judah who insisted on going to the land of Egypt to live there; in the land of Egypt they shall meet their end. They shall fall by the sword or be consumed by hunger. From the least to the greatest, they shall die by sword or hunger; they shall become a malediction, a horror, a curse, a reproach.* 13 Thus I will punish those who live in Egypt, just as I punished Jerusalem, with sword, hunger, and disease, 14 so that none of the remnant of Judah who came to live in the land of Egypt shall escape or survive.* No one shall return to the land of Judah. Even though they long to return and live there, they shall not return except as refugees.

15 They answered Jeremiah—all the men who knew that their wives were offering sacrifices to

† **44:2–30** Chronologically, these are the last of Jeremiah's words to his people. As the narrative ends, Jeremiah meets with rejection. According to tradition, recorded in a much later work, he was murdered in Egypt by fellow Judahites.

* **43:3** Jer 38:4. **43:4** Jer 41:16. **43:6** Jer 41:10. **43:7** Jer 42:13–14; 44:1. **43:10** Jer 27:6; Ez 29:19. **43:11** Jer 46:13; Ez 30:10. **43:12** Jer 46:25; Ez 30:13–14. **44:2** Jer 34:22; Lv 26:32–33. **44:3** Jer 11:17; Dt 32:17. **44:5** Jer 7:24, 26; 19:4. **44:8** Jer 25:6–7. **44:9** 1 Kgs 11:1, 8; Ezr 9:7, 14. **44:10** Jer 7:24. **44:12** Jer 42:15, 18, 22. **44:14** Jer 43:11.

other gods, all the women standing there in the
immense crowd, and all the people who lived in
Lower and Upper Egypt: 16“Regarding the word
you have spoken to us in the name of the LORD,
we are not listening to you.* 17Rather we will
go on doing what we proposed; we will offer
incense to the Queen of Heaven and pour out
libations to her, just as we have done, along with
our ancestors, our kings and princes, in the cities
of Judah and in the streets of Jerusalem. Then we
had plenty to eat, we prospered, and we suffered
no misfortune.* 18But ever since we stopped
offering sacrifices to the Queen of Heaven and
pouring out libations to her, we lack everything
and are being destroyed by sword and hunger.”
19And the women said, “When we offered sac-
rifices to the Queen of Heaven and poured out
libations to her, did we bake cakes in her image
and pour out libations to her without our hus-
bands’ consent?”*
20To all the people, men and women, who
gave him this answer, Jeremiah said: 21As for the
sacrifices you offered in the cities of Judah and
in the streets of Jerusalem—you, your ancestors,
your kings and princes, and the people of the
land—did not the LORD remember them? Did it
not enter his mind?* 22The LORD could no lon-
ger bear the evil of your deeds, the abominations
you were doing; then your land became a waste,
a horror, a curse, without even one inhabitant,
as it is today.* 23Because you offered sacrifice
and sinned against the LORD, not listening to
the voice of the LORD, not following his law, his
statutes, and his decrees, therefore this evil has
overtaken you, as it is today.*
24Jeremiah said to all the people and to all
the women: Hear the word of the LORD, all you
Judahites in the land of Egypt: 25Thus says the
LORD of hosts, the God of Israel: You and your
wives have carried out with your hands what
your mouths have spoken: “We will go on fulfill-
ing the vows we have made to offer sacrifice to
the Queen of Heaven and to pour out libations to
her.” Very well! keep your vows, fulfill your vows!
26And then listen to the word of the LORD, all you
Judahites living in Egypt; I swear by my own great
name, says the LORD: in the whole land of Egypt,
my name shall no longer be pronounced by the
lips of any Judahite, saying, “As the Lord GOD
lives.” 27I am watching over them for evil, not for
good. All the Judahites in Egypt shall come to an
end by sword or famine until they are completely
destroyed.* 28Those who escape the sword to
return from the land of Egypt to the land of Ju-
dah shall be few in number. The whole remnant
of Judah who came to Egypt to live shall know
whose word stands, mine or theirs.*
29And this shall be a sign to you—oracle of
the LORD—I will punish you in this place so
that you will know that my words stand solidly
against you for evil. 30Thus says the LORD: See! I
will hand over Pharaoh Hophra,† king of Egypt,
to his enemies, to those seeking his life, just as
I handed over Zedekiah, king of Judah, to his
enemy Nebuchadrezzar, king of Babylon, to the
one seeking his life.*

A Message to Baruch†

45 1The word that Jeremiah the prophet
spoke to Baruch, son of Neriah, when
he wrote on a scroll words from Jeremiah’s own
mouth in the fourth year of Jehoiakim, son of Jo-
siah, king of Judah:* 2Thus says the LORD, God of
Israel, to you, Baruch. 3You said, “Woe is me! the
LORD has added grief to my pain.* I have worn
myself out with groaning; rest eludes me.” 4You
must say this to him. Thus says the LORD: What
I have built, I am tearing down; what I have
planted, I am uprooting: all this land.* 5And
you, do you seek great things for yourself? Do
not seek them! I am bringing evil on all flesh—
oracle of the LORD—but I will grant you your life
as spoils of war, wherever you may go.*

VIII. Oracles Against the Nations†

46 1The word of the LORD that came to Jere-
miah the prophet concerning the nations.

Against Egypt

2Concerning Egypt. Against the army of Phar-
aoh Neco, king of Egypt, defeated at Carchemish
on the Euphrates† by Nebuchadrezzar, king of

† **44:30** *Hophra*: killed by his own people. Hophra’s successor, Amasis, ruled Egypt when Nebuchadnezzar took control of the country.

45:1–5 At the conclusion of his narrative, Baruch appends a message Jeremiah had given him when he first wrote down Jeremiah’s words (cf. 36:4). The future revealed by the prophet overwhelmed Baruch; now he learns his own safety is assured, even though the Lord will destroy Judah.

46:1–51:64 A collection of oracles against foreign nations constitutes the final section of the Hebrew text of Jeremiah; in the Greek text they follow 25:13. The oracles here appear to be arranged in loose chronological order: 46:2 mentions the fourth year of Jehoiakim; the oracles in 50:1–51:64 are evidently from the end of Jeremiah’s life.

46:2 *Carchemish on the Euphrates*: the western terminus of the Mesopotamian trade route, where Nebuchadnezzar defeated Pharaoh Neco in 605 B.C., thus gaining undisputed control of Syria and Palestine.

44:16 Jer 6:16–17.
44:17 Jer 5:3; 7:18.
44:19 Jer 7:18.
44:21 Jer 11:13.
44:22 Jer 15:6.
44:23 2 Kgs 17:15; Dn 9:11–12.
44:27 Ezr 7:3–7.
44:28 Dt 28:62; Is 10:22.
44:30 Jer 39:5–7; 46:25–26; Ez 29:3–4; 30:21.
45:1 Jer 36:4, 18, 32.
45:3 Lam 1:3; 5:5.
45:4 Jer 18:7; Is 5:5–6.
45:5 Jer 25:26–29.

Babylon, in the fourth year of Jehoiakim, son of Josiah, king of Judah:

3 Prepare buckler and shield!
move forward to battle!
4 Harness the horses,
charioteers, mount up!
Fall in, with helmets on;
polish your spears, put on your armor.
5 What do I see?
Are they panicking, falling apart?
Their warriors are hammered back,
They flee headlong
never making a stand.
Terror on every side—
oracle of the LORD! *
6 The swift cannot flee,
nor the warrior escape:
There up north, on the banks of the Euphrates
they stumble and fall.
7 Who is this? Like the Nile, it rears up;
like rivers, its waters surge.
8 Egypt rears up like the Nile,
like rivers, its waters surge.
"I will rear up," it says, "and cover the earth,
destroying the city and its people.*
9 Forward, horses!
charge, chariots!
March forth, warriors,
Cush and Put, bearing shields,
Archers of Lud, stretching bows!"
10 Today belongs to the Lord GOD of hosts,
a day of vengeance, vengeance on his foes!
The sword devours and is sated, drunk with their blood:
for the Lord GOD of hosts holds a sacrifice
in the land of the north, on the River Euphrates.*
11 Go up to Gilead, procure balm,
Virgin daughter Egypt!
No use to multiply remedies;
for you there is no healing.*
12 The nations hear your cries,
your screaming fills the earth.
Warrior stumbles against warrior,
both collapse together.*

13 * The word that the LORD spoke to Jeremiah the prophet when Nebuchadrezzar, king of Babylon, came to attack the land of Egypt:†

Did You Know?

Oracles Against the Nations

The Oracles Against the Nations, in Jeremiah, chapters 46–51, resemble the oracles in chapters 13–23 of Isaiah. In both, God's threats to destroy the enemies of Israel, as proclaimed by a prophet, reflect the bitterness that has welled up in the nation's heart during its long history of suffering.

Is God really as vengeful as the prophecies from Jeremiah suggest? We must balance our understanding of God's vengeance with Jesus' teachings—for example, Jesus' claim that God makes the "sun rise on the bad and the good" (Mt 5:45). The God whom Jesus called Abba is the parent of all nations, who wants enemies to be reconciled with one another. The Oracles Against the Nations challenge Christians to be the first to offer the handshake of forgiveness and break the cycle of violence.

▶ Jeremiah, chapters 46–51

JER

14 Proclaim in Egypt, announce in Migdol,
announce in Memphis and Tahpanhes!
Say: Fall in, get ready,
the sword has devoured your neighbors.*
15 Why has Apis† fled?
Your champion did not stand,
Because the LORD thrust him down;
16 he stumbled repeatedly then collapsed.
They said to each other,
"Get up! We must return to our own people,
To the land of our birth,
away from the destroying sword."*
17 Give Pharaoh, king of Egypt, the name
"Braggart-missed-his-chance."†
18 As I live, says the King
whose name is LORD of hosts,
Like Tabor above mountains,

46:13 In 601 B.C. Nebuchadnezzar advanced into Egypt itself, but finally had to withdraw to Syria.
46:15 *Apis*: the chief god of Memphis; the black bull honored as an incarnation of the god Ptah and, later, of the god Osiris.
46:17 *"Braggart-missed-his-chance"*: the Hebrew phrase may contain a pun on the Pharaoh's name or royal title.

46:5 Jer 6:25; 49:29.
46:8 Ez 29:3; 32:2.
46:10 Dt 32:42; Is 13:9; Ez 39:17–20.
46:11 Jer 8:22; 51:8; Ez 30:21–22.
46:12 Ez 32:9–12.
46:13 Jer 43:10–11; 44:30; Is 19:1.
46:14 Jer 44:1.
46:16 Lv 26:37.

like Carmel† above the sea, he comes.
19 Pack your bags for exile,
enthroned daughter Egypt;
Memphis shall become a wasteland,
an empty ruin.
20 Egypt is a beautiful heifer,
a horsefly from the north keeps coming.
21 Even the mercenaries in her ranks
are like fattened calves;
They too turn and flee together—
they do not stand their ground,
For their day of ruin comes upon them,
their time of punishment.
22 Her voice is like a snake!
Yes, they come in force;
They attack her with axes,
like those who fell trees.
23 They cut down her forest—oracle of the LORD—
impenetrable though it be;
More numerous than locusts,
they cannot be counted.
24 Shamed is daughter Egypt,
handed over to a people from the north.

25 The LORD of hosts, the God of Israel, has
said: See! I will punish Amon† of Thebes and
Egypt, gods, kings, Pharaoh, and those who trust
in him.* 26 I will hand them over to those who
seek their lives, to Nebuchadrezzar, king of Bab-
ylon, and to his officers. But later, Egypt shall
be inhabited again, as in days of old—oracle of
the LORD.*

27 But you, my servant Jacob, do not fear;
do not be dismayed, Israel!
Listen! I will deliver you from far-off lands;
your offspring, from the land of their exile.
Jacob shall again find rest,
secure, with none to frighten him.*
28 You, Jacob my servant, must not fear—oracle
of the LORD—
for I am with you;
I will make an end of all the nations
to which I have driven you,
But of you I will not make an end:
I will chastise you as you deserve,
I cannot let you go unpunished.*

Against the Philistines

47 1 The word of the LORD that came to Jere-
miah the prophet concerning the Philis-
tines, before Pharaoh attacked Gaza:*

2 Thus says the LORD:
†See: waters are rising from the north,
to become a torrent in flood;
They shall flood the land and all it contains,
the cities and their inhabitants.
People will howl and wail,
every inhabitant of the land.
3 At the noise of the pounding hooves of his
steeds,
the clanking chariots, the rumbling wheels,
Parents do not turn back for their children;
their hands hang helpless,
4 Because of the day that is coming
to destroy all the Philistines
And cut off from Tyre and Sidon†
the last of their allies.
Yes, the LORD is destroying the Philistines,
the remnant from the coasts of Caphtor.*
5 Baldness is visited upon Gaza,*
Ashkelon is reduced to silence;
Ashdod, remnant of their strength,
how long will you gash yourself?†
6 Ah! Sword of the LORD!
When will you find rest?
Return to your scabbard;
stop, be still!
7 How can it find rest
when the LORD has commanded it?
Against Ashkelon and the seacoast,
there he has appointed it.*

Against Moab†

48 1 Concerning Moab. Thus says the LORD of
hosts, the God of Israel:

Ah, Nebo! it is ravaged;
Kiriathaim is disgraced, captured;

---

† **46:18** *Tabor . . . Carmel*: mountains in Palestine that seem to tower over their surroundings as Nebuchadnezzar towers over the nations in his path as he makes his way toward Egypt.

46:25 *Amon*: the sun-god worshiped at Thebes in Upper Egypt.

47:2–7 Nebuchadnezzar's military campaign against Ashkelon in 604 B.C. may provide some historical background for this poem.

47:4 *Tyre and Sidon*: Phoenician seaports allied commercially with the Philistines and often rebelling against Nebuchadnezzar; cf. 27:1–4. After the capture of Jerusalem, Nebuchadnezzar carried out a partially successful thirteen-year siege of Tyre. *Caphtor*: Crete and other Aegean islands, points of origin for the Philistines and other sea peoples; cf. Am 9:7.

47:5 *Baldness . . . gash yourself*: close-cropped hair, silence, and ritual slashing of the body express mourning and grief and here represent the mourner's awareness that chaos has overcome order (cf. 41:5).

48:1–47 Moab, located east of the Dead Sea, was one of Israel's bitter enemies (cf., e.g., Is 15–16; Am 2:1–3). According to Flavius Josephus, Nebuchadnezzar conquered Moab and Ammon in his twenty-third year (582 B.C.), five years after the destruction of Jerusalem. This chapter is full of local place names in Moab.

---

* **46:25** Ez 30:15–16.
46:26 Jer 44:30; Ez 30:4; 32:11–12.
46:27 Jer 30:10; 43:5.
46:28 Jer 30:11.
47:1 Ez 25:15–16; Zep 2:4.
47:4 Jer 25:22; Ez 25:16–17; Am 1:8; 9:7.
47:5 Am 1:7.
47:7 Zep 2:5–6.

Disgraced and overthrown is the stronghold:
2 Moab's glory is no more.
In Heshbon they plot evil against her:
"Come! We will put an end to her as a nation."
You, too, Madmen,† shall be silenced;
you the sword stalks!
3 Listen! an outcry from Horonaim,*
"Ruin and great destruction!"
4 "Moab is crushed!"
their outcry is heard in Zoar.
5 Up the ascent of Luhith
they go weeping;
At the descent to Horonaim
they hear cries of anguish:
6 "Flee, save your lives!
Be like a wild donkey in the wilderness!"
7 Because you trusted in your works and your treasures,
you also shall be captured.
Chemosh† shall go into exile,
his priests and princes with him.*
8 The destroyer comes upon every city,
not a city escapes;
Ruined is the valley,
wasted the plateau—oracle of the LORD.
9 Set up a tombstone for Moab;
it will soon become a complete wasteland,
Its cities turned into ruins
where no one dwells.
10 Cursed are they who do the LORD's work carelessly,
cursed those who keep their sword from shedding blood.
11† Moab has been resting from its youth,
suspended above its dregs,
Never poured from flask to flask,
never driven into exile.
Thus it retained its flavor,
its bouquet is not lost.*

12 Be assured! The days are coming—oracle of
the LORD—when I will send him wine-makers
to decant the wine; they shall empty its flasks
and smash its jars. 13 Chemosh shall disappoint
Moab, just as the house of Israel was disap-
pointed by Bethel, in which they trusted.*

14 How can you say, "We are heroes,
mighty warriors"?
15 The one who ravages Moab and its cities comes up,
the best of its youth go down to slaughter—
oracle of the King, whose name is LORD of hosts.
16 Moab's ruin is near at hand,
its disaster approaches swiftly.
17 Mourn, all you neighbors,
all you who know its name!
Say: How the mighty scepter is broken,
the glorious staff!
18 Come down from glory, sit on the parched ground,
enthroned daughter Dibon;†
Moab's destroyer has fallen upon you,
has shattered your strongholds.*
19 Stand along the road, keep watch,
enthroned Aroer;
Ask the fleeing man, the escaping woman:
ask them what has happened.*
20 "Moab is put to shame, destroyed."
Wail and cry out,
Proclaim it at the Arnon:
"Moab is destroyed!"*

21 Judgment has come upon the plateau: on
Holon, Jahzah, and Mephaath,* 22 on Dibon,
Nebo, and Beth-diblathaim, 23 on Kiriathaim,
Beth-gamul, and Beth-meon, 24 on Kerioth and
on Bozrah: on all the cities of the land of Moab,
far and near.

25 The horn of Moab is cut off,
its arm is broken—oracle of the LORD.

26 Make him drunk because he set himself over
against the LORD; let Moab swim in his vomit and
become a laughingstock. 27 Has Israel not been
a laughingstock to you? Was he caught among
thieves that you wag your heads whenever you
speak of him?*

28 Abandon the cities, take shelter in the crags,
inhabitants of Moab.
Be like the dove that nests
in the walls of a gorge.
29 We have heard of the pride of Moab,*
pride beyond bounds:
His loftiness, his pride, his scorn,
his insolent heart.

†

48:2 *Madmen*: a place name, not mentioned elsewhere in the Old Testament.

48:7 *Chemosh*: chief god of Moab (cf. Nm 21:29).

48:11–12 Moabite wine was known for its high quality. Here the wine is a metaphor for Moab's complacency.

48:18 Dibon, the capital of Moab at that time, is situated on a height. The prophet here offers a personification of the city, pictured as a confident ruler.

*

48:3–5 Is 15:5.
48:7 Nm 21:29.
48:11 Zep 1:12.
48:13 Is 16:12.
48:18 Nm 21:30.
48:19 Dt 2:36.
48:20 Is 16:7.
48:21 Is 15:4.
48:27 Zep 2:8–10.
48:29–30 Is 16:6.

Cultural Connection

The Eagle

Jeremiah 48:40 portrays the punisher of Moab as an eagle. In the Bible, that is not an unusual description for this majestic bird (see also Jb 39:27, Is 40:31, Ez 17:3, Dn 7:4). Native American cultures admire the eagle as the strongest and bravest of all birds, and therefore view eagle feathers as a symbol of what is high and holy.

So, in some Native American tribes, when someone is honored for being brave, strong, and holy, an eagle feather is given to her or him. Native Americans also use eagle feathers for blessings. They hold or wave the feathers over a person's head as a prayer for peace and happiness. (*Note:* Native Americans are able to acquire feathers for use in their rituals. But keep in mind that it is generally illegal to hunt eagles or even to take a feather you find!)

The next time you see an eagle or a picture of an eagle, remember what its feathers symbolize, and pray about those ideals of honor, peace, protection, strength, courage, and holiness.

▶ Jer 48:40

30 I myself know his arrogance—oracle of the
Lord—
liar in word, liar in deed.
31 And so I wail over Moab,
over all Moab I cry,
over the people of Kir-heres I moan.*
32 More than for Jazer I weep for you,
vine of Sibmah.
Your tendrils trailed down to the sea,
as far as Jazer they stretched.
Upon your summer harvest and your vintage,
the destroyer has fallen.*
33 Joy and gladness are taken away
from the garden land, the land of Moab.
I dry up the wine from the wine vats,
the treader treads no more,
the vintage shout is stilled.

34 The cry of Heshbon and Elealeh is heard as
far as Jahaz; they call from Zoar to Horonaim
and to Eglath-shelishiyah; even the waters of
Nimrim turn into a wasteland.* 35 I will leave no
one in Moab—oracle of the Lord—to offer burnt
offerings on the high place or to make sacrifices
to their gods. 36 Hence my heart wails like a flute
for Moab; my heart wails like a flute for the peo-
ple of Kir-heres: the wealth they accumulated has
perished.* 37 Every head has been shaved bald,
every beard cut off; every hand gashed, and all
their loins are draped in sackcloth.* 38 On all
the rooftops of Moab and in all its squares there
is mourning. I have shattered Moab like a pot
that no one wants—oracle of the Lord. 39 How
terrified they are, how they wail! How Moab
turns its back in shame! Moab has become a
laughingstock and a horror to all its neighbors!

40 For thus says the Lord:
Look there! Like an eagle he swoops,
spreading his wings over Moab.*
41 Cities are captured,
strongholds seized:
On that day the hearts of Moab's warriors
become like the heart of a woman in labor.*
42 Moab shall be wiped out, a people no more,
because it set itself over against the Lord.*
43 Terror, pit, and trap be upon you,
enthroned Moab—oracle of the Lord.*
44 Those fleeing the terror
fall into the pit;
Those climbing out of the pit
are caught in the trap;
Ah, yes! I will bring these things upon Moab
in the year of their punishment—oracle of
the Lord.
45 In Heshbon's shadow the fugitives
stop short, exhausted;
For fire blazes up from Heshbon,
and flames up from the house of Sihon:
It consumes the forehead of Moab,
the scalp of the noisemakers.*

48:31 Is 16:7.
48:32 Is 16:8–9.
48:34 Is 15:4–5.
48:36 Is 16:11.
48:37 Jer 47:5; Is 15:2–3; Ez 7:18.
48:40 Jer 49:22.
48:41 Jer 6:24; 30:6.
48:42 Zep 2:9–10.
48:43 Is 24:17–18.
48:45 Nm 21:28–29.

46 Woe to you, Moab!
You are finished, people of Chemosh!
Your sons are taken into exile,
your daughters into captivity.
47 Yet I will restore the fortunes of Moab
in the days to come—oracle of the LORD.*

Thus far the judgment on Moab.

Against the Ammonites

49 1 Concerning the Ammonites. Thus says the LORD:

Has Israel no sons?
none to inherit?
Why has Milcom† disinherited Gad,
why are his people living in its cities?
2 Therefore the days are coming—oracle of the LORD—
when I will sound the battle alarm
against Rabbah of the Ammonites;
It shall become a mound of ruins,
and its villages destroyed by fire.
Israel shall then inherit those who disinherited it—
oracle of the LORD.*
3 Wail, Heshbon, "The ruin is destroyed!"
shriek, villages of Rabbah!
Put on sackcloth and lament!
Run back and forth in the sheepfolds.
For Milcom is going into exile,
taking priest and prince with him.*
4 Why boast in your strength,
your ebbing strength, rebellious daughter?
Why trust in your treasures, saying,
"Who would dare attack me?"
5 See, I am bringing terror upon you—
oracle of the Lord GOD of hosts—
from all around you;
You shall be scattered, each in headlong flight,
with no one to gather the fugitives.*
6 But afterward I will restore the fortunes
of the Ammonites—oracle of the LORD.

Against Edom†

7 Concerning Edom. Thus says the LORD of hosts:

Is there no more wisdom in Teman,†
has counsel perished from the prudent,
is their wisdom gone?
8 Flee, retreat, hide deep for lodging,
inhabitants of Dedan:
For I bring disaster upon Esau†
when I come to punish them.*
9 If vintagers came upon you,
they would leave no gleanings;
If thieves by night,
they would destroy as they pleased.*
10 So I myself will strip Esau;
I will uncover his lairs so he cannot hide.
Offspring and family are destroyed,
neighbors, too; he is no more.*
11 Leave your orphans behind, I will keep them alive;
your widows, let them trust in me.*

12 For thus says the LORD: Look, even those
not sentenced to drink the cup must drink it!
Shall you then go unpunished? You shall not!
You shall drink every bit of it!*
13 By myself I
have sworn—oracle of the LORD—Bozrah† shall
become an object of horror, a disgrace, a desolation, and a curse. Bozrah and all its cities shall
become ruins forever.*

14 I have heard a report from the LORD,
a herald has been sent among the nations:
"Gather together, move against it,
get ready for battle!"
15 I will make you the least among the nations,
despised by all people!*
16 The terror you spread,
the pride of your heart, beguiled you.
You denizens of rocks and crevices,
occupying towering peaks:
Though you build your nest high as the eagle,
from there I will bring you down—oracle of the LORD.*

17 Edom shall become an object of horror. Passersby recoil in terror, hissing at all its wounds.
18 As when Sodom, Gomorrah, and their neighbors were overthrown—oracle of the LORD—no
one shall live in it, nor anyone settle there.*

†

49:1 *Milcom*: chief god of the Ammonites (cf. 1 Kgs 11:5). The Ammonites shared a border with Gad, an Israelite tribe in Transjordan (Jos 13:8–10); the Ammonites occupied its territory after the collapse of the Northern Kingdom.

49:7–22 *Edom*: southeast of the Dead Sea, a traditional enemy who profited from Judah's downfall; cf. Ps 137:7; Lam 4:21–22; Ob 11–12.

49:7 Teman, a district of Edom (cf. Jb 2:11), represents the whole country, which was famous for the wisdom of its sages.

49:8 *Esau*: Jacob's brother, the traditional ancestor of the Edomites; cf. Gn 36:1.

49:13 *Bozrah*: capital of Edom.

*

48:47 Jer 49:39.
49:2 Am 1:14.
49:3 Is 15:2–5.
49:5 Jer 48:47.
49:8 Ez 25:13.
49:9 Ob 5.
49:10 Mal 1:3.
49:11 Dt 10:18; Ps 68:6.
49:12 Jer 25:15, 28; Lam 4:21–22.
49:13 Is 34:6; Ez 35:3–9; Ob 16.
49:15 Ob 2.
49:16 Jer 48:29–30.
49:18 Jer 50:40; Dt 29:23.

19 As when a lion comes up from a thicket of the Jordan
to a permanent pasture,
So in an instant, I will chase them off;
I will establish there whomever I choose.
For who is like me? Who holds me accountable?
What shepherd can stand against me?*
20 Therefore, listen to the strategy
the LORD devised for Edom;
The plans he has drawn up
against the inhabitants of Teman:
They shall be dragged away, even the smallest of the flock;
their pasture shall be aghast because of them.
21 With the din of their collapse the earth quakes,
to the Red Sea the outcry is heard!
22 Look! like an eagle he soars aloft,
and spreads his wings over Bozrah;
On that day the hearts of Edom's warriors become
like the heart of a woman in labor.*

Against Damascus

23 Concerning Damascus.

Hamath and Arpad† are shamed,
for they have heard bad news;
Anxious, they surge like the sea
which cannot calm down.*
24 Damascus loses heart, turns to flee;
panic has seized it.
Distress and pangs take hold,
like the pain of a woman in labor.
25 How can the glorious city be abandoned,
the town of joy!
26 But now its young men shall fall in its squares,
all the warriors destroyed on that day—
oracle of the LORD of hosts.
27 I will set fire to the wall of Damascus;
it shall devour the palaces of Ben-hadad.†

Against Arabia

28 About Kedar and the kingdoms of Hazor,
which Nebuchadnezzar, king of Babylon, de-
feated.

Thus says the LORD:
Rise up, attack Kedar,
destroy the people from the east.*
29 Their tents and flocks shall be taken away,
their tent curtains and all their goods;
Their camels they carry off,
they shout over them, "Terror on every side!"*
30 Flee! wander about, hide deep for lodging,
inhabitants of Hazor—oracle of the LORD;
For Nebuchadnezzar, king of Babylon, has devised a strategy against you,
drawn up a plan against you,
31 Get up! set out against a tranquil nation,
living in security—oracle of the LORD—
Without gates or bars,
dwelling alone.
32 Their camels shall become spoils,
their hordes of cattle, plunder;
I will scatter to the winds those who shave their temples;
from every side I will bring their ruin—
oracle of the LORD.*
33 Hazor shall become a haunt for jackals,
a wasteland forever,
Where no one lives,
no mortal stays.

Against Elam

34 The word of the LORD that came to Jeremiah
the prophet concerning Elam† at the beginning
of the reign of Zedekiah, king of Judah:

35 Thus says the LORD of hosts:
Look! I will break the bow of Elam,
the mainstay of their might.
36 I will bring upon Elam the four winds
from the four ends of the heavens:
I will scatter them to all these winds, until there is no nation
to which the outcasts of Elam have not gone.
37 I will terrify Elam before their foes,
those seeking their life;
I will bring evil upon them,
my burning wrath—oracle of the LORD.
I will send sword after them
until I have finished them off;
38 I will set up my throne in Elam
and destroy from there king and princes—
oracle of the LORD.
39 But at the end of days I will restore
the fortunes of Elam—oracle of the LORD.

---

†

49:23 *Hamath and Arpad*: independent Aramean states north of Damascus, the direction from which the invasion is coming. Cf. Is 10:9–10.

49:27 *Ben-hadad*: a dynastic name for some of the kings who ruled in Damascus; cf. 1 Kgs 15:18, 20.

49:34 *Elam*: an ancient kingdom east of Babylonia.

*

49:19 Jer 12:5; 25:9; 50:44–45.
49:22 Jer 4:13.
49:23 Is 36:19; 37:13.
49:28 Is 21:16.
49:29 Jer 4:20.
49:32 Jer 9:25.

The First Oracle Against Babylon

50 1The word the LORD spoke against Babylon,† against the land of the Chaldeans, through Jeremiah the prophet:*

2 Proclaim this among the nations,
announce it!
Announce it, do not hide it, but say:
Babylon is captured, Bel† put to shame,
Marduk terrified;
its images are put to shame, its idols
shattered.
3 A nation from the north advances against it,
making the land desolate
So that no one can live there;
human beings and animals have fled.*
4 In those days and at that time—oracle of the
LORD—
Israelite and Judahite shall come together,
Weeping as they come, to seek the LORD, their
God;*
5 They shall ask for Zion,
seeking out the way.
"Come, let us join ourselves to the LORD
in an everlasting covenant, never to be
forgotten."*
6 Lost sheep were my people,
their shepherds misled them,
leading them astray on the mountains;
From mountain to hill they wandered,
forgetting their fold.*
7 Whoever happened upon them devoured
them;
their enemies said, "We are not guilty,
Because they sinned against the LORD,
the abode of justice, the hope of their
ancestors."*
8 Flee from the midst of Babylon,
leave the land of the Chaldeans,
be like rams at the head of the flock.*
9 See, I am stirring up against Babylon
a band of great nations from the land of
the north;
They are arrayed against her,
from there she shall be taken.
Their arrows are like the arrows of a skilled
warrior
who never returns empty-handed.*
10 Chaldea shall become plunder;
all its plunderers shall be enriched—
oracle of the LORD.
11 Yes, rejoice and exult,
you that plunder my heritage;
Frisk like calves on the grass,
neigh like stallions!
12 Your mother will indeed be put to shame,
she that bore you shall be abashed;
See, the last of the nations,
a wilderness, a dry wasteland.*
13 Because of the LORD's wrath it shall be
uninhabited,
become an utter wasteland;
Everyone who passes by Babylon will be
appalled
and hiss at all its wounds.*
14 Take your posts encircling Babylon,
you who bend the bow;
Shoot at it, do not spare your arrows,*
15 raise the war cry against it on every side.
It surrenders, its bastions fall,
its walls are torn down:†
This is retribution from the LORD! Take
retribution on her,
as she has done, do to her;
for she sinned against the LORD.*
16 Cut off the sower from Babylon
and those who wield sickles at harvest
time!
Before the destroying sword,
all of them turn back to their own people,
all flee to their own land.*
17 Israel was a stray sheep
that lions pursued;
The king of Assyria once devoured him;
now Nebuchadnezzar of Babylon gnaws his
bones.*
18 Therefore, thus says the LORD of hosts, the
God of Israel:
I will punish the king of Babylon and his
land,
as I once punished the king of Assyria;*
19 But I will bring Israel back to its pasture,
to feed on Carmel and Bashan,
And on Mount Ephraim and Gilead,
until they have their fill.*

---

† **50:1–51:58** A collection of miscellaneous oracles against Babylon introducing the story in 51:59–64.

50:2 *Bel*: originally the title of the god of Nippur in Mesopotamia, later associated with *Merodach* (Marduk), chief god of Babylon (cf. Is 46:1).

50:15 *Its walls are torn down*: the prophet describes the downfall of Babylon in conventional language. Babylon surrendered peacefully to the Persians in 539 B.C.

* **50:1** Jer 51:1; Is 13:1–14; 21:1–10.
50:3 Jer 51:48; Is 13:17.
50:4 Jer 3:18; Ps 126:6.
50:5 Jer 31:31; 32:40.
50:6 Is 53:6; 1 Pt 2:25.
50:7 Jer 31:23.
50:8 Jer 51:6, 45; Is 48:20.
50:9 Jer 51:27.
50:12 Jer 51:43; Is 13:20–22.
50:13 Jer 25:12.
50:14 Jer 51:11; Is 21:2.
50:15 Jer 51:11, 44, 58; Ps 137:8.
50:16 Is 13:14.
50:17 2 Kgs 17:24; 18:14.
50:18 Is 10:12; 14:24–25.
50:19 Jer 23:3; Ez 34:13–14.

20 In those days, at that time—oracle of the LORD:

The guilt of Israel may be sought, but it no longer exists,
the sin of Judah, but it can no longer be found;
for I will forgive the remnant I preserve.*
21 Attack the land of Merathaim,
and those who live in Pekod;†
Slaughter and put them under the ban—
oracle of the LORD—
do all I have commanded you.
22 Battle alarm in the land,
great destruction!
23 How the hammer of the whole earth
has been cut off and broken!
What an object of horror
Babylon has become among the nations!*
24 You ensnared yourself and were caught,
Babylon, before you knew it!
You were discovered and seized,
because you challenged the LORD.*
25 The LORD opens his armory,
brings out the weapons of his wrath;
The Lord GOD of hosts has work to do
in the land of the Chaldeans.*
26 Come upon them from every side,
open their granaries,
Pile them up in heaps and put them under the ban;
do not leave a remnant.
27 Slay all the oxen,
take them down to slaughter;
Woe to them! their day has come,
the time of their punishment.
28 Listen! the fugitives, the refugees
from the land of Babylon:
They announce in Zion
the retribution of the LORD, our God.*
29 Call archers out against Babylon,
all who bend the bow;
Encamp around them;
let no one escape.
Repay them for their deeds;
what they have done, do to them,
For they insulted the LORD,
the Holy One of Israel.*
30 Therefore their young men shall fall in the squares,
all their warriors shall be stilled on that day—
oracle of the LORD.*
31 I am against you, O Insolence—
oracle of the Lord GOD of hosts;
For your day has come,
the time for me to punish you.
32 Insolence stumbles and falls;
there is no one to raise him up.
I will kindle a fire in his cities
to devour everything around him.
33 Thus says the LORD of hosts:
Oppressed are the people of Israel,
together with the people of Judah;
All their captors hold them fast
and refuse to let them go.
34 Strong is their Redeemer,
whose name is LORD of hosts,
The sure defender of their cause,
who gives rest to their land,
but unrest to those who live in Babylon.*
35 A sword upon the Chaldeans—oracle of the LORD—
upon the inhabitants of Babylon, her princes and sages!
36 A sword upon the soothsayers,
and they become fools!
A sword upon the warriors,
and they tremble;
37 A sword upon their motley throng,
and they become women!
A sword upon their treasures,
and they are plundered;*
38 A drought upon the waters,
and they dry up!
For it is a land of idols,
soon made frantic by phantoms.*
39 Hence, wildcats shall dwell there with hyenas,
and ostriches occupy it;
Never again shall it be inhabited or settled,
from age to age.*
40 As happened when God overturned Sodom
and Gomorrah and their neighbors—oracle of the LORD—
No one shall dwell there,
no mortal shall settle there.*
41 See, a people comes from the north,
a great nation, and mighty kings
rising from the ends of the earth.*
42 Bow and javelin they wield,

† **50:21** *Merathaim . . . Pekod*: "twice bitter," "punishment," symbolic terms for Babylon that recall the names of regions in the country.

* **50:20** Jer 31:34; Is 43:25; Mi 7:19.
50:23 Jer 51:20; Is 14:6.
50:24 Jer 51:57.
50:25 Jer 51:11–12; Is 13:5.
50:28 Jer 51:10–11.
50:29 Jer 51:56.
50:30 Jer 49:26; 51:4.
50:34 Jer 51:36.
50:37 Jer 51:30; Na 3:13.
50:38 Jer 51:32, 36.
50:39 Jer 51:37; Is 13:21–22.
50:40 Jer 51:43.
50:41 Jer 51:27–28.

cruel and pitiless are they;
They sound like the roaring sea,
as they ride forth on horses,
Each in place for battle
against you, daughter Babylon.
43 The king of Babylon hears news of them,
and his hands hang helpless;
Anguish takes hold of him,
like the pangs of a woman giving birth.*
44 As happens when a lion comes up from a thicket of the Jordan
to permanent pasture,
So I, in an instant, will chase them off,
and establish there whomever I choose!
For who is like me? Who can call me to account?
What shepherd can stand against me?*
45 Therefore, hear the strategy of the LORD,
which he has devised against Babylon;
Hear the plans drawn up
against the land of the Chaldeans:
They shall be dragged away, even the smallest sheep;
their own pasture aghast because of them.*
46 At the cry "Babylon is captured!" the earth quakes;
the outcry is heard among the nations.*

The Second Oracle Against Babylon

51 1 Thus says the LORD:
See! I rouse against Babylon,
and the inhabitants of Chaldea,
a destroyer wind.†
2 To Babylon I will send winnowers
to winnow and lay waste the land;
They shall besiege it on every side
on the day of affliction.*
3 How can the archers draw back their bows,
lift their armor?
Do not spare her young men,
put the entire army under the ban.*
4 The slain shall fall in the land of Chaldea,
the wounded, in its streets;*
5 For Israel and Judah are not left widowed
by their God, the LORD of hosts,
Even though the land is full of guilt
against the Holy One of Israel.
6 Flee from Babylon;
each of you save your own life,
do not perish because of her guilt;
This is a time of retribution from the LORD,

Did You Know?

Whatever Happened to Babylon?

In his time, Jeremiah prophesied about the destruction of Babylon, the powerful empire with the most glamorous and glittering capital in the Middle East (see Jeremiah, chapters 50–51). Not long afterward, in 587 BC, King Nebuchadrezzar (also called Nebuchadnezzar) of Babylon destroyed Jerusalem, blinded the king of Judah, and led the leaders of Judah off to exile. This seemed to be the end of Jerusalem and perhaps even the Israelites. However, the captives were eventually released when Persia defeated Babylon. Today, Jerusalem is a thriving city, and Judaism—as it emerged after the Exile—is a great religion. Babylon is long gone, and no one worships its chief god, Marduk.

Jeremiah saw past the immediate destruction of Jerusalem to the eventual doom of Babylon. He had a much broader vision of the future. Great cities come and go, but God is forever, and the people of God live on through all the ebbs and flows of history.

▶ **Jeremiah, chapter 51**

7 who pays out her due.*
Babylon was a golden cup in the hand of the LORD
making the whole earth drunk;
The nations drank its wine,
thus they have gone mad.*
8 Babylon suddenly falls and is broken:
wail over her!
Bring balm for her wounds,
in case she can be healed.*
9 "We have tried to heal Babylon,
but she cannot be healed.
Leave her, each of us must go to our own land."
The judgment against her reaches the heavens,
it touches the clouds.*
10 The LORD has brought forth our vindication;

† **51:1** The destroyer wind is the fierce dry wind from the east (cf. 4:11).

* **50:43** Is 13:7.
50:44 Jer 49:19.
50:45 Jer 51:12, 29.
50:46 Jer 51:29.
51:2 Jer 15:7; Is 41:16.
51:3 Jer 50:14, 29.
51:4 Jer 50:30.
51:7 Jer 50:8, 15, 29; Is 48:20.
51:7 Rev 14:8; 17:4.
51:8 Rev 18:9–18.
51:9 Is 13:14; Rev 18:5.

come, let us tell in Zion
what the LORD, our God, has done.*
11 Sharpen the arrows,
fill the quivers;
The LORD has stirred up the spirit of the kings of the Medes,†
for his resolve is Babylon's destruction.
Yes, it is retribution from the LORD,
retribution for his temple.*
12 Over the walls of Babylon raise a signal,
reinforce the watch;
Post sentries,
arrange ambushes!
For the LORD has both planned and carried out
what he spoke against the inhabitants of Babylon.
13 You who dwell by mighty waters,
rich in treasure,
Your end has come,
the time at which you shall be cut off!*
14 The LORD of hosts has sworn by himself:
I will fill you with people as numerous as locusts,
who shall raise over you a joyous shout!
15 He made the earth by his power,
established the world by wisdom,
and by his skill stretched out the heavens.*
16 When he thunders, the waters in the heavens roar,
he summons clouds from the ends of the earth,
Makes lightning flash in the rain,
and brings out winds from their storehouses.
17 Every man is stupid, ignorant;
every artisan is put to shame by his idol:
He molds a fraud,
without life-breath.
18 They are nothing, a ridiculous work,
that will perish at the time of punishment.
19 Jacob's portion is nothing like them:
he is the creator of all things.
Israel is his very own tribe;
LORD of hosts is his name.
20 You are my hammer,
a weapon for war;
With you I shatter nations,
with you I destroy kingdoms.
21 With you I shatter horse and rider,
with you I shatter chariot and driver.*
22 With you I shatter man and woman,
with you I shatter old and young,
with you I shatter the young man and young woman.*
23 With you I shatter shepherd and flock,
with you I shatter farmer and team,
with you I shatter governors and officers.
24 Thus I will repay Babylon,
all the inhabitants of Chaldea,
For all the evil they committed against Zion,
before your very eyes—oracle of the LORD.*
25 Beware! I am against you,
destroying mountain—oracle of the LORD—
destroyer of the entire earth,
I will stretch forth my hand against you,
roll you down over the cliffs,
and make you a burnt mountain:*
26 They will not take from you a cornerstone,
or a foundation stone;
You shall remain ruins forever—
oracle of the LORD.*
27 Raise a signal in the land,
sound the trumpet among the nations;
Dedicate nations for war against her,
summon against her the kingdoms:
Ararat, Minni, and Ashkenaz;†
Appoint a recruiting officer against her,
dispatch horses like bristling locusts.*
28 Dedicate nations for war against her:
the king of the Medes,
Its governors and all its officers,
every land in its domain.
29 The earth quakes and writhes,
the LORD's plan against Babylon is carried out,
Turning the land of Babylon
into a wasteland without inhabitants.
30 Babylon's warriors have ceased to fight,
they remain in their strongholds;
Dried up is their strength,
they have become women.
Burned down are their homes,
broken their gates.
31 One runner meets another,
herald meets herald,
Telling the king of Babylon
that his entire city has been taken.*
32 The fords have been seized,
marshes set on fire,
warriors panic.

---

† **51:11** *Kings of the Medes*: the Medes and the Persians lived in the area known today as Iran.

51:27 *Ararat, Minni, and Ashkenaz*: regions in eastern Asia Minor under the control of the Medes.

* **51:10** Jer 50:28.
51:11 2 Kgs 17:6; Is 13:17.
51:13 Na 2:1.
51:15 Jer 10:12.
51:21 Dn 7:7, 19, 23.
51:22 Is 13:16, 18.
51:24 Jer 25:14; 50:29; Ps 137:8.
51:25 Rev 8:7; 18:8–9.
51:26 Jer 25:12; Ps 118:22.
51:27 Na 3:17.
51:31 2 Chr 30:6; Jb 1:14–18.

[33] For thus says the LORD of hosts, the God of Israel:

Daughter Babylon is like a threshing floor
at the time of treading;
Yet a little while,
and the harvest time will come for her.*
[34] "He consumed me, defeated me,
Nebuchadnezzar, king of Babylon;
he left me like an empty vessel,
Swallowed me like a sea monster,
filled his belly with my delicacies and cast me out.
[35] Let my torn flesh be visited upon Babylon,"
says enthroned Zion;
"My blood upon the inhabitants of Chaldea,"
says Jerusalem.
[36] But now, thus says the LORD:
I will certainly defend your cause,
I will certainly avenge you;
I will dry up her sea,
and drain her fountain.
[37] Babylon shall become a heap of ruins,
a haunt of jackals;
A place of horror and hissing,
without inhabitants.*
[38] They roar like lions,
growl like lion cubs.*
[39] When they are parched, I will set drink before them
to make them drunk, that they may be overcome
with everlasting sleep, never to awaken—
oracle of the LORD.
[40] I will bring them down like lambs to slaughter,
like rams and goats.
[41] How she has been seized, taken captive,
the glory of the whole world!
What a horror Babylon has become among the nations:*
[42] against Babylon the sea rises,
she is overwhelmed by roaring waves!
[43] Her cities have become wasteland,
a parched and arid land
Where no one lives,
no one passes through.
[44] I will punish Bel in Babylon,
and make him vomit up what he swallowed;
nations shall no longer stream to him.
Even the wall of Babylon falls!
[45] Leave her, my people; each of you save your own life
from the burning wrath of the LORD.

[46] Do not be discouraged when rumors spread
through the land; this year one rumor comes,
next year another: "Violence in the land!" or
"Ruler against ruler!"* [47] Realize that the days
are coming when I will punish the idols of Bab-
ylon; the whole land shall be put to shame, all
her slain shall fall in her midst. [48] Then heaven
and earth and everything in them shall shout
over Babylon with joy, when the destroyers come
against her from the north—oracle of the LORD.*
[49] Babylon, too, must fall, you slain of Israel, be-
cause by the hand of Babylon the slain of all the
earth have fallen.

[50] You who have escaped the sword,
go, do not stand idle;
Remember the LORD from far away,
let Jerusalem come to mind.
[51] We are ashamed because we have heard taunts,
disgrace covers our faces;
strangers have entered sanctuaries in the LORD's house.*
[52] Therefore see, the days are coming—oracle of the LORD—
when I will punish her idols,
and throughout the land the wounded will groan.
[53] Though Babylon scale the heavens,
and make her strong heights inaccessible,
my destroyers shall reach her—oracle of the LORD.*
[54] A sound of crying from Babylon,
great destruction from the land of the Chaldeans;
[55] For the LORD lays Babylon waste,
silences her loud cry,
Waves roaring like mighty waters,
a clamor resounding.
[56] For the destroyer comes upon her, upon Babylon;
warriors are captured, their bows broken;
The LORD is a God of recompense,
he will surely repay.*

[57] I will make her princes and sages drunk, with her governors, officers, and warriors, so that they sleep an everlasting sleep, never to awaken—oracle of the King, whose name is LORD of hosts.

* **51:33** Rev 14:15.
51:37 Is 25:2.
51:38 Na 2:11–12.
51:41 Is 13:19.
51:46 Mt 24:6–7.
51:48 Rev 18:20.
51:51 Ps 44:16–17; 78:1–4.
51:53 Is 14:13.
51:56 Na 1:2.

JER

58 Thus says the LORD of hosts:
The walls of spacious Babylon shall be leveled
to the ground,
its lofty gates destroyed by fire.
The toil of the peoples is for nothing;
the nations weary themselves for what the
flames consume.*

The Prophecy Sent to Babylon

59 The mission Jeremiah the prophet gave to
Seraiah,† son of Neriah, son of Mahseiah, when
he went to Babylon with King Zedekiah, king
of Judah, in the fourth year of his reign; Seraiah
was chief quartermaster. 60 Jeremiah wrote down
on one scroll the disaster that would befall Bab-
ylon;† all these words were written against Bab-
ylon. 61 And Jeremiah said to Seraiah: "When you
reach Babylon, see that you read all these words
aloud,* 62 and then say: LORD, you yourself spoke
against this place in order to cut it down so that
nothing, human being or beast, could live in
it, because it is to remain a wasteland forever.
63 When you have finished reading this scroll, tie
a stone to it and throw it into the Euphrates,*
64 and say: Thus Babylon shall sink. It will never
rise, because of the disaster I am bringing upon
it." Thus far the words of Jeremiah.

IX. Historical Appendix†

Capture of Jerusalem

52 1 Zedekiah was twenty-one years old when
he became king; he reigned eleven years
in Jerusalem.* His mother's name was Hamutal,
daughter of Jeremiah from Libnah. 2 He did what
was evil in the sight of the LORD, just as Jehoia-
kim had done. 3 Indeed, the things done in Jeru-
salem and in Judah so angered the LORD that he
cast them out from his presence. Thus Zedekiah
rebelled against the king of Babylon. 4 * In the
tenth month of the ninth year of his reign, on the
tenth day of the month,† Nebuchadnezzar, king
of Babylon, and his entire army advanced against
Jerusalem, encamped around it, and built siege
walls on every side. 5 The siege of the city contin-
ued until the eleventh year of King Zedekiah.
6 On the ninth day of the fourth month, when
famine had gripped the city and the people had
no more bread, 7 the city walls were breached.
All the soldiers fled and left the city by night
through the gate between the two walls which
was near the king's garden. With the Chaldeans
surrounding the city, they went in the direction
of the Arabah. 8 But the Chaldean army pursued
the king and overtook Zedekiah in the wilderness
near Jericho; his whole army fled from him.
9 The king, therefore, was arrested and brought
to Riblah, in the land of Hamath, to the king of
Babylon, who pronounced judgment on him.
10 As Zedekiah looked on, the king of Babylon
slaughtered his sons before his eyes! All the no-
bles of Judah were slaughtered at Riblah. 11 And
the eyes of Zedekiah he then blinded, bound
him with chains, and the King of Babylon
brought him to Babylon and kept him in prison
until the day he died.

Destruction of Jerusalem

12 On the tenth day of the fifth month, this
was in the nineteenth year† of Nebuchadnezzar,
king of Babylon, Nebuzaradan, captain of the
bodyguard, came to Jerusalem as the represen-
tative of the king of Babylon. 13 He burned the
house of the LORD, the palace of the king, and all
the houses of Jerusalem; every large building he
destroyed with fire. 14 Then the Chaldean troops
with the captain of the guard tore down all the
walls that surrounded Jerusalem.
15 Nebuzaradan, captain of the guard, led into
exile the remnant of people left in the city, those
who had deserted to the king of Babylon, and the
rest of the artisans. 16 But Nebuzaradan, captain
of the guard, left behind some of the country's
poor as vinedressers and farmers.
17 The bronze pillars that belonged to the
house of the LORD, and the wheeled carts and
the bronze sea in the house of the LORD, the
Chaldeans broke into pieces; they carried away
all the bronze to Babylon. 18 They also took the
pots, shovels, snuffers, bowls, pans, and all the
bronze vessels used for service; 19 the basins, fire
holders, bowls, pots, lampstands, pans, the sac-
rificial bowls made of gold or silver. Along with
these furnishings the captain of the guard carried

†

51:59 *Seraiah*: the brother of Baruch; cf. 32:12. He may have gone to Babylon to explain away the presence of foreign ambassadors in Jerusalem that same year; cf. 27:3.

51:60 Jeremiah prophesied against Babylon, even as he foretold Judah's release from Babylon's power (3:14–18; 32:15; 33:6–9, 12–13); but his scroll against Babylon was thrown in the Euphrates (v. 63). Some of the preceding oracles may have been composed by later writers; see note on 50:1–51:58.

52:1–34 One of the editors of the Book of Jeremiah took most of this supplement from 2 Kgs 24:18–25:30 and placed it here to show the fulfillment of Jeremiah's prophecies. The supplement repeats part of the history given in Jeremiah 39–41, but omits the history of Gedaliah in 2 Kgs 25:22–26.

52:4 *In the tenth month of the ninth year of his reign, on the tenth day of the month*: January 15, 588 B.C. Cf. 39:1.

52:12 *On the tenth day of the fifth month . . . nineteenth year*: the tenth of Ab—July/August in 587/586 B.C.

*

51:58 Hb 2:13.
51:61 Jer 50:1–51.
51:63 Rev 18:21.
52:1–27 2 Kgs 24:18–25:21.
52:4–16 Jer 39:1–10.

off [20]the two pillars, the one sea and its base of twelve oxen cast in bronze, and the wheeled carts King Solomon had commissioned for the house of the LORD. The bronze from all these furnishings was impossible to weigh.

[21]As for the pillars, each of them was eighteen cubits high and twelve cubits in diameter; each was four fingers thick and hollow inside. [22]A bronze capital five cubits high crowned the one pillar, and a network with pomegranates encircled the capital, all of bronze; and so for the other pillar, with pomegranates. [23]There were ninety-six pomegranates on the sides, a hundred pomegranates surrounding the network.

[24]The captain of the guard also took Seraiah the high priest, Zephaniah the second priest, and the three keepers of the entrance. [25]From the city he took one courtier, a commander of soldiers, and seven men in the personal service of the king still in the city, the scribe of the army commander who mustered the people of the land, and sixty of the common people remaining in the city. [26]The captain of the guard, Nebuzaradan, arrested them and brought them to the king of Babylon at Riblah, [27]who had them struck down and executed in Riblah, in the land of Hamath. Thus Judah was exiled from the land. [28]† This is the number of people Nebuchadnezzar led away captive: in his seventh year, three thousand twenty-three people of Judah; [29]in the eighteenth year of Nebuchadnezzar, eight hundred thirty-two persons from Jerusalem; [30]in the twenty-third year of Nebuchadnezzar, Nebuzaradan, captain of the guard, deported seven hundred forty-five Judahites: four thousand six hundred persons in all.

Favor Shown to Jehoiachin†

[31]* In the thirty-seventh year of the exile of Jehoiachin, king of Judah, on the twenty-fifth day of the twelfth month, Evil-merodach, king of Babylon, in the inaugural year of his reign, raised up Jehoiachin, king of Judah, and released him from prison. [32]He spoke kindly to him and gave him a throne higher than the thrones of the other kings† who were with him in Babylon. [33]Jehoiachin took off his prison garb and ate at the king's table as long as he lived. [34]The allowance given him by the king of Babylon was a perpetual allowance, in fixed daily amounts, all the days of his life until the day of his death.

†

52:28–30 These verses, missing in the Greek text, do not come from 2 Kgs 25 but from a source using a different chronology. Besides the deportations of 598 and 587 B.C., this passage mentions a final deportation in 582/581, possibly a response to the murder of Gedaliah; cf. Jer 41:2.

52:31–34 In the year 561/560 B.C., Nebuchadnezzar's successor Awel-Marduk (Evil-merodach), who reigned only two years, released Jehoiachin. Babylonian records confirm that Jehoiachin and his family were supported at public expense.

52:32 *The other kings*: heads of state brought as captives to Babylon.

*

52:31–34 2 Kgs 25:27–30.

JER

The Book of Lamentations

If someone close to you has died, you know that the grief and sadness can be almost too much for words. At such times of deep emotion, many people resort to poetry or song to try to express their feelings. Written during the Babylonian Exile, the Book of Lamentations poetically expresses the overwhelming grief the Israelites felt over the loss of their homes, their freedom, their capital, and their Temple. Through its passages, the Book of Lamentations gives us insight into how devastating and destructive those days actually were.

At a Glance

I. The Desolation of Jerusalem (1:1–22).

II. The Lord's Wrath and Zion's Ruin (2:1–22).

III. The Voice of a Suffering Individual (3:1–66).

IV. Miseries of the Besieged City (4:1–22).

V. The Community's Lament to the Lord (5:1–22).

Quick Facts

Period Covered: the Babylonian Exile, from 587 to 538 BC
Inspired Authors: unknown
Theme: poems of grief over the destruction of Jerusalem and the hardships of the Exile

In Depth

The Book of Lamentations is a collection of five poem songs, each a separate chapter in the book. If you take a quick look, you will notice that each poem has twenty-two verses, except the third, which has sixty-six. This is not an accident. In the original Hebrew language, each verse of the first, second, and fourth poems begins with successive letters of the Hebrew alphabet, which has twenty-two letters. In the third poem, every set of three verses begins with a different letter of the alphabet. This poetic structure, called acrostic, cannot be successfully translated into English. It is found in several poetic sections of the Old Testament, including Psalm 119.

We are not sure why the Lamentation poems were written in this fashion. It may be because the structure made them easier to memorize. Some scholars believe that it may have been a mystical sign of order and completeness. Another possibility is that the poem's structure helped to give form to the people's grief, which is important because uncontrollable grief can keep people from moving on in life. Knowing that the poem had a definite end may have reminded them that their sorrow would also come to an end.

Through these beautiful poems, Israelites were able to grieve and acknowledge the sin that led to their destruction. By recalling their experience of the goodness of God in the past, they were also able to hope for the day when God would lead them back to their land to rebuild their lives in faithfulness to the covenant.

Lamentations

The Desolation of Jerusalem†

1 1 How solitary sits the city,
once filled with people.
She who was great among the nations
is now like a widow.
Once a princess among the provinces,
now a toiling slave.

2 She weeps incessantly in the night,
her cheeks damp with tears.
She has no one to comfort her
from all her lovers;†
Her friends have all betrayed her,
and become her enemies.*

3 Judah has gone into exile,
after oppression and harsh
labor;
She dwells among the nations,
yet finds no rest:*
All her pursuers overtake her
in the narrow straits.

4 The roads to Zion mourn,
empty of pilgrims to her feasts.
All her gateways are desolate,
her priests groan,
Her young women grieve;
her lot is bitter.*

5 Her foes have come out on top,
her enemies are secure;
Because the LORD has afflicted her
for her many rebellions.
Her children have gone away,
captive before the foe.

6 From daughter Zion has gone
all her glory:
Her princes have become like rams
that find no pasture.
They have gone off exhausted
before their pursuers.

7 Jerusalem remembers
in days of wretched homelessness,
All the precious things she once had
in days gone by.
But when her people fell into the hands of
the foe,
and she had no help,
Her foes looked on and laughed
at her collapse.

†

1:1–22 In this poem the poet first takes on the persona of an observer describing Jerusalem's abject state after the destruction wrought by the Babylonian army (vv. 1–11a); but the detached tone gives way to a more impassioned appeal when the city itself—personified as the grieving widow and mother Zion—abruptly intrudes upon this description (vv. 9c, 11c–16, 18–22) to demand that God look squarely at her misery.

1:2 *Lovers*: language of love was typically used to describe the relationship between treaty partners, thus here it connotes Judah's allies (see v. 19).

*

1:2 Jer 30:14; Ez 16:37.
1:3 Dt 28:65; Jer 45:3.
1:4 Is 33:8–9; Jer 14:2.

8 Jerusalem has sinned grievously,
therefore she has become a mockery;
Those who honored her now demean her,
for they saw her nakedness;
She herself groans out loud,
and turns away.*

9 Her uncleanness is on her skirt;
she has no thought of her future.
Her downfall is astonishing,
with no one to comfort her.
"Look, O LORD, at my misery;
how the enemy triumphs!"†

10 The foe stretched out his hands
to all her precious things;
She has seen the nations
enter her sanctuary,
Those you forbade to come
into your assembly.*

11 All her people groan,
searching for bread;
They give their precious things for food,
to retain the breath of life.
"Look, O LORD, and pay attention
to how I have been demeaned!

12 Come, all who pass by the way,
pay attention and see:
Is there any pain like my pain,
which has been ruthlessly inflicted upon me,
With which the LORD has tormented me
on the day of his blazing wrath?

13 From on high he hurled fire down
into my very bones;
He spread out a net for my feet,
and turned me back.
He has left me desolate,
in misery all day long.*

14 The yoke of my rebellions is bound together,
fastened by his hand.
His yoke is upon my neck;
he has made my strength fail.
The Lord has delivered me into the grip
of those I cannot resist.

15 All my valiant warriors
my Lord has cast away;
He proclaimed a feast against me
to crush my young men;
My Lord has trodden in the wine press
virgin daughter Judah.

16 For these things I weep—My eyes! My eyes!
They stream with tears!
How far from me is anyone to comfort,
anyone to restore my life.
My children are desolate;
the enemy has prevailed."*

17 Zion stretches out her hands,
with no one to comfort her;
The LORD has ordered against Jacob
his foes all around;
Jerusalem has become in their midst
a thing unclean.

18 "The LORD is in the right;
I had defied his command.
Listen, all you peoples,
and see my pain:
My young women and young men
have gone into captivity.*

19 I cried out to my lovers,
but they failed me.*
My priests and my elders
perished in the city;
How desperately they searched for food,
to save their lives!

20 Look, O LORD, at the anguish I suffer!
My stomach churns,
And my heart recoils within me:
How bitter I am!
Outside the sword bereaves—
indoors, there is death.*

21 Hear how I am groaning;
there is no one to comfort me.
All my enemies hear of my misery and rejoice
over what you have done.
Bring on the day you proclaimed,
and let them become like me!

22 Let all their evil come before you
and deal with them
As you have so ruthlessly dealt with me
for all my rebellions.

† **1:9** Zion breaks in on the poet's description in v. 9c, albeit briefly, to demand that the Lord face squarely her misery. She takes up the lament in a more sustained fashion in v. 11c.

* **1:8** Is 47:2–3; Jer 13:22, 26; Na 3:5.
1:10 Dt 23:3–6; Ps 74:4–8; Is 56:6; 66:20–21; Jer 51:51.
1:13 Ez 12:13.
1:16 Ps 69:21; Eccl 4:1; Jer 13:17; 14:17; Na 3:7.
1:18 Dt 28:41.
1:19 Jer 30:14.
1:20 Lam 2:11.

My groans are many,
 my heart is sick."*

The Lord's Wrath and Zion's Ruin†

2 [1] How the Lord in his wrath
 has abhorred daughter Zion,
Casting down from heaven to earth
 the glory of Israel,†
Not remembering his footstool
 on the day of his wrath!

2 The Lord has devoured without pity
 all of Jacob's dwellings;
In his fury he has razed
 daughter Judah's defenses,
Has brought to the ground in dishonor
 a kingdom and its princes.

3 In blazing wrath, he cut down entirely
 the horn† of Israel;
He withdrew the support of his right hand
 when the enemy approached;
He burned against Jacob like a blazing fire
 that consumes everything in its path.

4 He bent his bow like an enemy;
 the arrow in his right hand
Like a foe, he killed
 all those held precious;
On the tent of daughter Zion
 he poured out his wrath like fire.

5 The Lord has become the enemy,
 he has devoured Israel:
Devoured all its strongholds,
 destroyed its defenses,
Multiplied moaning and groaning
 throughout daughter Judah.

6 He laid waste his booth like a garden,
 destroyed his shrine;†
The LORD has blotted out in Zion
 feast day and sabbath,
Has scorned in fierce wrath
 king and priest.*

7 The Lord has rejected his altar,
 spurned his sanctuary;
He has handed over to the enemy
 the walls of its strongholds.
They shout in the house of the LORD
 as on a feast day.*

8 The LORD was bent on destroying
 the wall of daughter Zion:

Pray It!

Violence in Our City Streets

Poetic language is often used in the Bible to express the depth of human emotion that the author either feels or is trying to convey. When reading the Scriptures, we should be aware that poetic language often does not lend itself to a literal interpretation. Instead, we should open ourselves up to the spiritual and emotional truth this poetry contains.

The Book of Lamentations is a book of poetry that helps us reflect on the feelings and thoughts of the Jewish people in exile, who were suffering from the loss of their homes, freedom, security, and so much more. Verses 12 and 19 of the poem in chapter 2 of Lamentations both mention hunger and violence in the streets. Are things much different in our streets? In our own time, children are hungry, and people are being killed and violated. Our voice echoes the voice of this ancient prayer, calling out for God's mercy.

When will the violence stop, Lord? How many will die today from drug overdose and domestic abuse? How many children will go hungry because nobody took the time to care for them? Have mercy on your people, Lord!

▶ **Lamentations, chapter 2**

†

2:1–22 This chapter continues to move between the voice of the poet (vv. 1–20) and that of personified Zion (vv. 20–22). The persona of the poet, first portrayed in chap. 1 as a detached observer recounting both the desolation as well as the sins of the city, becomes in this chapter an advocate for Zion in her appeal to the Lord and never once mentions her sins.

2:1 *The glory of Israel*: the Temple. *His footstool*: the ark of the covenant (1 Chr 28:2; Ps 99:5; 132:7); or again, the Temple (Ez 43:7).

2:3 *Horn*: a symbol of power and strength; cf. v. 17; 1 Sm 2:1, 10; Ps 89:18, 25; 92:11; 112:9.

2:6 *Booth . . . shrine*: synonyms for the Temple; cf. Ps 27:5; 74:4, 8. The term for "shrine" in Hebrew (*mo'ed*) figures prominently in the pentateuchal expression "tent of meeting" (*'ohel mo'ed*).

*

1:22 Lam 3:64. **2:6** Is 1:13; 5:5. **2:7** Ez 24:21.

2:10

He stretched out the measuring line;†
did not hesitate to devour,
Brought grief on rampart and wall
till both succumbed.*

9 Her gates sank into the ground;
he smashed her bars to bits.
Her king and her princes are among the nations;
instruction is wanting,
Even her prophets do not obtain
any vision from the LORD.*

10 The elders of daughter Zion
sit silently on the ground;
They cast dust† on their heads
and dress in sackcloth;
The young women of Jerusalem
bow their heads to the ground.*

11 My eyes are spent with tears,
my stomach churns;†
My bile is poured out on the ground
at the brokenness of the daughter of my people,
As children and infants collapse
in the streets of the town.*

12 They cry out to their mothers,
"Where is bread and wine?"
As they faint away like the wounded
in the streets of the city,
As their life is poured out
in their mothers' arms.

13 To what can I compare you†—to what can I liken you—
O daughter Jerusalem?
What example can I give in order to comfort you,
virgin daughter Zion?
For your breach is vast as the sea;
who could heal you?*

14 Your prophets provided you visions
of whitewashed illusion;
They did not lay bare your guilt,
in order to restore your fortunes;
They saw for you only oracles
of empty deceit.*

15 All who pass by on the road,
clap their hands at you;
They hiss and wag their heads
over daughter Jerusalem:
"Is this the city they used to call
perfect in beauty and joy of all the earth?"*

16 They open their mouths against you,
all your enemies;
They hiss and gnash their teeth,
saying, "We have devoured her!
How we have waited for this day—
we have lived to see it!"*

17 The LORD has done what he planned.
He has fulfilled the threat

†

2:8 *The measuring line*: normally used for building, here employed ironically as an instrument of destruction; cf. Is 34:11; 2 Kgs 21:13.

2:10 *They cast dust*: as a sign of mourning; cf. Jos 7:6; Jb 2:12; Ez 27:30.

2:11 *My eyes are spent with tears, my stomach churns*: the poet appropriates the emotional language used by Zion in 1:16 and 1:20 to express a progressively stronger commitment to her cause. After describing the systematic dismantling of the city in vv. 5–9, the poet turns to the plight of the inhabitants in vv. 10–12. It is the description of children dying in the streets that finally brings about the poet's emotional breakdown, even as it did for Zion in 1:16.

2:13 *To what can I compare you . . . ?*: the author calls attention to the poetic task: to find language that speaks adequately of the atrocities and incomparable suffering experienced by Zion, and thus to attempt to offer comfort.

*

2:8 Jer 52:12–14.
2:9 Dt 28:36.
2:10 Is 3:26.
2:11 Lam 1:16, 20; 3:48; Jer 8:18.
2:13 Lam 1:12; Jer 8:21.
2:14 Is 58:1; Jer 2:8; 23:16; Ez 13:9; 22:28.
2:15 Ps 48:3; 50:12; Jer 18:16.
2:16 Lam 3:46.

Decreed from days of old,
destroying without pity!
He let the enemy gloat over you
and exalted the horn of your foes.*

18 Cry out to the Lord from your heart,
wall of daughter Zion!
Let your tears flow like a torrent
day and night;
Give yourself no rest,
no relief for your eyes.

19 Rise up! Wail in the night,
at the start of every watch;
Pour out your heart like water
before the Lord;
Lift up your hands to him
for the lives of your children,
Who collapse from hunger
at the corner of every street.†

20 "Look, O LORD, and pay attention:
to whom have you been so ruthless?
Must women eat their own offspring,†
the very children they have borne?
Are priest and prophet to be slain
in the sanctuary of the Lord?*

21 They lie on the ground in the streets,
young and old alike;
Both my young women and young men
are cut down by the sword;
You killed them on the day of your wrath,
slaughtered without pity.*

22 You summoned as to a feast day
terrors on every side;
On the day of the LORD's wrath,
none survived or escaped.
Those I have borne and nurtured,
my enemy has utterly destroyed."*

The Voice of a Suffering Individual†

3 1 I am one who has known affliction
under the rod of God's anger,*

2 One whom he has driven and forced to walk
in darkness, not in light;
3 Against me alone he turns his hand—
again and again all day long.

4 He has worn away my flesh and my skin,
he has broken my bones;*
5 He has besieged me all around
with poverty and hardship;
6 He has left me to dwell in dark places
like those long dead.*

7 He has hemmed me in with no escape,
weighed me down with chains;
8 Even when I cry for help,
he stops my prayer;*
9 He has hemmed in my ways with fitted stones,
and made my paths crooked.

10 He has been a bear lying in wait for me,
a lion in hiding!*
11 He turned me aside and tore me apart,
leaving me ravaged.*
12 He bent his bow, and set me up
as a target for his arrow.*

13 He pierced my kidneys
with shafts from his quiver.*
14 I have become a laughingstock to all my
people,
their taunt all day long;*
15 He has sated me with bitterness,
filled me with wormwood.*

16 He has made me eat gravel,
trampled me into the dust;
17 My life is deprived of peace,
I have forgotten what happiness is;
18 My enduring hope, I said,
has perished before the LORD.

19 The thought of my wretched homelessness
is wormwood and poison;
20 Remembering it over and over,
my soul is downcast.

†

2:19 The poet urges Zion to appeal to the Lord once more on behalf of her dying children. The image of Zion's children effectively condenses the metaphorical sense of all residents of the city (young and old alike) into the more poignant picture of actual children at the point of death. It was precisely this image, no doubt well known to survivors of besieged cities, that led to the emotional breakdown of both Zion (1:16) and the poet (2:11). The hope is that the Lord will be similarly affected by such a poignant image and respond with mercy.

2:20 *Must women eat their own offspring*: extreme famine in a besieged city sometimes led to cannibalism; this becomes a stereotypical way of expressing the nearly unthinkable horrors of war; cf. Lam 4:10; Dt 28:53; 2 Kgs 6:28–29; Bar 2:3; Ez 5:10.

3:1–66 This chapter is focused less on the destruction of Jerusalem than are chaps. 1 and 2 and more on the suffering of an individual. The identity of the individual is never given, and one probably should not search for a specific identification of the speaker. The figure of the representative sufferer makes concrete the pain of the people in a way similar to the personification of Zion as a woman in chaps. 1 and 2. Indeed, in vv. 40–48 the individual voice gives way to a communal voice, returning in vv. 49–66 to the individual sufferer.

*

2:17 Dt 28:15.
2:20 Lam 4:10.
2:21 Lam 3:43; 2 Chr 36:17; Jer 6:11.
2:22 Jer 42:17.
3:1 Jer 20:18.
3:4 Jb 30:30; Is 38:13.
3:6 Ps 143:3.
3:8 Ps 18:41; 22:2; 88:14–15.
3:10 Jb 10:16; Hos 13:8.
3:11 Lam 1:13.
3:12 Lam 2:4; Jb 16:12.
3:13 Jb 6:4; Ps 38:3.
3:14 Jb 30:9; Ps 69:13.
3:15 Jer 9:14; 23:15.

Live It!

Each New Day

The poems in Lamentations also have their hopeful side. They acknowledge that the favors of the Lord are not exhausted (see 3:22) and that the Israelites will not experience God's rejection forever (see verse 31). Verse 23 reminds the people that God's favors are renewed each morning.

Imagine that at the beginning of each day, you are given $86,400. You have the whole day to spend every last penny any way you want. Does that sound exciting? Well, God gives you 86,400 seconds every day to use however you like. Try making a one-day budget of the best ways to spend your 86,400 seconds. Remember, each day is a new gift filled with God's love. Make the most of it, and do so for God!

▶ Lam 3:22–33

LAM

21 But this I will call to mind;†
therefore I will hope:

22 The LORD's acts of mercy are not exhausted,
his compassion is not spent;*
23 They are renewed each morning—
great is your faithfulness!
24 The LORD is my portion, I tell myself,
therefore I will hope in him.*

25 The LORD is good to those who trust in him,
to the one that seeks him;*
26 It is good to hope in silence
for the LORD's deliverance.
27 It is good for a person, when young,
to bear the yoke,
28 To sit alone and in silence,
when its weight lies heavy,
29 To put one's mouth in the dust—†
there may yet be hope—
30 To offer one's cheek to be struck,
to be filled with disgrace.*

31 For the Lord does not
reject forever;*
32 Though he brings grief, he takes pity,
according to the abundance of his mercy;*
33 He does not willingly afflict
or bring grief to human beings.*

34 That someone tramples underfoot
all the prisoners in the land,
35 Or denies justice to anyone
in the very sight of the Most High,
36 Or subverts a person's lawsuit—
does the Lord not see?

37 Who speaks so that it comes to pass,
unless the Lord commands it?
38 Is it not at the word of the Most High
that both good and bad take place?*
39 What should the living complain about?
about their sins!

40† Let us search and examine our ways,
and return to the LORD!*
41 Let us lift up our hearts as well as our hands
toward God in heaven!
42 We have rebelled and been obstinate;
you have not forgiven us.

43 You wrapped yourself in wrath and pursued us,
killing without pity;*
44 You wrapped yourself in a cloud,
which no prayer could pierce.
45 You have made us filth and rubbish
among the peoples.*

46 They have opened their mouths against us,
all our enemies;
47 Panic and the pit have been our lot,
desolation and destruction;*
48† My eyes stream with tears over the destruction
of the daughter of my people.*

† **3:21–24** In the midst of a description of suffering, the speaker offers this brief but compelling statement of hope in God's ultimate mercy. It is a hard-won and precarious hope, nearly submerged by the volume and intensity of the surrounding lament, but it is hope nonetheless.

3:29 *To put one's mouth in the dust*: a sign of humiliation and submission; cf. v. 16; Ps 72:9.

3:40–66 The plural voice in this lament suggests that a communal lament begins here; it then continues in the singular voice in vv. 55–66.

3:48–51 These verses are more appropriate on the lips of the poet,

* **3:22** 1 Sm 20:15; Neh 9:31.
3:24 Ps 16:5; 73:26.
3:25 Ps 130:6; Is 30:18.
3:30 Is 50:6; Mt 5:39.
3:31 Ps 85:6; 103:9.
3:32 1 Sm 2:6–7; Tb 13:2; Is 54:8.
3:33 Ex 34:6–7.
3:38 Is 45:7.
3:40 Jl 2:12–13.
3:43 Lam 2:21.
3:45 1 Cor 4:13.
3:47 Is 24:17–18; Jer 48:43–44.
3:48 Lam 1:16; 2:11; Jer 8:23; 9:17.

49 My eyes will flow without ceasing,
without rest,
50 Until the LORD from heaven
looks down and sees.
51 I am tormented by the sight
of all the daughters of my city.

52 Without cause, my enemies snared me
as though I were a bird;
53 They tried to end my life in the pit,
pelting me with stones.
54 The waters flowed over my head:
and I said, "I am lost!"*

55 I have called upon your name, O LORD,*
from the bottom of the pit;
56 You heard me call, "Do not let your ear be deaf
to my cry for help."
57 You drew near on the day I called you;
you said, "Do not fear!"

58 You pleaded my case, Lord,
you redeemed my life.
59 You see, LORD, how I am wronged;
do me justice!*
60 You see all their vindictiveness,
all their plots against me.

61 You hear their reproach, LORD,
all their plots against me,
62 The whispered murmurings of my adversaries,
against me all day long;
63 Look! Whether they sit or stand,
I am the butt of their taunt.

64 Give them what they deserve, LORD,
according to their deeds;
65 Give them hardness of heart;
your curse be upon them;*
66 Pursue them in wrath and destroy them
from under the LORD's heaven!

Miseries of the Besieged City†

4 1 How the gold has lost its luster,
the noble metal changed;
Jewels† lie scattered
at the corner of every street.

2 And Zion's precious children,
worth their weight in gold—
How they are treated like clay jugs,
the work of any potter!*

3 Even jackals offer their breasts
to nurse their young;
But the daughter of my people is as cruel
as the ostrich† in the wilderness.*

4 The tongue of the infant cleaves
to the roof of its mouth in thirst;
Children beg for bread,
but no one gives them a piece.

5 Those who feasted on delicacies
are abandoned in the streets;
Those who reclined on crimson†
now embrace dung heaps.*

6 The punishment of the daughter of my people
surpassed the penalty of Sodom,
Which was overthrown in an instant
with no hand laid on it.*

7 Her princes were brighter than snow,
whiter than milk,
Their bodies more ruddy than coral,
their beauty like the sapphire.

8 Now their appearance is blacker than soot,
they go unrecognized in the streets;
Their skin has shrunk on their bones,
and become dry as wood.*

9 Better for those pierced by the sword
than for those pierced by hunger,
Better for those who bleed from wounds
than for those who lack food.

10 The hands of compassionate women
have boiled their own children!

LAM

† who speaks of "my city" (v. 51). *Daughters of my city*: here as elsewhere "daughter" may refer to villages dependent on a larger city.

4:1–22 This chapter returns to the focus of chaps. 1 and 2, namely the horrors of a siege. Unlike chaps. 1 and 2, however, the character of personified Zion never interrupts the voice of the poet to protest her abject state. As a result, the emotion of the poem is less intense, while at the same time seeming more grim on account of its lack of petition to the Lord.

4:1–2 *Jewels*: lit., "holy stones." These precious things designate the children who are abandoned, starving, and killed in the siege of Jerusalem (cf. Zec 9:16). Another explanation is that these are the stones of the destroyed Temple.

4:3 *Cruel as the ostrich*: see note on Jb 39:14–16. Jerusalem, in her distress, has abandoned her children.

4:5 *Crimson*: a sign of luxury. Tyrian purple, a red-purple or blue-purple dye produced from shellfish, was very expensive and the only colorfast dye in the ancient Near East. Thus purple or crimson cloth was available only to the wealthy.

* **3:54** Ps 69:2–3; 88:8; Jon 2:4.
3:55–56 Ps 130:1–2.
3:58–59 Ps 35:23–24; 43:1; 119:154.
3:65 Jer 11:20; 2 Tm 4:14.
4:2 Jer 19:11.
4:3 Jb 39:16.
4:5 Dt 28:56.
4:6 Gn 19:23–29; 2 Pt 2:6; Jude 7.
4:8 Lam 3:4.

Live It!

Growing Through Loss

One purpose of the poems in Lamentations is to help the ancient Israelites heal from the horrible tragedy of their loss. The poems accomplish this in three ways. First, in describing Israel's present loss and tragedy, they acknowledge that grief and mourning are needed. Second, they challenge Israel to look at its past, both to accept responsibility for its sin and to remember its great blessings from God. Finally, they encourage Israel to have hope for the future. In image after image, Israel is assured that the door to God's mercy is still open, in spite of great pain and loss.

So too must we allow ourselves to grieve when we have experienced the loss of someone we love. If we wall up our grief—and perhaps our guilt, because guilt often accompanies such a loss—we may at the same time shut out those who can help us heal. We must surround ourselves with family and friends who can be a source of comfort and support. We must also reclaim our memories of the person we lost, celebrating those of good times and healing those of hurtful times. Finally, as difficult as it may seem, we must open ourselves to the future, for God's love continues to be there for us, calling us to new life.

They became their food
when the daughter of my people was shattered.*

11 The LORD has exhausted his anger,
poured out his blazing wrath;
He has kindled a fire in Zion
that has consumed her foundations.*

12 The kings of the earth did not believe,
nor any of the world's inhabitants,
That foe or enemy could enter
the gates of Jerusalem.

13 Except for the sins of her prophets
and the crimes of her priests,
Who poured out in her midst
the blood of the just.*

14 They staggered blindly in the streets,
defiled with blood,
So that people could not touch
even their garments:*

15 "Go away! Unclean!" they cried to them,
"Away, away, do not touch!"
If they went away and wandered,
it would be said among the nations,
"They can no longer live here!

16 The presence of the LORD was their portion,
but he no longer looks upon them.
The priests are shown no regard,
the elders, no mercy.*

17 Even now our eyes are worn out,
searching in vain for help;
From our watchtower we have watched
for a nation† unable to save.

18 They dogged our every step,
we could not walk in our squares;
Our end drew near, our time was up;
yes, our end had come.

19 Our pursuers were swifter
than eagles in the sky,
In the mountains they were hot on our trail,
they ambushed us in the wilderness.*

20 The LORD's anointed—our very lifebreath!—†
was caught in their snares,
He in whose shade we thought
to live among the nations.*

21 Rejoice and gloat, daughter Edom,
dwelling in the land of Uz,†

---

† **4:17** *A nation*: probably Egypt, which failed to give effective aid against Babylon.

4:20 *Our very lifebreath*: lit., "the breath of our nostrils," that is, the king. This expression occurs in Egyptian texts of the late second millennium B.C., and may have survived as a royal epithet in the Jerusalem court. After the disaster of 598 B.C. (2 Kgs 24:1–17), Jerusalem could have hoped to live in peace amidst her neighbors; but they (vv. 21–22) as well as Babylon turned against her to ensure her total devastation in 587 B.C.

4:21 *Rejoice*: the address is sarcastic, since Edom (where Uz may have been located) ravaged the land after the fall of Jerusalem (cf. Ps 137).

4:10 Lam 2:20; Dt 28:56–57; 2 Kgs 6:29.
4:11 Jer 7:20; Ez 5:13.
4:13 Jer 6:13.
4:14 Dt 28:29; Is 59:10.
4:19 Jer 4:13; Hb 1:8.
4:20 Lam 2:9; Ez 19:4, 8.

The cup will pass to you as well;
you shall become drunk and strip yourself naked!*

22 Your punishment is completed, daughter Zion,
the Lord will not prolong your exile;
The Lord will punish your iniquity, daughter Edom,
will lay bare your sins.*

The Community's Lament to the Lord

5 1 Remember, LORD, what has happened to us,
pay attention, and see our disgrace:
2 Our heritage is turned over to strangers,
our homes, to foreigners.*
3 We have become orphans, without fathers;
our mothers are like widows.
4 We pay money to drink our own water,
our own wood comes at a price.
5 With a yoke on our necks, we are driven;
we are worn out, but allowed no rest.

6 We extended a hand to Egypt and Assyria,
to satisfy our need of bread.†
7 Our ancestors, who sinned, are no more;
but now we bear their guilt.
8 Servants† rule over us,
with no one to tear us from their hands.
9 We risk our lives just to get bread,
exposed to the desert heat;*
10 Our skin heats up like an oven,
from the searing blasts of famine.*
11 Women are raped in Zion,
young women in the cities of Judah;*
12 Princes have been hanged by them,
elders shown no respect.*
13 Young men carry millstones,
boys stagger under loads of wood;
14 The elders have abandoned the gate,†
the young men their music.

15 The joy of our hearts has ceased,
dancing has turned into mourning;*
16 The crown has fallen from our head:
woe to us that we sinned!
17 Because of this our hearts grow sick,
at this our eyes grow dim:
18 Because of Mount Zion, lying desolate,
and the jackals roaming there!

19 But you, LORD, are enthroned forever;
your throne stands from age to age.*
20† Why have you utterly forgotten us,
forsaken us for so long?*
21 Bring us back to you, LORD, that we may return:
renew our days as of old.*
22 For now you have indeed rejected us
and utterly turned your wrath against us.*

LAM

†

5:6 *Extended a hand*: that is, made an alliance. In its state of abjection, Judah was forced to depend on the major powers to the west and the east for subsistence.

5:8 *Servants*: the Hebrew word for "servant" is also the word used for an official of relatively high status (servant of the ruler; cf. 2 Kgs 25:24, where the term is used to refer to Babylonian rulers over occupied Jerusalem); the author doubtless intends the double meaning here.

5:14 *The gate*: a place of assembly, where city decisions were made and judgment given by the elders and other community leaders; see note on Ru 4:1.

5:20–22 Unlike most of the laments found in the Book of Psalms, the Book of Lamentations never moves from lament to thanksgiving. It ends with this question still unanswered by God: "Why have you utterly forgotten us?"

*

4:21 Lam 1:21; Jer 25:15.
4:22 Is 40:2.
5:2 Ps 79:1.
5:9 Lam 1:11.
5:10 Lam 4:8.
5:11 Zec 14:2.
5:12 Lam 4:16.
5:15 Jer 16:9; 25:10; Am 8:10.
5:19 Ps 9:8; 45:7; 102:13, 27.
5:20 Ps 13:2; 42:10; Is 49:14.
5:21 Ps 80:19–20.
5:22 Jer 14:19.

Perhaps you've seen them on the news—long lines of refugees leaving war-torn countries. Or the camps where they set up temporary homes, waiting to return to their homeland. The sad truth is many of them can never return home. They are faced with the difficult task of building new homes in a foreign land. The Book of Baruch was written in such a situation—after many Israelites were forced to relocate following the Babylonian invasion in 587 BC.

The Book of
Baruch

At a Glance

I. Letter to Jerusalem (1:1—3:8).
- A. Historical Setting (1:1–9).
- B. Confession of Guilt (1:10—2:10).
- C. Prayer for Deliverance (2:11—3:8).

II. Praise of Wisdom (3:9—4:4).
- A. Importance of Wisdom (3:9–23).
- B. Inaccessibility of Wisdom (3:24–36).
- C. Wisdom Contained in the Law (3:37—4:4).

III. Baruch's Poem of Consolation (4:5—5:9).
- A. Baruch Addresses Diaspora (4:5–9a).
- B. Jerusalem Addresses Neighbors (4:9b–16).
- C. Jerusalem Addresses Diaspora (4:17–29).
- D. Baruch Addresses Jerusalem (4:30—5:9).

IV. Letter of Jeremiah (6:1–72).

Quick Facts

Period Covered: The time of the author is probably from the second to the first centuries BC.

Inspired Author: an unknown compiler who attributed the book to Baruch, Jeremiah's secretary

Theme: Even in foreign lands, God's People can find hope in God's promises.

Of Note: Baruch is not found in every version of the Old Testament (see "The Case of the Missing Books," near Tb 1:16).

In Depth

In the ancient world, it was not uncommon for people to write books and letters in the name of famous ancestors or historical figures. Several Old and New Testament books, including Baruch, were written in this manner. An anonymous person collected a variety of independent writings and named them for Baruch, the famous secretary of the prophet Jeremiah, in order to emphasize their link with Jeremiah's tradition of prophecy.

The short Book of Baruch recalls the Babylonian conquest of Jerusalem in the sixth century BC. In doing so, it points out these lessons to be learned from the painful past:

- We do not gain anything when we sin. Instead, we invite suffering into our lives.
- No matter how difficult life gets, we can always rely on God's goodness.
- Believers can always approach God in prayer, even when their situation seems impossibly painful.
- The traditions we have inherited from our ancestors are a reliable guide in facing life's challenges.
- We should resist all cultural pressures to act in violation of God's will.
- God can return Diaspora Jews to the holy land just as God returned the Babylonian exiles.

The core truth Baruch addresses is that no matter where they are, God's People can lead happy and holy lives by admitting their sinfulness and committing themselves to the Lord. This is an important lesson for all believers to learn. Unless we learn from history, we will repeat its mistakes.

Baruch

I. Letter to Jerusalem

A. Historical Setting

1 [1]Now these are the words of the scroll which
Baruch, son of Neriah, son of Mahseiah, son of
Zedekiah, son of Hasadiah, son of Hilkiah, wrote
in Babylon,* [2]in the fifth year, on the seventh day
of the month,† at the time the Chaldeans took
Jerusalem and destroyed it with fire.* [3]* Baruch
read the words of this scroll in the hearing of Jeco-
niah, son of Jehoiakim, king of Judah, and all the
people who came to the reading:* [4]the nobles,
kings' sons, elders, and all the people, small and
great—all who lived in Babylon by the river Sud.†
[5]They wept, fasted, and prayed before the Lord,
[6]and collected such funds as each could afford.*
[7]These they sent to Jerusalem, to Jehoiakim the
priest, son of Hilkiah, son of Shallum, and to the
priests and the whole people who were with him
in Jerusalem. [8](At the same time he† received the
vessels of the house of the LORD that had been
removed from the temple, to restore them to the
land of Judah, on the tenth of Sivan. These silver
vessels Zedekiah, son of Josiah, king of Judah,
had had made [9]* after Nebuchadnezzar, king of
Babylon, carried off as captives Jeconiah and the
princes, the skilled workers, the nobles, and the
people of the land from Jerusalem, and brought
them to Babylon.)

B. Confession of Guilt

[10]The message was: "We send you funds, with
which you are to procure burnt offerings, sin of-
ferings, and frankincense, and to prepare grain
offerings; offer these† on the altar of the LORD our
God,* [11]and pray for the life of Nebuchadnezzar,
king of Babylon, and of Belshazzar, his son,† that
their lifetimes may be as the days of the heavens
above the earth.* [12]Pray that the LORD may give us
strength, and light to our eyes, that we may live
under the protective shadow of Nebuchadnezzar,
king of Babylon, and of Belshazzar, his son, to
serve them many days, and find favor in their

†

1:2 *In the fifth year, on the seventh day of the month*: Jerusalem fell on the seventh day of the fifth month in 587 B.C.; cf. 2 Kgs 25:8; Jer 52:12. Either the text read originally "the fifth month," or it refers to the observance of an anniversary of the fall of Jerusalem.

1:4 *The river Sud*: probably one of the Babylonian canals, not otherwise identified; or possibly a misreading of Ahava; cf. Ezr 8:21, 31.

1:8–9 *He*: apparently Baruch; less likely Jehoiakim the priest (v. 7). The silver vessels here described are distinct from the vessels referred to in 2 Kgs 25:14 and Ezr 1:7–9. The author of this note may have thought of the fifth year (v. 1) of Zedekiah, in view of Jer 28:1; 29:1–3. A "fifth year," again with no month mentioned, is given in Ez 1:2 for the inaugural vision of Ezekiel's prophetic career.

1:10 *Offer these*: since 2:26 suggests that the Temple is destroyed, the mention of sacrifices here may be an anachronism. Nevertheless, Jer 41:5 indicates that some people continued to worship at the Temple site after Nebuchadnezzar's destruction of the Temple.

1:11 *Nebuchadnezzar . . . Belshazzar, his son*: Belshazzar was the son of Nabonidus, the last king of Babylon, not of Nebuchadnezzar, the destroyer of Jerusalem. Belshazzar was co-regent for a few years while his father was away in Arabia. Later Jewish tradition seems to have simplified the end of the Babylonian empire (cf. Dn 5:1–2), for three kings came between Nebuchadnezzar and Nabonidus.

*

1:1 Jer 32:12; 36:4; 45:1–5.
1:2 2 Kgs 25:8–10.
1:3–4 2 Kgs 23:1–2.
1:3 2 Kgs 24:8–17; Jer 22:24–30; 27:20; 51:59–64.
1:6 Dt 16:17.
1:9 Jer 24:1.
1:10 Jer 17:26; 41:5.
1:11 Dt 11:21; Ps 89:30; Jer 29:7; Dn 5:1–2; 1 Tm 2:1–2.

sight. 13 Pray for us to the LORD, our God, for we
have sinned against the LORD, our God. Even to
this day the wrath of the LORD and his anger have
not turned away from us. 14 On the feast day and
during the days of assembly, read aloud in the
house of the LORD this scroll that we send you:*
15 † "To the Lord our God belongs justice; to
us, people of Judah and inhabitants of Jerusalem,
to be shamefaced, as on this day—* 16 to us, our
kings, rulers, priests, and prophets, and our ances-
tors. 17 We have sinned in the LORD's sight 18 and
disobeyed him. We have not listened to the voice
of the LORD, our God, so as to follow the precepts
the LORD set before us. 19 From the day the LORD
led our ancestors out of the land of Egypt until
the present day, we have been disobedient to
the LORD, our God, and neglected to listen to his
voice. 20 Even today evils cling to us, the curse the
LORD pronounced to Moses, his servant, at the
time he led our ancestors out of the land of Egypt
to give us a land flowing with milk and honey.*
21 For we did not listen to the voice of the LORD,
our God, in all the words of the prophets he sent
us, 22 but each of us has followed the inclinations
of our wicked hearts, served other gods, and done
evil in the sight of the LORD, our God.

2 1 "So the LORD carried out the warning he had
uttered against us: against our judges, who
governed Israel, against our kings and princes,
and against the people of Israel and Judah. 2 No-
where under heaven has anything been done
like what he did in Jerusalem, as was written
in the law of Moses:† * 3 that we would each
eat† the flesh of our sons, each the flesh of our
daughters. 4 He has made us subject to all the
kingdoms around us, an object of reproach and
horror among all the peoples around us, where
the LORD has scattered us.* 5 We are brought low,
not raised high,* because we sinned against the
LORD, our God, not listening to his voice.
6 "To the LORD, our God, belongs justice; to us
and to our ancestors, to be shamefaced, as on
this day.* 7 All the evils of which the LORD had
warned us have come upon us. 8 We did not en-
treat the favor of the LORD by turning, each one,
from the designs of our evil hearts. 9 The LORD
kept watch over the evils, and brought them
home to us; for the LORD is just in all the works
he commanded us to do,* 10 but we did not lis-
ten to his voice, or follow the precepts of the
LORD which he had set before us.

C. Prayer for Deliverance

11 † "And now, LORD, God of Israel, who led
your people out of the land of Egypt with a
strong hand, with signs and wonders and great
might, and with an upraised arm, so that you
have made for yourself a name to the present
day:* 12 we have sinned, we have committed
sacrilege, we have violated all your statutes, LORD,
our God.* 13 Withdraw your anger from us, for
we are left few in number among the nations
where you have scattered us. 14 Hear, LORD, our
prayer of supplication, and deliver us for your
own sake: grant us favor in the sight of those who
brought us into exile, 15 that the whole earth may
know that you are the LORD, our God, and that
Israel† and his descendants bear your name.*
16 LORD, look down from your holy dwelling
and take thought of us; LORD, incline your ear to
hear us.* 17 Open your eyes and see: it is not the
dead in Hades,† whose breath has been taken
from within them, who will declare the glory
and vindication to the LORD.* 18 The person who
is deeply grieved, who walks bowed and feeble,
with failing eyes and famished soul, will declare
your glory and justice, LORD!*
19 "Not on the just deeds of our ancestors
and our kings do we base our plea for mercy in
your sight, LORD, our God. 20 You have sent your
wrath and anger upon us, as you had warned us
through your servants the prophets: 21 Thus says
the LORD: Bend your necks and serve the king of
Babylon, that you may continue in the land I gave
your ancestors;* 22 † for if you do not listen to the
LORD's voice so as to serve the king of Babylon,
23 I will silence from the cities of Judah and from
the streets of Jerusalem the cry of joy and the cry
of gladness, the voice of the bridegroom and the
voice of the bride; and all the land shall be de-
serted, without inhabitants.* 24 But we did not

---

†

1:15–2:10 This confession of sin is similar to Dn 9:7–14, and echoes ideas from Deuteronomy and Jeremiah; cf. also Neh 9.

2:2 *Law of Moses*: cf. Dt 28:53–57.

2:3 *We would each eat*: such dreadful events were the result of the prolonged siege of Jerusalem; cf. Lam 2:20.

2:11–35 An earnest appeal for divine mercy, along with confession of sin; cf. Dn 9:15–19.

2:15 *Israel*: the Israelites claimed descent from the patriarch Jacob, who had received the name Israel in a mysterious encounter with God (Gn 32:29). Thus the Deity was sometimes referred to as "the God of Israel" (Gn 33:20; Ex 5:1).

2:17 *Hades*: this is the Greek translation of Hebrew *sheol*, the nether world.

2:22–24 These words are very similar to Jer 7:34; 27:9, 12.

*

1:14 Ex 23:14–17; Lv 23:35–36; Sir 50:6; Hos 9:5.
1:15 Bar 2:6; 3:8; Ezr 9:6–15; Neh 9:6–37; Dn 9:4–19.
1:20 Lv 26:14–39; Dt 28:15–68.
2:2–3 Dt 28:52–57; 2 Kgs 6:28–29; Jer 19:9; Lam 2:20; 4:10; Ez 5:10; Dn 9:12.
2:4 Jer 29:18; Dn 9:16.
2:5 Dt 28:13, 43–44.
2:6 Bar 1:15; Dn 9:7.
2:9 Jer 1:12; 31:28; 44:27; Dn 9:14.
2:11 Dt 6:21–22.
2:12 Ps 106:6.
2:15 Gn 33:20; Sir 36:11; Jer 14:9; 35:17.
2:16 Dt 26:15.
2:17 Ps 6:6; Is 38:18.
2:18 Zep 2:3.
2:21 Jer 27:12.
2:23 Jer 7:34.

listen to your voice, or serve the king of Babylon,
and you carried out the threats you had made
through your servants the prophets, that the
bones of our kings and the bones of our ancestors
would be brought out from their burial places.*
25 And indeed, they lie exposed† to the heat of
day and the frost of night. They died in great suf-
fering, by famine and sword and plague.* 26 And
you reduced the house which bears your name†
to what it is today, because of the wickedness of
the house of Israel and the house of Judah.*

God's Promises Recalled

27 "But with us, Lord, our God, you have dealt
in all your clemency and in all your great mercy.
28 † Thus you spoke through your servant Moses,
the day you ordered him to write down your law
in the presence of the Israelites: 29 'If you do not
listen to my voice, surely this great and numer-
ous throng will dwindle away among the nations
to which I will scatter them.* 30 For I know they
will not listen to me, because they are a stiff-
necked people. But in the land of their exile they
shall have a change of heart;* 31 they shall know
that I, the LORD, am their God. I will give them
a heart and ears that listen;* 32 and they shall
praise me in the land of their exile, and shall re-
member my name.* 33 Then they shall turn back
from their stiff-necked stubbornness, and from
their evil deeds, because they shall remember
the ways of their ancestors, who sinned against
the LORD.* 34 And I will bring them back to the
land I promised on oath to their ancestors, to
Abraham, Isaac, and Jacob; and they shall rule it.
I will make them increase; they shall not be few.
35 And I will establish for them an eternal cov-
enant: I will be their God, and they shall be my
people; and I will never again remove my people
Israel from the land I gave them.'*

3 1 "LORD Almighty, God of Israel, the an-
guished soul, the dismayed spirit cries out
to you. 2 Hear, LORD, and have mercy, for you
are a merciful God; have mercy on us, who have
sinned against you: 3 for you are enthroned for-
ever, while we are perishing forever.* 4 LORD Al-
mighty, God of Israel, hear the prayer of the dead
of Israel, children who sinned against you; they
did not listen to the voice of the LORD, their God,
and their evils cling to us.* 5 Do not remember
the wicked deeds of our ancestors, but remem-
ber at this time your power and your name, 6 for
you are the LORD our God; and you, LORD, we will
praise! 7 This is why you put into our hearts the
fear of you: that we may call upon your name,
and praise you in our exile, when we have re-
moved from our hearts all the wickedness of our
ancestors who sinned against you.* 8 See, today
we are in exile, where you have scattered us, an
object of reproach and cursing and punishment
for all the wicked deeds of our ancestors, who
withdrew from the LORD, our God."

II. Praise of Wisdom†

A. Importance of Wisdom

9 Hear, Israel, the commandments of life:
listen, and know prudence!*
10 How is it, Israel,
that you are in the land of your foes,
grown old in a foreign land,
11 Defiled with the dead,
counted among those destined for Hades?*
12 You have forsaken the fountain of wisdom!*
13 Had you walked in the way of God,
you would have dwelt in enduring peace.*

14 Learn where prudence is,
where strength, where understanding;
That you may know also
where are length of days, and life,
where light of the eyes, and peace.*
15 Who has found the place of wisdom?*
Who has entered into her treasuries?
16 Where are the rulers of the nations,
who lorded it over the wild beasts of the
earth,*
17 made sport of the birds in the heavens,
Who heaped up the silver,
the gold in which people trust,
whose possessions were unlimited,
18 Who schemed anxiously for money,
their doings beyond discovery?
19 They have vanished, gone down to Hades,

†

2:25 *They lie exposed*: Jeremiah's words threatened Jehoiakim with being left unburied (Jer 22:19; 36:30).

2:26 *The house which bears your name*: the Temple of Jerusalem; cf. Dt 12:11; Jer 7:11. *What it is today*: during the exile it lay in ruins.

2:28–35 These words do not actually quote anything Moses is recorded as having said, but they present the substance of a passage such as Dt 30:1–10, which envisions exile, repentance, and restoration.

3:9–4:4 This poem in praise of personified Wisdom utilizes the theme of Jb 28 (where is wisdom to be found?) and it identifies wisdom and law, as in Sir 24:22–23.

*

2:24 Jer 8:1–2.
2:25 Jer 7:34; 14:12; 31:30.
2:26 Jer 7:10–15; 11:17.
2:29 Lv 26:39.
2:30 Dt 30:1–2; 31:27.
2:31 Ps 40:7; Jer 24:7; Ez 36:26.
2:32 Tb 13:6.
2:33–35 Lv 26:42–45; Dt 30:1–10.
2:35 Jer 31:31; Lam 4:22.
3:3 Ps 29:10; 102:12–13.
3:4 Jer 31:29.
3:7 Jer 31:33.
3:9 Dt 6:4–5; Prv 4:20–22.
3:11 Ps 88:5.
3:12 Jer 2:13; Jn 4:10, 14.
3:13 Is 48:18.
3:14 Prv 3:2; 8:14.
3:15–37 Jb 28:1–28.
3:16 Jer 27:6; 1 Cor 1:20.

Live It!

The House of God

It is a warm, clear summer night. You and a good friend are sitting outside talking about the struggles both of you have been having with parents. Suddenly, you see a shooting star. Both of you spend a few moments gazing at the sky and marveling at how many stars there are and how clear the night is. The problems you were just discussing seem to pale in significance next to the vastness of the universe. And you realize that the two of you are seeing only one corner of the universe, "the dwelling of God" (Bar 3:24). You both feel a connection with the stars and the sky and with the God who created it all.

The author of Baruch 3:24–37 seems to be having a similar moment. This writer describes God's wisdom as vast and endless (see verse 25) and beyond any person's grasp (see verse 29), but given to Israel for salvation (see verse 37). The author is saying: "Be at ease. God is bigger than your problems and in control."

When struggling with life's problems, recall the beauty of the night sky in order to put them in perspective. Spend a few moments gazing at the stars, and remember who's really in control.

▶ Bar 3:24–37

and others have risen up in their stead.
20 Later generations have seen the light of day,
have dwelt on the earth,
But the way to understanding they have not known,
21 they have not perceived her paths or reached her;
their children remain far from the way to her.
22 She has not been heard of in Canaan,†
nor seen in Teman.*
23 The descendants of Hagar who seek knowledge on earth,
the merchants of Medan and Tema,*
the storytellers and those seeking knowledge—
These have not known the way to wisdom,
nor have they kept her paths in mind.

B. Inaccessibility of Wisdom

24 O Israel, how vast is the dwelling of God,†
how broad the scope of his dominion:
25 Vast and endless,
high and immeasurable!
26 In it were born the giants,†
renowned at the first,
huge in stature, skilled in war.*
27 These God did not choose,
nor did he give them the way of understanding;*
28 They perished for lack of prudence,
perished through their own folly.*
29 Who has gone up to the heavens and taken her,
bringing her down from the clouds?*
30 Who has crossed the sea and found her,
bearing her away rather than choice gold?
31 None knows the way to her,
nor has at heart her path.
32 But the one who knows all things knows her;
he has probed her by his knowledge—
The one who established the earth for all time,
and filled it with four-footed animals,
33 Who sends out the lightning, and it goes,
calls it, and trembling it obeys him;
34 Before whom the stars at their posts
shine and rejoice.
35 When he calls them, they answer, "Here we are!"
shining with joy for their Maker.*
36 Such is our God;
no other is to be compared to him:

C. Wisdom Contained in the Law

37† He has uncovered the whole way of understanding,
and has given her to Jacob, his servant,
to Israel, his beloved.*

†

3:22–23 Despite the renown for wisdom of the peoples of Canaan and Phoenicia (Ez 28:3–4), of Teman (Jer 49:7), of the descendants of Hagar or the Arabians of Medan and Tema, they did not possess true wisdom, which is found only in the law of God (Bar 4:1).

3:24 *The dwelling of God*: here, the whole universe; cf. Is 66:1.

3:26 *The giants*: Gn 6:1–4 reflects a tradition about giants who existed before the flood; this was developed in the non-canonical Book of Enoch.

3:37–38 As in Sir 24:8, Wisdom is given to Israel but also is said to live with all human beings (Prv 8:31).

*

3:22 Jb 2:11; Jer 49:7; Ez 28:4–5; Zec 9:2.
3:23 Gn 25:2, 15; Jb 6:19; Jer 25:23.
3:26 Gn 6:4; Wis 14:6; Sir 16:7.
3:27 1 Sm 16:7–10.
3:28 Sir 10:8.
3:29 Dt 30:12–13; Sir 24:4; Rom 10:6–7.
3:35 Jb 38:7; Ps 147:4; Is 40:26.
3:37 Ps 147:19; Sir 24:8–12.

38 Thus she has appeared on earth,
is at home with mortals.*

4 1† She is the book of the precepts of God,
the law that endures forever;
All who cling to her will live,
but those will die who forsake her.*
2 Turn, O Jacob, and receive her:
walk by her light toward splendor.*
3 Do not give your glory to another,
your privileges to an alien nation.
4 Blessed are we, O Israel;
for what pleases God is known to us!*

III. Baruch's Poem of Consolation†

A. Baruch Addresses Diaspora

5 Take courage, my people!
Remember, O Israel,
6 You were sold to the nations
not for destruction;
It was because you angered God
that you were handed over to your foes.*
7 For you provoked your Maker*
with sacrifices to demons and not to God;
8 You forgot the eternal God who nourished
you,
and you grieved Jerusalem who nurtured
you.
9 She indeed saw coming upon you
the wrath of God; and she said:

B. Jerusalem Addresses Neighbors

"Hear, you neighbors of Zion!
God has brought great mourning upon me,
10 For I have seen the captivity
that the Eternal One has brought
upon my sons and daughters.
11 With joy I nurtured them;
but with mourning and lament I sent them
away.
12 Let no one gloat over me,
a widow, bereft of many;
For the sins of my children I am left desolate,
because they turned from the law of God,*
13 and did not acknowledge his statutes;
In the ways of God's commandments they did
not walk,
nor did they tread the disciplined paths of
his justice.

Live It!

Stand Up!

The poem that begins with Baruch 4:5 has the nation of Israel speaking to the Jews in exile. After recalling that their disobedience brought on the exile, the author of the poem calls them to conversion. Worried that they may start worshiping the false gods of their new neighbors, the writer reminds them that if they are faithful to God, God will not abandon them.

It can be said that as Christians, we too live in a culture that is in some ways foreign to our values and beliefs. How easy is it to stand up against the pressures of peers, media values, and social standards that go against Christian values and beliefs? Are you confident enough to do what's right if others do not? It is important to find friends who share your values and look to your faith community for strength and courage.

▶ Bar 4:17–19

14 "Let Zion's neighbors come—
Remember the captivity of my sons and
daughters,
brought upon them by the Eternal One.
15 He has brought against them a nation from
afar,
a nation ruthless and of alien speech,
That has neither reverence for old age
nor pity for the child;*
16 They have led away this widow's beloved
sons,
have left me solitary, without daughters.

C. Jerusalem Addresses Diaspora

17 What can I do to help you?
18 The one who has brought this evil upon you
must himself deliver you from your
enemies' hands.*

†

4:1–4 The poem ends with the identification of Wisdom and Torah, as in Sir 24:22–23; cf. also Dt 4:5–8.

4:5–5:9 The poet addresses the exiles (vv. 5–9a), and then Zion personified is introduced, speaking to the nations and mourning the loss of her children (vv. 9b–16). She then addresses the exiles (vv. 17–29). Finally (4:30–5:9) the poet issues three calls to Jerusalem (4:30, 36; 5:5): she will see her children returning (4:22, 36–37; 5:5).

*

3:38 Wis 9:18; Jn 1:14.
4:1 Dt 4:6–8; Prv 8:35–36; Sir 24:22.
4:2 Prv 4:13, 19.
4:4 Dt 4:32–37; 33:29.
4:6 Jgs 2:14; Is 50:1; 52:3.
4:7–8 Dt 32:13–18; 1 Cor 10:20.
4:12 Lam 1:1, 2, 7.
4:15 Dt 28:49–50; Jer 5:15; 6:22–23.
4:18 Jer 32:42.

19 Farewell, my children, farewell;
I am left desolate.
20 I have taken off the garment of peace,
have put on sackcloth for my prayer of supplication;
while I live I will cry out to the Eternal One.*
21 "Take courage, my children; call upon God;
he will deliver you from oppression, from enemy hands.*
22 I have put my hope for your deliverance in the Eternal One,
and joy has come to me from the Holy One
Because of the mercy that will swiftly reach you
from your eternal Savior.
23 With mourning and lament I sent you away,
but God will give you back to me
with gladness and joy forever.*
24 As Zion's neighbors lately saw you taken captive,
so shall they soon see God's salvation come to you,
with great glory and the splendor of the Eternal One.*

25 "My children, bear patiently the wrath*
that has come upon you from God;
Your enemies have persecuted you,
but you will soon see their destruction
and trample upon their necks.†
26 My pampered children have trodden rough roads,
carried off by their enemies like sheep in a raid.*
27 Take courage, my children; call out to God!
The one who brought this upon you will remember you.*
28 As your hearts have been disposed to stray from God,
so turn now ten times the more to seek him;
29 For the one who has brought disaster upon you
will, in saving you, bring you eternal joy."*

D. Baruch Addresses Jerusalem

30 Take courage, Jerusalem!
The one who gave you your name will console you.*
31 Wretched shall be those who harmed you,
who rejoiced at your downfall;
32 Wretched shall be the cities where your children were enslaved,
wretched the city that received your children.*
33 As that city rejoiced at your collapse,*
and made merry at your downfall,
so shall she grieve over her own desolation.
34 I will take from her the rejoicing crowds,
and her exultation shall be turned to mourning:
35 For fire shall come upon her*
from the Eternal One, for many a day,
to be inhabited by demons for a long time.†
36 Look to the east, Jerusalem;
see the joy that comes to you from God!*
37 Here come your children whom you sent away,
gathered in from east to west
By the word of the Holy One,
rejoicing in the glory of God.

5 1 Jerusalem, take off your robe of mourning and misery;
put on forever the splendor of glory from God:*
2 Wrapped in the mantle of justice from God,
place on your head the diadem
of the glory of the Eternal One.*
3 For God will show your splendor to all under the heavens;
4 you will be named by God forever:
the peace of justice, the glory of God's worship.*

5 Rise up, Jerusalem! stand upon the heights;
look to the east and see your children
Gathered from east to west
at the word of the Holy One,
rejoicing that they are remembered by God.
6 Led away on foot by their enemies they left you:

† **4:25** *Trample upon their necks*: a sign of victory over the enemy (cf. Ps 44:6; Is 14:25). The Israelites considered their enemies to be God's enemies as well.
4:35 Deserts and desolate places were looked upon as the habitation of demons; cf. Tb 8:3; Lk 11:24.

* **4:20** Jdt 9:1; Est 4:16. **4:21** Jer 51:5. **4:23** Jer 31:12–13. **4:24** Is 60:1–7. **4:25** Is 51:23. **4:26** Lam 2:22. **4:27** Is 40:1. **4:29** Is 35:10. **4:30** Ps 46:5; Is 60:14. **4:32** Jer 51:43. **4:33–34** Is 13:20–22; 47:1–11; Jer 50:13. **4:35** Is 34:9–14. **4:36** Is 60:4–5. **5:1** Is 52:1. **5:2** Ex 39:30; Wis 18:24; Is 61:10; 62:3. **5:4** Is 1:26; 32:17; Jer 33:16.

BAR

but God will bring them back to you
carried high in glory as on royal thrones.*
7 For God has commanded
that every lofty mountain
and the age-old hills be made low,
That the valleys be filled to make level
ground,
that Israel may advance securely in the
glory of God.*
8 The forests and every kind of fragrant tree
have overshadowed Israel at God's
command;*
9 For God is leading Israel in joy
by the light of his glory,
with the mercy and justice that are his.

IV. Letter of Jeremiah

6 1A copy of the letter which Jeremiah sent
to those led captive to Babylon by the king
of the Babylonians, to tell them what God had
commanded him:*
For the sins you committed before God, you
are being led captive to Babylon by Nebuchad-
nezzar, king of the Babylonians. 2When you
reach Babylon you will be there many years, a
long time—seven generations;† after that I will
bring you back from there in peace. 3And now in
Babylon you will see gods of silver and gold and
wood, carried shoulder high, to cast fear upon
the nations.* 4† Take care that you yourselves
do not become like these foreigners and let not
such fear possess you. 5When you see the crowd
before them and behind worshiping them, say in
your hearts, "You, Lord, are the one to be wor-
shiped!"* 6For my angel† is with you, and he
will keep watch on you.*
7Their tongues are smoothed by woodworkers;
they are covered with gold and silver—but they
are frauds, and cannot speak.* 8People bring
gold, as though for a girl fond of dressing up,
9and prepare crowns for the heads of their gods.
Then sometimes the priests filch the gold and sil-
ver from their gods and spend it on themselves,
10or give part of it to harlots† in the brothel.
They dress them up in clothes like human
beings, these gods of silver and gold and wood.
11Though they are wrapped in purple clothing,
they are not safe from rust and corrosion. 12Their
faces are wiped clean of the cloud of dust which
is thick upon them. 13Each has a scepter, like the
human ruler of a district, but none can do away
with those that offend against it. 14Each has in
its right hand an ax or dagger, but it cannot save
itself from war or pillage. Thus it is known they
are not gods; do not fear them.
15As useless as a broken pot* 16are their
gods, set up in their temples, their eyes full of
dust from the feet of those who enter. 17Their

Pray It!

Lucky Charms?

The whole sixth chapter of Baruch points out the foolishness of people who worship statues of gods and goddesses. Some ancient peoples felt these images gave them luck or fertility or health. The author of this chapter is warning, "Just because you are in a foreign land, don't take up silly superstitions!"

Sometimes, modern people like to carry a special lucky charm in the belief that it will protect them or bring them good luck. Do you carry a rabbit's foot, wear a special piece of clothing for big events, or use some other good luck charm? If so, why?

Dear Lord, sometimes, when I feel like I can use every bit of luck I can get, a "lucky" object can be a comfort. Help me to remember, though, the true power over my life that comes from you.

▶ **Baruch, chapter 6**

6:2 *Seven generations*: this number may be symbolic. If it is not, it may indicate the date of this composition by an author writing for his contemporaries for whom the conditions of the exile were still realities. He has multiplied the seventy years of Jer 29:10 by three or four.

6:4–72 This whole chapter is a sustained argument against the temptation to worship Babylonian gods. A pattern is repeated throughout the chapter: various reasons are set forth to prove that the idols in the Babylonian temples are not gods (e.g., they are weak, helpless, attended by unworthy ministers); each section is followed by an exhortation not to be deceived, not to worship them. Note the refrain at vv. 14, 22, 28, 39, 44, 51, 56, 64. Israelite religion was aniconic, i.e., it prohibited images; as elsewhere in the Old Testament (e.g., Is 42:17; 44:9–20), the polemic against idols here oversimplifies by identifying the god worshiped with the image that represents it.

6:6 *My angel*: the prophet assures the people that God's watchful care is with them, just as he was with their ancestors during their journey to the promised land (Ex 23:20).

6:10 *Harlots*: cult prostitutes, common in some religions of the ancient Near East.

5:6 Is 49:22.
5:7 Is 40:3–4.
5:8 Is 41:19.
6:1 Jer 29:1.
6:3 Is 46:7; Jer 10:1–16.
6:5 Dt 6:13; 10:20; Mt 4:10; Lk 4:8.
6:6 Ex 23:20.
6:7 Ps 135:16.
6:15 Jer 22:28.

courtyards are walled in like those of someone
brought to execution for a crime against the king;
the priests reinforce their temples with gates and
bars and bolts, so they will not be carried off by
robbers. 18 They light more lamps for them than
for themselves, yet not one of these can they see.
19 They are like any timber in the temple; their
hearts, it is said, are eaten away. Though crawling
creatures from the ground consume them and
their garments, they do not feel it. 20 Their faces
become sooty from the smoke in the temple.
21 Bats and swallows alight on their bodies and
heads—any bird, and cats as well. 22 Know, there-
fore, that they are not gods; do not fear them.

23 Gold adorns them, but unless someone
wipes away the corrosion, they do not shine; they
felt nothing when they were molded. 24 They are
bought at whatever price, but there is no spirit in
them. 25 Since they have no feet, they are carried
shoulder high, displaying to all how worthless
they are; even those who worship them are put
to shame* 26 because, if they fall to the ground,
the worshipers must pick them up. They neither
move of themselves if one sets them upright, nor
come upright if they are tipped over; offerings
are set out for them as for the dead.* 27 † Their
priests sell their sacrifices for their own advan-
tage. Likewise their wives cure some of the meat,
but they do not share it with the poor and the
weak;* 28 women ritually unclean or at childbirth
handle their sacrifices. From such things, know
that they are not gods; do not fear them.

29 How can they be called gods? Women set
out the offerings for these gods of silver and gold
and wood, 30 and in their temples the priests
squat with torn tunic and with shaven hair and
beard, and with their heads uncovered.* 31 They
shout and wail before their gods as others do at
a funeral banquet. 32 The priests take some of the
clothing from their gods and put it on their wives
and children. 33 † Whether these gods are treated
well or badly by anyone, they cannot repay it.
They can neither set up nor remove a king.*
34 They cannot give anyone riches or pennies; if
one fails to fulfill a vow to them, they will not
exact it. 35 They neither save anyone from death,
nor deliver the weak from the strong,* 36 nor do
they restore sight to the blind, or rescue anyone
in distress. 37 The widow they do not pity, the
orphan they do not help. 38 These gilded and
silvered wooden statues are no better than stones
from the mountains; their worshipers will be
put to shame. 39 How then can it be thought or
claimed that they are gods?

40 Even the Chaldeans themselves have no re-
spect for them; for when they see a deaf mute,
unable to speak, they bring forward Bel† and
expect him to make a sound, as though he could
hear. 41 They themselves are unable to reflect
and abandon these gods, for they have no sense.
42 † And the women, with cords around them, sit
by the roads, burning chaff for incense;* 43 and
whenever one of them is taken aside by some
passerby who lies with her, she mocks her neigh-
bor who has not been thought thus worthy, and
has not had her cord broken. 44 All that is done
for these gods is a fraud; how then can it be
thought or claimed that they are gods?

45 They are produced by woodworkers and
goldsmiths; they are nothing other than what
these artisans wish them to be. 46 Even those who
produce them are not long-lived; 47 how then can
the things they have produced be gods? They have
left frauds and disgrace to their successors. 48 For
when war or disaster comes upon them, the priests
deliberate among themselves where they can hide
with them. 49 How then can one not understand
that these are not gods, who save themselves nei-
ther from war nor from disaster? 50 Beings that are
wooden, gilded and silvered, they will later be
known for frauds. To all nations and kings it will
be clear that they are not gods, but human hand-
iwork; and that God's work is not in them. 51 Is it
not obvious that they are not gods?

52 † They set no king over the land, nor do
they give rain. 53 They neither vindicate their
own rights, nor do they rescue anyone wronged,
for they are powerless. 54 They are like crows in
midair. For when fire breaks out in the temple of
these wooden or gilded or silvered gods, though
the priests flee and are safe, they themselves are
burned up in the fire like timbers. 55 They cannot
resist a king or enemy forces. 56 How then can it
be admitted or thought that they are gods?

†

6:27–31 From the viewpoint of Jewish ritual law, the practices named here were grotesque and depraved; cf. Lv 12:2–8; 15:19–23.

6:33–39 All that the Babylonian gods cannot do, the true God does; they have neither power nor inclination to save those in need, unlike the God of Israel, who champions the cause of the weak over the strong, and who defends the widow and the orphan. Cf. 1 Sm 2:7; Ps 68:6; 146:7–9; Is 35:4–5.

6:40 *Bel*: cf. note on Jer 50:2.

6:42–43 Perhaps a reference to the Babylonian practice of cultic prostitution mentioned by Herodotus, the fifth-century Greek historian. The unbroken cord was a sign that this service had not yet been rendered.

6:52–53 Unlike the God of Israel, the Babylonian gods are unable to set up and depose kings, or to provide life-giving rain.

*

6:25 Wis 13:16.
6:26 Sir 30:18–19.
6:27 Lv 12:4; 15:19–20; Dt 14:28–29.
6:30 Lv 10:6; 21:5, 10.
6:33 Dn 2:21.
6:35 Ps 68:6; 146:7–9.
6:42–43 Jer 3:2.

BAR

They are safe from neither thieves nor ban-
dits, these wooden and silvered and gilded gods.
57 Anyone who can will strip off the gold and the
silver, and go away with the clothing that was
on them; they cannot help themselves. 58 How
much better to be a king displaying his valor, or a
handy tool in a house, the joy of its owner, than
these false gods; better the door of a house, pro-
tecting whatever is within, than these false gods;
better a wooden post in a palace, than these
false gods!* 59 † The sun and moon and stars are
bright, obedient in the task for which they are
sent. 60 Likewise the lightning, when it flashes, is
a great sight; and the one wind blows over every
land. 61 The clouds, too, when commanded by
God to proceed across the whole world, fulfill
the command; 62 and fire, sent from on high to
burn up the mountains and the forests, carries
out its command. But these false gods are not
their equal, whether in appearance or in power.
63 So it is unthinkable, and cannot be claimed
that they are gods. They can neither execute judg-
ment, nor benefit anyone. 64 Know, therefore,
that they are not gods; do not fear them.

65 Kings they can neither curse nor bless. 66 They
show the nations no signs in the heavens, nor do
they shine like the sun, nor give light like the
moon. 67 The beasts are better than they—beasts
can help themselves by fleeing to shelter. 68 Thus
is it in no way apparent to us that they are gods;
so do not fear them.

69 For like a scarecrow in a cucumber patch,*
providing no protection, are their wooden, gild-
ed, silvered gods. 70 Just like a thornbush in a gar-
den on which perches every kind of bird, or like
a corpse hurled into darkness, are their wooden,
gilded, silvered gods. 71 From the rotting of the
purple and the linen upon them, you can know
that they are not gods; they themselves will in the
end be consumed, and be a disgrace in the land.
72 Better the just who has no idols; such shall be
far from disgrace!

†

6:59–62 The elements of nature, obedient to God's orders and accomplishing the divine purpose, are better than the Babylonian gods.

*

6:58 Wis 13:10–15; 15:7–17. **6:69** Jer 10:5.

The Book of

Ezekiel

Four-headed creatures, a strange craft made up of wheels within wheels, a being of light that appears out of the sky—the first chapter of the Book of Ezekiel sounds like a preview for a science fiction movie. Ezekiel, more than any other prophet, proclaims astonishing visions that are filled with bizarre images, symbols, and creatures.

At a Glance

I. **Call of the Prophet (1:1—3:27).**

II. **Before the Siege of Jerusalem (4:1—24:27).**

III. **Prophecies Against Foreign Nations (25:1—32:32).**

IV. **Hope for the Future (33:1—39:29).**

V. **The New Israel (40:1—48:35).**

Quick Facts

Period Covered: from 593 to 573 BC

Inspired Authors: Ezekiel, and the scribes who recorded his words and actions

Themes: Jerusalem is being punished for its sin. God's glory will be known to all the nations. God will restore the Temple.

In Depth

Ezekiel lived during the last days of Judah, just before it was destroyed by the Babylonians. He was probably among an early group of captives sent into exile in Babylon before Judah and the city of Jerusalem were demolished in 587 BC (see the timeline at the back of this Bible). He began his prophetic ministry in 593 BC, when he received a fantastic vision and call, described in chapters 1–3 of his book. We know that Ezekiel came from a priestly family (see 1:3) and that he was married (see 24:16–18).

Ezekiel preached many of the traditional themes of the other prophets but in a unique way. Note these examples:

The Lord's presence in the Temple. Possibly because of Ezekiel's priestly heritage, he gave God's presence—or lack of presence—in the Temple a more central role than did the other prophets. In his vision, the Temple will be the center of the new Israel, and a great priest will rule instead of a king.

The awesomeness of God. For Ezekiel, the Lord did not appear as a parent or someone to be argued with; rather, God was awesome and overpowering, beyond human explanations. Ezekiel often spoke of God's glory and holiness.

Personal responsibility. Ezekiel did not condemn the previous generation for the destruction of Judah, but preached that every generation is responsible for its own acts. Each individual can direct his or her life according to God's will.

Apocalyptic prophecy. Some of Ezekiel's prophecies take the form of symbolic images. The images are so mysterious they require special explanation by heavenly beings. The Books of Daniel and Revelation continue this type of writing, which is called apocalyptic literature.

Ezekiel

I. Call of the Prophet

The Vision: God on the Cherubim

1 [1] In the thirtieth year,† on the fifth day of the
fourth month, while I was among the exiles
by the river Chebar, the heavens opened, and I
saw divine visions.*— [2] On the fifth day of the
month—this was the fifth year† of King Jehoia-
chin's exile*— [3] the word of the LORD came to the
priest Ezekiel, the son of Buzi, in the land of the
Chaldeans by the river Chebar. There the hand of
the LORD came upon him.*
[4] As I watched, a great stormwind came from the
North,† a large cloud with flashing fire, a bright
glow all around it, and something like polished
metal gleamed at the center of the fire.* [5] From
within it figures in the likeness of four living crea-
tures† appeared. This is what they looked like:*
[6] They were in human form, but each had four faces
and four wings,* [7] and their legs were straight, the
soles of their feet like the hooves of a bull, gleam-
ing like polished brass.* [8] Human hands were
under their wings, and the wings of one touched
those of another.* [9] Their faces and their wings
looked out on all their four sides; they did not turn
when they moved, but each went straight ahead.*
[10] † Their faces were like this:* each of the four
had a human face, and on the right the face of
a lion, and on the left, the face of an ox, and
each had the face of an eagle. [11] Such were their
faces. Their wings were spread out above. On
each one, two wings touched one another, and
the other two wings covered the body.* [12] Each
went straight ahead. Wherever the spirit would
go, they went; they did not change direction
when they moved.* [13] † And the appearance of
the living creatures seemed like burning coals of
fire. Something indeed like torches moved back
and forth among the living creatures. The fire

†

1:1 *The thirtieth year,* which corresponds to the fifth year of exile (v. 2), has never been satisfactorily explained; possibly it refers to the prophet's age, or the anniversary of the finding of the book of the law in the Temple during Josiah's reform of 622 (2 Kgs 22:1–13). *The river Chebar*: probably a canal near Nippur, southeast of Babylon, one of the sites on which the Jewish exiles were settled.

1:2 *The fifth day . . . the fifth year*: the end of July, 593 B.C.; cf. v. 1.

1:4 *The North*: Zaphon, the traditional abode of the gods; see notes on Jb 37:22; Ps 48:3; Is 14:13–15.

1:5 *Four living creatures*: identified as cherubim in 10:1–2, 20. Known from Assyrian religion as minor guardian deities of palaces and temples, the cherubim were usually portrayed in gigantic sculpture with the bodies of bulls or lions, wings like an eagle and a human head. In the Jerusalem Temple, the Lord was enthroned above in the holy of holies (Is 6:1–2).

1:10 The four faces together represent animate creation: wild animals, domesticated livestock, birds, and human beings. Christian tradition associates them with the four evangelists: the lion with Mark, the ox with Luke, the eagle with John, and the man with Matthew.

1:13–14 The coals and flashing lightning moving among the four creatures and yet coming from them identify this vision as a theophany. See note on 10:2–13.

*

1:1 Ez 10:20; 11:24–25; 43:3; Ps 137:1.
1:2 2 Kgs 24:15.
1:3 Ez 3:14, 22; 8:1; 33:22; 37:1; 40:1; 2 Kgs 3:15; Is 8:11.
1:4 Ez 8:2; Jb 38:1.
1:5 Is 6:2.
1:6 Ez 10:14.
1:7 Rev 1:15.
1:8 Ez 10:8.
1:9 Ez 10:22.
1:10 Ez 10:14; Rev 4:6–7.
1:11 Is 6:2.
1:12 Ez 10:16–19.

Live It!

The Word Is Sweet

God called Ezekiel to speak God's word to the people. It was a tough job, for God's people weren't always willing to listen. But Ezekiel opened his mouth to receive the scroll containing God's word, and the scroll was sweet (see Ez 3:3).

God gave Ezekiel words to eat. God nourished Ezekiel so that Ezekiel could carry out his calling. In the same way, God gives us the Word to eat and nourishes us to carry out our calling. Jesus is often called the Word of God (see "The 'Cosmic Christ,'" near Jn 1:1–18).

At the Eucharist, we receive not only the Word of God when the Scriptures are proclaimed but also the Body of Christ when we come forward for Communion. With both Word and Sacrament, we are called to share the Good News of our faith with others.

- What are some ways we can bring this Good News to others?
- What are some things we might say or do to share our faith with the people we know?

▶ **Ez 2:1—3:11**

EZ

gleamed intensely, and from it lightning flashed.
14 The creatures darting back and forth flashed
like lightning.
15 † As I looked at the living creatures, I saw
wheels on the ground, one alongside each of the
four living creatures.* 16 The wheels and their
construction sparkled like yellow topaz, and all
four of them looked the same: their construction
seemed as though one wheel was inside the other.
17 When they moved, they went in any of the four
directions without veering as they moved. 18 * The
four of them had rims, high and fearsome—eyes
filled the four rims all around. 19 When the living
creatures moved, the wheels moved with them;
and when the living creatures were raised from
the ground, the wheels also were raised. 20 Wher-
ever the spirit would go, they went. And they were
raised up together with the living creatures, for
the spirit of the living creatures was in the wheels.
21 Wherever the living creatures moved, the wheels
moved; when they stood still, the wheels stood
still. When they were lifted up from the earth, the
wheels were lifted up with them.* For the spirit of
the living creatures was in the wheels.
22 † Above the heads of the living creatures
was a likeness of the firmament; it was awesome,
stretching upwards like shining crystal over their
heads.* 23 Beneath the firmament their wings
stretched out toward one another; each had two
wings covering the body. 24 Then I heard the
sound of their wings, like the roaring of mighty
waters, like the voice of the Almighty. When they
moved, the sound of the tumult was like the din
of an army. And when they stood still, they low-
ered their wings.* 25 While they stood with their
wings lowered, a voice came from above the
firmament over their heads.
26 Above the firmament over their heads was
the likeness of a throne that looked like sapphire;
and upon this likeness of a throne was seated,
up above, a figure that looked like a human
being.† * 27 And I saw something like polished
metal, like the appearance of fire enclosed on
all sides, from what looked like the waist up;
and from what looked like the waist down, I
saw something like the appearance of fire and
brilliant light surrounding him.* 28 Just like the
appearance of the rainbow in the clouds on a
rainy day so was the appearance of brilliance that
surrounded him. Such was the appearance of the
likeness of the glory of the LORD. And when I saw
it, I fell on my face and heard a voice speak.*

Eating of the Scroll

2 1 The voice said to me: Son of man,† stand
up! I wish to speak to you. 2 As he spoke to
me, the spirit† entered into me and set me on
my feet, and I heard the one who was speaking*

†

1:15–21 The repetitions and inconsistencies in the description of the wheels and the direction of their movements evoke the vision's mysterious quality and emphasize the difficulty of describing the divine world in human language.

1:22–23, 26 This symbolic description of God's throne is similar to that in Ex 24:9–10.

1:26 *Looked like a human being*: the God who transcends the powers of the human imagination is pictured here in the likeness of an enthroned human king.

2:1 *Son of man*: in Hebrew, "son/daughter of . . ." is a common idiom expressing affiliation in a group; in this case, "a human being." The title is God's habitual way of addressing the prophet throughout this book, probably used to emphasize the separation of the divine and the human.

2:2 *The spirit*: lit., wind, breath; a vital power, coming from God, which enables the prophet to hear the divine word; cf. 8:3; 11:1, 24.

*

1:15 Ez 10:2.
1:18 Ez 10:12; Rev 4:6, 8.
1:21 Ez 10:9–12.
1:22 Ez 10:1; Gn 1:6.
1:24 Ez 3:13; 10:5; 43:2; Rev 1:15.
1:26 Rev 1:13.
1:27 Ez 8:2.
1:28 Rev 4:2–3.
2:2 Ez 3:24; Dn 8:18.

3 say to me: Son of man, I am sending you to the
Israelites, a nation of rebels who have rebelled
against me; they and their ancestors have been in
revolt against me to this very day.* 4 Their chil-
dren are bold of face and stubborn of heart—to
them I am sending you. You shall say to them:
Thus says the Lord GOD.* 5 And whether they hear
or resist—they are a rebellious house—they shall
know that a prophet has been among them.*
6 But as for you, son of man, do not fear them or
their words. Do not fear, even though there are
briers or thorns and you sit among scorpions.†
Do not be afraid of their words or be terrified by
their looks for they are a rebellious house.* 7 You
must speak my words to them, whether they hear
or resist, because they are rebellious.* 8 But you,
son of man, hear me when I speak to you and do
not rebel like this rebellious house. Open your
mouth and eat what I am giving you.*
9 * It was then I saw a hand stretched out to me;
in it was a written scroll. 10 He unrolled it before
me; it was covered with writing front and back.
Written on it was: Lamentation, wailing, woe!*

3 1 He said to me: Son of man, eat what you
find here: eat this scroll, then go, speak to the
house of Israel. 2 So I opened my mouth, and he
gave me the scroll to eat. 3 * Son of man, he said
to me, feed your stomach and fill your belly with
this scroll I am giving you. I ate it, and it was as
sweet as honey† in my mouth. 4 Then he said to
me, Son of man, go now to the house of Israel,
and speak my words to them.
5 Not to a people with obscure speech and
difficult language am I sending you, but to the
house of Israel.* 6 Nor to many nations of ob-
scure speech and difficult language whose words
you cannot understand. For if I were to send
you to these, they would listen to you.* 7 But the
house of Israel will refuse to listen to you, since
they refuse to listen to me. For the whole house
of Israel is stubborn of brow and hard of heart.*
8 † Look! I make your face as hard as theirs,
and your brow as stubborn as theirs.* 9 Like
diamond, harder than flint, I make your brow.
Do not be afraid of them, or be terrified by their
looks, for they are a rebellious house.*
10 Then he said to me, Son of man, take into
your heart all my words that I speak to you; hear
them well. 11 Now go to the exiles, to your own
people, and speak to them. Say to them, whether
they hear or refuse to hear: Thus says the LORD
God!
12 Then the spirit lifted me up, and I heard be-
hind me a loud rumbling noise as the glory of
the LORD† rose from its place:* 13 the noise of the
wings of the living creatures beating against one
another, and the noise of the wheels alongside
them, a loud rumbling.* 14 And the spirit lifted
me up and took me away, and I went off, my
spirit angry and bitter, for the hand of the LORD

Introducing...

Ezekiel

Ezekiel's name means "God strengthens." He was a complex person: priest and prophet, poet and teacher, tender and angry. He experienced God in mysterious ways, often through visions that greatly influenced his life and prophetic ministry.

Ezekiel's vision of creatures from heaven in chapters 1–3 of his book was the basis for his call and prophetic ministry. His vision of the defilement of the Temple in chapters 8–11 was a major conversion experience. He, along with most of Israel, believed that God's glory resided in the Temple and that nothing could ever change that. The vision revealed corruption in Jerusalem and that the glory of God had left the Temple and had come to Babylon. His vision of dry bones coming to life in chapter 37 helped him understand that God would breathe new life into Israel. His final visions of a new Temple in chapters 40, 43, and 47 told him that God would restore Jerusalem and the Temple.

Besides having symbolic visions, Ezekiel also performed many dramatic, symbolic actions (see "Street Theater," near Ez 4:1—5:4). These were designed to catch people's attention and transmit God's message.

EZ

† **2:6** *And you sit among scorpions*: the prophet must be prepared for bitter opposition.
3:3 *As sweet as honey*: though the prophet must foretell terrible things, the word of God is sweet to the one who receives it.
3:8 Cf. Jer 1:18. The prophet must face fierce opposition with the determination and resistance shown by his opponents.
3:12 *The glory of the LORD*: the divine presence, manifested here in audible form. Cf. Ex 40:34; Lk 2:9.

* **2:3** Ez 20:8, 13.
2:4 Ex 32:9.
2:5 Ez 3:11, 27; 33:33.
2:6 Dt 31:6.
2:7 Ez 3:10–11; Jer 7:27.
2:8 Jer 15:16.
2:9 Ez 8:3; Rev 10:2.
2:10 Zec 5:3; Rev 5:1.
3:3 Jer 15:16; Rev 10:9–10.
3:5 Is 28:11.
3:6 cf. Mt 11:21.
3:7 Jer 7:27.
3:8 Jer 1:18.
3:9 Is 48:4.
3:12 Ez 8:3; 43:5.
3:13 Ez 10:16–17.

pressed hard on me. 15 Thus I came to the exiles who lived at Tel-abib† by the river Chebar; and there where they dwelt, I stayed among them distraught for seven days. 16 * At the end of the seven days, the word of the LORD came to me:

The Prophet as Sentinel†

17 Son of man, I have appointed you a sentinel for the house of Israel.* When you hear a word from my mouth, you shall warn them for me.

18 If I say to the wicked, You shall surely die—and you do not warn them or speak out to dissuade the wicked from their evil conduct in order to save their lives—then they shall die for their sin, but I will hold you responsible for their blood. 19 If, however, you warn the wicked and they still do not turn from their wickedness and evil conduct, they shall die for their sin, but you shall save your life.

20 But if the just turn away from their right conduct and do evil when I place a stumbling block before them, then they shall die. Even if you warned them about their sin, they shall still die, and the just deeds that they performed will not be remembered on their behalf. I will, however, hold you responsible for their blood.* 21 If, on the other hand, you warn the just to avoid sin, and they do not sin, they will surely live because of the warning, and you in turn shall save your own life.

Ezekiel Mute

22 The hand of the LORD came upon me there and he said to me: Get up and go out into the plain, where I will speak with you.* 23 * So I got up and went out into the plain. There it was! The glory of the LORD was standing there like the glory I had seen by the river Chebar. Then I fell on my face, 24 but the spirit entered into me, set me on my feet; he spoke to me, and said: Go, shut yourself in your house. 25 As for you, son of man, know that they will put ropes on you and bind you with them, so that you cannot go out among them.* 26 And I will make your tongue stick to the roof of your mouth so that you will be mute,† no longer one who rebukes them for being a rebellious house.* 27 Only when I speak to you and open your mouth, shall you say to them: Thus says the LORD God: Let those who hear, hear! Let those who resist, resist! They are truly a rebellious house.

II. Before the Siege of Jerusalem

Acts Symbolic of Siege and Exile

4 1 † You, son of man, take a clay tablet; place it in front of you, and draw on it a city, Jerusalem. 2 Lay siege to it: build up siege works, raise a ramp against it, pitch camps and set up battering rams all around it. 3 Then take an iron pan and set it up as an iron wall between you and the city. Set your face toward it and put it under siege. So you must lay siege to it as a sign for the house of Israel.* 4 Then lie down on your left side, while I place the guilt of the house of Israel upon you. As many days as you lie like this, you shall bear their guilt. 5 I allot you three hundred and ninety days† during which you must bear the guilt of the house of Israel, the same number of years they sinned. 6 When you have completed this, you shall lie down a second time, on your right side to bear the guilt of the house of Judah forty days; I allot you one day for each year.* 7 Turning your face toward the siege of Jerusalem, with bared arm† you shall prophesy against it. 8 See, I bind you with ropes so that you cannot turn from one side to the other until you have completed the days of your siege.*

9 † Then take wheat and barley, beans and lentils, millet and spelt; put them into a single pot and make them into bread. Eat it for as many days as you lie upon your side, three hundred and ninety days. 10 The food you eat shall be twenty shekels a day by weight; each day you shall eat it. 11 And the water you drink shall be the sixth of a hin† by measure; each day you shall drink it. 12 And the barley cake you eat you must bake on human excrement in the sight of all. 13 The LORD said: Thus the Israelites shall eat their food, unclean, among the nations where I drive them.* 14 "Oh no, Lord

3:15 *Tel-abib*: one of the sites where the exiles were settled, probably near Nippur.

3:17–21 This passage refers to the prophet's role as sentinel, placed here and in chap. 33 as introductions to sections containing judgment oracles and salvation oracles respectively; cf. Hb 2:1.

3:26–27 *Mute*: here the prophet's inability to speak to the people in exile while Jerusalem was being besieged is seen as a consequence of God's direct intervention (cf. 24:27).

4:1–5:4 The symbolic actions in this section prepare for the series of oracles that follow in 5:5–7:27.

4:5–6 *Three hundred and ninety days . . . forty days*: a symbol to represent the respective lengths of exile for the Northern Kingdom of Israel and the Southern Kingdom of Judah. Israel had already fallen to Assyria in 722/721 B.C. The numerical value of the Hebrew consonants in the phrase translated "the days of your siege" (v. 8) is three hundred and ninety. Forty years conventionally represents one generation.

4:7 *Bared arm*: a symbol of unrestrained power.

4:9–13 This action represents the scarcity of food during the siege of Jerusalem, and the consequent need to eat whatever is at hand. *Twenty shekels*: about nine ounces. *The sixth of a hin*: about one quart.

4:11 *Hin*: see note on 45:24.

3:16 Ez 33:7–9; cf. 18:5–18.
3:17 Is 52:8; Jer 1:17; Hb 2:1.
3:20 Is 8:14.
3:22 Ez 1:3; 8:4.
3:23 Ez 10:15; 40:3.
3:25 Ez 4:8.
3:26 Ps 22:15.
4:3 Is 8:18.
4:6 Dn 9:24–25; 12:11–12.
4:8 Ez 3:25.
4:13 Hos 9:4.

GOD," I protested. "Never have I defiled myself
nor have I eaten carrion flesh or flesh torn by
wild beasts, nor from my youth till now has any
unclean meat entered my mouth."* 15 Very well,
he replied, I will let you use cow manure in place
of human dung. You can bake your bread on that.
16 Then he said to me: Son of man, I am about to
break the staff of bread† in Jerusalem so they shall
eat bread which they have weighed out anxiously
and drink water which they have measured out
fearfully.* 17 Because they lack bread and water
they shall be devastated; each and every one will
waste away because of their guilt.*

5 1 Now you, son of man, take a sharp sword
and use it like a barber's razor, to shave your
head and your beard. Then take a balance scale
for weighing and divide the hair.* 2 Set a third on
fire within the city,† when the days of your siege
are completed; place another third around the
city and strike it with the sword; the final third
scatter to the wind and then unsheathe the sword
after it.* 3 But take a few of the hairs and tie them
in the hem of your garment. 4 Take some of these
and throw them into the fire and burn them in
the fire. Because of this, fire will flash out against
the whole house of Israel.

5 Thus says the Lord GOD: This is Jerusalem! I
placed it in the midst of the nations, surrounded
by foreign lands. 6 But it rebelled against my or-
dinances more wickedly than the nations, and
against my statutes more than the foreign lands
around it; they rejected my ordinances and did
not walk in my statutes.* 7 Therefore, thus says the
Lord GOD: Because you have caused more uproar
than the nations surrounding you, not living by
my statutes nor carrying out my judgments, nor
even living by the ordinances of the surrounding
nations; 8 therefore, thus says the Lord GOD: See,
I am coming against you!† I will carry out judg-
ments among you while the nations look on.*
9 Because of all your abominations I will do to you
what I have never done before, the like of which
I will never do again. 10 Therefore, parents will eat
their children in your midst, and children will eat
their parents.† I will inflict punishments upon
you and scatter all who remain to the winds.*

11 Therefore, as I live, says the Lord GOD,

Live It!

Street Theater

Look over what the prophet does in Ezekiel, chapters 3–5, to get people's attention before the fall of Jerusalem in 587 BC. He is speechless (see 3:22–27) as a sign that the people are rebellious and unwilling to hear God's word. He lies on his left side for days, and then his right (see 4:4–6), as a sign of the number of years the two kingdoms Israel and Judah will be in exile. He eats small amounts of food cooked on dung (see verses 10–15) as a sign of the shortage of food during the siege of the city. Ezekiel's "street theater" is a good way of making a point that everyone can understand.

Christians today need to use creative means to raise consciousness about the ways society violates human life and harms our world. Radio and television, the Internet, public prayer services, and rallies all help people get the message out. What does your church do to raise consciousness and move people to change their ways? What can you do?

▶ Ez 4:1—5:4

because you have defiled my sanctuary with all
your atrocities and all your abominations, I will
surely withdraw and not look upon you with pity
nor spare you.* 12 A third of your people shall die
of disease or starve to death within you; another
third shall fall by the sword all around you; a
third I will scatter to the winds and pursue them
with the sword.*

13 Thus my anger will spend itself; I will vent
my wrath against them until I am satisfied.
Then they will know that I the LORD spoke in my
passion when I spend my wrath upon them.*

EZ

4:16 *Break the staff of bread*: reducing the supply of bread that supports life as the walking staff supports a traveler; cf. 5:16; 14:13; Lv 26:26; Ps 105:16; Is 3:1.

5:2 *The city*: the one drawn on the tablet (4:1).

5:8 *I am coming against you*: an expression borrowed from the language of warfare in which an enemy attacked another with the sword. "You" in vv. 8–17 is Jerusalem.

5:10 *Parents will eat their children . . . parents*: the prophet describes the consequences of the prolonged Babylonian siege of Jerusalem in 587/586 B.C. See note on Lam 2:20.

4:14 Dn 1:8.
4:16 Ez 5:16; Lv 26:26.
4:17 Lv 26:39.
5:1 Is 7:20.
5:2 Jer 13:24.
5:6 Ez 16:47–51.
5:8 Jer 21:5.
5:10 Lv 26:29, 33; Dt 28:53; Jer 19:9.
5:11 Ez 7:4, 9; 8:18.
5:12 Ez 6:11–12; Rev 6:8.
5:13 Ez 16:42.

14 I will make you a desolation and a reproach among the nations around you, in the sight of every passerby.* 15 And you will be a reproach and a taunt, a warning and a horror to the nations around you when I execute judgments against you in angry wrath, with furious chastisements. I, the LORD, have spoken! 16 When I loose against you the deadly arrows of starvation that I am sending to destroy you, I will increase starvation and will break your staff of bread.* 17 I will send against you starvation and wild beasts who will leave you childless, while disease and bloodshed sweep through you. I will bring the sword against you. I, the LORD, have spoken.*

Against the Mountains of Israel

6 1 The word of the LORD came to me: 2 Son of man, set your face toward the mountains of Israel and prophesy against them:* 3 You shall say: Mountains of Israel, hear the word of the Lord GOD. Thus says the Lord GOD to the mountains and hills, to the ravines and valleys:* Pay attention! I am bringing a sword against you, and I will destroy your high places.† 4 Your altars shall be laid waste, your incense stands smashed, and I will throw your slain down in front of your idols. 5 Yes, I will lay the corpses of the Israelites in front of their idols, and scatter your bones around your altars.† * 6 Wherever you live, cities shall be ruined and high places laid waste, in order that your altars be laid waste and devastated, your idols broken and smashed, your incense altars hacked to pieces, and whatever you have made wiped out.* 7 The slain shall fall in your midst, and you shall know that I am the LORD.† * 8 But I will spare some of you from the sword to live as refugees among the nations when you are scattered to foreign lands. 9 Then your refugees will remember me among the nations to which they have been exiled, after I have broken their lusting hearts that turned away from me and their eyes that lusted after idols. They will loathe themselves for all the evil they have done, for all their abominations.* 10 Then they shall know that I the LORD did not threaten in vain to inflict this evil on them.

11 Thus says the Lord GOD: Clap your hands, stamp your feet,† and cry "Alas!" for all the evil abominations of the house of Israel! They shall fall by the sword, starvation, and disease.* 12 Those far off shall die of disease, those nearby shall fall by the sword, and those who survive and are spared shall perish by starvation; thus will I spend my fury upon them. 13 They shall know that I am the LORD, when their slain lie among their idols, all around their altars, on every high hill and mountaintop, beneath every green tree and leafy oak†—any place they offer sweet-smelling oblations to all their idols.* 14 I will stretch out my hand against them; I will make the land a desolate waste, from the wilderness to Riblah,† wherever they live. Thus they shall know that I am the LORD.*

The End Has Come

7 1 The word of the LORD came to me: 2 Son of man, now say: Thus says the Lord GOD to the land of Israel: An end! The end comes upon the four corners of the land!* 3 Now the end is upon you; I will unleash my anger against you, judge you according to your ways, and hold against you all your abominations. 4 My eye will not spare you, nor will I have pity; but I will hold your conduct against you, since your abominations remain within you; then shall you know that I am the LORD.*

5 Thus says the Lord GOD: Evil upon evil! See it coming! 6 An end is coming, the end is coming; it is ripe for you! See it coming! 7 The crisis has come for you who dwell in the land! The time has come, near is the day: panic, no rejoicing on the mountains.* 8 Soon now I will pour out my fury upon you and spend my anger against you; I will judge you according to your ways and hold against you all your abominations.* 9 My eye will not spare, nor will I take pity; I will hold your conduct against you since your abominations remain within you, then you shall know that it is I, the LORD, who strikes.*

EZ

†

6:3 *High places*: raised platforms usually built on hills outside towns for making sacrifices to the Lord or to Canaanite deities. They became synonymous with places of idolatry after the centralization of worship in the Jerusalem Temple.

6:5 *Scatter your bones . . . altars*: the bones of the dead defiled a place; cf. 2 Kgs 23:14.

6:7 *You shall know that I am the LORD*: this formula is repeated after most of Ezekiel's oracles from this point on. Whatever happens to Israel happens at the Lord's command; because the Lord uses the nations to punish or reward Israel for its behavior, Israel will learn that its God has sole rule over the nations and the universe, and will acknowledge that rule in obedience.

6:11 *Clap your hands, stamp your feet*: these gestures may express grief, even horror, at Israel's infidelities; in 25:6, they are signs of gloating.

6:13 *Every green tree and leafy oak*: trees often identified with fertility deities and the "tree of life"; sacred groves had a long history in Palestine and throughout the Mediterranean basin as places of worship; cf. Dt 12:2.

6:14 *From the wilderness to Riblah*: the whole land, from the far south to the far north.

*

5:14 Lv 26:32.
5:16 Ez 4:16; 14:13; Lv 26:26.
5:17 Lv 26:25.
6:2 Ez 36:1.
6:3 Ez 36:4; Lv 26:30.
6:5 Lv 26:30; Jer 8:12.
6:6 Lv 26:30.
6:7 Ez 11:10–12.
6:9 Ez 20:7, 24; Ps 137:1.
6:11 Ez 21:14–17.
6:13 Ez 20:28; Lv 26:30.
6:14 Jer 48:22.
7:2 Rev 7:1; 20:8.
7:4 Ez 5:11; Jer 13:14.
7:7 Ez 12:23; 30:3; Am 5:18–19; Zep 1:14.
7:8 Ez 20:8, 13, 21.
7:9 Ez 22:31; Jer 21:7.

10 The day is here! Look! it is coming! The cri-
sis has come! Lawlessness is blooming, insolence
budding; 11 the violent have risen up to wield a
scepter of wickedness. But none of them shall re-
main; none of their crowd, none of their wealth,
for none of them are innocent. 12 † The time
has come, the day dawns. The buyer must not
rejoice, nor the seller mourn, for wrath is com-
ing upon all the throng.* 13 Assuredly, the seller
shall not regain what was sold, as long as they
all live; for the vision is for the whole crowd: it
shall not be revoked! Yes, because of their guilt,
they shall not hold on to life. 14 They will sound
the trumpet and get everything ready, but no one
will go out to battle, for my wrath weighs upon
all the crowd.
15 The sword is outside; disease and hunger are
within. Whoever is in the fields will die by the
sword; whoever is in the city disease and hunger
will devour.* 16 If their survivors flee, they will
die on the mountains, moaning like doves of the
valley on account of their guilt. 17 All their hands
will hang limp, and all their knees† turn to wa-
ter.* 18 * They put on sackcloth, horror clothes
them; shame is on all their faces, all their heads
are shaved bald.† 19 They fling their silver into
the streets, and their gold is considered unclean.*
Their silver and gold cannot save them on the
day of the LORD's wrath. They cannot satisfy their
hunger or fill their bellies, for it has been the
occasion of their sin. 20 † In their beautiful orna-
ments they took pride; out of them they made
their abominable images, their detestable things.
For this reason I will make them unclean.* 21 I
will hand them over as spoils to foreigners, as
plunder to the wicked of the earth, so that they
may defile them. 22 I will turn my face away from
them. My treasure will be defiled; the violent will
enter and defile it.* 23 They will wreak slaughter,
for the land is filled with bloodshed and the city
with violence.* 24 I will bring in the worst of the
nations to take possession of their houses. I will
put an end to their proud strength,† and their
sanctuaries will be defiled.* 25 When anguish
comes, they will seek peace, but there is none.*
26 Disaster after disaster, rumor upon rumor.
They keep seeking a vision from the prophet; in-
struction from the priest is missing, and counsel
from the elders.* 27 The king mourns, the prince
is terror-stricken, the hands of the common peo-
ple tremble. I will deal with them according to
their ways, and according to their judgments I
will judge them. They shall know that I am the
LORD.

8 1 In the sixth year, on the fifth day of the
sixth month,† as I was sitting in my house,
with the elders of Judah sitting before me, the
hand of the Lord GOD fell upon me there.* 2 I
looked up and there was a figure that looked like
a man.† Downward from what looked like his
waist, there was fire; from his waist upward, like
the brilliance of polished bronze.*

Vision of Abominations in the Temple

3 He stretched out the form of a hand and
seized me by the hair of my head. The spirit lifted
me up† between earth and heaven and brought
me in divine vision to Jerusalem* to the entrance
of the inner gate facing north where the statue of
jealousy that provokes jealousy stood. 4 There I
saw the glory of the God of Israel, like the vision
I had seen in the plain.* 5 He said to me: Son
of man, lift your eyes to the north! I looked to
the north and there in the entry north of the al-
tar gate was this statue of jealousy.* 6 He asked,
Son of man, do you see what they are doing? Do
you see the great abominations that the house
of Israel is practicing here, so that I must depart
from my sanctuary? You shall see even greater
abominations!*
7 Then he brought me to the entrance of the
courtyard, and there I saw a hole in the wall. 8 Son
of man, he ordered, dig through the wall. I dug
through the wall—there was a doorway. 9 Go in,
he said to me, and see the evil abominations they

†

7:12–13 Normal affairs will cease to have any meaning in view of the disaster that is to come.

7:17 *Hands . . . knees*: image of profound terror; loss of control of body movement and functions.

7:18 *Shaved bald*: shaving the head was a sign of mourning.

7:20 Assyrian wall paintings show that statues of deities were often cast in precious metals and then decorated with jewelry. Cf. Is 40:19–20; 41:6–7; 44:9–20.

7:24 *Proud strength*: misplaced trust in the might and power of their kings and army. Cf. v. 22; 33:28 and related ideas in Is 2:12; 10:12; 13:11; Jer 48:29; Ez 24:21; 30:18.

8:1 *In the sixth year, on the fifth day of the sixth month*: September, 592 B.C.

8:2 *Looked like a man*: the divine presence which accompanies Ezekiel in these visions. Cf. 40:3–4.

8:3 *The spirit lifted me up*: the prophet is transported in vision from Babylon to Jerusalem. Ezekiel may be drawing on his memory of the Temple from before his exile in 598 B.C. *The statue of jealousy*: the statue which provokes the Lord's outrage against the insults of his own people; perhaps the statue of the goddess Asherah set up by Manasseh, king of Judah (cf. 2 Kgs 21:7; 2 Chr 33:7, 15). Although his successor, Josiah, had removed it (2 Kgs 23:6), the statue may have been set up again after his death.

*

7:12 Is 24:2; cf. Mt 24:17–18.
7:15 Dt 32:25.
7:17 Jer 47:3.
7:18 Is 15:2–3; Jer 4:8; 48:3.
7:19 Zep 1:7, 18; 2:2.
7:20 Jer 10:3–4.
7:22 Ps 74:7–8.
7:23 Ez 22:9; 24:6.
7:24 Lam 2:7.
7:25 Jer 6:1.
7:26 Jer 18:18; Mi 3:6–7.
8:1 Ez 14:1; 33:31.
8:2 Ez 1:4, 26–27.
8:3 Ez 2:9; 3:12; Dn 14:6.
8:4 Ez 3:22.
8:5 Ps 78:58.
8:6 Ps 78:60.

are doing here. 10 I went in and looked—figures of all kinds of creeping things and loathsome beasts,† all the idols of the house of Israel,* pictured around the wall. 11 Before them stood seventy of the elders of the house of Israel. Among them stood Jaazaniah, son of Shaphan, each with censer in hand; a cloud of incense drifted upward.* 12 Then he said to me: Do you see, son of man, what the elders of the house of Israel are doing in the dark, each in his idol chamber? They think: "The LORD cannot see us; the LORD has forsaken the land."* 13 He said: You will see them practicing even greater abominations.

14 Then he brought me to the entrance of the north gate of the house of the LORD. There women sat and wept for Tammuz.† * 15 He said to me: Do you see this, son of man? You will see other abominations, greater than these!

16 Then he brought me into the inner court of the house of the LORD. There at the door of the LORD's temple, between the porch and the altar, were about twenty-five men with their backs to the LORD's temple and their faces toward the east; they were bowing eastward† to the sun.* 17 He said: Do you see, son of man? Are the abominable things the house of Judah has done here so slight that they should also fill the land with violence, provoking me again and again? Now they are putting the branch to my nose!† 18 Therefore I in turn will act furiously: my eye will not spare, nor will I take pity. Even if they cry out in a loud voice for me to hear, I shall not listen to them.

Slaughter of the Idolaters

9 1 Then he cried aloud for me to hear: Come, you scourges of the city! 2 And there were six men coming from the direction of the upper gate which faces north, each with a weapon of destruction in his hand. In their midst was a man dressed in linen, with a scribe's case at his waist. They entered and stood beside the bronze altar.* 3 Then the glory of the God of Israel moved off the cherub and went up to the threshold of the temple. He called to the man dressed in linen with the scribe's case at his waist,* 4 * and the LORD said to him:† Pass through the city, through the midst of Jerusalem, and mark an X on the foreheads of those who grieve and lament over all the abominations practiced within it. 5 To the others he said in my hearing: Pass through the city after him and strike! Do not let your eyes spare; do not take pity. 6 Old and young, male and female, women and children—wipe them out! But do not touch anyone marked with the X. Begin at my sanctuary. So they began with the elders who were in front of the temple.* 7 Defile the temple, he said to them, fill its courts with the slain. Then go out and strike in the city.

8 As they were striking, I was left alone. I fell on my face, crying out, "Alas, Lord GOD! Will you destroy all that is left of Israel when you pour out your fury on Jerusalem?" 9 He answered me: The guilt of the house of Israel and the house of Judah is too great to measure; the land is filled with bloodshed, the city with lawlessness. They think that the LORD has abandoned the land, that he does not see them. 10 My eye, however, will not spare, nor shall I take pity, but I will bring their conduct down upon their heads.

11 Just then the man dressed in linen with the scribe's case at his waist made his report: "I have done as you commanded!"

10 1 Then I looked and there above the firmament over the heads of the cherubim was something like a sapphire, something that looked like a throne.* 2 † And he said to the man dressed in linen: Go within the wheelwork under the cherubim; fill both your hands with burning coals from the place among the cherubim, then scatter them over the city. As I watched, he entered.* 3 Now the cherubim were standing to the south of the temple when the man went in and a cloud filled the inner court. 4 The glory of the

†

8:10 *Creeping things and loathsome beasts*: perhaps images of Egyptian deities, often represented in animal form. During the last days of Jerusalem Zedekiah, king of Judah, was allied with Egypt, hoping for protection against the Babylonians.

8:14 *Wept for Tammuz*: the withering of trees and plants that began in late spring was attributed to the descent of Tammuz, the Mesopotamian god of fertility, to the world of the dead beneath the earth. During the fourth month of the year, female worshipers of Tammuz would wail and mourn the god's disappearance.

8:16 *Bowing eastward*: sun worship was perhaps introduced as a condition of alliance with other nations. While Josiah removed some elements of this worship (2 Kgs 23:11), Manasseh, for example, built altars to all the "hosts of heaven" in two Temple courtyards (2 Kgs 21:5).

8:17 *Putting the branch to my nose*: the meaning is uncertain. It may be connected with the social injustice mentioned in v. 17b and in 9:9, e.g., "with their violence they tweak my nose," i.e., "goad my fury." The Masoretic text reads "their noses" as a euphemism for "my nose," thus avoiding the impropriety of these idolaters coming into contact with God even figuratively.

9:4 Ezekiel emphasizes personal accountability; the innocent inhabitants of Jerusalem are spared while the idolatrous are punished. *An X*: lit., the Hebrew letter *taw*.

10:2–13 The burning coals, a sign of the divine presence (cf. 28:14; Ps 18:9), represent the judgment of destruction that God is visiting upon the city; they may also represent the judgment of purification that prepares the land to become the Lord's sanctuary (cf. Is 6:6–7).

*

8:10 Ez 23:14.
8:11 Nm 11:16.
8:12 Is 29:15.
8:14 cf. Dn 11:37.
8:16 Jb 31:26–28.
9:2 Ez 10:2; Dn 10:5; 12:6; Rev 8:2; 15:6.
9:3 Ez 11:22.
9:4 Ex 12:7; Rev 7:2–4; 13:16.
9:6 Gn 4:15; Ex 12:7.
10:1 Ex 24:10; Rev 4:2.
10:2 Rev 8:2.

LORD had moved off the cherubim to the thresh-
old of the temple; the temple was filled with the
cloud, the whole court brilliant with the glory of
the LORD. 5 The sound of the wings of the cheru-
bim could be heard as far as the outer court; it
was like the voice of God Almighty speaking.*
6 He commanded the man dressed in linen: Take
fire from within the wheelwork among the cher-
ubim. The man entered and stood by one of
the wheels. 7 Thereupon a cherub stretched out
a hand from among the cherubim toward the
fire in the midst of the cherubim, took some,
and put it in the hands of the one dressed in
linen. He took it and came out. 8 Something like
a human hand was visible under the wings of
the cherubim. 9 I also saw four wheels beside the
cherubim, one wheel beside each cherub, and
the wheels appeared to have the sparkle of yel-
low topaz. 10 And the appearance of the four all
seemed alike, as though one wheel were inside
the other. 11 When they moved, they went in any
of the four directions without veering as they
moved; in whatever direction the first cherub
faced, the others followed without veering as
they went. 12 Their entire bodies—backs, hands,
and wings—and wheels were covered with eyes
all around like the four wheels.* 13 I heard the
wheels called "wheelwork." 14 Each living crea-
ture had four faces: the first a cherub, the second
a human being, the third a lion, the fourth an
eagle.* 15 † When the cherubim rose up, they
were indeed the living creatures I had seen by the
river Chebar.* 16 When the cherubim moved, the
wheels went beside them; when the cherubim
lifted up their wings to rise from the earth, even
then the wheels did not leave their sides. 17 When
they stood still, the wheels stood still; when they
rose up, the wheels rose up with them, for the
spirit of the living creatures was in them. 18 Then
the glory of the LORD left the threshold of the tem-
ple and took its place upon the cherubim. 19 The
cherubim lifted their wings and rose up from the
earth before my eyes as they departed with the
wheels beside them. They stopped at the entrance
of the eastern gate of the LORD's house, and the
glory of the God of Israel was up above them.*
20 † These were the living creatures I had seen be-
neath the God of Israel by the river Chebar. Now
I knew they were cherubim.* 21 Each of them had
four faces and four wings, and something like
human hands under their wings. 22 Their faces
looked just like the faces I had seen by the river
Chebar; and each one went straight ahead.

Death for the Remnant in Jerusalem

11 1 The spirit lifted me up and brought me to
the east gate of the house of the LORD fac-
ing east. There at the entrance of the gate were
twenty-five men; among them I saw the public
officials Jaazaniah, son of Azzur, and Pelatiah,
son of Benaiah. 2 The LORD said to me: Son of
man, these are the men who are planning evil
and giving wicked counsel in this city. 3 They are
saying, "No need to build houses! The city is the
pot, and we are the meat."† * 4 Therefore proph-
esy against them, son of man, prophesy! 5 Then
the spirit of the LORD fell upon me and told me
to say: Thus says the LORD: This is how you talk,
house of Israel. I know the things that come into
your mind! 6 You have slain many in this city,
filled its streets with the slain. 7 Therefore thus
says the Lord GOD: The slain whom you piled up
in it, that is the meat, the pot is the city. But you
I will bring out of it.* 8 You fear the sword—that
sword I will bring upon you—oracle of the Lord
GOD.* 9 I will bring you out of the city, hand you
over to foreigners, and execute judgments against
you. 10 By the sword you shall fall. At the borders
of Israel I will judge you so that you will know
that I am the LORD. 11 The city shall not be a pot
for you, nor shall you be meat within it. At the
borders of Israel I will judge you,* 12 so you shall
know that I am the LORD, whose statutes you did
not follow, whose ordinances you did not keep.
Instead, you acted according to the ordinances of
the nations around you.

13 While I was prophesying, Pelatiah, the son
of Benaiah, dropped dead. I fell down on my face
and cried out in a loud voice: "Alas, Lord GOD!
You are finishing off what remains of Israel!"† *

---

†

10:15–19 The throne represents God's presence as ruler and protector of the land. In chap. 1, God is revealed as the lord of the world who can appear even in a far-off land; here God is about to abandon the Temple, that is, hand the city over to its enemies. God and the throne return again in 43:1–3.

10:20–22 The repetition of description from the preceding verses is a device intended to suggest the rapid, constantly changing motion of the vision and the difficulty of describing the divine in human language.

11:3 *No need to build houses . . . meat*: this advice is based on the conviction that invincible Jerusalem will protect its citizens from further danger just as a pot shields the meat inside from the fire. The poorer citizens of Jerusalem and the refugees from nearby villages can now appropriate the property abandoned by the city's wealthier upper class when they were deported (v. 15). The metaphor of the pot and its contents reappears in chap. 24.

11:13 In Ezekiel's vision Pelatiah represents the people left in Jerusalem, "the remnant of Israel." His sudden death in the vision, but not in reality, is a figure for the judgment described in vv. 8–10 and prompts Ezekiel's anguished question about the survival of the people left in the land after the deportations in 597.

---

*

10:5 Jb 40:9.
10:12 Ez 1:15–20; Rev 4:6–8.
10:14 cf. Gn 3:24.
10:15 Ps 137:1.
10:19 Ez 43:4.
10:20 Ez 1:1.
11:3 Ez 24:3; Jer 1:13.
11:7 Mi 3:2–3.
11:8 Lv 26:25.
11:11 2 Kgs 25:20–21.
11:13 Ez 9:8.

Pray It!

Have a Heart!

The Old Testament prophets are concerned about people's hearts. The ancient Israelites understood the heart as the center of intelligence, feelings, and human will. Jeremiah says the New Covenant will be written on people's hearts (see Jer 31:33), and Ezekiel says God will take away their stony hearts and give them natural hearts (see Ez 11:19).

In your prayer, reflect or journal on the following questions:

- What's the difference between having a natural, fleshy heart and a cold, stony heart?
- Why would a natural heart lead to obeying God (see verse 20)?
- When does your heart feel natural? When does it feel stony?

▶ **Ez 11:19–20**

Restoration for the Exiles

14 The word of the LORD came to me: 15 † Son
of man, the inhabitants of Jerusalem are saying
about all your relatives, the other exiles, and all
the house of Israel, "They are far away from the
LORD. The land is given to us as a possession."*
16 Therefore say: Thus says the Lord GOD: I have
indeed sent them far away among the nations,
scattered them over the lands, and have been but
little sanctuary for them in the lands to which
they have gone. 17 Therefore, thus says the Lord
GOD, I will gather you from the nations and collect you from the lands through which you were
scattered, so I can give you the land of Israel.*
18 They will enter it and remove all its atrocities
and abominations. 19 * And I will give them another heart and a new spirit I will put within
them. From their bodies I will remove the hearts
of stone, and give them hearts of flesh, 20 so that
they walk according to my statutes, taking care to
keep my ordinances. Thus they will be my people, and I will be their God.* 21 But as for those
whose hearts are devoted to their atrocities and
abominations, I will bring their conduct down
upon their heads—oracle of the Lord GOD.
22 Then the cherubim lifted their wings and the
wheels alongside them, with the glory of the God
of Israel above them.* 23 † The glory of the LORD
rose up from the middle of the city and came to
rest on the mountain east of the city.* 24 In a vision, the spirit lifted me up and brought me back
to the exiles in Chaldea, by the spirit of God. The
vision I had seen left me,* 25 and I told the exiles
everything the LORD had shown me.*

Acts Symbolic of the Exile

12 1 The word of the LORD came to me: 2 Son
of man, you live in the midst of a rebellious house; they have eyes to see, but do not see,
and ears to hear but do not hear. They are such
a rebellious house!* 3 Now, son of man, during
the day while they watch, pack a bag for exile,†
and again while they watch, go into exile from
your place to another place; perhaps they will see
that they are a rebellious house. 4 During the day,
while they watch, bring out your bag, an exile's
bag. In the evening, again while they watch, go
out as if into exile.* 5 While they watch, dig a
hole through the wall† and go out through it.
6 While they watch, shoulder your load and go
out in darkness. Cover your face so you cannot
see the land, for I am making you a sign for the
house of Israel!*
7 I did just as I was commanded. During the
day I brought out my bag, an exile's bag. In the
evening while they watched, I dug a hole through
the wall with my hands and set out in darkness,
shouldering my load.
8 In the morning, the word of the LORD came
to me: 9 Son of man, did not the house of Israel,
that house of rebels, say, "What are you doing?"*
10 Tell them: Thus says the Lord GOD: This load is
the prince in Jerusalem and the whole house of
Israel within it. 11 Say, I am a sign for you: just as I
have done, so it shall be done to them; into exile,
as captives they shall go.* 12 The prince among

†

11:15–21 Ezekiel insists that those who remained in Judah are doomed; the exiles, under a new covenant, will constitute a new Israel. Cf. chap. 36; Jer 24:7; 29.

11:23 The glory of the Lord departs toward the east, to the exiles in Babylon; it will return once the Temple is rebuilt (43:1–3).

12:3–10 An exile's bag contains bare necessities, probably no more than a bowl, a mat, and a waterskin. The prophet's action foreshadows the fate of ruler and people (vv. 11–14).

12:5 *Through the wall*: mud-brick outer wall of a private home. In this symbolic action, Ezekiel represents the enemy forces, and the house wall, the city wall of Jerusalem breached by the Babylonian army.

*

11:15 Ez 33:24.
11:17 Ez 34:13; 36:28.
11:19 Ez 18:31; 36:26; 2 Cor 3:3.
11:20 Ex 6:7; Jer 31:33; 32:38.
11:22 Ex 24:16.
11:23 Zec 14:4.
11:24 Ez 37:1.
11:25 Ez 3:4, 11.
12:2 Is 6:9–10; Jer 5:21; cf. Mt 13:15; Mk 4:12; 8:18.
12:4 2 Kgs 25:4.
12:6 Is 8:18.
12:9 Ez 20:49; 24:19.
12:11 2 Kgs 25:7; Jer 52:15.

them shall shoulder his load in darkness and go out through the hole they dug in the wall to bring him out. His face shall be covered so that he cannot even see the ground.* 13 * I will spread my net over him and he shall be caught in my snare. I will bring him into Babylon, to the land of the Chaldeans, though he shall not see it,† and there he shall die. 14 All his retinue, his aides and all his troops, I will scatter to the winds and pursue them with the sword.* 15 Then they shall know that I am the LORD, when I disperse them among the nations and scatter them throughout the lands.* 16 But I will let a few of them escape the sword, starvation, and plague, so that they may recount all their abominations among the nations to which they go. Thus they may know that I am the LORD.†

17 The word of the LORD came to me: 18 Son of man, eat your bread trembling and drink your water shaking with fear.* 19 And say to the people of the land:† Thus says the Lord GOD about the inhabitants of Jerusalem in the land of Israel: they shall eat their bread in fear and drink their water in horror, because the land will be emptied of what fills it—the lawlessness of all its inhabitants. 20 Inhabited cities shall be in ruins, the land a desolate place. Then you shall know that I am the LORD.

Prophecy Ridiculed

21 The word of the LORD came to me: 22 Son of man, what is this proverb you have in the land of Israel: "The days drag on, and every vision fails"?† * 23 Say to them therefore: Thus says the Lord GOD: I will put an end to that proverb; they shall never use it again in Israel. Say to them instead: "The days are at hand and every vision fulfilled."* 24 No longer shall there be any false visions or deceitful divinations within the house of Israel,* 25 for whatever word I speak shall happen without delay. In your days, rebellious house, whatever I speak I will bring about—oracle of the Lord GOD.*

26 The word of the LORD came to me: 27 Son of man, listen! The house of Israel is saying, "The vision he sees is a long time off; he prophesies for distant times!"* 28 Say to them therefore: Thus says the Lord GOD: None of my words shall be delayed any longer. Whatever I say is final; it shall be done—oracle of the Lord GOD.

Against the Prophets of Peace

13 1 The word of the LORD came to me: 2 Son of man, prophesy against the prophets of Israel, prophesy! Say to those who prophesy their own thoughts: Hear the word of the LORD!* 3 Thus says the Lord GOD: Woe to those prophets, the fools who follow their own spirit and see nothing.* 4 Like foxes among ruins are your prophets, Israel! 5 You did not step into the breach, nor repair the wall around the house of Israel so it would stand firm against attack on the day of the LORD. 6 False visions! Lying divinations! They say, "The oracle of the LORD," even though the LORD did not send them. Then they expect their word to be confirmed!* 7 Was not the vision you saw false? Did you not report a lying divination when you said, "Oracle of the LORD," even though I never spoke? 8 Therefore thus says the Lord GOD: Because you have spoken falsehood and seen lying visions, therefore, for certain I am coming at you—oracle of the Lord GOD. 9 My hand is against the prophets who see false visions and who make lying divinations. They shall not belong to the community of my people. They shall not be written in the register of the house of Israel, nor shall they enter the land of Israel. Thus you shall know that I am the LORD.*

10 Because they led my people astray, saying, "Peace!" when there is no peace, and when a wall is built, they cover it with whitewash,† 11 say then to the whitewashers: I will bring down a flooding rain; hailstones shall fall, and a stormwind shall break forth.* 12 When the wall has fallen, will you not be asked: "Where is the whitewash you spread on it?"

13 Therefore thus says the Lord GOD: In my fury I will let loose stormwinds; because of my anger there will be flooding rain, and hailstones will fall with destructive wrath.* 14 I will tear down the wall you whitewashed and level it to

EZ

†

12:13 *Though he shall not see it*: according to a Targum, an allusion to Nebuchadnezzar having Zedekiah blinded before deporting him to Babylonia (cf. 2 Kgs 25:7); according to the Septuagint, the king is ashamed of his flight from the city and disguises himself so others will not recognize him.

12:16 Both exiles and nations shall know that the exile is divine punishment for Israel's betrayal of the Lord and the covenant, not evidence that the Lord is too weak to fight off the Babylonian deity.

12:19 *The people of the land*: the exiles in Babylon who, ironically, are now outside the land.

12:22–28 This proverb conveys the skepticism the people of Jerusalem have; cf. Jer 20:7–9.

13:10 The false prophets contributed to popular illusions of security by predictions of peace, like those who whitewash a wall to conceal its defects.

*

12:12 Jer 23:33; 52:7.
12:13 Ez 17:20; 19:8; 32:3.
12:14 2 Kgs 25:5; Jer 21:7.
12:15 Lv 26:33.
12:18 Lam 5:9.
12:22 Ps 49:4.
12:23 Ez 7:7.
12:24 Ez 13:23; Jer 14:14; Zec 13:2–4.
12:25 Hb 2:3.
12:27 cf. Mt 24:48; 2 Pt 3:4.
13:2 Jer 23:16, 21–22; 28:15.
13:3 Ez 14:9; Nm 16:28; Is 32:6; Jer 23:1, 16, 25–40; Mi 2:11.
13:6 cf. Is 30:10.
13:9 Ex 32:32.
13:11 cf. Ps 18:7–15; 77:17–18.
13:13 Rev 11:19; 16:21.

the ground, laying bare its foundations. When it falls, you shall be crushed beneath it. Thus you shall know that I am the LORD. 15 When I have poured out my fury on the wall and its whitewashers, it will fall. Then I will say to you: No wall! No whitewashers— 16 the prophets of Israel who prophesy to Jerusalem and see visions of peace for it when there is no peace—oracle of the Lord GOD.*

Against Witches

17 As for you, son of man, now set your face against the daughters of your people who play the prophet from their own thoughts, and prophesy against them.* 18 You shall say, Thus says the Lord GOD: Woe to those who sew amulets for the wrists of every arm and make veils† for every head size to snare lives! You ensnare the lives of my people, even as you preserve your own lives! 19 You have profaned me among my people for handfuls of barley and crumbs of bread,† slaying those who should not be slain, and keeping alive those who should not live, lying to my people, who listen to lies. 20 Therefore thus says the Lord GOD: See! I am coming after your amulets by which you ensnare lives like prey. I will tear them from your arms and set free the lives of those you have ensnared like prey.* 21 I will tear off your veils and deliver my people from your power, so that they shall never again be ensnared by your hands. Thus you shall know that I am the LORD. 22 Because you discourage the righteous with lies when I did not want them to be distressed, and encourage the wicked so they do not turn from their evil ways and save their lives,* 23 therefore you shall no longer see false visions or practice divination again. I will deliver my people from your hand. Thus you shall know that I am the LORD.

Idolatry and Unfaithfulness

14 1 Some elders of Israel came and sat down before me.* 2 Then the word of the LORD came to me: 3 Son of man, these men keep the memory of their idols alive in their hearts, setting the stumbling block of their sin before them. Should I allow myself to be consulted by them? 4 Therefore say to them: Thus says the Lord GOD: If any of the house of Israel who keep the memory of their idols in their hearts, setting the stumbling block of their sin before them, come to a prophet, I the LORD will answer in person because of their many idols, 5 in order to catch the hearts of the house of Israel, estranged from me because of all their idols.

6 Therefore say to the house of Israel: Thus says the Lord GOD: Return, turn away from your idols; from all your abominations, turn your faces.* 7 For if anyone of the house of Israel or any alien residing in Israel who are estranged from me and who keep their idols in their hearts, setting the stumbling block of their sin before them, come to ask a prophet to consult me on their behalf, I the LORD will answer them in person. 8 I will set my face against them and make them a sign and a byword, and cut them off from the midst of my people. Thus you shall know that I am the LORD.

9 * As for the prophet, if he speaks a deceiving word, I the LORD am the one who deceives that prophet.† I will stretch out my hand against him and destroy him from the midst of my people Israel. 10 They will be punished for their own sins, the inquirer and the prophet alike, 11 so that the house of Israel may no longer stray from me, no longer defile themselves by all their sins. Then they shall be my people, and I shall be their God—oracle of the Lord GOD.

Just Cause†

12 The word of the LORD came to me: 13 * Son of man, if a land sins against me by breaking faith, and I stretch out my hand against it, breaking its staff of bread and setting famine loose upon it, cutting off from it human being and beast alike— 14 even if these three were in it, Noah, Daniel, and Job,† they could only save themselves by their righteousness—oracle of the Lord GOD.* 15 If I summoned wild beasts to prowl the land, depopulating it so that it became a wasteland which no one would cross because

†

13:18 *Sew amulets . . . make veils*: used by sorcerers to mark individuals for life or for death. For a small price (v. 19), these women promised protection for the wicked, who, in the Lord's estimation, "should not live" (v. 19), and death for the righteous, "who should not be slain" (v. 19). Both decisions belong to the Lord.

13:19 *Handfuls of barley and crumbs of bread*: payment for the amulets and scarves.

14:9 The ancient Israelites thought that God could use deception as a means of promoting divine justice; cf. 2 Sm 24:1–3; 1 Kgs 22:19–23.

14:12–23 According to Ezekiel, the people in Jerusalem deserve destruction because they are corrupt. Yet he admits an exception to the principle of individual responsibility when he affirms that some of those deserving death will survive and be reunited with family in exile. The depravity of Jerusalem testifies that the punishment of Jerusalem was just and necessary.

14:14 *Noah, Daniel, and Job*: righteous folk heroes whom Israel shared with other ancient Near Eastern cultures. Daniel was the just judge celebrated in Ugaritic literature, perhaps the model for the hero of Dn 13.

*

13:16 Jer 6:14.
13:17 Rev 2:20.
13:20 Ps 124:7.
13:22 Ez 18:21; 33:14–16.
14:1 Ez 8:1; 20:1.
14:6 Is 2:20; cf. Ez 18:30; 33:11.
14:9 cf. 1 Kgs 22:23; 2 Chr 18:22.
14:13 Lv 26:26.
14:14 Ez 28:3; Dn 1:6; cf. Gn 6:9; Jb 1:1.

of the wild beasts,* 16 and these three were in it,
as I live—oracle of the Lord GOD—I swear they
could save neither sons nor daughters; they alone
would be saved, but the land would become a
wasteland.* 17 Or if I bring the sword upon this
land, commanding the sword to pass through
the land cutting off from it human being and
beast alike,* 18 and these three were in it, as I
live—oracle of the Lord GOD—they could save
neither sons nor daughters; they alone would
be saved. 19 Or if I send plague into this land,
pouring out upon it my bloody wrath, cutting off
from it human being and beast alike, 20 even if
Noah, Daniel, and Job were in it, as I live—oracle
of the Lord GOD—they could save neither son
nor daughter; they would save only themselves
by their righteousness.
21 Thus says the Lord GOD: Even though I send
against Jerusalem my four evil punishments—
sword, famine, wild beasts, and plague—to cut
off from it human being and beast alike,* 22 there
will still be some survivors in it who will bring
out sons and daughters. When they come out to
you and you see their ways and their deeds, you
shall be consoled regarding the evil I brought on
Jerusalem, everything I brought upon it. 23 They
shall console you when you see their ways and
their deeds, and you shall know that not without
reason did I do to it everything I did—oracle of
the Lord GOD.*

Parable of the Vine

15 1 † The word of the LORD came to me:

2 Son of man,
what makes the wood of the vine
Better than the wood of branches
found on the trees in the forest?*
3 Can wood be taken from it
to make something useful?
Can someone make even a peg out of it
on which to hang a vessel?
4 Of course not! If it is fed to the fire for fuel,
and the fire devours both ends of it,
Leaving the middle charred,
is it useful for anything then?
5 Even when it is whole
it cannot be used for anything;
So when fire has devoured and charred it,
how useful can it be?
6 Therefore, thus says the Lord GOD:
Like vine wood among forest trees,
which I have given as fuel for fire,
So I will give the inhabitants of Jerusalem.
7 I will set my face against them:
Although they have escaped the fire,
the fire will still devour them;
You shall know that I am the LORD,
when I set my face against them.*
8 Yes, I will make the land desolate,
because they are so unfaithful—
oracle of the Lord GOD.

A Parable of Infidelity

16 1 The word of the LORD came to me: 2 Son
of man, make known to Jerusalem her
abominations.* 3 You shall say, Thus says the
Lord GOD to Jerusalem: By origin and birth you
belong to the land of the Canaanites; your father
was an Amorite, your mother a Hittite.† * 4 † As
for your birth, on the day you were born your
navel cord was not cut; you were not washed
with water or anointed; you were not rubbed
with salt or wrapped in swaddling clothes.* 5 No
eye looked on you with pity or compassion to
do any of these things for you. Rather, on the
day you were born you were left out in the field,
rejected.
6 Then I passed by and saw you struggling in
your blood, and I said to you in your blood,
"Live!" 7 I helped you grow up like a field plant,
so that you grew, maturing into a woman with
breasts developed and hair grown; but still you
were stark naked. 8 I passed by you again and
saw that you were now old enough for love. So I
spread the corner of my cloak† over you to cover
your nakedness; I swore an oath to you and en-
tered into covenant with you—oracle of the Lord
GOD—and you became mine.* 9 Then I bathed
you with water, washed away your blood, and

†

15:1–8 Verses 2–5 point out that the wood of the vinestock may be burned for fuel, fit only for destruction. In vv. 6–8 Ezekiel asserts that Jerusalem has the same destiny.

16:3–4 *By origin and birth . . . Hittite*: Jerusalem's pre-Israelite origins are the breeding ground for its inability to respond faithfully to the Lord's generosity.

16:4–5 In this chapter, Ezekiel represents Jerusalem and Samaria as unwanted, abandoned sisters whom the Lord rescues and cares for. Here the prophet depicts Jerusalem as a newborn female, abandoned and left to die, an accepted practice in antiquity for females, who were considered financial liabilities by their families. That the infant has no one, not even her mother, to tie off her umbilical cord, wash her clean, and wrap her in swaddling clothes emphasizes Jerusalem's death-like isolation and accentuates the Lord's gracious action in her behalf. The practice of rubbing the skin of newborns with salt is an attested Palestinian custom that survived into the twentieth century.

16:8 *I spread the corner of my cloak*: one way to acquire a woman for marriage; cf. Ru 3:9. In Dt 23:1 a son's illicit sexual relations with his father's wife is described as "uncovering the edge of the father's garment."

*

14:15 cf. Lv 26:22.
14:16 cf. Ez 18:20.
14:17 Lv 26:25.
14:21 cf. Rev 6:8.
14:23 Jer 22:8–9.
15:2 cf. Ps 80; Is 5:1–7.
15:7 Is 24:18; Am 9:1–4.
16:2 cf. Ez 8:17.
16:3 cf. Dt 26:5; Gn 23:10; 48:22.
16:4 cf. Lk 2:2.
16:8 cf. Ez 16:59; Ru 3:9.

anointed you with oil.* 10 I clothed you with an embroidered gown, put leather sandals on your feet; I gave you a fine linen sash and silk robes to wear.* 11 I adorned you with jewelry, putting bracelets on your arms, a necklace about your neck,* 12 a ring in your nose, earrings in your ears, and a beautiful crown on your head. 13 Thus you were adorned with gold and silver; your garments made of fine linen, silk, and embroidered cloth. Fine flour, honey, and olive oil were your food. You were very, very beautiful, fit for royalty.* 14 You were renowned among the nations for your beauty, perfected by the splendor I showered on you—oracle of the Lord GOD.

15 But you trusted in your own beauty and used your renown to serve as a prostitute. You poured out your prostitution on every passerby—let it be his.* 16 † You took some of your garments and made for yourself gaudy high places, where you served as a prostitute. It has never happened before, nor will it happen again!* 17 You took the splendid gold and silver ornaments that I had given you and made for yourself male images and served as a prostitute with them. 18 You took your embroidered garments to cover them; my oil and my incense you set before them; 19 the food I had given you, the fine flour, the oil, and the honey with which I fed you, you set before them as a pleasant odor, says the Lord GOD.* 20 † * The sons and daughters you bore for me you took and offered as sacrifices for them to devour! Was it not enough that you had become a prostitute? 21 * You slaughtered and immolated my children to them, making them pass through fire. 22 In all your abominations and prostitutions you did not remember the days of your youth when you were stark naked, struggling in your blood.*

23 Then after all your evildoing—woe, woe to you! oracle of the Lord GOD— 24 you built yourself a platform and raised up a dais† in every public place.* 25 * At every intersection you built yourself a dais so that you could degrade your beauty by spreading your legs for every passerby, multiplying your prostitutions. 26 You served as a prostitute with the Egyptians, your big-membered neighbors, and multiplied your prostitutions to provoke me. 27 Therefore I stretched out my hand against you and reduced your allotment, and delivered you over to the whim of your enemies, the Philistines,† who were revolted by your depraved conduct.* 28 You also served as a prostitute for the Assyrians, because you were not satisfied. Even after serving as a prostitute for them, you were still not satisfied.* 29 You increased your prostitutions again, now going to Chaldea, the land of traders; but despite this, you were still not satisfied.*

30 How wild your lust!—oracle of the Lord GOD—that you did all these works of a shameless prostitute, 31 when you built your platform at every intersection and set up your high place in every public square. But unlike a prostitute, you disdained payment. 32 Adulterous wife, taking strangers in place of her husband! 33 Prostitutes usually receive gifts. But you bestowed gifts on all your lovers, bribing them to come to you for prostitution from every side.* 34 Thus in your prostitution you were different from any other woman. No one solicited you for prostitution. Instead, you yourself offered payment; what a reversal!

35 Therefore, prostitute, hear the word of the LORD! 36 Thus says the Lord GOD: Because you poured out your lust and exposed your nakedness in your prostitution with your lovers and your abominable idols, because you gave the life-blood of your children to them, 37 * therefore, I will now gather together all your lovers with whom you found pleasure, both those you loved and those you hated; I will gather them against you from all sides and expose you naked for them to see. 38 † I will inflict on you the sentence of adultery and murder; I will bring on you bloody wrath and jealous anger.* 39 I will hand you over to them to tear down your platform and demolish your high place, to strip you of your garments and take away your splendid ornaments, leaving you stark naked.* 40 They shall lead an assembly against you to stone you and

†

16:16 In the allegory of this chapter the viewpoint often shifts from the figure (prostitution) to the reality (idolatry). A symbol of the woman's depravity supersedes her parents' cruel abandonment when she was an infant. It overrides the loyalty she owes her covenant partner and the care she owes their children.

16:20–21 Also a reference to the practice of child sacrifice introduced under Judah's impious kings; cf. 2 Kgs 16:3; 17:17; Jer 7:31; 19:5; 32:35.

16:24 *A platform . . . a dais*: associated with rituals borrowed from the Canaanites.

16:27 *Philistines*: lit., "daughters of the Philistines," a common expression when referring to the various towns that make up a territory.

16:38 As a jealous husband, Yhwh severely punishes Jerusalem for her adultery: i.e., her worship of idols. Adultery was considered a capital crime in ancient Israel; cf. Lv 20:10–14; Nm 5:11–28; Dt 22:22.

*

16:9 cf. Ru 3:3.
16:10 cf. Ps 45:14.
16:11 cf. Ez 23:40–42.
16:13 Dt 32:13–14; Hos 2:8.
16:15 Is 57:7–8.
16:16 cf. 2 Kgs 23:7.
16:19 Hos 2:13.
16:20 Jer 7:31; cf. Lv 18:21; Dt 18:10; 2 Kgs 21:6; 23:10.
16:21 cf. 2 Kgs 16:3; 17:17.
16:22 Jer 2:2; Hos 2:15; 11:1.
16:24 Is 57:7.
16:25 Jer 2:20; 3:2; 5:7; Hos 2:4.
16:27 cf. 2 Chr 28:18.
16:28 2 Kgs 16:7.
16:29 cf. Ez 23:14–17.
16:33 Hos 8:9–10.
16:37 cf. Ez 23:10, 22; Is 47:3; Rev 17:16.
16:38 Lv 20:10; Dt 22:22.
16:39 cf. 2 Kgs 18:11.

hack you to pieces with their swords.* [41] * They
shall set fire to your homes and inflict punish-
ments on you while many women watch. Thus
I will put an end to your prostitution, and you
shall never again offer payment. [42] When I have
spent my fury upon you I will stop being jealous
about you, and calm down, no longer angry.
[43] Because you did not remember the days of
your youth but enraged me with all these things,
see, I am bringing down your ways upon your
head—oracle of the Lord God. Have you not
added depravity to your other abominations?

[44] See, everyone who makes proverbs will
make this proverb about you, "Like mother, like
daughter." [45] Yes, you are truly the daughter of
your mother† who rejected her husband and
children: you are truly a sister to your sisters
who rejected their husbands and children—your
mother was a Hittite and your father an Amo-
rite.* [46] † Your elder sister was Samaria with her
daughters to the north of you; and your youn-
ger sister was Sodom and her daughters, south
of you.* [47] Not only did you walk in their ways
and act as abominably as they did, but in a very
short time you became more corrupt in all your
ways than they were.* [48] As I live—oracle of the
Lord God—I swear that your sister Sodom with
her daughters have not done the things you and
your daughters have done!* [49] * Now look at the
guilt of your sister Sodom: she and her daughters
were proud, sated with food, complacent in pros-
perity. They did not give any help to the poor
and needy. [50] Instead, they became arrogant and
committed abominations before me; then, as
you have seen, I removed them.* [51] Samaria did
not commit half the sins you did. You have done
more abominable things than they did. You even
made your sisters look righteous, with all the
abominations you have done. [52] You, then, must
bear your disgrace, for you have made a case for
your sisters! Because your sins are more abomi-
nable than theirs, they seem righteous compared
to you. Blush for shame, and bear the disgrace of
having made your sisters appear righteous.

[53] I will restore their fortunes, the fortunes of
Sodom and her daughters, the fortunes of Samaria
and her daughters—and your fortunes along with
them. [54] Thus you must bear your disgrace and be
ashamed of all you have done to bring them com-
fort. [55] Yes, your sisters, Sodom and her daugh-
ters, Samaria and her daughters, shall return to
the way they were,* and you and your daughters
shall return to the way you were. [56] Did you not
hold your sister Sodom in bad repute while you
felt proud of yourself, [57] before your evil was ex-
posed? Now you are like her, reproached by the
Arameans and all their neighbors, despised on all
sides by the Philistines.* [58] The penalty of your
depravity and your abominations—you must
bear it all—oracle of the Lord.

[59] For thus says the Lord God: I will deal with you
for what you did; you despised an oath by breaking
a covenant.* [60] But I will remember the covenant I
made with you when you were young; I will set up
an everlasting covenant† with you.* [61] Then you
shall remember your ways and be ashamed when
you receive your sisters, those older and younger
than you; I give them to you as daughters, but not
by reason of your covenant. [62] For I will re-establish
my covenant with you, that you may know that I
am the Lord,* [63] that you may remember and be
ashamed, and never again open your mouth be-
cause of your disgrace, when I pardon you for all
you have done—oracle of the Lord God.*

The Eagles and the Vine

17 [1] The word of the Lord came to me: [2] Son
of man, propose a riddle, and tell this
proverb to the house of Israel: [3] Thus says the
Lord God:

The great eagle, with wide wingspan
  and long feathers, with thick plumage,
  many-hued, came to Lebanon.
He plucked the crest of the cedar,*
4 broke off its topmost branch,
And brought it to a land of merchants,
  set it in a city of traders.
5 Then he took some native seed
  and planted it in fertile soil;
A shoot beside plentiful waters,
  like a willow he planted it,*

16:45 *Truly the daughter of your mother*: Jerusalem's depraved behavior follows from the bad behavior of its non-Israelite forebears; cf. v. 3.

16:46–47 Jerusalem is so much more corrupt than Samaria, the elder sister in size, and the smaller Sodom that both now appear just and righteous. Ezekiel's reference to Sodom indicates that the city's identification with wickedness and evil was already an established tradition in fifth century B.C. Judah.

16:60 *Everlasting covenant*: Ezekiel foresees God renewing the covenant of Sinai in a new and spirit-empowered way that will not be fatally broken as in the present exile or force God to abandon Israel again; cf. 11:19–21; 36:25–27; 37:26–28.

16:40 cf. Ez 23:47; Jn 8:5, 7.
16:41 2 Kgs 25:9; cf. Jgs 12:1; 15:6.
16:45 cf. Ez 23:2.
16:46 Jer 3:8–11; Rev 11:8.
16:47 cf. Dt 29:23; 32:32; Is 1:9–10.
16:48 cf. Gn 19:25; Mt 10:15; 11:23–24.
16:49 cf. Is 1:10; cf. Gn 49:24.
16:50 cf. Gn 18:20–21.
16:55 cf. Ez 36:11.
16:57 cf. Ez 25:12–14; 35:1–15; 2 Kgs 16:6.
16:59 cf. Ez 17:19.
16:60 cf. Ez 37:26; Is 55:3; Jer 32:40.
16:62 Dt 29:14.
16:63 Dn 9:7–8.
17:3 Dt 28:49; Jer 49:22; Dn 7:4.
17:5 cf. 2 Kgs 24:17.

6 That it might sprout and become a vine,
dense and low-lying,
With its branches turned toward him,
its roots beneath it.
Thus it became a vine, produced branches,
and put forth shoots.
7 Then another great eagle appeared,
with wide wingspan, rich in plumage,
And see! This vine bent its roots to him,
sent out branches for him to water.
From the bed where it was planted,*
8 it was transplanted to a fertile field
By abundant waters, to produce branches,
to bear fruit, to become a majestic vine.
9 Say: Thus says the Lord GOD: Can it thrive?
Will he not tear up its roots
and strip its fruit?
Then all its green leaves will wither—
neither strong arm nor mighty nation
is needed to uproot it.
10 True, it is planted; but will it thrive?
Will it not wither up
When the east wind strikes it,
wither in the very bed where it sprouted?*

11 † The word of the LORD came to me:

12 Now say to the rebellious house:
Do you not understand this? Tell them!
The king of Babylon came to Jerusalem
and took away its king and officials
and brought them to him in Babylon.*
13 After removing the nobles from the land,
he then took one of the royal line
And made a covenant with him,
binding him under oath,*
14 To be a humble kingdom,
without high aspirations,
to keep his covenant and so survive.
15 But this one rebelled against him
by sending envoys to Egypt
To obtain horses and a mighty army.
Can he thrive?
Can he escape if he does this?
Can he break a covenant and go free?*
16 As I live—oracle of the Lord GOD—
in the house of the king who set him up to
rule,
Whose oath he ignored and whose covenant
he broke,
there in Babylon I swear he shall die!*
17 Pharaoh shall not help him on the day of
battle,
with a great force and mighty horde,
When ramps are thrown up and siege works
built
for the cutting down of many lives.
18 He ignored his oath, breaking his covenant;
even though he gave his hand, he did all
these things—
he shall not escape!*
19 Therefore, thus says the Lord GOD:
As I live, my oath which he spurned,
And my covenant which he broke,
I will bring down on his head.
20 I will spread my net over him,
and he will be caught in my snare.
I will bring him to Babylon
to judge him there
because he broke faith with me.*
21 Any among his forces who escape
will fall by the sword,
And whoever might survive
will be scattered to the winds.*
Thus you will know that I the LORD have
spoken.
22 Thus says the Lord GOD:
I, too, will pluck from the crest of the cedar
the highest branch.
From the top a tender shoot
I will break off and transplant†
on a high, lofty mountain.
23 On the mountain height of Israel
I will plant it.
It shall put forth branches and bear fruit,
and become a majestic cedar.
Every small bird will nest under it,
all kinds of winged birds will dwell
in the shade of its branches.*
24 Every tree of the field will know
that I am the LORD.
I bring low the high tree,
lift high the lowly tree,
Wither up the green tree,
and make the dry tree bloom.*
As I, the LORD, have spoken, so will I do!

†

17:11–21 These verses explain the allegory in vv. 3–10. In 597 B.C., Nebuchadnezzar removed Jehoiachin from the throne and took him into exile; in his place he set Zedekiah, Jehoiachin's uncle, on the throne and received from him the oath of loyalty. But Zedekiah was persuaded to rebel by Pharaoh Hophra of Egypt and thus deserved punishment; cf. 2 Kgs 24:10–25:7.

17:22–23 The Lord will undo the actions of the Babylonian king by rebuilding the Davidic dynasty so the nations realize that only Israel's God can restore a people's destiny.

*

17:7 cf. Ez 31:4–5; Jer 37:5; 44:30.
17:10 cf. Ez 19:12.
17:12 2 Kgs 24:15.
17:13 2 Chr 36:13.
17:15 Jer 52:3.
17:16 2 Kgs 24:17; 25:7; Jer 52:11.
17:18 cf. 2 Kgs 10:15.
17:20 cf. Ez 12:13; 32:3.
17:21 Lv 26:33; 2 Kgs 25:5.
17:23 Dn 4:12; Hos 14:5–7.
17:24 Dn 5:21.

Personal Responsibility

18 1 The word of the LORD came to me: Son of
man, 2 what is the meaning of this proverb
you recite in the land of Israel:

"Parents eat sour grapes,*
but the children's teeth are set on edge"?†

3 As I live—oracle of the Lord GOD: I swear that
none of you will ever repeat this proverb in Is-
rael. 4 For all life is mine: the life of the parent is
like the life of the child, both are mine. Only the
one who sins shall die!

5 If a man is just—if he does what is right, 6 if he
does not eat on the mountains,† or raise his eyes
to the idols of the house of Israel; if he does not
defile a neighbor's wife, or have relations with a
woman during her period;* 7 * if he oppresses
no one, gives back the pledge received for a debt,
commits no robbery; gives food to the hungry
and clothes the naked; 8 if he does not lend at in-
terest or exact usury; if he refrains from evildoing
and makes a fair judgment between two oppo-
nents;* 9 if he walks by my statutes and is careful
to observe my ordinances, that man is just—he
shall surely live—oracle of the Lord GOD.*

10 But if he begets a son who is violent and
commits murder, or does any of these things,*
11 even though the father does none of them—a
son who eats on the mountains, defiles the wife
of his neighbor, 12 oppresses the poor and needy,
commits robbery, does not give back a pledge,
raises his eyes to idols, does abominable things,
13 lends at interest and exacts usury—this son
certainly shall not live. Because he practiced all
these abominations, he shall surely be put to
death; his own blood shall be on him.*

14 But, in turn, if he begets a son who sees all
the sins his father commits, yet fears and does
not imitate him— 15 a son who does not eat on
the mountains, or raise his eyes to the idols of
the house of Israel, or defile a neighbor's wife;
16 who does not oppress anyone, or exact a
pledge, or commit robbery; who gives his food
to the hungry and clothes the naked;* 17 who
refrains from evildoing, accepts no interest or
usury, but keeps my ordinances and walks in
my statutes—this one shall not die for the sins
of his father. He shall surely live! 18 Only the fa-
ther, since he committed extortion and robbed
his brother, and did what was not good among
his people—he will die because of his sin! 19 You
ask: "Why is not the son charged with the guilt of
his father?" Because the son has done what is just
and right and has been careful to observe all my
statutes—he shall surely live! 20 * Only the one
who sins shall die. The son shall not be charged
with the guilt of his father, nor shall the father be
charged with the guilt of his son. Justice belongs
to the just, and wickedness to the wicked.

21 But if the wicked man turns away from all
the sins he has committed, if he keeps all my
statutes and does what is just and right, he shall
surely live. He shall not die! 22 None of the crimes
he has committed shall be remembered against
him; he shall live because of the justice he has
shown. 23 * Do I find pleasure in the death of the
wicked—oracle of the Lord GOD? Do I not rejoice
when they turn from their evil way and live?

24 And if the just turn from justice and do evil,
like all the abominations the wicked do, can they
do this evil and still live? None of the justice they
did shall be remembered, because they acted
treacherously and committed these sins; because
of this, they shall die.* 25 * You say, "The LORD's
way is not fair!"† Hear now, house of Israel: Is it
my way that is unfair? Are not your ways unfair?
26 When the just turn away from justice to do
evil and die, on account of the evil they did they
must die. 27 But if the wicked turn from the wick-
edness they did and do what is right and just,
they save their lives; 28 since they turned away
from all the sins they committed, they shall live;
they shall not die. 29 But the house of Israel says,
"The Lord's way is not fair!" Is it my way that is
not fair, house of Israel? Is it not your ways that
are not fair?

30 * Therefore I will judge you, house of Israel,
all of you according to your ways—oracle of the
Lord GOD. Turn, turn back from all your crimes,
that they may not be a cause of sin for you ever
again. 31 Cast away from you all the crimes you
have committed, and make for yourselves a new
heart and a new spirit. Why should you die,
house of Israel?* 32 * For I find no pleasure in the

†

18:2 *Parents . . . on edge*: a proverb the people quoted to complain that they were being punished for their ancestors' sins; cf. Jer 31:29.

18:6 *Eat on the mountains*: take part in meals after sacrifice at the high places.

18:25 *The LORD's way is not fair*: this chapter rejects the idea that punishment is transferred from one generation to the next and emphasizes individual responsibility and accountability.

*

18:2 Jer 31:29; cf. Ez 21:19.
18:6 Lv 15:19–24; cf. Hos 4:13.
18:7 Ex 22:26; Is 58:7; Mt 25:35.
18:8 Ex 22:25; Lv 25:35–37; Dt 23:19–20.
18:9 Lv 18:5.
18:10 cf. Ez 22:6–9.
18:13 Ex 22:25; Lv 20:9–11.
18:16 cf. Ez 16:49; Is 58:7–10.
18:20 Dt 24:16; 2 Kgs 14:6; cf. Mt 16:27; Jn 9:2.
18:23 cf. Ez 33:11; 2 Pt 3:9.
18:24 cf. 2 Pt 2:20–22.
18:25 cf. Ez 33:20.
18:30 Jer 35:15; cf. Mt 3:2; Lk 3:3.
18:31 cf. Ez 11:19; 36:26.
18:32 cf. Ez 18:23; 33:11.

death of anyone who dies—oracle of the Lord GOD. Turn back and live!

Allegory of the Lions†

19 1 As for you, raise a lamentation over the
princes of Israel, 2 and say:

What a lioness was your mother,
a lion among lions!
She made her lair among young lions,
to raise her cubs;
3 One cub she raised up,
a young lion he became;
He learned to tear apart prey,
he devoured people.*
4 Nations heard about him;
in their pit he was caught;
They took him away with hooks
to the land of Egypt.† *
5 When she realized she had waited in vain,
she lost hope.
She took another of her cubs,
and made him a young lion.
6 He prowled among the lions,
became a young lion;
He learned to tear apart prey,
he devoured people.*
7 He ravaged their strongholds,
laid waste their cities.
The earth and everything in it were terrified
at the sound of his roar.
8 Nations laid out against him
snares all around;
They spread their net for him,
in their pit he was caught.*
9 They put him in fetters and took him away
to the king of Babylon,
So his roar would no longer be heard
on the mountains of Israel.

Allegory of the Vine Branch

10 Your mother was like a leafy vine†
planted by water,
Fruitful and full of branches
because of abundant water.
11 One strong branch grew
into a royal scepter.
So tall it towered among the clouds,
conspicuous in height,
with dense foliage.*
12 But she was torn out in fury
and flung to the ground;
The east wind withered her up,
her fruit was plucked away;
Her strongest branch dried up,
fire devoured it.*
13 Now she is planted in a wilderness,
in a dry, parched land.*
14 Fire flashed from her branch,
and devoured her shoots;
Now she does not have a strong branch,
a royal scepter!

This is a lamentation and serves as a lamentation.

Israel's History of Infidelity

20 1 In the seventh year, on the tenth day
of the fifth month,† some of the elders
of Israel came to consult the LORD and sat down
before me.* 2 Then the word of the LORD came
to me: 3 Son of man, speak to the elders of Israel
and say to them: Thus says the Lord GOD: Have
you come to consult me? As I live, I will not allow myself to be consulted by you!—oracle of
the Lord GOD.
4 Will you judge them? Will you judge, son
of man? Tell them about the abominations of
their ancestors,* 5 and say to them: Thus says
the Lord GOD: The day I chose Israel, I swore to
the descendants of the house of Jacob; I revealed
myself to them in the land of Egypt and swore to
them, saying: I am the LORD, your God. 6 That day
I swore to bring them out of the land of Egypt
to the land I had searched out for them, a land
flowing with milk and honey, a jewel among all
lands.* 7 Then I said to them: Throw away, each
of you, the detestable things† that held your
eyes; do not defile yourselves with the idols of
Egypt: I am the LORD, your God.*
8 But they rebelled and refused to listen to me;
none of them threw away the detestable things

†

19:1–9 Some commentators identify Jehoahaz and Zedekiah, sons of the same mother, as the "two young lions"; they were deported to Egypt and Babylon respectively. Cf. 2 Kgs 23:31–34; 24:18–20.

19:4 A common fate for royal prisoners: e.g., Assurbanipal claims he put a ring in the jaw of a captive king and a dog collar around his neck (cf. v. 9). A wall relief shows Esarhaddon holding two royal captives with ropes tied to rings in their lips.

19:10–14 *Vine*: Judah. *One strong branch*: the Davidic king. This allegory describes the deportation of the Davidic dynasty to Babylon and laments the destruction of the house of David. From Ezekiel's perspective, the arrogance of Judah's kings leads to this tragedy (vv. 12–14).

20:1 *The seventh year . . . the fifth month*: August 14, 591 B.C.

20:7 *Detestable things*: in the Book of Ezekiel, Israel's continued worship of idols in Egypt and in the wilderness, despite the Lord's powerful deeds on their behalf, is the reason God punishes them so severely; they must learn and acknowledge that he is their only Lord. Cf., e.g., Exodus (5:1–6:9; 14:10–30; 16:1–36) and Numbers (11:1–15; 14:1–12; 20:1–9), where the people's failure to trust Moses and the Lord brings punishment.

*

19:3 2 Kgs 23:31–34.
19:4 2 Chr 36:4.
19:6 2 Kgs 24:9.
19:8 2 Kgs 24:2–15.
19:11 Dn 4:11.
19:12 Hos 13:15.
19:13 cf. Ez 20:35.
20:1 cf. Ez 8:1.
20:4 cf. Ez 16:2; Mt 23:32.
20:6 Ex 3:8; 6:8; Dt 8:7–10.
20:7 Ex 20:2–4.

that held their eyes, nor did they abandon the
idols of Egypt. Then I considered pouring out my
fury and spending my anger against them there
in the land of Egypt.* 9 I acted for the sake of my
name, that it should not be desecrated in the eyes
of the nations among whom they were: in the
eyes of the nations I had made myself known to
them, to bring them out of the land of Egypt.*
10 Therefore I led them out of the land of Egypt
and brought them into the wilderness. 11 * Then
I gave them my statutes and made known to
them my ordinances, so that everyone who keeps
them has life through them. 12 * I also gave them
my sabbaths to be a sign between me and them,
to show that it is I, the LORD, who makes them
holy.

13 But the house of Israel rebelled against me in
the wilderness. They did not observe my statutes,
and they rejected my ordinances that bring life to
those who keep them. My sabbaths, too, they des-
ecrated grievously. Then I considered pouring out
my fury on them in the wilderness to put an end
to them,* 14 but I acted for the sake of my name,
so it would not be desecrated in the eyes of the
nations in whose sight I had brought them out.*
15 Nevertheless in the wilderness I swore to them
that I would not bring them into the land I had
given them—a land flowing with milk and honey,
a jewel among all the lands. 16 Their hearts fol-
lowed after their idols so closely that they did not
live by my statutes, but rejected my ordinances
and desecrated my sabbaths. 17 But I looked on
them with pity, not wanting to destroy them, so I
did not put an end to them in the wilderness.

18 Then I said to their children in the wilder-
ness: Do not follow the statutes of your parents.
Do not keep their ordinances. Do not defile
yourselves with their idols. 19 I am the LORD, your
God: follow my statutes and be careful to ob-
serve my ordinances; 20 keep holy my sabbaths
as a sign between me and you so that you may
know that I am the LORD, your God.* 21 But their
children rebelled against me: they did not follow
my statutes or keep my ordinances that bring life
to those who observe them; my sabbaths they
desecrated. Then I considered pouring out my
fury on them, spending my anger against them in
the wilderness; 22 but I stayed my hand, acting for
the sake of my name, lest it be desecrated in the
eyes of the nations, in whose sight I had brought
them out. 23 Nevertheless I swore to them in the
wilderness that I would disperse them among
the nations and scatter them in other lands, 24 be-
cause they did not carry out my ordinances, but
rejected my statutes and desecrated my sabbaths,
having eyes only for the idols of their ancestors.
25 Therefore I gave them statutes that were not
good,† and ordinances through which they could
not have life.* 26 I let them become defiled by
their offerings, by having them make a fiery of-
fering of every womb's firstborn, in order to ruin
them so they might know that I am the LORD.*

27 Therefore speak to the house of Israel, son
of man, and tell them: Thus says the Lord GOD:
In this way also your ancestors blasphemed me,
breaking faith with me. 28 When I brought them
to the land I had sworn to give them, and they
saw all its high hills and leafy trees, there they
offered sacrifices, there they made offerings to
provoke me, there they sent up sweet-smelling
oblations, there they poured out their libations.*
29 So I said to them, "What is this high place†
to which you go?" Thus its name became "high
place" even to this day.* 30 Therefore say to the
house of Israel: Thus says the Lord GOD: Will
you defile yourselves in the way your ancestors
did? Will you lust after their detestable idols?
31 By offering your gifts, by making your children
pass through the fire, you defile yourselves with
all your idols even to this day. Shall I let myself
be consulted by you, house of Israel? As I live—
oracle of the Lord GOD—I swear I will not let
myself be consulted by you!*

32 What has entered your mind shall never
happen: You are thinking, "We shall be like the
nations, like the peoples of foreign lands, serving
wood and stone." 33 As I live—oracle of the Lord
GOD—with mighty hand and outstretched arm,
with wrath poured out, I swear I will be king over
you!* 34 With mighty hand and outstretched arm,
with wrath poured out, I will bring you out from
the nations and gather you from the countries

†

20:25–26 *I gave them statutes that were not good*: because Israel rejected the Lord's life-giving laws, he "gave" laws (e.g., the sacrifice of every firstborn) that would lead only to death and destruction. Dt 12:29–31; Jer 7:31; 19:4–5 may address a popular assumption that the Lord accepted and perhaps required child sacrifice, especially as evidence of great trust during national emergencies (2 Kgs 3:27; Mi 6:7). By combining language from Ex 22:28 with the vocabulary of child sacrifice, Ezekiel suggests that firstborn sons were regularly sacrificed in Israel.

20:29 *High place*: a cultic site, originally a hilltop, but often a raised platform in a sacred area. Until Deuteronomy's insistence that official and legitimate worship of the Lord take place only in Jerusalem, these local shrines were popular places for worship (e.g., 1 Sm 9–10) or for consulting the Lord (1 Kgs 3:4–5). In order to unite the Kingdom of Judah politically and religiously, Dt 12:2 demands destruction of the high places. Ezekiel, like other prophets, condemns Israelite worship at these places and identifies this illegitimate worship as one reason for the punishment of exile.

*

20:8 cf. Ez 16:26; Ex 32:7.
20:9 cf. Ez 36:22.
20:11 Lv 18:5; Dt 4:7–8; Rom 10:5.
20:12 Ex 20:8, 10; 31:13; Dt 5:12; Neh 13:17–18.
20:13 Jer 11:7–8; 17:21–23.
20:14 Is 48:11.
20:20 Ex 31:13.
20:25 cf. Rom 1:28.
20:26 Lv 18:21.
20:28 Ps 78:57–58.
20:29 cf. Ez 16:16.
20:31 Ps 106:37–39.
20:33 Dt 4:34; 5:1.

over which you are scattered;* 35 † I will lead
you to the wilderness of the peoples and enter
into judgment with you face to face. 36 Just as I
entered into judgment with your ancestors in the
wilderness of the land of Egypt, so will I enter
into judgment with you—oracle of the Lord GOD.
37 Thus I will make you pass under the staff† and
will impose on you the terms of the covenant.*
38 I will sort out from you those who defied me
and rebelled against me; from the land where
they resided as aliens I will bring them out, but
they shall not return to the land of Israel. Thus
you shall know that I am the LORD.
39 As for you, house of Israel, thus says the
Lord GOD: Go! each of you, and worship your
idols. Listen to me! You shall never again des-
ecrate my holy name with your offerings and
your idols!* 40 For on my holy mountain,† on
the highest mountain in Israel—oracle of the
Lord GOD—there the whole house of Israel shall
worship me; there in the land I will accept them
all, there I will claim your tributes, the best of
your offerings, from all your holy things.* 41 As
a sweet-smelling oblation I will accept you,
when I bring you from among the nations and
gather you out of the lands over which you were
scattered; and through you I will manifest my
holiness in the sight of the nations.* 42 Thus you
shall know that I am the LORD, when I bring you
back to the soil of Israel, the land I swore to give
your ancestors. 43 There you shall remember your
ways, all the deeds by which you defiled your-
selves; and you shall loathe yourselves because
of all the evil you did.* 44 And you shall know
that I am the LORD when I deal with you thus, for
the sake of my name, not according to your evil
ways and wanton deeds, house of Israel—oracle
of the Lord GOD.*

The Sword of the Lord

21 1 The word of the LORD came to me: 2 † Son
of man, turn your face to the south: preach
against the south, prophesy against the forest
land in the south. 3 Say to the forest in the south:
Hear the word of the LORD! Thus says the Lord
GOD: See! I am kindling a fire in you that shall
devour every green tree as well as every dry tree.
The blazing flame shall not be quenched so that
from south to north every face shall be scorched
by it. 4 All flesh shall see that I, the LORD, have
kindled it; it shall not be quenched.*
5 But I said, "Ah! Lord GOD, they are saying
about me, 'Is not this the one who is forever
spinning parables?' " 6 Then the word of the LORD
came to me: 7 Son of man, turn your face toward
Jerusalem: preach against its sanctuary, proph-
esy against the land of Israel.* 8 Say to the land
of Israel: Thus says the LORD: See! I am coming
against you; I will draw my sword from its scab-
bard and cut off from you the righteous and the
wicked.† 9 Thus my sword shall come out from
its scabbard against all flesh from south to north
10 and all flesh shall know that I, the LORD, have
drawn my sword from its scabbard. It cannot re-
turn again.*

Act Symbolic of the City's Fall

11 As for you, son of man, groan! with shat-
tered loins and bitter grief, groan in their sight.
12 When they ask you, "Why are you groaning?"
you shall say: Because of what I heard!† When
it comes every heart shall melt, every hand fall
helpless; every spirit will grow faint, and ev-
ery knee run with water. See, it is coming, it is
here!—oracle of the Lord GOD.

Song of the Sword

13 The word of the LORD came to me:* 14 Son of
man, prophesy! say: Thus says the LORD:

A sword, a sword has been sharpened,
a sword, a sword has been burnished:*
15 Sharpened to make a slaughter,
burnished to flash lightning!
Why should I stop now?
You have rejected the rod and every
judgment!
16 I have given it over to the burnisher
that he might hold it in his hand,
A sword sharpened and burnished

---

† **20:35–38** Exile among other lands occasions a new exodus and a new wilderness journey back to Israel. The Lord will eliminate the rebellious, as he did on the first journey, and use the surviving remnant to reveal his power to the nations.

20:37 *Pass under the staff*: in Lv 27:32–33, a method of counting off animals to select those to be dedicated for the tithe. In Ezekiel, on the other hand, those who survive the selection process are marked for destruction for violating the covenant.

20:40 *Holy mountain*: the Temple mount and Jerusalem in contrast to "every high hill" in v. 28 (cf. the royal Zion theology in Ps 48:2). Acceptable worship takes place here among a restored people, a theme taken up in chaps. 40–48 (cf. 40:2).

21:2–4 In Babylon Ezekiel looks toward Judah, pictured as a forest about to be destroyed by fire.

21:8 *Cut off from you the righteous and the wicked*: a more complete devastation of Jerusalem than that described in 9:6.

21:12 *What I heard*: the news of the fall of Jerusalem; cf. 33:21–22.

20:34 Ps 106:47.
20:37 Lv 27:3; Jer 33:13.
20:39 Ex 20:7.
20:40 cf. Ps 2:6; Is 11:9; 56:7.
20:41 cf. 2 Cor 2:14.
20:43 Lv 26:41.
20:44 cf. Ez 36:22.
21:4 Lv 26:25.
21:7 Lv 26:36.
21:10 Is 34:5–6.
21:13 Gn 49:10.
21:14 cf. 2 Kgs 13:18–19.

to be put in the hands of an executioner.
17 Cry out and howl, son of man,
for it is destined for my people,
For all the princes of Israel,
victims of the sword with my people.
Therefore, slap your thigh,†
18 for it is tested, and why not?
Since you rejected my staff,
should it not happen?—
oracle of the Lord GOD.
19 As for you, son of man, prophesy,
and clap your hands!
Let the sword strike twice, a third time.
It is a sword of slaughter,
A sword for slaughtering,
whirling around them all,
20 That every heart may tremble;
for many will be made to stumble.
At all their gates
I have stationed the sword for slaughter,
Made it flash lightning,
drawn for slaughter.
21 Slash to the right!
turn to the left,
Wherever your edge is directed!*
22 Then I, too, shall clap my hands,†
and spend my fury.
I, the LORD, have spoken.

Nebuchadnezzar at the Crossroads

23 The word of the LORD came to me: 24 Son of
man, make for yourself two roads over which
the sword of the king of Babylon can come. Both
roads shall start out from the same land. Then
put a signpost at the head of each road 25 so the
sword can come to Rabbah of the Ammonites
or to Judah and its fortress, Jerusalem. 26 For the
king of Babylon is standing at the fork of the
two roads to read the omens:† he shakes out
the arrows, inquires of the teraphim, inspects
the liver.* 27 Into his right hand has fallen the
lot marked "Jerusalem":† to order the slaughter,
to raise the battle cry, to set the battering rams
against the gates, to throw up a ramp, to build
siege works. 28 In the eyes of those bound by oath
this seems like a false omen; yet the lot taken in
hand exposes the wickedness for which they, still
bound by oath, will be taken in hand.
29 Therefore thus says the Lord GOD: Because
your guilt has been exposed, your crimes laid
bare, your sinfulness revealed in all your deeds—
because you have been exposed, you shall be
taken in hand.* 30 And as for you, depraved and
wicked prince of Israel, a day is coming to end
your life of crime.* 31 Thus says the Lord GOD: Off
with the turban and away with the crown! Noth-
ing shall be as it was! Exalt the lowly and bring
the exalted low! 32 A ruin, a ruin, a ruin, I shall
make it! Nothing will be the same until the one
comes to whom I have given it for judgment.*

To the Ammonites†

33 As for you, son of man, prophesy: Thus
says the Lord GOD to the Ammonites and their
insults:

O sword, sword drawn for slaughter,
burnished to consume, to flash lightning!
34 Your false visions and lying omens,
Set you over the necks of the slain,
the wicked whose day had come—
an end to their life of crime.
35 Return to your scabbard!
In the place you were created,
In the land of your origin,
I will judge you.
36 I will pour out my anger upon you,
breathing my fiery wrath against you;
I will hand you over to ravagers,
artisans of destruction!
37 You shall be fuel for the fire,
your blood shall flow throughout the land;
You shall not be remembered,
for I, the LORD, have spoken.

Crimes of Jerusalem

22 1 The word of the LORD came to me:
2 You,† son of man, will you judge? will
you judge the city of bloodshed? Then make
known all its abominations, 3 and say: Thus says
the Lord GOD: O city that sheds blood within
itself so that its time has come, that has made

† **21:17** *Slap your thigh*: a gesture signifying grief and dread; cf. Jer 31:19.

21:22 *Clap my hands*: the Lord declares himself no longer responsible for Judah; cf. 22:13; Nm 24:10; Jb 27:23; Lam 2:15.

21:26 Three forms of divination are mentioned: arrow divination, consisting in the use of differently marked arrows extracted or shaken from a case at random; the consultation of the teraphim or household idols; and liver divination, scrutiny of the configurations of the livers of newly slaughtered animals, a common form of divination in Mesopotamia.

21:27–28 A lot marked "Jerusalem" falls out, which marks the guilt of the city's inhabitants.

21:33–37 In vv. 23–32 Ezekiel imagines Nebuchadnezzar deciding whether to attack Jerusalem or Rabbath-Ammon. As it happened, the Babylonians decided to attack Jerusalem first. Here (vv. 33–37) Ezekiel prophesies to the Ammonites that a nation which serves as an instrument of the Lord's judgment will itself be judged.

22:2–16 This first oracle focuses on Jerusalem as a "city of bloodshed" (cf. Na 3:1). Here transgressions involving blood, the oppression of the poor, and improper cultic practices are seen as interrelated, for blood as the carrier of life is fundamental to both the cultic and social spheres of life.

* **21:21** Prv 16:33; Zec 10:2. **21:26** Is 28:5; Ps 75:8. **21:29** Jer 8:11–12; 27:9–10. **21:30** cf. Ez 16:3. **21:32** Mal 3:19.

idols for its own defilement: 4 By the blood you
shed you have become guilty, and by the idols
you made you have become defiled. You have
brought on your day, you have come to the end
of your years. Therefore I make you an object of
scorn for the nations and a laughingstock for all
lands.* 5 Those near and those far off will mock
you: "Defiled of Name! Queen of Tumult!"
6 See! the princes of Israel within you use their
power to shed blood.† 7 Within you, father and
mother are dishonored; they extort the resident
alien in your midst; within you, they oppress
orphans and widows.* 8 What I consider holy
you have rejected, and my sabbaths you have
desecrated. 9 † In you are those who slander to
cause bloodshed; within you are those who feast
on the mountains; in your midst are those whose
actions are depraved.* 10 In you are those who
uncover the nakedness of their fathers; in you
those who coerce women to intercourse during
their period.* 11 * There are those in you who do
abominable things with their neighbors' wives,
men who defile their daughters-in-law by incest,
men who coerce their sisters to intercourse, the
daughters of their own fathers. 12 There are those
in you who take bribes to shed blood. You exact
interest and usury; you extort profit from your
neighbor by violence. But me you have forgot-
ten—oracle of the Lord God.*

13 See, I am clapping my hands because of the
profits you extorted and the blood shed in your
midst. 14 Will your heart remain firm, will your
hands be strong, in the days when I deal with
you? I am the Lord; I have spoken, and I will act!
15 I will disperse you among the nations and scat-
ter you over other lands, so that I may purge your
filth. 16 In you I will allow myself to be desecrated
in the eyes of the nations; thus you shall know
that I am the Lord.

17 The word of the Lord came to me: 18 † Son of
man, the house of Israel has become dross to me.
All of them are copper, tin, iron, and lead within a
furnace; they have become the dross from silver.*
19 Therefore thus says the Lord God: Because all of
you have become dross, See! I am gathering you
within Jerusalem. 20 Just as silver, copper, iron,
lead, and tin are gathered within a furnace to be
blasted with fire to smelt it, so I will gather you to-
gether in my furious wrath, put you in, and smelt
you.* 21 When I have assembled you, I will blast
you with the fire of my anger and smelt you with
it. 22 Just as silver is smelted in a furnace, so you
shall be smelted in it. Thus you shall know that I,
the Lord, have poured out my fury on you.

23 The word of the Lord came to me: 24 † Son of
man, say to her: You are an unclean land receiving
no rain at the time of my fury. 25 A conspiracy of
its princes is like a roaring lion tearing prey; they
devour people, seizing their wealth and precious
things, making many widows within her.* 26 Her
priests violate my law and desecrate what I con-
sider holy; they do not distinguish between holy
and common, nor teach the difference between
unclean and clean; they pay no attention to my
sabbaths, so that I have been desecrated in their
midst.* 27 * Within her, her officials are like wolves
tearing prey, shedding blood and destroying lives
to extort profit. 28 * And her prophets cover them
with whitewash, seeing false visions and perform-
ing lying divinations, saying, "Thus says the Lord
God," although the Lord has not spoken. 29 The
people of the land practice extortion and commit
robbery; they wrong the poor and the needy, and
oppress the resident alien without justice. 30 Thus
I have searched among them for someone who
would build a wall or stand in the breach before
me to keep me from destroying the land; but
I found no one. 31 Therefore I have poured out
my fury upon them; with my fiery wrath I have
consumed them, bringing down their ways upon
their heads—oracle of the Lord God.

The Two Sisters

23 1 * The word of the Lord came to me: 2 Son
of man, there were two women, daugh-
ters of the same mother.* 3 Even as young girls,
they were prostitutes, serving as prostitutes in
Egypt. There the Egyptians fondled their breasts
and caressed their virgin nipples.* 4 Oholah was
the name of the elder, and the name of her sis-
ter was Oholibah.† They became mine and gave
birth to sons and daughters.* As for their names:

†

22:6 *To shed blood*: a very serious charge in light of the solemn command of God to Noah in Gn 9:6 against human bloodshed.

22:9–11 The charges against Jerusalem echo the commandments of Lv 20:10–18.

22:18–22 The image of smelting metals for purifying the people by the attacks of their enemies is common among the prophets; cf. Is 1:22, 25; Jer 6:27–30.

22:24–31 For a similar oracle, cf. Zep 3:1–8.

23:4 *Oholah . . . Oholibah*: symbolic names for Samaria, "her own tent," and Jerusalem, "my tent is in her." Cf. Ps 15:1 where "tent" is a synonym for "holy mountain." The names refer to the temple set up in the Northern Kingdom of Samaria (1 Kgs 12:28–29) and the Jerusalem Temple.

*

22:4 Ps 44:13–14.
22:7 Ex 22:21–22; 23:9; Dt 5:16.
22:9 cf. Ez 18:11.
22:10 Lv 18:7–8, 19.
22:11 Lv 18:7–20; 20:10–21; Dt 23:1–30; Jer 5:8.
22:12 Ez 18:8; Dt 27:25; Am 5:12.
22:18 Is 1:21–26; 48:10; Jer 6:27–30.
22:20 Hos 8:10; Mal 3:2.
22:25 Jer 15:8.
22:26 Lv 20:25; Hg 2:11–14.
22:27 Mi 3:11; Zep 3:3.
22:28–29 cf. Ez 13:2–10.
23:1 cf. Ez 16.
23:2 Jer 3:7.
23:3 Is 1:21.
23:4 Jer 3:6–12.

Samaria was Oholah and Jerusalem, Oholibah.
5 * Oholah became a prostitute while married to
me and lusted after her lovers, the Assyrians: war-
riors 6 dressed in purple, governors and officers,
all of them handsome young soldiers, mounted
on horses. 7 She gave herself as a prostitute to
them, to all the Assyrian elite; with all those for
whom she lusted, she also defiled herself with
their idols. 8 She did not abandon the prostitu-
tion she had begun with the Egyptians, who had
lain with her when she was young, fondling her
virgin breasts and pouring out their lust upon
her.* 9 Therefore I handed her over to her lovers,
to the Assyrians for whom she lusted. 10 * They
exposed her nakedness; her sons and daughters
they took away, and her they killed with the
sword. She became a byword for women because
of the sentence carried out against her.
11 Although her sister Oholibah saw all this,
her lust was more depraved than her sister's; she
outdid her in prostitution.* 12 She too lusted af-
ter the Assyrians, governors and officers, warriors
impeccably clothed, mounted on horses, all of
them handsome young soldiers.* 13 I saw that
she had defiled herself—now both had gone
down the same path. 14 She went further in her
prostitution: She saw male figures drawn on the
wall, images of Chaldeans drawn with vermilion,
15 with sashes tied about their waists, flowing tur-
bans on their heads, all looking like chariot war-
riors, images of Babylonians, natives of Chaldea.
16 As soon as she set eyes on them she lusted for
them, and she sent messengers to them in Chal-
dea.* 17 The Babylonians came to her, to her love
couch; they defiled her with their impurities. But
as soon as they had defiled her, she recoiled from
them. 18 When her prostitution was discovered
and her shame revealed, I recoiled from her as I
had recoiled from her sister. 19 But she increased
her prostitution, recalling the days of her youth
when she had served as a prostitute in the land
of Egypt. 20 She lusted for the lechers of Egypt,
whose members are like those of donkeys, whose
thrusts are like those of stallions.
21 You reverted to the depravity of your youth,
when Egyptians fondled your breasts, caressing
your young nipples. 22 Therefore, Oholibah, thus
says the Lord GOD: I will now stir up your lovers
against you, those from whom you recoiled, and
I will bring them against you from every side:
23 the men of Babylon and all of Chaldea, Pekod,
Shoa and Koa,† along with all the Assyrians,
handsome young soldiers, all of them governors
and officers, charioteers and warriors, all of them
horsemen. 24 They shall invade you with armor,
chariots and wagons, a horde of peoples; they
will array against you on every side bucklers and
shields and helmets. I will give them the right
of judgment, and they will judge you according
to their standards.* 25 I will direct my jealousy
against you, so that they deal with you in fury,
cutting off your nose and ears; what is left of you

Live It!

Irresponsible Children

Raising children is a demanding job. In teaching their children about life, parents try to help them be responsible—to accept the consequences of their actions. For example, a parent might say: "You threw the ball and broke the window. The wind had nothing to do with it! Now, what are you going to do about it?"

Chapters 13–24 of Ezekiel contain prophecies, allegories, fables, and symbolic actions, all intended to encourage the people of Judah to take responsibility for their sinful actions. In a graphic allegory in chapter 23, the northern and southern kingdoms are compared to promiscuous daughters who will sleep with almost anyone who comes their way. God is using just about every possible means to say, "Take responsibility for your actions, my children, and live with the consequences!"

We are all like little children in that we are often tempted to ignore the consequences of our actions. For instance, we may think of cheating on homework as just a little wrong. But that wrong will catch up with us. It will lead to more cheating, in bigger things. By then, our "little" wrong could mean losing a job or destroying a relationship. If you want to please God, be honest in looking at the consequences of your actions and choose responsibly!

► Ez 23:1–21

EZ

† **23:23** *Pekod, Shoa and Koa*: nations along the Tigris River, part of "greater Babylonia."

* **23:5** Hos 5:3; 8:9.
23:8 cf. Ez 20:5–8.
23:10 cf. Ez 16:37.
23:11 Jer 3:8–11.
23:12 2 Kgs 16:7–15; 2 Chr 28:16.
23:16 Is 57:8–9.
23:24 Jer 30:5–6.

shall fall by the sword. They shall take away your
sons and daughters, and what is left of you shall
be devoured by fire. 26 They shall strip off your
clothes and seize your splendid jewelry. 27 I will
put an end to your depravity and to your prosti-
tution from the land of Egypt; you shall no longer
look to them, nor even remember Egypt again.
28 For thus says the Lord GOD: I am now hand-
ing you over to those whom you hate, to those
from whom you recoil. 29 They shall treat you
with hatred, seizing all that you worked for and
leaving you stark naked, so that your indecent
nakedness is exposed.* Your depravity and pros-
titution 30 brought these things upon you be-
cause you served as a prostitute for the nations,
defiling yourself with their idols.*
31 Because you followed your sister's path, I
will put her cup into your hand.† *

32 Thus says the Lord GOD:*
The cup of your sister you shall drink,
  deep and wide;
It brings ridicule and mockery,
  it holds so much;
33 You will be filled with drunkenness and grief—
  A cup of horror and devastation,
  the cup of your sister Samaria;
34 You shall drink it dry,
  its very sherds you will gnaw;
And you shall tear out your breasts;
  for I have spoken—oracle of the Lord GOD.

35 Therefore thus says the Lord GOD: You have
forgotten me and cast me behind your back; now
suffer for your depravity and prostitution.
36 † Then the LORD said to me: Son of man,
would you judge Oholah and Oholibah? Then
make known to them their abominations.* 37 For
they committed adultery, and blood covers their
hands. They committed adultery with their idols;
even the children they bore for me they burnt as
food for them. 38 And they also did this to me: on
that day, they defiled my sanctuary and desecrated
my sabbaths. 39 On the very day they slaughtered
their children for their idols, they entered my
sanctuary to desecrate it. Thus they acted within
my house!* 40 Moreover, they sent for men who
had to come from afar; when a messenger was
sent to them, they came. On their account you
bathed, painted your eyes, and put on jewelry.*
41 You sat on a magnificent couch, set before it a
table, on which to lay my incense and oil. 42 The
cries of a mob! The shouts of men coming in from
the wilderness! They put bracelets on the women's
arms and splendid crowns on their heads. 43 I said:
"That worn-out one still has adulteries in her!
Now they engage her as a prostitute and she . . .
44 And indeed they did come in to her as men
come in to a prostitute. Thus they came to Oholah
and Oholibah, the depraved women. 45 The righ-
teous shall certainly punish them with sentences
given to adulterers and murderers, for they com-
mitted adultery, and blood is on their hands.*
46 Indeed, thus says the Lord GOD: Raise up an
army against them and hand them over to terror
and plunder. 47 The army will stone them and
hack them to pieces with their swords. They will
kill their sons and daughters and set fire to their
houses. 48 Thus I will put an end to depravity in
the land, and all women will be warned not to
imitate your depravity. 49 They shall inflict on
you the penalty of your depravity, and you shall
pay for your sins of idolatry. Then you shall
know that I am the Lord GOD.*

Allegory of the Pot†

24 1 On the tenth day of the tenth month,
in the ninth year,† the word of the LORD
came to me:* 2 Son of man, write down today's
date this very day, for on this very day the king of
Babylon lays siege to Jerusalem. 3 * Propose this
parable to the rebellious house and say to them:
Thus says the Lord GOD:

Put the pot on, put it on!
  Pour in some water;
4 Add to it pieces of meat,
  all choice pieces;
With thigh and shoulder,
  with choice cuts fill it.

†

23:31 The cup is a metaphor for divine punishment, the lot of all who rebel against the Lord (cf. Ps 75:9; Jer 25:15–16; 51:7; Is 51:21–23; Lam 4:21; Hb 2:15–16).

23:36–49 Unlike vv. 1–35, this short poem juxtaposes the careers of the two sisters and looks to a future punishment. The male lovers of the first poem become the sisters' executioners, and the guests at the love feast a lynch mob. So corrupt and depraved are the two sisters that their executioners win the esteemed title "righteous," for they have acted appropriately as agents of the Lord's judgment.

24:1–14 As the Babylonian siege of Jerusalem begins (588 B.C.), Ezekiel uses allegory to depict Jerusalem and its over-confident inhabitants as a pot of meat set on the fire for boiling (vv. 3–5; cf. 11:3) and left there until only burnt bones remain (v. 10). In vv. 6–8, the innocent blood shed by Jerusalem's inhabitants is the rust that, despite efforts to remove it, coats the interior of the pot filled with meat. Once emptied (v. 8), the rust-encrusted pot is set on hot coals (v. 11), but the rust remains (v. 12). Only the brunt of the Lord's fury can cleanse Jerusalem of its guilt (vv. 13–14).

24:1 *The tenth day . . . the ninth year*: January 15, 588 B.C. The same wording appears in 2 Kgs 25:1 (Jer 52:4).

*

23:29 Jer 13:27; Mi 1:11.
23:30 Ps 106:37–38.
23:31 Ps 75:8; Ob 16; Mt 20:22; Rev 14:10.
23:32–33 Jer 25:15–16.
23:36 Is 58:1; Mi 3:8.
23:39 2 Kgs 21:4.
23:40 Jer 27:3.
23:45 Lv 20:10.
23:49 cf. Ez 24:13.
24:1 cf. Ez 8:1.
24:3–6 cf. Ez 11:3–12.

5 Choose the pick of the flock,
then pile logs beneath it;
Bring it to a boil,
cook all the pieces in it.*
6 Therefore thus says the Lord GOD:
Woe to the city full of blood!*
A pot containing filth,
whose filth cannot be removed!
Take out its pieces one by one,
for no lot has fallen on their behalf.
7 For her blood is still in her midst;
on a bare rock she left it;
She did not pour it on the ground
to be covered with dirt.†
8 To arouse wrath, to exact vengeance,
I have left her blood on bare rock
not to be covered.
9 Therefore, thus says the Lord GOD:
Woe to the city full of blood!
I will make the pyre great!
10 Pile on the wood, kindle the fire.
Cook the meat, stir the spicy mixture,
char the bones!
11 Then set it empty on the coals,
to heat up until its copper glows,
So its impurities melt,
its filth disappears.
12† The toil is exhausting,
but the great filth will not come out—
Filth, even with fire.
13 Even in defiling yourself with depravity
I would still have cleansed you,
but you would not have your impurity
cleansed.
You will not be cleansed now
until I wreak my fury on you.*
14 I, the LORD, have spoken;
it will happen!
I will do it and not hold back!
I will not have pity or relent.
By your conduct and deeds you shall be
judged—
oracle of the Lord GOD.

Ezekiel as a Sign for the Exiles

15 The word of the LORD came to me: 16 Son of
man, with a sudden blow I am taking away from
you the delight of your eyes, but do not mourn or
weep or shed any tears.* 17 Groan, moan for the
dead, but make no public lament; bind on your
turban, put your sandals on your feet, but do not
cover your beard or eat the bread of mourners.†
18 I spoke to the people in the morning. In the
evening my wife died. The next morning I did
as I had been commanded.* 19 Then the people
asked me, "Will you not tell us what all these
things you are doing mean for us?" 20 I said to
them, The word of the LORD came to me: 21 Say to
the house of Israel: Thus says the Lord GOD: I will
now desecrate my sanctuary, the pride of your
strength, the delight of your eyes, the concern of
your soul. The sons and daughters you left be-
hind shall fall by the sword.* 22 † Then you shall
do as I have done, not covering your beards nor
eating the bread of mourning. 23 * Your turbans
shall remain on your heads, your sandals on
your feet. You shall not mourn or weep, but you
shall waste away because of your sins and groan
to one another. 24 Ezekiel shall be a sign for you:
everything he did, you shall do. When it hap-
pens, you shall know that I am the Lord GOD.

End of Ezekiel's Muteness

25 * As for you, son of man, truly, on the very
day I take away from them their strength, their
glorious joy, the delight of their eyes, the de-
sire of their soul, the pride of their hearts, their
sons and daughters, 26 on that day a survivor will
come to you so that you may hear it with your
own ears.* 27 On that day, with the survivor, your
mouth shall be opened; you shall speak and be
mute† no longer. You shall be a sign to them,
and they shall know that I am the LORD.

III. Prophecies Against Foreign Nations†

Against Ammon

25 †1 The word of the LORD came to me: 2 Son
of man, turn toward the Ammonites and
prophesy against them.* 3 Say to the Ammonites:
Hear the word of the LORD! Thus says the Lord
GOD: Because you jeered at my sanctuary when
it was desecrated, at the land of Israel when it

---

† **24:7** *Blood . . . to be covered with dirt*: since blood was sacred to God, it had to be covered with earth (Gn 37:26; Lv 17:13); the blood of innocent victims left uncovered cried out for vengeance; cf. Gn 4:10; Jb 16:18; Is 26:21.

24:12 A cryptic line in Hebrew.

24:17 *The bread of mourners*: a post-burial meal that mourners shared to comfort one another; cf. 2 Sm 3:35; Jer 16:7. The other gestures mentioned here were also popular mourning customs. Because Ezekiel does not observe any of the mourning customs mentioned, the people are puzzled and ask him to explain.

24:22–24 The fall of the city will be so sudden and final that the exiles will have no time to go into mourning.

24:27 *Mute*: unable to preach anything but the Lord's judgment against Judah and Jerusalem; cf. 3:27 and note on 33:21–22.

25:1–32:32 These chapters form a body of oracles directed against foreign nations. They follow the prophet's condemnation of

---

* **24:5** Jer 52:24–27.
24:6 Na 3:1; Hb 2:12.
24:13 Is 22:14; Jer 6:28–30.
24:16 Jer 16:5–7.
24:18 cf. Ez 12:9.
24:21 Lv 26:31.
24:23–24 Is 20:2–3.
24:25 cf. Ez 3:22–27.
24:26 cf. Ez 33:22.
25:2 Jer 49:1–6; Am 1:13–15; Zep 2:8–11.

was destroyed, and at the house of Judah when they went into exile, 4 therefore I am giving you to people from the east† as a possession. They shall set up their encampments among you and pitch their tents in your midst; they shall eat your produce and drink your milk.* 5 And I will turn Rabbah into a pasture for camels and all of Ammon into a grazing place for flocks. Then you shall know that I am the LORD.

6 For thus says the Lord GOD: Because you rejoiced over the land of Israel with scorn in your heart, clapping your hands and stamping your feet, 7 therefore, see, I am stretching out my hand against you and giving you up as plunder to the nations. I will cut you off from the peoples and wipe you out of the lands. I will destroy you, and you shall know that I am the LORD.*

Against Moab

8 * Thus says the Lord GOD: Because Moab said, "See! the house of Judah is like all the other nations," 9 therefore, I am exposing the whole flank of Moab† with its cities, the jewels of its land: Beth-jesimoth, Baalmeon, and Kiriathaim. 10 I will hand it over, along with the Ammonites, to the people from the east that it may not be remembered among the nations. 11 I will execute judgment upon Moab that they may know that I am the LORD.*

Against Edom

12 * Thus says the Lord GOD: Because Edom took vengeance on the house of Judah and incurred terrible guilt by taking vengeance on them, 13 therefore thus says the Lord GOD: I will stretch out my hand against Edom and cut off from it human being and beast alike. I will turn it into ruins from Teman to Dedan; they shall fall by the sword.* 14 I will put my vengeance against Edom into the hands of my people Israel; they will deal with Edom in accord with my furious anger. Thus they shall know my vengeance!—oracle of the Lord GOD.*

Against the Philistines

15 Thus says the Lord GOD: Because the Philistines acted vengefully and exacted vengeance with intentional malice, destroying with undying hostility,* 16 therefore thus says the Lord GOD: See! I am stretching out my hand against the Philistines, and I will cut off the Cherethites† and wipe out the remnant on the seacoast. 17 Thus I will execute great acts of vengeance on them, punishing them furiously. Then they shall know that I am the LORD, when I wreak my vengeance on them.

Against the City of Tyre

26 1 † On the first day of the eleventh month of the eleventh year, the word of the LORD came to me:

2† Son of man, because Tyre said of Jerusalem:
"Aha! The gateway of the peoples is smashed!
It has been turned over to me;
I will be enriched by its ruin!"*
3 therefore thus says the Lord GOD:
See! I am coming against you, Tyre;
I will churn up against you many nations,
just as the sea churns up its waves.
4 They will destroy the walls of Tyre
and tear down its towers;
I will scrape off its debris
and leave it a bare rock.†
5 It will become a place for drying nets
in the midst of the sea.
For I have spoken—oracle of the Lord GOD:
she will become plunder for the nations.
6 Her daughter cities† on the mainland
will be slaughtered by the sword;
then they shall know that I am the LORD.
7† Indeed thus says the Lord GOD:
I am bringing up against Tyre
from the north, Nebuchadnezzar,
King of Babylon, king of kings,
with horses and chariots, with cavalry,

† Judah and oracles announcing its destruction. The unit precedes the announcement of Judah's salvation in chaps. 33–48.

25:1–17 Ezekiel condemns four nations for their reactions to Judah's destruction and exile: Ammon to the east (vv. 2–7); Moab to the southeast (vv. 8–11); Edom to the south (vv. 12–14); Philistia to the west (vv. 15–17). Their hostility was not unprovoked; at one time or another, each one either lost territory to Israel or had been under Israelite control.

25:4 *People from the east*: nomadic tribes from the desert east of Ammon and Moab (cf. Is 11:14; Jer 49:28), often a threat to outlying towns and villages.

25:9 *The whole flank of Moab*: the eastern edge of the Moabite plateau, perhaps lightly fortified because the vast desert to the east provided a natural barrier to invasion.

25:16 *Cherethites*: people from the island of Crete in the Aegean, the Philistines' point of origin. In Zep 2:5, the terms "Philistines," "Cherethites," and "seacoast people" describe the same group of people.

26:1 The Hebrew text does not give a number with the month. This translation assumes a scribal error, the omission of the second occurrence of the number eleven.

26:2 Tyre is pictured rejoicing over Jerusalem's fall to Babylon because now the wealth from caravans and other trade will go to Tyrian merchants.

26:4–5 *A bare rock*: the Tyre of Ezekiel's time was situated on a rocky island just off the Phoenician coast. During the time of Alexander the Great a causeway was built to connect it to the mainland.

26:6 *Daughter cities*: tributary towns and villages on the mainland.

* **25:4** Dt 28:33, 51.
25:7 Am 1:14–15.
25:8 Sir 50:26; Is 15–16; Jer 48; Am 2:1–3.
25:11 Am 2:1–3.
25:12 2 Sm 8:13–14; 2 Chr 28:17; Ob 11–14.
25:13 cf. Ez 35; Is 34:5–17; 63:1–6; Jer 49:7–11.
25:14 cf. Ez 35:11.
25:15 Is 14:29–31; Jer 47:1–7; Am 1:6–8; Zep 2:4–7.
26:2 Is 23:1–18; Jl 3:4–5; Am 1:9–10; Zec 9:2–4.

and a mighty horde of troops.*
8 Your daughter cities on the mainland
he shall slay with the sword.
He shall build a siege wall around you,
throw up a ramp against you,
and raise his shields about you.
9 He shall pound your walls with battering-rams
and break down your towers with his axes.
10 From the surging of his horses
he will cover you with dust;
from the noise of warhorses,
wheels and chariots.
Your walls will shake
when he enters your gates,
even as one enters a city that is breached.
11 With the hooves of his horses
he will trample all your streets;
Your people he will slay by the sword;
your mighty pillars will collapse.*
12 They shall plunder your wealth
and pillage your goods;
They will tear down your walls
and demolish your splendid houses.
Your stones, timbers, and debris
they will cast into the sea.
13 I will bring an end to the noise of your songs;
the music of your lyres will be heard no more.
14 I will turn you into bare rock,
you will become a place for drying nets.
You shall never be rebuilt,
for I the LORD have spoken—
oracle of the Lord GOD.
15 Thus says the Lord GOD to Tyre:
At the sound of your downfall,
at the groaning of the wounded,
When victims are slain within you,
will the islands not quake?
16 All the princes of the sea†
will step down from their thrones,
Lay aside their robes,
and strip off their embroidered garments.
Clothed in mourning,
they will sit on the ground
And tremble, horror-struck
and appalled at you.*
17 They will raise lament† over you
and say to you:
How you have perished,
gone from the seas,
Renowned City!
Once she was mighty on the sea,
she and her inhabitants,
Those who spread their terror
to all who dwelt nearby.*
18 On this, the day of your fall,
the islands quake!
The islands in the sea
are terrified at your passing.
19 Indeed thus says the Lord GOD:
When I make you a ruined city
like cities no longer inhabited,
When I churn up the deep
and its mighty waters cover you,
20 Then I will thrust you down
with those who go down to the pit,†
to those of the bygone age;
I will make you dwell in the netherworld,
in the everlasting ruins,
with those who have gone down to the pit,
So you will never return
or have a place in the land of the living.*
21 I will make you a horror,
and you shall be no more;
You shall be sought for,
but never found again—
oracle of the Lord GOD.

The Ship Tyre

27 1 The word of the LORD came to me: 2 You,
son of man, raise a lament over Tyre,
3 and say to Tyre, who sits at the entrance to the
sea, trader to peoples on many coastlands, Thus
says the Lord GOD:

Tyre, you said, "I am a ship,
perfect in beauty;*
4 In the heart of the sea was your territory;
your builders perfected your beauty.*
5 With juniper wood from Senir†
they built all your decks;
A cedar from Lebanon they took
to make you a mast.
6 With oaks of Bashan†
they fashioned your oars,
Your bridge, of ivory-inlaid cypress wood
from the coasts of Kittim.
7 Fine embroidered linen from Egypt

EZ

† **26:16** *The princes of the sea*: the rulers of the islands and coastal cities leagued commercially with Tyre.

26:17 *Lament*: the princes sing a funeral dirge at the burial of the personified Tyre; cf. the similar lamentation over Egypt in 32:3–8.

26:20 *Those who go down to the pit*: the dead, pictured as dwelling in Sheol, a place or cave of darkness. Cf. 32:17–32; Is 14:4–21 for other examples.

27:5 *Senir*: another name for Mount Hermon; cf. Dt 3:9.

27:6 *Bashan*: an area in northern Transjordan, noted for its lush growth and great forests (cf. Is 2:13). *Kittim*: here, probably Cyprus.

* **26:7** Jer 27:6; Na 2:3–4.
26:11 Na 3:11.
26:16 cf. Ez 32:10.
26:17 cf. Ez 19:1.
26:20 cf. Ez 31:14; 32:18, 24, 30.
27:3 Is 23:9.
27:4 cf. Ez 28:1.

became your sail;
Your awnings were made of purple and scarlet
from the coasts of Elishah.† *
8 Inhabitants of Sidon† and Arvad
were your oarsmen;
Your own sages, Tyre, were on board,
serving as your sailors.*
9 The elders and sages of Gebal
were with you to caulk your seams.
Every ship and sailor on the sea
came to you to carry on trade.*
10 Persia and Lud and Put
were warriors in your army;
Shield and helmet they hung on you
to enhance your splendor.
11 The men of Arvad and Helech†
were on your walls all around
And Gamadites on your towers;
they hung their shields around your walls,
they made your beauty perfect.
12 Tarshish traded with you,
so great was your wealth,
Exchanging for your wares
silver, iron, tin, and lead.
13 Javan, Tubal, and Meshech
also traded with you,
Exchanging slaves and bronze vessels
for your merchandise.*
14 Horses, steeds, and mules from Beth-togarmah
were exchanged for your wares.
15 Men of Rhodes trafficked with you;
many coastlands were your agents;
Ivory tusks and ebony wood
they brought back as your payment.
16 Edom traded with you for your many wares:
garnets, purple dye, embroidered cloth,
Fine linen, coral, and rubies
they gave you as merchandise.
17 Judah and the land of Israel
trafficked with you:
Minnith wheat, grain,† honey, oil, and balm*
they gave you as merchandise.
18 Damascus traded with you for your many
wares,
so great was your wealth,
exchanging Helbon wine and Zahar wool.
19 Javan exchanged wrought iron, cassia, and
aromatic cane
from Uzal for your wares.
20 Dedan traded with you for riding gear.*
21 Arabia and the sheikhs of Kedar were your
agents,
dealing in lambs, rams, and goats.*
22 The merchants of Sheba and Raamah also
traded with you,
exchanging for your wares the very best
spices,
all kinds of precious stones, and gold.
23 Haran, Canneh, and Eden,
the merchants of Sheba, Asshur, and
Chilmad,
24 Traded with you, marketing rich garments,
purple cloth, embroidered fabric,
varicolored carpets, and braided cords.
25 The ships of Tarshish sailed for you with your
goods;
You were full and heavily laden
in the heart of the sea.
26 Out into deep waters
your oarsmen brought you;
The east wind shattered you
in the heart of the sea.*
27 Your wealth, your goods, your wares,
your sailors, your crew,
The caulkers of your seams,
those who traded for your goods,
All the warriors with you,
the whole crowd with you
Sank into the heart of the sea
on the day of your downfall.*
28 At the sound of your sailors' shouts
the waves shudder,*
29 Down from their ships
come all who ply the oars;
Sailors, all the seafaring crew,
stand on the shore.
30 They raise their voices over you
and shout their bitter cries;
They pour dust on their heads
and cover themselves with ashes.
31 For you they shave their heads bald
and put on sackcloth;
For you they weep bitterly,
in anguished lament.*
32 They raise a lament for you;
they wail over you:
"Who was ever destroyed like Tyre
in the midst of the sea?"*
33 By exporting your goods by sea
you satisfied many peoples,

EZ

†

27:7 *Elishah*: perhaps another term for Cyprus.
27:8–9 *Sidon . . . Gebal*: Phoenician cities in Tyre's orbit of influence; Gebal is classical Byblos.
27:11 *Helech*: perhaps in Asia Minor; otherwise unknown.
27:17 *Grain*: most commentators have read "figs," but Hebrew *panag* more properly describes milled grains or prepared meal.

*

27:7 Is 19:9–10.
27:8 cf. Ez 28:20–23.
27:9 Ps 104:26.
27:13 cf. Ez 38:2; 39:1.
27:17 1 Kgs 5:9.
27:20 Is 21:13.
27:21 Is 21:17; Jer 49:28.
27:26 Ps 48:7; Jer 18:17.
27:27 cf. Ez 28:8.
27:28 Jer 49:21.
27:31 Is 15:2; Jer 48:37.
27:32 Is 23:1–6.

With your great wealth and merchandise
you enriched the kings of the earth.*
34 Now you are wrecked in the sea,
in the watery depths;
Your wares and all your crew
have fallen down with you.
35 All who dwell on the coastlands
are aghast over you;
Their kings are terrified,
their faces distorted.
36 The traders among the peoples
now hiss at you;
You have become a horror,
you shall be no more.

The Prince of Tyre

28 1 † The word of the LORD came to me:
2 Son of man, say to the prince of Tyre:
Thus says the Lord GOD:

Because you are haughty of heart,
you say, "I am a god!
I sit on a god's throne
in the heart of the sea!"
But you are a man, not a god;
yet you pretend
you are a god at heart!
3 Oh yes, you are wiser than Daniel,†
nothing secret is too obscure for you!*
4 By your wisdom and intelligence
you made yourself rich,
filling your treasuries with gold and silver.
5 Through your great wisdom in trading
you heaped up riches for yourself—
your heart is haughty because of your riches.
6 Therefore thus says the Lord GOD:
Because you pretend you are a god at heart,
7 Therefore, I will bring against you
strangers, the most bloodthirsty of nations.
They shall draw their swords
against your splendid wisdom,
and violate your radiance.*
8 They shall thrust you down into the pit:
you shall die a violent death
in the heart of the sea.
9 Then, face to face with your killers,
will you still say, "I am a god"?
No, you are a man, not a god,
handed over to those who slay you.
10 You shall die the death of the uncircumcised
handed over to strangers,
for I have spoken—oracle of the Lord GOD.*

11 The word of the LORD came to me: 12 Son of
man, raise a lament over the king of Tyre, and say
to him: Thus says the Lord GOD:

†You were a seal of perfection,
full of wisdom, perfect in beauty.*
13 In Eden, the garden of God, you lived;
precious stones of every kind were your
covering:
Carnelian, topaz, and beryl,
chrysolite, onyx, and jasper,
sapphire, garnet, and emerald.
Their mounts and settings
were wrought in gold,
fashioned for you the day you were created.*
14 With a cherub I placed you;
I put you on the holy mountain of God,†
where you walked among fiery stones.
15 Blameless were you in your ways
from the day you were created,
Until evil was found in you.
16 Your commerce was full of lawlessness, and
you sinned.
Therefore I banished you from the mountain
of God;
the cherub drove you out
from among the fiery stones.*
17 Your heart had grown haughty
because of your beauty;
You corrupted your wisdom
because of your splendor.
I cast you to the ground,
I made you a spectacle
in the sight of kings.*
18 Because of the enormity of your guilt,
and the perversity of your trade,
you defiled your sanctuary.
I brought fire out of you;
it devoured you;
I made you ashes on the ground
in the eyes of all who see you.*
19 All the nations who knew you
are appalled on account of you;
You have become a horror,
never to be again.*

EZ

†

28:1–10 Ezekiel mocks the arrogance of Tyre's leader, who mistakes the city's commercial success for evidence of his divinity. At the hands of a foreign army, commissioned by the only God worthy of the name, this leader dies a humiliating, unceremonious death.

28:3 *Wiser than Daniel*: see note on 14:14.

28:12–19 Ezekiel describes the leader of Tyre in language that recalls the imagery of Gn 2–3.

28:14 *The holy mountain of God*: the residence of gods in Israelite and non-Israelite myth; cf. Is 14:13. *Fiery stones*: associated with the divine presence; cf. Ez 1:13; Ps 18:13.

*

27:33 cf. Ez 28:4–5.
28:3 cf. Ez 14:14; Dn 1:20; 2:20–23.
28:7 cf. Ez 30:11; 31:12; 32:12.
28:10 cf. Ez 32:19, 24.
28:12 Is 14:12–15.
28:13 cf. Ez 31:8–9; Gn 2:8, 15.
28:16 Gn 3:24.
28:17 Is 10:12.
28:18 Ob 18.
28:19 Lv 26:12.

Against Sidon

20 The word of the LORD came to me: 21 Son of
man, turn your face toward Sidon and prophesy
against it. 22 Thus says the Lord GOD:

Watch out! I am against you, Sidon;
I will win glory for myself in your midst.
They shall know that I am the LORD,
when I deliver judgment upon it
and manifest my holiness in it.
23 I will send disease into it;
blood will fill its streets,
Within it shall fall
those slain by the sword
raised against it on every side.
Then they shall know that I am the LORD.
24 No longer will there be a thorn that tears
or a brier that scratches for the house of Israel
From the surrounding neighbors
who despise them;
thus they shall know that I am the LORD.*

25 Thus says the Lord GOD: When I gather the
house of Israel from the peoples among whom
they are scattered, and I manifest my holiness
through them in the sight of the nations, then
they shall live on the land I gave my servant Ja-
cob.* 26 They shall dwell on it securely, building
houses and planting vineyards. They shall dwell
securely while I execute judgment on all their
neighbors who treated them with contempt; then
they shall know that I, the LORD, am their God.*

Egypt the Crocodile

29 1 In the tenth year, on the twelfth day of
the tenth month,† the word of the LORD
came to me: 2 Son of man, turn your face toward
Pharaoh, king of Egypt, and prophesy against
him and against all Egypt.†* 3 Say to him: Thus
says the Lord GOD:

Pay attention! I am against you,
Pharaoh, king of Egypt,
Great dragon† crouching
in the midst of the Nile,
Who says, "The Nile belongs to me;
I made it myself!"*
4† I will put hooks in your jaws
and make all the fish of your Nile
Cling to your scales;
I will drag you up from your Nile,
With all the fish of your Nile
clinging to your scales.*
5 I will hurl you into the wilderness,
you and all the fish of your Nile.
You will fall into an open field,
you will not be picked up or gathered together.
To the beasts of the earth
and the birds of the sky
I give you as food.*
6 * Then all the inhabitants of Egypt
will know that I am the LORD.
Because you were a staff of reeds†
for the house of Israel:
7 When they took hold of you, you would splinter,
throwing shoulders out of joint.
When they leaned on you, you would break,
pitching them down headlong.
8 Therefore thus says the Lord GOD:
Look! I am bringing the sword against you
to cut off from you people and animals.
9 The land of Egypt shall become a desolate waste;
then they shall know that I am the LORD.
Because you said, "The Nile belongs to me;
I made it!"
10 Beware! I am against you
and against your Nile.
I will turn the land of Egypt into ruins,
into a dry, desolate waste,
From Migdol to Syene,†
up to the border of Ethiopia.*
11 No foot shall pass through it,
no human being or beast cross it;
it will remain uninhabited for forty years.
12 I will make the land of Egypt the most desolate
among desolate lands;

---

† **29:1** The date is calculated to be January 7, 587 B.C. The siege of Jerusalem had begun a year earlier; cf. 24:1.

29:2 Egypt was allied with Judah against the Babylonians.

29:3 *Dragon*: Hebrew reads *tannim*, usually translated "jackals," here a byform of *tannin*, the mythical dragon, or sea monster, representing chaos (cf. Is 27:1; 51:9; Jer 51:34; Ps 91:13; Jb 7:12), and the crocodile native to the Nile. *Nile*: the many rivulets of the Nile that branch out into the Delta.

29:4–5 Ezekiel's repetition of detail creates a vivid picture of Egypt's destruction: God hauls the crocodile (Pharaoh) and the fish clinging to it for protection (the Egyptian populace) out of the Nile and lands them in an open field, where their corpses are torn apart by wildlife rather than being properly buried (cf. Dt 28:26; 2 Kgs 9:36–37; Jer 34:20; Ez 39:17–20).

29:6 *Staff of reeds*: Pharaoh is like a reed that looks sturdy but breaks under pressure. For a similar image, cf. 2 Kgs 18:21 (Is 36:6).

29:10 *From Migdol to Syene*: from the northeastern to the southern limits of Egypt. Syene is the modern Aswan, at the first cataract of the Nile; Ethiopia (Heb. *kush*) is the territory south of Aswan.

---

* **28:24** Nm 33:55.
28:25 cf. Ez 20:41.
28:26 Lv 25:18–19; Jer 23:6.
29:2 Is 19:1–17; Jer 25:19.
29:3 cf. Ez 32:2.
29:4 Is 19:5.
29:5 Jer 7:33.
29:6–7 2 Kgs 18:21; Is 36:6.
29:10 cf. Ez 30:4, 6.

Its cities, the most deserted
among deserted cities for forty years;
I will scatter the Egyptians among the nations
and disperse them throughout other
lands.*
13 But thus says the Lord GOD:
At the end of forty years
I will gather the Egyptians
from among the peoples
where they are scattered;
14 I will restore Egypt's fortunes,
bringing them back to the land of Pathros,†
the land of their origin.
But there it will be a lowly kingdom,
15 lower than any other kingdom,
no longer able to set itself above the
nations.
I will make them few in number,
so they cannot rule other nations.
16 No longer shall they be security
for the house of Israel,
But a reminder of its iniquity
in turning away to follow them.
Then they shall know that I am the Lord
GOD.*

Wages for Nebuchadnezzar

17 In the twenty-seventh year on the first day of
the first month,† the word of the LORD came to
me: 18 Son of man, Nebuchadnezzar, the king of
Babylon, has made his army wage a hard cam-
paign against Tyre;† their heads grew bald, their
shoulders rubbed raw, yet neither he nor his
army received compensation from Tyre for all
the effort they expended against it.* 19 Therefore
thus says the Lord GOD:* See! I am giving to Neb-
uchadnezzar, king of Babylon, the land of Egypt!
He will carry off its wealth, plundering and pil-
laging whatever he can find to provide pay for
his army. 20 As payment for his toil I give him the
land of Egypt—oracle of the Lord GOD.
21 On that day I will make a horn† sprout for
the house of Israel, and I will let you again open
your mouth in their midst; then they shall know
that I am the LORD.*

The Day of the Lord Against Egypt

30 1 The word of the LORD came to me: 2 Son
of man, prophesy and say: Thus says the
Lord GOD:

Wail: "Alas the day!"
3 Yes, a day approaches,
a day of the Lord approaches:
A day of dark cloud,
a time appointed for the nations.*
4 A sword will come against Egypt,
there will be anguish in Ethiopia,
When the slain fall in Egypt
when its hordes are seized,
its foundations razed.*
5 Ethiopia, Put, and Lud,
all the mixed rabble† and Kub,
and the people of allied lands
shall fall by the sword with them.
6 Thus says the LORD:
The pillars of Egypt shall fall,
and its proud strength sink;
From Migdol to Syene,
its people will fall by the sword—
oracle of the Lord GOD.*
7 It shall be the most desolate
among desolate lands,
Its cities the most ruined
among ruined cities.
8 They shall know that I am the LORD,
when I set fire to Egypt,
and all its allies are shattered.*
9 On that day, messengers from me
will go forth in ships
to terrorize confident Ethiopia.
Anguish will be among them
on Egypt's day—it is certainly coming!†
10 Thus says the Lord GOD:
I will put an end to Egypt's hordes
by the hand of Nebuchadnezzar, king of
Babylon:
11 He and his army with him,
the most ruthless of nations,
will be brought in to devastate the land.

†

29:14 *Pathros*: an Egyptian word for upper, i.e., southern, Egypt, above Memphis/Thebes. As silt filled the Delta region and richer land became available there, the population spread north, creating the tradition of a migration from the south (Is 11:11; Jer 44:1, 15).

29:17 *In the twenty-seventh year on the first day of the first month*: April 26, 571 B.C. This is the latest date attached to any of Ezekiel's prophecies.

29:18–19 Nebuchadnezzar's thirteen-year siege (587–574 B.C.) ended with Tyre's surrender on the condition that the Babylonian army would not loot and pillage (*pace* 26:3–14). According to Ezekiel, Nebuchadnezzar and his army should collect their wages for serving as God's instrument in Tyre's punishment, by plundering and controlling Egypt.

29:21 *A horn*: God will give Israel renewed strength. For horn as a symbol of strength, cf. Dt 33:17; Ps 92:11; 132:17. Ezekiel suggests that the Babylonian conquest of Egypt precedes Israel's restoration, an event he expects to witness and acknowledge when God removes his muteness.

30:5 *Mixed rabble*: mercenaries.

30:9 God spreads panic throughout Ethiopia, ancient Cush, by sending messengers with news of Egypt's fall. Rivers at its borders insulated Ethiopia and made it inaccessible except by boat.

*

29:12 Jer 46:19.
29:16 Ps 40:5; Is 20:5.
29:18 Is 26:7–14.
29:19 Is 19:4.
29:21 Ps 132:17; Lk 1:69.
30:3 cf. Ez 7:7; Is 13:6.
30:4 Jer 25:19–20.
30:6 cf. Ez 29:10.
30:8 Jer 49:27.

They will draw their swords against Egypt
and fill the land with the slain.
12 Then I will dry up the streams of the Nile,
and sell the land into evil hands;
By the hand of foreigners I will devastate
the land and everything in it.
I, the LORD, have spoken.*
13† Thus says the Lord GOD:
I will destroy idols,
and put an end to images in Memphis.
There will never again be a prince
over the land of Egypt.
Instead, I will spread fear
throughout the land of Egypt.*
14 I will devastate Pathros,
set fire to Zoan,
and execute judgment against Thebes.*
15 I will pour out my wrath on Pelusium,
the fortress of Egypt,
and cut off the troops of Thebes.
16 I will set fire to Egypt;
Pelusium will writhe in anguish,
Thebes will be breached,
and Memphis besieged in daylight.
17 The warriors of On and Pi-beseth
will fall by the sword,
the cities taken captive.
18 In Tahpanhes, the day will turn dark
when I break the scepter of Egypt there
and put an end to its proud strength.
Dark clouds will cover it,
and its women will go into captivity.*
19 I will execute judgment against Egypt
that they may know that I am the LORD.

Pharaoh's Broken Arm

20 On the seventh day of the first month in
the eleventh year,† the word of the LORD came
to me: 21 † Son of man, I have broken the arm
of Pharaoh, king of Egypt. See! It has not been
immobilized for healing, nor set with a splint
to make it strong enough to grasp a sword.*
22 Therefore thus says the Lord GOD: See! I am
coming against Pharaoh, king of Egypt. I will
break both his arms, the strong one and the bro-
ken one, making the sword fall from his hand.
23 I will scatter the Egyptians among the nations
and disperse them throughout other lands. 24 I
will, however, strengthen the arms of the king of
Babylon and put my sword in his hand so he can
bring it against Egypt for plunder and pillage.*
25 When I strengthen the arms of the king of
Babylon, and the arms of Pharaoh collapse, they
shall know that I am the LORD, because I put my
sword into the hand of the king of Babylon to
wield against the land of Egypt. 26 When I scatter
the Egyptians among the nations and disperse
them throughout other lands, they shall know
that I am the LORD.

Allegory of the Cedar

31 1 On the first day of the third month in the
eleventh year,† the word of the LORD came
to me: 2 Son of man, say to Pharaoh, the king
of Egypt, and to his hordes: In your greatness,
whom do you resemble?

3 Assyria! It is Assyria!†
A cedar of Lebanon—
Beautiful branches,
thick shade,
Towering heights,
its crown in the clouds!*
4 The waters made it grow,
the deep made it tall,
Letting its currents flow
around the place it was planted,
Then sending its channels
to all the other trees of the field.*
5 Thereupon it towered in height
above all the trees in the field;
Its branches were numerous
and its boughs long,
Because of the many waters
sent to its shoots.
6 In its branches nested
all the birds of the sky;
Under its boughs all the wild animals
gave birth,
And in its shade† dwelt
all the mighty nations.*
7 It was magnificent in size

†

30:13–19 The prophet enumerates a list of major Egyptian cities that shall each bear the judgment proclaimed in the previous oracle, vv. 1–12.

30:20 *The seventh day of the first month in the eleventh year*: April 29, 587 B.C.

30:21–26 This oracle was delivered more than a year into the siege of Jerusalem (24:1). When Pharaoh Hophra came to help Jerusalem, the Babylonians temporarily lifted the siege; cf. Jer 34:21; 37:6–7. In Ezekiel's eyes, Hophra was interfering with the punishment God intended the Babylonians to inflict on Judah. The Babylonians routed the Egyptians, who could not offer Jerusalem any more help; cf. chap. 31.

31:1 *The first day of the third month in the eleventh year*: June 21, 587 B.C.

31:3 *Assyria*: this translates *te'ashshur*, which some interpret as "cypress tree." The oracle, however, compares the fate of Pharaoh to the terrible demise of Assyria because of its arrogant pride (cf. Na 1–3). Ezekiel may have drawn on an ancient myth of a cosmic tree of life to emphasize the greatness of Egypt's fall.

31:6 *Shade*: a metaphor for protection (cf. Lam 4:20).

*

30:12 Is 19:6.
30:13 Is 19:13.
30:14 Is 19:11, 13; Jer 46:25.
30:18 Jer 43:4–7.
30:21 Jer 37:10; 44:30; 48:25.
30:24 cf. Ez 21:14.
31:3 Ps 92:12; Jer 50:18.
31:4 Dn 4:10.
31:6 Dn 4:12; cf. Mt 13:32.

and in the length of its branches,
For its roots reached down
to the many waters.
8 In the garden of God,
no cedars could rival it,
No juniper could equal its branches,
no plane tree match its boughs.
No tree in the garden of God
could match its beauty.*
9 I made it beautiful
with abundant foliage,
So that all the trees in Eden
were envious of it.†
10 Therefore, thus says the Lord GOD:
Because it was arrogant about its height,
lifting its crown among the clouds
and exalting itself because of its size,*
11 I handed it over to a ruler of nations
to deal with it according to its evil.
I have cast it off,
12 and foreigners have cut it down,
The most ruthless nations,
have hurled it on the mountains.
Its boughs fell into every valley
and its branches lay broken
in every ravine in the land.
All the peoples of the earth
departed from its shade
when it was hurled down.*
13 On its fallen trunk
sit all the birds of the sky;
Beside its fallen branches,
are found all the beasts of the field.
14 This has happened so no well-watered tree
will gain such lofty height,
or lift its crown to the clouds.
Not one of those fed by water
will tower in height over the rest.
For all of them are destined for death,
for the underworld, among mere mortals,
with those who go down to the pit.
15 Thus says the Lord GOD:
On the day it went down to Sheol,
I made the deep close up
in mourning for it.
I restrained the currents of the deep,
and held back the many waters.
I darkened Lebanon because of it,
and all the trees of the field
languished because of it.
16 At the sound of its fall,
I made nations shudder,
When I cast it down to Sheol
with those who go down to the pit.
In the underworld
all the trees of Eden took comfort:
Lebanon's choicest and best,
all that were fed by the waters.*
17 They too will go down to Sheol,
to those slain by the sword,
Its allies† who dwelt
in its shade among the nations.
18 To whom among the trees of Eden
do you compare in glory and greatness?
You will be brought down
with the trees of Eden to the underworld,
And lie among the uncircumcised,
with those slain by the sword.
Such is Pharaoh and all his hordes—
oracle of the Lord GOD.

Lament over Pharaoh

32 1 On the first day of the twelfth month in
the twelfth year,† the word of the LORD
came to me: 2 Son of man, utter a lament over
Pharaoh, the king of Egypt, and say to him:

You liken yourself to a lion among nations,
but you are like the monster in the sea!
Thrashing about in your streams,
churning the water with your feet,
polluting the streams.*
3 Thus says the Lord GOD:
I will cast my net over you
by assembling many armies,
and I will hoist you up in my mesh.
4 I will hurl you onto the land,
cast you into an open field.
I will make all the birds of the sky
roost upon you,
The beasts of the whole earth
gorge themselves on you.
5 I will strew your flesh on the mountains,
and fill the valleys with your corpse.*
6 I will drench the land,
pouring out your blood on the mountain;
filling up the ravines with you.
7 When I extinguish you,
I will cover the heavens
and darken all its stars.
The sun I will cover with clouds;
the moon will not give light.*

†
31:9 Here Israel's God is responsible for Assyria's splendor, whereas in Is 10:13 Assyria claims to have created its own might.
31:17 *Allies*: lit., "arm."
32:1 *The first day of the twelfth month in the twelfth year*: March 3, 585 B.C.

*
31:8 Ps 80:10.
31:10 Is 2:11.
31:12 Dn 4:14.
31:16 Is 14:8, 15.
32:2 cf. Ez 19:1; 20:3.
32:5 Is 34:3.
32:7 Is 3:10.

EZ

8 All the shining lights in the heavens
I will darken over you;
I will spread darkness over your land—
oracle of the Lord GOD.
9 I will trouble the hearts
of many peoples,
When I bring you captive
among the nations,
to lands you do not know.
10 I will fill many nations with horror;
their kings will shudder at you,
when I brandish my sword in their faces.
They will tremble violently
fearing for their lives on the day of your fall.*
11 For thus says the Lord GOD:
The sword of the king of Babylon
will come against you.
12 I will cut down your hordes
with the swords of warriors,
all of them, ruthless nations;
They will lay waste the glory of Egypt,
and all its hordes will be destroyed.*
13 I will wipe out all the livestock
from the banks of its many waters;
No human foot will disturb them again,
no animal hoof stir them up.
14 Then I will make their waters clear
and their streams flow like oil—
oracle of the Lord GOD.
15 When I make Egypt a wasteland
and the land destitute of everything,
When I strike down all its inhabitants
they shall know that I am the LORD.
16 This is the lamentation
women of all nations will chant;
They will raise it over Egypt;
over all its hordes they will chant it—
oracle of the Lord GOD.

Another Lament over Egypt

17 † On the fifteenth day of that month in the
twelfth year, the word of the LORD came to me:

18 Son of man, wail over the hordes of Egypt—
you and the women of mighty nations—
Send them down to the underworld,
with those who go down into the pit.
19 Whom do you excel in beauty? Go down!
Be laid to rest with the uncircumcised!
20 Among those slain by the sword they will fall,
for the sword has been appointed!
Seize Egypt and all its hordes.*
21 Out of Sheol the mighty warriors
will speak to him and his allies:
Let them descend and lie down among the
uncircumcised,
those slain by the sword!*
22 There is Assyria and all its company,
around it are its graves,
all of them slain, fallen by the sword.
23 The graves are set
in the recesses of the pit;
Its company is assembled
around its grave,
All of them slain, fallen by the sword,
those who spread terror in the land of the
living.*
24 There is Elam and all its horde
around its grave,
All of them slain, fallen by the sword;
they descended uncircumcised
into the underworld,
Those who spread their terror
in the land of the living.
They bear their disgrace
with those who go down into the pit.
25 Among the slain is set its bed,
with all its horde around its grave;
All of them uncircumcised,
slain by the sword
Because of the terror they spread
in the land of the living.
They bear their disgrace
with those who go down into the pit.
Among the slain it is set!
26 There is Meshech and Tubal† and all the hordes
surrounding it with their graves.
All of them uncircumcised,
slain by the sword
Because they spread their terror
in the land of the living.*
27 They do not rest with the warriors
who fell in ancient times,
who went down to Sheol fully armed.
Their swords were placed under their heads
and their shields laid over their bones;
For there was terror of these warriors
in the land of the living.
28 But as for you, among the uncircumcised
you will be broken and laid to rest

† **32:17–32** The description of Pharaoh in Sheol shifts rapidly between the single individual and the collective body, between corpses speaking and corpses lying inert, between singular (his, hers, its) and plural (them, theirs) pronouns to emphasize that all the enemies of Israel come to the same end.

32:26 *Meshech and Tubal*: see note on 38:2.

* **32:10** Rev 18:9–10; 32:12; cf. Ez 31:11–12.
32:12 cf. Ez 3:11–12.
32:20 cf. Ez 31:17–18.
32:21 Is 14:9.
32:23 Is 14:15.
32:26 cf. Ez 27:13.

with those slain by the sword.
29 There is Edom, all its kings and princes,
who, despite their might,
are put with those slain by the sword.
They lie among the uncircumcised,
with those who go down into the pit.*
30 There are the generals of the north
and all the Sidonians
Who have gone down with the slain,
because of the terror their might inspired.
They lie uncircumcised
with those slain by the sword,
And bear their shame with those
who have gone down into the pit.*
31 When Pharaoh sees them,
he will be consoled on behalf of all his
hordes,
slain by the sword—
Pharaoh and all his army—
oracle of the Lord God.
32 I spread terror of him
in the land of the living;
Now he is laid among the uncircumcised,
with those slain by the sword—
Pharaoh and all his horde—
oracle of the Lord God.

IV. Hope for the Future

The Prophet as Sentinel

33 1 The word of the Lord came to me: 2 Son
of man, speak to your people and tell
them: When I bring the sword against a land,
if the people of that land select one of their
number as a sentinel† for them,* 3 and the sen-
tinel sees the sword coming against the land, he
should blow the trumpet to warn the people.*
4 If they hear the trumpet but do not take the
warning and a sword attacks and kills them, their
blood will be on their own heads.* 5 They heard
the trumpet blast but ignored the warning; their
blood is on them. If they had heeded the warn-
ing, they could have escaped with their lives. 6 If,
however, the sentinel sees the sword coming and
does not blow the trumpet, so that the sword
attacks and takes someone's life, his life will be
taken for his own sin, but I will hold the sentinel
responsible for his blood.
7 * You, son of man—I have appointed you as
a sentinel for the house of Israel; when you hear
a word from my mouth, you must warn them for
me. 8 When I say to the wicked, "You wicked, you
must die," and you do not speak up to warn the
wicked about their ways, they shall die in their
sins, but I will hold you responsible for their
blood. 9 If, however, you warn the wicked to turn
from their ways, but they do not, then they shall
die in their sins, but you shall save your life.

Individual Retribution

10 As for you, son of man, speak to the house of
Israel: You people say, "Our crimes and our sins
weigh us down; we are rotting away because of
them. How can we survive?"* 11 * Answer them:
As I live—oracle of the Lord God—I swear I take
no pleasure in the death of the wicked, but rather
that they turn from their ways and live. Turn,
turn from your evil ways! Why should you die,
house of Israel?
12 As for you, son of man, say to your people:
The justice of the just will not save them on the
day they sin; the wickedness of the wicked will
not bring about their downfall on the day they
turn from their wickedness. No, the just can-
not save their lives on the day they sin.* 13 Even
though I say to the just that they shall surely live,
if they, relying on their justice, do wrong, none
of their just deeds shall be remembered; because
of the wrong they have done, they shall die.*
14 And though I say to the wicked that they shall
die, if they turn away from sin and do what is just
and right— 15 returning pledges, restoring stolen
goods, walking by statutes that bring life, doing
nothing wrong—they shall surely live; they shall
not die.* 16 None of the sins they committed
shall be remembered against them. If they do
what is right and just, they shall surely live.
17 Your people say, "The way of the Lord is not
fair!" But it is their way that is not fair. 18 When
the just turn away from justice and do wrong,
they shall die for it.* 19 When the wicked turn
away from wickedness and do what is right and
just, because of this they shall live. 20 But still
you say, "The way of the Lord is not fair!" I will
judge each of you according to your ways, house
of Israel.

The Survivor from Jerusalem

21 On the fifth day of the tenth month,† in the
twelfth year of our exile, the survivor came to me

33:2 *Sentinel*: the theme of the sentinel's duty initiates a new commission to announce salvation (chaps. 33–48), just as the same command (3:17–21) opened Ezekiel's ministry to announce judgment (chaps. 3–24).

33:21–22 *The fifth day of the tenth month*: January 8, 585 B.C. According to Jeremiah (39:2), Jerusalem was taken in July, 587. Some manuscripts read "eleventh" for "twelfth" year (January, 586); even so, there was ample time between the fall of Jerusalem and the arrival

32:29 Is 34:5–15.
32:30 Jer 25:26.
33:2 Lv 26:25.
33:3 Hos 5:8; 8:1.
33:4 Lv 20:9; Jer 6:17.
33:7 Jer 1:17.
33:10 Lv 26:16, 39.
33:11 Jer 44:7–8; cf. Ez 18:23.
33:12 cf. Ez 3:20.
33:13 Heb 10:38.
33:15 Ex 22:1–4, 26.
33:18 Jer 18:7–10.

from Jerusalem and said, "The city is taken!"*
22 The hand of the LORD had come upon me the
evening before the survivor arrived and opened my
mouth when he reached me in the morning. My
mouth was opened, and I was mute no longer.*

Those Left in Judah†

23 The word of the LORD came to me: 24 Son
of man, these who live among the ruins in the
land of Israel are saying: "Abraham was only one
person, yet he was given possession of the land.
Since we are many, the land must be given to
us as our possession."* 25 Therefore say to them:
Thus says the Lord GOD: You eat on the mountains, you raise your eyes to your idols, you shed
blood—yet you would keep possession of the
land?* 26 You rely on your swords, you commit
abominations, each defiles his neighbor's wife—
yet you would keep possession of the land? 27 Say
this to them: Thus says the Lord GOD: As I live,
those among the ruins shall fall by the sword;
those in the open field I have made food for the
wild beasts; and those in rocky hideouts and
caves shall die by the plague. 28 I will make the
land a desolate waste, so that its proud strength
will come to an end, and the mountains of Israel
shall be so desolate that no one will cross them.
29 Thus they shall know that I am the LORD, when
I make the land a desolate waste because of all
the abominations they committed.

Popular Misunderstanding

30 As for you, son of man, your people are talking about you beside the walls and in the doorways of houses. They say to one another, "Let's
go hear the latest word that comes from the
LORD." 31 My people come to you, gathering as
a crowd and sitting in front of you to hear your
words, but they will not act on them. Love songs
are on their lips, but in their hearts they pursue dishonest gain.* 32 For them you are only a
singer† of love songs, with a pleasant voice and a
clever touch. They listen to your words, but they
do not obey them. 33 But when it comes—and
it is surely coming!—they shall know that there
was a prophet among them.

Parable of the Shepherds

34 1 The word of the LORD came to me: 2 Son
of man, prophesy against the shepherds†
of Israel. Prophesy and say to them: To the
shepherds, thus says the Lord GOD: Woe to the
shepherds of Israel who have been pasturing
themselves!* Should not shepherds pasture the
flock? 3 You consumed milk, wore wool, and
slaughtered fatlings, but the flock you did not
pasture.* 4 You did not strengthen the weak nor
heal the sick nor bind up the injured. You did not
bring back the stray or seek the lost but ruled them
harshly and brutally.* 5 So they were scattered for
lack of a shepherd, and became food for all the
wild beasts. They were scattered* 6 and wandered
over all the mountains and high hills; over the entire surface of the earth my sheep were scattered.
No one looked after them or searched for them.

7 Therefore, shepherds, hear the word of the
LORD: 8 As I live—oracle of the Lord GOD—
because my sheep became plunder, because my
sheep became food for wild beasts, for lack of a
shepherd, because my shepherds did not look
after my sheep, but pastured themselves and did
not pasture my sheep,* 9 therefore, shepherds,
hear the word of the LORD: 10 Thus says the Lord
GOD: Look! I am coming against these shepherds.
I will take my sheep out of their hand and put a
stop to their shepherding my flock, so that these
shepherds will no longer pasture them. I will
deliver my flock from their mouths so it will not
become their food.*

11 For thus says the Lord GOD: Look! I myself
will search for my sheep and examine them. 12 As
a shepherd examines his flock while he himself is
among his scattered sheep, so will I examine my
sheep. I will deliver them from every place where
they were scattered on the day of dark clouds.*
13 I will lead them out from among the peoples
and gather them from the lands; I will bring them
back to their own country and pasture them upon
the mountains of Israel, in the ravines and every
inhabited place in the land.* 14 In good pastures
I will pasture them; on the mountain heights of
Israel will be their grazing land. There they will

---

† of the survivor from that city to journey to Babylon. However, this is the survivor sent to fulfill the promise of Ez 24:25–27, the eyewitness whose arrival would release Ezekiel from his muteness; cf. 3:26–27.

33:23–29 News brought by the survivor furnished the occasion for this prophecy. Like Jeremiah, Ezekiel rejects the idea that those left in Judah have any claim to the land. The new Israel is to be formed from the exiles.

33:32 *Singer*: perhaps the term indicates an entertainer whom one enjoys and then forgets.

34:2 *Shepherds*: the leaders of the people. A frequent title for kings and deities in the ancient Near East; the ideal ruler took care of his subjects and anticipated their needs. Ezekiel's oracle broadens the reference to include the whole class of Jerusalem's leaders (v. 17). The prophet assures his audience, the exiles in Babylon, that God holds these leaders responsible for what has happened to Jerusalem and will give Israel a new shepherd worthy of the title.

---

* **33:21** 2 Kgs 25:4, 10; Is 39:1–2.
33:22 cf. Ez 3:26–27.
33:24 Is 51:2.
33:25 Gn 9:4; Jer 7:9–10.
33:31 cf. Ez 8:1; Mt 13:22.
34:2 Ps 78:70–72; Jn 10:11.
34:3 Is 56:11.
34:4 Ex 1:13; Zec 11:15–17; Mt 18:12–14.
34:5 cf. Mk 6:34.
34:8 Jude 12.
34:10 Ps 72:14.
34:12 Is 40:11; Lk 19:10.
34:13 cf. Ez 36:24, 29–30.

lie down on good grazing ground; in rich pas-
tures they will be pastured on the mountains of
Israel.* 15 I myself will pasture my sheep; I myself
will give them rest—oracle of the Lord God. 16 The
lost I will search out, the strays I will bring back,
the injured I will bind up, and the sick I will heal;
but the sleek and the strong I will destroy. I will
shepherd them in judgment.

Separation of the Sheep

17 As for you, my flock, thus says the Lord God:
I will judge between one sheep and another, be-
tween rams and goats.* 18 Was it not enough for
you to graze on the best pasture, that you had
to trample the rest of your pastures with your
hooves? Or to drink the clearest water, that you
had to pollute the rest with your hooves? 19 Thus
my flock had to graze on what your hooves had
trampled and drink what your hooves had pol-
luted. 20 Therefore thus says the Lord God: Now
I will judge between the fat and the lean. 21 Be-
cause you push with flank and shoulder, and
butt all the weak sheep with your horns until you
drive them off, 22 I will save my flock so they can
no longer be plundered; I will judge between one
sheep and another. 23 * I will appoint one shep-
herd† over them to pasture them, my servant Da-
vid; he shall pasture them and be their shepherd.
24 I, the Lord, will be their God, and my servant
David will be prince in their midst. I, the Lord,
have spoken.*
25 I will make a covenant of peace with them
and rid the country of wild beasts so they will
dwell securely in the wilderness and sleep in the
forests.* 26 I will settle them around my hill and
send rain in its season, the blessing of abundant
rain. 27 The trees of the field shall bear their fruits,
and the land its crops, and they shall dwell se-
curely on their own soil. They shall know that I
am the Lord when I break the bars of their yoke
and deliver them from the power of those who
enslaved them.* 28 They shall no longer be plun-
dered by the nations nor will wild beasts devour
them, but they shall dwell securely, with no
one to frighten them.* 29 I will prepare for them
peaceful fields for planting so they are never
again swept away by famine in the land or bear
taunts from the nations. 30 Thus they shall know

Pray It!

The Good Shepherd

The theme of the good shepherd is common in the Bible. Psalm 23 compares God to a protective shepherd. Ezekiel, chapter 34, describes bad shepherds and contrasts them with God, the true shepherd, who feeds the flock with justice. In John 10:1–18, Jesus compares himself to a good shepherd.

God, the true shepherd, thank you for your care and protection. Today, I will do what I can to help your work. Make me aware of the people in my life who are weak, injured, straying, or lost. With your help, I will do what I can to strengthen them, heal them, and bring them back to you. Help me to be more like a shepherd than like a sheep that merely follows!

▶ **Ezekiel, chapter 34**

that I, the Lord, their God, am with them, and
that they are my people, the house of Israel—
oracle of the Lord God.* 31 Yes, you are my flock:
you people are the flock of my pasture, and I am
your God—oracle of the Lord God.*

Against Edom†

35 1 The word of the Lord came to me: 2 Son
of man, set your face against Mount Seir
and prophesy against it. 3 Say to it: Thus says the
Lord God: Watch out! I am against you, Mount
Seir. I will stretch out my hand against you and
turn you into a desolate waste.* 4 Your cities I
will turn into ruins, and you shall be a desola-
tion; then you shall know that I am the Lord.*
5 Because you nursed a long-standing hatred
and handed the Israelites over to the sword at
the time of their collapse, at the time of their
final punishment,† * 6 therefore, as I live—oracle

EZ

†

34:23 *One shepherd*: a future king to rule over a unified, restored Israel, in the image of the idealized David present in the Book of Kings (cf., e.g., 1 Kgs 3:3; 11:38; 2 Kgs 14:3; 22:2). *My servant David*: a common characterization of David; e.g., 1 Kgs 11:34, 36, 38; 2 Kgs 8:19; Ps 36:1; 78:70. See Ez 37:25.

35:1–15 After the fall of Jerusalem, Edom assisted the Babylonians in devastating the land and subduing the population in order to occupy part of Judah's former territory. For this reason these oracles against Edom are found in the context of the city's fall.

35:5 *Final punishment*: throughout this oracle the prophet echoes the threat against the mountains of Israel found in chaps. 6–7.

*

34:14 Ps 23:2; Is 40:11.
34:17 Mt 25:32–33.
34:23 Ps 89:4, 20; Jer 23:5–6.
34:24 cf. Ez 36:28; Ps 89:49; Jn 10:16.
34:25 Is 11:6–9.
34:27 Lv 26:13; Ps 72:16; Jer 28:10–13.
34:28 Jer 30:10.
34:30 Ex 6:7.
34:31 Ps 28:9.
35:3 cf. Ez 25:12–14.
35:4 Ob 13.
35:5 Ob 11–15.

of the Lord GOD—you are guilty of blood, and
blood, I swear, shall pursue you. 7 I will make
Mount Seir a desolate waste and cut off from it
anyone who travels across it and back.* 8 I will
fill its mountains with the slain; those slain by
the sword shall fall on your hills, into your val-
leys and all your ravines.

9 I will make you a desolation forever,
your cities will not be inhabited,
and you shall know that I am the LORD.*

10 Because you said: The two nations and the
two lands† belong to me; let us take possession
of them—although the LORD was there— 11 there-
fore, as I live—oracle of the Lord GOD—I will
deal with you according to the anger and envy
you dealt out to them in your hatred, and I will
make myself known to them when I execute
judgment on you,* 12 then you shall know that I
am the LORD.

I have heard all the insults you spoke against
the mountains of Israel, saying: They are deso-
late; they have been given to us to devour. 13 You
boasted against me with your mouths and used
insolent words against me. I heard everything!
14 Thus says the Lord GOD: Because you rejoiced
that the whole land was desolate, so I will do to
you. 15 As you rejoiced over the devastation of
the heritage of the house of Israel, the same I will
do to you: you will become a ruin, Mount Seir,
and the whole of Edom, all of it! Then they shall
know that I am the LORD.*

Regeneration of the Land

36 1 As for you, son of man, prophesy to the
mountains of Israel and say: Mountains
of Israel, hear the word of the LORD! 2 Thus says
the Lord GOD: Because the enemy said about you,
"Ha! the ancient heights have become our posses-
sion," 3 therefore prophesy and say: Thus says the
Lord GOD: because you have been ridiculed and
hounded on all sides for becoming a possession
for the remaining nations and have become a by-
word and a popular jeer,* 4 therefore, mountains
of Israel, hear the word of the Lord GOD: Thus
says the Lord GOD to the mountains and hills, to
the ravines and valleys, to the desolate ruins and
abandoned cities, plundered and mocked by the
nations remaining around you:* 5 therefore thus
says the Lord GOD: Truly, with burning jealousy I
speak against the remaining nations and against
Edom; they all took possession of my land for
plunder with wholehearted joy and utter con-
tempt. 6 Therefore, prophesy concerning the land
of Israel and say to the mountains and hills, to the
ravines and valleys: Thus says the Lord GOD: See!
in my jealous fury I speak, because you endured
the reproach of the nations. 7 Therefore, thus says
the Lord GOD: I raise my hand and swear: the na-
tions around you shall bear their own reproach.

8 But you, mountains of Israel, you will sprout
branches and bear fruit for my people Israel, for
they are coming soon.* 9 Look! I am for you! I
will turn my face toward you; you will be plowed
and planted.* 10 Upon you I will multiply the
whole house of Israel; cities shall be resettled and
ruins rebuilt.* 11 Upon you I will multiply people
and animals so they can multiply and be fruitful.
I will resettle you as in the past, and make you
more prosperous than at your beginning; then
you shall know that I am the LORD.*

12 Upon you I will have them walk, my people
Israel. They shall possess you, and you shall be
their heritage. Never again shall you rob them of
their children.

13 Thus says the Lord GOD: Because they say of
you, "You devour your own people,† you rob
your nation of its children,"* 14 therefore, you
shall never again devour your people or rob your
nation of its children—oracle of the Lord GOD. 15 I
will no longer make you listen to the reproach of
nations. You will never again endure insults from
the peoples. Never again shall you rob your na-
tion of its children—oracle of the Lord GOD.

Regeneration of the People

16 The word of the LORD came to me: 17 Son of
man, when the house of Israel lived in its land,
they defiled it with their behavior and their
deeds. In my sight their behavior was like the
impurity of a woman in menstruation.* 18 So I
poured out my fury upon them for the blood
they poured out on the ground and for the idols
with which they defiled it. 19 I scattered them
among the nations, and they were dispersed

†

35:10 *The two nations and the two lands*: by presenting Edom's excursion into the southern territory of Judah as its claim to both kingdoms, Ezekiel exaggerates Edom's greed and arrogance. *LORD was there*: Edom's betrayal of Judah becomes an attack on Judah's God, the land's sovereign. In 11:15 and 33:24, Ezekiel condemns Judahites who annex land that does not belong to them. Now the exiles in Babylon learn that even though God had left Jerusalem (chap. 11), he witnesses Edom's insolence and pronounces judgment against it. Cf. 48:35, "The LORD is there!"

36:13 *You devour your own people*: i.e., the land destroys its own population; this phrase also occurs in Nm 13:32, where Israelite spies describe Canaan as "a land that devours its inhabitants."

*

35:7 Jer 46:19.
35:9 Is 34:5–6; Ob 10.
35:11 Ob 15.
35:15 Is 34:11; Ob 12.
36:3 Ob 13.
36:4 cf. Ez 6:3.
36:8 Lv 26:3–5.
36:9 Lv 26:9.
36:10 Is 49:8, 17–23.
36:11 cf. Gn 1:22, 28.
36:13 Nm 13:32.
36:17 Ps 106:37–38.

Cultural Connection

You Will Be Cleansed

The sweat lodge ceremony is a Native American tradition that is still used today. It is performed whenever there is a need to be purified in order to prepare for God's blessings or ask for God's help.

This ceremony is held in a shelter of poles and blankets that is made over a pit, with the door flap facing west, the direction the rains come from. Heated rocks fill the pit, and steam is formed when water is poured on the rocks. The ceremony consists of entering the shelter and sitting in a circle, passing a pipe, making steam, and praying toward the four directions for guidance and blessings and for maintaining an attitude of thankfulness.

This tradition ritualizes the cleansing and conversion Ezekiel proclaims in Ezekiel 36:25–26. It reflects a faith that the Great Spirit, or God, will cleanse us with waters and give us a new heart and spirit.

► Ez 36:25–26

through other lands; according to their behavior
and their deeds I carried out judgment against
them.* 20 † But when they came to the nations,
where they went, they desecrated my holy name,
for people said of them: "These are the people of
the LORD, yet they had to leave their land." 21 So
I relented because of my holy name which the
house of Israel desecrated among the nations to
which they came. 22 Therefore say to the house of
Israel: Thus says the Lord GOD: Not for your sake
do I act, house of Israel, but for the sake of my
holy name, which you desecrated among the na-
tions to which you came.* 23 But I will show the
holiness of my great name, desecrated among the
nations, in whose midst you desecrated it. Then
the nations shall know that I am the LORD—ora-
cle of the Lord GOD—when through you I show
my holiness before their very eyes.* 24 I will take
you away from among the nations, gather you
from all the lands, and bring you back to your
own soil. 25 † * I will sprinkle clean water over
you to make you clean; from all your impurities
and from all your idols I will cleanse you. 26 * I
will give you a new heart, and a new spirit I will
put within you. I will remove the heart of stone
from your flesh and give you a heart of flesh.*
27 I will put my spirit within you so that you
walk in my statutes, observe my ordinances, and
keep them.* 28 You will live in the land I gave to
your ancestors; you will be my people, and I will
be your God.* 29 I will deliver you from all your
impurities. I will summon the grain and make
it plentiful; I will not send famine against you.
30 I will increase the fruit on your trees and the
crops in your fields so that you no longer endure
reproach from the nations because of famine.*
31 Then you will remember your evil behavior
and your deeds that were not good; you will
loathe yourselves for your sins and your abom-
inations. 32 Not for your sake do I act—oracle
of the Lord GOD. Let this be known to you! Be
ashamed and humbled because of your behav-
ior, house of Israel.
33 Thus says the Lord GOD: When I cleanse you
of all your guilt, I will resettle the cities and the
ruins will be rebuilt.* 34 The desolate land will be
tilled—once a wasteland in the eyes of every pass-
erby. 35 They will say, "This once-desolate land
has become like the garden of Eden. The cities
once ruined, laid waste and destroyed, are now
resettled and fortified."* 36 Then the surrounding
nations that remain shall know that I, the LORD,

† **36:20–24** These verses make clear that Israel's restoration is God's initiative, independent of the people's shame and repentance (v. 31). By their wickedness, Israel provoked the exile; its presence among the nations gave the impression that God could not protect his people. God's gracious return of Israel to its land will restore his honor among these same nations.

36:25–26 God's initiative to cleanse Israel (cf. 24:13–14) is the first act in the creation of a new people, no longer disposed to repeating Israel's wicked past (chap. 20). To make this restoration permanent, God replaces Israel's rebellious and obdurate interiority ("heart of stone") with an interiority ("heart of flesh") susceptible to and animated by God's intentions ("my spirit," v. 27).

* **36:19** Lv 18:24–28.
36:22 cf. Ez 20:44; Dt 9:4–6; Is 37:35.
36:23 cf. Ez 20:41; Is 37:23.
36:25 Ezr 6:21; Ps 51:2–7.
36:26–27 Jer 31:33–34.
36:26 cf. Rom 8:5–8.
36:27 Ps 51:7–11.
36:28 Jer 30:22; 31:33.
36:30 Lv 26:4–5.
36:33 Lv 26:31.
36:35 cf. Ez 28:13; 31:9.

Did You Know?

Wind, Breath, and Spirit

In English, the words *wind, breath,* and *spirit* have three different meanings. Hebrew has only one word for all three meanings: *ruah.* The "mighty wind sweeping over the waters" at Creation (Gn 1:2) is *ruah.* The "breath of life" that God blows into the lifeless clay of the first human (Gn 2:7) is *ruah.* And the "spirit of the LORD [that] rushed upon David" at his anointing (1 Sm 16:13) is *ruah.*

In Ezekiel 37:1–14, all three meanings of the word *ruah* come into play. Ezekiel cries out, "Thus says the Lord GOD: From the four winds come, O breath, and breathe into these slain that they may come to life" (verse 9). In the prophet's vision, the bones scattered across the battlefield are the exiled people of God, who have experienced the "death" of defeat and humiliation. God promises that the spirit *(ruah)* of God (see verse 14) will bring the people of Israel back from the Exile and restore them to their land.

▶ **Ez 37:1–14**

EZ

have rebuilt what was destroyed and replanted
what was desolate. I, the LORD, have spoken: I will
do it. 37 Thus says the Lord GOD: This also I will be
persuaded to do for the house of Israel: to mul-
tiply them like sheep. 38 Like sheep for sacrifice,
like the sheep of Jerusalem on its feast days, the
ruined cities shall be filled with flocks of people;
then they shall know that I am the LORD.*

Vision of the Dry Bones†

37 1 The hand of the LORD came upon me,
and he led me out in the spirit of the LORD
and set me in the center of the broad valley. It
was filled with bones. 2 He made me walk among
them in every direction. So many lay on the sur-
face of the valley! How dry they were! 3 He asked
me: Son of man, can these bones come back to
life? "Lord GOD," I answered, "you alone know
that."* 4 Then he said to me: Prophesy over these
bones, and say to them: Dry bones, hear the word
of the LORD! 5 Thus says the Lord GOD to these
bones: Listen! I will make breath enter you so
you may come to life. 6 I will put sinews on you,
make flesh grow over you, cover you with skin,
and put breath into you so you may come to
life. Then you shall know that I am the LORD. 7 I
prophesied as I had been commanded. A sound
started up, as I was prophesying, rattling like
thunder. The bones came together, bone join-
ing to bone. 8 As I watched, sinews appeared on
them, flesh grew over them, skin covered them
on top, but there was no breath in them. 9 Then
he said to me: Prophesy to the breath, prophesy,
son of man! Say to the breath: Thus says the Lord
GOD: From the four winds come, O breath, and
breathe into these slain that they may come to
life.† * 10 I prophesied as he commanded me, and
the breath entered them; they came to life and
stood on their feet, a vast army.* 11 He said to me:
Son of man, these bones are the whole house of
Israel! They are saying, "Our bones are dried up,
our hope is lost, and we are cut off." 12 Therefore,
prophesy and say to them: Thus says the Lord
GOD: Look! I am going to open your graves; I will
make you come up out of your graves, my people,
and bring you back to the land of Israel.* 13 You
shall know that I am the LORD, when I open your
graves and make you come up out of them, my
people! 14 I will put my spirit in you that you may
come to life, and I will settle you in your land.
Then you shall know that I am the LORD. I have
spoken; I will do it—oracle of the LORD.*

The Two Sticks

15 † Thus the word of the LORD came to me:
16 As for you, son of man, take one stick and
write on it, "Judah and those Israelites associated

†

37:1–14 This account is a figurative description of God's creation of a new Israel. Even though that creation begins with the remains of the old Israel, the exiles under the image of dry bones, depicting a totally hopeless situation, the new Israel is radically different: it is an ideal people, shaped by God's spirit to live the covenant faithfully, something the old Israel, exiles included, were unable to do. While this passage in its present context is not about the doctrine of individual or communal resurrection, many Jewish and Christian commentators suggest that the doctrine is foreshadowed here.

37:9 The Hebrew word *rûah* has multiple related meanings expressed by different English words: wind, spirit, breath. In this translation, *rûah* is rendered "spirit," a powerful force that creates vision and insight (v. 1); "breath," physical energy that quickens and enlivens (vv. 5–6); "wind," invisible physical energy, sometimes destructive, sometimes invigorating (e.g., the rain-bearing winter winds), also a metaphor for restoration and new life (vv. 9–10); "my spirit," a share in God's power so the people observe the law that assures them life in the land (v. 14).

37:15–22 The symbolic action of joining two sticks into one continues Ezekiel's description of God's future saving action: the unification of Judah and Israel under an ideal ruler.

*

36:38 1 Kgs 8:63.
37:3 Is 26:19.
37:9 Ps 104:30; Is 32:15; Dn 7:2.
37:10 cf. Rev 11:11.
37:12 Is 26:19; Jer 19:14.
37:14 cf. Ez 36:27–28; Jer 43:2; Jl 3:1–2.

with it." Then take another stick and write on it: "Joseph, Ephraim's stick, and the whole house of Israel associated with it." 17 Join the two sticks together so they become one stick in your hand. 18 When your people ask you, "Will you not tell us what you mean by all this?" 19 answer them: Thus says the Lord GOD: I will take the stick of Joseph, now in Ephraim's hand, and the tribes of Israel associated with it, and join to it the stick of Judah, making them one stick; they shall become one in my hand.* 20 The sticks on which you write, you must hold in your hand in their sight. 21 Say to them: Thus says the Lord GOD: I will soon take the Israelites from among the nations to which they have gone and gather them from all around to bring them back to their land. 22 I will make them one nation in the land, upon the mountains of Israel, and there shall be one king for them all. They shall never again be two nations, never again be divided into two kingdoms.*

23 No longer shall they defile themselves with their idols, their abominations, and all their transgressions. I will deliver them from all their apostasy through which they sinned. I will cleanse them so that they will be my people, and I will be their God.* 24 * David my servant shall be king over them; they shall all have one shepherd. They shall walk in my ordinances, observe my statutes, and keep them. 25 They shall live on the land I gave to Jacob my servant, the land where their ancestors lived; they shall live on it always, they, their children, and their children's children, with David my servant as their prince forever. 26 * I will make a covenant of peace with them; it shall be an everlasting covenant with them. I will multiply them and put my sanctuary among them forever. 27 My dwelling shall be with them; I will be their God, and they will be my people.* 28 Then the nations shall know that I, the LORD, make Israel holy, by putting my sanctuary among them forever.

First Prophecy Against Gog

38 1 The word of the LORD came to me:† 2 Son of man, turn your face against Gog† of the land of Magog, the chief prince of Meshech and Tubal, and prophesy against him.* 3 Say: Thus says the Lord GOD: See! I am coming against you, Gog, chief prince of Meshech and Tubal. 4 I will turn you around and put hooks in your jaws to lead you out with all your army, horses and riders, all well armed, a great company, all of them with bucklers and shields, carrying swords: 5 * Persia, Cush, and Put with them, all with shields and helmets; 6 Gomer and all its troops, Beth-togarmah from the recesses of Zaphon and all its troops—many nations will accompany you. 7 Prepare and get ready, you and the company mobilized for you, but in my service. 8 After many days you will be called to battle; in the last

Live It!

Bone Dry

When have you felt dry and lifeless, like the collection of dry bones Ezekiel sees in his vision in Ezekiel 37:1–2? What helps you to re-energize, to put muscle and flesh back on your tired bones? What winds blow life through you to give you breath again, to make you new again?

Bones are our body's support structure, and prayer is our soul's support structure. In verse 14, God's Spirit brings life. We need to pray for God's Spirit—the Holy Spirit—to fill us in order to avoid shriveling up and becoming parched and lifeless. And we need to share God's Spirit with others, to breathe life into the dry bones around us—the people who seem to have no energy or hope.

What are the dry bones in your life? What can you do to be re-energized by God when you feel like dry bones? How can you help to energize others who seem dry and lifeless?

▶ **Ezekiel, chapter 37**

EZ

† **38:1–39:20** These three oracles against Gog (38:2–13; 14–23; 39:1–20) describe a mythic attack of God against a final enemy of his people sometime in the future. Like the oracles against the nations, their purpose is to strengthen Israel's hope in God, since they end with God's triumph on behalf of the people.

38:2 *Gog*: the name is symbolic, probably derived from Gyges, king of Lydia. The gloss Magog may be an Akkadian expression, *mat-Gog*, "the land of Gog." Meshech and Tubal, as well as Gomer and Beth-togarmah (v. 6), were countries around the Black Sea, the northernmost countries known to the Israelites. The north was the traditional direction from which invasion was expected; cf. Jer 1:13–15.

37:19 Zec 10:6.
37:22 cf. Ez 17:22; 34:13–14.
37:23 cf. Ez 11:18; 36:28; Na 2:2.
37:24 Ps 78:70–71; Is 55:4.
37:26 Gn 9:16; Nm 25:12; Heb 13:20.
37:27 Lv 26:11.
38:2 cf. Gn 10:2; Ez 27:13.
38:5–6 Gn 10:2–3, 6.

years you will invade a land that has survived the
sword—a people gathered from many nations
back to the long-deserted mountains of Israel,
brought forth from the nations to dwell se-
curely.* 9 You shall come up like a sudden storm,
covering the land like a cloud, you and all your
troops and the many nations with you.*
10 Thus says the Lord GOD: On that day
thoughts shall cross your mind, and you shall
devise an evil plan. 11 You will say, "I will invade
a land of open villages and attack a peaceful peo-
ple who live in security—all of them living with-
out city walls, bars, or gates"—* 12 in order to
plunder and pillage, turning your hand against
resettled ruins, against a people gathered from
the nations, a people whose concern is cattle
and goods, dwelling at the center† of the earth.
13 Sheba and Dedan, the merchants of Tarshish
and all its "young lions" shall ask you: "Have
you come here to plunder? Have you summoned
your army for pillage, to carry off silver and gold,
to take away cattle and goods, to seize much
plunder?"*

Second Prophecy Against Gog

14 Therefore, prophesy, son of man, and say to
Gog: Thus says the Lord GOD: On that day, when
my people Israel dwell securely, will you not
take action, 15 leaving your base in the recesses
of Zaphon,† you and many nations with you, all
mounted on horses, a great company, a mighty
army?* 16 You shall rise up over my people Israel
like a cloud covering the land. In those last days,
I will let you invade my land so that the nations
acknowledge me, when in their sight I show my
holiness through you, Gog.
17 Thus says the Lord GOD: About you I spoke
in earlier times through my servants, the proph-
ets of Israel, who prophesied at that time that I
would let you invade them. 18 But on that day,
the day Gog invades the land of Israel—oracle
of the Lord GOD—my fury will flare up in my
anger, 19 and in my jealousy, with fiery wrath, I
swear on that day there will be a great earthquake
in the land of Israel.* 20 Before me will tremble
the fish of the sea and the birds of the air, the
beasts of the field and everything that crawls
on the ground, and everyone on the face of the
earth. Mountains will be overturned, terraces will
collapse, and every wall will fall to the ground.*
21 Against him I will summon every terror—
oracle of the Lord GOD; every man's sword will
be raised against his brother.* 22 I will execute
judgment on him: disease and bloodshed; flood-
ing rain and hailstones, fire and brimstone, I
will rain down on him, on his troops and on the
many nations with him.* 23 And so I will show
my greatness and holiness and make myself
known in the sight of many nations. Then they
shall know that I am the LORD.*

Third Prophecy Against Gog

39 1 You, son of man, prophesy against Gog,
saying: Thus says the Lord GOD: Here
I am, Gog, coming at you, chief prince of Me-
shech and Tubal. 2 I will turn you around, even
though I urged you on and brought you up from
the recesses of Zaphon and let you attack the
mountains of Israel.* 3 Then I will strike the bow
from your left hand and make the arrows drop
from your right. 4 Upon the mountains of Israel
you shall fall, you and all your troops and the
peoples with you. I will give you as food to birds
of prey of every kind and to wild beasts to be
eaten. 5 In the open field you shall fall, for I have
spoken—oracle of the Lord GOD.*
6 I will send fire against Magog and against
those who live securely on the seacoast, and they
will know that I am the LORD.* 7 I will reveal my
holy name among my people Israel, and I will
never again allow my holy name to be defiled.
Then the nations shall know that I am the LORD,
the Holy One of Israel.* 8 Yes, it is coming! It
shall happen—oracle of the Lord GOD. This is the
day I decreed.
9 Everyone living in the cities of Israel shall
go out and set fire to the weapons, buckler and
shield, bows and arrows, clubs and spears; for
seven years they shall make fires with them.*
10 They will not need to bring in wood from the
fields or cut down trees in the forests, for they
will make fires with the weapons, plundering
those who plundered them, pillaging those who
pillaged them—oracle of the Lord GOD.
11 On that day I will give Gog a place for his
tomb in Israel, the Valley of Abarim,† east of
the sea. It will block the way of travelers. There
Gog shall be buried with all his horde; it shall
be called "Valley of Hamon-Gog."* 12 For seven
months the house of Israel shall bury them in

EZ

† **38:12** *Center*: lit., "navel." Many ancient peoples spoke of their own homelands as "the navel," that is, the center of the earth.
38:15 *Zaphon*: cf. note on Jb 37:22.
39:11 *The Valley of Abarim*: in the Abarim mountains, east of the Jordan. "Abarim" plays on the word *'oberim*, "travelers." *Hamon-Gog*: "the horde of Gog."

* **38:8** Is 24:22.
38:9 Is 25:4; Jer 4:13; Rev 20:8.
38:11 Zec 2:4–5.
38:13 Gn 10:4, 7.
38:15 cf. Ez 39:2.
38:19 Is 24:18; Rev 6:12.
38:20 Is 42:15.
38:21 Is 34:5–6; 66:16.
38:22 cf. Rev 9:17; 16:21.
38:23 Rev 20:8.
39:2 cf. Ez 32:30; 38:6, 15.
39:5 cf. Ez 32:4.
39:6 Rev 20:9.
39:7 Is 12:6.
39:9 Ps 46:9; 76:3.
39:11 cf. Ez 38:2.

order to cleanse the land. 13 All the people of the land shall take part in the burials, making a name for themselves on the day I am glorified—oracle of the Lord GOD. 14 Men shall be permanently assigned to pass through the land, burying those who lie unburied in order to cleanse the land. For seven months they shall keep searching. 15 When these pass through the land and see a human bone, they must set up a marker beside it, until the gravediggers bury it in the Valley of Hamon-Gog. 16 Also the name of the city is Hamonah. Thus the land will be cleansed.

17 As for you, son of man, thus says the Lord GOD: Say to birds of every kind and to every wild beast: "Assemble! Come from all sides for the sacrifice I am making for you, a great slaughter on the mountains of Israel. You shall eat flesh and drink blood! 18 You shall eat the flesh of warriors and drink the blood of the princes of the earth: rams, lambs, and goats, bulls and fatlings from Bashan, all of them.* 19 From the sacrifice I slaughtered for you, you shall eat fat until you are sated and drink blood until you are drunk. 20 At my table you shall be sated with horse and rider, with warrior and soldier of every kind—oracle of the Lord GOD.

Israel's Return

21 Then I will display my glory among the nations, and all the nations will see the judgment I executed, the hand I laid upon them. 22 From that day forward the house of Israel shall know that I am the LORD, their God. 23 The nations shall know that the house of Israel went into exile because of its sins. Because they betrayed me, I hid my face from them, handing them over to their foes, so they all fell by the sword.* 24 According to their defilement and their crimes I dealt with them, hiding my face from them.*

25 Therefore, thus says the Lord GOD: Now I will restore the fortunes of Jacob and take pity on the whole house of Israel; I am zealous for my holy name.* 26 They will forget their shame and all the infidelities they committed against me when they live securely on their own land with no one to frighten them. 27 When I bring them back from the nations and gather them from the lands of their enemies, I will show my holiness through them in the sight of many nations.* 28 Thus they shall know that I, the LORD, am their God, since I who exiled them among the nations will gather them back to their land, not leaving any of them behind. 29 I will no longer hide my face from them once I pour out my spirit upon the house of Israel—oracle of the Lord GOD.*

V. The New Israel†

The New Temple

The Man with a Measure

40 1 In the twenty-fifth year of our exile, at the beginning of the year, on the tenth day of the month, fourteen years after the city had been captured, on that very day the hand of the LORD came upon me and brought me back there.* 2 In a divine vision he brought me to the land of Israel, where he set me down on a very high mountain. In front of me, there was something like a city built on it.* 3 He brought me there, and there standing in the gateway was a man whose appearance was like bronze! He held in his hand a linen cord and a measuring rod.* 4 The man said to me, "Son of man, look carefully and listen intently. Pay strict attention to everything I show you, for you have been brought here so that I might show it to you. Then you must tell the house of Israel everything you see." 5 There an outer wall completely surrounded the temple. The measuring rod in the man's hand was six cubits long, each cubit being a cubit plus a handbreadth;† he measured the width of the structure, one rod, and its height, one rod.

The East Gate†

6 Going to the gate facing east, he climbed its steps and measured the threshold of the outer gateway as one rod wide.* 7 Each cell was one rod long and one rod wide, and there were five cubits between the cells; the threshold of the inner gateway adjoining the vestibule of the gate facing the temple was one rod wide. 8 He also measured

EZ

†

40:1–48:35 This lengthy vision of a new Temple and a restored Israel is dated in v. 1 to April 28, 573 B.C. The literary form of the vision is sometimes compared to a mandala, a sacred model through which one can move symbolically to reach the world of the divine. Ezekiel describes the Temple through its boundaries, entrances, and exits in chaps. 40–43; by its sacred and profane use and space in 44–46; and by its central place within the land itself in 47–48. The prophet could not have expected a literal fulfillment of much of what he described. The passage doubtless went through several editorial stages, both from the prophet and from later writers.

40:5 *A cubit plus a handbreadth*: a great cubit. The ordinary cubit consisted of six handbreadths; the great cubit, of seven. In measuring the Temple, a rod six great cubits long was used. The ordinary cubit was about one and a half feet, or, more exactly, 17.5 inches; the large cubit, 20.4 inches.

40:6–16 The gate facing east, leading into the outer court of the Temple, is described more fully than the north and south gates, which, however, have the same dimensions. On the west side of the outer court there is a large building instead of a gate (cf. 41:12).

*

39:18 Jer 51:40; Rev 19:17–21.
39:23 Ps 30:7; Is 54:8.
39:24 2 Kgs 17:23.
39:25 Is 27:13.
39:27 cf. Ez 20:41.
39:29 cf. Ez 37:9; Is 11:2.
40:1 2 Kgs 25:7; Jer 39:1–10; 52:4–11.
40:2 Is 2:2; Mi 4:1; Zec 14:10; cf. Rev 21:10.
40:3 Zec 2:1–2; Rev 1:15; 11:1; 21:15.
40:6 cf. Ez 8:16.

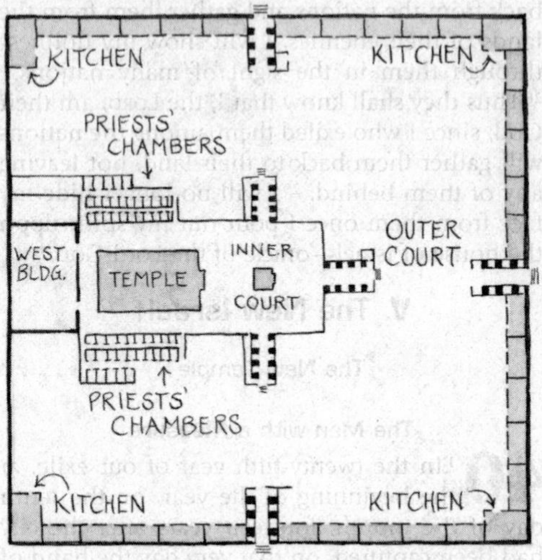

Chapter 40

the vestibule of the inner gate, 9 eight cubits, and
its posts, two cubits each. The vestibule faced the
inside. 10 On each side of the east gatehouse were
three cells, all the same size; their posts were all
the same size. 11 He measured the width of the
gate's entryway, ten cubits, and the length of the
gate itself, thirteen cubits. 12 The borders in front
of the cells on both sides were one cubit, while
the cells themselves measured six cubits by six
cubits from one opening to the next. 13 Next he
measured the gatehouse from the back wall of
one cell to the back wall of the cell on the oppo-
site side through the openings facing each other,
a width of twenty-five cubits. 14 All around the
courtyard of the gatehouse were posts six cubits
high. 15 From the front of the gatehouse at its
outer entry to the gateway of the porch facing
inward, the length was fifty cubits. 16 There were
recessed windows in the cells on all sides and in
the posts on the inner side of the gate. Posts and
windows were all around the inside, with palm
trees decorating the posts.*

The Outer Court

17 Then he brought me to the outer court,†
where there were chambers and pavement laid
all around the courtyard: thirty chambers facing
the pavement.* 18 The pavement lay alongside
the gatehouses, the same length as the gates;
this was the lower pavement. 19 He measured
the length of the pavement from the front of the
lower gate to the outside of the inner gate, one
hundred cubits. He then moved from the east to
the north side.

The North Gate

20 He measured the length and width of the
north gate of the outer courtyard. 21 Its cells, three
on each side, its posts, and its vestibule had the
same measurements as those of the first gate,
fifty cubits long and twenty-five cubits wide.
22 Its windows, its vestibule, and its palm deco-
rations had the same proportions as those of the
gate facing east. Seven steps led up to it, and its
vestibule faced the inside. 23 The inner court had
a gate opposite the north gate, just as at the east
gate; he measured one hundred cubits from one
gate to the other.

The South Gate

24 Then he led me to the south. There, too,
facing south, was a gate! He measured its posts
and vestibule; they were the same size as the
others. 25 The gate and its vestibule had windows
on both sides, like the other windows, fifty cu-
bits long and twenty-five cubits wide. 26 Seven
steps led up to it, its vestibule faced inside; and
palms decorated each of the posts opposite one
another. 27 The inner court also had a gate facing
south. He measured it from gate to gate, facing
south, one hundred cubits.

Gates of the Inner Court†

28 Then he brought me to the inner courtyard
by the south gate, where he measured the south
gateway; its measurements were the same as the
others. 29 Its cells, posts, and vestibule were the
same size as the others, fifty cubits long and
twenty-five cubits wide. 30 † The vestibules all
around were twenty-five cubits long and five
cubits wide. 31 Its vestibule faced the outer court;
palms decorated its posts, and its stairway had
eight steps. 32 Then he brought me to the inner
courtyard on the east and measured the gate
there; its dimensions were the same as the oth-
ers. 33 Its cells, posts, and vestibule were the same
size as the others. The gate and its vestibule had
windows on both sides, fifty cubits long and
twenty-five cubits wide. 34 Its vestibule faced the

†

40:17 *The outer court*: the court outside the Temple area proper, which had its own inner court (vv. 28–37).

40:28–37 The gates leading into the inner court of the Temple area correspond to the gates leading into the outer court, with the exception that their vestibules are on the outer rather than the inner side.

40:30 The reference to vestibules all around is uncertain, and the verse may have arisen as a partial repetition of v. 29.

40:16 1 Kgs 6:29, 32, 35. **40:17** cf. Ez 41:6; 42:1.

outer court, palms decorated the posts opposite
each other, and it had a stairway of eight steps.
35 Then he brought me to the north gate,* where
he measured the dimensions 36 of its cells, posts,
and vestibule; they were the same. The gate and
its vestibule had windows on both sides, fifty
cubits long and twenty-five cubits wide. 37 Its
vestibule faced the outer court; palm trees deco-
rated its posts opposite each other, and it had a
stairway of eight steps.

Side Rooms

38 There was a chamber opening off the ves-
tibule of the gate where burnt offerings were
washed.* 39 In the vestibule of the gate there were
two tables on either side for slaughtering the
burnt offerings, purification offerings, and repa-
ration offerings.* 40 Two more tables stood along
the wall of the vestibule by the entrance of the
north gate, and two tables on the other side of
the vestibule of the gate. 41 There were thus four
tables on one side of the gate and four tables on
the other side, eight tables in all, for slaughtering.
42 The four tables for burnt offerings were made
of cut stone, one and a half cubits long, one and
a half cubits wide, and one cubit high; the in-
struments used for slaughtering burnt offerings
and other sacrifices were kept 43 on shelves the
width of one hand, fixed all around the room;
but on the tables themselves was the meat for the
sacrifices. 44 Outside the inner gatehouse there
were two rooms on the inner courtyard, one be-
side the north gate, facing south, and the other
beside the south gate, facing north. 45 He said to
me, "This chamber facing south is reserved for
the priests who have charge of the temple area,
46 while this chamber facing north is reserved for
the priests who have charge of the altar; they are
the sons of Zadok,† the only Levites who may
come near to minister to the LORD." 47 He mea-
sured the courtyard, a square one hundred cubits
long and a hundred cubits wide, with the altar
standing in front of the temple.*

The Temple Building†

48 * Then he brought me into the vestibule of
the temple and measured the posts, five cubits
on each side. The gateway was fourteen cubits
wide, its side walls three cubits. 49 The vestibule
was twenty cubits long and twelve cubits wide;
ten steps led up to it, and there were columns by
the posts, one on each side.

41 1 Then he brought me to the nave and
measured the posts; each was six cubits
wide.* 2 The width of the entrance was ten cu-
bits, and the walls on either side measured five
cubits. He measured the nave, forty cubits long
and twenty cubits wide.
3 Then he went inside and measured the posts
at the other entrance, two cubits wide. The en-
trance was six cubits wide, with walls seven cu-
bits long on each side. 4 Next he measured the
length and width of the room beyond the nave,
twenty cubits long and twenty cubits wide. He
said to me, "This is the holy of holies."† *
5 Then he measured the wall of the temple,
six cubits wide, and the width of the side cham-
bers stretching all around the temple, four cu-
bits each. 6 † There were thirty side chambers,
chamber upon chamber in three stories; terraces
on the outside wall of the temple enclosing
the side chambers provided support, but there
were no supports for the temple wall itself. 7 A
broad passageway led up the side chambers, for
the house was enclosed all the way up and all
the way around. Thus the temple was widened
by the ascent that went from the lowest story
through the middle one to the highest story.* 8 I
saw a raised platform all around the temple, the
foundation for the side chambers; the width of
this terrace was a full rod, six cubits. 9 The width
of the outside wall enclosing the side chambers
was five cubits. There was an open space between
the side chambers of the temple 10 and the other
chambers that measured twenty cubits around
the temple on all sides. 11 The side chambers had
entrances to the open space, one entrance on
the north and the other on the south. The width
of the wall surrounding the open space was five
cubits. 12 The building† opposite the restricted
area on the west side was seventy cubits long and
ninety cubits wide, with walls five cubits thick
all around it. 13 Thus he measured the temple,

40:46 *Sons of Zadok*: descendants of the priestly line of Zadok; cf. 2 Sm 15:24–29; 1 Kgs 1:32–34; 2:35.

40:48–41:15 The description of Ezekiel's visionary Temple closely follows the description of the Temple of Solomon (1 Kgs 6), along with some crucial differences.

40:49–41:4 *Vestibule . . . nave . . . holy of holies*: the three divisions of the Temple building in progressing order of sanctity. The last is called "the inner sanctuary" in 1 Kgs 6.

41:6 The description of the three stories of rooms surrounding the Temple building can be compared with Solomon's Temple in 1 Kgs 6:6; there a step-like or terraced retaining wall supported the Temple building so no beams or nails from these chambers would enter the Temple wall itself.

41:12 *The building*: the function of this structure behind the Temple is never specified.

40:35 cf. Ez 44:4; 47:2.
40:38 2 Chr 4:6.
40:39 cf. Ez 46:2.
40:47 cf. Ez 41:13–14; 43:14–17.
40:48 1 Kgs 6:2.
41:1 1 Kgs 6:3–5.
41:4 1 Kgs 6:20; cf. Ex 26:33; Heb 9:3–8.
41:7 1 Kgs 6:8.

one hundred cubits long. The restricted area, its building and walls, measured a hundred cubits in length. 14 The temple facade, along with the restricted area to the east, was also one hundred cubits wide. 15 He then measured the building opposite the restricted area which was behind it, together with its terraces on both sides, one hundred cubits.

Interior of the Temple

The inner nave and the outer vestibule 16 were paneled; the windows had recesses and precious wood trim around all three sides except the sill. Paneling covered the walls from the floor up to the windows and even the window sections.* 17 Even above the doorway and in the inner part of the temple and outside as well, around all the walls inside and out, 18 were figures of cherubim and palm trees: a palm tree between each pair of cherubim. Each cherub had two faces:* 19 the face of a human being looked toward one palm tree and the face of a lion looked toward the other palm tree. Thus the figures covered all the walls around the temple. 20 From the floor to the lintel of the door, cherubim and palm trees decorated the walls. 21 The nave had a square door frame, and inside facing the holy place was something that looked like 22 a wooden altar,† three cubits high, two cubits long, and two cubits wide. It had corners and a wooden base and sides. He said to me, "This is the table that stands before the LORD."* 23 The nave had a double door,* and the holy place 24 also had a double door; each door had two sections that could move; two sections on one door, and two on the other.* 25 Cherubim and palm trees decorated the doors of the nave like the decoration on the walls. Outside a wooden lattice faced the vestibule. 26 There were recessed windows and palm trees on the side walls of the vestibule. The side chambers of the temple also had latticework.

Other Structures

42 1 Then he led me north to the outer court, bringing me to some chambers on the north side opposite the restricted area and the north building.* 2 They were a hundred cubits long on the north side and fifty cubits wide. 3 Built in rows at three different levels, they stood between the twenty cubits of the inner court and the pavement of the outer court. 4 In front of the chambers was a walkway ten cubits wide on the inside of a wall one cubit wide. The doorways faced north. 5 † The upper chambers were shorter because they lost space to the lower and middle tiers of the building. 6 Because they were in three tiers, they did not have foundations like the court, but were set back from the lower and middle levels from the ground up. 7 The outside walls ran parallel to the chambers along the outer court, a length of fifty cubits. 8 The chambers facing the outer court were fifty cubits long; thus the wall along the nave was a hundred cubits. 9 At the base of these chambers, there was an entryway from the east so that one could enter from the outer court 10 where the wall of the court began.

To the south along the side of the restricted area and the building there were also chambers 11 with a walkway in front of them. They looked like the chambers on the north side in length and width, in their exits, their design, and their doorways. 12 At the base of the chambers on the south side there was an entry at the end of a walkway in front of the protective wall by which one could enter from the east. 13 He said to me, "The north and south chambers facing the restricted area are the chambers of the holy place where the priests who approach the LORD shall eat the most holy meals. Here they shall place the most holy offerings: the grain offerings, the purification offerings, and the reparation offerings; for the place is holy.† * 14 When the priests have entered, they must not go out again from the holy place into the outer court without leaving the garments in which they ministered because they are holy. They shall put on other garments before approaching the area for the people."*

Measuring the Outer Court

15 When he finished measuring the interior of the temple area, he brought me out by way of the gate facing east and measured all around it. 16 He measured the east side, five hundred cubits by his measuring rod. Then he turned 17 and measured the north side: five hundred cubits by his measuring rod. He turned 18 and measured the south side, five hundred cubits by his measuring rod. 19 He turned and measured the west side, also five hundred cubits by his measuring rod. 20 Thus he measured it on the four sides. It was

41:22 *A wooden altar*: the altar of incense, standing in the nave at the entrance to the holy of holies.

42:5–6 The three rows of identical chambers, on different ground levels, necessarily had roofs on correspondingly different levels.

42:13 The function of these chambers is explained again in 46:19–20.

41:16 1 Kgs 6:4, 15.
41:18 1 Kgs 6:18, 29; 7:36.
41:22 Ex 25:23; Lv 24:5–9.
41:23 1 Kgs 6:32.
41:24 1 Kgs 6:34.
42:1 Ex 27:9.
42:13 Lv 10:12–13, 17.
42:14 Ex 29:9; Lv 8:7–9.

surrounded by a wall five hundred cubits long
and five hundred cubits wide, to separate the sa-
cred from the profane.

Restoration of the Temple

The Glory of the Lord Returns

43 1Then he led me to the gate facing east,*
2and there was the glory of the God of Is-
rael coming from the east! His voice was like the
roar of many waters, and the earth shone with
his glory. 3The vision I saw was like the vision I
had seen when he came to destroy the city and
like the vision I had seen by the river Chebar—I
fell on my face. 4The glory of the LORD entered
the temple by way of the gate facing east.* 5Then
the spirit lifted me up and brought me to the in-
ner court. And there the glory of the LORD filled
the temple!* 6I heard someone speaking to me
from the temple, but the man was standing be-
side me. 7The voice said to me: Son of man, do
you see the place for my throne, and the place
for the soles of my feet? Here I will dwell among
the Israelites forever. The house of Israel, nei-
ther they nor their kings, will never again defile
my holy name, with their prostitutions and the
corpses of their kings at their death.* 8When they
placed their threshold against my threshold†
and their doorpost next to mine, with only a
wall between me and them, they defiled my holy
name by the abominations they committed, and
I devoured them in my wrath.* 9From now on,
let them put their prostitution and the corpses of
their kings far from me, and I will dwell in their
midst forever.*

The Law of the Temple

10As for you, son of man, describe the temple
to the house of Israel so they are ashamed for
their sins. Let them measure its layout. 11If they
are ashamed for all they have done, tell them
about the layout and design of the temple, its
exits and entrances, with all its regulations and
instructions; write it down for them to see, that
they may carefully observe all its laws and stat-
utes. 12This is the law for the temple: the entire
area on top of the mountain all around will be a
most holy place. This is the law for the temple.

Live It!

God's Dwelling Place

Ezekiel's vision of God returning to the Temple in Ezekiel 43:1–5 completes the circle of his prophecy. Earlier, as described in chapter 10, he had a unique vision of God's glory leaving the Temple and coming to rest in Babylon. For Ezekiel, the Temple represents the heart of Israel's relationship with God, and it is important that God's presence will return to it. This probably explains why Ezekiel carefully records the specifics of the new Temple in the remaining chapters of his book—to help make it more real.

The early Christians learned from Jesus that God's presence isn't limited to the Temple. The good news is that God is present in every person! First Corinthians 3:16 says, "Do you not know that you are the temple of God, and that the Spirit of God dwells in you?" The basis for our self-worth should be knowing that God's Spirit dwells within us. If that doesn't make us special, what will?

► Ez 43:1–5

The Altar

13These were the dimensions of the altar†
in cubits, a cubit being one cubit plus a hand-
breadth. The channel was one cubit deep by one
cubit wide, and its rim had a lip one span wide
all around it.* The height of the altar itself was
as follows: 14from the channel at floor level up
to the lower ledge was two cubits, with the ledge
one cubit wide; from the lower ledge to the up-
per ledge, four cubits, with the ledge one cubit
wide. 15The altar hearth was four cubits high,
and extending up from the top of the hearth were
four horns. 16The hearth was twelve cubits long
and twelve cubits wide, a square with four equal

† **43:8** *They placed their threshold against my threshold*: in preexilic Jerusalem, the Temple and the palace belonged to the same complex of buildings; kings like Ahaz and Manasseh treated it as their private chapel for the religious practices Ezekiel condemns. In the new Israel the Temple is free, even spatially, from civil jurisdiction; cf. 45:7–8. This is an instance of Ezekiel's broader program to separate the sacred from the secular.

43:13–17 *The altar*: like altars from Assyria and other parts of the ancient Near East, this altar has three parts: a base, a pedestal, and an upper block with a channel cut into the surface on all sides. The rim around the upper block (v. 17) stopped blood and other sacrificial material from falling to the ground.

* **43:1** 1 Chr 9:18.
43:4 cf. Ez 10:19.
43:5 cf. Ez 11:24.
43:7 1 Chr 28:2; Ps 132:7; Is 6:1; Jer 3:17.
43:8 1 Kgs 7:1–12.
43:9 cf. Ez 37:26–28.
43:13 cf. Ex 20:24.

sides. 17 The upper ledge was fourteen cubits long and fourteen cubits wide on all four sides. The rim around it was half a cubit, with a channel one cubit all around. The steps faced east.*

18 Then he said to me: Son of man, thus says the Lord GOD: These are the statutes for the altar when it is set up for sacrificing burnt offerings and splashing blood on it.* 19 A young bull must be brought as a purification offering to the priests, the Levites descended from Zadok, who come near to serve me—oracle of the Lord GOD.* 20 You shall take some of its blood and smear it on the four horns of the altar, and on the four corners of the ledge, and all around its rim. Thus you shall purify and purge it.* 21 Then take the bull as purification offering and burn it in the appointed place outside the sanctuary.* 22 On the second day present an unblemished male goat as a purification offering, to purify the altar as you did with the bull. 23 When you have completed the purification,* you must bring an unblemished young bull and an unblemished ram from the flock 24 and present them before the LORD. The priests shall throw salt on them and sacrifice them as burnt offerings to the LORD. 25 Daily for seven days you shall give a male goat as a purification offering; and a young bull and a ram from the flock, all unblemished,* shall be offered 26 for seven days. Thus they shall purge the altar, in order to cleanse and dedicate it. 27 And when these days are over, from the eighth day on, the priests shall sacrifice your burnt offerings and communion offerings on the altar. Then I will be pleased with you—oracle of the Lord GOD.

The Closed Gate

44 1 Then he brought me back to the outer gate of the sanctuary facing east, but it was closed. 2 The LORD said to me: This gate must remain closed; it must not be opened, and no one should come through it. Because the LORD, the God of Israel, came through it, it must remain closed. 3 Only the prince may sit in it to eat a meal in the presence of the LORD; he must enter through the vestibule of the gate and leave the same way.† *

The New Law

Admission to the Temple

4 Then he brought me by way of the north gate to the facade of the temple. I looked—and the glory of the LORD filled the LORD's house! I fell on my face.* 5 The LORD said to me: Son of man, pay close attention, look carefully, and listen intently to everything I tell you about all the statutes and laws of the LORD's house. Pay close attention to the entrance into the temple and all the exits of the sanctuary. 6 Say to that rebellious house, the house of Israel: Thus says the Lord GOD: Enough of all your abominations, house of Israel! 7 You have admitted foreigners, uncircumcised in heart and flesh, into my sanctuary to profane it when you offered me food, the fat and blood.† Thus you have broken my covenant by all your abominations.* 8 Instead of caring for the service of my sanctuary, you appointed these foreigners to care for the service of my sanctuary. 9 Thus says the Lord GOD: No foreigners, uncircumcised in heart and flesh, shall ever enter my sanctuary: not even any of the foreigners who live among the Israelites.*

Levites

10 As for the Levites who went far away from me when Israel strayed from me after their idols, they will bear the consequences of their sin. 11 They will serve in my sanctuary only as gatekeepers and temple servants; they will slaughter burnt offerings and sacrifices for the people. They will stand before the people to serve them.* 12 Because they used to serve them before their idols, thus becoming a stumbling block to the house of Israel, therefore I have sworn an oath against them, says the Lord GOD, and they will bear the consequences of their sin. 13 They shall no longer come near to serve as my priests, nor shall they touch any of my sacred things or my most sacred offerings, for they must bear their shame, the abominations they committed. 14 Instead I will make them responsible for the service of the temple and all its work, for everything that must be done in it.*

†

44:3 Ezekiel imagines a scene like this: The prince stands at the eastern gate of the inner court while his sacrifice is being offered (46:2); he then goes to the vestibule of the outer court to eat the sacrificial meal. The closed outer gate on the eastern side signifies that the Lord has entered the Temple permanently, not to depart again.

44:7–14 According to Ezekiel, the Levites' priestly role is reduced to the performance of menial tasks as punishment for their misdeeds (cf. vv. 10–14). This demotion was enforced during the restoration of Temple worship under Ezra and Nehemiah; this may explain the small number of Levites willing to return to Jerusalem after the exile.

*

43:17 Ex 20:26.
43:18 Ex 29:16; Lv 4:6; 5:9.
43:19 Lv 4:3.
43:20 Lv 4:7.
43:21 Ex 29:14; Lv 4:12; 8:17; cf. Heb 13:11–13.
43:23 Ex 29:1.
43:25 Ex 29:37; Lv 8:33.
44:3 Ex 24:9–11; 2 Chr 26:16–20.
44:4 Is 6:4; Rev 15:8.
44:7 Lv 26:41.
44:9 Jl 4:17; Neh 13:8.
44:11 Nm 3:5–37; 1 Chr 26:12–19.
44:14 1 Chr 23:28–32.

Priests

15 As for the levitical priests, sons of Zadok,
who took charge of my sanctuary when the Isra-
elites strayed from me, they may approach me to
serve me and stand before me to offer the fat and
the blood—oracle of the Lord GOD.* 16 They may
enter my sanctuary; they may approach my table
to serve me and carry out my service.* 17 When-
ever they enter the gates of the inner court, they
shall wear linen garments; they shall not put on
anything woolen when they serve at the gates of
the inner court or within the temple. 18 * They
shall have linen turbans on their heads and linen
undergarments on their loins; they shall not
gird themselves with anything that causes sweat.
19 * And when they go out to the people in the
outer court, they shall take off the garments in
which they served and leave them in the rooms
of the sanctuary, and put on other garments so
they do not transmit holiness to the people† by
their garments.
20 * They shall not shave their heads nor let
their hair hang loose, but they shall keep their
hair carefully trimmed. 21 No priest shall drink
wine before he enters the inner court. 22 * They
shall not take as wives either widows or divorced
women, but only unmarried women from the
line of Israel; however, they may take as wives
widows who are widows of priests. 23 * They
shall teach my people to distinguish between
sacred and profane and make known to them
the difference between clean and unclean. 24 * In
legal cases they shall stand as judges, judging ac-
cording to my ordinances. They shall observe all
my laws and statutes regarding all my appointed
feasts, and they shall keep my sabbaths holy.
25 * They shall not make themselves unclean
by going near a dead body; only for their father,
mother, son, daughter, brother, or unmarried
sister may they make themselves unclean. 26 Af-
ter he is again clean, he must wait an additional
seven days; 27 on the day he enters the inner
court to serve in the sanctuary, he shall present
a purification offering for himself—oracle of the
Lord GOD. 28 * I will be their heritage: I am their
heritage! You shall not give them any property
in Israel, for I am their property! 29 * They shall
eat grain offerings, purification offerings, and
reparation offerings; anything under the ban† in
Israel belongs to them; 30 * all the choicest first
fruits of every kind and all the best of your of-
ferings of every kind shall belong to the priests;
the best of your dough you shall also give to
the priests to bring a blessing upon your house.
31 * The priests shall not eat anything, whether
bird or animal, that died naturally or was killed
by wild beasts.

The Holy Portion

45 1 When you apportion the land heritage
by heritage, you shall set apart a holy
portion for the LORD, holier than the rest of
the land—twenty-five thousand cubits long and
twenty thousand cubits wide; the entire area
shall be holy. 2 Of this land a square plot, five
hundred by five hundred cubits, shall be as-
signed to the sanctuary, with fifty cubits of free
space around it. 3 From this tract also measure
off a length of twenty-five thousand cubits and
a width of ten thousand cubits; on it the sanc-
tuary, the holy of holies, shall stand. 4 This shall
be the sacred part of the land belonging to the
priests, the ministers of the sanctuary, who draw
near to minister to the LORD; it shall be a place
for their homes and an area set apart for the
sanctuary. 5 There shall also be a strip twenty-five
thousand cubits long and ten thousand wide for
the Levites, the ministers of the temple, so they
have cities to live in. 6 You shall assign a strip five
thousand cubits wide and twenty-five thousand
long as the property of the city parallel to the
sacred tract; this shall belong to the whole house
of Israel. 7 A section shall belong to the prince,
bordering both sides of the sacred tract and city
combined, extending westward on the west side
and eastward on the east side, corresponding in
length to one of the tribal portions from the west
boundary to the east boundary 8 of the land. This
shall be his property in Israel so that my princes
will no longer oppress my people, but will leave
the land to the house of Israel according to its
tribes. 9 Thus says the Lord GOD: Enough, you
princes of Israel! Put away violence and oppres-
sion, and do what is just and right! Stop evicting
my people!—oracle of the Lord GOD.

EZ

44:19 *Transmit holiness to the people*: holiness was considered to have a physical quality that could be communicated from person to person. It is a danger to those who have not prepared themselves to be in God's presence. The priests remove their ceremonial garments out of concern for the people.

44:29 *Under the ban*: dedicated to the Lord.

44:15 1 Chr 6:50–53.
44:16 Lv 3:16–17.
44:18 Ex 28:39, 42.
44:19 Ex 39:27–29; Lv 6:10–11.
44:20 Lv 21:5.
44:22 Lv 21:7.
44:23 Hg 2:10–13.
44:24 Dt 17:8–9.
44:25 Lv 21:1–4.
44:28 Nm 18:23–24; Dt 18:1–2.
44:29 Lv 6:16; 27:28.
44:30 Nm 15:18–21; 18:12–13.
44:31 Lv 11:39.

Weights and Measures†

10 * You shall have honest scales, an honest ephah, and an honest bath. 11 The ephah and the bath shall be the same size: the bath equal to one tenth of a homer, and the ephah equal to one tenth of a homer; their capacity is based on the homer. 12 The shekel shall be twenty gerahs. Twenty shekels plus twenty-five shekels plus fifteen shekels make up a mina† for you.

Offerings

13 This is the offering you must make: one sixth of an ephah from each homer of wheat and one sixth of an ephah from each homer of barley. 14 This is the regulation for oil: for every bath of oil, one tenth of a bath, computed by the kor,† made up of ten baths, that is, a homer, for ten baths make a homer. 15 Also, one sheep from the flock for every two hundred from the pasture land of Israel, for the grain offering, the burnt offering, and communion offerings, to make atonement on their behalf—oracle of the Lord GOD.* 16 All the people of the land shall be responsible for these offerings to the prince in Israel. 17 It shall be the duty of the prince to provide burnt offerings, grain offerings, and libations on feast days, new moons, and sabbaths, on all the festivals of the house of Israel. He shall provide the purification offering, grain offering, burnt offering, and communion offerings, to make atonement on behalf of the house of Israel.*

The Passover

18 Thus says the Lord GOD: On the first day of the first month you shall take an unblemished young bull to purify the sanctuary.* 19 The priest shall take some of the blood from the purification offering and smear it on the doorposts of the house, on the four corners of the ledge of the altar, and on the doorposts of the gates of the inner courtyard.* 20 You shall repeat this on the seventh day of the month for those who have sinned inadvertently or out of ignorance; thus you shall purge the temple.* 21 On the fourteenth day of the first month you shall observe the feast of Passover; for seven days unleavened bread must be eaten. 22 On that day the prince shall sacrifice, on his own behalf and on behalf of all the people of the land, a bull as a purification offering. 23 On each of the seven days of the feast he shall sacrifice, as a burnt offering to the LORD, seven bulls and seven rams without blemish, and as a purification offering he shall sacrifice one male goat each day.* 24 As a grain offering he shall offer one ephah for each bull and one ephah for each ram and one hin† of oil for each ephah.*

The Feast of Booths

25 In the seventh month, on the fifteenth day of the seventh month, on the feast day and for the next seven days, he shall make the same offerings: the same purification offerings, burnt offerings, grain offerings, and offerings of oil.*

Sabbaths

46 1 Thus says the Lord GOD: The gate of the inner court facing east shall remain closed throughout the six working days, but on the sabbath and on the day of the new moon it shall be open. 2 † Then the prince shall enter from outside by way of the vestibule of the gate and remain standing at the doorpost of the gateway while the priests sacrifice his burnt offerings and communion offerings; then he shall bow down in worship at the opening of the gate and leave. But the gate shall not be closed until evening. 3 The people of the land also shall bow down in worship before the LORD at the opening of this gate on the sabbaths and new moons. 4 The burnt offerings which the prince sacrifices to the LORD on the sabbath shall consist of six unblemished lambs and an unblemished ram, 5 together with a grain offering of one ephah for the ram and whatever he pleases for the lambs, and a hin of oil for each ephah. 6 * On the day of the new moon, he shall provide an unblemished young bull, six lambs, and a ram without blemish, 7 with a grain offering of one ephah for the bull and an ephah for the ram, and for the lambs whatever he can, and for each ephah a hin of oil.*

---

†

45:10–12 Besides the land monopoly fostered by royal greed and collusion with the wealthy (Mi 2:2; Is 3:12–15; 5:8–10), one grave social evil of preexilic Israel was dishonesty in business; cf. Hos 12:8; Am 8:5. *Ephah, bath*: see note on Is 5:10.

45:12 *Mina*: before the exile, a mina was worth fifty shekels; later, in imitation of Babylonian practice, its value increased to sixty shekels. A shekel weighed slightly less than half an ounce. A shekel's monetary value depended on whether it was gold or silver.

45:14 *Kor*: a liquid and a dry measure, equal to a homer.

45:24 *Hin*: one sixth of the liquid measure known as a bath.

46:2–12 The prophet describes the inner eastern gateway opening on the inner court of the priests in front of the Temple itself where the altar of sacrifice stands. The people may watch the priests making offerings on sabbaths and feast days only by looking through the open gate; the prince, however, may stand inside the gate, in the vestibule on the edge of the inner court, to observe the offerings. Only priests could stand in the court itself.

---

*

45:10 Lv 19:35–36; Dt 25:13–16; Mi 6:10–12.
45:15 Lv 1:4; 6:23.
45:17 cf. Ez 46:4–12.
45:18 Lv 16:33.
45:19 Lv 16:18–19.
45:20 Lv 4:27.
45:23 Nm 22:40; 28:16–25.
45:24 Nm 28:12–13.
45:25 Ex 23:16; 34:22; Lv 23:34–43; Nm 29:12–38.
46:6 Lv 22:20.
46:7 cf. Nm 28:12.

Ritual Laws

8 When the prince enters, he shall always enter and depart by the vestibule of the gate. 9 When the people of the land come before the LORD to bow down on the festivals, if they enter by the north gate they shall leave by the south gate, and if they enter by the south gate they shall leave by the north gate. They shall not go back by the gate through which they entered; everyone shall leave by the opposite gate. 10 When they come in, the prince shall be with them; he shall also leave with them. 11 On feasts and festivals, the grain offering shall be an ephah for a bull, an ephah for a ram, but for the lambs whatever they please, and a hin of oil with each ephah. 12 When the prince makes a freewill offering to the LORD, whether a burnt offering or communion offering, the gate facing east shall be opened for him, and he shall bring his burnt offering or peace offering as he does on the sabbath. Then he shall leave, and the gate shall be closed after his departure. 13 * Every day you shall bring as a burnt offering to the LORD an unblemished year-old lamb; you shall offer it every morning, 14 and with it every morning a grain offering of one sixth of an ephah, with a third of a hin of oil to moisten the fine flour. This grain offering for the LORD is a perpetual statute. 15 * The lamb, the grain offering, and the oil you must bring every morning as a perpetual burnt offering.

The Prince and the Land

16 Thus says the Lord GOD: If the prince makes a gift of part of his heritage to any of his sons, it belongs to his sons; that property is their heritage. 17 But if he makes a gift of part of his heritage to one of his servants, it belongs to him until the year of release;† then it reverts to the prince. Only the heritage given to his sons belongs to him.* 18 The prince shall not seize any part of the heritage of the people by forcing them off their property. From his own property he shall provide heritage for his sons, so that none of my people will be driven off their property.

The Temple Kitchens

19 Then he brought me through the entrance at the side of the gateway to the chambers reserved for the priests, which faced north. There I saw a place at the far west end, 20 about which he said to me, "This is the place where the priests cook the reparation offerings and the purification offerings and bake the grain offerings, so they do not have to bring them into the outer court and so transmit holiness to the people."† * 21 Then he led me into the outer court and had me cross to the four corners of the court, and there, in each corner, was another court! 22 In all four corners of the courtyard there were courts set off, each forty cubits long by thirty cubits wide, all four of them the same size. 23 A stone wall surrounded them on four sides, and ovens were built along the bottom of the walls all the way around. 24 He said to me, "These are the kitchens where the temple ministers cook the sacrifices of the people."

The Wonderful Stream†

47 1 Then he brought me back to the entrance of the temple, and there! I saw water flowing out from under the threshold of the temple toward the east, for the front of the temple faced east. The water flowed out toward the right side of the temple to the south of the altar.* 2 He brought me by way of the north gate and around the outside to the outer gate facing east; there I saw water trickling from the southern side. 3 When he continued eastward with a measuring cord in his hand, he measured off a thousand cubits and had me wade through the water; it was ankle-deep. 4 He measured off another thousand cubits and once more had me wade through the water; it was up to the knees. He measured another thousand cubits and had me wade through the water; it was up to my waist. 5 Once more he measured off a thousand cubits. Now it was a river I could not wade across. The water had risen so high, I would have to swim—a river that was impassable. 6 Then he asked me, "Do you see this, son of man?" He brought me to the bank of the river and had me sit down. 7 As I was returning, I saw along the bank of the river a great many trees on each side.* 8 He said to me, "This water flows out into the eastern district, runs down into the Arabah and empties into the polluted waters of the sea† to freshen them.* 9 Wherever it flows, the river teems with every kind of living creature; fish will abound.

EZ

46:17 *The year of release*: the jubilee year; cf. Lv 25:23–55.
46:20 Cf. note on 44:19.
47:1–12 The life and refreshment produced wherever the Temple stream flows evoke the order and abundance of paradise (cf. Gn 1:20–22; 2:10–14; Ps 46:5) and represent the coming transformation Ezekiel envisions for the exiles and their land. Water signifies great blessings and evidence of the Lord's presence (cf. Jl 2:14).
47:8 *The sea*: the Dead Sea, in which nothing can live. This vision of the Temple stream which transforms places of death into places of life is similar in purpose to the oracle of dry bones in 37:1–14: it offers the exiles hope for the future.

46:13 Ex 29:38; Nm 28:3–8.
46:15 Ex 29:42; Nm 28:5–6.
46:17 Lv 25:8–17.
46:20 Lv 6:20.
47:1 cf. Gn 2:10; Ps 46:4; Rev 22:1.
47:7 Rev 22:2.
47:8 Zec 14:8.

Where these waters flow they refresh; everything
lives where the river goes. 10 Fishermen will stand
along its shore from En-gedi to En-eglaim;† it
will become a place for drying nets, and it will
abound with as many kinds of fish as the Great
Sea.* 11 Its marshes and swamps shall not be
made fresh, but will be left for salt. 12 Along each
bank of the river every kind of fruit tree will
grow; their leaves will not wither, nor will their
fruit fail. Every month they will bear fresh fruit
because the waters of the river flow out from the
sanctuary. Their fruit is used for food, and their
leaves for healing."*

The New Israel

Boundaries of the Land†

13 Thus says the Lord GOD: These are the
boundaries of the land which you shall ap-
portion among the twelve tribes of Israel, with
Joseph having two portions.* 14 You shall appor-
tion it equally because I swore to give it to your
ancestors as a heritage; this land, then, is your
heritage.* 15 * These are the borders of the land:
on the northern side, from the Great Sea in the
direction of Hethlon, Lebo-hamath to Zedad,
16 Berothah, and Sibraim, along the frontiers of
Damascus and Hamath, to Hazar-enon, on the
border of Hauran.* 17 Thus the border extends
from the sea to Hazar-enon, north of the border
of Damascus, the frontier of Hamath to the north.
This is the northern boundary. 18 The eastern bor-
der shall be between Damascus and Hauran,
while the Jordan will form the border between
Gilead and the land of Israel down to the eastern
sea as far as Tamar. This is the eastern boundary.
19 The southern border shall go southward from
Tamar to the waters of Meribath-kadesh, on to
the Wadi of Egypt, and into the Great Sea. This
is the southern boundary.* 20 The western border
shall have the Great Sea as a boundary as far as a
point opposite Lebo-hamath. This is the western
boundary.

The Northern Portions

21 You shall divide this land according to the
tribes of Israel. 22 * You shall allot it as heritage
for yourselves and for the resident aliens in your
midst who have fathered children among you.
You shall treat them like native Israelites; along
with you they shall receive a heritage among the
tribes of Israel. 23 In whatever tribe the resident
alien lives, there you shall assign his heritage—
oracle of the Lord GOD.

48 1 These are the names† of the tribes:
At the northern end, along the side of the
way to Hethlon, Lebo-hamath, and Hazar-enon,
the border of Damascus, and northward up to
the frontier with Hamath, from the eastern bor-
der to the western: Dan, one portion. 2 Along the
territory of Dan from the eastern border to the
western border: Asher, one portion.* 3 Along
the territory of Asher from the eastern border
to the western border: Naphtali, one portion.*
4 Along the territory of Naphtali from the east-
ern border to the western border: Manasseh,
one portion.* 5 Along the territory of Manasseh
from the eastern border to the western border:
Ephraim, one portion.* 6 Along the territory of
Ephraim from the eastern border to the western
border: Reuben, one portion.* 7 Along the terri-
tory of Reuben from the eastern border to the
western border: Judah, one portion.*

The Sacred Tract

8 Along the territory of Judah from the eastern
border to the western border is the tract you shall
set apart, twenty-five thousand cubits wide and
as long as one of the portions from the eastern
border to the western border. The sanctuary shall
stand in the center of the tract. 9 The tract you
set apart for the LORD shall be twenty-five thou-
sand cubits long by twenty thousand wide. 10 The
sacred tract will be given to the following: the
priests shall have twenty-five thousand cubits on
the north, ten thousand on the west, ten thou-
sand on the east, and twenty-five thousand on
the south. The sanctuary of the LORD shall be in its
center. 11 The consecrated priests, the Zadokites,
who fulfilled my service and did not stray with
the Israelites as the Levites did, 12 shall have their
own tract set apart, next to the territory of the Le-
vites, separate from the most holy tract. 13 The Le-

EZ

† **47:10** *From En-gedi to En-eglaim*: En-gedi is about halfway down the western shore of the Dead Sea; En-eglaim may have been at its northern end.

47:13–20 These boundaries for a restored Israel correspond to the boundaries of the Davidic kingdom at its fullest extent; they are the "ideal boundaries" of the promised land; cf. Nm 34:3–12.

48:1–29 This distribution of the land among the tribes does not correspond to the geographical realities of Palestine. It is another idealizing element in Ezekiel's representation of a restored and transformed Israel.

* **47:10** Ps 104:25. **47:12** Ps 1:3; Jer 17:8. **47:13** Gn 48:16; Nm 34:2–12. **47:14** Gn 12:7; 15:9–21. **47:15** Nm 34:1–12. **47:16** 2 Sm 8:8. **47:19** Nm 34:4; Dt 32:51. **47:22** Lv 24:22; Nm 15:29; 26:55–56; Is 56:6–7. **48:2** Jos 19:24–31. **48:3** Jos 19:32–39. **48:4** Jos 17:1–11. **48:5** Jos 16:5–9. **48:6** Jos 13:15–21. **48:7** Jos 15:1–63.

vites shall have territory corresponding to that of
the priests, twenty-five thousand cubits long and
ten thousand cubits wide. The whole tract shall
be twenty-five thousand cubits long and twenty
thousand wide. 14 They may not sell or exchange
or transfer any of it, the best part of the land,
for it is sacred to the LORD. 15 The remaining sec-
tion, five thousand cubits long and twenty-five
thousand cubits wide, is profane land, assigned
to the city for dwellings and pasture. The city is
at its center. 16 These are the dimensions of the
city: the north side, forty-five hundred cubits;
the south side, forty-five hundred cubits; the
east side, forty-five hundred cubits; and the west
side, forty-five hundred cubits.* 17 The pasture
land for the city extends north two hundred fifty
cubits, south two hundred fifty cubits, east two
hundred fifty cubits, and west two hundred fifty
cubits. 18 The remaining section runs eastward
along the sacred tract for ten thousand cubits
and westward ten thousand cubits. Its produce
shall provide food for the workers of the city.
19 The workers of the city, from all the tribes of
Israel, shall cultivate it. 20 The entire sacred tract
measures twenty-five thousand by twenty-five
thousand cubits; as a square you shall set apart
the sacred tract together with the city property.

21 The remaining land on both sides of the
sacred tract and the property of the city shall
belong to the prince, extending eastward twenty-
five thousand cubits up to the eastern boundary,
and westward twenty-five thousand cubits to the
western boundary. This portion belongs to the
prince and corresponds to the tribal portions.
The sacred tract and the sanctuary of the temple
shall be in the middle. 22 Except for the Levites'
property and the city's property, which are in
the middle of the prince's property, the territory
between the portion of Judah and the portion of
Benjamin shall belong to the prince.

The Southern Portions

23 These are the remaining tribes:
From the eastern border to the western border:
Benjamin, one portion.* 24 Along the territory of
Benjamin from the eastern border to the western
border: Simeon, one portion.* 25 Along the ter-
ritory of Simeon from the eastern border to the
western border: Issachar, one portion.* 26 Along
the territory of Issachar from the eastern border
to the western border: Zebulun, one portion.*
27 Along the territory of Zebulun from the eastern
border to the western border: Gad, one portion.*
28 Along the territory of Gad shall be the southern
border. This boundary shall extend from Tamar
to the waters of Meribath-kadesh, and along the
Wadi of Egypt to the Great Sea. 29 This is the land
you shall apportion as a heritage among the
tribes of Israel, and these are their portions—
oracle of the Lord GOD.

The Gates of the City

30 These are the exits from the city: On the
north side, measuring forty-five hundred cu-
bits— 31 the gates are named after the tribes of
Israel—on the north, three gates: the gate of
Reuben, one; the gate of Judah, one; and the
gate of Levi, one. 32 On the east side, measuring
forty-five hundred cubits, three gates: the gate of
Joseph, one; the gate of Benjamin, one; and the
gate of Dan, one. 33 On the south side, measuring
forty-five hundred cubits, three gates: the gate of
Simeon, one; the gate of Issachar, one; and the
gate of Zebulun, one. 34 On the west side, meas-
uring forty-five hundred cubits, three gates: the
gate of Gad, one; the gate of Asher, one; and the
gate of Naphtali, one.* 35 The circuit of the city
shall be eighteen thousand cubits. From now on
the name of the city is "The LORD is there."*

48:16 Rev 21:16.
48:23 Jos 18:11–28.
48:24 Jos 19:1–9.
48:25 Jos 19:17–23.
48:26 Jos 19:10–16.
48:27 Jos 13:24–28.
48:34 Rev 21:12–13.
48:35 Is 2:6; Rev 3:12; 21:3.

Do you have a favorite superhero from television or comic books? One characteristic of these larger-than-life heroes is their commitment to their own values and to saving victims of injustice. The Book of Daniel portrays just such a hero. Daniel's powers are his courage to remain faithful to God despite the threat of punishment, and his special visions, which foresee how things will turn out good even though the present situation seems far from hopeful. These powers enable him to lead his people on the right path in a foreign land filled with persecution and idolatry.

The Book of

Daniel

At a Glance

I. Daniel and the Kings of Babylon (1:1—6:29).

II. Daniel's Visions (7:1—12:13).

III. Appendix: Susanna, Bel, and the Dragon (13:1—14:42).

Quick Facts

Period Covered: from the Babylonian Exile in the sixth century to the second century BC

Inspired Author: unknown, writing around 167–164 BC, during the persecution of Israel by Antiochus IV Epiphanes

Theme: to give hope to those experiencing oppression and persecution; God's reign will ultimately triumph

In Depth

Daniel represents the ideal leader with the spiritual and prophetic insight to lead people through troubled times. Scholars question whether he was an actual person. If he was, he lived in the sixth century BC—but the Book of Daniel was written four hundred years later, during the reign of an evil Greek-Syrian king, Antiochus IV Epiphanes. This was also the time of the Maccabean revolt told about in First and Second Maccabees (see the timeline at the back of this Bible). King Antiochus desecrated the Temple and attempted to erase many of Israel's religious practices. To many in Israel, this seemed like the end of the world.

The author of the Book of Daniel writes about the great hero Daniel to give the people hope during this persecution. Chapters 1–6 present six stories of Daniel and three friends living their faith during the Babylonian Exile. Chapters 7–12 tell of Daniel's four visions about the empires that dominated Israel after the Exile: Media, Persia, and Greece. The visions are full of strange symbols meant to be understood by the Israelites but not the Greek rulers of the author's time.

As you read the Book of Daniel, you will find themes familiar from other biblical books. Like Baruch, it describes living faithfully in a strange land. Like First and Second Maccabees, the book shows the courage of Israelites willing to die for their beliefs. And it declares even more clearly than Second Maccabees and Wisdom of Solomon the belief in life after death. Daniel is shown as the ideal Jew—the embodiment of all the best of the people in exile. In the face of unjust persecution and oppression, he leads his people in faithfulness to God, even through death itself.

Daniel

5:5

I. Daniel and the Kings of Babylon

The Food Test

1 1 In the third year of the reign of Jehoiakim,†
king of Judah, King Nebuchadnezzar of Bab-
ylon came and laid siege to Jerusalem.* 2 * The
Lord handed over to him Jehoiakim, king of
Judah, and some of the vessels of the temple of
God, which he carried off to the land of Shinar†
and placed in the temple treasury of his god.
3 The king told Ashpenaz,† his chief chamber-
lain, to bring in some of the Israelites, some of
the royal line and of the nobility. 4 They should
be young men without any defect, handsome,
proficient in wisdom, well informed, and in-
sightful, such as could take their place in the
king's palace; he was to teach them the language
and literature of the Chaldeans. 5 The king al-
lotted them a daily portion of food and wine
from the royal table. After three years' training
they were to enter the king's service. 6 Among
these were Judeans, Daniel, Hananiah, Mishael,
and Azariah. 7 † The chief chamberlain changed
their names: Daniel to Belteshazzar, Hananiah
to Shadrach, Mishael to Meshach, and Azariah
to Abednego.
8 But Daniel was resolved not to defile himself
with the king's food or wine; so he begged the
chief chamberlain to spare him this defilement.†
9 Though God had given Daniel the favor and
sympathy of the chief chamberlain, 10 he said to
Daniel, "I am afraid of my lord the king, who
allotted your food and drink. If he sees that
you look thinner in comparison to the other
young men of your age, you will endanger my
life with the king." 11 Then Daniel said to the
guardian whom the chief chamberlain had put
in charge of Daniel, Hananiah, Mishael, and Aza-
riah, 12 "Please test your servants for ten days. Let
us be given vegetables to eat and water to drink.
13 Then see how we look in comparison with the
other young men who eat from the royal table,
and treat your servants according to what you
see." 14 He agreed to this request, and tested them
for ten days; 15 after ten days they looked healthier
and better fed than any of the young men who ate
from the royal table. 16 So the steward continued
to take away the food and wine they were to re-
ceive, and gave them vegetables.

1:1 According to 2 Kgs 24, the siege of Jerusalem took place after the death of Jehoiakim, but 2 Chr 36:5–8 says that Jehoiakim was taken to Babylon.

1:2 *Shinar*: ancient name for Babylonia, a deliberate archaism in this text; cf. Gn 10:10; 11:2.

1:3 The proper name Ashpenaz is sometimes taken as a title, major-domo.

1:7 Other prominent Jews with Babylonian names include Sheshbazzar and Zerubabbel, who were leaders of the postexilic community.

1:8 *This defilement*: the bread, meat, and wine of the Gentiles were unclean (Hos 9:3; Tb 1:12; Jdt 10:5; 12:1–2) because they might have been offered to idols; and the meat may not have been drained of blood, as Jewish dietary law requires. This test relates to the attempt of Antiochus to force Jews to eat forbidden foods in contempt of their religion (1 Mc 1:62–63; 2 Mc 6:18; 7:1).

1:1 2 Kgs 24:1; 2 Chr 36:6; Jer 25:1. **1:2** Dn 5:2; 2 Chr 36:7; Gn 10:10.

17 To these four young men God gave knowl-
edge and proficiency in all literature and wis-
dom, and to Daniel the understanding of all
visions and dreams. 18 At the end of the time
the king had specified for their preparation, the
chief chamberlain brought them before Nebu-
chadnezzar. 19 When the king had spoken with
all of them, none was found equal to Daniel,
Hananiah, Mishael, and Azariah; and so they
entered the king's service. 20 In any question of
wisdom or understanding which the king put to
them, he found them ten times better than any
of the magicians and enchanters in his kingdom.
21 * Daniel remained there until the first year of
King Cyrus.†

Nebuchadnezzar's Dream†

2 1 In the second year of his reign, King Nebu-
chadnezzar had a dream which left his spirit
no rest and robbed him of his sleep. 2 So he or-
dered that the magicians, enchanters, sorcerers,
and Chaldeans† be summoned to interpret the
dream for him. When they came and presented
themselves to the king, 3 he said to them, "I had
a dream which will allow my spirit no rest until I
know what it means." 4 The Chaldeans answered
the king in Aramaic:† "O king, live forever! Tell
your servants the dream and we will give its
meaning." 5 The king answered the Chaldeans,
"This is what I have decided: unless you tell me
the dream and its meaning, you shall be cut to
pieces and your houses made into a refuse heap.
6 But if you tell me the dream and its meaning,
you shall receive from me gifts and presents and
great honors. Therefore tell me the dream and its
meaning."
7 Again they answered, "Let the king tell his
servants the dream and we will give its mean-
ing." 8 But the king replied: "I know for certain
that you are bargaining for time, since you know
what I have decided. 9 If you do not tell me the
dream, there can be but one decree for you. You
have conspired to present a false and deceitful in-
terpretation to me until the crisis is past. Tell me
the dream, therefore, that I may be sure that you
can also give its correct interpretation."
10 The Chaldeans answered the king: "There is
not a man on earth who can do what you ask,
O king; never has any king, however great and
mighty, asked such a thing of any magician,
enchanter, or Chaldean. 11 What you demand,
O king, is too difficult; there is no one who can
tell it to the king except the gods, who do not
dwell among people of flesh." 12 At this the king
became violently angry and ordered all the wise
men† of Babylon to be put to death. 13 When
the decree was issued that the wise men should
be slain, Daniel and his companions were also
sought out.
14 Then Daniel prudently took counsel with
Arioch, the chief of the king's guard, who had set
out to kill the wise men of Babylon. 15 He asked
Arioch, the officer of the king, "What is the rea-
son for this harsh order from the king?" When
Arioch told him, 16 Daniel went and asked for
time from the king, that he might give him the
interpretation.
17 Daniel went home and informed his com-
panions Hananiah, Mishael, and Azariah, 18 that
they might implore the mercy of the God of
heaven in regard to this mystery, so that Daniel
and his companions might not perish with the
rest of the wise men of Babylon. 19 During the
night the mystery was revealed to Daniel in a vi-
sion, and he blessed the God of heaven:

20 "Blessed be the name of God forever and ever,
for wisdom and power are his.
21 He causes the changes of the times and
seasons,
establishes kings and deposes them.
He gives wisdom to the wise
and knowledge to those who understand.
22 He reveals deep and hidden things
and knows what is in the darkness,
for the light dwells with him.*
23 To you, God of my ancestors,
I give thanks and praise,
because you have given me wisdom and
power.
Now you have shown me what we asked of
you,
you have made known to us the king's
dream."

†

1:21 *The first year of King Cyrus*: the year of this Persian king's conquest of Babylon, 539/538 B.C.

2:1–49 The chronology of v. 1 is in conflict with that of 1:5, 18, and in 2:25 Daniel appears to be introduced to the king for the first time. It seems that the story of this chapter was originally entirely independent of chap. 1 and later retouched slightly to fit its present setting. The Septuagint (Papyrus 967) reads the twelfth year instead of the second.

2:2 *Chaldeans*: because the Babylonians gave serious study to the stars and planets, "Chaldeans" were identified with astrologers throughout the Hellenistic world.

2:4 *Aramaic*: a gloss to indicate that at this point the text switches from Hebrew to Aramaic, which continues through the end of chap. 7; at 8:1, the text switches back to Hebrew.

2:12 *Wise men*: the satire, although directed against the Babylonian diviners in the text, refers to the Hellenistic Greeks, who made special claims to wisdom; the assertion here is that true wisdom comes from God and resides with the Jews. Cf. also chap. 5.

*

1:21 Dn 6:29.

2:22 Jn 1:9; 8:12; 1 Cor 4:5; 1 Jn 1:6.

24 So Daniel went to Arioch, whom the king had appointed to destroy the wise men of Babylon, and said to him, "Do not put the wise men of Babylon to death. Bring me before the king, and I will tell him the interpretation of the dream." Arioch quickly brought Daniel to the king and said, 25 "I have found a man among the Judean exiles who can give the interpretation to the king." 26 The king asked Daniel, whose name was Belteshazzar, "Can you tell me the dream that I had and its meaning?" 27 In the king's presence Daniel made this reply:

"The mystery about which the king has inquired, the wise men, enchanters, magicians, and diviners could not explain to the king. 28 But there is a God in heaven who reveals mysteries, and he has shown King Nebuchadnezzar what is to happen in the last days; this was your dream, the visions† you saw as you lay in bed. 29 To you in your bed there came thoughts about what should happen in the future, and he who reveals mysteries showed you what is to be. 30 To me also this mystery has been revealed; not that I am wiser than any other living person, but in order that its meaning may be made known to the king, that you may understand the thoughts of your own mind.

31 "In your vision, O king, you saw a statue, very large and exceedingly bright, terrifying in appearance as it stood before you. 32 Its head was pure gold, its chest and arms were silver, its belly and thighs bronze, 33 its legs iron, its feet partly iron and partly clay.† 34 While you watched, a stone was hewn from a mountain without a hand being put to it, and it struck its iron and clay feet, breaking them in pieces. 35 The iron, clay, bronze, silver, and gold all crumbled at once, fine as the chaff on the threshing floor in summer, and the wind blew them away without leaving a trace. But the stone that struck the statue became a great mountain and filled the whole earth.

36 † "This was the dream; the interpretation we shall also give in the king's presence. 37 You, O king, are the king of kings; to you the God of heaven has given dominion and strength, power and glory; 38 human beings, wild beasts, and birds of the air, wherever they may dwell, he has handed over to you, making you ruler over them all; you are the head of gold. 39 Another kingdom shall take your place, inferior to yours, then a third kingdom, of bronze, which shall rule over the whole earth. 40 There shall be a fourth kingdom, strong as iron; it shall break in pieces and subdue all these others, just as iron breaks in pieces and crushes everything else. 41 The feet and toes you saw, partly of clay and partly of iron, mean that it shall be a divided kingdom, but yet have some of the hardness of iron. As you saw the iron mixed with clay tile, 42 and the toes partly iron and partly clay, the kingdom shall be partly strong and partly fragile. 43 The iron mixed with clay means that they shall seal their alliances by intermarriage, but they shall not stay united, any more than iron mixes with clay. 44 In the lifetime of those kings the God of heaven will set up a kingdom that shall never be destroyed or delivered up to another people; rather, it shall break in pieces all these kingdoms and put an end to them, and it shall stand forever. 45 * That is the meaning of the stone you saw hewn from the mountain without a hand being put to it, which broke in pieces the iron, bronze, clay, silver, and gold. The great God has revealed to the king what shall be in the future; this is exactly what you dreamed, and its meaning is sure."

46 Then King Nebuchadnezzar fell down and worshiped Daniel and ordered sacrifice and incense offered to him. 47 To Daniel the king said, "Truly your God is the God of gods and Lord of kings and a revealer of mysteries; that is why you were able to reveal this mystery." 48 He advanced Daniel to a high post, gave him many generous presents, made him ruler of the whole province of Babylon and chief prefect over all the wise men of Babylon. 49 At Daniel's request the king made Shadrach, Meshach, and Abednego administrators of the province of Babylon, while Daniel himself remained at the king's court.

The Fiery Furnace

3 1 King Nebuchadnezzar had a golden statue made, sixty cubits high and six cubits wide, which he set up in the plain of Dura† in the

2:28 *The visions*: lit., "the visions of your head," a phrasing which distinguishes visionary experiences that are personal from those that are observable by others (see 4:2, 7, 10). That Daniel, unlike the Chaldeans, has access to these visions testifies to his God-given wisdom. Actually, this "dream" is more properly an apocalyptic vision; cf. the very similar message in Daniel's vision of chap. 7.

2:33 *Clay*: it has been suggested that the motif of iron mixed with clay implies a hollow metal statue packed with clay to stabilize it. In the interpretation of the dream, however, the mixture is taken as a sign of weakness.

2:36–45 The four successive kingdoms in this apocalyptic perspective are the Babylonian (gold), the Median (silver), the Persian (bronze), and the Hellenistic (iron). The last, after Alexander's death, was divided among his generals (vv. 41–42). Of the kingdoms which emerged from this partitioning, the two that most affected the Jews were the dynasties of the Ptolemies in Egypt and the Seleucids in Syria. They tried in vain, by war and through intermarriage, to restore the unity of Alexander's empire (v. 43). The stone hewn from the mountain is the kingdom of God awaited by the Jews (vv. 44–45). Compare the image of the stone applied to Jesus in Luke 20:17–18.

3:1 *Dura*: several places in Babylonia bore this name. Probably the present reference is to one located close to Babylon. Giant statues of the type mentioned here were not uncommon in antiquity; a cubit

2:45 Mt 21:44; Lk 20:18.

Live It!

Doing the Right Thing

Chapter 3 of Daniel tells us of Shadrach, Meshach, and Abednego, three companions of Daniel's who refuse to compromise their religious beliefs. Even in the face of death, they will not denounce the Lord and worship the god of Nebuchadnezzar (also called Nebuchadrezzar).

The pressure to do what we know is wrong takes many forms. For teens in particular, numerous temptations—drugs, alcohol, sex, shoplifting, and many more—can create an overwhelming amount of pressure in their lives. Caving in to that pressure typically leads people to suffering, because by definition, sin leads to unhappy and unhealthy consequences. It may offer some short-term satisfaction, but denying what we know is right is ultimately denying God and the fullness of life God has planned for us.

Follow Shadrach, Meshach, and Abednego's example and stand up for what is right. Stand up for God!

▶ Dn 3:1–24

province of Babylon. [2]He then ordered the satraps,† prefects, and governors, the counselors, treasurers, judges, magistrates and all the officials of the provinces to be summoned to the dedication of the statue which he had set up. [3]The satraps, prefects, and governors, the counselors, treasurers, judges, magistrates and all the officials of the provinces came together for the dedication and stood before the statue which King Nebuchadnezzar had set up. [4]A herald cried out: "Nations and peoples of every language, [5]† when you hear the sound of the horn, pipe, zither, dulcimer, harp, double-flute, and all the other musical instruments, you must fall down and worship the golden statue which King Nebuchadnezzar has set up. [6]Whoever does not fall down and worship shall be instantly cast into a white-hot furnace." [7]Therefore, as soon as they heard the sound of the horn, pipe, zither, dulcimer, harp, double-flute, and all the other musical instruments, the nations and peoples of every language all fell down and worshiped the golden statue which King Nebuchadnezzar had set up.

[8]At that point, some of the Chaldeans came and accused the Jews [9]to King Nebuchadnezzar: "O king, live forever! [10]O king, you issued a decree that everyone who heard the sound of the horn, pipe, zither, dulcimer, harp, and double-flute, and all the other musical instruments should fall down and worship the golden statue; [11]whoever did not was to be cast into a white-hot furnace. [12]There are certain Jews whom you have made administrators of the province of Babylon: Shadrach, Meshach, and Abednego; these men, O king, have paid no attention to you; they will not serve your god or worship the golden statue which you set up."

[13]Nebuchadnezzar flew into a rage and sent for Shadrach, Meshach, and Abednego, who were promptly brought before the king. [14]King Nebuchadnezzar questioned them: "Is it true, Shadrach, Meshach, and Abednego, that you will not serve my god, or worship the golden statue that I set up? [15]Now, if you are ready to fall down and worship the statue I made, whenever you hear the sound of the horn, pipe, zither, dulcimer, harp, double-flute, and all the other musical instruments, then all will be well;† if not, you shall be instantly cast into the white-hot furnace; and who is the God who can deliver you out of my hands?" [16]Shadrach, Meshach, and Abednego answered King Nebuchadnezzar, "There is no need for us to defend ourselves before you in this matter. [17]If our God, whom we serve, can save us† from the white-hot furnace and from your hands, O king, may he save us! [18]But even if he will not, you should know, O king, that we will not serve your god or worship the golden statue which you set up."

[19]Nebuchadnezzar's face became livid with utter rage against Shadrach, Meshach, and Abednego. He ordered the furnace to be heated seven times more than usual [20]and had some of the strongest men in his army bind Shadrach, Meshach, and Abednego and cast them into the white-hot furnace. [21]They were bound and cast into the white-hot furnace with their trousers, shirts, hats and other garments, [22]for the king's order was urgent. So huge a fire was kindled in

† was about a foot and a half. The unrealistic proportions of this statue suggest a comic effect.

3:2 *Satraps*: Persian provincial governors.

3:5 The precise identification of the instruments is disputed. Several of the names are Greek.

3:15 *Then all will be well*: lacking in Aramaic; this phrase is supplied from the context.

3:17 *If our God . . . can save us*: the youths do not question the efficacy of the divine power, but whether it will be exercised (v. 18).

DN

the furnace that the flames devoured the men who threw Shadrach, Meshach, and Abednego into it. 23 But these three fell, bound, into the midst of the white-hot furnace.

Prayer of Azariah†

24 They walked about in the flames, singing to God and blessing the Lord. 25 Azariah† stood up in the midst of the fire and prayed aloud:

26 "Blessed are you, and praiseworthy,
O Lord, the God of our ancestors,
and glorious forever is your name.
27 For you are just in all you have done;
all your deeds are faultless, all your ways right,
and all your judgments proper.
28 You have executed proper judgments
in all that you have brought upon us
and upon Jerusalem, the holy city of our ancestors.
By a proper judgment you have done all this
because of our sins;
29 For we have sinned and transgressed
by departing from you,
and we have done every kind of evil.
30 Your commandments we have not heeded or observed,
nor have we done as you ordered us for our good.
31 Therefore all you have brought upon us,
all you have done to us,
you have done by a proper judgment.
32 You have handed us over to our enemies,
lawless and hateful rebels;
to an unjust king, the worst in all the world.
33 Now we cannot open our mouths;
shame and reproach have come upon us,
your servants, who revere you.
34 For your name's sake, do not deliver us up forever,
or make void your covenant.
35 Do not take away your mercy from us,
for the sake of Abraham, your beloved,
Isaac your servant, and Israel your holy one,
36 To whom you promised to multiply their offspring
like the stars of heaven,
or the sand on the shore of the sea.
37 For we are reduced, O Lord, beyond any other nation,
brought low everywhere in the world this day
because of our sins.
38 We have in our day no prince, prophet, or leader,
no burnt offering, sacrifice, oblation, or incense,
no place to offer first fruits, to find favor with you.
39 But with contrite heart and humble spirit
let us be received;
As though it were burnt offerings of rams and bulls,
or tens of thousands of fat lambs,
40 So let our sacrifice be in your presence today
and find favor before you;
for those who trust in you cannot be put to shame.
41 And now we follow you with our whole heart,
we fear you and we seek your face.
Do not put us to shame,
42 but deal with us in your kindness and great mercy.
43 Deliver us in accord with your wonders,
and bring glory to your name, O Lord:
44 Let all those be put to shame
who inflict evils on your servants;
Let them be shamed and powerless,
and their strength broken;
45 Let them know that you alone are the Lord God,
glorious over the whole world."

46 Now the king's servants who had thrown
them in continued to stoke the furnace with
naphtha, pitch, tow, and brush. 47 The flames
rose forty-nine cubits above the furnace, 48 and
spread out, burning the Chaldeans that it caught
around the furnace. 49 But the angel of the Lord
went down into the furnace with Azariah and
his companions, drove the fiery flames out of
the furnace, 50 and made the inside of the furnace as though a dew-laden breeze were blowing
through it. The fire in no way touched them or
caused them pain or harm. 51 Then these three in
the furnace with one voice sang, glorifying and
blessing God:

52 "Blessed are you, O Lord, the God of our ancestors,
praiseworthy and exalted above all forever;
And blessed is your holy and glorious name,

DN

† **3:24–90** These verses are additions to the Aramaic text of Daniel, translated from the Greek form of the book. They were probably first composed in Hebrew or Aramaic, but are no longer extant in the original language. The Roman Catholic Church has always regarded them as part of the canonical Scriptures.

3:25 *Azariah*: i.e., Abednego; cf. Dn 1:7.

praiseworthy and exalted above all for all
ages.
53 Blessed are you in the temple of your holy
glory,
praiseworthy and glorious above all forever.
54 Blessed are you on the throne of your
kingdom,
praiseworthy and exalted above all forever.
55 Blessed are you who look into the depths
from your throne upon the cherubim,
praiseworthy and exalted above all forever.
56 Blessed are you in the firmament of heaven,
praiseworthy and glorious forever.
57 Bless the Lord, all you works of the Lord,
praise and exalt him above all forever.
58 Angels of the Lord, bless the Lord,
praise and exalt him above all forever.
59 You heavens, bless the Lord,
praise and exalt him above all forever.*
60 All you waters above the heavens, bless the
Lord,
praise and exalt him above all forever.
61 All you powers, bless the Lord;
praise and exalt him above all forever.
62 Sun and moon, bless the Lord;
praise and exalt him above all forever.
63 Stars of heaven, bless the Lord;
praise and exalt him above all forever.
64 Every shower and dew, bless the Lord;
praise and exalt him above all forever.
65 All you winds, bless the Lord;
praise and exalt him above all forever.
66 Fire and heat, bless the Lord;
praise and exalt him above all forever.
67 Cold and chill, bless the Lord;
praise and exalt him above all forever.
68 Dew and rain, bless the Lord;
praise and exalt him above all forever.
69 Frost and chill, bless the Lord;
praise and exalt him above all forever.
70 Hoarfrost and snow, bless the Lord;
praise and exalt him above all forever.
71 Nights and days, bless the Lord;
praise and exalt him above all forever.
72 Light and darkness, bless the Lord;
praise and exalt him above all forever.
73 Lightnings and clouds, bless the Lord;
praise and exalt him above all forever.
74 Let the earth bless the Lord,
praise and exalt him above all forever.
75 Mountains and hills, bless the Lord;
praise and exalt him above all forever.
76 Everything growing on earth, bless the Lord;
praise and exalt him above all forever.
77 You springs, bless the Lord;
praise and exalt him above all forever.
78 Seas and rivers, bless the Lord;
praise and exalt him above all forever.
79 You sea monsters and all water creatures,
bless the Lord;
praise and exalt him above all forever.
80 All you birds of the air, bless the Lord;
praise and exalt him above all forever.
81 All you beasts, wild and tame, bless the Lord;
praise and exalt him above all forever.
82 All you mortals, bless the Lord;
praise and exalt him above all forever.
83 O Israel, bless the Lord;
praise and exalt him above all forever.
84 Priests of the Lord, bless the Lord;
praise and exalt him above all forever.
85 Servants of the Lord, bless the Lord;
praise and exalt him above all forever.
86 Spirits and souls of the just, bless the Lord;
praise and exalt him above all forever.
87 Holy and humble of heart, bless the Lord;
praise and exalt him above all forever.
88 Hananiah, Azariah, Mishael, bless the Lord;
praise and exalt him above all forever.
For he has delivered us from Sheol,
and saved us from the power of death;
He has freed us from the raging flame
and delivered us from the fire.
89 Give thanks to the Lord, who is good,
whose mercy endures forever.
90 Bless the God of gods, all you who fear the
Lord;
praise and give thanks,
for his mercy endures forever."

Deliverance from the Furnace

91 Then King Nebuchadnezzar was startled and
rose in haste, asking his counselors, "Did we not
cast three men bound into the fire?" "Certainly,
O king," they answered. 92 "But," he replied, "I
see four men unbound and unhurt, walking in
the fire, and the fourth looks like a son of God."
93 Then Nebuchadnezzar came to the opening of
the white-hot furnace and called: "Shadrach, Me-
shach, and Abednego, servants of the Most High
God, come out." Thereupon Shadrach, Meshach,
and Abednego came out of the fire. 94 When the
satraps, prefects, governors, and counselors of
the king came together, they saw that the fire
had had no power over the bodies of these men;
not a hair of their heads had been singed, nor
were their garments altered; there was not even
a smell of fire about them. 95 Nebuchadnezzar
exclaimed, "Blessed be the God of Shadrach,
Meshach, and Abednego, who sent his angel

*3:59 Ps 148:4.

to deliver the servants that trusted in him; they
disobeyed the royal command and yielded their
bodies rather than serve or worship any god ex-
cept their own God. [96]Therefore I decree for na-
tions and peoples of every language that whoever
blasphemes the God of Shadrach, Meshach, and
Abednego shall be cut to pieces and his house
made into a refuse heap. For there is no other
God who can rescue like this." [97]Then the king
promoted Shadrach, Meshach, and Abednego in
the province of Babylon.

[98]† King Nebuchadnezzar to the nations and
peoples of every language, wherever they dwell
on earth: May your peace abound! [99]It has
seemed good to me to publish the signs and
wonders which the Most High God has accom-
plished in my regard.

100 How great are his signs, how mighty his
wonders;
his kingship is an everlasting kingship,
and his dominion endures through all
generations.*

Nebuchadnezzar's Madness

4 [1]I, Nebuchadnezzar, was at home in my
palace, content and prosperous. [2]I had a
terrifying dream as I lay in bed, and the images
and my visions frightened me. [3]So I issued a
decree that all the wise men of Babylon should
be brought before me to give the interpretation
of the dream. [4]When the magicians, enchanters,
Chaldeans, and diviners had come in, I related
the dream before them; but none of them could
tell me its meaning. [5]Finally there came before
me Daniel, whose name is Belteshazzar after the
name of my god,† and in whom is a spirit of the
holy gods.* I repeated the dream to him: [6]"Bel-
teshazzar, chief of the magicians, I know that a
spirit of the holy gods is in you and no mystery is
too difficult for you; this is the dream that I saw,
tell me its meaning.

[7]"These were the visions I saw while in bed:
I saw a tree of great height at the center of the
earth. [8]It was large and strong, with its top touch-
ing the heavens, and it could be seen to the ends
of the earth. [9]Its leaves were beautiful, its fruit
abundant, providing food for all. Under it the
wild beasts found shade, in its branches the birds
of the air nested; all flesh ate of it. [10]In the vision

Pray It!

King Nebuchadnezzar's Conversion

Sometimes, it seems God has to go to extremes to get our attention. In Daniel, chapter 4 (written like a letter from the king to his subjects), King Nebuchadnezzar tells how he had to go through some pretty intense humiliation—acting like a wild animal (see verses 29–30)—before God got his attention. Even Daniel's prior warning didn't rein in his ego and bring him to his senses (see verses 23–24). After Nebuchadnezzar's reason returned, he realized the power of God and turned to praise and honor God.

Many people go through a conversion—a turning toward God—after they have suffered the consequences of their sinful actions. For others, the catalyst might be an illness or the death of a close friend or family member. Why does it take a crisis for us to realize our need for God? Maybe because during such a time, we realize that we cannot control life and that we need God's loving presence.

In your prayer, reflect or journal on the following questions:

- Where do you recognize your need for God?
- Is a conversion toward God in a crisis only a temporary thing, or can it lead to a lifelong commitment? Why?

▶ **Daniel, chapter 4**

I saw while in bed, a holy watcher† came down
from heaven [11]and cried aloud in these words:

'Cut down the tree and lop off its branches,
strip off its leaves and scatter its fruit;
Let the beasts flee from beneath it, and the
birds from its branches,
12 but leave its stump in the earth.
Bound with iron and bronze,
let him be fed with the grass of the field

† **3:98–4:34** This section has the form of a letter written by Nebuchadnezzar to his subjects.

4:5 *After the name of my god*: Belteshazzar, the Babylonian name given to Daniel at the king's orders (1:7), is *Balāṭ-šu-uṣur*, "protect his life." This passage implies a name connected with Bel, a Babylonian god. *A spirit of the holy gods*: or a holy divine spirit; or spirit of a holy God. See also vv. 6, 15; 5:11–12, 14; 6:4.

4:10 *A holy watcher*: lit., "a watcher and a holy one." Two terms for angels. The term watcher is found in the Bible only in this chapter of Daniel, but it is common in extra-canonical Jewish literature. In 1 Enoch, the fallen angels are called watchers.

* **3:100** Dn 4:31; 7:14. **4:5** Gn 41:38.

and bathed with the dew of heaven;
let his lot be with the beasts in the grass of
the earth.
13 Let his mind be changed from a human one;
let the mind of a beast be given him,
till seven years pass over him.
14 By decree of the watchers is this proclamation,
by order of the holy ones, this sentence;
That all who live may know
that the Most High is sovereign over
human kingship,
Giving it to whom he wills,
and setting it over the lowliest of mortals.'*

15 "This is the dream that I, King Nebuchadnez-
zar, had. Now, Belteshazzar, tell me its meaning.
None of the wise men in my kingdom can tell
me the meaning, but you can, because the spirit
of the holy gods is in you."
16 Then Daniel, whose name was Belteshazzar,
was appalled for a time, dismayed by his thoughts.
"Belteshazzar," the king said to him, "do not let
the dream or its meaning dismay you." "My
lord," Belteshazzar replied, "may this dream be
for your enemies, and its meaning for your foes.
17 The tree that you saw, large and strong, its top
touching the heavens, that could be seen by the
whole earth, 18 its leaves beautiful, its fruit abun-
dant, providing food for all, under which the wild
beasts lived, and in whose branches the birds of
the air dwelt— 19 you are that tree, O king, large
and strong! Your majesty has become so great as
to touch the heavens, and your rule reaches to the
ends of the earth. 20 As for the king's vision of a
holy watcher, who came down from heaven and
proclaimed: 'Cut down the tree and destroy it,
but leave its stump in the earth. Bound with iron
and bronze, let him be fed with the grass of the
field, and bathed with the dew of heaven; let his
lot be with wild beasts till seven years pass over
him'— 21 here is its meaning, O king, here is the
sentence that the Most High has passed upon my
lord king: 22 * You shall be cast out from human
society and dwell with wild beasts; you shall be
given grass to eat like an ox and be bathed with
the dew of heaven; seven years shall pass over
you, until you know that the Most High is sover-
eign over human kingship and gives it to whom
he will. 23 The command that the stump of the
tree is to be left means that your kingdom shall
be preserved for you, once you have learned that
heaven is sovereign. 24 Therefore, O king, may my
advice be acceptable to you; atone for your sins
by good deeds,† and for your misdeeds by kind-
ness to the poor; then your contentment will be
long lasting."
25 All this happened to King Nebuchadnezzar.
26 Twelve months later, as he was walking on the
roof of the royal palace in Babylon, 27 the king
said, "Babylon the great! Was it not I, with my
great strength, who built it as a royal residence
for my splendor and majesty?" 28 While these
words were still on the king's lips, a voice spoke
from heaven, "It has been decreed for you, King
Nebuchadnezzar, that your kingship is taken
from you! 29 You shall be cast out from human
society, and shall dwell with wild beasts; you
shall be given grass to eat like an ox, and seven
years shall pass over you, until you learn that
the Most High is sovereign over human kingship
and gives it to whom he will." 30 † At once this
was fulfilled. Nebuchadnezzar was cast out from
human society, he ate grass like an ox, and his
body was bathed with the dew of heaven, until
his hair grew like the feathers of an eagle, and his
nails like the claws of a bird.
31 When this period was over, I, Nebuchad-
nezzar, raised my eyes to heaven; my reason was
restored to me, and I blessed the Most High, I
praised and glorified the One who lives forever,

Whose dominion is an everlasting dominion,
and whose kingdom endures through all
generations.*
32 All who live on the earth are counted as
nothing;
he does as he wills with the powers of
heaven
and with those who live on the earth.
There is no one who can stay his hand
or say to him, "What have you done?"

33 At the same time my reason returned to me,
and for the glory of my kingdom, my majesty
and my splendor returned to me. My counselors
and nobles sought me out; I was restored to my
kingdom and became much greater than before.
34 Now, I, Nebuchadnezzar, praise and exalt and

†

4:24 *Good deeds*: the Aramaic word *ṣidqâ* has the root meaning of "righteousness," but in a late text such as this could mean "almsgiving."

4:30–32 There is no historical record that these events happened to Nebuchadnezzar. Scholars have long suspected that the story originally involved Nabonidus, the father of Belshazzar, who was absent from Babylon and lived at Teima in the Arabian desert for a number of years. This suggestion is now strengthened by the Prayer of Nabonidus, found at Qumran, which is closely related to chap. 4. The biblical author's chief interest was not in the historicity of this popular tale, but in the object lesson it contained for the proud "divine" kings of the Seleucid dynasty.

4:14 1 Sm 2:8.
4:22 Dn 5:21.
4:31 Dn 3:33; 7:14.

glorify the King of heaven, all of whose works are
right and ways just; and who is able to humble
those who walk in pride.

The Writing on the Wall

5 1 King Belshazzar gave a great banquet for a
thousand of his nobles, with whom he drank.
2 Under the influence of the wine, he ordered the
gold and silver vessels which Nebuchadnezzar,
his father,† had taken from the temple in Jerusa-
lem, to be brought in so that the king, his nobles,
his consorts, and his concubines might drink
from them. 3 When the gold vessels taken from
the temple, the house of God in Jerusalem, had
been brought in, and while the king, his nobles,
his consorts, and his concubines were drinking
4 wine from them, they praised their gods of gold
and silver, bronze and iron, wood and stone.

5 Suddenly, opposite the lampstand, the fin-
gers of a human hand appeared, writing on the
plaster of the wall in the king's palace. When
the king saw the hand that wrote, 6 his face be-
came pale; his thoughts terrified him, his hip
joints shook, and his knees knocked. 7 The king
shouted for the enchanters, Chaldeans, and di-
viners to be brought in. "Whoever reads this
writing and tells me what it means," he said to
the wise men of Babylon, "shall be clothed in
purple, wear a chain of gold around his neck,
and be third in governing the kingdom." 8 But
though all the king's wise men came in, none of
them could either read the writing or tell the king
what it meant. 9 Then King Belshazzar was greatly
terrified; his face became pale, and his nobles
were thrown into confusion.

10 When the queen heard of the discussion be-
tween the king and his nobles, she entered the
banquet hall and said, "O king, live forever! Do
not let your thoughts terrify you, or your face be-
come so pale! 11 There is a man in your kingdom
in whom is a spirit of the holy gods; during the
lifetime of your father he showed brilliant insight
and god-like wisdom. King Nebuchadnezzar,
your father, made him chief of the magicians,
enchanters, Chaldeans, and diviners. 12 Because
this Daniel, whom the king named Belteshazzar,
has shown an extraordinary spirit, knowledge,
and insight in interpreting dreams, explaining
riddles and solving problems, let him now be
summoned to tell you what this means."

13 Then Daniel was brought into the presence
of the king. The king asked him, "Are you the
Daniel, one of the Jewish exiles, whom my fa-
ther, the king, brought from Judah? 14 I have
heard that the spirit of the gods is in you, that
you have shown brilliant insight and extraordi-
nary wisdom. 15 The wise men and enchanters
were brought in to me to read this writing and
tell me its meaning, but they could not say what
the words meant. 16 But I have heard that you can
give interpretations and solve problems; now, if
you are able to read the writing and tell me what
it means, you shall be clothed in purple, wear a
chain of gold around your neck, and be third in
governing the kingdom."

17 Daniel answered the king: "You may keep
your gifts, or give your presents to someone
else; but the writing I will read for the king, and
tell what it means. 18 The Most High God gave
your father Nebuchadnezzar kingship, greatness,
splendor, and majesty. 19 Because he made him
so great, the nations and peoples of every lan-
guage dreaded and feared him. Whomever he
willed, he would kill or let live; whomever he
willed, he would exalt or humble. 20 But when
his heart became proud and his spirit hardened
by insolence, he was put down from his royal
throne and deprived of his glory; 21 * he was cast
out from human society and his heart was made
like that of a beast; he lived with wild asses, and
ate grass like an ox; his body was bathed with
the dew of heaven, until he learned that the Most
High God is sovereign over human kingship and
sets over it whom he will. 22 You, his son, Bel-
shazzar, have not humbled your heart, though
you knew all this; 23 you have rebelled against the
Lord of heaven. You had the vessels of his temple
brought before you, so that you and your nobles,
your consorts and your concubines, might drink
wine from them; and you praised the gods of sil-
ver and gold, bronze and iron, wood and stone,
that neither see nor hear nor have intelligence.
But the God in whose hand is your very breath
and the whole course of your life, you did not
glorify. 24 By him was the hand sent, and the
writing set down.

25 "This is the writing that was inscribed: MENE,
TEKEL, and PERES.† These words mean: 26 † MENE,
God has numbered your kingdom and put an
end to it; 27 TEKEL, you have been weighed on the

5:2 *Nebuchadnezzar, his father*: between Nebuchadnezzar and Belshazzar several kings ruled in Babylon. Belshazzar was the son of Nabonidus, and he acted as regent in Babylon during his father's absence.

5:25 *MENE, TEKEL, and PERES*: these seem to be the Aramaic names of weights and monetary values: the mina, the shekel (the sixtieth part of a mina), and the parsu (a half-mina).

5:26–28 Daniel interprets these three terms by a play on the words: *MENE*, connected with the verb meaning to number; *TEKEL*, with the verb meaning to weigh; *PERES*, with the verb meaning to divide. There is also a play on the last term with the word for Persians.

5:21 Dn 4:22.

scales and found wanting; 28 PERES, your kingdom has been divided and given to the Medes and Persians."

29 Then by order of Belshazzar they clothed Daniel in purple, with a chain of gold around his neck, and proclaimed him third in governing the kingdom. 30 That very night Belshazzar, the Chaldean king, was slain:

6 1 And Darius the Mede† succeeded to the kingdom at the age of sixty-two.

The Lions' Den

2 Darius decided to appoint over his entire kingdom one hundred and twenty satraps. 3 These were accountable to three ministers, one of whom was Daniel; the satraps reported to them, so that the king should suffer no loss. 4 Daniel outshone all the ministers and satraps because an extraordinary spirit was in him, and the king considered setting him over the entire kingdom. 5 Then the ministers and satraps tried to find grounds for accusation against Daniel regarding the kingdom. But they could not accuse him of any corruption. Because he was trustworthy, no fault or corruption was to be found in him. 6 Then these men said to themselves, "We shall find no grounds for accusation against this Daniel except in connection with the law of his God." 7 So these ministers and satraps stormed in to the king and said to him, "King Darius, live forever! 8 †* All the ministers of the kingdom, the prefects, satraps, counselors, and governors agree that the following prohibition ought to be put in force by royal decree: for thirty days, whoever makes a petition to anyone, divine or human, except to you, O king, shall be thrown into a den of lions. 9 Now, O king, let the prohibition be issued over your signature, immutable and irrevocable† according to the law of the Medes and Persians." 10 So King Darius signed the prohibition into law.

11 Even after Daniel heard that this law had been signed, he continued his custom of going home to kneel in prayer and give thanks to his God in the upper chamber three times a day, with the windows open toward Jerusalem. 12 So these men stormed in and found Daniel praying and pleading before his God. 13 Then they went to remind the king about the prohibition: "Did you not sign a decree, O king, that for thirty days, whoever makes a petition to anyone, divine or human, except to you, O king, shall be cast into a den of lions?" The king answered them, "The decree is absolute, irrevocable under the law of the Medes and Persians." 14 To this they replied, "Daniel, one of the Jewish exiles, has paid no attention to you, O king, or to the prohibition you signed; three times a day he offers his prayer." 15 The king was deeply grieved at this news and he made up his mind to save Daniel; he worked till sunset to rescue him. 16 But these men pressed the king. "Keep in mind, O king," they said, "that under the law of the Medes and Persians every royal prohibition or decree is irrevocable." 17 So the king ordered Daniel to be brought and cast into the lions' den.† To Daniel he said, "Your God, whom you serve so constantly, must save you." 18 To forestall any tampering, the king sealed with his own ring and the rings of the lords the stone that had been brought to block the opening of the den.

19 Then the king returned to his palace for the night; he refused to eat and he dismissed the entertainers. Since sleep was impossible for him, 20 the king rose very early the next morning and hastened to the lions' den. 21 As he drew near, he cried out to Daniel sorrowfully, "Daniel, servant of the living God, has your God whom you serve so constantly been able to save you from the lions?" 22 Daniel answered the king: "O king, live forever! 23 My God sent his angel and closed the lions' mouths so that they have not hurt me.* For I have been found innocent before him; neither have I done you any harm, O king!" 24 This gave the king great joy. At his order Daniel was brought up from the den; he was found to be unharmed because he trusted in his God. 25 The king then ordered the men who had accused Daniel, along with their children and their wives, to be cast into the lions' den. Before they reached the bottom of the den, the lions overpowered them and crushed all their bones.

26 Then King Darius wrote to the nations and

---

†

6:1 *Darius the Mede*: unknown outside of the Book of Daniel. The Median kingdom did not exist at this time because it had already been conquered by Cyrus the Persian. Apparently the author of Daniel is following an apocalyptic view of history, linked to prophecy (cf. Is 13:17–19; Jer 51:11, 28–30), according to which the Medes formed the second of four world kingdoms preceding the messianic times; see note on Dn 2:36–45. The character of Darius the Mede has probably been modeled on that of the Persian king Darius the Great (522–486 B.C.), the second successor of Cyrus. The Persian Darius did appoint satraps over his empire.

6:8–11 The Jews of the second century B.C. could relate the king's attempt to force upon them, under pain of death, the worship of a foreign deity to the decrees of Antiochus IV; cf. 1 Mc 1:41–50.

6:9 *Immutable and irrevocable*: Est 1:19 and 8:8 also refer to the immutability of Medo-Persian laws. The same idea is found in the historian Diodorus Siculus with reference to the time of Darius III (335–331 B.C.), the last of the Persian kings. Cf. Dn 6:13, 16.

6:17 *The lions' den*: a pit too deep to be easily scaled; its opening was blocked with a stone (v. 18).

*

6:8 Est 1:19. **6:23** 1 Mc 2:60.

peoples of every language, wherever they dwell
on the earth: "May your peace abound! 27 I de-
cree that throughout my royal domain the God
of Daniel is to be reverenced and feared:

"For he is the living God, enduring forever,
whose kingdom shall not be destroyed,
whose dominion shall be without end,
28 A savior and deliverer,
working signs and wonders in heaven and
on earth,
who saved Daniel from the lions' power."

29 So Daniel fared well during the reign of Da-
rius and the reign of Cyrus the Persian.*

II. Daniel's Visions

The Beasts and the Judgment†

7 1 In the first year of King Belshazzar of Bab-
ylon, as Daniel lay in bed he had a dream,
visions in his head. Then he wrote down the
dream; the account began: 2 In the vision I saw
during the night, suddenly the four winds of
heaven stirred up the great sea,† 3 from which
emerged four immense beasts,* each different
from the others. 4 The first was like a lion, but
with eagle's wings.† While I watched, the wings
were plucked; it was raised from the ground to
stand on two feet like a human being, and given
a human mind. 5 The second beast was like a
bear;† it was raised up on one side, and among
the teeth in its mouth were three tusks. It was
given the order, "Arise, devour much flesh." 6 Af-
ter this I looked and saw another beast, like a
leopard;† on its back were four wings like those
of a bird, and it had four heads. To this beast do-
minion was given. 7 † After this, in the visions of
the night I saw a fourth beast, terrifying, horrible,
and of extraordinary strength; it had great iron

Did You Know?

Apocalyptic Literature

As you read chapters 7–10 of Daniel, you might ask, What's with the four beasts in chapter 7, and the goat with the horn in chapter 8, and the man with a face like lightning in chapter 10? These are all examples of apocalyptic literature. *Apocalypse* is a Greek word meaning "to uncover or reveal." Apocalyptic literature is written to sound like an attempt to foretell the future by using symbols and visions. But the symbols are often codes for people and events in the present. This type of literature frequently is produced during a time of persecution, when using real names could get a person into trouble or even killed. Apocalyptic literature developed in Israel around 200 BC when the country was enduring great persecution and suffering. The Book of Revelation in the New Testament is another example of apocalyptic literature.

The Book of Daniel contains some explanation of the visions it describes. But sometimes, you will have to consult a good Bible commentary (a book that gives additional background on Bible passages) to completely understand the symbols. For instance, you might need help recognizing that the four beasts in chapter 7 are symbols for Babylon, Media, Persia, and Greece—the four nations that ruled over Israel but would pass away. Or that the arrogant eleventh horn on the fourth beast's head is a symbol for Antiochus IV Epiphanes, the king who persecuted the Jews during the time Daniel was written.

Apocalyptic literature assured the people of Israel that God would triumph and the present evil would eventually pass away. It was one more way to reinforce the belief that evil would be punished and good rewarded, even when it didn't look that way at the moment.

▶ **Daniel, chapters 7–10**

†

7:1–27 This vision continues the motif of the four kingdoms from chap. 2; see note on 2:36–45. To the four succeeding world kingdoms, Babylonian, Median, Persian, and Greek, is opposed the heavenly kingdom of God and the kingdom of God's people on earth. The beast imagery of this chapter has been used extensively in the Book of Revelation, where it is applied to the Roman empire, the persecutor of the Church.

7:2 *The great sea*: the primordial ocean beneath the earth, according to ancient Near Eastern cosmology (Gn 7:11; 49:25). It was thought to contain various monsters (Is 27:1; Jb 7:12), and in particular mythological monsters symbolizing the chaos which God had vanquished in primordial times (Jb 9:13; 26:12; Is 51:9–10; etc.).

7:4 In ancient times the Babylonian empire was commonly represented as a winged lion, in the rampant position (raised up on one side). The two wings that were plucked may represent Nebuchadnezzar and Belshazzar. *On two feet like a human being . . . a human mind*: contrasts with what is said in 4:13, 30.

7:5 *A bear*: represents the Median empire, its three tusks symbolizing its destructive nature; hence, the command: "Arise, devour much flesh."

7:6 *A leopard*: used to symbolize the swiftness with which Cyrus the Persian established his kingdom. *Four heads*: corresponding to the four Persian kings of 11:2.

7:7–8 Alexander's empire was different from all the others in that it was Western rather than Eastern in inspiration, and far exceeded

*

6:29 Dn 1:21. **7:3** Rev 13:1.

teeth with which it devoured and crushed, and
it trampled with its feet what was left. It differed
from the beasts that preceded it. It had ten horns.
8 I was considering the ten horns it had, when
suddenly another, a little horn, sprang out of
their midst, and three of the previous horns were
torn away to make room for it. This horn had
eyes like human eyes, and a mouth that spoke
arrogantly. 9 † As I watched,

Thrones were set up
and the Ancient of Days took his throne.
His clothing was white as snow,
the hair on his head like pure wool;
His throne was flames of fire,
with wheels of burning fire.
10 A river of fire surged forth,
flowing from where he sat;
Thousands upon thousands were ministering
to him,
and myriads upon myriads stood before
him.*

The court was convened, and the books were
opened. 11 I watched, then, from the first of the
arrogant words which the horn spoke, until
the beast was slain and its body destroyed and
thrown into the burning fire. 12 As for the other
beasts, their dominion was taken away, but they
were granted a prolongation of life for a time and
a season. 13 As the visions during the night contin-
ued, I saw coming with the clouds of heaven*

One like a son of man.†
When he reached the Ancient of Days
and was presented before him,
14 He received dominion, splendor, and kingship;
all nations, peoples and tongues will serve
him.
His dominion is an everlasting dominion
that shall not pass away,
his kingship, one that shall not be
destroyed.*

15 Because of this, my spirit was anguished
and I, Daniel, was terrified by my visions. 16 I ap-
proached one of those present and asked him the
truth of all this; in answer, he made known to me
its meaning: 17 "These four great beasts stand for
four kings which shall arise on the earth. 18 But
the holy ones† of the Most High shall receive the
kingship, to possess it forever and ever."

19 Then I wished to make certain about the
fourth beast, so very terrible and different from
the others, devouring and crushing with its iron
teeth and bronze claws, and trampling with its
feet what was left; 20 and about the ten horns on
its head, and the other one that sprang up, before
which three horns fell; and about the horn with
the eyes and the mouth that spoke arrogantly,
which appeared greater than its fellows. 21 For,
as I watched, that horn made war against the
holy ones and was victorious 22 until the Ancient
of Days came, and judgment was pronounced
in favor of the holy ones of the Most High, and
the time arrived for the holy ones to possess the
kingship. 23 He answered me thus:

"The fourth beast shall be a fourth kingdom
on earth,
different from all the others;
The whole earth it shall devour,
trample down and crush.
24 The ten horns shall be ten kings
rising out of that kingdom;
another shall rise up after them,
Different from those before him,
who shall lay low three kings.
25 He shall speak against the Most High
and wear down the holy ones of the Most
High,
intending to change the feast days and the
law.†
They shall be handed over to him
for a time, two times, and half a time.
26 But when the court is convened,
and his dominion is taken away

† the others in power. The ten horns represent the kings of the Seleucid dynasty, the only part of the Hellenistic empire that concerned the author. The little horn is Antiochus IV Epiphanes (175–164 B.C.), who usurped the throne and persecuted the Jews.

7:9–10 A vision of the heavenly throne of God (the Ancient of Days), who sits in judgment over the nations. Some of the details of the vision, depicting the divine majesty and omnipotence, are to be found in Ezekiel 1. Others are paralleled in 1 Enoch, a contemporary Jewish apocalypse.

7:13–14 *One like a son of man*: In contrast to the worldly kingdoms opposed to God, which are represented as grotesque beasts, the coming Kingdom of God is represented by a human figure. Scholars disagree as to whether this figure should be taken as a collective symbol for the people of God (cf. 7:27) or identified as a particular individual, e.g., the archangel Michael (cf. 12:1) or the messiah. The phrase "Son of Man" becomes a title for Jesus in the gospels, especially in passages dealing with the Second Coming (Mk 13 and parallels).

7:18 "Holy ones" in Hebrew and Aramaic literature are nearly always members of the heavenly court or angels (cf. 4:10, 14, 20; 8:13), though here the term is commonly taken to refer to Israel.

7:25 The reference is to the persecution of Antiochus IV and specifically to the disruption of the Temple cult (1 Mc 1:41–64). *A time, two times, and half a time*: an indefinite, evil period of time. Probably here, three and a half years, which becomes the standard period of tribulation in apocalyptic literature (Rev 11:2; 13:5 [in months]; 11:3 [in days]; and cf. 12:14). As seven is the Jewish "perfect" number, half of it signifies great imperfection. Actually, the Temple was desecrated for three years (1 Mc 4:52–54). The duration of the persecution was a little longer, since it was already under way before the Temple was desecrated.

* **7:10** Rev 5:11. **7:13** Mk 13:26; 14:62. **7:14** Dn 3:33; 4:31.

to be abolished and completely destroyed,
27 Then the kingship and dominion and majesty
of all the kingdoms under the heavens
shall be given to the people of the holy
ones of the Most High,
Whose kingship shall be an everlasting
kingship,
whom all dominions shall serve and obey."

28This is the end of the report. I, Daniel, was
greatly terrified by my thoughts, and my face be-
came pale, but I kept the matter to myself.†

The Ram and the He-goat†

8 1After this first vision, I, Daniel, had another,
in the third year of the reign of King Belshaz-
zar. 2In my vision I saw myself in the fortress of
Susa† in the province of Elam; I was beside the
river Ulai. 3I looked up and saw standing by the
river a ram with two great horns, the one larger
and newer than the other. 4I saw the ram butt-
ing toward the west, north, and south. No beast
could withstand it or be rescued from its power;
it did what it pleased and grew powerful.
5As I was reflecting, a he-goat with a promi-
nent horn on its forehead suddenly came from
the west across the whole earth without touching
the ground. 6It came to the two-horned ram I
had seen standing by the river, and rushed to-
ward it with savage force. 7I saw it reach the ram;
enraged, the he-goat attacked and shattered both
its horns. The ram did not have the strength to
withstand it; the he-goat threw the ram to the
ground and trampled upon it. No one could res-
cue the ram from its power.
8The he-goat grew very powerful, but at the
height of its strength the great horn was shat-
tered, and in its place came up four others, facing
the four winds of heaven. 9Out of one of them
came a little horn† which grew and grew toward
the south, the east, and the glorious land. 10It
grew even to the host of heaven,† so that it cast
down to earth some of the host and some of the
stars and trampled on them. 11It grew even to
the Prince of the host, from whom the daily sac-
rifice was removed, and whose sanctuary was cast
down. 12The host was given over together with
the daily sacrifice in the course of transgression.
It cast truth to the ground, and was succeeding in
its undertaking.
13I heard a holy one speaking, and another
said to whichever one it was that spoke, "How
long shall the events of this vision last concern-
ing the daily sacrifice, the desolating sin,† the
giving over of the sanctuary and the host for
trampling?" 14He answered him, "For two thou-
sand three hundred evenings and mornings; then
the sanctuary shall be set right."
15While I, Daniel, sought the meaning of the
vision I had seen, one who looked like a man
stood before me, 16and on the Ulai I heard a hu-
man voice that cried out, "Gabriel,† explain the
vision to this man." 17When he came near where
I was standing, I fell prostrate in terror. But he
said to me, "Understand, O son of man, that the
vision refers to the end time."† 18As he spoke to
me, I fell forward unconscious; he touched me
and made me stand up. 19"I will show you," he
said, "what is to happen in the last days of wrath;
for it is for the appointed time of the end.
20"The two-horned ram you saw represents the
kings of the Medes and Persians.† 21The he-goat
is the king of the Greeks, and the great horn on
its forehead is the first king. 22The four that rose
in its place when it was shattered are four king-
doms that will issue from his nation, but without
his strength.

23 "At the end of their reign,
when sinners have reached their measure,
There shall arise a king,
impudent, and skilled in intrigue.
24 He shall be strong and powerful,
bring about fearful ruin,
and succeed in his undertaking.
He shall destroy powerful peoples;

†

7:28 This verse ends the Aramaic part of the Book of Daniel.

8:1–27 This vision continues images of the preceding one, and develops it in more detail. As explained in vv. 20–22 the two-horned ram represents the combined kingdom of the Medes and Persians, destroyed by Alexander's Hellenistic empire originating in the west. Once again the author is interested only in the Seleucid dynasty, which emerged from the dissolution of Alexander's empire after his death in 323 B.C.

8:2 *The fortress of Susa*: the royal palace of the Persian kings in the ancient territory of Elam, east of Babylonia. *The river Ulai*: a canal along the northern side of Susa. Some scholars argue that the Hebrew word understood as "river" here should instead be translated "gate."

8:9 *A little horn*: as in chap. 7, Antiochus IV. *The glorious land*: Israel.

8:10–12 *The host of heaven*: the angelic host, symbolized by the stars. *The Prince of the host*: the Most High God, whose worship Antiochus suppressed (1 Mc 1:45).

8:13 *The desolating sin*: the Hebrew contains a wordplay (*shomem*) on the name Baal Shamem ("lord of the heavens," identified by some as the Greek Zeus Olympios). The reference is to some object with which Antiochus profaned the Temple of Jerusalem (2 Mc 6:2), most probably a pagan altar.

8:16 The angel Gabriel is mentioned here for the first time in the Bible. There is wordplay in the preceding verse on *geber*, "manlike figure."

8:17 *The end time*: the time when God sits in judgment on the wicked (v. 19).

8:20 *The Medes and Persians*: the Medes had been allies of the Babylonians in destroying the Assyrian empire (late seventh century B.C.), and Cyrus the Persian defeated the Medes en route to conquering the Babylonians. The Book of Daniel, however, treats the Medes and Persians as a dual kingdom; cf. also 5:28; 6:9; and note on 6:1.

Pray It!

A Closer Look

Let's look closely at the prayer in chapter 9 of Daniel. Here, the prophet uses four types of prayer:

- *intercession*, because he prays on behalf of the people
- *praise*, because he proclaims God to be awesome and great
- *sorrow*, because he expresses sadness for past sinfulness and asks for forgiveness
- *petition*, because he asks God for help

Daniel gives us a great example of the various ways we can pray to God. When you have a moment, pray by yourself or with a friend, trying to incorporate all four of these types into your prayer.

▶ **Daniel, chapter 9**

25 his cunning shall be against the holy ones,
his treacherous conduct shall succeed.
He shall be proud of heart
and destroy many by stealth.
But when he rises against the Prince of princes,
he shall be broken without a hand being
raised.
26 As for the vision of the evenings and the
mornings,
what was spoken is true.
But you, keep this vision secret:
it is for the distant future."

27 I, Daniel, was weak and ill for some days;
then I arose and took care of the king's affairs.
But the vision left me desolate, without understanding.

The Seventy Weeks of Years

9 1 It was the first year that Darius,† son of
Ahasuerus, of the race of the Medes, reigned
over the kingdom of the Chaldeans; 2 * in the
first year of his reign, I, Daniel, perceived in the
books the number of years the LORD had decreed
to the prophet Jeremiah: Jerusalem was to lie in
ruins for seventy years.†

3 I turned to the Lord God, to seek help, in
prayer and petition, with fasting, sackcloth, and
ashes. 4 * I prayed to the LORD, my God, and
confessed, "Ah, Lord, great and awesome God,
you who keep your covenant and show mercy
toward those who love you and keep your
commandments and your precepts! 5 We have
sinned, been wicked and done evil; we have rebelled and turned from your commandments
and your laws. 6 We have not obeyed your servants the prophets, who spoke in your name to
our kings, our princes, our ancestors, and all the
people of the land. 7 Justice, O Lord, is on your
side; we are shamefaced even to this day: the
men of Judah, the residents of Jerusalem, and all
Israel, near and far, in all the lands to which you
have scattered them because of their treachery
toward you. 8 O LORD, we are ashamed, like our
kings, our princes, and our ancestors, for having
sinned against you. 9 But to the Lord, our God,
belong compassion and forgiveness, though we
rebelled against him 10 and did not hear the voice
of the LORD, our God, by walking in his laws
given through his servants the prophets. 11 * The
curse and the oath written in the law of Moses,
the servant of God, were poured out over us for
our sins, because all Israel transgressed your law
and turned aside, refusing to hear your voice.
12 He fulfilled the words he spoke against us and
against those who ruled us, by bringing upon
us an evil—no evil so great has happened under heaven as happened in Jerusalem. 13 As it is
written† in the law of Moses, this evil has come
upon us. We did not appease the LORD, our God,
by turning back from our wickedness and acting
according to your truth, 14 so the LORD kept watch
over the evil and brought it upon us. The LORD,
our God, is just in all that he has done: we did
not listen to his voice.

15 "Now, Lord, our God, who led your people
out of the land of Egypt with a strong hand, and
made a name for yourself even to this day, we
have sinned, we are guilty. 16 Lord, in keeping
with all your just deeds, let your anger and your

†

9:1 *Darius*: see note on 6:1.

9:2 *Seventy years*: Jeremiah was understood to prophesy a Babylonian captivity of seventy years, a round number signifying the complete passing away of the existing generation (Jer 25:11; 29:10). On this view Jeremiah's prophecy was seen to be fulfilled in the capture of Babylon by Cyrus and the subsequent return of the Jews to Palestine. However, the author of Daniel, living during the persecution of Antiochus, extends Jeremiah's number to seventy weeks of years (Dn 9:24), i.e., seven times seventy years, to encompass the period of Seleucid persecution.

9:13 *As it is written*: the first time that this formula of Scriptural citation is used in the Bible. The reference (v. 11) is to the sanctions of Lv 26:14–16; Dt 28:15–17.

*

9:2 Jer 25:11; 29:10.
9:4 Ezr 9:6–14; Neh 9:6–37.
9:11 Dt 27:15.

wrath be turned away from your city Jerusalem,
your holy mountain. On account of our sins
and the crimes of our ancestors, Jerusalem and
your people have become the reproach of all
our neighbors. 17 Now, our God, hear the prayer
and petition of your servant; and for your own
sake, Lord, let your face shine upon your deso-
late sanctuary. 18 Give ear, my God, and listen;
open your eyes and look upon our desolate city
upon which your name is invoked. When we
present our petition before you, we rely not on
our just deeds, but on your great mercy. 19 Lord,
hear! Lord, pardon! Lord, be attentive and act
without delay, for your own sake, my God, be-
cause your name is invoked upon your city and
your people!"

20 I was still praying to the LORD, my God,
confessing my sin and the sin of my people Is-
rael, presenting my petition concerning the holy
mountain of my God— 21 I was still praying,
when the man, Gabriel, whom I had seen in
vision before, came to me in flight at the time
of the evening offering.† 22 He instructed me in
these words: "Daniel, I have now come to give
you understanding. 23 When you began your pe-
tition, an answer was given which I have come to
announce, because you are beloved. Therefore,
mark the answer and understand the vision.

24 "Seventy weeks† are decreed
for your people and for your holy city:
Then transgression will stop and sin will end,
guilt will be expiated,
Everlasting justice will be introduced,
vision and prophecy ratified,
and a holy of holies will be anointed.
25 Know and understand:
From the utterance of the word
that Jerusalem was to be rebuilt†
Until there is an anointed ruler,
there shall be seven weeks.
In the course of sixty-two weeks
it shall be rebuilt,
With squares and trenches,
in time of affliction.
26 After the sixty-two weeks
an anointed one† shall be cut down
with no one to help him.
And the people of a leader who will come
shall destroy the city and the sanctuary.
His end shall come in a flood;
until the end of the war, which is decreed,
there will be desolation.
27 For one week† he shall make
a firm covenant with the many;
Half the week
he shall abolish sacrifice and offering;
In their place shall be the desolating
abomination
until the ruin that is decreed
is poured out upon the desolator."*

An Angelic Vision†

10 1 In the third year of Cyrus, king of Persia,
a revelation was given to Daniel, who had
been named Belteshazzar. The revelation was
certain: a great war;† he understood this from the
vision. 2 In those days, I, Daniel, mourned three
full weeks. 3 I ate no savory food, took no meat
or wine, and did not anoint myself at all until the
end of the three weeks.
4 On the twenty-fourth day of the first month†
I was on the bank of the great river, the Tigris.
5 As I looked up, I saw a man† dressed in linen
with a belt of fine gold around his waist.* 6 His
body was like chrysolite, his face shone like light-
ning, his eyes were like fiery torches, his arms
and feet looked like burnished bronze, and the
sound of his voice was like the roar of a multi-
tude. 7 I alone, Daniel, saw the vision; but great
fear seized those who were with me; they fled
and hid themselves, although they did not see

†

9:21 *At the time of the evening offering*: between three and four in the afternoon.

9:24 *Seventy weeks*: i.e., of years. Just as Jeremiah's seventy years was an approximation (see note on v. 2), the four hundred and ninety years here is not to be taken literally. Similarly, the distribution of the "weeks" in the following verses indicates only relative proportions of the total figure. *A holy of holies*: or "most holy"; could be understood as a place (e.g., the Jerusalem Temple) or a person (cf. 1 Chr 23:13).

9:25 *From the utterance . . . to be rebuilt*: from the time of Jeremiah's prophecy. *Anointed ruler*: either Cyrus, who was called the anointed of the Lord to end the exile (Is 45:1), or the high priest Jeshua who presided over the rebuilding of the altar of sacrifice after the exile (Ezr 3:2). *Seven weeks*: forty-nine years, an approximation of the time of the exile. *In the course of sixty-two weeks . . . rebuilt*: a period of four hundred thirty-four years, roughly approximating the interval between the rebuilding of Jerusalem after the exile and the beginning of the Seleucid persecution.

9:26 *An anointed one*: the high priest Onias III, murdered in 171 B.C., from which the author dates the beginning of the persecution. Onias was in exile when he was killed. *A leader*: Antiochus IV.

9:27 *One week*: the final phase of the period in view, the time of Antiochus' persecution. *He*: Antiochus himself. *The many*: the faithless Jews who allied themselves with the Seleucids; cf. 1 Mc 1:11–13. *Half the week*: three and a half years; the Temple was desecrated by Antiochus from 167 to 164 B.C. *The desolating abomination*: see note on 8:13; probably a pagan altar. Jesus refers to this passage in his prediction of the destruction of Jerusalem in Mt 24:15.

10:1–12:13 This final vision is concerned with history from the time of Cyrus to the death of Antiochus Epiphanes.

10:1 *A great war*: or "the service was great," or "a mighty host." The Hebrew is ambiguous.

10:4 *The first month*: the month Nisan (mid-March to mid-April).

10:5–6 The heavenly person of the vision is probably the angel Gabriel, as in 9:21. *Chrysolite*: or topaz, a yellowish precious stone. Cf. the visions in Ez 1 and 8.

9:27 Mt 24:15; 1 Mc 1:54. **10:5** Ez 10:2.

the vision. 8 So I was left alone to see this great
vision. No strength remained in me; I turned
the color of death and was powerless. 9 When I
heard the sound of his voice, I fell face forward
unconscious.
10 But then a hand touched me, raising me to
my hands and knees. 11 "Daniel, beloved," he
said to me, "understand the words which I am
speaking to you; stand up, for my mission now
is to you." When he said this to me, I stood up
trembling. 12 "Do not fear, Daniel," he contin-
ued; "from the first day you made up your mind
to acquire understanding and humble yourself
before God, your prayer was heard. Because of it
I started out, 13 but the prince of the kingdom of
Persia† stood in my way for twenty-one days, un-
til finally Michael, one of the chief princes, came
to help me. I left him there with the prince of
the kingdom of Persia, 14 and came to make you
understand what shall happen to your people in
the last days; for there is yet a vision concerning
those days."
15 While he was speaking thus to me, I fell for-
ward and kept silent. 16 Then something like a
hand touched my lips; I opened my mouth and
said to the one standing before me, "My lord,
I was seized with pangs at the vision and I was
powerless. 17 How can my lord's servant speak
with you, my lord? For now no strength or even
breath is left in me." 18 The one who looked like
a man touched me again and strengthened me,
saying, 19 "Do not fear, beloved. Peace! Take
courage and be strong." When he spoke to me,
I grew strong and said, "Speak, my lord, for you
have strengthened me." 20 "Do you know," he
asked, "why I have come to you? Soon I must
fight the prince of Persia again. When I leave,
the prince of Greece will come; 21 but I shall tell
you what is written in the book of truth.† No
one supports me against these except Michael,*
your prince, 11:1 and in the first year of Darius
the Mede I stood to strengthen him and be his
refuge.

The Hellenistic Age

11 2 "Now I shall tell you the truth.
"Three kings of Persia† are yet to appear;
and a fourth shall acquire the greatest riches of
all. Strengthened by his riches, he shall stir up all
kingdoms, even that of Greece. 3 But a powerful
king† shall appear and rule with great might,
doing as he wills. 4 No sooner shall he appear
than his kingdom shall be broken and divided
in four directions under heaven; but not among
his descendants or in keeping with his mighty
rule, for his kingdom shall be torn to pieces and
belong to others.
5 † "The king of the south shall grow strong,
but one of his princes shall grow stronger still
and govern a domain greater than his. 6 † After
some years they shall become allies: the daughter
of the king of the south shall come to the king
of the north to carry out the alliance. But she
shall not retain power: and his offspring shall
not survive, and she shall be given up, together
with those who brought her, her son, and her
supporter in due time. 7 A descendant of her line
shall succeed to his place, and shall come against
the army, enter the stronghold of the king of
the north, attack and conquer them. 8 Even their
gods, with their molten images and their precious
vessels of silver and gold, he shall carry away as
spoils of war into Egypt. For years he shall have
nothing to do with the king of the north. 9 Then
the latter shall invade the land of the king of the
south, and return to his own country.
10 "But his sons shall be aroused and assemble
a great armed host, which shall pass through like
a flood and again surge around the stronghold.
11 † The king of the south, enraged, shall go out
to fight against the king of the north, who shall
field a great host, but the host shall be given into
his hand. 12 When the host is carried off, in the
pride of his heart he shall bring down tens of
thousands, but he shall not triumph. 13 † For the
king of the north shall raise another army, greater

10:13 *The prince of the kingdom of Persia*: the angelic guardian of Persia. Where older texts speak of the gods of various countries (Dt 32:8), Daniel speaks of "princes." *Michael*: the patron angel of Israel (v. 21).

10:21 *The book of truth*: a heavenly book in which future events are already recorded; cf. 7:10; 12:1.

11:2 *Three kings of Persia*: it is unclear which kings are intended because there were more than three Persian kings between Cyrus and the dissolution of the kingdom. The fourth is Xerxes I (486–465 B.C.), the great campaigner against Greece.

11:3 *A powerful king*: Alexander the Great, who broke Persian dominance by his victory at Issus in 333 B.C.

11:5–45 These verses describe the dynastic histories of the Ptolemies in Egypt (the king of the south) and the Seleucids in Syria (the king of the north), the two divisions of the Hellenistic empire that were of interest to the author (v. 6). Verses 10–20 describe the struggle between the two kingdoms for the control of Palestine; the Seleucids were eventually victorious.

11:6 The marriage of Antiochus II Theos and Berenice of Egypt about 250 B.C., which ended in tragedy.

11:11 The battle of Raphia (217 B.C.), in which Egypt defeated Syria.

11:13 Syria defeated Egypt at the battle of Paneas in 200 B.C. Judea then passed under Syrian rule.

10:21 Rev 12:7.

than before; after some years he shall attack with this large army and great resources. 14 In those times many shall resist the king of the south, and violent ones among your people shall rise up in fulfillment of vision, but they shall stumble. 15 † When the king of the north comes, he shall set up siegeworks and take the fortified city by storm. The forces of the south shall not withstand him, and not even his picked troops shall have the strength to withstand. 16 The invader shall do as he wills, with no one to withstand him. He shall stop in the glorious land, and it shall all be in his power. 17 † He shall resolve to come with the entire strength of his kingdom. He shall make an alliance with him and give him a daughter in marriage in order to destroy him, but this shall not stand. 18 † He shall turn to the coastland and take many prisoners, but a commander shall put an end to his shameful conduct, so that he cannot retaliate. 19 He shall turn to the strongholds of his own land, but shall stumble and fall, to be found no more. 20 † In his stead one shall arise who will send a collector of tribute through the glorious kingdom, but he shall soon be destroyed, though not in conflict or in battle.

21 † "There shall arise in his place a despicable person, to whom the royal insignia shall not be given. He shall enter by stealth and seize the kingdom by fraud. 22 Armed forces shall be completely overwhelmed by him and crushed, even the prince of the covenant.† 23 After making alliances, he shall treacherously rise to power with only a few supporters. 24 By stealth he shall enter prosperous provinces and do that which his fathers or grandfathers never did; he shall distribute spoil, plunder, and riches among them and devise plots against their strongholds. 25 He shall rouse his strength and courage to meet the king of the south with a great army; the king of the south shall go into battle with a very large and strong army, but he shall not stand because of the plots devised against him. 26 Even his table companions shall seek to destroy him, his army shall be overwhelmed, and many shall be struck down. 27 The two kings, resolved on evil, shall sit at table together and exchange lies, but they shall have no success, because the appointed end is not yet.

28 "He† shall turn back toward his land with great riches, his mind set against the holy covenant; he shall take action and return to his land. 29 At the time appointed he shall come again to the south, but this time it shall not be as before. 30 When ships of the Kittim† confront him, he shall lose heart and retreat. Then he shall rage against the holy covenant and take action; he shall again favor those who forsake the holy covenant. 31 Armed forces shall rise at his command and defile the sanctuary stronghold, abolishing the daily sacrifice and setting up the desolating abomination. 32 By his deceit he shall make some who were disloyal forsake the covenant; but those who remain loyal to their God shall take strong action. 33 Those with insight among the people shall instruct the many; though for a time the sword, flames, exile, and plunder will cause them to stumble. 34 When they stumble, they will be helped,† but only a little; many shall join them, but out of treachery. 35 Some of those with insight shall stumble so that they may be tested, refined, and purified, until the end time which is still appointed to come.

36 "The king shall do as he wills, exalting himself and making himself greater than any god; he shall utter dreadful blasphemies against the God of gods. He shall prosper only till the wrath is finished, for what is determined must take place. 37 He shall have no regard for the gods of his ancestors or for the one in whom women delight;† for no god shall he have regard, because he shall make himself greater than all. 38 Instead, he shall give glory to the god of strongholds;† a god unknown to his ancestors he shall glorify with gold, silver, precious stones, and other treasures. 39 He shall act for those who fortify strongholds, a people of a foreign god, whom he has recognized. He shall greatly honor them; he shall make them rule over the many and distribute the land as a reward.

11:15 The siege of Sidon after the battle of Paneas.

11:17 Antiochus III, the Great, betrothed his daughter to Ptolemy Epiphanes in 197 B.C.

11:18 The Roman general Scipio defeated Antiochus at Magnesia in 190 B.C.

11:20 Seleucus IV, who sent Heliodorus to Jerusalem (cf. 2 Mc 3).

11:21 Here begins the career of Antiochus IV Epiphanes.

11:22 *The prince of the covenant*: the high priest Onias III, who was murdered.

11:28 *He*: the king of the north, probably Antiochus IV.

11:30 *Kittim*: originally this word meant Cypriots or other westerners. It is sometimes used for the Greeks (1 Mc 1:1). Here it refers to the Romans, who forced Antiochus to withdraw from Egypt during his second campaign there.

11:34 *Helped*: this may be a reference to the Maccabean revolt. The apocalyptic author expects deliverance from God and has little regard for human efforts. In fact, the Maccabees routed the Syrian troops, recaptured Jerusalem, purified and rededicated the Temple, and brought to an end the Syrian persecution.

11:37 *The one in whom women delight*: Tammuz. Antiochus favored the cult of Zeus. Daniel takes this to imply the neglect of all other gods, although this does not appear to have been the case.

11:38 *The god of strongholds*: the god worshiped in the fortress Akra, which Antiochus established in Jerusalem.

Did You Know?

Resurrection

Most of the Old Testament contains no indication of a belief in life after death. Daniel, however, speaks of individual resurrection, or rising to life from death. This goes beyond the less specific belief in life after death expressed in the Wisdom of Solomon 5:15 and is similar to the belief expressed in 2 Maccabees 7:23. The understanding of personal resurrection developed quite late in Israel's existence. It is described as the complete transformation of the human being, body and spirit, after death. Daniel 12:3 says the resurrected will shine like stars.

▶ Dn 12:1–3

40 † "At the end time the king of the south
shall engage him in battle but the king of the
north shall overwhelm him with chariots and
horsemen and a great fleet, passing through the
lands like a flood. 41 He shall enter the glorious
land and many shall fall, except Edom, Moab,
and the chief part of Ammon, which shall escape
his power. 42 He shall extend his power over the
land, and not even Egypt shall escape. 43 He shall
control the riches of gold and silver and all the
treasures of Egypt; Libya and Ethiopia shall be
in his entourage. 44 When reports from the east
and the north disturb him, he shall set out with
great fury to destroy many, putting them under
the ban. 45 He shall pitch the tents of his royal
pavilion between the sea and the glorious holy
mountain, but he shall come to his end with
none to help him.

The Resurrection

12 1 "At that time there shall arise Michael,*
the great prince,
guardian of your people;
It shall be a time unsurpassed in distress
since the nation began until that time.
At that time your people shall escape,
everyone who is found written in the
book.†
2 Many of those who sleep†
in the dust of the earth shall awake;
Some to everlasting life,
others to reproach and everlasting
disgrace.*
3 But those with insight shall shine
brightly
like the splendor of the firmament,
And those who lead the many to justice
shall be like the stars† forever.*

4 "As for you, Daniel, keep secret the message
and seal the book until the end time; many shall
wander aimlessly and evil shall increase."
5 I, Daniel, looked and saw two others, one
standing on either bank of the river. 6 One of
them said to the man clothed in linen, who
was upstream, "How long shall it be to the end
of these appalling things?" 7 The man clothed
in linen,* who was upstream, lifted his hands
to heaven; and I heard him swear by him who
lives forever that it should be for a time, two
times, and half a time;† and that, when the
power of the destroyer of the holy people was
brought to an end, all these things should end.
8 I heard, but I did not understand; so I asked,
"My lord, what follows this?" 9 "Go, Daniel,"
he said, "because the words are to be kept
secret and sealed until the end time. 10 Many
shall be refined, purified, and tested, but the
wicked shall prove wicked; the wicked shall
have no understanding, but those with insight
shall. 11 † From the time that the daily sacrifice
is abolished and the desolating abomination is
set up, there shall be one thousand two hun-
dred and ninety days. 12 Blessed are they who
have patience and persevere for the one thou-
sand three hundred and thirty-five days. 13 Go,
take your rest, you shall rise for your reward at
the end of days."

†

11:40–45 In these concluding verses, the events described no longer correspond to the history of the Maccabean period. Daniel imagines the death of Antiochus on the model of Gog in Ez 38–39. Antiochus actually died in Persia.

12:1 *Written in the book*: cf. 10:21.

12:2 *Many of those who sleep*: Daniel does not envisage the universal resurrection as later developed. Two groups are distinguished, one that rises to eternal life, the other to reproach and disgrace. Then "those with insight" (11:33–35) are singled out for special honor.

12:3 *Like the stars*: like the heavenly host, or angels. Cf. Mt 22:30.

12:7 *A time, two times, and half a time*: see note on 7:25.

12:11 The specific numbers of days given in vv. 11–12 represent attempts to calculate the precise duration of the three and a half years. Most probably, when the first date (1,290 days) passed, the author attempted another calculation. Another, earlier calculation is preserved in 8:14. It is noteworthy, however, that the contradictory numbers were allowed to stand in the text; this is a reminder that it is not possible to calculate a precise date for God's judgment; cf. Mk 13:32.

*

12:1 Rev 12:7.
12:2 Is 66:24; Mt 25:46; Jn 5:29.
12:3 Wis 3:7.
12:7 Rev 10:5–6.

III. Appendix: Susanna, Bel, and the Dragon†

Susanna

13 1 In Babylon there lived a man named
Joakim, 2 who married a very beautiful
and God-fearing woman, Susanna, the daugh-
ter of Hilkiah; 3 her parents were righteous and
had trained their daughter according to the law
of Moses. 4 Joakim was very rich and he had a
garden near his house. The Jews had recourse to
him often because he was the most respected of
them all.
5 That year, two elders of the people were ap-
pointed judges, of whom the Lord said, "Lawless-
ness has come out of Babylon, that is, from the
elders who were to govern the people as judges."
6 These men, to whom all brought their cases, fre-
quented the house of Joakim. 7 When the people
left at noon, Susanna used to enter her husband's
garden for a walk. 8 When the elders saw her en-
ter every day for her walk, they began to lust for
her. 9 They perverted their thinking; they would
not allow their eyes to look to heaven, and did
not keep in mind just judgments. 10 Though both
were enamored of her, they did not tell each
other their trouble, 11 for they were ashamed to
reveal their lustful desire to have her. 12 Day by
day they watched eagerly for her. 13 One day they
said to each other, "Let us be off for home, it is
time for the noon meal." So they went their sep-
arate ways. 14 But both turned back and arrived at
the same spot. When they asked each other the
reason, they admitted their lust, and then they
agreed to look for an occasion when they could
find her alone.
15 One day, while they were waiting for the
right moment, she entered as usual, with two
maids only, wanting to bathe in the garden, for
the weather was warm. 16 Nobody else was there
except the two elders, who had hidden them-
selves and were watching her. 17 "Bring me oil
and soap," she said to the maids, "and shut the
garden gates while I bathe." 18 They did as she
said; they shut the garden gates and left by the
side gate to fetch what she had ordered, unaware
that the elders were hidden inside.
19 As soon as the maids had left, the two old
men got up and ran to her. 20 "Look," they said,
"the garden doors are shut, no one can see us,
and we want you. So give in to our desire, and

Pray It!

Susanna

Daniel is called the hero of chapter 13 of his book. But don't forget Susanna. A real hero, Susanna chooses to risk death rather than submitting to sin. Her prayer demanding God's justice causes the Holy Spirit to stir Daniel into action.

Through prayer, we have a similar opportunity to cry out to God for justice. Every day, the news is filled with stories of violence, injustice, and oppression. Although we typically can't directly change these situations, we can offer our prayers up to God in solidarity with those who suffer, hoping that the Holy Spirit will inspire a just response to these social sins.

- What injustices might you pray about?
- Whose attention do you need to get?

▶ Daniel, chapter 13

lie with us. 21 If you refuse, we will testify against
you that a young man was here with you and
that is why you sent your maids away."
22 "I am completely trapped," Susanna groaned.
"If I yield, it will be my death; if I refuse, I cannot
escape your power. 23 Yet it is better for me not
to do it and to fall into your power than to sin
before the Lord." 24 Then Susanna screamed, and
the two old men also shouted at her, 25 as one of
them ran to open the garden gates. 26 When the
people in the house heard the cries from the gar-
den, they rushed in by the side gate to see what
had happened to her. 27 At the accusations of the
old men, the servants felt very much ashamed,
for never had any such thing been said about
Susanna.
28 When the people came to her husband Joa-
kim the next day, the two wicked old men also
came, full of lawless intent to put Susanna to
death. 29 Before the people they ordered: "Send
for Susanna, the daughter of Hilkiah, the wife of
Joakim." When she was sent for, 30 she came with

† **13:1–14:42** The short stories in these two chapters exist now only in Greek and other translations, but probably were first composed in Hebrew or Aramaic. They were never part of the Hebrew-Aramaic Book of Daniel, or of the Hebrew Bible. They are excluded from the Protestant canon of Scripture, but the Catholic Church has always included them among the inspired writings; they existed in the Septuagint, which was used as its Bible by the early church.

Cultural Connection

Called to Be Prophets

The following excerpt from *Prophetic Voices* reveals how Hispanic young people express their prophetic mission:

> As Hispanic young people, as members of the Catholic Church, we wish to raise our prophetic voice in order to announce the values of the Gospel, to denounce sin, to invite all youth to struggle for the Kingdom of God.
>
> First of all, we announce the option for peace as against violence (see Mt 26:51–52, 2 Cor 5:18); for love as against injustice (see Jn 15:17); for good as against evil (see Dt 30:15); for the family as a fundamental value through which faith is transmitted (see Eph 6:4); and for maintaining one's own culture.
>
> Likewise, we denounce materialism, which leads us to believe that the important thing in life is to have more and more in contrast to the teachings of the Gospel (see Mt 6:25–30; *Populorum Progressio* 19).
>
> We denounce the injustice and oppression that Latin America suffers as a result of the cultural, economic, military, and political intervention of wealthy nations. . . .
>
> We denounce the Melting Pot theory and make an option for learning the culture of this country without forgetting our own (*Evangelii Nuntiandi* 20). We denounce abortion, the abuse of drugs and alcohol, and the negative and manipulative influence of commercial propaganda that creates false needs.
>
> We do not just denounce these injustices, we also feel ourselves called to struggle for peace in the world, to live a more simple lifestyle in solidarity with our poor brothers and sisters. . . .
>
> Let us be aware that we can change the world with our way of life today.
>
> (Secretariat for Hispanic Affairs, p. 12)

her parents, children and all her relatives. 31 Su-
sanna, very delicate and beautiful, 32 was veiled;
but those transgressors of the law ordered that
she be exposed so as to sate themselves with her
beauty. 33 All her companions and the onlookers
were weeping.

34 In the midst of the people the two old men
rose up and laid their hands on her head. 35 As
she wept she looked up to heaven, for she trusted
in the Lord wholeheartedly. 36 The old men said,
"As we were walking in the garden alone, this
woman entered with two servant girls, shut the
garden gates and sent the servant girls away. 37 A
young man, who was hidden there, came and lay
with her. 38 When we, in a corner of the garden,
saw this lawlessness, we ran toward them. 39 We
saw them lying together, but the man we could
not hold, because he was stronger than we; he
opened the gates and ran off. 40 Then we seized
this one and asked who the young man was,
41 but she refused to tell us. We testify to this."
The assembly believed them, since they were
elders and judges of the people, and they con-
demned her to death.

42 But Susanna cried aloud: "Eternal God, you
know what is hidden and are aware of all things
before they come to be: 43 you know that they
have testified falsely against me. Here I am about
to die, though I have done none of the things for
which these men have condemned me."

44 The Lord heard her prayer. 45 As she was
being led to execution, God stirred up the holy
spirit of a young boy named Daniel, 46 and he
cried aloud: "I am innocent of this woman's
blood." 47 All the people turned and asked him,
"What are you saying?" 48 He stood in their midst
and said, "Are you such fools, you Israelites, to
condemn a daughter of Israel without investi-
gation and without clear evidence? 49 Return to
court, for they have testified falsely against her."

50 Then all the people returned in haste. To
Daniel the elders said, "Come, sit with us and in-
form us, since God has given you the prestige of
old age." 51 But he replied, "Separate these two far
from one another, and I will examine them."

52 After they were separated from each other,
he called one of them and said: "How you have
grown evil with age! Now have your past sins
come to term: 53 passing unjust sentences, con-
demning the innocent, and freeing the guilty,*
although the Lord says, 'The innocent and the

* 13:53 Ex 23:7.

just you shall not put to death.' [54]Now, then, if
you were a witness, tell me under what tree you
saw them together." [55]"Under a mastic tree,"†
he answered. "Your fine lie has cost you your
head," said Daniel; "for the angel of God has al-
ready received the sentence from God and shall
split you in two." [56]Putting him to one side, he
ordered the other one to be brought. "Offspring
of Canaan, not of Judah," Daniel said to him,
"beauty has seduced you, lust has perverted your
heart. [57]This is how you acted with the daughters
of Israel, and in their fear they yielded to you;
but a daughter of Judah did not tolerate your
lawlessness. [58]Now, then, tell me under what
tree you surprised them together." [59]"Under an
oak," he said. "Your fine lie has cost you also
your head," said Daniel; "for the angel of God
waits with a sword to cut you in two so as to de-
stroy you both."

[60]The whole assembly cried aloud, blessing
God who saves those who hope in him. [61]They
rose up against the two old men, for by their own
words Daniel had convicted them of bearing false
witness.* They condemned them to the fate they
had planned for their neighbor: [62]in accordance
with the law of Moses they put them to death.
Thus was innocent blood spared that day.

[63]Hilkiah and his wife praised God for their
daughter Susanna, with Joakim her husband
and all her relatives, because she was found in-
nocent of any shameful deed. [64]And from that
day onward Daniel was greatly esteemed by the
people.

Bel and the Dragon†

14 [1]After King Astyages† was gathered to his
ancestors, Cyrus the Persian succeeded to
his kingdom. [2]Daniel was a companion of the
king and was held in higher honor than any of
the Friends of the King. [3]The Babylonians had an
idol called Bel,† and every day they provided for
it six bushels of fine flour, forty sheep, and six
measures of wine. [4]The king revered it and went
every day to worship it; but Daniel worshiped
only his God. [5]When the king asked him, "Why
do you not worship Bel?" Daniel replied, "Be-
cause I do not revere idols made with hands, but
only the living God who made heaven and earth
and has dominion over all flesh." [6]Then the king
continued, "You do not think Bel is a living god?
Do you not see how much he eats and drinks
every day?" [7]Daniel began to laugh. "Do not be
deceived, O king," he said; "it is only clay inside
and bronze outside; it has never eaten or drunk
anything." [8]Enraged, the king called his priests
and said to them, "Unless you tell me who it is
that consumes these provisions, you shall die.
But if you can show that Bel consumes them,
Daniel shall die for blaspheming Bel." [9]Daniel
said to the king, "Let it be as you say!"

There were seventy priests of Bel, besides their
wives and children. [10]† When the king went with
Daniel into the temple of Bel, [11]the priests of Bel
said, "See, we are going to leave. You, O king, set
out the food and prepare the wine; then shut the
door and seal it with your ring. [12]† If you do not
find that Bel has eaten it all when you return in
the morning, we are to die; otherwise Daniel shall
die for his lies against us." [13]They were not per-
turbed, because under the table they had made a
secret entrance through which they always came
in to consume the food. [14]After they departed the
king set the food before Bel, while Daniel ordered
his servants to bring some ashes, which they scat-
tered through the whole temple; the king alone
was present. Then they went outside, sealed the
closed door with the king's ring, and departed.
[15]† The priests entered that night as usual, with

†

13:55–59 The contrast between the mastic tree, which is small, and the majestic oak emphasizes the contradiction between the statements of the two elders. In the Greek text there is a play on words between the names of these two trees and the mortal punishment decreed by Daniel for the elders. The mastic tree (*schinon*) sounds like the verb "to split" (*schisai*). The oak tree (*prinon*) suggests a play on *poisai* (to saw).

14:1–22 In chap. 14, readings in the Septuagint differ markedly from those in Theodotion, which is followed here. See individual notes on 1–3a, 10–11, 12–14, 15–17 and 21–22; the translation is that of Collins, *Daniel*, pp. 405ff, with brackets indicating additions to the Septuagint according to Collins.

14:1–3a These verses in the Septuagint Greek text read: "From the prophecy of Habakkuk, son of Joshua, of the tribe of Levi. [2] There was a certain man, a priest, whose name was Daniel, son of Abal, a companion of the king of Babylon. [3] There was an idol, Bel, which the Babylonians revered, . . ." This may represent an earlier form of the story, before it was attached to the Book of Daniel. *King Astyages*: the last of the Median kings, defeated by Cyrus in 550 B.C. This story preserves the fiction of a successive Median and Persian rule of Babylon.

14:3 *Bel*: see note on 4:5.

14:10–11 These verses in the Septuagint Greek text read: "(Now, there were seventy priests of Bel, apart from women and children.) They led the king to the idol shrine. [11] The food was set out in the presence of the king and of Daniel, and mixed wine was brought in and set before Bel. Daniel said, 'You yourself see that these things are laid out, O king. You, therefore, seal the door of temple when it is closed.' [The word pleased the king.]"

14:12–14 Theodotion's vv. 12–13 and 14's "After they departed the king set the food before Bel" are lacking in the Septuagint Greek text, which continues vv. 15–17 from v. 11 as follows: "Then Daniel commanded his attendants to make everyone go out from the temple and sprinkle the whole temple with ashes, unknown to anyone outside. Then he ordered them to apply the seal with the king's ring [and the seals of certain illustrious priests, and so it was done]."

14:15–17 These verses in the Septuagint Greek text read: "[15] On the next day they came to the place. But the priests of Bel had entered through false doors and had eaten all that was set forth for Bel and drunk the wine. Daniel said, 'See whether your seals remain, O priests, and you, O king, see that nothing has happened that seems improper to you.' They found the seal as it had been, and they removed the seal."

*

13:61 Dt 19:18–19.

their wives and children, and they ate and drank everything.

16 Early the next morning, the king came with Daniel. 17 "Are the seals unbroken, Daniel?" he asked. And Daniel answered, "They are unbroken, O king." 18 As soon as he had opened the door, the king looked at the table and cried aloud, "You are great, O Bel; there is no deceit in you." 19 † But Daniel laughed and kept the king from entering. He said, "Look at the floor and consider whose footprints these are." 20 "I see the footprints of men, women, and children!" said the king. 21 † In his wrath the king arrested the priests, their wives, and their children. They showed him the secret door by which they used to enter to consume what was on the table. 22 The king put them to death, and handed Bel over to Daniel, who destroyed it and its temple.

23 There was a great dragon† which the Babylonians revered. 24 The king said to Daniel, "You cannot deny that this is a living god, so worship it." 25 But Daniel answered, "I worship the Lord, my God, for he is the living God. 26 Give me permission, O king, and I will kill this dragon without sword or club." "I give you permission," the king said. 27 Then Daniel took some pitch, fat, and hair; these he boiled together and made into cakes. He put them into the mouth of the dragon, and when the dragon ate them, he burst. "This," he said, "is what you revered."

28 When the Babylonians heard this, they were angry and turned against the king. "The king has become a Jew," they said; "he has destroyed Bel, killed the dragon, and put the priests to death." 29 They went to the king and demanded: "Hand Daniel over to us, or we will kill you and your family." 30 When he saw himself threatened with violence, the king was forced to hand Daniel over to them. 31 They threw Daniel into a lions' den,† where he remained six days. 32 In the den were seven lions. Two carcasses and two sheep had been given to them daily, but now they were given nothing, so that they would devour Daniel.

33 The prophet Habakkuk was in Judea. He mixed some bread in a bowl with the stew he had boiled, and was going to bring it to the reapers in the field, 34 when an angel of the Lord told him, "Take the meal you have to Daniel in the lions' den at Babylon." 35 But Habakkuk answered, "Sir, I have never seen Babylon, and I do not know the den!" 36 The angel of the Lord seized him by the crown of his head and carried him by the hair;* with the speed of the wind, he set him down in Babylon above the den. 37 "Daniel, Daniel," cried Habakkuk, "take the meal God has sent you." 38 "You have remembered me, O God," said Daniel; "you have not forsaken those who love you." 39 So Daniel ate, but the angel of God at once brought Habakkuk back to his own place.

40 On the seventh day the king came to mourn for Daniel. As he came to the den and looked in, there was Daniel, sitting there. 41 The king cried aloud, "You are great, O Lord, the God of Daniel, and there is no other besides you!" 42 He brought Daniel out, but those who had tried to destroy him he threw into the den, and they were devoured in a moment before his eyes.

†

14:19 Note that here the king seems unaware of Daniel's ruse.

14:21–22 These verses in the Septuagint Greek text read: "21 And he went to the house where the priests had come, and he found Bel's food and the wine, and Daniel showed the king the false doors through which the priests entered and consumed what had been set before Bel. 22 The king led them out of the temple of Bel and gave them over to Daniel. He gave Daniel what was expended on him and destroyed Bel."

14:23 *Dragon*: or "serpent," and see v. 27. Sacred snakes are well attested in the ancient world (e.g., in the temple of the god of healing Asclepius at Epidaurus), though evidence for their veneration in Babylon is doubtful.

14:31 *A lions' den*: this story provides a different account from chap. 6 as to why Daniel was associated with the lions' den.

*

14:36 Ez 8:3.

"Go marry a prostitute." "Say what, God?" A picture is worth a thousand words, and Hosea's family life was a living picture of Israel's infidelity and God's continuing faithfulness. The Book of Hosea captures this faithful prophet's commitment to God and his loving faithfulness to his straying wife.

The Book of Hosea

In Depth

Hosea preached to the northern kingdom of Israel before it was conquered by the Assyrians in 721 BC. As we learn from Hosea's speeches, the situation in the northern kingdom was not good. Over twenty-five years, Hosea saw seven kings come and go, most of them corrupt (see the timeline at the back of this Bible, and 2 Kings 14:23—17:23). Pursuing their own greedy ends and trying to play power politics, the ruling class overlooked the poor and the needy in their midst and led the people into idolatry. Through Hosea, God proclaimed, "I, the Lord, am your God, / since the land of Egypt" (Hos 13:4).

Even more powerful than Hosea's words was the living symbol of his marriage. Early in Hosea's preaching, God commanded him to marry a prostitute and have children by her. Hosea remained faithful to her, loving her even when she wandered to other men. Hosea used the image of his own marriage to preach his message to Israel. As Hosea's wife was unfaithful to him, so too was Israel unfaithful to God, wandering off in worship of other gods. However, just as Hosea was faithful to his wife and awaited her return, so too God was faithful to Israel and awaited its return from the distractions of power, wealth, and other gods.

Hosea and Amos were prophets in the northern kingdom at about the same time. But Amos had come from the southern kingdom and was more distant and cynical in describing the sins of the ruling class (see his description of well-off women in Am 4:1–3). Hosea was from the northern kingdom—these people were his people! He took their sins personally and passionately. Initially, he had hopes that the people would repent and return to God (see Hos 2:16–23). But after a succession of selfish and violent rulers, he prophesied against his people with all the passion of a scorned lover (see 13:7–11). Still, at the end, he hoped for Israel's return to God (see 14:2–3).

At a Glance

- **I. The Prophet's Marriage and Its Symbolism (1:2—3:5).**
- **II. Israel's Guilt, Punishment, and Restoration (4:1—14:9).**

Quick Facts

Period Covered: from 750 to after 732 BC

Inspired Authors: Hosea and later scribes

Themes: God's faithful love for Israel, the image of God as a loving parent

Hosea

3:1

1 1 † The word of the LORD that came to Hosea
son of Beeri, in the days of Uzziah, Jotham,
Ahaz, Hezekiah, kings of Judah, and in the days of
Jeroboam, son of Joash, king of Israel.†

I. The Prophet's Marriage and Its Symbolism

Marriage of Hosea and Gomer

2 When the LORD began to speak with Hosea,
the LORD said to Hosea: Go, get for yourself a
woman of prostitution† and children of prostitu-
tion, for the land prostitutes itself,* turning away
from the LORD.
3 So he went and took Gomer, daughter of
Diblaim; and she conceived and bore him a son.
4 Then the LORD said to him: Give him the name
"Jezreel,"† for in a little while I will punish the
house of Jehu for the bloodshed at Jezreel and
bring to an end the kingdom of the house of Is-
rael; 5 on that day I will break the bow of Israel in
the valley of Jezreel.
6 She conceived again and bore a daughter. The
LORD said to him: Give her the name "Not-Pit-
ied,"† for I will no longer feel pity for the house
of Israel: rather, I will utterly abhor them. 7 † Yet
for the house of Judah I will feel pity; I will save
them by the LORD, their God; but I will not save
them by bow or sword, by warfare, by horses or
horsemen.*
8 After she weaned Not-Pitied, she conceived
and bore a son. 9 Then the LORD said: Give him
the name "Not-My-People,"† for you are not my
people, and I am not "I am" for you.

2 1† The number of the Israelites
will be like the sand of the sea,
which can be neither measured nor counted.*

1:1–3 This section begins with Hosea's marriage to Gomer, which symbolizes Israel's relationship to God. Hence the symbolic names of Hosea's children and their later renaming (1:2–9; 2:1–3). The prophet foresees God's punishment for the unfaithful covenant partner, but knows that God's last word is always hope (2:4–25).

1:1 This superscription is from a Judean editor, who lists the kings of Judah in the south first, even though Hosea preached in the Northern Kingdom of Israel.

1:2 *A woman of prostitution*: this does not necessarily mean that Gomer was a prostitute when Hosea married her; the verse describes the event in its final consequences. Prostitution here may refer to Gomer's participation in the worship of other gods.

1:4 *Give him the name "Jezreel"*: the names of the three children are symbolic, and predict God's punishment in a crescendo. These names are frequently repeated in chaps. 1–2. *Jezreel*: (lit., "God will sow") the strategic valley in northern Israel where Jehu brought the dynasty of Omri to an end through bloodshed (2 Kgs 9–10). Jeroboam II was the next to the last king of the house of Jehu. The prophecy in this verse of the end of the house of Jehu was fulfilled by the murder of Zechariah, son of Jeroboam II (2 Kgs 15:8–10).

1:6 *"Not-Pitied"*: in Hebrew *lo-ruhama*.

1:7 Probably written by a later editor when the prophecies of Hosea circulated in the south, after the dissolution of the Northern Kingdom had occurred. The second part of the verse emphasizes the power of the Lord, who needs no human agents to fulfill the divine will. It may refer to the deliverance of Jerusalem from the siege of Sennacherib in 701 (2 Kgs 19:35–37).

1:9 *"Not-My-People"*: in Hebrew *lo-ammi*. *I am not "I am" for you*: a reference to the divine name revealed to Moses, "I am" (Ex 3:14). This reversal of the relationship marks the end of the covenant (Ex 6:7).

2:1–3 These verses abruptly reverse the tone of the judgments of 1:2–9 with words of hope for the covenant people: the name Jezreel is given a positive interpretation in contrast to its negative meaning in

1:2 Jer 2:20, 23; Ez 23:3.
1:7 Zec 4:6.
2:1 Gn 15:5; 22:17; 32:13.

Instead of being told,
"You are Not-My-People,"
They will be called,
"Children of the living God."*
2 Then the people of Judah and of Israel
will gather together;
They will appoint for themselves one head
and rise up from the land;
great indeed shall be the day of Jezreel!
3 Say to your brothers, "My People,"
and to your sisters, "Pitied."

The Lord and Israel His Spouse†

4 Accuse your mother, accuse!
for she is not my wife,
and I am not her husband.†
Let her remove her prostitution from her face.
her adultery from between her breasts,
5 Or I will strip her naked,†
leaving her as on the day of her birth;
I will make her like the wilderness,
make her like an arid land,
and let her die of thirst.
6 I will have no pity on her children,
for they are children of prostitution.
7 Yes, their mother has prostituted herself;
she who conceived them has acted
shamefully.
For she said, "I will go after my lovers,†
who give me my bread and my water,
my wool and my flax, my oil and my
drink."*
8† Therefore, I will hedge in her way with thorns
and erect a wall against her,
so that she cannot find her paths.
9 If she runs after her lovers, she will not
overtake them;
if she seeks them she will not find them.
Then she will say,
"I will go back to my first husband,
for I was better off then than now."*
10 She did not know
that it was I who gave her
the grain, the wine, and the oil,
I who lavished upon her silver,
and gold, which they used for Baal.†
11 Therefore I will take back my grain in its time,
and my wine in its season;
I will snatch away my wool and my flax,
which were to cover her nakedness.
12 Now I will lay bare her shame
in full view of her lovers,*
and no one can deliver her out of my
hand.*
13 I will put an end to all her joy,
her festivals, her new moons, her sabbaths—
all her seasonal feasts.
14 I will lay waste her vines and fig trees,
of which she said, "These are the fees
my lovers have given me";
I will turn them into rank growth
and wild animals shall devour them.
15 I will punish her for the days of the Baals,†
for whom she burnt incense,
When she decked herself out with her rings
and her jewelry,
and went after her lovers—
but me she forgot—oracle of the LORD.*
16 Therefore,† I will allure her now;
I will lead her into the wilderness*
and speak persuasively to her.
17 Then I will give her the vineyards she had,
and the valley of Achor† as a door of
hope.*
There she will respond as in the days of her
youth,
as on the day when she came up from the
land of Egypt.

18 On that day—oracle of the LORD—
You shall call me "My husband,"
and you shall never again call me "My
baal."†

---

† 1:4; the child named "Not-Pitied" in 1:6 is renamed "Pitied" in 2:3; the child named "Not-My-People" is renamed "My People." The reversal of these names occurs again in 2:25.

2:4–25 The section contains three oracles of doom (vv. 4–6, 7–9, 10–15), a transition (vv. 16–17), and three oracles of salvation (vv. 18–19, 20–22, 23–25).

2:4 The Lord speaks of Israel, still using the example of Hosea's wife.

2:5 *I will strip her naked*: it was the husband's responsibility to provide food and clothing for his wife (Ex 21:10) and now, because of her adultery, he takes back his support.

2:7 *My lovers*: even though Israel had experienced the Lord as the God of the desert, covenant and conquest, the people were inclined to turn to the local fertility deities, the Baals, who were believed to be responsible for agricultural success. They easily forgot that the Lord provides them with everything (v. 10; cf. Dt 7:13), and thus prostituted themselves by worshiping other gods.

2:8 The crop failures sent by the Lord are meant to make Israel see the folly of its ways.

2:10 *For Baal*: as an offering to Baal or to make statues of Baal.

2:15 *The days of the Baals*: feast days of the Baal cult (v. 13), or the whole period of Israel's apostasy.

2:16 *Therefore*: this word in Hebrew normally introduces an oracle of doom; here, surprisingly, it leads to hope. *Allure*: as though seducing a virgin (Ex 22:15–16). Ordinarily this word connotes deception (Jgs 14:15; 16:5; 1 Kgs 22:20–22).

2:17 *Valley of Achor*: lit., valley of trouble (Jos 7:26). Here this valley becomes a valley of hope, a new entry into the promised land.

2:18–19 *Baal*: the word means "lord, master." It was commonly used by women of their husbands, but it is to be shunned as a title for the Lord because of its association with the fertility gods, the Baals.

---

* **2:1** Rom 9:26–27. **2:7** Jer 2:25. **2:9** Lk 15:17–18. **2:12** Ez 16:37. **2:12** Jn 10:29. **2:15** Jer 2:32. **2:16** Jer 2:2–7. **2:17** Jos 7:24–26.

Live It!

Unconditional Faithfulness

We don't know all the details of Hosea's relationship with his wife, Gomer. But most people understand Hosea 3:1–3 to mean that Hosea accepted her back after she was unfaithful to him. We can only hope that Gomer was so touched by Hosea's unconditional forgiveness that she turned her life around and was faithful to him in return.

It is hard to be faithful to someone who is unfaithful to you. The other person doesn't have to be an adulterous spouse. She or he can be a friend who starts spending time with someone else instead of you, or a family member who keeps breaking promises to be with you. A natural reaction is to return the hurt in some way. How much harder—and more Christlike—it is to keep being faithful and friendly.

- Have you ever been hurt by someone's unfaithful behavior? If so, how did you react?
- How can you address a friend's or family member's unfaithful behavior and still remain faithful and loving yourself?

▶ **Hos 3:1–3**

19 I will remove from her mouth the names of
the Baals;
they shall no longer be mentioned by their
name.

20 I will make a covenant for them on that day,*
with the wild animals,
With the birds of the air,
and with the things that crawl on the ground.
Bow and sword and warfare
I will destroy from the land,
and I will give them rest in safety.

21 I will betroth you to me forever:
I will betroth you to me with† justice and
with judgment,
with loyalty and with compassion;
22 I will betroth you to me with fidelity,
and you shall know the LORD.

23 On that day I will respond—oracle of the
LORD—
I will respond to the heavens,
and they will respond to the earth;
24 The earth will respond to the grain, and wine,
and oil,
and these will respond to Jezreel.
25 I will sow her for myself in the land,
and I will have pity on Not-Pitied.
I will say to Not-My-People, "You are my
people,"*
and he will say, "My God!"

Hosea and His Wife Reunited†

3 1 Again the LORD said to me:

Go, love a woman
who is loved by her spouse but commits
adultery;
Just as the LORD loves the Israelites,
though they turn to other gods
and love raisin cakes.†

2 † So I acquired her for myself for fifteen
pieces of silver and a homer and a lethech of bar-
ley. 3 Then I said to her:

"You will wait for me for many days;
you will not prostitute yourself
Or belong to any man;
I in turn will wait for you."

4 † For the Israelites will remain many days

† Many Israelites saw little if any difference between the worship of the Lord and the worship of the Baals, thereby dishonoring the true source of the land's fertility.

2:21–22 *Betroth . . . with*: the betrothal was the legal moment before cohabitation when the dowry was paid to the father of the bride. In this remarriage the Lord gives the bride price to Israel herself "forever." *Justice . . . judgment*: refer to equity and fairness of conduct. The next two terms, "loyalty" (*hesed*), the steadfast love between the covenant partners, and "compassion," maternal love (cf. 1:6; 2:3, 25) are characteristic of Hosea. *You shall know*: not an abstract but a practical knowledge which means acknowledgment of God's will and obedience to his law (4:1; 5:4; 6:3, 6).

3:1–5 Just as the Lord is ready to take Israel back, Hosea takes his wife back. She must undergo a period of purification, just as Israel must experience purification before the restoration of the covenant relationship.

3:1 *Raisin cakes*: offerings to the fertility goddess Asherah, the female counterpart of Baal, cf. Jer 7:18; 44:19; Dn 14:5–8.

3:2 Just as the Lord offered a new bride price to Israel (2:21–22), so Hosea offers a new bride price to his wife. He returns to her what he has taken away from her (2:5): "fifteen (shekels) of silver"; "a homer of barley," a unit of dry measurement, which according to the etymology means "a mule load"; and "a lethech of barley," which is a half-homer.

3:4 Israel will lose its political and cultic institutions. *Sacred pillar*: originally perhaps a phallic symbol, representing Baal. These were also used in Israelite worship (cf. notes on Gn 28:18; Ex 34:13). *Ephod*: an instrument used in consulting the deity (1 Sm 23:6–12; 30:7; cf. notes on Ex 28:6, 15–30). *Household gods*: in Hebrew, *teraphim*; images regarded as the tutelary deities of the household (Gn 31:19; Jgs 17:5; 18:14, 17–18).

* **2:20** Gn 9:8–11; Ez 34:25; Jb 5:23. **2:25** Rom 9:25–26; 1 Pt 2:10.

without king or prince,
Without sacrifice or sacred pillar,
without ephod or household gods.
5 Afterward the Israelites will turn back
and seek the LORD, their God,
and David, their king;† *
They will come trembling to the LORD
and to his bounty, in the last days.

II. Israel's Guilt, Punishment, and Restoration

Indictment of Israel†

4 1 Hear the word of the LORD, Israelites,
for the LORD has a dispute
with the inhabitants of the land:*
There is no fidelity, no loyalty,
no knowledge of God in the land.
2 Swearing, lying, murder,
stealing and adultery break out;†
bloodshed follows bloodshed.*
3 Therefore the land dries up,
and everything that dwells in it languishes:
The beasts of the field,
the birds of the air,
and even the fish of the sea perish.*

Guilt of Priest and of People

4 But let no one accuse, let no one rebuke;
with you is my dispute, priest!†
5 You will stumble in the day,
and the prophet will stumble with you at night;
I will make an end of your mother.†
6 My people are ruined for lack of knowledge!
Since you have rejected knowledge,
I will reject you from serving as my priest;
Since you have forgotten the law of your God,
I will also forget your children.

7 The more they multiplied, the more they sinned against me,
I will change their glory† into shame.*
8 They feed on the sin of my people,
and are greedy for their iniquity.†
9 Like people, like priest:*
I will punish them for their ways,
and repay them for their deeds.
10 They will eat but not be satisfied,*
they will promote prostitution† but not increase,
Because they have abandoned the LORD,
devoting themselves
11 to prostitution.
Aged wine and new wine
take away understanding.*
12 My people consult their piece of wood,†
and their wand makes pronouncements for them,
For the spirit of prostitution has led them astray;
they prostitute themselves, forsaking their God.
13 On the mountaintops they offer sacrifice
and on the hills they burn incense,
Beneath oak and poplar and terebinth,
because of their pleasant shade.†
Therefore your daughters prostitute themselves,
and your daughters-in-law commit adultery.
14 I will not punish your daughters for their prostitution,
nor your daughters-in-law for their adultery,
Because the men themselves consort with prostitutes,
and with temple women† they offer sacrifice!
Thus a people without understanding comes to ruin.

15 Though you prostitute yourself, Israel,
do not let Judah become guilty!

†

3:5 *David, their king*: the king belonging to the line of David who will restore the Israelite nation (Jer 23:5; Ez 34:23, 24). *The last days*: a future time of transformation.

4:1–3 The introduction to the oracles (chaps. 4–11) which begin with "Hear the word of the Lord" (4:1) and end with "oracle of the Lord" (11:11).

4:2 Similar to the decalogue (Ex 20:1–17; cf. Jer 7:9).

4:4–6 Hosea is particularly severe with the priests in the Northern Kingdom who had led the way in the general apostasy from God's law. The prophets here associated with the priests (v. 5) were doubtless cult prophets; cf. Jer 2:8; 4:9–10; 6:13–14; 23:9–40.

4:5 *Your mother*: the one who gave life to the priest, understood here as an extension of the punishment to his whole family (Am 7:17), or "mother" taken as a metaphor for the community of Israel, of which the priest is a member (Hos 2:4).

4:7 *Their glory*: possibly connoting "their children." See 9:11: Is 22:24. Or "Glory" may refer to the Lord in contrast to Ba'al. The Hebrew word for shame, *bosheth*, is often substituted for Ba'al in biblical names. See Ishbaal (Heb. *Ishbosheth*, 2 Sm 2:8, 10, 12, 15) and Meribaal (Heb. *Mephibosheth*, 2 Sm 9:6, 10–13).

4:8 The priest receives part of the sacrifice (Lv 6:19; 7:7).

4:10–11 *Prostitution*: often a synonym for idolatry. The covenant bond was symbolized as the relationship between husband and wife (see chaps. 1–2). Thus, abandoning the Lord for a foreign god was called prostitution or adultery.

4:12 *Piece of wood*: a derogatory term for an idol. *Wand*: a sacred wooden object, perhaps some kind of staff, used for divination.

4:13 The shrines on the "high places" typically had an altar, a grove of trees, and a stone pillar representing a god (Dt 12:2; Jer 2:20).

4:14 *Temple women*: plural of Heb. *qedesha*; the exact import of the term is disputed. See notes on Gn 38:21 and Dt 23:18–19.

3:5 Jer 30:9; Ez 34:23.
4:1 Is 3:10–15; Mi 6:1–5.
4:2 Ex 20:13–17.
4:3 Is 24:4–7; Zep 1:2–3.
4:7 Jer 2:11; Ps 106:20.
4:9 Is 24:2.
4:10 Mi 6:14.
4:11 Is 28:7.

Do not come to Gilgal,†
do not go up to Beth-aven,*
do not swear, "As the Lord lives!"*
16 For like a stubborn cow,
Israel is stubborn;
Will the LORD now pasture them,
like lambs in a broad meadow?
17 Ephraim† is bound to idols,
let him alone!
18† When their drinking is over,
they give themselves to prostitution;*
they love shame more than their honor.
19 A wind† has bound them up in its wings;*
they shall be ashamed because of their
altars.*

Guilt of the Religious and Political Leaders

5 1 Hear this, priests,
Pay attention, house of Israel,
Household of the king, give ear!*
For you are responsible for judgment.†
But you have been a snare at Mizpah,†
a net spread upon Tabor,
2 a pit dug deep in Shittim.
Now I will discipline them all.

3 I know Ephraim,
and Israel is not hidden from me:
Now, Ephraim, you have practiced prostitution,
Israel is defiled.
4 Their deeds do not allow them
to return to their God;*
For the spirit of prostitution is in them,
and they do not know the LORD.

5 The arrogance of Israel bears witness against
him;
Israel and Ephraim stumble because of
their iniquity,
and Judah stumbles with them.
6 With their flocks and herds they will go
to seek the LORD, but will not find him;*
he has withdrawn from them.
7 They have betrayed the LORD,
for they have borne illegitimate children;
Now the new moon† will devour them
together with their fields.

Political Upheavals†

8 Blow the ram's horn in Gibeah,
the trumpet in Ramah!
Sound the alarm in Beth-aven:*
"Look behind you, Benjamin!"†
9 Ephraim shall become a wasteland
on the day of punishment:
Among the tribes of Israel
I announce what is sure to be.
10 The princes of Judah have become
like those who move a boundary line;† *
Upon them I will pour out
my wrath like water.
11 Ephraim is oppressed, crushed by
judgment,
for he has willingly gone after filth!†
12 I am like a moth for Ephraim,*
like rot for the house of Judah.
13 When Ephraim saw his infirmity,
and Judah his sore,
Ephraim went to Assyria,
and sent to the great king.† *
But he cannot heal you,
nor take away your sore.
14 For I am like a lion to Ephraim,
like a young lion to the house of Judah;*

†

4:15 *Gilgal*: close to Jericho (Jos 4:19–20; 5:2–9). *Beth-aven*: (lit., "house of iniquity") Hosea's derogatory term for the sanctuary of Bethel (lit., "house of God"), the major shrine of the Northern Kingdom (10:5, 8; cf. Am 5:5). *As the Lord lives*: a legitimate oath formula (1 Sm 26:10, 16), but unacceptable here because Israel is guilty of religious syncretism and the idolatrous worship of other gods.

4:17 *Ephraim*: the name of one of the sons of Joseph, son of Jacob (Gn 41:52), also used to designate one of the tribes living in the heartland of the Northern Kingdom. Hosea often uses the name Ephraim to refer to the whole Northern Kingdom of Israel. During the latter part of his ministry, after the Assyrians occupied Galilee, Ephraim was all that remained of Israel.

4:18 Cf. v. 11.

4:19 *A wind*: (Heb. *ruah*), a metaphor for Israel's addiction to the Baal cult, which is nothing but wind, a "spirit (*ruah*) of prostitution" (v. 12).

5:1 *For you . . . judgment*: possibly "for you are called to judgment."

5:1–2 *Mizpah*: several places bear this name; the best known is in Benjamin (1 Sm 7:6, 16; 10:17). Perhaps this is a wordplay on *mishpat*, "justice," "judgment." *Tabor*: the mountain that dominates the valley of Jezreel. *Shittim*: in Transjordan, where Israel committed its first act of idolatry with the Baal of Peor (9:10; cf. Nm 25). At these three places the leaders had misled the people by an idolatrous cult or by an abuse of justice.

5:7 *New moon*: normally a feast day of joy (2:13), but, because of infidelity, it will be a day of destruction.

5:8–14 This passage describes political and military conflict between Judah and Israel. Perhaps some allusion is made to the Syro-Ephraimite war of 735–734 B.C., when a coalition of Arameans and Israelites attempted to dethrone the king of Judah (2 Kgs 16:5; Is 7:1–9). Judah repulsed the attempt with the aid of Assyria, and the latter devastated both Aram and Israel.

5:8 A vision of invasion, from Gibeah and Ramah in northern Judah, into Israel.

5:10 *Move a boundary line*: invasion by Judah (v. 8) is compared to a case of social injustice (Dt 19:14; 27:17; Prv 23:10–11).

5:11 *Filth*: Ephraim's reliance on foreign nations and their gods.

5:13 *Ephraim went . . . . king*: in 738 the Israelite king Menahem had to pay tribute to the Assyrian king Tiglath-pileser III, whose vassal he became (2 Kgs 15:19–20). Under the threat of the Syro-Ephraimite invasion King Ahaz of Judah also submitted to Tiglath-pileser (2 Kgs 16:7–9). *Great king*: Heb. *melek-yarev*; may be a proper name: King Yarev, but unknown; or "the defender king": irony about the great king of Assyria (see note on 10:6).

*

4:15 Am 4:4.
4:15 Am 8:14.
4:18 Am 2:8.
4:19 Jer 4:11–12.
4:19 Is 1:29.
5:1 Mi 3:1.
5:4 Jer 13:23.
5:6 Is 55:6; Jer 29:13; Am 5:4–6; 8:12; Jn 7:34.
5:8 Jer 4:5; Jl 2:1.
5:10 Dt 19:14; 27:17.
5:12 Is 50:9.
5:13 2 Kgs 15:19–20; 16:7–9.
5:14 Is 5:29; Am 1:2; 3:12.

It is I who tear the prey and depart,
I carry it away and no one can save it.*

Insincere Conversion

15 I will go back to my place
until they make reparation
and seek my presence.
In their affliction, they shall look for me.*

6 1 "Come, let us return to the LORD,*
For it is he who has torn, but he will heal us;
he has struck down, but he will bind our wounds.
2 He will revive us after two days;
on the third day† he will raise us up,*
to live in his presence.
3 Let us know, let us strive to know the LORD;
as certain as the dawn is his coming.
He will come to us like the rain,
like spring rain that waters the earth."*

4 What can I do with you, Ephraim?
What can I do with you, Judah?
Your loyalty is like morning mist,
like the dew that disappears early.
5 For this reason I struck them down through the prophets,
I killed them by the words of my mouth;†*
my judgment shines forth like the light.
6 For it is loyalty that I desire, not sacrifice,
and knowledge of God rather than burnt offerings.*

Further Crimes of Israel

7 But they, at Adam,† violated the covenant;
there they betrayed me.

8 Gilead† is a city of evildoers,
tracked with blood.
9 Like brigands lying in wait
is the band of priests.
They murder on the road to Shechem,†
indeed they commit a monstrous crime.
10 In the house of Israel I have seen a horrible thing:
there is found Ephraim's prostitution,
Israel is defiled.
11 For you also, Judah,
a harvest† has been appointed!

7 When I would have restored the fortunes of my people,
1 when I would have healed Israel,
The guilt of Ephraim was revealed,
the wickedness of Samaria:
They practiced falsehood.
Thieves break in,
bandits roam outside.
2 Yet they do not call to mind
that I remember all their wickedness.*
Now their crimes surround them,
present to my sight.*

Israel's Domestic Politics†

3 With their wickedness they make the king rejoice,
the princes too, with their treacherous deeds.
4 They are all adulterers,†
like a blazing oven,
Which the baker quits stoking,
after the dough's kneading until its rising.
5 On the day of our king,
they made the princes sick with poisoned wine;
he extended his hand to the scoffers.
6 For they draw near in ambush
with their hearts like an oven.
All the night their anger sleeps;
in the morning it flares like a blazing fire.
7 They are all heated like ovens,
and consume their rulers.
All their kings have fallen;
none of them calls upon me.

Israel's Foreign Politics

8 Ephraim is mixed with the nations,†
Ephraim is an unturned cake.

†

6:2 *After two days; on the third day*: presumptuous Israel expects that soon God will renew them (cf. Ez 37).

6:5 The word of God proclaimed by the prophets is effective, it accomplished what it promised: punishment.

6:7 *At Adam*: the violation of the covenant at Adam is mentioned nowhere else in the Bible. The place Adam, the location of which is unknown, may be referred to in Jos 3:16.

6:8 *Gilead*: city in Transjordan (Gn 31:46–48; 2 Kgs 15:25).

6:9 *Shechem*: an important ancient religious and political center (Jos 24).

6:11 *Harvest*: God's judgment, when Judah will reap what it has sown.

7:3–7 This passage perhaps refers to a conspiracy at the royal court. Between the death of Jeroboam II (743 B.C.) and the fall of Samaria (722/721), nearly all the kings were murdered (2 Kgs 15:10, 14, 25, 30).

7:4 *Adulterers*: the unfaithful nobles who kill the king. Their passion is compared to the fire of the oven. The point of the metaphor is that, like this oven whose fire is always ready to blaze up again, the conspirators are always ready for rebellion.

7:8 *Is mixed with the nations*: the people reject exclusive allegiance to the Lord, and they now try to find their salvation in alliances with foreign nations. *An unturned cake*: burnt on one side, but not baked at all on the other, and thus worthless.

*

5:14 Dt 32:39.
5:15 Jer 29:13; Ps 78:34.
6:1 Lam 3:40.
6:2 Lk 24:7, 46; 1 Cor 15:4.
6:3 Dt 11:14; Ps 72:6.
6:5 Is 11:4; 49:2; Jer 5:14; Heb 4:12–13.
6:6 1 Sm 15:22; Am 5:22–24; Mi 6:6–8; Eccl 4:17; Mt 9:13; 12:7.
7:2 Ps 10:11.
7:2 Prv 5:21–22.

9 Strangers have consumed his strength,
but he does not know it;*
Gray hairs are strewn on his head,
but he takes no notice of it.
10 The arrogance of Israel bears witness against him;
yet they do not return to the LORD, their God,
nor seek him, despite all this.*
11 Ephraim is like a dove,
silly and senseless;
They call upon Egypt,
they go to Assyria.
12 When they go I will spread my net around them,
like birds in the air I will bring them down.*
I will chastise them when I hear of their assembly.
13 Woe to them, for they have strayed from me!
Ruin to them, for they have rebelled against me!
Though I wished to redeem them,
they spoke lies against me.
14 They have not cried to me from their hearts
when they wailed upon their beds;
For wheat and wine they lacerated themselves;†
they rebelled against me.
15 Though I trained and strengthened their arms,
yet they devised evil against me.
16 They have again become useless,
they have been like a treacherous bow.*
Their princes shall fall by the sword
because of the insolence of their tongues;
thus they shall be mocked in the land of Egypt.

Corruption of Cult, Domestic and Foreign Politics

8 1 Put the trumpet to your lips!*
One like an eagle† is over the house of the LORD!
Because they have violated my covenant,
and rebelled against my law,
2 They cry out to me,
"My God! We know you!"
3 But Israel has rejected what is good;
the enemy† shall pursue him.
4† They made kings, but not by my authority;
they established princes, but without my knowledge.
With their silver and gold
they made idols for themselves,
to their own destruction.
5 He has rejected your calf,† Samaria!*
My wrath is kindled against them;
How long will they be incapable of innocence in Israel?
6 An artisan made it,
it is no god at all.*
The calf of Samaria
will be dashed to pieces.
7 When they sow the wind,
they will reap the whirlwind;*
The stalk of grain that forms no head
can yield no flour;
Even if it could,
strangers would swallow it.
8 Israel is swallowed up;
now they are among the nations,
like a useless vessel.
9 For they went up to Assyria—†
a wild ass off on its own—
Ephraim bargained for lovers.*
10 Even though they bargain with the nations,
I will now gather them† together;
They will soon succumb
under the burden of king and princes.
11† When Ephraim made many altars to expiate sin,
they became altars for sinning.
12 Though I write for him my many instructions,
they are considered like a stranger's.
13 They love sacrifice,
they sacrifice meat and eat it,
but the LORD is not pleased with them.*
Now he will remember their guilt
and punish their sins;*

HOS

†

7:14 *Lacerated themselves*: a ritual to obtain a good harvest from Baal (2:7–10; 1 Kgs 18:28; Jer 16:6; 41:5). This practice was forbidden (Lv 19:28; Dt 14:1).

8:1 *Eagle*: perhaps an image for Tiglath-pileser III of Assyria, who overran the land of Israel in 733 B.C. (Jer 48:40; 49:22; Ez 17:3).

8:3 *Enemy*: Assyria.

8:4 Hosea is not against the monarchy, but against the conspiracies at the royal court (see note on 7:3–7). The king should be chosen by God (1 Kgs 19:15–16).

8:5 *Calf*: a cultic object introduced by Jeroboam I after the separation of the Northern Kingdom from the Southern Kingdom (1 Kgs 12:26–30; cf. Ex 32).

8:9 *They went up to Assyria*: a reference to the politics of appealing to Assyria (cf. 5:13; 7:11). There is a play on the Hebrew word for "wild ass" (*pere*) and "Ephraim."

8:10 *I will now gather them*: for judgment and for deportation.

8:11 The altars had become places of self-serving worship (cf. v. 13).

7:9 Jer 5:3; Rev 3:17.
7:10 Is 9:12; Am 4:6.
7:12 Ez 12:13; 32:3.
7:16 Ps 78:57.
8:1 Jl 2:1.
8:5 1 Kgs 12:28.
8:6 Ex 20:4; 34:17; Is 40:19–20; 44:9–20; Jer 10:1–16.
8:7 Jb 4:8; Prv 22:8; 2 Cor 9:6; Gal 6:7–8.
8:9 Ez 16:32–34.
8:13 Am 5:22.
8:13 Jer 14:10.

they shall return to Egypt.† *
14 Israel has forgotten his maker*
and has built palaces.
Judah, too, has fortified many cities,
but I will send fire upon his cities,
to devour their strongholds.*

From Days of Celebration to Days of Punishment

9 1 Do not rejoice, Israel,
do not exult like the nations!
For you have prostituted yourself, abandoning your God,
loving a prostitute's fee
upon every threshing floor.†
2 Threshing floor and wine press will not nourish them,
the new wine will fail them.

3 They will not dwell in the LORD's land;
Ephraim will return to Egypt,
and in Assyria they will eat unclean food.
4 They will not pour libations of wine to the LORD,
and their sacrifices will not please him.
Their bread will be like mourners' bread,† *
that makes unclean all who eat of it;
Their food will be for their own appetites;
it cannot enter the house of the LORD.

5 What will you do on the festival day,
the day of the LORD's feast?†
6† When they flee from the devastation,
Egypt will gather them, Memphis will bury them.
Weeds will overgrow their silver treasures,
and thorns, their tents.

7 They have come, the days of punishment!
they have come, the days of recompense!
Let Israel know it!
"The prophet is a fool,*
the man of the spirit is mad!"
Because your iniquity is great,
great, too, is your hostility.

Pray It!

Reaping the Whirlwind

Hosea uses lots of metaphors, or symbols, in describing Israel's relationship with God. Hosea 8:7 gives one of those metaphors, saying the Israelites have sowed the wind and will reap the whirlwind. The wind is their political scheming, injustice, and idolatry; the whirlwind is violence and injustice that will destroy the whole country.

Like Israel, we are free to reject or accept God, but we will have to reap the consequences of our choices.

In your prayer, reflect or journal on the following questions:

- What significant decisions have you made recently?
- What consequences are likely to follow as a result of each decision?
- Were your choices the ones that God wanted you to make? How do you know this?

▶ **Hos 8:7**

8† The watchman of Ephraim, the people of my God, is the prophet;*
yet a fowler's snare is on all his ways,
hostility in the house of his God.
9 They have sunk to the depths of corruption,
as in the days of Gibeah;† *
God will remember their iniquity
and punish their sins.

From Former Glory to a History of Corruption

10 Like grapes in the desert,
I found Israel;

H O S

†

8:13 *Return to Egypt*: to punish their violation of the covenant they will experience a reversal of the exodus.

9:1 *Threshing floor*: an allusion to harvest festivals in honor of Baal, to whom the Israelites had attributed the fertility of the land; cf. 2:7.

9:4 *Mourners' bread*: bread eaten at funeral rites (Dt 26:14). The presence of a corpse also made all food prepared in that house unclean (Jer 16:5–7).

9:5 *The LORD's feast*: probably the important autumn feast of Booths, the most important of the Israelite public celebrations (Lv 23:34).

9:6 Instead of gathering for celebration (v. 5), they will be gathered for death. *Memphis*: known for the monumental pyramid tombs. *Silver treasures*: the silver statues of Baal (8:4).

9:8 Prophets, like Hosea himself, are called to be sentinels for Israel, warning Israel of God's coming wrath (see Ez 3:17; 33:7), but often meet rejection.

9:9 *The days of Gibeah*: the precise allusion is not clear. Perhaps it is a reference to the outrage committed at Gibeah in the days of the judges (Jgs 19–21), or to questions surrounding Saul's kingship at Gibeah (1 Sm 10:26; 14:2; 22:6).

*

8:13 Dt 28:68.
8:14 Dt 32:15, 18; Is 51:13.
8:14 Am 1:7, 10, 12, 14; 2:2, 5.
9:4 Dt 26:14.
9:7 2 Kgs 9:11; Jn 10:20.
9:8 Jer 6:17; Ez 3:17; 33:2, 6, 7.
9:9 Jgs 19–21.

Like the first fruits of the fig tree, its first to
ripen,*
I looked on your ancestors.
But when they came to Baal-peor† *
and consecrated themselves to the
Shameful One,
they became as abhorrent as the thing they
loved.
11 Ephraim is like a bird:
their glory flies away—
no birth, no pregnancy, no conception.*
12 Even though they bring up their children,
I will make them childless, until no one is
left.
Indeed, woe to them
when I turn away from them!
13 Ephraim, as I saw, was a tree
planted in a meadow;
But now Ephraim will bring out
his children to the slaughterer!
14 Give them, LORD!
give them what?
Give them a miscarrying womb,
and dry breasts!*
15 All their misfortune began in Gilgal;†
yes, there I rejected them.
Because of their wicked deeds
I will drive them out of my house.
I will love them no longer;
all their princes are rebels.
16† Ephraim is stricken,
their root is dried up;*
they will bear no fruit.*
Were they to bear children,
I would slay the beloved of their womb.
17 My God will disown them
because they have not listened to him;
they will be wanderers among the nations.*

Destruction of Idolatrous Cultic Objects

10 1 * Israel is a luxuriant vine
whose fruit matches its growth.
The more abundant his fruit,
the more altars he built;
The more productive his land,
the more sacred pillars† he set up.
2 Their heart is false!
Now they will pay for their guilt:
God will break down their altars
and destroy their sacred pillars.
3 For now they will say,
"We have no king!†
Since we do not fear the LORD,
the king—what could he do for us?"
4 They make promises,
swear false oaths, and make covenants,
While lawsuits sprout
like poisonous weeds† in the furrows of a
field!

5 The inhabitants of Samaria are afraid
for the calf of Beth-aven;†
Its people mourn for it
and its idolatrous priests wail over it,
—over its glory which has departed from it.*
6 It too will be carried to Assyria,
as an offering to the great king.† *
Ephraim will be put to shame,
Israel will be shamed by his schemes.

7 Samaria and her king will disappear,
like a twig upon the waters.
8 The high places of Aven† will be destroyed,
the sin of Israel;
thorns and thistles will overgrow their
altars.
Then they will cry out to the mountains,
"Cover us!"
and to the hills, "Fall upon us!"*

War Because of Israel's Wickedness

9 Since the days of Gibeah*
you have sinned, Israel.
There they took their stand;
will war not reach them in Gibeah?
Against a perverse people
10 I came and I chastised them;
Peoples will be gathered against them

†

9:10 *Baal-peor*: where the Israelites consecrated themselves for the first time to Baal (Nm 25; see note on Hos 5:1–2). Baal is here called the Shameful One.

9:15 *Gilgal*: possibly a reference to Saul's disobedience to Samuel (1 Sm 13:7–14; 15), or to the idolatry practiced in that place (see note on Hos 4:15).

9:16 Wordplay on the Hebrew word for "fruit" (*peri*) and Ephraim (see note on 8:9). The whole passage (vv. 10–17) presents a reversal of Ephraim's name (Gn 41:52). He will have no fruit, a condition which will result in extinction.

10:1 *Sacred pillars*: see note on 3:4.

10:3 *No king*: the instability of the monarchy (7:3–7) and its vassalage to foreign kings (7:8–16) render the monarchy ineffective. The kings do the opposite of what they are supposed to do (10:4).

10:4 *Lawsuits . . . like poisonous weeds*: the administration of justice, which should have been the mainstay of the people, has in corrupt hands become another instrument of oppression; cf. Am 6:12.

10:5 *The calf of Beth-aven*: see note on 4:15.

10:6 *The great king*: a title used by the Assyrian kings. See also note on 5:13.

10:8 *Aven*: wickedness, first of all at Bethel (v. 5), but also at all the high places.

*

9:10 Is 28:4; Jer 2:2.
9:10 Nm 25.
9:11 Dt 28:18.
9:14 Jb 3:11–12; Lk 23:29.
9:16 Am 2:9.
9:16 Mt 21:19.
9:17 Gn 4:12, 14; Dt 28:64–65.
10:1 Is 5:1–7.
10:5 1 Sm 4:21–22.
10:6 Am 5:27.
10:8 Is 2:10, 19; Lk 23:30; Rev 6:16.
10:9 Jgs 19–21.

HOS

when I bind them to their two crimes.†
11 Ephraim was a trained heifer,
that loved to thresh;
I myself laid a yoke
upon her beautiful neck;
I will make Ephraim break ground, Judah
must plow,
Jacob must harrow for himself:
12 "Sow for yourselves justice,
reap the reward of loyalty;
Break up for yourselves a new field,*
for it is time to seek the LORD,
till he comes and rains justice upon you."*
13 But you have plowed wickedness,
reaped perversity,
and eaten the fruit of falsehood.
Because you have trusted in your own power,
and in your many warriors,*
14 The clamor of war shall break out among
your people
and all your fortresses shall be ravaged
As Salman ravaged Beth-arbel† on the day of
war,
smashing mothers along with their
children.*
15 So it will be done to you, Bethel,
because of your utter wickedness:
At dawn† the king of Israel
will utterly disappear.

The Disappointment of a Parent

11 1† When Israel was a child I loved him,*
out of Egypt† I called my son.*
2 The more I called them,
the farther they went from me,
Sacrificing to the Baals
and burning incense to idols.
3 Yet it was I who taught Ephraim to walk,
who took them in my arms;*
but they did not know that I cared for them.
4 I drew them with human cords,
with bands of love;†
I fostered them like those
who raise an infant to their cheeks;
I bent down to feed them.*

A Parent's Love

Hosea, chapter 11, describes God as a loving parent. This is one of the most touching passages of the Old Testament. Despite God's tenderness and care, Israel behaves as a rebellious child. God is heartbroken by Israel's rejection, but is compassionate in calling for its return.

God, loving father and mother, thank you for your generous and unconditional love. Let me remember that you always love me, even when I have done something wrong. Help me to return your love by living in a way that is pleasing to you. Amen.

▶ **Hos 11:1–7**

5 He shall return to the land of Egypt,*
Assyria shall be his king,
because they have refused to repent.
6 The sword shall rage in his cities:
it shall destroy his diviners,
and devour them because of their
schemings.
7 My people have their mind set on apostasy;
though they call on God in unison,
he shall not raise them up.

But Love Is Stronger and Restores

8 How could I give you up, Ephraim,
or deliver you up, Israel?
How could I treat you as Admah,
or make you like Zeboiim?† *
My heart is overwhelmed,
my pity is stirred.
9 I will not give vent to my blazing anger,

†

10:10 *Two crimes*: the allusion is not clear; a possible reference is the outrage described in Jgs 19.

10:14 *As Salman ravaged Beth-arbel*: perhaps Salamanu, king of Moab, mentioned in an inscription of Tiglath-pileser III, after an invasion in Gilead (Transjordan), where there was a Beth-arbel, close to present Irbid.

10:15 *At dawn*: normally the moment of God's victory over Israel's enemies, and thus his salvation (Is 17:14; Ps 46:6). Here it is a reversal of this expectation.

11:1–3 After the image of husband-wife (chaps. 1–3), Hosea uses the image of parent-child (Ex 4:22; Is 1:2; Jer 3:19).

11:1 *Out of Egypt*: Hosea dates the real beginning of Israel from the time of the exodus. Mt 2:15 applies this text to the return of Jesus from Egypt.

11:4 *I drew them . . . with bands of love*: perhaps a reversal of the yoke imagery of the previous chapter, i.e., not forcing them like draft animals, but drawing them with kindness and affection.

11:8 *Admah . . . Zeboiim*: cities in the vicinity of Sodom and Gomorrah (Gn 14:2, 8) and destroyed with them (Gn 19:24–25; Dt 29:22).

*

10:12 Jer 4:3.
10:12 Is 45:8; Jl 2:23.
10:13 Is 31:1.
10:14 Ps 137:9; Am 1:13.
11:1 Dt 7:8; 10:15; Jer 2:1–9.
11:1 Ex 4:22; Mt 2:15.
11:3 Dt 1:31; 8:5.
11:4 Dt 8:16.
11:5 Dt 17:16.
11:8 Dt 29:22.

Cultural Connection

I Therefore Commit

This prayer from Elizabeth S. Tapia of the Philippines could have been written in response to Hosea's call to live justly, to live the spirit of being a holy people of God:

We should not oppress children, indigenous people,
women, the homeless, refugees and victims of war.
We need to live in defense of peoples and creation.
For I believe in the interwovenness of life.
Creator and Creatures. Cosmic and Individual.
West, North, East, South. Rest and Prayer.
Food and Freedom. Theology and Ecology.
I therefore commit myself, together with you,
to take care of mother earth.
To advocate for peace and justice.
To choose and celebrate life!
These things I believe. Amen.

("Earth Credo," from *A Time to Speak*)

▶ Hos 12:3–7

I will not destroy Ephraim again;
For I am God and not a man,*
the Holy One present among you;
I will not come in wrath.
10 They shall follow the LORD,
who roars like a lion;*
When he roars,
his children shall come frightened from the west,
11 Out of Egypt they shall come trembling, like birds,
like doves, from the land of Assyria;
And I will resettle them in their homes,
oracle of the LORD.

Infidelity of Israel†

12 [1] Ephraim has surrounded me with lies,
the house of Israel, with deceit;
Judah still wanders about with gods,
and is faithful to holy ones.†
2† Ephraim shepherds the wind,
and pursues the east wind all day long.
He multiplies lies and violence:
They make a covenant with Assyria,
and oil is carried to Egypt.

3 The LORD has a dispute with Judah,
and will punish Jacob† for his conduct,
and repay him for his deeds.
4 In the womb he supplanted his brother,*
and in his vigor he contended with a divine being;
5 He contended with an angel and prevailed,*
he wept and entreated him.
At Bethel he met with him,
and there he spoke with him.*
6 The LORD is the God of hosts,
the LORD is his name!*
7 You must return to your God.
Maintain loyalty and justice
and always hope in your God.

8 A merchant who holds a false balance,
he loves to extort!
9 Ephraim has said,
"How rich I have become;
I have made a fortune!"*
All his gain will not suffice
for the guilt of his sin.
10 I the LORD have been your God,
since the land of Egypt;*
I will again have you live in tents,
as on feast days.
11 I spoke to the prophets,
I granted many visions,*
and through the prophets I told parables.
12 In Gilead is falsehood, they have come to nothing;
in Gilgal they sacrifice bulls,

†

12:1–15 This chapter draws a parallel between the history of Israel and events in the life of Jacob-Israel, the ancestor.

12:1 An attack on the idolatry of both kingdoms, Israel and Judah. *Holy ones*: subordinate gods, members of the divine council.

12:2 Hosea frequently condemns the alliances with Assyria and Egypt, the two world powers (7:8–16).

12:3 *Jacob*: whose name was changed to Israel (Gn 35:10).

*

11:9 Nm 23:19; Is 31:3; Ez 28:2.
11:10 Jl 4:16; Am 1:2; Jer 25:30.
12:4 Gn 25:26; 27:35–36.
12:5 Gn 32:25–30.
12:5 Gn 28:12–19; 35:15.
12:6 Ex 3:15; Am 4:13.
12:9 Rev 3:17.
12:10 Ex 20:2.
12:11 Ps 74:9.

But their altars are like heaps of stones*
in the furrows of the field.
13 Jacob fled to the land of Aram,
and Israel served for a wife;
for a wife he tended sheep.*
14 But by a prophet† the LORD brought Israel out of Egypt,
and by a prophet Israel was tended.*
15 Ephraim has aroused bitter anger,
so his Lord shall cast his bloodguilt upon him
and repay him for his scorn.

The Death of Ephraim

13 1 When Ephraim spoke there was terror;
he was exalted in Israel;†
but he became guilty through Baal and died.

2 Now they continue to sin,
making for themselves molten images,
Silver idols according to their skill,*
all of them the work of artisans.
"To these, offer sacrifice," they say.
People kiss calves!†*
3 Therefore, they will be like a morning cloud
or like the dew that vanishes with the dawn,
Like chaff storm-driven from the threshing floor*
or like smoke out of the window.

4 I, the LORD, am your God,
since the land of Egypt;†*
Gods apart from me you do not know;
there is no savior but me.*
5 I fed you in the wilderness,
in the parched land.
6 When I fed them, they were satisfied;
when satisfied, they became proud,
therefore they forgot me.
7 So, I will be like a lion to them,
like a leopard by the road I will keep watch.
8 * I will attack them like a bear robbed of its young,
and tear their hearts from their breasts;
I will devour them on the spot like a lion,
as a wild animal would rip them open.

9† I destroy you, Israel!
who is there to help you?
10 Where now is your king,
that he may rescue you?
And all your princes,
that they may defend you?
Of whom you said,
"Give me a king and princes"?*
11 I give you a king in my anger,
and I take him away in my wrath.†

12 The guilt of Ephraim is wrapped up,
his sin is stored away.
13† The birth pangs will come for him,*
but this is an unwise child,
Who, when it is time, does not present himself
at the mouth of the womb.*
14† Shall I deliver them from the power of Sheol?
shall I redeem them from death?
Where are your plagues, O death!
where is your sting, Sheol!*
Compassion is hidden from my eyes.

15 Though Ephraim† may flourish among his brothers,
an east wind* will come, a wind from the LORD,
rising from the wilderness,
That will dry up his spring,
and leave his fountain dry.
It will loot his treasury
of every precious thing.

14 1 Samaria† has become guilty,
for she has rebelled against her God.

12:14 *A prophet*: Moses.

13:1 *Exalted in Israel*: Ephraim enjoyed a privileged position in Israel (Gn 48:14–19).

13:2 *Kiss calves*: apparently a reference to a ritual gesture associated with the worship of Baal represented as a calf (1 Kgs 19:18).

13:4 *I, the LORD . . . land of Egypt*: according to 1 Kgs 12:28, Jeroboam introduced the calves used in the worship at the sanctuaries in Bethel and Dan with the words: "Here are your gods, O Israel, who brought you up from the land of Egypt."

13:9–10 Only God can save Israel, not the king, whom Israel had requested from the Lord (1 Sm 8:1–9).

13:11 *I give you a king . . . in my wrath*: the Lord punished the people of the Northern Kingdom by giving them kings who were soon deposed (see notes on 7:3–7 and 8:4).

13:13 Ephraim will die along with its stored-up sin, just as a mother dies along with a child that she cannot deliver.

13:14 God calls upon "death" and "Sheol" to send their auxiliaries, "plagues" and "sting," to punish Israel (Hb 3:5; Ps 91:6). Paul uses this text in a different way to speak about the victory over death (1 Cor 15:54–55).

13:15 Although "Ephraim" is not explicitly mentioned in the text (the Hebrew text has the word "he"), the wordplay with the Hebrew word for "flourish" (*yaphrî*) suggests the use of "Ephraim" in the translation. *Wind*: possibly Assyria.

14:1 *Samaria*: the capital of the Northern Kingdom will fall; this is the punishment predicted for Ephraim, the Northern Kingdom.

12:12 Gn 31:45–54; Jos 4–5.
12:13 Gn 28:5; 29:15–30; 30:31.
12:14 Ex 3:7–10; Dt 18:18.
13:2 Is 40:19–20; 44:9–20.
13:2 1 Kgs 19:18.
13:3 Is 17:13; Zep 2:2; Ps 1:4.
13:4 Ex 20:2.
13:4 Is 43:11.
13:8 2 Sm 17:8.
13:10 1 Sm 8:5.
13:13 Is 26:17–18; Jer 6:24; 22:23.
13:13 Is 37:3.
13:14 1 Cor 15:55.
13:15 Ez 19:12.

They shall fall by the sword,
their infants shall be dashed to pieces,*
their pregnant women shall be ripped open.*

"Return, Israel, to the LORD, your God; you have stumbled because of your iniquity."
(Hos 14:2)

Sincere Conversion and New Life

2 Return, Israel, to the LORD, your God;
you have stumbled because of your iniquity.
3 Take with you words,
and return to the LORD;
Say to him, "Forgive all iniquity,
and take what is good.
Let us offer the fruit of our lips.*
4† Assyria will not save us,
nor will we mount horses;*
We will never again say, 'Our god,'
to the work of our hands;
for in you the orphan finds compassion."*
5 I will heal their apostasy,
I will love them freely;
for my anger is turned away from them.
6 I will be like the dew for Israel:*
he will blossom like the lily;
He will strike root like the Lebanon cedar,
7 and his shoots will go forth.*
His splendor will be like the olive tree
and his fragrance like Lebanon cedar.*
8 Again they will live in his shade;
they will raise grain,
They will blossom like the vine,
and his renown will be like the wine of Lebanon.
9 Ephraim! What more have I to do with idols?*
I have humbled him, but I will take note of him.
I am like a verdant cypress tree.†
From me fruit will be found for you!

Epilogue

10† Who is wise enough to understand these things?*
Who is intelligent enough to know them?
Straight are the paths of the LORD,*
the just walk in them,*
but sinners stumble in them.

14:4 These good intentions promise a reversal of Israel's sins: no more reliance on "Assyria," i.e., on foreign alliances (see notes on 8:9 and 12:2), on "horses," i.e., on human power (10:13), and on idolatry (8:4–6; 13:2). Israel will trust in the Lord alone.

14:9 *Verdant cypress tree*: the symbol of lasting life, the opposite of the sacred trees of the Baal cult (4:13). The Lord provides the "fruit" (*peri*) to Israel (2:7, 10), another instance of the wordplay on Ephraim (see notes on 9:16 and 13:15).

14:10 A challenge to the reader in the style of the wisdom literature.

14:1 Ps 137:9.
14:1 Am 1:13.
14:3 Heb 13:15.
14:4 Is 31:1.
14:4 Lam 5:3.
14:6 Is 26:19.
14:7 Is 27:6.
14:7 Sg 4:11.
14:9 2 Cor 6:16.
14:10 Ps 107:43; Jer 9:11; Eccl 8:1.
14:10 Dt 32:4.
14:10 Dt 8:6; 11:22; Mi 6:8.

You're just cruising along, in the groove, and everything is going your way. Then it happens. You hit a major bump in the road, and everything starts falling apart. This appears to have been the situation in Joel's time, when a major plague of locusts was causing widespread destruction. Joel took it as a wake-up sign, calling Israel to rely totally on God no matter what happened.

At a Glance

I. **Announcement of Unprecedented Disaster (1:2–20).**

II. **The Day of the Lord (2:1–27).**

III. **The Lord's Final Judgment (3:1—4:21).**

Quick Facts

Period Covered: after the rebuilding of the Temple (515 BC) and before the destruction of Sidon (343 BC)

Inspired Authors: Joel and scribes, writing around 450–400 BC

Theme: a plague of locusts as an occasion to call for Israel to repent and turn to the Lord

In Depth

The Book of Joel does not state clearly when it was written, but it gives several clues that lead biblical scholars to believe it was written after the Babylonian Exile. During this time, Israel was ruled by the Greeks and did not have a king. The Temple and Jerusalem had been rebuilt, and Israel enjoyed relative peace, along with a growing expectancy for the coming of a messiah, a savior.

In this period, a natural disaster, perhaps a plague of locusts, occurred. In the first part of the book, Joel uses this tragedy to call Israel's attention toward God and renew its faith. He compares the plague of locusts to an invading army that brings devastation to a city. Eventually, prayer and penance end the plague and bring rain for new crops. More important, the gift of the Spirit renews the people of God (see Jl 3:1–2).

A major element of this book is a warrior-type song in which Joel speaks of the coming of the day of the Lord (see 2:1–17). He describes this as the day when judgment will be delivered against the nations that have destroyed Israel. The day of the Lord is a theme that runs throughout the Bible. It is sometimes described as a joyful time of celebration (see Is 9:2), and other times as a day of punishment and destruction (see Am 5:18–27). Initially, writers of the Scriptures applied the term *day of the Lord* only to Israel; Joel applied it to all nations. Gradually, it became connected to the final judgment (see Mt 25:31–46).

The Book of Joel ends by affirming that the Lord dwells in Zion (Jerusalem) and the land will be fruitful once more. This is Joel's central message: Despite plagues and even war, God is present in Judah, and there is reason for hope.

The Book of Joel

Joel

1 [1]The word of the LORD which came to Joel, the son of Pethuel.

I. Announcement of Unprecedented Disaster

2 Listen to this, you elders!
Pay attention, all who dwell in the land!
Has anything like this ever happened in your lifetime,
or in the lifetime of your ancestors?
3 Report it to your children.
Have your children report it to their children,
and their children to the next generation.
4 What the cutter left,
the swarming locust has devoured;
What the swarming locust left,
the hopper has devoured;
What the hopper left,
the consuming locust† has devoured.
5 Wake up, you drunkards,† and weep;
wail, all you wine drinkers,
Over the new wine,
taken away from your mouths.
6 For a nation† invaded my land,
powerful and past counting,
With teeth like a lion's,
fangs like those of a lioness.
7 It has stripped bare my vines,
splintered my fig tree,
Shearing off its bark and throwing it away,
until its branches turn white.
8 Wail like a young woman† dressed in sackcloth
for the husband of her youth.
9 Grain offering and libation are cut off
from the house of the LORD;
In mourning are the priests,
the ministers of the LORD.
10 The field is devastated;
the farmland mourns,†
Because the grain is devastated,
the wine has dried up,
the oil has failed.
11 Be appalled, you farmers!
wail, you vinedressers,
Over the wheat and the barley,
because the harvest in the field is ruined.
12 The vine has dried up,
the fig tree has withered;

†

1:4 *Cutter . . . swarming locust . . . hopper . . . consuming locust*: these names may refer to various species of locusts, or to some phases in the insect's life cycle, or to successive waves of locusts ravaging the countryside.

1:5 *Drunkards*: this metaphor expresses both the urgency behind Joel's preaching and his ironic assessment of his audience. There are no grapes to process into new wine, yet people view their situation as just another agricultural crisis. Joel argues that the problems they now face are lessons the Lord is using to provide the knowledge they lack.

1:6 *A nation*: the locusts are compared to an invading army, whose numbers are overwhelming. The ravaged landscape resembles the wasteland left behind by marauding troops; the order and peace associated with agricultural productivity (1 Kgs 5:5; Mi 4:4) has been destroyed.

1:8 *Like a young woman*: this simile personifies Jerusalem as a youthful widow, left unprotected and without resources by her husband's sudden death.

1:10 *The farmland mourns*: or "the farmland is dried up."

The pomegranate, even the date palm and the
apple—
every tree in the field has dried up.
Joy itself has dried up
among the people.

Cry Out to the Lord

13† Gird yourselves and lament, you priests!
wail, ministers of the altar!
Come, spend the night in sackcloth,
ministers of my God!
For the grain offering and the libation
are withheld from the house of your God.*
14 Proclaim a holy fast!
Call an assembly!
Gather the elders,
all who dwell in the land,
To the house of the LORD, your God,
and cry out to the LORD!*
15 O! The day!†
For near is the day of the LORD,
like destruction from the Almighty it is
coming!*
16 Before our very eyes†
has not food been cut off?
And from the house of our God,
joy and gladness?
17 The seed lies shriveled beneath clods of dirt;†
the storehouses are emptied.
The granaries are broken down,
for the grain is dried up.
18† How the animals groan!
The herds of cattle are bewildered!
Because they have no pasture,
even the flocks of sheep are starving.
19 To you, LORD, I cry!
for fire has devoured the wilderness
pastures,
flame has scorched all the trees in the field.
20 Even the animals in the wild
cry out to you;
For the streams of water have run dry,
and fire has devoured the wilderness
pastures.*

II. The Day of the Lord

The Day Approaches

2 1† Blow the horn in Zion,
sound the alarm on my holy mountain!
Let all the inhabitants of the land tremble,
for the day of the LORD is coming!*
Yes, it approaches,
2 a day of darkness and gloom,
a day of thick clouds!
Like dawn† spreading over the mountains,
a vast and mighty army!
Nothing like it has ever happened in ages past,
nor will the future hold anything like it,
even to the most distant generations.*
3 Before it,† fire devours,
behind it flame scorches.
The land before it is like the garden of Eden,
and behind it, a desolate wilderness;
from it nothing escapes.*
4 Their appearance is that of horses;
like war horses they run.
5 Like the rumble of chariots
they hurtle across mountaintops;
Like the crackling of fiery flames
devouring stubble;
Like a massive army
in battle formation.*
6 Before them peoples tremble,
every face turns pale.*
7 Like warriors they run,
like soldiers they scale walls,
Each advancing in line,
without swerving from the course.
8 No one crowds the other;
each advances in its own track;
They plunge through the weapons;
they are not checked.
9 They charge the city,

---

† **1:13** Judah's situation is so grave and the day of the Lord so imminent that priests must lament day and night if they hope to reverse the divine punishment.

1:15 As in Am 5:18–20, the day of the Lord in Joel's first speech brings punishment, not victory, for Judah. In his second speech, this event means victory for those faithful to the Lord and death for the nations who are the Lord's enemies. *Almighty*: Hebrew *shaddai*. There is wordplay between *shod* ("destruction") and *shaddai*.

1:16 *Before our very eyes*: Joel's audience should have discerned the significance of the winter drought and the locust invasion they witnessed. *Joy and gladness*: the loss of field crops has reduced Joel's audience to subsistence living, with no means for liturgical or personal celebration, as in v. 12.

1:17 *The seed . . . clods of dirt*: the meaning of the Hebrew is uncertain. Most commentators use the translation given here, since it fits the prophet's description of an agricultural year plagued by winter drought and a spring locust infestation.

1:18–19 In figurative language, Joel describes how the insufficient winter rain, the locust invasions, and summer's heat on pasture lands and water sources drive domestic and wild animals to cry out for rain.

2:1–11 Joel warns the people about the destruction he sees galloping toward Jerusalem. He combines the imagery of the locust invasion (chap. 1) with language from the holy war tradition in order to describe the Lord leading a heavenly army against the enemy, in this case, Jerusalem.

2:2 *Like dawn*: from the east comes dark destruction rather than a new day's light.

2:3 *Before it*: fire precedes and follows the army's advance. Even the ravaged landscape of chap. 1 looks like a lush garden compared to the devastation this army leaves behind.

---

* **1:13** Jer 4:8.
1:14 Jl 2:15.
1:15 Is 13:6; Ez 30:2–3; Ob 15; Zep 1:7.
1:20 Ps 42:2.
2:1 Is 13:9; Jer 4:5; 6:1; 51:27; Hos 5:8; Zep 1:16.
2:2 Is 13:14; Zep 1:4–15.
2:3 Is 13:9; 51:3; Ez 36:35.
2:5 Jer 6:23.
2:6 Na 2:11.

they run upon the wall,
they climb into the houses;
Through the windows
they enter like thieves.

10 Before them the earth trembles;
the heavens shake;
Sun and moon are darkened,
and the stars withhold their brightness.*
11 The LORD raises his voice
at the head of his army;
How immense is his host!
How numerous those who carry out his command!
How great is the day of the LORD!
Utterly terrifying! Who can survive it?*

Return to the Lord

12 Yet even now—oracle of the LORD—
return to me with your whole heart,
with fasting, weeping, and mourning.
13 Rend your hearts, not your garments,
and return to the LORD, your God,
For he is gracious and merciful,
slow to anger, abounding in steadfast love,
and relenting in punishment.*
14 Perhaps he will again relent
and leave behind a blessing,†
Grain offering and libation
for the LORD, your God.*
15 Blow the horn in Zion!
Proclaim a fast,
call an assembly!*
16 Gather the people,
sanctify the congregation;
Assemble the elderly;
gather the children,
even infants nursing at the breast;
Let the bridegroom leave his room,
and the bride† her bridal tent.
17 Between the porch and the altar†
let the priests weep,
let the ministers of the LORD weep and say:
"Spare your people, LORD!
do not let your heritage become a disgrace,
a byword among the nations!
Why should they say among the peoples,
'Where is their God?' "*

The Lord Relents

18 Then the LORD grew jealous† for his land and
took pity on his people. 19 In response the LORD
said to his people:

I am sending you
grain, new wine, and oil,
and you will be satisfied by them;
Never again will I make you
a disgrace among the nations.
20 The northerner† I will remove far from you,
driving them out into a dry and desolate land,
Their vanguard to the eastern sea,
their rearguard to the western sea,
And their stench will rise,
their stink will ascend,
What great deeds the Lord has done!
21 Do not fear, O land!
delight and rejoice,
for the LORD has done great things!*
22 Do not fear, you animals in the wild,
for the wilderness pastures sprout green grass.
The trees bear fruit,
the fig tree and the vine produce their harvest.
23 Children of Zion, delight
and rejoice in the LORD, your God!
For he has faithfully given you the early rain,†
sending rain down on you,
the early and the late rains as before.*
24 The threshing floors will be full of grain,
the vats spilling over with new wine and oil.

2:14 *Blessing*: the rain that makes possible the grapes and grain (v. 19) that workers will process into Temple offerings.

2:16 *Elderly . . . infants . . . bridegroom . . . bride*: Jerusalem is in such great danger that even those normally excused from fasting or working are called upon to participate in activities to ward off the imminent catastrophe.

2:17 *Between the porch and the altar*: the priests stood in the open space between the outdoor altar for burnt offerings and the Temple building.

2:18 *Jealous*: the Hebrew word describes the passionate empathetic bond the Lord has with Israel. The people's wholehearted participation in Joel's call for fasting and prayer sparks the Lord's longing to protect and love his people Israel. This desire moves him to withhold punishment and to send the blessing of v. 14 instead.

2:20 *The northerner*: the locusts, pictured as an invading army, which traditionally came from the north (Jer 1:14–15; Ez 26:7; 38:6, 15). Locusts are not usually an annual threat in Palestine, nor are they often associated with the north. However, to demonstrate the extent of the Lord's care for Judah and control over what happens within its borders, Joel assures his audience that the Lord will quickly drive the locusts out of Judah the coming spring, should they reappear. Dead locusts will litter the shores of the "eastern" (the Dead Sea) and the "western" (the Mediterranean) seas.

2:23 This autumn rain teaches the people to recognize God's compassionate presence in nature and history. There is a play on the double meaning of the Hebrew word *moreh*: "early rain" and "teacher." In the Dead Sea Scrolls, the word is used in the phrase "teacher (= *moreh*) of righteousness."

2:10 Jl 4:15; Is 13:10, 13; Ez 32:7–8; Mt 24:29; Mk 13:24; Lk 21:25–26.
2:11 Jer 30:7; Am 5:18; Zep 1:15.
2:13 Ex 34:6; Ps 86:5; Jon 4:2.
2:14 Jon 3:9.
2:15 Jl 1:14.
2:17 Ps 42:4, 11; 79:10; 115:2.
2:21 Ps 126:3.
2:23 Hos 10:12.

Cultural Connection

Vision Quest

Joel 3:1 mentions young men having visions. Vision quests are a Native American tradition. A young man with only a blanket is led by a holy person to a hill to be on his own for several days. During that time, he refrains from eating and drinking and tries to focus on being very still, believing he will receive a personal vision. That vision will give shape to his life and help him know his place in the world. The key is in the waiting. When the young man returns from his vision quest, he is considered a man and can become the person he is destined to become. He now has a vision to live out.

Jesus went on something like a vision quest before he began his public ministry. He went into the wilderness, fasted, and wrestled with the demons.

Joel 3:1–5 is read at Pentecost—the Church feast day that celebrates the coming of the Holy Spirit. You can let the Holy Spirit help you discern the path for your life through a personal retreat, guided by a spiritual director in the Christian tradition.

Jl 3:1–5

25 I will repay you double
what the swarming locust has eaten,
The hopper, the consuming locust, and the cutter,
my great army I sent against you.*
26 You will eat until you are fully satisfied,
then you will praise the name of the LORD, your God,
Who acts so wondrously on your behalf!
My people will never again be put to shame.
27 Then you will know that I am in the midst of Israel:
I, the LORD, am your God, and there is no other;
my people will never again be put to shame.*

III. The Lord's Final Judgment

The Day of the Lord*

3 1† It shall come to pass
I will pour out my spirit upon all flesh.
Your sons and daughters will prophesy,
your old men will dream dreams,
your young men will see visions.
2 Even upon your male and female servants,
in those days, I will pour out my spirit.
3 I will set signs in the heavens and on the earth,
blood, fire, and columns of smoke;
4 The sun will darken,
the moon turn blood-red,
Before the day of the LORD arrives,
that great and terrible day.*
5 Then everyone who calls upon the name of the LORD
will escape harm.
For on Mount Zion there will be a remnant,
as the LORD has said,
And in Jerusalem survivors
whom the LORD will summon.*

The Lord's Case Against the Nations

4 1 For see, in those days and at that time,*
when I restore the fortunes
of Judah and Jerusalem,
2 I will gather all the nations
and bring them down to the Valley of Jehoshaphat.†
There I will enter into judgment with them
on behalf of my people, my heritage, Israel;
Because they scattered them among the nations,

†

3:1–5 In many places in the Old Testament, Hebrew *ruah* is God's power, or spirit, bestowed on chosen individuals. The word can also mean "breath" or "wind." In this summary introduction to his second speech, Joel anticipates that the Lord will someday renew faithful Judahites with the divine spirit. In Acts 2:17–21 the author has Peter cite Joel's words to suggest that the newly constituted Christian community, filled with divine life and power, inaugurates the Lord's Day, understood as salvation for all who believe that Jesus of Nazareth is the Christ.

4:2 *Valley of Jehoshaphat*: one of the symbolic names of the place of punishment for Judah's enemies; the other is "Valley of Decision" (v. 14). The name Jehoshaphat means "the Lord judges." If the popular identification of this place as the Kidron Valley is accurate, Joel may imagine the Lord seated above the valley on Mount Zion directing his troops in the destruction of nations in the valley below.

*

2:25 Jer 5:17.
2:27 Is 45:5–6, 18; 46:9.
3:1 Is 44:3; Ez 39:28–29; Acts 2:17–21.
3:4 Jl 2:10; Mal 3:23.
3:5 Ob 17–18; Rom 10:13.
4:1 Jer 33:15; 50:4, 20.

they divided up my land.*
3 For my people they cast lots,
trading a young boy for the price of a prostitute,
exchanging a young girl for the wine they drank.*

4 † Moreover, what are you doing to me, Tyre
and Sidon, and all the regions of Philistia? Are
you paying me back for something? If you are, I
will very quickly turn your deeds back upon your
own head.* 5 You took my silver and my gold
and brought my priceless treasures into your
temples! 6 You sold the people of Judah and Je-
rusalem to the Greeks, taking them far from their
own country! 7 Look! I am rousing them from
the place to which you sold them, and I will turn
your deeds back upon your own head. 8 I will sell
your sons and daughters to the Judahites who
will sell them to the Sabeans,† a distant nation.
The LORD has spoken!

The Nations Destroyed

9 Announce this to the nations:
Proclaim a holy war!
Alert the warriors!
Let all the soldiers
report and march!*
10† Beat your plowshares into swords,
and your pruning knives into spears;
let the weakling boast, "I am a warrior!"*

11 Hurry and come, all you neighboring peoples,
assemble there!
Bring down, LORD, your warriors!
12 Let the nations rouse themselves and come up
to the Valley of Jehoshaphat;
For there I will sit in judgment
upon all the neighboring nations.

13 Wield the sickle,*
for the harvest is ripe;
Come and tread,
for the wine press is full;
The vats overflow,
for their crimes are numerous.†
14 Crowds upon crowds
in the Valley of Decision;
For near is the day of the LORD
in the Valley of Decision.*
15 Sun and moon are darkened,
and the stars withhold their brightness,*
16 The LORD roars from Zion,
and from Jerusalem raises his voice,*
The heavens and the earth quake,
but the LORD will be a shelter for his people,
a fortress for the people of Israel.

A Secure Future for Judah

17 Then you will know† that I the LORD am your God,*
dwelling on Zion, my holy mountain;
Jerusalem will be holy,
and strangers will never again travel through her.
18† On that day
the mountains will drip new wine,
and the hills flow with milk,
All the streams of Judah
will flow with water.
A spring will rise from the house of the LORD,
watering the Valley of Shittim.*
19 Egypt will be a waste,
Edom a desolate wilderness,
Because of violence done to the Judahites,
because they shed innocent blood in their land.*
20 But Judah will be inhabited forever,
and Jerusalem for all generations.
21 I will avenge their blood,
and I will not acquit the guilt.
The LORD dwells in Zion.

†

4:4–8 This prose material may be a later addition to the book. It illustrates a common biblical theme (cf. Ps 7:16; 9:16; 35:8; 37:14–15; 57:7), having one's evil deed (selling Judahites into slavery) turned into one's own punishment (being sold into slavery by the Judahites).

4:8 *Sabeans*: traders from the southwestern tip of the Arabian peninsula, present-day Yemen (cf. 1 Kgs 10:1–2; Ps 72:10; Jer 6:20).

4:10 The Lord directs the troops to forge military weapons out of the agricultural tools necessary for life during peacetime. In Is 2:4 and Mi 4:3, both in contexts presuming the defeat of Israel's enemies, this imagery is reversed.

4:13 *Their crimes are numerous*: the nations are ripe for punishment. Joel uses the vocabulary of the autumn grape harvest to describe the assault of the Lord's army against these nations. In Is 63:1–6, grape harvest imagery also controls the description of the Lord's return from Edom with blood-spattered clothing after having trod his enemies into the ground as if they were grapes (cf. Jer 25:30).

4:17 *Then you will know*: this verse further develops the motif of knowledge introduced in 2:27. The Judahites will learn that the Lord is present in their economic prosperity and political autonomy, even though they did not associate God's presence with their crop failure.

4:18 Images of agricultural abundance illustrate the harmony and order Joel expects the Lord to establish in Judah; like 2:18–27, this section reverses the deprivation and drought of chap. 1. *A spring . . . house of the LORD*: streams of water flowing from the Temple of an ideal Jerusalem also appear in Ez 47:1. *The Valley of Shittim*: or "the ravine of the acacia trees"; while there is a Shittim east of the Jordan, the reference here is probably to that rocky part of the Kidron Valley southeast of Jerusalem, an arid region where acacia trees flourished.

*

4:2 Is 66:18; Zec 14:2.
4:3 Ob 11, 16.
4:4 Ob 15.
4:9 Jer 6:4.
4:10 Is 2:4; Mi 4:3.
4:13 Is 63:1–6; Rev 14:15.
4:14 Ob 15.
4:15 Jl 2:10; 3:4.
4:16 Jer 25:30; Am 1:2.
4:17 Ob 17; Na 2:1.
4:18 Ez 47:1–12; Am 9:13; Zec 14:8.
4:19 Ob 10.

You've probably run across people who bluntly state what they see going on. They don't seem to care too much about what other people think. They say, "I just tell it like it is." The prophet Amos was like that. He didn't pull any punches in describing the wealthy class's sins or the destruction that God had planned for Israel. He was a powerful voice calling for justice in God's plan of salvation.

The Book of Amos

At a Glance

I. Editorial Introduction (1:1–2).

II. Oracles against the Nations (1:3—2:16).

III. Threefold Summons to Hear the Word of the Lord (3:1—5:9).

IV. Three Woes (5:7—6:14).

V. Symbolic Visions (7:1—9:10).

VI. Epilogue: Restoration Under a Davidic King (9:11–15).

Quick Facts

Period Covered: from 760 to 750 BC

Inspired Authors: Compiled by Amos or his disciples

Theme: God's destruction of Israel because of the injustice and hypocrisy of the wealthy and the ruling class

In Depth

Amos lived when there were two separate kingdoms of Israelites: a northern kingdom, named Israel, and a southern kingdom, named Judah. He was born in the southern kingdom and worked as a shepherd and tree trimmer (see Am 7:14). But God called him to preach to the northern kingdom. Amos was not an official prophet of the king's court, so he was free to speak against the king and the court and to be brutally honest in delivering God's message.

Among the Old Testament prophecies, Amos's are the least hopeful. Amos stresses that Israel's destruction, complete and total, is certain. He condemns Israel for its failure to be faithful to the covenant, but he has a special anger toward the king, the priests, and the wealthy class. He accuses them of being hypocrites who lead the people of Israel astray while pretending to be faithful themselves.

What was Amos's evidence? First, the covenant demanded special care for the poor, the outcast, and the marginalized. The king, the wealthy, and some of the priests were ignoring this demand. Instead of caring for the poor and the lowly, the wealthy were cheating them and treating them unjustly (see 2:6–8).

Second, with the monies they cheated out of the poor, the ruling class and the wealthy staged lavish ceremonies to God that were modeled on ceremonies honoring foreign gods. They went through the motions of worshiping God, but they ignored the demand to care for their neighbor (see 5:21–24). For Amos, this was the heart of Israel's hypocrisy—its sinful habit of separating its religious rituals from concern for its citizens. This phoniness was repulsive to God, and because of Israel's sin, God would bring it to destruction. Amos is rightly called the prophet of the Lord's justice.

Amos

I. Editorial Introduction

1 [1]The words of Amos, who was one of the sheepbreeders from Tekoa,* which he received in a vision concerning Israel in the days of Uzziah, king of Judah, and in the days of Jeroboam, son of Joash, king of Israel, two years before the earthquake.† [2]He said:

The LORD roars from Zion,†
and raises his voice from Jerusalem;
The pastures of the shepherds languish,
and the summit of Carmel withers.*

II. Oracles Against the Nations†

Aram

[3]Thus says the LORD:

For three crimes of Damascus, and now four—†
I will not take it back—
Because they threshed Gilead
with sledges of iron,
4 I will send fire upon the house of Hazael,
and it will devour the strongholds of
Ben-hadad.† *
5 I will break the barred gate of Damascus;
From the Valley of Aven† I will cut off the
one enthroned,
And the sceptered ruler from Beth-eden;
the people of Aram shall be exiled to Kir,*
says the LORD.

Philistia

[6]Thus says the LORD:

For three crimes of Gaza, and now four—
I will not take it back—
Because they exiled an entire population,
handing them over to Edom,
7 I will send fire upon the wall of Gaza,
and it will devour its strongholds;

†

1:1 *The earthquake*: a major earthquake during the reign of Uzziah (ca. 783–742 B.C.), so devastating that it was remembered long afterwards (cf. Zec 14:5). See the description of an earthquake in Amos's final vision (9:1).

1:2 Significantly, the roar comes to the Northern Kingdom from Jerusalem. This verse, perhaps an editorial remark, sets the tone of Amos's message.

1:3–2:16 All the nations mentioned here may have been part of the ideal empire of David-Solomon (cf. 1 Kgs 5:1; 2 Kgs 14:25). Certain standards of conduct were expected not only in their relations with Israel but also with one another.

1:3 *For three crimes . . . and now four*: this formula (N, N+1) is frequent in poetry (e.g., Prv 6:16–19; 30:18–19). The progression "three" followed by "four" here suggests a climax. The fourth crime is one too many and exhausts the Lord's forbearance.

1:4 *Hazael . . . Ben-hadad*: kings of the Arameans whose capital was Damascus (v. 5); they fought against Israel (2 Kgs 13:3) and had long occupied the region of Gilead (v. 3) in Transjordan.

1:5 *Valley of Aven*: lit., "valley of wickedness," perhaps a distortion of a place name in Aramean territory, identity unknown. *Beth-eden*: an Aramean city-state on the Euphrates, about two hundred miles northeast of Damascus, called *Bit-adini* in Assyro-Babylonian texts. *Kir*: cf. 9:7; probably to be identified with the city of Emar on the Euphrates, a major Aramean center in the Late Bronze Age. One text from this site calls the king of Emar "the king of the people of the land of Kir."

*

1:1 Zec 14:5.
1:2 Jer 25:30; Jl 4:16.
1:4 2 Kgs 13:3–7; Hos 8:14.
1:5 2 Kgs 16:9.

8 From Ashdod I will cut off the one enthroned
and the sceptered ruler from Ashkelon;
I will turn my hand against Ekron,
and the last of the Philistines shall perish,
says the Lord GOD.

Tyre

9 Thus says the LORD:

For three crimes of Tyre, and now four—
I will not take it back—
Because they handed over an entire
population to Edom,
and did not remember their covenant of
brotherhood,†
10 I will send fire upon the wall of Tyre,
and it will devour its strongholds.

Edom

11 Thus says the LORD:

For three crimes of Edom, and now four—
I will not take it back—
Because he pursued his brother† with the
sword,
suppressing all pity,
Persisting in his anger,
his wrath raging without end,
12 I will send fire upon Teman,
and it will devour the strongholds of Bozrah.†

Ammon

13 Thus says the LORD:

For three crimes of the Ammonites, and now
four—
I will not take it back—
Because they ripped open pregnant women in
Gilead,*
in order to extend their territory,
14 I will kindle a fire upon the wall of Rabbah,†
and it will devour its strongholds
Amid war cries on the day of battle,
amid stormwind on the day of tempest.
15 Their king shall go into exile,
he and his princes with him, says the LORD.

Moab

2 1 Thus says the LORD:

For three crimes of Moab, and now four—
I will not take it back—
Because he burned to ashes†
the bones of Edom's king,
2 I will send fire upon Moab,
and it will devour the strongholds of Kerioth;
Moab shall meet death amid uproar,
battle cries and blasts of the ram's horn.
3 I will cut off the ruler from its midst,
and all the princes I will slay with him, says
the LORD.

Judah

4 † Thus says the LORD:

For three crimes of Judah, and now four—
I will not take it back—
Because they spurned the instruction of the
LORD,*
and did not keep his statutes;
Because the lies† which their ancestors followed
have led them astray,
5 I will send fire upon Judah,
and it will devour the strongholds of
Jerusalem.

Israel

6 Thus says the LORD:

For three crimes of Israel,† and now four—
I will not take it back—
Because they hand over the just for silver,
and the poor for a pair of sandals;*
7 They trample the heads of the destitute
into the dust of the earth,
and force the lowly out of the way.
Son and father sleep with the same girl,†
profaning my holy name.

†

1:9 *Did not remember their covenant of brotherhood*: standard diplomatic language of this period, meaning "violated the treaty." The violation may not have been against Israel itself but against a fellow "subject" nation of the ideal Davidic-Solomonic empire (cf. 2:1).

1:11 *Pursued his brother*: "brother" here may denote a fellow vassal or subject of Israel.

1:12 *Teman . . . Bozrah*: two of the chief cities of Edom; cf. Jer 49:20.

1:14 *Rabbah*: now called Amman, the modern capital of Jordan.

2:1 *He burned to ashes*: to the peoples of the Near East, burning the bones of the dead was a particularly heinous crime, as it was believed to cause the spirits of these dead to wander without any hope of interment in their graves, where they could rest in peace.

2:4–8, 12 Unlike the crimes of the nations detailed in this section, which are wrongs against other nations, those of Judah and Israel named here are violations of the Lord's demands.

2:4 *The lies*: false gods worshiped by the Judahites.

2:6 *Israel*: Amos's audience would applaud his condemnation of foreign kingdoms in the foregoing seven oracles, especially of Judah. But now he adds an eighth, unexpected oracle—against Israel itself. This is the real "punch line" of this whole section, to which the preceding oracles serve mainly as introduction.

2:7 *Son and father sleep with the same girl*: the crime condemned here may be the misuse of power by the rich who take unfair advantage of young women from the ranks of the poor and force themselves on them, thus adding oppression to the sin of impurity.

1:13 2 Kgs 8:12; 15:16. **2:6** Am 8:6; Sir 46:19.
2:4 Is 5:24.

8 Upon garments taken in pledge
they recline beside any altar.†*
Wine at treasury expense
they drink in their temples.
9 Yet it was I who destroyed the Amorites
before them,
who were as tall as cedars,
and as strong as oak trees.
I destroyed their fruit above
and their roots beneath.*
10 It was I who brought you up from the land of
Egypt,
and who led you through the desert for
forty years,
to occupy the land of the Amorites;
11 I who raised up prophets among your children,
and nazirites† among your young men.
Is this not so, Israelites?—
oracle of the LORD.
12 But you made the nazirites drink wine,
and commanded the prophets, "Do not
prophesy!"*
13 Look, I am groaning beneath you,
as a wagon groans when laden with sheaves.
14 Flight shall elude the swift,
and the strong shall not retain strength;*
The warrior shall not save his life,
15 nor shall the archer stand his ground;
The swift of foot shall not escape,
nor shall the horseman save his life.
16 And the most stouthearted of warriors
shall flee naked on that day—
oracle of the LORD.

III. Threefold Summons to Hear the Word of the Lord

First Summons

3 1 Hear this word, Israelites, that the LORD
speaks concerning you,
concerning the whole family I brought up
from the land of Egypt:
2 You alone I have known,†
among all the families of the earth;*
Therefore I will punish you
for all your iniquities.
3† Do two journey together
unless they have agreed?
4 Does a lion roar in the forest
when it has no prey?
Does a young lion cry out from its den
unless it has seized something?
5 Does a bird swoop down on a trap on the
ground
when there is no lure for it?
Does a snare spring up from the ground
without catching anything?
6 Does the ram's horn sound in a city
without the people becoming frightened?
Does disaster befall a city
unless the LORD has caused it?*

7 (Indeed, the Lord GOD does nothing without re-
vealing his plan to his servants the prophets.)

8 The lion has roared,
who would not fear?*
The Lord GOD has spoken,
who would not prophesy?

9 Proclaim this in the strongholds of Assyria,†
in the strongholds of the land of Egypt:
"Gather on the mount of Samaria,
and see the great disorders within it,
the oppressions within its midst."†
10 They do not know how to do what is right—
oracle of the LORD—
Storing up in their strongholds
violence and destruction.
11 Therefore thus says the Lord GOD:
An enemy shall surround the land,
tear down your fortresses,
and pillage your strongholds.
12 Thus says the LORD:
As the shepherd rescues from the mouth of
the lion
a pair of sheep's legs or the tip of an ear,

†

2:8 *Upon garments . . . any altar*: creditors kept the garments taken as pledges from the poor instead of returning them to their owners before nightfall as the law commanded (Ex 22:25; cf. Dt 24:12). *Wine . . . in their temples*: lavish feasts for the rich, serving the finest wines in great abundance (see 6:4–7) and funded by the treasuries of local temples (e.g., at Dan and Bethel). The Hebrew in this verse is difficult. Another possible translation would be: "And the wine of those who have been fined / they drink in the house of their god."

2:11 *Nazirites*: see note on Nm 6:2–21. *Oracle of the LORD*: a phrase used extensively in prophetic books to indicate divine speech.

3:2 *You alone I have known*: precisely because Israel enjoyed a special status among the nations of the world in the eyes of the Lord (but see 9:7) it was called to a high degree of fidelity to God. Because Israel has failed in this expectation, it must experience God's punishment.

3:3–8 The metaphors in these sayings illustrate the principle of cause and effect, and lead up to the conclusion in v. 8.

3:9 *Assyria*: following the Greek version, the Hebrew text has "Ashod." It is supposed that this was a copyist's error: "Assyria" seems intended, in order to parallel "Egypt" in the next line.

3:9 With a keen sense of irony, Amos invites the most powerful oppressors in Israel's memory, past and present—Egypt and Assyria—to see and marvel at the great oppression and injustice being wrought within Samaria by the people of Israel.

*

2:8 Dt 24:12–13.
2:9 Nm 21:21–32; Dt 2:24–37; Jb 18:16; Hos 9:16.
2:12 Am 7:13; Nm 6:1–4; Is 30:10; Jer 11:21.
2:14 Ps 33:16.
3:2 Gn 18:19; Dt 7:6.
3:6 Jl 2:1.
3:8 Am 1:2.

So shall the Israelites escape,
those who dwell in Samaria,
With the corner of a couch
or a piece of a cot.†
13 Hear and bear witness against the house of Jacob—
an oracle of the Lord GOD, the God of hosts:
14 On the day when I punish Israel for its crimes,
I will also punish the altars of Bethel;
The horns of the altar shall be broken off
and fall to the ground.†*
15 I will strike the winter house
and the summer house;
The houses of ivory shall lie in ruin,
and their many rooms shall be no more—
oracle of the LORD.

Second Summons

4 1 Hear this word, you cows of Bashan,†
who live on the mount of Samaria:
Who oppress the destitute
and abuse the needy;
Who say to your husbands,
"Bring us a drink!"
2 The Lord GOD has sworn by his holiness:
Truly days are coming upon you
when they shall drag you away with ropes,
your children with fishhooks;
3 You shall go out through the breached walls
one in front of the other,
And you shall be exiled to Harmon—†
oracle of the LORD.
4 Come to Bethel† and sin,
to Gilgal and sin all the more!
Each morning bring your sacrifices,
every third day your tithes;
5 Burn leavened bread as a thanksgiving sacrifice,
proclaim publicly your voluntary offerings,
For so you love to do, Israelites—
oracle of the Lord GOD.
6 Though I made your teeth
clean of food in all your cities,
and made bread scarce in all your dwellings,
Yet you did not return to me—
oracle of the LORD.*

Did You Know?

AM

The Remnant

Does Amos feel that Israel is so corrupt that God will destroy it entirely? Apparently not, because he refers in several places to a tiny portion that will be saved (see Am 3:12). The idea that God will save a remnant—a small part—of the Jewish people gets picked up by others who prophesy after Amos (see Is 10:20–22, Jer 23:3, Mi 5:7–8, Zep 3:12).

The remnant that will be saved becomes an important biblical symbol of God's plan not to let Israel be completely destroyed. It will be known as a holy group because of its faith, repentance, purification, and willingness to be God's servant.

► Am 3:12

7 * And I withheld the rain from you
when the harvest was still three months away;
I sent rain upon one city
but not upon another;
One field was watered by rain,
but the one I did not water dried up;
8 Two or three cities staggered to another to drink water
but were not satisfied;
Yet you did not return to me—
oracle of the LORD.
9 I struck you with blight and mildew;
locusts devoured your gardens and vineyards,
the caterpillar consumed your fig trees and olive trees;
Yet you did not return to me—
oracle of the LORD.*
10 I sent upon you pestilence like that of Egypt;*
with the sword I killed your young men
and your captured horses,
and to your nostrils I brought the stench of your camps;

†

3:12 The "escape" is clearly a disaster, not a deliverance.

3:14 On Bethel, see also 4:4; 5:5–6; and 7:13. The prophet is condemning the religiosity and formalism of the worship by Israel's leaders.

4:1 *Cows of Bashan*: the pampered women of Samaria; Bashan was a region east of the Sea of Galilee, famous for its rich pasture and fattened herds.

4:3 *Harmon*: or perhaps "Mount Mon"; an unidentified site, probably far to the north of Israel, under the control of Assyria.

4:4 *Come to Bethel*: Amos's invitation to the people to come and "sin" at two of the major religious centers in Samaria is sarcastic. His point is that sacrifice and worship without justice is an abomination to the God of Israel; cf. 5:21–24.

3:14 Am 9:1; 1 Kgs 13:1–5.
4:6 Wis 12:2, 10.
4:7 Jer 14:1–6.
4:9 Dt 28:22; Jl 1:4; 2:25; Hg 2:17.
4:10 Dt 7:15; 28:27.

Pray It!

Prayer That Does Justice

In Amos 5:21–24, Amos again has harsh words, this time for the people who attend lavish religious ceremonies but don't practice justice in their life. To God and the prophets, justice is about living in right relationship with our fellow brothers and sisters, making sure that the dignity of all is protected and that the basic needs of all are met. Without a commitment to justice, the people's festivals, assemblies, and offerings will remain meaningless noise to God.

Amos's harsh words challenge us too. What does it mean to act justly as a teenager in today's world? Think about how you treat other people, especially people who are in need. How are you responding to these needs? Have you ever been wasteful, or consumed too much while others go in need of basic resources? What changes can you make in your life in order to live more justly? Pray today for all those who suffer from injustice in our world, and for the courage to personally respond by acting more justly in your own life.

▶ **Am 5:21–24**

Yet you did not return to me—
oracle of the LORD.
11 I overthrew you
as when God overthrew Sodom and Gomorrah;
you were like a brand plucked from the fire,*
Yet you did not return to me—
oracle of the LORD.
12 Therefore thus I will do to you,† Israel:
and since I will deal thus with you,
prepare to meet your God, O Israel!
13 The one who forms mountains and creates winds,
and declares to mortals their thoughts;
Who makes dawn into darkness
and strides upon the heights of the earth,
the LORD, the God of hosts, is his name!

Third Summons†

5 1 Hear this word which I utter concerning you,
this dirge, house of Israel:
2 She is fallen, to rise no more,
virgin Israel;
She lies abandoned on her land,
with no one to raise her up.*
3 For thus says the Lord GOD
to the house of Israel:
The city that marched out with a thousand
shall be left with a hundred,
Another that marched out with a hundred
shall be left with ten.
4 For thus says the LORD†
to the house of Israel:
Seek me, that you may live,*
5 but do not seek Bethel;
Do not come to Gilgal,
and do not cross over to Beer-sheba;
For Gilgal shall be led into exile
and Bethel shall be no more.
6† Seek the LORD, that you may live,
lest he flare up against the house of Joseph† like a fire
that shall consume the house of Israel, with no one to quench it.
8 The one who made the Pleiades and Orion,
who turns darkness into dawn,
and darkens day into night;
Who summons the waters of the sea,
and pours them out on the surface of the earth;*
9 Who makes destruction fall suddenly upon the stronghold
and brings ruin upon the fortress,
the LORD is his name.

† **4:12** *Therefore thus I will do to you*: this climax of vv. 6–12, announcing the sentence the Lord intends to pass on Israel, is open-ended.

5:1–17 These verses form a chiastic section beginning and ending with a lament over Israel (vv. 2, 16–17) and containing a double appeal to "seek" the Lord (vv. 4, 14). This editorial arrangement gives the whole section a negative cast, in effect nullifying the only hopeful verse in Amos (v. 15). Israel is as good as dead.

5:4–5 *For thus says the LORD . . . Bethel shall be no more*: these two verses continue the sarcasm of 4:4–5, verses in which Amos invites the people to come and "sin" at Bethel and Gilgal. The cult cities of Samaria should have been places where God could be "sought" but, because of the sins of the Northern Kingdom, these cities would cease to exist.

5:6 These verses have been rearranged to achieve the proper sequence according to the best possible manuscript tradition. Cf. the Textual Notes accompanying the translation.

5:6 *House of Joseph*: the kingdom of Israel or Northern Kingdom, the chief tribes of which were descended from Ephraim and Manasseh, the sons of Joseph; cf. 5:15; 6:6.

* **4:11** Gn 19:24–25; Zec 3:2. **5:2** Am 8:13. **5:4** Hos 5:6; 10:12. **5:8** Am 9:6; Jb 9:9; 38:31.

AM

IV. Three Woes

First Woe

7 Woe to those who turn justice into wormwood
and cast righteousness to the ground,
10 They hate those who reprove at the gate
and abhor those who speak with integrity;
11 Therefore, because you tax the destitute
and exact from them levies of grain,
Though you have built houses of hewn stone,
you shall not live in them;
Though you have planted choice vineyards,
you shall not drink their wine.*
12 Yes, I know how many are your crimes,
how grievous your sins:
Oppressing the just, accepting bribes,
turning away the needy at the gate.
13 (Therefore at this time the wise are struck dumb
for it is an evil time.)

14 Seek good and not evil,
that you may live;
Then truly the LORD, the God of hosts,
will be with you as you claim.
15 Hate evil and love good,
and let justice prevail at the gate;
Then it may be that the LORD, the God of hosts,
will have pity on the remnant of Joseph.*

16 Therefore, thus says the LORD,
the God of hosts, the Lord:
In every square there shall be lamentation,
and in every street they shall cry, "Oh, no!"
They shall summon the farmers to wail
and the professional mourners to lament.
17 And in every vineyard there shall be
lamentation
when I pass through your midst, says the
LORD.

Second Woe

18 Woe to those who yearn
for the day of the LORD!†
What will the day of the LORD mean for you?
It will be darkness, not light!*
19 As if someone fled from a lion
and a bear met him;
Or as if on entering the house
he rested his hand against the wall,
and a snake bit it.
20 Truly, the day of the LORD will be darkness,
not light,
gloom without any brightness!

21† * I hate, I despise your feasts,
I take no pleasure in your solemnities.
22 Even though you bring me your burnt
offerings and grain offerings
I will not accept them;
Your stall-fed communion offerings,
I will not look upon them.
23 Take away from me
your noisy songs;
The melodies of your harps,
I will not listen to them.

"Rather let justice surge like waters, and righteousness like an unfailing stream."
(Am 5:24)

24 Rather let justice surge like waters,
and righteousness like an unfailing
stream.
25 * Did you bring me sacrifices and grain
offerings
for forty years in the desert, O house of
Israel?*
26 Yet you will carry away Sukuth,† your king,
and Kaiwan, your star-image,
your gods that you have made for
yourselves,*

† **5:18** *The day of the LORD*: first mentioned in Amos, this refers to a specific time in the future, known to the Lord alone, when God's enemies would be decisively defeated. The common assumption among Israelites was that the Lord's foes and Israel's foes were one and the same. But Amos makes it clear that because the people have become God's enemies by refusing to heed the prophetic word, they too would experience the divine wrath on that fateful day. However, during the exile this expression comes to mean a time when God would avenge Israel against its oppressors and bring about its restoration (Jer 50:27; Ez 30:3–5).

5:21–27 The prophet does not condemn cultic activity as such but rather the people's attempt to offer worship with hands unclean from oppression of their fellow Israelites (cf. Ps 15:2–5; 24:3–4). But worship from those who disregard justice and righteousness (v. 24) is never acceptable to the God of Israel. Through the Sinai covenant the love of God and the love of neighbor are inextricably bound together.

5:26 *Sukuth*: probably a hebraized form of Assyro-Babylonian *Shukudu* ("the Arrow"), a name of Sirius, the brightest star in the night sky. It was associated with the god Ninurta, who was widely worshiped in Mesopotamia. According to 2 Kgs 17:30 the cult of Sirius was introduced into Samaria by deportees from Babylonia. *Kaiwan:* a hebraized form of an Akkadian name for the planet Saturn, also worshiped as a deity in Mesopotamia.

* **5:11** Am 9:14; Dt 28:30; Zep 1:13. **5:15** Jl 2:14; Rom 12:9. **5:18** Jer 14:16; Jl 2:1–2, 11; Zep 1:14–18. **5:21–24** Is 1:10–17; Jer 6:20. **5:25–26** Acts 7:42–43. **5:25** Jer 7:21–26. **5:26** 2 Kgs 17:30; Jer 2:28.

27 As I exile you beyond Damascus,
says the LORD,
whose name is the God of hosts.

Third Woe

6 1 Woe to those who are complacent in Zion,
secure on the mount of Samaria,
Leaders of the first among nations,
to whom the people of Israel turn.
2 Pass over to Calneh and see,
go from there to Hamath the great,
and down to Gath† of the Philistines.
Are you better than these kingdoms,
or is your territory greater than theirs?
3 You who would put off the day of disaster,
yet hasten the time of violence!
4 Those who lie on beds of ivory,
and lounge upon their couches;
Eating lambs taken from the flock,
and calves from the stall;
5 Who improvise to the music of the harp,
composing on musical instruments like
David,
6 Who drink wine from bowls,
and anoint themselves with the best oils,
but are not made ill by the collapse of
Joseph;
7 Therefore, now they shall be the first to go
into exile,
and the carousing of those who lounged
shall cease.

8 The Lord GOD has sworn by his very self—
an oracle of the LORD, the God of hosts:
I abhor the pride of Jacob,
I hate his strongholds,
and I will hand over the city with
everything in it;*
9 Should there remain ten people
in a single house, these shall die.
10 When a relative or one who prepares the body
picks up the remains
to carry them out of the house,
If he says to someone in the recesses of the
house,
"Is anyone with you?" and the answer is,
"No one,"
Then he shall say, "Silence!"
for no one must mention the name of the
LORD.†*
11 Indeed, the LORD has given the command
to shatter the great house to bits,
and reduce the small house to rubble.
12 Can horses run over rock,
or can one plow the sea with oxen?
Yet you have turned justice into gall,
and the fruit of righteousness into
wormwood,*
13 You who rejoice in Lodebar,
and say, "Have we not, by our own strength,
seized Karnaim† for ourselves?"
14 Look, I am raising up against you, house of
Israel—
oracle of the LORD, the God of hosts—
A nation† that shall oppress you
from Lebo-hamath even to the Wadi
Arabah.

V. Symbolic Visions

First Vision: The Locust Swarm

7 1 This is what the Lord GOD showed me: He
was forming a locust swarm when the late
growth began to come up (the late growth after
the king's mowing†). 2 When they had finished
eating the grass in the land, I said:

Forgive, O Lord GOD!
Who will raise up Jacob?
He is so small!

3 The LORD relented concerning this. "This shall
not be," said the Lord GOD.

Second Vision: The Rain of Fire

4 This is what the Lord GOD showed me: He
was summoning a rain of fire. It had devoured
the great abyss and was consuming the fields.
5 Then I said:

Cease, O Lord GOD!
Who will raise up Jacob?
He is so small!

6 The LORD relented concerning this. "This also
shall not be," said the Lord GOD.

---

† **6:2** *Calneh . . . Hamath . . . Gath*: city-states overcome by the Assyrians in the eighth century B.C., whose fate should be a lesson to the Israelites. The prophet castigates the leaders for being more intent on pursuing a luxurious lifestyle (vv. 1, 4–6) than reading the signs of the times.

6:10 In this desperate situation there seems to be a profound fear of the Lord, who is the cause of the deaths (cf. 3:6).

6:13 *Lodebar . . . Karnaim*: two towns recaptured from Judah by Israelite forces during the reign of Jeroboam II (see 2 Kgs 14:25). Some mockery of at least the first of these victories is probably intended by the prophet here, as Lodebar can be translated "nothing."

6:14 *A nation*: Assyria. *Lebo-hamath . . . Wadi Arabah*: the territorial limits of Solomon's kingdom, north and south respectively, as re-established by Jeroboam II (see 2 Kgs 14:25).

7:1 *The king's mowing*: the first harvesting of the crops apparently belonged to the king as a kind of tax.

6:8 Is 28:1–4; Jer 51:14.
6:10 Zep 1:7.
6:12 Am 5:7.

Third Vision: The Plummet

7 * This is what the Lord GOD showed me: He
was standing, plummet in hand, by a wall built
with a plummet.† 8 The Lord GOD asked me,
"What do you see, Amos?" And I answered, "A
plummet." Then the LORD said:

See, I am laying the plummet
in the midst of my people Israel;
I will forgive them no longer.
9 The high places of Isaac shall be laid waste,
and the sanctuaries of Israel made desolate;
and I will attack the house of Jeroboam
with the sword.

Biographical Interlude: Amos and Amaziah

10 Amaziah, the priest of Bethel, sent word to
Jeroboam, king of Israel: "Amos has conspired
against you within the house of Israel; the coun-
try cannot endure all his words. 11 For this is what
Amos says:

'Jeroboam shall die by the sword,
and Israel shall surely be exiled from its
land.'"

12 To Amos, Amaziah said: "Off with you, seer,
flee to the land of Judah and there earn your
bread by prophesying! 13 But never again proph-
esy in Bethel;* for it is the king's sanctuary and a
royal temple." 14 Amos answered Amaziah, "I am
not a prophet,† nor do I belong to a company
of prophets. I am a herdsman and a dresser of
sycamores,* 15 but the LORD took me from fol-
lowing the flock, and the LORD said to me, 'Go,
prophesy to my people Israel.'* 16 Now hear the
word of the LORD:

You say: 'Do not prophesy against Israel,
do not preach against the house of Isaac.'
17 Therefore thus says the LORD:
Your wife shall become a prostitute in the
city,
and your sons and daughters shall fall by
the sword.
Your land shall be parcelled out by measuring
line,
and you yourself shall die in an unclean
land;
and Israel shall be exiled from its land."

Fourth Vision: The Summer Fruit

8 1 This is what the Lord GOD showed me: a
basket of end-of-summer fruit.† 2 He asked,
"What do you see, Amos?" And I answered, "A
basket of end-of-summer fruit." And the LORD
said to me:

The end has come for my people Israel;
I will forgive them no longer.
3 The temple singers will wail on that day—
oracle of the Lord GOD.
Many shall be the corpses,
strewn everywhere—Silence!*

4 Hear this, you who trample upon the needy
and destroy the poor of the land:
5 "When will the new moon be over," you ask,
"that we may sell our grain,
And the sabbath,
that we may open the grain-bins?
We will diminish the ephah,†
add to the shekel,
and fix our scales for cheating!*
6 We will buy the destitute for silver,
and the poor for a pair of sandals;*
even the worthless grain we will sell!"
7 The LORD has sworn by the pride of Jacob:
Never will I forget a thing they have done!
8 Shall not the land tremble because of this,
and all who dwell in it mourn?
It will all rise up and toss like the Nile,
and subside like the river of Egypt.*
9 On that day—oracle of the Lord GOD—
I will make the sun set at midday
and in broad daylight cover the land with
darkness.
10 I will turn your feasts into mourning
and all your songs into dirges.
I will cover the loins of all with sackcloth
and make every head bald.

†

7:7 *A plummet*: with this vision, the pleas of the prophet (vv. 1–6) disappear, and disaster is announced. One use of the plummet in ancient times was to see how far out of line a wall or building had become, to determine whether it could be repaired or would have to be torn down. Like a structure that had become architecturally unsound, Israel was unsalvageable and would have to be demolished (cf. 2 Kgs 21:13; Is 34:11; Lam 2:8).

7:14 *I am not a prophet*: Amos reacts strongly to Amaziah's attempt to classify him as a "prophet-for-hire" who "earns [his] bread" by giving oracles in exchange for payment (cf. 1 Sm 9:3–10; Mi 3:5). To disassociate himself from this kind of "professional" prophet, Amos rejects outright the title of *nabi'* ("prophet"). By profession he is a herdsman/sheepbreeder and a dresser of sycamore trees, but God's call has commissioned him to prophesy to Israel.

8:1–2 *End-of-summer fruit . . . the end has come*: the English translation attempts to capture the wordplay of the Hebrew. The Hebrew word for "fruit picked late in the season" is *qayis*, while the word for "end" is *qes*.

8:5 *Ephah*: see note on Is 5:10.

*

7:7–8 Jer 1:11–14.
7:13 Am 2:12.
7:14 Am 1:1; 2 Sm 7:8.
7:15 Am 3:8.
8:3 Am 6:10.
8:5 Dt 25:13; Hos 12:8.
8:6 Am 2:6.
8:8 Am 1:1; 9:1, 5.

AM

Catholic Social Teaching

Stand Up and Be Counted!

In a small-town newspaper's opinion page, a reader complains about homeless people on the streets of his town. The reader writes: "These people are ruining our quality of life. They should get a job and get off our streets! Stand up and be counted and do not let this happen anymore in our town!"

Amos would have had a harsh reply for the author of that letter. Read 8:4–10 for his words condemning the people of his time who had no care or thought for the poor. Amos says that the more we choose to think of ourselves, rather than those who are needy, the closer we come to our own destruction. Jesus later echoes Amos in teaching that God's Reign of peace and justice will come through our efforts to support the weaker and less fortunate people in our world (see "Jesus' Preference for the Poor" near Lk 6:17–49). It is our responsibility as Christians to care for and protect those who are most in need in our world.

Let's be examples of God's care for those who are poor, until all opinion-page letters read: "Stand up and be counted! Let's work to end poverty and until then welcome the people who are poor among us!"

Am 8:4–10

Option for the Poor and Vulnerable

I will make it like the time of mourning for
an only child,
and its outcome like a day of bitter
weeping.*

11 See, days are coming—oracle of the Lord God—
when I will send a famine upon the land:
Not a hunger for bread, or a thirst for water,
but for hearing the word of the Lord.
12 They shall stagger from sea to sea
and wander from north to east
In search of the word of the Lord,
but they shall not find it.*

13 On that day, beautiful young women and
young men
shall faint from thirst,
14 Those who swear by Ashima of Samaria,†*
and who say, "By the life of your god,
O Dan,"
"By the life of the Power of Beer-sheba!"
They shall fall, never to rise again.

Fifth Vision: The Destruction of the Sanctuary

9 1 I saw the Lord standing beside the altar.
And he said:

Strike the capitals
so that the threshold shakes!
Break them off on the heads of them all!
Those who are left I will slay with the sword.
Not one shall get away,
no survivor shall escape.†*
2 Though they dig down to Sheol,
even from there my hand shall take them;
Though they climb to the heavens,
even from there I shall bring them down.*
3 Though they hide on the summit of Carmel,
there too I will hunt them down and take
them;
Though they hide from my gaze at the bottom
of the sea,
there I will command the serpent† to bite
them.*

† **8:14** *Ashima of Samaria*: a high-ranking goddess worshiped in Hamath, whose cult was transplanted by the people of that city when they were deported to Samaria by the Assyrians (2 Kgs 17:30). *The Power of Beer-sheba*: possibly an epithet of a deity worshiped in Beer-sheba, either a syncretistic form of the worship of Israel's God or of another god. *Dan . . . Beer-sheba*: the traditional designation for the northern and southern limits of Israel to which the Israelites made pilgrimages.

9:1 This vision may describe the destruction of the temple at Bethel and the fulfillment of the oracle in 3:14, linking God's judgment upon Israel with the "punishment" of the altars of Bethel. This dramatic event (perhaps to be identified with the earthquake mentioned in 1:1) symbolizes the end of the Northern Kingdom as the Lord's people, the consequence of their steadfast refusal to heed the prophetic word and return to the God of Israel.

9:3 *The serpent*: a name for the primeval chaos monster, vanquished by God at the time of creation but not annihilated. He was a personification of the sea, another primary archetype of chaos in the ancient Near East.

* **8:10** Tb 2:6; Zec 12:10.
8:12 Hos 5:6.
8:14 2 Kgs 17:30.
9:1 Am 2:13–16.
9:2 Ps 139:7–12; Jb 20:6.
9:3 Jb 7:12; Is 27:1.

4 Though they go into captivity before their
enemies,
there I will command the sword to slay
them.
I will fix my gaze upon them
for evil and not for good.

5 The Lord GOD of hosts,
Who melts the earth with his touch,
so that all who dwell on it mourn,
So that it will all rise up like the Nile,
and subside like the river of Egypt;*
6 Who has built his upper chamber in heaven,
and established his vault over the earth;
Who summons the waters of the sea
and pours them upon the surface of the
earth—
the LORD is his name.*

7 Are you not like the Ethiopians to me,
O Israelites?—oracle of the LORD—
Did I not bring the Israelites from the land of
Egypt
as I brought the Philistines from Caphtor
and the Arameans† from Kir?
8 See, the eyes of the Lord GOD are on this
sinful kingdom,
and I will destroy it from the face of the
earth—
But I will not destroy the house of Jacob
completely—
oracle of the LORD.
9 For see, I have given the command
to sift the house of Israel among all the
nations,
As one sifts with a sieve,
letting no pebble fall to the ground.
10 All sinners among my people shall die by the
sword,
those who say, "Disaster will not reach or
overtake us."*

VI. Epilogue: Restoration Under a Davidic King

11† On that day I will raise up
the fallen hut of David;
I will wall up its breaches,
raise up its ruins,
and rebuild it as in the days of old,*
12 That they may possess the remnant of Edom,
and all nations claimed in my name—
oracle of the LORD, the one who does this.
13 Yes, days are coming—
oracle of the LORD—
When the one who plows shall overtake the
one who reaps
and the vintager, the sower of the seed;
The mountains shall drip with the juice of
grapes,
and all the hills shall run with it.*
14 I will restore my people Israel,
they shall rebuild and inhabit their ruined
cities,
Plant vineyards and drink† the wine,
set out gardens and eat the fruits.*
15 I will plant them upon their own ground;
never again shall they be plucked
From the land I have given them—
the LORD, your God, has spoken.

†

9:7 *The Ethiopians . . . the Philistines . . . the Arameans*: although Israel's relationship to the Lord was special, even unique in some respects (3:2), Israel was not the only people on earth that God cared for. Striking here is the reference to divine intervention in the history of the Philistines and Arameans, not unlike the Lord's saving intervention to bring Israel out of Egypt. *Caphtor*: the island of Crete.

9:11–15 These verses are most likely an editorial supplement to Amos, added to bring the book into harmony with the positive thrust of the prophetic books in general, especially those written after the exile, when the final edition of Amos was probably completed. The editors would have seen the destruction of Samaria in 722/721 B.C. as the fulfillment of Amos's prophecies, but in this epilogue they express the view that destruction was not the Lord's final word for Israel. In Acts 15:15–17, James interprets this passage in a messianic sense. *The fallen hut of David*: the Davidic kingdom, which included what later became the divided Northern and Southern Kingdoms. *All nations claimed in my name*: lit., "all nations over whom my name has been pronounced." This idiom denotes ownership.

9:14 *Rebuild . . . inhabit . . . plant . . . drink*: in this era of restoration, the Lord nullifies the curse of 5:11, which uses these same four verbs, and turns it into a blessing for Israel.

*

9:5 Am 8:8.
9:6 Am 5:8.
9:10 Jer 5:12; 23:17.
9:11 Acts 15:16–17.
9:13 Jl 4:18.
9:14 Is 65:21–22.

A betrayal is always difficult, and a betrayal by someone who is related to you is a particularly hard pill to swallow. This is perhaps most true in abusive relationships where one person, through his or her words and actions, mistreats another. It can take a long time to heal these divisions and restore a sense of trust in the relationship. The Book of Obadiah has angry words against the nation of Edom, whose people were related to the Israelites. It should remind us that when the people we expect to care for us instead take advantage of us, the wound is especially painful.

The Book of Obadiah

At a Glance

I. **Edom's Fall Decreed (1–7).**

II. **Edom's Betrayal of Judah (8–14).**

III. **Edom's Fall and Judah's Restoration (15–21).**

Quick Facts

Period Covered: after the Babylonian Exile, sometime in the fifth century BC

Inspired Author: Obadiah

Theme: God will punish Edom for its abuse of Judah.

Of Note: *Obadiah* means "servant" or "worshiper of the Lord."

In Depth

The Book of Genesis records a conflict between Jacob (the father of the nation of Israel) and his brother Esau (the father of the nation of Edom, later called Idumea). Hundreds of years later, the Israelites still fought with the Edomites (see map 4, "The Kingdom Years"). In the Book of Obadiah, the bitterness deepens.

In 587 BC, Jerusalem was destroyed by the Babylonians. Apparently, the Edomites not only did not aid their "brother" (Obadiah, verse 10), but took advantage of Israel's situation by gloating (see verse 12), looting (see verse 13), and raiding its territory (see verse 14). Because of the Edomites' cruelty, the prophet Obadiah prophesied the destruction of Edom by another country (see verse 15).

Like many of the Old Testament prophets, Obadiah ultimately saw a hopeful future for Israel. All Israel's enemies would wither before the strong arm of the Lord. And there would come a day—"the day of the LORD" (verse 15)—when all Jews would unite and return to Mount Zion (the place where the Temple stood in Jerusalem). Mount Zion would "rule mount Esau" and that new "kingship shall be the LORD's" (verse 21).

We are given no clues about the identity or life of the prophet Obadiah. We know only that he wrote the shortest book in the Old Testament—just one chapter long.

Obadiah

Edom's Fall Decreed

1 The vision of Obadiah.
Thus says the Lord GOD concerning Edom:
We have heard a message from the LORD,
and a herald has been sent among the nations:
"Rise up, so we may go to war against it!"*
2 Now I make you least among the nations;
you are utterly contemptible.
3 The pride of your heart has deceived you—
you who dwell in mountain crevices,
in your lofty home,†
Who say in your heart,
"Who will bring me down to earth?"
4 Though you soar like the eagle,
and your nest is set among the stars,
From there I will bring you down—
oracle of the LORD.
5 If thieves came to you, robbers by night
—how you have been destroyed!—
would they not steal merely till they had enough?
If grape pickers came to you,
would they not leave some gleanings?†*
6† How Esau has been searched out,
his treasures hunted down!
7 To the border they have driven you—
all your allies;
Your partners have deceived you,
they have overpowered you;
Those who eat your bread†
will replace you with foreigners,
who have no understanding.

Edom's Betrayal of Judah

8 On that day—oracle of the LORD—will I not
make the wise disappear from Edom,
and understanding from Mount Esau?*
9 Teman,† your warriors will be terror-stricken,
so that everyone on Mount Esau will be cut down.
10 Because of violence to your brother† Jacob,
disgrace will cover you,
you will be done away with forever!*
11 On the day you stood by,

†

3 Edom occupied the mountains southeast of Israel and the Dead Sea.

5 Something of value may escape the thief, and the grape picker always leaves something for the gleaners, but God's devastation of Edom will be complete.

6 With the past tense in vv. 5–7, the prophet presents a future event as if it had already happened.

7 *Those who eat your bread*: alliances were often established by covenant meals (cf. Gn 31:44–46). When Edom is destroyed, foreigners will replace the Edomites, who were known for wisdom (cf. v. 8; Jer 49:7; Jb 2:11).

9 *Teman*: a synonym for Edom; perhaps the name of a region or a city, the part representing the whole. *Mount Esau*: whatever its geographic reference, the phrase is an effective representation of Edom's arrogance.

10 *Your brother*: used with a double meaning referring to the common lineage of Israel and Edom, in which their ancestors were brothers, Jacob and Esau (Gn 25:19–26), and referring also to their political alliance, in which allies were called brothers (cf. Am 1:9, 11).

1:1–4 Jer 49:14–16.
1:5 Jer 49:9.
1:8 Is 29:14; 1 Cor 1:19.
1:10 Gn 27:41–45; Ez 25:12–14.

Catholic Social Teaching

What Goes Around

"What goes around comes around." Have you ever heard that saying? Isn't that exactly what Obadiah is saying in verse 15 when he states, "Your conduct will come back upon your own head"?

Whatever you do comes back to affect you eventually. This is especially true when we consider our care for God's creation. Catholic social teaching reminds us that we have a moral obligation to protect the earth on which we live. Care for the earth is a *responsibility* of our faith, not an option we can choose to ignore. God has made us co-creators, entrusted with the stewardship of all that God has created. To be good stewards, we must work to create a world where God's creation is always respected and protected. This means speaking out against individuals, governments, and corporations that pollute and destroy our environment. In a more personal way, it means we must never litter and must be committed to recycling and reducing consumption.

The ongoing destruction of our environment may not ever affect our lives directly, but it will negatively affect the lives of our children and grandchildren, and the generations that follow them. In this way, the decisions we make today will come back around to impact both our family and the larger human family.

Think about what individual changes you can make to be a better steward of the environment.

- In what ways are you being wasteful with the world's natural resources?
- How can you show more concern in your life for the gift of God's creation?

Obadiah, verse 15

Care for God's Creation

the day strangers carried off his possessions,
And foreigners entered his gates
and cast lots for Jerusalem,
you too were like one of them.† *

12† Do not gloat over the day of your brother,
the day of his disaster;
Do not exult over the people of Judah
on the day of their ruin;
Do not speak haughtily
on the day of distress!
13 Do not enter the gate of my people
on the day of their calamity;
Do not gloat—especially you—over his
misfortune
on the day of his calamity;
Do not lay hands upon his possessions
on the day of his calamity!
14 Do not stand at the crossroads
to cut down his survivors;
Do not hand over his fugitives
on the day of distress!

Edom's Fall and Judah's Restoration

15 Near is the day of the LORD*
against all the nations!
As you have done, so will it be done to you,
your conduct will come back upon your
own head;
16 As you drank† upon my holy mountain,
so will all the nations drink continually.
Yes, they will drink and swallow,
and will become as though they had not
been.
17 But on Mount Zion there will be some who
escape;†
the mountain will be holy,
And the house of Jacob will take possession

†

11 In 587 B.C., Edomites joined the invading Babylonian forces (v. 13) and captured escaping Judahites. The destruction of Jerusalem strengthened and expanded Edom's hold on Judah's southern territory.

12–14 The commands in vv. 12–14 are not to be understood as future prohibitions but as descriptions of crimes Edom in fact already committed on the day of Jerusalem's fall described in v. 11.

16 *As you drank*: i.e., Judah has suffered the punishment of divine wrath in 587 B.C. The oracle promises a similar fate for the nations, especially Edom (v. 18). The metaphor "drinking the cup of God's wrath" occurs often in the Bible; cf. Jb 21:20; Is 51:17–23; Jer 25:15–16; Rev 14:10.

17–19 The Israelites will be restored and will occupy the lands of those who oppressed them. The survivors of Judah will be rejoined by the returned exiles from northern Israel.

1:11 Ps 137:7. **1:15** Jl 4:11–12, 14.

of those who dispossessed them.*
18 The house of Jacob will be a fire,
the house of Joseph a flame,
and the house of Esau stubble.
They will set it ablaze and devour it;
none will survive of the house of Esau,
for the LORD has spoken.

19 They will take possession of the Negeb,†
Mount Esau, the Shephelah, and Philistia, pos-
sess the countryside of Ephraim, the countryside
of Samaria, Benjamin, and Gilead.* 20 The exiles
of this Israelite army will possess the Canaan-
ite land as far as Zarephath,† and the exiles of
Jerusalem who are in Sepharad will possess the
cities of the Negeb. 21 And deliverers† will ascend
Mount Zion to rule Mount Esau, and the king-
ship shall be the LORD's.

†

19 *Negeb*: the area south of Judah and west of Edom. *Gilead*: east of the Jordan River.

20 *Zarephath*: a town in Phoenicia, north of Tyre; cf. 1 Kgs 17:10. *Sepharad*: perhaps Sardis in western Asia Minor. The later rabbis thought it was Spain.

21 *Deliverers*: the victorious Israelites who will rule over their enemies, as the ancient judges did; cf. Jgs 3:9, 15, 31; 10:1.

1:17 Jer 49:2. **1:19** Jer 50:19.

You're watching a comedy show where someone dressed like a doctor starts making outrageous comments about a person's health. You laugh, not because sickness is funny, but because doctors are supposed to be sensitive and caring. That's the basis of satire—that someone or something that is supposed to act one way acts another way. You're about to read a biblical satire about Jonah the prophet. The Book of Jonah uses humor to make an important point—God is the God of all people, even those we consider our enemies.

The Book of

Jonah

In Depth

This story was written after the Jews returned from their exile in Babylon. Jewish leaders encouraged Jewish people to stay away from non-Jewish people (see Ezra, chapter 9) in order to avoid falling into idolatry again. A result was a religious bigotry against other nations—a belief that God was against every nation that opposed Israel. The Book of Jonah was written to correct that narrow attitude. Through satire, this fictional short story gently pokes fun at Israel's religious self-righteousness.

How is the book funny? Well, right off the bat, Jonah is called by God and immediately takes off in the opposite direction (see Jon 1:1–3). What kind of prophet is this? When God tries to get his attention with a storm, it's the non-Jewish sailors who get the point (see verse 14). Just as the reader is probably wondering how God is going to get Jonah to Nineveh, along comes a taxi in the form of a large fish's stomach (see 2:1).

There's more. Readers from the author's time would have expected Jonah to be ignored at best, more likely beaten or killed by the people of Nineveh. After all, these were Israel's mortal enemies. Instead, the Ninevites immediately respond to Jonah's message and repent, even the animals (see 3:8)! At this point, the reader is giggling at the goofiness of pigs and sheep in sackcloth, but getting the message about God's salvation being for all nations.

Jonah is angry and upset. He didn't expect the Ninevites to convert—he wanted them punished. He goes outside the city to mope, and his favorite plant dies. The book ends with God's chiding Jonah for his bigoted anger. If Jonah is so concerned for his little plant (see 4:6–8), shouldn't God be concerned for the great city of Nineveh with its thousands of people (see verse 11)? The point is driven home, and the humor has helped to make a challenging message easier to accept.

At a Glance

I. **Jonah's Disobedience and Flight (1:1–16).**

II. **Jonah's Prayer (2:1–11).**

III. **Jonah's Obedience and the Ninevites' Repentance (3:1–10).**

IV. **Jonah's Anger and God's Reproof (4:1–11).**

Quick Facts

Period Covered: eighth century BC

Inspired Author: unknown, probably writing in the fifth century BC

Theme: a fictional short story showing that God cares for all people, including Israel's enemies

Jonah

Chapter 3

Jonah's Disobedience and Flight

1 1 The word of the LORD came to Jonah,* son of
Amittai:† 2 Set out for the great city† of Nin-
eveh, and preach against it; for their wickedness
has come before me.* 3 But Jonah made ready to
flee to Tarshish,† away from the LORD. He went
down to Joppa, found a ship going to Tarshish,
paid the fare, and went down in it to go with
them to Tarshish, away from the LORD.
4 * The LORD, however, hurled a great wind
upon the sea, and the storm was so great that
the ship was about to break up. 5 Then the sail-
ors were afraid and each one cried to his god.
To lighten the ship for themselves, they threw its
cargo into the sea. Meanwhile, Jonah had gone
down into the hold of the ship, and lay there fast
asleep. 6 The captain approached him and said,
"What are you doing asleep? Get up, call on your
god! Perhaps this god will be mindful of us so
that we will not perish."
7 Then they said to one another, "Come, let us
cast lots to discover on whose account this evil
has come to us." So they cast lots, and the lot fell
on Jonah.* 8 They said to him, "Tell us why this
evil has come to us! What is your business? Where
do you come from? What is your country, and to
what people do you belong?" 9 "I am a Hebrew,"
he replied; "I fear the LORD, the God of heaven,
who made the sea and the dry land."
10 Now the men were seized with great fear and
said to him, "How could you do such a thing!"—
They knew that he was fleeing from the LORD,
because he had told them. 11 They asked, "What
shall we do with you, that the sea may calm down
for us?" For the sea was growing more and more
stormy. 12 Jonah responded, "Pick me up and hurl
me into the sea and then the sea will calm down
for you. For I know that this great storm has come
upon you because of me."
13 Still the men rowed hard to return to dry
land, but they could not, for the sea grew more
and more stormy. 14 Then they cried to the LORD:
"Please, O LORD, do not let us perish for taking
this man's life; do not charge us with shedding
innocent blood, for you, LORD, have accomplished
what you desired."† 15 Then they picked up Jonah
and hurled him into the sea, and the sea stopped
raging. 16 Seized with great fear of the LORD, the
men offered sacrifice to the LORD and made vows.

†

1:1 *Jonah, son of Amittai*: a prophet of this name lived at the time of Jeroboam II (786–746 B.C.).

1:2 *Great city*: exaggeration is characteristic of this book; the word "great" (Heb. *gadol*) occurs fourteen times.

1:3 *Tarshish*: identified by many with Tartessus, an ancient Phoenician colony in southwest Spain; precise identification with any particular Phoenician center in the western Mediterranean is uncertain. To the Israelites it stood for the far west.

1:14 Aware that this disaster is a divine punishment on Jonah, the sailors ask that in ridding themselves of him they not be charged with the crime of murder.

1:1 2 Kgs 14:25.
1:2 Jon 3:3; 4:11.
1:4–6 Mk 4:37–38.
1:7 Jos 7:16–18; 1 Sm 14:40–42.

Jesus and Jonah

Do you see any similarities between Jonah and Jesus? Jonah is in the darkness of a fish's belly for three days before the Lord commands the fish to spit him out. Jesus experiences the darkness of death for three days before he bursts from the tomb in resurrected glory. In Matthew 16:4 and Luke 11:29, Jesus even refers to "the sign of Jonah" in relation to his own ministry.

Jonah's prayer in Jonah 2:3–10 could well have been Jesus' prayer before his death. It reminds us that salvation comes from God when we are experiencing dark times. When you are going through a difficult time, use Jonah's prayer as a model for writing your own prayer of trust. Describe your difficulties and your situation, and end by expressing your ultimate trust in God. Then say your prayer until the difficulty passes. It could make a difference!

▶ **Jon 2:3–10**

Jonah's Prayer

2 [1]But the LORD sent a great fish to swallow Jo-
nah, and he remained in the belly of the fish
three days and three nights.* [2]Jonah prayed to
the LORD, his God, from the belly of the fish:

3† Out of my distress I called to the LORD,
and he answered me;
From the womb of Sheol† I cried for help,
and you heard my voice.*
4 You cast me into the deep, into the heart of
the sea,
and the flood enveloped me;
All your breakers and your billows
passed over me.*
5 Then I said, "I am banished from your sight!
How will I again look upon your holy
temple?"*
6 The waters surged around me up to my neck;
the deep enveloped me;
seaweed wrapped around my head.*
7 I went down to the roots of the mountains;
to the land whose bars closed behind me
forever,
But you brought my life up from the pit,
O LORD, my God.*

8 When I became faint,
I remembered the LORD;
My prayer came to you
in your holy temple.*
9 Those who worship worthless idols
abandon their hope for mercy.*
10 But I, with thankful voice,
will sacrifice to you;
What I have vowed I will pay:
deliverance is from the LORD.*

[11]Then the LORD commanded the fish to vomit
Jonah upon dry land.

Jonah's Obedience and the Ninevites' Repentance

3 [1]The word of the LORD came to Jonah a sec-
ond time: [2]Set out for the great city of Nin-
eveh, and announce to it the message that I will
tell you. [3]So Jonah set out for Nineveh, in accord
with the word of the LORD. Now Nineveh was an
awesomely great city; it took three days to walk
through it. [4]Jonah began his journey through the
city, and when he had gone only a single day's
walk announcing, "Forty days more and Nineveh
shall be overthrown," [5]the people of Nineveh
believed God; they proclaimed a fast and all of
them, great and small,† put on sackcloth.*
[6]When the news reached the king of Nineveh,
he rose from his throne, laid aside his robe, cov-
ered himself with sackcloth, and sat in ashes.
[7]Then he had this proclaimed throughout Nin-
eveh:† "By decree of the king and his nobles,
no man or beast, no cattle or sheep, shall taste
anything; they shall not eat, nor shall they drink

†

2:3–10 These verses, which may have originally been an independent composition, are a typical example of a song of thanksgiving, a common psalm genre (e.g., Ps 116; Is 38:9–20). Such a song is relevant here, since Jonah has not drowned, and the imagery of vv. 4, 6 is appropriate.

2:3 *Sheol*: Cf. note on Ps 6:6.

3:5 *Great and small*: the contrast can refer to distinctions of social class (prominent citizens and the poor).

3:7–8 Fasting and wearing sackcloth are signs of human repentance; here they are legislated even for the animals—a humorous touch, perhaps anticipating 4:11.

*

2:1 Mt 12:40; 16:4; Lk 11:30; 1 Cor 15:4.
2:3 Ps 18:7; 120:1.
2:4 Ps 42:8.
2:5 Ps 31:23; Is 38:11.
2:6 Ps 18:5; 69:2.
2:7 Ps 16:10; 30:4.
2:8 Ps 5:8; 18:7; 88:3.
2:9 Ps 31:7.
2:10 Ps 50:14.
3:5 Mt 12:41; Lk 11:32.

water. 8 Man and beast alike must be covered
with sackcloth and call loudly to God; they all
must turn from their evil way and from the vio-
lence of their hands. 9 † Who knows? God may
again repent and turn from his blazing wrath,
so that we will not perish."* 10 When God saw
by their actions how they turned from their evil
way, he repented of the evil he had threatened to
do to them; he did not carry it out.

Jonah's Anger and God's Reproof

4 1 But this greatly displeased Jonah, and he
became angry.† 2 He prayed to the LORD, "O
LORD, is this not what I said while I was still in
my own country? This is why I fled at first to-
ward Tarshish. I knew that you are a gracious
and merciful God, slow to anger, abounding in
kindness, repenting of punishment.†* 3 So now,
LORD, please take my life from me; for it is better
for me to die than to live."* 4 But the LORD asked,
"Are you right to be angry?"†
5 Jonah then left the city for a place to the east
of it, where he built himself a hut and waited†
under it in the shade, to see what would happen
to the city. 6 Then the LORD God provided a gourd
plant.† And when it grew up over Jonah's head,
giving shade that relieved him of any discomfort,
Jonah was greatly delighted with the plant. 7 But
the next morning at dawn God provided a worm
that attacked the plant, so that it withered. 8 And
when the sun arose, God provided a scorching
east wind; and the sun beat upon Jonah's head
till he became faint. Then he wished for death,
saying, "It is better for me to die than to live."
9 But God said to Jonah, "Do you have a
right to be angry over the gourd plant?" Jonah
answered, "I have a right to be angry—angry
enough to die." 10 Then the LORD said, "You are
concerned† over the gourd plant which cost you
no effort and which you did not grow; it came
up in one night and in one night it perished.
11 And should I not be concerned over the great
city of Nineveh, in which there are more than a
hundred and twenty thousand persons who can-
not know their right hand from their left, not to
mention all the animals?"†

Live It!

Mistaken Loyalties

When God spares Nineveh, Jonah is angry! He is so angry he is willing to let his anger destroy him. And all because of mistaken loyalty. Jonah thought he was loyal to God (which is funny because at first, he tried to run away from God), and he feels that God is being disloyal to him by not destroying Nineveh. Jonah lacks empathy. He does not—or will not—understand that God's loyalty is to the whole human race, not just to Jonah's desires.

Are you ever angry with God because things don't go your way? Maybe your anger is about mistaken loyalties. If you didn't get picked for the lead part, that doesn't mean God is being disloyal to you. God is God over everyone—which sometimes means that you will not get what you want so that other people can receive what they need. We must never be selfish, striving instead to have empathy—true understanding of another—at all times.

The next time you are angry at God, ask yourself: Am I willing to see things from a large enough perspective? Am I expecting to receive God's favor at someone else's expense?

▶ **Jon 4:1–8**

JON

†

3:9–10 Scripture frequently presents the Lord as repenting (or, changing his mind) of the evil that he threatens; e.g., Gn 6:6–7; Jer 18:8.

4:1 *He became angry*: because of his narrow vindictiveness, Jonah did not wish the Lord to forgive the Ninevites.

4:2 *Punishment*: lit., "evil"; see 1:2, 7, 8; 3:8, 10; 4:1.

4:4 The Lord's question is as unexpected as it is pithy. It is also a mysterious reply to Jonah's wish to die; perhaps it serves to invite Jonah to think over his situation. However, it goes unanswered, and the request and reply will be repeated in vv. 8–9.

4:5 *Waited*: Jonah still hopes his threat of doom will be fulfilled.

4:6 *Gourd plant*: the Hebrew word, *qiqayon*, means here a wide-leafed plant of the cucumber or castor-bean variety.

4:10 *Concerned*: the meaning of the Hebrew verb suggests "pity, care for," and this appears in the Lord's attitude to Nineveh in v. 11. Jonah has shown only a selfish concern over the plant in contrast to the Lord's true "concern" for his creatures.

4:11 A selfish Jonah bemoans his personal loss of a gourd plant for shade without any concern over the threat of loss of life to the Ninevites through the destruction of their city. If a solicitous God provided the plant for a prophet without the latter's effort or merit, how much more is God disposed to show love and mercy toward all people, Jew and Gentile, when they repent of their sins and implore divine pardon. God's care goes beyond human beings to all creation, as in Job 38.

*

3:9 Jl 2:14.
4:2 Ex 34:6–7; Ps 86:5; Jl 2:13.
4:3 1 Kgs 19:4.

The Book of Micah

Oftentimes it takes someone from outside our local community to help us see things from a new perspective. We are so used to seeing things as they are that we sometimes fail to envision what could be until a new voice with unique insights comes along. Indeed, people who visit the places we live in often see things we have overlooked or taken for granted. The prophet Micah was like such a visitor. His home was a small village, but he prophesied in the big capital city of Jerusalem. God uses Micah's unique perspective to communicate warnings and promises to the people of Israel and to us.

In Depth

The Book of Micah is a collection of oracles (poem-like prophetic messages) taking different forms. Some of the oracles are harsh judgments (see 1:8—2:11), some are comforting promises that God will not desert the people (see chapter 4), and some are the prophet's own confessions of faith (see 3:8, 7:7). The Book of Micah shows us a God who is passionate for justice and fairness (see 3:9).

Perhaps because of his rural background, the prophet Micah has a special connection to the land and the people who work it. He speaks against those who covet and seize fields and homes (see 2:2). He describes the destruction of Zion (Jerusalem) as plowing a field (see 3:12). He represents the Ideal Kingdom as a place where all the people have their own grapevines and fig trees (see 4:4).

The Book of Micah shows signs of being extensively edited and revised to keep the prophet's message relevant during changing times. This is particularly true in chapters 4 and 5, which were added after the Babylonian Exile to give hope following the nation's great tragedy. In 4:3, the prophet envisions a day when nations will "beat their swords into plowshares" and when "nation shall not raise the sword against another, / nor shall they train for war again."

Micah prophesied at about the same time as First Isaiah (see the timeline at the back of this Bible), during the days of Kings Jotham, Ahaz, and Hezekiah (see 2 Chr 27:1—31:21). But whereas Isaiah was a member of the upper class, defending the rights of the poor, Micah was a poor person, suffering with the poor. That is why he speaks so passionately about their mistreatment (see Mi 3:1–3). Even though his message went unheeded at the time, he models for us trust in the Lord's saving power (see 7:7).

At a Glance

I. **Oracles of Punishment (1:2—3:12).**
II. **Oracles of Salvation (4:1—5:14).**
III. **Announcement of Judgment (6:1—7:6).**
IV. **Confidence in God's Future (7:7–20).**

Quick Facts

Period Covered: late eighth century BC

Inspired Authors: Micah and later editors

Themes: warnings against injustice and idolatry, promises of a new future, God's faithfulness to the covenant

Micah

4:3

1 [1]The word of the LORD which came to Micah of Moresheth in the days of Jotham, Ahaz, and Hezekiah, kings of Judah, which he saw concerning Samaria and Jerusalem.

I. Oracles of Punishment

2 Hear, O peoples, all of you,
give heed, O earth, and all that is in it!*
Let the Lord GOD be witness against you,
the Lord from his holy temple!†
3 For see, the LORD goes out from his place*
and descending, treads upon the heights of the earth.†
4 The mountains melt under him
and the valleys split open,
Like wax before the fire,
like water poured down a slope.
5 All this is for the crime of Jacob,
for the sins of the house of Israel.†
What is the crime of Jacob? Is it not Samaria?
And what is the sin of the house of Judah?
Is it not Jerusalem?
6 So I will make Samaria a ruin in the field,
a place to plant vineyards;
I will throw its stones into the valley,
and lay bare its foundations.†
7 All its carved figures shall be broken to pieces,*
all its wages shall be burned in the fire,
and all its idols I will destroy.
As the wages of a prostitute† it gathered them,
and to the wages of a prostitute they shall return.

8† For this I will lament and wail,
go barefoot and naked;
I will utter lamentation like the jackals,
mourning like the ostriches,*
9 For her wound is incurable;
it has come even to Judah.
It has reached to the gate of my people,
even to Jerusalem.

10† Do not announce it in Gath,
do not weep at all;

---

† **1:2** The prophet summons all the peoples to hear the divine accusations against them. What follows in 1:2–3:12 is a series of prophecies of punishment addressed to the capital cities of both the Northern and Southern Kingdoms, Samaria and Jerusalem. The prophecies indict the leaders and main officials, including prophets. Because of the corruption and selfishness of their leaders, Samaria and Jerusalem will fall to their enemies.

1:3 The Lord comes in a theophany which has devastating effects on the natural world (1:4).

1:5 Although the summons (1:2) had been addressed to all people, the Lord speaks against Israel and Judah, identifying their crimes with the respective capital cities of Samaria and Jerusalem. Only Samaria, however, is scheduled for destruction in the announcement of punishment (vv. 6–7).

1:6 The punishment of Samaria will be a military disaster such as the one that actually came at the hands of the Assyrian army in 722/721 B.C.

1:7 *The wages of a prostitute*: as often in the prophets, prostitution is a metaphor for idolatry (Hos 1–3; 4:14). *They shall return*: i.e., Samaria's idols shall come to nothing just as the wages of a prostitute are counted as nothing.

1:8–16 The prophet laments and wails, singing a funeral song or dirge over the city of Jerusalem. Finally (1:16) he calls upon the people of Jerusalem to join in the mourning.

1:10–15 Not all of the cities and villages in this long list can be

---

* **1:2** Dt 32:1; Is 1:2. **1:3–4** Is 26:21; Na 1:5; Hb 3:10. **1:7** Hos 9:1. **1:8** Jb 30:29.

Did You Know?

Micah Challenges Us to Fight Injustice

In chapter 2, the prophet Micah challenges the people to take an honest look at their behavior. In harsh images and language, he articulates how greed and injustice have destroyed the well-being of the nation. In verse 3, Micah implies that because of their injustice, the people will be like oxen whose necks are confined to yokes that hold their heads down in shame. Micah's message is that injustice forces all in the community and nation to carry a heavy burden.

This theme of examining injustices in the world has been repeated numerous times throughout the Scriptures. And to this very day, we continue to hear similar teachings coming out of the Church. What are we doing in our communities and in our country to fight against modern instances of injustice, such as racism, hunger, poverty, abortion, capital punishment, violence, and destruction of the natural environment? What injustices do you see in your own actions and in your own community? What can you do to stop injustices from happening so that our communities and nation can live freely in peace?

▶ **Micah, chapter 2**

In Beth-leaphrah
roll in the dust.*
11 Pass by,
you who dwell in Shaphir!
The inhabitants of Zaanan
do not come forth from their city.
There is lamentation in Beth-ezel.
It will withdraw its support from you.
12 The inhabitants of Maroth
hope for good,
But evil has come down from the LORD
to the gate of Jerusalem.
13 Harness steeds to the chariots,
inhabitants of Lachish;
You are the beginning of sin
for daughter Zion,
For in you were found
the crimes of Israel.
14 Therefore you must give back the dowry
to Moresheth-gath;
The houses of Achzib† are a dry stream bed
to the kings of Israel.
15 Again I will bring the conqueror to you,
inhabitants of Mareshah;
The glory of Israel shall come
even to Adullam.
16 Make yourself bald, cut off your hair,
for the children whom you cherish;
Make yourself bald as a vulture,
for they are taken from you into exile.†

2 1† Ah! you plotters of iniquity,
who work out evil on your beds!
In the morning light you carry it out
for it lies within your power.
2† You covet fields, and seize them;
houses, and take them;
You cheat owners of their houses,
people of their inheritance.

3 Therefore thus says the LORD:
Look, I am planning against this family an evil
from which you cannot free your necks;
Nor shall you walk with head held high,
for it will be an evil time.
4 On that day you shall be mocked,
and there will be bitter lament:

---

† located with certainty. However, those which can be identified, including the prophet's hometown, lie southwest of Jerusalem. In the Hebrew, wordplays on the names of these cities abound. The territory involved corresponds to that decimated by the Assyrian king Sennacherib in 701 B.C., during the reign of Hezekiah. *Do not weep at all*: some commentators and translators understand the Hebrew differently. They argue that the translation "in (unknown place name) weep!" fits the context better.

1:14 *The houses of Achzib*: there is a wordplay here. In the Hebrew, the word translated here as "dry stream bed" is *'achzab*; this word is sometimes translated as "deception" or "disappointment."

1:16 Shaving the head was a sign of mourning; cf. Is 3:24; Am 8:10.

2:1–5 The cry "Ah" (*hoy*) begins a typical prophetic speech that is usually continued, as here (vv. 1–2), by a description of the addressees in terms of their unrighteous activities. This description is an indictment which gives the reasons for punishment announced to a particular group of people (vv. 3–5). The prophet spells out the crimes; the Lord announces the punishment, which corresponds to the crime: those who take the land of others will have their own land taken.

Those who plot iniquity and have the power to do it are wealthy landowners. The evil which they do consists in coveting the fields and houses of others and taking them.

2:2 To covet the "house" and other property of the neighbor was a violation of the Decalogue (Ex 20:17; 34:24; Dt 5:21).

The Lord, as owner of the earth, allotted the land by tribes and families to the people of Israel (Jos 13–19). Losing one's inheritance diminished one's place in the community and threatened the family's economic viability and existence. According to Micah, those who used their power to expand their estates at the expense of weaker Israelites took more than land from them: they were tampering with the divine order.

---

* **1:10** 2 Sm 1:20.

"Our ruin is complete,
our fields are divided among our captors,
The fields of my people are measured out,
and no one can get them back!"†
5 Thus you shall have no one
in the assembly of the LORD
to allot to you a share of land.

6† "Do not preach," they preach,
"no one should preach of these things!
Shame will not overtake us."
7 How can it be said, house of Jacob,
"Is the LORD short of patience;
are these the Lord's deeds?"
Do not my words promise good
to the one who walks in justice?
8 But you rise up against my people as an enemy:
you have stripped off the garment from the peaceful,
From those who go their way in confidence,
as though it were spoils of war.
9 The women of my people you drive out
from their pleasant houses;
From their children you take away
forever the honor I gave them.

10† "Get up! Leave,
this is no place to rest";
Because of uncleanness that destroys
with terrible destruction.
11 If one possessed of a lying spirit*
speaks deceitfully, saying,
"I will preach to you wine and strong drink,"
that one would be the preacher for this people.

12† I will gather you, Jacob, each and every one,
I will assemble all the remnant of Israel;
I will group them like a flock in the fold,
like a herd in its pasture;
the noise of the people will resound.
13 The one who makes a breach goes up before them;
they make a breach and pass through the gate;
Their king shall go through before them,
the LORD at their head.

3

1† And I said:
Hear, you leaders of Jacob,
rulers of the house of Israel!
Is it not your duty to know what is right,
2 you who hate what is good, and love evil?
You who tear their skin from them,
and their flesh from their bones;*
3 Who eat the flesh of my people,
flay their skin from them,
and break their bones;
Who chop them in pieces like flesh in a kettle,
like meat in a pot.
4 When they cry to the LORD,
he will not answer them;
He will hide his face from them at that time,
because of the evil they have done.

5† Thus says the LORD regarding the prophets:
O you who lead my people astray,
When your teeth have something to bite
you announce peace,
But proclaim war against the one
who fails to put something in your mouth.*
6 Therefore you shall have night, not vision,
darkness, not divination;
The sun shall go down upon the prophets,
and the day shall be dark for them.*
7 Then the seers shall be put to shame,
and the diviners confounded;
They shall all cover their lips,
because there is no answer from God.
8 But as for me, I am filled with power,
with the spirit of the LORD,
with justice and with might;

2:4 Those who take land from the less powerful will in turn have their land taken away by invaders.

2:6–11 This unit is a disputation, an argument in which the prophet is debating with his opponents. The words of the opponents are given to us only as the prophet quotes them. The opponents accuse Micah of being a false prophet, and he reacts by accusing them of injustice and of preferring prophets and preachers who speak lies (v. 11).

2:10 The meaning of the Hebrew is uncertain.

2:12–13 This announcement of salvation to the "remnant of Israel" stands out dramatically in the context, and is probably a later addition to the words of Micah, coming from the time of the Babylonian exile. The content of the promise and the images are similar to those found in Second Isaiah, the great poet of Israel's salvation and restoration (see Is 40:11; 43:5).

3:1–4 This prophecy of punishment has an introductory call to hear (v. 1a–b) and two major parts, the indictment or reasons for punishment (vv. 1c–3) and the announcement of judgment (v. 4). The prophet accuses the leaders and rulers of Israel of treating the people so badly that their actions are comparable to cannibalism. Those who, above all, should know and maintain justice are the most corrupt of all. In the time of trouble the Lord will withdraw (v. 4); that is, God will abandon the leaders to their fate and refuse to answer their prayers.

3:5–8 This prophecy of punishment concerns and is addressed to false prophets. The prophets in Jerusalem who mislead the people are corrupt because their word can be bought (v. 5). Therefore such prophets, seers, and diviners shall be disgraced, put to shame, left in the dark without vision or answer (vv. 6–7). But Micah is convinced that he is filled with power and the spirit of the Lord, which corresponds to justice and might (v. 8).

2:11 1 Kgs 22:22–23.
3:2 Am 2:7.
3:5 Ez 13:10.
3:6 Jer 15:9; Am 8:9; Zec 13:3.

To declare to Jacob his crimes
and to Israel his sins.

9† Hear this, you leaders of the house of Jacob,
you rulers of the house of Israel!
You who abhor justice,
and pervert all that is right;
10 Who build up Zion with bloodshed,
and Jerusalem with wickedness!
11 Its leaders render judgment for a bribe,
the priests teach for pay,
the prophets divine for money,
While they rely on the LORD, saying,
"Is not the LORD in the midst of us?
No evil can come upon us!"*
12 Therefore, because of you,
Zion shall be plowed like a field,
and Jerusalem reduced to rubble,
And the mount of the temple
to a forest ridge.*

II. Oracles of Salvation

4 1† In days to come
the mount of the LORD's house
Shall be established as the highest mountain;
it shall be raised above the hills,
And peoples shall stream to it:*
2 Many nations shall come, and say,
"Come, let us climb the LORD's mountain,
to the house of the God of Jacob,
That he may instruct us in his ways,
that we may walk in his paths."
For from Zion shall go forth instruction,
and the word of the LORD from Jerusalem.
3 He shall judge between many peoples
and set terms for strong and distant nations;
They shall beat their swords into plowshares,
and their spears into pruning hooks;
One nation shall not raise the sword against
another,
nor shall they train for war again.
4 They shall all sit under their own vines,
under their own fig trees, undisturbed;
for the LORD of hosts has spoken.*
5 Though all the peoples walk,
each in the name of its god,
We will walk in the name of the LORD,
our God, forever and ever.

6† On that day—oracle of the LORD—
I will gather the lame,
And I will assemble the outcasts,
and those whom I have afflicted.
7 I will make of the lame a remnant,
and of the weak a strong nation;
The LORD shall be king over them on Mount
Zion,
from now on and forever.*

8 And you, O tower of the flock,†
hill of daughter Zion!
To you it shall come:
the former dominion shall be restored,
the reign of daughter Jerusalem.

9 Now why do you cry out so?
Are you without a king?
Or has your adviser perished,
That you are seized with pains
like a woman in labor?
10† Writhe, go into labor,
O daughter Zion,
like a woman giving birth;
For now you shall leave the city
and camp in the fields;
To Babylon you shall go,
there you shall be rescued.
There the LORD shall redeem you
from the hand of your enemies.

11† And now many nations are gathered against
you!
They say, "Let her be profaned,
let our eyes see Zion's downfall!"
12 But they do not know the thoughts of the LORD,
nor understand his plan:

3:9–12 This is the most comprehensive of Micah's prophecies of punishment concerning the leaders in Jerusalem. The indictment (vv. 9–11) includes all political and religious leaders. They combine corruption and greed with a false confidence that the Lord is on their side. But the announcement of judgment (v. 12) is not limited to the punishment of the leaders but includes Mount Zion where the Temple stands and the entire city, thus encompassing the entire population.

4:1–4 This magnificent prophecy of salvation is almost identical to Is 2:2–5, with the exception of its last verse. See also Jl 4:9–10, which transforms the promise into a call to war. It is not known if Micah or an editor of the book picked up the announcement from his contemporary Isaiah or if Isaiah borrowed it from Micah. Perhaps both Isaiah and Micah depended upon another, more ancient tradition. The ground of the prophetic hope voiced here is the justice and grace of the God who has chosen Israel. The basis for peace shall be a just order where all are obedient to the divine will. While the vision is a universal one, including all peoples and nations (vv. 3–4), its center and wellspring is the Temple of the Lord of Israel on Mount Zion in Jerusalem.

4:6–8 An announcement of salvation proclaiming that the Lord will restore the lame and afflicted people of God as a nation on Mount Zion. *Oracle of the LORD*: a phrase used extensively in prophetic books to indicate divine speech.

4:8 *Tower of the flock*: in Hebrew *migdal-eder*, a place name in Gn 35:21.

4:10 Frequently the prophets personify the city of Jerusalem as a woman, and here as a woman in labor.

4:11–13 The nations who have ridiculed Zion (v. 11) will be threshed like grain (v. 13).

3:11 Ez 22:27; Zep 3:3.
3:12 Jer 26:18.
4:1–3 Is 2:2–4.
4:4 Hos 14:8; Am 9:14.
4:7 Is 6:13; Dn 7:14; Zep 3:19; Lk 1:32.

He has gathered them
like sheaves to the threshing floor.
13 Arise and thresh, O daughter Zion;
your horn I will make iron
And your hoofs I will make bronze,
that you may crush many peoples;
You shall devote their spoils to the LORD,†
their riches to the Lord of the whole earth.*

14 Now grieve, O grieving daughter!†
"They have laid siege against us!"
With the rod they strike on the cheek
the ruler of Israel.

5 1† But you, Bethlehem-Ephrathah*
least among the clans of Judah,
From you shall come forth for me
one who is to be ruler in Israel;
Whose origin is from of old,
from ancient times.
2 Therefore the Lord will give them up, until
the time
when she who is to give birth has borne,†
Then the rest of his kindred shall return
to the children of Israel.*
3 He shall take his place as shepherd
by the strength of the LORD,
by the majestic name of the LORD, his God;
And they shall dwell securely, for now his
greatness
shall reach to the ends of the earth:
4 he shall be peace.†
If Assyria invades our country
and treads upon our land,
We shall raise against it seven shepherds,
eight of royal standing;
5 They shall tend the land of Assyria with the
sword,
and the land of Nimrod† with the drawn
sword;
They will deliver us from Assyria,
when it invades our land,
when it treads upon our borders.

6 The remnant of Jacob shall be
in the midst of many peoples,

Pray It!

From Humble Beginnings

As a country boy, Micah has a different vision than do some of the other prophets. He doesn't see the Ideal Ruler coming out of a big city like Jerusalem. No, he sees this great person coming from Bethlehem—a tiny, insignificant city, but also a place free from political corruption. The Gospel of Matthew shows Micah's prophecy being fulfilled in the birth of Jesus (see Mt 2:5–6).

Often in the Bible, we hear of God's accomplishing huge feats with small and humble people and things. In your prayer, reflect or journal on the following questions:

- What famous people started from humble beginnings?
- Why does God often use small and hidden people or things to accomplish God's purposes?
- What small or hidden gifts do you have to offer God to work with?

▶ **Mi 5:2–5**

Like dew coming from the LORD,
like showers on the grass,
Which wait for no one,
delay for no human being.
7 And the remnant of Jacob shall be among the
nations,
in the midst of many peoples,
Like a lion among beasts of the forest,
like a young lion among flocks of sheep;
When it passes through it tramples;
it tears and no one can rescue.
8 Your hand shall be lifted above your foes,
and all your enemies shall be cut down.

†

4:13 *Devote their spoils to the LORD*: the fulfillment of the ancient ordinance of the holy war in which all plunder taken in the war was "put under the ban," i.e., belonged to the Lord.

4:14 *Grieve, O grieving daughter!*: the Hebrew actually reflects the ancient Near Eastern mourning practice of afflicting oneself with cuts and gashes, as evidence of grief. A literal rendering would be "gash yourself, O woman who gashes."

5:1–6 Salvation will come through a "messiah," an anointed ruler. The Book of Micah shares with Isaiah the expectation that God will deliver Israel through a king in the line of David. Bethlehem-Ephrathah is the home of the Davidic line.

5:2 These words are sometimes understood as a reference to Isaiah's Emmanuel oracle, given some thirty years earlier (Is 7:14). The Gospel of Matthew reports that the chief priests and scribes cite this passage as the ancient promise of a messiah in the line of David to be born in Bethlehem (Mt 2:5–6).

5:4 *Peace*: he will not only symbolize but also bring about harmony and wholeness.

5:5 *Nimrod*: the legendary ancestor of the Mesopotamians; cf. Gn 10:10–12.

4:13 Is 41:15; Hos 10:11. **5:1** Ru 1:2; 1 Sm 17:12; Mt 2:6; Jn 7:42. **5:2–3** Is 7:14; 11:1–2.

Catholic Social Teaching

"To Love Kindness"

Perhaps you have heard the expression, "Perform a random act of kindness." This statement is commonly seen as an invitation to do something nice and unexpected for another person. Kindness, however, shouldn't be a random thing we do; rather, kindness is something that should be integrated into our lives at all times, not just at random moments. Imagine what our world would be like if every day, each of us were consistently kind to each person we encountered, whether we knew the person or not. Imagine if kindness were seen as a responsibility of all people, and not just as something done randomly!

Just as violence leads to more violence, so also can kindness create more kindness. This is why Micah includes kindness in his simple formula for doing God's will—it is not meant to be a random choice, but a human responsibility.

Consider these questions:

- What are some of the specific responsibilities all people have in our world today?
- Whom or what are we responsible for?
- When, if ever, does our responsibility to the rest of the world end?

Mi 6:8

Rights and Responsibilities

9† On that day—oracle of the LORD—
I will destroy the horses from your midst
and ruin your chariots;
10 I will destroy the cities of your land
and tear down all your fortresses.
11 I will destroy the sorcery you practice,
and there shall no longer be soothsayers
among you.
12 I will destroy your carved figures
and the sacred stones† from your midst;
And you shall no longer worship
the works of your hands.*
13 I will tear out the asherahs from your midst,
and destroy your cities.
14 I will wreak vengeance in anger and wrath
upon the nations that have not listened.

III. Announcement of Judgment

6 1† Hear, then, what the LORD says:
Arise, plead your case before the mountains,
and let the hills hear your voice!*
2 Hear, O mountains, the LORD's case,
pay attention, O foundations of the earth!
For the LORD has a case against his people;
he enters into trial with Israel.
3 My people, what have I done to you?
how have I wearied you? Answer me!*
4 I brought you up from the land of Egypt,
from the place of slavery I ransomed you;
And I sent before you Moses,
Aaron, and Miriam.*
5† My people, remember what Moab's King
Balak planned,
and how Balaam, the son of Beor,
answered him.
Recall the passage from Shittim to Gilgal,
that you may know the just deeds of the
LORD.*
6† With what shall I come before the LORD,
and bow before God most high?
Shall I come before him with burnt offerings,
with calves a year old?*

†

5:9–13 The Lord will destroy all those features of the nation's life that have stood between the people and their God. These false supports include horses, chariots, fortifications, and forbidden practices such as sorcery and idolatry.

5:12–13 *Sacred stones . . . asherahs*: the Hebrew *asherah* is a sacred pole. All forms of idolatry (standing stones and sacred poles were part of forbidden cult practices) were violations of Israel's covenant with the Lord.

6:1–5 The Lord, through the prophet, initiates a legal case against the people. The initial calls (vv. 1–2) signal the beginning of a trial, and the proclamation that the Lord intends to enter into a legal dispute with Israel. One would expect accusations to follow such an introduction, but instead the Lord speaks in self-defense, reciting mighty acts done in behalf of Israel (vv. 3–5).

6:5 The Lord calls for the people to remember the saving events of the past, from the encounters with Balak and Balaam (Nm 22:23) during the wandering in the wilderness to the entrance into the promised land ("from Shittim to Gilgal," Jos 3–5).

6:6–8 These verses continue the previous unit (6:1–5), the dialogue between the Lord and the people in the pattern of a trial. The Lord has initiated proceedings against them, and they ask how to re-establish the broken relationship with God (vv. 6–7), and are given an answer (v. 8). The form of the passage borrows from a priestly liturgical pattern. When worshipers came to the temple, they inquired

*

5:12 Hos 3:4; 10:1–2.
6:1 Is 6:2; Ob 1.
6:3 Jer 2:5.
6:4 Ex 15:20.
6:5 Nm 22:23; Jos 3–5.
6:6–7 Hos 6:6; 8:13; Am 5:21.

7 Will the LORD be pleased with thousands of rams,
with myriad streams of oil?
†Shall I give my firstborn for my crime,
the fruit of my body for the sin of my soul?
8† You have been told, O mortal, what is good,
and what the LORD requires of you:
Only to do justice and to love goodness,
and to walk humbly with your God.*

You have been told, O mortal, what is good, and what the LORD requires of you: Only to do justice and to love goodness, and to walk humbly with your God."
(Mi 6:8)

9† The LORD cries aloud to the city
(It is prudent to fear your name!):
Hear, O tribe and city assembly,
10 Am I to bear criminal hoarding
and the accursed short ephah?†
11 Shall I acquit crooked scales,
bags of false weights?
12 You whose wealthy are full of violence,
whose inhabitants speak falsehood
with deceitful tongues in their mouths!
13 I have begun to strike you
with devastation because of your sins.
14 You shall eat, without being satisfied,
food that will leave you empty;
What you acquire, you cannot save;
what you do save, I will deliver up to the sword.*
15 You shall sow, yet not reap,
tread out the olive, yet pour no oil,
crush the grapes, yet drink no wine.*
16 You have kept the decrees of Omri,
and all the works of the house of Ahab,
and you have walked in their counsels;
Therefore I will deliver you up to ruin,
and your citizens to derision;
and you shall bear the reproach of the nations.

7 1 Woe is me! I am like the one who gathers summer fruit,
when the vines have been gleaned;
There is no cluster to eat,
no early fig that I crave.
2 The faithful have vanished from the earth,
no mortal is just!
They all lie in wait to shed blood,
each one ensnares the other.*
3 Their hands succeed at evil;
the prince makes demands,
The judge is bought for a price,
the powerful speak as they please.*
4 The best of them is like a brier,
the most honest like a thorn hedge.
The day announced by your sentinels!
Your punishment has come;
now is the time of your confusion.
5 Put no faith in a friend,
do not trust a companion;
With her who lies in your embrace
watch what you say.*
6 For the son belittles his father,
the daughter rises up against her mother,
The daughter-in-law against her mother-in-law,
and your enemies are members of your household.*

IV. Confidence in God's Future

7 But as for me, I will look to the LORD,
I will wait for God my savior;
my God will hear me!*
8† Do not rejoice over me, my enemy!†
though I have fallen, I will arise;

† of the priest concerning the appropriate offering or sacrifice, and the priest answered them (see Ps 15; 24; Is 1:10–17; Am 5:21–24).

6:7 The questions reach their climax with the possibility of child sacrifice, a practice known in antiquity (cf. 2 Kgs 16:3; 21:6).

6:8 *To do justice* refers to human behavior in relationship to others. *To love goodness* refers to the kind of love and concern which is at the heart of the covenant between the Lord and Israel; it is persistently faithful. *To walk humbly with your God* means to listen carefully to the revealed will of God.

6:9–16 The language of the trial resumes as the Lord accuses the people of their sins (vv. 9–12, 16a) and announces their punishment (vv. 13–15, 16b). The city is Jerusalem, and those addressed are its inhabitants. Their wickedness includes cheating in business with false weights and measures, violence, lies, and following the practices of the Israelite kings Omri and Ahab (v. 16a), whose reigns came to symbolize a time of syncretistic worship. The punishment, which has already begun, will include a series of disasters. Finally, the Lord will destroy the city and see that its inhabitants are ridiculed (v. 16b).

6:10 *Ephah*: see note on Is 5:10.

7:8–20 The book concludes with a collection of confident prayers for deliverance, affirmations of faith, and announcements of salvation. Most of these verses bear the marks of use in worship, and probably arose in the exilic or postexilic periods.

7:8–10 An individual, possibly personified Jerusalem, expresses confidence that the Lord will deliver her from her enemy (cf. Ps 23).

* **6:8** Dt 26:16; Zec 7:9; Mt 23:23.
6:14 Dt 28:38; Am 5:11; Hg 1:6.
6:15 Hos 4:10.
7:2 Is 1:21; Hos 4:2.
7:3 Is 1:23.
7:5 Jer 9:3.
7:6 Mt 10:35–36.
7:7 Is 8:17.

though I sit in darkness, the LORD is my
light.
9 I will endure the wrath of the LORD
because I have sinned against him,
Until he pleads my case,
and establishes my right.
He will bring me forth to the light;
I will see his righteousness.
10 When my enemy sees this,
shame shall cover her:
She who said to me,
"Where is the LORD, your God?"
My eyes shall see her downfall;
now she will be trampled† underfoot,
like mud in the streets.
11† It is the day for building your walls;
on that day your boundaries shall be
enlarged.
12 It is the day when those from Assyria to Egypt
shall come to you,
And from Tyre even to the River,
from sea to sea, and from mountain to
mountain;*
13 And the earth shall be a waste
because of its inhabitants,
as a result of their deeds.

14† Shepherd your people with your staff,
the flock of your heritage,
That lives apart* in a woodland,
in the midst of an orchard.
Let them feed in Bashan and Gilead,
as in the days of old;
15 As in the days when you came from the land
of Egypt,
show us wonderful signs.
16 The nations will see and will be put to
shame,
in spite of all their strength;
They will put their hands over their mouths;
their ears will become deaf.
17 They will lick the dust like a snake,
like crawling things on the ground;
They will come quaking from their
strongholds;
they will tremble in fear of you, the LORD,
our God.
18† Who is a God like you, who removes guilt
and pardons sin for the remnant of his
inheritance;
Who does not persist in anger forever,
but instead delights in mercy,*
19 And will again have compassion on us,
treading underfoot our iniquities?
You will cast into the depths of the sea all our
sins;
20 You will show faithfulness to Jacob,
and loyalty to Abraham,
As you have sworn to our ancestors
from days of old.*

†

7:10 *She who said . . . she will be trampled*: in the Old Testament, cities are often personified as women. Here, the prophet is speaking of the enemies' cities.

7:11–13 An announcement of salvation to Zion. The walls of Jerusalem will be rebuilt, its inhabitants who are now scattered from Assyria to Egypt shall return, but the other peoples will suffer for their evil deeds.

7:14–17 A prayer that God will care for the people as in ancient days (v. 14) is answered (vv. 15–17) when the Lord promises to do marvelous things. The nations shall be afraid and turn to the Lord.

7:18–20 The final lines of the book contain a hymn of praise for the incomparable God, who pardons sin and delights in mercy. Thus the remnant, those left after the exile, is confident in God's compassion and in the ancient promises sworn to the ancestors.

*

7:12 Zec 14:16.
7:14 Nm 23:9.
7:18 Jer 10:6; Acts 10:43.
7:20 Ps 105:6; Is 41:8; 63:16.

Devastation, desolation, and destruction! If the Book of Nahum were made into a movie, it would have to be rated R for graphic violence. You are about to read some angry words. They portray a vengeful God bringing destruction upon Israel's enemies. What could make the prophet Nahum so angry? What could make God so angry?

In Depth

At the time Nahum was written, the Assyrian Empire had been the terror of the Middle East for several centuries. In 721 BC, it destroyed the northern part of Israel, called Israel. In 701 BC, it invaded the southern part of Israel, called Judah, and laid siege to Jerusalem (see the timeline and map 5, "The Assyrian Empire," at the back of this Bible). The siege broke off, and Jerusalem did not fall, but the Chosen People of God got a gruesome taste of Assyria's savage cruelty.

The sole concern of the prophet Nahum is the destruction of this evil world power. In the first chapter of his book, he declares the coming wrath of God, and in chapters 2–3, he describes the destruction of Nineveh (the Assyrian capital). We shouldn't be too surprised that when Assyria falls in 612 BC, Nahum sees the justice of God being worked out: the Assyrians are finally getting a taste of their own medicine! Nahum seems almost to be gloating in 3:19:

> All who hear this news of you
> clap their hands over you;
> For who has not suffered
> under your endless malice?

Hidden among the threats and violence against Assyria, we also find words of comfort for God's Chosen People: the awesome war with which God will avenge them because their enemies are God's enemies (see 1:2); good news and peace are coming for Judah (see 2:1); the Lord will restore Israel to its original majesty (see 2:3). We even find some wonderful reminders of God's love and protection, which balance the image of the God of vengeance and destruction: "The LORD is slow to anger, yet great in power" (1:3); "The LORD is good" (1:7); God is "a refuge on the day of distress" (1:7); God takes "care of those who look to him for protection" (1:7). Nahum reminds us that God has many sides and is always more than we can imagine.

At a Glance

I. **God's Terrifying Appearance (1:2–8).**

II. **Nineveh's Judgment and Judah's Restoration (1:9—2:1).**

III. **The Attack on Nineveh (2:2—3:7).**

IV. **Nineveh's Inescapable Fate (3:8–19).**

Quick Facts

Period Covered: from 622 to 609 BC

Inspired Author: Nahum

Theme: God will avenge Israel and destroy its cruel enemies, the Assyrians.

The Book of **Nahum**

Nahum

1 [1] Oracle† concerning Nineveh. The book of the vision of Nahum of Elkosh.

God's Terrifying Appearance

2† A jealous and avenging God† is the LORD,
an avenger is the LORD, full of wrath;
The LORD takes vengeance on his adversaries,
and rages against his enemies;
3 The LORD is slow to anger, yet great in power;
the LORD will not leave the guilty
unpunished.*
In stormwind† and tempest he comes,
and clouds are the dust at his feet;
4 He roars at the sea and leaves it dry,
and all the rivers he dries up.
Laid low are Bashan and Carmel,
and the bloom of Lebanon withers;†
5 The mountains quake before him,
and the hills dissolve;
The earth is laid waste before him,
the world and all who dwell in it.
6† Before his wrath, who can stand firm,
and who can face his blazing anger?*
His fury is poured out like fire,
and boulders break apart before him.
7 The LORD is good to those who wait for him,
a refuge on the day of distress,
Taking care of those who look to him for
protection,
8 when the flood rages;
He makes an end of his opponents,
and pursues his enemies into darkness.

Nineveh's Judgment and Judah's Restoration

9 What do you plot against the LORD,
the one about to bring total destruction?
No opponent rises a second time!
10† Like a thorny thicket, they are tangled,
and like drunkards, they are drunk;
like dry stubble, they are utterly
consumed.
11 From you has come
one plotting evil against the LORD,
one giving sinister counsel.†
12 Thus says the LORD:
though fully intact and so numerous,

†

1:1 *Oracle*: (Heb. *Massa'*) a word used frequently to describe a prophetic statement against a foreign nation or occasionally Israel; it is used favorably for Israel in Zec 12:1 and Mal 1:1. *Nahum of Elkosh*: Nahum means "comfort." Elkosh is a clan or village of unknown location, perhaps in southern Judah.

1:2–8 A poem written in the style of the alphabetic psalms (cf. Ps 9; 25; 111; 119) in which each verse unit begins with a successive letter of the Hebrew alphabet. The second half of the alphabet is not represented here.

1:2 *A jealous . . . God*: see note on Ex 20:5.

1:3–6 *In stormwind*: the power of God is often pictured by natural forces and cosmic disruption (Ex 19:9–25; Ps 18:8–16; 104:1–9).

1:4 Bashan, Carmel, and Lebanon were famous for their mountainous terrain and lush forests.

1:6–7 When God comes in judgment those who oppose God will be destroyed, and those who trust in God will be saved.

1:10 Thorns (Is 34:13), drunkenness (Lam 4:21; Na 3:11), and burning stubble (Ob 18) are all images of the judgment of God's enemies.

1:11 *From you . . . giving sinister counsel*: addressed to Nineveh, the capital city of Sennacherib, king of Assyria, who besieged Jerusalem ca. 700 B.C.

*

1:3 Ex 34:6–7; Jl 2:13.   **1:6** Is 30:27–28; Zep 1:15.

they† shall be mown down and disappear.
Though I have humbled you,
I will humble you no more.
13 Now I will break his yoke off of you,
and tear off your bonds.*

14 The LORD has commanded regarding you:†
no descendant will again bear your name;
From the house of your gods I will abolish
the carved and the molten image;
I will make your grave a dung heap.

2 1 At this moment on the mountains
the footsteps of one bearing good news,
of one announcing peace!*
Celebrate your feasts, Judah,
fulfill your vows!
For never again will destroyers invade you;†
they are completely cut off.

The Attack on Nineveh

2 One who scatters has come up against you;†
guard the rampart,
Watch the road, brace yourselves,
marshal all your strength!
3† The LORD will restore the vine of Jacob,
the honor of Israel,
Because ravagers have ravaged them
and ruined their branches.
4 The shields of his warriors are crimsoned,
the soldiers clad in scarlet;
Like fire are the trappings of the chariots
on the day he prepares for war;
the cavalry is agitated!
5 The chariots dash madly through the streets
and wheel in the squares,
Looking like torches,
bolting like lightning.
6 His picked troops are called,
ranks break at their charge;
To the wall they rush,
their screen† is set up.
7 The river gates† are opened,

Chapter 2

the palace is washed away.
8 The mistress is led forth captive,
and her maidservants† led away,
Moaning like doves,
beating their breasts.
9 Nineveh is like a pool
whose waters escape;
"Stop! Stop!"
but none turns back.*
10 "Plunder the silver, plunder the gold!"
There is no end to the treasure,
to wealth in every precious thing!

11 Emptiness, desolation, waste;
melting hearts and trembling knees,
Churning in every stomach,
every face turning pale!*
12 Where is the lionesses' den,
the young lions' cave,
Where the lion† went in and out,
and the cub, with no one to disturb them?*
13 The lion tore apart enough for his cubs,
and strangled for his lionesses;
He filled his lairs with prey,
and his dens with torn flesh.
14 I now come against you—
oracle of the LORD of hosts—

†

1:12–13 *They*: the enemies of Judah. *You*: Judah. *His yoke*: the dominion of the Assyrian king over Judah.

1:14 *You*: the king of Assyria.

2:1 *For never again will destroyers invade you*: prophets are not always absolutely accurate in the things they foresee. Nineveh was destroyed, as Nahum expected, but Judah was later invaded by the Babylonians and (much later) by the Romans. The prophets were convinced that Israel held a key place in God's plan and looked for the people to survive all catastrophes, always blessed by the Lord, though the manner was not always as they expected; the "fallen hut of David" was not rebuilt as Am 9:11 suggests, except in the coming of Jesus, and in a way far different than the prophet expected. Often the prophet speaks in hyperbole, as when Second Isaiah speaks of the restored Jerusalem being built with precious stones (Is 54:12) as a way of indicating a glorious future.

2:2 *One who scatters has come up against you*: the enemy is about to crush Nineveh, dispersing and deporting its people (v. 8; 3:18).

2:3 This verse does not fit its context well; it may have been the conclusion for the preceding section and have once followed v. 1, or it may be a later scribal addition.

2:6 *Their screen*: that is, a mantelet, a movable military shelter protecting the besiegers.

2:7 *River gates*: a network of canals brought water into Nineveh from the Tigris and Khosr Rivers on which the city was located.

2:8 *Mistress . . . and her maidservants*: either the queen of Nineveh with the ladies of her court, or the city of Nineveh itself, pictured as a noblewoman (3:4).

2:12 *The lion*: the king of Assyria.

*

1:13 Is 9:4; 10:27.
2:1 Is 52:7; Rom 10:15.
2:9 Is 8:7–8.
2:11 Jl 2:6.
2:12 Ez 19:2–7.

I will consume your chariots in smoke,
and the sword will devour your young lions;
Your preying on the land I will bring to an end,
the cry of your lionesses will be heard no more.

3 1 Ah! The bloody city,
all lies,
Full of plunder,
whose looting never stops!*
2 The crack of the whip,
the rumbling of wheels;
Horses galloping,
chariots bounding,
3 Cavalry charging,
the flash of the sword,
the gleam of the spear;
A multitude of slain,
a mass of corpses,
Endless bodies
to stumble upon!
4 For the many debaucheries of the prostitute,
a charming mistress of witchcraft,
Who enslaved nations with her prostitution,
and peoples by her witchcraft:*
5† I now come against you—
oracle of the LORD of hosts—
and I will lift your skirt above your face;
I will show your nakedness to the nations,
to the kingdoms your shame!*
6 I will cast filth upon you,
disgrace you and make you a spectacle;
7 Until everyone who sees you
runs from you saying,
"Nineveh is destroyed;
who can pity her?
Where can I find
any to console you?"

Nineveh's Inescapable Fate

8 Are you better than No-amon† *
that was set among the Nile's canals,
Surrounded by waters,
with the river for her rampart
and water for her wall?
9 Ethiopia was her strength,
and Egypt without end;
Put† and the Libyans
were her allies.
10 Yet even she became an exile,
and went into captivity;
Even her little ones were dashed to pieces
at the corner of every street;
For her nobles they cast lots,

Live It!

Images of God

"A multitude of slain, a mass of corpses, / Endless bodies to stumble upon!" (Na 3:3). The descriptions of God's vengeance on the Assyrians throughout chapters 2 and 3 of Nahum seem contradictory to Jesus' command to love one's enemies (see Mt 5:43–48). Was God different back in Old Testament times? or was Nahum just mistaken? These are difficult but important questions!

In understanding Nahum's message, it helps to keep in mind three things. First, throughout the Bible, there is a strong theme of divine hatred for all sin. In the New Testament, though, a distinction emerges that although God hates the sin, God still loves the sinner. Nahum doesn't make that distinction.

Second, Christians today make a distinction between God's directly causing something to happen and God's allowing something to occur—usually as a result of human limitations, people's poor choices, or natural phenomena. Again, Nahum doesn't make this distinction—for Nahum, if something happens, God is the direct cause.

Finally, we have to keep in mind that all our attempts to understand God will fall short. God is beyond human understanding. That is why the Bible's authors, including Nahum, describe God in many different—and often seemingly contradictory—ways.

How do you see God? as a vengeful fire (see Na 1:6) or as a stronghold of protection (see verse 7)? Are you comfortable imagining God in different—even opposite—ways?

▶ Na 2:1—3:3

† 3:5–6 The punishment for adulterous women.
3:8 *No-amon*: "No" was the Egyptian name of the capital of Upper Egypt, called Thebes by the Greeks; its patron deity was Amon. This great city was destroyed by the Assyrians in 663 B.C.
3:9 *Put*: a North African people often associated with Egypt and Ethiopia (Jer 46:8–9).

3:1 Is 10:13–14; Hb 2:12.
3:4 Mi 1:7; Rev 17:1.
3:5 Is 47:3; Jer 13:26.
3:8 Jer 46:25.

and all her great ones were put into
chains.
11 You, too, will drink of this;
you will be overcome;*
You, too, will seek
a refuge from the foe.
12 But all your fortresses are fig trees,
bearing early figs;†
When shaken, they fall
into the devourer's mouth.
13 Indeed your troops
are women in your midst;
To your foes are open wide
the gates of your land,
fire has consumed their bars.

14 Draw water for the siege,†
strengthen your fortresses;
Go down into the mud
and tread the clay,
take hold of the brick mold!
15 There the fire will consume you,
the sword will cut you down;
it will consume you like the
grasshoppers.
Multiply like the grasshoppers,
multiply like the locusts!*
16 You have made your traders† more numerous
than the stars of the heavens;
like grasshoppers that shed their skins and
fly away.
17 Your sentries are like locusts,
and your scribes like locust swarms
Gathered on the rubble fences
on a cold day!
Yet when the sun rises, they vanish,
and no one knows where they have gone.

18 Your shepherds slumber,
O king of Assyria,
your nobles have gone to rest;
Your people are scattered upon the
mountains,
with none to gather them.
19 There is no healing for your hurt,
your wound is fatal.
All who hear this news of you
clap their hands over you;
For who has not suffered
under your endless malice?

† **3:12** *Early figs*: the refugees from Nineveh who escape to presumably secure fortresses.
3:14 An ironic exhortation to prepare the city for a futile defense. *Go down . . . brick mold*: make bricks for the city walls.
3:16 *Traders*: agents of the economic exploitation that sustained and enriched the Assyrian empire.

* **3:11** Jer 25:15–16; Ob 16. **3:15** Jer 46:23.

God, why aren't you answering our cries for help? How long must we endure this trial? Most people have wondered this at times. Why does our good, all-powerful God let suffering or injustice go on? The prophet Habakkuk struggled with these same painful and disturbing questions. His hope in God's justice is a model of faith amid doubt.

At a Glance

I. Habakkuk's First Complaint (1:2–4).

II. God's Response (1:5–11).

III. Habakkuk's Second Complaint (1:12—2:1).

IV. God's Response (2:2–4).

V. Sayings Against Tyrants (2:5–20).

VI. Hymn About God's Reign (3:1–19).

Quick Facts

Period Covered: probably the reign of King Jehoiakim, from 605 to 587 BC (2 Kgs 23:36—24:7)

Inspired Author: Habakkuk

Theme: The answer to evil is faith in God's justice.

In Depth

Habakkuk was the first prophet who dared to ask God about God's behavior. He looked around at all the terrible things that were happening to his people and cried out: God, where are you? Do you even care about us? Why do you allow evil people to oppress us?

We know little about Habakkuk except that he was a prophet in the southern kingdom of Judah in the late seventh century BC. The Chaldeans (another name for the Babylonians) and the corrupt king of Judah, Jehoiakim, were causing so much trouble that Habakkuk was ready to despair. God answered him in a most surprising way, saying that the Chaldeans—as bad as they were—were chosen as God's instrument to punish the wicked all over the earth. Habakkuk was not satisfied. He asked why God was silent while the wicked destroyed the righteous. God then spoke to him in a vision (see Hb 2:2), saying that justice would come to the wicked in its own time, but the "just one who is righteous because of faith shall live" (Hb 2:4). Later, Paul would use these same words to describe the Christians (see Rom 1:17, Gal 3:11). For Habakkuk, faith in God and hope in God's justice were the same thing.

The short Book of Habakkuk is unique among the prophetic books in the variety of its writings. Its reflections about the problem of evil in the world resemble the wisdom literature. Its dialogues with God (see 1:2) are similar to Jeremiah's confessions (see Jer 12:1–6). Habakkuk, chapter 3 is a canticle (song).

The prophet's concluding canticle is a prayer of confidence in God's power to save the people. We too can pray in confidence because God is just and will save us in our time of need.

Habakkuk

1 [1]The oracle which Habakkuk the prophet received in a vision.

Habakkuk's First Complaint

2 How long, O LORD, must I cry for help†
and you do not listen?*
Or cry out to you, "Violence!"
and you do not intervene?
3 Why do you let me see iniquity?
why do you simply gaze at evil?
Destruction and violence are before me;*
there is strife and discord.
4 This is why the law is numb†
and justice never comes,
For the wicked surround the just;*
this is why justice comes forth perverted.

God's Response

5† Look over the nations and see!
Be utterly amazed!
For a work is being done in your days
that you would not believe, were it told.*
6 For now I am raising up the Chaldeans,*
that bitter and impulsive people,
Who march the breadth of the land
to take dwellings not their own.
7 They are terrifying and dreadful;
their right and their exalted position are of
their own making.
8 Swifter than leopards are their horses,
and faster than desert wolves.
Their horses spring forward;
they come from far away;
they fly like an eagle hastening to devour.
9 All of them come for violence,
their combined onslaught, a stormwind
to gather up captives like sand.
10 They scoff at kings,
ridicule princes;
They laugh at any fortress,
heap up an earthen ramp, and conquer it.
11 Then they sweep through like the wind and
vanish—
they make their own strength their god!†

Habakkuk's Second Complaint

12 Are you not from of old, O LORD,
my holy God, immortal?*

---

† **1:2–4** The prophet complains about God's apparent disregard for Judah's internal evils in language that echoes the preaching of prophets like Amos, Isaiah, and Jeremiah.

1:4 *The law is numb*: because the Lord has been silent, the Law, whether in the form of the scroll found in the Temple in the time of Josiah (2 Kgs 22) or in the form of divine instruction given by priests and prophets, has proved ineffective and so appeared to be cold, unreceptive, and powerless. For the Law to be credible, the Lord must see to it that the wicked are punished and the just rewarded.

1:5–7 Habakkuk interprets the Babylonian defeat of Egypt at Carchemish (605 B.C.) as the answer to his complaint: the Lord will send the Chaldean empire against Judah as punishment for their sins.

1:11 The primary aim of military campaigns by ancient Near Eastern rulers was usually the gathering of spoils and the collection of tribute rather than the annexation of territory. However, in the eighth century B.C., the Assyrians began to administer many conquered territories as provinces.

---

* **1:2** Ps 13:2.
1:3 Ez 45:9.
1:4 Is 29:20–21.
1:5 Acts 13:41.
1:6 Jer 32:28.
1:12 Ps 90:2.

LORD, you have appointed them for
judgment,†
O Rock,† you have set them in place to
punish!
13 Your eyes are too pure to look upon wickedness,
and the sight of evil you cannot endure.
Why, then, do you gaze on the faithless in
silence
while the wicked devour those more just
than themselves?
14 You have made mortals like the fish in the sea,
like creeping things without a leader.
15 He† brings them all up with a hook,
and hauls them away with his net;
He gathers them in his fishing net,
and then rejoices and exults.
16 Therefore he makes sacrifices to his net,†
and burns incense to his fishing net;
For thanks to them his portion is rich,
and his meal lavish.
17 Shall they, then, keep on drawing his sword
to slaughter nations without mercy?

2 1 I will stand at my guard post,
and station myself upon the rampart;*
I will keep watch to see what he will say to me,
and what answer he will give to my
complaint.

God's Response

2 Then the LORD answered me and said:
Write down the vision;† *
Make it plain upon tablets,
so that the one who reads it may run.
3 For the vision is a witness for the appointed
time,
a testimony to the end; it will not disappoint.
If it delays, wait for it,
it will surely come, it will not be late.
4 See, the rash have no integrity;
but the just one who is righteous because
of faith shall live.† *

Sayings Against Tyrants

5† Indeed wealth is treacherous;
a proud man does not succeed.
He who opens wide his throat like Sheol,
and is insatiable as death,
Who gathers to himself all the nations,

Live It!

Now!

"I want it all, and I want it now!" That statement could sum up the ambitions of a lot of people. It is how they define success. The key word in their goal is *now*. They don't like to wait in lines; they want instant service and immediate gratification. Think about your own frustration if the internet connection you're using is too slow, or if you can't immediately reach a friend on her or his cell phone. We have grown used to getting things right away, and we become impatient when our expectations are not met.

There is a temptation to apply this goal to our spiritual lives, hoping for an immediate and fulfilling relationship with God. But the spiritual life does not work that way. Recall these words from the Book of Ecclesiastes: "There is an appointed time for everything, / and a time for every affair under the heavens" (3:1). We have to remind ourselves that many valuable things take time. Our growth in faith will take time. We need to be open, patient, and trusting. As God reminds Habakkuk in his vision in Habakkuk 2:3, "If it delays, wait for it, / it will surely come, it will not be late."

Consider these questions:

- What are your goals for your relationship with God?
- How patient are you with your spiritual growth? How do you nurture it day by day?

▶ Hb 2:3

†

1:12–2:1 *Appointed them for judgment*: this complaint is directed against the violent Babylonians, the very nation God chose to punish Judah.

1:12 *Rock*: an ancient title celebrating the Lord's power and fidelity; cf. Dt 32:4; Is 26:4; 30:29; Ps 18:3, 32, 47; 95:1.

1:15 *He*: the Babylonian king (cf. vv. 6, 13), who easily conquers other nations and treats them as objects for his entertainment and enrichment.

1:16 *He makes sacrifices to his net*: the leader attributes victory to the military weapons he wields; he and his weapons have won victory, not any god.

2:2 *Write down the vision*: the vision is written down for two reasons: so that a herald may carry and proclaim its contents to the people, and so that the reception of the vision and its truth can be verified by its fulfillment (v. 3).

2:4 *The just one who is righteous because of faith shall live*: the faithful survive the impending doom because they trust in God's justice and wait patiently for God to carry it out. Several New Testament passages cite these words (Rom 1:17; Gal 3:11; cf. Heb 10:38) to confirm the teaching that people receive justification and supernatural life through faith in Christ.

2:5 This verse describes any tyrant who, like the Babylonians, possesses insatiable greed.

2:1 Is 21:8.
2:2 Is 30:8.
2:4 Rom 1:17; Gal 3:11; Heb 10:38.

and collects for himself all the peoples—
6 Shall not all these take up a taunt against him,*
and make a riddle about him, saying:

Ah! you who store up what is not yours
—how long can it last!—
you who load yourself down with collateral.
7 Will your debtors† not rise suddenly?
Will they not awake, those who make you tremble?
You will become their spoil!
8 Because you plundered many nations,
the remaining peoples shall plunder you;
Because of the shedding of human blood,
and violence done to the land,
to the city and to all who live in it.

9 Ah! you who pursue evil gain for your household,
setting your nest on high
to escape the reach of misfortune!
10 You have devised shame for your household,
cutting off many peoples, forfeiting your own life;
11 For the stone in the wall shall cry out,†
and the beam in the frame shall answer it!

12 Ah! you who build a city by bloodshed,
and who establish a town with injustice!*
13 Is this not from the LORD of hosts:
peoples toil† for what the flames consume,
and nations grow weary for nothing!
14 But the earth shall be filled
with the knowledge of the LORD's glory,
just as the water covers the sea.*

15 Ah! you who give your neighbors
the cup of your wrath to drink, and make them drunk,
until their nakedness is seen!*
16 You are filled with shame instead of glory;
drink, you too, and stagger!
The cup from the LORD's right hand shall come around to you,
and utter shame shall cover your glory.
17 For the violence done to Lebanon† shall cover you,*
and the destruction of the animals shall terrify you;
Because of the shedding of human blood,
and violence done to the land,
to the city and to all who live in it.

18 Of what use is the carved image,†
that its maker should carve it?
Or the molten image, the lying oracle,
that its very maker should trust in it,
and make mute idols?
19 Ah! you who say to wood, "Awake!"
to silent stone, "Arise!"
Can any such thing give oracles?*
It is only overlaid with gold and silver,
there is no breath in it at all.
20 But the LORD is in his holy temple;
silence before him, all the earth!*

Hymn About God's Reign

3 1 Prayer of Habakkuk, the prophet. According to Shigyonot.†

2 O LORD, I have heard your renown,
and am in awe, O LORD, of your work.
In the course of years revive it,†
in the course of years make yourself known;
in your wrath remember compassion!

3† God came from Teman,†
the Holy One from Mount Paran.*
Selah
His glory covered the heavens,
and his praise filled the earth;

HB

†

2:7 *Debtors*: the Hebrew term can mean either debtors or creditors, and this double meaning is likely intended: the debtor nations rise up against their creditor nation and become its creditors in the reversal of affairs described here.

2:11–12 The palaces, built at the expense of gross injustice (vv. 6–10), call down vengeance on their builders. This is typical prophetic language for the condemnation of social crimes within Israel and Judah.

2:13 *Peoples toil*: those oppressed by the Babylonians do not benefit from their work. Verses 13–14 break the pattern of reversal in the oracles that precede and may have been added by an editor.

2:17 *The violence done to Lebanon*: the destruction of the cedar forests of Lebanon, used in lavish building projects by the great conquerors; cf. Is 14:8; 37:24. *The destruction of the animals*: the killing off of the wild animals through excessive hunting by the same conquerors; cf. Bar 3:16.

2:18–20 Idolatrous worship is here shown to be folly by contrasting idols with the majesty of the one true God. Verse 18 may originally have followed v. 19, since the term "Ah!" begins each new saying in this section.

3:1 *Shigyonot*: a Hebrew technical term no longer understood, but probably a musical notation regarding the following hymn. This term, the references to the leader and stringed instruments at the end of the hymn (v. 19), and the use of the term *selah* in vv. 3, 9, and 13 are found elsewhere in the Bible only in the Psalter, and they indicate that, like the psalms, this poem was once used in worship.

3:2 *In the course of years revive it*: a plea for God to renew the works of the past.

3:3–15 Cf. the theophanies in Dt 33:2–3; Jgs 5:4–5; Ps 18:8–16; 68:8–9; 77:17–21; 97:1–5; Na 1:3–6, etc. Conventional language is employed to describe the appearance of the Lord, as in Ex 19:16–19.

3:3 *Teman*: a region in Edom. *Mount Paran*: in the territory of Edom, or the northern part of the Sinai peninsula.

*

2:6 Is 14:4.
2:12 Ez 24:6; Mi 3:10; Na 3:1.
2:14 Is 11:9.
2:15 Jer 51:7; Lam 4:21.
2:17 Is 14:8.
2:19 Is 44:18–19.
2:20 Ps 11:4.
3:3 Dt 33:2.

4 his splendor spread like the light.
He raised his horns high,*
he rejoiced on the day of his strength.
5 Before him went pestilence,
and plague† followed in his steps.
6 He stood and shook the earth;
he looked and made the nations tremble.
Ancient mountains were shattered,
the age-old hills bowed low,
age-old orbits† collapsed.

7 The tents of Cushan trembled,
the pavilions of the land of Midian.†
8 Was your anger against the rivers, O LORD?
your wrath against the rivers,
your rage against the sea,†*
That you mounted your steeds,
your victorious chariot?
9 You readied your bow,
you filled your bowstring with arrows.
Selah

You split the earth with rivers;
10 at the sight of you the mountains writhed.
The clouds poured down water;
the deep roared loudly.
The sun† forgot to rise,
11 the moon left its lofty station,*
At the light of your flying arrows,
at the gleam of your flashing spear.

12 In wrath you marched on the earth,
in fury you trampled the nations.
13 You came forth to save your people,
to save your anointed one.†
You crushed the back of the wicked,
you laid him bare, bottom to neck.
Selah

14† You pierced his head with your shafts;
his princes you scattered with your
stormwind,
as food for the poor in unknown places.
15 You trampled the sea with your horses
amid the churning of the deep waters.

16 I hear, and my body trembles;
at the sound, my lips quiver.
Decay invades my bones,
my legs tremble beneath me.
I await the day of distress
that will come upon the people who
attack us.

17 For though the fig tree does not blossom,
and no fruit appears on the vine,
Though the yield of the olive fails
and the terraces produce no nourishment,
Though the flocks disappear from the fold
and there is no herd in the stalls,
18 Yet I will rejoice in the LORD
and exult in my saving God.
19 GOD, my Lord, is my strength;
he makes my feet swift as those of deer
and enables me to tread upon the
heights.†*

For the leader; with stringed instruments.

†

3:5 *Pestilence . . . plague*: these may be figures who are part of the heavenly armies God leads into battle.

3:6 *Age-old orbits*: the regular paths through the skies of heavenly bodies are disrupted at the appearance of the divine warrior, as are the ancient mountains on earth. Such cosmic disruption is typical of divine appearances (Ps 18:8; Na 1:5).

3:7 *Cushan . . . Midian*: the inhabitants of the area southeast of Judah where the divine march originates (Teman, Mount Paran), who are shaken, together with the cosmos, at God's appearance.

3:8 *Rivers . . . sea*: the forces of chaos personified as *yam* (Sea) and *nahar* (River) try to destroy the order God imposed at creation by sweeping past their boundaries and covering the earth. Their mention here and in v. 15 emphasizes that God is both creator and deliverer, subduing historical enemies and cosmic forces.

3:10–11 *Sun . . . moon*: heavenly figures who, like pestilence and plague (v. 5), serve in God's army, or are startled at God's appearance, as are the ancient constellations (v. 6).

3:13 *Your anointed one*: the theocratic king, the head of God's people. *The back of the wicked*: this may refer both to God's cosmic enemy, River/Sea, and to the leader of Israel's historical enemy.

3:14 The last two lines of this verse are obscure in Hebrew and difficult to translate.

3:19 *The heights*: this term can also mean "backs" and may be an image of conquest over the poet's foes.

*

3:4 Ps 18:3.
3:8 Ps 74:13; 89:11; Is 51:9; Na 1:4.
3:11 Jos 10:12–13.
3:19 Ps 18:32–34.

During childhood, we usually have to clean up messes, take time-outs, or lose privileges as consequences for poor choices we have made. As we get older, we learn that our wrongdoing has more personal and painful consequences: perhaps a parent's refusal to trust us, a friend's anger, or our pain after hurting someone we love. The prophet Zephaniah warned the people of Judah of the severe consequences of their sin against the Lord.

The Book of Zephaniah

At a Glance

I. **The Day of the Lord: Judgment on Judah (1:2—2:3).**

II. **Judgment on the Nations (2:4–15).**

III. **Jerusalem Reproached (3:1–7).**

IV. **The Nations Punished and Jerusalem Restored (3:8–20).**

Quick Facts

Period Covered: approximately 640–609 BC

Inspired Author: Zephaniah (and perhaps a later editor)

Theme: Judah and its neighbors will experience the consequences of their sinfulness.

In Depth

The Book of Zephaniah gives us few clues about the prophet Zephaniah's identity. We do know that he preached in the southern kingdom of Judah during the reign of King Josiah (see 2 Chronicles, chapters 34–35), around 640–609 BC. He followed First Isaiah and Micah, and came a little before Habakkuk, during the time of Nahum.

Zephaniah follows the footsteps of the classical Old Testament prophets in denouncing the wrongdoing of society. His main contribution is considering pride (see 1:6, 2:10, 3:11) as the source of problems such as smugness (see 1:12), rebellion (see 3:2), and treachery (see 3:11). All these attitudes toward God lead to idolatry and social sin. Although all people sin, leaders have a greater responsibility, and their sins will provoke a harsh judgment during the coming day of the Lord (see 1:14). Only those who worship God humbly and who seek justice will be spared. Zephaniah calls them the remnant (see 3:12–13), meaning "a little piece that is left over." They are the ones who will stay faithful to God through both good times and bad.

The book ends with a song of joy reassuring the people of Jerusalem that God still loves them and will save them in the end. We are not sure whether the song is from Zephaniah himself or is the addition of a later editor. It is as if the writer knows that when people are experiencing the negative results of sinful actions, they need to be reassured they are still loved. God's punishment is to teach us, not to destroy us. Therefore, God's People should not despair but keep their trust in God.

Zephaniah

2:13–15

1 [1]The word of the LORD which came to Zeph-
aniah, the son of Cushi, the son of Gedaliah,
the son of Amariah, the son of Hezekiah,† in the
days of Josiah, the son of Amon, king of Judah.

The Day of the Lord: Judgment on Judah

2 I will completely sweep away all things
from the face of the land—oracle of the LORD.
3 I will sweep away human being and beast
alike,
I will sweep away the birds of the sky,
and the fish of the sea.
I will make the wicked stumble;
I will eliminate the people
from the face of the land—oracle of the
LORD.*
4 I will stretch out my hand against Judah,
and against all the inhabitants of Jerusalem;
I will eliminate from this place
the last vestige of Baal,
the name of the idolatrous priests.
5 And those who bow down on the roofs
to the host of heaven,†
And those who bow down to the LORD
but swear by Milcom;*
6 And those who have turned away from the LORD,
and those who have not sought the LORD,
who have not inquired of him.

7 Silence in the presence of the Lord GOD!
for near is the day of the LORD,
Yes, the LORD has prepared a sacrifice,
he has consecrated his guests.†*
8 On the day of the LORD's sacrifice
I will punish the officials and the king's sons,
and all who dress in foreign apparel.
9 I will punish, on that day,
all who leap over the threshold,†
Who fill the house of their master
with violence and deceit.
10 On that day—oracle of the LORD—
A cry will be heard from the Fish Gate,
a wail from the Second Quarter,†
loud crashing from the hills.
11 Wail, O inhabitants of Maktesh!
for all the merchants are destroyed,
all who weigh out silver, done away with.

12 At that time,
I will search Jerusalem with lamps,

†

1:1 *Hezekiah*: it is possible, but not certain, that Zephaniah's ancestor was King Hezekiah who reigned in Judah from 715 to 687 B.C. (2 Kgs 18–20).

1:5 *The host of heaven*: the sun, moon, planets, and stars, the worship of which became widespread in Judah under Assyrian influence. *Milcom*: the god of the Ammonites; cf. 1 Kgs 11:5, 7, 33; 2 Kgs 23:13.

1:7 *He has consecrated his guests*: God has consecrated the troops, presumably foreign, who have been invited to share in the spoil on the day of slaughter.

1:9 *Leap over the threshold*: the reference may be to a religious ritual like that practiced by the priests of the Philistine deity Dagon (1 Sm 5:5).

1:10–11 *The Second Quarter . . . Maktesh*: sections of Jerusalem (cf. 2 Kgs 22:14).

*

1:3 Hos 4:3.
1:5 Jer 8:2; 2 Kgs 23:13.
1:7 Is 34:6; Am 5:18.

I will punish the people
who settle like dregs in wine,†
Who say in their hearts,
"The Lord will not do good,
nor will he do harm."
13 Their wealth shall be given to plunder
and their houses to devastation;
They will build houses,
but not dwell in them;
They will plant vineyards,
but not drink their wine.*
14 Near is the great day of the LORD,
near and very swiftly coming.
The sound of the day of the LORD! Piercing—
there a warrior shrieks!
15 A day of wrath is that day,
a day of distress and anguish,
a day of ruin and desolation,
A day of darkness and gloom,
a day of thick black clouds,*
16 A day of trumpet blasts and battle cries
against fortified cities,
against lofty battlements.*
17 I will hem the people in
till they walk like the blind,
because they have sinned against the LORD;
And their blood shall be poured out like dust,
and their bowels like dung.
18 Neither their silver nor their gold
will be able to save them.
On the day of the LORD's wrath,
in the fire of his passion,
all the earth will be consumed.
For he will make an end, yes, a sudden end,
of all who live on the earth.*

2

1† Gather, gather yourselves together,
O nation without shame!
2 Before you are driven away,
like chaff that disappears;
Before there comes upon you
the blazing anger of the LORD;
Before there comes upon you
the day of the LORD's anger.
3 Seek the LORD,
all you humble of the land,
who have observed his law;
Seek justice,
seek humility;
Perhaps you will be sheltered
on the day of the LORD's anger.*

Judgment on the Nations

4 For Gaza shall be forsaken,
and Ashkelon shall be a waste,
Ashdod they shall drive out at midday,
and Ekron† shall be uprooted.*
5 Ah! You who dwell by the seacoast,
the nation of Cherethites,†
the word of the LORD is against you!
O Canaan, land of the Philistines,
I will leave you to perish without an
inhabitant!
6 You shall become fields for shepherds,
and folds for flocks.
7 The seacoast shall belong
to the remnant of the house of Judah;
by the sea they shall pasture.
In the houses of Ashkelon
they shall lie down in the evening.
For the LORD their God will take care of them,
and bring about their restoration.

8 I have heard the taunts uttered by Moab,
and the insults of the Ammonites,†
When they taunted my people
and made boasts against their territory.*
9 Therefore, as I live—
oracle of the LORD of hosts—
the God of Israel,
Moab shall become like Sodom,
the Ammonites like Gomorrah:
A field of weeds,
a salt pit,
a waste forever.
The remnant of my people shall plunder them,
the survivors of my nation dispossess them.
10 This will be the recompense for their pride,
because they taunted and boasted against
the people of the LORD of hosts.
11 The LORD shall inspire them with terror
when he makes all the gods of earth waste
away;
Then the distant shores of the nations,
each from its own place,
shall bow down to him.

ZEP

†

1:12 *Settle like dregs in wine*: those who are overconfident because, like the sediment that settles to the bottom of a bottle of wine, they have remained at peace and undisturbed for a long time.

2:1–3 This oracle is a classic description of the day of the Lord as an overwhelming disaster, concluding with a call for repentance and reform. *Nation without shame*: Judah.

2:4 *Gaza . . . Ashkelon . . . Ashdod . . . Ekron*: cities of the Philistine confederation.

2:5 *Cherethites*: a synonym for, or subgroup of, the Philistines, which may be associated with Crete, a part of the larger Aegean area from which the Philistines came.

2:8 *Moab . . . Ammonites*: Judah's neighbors to the East across the Jordan.

*

1:13 Am 5:11.
1:15 Is 13:9; Jl 2:1–2.
1:16 Am 2:2.
1:18 Zep 3:8; Jer 4:26–27.
2:3 Am 5:14–15.
2:4 Jer 47:5; Am 1:6–8.
2:8 Jer 48:1; 49:1.

Cultural Connection

Material Poverty and Spiritual Poverty

In the Bible, God is always opposed to material poverty and misery. Over and over in the Old Testament, wealth is called a blessing and poverty a curse. The laws of the covenant assert that poverty should not exist in Israel. Rich people are commanded to periodically forgive the debts of the poor and return land taken as payment of debt to the land's original owners (see Lv 25:8). Selfishness leads to injustice, and injustice leads to tragedy, violence, and despair.

Zephaniah gives a spiritual connotation to the word *poor* (translated as "lowly" in Zephaniah 3:12). He relates poverty to humility. In this sense, to be poor is to be empty of egoism and pride, and therefore open to God's action in us. Zephaniah believes a small group of spiritually poor people, known as the remnant of Israel or the poor of God, will keep the covenant alive.

Hispanic spirituality is deeply rooted in this concept of the poor, and the Virgin Mary is the culture's supreme example of it. To be spiritually poor is to be receptive to the Holy Spirit, to be generous with others, to trust in God's providence, and to accept suffering without losing hope.

- How will you live out the call to be spiritually poor, free of material goods beyond what is necessary to live?
- Ask God to give you the strength to respond to this call, which is so necessary in this world of pride, injustice, and materialism.

▶ **Zep 3:11–13**

12 You too, O Cushites,†
shall be slain by the sword of the LORD.*
13 He will stretch out his hand against the north,
to destroy Assyria;
He will make Nineveh a waste,
dry as the desert.*
14 In her midst flocks shall lie down,
all the wild life of the hollows;
The screech owl and the desert owl
shall roost in her columns;
The owl shall hoot from the window,
the raven croak from the doorway.*
15 Is this the exultant city†
that dwelt secure,
That told itself,
"I and there is no one else"?
How it has become a waste,
a lair for wild animals!
Those who pass by it
hiss, and shake their fists!

Jerusalem Reproached

3 1 Ah! Rebellious and polluted,
the tyrannical city!†
2 It listens to no voice,
accepts no correction;
In the LORD it has not trusted,
nor drawn near to its God.*
3 Its officials within it
are roaring lions;
Its judges are desert wolves
that have no bones to gnaw by morning.*
4 Its prophets are reckless,
treacherous people;
Its priests profane what is holy,
and do violence to the law.*
5 But the LORD in its midst is just,
doing no wrong;
Morning after morning rendering judgment
unfailingly, at dawn;
the wicked, however, know no shame.

6 I have cut down nations,
their battlements are laid waste;
I have made their streets deserted,
with no one passing through;
Their cities are devastated,
with no one dwelling in them.*

ZEP

†

2:12 *Cushites*: the Ethiopians, who had ruled Egypt a generation before Zephaniah's career.

2:15 *The exultant city*: Nineveh. *Hiss, and shake their fists*: gestures of derision.

3:1 *The tyrannical city*: Jerusalem.

*

2:12 2 Chr 14:7–14.
2:13 Na 3:7.
2:14 Is 34:11.
3:2 Jer 2:30; 7:28.
3:3 Ez 22:27; Mi 3:11.
3:4 Ez 22:26; Hb 1:4.
3:6 Jer 2:15.

7 I said, "Surely now you will fear me,
you will accept correction;
They cannot fail to see
all I have brought upon them."
Yet the more eagerly they have done
all their corrupt deeds.

The Nations Punished and Jerusalem Restored

8 Therefore, wait for me—oracle of the LORD—
until the day when I arise as accuser;
For it is my decision to gather nations,
to assemble kingdoms,
In order to pour out upon them my wrath,
all my blazing anger;
For in the fire of my passion
all the earth will be consumed.*

9 For then I will make pure
the speech of the peoples,
That they all may call upon the name of the LORD,
to serve him with one accord;
10 From beyond the rivers of Ethiopia
and as far as the recesses of the North,
they shall bring me offerings.

11 On that day
You will not be ashamed
of all your deeds,
when you rebelled against me;
For then I will remove from your midst
the proud braggarts,
And you shall no longer exalt yourself
on my holy mountain.
12 But I will leave as a remnant in your midst
a people humble and lowly,
Who shall take refuge in the name of the LORD—*
13 the remnant of Israel.
They shall do no wrong
and speak no lies;
Nor shall there be found in their mouths
a deceitful tongue;
They shall pasture and lie down
with none to disturb them.*
14 Shout for joy, daughter Zion!
sing joyfully, Israel!
Be glad and exult with all your heart,
daughter Jerusalem!*
15 The LORD has removed the judgment against you,
he has turned away your enemies;
The King of Israel, the LORD, is in your midst,
you have no further misfortune to fear.
16 On that day, it shall be said to Jerusalem:
Do not fear, Zion,
do not be discouraged!
17 The LORD, your God, is in your midst,
a mighty savior,
Who will rejoice over you with gladness,
and renew you in his love,
Who will sing joyfully because of you,*
18 as on festival days.

I will remove disaster from among you,
so that no one may recount your disgrace.
19 At that time I will deal
with all who oppress you;
I will save the lame,
and assemble the outcasts;
I will give them praise and renown
in every land where they were shamed.*
20 At that time I will bring you home,
and at that time I will gather you;
For I will give you renown and praise,
among all the peoples of the earth,
When I bring about your restoration
before your very eyes, says the LORD.*

3:8 Zep 1:18; Jl 4:2.
3:12 Is 57:13; Ob 17.
3:13 Mi 4:4.
3:14 Zec 9:9.
3:17 Jl 2:27.
3:19 Mi 4:6.
3:20 Jl 4:1.

Imagine that you've been saving for months for a new stereo system. Just when you are about to purchase it, a good friend's family has a major house fire. Unfortunately, they were not insured, so the community is taking up a collection to help them rebuild. Now you are faced with a decision: Will you buy the new stereo or help your friend's family? The Jews at the time of the prophet Haggai faced an even more difficult decision: Returning to Jerusalem after the Babylonian Exile, which would they rebuild first—their homes or God's Temple?

The Book of
Haggai

At a Glance

I. The Restoration of the Temple (1:1–15).

II. Oracles of Encouragement (2:1–23).

Quick Facts

Period Covered: approximately 520 BC

Inspired Author: Haggai

Theme: rebuilding God's Temple

In Depth

When the people of ancient Judah lost their Temple in 587 BC and were deported to a strange land, they experienced a crisis in faith. Had God abandoned them? Were they no longer God's People? Was God punishing them for their sins? Some of them dreamed of a time when they could return to their land and rebuild God's Temple. However, when they finally were able to return in 538 BC, things weren't as easy as they had hoped. Suffering from poverty, droughts, and crop failures (see Hg 1:10–11), they put off rebuilding the Temple. Into this scene came the prophet Haggai. He told the people that God was still with them, and life was so difficult because they didn't seem to care that God's house was in ruins (see verse 9). They had to get their priorities in order!

The people heard God's word spoken through Haggai and immediately began working on the Temple. In their minds, they knew the new Temple would never be as beautiful as the original one (see 2:3). Haggai used this opportunity to prophesy about a future Temple that would be filled with God's glory (see verse 7), a time when God would again bless these people and make their offerings holy. God would establish Judah as a powerful nation, and Zerubbabel (a descendant of David) would be its anointed king.

Haggai

Prophetic Call To Work on the Temple

1 [1]On the first day of the sixth month in the
second year† of Darius the king, the word of
the LORD came through Haggai the prophet to the
governor of Judah, Zerubbabel,* son of Shealtiel,
and to the high priest Joshua, son of Jehozadak:*
[2]Thus says the LORD of hosts: This people has
said: "Now is not the time to rebuild the house
of the LORD."
[3]Then the word of the LORD came through Hag-
gai the prophet: [4]Is it time for you to dwell in your
paneled houses while this house lies in ruins?† *

5 Now thus says the LORD of hosts:
Reflect on your experience!†
6 You have sown much, but have brought in little;
you have eaten, but have not been satisfied;*
You have drunk, but have not become intoxicated;
you have clothed yourselves, but have not been warmed;
And the hired worker labors for a bag full of holes.

7 Thus says the LORD of hosts:

Reflect on your experience!
8 Go up into the hill country;
bring timber, and build the house
that I may be pleased with it,
and that I may be glorified,† says the LORD.
9 You expected much, but it came to little;
and what you brought home, I blew away.
Why is this?—oracle of the LORD† of hosts—
Because my house is the one which lies in ruins,
while each of you runs to your own house.
10 Therefore, the heavens withheld the dew,
and the earth its yield.
11 And I have proclaimed a devastating heat†
upon the land and upon the mountains,
Upon the grain, the new wine, and the olive oil,
upon all that the ground brings forth;

† **1:1** *First day of the sixth month in the second year*: August 29, 520 B.C. This is the first of six chronological indicators in Haggai. *Darius*: Darius I, emperor of Persia from 522 to 486 B.C. *Governor*: term used for local rulers of provinces in the Persian imperial structure. *Zerubbabel*: grandson of King Jehoiachin (cf. 2 Kgs 24:8–17).

1:4 *Your paneled houses . . . house lies in ruins*: the contrast here is between the unfinished Temple and the completed houses of the Judeans.

1:5 *Reflect on your experience*: the prophet exhorts the people to consider the futility of their efforts as a result of their neglecting work on the Temple. The following verses call attention to harsh conditions in Judah after the return from exile and the preoccupation of the people with their personal concerns.

1:8 *That I may be glorified*: for the prophet, the rebuilding of the Temple restores the glory God had lost in the eyes of the nations by the Temple's destruction.

1:9 *Oracle of the LORD*: a phrase used extensively in prophetic books to indicate divine speech.

1:11 *Devastating heat*: this pronouncement of natural disaster, which functions as a warning to the people for their failure to rebuild the Temple, concludes the opening oracular section of Haggai.

* **1:1** Zec 4:6–10.
1:1 Zec 3:1–10.
1:4 2 Sm 7:2.
1:6 Lv 26:26; Hos 4:10.

...nter

The people of Haggai's time thought they did not have enough wealth to rebuild the Temple (see Hg 1:2). God told them they were poor and unsuccessful because they had not rebuilt it (see verse 9). They needed to trust that if they put their priorities in the right order, God would provide.

Perhaps Haggai's people had forgotten what the true riches in life are. One of the first things many poor European immigrants settling in the United States did was to build a church (and often a school). They did this at a great sacrifice of time and materials. The church was more than a building; it was a symbol of their willingness to work together and a symbol of their common faith. It is in things like this that true wealth is found.

God, help me and my family, friends, and community to put you and the building of your Reign first in our lives. Give us the true wealth that comes from working with others for the good of all. Amen.

▶ **Haggai, chapter 1**

Upon human being and beast alike,
  and upon all they produce.

Response of Leaders and People

12 Then Zerubbabel, son of Shealtiel, and the
high priest Joshua, son of Jehozadak, and all
the remnant of the people† obeyed the LORD
their God, and the words of Haggai the prophet,
since the LORD their God had sent him; thus the
people feared the LORD. 13 Then Haggai, the mes-
senger of the LORD, proclaimed to the people as
the message of the LORD: I am with you!—oracle
of the LORD.

14 And so the LORD stirred up the spirit of the
governor of Judah, Zerubbabel, son of Shealtiel,
and the spirit of the high priest Joshua, son of
Jehozadak, and the spirit of all the remnant of
the people,* so that they came to do the work
in the house of the LORD of hosts, their God, 15 on
the twenty-fourth day of the sixth month in the
second year† of Darius the king.

Assurance of God's Presence

2 1 On the twenty-first day of the seventh
month,† the word of the LORD came through
Haggai the prophet: 2 Speak to the governor of
Judah, Zerubbabel, son of Shealtiel, and to the
high priest Joshua, son of Jehozadak, and to the
remnant of the people:

3 Who is left among you†
  who saw this house in its former glory?
And how do you see it now?
  Does it not seem like nothing in your
    eyes?*
4 Now be strong, Zerubbabel—oracle of the
    LORD—
  be strong, Joshua, son of Jehozadak, high
    priest,
Be strong, all you people of the land—oracle
    of the LORD—
  and work! For I am with you—oracle of the
    LORD of hosts.
5 This is the commitment I made to you
  when you came out of Egypt.
My spirit remains in your midst;
  do not fear!

6 For thus says the LORD of hosts:†

In just a little while,
  I will shake the heavens and the
    earth,*

† **1:12** *The remnant of the people*: here the phrase appears to refer to the prophet's audience, but the "remnant" theme, though often in different Hebrew terminology, suggesting especially those whom the Lord will call back from exile and re-establish as his people, is important in the prophets (cf. Is 4:3; 37:31–32; Jl 3:5; Mi 4:7; Ob 17) and in the New Testament (cf. Rom 11:1–10).

1:15 *Twenty-fourth day of the sixth month in the second year*: September 21, 520 B.C. The resumption of work on the Temple occurred twenty-three days from the beginning of Haggai's prophecy. This date formula repeats in reverse order the formula of v. 1, thereby bringing to conclusion chap. 1; it also initiates the next unit in 2:1.

2:1 *Twenty-first day of the seventh month*: October 17, 520 B.C.

2:3 *Who is left among you*: i.e., who is old enough to have seen the first Temple prior to its destruction in 587 B.C.? Compare the reaction of priests who were alive then (Ezr 3:12–13).

2:6–9 These verses emphasize that the total fulfillment of God's promises to Israel is on the horizon. Such an eschatological event, which will shake the nations (v. 6; cf. v. 21), finds an echo not only in the political revolts in the Persian empire in 521 but also in the formative events of Israel's history (Ex 19:18; Jgs 5:4; Ps 68:8–9) when God intervened on behalf of the Israelites. The bringing of treasures of all the nations (v. 7) to Jerusalem recalls the visionary passages of Isaiah of the pilgrimage of all nations to Jerusalem (Is 2:2–4; 60:6–9).

1:14 Ezr 1:5; 5:1–2.
2:3 Ezr 3:10–13.
2:6 Heb 12:26.

the sea and the dry land.
7 I will shake all the nations,
so that the treasures of all the nations will
come in.
And I will fill this house with glory—
says the LORD of hosts.*

8 Mine is the silver and mine the gold—oracle of
the LORD of hosts.

9 Greater will be the glory of this house*
the latter more than the former—says the
LORD of hosts;
And in this place I will give you peace—†
oracle of the LORD of hosts.

Priestly Ruling with Prophetic Interpretation†

10 On the twenty-fourth day of the ninth month
in the second year† of Darius, the word of the
LORD came to Haggai the prophet: 11 Thus says
the LORD of hosts: Ask the priests for a ruling:†
12 If someone carries sanctified meat in the fold
of a garment and the fold touches bread, soup,
wine, oil, or any other food, do they become
sanctified? "No," the priests answered. 13 Then
Haggai asked: "If a person defiled from contact
with a corpse touches any of these, do they be-
come defiled?" The priests answered, "They be-
come defiled."* 14 Then Haggai replied:

So is this people,† and so is this nation
in my sight—oracle of the LORD—
And so is all the work of their hands;
what they offer there is defiled.

15 Now reflect,† from this day forward—before
you set stone to stone in the temple of the LORD,
16 what was your experience?
When one went to a heap of grain
ephahs,
there were only ten;
When one went to a vat to draw fifty ephahs,
there were only twenty.*
17 I struck you, and all the work of your hands,
with searing wind, blight, and hail,
yet you did not return to me—oracle of the
LORD.*

18 Reflect from this day forward, from the
twenty-fourth day of the ninth month.† From
the day on which the temple of the LORD was
founded, reflect!

19 Is there still seed in the storehouse?
Have the vine, the fig, the pomegranate,
and the olive tree still not borne fruit?
From this day, I will bless you.†

Future Hope†

20 The word of the LORD came a second time to
Haggai on the twenty-fourth day of the month:†
21 Speak to Zerubbabel, the governor of Judah:

I will shake the heavens and the earth;
22 I will overthrow the thrones of kingdoms,
and destroy the power of the kingdoms of
the nations.
I will overthrow the chariots and their riders,
and the riders with their horses
will fall by each other's swords.*

23 On that day—oracle of the LORD of hosts—I
will take you, my servant, Zerubbabel, son of
Shealtiel—oracle of the LORD—and I will make
you like a signet ring,† for I have chosen you—
oracle of the LORD of hosts.*

†

2:9 *Peace*: after God's presence or glory has returned to the Temple, Jerusalem will receive the treasures from the nations, making the Temple more glorious than ever; and from that place God will extend *shalom*, a peace which embraces prosperity, well-being, harmony.

2:10–14 A request for a priestly ruling (Heb. *torah*) is made in the form of a dialogue between Haggai and the priests. Explicit examples where such priestly rulings are quoted are rare in prophetic books. The interchange illustrates an essential role of the priesthood: the interpretation of God's law (cf. Lv 10:9–11).

2:10 *Twenty-fourth day of the ninth month in the second year*: December 18, 520 B.C.

2:11 *Ask the priests for a ruling*: i.e., a determination on whether defilement and sanctity can be physically transmitted. The priests are expected to make a legal decision. The answer is that sanctity cannot be transmitted (v. 12) but defilement can (v. 13). Priestly duties are enumerated in Lv 10:10–20.

2:14 *So is this people*: the prophet's interpretation is that the restored sacrifices were not acceptable because the people's behavior was tainted.

2:15–19 This prophecy is retrospective and should be read with 1:5–11, a description of the conditions of economic deprivation before the rebuilding of the Temple.

2:16 *Ephahs*: see note on Is 5:10.

2:18 *Twenty-fourth day of the ninth month*: December 18, 520 B.C., the date of the refounding of the Temple (vv. 10, 20), the central date in Haggai.

2:19 *I will bless you*: from the day of the refounding of the Temple, agricultural plenty and fertility are assured. This link between temple and prosperity is part of the ancient Near Eastern temple ideology that underlies Haggai and Zec 1–8.

2:20–23 This final oracle of hope is uttered on the day of the refounding of the Temple. Unlike the other oracles it is addressed to Zerubbabel alone, who, as a Davidic descendant, will have a servant role in God's future Israelite kingdom to be established when God intervenes to overthrow the nations.

2:20 *Twenty-fourth day of the month*: December 18, 520 B.C. (as in v. 18).

2:23 *Like a signet ring*: this promise to Zerubbabel reverses the punishment of his grandfather (Jer 22:23–25). A signet is a ring or other instrument used to mark documents or materials with the equivalent of an official signature. A lower official could thus be authorized to act on behalf of a higher official. Like a signet ring, Zerubbabel represents the Lord.

*

2:7 Is 60:7–11.
2:9 1 Kgs 8:11.
2:13 Lv 22:4–7.
2:16 Hos 4:3a.
2:17 Am 4:9.
2:22 Sir 49:11.
2:23 Zec 6:12–13.

The Book of Zechariah

Haggai 2:

r twenty

o you do when life is difficult and things seem to just be getting ? Some people dream about the future. They imagine a time when es have ended and life is happy again. If their trouble is caused by e, they may imagine how these people eventually pay for their wrong- ook of Zechariah looks at Israel's future in exactly these two ways.

At a Glance

I. First Zechariah.
   A. Introductory Unit (1:1-6).
   B. Visionary Unit (1:7—6:15).
   C. Address to Delegation from Bethel and Oracles (7:1—8:23).
II. Second Zechariah (chapters 9–14).

Quick Facts

Period Covered: First Zechariah around 520 BC, Second Zechariah sometime after 333 BC

Inspired Authors: the original Zechariah, and an unknown prophet or prophets writing much later

Themes: a command to rebuild the Temple, the message that God will win the final victory

Of Note: The prophecies of Zechariah are quoted in the New Testament because they were understood by the early Church to have been fulfilled in Jesus Christ.

In Depth

Like the Book of Isaiah, the Book of Zechariah was written by at least two prophets. The original Zechariah—we'll call him First Zechariah—lived around the same time as Haggai, after the exiled Israelites returned to Jerusalem from Babylon (see the timeline at the back of this Bible). Second Zechariah, who may have been one or more prophets, wrote about two hundred years later.

The optimistic message of the first prophet in chapters 1–8 of Zechariah is centered on two concerns: the rebuilding of the Temple and the end of time. First Zechariah saw that a rebuilt Temple was needed to restore the people's unity, identity, and relationship with God. Through a series of visions (see "Apocalyptic Literature," near Daniel, chapters 7–10), he announced his message: under the guidance of the priest Joshua and the prince Zerubbabel (a descendant of King David), Israel would be restored. It would become a nation of justice, faith, love, mercy, and truth where the Lord would dwell. Even the Gentiles (non-Jews) would come from faraway lands to worship God.

Second Zechariah wrote later, when Israel was under Greek domination (see the timeline at the back of this Bible). He preached not through visions, but through oracles (prophetic speeches) of warning, violence, and also promise. He talked about a great battle that was about to take place between the forces of good and the forces of evil. This was the final war, which would bring an end to the present-day evil and corrupt world. But Second Zechariah also proclaimed the coming of a humble king who would bring peace to all nations. Jerusalem would be purified and would become victorious as the city where God reigns as the highest power for good.

Zechariah

11:7

Call for Obedience

1 [1]In the second year of Darius,† in the eighth
month, the word of the LORD came to the
prophet Zechariah, son of Berechiah, son of Iddo:
[2]The LORD was very angry with your ancestors.† *
[3]Say to them: Thus says the LORD of hosts, Return
to me—oracle of the LORD† of hosts—and I will
return to you, says the LORD of hosts. [4]Do not be
like your ancestors to whom the earlier proph-
ets† proclaimed: Thus says the LORD of hosts:
Turn from your evil ways and from your wicked
deeds.* But they did not listen or pay attention
to me*—oracle of the LORD.—[5]Your ancestors,
where are they? And the prophets, can they live
forever? [6]But my words and my statutes, with
which I charged my servants the prophets, did
these not overtake your ancestors?* Then they re-
pented† and admitted: "Just as the LORD of hosts
intended to treat us according to our ways and
deeds, so the LORD has done."

First Vision: Horses Patrolling the Earth*

[7]In the second year of Darius, on the twenty-
fourth day of Shebat, the eleventh month,† the
word of the LORD came to the prophet Zechariah,
son of Berechiah, son of Iddo:
[8]† I looked out in the night,† and there was
a man mounted on a red horse standing in the
shadows among myrtle trees; and behind him
were red, sorrel, and white horses. [9]I asked, "What
are these, my lord?"† Then the angel who spoke
with me answered, "I will show you what these
are." [10]Then the man who was standing among
the myrtle trees spoke up and said, "These are
the ones whom the LORD has sent to patrol the
earth."* [11]And they answered the angel of the
LORD,† who was standing among the myrtle trees:

†

1:1 *Darius*: Darius I, emperor of Persia from 522 to 486 B.C. *The second year . . . eighth month*: October/November 520 B.C., i.e., prior to the latest date in Haggai (Dec. 18, 520 B.C., Hg 2:10). Unlike other prophets, Haggai and Zechariah 1–8 contain specific chronological information, probably because they were sensitive to the imminent end of the expected seventy years of exile. See note on Zec 1:12.

1:2 *Your ancestors*: refers to the preexilic people of Judah, who were subjected to Babylonian destruction and exile.

1:3 *Oracle of the LORD*: a phrase used extensively in prophetic books to indicate divine speech.

1:4 *Earlier prophets*: preexilic prophets of the Lord. There are many allusions to them in Zechariah, indicating their influence on the postexilic community (see 7:7, 12).

1:6 *Repented*: the Hebrew word *shub* literally means "turn back." This term is often used to speak of repentance as a return to the covenantal relationship between Israel and the Lord.

1:7 *The second year . . . eleventh month*: February 15, 519 B.C. The largest set of visions (1:7–6:15) is dated to a time just prior to the beginning of the new year in the spring.

1:8–11 Four riders on horses of three different colors are sent by God to patrol the four corners of the earth. Compare the four chariots of the seventh vision, 6:1–8.

1:8 *In the night*: nighttime, or this night. This setting of darkness is meant only for the first vision.

1:9 *My lord*: this expression in Hebrew (*'adoni*) is used as a polite form of address. *Angel who spoke with me*: angelic being (not identical to the angel of the Lord who is one of the four horsemen) who serves as an interpreter, bringing a message from God to the prophet, who himself is a messenger of God.

1:11 *Angel of the LORD*: chief angelic figure in God's heavenly court, and perhaps the "man" of 1:8.

*

1:2 Mi 3:7.
1:4 Is 55:7.
1:4 Lk 20:15.
1:6 Zec 7:7–14.
1:7 Zec 6:1–7; Rev 5:6; 6:1–9.
1:10 Zec 7:5; Jer 25:11–12; 29:10.

Cultural Connection

Four Winds, Four Directions

To many Native American peoples, the repeated emphasis on the number four in the visions of Zechariah could have a special meaning. In these visions are four horns representing the nations that oppressed Israel (see Zec 2:1), four blacksmiths to beat those horns down (see verse 3), and four chariots sent out to the four directions of the world (see 6:1–8).

Native Americans see the number four as special because it is repeated often in nature. There are four compass directions, four chambers of the human heart, four seasons, four phases of human life (child, youth, adult, and elder), and four basic elements (fire, water, rock, and air).

When Native Americans offer a formal prayer, they often do so facing the four directions, each with its own traditional color and emphasis:

- east (yellow), where the sun rises; the direction of light and wisdom
- south (white), where the warmth is; the direction of life
- west (black), where the sun sets; the direction of water and cleansing
- north (red), where the cold is; the direction of strength in hardship

Sometimes, two more directions are added: up, toward Father Sky (blue), and down, toward Mother Earth (green).

▶ Zec 2:1–4

"We have been patrolling the earth, and now the
whole earth rests quietly." 12 Then the angel of
the LORD replied, "LORD of hosts, how long will
you be without mercy for Jerusalem and the cities
of Judah that have felt your anger these seventy
years?"† * 13 To the angel who spoke with me, the
LORD replied favorably, with comforting words.

Oracular Response

14 The angel who spoke with me then said to
me, Proclaim: Thus says the LORD of hosts:

I am jealous for Jerusalem
 and for Zion† intensely jealous.*
15 I am consumed with anger
 toward the complacent nations;†
When I was only a little angry,
 they compounded the disaster.*
16 Therefore, thus says the LORD:
I return to Jerusalem in mercy;*
 my house† will be rebuilt there*—oracle of
  the LORD of hosts—
 and a measuring line will be stretched over
  Jerusalem.
17 Proclaim further: Thus says the LORD of hosts:
My cities will again overflow with prosperity;
 the LORD will again comfort Zion,
 and will again choose Jerusalem.*

Second Vision: The Four Horns and the Four Smiths

2 1 I raised my eyes and looked and there were
four horns.† 2 Then I asked the angel who
spoke with me, "What are those?" He answered,
"Those are the horns that scattered† Judah, Israel, and Jerusalem."*

† **1:12** *These seventy years*: allusion to the period of divine anger mentioned in Jer 25:11–12 and 29:10. Here the symbolic number seventy is understood to mark the period without a Temple in Jerusalem. Since these seventy years would have been almost over at this point, this symbolic number would have provided motivation for rebuilding the Temple as a sign of the end of the exile.

1:14 *For Jerusalem and for Zion*: rather than the usual order, Zion and Jerusalem, elsewhere in the Bible. The reversal highlights the centrality of Jerusalem, which is mentioned in all three of the brief oracles of 1:14–17.

1:15 *Complacent nations*: probably a reference to the Persian empire, which in its imperial extent included many national groups that maintained separate identities. *Compounded the disaster*: the surrounding nations took advantage of the Lord's anger against Judah to further their own interests.

1:16 *My house*: the Temple. See note on Hg 1:4. *Measuring line*: a builder's string, not for devastation, as in Is 34:11, but for reconstruction.

2:1 *Four horns*: symbols of the total political and military might of Judah's imperial adversaries, probably representing Assyria, Babylonia, and Persia. The number four represents universality rather than any specific number of foes.

2:2 *Scattered*: sent part of the population into exile. This was standard imperial policy initiated in the ancient Near East by the Assyrians for dealing with a conquered state.

* **1:12** Rev 6:10. **1:14** Zec 8:2. **1:15** Is 47:6. **1:16** Is 54:6–10. **1:16** Zec 2:5–9. **1:17** Zec 2:15; 13:9. **2:2** Dt 33:17; Dn 7:8.

3 Then the LORD showed me four workmen.†
4 And I said, "What are these coming to do?" And
the LORD said, "Those are the horns that scattered
Judah, so that none could raise their heads any
more;* and these have come to terrify them—to
cut down the horns of the nations that raised
their horns to scatter the land of Judah."

Third Vision: The Man with the Measuring Cord

5 I raised my eyes and looked, and there was
a man with a measuring cord† in his hand.* 6 I
asked, "Where are you going?" And he said, "To
measure Jerusalem—to see how great its width is
and how great its length."
7 Then the angel who spoke with me advanced
as another angel came out to meet him 8 and he
said to the latter, "Run, speak to that official:†
Jerusalem will be unwalled, because of the abun-
dance of people and beasts in its midst.* 9 I will
be an encircling wall of fire† for it—oracle of the
LORD—and I will be the glory in its midst."*

Expansion on the Themes of the First Three Visions

10 Up! Up! Flee from the land of the north†—
oracle of the LORD;—For like the four winds of
heaven I have dispersed you—oracle of the LORD.*
11 Up, Zion! Escape, you who dwell in daughter
Babylon! 12 For thus says the LORD of hosts after
the LORD's glory had sent me, concerning the na-
tions that have plundered you: Whoever strikes
you strikes me directly in the eye.* 13 Now I wave
my hand over them, and they become plunder
for their own servants.* Thus you shall know
that the LORD of hosts has sent me. 14 Sing and
rejoice, daughter Zion! Now, I am coming to
dwell in your midst—oracle of the LORD. 15 Many
nations will bind themselves to the LORD on that
day.* They will be my people,† and I will dwell
in your midst. Then you shall know that the LORD
of hosts has sent me to you. 16 The LORD will in-
herit Judah* as his portion of the holy land,† and
the LORD will again choose Jerusalem. 17 Silence,
all people, in the presence of the LORD, who stirs
forth from his holy dwelling.*

Prophetic Vision: Joshua the High Priest

3 1 Then he showed me Joshua the high priest
standing before the angel of the LORD, while
the adversary† stood at his right side to accuse
him.* 2 And the angel of the LORD said to the
adversary, "May the LORD rebuke you, O adver-
sary; may the LORD who has chosen Jerusalem
rebuke you!* Is this not a brand plucked from
the fire?"*
3 † Now Joshua was standing before the angel,
clad in filthy garments. 4 Then the angel said to
those standing before him, "Remove his filthy
garments."* And to him he said, "Look, I have
taken your guilt from you,* and I am clothing
you in stately robes." 5 Then he said, "Let them
put a clean turban on his head." And they put
a clean turban on his head and clothed him
with the garments while the angel of the LORD
was standing by. 6 Then the angel of the LORD
charged Joshua: 7 "Thus says the LORD of hosts:
If you walk in my ways and carry out my charge,
you will administer my house and watch over
my courts;† and I will give you access to those
standing here."

Supplementary Oracle

8 "Hear, O Joshua, high priest! You and your
associates who sit before you! For they are signs
of things to come!† * I will surely bring my ser-
vant the Branch. 9 Look at the stone* that I have

†

2:3 *Four workmen*: four agents of God's power. The imagery follows that of four horns: the workers cut down, or make ineffectual, the horns, i.e., enemy.

2:5 *Measuring cord*: a string for measuring, as opposed to a builder's string, 1:16.

2:8 *That official*: probably the man with the measuring cord of v. 5.

2:9 *Encircling wall of fire*: divine protection for an unwalled Jerusalem. Urban centers were generally walled, and Jerusalem's walls were eventually rebuilt in the late fifth century B.C. (Neh 2:17–20).

2:10 *Land of the north*: refers to Babylon (v. 11), in a geographic rather than a political sense, as the place from which exiles will return. The designation is "north" because imperial invaders historically entered Palestine from that direction (see Jer 3:18; 23:8).

2:15 *Many nations . . . my people*: a way of expressing God's relationship to people in covenant language. The covenant between God and Israel (see Jer 31:33; 32:38) is here universalized to include all nations.

2:16 *The holy land*: the Lord's earthly territory, a designation found only rarely in the Old Testament.

3:1 *Adversary*: Hebrew *satan*, here, the prosecuting attorney, a figure in the Lord's heavenly courtroom. Cf. Jb 1:6–2:7. Later tradition understands this figure to be Satan.

3:3–4 The filthy garments of Joshua symbolized the guilt of the Israelite people who have become unclean by going into exile. The angel of the Lord purifies the high priest by the removal of his garments.

3:7 *If you walk . . . watch over my courts*: four components of priestly activity: (1) following God's commandments and teaching them to the people, (2) carrying out cultic functions, (3) participating in the judicial system in certain difficult cases, and (4) administering the laborers and lands in the Temple's domain.

3:8 *Signs of things to come*: the restoration of the priesthood is a sign of the expected restoration of the Davidic line. *The Branch*: a tree metaphor for the expected future ruler as a descendant of the Davidic dynasty. This imagery also appears in Is 11:1, 10; Jer 23:5; 33:15; and Zec 6:12.

*

2:4 Jer 48:25.
2:5 Jer 31:38–39; Ez 41:13; Rev 11:1; 21:15.
2:8 Is 49:19–20; 54:2–3; Jer 31:27; Ez 38:11.
2:9 Rev 21:23; 22:3–5.
2:10 Zec 6:5; Is 48:20; Jer 50:8; 51:6.
2:12 Dt 32:10; Ps 17:8.
2:13 Is 14:2; Zep 3:15.
2:15 Is 56:6; 66:18.
2:16 Zec 1:17.
2:17 Hb 2:20; Zep 1:7; Rev 8:1a.
3:1 Jb 1:6–2:7; 1 Chr 21:1.
3:2 Jude 9.
3:2 Am 4:11.
3:4 Lk 15:22; Rev 19:8.
3:4 Is 6:7; Jer 31:34; Ez 36:33.
3:8 Is 8:18.
3:9 Zec 4:7, 10; Is 28:16.

placed before Joshua. On this one stone with
seven facets† * I will engrave its inscription—
oracle of the LORD of hosts—and I will take away
the guilt of that land in one day. 10 On that day—
oracle of the LORD of hosts—you will invite one
another under your vines and fig trees."*

Fourth Vision: The Lampstand and the Two Olive Trees

4 1 Then the angel who spoke with me returned
and aroused me, like one awakened from
sleep. 2 He said to me, "What do you see?" I re-
plied, "I see a lampstand† all of gold,* with a
bowl on top of it. There are seven lamps on it,
with seven spouts on each of the lamps that are
on top of it. 3 And beside it are two olive trees,†
one on the right of the bowl and one to its left."
4 Then I said to the angel who spoke with me,
"What are these things, my lord?" 5 And the angel
who spoke with me replied, "Do you not know
what these things are?" I said, "No, my lord."

An Oracle

6 Then he said to me: "This is the word of
the LORD to Zerubbabel: Not by might, and not
by power, but by my spirit,† * says the LORD of
hosts. 7 Who are you, O great mountain?† Before
Zerubbabel you become a plain. He will bring
forth the first stone amid shouts of 'Favor, favor
be upon it!' "
8 Then the word of the LORD came to me: 9 The
hands of Zerubbabel have laid the foundations
of this house, and his hands will finish it. Thus
you shall know that the LORD of hosts has sent
me to you. 10 For whoever has scorned such a day
of small things will rejoice to see the capstone†
in the hand of Zerubbabel.

Resumption of the Vision: Explanation of Lamps and Trees

"These seven are the eyes of the LORD that
range over the whole earth."* 11 I then asked him,
"What are these two olive trees, on the right of
the lampstand and on its left?" 12 A second time I
asked, "What are the two streams from the olive
trees that pour out golden oil through two taps of
gold?" 13 He said to me, "Do you not know what
these are?" I answered, "No, my lord." 14 Then
he said, "These are the two anointed ones† who
stand by the Lord of the whole earth."*

Fifth Vision: The Flying Scroll

5 1 Then I raised my eyes again and saw a fly-
ing scroll. 2 He asked me, "What do you see?"
I answered, "I see a flying scroll, twenty cubits
long and ten cubits wide."† * 3 Then he said to
me: "This is the curse which is to go forth over
the whole land. According to it, every thief and
every perjurer† will be expelled. 4 I will send it
forth—oracle of the LORD of hosts—so that it
will come to the house of the thief, and into
the house of the one who swears falsely by my
name.* It shall lodge within each house, con-
suming it, timber and stones."

Sixth Vision: The Basket of Wickedness

5 Then the angel who spoke with me came for-
ward and said to me, "Raise your eyes and look.
What is this that comes forth?" 6 I said, "What is
it?" And he answered, "This is the basket† that is

---

† **3:9** *Stone with seven facets*: represents both the precious stones that were part of the high priest's apparel and the building stone (see 4:7, 10) that initiated a major construction project. The seven facets (or "eyes") indicate the totality of its role as an instrument of God's vigilance and action. *Inscription*: can refer both to words engraved on the high priest's apparel (Ex 28:9, 11) and to words chiseled on a cornerstone.

4:2 *Lampstand*: receptacle for lamps and one of the furnishings of the main room of the Temple. This visionary object does not correspond to the biblical descriptions of the menorah in either the tabernacle (Ex 25:31–40) or the Solomonic Temple (1 Kgs 7:49) but rather has properties of both. *Seven lamps . . . seven spouts*: seven lamps, each with seven pinched wick holes. Such objects were part of the repertoire of cultic vessels throughout the Old Testament period. Here they symbolize God's eyes, i.e., divine omniscience; see v. 10.

4:3 *Olive trees*: visionary image that picks up the botanical language describing the Israelite cultic lampstands, with the olive trees specifically connoting fertility, permanence, and righteousness.

4:6 *Not by might . . . my spirit*: one of the most quoted verses from the Old Testament, particularly in Jewish tradition, which connects it with the theme of Hanukkah, sometimes called the Festival of Lights.

4:7 *Great mountain*: part of symbolic imagery for the Temple on Mount Zion, as embodiment of the cosmic mountain where heaven and earth connect. *Plain*: leveled ground serving as the foundation area for the construction of the Temple, and symbolizing the foundation of the cosmos. *First stone*: foundation stone of a major public building. Such stones were laid with great ceremony in foundation rituals when monumental buildings were newly built or rebuilt in the biblical world.

4:10 *Capstone*: topmost stone of a structure, which finishes the construction. This translation is based on the context. Other translations read: "stone of distinction," "plummet," "tin-stone."

4:14 *Two anointed ones*: two leadership positions in the ideal restored nation. The concept of a state headed by both priestly and political leaders harks back to premonarchic traditions (Aaron and Moses) and finds an echo in the two messianic figures—a Davidic and a levitical messiah—in the Dead Sea Scrolls and in apocryphal literature. See also the two crowns of 6:11–14.

5:2 *Twenty cubits long and ten cubits wide*: ca. thirty feet by fifteen feet. These dimensions may represent the ratio of height to width in the exposed portion of a scroll being opened for liturgical reading; at the same time it may symbolize the approach to God's presence since the entryway to the Temple has the same measurements (1 Kgs 6:3). The scroll itself may represent God's covenant with the people, insofar as it contains curses against those who break the law.

5:3 *Thief . . . perjurer*: a pair of miscreants representing all those who disobey God's covenant (see note on v. 2) and who must therefore be punished according to covenant curses.

5:6 *Basket*: literally, ephah, a dry measure; see note on Is 5:10.

---

* **3:9** Rev 5:6.
3:10 1 Kgs 5:5; Mi 4:4.
4:2 Ex 25:31–40; 1 Kgs 7:49; Rev 11:4.
4:6 Hos 1:7.
4:10 Zec 1:11; 6:7; Rev 5:6.
4:14 Jos 3:11; Mi 4:13; Rev 11:4.
5:2 Ez 2:9–10; Rev 10:9–11.
5:4 Ex 20:7, 16.

coming." And he said, "This is their guilt in all
the land." 7Then a leaden cover was lifted, and
there was a woman sitting inside the basket.†
8He said, "This is Wickedness," and he thrust her
inside the basket, pushing the leaden weight into
the opening.
9Then I raised my eyes and saw two women
coming forth with wind under their wings†—
they had wings like the wings of a stork—and
they lifted the basket into the air. 10I said to the
angel who spoke with me, "Where are they tak-
ing the basket?" 11He replied, "To build a temple
for it in the land of Shinar.† When the temple is
constructed, they will set it there on its base."

Seventh Vision: Four Chariots*

6 1Again I raised my eyes and saw four chari-
ots† coming out from between two moun-
tains; and the mountains were of bronze. 2The
first chariot had red horses, the second chariot
black horses, 3the third chariot white horses,
and the fourth chariot dappled horses—all of
them strong horses. 4I asked the angel who
spoke with me, "What are these, my lord?" 5The
angel answered me, "These are the four winds
of the heavens,† which are coming forth after
presenting themselves before the LORD of all the
earth.* 6The one with the black horses is going
toward the land of the north, and the white
horses go toward the west, and the dappled ones
go toward the land of the south." 7These strong
horses went out, eager to set about patrolling the
earth, for he said, "Go, patrol the earth!" So they
patrolled the earth. 8Then he cried out to me and
said, "See, those who go forth to the land of the
north provide rest for my spirit in the land of
the north."†

The Crowning

9Then the word of the LORD came to me:
10Take from the exiles—Heldai, Tobijah, Je-
daiah—and go the same day to the house of

6:1

Josiah, son of Zephaniah. (These had come from
Babylon.) 11You will take silver and gold, and
make crowns;† place one on the head of Joshua,
son of Jehozadak, the high priest. 12And say to
him: Thus says the LORD of hosts: There is a man
whose name is Branch†*—and from his place
he will branch out and he will build the temple
of the LORD. 13He will build the temple of the
LORD, and taking up the royal insignia, he will sit
as ruler upon his throne. The priest will be at his
right hand, and between the two of them there
will be peaceful understanding.†* 14The other
crown will be in the temple of the LORD as a gra-
cious reminder to Heldai, Tobijah, Jedaiah, and
the son of Zephaniah. 15And they who are from
afar will come and build the temple of the LORD,
and you will know that the LORD of hosts has sent
me to you. This will happen if you truly obey the
LORD your God.*

A Question About Fasting

7 1In the fourth year of Darius the king, the
word of the LORD came to Zechariah, on the
fourth day of the ninth month, Kislev.† 2Beth-
elsarezer sent Regem-melech and his men to

†

5:7 *Woman sitting inside the basket*: figure representing wickedness or foreign idolatry being transported back to Babylonia (vv. 1–11). Returning exiles were apparently worshiping deities they had learned to accept in Babylonia, and that "wickedness" (v. 8) must be removed.

5:9 *Two women . . . wings*: composite beings, part human and part animal, similar to the cherubim flanking the holy ark (Ex 25:18–22; 1 Kgs 6:23–28; Ez 10:18–22). Such creatures accompany foreign deities as here, or the biblical God.

5:11 *Shinar*: land of Babylonia; this name for Babylonia is found also in Gn 1:10; 11:2; 14:1; Is 11:11; and Dn 1:2.

6:1 *Four chariots*: vehicles with horses of four different colors (vv. 2–3) represent God's presence throughout the world and correspond to the four horses of 1:7–11.

6:5 *Four winds of the heavens*: four compass directions and therefore the whole world.

6:8 *Land of the north*: the enemy (cf. 2:10). This emphasis on the land of the north refers to the fact that God will deal with Israel's foes and order will be re-established.

6:11 *Crowns*: two crowns made of precious metals and representing two high offices (compare the symbolism of the two olive trees in 4:14). One crown is for the high priest Joshua, who, with the governor Zerubbabel, was one of the recognized rulers of the Persian province of Judah. The other crown would have been for a royal ruler, a Davidic descendant. Zerubbabel was a Davidide but could not be king because the Persians would not allow such autonomy. The second crown was thus put in storage in the Temple (v. 14) for the crowning of a future king, or "branch" (see 3:8), from the house of David.

6:12 *Branch*: future Davidic ruler. See note on 3:8.

6:13 *Peaceful understanding*: harmonious rule of both the high priest and the king.

7:1 *The fourth year of Darius . . . the ninth month, Kislev*: December 7, 518 B.C., the last chronological heading in Zechariah.

6:1 Rev 6:2–8.
6:5 Rev 7:1.
6:12 Zec 3:8; Jer 23:5.
6:13 Zec 4:14.
6:15 Dt 28:1.

implore the favor of the LORD 3 and to ask the
priests of the house of the LORD of hosts, and
the prophets, "Must I weep and abstain in the
fifth month† as I have been doing these many
years?" 4 Then the word of the LORD of hosts came
to me: 5 Say to all the people of the land and to
the priests: When you fasted and lamented in
the fifth and in the seventh month† these sev-
enty years, was it really for me that you fasted?*
6 When you were eating and drinking, was it not
for yourselves that you ate and for yourselves
that you drank?

7 Are these not the words which the LORD pro-
claimed through the earlier prophets,† when Je-
rusalem and its surrounding cities were inhabited
and secure, when the Negeb and the Shephelah
were inhabited? 8 The word of the LORD came to
Zechariah: 9 Thus says the LORD of hosts: Judge
with true justice, and show kindness and com-
passion toward each other.* 10 Do not oppress
the widow or the orphan, the resident alien or
the poor;† do not plot evil against one another
in your hearts.* 11 But they refused to listen; they
stubbornly turned their backs and stopped their
ears so as not to hear.* 12 And they made their
hearts as hard as diamond* so as not to hear the
instruction and the words that the LORD of hosts
had sent by his spirit through the earlier proph-
ets. So great anger came from the LORD of hosts:
13 Just as when I called out and they did not
listen, so they will call out and I will not listen,
says the LORD of hosts. 14 And I will scatter them
among all the nations that they do not know.*
So the land was left desolate behind them with
no one moving about, and they made a pleasant
land into a wasteland.

Seven Oracles: Judah and Zion Restored

8 1 Then the word of the LORD of hosts came:
2 Thus says the LORD of hosts:

I am intensely jealous for Zion,*
stirred to jealous wrath for her.

3 Thus says the LORD:

I have returned to Zion,
and I will dwell within Jerusalem;
Jerusalem will be called the faithful city,† *
and the mountain of the LORD of hosts, the
holy mountain.

4 Thus says the LORD of hosts:
Old men and old women will again sit in the
streets of Jerusalem, each with staff in hand be-
cause of old age.* 5 The city will be filled with
boys and girls playing in its streets.
6 Thus says the LORD of hosts:
Even if this should seem impossible in the
eyes of the remnant of this people in those days,
should it seem impossible in my eyes also?*—
oracle of the LORD of hosts.
7 Thus says the LORD of hosts:
I am going to rescue my people from the land
of the rising sun, and from the land of the setting
sun. 8 I will bring them back to dwell within Jeru-
salem. They will be my people, and I will be their
God,* in faithfulness and justice.
9 Thus says the LORD of hosts:
Let your hands be strong, you who now hear
these words which were spoken by the prophets
when the foundation of the house of the LORD of
hosts was laid† for the building of the temple.*
10 For before those days, there were no wages for
people, nor hire for animals. Those who came
and went were not safe from the enemy, for I set
neighbor against neighbor. 11 But now I will not
deal with the remnant of this people as in former
days—oracle of the LORD of hosts.

12 For there will be a sowing of peace:
the vine will yield its fruit,
the land will yield its crops,
and the heavens† will yield their dew.

I will give all these things to the remnant of this
people to possess. 13 Just as you became a curse

---

† **7:3** *Weep . . . fifth month*: a mourning ritual commemorating the destruction of Jerusalem and the Temple on the seventh day of the fifth month in the nineteenth year of Nebuchadnezzar's reign (ca. 587/586 B.C.; see 2 Kgs 25:8).

7:5 *Seventh month*: the time of a fast in memory of the murder of Gedaliah, the governor installed by the Babylonians after they conquered Jerusalem (see 2 Kgs 25:25; Jer 41:1–3). *Seventy years*: see note on 1:12.

7:7, 12 *Earlier prophets*: see note on 1:4.

7:10 *Widow . . . orphan . . . resident alien . . . poor*: four categories of socially and economically marginalized persons. Concern for their well-being is commanded in both pentateuchal and prophetic literature.

8:3 *Faithful city*: a unique biblical epithet for Jerusalem, signaling the importance of the holy city and its leaders for establishing justice in society (see also vv. 8, 16, 19). *Holy mountain*: Jerusalem and its Temple, the sacred center of the holy land (2:16) and of the whole world.

8:9 *When the foundation . . . was laid*: December 18, 520 B.C., the date of the Temple refoundation ceremony, marking the beginning of the project to restore the Temple (see Hg 2:10, 18, 20).

8:12 *Vine . . . land . . . heavens*: future prosperity, reversing the hardships of Hg 1:10.

---

* **7:5** Am 5:21.
7:9 Is 1:17; 58:6.
7:10 Ex 22:20–24; Dt 24:17; Jer 5:28; Mi 2:1.
7:11 Ex 32:9; Is 48:4.
7:12 Ez 11:19.
7:14 Dt 4:27.
8:2 Zec 1:14.
8:3 Is 1:26.
8:4 Dt 4:40.
8:6 Jer 32:27.
8:8 Zec 13:9; Jer 31:33.
8:9 Hg 1:14.

among the nations, O house of Judah and house
of Israel, so will I save you that you may be a
blessing.* Do not fear; let your hands be strong.
14 Thus says the LORD of hosts:
Just as I intended to harm you when your an-
cestors angered me—says the LORD of hosts—and
I did not relent, 15 so again in these days I intend
to favor Jerusalem and the house of Judah; do
not fear! 16 These then are the things you must
do: Speak the truth to one another;* judge with
honesty and complete justice in your gates.† *
17 Let none of you plot evil against another in
your heart, nor love a false oath. For all these
things I hate—oracle of the LORD.

Three Oracles: Judah and the Nations

18 The word of the LORD of hosts came to me:
19 Thus says the LORD of hosts:
The fast days of the fourth, the fifth, the sev-
enth, and the tenth months† * will become oc-
casions of joy and gladness, and happy festivals
for the house of Judah.* So love faithfulness and
peace!
20 Thus says the LORD of hosts:
There will yet come peoples and inhabitants
of many cities;* 21 and the inhabitants of one city
will approach those of another, and say, "Come!
let us go to implore the favor of the LORD and to
seek the LORD of hosts. I too am going." 22 Many
peoples and strong nations will come to seek the
LORD of hosts in Jerusalem and to implore the
favor of the LORD.
23 Thus says the LORD of hosts:
In those days ten people from nations of every
language will take hold,* yes, will take hold of
the cloak of every Judahite and say, "Let us go
with you, for we have heard that God is with
you."

Restoration of the Land of Israel†

9 1 An oracle:† the word of the LORD is against
the land of Hadrach,
and Damascus is its destination,
For the cities of Aram are the LORD's,
as are all the tribes of Israel.
2 Hamath also on its border,
Tyre too, and Sidon, no matter how clever
they be.
3 Tyre built itself a stronghold,
and heaped up silver like dust,
and gold like the mud of the streets.
4 But now the Lord will dispossess it,
and cast its wealth into the sea,
and it will be devoured by fire.
5 Ashkelon will see it and be afraid;
Gaza too will be in great anguish;
Ekron also, for its hope will wither.

Live It!

Thumbs Up!

"So will I save you that you may be a blessing. Do not fear; but let your hands be strong" (Zec 8:13). These words are a promise that God will bring the people of Israel out of hard times into good times. They are also an encouragement to us.

A young woman named Ana was in a car accident in which the driver lost control and three people were killed. Ana was severely hurt and faced months of rehabilitation. Ana, who once hoped to play college softball, now needed to learn to walk and talk again.

Ana knew that for some reason, God spared her life. She knew that her rehabilitation was not going to be easy and would take hard work. She was motivated by her faith and the feeling that God was there helping her. Her attitude and ambition came out every time she was asked how she was doing. She raised her hand and lifted her thumb and said faintly, "Thumbs up."

- How would you react in a situation like this?
- How can you be more like Ana?

▶ Zec 8:9–17

†

8:16 *Gates*: important gathering places in ancient Near Eastern cities, where legal proceedings were often carried out.

8:19 *Fast days of the fourth, the fifth, the seventh, and the tenth months*: all these fast days were probably held in connection with Jerusalem's demise. The fasts of the fourth month (commemorating the departure of Judahite leadership from Jerusalem, 2 Kgs 25:3–7) and of the tenth month (marking the beginning of the siege of Jerusalem, 2 Kgs 25:1) were added to the fasts of the fifth and seventh months mentioned in Zec 7:3 and 5 (see notes).

9:1–8 The opening verses of Second Zechariah delineate the ideal boundaries of a restored Israel. Echoing the ideas of Haggai and First Zechariah (chaps. 1–8), the prophet reiterates the notion that the rebuilt Temple will bring about peace. The areas to be returned to Israel include Syria (Aram), with the cities of Hadrach and Damascus; Phoenicia, with the cities of Tyre and Sidon; and Philistia, with the cities of Ashkelon, Gaza, Ekron, and Ashdod.

9:1 *An oracle*: this designation also introduces Zec 12:1 and Mal 1:1, suggesting a connection among the three units. The term functions as both a title to the larger literary unit (Zec 9–11) and a part of the message of the opening oracular statement.

*

8:13 Gn 12:3; Ps 72:17.
8:16 Eph 4:25.
8:16 Zec 7:9; Dt 21:19; 22:24; Ru 4:1, 11.
8:19 Zec 7:1–3; Mt 9:14–15.
8:19 Is 35:10; Jer 31:13.
8:20 1 Kgs 8:43.
8:23 1 Sm 15:27; Tb 13:11.

The king will disappear from Gaza,
Ashkelon will not be inhabited,
6 and the illegitimate will rule in Ashdod.
I will destroy the pride of the Philistines
7 and take from their mouths their bloody prey,
their disgusting meat from between their teeth.
They will become merely a remnant for our God,*
and will be like a clan in Judah;
Ekron will be like the Jebusites.†
8 I will encamp at my house,
a garrison against invaders;
No oppressor will overrun them again,
for now I have seen their affliction.

The King's Entry into Jerusalem†

9 Exult greatly, O daughter Zion!
Shout for joy, O daughter Jerusalem!
Behold: your king† is coming to you,
a just savior is he,
Humble, and riding on a donkey,
on a colt, the foal of a donkey.*
10 He shall banish the chariot from Ephraim,*
and the horse from Jerusalem;
The warrior's bow will be banished,
and he will proclaim peace to the nations.*
His dominion will be from sea to sea,
and from the River† to the ends of the earth.*

Restoration of the People

11 As for you, by the blood of your covenant,† *
I have freed your prisoners from a waterless pit.
12 Return to a fortress,†
O prisoners of hope;
This very day, I announce
I am restoring double to you.
13 For I have bent Judah as my bow,
I have set Ephraim as its arrow;
I will arouse your sons, O Zion,
against your sons, O Yavan,†
and I will use you as a warrior's sword.
14 The LORD will appear over them,
God's arrow will shoot forth as lightning;
The Lord GOD will sound the ram's horn,
and come in a storm from the south.*
15 The LORD of hosts will protect them;
they will devour and conquer with sling stones,
they will drink and become heated as with wine;
they will be full like bowls—like the corners of the altar.*
16 And the LORD their God will save them:
the people, like a flock on that day;*
For like gemstones of a crown†
they will shine on the land.
17 Then how good and how lovely!
Grain will make the young men flourish,
and new wine the young women.*

The Lord Strengthens Judah and Rescues Ephraim

10 1 Ask the LORD for rain in the spring season,*
the LORD who brings storm clouds, and heavy rains,*
who gives to everyone grain in the fields.
2 For the teraphim† have spoken nonsense,*
the diviners have seen false visions;
Deceitful dreams they have told,
empty comfort they have offered.
This is why they wandered like sheep,
wretched, for they have no shepherd.*
3 My wrath is kindled against the shepherds,†
and I will punish the leaders.
For the LORD of hosts attends to the flock, the house of Judah,

---

† **9:7** *The Jebusites*: the pre-Israelite inhabitants of Jerusalem, conquered by David and incorporated into Israel.

9:9–10 These two verses form the centerpiece of chap. 9. The restoration of a royal figure connects the first part of the chapter (vv. 1–8), which depicts the restored land of Israel, with the second part (vv. 11–17), which concerns the restoration of the people Israel.

9:9 *Your king*: a just savior, a figure of humble demeanor, but riding on a donkey like royalty in the ancient Near East (Gn 49:11; Jgs 5:10; 10:4). The announcement of the coming of such a king marks a departure from the view of the royal figure as a conquering warrior. This depiction is in keeping with the tone of First Zechariah (3:8; 4:6–10; 6:12) but contrasts with Haggai (2:20–23). New Testament authors apply this prophecy to Jesus' triumphant entry into Jerusalem (Mt 21:4–5; Jn 12:14–15).

9:10 *The River*: probably the Euphrates; see note on Ps 72:8.

9:11 *The blood of your covenant*: the covenant between the Lord and Israel sealed with sacrificial blood (Ex 24:8).

9:12 *Fortress*: the Hebrew word for "fortress" (*bissaron*) plays upon the Hebrew word for Zion (*siyyon*). Those who return to Zion will be protected by the Lord. *O prisoners of hope*: imagery of exile, conveying a sense that the future in Israel will be better.

9:13 *Your sons, O Yavan*: the reference is to the Greeks and their struggle with the Persians for control of Syria-Palestine and the eastern Mediterranean in the mid-fifth century B.C.

9:16 *Like gemstones of a crown*: imagery reminiscent of First Zechariah (3:9; 4:7, 10; 6:11, 14) and evocative of the Temple and the priestly headgear (cf. Ex 29:6 and Lv 8:9).

10:2 *Teraphim*: household idols or cult objects (see Gn 31:19, 30–35; Jgs 17:5; 1 Sm 19:11–17), or ancestor statuettes (see 2 Kgs 23:24; Hos 3:4).

10:3 *Against the shepherds*: bad leaders or false prophets.

9:7 Is 4:3.
9:9 Is 9:6; 62:11; Jer 23:5; Mt 21:5; Jn 12:15.
9:10 Mi 5:9.
9:10 Is 2:4; 11:6; Hos 2:20; Eph 2:17.
9:10 Ps 72:8.
9:11 Ex 24:4–8; Mt 26:28; Heb 13:20.
9:14 Dt 33:2; Ps 18:14; Hb 3:4.
9:15 Ex 27:3; 38:3; Nm 4:14.
9:16 Ez 34:11.
9:17 Jer 31:12–13.
10:1 Dt 11:14.
10:1 Ps 135:7.
10:2 1 Sm 15:23.
10:2 Ez 34:5; Mt 9:36.

and will make them like a splendid horse
in battle.
4 From them will come the tower,
from them the tent peg,
from them the bow of war,
from them every officer.
5 Together they will be like warriors,
trampling the mud of the streets in battle.
They will wage war because the LORD is with
them,
and will put the horsemen to shame.
6 I will strengthen the house of Judah,*
the house of Joseph† I will save;
I will bring them back, because I have mercy
on them;
they will be as if I had never cast them off,
for I am the LORD their God, and I will
answer them.*
7 Then Ephraim will be like a hero,
and their hearts will be cheered as by
wine.*
Their children will see and rejoice—
their hearts will exult in the LORD.
8 I will whistle for them and gather them in;
for I will redeem them
and they will be as numerous as before.†
9 I sowed them among the nations,
yet in distant lands they will remember me;
they will bear their children and return.*
10 I will bring them back from the land of
Egypt,
and gather them from Assyria.
To the land of Gilead and to Lebanon I will
bring them,
until no room is found for them.
11 I will cross over to Egypt
and smite the waves of the sea,
and all the depths of the Nile will dry up.
The pride of Assyria will be cast down,
and the scepter of Egypt disappear.
12 I will strengthen them in the LORD,*
in whose name they will walk—oracle of
the LORD.

The Cry of Trees, Shepherds, and Lions

11 1 Open your doors, Lebanon,
that fire may devour your cedars!
2 Wail, cypress trees,
for the cedars are fallen,
the mighty are destroyed!
Wail, oaks of Bashan,
for the dense forest is cut down!
3 Listen! the wailing of shepherds,
their glory has been destroyed.
Listen! the roaring of young lions,
the thickets of the Jordan are destroyed.

The Shepherd Narrative† *

4 Thus says the LORD, my God: Shepherd the
flock to be slaughtered.* 5 For they who buy
them slay them and are not held accountable;
while those who sell them say, "Blessed be the
LORD, I have become rich!" Even their own shep-
herds will not pity them. 6 For I will no longer
pity the inhabitants of the earth—oracle of the
LORD.—Yes, I will deliver them into each other's
power, or into the power of their kings; they will
crush the earth, and I will not deliver it out of
their power.

7 So I shepherded the flock to be slaughtered
for the merchants of the flock. I took two staffs:
one I called Delight, and the other Union. Thus
I shepherded the flock. 8 In a single month, I did
away with the three shepherds, for I wearied of
them, and they disdained me. 9 "I will not shep-
herd you," I said. "Whoever is to die shall die;
whoever is to be done away with shall be done
away with; and those who are left shall devour
one another's flesh."

10 Then I took my staff Delight and snapped it
in two, breaking my covenant which I had made
with all peoples. 11 So it was broken on that day.
The merchants of the flock, who were watching
me, understood that this was the word of the
LORD. 12 Then I said to them, "If it seems good
to you, give me my wages; but if not, withhold

† **10:6** *The house of Joseph*: represents the Northern Kingdom (Israel), as does Ephraim in v. 7 below.

10:8 *Gather them in . . . be as numerous as before*: God's intention is to bring back the exiles and redeem them as at the time of the exodus. This image, resumed in vv. 10–11, anticipates an expanded population, echoes the ancestral promise (Gn 1:22, 28; 9:1, 7; 35:11), and also suggests an awareness of the acute demographic decline of Jews in Palestine in the Persian period.

11:4–17 This narrative has features of an allegory, a parable, and a commissioning narrative. The use of a symbolic action (vv. 7, 10, 14), however, places this text squarely in the tradition of classical prophecy. For example, the staff "Delight" signifies the Mosaic covenant, and the staff "Union" signifies the union of Israel and Judah. Breaking the staffs signifies the breaking of the Mosaic covenant (resulting in the destruction of Jerusalem and the exile) and the historical schism between north and south. In this narrative the prophet is the "shepherd" of God's flock, which is to be slaughtered. The "three shepherds" of v. 8 represent either leaders responsible for the decay in Israelite society or false prophets (cf. vv. 15, 17 and 13:2–6). The service of the good shepherd is contemptuously valued at thirty pieces of silver, the legal indemnity for a gored slave (Ex 21:32). The prophet throws the money into the Temple treasury, showing how poorly God's love is requited (cf. Mt 26:14–16; 27:5). With great rhetorical irony, payment is rejected. The entire wage-payment scenario may be regarded as another symbolic action, embedded within the primary action.

10:6 Zec 12:5.
10:6 Is 41:17.
10:7 Ps 104:15.
10:9 Dt 30:1–3; Bar 2:30–32.
10:12 Zec 12:5.
11:4 Ez 34:1.
11:4 Jer 12:3.

Cultural Connection

The Principle of *Umoja*

Chapter 11 of Zechariah contains several allegorical images that represent the breakdown of the Israelite nation. In one, a shepherd's staff named Unity, or Bonds (see verse 7), is broken—symbolizing that the people have lost the unity that bound them together.

Unity is vital to the success of any people. For example, African Americans rely on the Kwanzaa principle of unity, called *umoja* (see "Kwanzaa as a Way of Life," near Dt 10:12–22). *Umoja* signifies unity in the family, community, nation, and race. This unity keeps brothers from killing brothers and sisters from killing sisters. This unity keeps families together even when the going gets tough.

Any race or culture can and often does experience difficulty maintaining and promoting *umoja*, especially a race or culture facing injustice, racism, or prejudice. With these elements present, a race or culture can be negatively affected as individuals, young and old, are tempted to come together in attitudes and behaviors that are selfish and destructive.

All of us are called to live in unity. All of us are called to foster unity and to direct our efforts toward bringing our families, communities, races, and nations together.

Keep the Kwanzaa principle of *umoja* alive! Be united in making the honor roll. Be united in respecting and protecting one another. Be united in putting an end to the problems that plague our cities and nation. Be united in being the best you can be!

▶ Zec 11:4–17

them."* And they counted out my wages,* thirty
pieces of silver. 13 Then the LORD said to me,
Throw it in the treasury—the handsome price at
which they valued me. So I took the thirty pieces
of silver and threw them into the treasury in the
house of the LORD. 14 Then I snapped in two my
second staff, Union, breaking the kinship between Judah and Israel.

15 The LORD said to me: This time take the gear
of a foolish shepherd.* 16 For I am raising up a
shepherd in the land who will take no note of
those that disappear, nor seek the strays, nor
heal the injured,* nor feed the exhausted; but
he will eat the flesh of the fat ones and tear off
their hoofs!

Oracle to the Worthless Shepherd

17 Ah! my worthless shepherd
who forsakes the flock!*
May the sword fall upon his arm
and upon his right eye;
His arm will surely wither,
and his right eye surely go blind!

Oracles Concerning the Nations and Judah†

12 1 An oracle:† The word of the LORD concerning Israel—oracle of the LORD, who
spreads out the heavens, lays the foundations of
the earth, and fashions the human spirit within:*
2 See, I will make Jerusalem a cup of reeling†
for all peoples round about.* Judah will be besieged, even Jerusalem. 3 On that day I will make
Jerusalem a heavy stone for all peoples. All who
attempt to lift it will injure themselves badly,
though all the nations of the earth will gather
against it. 4 On that day—oracle of the LORD—I
will strike every horse with fright, and its rider
with madness. But over the house of Judah I will
keep watch, while I strike blind all the horses of
the peoples. 5 Then the clans of Judah will say to
themselves, "The inhabitants of Jerusalem have
their strength in the LORD of hosts, their God."*

† **12:1–10** The oracles deal with (1) the status of Judah in relation to other political powers in the world that threaten its existence and (2) the reordering of Judah's internal structures so that its future can be realized. That future is linked to the fortunes of the house of David, which is mentioned five times between 12:7 and 13:1 (12:7, 8, 10, 12; 13:1).

12:1 *An oracle*: part two of Second Zechariah begins with the same heading as that of part one (9:1; also Mal 1:1), suggesting two distinct blocks of material. The unusual cluster of introductory terms that follow the heading greatly intensifies the claim of prophetic authority, apparently an issue in postexilic prophecy.

12:2 *Cup of reeling*: like a cup filled with intoxicating drink, Jerusalem will cause the nations to stumble and fall (cf. Is 51:17, 22; Jer 25:15; 49:12; Lam 4:21).

* **11:12** Mt 27:3–10.
11:12 2 Kgs 12:11; 22:4.
11:15 Ez 34:1–10.
11:16 Is 42:3; Mt 12:20.
11:17 Jer 23:1; Jn 10:12–13.
12:1 Gn 2:7; Is 42:5.
12:2 Is 51:17.
12:5 Zec 10:6, 12.

Old Testament Biblical Images

This statue of Ramses III, an **Egyptian Pharaoh,** was found in the ancient Canaanite city of Bet She'an, located on the Jordan River. The Egyptian Empire controlled Palestine for many centuries before the Kingdom of Israel was formed.

This massive stone structure was discovered in recent excavations of the **City of David.** Dating back to around the 10th century BCE, it is possibly a public building that existed during the time of the united kingdom of David and Solomon (2 Sm 5:6–10).

In anticipation of the Assyrian assault on Jerusalem, Hezekiah had a tunnel cut through solid rock from outside the city walls to bring water into the city. This photo shows the entrance to **Hezekiah's tunnel** at the **Spring of Gihon** (2 Chr 32:30).

The **Sinai Desert** is on a triangle-shaped peninsula located between the Mediterranean Sea and the Red Sea. In the Scriptures it is often referred to as Horeb, meaning waste or wilderness (Ex 17:6). Moses and the Israelites wandered in the desert for forty years before reaching the Promised Land.

During Hezekiah's reforms all **high places** and **pagan altars,** similar to the one pictured in the photo were destroyed (2 Kgs 18:1–4; 2 Chr 31:1).

During the reign of Zedekiah, Nebuchadrezzar and his army destroyed the Temple and the city of Jerusalem and exiled the Israelites to Babylon, where they remained in **Babylonian captivity** for over a generation (Jer 52:1–30).

The Names of God in the Old Testament

The Judean theology flowered from its Semitic roots where El was a generic term for all the deities of Canaan. El and its derivatives later revealed Yahweh as El—the one true God.

Name	Significance	Reference
El (God)	A generic Semitic title for deity; the mighty powerful Creator; God of the Covenant; the protector	Gn 1:1,3,4,22; 17:7; 31:24; Is 44:24
Eloah; El Echad (the one God)	A generic name for deity; the one God who is savior, redeemer, and deliverer; the source of living water	Gn 45:5–6; Nm 23:22; Is 41:14; 43:3; 45:21; Jer 2:13; Mal 2:10
El Shaddai (God Almighty)	El Shaddai is a title of respect for the gods in the Canaanite pantheon; later became a name for Yahweh of Israel	Gn 17:1,7; 28:3; 35:11; 49:25; Ru 1:20– 21; Ezr 1:2–4; 6:3; Ps 91:1; Is 9:6
El Rachum (God of compassion)	God, the compassionate one who suffers with the child in the "womb" (rechem in Hebrew means womb)	Dt 4:31; Neh 9:17
El Elyon (God most high)	Pre-Davidic God of Jerusalem; the faithful God; the most high	Gn 14:19–20; Nm 24:16; Dt 7:9; Ps 47:2–3
El Olam (God everlasting)	Eternal God of the universe; God of refuge and truth; originally a name for the Canaanite god of Beer-sheba but later became a name for Yahweh	Gn 21:33; Pss 31:5–6; 90:1–3; 93:2; 106:48; Is 26:4
El Yisrael; Hai; Elohe (God of Israel)	The living God; the Lord God of Israel; the holy one	Gn 33:20; Dt 5:26; 1 Sm 23:10; Ps 68:36; Is 5:16
El Gibbor (mighty God)	The God of war and strength; Lord; savior	Ex 15:2–3; Is 9:6
El Berith (God of the Covenant)	Pre-Israelite title for the Canaanite god of Shechem; later became a name for Yahweh	Jos 23:16; Jgs 9:46
Elohim (the single God)	Generic title for deity; signifies the singular, majestic God of Israel; plural form of El or Eloah—sons of heaven; can refer to Israel's God or to false gods	Gn 1:1,26; 6:2; 17:19; Ex 3:6; 20:3
Yahweh (life, existence, to be, Lord)	Personal name for God; I am who I am; the Creator; ruler of history; the deliverer; the tetragrammaton YHWH (pronounced Yahweh) was not spoken but was substituted with the word Adonai	Gn 4:26; 49:24–25; Ex 3:13–15; 2 Sm 22:2; Prv 9:10
Adonai (my great Lord)	Used as a substitute for Yahweh; also commonly used as a title of respect for a significant male, a lower Lord, a social superior, a king, husband, father, or slave master	Ps 11:7; Jer 31:32; Hos 2:18; Mal 1:6
Yahweh Sabaoth (Lord of hosts)	Lord Almighty; conqueror and ruler of angels and deities; king of glory	Neh 9:6; Pss 24:10; 89:9–19; Is 1:24
Immanuel (Emmanuel); **Yireh; El Roi** (God with us)	A child who is a sign of God's presence; the one who sees all, hears the cries of his people, knows the affliction of slavery, and saves	Gn 16:13–14;22:13–14; Dt 11:12; 2Chr 16:9; 42:1; Jb 34:21–22; Is 7:10–17

Sacred Time: Festivals, Feasts, and Fasts that Mark Biblical Events

Festivals include feasts to celebrate fertility, happiness, commitment, births, marriages, or victories. Times of fasting include penance and periods when feasting is forbidden.

Event	Significance and Reference
Sabbath	The seventh day is a day of rest to honor God and family. No work is permitted (Ex 20:8–11; Lv 23:1–3; Dt 5:12–15). Christians celebrate the Sabbath on Sunday to honor the Paschal mystery of Christ's life, death, and Resurrection (Mt 28:1–10; Mk 16:1–8; Lk 24:1–12; Jn 21:1–14).
Trumpets	New moon festival honors forty days of repentance and joy (Lv 23:23–25; Nm 28:11–15; Am 8:5).
New Year	Rosh Hashanah marks the New Year with prayers and rest. It anticipates the return of the Messiah and is a day of trumpets (Nm 29:1–6).
Yom Kippur or Day of Atonement	Ten days after the New Year, the Day of Awe marks the end of Trumpets and honors the ancestors. Repentance is symbolized by a scapegoat driven into the wilderness (Lv 16:29; 23:27; Nm 29:7–11). Christians associate the Day of Atonement with Jesus' sacrifice on the cross (Mt 26:28; Mk 14:24; Jn 8:12; Heb 9:11—10:18).
Sabbatical year	Every seven years the land rests, slaves are freed, and all debts are suspended or erased (Ex 21:2; 23:10–11; Lv 25:1–7; Dt 15:1–6).
Jubilee (fiftieth year)	The seventh sabbatical year is honored with compassion to the poor, the freedom of slaves, erasure of debts, the return of property to its original owner, and resting the land (Lv 25:8–22; 2 Chr 36:21; Is 61:1–2).
Pilgrimage festivals	The feasts of Passover, Unleavened Bread, Weeks, Booths (or Tabernacles), and the harvest were marked with pilgrimages to the sanctuary or Temple in Jerusalem (Ex 23:14–17; 34:22–23; Dt 16:16–17).
Feast of Passover or Unleavened Bread	The memorial of the Exodus from Egypt is honored in a seder meal in which prayers and blessings are offered for Jews across the world (Ex 12:1–28; 34:18,25; Lv 23:4–14; Nm 9:1–14; 28:16–25; Dt 16:1–8; Ez 45:18–24). Jesus memorialized Passover as he offered himself as the bread of life (or the Eucharist) (Mt 26:17–19,26–29; 1 Cor 10:1; 11:23–26; Eph 2:19–20).
Feast of Weeks	The seven weeks of harvest after the blessing of the first sheaf of barley in the rite of Omer during Pentecost (Ex 23:16; 34:22; Lv 23:15; Nm 28:26–31; Dt 16:9–10).
Pentecost	Pentecost concludes seven weeks after the rite of Omer as the first sheaf of grain is offered in thanks for the harvest. The feast of Weeks or Shavuot marks fifty days after Passover (Lv 23:15–22; Nm 28:26–31). Pentecost, for Christians, marks the descent of the Holy Spirit and reveals Christ's church (Acts 2:1–11; 20:16; 1 Cor 16:8).
Feast of Tabernacles or Booths	Autumn feast; gathering of the harvest on the fifteenth to the twenty-first days of the seventh month. The ingathering of the harvest marks Sukkoth, when Israel lived in the wilderness (Lv 23:33–43; Nm 29:12–39; Dt 16:13–17; Ez 45:25; Zec 14:16–19). The Transfiguration of Jesus took place at the feast of Tabernacles (feast of Booths) (Lk 9:33; Jn 7:2,37).
Feast of Shiloh	A version of Tabernacles or Booths during which families made pilgrimages to Shiloh (Jgs 21:19; 1 Sm 1:1–7)
Purim	Holy day that marks the defeat of Haman of Persia by Esther and honors Mordecai's faith. The feast includes drama, fasting, feasting, and prayers for Israel (Est 9:20–32).
Hanukkah	The dedication of the second Temple and the defeat of Antiochus IV (167 BCE) by the Maccabean Wars is the mythic source of Hanukkah. The festival includes gift giving, feasting, and celebrations (1 Mc 4:1–59; 2 Mc 10:1–8; Jn 10:22).

Prophets and the Kings (1050 – 571 BCE)

The Hebrew prophets proclaimed the will of God as the highest authority for honor and morality. The kings were anointed to lead the people with covenant values of monotheism and justice. Some were great sages, brave warriors, and brilliant statesmen. Others were idolatrous despots who abandoned their call for power and lust. The Scripture writers of the ancient world hailed or condemned their kings based on how they heeded the word of God offered by the prophets. (All dates are approximate.)

Prophets

Samuel (1050–1030): Last judge, first prophet (1 Sm 3:20; 10:1; 16:13)

Gad (995): Counseled David (1 Sm 22:5; 2 Sm 24:11–19)

Nathan (975): Seer of David and Solomon; revealed the Temple and the dynasty of David (2 Sm 7:12–13,17; 12:1–15; 1 Chr 29:29; 2 Chr 9:29)

Ahijah (924): Seer of Shiloh who, upon meeting Jeroboam, tore his cloak into twelve pieces to ritualize the civil war and the reign of Jeroboam as king of Israel (1 Kgs 11:29–35)

Jehu (902–884): Israelite prophet, son of Hanani, who condemned Baasha's idolatry and murder of Nadab (1 Kgs 16:7)

Elijah (865–842): Israelite wonder worker (1 Kgs 17:7–24); defeated the prophets of Baal and Asherah; reinstated faith in Yahweh (1 Kgs 18:36–40). He defeated the sons of Ahab and Jezebel (1 Kgs 17:1); made Elisha his successor and was taken to heaven in a fiery chariot (2 Kgs 2:11–15).

Kings of the United Monarchy

Saul (1020–1000): Warrior of the tribe of Benjamin who contained the Philistines but disobeyed the Lord's command (1 Sm 9:1–2,15–16; 13:10–14)

David (1010–961): Greatest king of Israel. Hero, warrior, man of repentance and faith. Husband of Bathsheba, father of Solomon (1 Sm 16:1—1 Kgs 2:11)

Solomon (961–922): Son of David and Bathsheba who built the Temple. His reign was marked by idolatry, taxes, and forced labor (1 Kgs 1:1—11:43). His cruel son Rehoboam led to the destruction of the United Monarchy.

Kings of Judah

Rehoboam (922–915): Idolatrous son of Solomon. His taxation fueled the civil war (1 Kgs 12:1–25; Sir 47:23–25)

Abijam (915–913): Idolater who inflicted war with Jeroboam (1 Kgs 14:31—15:8)

Asa (913–873): Loyal son of Abijam faithful to God (1 Kgs 15:8–24)

Jehoshaphat (873–849): Diplomatic son of Asa who worked for peace with Israel (1 Kgs 22:41–51)

Jehoram (Joram) (849–842): Serial murderer; son of Jehoshaphat; married Athaliah (843–837), daughter of Ahab and Jezebel (2 Kgs 8:16–24)

Ahaziah (842): Son of Jehoram and Athaliah (843–837), killed by Jeru. His widowed queen murdered all his male heirs but Joash (2 Kgs 8:25; 9:29; 11:1–20).

Athaliah (844-837): Daughter of Jezebel and Ahab, she was the only ruling queen of Judah (2 Kgs 11:1–20).

Joash (Jehoash) (837–800): Son of Ahaziah who survived the murderous reign of Athaliah, protected by his aunt Jehosheba. His reign ended with his murder (2 Kgs 11:1–20; 12:21).

Kings of Israel

Jeroboam (922–901): Israelite king who worshiped the golden calf of Samaria (1 Kgs 12:26–28; 14:20)

Nadab (901–900): Idolatrous son of Jeroboam (1 Kgs 15:25–31)

Baasha (900–877): Built citadels and honored idols in Tirzah (1 Kgs 15:33–34)

Elah (877–876): Son of Baasha, murdered by his servant Zimri (1 Kgs 16:8–14)

Zimri (876): Charioteer who murdered Elah, his family, and himself (1 Kgs 16:9–20)

Omri (876–869): Commander and first king of the Omride dynasty (1 Kgs 16:15–28)

Ahab (869–850): King who, along with Jezebel, served Baal, offered human sacrifice, and killed the prophets of God (1 Kgs 16:28—22:40)

Ahaziah (850–849): Son of Ahab and Jezebel (1 Kgs 22:52–53), he was a devotee of Baalzebub, god of Ekron. His death was prophesied by Elijah (2 Kgs 1:2–18).

Jehoram (Joram) (849–842): Son of Ahab, brother-in-law of Jehoram of Judah who succeeded Ahaziah on the throne (2 Kgs 3:1). The last of the Omride dynasty (2 Kgs 1:1–18)

Prophets

Elisha (850–800): Israelite prophet and miracle worker who served Elijah and followed as his successor (1 Kgs 19:19–21; 2 Kgs 2:9–22). He miraculously provided the poor with oil and bread; cured the leper; astounded the proud; raised the dead; offered hope; and anointed kings (2 Kgs 4:1—5:27).

Amos (760–745): Judean farm laborer in Israel (Am 7:14–15) who condemned treatment of workers (Am 5:7–17)

Hosea (755): An Israelite prophet of Judea; his marriage to the adulterous Gomer became an allegory for the love of God for the unfaithful Israel (Hos 3:1).

Isaiah of Jerusalem (740–700): Mystic who lived with a prophetess wife; served in the Temple of Jerusalem as Assyria pillaged Israel (Is 6:1–13; 8:3). He revealed the birth of a child, Immanuel (meaning God with us), who would save Israel (Is 7:14; 8:6–10). The book that carries his name represents two hundred years of Judean history.

Kings of Judah

Amaziah (800–783): Son of Joash who took the throne after his father's murder (2 Kgs 14:1–20)

Uzziah (Azariah) (783–745): Faithful son of Amaziah who came to rule at age sixteen. His reign was stable and victorious (2 Kgs 14:21; 15:1–7)

Jotham (750–735): Reigned eight years as regent, eight years as king, and left the high places intact (2 Kgs 15:32–38)

Ahaz (735–715): Idolatrous king who sacrificed his own son in the fires of Molech. He practiced the rites of Canaan on the high places; refused to join the anti-Assyrian alliance and became an Assyrian vassal (2 Kgs 16:1–20).

Kings of Israel

Jehu (842–815): Defeated the house of Ahab and removed Baal of Tyre from Israel. Jehu worshiped the golden calves of Samaria (2 Kgs 9:1—10:36).

Jehoahaz (815–801): Warring king who mixed worship of Yahweh with false gods (2 Kgs 13:1–9)

Jehoash (Joash) (801–786): Son of Jehoahaz who persisted in the sins began by Jeroboam. He was an adversary of Amaziah, king of Judah (2 Kgs 13:10–13).

Jeroboam II (786–746): A prosperous and unjust king, he worshiped the golden calves of Samaria (2 Kgs 14:23–29).

Zechariah (746–745): The last in the line of Jehu, whose six month rule was marked by injustice (2 Kgs 15:8–12)

Shallum (745): Murdered Zechariah and was assassinated within one month (2 Kgs 15:10–15)

Menahem (745–738): Much hated puppet ruler of the Assyrians who killed Shallum (2 Kgs 15:14–22)

Pekahiah (738–737): Pro-Assyrian son of Menahem who escalated the war (2 Kgs 15:22–26)

Pekah (737–732): After killing Pekahiah, he became king. He joined Damascus, Tyre, and Philistia against Assyria (2 Kgs 15:25–31).

Hoshea (732–724): Son of Elah, vassal to Shalmaneser of Assyria, who refused to pay the annual tribute. He was imprisoned and exiled with the Samarian people (2 Kgs 17:1–6). Last king of Israel.

Prophet of the Assyrian Destruction

Micah (720–701): Judean prophet of the Assyrian conquest who taught that sin hides the truth and leads to economic collapse and war (Mi 1:1; 2:1–10). He envisioned a new Israel and foretold of the royal shepherd of Bethlehem who would bring peace to the earth (Mi 4:1–7; 5:1–4).

Prophets of Judah

Zephaniah (640–609): He served in Jerusalem during the reign of Josiah (Zep 1:1–18; 3:14–20)

Nahum (612): Prophesied the destruction of Nineveh (Na 1:1–6)

Habakkuk (605–597): Revealed God's lament over Judah's sin (Hb 2:1–20)

Jeremiah (626–582): Called to be a prophet as a child, he advised the King and identified the Babylonian destruction and exile as sin (Jer 1:1–10; 26:1–16).

Ezekiel (593–571): Prophesying from Babylon, his strange visions warn of Jerusalem's fall (Ez 4:1—24:27).

Kings of Judah after the Assyrian Destruction of Israel

Hezekiah (715–687): Son of Ahaz; faithful ruler who healed ancient wounds. He dug the tunnel of Siloam to protect the city's water supply from the Assyrians (2 Kgs 18:1—20:21).

Manasseh (687–642): Sacrificed his son to Baal and was taken captive by Assyria (2 Chr 33:1–25; 2 Kgs 21:1–18)

Amon (642–640): Evil adulterer who was murdered (2 Kgs 21:19–26)

Josiah (640–609): Great reformer who renewed the Covenant and restored the Temple (2 Kgs 21:26—23:30)

Jehoahaz (609): Idolatrous son of Josiah who reigned three months then was taken prisoner by Pharaoh Neco. He died in Egypt (2 Kgs 23:30–33).

Jehoiakim (609–598): Son of Josiah named Eliakim. At age twenty-five Pharoah Neco renamed him Jehoiakim and made him king of Judah and a vassal to Egypt (2 Kgs 23:33–37).

Jehoiachin (597): Son of Jehoiakim. He was exiled to Babylon (2 Kgs 24:6–16; 25:27–30).

Zedekiah (Mattaniah) (597–587): Jehoiachin's uncle; Nebuchadnezzar murdered his family and gouged out his eyes. He was led to Babylon in chains and died in the shame of Exile (2 Kgs 24:17—25:11; Jer 52:1–11). He was the last pre-exilic king of Judah.

New Testament Biblical Images

The **Sea of Galilee** is where Jesus began his ministry and first called his disciples (Mt 4:12–22).

The Second **Temple** is presented here in a scale model as it would have appeared in Jerusalem at about the year AD 20. The Second Temple is where Mary and Joseph found the twelve-year-old Jesus conversing with the teachers (Lk 2:41–52) and where Jesus upset the trading of the money changers and the vendors (Mt 21:12–17; Mk 11:15–19; Lk 19:45–47; Jn 2:12–25). It was built to replace Solomon's Temple when the people of Israel returned from exile.

The **Mount of Olives** is directly across the Kidron Valley from the City of Jerusalem. This is where Jesus went to pray with his disciples before his arrest (Mt 26:36–46; Mk 14:32–42; Lk 22:39–46).

An **ablution basin** was used for ritual washing. This basin is in the Church of Saint Peter in Gallicantu on Mount Zion outside Jerusalem. Gallicantu is Latin for "cock crow". The church commemorates Peter's denial of Jesus and his subsequent repentance. How do you express sorrow for your sins?

This ancient **amphitheater at Caesarea** was built by Herod the Great and had a seating capacity of 3,500. All that remains is the seating and backstage area of this once magnificent theatre. But these were so well constructed that it is used for performances today! Caesarea was the center of Roman government in Palestine for over six hundred years. Both Philip and Peter preached the message of Jesus Christ to the people of Caesarea (Acts 8:40; 10:1—11:18).

This is an entrance to a **burial tomb** carved out of rock. The round stone is rolled in front of the opening to seal the tomb. The tomb Jesus was buried in was probably similar to this (Mt 27:57–61).

Titles of Jesus of Nazareth

Christology attempts to give language to the great mystery of Jesus, the Christ. Those who wrote the Gospels hoped to honor him with names, words, and titles that speak to our faith in Jesus.

Title	Significance and Reference
Jesus	*Yeshua* (or Joshua) in Hebrew, it means "God saves" (Mt 1:21; Lk 1:31).
Son of Mary	Identifies Jesus as born of woman and fully human (Mt 1:18; Lk 1:26–31)
Rabbi or Rabbouni	Jesus was a Jewish wisdom teacher, healer, and scholar of the Torah. His disciples honored him as Master (Mk 9:5; 10:51; Jn 3:2; 20:16).
Carpenter	Jesus was a craftsman who served with his father Joseph (Mt 13:55; Mk 6:3).
Messiah (Christ in Greek)	Christ (*Mashia* in Hebrew) means "anointed one" and is a title used for kings, prophets, and war heroes. Jesus was the Messiah who freed humanity from the bondage of slavery and from the pain and despair of sin. Over the centuries, this title honored Jesus' divinity (Mt 1:1,18; 16:16; Mk 1:1; 8:29; Jn 4:25–26; Acts 2:38).
King of the Jews	Jesus was born of David's royal line. Angels, shepherds, and the Magi adored the newborn king. Pilate mocked him with this title that he nailed to the cross of Christ (Mt 2:2; Mk 15:2; Lk 23:38; Jn 19:19).
Son (Root) of David	Jesus is a descendant of Israel's great King David, the fulfillment of the prophecy of Nathan who said the Covenant would remain with the house of David (2 Sm 7:11–16; Mt 1:1; 12:23; Lk 18:38; Rev 5:5).
Son of Abraham	Jesus is the descendant of Israel's great patriarch and shares in the election of Israel and the eternal covenant (Mt 1:1; Lk 3:34; Jn 8:58).
Son of Man *Bar Nasa*	*Bar Nasa* is Aramaic for Son of Man. Jesus and the evangelists of the Gospels used this divine title to describe Jesus' triune relationship in God (Mt 12:8; 16:13–16; Lk 6:5).
	Jesus used this title for himself when he spoke of his mission and of his Passion to come (Mt 8:20; 17:9; 19:28; Lk 9:22,58; 18:8).
	The Son of Man came as the "human one" from heaven with the authority to forgive sin (Mt 9:6; 12:32; Mk 2:10; Lk 5:24; 12:10; Jn 3:13).
	The Son of Man will be betrayed and handed over (Mt 17:12,22–23; 26:24).
	The Son of Man will be condemned, die, be buried, and offer his life to redeem many (Mt 20:18–19,28; Mk 9:31).
	The Son of Man will rise from the dead (Mk 9:9).
	There will be signs of the coming of the Son of Man (Mt 24:27,37,39,44).
	The Son of Man will be glorified, honored before angels, and send angels to earth (Mt 13:41; 16:27; 25:31; Lk 12:8; Jn 1:51; 12:23; 13:31).
	The Son of Man will judge the living and the dead and herald in a new age in glory (Mt 19:28, 26:64; Lk 22:69; Jn 5:26–29).
Son of God	Jesus is the Incarnation of the divine—Son of the Most High (Mt 4:3; 14:33; 27:54; Mk 3:11; Lk 1:32; Jn 20:31).
Savior	Jesus is savior of the world; the one who releases humanity from bondage, from sin and death, a form of Messiah or Christ (Lk 2:11; Jn 4:42).
	Israel's deliverer; the Redeemer; the God of history and of Israel revealed in Christ (Acts 13:23).
	As savior, Jesus grants forgiveness of sin (Acts 5:31).
The Lord; I am	Jesus Christ is Lord, the Glory of God, the manifestation of Yahweh among us. Jesus is the perfect image of true humanity. The one who calls us into eternal life (Mt 1:23; Lk 1:66; Jn 11:25–27; 20:28–29; Acts 2:36; Col 2:9–10; Phil 2:11).
	Jesus is the "I am" of Yahweh; the bread of life; the light of the world; the door, the gate; the Good Shepherd; the resurrection and life; the way, the truth, and the life (Jn 6:35; 8:12; 10:7,11; 11:25; 14:6).
Lamb of God	The worthy sacrifice who frees humanity from sin, who was slain, and who takes away grief (Jn 1:29,36; Rev 5:6; 17:14)
Word of God	Jesus is the word (logos) of God in the flesh. Jesus is the alpha and the omega; the beginning and end of all creation, the pre-existent one (Jn 1:1–3; Rev 19:13; 21:6).

Gospel Comparisons

	Mark	Matthew	Luke	John
Writer	Mark: A second generation Christian, possibly a follower of Peter; traditionally the John Mark of Acts	Matthew: An unknown Jewish Christian, traditionally the Apostle Matthew	Luke: A Gentile Christian, traditionally Luke the physician and Paul's traveling companion	John: The beloved disciple, the Apostle John, or his disciple
Date Written	65–70 CE	75–80 CE	80–85 CE	90–110 CE
Images of Christ	The suffering servant of God, Son of Man, Son of God, Messiah, and Lord	Teacher and prophet like Moses, Son of God, Son of Man, Messiah, and Lord	Great healer, merciful, compassion for the poor, Son of God, Son of Man, Messiah, and Lord	Logos, word of God, Son of God, Son of Man, lamb of God, Redeemer, Messiah, and Lord
The Author's Community	A Gentile Christian community in Rome undergoing persecution	A Jewish Christian community in Antioch, Syria	Written to Theophilus (meaning "lover of God"), who possibly represents any Christian (Greece)	Community of Jews, Gentiles, and Samaritans of Ephesus in Turkey
Theological Themes	Jesus shows that the suffering in our lives can be a source of grace when united to the sufferings of Christ.	Jesus teaches what it means to be a member of the Kingdom of heaven. He prepares his followers to continue his teaching and ministry.	Jesus heals long-standing divisions among people. He calls his followers to have a special compassion for those excluded from wealth and power.	Jesus is the divine Son of God, the image of God in flesh. Salvation is available for those who believe in Jesus and commit their lives to him.
Historical Situation	The Romans subdue armed Jewish rebellions. Christians experience persecution in Rome.	Written after Romans had destroyed all of Jerusalem, including the Temple of Herod	Written when the persecution of Jews and Christians was intensifying	Emperor Domitian deified himself and mandated that all people worship him. Jewish leaders banned Christians from the synagogues.
Caesars	Nero (54–68 CE)	Vespasian and Titus (70–81 CE)	Domitian (81–96 CE)	Domitian (81–96 CE), Nerva (96–98 CE), Trajan (98–117 CE)

6 On that day I will make the clans of Judah like
a brazier of fire in the woodland and like a burn-
ing torch among sheaves, and they will devour
right and left all the surrounding peoples; but
Jerusalem will again inhabit its own place.*
7 The LORD will save the tents of Judah first,
that the glory of the house of David and the
glory of the inhabitants of Jerusalem may not be
exalted over Judah. 8 On that day the LORD will
shield the inhabitants of Jerusalem, so that the
weakest among them will be like David on that
day; and the house of David will be like God, like
the angel of the LORD before them.
9 On that day I will seek the destruction of
all nations that come against Jerusalem.* 10 I
will pour out on the house of David and on the
inhabitants of Jerusalem a spirit of mercy and
supplication, so that when they look on him
whom they have thrust through,† * they will
mourn for him as one mourns for an only child,
and they will grieve for him as one grieves over
a firstborn.*

Catalogue of Mourners

11 On that day the mourning in Jerusalem will
be as great as the mourning for Hadadrimmon
in the plain of Megiddo.† 12 And the land shall
mourn, each family apart: the family of the
house of David, and their women; the family of
the house of Nathan, and their women; 13 the
family of the house of Levi, and their women;
the family of Shimei, and their women; 14 and
all the rest of the families, each family apart, and
the women apart.

Oracles Concerning the End of False Prophecy†

13 1 On that day a fountain will be opened for
the house of David† and the inhabitants of
Jerusalem, to purify from sin and uncleanness.*
2 On that day—oracle of the LORD of hosts—I
will destroy the names of the idols from the land,
so that they will be mentioned no more; I will
also remove the prophets and the spirit of un-
cleanness from the land. 3 If any still prophesy,
their father and mother who bore them will say,
"You will not live, because you have spoken a
lie in the name of the LORD." Their father and
mother who bore them will thrust them through
when they prophesy.*
4 On that day, all prophets will be ashamed
of the visions they prophesy; and they will not
put on the hairy mantle† to mislead,* 5 but each

Did You Know?

Prophecies of God's Victory

Zechariah, chapters 12–14, has several of Second Zechariah's prophecies on the final judgment, the restoration of Israel, and the Reign of God. Many of these prophecies were applied to Jesus by the first Christians.

For example, Zechariah foretells a time of mourning for "him whom they have thrust through" (Zec 12:10); the Gospel of John applies this verse to Jesus' death on the cross (see Jn 19:37). Zechariah says the sheep will be dispersed when the shepherd is struck (see Zec 13:7); the Gospel of Matthew uses this verse to describe the disciples' deserting Jesus (see Mt 26:31). And passages from Zechariah's description of the day of the Lord (see Zec 14:6–9) show up in the Book of Revelation's description of the new Jerusalem (see Rev 11:15, 21:23).

These beautiful prophecies assured Israel's people of God's love and mercy. For Christians, they have additional meaning. They also describe Jesus Christ, whose death is our salvation and whose Resurrection is the promise of the fullness of God's Reign!

▶ **Zechariah, chapters 12–14**

†

12:10 *They look on him . . . thrust through*: another possible rendering is "they shall look to me concerning him . . . thrust through." In either case, the victim is an enigmatic figure, perhaps referring to a Davidic descendant, a priestly leader, or even a true prophet. Some historical event, unknown to us from any surviving source, may underlie this reference. The Gospel of John applies this text to the piercing of Christ's side after his death (19:37).

12:11 The mourning for the pierced victim in Jerusalem is compared to the annual ritual mourning in the plain of Megiddo over the death of the Phoenician fertility god, Hadadrimmon. According to others, Hadadrimmon is the name of a place near Megiddo, and the reference would then be to the mourning over the death of King Josiah at the hands of Pharaoh Neco in 609 B.C.; cf. 2 Kgs 23:29–30; 2 Chr 35:22–25.

13:1–6 False prophecy is a major theme of Second Zechariah (chaps. 9–14) and figures in many other passages (10:1–2; 11; 12:10). Problems of idolatry and false prophecy occurred in postexilic Judah as they had in preexilic times. The understanding of the role of the prophet as an intermediary was challenged because (1) there was no king in Jerusalem, and (2) the texts of earlier prophets were beginning to be accorded the authority of prophetic tradition.

13:1 *For the house of David*: anticipation that a cleansed leadership will enable the re-established monarchy to be rid of the misdeeds of its past.

13:4 *Hairy mantle*: worn by prophets as a sign of their calling,

*

12:6 Zec 14:10.
12:9 Zec 14:3.
12:10 Jn 19:37; Rev 1:7.
12:10 Am 8:10.
13:1 Ez 36:25; 47:1; Jn 7:38.
13:3 Jn 19:34.
13:4 2 Kgs 1:8; Mt 3:4.

will say, "I am not a prophet. I am a tiller of the soil, for I have owned land since my youth."* 6 And if anyone asks, "What are these wounds on your chest?"† each will answer, "I received these wounds in the house of my friends."*

The Song of the Sword

7 Awake, O sword, against my shepherd,
against the one who is my associate
—oracle of the LORD of hosts.
Strike the shepherd
that the sheep may be scattered;† *
I will turn my hand against the little ones.
8 In all the land—oracle of the LORD—
two thirds of them will be cut off and perish,
and one third will be left.
9 I will bring the one third through the fire;
I will refine them as one refines silver,*
and I will test them as one tests gold.
They will call upon my name, and I will answer them;*
I will say, "They are my people,"*
and they will say, "The LORD is my God."

Devastation and Rescue of Jerusalem

14 1 † A day is coming for the LORD when the spoils taken from you will be divided in your midst. 2 And I will gather all the nations against Jerusalem for battle: The city will be taken, houses will be plundered, women raped; half the city will go into exile, but the rest of the people will not be removed from the city. 3 Then the LORD will go forth and fight against those nations, fighting as on a day of battle.* 4 On that day God's feet will stand† on the Mount of Olives, which is opposite Jerusalem to the east. The Mount of Olives will be split in two from east to west by a very deep valley,* and half of the mountain will move to the north and half of it to the south. 5 You will flee by the valley between the mountains, for the valley between the mountains will reach to Azal. Thus you will flee as you fled because of the earthquake† in the days of Uzziah king of Judah.* Then the LORD, my God, will come, and all his holy ones with him.*

Jerusalem Restored

6 On that day there will no longer be cold or frost. 7 There will be one continuous day—it is known to the LORD—not day and night, for in the evening there will be light. 8 On that day, fresh water will flow from Jerusalem,* half to the eastern sea, and half to the western sea. This will be so in summer and in winter. 9 The LORD will be king over the whole earth;* on that day the LORD will be the only one, and the LORD's name the only one. 10 All the land will turn into a plain, from Geba to Rimmon, south of Jerusalem, which will stand exalted in its place—from the Gate of Benjamin to the place of the first gate, to the Corner Gate and from the Tower of Hananel to the king's wine presses. 11 The city will be inhabited; never again will it be doomed. Jerusalem will dwell securely.*

The Fate of Jerusalem's Foes

12 And this will be the plague with which the LORD will strike all the peoples that have fought against Jerusalem: their flesh will rot while they stand on their feet, and their eyes will rot in their sockets, and their tongues will rot in their mouths.* 13 On that day a great panic from the LORD will be upon them.* They will seize each other's hands, and their hands will be raised against each other. 14 Even Judah will fight against Jerusalem. The riches of all the surrounding nations will be gathered together—gold, silver, and garments—in great abundance. 15 Like the plague on human beings will be the plague

---

† for example, Elijah (1 Kgs 19:13; 2 Kgs 1:8) and John the Baptist (Mt 3:4).

13:6 *Wounds on your chest*: lit., "wounds between your hands." The false prophets, like the prophets of Baal (1 Kgs 18:28), apparently inflicted wounds on themselves. Here it seems that persons accused of false prophecy deny having inflicted wounds on themselves and instead claim that they have received them at the houses of their friends.

13:7 *Strike the shepherd . . . may be scattered*: in Matthew's Gospel (26:31) Jesus makes use of this text before his arrest in the Garden of Gethsemane and the flight of the disciples.

14:1–21 The marked eschatological thrust of Zec 9–14 culminates in this apocalyptic description, with its astonishing images of the day of the Lord. This last and longest chapter focuses on the restoration of Jerusalem and the return of the people of Zion so that the rest of the world will acknowledge God's sovereignty. Four units constitute this chapter: vv. 1–5 concentrate on the destruction and rescue of Jerusalem and the escape of a remnant; vv. 6–11 describe the transformation of the climate and the topography of Jerusalem; vv. 12–15 depict the defeat of Jerusalem's enemies; and vv. 16–21 outline a vision for the end time, in which even foreign nations will make the pilgrimage to Jerusalem to acknowledge God's universal reign.

14:4 *God's feet will stand*: a remarkable anthropomorphic image adds emphasis to the traditional Old Testament scene of God appearing on a mountain and causing extreme reactions such as quaking, melting, shattering (see Ex 19:18; Ps 97:5; Hb 3:6). The Mount of Olives is split, which opens a way for those fleeing from the Lord's appearance to escape from Jerusalem.

14:5 *Earthquake*: Amos 1:1 mentions an earthquake in the time of King Uzziah (cf. Is 6:4).

13:5 Am 7:14.
13:6 1 Kgs 18:28.
13:7 Ez 34:1–8; Mt 26:31.
13:9 Is 1:25; 48:10.
13:9 Ps 91:15; Is 65:24.
13:9 Zec 8:8; Jer 31:31.
14:3 Is 31:4.
14:4 Mi 1:4.
14:5 Am 1:1.
14:5 Dt 33:2–3; Mt 16:27; 1 Thes 3:13.
14:8 Zec 13:1; Ez 47:1–8; Jl 4:18.
14:9 Ps 96:7–10; 97:1; 98:4–6; Rev 11:15.
14:11 Dt 33:28; Jer 31:40; Rev 22:3.
14:12 Is 66:24.
14:13 1 Sm 5:9, 11; 14:18–20; Is 22:5.

upon the horses, mules, camels, donkeys, and
upon all the beasts that are in those camps.

The Future: Jerusalem, Judah, and the Nations

16 Everyone who is left of all the nations that
came against Jerusalem will go up year after year
to bow down to the King, the LORD of hosts, and
to celebrate the feast of Booths.† * 17 Should any
of the families of the earth* not go up to Jerusa-
lem to bow down to the King, the LORD of hosts,
then there will be no rain for them. 18 And if the
family of Egypt does not go up or enter, upon
them will fall the plague,* with which the LORD
strikes the nations that do not go up to celebrate
the feast of Booths. 19 This will be the punish-
ment of Egypt and the punishment of all the
nations that do not go up to celebrate the feast
of Booths.
20 On that day, "Holy to the LORD"* will be
written on the horses' bells.† The pots in the
house of the LORD will be as the basins before
the altar. 21 Every pot† in Jerusalem and in Judah
will be holy to the LORD of hosts. All who come
to sacrifice will take them and cook in them. No
longer will there be merchants in the house of
the LORD of hosts on that day.

† **14:16** *Feast of Booths*: fall harvest festival, also known as the "festival of Ingathering" (Ex 23:16; 34:22) or "Booths" (Lv 23:33–36; Dt 16:13–15; 31:9–13). The singling out of this festival indicates its special status in the sacred calendar; it is frequently referred to as "the feast" (1 Kgs 8:1–2; 2 Chr 5:3; Ez 45:25).

14:20 *Horses' bells*: even these bells, part of the trappings of animals used for war, will become holy in the end time, like the bells of the high priest's garb (cf. Ex 28:34).

14:21 *Every pot*: vessels used for mundane food preparation will, in the end time, be as holy as Temple vessels.

* **14:16** Lv 23:33–36; Dt 16:13–15. **14:17** Zec 8:20–23; Is 2:1–4; Mi 4:1–3. **14:18** Ex 5:3; 9:15. **14:20** Lv 23:20; 27:30, 32.

The Book of

Malachi

"You promised me!" These three words speak volumes when they're used against us. A promise is a sacred thing, and breaking promises hurts and destroys relationships. The last book of the Old Testament, Malachi, focuses on promises with God that have been broken. At the time of its writing, priests had broken the covenant by offering inferior sacrifices, and men had broken the covenant by marrying foreign women and divorcing their Jewish wives. The prophet Malachi predicts that someone is coming who will purify the people, punishing the wicked and rewarding the righteous.

In Depth

The author of the Book of Malachi wrote just before the reforms of Ezra and Nehemiah, starting around 458 BC (see the timeline at the back of this Bible). The Temple had been rebuilt (see the Books of Haggai and Zechariah), and Temple worship had been restored, but serious violations of the covenantal law existed.

The Book of Malachi addresses two main problems. The first is the failure of Israel's priests to provide good leadership. Through a series of questions and answers, the prophet Malachi speaks harsh words against the priests of the Temple for failing to live up to their calling to honor God. They offer inferior sacrifices on the altar of the Temple, thinking that God won't notice. The prophet compares these priests with their ancestor Levi, who offered only the finest gifts to God. Levi was a good and honest man who kept God's Covenant; these priests are not.

The second problem has to do with marriage and divorce. Evidently, many men are marrying non-Jewish women and divorcing their Jewish wives. It's not clear why they are doing this, but maybe they are trying to climb the social ladder. The prophet challenges the people to be faithful to one another because their marriages are a reminder of God's Covenant with the people of Judah.

The book ends with a prophecy that forms a bridge to the New Testament and the coming of Jesus. It says that God will send a messenger, the prophet Elijah, before the day of judgment. His job will be to prepare the way for God. Those who repent will enjoy God's blessings; those who do not will be punished by God. New Testament writers saw this prophecy fulfilled by John the Baptist, who prepared the way for the coming of the Messiah, Jesus of Nazareth.

At a Glance

I. **Israel Preferred to Edom (1:2–5).**
II. **Offense in Sacrifice and Priestly Duty (1:6—2:9).**
III. **Marriage and Divorce (2:10–16).**
IV. **Purification and Just Judgment (2:17).**
V. **The Messenger of the Covenant (3:1–5).**
VI. **Gifts for God, Blessings for the People (3:6–12).**
VII. **The Need To Serve God (3:13–21).**
VIII. **Moses and Elijah (3:22–24).**

Quick Facts

Period Covered: around 455 BC
Inspired Author: unknown
Theme: calls for priestly reform and faithfulness in marriage; God sends the messenger to prepare the way for the Savior

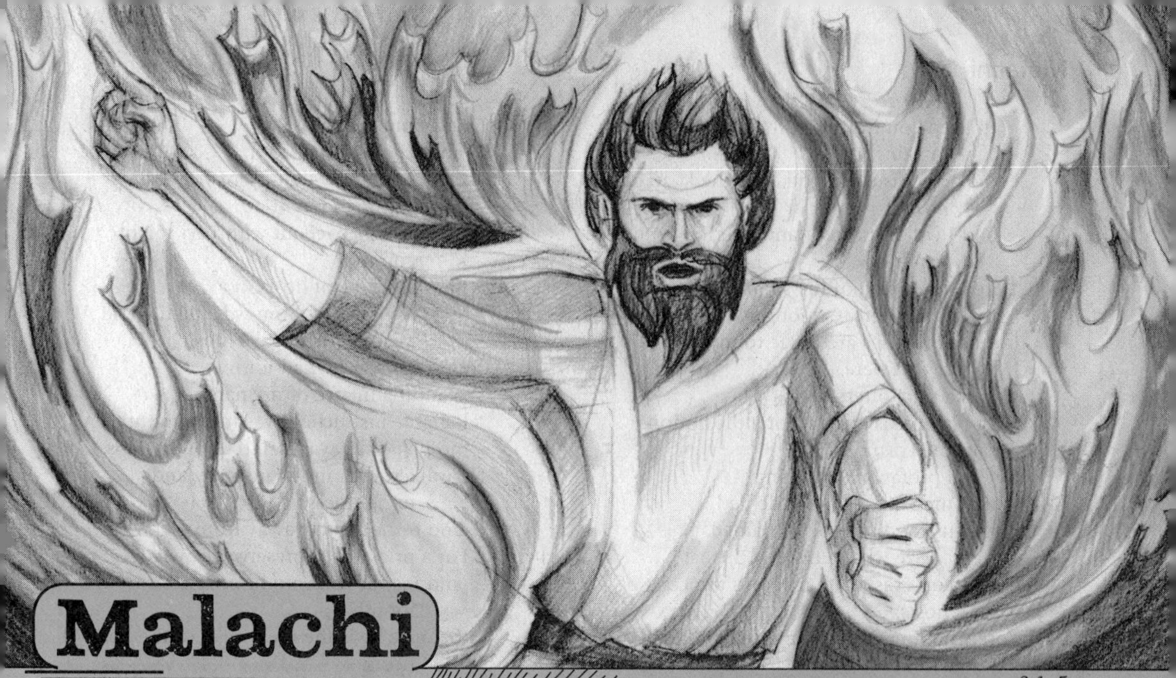

Malachi

3:1–5

1 [1] † An oracle. The word of the LORD to Israel
through Malachi.

Israel Preferred to Edom

2 * I love you, says the LORD;
but you say, "How do you love us?"
3† * Was not Esau Jacob's brother?—oracle of the
LORD.
I loved Jacob, but rejected Esau;
I made his mountains a waste,
his heritage a desert for jackals.
4 * If Edom says, "We have been crushed,
but we will rebuild the ruins,"
Thus says the LORD of hosts:
They indeed may build, but I will tear down,
And they shall be called "territory of wickedness,"
the people with whom the LORD is angry
forever.
5 * Your own eyes will see it, and you will say,
"Great is the LORD, even beyond the territory
of Israel."

Offense in Sacrifice and Priestly Duty

6 * A son honors his father,
and a servant fears his master;
If, then, I am a father,
where is the honor due to me?
And if I am a master,
where is the fear due to me?
So says the LORD of hosts to you, O priests,
who disdain my name.
But you ask, "How have we disdained your
name?"
7 By offering defiled food on my altar!
You ask, "How have we defiled it?"
By saying that the table of the LORD may be
disdained!
8† * When you offer a blind animal for sacrifice,
is there no wrong in that?
When you offer a lame or sick animal,
is there no wrong in that?
Present it to your governor!
Will he be pleased with you—or show you
favor?
says the LORD of hosts.
9 So now implore God's favor, that he may have
mercy on us!
You are the ones who have done this;
Will he show favor to any of you?
says the LORD of hosts.
10† Oh, that one of you would just shut the
temple gates

†

1:1 See note on Zec 9:1.

1:3–5 The thought passes from the person Esau to his descendants, Edom, and from the person Jacob to his descendants, Israel; cf. Gn 25:21–23. In the New Testament, Paul uses this passage as an example of God's freedom of choice in calling the Gentiles to faith (Rom 9:13).

1:8 The sacrificial offering of a lame, sick, or blind animal was forbidden in the law (Lv 22:17–25; Dt 17:1).

1:10–11 The imperfect sacrifices offered by the people of Judah are displeasing to the Lord. *Kindling fire on my altar*: kindle the altar

1:2 Dt 7:8; Ez 16; Hos 11:1; Am 1:11.
1:3 Gn 25:23; Rom 9:13.
1:4 Is 34:2–15; 63:1–6; Jer 49:7–22; Ob 21.
1:5 Is 60.
1:6 Prv 1:7; Is 29:13.
1:8 Lv 22:17–25; Dt 15:21; 17:1.

to keep you from kindling fire on my altar
in vain!
I take no pleasure in you, says the LORD of
hosts;
and I will not accept any offering from your
hands!
11 * From the rising of the sun to its setting,
my name is great among the nations;
Incense offerings are made to my name
everywhere,
and a pure offering;
For my name is great among the nations,
says the LORD of hosts.
12 But you profane it by saying
that the LORD's table is defiled,
and its food may be disdained.
13 You say, "See what a burden this is!"
and you exasperate me, says the LORD of
hosts;
You bring in what is mutilated, or lame, or
sick;
you bring it as an offering!
Will I accept it from your hands?
says the LORD.
14 Cursed is the cheat who has in his flock an
intact male,
and vows it, but sacrifices to the LORD a
defective one instead;
For a great king am I, says the LORD of hosts,
and my name is feared among the nations.

2 1 And now, priests, this commandment is for
you:
If you do not listen,
2 * And if you do not take to heart
giving honor to my name, says the LORD of
hosts,
I will send a curse upon you
and your blessing I will curse.
In fact, I have already cursed it,
because you do not take it to heart.
3 I will rebuke your offspring;
I will spread dung on your faces,
Dung from your feasts,
and will carry you to it.
4 You should know that I sent you this
commandment
so that my covenant with Levi might
endure,
says the LORD of hosts.
5 * My covenant with him was the life and
peace which I gave him,
and the fear he had for me,
standing in awe of my name.
6 * Reliable instruction was in his mouth,
no perversity was found upon his lips;
He walked with me in integrity and
uprightness,
and turned many away from evil.
7 * For a priest's lips preserve knowledge,
and instruction is to be sought from his
mouth,
because he is the messenger of the LORD of
hosts.
8 But you have turned aside from the way,
and have caused many to stumble by your
instruction;
You have corrupted the covenant of Levi,†
says the LORD of hosts.
9 I, therefore, have made you contemptible
and base before all the people,
For you do not keep my ways,
but show partiality in your instruction.

Marriage and Divorce

10† * Have we not all one father?
Has not one God created us?
Why, then, do we break faith with each other,
profaning the covenant of our ancestors?
11 * Judah has broken faith; an abominable
thing
has been done in Israel and in Jerusalem.
Judah has profaned the LORD's holy place,
which he loves,
and has married a daughter of a foreign
god.†

fire for sacrifice. In contrast, the Lord is pleased with the sacrifices offered by other peoples in other places (*the rising of the sun*: the far east; *its setting*: the far west). Since the people of other nations could not be expected to know the Lord's name as did the people of Judah, the rhetorical purpose of this statement is to shame the latter. *Incense offerings*: in the ancient world, the hallmark of an offering made to a god was the smoke it produced on an altar. In the Old Testament, this was true not only of animals (Lv 8:20–21) but also of incense (Ex 30:7), suet (Lv 3:11), and grain offerings (Lv 6:8). In a Christian interpretation of Mal 1:10–11, the "pure offering" of Mal 1:11 is seen as a reference to sacrifice in the Messianic Age. The Council of Trent endorsed this interpretation (DS 1724).

2:8 *The covenant of Levi*: not mentioned elsewhere in the Bible. The covenant with Phinehas the grandson of Aaron (Nm 25:11–13) and the Blessing of Levi (Dt 33:8–11) may lie in the background.

2:10–16 Intermarriage of Israelites with foreigners was forbidden according to Dt 7:1–4. After the exile, attempts were made to enforce this law (Ezr 9–10). Foreign marriages are here portrayed as a covenantal violation (v. 10). They were all the more reprehensible when they were accompanied by the divorce of Israelite wives (vv. 14–16), and God finds their sacrifices unacceptable (vv. 13–14). In Mk 10:2–12, Jesus forbids divorce; in Mt 19:3–12, this ideal is maintained with the provision that unlawful marriage may be grounds for divorce (see 1 Cor 7:10–16). *You should be on guard, then, for your life*: a warning of punishment for failure to obey God (cf. Dt 4:9; Jos 23:11; Jer 17:21).

2:11 *Daughter of a foreign god*: this unusual phrase connotes a woman who does not share the same father/creator (v. 10), since she does not share the same covenant.

1:11 Ps 113:3; Is 59:19.
2:2 Lv 26:14–45; Dt 28:15.
2:5 Ez 37:26.
2:6 Dt 33:8–11.
2:7 Lv 10:10–11; Dt 17:9–10; Hg 2:11–13.
2:10 Dt 32:6; Jb 31:15; Mt 23:9; Eph 4:6.
2:11 Ezr 9:2; Neh 13:25.

12 May the LORD cut off from the man who does this
both witness and advocate from the tents of Jacob,
and anyone to bring an offering to the LORD of hosts!
13 This also you do: the altar of the LORD you cover
with tears, weeping, and groaning,
Because the Lord no longer takes note of your offering
or accepts it favorably from your hand.
14 * And you say, "Why?"—
Because the LORD is witness
between you and the wife of your youth
With whom you have broken faith,
though she is your companion, your covenanted wife.†
15 * Did he not make them one, with flesh and spirit?
And what does the One require? Godly offspring!
You should be on guard, then, for your life,
and do not break faith with the wife of your youth.
16 For I hate divorce,
says the LORD, the God of Israel,
And the one who covers his garment with violence,
says the LORD of hosts.
You should be on guard, then, for your life,
and you must not break faith.

> **"Now, I am sending my messenger. . . . But who can endure the day of his coming?"**
> (Mal 3:1–2)

Purification and Just Judgment

17 You have wearied the LORD with your words,
yet you say, "How have we wearied him?"
By saying, "All evildoers
are good in the sight of the LORD,

Live It!

Prepare the Way

Malachi 3:1–2 talks about the sending of a messenger to prepare for God's coming. That arrival will mark a day of purification, when anything that isn't of value will be burnt away. In Matthew's Gospel, Jesus states that it is John the Baptist who fulfills this prophecy (see Mt 11:10–14). What does that have to do with you? Well, John the Baptist wasn't the only one entrusted with the task of preparing for the Lord's coming. As followers of Christ, we all continue to share in that role today.

So how do we do this? Where do we start? We start by listening to Jesus and nurturing our relationship with God through prayer and the sacraments. We must also share what we believe with others so that they too can find their way. By growing in faith and helping others to do the same, we will be a light for the world, preparing the way for Christ's return.

▶ **Mal 3:1–7**

And he is pleased with them,"
or "Where is the just God?"

The Messenger of the Covenant

3 1* Now I am sending my messenger—
he will prepare the way before me;†
And the lord whom you seek will come
suddenly to his temple;
The messenger of the covenant whom you desire—
see, he is coming! says the LORD of hosts.
2 But who can endure the day of his coming?
Who can stand firm when he appears?
For he will be like a refiner's fire,
like fullers' lye.
3 * He will sit refining and purifying silver,
and he will purify the Levites,

---

† **2:14** *Companion . . . covenanted wife*: the Hebrew word *haberet* signifies an equal, a partner. This woman, in contrast to the daughter of a foreign god, shares with her husband the same covenant with the Lord.

3:1 *My messenger . . . before me*: Mt 11:10 applies these words to John the Baptist; Mt 11:14 further identifies John as Elijah (see Mal 3:23). Some take God's messenger in v. 1a to be a person distinct from "the lord" and "the messenger of the covenant" in v. 1b; others hold that they are one and the same person. Some consider "the lord" and "the messenger of the covenant" to be divine, while others hold that in the text's literal sense he is a messianic earthly ruler.

---

* **2:14** Gn 31:49–50; Prv 5:18–19.
2:15 Gn 2:7, 22–24.
3:1 Ex 23:20–22; Is 40:3; Mt 11:10; Mk 1:2; Lk 1:17; 7:27.
3:3 Is 1:25; Zec 13:9.

Refining them like gold or silver,
that they may bring offerings to the LORD in righteousness.
4 Then the offering of Judah and Jerusalem
will please the LORD,
as in ancient days, as in years gone by.
5 I will draw near to you for judgment,
and I will be swift to bear witness
Against sorcerers, adulterers, and perjurers,
those who deprive a laborer of wages,
Oppress a widow or an orphan,
or turn aside a resident alien,
without fearing me, says the LORD of hosts.

Gifts for God, Blessings for the People

6 For I, the LORD, do not change,†
and you, sons of Jacob, do not cease to be.
7 * Since the days of your ancestors you have turned aside
from my statutes and have not kept them.
Return to me, that I may return to you,
says the LORD of hosts.
But you say, "Why should we return?"
8 * Can anyone rob God? But you are robbing me!
And you say, "How have we robbed you?"
Of tithes and contributions!
9 You are indeed accursed,
for you, the whole nation, rob me.
10 * Bring the whole tithe
into the storehouse,†
That there may be food in my house.
Put me to the test, says the LORD of hosts,
And see if I do not open the floodgates of heaven for you,
and pour down upon you blessing without measure!
11 I will rebuke the locust for you
so that it will not destroy your crops,
And the vine in the field will not be barren,
says the LORD of hosts.
12 * All the nations will call you blessed,
for you will be a delightful land,
says the LORD of hosts.

The Need To Serve God

13 Your words are too much for me, says the LORD.
You ask, "What have we spoken against you?"
14 * You have said, "It is useless to serve God;
what do we gain by observing God's requirements,
And by going about as mourners†
before the LORD of hosts?
15 But we call the arrogant blessed;
for evildoers not only prosper
but even test God and escape."
16 * Then those who fear the LORD spoke with one another,
and the LORD listened attentively;
A record book† was written before him
of those who fear the LORD and esteem his name.
17 * They shall be mine, says the LORD of hosts,
my own special possession, on the day when I take action.
And I will have compassion on them,
as a man has compassion on his son who serves him.
18 Then you will again distinguish
between the just and the wicked,
Between the person who serves God,
and the one who does not.
19 * For the day is coming, blazing like an oven,
when all the arrogant and all evildoers will be stubble,
And the day that is coming will set them on fire,
leaving them neither root nor branch,
says the LORD of hosts.
20 * But for you who fear my name, the sun of justice
will arise with healing in its wings;†
And you will go out leaping like calves from the stall
21 and tread down the wicked;
They will become dust under the soles of your feet,
on the day when I take action, says the LORD of hosts.

Moses and Elijah

22 * Remember the law of Moses my servant,
whom I charged at Horeb

†

3:6–7 *Not change*: God remains faithful to the covenant even when the human partners break it.

3:10 *Storehouse*: the temple treasury.

3:14 *As mourners*: the adverb translated "as mourners" means something like "with a long face."

3:16 *Record book*: see note on Ex 32:32.

3:20 *Wings*: a common symbol of the manifestation of a god in the ancient Near East is the winged sun disk found, for example, on premonarchic jar handles. Cf. Nm 6:25; Ps 4:7; 31:17; 34:6; 84:12.

*

3:7 Zec 1:3–4; Acts 7:51.
3:8 Neh 13:10–14.
3:10 Dt 28:2, 12; 2 Chr 31:10–11; Neh 10:38; 13:12; Prv 3:9–10.
3:12 Dt 28:10; Is 61:9.
3:14 Jb 21:14–15; 22:17; Ps 73:11–12; Is 58:3; Zec 7:2–7.
3:16 Rev 20:12.
3:17 Ex 19:5; Dt 7:6; Ps 103:13; 135:4.
3:19 Is 13:9; 34:8; Jl 3:3; Zep 1:18; 2 Pt 3:7.
3:20 Lk 1:78–79.
3:22 Ex 20; Lv 26; Dt 4:1, 5–6.

With statutes and ordinances
for all Israel.
23 * Now I am sending to you
Elijah† the prophet,
Before the day of the LORD comes,
the great and terrible day;
24 He will turn the heart of fathers to their sons,
and the heart of sons to their fathers,
Lest I come and strike
the land with utter destruction.

† **3:23** *Elijah*: taken up in a whirlwind, according to 2 Kgs 2:11. Here his return seems to be foretold. A Jewish tradition interpreted this literally; the gospels saw Elijah in the person of John the Baptist (Mt 11:13–14; 17:10–13; Mk 9:9–13).

* **3:23** 2 Kgs 2:10–12; Sir 48:10; Mt 11:13–14; 17:10–13; Mk 9:9–13; Lk 1:17.

The New Testament

Preface to the New American Bible First Edition of the New Testament

The New Testament translation has been approached with essentially the same fidelity to the thought and individual style of the biblical writers as was applied in the Old Testament. In some cases, however, the problem of marked literary peculiarities had to be met. What by any Western standard are the limited vocabularies and stylistic infelicities of the evangelists cannot be retained in the exact form in which they appear in the originals without displeasing the modern ear. A compromise is here attempted whereby some measure of the poverty of the evangelists' expression is kept and placed at the service of their message in its richness. Similarly, the syntactical shortcomings of Paul, his frequent lapses into anacoluthon, and the like, are rendered as they occur in his epistles rather than "smoothed out." Only thus, the translators suppose, will contemporary readers have some adequate idea of the kind of writing they have before them. When the prose of the original flows more smoothly, as in Luke, Acts, and Hebrews, it is reflected in the translation.

The Gospel according to John comprises a special case. Absolute fidelity to his technique of reiterated phrasing would result in an assault on the English ear, yet the softening of the vocal effect by substitution of other words and phrases would destroy the effectiveness of his poetry. Again, resort is had to compromise. This is not an easy matter when the very repetitiousness which the author deliberately employed is at the same time regarded by those who read and speak English to be a serious stylistic defect. Only those familiar with the Greek originals can know what a relentless tattoo Johannine poetry can produce. A similar observation could be made regarding other New Testament books as well. Matthew and Mark are given to identical phrasing twice and three times in the same sentence. As for the rhetorical overgrowth and mixed figures of speech in the letters of Peter, James, and Jude, the translator must resist a powerful compulsion to tidy them up if only to render these letters intelligibly.

Without seeking refuge in complaints against the inspired authors, however, the translators of *The New American Bible* here state that what they have attempted is a translation rather than a paraphrase. To be sure, all translation can be called paraphrase by definition. Any striving for complete fidelity will shortly end in infidelity. Nonetheless, it must be pointed out that the temptation to improve overladen sentences by the consolidation or elimination of multiplied adjectives, or the simplification of clumsy hendiadys, has been resisted here. For the most part, rhetorically ineffective words and phrases are retained in this translation in some form, even when it is clear that a Western contemporary writer would never have employed them.

The spelling of proper names in *The New American Bible* follows the customary forms found in most English Bibles since the Authorized Version.

Despite the arbitrary character of the divisions into numbered verses (a scheme which in its present form is only four centuries old), the translators have made a constant effort to keep within an English verse the whole verbal content of the Greek verse. At times the effort has not seemed worth the result since it often does violence to the original author's flow of expression, which preceded it by so many centuries. If this translation had been prepared for purposes of public reading only, the editors would have foregone the effort at an early stage. But since they never departed from the threefold objective of preparing a translation suitable for liturgical use, private reading, and the purposes of students, the last-named consideration prevailed. Those familiar with Greek should be able to discover how the translators of the New Testament have rendered any given original verse of scripture, if their exegetical or theological tasks require them to know this. At the same time, the fact should be set down here that the editors did not commit themselves in the synoptic gospels to rendering repeated words or phrases identically.

This leads to a final consideration: the Greek text used for the New Testament. Here, punctuation and verse division are at least as important as variant readings. In general, Nestle-Aland's *Novum Testamentum Graece* (25th edition, 1963) was followed. Additional help was derived from *The Greek New Testament* (Aland, Black, Metzger, Wikgren), produced for the use of translators by the United Bible Societies in 1966. However, the editors did not confine themselves strictly to these texts; at times, they inclined toward readings otherwise attested. The omission of alternative translations does not mean that the translators think them without merit, but only that in every case they had to make a choice.

Poorly attested readings do not occur in this translation. Doubtful readings of some merit appear within brackets; public readers may include such words or phrases, or omit them entirely without any damage to sense. Parentheses are used, as ordinarily in English, as a punctuation device. Material they enclose is in no sense textually doubtful. It is simply thought to be parenthetical in the intention of the biblical author, even though there is no such punctuation mark in Greek. The difficulty in dealing with quotation marks is well known. Since they do not appear in any form in the original text, wherever they occur here they constitute an editorial decision.

Preface to the Revised Edition

The New Testament of *The New American Bible*, a fresh translation from the Greek text, was first published in complete form in 1970, together with the Old Testament translation that had been completed the previous year. Portions of the New Testament had appeared earlier, in somewhat different form, in the provisional Mass lectionary of 1964 and in the *Lectionary for Mass* of 1970.

Since 1970 many different printings of the New Testament have been issued by a number of publishers, both separately and in complete Bibles, and the text has become widely known both in the United States and in other English-speaking countries. Most American Catholics have been influenced by it because of its widespread use in the liturgy, and it has received a generally favorable reception from many other Christians as well. It has taken its place among the standard contemporary translations of the New Testament, respected for its fidelity to the original and its attempt to render this into current American English.

Although the scriptures themselves are timeless, translations and explanations of them quickly become dated in an era marked by rapid cultural change to a degree never previously experienced. The explosion of biblical studies that has taken place in our century and the changing nature of our language itself require periodic adjustment both in translations and in the accompanying explanatory materials. The experience of actual use of the New Testament of *The New American Bible*, especially in oral proclamation, has provided a basis for further improvement. Accordingly, it was decided in 1978 to proceed with a thorough revision of the New Testament to reflect advances in scholarship and to satisfy needs identified through pastoral experience.

For this purpose a steering committee was formed to plan, organize, and direct the work of revision, to engage collaborators, and to serve as an editorial board to coordinate the work of the various revisers and to determine the final form of the text and the explanatory materials. Guidelines were drawn up and collaborators selected in 1978 and early 1979, and November of 1980 was established as the deadline for manuscripts. From December 1980 through September 1986 the editorial board met a total of fifty times and carefully reviewed and revised all the material in order to ensure accuracy and consistency of approach. The editors also worked together with the bishops' ad hoc committee that was appointed by the National Conference of Catholic Bishops in 1982 to oversee the revision.

The threefold purpose of the translation that was expressed in the preface to the first edition has been maintained in the revision: to provide a version suitable for liturgical proclamation, for private reading, and for purposes of study. Special attention has been given to the first of these purposes, since oral proclamation demands special qualities in a translation, and experience had provided insights and suggestions that could lead to improvement in this area. Efforts have also been made, however, to facilitate devotional reading by providing suitable notes and introductory materials, and to assist the student by achieving greater accuracy and consistency in the translation and supplying more abundant information in the introductions and notes.

The primary aim of the revision is to produce a version as accurate and faithful to the meaning of the Greek original as is possible for a translation. The editors have consequently moved in the direction of a formal-equivalence approach to translation, matching the vocabulary, structure, and even word order of the original as closely as possible in the receptor language. Some other contemporary biblical versions have adopted, in varying degrees, a dynamic-equivalence approach, which attempts to respect the individuality of each language by expressing the meaning of the original in a linguistic structure suited to English, even though this may be very different from the corresponding Greek structure. While this approach often results in fresh and brilliant renderings, it has the disadvantages of more or less radically abandoning traditional biblical and liturgical terminology and phraseology, of expanding the text to include what more properly belongs in notes, commentaries, or preaching, and of tending toward paraphrase. A more formal approach seems better suited to the specific purposes intended for this translation.

At the same time, the editors have wished to produce a version in English that reflects contemporary American usage and is readily understandable to ordinary educated people, but one that will be recognized as dignified speech, on the level of formal rather than colloquial usage. These aims are not in fact contradictory, for there are different levels of language in current use: the language of formal situations is not that of colloquial conversation, though people understand both and may pass from one to the other without adverting to the transition. The liturgy is a formal situation that requires a level of discourse more dignified, formal, and hieratic than the world of business, sport, or informal communication. People readily understand this more formal level even though they may not often use it; our passive vocabulary is much larger than our active vocabulary. Hence this revision, while avoiding archaisms, does not shrink from traditional biblical terms that are easily understood even though not in common use in everyday speech. The level of language consciously aimed at is one appropriate for liturgical proclamation; this may also permit the translation to serve the purposes of devotional reading and serious study.

A particular effort has been made to insure consistency of vocabulary. Always to translate a given Greek word by the same English equivalent would lead to ludicrous results and to infidelity to the meaning of the text. But in passages where a particular Greek term retains the same meaning, it has been rendered in the same way insofar as this has been feasible; this is particularly significant in the case of terms that have a specific theological meaning. The synoptic gospels have been carefully translated so as to reveal both the similarities and the differences of the Greek.

An especially sensitive problem today is the question of discrimination in language. In recent years there has been much discussion about allegations of anti-Jewish expressions in the New Testament and of language that discriminates against various minorities. Above all, however, the question of discrimination against women affects the largest number of people and arouses the greatest degree of interest and concern. At present there is little agreement about these problems or about the best way to deal with them. In all these areas the present translation attempts to display a sensitivity appropriate to the present state of the questions under discussion, which are not yet resolved and in regard to which it is impossible to please everyone, since intelligent and sincere participants in the debate hold mutually contradictory views.

The primary concern in this revision is fidelity to what the text says. When the meaning of the Greek is inclusive of both sexes, the translation seeks to reproduce such inclusivity insofar as this is possible in normal English usage, without resort to inelegant circumlocutions or neologisms that would offend against the dignity of the language. Although the generic sense of *man* is traditional in English, many today reject it; its use has therefore generally been avoided, though it is retained in cases where no fully satisfactory equivalent could be found. English does not possess a gender-inclusive third personal pronoun in the singular, and this translation continues to use the masculine resumptive pronoun after *everyone* or *anyone,* in the traditional way, where this cannot be avoided without infidelity to the meaning.

The translation of the Greek word *adelphos,* particularly in the plural form *adelphoi,* poses an especially delicate problem. While the term literally means *brothers* or other male blood relatives, even in profane Greek the plural can designate two persons, one of either sex, who were born of the same parents. It was adopted by the early Christians to designate, in a figurative sense, the members of the Christian community, who were conscious of a new familial relationship to one another by reason of their adoption as children of God. They are consequently addressed as *adelphoi.* This has traditionally been rendered into

English by *brothers* or, more archaically, *brethren.* There has never been any doubt that this designation includes *all* the members of the Christian community, both male and female. Given the absence in English of a corresponding term that explicitly includes both sexes, this translation retains the usage of *brothers,* with the inclusive meaning that has been traditionally attached to it in this biblical context.

Since the New Testament is the product of a particular time and culture, the views expressed in it and the language in which they are expressed reflect a particular cultural conditioning, which sometimes makes them quite different from contemporary ideas and concerns. Discriminatory language should be eliminated insofar as possible whenever it is unfaithful to the meaning of the New Testament, but the text should not be altered in order to adjust it to contemporary concerns. This translation does not introduce any changes, expansions, additions to, or subtractions from the text of scripture. It further retains the traditional biblical ways of speaking about God and about Christ, including the use of masculine nouns and pronouns.

The Greek text followed in this translation is that of the third edition of *The Greek New Testament,* edited by Kurt Aland, Matthew Black, Carlo Martini, Bruce Metzger, and Allen Wikgren, and published by the United Bible Societies in 1975. The same text, with a different critical apparatus and variations in punctuation and typography, was published as the twenty-sixth edition of the Nestle-Aland *Novum Testamentum Graece* in 1979 by the Deutsche Bibelstiftung, Stuttgart. This edition has also been consulted. When variant readings occur, the translation, with few exceptions, follows the reading that was placed in the text of these Greek editions, though the occurrence of the principal variants is pointed out in the notes.

The editors of the Greek text placed square brackets around words or portions of words of which the authenticity is questionable because the evidence of textual witnesses is inconclusive. The same has been done in the translation insofar as it is possible to reproduce this convention in English. It should be possible to read the text either with or without the disputed words, but in English it is not always feasible to provide this alternative, and in some passages the bracketed words must be included to make sense. As in the first edition, parentheses do not indicate textual uncertainty, but are simply a punctuation device to indicate a passage that in the editors' judgment appears parenthetical to the thought of the author.

Citations from the Old Testament are placed within quotation marks; longer citations are set off as block quotations in a separate indented paragraph. The sources of such citations, as well as those of many more or less subtle allusions to the Old Testament, are identified in the biblical cross-reference section at the bottom of each page. Insofar as possible, the translation of such Old Testament citations agrees with that of *The New American Bible* Old Testament whenever the underlying Greek agrees with the Hebrew (or, in some cases, the Aramaic or Greek) text from which the Old Testament translation was made. But citations in the New Testament frequently follow the Septuagint or some other version, or were made from memory; hence, in many cases the translation in the New Testament passage will not agree with what appears in the Old Testament. Some of these cases are explained in the notes.

It is a further aim of the revised edition to supply explanatory materials more abundantly than in the first edition. In most cases the introductions and notes have been entirely rewritten and expanded, and the cross-references checked and revised. It is intended that these materials should reflect the present state of sound biblical scholarship and should be presented in such a form that they can be assimilated by the ordinary intelligent reader without specialized biblical training. While they have been written with the ordinary educated Christian in mind, not all technical vocabulary can be entirely dispensed with in approaching the Bible, any more than in any other field. It is the hope of the editors that these materials, even if they sometimes demand an effort, will help the reader to a fuller and more intelligent understanding of the New Testament and a fruitful appropriation of its meaning for personal spiritual growth.

The New American Bible is a Roman Catholic translation. This revision, however, like the first edition, has been accomplished with the collaboration of scholars from other Christian churches, both among the revisers and on the editorial board, in response to the encouragement of Vatican Council II (*Dei Verbum,* 22). The editorial board expresses gratitude to all who have collaborated in the revision: to all the revisers, consultants, and bishops who contributed to it, to reviewers of the first edition, and to those who voluntarily submitted suggestions. May this translation fulfill its threefold purpose, "so that the word of the Lord may speed forward and be glorified" (2 Thes 3:1).

September 30, 1986
The Feast of St. Jerome

Introduction to the Gospels and the Acts of the Apostles

If you have ever written a research paper for a class project, you know how important it is to have good sources. You want sources that have the most insight into your chosen topic, sources that provide inspiration. The books of the New Testament are those sources for the Christian faith. The Gospels of Matthew, Mark, Luke, and John lay the foundation for understanding the message and the mission of Jesus, the center of the Christian faith. The Acts of the Apostles continues with an inspiring account of how the earliest Christians continued Jesus' mission despite conflicts and persecution. The Good News in these books invites a response from us: to accept Jesus as the promised Messiah, the Son of God, the Savior of the world.

In Depth

The books of the New Testament continue the Old Testament's revelation of God's saving work in the world. Their focus is on Jesus Christ—the hoped-for Messiah, the Savior. Jesus Christ is revealed as God's Son, being both fully human and fully divine. In Jesus, God's promises to Abraham, Moses, and David were fulfilled. In Jesus, God's Covenant is expanded beyond Judaism to include all peoples. In Jesus lie the forgiveness of sins and a new life of love and freedom for anyone who believes.

The New Testament tells of this Good News through four different types of books: (1) four similar but unique views of Jesus' life and teaching in books called Gospels, (2) stories on how the Apostles spread the Good News of Jesus in the Acts of the Apostles, (3) letters from early Christian leaders to the first Christians and Christian communities, and (4) apocalyptic writings in the Book of Revelation. This introduction covers the four Gospels and the Acts of the Apostles; another introduction will give further background on the letters and Revelation.

The Gospels of Matthew, Mark, Luke, and John tell the story of Jesus from four different perspectives. They are not historical biographies or documentaries like you might read today. They grew out of the teaching and preaching about Jesus in different early Christian communities. They reflect these early Christian communities' beliefs about Jesus, but they do not tell us exactly what Jesus said and did in his life on earth. Inspired by God, the authors of the Gospels arranged the stories to bring out a particular understanding of Jesus that had great importance in their Christian communities. Because of God's inspiration, the Gospels are without error in teaching us the truth about Christ's message, mission, and identity.

The Gospels of Matthew, Mark, and Luke are similar in their style and share much of the same content. They are called synoptic (from a Greek word that means "seeing the whole together") Gospels. It is likely that Mark was written first and the authors of Matthew and Luke used Mark as a source in creating their own Gospels (Lk 1:1

mentions other accounts of Jesus). The Gospel of John is quite different from the synoptic Gospels. It was written later and is more symbolic in its expression of who Jesus is.

The Acts of the Apostles is a continuation of Luke's Gospel (Acts 1:1). However, it is not itself a Gospel. It picks up where the Gospel of Luke ends, telling the story of the origins of Christianity after the death and Resurrection of Jesus, covering the period from about AD 30 to 64. Although Acts gives us a good deal of information about early Church leaders like Peter and Paul, its purpose is not to tell us their biographies. Rather, it gives us an interpretation of the events of the beginnings of Christianity that emphasizes God's saving purpose. The Book of Acts explains how Christianity, which began as an offshoot of the Jewish faith, gradually spread beyond Judaism into the Gentile, or non-Jewish, world.

The original Greek word for *gospel* is *euangelion,* which means "big or important news" (sometimes translated as "good news"). The authors of the Gospels wanted to share with others the important news of Jesus Christ. When you read these powerful stories of faith, let God use them to inspire and strengthen your faith in Jesus.

Other Background

- The Gospel of Matthew emphasizes Jesus as the promised Messiah of the Jewish people. Jesus is portrayed as the greatest prophet, teaching the New Law and calling people to be faithful to God.
- The Gospel of Mark was probably the first of the four Gospels to be written. It portrays Jesus as an active healer and miracle worker who accepts loneliness and suffering as the cost of obedience to God's will.
- The Gospel of Luke is a clear, orderly presentation of Jesus' mission to all people, Jews and Gentiles. This Gospel emphasizes Jesus' mercy, compassion, and concern for poor people.
- The Gospel of John was the last Gospel written and seeks to show Jesus as the unique Son of God. This Gospel portrays Jesus as noble and powerful, fully in control of his own destiny.
- The Acts of the Apostles was written by the author of the Gospel of Luke. It shows God at work in the growth of the early Christian communities, particularly through the efforts of Peter and Paul.

The Gospel According to

Matthew

Does your family have a traditional way of celebrating a holiday? Family traditions are usually handed down from one generation to the next. They give meaning to our special celebrations and help us know where we came from. The Gospel of Matthew presents Jesus as the promised Messiah and highlights Jesus' Jewish origins. The author wanted Jewish-Christian readers to know that believing in Jesus as the Son of God was not a break with their tradition but the fulfillment of it.

In Depth

The author of Matthew was probably a Jewish Christian writing for a community of Jewish Christians. This community's main mission was to bring the gospel message to its Jewish brothers and sisters (see 10:6) but there are also indications that this mission was beginning to be spread to the Gentile world (see 4:12–25). In defense of the community's belief in Jesus, the Gospel of Matthew links Jesus to important Jewish traditions and gives them new meanings. The Gospel begins with a list of Jesus' Jewish ancestors, connecting Jesus to Abraham, the father of Judaism, and David, Israel's greatest king. Then it makes frequent references to Old Testament laws, prophecies, and events that Jesus fulfills or completes.

The author of Matthew also wanted to show how Jesus broke with certain Jewish beliefs—no doubt to help explain why his community of Jewish Christians was protesting against the Jewish religious establishment that it considered corrupt and wayward. So in the Sermon on the Mount (see 5:1—7:29), the Gospel has Jesus giving a deeper interpretation to Jewish laws. And Jesus is frequently in conflict with the scribes and Pharisees over things like healing on the Sabbath (see 12:9–14). Such incidents probably reflect the experience of the author's community with Jewish leaders as much as Jesus' own conflicts.

Gradually, the Gospel of Matthew paints a picture of Jesus as the promised Son of David who would reign as king forever and a prophet / teacher like Moses, the true law giver. He is the Messiah, the fulfillment of all that the Jewish people have been waiting for, the one who will bring their liberation and salvation. This Good News should be proclaimed to Jews and non-Jews alike. And so the Gospel ends with the risen Jesus telling his disciples, "Go, therefore, and make disciples of all nations" (28:19).

At a Glance

- **I. The Infancy Narrative (1:1—2:23).**
- **II. The Proclamation of the Kingdom (3:1—7:29).**
- **III. Ministry and Mission in Galilee (8:1—11:1).**
- **IV. Opposition from Israel (11:2—13:53).**
- **V. Jesus, the Kingdom, and the Church (13:54—18:35).**
- **VI. Ministry in Judea and Jerusalem (19:1—25:46).**
- **VII. The Passion and Resurrection (26:1—28:20).**

Quick Facts

Inspired Author: unknown; traditionally associated with the Apostle Matthew

Date Written: approximately AD 85

Audience: Christian Jews

Image of Jesus: the greatest prophet, who brings the New Law

Matthew

2:1–12

I: The Infancy Narrative†

The Genealogy of Jesus

1 [1]* The book of the genealogy of Jesus Christ,
the son of David, the son of Abraham.†
[2]* Abraham became the father of Isaac, Isaac
the father of Jacob, Jacob the father of Judah and
his brothers.* [3]* Judah became the father of Perez
and Zerah, whose mother was Tamar. Perez be-
came the father of Hezron, Hezron the father of
Ram, [4]* Ram the father of Amminadab. Ammin-
adab became the father of Nahshon, Nahshon
the father of Salmon, [5]* Salmon the father of
Boaz, whose mother was Rahab. Boaz became the
father of Obed, whose mother was Ruth. Obed
became the father of Jesse, [6]* Jesse the father of
David the king.

David became the father of Solomon, whose
mother had been the wife of Uriah. [7]*† Solo-
mon became the father of Rehoboam, Rehoboam
the father of Abijah, Abijah the father of Asaph.
[8]Asaph became the father of Jehoshaphat, Je-
hoshaphat the father of Joram, Joram the father
of Uzziah. [9]Uzziah became the father of Jotham,
Jotham the father of Ahaz, Ahaz the father of
Hezekiah. [10]† Hezekiah became the father of
Manasseh, Manasseh the father of Amos, Amos

† **1:1—2:23** The infancy narrative forms the prologue of the gospel. Consisting of a genealogy and five stories, it presents the coming of Jesus as the climax of Israel's history, and the events of his conception, birth, and early childhood as the fulfillment of Old Testament prophecy. The genealogy is probably traditional material that Matthew edited. In its first two sections (1:2–11) it was drawn from Ru 4:18–22 and 1 Chr 1–3. Except for Jechoniah, Shealtiel, and Zerubbabel, none of the names in the third section (1:12–16) is found in any Old Testament genealogy. While the genealogy shows the continuity of God's providential plan from Abraham on, discontinuity is also present. The women Tamar (1:3), Rahab and Ruth (1:5), and the wife of Uriah, Bathsheba (1:6), bore their sons through unions that were in varying degrees strange and unexpected. These "irregularities" culminate in the supreme "irregularity" of the Messiah's birth of a virgin mother; the age of fulfillment is inaugurated by a creative act of God.

Drawing upon both biblical tradition and Jewish stories, Matthew portrays Jesus as reliving the Exodus experience of Israel and the persecutions of Moses. His rejection by his own people and his passion are foreshadowed by the troubled reaction of "all Jerusalem" to the question of the magi who are seeking the "newborn king of the Jews" (2:2–3), and by Herod's attempt to have him killed. The magi who do him homage prefigure the Gentiles who will accept the preaching of the gospel. The infancy narrative proclaims who Jesus is, the savior of his people from their sins (1:21), Emmanuel in whom "God is with us" (1:23), and the Son of God (2:15).

1:1 *The Son of David, the son of Abraham:* two links of the genealogical chain are singled out. Although the later, David is placed first in order to emphasize that Jesus is the royal Messiah. The mention of Abraham may be due not only to his being the father of the nation Israel but to Matthew's interest in the universal scope of Jesus' mission; cf Gn 22:18, ". . . in your descendants all the nations of the earth shall find blessing."

1:7 The successor of Abijah was not Asaph but Asa (see 1 Chr 3:10). Some textual witnesses read the latter name; however, *Asaph* is better attested. Matthew may have deliberately introduced the psalmist Asaph into the genealogy (and in v 10 the prophet Amos) in order to show that Jesus is the fulfillment not only of the promises made to David (see 2 Sm 7) but of all the Old Testament.

1:10 *Amos:* some textual witnesses read *Amon,* who was the actual successor of Manasseh (see 1 Chr 3:14).

1:1 Gn 5:1; 1 Chr 17:11; Gn 22:18.
1:2–17 Lk 3:23–38.
1:2 Gn 21:3; 25:26; 29:35; 1 Chr 2:1.
1:3 Gn 38:29–30; Ru 4:18; 1 Chr 2:4–9.
1:4 Ru 4:19–20; 1 Chr 2:10–11.
1:5 Ru 4:21–22; 1 Chr 2:11–12.
1:6 2 Sm 12:24; 1 Chr 2:15; 3:5.
1:7–11 2 Kgs 25:1–21; 1 Chr 3:10–15.

the father of Josiah. 11 Josiah became the father
of Jechoniah and his brothers at the time of the
Babylonian exile.
12* After the Babylonian exile, Jechoniah be-
came the father of Shealtiel, Shealtiel the father
of Zerubbabel, 13 Zerubbabel the father of Abiud.
Abiud became the father of Eliakim, Eliakim the
father of Azor, 14 Azor the father of Zadok. Zadok
became the father of Achim, Achim the father
of Eliud, 15 Eliud the father of Eleazar. Eleazar
became the father of Matthan, Matthan the fa-
ther of Jacob, 16 Jacob the father of Joseph, the
husband of Mary. Of her was born Jesus who is
called the Messiah.
17† Thus the total number of generations
from Abraham to David is fourteen generations;
from David to the Babylonian exile, fourteen
generations; from the Babylonian exile to the
Messiah, fourteen generations.

The Birth of Jesus

18† Now this is how the birth of Jesus Christ
came about. When his mother Mary was be-
trothed to Joseph,† but before they lived to-
gether, she was found with child through the
holy Spirit. 19† Joseph her husband, since he
was a righteous man, yet unwilling to expose
her to shame, decided to divorce her quietly.
20*† Such was his intention when, behold, the
angel of the Lord appeared to him in a dream
and said, "Joseph, son of David, do not be
afraid to take Mary your wife into your home.
For it is through the holy Spirit that this child
has been conceived in her. 21† She will bear a
son and you are to name him Jesus, because
he will save his people from their sins." 22 All
this took place to fulfill what the Lord had said
through the prophet:

Did You Know?

Jesus' Family Tree

In the first two chapters of Matthew, the author begins to reveal the unique focus of the Gospel. He starts by tracing Jesus' family tree, making his case that Jesus was the Messiah who would restore the covenant promised to Abraham, the father of the Jewish people. He also traces Jesus' ancestry back to David to show that Jesus is the fulfillment of the promises made to David (see 2 Samuel, chapter 7).

Things get even more interesting with a closer look at all the people mentioned in the list. There is a wide assortment of groups and social classes: patriarchs and slaves, kings and peasants, men and women, Jews and non-Jews. This genealogy is based on clan relations where non-Jews are included because they have been incorporated into the clan that traces itself back to David and Abraham. Essentially, this genealogy demonstrates that God has been at work from the call of Abraham, the "father" of Judaism, through the high point of their history (David), and even through their darkest times (the Babylonian Exile). And "God is with us" still in Jesus (Mt 1:23).

▶ **Mt 1:1–17**

†

1:17 Matthew is concerned with fourteen generations, probably because fourteen is the numerical value of the Hebrew letters forming the name of David. In the second section of the genealogy (6b–11), three kings of Judah, Ahaziah, Joash, and Amaziah, have been omitted (see 1 Chr 3:11–12), so that there are fourteen generations in that section. Yet the third (12–16) apparently has only thirteen. Since Matthew here emphasizes that each section has fourteen, it is unlikely that the thirteen of the last was due to his oversight. Some scholars suggest that *Jesus who is called the Messiah* (16b) doubles the final member of the chain: *Jesus,* born within the family of David, opens up the new age as *Messiah,* so that in fact there are fourteen generations in the third section. This is perhaps too subtle, and the hypothesis of a slip not on the part of Matthew but of a later scribe seems likely. On *Messiah,* see the note on Lk 2:11.

1:18–25 This first story of the infancy narrative spells out what is summarily indicated in v 16. The virginal conception of Jesus is the work of the Spirit of God. Joseph's decision to divorce Mary is overcome by the heavenly command that he take her into his home and accept the child as his own. The natural genealogical line is broken but the promises to David are fulfilled; through Joseph's adoption the child belongs to the family of David. Matthew sees the virginal conception as the fulfillment of Is 7:14.

1:18 *Betrothed to Joseph:* betrothal was the first part of the marriage, constituting a man and woman as husband and wife. Subsequent infidelity was considered adultery. The betrothal was followed some months later by the husband's taking his wife into his home, at which time normal married life began.

1:19 *A righteous man:* as a devout observer of the Mosaic law, Joseph wished to break his union with someone whom he suspected of gross violation of the law. It is commonly said that the law required him to do so, but the texts usually given in support of that view, e.g., Dt 22:20–21, do not clearly pertain to Joseph's situation. *Unwilling to expose her to shame:* the penalty for proved adultery was death by stoning; cf Dt 22:21–23.

1:20 *The angel of the Lord:* in the Old Testament a common designation of God in communication with a human being. *In a dream:* see 2:13, 19, 22. These dreams may be meant to recall the dreams of Joseph, son of Jacob the patriarch (Gn 37:5–11, 19). A closer parallel is the dream of Amram, father of Moses, related by Josephus (*Antiquities* 2:9, 3 §§212:215–16).

1:21 *Jesus:* in first-century Judaism the Hebrew name Joshua (Greek *Iēsous*) meaning "Yahweh helps" was interpreted as "Yahweh saves."

1:12–16 1 Chr 3:16–19. **1:20** Mt 2:13, 19; Lk 1:35.

23*† "Behold, the virgin shall be with child and
bear a son,
and they shall name him Emmanuel,"

which means "God is with us." 24 When Joseph awoke, he did as the angel of the Lord had commanded him and took his wife into his home. 25*† He had no relations with her until she bore a son, and he named him Jesus.

The Visit of the Magi

2 1† When Jesus was born in Bethlehem of Judea, in the days of King Herod,† behold, magi from the east arrived in Jerusalem, 2*† saying, "Where is the newborn king of the Jews? We saw his star at its rising and have come to do him homage." 3 When King Herod heard this, he was greatly troubled, and all Jerusalem with him. 4† Assembling all the chief priests and the scribes of the people, he inquired of them where the Messiah was to be born. 5* They said to him, "In Bethlehem of Judea, for thus it has been written through the prophet:

6 'And you, Bethlehem, land of Judah,
are by no means least among the rulers
of Judah;
since from you shall come a ruler,
who is to shepherd my people Israel.' "

7 Then Herod called the magi secretly and ascertained from them the time of the star's appearance. 8 He sent them to Bethlehem and said, "Go and search diligently for the child. When you have found him, bring me word, that I too may go and do him homage." 9 After their audience with the king they set out. And behold, the star that they had seen at its rising preceded them, until it came and stopped over the place where the child was.

Did You Know?

Jesus, Emmanuel

In announcing Jesus' birth, the Gospel of Matthew quotes Isaiah 7:14, in which Isaiah tells King Ahaz that his young wife will conceive a son and they will name him Emmanuel, which means "God is with us" (Mt 1:23). This is the perfect description for Jesus, the Son of God, who fully shares our humanity. The Gospel ends with the same promise, when the risen Jesus tells his disciples, "I am with you always" (28:20).

Mt 1:23

10 They were overjoyed at seeing the star, 11*† and on entering the house they saw the child with Mary his mother. They prostrated themselves and did him homage. Then they opened their treasures and offered him gifts of gold, frankincense, and myrrh. 12 And having been warned in a dream not to return to Herod, they departed for their country by another way.

The Flight to Egypt

13† When they had departed, behold, the angel of the Lord appeared to Joseph in a dream and said, "Rise, take the child and his mother, flee to Egypt,† and stay there until I tell you. Herod is going to search for the child to destroy him." 14 Joseph rose and took the child and his mother by night and departed for Egypt. 15*† He stayed

†

1:23 *God is with us:* God's promise of deliverance to Judah in Isaiah's time is seen by Matthew as fulfilled in the birth of Jesus, in whom God is with his people. The name Emmanuel is alluded to at the end of the gospel where the risen Jesus assures his disciples of his continued presence, ". . . I am with you always, until the end of the age" (28:20).

1:25 *Until she bore a son:* the evangelist is concerned to emphasize that Joseph was not responsible for the conception of Jesus.The Greek word translated "until" does not imply normal marital conduct after Jesus' birth, nor does it exclude it.

2:1–12 The future rejection of Jesus by Israel and his acceptance by the Gentiles are retrojected into this scene of the narrative.

2:1 *In the days of King Herod:* Herod reigned from 37 to 4 B.C. *Magi:* originally a designation of the Persian priestly caste, the word became used of those who were regarded as having more than human knowledge. Matthew's magi are astrologers.

2:2 *We saw his star:* it was a common ancient belief that a new star appeared at the time of a ruler's birth. Matthew also draws upon the Old Testament story of Balaam, who had prophesied that "A star shall advance from Jacob" (Nm 24:17), though there the star means not an astral phenomenon but the king himself.

2:4 Herod's consultation with the chief priests and scribes has some similarity to a Jewish legend about the child Moses in which the "sacred scribes" warn Pharaoh about the imminent birth of one who will deliver Israel from Egypt and the king makes plans to destroy him.

2:11 Cf Ps 72:10, 15; Is 60:6. These Old Testament texts led to the interpretation of the magi as kings.

2:13–23 Biblical and nonbiblical traditions about Moses are here applied to the child Jesus, though the dominant Old Testament type is not Moses but Israel (see v 15).

2:13 *Flee to Egypt:* Egypt was a traditional place of refuge for those fleeing from danger in Palestine (see 1 Kgs 11:40; Jer 26:21), but the main reason why the child is to be taken to Egypt is that he may relive the Exodus experience of Israel.

2:15 The fulfillment citation is taken from Hos 11:1. Israel, God's son, was called out of Egypt at the time of the Exodus; Jesus, the Son of God, will similarly be called out of that land in a new exodus. The father-son relationship between God and the nation is set in a higher key. Here the son is not a group adopted as "son of God," but the child who, as conceived by the holy Spirit, stands in unique relation to God. He is son of David and of Abraham, of Mary and of Joseph, but, above all, of God.

*

1:23 Is 7:14 LXX.
1:25 Lk 2:7.
2:2 Nm 24:17.
2:5–6 Mi 5:1; 2 Sm 5:2.
2:11 Ps 72:10–11, 15; Is 60:6.
2:15 Hos 11:1.

MT

Cultural Connection

Jesus Brought the Good News of Salvation to People of All Races

The wise men from another culture, who came to offer Jesus gifts for a royal messiah, symbolize that Jesus came as the savior of all races and cultures. Matthew 2:1–12 is the biblical basis for the religious feast day of Epiphany, which officially is January 6 but is celebrated on the first Sunday after the New Year.

In some Latin American traditions, children receive gifts on Epiphany, in remembrance of the gifts the wise men offered to Jesus. The evening before, at parties celebrated in homes and offices, a special bread is shared, known as *La Rosca*, that has a figure of the baby Jesus baked inside of it. Whoever finds the figure of the baby Jesus in a piece of bread has to host a party to celebrate Jesus' presentation in the Temple (see Lk 2:22–24). The Church celebrates this feast on February 2.

- How do you accept and celebrate people of different cultures?
- Think of spiritual gifts you have received from other people. Express your gratitude to God for those gifts.

Mt 2:1–12

there until the death of Herod, that what the
Lord had said through the prophet might be fulfilled, "Out of Egypt I called my son."

The Massacre of the Infants

16 When Herod realized that he had been de-
ceived by the magi, he became furious. He or-
dered the massacre of all the boys in Bethlehem
and its vicinity two years old and under, in accor-
dance with the time he had ascertained from the
magi. 17 Then was fulfilled what had been said
through Jeremiah the prophet:

18*† "A voice was heard in Ramah,
sobbing and loud lamentation;
Rachel weeping for her children,
and she would not be consoled,
since they were no more."

The Return from Egypt

19 When Herod had died, behold, the angel
of the Lord appeared in a dream to Joseph in
Egypt 20*† and said, "Rise, take the child and
his mother and go to the land of Israel, for
those who sought the child's life are dead."
21 He rose, took the child and his mother, and
went to the land of Israel. 22† But when he
heard that Archelaus was ruling over Judea in
place of his father Herod, he was afraid to go
back there. And because he had been warned in
a dream, he departed for the region of Galilee.
23*† He went and dwelt in a town called Naza-
reth, so that what had been spoken through the
prophets might be fulfilled, "He shall be called
a Nazorean."

II: The Proclamation of the Kingdom

The Preaching of John the Baptist

3 1*† In those days John the Baptist appeared,
preaching in the desert of Judea† 2*† [and]

†

2:18 Jer 31:15 portrays Rachel, wife of the patriarch Jacob, weeping for her children taken into exile at the time of the Assyrian invasion of the northern kingdom (722–21 B.C.). Bethlehem was traditionally identified with Ephrath, the place near which Rachel was buried (see Gn 35:19; 48:7), and the mourning of Rachel is here applied to her lost children of a later age. *Ramah:* about six miles north of Jerusalem. The lamentation of Rachel is so great as to be heard at a far distance.

2:20 *For those who sought the child's life are dead:* Moses, who had fled from Egypt because the Pharaoh sought to kill him (see Ex 2:15), was told to return there, "for all the men who sought your life are dead" (Ex 4:19).

2:22 With the agreement of the emperor Augustus, Archelaus received half of his father's kingdom, including Judea, after Herod's death. He had the title "ethnarch" (i.e., "ruler of a nation") and reigned from 4 B.C. to A.D. 6.

2:23 *Nazareth . . . He shall be called a Nazorean:* the tradition of Jesus' residence in Nazareth was firmly established, and Matthew sees it as being in accordance with the foreannounced plan of God. The town of Nazareth is not mentioned in the Old Testament, and no such prophecy can be found there. The vague expression "through the prophets" may be due to Matthew's seeing a connection between Nazareth and certain texts in which there are words with a remote similarity to the name of that town. Some such Old Testament texts are Is 11:1 where the Davidic king of the future is called "a bud" *(nēser)* that shall blossom from the roots of Jesse, and Jgs 13:5, 7 where Samson, the future deliverer of Israel from the Philistines, is called one who shall be consecrated (a *nāzîr*) to God.

3:1–12 Here Matthew takes up the order of Jesus' ministry found

2:18 Jer 31:15.
2:20 Ex 4:19.
2:23 Mt 13:54; Mk 1:9; Lk 2:39; 4:34; Jn 19:19.
3:1–12 Mk 1:2–8; Lk 3:2–17.
3:2 Mt 4:17; 10:7.

saying, "Repent, for the kingdom of heaven is at
hand!" 3*† It was of him that the prophet Isaiah
had spoken when he said:

"A voice of one crying out in the desert,
'Prepare the way of the Lord,
make straight his paths.' "

† in the gospel of Mark, beginning with the preparatory preaching of John the Baptist.

3:1 Unlike Luke, Matthew says nothing of the Baptist's origins and does not make him a relative of Jesus. *The desert of Judea:* the barren region west of the Dead Sea extending up the Jordan valley.

3:2 *Repent:* the Baptist calls for a change of heart and conduct, a turning of one's life from rebellion to obedience toward God. *The kingdom of heaven is at hand:* "heaven" (literally, "the heavens") is a substitute for the name "God" that was avoided by devout Jews of the time out of reverence. The expression "the kingdom of heaven" occurs only in the gospel of Matthew. It means the effective rule of God over his people. In its fullness it includes not only human obedience to God's word, but the triumph of God over physical evils, supremely over death. In the expectation found in Jewish apocalyptic, the kingdom was to be ushered in by a judgment in which sinners would be condemned and perish, an expectation shared by the Baptist. This was modified in Christian understanding where the kingdom was seen as being established in stages, culminating with the parousia of Jesus.

3:3 See the note on Jn 1:23.

* **3:3** Is 40:3.

Live It!

Jesus' Family Lives as Immigrants

Following an angel's order and facing the massacre of all boys under age two, Joseph takes Mary and Jesus to Egypt to protect them from Herod's threats. They become immigrants to avoid persecution.

Every year, millions of people in the world become immigrants, fleeing their countries because of hunger, poverty, or persecution. Often, they find themselves feeling like unwelcome strangers, not able to communicate in the language of their new land and even persecuted by its inhabitants—many who believe that these immigrants have come simply to take advantage of services provided by the government. Christians, however, should have a special compassion for immigrants because Jesus told us to love everyone, especially those who suffer. By honoring the plight of today's immigrants, we honor the Holy Family.

- Imagine Jesus, Mary, and Joseph exiled in this country. How would you treat them?
- What is your attitude toward refugees and immigrants in our country?
- Ask God to bless legislators with the love and wisdom to welcome immigrants, and to give your generation a courageous heart to seek justice and peace in the world.

▶ Mt 2:13

Did You Know?

Pharisees, Sadducees, and Scribes

In Jesus' day, several groups of Jews held positions of status or leadership. The *Pharisees* were devoted laymen who were scholars of the Law of Moses and experts at interpreting it, so as many as possible could obey it. People looked up to them for guidance about how they should live as good Jews. The Pharisees believed in the resurrection of the body at the end time. The *Sadducees* were associated with the Temple and the ruling class. They thought the well-being of the Jewish people was dependent on proper operation and support of the Temple. They did not believe in the resurrection of body as the Pharisees did. The *scribes* were skilled at reading and writing, and most likely performed those services for the ruling class and those who were able to pay them. Scribes were not a religious group within Judaism, but they would have been familiar with the Torah and other aspects of religious practice because they worked as secretaries for the Pharisees and Sadducees. Scribes probably were involved in copying some of the Old Testament manuscripts.

The negative reaction of John the Baptist to the Pharisees and Sadducees is typical in Matthew. But in general, the Pharisees, the Sadducees, and scribes were respected leaders during Jesus' time. The persecution later experienced by the community in which the author of Matthew lived probably affected his portrayal of them. (See "Introducing Jewish Sects," near the end of Second Maccabees, for more information on these groups.)

▶ Mt 3:7

Catholic Social Teaching

The Slaughter of the Innocents

The event described in Matthew 2:16–18 is often called the Slaughter of the Innocents. In many circumstances in history, innocent people, including infants and young children, have been victims of war and other acts of violence. Today, abortion has unfortunately continued this trend, prematurely ending the lives of innocent children. To many people, abortion is a simple solution to an unwanted pregnancy. The Church teaches, however, that human life begins at the moment of conception, and that these lives, no matter how small, are sacred and must always be protected. Abortion, therefore, is wrong in all circumstances.

Catholic social teaching extends this belief in the dignity of human life from "womb to tomb" to numerous other life issues, including capital punishment, war, and euthanasia. We, in turn, must reflect this consistent ethic of life in all that we believe, say, and do, working hard to ensure that human dignity is always upheld.

- How might we as individuals or communities support pregnant women to ensure they do not choose abortion?
- How difficult is it to have a truly consistent ethic of life in our world today?

Mt 2:16–18

Life and Dignity of the Human Person

4*† John wore clothing made of camel's hair and
had a leather belt around his waist. His food was
locusts and wild honey. 5 At that time Jerusalem,
all Judea, and the whole region around the Jor-
dan were going out to him 6† and were being
baptized by him in the Jordan River as they ac-
knowledged their sins.
7*† When he saw many of the Pharisees and
Sadducees coming to his baptism, he said to
them, "You brood of vipers! Who warned you to
flee from the coming wrath? 8 Produce good fruit
as evidence of your repentance. 9*And do not
presume to say to yourselves, 'We have Abraham
as our father.' For I tell you, God can raise up
children to Abraham from these stones. 10 Even
now the ax lies at the root of the trees. Therefore
every tree that does not bear good fruit will be
cut down and thrown into the fire. 11*† I am
baptizing you with water, for repentance, but
the one who is coming after me is mightier than
I. I am not worthy to carry his sandals. He will
baptize you with the holy Spirit and fire. 12*† His
winnowing fan is in his hand. He will clear his
threshing floor and gather his wheat into his
barn, but the chaff he will burn with unquench-
able fire."

The Baptism of Jesus

13*† Then Jesus came from Galilee to John at
the Jordan to be baptized by him. 14† John tried

†

3:4 The clothing of John recalls the austere dress of the prophet Elijah (2 Kgs 1:8). The expectation of the return of Elijah from heaven to prepare Israel for the final manifestation of God's kingdom was widespread, and according to Matthew this expectation was fulfilled in the Baptist's ministry (11:14; 17:11–13).

3:6 Ritual washing was practiced by various groups in Palestine between 150 B.C. and A.D. 250. John's baptism may have been related to the purificatory washings of the Essenes at Qumran.

3:7 *Pharisees and Sadducees:* the former were marked by devotion to the law, written and oral, and the scribes, experts in the law, belonged predominantly to this group. The Sadducees were the priestly aristocratic party, centered in Jerusalem. They accepted as scripture only the first five books of the Old Testament, followed only the letter of the law, rejected the oral legal traditions, and were opposed to teachings not found in the Pentateuch, such as the resurrection of the dead. Matthew links both of these groups together as enemies of Jesus (16:1, 6, 11, 12; cf Mk 8:11–13, 15). The threatening words that follow are addressed to them rather than to "the crowds" as in Lk 3:7. *The coming wrath:* the judgment that will bring about the destruction of unrepentant sinners.

3:11 *Baptize you with the holy Spirit and fire:* the water baptism of John will be followed by an "immersion" of the repentant in the cleansing power of the Spirit of God, and of the unrepentant in the destroying power of God's judgment. However, some see *the holy Spirit* and *fire* as synonymous, and the effect of this "baptism" as either purification or destruction. See the note on Lk 3:16.

3:12 The discrimination between the good and the bad is compared to the procedure by which a farmer separates wheat and chaff. The *winnowing fan* was a forklike shovel with which the threshed wheat was thrown into the air. The kernels fell to the ground; the light chaff, blown off by the wind, was gathered and burned up.

3:13–17 The baptism of Jesus is the occasion on which he is equipped for his ministry by the holy Spirit and proclaimed to be the Son of God.

3:14–15 This dialogue, peculiar to Matthew, reveals John's awareness of Jesus' superiority to him as the mightier one who is coming and who will baptize with the holy Spirit (11). His reluctance to admit Jesus among the sinners whom he is baptizing with water is overcome by Jesus' response. *To fulfill all righteousness:* in this gospel to *fulfill* usually refers to fulfillment of prophecy,

*

3:4 Mt 11:7–8; 2 Kgs 1:8; Zec 13:4.
3:7 Mt 12:34; 23:33; Is 59:5.
3:9 Jn 8:33, 39; Rom 9:7–8; Gal 4:21–31.
3:11 Jn 1:26–27, 33; Acts 1:5.
3:12 Mt 13:30; Is 41:16; Jer 15:7.
3:13–17 Mk 1:9–11; Lk 3:21–22; Jn 1:31–34.

to prevent him, saying, "I need to be baptized
by you, and yet you are coming to me?" 15 Jesus
said to him in reply, "Allow it now, for thus it is
fitting for us to fulfill all righteousness." Then he
allowed him. 16*† After Jesus was baptized, he
came up from the water and behold, the heavens
were opened [for him], and he saw the Spirit of
God descending like a dove [and] coming upon
him. 17*† And a voice came from the heavens,
saying, "This is my beloved Son, with whom I
am well pleased."

The Temptation of Jesus

4 1*† Then Jesus was led by the Spirit into the
desert to be tempted by the devil. 2*† He
fasted for forty days and forty nights, and after-
wards he was hungry. 3 The tempter approached
and said to him, "If you are the Son of God, com-
mand that these stones become loaves of bread."
4*† He said in reply, "It is written:

'One does not live by bread alone,
but by every word that comes forth from
the mouth of God.' "

5† Then the devil took him to the holy city, and
made him stand on the parapet of the temple,
6* and said to him, "If you are the Son of God,
throw yourself down. For it is written:

'He will command his angels concerning you'
and 'with their hands they will
support you,
lest you dash your foot against a stone.' "

7*Jesus answered him, "Again it is written, 'You
shall not put the Lord, your God, to the test.' "
8 Then the devil took him up to a very high
mountain, and showed him all the kingdoms of
the world in their magnificence, 9† and he said
to him, "All these I shall give to you, if you will
prostrate yourself and worship me." 10*At this,
Jesus said to him, "Get away, Satan! It is written:

'The Lord, your God, shall you worship
and him alone shall you serve.' "

Pray It!

Jesus' Temptations, My Temptations

"Command that these stones become loaves of bread" (4:3).

Jesus, you trusted God to provide your material needs. Help me to avoid placing my priorities on material things.

*"Throw yourself down. For it is written: . . .
'with their hands they will support you,
lest you dash your foot against a stone.' "
(Verse 6)*

Jesus, you resisted using your power for vain and foolish reasons. Help me to resist doing foolish things only to impress others.

*"All these I shall give to you, if you will prostrate yourself and worship me."
(Verse 9)*

Jesus, you refused to cooperate with the devil to achieve status and power. Help me to refuse to cooperate with evil and injustice in achieving my life's goals.

▶ **Mt 4:1–11**

† and *righteousness* to moral conduct in conformity with God's will. Here, however, as in 5:6 and 6:33, *righteousness* seems to mean the saving activity of God. *To fulfill all righteousness* is to submit to the plan of God for the salvation of the human race. This involves Jesus' identification with sinners; hence the propriety of his accepting John's baptism.

3:16 *The Spirit . . . coming upon him:* cf Is 42:1.

3:17 *This is my beloved Son:* the Marcan address to Jesus (Mk 1:11) is changed into a proclamation. The Father's voice speaks in terms that reflect Is 42:1; Ps 2:7; and Gn 22:2.

4:1–11 Jesus, proclaimed Son of God at his baptism, is subjected to a triple temptation. Obedience to the Father is a characteristic of true sonship, and Jesus is tempted by the devil to rebel against God, overtly in the third case, more subtly in the first two. Each refusal of Jesus is expressed in language taken from the Book of Deuteronomy (Dt 8:3; 6:13, 16). The testings of Jesus resemble those of Israel during the wandering in the desert and later in Canaan, and the victory of Jesus, the true Israel and the true Son, contrasts with the failure of the ancient and disobedient "son," the old Israel. In the temptation account Matthew is almost identical with Luke; both seem to have drawn upon the same source.

4:2 *Forty days and forty nights:* the same time as that during which Moses remained on Sinai (Ex 24:18). The time reference, however, seems primarily intended to recall the forty years during which Israel was tempted in the desert (Dt 8:2).

4:4 Cf Dt 8:3. Jesus refuses to use his power for his own benefit and accepts whatever God wills.

4:5–7 The devil supports his proposal by an appeal to the scriptures, Ps 91:11a, 12. Unlike Israel (Dt 6:16), Jesus refuses to "test" God by demanding from him an extraordinary show of power.

4:9 The worship of Satan to which Jesus is tempted is probably intended to recall Israel's worship of false gods. His refusal is expressed in the words of Dt 6:13.

3:16 Is 42:1.
3:17 Mt 12:18; 17:5; Gn 22:2; Ps 2:7; Is 42:1.
4:1–11 Mk 1:12–13; Lk 4:1–13.
4:2 Ex 24:18; Dt 8:2.
4:4 Dt 8:3.
4:6 Ps 91:11–12.
4:7 Dt 6:16.
4:10 Mt 16:23; Dt 6:13.

Catholic Connection

MT

Baptism

Imagine the scene . . . John the Baptist dressed in camel hair, standing by the Jordan River calling for people to turn from their sin and to be ritually washed (baptized) in water as a sign of their conversion. And who steps forward? Jesus, the Son of God, who is without sin! Jesus convinces John to baptize him as a sign of how fully Jesus embraces his humanity. As Jesus comes out of the water, God reveals Jesus' true identity to the world—"This is my beloved Son, with whom I am well pleased" (Mt 3:17)—thus beginning Jesus' public ministry leading toward his Passion, death, and Resurrection.

The sacrament of Baptism also serves as a beginning for all Catholics. As the first of the three sacraments of initiation, Baptism establishes our identity as adopted sons or daughters of God and makes us members of the Christian community.

Although many Catholics are baptized as infants, some young people and adults, referred to as catechumens, are baptized at the Easter Vigil each year. During the Baptism ritual, the person is immersed in water or has water poured over his or her head three times with the words: "I baptize you in the name of the Father, and of the Son, and of the Holy Spirit" (*Rite of Christian Initiation of Adults,* no. 226). By being washed in water, the person dies to sin and rises freed from sin, both original sin and personal sin, as a new creation in Christ. The individual is then anointed with chrism (sacred oil) to strengthen him or her to "remain for ever a member of Christ" (no. 228), who was anointed priest, prophet, and king. (In the Old Testament, such oil was used to anoint priests, prophets, and kings for service.) Afterward, a white garment is put on the newly baptized person, signifying his or her new life in Christ, and a candle is given to the person, calling him or her to always walk in the light of Christ and be a light to the world.

Together the sacraments of Baptism, Confirmation, and the Eucharist are a person's initiation into the Christian community. They call Christians to continual conversion in following Jesus.

Mt 3:13–17

Catechism, nos. 1213–1284

11 Then the devil left him and, behold, angels
came and ministered to him.

The Beginning of the Galilean Ministry

12 * † When he heard that John had been ar-
rested, he withdrew to Galilee. 13 * He left Naza-
reth and went to live in Capernaum by the sea, in
the region of Zebulun and Naphtali, 14 that what
had been said through Isaiah the prophet might
be fulfilled:

15 * "Land of Zebulun and land of Naphtali,
the way to the sea, beyond the Jordan,
Galilee of the Gentiles,
16 * the people who sit in darkness
have seen a great light,
on those dwelling in a land overshadowed
by death
light has arisen."

17 * † From that time on, Jesus began to preach
and say, "Repent, for the kingdom of heaven is
at hand."

The Call of the First Disciples

18 * † As he was walking by the Sea of Galilee,
he saw two brothers, Simon who is called Peter,
and his brother Andrew, casting a net into the
sea; they were fishermen. 19 He said to them,
"Come after me, and I will make you fishers of
men." 20 † At once they left their nets and fol-
lowed him. 21 He walked along from there and
saw two other brothers, James, the son of Zebe-
dee, and his brother John. They were in a boat,
with their father Zebedee, mending their nets.
He called them, 22 and immediately they left their
boat and their father and followed him.

Follow Me

As the first disciples chose to follow Jesus, what did they leave behind? Nets, boats, even parents—the very things they depended on for life and security! Knowing what you know of Jesus, what are you ready to "leave behind" in order to follow him and continue his mission?

Mt 4:18–22

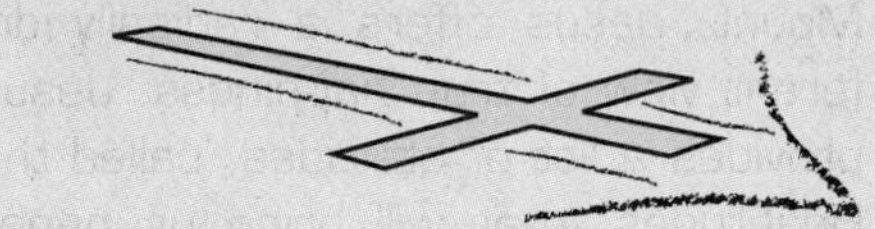

Ministering to a Great Multitude

23 * † He went around all of Galilee, teaching
in their synagogues,† proclaiming the gospel of
the kingdom, and curing every disease and illness
among the people. 24 † His fame spread to all of
Syria, and they brought to him all who were sick
with various diseases and racked with pain, those
who were possessed, lunatics, and paralytics, and
he cured them. 25 * † And great crowds from Gali-
lee, the Decapolis, Jerusalem, and Judea, and from
beyond the Jordan followed him.

The Sermon on the Mount

5 1 † When he saw the crowds,† he went up
the mountain, and after he had sat down,

---

†

4:12–17 Isaiah's prophecy of the light rising upon Zebulun and Naphtali (Is 8:23—9:1) is fulfilled in Jesus' residence at Capernaum. The territory of these two tribes was the first to be devastated (733–32 B.C.) at the time of the Assyrian invasion. In order to accommodate Jesus' move to Capernaum to the prophecy, Matthew speaks of that town as being "in the region of Zebulun and Naphtali" (13), whereas it was only in the territory of the latter, and he understands the sea of the prophecy, the Mediterranean, as the sea of Galilee.

4:17 At the beginning of his preaching Jesus takes up the words of John the Baptist (3:2) although with a different meaning; in his ministry the kingdom of heaven has already begun to be present (12:28).

4:18–22 The call of the first disciples promises them a share in Jesus' work and entails abandonment of family and former way of life. Three of the four, Simon, James, and John, are distinguished among the disciples by a closer relation with Jesus (17:1; 26:37).

4:20 Here and in v 22, as in Mark (1:16–20) and unlike the Lucan account (5:1–11), the disciples' response is motivated only by Jesus' invitation, an element that emphasizes his mysterious power.

4:23–25 This summary of Jesus' ministry concludes the narrative part of the first book of Matthew's gospel (chs 3–4). The activities of his ministry are teaching, proclaiming the gospel, and healing; cf 9:35.

4:23 *Their synagogues:* Matthew usually designates the Jewish synagogues as *their synagogue(s)* (9:35; 10:17; 12:9; 13:54) or, in address to Jews, *your synagogues* (23:34), an indication that he wrote after the break between church and synagogue.

4:24 *Syria:* the Roman province to which Palestine belonged.

4:25 *The Decapolis:* a federation of Greek cities in Palestine, originally ten in number, all but one east of the Jordan.

5:1—7:29 The first of the five discourses that are a central part of the structure of this gospel. It is the discourse section of the first book and contains sayings of Jesus derived from Q and from M. The Lucan parallel is in that gospel's "Sermon on the Plain" (Lk 6:20–49), although some of the sayings in Matthew's "Sermon on the Mount" have their parallels in other parts of Luke. The careful topical arrangement of the sermon is probably not due only to Matthew's editing; he seems to have had a structured discourse of Jesus as one of his sources. The form of that source may have been as follows: four beatitudes (5:3–4, 6, 11–12), a section on the new righteousness with illustrations (5:17, 20–24, 27–28, 33–48), a section on good works (6:1–6, 16–18), and three warnings (7:1–2, 15–21, 24–27).

5:1–2 Unlike Luke's sermon, this is addressed not only to the disciples but to the crowds (see 7:28).

*

4:12–13 Mk 1:14–15; Lk 4:14, 31.
4:13 Jn 2:12.
4:15–16 Is 8:23 LXX; 9:1.
4:16 Lk 1:79.
4:17 Mt 3:2.
4:18–22 Mk 1:16–20; Lk 5:1–11.
4:23 Mt 9:35; Mk 1:39; Lk 4:15, 44.
4:25 Mk 3:7–8; Lk 6:17–19.

MT

Catholic Connection

The Beatitudes

Have you ever thought if you only had the latest technology, or if only you were more popular, then you would be happy? Those feelings are natural, but in the Sermon on the Mount, Jesus offers a radically different view of true happiness. Jesus provides a list of attitudes, called the Beatitudes, that will bring us happiness. This list has nothing to do with material goods or popularity contests but focuses instead on our response to God's love and our love of neighbor. True happiness is found not here on earth, but in the gift of eternal reward in the kingdom of heaven.

Our desire for happiness was placed within us by God and can only be satisfied by loving God and doing God's will. Real happiness is attained not through the accumulation of possessions, but through the moral choices we make. The Beatitudes call us to turn from our desire for false or temporary happiness to seek the eternal happiness only God can give. By focusing on heaven, the decisions we make and the trials we endure on a daily basis are seen in a new light—the light of Christ's Passion and Resurrection.

Having heaven as our goal enables us to . . .

- realize that heaven is a gift from God that we receive only through God's grace
- find comfort when we mourn the loss of a loved one
- be humble
- desire righteousness (a right relationship with God and others) with every ounce of our being
- be merciful when others offend or harm us
- purify our heart so that we only desire God
- seek peace when conflict arises
- stick to our convictions when it is a question of right and wrong
- endure being made fun of or threatened because of our faith in Jesus Christ

Each and every day, God calls us to seek happiness by loving God and others generously, compassionately, humbly, with a hunger for justice, with a pure heart, and in a desire for peace. Make the Beatitudes part of your daily prayer, and know that you are not alone in the pursuit of happiness. You walk this journey with the Church, with Mary and the saints, who encourage you along the way!

Mt 5:1–12

Catechism, nos. 1716–1729

Catholic Social Teaching

An Upside-Down Kingdom

Read Matthew 5:1–12. These familiar words of Jesus, called the Beatitudes, begin what is called the Sermon on the Mount. In chapters 5–7, Jesus speaks about life in a way that challenged the attitudes of his listeners. Many thought it was enough to follow the letter of the law by performing minimal acts of caring for the poor, burying the dead, and giving alms. Jesus, however, turns their worldview upside down, asserting that they should do these things generously, compassionately, and humbly, with a hunger for justice, with a pure heart, and in a desire for peace.

Catholic social teaching promotes this same message, reminding us that God has a special love for those who are poor and those who are oppressed. If we are to be authentic Christians, we must show a similar love for those who are most in need in our world. Thankfully, our world has been blessed with numerous modern-day prophets who have shown us what it truly means to love and care for the poor. People like Archbishop Oscar Romero of El Salvador, who risked and eventually lost his own life because he was unafraid to speak out against the grave injustices being inflicted upon the poor in his country. Or Dorothy Day, who founded the Catholic Worker movement and devoted her adult life to promoting peace while serving the most poor and destitute. With these people and so many others as examples for us to follow, we too must always opt to love and serve the poor in our midst.

▶ **Mt 5:1–12**
Option for the Poor and Vulnerable

his disciples came to him. 2 He began to teach
them, saying:

The Beatitudes†

3* "Blessed are the poor in spirit,†
for theirs is the kingdom of heaven.
4*† Blessed are they who mourn,
for they will be comforted.
5*† Blessed are the meek,
for they will inherit the land.
6† Blessed are they who hunger and thirst
for righteousness,
for they will be satisfied.
7* Blessed are the merciful,
for they will be shown mercy.
8*† Blessed are the clean of heart,
for they will see God.
9 Blessed are the peacemakers,
for they will be called children of God.
10*† Blessed are they who are persecuted for the
sake of righteousness,
for theirs is the kingdom of heaven.

11*Blessed are you when they insult you and per-
secute you and utter every kind of evil against you
[falsely] because of me. 12*† Rejoice and be glad,
for your reward will be great in heaven. Thus they
persecuted the prophets who were before you.

† **5:3–12** The form *Blessed are (is)* occurs frequently in the Old Testament in the Wisdom literature and in the psalms. Although modified by Matthew, the first, second, fourth, and ninth beatitudes have Lucan parallels (5:3 // Lk 6:20; 5:4 // Lk 6:21b; 5:6 // Lk 6:21a; 5:11–12 // Lk 5:22–23). The others were added by the evangelist and are probably his own composition. A few manuscripts, Western and Alexandrian, and many versions and patristic quotations give the second and third beatitudes in inverted order.

5:3 *The poor in spirit:* in the Old Testament, the *poor (ʿanāwîm)* are those who are without material possessions and whose confidence is in God (see Is 61:1; Zep 2:3; in the NAB the word is translated *lowly* and *humble,* respectively, in those texts). Matthew added *in spirit* in order either to indicate that only the devout poor were meant or to extend the beatitude to all, of whatever social rank, who recognized their complete dependence on God. The same phrase *poor in spirit* is found in the Qumran literature (1QM 14:7).

5:4 Cf Is 61:2, "(The Lord has sent me) . . . to comfort all who mourn." *They will be comforted:* here the passive is a "theological passive" equivalent to the active "God will comfort them"; so also in vv 6 and 7.

5:5 Cf Ps 37:11, ". . . the poor will possess the land." In the psalm "the land" means the land of Palestine; here it means the kingdom.

5:6 *For righteousness:* a Matthean addition. For the meaning of *righteousness* here, see the note on 3:14–15.

5:8 Cf Ps 24:4. Only one "pure of heart" can take part in the temple worship. To be with God in the temple is described in Ps 42:3 as "see[ing] the face of God," but here the promise to *the clean of heart* is that they will *see God* not in the temple but in the coming kingdom.

5:10 *Righteousness* here, as usually in Matthew, means conduct in conformity with God's will.

5:12 *The prophets who were before you:* the disciples of Jesus stand in the line of the persecuted prophets of Israel. Some would see the expression as indicating also that Matthew considered all Christian disciples as prophets.

* **5:3–12** Lk 6:20–23.
5:4 Is 61:2–3; Rv 21:4.
5:5 Gn 13:15; Ps 37:11.
5:7 Mt 18:33; Jas 2:13.
5:8 Pss 24:4–5; 73:1.
5:10 1 Pt 2:20; 3:14; 4:14.
5:11 Mt 10:22; Acts 5:41.
5:12 2 Chr 36:16; Heb 11:32–38; Jas 5:10.

The Similes of Salt and Light†

13* "You are the salt of the earth. But if salt
loses its taste, with what can it be seasoned? It
is no longer good for anything but to be thrown
out and trampled underfoot.† 14* You are the
light of the world. A city set on a mountain
cannot be hidden. 15* Nor do they light a lamp
and then put it under a bushel basket; it is set
on a lampstand, where it gives light to all in the
house. 16* Just so, your light must shine before
others, that they may see your good deeds and
glorify your heavenly Father.

Teaching about the Law

17† "Do not think that I have come to abol-
ish the law or the prophets. I have come not
to abolish but to fulfill. 18* Amen, I say to you,
until heaven and earth pass away, not the small-
est letter or the smallest part of a letter will pass
from the law, until all things have taken place.
19† Therefore, whoever breaks one of the least of
these commandments and teaches others to do
so will be called least in the kingdom of heaven.
But whoever obeys and teaches these command-
ments will be called greatest in the kingdom of
heaven. 20 I tell you, unless your righteousness
surpasses that of the scribes and Pharisees, you
will not enter into the kingdom of heaven.

Teaching about Anger

21*† "You have heard that it was said to your
ancestors, 'You shall not kill; and whoever kills
will be liable to judgment.'† 22*† But I say to
you, whoever is angry with his brother will be
liable to judgment, and whoever says to his
brother, 'Raqa,' will be answerable to the Sanhe-
drin, and whoever says, 'You fool,' will be liable
to fiery Gehenna.† 23* Therefore, if you bring
your gift to the altar, and there recall that your
brother has anything against you, 24 leave your
gift there at the altar, go first and be reconciled
with your brother, and then come and offer your
gift. 25* Settle with your opponent quickly while
on the way to court with him. Otherwise your
opponent will hand you over to the judge, and
the judge will hand you over to the guard, and
you will be thrown into prison. 26 Amen, I say to
you, you will not be released until you have paid
the last penny.

Teaching about Adultery

27*† "You have heard that it was said, 'You
shall not commit adultery.' 28 But I say to you,
everyone who looks at a woman with lust has
already committed adultery with her in his
heart. 29*† If your right eye causes you to sin,
tear it out and throw it away. It is better for you
to lose one of your members than to have your
whole body thrown into Gehenna. 30 And if
your right hand causes you to sin, cut it off and
throw it away. It is better for you to lose one of
your members than to have your whole body go
into Gehenna.

---

†

5:13–16 By their deeds the disciples are to influence the world for good. They can no more escape notice than *a city set on a mountain.* If they fail in good works, they are as useless as flavorless salt or as a lamp whose light is concealed.

5:13 The unusual supposition of salt losing its flavor has led some to suppose that the saying refers to the salt of the Dead Sea that, because chemically impure, could lose its taste.

5:17–20 This statement of Jesus' position concerning the Mosaic law is composed of traditional material from Matthew's sermon documentation (see the note on 5:1—7:29), other Q material (cf 18 and Lk 16:17), and the evangelist's own editorial touches. *To fulfill* the law appears at first to mean a literal enforcement of the law in the least detail: *until heaven and earth pass away* nothing of the law *will pass* (18). Yet the "passing away" of heaven and earth is not necessarily the end of the world understood, as in much apocalyptic literature, as the dissolution of the existing universe. The "turning of the ages" comes with the apocalyptic event of Jesus' death and resurrection, and those to whom this gospel is addressed are living in the new and final age, prophesied by Isaiah as the time of "new heavens and a new earth" (Is 65:17; 66:22). Meanwhile, during Jesus' ministry when the kingdom is already breaking in, his mission remains within the framework of the law, though with significant anticipation of the age to come, as the following antitheses (vv 21–48) show.

5:19 Probably *these commandments* means those of the Mosaic law. But this is an interim ethic "until heaven and earth pass away."

5:21–48 Six examples of the conduct demanded of the Christian disciple. Each deals with a commandment of the law, introduced by *You have heard that it was said to your ancestors* or an equivalent formula, followed by Jesus' teaching in respect to that commandment, *But I say to you;* thus their designation as "antitheses." Three of them accept the Mosaic law but extend or deepen it (21–22; 27–28; 43–44); three reject it as a standard of conduct for the disciples (31–32; 33–37; 38–39).

5:21 Cf Ex 20:13; Dt 5:17. The second part of the verse is not an exact quotation from the Old Testament, but cf Ex 21:12.

5:22 Anger is the motive behind murder, as the insulting epithets are steps that may lead to it. They, as well as the deed, are all forbidden. *Raqa:* an Aramaic word *rēqā'* or *rēqâ* probably meaning "imbecile," "blockhead," a term of abuse. The ascending order of punishment, *judgment* (by a local council?), trial before *the Sanhedrin,* condemnation to *Gehenna,* points to a higher degree of seriousness in each of the offenses. *Sanhedrin:* the highest judicial body of Judaism. *Gehenna:* in Hebrew *gê-hinnōm,* "Valley of Hinnom," or *gê ben-hinnōm,* "Valley of the son of Hinnom," southwest of Jerusalem, the center of an idolatrous cult during the monarchy in which children were offered in sacrifice (see 2 Kgs 23:10; Jer 7:31). In Jos 18:16 (Septuagint, Codex Vaticanus) the Hebrew is transliterated into Greek as *gaienna,* which appears in the New Testament as *geenna.* The concept of punishment of sinners by fire either after death or after the final judgment is found in Jewish apocalyptic literature (e.g., Enoch 90:26) but the name *geenna* is first given to the place of punishment in the New Testament.

5:22–26 Reconciliation with an offended brother is urged in the admonition of vv 23–24 and the parable of vv 25–26 (// Lk 12:58–59). The severity of the judge in the parable is a warning of the fate of unrepentant sinners in the coming judgment by God.

5:27 See Ex 20:14; Dt 5:18.

5:29–30 No sacrifice is too great to avoid total destruction in *Gehenna.*

---

*

5:13 Mk 9:50; Lk 14:34–35.
5:14 Jn 8:12.
5:15 Mk 4:21; Lk 8:16; 11:33.
5:16 Jn 3:21.
5:18 Lk 16:17.
5:21 Ex 20:13; Dt 5:17.
5:22 Jas 1:19–20.
5:23 Mk 11:25.
5:25–26 Mt 18:34–35; Lk 12:58–59.
5:27 Ex 20:14; Dt 5:18.
5:29–30 Mt 18:8–9; Mk 9:43–47.

Teaching about Divorce

31*† "It was also said, 'Whoever divorces his wife must give her a bill of divorce.' 32* But I say to you, whoever divorces his wife (unless the marriage is unlawful) causes her to commit adultery, and whoever marries a divorced woman commits adultery.

Teaching about Oaths

33*† "Again you have heard that it was said to your ancestors, 'Do not take a false oath, but make good to the Lord all that you vow.' 34*† But I say to you, do not swear at all; not by heaven, for it is God's throne; 35 nor by the earth, for it is his footstool; nor by Jerusalem, for it is the city of the great King. 36 Do not swear by your head, for you cannot make a single hair white or black. 37† Let your 'Yes' mean 'Yes,' and your 'No' mean 'No.' Anything more is from the evil one.

Teaching about Retaliation

38*† "You have heard that it was said, 'An eye for an eye and a tooth for a tooth.' 39* But I say to you, offer no resistance to one who is evil. When someone strikes you on [your] right cheek, turn the other one to him as well. 40 If anyone wants to go to law with you over your tunic, hand him your cloak as well. 41*† Should anyone press you into service for one mile, go with him for two miles. 42* Give to the one who asks of you, and do not turn your back on one who wants to borrow.

Love of Enemies

43*† "You have heard that it was said, 'You shall love your neighbor and hate your enemy.'*

Pray It!

Christians and Revenge

For Jesus one way to love our enemies is to refuse to take revenge on those who have wronged us. Is this really possible to do?

Consider the case of a young woman named Julie Welch who was killed by a terrorist bombing in Oklahoma City. Julie's father worked unceasingly against the death penalty for the man responsible for the bombing. He knew that revenge would not bring his daughter back or make him feel better. He believed that Christians are obligated to always assume that for even the most heinous criminal, reconciliation and remorse are possible. Although his stance was not easy or popular, it illustrates what this passage teaches.

In your prayer, reflect or journal on the following questions:

- Who are your enemies?
- When they or someone else hurts you, what is your usual reaction?
- How hard is it to forgive someone who has hurt you?
- What is the greatest challenge for you in living out this teaching from Jesus?

▶ **Mt 5:38–48**

†

5:31–32 See Dt 24:1–5. The Old Testament commandment that a bill of divorce be given to the woman assumes the legitimacy of divorce itself. It is this that Jesus denies. *(Unless the marriage is unlawful)*: this "exceptive clause," as it is often called, occurs also in 19:9, where the Greek is slightly different. There are other sayings of Jesus about divorce that prohibit it absolutely (see Mk 10:11–12; Lk 16:18; cf 1 Cor 7:10, 11b), and most scholars agree that they represent the stand of Jesus. Matthew's "exceptive clauses" are understood by some as a modification of the absolute prohibition. It seems, however, that the unlawfulness that Matthew gives as a reason why a marriage must be broken refers to a situation peculiar to his community: the violation of Mosaic law forbidding marriage between persons of certain blood and/or legal relationship (Lv 18:6–18). Marriages of that sort were regarded as incest (*porneia*), but some rabbis allowed Gentile converts to Judaism who had contracted such marriages to remain in them. Matthew's "exceptive clause" is against such permissiveness for Gentile converts to Christianity; cf the similar prohibition of *porneia* in Acts 15:20, 29. In this interpretation, the clause constitutes no exception to the absolute prohibition of divorce when the marriage is lawful.

5:33 This is not an exact quotation of any Old Testament text, but see Ex 20:7, Dt 5:11, and Lv 19:12. The purpose of an oath was to guarantee truthfulness by one's calling on God as witness.

5:34–36 The use of these oath formularies that avoid the divine name is in fact equivalent to swearing by it, for all the things sworn by are related to God.

5:37 *Let your 'Yes' mean 'Yes,' and your 'No' mean 'No'*: literally, "let your speech be 'Yes, yes,' 'No, no.' " Some have understood this as a milder form of oath, permitted by Jesus. In view of v 34, "Do not swear at all," that is unlikely. *From the evil one:* i.e., from the devil. Oath-taking presupposes a sinful weakness of the human race, namely, the tendency to lie. Jesus demands of his disciples a truthfulness that makes oaths unnecessary.

5:38–42 See Lv 24:20. The Old Testament commandment was meant to moderate vengeance; the punishment should not exceed the injury done. Jesus forbids even this proportionate retaliation. Of the five examples that follow, only the first deals directly with retaliation for evil; the others speak of liberality.

5:41 Roman garrisons in Palestine had the right to requisition the property and services of the native population.

5:43–48 See Lv 19:18. There is no Old Testament commandment demanding hatred of one's enemy, but the "neighbor" of the love commandment was understood as one's fellow countryman. Both in the Old Testament (Ps 139:19–22) and at Qumran (1QS 9:21) hatred of evil persons is assumed to be right. Jesus extends the love commandment to the enemy and the persecutor. His disciples, as children of God, must imitate the example of their Father, who grants his gifts of sun and rain to both the good and the bad.

*

5:31 Mt 19:3–9; Dt 24:1.
5:32 Lk 16:18; 1 Cor 7:10–11.
5:33 Lv 19:12; Nm 30:3.
5:34–37 Ps 48:3; Sir 23:9; Is 66:1; Jas 5:12.
5:38 Ex 21:24; Lv 24:19–20.
5:39–42 Lk 6:29–30.
5:41 Lam 3:30.
5:42 Dt 15:7–8.
5:43–48 Lk 6:27, 32–36.
5:43 Lv 19:18.

Pray It!

Ash Wednesday

Matthew 6:1–18 is read on Ash Wednesday, the beginning of Lent. Lent is traditionally a forty-day period to examine and renew our spiritual lives. It is a time of prayer, service, and fasting. The forty days recall the forty years that the people of Israel wandered in the wilderness before arriving at the Promised Land and the forty days that Jesus spent in the wilderness after being baptized.

On Ash Wednesday, we receive ashes that remind us of our nature as created beings (see Gn 3:19). This practice echoes the Old Testament tradition of wearing ashes as a sign of anguish and repentance (see Jdt 4:11). As the ash cross is made on our foreheads, we hear words that echo John the Baptist's call to conversion: "Repent, and believe in the Gospel" (Roman Missal). We respond "Amen," meaning "So be it."

When Lent begins again, how will you use the forty days to strengthen your spiritual life? Make a special commitment and ask God for the grace to grow from it.

▶ **Mt 6:1–18**

44 But I say to you, love your enemies, and pray
for those who persecute you, 45 that you may be
children of your heavenly Father, for he makes
his sun rise on the bad and the good, and causes
rain to fall on the just and the unjust. 46† For if
you love those who love you, what recompense
will you have? Do not the tax collectors do the
same? 47† And if you greet your brothers only,
what is unusual about that? Do not the pagans
do the same? 48*† So be perfect, just as your
heavenly Father is perfect.

Teaching about Almsgiving

6 1*† "[But] take care not to perform righteous
deeds in order that people may see them;
otherwise, you will have no recompense from
your heavenly Father. 2*† When you give alms,
do not blow a trumpet before you, as the hypocrites do in the synagogues and in the streets to
win the praise of others. Amen, I say to you, they
have received their reward. 3 But when you give
alms, do not let your left hand know what your
right is doing, 4 so that your almsgiving may be
secret. And your Father who sees in secret will
repay you.

Teaching about Prayer

5 "When you pray, do not be like the hypocrites, who love to stand and pray in the synagogues and on street corners so that others may
see them. Amen, I say to you, they have received
their reward. 6 But when you pray, go to your
inner room, close the door, and pray to your Father in secret. And your Father who sees in secret
will repay you. 7† In praying, do not babble like
the pagans, who think that they will be heard
because of their many words.† 8 Do not be like
them. Your Father knows what you need before
you ask him.

The Lord's Prayer

9*† "This is how you are to pray:

Our Father in heaven,
hallowed be your name,†

5:46 *Tax collectors:* Jews who were engaged in the collection of indirect taxes such as tolls and customs. See the note on Mk 2:14.

5:47 Jesus' disciples must not be content with merely usual standards of conduct; see v 20 where the verb "surpass" (Greek *perisseuō*) is cognate with the *unusual* (*perisson*) of this verse.

5:48 *Perfect:* in the gospels this word occurs only in Matthew, here and in 19:21. The Lucan parallel (6:36) demands that the disciples be *merciful*.

6:1–18 The sermon continues with a warning against doing good in order to be seen and gives three examples, almsgiving (Mt 6:2–4), prayer (Mt 6:5–15), and fasting (Mt 6:16–18). In each, the conduct of the hypocrites (Mt 6:2) is contrasted with that demanded of the disciples. The sayings about reward found here and elsewhere (Mt 5:12, 46; 10:41–42) show that this is a genuine element of Christian moral exhortation. Possibly to underline the difference between the Christian idea of reward and that of the hypocrites, the evangelist uses two different Greek verbs to express the rewarding of the disciples and that of the hypocrites; in the latter case it is the verb *apechō*, a commercial term for giving a receipt for what has been paid in full (Mt 6:2, 5, 16).

6:2 *The hypocrites:* the scribes and Pharisees, see Mt 23:13, 15, 23, 25, 27, 29. The designation reflects an attitude resulting not only from the controversies at the time of Jesus' ministry but from the opposition between Pharisaic Judaism and the church of Matthew. *They have received their reward:* they desire praise and have received what they were looking for.

6:7–15 Matthew inserts into his basic traditional material an expansion of the material on prayer that includes the model prayer, the "Our Father." That prayer is found in Lk 11:2–4 in a different context and in a different form.

6:7 The example of what Christian prayer should be like contrasts it now not with the prayer of the hypocrites but with that of *the pagans*. Their babbling probably means their reciting a long list of divine names, hoping that one of them will force a response from the deity.

6:9–13 Matthew's form of the "Our Father" follows the liturgical tradition of his church. Luke's less developed form also represents

---

5:48 Lv 11:44; 19:2; Dt 18:13; Jas 1:4; 1 Pt 1:16; 1 Jn 3:3.
6:1 Mt 23:5.
6:2 Jn 12:43.
6:9–13 Lk 11:2–4.

10*† your kingdom come,
your will be done,
on earth as in heaven.
11*† Give us today our daily bread;
12*† and forgive us our debts,
as we forgive our debtors;
13*† and do not subject us to the final test,
but deliver us from the evil one.

14*† If you forgive others their transgressions,
your heavenly Father will forgive you. 15*But if
you do not forgive others, neither will your Father forgive your transgressions.

Teaching about Fasting

16† "When you fast, do not look gloomy like
the hypocrites. They neglect their appearance,
so that they may appear to others to be fasting.
Amen, I say to you, they have received their reward. 17 But when you fast, anoint your head and
wash your face, 18 so that you may not appear to
others to be fasting, except to your Father who is
hidden. And your Father who sees what is hidden will repay you.

Pray It!

A Lord's Prayer Reflection

In the Book of Matthew, Jesus teaches his followers the Lord's Prayer as an alternative to hypocritical and empty prayer. Most of us have memorized the Lord's Prayer. But although we know it by heart, we do not always pray it from the heart. It can easily become "many words" (6:7). Let this reflection help you to pray the Lord's Prayer thoughtfully:

Our Father in heaven,
hallowed be your name.
(Verse 9)

How do I honor God as creator of all things? How do I honor God in my thoughts, my words, and my actions?

your kingdom come,
your will be done,
on earth as in heaven.
(Verse 10)

How does my life reflect God's Reign of love, justice, and peace? Am I putting too much emphasis on material things?

Give us today our daily bread;
(Verse 11)

Can I trust God to provide for my daily physical, emotional, and spiritual needs?

and forgive us our debts,
as we forgive our debtors;
(Verse 12)

When I have sinned, do I admit my wrong, ask God's forgiveness, and start anew? When people have wronged me, do I hold a grudge? Am I able to forgive them as God forgives me?

and do not subject us to the final test,
but deliver us from the evil one.
(Verse 13)

What are the temptations I face in life? How do I rely on God for the strength to resist them?

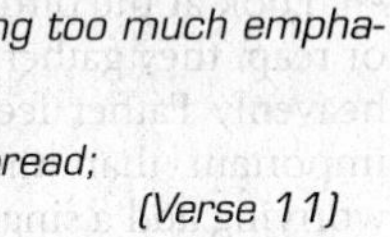

▶ Mt 6:5–15

† the liturgical tradition known to him, but it is probably closer than Matthew's to the original words of Jesus.

6:9 *Our Father in heaven:* this invocation is found in many rabbinic prayers of the post-New Testament period. *Hallowed be your name:* though the "hallowing" of the divine name could be understood as reverence done to God by human praise and by obedience to his will, this is more probably a petition that God hallow his own name, i.e., that he manifest his glory by an act of power (cf Ez 36:23), in this case, by the establishment of his kingdom in its fullness.

6:10 *Your kingdom come:* this petition sets the tone of the prayer, and inclines the balance toward divine rather than human action in the petitions that immediately precede and follow it. *Your will be done, on earth as in heaven:* a petition that the divine purpose to establish the kingdom, a purpose present now *in heaven,* be executed *on earth.*

6:11 *Give us today our daily bread:* the rare Greek word *epiousios,* here *daily,* occurs in the New Testament only here and in Lk 11:3. A single occurrence of the word outside of these texts and of literature dependent on them has been claimed, but the claim is highly doubtful. The word may mean *daily* or "future" (other meanings have also been proposed). The latter would conform better to the eschatological tone of the whole prayer. So understood, the petition would be for a speedy coming of the kingdom (*today*), which is often portrayed in both the Old Testament and the New under the image of a feast (Is 25:6; Mt 8:11; 22:1–10; Lk 13:29; 14:15–24).

6:12 *Forgive us our debts:* the word *debts* is used metaphorically of sins, "debts" owed to God (see Lk 11:4). The request is probably for forgiveness at the final judgment.

6:13 Jewish apocalyptic writings speak of a period of severe trial before the end of the age, sometimes called the "messianic woes." This petition asks that the disciples be spared that *final test.*

6:14–15 These verses reflect a set pattern called "Principles of Holy Law." Human action now will be met by a corresponding action of God at the final judgment.

6:16 The only fast prescribed in the Mosaic law was that of the Day of Atonement (Lv 16:31), but the practice of regular fasting was common in later Judaism; cf *Didache* 9:1.

* **6:10** Mt 26:42.
6:11 Prv 30:8–9.
6:12 Mt 18:21–22; Sir 28:2.
6:13 Jn 17:15; 2 Thes 3:3.
6:14 Mt 18:35; Sir 28:1–5; Mk 11:25.
6:15 Jas 2:13.

Treasure in Heaven

19*† "Do not store up for yourselves treasures
on earth, where moth and decay destroy, and
thieves break in and steal. 20* But store up trea-
sures in heaven, where neither moth nor decay de-
stroy, nor thieves break in and steal. 21 For where
your treasure is, there also will your heart be.

The Light of the Body

22*† "The lamp of the body is the eye. If your
eye is sound, your whole body will be filled with
light; 23 but if your eye is bad, your whole body
will be in darkness. And if the light in you is
darkness, how great will the darkness be.

God and Money

24*† "No one can serve two masters. He will
either hate one and love the other, or be devoted
to one and despise the other. You cannot serve
God and mammon.

Dependence on God

25*† "Therefore I tell you, do not worry about
your life, what you will eat [or drink], or about
your body, what you will wear. Is not life more
than food and the body more than clothing?
26* Look at the birds in the sky; they do not sow
or reap, they gather nothing into barns, yet your
heavenly Father feeds them. Are not you more
important than they? 27† Can any of you by
worrying add a single moment to your life-span?
28 Why are you anxious about clothes? Learn
from the way the wild flowers grow. They do
not work or spin. 29 But I tell you that not even
Solomon in all his splendor was clothed like one
of them. 30† If God so clothes the grass of the
field, which grows today and is thrown into the
oven tomorrow, will he not much more provide
for you, O you of little faith? 31 So do not worry
and say, 'What are we to eat?' or 'What are we
to drink?' or 'What are we to wear?' 32 All these
things the pagans seek. Your heavenly Father
knows that you need them all. 33† But seek first
the kingdom [of God] and his righteousness, and
all these things will be given you besides. 34 Do
not worry about tomorrow; tomorrow will take
care of itself. Sufficient for a day is its own evil.

Judging Others

7 1*† "Stop judging,† that you may not be
judged.* 2* For as you judge, so will you be
judged, and the measure with which you mea-
sure will be measured out to you. 3 Why do you
notice the splinter in your brother's eye, but
do not perceive the wooden beam in your own
eye? 4 How can you say to your brother, 'Let me
remove that splinter from your eye,' while the
wooden beam is in your eye? 5† You hypocrite,
remove the wooden beam from your eye first;
then you will see clearly to remove the splinter
from your brother's eye.

Pearls before Swine

6*† "Do not give what is holy to dogs, or throw
your pearls before swine, lest they trample them
underfoot, and turn and tear you to pieces.

The Answer to Prayers

7* "Ask and it will be given to you; seek and
you will find; knock and the door will be opened
to you.* 8* For everyone who asks, receives; and
the one who seeks, finds; and to the one who
knocks, the door will be opened. 9† Which one

---

† **6:19–34** The remaining material of this chapter is taken almost entirely from Q. It deals principally with worldly possessions, and the controlling thought is summed up in v 24: the disciple can serve only one master and must choose between God and wealth (*mammon*). See further the note on Lk 16:9.

6:22–23 In this context the parable probably points to the need for the disciple to be enlightened by Jesus' teaching on the transitory nature of earthly riches.

6:24 *Mammon:* an Aramaic word meaning wealth or property.

6:25–34 Jesus does not deny the reality of human needs (32), but forbids making them the object of anxious care and, in effect, becoming their slave.

6:27 *Life-span:* the Greek word can also mean "stature." If it is taken in that sense, the word here translated *moment* (literally, "cubit") must be translated literally as a unit not of time but of spatial measure. The cubit is about eighteen inches.

6:30 *Of little faith:* except for the parallel in Lk 12:28, the word translated *of little faith* is found in the New Testament only in Matthew. It is used by him of those who are disciples of Jesus but whose faith in him is not as deep as it should be (see Mt 8:26; 14:31; 16:8 and the cognate noun in 17:20).

6:33 *Righteousness:* see the note on 3:14–15.

7:1–12 In v 1 Matthew returns to the basic traditional material of the sermon (Lk 6:37–38, 41–42). The governing thought is the correspondence between conduct toward one's fellows and God's conduct toward the one so acting.

7:1 This is not a prohibition against recognizing the faults of others, which would be hardly compatible with vv 5 and 6, but against passing judgment in a spirit of arrogance, forgetful of one's own faults.

7:5 *Hypocrite:* the designation previously given to the scribes and Pharisees is here given to the Christian disciple who is concerned with the faults of another and ignores his own more serious offenses.

7:6 *Dogs* and *swine* were Jewish terms of contempt for Gentiles. This saying may originally have derived from a Jewish Christian community opposed to preaching the gospel (*what is holy . . . . pearls*) to Gentiles. In the light of 28:19 that can hardly be Matthew's meaning. He may have taken the saying as applying to a Christian dealing with an obstinately impenitent fellow Christian (18:17).

7:9–10 There is a resemblance between a stone and a round loaf of bread and between a serpent and the scaleless fish called *barbut.*

---

* **6:19** Jas 5:2–3.
6:20–21 Lk 12:33–34.
6:22–23 Lk 11:34–36.
6:24 Lk 16:13.
6:25–33 Lk 12:22–31.
6:26 Pss 145:15–16; 147:9.
7:1–5 Lk 6:37–38, 41–42.
7:1 Rom 2:1–2; 1 Cor 4:5.
7:2 Wis 12:22; Mk 4:24.
7:6 Prv 23:9.
7:7–11 Mk 11:24; Lk 11:9–13.
7:7 Mt 18:19.
7:8 Lk 18:1–8; Jn 14:13.

of you would hand his son a stone when he asks
for a loaf of bread, 10 or a snake when he asks for
a fish? 11* If you then, who are wicked, know
how to give good gifts to your children, how
much more will your heavenly Father give good
things to those who ask him.

The Golden Rule

12*† "Do to others whatever you would have
them do to you. This is the law and the proph-
ets.

The Narrow Gate

13*† "Enter through the narrow gate;† for the
gate is wide and the road broad that leads to
destruction, and those who enter through it are
many. 14 How narrow the gate and constricted
the road that leads to life. And those who find
it are few.

False Prophets

15*† "Beware of false prophets, who come to
you in sheep's clothing, but underneath are raven-
ous wolves. 16* By their fruits you will know them.
Do people pick grapes from thornbushes, or figs
from thistles? 17 Just so, every good tree bears good
fruit, and a rotten tree bears bad fruit. 18 A good
tree cannot bear bad fruit, nor can a rotten tree
bear good fruit. 19* Every tree that does not bear
good fruit will be cut down and thrown into the
fire. 20 So by their fruits you will know them.

The True Disciple

21*† "Not everyone who says to me, 'Lord,
Lord,' will enter the kingdom of heaven, but only
the one who does the will of my Father in heaven.
22* Many will say to me on that day, 'Lord, Lord,
did we not prophesy in your name? Did we not
drive out demons in your name? Did we not do
mighty deeds in your name?'* 23*† Then I will
declare to them solemnly, 'I never knew you. De-
part from me, you evildoers.'

Pray It!

The Gospel Call to Conversion

In closing the Sermon on the Mount, Jesus calls people to conversion. It is not enough to talk the talk; you must also walk the walk. As part of our conversion, Jesus commands the following:

- Those who are rich need to share their wealth with those who are poor.
- Those who have power need to serve those who do not have power.
- Priests need to serve all people without prejudice.
- Politicians need to govern with justice, taking into account the needs of people, especially those who are poor and powerless.
- Wise people need to express their knowledge in ways everyone can understand.

In your prayer, reflect or journal on the following:

- In the above list, what are some of the most needed areas of conversion in society today? in your local community? in your life?
- List some concrete ways you can make those conversions real.

▶ Mt 7:21–27

The Two Foundations

24*† "Everyone who listens to these words of
mine and acts on them will be like a wise man
who built his house on rock. 25* The rain fell, the
floods came, and the winds blew and buffeted

†

7:12 See Lk 6:31. This saying, known since the eighteenth century as the "Golden Rule," is found in both positive and negative form in pagan and Jewish sources, both earlier and later than the gospel. *This is the law and the prophets* is an addition probably due to the evangelist.

7:13–28 The final section of the discourse is composed of a series of antitheses, contrasting two kinds of life within the Christian community, that of those who obey the words of Jesus and that of those who do not. Most of the sayings are from Q and are found also in Luke.

7:13–14 The metaphor of the "two ways" was common in pagan philosophy and in the Old Testament. In Christian literature it is found also in the *Didache* (1–6) and the *Epistle of Barnabas* (18–20).

7:15–20 Christian disciples who claimed to speak in the name of God are called *prophets* (15) in 10:41 and in 23:34. They were presumably an important group within the church of Matthew. As in the case of the Old Testament prophets, there were both true and false ones, and for Matthew the difference could be recognized by the quality of their deeds, the *fruits* (16). The mention of *fruits* leads to the comparison with trees, some producing good fruit, others bad.

7:21–23 The attack on the false prophets is continued, but is broadened to include those disciples who perform works of healing and exorcism in the name of Jesus (*Lord*) but live evil lives. Entrance into the kingdom is only for those who do the will of the Father. On the day of judgment (*on that day*) the morally corrupt prophets and miracle workers will be rejected by Jesus.

7:23 *I never knew you:* cf 10:33. *Depart from me, you evildoers:* cf Ps 6:9.

7:24–27 The conclusion of the discourse (cf Lk 6:47–49). Here the relation is not between saying and doing as in vv 15–23 but between hearing and doing, and the words of Jesus are applied to every Christian (*everyone who listens*).

*

7:11 1 Jn 5:14–15.
7:12 Lk 6:31.
7:13 Lk 13:24.
7:15 2 Pt 2:1.
7:16–17 Mt 12:33; Lk 6:43–44.
7:19 Mt 3:10.
7:21 Is 29:13; Lk 6:46.
7:22–23 Lk 13:26–27.
7:22 Mt 25:11–12.
7:23 Pss 5:5; 6:9.
7:24–27 Lk 6:47–49.
7:25–26 Prv 10:25.

the house. But it did not collapse; it had been
set solidly on rock. 26 And everyone who listens
to these words of mine but does not act on them
will be like a fool who built his house on sand.
27 The rain fell, the floods came, and the winds
blew and buffeted the house. And it collapsed
and was completely ruined."
28† When Jesus finished these words, the
crowds were astonished at his teaching, 29*† for
he taught them as one having authority, and not
as their scribes.

III: Ministry and Mission in Galilee

The Cleansing of a Leper

8 1*† When Jesus came down from the moun-
tain, great crowds followed him. 2† And then
a leper approached, did him homage, and said,
"Lord, if you wish, you can make me clean."
3 He stretched out his hand, touched him, and
said, "I will do it. Be made clean." His leprosy
was cleansed immediately. 4*† Then Jesus said
to him, "See that you tell no one, but go show
yourself to the priest, and offer the gift that Mo-
ses prescribed; that will be proof for them."

The Healing of a Centurion's Servant†

5* When he entered Capernaum, a centurion†
approached him and appealed to him, 6 saying,
"Lord, my servant is lying at home paralyzed,
suffering dreadfully." 7 He said to him, "I will
come and cure him." 8† The centurion said in
reply, "Lord, I am not worthy to have you enter
under my roof; only say the word and my servant
will be healed. 9 For I too am a person subject to
authority, with soldiers subject to me. And I say

†

7:28–29 *When Jesus finished these words:* this or a similar formula is used by Matthew to conclude each of the five great discourses of Jesus (cf 11:1; 13:53; 19:1; 26:1).

7:29 *Not as their scribes:* scribal instruction was a faithful handing down of the traditions of earlier teachers; Jesus' teaching is based on his own authority. *Their scribes:* for the implications of *their,* see the note on 4:23.

8:1—9:38 This narrative section of the second book of the gospel is composed of nine miracle stories, most of which are found in Mark, although Matthew does not follow the Marcan order and abbreviates the stories radically. The stories are arranged in three groups of three, each group followed by a section composed principally of sayings of Jesus about discipleship. Verse 9:35 is an almost verbatim repetition of 4:23. Each speaks of Jesus' teaching, preaching, and healing. The teaching and preaching form the content of chs 5–7; the healing, that of chs 8–9. Some scholars speak of a portrayal of Jesus as "Messiah of the Word" in 5–7 and "Messiah of the Deed" in 8–9. That is accurate so far as it goes, but there is also a strong emphasis on discipleship in 8–9; these chapters have not only christological but ecclesiological import.

8:2 *A leper:* see the note on Mk 1:40.

8:4 Cf Lv 14:2–9. *That will be proof for them:* the Greek can also mean "that will be proof against them." It is not clear whether *them* refers to the priests or the people.

8:5–13 This story comes from Q (see Lk 7:1–10) and is also reflected in Jn 4:46–54. The similarity between the Q story and the Johannine is due to a common oral tradition, not to a common literary source. As in the later story of the daughter of the Canaanite woman (15:21–28) Jesus here breaks with his usual procedure of ministering only to Israelites and anticipates the mission to the Gentiles.

8:5 *A centurion:* a military officer commanding a hundred men. He was probably in the service of Herod Antipas, tetrarch of Galilee; see the note on 14:1.

8:8–9 Acquainted by his position with the force of a command, the centurion expresses faith in the power of Jesus' mere word.

7:29 Mk 1:22; Lk 4:32.
8:1–4 Mk 1:40–44; Lk 5:12–14.
8:4 Lv 14:2–32; Lk 17:14.
8:5–13 Lk 7:1–10; Jn 4:46–53.

Did You Know?

Miracles and the Reign of God

Matthew, chapters 8–9, describes ten miracles of Jesus intended as signs of the coming of the Reign of God. Most of Jesus' miracles are healings, but some also show his power over demons and nature. The Gospel of Mark records the most miracles (twenty-one), and the Gospel of John, the least (eight).

People today tend to view reports of miracles with suspicion. That's because our scientific minds want to believe that everything has a rational explanation. Because of this, we miss the point. People in Jesus' time were more concerned about what the miracle revealed than in the miracle itself or even the miracle worker. Other people besides Jesus were known to perform miracles. In fact, Jesus' healing miracles were not taken as proof of his divinity, only that he worked by the power of God.

In curing people of their illnesses and driving out demons, Jesus was revealing that the Reign of God is a place where suffering and evil are banished. By curing sinners, women, and foreigners, he showed that the Reign of God is also open to all, especially outcasts.

Miracles—then and now—point to God. Whether they are easily explained or beyond reasonable explanation does not matter. What matters is that they make us aware of God's loving presence in our lives. If we look at the events in our lives and ask ourselves what they point to and what they tell us about God's presence in the world, we might find ourselves utterly surrounded by miracles.

▶ Mt 8:1—9:34

to one, 'Go,' and he goes; and to another, 'Come here,' and he comes; and to my slave, 'Do this,' and he does it." 10† When Jesus heard this, he was amazed and said to those following him, "Amen, I say to you, in no one in Israel have I found such faith. 11*† I say to you, many will come from the east and the west, and will recline with Abraham, Isaac, and Jacob at the banquet in the kingdom of heaven, 12 but the children of the kingdom will be driven out into the outer darkness, where there will be wailing and grinding of teeth." 13 And Jesus said to the centurion, "You may go; as you have believed, let it be done for you." And at that very hour [his] servant was healed.

The Cure of Peter's Mother-in-Law

14*† Jesus entered the house of Peter, and saw his mother-in-law lying in bed with a fever. 15* He touched her hand, the fever left her, and she rose and waited on him.

Other Healings

16† When it was evening, they brought him many who were possessed by demons, and he drove out the spirits by a word and cured all the sick, 17*† to fulfill what had been said by Isaiah the prophet:

"He took away our infirmities
and bore our diseases."

The Would-be Followers of Jesus†

18* When Jesus saw a crowd around him, he gave orders to cross to the other side.† 19*† A scribe approached and said to him, "Teacher, I will follow you wherever you go." 20† Jesus answered him, "Foxes have dens and birds of the sky have nests, but the Son of Man has nowhere to rest his head." 21 Another of [his] disciples said to him, "Lord, let me go first and bury my father." 22† But Jesus answered him, "Follow me, and let the dead bury their dead."

The Calming of the Storm at Sea

23*† He got into a boat and his disciples followed him. 24† Suddenly a violent storm came up on the sea, so that the boat was being swamped by waves; but he was asleep. 25*† They came and woke him, saying, "Lord, save us! We are perishing!" 26† He said to them, "Why are you terrified, O you of little faith?" Then he got up, rebuked the winds and the sea, and there was great calm. 27 The men were amazed and said, "What sort of man is this, whom even the winds and the sea obey?"

The Healing of the Gadarene Demoniacs

28*† When he came to the other side, to the territory of the Gadarenes, two demoniacs who were coming from the tombs met him. They were so savage that no one could travel by that

---

8:10 *In no one in Israel:* there is good textual attestation (e.g., Codex Sinaiticus) for a reading identical with that of Lk 7:9, "not even in Israel." But that seems to be due to a harmonization of Matthew with Luke.

8:11–12 Matthew inserts into the story a Q saying (see Lk 13:28–29) about the entrance of Gentiles into the kingdom and the exclusion of those Israelites who, though descended from the patriarchs and members of the chosen nation (*the children of the kingdom*), refused to believe in Jesus. *There will be wailing and grinding of teeth:* the first occurrence of a phrase used frequently in this gospel to describe final condemnation (13:42, 50; 22:13; 24:51; 25:30). It is found elsewhere in the New Testament only in Lk 13:28.

8:14–15 Cf Mk 1:29–31. Unlike Mark, Matthew has no implied request by others for the woman's cure. Jesus acts on his own initiative, and the cured woman rises and waits not on "them" (Mk 1:31) but on *him.*

8:16 *By a word:* a Matthean addition to Mk 1:34; cf 8:8.

8:17 This fulfillment citation from Is 53:4 follows the MT, not the LXX. The prophet speaks of the Servant of the Lord who suffers vicariously for the sins ("infirmities") of others; Matthew takes the *infirmities* as physical afflictions.

8:18–22 This passage between the first and second series of miracles about following Jesus is taken from Q (see Lk 9:57–62). The third of the three sayings found in the source is absent from Matthew.

8:18 *The other side:* i.e., of the Sea of Galilee.

8:19 *Teacher:* for Matthew, this designation of Jesus is true, for he has Jesus using it of himself (10:24, 25; 23:8; 26:18), yet when it is used of him by others they are either his opponents (9:11; 12:38; 17:24; 22:16, 24, 36) or, as here and in 19:16, well-disposed persons who cannot see more deeply. Thus it reveals an inadequate recognition of who Jesus is.

8:20 *Son of Man:* see the note on Mk 8:31. This is the first occurrence in Matthew of a term that appears in the New Testament only in sayings of Jesus, except for Acts 7:56 and possibly 9:6 (// Mk 2:10; Lk 5:24). In Matthew it refers to Jesus in his ministry (seven times, as here), in his passion and resurrection (nine times, e.g., 17:22), and in his glorious coming at the end of the age (thirteen times, e.g., 24:30).

8:22 *Let the dead bury their dead:* the demand of Jesus overrides what both the Jewish and the Hellenistic world regarded as a filial obligation of the highest importance. See the note on Lk 9:60.

8:23 *His disciples followed him:* the first miracle in the second group (8:23—9:8) is introduced by a verse that links it with the preceding sayings by the catchword "follow." In Mark the initiative in entering the boat is taken by the disciples (Mk 4:35–41); here, Jesus enters first and the disciples follow.

8:24 *Storm:* literally, "earthquake," a word commonly used in apocalyptic literature for the shaking of the old world when God brings in his kingdom. All the synoptics use it in depicting the events preceding the parousia of the Son of Man (24:7; Mk 13:8; Lk 21:11). Matthew has introduced it here and in his account of the death and resurrection of Jesus (27:51–54; 28:2).

8:25 The reverent plea of the disciples contrasts sharply with their reproach of Jesus in Mk 4:38.

8:26 *You of little faith:* see the note on 6:30. *Great calm:* Jesus' calming the sea may be meant to recall the Old Testament theme of God's control over the chaotic waters (Pss 65:8; 89:10; 93:3–4; 107:29).

8:28 *Gadarenes:* this is the reading of Codex Vaticanus, supported by other important textual witnesses. The original reading of Codex Sinaiticus was Gazarenes, later changed to Gergesenes, and a few versions have Gerasenes. Each of these readings points to a different territory connected, respectively, with the cities Gadara, Gergesa, and Gerasa (modern Jerash). There is the same confusion of readings in the parallel texts, Mk 5:1 and Lk 8:26; there the best

---

8:11–12 Mt 13:42, 50; 22:13; 24:51; 25:30; Lk 13:28–29.
8:14–16 Mk 1:29–34; Lk 4:38–41.
8:15 Mt 9:25.
8:17 Is 53:4.
8:18 Mk 4:35.
8:19–22 Lk 9:57–60.
8:23–27 Mk 4:35–40; Lk 8:22–25.
8:25–26 Ps 107:28–29.
8:28–34 Mk 5:1–17; Lk 8:26–37.

Pray It!

Spiritual Paralysis

Jesus, healer, like the man you healed spiritually and physically, I too have experienced paralysis. Not a physical paralysis, but a spiritual paralysis that keeps me from walking with you.

This paralysis happens at times in school and in my neighborhood, when I know what the right thing to do is, but I am afraid to do it. I see someone discriminating against or abusing another person, but I stand by and do nothing. By my silence, I give my approval, but I am afraid to risk ridicule and rejection.

Forgive me of my sin of silence, Lord. Help me to overcome my fears so that I can stand up for what is right. Heal me of my spiritual paralysis so that I may walk with you. Amen.

▶ **Mt 9:1–8**

road. 29† They cried out, "What have you to do
with us, Son of God? Have you come here to tor-
ment us before the appointed time?" 30† Some
distance away a herd of many swine was feeding.
31* The demons pleaded with him, "If you drive
us out, send us into the herd of swine." 32 And
he said to them, "Go then!" They came out and
entered the swine, and the whole herd rushed
down the steep bank into the sea where they
drowned. 33 The swineherds ran away, and when
they came to the town they reported everything,
including what had happened to the demoniacs.
34 Thereupon the whole town came out to meet
Jesus, and when they saw him they begged him
to leave their district.

The Healing of a Paralytic

9 1*† He entered a boat, made the crossing,
and came into his own town. 2* And there
people brought to him a paralytic lying on a
stretcher. When Jesus saw their faith, he said
to the paralytic, "Courage, child, your sins are
forgiven." 3† At that, some of the scribes said to
themselves, "This man is blaspheming." 4 Jesus
knew what they were thinking, and said, "Why
do you harbor evil thoughts? 5 Which is easier,
to say, 'Your sins are forgiven,' or to say, 'Rise
and walk'? 6*† But that you may know that the
Son of Man has authority on earth to forgive
sins"—he then said to the paralytic, "Rise, pick
up your stretcher, and go home." 7 He rose and
went home. 8† When the crowds saw this they
were struck with awe and glorified God who had
given such authority to human beings.

The Call of Matthew

9*† As Jesus passed on from there, he saw a
man named Matthew† sitting at the customs
post. He said to him, "Follow me." And he got
up and followed him. 10*† While he was at ta-
ble in his house, many tax collectors and sinners
came and sat with Jesus and his disciples. 11† The
Pharisees saw this and said to his disciples, "Why
does your teacher eat with tax collectors and sin-
ners?" 12† He heard this and said, "Those who
are well do not need a physician, but the sick do.

---

† reading seems to be "Gerasenes," whereas "Gadarenes" is probably the original reading in Matthew. The town of Gadara was about five miles southeast of the Sea of Galilee, and Josephus (*Life* 9 §42) refers to it as possessing territory that lay on that sea. *Two demoniacs:* Mark (5:1–20) has one.

8:29 *What have you to do with us?:* see the note on Jn 2:4. *Before the appointed time:* the notion that evil spirits were allowed by God to afflict human beings until the time of the final judgment is found in Enoch 16:1 and Jubilees 10:7–10.

8:30 The tending of pigs, animals considered unclean by Mosaic law (Lv 11:6–7), indicates that the population was Gentile.

9:1 *His own town:* Capernaum; see 4:13.

9:3 *Scribes:* see the note on Mk 2:6. Matthew omits the reason given in the Marcan story for the charge of blasphemy: "Who but God alone can forgive sins?" (Mk 2:7).

9:6 It is not clear whether *"But that you may know . . . to forgive sins"* is intended to be a continuation of the words of Jesus or a parenthetical comment of the evangelist to those who would hear or read this gospel. In any case, Matthew here follows the Marcan text.

9:8 *Who had given such authority to human beings:* a significant difference from Mk 2:12 ("They . . . glorified God saying, 'We have never seen anything like this.' "). Matthew's extension to *human beings* of the authority to forgive sins points to the belief that such authority was being claimed by Matthew's church.

9:9–17 In this section the order is the same as that of Mk 2:13–22.

9:9 *A man named Matthew:* Mark names this tax collector Levi (2:14). No such name appears in the four lists of the twelve who were the closest companions of Jesus (10:2–4; Mk 3:16–19; Lk 6:14–16; Acts 1:13 [eleven, because of the defection of Judas Iscariot]), whereas all four list a Matthew, designated in 10:3 as "the tax collector." The evangelist may have changed the "Levi" of his source to *Matthew* so that this man, whose call is given special notice, like that of the first four disciples (4:18–22), might be included among the twelve. Another reason for the change may be that the disciple Matthew was the source of traditions peculiar to the church for which the evangelist was writing.

9:10 *His house:* it is not clear whether *his* refers to Jesus or Matthew. *Tax collectors:* see the note on 5:46. Table association with such persons would cause ritual impurity.

9:11 *Teacher:* see the note on 8:19.

9:12 See the note on Mk 2:17.

---

* **8:31** Lk 4:34, 41. **9:1–8** Mk 2:3–12; Lk 5:18–26. **9:2** Lk 7:48. **9:6** Jn 5:27. **9:9–13** Mk 2:14–17; Lk 5:27–32. **9:10** Mt 11:19; Lk 15:1–2.

13*† Go and learn the meaning of the words, 'I
desire mercy, not sacrifice.' I did not come to call
the righteous but sinners."

The Question about Fasting

14* Then the disciples of John approached
him and said, "Why do we and the Pharisees fast
[much], but your disciples do not fast?" 15† Jesus
answered them, "Can the wedding guests mourn
as long as the bridegroom is with them? The days
will come when the bridegroom is taken away
from them, and then they will fast. 16† No one
patches an old cloak with a piece of unshrunken
cloth, for its fullness pulls away from the cloak
and the tear gets worse. 17 People do not put
new wine into old wineskins. Otherwise the
skins burst, the wine spills out, and the skins are
ruined. Rather, they pour new wine into fresh
wineskins, and both are preserved."

The Official's Daughter and the Woman with a Hemorrhage

18*† While he was saying these things to them,
an official† came forward, knelt down before
him, and said, "My daughter has just died. But
come, lay your hand on her, and she will live."
19 Jesus rose and followed him, and so did his
disciples. 20† A woman suffering hemorrhages for
twelve years came up behind him and touched
the tassel on his cloak. 21* She said to herself,
"If only I can touch his cloak, I shall be cured."
22 Jesus turned around and saw her, and said,
"Courage, daughter! Your faith has saved you."
And from that hour the woman was cured.
23 When Jesus arrived at the official's house
and saw the flute players and the crowd who
were making a commotion, 24† he said, "Go
away! The girl is not dead but sleeping." And
they ridiculed him. 25 When the crowd was put
out, he came and took her by the hand, and
the little girl arose. 26 And news of this spread
throughout all that land.

The Healing of Two Blind Men

27*† And as Jesus passed on from there, two
blind men followed [him], crying out, "Son of
David,† have pity on us!"* 28 When he entered the
house, the blind men approached him and Jesus
said to them, "Do you believe that I can do this?"
"Yes, Lord," they said to him. 29 Then he touched
their eyes and said, "Let it be done for you ac-
cording to your faith." 30 And their eyes were
opened. Jesus warned them sternly, "See that no
one knows about this." 31 But they went out and
spread word of him through all that land.

The Healing of a Mute Person

32*† As they were going out, a demoniac who
could not speak was brought to him, 33* and
when the demon was driven out the mute per-
son spoke. The crowds were amazed and said,
"Nothing like this has ever been seen in Israel."
34*† But the Pharisees said, "He drives out de-
mons by the prince of demons."

The Compassion of Jesus

35*† Jesus went around to all the towns and vil-
lages, teaching in their synagogues, proclaiming

MT

†

9:13 *Go and learn . . . not sacrifice:* Matthew adds the prophetic statement of Hos 6:6 to the Marcan account (see also 12:7). If mercy is superior to the temple sacrifices, how much more to the laws of ritual impurity.

9:15 Fasting is a sign of mourning and would be as inappropriate at this time of joy, when Jesus is proclaiming the kingdom, as it would be at a marriage feast. Yet the saying looks forward to the time when Jesus will no longer be with the disciples visibly, the time of Matthew's church. *Then they will fast:* see *Didache* 8:1.

9:16–17 Each of these parables speaks of the unsuitability of attempting to combine the old and the new. Jesus' teaching is not a patching up of Judaism, nor can the gospel be contained within the limits of Mosaic law.

9:18–34 In this third group of miracles, the first (18–26) is clearly dependent on Mark (Mk 5:21–43). Though it tells of two miracles, the cure of the woman had already been included within the story of the raising of the official's daughter, so that the two were probably regarded as a single unit. The other miracles seem to have been derived from Mark and Q respectively, though there Matthew's own editing is much more evident.

9:18 *Official:* literally, "ruler." Mark calls him "one of the synagogue officials" (Mk 5:22). *My daughter has just died:* Matthew heightens the Marcan "my daughter is at the point of death" (Mk 5:23).

9:20 *Tassel:* possibly "fringe." The Mosaic law prescribed that tassels be worn on the corners of one's garment as a reminder to keep the commandments (see Nm 15:37–39; Dt 22:12).

9:24 *Sleeping:* sleep is a biblical metaphor for death (see Ps 87:6 LXX; Dn 12:2; 1 Thes 5:10). Jesus' statement is not a denial of the child's real death, but an assurance that she will be roused from her sleep of death.

9:27–31 This story was probably composed by Matthew out of Mark's story of the healing of a blind man named Bartimaeus (Mk 10:46–52). Mark places the event late in Jesus' ministry, just before his entrance into Jerusalem, and Matthew has followed his Marcan source at that point in his gospel also (see 20:29–34). In each of the Matthean stories the single blind man of Mark becomes two. The reason why Matthew would have given a double version of the Marcan story and placed the earlier one here may be that he wished to add a story of Jesus' curing the blind at this point in order to prepare for Jesus' answer to the emissaries of the Baptist (11:4–6) in which Jesus, recounting his works, begins with his giving sight to the blind.

9:27 *Son of David:* this messianic title is connected once with the healing power of Jesus in Mark (10:47–48) and Luke (18:38–39) but more frequently in Matthew (see also 12:23; 15:22; 20:30–31).

9:32–34 The source of this story seems to be Q (see Lk 11:14–15). As in the preceding healing of the blind, Matthew has two versions of this healing, the later in 12:22–24 and the earlier here.

9:34 This spiteful accusation foreshadows the growing opposition to Jesus in chs 11 and 12.

9:35 See the notes on 4:23–25 and 8:1—9:38.

*

9:13 Mt 12:7; Hos 6:6.
9:14–17 Mk 2:18–22; Lk 5:33–39.
9:18–26 Mk 5:22–43; Lk 8:41–56.
9:21 Mt 14:36; Nm 15:37.
9:27–31 Mt 20:29–34.
9:27 Mt 15:22.
9:32–34 Mt 12:22–24; Lk 11:14–15.
9:33 Mk 2:12; 7:37.
9:34 Mt 10:25; Mk 3:22.
9:35 Mt 4:23; Lk 8:1.

the gospel of the kingdom, and curing every dis-
ease and illness. 36*† At the sight of the crowds,
his heart was moved with pity for them because
they were troubled and abandoned, like sheep
without a shepherd. 37*† Then he said to his dis-
ciples, "The harvest is abundant but the laborers
are few; 38 so ask the master of the harvest to send
out laborers for his harvest."

The Mission of the Twelve

10 1*† Then he summoned his twelve dis-
ciples† and gave them authority over
unclean spirits to drive them out and to cure
every disease and every illness. 2† The names of
the twelve apostles are these: first, Simon called
Peter, and his brother Andrew; James, the son of
Zebedee, and his brother John; 3 Philip and Bar-
tholomew, Thomas and Matthew the tax collec-
tor; James, the son of Alphaeus, and Thaddeus;
4 Simon the Cananean, and Judas Iscariot who
betrayed him.

The Commissioning of the Twelve

5*† Jesus sent out these twelve after instructing
them thus, "Do not go into pagan territory or
enter a Samaritan town. 6* Go rather to the lost
sheep of the house of Israel. 7* As you go, make
this proclamation: 'The kingdom of heaven is at
hand.' 8† Cure the sick, raise the dead, cleanse
lepers, drive out demons. Without cost you have
received; without cost you are to give. 9* Do
not take gold or silver or copper for your belts;
10* no sack for the journey, or a second tunic, or
sandals, or walking stick. The laborer deserves
his keep. 11* Whatever town or village you en-
ter, look for a worthy person in it, and stay there
until you leave. 12 As you enter a house, wish it
peace. 13† If the house is worthy, let your peace
come upon it; if not, let your peace return to you.
14*† Whoever will not receive you or listen to
your words—go outside that house or town and
shake the dust from your feet. 15* Amen, I say
to you, it will be more tolerable for the land of
Sodom and Gomorrah on the day of judgment
than for that town.

Coming Persecutions

16* "Behold, I am sending you like sheep in
the midst of wolves; so be shrewd as serpents
and simple as doves. 17*† But beware of people,
for they will hand you over to courts and scourge
you in their synagogues,* 18 and you will be led
before governors and kings for my sake as a wit-
ness before them and the pagans. 19* When they
hand you over, do not worry about how you are
to speak or what you are to say. You will be given
at that moment what you are to say. 20 For it
will not be you who speak but the Spirit of your
Father speaking through you. 21*† Brother will
hand over brother to death, and the father his
child; children will rise up against parents and
have them put to death. 22† You will be hated by

---

†

9:36 See Mk 6:34; Nm 27:17; 1 Kgs 22:17.

9:37–38 This Q saying (see Lk 10:2) is only imperfectly related to this context. It presupposes that only God (*the master of the harvest*) can take the initiative in sending out preachers of the gospel, whereas in Matthew's setting it leads into ch 10, where Jesus does so.

10:1—11:1 After an introductory narrative (10:1–4), the second of the discourses of the gospel. It deals with the mission now to be undertaken by the disciples (5–15), but the perspective broadens and includes the missionary activity of the church between the time of the resurrection and the parousia.

10:1 *His twelve disciples:* although, unlike Mark (3:13–14) and Luke (6:12–16), Matthew has no story of Jesus' choosing the Twelve, he assumes that the group is known to the reader. The earliest New Testament text to speak of it is 1 Cor 15:5. The number probably is meant to recall the twelve tribes of Israel and implies Jesus' authority to call all Israel into the kingdom. While Luke (6:13) and probably Mark (4:10, 34) distinguish between the Twelve and a larger group also termed disciples, Matthew tends to identify the disciples and the Twelve. *Authority . . . every illness:* activities the same as those of Jesus; see 4:23; 9:35; 10:8. The Twelve also share in his proclamation of the kingdom (10:7). But although he teaches (4:23; 7:28; 9:35), they do not. Their commission to teach comes only after Jesus' resurrection, after they have been fully instructed by him (28:20).

10:2–4 Here, for the only time in Matthew, the Twelve are designated *apostles.* The word "apostle" means "one who is sent," and therefore fits the situation here described. In the Pauline letters, the place where the term occurs most frequently in the New Testament, it means primarily one who has seen the risen Lord and has been commissioned to proclaim the resurrection. With slight variants in Luke and Acts, the names of those who belong to this group are the same in the four lists given in the New Testament (see the note on 9:9). *Cananean:* this represents an Aramaic word meaning "zealot." The meaning of that designation is unclear (see the note on Lk 6:15).

10:5–6 Like Jesus (15:24), the Twelve are sent only to Israel. This saying may reflect an original Jewish Christian refusal of the mission to the Gentiles, but for Matthew it expresses rather the limitation that Jesus himself observed during his ministry.

10:8–11 The Twelve have received their own call and mission through God's gift, and the benefits they confer are likewise to be given freely. They are not to take with them money, provisions, or unnecessary clothing; their lodging and food will be provided by those who receive them.

10:13 The greeting of peace is conceived of not merely as a salutation but as an effective word. If it finds no worthy recipient, it will return to the speaker.

10:14 *Shake the dust from your feet:* this gesture indicates a complete disassociation from such unbelievers.

10:17 The persecutions attendant upon the post-resurrection mission now begin to be spoken of. Here Matthew brings into the discourse sayings found in Mk 13, which deals with events preceding the parousia.

10:21 See Mi 7:6, which is cited in vv 35, 36.

10:22 *To the end:* the original meaning was probably "until the parousia." But it is not likely that Matthew expected no missionary disciples to suffer death before then, since he envisages the martyrdom of other Christians (21). For him, *the end* is probably that of the individual's life (see 28).

---

*

9:36 Nm 27:17; 1 Kgs 22:17; Jer 50:6; Ez 34:5; Mk 6:34.
9:37–38 Lk 10:2; Jn 4:35.
10:1–4 Mk 3:14–19; Lk 6:13–16; Acts 1:13.
10:5–15 Mk 6:7–13; Lk 9:1–6.
10:6 Mt 15:24.
10:7 Mt 3:2; 4:17.
10:9–10 Mk 6:8–9; Lk 9:3; 10:4.
10:10 Lk 10:7; 1 Cor 9:14; 2 Tm 5:18.
10:11–15 Mk 6:10–11; Lk 9:4–5; 10:5–12.
10:14 Acts 13:51; 18:6.
10:15 Mt 11:24; Gn 19:1–29; Jude 7.
10:16 Lk 10:3.
10:17–22 Mk 13:9–13; Lk 21:12–19.
10:17 Acts 5:40.
10:19 Ex 4:11–12; Jer 1:6–10; Lk 12:11–12.
10:21–22 Mt 24:9, 13.

all because of my name, but whoever endures to
the end will be saved. 23† When they persecute
you in one town, flee to another. Amen, I say
to you, you will not finish the towns of Israel
before the Son of Man comes. 24* No disciple
is above his teacher, no slave above his master.
25† It is enough for the disciple that he become
like his teacher, for the slave that he become like
his master. If they have called the master of the
house Beelzebul, how much more those of his
household!

Courage under Persecution

26*† "Therefore do not be afraid of them.
Nothing is concealed that will not be revealed,
nor secret that will not be known.* 27 What I say
to you in the darkness, speak in the light; what
you hear whispered, proclaim on the housetops.
28* And do not be afraid of those who kill the
body but cannot kill the soul; rather, be afraid
of the one who can destroy both soul and body
in Gehenna. 29 Are not two sparrows sold for
a small coin? Yet not one of them falls to the
ground without your Father's knowledge. 30 Even
all the hairs of your head are counted. 31 So do
not be afraid; you are worth more than many
sparrows. 32† Everyone who acknowledges me
before others I will acknowledge before my heav-
enly Father. 33* But whoever denies me before
others, I will deny before my heavenly Father.

Jesus: A Cause of Division

34* "Do not think that I have come to bring
peace upon the earth. I have come to bring not
peace but the sword. 35 For I have come to set

a man 'against his father,
a daughter against her mother,
and a daughter-in-law against her mother-in-law;
36 and one's enemies will be those of
his household.'

Live It!

A Violent Jesus?

Jesus says a curious thing as he prepares the Twelve for their mission: "I have come to bring not peace but the sword" (Mt 10:34). This is one of the many hard sayings attributed to Jesus in the Gospels. Jesus is speaking metaphorically to emphasize the extreme demands of discipleship. He is not advocating violence but simply predicting how people will react to the new values and way of life of his followers. The author of Matthew lived in a community that knew living as Jesus' disciples is not always simple or easy. The people wished for peace, but living by Jesus' words brought them hatred and conflict with people in power.

At the time Matthew was written, Christians needed to be able to give up everything, including family attachments, in order to follow Jesus. Is it any different today? What attachments would it be difficult for you to leave behind?

▶ Mt 10:34–39

The Conditions of Discipleship

37* "Whoever loves father or mother more
than me is not worthy of me, and whoever loves
son or daughter more than me is not worthy
of me; 38† and whoever does not take up his
cross and follow after me is not worthy of me.
39*† Whoever finds his life will lose it, and who-
ever loses his life for my sake will find it.

†

10:23 *Before the Son of Man comes:* since the coming of the Son of Man at the end of the age had not taken place when this gospel was written, much less during the mission of the Twelve during Jesus' ministry, Matthew cannot have meant the coming to refer to the parousia. It is difficult to know what he understood it to be: perhaps the "proleptic parousia" of 28:16–20, or the destruction of the temple in A.D. 70, viewed as a coming of Jesus in judgment on unbelieving Israel.

10:25 *Beelzebul:* see 9:34 for the charge linking Jesus with "the prince of demons," who is named *Beelzebul* in 12:24. The meaning of the name is uncertain; possibly, "lord of the house."

10:26 The *concealed* and *secret* coming of the kingdom is to be proclaimed by them, and no fear must be allowed to deter them from that proclamation.

10:32–33 In the Q parallel (Lk 12:8–9), the Son of Man will acknowledge those who have acknowledged Jesus, and those who deny him will be denied (by the Son of Man) before the angels of God at the judgment. Here Jesus and the Son of Man are identified, and the acknowledgment or denial will be before his heavenly Father.

10:38 The first mention of the cross in Matthew, explicitly that of the disciple, but implicitly that of Jesus (*and follow after me*). Crucifixion was a form of capital punishment used by the Romans for offenders who were not Roman citizens.

10:39 One who denies Jesus in order to save one's earthly life will be condemned to everlasting destruction; loss of earthly life for Jesus' sake will be rewarded by everlasting life in the kingdom.

10:24–25 Lk 6:40; Jn 13:16; 15:20.
10:26–33 Lk 12:2–9.
10:26 Mk 4:22; Lk 8:17; 1 Tm 5:25.
10:28 Jas 4:12.
10:33 Mk 8:38; Lk 9:26; 2 Tm 2:12; Rv 3:5.
10:34–35 Lk 12:51–53.
10:37–39 Mt 16:24–25; Lk 14:26–27.
10:39 Mk 8:35; Lk 9:24; Jn 12:25.

Rewards

40*† "Whoever receives you receives me, and whoever receives me receives the one who sent me. 41† Whoever receives a prophet because he is a prophet will receive a prophet's reward, and whoever receives a righteous man because he is righteous will receive a righteous man's reward. 42* And whoever gives only a cup of cold water to one of these little ones to drink because he is a disciple—amen, I say to you, he will surely not lose his reward."

11 1† When Jesus finished giving these commands to his twelve disciples, he went away from that place to teach and to preach in their towns.

IV: Opposition from Israel

The Messengers from John the Baptist

2*† When John heard in prison† of the works of the Messiah, he sent his disciples to him 3† with this question, "Are you the one who is to come, or should we look for another?" 4 Jesus said to them in reply, "Go and tell John what you hear and see: 5*† the blind regain their sight, the lame walk, lepers are cleansed, the deaf hear, the dead are raised, and the poor have the good news proclaimed to them. 6 And blessed is the one who takes no offense at me."

Jesus' Testimony to John

7*† As they were going off, Jesus began to speak to the crowds about John, "What did you go out to the desert to see? A reed swayed by the wind? 8 Then what did you go out to see? Someone dressed in fine clothing? Those who wear fine clothing are in royal palaces. 9† Then why did you go out? To see a prophet? Yes, I tell you, and more than a prophet. 10* This is the one about whom it is written:

'Behold, I am sending my messenger ahead
of you;
he will prepare your way before you.'

11† Amen, I say to you, among those born of women there has been none greater than John the Baptist; yet the least in the kingdom of heaven is greater than he. 12*† From the days of John the Baptist until now, the kingdom of heaven suffers violence, and the violent are taking it by force. 13† All the prophets and the law prophesied up to the time of John. 14* And if you are willing to accept it, he is Elijah, the one who is to come. 15 Whoever has ears ought to hear.

16*† "To what shall I compare this generation? It is like children who sit in marketplaces and call to one another, 17 'We played the flute for you, but you did not dance, we sang a dirge but you did not mourn.' 18* For John came neither eating

---

†

10:40–42 All who receive the disciples of Jesus receive him, and God who sent him, and will be rewarded accordingly.

10:41 *A prophet:* one who speaks in the name of God; here, the Christian prophets who proclaim the gospel. *Righteous man:* since righteousness is demanded of all the disciples, it is difficult to take the *righteous man* of this verse and *one of these little ones* (42) as indicating different groups within the followers of Jesus. Probably all three designations are used here of Christian missionaries as such.

11:1 The closing formula of the discourse refers back to the original addressees, the Twelve.

11:2—12:50 The narrative section of the third book deals with the growing opposition to Jesus. It is largely devoted to disputes and attacks relating to faith and discipleship and thus contains much sayings-material, drawn in large part from Q.

11:2 *In prison:* see 4:12; 14:1–12. *The works of the Messiah:* the deeds of chs 8–9.

11:3 The question probably expresses a doubt of the Baptist that Jesus is *the one who is to come* (cf Mal 3:1) because his mission has not been one of fiery judgment as John had expected (3:2).

11:5–6 Jesus' response is taken from passages of Isaiah (26:19; 29:18–19; 35:5–6; 61:1) that picture the time of salvation as marked by deeds such as those that Jesus is doing. The beatitude is a warning to the Baptist not to disbelieve because his expectations have not been met.

11:7–19 Jesus' rebuke of John is counterbalanced by a reminder of the greatness of the Baptist's function (7–15) that is followed by a complaint about those who have heeded neither John nor Jesus (16–19).

11:9–10 In common Jewish belief there had been no prophecy in Israel since the last of the Old Testament prophets, Malachi. The coming of a new prophet was eagerly awaited, and Jesus agrees that John was such. Yet he was *more than a prophet,* for he was the precursor of the one who would bring in the new and final age. The Old Testament quotation is a combination of Mal 3:1 and Ex 23:20, with the significant change that the *before me* of Malachi becomes *before you.* The messenger now precedes not God, as in the original, but Jesus.

11:11 John's preeminent greatness lies in his function of announcing the imminence of the kingdom (3:1). But to be in the kingdom is so great a privilege that the least who has it is greater than the Baptist.

11:12 The meaning of this difficult saying is probably that the opponents of Jesus are trying to prevent people from accepting the kingdom and to snatch it away from those who have received it.

11:13 *All the prophets and the law:* Matthew inverts the usual order, "law and prophets," and says that both have *prophesied.* This emphasis on the prophetic character of the law points to its fulfillment in the teaching of Jesus and to the transitory nature of some of its commandments (see the note on 5:17–20).

11:16–19 See Lk 7:31–35. The meaning of the parable (16–17) and its explanation (18–19b) is much disputed. A plausible view is that the *children* of the parable are two groups, one of which proposes different entertainments to the other that will not agree with either proposal. The first represents John, Jesus, and their disciples; the second those who reject John for his asceticism and Jesus for his table association with those despised by the religiously observant. Verse 19c (*her works*) forms an inclusion with v 2 ("the works of the Messiah"). The original form of the saying is better preserved in Lk 7:35, ". . . wisdom is vindicated by all her children." There John and Jesus are the children of Wisdom; here the works of Jesus the Messiah are those of divine Wisdom, of which he is the embodiment. Some important textual witnesses, however, have essentially the same reading as in Luke.

10:40 Lk 10:16; Jn 12:44; 13:20.
10:42 Mt 25:40; Mk 9:41.
11:2–11 Lk 7:18–28.
11:5 Is 26:19; 29:18–19; 35:5–6; 61:1.
11:7 Mt 3:3, 5.
11:10 Ex 23:20; Mal 3:1; Mk 1:2; Lk 1:76.
11:12 Lk 16:16.
11:14 Mt 17:10–13; Mal 3:23; Lk 1:17.
11:16–19 Lk 7:31–35.
11:18 Lk 1:15.

nor drinking, and they said, 'He is possessed by
a demon.' 19* The Son of Man came eating and
drinking and they said, 'Look, he is a glutton and
a drunkard, a friend of tax collectors and sinners.'
But wisdom is vindicated by her works."

Reproaches to Unrepentant Towns

20* Then he began to reproach the towns
where most of his mighty deeds had been done,
since they had not repented. 21*† "Woe to you,
Chorazin! Woe to you, Bethsaida! For if the
mighty deeds done in your midst had been done
in Tyre and Sidon, they would long ago have re-
pented in sackcloth and ashes. 22 But I tell you, it
will be more tolerable for Tyre and Sidon on the
day of judgment than for you. 23*† And as for
you, Capernaum:

'Will you be exalted to heaven?
You will go down to the netherworld.'

For if the mighty deeds done in your midst had
been done in Sodom, it would have remained
until this day. 24* But I tell you, it will be more
tolerable for the land of Sodom on the day of
judgment than for you."

The Praise of the Father

25*† At that time Jesus said in reply, "I give
praise to you, Father, Lord of heaven and earth,
for although you have hidden these things from
the wise and the learned you have revealed them
to the childlike. 26 Yes, Father, such has been your
gracious will. 27* All things have been handed
over to me by my Father. No one knows the Son
except the Father, and no one knows the Father
except the Son and anyone to whom the Son
wishes to reveal him.

The Gentle Mastery of Christ

28† "Come to me, all you who labor and are
burdened,† and I will give you rest. 29*† Take
my yoke upon you and learn from me, for I am
meek and humble of heart; and you will find rest
for yourselves. 30 For my yoke is easy, and my
burden light."

Picking Grain on the Sabbath

12 1*† At that time Jesus was going through a
field of grain on the sabbath. His disciples
were hungry and began to pick the heads of grain
and eat them.*† 2 When the Pharisees saw this,
they said to him, "See, your disciples are doing
what is unlawful to do on the sabbath." 3*† He
said to them, "Have you not read what David
did when he and his companions were hungry,
4* how he went into the house of God and ate
the bread of offering, which neither he nor his
companions but only the priests could lawfully
eat? 5*† Or have you not read in the law that on
the sabbath the priests serving in the temple vio-
late the sabbath and are innocent? 6 I say to you,
something greater than the temple is here. 7*† If
you knew what this meant, 'I desire mercy, not
sacrifice,' you would not have condemned these
innocent men. 8*† For the Son of Man is Lord of
the sabbath."

The Man with a Withered Hand

9* Moving on from there, he went into their

†

11:21 Tyre and Sidon were pagan cities denounced for their wickedness in the Old Testament; cf Jl 4:4–7.

11:23 Capernaum's pride and punishment are described in language taken from the taunt song against the king of Babylon (Is 14:13–15).

11:25–27 This Q saying, identical with Lk 10:21–22 except for minor variations, introduces a joyous note into this section, so dominated by the theme of unbelief. While the *wise and the learned,* the scribes and Pharisees, have rejected Jesus' preaching and the significance of his mighty deeds, *the childlike* have accepted them. Acceptance depends upon the Father's revelation, but this is granted to those who are open to receive it and refused to the arrogant. Jesus can speak of all mysteries because he is *the Son* and there is perfect reciprocity of knowledge between him and the Father; what has been *handed over* to him is revealed only to those whom he wishes.

11:28–29 These verses are peculiar to Matthew and are similar to Ben Sirach's invitation to learn wisdom and submit to her yoke (Sir 51:23, 26).

11:28 *Who labor and are burdened:* burdened by the law as expounded by the scribes and Pharisees (23:4).

11:29 In place of the yoke of the law, complicated by scribal interpretation, Jesus invites the burdened to take the yoke of obedience to his word, under which they *will find rest;* cf Jer 6:16.

12:1–14 Matthew here returns to the Marcan order that he left in 9:18. The two stories depend on Mk 2:23–28 and 3:1–6, respectively, and are the only places in either gospel that deal explicitly with Jesus' attitude toward sabbath observance.

12:1–2 The picking of the heads of grain is here equated with reaping, which was forbidden on the sabbath (Ex 34:21).

12:3–4 See 1 Sm 21:2–7. In the Marcan parallel (2:25–26) the high priest is called Abiathar, although in 1 Samuel this action is attributed to Ahimelech. The Old Testament story is not about a violation of the sabbath rest; its pertinence to this dispute is that a violation of the law was permissible because of David's men being without food.

12:5–6 This and the following argument (7) are peculiar to Matthew. The temple service seems to be the changing of the showbread on the sabbath (Lv 24:8) and the doubling on the sabbath of the usual daily holocausts (Nm 28:9–10). The argument is that the law itself requires work that breaks the sabbath rest, because of the higher duty of temple service. If temple duties outweigh the sabbath law, how much more does the presence of Jesus, with his proclamation of the kingdom (*something greater than the temple*), justify the conduct of his disciples.

12:7 See the note on 9:13.

12:8 The ultimate justification for the disciples' violation of the sabbath rest is that Jesus, the Son of Man, has supreme authority over the law.

*

11:19 Mt 9:10–11.
11:20–24 Lk 10:12–15.
11:21 Jl 4:4–7.
11:23 Is 14:13–15.
11:24 Mt 10:15.
11:25–27 Lk 10:21–22.
11:27 Jn 3:35; 6:46; 7:28; 10:15.
11:29 Sir 51:26; Jer 6:16.
12:1–8 Mk 2:23–28; Lk 6:1–5.
12:1 Dt 23:26.
12:3–4 1 Sm 21:2–7.
12:4 Lv 24:5–9.
12:5 Lv 24:8; Nm 28:9–10.
12:7 Hos 6:6.
12:8 Jn 5:16–17.
12:9–15 Mk 3:1–6; Lk 6:6–11.

synagogue. 10† And behold, there was a man
there who had a withered hand. They questioned
him, "Is it lawful to cure on the sabbath?" so
that they might accuse him. 11† He said to them,
"Which one of you who has a sheep that falls
into a pit on the sabbath will not take hold of
it and lift it out? 12 How much more valuable a
person is than a sheep. So it is lawful to do good
on the sabbath." 13 Then he said to the man,
"Stretch out your hand." He stretched it out, and
it was restored as sound as the other. 14*† But the
Pharisees went out and took counsel against him
to put him to death.

The Chosen Servant†

15 When Jesus realized this, he withdrew from
that place. Many [people] followed him, and he
cured them all,† 16 but he warned them not to
make him known. 17 This was to fulfill what had
been spoken through Isaiah the prophet:

18* "Behold, my servant whom I have chosen,
my beloved in whom I delight;
I shall place my spirit upon him,
and he will proclaim justice to the Gentiles.
19† He will not contend or cry out,
nor will anyone hear his voice in
the streets.
20 A bruised reed he will not break,
a smoldering wick he will not quench,
until he brings justice to victory.
21† And in his name the Gentiles will hope."

Jesus and Beelzebul

22*† Then they brought to him a demoniac
who was blind and mute. He cured the mute
person so that he could speak and see. 23*† All
the crowd was astounded, and said, "Could this
perhaps be the Son of David?" 24*† But when
the Pharisees heard this, they said, "This man
drives out demons only by the power of Beel-
zebul, the prince of demons." 25*† But he knew
what they were thinking and said to them, "Ev-
ery kingdom divided against itself will be laid
waste, and no town or house divided against
itself will stand. 26 And if Satan drives out Satan,
he is divided against himself; how, then, will his
kingdom stand? 27† And if I drive out demons by
Beelzebul, by whom do your own people drive
them out? Therefore they will be your judges.
28*† But if it is by the Spirit of God that I drive
out demons, then the kingdom of God has come
upon you. 29† How can anyone enter a strong
man's house and steal his property, unless he
first ties up the strong man? Then he can plun-
der his house. 30*† Whoever is not with me is
against me, and whoever does not gather with
me scatters. 31*† Therefore, I say to you, every
sin and blasphemy will be forgiven people, but
blasphemy against the Spirit will not be forgiven.
32 And whoever speaks a word against the Son of
Man will be forgiven; but whoever speaks against
the holy Spirit will not be forgiven, either in this
age or in the age to come.

†

12:10 Rabbinic tradition later than the gospels allowed relief to be given to a sufferer on the sabbath if life was in danger. This may also have been the view of Jesus' Pharisaic contemporaries. But the case here is not about one in danger of death.

12:11 Matthew omits the question posed by Jesus in Mk 3:4 and substitutes one about rescuing a sheep on the sabbath, similar to that in Lk 14:5.

12:14 See Mk 3:6. Here the plan to bring about Jesus' death is attributed to the Pharisees only. This is probably due to the situation of Matthew's church, when the sole opponents were the Pharisees.

12:15–21 Matthew follows Mk 3:7–12 but summarizes his source in two verses (15, 16) that pick up the withdrawal, the healings, and the command for silence. To this he adds a fulfillment citation from the first Servant Song (Is 42:1–4) that does not correspond exactly to either the Hebrew or the LXX of that passage. It is the longest Old Testament citation in this gospel, emphasizing the meekness of Jesus, the Servant of the Lord, and foretelling the extension of his mission to the Gentiles.

12:15 Jesus' knowledge of the Pharisees' plot and his healing *all* are peculiar to Matthew.

12:19 The servant's not contending is seen as fulfilled in Jesus' withdrawal from the disputes narrated in 1–14.

12:21 Except for a minor detail, Matthew here follows the LXX, although the meaning of the Hebrew ("the coastlands will wait for his teaching") is similar.

12:22–32 For the exorcism, see the note on 9:32–34. The long discussion combines Marcan and Q material (Mk 3:22–30; Lk 11:19–20, 23; 12:10). Mk 3:20–21 is omitted, with a consequent lessening of the sharpness of 12:48.

12:23 See the note on 9:27.

12:24 See the note on 10:25.

12:25–26 Jesus' first response to the Pharisees' charge is that if it were true, Satan would be destroying his own kingdom.

12:27 Besides pointing out the absurdity of the charge, Jesus asks how the work of Jewish exorcists (*your own people*) is to be interpreted. Are they, too, to be charged with collusion with Beelzebul? For an example of Jewish exorcism see Josephus, *Antiquities* 8:2, 5 §§42–49.

12:28 The Q parallel (Lk 11:20) speaks of the "finger" rather than of the "spirit" of God. While the difference is probably due to Matthew's editing, he retains *the kingdom of God* rather than changing it to his usual "kingdom of heaven." *Has come upon you:* see 4:17.

12:29 A short parable illustrates what Jesus is doing. The *strong man* is Satan, whom Jesus has tied up and whose *house* he is plundering. Jewish expectation was that Satan would be chained up in the last days (Rv 20:2); Jesus' exorcisms indicate that those days have begun.

12:30 This saying, already attached to the preceding verses in Q (see Lk 11:23), warns that there can be no neutrality where Jesus is concerned. Its pertinence in a context where Jesus is addressing not the neutral but the bitterly opposed is not clear. The accusation of scattering, however, does fit the situation. Jesus is the shepherd of God's people (2:6), his mission is to the lost sheep of Israel (15:24); the Pharisees, who oppose him, are guilty of scattering the sheep.

12:31 *Blasphemy against the Spirit:* the sin of attributing to Satan (24) what is the work of the Spirit of God (28).

*

12:14 Jn 5:18.
12:18–21 Is 42:1–4.
12:22–24 Mt 9:32–34; Lk 11:14–15.
12:23 Mt 9:27.
12:24 Mt 10:25; Mk 3:22.
12:25–29 Mk 3:23–27; Lk 11:17–22.
12:28 Lk 11:20.
12:30 Lk 11:23.
12:31–32 Mk 3:28–30; Lk 12:10.

A Tree and Its Fruits

33*† "Either declare the tree good and its fruit
is good, or declare the tree rotten and its fruit is
rotten, for a tree is known by its fruit. 34*† You
brood of vipers, how can you say good things
when you are evil? For from the fullness of the
heart the mouth speaks. 35 A good person brings
forth good out of a store of goodness, but an
evil person brings forth evil out of a store of
evil. 36*† I tell you, on the day of judgment
people will render an account for every careless
word they speak. 37 By your words you will be
acquitted, and by your words you will be condemned."

The Demand for a Sign†

38* Then some of the scribes and Pharisees
said to him, "Teacher,† we wish to see a sign
from you." 39† He said to them in reply, "An
evil and unfaithful generation seeks a sign, but
no sign will be given it except the sign of Jonah
the prophet. 40† Just as Jonah was in the belly
of the whale three days and three nights, so will
the Son of Man be in the heart of the earth three
days and three nights. 41† At the judgment, the
men of Nineveh will arise with this generation
and condemn it, because they repented at the
preaching of Jonah; and there is something
greater than Jonah here. 42* At the judgment the
queen of the south will arise with this generation and condemn it, because she came from
the ends of the earth to hear the wisdom of
Solomon; and there is something greater than
Solomon here.

The Return of the Unclean Spirit

43*† "When an unclean spirit goes out of a
person it roams through arid regions searching

Live It!

Tripping over My Tongue

Just as a tree's fruit reveals whether the tree is good or bad, so also our words reveal much about our individual character. Unfortunately, swearing is all too common among young people today. For many it has become a habitual sin—a sin that is committed so frequently and casually that those who commit it sometimes don't even realize they're doing it! Yet, the words we choose to use say much about the person we are and the values that are at the core of our lives. When we swear, we carelessly neglect to honor the goodness that is inherent in our hearts, a goodness that has been within us since the moment we were created. Thus, we must strive to expand our vocabulary, choosing words that more fully reflect the treasure that is our life.

▶ Mt 12:33–37

for rest but finds none. 44 Then it says, 'I will return to my home from which I came.' But upon
returning, it finds it empty, swept clean, and put
in order. 45 Then it goes and brings back with itself seven other spirits more evil than itself, and
they move in and dwell there; and the last condition of that person is worse than the first. Thus
it will be with this evil generation."

12:33 *Declare:* literally, "make." The meaning of this verse is obscure. Possibly it is a challenge to the Pharisees either to declare Jesus and his exorcisms good or both of them bad. A tree is known by its fruit; if the fruit is good, so must the tree be. If the driving out of demons is good, so must its source be.

12:34 The admission of Jesus' goodness cannot be made by the Pharisees, for they are evil, and the words that proceed from their evil hearts cannot be good.

12:36–37 If on the day of judgment people will be held accountable for even their *careless* words, the vicious accusations of the Pharisees will surely lead to their condemnation.

12:38–42 This section is mainly from Q (see Lk 11:29–32). Mk 8:11–12, which Matthew has followed in 16:1–4, has a similar demand for a sign. The scribes and Pharisees refuse to accept the exorcisms of Jesus as authentication of his claims and demand a sign that will end all possibility of doubt. Jesus' response is that no such sign will be given. Because his opponents are evil and see him as an agent of Satan, nothing will convince them.

12:38 *Teacher:* see the note on 8:19. In 16:1 the request is for a sign "from heaven" (Mk 8:11).

12:39 *Unfaithful:* literally, "adulterous." The covenant between God and Israel was portrayed as a marriage bond, and unfaithfulness to the covenant as adultery; cf Hos 2:4–15; Jer 3:6–10.

12:40 See Jon 2:1. While in Q the sign was simply Jonah's preaching to the Ninevites (Lk 11:30, 32), Matthew here adds Jonah's sojourn *in the belly of the whale* for *three days and three nights,* a prefigurement of Jesus' sojourn in the abode of the dead and, implicitly, of his resurrection.

12:41–42 The Ninevites who *repented* (see Jon 3:1–10) and *the queen of the south* (i.e., of Sheba; see 1 Kgs 10:1–13) were pagans who responded to lesser opportunities than have been offered to Israel in the ministry of Jesus, *something greater than Jonah* or *Solomon.* At the final judgment they will condemn the faithless *generation* that has rejected him.

12:43–45 Another Q passage; cf 11:24–26. Jesus' ministry has broken Satan's hold over Israel, but the refusal of *this evil generation* to accept him will lead to a worse situation than what preceded his coming.

12:33–35 Lk 6:43–45. **12:34** Mt 3:7; 23:33; 15:11–12; Lk 3:7. **12:36–37** Jas 3:1–2. **12:38–42** Mt 16:1–4; Jon 2:1; 3:1–10; Mk 8:11–12; Lk 11:29–32. **12:42** 1 Kgs 10:1–10. **12:43–45** Lk 11:24–26.

The True Family of Jesus

46*† While he was still speaking to the crowds,
his mother and his brothers appeared outside,
wishing to speak with him. [47† Someone told
him, "Your mother and your brothers are stand-
ing outside, asking to speak with you."] 48 But
he said in reply to the one who told him, "Who
is my mother? Who are my brothers?" 49 And
stretching out his hand toward his disciples,
he said, "Here are my mother and my brothers.
50 For whoever does the will of my heavenly Fa-
ther is my brother, and sister, and mother."

The Parable of the Sower

13 1*† On that day, Jesus went out of the
house and sat down by the sea. 2 Such
large crowds gathered around him that he got
into a boat and sat down, and the whole crowd
stood along the shore. 3† And he spoke to them
at length in parables, saying: "A sower went out
to sow.† 4 And as he sowed, some seed fell on
the path, and birds came and ate it up. 5 Some
fell on rocky ground, where it had little soil. It
sprang up at once because the soil was not deep,
6 and when the sun rose it was scorched, and it
withered for lack of roots. 7 Some seed fell among
thorns, and the thorns grew up and choked it.
8 But some seed fell on rich soil, and produced
fruit, a hundred or sixty or thirtyfold. 9 Whoever
has ears ought to hear."

The Purpose of Parables

10 The disciples approached him and said,
"Why do you speak to them in parables?" 11† He
said to them in reply, "Because knowledge of
the mysteries of the kingdom of heaven has
been granted to you, but to them it has not been

Did You Know?

Parables

The Gospels frequently describe Jesus' teaching in parables. A parable is a literary form that uses a fictional story to make a point.

Many of Jesus' parables are like riddles. They have surprising or shocking endings designed to tease the people of his time into examining certain beliefs they took for granted. Unfortunately, the surprise of Jesus' parables is hard for some of us to understand today because we may be unfamiliar with the examples he used: baking bread, planting crops, herding sheep, or fishing for our supper.

Jesus also used parables to teach about God's Reign. These were often in the form of analogies comparing God's Reign to common things or events: "The kingdom of heaven is like . . ." Using parables, Jesus challenged powerful and educated people but was also understood by common people.

▶ Mt 13:10

†

12:46–50 See Mk 3:31–35. Matthew has omitted Mk 3:20–21, which is taken up in Mk 3:31 (see the note on 12:22–32), yet the point of the story is the same in both gospels: natural kinship with Jesus counts for nothing; only one who *does the will of* his *heavenly Father* belongs to his true family.

12:47 This verse is omitted in some important textual witnesses, including Codex Sinaiticus (original reading) and Codex Vaticanus.

13:1–53 The discourse in parables is the third great discourse of Jesus in Matthew and constitutes the second part of the third book of the gospel. Matthew follows the Marcan outline (Mk 4:1–35) but has only two of Mark's parables, the five others being from Q and M. In addition to the seven parables, the discourse gives the reason why Jesus uses this type of speech (10–15), declares the blessedness of those who understand his teaching (16–17), explains the parable of the sower (18–23) and of the weeds (36–43), and ends with a concluding statement to the disciples (51–52).

13:3 *In parables:* the word "parable" (Greek *parabolē*) is used in the LXX to translate the Hebrew *māshāl*, a designation covering a wide variety of literary forms such as axioms, proverbs, similitudes, and allegories. In the New Testament the same breadth of meaning of the word is found, but there it primarily designates stories that are illustrative comparisons between Christian truths and events of everyday life. Sometimes the event has a strange element that is quite different from usual experience (e.g., in v 33, the enormous amount of dough in the parable of the yeast); this is meant to sharpen the curiosity of the hearer. If each detail of such a story is given a figurative meaning, the story is an allegory. Those who maintain a sharp distinction between parable and allegory insist that a parable has only one point of comparison, and that while parables were characteristic of Jesus' teaching, to see allegorical details in them is to introduce meanings that go beyond their original intention and even falsify it. However, to exclude any allegorical elements from a parable is an excessively rigid mode of interpretation, now abandoned by many scholars.

13:3–8 Since in Palestine sowing often preceded plowing, much of the seed is scattered on ground that is unsuitable. Yet while much is wasted, the seed that falls on good ground bears fruit in extraordinarily large measure. The point of the parable is that, in spite of some failure because of opposition and indifference, the message of Jesus about the coming of the kingdom will have enormous success.

13:11 Since a parable is figurative speech that demands reflection for understanding, only those who are prepared to explore its meaning can come to know it. To understand is a gift of God, granted to the disciples but not to the crowds. In Semitic fashion, both the disciples' understanding and the crowd's obtuseness are attributed to God. The question of human responsibility for the obtuseness is not dealt with, although it is asserted in v 13. *The mysteries:* as in Lk 8:10; Mk 4:11 has "the mystery." The word is used in Dn 2:18, 19, 27 and in the Qumran literature (1QpHab 7:8; 1QS 3:23; 1QM 3:9) to designate a divine plan or decree affecting the course of history that can be known only when revealed. *Knowledge of the mysteries of the kingdom of heaven* means recognition that the kingdom has become present in the ministry of Jesus.

* **12:46–50** Mk 3:31–35; Lk 8:19–21. **13:1–15** Mk 4:1–12; Lk 8:4–10.

granted. 12*† To anyone who has, more will be
given and he will grow rich; from anyone who
has not, even what he has will be taken away.
13*† This is why I speak to them in parables, be-
cause 'they look but do not see and hear but do
not listen or understand.' 14* Isaiah's prophecy is
fulfilled in them, which says:

'You shall indeed hear but not understand,
you shall indeed look but never see.
15 Gross is the heart of this people,
they will hardly hear with their ears,
they have closed their eyes,
lest they see with their eyes
and hear with their ears
and understand with their heart and
be converted,
and I heal them.'

The Privilege of Discipleship

16*† "But blessed are your eyes, because they
see, and your ears, because they hear. 17 Amen, I
say to you, many prophets and righteous people
longed to see what you see but did not see it, and
to hear what you hear but did not hear it.

The Explanation of the Parable of the Sower

18*† "Hear then the parable of the sower. 19 The
seed sown on the path is the one who hears the
word of the kingdom without understanding it,
and the evil one comes and steals away what
was sown in his heart. 20 The seed sown on rocky
ground is the one who hears the word and re-
ceives it at once with joy. 21 But he has no root
and lasts only for a time. When some tribulation
or persecution comes because of the word, he
immediately falls away. 22 The seed sown among
thorns is the one who hears the word, but then
worldly anxiety and the lure of riches choke the
word and it bears no fruit. 23 But the seed sown
on rich soil is the one who hears the word and
understands it, who indeed bears fruit and yields
a hundred or sixty or thirtyfold."

Pray It!

The Kingdom Is Like . . .

In trying to get people to understand something as mystifying and overwhelming as the kingdom of heaven, Jesus used ordinary objects, like seeds and light, salt and yeast. He chose everyday actions like farming, fishing, and baking. And in doing so, he helped the people of his time to understand the new life that comes with the kingdom of heaven. Using these metaphors, Jesus is also clear that the kingdom of heaven is not a place we are trying to get to but a reality we have to work to create here on earth. Heaven is living in perfect communion with Christ and all who believe in him forever.

What does the kingdom mean to you? Based on what you read in Matthew 13:10–53, meditate on the following questions:

- What would our world look like if it truly reflected Jesus' vision for the kingdom of heaven?
- What object, action, or image best describes your understanding of the kingdom of heaven?

End your meditation with a prayer that your life will be a living sign to help others understand what the kingdom of heaven is all about.

▶ Mt 13:10–53

† **13:12** In the New Testament use of this axiom of practical "wisdom" (see 25:29; Mk 4:25; Lk 8:18; 19:26), the reference transcends the original level. God gives further understanding to one who accepts the revealed mystery; from the one who does not, he will take it away (note the "theological passive," *more will be given, what he has will be taken away*).

13:13 *Because 'they look . . . or understand':* Matthew softens his Marcan source, which states that Jesus speaks in parables so that the crowds may not understand (Mk 4:12), and makes such speaking a punishment given *because* they have not accepted his previous clear teaching. However, his citation of Is 6:9–10 in v 14 supports the harsher Marcan view.

13:16–17 Unlike the unbelieving crowds, the disciples have seen that which the *prophets* and the *righteous* of the Old Testament *longed to see* without having their longing fulfilled.

13:18–23 See Mk 4:14–20; Lk 8:11–15. In this explanation of the parable the emphasis is on the various types of soil on which the seed falls, i.e., on the dispositions with which the preaching of Jesus is received. The second and third types particularly are explained in such a way as to support the view held by many scholars that the explanation derives not from Jesus but from early Christian reflection upon apostasy from the faith that was the consequence of persecution and worldliness respectively. Others, however, hold that the explanation may come basically from Jesus even though it was developed in the light of later Christian experience. The four types of persons envisaged are (1) those who never accept *the word of the kingdom* (19); (2) those who believe for a while but fall away because of *persecution* (20–21); (3) those who believe, but in whom *the word* is choked by *worldly anxiety* and the seduction of *riches* (22); (4) those who respond to *the word* and produce *fruit* abundantly (23).

13:12 Mt 25:29; Mk 4:25; Lk 8:18; 19:26.
13:13 Jn 9:39.
13:14–15 Is 6:9–10; Jn 12:40; Acts 28:26–27; Rom 11:8.
13:16–17 Lk 10:23–24; 1 Pt 1:10–12.
13:18–23 Mk 4:13–20; Lk 8:11–15.

The Parable of the Weeds among the Wheat

24† He proposed another parable to them.
"The kingdom of heaven may be likened to a
man who sowed good seed in his field. 25† While
everyone was asleep his enemy came and sowed
weeds all through the wheat, and then went off.
26 When the crop grew and bore fruit, the weeds
appeared as well. 27 The slaves of the householder
came to him and said, 'Master, did you not sow
good seed in your field? Where have the weeds
come from?' 28 He answered, 'An enemy has done
this.' His slaves said to him, 'Do you want us to
go and pull them up?' 29 He replied, 'No, if you
pull up the weeds you might uproot the wheat
along with them. 30*† Let them grow together
until harvest; then at harvest time I will say to the
harvesters, "First collect the weeds and tie them
in bundles for burning; but gather the wheat into
my barn." ' "

The Parable of the Mustard Seed

31*† He proposed another parable to them.
"The kingdom of heaven is like a mustard seed
that a person took and sowed in a field. 32*† It is
the smallest of all the seeds, yet when full-grown
it is the largest of plants. It becomes a large bush,
and the 'birds of the sky come and dwell in its
branches.' "

The Parable of the Yeast

33*† He spoke to them another parable. "The
kingdom of heaven is like yeast that a woman
took and mixed with three measures of wheat
flour until the whole batch was leavened."

The Use of Parables

34*† All these things Jesus spoke to the crowds
in parables. He spoke to them only in parables,
35*† to fulfill what had been said through the
prophet:

"I will open my mouth in parables,
I will announce what has lain hidden from
the foundation [of the world]."

The Explanation of the Parable of the Weeds

36† Then, dismissing the crowds, he went into
the house. His disciples approached him and
said, "Explain to us the parable of the weeds in
the field." 37† He said in reply, "He who sows
good seed is the Son of Man, 38† the field is the
world, the good seed the children of the king-
dom. The weeds are the children of the evil one,
39† and the enemy who sows them is the devil.
The harvest is the end of the age, and the har-
vesters are angels. 40 Just as weeds are collected
and burned [up] with fire, so will it be at the
end of the age. 41† The Son of Man will send his
angels, and they will collect out of his kingdom
all who cause others to sin and all evildoers.
42* They will throw them into the fiery furnace,
where there will be wailing and grinding of teeth.
43*† Then the righteous will shine like the sun in
the kingdom of their Father. Whoever has ears
ought to hear.

---

† **13:24–30** This parable is peculiar to Matthew. The comparison in v 24 does not mean that *the kingdom of heaven may be likened* simply to the person in question but to the situation narrated in the whole story. The refusal of *the householder* to allow his *slaves* to separate *the wheat* from *the weeds* while they are still growing is a warning to the disciples not to attempt to anticipate the final judgment of God by a definitive exclusion of sinners from the kingdom. In its present stage it is composed of the good and the bad. The judgment of God alone will eliminate the sinful. Until then there must be patience and the preaching of repentance.

13:25 *Weeds:* darnel, a poisonous weed that in its first stage of growth resembles wheat.

13:30 *Harvest:* a common biblical metaphor for the time of God's judgment; cf Jer 51:33; Jl 4:13; Hos 6:11.

13:31–33 See Mk 4:30–32; Lk 13:18–21. The parables of the mustard seed and the yeast illustrate the same point: the amazing contrast between the small beginnings of the kingdom and its marvelous expansion.

13:32 See Dn 4:7–9, 17–19, where the birds nesting in the tree represent the people of Nebuchadnezzar's kingdom. See also Ez 17:23 and 31:6.

13:33 Except in this Q parable and in 16:12, *yeast* (or "leaven") is, in New Testament usage, a symbol of corruption (see 16:6, 11–12; Mk 8:15; Lk 12:1; 1 Cor 5:6–8; Gal 5:9). *Three measures:* an enormous amount, enough to feed a hundred people. The exaggeration of this element of the parable points to the greatness of the kingdom's effect.

13:34 *Only in parables:* see vv 10–15.

13:35 *The prophet:* some textual witnesses read "Isaiah the prophet." The quotation is actually from Ps 78:2; the first line corresponds to the LXX text of the psalm. The psalm's title ascribes it to Asaph, the founder of one of the guilds of temple musicians. He is called "the prophet" (NAB "the seer") in 2 Chr 29:30, but it is doubtful that Matthew averted to that; for him, any Old Testament text that could be seen as fulfilled in Jesus was prophetic.

13:36 *Dismissing the crowds:* the return of Jesus to the house marks a break with the crowds, who represent unbelieving Israel. From now on his attention is directed more and more to his disciples and to their instruction. The rest of the discourse is addressed to them alone.

13:37–43 In the explanation of the parable of the weeds emphasis lies on the fearful end of the wicked, whereas the parable itself concentrates on patience with them until judgment time.

13:38 *The field is the world:* this presupposes the resurrection of Jesus and the granting to him of "all power in heaven and on earth" (28:18).

13:39 *The end of the age:* this phrase is found only in Matthew (13:40, 49; 24:3; 28:20).

13:41 *His kingdom:* the *kingdom* of *the Son of Man* is distinguished from that of the Father (43); see 1 Cor 15:24–25. The church is the place where Jesus' kingdom is manifested, but his royal authority embraces the entire world; see the note on 13:38.

13:43 See Dn 12:3.

---

* **13:30** Mt 3:12.
13:31–32 Mk 4:30–32; Lk 13:18–19.
13:32 Ez 17:23; 31:6; Dn 4:7–9, 17–19.
13:33 Lk 13:20–21.
13:34–35 Mk 4:33–34.
13:35 Ps 78:2.
13:42 Mt 8:12; Rv 21:8.
13:43 Dn 12:3.

Cultural Connection

The Carpenter's Son

In Matthew 13:55, Jesus is called the carpenter's son. The carpenter is Saint Joseph, who has two feast days attributed to him—May 1 and March 19. In Sicily, there is a custom called Saint Joseph's Altar. The custom began during a time of severe drought and famine in the Middle Ages. The Sicilian people offered intercessory prayers to Saint Joseph for rain so that their crops would grow. Eventually, their prayers were answered, the crops grew, and they harvested grains, fruits, and vegetables in abundance. In thanksgiving to Saint Joseph, the people gathered to share their harvest with the poor people of the area. Bread, wine, vegetables, fruits, eggs, and fish were placed on an altar and then distributed to those in need. The altar filled with the harvest came to be known as Saint Joseph's Altar.

This event is now celebrated annually in Sicily on March 19. Throughout the year, Sicilians also direct many other intercessions toward Saint Joseph, their patron saint. The Sicilians pray not only for good weather and crops but also for health, for family members and friends, and for all kinds of other personal intentions. On March 19, they show their gratitude to Saint Joseph by preparing a Saint Joseph's Altar and by celebrating their good fortune with one another and the community.

▶ Mt 13:55

More Parables†

44* "The kingdom of heaven is like a treasure buried in a field,† which a person finds and hides again, and out of joy goes and sells all that he has and buys that field. 45 Again, the kingdom of heaven is like a merchant searching for fine pearls. 46 When he finds a pearl of great price, he goes and sells all that he has and buys it. 47 Again, the kingdom of heaven is like a net thrown into the sea, which collects fish of every kind. 48 When it is full they haul it ashore and sit down to put what is good into buckets. What is bad they throw away. 49 Thus it will be at the end of the age. The angels will go out and separate the wicked from the righteous 50 and throw them into the fiery furnace, where there will be wailing and grinding of teeth.

Treasures New and Old

51† "Do you understand all these things?" They answered, "Yes." 52† And he replied, "Then every scribe who has been instructed in the kingdom of heaven is like the head of a household who brings from his storeroom both the new and the old." 53 When Jesus finished these parables, he went away from there.

V: Jesus, the Kingdom, and the Church

The Rejection at Nazareth

54*† He came to his native place and taught the people in their synagogue. They were astonished† and said, "Where did this man get such wisdom and mighty deeds?* 55* Is he not the carpenter's

---

† **13:44–50** The first two of the last three parables of the discourse have the same point. The *person* who *finds* a buried *treasure* and the *merchant* who finds *a pearl of great price* sell *all* that they have to acquire these finds; similarly, the one who understands the supreme value of the kingdom gives up whatever he must to obtain it. The *joy* with which this is done is made explicit in the first parable, but it may be presumed in the second also. The concluding parable of the fishnet resembles the explanation of the parable of the weeds with its stress upon the final exclusion of evil persons from the kingdom.

13:44 In the unsettled conditions of Palestine in Jesus' time, it was not unusual to guard valuables by burying them in the ground.

13:51 Matthew typically speaks of the understanding of the disciples.

13:52 Since Matthew tends to identify the disciples and the Twelve (see the note on 10:1), this saying about the Christian *scribe* cannot be taken as applicable to all who accept the message of Jesus. While the Twelve are in many ways representative of all who believe in him, they are also distinguished from them in certain respects. The church of Matthew has leaders among whom are a group designated as "scribes" (23:34). Like the scribes of Israel, they are teachers. It is the Twelve and these their later counterparts to whom this verse applies. The *scribe . . . instructed in the kingdom of heaven* knows both the teaching of Jesus (*the new*) and the law and prophets (*the old*) and provides in his own teaching *both the new and the old* as interpreted and fulfilled by *the new*. On the translation *head of a household* (for the same Greek word translated *householder* in v 27), see the note on 24:45–51.

13:54—17:27 This section is the narrative part of the fourth book of the gospel.

13:54–58 After the Sermon on the Mount the crowds are in

13:44–45 Prv 2:4; 4:7.
13:54–58 Mk 6:1–6; Lk 4:16–30.
13:54 Mt 2:23; Jn 1:46; 7:15.
13:55 Mt 12:46; 27:56; Jn 6:42.

14:1–12

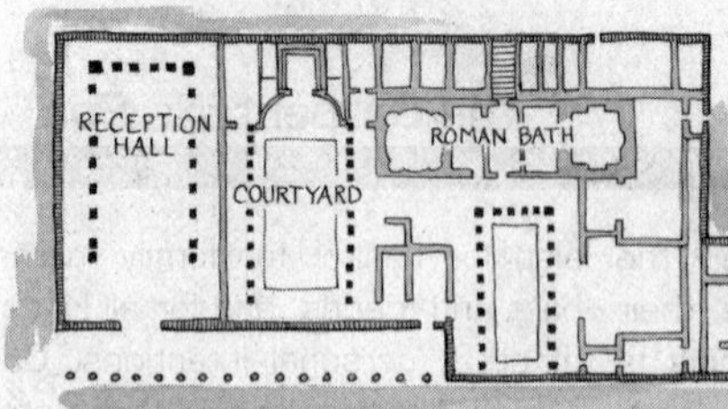

Herod's winter palace

son? Is not his mother named Mary and his broth-
ers James, Joseph, Simon, and Judas? 56 Are not
his sisters all with us? Where did this man get all
this?" 57* And they took offense at him. But Jesus
said to them, "A prophet is not without honor
except in his native place and in his own house."
58 And he did not work many mighty deeds there
because of their lack of faith.

Herod's Opinion of Jesus

14 1*† At that time Herod the tetrarch† *heard
of the reputation of Jesus* 2 and said to his
servants, "This man is John the Baptist. He has
been raised from the dead; that is why mighty
powers are at work in him."

The Death of John the Baptist

3*† Now Herod had arrested John, bound
[him], and put him in prison on account of Hero-
dias, the wife of his brother Philip, 4* for John had
said to him, "It is not lawful for you to have her."
5* Although he wanted to kill him, he feared the
people, for they regarded him as a prophet. 6 But
at a birthday celebration for Herod, the daughter
of Herodias performed a dance before the guests
and delighted Herod 7 so much that he swore to
give her whatever she might ask for. 8 Prompted
by her mother, she said, "Give me here on a plat-
ter the head of John the Baptist." 9 The king was
distressed, but because of his oaths and the guests
who were present, he ordered that it be given,
10 and he had John beheaded in the prison. 11 His
head was brought in on a platter and given to the
girl, who took it to her mother. 12 His disciples
came and took away the corpse and buried him;
and they went and told Jesus.

The Return of the Twelve and the Feeding of the Five Thousand

13*† When Jesus heard of it, he withdrew in a
boat to a deserted place by himself. The crowds
heard of this and followed him on foot from their
towns. 14 When he disembarked and saw the vast
crowd, his heart was moved with pity for them, and
he cured their sick. 15 When it was evening, the dis-
ciples approached him and said, "This is a deserted
place and it is already late; dismiss the crowds so
that they can go to the villages and buy food for
themselves." 16 [Jesus] said to them, "There is no
need for them to go away; give them some food
yourselves." 17 But they said to him, "Five loaves
and two fish are all we have here." 18 Then he said,
"Bring them here to me," 19† and he ordered the
crowds to sit down on the grass. Taking the five
loaves and the two fish, and looking up to heaven,
he said the blessing, broke the loaves, and gave
them to the disciples, who in turn gave them to the
crowds. 20† They all ate and were satisfied, and they
picked up the fragments left over—twelve wicker
baskets full. 21 Those who ate were about five thou-
sand men, not counting women and children.

---

† admiring astonishment at Jesus' teaching (7:28); here the astonishment is of those who take *offense at him.* Familiarity with his background and family leads them to regard him as pretentious. Matthew modifies his Marcan source (6:1–6). Jesus is not the carpenter but *the carpenter's son* (55), "and among his own kin" is omitted (57), *he did not work many mighty deeds* in face of such unbelief (58) rather than the Marcan ". . . he was not able to perform any mighty deed there" (6:5), and there is no mention of his amazement at his townspeople's lack of faith.

14:1–12 The murder of the Baptist by Herod Antipas prefigures the death of Jesus (see 17:12). The Marcan source (6:14–29) is much reduced and in some points changed. In Mark Herod reveres John as a holy man and the desire to kill him is attributed to Herodias (6:19, 20), whereas here that desire is Herod's from the beginning (5).

14:1 *Herod the tetrarch:* Herod Antipas, son of Herod the Great. When the latter died, his territory was divided among three of his surviving sons, Archelaus who received half of it (2:23), Herod Antipas who became ruler of Galilee and Perea, and Philip who became ruler of northern Transjordan. Since he received a quarter of his father's domain, Antipas is accurately designated *tetrarch* ("ruler of a fourth [part]"), although in v 9 Matthew repeats the "king" of his Marcan source (6:26).

14:3 Herodias was not the wife of Herod's half-brother Philip but of another half-brother, Herod Boethus. The union was prohibited by Lv 18:16; 20:21. According to Josephus (*Antiquities* 18:5, 2 §§116–19), Herod imprisoned and then executed John because he feared that the Baptist's influence over the people might enable him to lead a rebellion.

14:13–21 The feeding of the five thousand is the only miracle of Jesus that is recounted in all four gospels. The principal reason for that may be that it was seen as anticipating the Eucharist and the final banquet in the kingdom (8:11; 26:29), but it looks not only forward but backward, to the feeding of Israel with manna in the desert at the time of the Exodus (Ex 16), a miracle that in some contemporary Jewish expectation would be repeated in the messianic age (2 Baruch 29:8). It may also be meant to recall Elisha's feeding a hundred men with small provisions (2 Kgs 4:42–44).

14:19 The *taking,* saying the blessing, breaking, and giving to the disciples correspond to the actions of Jesus over the bread at the Last Supper (26:26). Since they were usual at any Jewish meal, that correspondence does not necessarily indicate a eucharistic reference here. Matthew's silence about Jesus' dividing the fish among the people (Mk 6:41) is perhaps more significant in that regard.

14:20 *The fragments left over:* as in Elisha's miracle, food was *left over* after all had been fed. The word *fragments* (Greek *klasmata*) is used, in the singular, of the broken bread of the Eucharist in *Didache* 9:3–4.

13:57 Jn 4:44.
14:1–12 Mk 6:14–29.
14:1 Lk 3:1.
14:1–2 Lk 9:7–9.
14:3–4 Lk 3:19–20.
14:4 Lv 18:16; 20:21.
14:5 Mt 21:26.
14:13–21 Mt 15:32–38; Mk 6:32–44; Lk 9:10–17; Jn 6:1–13.

The Walking on the Water

22*† Then he made the disciples get into the
boat and precede him to the other side, while
he dismissed the crowds. 23* After doing so, he
went up on the mountain by himself to pray.
When it was evening he was there alone. 24 Mean-
while the boat, already a few miles offshore, was
being tossed about by the waves, for the wind
was against it. 25† During the fourth watch of the
night, he came toward them, walking on the sea.
26 When the disciples saw him walking on the sea
they were terrified. "It is a ghost," they said, and
they cried out in fear. 27† At once [Jesus] spoke
to them, "Take courage, it is I; do not be afraid."
28 Peter said to him in reply, "Lord, if it is you,
command me to come to you on the water." 29 He
said, "Come." Peter got out of the boat and began
to walk on the water toward Jesus. 30* But when
he saw how [strong] the wind was he became
frightened; and, beginning to sink, he cried out,
"Lord, save me!" 31† Immediately Jesus stretched
out his hand and caught him, and said to him,
"O you of little faith, why did you doubt?" 32 Af-
ter they got into the boat, the wind died down.
33*† Those who were in the boat did him hom-
age, saying, "Truly, you are the Son of God."

The Healings at Gennesaret

34* After making the crossing, they came to
land at Gennesaret. 35 When the men of that
place recognized him, they sent word to all the
surrounding country. People brought to him all
those who were sick 36* and begged him that
they might touch only the tassel on his cloak,
and as many as touched it were healed.

The Tradition of the Elders

15 1*† Then Pharisees and scribes came to
Jesus from Jerusalem and said, 2*† "Why
do your disciples break the tradition of the elders?

Live It!

Do You Trust Jesus?

At this point in the Gospel of Matthew, different groups are beginning to line up for or against Jesus. The Pharisees, Sadducees, and scribes do not trust him. The disciples still follow Jesus, but they do not yet understand who he really is. In chapters 14–17, through several signs and wonders, the true identity of Jesus is revealed to the disciples. Peter in particular is being prepared for his role as leader.

Of the four Gospels, only Matthew includes the story of Peter's walking on the water. If you have gotten acquainted with Peter (see "Introducing Peter the Rock," near Mt 16:13–20), it will not surprise you that he was willing to take the risk. But why does Peter start to sink? When he is focused on Jesus, everything is fine. It is when he takes his eyes off Jesus, noticing the fierce wind, that he begins to sink.

Jesus invites you to risk a relationship with him. You have to step out in faith, maybe leaving some old ways of life behind. Learn from Peter to keep your focus on Jesus. As the disciples learned, this is no ordinary man but the Son of God! Following Jesus might get scary or difficult at times, but all great adventures involve some risk.

▶ **Mt 14:22–33**

---

† **14:22–33** The disciples, laboring against the turbulent sea, are saved by Jesus. For his power over the waters, see the note on 8:26. Here that power is expressed also by his *walking on the sea* (25; cf Ps 77:20; Jb 9:8). Matthew has inserted into the Marcan story (Mk 6:45–52) material that belongs to his special traditions on Peter (28–31).

14:25 *The fourth watch of the night:* between 3 a.m. and 6 a.m. The Romans divided the twelve hours between 6 p.m. and 6 a.m. into four equal parts called "watches."

14:27 *It is I:* see the note on Mk 6:50.

14:31 *You of little faith:* see the note on 6:30. *Why did you doubt?:* the verb is peculiar to Matthew and occurs elsewhere only in 28:17.

14:33 This confession is in striking contrast to the Marcan parallel (6:51) where the disciples are "completely astounded."

15:1–20 This dispute begins with the question of the Pharisees and scribes why Jesus' disciples are breaking *the tradition of the elders* about washing one's hands before eating (2). Jesus' counterquestion accuses his opponents of breaking *the commandment of God for the sake of* their *tradition* (3) and illustrates this by their interpretation of the commandment of the Decalogue concerning parents (4–6). Denouncing them as hypocrites, he applies to them a derogatory prophecy of Isaiah (7–8). Then with a wider audience (*the crowd,* 10) he goes beyond the violation of tradition with which the dispute has started. The parable (11) is an attack on the Mosaic law concerning clean and unclean foods, similar to those antitheses that abrogate the law (5:31–32, 33–34, 38–39). After a warning to his disciples not to follow the moral guidance of the Pharisees (13–14), he explains the *parable* (15) to them, saying that defilement comes not from what *enters the mouth* (17) but from the evil thoughts and deeds that rise from within, *from the heart* (18–20). The last verse returns to the starting point of the dispute (eating *with unwashed hands*). Because of Matthew's omission of Mk 7:19b, some scholars think that Matthew has weakened the Marcan repudiation of the Mosaic food laws. But that half verse is ambiguous in the Greek, which may be the reason for its omission here.

15:2 *The tradition of the elders:* see the note on Mk 7:5. The purpose of the handwashing was to remove defilement caused by contact with what was ritually unclean.

14:22–33 Mk 6:45–52; Jn 6:16–21.
14:23 Mk 1:35; Lk 5:16; 6:12.
14:30–31 Mt 8:25–26.
14:33 Mt 16:16.
14:34–36 Mk 6:53–56.
14:36 Mt 9:20–22.
15:1–20 Mk 7:1–23.
15:2 Lk 11:38.

Cultural Connection

A Prayer for Healing Humankind

In Matthew 15:1–20, Jesus addresses the hypocrisy of the Jewish leaders who manipulate the law to their own good. They and the people who follow them are blind to the results of their evil intentions. In this prayer, the Ojibwa (or Anishinabe) recognize the need for humans to overcome the evil that resides within the human heart:

Grandfather,
Look at our brokenness.
We know that in all creation
Only the human family
Has strayed from the Sacred
Way.
We know that we are the
ones
Who must come back
together
To walk in the Sacred Way.
Grandfather,
Sacred One,
Teach us love, compassion,
and honor
That we may heal the earth
And heal each other.

▶ **Mt 15:1–20**

They do not wash [their] hands when they eat a
meal." 3† He said to them in reply, "And why do
you break the commandment of God for the sake
of your tradition? 4* For God said, 'Honor your
father and your mother,' and 'Whoever curses
father or mother shall die.' 5† But you say, 'Who-
ever says to father or mother, "Any support you
might have had from me is dedicated to God,"
6 need not honor his father.' You have nullified
the word of God for the sake of your tradition.
7 Hypocrites, well did Isaiah prophesy about you
when he said:

8*† 'This people honors me with their lips,
but their hearts are far from me;
9* in vain do they worship me,
teaching as doctrines human precepts.'"

10* He summoned the crowd and said to them,
"Hear and understand. 11 It is not what enters
one's mouth that defiles that person; but what
comes out of the mouth is what defiles one."
12 Then his disciples approached and said to
him, "Do you know that the Pharisees took of-
fense when they heard what you said?" 13† He
said in reply, "Every plant that my heavenly
Father has not planted will be uprooted. 14* Let
them alone; they are blind guides [of the blind].
If a blind person leads a blind person, both will
fall into a pit." 15† Then Peter said to him in re-
ply, "Explain [this] parable to us." 16 He said to
them, "Are even you still without understand-
ing? 17 Do you not realize that everything that
enters the mouth passes into the stomach and is
expelled into the latrine? 18* But the things that
come out of the mouth come from the heart,
and they defile. 19† For from the heart come evil
thoughts, murder, adultery, unchastity, theft,
false witness, blasphemy. 20 These are what defile
a person, but to eat with unwashed hands does
not defile."

The Canaanite Woman's Faith

21*† Then Jesus went from that place and
withdrew to the region of Tyre and Sidon. 22 And
behold, a Canaanite woman of that district came
and called out, "Have pity on me, Lord, Son of
David! My daughter is tormented by a demon."
23 But he did not say a word in answer to her. His
disciples came and asked him, "Send her away,

† **15:3–4** For the commandment see Ex 20:12 (// Dt 5:16); 21:17. The honoring of one's parents had to do with supporting them in their needs.

15:5 See the note on Mk 7:11.

15:8 The text of Is 29:13 is quoted approximately according to the Septuagint.

15:13–14 Jesus leads his disciples away from the teaching authority of the Pharisees.

15:15 Matthew specifies *Peter* as the questioner, unlike Mk 7:17. Given his tendency to present the disciples as more understanding than in his Marcan source, it is noteworthy that here he retains the Marcan rebuke, although in a slightly milder form. This may be due to his wish to correct the Jewish Christians within his church who still held to the food laws and thus separated themselves from Gentile Christians who did not observe them.

15:19 The Marcan list of thirteen things that defile (7:21–22) is here reduced to seven that partially cover the content of the Decalogue.

15:21–28 See the note on 8:5–13.

* **15:4** Ex 20:12; 21:17; Lv 20:9; Dt 5:16; Prv 20:20.
15:8 Is 29:13 LXX.
15:9 Col 2:23.
15:10 Mk 7:14.
15:14 Mt 23:16, 19, 24; Lk 6:39; Jn 9:40.
15:18 Mt 12:34.
15:21–28 Mk 7:24–30.

for she keeps calling out after us." 24† He said in
reply, "I was sent only to the lost sheep of the
house of Israel." 25* But the woman came and
did him homage, saying, "Lord, help me." 26† He
said in reply, "It is not right to take the food of
the children and throw it to the dogs." 27 She
said, "Please, Lord, for even the dogs eat the
scraps that fall from the table of their masters."
28*† Then Jesus said to her in reply, "O woman,
great is your faith! Let it be done for you as you
wish." And her daughter was healed from that
hour.

The Healing of Many People

29 Moving on from there Jesus walked by the
Sea of Galilee, went up on the mountain, and sat
down there. 30* Great crowds came to him, hav-
ing with them the lame, the blind, the deformed,
the mute, and many others. They placed them at
his feet, and he cured them. 31 The crowds were
amazed when they saw the mute speaking, the
deformed made whole, the lame walking, and
the blind able to see, and they glorified the God
of Israel.

The Feeding of the Four Thousand

32*† Jesus summoned his disciples and said,
"My heart is moved with pity for the crowd, for
they have been with me now for three days and
have nothing to eat. I do not want to send them
away hungry, for fear they may collapse on the
way." 33 The disciples said to him, "Where could
we ever get enough bread in this deserted place
to satisfy such a crowd?" 34 Jesus said to them,
"How many loaves do you have?" "Seven," they
replied, "and a few fish." 35 He ordered the crowd
to sit down on the ground. 36† Then he took the
seven loaves and the fish, gave thanks, broke the
loaves, and gave them to the disciples, who in
turn gave them to the crowds. 37* They all ate
and were satisfied. They picked up the fragments
left over—seven baskets full. 38 Those who ate
were four thousand men, not counting women
and children. 39 And when he had dismissed the
crowds, he got into the boat and came to the dis-
trict of Magadan.

The Demand for a Sign

16 1*† The Pharisees and Sadducees came
and, to test him, asked him to show
them a sign from heaven. 2† He said to them
in reply, "[In the evening you say, 'Tomorrow
will be fair, for the sky is red'; 3* and, in the
morning, 'Today will be stormy, for the sky is
red and threatening.' You know how to judge
the appearance of the sky, but you cannot judge
the signs of the times.] 4*† An evil and unfaith-
ful generation seeks a sign, but no sign will be
given it except the sign of Jonah." Then he left
them and went away.

The Leaven of the Pharisees and Sadducees

5*† In coming to the other side of the sea, the
disciples had forgotten to bring bread. 6*† Jesus
said to them, "Look out, and beware of the
leaven of the Pharisees and Sadducees." 7† They
concluded among themselves, saying, "It is be-
cause we have brought no bread." 8 When Jesus
became aware of this he said, "You of little
faith, why do you conclude among yourselves
that it is because you have no bread? 9* Do you
not yet understand, and do you not remember
the five loaves for the five thousand, and how
many wicker baskets you took up? 10* Or the
seven loaves for the four thousand, and how
many baskets you took up? 11 How do you
not comprehend that I was not speaking to
you about bread? Beware of the leaven of the

†

15:24 See the note on 10:5–6.

15:26 *The children:* the people of Israel. *Dogs:* see the note on 7:6.

15:28 As in the case of the cure of the centurion's servant (8:10), Matthew ascribes Jesus' granting the request to the woman's *great faith,* a point not made equally explicit in the Marcan parallel (7:24–30).

15:32–39 Most probably this story is a doublet of that of the feeding of the five thousand (14:13–21). It differs from it notably only in that Jesus takes the initiative, not the disciples (32), and in the numbers: the crowd has been with Jesus *three days* (32), *seven loaves* are multiplied (36), *seven baskets* of *fragments* remain after the feeding (37), and *four thousand* men are fed (38).

15:36 *Gave thanks:* see 14:19, "said the blessing." There is no difference in meaning. The thanksgiving was a blessing of God for his benefits.

16:1 *A sign from heaven:* see the note on 12:38–42.

16:2–3 The answer of Jesus in these verses is omitted in many important textual witnesses, and it is very uncertain that it is an original part of this gospel. It resembles Lk 12:54–56 and may have been inserted from there. It rebukes the Pharisees and Sadducees who are able to read indications of coming weather but not the indications of the coming kingdom in the signs that Jesus does offer, his mighty deeds and teaching.

16:4 See the notes on 12:39, 40.

16:5–12 Jesus' warning his disciples against *the teaching of the Pharisees and Sadducees* comes immediately before his promise to confer on Peter the authority to bind and to loose on earth (Mt 16:19), an authority that will be confirmed in heaven. Such authority most probably has to do, at least in part, with teaching. The rejection of the teaching authority of the Pharisees (see also Mt 12:12–14) prepares for a new one derived from Jesus.

16:6 *Leaven:* see the note on Mt 13:33. *Sadducees:* Matthew's Marcan source speaks rather of "the leaven of Herod" (Mk 8:15).

16:7–11 The disciples, men *of little faith,* misunderstand Jesus' metaphorical use of *leaven,* forgetting that, as the feeding of the crowds shows, he is not at a loss to provide them with bread.

15:25 Mt 10:6.
15:28 Mt 8:10.
15:30 Is 35:5–6.
15:32–39 Mk 8:1–10.
15:37 Mt 16:10.
16:1–10 Mk 8:11–21.
16:3 Lk 12:54–56.
16:4 Mt 12:39; Jon 2:1.
16:5–12 Mk 8:14–21.
16:6 Lk 12:1.
16:9 Mt 14:17–21; Jn 6:9.
16:10 Mt 15:34–38.

Catholic Connection

The Church

Even after Jesus has been teaching and performing miracles for a while, people are still confused about his identity. So Jesus turns to the disciples and asks, "Who do you say that I am?" (Mt 16:15). Peter alone answers correctly, saying Jesus is the Messiah. As a result, Jesus tells Peter that he is clearly blessed and then proceeds to tell Peter that he will build the Church upon him and give him the keys to the kingdom of heaven!

Two thousand years later, the Catholic Church still recognizes the authority of Peter through Peter's successor the Pope, the Bishop of Rome. Just as Peter was the leader and sign of unity for the disciples, the Pope serves as the leader and sign of unity for the bishops and all the faithful. As the leader, the Pope has ultimate authority over the Church as both pastor and teacher. The Pope is also blessed just like Peter. For example, when the Pope makes an official declaration of doctrine addressing faith and morals, God ensures the truth of the doctrine. We call this papal infallibility.

As the Pope is the successor of Peter, the bishops are the successors of the Apostles. Each bishop is responsible for leading and ministering to the people within their own area, called a diocese. Under the authority of the bishop are the priests and deacons who aid him in his duties to care for the faithful. The bishops also work together in union with the Pope to address issues concerning the wider Church.

In addition to those already mentioned, the Catholic Church consists of people living a consecrated life. Those in consecrated life are not ordained but have dedicated their lives to a unique form of service to the Lord. Among them are nuns and brothers who have taken various vows, or promises, to live a certain lifestyle dedicated to Christ.

Finally, the main body of the Church, or the largest group, is the laity. The laity are those members who are not ordained or living a consecrated life. The laity has its own role to play in the mission of the Church. These individuals are called to seek the Reign of God in their everyday lives at school, work, or with family. They are called to proclaim the Good News and often may be the first or only ones able to bring the Good News to someone. By virtue of their Baptism, the laity are also able to bless the world by uniting their everyday lives to the sacrifice Christ made on the cross and by offering their lives to God.

Together all the different roles in the Church work together as one to bear witness that Jesus is the Son of God, the Messiah.

▶ **Mt 16:13–20**

Catechism, nos. 871–945

Pharisees and Sadducees." 12† Then they under-
stood that he was not telling them to beware of
the leaven of bread, but of the teaching of the
Pharisees and Sadducees.

Peter's Confession about Jesus†

13* When Jesus went into the region of Caes-
area Philippi† he asked his disciples, "Who do
people say that the Son of Man is?" 14*† They
replied, "Some say John the Baptist, others Eli-
jah, still others Jeremiah or one of the prophets."
15 He said to them, "But who do you say that I
am?" 16*† Simon Peter said in reply, "You are
the Messiah, the Son of the living God." 17† Jesus
said to him in reply, "Blessed are you, Simon son
of Jonah. For flesh and blood has not revealed
this to you, but my heavenly Father. 18*† And so
I say to you, you are Peter, and upon this rock I
will build my church, and the gates of the nether-
world shall not prevail against it. 19*† I will give

Introducing...

Peter the Rock

What images does the name Saint Peter bring to your mind? The simple fisherman named Simon who was among the first disciples called by Jesus (see Mt 4:18, Mk 1:16; Lk 5:10)? the hopeful believer who first recognized Jesus as the Messiah (see Mt 16:16, Mk 8:29, Lk 9:20)? the fearful friend who denied Jesus three times (see Mt 26:69–74, Mk 14:66–72, Lk 22:54–61, Jn 18:15–27)? the leader of the early Church, whom we recognize as the first Pope (see Jn 21:15, Acts 2:14)? Peter is all these things and more. The Bible paints a picture of a very human leader with sins and weaknesses along with many gifts and great faith.

The author of Matthew uses a play on words to make a statement about Peter as the foundation of the Church. The new name Jesus gives him—Peter—means "rock." So Jesus is saying, "You are a rock, and on this rock I will build my church" (see Mt 16:18). The Catholic Church uses this Scripture passage as support for its teaching on the Pope's position as the spiritual leader and highest authority of the Church. Peter's primacy as the first of Jesus' Apostles is understood to be passed on to the current Pope, through the succession of popes who go back to the beginnings of the Church at Rome.

▶ **Mt 16:13–20**

---

† **16:12** After his rebuke, the disciples understand that by *leaven* he meant the corrupting influence of *the teaching of the Pharisees and Sadducees.* The evangelist probably understands this *teaching* as common to both groups. Since at the time of Jesus' ministry the two differed widely on points of *teaching,* e.g., the resurrection of the dead, and at the time of the evangelist the Sadducee party was no longer a force in Judaism, the supposed common *teaching* fits neither period. The disciples' eventual understanding of Jesus' warning contrasts with their continuing obtuseness in the Marcan parallel (Mk 8:14–21).

16:13–20 The Marcan confession of Jesus as Messiah, made by Peter as spokesman for the other disciples (Mk 8:27–29; cf also Lk 9:18–20), is modified significantly here. The confession is of Jesus both as *Messiah* and as *Son of the living God* (Mt 16:16). Jesus' response, drawn principally from material peculiar to Matthew, attributes the confession to a divine revelation granted to Peter alone (Mt 16:17) and makes him the *rock* on which Jesus *will build* his *church* (Mt 16:18) and the disciple whose authority in the church *on earth* will be confirmed *in heaven,* i.e., by God (Mt 16:19).

16:13 *Caesarea Philippi:* situated about twenty miles north of the Sea of Galilee in the territory ruled by Philip, a son of Herod the Great, tetrarch from 4 B.C. until his death in A.D. 34 (see the note on Mt 14:1). He rebuilt the town of Paneas, naming it *Caesarea* in honor of the emperor, and *Philippi* ("of Philip") to distinguish it from the seaport in Samaria that was also called Caesarea. *Who do people say that the Son of Man is?:* although the question differs from the Marcan parallel (Mk 8:27: "Who . . . that I am?"), the meaning is the same, for Jesus here refers to himself as the *Son of Man* (cf Mt 16:15).

16:14 *John the Baptist:* see 14:2. *Elijah:* cf Mal 3:23–24; Sir 48:10; and see the note on 3:4. *Jeremiah:* an addition of Matthew to the Marcan source.

16:16 *The Son of the living God:* see 2:15; 3:17. The addition of this exalted title to the Marcan confession eliminates whatever ambiguity was attached to the title Messiah. This, among other things, supports the view proposed by many scholars that Matthew has here combined his source's confession with a post-resurrectional confession of faith in Jesus as *Son of the living God* that belonged to the appearance of the risen Jesus to Peter; cf 1 Cor 15:5; Lk 24:34.

16:17 *Flesh and blood:* a Semitic expression for human beings, especially in their weakness. *Has not revealed this . . . but my heavenly Father:* that Peter's faith is spoken of as coming not through human means but through a revelation from God is similar to Paul's description of his recognition of who Jesus was; see Gal 1:15–16, ". . . when [God] . . . was pleased to reveal his Son to me. . . ."

16:18 *You are Peter, and upon this rock I will build my church:* the Aramaic word *kēpā'* meaning *rock* and transliterated into Greek as *Kēphas* is the name by which Peter is called in the Pauline letters (1 Cor 1:12; 3:22; 9:5; 15:4; Gal 1:18; 2:9, 11, 14) except in Gal 2:7–8 ("Peter"). It is translated as *Petros* ("Peter") in Jn 1:42. The presumed original Aramaic of Jesus' statement would have been, in English, "You are the Rock (*Kēpā'*) and upon this rock (*kēpā'*) I will build my church." The Greek text probably means the same, for the difference in gender between the masculine noun *petros,* the disciple's new name, and the feminine noun *petra* (rock) may be due simply to the unsuitability of using a feminine noun as the proper name of a male. Although the two words were generally used with slightly different nuances, they were also used interchangeably with the same meaning, "rock." *Church:* this word (Greek *ekklēsia*) occurs in the gospels only here and in 18:17 (twice). There are several possibilities for an Aramaic original. Jesus' *church* means the community that he *will* gather and that, like a building, will have Peter as its solid foundation. That function of Peter consists in his being witness to Jesus as *the Messiah, the Son of the living God. The gates of the netherworld shall not prevail against it:* the netherworld (Greek *Hadēs,* the abode of the dead) is conceived of as a walled city whose *gates* will not close in upon the church of Jesus, i.e., it will not be overcome by the power of death.

16:19 *The keys to the kingdom of heaven:* the image of *the keys* is probably drawn from Is 22:15–25, where Eliakim, who succeeds Shebna as master of the palace, is given "the key of the House of David," which he authoritatively "opens" and "shuts" (22:22). *Whatever*

16:13–16 Mk 8:27–29; Lk 9:18–20.
16:14 Mt 14:2.
16:16 Jn 6:69.
16:18 Jn 1:42.
16:19 Is 22:22; Rv 3:7.

MT

Cultural Connection

The Principle of *Ujamaa*

A man who won't die for something is not fit to live.
(Martin Luther King Jr.)

Jesus tells us that we need to leave behind our old lives of selfishness and embrace a new way of life marked by caring about the needs of others. Only then can the Spirit of the Lord abound. Martin Luther King Jr. practiced this new way of life in his dream for a better day for African Americans—a dream he was willing to work and die for.

The Kwanzaa principle of *ujamaa*, or cooperative economics, requires this kind of selfless love for others. To practice *ujamaa* means to share resources with our brothers and sisters, to support one another's businesses, and to live so that everybody receives what they need to prosper. Jesus' words challenge us to build up our communities, preserving the gains we have made and laying foundations for the success of those who come after us. The cost is our me-first attitudes, but the reward is a new life of justice and freedom.

Dear God, my humanness wants to hoard myself; my spirit wants to give!

▶ Mt 16:25

you the keys to the kingdom of heaven. Whatever you bind on earth shall be bound in heaven;
and whatever you loose on earth shall be loosed
in heaven." 20* † Then he strictly ordered his disciples to tell no one that he was the Messiah.

The First Prediction of the Passion†

21* From that time on, Jesus began to show his
disciples that he† must go to Jerusalem and suffer greatly from the elders, the chief priests, and
the scribes, and be killed and on the third day be
raised.* 22† Then Peter took him aside and began
to rebuke him, "God forbid, Lord! No such thing
shall ever happen to you." 23*He turned and said
to Peter, "Get behind me, Satan! You are an obstacle to me. You are thinking not as God does,
but as human beings do."

The Conditions of Discipleship†

24* Then Jesus said to his disciples, "Whoever wishes to come after me must deny himself,† take up his cross, and follow me. 25*† For

you bind . . . loosed in heaven: there are many instances in rabbinic literature of the binding-loosing imagery. Of the several meanings given there to the metaphor, two are of special importance here: the giving of authoritative teaching, and the lifting or imposing of the ban of excommunication. It is disputed whether the image of *the keys* and that of binding and loosing are different metaphors meaning the same thing. In any case, the promise of the keys is given to Peter alone. In 18:18 all the disciples are given the power of binding and loosing, but the context of that verse suggests that there the power of excommunication alone is intended. That *the keys* are those to *the kingdom of heaven* and that Peter's exercise of authority in the church *on earth* will be confirmed *in heaven* show an intimate connection between, but not an identification of, the church and *the kingdom of heaven.*

16:20 Cf Mk 8:30. Matthew makes explicit that the prohibition has to do with speaking of Jesus as *the Messiah;* see the note on Mk 8:27–30.

16:21–23 This first prediction of the passion follows Mk 8:31–33 in the main and serves as a corrective to an understanding of Jesus' messiahship as solely one of glory and triumph. By his addition of *from that time on* (21) Matthew has emphasized that Jesus' revelation of his coming suffering and death marks a new phase of the gospel. Neither this nor the two later passion predictions (17:22–23; 20:17–19) can be taken as sayings that, as they stand, go back to Jesus himself. However, it is probable that he foresaw that his mission would entail suffering and perhaps death, but was confident that he would ultimately be vindicated by God (see 26:29).

16:21 *He:* the Marcan parallel (8:31) has "the Son of Man." Since Matthew has already designated Jesus by that title (13), its omission here is not significant. The Matthean prediction is equally about the sufferings of the Son of Man. *Must:* this necessity is part of the tradition of all the synoptics; cf Mk 8:31; Lk 9:21. *The elders, the chief priests, and the scribes:* see the note on Mk 8:31. *On the third day:* so also Lk 9:22, against the Marcan "after three days" (8:31). Matthew's formulation is, in the Greek, almost identical with the pre-Pauline fragment of the kerygma in 1 Cor 15:4, and also with Hos 6:2, which many take to be the Old Testament background to the confession that Jesus was raised *on the third day.* Josephus uses "after three days" and "on the third day" interchangeably (*Antiquities* 7, 11, 6 §§280–81; 8:8, 1–2 §§214, 218) and there is probably no difference in meaning between the two phrases.

16:22–23 Peter's refusal to accept Jesus' predicted suffering and death is seen as a satanic attempt to deflect Jesus from his God-appointed course, and the disciple is addressed in terms that recall Jesus' dismissal of the devil in the temptation account (4:10: "Get away, Satan!"). Peter's satanic purpose is emphasized by Matthew's addition to the Marcan source of the words *You are an obstacle to me.*

16:24–28 A readiness to follow Jesus even to giving up one's life for him is the condition for true discipleship; this will be repaid by him at the final judgment.

16:24 *Deny himself:* to deny someone is to disown him (see 10:33; 26:34–35) and to deny oneself is to disown oneself as the center of one's existence.

16:25 See the notes on 10:38, 39.

16:20 Mk 8:30; Lk 9:21.
16:21–28 Mk 8:31—9:1; Lk 9:22–27.
16:21 Mt 17:22–23; 20:17–19.
16:23 Mt 4:10.
16:24 Lk 14:27.
16:25 Lk 17:33; Jn 12:25.

whoever wishes to save his life will lose it, but
whoever loses his life for my sake will find it.
26 What profit would there be for one to gain
the whole world and forfeit his life? Or what
can one give in exchange for his life? 27*† For
the Son of Man will come with his angels in his
Father's glory, and then he will repay everyone
according to his conduct. 28† Amen, I say to you,
there are some standing here who will not taste
death until they see the Son of Man coming in
his kingdom."

The Transfiguration of Jesus†

17 1* After six days Jesus took Peter, James,
and John his brother, and led them up a
high mountain by themselves.† 2*† And he was
transfigured before them; his face shone like the
sun and his clothes became white as light. 3† And
behold, Moses and Elijah appeared to them,
conversing with him. 4† Then Peter said to Jesus
in reply, "Lord, it is good that we are here. If you
wish, I will make three tents here, one for you,
one for Moses, and one for Elijah." 5*† While
he was still speaking, behold, a bright cloud
cast a shadow over them, then from the cloud
came a voice that said, "This is my beloved Son,
with whom I am well pleased; listen to him."
6† When the disciples heard this, they fell pros-
trate and were very much afraid. 7 But Jesus came
and touched them, saying, "Rise, and do not
be afraid." 8 And when the disciples raised their
eyes, they saw no one else but Jesus alone.

The Coming of Elijah†

9* As they were coming down from the moun-
tain, Jesus charged them, "Do not tell the vision†
to anyone until the Son of Man has been raised
from the dead." 10*† Then the disciples asked
him, "Why do the scribes say that Elijah must
come first?" 11*† He said in reply, "Elijah will
indeed come and restore all things; 12* but I tell
you that Elijah has already come, and they did
not recognize him but did to him whatever they
pleased. So also will the Son of Man suffer at
their hands." 13† Then the disciples understood
that he was speaking to them of John the Bap-
tist.

The Healing of a Boy with a Demon

14*† When they came to the crowd a man
approached, knelt down before him, 15† and said,
"Lord, have pity on my son, for he is a lunatic and
suffers severely; often he falls into fire, and often
into water. 16 I brought him to your disciples, but

16:27 The parousia and final judgment are described in 25:31 in terms almost identical with these.

16:28 *Coming in his kingdom:* since the *kingdom* of *the Son of Man* has been described as "the world" and Jesus' sovereignty precedes his final coming in glory (13:38, 41), the *coming* in this verse is not the parousia as in the preceding but the manifestation of Jesus' rule after his resurrection; see the notes on 13:38, 41.

17:1–8 The account of the transfiguration confirms that Jesus is the *Son* of God (5) and points to fulfillment of the prediction that he will come *in his Father's glory* at the end of the age (16:27). It has been explained by some as a resurrection appearance retrojected into the time of Jesus' ministry, but that is not probable since the account lacks many of the usual elements of the resurrection-appearance narratives. It draws upon motifs from the Old Testament and noncanonical Jewish apocalyptic literature that express the presence of the heavenly and the divine, e.g., brilliant light, white garments, and the overshadowing cloud.

17:1 These three disciples are also taken apart from the others by Jesus in Gethsemane (26:37). *A high mountain:* this has been identified with Tabor or Hermon, but probably no specific mountain was intended by the evangelist or by his Marcan source (9:2). Its meaning is theological rather than geographical, possibly recalling the revelation to Moses on Mount Sinai (Ex 24:12–18) and to Elijah at the same place (1 Kgs 19:8–18; Horeb Sinai).

17:2 *His face shone like the sun:* this is a Matthean addition; cf Dn 10:6. *His clothes became white as light:* cf Dn 7:9, where the clothing of God appears "snow bright." For the *white* garments of other heavenly beings, see Rv 4:4; 7:9; 19:14.

17:3 See the note on Mk 9:5.

17:4 *Three tents:* the booths in which the Israelites lived during the feast of Tabernacles (cf Jn 7:2) were meant to recall their ancestors' dwelling in booths during the journey from Egypt to the promised land (Lv 23:39–42). The same Greek word, *skēnē,* here translated *tents,* is used in the LXX for the booths of that feast, and some scholars have suggested that there is an allusion here to that liturgical custom.

17:5 *Cloud cast a shadow over them:* see the note on Mk 9:7. *This is my beloved Son . . . listen to him:* cf 3:17. The voice repeats the baptismal proclamation about Jesus, with the addition of the command *listen to him.* The latter is a reference to Dt 18:15 in which the Israelites are commanded to *listen to* the prophet like Moses whom God will raise up for them. The command to *listen to* Jesus is general, but in this context it probably applies particularly to the preceding predictions of his passion and resurrection (16:21) and of his coming (16:27, 28).

17:6–7 A Matthean addition; cf Dn 10:9–10, 18–19.

17:9–13 In response to the disciples' question about the expected return of Elijah, Jesus interprets the mission of the Baptist as the fulfillment of that expectation. But that was not suspected by those who opposed and finally killed him, and Jesus predicts a similar fate for himself.

17:9 *The vision:* Matthew alone uses this word to describe the transfiguration. *Until the Son of Man has been raised from the dead:* only in the light of Jesus' resurrection can the meaning of his life and mission be truly understood; until then no testimony to *the vision* will lead people to faith.

17:10 See the notes on 3:4; 16:14.

17:11–12 The preceding question and this answer may reflect later controversy with Jews who objected to the Christian claims for Jesus that Elijah had not yet come.

17:13 See 11:14.

17:14–20 Matthew has greatly shortened the Marcan story (9:14–29). Leaving aside several details of the boy's illness, he concentrates on the need for faith, not so much on the part of the boy's father (as does Mark, for Matthew omits Mk 9:22b–24) but on that of his own disciples whose inability to drive out the demon is ascribed to their *little faith* (20).

17:15 *A lunatic:* this description of the boy is peculiar to Matthew. The word occurs in the New Testament only here and in 4:24 and means one affected or struck by the moon. The symptoms of the boy's illness point to epilepsy, and attacks of this were thought to be caused by phases of the moon.

16:27 Mt 25:31–33; Jb 34:11; Ps 62:13; Jer 17:10; 2 Thes 1:7–8.
17:1–8 Mk 9:2–8; Lk 9:28–36.
17:2 Mt 28:3; Dn 7:9; 10:6; Rv 4:4; 7:9; 19:14.
17:5 Mt 3:17; Dt 18:15; 2 Pt 1:17.
17:9–13 Mk 9:9–13.
17:10 Mal 3:23–24.
17:11 Lk 1:17.
17:12–13 Mt 11:14.
17:14–21 Mk 9:14–29; Lk 9:37–43.

MT

Catholic Connection

The Old Testament and the New Testament

The word *old* can often be taken to mean "outdated" or "no longer useful." Unfortunately, some people assume those meanings when they hear the words *Old Testament.* But the Gospel of Matthew is very clear that the Old Testament is indeed relevant (see 5:17–20) and that Jesus is its fulfillment.

Consider the story of the Transfiguration in Matthew's Gospel, which is packed with allusions and references to the Old Testament. According to the Gospel, the event took place on a mountain, which immediately calls to mind Moses' meeting with God and establishing the covenant on Mount Sinai (see Ex 24:12–18). The Gospel of Matthew also says that Moses (who represents the law) and Elijah (who represents the prophets) appeared with Jesus on the mountain; their presence highlights how Jesus' work is in agreement with the Old Testament law and prophets. Another allusion can be found in the cloud that accompanies God's presence during the scene, a cloud much like the one that led the Israelites during their wanderings in the desert (see Ex 40:34–37). A final reference to the Old Testament can be found in God's words commanding the disciples to listen to Jesus. This fulfills a prophecy in Deuteronomy, which states that God would deliver a prophet who would speak God's words and all are called to listen to him (see Dt 18:15–22).

From apostolic times to the present, the Catholic Church has continued to affirm the relevance and importance of the Old Testament. The Church teaches that from the beginning of creation to the sending of Jesus and the Holy Spirit, God gradually revealed himself and his plan for our salvation. Because God's one plan spans both the Old and New Testaments, the Church accepts and honors the natural unity of the two testaments. The Old Testament lays the foundation and prophesies the coming of Christ. The New Testament is the fulfillment of the prophecies and contains the story and teachings of Jesus Christ. Together the two testaments are read in light of each other, meaning we need to study both to fully understand God's plan for our salvation.

Mt 17:1–13

Catechism, nos. 120–137

they could not cure him." 17*† Jesus said in reply, "O faithless and perverse generation, how long will I be with you? How long will I endure you? Bring him here to me." 18† Jesus rebuked him and the demon came out of him, and from that hour the boy was cured. 19 Then the disciples approached Jesus in private and said, "Why could we not drive it out?" 20*† He said to them, "Because of your little faith. Amen, I say to you, if you have faith the size of a mustard seed, you will say to this mountain, 'Move from here to there,' and it will move. Nothing will be impossible for you." [21]†

The Second Prediction of the Passion

22*† As they were gathering in Galilee, Jesus said to them, "The Son of Man is to be handed over to men, 23 and they will kill him, and he will be raised on the third day." And they were overwhelmed with grief.

Payment of the Temple Tax†

24* When they came to Capernaum, the collectors of the temple tax† approached Peter and said, "Doesn't your teacher pay the temple tax?" 25† "Yes," he said. When he came into the house, before he had time to speak, Jesus asked him, "What is your opinion, Simon? From whom do the kings of the earth take tolls or census tax? From their subjects or from foreigners?" 26† When he said, "From foreigners," Jesus said to him, "Then the subjects are exempt. 27† But that we may not offend them, go to the sea, drop in a hook, and take the first fish that comes up. Open its mouth and you will find a coin worth twice the temple tax. Give that to them for me and for you."

The Greatest in the Kingdom

18 1*† At that time the disciples† approached Jesus and said, "Who is the greatest in the kingdom of heaven?" 2 He called a child over, placed it in their midst, 3*† and said, "Amen, I say to you, unless you turn and become like children, you will not enter the kingdom of heaven.

---

†

17:17 *Faithless and perverse:* so Matthew and Luke (9:41) against Mark's *faithless* (9:19). The Greek word here translated *perverse* is the same as that in Dt 32:5 LXX, where Moses speaks to his people. There is a problem in knowing to whom the reproach is addressed. Since the Matthean Jesus normally chides his disciples for their *little faith* (as in 20), it would appear that the charge of lack of faith could not be made against them and that the reproach is addressed to unbelievers among the Jews. However in v 20b (*if you have faith the size of a mustard seed*), which is certainly addressed to the disciples, they appear to have not even the smallest faith; if they had, they would have been able to cure the boy. In the light of v 20b the reproach of v 17 could have applied to the disciples. There seems to be an inconsistency between the charge of *little faith* in v 20a and that of not even a little in v 20b.

17:18 *The demon came out of him:* not until this verse does Matthew indicate that the boy's illness is a case of demoniacal possession.

17:20 The entire verse is an addition of Matthew who (according to the better attested text) omits the reason given for the disciples' inability in Mk 9:29. *Little faith:* see the note on 6:30. *Faith the size of a mustard seed . . . and it will move:* a combination of a Q saying (cf Lk 17:6) with a Marcan saying (cf Mk 11:23).

17:21 Some manuscripts add, "But this kind does not come out except by prayer and fasting"; this is a variant of the better reading of Mk 9:29.

17:22–23 The second passion prediction (cf 16:21–23) is the least detailed of the three and may be the earliest. In the Marcan parallel the disciples do not understand (9:32); here they understand and are *overwhelmed with grief* at the prospect of Jesus' death (23).

17:24–27 Like 14:28–31 and 16:16b–19, this episode comes from Matthew's special material on Peter. Although the question of *the collectors* concerns Jesus' payment of *the temple tax,* it is put to *Peter.* It is he who receives instruction from Jesus about freedom from the obligation of payment and yet why it should be made. The means of doing so is provided miraculously. The pericope deals with a problem of Matthew's church, whether its members should pay the temple tax, and the answer is given through a word of Jesus conveyed to Peter. Some scholars see here an example of the teaching authority of Peter exercised in the name of Jesus (see 16:19). The specific problem was a Jewish Christian one and may have arisen when the Matthean church was composed largely of that group.

17:24 *The temple tax:* before the destruction of the Jerusalem temple in A.D. 70 every male Jew above nineteen years of age was obliged to make an annual contribution to its upkeep (cf Ex 30:11–16; Neh 10:33). After the destruction the Romans imposed upon Jews the obligation of paying that tax for the temple of Jupiter Capitolinus. There is disagreement about which period the story deals with.

17:25 *From their subjects or from foreigners?:* the Greek word here translated *subjects* literally means "sons."

17:26 *Then the subjects are exempt:* just as *subjects* are not bound by laws applying to *foreigners,* neither are Jesus and his disciples, who belong to the kingdom of heaven, bound by the duty of paying the temple tax imposed on those who are not of the kingdom. If the Greek is translated "sons," the freedom of Jesus, the Son of God, and of his disciples, children ("sons") of the kingdom (cf 13:38), is even more clear.

17:27 *That we may not offend them:* though they are *exempt* (26), Jesus and his disciples are to avoid giving offense; therefore the tax is to be paid. *A coin worth twice the temple tax:* literally, "a stater," a Greek coin worth two double drachmas. Two double drachmas were equal to the Jewish shekel and the tax was a half-shekel. *For me and for you:* not only Jesus but Peter pays the tax, and this example serves as a standard for the conduct of all the disciples.

18:1–35 This discourse of the fourth book of the gospel is often called the "church order" discourse, but it lacks most of the considerations usually connected with church order, such as various offices in the church and the duties of each, and deals principally with the relations that must obtain among the members of the church. Beginning with the warning that greatness in *the kingdom of heaven* is measured not by rank or power but by childlikeness (1–5), it deals with the care that the disciples must take not to cause the *little ones to sin* or to neglect them if they stray from the community (6–14), the correction of members who sin (15–18), the efficacy of the prayer of the disciples because of the presence of Jesus (19–20), and the forgiveness that must be repeatedly extended to sinful members who repent (21–35).

18:1 The initiative is taken not by Jesus as in the Marcan parallel (9:33–34) but by the disciples. *Kingdom of heaven:* this may mean *the kingdom* in its fullness, i.e., after the parousia and the final judgment. But what follows about causes of sin, church discipline, and forgiveness, all dealing with the present age, suggests that the question has to do with rank also in the church, where *the kingdom* is manifested here and now, although only partially and by anticipation; see the notes on 3:2; 4:17.

18:3 *Become like children:* the child is held up as a model for the disciples not because of any supposed innocence of children but because of their complete dependence on, and trust in, their parents. So must the disciples be, in respect to God.

---

*

17:17 Dt 32:5 LXX.
17:20 Mt 21:21; Lk 17:6; 1 Cor 13:2.
17:22–23 Mt 16:21; 20:18–19.
17:24 Ex 30:11–16; Neh 10:33.
18:1–5 Mk 9:36–37; Lk 9:46–48.
18:3 Mt 19:14; Mk 10:15; Lk 18:17.

Cultural Connection

Santo Niño

The feast of Santo Niño, which means "Holy Child," is celebrated in the Philippines on the Sunday after the feast of the Baptism of the Lord. The beginning of chapter 18 of Matthew is one of the readings you might hear at Mass that day. The feast of Santo Niño celebrates Jesus as a child and is associated with a special statue. The statue portrays the child Jesus wearing a crown, red pants, and a white robe with a large triangular red collar flaring out from the shoulders. The statue can be found in many Philippine churches and on many car dashboards.

The original Santo Niño statue was made in Belgium and sent to a girl in the Philippines as a gift for her Baptism. Then it was lost for twenty-four years, until, during a battle, a soldier found it unharmed in the flaming ruins of a house. Folklore says that the statue once protected the island of Cebu from English invaders and that when the statue was placed in the sea during a drought, it miraculously began to rain.

The devotion to Santo Niño can help us to remember that Jesus was once a child who was taught and cared for by loving parents. In the spirit of Santo Niño, why not surprise a parent or grandparent with a love letter thanking him or her for all he or she has done for you?

Mt 18:1–11

4* Whoever humbles himself like this child is the
greatest in the kingdom of heaven. 5† And who-
ever receives one child such as this in my name
receives me.

Temptations to Sin

6*† "Whoever causes one of these little ones
who believe in me to sin, it would be better for
him to have a great millstone hung around his
neck and to be drowned in the depths of the
sea. 7† Woe to the world because of things that
cause sin! Such things must come, but woe to
the one through whom they come! 8*† If your
hand or foot causes you to sin, cut it off and
throw it away. It is better for you to enter into
life maimed or crippled than with two hands or
two feet to be thrown into eternal fire. 9 And if
your eye causes you to sin, tear it out and throw
it away. It is better for you to enter into life with
one eye than with two eyes to be thrown into
fiery Gehenna.

The Parable of the Lost Sheep†

10* "See that you do not despise one of these
little ones, for I say to you that their angels
in heaven always look upon the face of my

18:5 Cf 10:40.

18:6 *One of these little ones:* the thought passes from the child of vv 2–4 to the disciples, *little ones* because of their becoming *like children.* It is difficult to know whether this is a designation of all who are disciples or of those who are insignificant in contrast to others, e.g., the leaders of the community. Since apart from this chapter the designation *little ones* occurs in Matthew only in 10:42 where it means disciples as such, that is its more likely meaning here. *Who believe in me:* since discipleship is impossible without at least some degree of faith, this further specification seems superfluous. However, it serves to indicate that the warning against causing a *little one* to sin is principally directed against whatever would lead such a one to a weakening or loss of faith. The Greek verb *skandalizein,* here translated *causes . . . to sin,* means literally "causes to stumble"; what the stumbling is depends on the context. It is used of falling away from faith in 13:21. According to the better reading of Mk 9:42, *in me* is a Matthean addition to the Marcan source. *It would be better . . . depths of the sea:* cf Mk 9:42.

18:7 This is a Q saying; cf Lk 17:1. The inevitability of *things that cause sin* (literally, "scandals") does not take away the responsibility of *the one through whom they come.*

18:8–9 These verses are a doublet of 5:29–30. In that context they have to do with causes of sexual sin. As in the Marcan source from which they have been drawn (Mk 9:42–48), they differ from the first warning about scandal, which deals with causing another person to sin, for they concern what *causes* oneself *to sin* and they do not seem to be related to another's loss of faith, as the first warning is. It is difficult to know how Matthew understood the logical connection between these verses and vv 6–7.

18:10–14 The first and last verses are peculiar to Matthew The parable itself comes from Q; see Lk 15:3–7. In Luke it serves as justification for Jesus' table-companionship with sinners; here, it is an exhortation for the disciples to seek out fellow disciples who have gone *astray.* Not only must no one cause a fellow disciple to sin, but those who have strayed must be sought out and, if possible, brought back to the community. The joy of the shepherd on finding the sheep, though not absent in Matthew (13), is more emphasized in Luke. By his addition of vv 10 and 14, Matthew has drawn out explicitly the application of the parable to the care of the *little ones.*

18:4 Mt 23:12.
18:6–7 Mk 9:42; Lk 17:1–2.
18:8–9 Mt 5:29–30; Mk 9:43–47.
18:10–14 Ez 34:1–3, 16; Lk 15:3–7.

heavenly Father.† [11]*† 12 What is your opinion?
If a man has a hundred sheep and one of them
goes astray, will he not leave the ninety-nine in
the hills and go in search of the stray? 13 And if
he finds it, amen, I say to you, he rejoices more
over it than over the ninety-nine that did not
stray. 14 In just the same way, it is not the will
of your heavenly Father that one of these little
ones be lost.

A Brother Who Sins†

15* "If your brother† sins [against you], go and
tell him his fault between you and him alone.
If he listens to you, you have won over your
brother. 16*† If he does not listen, take one or
two others along with you, so that 'every fact may
be established on the testimony of two or three
witnesses.' 17*† If he refuses to listen to them,
tell the church. If he refuses to listen even to the
church, then treat him as you would a Gentile or
a tax collector. 18*† Amen, I say to you, whatever
you bind on earth shall be bound in heaven, and
whatever you loose on earth shall be loosed in
heaven. 19*† Again, [amen,] I say to you, if two
of you agree on earth about anything for which
they are to pray, it shall be granted to them by
my heavenly Father. 20*† For where two or three
are gathered together in my name, there am I in
the midst of them."

The Parable of the Unforgiving Servant

21*† Then Peter approaching asked him, "Lord,
if my brother sins against me, how often must I
forgive him? As many as seven times?" 22† Jesus
answered, "I say to you, not seven times but
seventy-seven times. 23* That is why the kingdom
of heaven may be likened to a king who decided
to settle accounts with his servants. 24† When he
began the accounting, a debtor was brought be-
fore him who owed him a huge amount. 25 Since
he had no way of paying it back, his master or-
dered him to be sold, along with his wife, his
children, and all his property, in payment of the
debt. 26† At that, the servant fell down, did him
homage, and said, 'Be patient with me, and I will
pay you back in full.' 27 Moved with compassion

†

18:10 *Their angels in heaven . . . my heavenly Father:* for the Jewish belief in angels as guardians of nations and individuals, see Dn 10:13, 20–21; Tb 5:4–7; 1QH 5:20–22; as intercessors who present the prayers of human beings to God, see Tb 13:12, 15. The high worth of the *little ones* is indicated by their being represented before God by these heavenly beings.

18:11 Some manuscripts add, "For the Son of Man has come to save what was lost"; cf 9:13. This is practically identical with Lk 19:10 and is probably a copyist's addition from that source.

18:15–20 Passing from the duty of Christian disciples toward those who have strayed from their number, the discourse now turns to how they are to deal with one who sins and yet remains within the community. First there is to be private correction (15); if this is unsuccessful, further correction before *two or three witnesses* (16); if this fails, the matter is to be brought before the assembled community (*the church*), and if the sinner refuses to attend to the correction of *the church,* he is to be expelled (17). The church's judgment will be ratified *in heaven,* i.e., by God (18). This three-step process of correction corresponds, though not exactly, to the procedure of the Qumran community; see 1QS 5:25–6:1; 6:24—7:25; CD 9:2–8. The section ends with a saying about the favorable response of God to prayer, even to that of a very small number, for Jesus is in the midst of any gathering of his disciples, however small (19–20). Whether this prayer has anything to do with the preceding judgment is uncertain.

18:15 *Your brother:* a fellow disciple; see 23:8. The bracketed words, *against you,* are widely attested but they are not in the important codices Sinaiticus and Vaticanus or in some other textual witnesses. Their omission broadens the type of sin in question. *Won over:* literally, "gained."

18:16 Cf Dt 19:15.

18:17 *The church:* the second of the only two instances of this word in the gospels; see the note on 16:18. Here it refers not to the entire *church* of Jesus, as in 16:18, but to the local congregation. *Treat him . . . a Gentile or a tax collector:* just as the observant Jew avoided the company of Gentiles and tax collectors, so must the congregation of Christian disciples separate itself from the arrogantly sinful member who refuses to repent even when convicted of his sin by the whole *church.* Such a one is to be set outside the fellowship of the community. The harsh language about *Gentile* and *tax collector* probably reflects a stage of the Matthean *church* when it was principally composed of Jewish Christians. That time had long since passed, but the principle of exclusion for such a sinner remained. Paul makes a similar demand for excommunication in 1 Cor 5:1–13.

18:18 Except for the plural of the verbs *bind* and *loose,* this verse is practically identical with 16:19b, and many scholars understand it as granting to all the disciples what was previously given to Peter alone. For a different view, based on the different contexts of the two verses, see the note on 16:19.

18:19–20 Some take these verses as applying to prayer on the occasion of the church's gathering to deal with the sinner of v 17. Unless an *a fortiori* argument is supposed, this seems unlikely. God's answer to the prayer of *two or three* envisages a different situation from one that involves the entire congregation. In addition, the object of this prayer is expressed in most general terms as *anything for which they are to pray.*

18:20 *For where two or three . . . midst of them:* the presence of Jesus guarantees the efficacy of the prayer. This saying is similar to one attributed to a rabbi executed in A.D. 135 at the time of the second Jewish revolt: ". . . When two sit and there are between them the words of the Torah, the divine presence *(Shekinah)* rests upon them" (*Pirqê 'Abôt* 3, 3).

18:21–35 The final section of the discourse deals with the forgiveness that the disciples are to give to their fellow disciples who sin against them. To the question of Peter how often forgiveness is to be granted (21), Jesus answers that it is to be given without limit (22) and illustrates this with the parable of the unmerciful servant (23–34), warning that his *heavenly Father* will give those who do not forgive the same treatment as that given to the unmerciful servant (35). Verses 21–22 correspond to Lk 17:4; the parable and the final warning are peculiar to Matthew. That the parable did not originally belong to this context is suggested by the fact that it really does not deal with repeated forgiveness, which is the point of Peter's question and Jesus' reply.

18:22 *Seventy-seven times:* the Greek corresponds exactly to the LXX of Gn 4:24. There is probably an allusion, by contrast, to the limitless vengeance of Lamech in the Genesis text. In any case, what is demanded of the disciples is limitless forgiveness.

18:24 *A huge amount:* literally, "ten thousand talents." The talent was a unit of coinage of high but varying value depending on its metal (gold, silver, copper) and its place of origin. It is mentioned in the New Testament only here and in 25:14–30.

18:26 *Pay you back in full:* an empty promise, given the size of the debt.

*

18:11 Lk 19:10.
18:15 Lv 19:17; Sir 19:13; Gal 6:1.
18:16 Dt 19:15; Jn 8:17; 1 Tm 5:19.
18:17 1 Cor 5:1–13.
18:18 Mt 16:19; Jn 20:23.
18:19 Mt 7:7–8; Jn 15:7.
18:20 1 Cor 5:4.
18:21–22 Mt 6:12; Lk 17:4.
18:23 Mt 25:19.

Pray It!

Forgive Us Our Debts

The parable of the unforgiving servant spells out clearly (and a bit harshly) what it means to ask God to "forgive us our debts, / as we forgive our debtors" (Mt 6:12).

Bring to mind a person who has hurt you or made you angry lately. Hold this person's image in your thoughts, and realize that Jesus is calling you to forgive her or him. Now, tell this person in your thoughts how she or he has hurt you. Finally, offer your forgiveness to the person so that you can let go of the burden of your hurt.

When you are done, imagine Jesus in your prayer and share with him something you have done that has hurt another person. Let Jesus forgive you in the same way you just forgave.

▶ Mt 18:21–35

the master of that servant let him go and forgave
him the loan. 28† When that servant had left,
he found one of his fellow servants who owed
him a much smaller amount. He seized him and
started to choke him, demanding, 'Pay back what
you owe.' 29 Falling to his knees, his fellow ser-
vant begged him, 'Be patient with me, and I will
pay you back.' 30 But he refused. Instead, he had
him put in prison until he paid back the debt.
31 Now when his fellow servants saw what had
happened, they were deeply disturbed, and went
to their master and reported the whole affair.
32 His master summoned him and said to him,
'You wicked servant! I forgave you your entire
debt because you begged me to. 33* Should you
not have had pity on your fellow servant, as I
had pity on you?' 34† Then in anger his master
handed him over to the torturers until he should
pay back the whole debt. 35*† So will my heav-
enly Father do to you, unless each of you forgives
his brother from his heart."

VI: Ministry in Judea and Jerusalem

Marriage and Divorce

19 1† When Jesus† finished these words,†
he left Galilee and went to the district of
Judea across the Jordan. 2 Great crowds followed
him, and he cured them there. 3*† Some Phari-
sees approached him, and tested him, saying, "Is
it lawful for a man to divorce his wife for any
cause whatever?" 4*† He said in reply, "Have
you not read that from the beginning the Cre-
ator 'made them male and female' 5* and said,
'For this reason a man shall leave his father and

†

18:28 *A much smaller amount:* literally, "a hundred denarii." A denarius was the normal daily wage of a laborer. The difference between the two debts is enormous and brings out the absurdity of the conduct of the Christian who has received the great forgiveness of God and yet refuses to forgive the relatively minor offenses done to him.

18:34 Since the debt is so great as to be unpayable, the punishment will be endless.

18:35 The Father's forgiveness, already given, will be withdrawn at the final judgment for those who have not imitated his forgiveness by their own.

19:1—23:39 The narrative section of the fifth book of the gospel. The first part (19:1—20:34) has for its setting the journey of Jesus from Galilee to Jerusalem; the second (21:1—23:39) deals with Jesus' ministry in Jerusalem up to the final great discourse of the gospel (chs 24–25). Matthew follows the Marcan sequence of events, though adding material both special to this gospel and drawn from Q. The second part ends with the denunciation of the scribes and Pharisees (23:1–36) followed by Jesus' lament over Jerusalem (37–39). This long and important speech raises a problem for the view that Matthew is structured around five other discourses of Jesus (see Introduction) and that this one has no such function in the gospel. However, it is to be noted that this speech lacks the customary concluding formula that follows the five discourses (see the note on 7:28), and that those discourses are all addressed either exclusively (chs 10:18:24–25) or primarily (chs 5–7:13) to the disciples, whereas this is addressed primarily to the scribes and Pharisees (13–36). Consequently, it seems plausible to maintain that the evangelist did not intend to give it the structural importance of the five other discourses, and that, in spite of its being composed of sayings-material, it belongs to the narrative section of this book. In that regard, it is similar to the sayings-material of 11:7–30. Some have proposed that Matthew wished to regard it as part of the final discourse of chs 24–25, but the intervening material (24:1–4) and the change in matter and style of those chapters do not support that view.

19:1–12 In giving Jesus' teaching on divorce (3–9), Matthew here follows his Marcan source (10:2–12) as he does Q in 5:31–32 (cf Lk 16:18). Verses 10–12 are peculiar to Matthew.

19:1 *When Jesus finished these words:* see the note on 7:28–29. *The district of Judea across the Jordan:* an inexact designation of the territory. Judea did not extend *across the Jordan;* the territory east of the river was Perea. The route to Jerusalem by way of Perea avoided passage through Samaria.

19:3 *Tested him:* the verb is used of attempts of Jesus' opponents to embarrass him by challenging him to do something they think impossible (16:1; Mk 8:11; Lk 11:16) or by having him say something that they can use against him (22:18, 35; Mk 10:2; 12:15). *For any cause whatever:* this is peculiar to Matthew and has been interpreted by some as meaning that Jesus was being asked to take sides in the dispute between the schools of Hillel and Shammai on the reasons for divorce, the latter holding a stricter position than the former. It is unlikely, however, that to ask Jesus' opinion about the differing views of two Jewish schools, both highly respected, could be described as "testing" him, for the reason indicated above.

19:4–6 Matthew recasts his Marcan source, omitting Jesus' question about Moses' command (Mk 10:3) and having him recall at once two Genesis texts that show the will and purpose of *the Creator* in making human beings *male and female* (Gn 1:27), namely, that *a man* may *be joined to his wife* in marriage in the intimacy of *one flesh* (Gn 2:24). *What God has* thus *joined* must not be separated by any *human being.* (The NAB translation of the Hebrew *bāśār* of Gn 2:24 as "body" rather than "flesh" obscures the reference of Matthew to that text.)

*

18:33 Sir 28:4.
18:35 Mt 6:15; Jas 2:13.
19:3–9 Mk 10:2–12.
19:4 Gn 1:27.
19:5 Gn 2:24; 1 Cor 6:16; Eph 5:31.

mother and be joined to his wife, and the two
shall become one flesh'? 6 So they are no lon-
ger two, but one flesh. Therefore, what God has
joined together, no human being must separate."
7*† They said to him, "Then why did Moses
command that the man give the woman a bill
of divorce and dismiss [her]?" 8 He said to them,
"Because of the hardness of your hearts Moses
allowed you to divorce your wives, but from the
beginning it was not so. 9*† I say to you, who-
ever divorces his wife (unless the marriage is un-
lawful) and marries another commits adultery."
10 [His] disciples said to him, "If that is the case
of a man with his wife, it is better not to marry."
11† He answered, "Not all can accept [this] word,
but only those to whom that is granted. 12† Some
are incapable of marriage because they were born
so; some, because they were made so by others;
some, because they have renounced marriage for
the sake of the kingdom of heaven. Whoever can
accept this ought to accept it."

Blessing of the Children

13*† Then children were brought to him that
he might lay his hands on them and pray. The
disciples rebuked them, 14* but Jesus said, "Let
the children come to me, and do not prevent
them; for the kingdom of heaven belongs to such
as these." 15 After he placed his hands on them,
he went away.

The Rich Young Man†

16* Now someone approached him and said,
"Teacher, what good must I do to gain eternal
life?"† 17† He answered him, "Why do you ask
me about the good? There is only One who is
good. If you wish to enter into life, keep the com-
mandments." 18*† He asked him, "Which ones?"
And Jesus replied, " 'You shall not kill; you shall
not commit adultery; you shall not steal; you
shall not bear false witness; 19 honor your fa-
ther and your mother'; and 'you shall love your
neighbor as yourself.' " 20† The young man said
to him, "All of these I have observed. What do I
still lack?" 21*† Jesus said to him, "If you wish
to be perfect, go, sell what you have and give to
[the] poor, and you will have treasure in heaven.
Then come, follow me." 22 When the young man
heard this statement, he went away sad, for he
had many possessions. 23† Then Jesus said to his
disciples, "Amen, I say to you, it will be hard for
one who is rich to enter the kingdom of heaven.
24* Again I say to you, it is easier for a camel
to pass through the eye of a needle than for

---

†

19:7 See Dt 24:1–4.

19:9 Moses' concession to human sinfulness (*the hardness of your hearts,* 8) is repudiated by Jesus, and the original will of the Creator is reaffirmed against that concession. *(Unless the marriage is unlawful):* see the note on 5:31–32. There is some evidence suggesting that Jesus' absolute prohibition of divorce was paralleled in the Qumran community (see 11QTemple 57:17–19; CD 4:12b—5:14). Matthew removes Mark's setting of this verse as spoken to the disciples alone "in the house" (Mk 10:10) and also his extension of the divorce prohibition to the case of a woman's divorcing her husband (10:12), probably because in Palestine, unlike the places where Roman and Greek law prevailed, the woman was not allowed to initiate the divorce.

19:11 *[This] word:* probably the disciples' *it is better not to marry* (10). Jesus agrees but says that celibacy is not for all but only for those *to whom that is granted* by God.

19:12 *Incapable of marriage:* literally, "eunuchs." Three classes are mentioned, eunuchs from birth, eunuchs by castration, and those who have voluntarily *renounced marriage* (literally, "have made themselves eunuchs") *for the sake of the kingdom,* i.e., to devote themselves entirely to its service. Some scholars take the last class to be those who have been divorced by their spouses and have refused to enter another marriage. But it is more likely that it is rather those who have chosen never to marry, since that suits better the optional nature of the decision: *Whoever can . . . ought to accept it.*

19:13–15 This account is understood by some as intended to justify the practice of infant baptism. That interpretation is based principally on the command not to *prevent* the children from coming, since that word sometimes has a baptismal connotation in the New Testament; see Acts 8:36.

19:16–30 Cf Mk 10:17–31. This story does not set up a "two-tier" morality, that of those who seek (only) *eternal life* (16) and that of those who *wish to be perfect* (21). It speaks rather of the obstacle that riches constitute for the following of Jesus and of the impossibility, humanly speaking, for one who has *many possessions* (22) *to enter the kingdom* (24). Actual renunciation of riches is not demanded of all; Matthew counts the rich Joseph of Arimathea as a disciple of Jesus (27:57). But only the poor in spirit (5:3) can *enter the kingdom* and, as here, such poverty may entail the sacrifice of one's *possessions.* The Twelve, who *have given up everything* (27) to follow Jesus, will have as their reward a share in Jesus' (the Son of Man's) *judging the twelve tribes of Israel* (28), and all who have similarly sacrificed family or property for his sake *will inherit eternal life* (29).

19:16 *Gain eternal life:* this is equivalent to "entering into life" (17) and "being saved" (25); the *life* is that of the new age after the final judgment (see 25:46). It probably is also equivalent here to "entering the kingdom of heaven" (23) or "the kingdom of God" (24), but see the notes on 3:2; 4:17; 18:1 for the wider reference of *the kingdom* in Matthew.

19:17 By Matthew's reformulation of the Marcan question and reply (Mk 10:17–18) Jesus' repudiation of the term "good" for himself has been softened. Yet the Marcan assertion that "no one is good but God alone" stands, with only unimportant verbal modification.

19:18–19 The first five commandments cited are from the Decalogue (see Ex 20:12–16; Dt 5:16–20). Matthew omits Mark's "you shall not defraud" (10:19; see Dt 24:14) and adds Lv 19:18. This combination of commandments of the Decalogue with Lv 19:18 is partially the same as Paul's enumeration of the demands of Christian morality in Rom 13:9.

19:20 *Young man:* in Matthew alone of the synoptics the questioner is said to be a *young man;* thus the Marcan "from my youth" (10:20) is omitted.

19:21 *If you wish to be perfect: to be perfect* is demanded of all Christians; see 5:48. In the case of this man, it involves selling his possessions and giving to the poor; only so can he *follow* Jesus.

19:23–24 Riches are an obstacle to entering *the kingdom* that cannot be overcome by human power. The comparison with the impossibility of a camel's passing *through the eye of a needle* should not be mitigated by such suppositions as that *the eye of a needle* means a low or narrow gate. *The kingdom of God:* as in 12:28; 21:31, 43, instead of Matthew's usual *kingdom of heaven.*

---

*

19:7 Dt 24:1–4.
19:9 Mt 5:32; Lk 16:18; 1 Cor 7:10–11.
19:13–15 Mk 10:13–16; Lk 18:15–17.
19:14 Mt 18:3; Acts 8:36.
19:16–30 Mk 10:17–31; Lk 18:18–30.
19:18–19 Ex 20:12–16; Dt 5:16–20; Lv 19:18; Rom 13:9.
19:21 Mt 5:48; 6:20.
19:24 Mt 7:14.

one who is rich to enter the kingdom of God."
25† When the disciples heard this, they were
greatly astonished and said, "Who then can be
saved?" 26* Jesus looked at them and said, "For
human beings this is impossible, but for God all
things are possible." 27* Then Peter said to him
in reply, "We have given up everything and fol-
lowed you. What will there be for us?" 28*† Jesus
said to them, "Amen, I say to you that you who
have followed me, in the new age, when the Son
of Man is seated on his throne of glory, will your-
selves sit on twelve thrones, judging the twelve
tribes of Israel. 29 And everyone who has given up
houses or brothers or sisters or father or mother
or children or lands for the sake of my name will
receive a hundred times more, and will inherit
eternal life. 30*† But many who are first will be
last, and the last will be first.

The Workers in the Vineyard

20 1† "The kingdom of heaven is like a
landowner who went out at dawn to hire
laborers for his vineyard. 2 After agreeing with
them for the usual daily wage, he sent them into
his vineyard. 3 Going out about nine o'clock,
he saw others standing idle in the marketplace,
4† and he said to them, 'You too go into my vine-
yard, and I will give you what is just.' 5 So they
went off. [And] he went out again around noon,
and around three o'clock, and did likewise. 6 Go-
ing out about five o'clock, he found others stand-
ing around, and said to them, 'Why do you stand
here idle all day?' 7 They answered, 'Because no
one has hired us.' He said to them, 'You too
go into my vineyard.' 8*† When it was evening
the owner of the vineyard said to his foreman,
'Summon the laborers and give them their pay,
beginning with the last and ending with the
first.' 9 When those who had started about five
o'clock came, each received the usual daily wage.
10 So when the first came, they thought that they
would receive more, but each of them also got
the usual wage. 11 And on receiving it they grum-
bled against the landowner, 12 saying, 'These last

Pray It!

Are You for Real?

Read Matthew 20:1–16 as an introduction to this prayer:

Lord, could you really be such a generous God? I have heard that you offer the same welcome to the sinner as to the saint. That you walk with the angry as well as the joyful, and can embrace the hurtful as well as the helpful. That you even offer the exact same love for the last to turn to you as you do for the first.

That's just not the way it is done around here, God, so excuse me if I have a hard time believing. But then, I've heard it said that you are as patient with the doubtful as you are with the faithful.

If you are this type of God, then please be with me right now. I need to talk to someone who understands and loves me despite my doubts and sin. I need a God who breaks the rules to let me know how much I am loved.

If you are indeed this kind of God, thanks! Thanks for being so crazy with your love that you would allow someone like me to hang around you. Promise to stay with me as I learn to trust in you and your acceptance of all people. Amen.

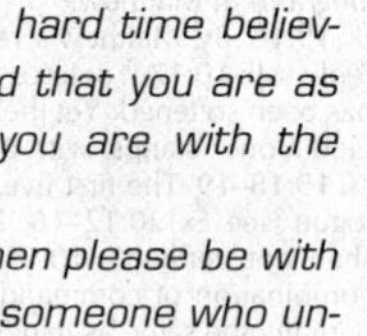

▶ Mt 20:1–16

† **19:25–26** See the note on Mk 10:23–27.

19:28 This saying, directed to the Twelve, is from Q; see Lk 22:29–30. *The new age:* the Greek word here translated "new age" occurs in the New Testament only here and in Ti 3:5. Literally, it means "rebirth" or "regeneration," and is used in Titus of spiritual rebirth through baptism. Here it means the "rebirth" effected by the coming of the kingdom. Since that coming has various stages (see the notes on 3:2; 4:17), *the new age* could be taken as referring to the time after the resurrection when the Twelve will govern the true Israel, i.e., the church of Jesus. (For "judge" in the sense of "govern," cf Jgs 12:8, 9, 11; 15:20; 16:31; Ps 2:10). But since it is connected here with the time when *the Son of Man* will be *seated on his throne of glory,* language that Matthew uses in 25:31 for the time of final judgment, it is more likely that what the Twelve are promised is that they will be joined with Jesus then in judging the people of Israel.

19:30 Different interpretations have been given to this saying, which comes from Mk 10:31. In view of Matthew's associating it with the following parable (20:1–15) and substantially repeating it (in reverse order) at the end of that parable (20:16), it may be that his meaning is that all who respond to the call of Jesus, at whatever time (*first* or *last*), will be the same in respect to inheriting the benefits of the kingdom, which is the gift of God.

20:1–16 This parable is peculiar to Matthew. It is difficult to know whether the evangelist composed it or received it as part of his traditional material and, if the latter is the case, what its original reference was. In its present context its close association with 19:30 suggests that its teaching is the equality of all the disciples in the reward of inheriting eternal life.

20:4 *What is just:* although the wage is not stipulated as in the case of those first hired, it will be fair.

20:8 *Beginning with the last . . . the first:* this element of the parable has no other purpose than to show how *the first* knew what *the last* were given (12).

* **19:26** Gn 18:14; Jb 42:2; Lk 1:37. **19:27** Mt 4:20, 22. **19:28** Mt 25:31; Dn 7:9, 22; Lk 22:30; Rv 3:21; 20:4. **19:30** Mt 20:16. **20:8** Lv 19:13; Dt 24:15.

Catholic Social Teaching

A Living Wage

In this parable, Jesus tells the story of a landowner who agrees on a daily wage with his workers and then pays them that established wage at the end of their work day. Because different workers were paid the same amount for varying amounts of work, some of the workers found the wage to be unfair, even though they received the amount they had agreed to when they were hired. Therein lies the difference between God's notion of fairness and justice. Fairness would mean paying the workers based on the hours they worked. Justice, however, means providing all people with what they need, as God, the landowner in this story, does. Such is the radical grace of God!

Throughout our world, many workers toil for long hours under brutal conditions for a wage that is not just. Even in the United States, a person working forty hours per week at minimum wage will rarely earn enough to cover all of life's basic needs—food, shelter, clothing, utilities, transportation, medical insurance—especially when caring for a family. Often, women and children suffer the most from unjust wage practices.

This is why Catholic social teaching asserts that we must advocate for a living wage for all workers. A living wage is the minimum hourly wage necessary for a person to achieve a basic standard of living above the poverty line. Paying higher wages is sometimes difficult for small business owners who fear it may raise operating costs and put them out of business. However, it is certainly no excuse for failing to give workers the wages they need to adequately survive.

Mt 20:1–16

The Dignity of Work and the Rights of Workers

ones worked only one hour, and you have made
them equal to us, who bore the day's burden and
the heat.' 13† He said to one of them in reply, 'My
friend, I am not cheating you. Did you not agree
with me for the usual daily wage? 14† Take what
is yours and go. What if I wish to give this last
one the same as you? 15 [Or] am I not free to do
as I wish with my own money? Are you envious
because I am generous?' 16† Thus, the last will be
first, and the first will be last."

The Third Prediction of the Passion

17*† As Jesus was going up to Jerusalem, he
took the twelve [disciples] aside by themselves,
and said to them on the way, 18 "Behold, we
are going up to Jerusalem, and the Son of Man
will be handed over to the chief priests and the
scribes, and they will condemn him to death,
19 and hand him over to the Gentiles to be
mocked and scourged and crucified, and he will
be raised on the third day."

The Request of James and John†

20* Then the mother† of the sons of Zebedee
approached him with her sons and did him
homage, wishing to ask him for something. 21 He
said to her, "What do you wish?" She answered
him, "Command that these two sons of mine sit,
one at your right and the other at your left, in
your kingdom." 22† Jesus said in reply, "You do

20:13 *I am not cheating you:* literally, "I am not treating you unjustly."

20:14–15 The owner's conduct involves no violation of justice (4, 13), and that all the workers receive the same wage is due only to his generosity to the latest arrivals; the resentment of the first comes from envy.

20:16 See the note on 19:30.

20:17–19 Cf Mk 10:32–34. This is the third and the most detailed of the passion predictions (16:21–23; 17:22–23). It speaks of Jesus' being *handed over to the Gentiles* (27:2), his being *mocked* (27:27–30), *scourged* (27:26), and *crucified* (27:31, 35). In all but the last of these points Matthew agrees with his Marcan source, but whereas Mark speaks of Jesus' being killed (10:34), Matthew has the specific *to be . . . crucified.*

20:20–28 Cf Mk 10:35–45. The request of the sons of Zebedee, made through their mother, for the highest places of honor in the *kingdom,* and the indignation of *the* other *ten* disciples at this request, show that neither *the two brothers* nor the others have understood that what makes for greatness in the kingdom is not lordly power but humble service. Jesus gives the example, and his ministry of service will reach its highest point when he gives his life for the deliverance of the human race from sin.

20:20–21 The reason for Matthew's making *the mother* the petitioner (cf Mk 10:35) is not clear. Possibly he intends an allusion to Bathsheba's seeking the kingdom for Solomon; see 1 Kgs 1:11–21. *Your kingdom:* see the note on 16:28.

20:22 *You do not know what you are asking:* the Greek verbs are plural and, with the rest of the verse, indicate that the answer is addressed not to the woman but to her sons. *Drink the cup:* see the note on Mk 10:38–40. Matthew omits the Marcan "or be baptized with the baptism with which I am baptized" (10:38).

20:17–19 Mt 16:21; 17:22–23; Mk 10:32–34; Lk 18:31–33.
20:20–28 Mk 10:35–45.

not know what you are asking. Can you drink the
cup that I am going to drink?" They said to him,
"We can." 23 He replied, "My cup you will indeed
drink, but to sit at my right and at my left [, this]
is not mine to give but is for those for whom it
has been prepared by my Father." 24* When the
ten heard this, they became indignant at the two
brothers. 25 But Jesus summoned them and said,
"You know that the rulers of the Gentiles lord it
over them, and the great ones make their author-
ity over them felt. 26 But it shall not be so among
you. Rather, whoever wishes to be great among
you shall be your servant; 27* whoever wishes to
be first among you shall be your slave. 28*† Just
so, the Son of Man did not come to be served
but to serve and to give his life as a ransom for
many."

The Healing of Two Blind Men

29*† As they left Jericho, a great crowd fol-
lowed him. 30*† Two blind men were sitting by
the roadside, and when they heard that Jesus was
passing by, they cried out, "[Lord,] Son of David,
have pity on us!" 31 The crowd warned them to
be silent, but they called out all the more, "Lord,
Son of David, have pity on us!" 32 Jesus stopped
and called them and said, "What do you want
me to do for you?" 33 They answered him, "Lord,
let our eyes be opened." 34 Moved with pity, Jesus
touched their eyes. Immediately they received
their sight, and followed him.

The Entry into Jerusalem†

21 1* When they drew near Jerusalem and
came to Bethphage† on the Mount of Ol-
ives, Jesus sent two disciples, 2† saying to them,
"Go into the village opposite you, and immediate-
ly you will find an ass tethered, and a colt with
her. Untie them and bring them here to me. 3 And

Live It!

True Greatness

What good parent does not want his or her son or daughter to find success in life? Like most people at the time of Jesus, the mother of James and John is confused about the Kingdom that Jesus had come to establish. She lobbies for her sons (see Mt 20:21), hoping they might be made "senior vice presidents" of the new "firm."

The resulting confusion and anger among the disciples allows Jesus the opportunity to remind them of how God defined true greatness. Jesus turns the tables on them by asking in a veiled way, "Can you drink the cup that I am going to drink?" (verse 22). He reminds them—and reminds us today—that true greatness is gained in serving others (see verses 26–27).

When you are in a position of leadership, do you see it as a chance to control others in order to gain power or social status, or do you see it as a chance to serve others and help them obtain what they need to live full and healthy lives? Why is it that wanting power for ourselves so often gets in the way of wanting to serve the needs of others?

▶ Mt 20:20–28

†

20:28 *Ransom:* this noun, which occurs in the New Testament only here and in the Marcan parallel (10:45), does not necessarily express the idea of liberation by payment of some price. The cognate verb is used frequently in the LXX of God's liberating Israel from Egypt or from Babylonia after the Exile; see Ex 6:6; 15:13; Ps 77 (76 LXX):16; Is 43:1; 44:22. The liberation brought by Jesus' death will be *for many;* cf Is 53:12. *Many* does not mean that some are excluded, but is a Semitism designating the collectivity who benefit from the service of the one, and is equivalent to "all." While there are few verbal contacts between this saying and the fourth Servant Song (Is 52:13—53:12), the ideas of that passage are reflected here.

20:29–34 The cure of the blind men is probably symbolic of what will happen to the disciples, now blind to the meaning of Jesus' passion and to the necessity of their sharing his suffering. As the men are given sight, so, after the resurrection, will the disciples come to see that to which they are now blind. Matthew has abbreviated his Marcan source (10:46–52) and has made Mark's one man two. Such doubling is characteristic of this gospel; see 8:28–34 (// Mk 5:1–20) and the note on 9:27–31.

20:30 [*Lord,*]: some important textual witnesses omit this, but that may be because copyists assimilated this verse to 9:27. *Son of David:* see the note on 9:27.

21:1–11 Jesus' coming to Jerusalem is in accordance with the divine will that he must go there (cf 16:21) to suffer, die, and be raised. He prepares for his entry into the city in such a way as to make it a fulfillment of the prophecy of Zec 9:9 (2) that emphasizes the humility of the *king* who *comes* (5). That prophecy, absent from the Marcan parallel account (11:1–11) although found also in the Johannine account of the entry (12:15), is the center of the Matthean story. During the procession from Bethphage to Jerusalem, Jesus is acclaimed as the Davidic messianic king by the crowds who accompany him (9). On his arrival *the whole city was shaken,* and to the inquiry of the amazed populace about Jesus' identity the crowds with him reply that he is *the prophet, from Nazareth in Galilee* (10, 11).

21:1 *Bethphage:* a village that can no longer be certainly identified. Mark mentions it before Bethany (11:1), which suggests that it lay to the east of the latter. *The Mount of Olives:* the hill east of Jerusalem that is spoken of in Zec 14:4 as the place where the Lord will come to rescue Jerusalem from the enemy nations.

21:2 *An ass tethered, and a colt with her:* instead of the one animal of Mk 11:2, Matthew has two, as demanded by his understanding of Zec 9:9.

*

20:24–27 Lk 22:25–27.
20:27 Mk 9:35.
20:28 Mt 26:28; Is 53:12; Rom 5:6; 1 Tm 2:6.
20:29–34 Mk 10:46–52; Lk 18:35–43.
20:30 Mt 9:27.
21:1–11 Mk 11:1–11; Lk 19:28–38; Jn 12:12–15.

if anyone should say anything to you, reply, 'The
master has need of them.' Then he will send them
at once." 4† This happened so that what had been
spoken through the prophet might be fulfilled:

5* "Say to daughter Zion,
'Behold, your king comes to you,
meek and riding on an ass,
and on a colt, the foal of a beast
of burden.' "

6 The disciples went and did as Jesus had ordered
them. 7† They brought the ass and the colt and
laid their cloaks over them, and he sat upon
them. 8*† The very large crowd spread their
cloaks on the road, while others cut branches
from the trees and strewed them on the road.
9*† The crowds preceding him and those following kept crying out and saying:

"Hosanna to the Son of David;
blessed is he who comes in the name of
the Lord;
hosanna in the highest."

10† And when he entered Jerusalem the whole
city was shaken and asked, "Who is this?"
11† And the crowds replied, "This is Jesus the
prophet, from Nazareth in Galilee."

The Cleansing of the Temple†

12* Jesus entered the temple area and drove
out all those engaged in selling and buying
there.* He overturned the tables of the money changers and the seats of those who were selling
doves.† 13*† And he said to them, "It is written:

'My house shall be a house of prayer,'
but you are making it a den of thieves."

14*† The blind and the lame approached him in
the temple area, and he cured them. 15† When
the chief priests and the scribes saw the wondrous things he was doing, and the children crying out in the temple area, "Hosanna to the Son
of David," they were indignant 16*† and said to
him, "Do you hear what they are saying?" Jesus

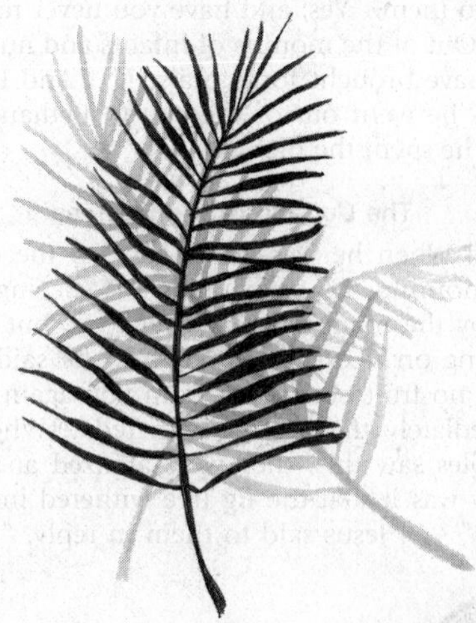

21:8

†

21:4–5 *The prophet:* this fulfillment citation is actually composed of two distinct Old Testament texts, Is 62:11 *(Say to daughter Zion)* and Zec 9:9. The *ass* and the *colt* are the same animal in the prophecy, mentioned twice in different ways, the common Hebrew literary device of poetic parallelism. That Matthew takes them as two is one of the reasons why some scholars think that he was a Gentile rather than a Jewish Christian who would presumably not make that mistake (see Introduction).

21:7 *Upon them:* upon the two animals; an awkward picture resulting from Matthew's misunderstanding of the prophecy.

21:8 *Spread . . . on the road:* cf 2 Kgs 9:13. There is a similarity between the cutting and strewing of the *branches* and the festivities of Tabernacles (Lv 23:39–40); see also 2 Mc 10:5–8 where the celebration of the rededication of the temple is compared to that of Tabernacles.

21:9 *Hosanna:* the Hebrew means "(O LORD) grant salvation"; see Ps 118:25, but that invocation had become an acclamation of jubilation and welcome. *Blessed is he . . . in the name of the Lord:* see Ps 118:26 and the note on Jn 12:13. *In the highest:* probably only an intensification of the acclamation, although *Hosanna in the highest* could be taken as a prayer, "May God save (him)."

21:10 *Was shaken:* in the gospels this verb is peculiar to Matthew where it is used also of the earthquake at the time of the crucifixion (27:51) and of the terror of the guards of Jesus' tomb at the appearance of the angel (28:4). For Matthew's use of the cognate noun, see the note on 8:24.

21:11 *The prophet:* see 16:14 ("one of the prophets") and 21:46.

21:12–17 Matthew changes the order of Mark (11:11, 12, 15) and places the cleansing of the temple on the same day as the entry into Jerusalem, immediately after it. The activities going on in *the temple area* were not secular but connected with the temple worship. Thus Jesus' attack on those so engaged and his charge that they were *making* God's *house of prayer a den of thieves* (12–13) constituted a claim to authority over the religious practices of Israel and were a challenge to the priestly authorities. Verses 14–17 are peculiar to Matthew. Jesus' healings and his countenancing the children's cries of praise rouse the indignation of *the chief priests and the scribes* (15). These two groups appear in the infancy narrative (2:4) and have been mentioned in the first and third passion predictions (16:21; 20:18). Now, as the passion approaches, they come on the scene again, exhibiting their hostility to Jesus.

21:12 These activities were carried on in the court of the Gentiles, the outermost court of *the temple area.* Animals for sacrifice were sold; the *doves* were for those who could not afford a more expensive offering; see Lv 5:7. *Tables of the money changers:* only the coinage of Tyre could be used for the purchases; other money had to be exchanged for that.

21:13 *'My house . . . prayer':* cf Is 56:7. Matthew omits the final words of the quotation, "for all peoples" ("all nations"), possibly because for him the worship of the God of Israel by all nations belongs to the time after the resurrection; see 28:19. *A den of thieves:* the phrase is taken from Jer 7:11.

21:14 *The blind and the lame:* according to 2 Sm 5:8 (LXX) *the blind and the lame* were forbidden to enter "the house of the Lord," the temple. These are the last of Jesus' healings in Matthew.

21:15 *The wondrous things:* the healings.

21:16 *'Out of the mouths . . . praise':* cf Ps 8:3 (LXX).

*

21:5 Is 62:11; Zec 9:9.
21:8 2 Kgs 9:13.
21:9 Ps 118:25–26.
21:12–17 Mk 11:15–19; Lk 19:45–48; Jn 2:14–22.
21:12 Lv 5:7.
21:13 Is 56:7; Jer 7:11.
21:14 2 Sm 5:8 LXX.
21:16 Ps 8:2 LXX; Wis 10:21.

said to them, "Yes; and have you never read the
text, 'Out of the mouths of infants and nurslings
you have brought forth praise'?" 17 And leaving
them, he went out of the city to Bethany, and
there he spent the night.

The Cursing of the Fig Tree

18*† When he was going back to the city in
the morning, he was hungry. 19* Seeing a fig
tree by the road, he went over to it, but found
nothing on it except leaves. And he said to it,
"May no fruit ever come from you again." And
immediately the fig tree withered. 20 When the
disciples saw this, they were amazed and said,
"How was it that the fig tree withered immedi-
ately?" 21*† Jesus said to them in reply, "Amen,
I say to you, if you have faith and do not waver,
not only will you do what has been done to the
fig tree, but even if you say to this mountain,
'Be lifted up and thrown into the sea,' it will be
done. 22* Whatever you ask for in prayer with
faith, you will receive."

The Authority of Jesus Questioned†

23* When he had come into the temple area,
the chief priests and the elders of the people
approached him as he was teaching and said,
"By what authority are you doing these things?†
And who gave you this authority?"* 24† Jesus
said to them in reply, "I shall ask you one ques-
tion, and if you answer it for me, then I shall tell
you by what authority I do these things. 25 Where
was John's baptism from? Was it of heavenly or
of human origin?" They discussed this among
themselves and said, "If we say 'Of heavenly or-
igin,' he will say to us, 'Then why did you not
believe him?' 26*† But if we say, 'Of human ori-
gin,' we fear the crowd, for they all regard John
as a prophet." 27† So they said to Jesus in reply,
"We do not know." He himself said to them,
"Neither shall I tell you by what authority I do
these things.

The Parable of the Two Sons

28† "What is your opinion? A man had two
sons. He came to the first and said, 'Son, go out

Did You Know?

Jesus and Civil Disobedience

The cleansing of the Temple is one of the few stories that occurs in all four Gospels. To fully understand Jesus' anger in this situation, we need to remember that the Jews were required to offer sacrificial animals as part of their religious obligation. Money exchange was a very necessary service for the proper operation of the Temple. Pilgrims needed Jewish coinage to pay the Temple tax. Likewise, buying animals for sacrifice at the Temple ensured that only the best would be offered to God. Jesus was angry because the religious and civil leaders were too concerned about these things, failing to remember that the Temple is God's house.

Jesus' clearing of the Temple was an act of religious and civil disobedience, challenging the highest members of Jewish society. His actions would have been viewed as an attack on the Temple. The Gospels of Luke and Mark both say that immediately after this event, Jewish leaders began looking for a way to kill Jesus. They waited because Jesus was so popular with the people (see Mk 11:18–19 and Lk 19:47–48). Jesus knew that his actions and teachings made these corrupt leaders angry and would ultimately lead to his death (see Mt 20:17–19).

Mt 21:12–13

†

21:18–22 In Mark the effect of Jesus' cursing the fig tree is not immediate; see 11:14, 20. By making it so, Matthew has heightened the miracle. Jesus' act seems arbitrary and ill-tempered, but it is a prophetic action similar to those of Old Testament prophets that vividly symbolize some part of their preaching; see, e.g., Ez 12:1–20. It is a sign of the judgment that is to come upon the Israel that with all its apparent piety lacks the fruit of good deeds (3:10) and will soon bear the punishment of its fruitlessness (43). Some scholars propose that this story is the development in tradition of a parable of Jesus about the destiny of a fruitless tree, such as Lk 13:6–9. Jesus' answer to the question of the amazed disciples (20) makes the miracle an example of the power of prayer made with unwavering *faith* (21–22).

21:21 See 17:20.

21:23–27 Cf Mk 11:27–33. This is the first of five controversies between Jesus and the religious authorities of Judaism in 21:23—22:46, presented in the form of questions and answers.

21:23 *These things:* probably his entry into the city, his cleansing of the temple, and his healings there.

21:24 To reply by counterquestion was common in rabbinical debate.

21:26 *We fear . . . as a prophet:* cf 14:5.

21:27 Since through embarrassment on the one hand and fear on the other the religious authorities claim ignorance of the origin of John's baptism, they show themselves incapable of speaking with authority; hence Jesus refuses to discuss with them the grounds of his authority.

21:28–32 The series of controversies is interrupted by three parables on the judgment of Israel (21:28—22:14) of which this, peculiar to Matthew, is the first. The second (21:33–46) comes from Mark (12:1–12), and the third (22:1–14) from Q; see Lk 14:15–24. This interruption of the controversies is similar to that in Mark, although

*

21:18–22 Mk 11:12–14, 20–24.
21:19 Jer 8:13; Lk 13:6–9.
21:21 Mt 17:20; Lk 17:6.
21:22 Mt 7:7; 1 Jn 3:22.
21:23–27 Mk 11:27–33; Lk 20:1–8.
21:23 Jn 2:18.
21:26 Mt 14:5.

and work in the vineyard today.' 29 He said in
reply, 'I will not,' but afterwards he changed his
mind and went. 30 The man came to the other
son and gave the same order. He said in reply,
'Yes, sir,' but did not go. 31 † Which of the two
did his father's will?" They answered, "The first."
Jesus said to them, "Amen, I say to you, tax col-
lectors and prostitutes are entering the kingdom
of God before you. 32 * † When John came to you
in the way of righteousness, you did not believe
him; but tax collectors and prostitutes did. Yet
even when you saw that, you did not later change
your minds and believe him.

The Parable of the Tenants†

33 * "Hear another parable. There was a land-
owner who planted a vineyard,* put a hedge
around it, dug a wine press in it, and built a
tower.† Then he leased it to tenants and went
on a journey. 34 † When vintage time drew near,
he sent his servants to the tenants to obtain his
produce. 35 But the tenants seized the servants
and one they beat, another they killed, and a
third they stoned. 36 Again he sent other servants,
more numerous than the first ones, but they
treated them in the same way. 37 Finally, he sent
his son to them, thinking, 'They will respect my
son.' 38 † But when the tenants saw the son, they
said to one another, 'This is the heir. Come, let us
kill him and acquire his inheritance.' 39 * † They
seized him, threw him out of the vineyard, and
killed him. 40 What will the owner of the vineyard
do to those tenants when he comes?" 41 † They
answered him, "He will put those wretched men
to a wretched death and lease his vineyard to
other tenants who will give him the produce at
the proper times." 42 * † Jesus said to them, "Did
you never read in the scriptures:

'The stone that the builders rejected
has become the cornerstone;
by the Lord has this been done,
and it is wonderful in our eyes'?

43 † Therefore, I say to you, the kingdom of God
will be taken away from you and given to a peo-
ple that will produce its fruit. [44 † The one who
falls on this stone will be dashed to pieces; and
it will crush anyone on whom it falls.]" 45 † When
the chief priests and the Pharisees heard his par-
ables, they knew that he was speaking about
them. 46 And although they were attempting to
arrest him, they feared the crowds, for they re-
garded him as a prophet.

Mark has only one parable between the first and second controversy. As regards Matthew's first parable, vv 28–30 if taken by themselves could point simply to the difference between saying and doing, a theme of much importance in this gospel (cf 7:21; 12:50); that may have been the parable's original reference. However, it is given a more specific application by the addition of vv 31–32. The two sons represent, respectively, the religious leaders and the religious outcasts who followed John's call to repentance. By the answer they give to Jesus' question (31) the leaders condemn themselves. There is much confusion in the textual tradition of the parable. Of the three different forms of the text given by important textual witnesses, one has the leaders answer that the son who agreed to go but did not was the one who did the father's will. Although some scholars accept that as the original reading, their arguments in favor of it seem unconvincing. The choice probably lies only between a reading that puts the son who agrees and then disobeys before the son who at first refuses and then obeys, and the reading followed in the present translation. The witnesses to the latter reading are slightly better than those that support the other.

21:31 *Entering . . . before you:* this probably means "they enter; you do not."

21:32 Cf Lk 7:29–30. Although the thought is similar to that of the Lucan text, the formulation is so different that it is improbable that the saying comes from Q. *Came to you . . . way of righteousness:* several meanings are possible: that John himself was righteous, that he taught righteousness to others, or that he had an important place in God's plan of salvation. For the last, see the note on 3:14–15.

21:33–46 Cf Mk 12:1–12. In this parable there is a close correspondence between most of the details of the story and the situation that it illustrates, the dealings of God with his people. Because of that heavy allegorizing, some scholars think that it does not in any way go back to Jesus, but represents the theology of the later church. That judgment applies to the Marcan parallel as well, although the allegorizing has gone farther in Matthew. There are others who believe that while many of the allegorical elements are due to church sources, they have been added to a basic parable spoken by Jesus. This view is now supported by the Gospel of Thomas, 65, where a less allegorized and probably more primitive form of the parable is found.

21:33 *Planted a vineyard . . . a tower:* cf Is 5:1–2. The *vineyard* is defined in Is 5:7 as "the house of Israel."

21:34–35 *His servants:* Matthew has two sendings of *servants* as against Mark's three sendings of a single servant (11:2–5a) followed by a statement about the sending of "many others" (11:2, 5b). That these *servants* stand for the prophets sent by God to Israel is clearly implied but not made explicit here, but see 23:37. *His produce:* cf Mk 12:2, "some of the produce." The *produce* is the good works demanded by God, and his claim to them is total.

21:38 *Acquire his inheritance:* if a Jewish proselyte died without heir, the tenants of his land would have final claim on it.

21:39 *Threw him out . . . and killed him:* the change in the Marcan order where the son is killed and his corpse then thrown out (12:8) was probably made because of the tradition that Jesus died outside the city of Jerusalem; see Jn 19:17; Heb 13:12.

21:41 *They answered:* in Mk 12:9 the question is answered by Jesus himself; here the leaders answer and so condemn themselves; cf v 31. Matthew adds that the new *tenants* to whom the vineyard will be transferred *will give* the owner *the produce at the proper times.*

21:42 Cf Ps 118:22–23. The psalm was used in the early church as a prophecy of Jesus' resurrection; see Acts 4:11; 1 Pt 2:7. If, as some think, the original parable ended at v 39, it was thought necessary to complete it by a reference to Jesus' vindication by God.

21:43 Peculiar to Matthew. *Kingdom of God:* see the note on 19:23–24. Its presence here instead of Matthew's usual "kingdom of heaven" may indicate that the saying came from Matthew's own traditional material. *A people that will produce its fruit:* believing Israelites and Gentiles, the church of Jesus.

21:44 The majority of textual witnesses omit this verse. It is probably an early addition to Matthew from Lk 20:18 with which it is practically identical.

21:45 *The Pharisees:* Matthew inserts into the group of Jewish leaders (23) those who represented the Judaism of his own time.

21:32 Lk 7:29–30.
21:33–46 Mk 12:1–12; Lk 20:9–19.
21:33 Is 5:1–27.
21:39 Heb 13:12.
21:42 Ps 118:22–23; Is 28:16; Acts 4:11; 1 Pt 2:7.

The Parable of the Wedding Feast

22 1*† Jesus again in reply spoke to them
in parables, saying, 2† "The kingdom of
heaven may be likened to a king who gave a
wedding feast for his son. 3† He dispatched his
servants to summon the invited guests to the
feast, but they refused to come. 4 A second time
he sent other servants, saying, 'Tell those invited:
"Behold, I have prepared my banquet, my calves
and fattened cattle are killed, and everything is
ready; come to the feast." ' 5 Some ignored the in-
vitation and went away, one to his farm, another
to his business. 6* The rest laid hold of his ser-
vants, mistreated them, and killed them. 7† The
king was enraged and sent his troops, destroyed
those murderers, and burned their city. 8 Then he
said to his servants, 'The feast is ready, but those
who were invited were not worthy to come. 9 Go
out, therefore, into the main roads and invite to
the feast whomever you find.' 10† The servants
went out into the streets and gathered all they
found, bad and good alike, and the hall was
filled with guests. 11† But when the king came
in to meet the guests he saw a man there not
dressed in a wedding garment. 12 He said to him,
'My friend, how is it that you came in here with-
out a wedding garment?' But he was reduced to
silence. 13*† Then the king said to his attendants,
'Bind his hands and feet, and cast him into the
darkness outside, where there will be wailing and
grinding of teeth.' 14 Many are invited, but few
are chosen."

Paying Taxes to the Emperor†

15* Then the Pharisees† went off and plotted
how they might entrap him in speech. 16† They
sent their disciples to him, with the Herodians,
saying, "Teacher, we know that you are a truth-
ful man and that you teach the way of God in
accordance with the truth. And you are not con-
cerned with anyone's opinion, for you do not
regard a person's status. 17† Tell us, then, what
is your opinion: Is it lawful to pay the census tax
to Caesar or not?" 18 Knowing their malice, Jesus
said, "Why are you testing me, you hypocrites?
19† Show me the coin that pays the census tax."
Then they handed him the Roman coin. 20 He
said to them, "Whose image is this and whose
inscription?" 21*† They replied, "Caesar's." At
that he said to them, "Then repay to Caesar what
belongs to Caesar and to God what belongs to
God." 22 When they heard this they were amazed,
and leaving him they went away.

The Question about the Resurrection†

23* On that day Sadducees approached him,
saying that there is no resurrection.† They put

---

† **22:1–14** This parable is from Q; see Lk 14:15–24. It has been given many allegorical traits by Matthew, e.g., the burning of the *city* of the guests who refused the invitation (7), which corresponds to the destruction of Jerusalem by the Romans in A.D. 70. It has similarities with the preceding parable of the tenants: the sending of two groups of *servants* (3, 4), the murder of the *servants* (6), the punishment of the *murderers* (7), and the entrance of a new group into a privileged situation of which the others had proved themselves unworthy (8–10). The parable ends with a section that is peculiar to Matthew (11–14), which some take as a distinct parable. Matthew presents the *kingdom* in its double aspect, already present and something that can be entered here and now (1–10), and something that will be possessed only by those present members who can stand the scrutiny of the final judgment (11–14). The parable is not only a statement of God's judgment on Israel but a warning to Matthew's church.

22:2 *Wedding feast:* the Old Testament's portrayal of final salvation under the image of a banquet (Is 25:6) is taken up also in 8:11; cf Lk 13:15.

22:3–4 *Servants . . . other servants:* probably Christian missionaries in both instances; cf 23:34.

22:7 See the note on vv 1–14.

22:10 *Bad and good alike:* cf 13:47.

22:11 *A wedding garment:* the repentance, change of heart and mind, that is the condition for entrance into the kingdom (3:2; 4:17) must be continued in a life of good deeds (7:21–23).

22:13 *Wailing and grinding of teeth:* the Christian who lacks the wedding garment of good deeds will suffer the same fate as those Jews who have rejected Jesus; see the note on 8:11–12.

22:15–22 The series of controversies between Jesus and the representatives of Judaism (see the note on 21:23–27) is resumed. As in the first (21:23–27), here and in the following disputes Matthew follows his Marcan source with few modifications.

22:15 *The Pharisees:* while Matthew retains the Marcan union of Pharisees and Herodians in this account, he clearly emphasizes the Pharisees' part. They alone are mentioned here, and the Herodians are joined with them only in a prepositional phrase of v 16. *Entrap him in speech:* the question that they will pose is intended to force Jesus to take either a position contrary to that held by the majority of the people or one that will bring him into conflict with the Roman authorities.

22:16 *Herodians:* see the note on Mk 3:6. They would favor payment of the tax; the Pharisees did not.

22:17 *Is it lawful:* the law to which they refer is the law of God.

22:19 *They handed him the Roman coin:* their readiness in producing the money implies their use of it and their acceptance of the financial advantages of the Roman administration in Palestine.

22:21 *Caesar's:* the emperor Tiberius (A.D. 14–37). *Repay to Caesar what belongs to Caesar:* those who willingly use the coin that is Caesar's should *repay* him in kind. The answer avoids taking sides in the question of the lawfulness of the tax. *To God what belongs to God:* Jesus raises the debate to a new level. Those who have hypocritically asked about tax in respect to its relation to the law of God should be concerned rather with repaying *God* with the good deeds that are his due; cf 21:41, 43.

22:23–33 Here Jesus' opponents are the *Sadducees,* members of the powerful priestly party of his time; see the note on 3:7. Denying the resurrection of the dead, a teaching of relatively late origin in Judaism (cf Dn 12:2), they appeal to a law of the Pentateuch (Dt 25:5–10) and present a case based on it that would make resurrection from the dead ridiculous (24–28). Jesus chides them for knowing neither *the scriptures* nor *the power of God* (29). His argument in respect to God's *power* contradicts the notion, held even by many proponents as well as by opponents of the teaching, that the life of those raised from the dead would be essentially a continuation of the type of life they had had before death (30). His argument based on the scriptures (31–32) is of a sort that was accepted as valid among Jews of the time.

22:23 *Saying that there is no resurrection:* in the Marcan parallel (12:18) the Sadducees are correctly defined as those "who say there is no resurrection"; see also Lk 20:27. Matthew's rewording of Mark can mean that these particular Sadducees deny the resurrection, which would imply that he was not aware that the denial was characteristic of the party. For some scholars this is an indication of his being a Gentile Christian; see the note on 21:4–5.

---

* **22:1–14** Lk 14:15–24.
22:6 Mt 21:35.
22:13 Mt 8:12; 25:30.
22:15–22 Mk 12:13–17; Lk 20:20–26.
22:21 Rom 13:7.
22:23–33 Mk 12:18–27; Lk 20:27–40.

this question to him, 24*† saying, "Teacher, Mo-
ses said, 'If a man dies without children, his
brother shall marry his wife and raise up descen-
dants for his brother.' 25 Now there were seven
brothers among us. The first married and died
and, having no descendants, left his wife to his
brother. 26 The same happened with the second
and the third, through all seven. 27 Finally the
woman died. 28 Now at the resurrection, of the
seven, whose wife will she be? For they all had
been married to her." 29† Jesus said to them
in reply, "You are misled because you do not
know the scriptures or the power of God. 30 At
the resurrection they neither marry nor are given
in marriage but are like the angels in heaven.
31† And concerning the resurrection of the dead,
have you not read what was said to you by God,
32* 'I am the God of Abraham, the God of Isaac,
and the God of Jacob'? He is not the God of the
dead but of the living." 33 When the crowds heard
this, they were astonished at his teaching.

The Greatest Commandment

34*† When the Pharisees heard that he had
silenced the Sadducees, they gathered together,
35† and one of them [a scholar of the law] tested
him by asking, 36† "Teacher, which command-
ment in the law is the greatest?" 37*† He said to
him, "You shall love the Lord, your God, with
all your heart, with all your soul, and with all
your mind. 38 This is the greatest and the first
commandment. 39*† The second is like it: You
shall love your neighbor as yourself. 40*† The
whole law and the prophets depend on these two
commandments."

Live It!

The Perfect Plan

Can you imagine a world where every person lives according to the two commandments Jesus gives in Matthew 22:34–40? where every word, thought, and action is motivated by a deep love for God and by a desire for the well-being of others? Sounds a bit like the Garden of Eden! Libraries are filled with volumes describing philosophies for achieving the ideal human society, yet Jesus articulates the perfect plan in a few short sentences. In fact, these two commands summarize the Ten Commandments and were long considered a summary of Mosaic Law.

The message of these two great commandments obviously remains real and relevant for us today. Following in the footsteps of the Apostles who first heard Jesus' words, it is now our responsibility to live out these commandments in our world—becoming living, breathing examples of what it means to love God, neighbor, and self.

▶ **Mt 22:34–40**

The Question about David's Son†

41* While the Pharisees were gathered together,

22:24 *'If a man dies . . . his brother'*: this is known as the "law of the levirate," from the Latin *levir*, "brother-in-law." Its purpose was to continue the family line of the deceased *brother* (Dt 25:6).

22:29 The sexual relationships of this world will be transcended; the risen body will be the work of the creative *power of God*.

22:31–32 Cf Ex 3:6. In the Pentateuch, which the Sadducees accepted as normative for Jewish belief and practice, God speaks even now (*to you*) of himself as the God of the patriarchs who died centuries ago. He identifies himself in relation to them, and because of their relation to him, the living God, they too are alive. This might appear no argument for the resurrection, but simply for life after death as conceived in Wis 3:1–3. But the general thought of early first-century Judaism was not influenced by that conception; for it human immortality was connected with the existence of the body.

22:34–40 The Marcan parallel (12:28–34) is an exchange between Jesus and a scribe who is impressed by the way in which Jesus has conducted himself in the previous controversy (12:28), who compliments him for the answer he gives him (12:32), and who is said by Jesus to be "not far from the kingdom of God" (12:34). Matthew has sharpened that scene. The questioner, as the representative of other Pharisees, tests Jesus by his question (34–35), and both his reaction to Jesus' reply and Jesus' commendation of him are lacking.

22:35 [*A scholar of the law*]: meaning "scribe." Although this reading is supported by the vast majority of textual witnesses, it is the only time that the Greek word so translated occurs in Matthew. It is relatively frequent in Luke, and there is reason to think that it may have been added here by a copyist since it occurs in the Lucan parallel (10:25–28). *Tested:* see the note on 19:3.

22:36 For the devout Jew all the commandments were to be kept with equal care, but there is evidence of preoccupation in Jewish sources with the question put to Jesus.

22:37–38 Cf Dt 6:5. Matthew omits the first part of Mark's fuller quotation (12:29; Dt 6:4–5), probably because he considered its monotheistic emphasis needless for his church. The love of God must engage the total person (*heart, soul, mind*).

22:39 Jesus goes beyond the extent of the question put to him and joins to *the greatest and the first commandment* a *second,* that of *love* of *neighbor,* Lv 19:18; see the note on 19:18–19. This combination of the two commandments may already have been made in Judaism.

22:40 The double commandment is the source from which *the whole law and the prophets* are derived.

22:41–46 Having answered the questions of his opponents in the preceding three controversies, Jesus now puts a question to them about the sonship of the Messiah. Their easy response (43a) is countered by his quoting a verse of Ps 110 that raises a problem for their response (43b–45). They are unable to solve it and *from that day on* their questioning of him is ended.

22:24 Gn 38:8; Dt 25:5–6.
22:32 Ex 3:6.
22:34–40 Mk 12:28–34; Lk 10:25–28.
22:37 Dt 6:5.
22:39 Lv 19:18; Jas 2:8.
22:40 Rom 13:8–10; Gal 5:14.
22:41–46 Mk 12:35–37; Lk 20:41–44.

Jesus questioned them,† 42† saying, "What is
your opinion about the Messiah? Whose son is
he?" They replied, "David's." 43 He said to them,
"How, then, does David, inspired by the Spirit,
call him 'lord,' saying:

44* 'The Lord said to my lord,
"Sit at my right hand
until I place your enemies under your feet"'?

45 † If David calls him 'lord,' how can he be his
son?" 46* No one was able to answer him a word,
nor from that day on did anyone dare to ask him
any more questions.

Pray It!

No Respect

The "woe" statements of Jesus in Matthew 23:1–36 may be his harshest words in all the Gospels. Scholars think the community in which the author of Matthew lived may have had negative experiences with certain Jewish leaders (see "Pharisees, Sadducees, and Scribes," near Mt 3:7), and their hard feelings are reflected in Jesus' words. We should take Matthew 23:3–24 not as a condemnation of Jewish people but as a call to do the following:

- practice what we preach (see verse 3)
- show compassion; don't burden others (see verse 4)
- practice religion not to look important but as an expression of faith (see verses 5–7)
- humbly respect the people who follow us (see verses 8–15)
- be guided by mercy and justice in our understanding of law (see verses 23–24)

Jesus' sharpest criticism here and in many other places in the Gospels is directed against hypocrisy—the act of pretending to be holy and just while actually doing sinful things.

In your prayer, reflect or journal on the following questions:

- How have I expressed my faith in my spoken words as well as in my inner thoughts?
- When has my life demonstrated what my faith is all about?
- When have I asked others to do something I was not willing to do myself? Why did I do that?
- When have I used any power or influence I might have in a way that was humble and served the needs of others? How did I do that?

Try looking at these same questions each week or month, and see if your answers change over time.

► **Mt 23:1–36**

Denunciation of the Scribes and Pharisees

23 1*† Then Jesus spoke to the crowds and to
his disciples, 2† saying, "The scribes and
the Pharisees have taken their seat on the chair

† **22:41** *The Pharisees . . . questioned them:* Mark is not specific about who are questioned (12:35).

22:42–44 *David's:* this view of the Pharisees was based on such Old Testament texts as Is 11:1–9; Jer 23:5; and Ez 34:23; see also the extrabiblical Psalms of Solomon 17:21. *How, then . . . saying:* Jesus cites Ps 110:1, accepting the Davidic authorship of the psalm, a common view of his time. The psalm was probably composed for the enthronement of a Davidic king of Judah. Matthew assumes that the Pharisees interpret it as referring to the Messiah, although there is no clear evidence that it was so interpreted in the Judaism of Jesus' time. It was widely used in the early church as referring to the exaltation of the risen Jesus. *My lord:* understood as the Messiah.

22:45 Since Matthew presents Jesus both as Messiah (16:16) and as Son of David (1:1; see also the note on 9:27), the question is not meant to imply Jesus' denial of Davidic sonship. It probably means that although he is the Son of David, he is someone greater, Son of Man and Son of God, and recognized as greater by David who calls him my *'lord.'*

23:1–39 The final section of the narrative part of the fifth book of the gospel is a denunciation by Jesus of the scribes and the Pharisees (see the note on 3:7). It depends in part on Mark and Q (cf Mk 12:38–39; Lk 11:37–52; 13:34–35), but in the main it is peculiar to Matthew. (For the reasons against considering this extensive body of sayings-material either as one of the structural discourses of this gospel or as part of the one that follows in chs 24–25, see the note on 19:1—23:39.) While the tradition of a deep opposition between Jesus and the Pharisees is well founded, this speech reflects an opposition that goes beyond that of Jesus' ministry and must be seen as expressing the bitter conflict between Pharisaic Judaism and the church of Matthew at the time when the gospel was composed. The complaint often made that the speech ignores the positive qualities of Pharisaism and of its better representatives is true, but the complaint overlooks the circumstances that gave rise to the invective. Nor is the speech purely anti-Pharisaic. The evangelist discerns in his church many of the same faults that he finds in its opponents and warns his fellow Christians to look to their own conduct and attitudes.

23:2–3 *Have taken their seat . . . Moses:* it is uncertain whether this is simply a metaphor for Mosaic teaching authority or refers to an actual *chair* on which the teacher sat. It has been proved that there was a seat so designated in synagogues of a later period than that of this gospel. *Do and observe . . . they tell you:* since the Matthean Jesus abrogates Mosaic law (5:31–42), warns his disciples against the teaching of the Pharisees (14:1–12), and, in this speech, denounces the Pharisees as blind guides in respect to their teaching on oaths (16–22), this commandment *to observe all things whatsoever they* (the scribes and Pharisees) *tell you* cannot be taken as the evangelist's understanding of the proper standard of conduct for his church. The saying may reflect a period when the Matthean community was largely Jewish Christian and was still seeking to avoid a complete break with the synagogue. Matthew has incorporated this traditional material into the speech in accordance with his view of the course of salvation history, in which he portrays the time of Jesus' ministry as marked by the fidelity to the law, although with significant pointers

22:44 Ps 110:1; Acts 2:35; Heb 1:13.
22:46 Lk 20:40.
23:1–39 Mk 12:38–39; Lk 11:37–52; 13:34–35.

of Moses. 3 Therefore, do and observe all things
whatsoever they tell you, but do not follow their
example. For they preach but they do not prac-
tice. 4*† They tie up heavy burdens [hard to carry]
and lay them on people's shoulders, but they will
not lift a finger to move them. 5*† All their works
are performed to be seen. They widen their phy-
lacteries and lengthen their tassels. 6*† They love
places of honor at banquets, seats of honor in
synagogues, 7 greetings in marketplaces, and the
salutation 'Rabbi.' 8† As for you, do not be called
'Rabbi.' You have but one teacher, and you are all
brothers. 9 Call no one on earth your father; you
have but one Father in heaven. 10 Do not be called
'Master'; you have but one master, the Messiah.
11* The greatest among you must be your servant.
12* Whoever exalts himself will be humbled; but
whoever humbles himself will be exalted.

13*† "Woe to you, scribes and Pharisees, you
hypocrites. You lock the kingdom of heaven†
before human beings. You do not enter your-
selves, nor do you allow entrance to those trying
to enter. [14]†

15† "Woe to you, scribes and Pharisees, you
hypocrites. You traverse sea and land to make
one convert, and when that happens you make
him a child of Gehenna twice as much as your-
selves.

16*† "Woe to you, blind guides, who say, 'If
one swears by the temple, it means nothing, but
if one swears by the gold of the temple, one is
obligated.' 17 Blind fools, which is greater, the
gold, or the temple that made the gold sacred?
18 And you say, 'If one swears by the altar, it
means nothing, but if one swears by the gift on
the altar, one is obligated.' 19 You blind ones,
which is greater, the gift, or the altar that makes
the gift sacred? 20* One who swears by the altar
swears by it and all that is upon it; 21 one who
swears by the temple swears by it and by him
who dwells in it; 22 one who swears by heaven
swears by the throne of God and by him who is
seated on it.

23*† "Woe to you, scribes and Pharisees, you
hypocrites. You pay tithes of mint and dill and
cummin, and have neglected the weightier things
of the law: judgment and mercy and fidelity.
[But] these you should have done, without ne-
glecting the others. 24*† Blind guides, who strain
out the gnat and swallow the camel!

M
T

†

to the new situation that would exist after his death and resurrection (see the note on 5:17–20). The crowds and the disciples (1) are exhorted not to *follow* the *example* of the Jewish leaders, whose deeds do not conform to their teaching (3).

23:4 *Tie up heavy burdens:* see the note on 11:28.

23:5 To the charge of preaching but not practicing (3), Jesus adds that of acting in order to earn praise. The disciples have already been warned against this same fault (see the note on 6:1–18). *Phylacteries:* the Mosaic law required that during prayer small boxes containing parchments on which verses of scripture were written be worn on the left forearm and the forehead (see Ex 13:9, 16; Dt 6:8; 11:18). *Tassels:* see the note on 9:20. The widening of *phylacteries* and the lengthening of *tassels* were for the purpose of making these evidences of piety more noticeable.

23:6–7 Cf Mk 12:38–39. *'Rabbi':* literally, "my great one," a title of respect for teachers and leaders.

23:8–12 These verses, warning against the use of various titles, are addressed to the disciples alone. While only the title *'Rabbi'* has been said to be used in addressing the scribes and Pharisees (7), the implication is that *Father* and *'Master'* also were. The prohibition of these titles to the disciples suggests that their use was present in Matthew's church. The Matthean Jesus forbids not only the titles but the spirit of superiority and pride that is shown by their acceptance. *Whoever exalts . . . will be exalted:* cf Lk 14:11.

23:13–36 This series of seven "woes," directed against the *scribes and Pharisees* and addressed to them, is the heart of the speech. The phrase *woe to* occurs often in the prophetic and apocalyptic literature, expressing horror of a sin and punishment for those who commit it. *Hypocrites:* see the note on 6:2. The hypocrisy of the *scribes and Pharisees* consists in the difference between their speech and action (3) and in demonstrations of piety that have no other purpose than to enhance their reputation as religious persons (5).

23:13 *You lock the kingdom of heaven:* cf 16:19 where Jesus tells Peter that he will give him the keys to *the kingdom of heaven.* The purpose of the authority expressed by that metaphor is to give entrance into the kingdom (the kingdom is closed only to those who reject the authority); here the charge is made that the authority of the *scribes and Pharisees* is exercised in such a way as to be an obstacle to entrance. Cf Lk 11:52 where the accusation against the "scholars of the law" (Matthew's *scribes*) is that they "have taken away the key of knowledge."

23:14 Some manuscripts add a verse here or after v 12, "Woe to you, scribes and Pharisees, you hypocrites. You devour the houses of widows and, as a pretext, recite lengthy prayers. Because of this, you will receive a very severe condemnation." Cf Mk 12:40; Lk 20:47. This "woe" is almost identical with Mk 12:40 and seems to be an interpolation derived from that text.

23:15 In the first century A.D. until the First Jewish Revolt against Rome (A.D. 66–70), many Pharisees conducted a vigorous missionary campaign among Gentiles. *Convert:* literally, "proselyte," a Gentile who accepted Judaism fully by submitting to circumcision and all other requirements of Mosaic law. *Child of Gehenna:* worthy of everlasting punishment; for *Gehenna,* see the note on 5:22. *Twice as much as yourselves:* possibly this refers simply to the zeal of the *convert,* surpassing that of the one who converted him.

23:16–22 An attack on the casuistry that declared some oaths binding (*one is obligated*) and others not (*it means nothing*) and held the binding oath to be the one made by something of lesser value (*the gold; the gift on the altar*). Such teaching, which inverts the order of values, reveals the teachers to be *blind guides;* cf 15:14. Since the Matthean Jesus forbids all oaths to his disciples (5:33–37), this *woe* does not set up a standard for Christian moral conduct, but ridicules the Pharisees on their own terms.

23:23 The Mosaic law ordered tithing of the produce of the land (Lv 27:30; Dt 14:22–23), and the scribal tradition is said here to have extended this law to even the smallest herbs. The practice is criticized not in itself but because it shows the Pharisees' preoccupation with matters of less importance while they neglect *the weightier things of the law.*

23:24 Cf Lv 11:41–45 that forbids the eating of any "swarming creature." The Pharisees' scrupulosity about minor matters and neglect of greater ones (23) is further brought out by this contrast between straining liquids that might contain a tiny "swarming creature" and yet swallowing *the camel.* The latter was one of the unclean animals forbidden by the law (Lv 11:4), but it is hardly possible that the scribes and Pharisees are being denounced as guilty of so gross a violation of the food laws. To *swallow the camel* is only a hyperbolic way of speaking of their neglect of what is important.

*

23:4 Lk 11:46.
23:5 Mt 6:1–6; Ex 13:9, 16; Nm 15:38–39; Dt 6:8; 11:18.
23:6–7 Mk 12:38–39; Lk 11:43; 20:46.
23:11 Mt 20:26.
23:12 Lk 14:11; 18:14.
23:13 Lk 11:52.
23:16 Mt 15:14.
23:20–22 Mt 5:34–35.
23:23 Lv 27:30; Dt 14:22; Lk 11:42.
23:24 Lv 11:41–45.

25*† "Woe to you, scribes and Pharisees, you hypocrites. You cleanse the outside of cup and dish, but inside they are full of plunder and self-indulgence. 26 Blind Pharisee, cleanse first the inside of the cup, so that the outside also may be clean.

27† "Woe to you, scribes and Pharisees, you hypocrites. You are like whitewashed tombs, which appear beautiful on the outside, but inside are full of dead men's bones and every kind of filth. 28* Even so, on the outside you appear righteous, but inside you are filled with hypocrisy and evildoing.

29† "Woe to you, scribes and Pharisees,† you hypocrites. You build the tombs of the prophets and adorn the memorials of the righteous, 30* and you say, 'If we had lived in the days of our ancestors, we would not have joined them in shedding the prophets' blood.' 31* Thus you bear witness against yourselves that you are the children of those who murdered the prophets; 32 now fill up what your ancestors measured out! 33* You serpents, you brood of vipers, how can you flee from the judgment of Gehenna? 34*† Therefore, behold, I send to you prophets and wise men and scribes; some of them you will kill and crucify, some of them you will scourge in your synagogues and pursue from town to town, 35 so that there may come upon you all the righteous blood shed upon earth, from the righteous blood of Abel to the blood of Zechariah, the son of Barachiah, whom you murdered between the sanctuary and the altar. 36 Amen, I say to you, all these things will come upon this generation.

The Lament over Jerusalem

37*† "Jerusalem, Jerusalem, you who kill the prophets and stone those sent to you, how many times I yearned to gather your children together, as a hen gathers her young under her wings, but you were unwilling!* 38* Behold, your house will be abandoned, desolate. 39* I tell you, you will not see me again until you say, 'Blessed is he who comes in the name of the Lord.' "

The Destruction of the Temple Foretold

24 1*† Jesus left the temple area and was going away, when his disciples approached him to point out the temple buildings. 2† He said to them in reply, "You see all these things, do you not? Amen, I say to you, there will not be left here a stone upon another stone that will not be thrown down."

23:25–26 The ritual washing of utensils for dining (cf Mk 7:4) is turned into a metaphor illustrating a concern for appearances while inner purity is ignored. The *scribes and Pharisees* are compared to cups carefully washed on the outside but filthy within. *Self-indulgence:* the Greek word here translated means lack of self-control, whether in drinking or in sexual conduct.

23:27–28 The sixth *woe,* like the preceding one, deals with concern for externals and neglect of what is *inside.* Since contact with dead bodies, even when one was unaware of it, caused ritual impurity (Nm 19:11–22), tombs were whitewashed so that no one would contract such impurity inadvertently.

23:29–36 The final *woe* is the most serious indictment of all. It portrays the *scribes and Pharisees* as standing in the same line as their *ancestors* who murdered *the prophets* and *the righteous.*

23:29–32 In spite of honoring the slain dead by building their *tombs* and adorning their *memorials,* and claiming that they would not have joined in their ancestors' crimes if they *had lived in* their *days,* the *scribes and Pharisees* are true *children* of their ancestors and are defiantly ordered by Jesus to *fill up* what those *ancestors measured out.* This order reflects the Jewish notion that there was an allotted measure of suffering that had to be completed before God's final judgment would take place.

23:34–36 There are important differences between the Matthean and the Lucan form of this Q material; cf Lk 11:49–51. In Luke the one who sends the emissaries is the "wisdom of God." If, as many scholars think, that is the original wording of Q, Matthew, by making Jesus the sender, has presented him as the personified divine wisdom. In Luke, wisdom's emissaries are the Old Testament "prophets" and the Christian "apostles." Matthew's *prophets and wise men and scribes* are probably Christian disciples alone; cf 10:41 and see the note on 13:52. *You will kill:* see 24:9. *Scourge in your synagogues . . . town to town:* see 10:17, 23 and the note on 10:17. *All the righteous blood shed upon the earth:* the slaying of the disciples is in continuity with all the shedding of *righteous blood* beginning with that *of Abel.* The persecution of Jesus' disciples by *this generation* involves the persecutors in the guilt of their murderous ancestors. *The blood of Zechariah:* see the note on Lk 11:51. By identifying him as *the son of Barachiah* Matthew understands him to be Zechariah the Old Testament minor prophet; see Zec 1:1.

23:37–39 Cf Lk 13:34–35. The denunciation of Pharisaic Judaism ends with this lament over *Jerusalem,* which has repeatedly rejected and murdered those whom God has *sent to* her. *How many times:* this may refer to various visits of Jesus to the city, an aspect of his ministry found in John but otherwise not in the synoptics. *As a hen . . . under her wings:* for imagery similar to this, see Pss 17:8; 91:4. *Your house . . . desolate:* probably an allusion to the destruction of the temple in A.D. 70. *You will not see me . . . in the name of the Lord:* Israel will not see Jesus again until he comes in glory for the final judgment. The acclamation has been interpreted in contrasting ways, as an indication that Israel will at last accept Jesus at that time, and as its troubled recognition of him as its dreaded judge who will pronounce its condemnation; in support of the latter view see 24:30.

24:1—25:46 The discourse of the fifth book, the last of the five around which the gospel is structured. It is called the "eschatological" discourse since it deals with the coming of the new age (the *eschaton*) in its fullness, with events that will precede it, and with how the disciples are to conduct themselves while awaiting an event that is as certain as its exact time is unknown to all but the Father (24:36). The discourse may be divided into two parts, 24:1–44 and 24:45—25:46. In the first, Matthew follows his Marcan source (13:1–37) closely. The second is drawn from Q and from the evangelist's own traditional material. Both parts show Matthew's editing of his sources by deletions, additions, and modifications. The vigilant waiting that is emphasized in the second part does not mean a cessation of ordinary activity and concentration only on what is to come, but a faithful accomplishment of duties at hand, with awareness that the end, for which the disciples must always be ready, will entail the great judgment by which the everlasting destiny of all will be determined.

24:2 As in Mark, Jesus predicts the destruction of the temple. By omitting the Marcan story of the widow's contribution (12:41–44) that immediately precedes the prediction in that gospel, Matthew has established a close connection between it and 23:38, ". . . your house will be abandoned desolate."

23:25–26 Mk 7:4; Lk 11:39.
23:28 Lk 16:15; 18:9.
23:30 Lk 11:47.
23:31 Acts 7:52.
23:33 Mt 3:7; 12:34.
23:34–36 Mt 5:12; Gn 4:8; 2 Chr 24:20–22; Zec 1:1; Lk 11:49–51; Rv 18:24.
23:37–39 Lk 13:34–35; 19:41–44.
23:37 Mt 21:35.
23:38 Jer 12:7.
23:39 Ps 118:26.
24:1–44 Mk 13:1–37; Lk 21:5–36.

The Beginning of Calamities

3† As he was sitting on the Mount of Olives,
the disciples approached him privately and said,
"Tell us, when will this happen, and what sign
will there be of your coming, and of the end of
the age?" 4† Jesus said to them in reply, "See that
no one deceives you. 5 For many will come in
my name, saying, 'I am the Messiah,' and they
will deceive many. 6*† You will hear of wars and
reports of wars; see that you are not alarmed,
for these things must happen, but it will not yet
be the end. 7* Nation will rise against nation,
and kingdom against kingdom; there will be
famines and earthquakes from place to place.
8† All these are the beginning of the labor pains.
9*† Then they will hand you over to persecution,
and they will kill you. You will be hated by all
nations because of my name. 10 And then many
will be led into sin; they will betray and hate
one another. 11 Many false prophets will arise
and deceive many; 12 and because of the increase
of evildoing, the love of many will grow cold.
13* But the one who perseveres to the end will be
saved. 14*† And this gospel of the kingdom will
be preached throughout the world as a witness to
all nations, and then the end will come.

The Great Tribulation†

15* "When you see the desolating abomina-
tion† spoken of through Daniel the prophet
standing in the holy place (let the reader under-
stand), 16† then those in Judea must flee to the
mountains, 17*† a person on the housetop must
not go down to get things out of his house, 18 a
person in the field must not return to get his
cloak. 19 Woe to pregnant women and nursing
mothers in those days. 20† Pray that your flight

24:3 *The Mount of Olives:* see the note on 21:1. *The disciples:* cf Mk 13:3–4 where only Peter, James, John, and Andrew put the question that is answered by the discourse. In both gospels, however, the question is put *privately:* the ensuing discourse is only for those who are *disciples* of Jesus. *When will this happen . . . end of the age?:* Matthew distinguishes carefully between the destruction of the temple (*this*) and the *coming* of Jesus that will bring *the end of the age.* In Mark the two events are more closely connected, a fact that may be explained by Mark's believing that the one would immediately succeed the other. *Coming:* this translates the Greek word *parousia,* which is used in the gospels only here and in vv 27:37, and 39. It designated the official visit of a ruler to a city or the manifestation of a saving deity, and it was used by Christians to refer to the final coming of Jesus in glory, a term first found in the New Testament with that meaning in 1 Thes 2:19. *The end of the age:* see the note on 13:39.

24:4–14 This section of the discourse deals with calamities in the world (6–7) and in the church (9–12). The former *must happen* before *the end* comes (6), but they are only *the beginning of the labor pains* (8). (It may be noted that the Greek word translated *the end* in v 6 and in vv 13–14 is not the same as the phrase "the end of the age" in v 3, although the meaning is the same.) The latter are sufferings of the church, both from within and without, that will last until the *gospel* is *preached . . . to all nations. Then the end will come* and those who have endured the sufferings with fidelity *will be saved* (13–14).

24:6–7 The disturbances mentioned here are a commonplace of apocalyptic language, as is the assurance that they *must happen* (see Dn 2:28 LXX), for that is the plan of God. *Kingdom against kingdom:* see Is 19:2.

24:8 *The labor pains:* the tribulations leading up to the end of the age are compared to the pains of a woman about to give birth. There is much attestation for rabbinic use of the phrase "the woes (or birth pains) of the Messiah" after the New Testament period, but in at least one instance it is attributed to a rabbi who lived in the late first century A.D. In this Jewish usage it meant the distress of the time preceding the coming of the Messiah; here, the *labor pains* precede the coming of the Son of Man in glory.

24:9–12 Matthew has used Mk 13:9–12 in his missionary discourse (10:17–21) and omits it here. Besides the sufferings, including death, and the hatred of *all nations* that the disciples will have to endure, there will be worse affliction within the church itself. This is described in vv 10–12, which are peculiar to Matthew. *Will be led into sin:* literally, "will be scandalized," probably meaning that they will become apostates; see 13:21 where "fall away" translates the same Greek word as here. *Betray:* in the Greek this is the same word as the *hand over* of v 9. The handing over to persecution and hatred from outside will have their counterpart within the church. *False prophets:* these are Christians; see the note on 7:15–20. *Evildoing:* see 7:23. Because of the apocalyptic nature of much of this discourse, the literal meaning of this description of the church should not be pressed too hard. However, there is reason to think that Matthew's addition of these verses reflects in some measure the condition of his community.

24:14 Except for the last part (*and then the end will come*), this verse substantially repeats Mk 13:10. The Matthean addition raises a problem since what follows in vv 15–23 refers to the horrors of the First Jewish Revolt including the destruction of the temple, and Matthew, writing after that time, knew that the parousia of Jesus was still in the future. A solution may be that the evangelist saw the events of those verses as foreshadowing the cosmic disturbances that he associates with the parousia (29) so that the period in which the former took place could be understood as belonging to *the end.*

24:15–28 Cf Mk 13:14–23; Lk 17:23–24, 37. A further stage in the tribulations that will precede the coming of the Son of Man, and an answer to the question of v 3a, "when will this (the destruction of the temple) happen?"

24:15 *The desolating abomination:* in 167 B.C. the Syrian king Antiochus IV Epiphanes desecrated the temple by setting up in it a statue of Zeus Olympios (see 1 Mc 1:54). That event is referred to in Dn 12:11 LXX as the "desolating abomination" (NAB "horrible abomination") and the same Greek term is used here; cf also Dn 9:27; 11:31. Although the desecration had taken place before Daniel was written, it is presented there as a future event, and Matthew sees that "prophecy" fulfilled in the desecration of the temple by the Romans. *In the holy place:* the temple; more precise than Mark's *where he should not* (13:14). *Let the reader understand:* this parenthetical remark, taken from Mk 13:14, invites *the reader* to realize the meaning of Daniel's "prophecy."

24:16 The tradition that the Christians of Jerusalem fled from that city to Pella, a city of Transjordan, at the time of the First Jewish Revolt is found in Eusebius (*Ecclesiastical History,* 3, 5, 3), who attributes the flight to "a certain oracle given by revelation before the war." The tradition is not improbable but the Matthean command, derived from its Marcan source, is vague in respect to the place of flight (*to the mountains*), although some scholars see it as applicable to the flight to Pella.

24:17–19 Haste is essential, and the journey will be particularly difficult for women who are burdened with unborn or infant children.

24:20 *On the sabbath:* this addition to *in winter* (cf Mk 13:18) has been understood as an indication that Matthew was addressed to a church still observing the Mosaic law of sabbath rest and the scribal limitations upon the length of journeys that might lawfully be made on that day. That interpretation conflicts with Matthew's view on sabbath observance (cf 12:1–14). The meaning of the addition may be that those undertaking on the sabbath a journey such as the one here ordered would be offending the sensibilities of law-observant Jews and would incur their hostility.

24:6 Dn 2:28 LXX.
24:7 Is 19:2.
24:9 Mt 10:17.
24:13 Mt 10:22.
24:14 Mt 28:19; Rom 10:18.
24:15 Dn 9:27; 11:31; 12:11; Mk 13:14.
24:17 Lk 17:31.

not be in winter or on the sabbath, 21*† for at
that time there will be great tribulation, such as
has not been since the beginning of the world
until now, nor ever will be. 22 And if those days
had not been shortened, no one would be saved;
but for the sake of the elect they will be short-
ened. 23* If anyone says to you then, 'Look, here
is the Messiah!' or, 'There he is!' do not believe
it. 24 False messiahs and false prophets will arise,
and they will perform signs and wonders so great
as to deceive, if that were possible, even the elect.
25 Behold, I have told it to you beforehand. 26† So
if they say to you, 'He is in the desert,' do not go
out there; if they say, 'He is in the inner rooms,'
do not believe it. 27* For just as lightning comes
from the east and is seen as far as the west, so will
the coming of the Son of Man be. 28 Wherever the
corpse is, there the vultures will gather.

The Coming of the Son of Man

29*† "Immediately after the tribulation of
those days,

the sun will be darkened,
and the moon will not give its light,
and the stars will fall from the sky,
and the powers of the heavens will
be shaken.

30*† And then the sign of the Son of Man will ap-
pear in heaven, and all the tribes of the earth will
mourn, and they will see the Son of Man coming
upon the clouds of heaven with power and great
glory. 31*† And he will send out his angels with a
trumpet blast, and they will gather his elect from
the four winds, from one end of the heavens to
the other.

The Lesson of the Fig Tree

32† "Learn a lesson from the fig tree. When its
branch becomes tender and sprouts leaves, you
know that summer is near. 33 In the same way,
when you see all these things, know that he is
near, at the gates. 34† Amen, I say to you, this gen-
eration will not pass away until all these things

Live It!

Look Busy!

Cardinal Francis Spellman, former archbishop of New York, was in his office when the phone rang. It was a receptionist from the chancery lobby who said, "Cardinal, there is a man here in the lobby claiming to be Jesus Christ. What should I do?" The Cardinal responded, "Look busy!"

Though the cardinal's response was meant to be a humorous one, the message should resonate with all of us. If Jesus were to return today, what would he say about our lives? What would he say about our world? Are we truly awake and ready for Jesus' return?

In this final teaching in Matthew, Jesus is speaking of the final coming of God. The Gospel reminds us that no one knows when Christ will come for us. Thus, it is foolish and dangerous to put off living a life committed to Christ. Instead, we should "look busy" every day of our lives, working hard to ensure that we are living as true disciples of Christ. We never know when that "unexpected hour" may arrive!

▶ Mt 24:36–44

† **24:21** For the unparalleled distress of that time, see Dn 12:1.

24:26–28 Claims that the Messiah is to be found in some distant or secret place must be ignored. *The coming of the Son of Man* will be as clear as *lightning* is to all and as *the corpse* of an animal is to *vultures;* cf Lk 17:24, 37. Here there is clear identification of *the Son of Man* and the Messiah; cf v 23.

24:29 The answer to the question of v 3b, "What sign will there be of your coming?" *Immediately after . . . those days:* the shortening of time between the preceding *tribulation* and the parousia has been explained as Matthew's use of a supposed device of Old Testament prophecy whereby certainty that a predicted event will occur is expressed by depicting it as imminent. While it is questionable that that is an acceptable understanding of the Old Testament predictions, it may be applicable here, for Matthew knew that the parousia had not come *immediately after* the fall of Jerusalem, and it is unlikely that he is attributing a mistaken calculation of time to Jesus. *The sun . . . be shaken:* cf Is 13:10, 13.

24:30 *The sign of the Son of Man:* perhaps this means *the sign* that is the glorious appearance *of the Son of Man;* cf 12:39–40 where "the sign of Jonah" is Jonah's being in the "belly of the whale." *Tribes of the earth will mourn:* peculiar to Matthew; cf Zec 12:12–14. *Coming upon the clouds . . . glory:* cf Dn 7:13, although there the "one like a son of man" comes to God to receive kingship; here *the Son of Man* comes from heaven for judgment.

24:31 *Send out his angels:* cf 13:41 where they are sent out to collect the wicked for punishment. *Trumpet blast:* cf Is 27:13; 1 Thes 4:16.

24:32–35 Cf Mk 13:28–31.

24:34 The difficulty raised by this verse cannot be satisfactorily removed by the supposition that *this generation* means the Jewish people throughout the course of their history, much less the entire human race. Perhaps for Matthew it means the *generation* to which he and his community belonged.

24:21 Dn 12:1.
24:23 Lk 17:23.
24:27–28 Lk 17:24, 37.
24:29 Is 13:10, 13; Ez 32:7; Am 8:9.
24:30 Dn 7:13; Zec 12:12–14; Rv 1:7.
24:31 Is 27:13; 1 Cor 15:52; 1 Thes 4:16.

have taken place. 35* Heaven and earth will pass away, but my words will not pass away.

The Unknown Day and Hour†

36* "But of that day and hour no one knows, neither the angels of heaven, nor the Son,† but the Father alone. 37*† For as it was in the days of Noah, so it will be at the coming of the Son of Man. 38 In [those] days before the flood, they were eating and drinking, marrying and giving in marriage, up to the day that Noah entered the ark. 39 They did not know until the flood came and carried them all away. So will it be [also] at the coming of the Son of Man. 40*† Two men will be out in the field; one will be taken, and one will be left. 41 Two women will be grinding at the mill; one will be taken, and one will be left. 42*† Therefore, stay awake! For you do not know on which day your Lord will come. 43* Be sure of this: if the master of the house had known the hour of night when the thief was coming, he would have stayed awake and not let his house be broken into. 44 So too, you also must be prepared, for at an hour you do not expect, the Son of Man will come.

The Faithful or the Unfaithful Servant†

45* "Who, then, is the faithful and prudent servant, whom the master has put in charge of his household to distribute to them their food at the proper time?† 46 Blessed is that servant whom his master on his arrival finds doing so. 47 Amen, I say to you, he will put him in charge of all his property. 48† But if that wicked servant says to himself, 'My master is long delayed,' 49 and begins to beat his fellow servants, and eat and drink with drunkards, 50 the servant's master will come on an unexpected day and at an unknown hour 51*† and will punish him severely and assign him a place with the hypocrites, where there will be wailing and grinding of teeth.

Pray It!

When Are You Coming?

I have accepted your invitation, Lord.
But when are you coming?
I need to be ready, Lord.
But when are you coming?
I want to share your love with others, Lord.
But when are you coming?
I will be prepared, Lord.
No matter when you are coming.

▶ Mt 25:1–13

The Parable of the Ten Virgins†

25 1 "Then† the kingdom of heaven will be like ten virgins who took their lamps and went out to meet the bridegroom. 2† Five of them were foolish and five were wise. 3 The foolish ones, when taking their lamps, brought no oil with them, 4 but the wise brought flasks of oil with their lamps. 5 Since the bridegroom was long delayed, they all became drowsy and fell asleep. 6 At midnight, there was a cry, 'Behold, the bridegroom! Come out to meet him!'

24:36–44 The statement of v 34 is now counterbalanced by one that declares that the exact time of the parousia is known only to *the Father* (36), and the disciples are warned to be always ready for it. This section is drawn from Mark and Q (cf Lk 17:26–27, 34–35; 12:39–40).

24:36 Many textual witnesses omit *nor the Son,* which follows Mk 13:32. Since its omission can be explained by reluctance to attribute this ignorance to *the Son,* the reading that includes it is probably original.

24:37–39 Cf Lk 17:26–27. *In the days of Noah:* the Old Testament account of the flood lays no emphasis upon what is central for Matthew, i.e., the unexpected coming of the flood upon those who were unprepared for it.

24:40–41 Cf Lk 17:34–35. *Taken . . . left:* the former probably means *taken* into the kingdom; the latter, *left* for destruction. People in the same situation will be dealt with in opposite ways. In this context, the discrimination between them will be based on their readiness for the coming of the Son of Man.

24:42–44 Cf Lk 12:39–40. The theme of vigilance and readiness is continued with the bold comparison of the Son of Man to a thief who comes to break into a house.

24:45–51 The second part of the discourse (see the note on 24:1—25:46) begins with this parable of *the faithful* or unfaithful *servant;* cf Lk 12:41–46. It is addressed to the leaders of Matthew's church; *the servant has* been *put in charge* of his master's *household* (45) even though that *household* is composed of those who are his *fellow servants* (49).

24:45 *To distribute . . . proper time:* readiness for the master's return means a vigilance that is accompanied by faithful performance of the duty assigned.

24:48 *My master . . . delayed:* the note of delay is found also in the other parables of this section; cf 25:5, 19.

24:51 *Punish him severely:* the Greek verb, found in the New Testament only here and in the Lucan parallel (12:46), means, literally, "cut in two." *With the hypocrites:* see the note on 6:2. Matthew classes the unfaithful Christian leader with the unbelieving leaders of Judaism. *Wailing and grinding of teeth:* see the note on 8:11–12.

25:1–13 Peculiar to Matthew.

25:1 *Then:* at the time of the parousia. *Kingdom . . . will be like:* see the note on 13:24–30.

25:2–4 *Foolish . . . wise:* cf the contrasted "wise man" and "fool" of 7:24, 26, where the two are distinguished by good deeds and lack of them, and such deeds may be signified by the *oil* of this parable.

*
24:35 Is 40:8.
24:36 Acts 1:7.
24:37–39 Gn 6:5—7:23; Lk 17:26–27; 2 Pt 3:6.
24:40–41 Lk 17:34–35.
24:42–44 Mt 25:13; Lk 12:39–40.
24:43 1 Thes 5:2.
24:45–51 Lk 12:41–46.
24:51 Mt 13:42; 25:30.

Cultural Connection

The Principle of *Kuumba*

I wish I had a great singing voice. I often daydream about belting out songs with the vocal power of the sister of soul, Aretha Franklin. Sure, I have other gifts, but more than anything else, I wish I could sing. Here I go again, neglecting what I do have as I yearn for what I lack. Why do I do that?

This attitude sounds a bit like that of the servant Jesus speaks of in Matthew 25:14–30, the parable of the talents, doesn't it? In the parable, the master gives the third servant a talent, but the servant keeps it hidden. And precisely because he keeps it hidden, the timid servant loses the one talent he does have.

Although a talent is actually a very large sum of money, many contemporary commentaries associate the word with abilities. God has given us our talents and abilities. The Kwanzaa principle of *kuumba* (creativity) calls us to use our talents creatively and boldly in the service of God. Don't second-guess the Lord by wanting something you do not have. Trust that God has blessed you with the gifts you need, and use them!

Dear God, thank you for what I have. Help me to use it to your glory. Amen.

▶ Mt 25:14–30

7 Then all those virgins got up and trimmed their
lamps. 8 The foolish ones said to the wise, 'Give
us some of your oil, for our lamps are going out.'
9 But the wise ones replied, 'No, for there may
not be enough for us and you. Go instead to the
merchants and buy some for yourselves.' 10 While
they went off to buy it, the bridegroom came
and those who were ready went into the wedding feast with him. Then the door was locked.
11*† Afterwards the other virgins came and said,
'Lord, Lord, open the door for us!' 12 But he said
in reply, 'Amen, I say to you, I do not know you.'
13*† Therefore, stay awake, for you know neither
the day nor the hour.

The Parable of the Talents†

14* "It will be as when a man who was going
on a journey† called in his servants and entrusted
his possessions to them. 15† To one he gave five
talents; to another, two; to a third, one—to each
according to his ability. Then he went away. Immediately 16 the one who received five talents
went and traded with them, and made another
five. 17 Likewise, the one who received two made
another two. 18† But the man who received one
went off and dug a hole in the ground and buried
his master's money. 19 After a long time the master
of those servants came back and settled accounts
with them. 20† The one who had received five talents came forward bringing the additional five.
He said, 'Master, you gave me five talents. See,
I have made five more.' 21* His master said to
him, 'Well done, my good and faithful servant.
Since you were faithful in small matters, I will
give you great responsibilities. Come, share your
master's joy.' 22 [Then] the one who had received
two talents also came forward and said, 'Master,
you gave me two talents. See, I have made two
more.' 23 His master said to him, 'Well done, my
good and faithful servant. Since you were faithful
in small matters, I will give you great responsibilities. Come, share your master's joy.' 24 Then
the one who had received the one talent came
forward and said, 'Master, I knew you were a

†

25:11–12 *Lord, Lord:* cf 7:21. *I do not know you:* cf 7:23, where the Greek verb is different but synonymous.

25:13 *Stay awake:* some scholars see this command as an addition to the original parable of Matthew's traditional material, since in v 5 all the virgins, wise and foolish, fall asleep. But the wise virgins are adequately equipped for their task, and *stay awake* may mean no more than to be prepared; cf 24:42, 44.

25:14–30 Cf Lk 19:12–27.

25:14 *It will be as when . . . journey:* literally, "For just as a man who was going on a journey." Although the comparison is not completed, the sense is clear; the kingdom of heaven is like the situation here described. Faithful use of one's gifts will lead to participation in the fullness of the kingdom, lazy inactivity to exclusion from it.

25:15 *Talents:* see the note on 18:24.

25:18 *Buried his master's money:* see the note on 13:44.

25:20–23 Although the first two servants have received and doubled large sums, their faithful trading is regarded by the master as fidelity *in small matters* only, compared with the *great responsibilities* now to be given to them. The latter are unspecified. *Share your master's joy:* probably the joy of the banquet of the kingdom; cf 8:11.

25:11–12 Mt 7:21, 23; Lk 13:25, 27.
25:13 Mt 24:42; Mk 13:33.
25:14–30 Lk 19:12–27.
25:21 Lk 16:10.

Catholic Social Teaching

"You Did It for Me"

We have all heard excuses for not helping those in need: "He got what he deserved!" "She is not my problem!" "If only they would have done this or that, they wouldn't be in the mess they're in!" These common misconceptions pacify the consciences of many people. Instead, Jesus says we shouldn't let people suffer; we must reach out to them. He is neither suggesting that we respond nor encouraging us to; he is demanding that we do. He also states quite clearly that we will be judged by God as to how well we care for those who are disadvantaged because that is where we encounter and minister to Christ.

Catholic social teaching teaches that all human beings have basic rights that need to be protected at all times. The United Nations' "Universal Declaration of Human Rights" gives a good starting point in determining what these basic rights might be, listing thirty human rights that should always be guaranteed for all members of the human family. These rights include the right to work, education, fair legal treatment, and ownership of property.

Corresponding to these rights are certain responsibilities, similar to what Jesus outlines for his disciples in this challenging passage—feeding the hungry, welcoming the stranger, clothing the naked, tending to the sick, and supporting those who have been imprisoned. These are the demands of our faith, if we want to call ourselves disciples. There is no option, only an obligation, as Jesus makes abundantly clear.

How does your local community respond to Jesus' call? Can hungry people get a free meal somewhere? Does your school or parish have food or clothing drives? How are shut-ins and terminally ill people cared for? Who visits or writes to the prisoners in the county jail? How does your community, school, or parish respond to refugees or immigrants? Who are the hungry, the thirsty, the strangers, the naked, the sick, or the imprisoned in your neighborhood or community? What can you do to help minister to them?

▶ **Mt 25:31–46**
Rights and Responsibilities

MT

demanding person, harvesting where you did not
plant and gathering where you did not scatter;
25 so out of fear I went off and buried your talent
in the ground. Here it is back.' 26† His master
said to him in reply, 'You wicked, lazy servant!
So you knew that I harvest where I did not plant
and gather where I did not scatter? 27 Should you
not then have put my money in the bank so that I
could have got it back with interest on my return?
28 Now then! Take the talent from him and give
it to the one with ten. 29*† For to everyone who
has, more will be given and he will grow rich; but
from the one who has not, even what he has will
be taken away. 30† And throw this useless servant
into the darkness outside, where there will be
wailing and grinding of teeth.'

The Judgment of the Nations†

31* "When the Son of Man comes in his glory,
and all the angels with him, he will sit upon his

†

25:26–28 *Wicked, lazy servant:* this man's inactivity is not negligible but seriously culpable. As punishment, he loses the gift he had received, that is now given to the first servant, whose possessions are already great.

25:29 See the note on 13:12 where there is a similar application of this maxim.

25:30 See the note on 8:11–12.

25:31–46 The conclusion of the discourse, which is peculiar to Matthew, portrays the final judgment that will accompany the parousia. Although often called a "parable," it is not really such, for the only parabolic elements are the depiction of *the Son of Man* as a *shepherd* and of *the righteous* and the wicked as *sheep* and *goats* respectively (32–33). The criterion of judgment will be the deeds of mercy that have been done for the *least* of Jesus' *brothers* (40). A difficult and important question is the identification of these *least brothers.* Are they all people who have suffered hunger, thirst, etc. (35, 36) or a particular group of such sufferers? Scholars are divided in their response and arguments can be made for either side. But leaving aside the problem of what the traditional material that Matthew edited may have meant, it seems that a stronger case can be made for the view that in the evangelist's sense the sufferers are Christians, probably Christian missionaries whose sufferings were brought upon them by their preaching of the gospel. The criterion of judgment for *all the nations* is their treatment of those who have borne to the world the message of Jesus, and this means ultimately their acceptance or rejection of Jesus himself; cf 10:40, "Whoever receives you, receives me."

*

25:29 Mt 13:12; Mk 4:25; Lk 8:18; 19:26. **25:31** Mt 16:27; Dt 33:2 LXX.

glorious throne,† 32*† and all the nations will
be assembled before him. And he will separate
them one from another, as a shepherd sepa-
rates the sheep from the goats. 33 He will place
the sheep on his right and the goats on his left.
34 Then the king will say to those on his right,
'Come, you who are blessed by my Father. In-
herit the kingdom prepared for you from the
foundation of the world. 35* For I was hungry
and you gave me food, I was thirsty and you
gave me drink, a stranger and you welcomed
me, 36 naked and you clothed me, ill and you
cared for me, in prison and you visited me.'
37† Then the righteous will answer him and
say, 'Lord, when did we see you hungry and
feed you, or thirsty and give you drink? 38 When
did we see you a stranger and welcome you, or
naked and clothe you? 39 When did we see you
ill or in prison, and visit you?' 40* And the king
will say to them in reply, 'Amen, I say to you,
whatever you did for one of these least broth-
ers of mine, you did for me.' 41*† Then he will
say to those on his left, 'Depart from me, you
accursed, into the eternal fire prepared for the
devil and his angels. 42* For I was hungry and
you gave me no food, I was thirsty and you gave
me no drink, 43 a stranger and you gave me no
welcome, naked and you gave me no clothing,
ill and in prison, and you did not care for me.'
44† Then they will answer and say, 'Lord, when
did we see you hungry or thirsty or a stranger
or naked or ill or in prison, and not minister to
your needs?' 45 He will answer them, 'Amen, I
say to you, what you did not do for one of these
least ones, you did not do for me.' 46* And these
will go off to eternal punishment, but the righ-
teous to eternal life."

VII: The Passion and Resurrection

The Conspiracy against Jesus

26 1† When Jesus finished all these words,†
he said to his disciples, 2* "You know
that in two days' time it will be Passover, and
the Son of Man will be handed over to be cruci-
fied." 3† Then the chief priests and the elders of
the people assembled in the palace of the high
priest, who was called Caiaphas, 4* and they con-
sulted together to arrest Jesus by treachery and
put him to death. 5† But they said, "Not during
the festival, that there may not be a riot among
the people."

The Anointing at Bethany

6*† Now when Jesus was in Bethany in the
house of Simon the leper, 7 a woman came up to
him with an alabaster jar of costly perfumed oil,
and poured it on his head while he was reclin-
ing at table. 8 When the disciples saw this, they
were indignant and said, "Why this waste? 9 It
could have been sold for much, and the money
given to the poor." 10 Since Jesus knew this, he
said to them, "Why do you make trouble for
the woman? She has done a good thing for me.
11* The poor you will always have with you;
but you will not always have me. 12† In pour-
ing this perfumed oil upon my body, she did it
to prepare me for burial. 13 Amen, I say to you,
wherever this gospel is proclaimed in the whole
world, what she has done will be spoken of, in
memory of her."

The Betrayal by Judas

14*† Then one of the Twelve, who was called

---

†

25:31 See the note on 16:27.

25:32 *All the nations:* before the end the gospel will have been preached throughout the world (24:14); thus the Gentiles will be judged on their response to it. But the phrase *all the nations* includes the Jews also, for at the judgment "the Son of Man . . . will repay everyone according to his conduct" (16:27).

25:37–40 *The righteous* will be astonished that in caring for the needs of the sufferers they were ministering to the *Lord* himself. *One of these least brothers of mine:* cf 10:42.

25:41 *Fire prepared . . . his angels:* cf 1 Enoch 10:13 where it is said of the evil angels and Semyaza, their leader, "In those days they will lead them into the bottom of the fire—and in torment—in the prison (where) they will be locked up forever."

25:44–45 The *accursed* (41) will be likewise astonished that their neglect of the sufferers was neglect of the *Lord* and will receive from him a similar answer.

26:1—28:20 The five books with alternating narrative and discourse (3:1—25:46) that give this gospel its distinctive structure lead up to the climactic events that are the center of Christian belief and the origin of the Christian church, the passion and resurrection of Jesus. In his passion narrative (chs 26–27) Matthew follows his Marcan source closely but with omissions (e.g., Mk 14:51–52) and additions (e.g., 27:3–10, 19). Some of the additions indicate that he utilized traditions that he had received from elsewhere; others are due to his own theological insight (e.g., 26:28, ". . . for the forgiveness of sins"; 27:52). In his editing Matthew also altered Mark in some minor details. But there is no need to suppose that he knew any passion narrative other than Mark's.

26:1–2 *When Jesus finished all these words:* see the note on 7:28–29. *"You know . . . crucified":* Matthew turns Mark's statement of the time (14:1) into Jesus' final prediction of his passion. *Passover:* see the note on Mk 14:1.

26:3 *Caiaphas* was high priest from A.D. 18 to 36.

26:5 *Not during the festival:* the plan to delay Jesus' arrest and execution until after *the festival* was not carried out, for according to the synoptics he was arrested on the night of Nisan 14 and put to death the following day. No reason is given why the plan was changed.

26:6–13 See the notes on Mk 14:3–9 and Jn 12:1–8.

26:12 *To prepare me for burial:* cf Mk 14:8. In accordance with the interpretation of this act as Jesus' *burial* anointing, Matthew, more consistent than Mark, changes the purpose of the visit of the women to Jesus' tomb; they do not go to anoint him (Mk 16:1) but "to see the tomb" (28:1).

26:14 *Iscariot:* see the note on Lk 6:16.

25:32 Ez 34:17.
25:35–36 Is 58:7; Ez 18:7.
25:40 Mt 10:40, 42.
25:41 Mt 7:23; Lk 13:27.
25:42–43 Jb 22:7; Jas 2:15–16.
25:46 Dn 12:2.
26:2–5 Mk 14:1–2; Lk 22:1–2.
26:4 Jn 11:47–53.
26:6–13 Mk 14:3–9; Jn 12:1–8.
26:11 Dt 15:11.
26:14–16 Mk 14:10–11; Lk 22:3–6.

Judas Iscariot, went to the chief priests 15*† and said, "What are you willing to give me if I hand him over to you?" They paid him thirty pieces of silver, 16 and from that time on he looked for an opportunity to hand him over.

Preparations for the Passover

17*† On the first day of the Feast of Unleavened Bread, the disciples approached Jesus and said, "Where do you want us to prepare for you to eat the Passover?"* 18† He said, "Go into the city to a certain man and tell him, 'The teacher says, "My appointed time draws near; in your house I shall celebrate the Passover with my disciples."'" 19 The disciples then did as Jesus had ordered, and prepared the Passover.

The Betrayer

20 When it was evening, he reclined at table with the Twelve. 21† And while they were eating, he said, "Amen, I say to you, one of you will betray me." 22 Deeply distressed at this, they began to say to him one after another, "Surely it is not I, Lord?" 23 He said in reply, "He who has dipped his hand into the dish with me is the one who will betray me. 24*† The Son of Man indeed goes, as it is written of him, but woe to that man by whom the Son of Man is betrayed. It would be better for that man if he had never been born." 25† Then Judas, his betrayer, said in reply, "Surely

26:26

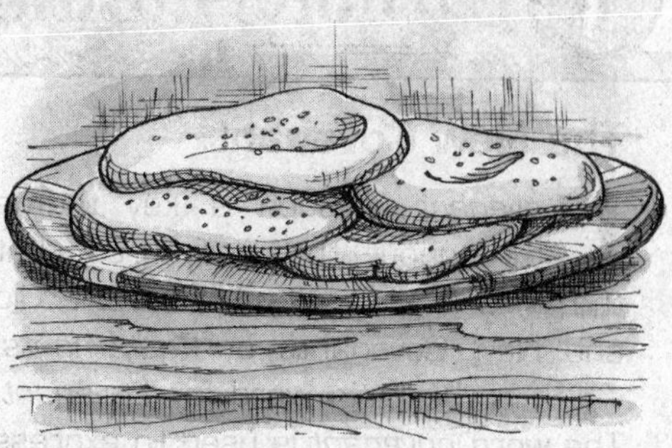

it is not I, Rabbi?" He answered, "You have said so."

The Lord's Supper

26*† While they were eating,* Jesus took bread, said the blessing, broke it, and giving it to his disciples said, "Take and eat; this is my body."† 27† Then he took a cup, gave thanks, and gave it to them, saying, "Drink from it, all of you, 28* for this is my blood of the covenant, which will be shed on behalf of many for the forgiveness of sins. 29† I tell you, from now on I shall not drink this fruit of the vine until the day when I drink it with you new in the kingdom of my Father." 30† Then, after singing a hymn, they went out to the Mount of Olives.

†

26:15 The motive of avarice is introduced by Judas's question about the price for betrayal, which is absent in the Marcan source (14:10–11). *Hand him over:* the same Greek verb is used to express the saving purpose of God by which Jesus is handed over to death (cf 17:22; 20:18; 26:2) and the human malice that hands him over. *Thirty pieces of silver:* the price of the betrayal is found only in Matthew. It is derived from Zec 11:12 where it is the wages paid to the rejected shepherd, a cheap price (Zec 11:13). That amount is also the compensation paid to one whose slave has been gored by an ox (Ex 21:32).

26:17 *The first day of the Feast of Unleavened Bread:* see the note on Mk 14:1. Matthew omits Mark's "when they sacrificed the Passover lamb."

26:18 By omitting much of Mk 14:13–15, adding *My appointed time draws near,* and turning the question into a statement, *in your house I shall celebrate the Passover,* Matthew has given this passage a solemnity and majesty greater than that of his source.

26:21 Given Matthew's interest in the fulfillment of the Old Testament, it is curious that he omits the Marcan designation of Jesus' betrayer as "one who is eating with me" (14:18), since that is probably an allusion to Ps 41:10. However, the shocking fact that the betrayer is one who shares table fellowship with Jesus is emphasized in v 23.

26:24 *It would be better . . . born:* the enormity of the deed is such that it would be better not to exist than to do it.

26:25 Peculiar to Matthew. *You have said so:* cf 26:64; 27:11. This is a half-affirmative. Emphasis is laid on the pronoun and the answer implies that the statement would not have been made if the question had not been asked.

26:26–29 See the note on Mk 14:22–24. The Marcan-Matthean is one of the two major New Testament traditions of the words of Jesus when instituting the Eucharist. The other (and earlier) is the Pauline-Lucan (1 Cor 11:23–25; Lk 22:19–20). Each shows the influence of Christian liturgical usage, but the Marcan-Matthean is more developed in that regard than the Pauline-Lucan. The words over the bread and cup succeed each other without the intervening meal mentioned in 1 Cor 11:25; Lk 22:20; and there is parallelism between the consecratory words (*this is my body . . . this is my blood*). Matthew follows Mark closely but with some changes.

26:26 See the note on 14:19. *Said the blessing:* a prayer blessing God. *Take and eat:* literally, *Take, eat. Eat* is an addition to Mark's "take it" (literally, "take"; 14:22). *This is my body:* the bread is identified with Jesus himself.

26:27–28 *Gave thanks:* see the note on 15:36. *Gave it to them . . . all of you:* cf Mk 14:23–24. In the Marcan sequence the disciples drink and then Jesus says the interpretative words. Matthew has changed this into a command to *drink* followed by those words. *My blood:* see Lv 17:11 for the concept that the *blood* is "the seat of life" and that when placed on the altar it "makes atonement." *Which will be shed:* the present participle, "being shed" or "going to be shed," is future in relation to the Last Supper. *On behalf of:* Greek *peri;* see the note on Mk 14:24. *Many:* see the note on 20:28. *For the forgiveness of sins:* a Matthean addition. The same phrase occurs in Mk 1:4 in connection with John's baptism but Matthew avoids it there (3:11). He places it here probably because he wishes to emphasize that it is the sacrificial death of Jesus that brings *forgiveness of sins.*

26:29 Although his death will interrupt the table fellowship he has had with the disciples, Jesus confidently predicts his vindication by God and a new table fellowship with them at the banquet of the kingdom.

26:30 See the note on Mk 14:26.

*

26:15 Zec 11:12.
26:17–25 Mk 14:12–21; Lk 22:7–23.
26:17 Ex 12:14–20.
26:24 Is 53:8–10.
26:26–30 Mk 14:22–26; Lk 22:14–23; 1 Cor 11:23–25.
26:26–27 1 Cor 10:16.
26:28 Ex 24:8; Is 53:12.

MT

Catholic Connection

The New Covenant

Covenant is such a key theme throughout the Scriptures that the Bible itself is often called the Old and New Covenants or *Testaments,* which is the Latin word for *covenant.* The word *covenant* is used to express the unique relationship between God and God's people. In the Old Testament, the laws and worship practices of the Israelites were a sign of this covenant relationship (see "Covenant," near Gn 17:1–27.) But during the Last Supper, Jesus catapults humanity into a new and dynamic dimension of the covenant relationship with God when he shares the cup and says, "Drink from it, all of you, for this is my blood of the covenant" (Mt 26:27–28). In Luke's Gospel, Jesus calls it "the new covenant in my blood" (Lk 22:20). Through Jesus' selfless love shown on the cross, our relationship with God is restored fully and completely and a new, eternal covenant is established with God.

Jesus Christ, the Word made flesh, initiated the New Covenant through his life offered up in sacrifice for all. In his teaching and ministry, Jesus reinterpreted the life of a covenant people. He taught that the true content of the covenant was in the commandments to love God totally and to love one another with the same unconditional love God has shown us. Practicing kindness, justice, forgiveness, and righteousness are the qualities that constitute the heart of the covenant. Jesus' disciples entered into this New Covenant when they partook of the Body and Blood of Christ at the Last Supper and actually became the Body of Christ, entering into the deepest kind of communion (relationship) with God.

This communion in the Body of Christ also speaks of the communion of all believers to one another—no matter how different we may be from one another in nationality, race, culture, or social status. Our communion as Christians, the covenant people of God, transcends any and all human division. As often as we partake in the Eucharist, we reaffirm the New Covenant in Jesus. Our hearts are cleansed and renewed by Jesus' self-offering upon the cross; and we pledge to share our lives together as a Christian community, to be an example for the world.

The covenant, which began with Abraham and was fully revealed in Jesus, is God's way of bringing us back to the source of our lives in God and into unity with one another. We enter into this New and Eternal Covenant through Baptism and keep it by remaining faithful to Christ. In the Eucharist, we are brought more deeply into communion with God and with one another and, through the power of the Holy Spirit, we are able to go forth and live the New Covenant.

► **Mt 26:26–29**

Catechism, nos. 68–73, 610, 613, 1365, 1405

Peter's Denial Foretold

[31]*† Then Jesus said to them, "This night all
of you will have your faith in me shaken, for it
is written:

'I will strike the shepherd,
and the sheep of the flock will
be dispersed';*

[32]but after I have been raised up, I shall go
before you to Galilee." [33]Peter said to him in
reply, "Though all may have their faith in you
shaken, mine will never be." [34]*† Jesus said to
him, "Amen, I say to you, this very night before
the cock crows, you will deny me three times."*
[35]Peter said to him, "Even though I should have
to die with you, I will not deny you." And all the
disciples spoke likewise.

The Agony in the Garden

[36]*† Then Jesus came with them to a place
called Gethsemane,† and he said to his disci-
ples,* "Sit here while I go over there and pray."
[37]*† He took along Peter and the two sons of
Zebedee, and began to feel sorrow and distress.
[38]*† Then he said to them, "My soul is sorrow-
ful even to death. Remain here and keep watch
with me." [39]*† He advanced a little and fell
prostrate in prayer, saying, "My Father, if it is
possible, let this cup pass from me; yet, not as I
will, but as you will." [40]When he returned to his
disciples he found them asleep. He said to Peter,
"So you could not keep watch with me for one
hour? [41]† Watch and pray that you may not un-
dergo the test. The spirit is willing, but the flesh

MT

†

26:31 *Will have . . . shaken:* literally, "will be scandalized in me"; see the note on 24:9–12. *I will strike . . . dispersed:* cf Zec 13:7.

26:34 *Before the cock crows:* see the note on 14:25. The third watch of the night was called "cockcrow." *Deny me:* see the note on 16:24.

26:36–56 Cf Mk 14:32–52. The account of Jesus in Gethsemane is divided between that of his agony (36–46) and that of his betrayal and arrest (47–56). Jesus' *sorrow and distress* (37) in face of death is unrelieved by the presence of his three disciples who, though urged to *watch with* him (38, 41), fall asleep (40, 43). He prays that *if . . . possible* his death may be avoided (39) but that his Father's will be done (39, 42, 44). Knowing then that his death must take place, he announces to his companions that *the hour* for his being *handed over* has come (45). Judas arrives with an armed band provided by the Sanhedrin and greets Jesus with a kiss, the prearranged sign for his identification (47–49). After his arrest, he rebukes a disciple who has attacked the *high priest's servant* with a *sword* (51–54), and chides those who have come out to seize him with *swords and clubs* as if he were *a robber* (55–56). In both rebukes Jesus declares that the treatment he is now receiving is the fulfillment of the scriptures (55, 56). The subsequent flight of *all the disciples* is itself the fulfillment of his own prediction (cf 31). In this episode, Matthew follows Mark with a few alterations.

26:36 *Gethsemane:* the Hebrew name means "oil press" and designates an olive orchard on the western slope of the Mount of Olives; see the note on 21:1. The name appears only in Matthew and Mark. The place is called a "garden" in Jn 18:1.

26:37 *Peter and the two sons of Zebedee:* cf 17:1.

26:38 Cf Ps 42:6, 12. In the Septuagint (Ps 41:5, 12) the same Greek word for *sorrowful* is used as here. *To death:* i.e., "enough to die"; cf Jon 4:9.

26:39 *My Father:* see the note on Mk 14:36. Matthew omits the Aramaic *'abba'* and adds the qualifier *my. This cup:* see the note on Mk 10:38–40.

26:41 *Undergo the test:* see the note on 6:13. In that verse "the final test" translates the same Greek word as is here translated *the test,* and these are the only instances of the use of that word in Matthew. It is possible that the passion of Jesus is seen here as an anticipation of the great tribulation that will precede the parousia (see the notes on 24:8; 24:21) to which 6:13 refers, and that just as Jesus prays to be delivered from death (39), so he exhorts the disciples to pray that they will not have to *undergo the* great *test* that his passion would be for them. Some scholars, however, understand *not undergo* (literally, "not enter") *the test* as meaning not that the disciples may be spared *the test* but that they may not yield to the temptation of falling away from Jesus because of his passion even though they will have to endure it.

*

26:31–35 Mk 14:7–31.
26:31 Zec 13:7; Jn 16:32.
26:34–35 Lk 22:33–34; Jn 13:37–38.
26:34 Mt 26:69–75.
26:36–46 Mk 14:32–42; Lk 22:39–46.
26:36 Jn 18:1.
26:37–39 Heb 5:7.
26:38 Ps 42:6, 12; Jon 4:9.
26:39 Jn 4:34; 6:38; Phil 2:8.

Live It!

Jesus' Imperfect Friends

Imagine that you are in the middle of a crisis and ask your best friends to stay with you while you prepare to face the situation. They all promise to be there for you. But one friend after another fails to come through, and you are left to face the predicament alone.

The friends of Jesus were no different. They were well intentioned and meant to stay awake with him. But in their tiredness, they let him down.

We recognize that the friends of Jesus, the Apostles in particular, were special and holy, but they were also human and had their own weaknesses. Even Peter, one of the greatest heroes of Christianity, lacked the courage to admit he knew Jesus, as we read in Matthew 26:69–75. Yet, Jesus loved his disciples despite their failings and even when they were disloyal.

- Is it easy for you to stay friends with those who let you down?
- Can you follow the example of Jesus?

▶ **Mt 26:36–45**

is weak." 42*† Withdrawing a second time, he
prayed again, "My Father, if it is not possible that
this cup pass without my drinking it, your will be
done!" 43 Then he returned once more and found
them asleep, for they could not keep their eyes
open. 44 He left them and withdrew again and
prayed a third time, saying the same thing again.
45* Then he returned to his disciples and said
to them, "Are you still sleeping and taking your
rest? Behold, the hour is at hand when the Son of
Man is to be handed over to sinners. 46 Get up, let
us go. Look, my betrayer is at hand."

The Betrayal and Arrest of Jesus

47* While he was still speaking, Judas, one
of the Twelve, arrived, accompanied by a large
crowd, with swords and clubs, who had come
from the chief priests and the elders of the peo-
ple. 48 His betrayer had arranged a sign with
them, saying, "The man I shall kiss is the one;
arrest him." 49† Immediately he went over to
Jesus and said, "Hail, Rabbi!" and he kissed him.
50 Jesus answered him, "Friend, do what you
have come for." Then stepping forward they laid
hands on Jesus and arrested him. 51 And behold,
one of those who accompanied Jesus put his
hand to his sword, drew it, and struck the high
priest's servant, cutting off his ear. 52 Then Jesus
said to him, "Put your sword back into its sheath,
for all who take the sword will perish by the
sword. 53 Do you think that I cannot call upon
my Father and he will not provide me at this mo-
ment with more than twelve legions of angels?
54 But then how would the scriptures be fulfilled
which say that it must come to pass in this way?"
55† At that hour Jesus said to the crowds, "Have
you come out as against a robber, with swords
and clubs to seize me? Day after day I sat teach-
ing in the temple area, yet you did not arrest me.
56* But all this has come to pass that the writings
of the prophets may be fulfilled." Then all the
disciples left him and fled.

Jesus before the Sanhedrin†

57* Those who had arrested Jesus led him
away to Caiaphas† the high priest, where the
scribes and the elders were assembled. 58 Peter
was following him at a distance as far as the high
priest's courtyard, and going inside he sat down
with the servants to see the outcome. 59† The
chief priests and the entire Sanhedrin kept trying
to obtain false testimony against Jesus in order
to put him to death, 60*† but they found none,
though many false witnesses came forward. Fi-
nally two came forward 61 who stated, "This man
said, 'I can destroy the temple of God and within
three days rebuild it.' " 62 The high priest rose and
addressed him, "Have you no answer? What are
these men testifying against you?" 63*† But Jesus
was silent. Then the high priest said to him, "I
order you to tell us under oath before the living
God whether you are the Messiah, the Son of
God." 64*† Jesus said to him in reply, "You have
said so. But I tell you:

From now on you will see 'the Son of Man
seated at the right hand of the Power'
and 'coming on the clouds of heaven.' "

26:42 *Your will be done:* cf 6:10.

26:49 *Rabbi:* see the note on 23:6–7. Jesus is so addressed twice in Matthew (cf 25), both times by Judas. For the significance of the closely related address "teacher" in Matthew, see the note on 8:19.

26:55 *Day after day . . . arrest me:* cf Mk 14:49. This suggests that Jesus had taught for a relatively long period in Jerusalem, whereas 21:1–11 puts his coming to the city for the first time only a few days before.

26:57–68 Following Mk 14:53–65, Matthew presents the nighttime appearance of Jesus before *the Sanhedrin* as a real trial. After *many false witnesses* bring charges against him that do not suffice for the death sentence (60), *two came forward* who charge him with claiming to be able to *destroy the temple . . . and within three days* to *rebuild it* (60–61). Jesus makes no answer even when challenged to do so by *the high priest,* who then orders him to declare *under oath . . . whether* he is *the Messiah, the Son of God* (62–63). Matthew changes Mark's clear affirmative response (14:62) to the same one as that given to Judas (cf 25), but follows Mark almost verbatim in Jesus' predicting that his judges will see him (*the Son of Man*) *seated at the right hand of* God *and coming on the clouds of heaven* (64). *The high priest* then charges him with blasphemy (65), a charge with which the other members of *the Sanhedrin* agree by declaring that *he deserves to die* (66). They then attack him (67) and mockingly demand that he *prophesy* (68). This account contains elements that are contrary to the judicial procedures prescribed in the Mishnah, the Jewish code of law that dates in written form from ca. A.D. 200, e.g., trial on a feast day, a night session of the court, pronouncement of a verdict of condemnation at the same session at which testimony was received. Consequently, some scholars regard the account entirely as a creation of the early Christians without historical value. However, it is disputable whether the norms found in the Mishnah were in force at the time of Jesus. More to the point is the question whether the Matthean-Marcan night trial derives from a combination of two separate incidents, a nighttime preliminary investigation (cf Jn 18:13, 19–24) and a formal trial on the following morning (cf Lk 22:66–71).

26:57 *Caiaphas:* see the note on 26:3.

26:59 *Sanhedrin:* see the note on Lk 22:66.

26:60–61 *Two:* cf Dt 19:15. *I can destroy . . . rebuild it:* there are significant differences from the Marcan parallel (14:58). Matthew omits "made with hands" and "not made with hands" and changes Mark's "will destroy" and "will build another" to *can destroy* and (can) *rebuild.* The charge is probably based on Jesus' prediction of the temple's destruction; see the notes on 23:37–39; 24:2; and Jn 2:19. A similar prediction by Jeremiah was considered as deserving death; cf Jer 7:1–15; 26:1–8.

26:63 *Silent:* possibly an allusion to Is 53:7. *I order you . . . living God:* peculiar to Matthew; cf Mk 14:61.

26:64 *You have said so:* see the note on 26:25. *From now on . . . heaven:* the Son of Man who is to be crucified (cf 20:19) will be seen in glorious majesty (cf Ps 110:1) and *coming on the clouds of heaven* (cf Dn 7:13). *The Power:* see the note on Mk 14:61–62.

26:42 Mt 6:10; Heb 10:9.
26:45 Jn 12:23; 13:1; 17:1.
26:47–56 Mk 14:43–50; Lk 22:47–53; Jn 18:3–11.
26:56 Mt 26:31.
26:57–68 Mk 14:53–65; Lk 22:54–55, 63–71; Jn 18:12–14, 19–24.
26:60–61 Dt 19:15; Jn 2:19; Acts 6:14.
26:63 Is 53:7.
26:64 Ps 110:1; Dn 7:13.

65† Then the high priest tore his robes and said,
"He has blasphemed! What further need have
we of witnesses? You have now heard the blas-
phemy; 66 what is your opinion?" They said in
reply, "He deserves to die!" 67*† Then they spat
in his face and struck him, while some slapped
him, 68 saying, "Prophesy for us, Messiah: who is
it that struck you?"

Peter's Denial of Jesus

69* Now Peter was sitting outside in the court-
yard. One of the maids came over to him and
said, "You too were with Jesus the Galilean."
70† But he denied it in front of everyone, saying,
"I do not know what you are talking about!" 71 As
he went out to the gate, another girl saw him
and said to those who were there, "This man was
with Jesus the Nazorean." 72 Again he denied it
with an oath, "I do not know the man!" 73† A
little later the bystanders came over and said
to Peter, "Surely you too are one of them; even
your speech gives you away." 74 At that he began
to curse and to swear, "I do not know the man."
And immediately a cock crowed. 75* Then Peter
remembered the word that Jesus had spoken:
"Before the cock crows you will deny me three
times." He went out and began to weep bitterly.

Jesus before Pilate

27 1*† When it was morning, all the chief
priests and the elders of the people took
counsel† against Jesus to put him to death. 2 They
bound him, led him away, and handed him over
to Pilate, the governor.

The Death of Judas

3*† Then Judas, his betrayer, seeing that Jesus
had been condemned, deeply regretted what he
had done. He returned the thirty pieces of silver

MT

Did You Know?

Judas's Suicide

The Gospel of Matthew presents Judas's suicide as the fulfillment of some Old Testament prophecies, but it does not tell us why Judas killed himself. We don't know the historical circumstances around this event, nor do we know what was in Judas's mind or what motivated him to do this or how this event would have been perceived at a different time and in a culture very different from our own. But some teenagers think suicide will end their pain, using it as a way out.

Unfortunately, suicide ends everything; not just the current pain but future possibilities for healing, for growth, for new relationships and good times. Consider that both Judas and Peter betrayed Jesus. But Judas ended his life, and Peter trusted in God's love and forgiveness and went on to become a great hero. Nothing you can do is so terrible that your only option is taking your life.

Do you ever have thoughts of suicide? If so, talk about them with someone you trust. Speak with a priest, a parent, a youth minister, a school counselor, a coach, or a trusted friend. Caring people will help you. Seeking their help is a better way out. (For more on suicide, see "Suicide Is Not an Answer," near 1 Sm 31:1–6.)

▶ Mt 27:3–10

†

26:65 *Blasphemed:* the punishment for *blasphemy* was death by stoning (see Lv 24:10–16). According to the Mishnah, to be guilty of *blasphemy* one had to pronounce "the Name itself," i.e. Yahweh; cf *Sanhedrin* 7:4, 5. Those who judge the gospel accounts of Jesus' trial by the later Mishnah standards point out that Jesus uses the surrogate "the Power," and hence no Jewish court would have regarded him as guilty of *blasphemy;* others hold that the Mishnah's narrow understanding of *blasphemy* was a later development.

26:67–68 The physical abuse, apparently done to Jesus by the members of the Sanhedrin themselves, recalls the sufferings of the Isaian Servant of the Lord; cf Is 50:6. The mocking challenge to *prophesy* is probably motivated by Jesus' prediction of his future glory (64).

26:70 *Denied it in front of everyone:* see 10:33. Peter's repentance (75) saves him from the fearful destiny of which Jesus speaks there.

26:73 *Your speech . . . away:* Matthew explicates Mark's "you too are a Galilean" (14:70).

27:1–31 Cf Mk 15:1–20. Matthew's account of the Roman trial before *Pilate* is introduced by a consultation of the Sanhedrin after which Jesus is *handed over to . . . the governor* (1–2). Matthew follows his Marcan source closely but adds some material that is peculiar to him, the death of *Judas* (3–10), possibly the name *Jesus* as the name of *Barabbas* also (16–17), the intervention of Pilate's *wife* (19), Pilate's washing *his hands* in token of his disclaiming responsibility for Jesus' death (24), and the assuming of that responsibility by *the whole people* (25).

27:1–2 There is scholarly disagreement about the meaning of the Sanhedrin's taking *counsel* (*symboulion elabon;* cf 12:14; 22:15; 27:7; 28:12); see the note on Mk 15:1. Some understand it as a discussion about the strategy for putting their death sentence against *Jesus* into effect since they lacked the right to do so themselves. Others see it as the occasion for their passing that sentence, holding that Matthew, unlike Mark (14:64), does not consider that it had been passed in the night session (26:66). Even in the latter interpretation, their handing *him over to Pilate* is best explained on the hypothesis that they did not have competence to put their sentence into effect, as is stated in Jn 18:31.

27:3 *The thirty pieces of silver:* see 26:15.

*

26:67 Wis 2:19; Is 50:6.
26:69–75 Mk 14:66–72; Lk 22:56–62; Jn 18:17–18, 25–27.
26:75 Mt 26:34.
27:1–2 Mk 15:1; Lk 23:1; Jn 18:28.
27:3–10 Acts 1:18–19.

Cultural Connection

Jesus Died on the Cross Because He Loves Us

Hispanics often identify more with the suffering and crucified Christ than with the risen Christ because of how much they and their ancestors have suffered oppression. In the cross, Hispanics find God's immense love for them. It is a redemptive love, one that brings peace and the strength to accept what cannot be changed and to continue the struggle out of poverty and oppression.

Hispanic young people learn from their families and culture that there is always suffering in life. When this suffering is not accepted, it is even worse. In contrast, when we accept suffering, it is bearable, and we have the inner peace needed to continue living and working for a better life. Suffering achieves its highest meaning when it is accepted out of love. That Jesus is capable of suffering gives witness to God's special love for those who suffer.

Finding God's life in the midst of suffering leads to generous sacrifices that are a source of life for those we love. Let's pray:

Jesus, help us to always remember that your commitment to your mission led to your death. Help us to understand that true life is always achieved through love. Help us to have love at the core of all we think and do. And help us to share your love, especially with those who need it the most, those who are poor and marginalized. Amen.

▶ Mt 27:24–56

M
T

to the chief priests and elders,* 4 saying, "I have
sinned in betraying innocent blood." They said,
"What is that to us? Look to it yourself." 5† Fling-
ing the money into the temple, he departed and
went off and hanged himself. 6 The chief priests
gathered up the money, but said, "It is not law-
ful to deposit this in the temple treasury, for it
is the price of blood." 7 After consultation, they
used it to buy the potter's field as a burial place
for foreigners. 8 That is why that field even today
is called the Field of Blood. 9† Then was ful-
filled what had been said through Jeremiah the
prophet, "And they took the thirty pieces of sil-
ver, the value of a man with a price on his head,
a price set by some of the Israelites, 10* and they
paid it out for the potter's field just as the Lord
had commanded me."

Jesus Questioned by Pilate

11*† Now Jesus stood before the governor,
and he questioned him, "Are you the king of the
Jews?" Jesus said, "You say so." 12*† And when
he was accused by the chief priests and elders, he
made no answer. 13 Then Pilate said to him, "Do
you not hear how many things they are testifying
against you?" 14 But he did not answer him one
word, so that the governor was greatly amazed.

The Sentence of Death

15*† Now on the occasion of the feast the

†

27:5–8 For another tradition about the death of Judas, cf Acts 1:18–19. The two traditions agree only in the purchase of a *field* with *the money* paid to Judas for his betrayal of Jesus and the name given to the *field, the Field of Blood.* In Acts Judas himself buys the field and its name comes from his own blood shed in his fatal accident on it. *The potter's field:* this designation of the field is based on the fulfillment citation in v 10.

27:9–10 Cf 26:15. Matthew's attributing this text to Jeremiah is puzzling, for there is no such text in that book, and *the thirty pieces of silver* thrown by Judas "into the temple" (5) recall rather Zec 11:12–13. It is usually said that the attribution of the text to Jeremiah is due to Matthew's combining the Zechariah text with texts from Jeremiah that speak of a *potter* (18:2–3), the buying of a *field* (32:6–9), or the breaking of a potter's flask at Topheth in the valley of Ben-Hinnom with the prediction that it will become a burial place (19:1–13).

27:11 *King of the Jews:* this title is used of Jesus only by pagans. The Matthean instances are, besides this verse, 2:2; 27:29, 37. Matthew equates it with "Messiah"; cf 2:2, 4 and 27:17, 22 where he has changed "the king of the Jews" of his Marcan source (15:9, 12) to "(Jesus) called Messiah." The normal political connotation of both titles would be of concern to the Roman *governor. You say so:* see the note on 26:25. An unqualified affirmative response is not made because Jesus' kingship is not what Pilate would understand it to be.

27:12–14 Cf 26:62–63. As in the trial before the Sanhedrin, Jesus' silence may be meant to recall Is 53:7. *Greatly amazed:* possibly an allusion to Is 52:14–15.

27:15–26 The choice that Pilate offers *the crowd* between *Barabbas* and *Jesus* is said to be in accordance with a custom of releasing at the Passover feast *one prisoner* chosen by *the crowd* (15). This custom is mentioned also in Mk 15:6 and Jn 18:39 but not in Luke; see the note on Lk 23:17. Outside of the gospels there is no direct attestation of it, and scholars are divided in their judgment of the historical reliability of the claim that there was such a practice.

27:3 Mt 26:15.
27:10 Zec 11:12–13.
27:11–14 Mk 15:2–5; Lk 23:2–3; Jn 18:29–38.
27:12 Is 53:7.
27:15–26 Mk 15:6–15; 23:17–25; Jn 18:39—19:16.

governor was accustomed to release to the crowd one prisoner whom they wished. 16† And at that time they had a notorious prisoner called [Jesus] Barabbas. 17 So when they had assembled, Pilate said to them, "Which one do you want me to release to you, [Jesus] Barabbas, or Jesus called Messiah?" 18† For he knew that it was out of envy that they had handed him over. 19† While he was still seated on the bench, his wife sent him a message, "Have nothing to do with that righteous man. I suffered much in a dream today because of him." 20* The chief priests and the elders persuaded the crowds to ask for Barabbas but to destroy Jesus. 21 The governor said to them in reply, "Which of the two do you want me to release to you?" They answered, "Barabbas!" 22† Pilate said to them, "Then what shall I do with Jesus called Messiah?" They all said, "Let him be crucified!" 23 But he said, "Why? What evil has he done?" They only shouted the louder, "Let him be crucified!" 24*† When Pilate saw that he was not succeeding at all, but that a riot was breaking out instead, he took water and washed his hands in the sight of the crowd, saying, "I am innocent of this man's blood. Look to it yourselves." 25 And the whole people said in reply, "His blood be upon us and upon our children." 26† Then he released Barabbas to them, but after he had Jesus scourged, he handed him over to be crucified.

Mockery by the Soldiers

27*† Then the soldiers of the governor took Jesus inside the praetorium and gathered the whole cohort around him. 28† They stripped off his clothes and threw a scarlet military cloak about him. 29*† Weaving a crown out of thorns, they placed it on his head, and a reed in his right hand. And kneeling before him, they mocked

Pray It!

Suffering Prayer

Jesus, anointed one, everyone endures some suffering in life. Some suffer in silence. Some loudly complain, making it known to all. Some bitterly blame everyone around them. You suffered ridicule, betrayal, persecution, Crucifixion, and death. Your burden was so great, yet you endured. Glorifying God, your sacrifice gives us the hope of eternal life.

Strengthen me to withstand the suffering I must face in my life. When I feel that I have more than I can take, fortify me with the endurance of Job. Give me the patience to suffer injustices without lashing out at others. Fill me with mercy to forgive those who persecute me. Fill me with your loving presence to be a faithful witness to the glory of God and to the promise of eternal life. Amen.

▶ Mt 27:27–44

MT

27:16–17 Jesus *Barabbas:* it is possible that the double name is the original reading; *Jesus* was a common Jewish name; see the note on 1:21. This reading is found in only a few textual witnesses, although its absence in the majority can be explained as an omission of *Jesus* made for reverential reasons. That name is bracketed because of its uncertain textual attestation. The Aramaic name *Barabbas* means "son of the father"; the irony of the choice offered between him and Jesus, the true son of the Father, would be evident to those addressees of Matthew who knew that.

27:18 Cf Mk 14:10. This is an example of the tendency, found in varying degree in all the gospels, to present Pilate in a relatively favorable light and emphasize the hostility of the Jewish authorities and eventually of the people.

27:19 Jesus' innocence is declared by a Gentile woman. *In a dream:* in Matthew's infancy narrative, dreams are the means of divine communication; cf 1:20; 2:12, 13, 19, 22.

27:22 *Let him be crucified:* incited by the chief priests and elders (20), the crowds demand that Jesus be executed by crucifixion, a peculiarly horrible form of Roman capital punishment. The Marcan parallel, "Crucify him" (15:3), addressed to Pilate, is changed by Matthew to the passive, probably to emphasize the responsibility of the crowds.

27:24–25 Peculiar to Matthew. *Took water . . . blood:* cf Dt 21:1–8, the handwashing prescribed in the case of a murder when the killer is unknown. The elders of the city nearest to where the corpse is found must wash their hands, declaring, "Our hands did not shed this blood." *Look to it yourselves:* cf v 4. *The whole people:* Matthew sees in those who speak these words *the entire people* (Greek *laos*) of Israel. *His blood . . . and upon our children:* cf Jer 26:15. The responsibility for Jesus' death is accepted by the nation that was God's special possession (Ex 19:5), his own *people* (Hos 2:25), and they thereby lose that high privilege; see 21:43 and the note on that verse. The controversy between Matthew's church and Pharisaic Judaism about which was the true people of God is reflected here. As the Second Vatican Council has pointed out, guilt for Jesus' death is not attributable to all the Jews of his time or to any Jews of later times.

27:26 *He had Jesus scourged:* the usual preliminary to crucifixion.

27:27 *The praetorium:* the residence of the Roman *governor.* His usual place of residence was at Caesarea Maritima on the Mediterranean coast, but he went to Jerusalem during the great feasts, when the influx of pilgrims posed the danger of a nationalistic riot. It is disputed whether *the praetorium* in Jerusalem was the old palace of Herod in the west of the city or the fortress of Antonia northwest of the temple area. *The whole cohort:* normally six hundred soldiers.

27:28 *Scarlet military cloak:* so Matthew as against the royal purple of Mk 15:17 and Jn 19:2.

27:29 *Crown out of thorns:* probably of long *thorns* that stood upright so that it resembled the "radiant" *crown,* a diadem with spikes worn by Hellenistic kings. The soldiers' purpose was mockery, not torture. *A reed:* peculiar to Matthew; a mock scepter.

27:20 Acts 3:14.
27:24 Dt 21:1–8.
27:27–31 Mk 15:16–20; Jn 19:2–3.
27:29 Mt 27:11.

him, saying, "Hail, King of the Jews!" 30*† They
spat upon him and took the reed and kept strik-
ing him on the head. 31 And when they had
mocked him, they stripped him of the cloak,
dressed him in his own clothes, and led him off
to crucify him.

The Way of the Cross

32*† As they were going out, they met a Cyre-
nian named Simon; this man they pressed into
service to carry his cross.

The Crucifixion

33* And when they came to a place called
Golgotha (which means Place of the Skull),
34*† they gave Jesus wine to drink mixed with
gall. But when he had tasted it, he refused to
drink. 35*† After they had crucified him, they
divided his garments by casting lots; 36 then
they sat down and kept watch over him there.
37† And they placed over his head the written
charge against him: This is Jesus, the King of
the Jews. 38† Two revolutionaries were crucified
with him, one on his right and the other on his
left. 39*† Those passing by reviled him, shaking
their heads 40* and saying, "You who would
destroy the temple and rebuild it in three days,
save yourself, if you are the Son of God, [and]
come down from the cross!" 41 Likewise the chief
priests with the scribes and elders mocked him
and said, 42† "He saved others; he cannot save
himself. So he is the king of Israel! Let him come
down from the cross now, and we will believe
in him. 43*† He trusted in God; let him deliver
him now if he wants him. For he said, 'I am the
Son of God.' " 44 The revolutionaries who were
crucified with him also kept abusing him in the
same way.

The Death of Jesus

45*† From noon onward,* darkness came over
the whole land until three in the afternoon.
46*† And about three o'clock Jesus cried out in
a loud voice, *"Eli, Eli, lema sabachthani?"* which

Did You Know?

The Dawn of a New Age

According to the Gospel of Matthew, some strange things happened when Jesus died. Each event tells us something about Jesus. The darkness that covered the land (see Mt 27:45) and the earthquake (see verse 51) show that all creation was aware that something significant had happened, a new age was dawning. The splitting of the sanctuary veil (see verse 51), which is the barrier that separated the holiest part of the Temple (where God was thought to dwell) from the rest of the Temple area, symbolizes that now God would be directly accessible to the people. And the dead saints who came out of their tombs to walk in the city symbolize God's triumph over death. These are all Old Testament signs of the end times (see Is 26:19, Ez 37:12, Jl 2:10, Na 1:5–6).

▶ **Mt 27:45–54**

27:30 *Spat upon him:* cf 26:67 where there also is a possible allusion to Is 50:6.

27:32 See the note on Mk 15:21. *Cyrenian named Simon:* Cyrenaica was a Roman province on the north coast of Africa and Cyrene was its capital city. The city had a large population of Greek-speaking Jews. *Simon* may have been living in Palestine or have come there for the Passover as a pilgrim. *Pressed into service:* see the note on 5:41.

27:34 *Wine . . . mixed with gall:* cf Mk 15:23 where the drink is "wine drugged with myrrh," a narcotic. Matthew's text is probably an inexact allusion to Ps 69:22. That psalm belongs to the class called the individual lament, in which a persecuted just man prays for deliverance in the midst of great suffering and also expresses confidence that his prayer will be heard. That theme of the suffering Just One is frequently applied to the sufferings of Jesus in the passion narratives.

27:35 The clothing of an executed criminal went to his executioner(s), but the description of that procedure in the case of Jesus, found in all the gospels, is plainly inspired by Ps 22:19. However, that psalm verse is quoted only in Jn 19:24.

27:37 The offense of a person condemned to death by crucifixion was written on a tablet that was displayed on his cross. The *charge* against *Jesus* was that he had claimed to be the *King of the Jews* (cf 11), i.e., the Messiah (cf 17, 22).

27:38 *Revolutionaries:* see the note on Jn 18:40 where the same Greek word as that found here is used for Barabbas.

27:39–40 *Reviled him . . . heads:* cf Ps 22:8. *You who would destroy . . . three days:* cf 26:61. *If you are the Son of God:* the same words as those of the devil in the temptation of Jesus; cf 4:3, 6.

27:42 *King of Israel:* in their mocking of Jesus the members of the Sanhedrin call themselves and their people not "the Jews" but *Israel.*

27:43 Peculiar to Matthew. *He trusted in God . . . wants him:* cf Ps 22:9. *He said . . . of God:* probably an allusion to Wis 2:12–20 where the theme of the suffering Just One appears.

27:45 Cf Amos 8:9 where on the day of the Lord "the sun will set at midday."

27:46 *Eli, Eli, lema sabachthani?:* Jesus cries out in the words of Ps 22:2a, a psalm of lament that is the Old Testament passage most frequently drawn upon in this narrative. In Mark the verse is cited entirely in Aramaic, which Matthew partially retains but changes the invocation of God to the Hebrew *Eli,* possibly because that is more easily related to the statement of the following verse about Jesus' calling for Elijah.

27:30 Is 50:6.
27:32 Mk 15:21; Lk 23:26.
27:33–44 Mk 15:22–32; Lk 23:32–38; Jn 19:17–19, 23–24.
27:34 Ps 69:21.
27:35 Ps 22:19.
27:39 Ps 22:8.
27:40 Mt 4:3, 6; 26:61.
27:43 Ps 22:9; Wis 2:12–20.
27:45–46 Mk 15:33–41; Lk 23:44–49; Jn 19:28–30.
27:45 Am 8:9.
27:46 Ps 22:2.

means, "My God, my God, why have you forsaken me?" 47† Some of the bystanders who heard it said, "This one is calling for Elijah." 48* Immediately one of them ran to get a sponge; he soaked it in wine, and putting it on a reed, gave it to him to drink. 49 But the rest said, "Wait, let us see if Elijah comes to save him." 50† But Jesus cried out again in a loud voice, and gave up his spirit. 51*† And behold, the veil of the sanctuary was torn in two from top to bottom. The earth quaked, rocks were split, 52* tombs were opened, and the bodies of many saints who had fallen asleep were raised. 53 And coming forth from their tombs after his resurrection, they entered the holy city and appeared to many. 54† The centurion and the men with him who were keeping watch over Jesus feared greatly when they saw the earthquake and all that was happening, and they said, "Truly, this was the Son of God!" 55† There were many women there, looking on from a distance, who had followed Jesus from Galilee, ministering to him. 56* Among them were Mary Magdalene and Mary the mother of James and Joseph, and the mother of the sons of Zebedee.

The Burial of Jesus

57*† When it was evening, there came a rich man from Arimathea named Joseph, who was himself a disciple of Jesus.* 58 He went to Pilate and asked for the body of Jesus; then Pilate ordered it to be handed over. 59 Taking the body, Joseph wrapped it [in] clean linen 60 and laid it in his new tomb that he had hewn in the rock. Then he rolled a huge stone across the entrance to the tomb and departed. 61 But Mary Magdalene and the other Mary remained sitting there, facing the tomb.

The Guard at the Tomb†

62 The next day, the one following the day of preparation,† the chief priests and the Pharisees gathered before Pilate 63* and said, "Sir, we

Did You Know?

Jesus Prays Psalm 22

The Gospel writer tells us that before Jesus gave up his spirit and breathed his last breath, he cried out, "My God, my God, why have you forsaken me?" Jesus was actually reciting and praying the opening lines of Psalm 22. This psalm begins in despair but ends in triumph and confidence through God's saving help. With this prayer to God, Jesus invites all people gathered at the Crucifixion to pray the entire psalm—not just the first words of despair but also the concluding words of hope.

Mt 27:46

MT

†

27:47 *Elijah:* see the note on 3:4. This prophet, taken up into heaven (2 Kgs 2:11), was believed to come to the help of those in distress, but the evidences of that belief are all later than the gospels.

27:50 *Gave up his spirit:* cf the Marcan parallel (15:37), "breathed his last." Matthew's alteration expresses both Jesus' control over his destiny and his obedient giving up of his life to God.

27:51–53 *Veil of the sanctuary . . . bottom:* cf Mk 15:38; Lk 23:45. Luke puts this event immediately before the death of Jesus. There were two veils in the Mosaic tabernacle on the model of which the temple was constructed, the outer one before the entrance of the Holy Place and the inner one before the Holy of Holies (see Ex 26:31–36). Only the high priest could pass through the latter and that only on the Day of Atonement (see Lv 16:1–18). Probably the *torn veil* of the gospels is the inner one. The meaning of the scene may be that now, because of Jesus' death, all people have access to the presence of God, or that the temple, its holiest part standing exposed, is now profaned and will soon be destroyed. *The earth quaked . . . appeared to many:* peculiar to Matthew. The earthquake, the splitting of the *rocks,* and especially the resurrection of the dead *saints* indicate the coming of the final age. In the Old Testament the coming of God is frequently portrayed with the imagery of an earthquake (see Pss 68:9; 77:19), and Jesus speaks of the earthquakes that will accompany the "labor pains" that signify the beginning of the dissolution of the old world (24:7–8). For the expectation of the resurrection of the dead at the coming of the new and final age, see Dn 12:1–3. Matthew knows that the end of the old age has not yet come (28:20), but the new age has broken in with the death (and resurrection; cf the earthquake in 28:2) of Jesus; see the note on 16:28. *After his resurrection:* this qualification seems to be due to Matthew's wish to assert the primacy of Jesus' *resurrection* even though he has placed the resurrection of the dead *saints* immediately after Jesus' death.

27:54 Cf Mk 15:39. The Christian confession of faith is made by Gentiles, not only *the centurion,* as in Mark, but the other soldiers *who were keeping watch over Jesus* (cf 36).

27:55–56 *Looking on from a distance:* cf Ps 38:12. *Mary Magdalene . . . Joseph:* these two women are mentioned again in v 61 and 28:1 and are important as witnesses of the reality of the empty tomb. A *James* and *Joseph* are referred to in 13:55 as brothers of Jesus.

27:57–61 Cf Mk 15:42–47. Matthew drops Mark's designation of *Joseph of Arimathea* as "a distinguished member of the council" (the Sanhedrin), and makes him *a rich man* and *a disciple of Jesus.* The former may be an allusion to Is 53:9 (the Hebrew reading of that text is disputed and the one followed in the NAB OT has nothing about the rich, but they are mentioned in the LXX version). That the tomb was the *new tomb of a rich man* and that it was seen by the women are indications of an apologetic intent of Matthew; there could be no question about the identity of Jesus' burial place. *The other Mary:* the mother of James and Joseph (56).

27:62–66 Peculiar to Matthew. The story prepares for 28:11–15 and the Jewish charge that the tomb was empty because the *disciples* had stolen the body of Jesus (28:13, 15).

27:62 *The next day . . . preparation:* the sabbath. According to the synoptic chronology, in that year *the day of preparation* (for the sabbath) was the Passover; cf Mk 15:42. *The Pharisees:* the principal opponents of Jesus during his ministry and, in Matthew's time, of the Christian church, join with *the chief priests* to guarantee against a possible attempt of Jesus' *disciples* to steal his body.

*

27:48 Ps 69:21.
27:51 Ex 26:31–36; Pss 68:9; 77:19.
27:52 Dn 12:1–3.
27:56 Mt 13:55.
27:57–61 Mk 15:42–47; Lk 23:50–56; Jn 19:38–42.
27:57 Is 53:9.
27:63 Mt 12:40; 16:21; 17:23; 20:19.

remember that this impostor while still alive
said, 'After three days I will be raised up.' 64† Give
orders, then, that the grave be secured until the
third day, lest his disciples come and steal him
and say to the people, 'He has been raised from
the dead.' This last imposture would be worse
than the first." 65† Pilate said to them, "The guard
is yours; go secure it as best you can." 66 So they
went and secured the tomb by fixing a seal to the
stone and setting the guard.

The Resurrection of Jesus

28 1*† After the sabbath, as the first day of
the week was dawning,† Mary Magdalene
and the other Mary came to see the tomb. 2*† And
behold, there was a great earthquake; for an angel
of the Lord descended from heaven, approached,
rolled back the stone, and sat upon it. 3* His ap-
pearance was like lightning and his clothing was
white as snow. 4 The guards were shaken with fear
of him and became like dead men. 5 Then the an-
gel said to the women in reply, "Do not be afraid!
I know that you are seeking Jesus the crucified.
6† He is not here, for he has been raised just as
he said. Come and see the place where he lay.
7* Then go quickly and tell his disciples, 'He has
been raised from the dead, and he is going before
you to Galilee; there you will see him.' Behold, I
have told you." 8† Then they went away quickly
from the tomb, fearful yet overjoyed, and ran to
announce this to his disciples. 9*† And behold,
Jesus met them on their way and greeted them.
They approached, embraced his feet, and did him
homage. 10 Then Jesus said to them, "Do not be
afraid. Go tell my brothers to go to Galilee, and
there they will see me."

The Report of the Guard

11† While they were going, some of the guard
went into the city and told the chief priests all
that had happened. 12 They assembled with the
elders and took counsel; then they gave a large
sum of money to the soldiers, 13 telling them,
"You are to say, 'His disciples came by night and
stole him while we were asleep.' 14 And if this gets
to the ears of the governor, we will satisfy [him]
and keep you out of trouble." 15 The soldiers took
the money and did as they were instructed. And
this story has circulated among the Jews to the
present [day].

The Commissioning of the Disciples†

16* The eleven† disciples went to Galilee,
to the mountain to which Jesus had ordered

---

†

27:64 *This last imposture . . . the first:* the claim that Jesus *has been raised from the dead* is clearly the *last imposture; the first* may be either his claim that he would *be raised up* (63) or his claim that he was the one with whose ministry the kingdom of God had come (see 12:28).

27:65 *The guard is yours:* literally, "have a guard" or "you have a guard." Either the imperative or the indicative could mean that Pilate granted the petitioners some Roman soldiers as guards, which is the sense of the present translation. However, if the verb is taken as an indicative it could also mean that Pilate told them to use their own Jewish guards.

28:1–20 Except for vv 1–8, based on Mk 16:1–8, the material of this final chapter is peculiar to Matthew. Even where he follows Mark, Matthew has altered his source so greatly that a very different impression is given from that of the Marcan account. The two points that are common to the resurrection testimony of all the gospels are that the tomb of Jesus had been found empty and that the risen Jesus had appeared to certain persons, or, in the original form of Mark, that such an appearance was promised as soon to take place (see Mk 16:7). On this central and all-important basis, Matthew has constructed an account that interprets the resurrection as the turning of the ages (2–4), shows the Jewish opposition to Jesus as continuing *to the present* in the claim that the resurrection is a deception perpetrated by the *disciples* who stole his body from the tomb (11–15), and marks a new stage in the mission of *the disciples* once limited to Israel (10:5–6); now they are to *make disciples of all nations.* In this work they will be strengthened by the presence of the exalted Son of Man, who will be with them *until* the kingdom comes in fullness at *the end of the age* (16–20).

28:1 *After the sabbath . . . dawning:* since the sabbath ended at sunset, this could mean in the early evening, for *dawning* can refer to the appearance of the evening star; cf Lk 23:54. However, it is probable that Matthew means the morning dawn of the day after the sabbath, as in the similar though slightly different text of Mark, "when the sun had risen" (16:2). *Mary Magdalene and the other Mary:* see the notes on 27:55–56; 57–61. *To see the tomb:* cf Mk 16:1–2 where the purpose of the women's visit is to anoint Jesus' body.

28:2–4 Peculiar to Matthew. *A great earthquake:* see the note on 27:51–53. *Descended from heaven:* this trait is peculiar to Matthew, although his interpretation of the "young man" of his Marcan source (16:5) as an *angel* is probably true to Mark's intention; cf Lk 24:23 where the "two men" of 24:4 are said to be "angels." *Rolled back the stone . . . upon it:* not to allow the risen Jesus to leave the tomb but to make evident that the tomb is empty (see 6). Unlike the apocryphal Gospel of Peter (9:35—11:44), the New Testament does not describe the resurrection of Jesus, nor is there anyone who sees it. *His appearance was like lightning . . . snow:* see the note on 17:2.

28:6–7 Cf Mk 16:6–7. *Just as he said:* a Matthean addition referring to Jesus' predictions of his resurrection, e.g., 16:21; 17:23; 20:19. *Tell his disciples:* like the angel of the Lord of the infancy narrative, the angel interprets a fact and gives a commandment about what is to be done; cf 1:20–21. Matthew omits Mark's "and Peter" (16:7); considering his interest in Peter, this omission is curious. Perhaps the reason is that the Marcan text may allude to a first appearance of Jesus to Peter alone (cf 1 Cor 15:5; Lk 24:34) which Matthew has already incorporated into his account of Peter's confession at Caesarea Philippi; see the note on 16:16. *He is going . . . Galilee:* like Mk 16:7, a reference to Jesus' prediction at the Last Supper (26:32; Mk 14:28). Matthew changes Mark's "as he told you" to a declaration of the angel.

28:8 Contrast Mk 16:8 where the women in their fear "said nothing to anyone."

28:9–10 Although these verses are peculiar to Matthew, there are similarities between them and Jn's account of the appearance of Jesus to Mary Magdalene (20:17). In both there is a touching of Jesus' body, and a command of Jesus to bear a message to his disciples, designated as his *brothers.* Matthew may have drawn upon a tradition that appears in a different form in John. Jesus' words to the women are mainly a repetition of those of the angel (5a; 7b).

28:11–15 This account indicates that the dispute between Christians and Jews about the empty tomb was not whether the tomb was empty but why.

28:16–20 This climactic scene has been called a "proleptic parousia," for it gives a foretaste of the final glorious coming of the Son of Man (26:64). Then his triumph will be manifest to all; now it is revealed only to *the disciples,* who are commissioned to announce it to *all nations* and bring them to belief in Jesus and obedience to his commandments.

28:16 *The eleven:* the number recalls the tragic defection of Judas

---

*

28:1–10 Mk 16:1–8; Lk 24:1–12; Jn 20:1–10.
28:2 Mt 25:51.
28:3 Mt 17:2.
28:7 Mt 26:32.
28:9–10 Jn 20:17.
28:16–20 Mk 16:14–16; Lk 24:36–49; Jn 20:19–23.

them. 17† When they saw him, they worshiped,
but they doubted. 18*† Then Jesus approached
and said to them, "All power in heaven and on
earth has been given to me. 19*† Go, therefore,
and make disciples of all nations, baptizing
them in the name of the Father, and of the Son,
and of the holy Spirit, 20*† teaching them to
observe all that I have commanded you. And
behold, I am with you always, until the end of
the age."

† Iscariot. *To the mountain . . . ordered them:* since the message to the *disciples* was simply that they were to go to Galilee (10), some think that *the mountain* comes from a tradition of the message known to Matthew and alluded to here. For the significance of *the mountain,* see the note on 17:1.

28:17 *But they doubted:* the Greek can also be translated, "but some doubted." The verb occurs elsewhere in the New Testament only in 14:31 where it is associated with Peter's being of "little faith." For the meaning of that designation, see the note on 6:30.

28:18 *All power . . . me:* the Greek word here translated *power* is the same as that found in the LXX translation of Dn 7:13–14 where one "like a son of man" is given *power* and an everlasting kingdom by God. The risen Jesus here claims universal power, i.e., *in heaven and on earth.*

28:19 *Therefore:* since universal power belongs to the risen Jesus (18), he gives the eleven a mission that is universal. They are to *make disciples of all nations.* While *all nations* is understood by some scholars as referring only *to all* Gentiles, it is probable that it included the Jews as well. *Baptizing them:* baptism is the means of entrance into the community of the risen one, the Church. *In the name of the Father . . . holy Spirit:* this is perhaps the clearest expression in the New Testament of trinitarian belief. It may have been the baptismal formula of Matthew's church, but primarily it designates the effect of baptism, the union of the one baptized with the Father, Son, and holy Spirit.

28:20 *All that I have commanded you:* the moral teaching found in this gospel, preeminently that of the Sermon on the Mount (chs 5–7). The commandments of Jesus are the standard of Christian conduct, not the Mosaic law as such, even though some of the Mosaic commandments have now been invested with the authority of Jesus. *Behold, I am with you always:* the promise of Jesus' real though invisible presence echoes the name Emmanuel given to him in the infancy narrative; see the note on 1:23. *End of the age:* see the notes on 13:39 and 24:3.

* **28:18** Dn 7:14 LXX.
28:19 Acts 1:8.
28:20 Mt 1:23; 13:39; 24:3.

M
T

The Gospel According to

Mark

Have you ever been ridiculed or rejected by others—maybe even your friends—for trying to do something good? Jesus would understand your feelings. In the Gospel of Mark, Jesus is misunderstood and abandoned by those closest to him. This Gospel was written for early Christians experiencing persecution or death for their faith. The author is reminding them and us to put our total trust in God as Jesus did, despite whatever difficulties we encounter in being a Christian.

In Depth

The Gospel of Mark is the shortest of the four Gospels and can be easily read in one sitting. It portrays Jesus as a man of action—human in his feelings, and always on the move fulfilling his mission. This Gospel answers two fundamental questions: Who is this Jesus called the Christ? and What does it mean to be his disciple? Because the people hearing this Gospel were being persecuted for believing in Jesus, those questions were a matter of life and death.

To answer the first question, the Gospel of Mark tells stories about Jesus' power to heal and about his compassion for suffering people. It tells about his conflicts with demons and with religious and civil authorities and how he was misunderstood by his own disciples. Through these stories, the reader learns that Jesus is the Son of God, the favored one who acts with God's authority because he is obedient to God's will. Jesus did not come as the victorious king as many Jews expected. Instead, he accepted the suffering that comes with doing God's will. His painful and shameful death was needed before his glory could be seen. Can we believe in a despised, suffering Messiah?

Mark answers the second question in surprising ways. The disciples Jesus called were initially eager to follow him, but they quickly became fearful. They wanted to be powerful and important, and they wanted the approval of their peers. Even when Jesus was arrested, they were so fearful that they ran away and left Jesus alone. But Jesus did not abandon them. After he was raised from the dead, he sent them a message that he would meet them again in Galilee. The Gospel of Mark also tells stories about a blind man, a leper, and Gentiles (non-Jews), all of whom were Jesus' disciples because they placed their total trust in him. Whether gradually or quickly, can we place our complete faith in Jesus, becoming his disciples?

At a Glance

Quick Facts

Inspired Author: a Gentile Christian, traditionally thought to be a disciple of Peter named John Mark
Date Written: from approximately AD 65 to 70; this was the first written Gospel
Audience: non-Jewish Christians (in Rome?) who were experiencing persecution because of their belief in Jesus
Image of Jesus: healer and miracle worker who accepts suffering as the cost for following God's will

Mark

15:25–27

I: The Preparation for the Public Ministry of Jesus†

1 [1]The beginning of the gospel of Jesus Christ
[the Son of God].†

The Preaching of John the Baptist

[2]*† As it is written in Isaiah the prophet:

"Behold, I am sending my messenger ahead
of you;
he will prepare your way.*
[3]* A voice of one crying out in the desert:
'Prepare the way of the Lord,
make straight his paths.' "

[4]John [the] Baptist appeared in the desert
proclaiming a baptism of repentance for the
forgiveness of sins. [5]People of the whole Judean
countryside and all the inhabitants of Jerusalem
were going out to him and were being baptized
by him in the Jordan River as they acknowledged
their sins. [6]† John was clothed in camel's hair,
with a leather belt around his waist. He fed on
locusts and wild honey. [7]And this is what he
proclaimed: "One mightier than I is coming af-
ter me. I am not worthy to stoop and loosen the
thongs of his sandals. [8]*† I have baptized you
with water; he will baptize you with the holy
Spirit."

The Baptism of Jesus

[9]* It happened in those days that Jesus came
from Nazareth of Galilee and was baptized in
the Jordan by John. [10]† On coming up out of
the water he saw the heavens being torn open
and the Spirit, like a dove, descending upon

†

1:1–13 The prologue of the Gospel according to Mark begins with the title (1) followed by three events preparatory to Jesus' preaching: (1) the appearance in the Judean wilderness of John, baptizer, preacher of repentance, and precursor of Jesus (2–8); (2) the baptism of Jesus, at which a voice from heaven acknowledges Jesus to be God's Son, and the holy Spirit descends on him (9–11); (3) the temptation of Jesus by Satan (12–13).

1:1 *The gospel of Jesus Christ [the Son of God]:* the "good news" of salvation in and through Jesus, crucified and risen, acknowledged by the Christian community as Messiah (8:29; 14:61–62) and Son of God (Mk 1:11; 9:7; 15:39), although some important manuscripts here omit *the Son of God.*

1:2–3 Although Mark attributes the prophecy to Isaiah, the text is a combination of Mal 3:1; Is 40:3; and Ex 23:20; cf Mt 11:10; Lk 7:27. John's ministry is seen as God's prelude to the saving mission of his Son. *The way of the Lord:* this prophecy of Deutero-Isaiah concerning the end of the Babylonian exile is here applied to the coming of Jesus; John the Baptist is to prepare the way for him.

1:6 *Clothed in camel's hair . . . waist:* the Baptist's garb recalls that of Elijah in 2 Kgs 1:8. Jesus speaks of the Baptist as Elijah who has already come (9:11–13; Mt 17:10–12; cf Mal 3:23–24; Lk 1:17).

1:8–9 Through the life-giving baptism with the holy Spirit (8), Jesus will create a new people of God. But first he identifies himself with the people of Israel in submitting to John's baptism of repentance and in bearing on their behalf the burden of God's decisive judgment (9; cf 4). As in the desert of Sinai, so here in the wilderness of Judea, Israel's sonship with God is to be renewed.

1:10–11 *He saw the heavens . . . and the Spirit . . . upon him:* indicating divine intervention in fulfillment of promise. Here the descent of the Spirit on Jesus is meant, anointing him for his ministry; cf Is 11:2; 42:1; 61:1; 63:9. *A voice . . . with you I am well pleased:* God's acknowledgment of Jesus as his unique Son, the object of his love. His approval of Jesus is the assurance that Jesus will fulfill his messianic mission of salvation.

1:2–8 Mt 3:1–11; Lk 3:2–16.
1:2 Mal 3:1.
1:3 Is 40:3; Jn 1:23.
1:8 Jn 1:27; Acts 1:5; 11:16.
1:9–11 Mt 3:13–17; Lk 3:21–23; Jn 1:32–33.

Cultural Connection

Spirits

Most Native American peoples would not be surprised by all the angels and spirits in the first chapter of Mark. Many Native American cultures believe in the presence of good and bad spirits in the world. They view good spirits as personal helpers and message bearers, like the angels who take care of Jesus in verse 13. They believe that spirits often appear as animals, much as the Holy Spirit appears as a dove in verse 10. And many believe that bad spirits influence and control people, just as the unclean spirit does in verse 23.

Isn't it interesting that different cultures can develop such parallel religious beliefs? Whether we call them angels and demons or good and bad spirits, we share a common understanding about unseen powers influencing our lives. It is an understanding of the world that is often rejected in our scientific, technology-filled culture.

▶ Mk 1:9–39

him. 11* And a voice came from the heavens,
"You are my beloved Son; with you I am well
pleased."

The Temptation of Jesus

12*† At once the Spirit drove him out into the
desert, 13 and he remained in the desert for forty
days, tempted by Satan. He was among wild
beasts, and the angels ministered to him.

II: The Mystery of Jesus

The Beginning of the Galilean Ministry

14*† After John had been arrested, Jesus came
to Galilee proclaiming the gospel of God:
15* "This is the time of fulfillment. The king-
dom of God is at hand. Repent, and believe in
the gospel."

The Call of the First Disciples

16*† As he passed by the Sea of Galilee, he
saw Simon and his brother Andrew casting
their nets into the sea; they were fishermen.
17 Jesus said to them, "Come after me, and I
will make you fishers of men." 18 Then they
abandoned their nets and followed him. 19 He
walked along a little farther and saw James, the
son of Zebedee, and his brother John. They too
were in a boat mending their nets. 20 Then he
called them. So they left their father Zebedee
in the boat along with the hired men and fol-
lowed him.

The Cure of a Demoniac

21*† Then they came to Capernaum, and on
the sabbath he entered the synagogue and taught.
22* The people were astonished at his teaching,
for he taught them as one having authority and
not as the scribes. 23† In their synagogue was
a man with an unclean spirit; 24† he cried out,
"What have you to do with us, Jesus of Nazareth?
Have you come to destroy us? I know who you

†

1:12–13 The same Spirit who descended on Jesus in his baptism now drives him into the desert for forty days. The result is radical confrontation and temptation by Satan who attempts to frustrate the work of God. The presence of wild beasts may indicate the horror and danger of the desert regarded as the abode of demons or may reflect the paradise motif of harmony among all creatures; cf Is 11:6–9. The presence of ministering angels to sustain Jesus recalls the angel who guided the Israelites in the desert in the first Exodus (14:19; 23:20) and the angel who supplied nourishment to Elijah in the wilderness (1 Kgs 19:5–7). The combined forces of good and evil were present to Jesus in the desert. His sustained obedience brings forth the new Israel of God there where Israel's rebellion had brought death and alienation.

1:14–15 *After John had been arrested:* in the plan of God, Jesus was not to proclaim the good news of salvation prior to the termination of the Baptist's active mission. *Galilee:* in the Marcan account, scene of the major part of Jesus' public ministry before his arrest and condemnation. *The gospel of God:* not only the good news from God but about God at work in Jesus Christ. *This is the time of fulfillment:* i.e., of God's promises. *The kingdom of God . . . Repent:* see the note on Mt 3:2.

1:16–20 These verses narrate the call of the first disciples. See the notes on Mt 4:18–22 and 4:20.

1:21–45 The account of a single day's ministry of Jesus on a sabbath in and outside the synagogue of Capernaum (21–31) combines teaching and miracles of exorcism and healing. Mention is not made of the content of the teaching but of the effect of astonishment and alarm on the people. Jesus' teaching with authority, making an absolute claim on the hearer, was in the best tradition of the ancient prophets, not of the scribes. The narrative continues with events that evening (32–34; see the notes on Mt 8:14–17) and the next day (35–39). The cleansing in vv 40–45 stands as an isolated story.

1:23 *An unclean spirit:* so called because of the spirit's resistance to the holiness of God. The spirit knows and fears the power of Jesus to destroy his influence; cf 32, 34; 3:11; 6:13.

1:24 *What have you to do with us?:* see the note on Jn 2:4.

*

1:11 Ps 2:7.
1:12–13 Mt 4:1–11; Lk 4:1–13.
1:14–15 Mt 4:12–17; Lk 4:14–15.
1:15 Mt 3:2.
1:16–20 Mt 4:18–22; Lk 5:2–11.
1:21–28 Lk 4:31–37.
1:22 Mt 7:28–29.

are—the Holy One of God!"† [25]Jesus rebuked him and said, "Quiet! Come out of him!" [26]The unclean spirit convulsed him and with a loud cry came out of him. [27]All were amazed and asked one another, "What is this? A new teaching with authority. He commands even the unclean spirits and they obey him." [28]His fame spread everywhere throughout the whole region of Galilee.

The Cure of Simon's Mother-in-Law

[29]* On leaving the synagogue he entered the house of Simon and Andrew with James and John. [30]Simon's mother-in-law lay sick with a fever. They immediately told him about her. [31]He approached, grasped her hand, and helped her up. Then the fever left her and she waited on them.

Other Healings

[32]When it was evening, after sunset, they brought to him all who were ill or possessed by demons. [33]The whole town was gathered at the door. [34]He cured many who were sick with various diseases, and he drove out many demons, not permitting them to speak because they knew him.

Jesus Leaves Capernaum

[35]* Rising very early before dawn, he left and went off to a deserted place, where he prayed. [36]Simon and those who were with him pursued him [37]and on finding him said, "Everyone is looking for you." [38]He told them, "Let us go on to the nearby villages that I may preach there also. For this purpose have I come." [39]So he went into their synagogues, preaching and driving out demons throughout the whole of Galilee.

The Cleansing of a Leper

[40]*† A leper came to him [and kneeling down] begged him and said, "If you wish, you can make me clean." [41]* Moved with pity, he stretched out his hand, touched him, and said to him, "I do will it. Be made clean." [42]* The leprosy left him immediately, and he was made clean. [43]Then, warning him sternly, he dismissed him at once. [44]* Then he said to him, "See that you tell no one anything, but go, show yourself to the priest and offer for your cleansing what Moses prescribed; that will be proof for them." [45]The man went away and began to publicize the whole matter. He spread the report abroad so that it was impossible for Jesus to enter a town openly. He remained outside in deserted places, and people kept coming to him from everywhere.

Live It!

Called to Follow Jesus

The response of Peter, Andrew, James, and John to Jesus is an example of obedience to God's call. Jesus calls them because he loves them and trusts them to share in his mission.

The Catholic Church believes that through Baptism, all Christians are called to be Jesus' disciples (followers) in whatever path their lives take. Most people are called to mission as laypersons. A few are called to serve through the priesthood, diaconate, or religious life. So whether you end up a priest or a plumber, married or single, poor or rich, faithfulness to God's call is the most important loyalty you can have.

It might be hard to imagine how school or a fast-food job is part of your call to follow Jesus. But attitude is everything! Do you see school as a necessary evil to get a high-paying job? or do you see it as preparation for a career that will allow you to serve others and contribute to society? If you work, do you approach your job halfheartedly, or are you enthusiastic, always giving your best effort? Do you treat coworkers and customers with warmth and respect? Jesus is calling you to be his disciple wherever you are and in whatever you might be doing.

▶ Mk 1:16–20

The Healing of a Paralytic

2 [1]*† When Jesus returned to Capernaum after some days, it became known that he was at

MK

† **1:24–25** *The Holy One of God:* not a confession but an attempt to ward off Jesus' power, reflecting the notion that use of the precise name of an opposing spirit would guarantee mastery over him. Jesus silenced the cry of the unclean spirit and drove him out of the man.

1:40 *A leper:* for the various forms of skin disease, see Lv 13:1–50 and the note on Lv 13:2–4. There are only two instances in the Old Testament in which God is shown to have cured a leper (Nm 12:10–15 and 2 Kgs 5:1–14). The law of Moses provided for the ritual purification of a leper. In curing the leper, Jesus assumes that the priests will reinstate the cured man into the religious community. See also the note on Lk 5:14.

2:1–3:6 This section relates a series of conflicts between Jesus and the scribes and Pharisees in which the growing opposition of the latter leads to their plot to put Jesus to death (3:6).

* **1:29–34** Mt 8:14–16; Lk 4:38–41.
1:35–39 Lk 4:42–44.
1:40–44 Mt 8:2–4; Lk 5:12–14.
1:41 Mk 5:30.
1:42 Lk 17:14.
1:44 Lv 14:2–32.
2:1–12 Mt 9:2–8; Lk 5:18–26.

Live It!

Sacramental Healing

The physical healing Jesus provides for the paralytic in this story is considered miraculous, and rightly so. What shouldn't get lost in the story, however, is that along with his physical healing, Jesus offers this man spiritual healing: the forgiveness of his sins. Imagine the sense of comfort this man must have felt as he walked away, his heart cleansed and his spirit lifted!

Reflecting the actions of Jesus in this story, the Catholic Church has two sacraments dedicated to healing. The sacrament of Penance and Reconciliation offers us personal healing if we are willing to be honest about the sinfulness in our lives. The sacrament of Anointing of the Sick offers hope, strength, and spiritual comfort to the seriously ill and aged. Each sacrament is a tangible sign of God's love for those who suffer in body and spirit, and is meant to empower us to share in Jesus' ministry of healing.

- When have you reconciled with those who are in need of forgiveness?
- In what ways can you bring comfort and hope to those who are in need of healing, either in body or spirit?

▶ **Mk 2:1–12**

home.† 2 Many gathered together so that there was no longer room for them, not even around the door, and he preached the word to them.
3 They came bringing to him a paralytic carried by four men. 4 Unable to get near Jesus because of the crowd, they opened up the roof above him. After they had broken through, they let down the mat on which the paralytic was lying. 5† When Jesus saw their faith, he said to the paralytic, "Child, your sins are forgiven." 6† Now some of the scribes were sitting there asking themselves, 7*† "Why does this man speak that way? He is blaspheming. Who but God alone can forgive sins?" 8 Jesus immediately knew in his mind what they were thinking to themselves, so he said, "Why are you thinking such things in your hearts? 9 Which is easier, to say to the paralytic, 'Your sins are forgiven,' or to say, 'Rise, pick up your mat and walk'? 10† But that you may know that the Son of Man has authority to forgive sins on earth"— 11 he said to the paralytic, "I say to you, rise, pick up your mat, and go home." 12 He rose, picked up his mat at once, and went away in the sight of everyone. They were all astounded and glorified God, saying, "We have never seen anything like this."

The Call of Levi

13*† Once again he went out along the sea. All the crowd came to him and he taught them. 14*† As he passed by, he saw Levi, son of Alphaeus, sitting at the customs post. He said to him, "Follow me." And he got up and followed him. 15† While he was at table in his house, many tax collectors and sinners sat with Jesus and his disciples; for there were many who followed him. 16† Some scribes who were Pharisees saw that he was eating with sinners and tax collectors and said to his disciples, "Why does he eat with tax collectors and sinners?" 17† Jesus heard this and said to them [that], "Those who are well do not need a physician, but the sick do. I did not come to call the righteous but sinners."

†

2:1–2 *He was at home:* to the crowds that gathered in and outside the house Jesus *preached the word,* i.e., the gospel concerning the nearness of the kingdom and the necessity of repentance and faith (1:14).

2:5 It was the faith of the paralytic and those who carried him that moved Jesus to heal the sick man. Accounts of other miracles of Jesus reveal more and more his emphasis on faith as the requisite for exercising his healing powers (5:34; 9:23–24; 10:52).

2:6 *Scribes:* trained in oral interpretation of the written law; in Mark's gospel, adversaries of Jesus, with one exception (12:28, 34).

2:7 *He is blaspheming:* an accusation made here and repeated during the trial of Jesus (14:60–64).

2:10 *But that you may know that the Son of Man . . . on earth:* although vv 8–9 are addressed to the scribes, the sudden interruption of thought and structure in v 10 seems not addressed to them nor to the paralytic. Moreover, the early public use of the designation "Son of Man" to unbelieving scribes is most unlikely. The most probable explanation is that Mark's insertion of v 10 is a commentary addressed to Christians for whom he recalls this miracle and who already accept in faith that Jesus is Messiah and Son of God.

2:13 *He taught them:* see the note on 1:21–45.

2:14 *As he passed by:* see the note on 1:16–20. *Levi, son of Alphaeus:* see the note on Mt 9:9. *Customs post:* such tax collectors paid a fixed sum for the right to collect customs duties within their districts. Since whatever they could collect above this amount constituted their profit, the abuse of extortion was widespread among them. Hence, Jewish customs officials were regarded as sinners (16), outcasts of society, and disgraced along with their families. *He got up and followed him:* i.e., became a disciple of Jesus.

2:15 *In his house:* cf v 1; Mt 9:10. Lk 5:29 clearly calls it Levi's house.

2:16–17 This and the following conflict stories reflect a similar pattern: a statement of fact, a question of protest, and a reply by Jesus.

2:17 *Do not need a physician:* this maxim of Jesus with its implied irony was uttered to silence his adversaries who objected that he ate with *tax collectors and sinners* (16). Because the scribes and Pharisees were self-righteous, they were not capable of responding to Jesus' call to repentance and faith in the gospel.

*

2:7 Is 43:25. **2:13** Mk 4:1. **2:14–17** Mt 9:9–13; Lk 5:27–32.

The Question about Fasting

18* † The disciples of John and of the Pharisees were accustomed to fast. People came to him and objected, "Why do the disciples of John and the disciples of the Pharisees fast, but your disciples do not fast?" 19† Jesus answered them, "Can the wedding guests fast while the bridegroom is with them? As long as they have the bridegroom with them they cannot fast. 20 But the days will come when the bridegroom is taken away from them, and then they will fast on that day. 21 No one sews a piece of unshrunken cloth on an old cloak. If he does, its fullness pulls away, the new from the old, and the tear gets worse. 22 Likewise, no one pours new wine into old wineskins. Otherwise, the wine will burst the skins, and both the wine and the skins are ruined. Rather, new wine is poured into fresh wineskins."

The Disciples and the Sabbath

23* † As he was passing through a field of grain on the sabbath, his disciples began to make a path while picking the heads of grain. 24* At this the Pharisees said to him, "Look, why are they doing what is unlawful on the sabbath?" 25† He said to them, "Have you never read what David did when he was in need and he and his companions were hungry? 26* How he went into the house of God when Abiathar was high priest and ate the bread of offering that only the priests could lawfully eat, and shared it with his companions?" 27* † Then he said to them, "The sabbath was made for man, not man for the sabbath. 28† That is why the Son of Man is lord even of the sabbath."

A Man with a Withered Hand

3 1* † Again he entered the synagogue. There was a man there who had a withered hand. 2 They watched him closely to see if he would

2:18–22 This conflict over the question of fasting has the same pattern as vv 16–17; see the notes on Mt 9:15 and 9:16–17.

2:19 *Can the wedding guests fast?:* the bridal metaphor expresses a new relationship of love between God and his people in the person and mission of Jesus to his disciples. It is the inauguration of the new and joyful messianic time of fulfillment and the passing of the old. Any attempt at assimilating the Pharisaic practice of fasting, or of extending the preparatory discipline of John's disciples beyond the arrival of the bridegroom, would be as futile as sewing *a piece of unshrunken cloth on an old cloak* or pouring *new wine into old wineskins* with the resulting destruction of both cloth and wine (21–22). Fasting is rendered superfluous during the earthly ministry of Jesus; cf v 20.

2:23–28 This conflict regarding the sabbath follows the same pattern as in vv 18–22.

2:25–26 *Have you never read what David did?:* Jesus defends the action of his disciples on the basis of 1 Sm 21:2–7 in which an exception is made to the regulation of Lv 24:9 because of the extreme hunger of David and his men. According to 1 Samuel, the priest who gave the bread to David was Ahimelech, father of Abiathar.

2:27 *The sabbath was made for man:* a reaffirmation of the divine intent of the sabbath to benefit Israel as contrasted with the restrictive Pharisaic tradition added to the law.

2:28 *The Son of Man is lord even of the sabbath:* Mark's comment on the theological meaning of the incident is to benefit his Christian readers; see the note on 2:10.

3:1–5 Here Jesus is again depicted in conflict with his adversaries over the question of sabbath-day observance. His opponents were already ill disposed toward him because they regarded Jesus as a violator of the sabbath. Jesus' question *Is it lawful to do good on the sabbath rather than to do evil?* places the matter in the broader theological context outside the casuistry of the scribes. The answer is obvious. Jesus heals the man with the withered hand in the sight of all and reduces his opponents to silence; cf Jn 5:17–18.

2:18–22 Mt 9:14–17; Lk 5:33–39.
2:23–28 Mt 12:1–8; Lk 6:1–5.
2:24 Dt 23:25.
2:26 1 Sm 21:2–7; Lv 24:5–9.
2:27 2 Mc 5:19.
3:1–6 Mt 12:9–14; Lk 6:6–11.

Live It!

Getting Personal

It is one thing to be seen hanging out with certain groups of people, but it is another to be seen eating with them. Jesus was often criticized for eating with the wrong kind of people, a charge he answers in Mark 2:13–17. He knew that the only way to help someone grow was to get to know him or her personally. This is why he consistently invited people to sit down and share a meal with him, in the same way we share meals with our family and friends.

Jesus' "meal ministry" throughout the Gospels is a reminder to us that we too must live in solidarity and friendship with all people in our world, especially those who are most in need. It did not matter to Jesus whether a person was rich or poor, well known or unknown, regarded as a saint or as a sinner. It did not matter to him whether a person was black or white, male or female, young or old. What did matter to Jesus was whether the person he approached was interested in getting to know him—and his heavenly Father—personally.

Are you ready to get to know Jesus personally? If so, take a few minutes to close your eyes and think about what this passage says. Talk to Jesus about what is going on in your life and in your family's life. When you are done talking, spend some time quietly listening for what Jesus has to say to you—personally.

▶ **Mk 2:13–17**

MK

cure him on the sabbath so that they might
accuse him. 3 He said to the man with the with-
ered hand, "Come up here before us." 4 Then
he said to them, "Is it lawful to do good on
the sabbath rather than to do evil, to save life
rather than to destroy it?" But they remained
silent. 5* Looking around at them with anger
and grieved at their hardness of heart, he said to
the man, "Stretch out your hand." He stretched
it out and his hand was restored. 6† The Phar-
isees went out and immediately took counsel
with the Herodians against him to put him to
death.

The Mercy of Jesus

7*† Jesus withdrew toward the sea with his
disciples. A large number of people [followed]
from Galilee and from Judea. 8 Hearing what he
was doing, a large number of people came to
him also from Jerusalem, from Idumea, from
beyond the Jordan, and from the neighborhood
of Tyre and Sidon. 9 He told his disciples to have
a boat ready for him because of the crowd, so
that they would not crush him. 10* He had cured
many and, as a result, those who had diseases
were pressing upon him to touch him. 11*† And
whenever unclean spirits saw him they would
fall down before him and shout, "You are the
Son of God." 12 He warned them sternly not to
make him known.

The Mission of the Twelve

13*† He went up the mountain and sum-
moned those whom he wanted and they came
to him. 14*† He appointed twelve [whom he
also named apostles] that they might be with
him and he might send them forth to preach
15 and to have authority to drive out demons:
16† [he appointed the twelve:] Simon, whom
he named Peter; 17* James, son of Zebedee, and
John the brother of James, whom he named
Boanerges, that is, sons of thunder; 18 Andrew,
Philip, Bartholomew, Matthew, Thomas, James
the son of Alphaeus; Thaddeus, Simon the
Cananean, 19 and Judas Iscariot who betrayed
him.

Live It!

Trusting God

In Mark 3:1–6, among those gathered in the synagogue is a man with a withered hand. There is no indication that he is seeking out Jesus or that he commands any special attention. Jesus notices him and invites him to come forward. Jesus then asks the man to stretch out his disfigured hand for all to see. The man, we might guess, probably did not feel proud of his hand. It certainly would be understandable if, when invited by Jesus to stretch out his hand for all to see, the man had stormed out of the synagogue in anger and shame. Instead, he did what Jesus asked, and through his trust in Jesus, his hand was restored to wholeness.

We are all "disfigured" in some way—whether physically, emotionally, or spiritually. We may feel a sense of shame or embarrassment at our imperfections and come to think of ourselves as less than what we were created to be. Jesus, however, invites us into relationship with him despite our limitations, offering us compassion, love, and mercy if we are willing to put our trust in him.

- What source of pain or shame in your own life might Jesus be inviting you to share with him?
- Can you risk becoming vulnerable and trusting him with it?

▶ **Mk 3:1–6**

---

† **3:6** In reporting the plot of the Pharisees and Herodians to put Jesus to death after this series of conflicts in Galilee, Mark uses a pattern that recurs in his account of later controversies in Jerusalem (11:17–18; 12:13–17). The help of the Herodians, supporters of Herod Antipas, tetrarch of Galilee and Perea, is needed to take action against Jesus. Both series of conflicts point to their gravity and to the impending passion of Jesus.

3:7–19 This overview of the Galilean ministry manifests the power of Jesus to draw people to himself through his teaching and deeds of power. The crowds of Jews from many regions surround Jesus (7–12). This phenomenon prepares the way for creating a new people of Israel. The choice and mission of the Twelve is the prelude (13–19).

3:11–12 See the note on 1:24–25.

3:13 *He went up the mountain:* here and elsewhere the mountain is associated with solemn moments and acts in the mission and self-revelation of Jesus (6:46; 9:2–8; 13:3). Jesus acts with authority as he *summoned those whom he wanted and they came to him.*

3:14–15 *He appointed twelve [whom he also named apostles] that they might be with him:* literally "he made," i.e., instituted them as apostles to extend his messianic mission through them (6:7–13). See the notes on Mt 10:1 and 10:2–4.

3:16 *Simon, whom he named Peter:* Mark indicates that Simon's name was changed on this occasion. Peter is first in all lists of the apostles (Mt 10:2; Lk 6:14; Acts 1:13; cf 1 Cor 15:5–8).

---

* **3:5** Lk 14:4.
3:7–12 Mt 4:23–25; 12:15; Lk 6:17–19.
3:10 Mk 5:30.
3:11 Mk 1:34; Lk 4:41.
3:13–19 Mt 10:1–4; Lk 6:12–16.
3:14 Mk 6:7.
3:17 Mt 16:18; Jn 1:42.

Catholic Connection

Holy Orders

God has a plan for each of us, if we just have the courage to follow it. Look at the Twelve Apostles Christ called to join him on the mountain. Each had the choice to go up the mountain or not, and each chose to go. Once on the mountain, Christ appointed them Apostles (which means "sent") to continue his mission. If the Apostles had answered "no" to Jesus' call, they may have been spared the heartbreak of witnessing the Crucifixion, but they also would have missed the joy of seeing Jesus after the Resurrection!

All God's people are invited to share in Christ's mission through the sacrament of Baptism in what is called the common priesthood. This means that all Christians are called to share in Christ's priesthood by living holy lives and spreading God's message of love. But just as Jesus singled out the Twelve Apostles to carry on his mission as leaders in the Church, some men are also invited to participate in the mission of Christ by answering the call to the ministerial priesthood. This differs from the common priesthood in that the ministerial priesthood is given a sacred power to serve the Church by helping all the faithful to live out their baptismal calling. Men who answer "yes" to the ministerial priesthood are ordained by receiving the sacrament of Holy Orders.

Through the sacrament, a man enters into one of three forms of ministry, becoming a bishop, priest, or deacon. Through the grace of ordination, bishops are the direct successors of the Apostles. Out of their love for Christ, they work with the Pope to lead, teach, and celebrate the sacraments. Priests are ordained as coworkers of the bishop and serve the Church especially through teaching the faithful and sacramental ministry. Deacons are ordained as helpers to the bishop, proclaiming the word and performing acts of charity. Together, through these three forms of ministry, these men show their love for Christ and through their work Christ shows his love for the Church.

The celebration of the sacrament of Holy Orders is always administered by a bishop and varies depending on the ministry the man is entering. During the rite, the men becoming bishops and priests are anointed with sacred chrism (oil) as a sign of the Holy Spirit who empowers them to fulfill their ministry. During the ordination of a deacon, the man has hands laid upon him by the bishop, who then prays for the gift of the Holy Spirit to empower and guide the new deacon's ministry.

▶ **Mk 3:13–19**

Catechism, nos. 1533–1600

Cultural Connection

Jesus Teaches Us Through Stories

In Mark, chapter 4, Jesus teaches about God's Reign through parables (see "Parables," near Mt 13:10). In some Hispanic families, it is customary for young people to hear their *abuelita* (grandmother) tell stories about their family history, traditions, and faith. Many of the stories are true; others may be created to give a moral teaching, like the parables.

Here is a true story: A little girl's father died, leaving her family in extreme poverty. Her mother never lost faith in God, daily prayed to the Divine Providence, and asked other people to pray with her. Her prayers were always answered: food appeared miraculously in front of the family's door, and her six children were accepted free in Catholic schools.

Eventually, the mother married a creative businessman. When the business prospered, she remembered the way God had moved the hearts of people so that her family could have food and education, and with great confidence in God, she started a boarding school for boys. Whenever there was not enough food, she prayed and invited other people to pray. The Divine Providence always responded. The school has sheltered and educated two hundred boys each year for the last seventy years.

- Which stories of faith, love, and service have marked the history of your family?
- How are you honoring your family's tradition of bringing the Gospel to people in need?

▶ Mk 4:1–34

M K

Blasphemy of the Scribes

20*† He came home.† Again [the] crowd gath-
ered, making it impossible for them even to eat.
21* When his relatives heard of this they set out to
seize him, for they said, "He is out of his mind."
22*† The scribes who had come from Jerusalem
said, "He is possessed by Beelzebul," and "By the
prince of demons he drives out demons."

Jesus and Beelzebul

23 Summoning them, he began to speak to them
in parables, "How can Satan drive out Satan? 24 If
a kingdom is divided against itself, that kingdom
cannot stand. 25 And if a house is divided against
itself, that house will not be able to stand. 26 And if
Satan has risen up against himself and is divided,
he cannot stand; that is the end of him. 27 But no
one can enter a strong man's house to plunder his
property unless he first ties up the strong man.
Then he can plunder his house. 28* Amen, I say
to you, all sins and all blasphemies that people
utter will be forgiven them. 29† But whoever blas-
phemes against the holy Spirit will never have for-
giveness, but is guilty of an everlasting sin." 30 For
they had said, "He has an unclean spirit."

Jesus and His Family

31* His mother and his brothers arrived. Stand-
ing outside they sent word to him and called
him. 32† A crowd seated around him told him,
"Your mother and your brothers [and your sis-
ters] are outside asking for you." 33 But he said
to them in reply, "Who are my mother and [my]
brothers?" 34 And looking around at those seated
in the circle he said, "Here are my mother and
my brothers. 35 [For] whoever does the will of
God is my brother and sister and mother."

3:20–35 Within the narrative of the coming of Jesus' relatives (20–21) is inserted the account of the unbelieving scribes from Jerusalem who attributed Jesus' power over demons to Beelzebul (22–30); see the note on 5:21–43. There were those even among the relatives of Jesus who disbelieved and regarded Jesus as *out of his mind* (21). Against this background, Jesus is informed of the arrival of his mother and brothers [and sisters] (32). He responds by showing that not family ties but doing God's will (35) is decisive in the kingdom; cf the note on Mt 12:46–50.

3:20 *He came home:* cf 2:1–2 and see the note on 2:15.

3:22 *By Beelzebul:* see the note on Mt 10:25. Two accusations are leveled against Jesus: (1) that *he is possessed* by an unclean spirit, and (2) *by the prince of demons he drives out demons.* Jesus answers the second charge by a parable (24–27) and responds to the first charge in vv 28–29.

3:29 *Whoever blasphemes against the holy Spirit:* this sin is called *an everlasting sin* because it attributes to Satan, who is the power of evil, what is actually the work of the holy Spirit, namely, victory over the demons.

3:32 *Your brothers:* see the note on 6:3.

3:20 Mk 2:2.
3:21 Jn 10:20.
3:22–30 Mt 12:24–32; Lk 11:15–22; 12:10.
3:28 Lk 12:10.
3:31–35 Mt 12:46–50; Lk 8:19–21.

The Parable of the Sower

4 1*† On another occasion he began to teach
by the sea.† A very large crowd gathered
around him so that he got into a boat on the sea
and sat down. And the whole crowd was beside
the sea on land.* 2 And he taught them at length
in parables, and in the course of his instruction
he said to them, 3† "Hear this! A sower went out
to sow. 4 And as he sowed, some seed fell on the
path, and the birds came and ate it up. 5 Other
seed fell on rocky ground where it had little soil.
It sprang up at once because the soil was not
deep. 6 And when the sun rose, it was scorched
and it withered for lack of roots. 7 Some seed
fell among thorns, and the thorns grew up and
choked it and it produced no grain. 8 And some
seed fell on rich soil and produced fruit. It came
up and grew and yielded thirty, sixty, and a hun-
dredfold." 9 He added, "Whoever has ears to hear
ought to hear."

The Purpose of the Parables

10 And when he was alone, those present along
with the Twelve questioned him about the para-
bles. 11† He answered them, "The mystery of the
kingdom of God has been granted to you. But
to those outside everything comes in parables,
12* so that

'they may look and see but not perceive,
and hear and listen but not understand,
in order that they may not be converted and
be forgiven.' "

13*† Jesus said to them, "Do you not understand
this parable? Then how will you understand any of
the parables? 14 The sower sows the word. 15 These
are the ones on the path where the word is sown.
As soon as they hear, Satan comes at once and
takes away the word sown in them. 16 And these
are the ones sown on rocky ground who, when
they hear the word, receive it at once with joy.
17 But they have no root; they last only for a time.
Then when tribulation or persecution comes be-
cause of the word, they quickly fall away. 18 Those
sown among thorns are another sort. They are the
people who hear the word, 19 but worldly anxiety,
the lure of riches, and the craving for other things
intrude and choke the word, and it bears no fruit.
20 But those sown on rich soil are the ones who
hear the word and accept it and bear fruit thirty
and sixty and a hundredfold."

Parable of the Lamp

21* He said to them, "Is a lamp brought in to
be placed under a bushel basket or under a bed,
and not to be placed on a lampstand?* 22* For
there is nothing hidden except to be made vis-
ible; nothing is secret except to come to light.
23 Anyone who has ears to hear ought to hear."
24* He also told them, "Take care what you hear.
The measure with which you measure will be
measured out to you, and still more will be given
to you. 25* To the one who has, more will be
given; from the one who has not, even what he
has will be taken away."

Seed Grows of Itself

26*† He said, "This is how it is with the king-
dom of God; it is as if a man were to scatter seed
on the land 27 and would sleep and rise night
and day and the seed would sprout and grow,
he knows not how. 28 Of its own accord the land
yields fruit, first the blade, then the ear, then
the full grain in the ear. 29 And when the grain is
ripe, he wields the sickle at once, for the harvest
has come."

MK

† **4:1–34** *In parables* (2): see the note on Mt 13:3. The use of parables is typical of Jesus' enigmatic method of teaching the crowds (2–9, 12) as compared with the interpretation of the parables he gives to his disciples (10–25, 33–34), to each group according to its capacity to understand (9–11). The key feature of the parable at hand is the sowing of the seed (3), representing the breakthrough of the kingdom of God into the world. The various types of soil refer to the diversity of response accorded the word of God (4–7). The climax of the parable is the harvest of thirty, sixty, and a hundredfold, indicating the consummation of the kingdom (8). Thus both the present and the future action of God, from the initiation to the fulfillment of the kingdom, is presented through this and other parables (26–29, 30–32).

4:1 *By the sea:* the shore of the Sea of Galilee or a boat near the shore (2:13; 3:7–8) is the place where Mark depicts Jesus teaching the crowds. By contrast the mountain is the scene of Jesus at prayer (6:46) or in the process of forming his disciples (3:13; 9:2).

4:3–8 See the note on Mt 13:3–8.

4:11–12 These verses are to be viewed against their background in 3:6, 22 concerning the unbelief and opposition Jesus encountered in his ministry. It is against this background that the distinction in Jesus' method becomes clear of presenting the kingdom to the disbelieving crowd in one manner and to the disciples in another. To the former it is presented in parables and the truth remains hidden; for the latter the parable is interpreted and the mystery is partially revealed because of their faith; see the notes on Mt 13:11 and 13:13.

4:13–20 See the note on Mt 13:18–23.

4:26–29 Only Mark records the parable of the seed's growth. Sower and harvester are the same. The emphasis is on the power of the seed to grow of itself without human intervention (27). Mysteriously it produces *blade* and *ear* and *full grain* (28). Thus the kingdom of God initiated by Jesus in proclaiming the word develops quietly yet powerfully until it is fully established by him at the final judgment (29); cf Rv 14:15.

* **4:1–12** Mt 13:1–13; Lk 8:4–10.
4:1 Mk 2:13; Lk 5:1.
4:12 Is 6:9; Jn 12:40; Acts 28:26; Rom 11:8.
4:13–20 Mt 13:18–23; Lk 8:11–15.
4:21–25 Lk 8:16–18.
4:21 Mt 5:15; Lk 11:33.
4:22 Mt 10:26; Lk 12:2.
4:24 Mt 7:2; Lk 6:38.
4:25 Mt 13:12; Lk 19:26.
4:26–29 Jas 5:7.

4:30–32

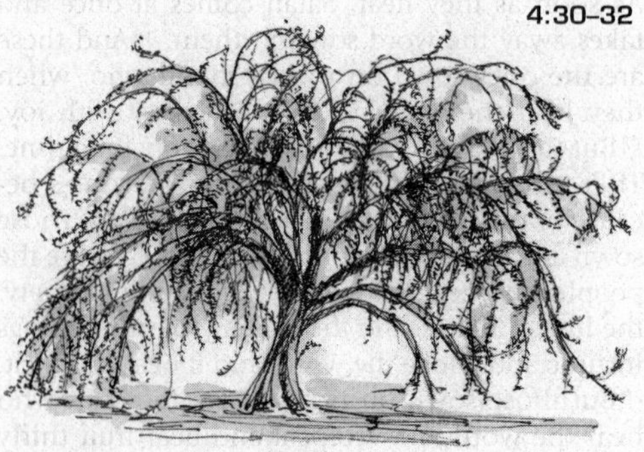

MK

The Mustard Seed

30* He said, "To what shall we compare the kingdom of God, or what parable can we use for it? 31 It is like a mustard seed that, when it is sown in the ground, is the smallest of all the seeds on the earth. 32† But once it is sown, it springs up and becomes the largest of plants and puts forth large branches, so that the birds of the sky can dwell in its shade." 33* With many such parables he spoke the word to them as they were able to understand it. 34 Without parables he did not speak to them, but to his own disciples he explained everything in private.

The Calming of a Storm at Sea

35*† On that day, as evening drew on, he said to them, "Let us cross to the other side." 36 Leaving the crowd, they took him with them in the boat just as he was. And other boats were with him. 37 A violent squall came up and waves were breaking over the boat, so that it was already filling up. 38 Jesus was in the stern, asleep on a cushion. They woke him and said to him, "Teacher, do you not care that we are perishing?" 39† He woke up, rebuked the wind, and said to the sea, "Quiet! Be still!" The wind ceased and there was great calm. 40 Then he asked them, "Why are you terrified? Do you not yet have faith?" 41*† They were filled with great awe and said to one another, "Who then is this whom even wind and sea obey?"

Pray It!

Life's Storms

Storms on the Sea of Galilee are a common occurrence. They are a fisher's nightmare, and the one described in Mark 4:35–41 was really bad! It is no wonder the Apostles felt fearful and powerless. As part of your prayer, try this meditation:

Begin by closing your eyes and relaxing. Then visualize yourself standing on the beach with Jesus and the disciples. Join them as they board the boat. When the squall comes, experience the rocking of the boat, the waves crashing on deck, and the winds blowing. Feel the disciples' anxiety and fear as the boat is tossed and water pours into the boat. Go with the disciples to wake Jesus, and watch as Jesus calms the storm. Now, experience the peacefulness and tranquility of the miracle you have witnessed.

All of us have storms we must face—that is, parts of our lives that are filled with anxiety or fear. Think about your life. What are the storms that batter and rock your world? Who in your family or in your community can calm your fears? How would you respond to Jesus' question, "Do you not yet have faith?" (Mk 4:40).

▶ Mk 4:35–41

The Healing of the Gerasene Demoniac

5 1*† They came to the other side of the sea, to the territory of the Gerasenes. 2† When he got out of the boat, at once a man from the tombs who had an unclean spirit met him. 3 The man had been dwelling among the tombs, and no one could restrain him any longer, even with a chain. 4 In fact, he had frequently been bound with

†

4:32 The universality of the kingdom of God is indicated here; cf Ez 17:23; 31:6; Dn 4:17–19.

4:35—5:43 After the chapter on parables, Mark narrates four miracle stories: 4:35–41; 5:1–20; and two joined together in 5:21–43. See also the notes on Mt 8:23–34 and 9:8–26.

4:39 *Quiet! Be still!:* as in the case of silencing a demon (1:25), Jesus rebukes the wind and subdues the turbulence of the sea by a mere word; see the note on Mt 8:26.

4:41 Jesus is here depicted as exercising power over wind and sea. In the Christian community this event was seen as a sign of Jesus' saving presence amid persecutions that threatened its existence.

5:1 *The territory of the Gerasenes:* the reference is to pagan territory; cf Is 65:1. Another reading is "Gadarenes"; see the note on Mt 8:28.

5:2–6 The man was an outcast from society, dominated by unclean spirits (8, 13), living among the tombs. The prostration before Jesus (6) indicates Jesus' power over evil spirits.

4:30–32 Mt 13:31–32; Lk 13:18–19.
4:33–34 Mt 13:34.
4:35–40 Mt 8:18, 23–37; Lk 8:22–25.
4:41 Mk 1:27.
5:1–20 Mt 8:28–34; Lk 8:26–39.

shackles and chains, but the chains had been
pulled apart by him and the shackles smashed,
and no one was strong enough to subdue him.
[5]Night and day among the tombs and on the
hillsides he was always crying out and bruising
himself with stones. [6]Catching sight of Jesus
from a distance, he ran up and prostrated himself
before him, [7]† crying out in a loud voice, "What
have you to do with me, Jesus, Son of the Most
High God? I adjure you by God, do not torment
me!" [8](He had been saying to him, "Unclean
spirit, come out of the man!") [9]*† He asked him,
"What is your name?" He replied, "Legion is my
name. There are many of us." [10]And he pleaded
earnestly with him not to drive them away from
that territory.
[11]† Now a large herd of swine was feeding
there on the hillside. [12]And they pleaded with
him, "Send us into the swine. Let us enter them."
[13]And he let them, and the unclean spirits came
out and entered the swine. The herd of about
two thousand rushed down a steep bank into the
sea, where they were drowned. [14]The swineherds
ran away and reported the incident in the town
and throughout the countryside. And people
came out to see what had happened. [15]As they
approached Jesus, they caught sight of the man
who had been possessed by Legion, sitting there
clothed and in his right mind. And they were
seized with fear. [16]Those who witnessed the in-
cident explained to them what had happened to
the possessed man and to the swine. [17]Then they
began to beg him to leave their district. [18]As he
was getting into the boat, the man who had been
possessed pleaded to remain with him. [19]† But
he would not permit him but told him instead,
"Go home to your family and announce to them
all that the Lord in his pity has done for you."
[20]Then the man went off and began to proclaim
in the Decapolis what Jesus had done for him;
and all were amazed.

Jairus's Daughter and the Woman with a Hemorrhage

[21]*† When Jesus had crossed again [in the
boat] to the other side, a large crowd gathered
around him, and he stayed close to the sea.
[22]* One of the synagogue officials, named Jai-
rus, came forward. Seeing him he fell at his feet
[23]† and pleaded earnestly with him, saying,
"My daughter is at the point of death. Please,
come lay your hands on her that she may get
well and live." [24]He went off with him, and a
large crowd followed him and pressed upon
him.
[25]There was a woman afflicted with hemor-
rhages for twelve years. [26]She had suffered
greatly at the hands of many doctors and had
spent all that she had. Yet she was not helped
but only grew worse. [27]She had heard about
Jesus and came up behind him in the crowd and

Did You Know?

Demon Possession

The Gospels of Matthew, Mark, and Luke all have stories about Jesus' curing people of unclean spirits, or demons. Many cultures believe in spirits, both good and bad (see "Spirits," near Mk 1:9–39), which can influence or even control people's decisions and actions. The first time a demon is mentioned in the Bible is in the Book of Tobit; however, the concept of demons is much older. Demons represented evil—mysterious powers hostile to God, health, and goodness. Jesus' ability to free people of demonic influence was a sign of the arrival of the Reign of God (see "Miracles and the Reign of God," near Mt 8:1—9:34).

The ancients believed that illness was caused by evil spirits. We don't hold that view today, but we do recognize that illness is a part of the spiritual reality that affects our lives.

Mk 1:23–34, 5:1–20

†

5:7 *What have you to do with me?:* cf 1:24 and see the note on Jn 2:4.

5:9 *Legion is my name:* the demons were numerous and the condition of the possessed man was extremely serious; cf Mt 12:45.

5:11 *Herd of swine:* see the note on Mt 8:30.

5:19 *Go home:* Jesus did not accept the man's request *to remain with him* as a disciple (18), yet invited him to announce to his own people what the Lord had done for him, i.e., proclaim the gospel message to his pagan family; cf 1:14, 39; 3:14; 13:10.

5:21–43 The story of the raising to life of Jairus's daughter is divided into two parts: vv 21–24 and 35–43. Between these two separated parts the account of the cure of the hemorrhage victim (25–34) is interposed. This technique of intercalating or sandwiching one story within another occurs several times in Mark: 3:19b–21 (22–30) 31–35; 6:6b–13 (14–29) 30; 11:12–14 (15–19) 20–25; 14:53 (54) 55–65 (66–73).

5:23 *Lay your hands on her:* this act for the purpose of healing is frequent in Mark (6:5; 7:32–35; 8:23–25; 16:18) and is also found in Mt 9:18; Lk 4:40; 13:13; Acts 9:17; 28:8.

*

5:9 Mt 12:45; Lk 8:2; 11:26. **5:21** Mk 2:13. **5:22–43** Mt 9:18–26; Lk 8:41–56.

Pray It!

Everyone's Welcome!

In Mark, chapters 5–8, Jesus expands his mission into Gentile territory, the region on the eastern side of the Sea of Galilee. Three miraculous healings of Gentiles—the Gerasene demoniac (see 5:1–13), the Syrophoenician's daughter (see 7:24–30), and the deaf man from Tyre (see 7:31–37)—extend the promises of the Reign of God to all who have faith in Jesus. In arranging these stories, the author of the Gospel emphasizes that God's salvation is available to everyone, not just to the Jews.

In your prayer, reflect or journal on the following questions:

- How do you treat people from a different race, culture, or religion?
- How could you be more welcoming toward them, more like Jesus?

Write a prayer expressing your desire to be more like Jesus.

► **Mk 5:1—8:30**

touched his cloak. 28† She said, "If I but touch
his clothes, I shall be cured." 29 Immediately her
flow of blood dried up. She felt in her body that
she was healed of her affliction. 30 Jesus, aware
at once that power had gone out from him,
turned around in the crowd and asked, "Who has
touched my clothes?" 31 But his disciples said to
him, "You see how the crowd is pressing upon
you, and yet you ask, 'Who touched me?' " 32 And
he looked around to see who had done it. 33 The
woman, realizing what had happened to her,
approached in fear and trembling. She fell down
before Jesus and told him the whole truth. 34* He
said to her, "Daughter, your faith has saved you.
Go in peace and be cured of your affliction."
35† While he was still speaking, people from
the synagogue official's house arrived and said,
"Your daughter has died; why trouble the teacher
any longer?" 36 Disregarding the message that
was reported, Jesus said to the synagogue official,
"Do not be afraid; just have faith." 37 He did not
allow anyone to accompany him inside except
Peter, James, and John, the brother of James.
38 When they arrived at the house of the syna-
gogue official, he caught sight of a commotion,
people weeping and wailing loudly. 39*† So he
went in and said to them, "Why this commotion
and weeping? The child is not dead but asleep."
40 And they ridiculed him. Then he put them all
out. He took along the child's father and mother
and those who were with him and entered the
room where the child was. 41† He took the child
by the hand and said to her, *"Talitha koum,"*
which means, "Little girl, I say to you, arise!"
42 The girl, a child of twelve, arose immediately
and walked around. [At that] they were utterly
astounded. 43 He gave strict orders that no one
should know this and said that she should be
given something to eat.

The Rejection at Nazareth

6 1*† He departed from there and came to his
native place, accompanied by his disciples.
2† When the sabbath came he began to teach in
the synagogue, and many who heard him were
astonished. They said, "Where did this man get
all this? What kind of wisdom has been given
him? What mighty deeds are wrought by his
hands! 3*† Is he not the carpenter, the son of
Mary, and the brother of James and Joses and

†

5:28 Both in the case of Jairus and his daughter (23) and in the case of the hemorrhage victim, the inner conviction that physical contact (30) accompanied by faith in Jesus' saving power could effect a cure was rewarded.

5:35 The faith of Jairus was put to a twofold test: (1) that his daughter might be cured and, now that she had died, (2) that she might be restored to life. His faith contrasts with the lack of faith of the crowd.

5:39 *Not dead but asleep:* the New Testament often refers to death as sleep (Mt 27:52; Jn 11:11; 1 Cor 15:6; 1 Thes 4:13–15); see the note on Mt 9:24.

5:41 *Arise:* the Greek verb *egeirein* is the verb generally used to express resurrection from death (6:14, 16; Mt 11:5; Lk 7:14) and Jesus' own resurrection (16:6; Mt 28:6; Lk 24:6).

6:1 *His native place:* the Greek word *patris* here refers to Nazareth (cf 1:9; Lk 4:16, 23–24), though it can also mean native land.

6:2–6 See the note on Mt 13:54–58.

6:3 *Is he not the carpenter?:* no other gospel calls Jesus a carpenter. Some witnesses have "the carpenter's son," as in Mt 13:55. *Son of Mary:* contrary to Jewish custom, which calls a man the son of his father, this expression may reflect Mark's own faith that God is the Father of Jesus (1:1, 11; 8:38; 13:32; 14:36). *The brother of James . . . Simon:* in Semitic usage, the terms 'brother,' 'sister' are applied not only to children of the same parents, but to nephews, nieces, cousins, half-brothers, and half-sisters; cf Gn 14:16; 29:15; Lv 10:4. While one cannot suppose that the meaning of a Greek word should be sought in the first place from Semitic usage, the Septuagint often translates the Hebrew *'āh* by the Greek word *adelphos,* "brother," as in the cited passages, a fact that may argue for a similar breadth of meaning in some New Testament passages. For instance, there is no doubt that in v 17, "brother" is used of Philip, who was actually the half-brother of Herod Antipas. On the other hand, Mark may have understood the terms literally; see also Mk 3:31–32; Mt 12:46; 13:55–56; Lk 8:19; Jn 7:3, 5. The question of meaning here would not have arisen but for the faith of the church in Mary's perpetual virginity.

*

5:34 Lk 7:30.
5:39–40 Acts 9:40.
6:1–6 Mt 13:54–58; Lk 4:16–30.
6:3 Mk 15:40; Mt 12:46; Jn 6:42.

Catholic Social Teaching

"The Carpenter?"

"Is he not the carpenter?" (Mk 6:3). The people of Nazareth were astounded by how a man, who in their minds was merely a carpenter, could speak and act with such wisdom and power. Perhaps they had low expectations of Jesus, given that his work was a humble trade, one that certainly was not associated with great wealth or prestige. Jesus shows us, however, that all workers, even those who engage in simple, unassuming work, are capable of great things.

This unique glimpse of Jesus, as the worker, is a reminder to us that Jesus was both a laborer and a minister to his people. We have a similar vocational call to be workers and ministers, no matter what kind of work we do. As Jesus did, we must ensure that the work we do is focused not on the acquisition of wealth, power, or social status but on the preservation of justice, fairness, and the dignity of all people. Catholic social teaching reminds us that all work inherently has dignity and that, consequently, all those who work deserve to be treated with dignity, whether that worker is an underpaid factory worker, an overworked migrant farmer, or even a humble carpenter.

▶ **Mk 6:1–6**
The Dignity of Work and the Rights of Workers

MK

Judas and Simon? And are not his sisters here
with us?" And they took offense at him. [4]*† Jesus
said to them, "A prophet is not without honor
except in his native place and among his own
kin and in his own house." [5]† So he was not able
to perform any mighty deed there, apart from
curing a few sick people by laying his hands on
them. [6]He was amazed at their lack of faith.

The Mission of the Twelve

He went around to the villages in the vicinity
teaching. [7]*† He summoned the Twelve and be-
gan to send them out two by two and gave them
authority over unclean spirits. [8]† He instructed
them to take nothing for the journey but a walk-
ing stick—no food, no sack, no money in their
belts. [9]They were, however, to wear sandals but
not a second tunic. [10]† He said to them, "Wher-
ever you enter a house, stay there until you leave
from there. [11]Whatever place does not welcome
you or listen to you, leave there and shake the
dust off your feet in testimony against them."
[12]So they went off and preached repentance.
[13]*† They drove out many demons, and they
anointed with oil many who were sick and cured
them.

Herod's Opinion of Jesus†

[14]* King Herod† heard about it, for his fame
had become widespread, and people were say-
ing, "John the Baptist has been raised from the
dead; that is why mighty powers are at work in
him."* [15]* Others were saying, "He is Elijah";
still others, "He is a prophet like any of the

†

6:4 *A prophet is not without honor except . . . in his own house:* a saying that finds parallels in other literatures, especially Jewish and Greek, but without reference to a prophet. Comparing himself to previous Hebrew prophets whom the people rejected, Jesus intimates his own eventual rejection by the nation especially in view of the dishonor his own relatives had shown him (3:21) and now his townspeople as well.

6:5 *He was not able to perform any mighty deed there:* according to Mark, Jesus' power could not take effect because of a person's lack of faith.

6:7–13 The preparation for the mission of the Twelve is seen in the call (1) of the first disciples to be fishers of men (1:16–20), (2) then of the Twelve set apart to be with Jesus and to receive authority to preach and expel demons (3:13–19). Now they are given the specific mission to exercise that authority in word and power as representatives of Jesus during the time of their formation.

6:8–9 In Mark the use of a *walking stick* (8) and *sandals* (9) is permitted, but not in Mt 10:10 nor in Lk 10:4. Mark does not mention any prohibition to visit pagan territory and to enter Samaritan towns. These differences indicate a certain adaptation to conditions in and outside of Palestine and suggest in Mark's account a later activity in the church. For the rest, Jesus required of his apostles a total dependence on God for food and shelter; cf vv 35–44; 8:1–9.

6:10–11 Remaining in the same house as a guest (10) rather than moving to another offering greater comfort avoided any impression of seeking advantage for oneself and prevented dishonor to one's host. Shaking the dust off one's feet served as testimony against those who rejected the call to repentance.

6:13 *Anointed with oil . . . cured them:* a common medicinal remedy, but seen here as a vehicle of divine power for healing.

6:14–16 The various opinions about Jesus anticipate the theme of his identity that reaches its climax in 8:27–30.

6:14 *King Herod:* see the note on Mt 14:1.

*

6:4 Jn 4:44.
6:7–11 Mt 10:1, 9–14; Lk 9:15; 10:4–11.
6:13 Jas 5:14.
6:14–16 Lk 9:7–8.
6:14–29 Mt 14:1–12.
6:15 Mt 16:14.

prophets." 16 But when Herod learned of it, he
said, "It is John whom I beheaded. He has been
raised up."

The Death of John the Baptist

17*† Herod was the one who had John arrested
and bound in prison on account of Herodias, the
wife of his brother Philip, whom he had married.
18* John had said to Herod, "It is not lawful for
you to have your brother's wife." 19† Herodias
harbored a grudge against him and wanted to
kill him but was unable to do so. 20 Herod feared
John, knowing him to be a righteous and holy
man, and kept him in custody. When he heard
him speak he was very much perplexed, yet he
liked to listen to him. 21 She had an opportunity
one day when Herod, on his birthday, gave a ban-
quet for his courtiers, his military officers, and the
leading men of Galilee. 22 Herodias's own daugh-
ter came in and performed a dance that delighted
Herod and his guests. The king said to the girl,
"Ask of me whatever you wish and I will grant it
to you." 23* He even swore [many things] to her,
"I will grant you whatever you ask of me, even to
half of my kingdom." 24 She went out and said to
her mother, "What shall I ask for?" She replied,
"The head of John the Baptist." 25 The girl hurried
back to the king's presence and made her request,
"I want you to give me at once on a platter the
head of John the Baptist." 26 The king was deeply
distressed, but because of his oaths and the guests
he did not wish to break his word to her. 27* So
he promptly dispatched an executioner with
orders to bring back his head. He went off and
beheaded him in the prison. 28 He brought in the
head on a platter and gave it to the girl. The girl in
turn gave it to her mother. 29 When his disciples
heard about it, they came and took his body and
laid it in a tomb.

The Return of the Twelve

30*† The apostles gathered together with Jesus
and reported all they had done and taught.
31*† He said to them, "Come away by yourselves
to a deserted place and rest a while." People
were coming and going in great numbers, and
they had no opportunity even to eat. 32* So they
went off in the boat by themselves to a deserted
place. 33 People saw them leaving and many
came to know about it. They hastened there on
foot from all the towns and arrived at the place
before them.

Did You Know?

Those Thickheaded Disciples

The disciples in the Gospel of Mark seem unable to do anything right. During a storm at sea, they fail to put their trust in Jesus (see Mk 4:35–41). Then they cannot understand about the miracle of the bread because their hearts are hardened (see 6:52). When Jesus gives them private tutoring sessions, they still fail to understand his teachings. Later, Peter proclaims that Jesus is the Messiah, but he ends up arguing with him after Jesus tells him that he will be a suffering Messiah (see 8:27–33). Finally, when Jesus is arrested, the disciples all desert him (see 14:50).

The author of Mark intentionally emphasizes the lack of faith of the original disciples in order to contrast it with the unexpected faith of people like the Syrophoenician woman in 7:24–30. The Gospel makes the point that Jesus' true disciples are the ones who hear Jesus and place their faith in him. But don't count out the original disciples. Their journey is like most of ours, a lifelong experience of growing in faith and understanding. The Acts of the Apostles tells how they fearlessly preached the news about the risen Christ. Despite their human weakness, God works through them. That goes for us too!

▶ Mk 6:30–52

†

6:17–29 Similarities are to be noted between Mark's account of the imprisonment and death of John the Baptist in this pericope, and that of the passion of Jesus (15:1–47). Herod and Pilate, each in turn, acknowledges the holiness of life of one over whom he unjustly exercises the power of condemnation and death (26–27; 15:9–10, 14–15). The hatred of Herodias toward John parallels that of the Jewish leaders toward Jesus. After the deaths of John and of Jesus, well-disposed persons request the bodies of the victims of Herod and of Pilate in turn to give them respectful burial (29; 15:45–46).

6:19 *Herodias:* see the note on Mt 14:3.

6:30 *Apostles:* here, and in some manuscripts at 3:14, Mark calls apostles (i.e., those sent forth) the Twelve whom Jesus sends as his emissaries, empowering them to preach, to expel demons, and to cure the sick (13). Only after Pentecost is the title used in the technical sense.

6:31–34 The withdrawal of Jesus with his disciples to a desert place to rest attracts a great number of people to follow them. Toward this people of the new exodus Jesus is moved with pity; he satisfies their spiritual hunger by teaching them many things, thus gradually showing himself the faithful shepherd of a new Israel; cf Nm 27:17; Ez 34:15.

*

6:17 Lk 3:19–20.
6:18 Lv 18:16.
6:23 Est 5:3.
6:27–28 Lk 9:9.
6:30 Lk 9:10.
6:31 Mk 3:20; Mt 14:13; Lk 9:10.
6:32–44 Mt 14:13–21; Lk 9:10–17; Jn 6:1–13.

The Feeding of the Five Thousand

34 When he disembarked and saw the vast crowd, his heart was moved with pity for them, for they were like sheep without a shepherd; and he began to teach them many things. 35† By now it was already late and his disciples approached him and said, "This is a deserted place and it is already very late. 36 Dismiss them so that they can go to the surrounding farms and villages and buy themselves something to eat." 37 He said to them in reply, "Give them some food yourselves." But they said to him, "Are we to buy two hundred days' wages worth of food and give it to them to eat?" 38 He asked them, "How many loaves do you have? Go and see." And when they had found out they said, "Five loaves and two fish." 39 So he gave orders to have them sit down in groups on the green grass. 40† The people took their places in rows by hundreds and by fifties. 41† Then, taking the five loaves and the two fish and looking up to heaven, he said the blessing, broke the loaves, and gave them to [his] disciples to set before the people; he also divided the two fish among them all. 42 They all ate and were satisfied. 43 And they picked up twelve wicker baskets full of fragments and what was left of the fish. 44 Those who ate [of the loaves] were five thousand men.

The Walking on the Water†

45* Then he made his disciples get into the boat and precede him to the other side toward Bethsaida,† while he dismissed the crowd. 46† And when he had taken leave of them, he went off to the mountain to pray. 47 When it was evening, the boat was far out on the sea and he was alone on shore. 48† Then he saw that they were tossed about while rowing, for the wind was against them. About the fourth watch of the night, he came towards them walking on the sea. He meant to pass by them. 49 But when they saw him walking on the sea, they thought it was a ghost and cried out. 50† They had all seen him and were terrified. But at once he spoke with them, "Take courage, it is I, do not be afraid!" 51 He got into the boat with them and the wind died down. They were [completely] astounded. 52*† They had not understood the incident of the loaves. On the contrary, their hearts were hardened.

The Healings at Gennesaret

53* After making the crossing, they came to land at Gennesaret and tied up there. 54 As they were leaving the boat, people immediately recognized him. 55 They scurried about the surrounding country and began to bring in the sick on mats to wherever they heard he was. 56* Whatever villages or towns or countryside he entered, they laid the sick in the marketplaces and begged him that they might touch only the tassel on his cloak; and as many as touched it were healed.

MK

The Tradition of the Elders

7 1*† Now when the Pharisees with some scribes who had come from Jerusalem gathered around him, 2 they observed that some of his disciples ate their meals with unclean, that is, unwashed, hands. 3† (For the Pharisees and, in fact, all Jews, do not eat without carefully washing their hands, keeping the tradition of the elders. 4 And on coming from the marketplace they do not eat without purifying themselves. And there are many other things that they have traditionally observed, the purification of cups

†

6:35–44 See the note on Mt 14:13–21. Compare this section with 8:1–9. The various accounts of the multiplication of loaves and fishes, two each in Mark and in Matthew and one each in Luke and in John, indicate the wide interest of the early church in their eucharistic gatherings; see, e.g., v 41; 8:6; 14:22; and recall also the sign of bread in Ex 16; Dt 8:3–16; Pss 78:24–25; 105:40; Wis 16:20–21.

6:40 *The people . . . in rows by hundreds and by fifties:* reminiscent of the groupings of Israelites encamped in the desert (Ex 18:21–25) and of the wilderness tradition of the prophets depicting the transformation of the wasteland into pastures where the true shepherd feeds his flock (Ez 34:25–26) and makes his people beneficiaries of messianic grace.

6:41 On the language of this verse as eucharistic (cf 14:22), see the notes on Mt 14:19, 20. Jesus observed the Jewish table ritual of blessing God before partaking of food.

6:45–52 See the note on Mt 14:22–33.

6:45 *To the other side toward Bethsaida:* a village at the northeastern shore of the Sea of Galilee.

6:46 *He went off to the mountain to pray:* see 1:35–38. In Jn 6:15 Jesus withdrew to evade any involvement in the false messianic hopes of the multitude.

6:48 *Walking on the sea:* see the notes on Mt 14:22–33 and on Jn 6:19.

6:50 *It is I, do not be afraid!:* literally, "I am." This may reflect the divine revelatory formula of Ex 3:14; Is 41:4, 10, 14; 43:1–3, 10, 13. Mark implies the hidden identity of Jesus as Son of God.

6:52 *They had not understood . . . the loaves:* the revelatory character of this sign and that of the walking on the sea completely escaped the disciples. *Their hearts were hardened:* in 3:5–6 hardness of heart was attributed to those who did not accept Jesus and plotted his death. Here the same disposition prevents the disciples from comprehending Jesus' self-revelation through signs; cf 8:17.

7:1–23 See the note on Mt 15:1–20. Against the Pharisees' narrow, legalistic, and external practices of piety in matters of purification (2–5), external worship (6–7), and observance of commandments, Jesus sets in opposition the true moral intent of the divine law (8–13). But he goes beyond contrasting the law and Pharisaic interpretation of it. The parable of vv 14–15 in effect sets aside the law itself in respect to clean and unclean food. He thereby opens the way for unity between Jew and Gentile in the kingdom of God, intimated by Jesus' departure for pagan territory beyond Galilee. For similar contrast see 2:1—3:6; 3:20–35; 6:1–6.

7:3 *Carefully washing their hands:* refers to ritual purification.

*

6:45–51 Mt 14:22–32; Jn 6:15–21.
6:52 Mk 4:13.
6:53–56 Mt 14:34–36.
6:56 Mk 5:27–28; Acts 5:15.
7:1–23 Mt 15:1–20.

Live It!

Sin's Source

Some people believe that spiritual depth is measured by how well certain rules or religious practices are followed. Jesus reminds us in Mark 7:14–15 that our greater concern ought to be with what is in our heart, because it is from there that both our good and bad actions originate. Ultimately, what is in our heart should have a greater effect on our spiritual lives than should outside sources, even though these external influences can often be powerful forces.

- What outside sources have the potential to negatively affect your spiritual life?

▶ Mk 7:14–23

and jugs and kettles [and beds].) 5† So the Phar-
isees and scribes questioned him, "Why do your
disciples not follow the tradition of the elders
but instead eat a meal with unclean hands?"
6* He responded, "Well did Isaiah prophesy
about you hypocrites, as it is written:

'This people honors me with their lips,
but their hearts are far from me;
7 In vain do they worship me,
teaching as doctrines human precepts.'

8You disregard God's commandment but cling
to human tradition." 9He went on to say, "How
well you have set aside the commandment of
God in order to uphold your tradition! 10* For
Moses said, 'Honor your father and your mother,'
and 'Whoever curses father or mother shall die.'
11† Yet you say, 'If a person says to father or
mother, "Any support you might have had from
me is *qorban*"' (meaning, dedicated to God),
12you allow him to do nothing more for his fa-
ther or mother. 13You nullify the word of God
in favor of your tradition that you have handed
on. And you do many such things." 14* He sum-
moned the crowd again and said to them, "Hear
me, all of you, and understand. 15Nothing that
enters one from outside can defile that person;
but the things that come out from within are
what defile." [16]†

17*† When he got home away from the crowd
his disciples questioned him about the para-
ble. 18He said to them, "Are even you likewise
without understanding? Do you not realize that
everything that goes into a person from outside
cannot defile, 19*† since it enters not the heart
but the stomach and passes out into the latrine?"
(Thus he declared all foods clean.) 20"But what
comes out of a person, that is what defiles.
21* From within people, from their hearts, come
evil thoughts, unchastity, theft, murder, 22adul-
tery, greed, malice, deceit, licentiousness, envy,
blasphemy, arrogance, folly. 23All these evils
come from within and they defile."

The Syrophoenician Woman's Faith

24*† From that place he went off to the district
of Tyre. He entered a house and wanted no one
to know about it, but he could not escape no-
tice. 25Soon a woman whose daughter had an
unclean spirit heard about him. She came and
fell at his feet. 26* The woman was a Greek, a
Syrophoenician by birth, and she begged him
to drive the demon out of her daughter. 27† He
said to her, "Let the children be fed first. For it
is not right to take the food of the children and
throw it to the dogs." 28She replied and said to
him, "Lord, even the dogs under the table eat the
children's scraps." 29Then he said to her, "For
saying this, you may go. The demon has gone

---

†

7:5 *Tradition of the elders:* the body of detailed, unwritten, human laws regarded by the scribes and Pharisees to have the same binding force as that of the Mosaic law; cf Gal 1:14.

7:11 *Qorban:* a formula for a gift to God, dedicating the offering to the temple, so that the giver might continue to use it for himself but not give it to others, even needy parents.

7:16 Verse 16, "Anyone who has ears to hear ought to hear," is omitted because it is lacking in some of the best Greek manuscripts and was probably transferred here by scribes from 4:(9), 23.

7:17 *Away from the crowd . . . the parable:* in this context of privacy the term *parable* refers to something hidden, about to be revealed to the disciples; cf 4:10–11, 34. Jesus sets the Mosaic food laws in the context of the kingdom of God where they are abrogated, and he declares moral defilement the only cause of uncleanness.

7:19 *(Thus he declared all foods clean.):* if this bold declaration goes back to Jesus, its force was not realized among Jewish Christians in the early church; cf Acts 10:1—11:18.

7:24–37 The withdrawal of Jesus to the district of Tyre may have been for a respite (24), but he soon moved onward to Sidon and, by way of the Sea of Galilee, to the Decapolis. These districts provided a Gentile setting for the extension of his ministry of healing because the people there acknowledged his power (29, 37). The actions attributed to Jesus (33–35) were also used by healers of the time.

7:27–28 The figure of a household in which children at table are fed first and then their leftover food is given to the dogs under the table is used effectively to acknowledge the prior claim of the Jews to the ministry of Jesus; however, Jesus accedes to the Gentile woman's plea for the cure of her afflicted daughter because of her faith.

7:6 Is 29:13.
7:10 Ex 21:17; Lv 20:9; Dt 5:16; Eph 6:2.
7:14–23 Mt 15:10–20.
7:17 Mk 4:10, 13.
7:19 Acts 10:15.
7:21 Jer 17:9.
7:24–30 Mt 15:21–28.
7:26 Mt 8:29.

out of your daughter." [30]When the woman went
home, she found the child lying in bed and the
demon gone.

The Healing of a Deaf Man

[31]* Again he left the district of Tyre and went
by way of Sidon to the Sea of Galilee, into the
district of the Decapolis. [32]And people brought
to him a deaf man who had a speech impedi-
ment and begged him to lay his hand on him.
[33]He took him off by himself away from the
crowd. He put his finger into the man's ears
and, spitting, touched his tongue; [34]then he
looked up to heaven and groaned, and said to
him, "*Ephphatha!*" (that is, "Be opened!") [35]And
[immediately] the man's ears were opened, his
speech impediment was removed, and he spoke
plainly. [36]† He ordered them not to tell anyone.
But the more he ordered them not to, the more
they proclaimed it. [37]* They were exceedingly as-
tonished and they said, "He has done all things
well. He makes the deaf hear and [the] mute
speak."

The Feeding of the Four Thousand

8 [1]*† In those days when there again was a
great crowd without anything to eat, he
summoned the disciples and said, [2]"My heart
is moved with pity for the crowd, because they
have been with me now for three days and have
nothing to eat. [3]If I send them away hungry to
their homes, they will collapse on the way, and
some of them have come a great distance." [4]His
disciples answered him, "Where can anyone get
enough bread to satisfy them here in this de-
serted place?" [5]Still he asked them, "How many
loaves do you have?" "Seven," they replied. [6]† He
ordered the crowd to sit down on the ground.
Then, taking the seven loaves he gave thanks,
broke them, and gave them to his disciples to
distribute, and they distributed them to the
crowd. [7]They also had a few fish. He said the
blessing over them and ordered them distributed
also. [8]They ate and were satisfied. They picked

8:8

up the fragments left over—seven baskets. [9]There
were about four thousand people.
He dismissed them [10]and got into the boat
with his disciples and came to the region of Dal-
manutha.

The Demand for a Sign

[11]*† The Pharisees came forward and began to
argue with him, seeking from him a sign from
heaven to test him.* [12]He sighed from the depth
of his spirit and said, "Why does this generation
seek a sign? Amen, I say to you, no sign will be
given to this generation." [13]Then he left them,
got into the boat again, and went off to the other
shore.

The Leaven of the Pharisees

[14]* They had forgotten to bring bread, and
they had only one loaf with them in the boat.
[15]† He enjoined them, "Watch out, guard against
the leaven of the Pharisees and the leaven of
Herod." [16]They concluded among themselves
that it was because they had no bread. [17]* When
he became aware of this he said to them, "Why
do you conclude that it is because you have no
bread? Do you not yet understand or compre-
hend? Are your hearts hardened? [18]* Do you
have eyes and not see, ears and not hear? And
do you not remember, [19]when I broke the five

†

7:36 *The more they proclaimed it:* the same verb *proclaim* attributed here to the crowd in relation to the miracles of Jesus is elsewhere used in Mark for the preaching of the gospel on the part of Jesus, of his disciples, and of the Christian community (1:14; 13:10; 14:9). Implied in the action of the crowd is a recognition of the salvific mission of Jesus; see the note on Mt 11:5–6.

8:1–10 The two accounts of the multiplication of loaves and fishes (8:1–10 and 6:31–44) have eucharistic significance. Their similarity of structure and themes but dissimilarity of detail are considered by many to refer to a single event that, however, developed in two distinct traditions, one Jewish Christian and the other Gentile Christian, since Jesus in Mark's presentation (7:24–37) has extended his saving mission to the Gentiles.

8:6 See the note on 6:41.

8:11–12 The objection of the Pharisees that Jesus' miracles are unsatisfactory for proving the arrival of God's kingdom is comparable to the request of the crowd for a sign in Jn 6:30–31. Jesus' response shows that a sign originating in human demand will not be provided; cf Nm 14:11, 22.

8:15 *The leaven of the Pharisees . . . of Herod:* the corruptive action of leaven (1 Cor 5:6–8; Gal 5:9) was an apt symbol of the evil dispositions both of the Pharisees (11–13; 7:5–13) and of Herod (6:14–29) toward Jesus. The disciples of Jesus are warned against sharing such rebellious attitudes toward Jesus; cf vv 17, 21.

*

7:31–37 Mt 15:29–31.
7:37 Mt 15:31.
8:1–10 Mk 6:34–44; Mt 15:32–39.
8:11–13 Mt 12:38–39; 16:1–4.
8:11 Lk 11:16.
8:14–21 Mt 16:5–12; Lk 12:1.
8:17 Mk 4:13.
8:18 Jer 5:21; Ez 12:2.

loaves for the five thousand, how many wicker
baskets full of fragments you picked up?" They
answered him, "Twelve." 20 "When I broke the
seven loaves for the four thousand, how many
full baskets of fragments did you pick up?" They
answered [him], "Seven." 21 He said to them, "Do
you still not understand?"

The Blind Man of Bethsaida

22† When they arrived at Bethsaida, they
brought to him a blind man and begged him
to touch him. 23* He took the blind man by the
hand and led him outside the village. Putting
spittle on his eyes he laid his hands on him and
asked, "Do you see anything?" 24 Looking up he
replied, "I see people looking like trees and walk-
ing." 25 Then he laid hands on his eyes a second
time and he saw clearly; his sight was restored
and he could see everything distinctly. 26 Then he
sent him home and said, "Do not even go into
the village."

III: The Mystery Begins to Be Revealed

Peter's Confession about Jesus

27*† Now Jesus and his disciples set out for
the villages of Caesarea Philippi. Along the way
he asked his disciples, "Who do people say that
I am?" 28 They said in reply, "John the Baptist,
others Elijah, still others one of the prophets."
29 And he asked them, "But who do you say that
I am?" Peter said to him in reply, "You are the
Messiah." 30 Then he warned them not to tell
anyone about him.

The First Prediction of the Passion

31*† He began to teach them that the Son of
Man must suffer greatly and be rejected by the
elders, the chief priests, and the scribes, and be
killed, and rise after three days. 32 He spoke this
openly. Then Peter took him aside and began
to rebuke him. 33 At this he turned around and,
looking at his disciples, rebuked Peter and said,
"Get behind me, Satan. You are thinking not as
God does, but as human beings do."

Live It!

Total Commitment

In Mark 8:34–38, Jesus calls for a total commitment requiring great sacrifice. He tells the disciples that to be truly alive, they must be willing to deny themselves and take up their own crosses. The cross symbolizes denying the way of the world and embracing the way of Jesus. It means tough self-sacrifice and, at times, a willingness to suffer for what is right.

But what does it mean to deny ourselves and take up our own crosses? When we deny ourselves, it means we cannot be fooled by what the world says about being truly alive. The world tells us to buy our happiness with wealth, power, prestige, or selfish pleasure. But those things actually make us feel less alive and more anxious.

Taking up our own crosses means being willing to cling to the right things—forgiveness, justice, service, and compassion for those who are poor and those who are unpopular—even if it brings us suffering and pain. Being committed to Jesus and these virtues or "right things" will bring us real life, true freedom, joy, and inner peace.

The way of the cross is the path to resurrection and eternal life.

▶ Mk 8:34–38

†

8:22–26 Jesus' actions and the gradual cure of the blind man probably have the same purpose as in the case of the deaf man (7:31–37). Some commentators regard the cure as an intended symbol of the gradual enlightenment of the disciples concerning Jesus' messiahship.

8:27–30 This episode is the turning point in Mark's account of Jesus in his public ministry. Popular opinions concur in regarding him as a prophet. The disciples by contrast believe him to be the Messiah. Jesus acknowledges this identification but prohibits them from making his messianic office known to avoid confusing it with ambiguous contemporary ideas on the nature of that office. See further the notes on Mt 16:13–20.

8:31 *Son of Man:* an enigmatic title. It is used in Dn 7:13–14 as a symbol of "the saints of the Most High," the faithful Israelites who receive the everlasting kingdom from the Ancient One (God). They are represented by a human figure that contrasts with the various beasts who represent the previous kingdoms of the earth. In the Jewish apocryphal books of 1 Enoch and 4 Ezra the "Son of Man" is not, as in Daniel, a group, but a unique figure of extraordinary spiritual endowments, who will be revealed as the one through whom the everlasting kingdom decreed by God will be established. It is possible though doubtful that this individualization of the Son of Man figure had been made in Jesus' time, and therefore his use of the title in that sense is questionable. Of itself, this expression means simply a human being, or, indefinitely, someone, and there are evidences of this use in pre-Christian times. Its use in the New Testament is probably due to Jesus' speaking of himself in that way, "a human being," and the later church's taking this in the sense of the Jewish apocrypha and applying it to him with that meaning. *Rejected by the elders, the chief priests, and the scribes:* the supreme council called the Sanhedrin was made up of seventy-one members of these three groups and presided over by the high priest. It exercised authority over the Jews in religious matters. See the note on Mt 8:20.

8:23 Mk 7:33; Jn 9:6.
8:27–30 Mt 16:13–20; Lk 9:18–21.
8:31–38 Mt 16:21–27; Lk 9:22–26.

The Conditions of Discipleship

34*† He summoned the crowd with his disci-
ples and said to them, "Whoever wishes to come
after me must deny himself, take up his cross,
and follow me. 35*† For whoever wishes to save
his life will lose it, but whoever loses his life
for my sake and that of the gospel will save it.
36 What profit is there for one to gain the whole
world and forfeit his life? 37 What could one give
in exchange for his life? 38* Whoever is ashamed
of me and of my words in this faithless and sin-
ful generation, the Son of Man will be ashamed
of when he comes in his Father's glory with the
holy angels."

9 1*† He also said to them, "Amen, I say to
you, there are some standing here who will
not taste death until they see that the kingdom of
God has come in power."

The Transfiguration of Jesus

2*† After six days Jesus took Peter, James, and
John and led them up a high mountain apart by
themselves. And he was transfigured before them,
3 and his clothes became dazzling white, such as
no fuller on earth could bleach them. 4 Then Eli-
jah appeared to them along with Moses, and they
were conversing with Jesus. 5† Then Peter said to
Jesus in reply, "Rabbi, it is good that we are here!
Let us make three tents: one for you, one for Mo-
ses, and one for Elijah." 6 He hardly knew what to
say, they were so terrified. 7† Then a cloud came,
casting a shadow over them; then from the cloud
came a voice, "This is my beloved Son. Listen to
him." 8 Suddenly, looking around, they no longer
saw anyone but Jesus alone with them.

The Coming of Elijah

9*† As they were coming down from the
mountain, he charged them not to relate what

MK

Live It!

The Transfiguration: On Top of the World

The story of the Transfiguration takes place after Jesus tells his disciples about his coming suffering, death, and Resurrection (see Mk 8:31). They need hope and a boost of faith. Jesus takes three disciples to a mountaintop to see the Reign of God coming in power. The three disciples see Jesus in a glorious state talking with Moses and Elijah.

God revealed the secret about Jesus to three of his disciples. The two Old Testament figures are key symbols: Moses represents the law, and Elijah, the prophets. The message is clear: Jesus is the person who fulfills the law and who realizes God's promises to the prophets. It was a profound religious experience. The disciples glimpsed Jesus' glory, but they could not understand it. Understanding came only after Jesus' Resurrection.

It is understandable to want to found our faith on mountaintop experiences (see "Spiritual Highs," near Lk 9:28–36). But though profound religious experiences enliven our faith, listening and following Jesus' words daily are what really fortify our faith and give us new life.

▶ **Mk 9:2–8**

---

† **8:34–35** This utterance of Jesus challenges all believers to authentic discipleship and total commitment to himself through self-renunciation and acceptance of the cross of suffering, even to the sacrifice of life itself. *Whoever wishes to save his life will lose it . . . will save it:* an expression of the ambivalence of life and its contrasting destiny. Life seen as mere self-centered earthly existence and lived in denial of Christ ends in destruction, but when lived in loyalty to Christ, despite earthly death, it arrives at fullness of life.

8:35 *For my sake and that of the gospel:* Mark here, as at 10:29, equates Jesus with the gospel.

9:1 *There are some standing . . . come in power:* understood by some to refer to the establishment by God's power of his kingdom on earth in and through the church; more likely, as understood by others, a reference to the imminent parousia.

9:2–8 Mark and Mt 17:1 place the transfiguration of Jesus six days after the first prediction of his passion and death and his instruction to the disciples on the doctrine of the cross; Lk 9:28 has "about eight days." Thus the transfiguration counterbalances the prediction of the passion by affording certain of the disciples insight into the divine glory that Jesus possessed. His glory will overcome his death and that of his disciples; cf 2 Cor 3:18; 2 Pt 1:16–19. The heavenly voice (7) prepares the disciples to understand that in the divine plan Jesus must die ignominiously before his messianic glory is made manifest; cf Lk 24:25–27. See further the note on Mt 17:1–8.

9:5 Moses and Elijah represent respectively law and prophecy in the Old Testament and are linked to Mt. Sinai; cf Ex 9:16—20:17; 1 Kgs 19:2, 8–14. They now appear with Jesus as witnesses to the fulfillment of the law and the prophets taking place in the person of Jesus as he appears in glory.

9:7 *A cloud came, casting a shadow over them:* even the disciples enter into the mystery of his glorification. In the Old Testament the cloud covered the meeting tent, indicating the Lord's presence in the midst of his people (Ex 40:34–35) and came to rest upon the temple in Jerusalem at the time of its dedication (1 Kgs 8:10).

9:9–13 At the transfiguration of Jesus his disciples had seen Elijah. They were perplexed because, according to the rabbinical interpretation of Mal 3:23–24, Elijah was to come first. Jesus' response shows that Elijah has come, in the person of John the Baptist, to prepare for the day of the Lord. Jesus *must suffer greatly and be treated with contempt* (12) like the Baptist (13); cf 6:17–29.

---

* **8:34** Mt 10:38–39; 16:24–27; Lk 14:26–27.
8:35 Jn 12:25.
8:38 Mt 10:33; Lk 12:8.
9:1 Mt 16:28; Lk 9:27.
9:2–13 Mt 17:1–13; Lk 9:28–36.
9:9 Mk 8:31.

Pray It!

"I Do Believe; Help My Unbelief!"

Saying that we believe in something may not be enough to prove that we truly believe. Faith in God means knowing that God is totally with us even when it doesn't seem that way!

When we have nagging doubts whether even God can help us in a particular situation—like the father in Mark 9:24—we can turn to God by praying for faith. We don't have to have our faith or our lives perfectly together before we ask God for help. The test of faith is trusting that God cares for us and provides what we need, even when our prayers are not answered in the way we desire.

► **Mk 9:14–29**

MK

they had seen to anyone, except when the Son
of Man had risen from the dead. 10 So they kept
the matter to themselves, questioning what rising
from the dead meant. 11* Then they asked him,
"Why do the scribes say that Elijah must come
first?" 12 He told them, "Elijah will indeed come
first and restore all things, yet how is it written
regarding the Son of Man that he must suffer
greatly and be treated with contempt? 13* But I
tell you that Elijah has come and they did to him
whatever they pleased, as it is written of him."

The Healing of a Boy with a Demon

14*† When they came to the disciples, they saw
a large crowd around them and scribes arguing
with them. 15 Immediately on seeing him, the
whole crowd was utterly amazed. They ran up to
him and greeted him. 16 He asked them, "What
are you arguing about with them?" 17 Someone
from the crowd answered him, "Teacher, I have
brought to you my son possessed by a mute
spirit. 18 Wherever it seizes him, it throws him
down; he foams at the mouth, grinds his teeth,
and becomes rigid. I asked your disciples to drive
it out, but they were unable to do so." 19 He said
to them in reply, "O faithless generation, how
long will I be with you? How long will I endure
you? Bring him to me." 20 They brought the boy
to him. And when he saw him, the spirit imme-
diately threw the boy into convulsions. As he fell
to the ground, he began to roll around and foam
at the mouth. 21 Then he questioned his father,
"How long has this been happening to him?" He
replied, "Since childhood. 22 It has often thrown
him into fire and into water to kill him. But if
you can do anything, have compassion on us
and help us." 23 Jesus said to him, " 'If you can!'
Everything is possible to one who has faith."
24 Then the boy's father cried out, "I do believe,
help my unbelief!" 25 Jesus, on seeing a crowd
rapidly gathering, rebuked the unclean spirit and
said to it, "Mute and deaf spirit, I command you:
come out of him and never enter him again!"
26 Shouting and throwing the boy into convul-
sions, it came out. He became like a corpse,
which caused many to say, "He is dead!" 27 But
Jesus took him by the hand, raised him, and he
stood up. 28 When he entered the house, his dis-
ciples asked him in private, "Why could we not
drive it out?" 29† He said to them, "This kind can
only come out through prayer."

The Second Prediction of the Passion

30* They left from there and began a journey
through Galilee, but he did not wish anyone
to know about it.* 31 He was teaching his disci-
ples and telling them, "The Son of Man is to be
handed over to men and they will kill him, and
three days after his death he will rise." 32 But they
did not understand the saying, and they were
afraid to question him.

IV: The Full Revelation of the Mystery

The Greatest in the Kingdom

33*† They came to Capernaum and, once in-
side the house, he began to ask them, "What
were you arguing about on the way?" 34 But
they remained silent. They had been discussing

†

9:14–29 The disciples' failure to effect a cure seems to reflect unfavorably on Jesus (14–18, 22). In response Jesus exposes their lack of trust in God (19) and scores their lack of prayer (29), i.e., of conscious reliance on God's power when acting in Jesus' name. For Matthew, see the note on 17:14–20. Lk 9:37–43 centers attention on Jesus' sovereign power.

9:29 *This kind can only come out through prayer:* a variant reading adds "and through fasting."

9:33–37 Mark probably intends this incident and the sayings that follow as commentary on the disciples' lack of understanding (32). Their role in Jesus' work is one of service, especially to the poor and lowly. Children were the symbol Jesus used for the *anawim,* the poor in spirit, the lowly in the Christian community.

*

9:11–12 Is 53:3; Mal 3:23.
9:13 1 Kgs 19:2–10.
9:14–29 Mt 17:14–21; Lk 9:37–43.
9:30 Jn 7:1.
9:30–32 Mk 8:31; Mt 17:22–23; Lk 9:43–45.
9:33–37 Mt 18:1–5; Lk 9:46–48.

among themselves on the way who was the greatest. 35* Then he sat down, called the Twelve, and said to them, "If anyone wishes to be first, he shall be the last of all and the servant of all." 36 Taking a child he placed it in their midst, and putting his arms around it he said to them, 37* "Whoever receives one child such as this in my name, receives me; and whoever receives me, receives not me but the One who sent me."

Another Exorcist

38*† John said to him, "Teacher, we saw someone driving out demons in your name, and we tried to prevent him because he does not follow us." 39 Jesus replied, "Do not prevent him. There is no one who performs a mighty deed in my name who can at the same time speak ill of me. 40* For whoever is not against us is for us. 41* Anyone who gives you a cup of water to drink because you belong to Christ, amen, I say to you, will surely not lose his reward.

Temptations to Sin

42* "Whoever causes one of these little ones who believe [in me] to sin, it would be better for him if a great millstone were put around his neck and he were thrown into the sea. 43† If your hand causes you to sin, cut it off. It is better for you to enter into life maimed than with two hands to go into Gehenna, into the unquenchable fire. [44]† 45 And if your foot causes you to sin, cut if off. It is better for you to enter into life crippled than with two feet to be thrown into Gehenna. [46]† 47 And if your eye causes you to sin, pluck it out. Better for you to enter into the kingdom of God with one eye than with two eyes to be thrown into Gehenna, 48* where 'their worm does not die, and the fire is not quenched.'

The Simile of Salt

49† "Everyone will be salted with fire. 50* Salt is good, but if salt becomes insipid, with what will you restore its flavor? Keep salt in yourselves and you will have peace with one another."

Marriage and Divorce

10 1 He set out from there and went into the district of Judea [and] across the Jordan. Again crowds gathered around him and, as was his custom, he again taught them. 2*† The Pharisees approached and asked, "Is it lawful for a husband to divorce his wife?" They were testing him. 3 He said to them in reply, "What did Moses command you?" 4* They replied, "Moses permitted him to write a bill of divorce and dismiss her." 5 But Jesus told them, "Because of the hardness of your hearts he wrote you this commandment. 6* But from the beginning of creation, 'God made them male and female. 7* For this reason a man shall leave his father and mother [and be joined to his wife], 8 and the two shall become one flesh.' So they are no longer two but one flesh. 9 Therefore what God has joined together, no human being must separate." 10 In the house the disciples again questioned him about this. 11* He said to them, "Whoever divorces his wife and marries another commits adultery against her; 12 and if she divorces her husband and marries another, she commits adultery."

Blessing of the Children

13* And people were bringing children to him that he might touch them, but the disciples rebuked them.* 14 When Jesus saw this he became indignant and said to them, "Let the children come to me; do not prevent them, for the kingdom of God belongs to such as these. 15*† Amen, I say to you, whoever does not accept the kingdom of God like a child will not enter it." 16 Then he embraced them and blessed them, placing his hands on them.

The Rich Man

17* As he was setting out on a journey, a man ran up, knelt down before him, and asked him,

---

† **9:38–41** Jesus warns against jealousy and intolerance toward others, such as exorcists who do *not follow us.* The saying in v 40 is a broad principle of the divine tolerance. Even the smallest courtesies shown to those who teach in Jesus' name do not go unrewarded.

9:43, 45, 47 *Gehenna:* see the note on Mt 5:22.

9:44, 46 These verses, lacking in some important early manuscripts, are here omitted as scribal additions. They simply repeat v 48, itself a modified citation of Is 66:24.

9:49 *Everyone will be salted with fire:* so the better manuscripts. Some add "every sacrifice will be salted with salt." The purifying and preservative use of salt in food (Lv 2:13) and the refinement effected through fire refer here to comparable effects in the spiritual life of the disciples of Jesus.

10:2–9 In the dialogue between Jesus and the Pharisees on the subject of divorce, Jesus declares that the law of Moses permitted divorce (Dt 24:1) only *because of the hardness of your hearts* (4–5). In citing Gn 1:27 and 2:24, Jesus proclaims permanence to be the divine intent from the beginning concerning human marriage (6–8). He reaffirms this with the declaration that *what God has joined together, no human being must separate* (9). See further the notes on Mt 5:31–32 and 19:3–9.

10:15 *Whoever does not accept the kingdom of God like a child:* i.e., in total dependence upon and obedience to the gospel; cf Mt 18:3–4.

---

* **9:35** Mt 20:27.
9:37 Mt 10:40; 18:5; Jn 13:20.
9:38–41 Nm 11:28; Lk 9:49–50; 1 Cor 12:3.
9:40 Mt 12:30.
9:41 Mt 10:42; 1 Cor 3:23.
9:42–47 Mt 5:29–30; 18:6–9; Lk 17:1–2.
9:48 Is 66:24.
9:50 Lv 2:13; Mt 5:13; Lk 14:34–35; Col 4:6.
10:2–12 Mt 19:3–9.
10:4 Dt 24:1–4.
10:6 Gn 1:27.
10:7–8 Gn 2:24; 1 Cor 6:16; Eph 5:31.
10:11–12 Mt 5:32; Lk 16:18; 1 Cor 7:10–11.
10:13–16 Mt 19:13–15; Lk 18:15–17.
10:13 Lk 9:47.
10:15 Mt 18:3.
10:17–31 Mt 19:16–30; Lk 18:18–30.

Catholic Connection

Marriage

Jesus always has a great way of seeing the good in everything. For example, when the Pharisees try to test Jesus with a question about divorce, Jesus speaks about marriage. Rather than focus on the negative, Jesus turns everyone's attention to the positive—the beauty of two people who "are no longer two but one flesh" (Mk 10:8).

The Catholic Church shares Jesus' positive view of marriage and celebrates it in the sacrament of Matrimony, one of the seven official sacraments of the Church. The Church teaches that through the sacrament, the couple's love for one another is sealed by God and actually becomes a part of God's love. As a result, the sacrament provides the couple with the grace necessary to love one another fully as God intends; helps them to welcome children joyfully as a gift from God; and gives them the strength to overcome the challenges that their life together may bring. The Church believes that in a Christian marriage, God's love and grace are present in a special way (see Eph 5:21–33).

When two Catholics are joined in Matrimony, it is usually celebrated during a Mass. When a Catholic marries a Christian of another faith or an unbaptized person, it is usually celebrated within the context of the liturgy of the word and prayer. During the liturgical celebration, the couple is questioned by the celebrant (either a priest or deacon) after the homily as to their desire to be married and to ensure that they are freely choosing to enter into this special union. Then the couple exchanges vows before God and the community, declaring their undying love and commitment to one another. During this exchange, the couple actually confers the sacrament upon one another, with the celebrant there as a witness for the Church. Afterwards, the celebrant declares, as Christ did, that what has been joined by God shall not be separated. The couple then exchanges rings as a sign of their everlasting commitment to one another. Finally, toward the conclusion of the liturgical celebration, the celebrant offers the nuptial blessing, which calls upon the Lord to watch over and guide the new couple as they begin their new life together as one.

Mk 10:1–12

Catechism, nos. 1601–1666

MK

"Good teacher, what must I do to inherit eter-
nal life?" 18† Jesus answered him, "Why do you
call me good? No one is good but God alone.
19* You know the commandments: 'You shall
not kill; you shall not commit adultery; you
shall not steal; you shall not bear false witness;
you shall not defraud; honor your father and
your mother.' " 20 He replied and said to him,
"Teacher, all of these I have observed from my
youth." 21 Jesus, looking at him, loved him and
said to him, "You are lacking in one thing. Go,
sell what you have, and give to [the] poor and
you will have treasure in heaven; then come, fol-
low me." 22 At that statement his face fell, and he
went away sad, for he had many possessions.
23*† Jesus looked around and said to his disci-
ples, "How hard it is for those who have wealth
to enter the kingdom of God!" 24 The disciples
were amazed at his words. So Jesus again said to
them in reply, "Children, how hard it is to enter
the kingdom of God! 25 It is easier for a camel to
pass through [the] eye of [a] needle than for one
who is rich to enter the kingdom of God." 26 They
were exceedingly astonished and said among
themselves, "Then who can be saved?" 27 Jesus
looked at them and said, "For human beings it is
impossible, but not for God. All things are pos-
sible for God." 28 Peter began to say to him, "We
have given up everything and followed you."
29 Jesus said, "Amen, I say to you, there is no one
who has given up house or brothers or sisters or
mother or father or children or lands for my sake
and for the sake of the gospel 30 who will not re-
ceive a hundred times more now in this present
age: houses and brothers and sisters and mothers
and children and lands, with persecutions, and
eternal life in the age to come. 31* But many that
are first will be last, and [the] last will be first."

The Third Prediction of the Passion

32* They were on the way, going up to Jerusa-
lem, and Jesus went ahead of them. They were
amazed, and those who followed were afraid.
Taking the Twelve aside again, he began to tell
them what was going to happen to him. 33 "Be-
hold, we are going up to Jerusalem, and the Son
of Man will be handed over to the chief priests
and the scribes, and they will condemn him to
death and hand him over to the Gentiles 34 who
will mock him, spit upon him, scourge him, and
put him to death, but after three days he will
rise."

Ambition of James and John

35* Then James and John, the sons of Zebedee,
came to him and said to him, "Teacher, we want
you to do for us whatever we ask of you." 36 He
replied, "What do you wish [me] to do for you?"
37 They answered him, "Grant that in your glory
we may sit one at your right and the other at your
left." 38*† Jesus said to them, "You do not know
what you are asking. Can you drink the cup that I
drink or be baptized with the baptism with which
I am baptized?" 39 They said to him, "We can."
Jesus said to them, "The cup that I drink, you will
drink, and with the baptism with which I am bap-
tized, you will be baptized; 40 but to sit at my right
or at my left is not mine to give but is for those
for whom it has been prepared." 41 When the ten
heard this, they became indignant at James and
John. 42*† Jesus summoned them and said to
them, "You know that those who are recognized
as rulers over the Gentiles lord it over them, and
their great ones make their authority over them
felt. 43 But it shall not be so among you. Rather,
whoever wishes to be great among you will be
your servant; 44 whoever wishes to be first among
you will be the slave of all. 45 For the Son of Man
did not come to be served but to serve and to give
his life as a ransom for many."

The Blind Bartimaeus

46*† They came to Jericho. And as he was
leaving Jericho with his disciples and a sizable

†

10:18 *Why do you call me good?:* Jesus repudiates the term "good" for himself and directs it to God, the source of all goodness who alone can grant the gift of eternal life; cf Mt 19:16–17.

10:23–27 In the Old Testament wealth and material goods are considered a sign of God's favor (Jb 1:10; Ps 128:1–2; Is 3:10). The words of Jesus in 23–25 provoke astonishment among the disciples because of their apparent contradiction of the Old Testament concept (24, 26). Since wealth, power, and merit generate false security, Jesus rejects them utterly as a claim to enter the kingdom. Achievement of salvation is beyond human capability and depends solely on the goodness of God who offers it as a gift (27).

10:38–40 *Can you drink the cup . . . I am baptized?:* the metaphor of drinking the cup is used in the Old Testament to refer to acceptance of the destiny assigned by God; see the note on Ps 11:6. In Jesus' case, this involves divine judgment on sin that Jesus the innocent one is to expiate on behalf of the guilty (14:24; Is 53:5). His baptism is to be his crucifixion and death for the salvation of the human race; cf Lk 12:50. The request of James and John for a share in the glory (35–37) must of necessity involve a share in Jesus' sufferings, the endurance of tribulation and suffering for the gospel (39). The authority of assigning places of honor in the kingdom is reserved to God (40).

10:42–45 Whatever authority is to be exercised by the disciples must, like that of Jesus, be rendered as service to others (45) rather than for personal aggrandizement (42–44). The service of Jesus is his passion and death for the sins of the human race (45); cf 14:24; Is 53:11–12; Mt 26:28; Lk 22:19–20.

10:46–52 See the notes on Mt 9:27–31 and 20:29–34.

10:19 Ex 20:12–16; Dt 5:16–21.
10:23 Prv 11:28.
10:31 Mt 19:30; Lk 13:30.
10:32–34 Mk 8:31; Mt 20:17–19; Lk 18:31–33.
10:35–45 Mt 20:20–28.
10:38 Lk 12:50.
10:42–45 Lk 22:25–27.
10:46–52 Mt 20:29–34; Lk 18:35–43.

crowd, Bartimaeus, a blind man, the son of Timaeus, sat by the roadside begging. [47] On hearing that it was Jesus of Nazareth, he began to cry out and say, "Jesus, son of David, have pity on me." [48] And many rebuked him, telling him to be silent. But he kept calling out all the more, "Son of David, have pity on me." [49] Jesus stopped and said, "Call him." So they called the blind man, saying to him, "Take courage; get up, he is calling you." [50] He threw aside his cloak, sprang up, and came to Jesus. [51] Jesus said to him in reply, "What do you want me to do for you?" The blind man replied to him, "Master, I want to see." [52] Jesus told him, "Go your way; your faith has saved you." Immediately he received his sight and followed him on the way.

MK

The Entry into Jerusalem

11 [1]*† When they drew near to Jerusalem, to Bethphage and Bethany at the Mount of Olives, he sent two of his disciples [2] and said to them, "Go into the village opposite you, and immediately on entering it, you will find a colt tethered on which no one has ever sat. Untie it and bring it here. [3] If anyone should say to you, 'Why are you doing this?' reply, 'The Master has need of it and will send it back here at once.' " [4] So they went off and found a colt tethered at a gate outside on the street, and they untied it. [5] Some of the bystanders said to them, "What are you doing, untying the colt?" [6] They answered them just as Jesus had told them to, and they permitted them to do it. [7] So they brought the colt to Jesus and put their cloaks over it. And he sat on it. [8] Many people spread their cloaks on the road, and others spread leafy branches that they had cut from the fields. [9]* Those preceding him as well as those following kept crying out:

"Hosanna!
Blessed is he who comes in the name of the Lord!
[10] Blessed is the kingdom of our father David that is to come!
Hosanna in the highest!"

[11]* He entered Jerusalem and went into the temple area. He looked around at everything and, since it was already late, went out to Bethany with the Twelve.

Jesus Curses a Fig Tree

[12]*† The next day as they were leaving Bethany he was hungry. [13] Seeing from a distance a fig tree in leaf, he went over to see if he could find anything on it. When he reached it he found nothing but leaves; it was not the time for figs. [14] And he said to it in reply, "May no one ever eat of your fruit again!" And his disciples heard it.

Cleansing of the Temple

[15]*† They came to Jerusalem, and on entering the temple area he began to drive out those selling and buying there. He overturned the tables of the money changers and the seats of those who were selling doves. [16] He did not permit anyone to carry anything through the temple area. [17]* Then he taught them saying, "Is it not written:

'My house shall be called a house of prayer
for all peoples'?
But you have made it a den of thieves."

[18] The chief priests and the scribes came to hear of it and were seeking a way to put him to death, yet they feared him because the whole crowd was astonished at his teaching. [19]* When evening came, they went out of the city.

The Withered Fig Tree

[20]* Early in the morning, as they were walking along, they saw the fig tree withered to its roots. [21] Peter remembered and said to him, "Rabbi, look! The fig tree that you cursed has withered." [22] Jesus said to them in reply, "Have faith in God. [23]* Amen, I say to you, whoever says to this mountain, 'Be lifted up and thrown into the sea,' and does not doubt in his heart but believes that what he says will happen, it shall be done for him. [24]* Therefore I tell you, all that you ask for in prayer, believe that you will receive it and it shall be yours. [25]* When you stand to pray, forgive anyone against whom you have a grievance, so that your heavenly Father may in turn forgive you your transgressions. [26]† "

---

†

11:1–11 In Mark's account Jesus takes the initiative in ordering the preparation for his entry into Jerusalem (1–6) even as he later orders the preparation of his last Passover supper (14:12–16). In vv 9–10 the greeting Jesus receives stops short of proclaiming him Messiah. He is greeted rather as the prophet of the coming messianic kingdom. Contrast Mt 21:9.

11:12–14 Jesus' search for fruit on the fig tree recalls the prophets' earlier use of this image to designate Israel; cf Jer 8:13; 29:17; Jl 1:7; Hos 9:10, 16. Cursing the fig tree is a parable in action representing Jesus' judgment (20) on barren Israel and the fate of Jerusalem for failing to receive his teaching; cf Is 34:4; Hos 2:14; Lk 13:6–9.

11:15–19 See the note on Mt 21:12–17.

11:26 This verse, which reads, "But if you do not forgive, neither

---

*

11:1–10 Mt 21:1–9; Lk 19:29–38; Jn 12:12–15.
11:9–10 2 Sm 7:16; Ps 118:26.
11:11 Mt 21:10, 17.
11:12–14 Mt 21:18–20; Lk 13:6–9.
11:15–18 Mt 21:12–13; Lk 19:45–46; Jn 2:14–16.
11:17 Is 56:7; Jer 7:11.
11:19 Lk 21:37.
11:20–24 Mt 21:20–22.
11:23 Mt 17:20–21; Lk 17:6.
11:24 Mt 7:7; Jn 11:22; 14:13.
11:25 Mt 6:14; 18:35.

The Authority of Jesus Questioned

27*† They returned once more to Jerusalem.
As he was walking in the temple area, the chief
priests, the scribes, and the elders approached
him 28 and said to him, "By what authority are
you doing these things? Or who gave you this au-
thority to do them?" 29 Jesus said to them, "I shall
ask you one question. Answer me, and I will tell
you by what authority I do these things. 30 Was
John's baptism of heavenly or of human origin?
Answer me." 31 They discussed this among them-
selves and said, "If we say, 'Of heavenly origin,'
he will say, '[Then] why did you not believe
him?' 32 But shall we say, 'Of human origin'?"—
they feared the crowd, for they all thought John
really was a prophet. 33 So they said to Jesus in
reply, "We do not know." Then Jesus said to
them, "Neither shall I tell you by what authority
I do these things."

Parable of the Tenants

12 1*† He began to speak to them in parables.
"A man planted a vineyard, put a hedge
around it, dug a wine press, and built a tower.
Then he leased it to tenant farmers and left on a
journey.* 2 At the proper time he sent a servant
to the tenants to obtain from them some of the
produce of the vineyard. 3 But they seized him,
beat him, and sent him away empty-handed.
4 Again he sent them another servant. And that
one they beat over the head and treated shame-
fully. 5 He sent yet another whom they killed. So,
too, many others; some they beat, others they
killed. 6 He had one other to send, a beloved son.
He sent him to them last of all, thinking, 'They
will respect my son.' 7 But those tenants said to
one another, 'This is the heir. Come, let us kill
him, and the inheritance will be ours.' 8 So they
seized him and killed him, and threw him out of
the vineyard. 9 What [then] will the owner of the
vineyard do? He will come, put the tenants to
death, and give the vineyard to others. 10* Have
you not read this scripture passage:

'The stone that the builders rejected
has become the cornerstone;
11 by the Lord has this been done,
and it is wonderful in our eyes'?"

† will your heavenly Father forgive your transgressions," is omitted in the best manuscripts. It was probably added by copyists under the influence of Mt 6:15.

11:27–33 The mounting hostility toward Jesus came from the chief priests, the scribes, and the elders (27); the Herodians and the Pharisees (12:13); and the Sadducees (12:18). By their rejection of God's messengers, John the Baptist and Jesus, they incurred the divine judgment implied in vv 27–33 and confirmed in the parable of the vineyard tenants (12:1–12).

12:1–12 The vineyard denotes Israel (Is 5:1–7). The tenant farmers are the religious leaders of Israel. God is the owner of the vineyard. His servants are his messengers, the prophets. The beloved son is Jesus (1:11; 9:7; Mt 3:17; 17:5; Lk 3:22; 9:35). The punishment of the tenants refers to the religious leaders, and the transfer of the vineyard to others refers to the people of the new Israel.

11:27–33 Mt 21:23–27; Lk 20:1–8.
12:1–12 Mt 21:33–46; Lk 20:9–19.
12:1 Is 5:1–7; Jer 2:21.
12:10–11 Ps 118:22–23; Is 28:16.

Pray It!

Unanswered Prayer

Did you ever want something so badly that you prayed for it?

Sometimes, when things turn out the way we want, we say that God has answered our prayers. But when things don't turn out the way we want, we say that God didn't answer our prayers.

In Mark 11:24, it seems that we have the power to obtain what we want from God just by stating our wishes. This is a dangerous thought, though, especially when someone else might be praying for the exact opposite of what we're praying for. Why should God answer our prayers and not someone else's? In addition, when something horrible happens despite all our prayers, it is incorrect to think that God willed such pain and suffering. For example, sometimes we hear people saying, "God must have wanted me to learn some lesson from this tragedy." God never causes tragedy. Tragedy just happens. Saying that such things are "God's will" or part of "God's plan" is dangerous, and not an accurate representation of the God we know—a God who loves us intimately and hates to see us suffering or in pain.

People often ask, and we may be asking ourselves, Why pray at all if it isn't going to change anything? God wants only the best for us and knows what we need before we ask. But God also waits for us to ask because of the freedom he has given us. In freedom we ask, and in love we await God's response.

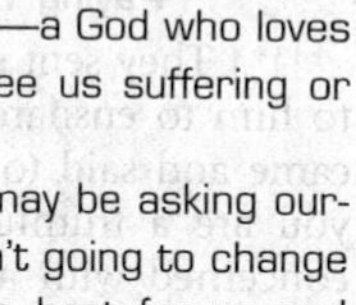

▶ **Mk 11:24**

MK

Pray It!

What Do You Want from Me?

Dear God, Jesus tells us to give to you what is yours. What do you want from me, God? What can I give to you?

As a young person still growing and developing, I don't have much to offer financially. I can make a small financial contribution to the church, to poor people, . . . but is it enough, Lord? What more can I give?

I can offer my time and talents to serve my faith community. I can sing, play an instrument, draw posters, greet visitors, clean, decorate, organize, cook, bake, and make phone calls. I can help teach children, lector, or usher, . . . but is it enough, Lord? What more can I give?

I can reach out to serve and share your love at home, in my neighborhood, my school, my community, . . . but is it enough, Lord? What more can I give?

I want to serve you better, Lord. Speak to me, and I will listen.
Amen.

▶ Mk 12:13–17

12They were seeking to arrest him, but they
feared the crowd, for they realized that he had
addressed the parable to them. So they left him
and went away.

Paying Taxes to the Emperor

13*† They sent some Pharisees and Herodians
to him to ensnare him* in his speech.† 14They
came and said to him, "Teacher, we know that
you are a truthful man and that you are not
concerned with anyone's opinion. You do not
regard a person's status but teach the way of God
in accordance with the truth. Is it lawful to pay
the census tax to Caesar or not? Should we pay or
should we not pay?" 15Knowing their hypocrisy
he said to them, "Why are you testing me? Bring
me a denarius to look at." 16They brought one
to him and he said to them, "Whose image and
inscription is this?" They replied to him, "Caesar's."
17* So Jesus said to them, "Repay to Caesar
what belongs to Caesar and to God what belongs
to God." They were utterly amazed at him.

The Question about the Resurrection

18† Some Sadducees, who say there is no resurrection,
came to him and put this question to
him, 19* saying, "Teacher, Moses wrote for us,
'If someone's brother dies, leaving a wife but no
child, his brother must take the wife and raise up
descendants for his brother.' 20Now there were
seven brothers. The first married a woman and
died, leaving no descendants. 21So the second
married her and died, leaving no descendants,
and the third likewise. 22And the seven left no
descendants. Last of all the woman also died.
23At the resurrection [when they arise] whose
wife will she be? For all seven had been married
to her." 24Jesus said to them, "Are you not misled
because you do not know the scriptures or the
power of God? 25When they rise from the dead,
they neither marry nor are given in marriage,
but they are like the angels in heaven. 26* As for
the dead being raised, have you not read in the
Book of Moses, in the passage about the bush,
how God told him, 'I am the God of Abraham,
[the] God of Isaac, and [the] God of Jacob'? 27He
is not God of the dead but of the living. You are
greatly misled."

The Greatest Commandment

28*† One of the scribes, when he came forward
and heard them disputing and saw how well he
had answered them, asked him, "Which is the
first of all the commandments?" 29Jesus replied,
"The first is this: 'Hear, O Israel! The Lord our
God is Lord alone! 30* You shall love the Lord
your God with all your heart, with all your soul,
with all your mind, and with all your strength.'
31* The second is this: 'You shall love your neighbor
as yourself.' There is no other commandment
greater than these." 32The scribe said to him,
"Well said, teacher. You are right in saying, 'He
is One and there is no other than he.' 33* And 'to
love him with all your heart, with all your understanding,
with all your strength, and to love
your neighbor as yourself' is worth more than

---

† **12:13–34** In the ensuing conflicts (cf also 2:1—3:6) Jesus vanquishes his adversaries by his responses to their questions and reduces them to silence (34).

12:13–17 See the note on Mt 22:15–22.

12:18–27 See the note on Mt 22:23–33.

12:28–34 See the note on Mt 22:34–40.

12:13–27 Mt 22:15–33; Lk 20:20–39.
12:13 Mk 3:6.
12:17 Rom 13:7.
12:19 Dt 25:5.
12:26 Ex 3:6.
12:28–34 Mt 22:34–40; Lk 10:25–28.
12:30 Dt 6:4–5.
12:31 Lv 19:18; Rom 13:9; Gal 5:14; Jas 2:8.
12:33 Dt 6:4; Ps 40:7–9.

all burnt offerings and sacrifices." 34* And when Jesus saw that [he] answered with understanding, he said to him, "You are not far from the kingdom of God." And no one dared to ask him any more questions.

The Question about David's Son

35*† As Jesus was teaching in the temple area he said, "How do the scribes claim that the Messiah is the son of David? 36* David himself, inspired by the holy Spirit, said:

> 'The Lord said to my lord,
> "Sit at my right hand
> until I place your enemies under your feet." '

37 David himself calls him 'lord'; so how is he his son?" [The] great crowd heard this with delight.

Denunciation of the Scribes

38*† In the course of his teaching he said, "Beware of the scribes, who like to go around in long robes and accept greetings in the marketplaces, 39 seats of honor in synagogues, and places of honor at banquets. 40 They devour the houses of widows and, as a pretext, recite lengthy prayers. They will receive a very severe condemnation."

The Poor Widow's Contribution

41*† He sat down opposite the treasury and observed how the crowd put money into the treasury. Many rich people put in large sums. 42 A poor widow also came and put in two small coins worth a few cents. 43 Calling his disciples to himself, he said to them, "Amen, I say to you, this poor widow put in more than all the other contributors to the treasury. 44 For they have all contributed from their surplus wealth, but she, from her poverty, has contributed all she had, her whole livelihood."

12:41–44

The Destruction of the Temple Foretold

13 1*† As he was making his way out of the temple area one of his disciples said to him, "Look, teacher, what stones and what buildings!" 2 Jesus said to him, "Do you see these great buildings? There will not be one stone left upon another that will not be thrown down."

The Signs of the End

3*† As he was sitting on the Mount of Olives opposite the temple area, Peter, James, John, and Andrew asked him privately, 4 "Tell us, when will this happen, and what sign will there be when all these things are about to come to an end?" 5* Jesus began to say to them, "See that no one deceives you. 6 Many will come in my name saying, 'I am he,' and they will deceive many. 7 When you hear of wars and reports of wars do not be alarmed; such things must happen, but it will not yet be the end. 8 Nation will rise against nation and kingdom against kingdom. There will

---

† **12:35–37** Jesus questions the claim of the scribes about the Davidic descent of the Messiah, not to deny it (Mt 1:1; Acts 2:20, 34; Rom 1:3; 2 Tm 2:8) but to imply that he is more than this. His superiority derives from his transcendent origin, to which David himself attested when he spoke of the Messiah with the name "Lord" (Ps 110:1). See also the note on Mt 22:41–46.

12:38–40 See the notes on 7:1–23 and Mt 23:1–39.

12:41–44 See the note on Lk 21:1–4.

13:1–2 The reconstructed temple with its precincts, begun under Herod the Great ca. 20 B.C., was completed only some seven years before it was destroyed by fire in A.D. 70 at the hands of the Romans; cf Jer 26:18; Mt 24:1–2. For the dating of the reconstruction of the temple, see further the note on Jn 2:20.

13:3–37 Jesus' prediction of the destruction of the temple (2) provoked questions that the four named disciples put to him in private regarding the time and the sign when all *these things are about to come to an end* (3–4). The response to their questions was Jesus' eschatological discourse prior to his imminent death. It contained instruction and consolation exhorting the disciples and the church to faith and obedience through the trials that would confront them (5–13). The sign is the presence of *the desolating abomination* (14; see Dn 9:27), i.e., of the Roman power profaning the temple. Flight from Jerusalem is urged rather than defense of the city through misguided messianic hope (14–23). Intervention will occur only after destruction (24–27), which will happen before the end of the first Christian generation (28–31). No one but the Father knows the precise time, or that of the parousia (32); hence the necessity of constant vigilance (33–37). Luke sets the parousia at a later date, after "the time of the Gentiles" (Lk 21:24). See also the notes on Mt 24:1—25:46.

---

* **12:34** Mt 22:46; Lk 20:40.
12:35–37 Mt 22:41–45; Lk 20:41–44.
12:36 Ps 110:1.
12:38–40 Mt 23:1–7; Lk 11:43; 20:45–47.
12:41–44 Lk 21:1–4.
13:1–2 Mt 24:1–2; Lk 21:5–6.
13:3–8 Mt 24:3–8; Lk 21:7–11.
13:5 Eph 5:6; 2 Thes 2:3.

Cultural Connection

Sacrificial Giving

Native Americans can appreciate the widow's offering in Mark 12:41–44. For example, the Lakota tribe has a custom called *otuhan*, or "giveaway." During important occasions, a person honors the other members of the tribe by giving away much of what she or he has. Sometimes, everything is given away. To be called stingy is the worst insult.

Think about your own circumstances. How easy would it be to share or give away your favorite possessions? Could you give away something you really value? Why or why not?

Many Native Americans believe that all we have belongs to the Great Spirit and is a gift to be shared with others. Make a decision! Follow the example of the widow, and be generous to others to the point of sacrifice.

Mk 12:41–44

be earthquakes from place to place and there
will be famines. These are the beginnings of the
labor pains.

The Coming Persecution

9* "Watch out for yourselves. They will hand
you over to the courts. You will be beaten in syn-
agogues. You will be arraigned before governors
and kings because of me, as a witness before
them. 10† But the gospel must first be preached
to all nations. 11* When they lead you away and
hand you over, do not worry beforehand about
what you are to say. But say whatever will be
given to you at that hour. For it will not be you
who are speaking but the holy Spirit. 12 Brother
will hand over brother to death, and the father
his child; children will rise up against parents
and have them put to death. 13 You will be hated
by all because of my name. But the one who per-
severes to the end will be saved.

The Great Tribulation

14*† "When you see the desolating abomina-
tion standing where he should not (let the reader
understand), then those in Judea must flee to the
mountains,* 15* [and] a person on a housetop
must not go down or enter to get anything out of
his house, 16 and a person in a field must not re-
turn to get his cloak. 17 Woe to pregnant women
and nursing mothers in those days. 18 Pray that
this does not happen in winter. 19* For those
times will have tribulation such as has not been
since the beginning of God's creation until now,
nor ever will be. 20 If the Lord had not shortened
those days, no one would be saved; but for the
sake of the elect whom he chose, he did shorten
the days. 21 If anyone says to you then, 'Look,
here is the Messiah! Look, there he is!' do not
believe it. 22 False messiahs and false prophets
will arise and will perform signs and wonders
in order to mislead, if that were possible, the
elect. 23 Be watchful! I have told it all to you be-
forehand.

The Coming of the Son of Man

24* "But in those days after that tribulation

the sun will be darkened,
and the moon will not give its light,*
25 and the stars will be falling from the sky,
and the powers in the heavens will be
shaken.

26*† And then they will see 'the Son of Man com-
ing in the clouds' with great power and glory,
27 and then he will send out the angels and gather
[his] elect from the four winds, from the end of
the earth to the end of the sky.

---

† **13:10** *The gospel . . . to all nations:* the period of the Christian mission.

13:14 The participle *standing* is masculine, in contrast to the neuter at Mt 24:15.

13:26 *Son of Man . . . with great power and glory:* Jesus cites this text from Dn 7:13 in his response to the high priest, *Are you the Messiah?* (14:61). In Ex 34:5; Lv 16:2; and Nm 11:25 the clouds indicate the presence of the divinity. Thus in his role of Son of Man, Jesus is a heavenly being who will come in power and glory.

13:9–13 Mt 24:9–14; Lk 21:12–19.
13:11–12 Mt 10:19–22; Lk 12:11–12.
13:14–23 Mt 24:15–22; Lk 21:20–24.
13:14 Dn 9:27; Mt 24:15.
13:15 Lk 17:31.
13:19 Dn 12:1.
13:24–27 Mt 24:29–31; Lk 21:25–27.
13:24 Is 13:10; Ez 32:7; Jl 2:10.
13:26 Mk 14:62; Dn 7:13–14.

The Lesson of the Fig Tree

28* "Learn a lesson from the fig tree. When its
branch becomes tender and sprouts leaves, you
know that summer is near. 29 In the same way,
when you see these things happening, know that
he is near, at the gates. 30 Amen, I say to you,
this generation will not pass away until all these
things have taken place. 31 Heaven and earth will
pass away, but my words will not pass away.

Need for Watchfulness

32 "But of that day or hour, no one knows, nei-
ther the angels in heaven, nor the Son, but only
the Father. 33* Be watchful! Be alert! You do not
know when the time will come. 34* It is like a man
traveling abroad. He leaves home and places his
servants in charge, each with his work, and orders
the gatekeeper to be on the watch. 35 Watch, there-
fore; you do not know when the lord of the house
is coming, whether in the evening, or at midnight,
or at cockcrow, or in the morning. 36 May he not
come suddenly and find you sleeping. 37 What I
say to you, I say to all: 'Watch!'"

The Conspiracy against Jesus

14 1*† The Passover and the Feast of Unleav-
ened Bread† were to take place in two
days' time. So the chief priests and the scribes
were seeking a way to arrest him by treachery and
put him to death. 2 They said, "Not during the
festival, for fear that there may be a riot among
the people."

The Anointing at Bethany

3*† When he was in Bethany reclining at table
in the house of Simon the leper, a woman came
with an alabaster jar of perfumed oil, costly gen-
uine spikenard. She broke the alabaster jar and
poured it on his head. 4 There were some who
were indignant. "Why has there been this waste
of perfumed oil? 5 It could have been sold for
more than three hundred days' wages and the
money given to the poor." They were infuriated
with her. 6 Jesus said, "Let her alone. Why do you
make trouble for her? She has done a good thing
for me. 7 The poor you will always have with
you, and whenever you wish you can do good
to them, but you will not always have me. 8 She
has done what she could. She has anticipated
anointing my body for burial. 9 Amen, I say to
you, wherever the gospel is proclaimed to the
whole world, what she has done will be told in
memory of her."

The Betrayal by Judas

10* Then Judas Iscariot, one of the Twelve,
went off to the chief priests to hand him over to

Did You Know?

Signs and Omens

The community for which the author of Mark's Gospel wrote saw its sufferings as part of the troubles that would come with the end time. However, the author didn't intend that his readers take Jesus' signs and omens of wars and earthquakes to mean that the end of the world was literally at hand; rather, these descriptions were used symbolically (see "Apocalyptic Literature," near Daniel, chapters 7–10) to help the community make sense of its persecutions. The message of this Gospel is that Christians who were getting beaten up and thrown in jail would be saved by God. And ultimately, human history would climax in the perfect Reign of God. It was their job to hang on and endure to the end. All they had to worry about was spreading the Good News of Jesus Christ, and God would take care of the rest.

▶ **Mark, chapter 13**

MK

†

14:1—16:8 In the movement of Mark's gospel the cross is depicted as Jesus' way to glory in accordance with the divine will. Thus the passion narrative is seen as the climax of Jesus' ministry.

14:1 *The Passover and the Feast of Unleavened Bread:* the connection between the two festivals is reflected in Ex 12:3–20; 34:18; Lv 23:4–8; Nm 9:2–14; 28:16–17; Dt 16:1–8. The Passover commemorated the redemption from slavery and the departure of the Israelites from Egypt by night. It began at sundown after the Passover lamb was sacrificed in the temple in the afternoon of the fourteenth day of the month of Nisan. With the Passover supper on the same evening was associated the eating of unleavened bread. The latter was continued through Nisan 21, a reminder of the affliction of the Israelites and of the haste surrounding their departure. Praise and thanks to God for his goodness in the past were combined at this dual festival with the hope of future salvation. *The chief priests . . . to death:* the intent to put Jesus to death was plotted for a long time but delayed for fear of the crowd (3:6; 11:18; 12:12).

14:3–9 At Bethany on the Mount of Olives, a few miles from Jerusalem, *in the house of Simon the leper,* Jesus defends a woman's loving action of anointing his head with perfumed oil in view of his impending death and burial as a criminal, in which case his body would not be anointed. See further the note on Jn 12:7. He assures the woman of the remembrance of her deed in the worldwide preaching of the good news.

*

13:28–32 Mt 24:32–36; Lk 21:29–33.
13:33–37 Mt 24:42; 25:13–15.
13:34 Mt 25:14–30; Lk 19:12–27.
14:1–2 Mt 26:2–5; Lk 22:1–2; Jn 11:45–53.
14:3–9 Mt 26:6–13; Jn 12:1–8.
14:10–11 Mt 26:14–16; Lk 22:3–6.

them. [11]When they heard him they were pleased
and promised to pay him money. Then he
looked for an opportunity to hand him over.

Preparations for the Passover

[12]*† On the first day of the Feast of Unleav-
ened Bread, when they sacrificed the Passover
lamb, his disciples said to him, "Where do you
want us to go and prepare for you to eat the Pass-
over?" [13]† He sent two of his disciples and said to
them, "Go into the city and a man will meet you,
carrying a jar of water. Follow him. [14]Wherever
he enters, say to the master of the house, 'The
Teacher says, "Where is my guest room where
I may eat the Passover with my disciples?"'
[15]Then he will show you a large upper room fur-
nished and ready. Make the preparations for us
there." [16]The disciples then went off, entered the
city, and found it just as he had told them; and
they prepared the Passover.

The Betrayer

[17]* When it was evening, he came with the
Twelve. [18]† And as they reclined at table and
were eating, Jesus said, "Amen, I say to you, one
of you will betray me, one who is eating with
me." [19]They began to be distressed and to say to
him, one by one, "Surely it is not I?" [20]He said to
them, "One of the Twelve, the one who dips with
me into the dish. [21]† For the Son of Man indeed
goes, as it is written of him, but woe to that man
by whom the Son of Man is betrayed. It would be
better for that man if he had never been born."

The Lord's Supper

[22]*† While they were eating, he took bread,
said the blessing, broke it, and gave it to them,
and said, "Take it; this is my body." [23]Then he
took a cup, gave thanks, and gave it to them, and
they all drank from it. [24]† He said to them, "This
is my blood of the covenant, which will be shed
for many. [25]Amen, I say to you, I shall not drink
again the fruit of the vine until the day when I
drink it new in the kingdom of God." [26]*† Then,
after singing a hymn, they went out to the Mount
of Olives.

Live It!

Mass Prayer

"Take it; this is my body. . . . This is my blood." Reading those words may sometimes make us feel guilty because we should be hearing them at Mass, and we are often good at finding excuses not to go to Mass: the church pews are uncomfortable, we'd rather sleep late, we don't like the music or the homily, it is too nice outside, it's boring.

Amidst the busyness of our lives and the excuses we make up, it is easy to forget that Jesus gave us a special invitation to share in the Eucharistic meal. Regularly celebrating the Eucharist gives us an opportunity to participate in Jesus' death and Resurrection, strengthen our faith, and renew our hope of sharing in God's Reign. It is a privilege to be invited to the Eucharistic table, to be nourished by Christ, and to connect with both the present Church and all the saints of the past who have shared this sacred meal. Although it's usually easier to make excuses, it is important for each of us to make Mass a priority in our lives. (For more on the Eucharist, see "The New Covenant," near Mt 26:26–29; "The Eucharist," near Lk 22:14–20; and "Feast of the Passover," near Jn 13:1–20.)

▶ **Mk 14:22–25**

†

14:12 *The first day of the Feast of Unleavened Bread . . . the Passover lamb:* a less precise designation of the day for sacrificing the Passover lamb as evidenced by some rabbinical literature. For a more exact designation, see the note on 14:1. It was actually Nisan 14.

14:13 *A man . . . carrying a jar of water:* perhaps a prearranged signal, for only women ordinarily carried water in jars. The Greek word used here, however, implies simply a person and not necessarily a male.

14:18 *One of you will betray me, one who is eating with me:* contrasts the intimacy of table fellowship at the Passover meal with the treachery of the traitor; cf Ps 41:10.

14:21 *The Son of Man indeed goes, as it is written of him:* a reference to Ps 41:10 cited by Jesus concerning Judas at the Last Supper; cf Jn 13:18–19.

14:22–24 The actions and words of Jesus express within the framework of the Passover meal and the transition to a new covenant the sacrifice of himself through the offering of his body and blood in anticipation of his passion and death. His *blood of the covenant* both alludes to the ancient rite of Ex 24:4–8 and indicates the new community that the sacrifice of Jesus will bring into being (Mt 26:26–28; Lk 22:19–20; 1 Cor 11:23–25).

14:24 *Which will be shed:* see the note on Mt 26:27–28. *For many:* the Greek preposition *hyper* is a different one from that at Mt 26:28 but the same as that found at Lk 22:19, 20 and 1 Cor 11:24. The sense of both words is vicarious, and it is difficult in Hellenistic Greek to distinguish between them. For *many* in the sense of "all," see the note on Mt 20:28.

14:26 *After singing a hymn:* Pss 114–118, thanksgiving songs concluding the Passover meal.

*

14:12–16 Mt 26:17–19; Lk 22:7–13.
14:17–21 Mt 26:20–24; Lk 22:21–23; Jn 13:21–26.
14:22–25 Mt 26:26–30; Lk 22:19–20; 1 Cor 11:23–25.
14:26–31 Mt 26:30–35; Lk 22:34, 39; Jn 13:36–38.

Peter's Denial Foretold

27*† Then Jesus said to them, "All of you will
have your faith shaken, for it is written:

'I will strike the shepherd,
and the sheep will be dispersed.'

28 But after I have been raised up, I shall go be-
fore you to Galilee." 29 Peter said to him, "Even
though all should have their faith shaken, mine
will not be." 30 Then Jesus said to him, "Amen, I
say to you, this very night before the cock crows
twice you will deny me three times." 31 But he
vehemently replied, "Even though I should have
to die with you, I will not deny you." And they
all spoke similarly.

The Agony in the Garden

32*† Then they came to a place named
Gethsemane, and he said to his disciples, "Sit
here while I pray."* 33 He took with him Peter,
James, and John, and began to be troubled and
distressed. 34 Then he said to them, "My soul is
sorrowful even to death. Remain here and keep
watch." 35 He advanced a little and fell to the
ground and prayed that if it were possible the
hour might pass by him; 36† he said, "Abba, Fa-
ther, all things are possible to you. Take this cup
away from me, but not what I will but what you
will." 37 When he returned he found them asleep.
He said to Peter, "Simon, are you asleep? Could
you not keep watch for one hour? 38*† Watch
and pray that you may not undergo the test. The
spirit is willing but the flesh is weak." 39 With-
drawing again, he prayed, saying the same thing.
40 Then he returned once more and found them
asleep, for they could not keep their eyes open
and did not know what to answer him. 41 He re-
turned a third time and said to them, "Are you
still sleeping and taking your rest? It is enough.
The hour has come. Behold, the Son of Man is
to be handed over to sinners. 42 Get up, let us go.
See, my betrayer is at hand."

The Betrayal and Arrest of Jesus

43* Then, while he was still speaking, Judas,
one of the Twelve, arrived, accompanied by a
crowd with swords and clubs who had come
from the chief priests, the scribes, and the elders.
44 His betrayer had arranged a signal with them,
saying, "The man I shall kiss is the one; arrest
him and lead him away securely." 45 He came
and immediately went over to him and said,
"Rabbi." And he kissed him. 46 At this they laid
hands on him and arrested him. 47 One of the by-
standers drew his sword, struck the high priest's
servant, and cut off his ear. 48 Jesus said to them
in reply, "Have you come out as against a robber,
with swords and clubs, to seize me? 49 Day after
day I was with you teaching in the temple area,
yet you did not arrest me; but that the scriptures
may be fulfilled." 50 And they all left him and
fled. 51 Now a young man followed him wearing
nothing but a linen cloth about his body. They
seized him, 52 but he left the cloth behind and
ran off naked.

Jesus before the Sanhedrin

53*† They led Jesus away to the high priest,
and all the chief priests and the elders and the
scribes came together. 54 Peter followed him at a
distance into the high priest's courtyard and was
seated with the guards, warming himself at the
fire. 55 The chief priests and the entire Sanhedrin
kept trying to obtain testimony against Jesus in
order to put him to death, but they found none.
56 Many gave false witness against him, but their
testimony did not agree. 57† Some took the
stand and testified falsely against him, alleging,
58* "We heard him say, 'I will destroy this temple
made with hands and within three days I will

---

†

14:27–31 Jesus predicted that the Twelve would waver in their faith, even abandon him, despite their protestations to the contrary. Yet he reassured them that after his resurrection he would regather them in Galilee (16:7; cf Mt 26:32; 28:7, 10, 16; Jn 21), where he first summoned them to be his followers as he began to preach the good news (1:14–20).

14:32–34 The disciples who had witnessed the raising to life of the daughter of Jairus (5:37) and the transfiguration of their Master (9:2) were now invited to witness his degradation and agony and to watch and pray with him.

14:36 *Abba, Father:* an Aramaic term, here also translated by Mark, Jesus' special way of addressing God with filial intimacy. The word *'abbā'* seems not to have been used in earlier or contemporaneous Jewish sources to address God without some qualifier. Cf Rom 8:15; Gal 4:6 for other occurrences of the Aramaic word in the Greek New Testament. *Not what I will but what you will:* note the complete obedient surrender of the human will of Jesus to the divine will of the Father; cf Jn 4:34; 8:29; Rom 5:19; Phil 2:8; Heb 5:8.

14:38 *The spirit is willing but the flesh is weak:* the spirit is drawn to what is good yet found in conflict with the flesh, inclined to sin; cf Ps 51:7, 12. Everyone is faced with this struggle, the full force of which Jesus accepted on our behalf and, through his bitter passion and death, achieved the victory.

14:53 *They led Jesus away . . . came together:* Mark presents a formal assembly of the whole Sanhedrin (chief priests, elders, and scribes) at night, leading to the condemnation of Jesus (64), in contrast to Lk 22:66, 71, where Jesus is condemned in a daytime meeting of the council; see also Jn 18:13, 19–24.

14:57–58 See the notes on Mt 26:60–61 and Jn 2:19.

*

14:27 Zec 13:7; Jn 16:32.
14:32–42 Mt 26:36–46; Lk 22:40–46.
14:32 Jn 18:1.
14:38 Rom 7:5.
14:43–50 Mt 26:47–56; Lk 22:47–53; Jn 18:3–11.
14:53–65 Mt 26:57–68; Lk 22:54–55, 63–65, 67–71; Jn 18:12–13.
14:58 Mk 15:29; 2 Cor 5:1.

Pray It!

Facing the Hard Times

Lord, you really do know what it is like to be beaten, teased, pushed around, and rejected. If you could put up with this torment, then maybe there is hope for others who feel the same way at times. Like when we are made fun of or rejected because of the way we look or act or for what we believe in. Or when we feel all alone or that no one understands what we are feeling.

But now I know that you understand, Lord. You took these difficult steps even before we did. You have been there. You show us a way through these tough times.

Teach me to pray as you did: "Abba, Father, all things are possible to you. Take this cup [suffering] away from me, but not what I will but what you will" (Mk 14:36). Give me the strength to overcome my despair. Give me faith to abandon myself in God's hands as you did. Give me hope to see a new life beyond these moments of pain and hopelessness. Amen.

▶ **Mk 15:16–20**

build another not made with hands.' " 59 Even so
their testimony did not agree. 60 The high priest
rose before the assembly and questioned Jesus,
saying, "Have you no answer? What are these
men testifying against you?" 61† But he was si-
lent and answered nothing. Again the high priest
asked him and said to him, "Are you the Mes-
siah, the son of the Blessed One?" 62* Then Jesus
answered, "I am;

and 'you will see the Son of Man
seated at the right hand of the Power
and coming with the clouds of heaven.' "

63 At that the high priest tore his garments and
said, "What further need have we of witnesses?
64 You have heard the blasphemy. What do you
think?" They all condemned him as deserving to
die. 65* Some began to spit on him. They blind-
folded him and struck him and said to him,
"Prophesy!" And the guards greeted him with
blows.

Peter's Denial of Jesus

66* While Peter was below in the courtyard,
one of the high priest's maids came along.
67 Seeing Peter warming himself, she looked in-
tently at him and said, "You too were with the
Nazarene, Jesus." 68† But he denied it saying, "I
neither know nor understand what you are talk-
ing about." So he went out into the outer court.
[Then the cock crowed.] 69 The maid saw him and
began again to say to the bystanders, "This man
is one of them." 70 Once again he denied it. A lit-
tle later the bystanders said to Peter once more,
"Surely you are one of them; for you too are a
Galilean." 71 He began to curse and to swear, "I
do not know this man about whom you are talk-
ing." 72* And immediately a cock crowed a sec-
ond time. Then Peter remembered the word that
Jesus had said to him, "Before the cock crows
twice you will deny me three times." He broke
down and wept.

Jesus before Pilate

15 1*† As soon as morning came,* the chief
priests with the elders and the scribes, that
is, the whole Sanhedrin, held a council. They
bound Jesus, led him away, and handed him
over to Pilate. 2† Pilate questioned him, "Are
you the king of the Jews?" He said to him in re-
ply, "You say so." 3 The chief priests accused him
of many things. 4 Again Pilate questioned him,
"Have you no answer? See how many things

---

† **14:61–62** *The Blessed One:* a surrogate for the divine name, which Jews did not pronounce. *I am:* indicates Jesus' acknowledgment that he is the Messiah and Son of God; cf 1:1. Contrast Mt 26:64 and Lk 22:67–70, in which Jesus leaves his interrogators to answer their own question. *You will see the Son of Man . . . with the clouds of heaven:* an allusion to Dn 7:13 and Ps 110:1, portending the enthronement of Jesus as judge in the transcendent glory of God's kingdom. *The Power:* another surrogate for the name of God.

14:68 [*Then the cock crowed*]: found in most manuscripts, perhaps in view of vv 30 and 72, but omitted in others.

15:1 *Held a council:* the verb here, *poieō,* can mean either "convene a council" or "take counsel." This reading is preferred to a variant "reached a decision" (cf 3:6), which 14:64 describes as having happened at the night trial; see the note on Mt 27:1–2. *Handed him over to Pilate:* lacking authority to execute their sentence of condemnation (14:64), the Sanhedrin had recourse to Pilate to have Jesus tried and put to death (15); cf Jn 18:31.

15:2 *The king of the Jews:* in the accounts of the evangelists a certain irony surrounds the use of this title as an accusation against Jesus (see the note on 15:26). While Pilate uses this term (2, 9, 12), he is aware of the evil motivation of the chief priests who handed Jesus over for trial and condemnation (10; Lk 23:14–16, 20; Mt 27:18, 24; Jn 18:38; 19:4, 6, 12).

---

* **14:62** Mk 13:26; Ps 110:1; Dn 7:13; Mt 24:30. **14:65** Lk 22:63–65. **14:66–72** Mt 26:69–75; Lk 22:56–62; Jn 18:16–18, 25–27. **14:72** Jn 13:38. **15:1–5** Mt 27:1–2, 11–14; Lk 23:1–3. **15:1** Jn 18:28.

they accuse you of." 5 Jesus gave him no further
answer, so that Pilate was amazed.

The Sentence of Death

6*† Now on the occasion of the feast he used
to release to them one prisoner whom they re-
quested. 7† A man called Barabbas was then in
prison along with the rebels who had committed
murder in a rebellion. 8 The crowd came forward
and began to ask him to do for them as he was
accustomed. 9 Pilate answered, "Do you want
me to release to you the king of the Jews?" 10 For
he knew that it was out of envy that the chief
priests had handed him over. 11 But the chief
priests stirred up the crowd to have him release
Barabbas for them instead. 12 Pilate again said
to them in reply, "Then what [do you want] me
to do with [the man you call] the king of the
Jews?" 13† They shouted again, "Crucify him."
14 Pilate said to them, "Why? What evil has he
done?" They only shouted the louder, "Crucify
him." 15† So Pilate, wishing to satisfy the crowd,
released Barabbas to them and, after he had Jesus
scourged, handed him over to be crucified.

Mockery by the Soldiers

16*† The soldiers led him away inside the pal-
ace, that is, the praetorium, and assembled the
whole cohort. 17 They clothed him in purple and,
weaving a crown of thorns, placed it on him.
18 They began to salute him with, "Hail, King of
the Jews!" 19 and kept striking his head with a
reed and spitting upon him. They knelt before
him in homage. 20 And when they had mocked
him, they stripped him of the purple cloak,
dressed him in his own clothes, and led him out
to crucify him.

The Way of the Cross

21*† They pressed into service a passer-by, Si-
mon, a Cyrenian, who was coming in from the
country, the father of Alexander and Rufus, to
carry his cross.

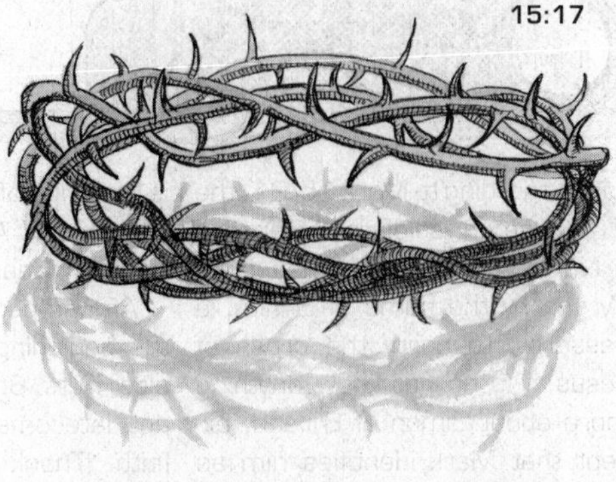

15:17

The Crucifixion

22* They brought him to the place of Golgotha
(which is translated Place of the Skull). 23 They
gave him wine drugged with myrrh, but he did
not take it. 24*† Then they crucified him and
divided his garments by casting lots for them to
see what each should take. 25† It was nine o'clock
in the morning when they crucified him. 26† The
inscription of the charge against him read, "The
King of the Jews." 27* With him they crucified
two revolutionaries, one on his right and one
on his left. [28]† 29*† Those passing by reviled
him, shaking their heads and saying, "Aha! You
who would destroy the temple and rebuild it
in three days, 30 save yourself by coming down
from the cross." 31 Likewise the chief priests, with
the scribes, mocked him among themselves and
said, "He saved others; he cannot save himself.
32* Let the Messiah, the King of Israel, come
down now from the cross that we may see and
believe." Those who were crucified with him also
kept abusing him.

The Death of Jesus

33 At noon darkness came over the whole land
until three in the afternoon. 34*† And at three
o'clock Jesus cried out in a loud voice, *"Eloi, Eloi,
lema sabachthani?"* which is translated, "My God,

†

15:6–15 See the note on Mt 27:15–26.

15:7 *Barabbas:* see the note on Mt 27:16–17.

15:13 *Crucify him:* see the note on Mt 27:22.

15:15 See the note on Mt 27:26.

15:16 *Praetorium:* see the note on Mt 27:27.

15:21 *They pressed into service . . . Simon, a Cyrenian:* a condemned person was constrained to bear his own instrument of torture, at least the crossbeam. The precise naming of Simon and his sons is probably due to their being known among early Christian believers to whom Mark addressed his gospel. See also the notes on Mt 27:32 and Lk 23:26–32.

15:24 See the notes on Mt 27:35 and Jn 19:23–25a.

15:25 *It was nine o'clock in the morning:* literally, "the third hour," thus between 9 a.m. and 12 noon. Cf vv 33, 34, 42 for Mark's chronological sequence, which may reflect liturgical or catechetical considerations rather than the precise historical sequence of events; contrast the different chronologies in the other gospels, especially Jn 19:14.

15:26 *The inscription . . . the King of the Jews:* the political reason for the death penalty falsely charged by the enemies of Jesus. See further the notes on Mt 27:37 and Jn 19:19.

15:28 This verse, "And the scripture was fulfilled that says, 'And he was counted among the wicked,' " is omitted in the earliest and best manuscripts. It contains a citation from Is 53:12, and was probably introduced from Lk 22:37.

15:29 See the note on Mt 27:39–40.

15:34 An Aramaic rendering of Ps 22:2. See also the note on Mt 27:46.

*

15:6–15 Mt 27:15–26; Lk 23:17–25; Jn 18:39–40.
15:16–20 Mt 27:27–31; Jn 19:2–3.
15:21 Mt 27:32; Lk 23:26.
15:22–38 Mt 27:33–51; Lk 23:32–46; Jn 19:17–30.
15:24 Ps 22:18.
15:27 Lk 23:33.
15:29 Jn 2:19.
15:32 Lk 23:39.
15:34 Ps 22:2.

Cultural Connection

We Were There

According to Mark 15:21, the Roman soldiers compelled a North African black man from Cyrene by the name of Simon, a passerby, to carry the cross of Jesus. We do not know anything more about Simon of Cyrene, except that Mark identifies him as the father of Alexander and Rufus. The reference to Simon's sons by name and the possibility that Rufus is the same person Paul greets in Romans 16:13 indicate that they were known among the early Christians. This is significant for African Americans because it is evidence of the prominence and influence of African people in the early Christian Church.

African people were there from the beginning of Christianity (see also Acts 8:26–40). They were not latecomers to the Christian faith. Thank God, somebody always remembers! African Americans and other people who have experienced oppression are in danger of forgetting who they are and where they come from—not because they are forgetful peoples, but because the oppressors have tried to erase their culture and identity to cripple and control them. Yet despite all this, somebody always remembers.

We praise you, God, for having African people there to minister to Jesus in his time of need. We praise you in knowing that people of all races will be with you at the end. Hallelujah. Amen!

Mk 15:21

MK

my God, why have you forsaken me?" 35† Some of the bystanders who heard it said, "Look, he is calling Elijah." 36 One of them ran, soaked a sponge with wine, put it on a reed, and gave it to him to drink, saying, "Wait, let us see if Elijah comes to take him down." 37 Jesus gave a loud cry and breathed his last. 38† The veil of the sanctuary was torn in two from top to bottom. 39*† When the centurion who stood facing him saw how he breathed his last he said, "Truly this man was the Son of God!" 40*† There were also women looking on from a distance. Among them were Mary Magdalene, Mary the mother of the younger James and of Joses, and Salome. 41 These women had followed him when he was in Galilee and ministered to him. There were also many other women who had come up with him to Jerusalem.

The Burial of Jesus

42* When it was already evening, since it was the day of preparation, the day before the sabbath, 43† Joseph of Arimathea, a distinguished member of the council, who was himself awaiting the kingdom of God, came and courageously went to Pilate and asked for the body of Jesus. 44 Pilate was amazed that he was already dead. He summoned the centurion and asked him if Jesus had already died. 45 And when he learned of it from the centurion, he gave the body to Joseph. 46 Having bought a linen cloth, he took him down, wrapped him in the linen cloth and laid him in a tomb that had been hewn out of the rock. Then he rolled a stone against the entrance to the tomb. 47 Mary Magdalene and Mary the mother of Joses watched where he was laid.

The Resurrection of Jesus

16 1*† When the sabbath was over, Mary Magdalene, Mary, the mother of James, and Salome bought spices so that they might go and anoint him.* 2 Very early when the sun had risen, on the first day of the week, they came to

†

15:35 *Elijah:* a verbal link with *Eloi* (34). See the note on 9:9–13; cf Mal 3:23–24. See also the note on Mt 27:47.

15:38 See the note on Mt 27:51–53.

15:39 The closing portion of Mark's gospel returns to the theme of its beginning in the Gentile centurion's climactic declaration of belief that Jesus *was the Son of God.* It indicates the fulfillment of the good news announced in the prologue (1:1) and may be regarded as the firstfruit of the passion and death of Jesus.

15:40–41 See the note on Mt 27:55–56.

15:43 *Joseph of Arimathea:* see the note on Mt 27:57–61.

16:1–8 The purpose of this narrative is to show that the tomb is empty and that Jesus *has been raised* (6) and *is going before you to Galilee* (7) in fulfillment of 14:28. The women find the tomb empty, and an angel stationed there announces to them what has happened. They are told to proclaim the news to Peter and the disciples in order to prepare them for a reunion with him. Mark's composition of the gospel ends at v 8 with the women telling no one, because they were afraid. This abrupt termination causes some to believe that the original ending of this gospel may have been lost. See the following note.

*

15:39–41 Mt 27:54–56; Lk 23:47–49.
15:40 Mk 6:3; Lk 8:2–3.
15:42–47 Mt 27:57–61; Lk 23:50–56; Jn 19:38–42.
16:1–8 Mt 28:1–8; Lk 24:1–10; Jn 20:1–10.
16:1–2 Mt 28:1; Lk 23:56.

the tomb. 3 They were saying to one another,
"Who will roll back the stone for us from the
entrance to the tomb?" 4 When they looked up,
they saw that the stone had been rolled back; it
was very large. 5* On entering the tomb they saw
a young man sitting on the right side, clothed in
a white robe, and they were utterly amazed. 6 He
said to them, "Do not be amazed! You seek Jesus
of Nazareth, the crucified. He has been raised;
he is not here. Behold, the place where they laid
him. 7* But go and tell his disciples and Peter,
'He is going before you to Galilee; there you will
see him, as he told you.' " 8 Then they went out
and fled from the tomb, seized with trembling
and bewilderment. They said nothing to anyone,
for they were afraid.

The Longer Ending

The Appearance to Mary Magdalene

[9*† When he had risen, early on the first day
of the week, he appeared first to Mary Magda-
lene, out of whom he had driven seven demons.
10* She went and told his companions who were

† **16:9–20** This passage, termed the Longer Ending to the Marcan gospel by comparison with a much briefer conclusion found in some less important manuscripts, has traditionally been accepted as a canonical part of the gospel and was defined as such by the Council of Trent. Early citations of it by the Fathers indicate that it was composed by the second century, although vocabulary and style indicate that it was written by someone other than Mark. It is a general resume

16:5 Jn 20:12. **16:7** Mk 14:28. **16:9–20** Mt 28:1–10; Jn 20:11–18. **16:10–11** Lk 24:10–11; Jn 20:18.

MK

Live It!

Alone!

Have you ever felt lost, afraid, or abandoned? Sometimes, we may actually be physically lost or abandoned, but more often these feelings are deeply emotional or spiritual as we struggle to find our way, feeling that there is no one in our lives who can fully help and support us.

Jesus may have had similar feelings. He may have felt lost, and he may have felt completely abandoned by his friends and even by God. He had to face his death alone. Can you imagine anything more lonely? His prayers did not change his circumstances but gave him a way to lament, to cry out to God to express his distress.

What makes you the most lonely and afraid? What is it like to be abandoned? In these situations of distress, it is always okay to lament. Crying out does not always change our circumstances, but it can help to remind us that we are not truly alone—God is with us.

▶ **Mk 15:33–34**

Live It!

Jesus Strengthens Our Faith

A group of faithful women accompany Jesus from afar when he dies on the cross, and they look to see where he is buried (see Mk 15:40–47). They are witnesses to the terrible violence of Jesus' death. Two days later, after the Sabbath, three of the women go to the tomb to anoint Jesus' body, giving him a proper burial. When they receive the news that Jesus is alive, they flee from the tomb terrified and amazed.

This is where the original Gospel of Mark ends. Immediately we want to ask lots of questions. What happened to the disciples? Did they go to Galilee? How did the word get out that Jesus had risen from the dead? Apparently, early Christians found this abrupt ending troublesome, so they added other endings similar to those of the other Gospels.

These additions, starting at Mark 16:9, emphasize the surprise of the disciples. It seems as if they are paralyzed. Only a strong scolding by Jesus and being commissioned to proclaim the Good News to the whole creation brings them around.

How do doubts and confusion paralyze you in living your faith? Pay attention to Jesus! Hear his voice! He is telling you to carry his message of love to other people. By doing so, you will strengthen your faith, and your life will be full of joy!

▶ **Mk 16:1–20**

Catholic Connection

Faith and Reason

When we hear a person make some incredible claim on television, we often want to see proof that the claim is true. This was also the case for the disciples after Jesus rose from the dead. Some saw the risen Lord and believed, but others refused to believe because they had not witnessed the risen Lord with their own eyes (see Mk 16:9–12). Jesus scolds these disciples for their lack of faith (see verse 14). If the disciples who were with Jesus throughout his ministry were slow to believe, how difficult then would it be for the rest of the world to believe? Perhaps that is why Mark's Gospel concludes by saying that Jesus himself confirms the message of the Good News with signs like healings and miracles.

Although that is the end of Mark's Gospel, the story has fortunately continued for over two thousand years. Countless people have come to faith in Jesus Christ through the ongoing preaching of the Good News and the signs that confirm Christ's message. Through this combination of the message and signs, we begin to see the natural relationship that exists between faith and reason.

To understand this relationship, we must begin by examining the Church's understanding of faith. First and foremost, faith is a gift from God. Through God's grace and the help of the Holy Spirit, our heart is turned toward God. Through this change, God then opens our minds so that we may accept and believe the truth. We too play an active role in receiving the gift of faith by welcoming God's grace and accepting the truth.

Our acceptance of the truth is not by blind faith; it involves our use of reason. And because God created everything, including both faith and reason, he did not create them to contradict one another but to work together to arrive at the truth. Therefore, God provides external proofs like the signs and miracles mentioned in the Gospel. But God also provides other more ordinary proofs like the existence and growth of the Church or the daily lives of saints and people of faith.

When our faith and reason work together, an interesting thing can occur. Our faith leads us to desire and know God better, so we then use our reason to learn more about God. Once we learn more about God, our faith is deepened and we then desire to know God even more! The use of faith and reason becomes a never ending circle that continues to draw us closer and closer to the God who we love and who loves us.

▶ **Mk 16:20**

Catechism, nos. 156–159

MK

mourning and weeping. 11 When they heard that
he was alive and had been seen by her, they did
not believe.

The Appearance to Two Disciples

12* After this he appeared in another form to
two of them walking along on their way to the
country. 13 They returned and told the others; but
they did not believe them either.

The Commissioning of the Eleven

14* [But] later, as the eleven were at table, he
appeared to them and rebuked them for their un-
belief and hardness of heart because they had not
believed those who saw him after he had been
raised. 15* He said to them, "Go into the whole
world and proclaim the gospel to every creature.
16 Whoever believes and is baptized will be saved;
whoever does not believe will be condemned.
17 These signs will accompany those who believe:
in my name they will drive out demons, they
will speak new languages. 18* They will pick up
serpents [with their hands], and if they drink any
deadly thing, it will not harm them. They will lay
hands on the sick, and they will recover."

The Ascension of Jesus

19* So then the Lord Jesus, after he spoke to
them, was taken up into heaven and took his seat
at the right hand of God. 20* But they went forth
and preached everywhere, while the Lord worked
with them and confirmed the word through ac-
companying signs.]

The Shorter Ending

[And they reported all the instructions briefly to Peter's companions. Afterwards Jesus himself, through them, sent forth from east to west the sacred and imperishable proclamation of eternal salvation. Amen.]

† of the material concerning the appearances of the risen Jesus, reflecting, in particular, traditions found in Luke (24) and John (20).

The Freer Logion: Found after v 14 in a fourth-fifth century manuscript preserved in the Freer Gallery of Art, Washington, DC, this ending was known to Jerome in the fourth century. It reads: "And they excused themselves, saying, 'This age of lawlessness and unbelief is under Satan, who does not allow the truth and power of God to prevail over the unclean things dominated by the spirits [or, does not allow the unclean things dominated by the spirits to grasp the truth and power of God]. Therefore reveal your righteousness now.' They spoke to Christ. And Christ responded to them, 'The limit of the years of Satan's power is completed, but other terrible things draw near. And for those who sinned I was handed over to death, that they might return to the truth and no longer sin, in order that they might inherit the spiritual and incorruptible heavenly glory of righteousness. But . . . .' "

16:20 The Shorter Ending: Found after v 8 before the Longer Ending in four seventh-to-ninth-century Greek manuscripts as well as in one Old Latin version, where it appears alone without the Longer Ending.

* **16:12–14** Lk 24:13–35. **16:14** Lk 24:36–49; 1 Cor 15:5. **16:15–16** Mk 13:10; Mt 28:18–20; Lk 24:47; Jn 20:21. **16:18** Mt 10:1; Lk 10:19; Acts 28:3–6. **16:19** Lk 24:50–53. **16:20** 1 Tm 3:16.

The Gospel According to Luke

Black and white. Male and female. Rich and poor. In our world today, we often divide ourselves into distinct categories instead of focusing on what unites us. These divisions can lead to discrimination, inequality, and injustice as one group is considered "less than" another. In the Gospel of Luke, Jesus asserts that such divisions have no place in the Kingdom of God. Outcasts, sinners, women, those who are poor—all are compassionately welcomed to be disciples.

At a Glance

I. The Prologue (1:1–4).
II. The Infancy Narrative (1:5—2:52).
III. The Preparation for the Public Ministry (3:1—4:13).
IV. The Ministry in Galilee (4:14—9:50).
V. The Journey to Jerusalem: Luke's Travel Narrative (9:51—19:27).
VI. The Teaching Ministry in Jerusalem (19:28—21:38).
VII. The Passion Narrative (22:1—23:56).
VIII. The Resurrection Narrative (24:1–53).

Quick Facts

Inspired Author: a Gentile Christian named Luke, traditionally thought to be a disciple of Paul (see Col 4:14)

Date Written: from approximately AD 80 to 90

Audience: Gentile (Greek) Christians represented by Theophilus (see Lk 1:3)

Of Note: Luke also wrote the Acts of the Apostles.

Image of Jesus: merciful, compassionate, with a special concern for poor people, women, and non-Jews

In Depth

The author of the Gospel of Luke was a Gentile (non-Jewish) convert to Christianity. So one of Luke's important concerns is to show how Gentiles came to be included in God's plan of salvation and among God's elect, which first belonged to the Jews alone. In Luke's Gospel, Jesus praises the faith of a centurion (see 7:1–10), who is a Gentile. Jesus also makes a Samaritan (Samaritans were considered foreigners by other Jews) the hero of a parable (see 10:25–37).

Other in-groups for Jesus in Luke's Gospel are women and poor people. Most women had little status in society at the time. But Luke includes many stories about women, including Mary's visit to her cousin Elizabeth before the births of their sons, Jesus and John the Baptist (see 1:39–66). This Gospel also shows how Jesus loved the poor and scolded the rich for their lack of concern for the poor. For example, it includes a story about a poor man named Lazarus, who begged for food at a rich man's door. God honored Lazarus with a special place in Abraham's bosom (Heaven) when he died (see 16:19–31), whereas the rich man suffered in Hades.

Finally, Luke's Gospel shows Jesus' compassion and forgiveness for outcasts and sinners. It includes stories about the tax collector Zacchaeus, who climbs a tree to see Jesus (see 19:1–10), the good Samaritan (see 10:25–37), and the penitent sinner who was crucified beside Jesus (see 23:39–43). In the Gospel of Luke, Jesus is also the prophet par excellence who will be rejected by his own people (see 4:16–30). The Gospel presents a vivid picture of how Jesus made the Reign of God present, inspiring his disciples to take the Gospel message to other lands and cultures.

Luke

2:6–7

I: The Prologue

1 1*† Since many have undertaken to compile a
narrative of the events that have been fulfilled
among us, 2* just as those who were eyewitnesses
from the beginning and ministers of the word have
handed them down to us, 3 I too have decided,
after investigating everything accurately anew, to
write it down in an orderly sequence for you, most
excellent Theophilus, 4 so that you may realize the
certainty of the teachings you have received.

II: The Infancy Narrative†

Announcement of the Birth of John

5* In the days of Herod, King of Judea,† there
was a priest named Zechariah of the priestly divi-
sion of Abijah; his wife was from the daughters
of Aaron, and her name was Elizabeth. 6 Both
were righteous in the eyes of God, observing all
the commandments and ordinances of the Lord
blamelessly. 7*† But they had no child, because
Elizabeth was barren and both were advanced in

†

1:1–4 The Gospel according to Luke is the only one of the synoptic gospels to begin with a literary prologue. Making use of a formal, literary construction and vocabulary, the author writes the prologue in imitation of Hellenistic Greek writers and, in so doing, relates his story about Jesus to contemporaneous Greek and Roman literature. Luke is not only interested in the words and deeds of Jesus, but also in the larger context of the birth, ministry, death, and resurrection of Jesus as the fulfillment of the promises of God in the Old Testament. As a second- or third-generation Christian, Luke acknowledges his debt to earlier *eyewitnesses* and *ministers of the word,* but claims that his contribution to this developing tradition is a complete and accurate account, told in an orderly manner, and intended to provide *Theophilus* ("friend of God," literally) and other readers with certainty about earlier teachings they have received.

1:5—2:52 Like the Gospel according to Matthew, this gospel opens with an infancy narrative, a collection of stories about the birth and childhood of Jesus. The narrative uses early Christian traditions about the birth of Jesus, traditions about the birth and circumcision of John the Baptist, and canticles such as the Magnificat (1:46–55) and Benedictus (1:67–79), composed of phrases drawn from the Greek Old Testament. It is largely, however, the composition of Luke who writes in imitation of Old Testament birth stories, combining historical and legendary details, literary ornamentation and interpretation of scripture, to answer in advance the question, "Who is Jesus Christ?" The focus of the narrative, therefore, is primarily christological. In this section Luke announces many of the themes that will become prominent in the rest of the gospel: the centrality of Jerusalem and the temple, the journey motif, the universality of salvation, joy and peace, concern for the lowly, the importance of women, the presentation of Jesus as savior, Spirit-guided revelation and prophecy, and the fulfillment of Old Testament promises. The account presents parallel scenes (diptychs) of angelic announcements of the birth of John the Baptist and of Jesus, and of the birth, circumcision, and presentation of John and Jesus. In this parallelism, the ascendency of Jesus over John is stressed: John is prophet of the Most High (1:76); Jesus is Son of the Most High (1:32). John is great in the sight of the Lord (1:15); Jesus will be Great (a LXX attribute, used absolutely, of God) (1:32). John will go before the Lord (1:16–17); Jesus will be Lord (1:43; 2:11).

1:5 *In the days of Herod, King of Judea:* Luke relates the story of salvation history to events in contemporary world history. Here and in 3:1–2, he connects his narrative with events in Palestinian history; in 2:1–2 and 3:1, he casts the Jesus story in the light of events of Roman history. Herod the Great, the son of the Idumean Antipater, was declared "King of Judea" by the Roman Senate in 40 B.C., but became the undisputed ruler of Palestine only in 37 B.C. He continued as king until his death in 4 B.C. *Priestly division of Abijah:* a reference to the eighth of the twenty-four divisions of priests who, for a week at a time, twice a year, served in the Jerusalem temple.

1:7 *They had no child:* though childlessness was looked upon in contemporaneous Judaism as a curse or punishment for sin, it is intended here to present Elizabeth in a situation similar to that of some of the great mothers of important Old Testament figures: Sarah (Gn 15:3; 16:1); Rebekah (Gn 25:21); Rachel (Gn 29:31; 30:1); the mother of Samson and wife of Manoah (Jgs 13:2–3); Hannah (1 Sm 1:2).

*

1:1–4 Acts 1:1; 1 Cor 15:3.
1:2 Lk 24:48; Jn 15:27; Acts 1:21–22.
1:5 1 Chr 24:10.
1:7 Gn 18:11; Jgs 13:2–5; 1 Sm 1:5–6.

years. [8] Once when he was serving as priest in his
division's turn before God, [9]* according to the
practice of the priestly service, he was chosen by
lot to enter the sanctuary of the Lord to burn in-
cense. [10] Then, when the whole assembly of the
people was praying outside at the hour of the in-
cense offering, [11] the angel of the Lord appeared
to him, standing at the right of the altar of in-
cense. [12] Zechariah was troubled by what he saw,
and fear came upon him. [13]*† But the angel said
to him, "Do not be afraid, Zechariah, because
your prayer has been heard. Your wife Elizabeth
will bear you a son, and you shall name him
John. [14] And you will have joy and gladness, and
many will rejoice at his birth, [15]*† for he will be
great in the sight of [the] Lord. He will drink nei-
ther wine nor strong drink. He will be filled with
the holy Spirit even from his mother's womb,
[16] and he will turn many of the children of Israel
to the Lord their God. [17]*† He will go before
him in the spirit and power of Elijah to turn the
hearts of fathers toward children and the disobe-
dient to the understanding of the righteous, to
prepare a people fit for the Lord." [18] Then Zech-
ariah said to the angel, "How shall I know this?
For I am an old man, and my wife is advanced
in years." [19]*† And the angel said to him in re-
ply, "I am Gabriel, who stand before God. I was
sent to speak to you and to announce to you this
good news. [20]*† But now you will be speechless
and unable to talk until the day these things take
place, because you did not believe my words,
which will be fulfilled at their proper time."
[21] Meanwhile the people were waiting for Zech-
ariah and were amazed that he stayed so long in
the sanctuary. [22] But when he came out, he was
unable to speak to them, and they realized that
he had seen a vision in the sanctuary. He was
gesturing to them but remained mute. [23] Then,
when his days of ministry were completed, he
went home. [24] After this time his wife Elizabeth
conceived, and she went into seclusion for five

Introducing...

Mary of Nazareth

Luke's Gospel makes it clear that Mary of Nazareth has a special place in God's plan of salvation. Beginning with Mary's humble acceptance of God's will revealed by the angel Gabriel (see Lk 1:26–38), Mary is presented as the true, first disciple who does the will of God. Her yes to God leads to Jesus' presence among us. She follows Jesus to the cross and is with the disciples in the upper room during the coming of the Holy Spirit (see Acts 1:14). Mary reveals to us the meaning of true faith—a willingness to accept God's call and to gradually discover the full meaning of God's will.

In choosing Mary to be the mother of Jesus, God selects not a rich queen but a poor young girl open to the action of the Holy Spirit in her life. In Mary, Luke emphasizes God's preference for the poor and the little ones (see "The *Magnificat*: The Prayer of the Poor" near Lk 1:39–56).

Besides being the mother of Jesus, Mary is presented in the Bible as the mother of the Church (see Jn 19:25–27). For this reason, Catholic Christians have a special devotion to Mary. They celebrate her virginal conception of Jesus on the feast of the Annunciation (March 25). They believe Mary was born free from original sin, and they celebrate this on the feast of the Immaculate Conception (December 8). They also believe she was taken into heaven, body and soul, at the end of her life, and they celebrate this on the feast of the Assumption (August 15). Catholics also have a special prayer form honoring Mary, called the rosary.

▶ Lk 1:26–56

†

1:13 *Do not be afraid:* a stereotyped Old Testament phrase spoken to reassure the recipient of a heavenly vision (Gn 15:1; Jos 1:9; Dn 10:12, 19 and elsewhere in 1:30; 2:10). *You shall name him John:* the name means "Yahweh has shown favor," an indication of John's role in salvation history.

1:15 *He will drink neither wine nor strong drink:* like Samson (Jgs 13:4–5) and Samuel (1 Sm 1:11 LXX and 4QSam^{a}), John is to be consecrated by Nazirite vow and set apart for the Lord's service.

1:17 *He will go before him in the spirit and power of Elijah:* John is to be the messenger sent before Yahweh, as described in Mal 3:1–2. He is cast, moreover, in the role of the Old Testament fiery reformer, the prophet Elijah, who according to Mal 3:23 (4:5) is sent before "the great and terrible day of the Lord comes."

1:19 *I am Gabriel:* "the angel of the Lord" is identified as Gabriel, the angel who in Dn 9:20–25 announces the seventy weeks of years and the coming of an anointed one, a prince. By alluding to Old Testament themes in vv 17 and 19, such as the coming of the day of the Lord and the dawning of the messianic era, Luke is presenting his interpretation of the significance of the births of John and Jesus.

1:20 *You will be speechless and unable to talk:* Zechariah's becoming mute is the sign given in response to his question in v 18. When Mary asks a similar question in 1:34, unlike Zechariah who was punished for his doubt, she, in spite of her doubt, is praised and reassured (35–37).

*

1:9 Ex 30:7.
1:13 Lk 1:57, 60, 63; Mt 1:20–21.
1:15 Lk 7:33; Nm 6:1–21; Jgs 13:4; 1 Sm 1:11 LXX.
1:17 Sir 48:10; Mal 3:1; 3:23–24; Mt 11:14; 17:11–13.
1:19 Dn 8:16; 9:21.
1:20 Lk 1:45.

Cultural Connection

The *Magnificat*: The Prayer of the Poor

Mary gives a testimony of her faith right after she receives the news that she will be the mother of God. During her visit to her cousin Elizabeth, she sings of God's salvation in a song known as the *Magnificat*, which means "[my soul] praises." This prayer is mainly made up of verses taken from the Psalms and the prophets. Mary first sings of her salvation; then she sings of God's salvation brought to the humble, the poor, and the hungry; and she finishes by singing of the salvation brought to all the people of God as promised to Abraham.

The *Magnificat* is an important prayer for Hispanic people. It is the song of the poor of God, those who expected salvation from God, not from people in power or through wars and conquests. The social consequences of God's salvation are clearly revealed in Mary's song. The prayer is directed to God and talks about God's care for the poor. Jesus is the one who acts as God's agent, accomplishing these things on God's behalf; he raises up the lowly and brings down the powerful to build the Reign of God.

- In a world marked by huge gaps between rich people and poor people, is it clear that Christians are in solidarity with the poor?
- How are you helping the poor now, and how are you planning to do so as an adult?
- Pray the *Magnificat* slowly, savoring what it says, letting it move to the core of your heart.

▶ Lk 1:39–56

months, saying, 25* "So has the Lord done for me
at a time when he has seen fit to take away my
disgrace before others."

Announcement of the Birth of Jesus

26† In the sixth month, the angel Gabriel was
sent from God to a town of Galilee called Naz-
areth, 27* to a virgin betrothed to a man named
Joseph, of the house of David, and the virgin's
name was Mary. 28* And coming to her, he said,
"Hail, favored one! The Lord is with you." 29 But
she was greatly troubled at what was said and
pondered what sort of greeting this might be.
30 Then the angel said to her, "Do not be afraid,
Mary, for you have found favor with God. 31* Be-
hold, you will conceive in your womb and bear
a son, and you shall name him Jesus. 32*† He
will be great and will be called Son of the Most
High, and the Lord God will give him the throne
of David his father, 33* and he will rule over the
house of Jacob forever, and of his kingdom there
will be no end." 34† But Mary said to the angel,
"How can this be, since I have no relations with a
man?" 35* And the angel said to her in reply, "The
holy Spirit will come upon you, and the power
of the Most High will overshadow you. Therefore
the child to be born will be called holy, the Son
of God. 36† And behold, Elizabeth, your relative,
has also conceived a son in her old age, and this
is the sixth month for her who was called bar-
ren; 37* for nothing will be impossible for God."
38 Mary said, "Behold, I am the handmaid of the
Lord. May it be done to me according to your
word." Then the angel departed from her.

Mary Visits Elizabeth

39 During those days Mary set out and trav-
eled to the hill country in haste to a town of

†

1:26–38 The announcement to Mary of the birth of Jesus is parallel to the announcement to Zechariah of the birth of John. In both the angel Gabriel appears to the parent who is troubled by the vision (11–12, 26–29) and then told by the angel not to fear (13, 30). After the announcement is made (14–17, 31–33) the parent objects (18, 34) and a sign is given to confirm the announcement (20, 36). The particular focus of the announcement of the birth of Jesus is on his identity as Son of David (32–33) and Son of God (32, 35).

1:32 *Son of the Most High:* cf 1:76 where John is described as "prophet of the Most High." "Most High" is a title for God commonly used by Luke (35, 76; 6:35; 8:28; Acts 7:48; 16:17).

1:34 Mary's questioning response is a denial of sexual relations and is used by Luke to lead to the angel's declaration about the Spirit's role in the conception of this child (35). According to Luke, the virginal conception of Jesus takes place through the holy Spirit, the power of God, and therefore Jesus has a unique relationship to Yahweh: he is Son of God.

1:36–37 The sign given to Mary in confirmation of the angel's announcement to her is the pregnancy of her aged relative Elizabeth. If a woman past the childbearing age could become pregnant, why, the angel implies, should there be doubt about Mary's pregnancy, for *nothing will be impossible for God.*

*

1:25 Gn 30:23.
1:27 Lk 2:5; Mt 1:16, 18.
1:28 Jgs 6:12; Ru 2:4; Jdt 13:18.
1:31 Gn 16:11; Jgs 13:3; Is 7:14; Mt 1:21–23.
1:32–33 2 Sm 7:12, 13, 16; Is 9:7.
1:33 Dn 2:44; 7:14; Mi 4:7; Mt 28:18.
1:35 Mt 1:20.
1:37 Gn 18:14; Jer 32:27; Mt 19:26.

Judah, 40 where she entered the house of Zecha-
riah and greeted Elizabeth. 41* When Elizabeth
heard Mary's greeting, the infant leaped in her
womb, and Elizabeth, filled with the holy Spirit,
42* cried out in a loud voice and said, "Most
blessed are you among women, and blessed
is the fruit of your womb. 43† And how does
this happen to me, that the mother of my Lord
should come to me? 44 For at the moment the
sound of your greeting reached my ears, the
infant in my womb leaped for joy. 45*† Blessed
are you who believed that what was spoken to
you by the Lord would be fulfilled."

The Canticle of Mary

46*† And Mary said:

"My soul proclaims the greatness of the
Lord;*
47* my spirit rejoices in God my savior.
48* For he has looked upon his handmaid's
lowliness;
behold, from now on will all ages call me
blessed.
49* The Mighty One has done great things
for me,
and holy is his name.
50* His mercy is from age to age
to those who fear him.
51* He has shown might with his arm,
dispersed the arrogant of mind and
heart.
52* He has thrown down the rulers from their
thrones
but lifted up the lowly.
53* The hungry he has filled with good things;
the rich he has sent away empty.
54* He has helped Israel his servant,
remembering his mercy,
55* according to his promise to our fathers,
to Abraham and to his descendants
forever."

56 Mary remained with her about three months
and then returned to her home.

The Birth of John

57† When the time arrived for Elizabeth to
have her child she gave birth to a son. 58* Her
neighbors and relatives heard that the Lord had
shown his great mercy toward her, and they re-
joiced with her. 59*† When they came on the
eighth day to circumcise the child, they were
going to call him Zechariah after his father,
60* but his mother said in reply, "No. He will
be called John." 61 But they answered her, "There
is no one among your relatives who has this
name." 62 So they made signs, asking his father
what he wished him to be called. 63 He asked for
a tablet and wrote, "John is his name," and all
were amazed. 64* Immediately his mouth was
opened, his tongue freed, and he spoke blessing
God. 65 Then fear came upon all their neighbors,
and all these matters were discussed throughout
the hill country of Judea. 66 All who heard these
things took them to heart, saying, "What, then,
will this child be?" For surely the hand of the
Lord was with him.

The Canticle of Zechariah

67 Then Zechariah his father, filled with the
holy Spirit, prophesied, saying:

†

1:43 Even before his birth, Jesus is identified in Luke as the Lord.

1:45 *Blessed are you who believed:* Luke portrays Mary as a believer whose faith stands in contrast to the disbelief of Zechariah (20). Mary's role as believer in the infancy narrative should be seen in connection with the explicit mention of her presence among "those who believed" after the resurrection at the beginning of the Acts of the Apostles (1:14).

1:46–55 Although Mary is praised for being the mother of the Lord and because of her belief, she reacts as the servant in a psalm of praise, the Magnificat. Because there is no specific connection of the canticle to the context of Mary's pregnancy and her visit to Elizabeth, the Magnificat (with the possible exception of v 48) may have been a Jewish Christian hymn that Luke found appropriate at this point in his story. Even if not composed by Luke, it fits in well with themes found elsewhere in Luke: joy and exultation in the Lord; the lowly being singled out for God's favor; the reversal of human fortunes; the fulfillment of Old Testament promises. The loose connection between the hymn and the context is further seen in the fact that a few Old Latin manuscripts identify the speaker of the hymn as Elizabeth, even though the overwhelming textual evidence makes Mary the speaker.

1:57–66 The birth and circumcision of John above all emphasize John's incorporation into the people of Israel by the sign of the covenant (Gn 17:1–12). The narrative of John's circumcision also prepares the way for the subsequent description of the circumcision of Jesus in 2:21. At the beginning of his two-volume work Luke shows those who play crucial roles in the inauguration of Christianity to be wholly a part of the people of Israel. At the end of the Acts of the Apostles (21:20; 22:3; 23:6–9; 24:14–16; 26:2–8, 22–23) he will argue that Christianity is the direct descendant of Pharisaic Judaism.

1:59 The practice of Palestinian Judaism at this time was to name the child at birth; moreover, though naming a male child after the father is not completely unknown, the usual practice was to name the child after the grandfather (see 61). The naming of the child John and Zechariah's recovery from his loss of speech should be understood as fulfilling the angel's announcement to Zechariah in 1:13 and 20.

*

1:41 Lk 1:15; Gn 25:22 LXX.
1:42 Lk 11:27–28; Jgs 5:24; Jdt 13:18; Dt 28:4.
1:45 Lk 1:20.
1:46–55 1 Sm 2:1–10.
1:46 Ps 35:9; Is 61:10; Hb 3:18.
1:47 Ti 3:4; Jude 25.
1:48 Lk 11:27; 1 Sm 1:11; 2 Sm 16:12; 2 Kgs 14:26; Ps 113:7.
1:49 Dt 10:21; Pss 71:19; 111:9; 126:2–3.
1:50 Pss 89:2; 103:13, 17.
1:51 Pss 89:10; 118:15; Jer 32:17 (39:17 LXX).
1:52 1 Sm 2:7; 2 Sm 22:28; Jb 5:11; 12:19; Ps 147:6; Sir 10:14; Jas 4:6; 1 Pt 5:5.
1:53 1 Sm 2:5; Ps 107:9.
1:54 Ps 98:3; Is 41:8–9.
1:55 Gn 13:15; 17:7; 18:18; 22:17–18; Mi 7:20.
1:58 Lk 1:14.
1:59 Lk 2:21; Gn 17:10, 12; Lv 12:3.
1:60 Lk 1:13.
1:64 Lk 1:20.

68*† "Blessed be the Lord, the God of Israel,
for he has visited and brought redemption
to his people.
69*† He has raised up a horn for our salvation
within the house of David his servant,
70 even as he promised through the mouth of
his holy prophets from of old:
71* salvation from our enemies and from the
hand of all who hate us,
72* to show mercy to our fathers
and to be mindful of his holy covenant*
73* and of the oath he swore to Abraham our
father,
and to grant us that, 74 rescued from the
hand of enemies,
without fear we might worship him 75* in
holiness and righteousness
before him all our days.
76*† And you, child, will be called prophet of the
Most High,
for you will go before the Lord to prepare
his ways,
77 to give his people knowledge of salvation
through the forgiveness of their sins,
78*† because of the tender mercy of our God
by which the daybreak from on high will
visit us*
79 to shine on those who sit in darkness and
death's shadow,
to guide our feet into the path of peace."

80* The child grew and became strong in spirit,
and he was in the desert until the day of his man-
ifestation to Israel.

The Birth of Jesus

2 1† In those days a decree went out from Cae-
sar Augustus† that the whole world should
be enrolled. 2 This was the first enrollment, when
Quirinius was governor of Syria. 3 So all went to be
enrolled, each to his own town. 4* And Joseph too
went up from Galilee from the town of Nazareth
to Judea, to the city of David that is called Bethle-
hem, because he was of the house and family of
David, 5* to be enrolled with Mary, his betrothed,
who was with child. 6 While they were there, the
time came for her to have her child, 7*† and she
gave birth to her firstborn son. She wrapped him
in swaddling clothes and laid him in a manger,
because there was no room for them in the inn.
8† Now there were shepherds in that region
living in the fields and keeping the night watch
over their flock. 9* The angel of the Lord ap-
peared to them and the glory of the Lord shone

†

1:68–79 Like the canticle of Mary (46–55) the canticle of Zechariah is only loosely connected with its context. Apart from vv 76–77, the hymn in speaking of *a horn for our salvation* (69) and *the daybreak from on high* (78) applies more closely to Jesus and his work than to John. Again like Mary's canticle, it is largely composed of phrases taken from the Greek Old Testament and may have been a Jewish Christian hymn of praise that Luke adapted to fit the present context by inserting vv 76–77 to give Zechariah's reply to the question asked in v 66.

1:69 *A horn for our salvation:* the horn is a common Old Testament figure for strength (Pss 18:3; 75:5–6; 89:18; 112:9; 148:14). This description is applied to God in Ps 18:3 and is here transferred to Jesus. The connection of the phrase with *the house of David* gives the title messianic overtones and may indicate an allusion to a phrase in Hannah's song of praise (1 Sm 2:10), "the horn of his anointed."

1:76 *You will go before the Lord:* here *the Lord* is most likely a reference to Jesus (contrast 15–17 where *Yahweh* is meant) and John is presented as the precursor of Jesus.

1:78 *The daybreak from on high:* three times in the LXX (Jer 23:5; Zec 3:8; 6:12), the Greek word used here for *daybreak* translates the Hebrew word for "scion, branch," an Old Testament messianic title.

2:1–2 Although universal registrations of Roman citizens are attested in 28 B.C., 8 B.C., and A.D. 14 and enrollments in individual provinces of those who are not Roman citizens are also attested, such a universal census of the Roman world under Caesar Augustus is unknown outside the New Testament. Moreover, there are notorious historical problems connected with Luke's dating the census *when Quirinius was governor of Syria,* and the various attempts to resolve the difficulties have proved unsuccessful. P. Sulpicius Quirinius became legate of the province of Syria in A.D. 6–7 when Judea was annexed to the province of Syria. At that time, a provincial census of Judea was taken up. If Quirinius had been legate of Syria previously, it would have to have been before 10 B.C. because the various legates of Syria from 10 B.C. to 4 B.C. (the death of Herod) are known, and such a dating for an earlier census under Quirinius would create additional problems for dating the beginning of Jesus' ministry (3:1, 23). A previous legateship after 4 B.C. (and before A.D. 6) would not fit with the dating of Jesus' birth in the days of Herod (1:5; Mt 2:1). Luke may simply be combining Jesus' birth in Bethlehem with his vague recollection of a census under Quirinius (see also Acts 5:37) to underline the significance of this birth for the whole Roman world: through this child born in Bethlehem peace and salvation come to the empire.

2:1 *Caesar Augustus:* the reign of the Roman emperor Caesar Augustus is usually dated from 27 B.C. to his death in A.D. 14. According to Greek inscriptions, Augustus was regarded in the Roman Empire as "savior" and "god," and he was credited with establishing a time of peace, the *pax Augusta,* throughout the Roman world during his long reign. It is not by chance that Luke relates the birth of Jesus to the time of Caesar Augustus: the real savior (11) and peace-bearer (14; see also 19:38) is the child born in Bethlehem. The great emperor is simply God's agent (like the Persian king Cyrus in Is 44:28—45:1) who provides the occasion for God's purposes to be accomplished. *The whole world:* that is, the whole Roman world: Rome, Italy, and the Roman provinces.

2:7 *Firstborn son:* the description of Jesus as *firstborn son* does not necessarily mean that Mary had other sons. It is a legal description indicating that Jesus possessed the rights and privileges of the firstborn son (Gn 27; Ex 13:2; Nm 3:12–13; 18:15–16; Dt 21:15–17). See the notes on Mt 1:25 and Mk 6:3. *Wrapped him in swaddling clothes:* there may be an allusion here to the birth of another descendant of David, his son Solomon, who though a great king was wrapped in swaddling clothes like any other infant (Wis 7:4–6). *Laid him in a manger:* a feeding trough for animals. A possible allusion to Is 1:3 LXX.

2:8–20 The annoucement of Jesus' birth to the shepherds is in keeping with Luke's theme that the lowly are singled out as the recipients of God's favors and blessings (see also 1:48, 52).

1:68 Lk 7:16; Pss 41:13; 72:18; 106:48; 111:9.
1:69 Ps 18:3.
1:71 Ps 106:10.
1:72 Ps 106:45–46.
1:72–73 Gn 17:7; Lv 26:42; Ps 105:8–9; Mi 7:20.
1:73–74 Gn 22:16–17.
1:75 Ti 2:12.
1:76 Is 40:3; Mal 3:1; Mt 3:3; 11:10.
1:78 Mal 3:20.
1:78–79 Is 60:1–2.
1:80 Lk 2:40; Mt 3:1.
2:4 Mi 5:2; Mt 2:6.
2:5 Lk 1:27; Mt 1:18.
2:7 Mt 1:25.
2:9 Lk 1:11, 26.

Cultural Connection

O Christmas Tree

Did you ever wonder where the tradition of the Christmas tree came from? It began in Germany, the country that also gave us the beautiful song "Silent Night." For hundreds of years, the Christmas tree has been the focal point and symbol of the Christmas season for the people of Germany.

In the year AD 350, Pope Julius declared December 25, which had been the day of the pagan feast of the sun god, a feast day in observance of the birth of the Son of God. Prior to AD 350, the German people had a tradition of keeping evergreen branches in the house to ward off evil spirits. This pagan tradition was exchanged for a Christian tradition of having branches in the house to symbolize the life that Jesus brought to the world. After some time, the branches themselves were exchanged for entire trees, which were brought into homes and decorated with candles. Centuries later, as the German people immigrated into North America, especially to the U.S. and Canada, they brought the lovely tradition of the Christmas tree with them.

Today, the Christmas tree is a central symbol of Christmas in the United States. Adding lights and decorations helps us to celebrate the birth of Jesus, the light of the world.

▶ Lk 2:1–14

L
K

around them, and they were struck with great
fear. 10 The angel said to them, "Do not be afraid;
for behold, I proclaim to you good news of great
joy that will be for all the people. 11*† For today
in the city of David a savior has been born for
you who is Messiah and Lord. 12 And this will be
a sign for you: you will find an infant wrapped in
swaddling clothes and lying in a manger." 13 And
suddenly there was a multitude of the heavenly
host with the angel, praising God and saying:

14*† "Glory to God in the highest
and on earth peace to those on whom his
favor rests."

The Visit of the Shepherds

15 When the angels went away from them to
heaven, the shepherds said to one another, "Let
us go, then, to Bethlehem to see this thing that
has taken place, which the Lord has made known
to us." 16 So they went in haste and found Mary
and Joseph, and the infant lying in the manger.
17 When they saw this, they made known the
message that had been told them about this
child. 18 All who heard it were amazed by what
had been told them by the shepherds. 19 And
Mary kept all these things, reflecting on them in
her heart. 20 Then the shepherds returned, glorify-
ing and praising God for all they had heard and
seen, just as it had been told to them.

The Circumcision and Naming of Jesus

21*† When eight days were completed for his
circumcision, he was named Jesus, the name
given him by the angel before he was conceived
in the womb.

2:11 The basic message of the infancy narrative is contained in the angel's announcement: this child is *savior, Messiah,* and *Lord.* Luke is the only synoptic gospel writer to use the title *savior* for Jesus (11; Acts 5:31; 13:23; see also 1:69; 19:9; Acts 4:12). As savior, Jesus is looked upon by Luke as the one who rescues humanity from sin and delivers humanity from the condition of alienation from God. The title *christos,* "Christ," is the Greek equivalent of the Hebrew *māšîah,* "Messiah," "anointed one." Among certain groups in first-century Palestinian Judaism, the title was applied to an expected royal leader from the line of David who would restore the kingdom to Israel (see Acts 1:6). The political overtones of the title are played down in Luke and instead the Messiah of the Lord (26) or the Lord's anointed is the one who now brings salvation to all humanity, Jew and Gentile (29–32). *Lord* is the most frequently used title for Jesus in Luke and Acts. In the New Testament it is also applied to Yahweh, as it is in the Old Testament. When used of Jesus it points to his transcendence and dominion over humanity.

2:14 *On earth peace to those on whom his favor rests:* the peace that results from the Christ event is for those whom God has favored with his grace. This reading is found in the oldest representatives of the Western and Alexandrian text traditions and is the preferred one; the Byzantine text tradition, on the other hand, reads: "on earth peace, good will toward men." The peace of which Luke's gospel speaks (14; 7:50; 8:48; 10:5–6; 19:38, 42; 24:36) is more than the absence of war of the *pax Augusta;* it also includes the security and well-being characteristic of peace in the Old Testament.

2:21 Just as John before him had been incorporated into the people of Israel through his circumcision, so too this child (see the note on 1:57–66).

2:11 Mt 1:21; 16:16; Jn 4:42; Acts 2:36; 5:31; Phil 2:11.
2:14 Lk 19:38.
2:21 Lk 1:31; Gn 17:12; Mt 1:21.

The Presentation in the Temple

22*† When the days were completed for their
purification† according to the law of Moses, they
took him up to Jerusalem to present him to the
Lord, 23* just as it is written in the law of the
Lord, "Every male that opens the womb shall
be consecrated to the Lord," 24 and to offer the
sacrifice of "a pair of turtledoves or two young
pigeons," in accordance with the dictate in the
law of the Lord.

25† Now there was a man in Jerusalem whose
name was Simeon. This man was righteous and
devout, awaiting the consolation of Israel, and
the holy Spirit was upon him. 26 It had been re-
vealed to him by the holy Spirit that he should
not see death before he had seen the Messiah of
the Lord. 27 He came in the Spirit into the tem-
ple; and when the parents brought in the child
Jesus to perform the custom of the law in regard
to him, 28 he took him into his arms and blessed
God, saying:

29 "Now, Master, you may let your servant go
in peace, according to your word,
30* for my eyes have seen your salvation,
31 which you prepared in sight of all the
peoples,
32* a light for revelation to the Gentiles,
and glory for your people Israel."

33 The child's father and mother were amazed
at what was said about him; 34* and Simeon
blessed them and said to Mary his mother, "Be-
hold, this child is destined for the fall and rise
of many in Israel, and to be a sign that will be
contradicted 35† (and you yourself a sword will
pierce) so that the thoughts of many hearts may

Live It!

Jesus' Birth: Good News to the Poor

On December 25, we celebrate Christmas, the birth of Jesus. We recall the moment of God's entering our world—a defining moment in the history of salvation. As Luke records the moment of the birth of the Messiah, who are the stars of the show? To whom do the angels appear to announce this remarkable event, this "good news of great joy that will be for all the people" (Lk 2:10)? the high priest? the rich and important residents of Bethlehem? No. The announcement is made to shepherds, poor workers living in the fields nearby.

Like Mary, the shepherds are people of little power and significance. Luke makes the point that sometimes what the world sees as unimportant, God honors. This is the justice of God. It is the same today. The poorest in our world, the most hidden people who have no power, hold a special place in the heart of God. And, like the shepherds, those who are poor often know God better than those who are rich or powerful by this world's standards.

This truth is a challenge but also good news for all of us, rich and poor alike. How do your attitudes and actions—even the way you celebrate Christmas—reflect God's special attention to those who are poor?

▶ Lk 2:8–20

L
K

†

2:22–40 The presentation of Jesus in the temple depicts the parents of Jesus as devout Jews, faithful observers of the law of the Lord (23, 24, 39), i.e., the law of Moses. In this respect, they are described in a fashion similar to the parents of John (1:6) and Simeon (25) and Anna (36–37).

2:22 *Their purification:* syntactically, *their* must refer to Mary and Joseph, even though the Mosaic law never mentions the purification of the husband. Recognizing the problem, some Western scribes have altered the text to read "his purification," understanding the presentation of Jesus in the temple as a form of purification; the Vulgate version has a Latin form that could be either "his" or "her." According to the Mosaic law (Lv 12:2–8), the woman who gives birth to a boy is unable for forty days to touch anything sacred or to enter the temple area by reason of her legal impurity. At the end of this period she is required to offer a year-old lamb as a burnt offering and a turtledove or young pigeon as an expiation of sin. The woman who could not afford a lamb offered instead two turtledoves or two young pigeons, as Mary does here. *They took him up to Jerusalem to present him to the Lord:* as the firstborn son (7) Jesus was consecrated to the Lord as the law required (Ex 13:2, 12), but there was no requirement that this be done at the temple. The concept of a presentation at the temple is probably derived from 1 Sm 1:24–28, where Hannah offers the child Samuel for sanctuary services. The law further stipulated (Nm 3:47–48) that the firstborn son should be redeemed by the parents through their payment of five shekels to a member of a priestly family. About this legal requirement Luke is silent.

2:25 *Awaiting the consolation of Israel:* Simeon here and later Anna who speak about the child to all who were awaiting the redemption of Jerusalem represent the hopes and expectations of faithful and devout Jews who at this time were looking forward to the restoration of God's rule in Israel. The birth of Jesus brings these hopes to fulfillment.

2:35 *(And you yourself a sword will pierce):* Mary herself will not be untouched by the various reactions to the role of Jesus (34). Her blessedness as mother of the Lord will be challenged by her son who describes true blessedness as "hearing the word of God and observing it" (8:20–21 and 11:27–28).

*

2:22–24 Lv 12:2–8. **2:23** Ex 13:2, 12. **2:30–31** Lk 3:6; Is 40:5 LXX; 52:10. **2:32** Is 42:6; 46:13; 49:6; Acts 13:47; 26:23. **2:34** Lk 12:51; Is 8:14; Jn 9:39; Rom 9:33; 1 Cor 1:23; 1 Pt 2:7–8.

be revealed." 36 There was also a prophetess,
Anna, the daughter of Phanuel, of the tribe of
Asher. She was advanced in years, having lived
seven years with her husband after her marriage,
37 and then as a widow until she was eighty-four.
She never left the temple, but worshiped night
and day with fasting and prayer. 38* And coming
forward at that very time, she gave thanks to God
and spoke about the child to all who were await-
ing the redemption of Jerusalem.

The Return to Nazareth

39* When they had fulfilled all the prescrip-
tions of the law of the Lord, they returned to
Galilee, to their own town of Nazareth. 40* The
child grew and became strong, filled with wis-
dom; and the favor of God was upon him.

The Boy Jesus in the Temple

41*† Each year his parents went to Jerusalem
for the feast of Passover, 42 and when he was
twelve years old, they went up according to festi-
val custom. 43 After they had completed its days,
as they were returning, the boy Jesus remained
behind in Jerusalem, but his parents did not
know it. 44 Thinking that he was in the caravan,
they journeyed for a day and looked for him
among their relatives and acquaintances, 45 but

† **2:41–52** This story's concern with an incident from Jesus' youth is unique in the canonical gospel tradition. It presents Jesus in the role of the faithful Jewish boy, raised in the traditions of Israel, and fulfilling all that the law requires. With this episode, the infancy narrative ends just as it began, in the setting of the Jerusalem temple.

2:38 Is 52:9.
2:39 Mt 2:23.
2:40 Lk 1:80; 2:52.
2:41 Ex 12:24–27; 23:15; Dt 16:1–8.

Introducing...

The Holy Family

On the first Sunday after Christmas, the Catholic Church celebrates the feast of the Holy Family: Jesus, Mary, and Joseph. The Bible does not tell us a lot about the Holy Family. We know that Joseph was a kind and compassionate man, eager to do God's will. He raised Jesus as his own son, even though he was not Jesus' biological father. Jesus was raised in a home in which love and faith were the norm.

We can be sure that the Holy Family had their moments of conflict and crisis—all families do. Luke's story of Jesus' getting separated from his parents demonstrates that. But we can also be sure that their love and faith helped them to survive such conflicts and grow stronger because of them. The Church holds the Holy Family up as a model of respect, compassion, love, and faith in family life.

How does your family express love and respect for one another? What crises and conflicts have you and your family survived? What can you do to bring the qualities of the Holy Family more fully into your family's life?

▶ Lk 2:41–52

Live It!

Jesus Grows in Age and Wisdom

Luke is the only New Testament Gospel that has any stories of Jesus' childhood. When Jesus was twelve, he came to Jerusalem with his family to celebrate the pilgrimage festival of Passover. He was left behind, and when Mary and Joseph searched for him, they found him in the Temple. At the Temple, Jesus listened to and questioned the teachers, trying to understand his faith better. His questions and his understanding—and, we can presume, his sincerity—amazed all who heard him.

Adolescence is an important time for exploring life's questions—including life's religious questions. Sometimes, young people are led to believe they shouldn't have any questions—which is a sad statement about adult leaders and teachers. Wise teachers—like those the young Jesus met in the Temple—welcome and encourage your questions, even your religious questions. So ask yourself: How well do I know my faith? What are my main questions? Who are the wise teachers I can go to for help in searching out the answers?

▶ Lk 2:41–52

not finding him, they returned to Jerusalem to
look for him. 46 After three days they found him
in the temple, sitting in the midst of the teachers,
listening to them and asking them questions,
47 and all who heard him were astounded at his
understanding and his answers. 48 When his par-
ents saw him, they were astonished, and his
mother said to him, "Son, why have you done
this to us? Your father and I have been looking
for you with great anxiety." 49† And he said to
them, "Why were you looking for me? Did you
not know that I must be in my Father's house?"
50 But they did not understand what he said to
them. 51* He went down with them and came to
Nazareth, and was obedient to them; and his
mother kept all these things in her heart. 52* And
Jesus advanced [in] wisdom and age and favor
before God and man.

III: The Preparation for the Public Ministry

The Preparation of John the Baptist†

3 1* In the fifteenth year of the reign of Tiber-
ius Caesar,† when Pontius Pilate was gover-
nor of Judea, and Herod was tetrarch of Galilee,
and his brother Philip tetrarch of the region of
Ituraea and Trachonitis, and Lysanias was te-
trarch of Abilene, 2*† during the high priesthood
of Annas and Caiaphas, the word of God came to

Introducing...

John the Baptist

Picture a man living in the desert, eating grasshoppers and wild honey, and wearing a camel hair coat. Does this sound like the person Jesus described as "among those born of women, no one is greater than John" (Lk 7:28)? The person Jesus is talking about is John the Baptist, and he plays an important role in all four Gospels. John is portrayed like an Old Testament prophet, calling people to repentance for their sins. Indeed, his ministry was so similar to Jesus' ministry that after Herod had John killed (see Mt 14:1–12), he thought that Jesus might have been John raised from the dead (see Lk 9:7–9). The power of John's preaching is demonstrated by Jesus' disciples still encountering John's followers years after John's death (see Acts 19:1–7).

John the Baptist was Jesus' cousin, and the Gospel of Luke presents many parallels between the two men. John's preaching gives us a preview into Jesus' message. John was preparing the way for Jesus. He was a humble servant "not worthy to loosen the thongs of [Jesus'] sandals" (Lk 3:16). He described his baptism as a baptism of water in contrast with Jesus' baptism with "the holy Spirit and fire" (verse 16).

John the Baptist is the model of how Christians should perform their prophetic mission, pointing others toward Jesus with passion and humility.

▶ Lk 3:1–20

LK

2:49 *I must be in my Father's house:* this phrase can also be translated, "I must be about my Father's work." In either translation, Jesus refers to God as his Father. His divine sonship, and his obedience to his heavenly Father's will, take precedence over his ties to his family.

3:1–20 Although Luke is indebted in this section to his sources, the Gospel of Mark and a collection of sayings of John the Baptist, he has clearly marked this introduction to the ministry of Jesus with his own individual style. Just as the gospel began with a long periodic sentence (1:1–4), so too this section (1–2). He casts the call of John the Baptist in the form of an Old Testament prophetic call (2) and extends the quotation from Isaiah found in Mk 1:3 (Is 40:3) by the addition of Is 40:4–5 in vv 5–6. In doing so, he presents his theme of the universality of salvation, which he has announced earlier in the words of Simeon (2:30–32). Moreover, in describing the expectation of the people (15), Luke is characterizing the time of John's preaching in the same way as he had earlier described the situation of other devout Israelites in the infancy narrative (2:25–26, 37–38). In vv 7–18 Luke presents the preaching of John the Baptist who urges the crowds to reform in view of the coming wrath (7, 9: eschatological preaching), and who offers the crowds certain standards for reforming social conduct (10–14: ethical preaching), and who announces to the crowds the coming of *one mightier than* he (15–18: messianic preaching).

3:1 *Tiberius Caesar:* Tiberius succeeded Augustus as emperor in A.D. 14 and reigned until A.D. 37. The fifteenth year of his reign, depending on the method of calculating his first regnal year, would have fallen between A.D. 27 and 29. *Pontius Pilate:* prefect of Judea from A.D. 26 to 36. The Jewish historian Josephus describes him as a greedy and ruthless prefect who had little regard for the local Jewish population and their religious practices (see 13:1). *Herod:* i.e., Herod Antipas, the son of Herod the Great. He ruled over Galilee and Perea from 4 B.C. to A.D. 39. His official title *tetrarch* means literally, "ruler of a quarter," but came to designate any subordinate prince. *Philip:* also a son of Herod the Great, tetrarch of the territory to the north and east of the Sea of Galilee from 4 B.C. to A.D. 34. Only two small areas of this territory are mentioned by Luke. *Lysanias:* nothing is known about this Lysanias who is said here to have been tetrarch of Abilene, a territory northwest of Damascus.

3:2 *During the high priesthood of Annas and Caiaphas:* after situating the call of John the Baptist in terms of the civil rulers of the period, Luke now mentions the religious leadership of Palestine (see the note on 1:5). Annas had been high priest A.D. 6–15. After being deposed by the Romans in A.D. 15 he was succeeded by various members of his family and eventually by his son-in-law, Caiaphas, who was high priest A.D. 18–36. Luke refers to Annas as high priest at this time (but see Jn 18:13, 19), possibly because of the continuing influence of Annas or because the title continued to be used for the ex-high priest. *The word of God came to John:* Luke is alone among the New Testament writers in associating the preaching of John with a call from God. Luke is thereby identifying John with the prophets

2:51 Lk 2:19.
2:52 Lk 1:80; 2:40; 1 Sm 2:26.
3:1–20 Mt 3:1–12; Mk 1:1–8; Jn 1:19–28.
3:2 Lk 1:80.

Did You Know?

The Liturgical Year

The story of Jesus' baptism is one of the readings for the feast of the Baptism of the Lord. The feast days and holy days celebrated by Catholics and other Christians follow a yearly pattern. This pattern is called the liturgical year; it is not the same as the calendar year. You can read more about Church feast days and see a diagram of the liturgical calendar on pages 1836–1837.

▶ Lk 3:15–22

John the son of Zechariah in the desert. 3*† He
went throughout [the] whole region of the Jordan, proclaiming a baptism of repentance for the
forgiveness of sins, 4*† as it is written in the book
of the words of the prophet Isaiah:

"A voice of one crying out in the desert:
'Prepare the way of the Lord,
make straight his paths.
5 Every valley shall be filled
and every mountain and hill shall be made low.
The winding roads shall be made straight,
and the rough ways made smooth,
6* and all flesh shall see the salvation of God.' "

7* He said to the crowds who came out to be baptized by him, "You brood of vipers! Who warned
you to flee from the coming wrath? 8* Produce
good fruits as evidence of your repentance; and do not begin to say to yourselves, 'We have Abraham as our father,' for I tell you, God can raise up children to Abraham from these stones.
9* Even now the ax lies at the root of the trees. Therefore every tree that does not produce good fruit will be cut down and thrown into the fire."
10 And the crowds asked him, "What then
should we do?" 11 He said to them in reply,
"Whoever has two cloaks should share with the person who has none. And whoever has food
should do likewise." 12* Even tax collectors came
to be baptized and they said to him, "Teacher,
what should we do?" 13 He answered them,
"Stop collecting more than what is prescribed."
14 Soldiers also asked him, "And what is it that we should do?" He told them, "Do not practice extortion, do not falsely accuse anyone, and be satisfied with your wages."
15* Now the people were filled with expectation, and all were asking in their hearts whether
John might be the Messiah. 16*† John answered
them all, saying, "I am baptizing you with water, but one mightier than I is coming. I am not worthy to loosen the thongs of his sandals. He will
baptize you with the holy Spirit and fire. 17*† His
winnowing fan is in his hand to clear his threshing floor and to gather the wheat into his barn, but the chaff he will burn with unquenchable
fire." 18 Exhorting them in many other ways, he
preached good news to the people. 19*† Now
Herod the tetrarch, who had been censured by him because of Herodias, his brother's wife, and because of all the evil deeds Herod had commit-
ted, 20 added still another to these by [also] putting John in prison.

The Baptism of Jesus

21*† After all the people had been baptized and Jesus also had been baptized and was

---

whose ministries began with similar calls. In 7:26 John will be described as "more than a prophet"; he is also the precursor of Jesus (7:27), a transitional figure inaugurating the period of the fulfillment of prophecy and promise.

3:3 See the note on Mt 3:2.

3:4 The Essenes from Qumran used the same passage to explain why their community was in the desert studying and observing the law and the prophets (1QS 8:12–15).

3:16 *He will baptize you with the holy Spirit and fire:* in contrast to John's baptism with water, Jesus is said to baptize with the holy Spirit and with fire. From the point of view of the early Christian community, the Spirit and fire must have been understood in the light of the fire symbolism of the pouring out of the Spirit at Pentecost (Acts 2:1–4); but as part of John's preaching, the Spirit and fire should be related to their purifying and refining characteristics (Ez 36:25–27; Mal 3:2–3). See the note on Mt 3:11.

3:17 *Winnowing fan:* see the note on Mt 3:12.

3:19–20 Luke separates the ministry of John the Baptist from that of Jesus by reporting the imprisonment of John before the baptism of Jesus (21–22). Luke uses this literary device to serve his understanding of the periods of salvation history. With John the Baptist, the time of promise, the period of Israel, comes to an end; with the baptism of Jesus and the descent of the Spirit upon him, the time of fulfillment, the period of Jesus, begins. In his second volume, the Acts of the Apostles, Luke will introduce the third epoch in salvation history, the period of the church.

3:21–22 This episode in Luke focuses on the heavenly message identifying Jesus as *Son* and, through the allusion to Is 42:1, as Servant of Yahweh. The relationship of Jesus to the Father has already been announced in the infancy narrative (1:32, 35; 2:49); it occurs here at the beginning of Jesus' Galilean ministry and will reappear in 9:35 before another major section of Luke's gospel, the travel narrative (9:51—19:27). Elsewhere in Luke's writings (4:18; Acts 10:38), this incident will be interpreted as a type of anointing of Jesus.

3:3 Acts 13:24; 19:4.
3:4–6 Is 40:3–5.
3:4 Jn 1:23.
3:6 Lk 2:30–31.
3:7 Mt 12:34.
3:8 Jn 8:39.
3:9 Mt 7:19; Jn 15:6.
3:12 Lk 7:29.
3:15–16 Acts 13:25.
3:16 Lk 7:19–20; Jn 1:27; Acts 1:5; 11:16.
3:17 Mt 3:12.
3:19–20 Mt 14:3–4; Mk 6:17–18.
3:21–22 Mt 3:13–17; Mk 1:9–11.

praying,† heaven was opened 22*† and the holy
Spirit descended upon him in bodily form like a
dove. And a voice came from heaven, "You are
my beloved Son; with you I am well pleased."

The Genealogy of Jesus

23*† When Jesus began his ministry he was
about thirty years of age. He was the son, as was
thought, of Joseph, the son of Heli,* 24 the son
of Matthat, the son of Levi, the son of Melchi,
the son of Jannai, the son of Joseph, 25 the son of
Mattathias, the son of Amos, the son of Nahum,
the son of Esli, the son of Naggai, 26 the son of
Maath, the son of Mattathias, the son of Semein,
the son of Josech, the son of Joda, 27* the son of
Joanan, the son of Rhesa, the son of Zerubbabel,
the son of Shealtiel, the son of Neri, 28 the son
of Melchi, the son of Addi, the son of Cosam,
the son of Elmadam, the son of Er, 29 the son
of Joshua, the son of Eliezer, the son of Jorim,
the son of Matthat, the son of Levi, 30 the son of
Simeon, the son of Judah, the son of Joseph, the
son of Jonam, the son of Eliakim, 31*† the son
of Melea, the son of Menna, the son of Mattatha,
the son of Nathan,* the son of David,* 32 the son
of Jesse, the son of Obed, the son of Boaz, the
son of Sala, the son of Nahshon, 33* the son of
Amminadab, the son of Admin, the son of Arni,
the son of Hezron, the son of Perez, the son of
Judah,* 34* the son of Jacob, the son of Isaac, the
son of Abraham, the son of Terah, the son of Na-
hor, 35 the son of Serug, the son of Reu, the son of
Peleg, the son of Eber, the son of Shelah, 36* the
son of Cainan, the son of Arphaxad, the son of
Shem, the son of Noah, the son of Lamech, 37 the
son of Methuselah, the son of Enoch, the son of
Jared, the son of Mahalaleel, the son of Cainan,
38* the son of Enos, the son of Seth, the son of
Adam, the son of God.

The Temptation of Jesus†

4 1* Filled with the holy Spirit,† Jesus returned
from the Jordan and was led by the Spirit
into the desert 2*† for forty days, to be tempted
by the devil. He ate nothing during those days,
and when they were over he was hungry. 3 The
devil said to him, "If you are the Son of God,
command this stone to become bread." 4* Jesus
answered him, "It is written, 'One does not live
by bread alone.' " 5 Then he took him up and
showed him all the kingdoms of the world in a
single instant. 6* The devil said to him, "I shall
give to you all this power and their glory; for it
has been handed over to me, and I may give it
to whomever I wish. 7 All this will be yours, if
you worship me." 8* Jesus said to him in reply,
"It is written:

'You shall worship the Lord, your God,
and him alone shall you serve.' "

9† Then he led him to Jerusalem, made him
stand on the parapet of the temple, and said to
him, "If you are the Son of God, throw yourself
down from here, 10* for it is written:

'He will command his angels concerning you,
to guard you,'

11* and:

'With their hands they will support you,
lest you dash your foot against a stone.' "

12* Jesus said to him in reply, "It also says, 'You
shall not put the Lord, your God, to the test.' "
13*† When the devil had finished every tempta-
tion, he departed from him for a time.

LK

†

3:21 *Was praying:* Luke regularly presents Jesus at prayer at important points in his ministry: here at his baptism; at the choice of the Twelve (6:12); before Peter's confession (9:18); at the transfiguration (9:28); when he teaches his disciples to pray (11:1); at the Last Supper (22:32); on the Mount of Olives (22:41); on the cross (23:46).

3:22 *You are my beloved Son; with you I am well pleased:* this is the best attested reading in the Greek manuscripts. The Western reading, "You are my Son, this day I have begotten you," is derived from Ps 2:7.

3:23–38 Whereas Mt 1:2 begins the genealogy of Jesus with Abraham to emphasize Jesus' bonds with the people of Israel, Luke's universalism leads him to trace the descent of Jesus beyond Israel to Adam and beyond that to God (38) to stress again Jesus' divine sonship.

3:31 *The son of Nathan, the son of David:* in keeping with Jesus' prophetic role in Luke and Acts (e.g., 7:16, 39; 9:8; 13:33; 24:19; Acts 3:22–23; 7:37) Luke traces Jesus' Davidic ancestry through the prophet Nathan (see 2 Sm 7:2) rather than through King Solomon, as Mt 1:6–7.

4:1–13 See the note on Mt 4:1–11.

4:1 *Filled with the holy Spirit:* as a result of the descent of the Spirit upon him at his baptism (3:21–22), Jesus is now equipped to overcome the devil. Just as the Spirit is prominent at this early stage of Jesus' ministry (1, 14, 18), so too it will be at the beginning of the period of the church in Acts (Acts 1:4; 2:4, 17).

4:2 *For forty days:* the mention of forty days recalls the forty years of the wilderness wanderings of the Israelites during the Exodus (Dt 8:2).

4:9 *To Jerusalem:* the Lucan order of the temptations concludes on the parapet of the temple in Jerusalem, the city of destiny in Luke-Acts. It is in Jerusalem that Jesus will ultimately face his destiny (9:51; 13:33).

4:13 *For a time:* the devil's opportune time will occur before the passion and death of Jesus (Lk 22:3, 31–32, 53).

*

3:22 Lk 9:35; Ps 2:7; Is 42:1; Mt 12:18; 17:5; Mk 9:7; Jn 1:32; 2 Pt 1:17.
3:23–38 Mt 1:1–17.
3:23 Lk 4:22; Jn 6:42.
3:27 1 Chr 3:17; Ez 3:2.
3:31 2 Sm 5:14.
3:31–32 1 Sm 16:1, 18.
3:31–33 Ru 4:17–22; 1 Chr 2:1–15.
3:33 Gn 29:35; 38:29.
3:34 Gn 21:3; 25:26; 1 Chr 1:34; 28:34.
3:34–36 Gn 11:10–26; 1 Chr 1:24–27.
3:36–38 Gn 4:25—5:32; 1 Chr 1:1–4.
4:1–13 Mt 4:1–11; Mk 1:12–13.
4:2 Heb 4:15.
4:4 Dt 8:3.
4:6 Jer 27:5; Mt 28:18.
4:8 Dt 6:13.
4:10 Ps 91:11.
4:11 Ps 91:12.
4:12 Dt 6:16; 1 Cor 10:9.
4:13 Lk 22:3; Jn 13:2, 27; Heb 4:15.

Catholic Connection

The Bible, Tradition, and Magisterium

Knowing the Scriptures and applying them to our lives is essential as Christians. Jesus himself often quoted the Sacred Scriptures during his ministry. In the story of Jesus' temptation in the wilderness, Jesus quotes the Scriptures several times as a means to refute the devil and his temptations. But the devil also quotes the Scriptures in an effort to lead Jesus astray. The confrontation ends with the departure of the devil and Jesus' holding fast to the truth of God's Revelation and, ultimately, his role as the obedient Son of God.

We should always be careful about misinterpreting the Bible. That is why the Catholic Church teaches that our faith is based on both the Bible and the Sacred Tradition handed down by the Apostles. The Sacred Scriptures are the inspired word of God—inspired in the sense that the Holy Spirit guided the many authors who wrote and compiled the books of both the Old and New Testaments. When we are interpreting the Scriptures, we must be mindful of what the human authors intended—which requires learning about the history, culture, literary expressions, and language of the time. In this way, we learn what God wanted communicated through the Scriptures.

Sacred Tradition is rooted in the teachings of the Apostles, refined and passed on through the teaching authority of the Church. It includes development of doctrine and morals. Together, Scripture and Tradition form the one sacred deposit of the word of God for the salvation of God's people.

The role of the Magisterium, or teaching authority of the Church, is to act as shepherd in service of the word of God (Scripture and Tradition). Under the guidance of the Holy Spirit, the bishops, in communion with the Pope, are entrusted with teaching what has been handed on through the Scriptures and Tradition.

Together the Bible, Tradition, and Magisterium help us discern God's Revelation in the world. All three are essential guides in our efforts to know Christ and our role as Christians.

Lk 4:1–13
Catechism, nos. 74–141

Cultural Connection

Free . . . to Be Tempted

African Americans have been struggling for freedom for a long time. They have sung about freedom. They have written poems about it. And they have had demonstrations over it. For most African Americans, freedom is the Promised Land, a place overflowing with milk and honey, a place like heaven where there is justice and peace.

After Jesus' baptism, he went out into the wilderness to be alone so he could discern what God wanted him to do. While he was out there, he realized he could still be tempted to make selfish choices. Read Luke 4:1–13. Imagine how tempting it might have been for Jesus to use his power to prove to the world how great he was, instead of how great and loving God is. But he never gave in!

Many people throughout history have faced the choice of using their newly won freedom for their own selfish interests or for the good of others. After securing their freedom, some slaves, like Harriet Tubman, decided to spend their lives helping others become free—often at great risk and sacrifice to themselves. You can be sure they were tempted to choose an easier and safer life.

If we want to be free, we will face temptation. And if we want to remain free, we must resist the temptation to choose selfishly. Once we give in to selfishness, we become less free to resist it the next time around. And before long, we will become slaves again—slaves to our own desires.

Lk 4:1–13

LK

IV: The Ministry in Galilee

The Beginning of the Galilean Ministry

14*† Jesus returned to Galilee in the power of
the Spirit, and news of him spread throughout
the whole region.* 15 He taught in their syna-
gogues and was praised by all.

The Rejection at Nazareth†

16* He came to Nazareth, where he had grown
up, and went according to his custom† into the
synagogue on the sabbath day. He stood up to
read 17 and was handed a scroll of the prophet
Isaiah. He unrolled the scroll and found the pas-
sage where it was written:

18*† "The Spirit of the Lord is upon me,
because he has anointed me
to bring glad tidings to the poor.
He has sent me to proclaim liberty to captives
and recovery of sight to the blind,
to let the oppressed go free,
19 and to proclaim a year acceptable to the Lord."

20 Rolling up the scroll, he handed it back to the
attendant and sat down, and the eyes of all in the
synagogue looked intently at him. 21† He said to
them, "Today this scripture passage is fulfilled in
your hearing." 22* And all spoke highly of him
and were amazed at the gracious words that came
from his mouth. They also asked, "Isn't this the
son of Joseph?" 23† He said to them, "Surely you

†

4:14 *News of him spread:* a Lucan theme; see v 37; 5:15; 7:17.

4:16–30 Luke has transposed to the beginning of Jesus' ministry an incident from his Marcan source, which situated it near the end of the Galilean ministry (Mk 6:1–6a). In doing so, Luke turns the initial admiration (22) and subsequent rejection of Jesus (28–29) into a foreshadowing of the whole future ministry of Jesus. Moreover, the rejection of Jesus in his own hometown hints at the greater rejection of him by Israel (Acts 13:46).

4:16 *According to his custom:* Jesus' practice of regularly attending synagogue is carried on by the early Christians' practice of meeting in the temple (Acts 2:46; 3:1; 5:12).

4:18 *The Spirit of the Lord is upon me, because he has anointed me:* see the note on 3:21–22. As this incident develops, Jesus is portrayed as a prophet whose ministry is compared to that of the prophets Elijah and Elisha. Prophetic anointings are known in first-century Palestinian Judaism from the Qumran literature that speaks of prophets as God's anointed ones. *To bring glad tidings to the poor:* more than any other gospel writer Luke is concerned with Jesus' attitude toward the economically and socially poor (see 6:20, 24; 12:16–21; 14:12–14; 16:19–26; 19:8). At times, the poor in Luke's gospel are associated with the downtrodden, the oppressed and afflicted, the forgotten and the neglected (18; 6:20–22; 7:22; 14:12–14), and it is they who accept Jesus' message of salvation.

4:21 *Today this scripture passage is fulfilled in your hearing:* this sermon inaugurates the time of fulfillment of Old Testament prophecy. Luke presents the ministry of Jesus as fulfilling Old Testament hopes and expectations (7:22); for Luke, even Jesus' suffering, death, and resurrection are done in fulfillment of the scriptures (24:25–27, 44–46; Acts 3:18).

4:23 *The things that we heard were done in Capernaum:* Luke's source for this incident reveals an awareness of an earlier ministry of Jesus in Capernaum that Luke has not yet made use of because of

*

4:14–15 Mt 4:12–17; Mk 1:14–15.
4:14 Lk 5:15; Mt 3:16.
4:16–30 Mt 13:53–58; Mk 6:1–6.
4:18–19 Is 61:1–2; 58:6.
4:22 Lk 3:23; Jn 6:42.

Catholic Social Teaching

Jesus Liberates People from Oppression

In the Gospel of Luke, Jesus begins his mission by referring to Isaiah's prophecy (see Is 61:1). In the Gospel, we see Jesus fulfilling this prophecy by:

- healing the sick, whose sickness is viewed as caused by demon possession
- touching and curing lepers, who are separated from the rest of society
- speaking to and spending time with Samaritans, who are looked down upon and rejected by the Jews
- accepting as disciples women, who are generally not accepted as equals, socially and religiously
- forgiving and eating with sinners, who are put down and discriminated against by leaders of the Temple

Throughout his ministry, Jesus treats with great respect all whom he encounters. He recognizes that all people possess dignity and that their lives, even when afflicted by sin, sickness, or poverty, are a reflection of God's own self. Catholic social teaching urges us to do the same in our world today. We must never discriminate against or marginalize someone because of his or her race, gender, health, or social status; rather, our actions must be directed toward protecting and enhancing the dignity that all have been blessed with from the moment of creation.

Consider these questions:

- How and where is human dignity being diminished in our world?
- Where is human dignity being uplifted and protected?
- How can we work to ensure the enhancement of the dignity of all people?

Lk 4:14–30
Life and Dignity of the Human Person

will quote me this proverb, 'Physician, cure your-
self,' and say, 'Do here in your native place the
things that we heard were done in Capernaum.' "
24 And he said, "Amen, I say to you, no prophet
is accepted in his own native place. 25*† Indeed,
I tell you, there were many widows in Israel in
the days of Elijah when the sky was closed for
three and a half years and a severe famine spread
over the entire land. 26*† It was to none of these
that Elijah was sent, but only to a widow in Zare-
phath in the land of Sidon. 27* Again, there were
many lepers in Israel during the time of Elisha
the prophet; yet not one of them was cleansed,
but only Naaman the Syrian." 28 When the peo-
ple in the synagogue heard this, they were all
filled with fury. 29 They rose up, drove him out
of the town, and led him to the brow of the hill
on which their town had been built, to hurl him
down headlong. 30 But he passed through the
midst of them and went away.

The Cure of a Demoniac

31*† Jesus then went down to Capernaum, a
town of Galilee.* He taught them on the sab-
bath, 32* and they were astonished at his teach-
ing because he spoke with authority. 33* In the
synagogue there was a man with the spirit of an
unclean demon, and he cried out in a loud voice,
34*† "Ha! What have you to do with us, Jesus of
Nazareth? Have you come to destroy us? I know
who you are—the Holy One of God!" 35 Jesus re-
buked him and said, "Be quiet! Come out of him!"
Then the demon threw the man down in front of
them and came out of him without doing him

his transposition of this Nazareth episode to the beginning of Jesus' Galilean ministry. It is possible that by use of the future tense *you will quote me. . . ,* Jesus is being portrayed as a prophet.

4:25–26 The references to Elijah and Elisha serve several purposes in this episode: they emphasize Luke's portrait of Jesus as a prophet like Elijah and Elisha; they help to explain why the initial admiration of the people turns to rejection; and they provide the scriptural justification for the future Christian mission to the Gentiles.

4:26 *A widow in Zarephath in the land of Sidon:* like Naaman the Syrian in v 27, a non-Israelite becomes the object of the prophet's ministry.

4:31–44 The next several incidents in Jesus' ministry take place in Capernaum and are based on Luke's source, Mk 1:21–39. To the previous portrait of Jesus as prophet (16–30) they now add a presentation of him as teacher (31–32), exorcist (32–37, 41), healer (38–40), and proclaimer of God's kingdom (43).

4:34 *What have you to do with us?:* see the note on Jn 2:4. *Have you come to destroy us?:* the question reflects the current belief that before the day of the Lord control over humanity would be wrested from the evil spirits, evil destroyed, and God's authority over humanity reestablished. The synoptic gospel tradition presents Jesus carrying out this task.

4:25 1 Kgs 17:1–7; 18:1; Jas 5:17.
4:26 1 Kgs 17:9.
4:27 2 Kgs 5:1–14.
4:31–37 Mk 1:21–28.
4:31 Mt 4:13; Jn 2:12.
4:32 Mt 7:28–29.
4:33–34 Lk 8:28; Mt 8:29; Mk 1:23–24; 5:7.
4:34 Lk 4:41; Jn 6:69.

any harm. 36 They were all amazed and said to one
another, "What is there about his word? For with
authority and power he commands the unclean
spirits, and they come out." 37 And news of him
spread everywhere in the surrounding region.

The Cure of Simon's Mother-in-Law

38*† After he left the synagogue, he entered
the house of Simon. Simon's mother-in-law
was afflicted with a severe fever, and they inter-
ceded with him about her. 39 He stood over her,
rebuked the fever, and it left her. She got up im-
mediately and waited on them.

Other Healings

40* At sunset, all who had people sick with
various diseases brought them to him. He laid
his hands on each of them and cured them.
41*† And demons also came out from many,
shouting, "You are the Son of God." But he re-
buked them and did not allow them to speak be-
cause they knew that he was the Messiah.

Jesus Leaves Capernaum

42*† At daybreak, Jesus left and went to a de-
serted place. The crowds went looking for him,
and when they came to him, they tried to prevent
him from leaving them. 43* But he said to them,
"To the other towns also I must proclaim the
good news of the kingdom of God, because for
this purpose I have been sent." 44† And he was
preaching in the synagogues of Judea.

The Call of Simon the Fisherman*†

5 1* While the crowd was pressing in on Jesus
and listening to the word of God, he was
standing by the Lake of Gennesaret. 2 He saw two
boats there alongside the lake; the fishermen had
disembarked and were washing their nets. 3 Get-
ting into one of the boats, the one belonging to
Simon, he asked him to put out a short distance
from the shore. Then he sat down and taught the
crowds from the boat. 4* After he had finished
speaking, he said to Simon, "Put out into deep

†

4:38 *The house of Simon:* because of Luke's arrangement of material, the reader has not yet been introduced to Simon (cf Mk 1:16–18, 29–31). Situated as it is before the call of Simon (5:1–11), it helps the reader to understand Simon's eagerness to do what Jesus says (5:5) and to follow him (5:11).

4:41 *They knew that he was the Messiah:* that is, the Christ (see the note on 2:11).

4:42 *They tried to prevent him from leaving them:* the reaction of these strangers in Capernaum is presented in contrast to the reactions of those in his hometown who rejected him (28–30).

4:44 *In the synagogues of Judea:* instead of *Judea,* which is the best reading of the manuscript tradition, the Byzantine text tradition and other manuscripts read "Galilee," a reading that harmonizes Luke with Mt 4:23 and Mk 1:39. Up to this point Luke has spoken only of a ministry of Jesus in Galilee. Luke may be using *Judea* to refer to the land of Israel, the territory of the Jews, and not to a specific portion of it.

5:1–11 This incident has been transposed from his source, Mk 1:16–20, which places it immediately after Jesus makes his appearance in Galilee. By this transposition Luke uses this example of Simon's acceptance of Jesus to counter the earlier rejection of him by his hometown people, and since several incidents dealing with Jesus' power and authority have already been narrated, Luke creates a plausible context for the acceptance of Jesus by Simon and his partners. Many commentators have noted the similarity between the wondrous catch of fish reported here (4–9) and the post-resurrectional appearance of Jesus in Jn 21:1–11. There are traces in Luke's story that the post-resurrectional context is the original one: in v 8 Simon addresses Jesus as *Lord* (a post-resurrectional title for Jesus—see 24:34; Acts 2:36—that has been read back into the historical ministry of Jesus) and recognizes himself as a sinner (an appropriate recognition for one who has denied knowing Jesus—22:54–62). As used by Luke, the incident looks forward to Peter's leadership in Luke-Acts (6:14; 9:20; 22:31–32; 24:34; Acts 1:15; 2:14–40; 10:11–18; 15:7–12) and symbolizes the future success of Peter as fisherman (Acts 2:41).

*

4:38–39 Mt 8:14–15; Mk 1:29–31.
4:40–41 Mt 8:16; Mk 1:32–34.
4:41 Lk 4:34; Mt 8:29; Mk 3:11–12.
4:42–44 Mk 1:35–39.
4:43 Lk 8:1; Mk 1:14–15.
5:1–11 Mt 4:18–22; Mk 1:16–20.
5:1–3 Mt 13:1–2; Mk 2:13; 3:9–10; 4:1–2.
5:4–9 Jn 21:1–11.

Live It!

Do Not Be Afraid

How would you respond if someone walked into the room right now and announced that God wanted to see you in the next room in five minutes? As astonishing as that would be, few of us would probably be anxious about running right in to see God. We would probably want a little more time to get some things in our lives "straightened out"!

The Gospel of Luke reveals something interesting when it describes a miraculous catch of fish and the call of the first disciples. Upon seeing the miraculous catch, Peter knows he is in the presence of God. He asks Jesus to leave because Peter is overwhelmed by his own sinfulness and he knows that no one can see the face of God and live (see Lk 5:8).

If we found ourselves in a boat with God, we might respond the same way. Jesus reassures Peter, uttering words so important that they are repeated six times in Luke: "Do not be afraid." God knows we are sinners too. Jesus came not to condemn us but to save us and to make God's love known to us. Jesus is also saying to us: "Do not be afraid. Come, follow me!"

▶ Lk 5:1–11

water and lower your nets for a catch." 5 Simon said in reply, "Master, we have worked hard all night and have caught nothing, but at your command I will lower the nets." 6 When they had done this, they caught a great number of fish and their nets were tearing. 7 They signaled to their partners in the other boat to come to help them. They came and filled both boats so that they were in danger of sinking. 8 When Simon Peter saw this, he fell at the knees of Jesus and said, "Depart from me, Lord, for I am a sinful man." 9 For astonishment at the catch of fish they had made seized him and all those with him, 10* and likewise James and John, the sons of Zebedee, who were partners of Simon. Jesus said to Simon, "Do not be afraid; from now on you will be catching men." 11*† When they brought their boats to the shore, they left everything and followed him.

The Cleansing of a Leper

12*† Now there was a man full of leprosy in one of the towns where he was; and when he saw Jesus, he fell prostrate, pleaded with him, and said, "Lord, if you wish, you can make me clean." 13 Jesus stretched out his hand, touched him, and said, "I do will it. Be made clean." And the leprosy left him immediately. 14*† Then he ordered him not to tell anyone, but "Go, show yourself to the priest and offer for your cleansing what Moses prescribed; that will be proof for them." 15 The report about him spread all the more, and great crowds assembled to listen to him and to be cured of their ailments, 16* but he would withdraw to deserted places to pray.

The Healing of a Paralytic

17*† One day as Jesus was teaching, Pharisees† and teachers of the law were sitting there who had come from every village of Galilee and Judea and Jerusalem, and the power of the Lord was with him for healing. 18 And some men brought on a stretcher a man who was paralyzed; they were trying to bring him in and set [him] in his presence. 19† But not finding a way to bring him in because of the crowd, they went up on the roof and lowered him on the stretcher through the tiles into the middle in front of Jesus. 20† When he saw their faith, he said, "As for you, your sins are forgiven." 21*† Then the scribes and Pharisees began to ask themselves, "Who is this who speaks blasphemies? Who but God alone can forgive sins?" 22* Jesus knew their thoughts and said to them in reply, "What are you thinking in your hearts? 23 Which is easier, to say, 'Your sins are forgiven,' or to say, 'Rise and walk'? 24*† But that you may know that the Son of Man has authority on earth to forgive sins"—he said to the man who was paralyzed, "I say to you, rise, pick up your stretcher, and go home." 25 He stood up immediately before them, picked up what he had been lying on, and went home, glorifying God. 26 Then astonishment seized them all and they glorified God, and, struck with awe, they said, "We have seen incredible things today."

The Call of Levi

27* After this he went out and saw a tax collector named Levi sitting at the customs post. He said to him, "Follow me." 28† And leaving everything behind, he got up and followed him. 29* Then Levi gave a great banquet for him in his house, and a large crowd of tax collectors and others were at table with them. 30 The Pharisees and their scribes complained to his disciples, saying, "Why do you eat and drink with tax collectors and sinners?" 31 Jesus said to them in reply, "Those who are healthy do not need a physician, but the sick do. 32 I have not come to call the righteous to repentance but sinners."

5:11 *They left everything:* in Mk 1:16–20 and Mt 4:18–22 the fishermen who follow Jesus leave their nets and their father; in Luke, they leave *everything* (see also 28; 12:33; 14:33; 18:22), an indication of Luke's theme of complete detachment from material possessions.

5:12 *Full of leprosy:* see the note on Mk 1:40.

5:14 *Show yourself to the priest . . . what Moses prescribed:* this is a reference to Lv 14:2–9 that gives detailed instructions for the purification of one who had been a victim of leprosy and thereby excluded from contact with others (see Lv 13:45–46, 49; Nm 5:2–3). *That will be proof for them:* see the note on Mt 8:4.

5:17—6:11 From his Marcan source, Luke now introduces a series of controversies with Pharisees: controversy over Jesus' power to forgive sins (17–26); controversy over his eating and drinking with tax collectors and sinners (27–32); controversy over not fasting (33–36); and finally two episodes narrating controversies over observance of the sabbath (1–11).

5:17 *Pharisees:* see the note on Mt 3:7.

5:19 *Through the tiles:* Luke has adapted the story found in Mark to his non-Palestinian audience by changing "opened up the roof" (Mk 2:4, a reference to Palestinian straw and clay roofs) to *through the tiles,* a detail that reflects the Hellenistic Greco-Roman house with tiled roof.

5:20 *As for you, your sins are forgiven:* literally, "O man, your sins are forgiven you." The connection between the forgiveness of sins and the cure of the paralytic reflects the belief of first-century Palestine (based on the Old Testament: Ex 20:5; Dt 5:9) that sickness and infirmity are the result of sin, one's own or that of one's ancestors (see also 13:2; Jn 5:14; 9:2).

5:21 *The scribes:* see the note on Mk 2:6.

5:24 See the notes on Mt 9:6 and Mk 2:10.

5:28 *Leaving everything behind:* see the note on 5:11.

5:10 Jer 16:16.
5:11 Mt 19:27.
5:12–16 Mt 8:2–4; Mk 1:40–45.
5:14 Lk 8:56; Lv 14:2–32; Mk 7:36.
5:16 Mk 1:35.
5:17–26 Mt 9:1–8; Mk 2:1–12.
5:21 Lk 7:49; Is 43:25.
5:22 Lk 6:8; 9:47.
5:24–25 Jn 5:8–9, 27.
5:27–32 Mt 9:9–13; Mk 2:13–17.
5:29–30 Lk 15:1–2.

The Question about Fasting

33* And they said to him, "The disciples of John fast often and offer prayers, and the disciples of the Pharisees do the same; but yours eat and drink." 34† Jesus answered them, "Can you make the wedding guests† fast while the bridegroom is with them? 35 But the days will come, and when the bridegroom is taken away from them, then they will fast in those days." 36† And he also told them a parable. "No one tears a piece from a new cloak to patch an old one. Otherwise, he will tear the new and the piece from it will not match the old cloak. 37 Likewise, no one pours new wine into old wineskins. Otherwise, the new wine will burst the skins, and it will be spilled, and the skins will be ruined. 38 Rather, new wine must be poured into fresh wineskins. 39† [And] no one who has been drinking old wine desires new, for he says, 'The old is good.' "

Debates about the Sabbath

6 1*† While he was going through a field of grain on a sabbath, his disciples were picking the heads of grain, rubbing them in their hands, and eating them.* 2 Some Pharisees said, "Why are you doing what is unlawful on the sabbath?" 3* Jesus said to them in reply, "Have you not read what David did when he and those [who were] with him were hungry? 4*† [How] he went into the house of God, took the bread of offering, which only the priests could lawfully eat, ate of it, and shared it with his companions." 5 Then he said to them, "The Son of Man is lord of the sabbath."

6* On another sabbath he went into the synagogue and taught, and there was a man there whose right hand was withered. 7* The scribes and the Pharisees watched him closely to see if he would cure on the sabbath so that they might discover a reason to accuse him. 8* But he realized their intentions and said to the man with the withered hand, "Come up and stand before us." And he rose and stood there. 9 Then Jesus said to them, "I ask you, is it lawful to do good on the sabbath rather than to do evil, to save life rather than to destroy it?" 10 Looking around at them all, he then said to him, "Stretch out your hand." He did so and his hand was restored. 11 But they became enraged and discussed together what they might do to Jesus.

The Mission of the Twelve†

12* In those days he departed to the mountain to pray, and he spent the night in prayer† to God. 13† When day came, he called his disciples to himself, and from them he chose Twelve, whom he also named apostles: 14*† Simon, whom he named Peter, and his brother Andrew, James, John, Philip, Bartholomew, 15† Matthew, Thomas, James the son of Alphaeus, Simon who was called a Zealot, 16† and Judas the son of James, and Judas Iscariot, who became a traitor.

Ministering to a Great Multitude

17*† And he came down with them and stood on a stretch of level ground. A great crowd of his disciples and a large number of the people from all Judea and Jerusalem and the coastal region of Tyre and Sidon 18 came to hear him and to be healed of their diseases; and even those who were tormented by unclean spirits were cured.

†

5:34–35 See the notes on Mt 9:15 and Mk 2:19.

5:34 *Wedding guests:* literally, "sons of the bridal chamber."

5:36–39 See the notes on Mt 9:16–17 and Mk 2:19.

5:39 *The old is good:* this saying is meant to be ironic and offers an explanation for the rejection by some of the new wine that Jesus offers: satisfaction with old forms will prevent one from sampling the new.

6:1–11 The two episodes recounted here deal with gathering grain and healing, both of which were forbidden on the sabbath. In his defense of his disciples' conduct and his own charitable deed, Jesus argues that satisfying human needs such as hunger and performing works of mercy take precedence even over the sacred sabbath rest. See also the notes on Mt 12:1–14 and Mk 2:25–26.

6:4 *The bread of offering:* see the note on Mt 12:5–6.

6:12–16 See the notes on Mt 10:1—11:1 and Mk 3:14–15.

6:12 *Spent the night in prayer:* see the note on 3:21.

6:13 *He chose Twelve:* the identification of this group as the *Twelve* is a part of early Christian tradition (see 1 Cor 15:5), and in Matthew and Luke, the Twelve are associated with the twelve tribes of Israel (22:29–30; Mt 19:28). After the fall of Judas from his position among the Twelve, the need is felt on the part of the early community to reconstitute this group before the Christian mission begins at Pentecost (Acts 1:15–26). From Luke's perspective, they are an important group who because of their association with Jesus from the time of his baptism to his ascension (Acts 1:21–22) provide the continuity between the historical Jesus and the church of Luke's day and who as the original eyewitnesses guarantee the fidelity of the church's beliefs and practices to the teachings of Jesus (1:1–4). *Whom he also named apostles:* only Luke among the gospel writers attributes to Jesus the bestowal of the name *apostles* upon the Twelve. See the note on Mt 10:2–4. "Apostle" becomes a technical term in early Christianity for a missionary sent out to preach the word of God. Although Luke seems to want to restrict the title to the Twelve (only in Acts 4:4, 14 are Paul and Barnabas termed apostles), other places in the New Testament show an awareness that the term was more widely applied (1 Cor 15:5–7; Gal 1:19; 1 Cor 1:1; 9:1; Rom 16:7).

6:14 *Simon, whom he named Peter:* see the note on Mk 3:16.

6:15 *Simon who was called a Zealot:* the Zealots were the instigators of the First Revolt of Palestinian Jews against Rome in A.D. 66–70. Because the existence of the Zealots as a distinct group during the lifetime of Jesus is the subject of debate, the meaning of the identification of Simon as a Zealot is unclear.

6:16 *Judas Iscariot:* the name *Iscariot* may mean "man from Kerioth."

6:17 *The coastal region of Tyre and Sidon:* not only Jews from Judea and Jerusalem, but even Gentiles from outside Palestine come to hear Jesus (see 2:31–32; 3:6; 4:24–27).

*

5:33–39 Mt 9:14–17; Mk 2:18–22.
6:1–5 Mt 12:1–8; Mk 2:23–28.
6:1 Dt 23:26.
6:3–4 1 Sm 21:1–6.
6:4 Lv 24:5–9.
6:6–11 Mt 12:9–14; Mk 3:1–6.
6:7 Lk 14:1.
6:8 Lk 5:22; 9:47.
6:12–16 Mt 10:1–4; Mk 3:13–19.
6:14–16 Acts 1:13.
6:17–19 Mt 4:23–25; Mk 3:7–10.

19 Everyone in the crowd sought to touch him
because power came forth from him and healed
them all.

Sermon on the Plain

20*† And raising his eyes toward his disciples
he said:

"Blessed are you who are poor,†
for the kingdom of God is yours.
21* Blessed are you who are now hungry,
for you will be satisfied.
Blessed are you who are now weeping,
for you will laugh.
22* Blessed are you when people hate you,
and when they exclude and insult you,
and denounce your name as evil
on account of the Son of Man.

23* Rejoice and leap for joy on that day! Behold,
your reward will be great in heaven. For their an-
cestors treated the prophets in the same way.

24* But woe to you who are rich,
for you have received your consolation.
25* But woe to you who are filled now,
for you will be hungry.
Woe to you who laugh now,
for you will grieve and weep.
26* Woe to you when all speak well of you,
for their ancestors treated the false prophets
in this way.

Love of Enemies

27*† "But to you who hear I say, love your en-
emies, do good to those who hate you,* 28* bless
those who curse you, pray for those who mistreat
you. 29 To the person who strikes you on one
cheek, offer the other one as well, and from the
person who takes your cloak, do not withhold
even your tunic. 30 Give to everyone who asks of

Pray It!

LK

Jesus' Preference for the Poor

In the Gospel of Luke, Jesus gives the Sermon on the Plain, which parallels the Sermon on the Mount in Matthew. Even more clearly than Matthew, Luke makes the point that God's justice has a preference for the poor and the little ones. So it's not surprising that the four Beatitudes (blessings) in Luke are balanced by four woes ("Woe!" is like saying, "Trouble ahead!"). For example, "Blessed are you who are poor" (Lk 6:20) is countered by "Woe to you who are rich" (verse 24). Jesus shows his care for both those who are rich and those who are poor by calling the rich to practice justice and the poor to have hope.

Unlike Matthew, Luke does not "spiritualize" the Beatitudes. Matthew says, "Blessed are the poor in spirit" (5:3), but Luke simply says, "Blessed are you who are poor" (6:20), meaning materially poor. Matthew is concerned for people's salvation; Luke is concerned about their salvation and their material needs.

How do you show special concern for those who are poor? Pray that God helps us to share God's love with those caught in the struggles of life.

▶ **Lk 6:17–49**

† **6:20–49** Luke's "Sermon on the Plain" is the counterpart to Matthew's "Sermon on the Mount" (Mt 5:1—7:27). It is addressed to the disciples of Jesus, and, like the sermon in Matthew, it begins with beatitudes (20–22) and ends with the parable of the two houses (46–49). Almost all the words of Jesus reported by Luke are found in Matthew's version, but because Matthew includes sayings that were related to specifically Jewish Christian problems (e.g., Mt 5:17–20; 6:1–8, 16–18) that Luke did not find appropriate for his predominantly Gentile Christian audience, the "Sermon on the Mount" is considerably longer. Luke's sermon may be outlined as follows: an introduction consisting of blessings and woes (20–26); the love of one's enemies (27–36); the demands of loving one's neighbor (37–42); good deeds as proof of one's goodness (43–45); a parable illustrating the result of listening to and acting on the words of Jesus (46–49). At the core of the sermon is Jesus' teaching on the love of one's enemies (27–36) that has as its source of motivation God's graciousness and compassion for all humanity (35–36) and Jesus' teaching on the love of one's neighbor (37–42) that is characterized by forgiveness and generosity.

6:20–26 The introductory portion of the sermon consists of blessings and woes that address the real economic and social conditions of humanity (the poor—the rich; the hungry—the satisfied; those grieving—those laughing; the outcast—the socially acceptable). By contrast, Matthew emphasizes the religious and spiritual values of disciples in the kingdom inaugurated by Jesus ("poor in spirit," Mt 5:3; "hunger and thirst for righteousness" 5:6). In the sermon, *blessed* extols the fortunate condition of persons who are favored with the blessings of God; the woes, addressed as they are to the disciples of Jesus, threaten God's profound displeasure on those so blinded by their present fortunate situation that they do not recognize and appreciate the real values of God's kingdom. In all the blessings and woes, the present condition of the persons addressed will be reversed in the future.

6:27–36 See the notes on Mt 5:43–48 and 5:48.

* **6:20–26** Mt 5:1–12. **6:21** Ps 126:5–6; Is 61:3; Jer 31:25; Rv 7:16–17. **6:22** Jn 15:19; 16:2; 1 Pt 4:14. **6:23** Lk 11:47–48; 2 Chr 36:16; Mt 23:30–31. **6:24** Jas 5:1. **6:25** Is 65:13–14. **6:26** Jas 4:4. **6:27–36** Mt 5:38–48. **6:27** Prv 25:21; Rom 12:20–21. **6:28** Rom 12:14; 1 Pt 3:9.

you, and from the one who takes what is yours
do not demand it back. 31* Do to others as you
would have them do to you. 32 For if you love
those who love you, what credit is that to you?
Even sinners love those who love them. 33 And if
you do good to those who do good to you, what
credit is that to you? Even sinners do the same.
34* If you lend money to those from whom you
expect repayment, what credit [is] that to you?
Even sinners lend to sinners, and get back the
same amount. 35* But rather, love your enemies
and do good to them, and lend expecting noth-
ing back; then your reward will be great and you
will be children of the Most High, for he himself
is kind to the ungrateful and the wicked. 36 Be
merciful, just as [also] your Father is merciful.

Judging Others†

37* "Stop judging and you will not be judged.
Stop condemning and you will not be con-
demned. Forgive and you will be forgiven.*
38* Give and gifts will be given to you; a good
measure, packed together, shaken down, and
overflowing, will be poured into your lap. For
the measure with which you measure will in
return be measured out to you." 39* And he
told them a parable, "Can a blind person guide
a blind person? Will not both fall into a pit?
40* No disciple is superior to the teacher; but
when fully trained, every disciple will be like his
teacher. 41 Why do you notice the splinter in your
brother's eye, but do not perceive the wooden
beam in your own? 42 How can you say to your
brother, 'Brother, let me remove that splinter
in your eye,' when you do not even notice the
wooden beam in your own eye? You hypocrite!
Remove the wooden beam from your eye first;
then you will see clearly to remove the splinter
in your brother's eye.

A Tree Known by Its Fruit

43*† "A good tree does not bear rotten fruit,
nor does a rotten tree bear good fruit. 44 For every
tree is known by its own fruit. For people do not
pick figs from thornbushes, nor do they gather
grapes from brambles. 45 A good person out of
the store of goodness in his heart produces good,
but an evil person out of a store of evil produces
evil; for from the fullness of the heart the mouth
speaks.

The Two Foundations

46* "Why do you call me, 'Lord, Lord,' but not
do what I command? 47*† I will show you what
someone is like who comes to me, listens to my
words, and acts on them. 48 That one is like a per-
son building a house, who dug deeply and laid
the foundation on rock; when the flood came,
the river burst against that house but could not
shake it because it had been well built. 49 But the
one who listens and does not act is like a person
who built a house on the ground without a foun-
dation. When the river burst against it, it col-
lapsed at once and was completely destroyed."

The Healing of a Centurion's Slave

7 1*† When he had finished all his words to
the people, he entered Capernaum.† 2† A
centurion there had a slave who was ill and
about to die, and he was valuable to him. 3 When
he heard about Jesus, he sent elders of the Jews
to him, asking him to come and save the life of
his slave. 4 They approached Jesus and strongly
urged him to come, saying, "He deserves to have
you do this for him, 5 for he loves our nation and
he built the synagogue for us." 6† And Jesus went
with them, but when he was only a short dis-
tance from the house, the centurion sent friends
to tell him, "Lord, do not trouble yourself, for I
am not worthy to have you enter under my roof.
7 Therefore, I did not consider myself worthy to
come to you; but say the word and let my ser-
vant be healed. 8 For I too am a person subject to
authority, with soldiers subject to me. And I say
to one, 'Go,' and he goes; and to another, 'Come
here,' and he comes; and to my slave, 'Do this,'
and he does it." 9 When Jesus heard this he was
amazed at him and, turning, said to the crowd

† **6:37–42** See the notes on Mt 7:1–12; 7:1; 7:5.

6:43–46 See the notes on Mt 7:15–20 and 12:33.

6:47–49 See the note on Mt 7:24–27.

7:1—8:3 The episodes in this section present a series of reactions to the Galilean ministry of Jesus and reflect some of Luke's particular interests: the faith of a Gentile (1–10); the prophet Jesus' concern for a widowed mother (11–17); the ministry of Jesus directed to the afflicted and unfortunate of Is 61:1 (18–23); the relation between John and Jesus and their role in God's plan for salvation (24–35); a forgiven sinner's manifestation of love (36–50); the association of women with the ministry of Jesus (8:1–3).

7:1–10 This story about the faith of the centurion, a Gentile who cherishes the Jewish nation (5), prepares for the story in Acts of the conversion by Peter of the Roman centurion Cornelius who is similarly described as one who is generous to the Jewish nation (Acts 10:2). See also Acts 10:34–35 in the speech of Peter: "God shows no partiality . . . whoever fears him and acts uprightly is acceptable to him." See also the notes on Mt 8:5–13 and Jn 4:43–54.

7:2 *A centurion:* see the note on Mt 8:5.

7:6 *I am not worthy to have you enter under my roof:* to enter the house of a Gentile was considered unclean for a Jew; cf Acts 10:28.

6:31 Mt 7:12.
6:34 Dt 15:7–8.
6:35 Lv 25:35–36.
6:37–42 Mt 7:1–5.
6:37 Mt 6:14; Jas 2:13.
6:38 Mk 4:24.
6:39 Mt 15:14; 23:16–17, 24.
6:40 Mt 10:24–25; Jn 13:16; 15:20.
6:43–45 Mt 7:16–20; 12:33, 35.
6:46 Mt 7:21; Rom 2:13; Jas 1:22.
6:47–49 Mt 7:24–27.
7:1–10 Mt 8:5–13; Jn 4:43–54.

Cultural Connection

The Reunion Dinner

The words of the centurion in Luke 7:6–7 are the basis for the words Catholics say before receiving the Holy Eucharist: "Lord, I am not worthy that you should enter under my roof, but only say the word and my soul shall be healed" (Roman Missal). These words indicate our humility and our willingness to accept God's forgiveness and healing in our lives. They remind us to receive Jesus in a state of peace with God and one another, especially by seeking reconciliation with family and friends.

The Chinese New Year's celebration includes a "reunion dinner." The whole family gathers at the home of the eldest family member. People travel from faraway cities, and even from other countries, to be together. The meal is not eaten until everyone is present, and no one eats until any disagreement or hurt is forgiven, and the family is at peace.

Lk 7:1–10

following him, "I tell you, not even in Israel have I found such faith." 10 When the messengers returned to the house, they found the slave in good health.

Raising of the Widow's Son

11*† Soon afterward he journeyed to a city called Nain, and his disciples and a large crowd accompanied him. 12* As he drew near to the gate of the city, a man who had died was being carried out, the only son of his mother, and she was a widow. A large crowd from the city was with her. 13 When the Lord saw her, he was moved with pity for her and said to her, "Do not weep." 14 He stepped forward and touched the coffin; at this the bearers halted, and he said, "Young man, I tell you, arise!" 15* The dead man sat up and began to speak, and Jesus gave him to his mother. 16* Fear seized them all, and they glorified God, exclaiming, "A great prophet has arisen in our midst," and "God has visited his people." 17 This report about him spread through the whole of Judea and in all the surrounding region.

The Messengers from John the Baptist

18*† The disciples of John told him about all these things. John summoned two of his disciples 19* and sent them to the Lord to ask, "Are you the one who is to come, or should we look for another?" 20 When the men came to him, they said, "John the Baptist has sent us to you to ask, 'Are you the one who is to come, or should we look for another?' " 21 At that time he cured many of their diseases, sufferings, and evil spirits; he also granted sight to many who were blind. 22* And he said to them in reply, "Go and tell John what you have seen and heard: the blind regain their sight, the lame walk, lepers are cleansed, the deaf hear, the dead are raised, the poor have the good news proclaimed to them. 23† And blessed is the one who takes no offense at me."

Jesus' Testimony to John

24*† When the messengers of John had left, Jesus began to speak to the crowds about John. "What did you go out to the desert to see—a reed swayed by the wind? 25 Then what did you go out

†

7:11–17 In the previous incident Jesus' power was displayed for a Gentile whose servant was dying; in this episode it is displayed toward a widowed mother whose only son has already died. Jesus' power over death prepares for his reply to John's disciples in v 22: "the dead are raised." This resuscitation in alluding to the prophet Elijah's resurrection of the only son of a widow of Zarephath (1 Kgs 7:18–24) leads to the reaction of the crowd: "A great prophet has arisen in our midst" (16).

7:18–23 In answer to John's question, *Are you the one who is to come?*—a probable reference to the return of the fiery prophet of reform, Elijah, "before the day of the LORD comes, the great and terrible day" (Mal 3:23)—Jesus responds that his role is rather to bring the blessings spoken of in Is 61:1 to the oppressed and neglected of society (22; cf 4:18).

7:23 *Blessed is the one who takes no offense at me*: this beatitude is pronounced on the person who recognizes Jesus' true identity in spite of previous expectations of what "the one who is to come" would be like.

7:24–30 In his testimony to John, Jesus reveals his understanding of the relationship between them: John is the precursor of Jesus (27); John is the messenger spoken of in Mal 3:1 who in Mal 3:23 is identified as Elijah. Taken with the previous episode, it can be seen that Jesus identifies John as precisely the person John envisioned Jesus to be: the Elijah who prepares the way for the coming of the day of the Lord.

7:11–17 Lk 4:25–26; 1 Kgs 17:17–24.
7:12 Lk 8:42; 1 Kgs 17:17.
7:15 1 Kgs 17:23; 2 Kgs 4:36.
7:16 Lk 1:68; 19:44.
7:18–23 Mt 11:2–6.
7:19 Mal 3:1; Rv 1:4, 8; 4:8.
7:22 Lk 4:18; Is 35:5–6; 61:1.
7:24–30 Mt 11:7–15.

to see? Someone dressed in fine garments? Those
who dress luxuriously and live sumptuously are
found in royal palaces. 26* Then what did you go
out to see? A prophet? Yes, I tell you, and more
than a prophet. 27* This is the one about whom
scripture says:

'Behold, I am sending my messenger ahead of
you,
he will prepare your way before you.'

28 I tell you, among those born of women, no one
is greater than John; yet the least in the kingdom
of God is greater than he." 29* (All the people
who listened, including the tax collectors, and
who were baptized with the baptism of John,
acknowledged the righteousness of God; 30 but
the Pharisees and scholars of the law, who were
not baptized by him, rejected the plan of God
for themselves.)

31*† "Then to what shall I compare the people
of this generation? What are they like? 32 They are
like children who sit in the marketplace and call
to one another,

'We played the flute for you, but you did not
dance.
We sang a dirge, but you did not weep.'

33 For John the Baptist came neither eating food
nor drinking wine, and you said, 'He is possessed
by a demon.' 34* The Son of Man came eating and
drinking and you said, 'Look, he is a glutton and
a drunkard, a friend of tax collectors and sinners.'
35 But wisdom is vindicated by all her children."

The Pardon of the Sinful Woman†

36* A Pharisee invited him to dine with him,
and he entered the Pharisee's house and reclined
at table.† 37* Now there was a sinful woman
in the city who learned that he was at table in
the house of the Pharisee. Bringing an alabaster
flask of ointment,* 38 she stood behind him at
his feet weeping and began to bathe his feet with
her tears. Then she wiped them with her hair,
kissed them, and anointed them with the oint-
ment. 39 When the Pharisee who had invited him
saw this he said to himself, "If this man were a
prophet, he would know who and what sort of
woman this is who is touching him, that she is
a sinner." 40 Jesus said to him in reply, "Simon, I
have something to say to you." "Tell me, teacher,"
he said. 41† "Two people were in debt to a certain
creditor; one owed five hundred days' wages and
the other owed fifty. 42 Since they were unable
to repay the debt, he forgave it for both. Which
of them will love him more?" 43 Simon said in
reply, "The one, I suppose, whose larger debt
was forgiven." He said to him, "You have judged
rightly." 44 Then he turned to the woman and said
to Simon, "Do you see this woman? When I en-
tered your house, you did not give me water for
my feet, but she has bathed them with her tears
and wiped them with her hair. 45 You did not give
me a kiss, but she has not ceased kissing my feet
since the time I entered. 46 You did not anoint my
head with oil, but she anointed my feet with oint-
ment. 47† So I tell you, her many sins have been
forgiven; hence, she has shown great love. But the
one to whom little is forgiven, loves little." 48* He
said to her, "Your sins are forgiven." 49* The oth-
ers at table said to themselves, "Who is this who
even forgives sins?" 50 But he said to the woman,
"Your faith has saved you; go in peace."

Galilean Women Follow Jesus

8 1*† Afterward he journeyed from one town
and village to another, preaching and pro-
claiming the good news of the kingdom of God.
Accompanying him were the Twelve 2* and some

LK

†

7:31–35 See the note on Mt 11:16–19.

7:36–50 In this story of the pardoning of the sinful woman Luke presents two different reactions to the ministry of Jesus. A Pharisee, suspecting Jesus to be a prophet, invites Jesus to a festive banquet in his house, but the Pharisee's self-righteousness leads to little forgiveness by God and consequently little love shown toward Jesus. The sinful woman, on the other hand, manifests a faith in God (50) that has led her to seek forgiveness for her sins, and because so much was forgiven, she now overwhelms Jesus with her display of love; cf the similar contrast in attitudes in 18:9–14. The whole episode is a powerful lesson on the relation between forgiveness and love.

7:36 *Reclined at table:* the normal posture of guests at a banquet. Other oriental banquet customs alluded to in this story include the reception by the host with a kiss (45), washing the feet of the guests (44), and the anointing of the guests' heads (46).

7:41 *Days' wages:* one denarius is the normal daily wage of a laborer.

7:47 *Her many sins have been forgiven; hence, she has shown great love:* literally, "her many sins have been forgiven, seeing that she has loved much." That the woman's sins have been forgiven is attested by the great love she shows toward Jesus. Her love is the consequence of her forgiveness. This is also the meaning demanded by the parable in vv 41–43.

8:1–3 Luke presents Jesus as an itinerant preacher traveling in the company of the Twelve and of the Galilean women who are sustaining them out of their means. These Galilean women will later accompany Jesus on his journey to Jerusalem and become witnesses to his death (23:49) and resurrection (24:9–11, where Mary Magdalene and Joanna are specifically mentioned; cf also Acts 1:14). The association of women with the ministry of Jesus is most unusual in the light of the attitude of first-century Palestinian Judaism toward women. The more common attitude is expressed in Jn 4:27, and early rabbinic documents caution against speaking with women in public.

*

7:26 Lk 1:76.
7:27 Mal 3:1 / Is 40:3.
7:29–30 Lk 3:7, 12; Mt 21:32.
7:31–35 Mt 11:16–19.
7:34 Lk 15:2.
7:36 Lk 11:37; 14:1.
7:37 Mt 26:7; Mk 14:3.
7:37–38 Jn 12:3.
7:48 Lk 5:20; Mt 9:20; Mk 2:5.
7:49 Lk 5:21.
8:1 Lk 4:43.
8:2–3 Lk 23:49; 24:10; Mt 27:55–56; Mk 15:40–41; Jn 19:5.

8:4–8

women who had been cured of evil spirits and infirmities, Mary, called Magdalene, from whom seven demons had gone out, 3 Joanna, the wife of Herod's steward Chuza, Susanna, and many others who provided for them out of their resources.

The Parable of the Sower

4*† When a large crowd gathered, with people from one town after another journeying to him, he spoke in a parable.† 5 "A sower went out to sow his seed. And as he sowed, some seed fell on the path and was trampled, and the birds of the sky ate it up. 6 Some seed fell on rocky ground, and when it grew, it withered for lack of moisture. 7 Some seed fell among thorns, and the thorns grew with it and choked it. 8* And some seed fell on good soil, and when it grew, it produced fruit a hundredfold." After saying this, he called out, "Whoever has ears to hear ought to hear."

The Purpose of the Parables

9* Then his disciples asked him what the meaning of this parable might be. 10* He answered, "Knowledge of the mysteries of the kingdom of God has been granted to you; but to the rest, they are made known through parables so that 'they may look but not see, and hear but not understand.'

The Parable of the Sower Explained

11*† "This is the meaning of the parable. The seed is the word of God.* 12 Those on the path are the ones who have heard, but the devil comes and takes away the word from their hearts that they may not believe and be saved. 13 Those on rocky ground are the ones who, when they hear, receive the word with joy, but they have no root; they believe only for a time and fall away in time of trial. 14 As for the seed that fell among thorns, they are the ones who have heard, but as they go along, they are choked by the anxieties and riches and pleasures of life, and they fail to produce mature fruit. 15 But as for the seed that fell on rich soil, they are the ones who, when they have heard the word, embrace it with a generous and good heart, and bear fruit through perseverance.

The Parable of the Lamp

16*† "No one who lights a lamp conceals it with a vessel or sets it under a bed; rather, he places it on a lampstand so that those who enter may see the light.* 17* For there is nothing hidden that will not become visible, and nothing secret that will not be known and come to light. 18* Take care, then, how you hear. To anyone who has, more will be given, and from the one

†

8:4–21 The focus in this section is on how one should hear the word of God and act on it. It includes the parable of the sower and its explanation (4–15), a collection of sayings on how one should act on the word that is heard (16–18), and the identification of the mother and brothers of Jesus as the ones who hear the word and act on it (19–21). See also the notes on Mt 13:1–53 and Mk 4:1–34.

8:4–8 See the note on Mt 13:3–8.

8:11–15 On the interpretation of the parable of the sower, see the note on Mt 13:18–23.

8:16–18 These sayings continue the theme of responding to the word of God. Those who hear the word must become a light to others (16); even the mysteries of the kingdom that have been made known to the disciples (9–10) must come to light (17); a generous and persevering response to the word of God leads to a still more perfect response to the word.

*

8:4–8 Mt 13:1–9; Mk 4:1–9. Mk 4:13–20.
8:8 Lk 14:35; Mt 11:15; 13:43; Mk 4:23.
8:9–10 Mt 13:10–13; Mk 4:10–12.
8:10 Is 6:9.
8:11–15 Mt 13:18–23;
8:11 1 Pt 1:23.
8:16–18 Mk 4:21–25.
8:16 Lk 11:33; Mt 5:15.
8:17 Lk 12:2; Mt 10:26.
8:18 Lk 19:26; Mt 13:12; 25:29.

who has not, even what he seems to have will be taken away."

Jesus and His Family

19*† Then his mother and his brothers came to him but were unable to join him because of the crowd. 20* He was told, "Your mother and your brothers are standing outside and they wish to see you." 21† He said to them in reply, "My mother and my brothers are those who hear the word of God and act on it."

The Calming of a Storm at Sea

22*† One day he got into a boat with his disciples and said to them, "Let us cross to the other side of the lake." So they set sail, 23 and while they were sailing he fell asleep. A squall blew over the lake, and they were taking in water and were in danger. 24 They came and woke him saying, "Master, master, we are perishing!" He awakened, rebuked the wind and the waves, and they subsided and there was a calm. 25 Then he asked them, "Where is your faith?" But they were filled with awe and amazed and said to one another, "Who then is this, who commands even the winds and the sea, and they obey him?"

The Healing of the Gerasene Demoniac

26*† Then they sailed to the territory of the Gerasenes, which is opposite Galilee. 27 When he came ashore a man from the town who was possessed by demons met him. For a long time he had not worn clothes; he did not live in a house, but lived among the tombs. 28* When he saw Jesus, he cried out and fell down before him; in a loud voice he shouted, "What have you to do with me, Jesus, son of the Most High God? I beg you, do not torment me!" 29 For he had ordered the unclean spirit to come out of the man. (It had taken hold of him many times, and he used to be bound with chains and shackles as a restraint, but he would break his bonds and be driven by the demon into deserted places.) 30† Then Jesus asked him, "What is your name?" He replied, "Legion," because many demons had entered him. 31† And they pleaded with him not to order them to depart to the abyss.

32 A herd of many swine was feeding there on the hillside, and they pleaded with him to allow them to enter those swine; and he let them. 33 The demons came out of the man and entered the swine, and the herd rushed down the steep bank into the lake and was drowned. 34 When the swineherds saw what had happened, they ran away and reported the incident in the town and throughout the countryside. 35† People came out to see what had happened and, when they approached Jesus, they discovered the man from whom the demons had come out sitting at his feet. He was clothed and in his right mind, and they were seized with fear. 36 Those who witnessed it told them how the possessed man had been saved. 37 The entire population of the region of the Gerasenes asked Jesus to leave them because they were seized with great fear. So he got into a boat and returned. 38 The man from whom the demons had come out begged to remain with him, but he sent him away, saying, 39 "Return home and recount what God has done for you." The man went off and proclaimed throughout the whole town what Jesus had done for him.

Jairus's Daughter and the Woman with a Hemorrhage

40*† When Jesus returned, the crowd welcomed him, for they were all waiting for him. 41 And a man named Jairus, an official of the synagogue, came forward. He fell at the feet of Jesus and begged him to come to his house, 42† because he had an only daughter, about

†

8:19 *His brothers:* see the note on Mk 6:3.

8:21 The family of Jesus is not constituted by physical relationship with him but by obedience to the word of God. In this, Luke agrees with the Marcan parallel (3:31–35), although by omitting Mk 3:33 and especially Mk 3:20–21 Luke has softened the Marcan picture of Jesus' natural family. Probably he did this because Mary has already been presented in 1:38 as the obedient handmaid of the Lord who fulfills the requirement for belonging to the eschatological family of Jesus; cf also 11:27–28.

8:22–56 This section records four miracles of Jesus that manifest his power and authority: (1) the calming of a storm on the lake (22–25); (2) the exorcism of a demoniac (26–39); (3) the cure of a hemorrhaging woman (40–48); (4) the raising of Jairus's daughter to life (49–56). They parallel the same sequence of stories at Mk 4:35—5:43.

8:26 *Gerasenes:* other manuscripts read Gadarenes or Gergesenes. See also the note on Mt 8:28. *Opposite Galilee:* probably Gentile territory (note the presence in the area of pigs—unclean animals to Jews) and an indication that the person who receives salvation (36) is a Gentile.

8:30 *What is your name?:* the question reflects the popular belief that knowledge of the spirit's name brought control over the spirit. *Legion:* to Jesus' question the demon replies with a Latin word transliterated into Greek. The Roman legion at this period consisted of 5,000 to 6,000 foot soldiers; hence the name implies a very large number of demons.

8:31 *Abyss:* the place of the dead (Rom 10:7) or the prison of Satan (Rv 20:3) or the subterranean "watery deep" that symbolizes the chaos before the order imposed by creation (Gn 1:2).

8:35 *Sitting at his feet:* the former demoniac takes the position of a disciple before the master (10:39; Acts 22:3).

8:40–56 Two interwoven miracle stories, one a healing and the other a resuscitation, present Jesus as master over sickness and death. In the Lucan account, faith in Jesus is responsible for the cure (48) and for the raising to life (50).

8:42 *An only daughter:* cf the son of the widow of Nain whom Luke describes as an "only" son (7:12; see also 9:38).

*

8:19–21 Mt 12:46–50; Mk 3:31–35.
8:20–21 Lk 11:27–28.
8:22–25 Mt 8:18, 23–27; Mk 4:35–41.
8:26–39 Mt 8:28–34; Mk 5:1–20.
8:28–29 Lk 4:33–35; Mt 8:29; Mk 1:23–24.
8:40–56 Mt 9:18–26; Mk 5:21–43.

Live It!

Mission Possible

Just like the director of operations in the movie *Mission Impossible*, Jesus, in Luke 9:1–6, seems to say to the disciples, "Your mission, should you choose to accept it. . . ." The director in the movie labeled his missions as impossible, but Jesus knew *his* missions were possible—though, in some cases, not always popular (see 10:10–11).

We too are asked to share in Jesus' mission. Sound easy? We know it is not. Doing what Jesus would do may mean sticking our necks out rather than following the crowd. The hardest part? Letting people know that the reason for our actions is our faith in Jesus Christ. It's not impossible, but it's certainly a challenge! Are you up to it? If you trust in God, you will be!

▶ Lk 9:1–6

twelve years old, and she was dying. As he
went, the crowds almost crushed him. 43† And
a woman afflicted with hemorrhages for twelve
years, who [had spent her whole livelihood on
doctors and] was unable to be cured by anyone,
44 came up behind him and touched the tassel
on his cloak. Immediately her bleeding stopped.
45 Jesus then asked, "Who touched me?" While all
were denying it, Peter said, "Master, the crowds
are pushing and pressing in upon you." 46* But
Jesus said, "Someone has touched me; for I know
that power has gone out from me." 47 When the
woman realized that she had not escaped notice, she came forward trembling. Falling down
before him, she explained in the presence of all
the people why she had touched him and how
she had been healed immediately. 48* He said
to her, "Daughter, your faith has saved you; go
in peace."
49 While he was still speaking, someone from
the synagogue official's house arrived and said,
"Your daughter is dead; do not trouble the
teacher any longer." 50 On hearing this, Jesus
answered him, "Do not be afraid; just have faith
and she will be saved." 51 When he arrived at the
house he allowed no one to enter with him except Peter and John and James, and the child's
father and mother. 52*† All were weeping and
mourning for her, when he said, "Do not weep
any longer, for she is not dead, but sleeping."
53 And they ridiculed him, because they knew
that she was dead. 54 But he took her by the hand
and called to her, "Child, arise!" 55 Her breath
returned and she immediately arose. He then directed that she should be given something to eat.
56 Her parents were astounded, and he instructed
them to tell no one what had happened.

The Mission of the Twelve

9 1*† He summoned the Twelve and gave
them power and authority over all demons
and to cure diseases, 2 and he sent them to proclaim the kingdom of God and to heal [the sick].
3† He said to them, "Take nothing for the journey, neither walking stick, nor sack, nor food,
nor money, and let no one take a second tunic.
4* Whatever house you enter, stay there and
leave from there. 5*† And as for those who do
not welcome you, when you leave that town,
shake the dust from your feet in testimony
against them." 6 Then they set out and went from
village to village proclaiming the good news and
curing diseases everywhere.

Herod's Opinion of Jesus

7*† Herod the tetrarch† heard about all that
was happening, and he was greatly perplexed
because some were saying, "John has been raised
from the dead";* 8 others were saying, "Elijah

†

8:43 *Afflicted with hemorrhages for twelve years:* according to the Mosaic law (Lv 15:25–30) this condition would render the woman unclean and unfit for contact with other people.

8:52 *Sleeping:* her death is a temporary condition; cf Jn 11:11–14.

9:1–6 Armed with the power and authority that Jesus himself has been displaying in the previous episodes, the Twelve are now sent out to continue the work that Jesus has been performing throughout his Galilean ministry: (1) proclaiming the kingdom (4:43; 8:1); (2) exorcising demons (4:33–37, 41; 8:26–39) and (3) healing the sick (4:38–40; 5:12–16, 17–26; 6:6–10; 7:1–10, 17, 22; 8:40–56).

9:3 *Take nothing for the journey:* the absolute detachment required of the disciple (14:33) leads to complete reliance on God (12:22–31).

9:5 *Shake the dust from your feet:* see the note on Mt 10:14.

9:7–56 This section in which Luke gathers together incidents that focus on the identity of Jesus is introduced by a question that Herod is made to ask in this gospel: *"Who then is this about whom I hear such things?"* (9). In subsequent episodes, Luke reveals to the reader various answers to Herod's question: Jesus is one in whom God's power is present and who provides for the needs of God's people (10–17); Peter declares Jesus to be "the Messiah of God" (18–21); Jesus says he is the suffering Son of Man (22, 43–45); Jesus is the Master to be followed, even to death (23–27); Jesus is God's Son, his Chosen One (28–36).

9:7 *Herod the tetrarch:* see the note on 3:1.

*

8:46 Lk 6:19.
8:48 Lk 7:50; 17:19; 18:42.
8:52 Lk 7:13.
9:1–6 Mt 10:1, 5–15; Mk 6:7–13.
9:4 Lk 10:5–7.
9:5 Lk 10:10–11; Acts 13:51.
9:7–9 Mt 14:1–12; Mk 6:14–29.
9:7–8 Lk 9:19; Mt 16:14; Mk 8:28.

has appeared"; still others, "One of the ancient
prophets has arisen." 9*† But Herod said, "John
I beheaded. Who then is this about whom I hear
such things?" And he kept trying to see him.

The Return of the Twelve and the Feeding of the Five Thousand

10* When the apostles returned, they explained
to him what they had done. He took them and
withdrew in private to a town called Bethsaida.
11 The crowds, meanwhile, learned of this and
followed him. He received them and spoke to
them about the kingdom of God, and he healed
those who needed to be cured. 12 As the day was
drawing to a close, the Twelve approached him
and said, "Dismiss the crowd so that they can go
to the surrounding villages and farms and find
lodging and provisions; for we are in a deserted
place here." 13* He said to them, "Give them
some food yourselves." They replied, "Five loaves
and two fish are all we have, unless we ourselves
go and buy food for all these people." 14 Now
the men there numbered about five thousand.
Then he said to his disciples, "Have them sit
down in groups of [about] fifty." 15 They did so
and made them all sit down. 16*† Then taking
the five loaves and the two fish, and looking up
to heaven, he said the blessing over them, broke
them, and gave them to the disciples to set before
the crowd. 17 They all ate and were satisfied. And
when the leftover fragments were picked up, they
filled twelve wicker baskets.

Peter's Confession about Jesus

18*† Once when Jesus was praying in soli-
tude,† and the disciples were with him, he
asked them, "Who do the crowds say that I am?"
19* They said in reply, "John the Baptist; others,
Elijah; still others, 'One of the ancient prophets
has arisen.' " 20† Then he said to them, "But who
do you say that I am?" Peter said in reply, "The
Messiah of God." 21 He rebuked them and di-
rected them not to tell this to anyone.

The First Prediction of the Passion

22* He said, "The Son of Man must suffer
greatly and be rejected by the elders, the chief
priests, and the scribes, and be killed and on the
third day be raised."

The Conditions of Discipleship

23*† Then he said to all, "If anyone wishes to
come after me, he must deny himself and take up
his cross daily and follow me.* 24* For whoever
wishes to save his life will lose it, but whoever
loses his life for my sake will save it. 25 What
profit is there for one to gain the whole world yet
lose or forfeit himself? 26* Whoever is ashamed
of me and of my words, the Son of Man will be
ashamed of when he comes in his glory and in
the glory of the Father and of the holy angels.
27 Truly I say to you, there are some standing here
who will not taste death until they see the king-
dom of God."

The Transfiguration of Jesus†

28* About eight days after he said this, he took
Peter, John, and James and went up the moun-
tain to pray.† 29 While he was praying his face
changed in appearance and his clothing became
dazzling white. 30† And behold, two men were
conversing with him, Moses and Elijah, 31*† who
appeared in glory and spoke of his exodus
that he was going to accomplish in Jerusalem.
32*† Peter and his companions had been over-
come by sleep, but becoming fully awake, they

†

9:9 *And he kept trying to see him:* this indication of Herod's interest in Jesus prepares for 13:31–33 and for 23:8–12 where Herod's curiosity about Jesus' power to perform miracles remains unsatisfied.

9:16 *Then taking . . . :* the actions of Jesus recall the institution of the Eucharist in 22:19; see also the note on Mt 14:19.

9:18–22 This incident is based on Mk 8:27–33, but Luke has eliminated Peter's refusal to accept Jesus as suffering Son of Man (Mk 8:32) and the rebuke of Peter by Jesus (Mk 8:33). Elsewhere in the gospel, Luke softens the harsh portrait of Peter and the other apostles found in his Marcan source (cf 22:39–46, which similarly lacks a rebuke of Peter that occurs in the source, Mk 14:37–38).

9:18 *When Jesus was praying in solitude:* see the note on 3:21.

9:20 *The Messiah of God:* on the meaning of this title in first-century Palestinian Judaism, see the notes on 2:11 and on Mt 16:13–20 and Mk 8:27–30.

9:23 *Daily:* this is a Lucan addition to a saying of Jesus, removing the saying from a context that envisioned the imminent suffering and death of the disciple of Jesus (as does the saying in Mk 8:34–35) to one that focuses on the demands of daily Christian existence.

9:28–36 Situated shortly after the first announcement of the passion, death, and resurrection, this scene of Jesus' transfiguration provides the heavenly confirmation to Jesus' declaration that his suffering will end in glory (32); see also the notes on Mt 17:1–8 and Mk 9:2–8.

9:28 *Up the mountain to pray:* the "mountain" is the regular place of prayer in Luke (see 6:12; 22:39–41).

9:30 *Moses and Elijah:* the two figures represent the Old Testament law and the prophets. At the end of this episode, the heavenly voice will identify Jesus as the one to be listened to now (35). See also the note on Mk 9:5.

9:31 *His exodus that he was going to accomplish in Jerusalem:* Luke identifies the subject of the conversation as the *exodus* of Jesus, a reference to the death, resurrection, and ascension of Jesus that will take place in Jerusalem, the city of destiny (see 9:51). The mention of *exodus,* however, also calls to mind the Israelite Exodus from Egypt to the promised land.

9:32 *They saw his glory:* the *glory* that is proper to God is here attributed to Jesus (see 24:26).

9:9 Lk 23:8.
9:10–17 Mt 14:13–21; Mk 6:30–44; Jn 6:1–14.
9:13–17 2 Kgs 4:42–44.
9:16 Lk 22:19; 24:30–31; Acts 2:42; 20:11; 27:35.
9:18–21 Mt 16:13–20; Mk 8:27–30.
9:19 Lk 9:7–8.
9:22 Lk 24:7, 26; Mt 16:21; 20:18–19; Mk 8:31; 10:33–34.
9:23–27 Mt 16:24–28; Mk 8:34—9:1.
9:23 Lk 14:27; Mt 10:38.
9:24 Lk 17:33; Mt 10:39; Jn 12:25.
9:26 Lk 12:9; Mt 10:33; 2 Tm 2:12.
9:28–36 Mt 17:1–8; Mk 9:2–8.
9:31 Lk 9:22; 13:33.
9:32 Jn 1:14; 2 Pt 1:16.

Catholic Connection

The Messiah

Have you ever noticed that when a dramatic event takes place, people want to gather and talk about it? The same was probably true when Jesus walked the earth teaching and performing miracles. It is not difficult to imagine people talking over dinner or in the public square about Jesus and the things he was doing. Jesus was probably aware of the talk when he turned to the disciples and asked them what the crowds were saying about him. The disciples replied that the people thought Jesus was John the Baptist or some other great hero brought back to life. The crowds were on the right track thinking Jesus was someone special, but only the disciples realized his true identity as the Messiah.

Ever since sin entered the world with Adam and Eve, humankind anxiously awaited the arrival of the Messiah. Throughout the Old Testament, God was laying the foundation for the coming of the Messiah. The prophecies in Isaiah tell us a lot about the identity and role of the Messiah. In Isaiah, the Messiah is described as fully possessing the gifts of the Holy Spirit (see "The Gifts of the Holy Spirit," near Is 11:1–2). The Messiah is the one who will usher in an era of peace that will be evident in all of God's creation (the lamb will lie down with the wolf), as it was intended before Adam and Eve fell into sin. In chapter 53 of Isaiah, the Messiah is described as God's servant who, even though he was without sin, willingly takes on the punishment for the sins of the world. His suffering and death would restore humankind's relationship with God.

Although Jesus is the Messiah hoped for in the Old Testament, many did not recognize him because they mistakenly thought the messiah was going to be a king who would establish his rule over Israel like Kings David and Solomon. They wanted a messiah who would do battle with earthly powers and save them from oppressive rulers. Jesus showed the world that the messiah was a king, but one who would usher in the Reign of God. Jesus is the Messiah, the Christ or anointed one, who must suffer and die for the sins of all just as Isaiah had prophesied. And when the time was right, Jesus willfully suffered Crucifixion and offered his life on our behalf. He did battle with the powers of darkness and saved us from oppression to sin. Jesus' death and Resurrection opened up for us the way to heaven, where the lamb and the wolf will lie together in peace.

Lk 9:18–20

Catechism, nos. 436–440, 711–716

saw his glory and the two men standing with
him. 33† As they were about to part from him,
Peter said to Jesus, "Master, it is good that we are
here; let us make three tents, one for you, one for
Moses, and one for Elijah." But he did not know
what he was saying. 34† While he was still speak-
ing, a cloud came and cast a shadow over them,
and they became frightened when they entered
the cloud. 35*† Then from the cloud came a voice
that said, "This is my chosen Son; listen to him."
36† After the voice had spoken, Jesus was found
alone. They fell silent and did not at that time tell
anyone what they had seen.

The Healing of a Boy with a Demon

37*† On the next day, when they came down
from the mountain, a large crowd met him.
38There was a man in the crowd who cried
out, "Teacher, I beg you, look at my son; he is
my only child. 39 For a spirit seizes him and he
suddenly screams and it convulses him until he
foams at the mouth; it releases him only with
difficulty, wearing him out. 40 I begged your dis-
ciples to cast it out but they could not." 41 Jesus
said in reply, "O faithless and perverse genera-
tion, how long will I be with you and endure
you? Bring your son here." 42 As he was coming
forward, the demon threw him to the ground
in a convulsion; but Jesus rebuked the unclean
spirit, healed the boy, and returned him to his
father. 43* And all were astonished by the maj-
esty of God.

The Second Prediction of the Passion

While they were all amazed at his every deed,
he said to his disciples, 44 "Pay attention to what
I am telling you. The Son of Man is to be handed
over to men." 45 But they did not understand
this saying; its meaning was hidden from them
so that they should not understand it, and they
were afraid to ask him about this saying.

The Greatest in the Kingdom

46*† An argument arose among the disciples
about which of them was the greatest.* 47 Jesus
realized the intention of their hearts and took
a child and placed it by his side 48* and said
to them, "Whoever receives this child in my
name receives me, and whoever receives me
receives the one who sent me. For the one who
is least among all of you is the one who is the
greatest."

---

†

9:33 *Let us make three tents:* in a possible allusion to the feast of Tabernacles, Peter may be likening his joy on the occasion of the transfiguration to the joyful celebration of this harvest festival.

9:34 *Over them:* it is not clear whether *them* refers to Jesus, Moses, and Elijah, or to the disciples. For the cloud casting its shadow, see the note on Mk 9:7.

9:35 Like the heavenly voice that identified Jesus at his baptism prior to his undertaking the Galilean ministry (3:22), so too here before the journey to the city of destiny is begun (51) the heavenly voice again identifies Jesus as Son. *Listen to him:* the two representatives of Israel of old depart (33) and Jesus is left alone (36) as the teacher whose words must be heeded (see also Acts 3:22).

9:36 *At that time:* i.e., before the resurrection.

9:37–43a See the note on Mk 9:14–29.

9:46–50 These two incidents focus on attitudes that are opposed to Christian discipleship: rivalry and intolerance of outsiders.

*

9:35 Lk 3:22; Dt 18:15; Ps 2:7; Is 42:1; Mt 3:17; 12:18; Mk 1:11; 2 Pt 1:17–18.
9:37–43 Mt 17:14–18; Mk 9:14–27.
9:43–45 Lk 18:32–34; Mt 17:22–23; Mk 9:30–32.
9:46–48 Mt 18:1–5; Mk 9:33–37.
9:46 Lk 22:24.
9:48 Lk 10:16; Mt 10:40; Jn 13:20.

Live It!

Spiritual Highs

Have you ever been on a great retreat, camping trip, or service trip? If so, you may have felt really close to God and to others who shared that experience with you. You may have even wished the experience did not have to end.

Peter, James, and John must have felt that way when they saw Jesus in his glory talking with Moses and Elijah on the mountaintop. Peter wanted to stay up on the mountain, but it quickly became clear that he could not do so.

Faith has its high moments as well as its low moments. It is unrealistic to think we can maintain some kind of spiritual high all the time—doing so may even be dangerous. The faith of those who depend on mountaintop experiences often fizzles out. The better challenge is to learn what it means to live as a Christian down in the thick of life. Remember, our faith is more than feelings. God's love and mercy do not depend on our ability to feel "warm fuzzies," as nice as those may be.

Recall a special time in your life when you felt on top of the world. Relive the moment in your mind, this time looking for how God was present in that experience. What direction was God inviting you to go after it was over? Are you there yet?

▶ **Lk 9:28–36**

Another Exorcist

49* Then John said in reply, "Master, we saw
someone casting out demons in your name and
we tried to prevent him because he does not fol-
low in our company." 50 Jesus said to him, "Do
not prevent him, for whoever is not against you
is for you."

V: The Journey to Jerusalem: Luke's Travel Narrative†

Departure for Jerusalem; Samaritan Inhospitality

51*† When the days for his being taken up†
were fulfilled, he resolutely determined to jour-
ney to Jerusalem, 52*† and he sent messengers
ahead of him. On the way they entered a Samar-
itan village to prepare for his reception there,
53 but they would not welcome him because
the destination of his journey was Jerusalem.
54* When the disciples James and John saw this
they asked, "Lord, do you want us to call down
fire from heaven to consume them?" 55 Jesus
turned and rebuked them, 56 and they journeyed
to another village.

The Would-be Followers of Jesus

57*† As they were proceeding on their jour-
ney someone said to him, "I will follow you
wherever you go." 58 Jesus answered him, "Foxes
have dens and birds of the sky have nests, but
the Son of Man has nowhere to rest his head."
59 And to another he said, "Follow me." But he
replied, "[Lord,] let me go first and bury my fa-
ther." 60† But he answered him, "Let the dead
bury their dead. But you, go and proclaim the
kingdom of God." 61* And another said, "I will
follow you, Lord, but first let me say farewell to
my family at home." 62 [To him] Jesus said, "No
one who sets a hand to the plow and looks to
what was left behind is fit for the kingdom of
God."

The Mission of the Seventy-two†

10 1* After this the Lord appointed seventy
[-two]† others whom he sent ahead of
him in pairs to every town and place he in-
tended to visit. 2* He said to them, "The harvest
is abundant but the laborers are few; so ask the
master of the harvest to send out laborers for his
harvest. 3* Go on your way; behold, I am send-
ing you like lambs among wolves. 4*† Carry no
money bag, no sack, no sandals;* and greet no
one along the way. 5† Into whatever house you
enter, first say, 'Peace to this household.' 6† If a
peaceful person lives there, your peace will rest
on him; but if not, it will return to you. 7* Stay in
the same house and eat and drink what is offered
to you, for the laborer deserves his payment. Do

†

9:51—18:14 The Galilean ministry of Jesus finishes with the previous episode and a new section of Luke's gospel begins, the journey to Jerusalem. This journey is based on Mk 10:1–52, but Luke uses his Marcan source only in 18:15—19:27. Before that point he has inserted into his gospel a distinctive collection of sayings of Jesus and stories about him that he has drawn from Q, a collection of sayings of Jesus used also by Matthew, and from his own special traditions. All of the material collected in this section is loosely organized within the framework of a journey of Jesus to Jerusalem, the city of destiny, where his exodus (suffering, death, resurrection, ascension) is to take place (9:31), where salvation is accomplished, and from where the proclamation of God's saving word is to go forth (24:47; Acts 1:8). Much of the material in the Lucan travel narrative is teaching for the disciples. During the course of this journey Jesus is preparing his chosen Galilean witnesses for the role they will play after his exodus (9:31): they are to be his witnesses to the people (Acts 10:39; 13:31) and thereby provide certainty to the readers of Luke's gospel that the teachings they have received are rooted in the teachings of Jesus (1:1–4).

9:51–55 Just as the Galilean ministry began with a rejection of Jesus in his hometown, so too the travel narrative begins with the rejection of him by Samaritans. In this episode Jesus disassociates himself from the attitude expressed by his disciples that those who reject him are to be punished severely. The story alludes to 2 Kgs 1:10, 12, where the prophet Elijah takes the course of action Jesus rejects, and Jesus thereby rejects the identification of himself with Elijah.

9:51 *Days for his being taken up:* like the reference to his exodus in v 31, this is probably a reference to all the events (suffering, death, resurrection, ascension) of his last days in Jerusalem. *He resolutely determined:* literally, "he set his face."

9:52 *Samaritan:* Samaria was the territory between Judea and Galilee west of the Jordan river. For ethnic and religious reasons, the Samaritans and the Jews were bitterly opposed to one another (see Jn 4:9).

9:57–62 In these sayings Jesus speaks of the severity and the unconditional nature of Christian discipleship. Even family ties and filial obligations, such as burying one's parents, cannot distract one no matter how briefly from proclaiming the kingdom of God. The first two sayings are paralleled in Mt 8:19–22; see also the notes there.

9:60 *Let the dead bury their dead:* i.e., let the spiritually dead (those who do not follow) bury their physically dead. See also the note on Mt 8:22.

10:1–12 Only the Gospel of Luke contains two episodes in which Jesus sends out his followers on a mission: the first (9:1–6) is based on the mission in Mk 6:6b–13 and recounts the sending out of the Twelve; here in vv 1–12 a similar report based on Q becomes the sending out of seventy-two in this gospel. The episode continues the theme of Jesus preparing witnesses to himself and his ministry. These witnesses include not only the Twelve but also the seventy-two who may represent the Christian mission in Luke's own day. Note that the instructions given to the Twelve and to the seventy-two are similar and that what is said to the seventy-two in v 4 is directed to the Twelve in 22:35.

10:1 *Seventy[-two:]* important representatives of the Alexandrian and Caesarean text types read "seventy," while other important Alexandrian texts and Western readings have "seventy-two."

10:4 *Carry no money bag . . . greet no one along the way:* because of the urgency of the mission and the singlemindedness required of missionaries, attachment to material possessions should be avoided and even customary greetings should not distract from the fulfillment of the task.

10:5 *First say, 'Peace to this household':* see the notes on 2:14 and Mt 10:13.

10:6 *A peaceful person:* literally, "a son of peace."

9:49–50 Mk 9:38–40.
9:51 Lk 9:53; 13:22, 33; 17:11; 18:31; 19:28; 24:51; Acts 1:2, 9–11, 22.
9:52 Mal 3:1.
9:54 2 Kgs 1:10, 12.
9:57–60 Mt 8:19–22.
9:61–62 1 Kgs 19:20.
10:1 Mk 6:7.
10:2 Mt 9:37–38; Jn 4:35.
10:3 Mt 10:16.
10:4 Lk 9:3; 2 Kgs 4:29.
10:4–11 Mt 10:7–14.
10:7 Lk 9:4; Mt 10:10; 1 Cor 9:6–14; 1 Tm 5:18.

not move about from one house to another.
8* Whatever town you enter and they welcome
you, eat what is set before you, 9* cure the sick
in it and say to them, 'The kingdom of God is at
hand for you.' 10* Whatever town you enter and
they do not receive you, go out into the streets
and say, 11* 'The dust of your town that clings to
our feet, even that we shake off against you.' Yet
know this: the kingdom of God is at hand. 12* I
tell you, it will be more tolerable for Sodom on
that day than for that town.

Reproaches to Unrepentant Towns

13*† "Woe to you, Chorazin! Woe to you,
Bethsaida!* For if the mighty deeds done in your
midst had been done in Tyre and Sidon, they
would long ago have repented, sitting in sack-
cloth and ashes. 14 But it will be more tolerable
for Tyre and Sidon at the judgment than for you.
15*† And as for you, Capernaum, 'Will you be
exalted to heaven? You will go down to the neth-
erworld.' " 16* Whoever listens to you listens to
me. Whoever rejects you rejects me. And whoever
rejects me rejects the one who sent me."

Return of the Seventy-two

17 The seventy[-two] returned rejoicing, and
said, "Lord, even the demons are subject to us
because of your name." 18*† Jesus said, "I have
observed Satan fall like lightning from the sky.
19* Behold, I have given you the power 'to tread
upon serpents' and scorpions and upon the full
force of the enemy and nothing will harm you.
20* Nevertheless, do not rejoice because the spir-
its are subject to you, but rejoice because your
names are written in heaven."

Praise of the Father

21*† At that very moment he rejoiced [in] the
holy Spirit and said, "I give you praise, Father,
Lord of heaven and earth, for although you
have hidden these things from the wise and the
learned you have revealed them to the childlike.
Yes, Father, such has been your gracious will.*
22* All things have been handed over to me by
my Father. No one knows who the Son is except
the Father, and who the Father is except the Son
and anyone to whom the Son wishes to reveal
him."

The Privileges of Discipleship

23* Turning to the disciples in private he said,
"Blessed are the eyes that see what you see. 24 For
I say to you, many prophets and kings desired to
see what you see, but did not see it, and to hear
what you hear, but did not hear it."

The Greatest Commandment

25*† There was a scholar of the law† who
stood up to test him and said, "Teacher, what
must I do to inherit eternal life?"* 26 Jesus said
to him, "What is written in the law? How do you
read it?" 27* He said in reply, "You shall love the
Lord, your God, with all your heart, with all your
being, with all your strength, and with all your
mind, and your neighbor as yourself." 28* He
replied to him, "You have answered correctly; do
this and you will live."

The Parable of the Good Samaritan

29 But because he wished to justify himself, he
said to Jesus, "And who is my neighbor?" 30 Jesus
replied, "A man fell victim to robbers as he went
down from Jerusalem to Jericho. They stripped
and beat him and went off leaving him half-
dead. 31† A priest happened to be going down
that road, but when he saw him, he passed by
on the opposite side. 32 Likewise a Levite came to
the place, and when he saw him, he passed by on
the opposite side. 33 But a Samaritan traveler who

10:13–16 The call to repentance that is a part of the proclamation of the kingdom brings with it a severe judgment for those who hear it and reject it.

10:15 *The netherworld:* the underworld, the place of the dead (Acts 2:27, 31), here contrasted with heaven; see also the note on Mt 11:23.

10:18 *I have observed Satan fall like lightning:* the effect of the mission of the seventy-two is characterized by the Lucan Jesus as a symbolic fall of Satan. As the kingdom of God is gradually being established, evil in all its forms is being defeated; the dominion of Satan over humanity is at an end.

10:21 *Revealed them to the childlike:* a restatement of the theme announced in 8:10: the mysteries of the kingdom are revealed to the disciples. See also the note on Mt 11:25–27.

10:25–37 In response to a question from a Jewish legal expert about inheriting eternal life, Jesus illustrates the superiority of love over legalism through the story of the good Samaritan. The law of love proclaimed in the "Sermon on the Plain" (6:27–36) is exemplified by one whom the legal expert would have considered ritually impure (see Jn 4:9). Moreover, the identity of the "neighbor" requested by the legal expert (29) turns out to be a Samaritan, the enemy of the Jew (see the note on 9:52).

10:25 *Scholar of the law:* an expert in the Mosaic law, and probably a member of the group elsewhere identified as the scribes (5:21).

10:31–32 *Priest . . . Levite:* those religious representatives of Judaism who would have been expected to be models of "neighbor" to the victim pass him by.

10:8 1 Cor 10:27.
10:9 Mt 3:2; 4:17; Mk 1:15.
10:10–11 Lk 9:5.
10:11 Acts 13:51; 18:6.
10:12 Mt 10:15; 11:24.
10:13–15 Mt 11:20–24.
10:13–14 Is 23; Ez 26–28; Jl 3:4–8; Am 1:1–10; Zec 9:2–4.
10:15 Is 14:13–15.
10:16 Mt 10:40; Jn 5:23; 13:20; 15:23.
10:18 Is 14:12; Jn 12:31; Rv 12:7–12.
10:19 Ps 19:13; Mk 16:18.
10:20 Ex 32:32; Dn 12:1; Mt 7:22; Phil 4:3; Heb 12:23; Rv 3:5; 21:27.
10:21–22 Mt 11:25–27.
10:21 1 Cor 1:26–28.
10:22 Jn 3:35; 10:15.
10:23–24 Mt 13:16–17.
10:25–28 Mt 22:34–40; Mk 12:28–34.
10:25 Lk 18:18; Mt 19:16; Mk 10:17.
10:27 Lv 19:18; Dt 6:5; 10:12; Jos 22:5; Mt 19:19; 22:37–39; Rom 13:9; Gal 5:14; Jas 2:8.
10:28 Lv 18:5; Prv 19:16; Rom 10:5; Gal 3:12.

Catholic Social Teaching

Discrimination in Jesus' Time

The good Samaritan is a popular Bible story with an obvious message: We must not only help others but also love the ones who hate us. In Jesus' day, the Samaritans were despised by Jews and vice versa, even though Abraham was the father of faith for both groups. Jesus' making a Samaritan the hero of the story would have given the lawyer and other people listening to Jesus something to think about.

The parable itself is told as a response to the question posed of Jesus, "Who is my neighbor?" The answer to this question? Everyone! Jesus reminds us that we are called to live in solidarity with all people, no matter what their race, religion, ethnicity, gender, or social status. We are also called to treat all people with great compassion, loving our neighbor as ourselves and welcoming the stranger into our midst.

Catholic social teaching further reminds us that we are, in fact, our brother's keeper, and that we have been entrusted with the responsibility of taking care of one another. Indeed, we are all called to stand united as one human family, even though we are often used to thinking in terms of what divides us rather than what brings us together.

Imagine that this story takes place in your community.

- Who are the Samaritans in your community—that is, the culture or people that others judge and reject?
- How does this reflection affect your understanding of discrimination and racism?
- What can you do to better live in solidarity with all people in your community?

▶ Lk 10:25–37

Solidarity

came upon him was moved with compassion at
the sight. 34 He approached the victim, poured oil
and wine over his wounds and bandaged them.
Then he lifted him up on his own animal, took
him to an inn and cared for him. 35 The next day
he took out two silver coins and gave them to the
innkeeper with the instruction, 'Take care of him.
If you spend more than what I have given you,
I shall repay you on my way back.' 36 Which of
these three, in your opinion, was neighbor to the
robbers' victim?" 37 He answered, "The one who
treated him with mercy." Jesus said to him, "Go
and do likewise."

Martha and Mary

38*† As they continued their journey he entered
a village where a woman whose name was Martha
welcomed him. 39† She had a sister named Mary
[who] sat beside the Lord at his feet listening to
him speak. 40 Martha, burdened with much serv-
ing, came to him and said, "Lord, do you not care
that my sister has left me by myself to do the serv-
ing? Tell her to help me." 41 The Lord said to her
in reply, "Martha, Martha, you are anxious and
worried about many things. 42† There is need of
only one thing. Mary has chosen the better part
and it will not be taken from her."

The Lord's Prayer

11 1*† He was praying in a certain place, and
when he had finished, one of his disci-
ples said to him, "Lord, teach us to pray just as
John taught his disciples." † 2† He said to them,
"When you pray, say:

10:38–42 The story of Martha and Mary further illustrates the importance of hearing the words of the teacher and the concern with women in Luke.

10:39 *Sat beside the Lord at his feet:* it is remarkable for first-century Palestinian Judaism that a woman would assume the posture of a disciple at the master's feet (see also 8:35; Acts 22:3), and it reveals a characteristic attitude of Jesus toward women in this gospel (see 8:2–3).

10:42 *There is need of only one thing:* some ancient versions read, "there is need of few things"; another important, although probably inferior, reading found in some manuscripts is, "there is need of few things, or of one."

11:1–13 Luke presents three episodes concerned with prayer. The first (1–4) recounts Jesus teaching his disciples the Christian communal prayer, the "Our Father"; the second (5–8), the importance of persistence in prayer; the third (9–13), the effectiveness of prayer.

11:1–4 The Matthean form of the "Our Father" occurs in the "Sermon on the Mount" (Mt 6:9–15); the shorter Lucan version is presented while Jesus is at prayer (see the note on 3:21) and his disciples ask him to teach them to pray just as John taught his disciples to pray. In answer to their question, Jesus presents them with an example of a Christian communal prayer that stresses the fatherhood of God and acknowledges him as the one to whom the Christian disciple owes daily sustenance (3), forgiveness (4), and deliverance from the final trial (4). See also the notes on Mt 6:9–13.

11:2 *Your kingdom come:* in place of this petition, some early church Fathers record: "May your holy Spirit come upon us and cleanse us," a petition that may reflect the use of the "Our Father" in a baptismal liturgy.

10:38–39 Jn 11:1; 12:2–3. **11:1–4** Mt 6:9–15.

Father, hallowed be your name,
your kingdom come.
3† Give us each day our daily bread
4 and forgive us our sins
for we ourselves forgive everyone in debt
to us,
and do not subject us to the final test."

Further Teachings on Prayer

5* And he said to them, "Suppose one of
you has a friend to whom he goes at midnight
and says, 'Friend, lend me three loaves of
bread, 6 for a friend of mine has arrived at my
house from a journey and I have nothing to
offer him,' 7 and he says in reply from within,
'Do not bother me; the door has already been
locked and my children and I are already in
bed. I cannot get up to give you anything.' 8 I
tell you, if he does not get up to give him the
loaves because of their friendship, he will get
up to give him whatever he needs because of
his persistence.

The Answer to Prayer

9* "And I tell you, ask and you will receive;
seek and you will find; knock and the door will
be opened to you.* 10 For everyone who asks,
receives; and the one who seeks, finds; and to
the one who knocks, the door will be opened.
11 What father among you would hand his son
a snake when he asks for a fish? 12 Or hand him
a scorpion when he asks for an egg? 13† If you
then, who are wicked, know how to give good
gifts to your children, how much more will the
Father in heaven give the holy Spirit to those
who ask him?"

Jesus and Beelzebul

14* He was driving out a demon [that was]
mute, and when the demon had gone out,
the mute person spoke and the crowds were
amazed. 15* Some of them said, "By the power
of Beelzebul, the prince of demons, he drives
out demons." 16* Others, to test him, asked
him for a sign from heaven. 17 But he knew their
thoughts and said to them, "Every kingdom di-
vided against itself will be laid waste and house

Pray It!

Too Busy to Be Still

Help me to slow down, Lord, right now, before I think of something else that I should be doing—as if it really is more important than you. Let me sit in the quiet peace of your presence and soak up all that you have to say to me. Give me the patience and perception to do nothing else for these next few moments except to be totally, completely, and wonderfully centered on you!

Lk 10:38–42

will fall against house. 18 And if Satan is divided
against himself, how will his kingdom stand?
For you say that it is by Beelzebul that I drive out
demons. 19† If I, then, drive out demons by Beel-
zebul, by whom do your own people drive them
out? Therefore they will be your judges. 20* But
if it is by the finger of God that I drive out de-
mons, then the kingdom of God has come upon
you. 21 When a strong man fully armed guards
his palace, his possessions are safe. 22† But when
one stronger than he attacks and overcomes him,
he takes away the armor on which he relied and
distributes the spoils. 23* Whoever is not with me
is against me, and whoever does not gather with
me scatters.

The Return of the Unclean Spirit

24* "When an unclean spirit goes out of some-
one, it roams through arid regions searching for
rest but, finding none, it says, 'I shall return to
my home from which I came.' 25 But upon re-
turning, it finds it swept clean and put in order.
26* Then it goes and brings back seven other
spirits more wicked than itself who move in and
dwell there, and the last condition of that person
is worse than the first."

LK

†

11:3–4 *Daily bread:* see the note on Mt 6:11. *The final test:* see the note on Mt 6:13.

11:13 *The holy Spirit:* this is a Lucan editorial alteration of a traditional saying of Jesus (see Mt 7:11). Luke presents the gift of the holy Spirit as the response of the Father to the prayer of the Christian disciple.

11:19 *Your own people:* the Greek reads "your sons." Other Jewish exorcists (see Acts 19:13–20), who recognize that the power of God is active in the exorcism, would themselves convict the accusers of Jesus. See also the note on Mt 12:27.

11:22 *One stronger:* i.e., Jesus. Cf 3:16 where John the Baptist identifies Jesus as "mightier than I."

*

11:5–8 Lk 18:1–5.
11:9–13 Mt 7:7–11.
11:9 Mt 21:22; Mk 11:24; Jn 14:13; 15:7; 1 Jn 5:14–15.
11:14–23 Mt 12:22–30; Mk 3:20–27.
11:15 Mt 9:34.
11:16 Mt 12:38; 16:1; Mk 8:11; 1 Cor 1:22.
11:20 Ex 8:19.
11:23 Lk 9:50; Mk 9:40.
11:24–26 Mt 12:43–45.
11:26 Jn 5:14.

Catholic Connection

The Lord's Prayer

Sometimes, asking the simplest question can make all the difference! The disciples had been traveling with Jesus for some time and no doubt began to notice how frequently Jesus prayed, especially before important events, like the Transfiguration. So, it is no wonder that after hearing Jesus pray to the Father about how only the Son can reveal the Father to the world that the disciples ask Jesus a simple question: Can you teach us how to pray? Jesus responds by teaching them the Lord's Prayer, also called the Our Father.

The disciples' simple question led to what is now the model for all Christian prayer. It is the perfect prayer in that it covers everything regarding our relationship with God and our needs as God's children. The structure of the prayer even helps us to put our lives in proper order. The prayer can be broken down into the opening address and seven petitions as follows:

Our Father who art in heaven,

1. Hallowed be thy name,

2. Thy kingdom come,

3. thy will be done, on earth as it is in heaven.

4. Give us this day our daily bread,

5. and forgive us our trespasses, as we forgive those who trespass against us,

6. and lead us not into temptation,

7. but deliver us from evil.

We begin with the opening address, by calling God "Father," which reflects our own identity as adopted daughters and sons of God through our Baptism. Then we focus our first three petitions on God: we acknowledge God's holiness, we express a desire for his Kingdom, and we seek to unite our will with God's. By placing our attention on God, we draw closer to God and begin to leave behind all that would hold us back from loving God. The final four petitions acknowledge our own weaknesses and call on God's mercy. They address our basic human need for nourishment, both physical and spiritual, and for forgiveness, for both ourselves and others. They also focus on our struggle to resist sin, our need for God's grace to persevere, and our hope in deliverance from all that would keep us from the eternal life already won by Christ. The Lord's Prayer teaches us how to love God and gives us the words to express and deepen that love. As followers of Jesus, we are called to not only pray the Lord's Prayer frequently but also to live it!

Lk 11:1–4

Catechism, nos. 2759–2776

True Blessedness

27*† While he was speaking, a woman from the crowd called out and said to him, "Blessed is the womb that carried you and the breasts at which you nursed." 28 He replied, "Rather, blessed are those who hear the word of God and observe it."

The Demand for a Sign

29*† While still more people gathered in the crowd, he said to them, "This generation is an evil generation; it seeks a sign, but no sign will be given it, except the sign of Jonah.* 30 Just as Jonah became a sign to the Ninevites, so will the Son of Man be to this generation. 31* At the judgment the queen of the south will rise with the men of this generation and she will condemn them, because she came from the ends of the earth to hear the wisdom of Solomon, and there is something greater than Solomon here. 32* At the judgment the men of Nineveh will arise with this generation and condemn it, because at the preaching of Jonah they repented, and there is something greater than Jonah here.

The Simile of Light

33* "No one who lights a lamp hides it away or places it [under a bushel basket], but on a lampstand so that those who enter might see the light. 34* The lamp of the body is your eye. When your eye is sound, then your whole body is filled with light, but when it is bad, then your body is in darkness. 35 Take care, then, that the light in you not become darkness. 36 If your whole body is full of light, and no part of it is in darkness, then it will be as full of light as a lamp illuminating you with its brightness."

Denunciation of the Pharisees and Scholars of the Law

37*† After he had spoken, a Pharisee invited him to dine at his home. He entered and reclined at table to eat.* 38* The Pharisee was amazed to see that he did not observe the prescribed washing before the meal. 39* The Lord said to him, "Oh you Pharisees! Although you cleanse the outside of the cup and the dish, inside you are filled with plunder and evil. 40 You fools! Did not the maker of the outside also make the inside? 41 But as to what is within, give alms, and behold, everything will be clean for you. 42* Woe to you Pharisees! You pay tithes of mint and of rue and of every garden herb, but you pay no attention to judgment and to love for God. These you should have done, without overlooking the others. 43* Woe to you Pharisees! You love the seat of honor in synagogues and greetings in marketplaces. 44*† Woe to you! You are like unseen graves over which people unknowingly walk."

45*† Then one of the scholars of the law said to him in reply, "Teacher, by saying this you are insulting us too." 46 And he said, "Woe also to

Live It!

Ask and You Shall Receive

Have you ever determinedly asked your parents for something? They may have replied, "Will you stop asking me?!"

This is one response you will never hear from God. In fact, Jesus tells us to always be persistent with God. God wants to hear from us! Too often we hesitate to bring everything inside of us to God. We sort through what we think God wants to hear. Don't be selective! Bring it *all* to God—the big stuff as well as the little stuff. Be persistent and relentless. God doesn't mind at all.

▶ Lk 11:5–13

LK

†

11:27–28 The beatitude in v 28 should not be interpreted as a rebuke of the mother of Jesus; see the note on 8:21. Rather, it emphasizes (like 2:35) that attentiveness to God's word is more important than biological relationship to Jesus.

11:29–32 The "sign of Jonah" in Luke is the preaching of the need for repentance by a prophet who comes from afar. Cf Mt 12:38–42 (and see the notes there) where the "sign of Jonah" is interpreted by Jesus as his death and resurrection.

11:37–54 This denunciation of the Pharisees (39–44) and the scholars of the law (45–52) is set by Luke in the context of Jesus' dining at the home of a Pharisee. Controversies with or reprimands of Pharisees are regularly set by Luke within the context of Jesus' eating with Pharisees (see 5:29–39; 7:36–50; 14:1–24). A different compilation of similar sayings is found in Mt 23 (see also the notes there).

11:44 *Unseen graves:* contact with the dead or with human bones or graves (see Nm 19:16) brought ritual impurity. Jesus presents the Pharisees as those who insidiously lead others astray through their seeming attention to the law.

11:45 *Scholars of the law:* see the note on 10:25.

*

11:27 Lk 1:28, 42, 48.
11:29–32 Mt 12:38–42; Mk 8:12.
11:29 Mt 16:1, 4; Jn 6:30; 1 Cor 1:22.
11:31 1 Kgs 10:1–10; 2 Chr 9:1–12.
11:32 Jon 3:8, 10.
11:33 Lk 8:16; Mt 5:15; Mk 4:21.
11:34–36 Mt 6:22–23.
11:37–54 Lk 20:45–47; Mt 23:1–36; Mk 12:38–40.
11:37 Lk 7:36; 14:1.
11:38 Mt 15:2; Mk 7:2–5.
11:39–41 Mt 23:25–26.
11:42 Lv 27:30; Mt 23:23.
11:43 Lk 20:46; Mt 23:6; Mk 12:38–39.
11:44 Mt 23:27.
11:45 Mt 23:4.

you scholars of the law! You impose on people
burdens hard to carry, but you yourselves do not
lift one finger to touch them. 47* Woe to you!
You build the memorials of the prophets whom
your ancestors killed. 48 Consequently, you bear
witness and give consent to the deeds of your
ancestors, for they killed them and you do the
building. 49*† Therefore, the wisdom of God
said, 'I will send to them prophets and apostles;
some of them they will kill and persecute' 50 in
order that this generation might be charged with
the blood of all the prophets shed since the foun-
dation of the world, 51*† from the blood of Abel
to the blood of Zechariah who died between the
altar and the temple building. Yes, I tell you,
this generation will be charged with their blood!
52* Woe to you, scholars of the law! You have
taken away the key of knowledge. You yourselves
did not enter and you stopped those trying to
enter." 53* When he left, the scribes and Phari-
sees began to act with hostility toward him and
to interrogate him about many things, 54* for
they were plotting to catch him at something he
might say.

LK

The Leaven of the Pharisees

12 1*† Meanwhile, so many people were
crowding together that they were tram-
pling one another underfoot. He began to speak,
first to his disciples, "Beware of the leaven—that
is, the hypocrisy—of the Pharisees.

Courage under Persecution

2*† "There is nothing concealed that will not
be revealed, nor secret that will not be known.*
3 Therefore whatever you have said in the dark-
ness will be heard in the light, and what you
have whispered behind closed doors will be pro-
claimed on the housetops. 4 I tell you, my friends,
do not be afraid of those who kill the body but
after that can do no more. 5† I shall show you
whom to fear. Be afraid of the one who after
killing has the power to cast into Gehenna; yes,
I tell you, be afraid of that one. 6† Are not five
sparrows sold for two small coins? Yet not one of
them has escaped the notice of God. 7* Even the
hairs of your head have all been counted. Do not
be afraid. You are worth more than many spar-
rows. 8 I tell you, everyone who acknowledges me
before others the Son of Man will acknowledge
before the angels of God. 9* But whoever denies
me before others will be denied before the an-
gels of God.

Sayings about the holy Spirit

10*† "Everyone who speaks a word against the
Son of Man will be forgiven, but the one who
blasphemes against the holy Spirit will not be for-
given. 11* When they take you before synagogues
and before rulers and authorities, do not worry
about how or what your defense will be or about
what you are to say. 12 For the holy Spirit will teach
you at that moment what you should say."

Saying against Greed

13† Someone in the crowd said to him,
"Teacher, tell my brother to share the inheri-
tance with me." 14* He replied to him, "Friend,
who appointed me as your judge and arbitra-
tor?" 15* Then he said to the crowd, "Take care to
guard against all greed, for though one may be
rich, one's life does not consist of possessions."

Parable of the Rich Fool

16 Then he told them a parable. "There was a
rich man whose land produced a bountiful har-
vest. 17 He asked himself, 'What shall I do, for I
do not have space to store my harvest?' 18 And he
said, 'This is what I shall do: I shall tear down my
barns and build larger ones. There I shall store all
my grain and other goods 19* and I shall say to
myself, "Now as for you, you have so many good

†

11:49 *I will send to them prophets and apostles:* Jesus connects the mission of the church (apostles) with the mission of the Old Testament prophets who often suffered the rebuke of their contemporaries.

11:51 *From the blood of Abel to the blood of Zechariah:* the murder of Abel is the first murder recounted in the Old Testament (Gn 4:8). The Zechariah mentioned here may be the Zechariah whose murder is recounted in 2 Chr 24:20–22, the last murder presented in the Hebrew canon of the Old Testament.

12:1 See the notes on Mk 8:15 and Mt 16:5–12.

12:2–9 Luke presents a collection of sayings of Jesus exhorting his followers to acknowledge him and his mission fearlessly and assuring them of God's protection even in times of persecution. They are paralleled in Mt 10:26–33.

12:5 *Gehenna:* see the note on Mt 5:22.

12:6 *Two small coins:* the Roman copper coin, the assarion (Latin *as*), was worth about one-sixteenth of a denarius (see the note on 7:41).

12:10–12 The sayings about the holy Spirit are set in the context of fearlessness in the face of persecution (2–9; cf Mt 12:31–32). The holy Spirit will be presented in Luke's second volume, the Acts of the Apostles, as the power responsible for the guidance of the Christian mission and the source of courage in the face of persecution.

12:13–34 Luke has joined together sayings contrasting those whose focus and trust in life is on material possessions, symbolized here by the rich fool of the parable (16–21), with those who recognize their complete dependence on God (21), those whose radical detachment from material possessions symbolizes their heavenly treasure (33–34).

*

11:47–48 Mt 23:29–32.
11:49–51 Mt 23:34–36.
11:51 Gn 4:8; 2 Chr 24:20–22.
11:52 Mt 23:13.
11:53 Lk 6:11; Mt 22:15–22.
11:54 Lk 20:20.
12:1 Mt 16:6; Mk 8:15.
12:2–9 Mt 10:26–33.
12:2 Lk 8:17; Mk 4:22.
12:7 Lk 12:24; 21:18; Acts 27:34.
12:9 Lk 9:26; Mk 8:38; 2 Tm 2:12.
12:10 Mt 12:31–32; Mk 3:28–29.
12:11–12 Lk 21:12–15; Mt 10:17–20; Mk 13:11.
12:14 Ex 2:14; Acts 7:27.
12:15 1 Tm 6:9–10.
12:19–21 Mt 6:19–21; 1 Tm 6:17.

things stored up for many years, rest, eat, drink,
be merry!" '* 20 But God said to him, 'You fool,
this night your life will be demanded of you;
and the things you have prepared, to whom will
they belong?' 21† Thus will it be for the one who
stores up treasure for himself but is not rich in
what matters to God."

Dependence on God

22* He said to [his] disciples, "Therefore I tell
you, do not worry about your life and what you
will eat, or about your body and what you will
wear. 23 For life is more than food and the body
more than clothing. 24* Notice the ravens: they
do not sow or reap; they have neither storehouse
nor barn, yet God feeds them. How much more
important are you than birds! 25 Can any of you
by worrying add a moment to your life-span? 26 If
even the smallest things are beyond your control,
why are you anxious about the rest? 27* Notice
how the flowers grow. They do not toil or spin.
But I tell you, not even Solomon in all his splen-
dor was dressed like one of them. 28 If God so
clothes the grass in the field that grows today
and is thrown into the oven tomorrow, will he
not much more provide for you, O you of little
faith? 29 As for you, do not seek what you are to
eat and what you are to drink, and do not worry
anymore. 30 All the nations of the world seek for
these things, and your Father knows that you
need them. 31 Instead, seek his kingdom, and
these other things will be given you besides.
32* Do not be afraid any longer, little flock, for
your Father is pleased to give you the kingdom.
33* Sell your belongings and give alms. Provide
money bags for yourselves that do not wear out,
an inexhaustible treasure in heaven that no thief
can reach nor moth destroy. 34 For where your
treasure is, there also will your heart be.

Vigilant and Faithful Servants

35*† "Gird your loins and light your lamps
36* and be like servants who await their master's
return from a wedding, ready to open immedi-
ately when he comes and knocks. 37 Blessed are
those servants whom the master finds vigilant
on his arrival. Amen, I say to you, he will gird
himself, have them recline at table, and proceed
to wait on them. 38 And should he come in the
second or third watch and find them prepared in
this way, blessed are those servants. 39* Be sure
of this: if the master of the house had known the
hour when the thief was coming, he would not
have let his house be broken into. 40 You also
must be prepared, for at an hour you do not ex-
pect, the Son of Man will come."
41 Then Peter said, "Lord, is this parable meant
for us or for everyone?" 42 And the Lord replied,
"Who, then, is the faithful and prudent steward
whom the master will put in charge of his ser-
vants to distribute [the] food allowance at the
proper time? 43 Blessed is that servant whom his
master on arrival finds doing so. 44 Truly, I say to
you, he will put him in charge of all his property.

Live It!

The Greed Trap

It is easy to regard possessions as treasures and to find so much pleasure in them that we want more and more. This is the greed trap Jesus warns against in Luke 12:13–21. How do we let ourselves fall into this trap? Certainly, advertisements play a role in convincing us we need to own everything that is new and improved (see "New and Improved!" near Eccl 1:1–11). Our own insecurities also play a role—the more we possess, the more important we tend to think we are. But as Luke 12:18 indicates, greed is a sin that is addictive. Instead of feeling fulfilled by attaining the thing we crave, we feel that what we have still isn't enough. It is a vicious cycle.

The solution to greed is simple. It's sharing—that value we learned when we were very small. Sharing our time and possessions makes us "rich in what matters to God" (verse 21). Where do you see the sin of greed at work in your world? Where and when could you, your friends, and your family share more? Don't fall into the greed trap. Share!

▶ **Lk 12:13–21**

LK

†

12:21 *Rich in what matters to God:* literally, "rich for God."

12:35–48 This collection of sayings relates to Luke's understanding of the end time and the return of Jesus. Luke emphasizes for his readers the importance of being faithful to the instructions of Jesus in the period before the parousia.

*

12:19–20 Sir 11:19.
12:22–32 Mt 6:25–34.
12:24 Lk 12:7.
12:27 1 Kgs 10:4–7; 2 Chr 9:3–6.
12:32 Lk 22:29; Rv 1:6.
12:33 Lk 18:22; Mt 6:20–21; Mk 10:21.
12:35–46 Mt 24:45–51.
12:36 Mt 25:1–13; Mk 13:35–37.
12:39–40 Mt 24:43–44; 1 Thes 5:2.

Live It!

The Anxiety Trap

Doesn't it seem a little naive to assume that if we just trust God, we will get what we need and that we shouldn't worry about the everyday things like clothing, food, and shelter, or even things like work, our grades in school, and relationships? That certainly seems risky.

Indeed, putting our faith in God is a risk, but it's one that comes with the potential for great reward. Jesus tells us to not worry so much about everyday needs. Instead, we should look around for the simple signs that show God's care for us. Of course we also need to recognize that God intends we use the gifts, creativity, and freedom he has given us to meet those needs. If we do so, we won't fail to notice the many ways God is already working in our lives. Life will surely be so much calmer and less stressful if we heed Jesus' message. Try it!

▶ Lk 12:22–34

LK

45† But if that servant says to himself, 'My mas-
ter is delayed in coming,' and begins to beat the
menservants and the maidservants, to eat and
drink and get drunk, 46 then that servant's master
will come on an unexpected day and at an un-
known hour and will punish him severely and
assign him a place with the unfaithful. 47* That
servant who knew his master's will but did not
make preparations nor act in accord with his will
shall be beaten severely; 48 and the servant who
was ignorant of his master's will but acted in a
way deserving of a severe beating shall be beaten
only lightly. Much will be required of the person
entrusted with much, and still more will be de-
manded of the person entrusted with more.

Jesus: A Cause of Division

49† "I have come to set the earth on fire, and
how I wish it were already blazing! 50*† There is
a baptism with which I must be baptized, and
how great is my anguish until it is accomplished!
51* Do you think that I have come to establish
peace on the earth? No, I tell you, but rather di-
vision.* 52 From now on a household of five will
be divided, three against two and two against
three; 53* a father will be divided against his son
and a son against his father, a mother against her
daughter and a daughter against her mother, a
mother-in-law against her daughter-in-law and a
daughter-in-law against her mother-in-law."

Signs of the Times

54* He also said to the crowds, "When you see
[a] cloud rising in the west you say immediately
that it is going to rain—and so it does; 55 and when
you notice that the wind is blowing from the south
you say that it is going to be hot—and so it is.
56 You hypocrites! You know how to interpret the
appearance of the earth and the sky; why do you
not know how to interpret the present time?

Settlement with an Opponent

57* "Why do you not judge for yourselves what
is right? 58 If you are to go with your opponent be-
fore a magistrate, make an effort to settle the mat-
ter on the way; otherwise your opponent will turn
you over to the judge, and the judge hand you
over to the constable, and the constable throw
you into prison. 59† I say to you, you will not be
released until you have paid the last penny."

A Call to Repentance†

13 1 At that time some people who were pres-
ent there told him about the Galileans
whose blood Pilate† had mingled with the blood

†

12:45 *My master is delayed in coming:* this statement indicates that early Christian expectations for the imminent return of Jesus had undergone some modification. Luke cautions his readers against counting on such a delay and acting irresponsibly. Cf the similar warning in Mt 24:48.

12:49–53 Jesus' proclamation of the kingdom is a refining and purifying fire. His message that meets with acceptance or rejection will be a source of conflict and dissension even within families.

12:50 *Baptism:* i.e., his death.

12:59 *The last penny:* Greek, *lepton,* a very small amount. Mt 5:26 has for "the last penny" the Greek word *kodrantēs* (Latin *quadrans,* "farthing").

13:1–5 The death of the Galileans at the hands of Pilate (1) and the accidental death of those on whom the tower fell (4) are presented by the Lucan Jesus as timely reminders of the need for all to repent, for the victims of these tragedies should not be considered outstanding sinners who were singled out for punishment.

13:1 The slaughter of the Galileans by Pilate is unknown outside Luke; but from what is known about Pilate from the Jewish historian Josephus, such a slaughter would be in keeping with the character of Pilate. Josephus reports that Pilate had disrupted a religious gathering of the Samaritans on Mt. Gerizim with a slaughter of the participants (*Antiquities* 18, 4, 1 §§86–87), and that on another occasion Pilate had killed many Jews who had opposed him when he appropriated money from the temple treasury to build an aqueduct in Jerusalem (*Jewish War* 2, 9, 4 §§175–77; *Antiquities* 18, 3, 2 §§60–62).

*

12:47 Jas 4:17.
12:50 Mk 10:38–39.
12:51–53 Mt 10:34–35.
12:51 Lk 2:14.
12:53 Mi 7:6.
12:54–56 Mt 16:2–3.
12:57–59 Mt 5:25–26.

of their sacrifices. 2* He said to them in reply, "Do you think that because these Galileans suffered in this way they were greater sinners than all other Galileans? 3* By no means! But I tell you, if you do not repent, you will all perish as they did! 4† Or those eighteen people who were killed when the tower at Siloam fell on them—do you think they were more guilty than everyone else who lived in Jerusalem? 5 By no means! But I tell you, if you do not repent, you will all perish as they did!"

The Parable of the Barren Fig Tree

6*† And he told them this parable: "There once was a person who had a fig tree planted in his orchard, and when he came in search of fruit on it but found none, 7 he said to the gardener, 'For three years now I have come in search of fruit on this fig tree but have found none. [So] cut it down. Why should it exhaust the soil?' 8 He said to him in reply, 'Sir, leave it for this year also, and I shall cultivate the ground around it and fertilize it; 9 it may bear fruit in the future. If not you can cut it down.' "

Cure of a Crippled Woman on the Sabbath

10† He was teaching in a synagogue on the sabbath. 11 And a woman was there who for eighteen years had been crippled by a spirit; she was bent over, completely incapable of standing erect. 12 When Jesus saw her, he called to her and said, "Woman, you are set free of your infirmity." 13 He laid his hands on her, and she at once stood up straight and glorified God. 14* But the leader of the synagogue, indignant that Jesus had cured on the sabbath, said to the crowd in reply, "There are six days when work should be done. Come on those days to be cured, not on the sabbath day." 15*† The Lord said to him in reply, "Hypocrites! Does not each one of you on the sabbath untie his ox or his ass from the manger and lead it out for watering? 16*† This daughter of Abraham, whom Satan has bound for eighteen years now, ought she not to have been set free on the sabbath day from this bondage?" 17 When he said this, all his adversaries were humiliated; and the whole crowd rejoiced at all the splendid deeds done by him.

The Parable of the Mustard Seed

18*† Then he said, "What is the kingdom of God like? To what can I compare it? 19* It is like a mustard seed that a person took and planted in the garden. When it was fully grown, it became a large bush and 'the birds of the sky dwelt in its branches.' "

The Parable of the Yeast

20* Again he said, "To what shall I compare the kingdom of God? 21 It is like yeast that a woman took and mixed [in] with three measures of wheat flour until the whole batch of dough was leavened."

The Narrow Door; Salvation and Rejection

22† He passed through towns and villages, teaching as he went and making his way to Jerusalem. 23 Someone asked him, "Lord, will only a few people be saved?" He answered them, 24* "Strive to enter through the narrow gate, for many, I tell you, will attempt to enter but will not be strong enough.* 25* After the master of the house has arisen and locked the door, then will you stand outside knocking and saying, 'Lord, open the door for us.' He will say to you in reply, 'I do not know where you are from.' 26 And you will say, 'We ate and drank in your company and you taught in our streets.' 27* Then he will say to

L K

†

13:4 Like the incident mentioned in v 1, nothing of this accident in Jerusalem is known outside Luke and the New Testament.

13:6–9 Following on the call to repentance in vv 1–5, the parable of the barren fig tree presents a story about the continuing patience of God with those who have not yet given evidence of their repentance (see 3:8). The parable may also be alluding to the delay of the end time, when punishment will be meted out, and the importance of preparing for the end of the age because the delay will not be permanent (8–9).

13:10–17 The cure of the crippled woman on the sabbath and the controversy that results furnishes a parallel to an incident that will be reported by Luke in 14:1–6, the cure of the man with dropsy on the sabbath. A characteristic of Luke's style is the juxtaposition of an incident that reveals Jesus' concern for a man with an incident that reveals his concern for a woman; cf, e.g., 7:11–17 and 8:49–56.

13:15–16 If the law as interpreted by Jewish tradition allowed for the untying of bound animals on the sabbath, how much more should this woman who has been bound by Satan's power be freed on the sabbath from her affliction.

13:16 *Whom Satan has bound:* affliction and infirmity are taken as evidence of Satan's hold on humanity. The healing ministry of Jesus reveals the gradual wresting from Satan of control over humanity and the establishment of God's kingdom.

13:18–21 Two parables are used to illustrate the future proportions of the kingdom of God that will result from its deceptively small beginning in the preaching and healing ministry of Jesus. They are paralleled in Mt 13:31–33 and Mk 4:30–32.

13:22–30 These sayings of Jesus follow in Luke upon the parables of the kingdom (18–21) and stress that great effort is required for entrance into the kingdom (24) and that there is an urgency to accept the present opportunity to enter because the narrow door will not remain open indefinitely (25). Lying behind the sayings is the rejection of Jesus and his message by his Jewish contemporaries (26) whose places at table in the kingdom will be taken by Gentiles from the four corners of the world (29). Those called last (the Gentiles) will precede those to whom the invitation to enter was first extended (the Jews). See also 14:15–24.

*

13:2 Jn 9:2.
13:3–5 Jn 8:24.
13:6–9 Jer 8:13; Hb 3:17; Mt 21:19; Mk 11:13.
13:14 Lk 6:7; 14:3; Ex 20:8–11; Dt 5:12–15; Mt 12:10; Mk 3:2–4; Jn 5:16; 7:23; 9:14, 16.
13:15 Lk 14:5; Dt 22:4; Mt 12:11.
13:16 Lk 19:9.
13:18–19 Mt 13:31–32; Mk 4:30–32.
13:19 Ez 17:23–24; 31:6.
13:20–21 Mt 13:33.
13:24–30 Mt 7:13–14, 21–23.
13:24 Mk 10:25.
13:25 Mt 25:10–12.
13:27 Ps 6:9; Mt 7:23; 25:41.

God's Invitation List

Jesus uses the image of a banquet to describe the Reign of God. Jesus' point is not about what is on the menu but who is on the invitation list: the weak, the poor, and the little ones. Who is on your "invitation list"—who are the people you reach out to and serve?

▶ Lk 14:7–24

you, 'I do not know where [you] are from. Depart
from me, all you evildoers!' 28* And there will
be wailing and grinding of teeth when you see
Abraham, Isaac, and Jacob and all the prophets in
the kingdom of God and you yourselves cast out.
29* And people will come from the east and the
west and from the north and the south and will
recline at table in the kingdom of God. 30* For
behold, some are last who will be first, and some
are first who will be last."

Herod's Desire to Kill Jesus

31 At that time some Pharisees came to him
and said, "Go away, leave this area because
Herod wants to kill you." 32† He replied, "Go
and tell that fox, 'Behold, I cast out demons and
I perform healings today and tomorrow, and on
the third day I accomplish my purpose. 33*† Yet
I must continue on my way today, tomorrow,
and the following day, for it is impossible that a
prophet should die outside of Jerusalem.'

The Lament over Jerusalem

34* "Jerusalem, Jerusalem, you who kill the
prophets and stone those sent to you, how many
times I yearned to gather your children together
as a hen gathers her brood under her wings, but
you were unwilling! 35* Behold, your house will
be abandoned. [But] I tell you, you will not see
me until [the time comes when] you say, 'Blessed
is he who comes in the name of the Lord.'"

Healing of the Man with Dropsy on the Sabbath

14 1*† On a sabbath he went to dine at the
home of one of the leading Pharisees, and
the people there were observing him carefully.*
2† In front of him there was a man suffering from
dropsy. 3* Jesus spoke to the scholars of the law
and Pharisees in reply, asking, "Is it lawful to
cure on the sabbath or not?" 4 But they kept si-
lent; so he took the man and, after he had healed
him, dismissed him. 5*† Then he said to them,
"Who among you, if your son or ox falls into a
cistern, would not immediately pull him out on
the sabbath day?" 6* But they were unable to an-
swer his question.

Conduct of Invited Guests and Hosts

7*† He told a parable to those who had been
invited, noticing how they were choosing the
places of honor at the table. 8* "When you are in-
vited by someone to a wedding banquet, do not
recline at table in the place of honor. A more dis-
tinguished guest than you may have been invited
by him, 9 and the host who invited both of you
may approach you and say, 'Give your place to
this man,' and then you would proceed with em-
barrassment to take the lowest place. 10 Rather,
when you are invited, go and take the lowest
place so that when the host comes to you he may
say, 'My friend, move up to a higher position.'
Then you will enjoy the esteem of your com-
panions at the table. 11* For everyone who exalts
himself will be humbled, but the one who hum-
bles himself will be exalted." 12* Then he said
to the host who invited him, "When you hold a
lunch or a dinner, do not invite your friends or
your brothers or your relatives or your wealthy

---

† **13:32** Nothing, not even Herod's desire to kill Jesus, stands in the way of Jesus' role in fulfilling God's will and in establishing the kingdom through his exorcisms and healings.

13:33 *It is impossible that a prophet should die outside of Jerusalem:* Jerusalem is the city of destiny and the goal of the journey of the prophet Jesus. Only when he reaches the holy city will his work be accomplished.

14:1–6 See the note on 13:10–17.

14:2 *Dropsy:* an abnormal swelling of the body because of the retention and accumulation of fluid.

14:5 *Your son or ox:* this is the reading of many of the oldest and most important New Testament manuscripts. Because of the strange collocation of *son* and *ox,* some copyists have altered it to "your ass or ox," on the model of the saying in 13:15.

14:7–14 The banquet scene found only in Luke provides the opportunity for these teachings of Jesus on humility and presents a setting to display Luke's interest in Jesus' attitude toward the rich and the poor (see the notes on 4:18; 6:20–26; 12:13–34).

13:28–29 Mt 8:11–12.
13:29 Ps 107:2–3.
13:30 Mt 19:20; 20:16; Mk 10:31.
13:33 Lk 2:38; Jn 6:30; 8:20.
13:34–35 Lk 19:41–44; Mt 23:37–39.
13:35 Lk 19:38; 1 Kgs 9:7–8; Ps 118:26; Jer 7:4–7, 13–15; 12:7; 22:5.
14:1–6 Lk 6:6–11; 13:10–17.
14:1 Lk 11:37.
14:3 Lk 6:9; Mk 3:4.
14:5 Lk 13:15; Dt 22:4; Mt 12:11.
14:6 Mt 22:46.
14:7 Lk 11:43; Mt 23:6; Mk 12:38–39.
14:8–10 Prv 25:6–7.
14:11 Lk 18:14.
14:12 Lk 6:32–35.

neighbors, in case they may invite you back and
you have repayment. 13 Rather, when you hold a
banquet, invite the poor, the crippled, the lame,
the blind; 14* blessed indeed will you be because
of their inability to repay you. For you will be re-
paid at the resurrection of the righteous."

The Parable of the Great Feast

15† One of his fellow guests on hearing this
said to him, "Blessed is the one who will dine
in the kingdom of God." 16* He replied to him,
"A man gave a great dinner to which he invited
many. 17 When the time for the dinner came, he
dispatched his servant to say to those invited,
'Come, everything is now ready.' 18 But one by
one, they all began to excuse themselves. The
first said to him, 'I have purchased a field and
must go to examine it; I ask you, consider me
excused.' 19 And another said, 'I have purchased
five yoke of oxen and am on my way to evaluate
them; I ask you, consider me excused.' 20 And
another said, 'I have just married a woman, and
therefore I cannot come.' 21 The servant went and
reported this to his master. Then the master of
the house in a rage commanded his servant, 'Go
out quickly into the streets and alleys of the town
and bring in here the poor and the crippled,
the blind and the lame.' 22 The servant reported,
'Sir, your orders have been carried out and still
there is room.' 23 The master then ordered the
servant, 'Go out to the highways and hedgerows
and make people come in that my home may be
filled. 24 For, I tell you, none of those men who
were invited will taste my dinner.' "

Sayings on Discipleship

25† Great crowds were traveling with him,
and he turned and addressed them, 26*† "If
anyone comes to me without hating his father
and mother, wife and children, brothers and
sisters, and even his own life, he cannot be my
disciple.* 27* Whoever does not carry his own
cross and come after me cannot be my disciple.
28 Which of you wishing to construct a tower
does not first sit down and calculate the cost to
see if there is enough for its completion? 29 Oth-
erwise, after laying the foundation and finding
himself unable to finish the work the onlookers
should laugh at him 30 and say, 'This one began
to build but did not have the resources to finish.'
31 Or what king marching into battle would not
first sit down and decide whether with ten thou-
sand troops he can successfully oppose another
king advancing upon him with twenty thousand
troops? 32 But if not, while he is still far away,
he will send a delegation to ask for peace terms.
33* In the same way, everyone of you who does
not renounce all his possessions cannot be my
disciple.

The Simile of Salt

34*† "Salt is good, but if salt itself loses its
taste, with what can its flavor be restored? 35* It
is fit neither for the soil nor for the manure pile;
it is thrown out. Whoever has ears to hear ought
to hear."

Pray It!

Making a Difference

Lord, I want to be where I can make a difference, where I can enrich and add flavor to another person's life by bringing him or her the Good News of your love and justice.

Help me to discover all the gifts you have graced me with so that I can help turn this world around—starting with my own life! Show me how to keep fresh in my commitment to serve you each day. Amen.

▶ **Lk 14:34–35**

LK

†

14:15–24 The parable of the great dinner is a further illustration of the rejection by Israel, God's chosen people, of Jesus' invitation to share in the banquet in the kingdom and the extension of the invitation to other Jews whose identification as the poor, crippled, blind, and lame (21) classifies them among those who recognize their need for salvation, and to Gentiles (23). A similar parable is found in Mt 22:1–10.

14:25–33 This collection of sayings, most of which are peculiar to Luke, focuses on the total dedication necessary for the disciple of Jesus. No attachment to family (26) or possessions (33) can stand in the way of the total commitment demanded of the disciple. Also, acceptance of the call to be a disciple demands readiness to accept persecution and suffering (27) and a realistic assessment of the hardships and costs (28–32).

14:26 *Hating his father . . . :* cf the similar saying in Mt 10:37. The disciple's family must take second place to the absolute dedication involved in following Jesus (see also 9:59–62).

14:34–35 The simile of salt follows the sayings of Jesus that demanded of the disciple total dedication and detachment from family and possessions and illustrates the condition of one who does not display this total commitment. The halfhearted disciple is like salt that cannot serve its intended purpose. See the simile of salt in Mt 5:13 and the note there.

*

14:14 Jn 5:29.
14:16–24 Mt 22:2–10.
14:26–27 Mt 10:37–38.
14:26 Lk 9:57–62; 18:29; Jn 12:25.
14:27 Lk 9:23; Mt 16:24; Mk 8:34.
14:33 Lk 5:11.
14:34 Mt 5:13; Mk 9:50.
14:35 Lk 8:8; Mt 11:15; 13:9; Mk 4:9, 23.

The Parable of the Lost Sheep

15 1*† The tax collectors and sinners were all
drawing near to listen to him, 2* but the
Pharisees and scribes began to complain, say-
ing, "This man welcomes sinners and eats with
them." 3 So to them he addressed this parable.
4* "What man among you having a hundred
sheep and losing one of them would not leave
the ninety-nine in the desert and go after the
lost one* until he finds it?* 5 And when he does
find it, he sets it on his shoulders with great joy
6 and, upon his arrival home, he calls together his
friends and neighbors and says to them, 'Rejoice
with me because I have found my lost sheep.' 7* I
tell you, in just the same way there will be more
joy in heaven over one sinner who repents than
over ninety-nine righteous people who have no
need of repentance.

The Parable of the Lost Coin

8† "Or what woman having ten coins and
losing one would not light a lamp and sweep
the house, searching carefully until she finds it?
9 And when she does find it, she calls together her
friends and neighbors and says to them, 'Rejoice
with me because I have found the coin that I
lost.' 10 In just the same way, I tell you, there will
be rejoicing among the angels of God over one
sinner who repents."

The Parable of the Lost Son

11 Then he said, "A man had two sons, 12 and
the younger son said to his father, 'Father, give
me the share of your estate that should come to
me.' So the father divided the property between
them. 13* After a few days, the younger son col-
lected all his belongings and set off to a distant
country where he squandered his inheritance
on a life of dissipation. 14 When he had freely
spent everything, a severe famine struck that
country, and he found himself in dire need. 15 So
he hired himself out to one of the local citizens
who sent him to his farm to tend the swine.
16 And he longed to eat his fill of the pods on
which the swine fed, but nobody gave him any.
17 Coming to his senses he thought, 'How many
of my father's hired workers have more than

† **15:1–32** To the parable of the lost sheep (1–7) that Luke shares with Matthew (Mt 18:12–14), Luke adds two parables (the lost coin, 8–10; the prodigal son, 11–32) from his own special tradition to illustrate Jesus' particular concern for the lost and God's love for the repentant sinner.

15:8 *Ten coins:* literally, "ten drachmas." A drachma was a Greek silver coin.

* **15:1–7** Mt 9:10–13.
15:2 Lk 5:30; 19:7.
15:4–7 Mt 18:12–14.
15:4–6 Lk 19:10.
15:4 Ez 34:11–12, 16.
15:7 Ez 18:23.
15:13 Prv 29:3.

L
K

Live It!

Lost and Found

Who hasn't been lost at some point in life? Everyone can identify with the frustration, fear, and loneliness that come with being lost . . . which means everyone can also identify with being found! What a wonderful feeling it is to finally see the familiar landmark or to make the right turn to the main road or to have someone help you get your life back on track.

If you identify with that lone sheep who strayed from the flock (see Lk 15:1–7), remember that God never stops looking for you. Maybe all you need to do is stop and listen for God's call so God can embrace you and celebrate your return.

Talk to God now about the recent experiences that have led you astray and have made you feel lost. Let God hold you tight and lift you high as the divine shepherd celebrates your return.

▶ Lk 15:1–7

15:1–7

enough food to eat, but here am I, dying from
hunger. [18] I shall get up and go to my father and
I shall say to him, "Father, I have sinned against
heaven and against you. [19] I no longer deserve to
be called your son; treat me as you would treat
one of your hired workers." ' [20] So he got up and
went back to his father. While he was still a long
way off, his father caught sight of him, and was
filled with compassion. He ran to his son, em-
braced him and kissed him. [21] His son said to
him, 'Father, I have sinned against heaven and
against you; I no longer deserve to be called
your son.' [22] But his father ordered his servants,
'Quickly bring the finest robe and put it on him;
put a ring on his finger and sandals on his feet.
[23] Take the fattened calf and slaughter it. Then let
us celebrate with a feast, [24] because this son of
mine was dead, and has come to life again; he
was lost, and has been found.' Then the celebra-
tion began. [25] Now the older son had been out in
the field and, on his way back, as he neared the
house, he heard the sound of music and danc-
ing. [26] He called one of the servants and asked
what this might mean. [27] The servant said to him,
'Your brother has returned and your father has
slaughtered the fattened calf because he has him
back safe and sound.' [28] He became angry, and
when he refused to enter the house, his father
came out and pleaded with him. [29] He said to his
father in reply, 'Look, all these years I served you
and not once did I disobey your orders; yet you
never gave me even a young goat to feast on with
my friends. [30] But when your son returns who
swallowed up your property with prostitutes, for
him you slaughter the fattened calf.' [31] He said
to him, 'My son, you are here with me always;
everything I have is yours. [32] But now we must
celebrate and rejoice, because your brother was
dead and has come to life again; he was lost and
has been found.' "

The Parable of the Dishonest Steward

16 [1] † Then he also said to his disciples, "A
rich man had a steward who was reported
to him for squandering his property. [2] He sum-
moned him and said, 'What is this I hear about
you? Prepare a full account of your stewardship,
because you can no longer be my steward.' [3] The
steward said to himself, 'What shall I do, now that
my master is taking the position of steward away
from me? I am not strong enough to dig and I am
ashamed to beg. [4] I know what I shall do so that,
when I am removed from the stewardship, they

Live It!

God's Limitless Love

We have all heard the story of the lost son (prodigal son). We have all heard about the older brother's envious reaction to his father's generosity. And it seems clear that the forgiving father represents God and the sons represent each of us at different points in our lives.

On second thought, perhaps there is more to this familiar parable than meets the eye. Think about the story for a moment. What does it really say about God? Not only is the father not upset about his son's wasting all his money, but the father is incredibly happy to see his son return home. He runs to meet him! Picture it—this man so eager to welcome his son that he runs down the road toward him and then hugs and kisses him. Doesn't this seem a bit excessive?

But it doesn't end there. Despite the son's apology, which the father ignores, the father tells his servants to throw a huge party, to go all out for his son. This seems almost too much to believe, doesn't it? Music, dancing, expensive robes and rings, and a feast for everyone! What's going on here?

Luke is trying to show us, in the most visual way possible, that there is simply no limit to God's love for us. It is not a conditional love. It is an extravagant, outrageous love. God doesn't hold back. How can we refuse such boundless love? How can we hold back from such divine eagerness? The next time you think you have separated yourself from God's love, picture yourself walking down a road, God running toward you with open arms. What is your response?

▶ Lk 15:11–32

L K

---

† **16:1–8a** The parable of the dishonest steward has to be understood in the light of the Palestinian custom of agents acting on behalf of their masters and the usurious practices common to such agents. The dishonesty of the steward consisted in the squandering of his master's property (1) and not in any subsequent graft. The master commends the dishonest steward who has forgone his own usurious commission on the business transaction by having the debtors write new notes that reflected only the real amount owed the master (i.e., minus the steward's profit). The dishonest steward acts in this way in order to ingratiate himself with the debtors because he knows he is being dismissed from his position (3). The parable, then, teaches the prudent use of one's material goods in light of an imminent crisis.

Did You Know?

Understanding Parables

In some of Jesus' parables, the characters represent someone else. For example, in the parable of the prodigal son (see Lk 15:11–32), the forgiving father represents God. In other parables, the characters are examples for us to follow, as in the parable of the good Samaritan (see 10:29–37). However, in some parables, the characters neither represent God nor are role models for us.

For example, in the parable of the dishonest manager (see 16:1–13), the master doesn't represent God. And Jesus is not encouraging us to be dishonest like the manager. Jesus is simply saying that we need to be even more clever than dishonest people in using our money and talents for the sake of the Gospel.

(For more on understanding the parables, see "Parables," near Mt 13:10.)

▶ Lk 16:1–13

may welcome me into their homes.' 5 He called
in his master's debtors one by one. To the first he
said, 'How much do you owe my master?' 6† He
replied, 'One hundred measures of olive oil.' He
said to him, 'Here is your promissory note. Sit
down and quickly write one for fifty.' 7† Then
to another he said, 'And you, how much do you
owe?' He replied, 'One hundred kors of wheat.' He
said to him, 'Here is your promissory note; write
one for eighty.' 8* And the master commended
that dishonest steward for acting prudently.

Application of the Parable†

"For the children of this world are more pru-
dent in dealing with their own generation than
are the children of light.† 9*† I tell you, make
friends for yourselves with dishonest wealth, so
that when it fails, you will be welcomed into
eternal dwellings. 10*† The person who is trust-
worthy in very small matters is also trustworthy
in great ones; and the person who is dishonest
in very small matters is also dishonest in great
ones. 11 If, therefore, you are not trustworthy with
dishonest wealth, who will trust you with true
wealth? 12 If you are not trustworthy with what
belongs to another, who will give you what is
yours? 13*† No servant can serve two masters. He
will either hate one and love the other, or be de-
voted to one and despise the other. You cannot
serve God and mammon."

A Saying against the Pharisees

14† The Pharisees, who loved money,† heard all
these things and sneered at him. 15* And he said to
them, "You justify yourselves in the sight of others,
but God knows your hearts; for what is of human
esteem is an abomination in the sight of God.

Sayings about the Law

16*† "The law and the prophets lasted until
John; but from then on the kingdom of God is
proclaimed, and everyone who enters does so
with violence. 17* It is easier for heaven and earth
to pass away than for the smallest part of a letter
of the law to become invalid.

Sayings about Divorce

18*"Everyone who divorces his wife and mar-
ries another commits adultery, and the one who

---

† **16:6** *One hundred measures:* literally, "one hundred baths." A bath is a Hebrew unit of liquid measurement equivalent to eight or nine gallons.

16:7 *One hundred kors:* a *kor* is a Hebrew unit of dry measure for grain or wheat equivalent to ten or twelve bushels.

16:8b–13 Several originally independent sayings of Jesus are gathered here by Luke to form the concluding application of the parable by the dishonest steward.

16:8b–9 The first conclusion recommends the prudent use of one's wealth (in the light of the coming of the end of the age) after the manner of the children of this world, represented in the parable by the dishonest steward.

16:9 *Dishonest wealth:* literally, "mammon of iniquity." *Mammon* is the Greek transliteration of a Hebrew or Aramaic word that is usually explained as meaning "that in which one trusts." The characterization of this wealth as *dishonest* expresses a tendency of wealth to lead one to dishonesty. *Eternal dwellings:* or, "eternal tents," i.e., heaven.

16:10–12 The second conclusion recommends constant fidelity to those in positions of responsibility.

16:13 The third conclusion is a general statement about the incompatibility of serving God and being a slave to riches. To be dependent upon wealth is opposed to the teachings of Jesus who counseled complete dependence on the Father as one of the characteristics of the Christian disciple (12:22–39). *God and mammon:* see the note on 16:9. Mammon is used here as if it were itself a god.

16:14–18 The two parables about the use of riches in ch 16 are separated by several isolated sayings of Jesus on the hypocrisy of the Pharisees (14–15), on the law (16–17), and on divorce (18).

16:14–15 The Pharisees are here presented as examples of those who are slaves to wealth (see 16:13) and, consequently, they are unable to serve God.

16:16 John the Baptist is presented in Luke's gospel as a transitional figure between the period of Israel, the time of promise, and the period of Jesus, the time of fulfillment. With John, the fulfillment of the Old Testament promises has begun.

---

* **16:8** Eph 5:8; 1 Thes 5:5.
16:9 Lk 12:33.
16:10 Lk 19:17; Mt 25:20–23.
16:13 Mt 6:24.
16:15 Lk 18:9–14.
16:16 Mt 11:12–13.
16:17 Mt 5:18.
16:18 Mt 5:32; 19:9; Mk 10:11–12; 1 Cor 7:10–11.

marries a woman divorced from her husband
commits adultery.

The Parable of the Rich Man and Lazarus†

19 "There was a rich man† who dressed in pur-
ple garments and fine linen and dined sumptu-
ously each day. 20 And lying at his door was a
poor man named Lazarus, covered with sores,
21* who would gladly have eaten his fill of the
scraps that fell from the rich man's table. Dogs
even used to come and lick his sores. 22 When the
poor man died, he was carried away by angels to
the bosom of Abraham. The rich man also died
and was buried, 23† and from the netherworld,
where he was in torment, he raised his eyes and
saw Abraham far off and Lazarus at his side.
24 And he cried out, 'Father Abraham, have pity
on me. Send Lazarus to dip the tip of his finger
in water and cool my tongue, for I am suffering
torment in these flames.' 25* Abraham replied,
'My child, remember that you received what was
good during your lifetime while Lazarus likewise
received what was bad; but now he is comforted
here, whereas you are tormented. 26 Moreover,
between us and you a great chasm is established
to prevent anyone from crossing who might
wish to go from our side to yours or from your
side to ours.' 27 He said, 'Then I beg you, father,
send him to my father's house, 28 for I have five
brothers, so that he may warn them, lest they too
come to this place of torment.' 29 But Abraham
replied, 'They have Moses and the prophets. Let
them listen to them.' 30† He said, 'Oh no, father
Abraham, but if someone from the dead goes to
them, they will repent.' 31* Then Abraham said,
'If they will not listen to Moses and the proph-
ets, neither will they be persuaded if someone
should rise from the dead.'"

Temptations to Sin

17 1* He said to his disciples, "Things that cause
sin will inevitably occur, but woe to the per-
son through whom they occur. 2 It would be better
for him if a millstone were put around his neck and
he be thrown into the sea than for him to cause one
of these little ones to sin. 3*† Be on your guard! If
your brother sins, rebuke him; and if he repents,
forgive him. 4* And if he wrongs you seven times
in one day and returns to you seven times saying, 'I
am sorry,' you should forgive him."

Saying of Faith

5 And the apostles said to the Lord, "Increase
our faith." 6* The Lord replied, "If you have faith

Live It!

The Great Chasm

In this famous parable about the rich man and poor Lazarus, Luke puts the following words in the mouth of Abraham: "Between us and you a great chasm is established to prevent anyone from crossing who might wish to go from our side to yours or from your side to ours" (Lk 16:26). Abraham is speaking metaphorically about heaven and hell, but he could just as easily be speaking about the gap between the "haves" and the "have-nots."

In our society and across the globe, the gap between those who are wealthy and those who are poor is indeed becoming a great chasm. It grows more and more difficult for those who are poor and destitute to improve their lot in life. Yet, we hear about millionaires becoming billionaires, many of whom seem to have little or no regard for the millions of people who go without in the world.

This parable speaks volumes to the inequities in our world and to our responsibility to be concerned for all the Lazaruses at our door.

- What are we doing now for those who are poor? What more could we be doing?
- How can we become more sensitive to the needs of those who are poor?

▶ Lk 16:19–31

L
K

†

16:19–31 The parable of the rich man and Lazarus again illustrates Luke's concern with Jesus' attitude toward the rich and the poor. The reversal of the fates of the rich man and Lazarus (22–23) illustrates the teachings of Jesus in Luke's "Sermon on the Plain" (6:20–21, 24–25).

16:19 The oldest Greek manuscript of Luke dating from ca. A.D. 175–225 records the name of the rich man as an abbreviated form of "Nineveh," but there is very little textual support in other manuscripts for this reading. "Dives" of popular tradition is the Latin Vulgate's translation for "rich man."

16:23 *The netherworld:* see the note on 10:15.

16:30–31 A foreshadowing in Luke's gospel of the rejection of the call to repentance even after Jesus' resurrection.

17:3a *Be on your guard:* the translation takes v 3a as the conclusion to the saying on scandal in vv 1–2. It is not impossible that it should be taken as the beginning of the saying on forgiveness in vv 3b–4.

*

16:21 Mt 15:27; Mk 7:28.
16:25 Lk 6:24–25.
16:31 Jn 5:46–47; 11:44–48.
17:1–2 Mt 18:6–7.
17:3 Mt 18:15.
17:4 Mt 6:14; 18:21–22, 35; Mk 11:25.
17:6 Mt 17:20; 21:21; Mk 11:23.

the size of a mustard seed, you would say to
[this] mulberry tree, 'Be uprooted and planted in
the sea,' and it would obey you.

Attitude of a Servant

7† "Who among you would say to your servant
who has just come in from plowing or tending
sheep in the field, 'Come here immediately and
take your place at table'? 8 Would he not rather
say to him, 'Prepare something for me to eat.
Put on your apron and wait on me while I eat
and drink. You may eat and drink when I am
finished'? 9 Is he grateful to that servant because
he did what was commanded? 10 So should it be
with you. When you have done all you have been
commanded, say, 'We are unprofitable servants;
we have done what we were obliged to do.' "

The Cleansing of Ten Lepers†

11* As he continued his journey to Jerusalem,
he traveled through Samaria and Galilee.† 12 As
he was entering a village, ten lepers met [him].
They stood at a distance from him 13* and raised
their voice, saying, "Jesus, Master! Have pity on
us!" 14*† And when he saw them, he said, "Go
show yourselves to the priests." As they were
going they were cleansed. 15 And one of them,
realizing he had been healed, returned, glorify-
ing God in a loud voice; 16 and he fell at the feet
of Jesus and thanked him. He was a Samaritan.
17 Jesus said in reply, "Ten were cleansed, were
they not? Where are the other nine? 18 Has none
but this foreigner returned to give thanks to
God?" 19* Then he said to him, "Stand up and
go; your faith has saved you."

The Coming of the Kingdom of God

20*† Asked by the Pharisees when the king-
dom of God would come, he said in reply, "The
coming of the kingdom of God cannot be ob-
served, 21*† and no one will announce, 'Look,
here it is,' or, 'There it is.' For behold, the king-
dom of God is among you."

The Day of the Son of Man

22 Then he said to his disciples, "The days will
come when you will long to see one of the days of
the Son of Man, but you will not see it. 23* There
will be those who will say to you, 'Look, there he
is,' [or] 'Look, here he is.' Do not go off, do not
run in pursuit. 24* For just as lightning flashes
and lights up the sky from one side to the other,
so will the Son of Man be [in his day]. 25* But
first he must suffer greatly and be rejected by this
generation. 26* As it was in the days of Noah, so
it will be in the days of the Son of Man; 27 they
were eating and drinking, marrying and giving
in marriage up to the day that Noah entered the
ark, and the flood came and destroyed them all.
28* Similarly, as it was in the days of Lot: they
were eating, drinking, buying, selling, planting,
building; 29 on the day when Lot left Sodom, fire
and brimstone rained from the sky to destroy
them all. 30 So it will be on the day the Son of
Man is revealed. 31* On that day, a person who
is on the housetop and whose belongings are in
the house must not go down to get them, and
likewise a person in the field must not return to
what was left behind.* 32 Remember the wife of
Lot. 33* Whoever seeks to preserve his life will
lose it, but whoever loses it will save it. 34 I tell
you, on that night there will be two people in
one bed; one will be taken, the other left. 35* And
there will be two women grinding meal together;
one will be taken, the other left. [36]† 37* They
said to him in reply, "Where, Lord?" He said to
them, "Where the body is, there also the vultures
will gather."

†

17:7–10 These sayings of Jesus, peculiar to Luke, which continue his response to the apostles' request to increase their faith (5–6), remind them that Christian disciples can make no claim on God's graciousness; in fulfilling the exacting demands of discipleship, they are only doing their duty.

17:11–19 This incident recounting the thankfulness of the cleansed Samaritan leper is narrated only in Luke's gospel and provides an instance of Jesus holding up a non-Jew (18) as an example to his Jewish contemporaries (cf 10:33 where a similar purpose is achieved in the story of the good Samaritan). Moreover, it is the faith in Jesus manifested by the foreigner that has brought him salvation (19; cf the similar relationship between faith and salvation in 7:50; 8:48, 50).

17:11 *Through Samaria and Galilee:* or, "between Samaria and Galilee."

17:14 See the note on 5:14.

17:20–37 To the question of the Pharisees about the time of the coming of God's kingdom, Jesus replies that the kingdom is *among you* (20–21). The emphasis has thus been shifted from an imminent observable coming of the kingdom to something that is already present in Jesus' preaching and healing ministry. Luke has also appended further traditional sayings of Jesus about the unpredictable suddenness of the day of the Son of Man, and assures his readers that in spite of the delay of that day (12:45), it will bring judgment unexpectedly on those who do not continue to be vigilant.

17:21 *Among you:* the Greek preposition translated as *among* can also be translated as "within." In the light of other statements in Luke's gospel about the presence of the kingdom (see 10:9, 11; 11:20) "among" is to be preferred.

17:36 The inclusion of v 36, "There will be two men in the field; one will be taken, the other left behind," in some Western manuscripts appears to be a scribal assimilation to Mt 24:40.

*

17:11 Lk 9:51–53; 13:22, 33; 18:31; 19:28; Jn 4:4.
17:13 Lk 18:38; Mt 9:27; 15:22.
17:14 Lk 5:14; Lv 14:2–32; Mt 8:4; Mk 1:44.
17:19 Lk 7:50; 18:42.
17:20 Jn 3:3.
17:21 Lk 17:23; Mt 24:23; Mk 13:21.
17:23 Lk 17:21; Mt 24:23, 26; Mk 13:21.
17:24 Mt 24:27.
17:25 Lk 9:22; 18:32–33; Mt 16:21; 17:22–23; 20:18–19; Mk 8:31; 9:31; 10:33–34.
17:26–27 Gn 6–8; Mt 24:37–39.
17:28–29 Gn 18:20–21; 19:1–29.
17:31 Mt 24:17–18; Mk 13:15–16.
17:31–32 Gn 19:17, 26.
17:33 Lk 9:24; Mt 10:39; 16:25; Mk 8:35; Jn 12:25.
17:35 Mt 24:40–41.
17:37 Jb 39:30; Mt 24:28.

The Parable of the Persistent Widow

18 1*† Then he told them a parable about
the necessity for them to pray always
without becoming weary. He said, 2 "There was
a judge in a certain town who neither feared
God nor respected any human being. 3 And a
widow in that town used to come to him and
say, 'Render a just decision for me against my
adversary.' 4 For a long time the judge was un-
willing, but eventually he thought, 'While it
is true that I neither fear God nor respect any
human being, 5*† because this widow keeps
bothering me I shall deliver a just decision for
her lest she finally come and strike me.' " 6 The
Lord said, "Pay attention to what the dishonest
judge says. 7 Will not God then secure the rights
of his chosen ones who call out to him day
and night? Will he be slow to answer them? 8 I
tell you, he will see to it that justice is done for
them speedily. But when the Son of Man comes,
will he find faith on earth?"

The Parable of the Pharisee and the Tax Collector

9* He then addressed this parable to those
who were convinced of their own righteous-
ness and despised everyone else. 10 "Two people
went up to the temple area to pray; one was a
Pharisee and the other was a tax collector. 11 The
Pharisee took up his position and spoke this
prayer to himself, 'O God, I thank you that I am
not like the rest of humanity—greedy, dishon-
est, adulterous—or even like this tax collector.
12* I fast twice a week, and I pay tithes on my
whole income.' 13* But the tax collector stood
off at a distance and would not even raise his
eyes to heaven but beat his breast and prayed,
'O God, be merciful to me a sinner.' 14* I tell
you, the latter went home justified, not the for-
mer; for everyone who exalts himself will be
humbled, and the one who humbles himself
will be exalted."

Pray It!

Can You Hear Me, Lord?

Dear God, Jesus had to remind people to pray always and not to lose hope when faced with injustice. I need to hear that too. Sometimes it seems like I pray and pray, but you are not answering.

I know I have to be willing to look and listen for your response. I know I have to pray always, not just in times of need. I know I need to share my daily life with you. Help me to do these things I know I need to do. Help me to pray, Lord. Amen.

▶ Lk 18:1–8

Saying on Children and the Kingdom

15*† People were bringing even infants to
him that he might touch them,† and when the
disciples saw this, they rebuked them. 16 Jesus,
however, called the children to himself and said,
"Let the children come to me and do not prevent
them; for the kingdom of God belongs to such
as these. 17* Amen, I say to you, whoever does
not accept the kingdom of God like a child will
not enter it."

The Rich Official

18* An official asked him this question, "Good
teacher, what must I do to inherit eternal life?"*
19 Jesus answered him, "Why do you call me good?
No one is good but God alone. 20* You know the
commandments, 'You shall not commit adultery;
you shall not kill; you shall not steal; you shall
not bear false witness; honor your father and your

18:1–14 The particularly Lucan material in the travel narrative concludes with two parables on prayer. The first (1–8) teaches the disciples the need of persistent prayer so that they not fall victims to apostasy (8). The second (9–14) condemns the self-righteous, critical attitude of the Pharisee and teaches that the fundamental attitude of the Christian disciple must be the recognition of sinfulness and complete dependence on God's graciousness. The second parable recalls the story of the pardoning of the sinful woman (7:36–50) where a similar contrast is presented between the critical attitude of the Pharisee Simon and the love shown by the pardoned sinner.

18:5 *Strike me:* the Greek verb translated as strike means "to strike under the eye" and suggests the extreme situation to which the persistence of the widow might lead. It may, however, be used here in the much weaker sense of "to wear one out."

18:15—19:27 Luke here includes much of the material about the journey to Jerusalem found in his Marcan source (10:1–52) and adds to it the story of Zacchaeus (19:1–10) from his own particular tradition and the parable of the gold coins *(minas)* (19:11–27) from Q, the source common to Luke and Matthew.

18:15–17 The sayings on children furnish a contrast to the attitude of the Pharisee in the preceding episode (9–14) and that of the wealthy official in the following one (18–23) who think that they can lay claim to God's favor by their own merit. The attitude of the disciple should be marked by the receptivity and trustful dependence characteristic of the child.

18:1 Rom 12:12; Col 4:2; 1 Thes 5:17.
18:5 Lk 11:8.
18:9 Lk 16:5; Mt 23:25–28.
18:12 Mt 23:23.
18:13 Ps 51:3.
18:14 Lk 14:11; Mt 23:12.
18:15–17 Mt 19:13–15; Mk 10:13–16.
18:17 Mt 18:3.
18:18–30 Mt 19:16–30; Mk 10:17–31.
18:18 Lk 10:25.
18:20 Ex 20:12–16; Dt 5:16–20.

Live It!

The Loaded Question

If you ask a loaded question, you should expect a loaded answer, especially if you're asking God! Picture the rich ruler in Luke 18:18–30, who devoutly followed the Commandments all his life. After hearing Jesus talk about the Reign of God, he eagerly asks Jesus, "What must I do to inherit eternal life?"

Jesus' answer, "Sell all that you have and distribute it to the poor" (verse 22), must have been like a blow. Jesus asked for a radical commitment from this rich ruler, just as Jesus asks for a radical commitment from us. As often happens in Luke's portrayal of Jesus, that radical commitment has something to do with wealth and those who are poor. If we dare to ask the loaded question—What must I do?—we must be prepared to unload something too. Our human tendency is to hoard our money and our material goods. But with God's help (see verse 27), we can become generous with those in need.

▶ Lk 18:18–30

mother.' " 21 And he replied, "All of these I have observed from my youth." 22*† When Jesus heard this he said to him, "There is still one thing left for you: sell all that you have and distribute it to the poor, and you will have a treasure in heaven. Then come, follow me." 23 But when he heard this he became quite sad, for he was very rich.

On Riches and Renunciation

24 Jesus looked at him [now sad] and said, "How hard it is for those who have wealth to enter the kingdom of God! 25 For it is easier for a camel to pass through the eye of a needle than for a rich person to enter the kingdom of God." 26 Those who heard this said, "Then who can be saved?" 27* And he said, "What is impossible for human beings is possible for God." 28 Then Peter said, "We have given up our possessions and followed you." 29* He said to them, "Amen, I say to you, there is no one who has given up house or wife or brothers or parents or children for the sake of the kingdom of God 30 who will not receive [back] an overabundant return in this present age and eternal life in the age to come."

The Third Prediction of the Passion

31*† Then he took the Twelve aside and said to them, "Behold, we are going up to Jerusalem and everything written by the prophets about the Son of Man will be fulfilled.† 32* He will be handed over to the Gentiles and he will be mocked and insulted and spat upon; 33 and after they have scourged him they will kill him, but on the third day he will rise." 34* But they understood nothing of this; the word remained hidden from them and they failed to comprehend what he said.

The Healing of the Blind Beggar

35* Now as he approached Jericho a blind man was sitting by the roadside begging, 36 and hearing a crowd going by, he inquired what was happening. 37 They told him, "Jesus of Nazareth is passing by." 38*† He shouted, "Jesus, Son of David, have pity on me!" 39 The people walking in front rebuked him, telling him to be silent, but he kept calling out all the more, "Son of David, have pity on me!" 40 Then Jesus stopped and ordered that he be brought to him; and when he came near, Jesus asked him, 41* "What do you want me to do for you?" He replied, "Lord, please let me see." 42* Jesus told him, "Have sight; your faith has saved you." 43 He immediately received his sight and followed him, giving glory to God. When they saw this, all the people gave praise to God.

---

†

18:22 Detachment from material possessions results in the total dependence on God demanded of one who would inherit eternal life. *Sell all that you have:* the original saying (cf Mk 10:21) has characteristically been made more demanding by Luke's addition of "all."

18:31–33 The details included in this third announcement of Jesus' suffering and death suggest that the literary formulation of the announcement has been directed by the knowledge of the historical passion and death of Jesus.

18:31 *Everything written by the prophets . . . will be fulfilled:* this is a Lucan addition to the words of Jesus found in the Marcan source (Mk 10:32–34). Luke understands the events of Jesus' last days in Jerusalem to be the fulfillment of Old Testament prophecy, but, as is usually the case in Luke-Acts, the author does not specify which Old Testament prophets he has in mind; cf 24:25, 27, 44; Acts 3:8; 13:27; 26:22–23.

18:38 *Son of David:* the blind beggar identifies Jesus with a title that is related to Jesus' role as Messiah (see the note on 2:11). Through this Son of David, salvation comes to the blind man. Note the connection between salvation and house of David mentioned earlier in Zechariah's canticle (1:69). See also the note on Mt 9:27.

•

18:22 Lk 12:33; Sir 29:11; Mt 6:20.
18:27 Mk 14:36.
18:29–30 Lk 14:26.
18:31–34 Lk 24:25–27, 44; Mt 20:17–19; Mk 10:32–34; Acts 3:18.
18:32–33 Lk 9:22, 44.
18:34 Mk 9:32.
18:35–43 Mt 20:29–34; Mk 10:46–52.
18:38–39 Lk 17:13; Mt 9:27; 15:22.
18:41 Mk 10:36.
18:42 Lk 7:50; 17:19.

Zacchaeus the Tax Collector

19 1 † He came to Jericho and intended to
pass through the town. 2 Now a man
there named Zacchaeus, who was a chief tax col-
lector and also a wealthy man, 3 was seeking to
see who Jesus was; but he could not see him be-
cause of the crowd, for he was short in stature.
4 So he ran ahead and climbed a sycamore tree
in order to see Jesus, who was about to pass that
way. 5 When he reached the place, Jesus looked
up and said to him, "Zacchaeus, come down
quickly, for today I must stay at your house."
6 And he came down quickly and received him
with joy. 7 * When they all saw this, they began
to grumble, saying, "He has gone to stay at
the house of a sinner." 8 * But Zacchaeus stood
there and said to the Lord, "Behold, half of my
possessions, Lord, I shall give to the poor, and
if I have extorted anything from anyone I shall
repay it four times over." 9 * † And Jesus said to
him, "Today salvation has come to this house
because this man too is a descendant of Abra-
ham. 10 * † For the Son of Man has come to seek
and to save what was lost."

The Parable of the Ten Gold Coins

11 * † While they were listening to him speak,
he proceeded to tell a parable because he was
near Jerusalem and they thought that the king-
dom of God would appear there immediately.
12 * So he said, "A nobleman went off to a dis-
tant country to obtain the kingship for himself
and then to return. 13 † He called ten of his
servants and gave them ten gold coins and told
them, 'Engage in trade with these until I return.'
14 His fellow citizens, however, despised him
and sent a delegation after him to announce,
'We do not want this man to be our king.' 15 But
when he returned after obtaining the kingship,
he had the servants called, to whom he had

Live It!

Look Up!

Jesus looked up. With this simple act, Jesus changed a man's life, inviting him down from the tree and into relationship with him. Why would Jesus choose Zacchaeus, who was hated and despised as a tax collector, to become a disciple? Besides that, he was pretty short and did not stand out in a crowd. Perhaps Luke is trying to tell us that our physical attributes, our past history, and other people's perceptions do not figure into God's equation.

When Jesus looks up and notices Zacchaeus, Zacchaeus ends up not only believing in Jesus but also doing something surprising. He gives away half of his money and possessions, perhaps to make up for all the times he cheated people. This is what conversion is—a change of heart and behavior. Conversion calls us to act in ways we would not have acted before.

- Jesus has been with you from the moment of your conception. How have you tried to know him better?
- How do you feel knowing that Jesus sees past externals and loves you for who you truly are?
- Whom in your own life have you been failing to notice by not taking the time to look up?

Lk 19:1–10

†

19:1–10 The story of the tax collector Zacchaeus is unique to this gospel. While a rich man (2), Zacchaeus provides a contrast to the rich man of 18:18–23 who cannot detach himself from his material possessions to become a follower of Jesus. Zacchaeus, according to Luke, exemplifies the proper attitude toward wealth: he promises to give half of his possessions to the poor (8) and consequently is the recipient of salvation (9–10).

19:9 *A descendant of Abraham:* literally, "a son of Abraham." The tax collector Zacchaeus, whose repentance is attested by his determination to amend his former ways, shows himself to be a true descendant of Abraham, the true heir to the promises of God in the Old Testament. Underlying Luke's depiction of Zacchaeus as a descendant of Abraham, the father of the Jews (1:73; 16:22–31), is his recognition of the central place occupied by Israel in the plan of salvation.

19:10 This verse sums up for Luke his depiction of the role of Jesus as savior in this gospel.

19:11–27 In this parable Luke has combined two originally distinct parables: (1) a parable about the conduct of faithful and productive servants (13, 15b–26) and (2) a parable about a rejected king (12, 14–15a, 27). The story about the conduct of servants occurs in another form in Mt 25:14–20. The story about the rejected king may have originated with a contemporary historical event. After the death of Herod the Great, his son Archelaus traveled to Rome to receive the title of king. A delegation of Jews appeared in Rome before Caesar Augustus to oppose the request of Archelaus. Although not given the title of king, Archelaus was made ruler over Judea and Samaria. As the story is used by Luke, however, it furnishes a correction to the expectation of the imminent end of the age and of the establishment of the kingdom in Jerusalem (11). Jesus is not on his way to Jerusalem to receive the kingly power; for that, he must go away and only after returning from the distant country (a reference to the parousia) will reward and judgment take place.

19:13 *Ten gold coins:* literally, "ten minas." A mina was a monetary unit that in ancient Greece was the equivalent of one hundred drachmas.

*

19:7 Lk 5:30; 15:2.
19:8 Ex 21:37; Nm 5:6–7; 2 Sm 12:6.
19:9 Lk 13:16; Mt 21:31.
19:10 Lk 15:4–10; Ez 34:16.
19:11–27 Mt 25:14–30.
19:12 Mk 13:34.

Cultural Connection

Jesus Goes to Jerusalem as the Messiah

As Jesus enters Jerusalem to celebrate the Passover, the crowd joyfully hails him as the king and Messiah returning to the City of David. He is the prophet who brings new hope and calls people to conversion.

On Palm Sunday—also known as Passion Sunday—we begin our preparation for Holy Week. At Mass we receive blessed branches of palms to symbolize our profession of Jesus as the Messiah, king of peace. In some Hispanic communities, the palms are woven into beautiful braids, crosses, and flowers. In others, people receive a small donkey made of palm leaves, as a remembrance of Jesus' riding the donkey into Jerusalem. Often, Jesus' entrance into Jerusalem is re-enacted. Hispanics use art, song, and drama to celebrate and express their faith.

- Picture yourself in the crowd welcoming Jesus. Does Jesus' arrival fill you with joy and hope?
- Next Palm Sunday, find a special place for your palm. Think of a concrete way you will live out your calling as a disciple of Jesus in the coming year. Each time you see the palm, remember your call, and pray for help to respond to it.

▶ Lk 19:28–40

given the money, to learn what they had gained
by trading. 16 The first came forward and said,
'Sir, your gold coin has earned ten additional
ones.' 17* He replied, 'Well done, good servant!
You have been faithful in this very small matter; take charge of ten cities.' 18 Then the second
came and reported, 'Your gold coin, sir, has
earned five more.' 19 And to this servant too he
said, 'You, take charge of five cities.' 20 Then the
other servant came and said, 'Sir, here is your
gold coin; I kept it stored away in a handkerchief, 21 for I was afraid of you, because you are
a demanding person; you take up what you did
not lay down and you harvest what you did not
plant.' 22 He said to him, 'With your own words
I shall condemn you, you wicked servant. You
knew I was a demanding person, taking up what
I did not lay down and harvesting what I did
not plant; 23 why did you not put my money in a
bank? Then on my return I would have collected
it with interest.' 24 And to those standing by he
said, 'Take the gold coin from him and give it to
the servant who has ten.' 25 But they said to him,
'Sir, he has ten gold coins.' 26* 'I tell you, to everyone who has, more will be given, but from
the one who has not, even what he has will be
taken away. 27 Now as for those enemies of mine
who did not want me as their king, bring them
here and slay them before me.' "

VI: The Teaching Ministry in Jerusalem

The Entry into Jerusalem

28*† After he had said this, he proceeded on
his journey up to Jerusalem. 29* As he drew near
to Bethphage and Bethany at the place called
the Mount of Olives, he sent two of his disciples. 30* He said, "Go into the village opposite
you, and as you enter it you will find a colt
tethered on which no one has ever sat. Untie it
and bring it here. 31 And if anyone should ask
you, 'Why are you untying it?' you will answer,
'The Master has need of it.' " 32* So those who
had been sent went off and found everything
just as he had told them. 33 And as they were
untying the colt, its owners said to them, "Why
are you untying this colt?" 34 They answered,
"The Master has need of it." 35* So they brought
it to Jesus, threw their cloaks over the colt, and
helped Jesus to mount. 36 As he rode along, the
people were spreading their cloaks on the road;

† **19:28—21:38** With the royal entry of Jesus into Jerusalem, a new section of Luke's gospel begins, the ministry of Jesus in Jerusalem before his death and resurrection. Luke suggests that this was a lengthy ministry in Jerusalem (19:47; 20:1; 21:37–38; 22:53) and it is characterized by Jesus' daily teaching in the temple (21:37–38). For the story of the entry of Jesus into Jerusalem, see also Mt 21:1–11; Mk 11:1–10; Jn 12:12–19 and the notes there.

* **19:17** Lk 16:10.
19:26 Lk 8:18; Mt 13:12; Mk 4:25.
19:28–40 Mt 21:1–11; Mk 11:1–11; Jn 12:12–19.
19:29 Zec 14:4.
19:30 Nm 19:2; Dt 21:3; 1 Sm 6:7; Zec 9:9.
19:32 Lk 22:13.
19:35–36 2 Kgs 9:13.

37 and now as he was approaching the slope of
the Mount of Olives, the whole multitude of his
disciples began to praise God aloud with joy for
all the mighty deeds they had seen. 38*† They
proclaimed:

"Blessed is the king who comes
in the name of the Lord.
Peace in heaven
and glory in the highest."

39† Some of the Pharisees in the crowd said to
him, "Teacher, rebuke your disciples." 40 He said
in reply, "I tell you, if they keep silent, the stones
will cry out!"

The Lament for Jerusalem

41*† As he drew near, he saw the city and
wept over it,* 42* saying, "If this day you only
knew what makes for peace—but now it is hid-
den from your eyes. 43*† For the days are com-
ing upon you when your enemies will raise a
palisade against you; they will encircle you and
hem you in on all sides. 44* They will smash you
to the ground and your children within you,
and they will not leave one stone upon another
within you because you did not recognize the
time of your visitation."

The Cleansing of the Temple

45*† Then Jesus entered the temple area and pro-
ceeded to drive out those who were selling things,*
46* saying to them, "It is written, 'My house shall
be a house of prayer, but you have made it a den
of thieves.' " 47* And every day he was teaching in
the temple area. The chief priests, the scribes, and
the leaders of the people, meanwhile, were seeking
to put him to death,* 48 but they could find no way
to accomplish their purpose because all the people
were hanging on his words.

Did You Know?

The Human Jesus

Have you ever been so disappointed in something that you just sat down and wept? That's what happened to Jesus. In Luke 19:41–42, we hear of his great disappointment and frustration that he cannot help Jerusalem and its people. The people of Jerusalem do not accept his message of justice and peace, so the Temple and Jerusalem are to be destroyed again. Jesus is so upset that he weeps.

We often forget that although Jesus is fully God, he is also fully human and experienced all the things that normal people experience. He enjoyed excitement, laughter, and fun times with friends. He also experienced fear, sadness, and frustration. He was completely human in all things but sin.

- What does it mean to you that Jesus shares our humanity?
- Why is Jesus' humanity an important part of the Christian message?

▶ **Lk 19:41–42**

The Authority of Jesus Questioned

20 1*† One day as he was teaching the peo-
ple in the temple area and proclaiming
the good news, the chief priests and scribes, to-
gether with the elders, approached him 2* and
said to him, "Tell us, by what authority are you
doing these things? Or who is the one who gave

†

19:38 *Blessed is the king who comes in the name of the Lord:* only in Luke is Jesus explicitly given the title *king* when he enters Jerusalem in triumph. Luke has inserted this title into the words of Ps 118:26 that heralded the arrival of the pilgrims coming to the holy city and to the temple. Jesus is thereby acclaimed as *king* (see 1:32) and as the one *who comes* (see Mal 3:1; Lk 7:19). *Peace in heaven . . . :* the acclamation of the disciples of Jesus in Luke echoes the announcement of the angels at the birth of Jesus (2:14). The peace Jesus brings is associated with the salvation to be accomplished here in Jerusalem.

19:39 *Rebuke your disciples:* this command, found only in Luke, was given so that the Roman authorities would not interpret the acclamation of Jesus as king as an uprising against them; cf 23:2–3.

19:41–44 The lament for Jerusalem is found only in Luke. By not accepting Jesus (the one who mediates peace), Jerusalem will not find peace but will become the victim of devastation.

19:43–44 Luke may be describing the actual disaster that befell Jerusalem in A.D. 70 when it was destroyed by the Romans during the First Revolt.

19:45–46 Immediately upon entering the holy city, Jesus in a display of his authority enters the temple (see Mal 3:1–3) and lays claim to it after cleansing it that it might become a proper place for his teaching ministry in Jerusalem (19:47; 20:1; 21:37; 22:53). See Mt 21:12–17; Mk 11:15–19; Jn 2:13–17 and the notes there.

20:1–47 The Jerusalem religious leaders or their representatives, in an attempt to incriminate Jesus with the Romans and to discredit him with the people, pose a number of questions to him (about his authority, 2; about payment of taxes, 22; about the resurrection, 28–33).

19:38 Lk 2:14; Ps 118:26.
19:41–44 Lk 13:34–35.
19:41 2 Kgs 8:11–12; Jer 14:17; 15:5.
19:42 Lk 8:10; Is 6:9–10; Mt 13:14; Mk 4:12; Acts 28:26–27; Rom 11:8, 10.
19:43 Is 29:3.
19:44 Lk 1:68; 21:6; Ps 137:9; Mt 24:2; Mk 13:2.
19:45–46 Mt 21:12–13; Mk 11:15–17; Jn 2:13–17.
19:45 Lk 3:1; Hos 9:15.
19:46 Is 56:7; Jer 7:11.
19:47–48 Lk 20:19; 22:2; Mt 21:46; Mk 11:18; 12:12; 14:1–2; Jn 5:18; 7:30.
19:47 Lk 21:37; 22:53; Jn 18:20.
20:1–8 Mt 21:23–27; Mk 11:27–33.
20:2 Acts 4:7.

Catholic Social Teaching

Sit and Stand Against Injustice

Jesus not only claimed to be God's son but also took an active stand against injustice, greed, and religious hypocrisy. This outraged the leaders of his time and put his life in danger.

Despite the risks, other people have followed Jesus' example of civil disobedience. On February 1, 1960, in Greensboro, North Carolina, four first-year college students began a sit-in at a diner that did not allow black people to eat there. These students' actions against injustice sparked similar sit-ins across the country. Thousands of courageous people protested against unfair and cruel policies that granted white people privileges that were denied to black people.

Another example of uncommon bravery occurred on December 1, 1955, in Selma, Alabama. Rosa Parks, a black woman, boarded a public bus and sat in one of the seats toward the front, where only white people were allowed to sit. For her bravery, she was arrested, jailed, and fined. This event triggered a bus boycott that lasted for months and finally put an end to that policy.

Civil disobedience continues today. Every year, busloads of people travel to Fort Benning, Georgia, to protest a U.S. military facility nicknamed "The School of the Assassins." This school teaches methods of torture and terrorism. Over the years, peaceful protesters have poured water on the grounds of the military base, held candles, sung songs, and sprawled themselves on the school grounds to re-enact scenes of death inflicted upon victims of the school's graduates. The protestors often end up in jail.

Catholic social teaching asserts that every person has a right and a duty to participate actively in shaping society and to promote the well-being of all, especially the poor and vulnerable. Not every Christian is called to participate in acts of civil disobedience, but we are all called to be aware of and speak out against situations that are racist, sexist, or unjust. As Jesus shows us, silence is not an acceptable option in the face of injustice.

▶ **Lk 19:45–48**
Call to Family, Community, and Participation

you this authority?" 3He said to them in re-
ply, "I shall ask you a question. Tell me, 4* was
John's baptism of heavenly or of human origin?"
5* They discussed this among themselves, and
said, "If we say, 'Of heavenly origin,' he will
say, 'Why did you not believe him?' 6But if we
say, 'Of human origin,' then all the people will
stone us, for they are convinced that John was a
prophet." 7So they answered that they did not
know from where it came. 8Then Jesus said to
them, "Neither shall I tell you by what authority
I do these things."

The Parable of the Tenant Farmers

9*† Then he proceeded to tell the people this
parable. "[A] man planted a vineyard, leased it
to tenant farmers, and then went on a journey
for a long time.* 10* At harvest time he sent a
servant to the tenant farmers to receive some
of the produce of the vineyard. But they beat
the servant and sent him away empty-handed.
11So he proceeded to send another servant, but
him also they beat and insulted and sent away
empty-handed. 12Then he proceeded to send a
third, but this one too they wounded and threw
out. 13* The owner of the vineyard said, 'What
shall I do? I shall send my beloved son; maybe
they will respect him.' 14But when the tenant
farmers saw him they said to one another, 'This
is the heir. Let us kill him that the inheritance
may become ours.' 15† So they threw him out of
the vineyard and killed him. What will the owner

† **20:9–19** This parable about an absentee landlord and a tenant farmers' revolt reflects the social and economic conditions of rural Palestine in the first century. The synoptic gospel writers use the parable to describe how the rejection of the landlord's son becomes the occasion for the vineyard to be taken away from those to whom it was entrusted (the religious leadership of Judaism that rejects the teaching and preaching of Jesus; 19).

20:15 *They threw him out of the vineyard and killed him:* cf Mk 12:8. Luke has altered his Marcan source and reports that the murder takes place outside the vineyard.

20:4 Lk 3:3, 16.
20:5 Mt 21:32.
20:9–19 Mt 21:33–46; Mk 12:1–12.
20:9 Is 5:1–7.
20:10–12 2 Chr 36:15–16.
20:13 Lk 3:22.

of the vineyard do to them? 16 He will come and put those tenant farmers to death and turn over the vineyard to others." When the people heard this, they exclaimed, "Let it not be so!" 17* But he looked at them and asked, "What then does this scripture passage mean:

'The stone which the builders rejected
has become the cornerstone'?

18 Everyone who falls on that stone will be dashed to pieces; and it will crush anyone on whom it falls." 19* The scribes and chief priests sought to lay their hands on him at that very hour, but they feared the people, for they knew that he had addressed this parable to them.

Paying Taxes to the Emperor

20*† They watched him closely and sent agents pretending to be righteous who were to trap him in speech,* in order to hand him over to the authority and power of the governor. 21* They posed this question to him, "Teacher, we know that what you say and teach is correct, and you show no partiality, but teach the way of God in accordance with the truth. 22† Is it lawful for us to pay tribute to Caesar or not?" 23 Recognizing their craftiness he said to them, 24† "Show me a denarius; whose image and name does it bear?" They replied, "Caesar's." 25* So he said to them, "Then repay to Caesar what belongs to Caesar and to God what belongs to God." 26 They were unable to trap him by something he might say before the people, and so amazed were they at his reply that they fell silent.

The Question about the Resurrection

27*† Some Sadducees, those who deny that there is a resurrection, came forward and put this question to him,* 28*† saying, "Teacher, Moses wrote for us, 'If someone's brother dies leaving a wife but no child, his brother must take the wife and raise up descendants for his brother.' 29 Now there were seven brothers; the first married a woman but died childless. 30 Then the second 31 and the third married her, and likewise all the seven died childless. 32 Finally the woman also died. 33 Now at the resurrection whose wife will that woman be? For all seven had been married to her." 34 Jesus said to them, "The children of this age marry and are given in marriage; 35 but those who are deemed worthy to attain to the coming age and to the resurrection of the dead neither marry nor are given in marriage. 36† They can no longer die, for they are like angels; and they are the children of God because they are the ones who will rise. 37* That the dead will rise even Moses made known in the passage about the bush, when he called 'Lord' the God of Abraham, the God of Isaac, and the God of Jacob; 38* and he is not God of the dead, but of the living, for to him all are alive." 39 Some of the scribes said in reply, "Teacher, you have answered well." 40* And they no longer dared to ask him anything.

The Question about David's Son

41*† Then he said to them, "How do they claim that the Messiah is the Son of David? 42* For David himself in the Book of Psalms says:

'The Lord said to my lord,
"Sit at my right hand
43 till I make your enemies your footstool."'

44 Now if David calls him 'lord,' how can he be his son?"

Denunciation of the Scribes

45* Then, within the hearing of all the people, he said to [his] disciples, 46* "Be on guard

---

† der of the son takes place outside the vineyard to reflect the tradition of Jesus' death outside the walls of the city of Jerusalem (see Heb 13:12).

20:20 *The governor:* i.e., Pontius Pilate, the Roman administrator responsible for the collection of taxes and maintenance of order in Palestine.

20:22 Through their question the agents of the Jerusalem religious leadership hope to force Jesus to take sides on one of the sensitive political issues of first-century Palestine. The issue of nonpayment of taxes to Rome becomes one of the focal points of the First Jewish Revolt (A.D. 66–70) that resulted in the Roman destruction of Jerusalem and the temple. See also the note on Mt 22:15–22.

20:24 *Denarius:* a Roman silver coin (see the note on 7:41).

20:27 *Sadducees:* see the note on Mt 3:7.

20:28–33 The Sadducees' question, based on the law of levirate marriage recorded in Dt 25:5–10, ridicules the idea of the resurrection. Jesus rejects their naive understanding of the resurrection (35–36) and then argues on behalf of the resurrection of the dead on the basis of the written law (37–38) that the Sadducees accept. See also the notes on Mt 22:23–33.

20:36 *Because they are the ones who will rise:* literally, "being sons of the resurrection."

20:41–44 After successfully answering the three questions of his opponents, Jesus now asks them a question. Their inability to respond implies that they have forfeited their position and authority as the religious leaders of the people because they do not understand the scriptures. This series of controversies between the religious leadership of Jerusalem and Jesus reveals Jesus as the authoritative teacher whose words are to be listened to (see 9:35). See also the notes on Mt 22:41–46.

* **20:17** Ps 118:22; Is 28:16.
20:19 Lk 19:47–48; 22:2; Mt 21:46; Mk 11:18; 12:12; 14:1–2; Jn 5:18; 7:30.
20:20–26 Mt 22:15–22; Mk 12:13–17.
20:20 Lk 11:54.
20:21 Jn 3:2.
20:25 Rom 13:6–7.
20:27–40 Mt 22:23–33; Mk 12:18–27.
20:27 Acts 23:8.
20:28 Gn 38:8; Dt 25:5.
20:37 Ex 3:2, 6, 15–16.
20:38 Rom 14:8–9.
20:40 Mt 22:46; Mk 12:34.
20:41–44 Mt 22:41–45; Mk 12:35–37.
20:42–43 Ps 110:1.
20:45–47 Lk 11:37–54; Mt 23:1–36; Mk 12:38–40.
20:46 Lk 14:7–11.

Live It!

Stewardship: Making a Contribution

In Luke 21:1–4, Jesus notices that the rich people gave from their excess wealth, but the widow gave from her limited budget. She actually contributed more meaningfully because she gave from what little she had.

God calls us to be contributing members of the faith community and the human family—even to the point of sacrifice. We are called to stewardship, which means giving our time, talents, and treasure to support the Church's mission to spread the Good News of Jesus Christ. We should also support other organizations that contribute to the positive welfare of people in need.

How are you responding to God's call to give? Pray for the generosity of the poor widow as you discern how much of your time, talents, and treasure you are being called to give.

▶ Lk 21:1–4

against the scribes, who like to go around in long
robes and love greetings in marketplaces, seats
of honor in synagogues, and places of honor at
banquets. 47 They devour the houses of widows
and, as a pretext, recite lengthy prayers. They will
receive a very severe condemnation."

The Poor Widow's Contribution

21 1*† When he looked up he saw some
wealthy people putting their offerings into
the treasury 2 and he noticed a poor widow
putting in two small coins. 3 He said, "I tell you
truly, this poor widow put in more than all the
rest; 4 for those others have all made offerings
from their surplus wealth, but she, from her pov-
erty, has offered her whole livelihood."

The Destruction of the Temple Foretold

5*† While some people were speaking about
how the temple was adorned with costly stones
and votive offerings, he said, 6* "All that you see
here—the days will come when there will not be
left a stone upon another stone that will not be
thrown down."

The Signs of the End

7* Then they asked him, "Teacher, when will
this happen? And what sign will there be when
all these things are about to happen?" 8*† He an-
swered, "See that you not be deceived, for many
will come in my name, saying, 'I am he,' and 'The
time has come.' Do not follow them! 9 When you
hear of wars and insurrections, do not be terri-
fied; for such things must happen first, but it will
not immediately be the end." 10* Then he said to
them, "Nation will rise against nation, and king-
dom against kingdom. 11 There will be powerful
earthquakes, famines, and plagues from place to
place; and awesome sights and mighty signs will
come from the sky.

The Coming Persecution

12*† "Before all this happens, however, they
will seize and persecute you, they will hand you
over to the synagogues and to prisons, and they
will have you led before kings and governors be-
cause of my name.* 13 It will lead to your giving
testimony. 14 Remember, you are not to prepare
your defense beforehand, 15*† for I myself shall
give you a wisdom in speaking that all your
adversaries will be powerless to resist or refute.
16* You will even be handed over by parents,
brothers, relatives, and friends, and they will put

† **21:1–4** The widow is another example of the poor ones in this gospel whose detachment from material possessions and dependence on God leads to their blessedness (6:20). Her simple offering provides a striking contrast to the pride and pretentiousness of the scribes denounced in the preceding section (20:45–47). The story is taken from Mk 12:41–44.

21:5–36 Jesus' eschatological discourse in Luke is inspired by Mk 13, but Luke has made some significant alterations to the words of Jesus found there. Luke maintains, though in a modified form, the belief in the early expectation of the end of the age (see 27, 28, 31, 32, 36), but, by focusing attention throughout the gospel on the importance of the day-to-day following of Jesus and by reinterpreting the meaning of some of the signs of the end from Mk 13, he has come to terms with what seemed to the early Christian community to be a delay of the parousia. Mark, for example, described the desecration of the Jerusalem temple by the Romans (Mk 13:14) as the apocalyptic symbol (see Dn 9:27; 12:11) accompanying the end of the age and the coming of the Son of Man. Luke (21:20–24), however, removes the apocalyptic setting and separates the historical destruction of Jerusalem from the signs of the coming of the Son of Man by a period that he refers to as "the times of the Gentiles" (21:24). See also the notes on Mt 24:1–36 and Mk 13:1–37.

21:8 *The time has come:* in Luke, the proclamation of the imminent end of the age has itself become a false teaching.

21:12 *Before all this happens . . . :* to Luke and his community, some of the signs of the end just described (10–11) still lie in the future. Now in dealing with the persecution of the disciples (12–19) and the destruction of Jerusalem (20–24) Luke is pointing to eschatological signs that have already been fulfilled.

21:15 *A wisdom in speaking:* literally, "a mouth and wisdom."

* **21:1–4** Mk 12:41–44.
21:5–6 Mt 24:1–2; Mk 13:1–2.
21:6 Lk 19:44.
21:7–19 Mt 24:3–14; Mk 13:3–13.
21:8 Lk 17:23; Mk 13:5, 6, 21; 1 Jn 2:18.
21:10 2 Chr 15:6; Is 19:2.
21:12–15 Lk 12:11–12; Mt 10:17–20; Mk 13:9–11.
21:12 Jn 16:2; Acts 25:24.
21:15 Acts 6:10.
21:16–18 Mt 10:21–22.

some of you to death.* [17] You will be hated by all because of my name, [18]* but not a hair on your head will be destroyed. [19]* By your perseverance you will secure your lives.

The Great Tribulation

[20]*† "When you see Jerusalem surrounded by armies, know that its desolation is at hand.* [21]* Then those in Judea must flee to the mountains. Let those within the city escape from it, and let those in the countryside not enter the city, [22] for these days are the time of punishment when all the scriptures are fulfilled. [23]* Woe to pregnant women and nursing mothers in those days, for a terrible calamity will come upon the earth and a wrathful judgment upon this people. [24]*† They will fall by the edge of the sword and be taken as captives to all the Gentiles; and Jerusalem will be trampled underfoot by the Gentiles until the times of the Gentiles are fulfilled.

The Coming of the Son of Man

[25]* "There will be signs in the sun, the moon, and the stars, and on earth nations will be in dismay, perplexed by the roaring of the sea and the waves.* [26]*† People will die of fright in anticipation of what is coming upon the world, for the powers of the heavens will be shaken. [27]* And then they will see the Son of Man coming in a cloud with power and great glory. [28]* But when these signs begin to happen, stand erect and raise your heads because your redemption is at hand."

The Lesson of the Fig Tree

[29]* He taught them a lesson. "Consider the fig tree and all the other trees. [30] When their buds burst open, you see for yourselves and know that summer is now near; [31] in the same way, when you see these things happening, know that the kingdom of God is near. [32]* Amen, I say to you, this generation will not pass away until all these things have taken place. [33]* Heaven and earth will pass away, but my words will not pass away.

Exhortation to be Vigilant

[34]* "Beware that your hearts do not become drowsy from carousing and drunkenness and the anxieties of daily life, and that day catch you by surprise [35] like a trap. For that day will assault everyone who lives on the face of the earth. [36]* Be vigilant at all times and pray that you have the strength to escape the tribulations that are imminent and to stand before the Son of Man."

Ministry in Jerusalem

[37]* During the day, Jesus was teaching in the temple area, but at night he would leave and stay at the place called the Mount of Olives. [38] And all the people would get up early each morning to listen to him in the temple area.

VII: The Passion Narrative†

The Conspiracy against Jesus

22 [1]* Now the feast of Unleavened Bread, called the Passover,† was drawing near, [2]* and the chief priests and the scribes were seeking a way to put him to death, for they were afraid of the people. [3]*† Then Satan entered into Judas, the one surnamed Iscariot, who was counted among the Twelve,* [4] and he went to the chief priests and temple guards to discuss a plan for handing him over to them. [5] They were pleased and agreed to pay him money.

L K

21:20–24 The actual destruction of Jerusalem by Rome in A.D. 70 upon which Luke and his community look back provides the assurance that, just as Jesus' prediction of Jerusalem's destruction was fulfilled, so too will be his announcement of their final redemption (27–28).

21:24 *The times of the Gentiles:* a period of indeterminate length separating the destruction of Jerusalem from the cosmic signs accompanying the coming of the Son of Man.

21:26 *The powers of the heavens:* the heavenly bodies mentioned in v 25 and thought of as cosmic armies.

22:1—23:56a The passion narrative. Luke is still dependent upon Mark for the composition of the passion narrative but has incorporated much of his own special tradition into the narrative. Among the distinctive sections in Luke are: (1) the tradition of the institution of the Eucharist (22:15–20); (2) Jesus' farewell discourse (22:21–38); (3) the mistreatment and interrogation of Jesus (22:63–71); (4) Jesus before Herod and his second appearance before Pilate (23:6–16); (5) words addressed to the women followers on the way to the crucifixion (23:27–32); (6) words to the penitent thief (23:39–41); (7) the death of Jesus (23:46, 47b-49). Luke stresses the innocence of Jesus (23:4, 14–15, 22) who is the victim of the powers of evil (22:3, 31, 53) and who goes to his death in fulfillment of his Father's will (22:42, 46). Throughout the narrative Luke emphasizes the mercy, compassion, and healing power of Jesus (22:51; 23:43) who does not go to death lonely and deserted, but is accompanied by others who follow him on the way of the cross (23:26–31, 49).

22:1 *Feast of Unleavened Bread, called the Passover:* see the note on Mk 14:1.

22:3 *Satan entered into Judas:* see the note on 4:13.

21:16 Lk 12:52–53.
21:18 Lk 12:7; 1 Sm 14:45; Mt 10:30; Acts 27:34.
21:19 Lk 8:15.
21:20–24 Mt 24:15–21; Mk 13:14–19.
21:20–22 Lk 19:41–44.
21:21 Lk 17:31.
21:23 1 Cor 7:26.
21:24 Tb 14:5; Ps 79:1; Is 63:18; Jer 21:7; Rom 11:25; Rv 11:2.
21:25–28 Mt 24:29–31; Mk 13:24–27.
21:25 Wis 5:22; Is 13:10; Ez 32:7; Jl 2:10; 3:3–4; 4:15; Rv 6:12–14.
21:26 Hg 2:6, 21.
21:27 Dn 7:13–14; Mt 26:64; Rv 1:7.
21:28 Lk 2:38.
21:29–33 Mt 24:32–35; Mk 13:28–31.
21:32 Lk 9:27; Mt 16:28.
21:33 Lk 16:17.
21:34 Lk 12:45–46; Mt 24:48–50; 1 Thes 5:3, 6–7.
21:36 Mk 13:33.
21:37 Lk 19:47; 22:39.
22:1–2 Mt 26:1–5; Mk 14:1–2; Jn 11:47–53.
22:2 Lk 19:47–48; 20:19; Mt 21:46; Mk 12:12; Jn 5:18; 7:30.
22:3–6 Mt 26:14–16; Mk 14:10–11; Jn 13:2, 27.
22:3 Acts 1:17.

Catholic Connection

The Eucharist

In Luke's Gospel, Jesus' words from the Last Supper, "Do this in memory of me" (22:19), invite us to enter into the mystery of Jesus' life, Passion, death, and Resurrection. These are not just separate events in Jesus' life but rather essential parts of the whole mystery of Christ's redemption and salvation, known as the Paschal mystery. Each Sunday, Catholics gather together with their parish community, the assembled Body of Christ, to celebrate this core mystery of our faith during the Eucharist.

To share in this mystery means we take on the pattern of Jesus' life, Passion, death, and Resurrection as the pattern for our own lives. When we celebrate the Eucharist, we are truly sharing in the sacrifice of Christ. Everything that happens in our lives we take with us to the Eucharist and offer up in the gifts of bread and wine. As the bread and wine become the Body and Blood of Christ, so are our lives transformed by the Spirit of God. As we leave Mass, we enter back into our everyday world more prepared to be Christ's presence for others.

To celebrate the Eucharist is to commit ourselves to a way of life based on the Paschal mystery. Over and over again, we commit ourselves to dying to self and living for others, to putting to death our old ways of sin and living a life of holiness, to embracing the cross so that we might be raised to new life in Christ. Each week, we strive to enter more fully into the Paschal mystery by pledging to live more like Christ the rest of the week ahead. That is why we need to celebrate and attend Mass every week. Each week, as the mystery of God's Revelation is shared and unpacked, we come to a deeper understanding of how pain and death, lovingly embraced, can result in growth and new life. This contradicts the cultural message that we should avoid pain at all costs. We cannot afford to delude ourselves into thinking that growth should be easy, that love should be painless, and that happiness should be constant. By embracing the Paschal mystery as a way of life, we will, more and more, come to live a life of real love.

For the short period of time we gather at the Eucharist each week, we are given time away from "practicing our faith" in order to just *be* the Body of Christ. It is the other 167 hours of the week that we are called to put into practice what we are when we are assembled at Mass. The Eucharist ends with a reminder of our purpose in life—to love and serve God by loving and serving one another as Christ did. Thus, the Eucharist never really ends, for we are always called to be a Eucharistic people.

Lk 22:14–20

Catechism, nos. 787–796, 1329, 1396

LK

6 He accepted their offer and sought a favorable
opportunity to hand him over to them in the ab-
sence of a crowd.

Preparations for the Passover

7* When the day of the feast of Unleavened
Bread arrived, the day for sacrificing the Passover
lamb,* 8 he sent out Peter and John, instructing
them, "Go and make preparations for us to eat
the Passover." 9 They asked him, "Where do you
want us to make the preparations?" 10† And he
answered them, "When you go into the city, a
man will meet you carrying a jar of water. Fol-
low him into the house that he enters 11 and
say to the master of the house, 'The teacher says
to you, "Where is the guest room where I may
eat the Passover with my disciples?"' 12 He will
show you a large upper room that is furnished.
Make the preparations there." 13* Then they went
off and found everything exactly as he had told
them, and there they prepared the Passover.

The Last Supper

14* When the hour came, he took his place
at table with the apostles. 15† He said to them,
"I have eagerly desired to eat this Passover with
you before I suffer, 16* for, I tell you, I shall not
eat it [again] until there is fulfillment in the
kingdom of God." 17† Then he took a cup, gave
thanks, and said, "Take this and share it among
yourselves; 18 for I tell you [that] from this time
on I shall not drink of the fruit of the vine until
the kingdom of God comes." 19*† Then he took
the bread, said the blessing, broke it, and gave it
to them, saying, "This is my body, which will be
given for you; do this in memory of me." 20* And
likewise the cup after they had eaten, saying,
"This cup is the new covenant in my blood,
which will be shed for you.

The Betrayal Foretold

21* "And yet behold, the hand of the one who
is to betray me is with me on the table; 22 for
the Son of Man indeed goes as it has been de-
termined; but woe to that man by whom he is
betrayed." 23 And they began to debate among
themselves who among them would do such a
deed.

The Role of the Disciples

24*† Then an argument broke out among them
about which of them should be regarded as the
greatest. 25*† He said to them, "The kings of the
Gentiles lord it over them and those in authority
over them are addressed as 'Benefactors'; 26* but
among you it shall not be so. Rather, let the
greatest among you be as the youngest, and the
leader as the servant. 27 For who is greater:
the one seated at table or the one who serves? Is
it not the one seated at table? I am among you as
the one who serves. 28 It is you who have stood
by me in my trials; 29* and I confer a kingdom on
you, just as my Father has conferred one on me,

Pray It!

Prayer of a Servant Leader

Dear Jesus, you made it clear that those who are greatest are the ones who serve, not the ones who have fame, fortune, or authority. Help me to adjust my priorities to put others first. Place within me a genuine desire to serve. Enable me to recognize the daily opportunities I have to reach out to those in need in my family, in my school, and in my community. Guide me as I strive to follow your example to become a servant leader.
Amen.

▶ Lk 22:24–27

†

22:10 *A man will meet you carrying a jar of water:* see the note on Mk 14:13.

22:15 *This Passover:* Luke clearly identifies this last supper of Jesus with the apostles as a Passover meal that commemorated the deliverance of the Israelites from slavery in Egypt. Jesus reinterprets the significance of the Passover by setting it in the context of the kingdom of God (16). The "deliverance" associated with the Passover finds its new meaning in the blood that will be shed (20).

22:17 Because of a textual problem in vv 19 and 20, some commentators interpret this cup as the eucharistic cup.

22:19c–20 *Which will be given . . . do this in memory of me:* these words are omitted in some important Western text manuscripts and a few Syriac manuscripts. Other ancient text types, including the oldest papyrus manuscript of Luke dating from the late second or early third century, contain the longer reading presented here. The Lucan account of the words of institution of the Eucharist bears a close resemblance to the words of institution in the Pauline tradition (see 1 Cor 11:23–26). See also the notes on Mt 26:26–29; 26:27–28; and Mk 14:22–24.

22:24–38 The Gospel of Luke presents a brief farewell discourse of Jesus; compare the lengthy farewell discourses and prayer in John, chs 13–17.

22:25 *'Benefactors':* this word occurs as a title of rulers in the Hellenistic world.

*

22:7–13 Mt 26:17–19; Mk 14:12–16.
22:7 Ex 12:6, 14–20.
22:13 Lk 19:32.
22:14–20 Mt 26:20, 26–30; Mk 14:17, 22–26; 1 Cor 11:23–25.
22:16 Lk 13:29.
22:19 Lk 24:30; Acts 27:35.
22:20 Ex 24:8; Jer 31:31; 32:40; Zec 9:11.
22:21–23 Ps 41:10; Mt 26:21–25; Mk 14:18–21; Jn 13:21–30.
22:24 Lk 9:46; Mt 18:1; Mk 9:34.
22:25–27 Mt 20:25–27; Mk 10:42–44; Jn 13:3–16.
22:26 Mt 23:11; Mk 9:35.
22:29 Lk 12:32.

22:39

30* that you may eat and drink at my table in my
kingdom; and you will sit on thrones judging the
twelve tribes of Israel.

Peter's Denial Foretold

31*† "Simon, Simon, behold Satan has de-
manded to sift all of you like wheat,*† 32 but
I have prayed† that your own faith may not
fail; and once you have turned back, you must
strengthen your brothers." 33* He said to him,
"Lord, I am prepared to go to prison and to die
with you." 34* But he replied, "I tell you, Peter,
before the cock crows this day, you will deny
three times that you know me."

Instructions for the Time of Crisis

35* He said to them, "When I sent you forth
without a money bag or a sack or sandals, were
you in need of anything?" "No, nothing," they
replied. 36*† He said to them, "But now one
who has a money bag should take it, and like-
wise a sack, and one who does not have a sword
should sell his cloak and buy one. 37* For I tell
you that this scripture must be fulfilled in me,
namely, 'He was counted among the wicked';
and indeed what is written about me is coming
to fulfillment." 38† Then they said, "Lord, look,
there are two swords here." But he replied, "It is
enough!"

The Agony in the Garden

39* Then going out he went, as was his cus-
tom, to the Mount of Olives, and the disciples
followed him. 40* When he arrived at the place
he said to them, "Pray that you may not undergo
the test." 41* After withdrawing about a stone's
throw from them and kneeling, he prayed,
42* saying, "Father, if you are willing, take this
cup away from me; still, not my will but yours be
done." [43† And to strengthen him an angel from
heaven appeared to him. 44 He was in such agony
and he prayed so fervently that his sweat be-
came like drops of blood falling on the ground.]
45 When he rose from prayer and returned to his
disciples, he found them sleeping from grief.
46* He said to them, "Why are you sleeping? Get
up and pray that you may not undergo the test."

The Betrayal and Arrest of Jesus

47* While he was still speaking, a crowd ap-
proached and in front was one of the Twelve,
a man named Judas. He went up to Jesus to
kiss him. 48 Jesus said to him, "Judas, are you
betraying the Son of Man with a kiss?" 49* His
disciples realized what was about to happen, and
they asked, "Lord, shall we strike with a sword?"
50* And one of them struck the high priest's ser-
vant and cut off his right ear. 51† But Jesus said in
reply, "Stop, no more of this!" Then he touched
the servant's ear and healed him. 52* And Jesus
said to the chief priests and temple guards and
elders who had come for him, "Have you come

†

22:31 *All of you:* literally, "you." The translation reflects the meaning of the Greek text that uses a second person plural pronoun here.

22:31–32 Jesus' prayer for Simon's faith and the commission to strengthen his brothers anticipates the post-resurrectional prominence of Peter in the first half of Acts, where he appears as the spokesman for the Christian community and the one who begins the mission to the Gentiles (Acts 10–11).

22:36 In contrast to the ministry of the Twelve and of the seventy-two during the period of Jesus (9:3; 10:4), in the future period of the church the missionaries must be prepared for the opposition they will face in a world hostile to their preaching.

22:38 *It is enough!:* the farewell discourse ends abruptly with these words of Jesus spoken to the disciples when they take literally what was intended as figurative language about being prepared to face the world's hostility.

22:43–44 These verses, though very ancient, were probably not part of the original text of Luke. They are absent from the oldest papyrus manuscripts of Luke and from manuscripts of wide geographical distribution.

22:51 *And healed him:* only Luke recounts this healing of the injured servant.

22:30 Mt 19:28.
22:31–34 Mt 26:33–35; Mk 14:29–31; Jn 13:37–38.
22:31 Jb 1:6–12; Am 9:9.
22:33 Lk 22:54.
22:34 Lk 22:54–62.
22:35 Lk 9:3; 10:4; Mt 10:9–10; Mk 6:7–9.
22:36 Lk 22:49.
22:37 Is 53:12.
22:39–46 Mt 26:30, 36–46; Mk 14:26, 32–42; Jn 18:1–2.
22:40 Lk 22:46.
22:41 Heb 5:7–8.
22:42 Mt 6:10.
22:46 Lk 22:40.
22:47–53 Mt 26:47–56; Mk 14:43–50; Jn 18:3–4.
22:49 Lk 22:36.
22:50 Jn 18:26.
22:52 Lk 22:37.

out as against a robber, with swords and clubs?
53* Day after day I was with you in the temple area, and you did not seize me; but this is your hour, the time for the power of darkness."

Peter's Denial of Jesus

54* After arresting him they led him away and took him into the house of the high priest; Peter was following at a distance.*
55 They lit a fire in the middle of the courtyard and sat around it, and Peter sat down with them.
56 When a maid saw him seated in the light, she looked intently at him and said, "This man too was with him."
57 But he denied it saying, "Woman, I do not know him."
58 A short while later someone else saw him and said, "You too are one of them"; but Peter answered, "My friend, I am not."
59 About an hour later, still another insisted, "Assuredly, this man too was with him, for he also is a Galilean."
60 But Peter said, "My friend, I do not know what you are talking about." Just as he was saying this, the cock crowed,
61*† and the Lord turned and looked at Peter; and Peter remembered the word of the Lord, how he had said to him, "Before the cock crows today, you will deny me three times."
62 He went out and began to weep bitterly.
63* The men who held Jesus in custody were ridiculing and beating him.
64 They blindfolded him and questioned him, saying, "Prophesy! Who is it that struck you?"
65 And they reviled him in saying many other things against him.

Jesus before the Sanhedrin†

66* When day came the council of elders of the people met, both chief priests and scribes,* and they brought him before their Sanhedrin.†
67* They said, "If you are the Messiah, tell us," but he replied to them, "If I tell you, you will not

†

22:61 Only Luke recounts that *the Lord turned and looked at Peter*. This look of Jesus leads to Peter's weeping bitterly over his denial (62).

22:66–71 Luke recounts one daytime trial of Jesus (66–71) and hints at some type of preliminary nighttime investigation (54–65). Mark (and Matthew who follows Mark) has transferred incidents of this day into the nighttime interrogation with the result that there appear to be two Sanhedrin trials of Jesus in Mark (and Matthew); see the note on Mk 14:53.

22:66 *Sanhedrin:* the word is a Hebraized form of a Greek word meaning a "council," and refers to the elders, chief priests, and scribes who met under the high priest's leadership to decide religious and legal questions that did not pertain to Rome's interests. Jewish sources are not clear on the competence of the Sanhedrin to sentence and to execute during this period.

*

22:53 Lk 19:47; 21:37; Jn 7:30; 8:20; Col 1:13.
22:54–62 Mt 26:57–58, 69–75; Mk 14:53–54, 66–72; Jn 18:12–18, 25–27.
22:54 Lk 22:33.
22:61 Lk 22:34.
22:63–65 Mt 26:67–68; Mk 14:65.
22:66–71 Mt 26:59–66; Mk 14:55–64.
22:66 Mt 27:1; Mk 15:1.
22:67 Jn 3:12; 8:45; 10:24.

Did You Know?

Luke's Account of Jesus' Death

The stories of Jesus' Passion—the name Christians use to describe his suffering and death—differ in all four Gospels. By comparing these stories, we get insight into the authors' portrayal of Jesus. Let's take a closer look at the perspective in the Gospel of Luke.

First, in Jesus' Passion, Luke describes the openness of Gentiles to Jesus' message of salvation. The Roman centurion who praises God at the moment of Jesus' death (see Lk 23:47) is an example.

Second, Luke emphasizes Jesus' compassion and forgiveness, even during his greatest suffering. While carrying the cross, Jesus shows his concern for the women who are following him (see verses 28–31). As he is nailed to the cross, he forgives those responsible (see verse 34). And when one of the criminals asks for Jesus to remember him, Jesus goes beyond that to promise him the first place in Paradise (see verse 43).

Third, whereas Mark portrays Jesus as abandoned in his Passion (see Mk 15:34), Luke surrounds Jesus with sympathetic people: a crowd including the women of Jerusalem (see Lk 23:27), the good thief (see verses 40–41), and the centurion (see verse 47). In Mark, Jesus feels God's absence (see Mk 15:34), but Luke presents Jesus as obedient even at his death, handing his spirit over to God (see Lk 23:46). Mark's emphasis is on Jesus' suffering and loss because he is writing to a community of Christians who are being persecuted. Luke's emphasis is on Jesus' obedience and love for those on the fringe of society because Luke's audience consists of Gentiles, considered outcasts in Jewish tradition. Luke is making it clear in his portrayal of Jesus' Passion that Jesus is the loving, forgiving savior of all humankind.

▶ **Lk 22:47—23:56**

Cultural Connection

Salubong

In the Philippines, Catholics celebrate the *Salubong*, the encounter between the risen Jesus and his sorrowful mother on Easter morning. This is based on a tradition that Mary was with the women mentioned in Luke 23:27,55; 24:1,10.

On the day of *Salubong*, at dawn, two groups of worshipers begin walking in two different directions. One group carries a statue of Jesus, and the other group carries a statue of Mary. Both statues are draped in black capes. The people walk through the town and meet on a main street, usually under an arch. A little robed "angel" (a small girl or boy) then removes the sorrowful black capes to reveal joyful white or golden robes on each statue, symbolizing the joy and glory of the Resurrection. Then the entire assembly returns to the church, and Easter Mass begins.

▶ Lk 23:26–31

believe, 68 and if I question, you will not respond.
69* But from this time on the Son of Man will be
seated at the right hand of the power of God."
70 They all asked, "Are you then the Son of God?"
He replied to them, "You say that I am." 71 Then
they said, "What further need have we for testimony? We have heard it from his own mouth."

Jesus before Pilate

23 1*† Then the whole assembly of them
arose and brought him before Pilate.
2* They brought charges against him, saying,
"We found this man misleading our people;
he opposes the payment of taxes to Caesar and
maintains that he is the Messiah, a king." 3* Pi-
late asked him, "Are you the king of the Jews?"
He said to him in reply, "You say so." 4* Pilate
then addressed the chief priests and the crowds,
"I find this man not guilty." 5 But they were adamant and said, "He is inciting the people with his teaching throughout all Judea, from Galilee where he began even to here."

Jesus before Herod

6† On hearing this Pilate asked if the man was
a Galilean; 7* and upon learning that he was un-
der Herod's jurisdiction, he sent him to Herod
who was in Jerusalem at that time. 8* Herod
was very glad to see Jesus; he had been wanting to see him for a long time, for he had heard about him and had been hoping to see him
perform some sign. 9* He questioned him at
length, but he gave him no answer. 10* The chief
priests and scribes, meanwhile, stood by accus-
ing him harshly. 11* [Even] Herod and his sol-
diers treated him contemptuously and mocked him, and after clothing him in resplendent garb,
he sent him back to Pilate. 12 Herod and Pilate
became friends that very day, even though they
had been enemies formerly. 13 Pilate then sum-
moned the chief priests, the rulers, and the
people 14* and said to them, "You brought this
man to me and accused him of inciting the people to revolt. I have conducted my investigation in your presence and have not found this man guilty of the charges you have brought against
him, 15 nor did Herod, for he sent him back to
us. So no capital crime has been committed by
him. 16* Therefore I shall have him flogged and
then release him." [17]†

23:1–5, 13–25 Twice Jesus is brought before Pilate in Luke's account, and each time Pilate explicitly declares Jesus innocent of any wrongdoing (4, 14, 22). This stress on the innocence of Jesus before the Roman authorities is also characteristic of John's gospel (Jn 18:38; 19:4, 6). Luke presents the Jerusalem Jewish leaders as theones who force the hand of the Roman authorities (1–2, 5, 10, 13, 18, 21, 23–25).

23:6–12 The appearance of Jesus before Herod is found only in this gospel. Herod has been an important figure in Luke (9:7–9; 13:31–33) and has been presented as someone who has been curious about Jesus for a long time. His curiosity goes unrewarded. It is faith in Jesus, not curiosity, that is rewarded (7:50; 8:48, 50; 17:19).

23:17 This verse, "He was obliged to release one prisoner for them at the festival," is not part of the original text of Luke. It is an explanatory gloss from Mk 15:6 (also Mt 27:15) and is not found in many early and important Greek manuscripts. On its historical background, see the notes on Mt 27:15–26.

22:69 Ps 110:1; Dn 7:13–14; Acts 7:56.
23:1–5 Mt 27:1–2, 11–14; Mk 15:1–5; Jn 18:28–38.
23:2 Lk 20:22–25; Acts 17:7; 24:5.
23:3 Lk 22:70; 1Tm 6:13.
23:4 Lk 23:14, 22, 41; Mt 27:24; Jn 19:4, 6; Acts 13:28.
23:7 Lk 3:1; 9:7.
23:8 Lk 9:9; Acts 4:27–28.
23:9 Mk 15:5.
23:10 Mt 27:12; Mk 15:3.
23:11 Mt 27:28–30; Mk 15:17–19; Jn 19:2–3.
23:14 Lk 23:4, 22, 41.
23:16 Lk 23:22; Jn 19:12–14.

Cultural Connection

Waiting in Darkness

The darkness before Jesus died symbolizes the coming of the day of the Lord (see the introduction to Joel). This Iroquois prayer expresses the feeling of that moment:

We wait in the darkness!
Come, all ye who listen,
Help in our night journey:
Now no sun is shining;
Now no star is glowing;
Come show us the pathway:
The night is not friendly;
The moon has forgot us,
We wait in the darkness!

▶ **Lk 23:44–46**

The Sentence of Death

18* But all together they shouted out, "Away with this man! Release Barabbas to us." 19 (Now Barabbas had been imprisoned for a rebellion that had taken place in the city and for murder.) 20 Again Pilate addressed them, still wishing to release Jesus, 21 but they continued their shouting, "Crucify him! Crucify him!" 22 Pilate addressed them a third time, "What evil has this man done? I found him guilty of no capital crime. Therefore I shall have him flogged and then release him." 23 With loud shouts, however, they persisted in calling for his crucifixion, and their voices prevailed. 24 The verdict of Pilate was that their demand should be granted. 25 So he released the man who had been imprisoned for rebellion and murder, for whom they asked, and he handed Jesus over to them to deal with as they wished.

The Way of the Cross

26*† As they led him away they took hold of a certain Simon, a Cyrenian, who was coming in from the country; and after laying the cross on him, they made him carry it behind Jesus. 27 A large crowd of people followed Jesus, including many women who mourned and lamented him. 28* Jesus turned to them and said, "Daughters of Jerusalem, do not weep for me; weep instead for yourselves and for your children, 29 for indeed, the days are coming when people will say, 'Blessed are the barren, the wombs that never bore and the breasts that never nursed.' 30* At that time people will say to the mountains, 'Fall upon us!' and to the hills, 'Cover us!' 31 for if these things are done when the wood is green what will happen when it is dry?" 32 Now two others, both criminals, were led away with him to be executed.

The Crucifixion

33* When they came to the place called the Skull, they crucified him and the criminals there, one on his right, the other on his left.* 34*† [Then Jesus said, "Father, forgive them, they know not what they do."] They divided his garments by casting lots. 35* The people stood by and watched; the rulers, meanwhile, sneered at him and said, "He saved others, let him save himself if he is the chosen one, the Messiah of God."* 36* Even the soldiers jeered at him. As they approached to offer him wine 37 they called out, "If you are King of the Jews, save yourself." 38 Above him there was an inscription that read, "This is the King of the Jews."

39† Now one of the criminals hanging there reviled Jesus, saying, "Are you not the Messiah? Save yourself and us." 40 The other, however, rebuking him, said in reply, "Have you no fear of God, for you are subject to the same condemnation?

LK

23:26–32 An important Lucan theme throughout the gospel has been the need for the Christian disciple to follow in the footsteps of Jesus. Here this theme comes to the fore with the story of Simon of Cyrene who takes up the cross and follows Jesus (see 9:23; 14:27) and with the large crowd who likewise follow Jesus on the way of the cross. See also the note on Mk 15:21.

23:34a [*Then Jesus said, "Father, forgive them, they know not what they do."*]: this portion of v 34 does not occur in the oldest papyrus manuscript of Luke and in other early Greek manuscripts and ancient versions of wide geographical distribution.

23:39–43 This episode is recounted only in this gospel. The penitent sinner receives salvation through the crucified Jesus. Jesus' words to the penitent thief reveal Luke's understanding that the destiny of the Christian is "to be with Jesus."

23:18–25 Mt 27:20–26; Mk 15:6–7, 11–15; Jn 18:38b–40; 19:14–16; Acts 3:13–14.
23:26–32 Mt 27:32, 38; Mk 15:21, 27; Jn 19:17.
23:28–31 Lk 19:41–44; 21:23–24.
23:30 Hos 10:8; Rv 6:16.
23:33–43 Mt 27:33–44; Mk 15:22–32; Jn 19:17–24.
23:33 Lk 22:37; Is 53:12.
23:34 Nm 15:27–31; Ps 22:19; Mt 5:44; Acts 7:60.
23:35–36 Ps 22:8–9.
23:35 Lk 4:23.
23:36 Ps 69:22; Mt 27:48; Mk 15:36.

Did You Know?

Resurrection Hope

Think about a time when you felt hopeless. Were you depressed? lonely? angry? afraid? These were probably some of the feelings of the women who approached Jesus' tomb on the Sunday morning after his death. Their leader, their teacher, their Lord had just been horribly executed before a huge crowd, and his wonderful vision of love, justice, and forgiveness had been shattered.

But what they encountered in that tomb likely changed their lives forever. The tomb was empty. Two dazzling men appeared and spoke to them. Jesus had indeed risen!

When you think that a situation is hopeless, that no end is in sight, that evil is winning out, remember this story. Along with the Resurrection stories in the other three Gospels, this story is proof that despair and death do not win, that God is at work in the most hopeless situations!

▶ Lk 24:1–12

41* And indeed, we have been condemned justly, for the sentence we received corresponds to our crimes, but this man has done nothing criminal." 42* Then he said, "Jesus, remember me when you come into your kingdom." 43* He replied to him, "Amen, I say to you, today you will be with me in Paradise."

The Death of Jesus

44*† It was now about noon* and darkness came over the whole land until three in the afternoon 45* because of an eclipse of the sun. Then the veil of the temple was torn down the middle. 46* Jesus cried out in a loud voice, "Father, into your hands I commend my spirit"; and when he had said this he breathed his last. 47† The centurion who witnessed what had happened glorified God and said, "This man was innocent beyond doubt." 48* When all the people who had gathered for this spectacle saw what had happened, they returned home beating their breasts; 49* but all his acquaintances stood at a distance, including the women who had followed him from Galilee and saw these events.

The Burial of Jesus

50* Now there was a virtuous and righteous man named Joseph who, though he was a member of the council, 51* had not consented to their plan of action. He came from the Jewish town of Arimathea and was awaiting the kingdom of God. 52 He went to Pilate and asked for the body of Jesus. 53* After he had taken the body down, he wrapped it in a linen cloth and laid him in a rock-hewn tomb in which no one had yet been buried. 54 It was the day of preparation, and the sabbath was about to begin. 55* The women who had come from Galilee with him followed behind, and when they had seen the tomb and the way in which his body was laid in it, 56* they returned and prepared spices and perfumed oils. Then they rested on the sabbath according to the commandment.

VIII: The Resurrection Narrative

The Resurrection of Jesus

24 1*† But at daybreak on the first day of the week they took the spices they had prepared and went to the tomb. 2 They found the stone rolled away from the tomb; 3 but when they entered, they did not find the body of the Lord Jesus. 4* While they were puzzling over this, behold, two men in dazzling garments appeared to them. 5* They were terrified and bowed their faces to the ground. They said to them, "Why do you seek the living one among the dead? 6† He

---

23:44 *Noon . . . three in the afternoon:* literally, the sixth and ninth hours. See the note on Mk 15:25.

23:47 *This man was innocent:* or, "This man was righteous."

24:1–53 The resurrection narrative in Luke consists of five sections: (1) the women at the empty tomb (23:56b–24:12); (2) the appearance to the two disciples on the way to Emmaus (24:13–35); (3) the appearance to the disciples in Jerusalem (24:36–43); (4) Jesus' final instructions (24:44–49); (5) the ascension (24:50–53). In Luke, all the resurrection appearances take place in and around Jerusalem; moreover, they are all recounted as having taken place on Easter Sunday. A consistent theme throughout the narrative is that the suffering, death, and resurrection of Jesus were accomplished in fulfillment of Old Testament promises and of Jewish hopes (19a, 21, 26–27, 44, 46). In his second volume, Acts, Luke will argue that Christianity is the fulfillment of the hopes of Pharisaic Judaism and its logical development (see Acts 24:10–21).

24:6a *He is not here, but he has been raised:* this part of the verse is omitted in important representatives of the Western text tradition, but its presence in other text types and the slight difference in wording from Mt 28:6 and Mk 16:6 argue for its retention.

23:41 Lk 23:4, 14, 22.
23:42 Lk 9:27; 23:2, 3, 38.
23:43 2 Cor 12:3; Rv 2:7.
23:44–49 Mt 27:45–56; Mk 15:33–41; Jn 19:25–30.
23:44–45 Am 8:9.
23:45 Ex 26:31–33; 36:35.
23:46 Ps 31:6; Acts 7:59.
23:48 Lk 18:13; Zec 12:10.
23:49 Lk 8:1–3; 23:55–56; 24:10; Ps 38:12.
23:50–56 Mt 27:57–61; Mk 15:42–47; Jn 19:38–42; Acts 13:29.
23:51 Lk 2:25, 38.
23:53 Lk 19:30; Acts 13:29.
23:55 Lk 8:2; 23:49; 24:10.
23:56 Ex 12:16; 20:10; Dt 5:14.
24:1–8 Mt 28:1–8; Mk 16:1–8; Jn 20:1–17.
24:4 2 Mc 3:26; Acts 1:10.
24:5 Acts 2:9.

is not here, but he has been raised. Remember
what he said to you while he was still in Gal-
ilee, 7* that the Son of Man must be handed
over to sinners and be crucified, and rise on the
third day." 8* And they remembered his words.
9*† Then they returned from the tomb and an-
nounced all these things to the eleven and to all
the others. 10* The women were Mary Magda-
lene, Joanna, and Mary the mother of James; the
others who accompanied them also told this to
the apostles, 11 but their story seemed like non-
sense and they did not believe them. 12*† But Pe-
ter got up and ran to the tomb, bent down, and
saw the burial cloths alone; then he went home
amazed at what had happened.

The Appearance on the Road to Emmaus

13*† Now that very day two of them were
going to a village seven miles† from Jerusalem
called Emmaus, 14 and they were conversing
about all the things that had occurred. 15 And it
happened that while they were conversing and
debating, Jesus himself drew near and walked
with them, 16*† but their eyes were prevented
from recognizing him. 17 He asked them, "What
are you discussing as you walk along?" They
stopped, looking downcast. 18 One of them,
named Cleopas, said to him in reply, "Are you
the only visitor to Jerusalem who does not know
of the things that have taken place there in these
days?" 19* And he replied to them, "What sort
of things?" They said to him, "The things that
happened to Jesus the Nazarene, who was a
prophet mighty in deed and word before God
and all the people, 20 how our chief priests and
rulers both handed him over to a sentence of
death and crucified him. 21* But we were hoping
that he would be the one to redeem Israel; and
besides all this, it is now the third day since this
took place. 22* Some women from our group,

Live It!

Jesus Is with Us!

A young man was at Mass when he heard Luke 24:13–35. "Pretty strange!" he thought. "Those two guys did not recognize Jesus after they had been with him for three years. I wonder if he looked different after the Resurrection. If I had been walking on the road to Emmaus, I wonder if I would have recognized him. I wonder if people would recognize him today if he came among us." He continued to ponder these thoughts as the Mass continued. He remembered his mother saying that Jesus is present among us every day—in the people we meet, when we gather to pray, and in the Eucharist.

Suddenly, the young man was aware of what the priest was saying: "This is my body which will be given up for you. This is the cup of my blood . . . it will be shed for you and for all. Do this in memory of me."

He looked around the church, noticing people he had not paid attention to before: the family who were refugees from a war-torn country, the little baby who had been born with severe disabilities, the woman who lived alone at ninety-six years old, some other teenagers who were sitting together in the front of church. Somehow, all these different people found love and acceptance in the parish family. "I think I understand now," he thought. "Jesus does look different, but he is here!"

When Jesus joined the disciples at their table and broke the bread, they recognized him. It was at the Eucharist that this young man recognized the presence of Jesus alive today. How about you? When and where do you recognize Jesus? Who in your community reminds you of him the most? How hard is it to recognize Jesus' presence in all people today?

► Lk 24:13–35

†

24:9 The women in this gospel do not flee from the tomb and tell no one, as in Mk 16:8, but return and tell the disciples about their experience. The initial reaction to the testimony of the women is disbelief (11).

24:12 This verse is missing from the Western textual tradition but is found in the best and oldest manuscripts of other text types.

24:13–35 This episode focuses on the interpretation of scripture by the risen Jesus and the recognition of him in the breaking of the bread. The references to the quotations of scripture and explanation of it (25–27), the kerygmatic proclamation (34), and the liturgical gesture (30) suggest that the episode is primarily catechetical and liturgical rather than apologetic.

24:13 *Seven miles:* literally, "sixty stades." A stade was 607 feet. Some manuscripts read "160 stades" or more than eighteen miles. The exact location of Emmaus is disputed.

24:16 A consistent feature of the resurrection stories is that the risen Jesus was different and initially unrecognizable (37; Mk 16:12; Jn 20:14; 21:4).

*

24:7 Lk 9:22, 44; 17:25; 18:32–33; Mt 16:21; 17:22–23; Mk 9:31; Acts 17:3.
24:8 Jn 2:22.
24:9–11 Mk 16:10–11; Jn 20:18.
24:10 Lk 8:2–3; Mk 16:9.
24:12 Jn 20:3–7.
24:13 Mk 16:12–13.
24:16 Jn 20:14; 21:4.
24:19 Mt 2:23; 21:11; Acts 2:22.
24:21 Lk 1:54, 68; 2:38.
24:22–23 Lk 24:1–11; Mt 28:1–8; Mk 16:1–8.

however, have astounded us: they were at the tomb early in the morning 23 and did not find his body; they came back and reported that they had indeed seen a vision of angels who announced that he was alive. 24* Then some of those with us went to the tomb and found things just as the women had described, but him they did not see." 25* And he said to them, "Oh, how foolish you are! How slow of heart to believe all that the prophets spoke! 26† Was it not necessary that the Messiah should suffer these things and enter into his glory?" 27* Then beginning with Moses and all the prophets, he interpreted to them what referred to him in all the scriptures. 28 As they approached the village to which they were going, he gave the impression that he was going on farther. 29 But they urged him, "Stay with us, for it is nearly evening and the day is almost over." So he went in to stay with them. 30 And it happened that, while he was with them at table, he took bread, said the blessing, broke it, and gave it to them. 31 With that their eyes were opened and they recognized him, but he vanished from their sight. 32 Then they said to each other, "Were not our hearts burning [within us] while he spoke to us on the way and opened the scriptures to us?" 33 So they set out at once and returned to Jerusalem where they found gathered together the eleven and those with them 34* who were saying, "The Lord has truly been raised and has appeared to Simon!" 35 Then the two recounted what had taken place on the way and how he was made known to them in the breaking of the bread.

The Appearance to the Disciples in Jerusalem

36*† While they were still speaking about this, he stood in their midst and said to them, "Peace be with you."* 37* But they were startled and terrified and thought that they were seeing a ghost. 38 Then he said to them, "Why are you troubled? And why do questions arise in your hearts? 39† Look at my hands and my feet, that it is I myself. Touch me and see, because a ghost does not have flesh and bones as you can see I have." 40* And as he said this, he showed them his hands and his feet. 41 While they were still incredulous for joy and were amazed, he asked them, "Have you anything here to eat?" 42* They gave him a piece of baked fish; 43 he took it and ate it in front of them.

44* He said to them, "These are my words that I spoke to you while I was still with you, that everything written about me in the law of Moses and in the prophets and psalms must be fulfilled." 45* Then he opened their minds to understand the scriptures. 46*† And he said to them, "Thus it is written that the Messiah would suffer and rise from the dead on the third day 47* and that repentance, for the forgiveness of sins, would be preached in his name to all the nations, beginning from Jerusalem. 48* You are witnesses of these things. 49*† And [behold] I am sending the promise of my Father upon you; but stay in the city until you are clothed with power from on high."

The Ascension

50*† Then he led them [out] as far as Bethany, raised his hands, and blessed them. 51 As he blessed them he parted from them and was taken up to heaven. 52* They did him homage and then returned to Jerusalem with great joy, 53† and they were continually in the temple praising God.

24:26 *That the Messiah should suffer . . . :* Luke is the only New Testament writer to speak explicitly of a suffering Messiah (26, 46; Acts 3:18; 17:3; 26:23). The idea of a suffering Messiah is not found in the Old Testament or in other Jewish literature prior to the New Testament period, although the idea is hinted at in Mk 8:31–33. See the notes on Mt 26:63 and 26:67–68.

24:36–43, 44–49 The Gospel of Luke, like each of the other gospels (Mt 28:16–20; Mk 16:14–15; Jn 20:19–23), focuses on an important appearance of Jesus to the Twelve in which they are commissioned for their future ministry. As in vv 6 and 12, so in vv 36 and 40 there are omissions in the Western text.

24:39–42 The apologetic purpose of this story is evident in the concern with the physical details and the report that Jesus ate food.

24:46 See the note on 24:26.

24:49 *The promise of my Father:* i.e., the gift of the holy Spirit.

24:50–53 Luke brings his story about the time of Jesus to a close with the report of the ascension. He will also begin the story of the time of the church with a recounting of the ascension. In the gospel, Luke recounts the ascension of Jesus on Easter Sunday night, thereby closely associating it with the resurrection. In Acts (1:3, 9–11; 13:31) he historicizes the ascension by speaking of a forty-day period between the resurrection and the ascension. The Western text omits some phrases in vv 51 and 52, perhaps to avoid any chronological conflict with Acts 1 about the time of the ascension.

24:53 The Gospel of Luke ends as it began (1:9), in the Jerusalem temple.

24:24 Jn 20:3–10.
24:25–26 Lk 9:22; 18:31; 24:44; Acts 3:24; 17:3.
24:27 Lk 24:44; Dt 18:25; Ps 22:1–18; Is 53; 1 Pt 1:10–11.
24:34 1 Cor 15:4–5.
24:36–53 Mk 16:14–19; Jn 20:19–20.
24:36 1 Cor 15:5.
24:37 Mt 14:26.
24:40–41 Jn 21:5, 9–10, 13.
24:42 Acts 10:41.
24:44 Lk 18:31; 24:27; Mt 16:21; Jn 5:39, 46.
24:45 Jn 20:9.
24:46 Lk 9:22; Is 53; Hos 6:2.
24:47 Mt 3:2; 28:19–20; Mk 16:15–16; Acts 10:41.
24:48 Acts 1:8.
24:49 Jn 14:26; Acts 1:4; 2:3–4.
24:50–51 Mk 16:19; Acts 1:9–11.
24:52 Acts 1:12.

The Gospel According to John

"We are like two peas in a pod." "She's a great shoulder to cry on." "Our friendship is as solid as a rock." People often use analogies or symbolic images in describing their closest relationships. The author of the Gospel of John does this. Throughout the Gospel, symbolic imagery is used to describe the Christian believer's relationship with Jesus. Very different in style from the other Gospels, John's Gospel also gives us the clearest picture of Jesus' unique relationship with God the Father.

At a Glance

I. **Prologue (1:1–18).**

II. **The Book of Signs (1:19—12:50).**

III. **The Book of Glory (13:1—20:31).**

IV. **Epilogue: The Resurrection Appearance in Galilee (21:1–25).**

Quick Facts

Inspired Author: a member of a Christian community possibly founded by the Beloved Disciple

Date Written: most likely from AD 90 to 100

Audience: a Jewish Christian community that may have admitted Gentiles and Samaritans

Image of Jesus: noble and powerful, one with the Father; fully in control of his destiny

In Depth

The Gospel of John begins with symbolic language describing Jesus as the Word, who was with God in the beginning of Creation and who became flesh to live among us. The author goes on to describe Jesus as the light that overcomes darkness. Those who believe in Jesus walk in the light—their lives have meaning and direction. Those who do not believe stumble in the darkness of confusion and sin. John is clear that Jesus is the divine Son of God and that to belong to God, we have to follow Jesus.

In addition to its symbolic language and stress on Jesus' unique relationship with God the Father, John's Gospel differs from the synoptic Gospels—Matthew, Mark, and Luke—in other ways:

- In the synoptic Gospels, Jesus' teaching focuses on the Kingdom (or Reign) of God. In John's Gospel, Jesus' teaching stresses relationships: Jesus' relationship with God the Father and our relationship with Jesus.
- In the synoptic Gospels, Jesus teaches with parables and performs many healings and miracles. In the Gospel of John, Jesus does not teach by parables. Instead, Jesus performs seven miraculous signs and teaches in long discourses.
- John's Gospel has several passages about the role of the Holy Spirit. The synoptic Gospels hardly mention the Holy Spirit.

John's story of Jesus climaxes with the coming of Jesus' "hour," a symbol for Jesus' death and execution. But in the Gospel of John, Jesus' death is not tragic at all—it is his glorious return to the Father. This Gospel assures us that trust in God will pay off in the end: "I will come back again and take you to myself, so that where I am you also may be" (14:3).

John

20:11–17

I: Prologue†

1 [1]*† In the beginning was the Word,
and the Word was with God,
and the Word was God.
2 He was in the beginning with God.
3*† All things came to be through him,
and without him nothing came to be.
What came to be 4* through him was life,
and this life was the light of the human race;
5*† the light shines in the darkness,
and the darkness has not overcome it.

6*† A man named John was sent from God.
7*† He came for testimony, to testify to the light,
so that all might believe through him. 8* He was
not the light, but came to testify to the light. 9* The
true light, which enlightens everyone, was coming
into the world.

10 He was in the world,
and the world came to be through him,
but the world did not know him.
11† He came to what was his own,
but his own people did not accept him.

12* But to those who did accept him he gave
power to become children of God, to those who
believe in his name, 13*† who were born not by
natural generation nor by human choice nor by a
man's decision but of God.

1:1–18 The prologue states the main themes of the gospel: life, light, truth, the world, testimony, and the preexistence of Jesus Christ, the incarnate *Logos,* who reveals God the Father. In origin, it was probably an early Christian hymn. Its closest parallel is in other christological hymns, Col 1:15–20 and Phil 2:6–11. Its core (1–5, 10–11, 14) is poetic in structure, with short phrases linked by "staircase parallelism," in which the last word of one phrase becomes the first word of the next. Prose inserts (at least 6–8 and 15) deal with John the Baptist.

1:1 *In the beginning:* also the first words of the Old Testament (Gn 1:1). *Was:* this verb is used three times with different meanings in this verse: existence, relationship, and predication. *The Word* (Greek *logos*): this term combines God's dynamic, creative word (Genesis), personified preexistent Wisdom as the instrument of God's creative activity (Proverbs), and the ultimate intelligibility of reality (Hellenistic philosophy). *With God:* the Greek preposition here connotes communication with another. *Was God:* lack of a definite article with "God" in Greek signifies predication rather than identification.

1:3 *What came to be:* while the oldest manuscripts have no punctuation here, the corrector of Bodmer Papyrus P75, some manuscripts, and the Ante-Nicene Fathers take this phrase with what follows, as staircase parallelism. Connection with v 3 reflects fourth-century anti-Arianism.

1:5 The ethical dualism of light and darkness is paralleled in intertestamental literature and in the Dead Sea Scrolls. *Overcome:* "comprehend" is another possible translation, but cf 12:35; Wis 7:29–30.

1:6 John was *sent* just as Jesus was "sent" (4:34) in divine mission. Other references to John the Baptist in this gospel emphasize the differences between them and John's subordinate role.

1:7 *Testimony:* the testimony theme of John is introduced, which portrays Jesus as if on trial throughout his ministry. All testify to Jesus: John the Baptist, the Samaritan woman, scripture, his works, the crowds, the Spirit, and his disciples.

1:11 *What was his own . . . his own people:* first a neuter, literally, "his own property/possession" (probably=Israel), then a masculine, "his own people" (the Israelites).

1:13 Believers in Jesus become children of God not through any of the three natural causes mentioned but through God who is the imme-

---

1:1 Jn 10:30; Gn 1:1–5; Jb 28:12–27; Prv 8:22–25; Wis 9:1–2; 1 Jn 1:1–2; Col 1:1, 15; Rv 3:14; 19:13.
1:3 Ps 33:9; Wis 9:1; Sir 42:15; 1 Cor 8:6; Col 1:16; Heb 1:2; Rv 3:14.
1:4 Jn 5:26; 8:12; 1 Jn 1:2.
1:5 Jn 3:19; 8:12; 9:5; 12:35, 46; Wis 7:29–30; 1 Thes 5:4; 1 Jn 2:8.
1:6 Mt 3:1; Mk 1:4; Lk 3:2–3.
1:7 Jn 1:19–34; 5:33.
1:8 Jn 5:35.
1:9 Jn 3:19; 8:12; 9:39; 12:46.
1:12 Jn 3:11–12; 5:43–44; 12:46–50; Gal 3:26; 4:6–7; Eph 1:5; 1 Jn 3:2.
1:13 Jn 3:5–6.

14*† And the Word became flesh
and made his dwelling among us,
and we saw his glory,
the glory as of the Father's only Son,
full of grace and truth.

15*† John testified to him and cried out, saying,
"This was he of whom I said, 'The one who is
coming after me ranks ahead of me because he
existed before me.' " 16† From his fullness we have
all received, grace in place of grace, 17* because
while the law was given through Moses, grace and
truth came through Jesus Christ. 18*† No one has
ever seen God. The only Son, God, who is at the
Father's side, has revealed him.

II: The Book of Signs

John the Baptist's Testimony to Himself

19† And this is the testimony of John. When
the Jews† from Jerusalem sent priests and Le-
vites [to him] to ask him, "Who are you?"
20*† he admitted and did not deny it, but ad-
mitted, "I am not the Messiah." 21*† So they
asked him, "What are you then? Are you Eli-
jah?" And he said, "I am not." "Are you the
Prophet?" He answered, "No." 22 So they said to
him, "Who are you, so we can give an answer to
those who sent us? What do you have to say for
yourself?" 23*† He said:

Live It!

The "Cosmic Christ"

Science fiction or fantasy movies and books often include important eternal beings or powers. The Star Wars series has "the Force." The Chronicles of Narnia, a fantasy series by C. S. Lewis, has Aslan, the noble lion who is the creator and savior of Narnia.

The poem that begins the Gospel of John reads like something from a great science fiction classic. Only in this case, the story is not fiction but God's Revelation! The poem presents Jesus as the Word, who has existed from all time, the one through whom all things came into being. The Scriptures tell us a great mystery here: the man named Jesus, who lived in Nazareth some two thousand years ago, is the creative power of God, who "became flesh / and made his dwelling among us" (Jn 1:14). No one has ever seen God. But Jesus, the perfect image of God, "has revealed him" (verse 18) in flesh and blood.

Many people in the Gospel of John do not recognize or accept Jesus, and many people still do not today.

- What does it mean for you to accept Jesus?
- Who or what has helped you to recognize or accept Jesus?

▶ Jn 1:1–18

†

diate cause of the new spiritual life. *Were born:* the Greek verb can mean "begotten" (by a male) or "born" (from a female or of parents). The variant "he who was begotten," asserting Jesus' virginal conception, is weakly attested in Old Latin and Syriac versions.

1:14 *Flesh:* the whole person, used probably against docetic tendencies (cf 1 Jn 4:2; 2 Jn 7). *Made his dwelling:* literally, "pitched his tent/tabernacle." Cf the tabernacle or tent of meeting that was the place of God's presence among his people (Ex 25:8–9). The incarnate Word is the new mode of God's presence among his people. The Greek verb has the same consonants as the Aramaic word for God's presence (Shekinah). *Glory:* God's visible manifestation of majesty in power, which once filled the tabernacle (Ex 40:34) and the temple (1 Kgs 8:10–11, 27), is now centered in Jesus. *Only Son:* Greek, *monogenēs,* but see the note on 1:18. *Grace and truth:* these words may represent two Old Testament terms describing Yahweh in covenant relationship with Israel (cf Ex 34:6), thus God's "love" and "fidelity." The Word shares Yahweh's covenant qualities.

1:15 This verse, interrupting vv 14 and 16, seems drawn from v 30.

1:16 *Grace in place of grace:* replacement of the Old Covenant with the New (cf 17). Other possible translations are "grace upon grace" (accumulation) and "grace for grace" (correspondence).

1:18 *The only Son, God:* while the vast majority of later textual witnesses have another reading, "the Son, the only one" or "the only Son," the translation above follows the best and earliest manuscripts, *monogenēs theos,* but takes the first term to mean not just "Only One" but to include a filial relationship with the Father, as at Lk 9:38 ("only child") or Heb 11:17 ("only son") and as translated at Jn 1:14. The Logos is thus "only Son" and God but not Father/God.

1:19–51 The testimony of John the Baptist about the Messiah and Jesus' self-revelation to the first disciples. This section constitutes the introduction to the gospel proper and is connected with the prose inserts in the prologue. It develops the major theme of testimony in four scenes: John's negative testimony about himself; his positive testimony about Jesus; the revelation of Jesus to Andrew and Peter; the revelation of Jesus to Philip and Nathanael.

1:19 *The Jews:* throughout most of the gospel, the "Jews" does not refer to the Jewish people as such but to the hostile authorities, both Pharisees and Sadducees, particularly in Jerusalem, who refuse to believe in Jesus. The usage reflects the atmosphere, at the end of the first century, of polemics between church and synagogue, or possibly it refers to Jews as representative of a hostile world (10–11).

1:20 *Messiah:* the anointed agent of Yahweh, usually considered to be of Davidic descent. See further the note on 1:41.

1:21 *Elijah:* the Baptist did not claim to be Elijah returned to earth (cf Mal 3:23; Mt 11:14). *The Prophet:* probably the prophet like Moses (Dt 18:15; cf Acts 3:22).

1:23 This is a repunctuation and reinterpretation (as in the

*

1:14 Ex 16:10; 24:17; 25:8–9; 33:22; 34:6; Sir 24:4, 8; Is 60:1; Ez 43:7; Jl 4:17; Hb 2:14; 1 Jn 1:2; 4:2; 2 Jn 7.
1:15 Jn 1:30; 3:27–30.
1:17 Jn 7:19; Ex 31:18; 34:28.
1:18 Jn 5:37; 6:46; Ex 33:20; Jgs 13:21–22; 1 Tm 6:16; 1 Jn 4:12.
1:20 Jn 3:28; Lk 3:15; Acts 13:25.
1:21 Dt 18:15, 18; 2 Kgs 2:11; Sir 48:10; Mal 3:1, 23; Mt 11:14; 17:11–13; Mk 9:13; Acts 3:22.
1:23 Is 40:3; Mt 3:3; Mk 1:2; Lk 3:4.

"I am 'the voice of one crying out in the desert,
"Make straight the way of the Lord," '

as Isaiah the prophet said." 24† Some Pharisees were also sent. 25* They asked him, "Why then do you baptize if you are not the Messiah or Elijah or the Prophet?" 26*† John answered them, "I baptize with water; but there is one among you whom you do not recognize, 27 the one who is coming after me, whose sandal strap I am not worthy to untie." 28† This happened in Bethany across the Jordan, where John was baptizing.

John the Baptist's Testimony to Jesus

29*† The next day he saw Jesus coming toward him and said, "Behold, the Lamb of God, who takes away the sin of the world. 30*† He is the one of whom I said, 'A man is coming after me who ranks ahead of me because he existed before me.' 31† I did not know him, but the reason why I came baptizing with water was that he might be made known to Israel." 32*† John testified further, saying, "I saw the Spirit come down like a dove from the sky and remain upon him. 33* I did not know him, but the one who sent me to baptize with water told me, 'On whomever you see the Spirit come down and remain, he is the one who will baptize with the holy Spirit.' 34*† Now I have seen and testified that he is the Son of God."

The First Disciples

35* The next day John was there again with two of his disciples, 36† and as he watched Jesus walk by, he said, "Behold, the Lamb of God." 37† The two disciples heard what he said and followed Jesus. 38 Jesus turned and saw them following him and said to them, "What are you looking for?" They said to him, "Rabbi" (which translated means Teacher), "where are you staying?" 39† He said to them, "Come, and you will see." So they went and saw where he was staying, and they stayed with him that day. It was about four in the afternoon. 40 Andrew, the brother of Simon Peter, was one of the two who heard John and followed Jesus. 41*† He first found his own brother Simon and told him, "We have found the Messiah" (which is translated Anointed). 42*† Then he brought him to Jesus. Jesus looked at him and said, "You are Simon the son of John; you will be called Cephas" (which is translated Peter).

43† The next day he decided to go to Galilee, and he found Philip. And Jesus said to him, "Follow me." 44 Now Philip was from Bethsaida, the town of Andrew and Peter. 45* Philip found Nathanael and told him, "We have found the one about whom Moses wrote in the law, and also the prophets, Jesus son of Joseph, from Nazareth." 46 But Nathanael said to him, "Can anything good come from Nazareth?" Philip

---

synoptic gospels and Septuagint) of the Hebrew text of Is 40:3, which reads, "A voice cries out: In the desert prepare the way of the LORD."

1:24 *Some Pharisees:* other translations, such as "Now they had been sent from the Pharisees," misunderstand the grammatical construction. This is a different group from that in v 19; the priests and Levites would have been Sadducees, not Pharisees.

1:26 *I baptize with water:* the synoptics add "but he will baptize you with the holy Spirit" (Mk 1:8) or ". . . holy Spirit and fire" (Mt 3:11; Lk 3:16). John's emphasis is on purification and preparation for a better baptism.

1:28 *Bethany across the Jordan:* site unknown. Another reading is "Bethabara."

1:29 *The Lamb of God:* the background for this title may be the victorious apocalyptic lamb who would destroy evil in the world (Rv 5–7; 17:14); the paschal lamb, whose blood saved Israel (Ex 12); and/or the suffering servant led like a lamb to the slaughter as a sin-offering (Is 53:7, 10).

1:30 *He existed before me:* possibly as Elijah (to come, 27); for the evangelist and his audience, Jesus' preexistence would be implied (see the note on 1:1).

1:31 *I did not know him:* this gospel shows no knowledge of the tradition (Lk 1) about the kinship of Jesus and John the Baptist. *The reason why I came baptizing with water:* in this gospel, John's baptism is not connected with forgiveness of sins; its purpose is revelatory, that Jesus may be made known to Israel.

1:32 *Like a dove:* a symbol of the new creation (Gn 8:8) or the community of Israel (Hos 11:11). *Remain:* the first use of a favorite verb in John, emphasizing the permanency of the relationship between Father and Son (as here) and between the Son and the Christian. Jesus is the permanent bearer of the Spirit.

1:34 *The Son of God:* this reading is supported by good Greek manuscripts, including the Chester Beatty and Bodmer Papyri and the Vatican Codex, but is suspect because it harmonizes this passage with the synoptic version: "This is my beloved Son" (Mt 3:17; Mk 1:11; Lk 3:22). The poorly attested alternate reading, "God's chosen One," is probably a reference to the Servant of Yahweh (Is 42:1).

1:36 John the Baptist's testimony makes his disciples' following of Jesus plausible.

1:37 *The two disciples:* Andrew (40) and, traditionally, John, son of Zebedee (see the note on 13:23).

1:39 *Four in the afternoon:* literally, the tenth hour, from sunrise, in the Roman calculation of time. Some suggest that the next day, beginning at sunset, was the sabbath; they would have stayed with Jesus to avoid travel on it.

1:41 *Messiah:* the Hebrew word *māšîaḥ,* "anointed one" (see the note on Lk 2:11), appears in Greek as the transliterated *messias* only here and in 4:25. Elsewhere the Greek translation *christos* is used.

1:42 *Simon, the son of John:* in Mt 16:17, Simon is called *Bariōna,* "son of Jonah," a different tradition for the name of Simon's father. *Cephas:* in Aramaic = the Rock; cf Mt 16:18. Neither the Greek equivalent *Petros* nor, with one isolated exception, *Cephas* is attested as a personal name before Christian times.

1:43 *He:* grammatically, could be Peter, but logically is probably Jesus.

1:25 Ez 36:25; Zec 13:1; Mt 16:14.
1:26 Mt 3:11; Mk 1:7–8; Lk 3:16; Acts 13:25.
1:29 Jn 1:36; Ex 12; Is 53:7; Rv 5–7; 17:14.
1:30 Jn 1:15; Mt 3:11; Mk 1:7; Lk 3:16.
1:32 Sg 5:2; Is 11:2; Hos 11:11; Mt 3:16; Mk 1:10; Lk 3:21–22.
1:33 Is 42:1; Mt 3:11; Mk 1:8; Lk 3:16.
1:34 Is 42:1; Mt 3:17; Mk 1:11; Lk 9:35.
1:35–51 Mt 4:18–22; Mk 1:16–20; Lk 5:1–11.
1:41 Jn 4:25.
1:42 Mt 16:18; Mk 3:16.
1:45 Jn 21:2.

said to him, "Come and see." 47† Jesus saw Na-
thanael coming toward him and said of him,
"Here is a true Israelite. There is no duplicity in
him." 48*† Nathanael said to him, "How do you
know me?" Jesus answered and said to him, "Be-
fore Philip called you, I saw you under the fig
tree." 49*† Nathanael answered him, "Rabbi, you
are the Son of God; you are the King of Israel."
50† Jesus answered and said to him, "Do you be-
lieve because I told you that I saw you under the
fig tree? You will see greater things than this."
51*† And he said to him, "Amen, amen, I say to
you, you will see the sky opened and the angels
of God ascending and descending on the Son of
Man."

The Wedding at Cana

2 1*† On the third day there was a wedding†
in Cana† in Galilee, and the mother of Jesus
was there. 2 Jesus and his disciples were also in-
vited to the wedding. 3 When the wine ran short,
the mother of Jesus said to him, "They have no
wine." 4*† [And] Jesus said to her, "Woman,
how does your concern affect me? My hour has
not yet come." 5* His mother said to the servers,
"Do whatever he tells you." 6*† Now there were
six stone water jars there for Jewish ceremonial
washings, each holding twenty to thirty gallons.
7 Jesus told them, "Fill the jars with water." So
they filled them to the brim. 8† Then he told
them, "Draw some out now and take it to the
headwaiter." So they took it. 9 And when the
headwaiter tasted the water that had become

Live It!

The First Sign

If there is one day that people want to go exactly as planned, it's usually a wedding day. Months of planning, and usually lots of money, go into ensuring the big day will go smoothly. Imagine if there wasn't enough food to feed everyone! How embarrassing! Imagine if the cake never arrived, or if there wasn't enough wine for all the guests!

This is exactly what happens at the wedding at Cana. Jesus is there, along with his followers and his mother, Mary. Mary mentions to Jesus that they are running out of wine. Take a moment to study Jesus' reaction to his mother's comment. Does it seem a bit strange? Why do you think Jesus hesitates? Why does Mary persist?

In the Gospel of John, this is the first of seven miracles, or as John calls them, signs, that Jesus performs. Why do you think this one is first? What happens because of this miracle? What might it be a sign of? As you read further in John's Gospel, pay attention to what each of Jesus' seven miracles teaches us about Jesus and his mission.

▶ **Jn 2:1–11**

1:47 *A true Israelite. There is no duplicity in him:* Jacob was the first to bear the name "Israel" (Gn 32:29), but Jacob was a man of duplicity (Gn 27:35–36).

1:48 *Under the fig tree:* a symbol of messianic peace (cf Mi 4:4; Zec 3:10).

1:49 *Son of God:* this title is used in the Old Testament, among other ways, as a title of adoption for the Davidic king (2 Sm 7:14; Pss 2:7; 89:27), and thus here, with *King of Israel,* in a messianic sense. For the evangelist, *Son of God* also points to Jesus' divinity (cf 20:28).

1:50 Possibly a statement: "You [singular] believe because I saw you under the fig tree."

1:51 The double "Amen" is characteristic of John. *You* is plural in Greek. The allusion is to Jacob's ladder (Gn 28:12).

2:1—6:71 Signs revealing Jesus as the Messiah to all Israel. "Sign" (*sēmeion*) is John's symbolic term for Jesus' wondrous deeds (see Introduction). The Old Testament background lies in the Exodus story (cf Dt 11:3; 29:2). John is interested primarily in what the *sēmeia* signify: God's intervention in human history in a new way through Jesus.

2:1–11 The first sign. This story of replacement of Jewish ceremonial washings (6) presents the initial revelation about Jesus at the outset of his ministry. He manifests his glory; the disciples believe. There is no synoptic parallel.

2:1 *Cana:* unknown from the Old Testament. *The mother of Jesus:* she is never named in John.

2:4 This verse may seek to show that Jesus did not work miracles to help his family and friends, as in the apocryphal gospels. *Woman:* a normal, polite form of address, but unattested in reference to one's mother. Cf also 19:26. *How does your concern affect me?:* literally, "What is this to me and to you?"—a Hebrew expression of either hostility (Jgs 11:12; 2 Chr 35:21; 1 Kgs 17:18) or denial of common interest (Hos 14:9; 2 Kgs 3:13). Cf Mk 1:24; 5:7, used by demons to Jesus. *My hour has not yet come:* the translation as a question ("Has not my hour now come?"), while preferable grammatically and supported by Greek Fathers, seems unlikely from a comparison with 7:6, 30. The "hour" is that of Jesus' passion, death, resurrection, and ascension (13:1).

2:6 *Twenty to thirty gallons:* literally, "two or three measures"; the Attic liquid measure contained 39.39 liters. The vast quantity recalls prophecies of abundance in the last days; cf Am 9:13–14; Hos 14:7; Jer 31:12.

2:8 *Headwaiter:* used of the official who managed a banquet, but there is no evidence of such a functionary in Palestine. Perhaps here a friend of the family acted as master of ceremonies; cf Sir 32:1.

1:48 Mi 4:4; Zec 3:10.
1:49 Jn 12:13; Ex 4:22; Dt 14:1; 2 Sm 7:14; Jb 1:6; 2:1; 38:7; Pss 2:7; 29:1; 89:27; Wis 2:18; Sir 4:10; Dn 3:25; Hos 11:1; Mt 14:33; 16:16; Mk 13:32.
1:51 Gn 28:10–17; Dn 7:13.
2:1 Jn 4:46; Jgs 14:12; Tb 11:8.
2:4 Jn 7:30; 8:20; 12:23; 13:1; Jgs 11:12; 1 Kgs 17:18; 2 Kgs 3:13; 2 Chr 35:21; Hos 14:9; Mk 1:24; 5:7; 7:30; 8:20; 12:23; 13:1.
2:5 Gn 41:55.
2:6 Jn 3:25; Lv 11:33; Am 9:13–14; Mt 15:2; 23:25–26; Mk 7:2–4; Lk 11:38.

J
N

wine, without knowing where it came from (al-
though the servers who had drawn the water
knew), the headwaiter called the bridegroom
10 and said to him, "Everyone serves good wine
first, and then when people have drunk freely,
an inferior one; but you have kept the good wine
until now." 11*† Jesus did this as the beginning
of his signs in Cana in Galilee and so revealed his
glory, and his disciples began to believe in him.
12† After this, he and his mother, [his] broth-
ers, and his disciples went down to Capernaum
and stayed there only a few days.†

Cleansing of the Temple

13*† Since the Passover† of the Jews was near,
Jesus went up to Jerusalem. 14*† He found in the
temple area those who sold oxen, sheep, and
doves,† as well as the money-changers seated
there. 15 He made a whip out of cords and drove
them all out of the temple area, with the sheep
and oxen, and spilled the coins of the money-
changers and overturned their tables, 16* and
to those who sold doves he said, "Take these
out of here, and stop making my Father's house
a marketplace." 17*† His disciples recalled the
words of scripture, "Zeal for your house will
consume me." 18* At this the Jews answered
and said to him, "What sign can you show us
for doing this?" 19*† Jesus answered and said to
them, "Destroy this temple and in three days I
will raise it up." 20† The Jews said, "This temple
has been under construction for forty-six years,

†

2:11 *The beginning of his signs:* the first of seven (see Introduction).

2:12—3:21 The next three episodes take place in Jerusalem. Only the first is paralleled in the synoptic gospels.

2:12 This transitional verse may be a harmonization with the synoptic tradition in Lk 4:31 and Mt 4:13. There are many textual variants. John depicts no extended ministry in Capernaum as do the synoptics.

2:13–22 This episode indicates the post-resurrectional replacement of the temple by the person of Jesus.

2:13 *Passover:* this is the first Passover mentioned in John; a second is mentioned in 6:4, a third in 13:1. Taken literally, they point to a ministry of at least two years.

2:14–22 The other gospels place the cleansing of the temple in the last days of Jesus' life (Matthew, on the day Jesus entered Jerusalem; Mark, on the next day). The order of events in the gospel narratives is often determined by theological motives rather than by chronological data.

2:14 *Oxen, sheep, and doves:* intended for sacrifice. The doves were the offerings of the poor (Lv 5:7). *Money-changers:* for a temple tax paid by every male Jew more than nineteen years of age, with a half-shekel coin (Ex 30:11–16), in Tyrian currency. See the note on Mt 17:24.

2:17 Ps 69:10, changed to future tense to apply to Jesus.

2:19 This saying about the destruction of the temple occurs in various forms (Mt 24:2; 27:40; Mk 13:2; 15:29; Lk 21:6; cf Acts 6:14). Mt 26:61 has: "I *can* destroy the temple of God . . ."; see the note there. In Mk 14:58, there is a metaphorical contrast with a new temple: "I will destroy this temple *made with hands* and within three days I will build another *not made with hands.*" Here it is symbolic of Jesus' resurrection and the resulting community (see 21 and Rv 21:2). *In three days:* an Old Testament expression for a short, indefinite period of time; cf Hos 6:2.

2:20 *Forty-six years:* based on references in Josephus (*Jewish Wars* 1, 21, 1 §§401; *Antiquities* 15, 11, 1 §380), possibly the spring of A.D. 28. Cf the note on Lk 3:1.

2:11 Jn 4:54.
2:13–22 Mt 21:12–13; Mk 11:15–17; Lk 19:45–46.
2:14 Ex 30:11–16; Lv 5:7.
2:16 Zec 14:21.
2:17 Ps 69:9.
2:18 Jn 6:30.
2:19 Mt 24:2; 26:61; 27:40; Mk 13:2; 14:58; 15:29; Lk 21:6; Acts 6:14.

2:1–12

Did You Know?

"The Jews" in the Gospel of John

When you read the Gospel of John, you may notice that the Gospel writer often makes references to "the Jews." They are often portrayed questioning (see Jn 2:18) or challenging Jesus. Around the time John was written, Christian Jews were being forcibly removed from Jewish synagogues (see 16:1–4). With this rivalry in the background, the Gospel writer sometimes lumps all Jews together, portraying them as the "bad guys." Christian churches teach that we should not take John's references to "the Jews" as a basis for prejudice or anger against Jewish people.

▶ Jn 2:18–20

and you will raise it up in three days?" 21 But he was speaking about the temple of his body. 22* Therefore, when he was raised from the dead, his disciples remembered that he had said this, and they came to believe the scripture and the word Jesus had spoken.

23* While he was in Jerusalem for the feast of Passover, many began to believe in his name when they saw the signs he was doing. 24 But Jesus would not trust himself to them because he knew them all, 25* and did not need anyone to testify about human nature. He himself understood it well.

Nicodemus†

3 1*† Now there was a Pharisee named Nicodemus, a ruler of the Jews. 2* He came to Jesus at night and said to him, "Rabbi, we know that you are a teacher who has come from God, for no one can do these signs that you are doing unless God is with him." 3† Jesus answered and said to him, "Amen, amen, I say to you, no one can see the kingdom of God without being born from above." 4* Nicodemus said to him, "How can a person once grown old be born again? Surely he cannot reenter his mother's womb and be born again, can he?" 5* Jesus answered, "Amen, amen, I say to you, no one can enter the kingdom of God without being born of water and Spirit. 6* What is born of flesh is flesh and what is born of spirit is spirit. 7 Do not be amazed that I told you, 'You must be born from above.' 8*† The wind blows where it wills, and you can hear the sound it makes, but you do not know where it comes from or where it goes; so it is with everyone who is born of the Spirit." 9 Nicodemus answered and said to him, "How can this happen?" 10 Jesus answered and said to him, "You are the teacher of Israel and you do not understand this? 11* Amen, amen, I say to you, we speak of what we know and we testify to what we have seen, but you people do not accept our testimony. 12* If I tell you about earthly things and you do not believe, how will you believe if I tell you about heavenly things? 13* No one has gone up to heaven except the one who has come down from heaven, the Son of Man. 14*† And just as Moses lifted up the serpent in the desert, so must the Son of Man be lifted up, 15† so that everyone who believes in him may have eternal life."

Live It!

Nic at Night

Nicodemus, a Jewish teacher with a high position of leadership, is meeting secretly with Jesus. Nicodemus has been waiting for a sign that God's promise of salvation through a savior will happen in his lifetime. He senses that maybe Jesus is this savior. But he does not yet believe in Jesus, as is emphasized by his coming to Jesus "at night" (Jn 3:2). Speaking symbolically, Jesus outlines what it takes for salvation: to believe in Jesus as the one sent by God and to be born again through baptism and the Holy Spirit. The same is true for people today.

Nicodemus most likely knew that to accept Jesus publicly would put him in bad standing with the other Jewish leaders. Sometimes, we must make choices that might make us look foolish to others.

- How hard would it be for you to express belief in Jesus publicly?
- Are you a believer in the night or in the light?

▶ **Jn 3:1–21**

†

3:1–21 Jesus instructs Nicodemus on the necessity of a new birth from above. This scene in Jerusalem at Passover exemplifies the faith engendered by signs (2:23). It continues the self-manifestation of Jesus in Jerusalem begun in ch 2. This is the first of the Johannine discourses, shifting from dialogue to monologue (11–15) to reflection of the evangelist (16–21). The shift from singular through v 10 to plural in v 11 may reflect the early church's controversy with the Jews.

3:1 *A ruler of the Jews:* most likely a member of the Jewish council, the Sanhedrin; see the note on Mk 8:31.

3:3 *Born:* see the note on 1:13. *From above:* the Greek adverb *anōthen* means both "from above" and "again." Jesus means "from above" (see 31), but Nicodemus misunderstands it as "again." This misunderstanding serves as a springboard for further instruction.

3:8 *Wind:* the Greek word *pneuma* (as well as the Hebrew *rûah*) means both "wind" and "spirit." In the play on the double meaning, "wind" is primary.

3:14 *Lifted up:* in Nm 21:9, Moses simply "mounted" a serpent upon a pole. John here substitutes a verb implying glorification. Jesus, exalted to glory at his cross and resurrection, represents healing for all.

3:15 *Eternal life:* used here for the first time in John, this term stresses quality of life rather than duration.

*

2:22 Jn 5:39; 12:16; 14:26; 20:9; Mt 12:6; Lk 24:6–8; Rv 21:22.
2:23 Jn 4:45.
2:25 1 Kgs 8:39; Pss 33:15; 94:11; Sir 42:18; Jer 17:10; 20:12.
3:1 Jn 7:50–51; 19:39.
3:2 Jn 9:4, 16, 33; 10:21; 11:10; 13:30; Mt 22:16; Mk 12:14; Lk 20:21.
3:4 Jn 1:13.
3:5 Jn 1:32; 7:39; 19:30, 34–35; Is 32:15; 44:3; Ez 36:25–27; Jl 3:1–2.
3:6 Jn 6:63; 1 Cor 15:44–50.
3:8 Eccl 11:4–5; Acts 2:2–4.
3:11 Jn 3:32, 34; 8:14; Mt 11:27.
3:12 Jn 6:62–65; Wis 9:16–17; 1 Cor 15:40; 2 Cor 5:1; Phil 2:10; 3:19–20.
3:13 Jn 1:18; 6:62; Dn 7:13; Rom 10:6; Eph 4:9.
3:14 Jn 8:28; 12:32, 34; Nm 21:4–9; Wis 16:5–7.

Pray It!

How Deep Is Your Well?

In John 4:1–42, Jesus engages a Samaritan woman in conversation. She has no idea who Jesus is and what living water he is referring to, but she stands and listens. She is changed as a result. She comes to believe in Jesus and goes to tell others about the Messiah. John uses her as a role model for those who believe.

Look inside the well of faith within you. How deep is that well? Do you thirst for a deeper relationship with Jesus? Are you ready to share the Good News with others? Jesus invites each of us to join with him in a personal relationship. All we have to do is ask. Begin your relationship with Jesus by praying:

Jesus, you are the Messiah, the anointed one. I am thirsty. . . . Quench my thirst.

▶ Jn 4:1–42

16*† For God so loved the world that he gave
his only Son, so that everyone who believes in
him might not perish but might have eternal life.
17*† For God did not send his Son into the world
to condemn the world, but that the world might
be saved through him. 18* Whoever believes in
him will not be condemned, but whoever does
not believe has already been condemned, be-
cause he has not believed in the name of the only
Son of God. 19*† And this is the verdict, that the
light came into the world, but people preferred
darkness to light, because their works were evil.
20* For everyone who does wicked things hates
the light and does not come toward the light,
so that his works might not be exposed. 21* But
whoever lives the truth comes to the light, so that
his works may be clearly seen as done in God.

Final Witness of the Baptist

22*† After this, Jesus and his disciples went
into the region of Judea, where he spent some
time with them baptizing. 23† John was also bap-
tizing in Aenon near Salim, because there was
an abundance of water there, and people came
to be baptized, 24*† for John had not yet been
imprisoned. 25† Now a dispute arose between
the disciples of John and a Jew about ceremonial
washings. 26* So they came to John and said to
him, "Rabbi, the one who was with you across
the Jordan, to whom you testified, here he is bap-
tizing and everyone is coming to him." 27* John
answered and said, "No one can receive anything
except what has been given him from heaven.
28* You yourselves can testify that I said [that] I
am not the Messiah, but that I was sent before
him. 29*† The one who has the bride is the bride-
groom; the best man, who stands and listens to
him, rejoices greatly at the bridegroom's voice.
So this joy of mine has been made complete.
30* He must increase; I must decrease."

The One from Heaven

31*† The one who comes from above is above
all. The one who is of the earth is earthly and
speaks of earthly things. But the one who comes
from heaven [is above all]. 32* He testifies to
what he has seen and heard, but no one accepts
his testimony. 33* Whoever does accept his tes-
timony certifies that God is trustworthy. 34† For
the one whom God sent speaks the words of
God. He does not ration his gift of the Spirit.
35* The Father loves the Son and has given ev-
erything over to him. 36* Whoever believes in

†

3:16 *Gave:* as a gift in the incarnation, and also "over to death" in the crucifixion; cf Rom 8:32.

3:17–19 *Condemn:* the Greek root means both judgment and condemnation. Jesus' purpose is to save, but his coming provokes judgment; some condemn themselves by turning from the light.

3:19 Judgment is not only future but is partially realized here and now.

3:22–26 Jesus' ministry in Judea is only loosely connected with 2:13—3:21; cf 1:19–36. Perhaps John the Baptist's further testimony was transposed here to give meaning to "water" in v 5. Jesus is depicted as baptizing (22); contrast 4:2.

3:23 *Aenon near Salim:* site uncertain, either in the upper Jordan valley or in Samaria.

3:24 A remark probably intended to avoid objections based on a chronology like that of the synoptics (Mt 4:12; Mk 1:14).

3:25 *A Jew:* some think Jesus is meant. Many manuscripts read "Jews."

3:29 *The best man:* literally, "the friend of the groom," the *shoshben* of Jewish tradition, who arranged the wedding. Competition between him and the groom would be unthinkable.

3:31–36 It is uncertain whether these are words by the Baptist, Jesus, or the evangelist. They are reflections on the two preceding scenes.

3:34 *His gift:* of God or to Jesus, perhaps both. This verse echoes vv 5 and 8.

*

3:16 1 Jn 4:9.
3:17 Jn 5:22, 30; 8:15–18; 12:47.
3:18 Jn 5:24; Mk 16:16.
3:19 Jn 1:5, 9–11; 8:12; 9:5.
3:20 Jb 24:13–17.
3:21 Gn 47:29 LXX; Jos 2:14 LXX; 2 Sm 2:6 LXX; 15:20 LXX; Tb 4:6 LXX; 13:6; Is 26:10 LXX; Mt 5:14–16.
3:22–23 Jn 4:1–2.
3:24 Mt 4:12; 14:3; Mk 1:14; 6:17; Lk 3:20.
3:26 Jn 1:26, 32–34, 36.
3:27 Jn 19:11; 1 Cor 4:7; 2 Cor 3:5; Heb 5:4.
3:28 Jn 1:20–23; Lk 3:15.
3:29 Jn 15:11; 17:13; Mt 9:15.
3:30 2 Sm 3:1.
3:31 Jn 8:23.
3:32 Jn 3:11.
3:33–34 Jn 8:26; 12:44–50; 1 Jn 5:10.
3:35 Jn 13:3; Mt 11:27; 28:18; Lk 10:22.
3:36 Jn 3:16; 1 Jn 5:13.

the Son has eternal life, but whoever disobeys
the Son will not see life, but the wrath of God
remains upon him.

4 1† Now when Jesus learned that the Pharisees
had heard that Jesus was making and baptiz-
ing more disciples than John 2† (although Jesus
himself was not baptizing, just his disciples), 3 he
left Judea and returned to Galilee.

The Samaritan Woman

4† He had to pass through Samaria. 5*† So he
came to a town of Samaria called Sychar, near
the plot of land that Jacob had given to his son
Joseph. 6 Jacob's well was there. Jesus, tired from
his journey, sat down there at the well. It was
about noon.
7 A woman of Samaria came to draw water.
Jesus said to her, "Give me a drink." 8 His disci-
ples had gone into the town to buy food. 9*† The
Samaritan woman said to him, "How can you, a
Jew, ask me, a Samaritan woman, for a drink?"
(For Jews use nothing in common with Samar-
itans.) 10*† Jesus answered and said to her, "If
you knew the gift of God and who is saying to
you, 'Give me a drink,' you would have asked
him and he would have given you living water."
11† [The woman] said to him, "Sir, you do not
even have a bucket and the well is deep; where
then can you get this living water? 12* Are you
greater than our father Jacob, who gave us this
well and drank from it himself with his children
and his flocks?" 13 Jesus answered and said to her,
"Everyone who drinks this water will be thirsty
again; 14* but whoever drinks the water I shall
give will never thirst; the water I shall give will
become in him a spring of water welling up to
eternal life." 15 The woman said to him, "Sir, give
me this water, so that I may not be thirsty or have
to keep coming here to draw water."
16 Jesus said to her, "Go call your husband
and come back." 17 The woman answered and
said to him, "I do not have a husband." Jesus
answered her, "You are right in saying, 'I do not
have a husband.' 18* For you have had five hus-
bands, and the one you have now is not your
husband. What you have said is true." 19* The
woman said to him, "Sir, I can see that you
are a prophet. 20*† Our ancestors worshiped

Did You Know?

Why Are the Disciples Surprised?

The disciples "were amazed that he [Jesus] was talking with a woman" (Jn 4:27). For several reasons, it was unusual for Jesus to be talking to her. First, in first-century Israel, men did not talk to women, especially strangers, in public places. Second, Jews did not talk to Samaritans (see "Who Belongs and Who Does Not?" near Ezra, chapters 9–10, and "Discrimination in Jesus' Time," near Lk 10:25–37), who were not considered to be real Jews (see Jn 4:20). And finally, the woman with whom Jesus was speaking was accused of having had five husbands. Some scholars think that "five husbands" is symbolic of the five books of the Torah that the Samaritans revered. On the other hand, most first-century women did not have the right to divorce, only their husbands did. So it may be that she was just terribly unlucky having been widowed or dismissed numerous times and now taken in as a servant in someone's household.

This episode is one more example in the Gospel of John that shows Jesus is not bound by customs and stereotypes when the message of the Gospel is at stake.

▶ **Jn 4:1–42**

JN

†

4:1–42 Jesus in Samaria. The self-revelation of Jesus continues with his second discourse, on his mission to "half-Jews." It continues the theme of replacement, here with regard to cult (21). *Water* (7–15) serves as a symbol (as at Cana and in the Nicodemus episode).

4:2 An editorial refinement of 3:22, perhaps directed against followers of John the Baptist who claimed that Jesus imitated him.

4:4 *He had to:* a theological necessity; geographically, Jews often bypassed Samaria by taking a route across the Jordan.

4:5 *Sychar:* Jerome identifies this with Shechem, a reading found in Syriac manuscripts.

4:9 *Samaritan* women were regarded by Jews as ritually impure, and therefore Jews were forbidden to drink from any vessel they had handled.

4:10 *Living water:* the water of life, i.e., the revelation that Jesus brings; the woman thinks of "flowing water," so much more desirable than stagnant cistern water. On John's device of such misunderstanding, cf the note on 3:3.

4:11 *Sir:* the Greek *kyrios* means "master" or "lord," as a respectful mode of address for a human being or a deity; cf 4:19. It is also the word used in the Septuagint for the Hebrew *adônai,* substituted for the tetragrammaton YHWH.

4:20 *This mountain:* Gerizim, on which a temple was erected in the fourth century B.C. by Samaritans to rival Mt. Zion in Jerusalem; cf Dt 27:4 (Mt. Ebal = the Jews' term for Gerizim).

*

4:5 Gn 33:18–19; 48:22; Jos 24:32.
4:9 Sir 50:25–26; Mt 10:5.
4:10 Sir 24:20–21; Is 55:1; Jer 2:13.
4:12 Jn 8:53; Mt 12:41.
4:14 Jn 6:35, 58; 7:37–39; Is 44:3; 49:10; Jl 4:18; Rv 7:16; 21:6.
4:18 2 Kgs 17:24–34.
4:19 Jn 9:17; Hos 1:3.
4:20 Dt 11:29; 27:4; Jos 8:33; Ps 122:1–5.

Cultural Connection

This Is Christmas

This poem, by Masao and Fumiko Takenaka of Japan, is a reflection on Jesus as "living water" (Jn 4:10):

One who said I am the
eternal water
Dwelt among us
Living with us
Sustaining us
This is Christmas.
To receive a cup of living
water
Is not only to cleanse
ourselves
But also to cleanse all the
waters,
River and well, lake and
ocean,
And to share them with all.
This is Christmas.

(From Tirabassi and Eddy, editors, *Gifts of Many Cultures*, p. 144)

Jn 4:1–15

on this mountain; but you people say that the
place to worship is in Jerusalem." 21 Jesus said
to her, "Believe me, woman, the hour is coming when you will worship the Father neither
on this mountain nor in Jerusalem. 22* You
people worship what you do not understand;
we worship what we understand, because salvation is from the Jews. 23† But the hour is
coming, and is now here, when true worshipers
will worship the Father in Spirit and truth; and
indeed the Father seeks such people to worship
him. 24* God is Spirit, and those who worship
him must worship in Spirit and truth." 25*† The
woman said to him, "I know that the Messiah
is coming, the one called the Anointed; when
he comes, he will tell us everything." 26*† Jesus
said to her, "I am he, the one who is speaking
with you."
27† At that moment his disciples returned,
and were amazed that he was talking with a
woman, but still no one said, "What are you
looking for?" or "Why are you talking with
her?" 28 The woman left her water jar and went
into the town and said to the people, 29 "Come
see a man who told me everything I have done.
Could he possibly be the Messiah?" 30 They went
out of the town and came to him. 31 Meanwhile,
the disciples urged him, "Rabbi, eat." 32 But he
said to them, "I have food to eat of which you
do not know." 33 So the disciples said to one
another, "Could someone have brought him
something to eat?" 34* Jesus said to them, "My
food is to do the will of the one who sent me
and to finish his work. 35*† Do you not say, 'In
four months the harvest will be here'? I tell you,
look up and see the fields ripe for the harvest.
36*† The reaper is already receiving his payment
and gathering crops for eternal life, so that the
sower and reaper can rejoice together. 37* For
here the saying is verified that 'One sows and another reaps.' 38 I sent you to reap what you have
not worked for; others have done the work, and
you are sharing the fruits of their work."
39† Many of the Samaritans of that town began to believe in him because of the word of the
woman who testified, "He told me everything
I have done." 40 When the Samaritans came to
him, they invited him to stay with them; and
he stayed there two days. 41 Many more began
to believe in him because of his word, 42* and
they said to the woman, "We no longer believe
because of your word; for we have heard for ourselves, and we know that this is truly the savior
of the world."

†

4:23 *In Spirit and truth:* not a reference to an interior worship within one's own spirit. The Spirit is the spirit given by God that reveals truth and enables one to worship God appropriately (14:16–17). Cf "born of water and Spirit" (3:5).

4:25 The expectations of the Samaritans are expressed here in Jewish terminology. They did not expect a messianic king of the house of David but a prophet like Moses (Dt 18:15).

4:26 *I am he:* it could also be translated "I am," an Old Testament self-designation of Yahweh (Is 43:3, etc.); cf 6:20; 8:24, 28, 58; 13:19; 18:5, 6, 8. See the note on Mk 6:50.

4:27 *Talking with a woman:* a religious and social restriction that Jesus is pictured treating as unimportant.

4:35 *'In four months . . .':* probably a proverb; cf Mt 9:37–38.

4:36 *Already:* this word may go with the preceding verse rather than with 36.

4:39 The woman is presented as a missionary, described in virtually the same words as the disciples are in Jesus' prayer (17:20).

*

4:22 2 Kgs 17:27; Ps 76:2–3.
4:24 2 Cor 3:17.
4:25 Jn 1:41.
4:26 Jn 9:37.
4:34 Jn 5:30, 36; 6:38; 9:4; 17:4.
4:35 Mt 9:37–38; Lk 10:2; Rv 14:15.
4:36 Ps 126:5–6; Am 9:13–14.
4:37 Dt 20:6; 28:30; Jb 31:8; Mi 6:15.
4:42 1 Jn 4:14.

Return to Galilee

43† After the two days, he left there for Galilee. 44*† For Jesus himself testified that a prophet has no honor in his native place. 45 When he came into Galilee, the Galileans welcomed him, since they had seen all he had done in Jerusalem at the feast; for they themselves had gone to the feast.

Second Sign at Cana

46*† Then he returned to Cana in Galilee, where he had made the water wine. Now there was a royal official whose son was ill in Capernaum. 47 When he heard that Jesus had arrived in Galilee from Judea, he went to him and asked him to come down and heal his son, who was near death. 48* Jesus said to him, "Unless you people see signs and wonders, you will not believe." 49 The royal official said to him, "Sir, come down before my child dies." 50* Jesus said to him, "You may go; your son will live." The man believed what Jesus said to him and left. 51 While he was on his way back, his slaves met him and told him that his boy would live. 52 He asked them when he began to recover. They told him, "The fever left him yesterday, about one in the afternoon." 53 The father realized that just at that time Jesus had said to him, "Your son will live," and he and his whole household came to believe. 54* [Now] this was the second sign Jesus did when he came to Galilee from Judea.

Cure on a Sabbath

5 1*† After this, there was a feast† of the Jews, and Jesus went up to Jerusalem. 2*† Now there is in Jerusalem at the Sheep [Gate] a pool called in Hebrew Bethesda, with five porticoes. 3† In these lay a large number of ill, blind, lame, and crippled. [4]† 5 One man was there who had been ill for thirty-eight years. 6 When Jesus saw him lying there and knew that he had been ill for a long time, he said to him, "Do you want to be well?" 7 The sick man answered him, "Sir, I have no one to put me into the pool when the water is stirred up; while I am on my way, someone else gets down there before me." 8* Jesus said to him, "Rise, take up your mat, and walk." 9* Immediately the man became well, took up his mat, and walked.

Now that day was a sabbath. 10* So the Jews said to the man who was cured, "It is the sabbath, and it is not lawful for you to carry your mat." 11 He answered them, "The man who made me well told me, 'Take up your mat and walk.' " 12 They asked him, "Who is the man who told you, 'Take it up and walk'?" 13* The man who was healed did not know who it was, for Jesus had slipped away, since there was a crowd there. 14*† After this Jesus found him in the temple area and said to him, "Look, you are well; do not sin any more, so that nothing worse may happen to you." 15 The man went and told the Jews that Jesus was the one who had made him well. 16* Therefore, the Jews began to persecute Jesus because he did this on a sabbath. 17*† But

†

4:43–54 Jesus' arrival in Cana in Galilee; the second sign. This section introduces another theme, that of the life-giving word of Jesus. It is explicitly linked to the first sign (2:11). The royal official believes (50). The natural life given his son is a sign of eternal life.

4:44 Probably a reminiscence of a tradition as in Mk 6:4. Cf Gospel of Thomas 31: "No prophet is acceptable in his village, no physician heals those who know him."

4:46–54 The story of the cure of the royal official's son may be a third version of the cure of the centurion's son (Mt 8:5–13) or servant (Lk 7:1–10). Cf also Mt 15:21–28 // Mk 7:24–30.

5:1–47 The self-revelation of Jesus continues in Jerusalem at a feast. The third sign (cf 2:11; 4:54) is performed, the cure of a paralytic by Jesus' life-giving word. The water of the pool fails to bring life; Jesus' word does.

5:1 The reference in vv 45–46 to Moses suggests that the feast was Pentecost. The connection of that feast with the giving of the law to Moses on Sinai, attested in later Judaism, may already have been made in the first century. The feast could also be Passover (cf 6:4). John stresses that the day was a sabbath (9).

5:2 There is no noun with *Sheep.* "Gate" is supplied on the grounds that there must have been a gate in the NE wall of the temple area where animals for sacrifice were brought in; cf Neh 3:1, 32; 12:39. *Hebrew:* more precisely, Aramaic. *Bethesda:* preferred to variants "Be(th)zatha" and "Bethsaida"; *bêt-eˆsdatayin* is given as the name of a double pool northeast of the temple area in the Qumran Copper Roll. *Five porticoes:* a pool excavated in Jerusalem actually has five porticoes.

5:3 The Caesarean and Western recensions, followed by the Vulgate, add "waiting for the movement of the water." Apparently an intermittent spring in the pool bubbled up occasionally (see 7). This turbulence was believed to cure.

5:4 Toward the end of the second century in the West and among the fourth-century Greek Fathers, an additional verse was known: "For from time to time an angel of the Lord used to come down into the pool; and the water was stirred up, so the first one to get in after the stirring of the water was healed of whatever disease afflicted him." The angel was a popular explanation of the turbulence and the healing powers attributed to it. This verse is missing from all early Greek manuscripts and the earliest versions, including the original Vulgate. Its vocabulary is markedly non-Johannine.

5:14 While the cure of the paralytic in Mk 2:1–12 is associated with the forgiveness of sins, Jesus never drew a one-to-one connection between sin and suffering (cf 9:3; Lk 12:1–5), as did Ez 18:20.

5:17 Sabbath observance (10) was based on God's resting on the seventh day (cf Gn 2:2–3; Ex 20:11). Philo and some rabbis insisted that God's providence remains active on the sabbath, keeping all things in existence, giving life in birth and taking it away in death. Other rabbis taught that God rested from creating, but not from judging (= ruling, governing). Jesus here claims the same authority to work as the Father, and, in the discourse that follows, the same divine prerogatives: power over life and death (21, 24–26) and judgment (22, 27).

4:44 Mt 13:57; Mk 6:4; Lk 4:24.
4:46–54 Jn 2:1–11; Mt 8:5–13; 15:21–28; Mk 7:24–30; Lk 7:1–10.
4:48 Jn 2:18, 23; Wis 8:8; Mt 12:38; 1 Cor 1:22.
4:50 1 Kgs 17:23.
4:54 Jn 2:11.
5:1 Jn 6:4.
5:2 Neh 3:1, 32; 12:39.
5:8 Mt 9:6; Mk 2:11; Lk 5:24; Acts 3:6.
5:9 Mk 2:12; Lk 5:25; 9:14.
5:10 Ex 20:8; Jer 17:21–27; Mk 3:2; Lk 13:10; 14:1.
5:13 Mt 8:18; 13:36; Mk 4:36; 7:17.
5:14 Jn 8:11; 9:2; Ez 18:20.
5:16 Jn 7:23; Mt 12:8.
5:17 Ex 20:11.

Did You Know?

"I Am" Sayings of Jesus

The Gospel of John contains a whole series of "I am" sayings as a way for Jesus to explain his role as the Messiah. For example:

- "I am the bread of life" (6:35).
- "I am the light of the world" (8:12).
- "I am the gate for the sheep" (10:7).
- "I am the good shepherd" (10:11).
- "I am the resurrection and the life" (11:25).
- "I am the way and the truth and the life" (14:6).
- "I am the vine, you are the branches" (15:5).

The "I am" sayings are also a means of establishing the divine nature of Jesus. Jesus' use of "I am" is similar to the revelation of God's name to Moses at the burning bush (see Ex 3:14). Ironically, in John, the Jewish leaders are correct in thinking that Jesus is equating himself with God (see 5:18). But they are wrong in not recognizing that Jesus is right!

▶ Jn 5:16–18

JN

Jesus answered them, "My Father is at work until
now, so I am at work." 18* For this reason the
Jews tried all the more to kill him, because he not
only broke the sabbath but he also called God
his own father, making himself equal to God.

The Work of the Son

19*† Jesus answered and said to them, "Amen,
amen, I say to you, a son cannot do anything on
his own, but only what he sees his father doing;
for what he does, his son will do also. 20* For
the Father loves his Son and shows him every-
thing that he himself does, and he will show
him greater works than these, so that you may
be amazed. 21*† For just as the Father raises the
dead and gives life, so also does the Son give life
to whomever he wishes. 22*† Nor does the Father
judge anyone, but he has given all judgment to
his Son, 23 so that all may honor the Son just as
they honor the Father. Whoever does not honor
the Son does not honor the Father who sent him.
24* Amen, amen, I say to you, whoever hears my
word and believes in the one who sent me has
eternal life and will not come to condemnation,
but has passed from death to life. 25* Amen,
amen, I say to you, the hour is coming and is
now here when the dead will hear the voice of
the Son of God, and those who hear will live.
26* For just as the Father has life in himself, so
also he gave to his Son the possession of life in
himself. 27* And he gave him power to exercise
judgment, because he is the Son of Man. 28*† Do
not be amazed at this, because the hour is com-
ing in which all who are in the tombs will hear
his voice 29* and will come out, those who have
done good deeds to the resurrection of life, but
those who have done wicked deeds to the resur-
rection of condemnation.
30* "I cannot do anything on my own; I judge
as I hear, and my judgment is just, because I do
not seek my own will but the will of the one who
sent me.

Witnesses to Jesus

31* "If I testify on my own behalf, my testi-
mony cannot be verified. 32† But there is another
who testifies on my behalf, and I know that the
testimony he gives on my behalf is true. 33* You
sent emissaries to John, and he testified to the
truth. 34* I do not accept testimony from a hu-
man being, but I say this so that you may be
saved. 35*† He was a burning and shining lamp,
and for a while you were content to rejoice in
his light. 36* But I have testimony greater than
John's. The works that the Father gave me to
accomplish, these works that I perform tes-
tify on my behalf that the Father has sent me.

---

† **5:19** This proverb or parable is taken from apprenticeship in a trade: the activity of a son is modeled on that of his father. Jesus' dependence on the Father is justification for doing what the Father does.

5:21 *Gives life:* in the Old Testament, a divine prerogative (Dt 32:39; 1 Sm 2:6; 2 Kgs 5:7; Tb 13:2; Is 26:19; Dan 12:2).

5:22 *Judgment:* another divine prerogative, often expressed as acquittal or condemnation (Dt 32:36; Ps 43:1).

5:28–29 While vv 19–27 present realized eschatology, vv 28–29 are future eschatology; cf Dn 12:2.

5:32 *Another:* likely the Father, who in four different ways gives testimony to Jesus, as indicated in the verse groupings 33–34, 36, 37–38, 39–40.

5:35 *Lamp:* cf Ps 132:17: "I will place a lamp for my anointed (= David)," and possibly the description of Elijah in Sir 48:1. But only *for a while,* indicating the temporary and subordinate nature of John's mission.

---

* **5:18** Jn 7:1, 25; 8:37, 40; 10:33, 36; 14:28; Gn 3:5–6; Wis 2:16; Mt 26:4; 2 Thes 2:4.
5:19 Jn 3:34; 8:26; 9:4; 10:30; 12:49.
5:20 Jn 3:35.
5:21 Jn 11:25; Dt 32:39; 1 Sm 2:6; 2 Kgs 5:7; Tb 13:2; Wis 16:13; Is 26:19; Dn 7:10, 13; 12:2; Rom 4:17; 2 Cor 1:9.
5:22 Acts 10:42; 17:31.
5:24 Jn 3:18; 8:51; 1 Jn 3:14.
5:25 Jn 5:28; 8:51; 11:25–26; Eph 2:1; 5:14; Rv 3:1.
5:26 Jn 1:4; 1 Jn 5:11.
5:27 Jn 5:22; Dn 7:13, 22; Mt 25:31; Lk 21:36.
5:28 Jn 11:43.
5:29 Dn 12:2; Mt 16:27; 25:46; Acts 24:15; 2 Cor 5:10.
5:30 Jn 6:38.
5:31–32 Jn 8:13–14, 18.
5:33 Jn 1:19–27; Mt 11:10–11.
5:34 1 Jn 5:9.
5:35 Jn 1:8; Ps 132:17; Sir 48:1.
5:36 Jn 10:25.

37* Moreover, the Father who sent me has testified on my behalf. But you have never heard his voice nor seen his form, 38* and you do not have his word remaining in you, because you do not believe in the one whom he has sent. 39*† You search the scriptures, because you think you have eternal life through them; even they testify on my behalf. 40 But you do not want to come to me to have life.

Unbelief of Jesus' Hearers

41† "I do not accept human praise; 42* moreover, I know that you do not have the love of God in you. 43* I came in the name of my Father, but you do not accept me; yet if another comes in his own name, you will accept him. 44* How can you believe, when you accept praise from one another and do not seek the praise that comes from the only God? 45* Do not think that I will accuse you before the Father: the one who will accuse you is Moses, in whom you have placed your hope. 46* For if you had believed Moses, you would have believed me, because he wrote about me. 47 But if you do not believe his writings, how will you believe my words?"

Multiplication of the Loaves†

6 1* After this, Jesus went across the Sea of Galilee [of Tiberias].† 2 A large crowd followed him, because they saw the signs he was performing on the sick. 3 Jesus went up on the mountain, and there he sat down with his disciples. 4* The Jewish feast of Passover was near. 5*† When Jesus raised his eyes and saw that a large crowd was coming to him, he said to Philip, "Where can we buy enough food for them to eat?" 6† He said this to test him, because he himself knew what he was going to do. 7*† Philip answered him, "Two hundred days' wages worth of food would not be enough for each of them to have a little [bit]." 8 One of his disciples, Andrew, the brother of Simon Peter, said to him, 9*† "There is a boy here who has five barley loaves and two fish; but what good are these for so many?" 10*† Jesus said, "Have the people recline." Now there was a great deal of grass in that place. So the men reclined, about five thousand in number. 11* Then Jesus took the loaves, gave thanks, and distributed them to those who were reclining,

Pray It!

A Little Gift Goes a Long Way

God, could you use me like the boy who helped feed the five thousand? Out of the thousands of people gathered to see you, you chose a young person, took his five loaves and two fish, and made sure thousands had more than their fill to eat (see Jn 6:1–14).

I wonder how those people felt when that little bit of food was offered by a youth? Were they embarrassed by the boy's foolishness? Or did they feel guilty that they had not offered their own food? Regardless, you accepted the gift and did fantastic things with it.

Could you do the same with me? Could you take my simple gifts and do wondrous things with them? I'm just afraid that my gifts will be rejected.

Help me to take the risk and let you use the gifts I have, trusting that it doesn't matter what other people think. Even if things don't work out as I plan, I'll trust that you are in charge and know better than I do. Amen.

▶ **Jn 6:1–14**

JN

†

5:39 *You search:* this may be an imperative: "Search the scriptures, because you think that you have eternal life through them."

5:41 *Praise:* the same Greek word means "praise" or "honor" (from others) and "glory" (from God). There is a play on this in v 44.

6:1–15 This story of the multiplication of the loaves is the fourth sign (cf the note on 5:1–47). It is the only miracle story found in all four gospels (occurring twice in Mark and Matthew). See the notes on Mt 14:13–21 and 15:32–39. John differs on the roles of Philip and Andrew, the proximity of Passover (4), and the allusion to Elisha (see 9). The story here symbolizes the food that is really available through Jesus. It connotes a new exodus and has eucharistic overtones.

6:1 [*Of Tiberias*]: the awkward apposition represents a later name of the Sea of Galilee. It was probably originally a marginal gloss.

6:5 Jesus takes the initiative (in the synoptics, the disciples do), possibly pictured as (cf 14) the new Moses (cf Nm 11:13).

6:6 Probably the evangelist's comment; in this gospel Jesus is never portrayed as ignorant of anything.

6:7 *Days' wages:* literally, "denarii"; a Roman denarius is a day's wage in Mt 20:2.

6:9 *Barley loaves:* the food of the poor. There seems an allusion to the story of Elisha multiplying the barley bread in 2 Kgs 4:42–44.

6:10 *Grass:* implies springtime, and therefore Passover. *Five thousand:* so Mk 6:39, 44 and parallels.

*

5:37 Jn 8:18; Dt 4:12, 15; 1 Jn 5:9.
5:38 1 Jn 2:14.
5:39 Jn 12:16; 19:28; 20:9; Lk 24:27, 44; 1 Pt 1:10.
5:42 1 Jn 2:15.
5:43 Mt 24:5, 24.
5:44 Jn 12:43.
5:45 Dt 31:26.
5:46 Jn 5:39; Dt 18:15; Lk 16:31; 24:44.
6:1–13 Mt 14:13–21; Mk 6:32–44; Lk 9:10–17.
6:4 Jn 2:13; 11:55.
6:5 Nm 11:13.
6:7 Mt 20:2.
6:9 2 Kgs 4:42–44.
6:10 Mt 14:21; Mk 6:44.
6:11 Jn 21:13.

and also as much of the fish as they wanted.
12 When they had had their fill, he said to his
disciples, "Gather the fragments left over, so that
nothing will be wasted." 13† So they collected
them, and filled twelve wicker baskets with frag-
ments from the five barley loaves that had been
more than they could eat. 14*† When the people
saw the sign he had done, they said, "This is truly
the Prophet, the one who is to come into the
world." 15* Since Jesus knew that they were going
to come and carry him off to make him king, he
withdrew again to the mountain alone.

Walking on the Water

16*† When it was evening, his disciples went
down to the sea, 17 embarked in a boat, and
went across the sea to Capernaum. It had already
grown dark, and Jesus had not yet come to them.
18 The sea was stirred up because a strong wind
was blowing. 19*† When they had rowed about
three or four miles, they saw Jesus walking on the
sea and coming near the boat, and they began
to be afraid. 20† But he said to them, "It is I. Do
not be afraid." 21 They wanted to take him into
the boat, but the boat immediately arrived at the
shore to which they were heading.

The Bread of Life Discourse

22† The next day, the crowd that remained
across the sea saw that there had been only one
boat there, and that Jesus had not gone along
with his disciples in the boat, but only his disci-
ples had left. 23† Other boats came from Tiberias
near the place where they had eaten the bread
when the Lord gave thanks. 24 When the crowd
saw that neither Jesus nor his disciples were
there, they themselves got into boats and came
to Capernaum looking for Jesus. 25 And when
they found him across the sea they said to him,
"Rabbi, when did you get here?" 26 Jesus answered
them and said, "Amen, amen, I say to you, you
are looking for me not because you saw signs
but because you ate the loaves and were filled.
27*† Do not work for food that perishes but for
the food that endures for eternal life, which the
Son of Man will give you. For on him the Father,
God, has set his seal." 28 So they said to him,
"What can we do to accomplish the works of

Pray It!

The Eucharist

Jesus calls himself the "bread of life" (Jn 6:35). Some type of bread is part of the basic diet of almost every culture. Thus, in a symbolic way, Jesus is telling us that he is part of the basic diet for spiritual life. And just as bread is shared and valued in every culture, Jesus shares himself with all people who are willing to believe.

Many of Jesus' early followers were troubled when he taught that they must eat his flesh and drink his blood in order to have true life (see verses 56–60). The confusion and arguing among his listeners are understandable; his words must have sounded strange. Yet, this teaching about the Body and Blood of Christ (which is portrayed in the Last Supper in Matthew, Mark, and Luke) is central to the Catholic faith. Catholics believe that Jesus is really present with us and nourishes us when we celebrate the Eucharist together, the bread and wine being changed into the Body and Blood of Christ.

In your prayer, reflect or journal on the following questions:

- How is Jesus a source of nourishment for you?
- How does celebrating the Eucharist help you to recognize more clearly Jesus' presence?
- How are you called to be the Body and Blood of Christ to the world around you?

▶ John, chapter 6

†

6:13 *Baskets:* the word describes the typically Palestinian wicker basket, as in Mk 6:43 and parallels.

6:14 *The Prophet:* probably the prophet like Moses (see the note on 1:21). *The one who is to come into the world:* probably Elijah; cf Mal 3:1; 4:5.

6:16–21 The fifth sign is a nature miracle, portraying Jesus sharing Yahweh's power. Cf the parallel stories following the multiplication of the loaves in Mk 6:45–52 and Mt 14:22–33.

6:19 *Walking on the sea:* although the Greek (cf 16) could mean "on the seashore" or "by the sea" (cf 21:1), the parallels, especially Mt 14:25, make clear that Jesus walked upon the water. John may allude to Job 9:8: God "treads upon the crests of the sea."

6:20 *It is I:* literally, "I am." See also the notes on 4:26 and Mk 6:50.

6:22–71 Discourse on the bread of life; replacement of the manna. Verses 22–34 serve as an introduction, vv 35–59 constitute the discourse proper, vv 60–71 portray the reaction of the disciples and Peter's confession.

6:23 Possibly a later interpolation, to explain how the crowd got to Capernaum.

6:27 *The food that endures for eternal life:* cf 4:14, on water "springing up to eternal life."

6:14 Dt 18:15, 18; Mal 3:1, 23; Acts 3:22.
6:15 Jn 18:36.
6:16–21 Mt 14:22–27; Mk 6:45–52.
6:19 Jb 9:8; Pss 29:3–4; 77:20; Is 43:16.
6:27 Jn 6:50, 51, 54, 58.

God?" [29] Jesus answered and said to them, "This
is the work of God, that you believe in the one
he sent." [30]* So they said to him, "What sign
can you do, that we may see and believe in you?
What can you do? [31]*† Our ancestors ate manna
in the desert, as it is written:

'He gave them bread from heaven to eat.' "

[32]* So Jesus said to them, "Amen, amen, I say to
you, it was not Moses who gave the bread from
heaven; my Father gives you the true bread from
heaven. [33] For the bread of God is that which comes
down from heaven and gives life to the world."
[34]* So they said to him, "Sir, give us this bread
always." [35]*† Jesus said to them, "I am the bread
of life; whoever comes to me will never hunger,
and whoever believes in me will never thirst.
[36]* But I told you that although you have seen
[me], you do not believe. [37] Everything that the
Father gives me will come to me, and I will not
reject anyone who comes to me, [38]* because I
came down from heaven not to do my own will
but the will of the one who sent me. [39]* And this
is the will of the one who sent me, that I should
not lose anything of what he gave me, but that I
should raise it [on] the last day. [40]* For this is the
will of my Father, that everyone who sees the Son
and believes in him may have eternal life, and I
shall raise him [on] the last day."
[41] The Jews murmured about him because
he said, "I am the bread that came down from
heaven," [42]* and they said, "Is this not Jesus,
the son of Joseph? Do we not know his father
and mother? Then how can he say, 'I have come
down from heaven'?" [43]*† Jesus answered and
said to them, "Stop murmuring among your-
selves. [44] No one can come to me unless the Fa-
ther who sent me draw him, and I will raise him
on the last day. [45]* It is written in the prophets:

'They shall all be taught by God.'

Everyone who listens to my Father and learns
from him comes to me. [46]* Not that anyone has
seen the Father except the one who is from God;
he has seen the Father. [47] Amen, amen, I say to
you, whoever believes has eternal life. [48] I am the
bread of life. [49]* Your ancestors ate the manna in
the desert, but they died; [50] this is the bread that
comes down from heaven so that one may eat it
and not die. [51]* I am the living bread that came

†

6:31 *Bread from heaven:* cf Ex 16:4, 15, 32–34 and the notes there; Ps 78:24. The manna, thought to have been hidden by Jeremiah (2 Mc 2:5–8), was expected to reappear miraculously at Passover, in the last days.

6:35–59 Up to v 50, "bread of life" is a figure for God's revelation in Jesus; in vv 51–58, the eucharistic theme comes to the fore. There may thus be a break between vv 50 and 51.

6:43 *Murmuring:* the word may reflect the Greek of Ex 16:2, 7, 8.

*

6:30 Mt 16:1–4; Lk 11:29–30.
6:31 Ex 16:4–5; Nm 11:7–9; Ps 78:24.
6:32 Mt 6:11.
6:34 Jn 4:15.
6:35 Is 55:1–3; Am 8:11–13.
6:36 Jn 20:29.
6:38 Jn 4:34; Mt 26:39; Heb 10:9.
6:39 Jn 10:28–29; 17:12; 18:9.
6:40 1 Jn 2:25.
6:42 Mt 13:54–57; Mk 6:1–4; Lk 4:22.
6:43 Ex 16:2, 7, 8; Lk 4:22.
6:45 Is 54:13; Jer 31:33–34.
6:46 Jn 1:18; 7:29; Ex 33:20.
6:49 1 Cor 10:3, 5.
6:51 Mt 26:26–27; Lk 22:19.

Did You Know?

Jesus Fulfills Jewish Feasts

In John, chapters 5–10, several references are made to four Old Testament feasts, which are also called festivals. On each feast, the author of John has Jesus say or do something that cleverly indicates he is the fulfillment of the feast's intent.

In chapter 5, after healing on the *Sabbath*, Jesus says, "My Father is at work until now, so I am at work" (verse 17). Essentially, he is declaring himself equal to God. In chapter 6, near the feast of the *Passover* (see "The Passover," near Ex 12:14–28), Jesus feeds five thousand people and teaches that he is the bread of life. The implication is that although Moses gave the Israelites manna during the Exodus, God gives a greater gift in Jesus, who is the bread of everlasting life—the Eucharist.

Chapters 7–9 of John refer to the *feast of Booths*, also called Tabernacles. This is a harvest festival that lasts a whole week. Two of the main symbols of the feast of Booths are water and light. Jesus proclaims himself living water (see 7:36) and the light of the world (see 8:12).

Finally, the *feast of the Dedication*, sometimes called Hanukkah (see "Hanukkah," near 1 Mc 4:52–59), is mentioned in chapter 10. During this festival, which celebrates the dedication of the Temple, Jesus claims to be the one who is consecrated and sent into the world (see verse 36). In fulfilling these feasts, Jesus' saving mission is made clear. But his actions also lead to continued conflicts with the Jewish leaders.

▶ John, chapters 5–10

down from heaven; whoever eats this bread will
live forever; and the bread that I will give is my
flesh for the life of the world."
52 The Jews quarreled among themselves, say-
ing, "How can this man give us [his] flesh to
eat?" 53 Jesus said to them, "Amen, amen, I say to
you, unless you eat the flesh of the Son of Man
and drink his blood, you do not have life within
you. 54† Whoever eats my flesh and drinks my
blood has eternal life, and I will raise him on
the last day. 55 For my flesh is true food, and my
blood is true drink. 56 Whoever eats my flesh and
drinks my blood remains in me and I in him.
57* Just as the living Father sent me and I have
life because of the Father, so also the one who
feeds on me will have life because of me. 58 This
is the bread that came down from heaven. Un-
like your ancestors who ate and still died, who-
ever eats this bread will live forever." 59 These
things he said while teaching in the synagogue
in Capernaum.

The Words of Eternal Life

60† Then many of his disciples who were lis-
tening said, "This saying is hard; who can accept
it?" 61 Since Jesus knew that his disciples were
murmuring about this, he said to them, "Does
this shock you? 62† What if you were to see the
Son of Man ascending to where he was before?
63† It is the spirit that gives life, while the flesh is
of no avail. The words I have spoken to you are
spirit and life. 64* But there are some of you who
do not believe." Jesus knew from the beginning
the ones who would not believe and the one
who would betray him. 65 And he said, "For this
reason I have told you that no one can come to
me unless it is granted him by my Father."
66 As a result of this, many [of] his disciples
returned to their former way of life and no lon-
ger accompanied him. 67 Jesus then said to the
Twelve, "Do you also want to leave?" 68 Simon
Peter answered him, "Master, to whom shall we
go? You have the words of eternal life. 69* We
have come to believe and are convinced that
you are the Holy One of God." 70 Jesus answered
them, "Did I not choose you twelve? Yet is not
one of you a devil?" 71* He was referring to Ju-
das, son of Simon the Iscariot; it was he who
would betray him, one of the Twelve.

The Feast of Tabernacles

7 1* After this, Jesus moved about within Gal-
ilee; but he did not wish to travel in Judea,
because the Jews were trying to kill him. 2* But
the Jewish feast of Tabernacles was near. 3† So
his brothers said to him, "Leave here and go to
Judea, so that your disciples also may see the
works you are doing. 4* No one works in secret
if he wants to be known publicly. If you do these
things, manifest yourself to the world." 5 For his
brothers did not believe in him. 6† So Jesus said
to them, "My time is not yet here, but the time
is always right for you. 7* The world cannot hate
you, but it hates me, because I testify to it that
its works are evil. 8† You go up to the feast. I am
not going up to this feast, because my time has
not yet been fulfilled." 9 After he had said this, he
stayed on in Galilee.
10 But when his brothers had gone up to the
feast, he himself also went up, not openly but
[as it were] in secret. 11 The Jews were looking for
him at the feast and saying, "Where is he?" 12 And
there was considerable murmuring about him
in the crowds. Some said, "He is a good man,"

†

6:54–58 *Eats:* the verb used in these verses is not the classical Greek verb used of human eating, but that of animal eating: "munch," "gnaw." This may be part of John's emphasis on the reality of the flesh and blood of Jesus (cf 55), but the same verb eventually became the ordinary verb in Greek meaning "eat."

6:60–71 These verses refer more to themes of vv 35–50 than to those of 51–58 and seem to be addressed to members of the Johannine community who found it difficult to accept the high christology reflected in the bread of life discourse.

6:62 This unfinished conditional sentence is obscure. Probably there is a reference to vv 49–51. Jesus claims to be *the bread that comes down from heaven* (50); this claim provokes incredulity (60); and so Jesus is pictured as asking what his disciples will say when he goes up to heaven.

6:63 *Spirit . . . flesh:* probably not a reference to the eucharistic body of Jesus but to the supernatural and the natural, as in 3:6. *Spirit and life:* all Jesus said about the bread of life is the revelation of the Spirit.

7–8 These chapters contain events about the feast of Tabernacles (Sukkoth, Ingathering: Ex 23:16; Tents, Booths: Dt 16:13–16), with its symbols of booths (originally built to shelter harvesters), rain (water from Siloam poured on the temple altar), and lights (illumination of the four torches in the Court of the Women). They continue the theme of the replacement of feasts (Passover, 2:13; 6:4; Hanukkah, 10:22; Pentecost, 5:1), here accomplished by Jesus as the Living Water. These chapters comprise seven miscellaneous controversies and dialogues. There is a literary inclusion with Jesus in hiding in 7:4, 10 and 8:59. There are frequent references to attempts on his life: 7:1, 13, 19, 25, 30, 32, 44; 8:37, 40, 59.

7:3 *Brothers:* these relatives (cf 2:12 and see the note on Mk 6:3) are never portrayed as disciples until after the resurrection (Acts 1:14). Mt 13:55 and Mk 6:3 give the names of four of them. Jesus has already performed works/signs in Judea; cf 2:23; 3:2; 4:45; 5:8.

7:6 *Time:* the Greek word means "opportune time," here a synonym for Jesus' "hour" (see the note on 2:4), his death and resurrection. In the wordplay, any time is suitable for Jesus' brothers, because they are not dependent on God's will.

7:8 *I am not going up:* an early attested reading "not yet" seems a correction, since Jesus in the story does go up to the feast. "Go up," in a play on words, refers not only to going up to Jerusalem but also to exaltation at the cross, resurrection, and ascension; cf 3:14; 6:62; 20:17.

*

6:57 Jn 5:26.
6:64 Jn 13:11.
6:69 Jn 11:27; Mt 16:16; Mk 1:24; Lk 4:34.
6:71 Jn 12:4; 13:2, 27.
7:1 Jn 5:18; 8:37, 40.
7:2 Ex 23:16; Lv 23:34; Nm 29:12; Dt 16:13–16; Zec 14:16–19.
7:4 Jn 14:22.
7:7 Jn 15:18.

[while] others said, "No; on the contrary, he mis-
leads the crowd." 13* Still, no one spoke openly
about him because they were afraid of the Jews.

The First Dialogue

14† When the feast was already half over,
Jesus went up into the temple area and began
to teach. 15* † The Jews were amazed and said,
"How does he know scripture without having
studied?" 16 Jesus answered them and said, "My
teaching is not my own but is from the one who
sent me. 17*† Whoever chooses to do his will
shall know whether my teaching is from God or
whether I speak on my own. 18 Whoever speaks
on his own seeks his own glory, but whoever
seeks the glory of the one who sent him is
truthful, and there is no wrong in him. 19* Did
not Moses give you the law? Yet none of you
keeps the law. Why are you trying to kill me?"
20*† The crowd answered, "You are possessed!
Who is trying to kill you?" 21*† Jesus answered
and said to them, "I performed one work and
all of you are amazed 22* because of it. Moses
gave you circumcision—not that it came from
Moses but rather from the patriarchs—and you
circumcise a man on the sabbath. 23* If a man
can receive circumcision on a sabbath so that
the law of Moses may not be broken, are you
angry with me because I made a whole person
well on a sabbath? 24* Stop judging by appear-
ances, but judge justly."
25 So some of the inhabitants of Jerusalem
said, "Is he not the one they are trying to kill?
26† And look, he is speaking openly and they
say nothing to him. Could the authorities have
realized that he is the Messiah? 27* But we know
where he is from. When the Messiah comes, no
one will know where he is from." 28* So Jesus
cried out in the temple area as he was teaching
and said, "You know me and also know where
I am from. Yet I did not come on my own, but
the one who sent me, whom you do not know,
is true. 29* I know him, because I am from him,
and he sent me." 30* So they tried to arrest him,
but no one laid a hand upon him, because his
hour had not yet come. 31* But many of the
crowd began to believe in him, and said, "When
the Messiah comes, will he perform more signs
than this man has done?"

Officers Sent to Arrest Jesus

32† The Pharisees heard the crowd murmuring
about him to this effect, and the chief priests and
the Pharisees sent guards to arrest him. 33* So
Jesus said, "I will be with you only a little while
longer, and then I will go to the one who sent
me. 34* You will look for me but not find [me],
and where I am you cannot come." 35† So the
Jews said to one another, "Where is he going
that we will not find him? Surely he is not going
to the dispersion among the Greeks to teach the
Greeks, is he? 36 What is the meaning of his say-
ing, 'You will look for me and not find [me], and
where I am you cannot come'?"

Rivers of Living Water

37*† On the last and greatest day of the feast,
Jesus stood up and exclaimed, "Let anyone who
thirsts come to me and drink. 38*† Whoever be-
lieves in me, as scripture says:

> 'Rivers of living water will flow from within
> him.' "

39*† He said this in reference to the Spirit that
those who came to believe in him were to re-
ceive. There was, of course, no Spirit yet, because
Jesus had not yet been glorified.

†

7:14–31 Jesus teaches in the temple; debate with the Jews.

7:15 *Without having studied:* literally, "How does he know letters without having learned?" Children were taught to read and write by means of the scriptures. But here more than Jesus' literacy is being discussed; the people are wondering how he can teach like a rabbi. Rabbis were trained by other rabbis and traditionally quoted their teachers.

7:17 *To do his will:* presumably a reference back to the "work" of 6:29: belief in the one whom God has sent.

7:20 *You are possessed:* literally, "You have a demon." The insane were thought to be possessed by a demoniacal spirit.

7:21 *One work:* the cure of the paralytic (5:1–9) because of the reference to the sabbath (22; 5:9–10).

7:26 *The authorities:* the members of the Sanhedrin (same term as 3:1).

7:32–36 Jesus announces his approaching departure (cf also 8:21; 12:36; 13:33) and complete control over his destiny.

7:35 *Dispersion:* or "diaspora": Jews living outside Palestine. *Greeks:* probably refers to the Gentiles in the Mediterranean area; cf 12:20.

7:37–39 Promise of living water through the Spirit.

7:38 *Living water:* not an exact quotation from any Old Testament passage; in the gospel context the gift of the Spirit is meant; cf 3:5. *From within him:* either Jesus or the believer; if Jesus, it continues the Jesus-Moses motif (water from the rock, Ex 17:6; Nm 20:11) as well as Jesus as the new temple (cf Ez 47:1). Grammatically, it goes better with the believer.

7:39 *No Spirit yet:* Codex Vaticanus and early Latin, Syriac, and Coptic versions add "given." In this gospel, the sending of the Spirit cannot take place until Jesus' glorification through his death, resurrection, and ascension; cf 20:22.

*

7:13 Jn 9:22; 19:38; 20:19.
7:15 Lk 2:47.
7:17 Jn 6:29.
7:19 Acts 7:53.
7:20 Jn 8:48–49; 10:20.
7:21 Jn 5:1–9.
7:22 Gn 17:10; Lv 12:3.
7:23 Jn 5:2–9, 16; Mt 12:11–12; Lk 14:5.
7:24 Jn 8:15; Lv 19:15; Is 11:3–4.
7:27 Heb 7:3.
7:28 Jn 8:19.
7:29 Jn 6:46; 8:55.
7:30 Jn 7:44; 8:20; Lk 4:29–30.
7:31 Jn 2:11; 10:42; 11:45.
7:33 Jn 13:33; 16:16.
7:34 Jn 8:21; 12:36; 13:33, 36; 16:5; Dt 4:29; Prv 1:28; Is 55:6; Hos 5:6.
7:37 Rv 21:6.
7:38 Jn 4:10, 14; 19:34; Is 12:3; Ez 47:1.
7:39 Jn 16:7.

JN

Live It!

Divine Compassion

Jesus was great at turning the tables on those who considered themselves his enemies. In John 8:2–11, the scribes and Pharisees think they have come up with a perfect trap. They want Jesus to save the woman from being stoned by giving a "wrong" interpretation of the law. Making such a wrong judgment publicly would cause Jesus to lose his credibility quickly.

With one amazing sentence, Jesus redefines the game. The focus moves away from the woman and onto the accusers, who cannot deny that they too are guilty of sin. The trap fails miserably, and the humbled religious leaders leave in silence.

We are often quick to notice the sinfulness of others while minimizing our own guilt. Jesus reminds us to be compassionate toward the sins of others. And notice how tenderly Christ dealt with the woman, whose dignity and reputation had been trampled on. When you recognize your own guilt and stand exposed and shamed before God and others, remember that God is just as tender and compassionate toward you.

▶ **Jn 8:2–11**

Discussion about the Origins of the Messiah

40*† Some in the crowd who heard these
words said, "This is truly the Prophet." 41 Others
said, "This is the Messiah." But others said, "The
Messiah will not come from Galilee, will he?
42* Does not scripture say that the Messiah will
be of David's family and come from Bethlehem,
the village where David lived?" 43 So a division
occurred in the crowd because of him. 44 Some
of them even wanted to arrest him, but no one
laid hands on him.
45 So the guards went to the chief priests and
Pharisees, who asked them, "Why did you not
bring him?" 46 The guards answered, "Never be-
fore has anyone spoken like this one." 47 So the
Pharisees answered them, "Have you also been
deceived? 48* Have any of the authorities or the
Pharisees believed in him? 49 But this crowd,
which does not know the law, is accursed."
50* Nicodemus, one of their members who had
come to him earlier, said to them, 51* "Does
our law condemn a person before it first hears
him and finds out what he is doing?" 52 They an-
swered and said to him, "You are not from Gal-
ilee also, are you? Look and see that no prophet
arises from Galilee."

A Woman Caught in Adultery

8 [7:53† Then each went to his own house,
1*† while Jesus went to the Mount of Olives.
2 But early in the morning he arrived again in
the temple area, and all the people started com-
ing to him, and he sat down and taught them.
3 Then the scribes and the Pharisees brought a
woman who had been caught in adultery and
made her stand in the middle. 4 They said to him,
"Teacher, this woman was caught in the very act
of committing adultery. 5*† Now in the law,
Moses commanded us to stone such women. So
what do you say?" 6† They said this to test him,
so that they could have some charge to bring
against him. Jesus bent down and began to write
on the ground with his finger. 7*† But when they
continued asking him, he straightened up and
said to them, "Let the one among you who is
without sin be the first to throw a stone at her."
8 Again he bent down and wrote on the ground.
9 And in response, they went away one by one,
beginning with the elders. So he was left alone
with the woman before him. 10* Then Jesus
straightened up and said to her, "Woman, where
are they? Has no one condemned you?" 11* She
replied, "No one, sir." Then Jesus said, "Neither

†

7:40–53 Discussion of the Davidic lineage of the Messiah.

7:53—8:11 The story of the woman caught in adultery is a later insertion here, missing from all early Greek manuscripts. A Western text-type insertion, attested mainly in Old Latin translations, it is found in different places in different manuscripts: here, or after 7:36, or at the end of this gospel, or after Lk 21:38, or at the end of that gospel. There are many non-Johannine features in the language, and there are also many doubtful readings within the passage. The style and motifs are similar to those of Luke, and it fits better with the general situation at the end of Lk 21, but it was probably inserted here because of the allusion to Jer 17:13 (cf the note on 8:6) and the statement, "I do not judge anyone," in 8:15. The Catholic Church accepts this passage as canonical scripture.

8:1 *Mount of Olives:* not mentioned elsewhere in the gospel tradition outside of passion week.

8:5 Lv 20:10 and Dt 22:22 mention only death, but Dt 22:23–24 prescribes stoning for a betrothed virgin.

8:6 Cf Jer 17:13 (RSV): "Those who turn away from thee shall be written in the earth, for they have forsaken the LORD, the fountain of living water"; cf 7:38.

8:7 The first stones were to be thrown by the witnesses (Dt 17:7).

*

7:40 Dt 18:15, 18.
7:42 2 Sm 7:12–14; Pss 89:3–4; 132:11; Mi 5:1; Mt 2:5–6.
7:48 Jn 12:42.
7:50 Jn 3:1; 19:39.
7:51 Dt 1:16–17.
8:1–2 Lk 21:37–38.
8:5 Lv 20:10; Dt 22:22–29.
8:7 Dt 17:7.
8:10 Ez 33:11.
8:11 Jn 5:14.

Cultural Connection

The Sun Gives Life

The Sun, the Light of the world,
I hear Him coming,
I see His Face as He comes.
He makes the beings on earth happy,
And they rejoice.
O Wakan-Tanka, I offer to You this world of light . . .
I offer all to You. . . .
May all be attentive and behold! . . . that they may live.

(In Brown, *The Sacred Pipe*, University of Oklahoma Press)

For many Native Americans, the sun is a symbol of the Great Spirit, or *Wakan-Tanka*. Black Elk's poem prayer has a strong parallel in the Gospel of John. When Jesus reveals that he is "the light of the world" (8:12), he is saying that those who walk in the light (believe) enjoy eternal life and those who walk in darkness or avoid the light (refuse to believe) are condemned. In Christian spirituality, Jesus is sometimes called the Sun (or Son) of Righteousness.

▶ Jn 8:12–20

do I condemn you. Go, [and] from now on do
not sin any more."]

The Light of the World

12* † Jesus spoke to them again, saying, "I am
the light of the world. Whoever follows me will
not walk in darkness, but will have the light of
life." 13 So the Pharisees said to him, "You testify
on your own behalf, so your testimony cannot
be verified." 14* † Jesus answered and said to
them, "Even if I do testify on my own behalf, my
testimony can be verified, because I know where
I came from and where I am going. But you do
not know where I come from or where I am go-
ing. 15* † You judge by appearances, but I do not
judge anyone. 16* And even if I should judge, my
judgment is valid, because I am not alone, but
it is I and the Father who sent me. 17* † Even in
your law it is written that the testimony of two
men can be verified. 18* I testify on my behalf
and so does the Father who sent me." 19* So they
said to him, "Where is your father?" Jesus an-
swered, "You know neither me nor my Father. If
you knew me, you would know my Father also."
20* He spoke these words while teaching in the
treasury in the temple area. But no one arrested
him, because his hour had not yet come.

Jesus, the Father's Ambassador†

21* He said to them again, "I am going away
and you will look for me, but you will die in your
sin.† Where I am going you cannot come." 22† So
the Jews said, "He is not going to kill himself, is
he, because he said, 'Where I am going you can-
not come'?" 23* He said to them, "You belong
to what is below, I belong to what is above. You
belong to this world, but I do not belong to this
world. 24* † That is why I told you that you will
die in your sins. For if you do not believe that
I AM, you will die in your sins." 25* † So they

†

8:12–20 Jesus the light of the world. Jesus replaces the four torches of the illumination of the temple as the light of joy.

8:14 *My testimony can be verified:* this seems to contradict 5:31, but the emphasis here is on Jesus' origin from the Father and his divine destiny. *Where I am going:* indicates Jesus' passion and glorification.

8:15 *By appearances:* literally, "according to the flesh." *I do not judge anyone:* superficial contradiction of 5:22, 27, 30; here the emphasis is that the judgment is not by material standards.

8:17 *Your law:* a reflection of later controversy between church and synagogue.

8:21–30 He whose ambassador I am is with me. Jesus' origin is from God; he can reveal God.

8:21 *You will die in your sin:* i.e., of disbelief; cf v 24. *Where I am going you cannot come:* except through faith in Jesus' passion-resurrection.

8:22 The Jews suspect that he is referring to his death. Johannine irony is apparent here; Jesus' death will not be self-inflicted but destined by God.

8:24, 28 *I AM:* an expression that late Jewish tradition understood as Yahweh's own self-designation (Is 43:10); see the note on 4:26. Jesus is here placed on a par with Yahweh.

8:25 *What I told you from the beginning:* this verse seems textually corrupt, with several other possible translations: "(I am) what I say to you"; "Why do I speak to you at all?" The earliest attested reading (Bodmer Papyrus P66) has (in a second hand), "I told you at the beginning what I am also telling you (now)." The answer here (cf Prv 8:22) seems to hinge on a misunderstanding of v 24 "*that* I AM" as "*what* I am."

*

8:12 Jn 1:4–5, 9; 12:46; Ex 13:22; Is 42:6; Zec 14:8.
8:14 Jn 5:31.
8:15 Jn 12:47; 1 Sm 16:7.
8:16 Jn 5:30.
8:17 Dt 17:6; 19:15; Nm 35:30.
8:18 Jn 5:23, 37.
8:19 Jn 7:28; 14:7; 15:21.
8:20 Jn 7:30.
8:21 Jn 7:34; 13:33.
8:23 Jn 3:31; 17:14; 18:36.
8:24 Ex 3:14; Dt 32:39; Is 43:10.
8:25 Jn 10:24.

Cultural Connection

Jesus Is the Light of Life

Once again, the Gospel of John creates a sharp distinction between light and darkness, belief and unbelief. Those who follow Jesus will never walk in darkness but will have the light of life. Light is a symbol of belief that results in life, happiness, and the joy of salvation and liberation in Christ. Darkness is a symbol of unbelief that results in death, disgrace, and condemnation.

Hispanics have a long tradition of lighting candles in church, at home, and at job sites. The candles symbolize the light that comes from Christ and guides us to true life.

We need the light of Christ to live with wholeness and integrity, and to give a proper value and place to material things and human activities. The light of Christ can direct us in our journey to God. Religious symbols and rituals are privileged means to help us to remember the Gospel, to give witness of the Gospel with our own lives, and to radiate God's love to those around us.

- How do you transmit the light of Christ to others today?
- Where in your life do you need the light of Christ?
- Give thanks to Jesus for inviting you to share in the life of God.

▶ Jn 8:12–59

said to him, "Who are you?" Jesus said to them,
"What I told you from the beginning. 26* I have
much to say about you in condemnation. But the
one who sent me is true, and what I heard from
him I tell the world." 27 They did not realize that
he was speaking to them of the Father. 28* So
Jesus said [to them], "When you lift up the Son
of Man, then you will realize that I AM, and that
I do nothing on my own, but I say only what the
Father taught me. 29 The one who sent me is with
me. He has not left me alone, because I always
do what is pleasing to him." 30 Because he spoke
this way, many came to believe in him.

Jesus and Abraham†

31 Jesus then said to those Jews who believed
in him,† "If you remain in my word, you will
truly be my disciples, 32* and you will know the
truth, and the truth will set you free." 33*† They
answered him, "We are descendants of Abraham
and have never been enslaved to anyone. How
can you say, 'You will become free'?" 34* Jesus
answered them, "Amen, amen, I say to you,
everyone who commits sin is a slave of sin.
35*† A slave does not remain in a household forever, but a son always remains. 36 So if a son frees
you, then you will truly be free. 37 I know that
you are descendants of Abraham. But you are
trying to kill me, because my word has no room
among you. 38† I tell you what I have seen in the
Father's presence; then do what you have heard
from the Father."
39*† They answered and said to him, "Our
father is Abraham." Jesus said to them, "If you
were Abraham's children, you would be doing
the works of Abraham. 40 But now you are trying
to kill me, a man who has told you the truth
that I heard from God; Abraham did not do this.
41* You are doing the works of your father!" [So]
they said to him, "We are not illegitimate. We
have one Father, God." 42* Jesus said to them, "If
God were your Father, you would love me, for I
came from God and am here; I did not come on
my own, but he sent me. 43 Why do you not understand what I am saying? Because you cannot
bear to hear my word. 44* You belong to your

† **8:31–59** Jesus' origin ("before Abraham") and destiny are developed; the truth will free them from sin (34) and death (51).

8:31 *Those Jews who believed in him:* a rough editorial suture, since in v 37 they are described as trying to kill Jesus.

8:33 *Have never been enslaved to anyone:* since, historically, the Jews were enslaved almost continuously, this verse is probably Johannine irony, about slavery to sin.

8:35 *A slave . . . a son:* an allusion to Ishmael and Isaac (Gn 16 and 21), or to the release of a slave after six years (Ex 21:2; Dt 15:12).

8:38 *The Father:* i.e., God. It is also possible, however, to understand the second part of the verse as a sarcastic reference to descent of the Jews from the devil (44), "You do what you have heard from [your] father."

8:39 *The works of Abraham:* Abraham believed; cf Rom 4:11–17; Jas 2:21–23.

* **8:26** Jn 12:44–50.
8:28 Jn 3:14; 12:32, 34.
8:32 Is 42:7; Gal 4:31.
8:33 Mt 3:9.
8:34 Rom 6:16–17.
8:35 Gn 21:10; Gal 4:30; Heb 3:5–6.
8:39 Gn 26:5; Rom 4:11–17; Jas 2:21–23.
8:41 Mal 2:10.
8:42 1 Jn 5:1.
8:44 Gn 3:4; Wis 1:13; 2:24; Acts 13:10; 1 Jn 3:8–15.

father the devil and you willingly carry out your
father's desires. He was a murderer from the
beginning and does not stand in truth, because
there is no truth in him. When he tells a lie, he
speaks in character, because he is a liar and the
father of lies. 45 But because I speak the truth, you
do not believe me. 46* Can any of you charge me
with sin? If I am telling the truth, why do you not
believe me? 47* Whoever belongs to God hears
the words of God; for this reason you do not lis-
ten, because you do not belong to God."
48† The Jews answered and said to him, "Are
we not right in saying that you are a Samaritan
and are possessed?" 49 Jesus answered, "I am not
possessed; I honor my Father, but you dishonor
me. 50* I do not seek my own glory; there is
one who seeks it and he is the one who judges.
51* Amen, amen, I say to you, whoever keeps my
word will never see death." 52 [So] the Jews said
to him, "Now we are sure that you are possessed.
Abraham died, as did the prophets, yet you say,
'Whoever keeps my word will never taste death.'
53*† Are you greater than our father Abraham,
who died? Or the prophets, who died? Who do
you make yourself out to be?" 54 Jesus answered,
"If I glorify myself, my glory is worth nothing;
but it is my Father who glorifies me, of whom
you say, 'He is our God.' 55* You do not know
him, but I know him. And if I should say that I
do not know him, I would be like you a liar. But I
do know him and I keep his word. 56*† Abraham
your father rejoiced to see my day; he saw it and
was glad. 57† So the Jews said to him, "You are
not yet fifty years old and you have seen Abra-
ham?" 58*† Jesus said to them, "Amen, amen, I
say to you, before Abraham came to be, I AM."
59* So they picked up stones to throw at him; but
Jesus hid and went out of the temple area.

The Man Born Blind

9 1*† As he passed by he saw a man blind from
birth. 2*† His disciples asked him, "Rabbi,
who sinned, this man or his parents, that he was

Pray It!

Seeing with God's Eyes

Lord, can you fix my eyesight like you did for the blind man?

I want to see with your eyes those who are teased for being different at school.

I want to see with your eyes the homeless person on a park bench.

I want to see with your eyes people from other races and cultures.

I want to see more than people who think that being thinner or stronger makes you more lovable.

I want to see more than people who look at wealth and think that's what life is all about.

Help me to see with your eyes, Lord! Blind me to the way the world sees so that I won't give in to judging people on their looks or skin color or possessions or personality.

Help me to see, and to love, as you love, Lord—with eyes so wide open that they see past the outside and right into the heart of another.

▶ John, chapter 9

born blind?" 3* Jesus answered, "Neither he nor
his parents sinned; it is so that the works of God
might be made visible through him. 4* We have
to do the works of the one who sent me while it
is day. Night is coming when no one can work.
5* While I am in the world, I am the light of the
world." 6* When he had said this, he spat on
the ground and made clay with the saliva, and
smeared the clay on his eyes, 7*† and said to

JN

8:48 *Samaritan:* therefore interested in magical powers; cf Acts 7:14–24.

8:53 *Are you greater than our father Abraham?:* cf 4:12.

8:56 *He saw it:* this seems a reference to the birth of Isaac (Gn 17:7; 21:6), the beginning of the fulfillment of promises about Abraham's seed.

8:57 The evidence of the third-century Bodmer Papyrus P^{75} and the first hand of Codex Sinaiticus indicates that the text originally read: "How can Abraham have seen you?"

8:58 *Came to be, I AM:* the Greek word used for "came to be" is the one used of all creation in the prologue, while the word used for "am" is the one reserved for the Logos.

9:1—10:21 Sabbath healing of the man born blind. This sixth sign is introduced to illustrate the saying, "I am the light of the world" (8:12; 9:5). The narrative of conflict about Jesus contrasts Jesus (light) with the Jews (blindness, 39–41). The theme of water is reintroduced in the reference to the pool of Siloam. Ironically, Jesus is being judged by the Jews, yet the Jews are judged by the Light of the world; cf 3:19–21.

9:2 See the note on 5:14, and Ex 20:5, that parents' sins were visited upon their children. Jesus denies such a cause and emphasizes the purpose: the infirmity was providential.

9:7 *Go wash:* perhaps a test of faith; cf 2 Kgs 5:10–14. The water tunnel Siloam (= Sent) is used as a symbol of Jesus, sent by his Father.

8:46 Heb 4:15; 1 Pt 2:22; 1 Jn 3:5.
8:47 Jn 10:26; 1 Jn 4:6.
8:50 Jn 7:18.
8:51 Jn 5:24–29; 6:40, 47; 11:25–26.
8:53 Jn 4:12.
8:55 Jn 7:28–29.
8:56 Gn 17:17; Mt 13:17; Lk 17:22.
8:58 Jn 1:30; 17:5.
8:59 Jn 10:31, 39; 11:8; Lk 4:29–30.
9:1–2 Is 42:7.
9:2 Ex 20:5; Ez 18:20; Lk 13:2.
9:3 Jn 5:14; 11:4.
9:4 Jn 11:9–10; 12:35–36.
9:5 Jn 8:12.
9:6 Jn 5:11; Mk 7:33; 8:23.
9:7 2 Kgs 5:10–14.

him, "Go wash in the Pool of Siloam" (which
means Sent). So he went and washed, and came
back able to see.
8 His neighbors and those who had seen him
earlier as a beggar said, "Isn't this the one who
used to sit and beg?" 9 Some said, "It is," but oth-
ers said, "No, he just looks like him." He said, "I
am." 10 So they said to him, "[So] how were your
eyes opened?" 11 He replied, "The man called
Jesus made clay and anointed my eyes and told
me, 'Go to Siloam and wash.' So I went there and
washed and was able to see." 12 And they said to
him, "Where is he?" He said, "I don't know."
13 They brought the one who was once blind
to the Pharisees. 14*† Now Jesus had made clay
and opened his eyes on a sabbath. 15 So then the
Pharisees also asked him how he was able to see.
He said to them, "He put clay on my eyes, and I
washed, and now I can see." 16* So some of the
Pharisees said, "This man is not from God, be-
cause he does not keep the sabbath." [But] others
said, "How can a sinful man do such signs?" And
there was a division among them. 17* So they
said to the blind man again, "What do you have
to say about him, since he opened your eyes?"
He said, "He is a prophet."
18 Now the Jews did not believe that he had
been blind and gained his sight until they sum-
moned the parents of the one who had gained his
sight. 19 They asked them, "Is this your son, who
you say was born blind? How does he now see?"
20 His parents answered and said, "We know that
this is our son and that he was born blind. 21 We
do not know how he sees now, nor do we know
who opened his eyes. Ask him, he is of age; he
can speak for himself." 22*† His parents said this
because they were afraid of the Jews, for the Jews
had already agreed that if anyone acknowledged
him as the Messiah, he would be expelled from
the synagogue. 23* For this reason his parents
said, "He is of age; question him."
24*† So a second time they called the man
who had been blind and said to him, "Give God
the praise! We know that this man is a sinner."
25 He replied, "If he is a sinner, I do not know.
One thing I do know is that I was blind and
now I see." 26 So they said to him, "What did he
do to you? How did he open your eyes?" 27 He
answered them, "I told you already and you did
not listen. Why do you want to hear it again? Do
you want to become his disciples, too?" 28 They
ridiculed him and said, "You are that man's disci-
ple; we are disciples of Moses! 29* We know that
God spoke to Moses, but we do not know where
this one is from." 30 The man answered and said
to them, "This is what is so amazing, that you do
not know where he is from, yet he opened my
eyes. 31* We know that God does not listen to
sinners, but if one is devout and does his will,
he listens to him. 32† It is unheard of that any-
one ever opened the eyes of a person born blind.
33* If this man were not from God, he would
not be able to do anything." 34 They answered
and said to him, "You were born totally in sin,
and are you trying to teach us?" Then they threw
him out.
35 When Jesus heard that they had thrown him
out, he found him and said, "Do you believe in
the Son of Man?" 36 He answered and said, "Who
is he, sir, that I may believe in him?" 37* Jesus
said to him, "You have seen him and the one
speaking with you is he." 38 He said, "I do be-
lieve, Lord," and he worshiped him. 39*† Then
Jesus said, "I came into this world for judgment,
so that those who do not see might see, and
those who do see might become blind."
40* Some of the Pharisees who were with him
heard this and said to him, "Surely we are not
also blind, are we?" 41* Jesus said to them, "If
you were blind, you would have no sin; but now
you are saying, 'We see,' so your sin remains.

The Good Shepherd

10 1*† "Amen, amen, I say to you, whoever
does not enter a sheepfold† through the
gate but climbs over elsewhere is a thief and a

†

9:14 In using spittle, kneading clay, and healing, Jesus had broken the sabbath rules laid down by Jewish tradition.

9:22 This comment of the evangelist (in terms used again in 12:42 and 16:2) envisages a situation after Jesus' ministry. Rejection/excommunication from the synagogue of Jews who confessed Jesus as Messiah seems to have begun ca. A.D. 85, when the curse against the *mînîm* or heretics was introduced into the "Eighteen Benedictions."

9:24 *Give God the praise!:* an Old Testament formula of adjuration to tell the truth; cf Jos 7:19; 1 Sm 6:5 LXX. Cf 5:41.

9:32 *A person born blind:* the only Old Testament cure from blindness is found in Tobit (cf Tb 7:7; 11:7–13; 14:1–2), but Tobit was not born blind.

9:39–41 These verses spell out the symbolic meaning of the cure; the Pharisees are not the innocent blind, willing to accept the testimony of others.

10:1–21 The good shepherd discourse continues the theme of attack on the Pharisees that ends ch 9. The figure is allegorical: the hired hands are the Pharisees who excommunicated the cured blind man. It serves as a commentary on ch 9. For the shepherd motif, used of Yahweh in the Old Testament, cf Ex 34; Gn 48:15; 49:24; Mi 7:14; Pss 23:1–4; 80:1.

10:1 *Sheepfold:* a low stone wall open to the sky.

*

9:14 Jn 5:9.
9:16 Jn 3:2; Mt 12:10–11; Lk 13:10–11; 14:1–4.
9:17 Jn 4:19.
9:22 Jn 7:13; 12:42; 16:2; 19:38.
9:23 Jn 12:42.
9:24 Jos 7:19; 1 Sm 6:5 LXX.
9:29 Ex 33:11.
9:31 Jn 10:21; Pss 34:16; 66:18; Prv 15:29; Is 1:15.
9:33 Jn 3:2.
9:37 Jn 4:26; Dn 7:13.
9:39 Mt 13:33–35.
9:40 Mt 15:14; 23:26; Rom 2:19.
9:41 Jn 15:22.
10:1–5 Gn 48:15; 49:24; Pss 23:1–4; 80:2; Jer 23:1–4; Ez 34:1–31; Mi 7:14.

robber. 2 But whoever enters through the gate
is the shepherd of the sheep. 3 The gatekeeper
opens it for him, and the sheep hear his voice, as
he calls his own sheep by name and leads them
out. 4*† When he has driven out all his own, he
walks ahead of them, and the sheep follow him,
because they recognize his voice. 5 But they will
not follow a stranger; they will run away from
him, because they do not recognize the voice of
strangers." 6† Although Jesus used this figure of
speech, they did not realize what he was trying
to tell them.

7† So Jesus said again, "Amen, amen, I say
to you, I am the gate for the sheep. 8† All who
came [before me] are thieves and robbers, but
the sheep did not listen to them. 9 I am the gate.
Whoever enters through me will be saved, and
will come in and go out and find pasture. 10 A
thief comes only to steal and slaughter and de-
stroy; I came so that they might have life and
have it more abundantly. 11* I am the good shep-
herd. A good shepherd lays down his life for the
sheep. 12* A hired man, who is not a shepherd
and whose sheep are not his own, sees a wolf
coming and leaves the sheep and runs away,
and the wolf catches and scatters them. 13 This
is because he works for pay and has no concern
for the sheep. 14 I am the good shepherd, and I
know mine and mine know me, 15* just as the
Father knows me and I know the Father; and I
will lay down my life for the sheep. 16*† I have
other sheep that do not belong to this fold. These
also I must lead, and they will hear my voice, and
there will be one flock, one shepherd. 17* This
is why the Father loves me, because I lay down
my life in order to take it up again. 18*† No one
takes it from me, but I lay it down on my own.
I have power to lay it down, and power to take
it up again. This command I have received from
my Father."

19* Again there was a division among the Jews
because of these words. 20* Many of them said,
"He is possessed and out of his mind; why lis-
ten to him?" 21* Others said, "These are not the
words of one possessed; surely a demon cannot
open the eyes of the blind, can he?"

Pray It!

Jesus, the Good Shepherd

The theme of shepherds and sheep is a recurring one in the Bible. In the Old Testament, God is sometimes portrayed as a shepherd. For example, see Psalm 23 and Ezekiel, chapter 34. David, the greatest king of Israel, is also portrayed as a shepherd in Psalm 78:70–72. In passages like Jeremiah 23:1–6, God promises to raise up new shepherds who will follow in David's legacy. So it is natural that Jesus compares himself to a shepherd in John 10:1–18.

Being a shepherd is not an easy job. Sheep are pretty defenseless creatures, and shepherds have to protect them from predators like lions and wolves. Sheep also have a tendency to stray from the flock, making them especially vulnerable. Shepherds endure the hardships of being away from their homes and putting up with simple food and harsh weather while pasturing sheep. Their lives can be endangered when confronted by desperate predators. Sheep learn to recognize their shepherd's voice, which makes it easier to separate different flocks when flocks are mixed together for grazing or protection.

In your prayer, reflect or journal on the following questions:

- How do you relate to Jesus as the good shepherd?
- When is it reassuring to know that Jesus is watching out for you? How do you see yourself helping to "shepherd" other people as a follower of Jesus?

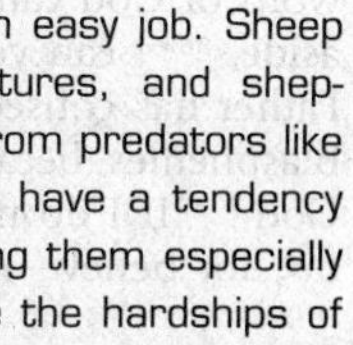

▶ Jn 10:1–18

†

10:4 *Recognize his voice:* the Pharisees do not recognize Jesus, but the people of God, symbolized by the blind man, do.

10:6 *Figure of speech:* John uses a different word for illustrative speech than the "parable" of the synoptics, but the idea is similar.

10:7–10 In vv 7–8, the figure is of a gate for the shepherd to come to the sheep; in vv 9–10, the figure is of a gate for the sheep to *come in and go out*.

10:8 *[Before me]*: these words are omitted in many good early manuscripts and versions.

10:16 *Other sheep:* the Gentiles, possibly a reference to "God's dispersed children" of 11:52 destined to be gathered into one, or "apostolic Christians" at odds with the community of the beloved disciple.

10:18 *Power to take it up again:* contrast the role of the Father as the efficient cause of the resurrection in Acts 2:24; 4:10; etc.; Rom 1:4; 4:24. Yet even here is added: *This command I have received from my Father.*

*

10:4 Mi 2:12–13.
10:11 Ps 23:1–4; Is 40:11; 49:9–10; Heb 13:20; Rv 7:17.
10:12 Zec 11:17.
10:15 Jn 15:13; 1 Jn 3:16.
10:16 Jn 11:52; Is 56:8; Jer 23:3; Ez 34:23; 37:24; Mi 2:12.
10:17 Heb 10:10.
10:18 Jn 19:11.
10:19 Jn 7:43; 9:16.
10:20 Jn 7:20; 8:48.
10:21 Jn 3:2.

J
N

Feast of the Dedication

22*† The feast of the Dedication was then tak-
ing place in Jerusalem. It was winter. 23† And
Jesus walked about in the temple area on the
Portico of Solomon. 24*† So the Jews gathered
around him and said to him, "How long are you
going to keep us in suspense? If you are the Mes-
siah, tell us plainly." 25*† Jesus answered them,
"I told you and you do not believe. The works I
do in my Father's name testify to me. 26* But you
do not believe, because you are not among my
sheep. 27 My sheep hear my voice; I know them,
and they follow me. 28* I give them eternal life,
and they shall never perish. No one can take
them out of my hand. 29*† My Father, who has
given them to me, is greater than all, and no one
can take them out of the Father's hand. 30*† The
Father and I are one."
31* The Jews again picked up rocks to stone
him. 32 Jesus answered them, "I have shown you
many good works from my Father. For which
of these are you trying to stone me?" 33* The
Jews answered him, "We are not stoning you
for a good work but for blasphemy. You, a man,
are making yourself God." 34*† Jesus answered
them, "Is it not written in your law, 'I said, "You
are gods"'? 35 If it calls them gods to whom the
word of God came, and scripture cannot be set
aside, 36*† can you say that the one whom the
Father has consecrated and sent into the world
blasphemes because I said, 'I am the Son of
God'? 37 If I do not perform my Father's works,
do not believe me; 38* but if I perform them,
even if you do not believe me, believe the works,
so that you may realize [and understand] that the
Father is in me and I am in the Father." 39 [Then]
they tried again to arrest him; but he escaped
from their power.
40* He went back across the Jordan to the
place where John first baptized, and there he re-
mained. 41† Many came to him and said, "John
performed no sign, but everything John said
about this man was true." 42* And many there
began to believe in him.

The Raising of Lazarus

11 1*† Now a man was ill, Lazarus from Beth-
any, the village of Mary and her sister Mar-
tha. 2 Mary was the one who had anointed the
Lord with perfumed oil and dried his feet with
her hair; it was her brother Lazarus who was ill.
3 So the sisters sent word to him, saying, "Master,
the one you love is ill." 4*† When Jesus heard
this he said, "This illness is not to end in death,
but is for the glory of God, that the Son of God
may be glorified through it." 5 Now Jesus loved
Martha and her sister and Lazarus. 6 So when he
heard that he was ill, he remained for two days
in the place where he was. 7 Then after this he
said to his disciples, "Let us go back to Judea."
8* The disciples said to him, "Rabbi, the Jews
were just trying to stone you, and you want to
go back there?" 9* Jesus answered, "Are there not
twelve hours in a day? If one walks during the
day, he does not stumble, because he sees the
light of this world.* 10† But if one walks at night,
he stumbles, because the light is not in him."

10:22 *Feast of the Dedication:* an eight-day festival of lights (Hebrew, Hanukkah) held in December, three months after the feast of Tabernacles (7:2), to celebrate the Maccabees' rededication of the altar and reconsecration of the temple in 164 B.C., after their desecration by Antiochus IV Epiphanes (Dn 8:13; 9:27; cf 1 Mc 4:36–59; 2 Mc 1:18—2:19; 10:1–8).

10:23 *Portico of Solomon:* on the east side of the temple area, offering protection against the cold winds from the desert.

10:24 *Keep us in suspense:* literally, "How long will you take away our life?" Cf 11:48–50. *If you are the Messiah, tell us plainly:* cf Lk 22:67. This is the climax of Jesus' encounters with the Jewish authorities. There has never yet been an open confession before them.

10:25 *I told you:* probably at 8:25, which was an evasive answer.

10:29 The textual evidence for the first clause is very divided; it may also be translated: "As for the Father, what he has given me is greater than all," or "My Father is greater than all, in what he has given me."

10:30 This is justification for v 29; it asserts unity of power and reveals that the words and deeds of Jesus are the words and deeds of God.

10:34 This is a reference to the judges of Israel who, since they exercised the divine prerogative to judge (Dt 1:17), were called "gods"; cf Ex 21:6, besides Ps 82:6, from which the quotation comes.

10:36 *Consecrated:* this may be a reference to the rededicated altar at the Hanukkah feast; see the note on 10:22.

10:41 *Performed no sign:* this is to stress the inferior role of John the Baptist. The Transjordan topography recalls the great witness of John the Baptist to Jesus, as opposed to the hostility of the authorities in Jerusalem.

11:1–44 The raising of Lazarus, the longest continuous narrative in John outside of the Passion account, is the climax of the signs. It leads directly to the decision of the Sanhedrin to kill Jesus. The theme of life predominates. Lazarus is a token of the real life that Jesus dead and raised will give to all who believe in him. Johannine irony is found in the fact that Jesus' gift of life leads to his own death. The story is not found in the synoptics, but cf Mk 5:21 and parallels; Lk 7:11–17. There are also parallels between this story and Luke's parable of the rich man and poor Lazarus (Lk 16:19–31). In both a man named Lazarus dies; in Luke, there is a request that he return to convince his contemporaries of the need for faith and repentance, while in John, Lazarus does return and some believe but others do not.

11:4 *Not to end in death:* this is misunderstood by the disciples as referring to physical death, but it is meant as spiritual death.

11:10 *The light is not in him:* the ancients apparently did not grasp clearly the entry of light *through* the eye; they seem to have thought of it as being *in* the eye; cf Lk 11:34; Mt 6:23.

10:22 1 Mc 4:54, 59.
10:24 Lk 22:67.
10:25 Jn 8:25 / Jn 5:36; 10:38.
10:26 Jn 8:45, 47.
10:28 Dt 32:39.
10:29 Wis 3:1; Is 43:13.
10:30 Jn 1:1; 12:45; 14:9; 17:21.
10:31 Jn 8:59.
10:33 Jn 5:18; 19:7; Lv 24:16.
10:34 Ps 82:6.
10:36 Jn 5:18.
10:38 Jn 14:10–11, 20.
10:40 Jn 1:28.
10:42 Jn 2:23; 7:31; 8:30.
11:1–2 Jn 12:1–8; Lk 10:38–42; 16:19–31.
11:4 Jn 9:3, 24.
11:8 Jn 8:59; 10:31.
11:9 Jn 8:12; 9:4.
11:9–10 Jn 12:35; 1 Jn 2:10.

JN

11 He said this, and then told them, "Our friend
Lazarus is asleep, but I am going to awaken
him." 12 So the disciples said to him, "Master, if
he is asleep, he will be saved." 13* But Jesus was
talking about his death, while they thought that
he meant ordinary sleep. 14 So then Jesus said to
them clearly, "Lazarus has died. 15 And I am glad
for you that I was not there, that you may be-
lieve. Let us go to him." 16*† So Thomas, called
Didymus, said to his fellow disciples, "Let us also
go to die with him."

17 When Jesus arrived, he found that Lazarus
had already been in the tomb for four days.
18† Now Bethany was near Jerusalem, only about
two miles away. 19* And many of the Jews had
come to Martha and Mary to comfort them about
their brother. 20 When Martha heard that Jesus
was coming, she went to meet him; but Mary sat
at home. 21* Martha said to Jesus, "Lord, if you
had been here, my brother would not have died.
22 [But] even now I know that whatever you ask
of God, God will give you." 23 Jesus said to her,
"Your brother will rise." 24* Martha said to him,
"I know he will rise, in the resurrection on the
last day." 25* Jesus told her, "I am the resurrec-
tion and the life; whoever believes in me, even if
he dies, will live, 26 and everyone who lives and
believes in me will never die. Do you believe
this?" 27*† She said to him, "Yes, Lord. I have
come to believe that you are the Messiah, the Son
of God, the one who is coming into the world."

28 When she had said this, she went and called
her sister Mary secretly, saying, "The teacher is
here and is asking for you." 29 As soon as she
heard this, she rose quickly and went to him.
30 For Jesus had not yet come into the village, but
was still where Martha had met him. 31 So when
the Jews who were with her in the house com-
forting her saw Mary get up quickly and go out,
they followed her, presuming that she was going
to the tomb to weep there. 32 When Mary came to
where Jesus was and saw him, she fell at his feet
and said to him, "Lord, if you had been here, my
brother would not have died." 33† When Jesus
saw her weeping and the Jews who had come
with her weeping, he became perturbed and
deeply troubled, 34 and said, "Where have you
laid him?" They said to him, "Sir, come and see."
35* And Jesus wept. 36 So the Jews said, "See how
he loved him." 37 But some of them said, "Could
not the one who opened the eyes of the blind
man have done something so that this man
would not have died?"

38 So Jesus, perturbed again, came to the tomb.

†

11:16 *Called Didymus: Didymus* is the Greek word for twin. Thomas is derived from the Aramaic word for twin; in an ancient Syriac version and in the Gospel of Thomas (80:11–12) his given name, Judas, is supplied.

11:18 *About two miles:* literally, "about fifteen stades"; a stade was 607 feet.

11:27 The titles here are a summary of titles given to Jesus earlier in the gospel.

11:33 *Became perturbed:* a startling phrase in Greek, literally, "He snorted in spirit," perhaps in anger at the presence of evil (death).

*

11:13 Mt 9:24.
11:16 Jn 14:5, 22.
11:19 Jn 12:9, 17–18.
11:21 Jn 11:32.
11:24 Jn 5:29; 6:39–40, 44, 54; 12:48; Is 2:2; Mi 4:1; Acts 23:8; 24:15.
11:25 Jn 5:24; 8:51; 14:6; Dn 12:2.
11:27 Jn 1:9; 6:69.
11:35 Lk 19:41.

Live It!

Alive Again!

"Jesus wept" (Jn 11:35). Why does Jesus weep? Scholars are not exactly sure what causes Jesus to weep. But it might be plausible that when Jesus sees his dear friend Mary crying because of the death of her brother Lazarus, Jesus cannot help himself and cries too, expressing both compassion for Mary and his own grief at the loss of his friend Lazarus. What a beautiful, powerful expression of Jesus' humanity!

What follows next is a powerful expression of Jesus' impending death and Resurrection—his glorification. It is the seventh and final sign in John's Gospel. What a dramatic moment, as Jesus steps into the tomb of a man who has been dead for four days. He calls to Lazarus and asks him to come out—and Lazarus, bound in burial cloth, indeed comes out! He is alive again. Imagine how astonished the onlookers must have been and how grateful Martha and Mary would have been to have their brother alive again.

It does make one wonder what it would feel like to be alive again after being in the grave for four days. How do people react to this man who is alive once again? Why do you think John chose this as the last sign of Jesus' power? Notice that this event occurs about a week before the last days of Jesus' life. Why is this sign such a threat to the ruling officials of Jerusalem?

▶ **Jn 11:1–44**

Pray It!

A God Who Cries

Lord, have I ever made you cry? angry enough to yell? tickled enough to laugh? proud enough to burst? I hope so. I hope you know me so well that my every movement, my every breath, is noticed by you. I want to believe that about you, Jesus, because that is the image of you I can talk to—the image of a God who can relate to me and accept me in all that I do, a God who understands the real emotions I feel, a God who knows what it means to be human, a God who is not afraid to cry. Amen.

► Jn 11:35

It was a cave, and a stone lay across it. 39 Jesus
said, "Take away the stone." Martha, the dead
man's sister, said to him, "Lord, by now there
will be a stench; he has been dead for four days."
40 Jesus said to her, "Did I not tell you that if you
believe you will see the glory of God?" 41† So
they took away the stone. And Jesus raised his
eyes and said, "Father, I thank you for hearing
me. 42* I know that you always hear me; but be-
cause of the crowd here I have said this, that they
may believe that you sent me." 43† And when he
had said this, he cried out in a loud voice, "Laz-
arus, come out!" 44 The dead man came out, tied
hand and foot with burial bands, and his face
was wrapped in a cloth. So Jesus said to them,
"Untie him and let him go."

Session of the Sanhedrin

45* Now many of the Jews who had come
to Mary and seen what he had done began to
believe in him. 46 But some of them went to the
Pharisees and told them what Jesus had done.
47* So the chief priests and the Pharisees con-
vened the Sanhedrin and said, "What are we
going to do? This man is performing many signs.
48† If we leave him alone, all will believe in him,
and the Romans will come and take away both
our land and our nation." 49*† But one of them,
Caiaphas, who was high priest that year, said to
them, "You know nothing, 50 nor do you con-
sider that it is better for you that one man should
die instead of the people, so that the whole na-
tion may not perish." 51 He did not say this on
his own, but since he was high priest for that
year, he prophesied that Jesus was going to die
for the nation, 52† and not only for the nation,
but also to gather into one the dispersed children
of God. 53* So from that day on they planned to
kill him.
54† So Jesus no longer walked about in public
among the Jews, but he left for the region near
the desert, to a town called Ephraim, and there
he remained with his disciples.

The Last Passover

55*† Now the Passover of the Jews was near,
and many went up from the country to Jerusa-
lem before Passover to purify themselves. 56 They
looked for Jesus and said to one another as they
were in the temple area, "What do you think?
That he will not come to the feast?" 57 For the
chief priests and the Pharisees had given orders
that if anyone knew where he was, he should in-
form them, so that they might arrest him.

The Anointing at Bethany

12 1*† Six days before Passover Jesus came
to Bethany, where Lazarus was, whom
Jesus had raised from the dead.* 2* They gave a
dinner for him there, and Martha served, while
Lazarus was one of those reclining at table with
him. 3*† Mary took a liter of costly perfumed oil
made from genuine aromatic nard and anointed
the feet of Jesus and dried them with her hair;

† **11:41** *Father:* in Aramaic, *'abbā.'* See the note on Mk 14:36.

11:43 *Cried out in a loud voice:* a dramatization of 5:28: "the hour is coming when all who are in the tombs will hear his voice."

11:48 *The Romans will come:* Johannine irony; this is precisely what happened after Jesus' death.

11:49 *That year:* emphasizes the conjunction of the office and the year. Actually, Caiaphas was high priest A.D. 18–36. The Jews attributed a gift of prophecy, sometimes unconscious, to the high priest.

11:52 *Dispersed children of God:* perhaps the "other sheep" of 10:16.

11:54 *Ephraim* is usually located about twelve miles northeast of Jerusalem, where the mountains descend into the Jordan valley.

11:55 *Purify:* prescriptions for purity were based on Ex 19:10–11, 15; Nm 9:6–14; 2 Chr 30:1–3, 15–18.

12:1–8 This is probably the same scene of anointing found in Mk 14:3–9 (see the note there) and Mt 26:6–13. The anointing by a penitent woman in Lk 7:36–38 is different. Details from these various episodes have become interchanged.

12:3 *The feet of Jesus:* so Mk 14:3; but in Mt 26:6, Mary anoints Jesus' head as a sign of regal, messianic anointing.

* **11:42** Jn 12:30.
11:45 Lk 16:31.
11:47 Jn 12:19; Mt 26:3–5; Lk 22:2; Acts 4:16.
11:49–50 Jn 18:13–14.
11:53 Jn 5:18; 7:1; Mt 12:14.
11:55 Jn 2:13; 5:1; 6:4; 18:28; Ex 19:10–11, 15; Nm 9:6–14; 19:12; Dt 16:6; 2 Chr 30:1–3, 15–18.
12:1–11 Mt 26:6–13; Mk 14:3–9.
12:1–2 Jn 11:1.
12:2 Lk 10:38–42.
12:3 Jn 11:2.

the house was filled with the fragrance of the
oil. 4 Then Judas the Iscariot, one [of] his disci-
ples, and the one who would betray him, said,
5 † "Why was this oil not sold for three hundred
days' wages and given to the poor?" 6 * He said
this not because he cared about the poor but be-
cause he was a thief and held the money bag and
used to steal the contributions. 7 † So Jesus said,
"Leave her alone. Let her keep this for the day of
my burial. 8 * You always have the poor with you,
but you do not always have me."
9 * [The] large crowd of the Jews found out
that he was there and came, not only because
of Jesus, but also to see Lazarus, whom he had
raised from the dead. 10 And the chief priests
plotted to kill Lazarus too, 11 * because many of
the Jews were turning away and believing in Jesus
because of him.

The Entry into Jerusalem

12 * † On the next day, when the great crowd
that had come to the feast heard that Jesus
was coming to Jerusalem, 13 * † they took palm
branches and went out to meet him, and cried
out:

"Hosanna!
Blessed is he who comes in the name of the
Lord,
[even] the king of Israel."

14 Jesus found an ass and sat upon it, as is writ-
ten:

15 * † "Fear no more, O daughter Zion;
see, your king comes, seated upon an ass's colt."

16 * † His disciples did not understand this at first,
but when Jesus had been glorified they remem-
bered that these things were written about him
and that they had done this for him. 17 † So the
crowd that was with him when he called Lazarus
from the tomb and raised him from death con-
tinued to testify. 18 This was [also] why the crowd
went to meet him, because they heard that he
had done this sign. 19 * † So the Pharisees said to
one another, "You see that you are gaining noth-
ing. Look, the whole world has gone after him."

The Coming of Jesus' Hour†

20 * Now there were some Greeks† among
those who had come up to worship at the feast.
21 * † They came to Philip, who was from Bethsa-
ida in Galilee, and asked him, "Sir, we would like
to see Jesus." 22 * Philip went and told Andrew;
then Andrew and Philip went and told Jesus.
23 * † Jesus answered them, "The hour has come
for the Son of Man to be glorified. 24 * † Amen,
amen, I say to you, unless a grain of wheat falls
to the ground and dies, it remains just a grain
of wheat; but if it dies, it produces much fruit.
25 * † Whoever loves his life loses it, and whoever
hates his life in this world will preserve it for eter-
nal life. 26 * Whoever serves me must follow me,
and where I am, there also will my servant be.
The Father will honor whoever serves me.
27 * † "I am troubled now. Yet what should I

JN

†

12:5 *Days' wages:* literally, "denarii." A denarius is a day's wage in Mt 20:2; see the note on 6:7.

12:7 Jesus' response reflects the rabbinical discussion of what was the greatest act of mercy, almsgiving or burying the dead. Those who favored proper burial of the dead thought it an essential condition for sharing in the resurrection.

12:12–19 In John, the entry into Jerusalem follows the anointing whereas in the synoptics it precedes. In John, the crowd, not the disciples, are responsible for the triumphal procession.

12:13 *Palm branches:* used to welcome great conquerors; cf 1 Mc 13:51; 2 Mc 10:7. They may be related to the *lûlāb,* the twig bundles used at the feast of Tabernacles. *Hosanna:* see Ps 118:25–26. The Hebrew word means: "(O Lord), grant salvation." *He who comes in the name of the Lord:* referred in Ps 118:26 to a pilgrim entering the temple gates, but here a title for Jesus (see the notes on Mt 11:3 and Jn 6:14; 11:27). *The king of Israel:* perhaps from Zep 3:14–15, in connection with the next quotation from Zec 9:9.

12:15 *Daughter Zion:* Jerusalem. *Ass's colt:* symbol of peace, as opposed to the war-horse.

12:16 *They had done this:* the antecedent of *they* is ambiguous.

12:17–18 There seem to be two different crowds in these verses. There are some good witnesses to the text that have another reading for v 17: "Then the crowd that was with him began to testify that he had called Lazarus out of the tomb and raised him from the dead."

12:19 *The whole world:* the sense is that everyone is following Jesus, but John has an ironic play on *world;* he alludes to the universality of salvation (3:17; 4:42).

12:20–36 This announcement of glorification by death is an illustration of "the whole world" (19) going after him.

12:20 *Greeks:* not used here in a nationalistic sense. These are probably Gentile proselytes to Judaism; cf 7:35.

12:21–22 *Philip . . . Andrew:* the approach is made through disciples who have distinctly Greek names, suggesting that access to Jesus was mediated to the Greek world through his disciples. Philip and Andrew were from Bethsaida (1:44); Galileans were mostly bilingual. *See:* here seems to mean "have an interview with."

12:23 Jesus' response suggests that only after the crucifixion could the gospel encompass both Jew and Gentile.

12:24 This verse implies that through his death Jesus will be accessible to all. *It remains just a grain of wheat:* this saying is found in the synoptic triple and double traditions (Mk 8:35 // Mt 16:25 // Lk 9:24; Mt 10:39 // Lk 17:33). John adds the phrases (25) *in this world* and *for eternal life.*

12:25 *His life:* the Greek word *psychē* refers to a person's natural life. It does not mean "soul," for Hebrew anthropology did not postulate body/soul dualism in the way that is familiar to us.

12:27 *I am troubled:* perhaps an allusion to the Gethsemane agony scene of the synoptics.

12:6 Jn 13:29.
12:8 Dt 15:11.
12:9 Jn 11:19.
12:11 Jn 11:45.
12:12–19 Mt 21:1–16; Mk 11:1–10; Lk 19:28–40.
12:13 Jn 1:49; Lv 23:40; 1 Mc 13:51; 2 Mc 10:7; Rv 7:9.
12:15 Is 40:9; Zec 9:9.
12:16 Jn 2:22.
12:19 Jn 11:47–48.
12:20 Acts 10:2.
12:21 Jn 1:44.
12:22 Jn 1:40.
12:23 Jn 2:4.
12:24 Is 53:10–12; 1 Cor 15:36.
12:25 Mt 10:39; 16:25; Mk 8:35; Lk 9:24; 17:33.
12:26 Jn 14:3; 17:24; Mt 16:24; Mk 8:34; Lk 9:23.
12:27 Jn 6:38; 18:11; Mt 26:38–39; Mk 14:34–36; Lk 22:42; Heb 5:7–8.

say? 'Father, save me from this hour'? But it was
for this purpose that I came to this hour. 28* Fa-
ther, glorify your name." Then a voice came from
heaven, "I have glorified it and will glorify it
again." 29* The crowd there heard it and said it
was thunder; but others said, "An angel has spo-
ken to him." 30* Jesus answered and said, "This
voice did not come for my sake but for yours.
31*† Now is the time of judgment on this world;
now the ruler of this world will be driven out.
32* And when I am lifted up from the earth, I will
draw everyone to myself." 33 He said this indicat-
ing the kind of death he would die. 34*† So the
crowd answered him, "We have heard from the
law that the Messiah remains forever. Then how
can you say that the Son of Man must be lifted
up? Who is this Son of Man?" 35* Jesus said to
them, "The light will be among you only a lit-
tle while. Walk while you have the light, so that
darkness may not overcome you. Whoever walks
in the dark does not know where he is going.
36* While you have the light, believe in the light,
so that you may become children of the light."

Unbelief and Belief among the Jews

After he had said this, Jesus left and hid from
them. 37*† Although he had performed so many
signs in their presence they did not believe in
him, 38*† in order that the word which Isaiah the
prophet spoke might be fulfilled:

"Lord, who has believed our preaching,
to whom has the might of the Lord been
revealed?"

39 For this reason they could not believe, be-
cause again Isaiah said:

40* "He blinded their eyes
and hardened their heart,
so that they might not see with their eyes
and understand with their heart and be
converted,
and I would heal them."

41*† Isaiah said this because he saw his glory and
spoke about him. 42* Nevertheless, many, even
among the authorities, believed in him, but be-
cause of the Pharisees they did not acknowledge
it openly in order not to be expelled from the
synagogue. 43* For they preferred human praise
to the glory of God.

Pray It!

Dying for New Life

In John 12:24–26, Jesus is describing what Christians call the *Paschal mystery*. It is the belief that God brings new life out of suffering and death. The ultimate expression of the Paschal mystery is Jesus' own death and Resurrection. God used Christ's sacrifice to free us from the bonds of sin, and Christ's Resurrection to open the path to new life. This belief that new life can come out of sin and death is a continuously unfolding mystery that no one can fully explain, and yet it is perhaps the most essential foundation of our faith.

Like the grain of wheat in this Gospel passage, in death we bear the fruit of new life. The path to new life is through sacrifice and death. By dying to our selfishness and focusing on loving others, we experience the fullness of life in Christ Jesus.

In your prayer, reflect or journal on the following questions:

- What does the Paschal mystery mean to you?
- What kinds of attitudes, desires, or actions must be let go of in your life?

Write a prayer asking God to give you the courage to let go of the things that keep you from fullness of life.

▶ **Jn 12:24–26**

JN

† **12:31** *Ruler of this world:* Satan.

12:34 There is no passage in the Old Testament that states precisely that *the Messiah remains forever.* Perhaps the closest is Ps 89:37.

12:37–50 These verses, on unbelief of the Jews, provide an epilogue to the Book of Signs.

12:38–41 John gives a historical explanation of the disbelief of the Jewish people, not a psychological one. The Old Testament had to be fulfilled; the disbelief that met Isaiah's message was a foreshadowing of the disbelief that Jesus encountered. In v 42 and also in 3:20, we see that there is no negation of freedom.

12:41 *His glory:* Isaiah saw the glory of Yahweh enthroned in the heavenly temple, but in John the antecedent of *his* is Jesus.

* **12:28** Jn 2:11; 17:5; Dn 4:31, 34.
12:29 Ex 9:28; 2 Sm 22:14; Jb 37:4; Ps 29:3; Lk 22:43; Acts 23:9.
12:30 Jn 11:42.
12:31 Jn 16:11; Lk 10:18; Rv 12:9.
12:32 Jn 3:14; 8:28; Is 52:13.
12:34 Pss 89:5; 110:4; Is 9:7; Dn 7:13–14; Rv 20:1–6.
12:35 Jn 9:4; 11:10; Jb 5:14.
12:36 Eph 5:8.
12:37–43 Dt 29:2–4; Mk 4:11–12; Rom 9–11.
12:38 Is 53:1; Rom 10:16.
12:40 Is 6:9–10; Mt 13:13–15; Mk 4:12.
12:41 Jn 5:39; Is 6:1, 4.
12:42 Jn 9:22.
12:43 Jn 5:44.

Recapitulation

44* Jesus cried out and said, "Whoever believes
in me believes not only in me but also in the one
who sent me, 45* and whoever sees me sees the
one who sent me. 46* I came into the world as
light, so that everyone who believes in me might
not remain in darkness. 47* And if anyone hears
my words and does not observe them, I do not
condemn him, for I did not come to condemn
the world but to save the world. 48* Whoever
rejects me and does not accept my words has
something to judge him: the word that I spoke,
it will condemn him on the last day, 49* because
I did not speak on my own, but the Father who
sent me commanded me what to say and speak.
50 And I know that his commandment is eternal
life. So what I say, I say as the Father told me."

III: The Book of Glory†

The Washing of the Disciples' Feet†

13 1* Before the feast of Passover,† Jesus knew
that his hour had come to pass from this
world to the Father. He loved his own in the
world and he loved them to the end. 2*† The
devil had already induced Judas, son of Simon
the Iscariot, to hand him over. So, during supper,
3* fully aware that the Father had put everything
into his power and that he had come from God
and was returning to God, 4 he rose from sup-
per and took off his outer garments. He took a
towel and tied it around his waist. 5*† Then he
poured water into a basin and began to wash
the disciples' feet and dry them with the towel
around his waist. 6 He came to Simon Peter, who
said to him, "Master, are you going to wash my
feet?" 7 Jesus answered and said to him, "What
I am doing, you do not understand now, but
you will understand later." 8* Peter said to him,
"You will never wash my feet." Jesus answered
him, "Unless I wash you, you will have no in-
heritance with me." 9 Simon Peter said to him,
"Master, then not only my feet, but my hands
and head as well." 10*† Jesus said to him, "Who-
ever has bathed has no need except to have his
feet washed, for he is clean all over; so you are

†

13:1—19:42 The Book of Glory. There is a major break here; the word "sign" is used again only in 20:30. In this phase of Jesus' return to the Father, the discourses (chs 13–17) precede the traditional narrative of the passion (chs 18–20) to interpret them for the Christian reader. This is the only extended example of esoteric teaching of disciples in John.

13:1–20 Washing of the disciples' feet. This episode occurs in John at the place of the narration of the institution of the Eucharist in the synoptics. It may be a dramatization of Lk 22:27: "I am your servant." It is presented as a "model" ("pattern") of the crucifixion. It symbolizes cleansing from sin by sacrificial death.

13:1 *Before the feast of Passover:* this would be Thursday evening, before the day of preparation; in the synoptics, the Last Supper is a Passover meal taking place, in John's chronology, on Friday evening. *To the end:* or, "completely."

13:2 *Induced:* literally, "The devil put into the heart that Judas should hand him over."

13:5 The act of washing another's feet was one that could not be required of the lowliest Jewish slave. It is an allusion to the humiliating death of the crucifixion.

13:10 *Bathed:* many have suggested that this passage is a symbolic reference to baptism. The Greek root involved is used in baptismal contexts in 1 Cor 6:11; Eph 5:26; Ti 3:5; Heb 10:22.

*

12:44 Jn 13:20; 14:1.
12:45 Jn 14:7–9.
12:46 Jn 1:9; 8:12.
12:47 Jn 3:17.
12:48 Lk 10:16; Heb 4:12.
12:49 Jn 14:10, 31; Dt 18:18–19.
13:1 Jn 2:4; 7:30; 8:20; Mt 26:17, 45; Mk 14:12, 41; Lk 22:7.
13:2 Jn 6:71; 17:12; Mt 26:20–21; Mk 14:17–18; Lk 22:3.
13:3 Jn 3:35.
13:5 1 Sm 25:41.
13:8 2 Sm 20:1.
13:10 Jn 15:3.

Did You Know?

Feast of the Passover

Chapter 13 is the beginning of the second part of the Gospel of John, sometimes called the Book of Glory. Its central theme is how Jesus is glorified through his Passion, death, and Resurrection. It begins with Jesus' washing the disciples' feet at the Last Supper, before the Passover.

The Jewish feast of Passover, also called the feast of Unleavened Bread, reminds us of how God rescued the Israelites from slavery in Egypt by killing the firstborn Egyptians and "passing over" the homes of the Israelites (about 1250 BC). The feast was traditionally celebrated with a meal of lamb, bitter herbs, and unleavened bread (see "The Passover," near Ex 12:14–28). It was the blood of a lamb, smeared on the doorposts of the Israelites' houses, that signaled the angel of death to spare the firstborn of God's people.

In the other Gospels, the last meal that Jesus shares with his disciples is the Passover meal. However, in the Gospel of John, Jesus is arrested before Passover. He is crucified on the preparation day of the feast of Unleavened Bread, at the same time that the lambs are being sacrificed in the Temple. The symbolism would not be missed by the readers of John: Jesus is the new and perfect Passover lamb.

▶ Jn 13:1–20

JN

Cultural Connection

The *Indriappam*

In the province of Kerala, in India, about 80 percent of the population is Catholic and celebrates the Lord's Passion with special time-honored customs. One such custom takes place on Holy Thursday. On that day, nearly all the villagers or townspeople attend morning Mass. During the Eucharist, the ritual of foot washing occurs, the priest washing the feet of twelve children chosen from among those who are poor. Then, after dinner that evening, the people gather again for the stations of the cross and prayers. They return home around nine or ten o'clock for a special Passover meal.

The Passover meal consists of bread baked only on Holy Thursday and a special drink of coconut milk mixed with brown sugar and spices. This Passover bread, or *indriappam*, is baked with a cross of palm on top, which is placed there by the oldest woman of the family. At the meal, the oldest man cuts the bread and passes a piece to each person, beginning with the oldest and working down to the youngest. Often, families visit one another and share this tradition throughout the evening. And if a death has occurred in any family that year, the other households of the village provide the *indriappam* for them.

On Good Friday, which is a national holiday in India despite the fact that India is a primarily Hindu country, the leftover bread and milk are served to the servants and those of the village who are poor and needy. This custom of *indriappam* combines devotion to Christ in the Eucharist with a reminder of the service we are obliged to offer to those who are needy and poor.

- What customs and traditions does your family or parish take part in to commemorate the gift of the Eucharist given at the Last Supper?

▶ Jn 13:1–17

clean, but not all." [11]* For he knew who would
betray him; for this reason, he said, "Not all of
you are clean."
[12]So when he had washed their feet [and]
put his garments back on and reclined at table
again, he said to them, "Do you realize what I
have done for you? [13]* You call me 'teacher' and
'master,' and rightly so, for indeed I am. [14]If I,
therefore, the master and teacher, have washed
your feet, you ought to wash one another's feet.
[15]* I have given you a model to follow, so that
as I have done for you, you should also do.
[16]*† Amen, amen, I say to you, no slave is greater
than his master nor any messenger greater than
the one who sent him. [17]If you understand this,
blessed are you if you do it. [18]* I am not speaking
of all of you. I know those whom I have chosen.
But so that the scripture might be fulfilled, 'The
one who ate my food has raised his heel against
me.' [19]From now on I am telling you before it
happens, so that when it happens you may be-
lieve that I AM. [20]* Amen, amen, I say to you,
whoever receives the one I send receives me,
and whoever receives me receives the one who
sent me."

Announcement of Judas's Betrayal

[21]* When he had said this, Jesus was deeply
troubled and testified, "Amen, amen, I say to
you, one of you will betray me." [22]The disciples
looked at one another, at a loss as to whom he
meant. [23]*† One of his disciples, the one whom
Jesus loved, was reclining at Jesus' side. [24]So Si-
mon Peter nodded to him to find out whom he
meant. [25]* He leaned back against Jesus' chest
and said to him, "Master, who is it?" [26]† Jesus an-
swered, "It is the one to whom I hand the morsel
after I have dipped it." So he dipped the morsel

†

13:16 *Messenger:* the Greek has *apostolos,* the only occurrence of the term in John. It is not used in the technical sense here.

13:23 *The one whom Jesus loved:* also mentioned in 19:26; 20:2; 21:7. A disciple, called "another disciple" or "the other disciple," is mentioned in 18:15 and 20:2; in the latter reference he is identified with the disciple whom Jesus loved. There is also an unnamed disciple in 1:35–40; see the note on 1:37.

13:26 *Morsel:* probably the bitter herb dipped in salt water.

*

13:11 Jn 6:70.
13:13 Mt 23:8, 10.
13:15 Lk 22:27; 1 Pt 2:21.
13:16 Jn 15:20; Mt 10:24; Lk 6:40.
13:18 Ps 41:10.
13:20 Mt 10:40; Mk 9:37; Lk 9:48.
13:21–30 Mt 26:21–25; Mk 14:18–21; Lk 22:21–23.
13:23 Jn 19:26; 20:2; 21:7, 20; Mt 10:37.
13:25 Jn 21:20.

and [took it and] handed it to Judas, son of Si-
mon the Iscariot. 27* After he took the morsel,
Satan entered him. So Jesus said to him, "What
you are going to do, do quickly." 28 [Now] none
of those reclining at table realized why he said
this to him. 29* Some thought that since Judas
kept the money bag, Jesus had told him, "Buy
what we need for the feast," or to give something
to the poor. 30 So he took the morsel and left at
once. And it was night.

The New Commandment

31† When he had left, Jesus said,† "Now is the
Son of Man glorified, and God is glorified in
him. 32* [If God is glorified in him,] God will
also glorify him in himself, and he will glorify
him at once. 33* My children, I will be with you
only a little while longer. You will look for me,
and as I told the Jews, 'Where I go you cannot
come,' so now I say it to you. 34*† I give you a
new commandment: love one another. As I have
loved you, so you also should love one another.
35 This is how all will know that you are my disci-
ples, if you have love for one another."

Peter's Denial Predicted

36* Simon Peter said to him, "Master, where
are you going?" Jesus answered [him], "Where

† **13:31—17:26** Two farewell discourses and a prayer. These seem to be Johannine compositions, including sayings of Jesus at the Last Supper and on other occasions, modeled on similar farewell discourses in Greek literature and the Old Testament (of Moses, Joshua, David).

13:31–38 Introduction: departure and return. Terms of coming and going predominate. These verses form an introduction to the last discourse of Jesus, which extends through chs 14 to 17. In it John has collected Jesus' words to *his own* (13:1). There are indications that several speeches have been fused together, e.g., in 14:31 and 17:1.

13:34 *I give you a new commandment:* this puts Jesus on a par with Yahweh. The commandment itself is not new; cf Lv 19:18 and the note there.

* **13:27** Jn 13:2; Lk 22:3. **13:29** Jn 12:5–6. **13:32** Jn 17:1–5. **13:33** Jn 7:33; 8:21. **13:34** Jn 15:12–13, 17; Lv 19:18; 1 Thes 4:9; 1 Jn 2:7–10; 3:23; 2 Jn 5. **13:36** Mk 14:27; Lk 22:23.

Live It!

Jesus Models Service to Others

In Matthew, Mark, and Luke, the focus of the Last Supper is on the institution of the Eucharist. But in John, the focus is on Jesus' washing his disciples' feet (see 13:1–17). John makes the point that serving others is at the heart of being a follower of Jesus. In Holy Thursday Mass, we celebrate both traditions, indicating that service is a necessary part of living the Paschal mystery that we celebrate in the Eucharist.

- Read John 13:1–17. Reflect on and listen to Jesus' message to you.
- How is Jesus calling you to serve others, humbly and compassionately?

For more on the Eucharist, see "The New Covenant," near Matthew 26:26–29; "The Eucharist," near Luke 22:14–20; and "Feast of the Passover," near John 13:1–20.

▶ Jn 13:1–17

Introducing...

The Beloved Disciple

In the Last Supper scene, we are introduced to a mysterious character found only in the Gospel of John, described as the disciple "whom Jesus loved" (Jn 13:23). He is mentioned several more times in John: at the foot of the cross with Jesus' mother (see 19:25–27), on Easter morning when he enters the empty tomb with Peter (see 20:2–10), and after the Resurrection when he identifies Jesus from the boat (see 21:7,20). He is always with Peter or where Peter should be (at the cross).

So who is the mystery man? Traditionally, he has been identified as John, the son of Zebedee and one of the Twelve Apostles, and as the writer of the Gospel of John. But if that is true, why does he refer to himself so strangely? Many scholars today believe that the Beloved Disciple was a lesser-known follower of Jesus who was the founder of the Christian community that ultimately produced the Gospel of John. They think his eyewitness accounts (see 21:24) were passed on and are the basis for the Gospel we have today.

▶ Jn 13:23–25

Catholic Connection

Easter Triduum

In the Gospel of John, the beloved disciple was with Jesus in the upper room at the Last Supper, stood at the foot of the cross during Jesus' Crucifixion (see Jn 19:26), and was there to examine the empty tomb (see 20:1–10). It is no surprise then that roughly more than a third of the Gospel of John is devoted to detailing the events in the upper room and the subsequent Passion, death, and Resurrection of Jesus. John's Gospel progressively reveals the glory of God's only Son, who reveals the Father and then reveals the disciples' place in God's plan of salvation. These events changed our world and our relationship with God.

The importance and meaning of these events also serve as the focus for the greatest feast in the liturgical year, the Easter Triduum. The Easter Triduum consists of three holy days that celebrate Jesus' Passion, death, and Resurrection. The Triduum begins on Holy Thursday, the Thursday before Easter. The reading for the day recounts the Last Supper and Christ's humility when washing the disciples' feet (see 13:1–15). Holy Thursday is followed by Good Friday, during which John's account of Jesus' Passion (see chapters 18–19) is read. In the course of the service, Catholics venerate (honor) the cross, recalling Jesus' painful sacrifice that opened the way to our salvation.

The climax of the Triduum is the Easter Vigil held on Saturday evening, beginning after nightfall. This celebration incorporates a dramatic ceremony of light in which the Easter fire is lit, followed by the lighting of the Paschal (Jesus) candle and a candle for every person in the church. During the Mass, seven readings from the Old Testament and one epistle from the New Testament are proclaimed. These readings highlight important events that have shaped our salvation history. The readings culminate with a reading from John's Gospel that recounts the story of Jesus' Resurrection (see 20:1–9). Then those who have been preparing to join the church are baptized, confirmed, and welcomed to receive the Eucharist.

The Easter Triduum, although celebrated over three days, is actually one celebration, from the opening song on Holy Thursday to the closing song of the Easter Vigil.

▶ **Jn 13:1—20:18**

Catechism, nos. 1168–1171

JN

Cultural Connection

The Way and the Truth and the Life

Catholics from the country of Laos often point to John 14:6 as a significant connection between the Buddhist religion and their Catholic faith. There is a Buddhist tradition of honoring the way and the truth. Becoming a Catholic and knowing the risen Christ bring a deeper appreciation of everlasting life. This completes the triangle of "the way and the truth and the life."

▶ Jn 14:6–7

I am going, you cannot follow me now, though
you will follow later." 37 Peter said to him, "Mas-
ter, why can't I follow you now? I will lay down
my life for you." 38* Jesus answered, "Will you
lay down your life for me? Amen, amen, I say to
you, the cock will not crow before you deny me
three times."

Last Supper Discourses

14 1† "Do not let your hearts be troubled.
You have faith† in God; have faith also
in me. 2 In my Father's house there are many
dwelling places. If there were not, would I have
told you that I am going to prepare a place for
you? 3*† And if I go and prepare a place for you,
I will come back again and take you to myself,
so that where I am you also may be. 4† Where
[I] am going you know the way." 5 Thomas said
to him, "Master, we do not know where you are
going; how can we know the way?" 6*† Jesus said
to him, "I am the way and the truth and the life.
No one comes to the Father except through me.
7*† If you know me, then you will also know
my Father. From now on you do know him and
have seen him." 8*† Philip said to him, "Master,
show us the Father, and that will be enough for
us." 9* Jesus said to him, "Have I been with you
for so long a time and you still do not know
me, Philip? Whoever has seen me has seen the
Father. How can you say, 'Show us the Father'?
10* Do you not believe that I am in the Father
and the Father is in me? The words that I speak
to you I do not speak on my own. The Father
who dwells in me is doing his works. 11* Believe
me that I am in the Father and the Father is in
me, or else, believe because of the works them-
selves. 12* Amen, amen, I say to you, whoever
believes in me will do the works that I do, and
will do greater ones than these, because I am
going to the Father. 13* And whatever you ask
in my name, I will do, so that the Father may be
glorified in the Son. 14 If you ask anything of me
in my name, I will do it.

The Advocate

15* "If you love me, you will keep my com-
mandments. 16*† And I will ask the Father, and
he will give you another Advocate to be with you
always, 17*† the Spirit of truth, which the world
cannot accept, because it neither sees nor knows
it. But you know it, because it remains with
you, and will be in you. 18† I will not leave you

JN

†

14:1–31 Jesus' departure and return. This section is a dialogue marked off by a literary inclusion in vv 1 and 27: "Do not let your hearts be troubled."

14:1 *You have faith:* could also be imperative: "Have faith."

14:3 *Come back again:* a rare Johannine reference to the parousia; cf 1 Jn 2:28.

14:4 *The way:* here, of Jesus himself; also a designation of Christianity in Acts 9:2; 19:9, 23; 22:4; 24:14, 22.

14:6 *The truth:* in John, the divinely revealed reality of the Father manifested in the person and works of Jesus. The possession of truth confers knowledge and liberation from sin (8:32).

14:7 An alternative reading, "If you knew me, then you would have known my Father also," would be a rebuke, as in 8:19.

14:8 *Show us the Father:* Philip is pictured asking for a theophany like Ex 24:9–10; 33:18.

14:16 *Another Advocate:* Jesus is the first advocate (paraclete); see 1 Jn 2:1, where Jesus is an advocate in the sense of intercessor in heaven. The Greek term derives from legal terminology for an advocate or defense attorney, and can mean spokesman, mediator, intercessor, comforter, consoler, although no one of these terms encompasses the meaning in John. The Paraclete in John is a teacher, a witness to Jesus, and a prosecutor of the world, who represents the continued presence on earth of the Jesus who has returned to the Father.

14:17 *The Spirit of truth:* this term is also used at Qumran, where it is a moral force put into a person by God, as opposed to the spirit of perversity. It is more personal in John; it will teach the realities of the new order (26), and testify to the truth (6). While it has been customary to use masculine personal pronouns in English for the Advocate, the Greek word for "spirit" is neuter, and the Greek text and manuscript variants fluctuate between masculine and neuter pronouns.

14:18 *I will come to you:* indwelling, not parousia.

*

13:38 Jn 18:27; Mt 26:33–35; Mk 14:29–31; Lk 22:33–34.
14:3 Jn 12:26; 17:24; 1 Jn 2:28.
14:6 Jn 8:31–47.
14:7 Jn 8:19; 12:45.
14:8 Ex 24:9–10; 33:18.
14:9 Jn 1:18; 10:30; 12:45; 2 Cor 4:4; Col 1:15; Heb 1:3.
14:10 Jn 1:1; 10:37–38; 12:49.
14:11 Jn 10:38.
14:12 Jn 1:50; 5:20.
14:13 Jn 15:7, 16; 16:23–24; Mt 7:7–11.
14:15 Jn 15:10; Dt 6:4–9; Ps 119; Wis 6:18; 1 Jn 5:3; 2 Jn 6.
14:16 Jn 15:26; Lk 24:49; 1 Jn 2:1.
14:17 Jn 16:13; Mt 28:20; 2 Jn 1–2.

Live It!

The Holy Spirit Guides Us into All Truth

Jesus told his disciples that after his death, God would send the Spirit of Truth to be with them forever. Jesus calls the Holy Spirit the Advocate (see Jn 16:7), the one who defends us from sin. The Holy Spirit also guides us into all Truth, helping us to grasp the meaning of Jesus' words, actions, and miracles. As we live out our faith, it is the Spirit that animates us as disciples, empowering us to use our unique gifts to make a difference in our world.

- Jesus promises his followers that the Holy Spirit will abide in us (see 14:17). How are you aware of the Holy Spirit's presence in your life?
- Place yourself in the hands of the Most Holy Trinity and call upon the Holy Spirit to protect you from all sin and evil and to bring you peace.

▶ Jn 14:15–31, 16:5–15

orphans; I will come to you. 19* In a little while
the world will no longer see me, but you will see
me, because I live and you will live. 20* On that
day you will realize that I am in my Father and
you are in me and I in you. 21* Whoever has my
commandments and observes them is the one
who loves me. And whoever loves me will be
loved by my Father, and I will love him and re-
veal myself to him." 22*† Judas, not the Iscariot,
said to him, "Master, [then] what happened
that you will reveal yourself to us and not to
the world?" 23* Jesus answered and said to him,
"Whoever loves me will keep my word, and my
Father will love him, and we will come to him
and make our dwelling with him. 24 Whoever
does not love me does not keep my words; yet
the word you hear is not mine but that of the
Father who sent me.
25 "I have told you this while I am with you.
26* The Advocate, the holy Spirit that the Father
will send in my name—he will teach you ev-
erything and remind you of all that I told you.
27*† Peace I leave with you; my peace I give to
you. Not as the world gives do I give it to you.
Do not let your hearts be troubled or afraid.
28*† You heard me tell you, 'I am going away and
I will come back to you.' If you loved me, you
would rejoice that I am going to the Father; for
the Father is greater than I. 29* And now I have
told you this before it happens, so that when it
happens you may believe. 30† I will no longer
speak much with you, for the ruler of the world
is coming. He has no power over me, 31* but the
world must know that I love the Father and that
I do just as the Father has commanded me. Get
up, let us go.

The Vine and the Branches

15 1*† "I am the true vine,† and my Father
is the vine grower. 2† He takes away every
branch in me that does not bear fruit, and every
one that does he prunes so that it bears more
fruit. 3* You are already pruned because of the
word that I spoke to you. 4 Remain in me, as I
remain in you. Just as a branch cannot bear fruit
on its own unless it remains on the vine, so nei-
ther can you unless you remain in me. 5 I am the
vine, you are the branches. Whoever remains in
me and I in him will bear much fruit, because
without me you can do nothing. 6*† Anyone
who does not remain in me will be thrown out
like a branch and wither; people will gather

14:22 *Judas, not the Iscariot:* probably not the brother of Jesus in Mk 6:3 // Mt 13:55 or the apostle named Jude in Lk 6:16, but Thomas (see the note on 11:16), although other readings have "Judas the Cananean."

14:27 *Peace:* the traditional Hebrew salutation *šālôm;* but Jesus' "Shalom" is a gift of salvation, connoting the bounty of messianic blessing.

14:28 *The Father is greater than I:* because he *sent, gave,* etc., and Jesus is "a man who has told you the truth that I heard from God" (8:40).

14:30 *The ruler of the world:* Satan; cf 12:31; 16:11.

15:1–16:4 Discourse on the union of Jesus with his disciples. His words become a monologue and go beyond the immediate crisis of the departure of Jesus.

15:1–17 Like 10:1–5, this passage resembles a parable. Israel is spoken of as a vineyard at Is 5:1–7; Mt 21:33–46 and as a vine at Ps 80:9–17; Jer 2:21; Ez 15:2; 17:5–10; 19:10; Hos 10:1. The identification of the vine as the Son of Man in Ps 80:16, and Wisdom's description of herself as a vine in Sir 24:17, are further background for portrayal of Jesus by this figure. There may be secondary eucharistic symbolism here; cf Mk 14:25, "the fruit of the vine."

15:2 *Takes away . . . prunes:* in Greek there is a play on two related verbs.

15:6 Branches were cut off and dried on the wall of the vineyard for later use as fuel.

14:19 Jn 16:16.
14:20 Jn 10:38; 17:21; Is 2:17; 4:2–3.
14:21 Jn 16:27; 1 Jn 2:5; 3:24.
14:22 Jn 7:4; Acts 10:40–41.
14:23 Rv 3:20.
14:26 Jn 15:26; 16:7, 13–14; Ps 51:13; Is 63:10.
14:27 Jn 16:33; Eph 2:14–18.
14:28 Jn 8:40.
14:29 Jn 13:19; 16:4.
14:31 Jn 6:38.
15:1 Ps 80:9–17; Is 5:1–7; Jer 2:21; Ez 15:2; 17:5–10; 19:10.
15:3 Jn 13:10.
15:6 Ez 15:6–7; 19:10–14.

them and throw them into a fire and they will
be burned. 7* If you remain in me and my words
remain in you, ask for whatever you want and
it will be done for you. 8* By this is my Father
glorified, that you bear much fruit and become
my disciples. 9* As the Father loves me, so I also
love you. Remain in my love. 10* If you keep my
commandments, you will remain in my love,
just as I have kept my Father's commandments
and remain in his love.
11* "I have told you this so that my joy might
be in you and your joy might be complete.
12* This is my commandment: love one another
as I love you. 13*† No one has greater love than
this, to lay down one's life for one's friends.
14 You are my friends if you do what I command
you. 15*† I no longer call you slaves, because a
slave does not know what his master is doing. I
have called you friends, because I have told you
everything I have heard from my Father. 16* It
was not you who chose me, but I who chose you
and appointed you to go and bear fruit that will
remain, so that whatever you ask the Father in
my name he may give you. 17* This I command
you: love one another.

The World's Hatred

18*† "If the world hates you, realize that it
hated me first. 19* If you belonged to the world,
the world would love its own; but because
you do not belong to the world, and I have
chosen you out of the world, the world hates
you. 20*† Remember the word I spoke to you,
'No slave is greater than his master.' If they

†

15:13 *For one's friends:* or: "those whom one loves." In 9–13a, the words for love are related to the Greek *agapaō.* In 13b–15, the words for love are related to the Greek *phileō.* For John, the two roots seem synonymous and mean "to love"; cf also 21:15–17. The word *philos* is used here.

15:15 *Slaves . . . friends:* in the Old Testament, Moses (Dt 34:5), Joshua (Jos 24:29), and David (Ps 89:21) were called "servants" or "slaves of Yahweh"; only Abraham (Is 41:8; 2 Chr 20:7; cf Jas 2:23) was called a "friend of God."

15:18—16:4 The hostile reaction of the world. There are synoptic parallels, predicting persecution, especially at Mt 10:17–25; 24:9–10.

15:20 *The word I spoke to you:* a reference to 13:16.

15:7 Jn 14:13; Mt 7:7; Mk 11:24; 1 Jn 5:14.
15:8 Mt 5:16.
15:9 Jn 17:23.
15:10 Jn 8:29; 14:15.
15:11 Jn 16:22; 17:13.
15:12 Jn 13:34.
15:13 Rom 5:6–8; 1 Jn 3:16.
15:15 Dt 34:5; Jos 24:29; 2 Chr 20:7; Ps 89:21; Is 41:8; Rom 8:15; Gal 4:7; Jas 2:23.
15:16 Jn 14:13; Dt 7:6.
15:17 Jn 13:34; 1 Jn 3:23; 4:21.
15:18 Jn 7:7; 14:17; Mt 10:22; 24:9; Mk 13:13; Lk 6:22; 1 Jn 3:13.
15:19 Jn 17:14–16; 1 Jn 4:5.
15:20 Jn 13:16; Mt 10:24.

Make Your Home with Jesus

Jesus calls himself the true vine, and us the branches (see Jn 15:5). What does this mean for us? First, it means that apart from Jesus, we can produce no fruit—that is, we have nothing of ultimate value to offer others. It also means that to stay alive, we must "remain" in Jesus (verse 4). To remain, in this sense, means to stay or make our home with. How at home are you with Jesus?

▶ Jn 15:1–11

Pray It!

Not of This World

It is easy to get caught up in the pressures put on us by our society. It seems that we have to dress a certain way, have certain possessions, and live in a certain kind of house just to be considered average. People who resist those pressures are often labeled weird or different. They often feel out of place, not of this world.

The community from which the Gospel of John emerged did not feel at home in the world either. Their message of the divine Jesus had been rejected by Jews, Gentiles, and perhaps even other early Christians. No wonder the author has Jesus emphasize, "Because you do not belong to the world, . . . the world hates you" (15:19).

In your prayer, reflect or journal on the following questions:

- How might Christians today be considered not of this world?
- What societal pressures do you need to resist?
- How does Jesus' warning to his disciples about the world's hatred (see verses 18–25) apply to Christians today?

▶ Jn 15:18–25

Cultural Connection

Race Relations

On April 4, 2001, the thirty-third anniversary of the death of Martin Luther King Jr., Cardinal George of the Archdiocese of Chicago published a letter to the faithful, titled "Dwell in My Love." In it Cardinal George challenges us to look at John 15:7–10, in which Jesus invites us to dwell in his love. Cardinal George makes the point that all people, races, cultures, and nationalities are part of the human family and that Jesus invites us to be unified in his love.

Race is a gift from God that underscores our uniqueness. It is important for us to celebrate our differences in a way that brings us together as followers of Jesus. The bottom line of Cardinal George's letter is that our diversity enriches us, making life more full and interesting.

Think of all the ways in which people of different races, cultures, and nationalities have brought richness to your community, family, parish, and school.

▶ Jn 15:7–10

persecuted me, they will also persecute you. If they kept my word, they will also keep yours. 21*† And they will do all these things to you on account of my name, because they do not know the one who sent me. 22*† If I had not come and spoken to them, they would have no sin; but as it is they have no excuse for their sin. 23* Whoever hates me also hates my Father. 24* If I had not done works among them that no one else ever did, they would not have sin; but as it is, they have seen and hated both me and my Father. 25*† But in order that the word written in their law might be fulfilled, 'They hated me without cause.'

26*† "When the Advocate comes whom I will send you from the Father, the Spirit of truth that proceeds from the Father, he will testify to me. 27* And you also testify, because you have been with me from the beginning.

16 1 "I have told you this so that you may not fall away. 2*† They will expel you from the synagogues; in fact, the hour is coming when everyone who kills you will think he is offering worship to God. 3* They will do this because they have not known either the Father or me. 4*† I have told you this so that when their hour comes you may remember that I told you.

Jesus' Departure; Coming of the Advocate

"I did not tell you this from the beginning, because I was with you. 5*† But now I am going to the one who sent me, and not one of you asks me, 'Where are you going?' 6 But because I told you this, grief has filled your hearts. 7* But I tell you the truth, it is better for you that I go. For if I do not go, the Advocate will not come to you. But if I go, I will send him to you. 8† And when he comes he will convict the world in regard to sin

---

15:21 *On account of my name:* the idea of persecution for Jesus' name is frequent in the New Testament (Mt 10:22; 24:9; Acts 9:14). For John, association with Jesus' name implies union with Jesus.

15:22, 24 Jesus' words (*spoken*) and deeds (*works*) are the great motives of credibility. *They have seen and hated:* probably means that they have seen his works and still have hated; but the Greek can be read: "have seen both me and my Father and still have hated both me and my Father." *Works . . . that no one else ever did:* so Yahweh in Dt 4:32–33.

15:25 *In their law:* law is here used as a larger concept than the Pentateuch, for the reference is to Ps 35:19 or 69:5. See the notes on 10:34; 12:34. *Their* law reflects the argument of the church with the synagogue.

15:26 *Whom I will send:* in 14:16, 26, the Paraclete is to be sent by the Father, at the request of Jesus. Here the Spirit comes from both Jesus and the Father in mission; there is no reference here to the eternal procession of the Spirit.

16:2 *Hour:* of persecution, not Jesus' "hour" (see the note on 2:4).

16:4b–33 A duplicate of 14:1–31 on departure and return.

16:5 *Not one of you asks me:* the difficulty of reconciling this with Simon Peter's question in 13:36 and Thomas' words in 14:5 strengthens the supposition that the last discourse has been made up of several collections of Johannine material.

16:8–11 These verses illustrate the forensic character of the Paraclete's role: in the forum of the disciples' conscience he prosecutes the world. He leads believers to see (a) that the basic sin was and is refusal to believe in Jesus; (b) that, although Jesus was found guilty and apparently died in disgrace, in reality righteousness has triumphed, for Jesus has returned to his Father; (c) finally, that it is *the ruler of this world,* Satan, who has been condemned through Jesus' death (12:32).

15:21 Jn 8:19; 16:3.
15:22 Jn 8:21, 24; 9:41.
15:23 Jn 5:23; Lk 10:16; 1 Jn 2:23.
15:24 Jn 3:2; 9:32; Dt 4:32–33.
15:25 Pss 35:19; 69:4.
15:26 Jn 14:16, 26; Mt 10:19–20.
15:27 Lk 1:2; Acts 1:8.
16:2 Jn 9:22; 12:42; Mt 10:17; Lk 21:12; Acts 26:11.
16:3 Jn 15:21.
16:4 Jn 13:19; 14:29.
16:5 Jn 7:33; 13:36; 14:5.
16:7 Jn 7:39; 14:16–17, 26; 15:26.

Cultural Connection
Christ Lives in Us Through the Holy Spirit

In his farewell speech to his disciples, Jesus tells them he will return to the Father but will not leave them orphaned (see Jn 14:18). The Father will give them another Advocate—the Holy Spirit. We also receive the Holy Spirit, through our Baptism and our Confirmation. Hispanic spirituality emphasizes the Spirit's gifts of love, freedom, truth, life, and hope.

- *Love* lets us find joy in the midst of suffering and pain. Christ did not end human suffering; instead, he showed how suffering for those we love can bring new life to them.
- *Freedom* from material goods, false gratification, and addictions nurtures the lifestyle we adopt as disciples of Jesus.
- *Truth* about God, us, and history can be achieved only through God's Revelation. The Spirit gives us the light to discover this truth and the strength to direct our lives by it.
- *God's life* in us helps us to overcome prejudices, promote reconciliation, foster unity in diversity, and work for justice and peace.
- *Hope* in being forever with God and the people we love is continuously nourished by the Spirit, who gives us a glimpse of the glory to come despite our earthly limitations.

▶ Jn 14:12–21, 16:12–15

and righteousness and condemnation: [9]* sin, be-
cause they do not believe in me; [10] righteousness,
because I am going to the Father and you will no
longer see me; [11]* condemnation, because the
ruler of this world has been condemned.
[12] "I have much more to tell you, but you can-
not bear it now. [13]*† But when he comes, the
Spirit of truth, he will guide you to all truth. He
will not speak on his own, but he will speak what
he hears, and will declare to you the things that
are coming. [14] He will glorify me, because he will
take from what is mine and declare it to you.
[15] Everything that the Father has is mine; for this
reason I told you that he will take from what is
mine and declare it to you.
[16]* "A little while and you will no longer see
me, and again a little while later and you will
see me." [17] So some of his disciples said to one
another, "What does this mean that he is saying
to us, 'A little while and you will not see me,
and again a little while and you will see me,'
and 'Because I am going to the Father'?" [18] So
they said, "What is this 'little while' [of which
he speaks]? We do not know what he means."
[19] Jesus knew that they wanted to ask him, so
he said to them, "Are you discussing with one
another what I said, 'A little while and you will
not see me, and again a little while and you
will see me'? [20]* Amen, amen, I say to you, you
will weep and mourn, while the world rejoices;
you will grieve, but your grief will become joy.
[21]* When a woman is in labor, she is in anguish
because her hour has arrived; but when she has
given birth to a child, she no longer remembers
the pain because of her joy that a child has been
born into the world. [22]* So you also are now in
anguish. But I will see you again, and your hearts
will rejoice, and no one will take your joy away
from you. [23]* On that day you will not question
me about anything. Amen, amen, I say to you,
whatever you ask the Father in my name he will
give you. [24] Until now you have not asked any-
thing in my name; ask and you will receive, so
that your joy may be complete.
[25]*† "I have told you this in figures of speech.
The hour is coming when I will no longer speak
to you in figures but I will tell you clearly about
the Father. [26]* On that day you will ask in my
name, and I do not tell you that I will ask the
Father for you. [27] For the Father himself loves
you, because you have loved me and have come
to believe that I came from God. [28]* I came from

†

16:13 *Declare to you the things that are coming:* not a reference to new predictions about the future, but interpretation of what has already occurred or been said.

16:25 See the note on 10:6. Here, possibly a reference to 15:1–16 or 16:21.

*

16:9 Jn 8:21–24; 15:22.
16:11 Jn 12:31.
16:13 Jn 14:17, 26; 15:26; Pss 25:5; 143:10; 1 Jn 2:27; Rv 7:17.
16:16 Jn 7:33; 14:19.
16:20 Ps 126:6.
16:21 Is 26:17–18; Jer 31:13; Mi 4:9.
16:22 Jn 14:19; 15:11; 20:20.
16:23 Jn 14:13.
16:25 Mt 13:34–35.
16:26 Jn 14:13.
16:28 Jn 1:1.

Pray It!

A Prayer for Friends

In John, chapter 17, Jesus prays for his friends, the disciples. And he also prays for us, his future disciples (see verse 20)! Here is a prayer you can say for your friends:

Dear Jesus, thank you for my true friends. They accept me for who I am. With them, I don't have to pretend to be someone else. They support me when I feel that the world is crumbling around me. They are honest with me even if what they say is not what I want to hear. They offer their sense of humor so that we can laugh together.

Spirit of Jesus, watch over these friends just as you watch over me. Show them your loving acceptance and support. Help them to honestly look at themselves and the decisions they are making. If they experience pain, frustration, or failure, give them strength to lean on you. Fill their days with laughter and love. Protect them and keep them safe all the days of their lives. Amen.

▶ **John, chapter 17**

JN

the Father and have come into the world. Now I
am leaving the world and going back to the Fa-
ther." 29 His disciples said, "Now you are talking
plainly, and not in any figure of speech. 30† Now
we realize that you know everything and that
you do not need to have anyone question you.
Because of this we believe that you came from
God." 31 Jesus answered them, "Do you believe
now? 32*† Behold, the hour is coming and has
arrived when each of you will be scattered to his
own home and you will leave me alone. But I am
not alone, because the Father is with me. 33* I
have told you this so that you might have peace
in me. In the world you will have trouble, but
take courage, I have conquered the world."

The Prayer of Jesus†

17 1* When Jesus had said this, he raised his
eyes to heaven† and said, "Father, the hour
has come. Give glory to your son, so that your
son may glorify you, 2*† just as you gave him
authority over all people, so that he may give
eternal life to all you gave him. 3*† Now this is
eternal life, that they should know you, the only
true God, and the one whom you sent, Jesus
Christ. 4 I glorified you on earth by accomplish-
ing the work that you gave me to do. 5* Now
glorify me, Father, with you, with the glory that I
had with you before the world began.

6† "I revealed your name to those whom you
gave me out of the world. They belonged to you,
and you gave them to me, and they have kept
your word. 7 Now they know that everything
you gave me is from you, 8 because the words
you gave to me I have given to them, and they
accepted them and truly understood that I came
from you, and they have believed that you sent
me. 9* I pray for them. I do not pray for the
world but for the ones you have given me, be-
cause they are yours, 10* and everything of mine
is yours and everything of yours is mine, and I
have been glorified in them. 11 And now I will
no longer be in the world, but they are in the
world, while I am coming to you. Holy Father,
keep them in your name that you have given me,
so that they may be one just as we are. 12* When
I was with them I protected them in your name
that you gave me, and I guarded them, and none
of them was lost except the son of destruction, in
order that the scripture might be fulfilled. 13* But

†

16:30 The reference is seemingly to the fact that Jesus could anticipate their question in v 19. The disciples naively think they have the full understanding that is the climax of "the hour" of Jesus' death, resurrection, and ascension (25), but the only part of the hour that is at hand for them is their share in the passion (32).

16:32 *You will be scattered:* cf Mk 14:27 and Mt 26:31, where both cite Zec 13:7 about the sheep being dispersed.

17:1–26 Climax of the last discourse(s). Since the sixteenth century, this chapter has been called the "high priestly prayer" of Jesus. He speaks as intercessor, with words addressed directly to the Father and not to the disciples, who supposedly only overhear. Yet the prayer is one of petition, for immediate (6–19) and future (20–21) disciples. Many phrases reminiscent of the Lord's Prayer occur. Although still in the world (13), Jesus looks on his earthly ministry as a thing of the past (4, 12). Whereas Jesus has up to this time stated that the disciples could follow him (13:33, 36), now he wishes them to be with him in union with the Father (12–14).

17:1 The action of looking up to heaven and the address *Father* are typical of Jesus at prayer; cf 11:41 and Lk 11:2.

17:2 Another possible interpretation is to treat the first line of the verse as parenthetical and the second as an appositive to the clause that ends v 1: *so that your son may glorify you (just as . . . all people), so that he may give eternal life. . . .*

17:3 This verse was clearly added in the editing of the gospel as a reflection on the preceding verse; Jesus nowhere else refers to himself as Jesus Christ.

17:6 *I revealed your name:* perhaps the name *I AM;* cf 8:24, 28, 58; 13:19.

16:32 Jn 8:29; Zec 13:7; Mt 26:31; Mk 14:27.
16:33 Jn 14:27.
17:1 Jn 13:31.
17:2 Jn 3:35; Mt 28:18.
17:3 Jn 1:17; Wis 14:7; 15:3; 1 Jn 5:20.
17:5 Jn 1:1, 2; 12:28; Phil 2:6, 9–11.
17:9 Jn 17:20.
17:10 Jn 16:15; 2 Thes 1:10, 12.
17:12 Jn 13:18; 18:9; Ps 41:10; Mt 26:24; Acts 1:16.
17:13 Jn 15:11.

now I am coming to you. I speak this in the
world so that they may share my joy completely.
14* I gave them your word, and the world hated
them, because they do not belong to the world
any more than I belong to the world. 15*† I do
not ask that you take them out of the world but
that you keep them from the evil one. 16 They do
not belong to the world any more than I belong
to the world. 17* Consecrate them in the truth.
Your word is truth. 18* As you sent me into the
world, so I sent them into the world. 19 And I
consecrate myself for them, so that they also may
be consecrated in truth.

20 "I pray not only for them, but also for those
who will believe in me through their word, 21* so
that they may all be one, as you, Father, are in
me and I in you, that they also may be in us, that
the world may believe that you sent me. 22 And I
have given them the glory you gave me, so that
they may be one, as we are one, 23 I in them and
you in me, that they may be brought to perfec-
tion as one, that the world may know that you
sent me, and that you loved them even as you
loved me. 24*† Father, they are your gift to me. I
wish that where I am they also may be with me,
that they may see my glory that you gave me, be-
cause you loved me before the foundation of the
world. 25* Righteous Father, the world also does
not know you, but I know you, and they know
that you sent me. 26† I made known to them
your name and I will make it known, that the
love with which you loved me may be in them
and I in them."

Jesus Arrested†

18 1* When he had said this, Jesus went out†
with his disciples across the Kidron valley
to where there was a garden, into which he and
his disciples entered. 2 Judas his betrayer also
knew the place, because Jesus had often met there
with his disciples. 3*† So Judas got a band of sol-
diers and guards from the chief priests and the

Did You Know?

The Triumph of Jesus

The Gospel of John most closely resembles the other three Gospels in its stories of Jesus' trial, death, and Resurrection. But even here, John's unique portrayal of Jesus is seen. The most obvious difference is that in John, Jesus is clearly in charge and in his glory from the moment he is arrested. There is no agony in the garden. When the soldiers and police come to arrest Jesus, they fall to the ground as he speaks (see Jn 18:6). He teaches Pilate about his identity and mission, in essence putting Pilate on trial (see verses 33–38). Jesus brings together his mother and the Beloved Disciple (see 19:26–27). Jesus is not the victim; rather, he decides the moment of his death when he gives up his spirit (see verse 30).

John is also careful to show in detail the ways Jesus' Crucifixion fulfills Old Testament prophecies of the Messiah. He identifies Jesus with the just man who was persecuted in Psalms 22 and 69. He does this by connecting the gambling for Jesus' seamless tunic (see Jn 19:24) with Psalm 22:19, and the offering of sour wine (see Jn 19:29) with Psalm 69:22. Jesus' unbroken legs (see Jn 19:33) are a reference to the Paschal lamb in Exodus 12:46, and his pierced side (see Jn 19:34) is seen as the fulfillment of Zechariah 12:10.

John wants us to know that these events are the central "Hour" in the world's history and the time of Jesus' triumph. For the author of John, Jesus is clearly the divine Son of God, and by Jesus' self-sacrifice, God brings salvation to the entire world. The author of John wants us to focus not on the tragedy but on God's power at work in Jesus.

▶ John, chapters 18–19

J N

†

17:15 Note the resemblance to the petition of the Lord's Prayer, "deliver us from the evil one." Both probably refer to the devil rather than to abstract evil.

17:24 *Where I am:* Jesus prays for the believers ultimately to join him in heaven. Then they will not see his glory as in a mirror but clearly (2 Cor 3:18; 1 Jn 3:2).

17:26 *I will make it known:* through the Advocate.

18:1–14 John does not mention the agony in the garden and the kiss of Judas, nor does he identify the place as Gethsemane or the Mount of Olives.

18:1 *Jesus went out:* see 14:31, where it seems he is leaving the supper room. *Kidron valley:* literally, "the winter-flowing Kidron"; this wadi has water only during the winter rains.

18:3 *Band of soldiers:* seems to refer to Roman troops, either the full cohort of 600 men (1/10 of a legion), or more likely the maniple of 200 under their tribune (12). In this case, John is hinting at Roman collusion in the action against Jesus before he was brought to Pilate. The *lanterns* and *torches* may be symbolic of the hour of darkness.

*

17:14 Jn 15:19.
17:15 Mt 6:13; 2 Thes 3:3; 1 Jn 5:18.
17:17 1 Pt 1:22.
17:18 Jn 20:21–22.
17:21 Jn 10:30; 14:10–11, 20.
17:24 Jn 14:3; 1 Thes 4:17.
17:25 Jn 1:10.
18:1 2 Sm 15:23; Mt 26:30, 36; Mk 14:26, 32; Lk 22:39.
18:3 Mt 26:47–51; Mk 14:43–44; Lk 22:47.

Catholic Connection

The Trinity

If you knew you were about to die, how would you spend your final moments with your friends? The Gospel of John (see 13:1—17:26) gives us a window into Jesus' final moments with his disciples right before his arrest and Crucifixion. During his time with them, Jesus washes their feet, tells them about the promise of the Holy Spirit, and shares his hopes for them. Jesus concludes his last moments with them with a prayer that reveals and reflects on the unity that exists between Jesus, God the Father, and his disciples. The unity between the Father and the Son, which Jesus refers to in his prayer, points to one of the greatest mysteries of the Christian faith: that there is only one God in three persons—the Father, the Son, and the Holy Spirit. We call this mystery the Trinity.

This mystery is known only because God chose to reveal it to the world. A glimpse of it can be seen in God's actions over the course of salvation history. In the Old Testament, God revealed himself as the Father of all creation. In the New Testament, God revealed himself as Father in relationship to the Son, as Son in the person of Jesus Christ, and as Holy Spirit sent from the Father and the Son. United as one God, the Father, Son, and Holy Spirit worked together to bring about our salvation.

The Church teaches that each person of the Trinity—Father, Son, and Holy Spirit—is fully divine in and of themselves. In other words, the Father is God, Jesus is God, and the Holy Spirit is God, and together they are the one God. The Church also teaches that each person of the Trinity is truly distinct from the others and each person's true distinction lies in the relationship among all three as Father, Son, and Holy Spirit—meaning they are not just a way to name the different ways God acts in the world. Because of their unity, each person of the Trinity is entirely in the other two and all work together. For example, when we follow the Son, we are doing so because the Father invited us and the Holy Spirit moved us to do so.

Jesus' prayer calls us to share in and reflect the unity that exists in the Trinity. When we are baptized in the name of the Father, Son, and Holy Spirit, we enter into the life and mystery of the Trinity. Every time we make the sign of the cross, we are reminded of the Trinity. As believers in the Triune God, we are called to reflect God's unity in our relationships with one another by working together to help all people find salvation in God the Father, Son, and Holy Spirit.

▶ **Jn 17:20–26**

Catechism, nos. 232–267

Pharisees and went there with lanterns, torches, and weapons. 4 Jesus, knowing everything that was going to happen to him, went out and said to them, "Whom are you looking for?" 5† They answered him, "Jesus the Nazorean." He said to them, "I AM." Judas his betrayer was also with them. 6 When he said to them, "I AM," they turned away and fell to the ground. 7 So he again asked them, "Whom are you looking for?" They said, "Jesus the Nazorean." 8 Jesus answered, "I told you that I AM. So if you are looking for me, let these men go." 9*† This was to fulfill what he had said, "I have not lost any of those you gave me." 10† Then Simon Peter, who had a sword, drew it, struck the high priest's slave, and cut off his right ear. The slave's name was Malchus. 11*† Jesus said to Peter, "Put your sword into its scabbard. Shall I not drink the cup that the Father gave me?"

12* So the band of soldiers, the tribune, and the Jewish guards seized Jesus, bound him, 13*† and brought him to Annas first. He was the father-in-law of Caiaphas, who was high priest that year. 14* It was Caiaphas who had counseled the Jews that it was better that one man should die rather than the people.

Peter's First Denial

15*† Simon Peter and another disciple followed Jesus. Now the other disciple was known to the high priest, and he entered the courtyard of the high priest with Jesus. 16 But Peter stood at the gate outside. So the other disciple, the acquaintance of the high priest, went out and spoke to the gatekeeper and brought Peter in. 17 Then the maid who was the gatekeeper said to Peter, "You are not one of this man's disciples, are you?" He said, "I am not." 18 Now the slaves and the guards were standing around a charcoal fire that they had made, because it was cold, and were warming themselves. Peter was also standing there keeping warm.

The Inquiry before Annas

19* The high priest questioned Jesus about his disciples and about his doctrine. 20*† Jesus answered him, "I have spoken publicly to the world. I have always taught in a synagogue or in the temple area where all the Jews gather, and in secret I have said nothing. 21 Why ask me? Ask those who heard me what I said to them. They know what I said." 22* When he had said this, one of the temple guards standing there struck Jesus and said, "Is this the way you answer the high priest?" 23 Jesus answered him, "If I have spoken wrongly, testify to the wrong; but if I have spoken rightly, why do you strike me?" 24*† Then Annas sent him bound to Caiaphas the high priest.

Peter Denies Jesus Again

25* Now Simon Peter was standing there keeping warm. And they said to him, "You are not one of his disciples, are you?" He denied it and said, "I am not." 26 One of the slaves of the high priest, a relative of the one whose ear Peter had cut off, said, "Didn't I see you in the garden with him?" 27† Again Peter denied it. And immediately the cock crowed.

The Trial before Pilate

28*† Then they brought Jesus from Caiaphas to the praetorium. It was morning. And they themselves did not enter the praetorium, in order not to be defiled so that they could eat the Passover. 29 So Pilate came out to them and said, "What charge do you bring [against] this man?" 30 They answered and said to him, "If he were not a criminal, we would not have handed him over to you." 31† At this, Pilate said to them, "Take him

†

18:5 *Nazorean:* the form found in Mt 26:71 (see the note on Mt 2:23) is here used, not *Nazarene* of Mark. *I AM:* or "I am he," but probably intended by the evangelist as an expression of divinity (cf their appropriate response in 6); see the note on 8:24. John sets the confusion of the arresting party against the background of Jesus' divine majesty.

18:9 The citation may refer to 6:39; 10:28; or 17:12.

18:10 Only John gives the names of the two antagonists; both John and Luke mention the right ear.

18:11 The theme of the cup is found in the synoptic account of the agony (Mk 14:36 and parallels).

18:13 *Annas:* only John mentions an inquiry before Annas; cf 16, 19–24; see the note on Lk 3:2. It is unlikely that this nighttime interrogation before Annas is the same as the trial before Caiaphas placed by Matthew and Mark at night and by Luke in the morning.

18:15–16 *Another disciple . . . the other disciple:* see the note on 13:23.

18:20 *I have always taught . . . in the temple area:* cf Mk 14:49 for a similar statement.

18:24 *Caiaphas:* see Mt 26:3, 57; Lk 3:2; and the notes there. John may leave room here for the trial before Caiaphas described in the synoptic gospels.

18:27 Cockcrow was the third Roman division of the night, lasting from midnight to 3 a.m.

18:28 *Praetorium:* see the note on Mt 27:27. *Morning:* literally, "the early hour," or fourth Roman division of the night, 3 to 6 a.m. *The Passover:* the synoptic gospels give the impression that the Thursday night supper was the Passover meal (Mk 14:12); for John that meal is still to be eaten Friday night.

18:31 *We do not have the right to execute anyone:* only John gives this reason for their bringing Jesus to Pilate. Jewish sources are not clear on the competence of the Sanhedrin at this period to sentence and to execute for political crimes.

*

18:9 Jn 6:39; 10:28; 17:12.
18:11 Mt 20:22; 26:39; Mk 10:38; Lk 22:42.
18:12–14 Mt 26:57–58; Mk 14:53–54; Lk 22:54–55.
18:13 Lk 3:2.
18:14 Jn 11:49–50.
18:15–18 Mt 26:58, 69–70; Mk 14:54, 66–68; Lk 22:54–57.
18:19–24 Mt 26:59–66; Mk 14:55–64; Lk 22:66–71.
18:20 Jn 6:59; 7:14, 26; Is 48:16; Mt 26:55; Mk 4:23; Lk 19:47; 22:53.
18:22 Acts 23:2.
18:24 Mt 26:57.
18:25–27 Mt 26:71–75; Mk 14:69–72; Lk 22:58–62.
18:28–38a Mt 27:1–2, 11–25; Mk 15:1–5; Lk 23:1–5.

19:2

yourselves, and judge him according to your law."
The Jews answered him, "We do not have the right
to execute anyone," 32*† in order that the word
of Jesus might be fulfilled that he said indicating
the kind of death he would die. 33 So Pilate went
back into the praetorium and summoned Jesus
and said to him, "Are you the King of the Jews?"
34 Jesus answered, "Do you say this on your own
or have others told you about me?" 35* Pilate an-
swered, "I am not a Jew, am I? Your own nation
and the chief priests handed you over to me. What
have you done?" 36* Jesus answered, "My kingdom
does not belong to this world. If my kingdom did
belong to this world, my attendants [would] be
fighting to keep me from being handed over to the
Jews. But as it is, my kingdom is not here." 37*† So
Pilate said to him, "Then you are a king?" Jesus an-
swered, "You say I am a king. For this I was born
and for this I came into the world, to testify to the
truth. Everyone who belongs to the truth listens to
my voice." 38* Pilate said to him, "What is truth?"
When he had said this, he again went out to
the Jews and said to them, "I find no guilt in
him. 39† But you have a custom that I release one
prisoner to you at Passover. Do you want me to
release to you the King of the Jews?" 40† They
cried out again, "Not this one but Barabbas!"
Now Barabbas was a revolutionary.

19 1*† Then Pilate took Jesus and had him
scourged. 2 And the soldiers wove a crown
out of thorns and placed it on his head, and
clothed him in a purple cloak, 3 and they came
to him and said, "Hail, King of the Jews!" And
they struck him repeatedly. 4* Once more Pilate
went out and said to them, "Look, I am bringing
him out to you, so that you may know that I find
no guilt in him." 5* So Jesus came out, wearing
the crown of thorns and the purple cloak. And
he said to them, "Behold, the man!" 6* When
the chief priests and the guards saw him they
cried out, "Crucify him, crucify him!" Pilate said
to them, "Take him yourselves and crucify him.
I find no guilt in him." 7*† The Jews answered,
"We have a law, and according to that law he
ought to die, because he made himself the Son
of God." 8 Now when Pilate heard this statement,
he became even more afraid, 9* and went back
into the praetorium and said to Jesus, "Where are
you from?" Jesus did not answer him. 10 So Pilate
said to him, "Do you not speak to me? Do you
not know that I have power to release you and I
have power to crucify you?" 11* Jesus answered
[him], "You would have no power over me if it
had not been given to you from above. For this
reason the one who handed me over to you has
the greater sin." 12*† Consequently, Pilate tried
to release him; but the Jews cried out, "If you re-
lease him, you are not a Friend of Caesar. Every-
one who makes himself a king opposes Caesar."
13† When Pilate heard these words he brought

†

18:32 The Jewish punishment for blasphemy was stoning (Lv 24:16). In coming to the Romans to ensure that Jesus would be crucified, the Jewish authorities fulfilled his prophecy that he would be *exalted* (3:14; 12:32–33). There is some historical evidence, however, for Jews crucifying Jews.

18:37 *You say I am a king:* see Mt 26:64 for a similar response to the high priest. It is at best a reluctant affirmative.

18:39 See the note on Mt 27:15.

18:40 *Barabbas:* see the note on Mt 27:16–17. *Revolutionary:* a guerrilla warrior fighting for nationalistic aims, though the term can also denote a robber. See the note on Mt 27:38.

19:1 Luke places the mockery of Jesus at the midpoint in the trial when Jesus was sent to Herod. Mark and Matthew place the scourging and mockery at the end of the trial after the sentence of death. Scourging was an integral part of the crucifixion penalty.

19:7 *Made himself the Son of God:* this question was not raised in John's account of the Jewish interrogations of Jesus as it was in the synoptic account. Nevertheless, see 5:18; 8:53; 10:36.

19:12 *Friend of Caesar:* a Roman honorific title bestowed upon high-ranking officials for merit.

19:13 *Seated him:* others translate "(Pilate) sat down." In John's thought, Jesus is the real judge of the world, and John may here be portraying him seated on the judgment bench. *Stone Pavement:* in Greek *lithostrotos;* under the fortress Antonia, one of the conjectured locations of the praetorium, a massive stone pavement has been excavated. *Gabbatha* (Aramaic rather than Hebrew) probably means "ridge, elevation."

*

18:32 Jn 3:14; 8:28; 12:32–33.
18:35 Jn 1:11.
18:36 Jn 1:10; 8:23.
18:37 Jn 8:47; 1 Tm 6:13.
18:38b–40 Mt 27:15–26; Mk 15:6–15; Lk 23:18–25; Acts 3:14.
19:1–16 Mt 27:27–31; Mk 15:16–20; Lk 23:13–25.
19:4 Jn 18:38.
19:5 Is 52:14.
19:6 Jn 18:31; 19:15.
19:7 Jn 10:33–36; Lv 24:16.
19:9 Jn 7:28.
19:11 Jn 3:27; 10:18; Rom 13:1.
19:12 Acts 17:7.

Jesus out and seated him on the judge's bench
in the place called Stone Pavement, in Hebrew,
Gabbatha. 14† It was preparation day for Pass-
over, and it was about noon. And he said to
the Jews, "Behold, your king!" 15They cried out,
"Take him away, take him away! Crucify him!"
Pilate said to them, "Shall I crucify your king?"
The chief priests answered, "We have no king but
Caesar." 16† Then he handed him over to them
to be crucified.

The Crucifixion of Jesus

So they took Jesus, 17*† and carrying the cross
himself he went out to what is called the Place
of the Skull, in Hebrew, Golgotha. 18There they
crucified him, and with him two others, one on
either side, with Jesus in the middle. 19† Pilate
also had an inscription written and put on the
cross. It read, "Jesus the Nazorean, the King of
the Jews." 20Now many of the Jews read this
inscription, because the place where Jesus was
crucified was near the city; and it was written in
Hebrew, Latin, and Greek. 21* So the chief priests
of the Jews said to Pilate, "Do not write 'The King
of the Jews,' but that he said, 'I am the King of the
Jews.' " 22Pilate answered, "What I have written,
I have written."

23*† When the soldiers had crucified Jesus,
they took his clothes and divided them into four
shares, a share for each soldier.* They also took
his tunic, but the tunic was seamless, woven in
one piece from the top down. 24So they said to
one another, "Let's not tear it, but cast lots for it
to see whose it will be," in order that the passage
of scripture might be fulfilled [that says]:

"They divided my garments among them,
and for my vesture they cast lots."

This is what the soldiers did. 25*† Standing by the
cross of Jesus were his mother and his mother's

Did You Know?

The Words on the Cross

In the Gospel of John, Pontius Pilate acts as a mediator between two worlds—the outside world of darkness and unbelief and the inner world of light and truth. During Jesus' trial, Pilate goes back and forth between the Jewish religious authorities who are outside (in the dark) and Jesus, who is inside Pilate's headquarters (in the light).

Does Pilate know the truth about Jesus? When he writes out the charges to be placed on the cross, "the Jews" (see "'The Jews' in the Gospel of John," near Jn 2:18–20) argue with him about the wording. He answers by saying, "What I have written, I have written" (19:22)—that is, "These words are the truth about Jesus." The words he writes are "Jesus the Nazorean, the King of the Jews" (verse 19). In Latin, they read, *"Iesus Nazarenus Rex Iudaeorum."* When artists draw or sculpt the Crucifixion scene, they often include this Latin phrase in abbreviated form above the cross: *INRI*.

In another of the Gospel's ironies, Pilate recognizes what the Jewish leaders rejected—Jesus Christ is a king. Christians believe a deeper truth—Christ is king of not only the Jews but of all creation! On the last Sunday of the liturgical year, the Catholic Church celebrates this in the feast of Christ the King.

Jn 19:19–22

JN

†

19:14 *Noon:* Mk 15:25 has Jesus crucified "at the third hour," which means either 9 a.m. or the period from 9 to 12. Noon, the time when, according to John, Jesus was sentenced to death, was the hour at which the priests began to slaughter Passover lambs in the temple; see Jn 1:29.

19:16 *He handed him over to them to be crucified:* in context this would seem to mean "handed him over to the chief priests." Lk 23:25 has a similar ambiguity. There is a polemic tendency in the gospels to place the guilt of the crucifixion on the Jewish authorities and to exonerate the Romans from blame. But John later mentions the Roman soldiers (23), and it was to these soldiers that Pilate handed Jesus over.

19:17 *Carrying the cross himself:* a different picture from that of the synoptics, especially Lk 23:26, where Simon of Cyrene is made to carry the cross, walking behind Jesus. In John's theology, Jesus remained in complete control and master of his destiny (cf 10:18). *Place of the Skull:* the Latin word for skull is *Calvaria;* hence "Calvary." *Golgotha* is actually an Aramaic rather than a Hebrew word.

19:19 The inscription differs with slightly different words in each of the four gospels. John's form is fullest and gives the equivalent of the Latin *INRI = Jesus Nazarenus Rex Iudaeorum.* Only John mentions its polyglot character (20) and Pilate's role in keeping the title unchanged (21–22).

19:23–25a While all four gospels describe the soldiers casting lots to divide Jesus' garments (see the note on Mt 27:35), only John quotes the underlying passage from Ps 22:19, and only John sees each line of the poetic parallelism literally carried out in two separate actions (23a; 23b–24).

19:25 It is not clear whether four women are meant, or three (i.e., *Mary the wife of Cl[e]opas* [cf Lk 24:18] is in apposition with *his mother's sister*) or two (his mother and his mother's sister, i.e., Mary of Cl[e]opas and Mary of Magdala). Only John mentions the mother of Jesus here. The synoptics have a group of women looking on from a distance at the cross (Mk 15:40).

19:17–22 Mt 27:32–37; Mk 15:21–26; Lk 23:26–35.
19:21 Jn 18:33; Lk 19:14.
19:23–27 Mt 27:38–44; Mk 15:27–32; Lk 23:36–43.
19:23–24 Ps 22:19; Mt 27:35; Mk 15:24; Lk 23:34.
19:25 Mt 27:55; Mk 15:40–41; Lk 8:2; 23:49.

Cultural Connection

Our Mother of Guadalupe: A Gift from God

Devotion to Mary as mother of God and mother of the Church has been a consistent dimension of Christian faith. From Jesus' words on the cross in John 19:25–27, Christians have identified with the Beloved Disciple and seen Mary as their mother. This experience has led Catholics of many countries to name Mary as their patroness (advocate, protector, supporter, mother): for instance, they call her Virgin of the Immaculate Conception in the United States and Chile, Virgin of Lourdes in France, and Virgin of Fátima in Portugal. The strong devotion of Latin American countries to Mary as a mother who protects and assists her children is revealed in their titles for her: Our Lady of Mercy in the Dominican Republic, Our Lady of Caridad del Cobre (charity) in Cuba, Our Lady of Divine Providence in Puerto Rico, and Our Lady of Help in Guatemala, to name a few.

But Mexico developed the strongest devotion to Mary as mother of a nation. The Virgin of Guadalupe appeared to Saint Juan Diego, a humble native from Tenochtitlán, near Mexico City. She had the face of the mestizo people (the descendants of native and Spanish peoples), and her words to Juan Diego were those of a caring mother, especially for her children who are suffering, poor, or oppressed:

> Here I wish to hear and help you, and all who dwell in this land and all those who love me, and invoke and place their confidence in me; and to hear your complaints and remedy all your sorrows, hardships, and suffering. . . .
> Listen and understand well my son, smallest of all, that you have no cause to be frightened. . . . Is this not your mother here next to you? Are you not here in the shelter of my loving shadow? . . . Let nothing worry or afflict you further. . . .
> (Office of Religious Education, *A Handbook on Guadalupe*, pp. 148, 152)

► Jn 19:25–27

sister, Mary the wife of Clopas, and Mary of
Magdala. 26*† When Jesus saw his mother and
the disciple there whom he loved, he said to his
mother, "Woman, behold, your son." 27 Then
he said to the disciple, "Behold, your mother."
And from that hour the disciple took her into
his home.
28*† After this, aware that everything was now
finished, in order that the scripture might be
fulfilled, Jesus said, "I thirst."* 29† There was a
vessel filled with common wine. So they put a
sponge soaked in wine on a sprig of hyssop and
put it up to his mouth. 30*† When Jesus had
taken the wine, he said, "It is finished." And
bowing his head, he handed over the spirit.

The Blood and Water

31* Now since it was preparation day, in order
that the bodies might not remain on the cross
on the sabbath, for the sabbath day of that week
was a solemn one, the Jews asked Pilate that their
legs be broken and they be taken down. 32 So the
soldiers came and broke the legs of the first and
then of the other one who was crucified with
Jesus. 33 But when they came to Jesus and saw
that he was already dead, they did not break his

† **19:26–27** This scene has been interpreted literally, of Jesus' concern for his mother; and symbolically, e.g., in the light of the Cana story in ch 2 (the presence of the mother of Jesus, the address *woman,* and the mention of the *hour*) and of the upper room in ch 13 (the presence of the beloved disciple; the *hour*). Now that the hour has come (28), Mary (a symbol of the church?) is given a role as the mother of Christians (personified by the beloved disciple); or, as a representative of those seeking salvation, she is supported by the disciple who interprets Jesus' revelation; or Jewish and Gentile Christianity (or Israel and the Christian community) are reconciled.

19:28 *The scripture . . . fulfilled:* either in the scene of vv 25–27, or in the *I thirst* of v 28. If the latter, Pss 22:16 and 69:22 deserve consideration.

19:29 *Wine:* John does not mention the drugged wine, a narcotic that Jesus refused as the crucifixion began (Mk 15:23), but only this final gesture of kindness at the end (Mk 15:36). *Hyssop,* a small plant, is scarcely suitable for carrying a sponge (Mark mentions a reed) and may be a symbolic reference to the *hyssop* used to daub the blood of the paschal lamb on the doorpost of the Hebrews (Ex 12:22).

19:30 *Handed over the spirit:* there is a double nuance of dying (giving up the last breath or spirit) and that of passing on the holy Spirit; see 7:39, which connects the giving of the Spirit with Jesus' glorious return to the Father, and 20:22, where the author portrays the conferral of the Spirit.

19:26 Jn 13:23.
19:28–30 Mt 27:45–56; Mk 15:33–41; Lk 23:44–49.
19:28 Pss 22:16; 69:22.
19:30 Jn 4:34; 10:18; 17:4; Lk 23:46.
19:31 Ex 12:16; Dt 21:23.

legs, 34*† but one soldier thrust his lance into his
side, and immediately blood and water flowed
out. 35*† An eyewitness has testified, and his tes-
timony is true; he knows that he is speaking the
truth, so that you also may [come to] believe.
36* For this happened so that the scripture pas-
sage might be fulfilled:

"Not a bone of it will be broken."

37* And again another passage says:

"They will look upon him whom they have
pierced."

The Burial of Jesus

38*† After this, Joseph of Arimathea, secretly a
disciple of Jesus for fear of the Jews, asked Pilate
if he could remove the body of Jesus. And Pi-
late permitted it. So he came and took his body.
39* Nicodemus, the one who had first come to
him at night, also came bringing a mixture of
myrrh and aloes weighing about one hundred
pounds. 40 They took the body of Jesus and
bound it with burial cloths along with the spices,
according to the Jewish burial custom. 41 Now in
the place where he had been crucified there was a
garden, and in the garden a new tomb, in which
no one had yet been buried. 42 So they laid Jesus
there because of the Jewish preparation day; for
the tomb was close by.

The Empty Tomb†

20 1*† On the first day of the week, Mary
of Magdala came to the tomb early in
the morning, while it was still dark,† and saw
the stone removed from the tomb.* 2† So she
ran and went to Simon Peter and to the other
disciple whom Jesus loved, and told them, "They
have taken the Lord from the tomb, and we don't
know where they put him." 3† So Peter and the
other disciple went out and came to the tomb.
4 They both ran, but the other disciple ran faster
than Peter and arrived at the tomb first; 5 he bent
down and saw the burial cloths there, but did
not go in. 6*† When Simon Peter arrived after
him, he went into the tomb and saw the burial

Introducing...

Mary Magdalene

Like the Samaritan woman, who is the first to spread the word that Jesus is the Messiah (see Jn 4:1–42), Mary Magdalene is the first to announce that Jesus has been raised from the dead. She comes to the tomb while it is still dark (symbolizing unbelief). Later, she encounters the risen Jesus and begins to see with eyes of faith. Belief prompts her to action, and so she goes to tell the others, "I have seen the Lord" (20:18).

Mary Magdalene is first in every listing of Jesus' female disciples (see Mt 27:55–56, Mk 15:40–41, Lk 8:2–3). She seems to have been the leader of a group of women who followed Jesus from the beginning of his ministry, through his death and beyond. Luke indicates that Jesus cured her of seven demons (see Lk 8:2). All four Gospels name her as one of the first eyewitnesses of Jesus' Resurrection. From all this, we can presume that she was a special friend and disciple of Jesus and an important leader among the first Christians.

▶ Jn 20:1–18

JN

†

19:34–35 John probably emphasizes these verses to show the reality of Jesus' death, against the docetic heretics. In the blood and water there may also be a symbolic reference to the Eucharist and baptism.

19:35 *He knows:* it is not certain from the Greek that this *he* is the *eyewitness* of the first part of the sentence. *May [come to] believe:* see the note on 20:31.

19:38–42 In the first three gospels there is no anointing on Friday. In Matthew and Luke, the women come to the tomb on Sunday morning precisely to anoint Jesus.

20:1–31 The risen Jesus reveals his glory and confers the Spirit. This story fulfills the basic need for testimony to the resurrection. What we have here is not a record but a series of single stories.

20:1–10 The story of the empty tomb is found in both the Matthean and the Lucan traditions; John's version seems to be a fusion of the two.

20:1 *Still dark:* according to Mark the sun had risen, Matthew describes it as "dawning," and Luke refers to early dawn. Mary sees the stone removed, not the empty tomb.

20:2 Mary runs away, not directed by an angel/young man as in the synoptic accounts. The plural "we" in the second part of her statement might reflect a tradition of more women going to the tomb.

20:3–10 The basic narrative is told of Peter alone in Lk 24:12, a verse missing in important manuscripts and which may be borrowed from tradition similar to John. Cf also Lk 24:24.

20:6–8 Some special feature about the state of the burial cloths caused the beloved disciple to believe. Perhaps the details emphasized that the grave had not been robbed.

•

19:34 Nm 20:11; 1 Jn 5:6.
19:35 Jn 7:37–39; 21:24.
19:36 Ex 12:46; Nm 9:12; Ps 34:21.
19:37 Nm 21:9; Zec 12:10; Rv 1:7.
19:38–42 Mt 27:57–60; Mk 15:42–46; Lk 34:50–54.
19:39 Jn 3:1–2; 7:50; Ps 45:9.
20:1–10 Mt 28:1–10; Mk 16:1–11; Lk 24:1–12.
20:1 Jn 19:25.
20:6 Lk 24:12.

cloths there, 7* and the cloth that had covered
his head, not with the burial cloths but rolled up
in a separate place. 8 Then the other disciple also
went in, the one who had arrived at the tomb
first, and he saw and believed. 9*† For they did
not yet understand the scripture that he had to
rise from the dead. 10 Then the disciples returned
home.

The Appearance to Mary of Magdala

11*† But Mary stayed outside the tomb weep-
ing. And as she wept, she bent over into the tomb
12 and saw two angels in white sitting there, one
at the head and one at the feet where the body of
Jesus had been. 13 And they said to her, "Woman,
why are you weeping?" She said to them, "They
have taken my Lord, and I don't know where
they laid him." 14* When she had said this, she
turned around and saw Jesus there, but did not
know it was Jesus. 15* Jesus said to her, "Woman,
why are you weeping? Whom are you looking
for?" She thought it was the gardener and said to
him, "Sir, if you carried him away, tell me where
you laid him, and I will take him." 16† Jesus said
to her, "Mary!" She turned and said to him in
Hebrew, "Rabbouni," which means Teacher.
17*† Jesus said to her, "Stop holding on to me,
for I have not yet ascended to the Father. But
go to my brothers and tell them, 'I am going to
my Father and your Father, to my God and your
God.' " 18 Mary of Magdala went and announced
to the disciples, "I have seen the Lord," and what
he told her.

Appearance to the Disciples

19*† On the evening of that first day of the
week, when the doors were locked, where the
disciples† were, for fear of the Jews, Jesus came
and stood in their midst and said to them,
"Peace be with you." 20*† When he had said
this, he showed them his hands and his side.
The disciples rejoiced when they saw the Lord.
21*† [Jesus] said to them again, "Peace be with
you. As the Father has sent me, so I send you."
22*† And when he had said this, he breathed on
them and said to them, "Receive the holy Spirit.
23*† Whose sins you forgive are forgiven them,
and whose sins you retain are retained."

Thomas

24 Thomas, called Didymus, one of the Twelve,
was not with them when Jesus came. 25* So the
other disciples said to him, "We have seen the
Lord." But he said to them, "Unless I see the mark
of the nails in his hands and put my finger into
the nailmarks and put my hand into his side, I
will not believe." 26* Now a week later his disci-
ples were again inside and Thomas was with
them. Jesus came, although the doors were locked,
and stood in their midst and said, "Peace be with
you." 27 Then he said to Thomas, "Put your finger
here and see my hands, and bring your hand and
put it into my side, and do not be unbelieving,
but believe." 28*† Thomas answered and said to
him, "My Lord and my God!" 29*† Jesus said to
him, "Have you come to believe because you

†

20:9 Probably a general reference to the scriptures is intended, as in Lk 24:26 and 1 Cor 15:4. Some individual Old Testament passages suggested are Ps 16:10; Hos 6:2; Jon 2:1, 2, 11.

20:11–18 This appearance to Mary is found only in John, but cf Mt 28:8–10 and Mk 16:9–11.

20:16 *Rabbouni:* Hebrew or Aramaic for "my master."

20:17 *Stop holding on to me:* see Mt 28:9, where the women take hold of his feet. *I have not yet ascended:* for John and many of the New Testament writers, the ascension in the theological sense of going to the Father to be glorified took place with the resurrection as one action. This scene in John dramatizes such an understanding, for by Easter night Jesus is glorified and can give the Spirit. Therefore his ascension takes place immediately after he has talked to Mary. In such a view, the ascension after forty days described in Acts 1:1–11 would be simply a termination of earthly appearances or, perhaps better, an introduction to the conferral of the Spirit upon the early church, modeled on Elisha's being able to have a (double) share in the spirit of Elijah if he saw him being taken up (same verb as ascending) into heaven (2 Kgs 2:9–12). *To my Father and your Father, to my God and your God:* this echoes Ru 1:16: "Your people shall be my people, and your God my God." The Father of Jesus will now become the Father of the disciples because, once ascended, Jesus can give them the Spirit that comes from the Father and they can be reborn as God's children (3:5). That is why he calls them *my brothers.*

20:19–29 The appearances to the disciples, without or with Thomas (cf 11:16; 14:5), have rough parallels in the other gospels only for vv 19–23; cf Lk 24:36–39; Mk 16:14–18.

20:19 *The disciples:* by implication from v 24, this means ten of the Twelve, presumably in Jerusalem. *Peace be with you:* although this could be an ordinary greeting, John intends here to echo 14:27. The theme of rejoicing in v 20 echoes 16:22.

20:20 *Hands and . . . side:* Lk 24:39–40 mentions "hands and feet," based on Ps 22:17.

20:21 By means of this sending, the Eleven were made apostles, that is, "those sent" (cf 17:18), though John does not use the noun in reference to them (see the note on 13:16). A solemn mission or "sending" is also the subject of the post-resurrection appearances to the Eleven in Mt 28:19; Lk 24:47; Mk 16:15.

20:22 This action recalls Gn 2:7, where God breathed on the first man and gave him life; just as Adam's life came from God, so now the disciples' new spiritual life comes from Jesus. Cf also the revivification of the dry bones in Ez 37. This is the author's version of Pentecost. Cf also the note on 19:30.

20:23 The Council of Trent defined that this power to forgive sins is exercised in the sacrament of penance. See Mt 16:19 and 18:18.

20:28 *My Lord and my God:* this forms a literary inclusion with the first verse of the gospel: "and the Word was God."

20:29 This verse is a beatitude on future generations; faith, not sight, matters.

20:7 Jn 11:44; 19:40.
20:9 Acts 2:26–27; 1 Cor 15:4.
20:11–18 Mk 16:9–11.
20:14 Jn 21:4; Mk 16:12; Lk 24:16; 1 Cor 15:43–44.
20:15–17 Mt 28:9–10.
20:17 Acts 1:9.
20:19–23 Mt 28:16–20; Mk 16:14–18; Lk 24:36–44.
20:20 Jn 14:27.
20:21 Jn 17:18; Mt 28:19; Mk 16:15; Lk 24:47–48.
20:22 Gn 2:7; Ez 37:9; 1 Cor 15:45.
20:23 Mt 16:19; 18:18.
20:25 1 Jn 1:1.
20:26 Jn 21:14.
20:28 Jn 1:1.
20:29 Jn 4:48; Lk 1:45; 1 Pt 1:8.

Catholic Connection

Sacrament of Penance and Reconciliation

Imagine the disciples locked in a room, full of fear. Then Jesus miraculously appears, showing them that neither fear nor human obstacles can keep out Christ and his offer of peace. The disciples' fear is suddenly turned into rejoicing. Jesus hands on his mission to the disciples and gives them the Holy Spirit so that they may reconcile people to the Father by forgiving sins in God's name just as Jesus had done.

The Church continues Jesus' ministry of reconciling people to God in a special way through the sacrament of Penance and Reconciliation. Although Baptism takes away original sin, it does not remove its effects, namely our tendency to sin. Because we are members of the Church, our sin not only offends God but also harms the community. Therefore, we need to be reconciled to God and the Church. Celebrating the sacrament of Penance and Reconciliation helps us to do that.

The sacrament of Penance and Reconciliation, which is sometimes called Confession, because a person confesses his or her sins, is generally administered by a priest who represents Christ and the Church. As Christ's representative, the priest acts as the servant of God's mercy and forgiveness. Through the actions of the priest, the individual receiving the sacrament truly experiences the peace of Christ's redeeming love.

The sacrament takes place between a baptized individual (penitent) and a priest. The rite begins with the priest's greeting the penitent and the penitent's responding by making the sign of the cross. The priest invites the penitent to trust in God's mercy and may choose to read a passage from the Scriptures. Then the penitent confesses his or her sins and the priest gives him or her a penance. A penance is something the penitent will later say or do that will help to repair the harm his or her sins have caused. It also can strengthen the penitent and help him or her to avoid the sin in the future. Next, the penitent will say an Act of Contrition—a prayer that admits guilt and expresses the penitent's desire to do better with God's help. The priest, in the name of Christ and his Church, then offers a prayer of absolution, which frees the penitent from all sin and reconciles him or her to God and the Church. Concluding the sacrament, the penitent gives praise to God for his mercy, and the priest tells the penitent to go forth in peace.

When was the last time you experienced God's love and mercy in the sacrament of Penance and Reconciliation? Even if it has been a while, God and the Church are always there waiting with open arms. So consider making time this week to be reconciled and renewed.

Jn 20:19–23

Catechism, nos. 1420–1470

Cultural Connection

The Blessing of Baskets

It's early Holy Saturday morning, and the priest of the parish arrives to open the church for a special event. As he draws near the front door, the smell of eggs, sausages, freshly baked bread, and other breakfast foods wafts from the baskets of those already gathered. As people enter the church, they place their baskets on a table before the altar. The priest begins Mass with a prayer and then blesses the baskets of food with holy water and the sign of the cross:

Blessed are you, O God! In your bounty you provide for your people. As we prepare to celebrate the Resurrection of your Son, bless these Easter foods, and strengthen your people that they may be true witnesses to the new life offered in Christ Jesus, our Lord. Amen.

This custom originated in Eastern Europe and can be found today in many churches around the world. The blessing of baskets reminds us that Jesus' death and Resurrection should touch every aspect of the lives of the faithful. Especially after a long Lent of fasting and self-denial, the rich foods of the Easter table call to mind that Good Friday's sacrifice culminated in Easter glory—a time for celebration and feasting.

▶ Jn 21:1–14

have seen me? Blessed are those who have not
seen and have believed."

Conclusion

30*† Now Jesus did many other signs in the
presence of [his] disciples that are not written in
this book. 31* But these are written that you may
[come to] believe that Jesus is the Messiah, the
Son of God, and that through this belief you may
have life in his name.

IV: Epilogue

The Resurrection Appearance in Galilee

The Appearance to the Seven Disciples

21 1*† After this, Jesus revealed himself again
to his disciples at the Sea of Tiberias. He
revealed himself in this way. 2† Together were
Simon Peter, Thomas called Didymus, Nathanael from Cana in Galilee, Zebedee's sons, and
two others of his disciples. 3*† Simon Peter said
to them, "I am going fishing." They said to him,
"We also will come with you." So they went out
and got into the boat, but that night they caught
nothing. 4* When it was already dawn, Jesus was
standing on the shore; but the disciples did not
realize that it was Jesus. 5* Jesus said to them,
"Children, have you caught anything to eat?"
They answered him, "No." 6 So he said to them,
"Cast the net over the right side of the boat and
you will find something." So they cast it, and
were not able to pull it in because of the number
of fish. 7 So the disciple whom Jesus loved said to
Peter, "It is the Lord." When Simon Peter heard
that it was the Lord, he tucked in his garment,
for he was lightly clad, and jumped into the sea.
8 The other disciples came in the boat, for they
were not far from shore, only about a hundred

†

20:30–31 These verses are clearly a conclusion to the gospel and express its purpose. While many manuscripts read *come to believe,* possibly implying a missionary purpose for John's gospel, a small number of quite early ones read "continue to believe," suggesting that the audience consists of Christians whose faith is to be deepened by the book; cf 19:35.

21:1–23 There are many non-Johannine peculiarities in this chapter, some suggesting Lucan Greek style; yet this passage is closer to John than 7:53—8:11. There are many Johannine features as well. Its closest parallels in the synoptic gospels are found in Lk 5:1–11 and Mt 14:28–31. Perhaps the tradition was ultimately derived from John but preserved by some disciple other than the writer of the rest of the gospel. The appearances narrated seem to be independent of those in ch 20. Even if a later addition, the chapter was added before publication of the gospel, for it appears in all manuscripts.

21:2 *Zebedee's sons:* the only reference to James and John in this gospel (but see the note on 1:37). Perhaps the phrase was originally a gloss to identify, among the five, the *two others of his disciples.* The anonymity of the latter phrase is more Johannine (1:35). The total of seven may suggest the community of the disciples in its fullness.

21:3–6 This may be a variant of Luke's account of the catch of fish; see the note on Lk 5:1–11.

*

20:30 Jn 21:25.
20:31 Jn 3:14, 15; 1 Jn 5:13.
21:1 Mt 26:32; 28:7.
21:3 Mt 4:18; Lk 5:4–10.
21:4 Jn 20:14; Mt 28:17; Lk 24:16.
21:5 Lk 24:41.

yards, dragging the net with the fish. 9*† When
they climbed out on shore, they saw a charcoal
fire with fish on it and bread. 10 Jesus said to
them, "Bring some of the fish you just caught."
11*† So Simon Peter went over and dragged the
net ashore full of one hundred fifty-three large
fish. Even though there were so many, the net
was not torn. 12† Jesus said to them, "Come, have
breakfast." And none of the disciples dared to
ask him, "Who are you?" because they realized
it was the Lord. 13* Jesus came over and took the
bread and gave it to them, and in like manner
the fish. 14*† This was now the third time Jesus
was revealed to his disciples after being raised
from the dead.

Jesus and Peter

15† When they had finished breakfast, Jesus
said to Simon Peter, "Simon, son of John, do
you love me more than these?" †He said to him,
"Yes, Lord, you know that I love you." He said to
him, "Feed my lambs."† 16 He then said to him
a second time, "Simon, son of John, do you love
me?" He said to him, "Yes, Lord, you know that
I love you." He said to him, "Tend my sheep."
17* He said to him the third time, "Simon, son

†

21:9, 12–13 It is strange that Jesus already has fish since none have yet been brought ashore. This meal may have had eucharistic significance for early Christians since v 13 recalls Jn 6:11, which uses the vocabulary of Jesus' action at the Last Supper; but see also the note on Mt 14:19.

21:11 The exact number 153 is probably meant to have a symbolic meaning in relation to the apostles' universal mission; Jerome claims that Greek zoologists catalogued 153 species of fish. Or 153 is the sum of the numbers from 1 to 17. Others invoke Ez 47:10.

21:12 *None . . . dared to ask him:* is Jesus' appearance strange to them? Cf Lk 24:16; Mk 16:12; Jn 20:14. The disciples do, however, recognize Jesus before the breaking of the bread (opposed to Lk 24:35).

21:14 This verse connects chs 20 and 21; cf 20:19, 26.

21:15–23 This section constitutes Peter's rehabilitation and emphasizes his role in the church.

21:15–17 In these three verses there is a remarkable variety of synonyms: two different Greek verbs for *love* (see the note on 15:13); two verbs for *feed/tend;* two nouns for *sheep;* two verbs for *know.* But apparently there is no difference of meaning. The threefold confession of Peter is meant to counteract his earlier threefold denial (18:17, 25, 27). The First Vatican Council cited these verses in defining that Jesus after his resurrection gave Peter the jurisdiction of supreme shepherd and ruler over the whole flock.

21:15 *More than these:* probably "more than these disciples do" rather than "more than you love them" or "more than you love these things [fishing, etc.]."

*

21:9 Lk 24:41–43.
21:11 2 Chr 2:16.
21:13 Lk 24:42.
21:14 Jn 20:19, 26.
21:17 Jn 13:37–38; 18:15–18, 25–27; Mt 26:69–75; Mk 14:66–72; Lk 22:55–62.

Did You Know?

Resurrection Stories

There are fourteen stories about Jesus' Resurrection in the four Gospels. None of the stories describes the actual Resurrection or the physical appearance of the resurrected Christ. Matthew emphasizes God's power with dramatic symbols like earthquakes and lightning (see Mt 28:2–3). Mark, in its original ending, focuses on the empty tomb (see Mk 16:1–8). Luke emphasizes the living presence of Jesus in the Scriptures and the Eucharist (see Lk 24:13–35). John brings out the authority of the leaders of the early Church, especially Peter's role as shepherd of the Church (see Jn 20:19–23, 21:15–19).

Together, all these stories convey the faith of the disciples that Jesus is alive. Through God's power, life has triumphed over death. The disciples' mission is to communicate this Good News. And that's our mission too!

▶ Jn 21:15–19

The Gospel According To . . .

The Gospel of John ends by saying that if everything Jesus did were to be written down, the entire world could not contain it. Sounds like a challenge, doesn't it? Perhaps the author was thinking of all the things the risen Christ continues to do in the lives of believers. If you were to write your own Gospel story, one based on the risen Jesus at work in your life, what marvelous stories would it hold? What messages and teachings would you offer to the people of today? How has your life revealed and reflected the Good News of Jesus?

▶ Jn 21:24–25

of John, do you love me?" Peter was distressed
that he had said to him a third time, "Do you
love me?" and he said to him, "Lord, you know
everything; you know that I love you." [Jesus]
said to him, "Feed my sheep. 18*† Amen, amen,
I say to you, when you were younger, you used
to dress yourself and go where you wanted; but
when you grow old, you will stretch out your
hands, and someone else will dress you and lead
you where you do not want to go." 19* He said
this signifying by what kind of death he would
glorify God. And when he had said this, he said
to him, "Follow me."

The Beloved Disciple

20* Peter turned and saw the disciple follow-
ing whom Jesus loved, the one who had also
reclined upon his chest during the supper and
had said, "Master, who is the one who will betray
you?" 21 When Peter saw him, he said to Jesus,
"Lord, what about him?" 22*† Jesus said to him,
"What if I want him to remain until I come?
What concern is it of yours? You follow me."
23† So the word spread among the brothers that
that disciple would not die. But Jesus had not
told him that he would not die, just "What if I
want him to remain until I come? [What concern
is it of yours?]"

Conclusion

24*† It is this disciple who testifies to these things
and has written them, and we know that his testi-
mony is true. 25* There are also many other things
that Jesus did, but if these were to be described in-
dividually, I do not think the whole world would
contain the books that would be written.

†

21:18 Originally probably a proverb about old age, now used as a figurative reference to the crucifixion of Peter.

21:22 *Until I come:* a reference to the parousia.

21:23 This whole scene takes on more significance if the disciple is already dead. The death of the apostolic generation caused problems in the church because of a belief that Jesus was to have returned first. Loss of faith sometimes resulted; cf 2 Pt 3:4.

21:24 *Who . . . has written them:* this does not necessarily mean he wrote them with his own hand. The same expression is used in 19:22 of Pilate, who certainly would not have written the inscription himself. *We know:* i.e., the Christian community; cf 1:14, 16.

*

21:18 Acts 21:11, 14; 2 Pt 1:14.
21:19 Jn 13:36.
21:20 Jn 13:25.
21:22 Mt 16:28.
21:24 Jn 19:35.
21:25 Jn 20:30.

In your history classes in school, you probably studied stories about the heroic men and women who helped create the United States: George Washington, Benjamin Franklin, Harriet Tubman, Susan B. Anthony, and Harry S. Truman to name a few. The stories about these famous people are an important part of our national identity. The Acts of the Apostles is a book containing stories like these, but these stories are inspired by God. It continues the account of salvation history by telling about the beginnings of the Christian movement, primarily through stories about two of its most important missionaries, Peter and Paul.

In Depth

The Acts of the Apostles—sometimes simply called Acts—was written by the same author as the Gospel of Luke. So Acts is really the second volume of a two-volume history. Like the Gospels, it is not a history in the sense of an eyewitness account of the beginnings of Christianity; rather, it is an interpretation of this history, explaining how Christianity spread outside of Judaism to the Gentile world under the direction of the Holy Spirit.

At a Glance

I. **The Preparation for the Christian Mission (1:1—2:13).**

II. **The Mission in Jerusalem (2:14—8:3).**

III. **The Mission in Judea and Samaria (8:4—9:43).**

IV. **The Inauguration of the Gentile Mission (10:1—15:35).**

V. **The Mission of Paul to the Ends of the Earth (15:36—28:31).**

Quick Facts

Inspired Author: often identified as Luke, who also wrote the Gospel of Luke

Date Written: approximately AD 80

Audience: Gentile (Greek) Christians represented by Theophilus (see Acts 1:1)

Lots of great stories are in the Acts of the Apostles. We read about the descent of the Holy Spirit on the Apostles (see 2:1–41), Paul's conversion to the Christian way (see 9:1–19), and some miraculous escapes from prisons and riots (see 12:6–11, 16:16–40). We learn about the first church council in Jerusalem, where a decision was made to accept Gentiles (non-Jews) as Christians without requiring that they also become practicing Jews (see 15:1–35). Acts continuously emphasizes how faith in Christ is shared and supported through Christian community.

The Acts of the Apostles gives us information about how Christians lived in the years after Jesus' Resurrection and Ascension. We learn how the believers celebrated the Eucharist together and shared their belongings (see 2:42–47). We learn how the Gospel message was preached, first to Jews in the synagogues and later to Gentiles. We learn how traveling missionaries like Paul went on long journeys and suffered many hardships to form new groups of believers across the Roman Empire. Under the guidance of the Holy Spirit, the church miraculously went from a small group of disciples in Jerusalem to a movement spreading across the entire Roman Empire, even to Rome itself.

Acts

I: The Preparation for the Christian Mission

The Promise of the Spirit

1 [1]*† In the first book, Theophilus, I dealt with
all that Jesus did and taught [2]* until the day
he was taken up, after giving instructions through
the holy Spirit to the apostles whom he had cho-
sen. [3]*† He presented himself alive to them by
many proofs after he had suffered, appearing to
them during forty days and speaking about the
kingdom of God. [4]*† While meeting with them,
he enjoined them not to depart from Jerusalem,
but to wait for "the promise of the Father about
which you have heard me speak; [5]* for John bap-
tized with water, but in a few days you will be
baptized with the holy Spirit."

The Ascension of Jesus

[6]† When they had gathered together they
asked him, "Lord, are you at this time going to
restore the kingdom to Israel?" [7]*† He answered
them, "It is not for you to know the times or sea-
sons that the Father has established by his own
authority. [8]*† But you will receive power when
the holy Spirit comes upon you, and you will
be my witnesses in Jerusalem, throughout Ju-
dea and Samaria, and to the ends of the earth."
[9]* When he had said this, as they were looking

†

1:1–26 This introductory material (1–2) connects Acts with the Gospel of Luke, shows that the apostles were instructed by the risen Jesus (3–5), points out that the parousia or second coming in glory of Jesus will occur as certainly as his ascension occurred (6–11), and lists the members of the Twelve, stressing their role as a body of divinely mandated witnesses to his life, teaching, and resurrection (12–26).

1:3 *Appearing to them during forty days:* Luke considered especially sacred the interval in which the appearances and instructions of the risen Jesus occurred and expressed it therefore in terms of the sacred number forty (cf Dt 8:2). In his gospel, however, Luke connects the ascension of Jesus with the resurrection by describing the ascension on Easter Sunday evening (Lk 24:50–53). What should probably be understood as one event (resurrection, glorification, ascension, sending of the Spirit—the paschal mystery) has been historicized by Luke when he writes of a visible ascension of Jesus after forty days and the descent of the Spirit at Pentecost. For Luke, the ascension marks the end of the appearances of Jesus except for the extraordinary appearance to Paul. With regard to Luke's understanding of salvation history, the ascension also marks the end of the time of Jesus (Lk 24:50–53) and signals the beginning of the time of the church.

1:4 *The promise of the Father:* the holy Spirit, as is clear from the next verse. This gift of the Spirit was first promised in Jesus' final instructions to his chosen witnesses in Luke's gospel (Lk 24:49) and formed part of the continuing instructions of the risen Jesus on the kingdom of God, of which Luke speaks in v 3.

1:6 The question of the disciples implies that in believing Jesus to be the Christ (see the note on Lk 2:11) they had expected him to be a political leader who would restore self-rule to Israel during his historical ministry. When this had not taken place, they ask if it is to take place at this time, the period of the church.

1:7 This verse echoes the tradition that the precise time of the parousia is not revealed to human beings; cf Mk 13:32; 1 Thes 5:1–3.

1:8 Just as Jerusalem was the city of destiny in the Gospel of Luke (the place where salvation was accomplished), so here at the beginning of Acts, Jerusalem occupies a central position. It is the starting point for the mission of the Christian disciples to "the ends of the earth," the place where the apostles were situated and the doctrinal focal point in the early days of the community (15:2, 6). *The ends of the earth:* for Luke, this means Rome.

1:1 Lk 1:1–4.
1:2 Mt 28:19–20; Lk 24:44–49; Jn 20:22; 1 Tm 3:16.
1:3 Acts 10:41; 13:31.
1:4 Jn 14:16, 17, 26.
1:5 Acts 11:16; Mt 3:11; Mk 1:8; Lk 3:16; Jn 1:26; Eph 1:13.
1:7 Mt 24:36; 1 Thes 5:1–2.
1:8 Acts 2:1–13; 10:39; Is 43:10; Mt 28:19; Lk 24:47–48.
1:9 2 Kgs 2:11; Mk 16:19; Lk 24:51.

on, he was lifted up, and a cloud took him
from their sight. 10* While they were looking
intently at the sky as he was going, suddenly
two men dressed in white garments stood be-
side them. 11* They said, "Men of Galilee, why
are you standing there looking at the sky? This
Jesus who has been taken up from you into
heaven will return in the same way as you have
seen him going into heaven." 12* Then they
returned to Jerusalem from the mount called
Olivet, which is near Jerusalem, a sabbath day's
journey away.

The First Community in Jerusalem

13 When they entered the city they went to
the upper room where they were staying, Peter
and John and James and Andrew, Philip and
Thomas, Bartholomew and Matthew, James
son of Alphaeus, Simon the Zealot, and Judas
son of James. 14* All these devoted themselves
with one accord to prayer, together with some
women, and Mary the mother of Jesus, and his
brothers.

The Choice of Judas's Successor

15 During those days Peter stood up in the
midst of the brothers (there was a group of
about one hundred and twenty persons in the
one place). He said, 16* "My brothers, the scrip-
ture had to be fulfilled which the holy Spirit
spoke beforehand through the mouth of David,
concerning Judas, who was the guide for those
who arrested Jesus. 17 He was numbered among
us and was allotted a share in this ministry.
18*† He bought a parcel of land with the wages
of his iniquity, and falling headlong, he burst
open in the middle, and all his insides spilled
out. 19 This became known to everyone who
lived in Jerusalem, so that the parcel of land
was called in their language 'Akeldama,' that is,
Field of Blood. 20* For it is written in the Book
of Psalms:

> 'Let his encampment become desolate,
> and may no one dwell in it.'

And:

> 'May another take his office.'

Pray It!

Send Us Your Spirit

After Jesus was taken up to heaven, the Apostles, Mary, and other women and men gathered to pray together. They knew they needed the Holy Spirit, promised by Jesus, to begin the difficult task of giving witness to the Reign of God. Today, we continue to pray:

Jesus, send us your Spirit, and renew the face of the earth. You know our strengths and weaknesses. Transform us into messengers of your Gospel for those who yearn for you.

Jesus, send us your Spirit, and renew the face of the earth. You know our history, with its beautiful and painful experiences. Help us to be untiring promoters of a society based on love, justice, and peace.

Jesus, send us your Spirit, and renew the face of the earth. You know our longing for love and community. Make us instruments of unity and service, especially for those who are weak and those who are lonely. Amen.

▶ Acts 1:1–14

21 Therefore, it is necessary that one of the men
who accompanied us the whole time the Lord
Jesus came and went among us, 22* beginning
from the baptism of John until the day on
which he was taken up from us, become with
us a witness to his resurrection." 23 So they pro-
posed two, Joseph called Barsabbas, who was
also known as Justus, and Matthias. 24 Then they
prayed, "You, Lord, who know the hearts of all,
show which one of these two you have chosen
25 to take the place in this apostolic ministry
from which Judas turned away to go to his own
place." 26*† Then they gave lots to them, and the
lot fell upon Matthias, and he was counted with
the eleven apostles.

1:18 Luke records a popular tradition about the death of Judas that differs from the one in Mt 27:5, according to which Judas hanged himself. Here, although the text is not certain, Judas is depicted as purchasing a piece of property with the betrayal money and being killed on it in a fall.

1:26 The need to replace Judas was probably dictated by the symbolism of the number twelve, recalling the twelve tribes of Israel. This symbolism also indicates that for Luke (see Lk 22:30) the Christian church is a reconstituted Israel.

1:10 Jn 20:17.
1:11 Lk 24:51; Eph 4:8–10; 1 Pt 3:22; Rv 1:7.
1:12–14 Lk 6:14–16.
1:14 Lk 23:49.
1:16 Ps 41:10; Lk 22:47.
1:18 Mt 27:3–10.
1:20 Pss 69:26; 109:8; Jn 17:12.
1:22 Acts 1:8–9; 10:39.
1:26 Prv 16:33.

The Coming of the Spirit

2 1*† When the time for Pentecost was ful-
filled, they were all in one place together.
2*† And suddenly there came from the sky a
noise like a strong driving wind, and it filled
the entire house in which they were. 3*† Then
there appeared to them tongues as of fire, which
parted and came to rest on each one of them.
4*† And they were all filled with the holy Spirit
and began to speak in different tongues, as the
Spirit enabled them to proclaim.
5 Now there were devout Jews from every na-
tion under heaven staying in Jerusalem. 6 At this
sound, they gathered in a large crowd, but they
were confused because each one heard them
speaking in his own language. 7* They were as-
tounded, and in amazement they asked, "Are
not all these people who are speaking Galileans?
8 Then how does each of us hear them in his own
native language? 9 We are Parthians, Medes, and
Elamites, inhabitants of Mesopotamia, Judea
and Cappadocia, Pontus and Asia, 10 Phrygia
and Pamphylia, Egypt and the districts of Libya
near Cyrene, as well as travelers from Rome,
11* both Jews and converts to Judaism, Cretans
and Arabs, yet we hear them speaking in our
own tongues of the mighty acts of God." 12 They
were all astounded and bewildered, and said to
one another, "What does this mean?" 13* But
others said, scoffing, "They have had too much
new wine."

II: The Mission in Jerusalem

Peter's Speech at Pentecost

14† Then Peter stood up with the Eleven, raised
his voice, and proclaimed to them, "You who are
Jews, indeed all of you staying in Jerusalem. Let
this be known to you, and listen to my words.
15 These people are not drunk, as you suppose, for
it is only nine o'clock in the morning. 16 No, this is
what was spoken through the prophet Joel:

17* 'It will come to pass in the last days,' God says,
'that I will pour out a portion of my spirit upon all flesh.
Your sons and your daughters shall prophesy,
your young men shall see visions,
your old men shall dream dreams.
18 Indeed, upon my servants and my handmaids
I will pour out a portion of my spirit in those days,
and they shall prophesy.
19 And I will work wonders in the heavens above
and signs on the earth below:
blood, fire, and a cloud of smoke.
20 The sun shall be turned to darkness,
and the moon to blood,
before the coming of the great and splendid day of the Lord,
21* and it shall be that everyone shall be saved
who calls on the name of the Lord.'

22* You who are Israelites, hear these words.
Jesus the Nazorean was a man commended to
you by God with mighty deeds, wonders, and
signs, which God worked through him in your
midst, as you yourselves know. 23* This man,
delivered up by the set plan and foreknowledge
of God, you killed, using lawless men to crucify
him. 24* But God raised him up, releasing him
from the throes of death, because it was impos-
sible for him to be held by it. 25* For David says
of him:

'I saw the Lord ever before me,
with him at my right hand I shall not be disturbed.
26 Therefore my heart has been glad and my tongue has exulted;
my flesh, too, will dwell in hope,
27* because you will not abandon my soul to the nether world,
nor will you suffer your holy one to see corruption.

†

2:1–41 Luke's pentecostal narrative consists of an introduction (1–13), a speech ascribed to Peter declaring the resurrection of Jesus and its messianic significance (14–36), and a favorable response from the audience (37–41). It is likely that the narrative telescopes events that took place over a period of time and on a less dramatic scale. The Twelve were not originally in a position to proclaim publicly the messianic office of Jesus without incurring immediate reprisal from those religious authorities in Jerusalem who had brought about Jesus' death precisely to stem the rising tide in his favor.

2:2 *There came from the sky a noise like a strong driving wind:* wind and spirit are associated in Jn 3:8. The sound of a great rush of wind would herald a new action of God in the history of salvation.

2:3 *Tongues as of fire:* see Ex 19:18 where fire symbolizes the presence of God to initiate the covenant on Sinai. Here the holy Spirit acts upon the apostles, preparing them to proclaim the new covenant with its unique gift of the Spirit (38).

2:4 *To speak in different tongues:* ecstatic prayer in praise of God, interpreted in vv 6 and 11 as speaking in foreign languages, symbolizing the worldwide mission of the church.

2:14–36 The first of six discourses in Acts (along with 3:12–26; 4:8–12; 5:29–32; 10:34–43; 13:16–41) dealing with the resurrection of Jesus and its messianic import. Five of these are attributed to Peter, the final one to Paul. Modern scholars term these discourses in Acts the "kerygma," the Greek word for proclamation (cf 1 Cor 15:11).

2:1 Lv 23:15–21; Dt 16:9–11.
2:2–3 Jn 3:8.
2:3 Lk 3:16.
2:4 Acts 1:5; 4:31; 8:15, 17; 10:44; 11:15–16; 15:8; 19:6; Ps 104:30; Jn 20:33.
2:7 Acts 1:11.
2:11 Acts 10:46.
2:13 1 Cor 14:23.
2:17 Is 2:2; 44:3; Jl 3:1–5.
2:21 Rom 10:13.
2:22 Acts 10:38; Lk 24:19.
2:23 1 Thes 2:15.
2:24 Acts 13:34.
2:25–28 Ps 16:8–11.
2:27 Acts 13:35.

Catholic Connection

Confirmation

After Jesus' Ascension, the Apostles eagerly awaited the promised arrival of the Holy Spirit. What an arrival it was! The loud noise and tongues of fire were only the beginning of the amazing work the Holy Spirit initiated that day. Filled with the Holy Spirit, the Apostles suddenly had abilities and courage they never had before. The Holy Spirit began to guide and empower each of them, leading the Apostles to proclaim Christ's Resurrection to all who had ears to hear.

Following Pentecost, the Apostles began to baptize and lay hands on each new convert so that they too could receive the gift of the Holy Spirit. The laying on of hands and the prayer for the Holy Spirit was a part of one's initiation into the Church and continues to be celebrated in the sacrament of Confirmation today. The Church teaches that through the sacrament of Confirmation, one is given a special outpouring of the Holy Spirit and is thereby given special strength (see "The Gifts of the Holy Spirit," near Is 11:1–2) to spread the Gospel.

Confirmation is ordinarily administered by a bishop as a sign of the connection between the Apostles' experience of receiving the Holy Spirit and the recipient's initiation into the Church. During the rite, the bishop extends his hands over the candidates and prays for the coming of the Holy Spirit. Then each candidate is presented to the bishop by her or his sponsor, who is a representative from the Catholic community. The bishop uses chrism (sacred oil) and traces the sign of the cross on the candidate's forehead with the words, "Be sealed with the gift of the Holy Spirit." The candidate responds "Amen" (*Rite of Confirmation,* no. 27). Then the bishop and candidate exchange an offering of Christ's peace to each other. The rite ends with a final blessing, asking God to keep the Spirit active in the hearts of all believers so they will never be ashamed to proclaim Christ to the world.

Together the sacraments of Baptism, Confirmation, and the Eucharist are a person's initiation into the Church.

Acts 2:1–13

Catechism, nos. 1285–1321

Catholic Connection

Pentecost

Another promise kept. On Pentecost, fifty days after his Resurrection, Jesus fulfilled his promise to his disciples by sending the Holy Spirit, or the Advocate (see Jn 14:26). Before returning to his father, Jesus told his followers that the Holy Spirit would guide them in truth and give them power from heaven. The dramatic descent of the Holy Spirit on Pentecost brought about more than the disciples could have ever imagined. The Spirit enabled them to speak in languages that everyone could understand and transformed their fears so they were able to proclaim God's salvation in Jesus Christ with courage, confidence, and zeal. And that was just on day one!

The descent of the Holy Spirit on Pentecost also brought about several interesting events in the history of the world. First, Pentecost marks the day the Trinity was made fully known. Second, it marks the day the Reign of God was first made available to all who believed in Jesus Christ. And finally, in a sense, the world entered into what is called the time of the Church or final days when God's Reign is, in part, here on earth.

By ushering in the time of the Church, Pentecost is considered the birthday of the Christian Church. The Catholic Church traditionally celebrates the feast of Pentecost on the second Sunday after Ascension Thursday, which is approximately fifty days after Easter (the term *pente* means "fifty"). It continues to be an important feast to celebrate the unity of all Christians.

Since Pentecost, the Holy Spirit has been guiding the Church in carrying out its mission to lead people to salvation through Jesus Christ for over two thousand years. At Mass it is the Holy Spirit who prepares those gathered to receive Christ, transforms the bread and wine into the Body and Blood of Jesus Christ, and transforms the community in the process. It is through the prompting of the Holy Spirit that the Church and its members are formed in a life of prayer. The Holy Spirit also guides the Church so that it can teach about faith and morals without error.

The Holy Spirit that worked wonders through the disciples and continues to guide the Church today can also work wonders through each of us. Through the power of the Holy Spirit, we too can find the courage, confidence, and zeal to boldly share our faith and follow God's will. All we need to do is ask, knowing that Jesus always keeps his promises, often in ways we never could have dreamed!

Acts 2:1–13

Catechism, nos. 731–741, 1108–1112

Catholic Social Teaching

Christian Community

In the famous passage of Acts of the Apostles 2:42–47, the ideal Christian community is portrayed as open to the Holy Spirit. The people shared everything in common, including prayer, meals, and possessions. No one went in need. Sound impossible?

One of the principles of Catholic social teaching, *Call to Family, Community, and Participation*, invites us to be mindful of the fact that families are at the heart of the community. Programs and policies of our society should demonstrate support and respect for the family. The U.S. bishops call us to be concerned for those who are at risk and vulnerable, not only in our own country but also in the global community. They speak about the importance of supporting policies that address the needs of families, specifically the rights of children, who often are the most vulnerable, to adequate food, shelter, healthcare, quality education, and a safe environment in which to flourish.

Our faith teaches us to respect the dignity of the human person. This passage from Acts of the Apostles reminds us that the early Christian community tried very hard to live as a community that cared for one another and made sure that everyone felt respected and had their basic needs met. We are also called to be participants in helping to promote this reality in the world today. It is not always easy, but we can find ways to do what we can to share in that vision.

- What do you think society would be like today if everyone lived as the early Christian community tried to live?

Acts 2:42–47
Call to Family, Community, and Participation

28 You have made known to me the paths of life;
you will fill me with joy in your presence.'

29 My brothers, one can confidently say to you
about the patriarch David that he died and was
buried, and his tomb is in our midst to this day.
30* But since he was a prophet and knew that
God had sworn an oath to him that he would
set one of his descendants upon his throne,
31* he foresaw and spoke of the resurrection of
the Messiah, that neither was he abandoned to
the netherworld nor did his flesh see corruption.
32 God raised this Jesus; of this we are all wit-
nesses. 33*† Exalted at the right hand of God, he
received the promise of the holy Spirit from the
Father and poured it forth, as you [both] see and
hear. 34* For David did not go up into heaven,
but he himself said:

'The Lord said to my Lord,
"Sit at my right hand
35 until I make your enemies your footstool." '

36* Therefore let the whole house of Israel know
for certain that God has made him both Lord
and Messiah, this Jesus whom you crucified."
37* Now when they heard this, they were cut
to the heart, and they asked Peter and the other
apostles, "What are we to do, my brothers?"
38*† Peter [said] to them, "Repent and be bap-
tized, every one of you, in the name of Jesus
Christ for the forgiveness of your sins; and you
will receive the gift of the holy Spirit. 39* For
the promise is made to you and to your chil-
dren and to all those far off, whomever the Lord
our God will call." 40* He testified with many
other arguments, and was exhorting them,
"Save yourselves from this corrupt generation."
41* Those who accepted his message were bap-
tized, and about three thousand persons were
added that day.

ACTS

† **2:33** *At the right hand of God:* or "by the right hand of God."
2:38 *Repent and be baptized:* repentance is a positive concept, a change of mind and heart toward God reflected in the actual goodness of one's life. It is in accord with the apostolic teaching derived from Jesus (42) and ultimately recorded in the four gospels. Luke presents baptism in Acts as the expected response to the apostolic preaching about Jesus and associates it with the conferring of the Spirit (1:5; 10:44–48; 11:16).

2:30 2 Sm 7:12; Ps 132:11.
2:31 Acts 13:35; Ps 16:10.
2:33 Acts 1:4–5.
2:34–35 Ps 110:1.
2:36 Acts 9:22; Rom 10:9; Phil 2:11.
2:37 Lk 3:10.
2:38 Acts 3:19; 16:31; Lk 3:3.
2:39 Is 57:19; Jl 3:5; Eph 2:17.
2:40 Dt 32:5; Ps 78:8; Lk 9:41; Phil 2:15.
2:41 Acts 2:47; 4:4; 5:14; 6:7; 11:21, 24; 21:20.

Live It!

Share Christ

As is true in our own cities today, it was not uncommon to encounter beggars on the streets in Jerusalem during the first century. And probably, like today, some people averted their eyes and walked by while others stopped to offer a few coins.

When Peter and John encounter a beggar in Acts of the Apostles 3:3, they don't have a whole lot of money to share with him, but they stop just the same. Looking him in the eye, Peter offers the lame man the one thing of value he does have: the powerful gift of healing found in the name of Jesus Christ.

You may not have the gift of healing or lots of extra money to give to those in need. But Peter and John remind us that knowing Jesus is the greatest treasure one can acquire in life, and that this treasure has been given to us freely. Don't forget to share it with others!

▶ Acts 3:1–10

Communal Life

42*† They devoted themselves to the teach-
ing of the apostles and to the communal life, to
the breaking of the bread and to the prayers.*
43* Awe came upon everyone, and many wonders
and signs were done through the apostles. 44* All
who believed were together and had all things in
common; 45 they would sell their property and
possessions and divide them among all accord-
ing to each one's need. 46 Every day they devoted
themselves to meeting together in the temple
area and to breaking bread in their homes. They
ate their meals with exultation and sincerity of
heart, 47 praising God and enjoying favor with
all the people. And every day the Lord added to
their number those who were being saved.

Cure of a Crippled Beggar

3 1† Now Peter and John were going up to
the temple area for the three o'clock hour
of prayer.† 2* And a man crippled from birth
was carried and placed at the gate of the temple
called "the Beautiful Gate" every day to beg for
alms from the people who entered the temple.
3 When he saw Peter and John about to go into
the temple, he asked for alms. 4 But Peter looked
intently at him, as did John, and said, "Look at
us." 5 He paid attention to them, expecting to
receive something from them. 6*† Peter said, "I
have neither silver nor gold, but what I do have
I give you: in the name of Jesus Christ the Naz-
orean, [rise and] walk." 7 Then Peter took him
by the right hand and raised him up, and im-
mediately his feet and ankles grew strong. 8* He
leaped up, stood, and walked around, and went
into the temple with them, walking and jumping
and praising God. 9 When all the people saw him
walking and praising God, 10 they recognized
him as the one who used to sit begging at the
Beautiful Gate of the temple, and they were filled
with amazement and astonishment at what had
happened to him.

Peter's Speech

11* As he clung to Peter and John, all the peo-
ple hurried in amazement toward them in the
portico called "Solomon's Portico." 12* When
Peter saw this, he addressed the people, "You Is-
raelites, why are you amazed at this, and why do

---

† **2:42–47** The first of three summary passages (along with 4:32–37 and 5:12–16) that outline, somewhat idyllically, the chief characteristics of the Jerusalem community: adherence to the teachings of the Twelve and the centering of its religious life in the eucharistic liturgy (42); a system of distribution of goods that led wealthier Christians to sell their possessions when the needs of the community's poor required it (44 and the note on 4:32–37); and continued attendance at the temple, since in this initial stage there was little or no thought of any dividing line between Christianity and Judaism (46).

3:1–4:31 This section presents a series of related events: the dramatic cure of a lame beggar (3:1–10) produces a large audience for the kerygmatic discourse of Peter (3:11–26). The Sadducees, taking exception to the doctrine of resurrection, have Peter, John, and apparently the beggar as well, arrested (4:1–4) and brought to trial before the Sanhedrin. The issue concerns the authority by which Peter and John publicly teach religious doctrine in the temple (4:5–7). Peter replies with a brief summary of the kerygma, implying that his authority is prophetic (4:8–12). The court warns the apostles to abandon their practice of invoking prophetic authority in the name of Jesus (4:13–18). When Peter and John reply that the prophetic role cannot be abandoned to satisfy human objections, the court nevertheless releases them, afraid to do otherwise since the beggar, lame from birth and over forty years old, is a well-known figure in Jerusalem and the facts of his cure are common property (4:19–22).

The narrative concludes with a prayer of the Christian community imploring divine aid against threats of persecution (4:23–31).

3:1 *For the three o'clock hour of prayer:* literally, "at the ninth hour of prayer." With the day beginning at 6 a.m., the ninth hour would be 3 p.m.

3:6–10 The miracle has a dramatic cast; it symbolizes the saving power of Christ and leads the beggar to enter the temple, where he hears Peter's proclamation of salvation through Jesus.

---

* **2:42–47** Acts 4:32–35. **2:42** Acts 1:14; 6:4. **2:43** Acts 5:12–16. **2:44** Acts 4:32, 34–35. **3:2–8** Acts 14:8–10. **3:6** Acts 4:10. **3:8** Is 35:6; Lk 7:22. **3:11** Acts 5:12; Jn 10:23. **3:12** Acts 14:15.

you look so intently at us as if we had made him
walk by our own power or piety? 13*† The God
of Abraham, [the God] of Isaac, and [the God]
of Jacob, the God of our ancestors, has glorified
his servant Jesus whom you handed over and
denied in Pilate's presence, when he had decided
to release him. 14*† You denied the Holy and
Righteous One and asked that a murderer be
released to you. 15*† The author of life you put
to death, but God raised him from the dead; of
this we are witnesses. 16 And by faith in his name,
this man, whom you see and know, his name has
made strong, and the faith that comes through
it has given him this perfect health, in the pres-
ence of all of you. 17*† Now I know, brothers,
that you acted out of ignorance, just as your
leaders did; 18*† but God has thus brought to
fulfillment what he had announced beforehand
through the mouth of all the prophets, that his
Messiah would suffer. 19* Repent, therefore, and
be converted, that your sins may be wiped away,
20† and that the Lord may grant you times of
refreshment and send you the Messiah already
appointed for you, Jesus, 21† whom heaven must
receive until the times of universal restoration of
which God spoke through the mouth of his holy
prophets from of old. 22*† For Moses said:

'A prophet like me will the Lord, your God,
raise up for you
from among your own kinsmen;
to him you shall listen in all that he may say
to you.
23* Everyone who does not listen to that prophet
will be cut off from the people.'

24 Moreover, all the prophets who spoke, from
Samuel and those afterwards, also announced
these days. 25* You are the children of the proph-
ets and of the covenant that God made with your
ancestors when he said to Abraham, 'In your
offspring all the families of the earth shall be
blessed.' 26* For you first, God raised up his ser-
vant and sent him to bless you by turning each of
you from your evil ways."

4 1† While they were still speaking to the
people, the priests, the captain of the tem-
ple guard, and the Sadducees confronted them,
2* disturbed that they were teaching the people
and proclaiming in Jesus the resurrection of the
dead. 3 They laid hands on them and put them
in custody until the next day, since it was already
evening. 4 But many of those who heard the word
came to believe and [the] number of men grew
to [about] five thousand.

Before the Sanhedrin

5 On the next day, their leaders, elders, and
scribes were assembled in Jerusalem, 6 with An-
nas the high priest, Caiaphas, John, Alexander,
and all who were of the high-priestly class. 7 They
brought them into their presence and questioned
them, "By what power or by what name have you
done this?" 8* Then Peter, filled with the holy
Spirit, answered them, "Leaders of the people

3:13 *Has glorified:* through the resurrection and ascension of Jesus, God reversed the judgment against him on the occasion of his trial. *Servant:* the Greek word can also be rendered as "son" or even "child" here and also in 3:26; 4:25 (applied to David); 4:27; and 4:30. Scholars are of the opinion, however, that the original concept reflected in the words identified Jesus with the suffering Servant of the Lord of Is 52:13—53:12.

3:14 *The Holy and Righteous One:* so designating Jesus emphasizes his special relationship to the Father (see Lk 1:35; 4:34) and emphasizes his sinlessness and religious dignity that are placed in sharp contrast with the guilt of those who rejected him in favor of Barabbas.

3:15 *The author of life:* other possible translations of the Greek title are "leader of life" or "pioneer of life." The title clearly points to Jesus as the source and originator of salvation.

3:17 *Ignorance:* a Lucan motif, explaining away the actions not only of the people but also of their leaders in crucifying Jesus. On this basis the presbyters in Acts could continue to appeal to the Jews in Jerusalem to believe in Jesus, even while affirming their involvement in his death because they were unaware of his messianic dignity. See also 13:27 and Lk 23:34.

3:18 *Through the mouth of all the prophets:* Christian prophetic insight into the Old Testament saw the crucifixion and death of Jesus as the main import of messianic prophecy. The Jews themselves did not anticipate a suffering Messiah; they usually understood the Servant Song in Is 52:13—53:12 to signify their own suffering as a people. In his typical fashion (cf Lk 18:31; 24:25, 27, 44), Luke does not specify the particular Old Testament prophecies that were fulfilled by Jesus. See also the note on Lk 24:26.

3:20 *The Lord . . . and send you the Messiah already appointed for you, Jesus:* an allusion to the parousia or second coming of Christ, judged to be imminent in the apostolic age. This reference to its nearness is the only explicit one in Acts. Some scholars believe that this verse preserves a very early christology, in which the title "Messiah" (Greek "Christ") is applied to him as of his parousia, his second coming (contrast 2:36). This view of a future messiahship of Jesus is not found elsewhere in the New Testament.

3:21 *The times of universal restoration:* like "the times of refreshment" (20), an apocalyptic designation of the messianic age, fitting in with the christology of v 20 that associates the messiahship of Jesus with his future coming.

3:22 A loose citation of Dt 18:15, which teaches that the Israelites are to learn the will of Yahweh from no one but their prophets. At the time of Jesus, some Jews expected a unique prophet to come in fulfillment of this text. Early Christianity applied this tradition and text to Jesus and used them especially in defense of the divergence of Christian teaching from traditional Judaism.

4:1 *The priests, the captain of the temple guard, and the Sadducees:* the priests performed the temple liturgy; the temple guard was composed of Levites, whose captain ranked next after the high priest. The Sadducees, a party within Judaism at this time, rejected those doctrines, including bodily resurrection, which they believed alien to the ancient Mosaic religion. The Sadducees were drawn from priestly families and from the lay aristocracy.

3:13 Ex 3:6, 15; Is 52:13; Lk 23:14–25.
3:14 Mt 27:20–21; Mk 15:11; Lk 23:18; Jn 18:40.
3:15 Acts 4:10; 5:31 / Acts 1:8; 2:32.
3:17 Acts 13:27; Lk 23:34; 1 Cor 2:8; 1 Tm 1:13.
3:18 Lk 18:31.
3:19 Acts 2:38.
3:22 Acts 7:37; Dt 18:15, 18.
3:23 Lv 23:29; Dt 18:19.
3:25 Gn 12:3; 18:18; 22:18; Sir 44:19–21; Gal 3:8–9.
3:26 Acts 13:46; Rom 1:16.
4:2 Acts 23:6–8; 24:21.
4:8 Mt 10:20.

and elders: [9]If we are being examined today
about a good deed done to a cripple, namely, by
what means he was saved, [10]then all of you and
all the people of Israel should know that it was
in the name of Jesus Christ the Nazorean whom
you crucified, whom God raised from the dead;
in his name this man stands before you healed.
[11]*† He is 'the stone rejected by you, the builders,
which has become the cornerstone.' [12]*† There is
no salvation through anyone else, nor is there
any other name under heaven given to the human race by which we are to be saved."
[13]Observing the boldness of Peter and John
and perceiving them to be uneducated, ordinary
men, they were amazed, and they recognized
them as the companions of Jesus. [14]Then when
they saw the man who had been cured standing
there with them, they could say nothing in reply.
[15]So they ordered them to leave the Sanhedrin,
and conferred with one another, saying, [16]"What
are we to do with these men? Everyone living in
Jerusalem knows that a remarkable sign was done
through them, and we cannot deny it. [17]* But so
that it may not be spread any further among the
people, let us give them a stern warning never
again to speak to anyone in this name."
[18]So they called them back and ordered them
not to speak or teach at all in the name of Jesus.
[19]* Peter and John, however, said to them in reply, "Whether it is right in the sight of God for us
to obey you rather than God, you be the judges.
[20]It is impossible for us not to speak about what
we have seen and heard." [21]After threatening
them further, they released them, finding no way
to punish them, on account of the people who
were all praising God for what had happened.
[22]For the man on whom this sign of healing had
been done was over forty years old.

Prayer of the Community

[23]After their release they went back to their
own people and reported what the chief priests
and elders had told them. [24]And when they
heard it, they raised their voices to God with
one accord and said, "Sovereign Lord, maker of
heaven and earth and the sea and all that is in
them, [25]* you said by the holy Spirit through the
mouth of our father David, your servant:

'Why did the Gentiles rage
 and the peoples entertain folly?
[26] The kings of the earth took their stand
 and the princes gathered together
  against the Lord and against his
  anointed.'

Pray It!

I Believe! The Apostles' Creed

In Acts of the Apostles 4:5–12, Peter stands up before the Jewish rulers and elders of the Temple and boldly proclaims his faith in Jesus as healer and Messiah. Every Sunday at Mass, Catholic Christians also profess their faith when they pray the Nicene Creed. (A creed is a type of prayer that expresses faith beliefs.) Did you know there is also a shorter creed called the Apostles' Creed? The Apostles' Creed is based on the teachings and beliefs of the earliest Christians.

Take a moment to pray the Apostles' Creed:

I believe in God, the Father almighty, Creator of heaven and earth, and in Jesus Christ, his only Son, our Lord, who was conceived by the Holy Spirit, born of the Virgin Mary, suffered under Pontius Pilate, was crucified, died and was buried; he descended into hell; on the third day he rose again from the dead; he ascended into heaven, and is seated at the right hand of God the Father almighty; from there he will come to judge the living and the dead. I believe in the Holy Spirit, the holy catholic Church, the communion of saints, the forgiveness of sins, the resurrection of the body, and life everlasting. Amen.

Then reflect or journal on the following questions:

- Which statements of the creed do you have questions about?
- How hard would it be for you to express your faith beliefs to people who don't believe in Jesus?
- To what actions does a faith like this call us?

Acts 4:5–12

† **4:11** Early Christianity applied this citation from Ps 118:22 to Jesus; cf Mk 12:10; 1 Pt 2:7.

4:12 In the Roman world of Luke's day, salvation was often attributed to the emperor who was hailed as "savior" and "god." Luke, in the words of Peter, denies that deliverance comes through anyone other than Jesus.

4:11 Ps 118:22; Is 28:16; Mt 21:42; Mk 12:10; Lk 20:17; Rom 9:33; 1 Pt 2:7.
4:12 Mt 1:21; 1 Cor 3:11.
4:17 Acts 5:28.
4:19 Acts 5:29–32.
4:25–26 Ps 2:1–2.

27*† Indeed they gathered in this city against
your holy servant Jesus whom you anointed,
Herod and Pontius Pilate, together with the Gen-
tiles and the peoples of Israel, 28 to do what your
hand and [your] will had long ago planned to
take place. 29 And now, Lord, take note of their
threats, and enable your servants to speak your
word with all boldness, 30 as you stretch forth
[your] hand to heal, and signs and wonders are
done through the name of your holy servant
Jesus." 31*† As they prayed, the place where they
were gathered shook, and they were all filled
with the holy Spirit and continued to speak the
word of God with boldness.

Life in the Christian Community

32† The community of believers was of one
heart and mind, and no one claimed that any of
his possessions was his own, but they had every-
thing in common. 33 With great power the apos-
tles bore witness to the resurrection of the Lord
Jesus, and great favor was accorded them all.
34* There was no needy person among them, for
those who owned property or houses would sell
them, bring the proceeds of the sale, 35 and put
them at the feet of the apostles, and they were
distributed to each according to need.

36* Thus Joseph, also named by the apostles
Barnabas (which is translated "son of encour-
agement"), a Levite, a Cypriot by birth, 37 sold a
piece of property that he owned, then brought
the money and put it at the feet of the apostles.

Ananias and Sapphira

5 1† A man named Ananias, however, with his
wife Sapphira, sold a piece of property. 2 He
retained for himself, with his wife's knowledge,
some of the purchase price, took the remainder,
and put it at the feet of the apostles. 3* But Peter
said, "Ananias, why has Satan filled your heart
so that you lied to the holy Spirit and retained
part of the price of the land? 4 While it remained
unsold, did it not remain yours? And when it was
sold, was it not still under your control? Why
did you contrive this deed? You have lied not
to human beings, but to God." 5 When Ananias
heard these words, he fell down and breathed his
last, and great fear came upon all who heard of
it. 6 The young men came and wrapped him up,
then carried him out and buried him.

7 After an interval of about three hours, his
wife came in, unaware of what had happened.
8 Peter said to her, "Tell me, did you sell the land
for this amount?" She answered, "Yes, for that

Did You Know?

Stewardship

Acts of the Apostles 4:32–37 describes the value of stewardship. Stewardship involves sharing the gifts of time, talents, and treasure that God has placed in your care (see "Stewardship: Making a Contribution," near Lk 21:1–4). It is key to the life of any Christian community.

Sharing our treasure and giving money are the most obvious ways of sharing. Consider the disciple named in the passage, Joseph Barnabas. How did he share? Can you think of things you spend money on—a CD, new jeans, a movie—and make a commitment to give some of that money to a charitable organization?

But giving money isn't the only way to share with others. Think about your own gifts. What are you good at that you could share with your parish, school, or community? Do not discount even the simplest ability. For example, maybe you are persistent; this talent can help with the success of any project. Or perhaps you love children and can baby-sit for overwhelmed parents.

How are you a good steward of your time, talents, and treasure? Think about it!

▶ Acts 4:32–37

ACTS

4:27 *Herod:* Herod Antipas, ruler of Galilee and Perea from 4 B.C. to A.D. 39, who executed John the Baptist and before whom Jesus was arraigned; cf Lk 23:6–12.

4:31 *The place . . . shook:* the earthquake is used as a sign of the divine presence in Ex 19:18; Is 6:4. Here the shaking of the building symbolizes God's favorable response to the prayer. Luke may have had as an additional reason for using the symbol in this sense the fact that it was familiar in the Hellenistic world. Ovid and Virgil also employ it.

4:32–37 This is the second summary characterizing the Jerusalem community (see the note on 2:42–47). It emphasizes the system of the distribution of goods and introduces Barnabas, who appears later in Acts as the friend and companion of Paul, and who, as noted here (37), endeared himself to the community by a donation of money through the sale of property. This sharing of material possessions continues a practice that Luke describes during the historical ministry of Jesus (Lk 8:3) and is in accord with the sayings of Jesus in Luke's gospel (Lk 12:33; 16:9, 11, 13).

5:1–11 The sin of Ananias and Sapphira did not consist in the withholding of part of the money but in their deception of the community. Their deaths are ascribed to a lie to the holy Spirit (3, 9), i.e., they accepted the honor accorded them by the community for their generosity, but in reality they were not deserving of it.

4:27 Lk 23:12–13.
4:31 Acts 2:4.
4:34–35 Acts 2:44–45.
4:36–37 Acts 9:27; 11:22, 30; 12:25; 13:15; 1 Cor 9:6; Gal 2:1, 9, 13; Col 4:10.
5:3 Lk 22:3; Jn 13:2.

Live It!

Pop Quiz

The scene. The disciples, who are spreading the Good News of Jesus Christ, are taken before the Jewish council to explain their motives and reasons for this work.

The test. Gamaliel, a wise Jewish leader, talks the rest of the council out of killing the disciples, whose profession of faith in Jesus was considered blasphemy, by using the following reasoning: If the disciples' mission is from God, it will succeed despite anything the council does. But if it is not of God's design, it will fail and Jesus' followers will eventually disappear anyway.

The question. If you were brought before a similar council, would your life's mission pass or fail this test? Would your words and actions in the past week reflect Jesus' attitudes, actions, and mission?

▶ Acts 5:27–39

amount." 9 Then Peter said to her, "Why did you
agree to test the Spirit of the Lord? Listen, the
footsteps of those who have buried your hus-
band are at the door, and they will carry you
out." 10 At once, she fell down at his feet and
breathed her last. When the young men entered
they found her dead, so they carried her out and
buried her beside her husband. 11* And great fear
came upon the whole church and upon all who
heard of these things.

Signs and Wonders of the Apostles

12*† Many signs and wonders were done
among the people at the hands of the apostles.
They were all together in Solomon's portico.
13 None of the others dared to join them, but the
people esteemed them. 14 Yet more than ever,
believers in the Lord, great numbers of men and
women, were added to them. 15* Thus they even
carried the sick out into the streets and laid them
on cots and mats so that when Peter came by, at
least his shadow might fall on one or another
of them. 16 A large number of people from the
towns in the vicinity of Jerusalem also gathered,
bringing the sick and those disturbed by unclean
spirits, and they were all cured.

Trial before the Sanhedrin

17*† Then the high priest rose up and all his
companions, that is, the party of the Sadducees,
and, filled with jealousy, 18 laid hands upon the
apostles and put them in the public jail. 19* But
during the night, the angel of the Lord opened
the doors of the prison, led them out, and said,
20 "Go and take your place in the temple area,
and tell the people everything about this life."
21 When they heard this, they went to the tem-
ple early in the morning and taught. When the
high priest and his companions arrived, they
convened the Sanhedrin, the full senate of the
Israelites, and sent to the jail to have them
brought in. 22 But the court officers who went
did not find them in the prison, so they came
back and reported, 23 "We found the jail securely
locked and the guards stationed outside the
doors, but when we opened them, we found no
one inside." 24 When they heard this report, the
captain of the temple guard and the chief priests
were at a loss about them, as to what this would
come to. 25 Then someone came in and reported
to them, "The men whom you put in prison are
in the temple area and are teaching the people."
26* Then the captain and the court officers went
and brought them in, but without force, because
they were afraid of being stoned by the people.
27 When they had brought them in and made
them stand before the Sanhedrin, the high priest
questioned them, 28* "We gave you strict orders
[did we not?] to stop teaching in that name. Yet
you have filled Jerusalem with your teaching and
want to bring this man's blood upon us." 29* But

†

5:12–16 This, the third summary portraying the Jerusalem community, underscores the Twelve as its bulwark, especially because of their charismatic power to heal the sick; cf 2:42–47; 4:32–37.

5:17–42 A second action against the community is taken by the Sanhedrin in the arrest and trial of the Twelve; cf 4:1–3. The motive is the jealousy of the religious authorities over the popularity of the apostles (17) who are now charged with the defiance of the Sanhedrin's previous order to them to abandon their prophetic role (28; cf 4:18). In this crisis the apostles are favored by a miraculous release from prison (18–24). (For similar incidents involving Peter and Paul, see 12:6–11; 16:25–29.) The real significance of such an event, however, would be manifest only to people of faith, not to unbelievers; since the Sanhedrin already judged the Twelve to be inauthentic prophets, it could disregard reports of their miracles. When the Twelve immediately resumed public teaching, the Sanhedrin determined to invoke upon them the penalty of death (33) prescribed in Dt 13:6–10. Gamaliel's advice against this course finally prevailed, but it did not save the Twelve from the punishment of scourging (40) in a last endeavor to shake their conviction of their prophetic mission.

*

5:11 Acts 2:43; 5:5; 19:17.
5:12 Acts 2:43; 6:8; 14:3; 15:12.
5:15 Acts 19:11–12; Mk 6:56.
5:17 Acts 4:1–3, 6.
5:19 Acts 12:7–10; 16:25–26.
5:26 Lk 20:19.
5:28 Mt 27:25.
5:29 Acts 4:19.

Catholic Practices and Prayers

Being Catholic

There are an estimated one billion Catholics living in the world. That is about 17 percent of the world's population. There are more Catholics than there are people in any other Christian denomination. There are also more Catholics than there are Jews, Hindus, or Buddhists—only Muslims have more members. The great number of Catholics in the world testifies to Catholicism's universal appeal and to the power that the Catholic faith has in people's lives.

This section of The Catholic Youth Bible® provides only a quick view of Catholic beliefs, practices, and attitudes. It does not offer in-depth explanation as to why Catholics believe or practice what they do. For an in-depth exploration of the Catholic faith, you may wish to purchase The Catholic Faith Handbook for Youth, Second Edition, by Brian Singer-Towns (Saint Mary's Press, 2008) from which the content of this section has been adapted.

Core Catholic Beliefs

- God created human beings to be in perfect union with God and one another. However, the sin of our first parents—original sin—deprived the human race of our original holiness and justice.

- Throughout human history, God worked to restore the relationship of love and trust that was lost through original sin. God did this by entering into covenants—

special relationships based on mutual promises—with Noah, Abraham and Sarah, and the people of Israel. But the people often broke their covenant promises.

- Ultimately God sent God's only begotten son, Jesus Christ, as savior for the human race. Christ was both fully God and fully man. He became the perfect sacrifice for the forgiveness of sins and the restoration of the relationship of love and trust between God and humankind.
- Following his death, Jesus was brought back to life in the Resurrection! Christ overcame death and opened heaven's gates for all the just.
- The Holy Spirit has been at work in the world from the beginning of creation to the present day. The Holy Spirit is one with the Father and the Son, and is also called the Advocate (Paraclete) and the Spirit of Truth.
- God has revealed God's self to be Trinity—that is, the mystery of one God in three divine persons: Father, Son, and Holy Spirit. This mystery cannot be arrived at by reason but was revealed by Jesus Christ.
- Christ established the Catholic Church on the foundation of the Apostles. Christ and the Holy Spirit revealed the fullness of religious truth to the Apostles. The fullness of God's revealed truth is called Sacred Tradition and is entrusted to the Apostles' successors, the bishops of the Church.
- The Bible, or the Sacred Scriptures, is another source of God's revealed truth for Catholics. The Bible is closely connected to Sacred Tradition. The Holy Spirit inspired the authors of the Bible to write what God wants us to know for our salvation.
- All people are destined for eternal life after death. The baptized who have put their faith in Jesus Christ as their savior will find their eternal reward in heaven. Those who have rejected Christ will find their eternal punishment in hell.

Core Catholic Practices

- Catholics celebrate seven sacraments that form the basis of their worship, or communal prayer, together. The seven sacraments were instituted by Christ and entrusted to the Church to make the love of God real and present in the world.
- The sacrament of the Eucharist is the heart of the Catholic Church's life. In the sacrament, Catholics literally receive the Body and Blood of Christ in the appearance of bread and wine.

"Come, Holy Spirit,
fill the hearts of your faithful."

- Sunday, or the "Lord's Day," is the principal day for the celebration of the Eucharist. Catholics keep the day holy by attending Mass and resting from work, in honor of Christ's Resurrection.
- Catholics follow a special calendar with all the feasts and holy days of the liturgical year. The special seasons of Advent and Lent prepare them to understand God's great love, which is celebrated at Christmas and Easter.
- Catholics place a strong emphasis on living morally, because they believe they are called to new life in the Holy Spirit. The moral code for this new life is based on the Ten Commandments and the Beatitudes.
- Catholics defend the dignity of human life, and Catholic morality is often described as pro-life. Catholics are opposed to anything that threatens the sanctity of human life, including abortion, euthanasia, capital punishment, and human cloning.
- Serving people in need and working to transform society are essential elements of Catholic life. The Church is called to be a sign of God's Perfect Kingdom yet to come, by working for justice and human rights in this life.
- Catholics honor the great people of faith who have preceded them: the saints, and in a dear and special way, Mary, the mother of Jesus.

Core Catholic Attitudes

- Catholics recognize that God is present to, in, and through all creation—including the natural world, persons, communities, and historical events. For Catholics all creation is sacred and has the potential to be a source of God's grace.
- Catholics place their trust in the essential goodness of the human person, who is made in the image of God, even though flawed by the effect of original sin.
- Catholics appreciate both faith and reason, both religion and science. Reason can lead to faith.
- Although the fullness of truth resides in the Catholic Church, Catholics seek to recognize and affirm the aspects of God's revealed truth that is shared with other religions and all people of good will.
- Because the human person is saved by participating in the community of faith—that is, the Church—rather than by existing as an isolated individual, Catholics emphasize community life and communal worship.
- Catholicism respects the great diversity of cultures in the world and is committed to proclaiming the message of Jesus to all people in all cultures at all times.
- Catholics respect and embrace a wide variety of spiritualities and prayer forms.

Core Catholic Spirituality and Prayers

Two Great Commandments

- "You shall love the Lord your God with all your heart, with all your soul, and all your mind, and with all your strength."
- "You shall love your neighbor as yourself."

(Mt 22:37–40, Mk 12:29–31, Lk 10:27)

Ten Commandments

1. I am the Lord your God: you shall not have strange gods before me.
2. You shall not take the name of the Lord, your God, in vain.
3. Remember to keep holy the Lord's Day.
4. Honor your father and mother.
5. You shall not kill.
6. You shall not commit adultery.
7. You shall not steal.
8. You shall not bear false witness against your neighbor.
9. You shall not covet your neighbor's wife.
10. You shall not covet your neighbor's goods.

Beatitudes

- Blessed are the poor in spirit, the kingdom of heaven is theirs.
- Blessed are they who mourn, they will be comforted.
- Blessed are the meek, they will inherit the earth.
- Blessed are they who hunger and thirst for righteousness, they will be satisfied.
- Blessed are the merciful, they will be shown mercy.
- Blessed are the clean of heart, they will see God.
- Blessed are the peacemakers, they will be called children of God.
- Blessed are they who are persecuted for the sake of righteousness, the kingdom of heaven is theirs.

Corporal Works of Mercy

- Feed the hungry.
- Give drink to the thirsty.
- Shelter the homeless.
- Clothe the naked.
- Care for the sick.
- Help the imprisoned.
- Bury the dead.

Spiritual Works of Mercy

- Share knowledge.
- Give advice to those who need it.
- Comfort those who suffer.
- Be patient with others.
- Forgive those who hurt you.
- Give correction to those who need it.
- Pray for the living and the dead.

Theological Virtues

- Faith
- Hope
- Love

Cardinal Virtues

- Prudence
- Justice
- Fortitude
- Temperance

Seven Gifts of the Holy Spirit

- Wisdom
- Understanding
- Right judgment
- Courage
- Knowledge
- Reverence
- Wonder and awe

Fruits of the Holy Spirit

- Charity
- Joy
- Peace
- Patience
- Goodness
- Kindness
- Long suffering
- Humility
- Faithfulness
- Modesty
- Continence
- Chastity

Four Marks of the Catholic Church

- One
- Holy
- Catholic
- Apostolic

Seven Sacraments

- Baptism
- Confirmation
- The Eucharist
- Penance and Reconciliation
- Anointing of the Sick
- Matrimony
- Holy Orders

Precepts of the Church

1. To keep holy the day of the Lord's Resurrection; to worship God by participating in Mass every Sunday and on the holy days of obligation; to avoid those activities that would hinder renewal of the soul and body on the Sabbath (for example, needless work or unnecessary shopping).
2. To lead a sacramental life; to receive Holy Communion frequently and the sacrament of Penance and Reconciliation regularly—minimally, to receive the sacrament of Penance and Reconciliation at least once a year (annual confession is obligatory only if serious sin is involved); minimally also, to receive Holy Communion at least once a year between the first Sunday of Lent and Trinity Sunday.
3. To study Catholic teaching in preparation for the sacrament of Confirmation, to be confirmed, and then to continue to study and advance the cause of Christ.
4. To observe the marriage laws of the Church; to give religious training, by example and word, to one's children; to use parish schools and catechetical programs.
5. To strengthen and support the Church—one's own parish community and parish priests, the worldwide Church, and the Pope.
6. To do penance, including abstaining from meat and fasting from food on the appointed days.
7. To join in the missionary spirit and apostolate (work) of the Church.

Holy Days of Obligation

- Christmas (December 25)
- Solemnity of the Blessed Virgin Mary, the Mother of God (January 1)
- Ascension of the Lord (the Sunday that follows forty days after Easter)
- Assumption of the Blessed Virgin Mary (August 15)
- All Saints (November 1)
- Immaculate Conception of the Blessed Virgin Mary (December 8)

Catholic Prayers and Devotions

Act of Contrition

My God, I am sorry for my sins
with all my heart, and I detest them.
In choosing to do wrong and failing to
do good, I have sinned against you,
whom I should love above all things.
I firmly intend, with your help,
to do penance, to sin no more,
and to avoid whatever
leads me to sin.
Our savior Jesus Christ
suffered and died for us.
In his name, my God,
have mercy.

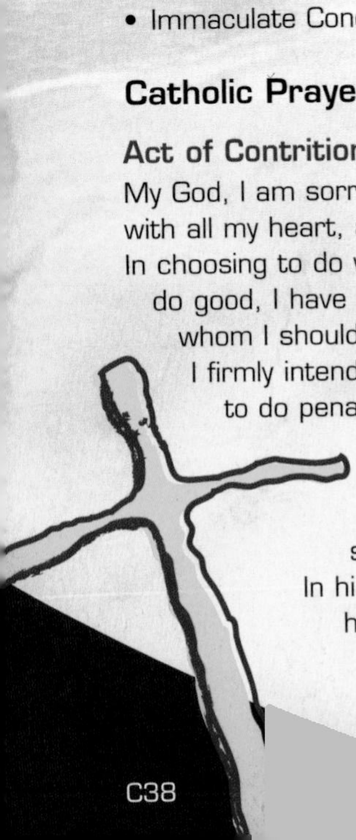

Act of Faith

My God, I firmly believe you are one God in three Divine Persons, Father, Son, and Holy Spirit.

I believe in Jesus Christ, your son, who became man and died for our sins, and who will come to judge the living and the dead.

I believe these and all the truths which the Holy Catholic Church teaches, because you have revealed them, who can neither deceive nor be deceived. Amen.

Act of Hope

O my God, trusting in your infinite goodness and promises, I hope to obtain pardon of my sins, the help of your grace, and life everlasting, through the merits of Jesus Christ, my Lord and redeemer. Amen.

Act of Love

My God, I love you above all things, with my whole heart and soul, because you are all-good and worthy of all my love. I love my neighbor as myself for love of you. I forgive all who have injured me, and I ask pardon of all whom I have injured. Amen.

Apostles' Creed

I believe in God, the Father almighty, Creator of heaven and earth, and in Jesus Christ, his only Son, our Lord, who was conceived by the Holy Spirit, born of the Virgin Mary, suffered under Pontius Pilate, was crucified, died and was buried; he descended into hell; on the third day he rose again from the dead; he ascended into heaven, and is seated at the right hand of God the Father almighty; from there he will come to judge the living and the dead.

I believe in the Holy Spirit, the holy catholic Church, the communion of saints, the forgiveness of sins, the resurrection of the body, and life everlasting. Amen.

Glory Be

Glory be to the Father, and to the Son, and to the Holy Spirit, as it was in the beginning, is now, and will be forever. Amen.

Grace After Meals

We give you thanks, almighty God,
for these and all your gifts
which we have received
through Christ our Lord. Amen.

The Lord's Prayer (also called the Our Father)

Our Father who art in heaven,
hallowed be thy name.
Thy kingdom come.
Thy will be done on earth, as it is in heaven.
Give us this day our daily bread,
and forgive us our trespasses,
as we forgive those who trespass against us,
and lead us not into temptation,
but deliver us from evil. Amen.

Grace Before Meals

Bless us, O Lord, and these your gifts,
which we are about to receive
from your bounty,
through Christ our Lord. Amen.

Hail Mary

Hail Mary, full of grace,
the Lord is with you;
blessed are you among women,
and blessed is the fruit of your womb, Jesus.

Holy Mary, Mother of God,
pray for us sinners
now and at the hour of our death.
Amen.

Mysteries of the Rosary

Joyful Mysteries

- The Annunciation
- The Visitation
- The Birth of Our Lord
- The Presentation of Jesus in the Temple
- The Finding of Jesus in the Temple

(continued on next page)

(Mysteries of the Rosary continued)

Sorrowful Mysteries

- The Agony of Jesus in the Garden
- The Scourging at the Pillar
- The Crowning of Thorns
- The Carrying of the Cross
- The Crucifixion

Glorious Mysteries

- The Resurrection of Jesus
- The Ascension of Jesus into Heaven
- The Descent of the Holy Spirit on the Apostles (Pentecost)
- The Assumption of Mary into Heaven
- The Crowning of Mary as Queen of Heaven

Luminous Mysteries

- The Baptism of Jesus
- Jesus Reveals Himself in the Miracle at Cana
- Jesus Proclaims the Good News of the Kingdom of God
- The Transfiguration of Jesus
- The Institution of the Eucharist

Prayer to the Holy Spirit

Come, Holy Spirit, fill the hearts of your faithful. Enkindle in them the fire of your love. Send forth your Spirit, and they will be created. And you will renew the face of the earth.

Let us pray:
Lord, by the light of the Holy Spirit, you have taught the hearts of the faithful. In the same Spirit, help to us relish what is right and always rejoice in your consolation.
We ask this through Christ our Lord. Amen.

Stations of the Cross

1. Jesus is condemned to death.
2. Jesus takes up his cross.
3. Jesus falls the first time.
4. Jesus meets his mother.
5. Simon helps Jesus carry the cross.
6. Veronica wipes the face of Jesus.
7. Jesus falls the second time.
8. Jesus meets the women of Jerusalem.
9. Jesus falls the third time.
10. Jesus is stripped of his garments.
11. Jesus is nailed to the cross.
12. Jesus dies on the cross.
13. Jesus is taken down from the cross.
14. Jesus is laid in the tomb.

Peter and the apostles said in reply, "We must
obey God rather than men. 30*† The God of our
ancestors raised Jesus, though you had him killed
by hanging him on a tree. 31*† God exalted him
at his right hand as leader and savior to grant
Israel repentance and forgiveness of sins. 32* We
are witnesses of these things, as is the holy Spirit
that God has given to those who obey him."
33 When they heard this, they became infuri-
ated and wanted to put them to death. 34*† But
a Pharisee in the Sanhedrin named Gamaliel, a
teacher of the law, respected by all the people,
stood up, ordered the men to be put outside for a
short time, 35 and said to them, "Fellow Israelites,
be careful what you are about to do to these men.
36† Some time ago, Theudas appeared, claiming
to be someone important, and about four hun-
dred men joined him, but he was killed, and all
those who were loyal to him were disbanded
and came to nothing. 37 After him came Judas
the Galilean at the time of the census. He also
drew people after him, but he too perished and
all who were loyal to him were scattered. 38 So
now I tell you, have nothing to do with these
men, and let them go. For if this endeavor or this
activity is of human origin, it will destroy itself.
39 But if it comes from God, you will not be able
to destroy them; you may even find yourselves
fighting against God." They were persuaded by
him. 40* After recalling the apostles, they had
them flogged, ordered them to stop speaking in
the name of Jesus, and dismissed them. 41* So
they left the presence of the Sanhedrin, rejoicing
that they had been found worthy to suffer dis-
honor for the sake of the name. 42* And all day
long, both at the temple and in their homes,
they did not stop teaching and proclaiming the
Messiah, Jesus.

The Need for Assistants

6 1*† At that time, as the number of dis-
ciples continued to grow, the Hellenists
complained against the Hebrews because their
widows were being neglected in the daily dis-
tribution. 2† So the Twelve called together the
community of the disciples and said, "It is not
right for us to neglect the word of God to serve
at table.† 3 Brothers, select from among you
seven reputable men, filled with the Spirit and
wisdom, whom we shall appoint to this task,
4 whereas we shall devote ourselves to prayer
and to the ministry of the word." 5 The proposal
was acceptable to the whole community, so they
chose Stephen, a man filled with faith and the
holy Spirit, also Philip, Prochorus, Nicanor, Ti-
mon, Parmenas, and Nicholas of Antioch, a con-
vert to Judaism. 6*† They presented these men to
the apostles who prayed and laid hands on them.
7* The word of God continued to spread, and the
number of the disciples in Jerusalem increased
greatly; even a large group of priests were becom-
ing obedient to the faith.

Accusation against Stephen

8† Now Stephen, filled with grace and
power, was working great wonders and signs

5:30 *Hanging him on a tree:* that is, crucifying him (cf also Gal 3:13).

5:31 *At his right hand:* see the note on 2:33.

5:34 *Gamaliel:* in 22:3, Paul identifies himself as a disciple of this Rabbi Gamaliel I who flourished in Jerusalem between A.D. 25 and 50.

5:36–37 Gamaliel offers examples of unsuccessful contemporary movements to argue that if God is not the origin of this movement preached by the apostles it will perish by itself. The movement initiated by Theudas actually occurred when C. Cuspius Fadus was governor, A.D. 44–46. Luke's placing of Judas the Galilean after Theudas and at the time of the census (see the note on Lk 2:1–2) is an indication of the vagueness of his knowledge of these events.

6:1–7 *The Hellenists . . . the Hebrews:* the Hellenists were not necessarily Jews from the diaspora, but were more probably Palestinian Jews who spoke only Greek. The Hebrews were Palestinian Jews who spoke Hebrew or Aramaic and who may also have spoken Greek. Both groups belong to the Jerusalem Jewish Christian community. The conflict between them leads to a restructuring of the community that will better serve the community's needs. The real purpose of the whole episode, however, is to introduce Stephen as a prominent figure in the community whose long speech and martyrdom will be recounted in ch 7.

6:2–4 The essential function of the Twelve is the "service of the word," including development of the kerygma by formulation of the teachings of Jesus.

6:2 *To serve at table:* some commentators think that it is not the serving of food that is described here but rather the keeping of the accounts that recorded the distribution of food to the needy members of the community. In any case, after Stephen and the others are chosen, they are never presented carrying out the task for which they were appointed (2–3). Rather, two of their number, Stephen and Philip, are presented as preachers of the Christian message. They, the Hellenist counterpart of the Twelve, are active in the ministry of the word.

6:6 *They . . . laid hands on them:* the customary Jewish way of designating persons for a task and invoking upon them the divine blessing and power to perform it.

6:8—8:1 The summary (6:7) on the progress of the Jerusalem community, illustrated by the conversion of the priests, is followed by a lengthy narrative regarding Stephen. Stephen's defense is not a response to the charges made against him but takes the form of a discourse that reviews the fortunes of God's word to Israel and leads to a prophetic declaration: a plea for the hearing of that word as announced by Christ and now possessed by the Christian community. The charges that Stephen depreciated the importance of the temple and the Mosaic law and elevated Jesus to a stature above Moses (6:13–14) were in fact true. Before the Sanhedrin, no defense against them was possible. With Stephen, who thus perceived the fuller implications of the teachings of Jesus, the differences between Judaism and Christianity began to appear. Luke's account of Stephen's martyrdom and its aftermath shows how the major impetus behind the Christian movement passed from Jerusalem, where the temple and law prevailed, to Antioch in Syria, where these influences were less pressing.

5:30 Acts 2:23–24.
5:31 Acts 2:38.
5:32 Lk 24:48; Jn 15:26.
5:34 Acts 22:3.
5:40 Mt 10:17; Acts 4:17–18.
5:41 Mt 5:10–11; 1 Pt 4:13.
5:42 Acts 2:46; 5:20–21, 25; 8:35; 17:3; 18:5, 28; 19:4–5.
6:1 Acts 2:45; 4:34–35.
6:6 Acts 1:24; 13:3; 14:23.
6:7 Acts 9:31; 12:24; 16:5; 19:20; 28:30–31.

Cultural Connection

Don't Forget the Shoulders You Stand On

Take a few minutes to read about the martyrdom of Stephen, in Acts of the Apostles 6:8—7:60. There is perhaps no more touching story in the New Testament than this young man's brave defense of his faith as he followed in his Lord's footsteps. He knew his history and his ancestors, and they gave him divine courage in the face of death.

People of all ages and cultures need to respect and honor the faith and sacrifices of their ancestors. For example, the *Eyes on the Prize* video series is a reminder for all Americans of the debt owed to African Americans of a previous generation. This documentation of the civil rights movement immortalizes the faith of countless people who were brave enough to protest the injustice of racism.

Today is a gift from them. Somebody died so that all Americans might live freely. Somebody suffered so that all Americans could enjoy civil rights. Somebody accepted persecution to call all Americans to respect God's justice.

How many youth today would be willing to make similar sacrifices in the struggle for freedom and equality—signs of the Reign of God?

Dear God, help me to treasure my ancestors' sacrifice and bravery. Help me to follow their example in working for justice with love and courage. Amen.

▶ Acts 6:8—7:60

among the people. 9 Certain members of the
so-called Synagogue of Freedmen, Cyrenians,
and Alexandrians, and people from Cilicia
and Asia, came forward and debated with Ste-
phen, 10* but they could not withstand the
wisdom and the spirit with which he spoke.
11* Then they instigated some men to say, "We
have heard him speaking blasphemous words
against Moses and God." 12 They stirred up the
people, the elders, and the scribes, accosted
him, seized him, and brought him before the
Sanhedrin. 13† They presented false witnesses
who testified, "This man never stops saying
things against [this] holy place and the law.
14* For we have heard him claim that this
Jesus the Nazorean will destroy this place and
change the customs that Moses handed down
to us." 15 All those who sat in the Sanhedrin
looked intently at him and saw that his face
was like the face of an angel.

Stephen's Discourses

7 1 Then the high priest asked, "Is this so?"
2*† And he replied, "My brothers and fathers,
listen. The God of glory appeared to our father
Abraham while he was in Mesopotamia,† before
he had settled in Haran, 3* and said to him, 'Go
forth from your land and [from] your kinsfolk
to the land that I will show you.' 4* So he went
forth from the land of the Chaldeans and settled
in Haran. And from there, after his father died,
he made him migrate to this land where you
now dwell. 5* Yet he gave him no inheritance in
it, not even a foot's length, but he did promise
to give it to him and his descendants as a posses-
sion, even though he was childless. 6* And God
spoke thus, 'His descendants shall be aliens in a
land not their own, where they shall be enslaved
and oppressed for four hundred years; 7* but I
will bring judgment on the nation they serve,'

†

6:13 *False witnesses:* here, and in his account of Stephen's execution (7:54–60), Luke parallels the martyrdom of Stephen with the death of Jesus.

7:2–53 Stephen's speech represents Luke's description of Christianity's break from its Jewish matrix. Two motifs become prominent in the speech: (1) Israel's reaction to God's chosen leaders in the past reveals that the people have consistently rejected them; and (2) Israel has misunderstood God's choice of the Jerusalem temple as the place where he is to be worshiped.

7:2 *God . . . appeared to our father Abraham . . . in Mesopotamia:* the first of a number of minor discrepancies between the data of the Old Testament and the data of Stephen's discourse. According to Gn 12:1, God first spoke to Abraham in Haran. The main discrepancies are these: in v 16 it is said that Jacob was buried in Shechem, whereas Gn 50:13 says he was buried at Hebron; in the same verse it is said that the tomb was purchased by Abraham, but in Gn 33:19 and Jos 24:32 the purchase is attributed to Jacob himself.

*

6:10 Lk 21:15.
6:11 Mt 26:59–61; Mk 14:55–58; Acts 21:21.
6:14 Mt 26:59–61; 27:40; Jn 2:19.
7:2 Gn 11:31; 12:1; Ps 29:3.
7:3 Gn 12:1.
7:4 Gn 12:5; 15:7.
7:5 Gn 12:7; 13:15; 15:2; 16:1; Dt 2:5.
7:6–7 Gn 15:13–14.
7:7 Ex 3:12.

God said, 'and after that they will come out and worship me in this place.' 8* Then he gave him the covenant of circumcision, and so he became the father of Isaac, and circumcised him on the eighth day, as Isaac did Jacob, and Jacob the twelve patriarchs.

9* "And the patriarchs, jealous of Joseph, sold him into slavery in Egypt; but God was with him 10* and rescued him from all his afflictions. He granted him favor and wisdom before Pharaoh, the king of Egypt, who put him in charge of Egypt and [of] his entire household. 11* Then a famine and great affliction struck all Egypt and Canaan, and our ancestors could find no food; 12* but when Jacob heard that there was grain in Egypt, he sent our ancestors there a first time. 13* The second time, Joseph made himself known to his brothers, and Joseph's family became known to Pharaoh. 14* Then Joseph sent for his father Jacob, inviting him and his whole clan, seventy-five persons; 15* and Jacob went down to Egypt. And he and our ancestors died 16* and were brought back to Shechem and placed in the tomb that Abraham had purchased for a sum of money from the sons of Hamor at Shechem.

17* "When the time drew near for the fulfillment of the promise that God pledged to Abraham, the people had increased and become very numerous in Egypt, 18* until another king who knew nothing of Joseph came to power [in Egypt]. 19 He dealt shrewdly with our people and oppressed [our] ancestors by forcing them to expose their infants, that they might not survive. 20* At this time Moses was born, and he was extremely beautiful. For three months he was nursed in his father's house; 21* but when he was exposed, Pharaoh's daughter adopted him and brought him up as her own son. 22 Moses was educated [in] all the wisdom of the Egyptians and was powerful in his words and deeds.

23* "When he was forty years old, he decided to visit his kinsfolk, the Israelites. 24 When he saw one of them treated unjustly, he defended and avenged the oppressed man by striking down the Egyptian. 25 He assumed [his] kinsfolk would understand that God was offering them deliverance through him, but they did not understand. 26* The next day he appeared to them as they were fighting and tried to reconcile them peacefully, saying, 'Men, you are brothers. Why are you harming one another?' 27 Then the one who was harming his neighbor pushed him aside, saying, 'Who appointed you ruler and judge over us? 28 Are you thinking of killing me as you killed the Egyptian yesterday?' 29* Moses fled when he heard this and settled as an alien in the

Did You Know?

Martyrs

The stoning of Stephen is a turning point in Luke's account of the first Christians. Symbolically, Stephen marks the beginning of the phenomenon of martyrdom—dying for one's faith—but historically, we don't actually know that he was the first martyr. Luke makes it clear that Stephen's death, rather than causing the Christian movement to fall apart now that the stakes were higher, actually strengthened the Church. His heroic sacrifice is even presented as a model for Christians—notice all the similarities between his death and Jesus'.

It is easy for North Americans to assume that religious persecution does not exist today. We do not normally hear stories of people being killed for their beliefs in Jesus or Christianity. Not so for people on other continents. All around the world, including places close to home, people are mistreated, and even killed, because of their religious beliefs.

For example, Archbishop Oscar Romero of El Salvador was shot to death because he challenged the wealthy and powerful people in his country to change their ways so the poor people could have a better quality of life. Archbishop Romero, like Stephen, was killed for being a faithful Christian.

Stephen was convinced that following the teachings of Jesus was the most important way to live. He died for his beliefs, and the Church became stronger because of his faith and heroism. What would you die for?

▶ Acts 6:8—8:1

7:8 Gn 17:10–14; 21:2–4.
7:9 Gn 37:11, 28; 39:2, 3, 21, 23.
7:10 Gn 41:37–43; Ps 105:21; Wis 10:13–14.
7:11 Gn 41:54–57; 42:5.
7:12 Gn 42:1–2.
7:13 Gn 45:3–4, 16.
7:14 Gn 45:9–11, 18–19; 46:27; Ex 1:5 LXX; Dt 10:22.
7:15 Gn 46:5–6; 49:33.
7:16 Gn 23:3–20; 33:19; 49:29–30; 50:13; Jos 24:32.
7:17 Ex 1:7.
7:18 Ex 1:8.
7:20 Ex 2:2; Heb 11:23.
7:21 Ex 2:3–10.
7:23–24 Ex 2:11–12.
7:26–28 Ex 2:13–14.
7:29 Ex 2:15, 21–22; 18:3–4.

land of Midian, where he became the father of two sons.

30* "Forty years later, an angel appeared to him in the desert near Mount Sinai in the flame of a burning bush. 31 When Moses saw it, he was amazed at the sight, and as he drew near to look at it, the voice of the Lord came, 32 'I am the God of your fathers, the God of Abraham, of Isaac, and of Jacob.' Then Moses, trembling, did not dare to look at it. 33 But the Lord said to him, 'Remove the sandals from your feet, for the place where you stand is holy ground. 34 I have witnessed the affliction of my people in Egypt and have heard their groaning, and I have come down to rescue them. Come now, I will send you to Egypt.' 35* This Moses, whom they had rejected with the words, 'Who appointed you ruler and judge?' God sent as [both] ruler and deliverer, through the angel who appeared to him in the bush. 36* This man led them out, performing wonders and signs in the land of Egypt, at the Red Sea, and in the desert for forty years. 37* It was this Moses who said to the Israelites, 'God will raise up for you, from among your own kinsfolk, a prophet like me.' 38* It was he who, in the assembly in the desert, was with the angel who spoke to him on Mount Sinai and with our ancestors, and he received living utterances to hand on to us.

39* "Our ancestors were unwilling to obey him; instead, they pushed him aside and in their hearts turned back to Egypt, 40* saying to Aaron, 'Make us gods who will be our leaders. As for that Moses who led us out of the land of Egypt, we do not know what has happened to him.' 41* So they made a calf in those days, offered sacrifice to the idol, and reveled in the works of their hands. 42* Then God turned and handed them over to worship the host of heaven, as it is written in the book of the prophets:

'Did you bring me sacrifices and offerings
for forty years in the desert, O house of Israel?*
43 No, you took up the tent of Moloch
and the star of [your] god Rephan,
the images that you made to worship.
So I shall take you into exile beyond Babylon.'

44* Our ancestors had the tent of testimony in the desert just as the One who spoke to Moses directed him to make it according to the pattern he had seen. 45* Our ancestors who inherited it brought it with Joshua when they dispossessed the nations that God drove out from before our ancestors, up to the time of David, 46* who found favor in the sight of God and asked that he might find a dwelling place for the house of Jacob. 47* But Solomon built a house for him. 48* Yet the Most High does not dwell in houses made by human hands. As the prophet says:

49* 'The heavens are my throne,
the earth is my footstool.
What kind of house can you build for me?
says the Lord,
or what is to be my resting place?
50 Did not my hand make all these things?'

Conclusion

51 "You stiff-necked people, uncircumcised in heart and ears, you always oppose the holy Spirit; you are just like your ancestors. 52* Which of the prophets did your ancestors not persecute? They put to death those who foretold the coming of the righteous one, whose betrayers and murderers you have now become. 53* You received the law as transmitted by angels, but you did not observe it."

Stephen's Martyrdom

54 When they heard this, they were infuriated, and they ground their teeth at him. 55*† But he, filled with the holy Spirit, looked up intently to heaven and saw the glory of God and Jesus standing at the right hand of God, 56 and he said, "Behold, I see the heavens opened and the Son of Man standing at the right hand of God." 57† But they cried out in a loud voice, covered their ears, and rushed upon him together. 58* They threw him out of the city, and began to stone him. The witnesses laid down their cloaks at the feet of a young man named Saul. 59*† As they were

†

7:55 *He . . . saw . . . Jesus standing at the right hand of God:* Stephen affirms to the Sanhedrin that the prophecy Jesus made before them has been fulfilled (Mk 14:62).

7:57 *Covered their ears:* Stephen's declaration, like that of Jesus, is a scandal to the court, which regards it as blasphemy.

7:59 Compare Lk 23:[34], 46.

*

7:30–34 Ex 3:2–3.
7:35 Ex 2:14.
7:36 Ex 7:3, 10; 14:21; Nm 14:33.
7:37 Dt 18:15; Acts 3:22.
7:38 Ex 19:3; 20:1–17; Dt 5:4–22; 6:4–25.
7:39 Nm 14:3.
7:40 Ex 32:1, 23.
7:41 Ex 32:4–6.
7:42–43 Am 5:25–27.
7:42 Jer 7:18; 8:2; 19:13.
7:44 Ex 25:9, 40.
7:45 Jos 3:14–17; 18:1; 2 Sm 7:5–7.
7:46 2 Sm 7:1–2; 1 Kgs 8:17; Ps 132:1–5.
7:47 1 Kgs 6:1; 1 Chr 17:12.
7:48 Acts 17:24.
7:49 Is 66:1–2.
7:52 2 Chr 36:16; Mt 23:31, 34.
7:53 Gal 3:19; Heb 2:2.
7:55–56 Mt 26:64; Mk 14:62; Lk 22:69; Acts 2:34.
7:58 Acts 22:20.
7:59 Ps 31:6; Lk 23:46.

stoning Stephen, he called out, "Lord Jesus, re-
ceive my spirit." 60* Then he fell to his knees and
cried out in a loud voice, "Lord, do not hold this
sin against them"; and when he said this, he fell
asleep.

8 1*† Now Saul was consenting to his execu-
tion.

Persecution of the Church

On that day, there broke out a severe perse-
cution of the church in Jerusalem, and all were
scattered throughout the countryside of Judea
and Samaria, except the apostles.† 2 Devout men
buried Stephen and made a loud lament over
him. 3*† Saul, meanwhile, was trying to destroy
the church; entering house after house and drag-
ging out men and women, he handed them over
for imprisonment.

III: The Mission in Judea and Samaria

Philip in Samaria

4* Now those who had been scattered went
about preaching the word. 5* Thus Philip went
down to [the] city of Samaria and proclaimed
the Messiah to them. 6 With one accord, the
crowds paid attention to what was said by Philip
when they heard it and saw the signs he was do-
ing. 7* For unclean spirits, crying out in a loud
voice, came out of many possessed people, and
many paralyzed and crippled people were cured.
8 There was great joy in that city.

†

8:1–40 Some idea of the severity of the persecution that now breaks out against the Jerusalem community can be gathered from 22:4 and 26:9–11. Luke, however, concentrates on the fortunes of the word of God among people, indicating how the dispersal of the Jewish community resulted in the conversion of the Samaritans (4–17, 25). His narrative is further expanded to include the account of Philip's acceptance of an Ethiopian (26–39).

8:1 *All were scattered . . . except the apostles:* this observation leads some modern scholars to conclude that the persecution was limited to the Hellenist Christians and that the Hebrew Christians were not molested, perhaps because their attitude toward the law and temple was still more in line with that of their fellow Jews (see the charge leveled against the Hellenist Stephen in 6:13–14). Whatever the facts, it appears that the Twelve took no public stand regarding Stephen's position, choosing, instead, to await the development of events.

8:3 *Saul . . . was trying to destroy the church:* like Stephen, Saul was able to perceive that the Christian movement contained the seeds of doctrinal divergence from Judaism. A pupil of Gamaliel, according to 22:3, and totally dedicated to the law as the way of salvation (Gal 1:13–14), Saul accepted the task of crushing the Christian movement, at least insofar as it detracted from the importance of the temple and the law. His vehement opposition to Christianity reveals how difficult it was for a Jew of his time to accept a messianism that differed so greatly from the general expectation.

*

7:60 Mt 27:46, 50; Mk 15:34; Lk 23:46.
8:1 Acts 22:20.
8:3 Acts 9:1, 13; 22:4; 26:9–11; 1 Cor 5:9; Gal 1:13.
8:4 Acts 11:19.
8:5 Acts 6:5; 21:8–9.
8:7 Mk 16:17.

Introducing...

Saint Paul

As Stephen is stoned to death, Acts of the Apostles introduces a person who will become the major character in the second half of the book, Saul of Tarsus, also known as Paul. Paul begins as a persecutor of the early Christians. He is a member of the Pharisees, a group that holds to a rigid interpretation of Jewish Law (see Acts 26:4–5). He probably sees the Christians as a threat to the Jewish faith. But after a profound experience of the risen Christ, Paul is converted to the Christian faith. Paul is initially distrusted by other Christians who remember his persecution of them. However, another early Christian leader, Barnabas, becomes Paul's companion and advocate (see 9:27).

Paul's major insight is that God has made salvation available to everyone, Jews and Gentiles alike. He also knows that God's offer of salvation is a free gift, that no one could do anything to actually earn it. But many of the early Christians, who are former Jews, disagree with him. This conflict comes to a head at the Council of Jerusalem (see Acts of the Apostles, chapter 15), where Paul stands toe to toe with Peter and James (see Gal 2:1–10) and argues that the Gentiles can become Christians without following Jewish laws and customs, including circumcision.

Paul took it upon himself to spread the Good News of God's salvation in Jesus to the Gentiles. During three different missionary journeys, he was instrumental in founding new Christian communities in what is now the Middle East and Western Europe. He stayed in touch with those communities through letters, some of which are included as books in the New Testament. Paul's impact in spreading Christianity was so great that he is sometimes called the second founder of Christianity.

▶ **Acts 8:1–3**

Chapter 8

Early Christian symbols representing Jesus Christ

Simon the Magician

9† A man named Simon used to practice magic
in the city and astounded the people of Samar-
ia, claiming to be someone great. 10 All of them,
from the least to the greatest, paid attention to
him, saying, "This man is the 'Power of God' that
is called 'Great.' " 11 They paid attention to him
because he had astounded them by his magic for
a long time, 12* but once they began to believe
Philip as he preached the good news about the
kingdom of God and the name of Jesus Christ,
men and women alike were baptized. 13 Even Si-
mon himself believed and, after being baptized,
became devoted to Philip; and when he saw the
signs and mighty deeds that were occurring, he
was astounded.

14 Now when the apostles in Jerusalem heard
that Samaria had accepted the word of God, they
sent them Peter and John, 15 who went down and
prayed for them, that they might receive the holy
Spirit, 16† for it had not yet fallen upon any of
them; they had only been baptized in the name
of the Lord Jesus. 17* Then they laid hands on
them and they received the holy Spirit.

18† When Simon saw that the Spirit was con-
ferred by the laying on of the apostles' hands, he
offered them money 19 and said, "Give me this
power too, so that anyone upon whom I lay my
hands may receive the holy Spirit." 20 But Peter said
to him, "May your money perish with you, because
you thought that you could buy the gift of God with
money. 21 You have no share or lot in this matter,
for your heart is not upright before God. 22 Repent
of this wickedness of yours and pray to the Lord
that, if possible, your intention may be forgiven.
23 For I see that you are filled with bitter gall and are
in the bonds of iniquity." 24 Simon said in reply,
"Pray for me to the Lord, that nothing of what you
have said may come upon me." 25 So when they
had testified and proclaimed the word of the Lord,
they returned to Jerusalem and preached the good
news to many Samaritan villages.

Philip and the Ethiopian

26† Then the angel of the Lord spoke to Philip,
"Get up and head south on the road that goes
down from Jerusalem to Gaza, the desert route."
27*† So he got up and set out. Now there was an
Ethiopian eunuch, a court official of the Candace,
that is, the queen of the Ethiopians, in charge of
her entire treasury, who had come to Jerusalem
to worship, 28 and was returning home. Seated in
his chariot, he was reading the prophet Isaiah.
29 The Spirit said to Philip, "Go and join up with
that chariot." 30† Philip ran up and heard him
reading Isaiah the prophet and said, "Do you un-
derstand what you are reading?" 31* He replied,
"How can I, unless someone instructs me?" So he
invited Philip to get in and sit with him. 32* This
was the scripture passage he was reading:

8:9–13, 18–24 Sorcerers were well known in the ancient world. Probably the incident involving Simon and his altercation with Peter is introduced to show that the miraculous charisms possessed by members of the Christian community (6–7) were not to be confused with the magic of sorcerers.

8:16 Here and in 10:44–48 and 19:1–6, Luke distinguishes between baptism in the name of the Lord Jesus and the reception of the Spirit. In each case, the Spirit is conferred through members of the Twelve (Peter and John) or their representative (Paul). This may be Luke's way of describing the role of the church in the bestowal of the Spirit. Elsewhere in Acts, baptism and the Spirit are more closely related (1:5; 11:16).

8:18–20 Simon attempts to buy the gift of God (20) with money. Peter's cursing of Simon's attempt so to use his money expresses a typically Lucan attitude toward material wealth (cf Lk 6:24; 12:16–21; 16:13).

8:26–40 In the account of the conversion of the Ethiopian eunuch, Luke adduces additional evidence to show that the spread of Christianity outside the confines of Judaism itself was in accord with the plan of God. He does not make clear whether the Ethiopian was originally a convert to Judaism or, as is more probable, a "God-fearer" (10:1), i.e., one who accepted Jewish monotheism and ethic and attended the synagogue but did not consider himself bound by other regulations such as circumcision and observance of the dietary laws. The story of his conversion to Christianity is given a strong supernatural cast by the introduction of an angel (26), instruction from the holy Spirit (29), and the strange removal of Philip from the scene (39).

8:27 *The Candace:* Candace is not a proper name here but the title of a Nubian queen.

8:30–34 Philip is brought alongside the carriage at the very moment when the Ethiopian is pondering the meaning of Is 53:7–8, a passage that Christianity, from its earliest origins, has applied to Jesus; cf the note on 3:13.

8:12 Acts 1:3; 19:8; 28:23, 31.
8:17 Acts 2:4; 4:31; 10:44–47; 15:8–9; 19:2, 6.
8:27 Is 56:3–5.
8:31 Jn 16:13.
8:32–33 Is 53:7–8 LXX.

"Like a sheep he was led to the slaughter,
and as a lamb before its shearer is silent,
so he opened not his mouth.
33 In [his] humiliation justice was denied him.
Who will tell of his posterity?
For his life is taken from the earth."

34 Then the eunuch said to Philip in reply, "I beg
you, about whom is the prophet saying this?
About himself, or about someone else?" 35 Then
Philip opened his mouth and, beginning with
this scripture passage, he proclaimed Jesus to him.
36* As they traveled along the road they came to
some water, and the eunuch said, "Look, there is
water. What is to prevent my being baptized?"
[37]† 38 Then he ordered the chariot to stop, and
Philip and the eunuch both went down into the
water, and he baptized him. 39* When they came
out of the water, the Spirit of the Lord snatched
Philip away, and the eunuch saw him no more,
but continued on his way rejoicing. 40* Philip
came to Azotus, and went about proclaiming
the good news to all the towns until he reached
Caesarea.

Saul's Conversion

9 1*† Now Saul, still breathing murderous
threats against the disciples of the Lord, went
to the high priest* 2† and asked him for letters to
the synagogues in Damascus, that, if he should
find any men or women who belonged to the
Way, he might bring them back to Jerusalem
in chains. 3* On his journey, as he was nearing
Damascus, a light from the sky suddenly flashed
around him. 4* He fell to the ground and heard
a voice saying to him, "Saul, Saul, why are you
persecuting me?" 5* He said, "Who are you, sir?"
The reply came, "I am Jesus, whom you are perse-
cuting. 6* Now get up and go into the city and you
will be told what you must do." 7* The men who
were traveling with him stood speechless, for they
heard the voice but could see no one. 8*† Saul got
up from the ground, but when he opened his eyes
he could see nothing; so they led him by the hand

Live It!

Bearing Good News

Acts of the Apostles 8:26–40 tells the story of an Ethiopian (African) eunuch. A eunuch is a man who has been castrated, either by accident or by design. Eunuchs often served as guards of the harems of kings. This eunuch was reading a text from Isaiah while returning from a visit to Jerusalem. The Holy Spirit moved the missionary Philip to explain to him how Isaiah's prophecies pointed to Jesus. And the eunuch believed and was baptized. From a cultural point of view, this story is significant because the eunuch was presumably African.

The eunuch's faith was dependent on the interaction of three characters: himself, the searching eunuch; Philip, bearing the Good News; and the Holy Spirit, who brought them together. Reflect for a moment on the following questions:

- How are you like the Ethiopian? What are you searching for in your faith?
- How are you like Philip? How do you share the Good News with others?
- How can you share in the work of the Holy Spirit? How can you motivate other young people to become bearers of the Good News?

As Philip baptized the eunuch, geographical, ethnic, and legal barriers were washed away. Praise God for the salvation brought by Jesus to all people!

Acts 8:26–40

†

8:37 The oldest and best manuscripts of Acts omit this verse, which is a Western text reading: "And Philip said, 'If you believe with all your heart, you may.' And he said in reply, 'I believe that Jesus Christ is the Son of God.' "

9:1–19 This is the first of three accounts of Paul's conversion (with 22:3–16 and 26:2–18) with some differences of detail owing to Luke's use of different sources. Paul's experience was not visionary but was precipitated by the appearance of Jesus, as he insists in 1 Cor 15:8. The words of Jesus, "Saul, Saul, why are you persecuting me?" related by Luke with no variation in all three accounts, exerted a profound and lasting influence on the thought of Paul. Under the influence of this experience he gradually developed his understanding of justification by faith (see the letters to the Galatians and Romans) and of the identification of the Christian community with Jesus Christ (see 1 Cor 12:27). That Luke would narrate this conversion three times is testimony to the importance he attaches to it. This first account occurs when the word is first spread to the Gentiles. At this point, the conversion of the hero of the Gentile mission is recounted. The emphasis in the account is on Paul as a divinely chosen instrument (15).

9:2 *The Way:* a name used by the early Christian community for itself (18:26; 19:9, 23; 22:4; 24:14, 22). The Essene community at Qumran used the same designation to describe its mode of life.

9:8 *He could see nothing:* a temporary blindness (18) symbolizing the religious blindness of Saul as persecutor (cf 26:18).

*

8:36 Acts 10:47.
8:39 1 Kgs 18:12.
8:40 Acts 21:8.
9:1 Acts 8:3; 9:13; 22:4; 1 Cor 15:9; Gal 1:13–14.
9:1–2 Acts 9:14; 26:10.
9:3 1 Cor 9:1; 15:8; Gal 1:16.
9:4 Acts 22:6; 26:14.
9:5 Acts 22:8; 26:15; Mt 25:40.
9:6 Acts 22:10; 26:16.
9:7 Acts 22:9; 26:13–14.
9:8 Acts 22:11.

ACTS

Pray It!

Conversion

Saul (or Paul) experienced some dramatic events that converted him from a persecutor of Christians to a believer in Jesus Christ. He had a powerful experience of the risen Christ during which he was blinded. His physical blindness is symbolic of his previous spiritual blindness. For three days, Paul was practically lifeless—not seeing, not eating, not drinking. This period reminds us of Jesus' three days in the tomb. In many ways, going through a conversion is like dying—dying to old ways of thinking and acting. But after three days, Paul's blindness was lifted, and he was filled with the Holy Spirit.

No longer a persecutor of Christians, Paul was a new person. He now felt compelled to learn more about Jesus and to share the Good News with other people. Paul's change told the early Christians that even the most unlikely person can be called by God and radically changed.

In our own lives, conversions can also happen in more subtle, ordinary ways. Sometimes, in the midst of our days, we come to a new realization about how we should live as Jesus did, or how we might be kinder to others or sacrifice some of our needs to help someone else—even when that may seem difficult.

In your prayer, reflect or journal on the following questions:

- Have you ever been suddenly aware of God's presence and calling in your life?
- What plans do you think God might have for your life?
- How will you respond?

Then close with these words:

Dear Jesus, following you is a lifelong journey where we come to learn more about how we can follow your ways. Sometimes, it is an easy journey; sometimes, it is a struggle. Help me to be open to your light in the Scriptures, in others, and within myself.
Amen.

Acts 9:1–19

and brought him to Damascus. [9] For three days he
was unable to see, and he neither ate nor drank.

Saul's Baptism

[10]* There was a disciple in Damascus named
Ananias, and the Lord said to him in a vision, "An-
anias." He answered, "Here I am, Lord." [11]* The
Lord said to him, "Get up and go to the street
called Straight and ask at the house of Judas for
a man from Tarsus named Saul. He is there pray-
ing, [12] and [in a vision] he has seen a man named
Ananias come in and lay [his] hands on him,
that he may regain his sight." [13]*† But Ananias
replied, "Lord, I have heard from many sources
about this man, what evil things he has done to
your holy ones in Jerusalem. [14]* And here he has
authority from the chief priests to imprison all
who call upon your name." [15]* But the Lord said
to him, "Go, for this man is a chosen instrument
of mine to carry my name before Gentiles, kings,
and Israelites, [16] and I will show him what he will
have to suffer for my name." [17] So Ananias went
and entered the house; laying his hands on him,
he said, "Saul, my brother, the Lord has sent me,
Jesus who appeared to you on the way by which
you came, that you may regain your sight and be
filled with the holy Spirit." [18] Immediately things
like scales fell from his eyes and he regained his
sight. He got up and was baptized, [19]† and when
he had eaten, he recovered his strength.

Saul Preaches in Damascus

He stayed some days with the disciples in Da-
mascus, [20]† and he began at once to proclaim
Jesus in the synagogues, that he is the Son of
God. [21] All who heard him were astounded and
said, "Is not this the man who in Jerusalem rav-
aged those who call upon this name, and came
here expressly to take them back in chains to the
chief priests?" [22] But Saul grew all the stronger
and confounded [the] Jews who lived in Damas-
cus, proving that this is the Messiah.

Saul Visits Jerusalem

[23] After a long time had passed, the Jews con-
spired to kill him, [24]* but their plot became

9:13 *Your holy ones:* literally, "your saints."

9:19–30 This is a brief resume of Paul's initial experience as an apostolic preacher. At first he found himself in the position of being regarded as an apostate by the Jews and suspect by the Christian community of Jerusalem. His acceptance by the latter was finally brought about through his friendship with Barnabas (27).

9:20 *Son of God:* the title "Son of God" occurs in Acts only here, but cf the citation of Ps 2:7 in Paul's speech at Antioch in Pisidia (13:33).

9:10–19 Acts 22:12–16.
9:11 Acts 21:39.
9:13 Acts 8:3; 9:1.
9:14 Acts 9:1–2; 26:10; 1 Cor 1:2; 2 Tm 2:22.
9:15 Acts 22:15; 26:1; 27:24.
9:24–25 2 Cor 11:32–33.

known to Saul. Now they were keeping watch on the gates day and night so as to kill him, 25 but his disciples took him one night and let him down through an opening in the wall, lowering him in a basket.

26*† When he arrived in Jerusalem he tried to join the disciples, but they were all afraid of him, not believing that he was a disciple. 27 Then Barnabas took charge of him and brought him to the apostles, and he reported to them how on the way he had seen the Lord and that he had spoken to him, and how in Damascus he had spoken out boldly in the name of Jesus. 28 He moved about freely with them in Jerusalem, and spoke out boldly in the name of the Lord. 29† He also spoke and debated with the Hellenists, but they tried to kill him. 30* And when the brothers learned of this, they took him down to Caesarea and sent him on his way to Tarsus.

The Church at Peace

31† The church throughout all Judea, Galilee, and Samaria was at peace. It was being built up and walked in the fear of the Lord, and with the consolation of the holy Spirit it grew in numbers.

Peter Heals Aeneas at Lydda

32 As Peter was passing through every region, he went down to the holy ones living in Lydda. 33 There he found a man named Aeneas, who had been confined to bed for eight years, for he was paralyzed. 34 Peter said to him, "Aeneas, Jesus Christ heals you. Get up and make your bed." He got up at once. 35 And all the inhabitants of Lydda and Sharon saw him, and they turned to the Lord.

Peter Restores Tabitha to Life

36† Now in Joppa there was a disciple named Tabitha (which translated means Dorcas). She was completely occupied with good deeds and almsgiving. 37 Now during those days she fell sick and died, so after washing her, they laid [her] out in a room upstairs. 38 Since Lydda was near Joppa, the disciples, hearing that Peter was there, sent two men to him with the request, "Please come to us without delay." 39 So Peter got up and went with them. When he arrived, they took him to the room upstairs where all the widows came to him weeping and showing him the tunics and cloaks that Dorcas had made while she was with them. 40* Peter sent them all out and knelt down and prayed. Then he turned to her body and said, "Tabitha, rise up." She opened her eyes, saw Peter, and sat up. 41 He gave her his hand and raised her up, and when he had called the holy ones and the widows, he presented her alive. 42 This became known all over Joppa, and many came to believe in the Lord. 43*† And he stayed a long time in Joppa with Simon, a tanner.

IV: The Inauguration of the Gentile Mission

The Vision of Cornelius

10 1*† Now in Caesarea there was a man named Cornelius, a centurion of the Cohort called the Italica,† 2† devout and God-fearing along with his whole household, who used to give alms generously to the Jewish people and pray to God constantly. 3† One afternoon about three o'clock, he saw plainly in a vision an angel of God come in to him and say to him, "Cornelius." 4 He looked intently at him and, seized with fear, said, "What is it, sir?" He said to him, "Your prayers and almsgiving have ascended as a memorial offering before God. 5 Now send some men to Joppa and summon one Simon who is called Peter. 6* He is staying with another Simon, a tanner, who has a house by the sea." 7† When the angel who spoke to him had left, he called

ACTS

9:26 This visit of Paul to Jerusalem is mentioned by Paul in Gal 1:18.

9:29 *Hellenists:* see the note on 6:1–7.

9:31–43 In the context of the period of peace enjoyed by the community through the cessation of Paul's activities against it, Luke introduces two traditions concerning the miraculous power exercised by Peter as he was making a tour of places where the Christian message had already been preached. The towns of Lydda, Sharon, and Joppa were populated by both Jews and Gentiles and their Christian communities may well have been mixed.

9:36 *Tabitha* (*Dorcas*), respectively the Aramaic and Greek words for "gazelle," exemplifies the right attitude toward material possessions expressed by Jesus in the Lucan Gospel (Lk 6:30; 11:41; 12:33; 18:22; 19:8).

9:43 The fact that Peter lodged with a tanner would have been significant to both the Gentile and Jewish Christians, for Judaism considered the tanning occupation unclean.

10:1–48 The narrative centers on the conversion of Cornelius, a Gentile and a "God-fearer" (see the note on 8:26–40). Luke considers the event of great importance, as is evident from his long treatment of it. The incident is again related in 11:1–18 where Peter is forced to justify his actions before the Jerusalem community and alluded to in 15:7–11 where at the Jerusalem "Council" Peter supports Paul's missionary activity among the Gentiles. The narrative divides itself into a series of distinct episodes, concluding with Peter's presentation of the Christian kerygma (34–43) and a pentecostal experience undergone by Cornelius' household preceding their reception of baptism (44–48).

10:1 *The Cohort called the Italica:* this battalion was an auxiliary unit of archers formed originally in Italy but transferred to Syria shortly before A.D. 69.

10:2 *Used to give alms generously:* like Tabitha (9:36), Cornelius exemplifies the proper attitude toward wealth (see the note on 9:36).

10:3 *About three o'clock:* literally, "about the ninth hour." See the note on 3:1.

10:7 *A devout soldier:* by using this adjective, Luke probably intends to classify him as a "God-fearer" (see the note on 8:26–40).

9:26–27 Gal 1:18.
9:30 Acts 11:25.
9:40 Mk 5:40–41.
9:43 Acts 10:6.
10:1–8 Acts 10:30–33.
10:6 Acts 9:43.

two of his servants and a devout soldier from his staff, 8 explained everything to them, and sent them to Joppa.

The Vision of Peter

9† The next day, while they were on their way and nearing the city, Peter went up to the roof terrace to pray at about noontime.† 10 He was hungry and wished to eat, and while they were making preparations he fell into a trance. 11* He saw heaven opened and something resembling a large sheet coming down, lowered to the ground by its four corners. 12 In it were all the earth's four-legged animals and reptiles and the birds of the sky. 13 A voice said to him, "Get up, Peter. Slaughter and eat." 14* But Peter said, "Certainly not, sir. For never have I eaten anything profane and unclean." 15* The voice spoke to him again, a second time, "What God has made clean, you are not to call profane." 16 This happened three times, and then the object was taken up into the sky.

17† While Peter was in doubt about the meaning of the vision he had seen, the men sent by Cornelius asked for Simon's house and arrived at the entrance. 18 They called out inquiring whether Simon, who is called Peter, was staying there. 19* As Peter was pondering the vision, the Spirit said [to him], "There are three men here looking for you. 20 So get up, go downstairs, and accompany them without hesitation, because I have sent them." 21 Then Peter went down to the men and said, "I am the one you are looking for. What is the reason for your being here?" 22* They answered, "Cornelius, a centurion, an upright and God-fearing man, respected by the whole Jewish nation, was directed by a holy angel to summon you to his house and to hear what you have to say." 23 So he invited them in and showed them hospitality.

The next day he got up and went with them, and some of the brothers from Joppa went with him. 24† On the following day he entered Caesarea. Cornelius was expecting them and had called together his relatives and close friends. 25* When Peter entered, Cornelius met him and, falling at his feet, paid him homage. 26 Peter, however, raised him up, saying, "Get up. I myself am also a human being." 27 While he conversed with him, he went in and found many people gathered together 28*† and said to them, "You know that it is unlawful for a Jewish man to associate with, or visit, a Gentile, but God has shown me that I should not call any person profane or unclean. 29 And that is why I came without objection when sent for. May I ask, then, why you summoned me?"

30† Cornelius replied, "Four days ago at this hour, three o'clock in the afternoon, I was at prayer in my house when suddenly a man in dazzling robes stood before me and said, 31 'Cornelius, your prayer has been heard and your almsgiving remembered before God. 32 Send therefore to Joppa and summon Simon, who is called Peter. He is a guest in the house of Simon, a tanner, by the sea.' 33 So I sent for you immediately, and you were kind enough to come. Now therefore we are all here in the presence of God to listen to all that you have been commanded by the Lord."

Peter's Speech†

34* Then Peter proceeded to speak and said,† "In truth, I see that God shows no partiality. 35 Rather, in every nation whoever fears him and acts uprightly is acceptable to him. 36*† You know the word [that] he sent to the Israelites† as he proclaimed peace through Jesus Christ, who is Lord of all, 37* what has happened all over Judea, beginning in Galilee after the baptism that John

---

†

10:9–16 The vision is intended to prepare Peter to share the food of Cornelius' household without qualms of conscience (48). The necessity of such instructions to Peter reveals that at first not even the apostles fully grasped the implications of Jesus' teaching on the law. In Acts, the initial insight belongs to Stephen.

10:9 *At about noontime:* literally, "about the sixth hour."

10:17–23 The arrival of the Gentile emissaries with their account of the angelic apparition illuminates Peter's vision: he is to be prepared to admit Gentiles, who were considered unclean like the animals of his vision, into the Christian community.

10:24–27 So impressed is Cornelius with the apparition that he invites close personal friends to join him in his meeting with Peter. But his understanding of the person he is about to meet is not devoid of superstition, suggested by his falling down before him. For a similar experience of Paul and Barnabas, see 14:11–18.

10:28 Peter now fully understands the meaning of his vision; see the note on 10:17–23.

10:30 *Four days ago:* literally, "from the fourth day up to this hour."

10:34–43 Peter's speech to the household of Cornelius typifies early Christian preaching to Gentiles.

10:34–35 The revelation of God's choice of Israel to be the people of God did not mean he withheld the divine favor from other people.

10:36–43 These words are more directed to Luke's Christian readers than to the household of Cornelius, as indicated by the opening words, "You know." They trace the continuity between the preaching and teaching of Jesus of Nazareth and the proclamation of Jesus by the early community. The emphasis on this divinely ordained continuity (41) is meant to assure Luke's readers of the fidelity of Christian tradition to the words and deeds of Jesus.

10:36 *To the Israelites:* Luke, in the words of Peter, speaks of the prominent position occupied by Israel in the history of salvation.

10:11–20 Acts 11:5–12.
10:14 Lv 11:1–47; Ez 4:14.
10:15 Mk 7:15–19; Gal 2:12.
10:19 Acts 13:2.
10:22 Lk 7:4–5.
10:25–26 Acts 14:13–15; Rv 19:10.
10:28 Gal 2:11–16.
10:34 Dt 17:2; 2 Chr 19:7; Jb 34:19; Wis 6:7; Rom 2:11; Gal 2:6; Eph 6:9; 1 Pt 1:17.
10:36 Is 52:7; Na 2:1.
10:37 Mt 4:12; Mk 1:14; Lk 4:14.

Cultural Connection

Here Comes Everybody

The word *catholic* means "universal." Someone once described being Catholic as, "Here comes everybody!"

In Acts of the Apostles 10:34–36, we hear that God shows no partiality; neither should we. Even so, it is sometimes easier to stick with people who are similar to us. They understand us and know where we are coming from. There's less explaining to do. Right?

But being catholic means reaching out of our familiar circle of friends and including in our group people of different cultures and religions.

Have you ever seen a Native American blanket? Threads of various colors are woven together to form an intricate, new pattern. Each blanket is completely different from every other blanket. By building relationships with people of different cultures and embracing their diversity, we become like one of the threads in such a blanket, weaving our uniquenesses in a new and beautiful pattern. The result is different and enriching, and then we become truly catholic.

▶ **Acts 10:34–36**

preached, [38]*† how God anointed Jesus of Naz-
areth with the holy Spirit and power. He went
about doing good and healing all those oppressed
by the devil, for God was with him. [39]† We are wit-
nesses of all that he did both in the country of the
Jews and [in] Jerusalem. They put him to death by
hanging him on a tree. [40]This man God raised [on]
the third day and granted that he be visible, [41]* not
to all the people, but to us, the witnesses chosen by
God in advance, who ate and drank with him after
he rose from the dead. [42]*† He commissioned us
to preach to the people and testify that he is the
one appointed by God as judge of the living and
the dead. [43]To him all the prophets bear witness,
that everyone who believes in him will receive for-
giveness of sins through his name."

The Baptism of Cornelius

[44]*† While Peter was still speaking these
things, the holy Spirit fell upon all who were
listening to the word. [45]The circumcised believ-
ers who had accompanied Peter were astounded
that the gift of the holy Spirit should have been
poured out on the Gentiles also, [46]for they could
hear them speaking in tongues and glorifying
God. Then Peter responded, [47]* "Can anyone
withhold the water for baptizing these people,
who have received the holy Spirit even as we
have?" [48]He ordered them to be baptized in the
name of Jesus Christ. [49]Then they invited him to
stay for a few days.

The Baptism of the Gentiles Explained

11 [1]† Now the apostles and the brothers who
were in Judea heard that the Gentiles too
had accepted the word of God. [2]So when Peter
went up to Jerusalem the circumcised believers
confronted him, [3]† saying, "You entered the
house of uncircumcised people and ate with
them." [4]Peter began and explained it to them

†

10:38 *Jesus of Nazareth:* God's revelation of his plan for the destiny of humanity through Israel culminated in Jesus of Nazareth. Consequently, the ministry of Jesus is an integral part of God's revelation. This viewpoint explains why the early Christian communities were interested in conserving the historical substance of the ministry of Jesus, a tradition leading to the production of the four gospels.

10:39 *We are witnesses:* the apostolic testimony was not restricted to the resurrection of Jesus but also included his historical ministry. This witness, however, was theological in character; the Twelve, divinely mandated as prophets, were empowered to interpret his sayings and deeds in the light of his redemptive death and resurrection. The meaning of these words and deeds was to be made clear to the developing Christian community as the bearer of the word of salvation (cf 1:21–26). *Hanging him on a tree:* see the note on 5:30.

10:42 *As judge of the living and the dead:* the apostolic preaching to the Jews appealed to their messianic hope, while the preaching to Gentiles stressed the coming divine judgment; cf 1 Thes 1:10.

10:44 Just as the Jewish Christians received the gift of the Spirit, so too do the Gentiles.

11:1–18 The Jewish Christians of Jerusalem were scandalized to learn of Peter's sojourn in the house of the Gentile Cornelius. Nonetheless, they had to accept the divine directions given to both Peter and Cornelius. They concluded that the setting aside of the legal barriers between Jew and Gentile was an exceptional ordinance of God to indicate that the apostolic kerygma was also to be directed to the Gentiles. Only in ch 15 at the "Council" in Jerusalem does the evangelization of the Gentiles become the official position of the church leadership in Jerusalem.

11:3 *You entered . . . :* alternatively, this could be punctuated as a question.

10:38 Is 61:1; Lk 4:18.
10:41 Lk 24:41–43.
10:42 Acts 1:8; 3:15; 17:31; Lk 24:48; Rom 14:9; 2 Tm 4:1.
10:44 Acts 11:15; 15:8.
10:47 Acts 8:36.

Introducing...

Barnabas

We first met Barnabas defending Paul after Paul's conversion in Acts of the Apostles, chapter 9. Now, in chapter 11, we are told that Barnabas "was a good man, filled with the holy Spirit and faith" (verse 24). Barnabas's name literally means "son of encouragement." And encouraging others seemed to be Barnabas's gift. He recognized Paul's gifts and brought Paul to Antioch to minister to the new Christians there when no one else trusted Paul. Later, Barnabas reached out to Mark, disagreeing with Paul on whether to give Mark a second chance to travel with them (see 15:36–39). Barnabas sounds like the friend we would all like to have, someone who would believe in us through good times and bad.

Have you had a Barnabas in your life, someone who encouraged you and believed in you even after you made mistakes? Can you be that kind of encouraging friend to others?

▶ Acts 11:19–26

step by step, saying, 5* "I was at prayer in the city
of Joppa when in a trance I had a vision, some-
thing resembling a large sheet coming down,
lowered from the sky by its four corners, and it
came to me. 6 Looking intently into it, I observed
and saw the four-legged animals of the earth, the
wild beasts, the reptiles, and the birds of the sky.
7 I also heard a voice say to me, 'Get up, Peter.
Slaughter and eat.' 8 But I said, 'Certainly not, sir,
because nothing profane or unclean has ever en-
tered my mouth.' 9 But a second time a voice from
heaven answered, 'What God has made clean, you
are not to call profane.' 10 This happened three
times, and then everything was drawn up again
into the sky. 11 Just then three men appeared at
the house where we were, who had been sent
to me from Caesarea. 12† The Spirit told me to
accompany them without discriminating. These
six brothers also went with me, and we entered
the man's house. 13* He related to us how he had
seen [the] angel standing in his house, saying,
'Send someone to Joppa and summon Simon,
who is called Peter, 14 who will speak words to
you by which you and all your household will be
saved.' 15* As I began to speak, the holy Spirit fell
upon them as it had upon us at the beginning,
16* and I remembered the word of the Lord, how
he had said, 'John baptized with water but you
will be baptized with the holy Spirit.' 17* If then
God gave them the same gift he gave to us when
we came to believe in the Lord Jesus Christ, who
was I to be able to hinder God?" 18 When they
heard this, they stopped objecting and glorified
God, saying, "God has then granted life-giving
repentance to the Gentiles too."

The Church at Antioch

19*† Now those who had been scattered by
the persecution that arose because of Stephen
went as far as Phoenicia, Cyprus, and Antioch,
preaching the word to no one but Jews. 20 There
were some Cypriots and Cyrenians among them,
however, who came to Antioch and began to
speak to the Greeks as well, proclaiming the Lord
Jesus. 21 The hand of the Lord was with them and
a great number who believed turned to the Lord.
22 The news about them reached the ears of the
church in Jerusalem, and they sent Barnabas [to
go] to Antioch. 23 When he arrived and saw the
grace of God, he rejoiced and encouraged them
all to remain faithful to the Lord in firmness of
heart, 24 for he was a good man, filled with the
holy Spirit and faith. And a large number of
people was added to the Lord. 25 Then he went
to Tarsus to look for Saul, 26† and when he had
found him he brought him to Antioch. For a
whole year they met with the church and taught
a large number of people, and it was in Antioch
that the disciples were first called Christians.

The Prediction of Agabus

27† At that time some prophets came down
from Jerusalem to Antioch, 28* and one of them

11:12 *These six brothers:* companions from the Christian community of Joppa (see 10:23).

11:19–26 The Jewish Christian antipathy to the mixed community was reflected by the early missionaries generally. The few among them who entertained a different view succeeded in introducing Gentiles into the community at Antioch (in Syria). When the disconcerted Jerusalem community sent Barnabas to investigate, he was so favorably impressed by what he observed that he persuaded his friend Saul to participate in the Antioch mission.

11:26 *Christians:* "Christians" is first applied to the members of the community at Antioch because the Gentile members of the community enable it to stand out clearly from Judaism.

11:27–30 It is not clear whether the prophets from Jerusalem

11:5–12 Acts 10:11–20. **11:13** Acts 10:3–5, 22, 30–32. **11:15** Acts 10:44. **11:16** Acts 1:5; 19:4; Lk 3:16. **11:17** Acts 15:8–9. **11:19** Acts 8:1–4. **11:28** Acts 21:10.

named Agabus stood up and predicted by the
Spirit that there would be a severe famine all
over the world, and it happened under Claudius.
29* So the disciples determined that, according
to ability, each should send relief to the brothers
who lived in Judea. 30† This they did, sending it
to the presbyters in care of Barnabas and Saul.

Herod's Persecution of the Christians

12 1† About that time King Herod laid hands
upon some members of the church to
harm them. 2† He had James, the brother of
John, killed by the sword, 3† and when he saw
that this was pleasing to the Jews he proceeded to
arrest Peter also. (It was [the] feast of Unleavened
Bread.) 4 He had him taken into custody and put
in prison under the guard of four squads of four
soldiers each. He intended to bring him before
the people after Passover. 5* Peter thus was be-
ing kept in prison, but prayer by the church was
fervently being made to God on his behalf.
6 On the very night before Herod was to bring
him to trial, Peter, secured by double chains, was
sleeping between two soldiers, while outside the
door guards kept watch on the prison. 7 Suddenly
the angel of the Lord stood by him and a light
shone in the cell. He tapped Peter on the side
and awakened him, saying, "Get up quickly."
The chains fell from his wrists. 8 The angel said
to him, "Put on your belt and your sandals."
He did so. Then he said to him, "Put on your
cloak and follow me." 9 So he followed him out,
not realizing that what was happening through
the angel was real; he thought he was seeing a
vision. 10 They passed the first guard, then the
second, and came to the iron gate leading out to
the city, which opened for them by itself. They
emerged and made their way down an alley,
and suddenly the angel left him. 11 Then Peter
recovered his senses and said, "Now I know for
certain that [the] Lord sent his angel and rescued
me from the hand of Herod and from all that the
Jewish people had been expecting." 12* When he
realized this, he went to the house of Mary, the
mother of John who is called Mark, where there
were many people gathered in prayer. 13 When
he knocked on the gateway door, a maid named
Rhoda came to answer it. 14 She was so overjoyed
when she recognized Peter's voice that, instead of
opening the gate, she ran in and announced that
Peter was standing at the gate. 15 They told her,
"You are out of your mind," but she insisted that
it was so. But they kept saying, "It is his angel."
16 But Peter continued to knock, and when they
opened it, they saw him and were astounded.
17† He motioned to them with his hand to be
quiet and explained [to them] how the Lord had
led him out of the prison, and said, "Report this
to James and the brothers." Then he left and
went to another place. 18* At daybreak there was
no small commotion among the soldiers over
what had become of Peter. 19 Herod, after insti-
tuting a search but not finding him, ordered the
guards tried and executed. Then he left Judea to
spend some time in Caesarea.

> **Pray It!**
>
> ## What Imprisons You?
>
> *Holy Spirit, come! Open my mind to seek the truth. Break down the barriers that imprison me. Empower me to overcome any guilt by asking for forgiveness. Enable me to forgive others and release my past hurt and anger. Open my eyes to vices, habits, and attitudes that are destructive to me and to others. Guide me to true freedom with your word. Amen.*
>
> 
>
> ▶ **Acts 12:6–19**

† came to Antioch to request help in view of the coming famine or whether they received this insight during their visit there. The former supposition seems more likely. Suetonius and Tacitus speak of famines during the reign of Claudius (A.D. 41–54), while the Jewish historian Josephus mentions a famine in Judea in A.D. 46–48. Luke is interested, rather, in showing the charity of the Antiochene community toward the Jewish Christians of Jerusalem despite their differences on mixed communities.

11:30 *Presbyters:* this is the same Greek word that elsewhere is translated "elders," primarily in reference to the Jewish community.

12:1–19 Herod Agrippa ruled Judea A.D. 41–44. While Luke does not assign a motive for his execution of James and his intended execution of Peter, the broad background lies in Herod's support of Pharisaic Judaism. The Jewish Christians had lost the popularity they had had in Jerusalem (2:47), perhaps because of suspicions against them traceable to the teaching of Stephen.

12:2 *James, the brother of John:* this James, the son of Zebedee, was beheaded by Herod Agrippa ca. A.D. 44.

12:3, 4 *Feast of Unleavened Bread . . . Passover:* see the note on Lk 22:1.

12:17 *To James:* this James is not the son of Zebedee mentioned in v 2, but is James, the "brother of the Lord" (Gal 1:19), who in chs 15 and 21 is presented as leader of the Jerusalem Christian community. *He left and went to another place:* the conjecture that Peter left for Rome at this time has nothing to recommend it. His chief responsibility was still the leadership of the Jewish Christian community in Palestine (see Gal 2:7). The concept of the great missionary effort of the church was yet to come (see 13:1–3).

11:29–30 Acts 12:25. **12:5** Jas 5:16. **12:12** Acts 12:25; 15:37. **12:18** Acts 5:22–24.

Herod's Death

20† He had long been very angry with the peo-
ple of Tyre and Sidon, who now came to him
in a body. After winning over Blastus, the king's
chamberlain, they sued for peace because their
country was supplied with food from the king's
territory. 21 On an appointed day, Herod, attired
in royal robes, [and] seated on the rostrum, ad-
dressed them publicly. 22 The assembled crowd
cried out, "This is the voice of a god, not of a
man." 23 At once the angel of the Lord struck him
down because he did not ascribe the honor to
God, and he was eaten by worms and breathed
his last. 24* But the word of God continued to
spread and grow.

Mission of Barnabas and Saul

25*† After Barnabas and Saul completed their
relief mission, they returned to Jerusalem, taking
with them John, who is called Mark.
13 1† Now there were in the church at An-
tioch prophets and teachers: Barnabas,
Symeon who was called Niger, Lucius of Cyrene,
Manaen who was a close friend of Herod the
tetrarch, and Saul. 2 While they were worshiping
the Lord and fasting, the holy Spirit said, "Set
apart for me Barnabas and Saul for the work to
which I have called them." 3 Then, completing
their fasting and prayer, they laid hands on them
and sent them off.

First Mission Begins in Cyprus

4† So they, sent forth by the holy Spirit, went
down to Seleucia and from there sailed to Cy-
prus. 5† When they arrived in Salamis, they
proclaimed the word of God in the Jewish syn-
agogues. They had John also as their assistant.
6† When they had traveled through the whole
island as far as Paphos, they met a magician
named Bar-Jesus who was a Jewish false prophet.
7 He was with the proconsul Sergius Paulus, a
man of intelligence, who had summoned Bar-
nabas and Saul and wanted to hear the word of
God. 8 But Elymas the magician (for that is what
his name means) opposed them in an attempt to
turn the proconsul away from the faith. 9† But
Saul, also known as Paul, filled with the holy
Spirit, looked intently at him 10 and said, "You
son of the devil, you enemy of all that is right,
full of every sort of deceit and fraud. Will you
not stop twisting the straight paths of [the] Lord?
11 Even now the hand of the Lord is upon you.
You will be blind, and unable to see the sun for
a time." Immediately a dark mist fell upon him,
and he went about seeking people to lead him by
the hand. 12 When the proconsul saw what had
happened, he came to believe, for he was aston-
ished by the teaching about the Lord.

Paul's Arrival at Antioch in Pisidia

13* From Paphos, Paul and his companions
set sail and arrived at Perga in Pamphylia. But
John left them and returned to Jerusalem. 14 They
continued on from Perga and reached Antioch in
Pisidia. On the sabbath they entered [into] the
synagogue and took their seats. 15 After the read-
ing of the law and the prophets, the synagogue
officials sent word to them, "My brothers, if one
of you has a word of exhortation for the people,
please speak."

Paul's Address in the Synagogue

16† So Paul got up, motioned with his hand,
and said, "Fellow Israelites and you others who
are God-fearing,† listen. 17* The God of this peo-
ple Israel chose our ancestors and exalted the
people during their sojourn in the land of Egypt.
With uplifted arms he led them out of it 18*† and
for about forty years he put up with them in the

†

12:20–23 Josephus gives a similar account of Herod's death that occurred in A.D. 44. Early Christian tradition considered the manner of it to be a divine punishment upon his evil life. See 2 Kgs 19:35 for the figure of the angel of the Lord in such a context.

12:25 *They returned to Jerusalem:* many manuscripts read "from Jerusalem," since 11:30 implies that Paul and Barnabas are already in Jerusalem. This present verse could refer to a return visit or subsequent relief mission.

13:1–3 The impulse for the first missionary effort in Asia Minor is ascribed to the prophets of the Antiochene community, under the inspiration of the holy Spirit. Just as the Jerusalem community had earlier been the center of missionary activity, so too Antioch becomes the center from which the missionaries Barnabas and Saul are sent out.

13:4–14, 27 The key event in Luke's account of the first missionary journey is the experience of Paul and Barnabas at Pisidian Antioch (13:14–52). The Christian kerygma proclaimed by Paul in the synagogue was favorably received. Some Jews and "God-fearers" (see the note on 8:26–40) became interested and invited the missionaries to speak again on the following sabbath (13:42). By that time, however, the appearance of a large number of Gentiles from the city had so disconcerted the Jews that they became hostile toward the apostles (13:44–50). This hostility of theirs appears in all three accounts of Paul's missionary journeys in Acts, the Jews of Iconium (14:1–2) and Beroea (17:11) being notable exceptions.

13:5 *John:* that is, John Mark (see 12:12, 25).

13:6 *A magician named Bar-Jesus who was a Jewish false prophet:* that is, he posed as a prophet. Again Luke takes the opportunity to dissociate Christianity from the magical acts of the time (7–11); see also 8:18–24.

13:9 *Saul, also known as Paul:* there is no reason to believe that his name was changed from Saul to Paul upon his conversion. The use of a double name, one Semitic (Saul), the other Greco-Roman (Paul), is well attested (cf 1:23, Joseph Justus; 12:12, 25, John Mark).

13:16–41 This is the first of several speeches of Paul to Jews proclaiming that the Christian church is the logical development of Pharisaic Judaism (see also 24:10–21; 26:2–23).

13:16 *Who are God-fearing:* see the note on 8:26–40.

13:18 *Put up with:* some manuscripts read "sustained."

*

12:24 Acts 6:7.
12:25 Acts 11:29–30.
13:13 Acts 15:38.
13:17 Ex 6:1, 6; 12:51.
13:18 Ex 16:1, 35; Nm 14:34.

desert. [19]* When he had destroyed seven nations in the land of Canaan, he gave them their land as an inheritance [20]*† at the end of about four hundred and fifty years. After these things he provided judges up to Samuel [the] prophet. [21]* Then they asked for a king. God gave them Saul, son of Kish, a man from the tribe of Benjamin, for forty years. [22]* Then he removed him and raised up David as their king; of him he testified, 'I have found David, son of Jesse, a man after my own heart; he will carry out my every wish.' [23]* From this man's descendants God, according to his promise, has brought to Israel a savior, Jesus. [24]* John heralded his coming by proclaiming a baptism of repentance to all the people of Israel; [25]* and as John was completing his course, he would say, 'What do you suppose that I am? I am not he. Behold, one is coming after me; I am not worthy to unfasten the sandals of his feet.'

[26] "My brothers, children of the family of Abraham, and those others among you who are God-fearing, to us this word of salvation has been sent. [27] The inhabitants of Jerusalem and their leaders failed to recognize him, and by condemning him they fulfilled the oracles of the prophets that are read sabbath after sabbath. [28]* For even though they found no grounds for a death sentence, they asked Pilate to have him put to death, [29]* and when they had accomplished all that was written about him, they took him down from the tree and placed him in a tomb. [30]* But God raised him from the dead, [31]*† and for many days he appeared to those who had come up with him from Galilee to Jerusalem. These are [now] his witnesses before the people. [32] We ourselves are proclaiming this good news to you that what God promised our ancestors [33]* he has brought to fulfillment for us, [their] children, by raising up Jesus, as it is written in the second psalm, 'You are my son; this day I have be- gotten you.' [34]* And that he raised him from the dead never to return to corruption he declared in this way, 'I shall give you the benefits assured to David.' [35]* That is why he also says in another psalm, 'You will not suffer your holy one to see corruption.' [36]* Now David, after he had served the will of God in his lifetime, fell asleep, was gathered to his ancestors, and did see corruption. [37] But the one whom God raised up did not see corruption. [38]† You must know, my

Did You Know?

The Journeys of Paul

According to the way Luke constructed Paul's story, Paul made three missionary journeys over a ten-year period to spread the Gospel message. The details of his first journey are covered in chapters 13–14. The second journey is reported in chapters 16–18. The third journey is described in chapters 19–21. Paul himself may have seen these not as three separate journeys but as one continuous missionary activity. On these journeys, Paul made converts and started Christian communities. On the second and third journeys, he also visited established communities to give them guidance and support. See maps 8 and 9 for the routes of Paul's journeys.

Paul's third journey landed him back in Jerusalem, where some Jews had him arrested. On the basis of his Roman citizenship, Paul appealed to the emperor. So he was transported to Rome (this trip is referred to as his fourth journey). He probably died there as a martyr around AD 65. Some traditions say that Paul wasn't martyred there but went on to evangelize in Spain.

Acts of the Apostles, chapters 13–21

ACTS

13:20 *At the end of about four hundred and fifty years:* the manuscript tradition makes it uncertain whether the mention of four hundred and fifty years refers to the sojourn in Egypt before the Exodus, the wilderness period and the time of the conquest (see Ex 12:40–41), as the translation here suggests, or to the time between the conquest and the time of Samuel, the period of the judges, if the text is read, "After these things, for about four hundred and fifty years, he provided judges."

13:31 The theme of the Galilean witnesses is a major one in the Gospel of Luke and in Acts and is used to signify the continuity between the teachings of Jesus and the teachings of the church and to guarantee the fidelity of the church's teachings to the words of Jesus.

13:38–39 *Justified:* the verb is the same as that used in Paul's letters to speak of the experience of justification and, as in Paul, is here connected with the term "to have faith" ("every believer"). But this seems the only passage about Paul in Acts where justification is mentioned. In Lucan fashion it is paralleled with "forgiveness of

---

13:19 Dt 7:1; Jos 14:1–2.
13:20 Jgs 2:16; 1 Sm 3:20.
13:21 1 Sm 8:5, 19; 9:16; 10:1, 20–21, 24; 11:15.
13:22 1 Sm 13:14; 16:12–13; Ps 89:20–21.
13:23 Is 11:1.
13:24 Mt 3:1–2; Mk 1:4–5; Lk 3:2–3.
13:25 Mt 3:11; Mk 1:7; Lk 3:16; Jn 1:20, 27.
13:28 Mt 27:20, 22–23; Mk 15:13–14; Lk 23:4, 14–15, 21–23; Jn 19:4–6, 15.
13:29 Mt 27:59–60; Mk 15:46; Lk 23:53; Jn 19:38, 41–42.
13:30 Acts 2:24, 32; 3:15; 4:10; 17:31.
13:31 Acts 1:3, 8; 10:39, 41; Mt 28:8–10, 16–20; Mk 16:9, 12–20; Lk 24:13–53; Jn 20:11–29; 21:1–23.
13:33 Ps 2:7.
13:34 Is 55:3.
13:35 Ps 16:10.
13:36 Acts 2:29; 1 Kgs 2:10.

brothers, that through him forgiveness of sins is
being proclaimed to you, [and] in regard to ev-
erything from which you could not be justified
under the law of Moses, 39* in him every believer
is justified. 40 Be careful, then, that what was said
in the prophets not come about:

41* 'Look on, you scoffers,
be amazed and disappear.
For I am doing a work in your days,
a work that you will never believe even if
someone tells you.' "

42 As they were leaving, they invited them to
speak on these subjects the following sabbath.
43 After the congregation had dispersed, many
Jews and worshipers who were converts to Juda-
ism followed Paul and Barnabas, who spoke to
them and urged them to remain faithful to the
grace of God.

Address to the Gentiles

44 On the following sabbath almost the whole
city gathered to hear the word of the Lord. 45 When
the Jews saw the crowds, they were filled with jeal-
ousy and with violent abuse contradicted what
Paul said. 46*† Both Paul and Barnabas spoke out
boldly and said, "It was necessary that the word
of God be spoken to you first, but since you reject
it and condemn yourselves as unworthy of eternal
life, we now turn to the Gentiles. 47* For so the
Lord has commanded us, 'I have made you a light
to the Gentiles, that you may be an instrument of
salvation to the ends of the earth.' "
48 The Gentiles were delighted when they heard
this and glorified the word of the Lord. All who
were destined for eternal life came to believe,
49 and the word of the Lord continued to spread
through the whole region. 50 The Jews, however,
incited the women of prominence who were wor-
shipers and the leading men of the city, stirred
up a persecution against Paul and Barnabas, and
expelled them from their territory. 51*† So they
shook the dust from their feet in protest against
them and went to Iconium. 52 The disciples were
filled with joy and the holy Spirit.

Paul and Barnabas at Iconium

14 1 In Iconium they entered the Jewish syn-
agogue together and spoke in such a way
that a great number of both Jews and Greeks
came to believe, 2 although the disbelieving Jews
stirred up and poisoned the minds of the Gen-
tiles against the brothers. 3* So they stayed for a
considerable period, speaking out boldly for the
Lord, who confirmed the word about his grace
by granting signs and wonders to occur through
their hands. 4 The people of the city were divided:
some were with the Jews; others, with the apos-
tles. 5* When there was an attempt by both the
Gentiles and the Jews, together with their leaders,
to attack and stone them, 6 they realized it and
fled to the Lycaonian cities of Lystra and Derbe
and to the surrounding countryside, 7 where they
continued to proclaim the good news.

Paul and Barnabas at Lystra

8† At Lystra there was a crippled man, lame
from birth, who had never walked. 9 He listened
to Paul speaking, who looked intently at him, saw
that he had the faith to be healed, 10 and called
out in a loud voice, "Stand up straight on your
feet." He jumped up and began to walk about.
11* When the crowds saw what Paul had done,
they cried out in Lycaonian, "The gods have come
down to us in human form." 12† They called Bar-
nabas "Zeus" and Paul "Hermes," because he was
the chief speaker. 13 And the priest of Zeus, whose
temple was at the entrance to the city, brought
oxen and garlands to the gates, for he together
with the people intended to offer sacrifice.
14† The apostles Barnabas and Paul tore their
garments when they heard this and rushed out
into the crowd, shouting, 15*† "Men, why are
you doing this? We are of the same nature as
you, human beings. We proclaim to you good

sins" (a theme at 2:38; 3:19; 5:31; 10:43) based on Jesus' resurrection (37) rather than his cross, and is put negatively (38). Therefore, some would translate, "in regard to everything from which you could not be acquitted . . . every believer is acquitted."

13:46 The refusal to believe frustrates God's plan for his chosen people; however, no adverse judgment is made here concerning their ultimate destiny. Again, Luke, in the words of Paul, speaks of the priority of Israel in the plan for salvation (see 10:36).

13:51 See the note on Lk 9:5.

14:8–18 In an effort to convince his hearers that the divine power works through his word, Paul cures the cripple. However, the pagan tradition of the occasional appearance of gods among human beings leads the people astray in interpreting the miracle. The incident reveals the cultural difficulties with which the church had to cope. Note the similarity of the miracle worked here by Paul to the one performed by Peter in 3:2–10.

14:12 *"Zeus" . . . "Hermes":* in Greek religion, Zeus was the chief of the Olympian gods, the "father of gods and men"; Hermes was a son of Zeus and was usually identified as the herald and messenger of the gods.

14:14 *Tore their garments:* a gesture of protest.

14:15–17 This is the first speech of Paul to Gentiles recorded by Luke in Acts (cf 17:22–31). Rather than showing how Christianity is the logical outgrowth of Judaism, as he does in speeches before Jews, Luke says that God excuses past Gentile ignorance and then presents a natural theology arguing for the recognition of God's existence and presence through his activity in natural phenomena.

13:39 Rom 3:20.
13:41 Hb 1:5.
13:46 Acts 3:26; Rom 1:16.
13:47 Is 49:6.
13:51 Mt 10:14; Mk 6:11; Lk 9:5; 10:11.
14:3 Mk 16:17–20.
14:5 2Tm 3:11.
14:11 Acts 28:6.
14:15 Acts 3:12; 10:26; Ex 20:11; Ps 146:6.

news that you should turn from these idols to the
living God, 'who made heaven and earth and sea
and all that is in them.' 16* In past generations he
allowed all Gentiles to go their own ways; 17* yet,
in bestowing his goodness, he did not leave
himself without witness, for he gave you rains
from heaven and fruitful seasons, and filled you
with nourishment and gladness for your hearts."
18 Even with these words, they scarcely restrained
the crowds from offering sacrifice to them.

19* However, some Jews from Antioch and
Iconium arrived and won over the crowds. They
stoned Paul and dragged him out of the city,
supposing that he was dead. 20 But when the
disciples gathered around him, he got up and en-
tered the city. On the following day he left with
Barnabas for Derbe.

End of the First Mission

21 After they had proclaimed the good news
to that city and made a considerable number of
disciples, they returned to Lystra and to Iconium
and to Antioch. 22* They strengthened the spirits
of the disciples and exhorted them to persevere in
the faith, saying, "It is necessary for us to undergo
many hardships to enter the kingdom of God."
23† They appointed presbyters for them in each
church and, with prayer and fasting, commended
them to the Lord in whom they had put their
faith. 24 Then they traveled through Pisidia and
reached Pamphylia. 25 After proclaiming the word
at Perga they went down to Attalia. 26* From there
they sailed to Antioch, where they had been com-
mended to the grace of God for the work they had
now accomplished. 27 And when they arrived, they
called the church together and reported what God
had done with them and how he had opened the
door of faith to the Gentiles. 28 Then they spent no
little time with the disciples.

Council of Jerusalem

15 1*† Some who had come down from Ju-
dea were instructing the brothers, "Unless
you are circumcised according to the Mosaic
practice,* you cannot be saved."† 2 Because there
arose no little dissension and debate by Paul and
Barnabas with them, it was decided that Paul,
Barnabas, and some of the others should go up
to Jerusalem to the apostles and presbyters about
this question. 3 They were sent on their journey
by the church, and passed through Phoenicia
and Samaria telling of the conversion of the Gen-
tiles, and brought great joy to all the brothers.
4 When they arrived in Jerusalem, they were wel-
comed by the church, as well as by the apostles
and the presbyters, and they reported what God
had done with them. 5 But some from the party
of the Pharisees who had become believers stood
up and said, "It is necessary to circumcise them
and direct them to observe the Mosaic law."

6† The apostles and the presbyters met to-
gether to see about this matter. 7*† After much

Live It!

A Courageous Stance

One thing is clear about taking a stand and spreading the Gospel—it takes great courage. The story of Paul and Barnabas in Iconium is further evidence of how the early disciples risked their own lives to preach the Good News. It seems the Good News is not easy for some people to hear or accept.

In your prayer, reflect or journal on the following questions:

- In what ways is God inviting you to speak and act boldly to spread the Good News in your school? your home? your neighborhood and community?
- What keeps you from responding?

▶ Acts 14:1–7

14:23 *They appointed presbyters:* the communities are given their own religious leaders by the traveling missionaries. The structure in these churches is patterned on the model of the Jerusalem community (11:30; 15:2, 5, 22; 21:18).

15:1–35 The Jerusalem "Council" marks the official rejection of the rigid view that Gentile converts were obliged to observe the Mosaic law completely. From here to the end of Acts, Paul and the Gentile mission become the focus of Luke's writing.

15:1–5 When some of the converted Pharisees of Jerusalem discover the results of the first missionary journey of Paul, they urge that the Gentiles be taught to follow the Mosaic law. Recognizing the authority of the Jerusalem church, Paul and Barnabas go there to settle the question of whether Gentiles can embrace a form of Christianity that does not include this obligation.

15:6–12 The gathering is possibly the same as that recalled by Paul in Gal 2:1–10. Note that in v 2 it is only the apostles and presbyters, a small group, with whom Paul and Barnabas are to meet. Here Luke gives the meeting a public character because he wishes to emphasize its doctrinal significance (see 22).

15:7–11 Paul's refusal to impose the Mosaic law on the Gentile Christians is supported by Peter on the ground that within his own experience God bestowed the holy Spirit upon Cornelius and his household without preconditions concerning the adoption of the Mosaic law (see 10:44–47).

14:16 Acts 17:30.
14:17 Wis 13:1.
14:19–20 2 Cor 11:25; 2 Tm 3:11.
14:22 1 Thes 3:3.
14:26 Acts 13:1–3.
15:1–4 Gal 2:1–9.
15:1 Lv 12:3; Gal 5:2.
15:7 Acts 10:27–43.

Catholic Connection

Ministry in the Church

This was not your typical road trip! Paul and Barnabas had been sent forth by the Church in Antioch to spread the Gospel message. While traveling and preaching about Jesus, they were persecuted, falsely worshiped as gods, and nearly stoned to death! But that did not stop them. They bravely returned to each city to encourage those who had converted and to appoint elders, or presbyters. These leaders were selected through prayers and fasting to lead the community and guard against those who would twist and distort the Gospel. At the conclusion of their trip, Paul and Barnabas returned home to share the joys of their success and the thrills of a few heroic moments.

Paul and Barnabas's journeys to local churches give us great insight into the origins and development of ministry within the Catholic Church. From the leaders or overseers (see Acts 20:28) Paul and Barnabas appointed to guard and teach the faith, we get a glimpse at the origins of the role of bishops, the successors of the Apostles. The leaders who assisted the bishops became known as priests, or presbyters. Finally, those who were specifically set aside for service to the community and who aided the bishops and priests were called deacons (see 1 Tm 3:8–13).

There are numerous ways a person can answer her or his baptismal call to serve and take part in the ministry of the Church today. Some men choose to answer the call through ordained ministry as bishops, priests, or deacons. Other women and men may discern a call to the religious life as sisters or brothers. Finally, some men and women choose to use their gifts to serve the community as lay ecclesial ministers. Lay ecclesial ministry is very broad and includes youth ministers, catechists, liturgical ministers, outreach ministers, and so on. All the various ministries work together under the direction of the bishop and pastors. By using all the various gifts of its members, the Church is able to spread the Gospel with courage and perseverance as Paul and Barnabas did so long ago.

Acts 14:21–28
Catechism, nos. 871–945

debate had taken place, Peter got up and said to
them, "My brothers, you are well aware that from
early days God made his choice among you that
through my mouth the Gentiles would hear the
word of the gospel and believe. 8* And God, who
knows the heart, bore witness by granting them
the holy Spirit just as he did us. 9* He made no
distinction between us and them, for by faith he
purified their hearts. 10* Why, then, are you now
putting God to the test by placing on the shoulders
of the disciples a yoke that neither our ancestors
nor we have been able to bear? 11*† On the
contrary, we believe that we are saved through
the grace of the Lord Jesus, in the same way as
they." 12 The whole assembly fell silent, and they
listened while Paul and Barnabas described the
signs and wonders God had worked among the
Gentiles through them.

James on Dietary Law

13† After they had fallen silent, James responded,
"My brothers, listen to me. 14† Symeon
has described how God first concerned himself
with acquiring from among the Gentiles a people
for his name. 15 The words of the prophets agree
with this, as is written:

16* 'After this I shall return
and rebuild the fallen hut of David;
from its ruins I shall rebuild it
and raise it up again,
17 so that the rest of humanity may seek out the
Lord,
even all the Gentiles on whom my name is
invoked.
Thus says the Lord who accomplishes these
things,
18 known from of old.'

19* It is my judgment, therefore, that we ought
to stop troubling the Gentiles who turn to God,
20* but tell them by letter to avoid pollution
from idols, unlawful marriage, the meat of
strangled animals, and blood. 21 For Moses, for

†

15:11 In support of Paul, Peter formulates the fundamental meaning of the gospel: that all are invited to be saved through faith in the power of Christ.

15:13–35 Some scholars think that this apostolic decree suggested by James, the immediate leader of the Jerusalem community, derives from another historical occasion than the meeting in question. This seems to be the case if the meeting is the same as the one related in Gal 2:1–10. According to that account, nothing was imposed upon Gentile Christians in respect to Mosaic law; whereas the decree instructs Gentile Christians of mixed communities to abstain from meats sacrificed to idols and from blood-meats, and to avoid marriage within forbidden degrees of consanguinity and affinity (Lv 18), all of which practices were especially abhorrent to Jews. Luke seems to have telescoped two originally independent incidents here: the first a Jerusalem "Council" that dealt with the question of circumcision, and the second a Jerusalem decree dealing mainly with Gentile observance of dietary laws (see 21:25 where Paul seems to be learning of the decree for the first time).

15:14 *Symeon:* elsewhere in Acts he is called either Peter or Simon. The presence of the name Symeon here suggests that, in the source Luke is using for this part of the Jerusalem "Council" incident, the name may have originally referred to someone other than Peter (see 13:1 where the Antiochene Symeon Niger is mentioned). As the text now stands, however, it is undoubtedly a reference to Simon Peter (7).

*

15:8 Acts 10:44–48.
15:9 Acts 10:34–35.
15:10 Mt 23:4; Gal 5:1.
15:11 Gal 2:16; 3:11; Eph 2:5–8.
15:16–17 Am 9:11–12.
15:19–20 Acts 15:28–29; 21:25.
15:20 Gn 9:4; Lv 3:17; 17:10–14.

Live It!

Unity in Faith and Love

When Paul and Barnabas were in Antioch, a controversy arose regarding the need for Gentiles to be circumcised and to follow certain Jewish laws and holidays. The earliest Christians were Jews. They believed in Jesus and continued to follow the rules of the Jewish faith as a sign that they were a covenant people. But with Gentiles becoming Christians, new questions were raised: Do Gentiles have to follow all the Jewish rules? Do Gentiles need to be circumcised as a sign of the covenant? Circumcision is the surgical removal of the foreskin from the penis, and the Gentile converts did not see the need for it.

Paul and Barnabas insisted that Christians were free from such Jewish laws; they went to Jerusalem to meet with the other Apostles to defend their position. With Peter's support, the community decided that Paul and Barnabas were right. And so the Apostles at the council agreed that the center of the Christian faith was believing in the risen Christ, not conforming to specific Jewish rituals. This meeting of the Apostles is called the Council of Jerusalem and was a pivotal point in the history of the Church.

How does your youth group or parish handle conflict? Does it handle it better when members remind themselves that they are united by their faith in Jesus?

▶ Acts 15:1–35

generations now, has had those who proclaim
him in every town, as he has been read in the
synagogues every sabbath."

Letter of the Apostles

22 Then the apostles and presbyters, in agree-
ment with the whole church, decided to choose
representatives and to send them to Antioch with
Paul and Barnabas. The ones chosen were Judas,
who was called Barsabbas, and Silas, leaders
among the brothers. 23 This is the letter deliv-
ered by them: "The apostles and the presbyters,
your brothers, to the brothers in Antioch, Syria,
and Cilicia of Gentile origin: greetings. 24 Since
we have heard that some of our number [who
went out] without any mandate from us have
upset you with their teachings and disturbed
your peace of mind, 25 we have with one accord
decided to choose representatives and to send
them to you along with our beloved Barnabas
and Paul, 26 who have dedicated their lives to
the name of our Lord Jesus Christ. 27 So we are
sending Judas and Silas who will also convey
this same message by word of mouth: 28* 'It is
the decision of the holy Spirit and of us not to
place on you any burden beyond these necessi-
ties, 29* namely, to abstain from meat sacrificed
to idols, from blood, from meats of strangled an-
imals, and from unlawful marriage. If you keep
free of these, you will be doing what is right.
Farewell.'"

Delegates at Antioch

30 And so they were sent on their journey.
Upon their arrival in Antioch they called the as-
sembly together and delivered the letter. 31 When
the people read it, they were delighted with the
exhortation. 32 Judas and Silas, who were them-
selves prophets, exhorted and strengthened the
brothers with many words. 33 After they had
spent some time there, they were sent off with
greetings of peace from the brothers to those
who had commissioned them. [34]† 35 But Paul
and Barnabas remained in Antioch, teaching
and proclaiming with many others the word of
the Lord.

V: The Mission of Paul to the Ends of the Earth

Paul and Barnabas Separate

36† After some time, Paul said to Barnabas,
"Come, let us make a return visit to see how the
brothers are getting on in all the cities where
we proclaimed the word of the Lord." 37 Barna-
bas wanted to take with them also John, who
was called Mark, 38* but Paul insisted that they
should not take with them someone who had de-
serted them at Pamphylia and who had not con-
tinued with them in their work. 39 So sharp was
their disagreement that they separated. Barnabas
took Mark and sailed to Cyprus. 40 But Paul chose
Silas and departed after being commended by
the brothers to the grace of the Lord. 41 He trav-
eled through Syria and Cilicia bringing strength
to the churches.

Paul in Lycaonia: Timothy

16 1* He reached [also] Derbe and Lystra
where there was a disciple named Tim-
othy, the son of a Jewish woman who was a
believer, but his father was a Greek. 2* The broth-
ers in Lystra and Iconium spoke highly of him,
3† and Paul wanted him to come along with him.
On account of the Jews of that region, Paul had
him circumcised, for they all knew that his father
was a Greek. 4 As they traveled from city to city,
they handed on to the people for observance the
decisions reached by the apostles and presbyters
in Jerusalem. 5 Day after day the churches grew
stronger in faith and increased in number.

Through Asia Minor

6 They traveled through the Phrygian and Gala-
tian territory because they had been prevented
by the holy Spirit from preaching the message
in the province of Asia. 7† When they came to
Mysia, they tried to go on into Bithynia, but

15:34 Some manuscripts add, in various wordings, "But Silas decided to remain there."

15:36—18:22 This continuous narrative recounts Paul's second missionary journey. On the internal evidence of the Lucan account, it lasted about three years. Paul first visited the communities he had established on his first journey (16:1–5), then pushed on into Macedonia, where he established communities at Philippi, Thessalonica, and Beroea (16:7—17:5). To escape the hostility of the Jews of Thessalonica, he left for Greece and while resident in Athens attempted, without success, to establish an effective Christian community there. From Athens he proceeded to Corinth and, after a stay of a year and a half, returned to Antioch by way of Ephesus and Jerusalem (17:16—18:22). Luke does not concern himself with the structure or statistics of the communities but aims to show the general progress of the gospel in the Gentile world as well as its continued failure to take root in the Jewish community.

16:3 *Paul had him circumcised:* he did this in order that Timothy might be able to associate with the Jews and so perform a ministry among them. Paul did not object to the Jewish Christians' adherence to the law. But he insisted that the law could not be imposed on the Gentiles. Paul himself lived in accordance with the law, or as exempt from the law, according to particular circumstances (see 1 Cor 9:19–23).

16:7 *The Spirit of Jesus:* this is an unusual formulation in Luke's writings. The parallelism with v 6 indicates its meaning, the holy Spirit.

15:28–29 Acts 15:19–20. **15:29** Gn 9:4; Lv 3:17; 17:10–14. **15:38** Acts 13:13. **16:1** 1 Tm 1:2; 2 Tm 1:5. **16:2** Phil 2:20.

the Spirit of Jesus did not allow them, 8 so they
crossed through Mysia and came down to Troas.
9 During [the] night Paul had a vision. A Mace-
donian stood before him and implored him with
these words, "Come over to Macedonia and help
us." 10† When he had seen the vision, we sought
passage to Macedonia at once, concluding that
God had called us to proclaim the good news
to them.

Into Europe

11† We set sail from Troas, making a straight
run for Samothrace, and on the next day to
Neapolis, 12 and from there to Philippi, a lead-
ing city in that district of Macedonia and a Ro-
man colony. We spent some time in that city.
13 On the sabbath we went outside the city gate
along the river where we thought there would
be a place of prayer. We sat and spoke with the
women who had gathered there. 14† One of
them, a woman named Lydia, a dealer in purple
cloth, from the city of Thyatira, a worshiper of
God, listened, and the Lord opened her heart to
pay attention to what Paul was saying. 15 After
she and her household had been baptized, she
offered us an invitation, "If you consider me a
believer in the Lord, come and stay at my home,"
and she prevailed on us.

Imprisonment at Philippi

16† As we were going to the place of prayer,
we met a slave girl with an oracular spirit, who
used to bring a large profit to her owners through
her fortune-telling. 17 She began to follow Paul
and us, shouting, "These people are slaves of the
Most High God, who proclaim to you a way of
salvation." 18 She did this for many days. Paul
became annoyed, turned, and said to the spirit,
"I command you in the name of Jesus Christ to
come out of her." Then it came out at that mo-
ment.
19 When her owners saw that their hope of
profit was gone, they seized Paul and Silas and
dragged them to the public square before the
local authorities. 20† They brought them before
the magistrates and said, "These people are Jews
and are disturbing our city 21 and are advocating
customs that are not lawful for us Romans to
adopt or practice." 22* The crowd joined in the
attack on them, and the magistrates had them
stripped and ordered them to be beaten with
rods. 23 After inflicting many blows on them, they
threw them into prison and instructed the jailer
to guard them securely. 24 When he received these
instructions, he put them in the innermost cell
and secured their feet to a stake.

Deliverance from Prison

25 About midnight, while Paul and Silas were
praying and singing hymns to God as the prison-
ers listened, 26 there was suddenly such a severe
earthquake that the foundations of the jail shook;
all the doors flew open, and the chains of all were

Introducing...

Lydia and Priscilla

Women were a crucial part of Christianity from its beginnings. The Acts of the Apostles names two women who were instrumental in Paul's missionary journeys: Lydia and Priscilla. Lydia (see Acts 16:11–15) was Paul's first convert in Philippi, which is part of modern-day Europe. She was a textile merchant and was wealthy enough to support a household and open her home to Paul and Silas to stay for an extended time.

In chapter 18, we meet Priscilla and her husband, Aquila. This family hosted Paul in Corinth. Later, they accompanied him from Corinth to Antioch. While there they instructed Apollos in the "Way [of God]" (18:26). Luke's inclusion of these women indicates that women were active in the early Church, not only supporting the missionary work of Paul but also leading and teaching.

▶ Acts 16:14–15, 18:1–26

†

16:10–17 This is the first of the so-called "we-sections" in Acts, where Luke writes as one of Paul's companions. The other passages are 20:5–15; 21:1–18; 27:1—28:16. Scholars debate whether Luke may not have used the first person plural simply as a literary device to lend color to the narrative. The realism of the narrative, however, lends weight to the argument that the "we" includes Luke or another companion of Paul whose data Luke used as a source.

16:11–40 The church at Philippi became a flourishing community to which Paul addressed one of his letters (see Introduction to the Letter to the Philippians).

16:14 *A worshiper of God:* a "God-fearer." See the note on 8:26–40.

16:16 *With an oracular spirit:* literally, "with a Python spirit." The Python was the serpent or dragon that guarded the Delphic oracle. It later came to designate a "spirit that pronounced oracles" and also a ventriloquist who, it was thought, had such a spirit in the belly.

16:20 *Magistrates:* in Greek, *stratēgoi,* the popular designation of the *duoviri,* the highest officials of the Roman colony of Philippi.

16:22–23 2 Cor 11:25; Phil 1:30; 1 Thes 2:2.

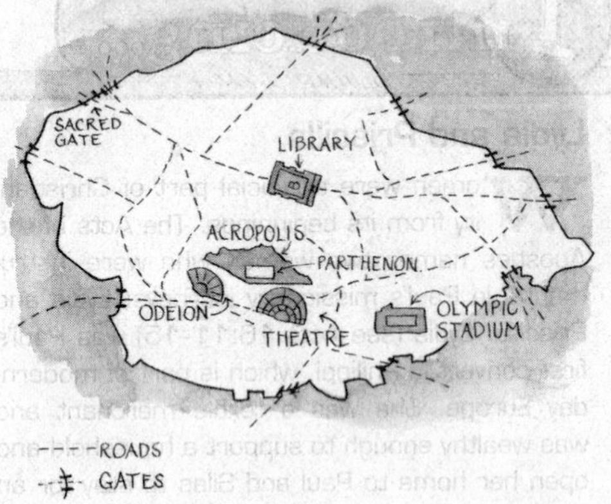

Map of first-century Athens **17:16–34**

pulled loose. 27 When the jailer woke up and saw the prison doors wide open, he drew [his] sword and was about to kill himself, thinking that the prisoners had escaped. 28 But Paul shouted out in a loud voice, "Do no harm to yourself; we are all here." 29 He asked for a light and rushed in and, trembling with fear, he fell down before Paul and Silas. 30 Then he brought them out and said, "Sirs, what must I do to be saved?" 31 And they said, "Believe in the Lord Jesus and you and your household will be saved." 32 So they spoke the word of the Lord to him and to everyone in his house. 33 He took them in at that hour of the night and bathed their wounds; then he and all his family were baptized at once. 34 He brought them up into his house and provided a meal and with his household rejoiced at having come to faith in God.

35† But when it was day, the magistrates sent the lictors with the order, "Release those men." 36 The jailer reported the[se] words to Paul, "The magistrates have sent orders that you be released. Now, then, come out and go in peace." 37*† But Paul said to them, "They have beaten us publicly, even though we are Roman citizens and have not been tried, and have thrown us into prison. And now, are they going to release us secretly? By no means. Let them come themselves and lead us out." 38* The lictors reported these words to the magistrates, and they became alarmed when they heard that they were Roman citizens. 39 So they came and placated them, and led them out and asked that they leave the city. 40 When they had come out of the prison, they went to Lydia's house where they saw and encouraged the brothers, and then they left.

Paul in Thessalonica

17 1* When they took the road through Amphipolis and Apollonia, they reached Thessalonica, where there was a synagogue of the Jews. 2 Following his usual custom, Paul joined them, and for three sabbaths he entered into discussions with them from the scriptures, 3* expounding and demonstrating that the Messiah had to suffer and rise from the dead, and that "This is the Messiah, Jesus, whom I proclaim to you." 4 Some of them were convinced and joined Paul and Silas; so, too, a great number of Greeks who were worshipers, and not a few of the prominent women. 5* But the Jews became jealous and recruited some worthless men loitering in the public square, formed a mob, and set the city in turmoil. They marched on the house of Jason, intending to bring them before the people's assembly. 6† When they could not find them, they dragged Jason and some of the brothers before the city magistrates, shouting, "These people who have been creating a disturbance all over the world have now come here, 7*† and Jason has welcomed them. They all act in opposition to the decrees of Caesar and claim instead that there is another king, Jesus." 8 They stirred up the crowd and the city magistrates who, upon hearing these charges, 9 took a surety payment from Jason and the others before releasing them.

Paul in Beroea

10 The brothers immediately sent Paul and Silas to Beroea during the night. Upon arrival they went to the synagogue of the Jews. 11* These Jews were more fair-minded than those in Thessalonica, for they received the word with all willingness and examined the scriptures daily to determine whether these things were so. 12 Many of them became believers, as did not a few of the influential Greek women and men. 13 But when the Jews of Thessalonica learned that the word of God had now been proclaimed by Paul in Beroea also, they came there too to cause a commotion

†

16:35 *The lictors:* the equivalent of police officers, among whose duties were the apprehension and punishment of criminals.

16:37 Paul's Roman citizenship granted him special privileges in regard to criminal process. Roman law forbade under severe penalty the beating of Roman citizens (see also 22:25).

17:6–7 The accusations against Paul and his companions echo the charges brought against Jesus in Lk 23:2.

17:7 *There is another king, Jesus:* a distortion into a political sense of the apostolic proclamation of Jesus and the kingdom of God (see 8:12).

*

16:37 Acts 22:25.
16:38 Acts 22:29.
17:1 1 Thes 2:1–2.
17:3 Acts 3:18; Lk 24:25–26, 46.
17:5 Rom 16:21.
17:7 Lk 23:2; Jn 19:12–15.
17:11 Jn 5:39.

ACTS

and stir up the crowds. 14* So the brothers at once sent Paul on his way to the seacoast, while Silas and Timothy remained behind. 15 After Paul's escorts had taken him to Athens, they came away with instructions for Silas and Timothy to join him as soon as possible.

Paul in Athens

16† While Paul was waiting for them in Athens, he grew exasperated at the sight of the city full of idols. 17 So he debated in the synagogue with the Jews and with the worshipers, and daily in the public square with whoever happened to be there. 18† Even some of the Epicurean and Stoic philosophers engaged him in discussion. Some asked, "What is this scavenger trying to say?" Others said, "He sounds like a promoter of foreign deities," because he was preaching about 'Jesus' and 'Resurrection.' 19*† They took him and led him to the Areopagus and said, "May we learn what this new teaching is that you speak of? 20 For you bring some strange notions to our ears; we should like to know what these things mean." 21 Now all the Athenians as well as the foreigners residing there used their time for nothing else but telling or hearing something new.

Paul's Speech at the Areopagus

22† Then Paul stood up at the Areopagus and said:

"You Athenians, I see that in every respect you are very religious. 23† For as I walked around looking carefully at your shrines, I even discovered an altar inscribed, 'To an Unknown God.' What therefore you unknowingly worship, I proclaim to you. 24* The God who made the world and all that is in it, the Lord of heaven and earth,

Pray It!

Help Us to Evangelize

Paul was wonderfully gifted for his work as an evangelist. He had the ability to communicate with both common people and intellectuals. He was familiar with three cultures—Jewish, Greek, and Roman—and proclaimed the Gospel message in ways all three could understand. He was skilled at building Christian communities. And he was absolutely fearless in preaching about Jesus Christ. Let's pray for these gifts in ourselves so that we can continue the Church's mission of evangelization, particularly to young people.

O God, how I admire Paul! I too want to share your Good News with others. So let your Holy Spirit bless me with the gift of evangelization. Help me to reach out to other young people no matter what clique or group they belong to. Help me to bring out the best in our culture and to challenge that which is wrong or misleading. Give me courage to speak fearlessly about my faith in Jesus when it is right to do so. And let me be your instrument in building communities of faith, hope, and love. Amen.

▶ **Acts of the Apostles, chapter 17**

ACTS

†

17:16–21 Paul's presence in Athens sets the stage for the great discourse before a Gentile audience in vv 22–31. Although Athens was a politically insignificant city at this period, it still lived on the glories of its past and represented the center of Greek culture. The setting describes the conflict between Christian preaching and Hellenistic philosophy.

17:18 *Epicurean and Stoic philosophers:* for the followers of Epicurus (342–271 B.C.), the goal of life was happiness attained through sober reasoning and the searching out of motives for all choice and avoidance. The Stoics were followers of Zeno, a younger contemporary of Alexander the Great. Zeno and his followers believed in a type of pantheism that held that the spark of divinity was present in all reality and that, in order to be free, each person must live "according to nature." *This scavenger:* literally, "seed-picker," as of a bird that picks up grain. The word is later used of scrap collectors and of people who take other people's ideas and propagate them as if they were their own. *Promoter of foreign deities:* according to Xenophon, Socrates was accused of promoting new deities. The accusation against Paul echoes the charge against Socrates. *'Jesus' and 'Resurrection':* the Athenians are presented as misunderstanding Paul from the outset; they think he is preaching about Jesus and a goddess named *Anastasis,* i.e., Resurrection.

17:19 *To the Areopagus:* the "Areopagus" refers either to the Hill of Ares west of the Acropolis or to the Council of Athens, which at one time met on the hill but which at this time assembled in the Royal Colonnade (*Stoa Basileios*).

17:22–31 In Paul's appearance at the Areopagus he preaches his climactic speech to Gentiles in the cultural center of the ancient world. The speech is more theological than christological. Paul's discourse appeals to the Greek world's belief in divinity as responsible for the origin and existence of the universe. It contests the common belief in a multiplicity of gods supposedly exerting their powers through their images. It acknowledges that the attempt to find God is a constant human endeavor. It declares, further, that God is the judge of the human race, that the time of the judgment has been determined, and that it will be executed through a man whom God raised from the dead. The speech reflects sympathy with pagan religiosity, handles the subject of idol worship gently, and appeals for a new examination of divinity, not from the standpoint of creation but from the standpoint of judgment.

17:23 *'To an Unknown God':* ancient authors such as Pausanias, Philostratus, and Tertullian speak of Athenian altars with no specific dedication as altars of "unknown gods" or "nameless altars."

17:14 1 Thes 3:1–2.
17:19 1 Cor 1:22.
17:24 Acts 7:48–50; Gn 1:1; 1 Kgs 8:27; Is 42:5.

does not dwell in sanctuaries made by human hands, 25 nor is he served by human hands because he needs anything. Rather it is he who gives to everyone life and breath and everything. 26† He made from one the whole human race to dwell on the entire surface of the earth, and he fixed the ordered seasons and the boundaries of their regions, 27* so that people might seek God, even perhaps grope for him and find him, though indeed he is not far from any one of us. 28† For 'In him we live and move and have our being,' as even some of your poets have said, 'For we too are his offspring.' 29* Since therefore we are the offspring of God, we ought not to think that the divinity is like an image fashioned from gold, silver, or stone by human art and imagination. 30 God has overlooked the times of ignorance, but now he demands that all people everywhere repent 31* because he has established a day on which he will 'judge the world with justice' through a man he has appointed, and he has provided confirmation for all by raising him from the dead."

32 When they heard about resurrection of the dead, some began to scoff, but others said, "We should like to hear you on this some other time." 33 And so Paul left them. 34 But some did join him, and became believers. Among them were Dionysius, a member of the Court of the Areopagus, a woman named Damaris, and others with them.

Paul in Corinth

ACTS

18 1 After this he left Athens and went to Corinth. 2*† There he met a Jew named Aquila, a native of Pontus, who had recently come from Italy with his wife Priscilla because Claudius had ordered all the Jews to leave Rome. He went to visit them 3 and, because he practiced the same trade, stayed with them and worked, for they were tentmakers by trade. 4 Every sabbath, he entered into discussions in the synagogue, attempting to convince both Jews and Greeks.

5 When Silas and Timothy came down from Macedonia, Paul began to occupy himself totally with preaching the word, testifying to the Jews that the Messiah was Jesus. 6*† When they opposed him and reviled him, he shook out his garments and said to them, "Your blood be on your heads! I am clear of responsibility. From now on I will go to the Gentiles." 7*† So he left there and went to a house belonging to a man named Titus Justus, a worshiper of God; his house was next to a synagogue. 8*† Crispus, the synagogue official, came to believe in the Lord along with his entire household, and many of the Corinthians who heard believed and were baptized. 9* One night in a vision the Lord said to Paul, "Do not be afraid. Go on speaking, and do not be silent, 10 for I am with you. No one will attack and harm you, for I have many people in this city." 11 He settled there for a year and a half and taught the word of God among them.

Accusations before Gallio

12† But when Gallio was proconsul of Achaia, the Jews rose up together against Paul and brought him to the tribunal, 13† saying, "This man is inducing people to worship God contrary to the law." 14 When Paul was about to reply, Gallio spoke to the Jews, "If it were a matter of some crime or malicious fraud, I should with reason hear the complaint of you Jews; 15 but since it is a question of arguments over doctrine and titles and your own law, see to it yourselves. I do not wish to be a judge of such matters." 16 And he drove them away from the tribunal. 17 They all seized Sosthenes, the synagogue official, and beat him in full view of the tribunal. But none of this was of concern to Gallio.

Return to Syrian Antioch

18*† Paul remained for quite some time, and after saying farewell to the brothers he sailed for Syria, together with Priscilla and Aquila. At

†

17:26 *From one:* many manuscripts read "from one blood." *Fixed . . . seasons:* or "fixed limits to the epochs."

17:28 *'In him we live and move and have our being':* some scholars understand this saying to be based on an earlier saying of Epimenides of Knossos (6th century B.C.). *'For we too are his offspring':* here Paul is quoting Aratus of Soli, a third-century B.C. poet from Cilicia.

18:2 *Aquila . . . Priscilla:* both may already have been Christians at the time of their arrival in Corinth (see 26). According to 1 Cor 16:19, their home became a meeting place for Christians. *Claudius:* the Emperor Claudius expelled the Jews from Rome ca. A.D. 49. The Roman historian Suetonius gives as reason for the expulsion disturbances among the Jews "at the instigation of Chrestos," probably meaning disputes about the messiahship of Jesus.

18:6 *Shook out his garments:* a gesture indicating Paul's repudiation of his mission to the Jews there; cf 28:17–31.

18:7 *A worshiper of God:* see the note on 8:26–40.

18:8 *Crispus:* in 1 Cor 1:14, Paul mentions that Crispus was one of the few he himself baptized at Corinth.

18:12 *When Gallio was proconsul of Achaia:* Gallio's proconsulship in Achaia is dated to A.D. 51–52 from an inscription discovered at Delphi. This has become an important date in establishing a chronology of the life and missionary work of Paul.

18:13 *Contrary to the law:* Gallio (15) understands this to be a problem of Jewish, not Roman, law.

18:18 *He had his hair cut because he had taken a vow:* a reference to a Nazirite vow (see Nm 6:1–21, especially, 6:18) taken by Paul (see also 21:23–27).

17:27 Jer 23:23; Wis 13:6; Rom 1:19.
17:29 Acts 19:26; Is 40:18–20; 44:10–17; Rom 1:22–23.
17:31 Acts 10:42.
18:2 Rom 16:3.
18:6 Acts 13:51; Mt 10:14; 27:24–25; Mk 6:11; Lk 9:5; 10:10–11.
18:7 Acts 13:46–47; 28:28.
18:8 1 Cor 1:14.
18:9–10 Jer 1:8.
18:18 Acts 21:24; Nm 6:18.

Cenchreae he had his hair cut because he had
taken a vow. 19 When they reached Ephesus, he
left them there, while he entered the synagogue
and held discussions with the Jews. 20 Although
they asked him to stay for a longer time, he did
not consent, 21 but as he said farewell he prom-
ised, "I shall come back to you again, God will-
ing." Then he set sail from Ephesus. 22† Upon
landing at Caesarea, he went up and greeted the
church and then went down to Antioch. 23† After
staying there some time, he left and traveled in
orderly sequence through the Galatian country
and Phrygia, bringing strength to all the disci-
ples.

Apollos

24*† A Jew named Apollos, a native of Alex-
andria, an eloquent speaker, arrived in Ephesus.
He was an authority on the scriptures. 25 He had
been instructed in the Way of the Lord and, with
ardent spirit, spoke and taught accurately about
Jesus, although he knew only the baptism of
John. 26† He began to speak boldly in the syn-
agogue; but when Priscilla and Aquila heard
him, they took him aside and explained to him
the Way [of God] more accurately. 27 And when
he wanted to cross to Achaia, the brothers en-
couraged him and wrote to the disciples there
to welcome him. After his arrival he gave great
assistance to those who had come to believe
through grace. 28 He vigorously refuted the Jews
in public, establishing from the scriptures that
the Messiah is Jesus.

Paul in Ephesus

19 1† While Apollos was in Corinth, Paul
traveled through the interior of the
country and came [down] to Ephesus where
he found some disciples. 2 He said to them,
"Did you receive the holy Spirit when you be-
came believers?" They answered him, "We have
never even heard that there is a holy Spirit."
3 He said, "How were you baptized?" They re-
plied, "With the baptism of John." 4* Paul then
said, "John baptized with a baptism of repen-
tance, telling the people to believe in the one
who was to come after him, that is, in Jesus."
5 When they heard this, they were baptized
in the name of the Lord Jesus. 6* And when
Paul laid [his] hands on them, the holy Spirit
came upon them, and they spoke in tongues
and prophesied. 7 Altogether there were about
twelve men.

8 He entered the synagogue, and for three
months debated boldly with persuasive argu-
ments about the kingdom of God. 9 But when
some in their obstinacy and disbelief dispar-
aged the Way before the assembly, he withdrew
and took his disciples with him and began to
hold daily discussions in the lecture hall of
Tyrannus. 10 This continued for two years with
the result that all the inhabitants of the prov-
ince of Asia heard the word of the Lord, Jews
and Greeks alike. 11 So extraordinary were the
mighty deeds God accomplished at the hands
of Paul 12* that when face cloths or aprons that
touched his skin were applied to the sick, their
diseases left them and the evil spirits came out
of them.

The Jewish Exorcists

13 Then some itinerant Jewish exorcists tried
to invoke the name of the Lord Jesus over those
with evil spirits, saying, "I adjure you by the Jesus
whom Paul preaches." 14 When the seven sons of
Sceva, a Jewish high priest, tried to do this, 15 the
evil spirit said to them in reply, "Jesus I recog-
nize, Paul I know, but who are you?" 16 The per-
son with the evil spirit then sprang at them and
subdued them all. He so overpowered them that
they fled naked and wounded from that house.
17 When this became known to all the Jews and
Greeks who lived in Ephesus, fear fell upon them
all, and the name of the Lord Jesus was held in
great esteem. 18 Many of those who had become
believers came forward and openly acknowledged
their former practices. 19 Moreover, a large number
of those who had practiced magic collected their
books and burned them in public. They calculated
their value and found it to be fifty thousand silver
pieces. 20 Thus did the word of the Lord continue
to spread with influence and power.

†

18:22 *He went up and greeted the church:* "going up" suggests a visit to the church in Jerusalem.

18:23—21:16 Luke's account of Paul's third missionary journey devotes itself mainly to his work at Ephesus (19:1—20:1). There is a certain restiveness on Paul's part and a growing conviction that the Spirit bids him return to Jerusalem and prepare to go to Rome (19:21).

18:24–25 Apollos appears as a preacher who knows the teaching of Jesus in the context of John's baptism of repentance. Aquila and Priscilla instruct him more fully. He is referred to in 1 Cor 1:12; 3:5–6, 22.

18:26 *The Way [of God]:* for the Way, see the note on 9:2. Other manuscripts here read "the Way of the Lord," "the word of the Lord," or simply "the Way."

19:1–6 Upon his arrival in Ephesus, Paul discovers other people at the same religious stage as Apollos, though they seem to have considered themselves followers of Christ, not of the Baptist. On the relation between baptism and the reception of the Spirit, see the note on 8:16.

*

18:24 1 Cor 1:12.
19:4 Acts 1:5; 11:16; 13:24–25; Mt 3:11; Mk 1:8; Lk 3:16.
19:6 Acts 8:15–17; 10:44, 46.
19:12 Acts 5:15–16; Lk 8:44–47.

19:23–40

The temple of the goddess Artemis

Paul's Plans

21* When this was concluded, Paul made up
his mind to travel through Macedonia and
Achaia, and then to go on to Jerusalem, say-
ing, "After I have been there, I must visit Rome
also." 22 Then he sent to Macedonia two of his
assistants, Timothy and Erastus, while he himself
stayed for a while in the province of Asia.

The Riot of the Silversmiths

23 About that time a serious disturbance broke
out concerning the Way. 24† There was a silver-
smith named Demetrius who made miniature
silver shrines of Artemis and provided no little
work for the craftsmen. 25 He called a meeting of
these and other workers in related crafts and said,
"Men, you know well that our prosperity derives
from this work. 26* As you can now see and hear,
not only in Ephesus but throughout most of the
province of Asia this Paul has persuaded and
misled a great number of people by saying that
gods made by hands are not gods at all. 27 The
danger grows, not only that our business will be
discredited, but also that the temple of the great
goddess Artemis will be of no account, and that
she whom the whole province of Asia and all
the world worship will be stripped of her mag-
nificence."
28 When they heard this, they were filled with
fury and began to shout, "Great is Artemis of
the Ephesians!" 29* The city was filled with
confusion, and the people rushed with one
accord into the theater, seizing Gaius and Aris-
tarchus, the Macedonians, Paul's traveling com-
panions. 30 Paul wanted to go before the crowd,
but the disciples would not let him, 31† and even
some of the Asiarchs who were friends of his sent
word to him advising him not to venture into
the theater. 32 Meanwhile, some were shouting
one thing, others something else; the assembly
was in chaos, and most of the people had no
idea why they had come together. 33 Some of the
crowd prompted Alexander, as the Jews pushed
him forward, and Alexander signaled with his
hand that he wished to explain something to the
gathering. 34 But when they recognized that he
was a Jew, they all shouted in unison, for about
two hours, "Great is Artemis of the Ephesians!"
35† Finally the town clerk restrained the crowd
and said, "You Ephesians, what person is there
who does not know that the city of the Ephe-
sians is the guardian of the temple of the great
Artemis and of her image that fell from the sky?
36 Since these things are undeniable, you must
calm yourselves and not do anything rash. 37 The
men you brought here are not temple robbers,
nor have they insulted our goddess. 38 If Deme-
trius and his fellow craftsmen have a complaint
against anyone, courts are in session, and there
are proconsuls. Let them bring charges against
one another. 39 If you have anything further to
investigate, let the matter be settled in the law-
ful assembly, 40† for, as it is, we are in danger
of being charged with rioting because of today's
conduct. There is no cause for it. We shall [not]
be able to give a reason for this demonstration."
With these words he dismissed the assembly.

Journey to Macedonia and Greece

20 1* When the disturbance was over, Paul
had the disciples summoned and, after
encouraging them, he bade them farewell and
set out on his journey to Macedonia. 2 As he
traveled throughout those regions, he provided
many words of encouragement for them. Then
he arrived in Greece, 3 where he stayed for three
months. But when a plot was made against him

†

19:24 *Miniature silver shrines of Artemis:* the temple of Artemis at Ephesus was one of the seven wonders of the ancient world. Artemis, originally the Olympian virgin hunter, moon goddess, and goddess of wild nature, was worshiped at Ephesus as an Asian mother goddess and goddess of fertility. She was one of the most widely worshiped female deities in the Hellenistic world (see 18:27).

19:31 *Asiarchs:* the precise status and role of the Asiarchs is disputed. They appear to have been people of wealth and influence who promoted the Roman imperial cult and who may also have been political representatives in a league of cities in the Roman province of Asia.

19:35 *Guardian of the temple:* this title was accorded by Rome to cities that provided a temple for the imperial cult. Inscriptional evidence indicates that Ephesus was acknowledged as the temple keeper of Artemis and of the imperial cult. *That fell from the sky:* many scholars think that this refers to a meteorite that was worshiped as an image of the goddess.

19:40 Some manuscripts omit the negative in [*not*] *be able,* making the meaning, "There is no cause for which we shall be able to give a reason for this demonstration."

19:21 Acts 23:11; Rom 1:13; 15:22–32.
19:26 Acts 17:29.
19:29 Col 4:10.
20:1 1 Cor 16:1.

by the Jews as he was about to set sail for Syria,
he decided to return by way of Macedonia.

Return to Troas

4* Sopater, the son of Pyrrhus, from Beroea, ac-
companied him, as did Aristarchus and Secundus
from Thessalonica, Gaius from Derbe, Timothy,
and Tychicus and Trophimus from Asia 5*† who
went on ahead and waited for us at Troas. 6† We
sailed from Philippi after the feast of Unleavened
Bread, and rejoined them five days later in Troas,
where we spent a week.

Eutychus Restored to Life

7† On the first day of the week when we gath-
ered to break bread, Paul spoke to them because
he was going to leave on the next day, and he
kept on speaking until midnight. 8 There were
many lamps in the upstairs room where we were
gathered, 9 and a young man named Eutychus
who was sitting on the window sill was sink-
ing into a deep sleep as Paul talked on and on.
Once overcome by sleep, he fell down from the
third story and when he was picked up, he was
dead. 10*† Paul went down, threw himself upon
him, and said as he embraced him, "Don't be
alarmed; there is life in him." 11 Then he returned
upstairs, broke the bread, and ate; after a long
conversation that lasted until daybreak, he de-
parted. 12 And they took the boy away alive and
were immeasurably comforted.

Journey to Miletus

13 We went ahead to the ship and set sail for
Assos where we were to take Paul on board, as
he had arranged, since he was going overland.
14 When he met us in Assos, we took him aboard
and went on to Mitylene. 15 We sailed away from
there on the next day and reached a point off
Chios, and a day later we reached Samos, and on
the following day we arrived at Miletus. 16† Paul
had decided to sail past Ephesus in order not
to lose time in the province of Asia, for he was
hurrying to be in Jerusalem, if at all possible, for
the day of Pentecost.

Paul's Farewell Speech at Miletus

17 From Miletus he had the presbyters of the
church at Ephesus summoned. 18 When they
came to him, he addressed them, "You know
how I lived among you the whole time from the
day I first came to the province of Asia. 19 I served
the Lord with all humility and with the tears and
trials that came to me because of the plots of the
Jews, 20 and I did not at all shrink from telling
you what was for your benefit, or from teaching
you in public or in your homes. 21 I earnestly
bore witness for both Jews and Greeks to repen-
tance before God and to faith in our Lord Jesus.
22 But now, compelled by the Spirit, I am going
to Jerusalem. What will happen to me there I do
not know, 23* except that in one city after an-
other the holy Spirit has been warning me that
imprisonment and hardships await me. 24* Yet
I consider life of no importance to me, if only I
may finish my course and the ministry that I re-
ceived from the Lord Jesus, to bear witness to the
gospel of God's grace.

25 "But now I know that none of you to whom
I preached the kingdom during my travels will
ever see my face again. 26 And so I solemnly
declare to you this day that I am not responsi-
ble for the blood of any of you, 27 for I did not
shrink from proclaiming to you the entire plan
of God. 28*† Keep watch over yourselves and
over the whole flock of which the holy Spirit has
appointed you overseers, in which you tend the
church of God that he acquired with his own
blood. 29* I know that after my departure savage
wolves will come among you, and they will not
spare the flock. 30* And from your own group,
men will come forward perverting the truth to
draw the disciples away after them. 31* So be
vigilant and remember that for three years, night
and day, I unceasingly admonished each of you
with tears. 32 And now I commend you to God

†

20:5 The second "we-section" of Acts begins here. See the note on 16:10–17.

20:6 *Feast of Unleavened Bread:* see the note on Lk 22:1.

20:7 *The first day of the week:* the day after the sabbath and the first day of the Jewish week, apparently chosen originally by the Jerusalem community for the celebration of the liturgy of the Eucharist in order to relate it to the resurrection of Christ.

20:10 The action of Paul in throwing himself upon the dead boy recalls that of Elijah in 1 Kgs 17:21 where the son of the widow of Zarephath is revived and that of Elisha in 2 Kgs 4:34 where the Shunamite woman's son is restored to life.

20:16–35 Apparently aware of difficulties at Ephesus and neighboring areas, Paul calls the presbyters together at Miletus, about thirty miles from Ephesus. He reminds them of his dedication to the gospel (18–21), speaks of what he is about to suffer for the gospel (22–27), and admonishes them to guard the community against false prophets, sure to arise upon his departure (28–31). He concludes by citing a saying of Jesus (35) not recorded in the gospel tradition. Luke presents this farewell to the Ephesian presbyters as Paul's last will and testament.

20:28 *Overseers:* see the note on Phil 1:1. *The church of God:* because the clause "that he acquired with his own blood" following "the church of God" suggests that "his own blood" refers to God's blood, some early copyists changed "the church of God" to "the church of the Lord." Some prefer the translation "acquired with the blood of his own," i.e., Christ.

20:4 Rom 16:21.
20:5 Acts 21:29; 2 Tm 4:20.
20:10 1 Kgs 17:17–24; 2 Kgs 4:30–37; Mt 9:24; Mk 5:39; Lk 8:52.
20:23 Acts 9:16.
20:24 2 Tm 4:7.
20:28 Jn 21:15–17; 1 Pt 5:2.
20:29 Jn 10:12.
20:30 Mt 7:15; 2 Pt 2:1–3; 1 Jn 2:18–19.
20:31 1 Thes 2:11.

Pray It!

Good-Bye to a Friend

As Paul prepares to leave Ephesus in Acts of the Apostles 20:36–38, we hear that the members of the Christian community there are experiencing feelings of sadness as they say good-bye to Paul. He has been an important person in their lives, and they have come to depend on him. Their grief overwhelms them, and they all experience great pain over his departure.

When we have to say good-bye to someone we care for deeply, we go through a grieving process. We feel sad and mad at the same time. Even after our friend has been gone for a long time, our heart has an empty space that our friend used to fill.

Lord, it is so difficult to say good-bye to my friend. We have shared so much together. I thank you for blessing me with this friendship. As we depart in separate directions, be our constant guardian and companion. Guide each of us safely to our destination. And until our paths cross again, surround us with your loving and protective embrace. Amen.

▶ **Acts 20:36–38**

ACTS

and to that gracious word of his that can build
you up and give you the inheritance among
all who are consecrated. 33 I have never wanted
anyone's silver or gold or clothing. 34* You know
well that these very hands have served my needs
and my companions. 35* In every way I have
shown you that by hard work of that sort we
must help the weak, and keep in mind the words
of the Lord Jesus who himself said, 'It is more
blessed to give than to receive.' "
36 When he had finished speaking he knelt down
and prayed with them all. 37 They were all weeping
loudly as they threw their arms around Paul and
kissed him, 38 for they were deeply distressed that
he had said that they would never see his face
again. Then they escorted him to the ship.

Arrival at Tyre

21 1† When we had taken leave of them we
set sail, made a straight run for Cos, and
on the next day for Rhodes, and from there to
Patara. 2 Finding a ship crossing to Phoenicia, we
went on board and put out to sea. 3 We caught
sight of Cyprus but passed by it on our left and
sailed on toward Syria and put in at Tyre where
the ship was to unload cargo. 4 There we sought
out the disciples and stayed for a week. They kept
telling Paul through the Spirit not to embark for
Jerusalem. 5 At the end of our stay we left and
resumed our journey. All of them, women and
children included, escorted us out of the city,
and after kneeling on the beach to pray, 6 we
bade farewell to one another. Then we boarded
the ship, and they returned home.

Arrival at Ptolemais and Caesarea

7 We continued the voyage and came from Tyre
to Ptolemais, where we greeted the brothers and
stayed a day with them. 8*† On the next day we
resumed the trip and came to Caesarea, where
we went to the house of Philip the evangelist,
who was one of the Seven, and stayed with him.
9 He had four virgin daughters gifted with proph-
ecy. 10† We had been there several days when a
prophet named Agabus came down from Judea.
11*† He came up to us, took Paul's belt, bound
his own feet and hands with it, and said, "Thus
says the holy Spirit: This is the way the Jews
will bind the owner of this belt in Jerusalem,
and they will hand him over to the Gentiles."
12 When we heard this, we and the local residents
begged him not to go up to Jerusalem. 13* Then
Paul replied, "What are you doing, weeping and
breaking my heart? I am prepared not only to be
bound but even to die in Jerusalem for the name
of the Lord Jesus." 14*† Since he would not be
dissuaded we let the matter rest, saying, "The
Lord's will be done."

Paul and James in Jerusalem

15 After these days we made preparations for
our journey, then went up to Jerusalem. 16 Some

† **21:1–18** The third "we-section" of Acts (see the note on 16:10–17).

21:8 *One of the Seven:* see the note on 6:2–4.

21:10 *Agabus:* mentioned in 11:28 as the prophet who predicted the famine that occurred when Claudius was emperor.

21:11 The symbolic act of Agabus recalls those of Old Testament prophets. Compare Is 20:2; Ez 4:1; Jer 13:1.

21:14 The Christian disciples' attitude reflects that of Jesus (see Lk 22:42).

* **20:34** 1 Cor 4:12; 1 Thes 2:9; 2 Thes 3:8.
20:35 Sir 4:31.
21:8 Acts 6:5; 8:5–6.
21:11 Acts 11:28; 20:23.
21:13 Acts 19:15–16.
21:14 Mt 6:10; 26:39; Mk 14:36; Lk 22:42.

of the disciples from Caesarea came along to
lead us to the house of Mnason, a Cypriot, a
disciple of long standing, with whom we were to
stay. 17† When we reached Jerusalem the broth-
ers welcomed us warmly. 18 The next day, Paul
accompanied us on a visit to James, and all the
presbyters were present. 19 He greeted them, then
proceeded to tell them in detail what God had
accomplished among the Gentiles through his
ministry. 20 They praised God when they heard
it but said to him, "Brother, you see how many
thousands of believers there are from among
the Jews, and they are all zealous observers of
the law. 21 They have been informed that you
are teaching all the Jews who live among the
Gentiles to abandon Moses and that you are tell-
ing them not to circumcise their children or to
observe their customary practices. 22 What is to
be done? They will surely hear that you have ar-
rived. 23*† So do what we tell you. We have four
men who have taken a vow. 24† Take these men
and purify yourself with them, and pay their ex-
penses that they may have their heads shaved. In
this way everyone will know that there is nothing
to the reports they have been given about you but
that you yourself live in observance of the law.
25*† As for the Gentiles who have come to be-
lieve, we sent them our decision that they abstain
from meat sacrificed to idols, from blood, from
the meat of strangled animals, and from unlaw-
ful marriage." 26* So Paul took the men, and on
the next day after purifying himself together with
them entered the temple to give notice of the day
when the purification would be completed and
the offering made for each of them.

Paul's Arrest

27 When the seven days were nearly completed,
the Jews from the province of Asia noticed him in
the temple, stirred up the whole crowd, and laid
hands on him, 28*† shouting, "Fellow Israelites,
help us. This is the man who is teaching everyone
everywhere against the people and the law and

Did You Know?

Who Are Paul's Opponents?

As you read about Paul's return to Jerusalem, it may become confusing to keep track of the main characters. To help you keep it straight, here are some clues:

- One group is the Jewish Christians, represented by James and the elders (see Acts 21:17–26). Although the Jewish Christians might be suspicious of Paul's defense of the Gentile Christians, they support Paul and come up with a plan for him to try to prove his Jewish loyalty.
- Another group is the Jews who don't believe in Jesus. These Jews see the rise of the Jesus movement as a threat to Judaism, and Paul is the most well-known representative of that movement. They attempt to arrest him and have him killed in a mob scene (see verses 27–36).
- The third group is the Roman rulers. The Romans probably have no interest in this conflict except to keep the peace. The Roman tribune (governor) thinks he can keep the Jews happy by having Paul flogged (see 22:22–29). But surprise! Paul is a Roman citizen and has civil rights that the tribune must honor.

So who are Paul's—and Christianity's—opponents? Luke tells us that at first they are the Jewish Christians. Later, they are the Jews who don't believe in Jesus. Still later—after this story occurs—they will be the Romans. Luke knows all this in hindsight and brings all of Paul's opponents into play in describing Paul's arrest and imprisonment.

▶ **Acts 21:17–26**

ACTS

†

21:17–26 The leaders of the Jewish Christians of Jerusalem inform Paul that the Jews there believe he has encouraged the Jews of the diaspora to abandon the Mosaic law. According to Acts, Paul had no objection to the retention of the law by the Jewish Christians of Jerusalem and left the Jews of the diaspora who accepted Christianity free to follow the same practice.

21:23–26 The leaders of the community suggest that Paul, on behalf of four members of the Jerusalem community, make the customary payment for the sacrifices offered at the termination of the Nazirite vow (see Nm 6:1–24) in order to impress favorably the Jewish Christians in Jerusalem with his high regard for the Mosaic law. Since Paul himself had once made this vow (18:18), his respect for the law would be on public record.

21:24 *Pay their expenses:* according to Nm 6:14–15 the Nazirite had to present a yearling lamb for a holocaust, a yearling ewe lamb for a sin offering, and a ram for a peace offering, along with food and drink offerings, upon completion of the period of the vow.

21:25 Paul is informed about the apostolic decree, seemingly for the first time (see the note on 15:13–35). The allusion to the decree was probably introduced here by Luke to remind his readers that the Gentile Christians themselves were asked to respect certain Jewish practices deriving from the law.

21:28 The charges against Paul by the diaspora Jews are identical to the charges brought against Stephen by diaspora Jews in 6:13. *Brought Greeks into the temple:* non-Jews were forbidden, under penalty of death, to go beyond the Court of the Gentiles. Inscriptions in Greek and Latin on a stone ballustrade marked off the prohibited area.

*

21:23–27 Acts 18:18; Nm 6:1–21. **21:25** Acts 15:19–20, 28–29. **21:26** 1 Cor 9:20. **21:28** Rom 15:31.

Live It!

Sharing Your Story

Have you ever heard a dramatic conversion story? Sometimes, on religious television programs or at large youth rallies, individuals share personal stories of their belief in God helping them to overcome addictions, terrible problems, or great sin. Or they tell of how they came to recognize and accept God in their lives as a result of a serious illness or the death of a close friend or family member. Listening to these dramatic stories may make us feel that our own journey as a follower of Jesus—our own story—does not quite measure up. Nothing could be further from the truth in God's eyes.

We all have our own conversion stories—those moments of turning to God, of receiving a special call to serve others. And though our personal story might not be as dramatic as other people's stories, God will use it to encourage others to put their faith in Christ and dedicate their lives to his mission. Are you willing to share your story of faith with others?

► **Acts 22:6–16**

ACTS

this place, and what is more, he has even brought
Greeks into the temple and defiled this sacred
place." 29 For they had previously seen Trophimus
the Ephesian in the city with him and supposed
that Paul had brought him into the temple. 30 The
whole city was in turmoil with people rushing
together. They seized Paul and dragged him out
of the temple, and immediately the gates were
closed. 31† While they were trying to kill him, a
report reached the cohort commander that all
Jerusalem was rioting. 32 He immediately took
soldiers and centurions and charged down on
them. When they saw the commander and the
soldiers they stopped beating Paul. 33 The cohort
commander came forward, arrested him, and
ordered him to be secured with two chains; he
tried to find out who he might be and what he
had done. 34 Some in the mob shouted one thing,
others something else; so, since he was unable
to ascertain the truth because of the uproar, he
ordered Paul to be brought into the compound.
35 When he reached the steps, he was carried by
the soldiers because of the violence of the mob,
36*† for a crowd of people followed and shouted,
"Away with him!"
37 Just as Paul was about to be taken into the
compound, he said to the cohort commander,
"May I say something to you?" He replied, "Do
you speak Greek? 38*† So then you are not the
Egyptian who started a revolt some time ago and
led the four thousand assassins into the desert?"
39 Paul answered, "I am a Jew, of Tarsus in Cilicia,
a citizen of no mean city; I request you to permit
me to speak to the people." 40† When he had
given his permission, Paul stood on the steps and
motioned with his hand to the people; and when
all was quiet he addressed them in Hebrew.

Paul's Defense before the Jerusalem Jews

22 1† "My brothers and fathers, listen to
what I am about to say to you in my de-
fense." 2 When they heard him addressing them
in Hebrew they became all the more quiet. And
he continued, 3* "I am a Jew, born in Tarsus in
Cilicia, but brought up in this city. At the feet of
Gamaliel I was educated strictly in our ancestral
law and was zealous for God, just as all of you are
today. 4* I persecuted this Way to death, binding
both men and women and delivering them to
prison. 5 Even the high priest and the whole coun-
cil of elders can testify on my behalf. For from
them I even received letters to the brothers and
set out for Damascus to bring back to Jerusalem
in chains for punishment those there as well.
6* "On that journey as I drew near to Da-
mascus, about noon a great light from the sky

† **21:31** *Cohort commander:* literally, "the leader of a thousand in a cohort." At this period the Roman cohort commander usually led six hundred soldiers, a tenth of a legion; but the number in a cohort varied.

21:36 *"Away with him!":* at the trial of Jesus before Pilate in Lk 23:18, the people similarly shout, "Away with this man."

21:38 *The Egyptian:* according to the Jewish historian Josephus, an Egyptian gathered a large crowd on the Mount of Olives to witness the destruction of the walls of Jerusalem that would fall at the Egyptian "prophet's" word. The commotion was put down by the Roman authorities and the Egyptian escaped, but only after thousands had been killed. *Four thousand assassins:* literally, *sicarii.* According to Josephus, these were political nationalists who removed their opponents by assassination with a short dagger, called in Latin a *sica.*

21:40 *In Hebrew:* meaning, perhaps, in Aramaic, which at this time was the Semitic tongue in common use.

22:1–21 Paul's first defense speech is presented to the Jerusalem crowds. Luke here presents Paul as a devout Jew (3) and zealous persecutor of the Christian community (4–5), and then recounts the conversion of Paul for the second time in Acts (see the note on 9:1–19).

* **21:36** Lk 23:18; Jn 19:15; Acts 22:22.
21:38 Acts 5:36–37.
22:3 Acts 5:34; 26:4–5; 2 Cor 11:22; Gal 1:13–14; Phil 3:5–6.
22:4 Acts 8:3; 9:1–2; 22:19; 26:9–11; Phil 3:6.
22:6 Acts 9:3; 26:13; 1 Cor 15:8.

suddenly shone around me. 7* I fell to the ground and heard a voice saying to me, 'Saul, Saul, why are you persecuting me?' 8* I replied, 'Who are you, sir?' And he said to me, 'I am Jesus the Nazorean whom you are persecuting.' 9* My companions saw the light but did not hear the voice of the one who spoke to me. 10* I asked, 'What shall I do, sir?' The Lord answered me, 'Get up and go into Damascus, and there you will be told about everything appointed for you to do.' 11* Since I could see nothing because of the brightness of that light, I was led by hand by my companions and entered Damascus.

12* "A certain Ananias, a devout observer of the law, and highly spoken of by all the Jews who lived there, 13 came to me and stood there and said, 'Saul, my brother, regain your sight.' And at that very moment I regained my sight and saw him. 14 Then he said, 'The God of our ancestors designated you to know his will, to see the Righteous One, and to hear the sound of his voice; 15† for you will be his witness before all to what you have seen and heard. 16 Now, why delay? Get up and have yourself baptized and your sins washed away, calling upon his name.'

17 "After I had returned to Jerusalem and while I was praying in the temple, I fell into a trance 18 and saw the Lord saying to me, 'Hurry, leave Jerusalem at once, because they will not accept your testimony about me.' 19* But I replied, 'Lord, they themselves know that from synagogue to synagogue I used to imprison and beat those who believed in you. 20* And when the blood of your witness Stephen was being shed, I myself stood by giving my approval and keeping guard over the cloaks of his murderers.' 21*† Then he said to me, 'Go, I shall send you far away to the Gentiles.' "

Paul Imprisoned

22*† They listened to him until he said this, but then they raised their voices and shouted, "Take such a one as this away from the earth. It is not right that he should live." 23 And as they were yelling and throwing off their cloaks and flinging dust into the air, 24 the cohort commander ordered him to be brought into the compound and gave instruction that he be interrogated under the lash to determine the reason why they were making such an outcry against him. 25*† But when they had stretched him out for the whips, Paul said to the centurion on duty, "Is it lawful for you to scourge a man who is a Roman citizen and has not been tried?" 26 When the centurion heard this, he went to the cohort commander and reported it, saying, "What are you going to do? This man is a Roman citizen." 27 Then the commander came and said to him, "Tell me, are you a Roman citizen?" "Yes," he answered. 28 The commander replied, "I acquired this citizenship for a large sum of money." Paul said, "But I was born one." 29 At once those who were going to interrogate him backed away from him, and the commander became alarmed when he realized that he was a Roman citizen and that he had had him bound.

Paul before the Sanhedrin

30 The next day, wishing to determine the truth about why he was being accused by the Jews, he freed him and ordered the chief priests and the whole Sanhedrin to convene. Then he brought Paul down and made him stand before them.

23 1* Paul looked intently at the Sanhedrin and said, "My brothers, I have conducted myself with a perfectly clear conscience before God to this day." 2† The high priest Ananias ordered his attendants to strike his mouth. 3*† Then Paul said to him, "God will strike you, you whitewashed wall. Do you indeed sit in judgment upon me according to the law and yet in violation of the law order me to be struck?" 4 The attendants said, "Would you revile God's high priest?" 5*† Paul answered, "Brothers, I did not realize he was the high priest. For it is written, 'You shall not curse a ruler of your people.' "

6* Paul was aware that some were Sadducees and some Pharisees, so he called out before the

---

22:15 *His witness:* like the Galilean followers during the historical ministry of Jesus, Paul too, through his experience of the risen Christ, is to be a witness to the resurrection (compare 1:8; 10:39–41; Lk 24:48).

22:21 Paul endeavors to explain that his position on the law has not been identical with that of his audience because it has been his prophetic mission to preach to the Gentiles to whom the law was not addressed and who had no faith in it as a way of salvation.

22:22 Paul's suggestion that his prophetic mission to the Gentiles did not involve his imposing the law on them provokes the same opposition as occurred in Pisidian Antioch (13:45).

22:25 *"Is it lawful for you to scourge a man who is a Roman citizen and has not been tried?":* see the note on 16:37.

23:2 *The high priest Ananias:* Ananias, son of Nedebaeus, was high priest from A.D. 47 to 59.

23:3 *God will strike you:* Josephus reports that Ananias was later assassinated in A.D. 66 at the beginning of the First Revolt.

23:5 Luke portrays Paul as a model of one who is obedient to the Mosaic law. Paul, because of his reverence for the law (Ex 22:27), withdraws his accusation of hypocrisy, "whitewashed wall" (cf Mt 23:27), when he is told Ananias is the high priest.

22:7 Acts 9:4; 26:14.
22:8 Mt 25:40; Acts 9:5; 26:15.
22:9 Acts 9:7; 26:13–14.
22:10 Acts 9:6; 26:16.
22:11 Acts 9:8.
22:12–16 Acts 9:10–19.
22:19 Acts 8:3; 9:1–2; 22:4–5; 26:9–11.
22:20 Acts 7:58; 8:1.
22:21 Acts 9:15; Gal 2:7–9.
22:22 Acts 21:36; Lk 23:18; Jn 19:15.
22:25 Acts 16:37.
23:1 Acts 24:16.
23:3 Ez 13:10–15; Mt 23:27.
23:5 Ex 22:27.
23:6 Acts 24:15, 21; 26:5; Phil 3:5.

Did You Know?

What About the Jews?

The earliest Christians were Jews. It was agonizing to them that so many of their Jewish friends wouldn't believe in Jesus. Indeed, not only did those friends not believe in Jesus, but some tried to stop the spread of Christianity because they viewed Christian beliefs as blasphemy. Acts of the Apostles, chapters 22–28, tells of Jewish attacks against Paul, which ultimately end with Paul's traveling to Rome to make his case before the emperor.

But the questions remain: If the Jews are God's People, why don't they believe that Jesus was the Jewish Messiah? Couldn't God make it easier for them to believe? Does God cause their lack of faith in Jesus? Who is ultimately responsible for anyone's faith? If you are interested, read Romans, chapters 9–11, where Paul tries to answer those questions.

▶ Acts 22:30—28:31

Sanhedrin, "My brothers, I am a Pharisee, the
son of Pharisees; I am on trial for hope in the
resurrection of the dead." 7 When he said this, a
dispute broke out between the Pharisees and
Sadducees, and the group became divided. 8* For
the Sadducees say that there is no resurrection or
angels or spirits, while the Pharisees acknowledge all three. 9 A great uproar occurred, and
some scribes belonging to the Pharisee party
stood up and sharply argued, "We find nothing
wrong with this man. Suppose a spirit or an angel has spoken to him?" 10 The dispute was so
serious that the commander, afraid that Paul
would be torn to pieces by them, ordered his
troops to go down and rescue him from their
midst and take him into the compound. 11*† The
following night the Lord stood by him and said,
"Take courage. For just as you have borne witness
to my cause in Jerusalem, so you must also bear
witness in Rome."

Transfer to Caesarea

12 When day came, the Jews made a plot and
bound themselves by oath not to eat or drink
until they had killed Paul. 13 There were more
than forty who formed this conspiracy. 14 They
went to the chief priests and elders and said,
"We have bound ourselves by a solemn oath to
taste nothing until we have killed Paul. 15 You,
together with the Sanhedrin, must now make an
official request to the commander to have him
bring him down to you, as though you meant
to investigate his case more thoroughly. We on
our part are prepared to kill him before he arrives." 16 The son of Paul's sister, however, heard
about the ambush; so he went and entered the
compound and reported it to Paul. 17† Paul then
called one of the centurions and requested, "Take
this young man to the commander; he has something to report to him." 18 So he took him and
brought him to the commander and explained,
"The prisoner Paul called me and asked that I
bring this young man to you; he has something
to say to you." 19 The commander took him by
the hand, drew him aside, and asked him privately, "What is it you have to report to me?"
20 He replied, "The Jews have conspired to ask
you to bring Paul down to the Sanhedrin tomorrow, as though they meant to inquire about him
more thoroughly, 21 but do not believe them.
More than forty of them are lying in wait for
him; they have bound themselves by oath not
to eat or drink until they have killed him. They
are now ready and only wait for your consent."
22 As the commander dismissed the young man
he directed him, "Tell no one that you gave me
this information."

23† Then he summoned two of the centurions
and said, "Get two hundred soldiers ready to go
to Caesarea by nine o'clock tonight, along with
seventy horsemen and two hundred auxiliaries.
24 Provide mounts for Paul to ride and give him
safe conduct to Felix the governor." 25 Then
he wrote a letter with this content: 26† "Claudius Lysias to his excellency the governor Felix,

ACTS

23:11 The occurrence of the vision of Christ consoling Paul and assuring him that he will be his witness in Rome prepares the reader for the final section of Acts: the journey of Paul and the word he preaches to Rome under the protection of the Romans.

23:17 *Centurions:* a centurion was a military officer in charge of one hundred soldiers.

23:23 *By nine o'clock tonight:* literally, "by the third hour of the night." The night hours began at 6 p.m. *Two hundred auxiliaries:* the meaning of the Greek is not certain. It seems to refer to spearmen from the local police force and not from the cohort of soldiers, which would have numbered only 500–1000 men.

23:26–30 The letter emphasizes the fact that Paul is a Roman citizen and asserts the lack of evidence that he is guilty of a crime against the empire. The tone of the letter implies that the commander became initially involved in Paul's case because of his Roman citizenship, but this is not an exact description of what really happened (see 21:31–33; 22:25–29).

23:8 Mt 22:23; Lk 20:27. **23:11** Acts 19:21.

greetings.† [27]* This man, seized by the Jews and
about to be murdered by them, I rescued after
intervening with my troops when I learned that
he was a Roman citizen. [28] I wanted to learn
the reason for their accusations against him so
I brought him down to their Sanhedrin. [29]* I
discovered that he was accused in matters of con-
troversial questions of their law and not of any
charge deserving death or imprisonment. [30] Since
it was brought to my attention that there will be
a plot against the man, I am sending him to you
at once, and have also notified his accusers to
state [their case] against him before you."
[31] So the soldiers, according to their orders,
took Paul and escorted him by night to An-
tipatris. [32] The next day they returned to the
compound, leaving the horsemen to complete
the journey with him. [33] When they arrived in
Caesarea they delivered the letter to the governor
and presented Paul to him. [34] When he had read
it and asked to what province he belonged, and
learned that he was from Cilicia, [35] he said, "I
shall hear your case when your accusers arrive."
Then he ordered that he be held in custody in
Herod's praetorium.

Trial before Felix

24 [1] Five days later the high priest Ananias
came down with some elders and an ad-
vocate, a certain Tertullus, and they presented
formal charges against Paul to the governor.
[2] When he was called, Tertullus began to accuse
him, saying, "Since we have attained much peace
through you, and reforms have been accom-
plished in this nation through your provident
care, [3] we acknowledge this in every way and
everywhere, most excellent Felix, with all grati-
tude. [4] But in order not to detain you further, I
ask you to give us a brief hearing with your cus-
tomary graciousness. [5]*† We found this man to
be a pest; he creates dissension among Jews all
over the world and is a ringleader of the sect of
the Nazoreans. [6]* He even tried to desecrate our
temple, but we arrested him. [7]† [8] If you examine
him you will be able to learn from him for your-
self about everything of which we are accusing
him." [9] The Jews also joined in the attack and
asserted that these things were so.
[10]† Then the governor motioned to him to
speak and Paul replied, "I know that you have
been a judge over this nation for many years
and so I am pleased to make my defense before
you. [11] As you can verify, not more than twelve
days have passed since I went up to Jerusalem
to worship. [12] Neither in the temple, nor in the
synagogues, nor anywhere in the city did they
find me arguing with anyone or instigating a riot
among the people. [13] Nor can they prove to you
the accusations they are now making against me.
[14]* But this I do admit to you, that according to
the Way, which they call a sect, I worship the
God of our ancestors and I believe everything
that is in accordance with the law and written in
the prophets. [15]* I have the same hope in God
as they themselves have that there will be a res-
urrection of the righteous and the unrighteous.
[16]* Because of this, I always strive to keep my
conscience clear before God and man. [17]* After
many years, I came to bring alms for my nation
and offerings. [18]* While I was so engaged, they
found me, after my purification, in the temple
without a crowd or disturbance. [19] But some
Jews from the province of Asia, who should be
here before you to make whatever accusation
they might have against me— [20] or let these men
themselves state what crime they discovered
when I stood before the Sanhedrin, [21]* unless it
was my one outcry as I stood among them, that 'I
am on trial before you today for the resurrection
of the dead.' "
[22] Then Felix, who was accurately informed
about the Way, postponed the trial, saying,
"When Lysias the commander comes down, I
shall decide your case." [23] He gave orders to the
centurion that he should be kept in custody
but have some liberty, and that he should not
prevent any of his friends from caring for his
needs.

Captivity in Caesarea

[24]† Several days later Felix came with his
wife Drusilla, who was Jewish. He had Paul

†

23:26 M. Antonius Felix was procurator of Judea from A.D. 52 to 60. His procuratorship was marked by cruelty toward and oppression of his Jewish subjects.

24:5 *Nazoreans:* that is, followers of Jesus of Nazareth.

24:7 The Western text has added here a verse (really 6b–8a) that is not found in the best Greek manuscripts. It reads, "and would have judged him according to our own law, but the cohort commander Lysias came and violently took him out of our hands and ordered his accusers to come before you."

24:10–21 Whereas the advocate Tertullus referred to Paul's activities on his missionary journeys, the apostle narrowed the charges down to the riot connected with the incident in the temple (see 21:27–30; 24:17–20). In his defense, Paul stresses the continuity between Christianity and Judaism.

24:24–25 The way of Christian discipleship greatly disquiets Felix, who has entered into an adulterous marriage with Drusilla, daughter of Herod Agrippa I. This marriage provides the background for the topics Paul speaks about and about which Felix does not want to hear.

*

23:27 Acts 21:30–34; 22:27.
23:29 Acts 18:14–15; 25:18–19.
24:5 Acts 24:14; Lk 23:2.
24:6 Acts 21:28.
24:14 Acts 24:5.
24:15 Dn 12:2; Jn 5:28–29.
24:16 Acts 23:1.
24:17 Rom 15:25–26; Gal 2:10.
24:18–19 Acts 21:26–30.
24:21 Acts 23:6; 24:15.

ACTS

summoned and listened to him speak about
faith in Christ Jesus. 25 But as he spoke about
righteousness and self-restraint and the coming
judgment, Felix became frightened and said,
"You may go for now; when I find an opportu-
nity I shall summon you again." 26 At the same
time he hoped that a bribe would be offered him
by Paul, and so he sent for him very often and
conversed with him.
27† Two years passed and Felix was succeeded
by Porcius Festus. Wishing to ingratiate himself
with the Jews, Felix left Paul in prison.

Appeal to Caesar

25 1 Three days after his arrival in the prov-
ince, Festus went up from Caesarea to
Jerusalem 2† where the chief priests and Jew-
ish leaders presented him their formal charges
against Paul. They asked him 3 as a favor to have
him sent to Jerusalem, for they were plotting to
kill him along the way. 4 Festus replied that Paul
was being held in custody in Caesarea and that
he himself would be returning there shortly. 5 He
said, "Let your authorities come down with me,
and if this man has done something improper,
let them accuse him."
6 After spending no more than eight or ten
days with them, he went down to Caesarea, and
on the following day took his seat on the tribu-
nal and ordered that Paul be brought in. 7 When
he appeared, the Jews who had come down from
Jerusalem surrounded him and brought many
serious charges against him, which they were un-
able to prove. 8 In defending himself Paul said,
"I have committed no crime either against the
Jewish law or against the temple or against Cae-
sar." 9† Then Festus, wishing to ingratiate himself
with the Jews, said to Paul in reply, "Are you will-
ing to go up to Jerusalem and there stand trial
before me on these charges?" 10 Paul answered,
"I am standing before the tribunal of Caesar;
this is where I should be tried. I have commit-
ted no crime against the Jews, as you very well
know. 11 If I have committed a crime or done
anything deserving death, I do not seek to escape
the death penalty; but if there is no substance to
the charges they are bringing against me, then
no one has the right to hand me over to them. I
appeal to Caesar." 12 Then Festus, after conferring
with his council, replied, "You have appealed to
Caesar. To Caesar you will go."

Paul before King Agrippa

13† When a few days had passed, King Agrippa
and Bernice arrived in Caesarea on a visit to
Festus. 14* Since they spent several days there,
Festus referred Paul's case to the king, saying,
"There is a man here left in custody by Felix.
15 When I was in Jerusalem the chief priests and
the elders of the Jews brought charges against
him and demanded his condemnation. 16 I an-
swered them that it was not Roman practice to
hand over an accused person before he has faced
his accusers and had the opportunity to defend
himself against their charge. 17 So when [they]
came together here, I made no delay; the next
day I took my seat on the tribunal and ordered
the man to be brought in. 18* His accusers stood
around him, but did not charge him with any of
the crimes I suspected. 19 Instead they had some
issues with him about their own religion and
about a certain Jesus who had died but who Paul
claimed was alive. 20 Since I was at a loss how to
investigate this controversy, I asked if he were
willing to go to Jerusalem and there stand trial
on these charges. 21 And when Paul appealed that
he be held in custody for the Emperor's decision,
I ordered him held until I could send him to Cae-
sar." 22 Agrippa said to Festus, "I too should like
to hear this man." He replied, "Tomorrow you
will hear him."
23 The next day Agrippa and Bernice came with
great ceremony and entered the audience hall
in the company of cohort commanders and the
prominent men of the city and, by command of
Festus, Paul was brought in. 24 And Festus said,
"King Agrippa and all you here present with us,
look at this man about whom the whole Jewish
populace petitioned me here and in Jerusalem,
clamoring that he should live no longer. 25 I
found, however, that he had done nothing de-
serving death, and so when he appealed to the
Emperor, I decided to send him. 26 But I have
nothing definite to write about him to our sover-
eign; therefore I have brought him before all of
you, and particularly before you, King Agrippa,

ACTS

†

24:27 Very little is known of Porcius Festus who was a procurator of Judea from A.D. 60 to 62.

25:2 Even after two years the animosity toward Paul in Jerusalem had not subsided (see 24:27).

25:9–12 Paul refuses to acknowledge that the Sanhedrin in Jerusalem has any jurisdiction over him now (11). Paul uses his right as a Roman citizen to appeal his case to the jurisdiction of the Emperor (Nero, ca. A.D. 60) (12). This move broke the deadlock between Roman protective custody of Paul and the plan of his enemies to kill him (3).

25:13 *King Agrippa and Bernice:* brother and sister, children of Herod Agrippa I whose activities against the Jerusalem community are mentioned in 12:1–19. Agrippa II was a petty ruler over small areas in northern Palestine and some villages in Perea. His influence on the Jewish population of Palestine was insignificant.

25:14 Acts 24:27. **25:18–19** Acts 18:14–15; 23:29.

Cultural Connection

Paul Teaches Us How to Live Our Faith

Reporters *Marisa and Ricardo.* [Speaking into their microphones] We're here, live, in Caesarea, where Paul of Tarsus has just spoken with King Agrippa and Governor Festus. Here comes Paul now. Let's see what he has to say. Paul, why has your message caused so much controversy?

Paul. It was never my intention to cause strife or conflict. But I must speak the truth, and the truth is that God has revealed his salvation for us in Jesus Christ. In Jesus, salvation is available to everyone—Jews and Gentiles, slaves and free people, men and women—and we are all equal as sons and daughters of God. Unfortunately, this truth is upsetting to some people, and they have gone to great lengths to try to get rid of me.

Marisa and Ricardo. But hasn't your message been well received by many people—including many different types of people?

Paul. Yes, it has. I think this is because Jesus taught us always to respect every person as a son or daughter of God regardless of his or her culture or social class. Under the guidance of the Holy Spirit, Christian communities allow for diversity while keeping a common unity in Jesus Christ. I think people are hungry for this.

Marisa and Ricardo. Soon you will be heading for Rome, where you will be on trial for alleged crimes against the empire. Are you worried?

Paul. [Smiling] Why be worried? No one has ultimate power over me except my Lord Jesus Christ. I only need to be faithful to my calling, and I will receive my prize—eternal life with God. Plus I have the prayers and support of many close friends. But thank you for your concern. God's grace and peace be with you.

Marisa and Ricardo. And thank you, Paul.

Acts of the Apostles, chapter 26

so that I may have something to write as a result
of this investigation. 27 For it seems senseless to
me to send up a prisoner without indicating the
charges against him."

King Agrippa Hears Paul

26 1 Then Agrippa said to Paul, "You may
now speak on your own behalf." So Paul
stretched out his hand and began his defense.
2† "I count myself fortunate, King Agrippa, that
I am to defend myself before you today against
all the charges made against me by the Jews, 3 es-
pecially since you are an expert in all the Jewish
customs and controversies. And therefore I beg
you to listen patiently. 4† My manner of living
from my youth, a life spent from the beginning
among my people and in Jerusalem, all [the]
Jews know. 5* They have known about me from
the start, if they are willing to testify, that I have
lived my life as a Pharisee, the strictest party of
our religion. 6* But now I am standing trial be-
cause of my hope in the promise made by God to
our ancestors. 7 Our twelve tribes hope to attain
to that promise as they fervently worship God
day and night; and on account of this hope I am
accused by Jews, O king. 8 Why is it thought un-
believable among you that God raises the dead?
9* I myself once thought that I had to do many
things against the name of Jesus the Nazorean,
10* and I did so in Jerusalem. I imprisoned many
of the holy ones with the authorization I received
from the chief priests, and when they were to be
put to death I cast my vote against them. 11 Many
times, in synagogue after synagogue, I punished
them in an attempt to force them to blaspheme; I
was so enraged against them that I pursued them
even to foreign cities.
12 "On one such occasion I was traveling to
Damascus with the authorization and commis-
sion of the chief priests. 13* At midday, along the

† **26:2–23** Paul's final defense speech in Acts is now made before a king (see 9:15). In the speech Paul presents himself as a zealous Pharisee and Christianity as the logical development of Pharisaic Judaism. The story of his conversion is recounted for the third time in Acts in this speech (see the note on 9:1–19).

26:4 *Among my people:* that is, among the Jews.

26:5 Phil 3:5–6; Gal 1:13–14; 2 Cor 11:22.
26:6–8 Acts 23:6; 24:15, 21; 28:20.
26:9–11 Acts 8:3; 9:1–2; 22:19; Phil 3:6.
26:10 Acts 9:14.
26:13–14 Acts 9:7.

ACTS

way, O king, I saw a light from the sky, brighter
than the sun, shining around me and my travel-
ing companions.* 14*† We all fell to the ground
and I heard a voice saying to me in Hebrew,
'Saul, Saul, why are you persecuting me? It is
hard for you to kick against the goad.' 15* And I
said, 'Who are you, sir?' And the Lord replied, 'I
am Jesus whom you are persecuting. 16*† Get up
now, and stand on your feet. I have appeared to
you for this purpose, to appoint you as a servant
and witness of what you have seen [of me] and
what you will be shown. 17* I shall deliver you
from this people and from the Gentiles to whom
I send you, 18*† to open their eyes that they may
turn from darkness to light and from the power
of Satan to God, so that they may obtain forgive-
ness of sins and an inheritance among those who
have been consecrated by faith in me.'

19 "And so, King Agrippa, I was not disobedi-
ent to the heavenly vision. 20 On the contrary,
first to those in Damascus and in Jerusalem and
throughout the whole country of Judea, and then
to the Gentiles, I preached the need to repent and
turn to God, and to do works giving evidence of
repentance. 21* That is why the Jews seized me
[when I was] in the temple and tried to kill me.
22*† But I have enjoyed God's help to this very
day, and so I stand here testifying to small and
great alike, saying nothing different from what
the prophets and Moses foretold, 23*† that the
Messiah must suffer and that, as the first to rise
from the dead, he would proclaim light both to
our people and to the Gentiles."

Reactions to Paul's Speech

24 While Paul was so speaking in his defense,
Festus said in a loud voice, "You are mad, Paul;
much learning is driving you mad." 25 But Paul
replied, "I am not mad, most excellent Festus; I
am speaking words of truth and reason. 26† The
king knows about these matters and to him I
speak boldly, for I cannot believe that [any] of
this has escaped his notice; this was not done
in a corner. 27† King Agrippa, do you believe the
prophets? I know you believe." 28 Then Agrippa
said to Paul, "You will soon persuade me to play
the Christian." 29 Paul replied, "I would pray to
God that sooner or later not only you but all who
listen to me today might become as I am except
for these chains."

30 Then the king rose, and with him the gov-
ernor and Bernice and the others who sat with
them. 31† And after they had withdrawn they
said to one another, "This man is doing nothing
[at all] that deserves death or imprisonment."
32* And Agrippa said to Festus, "This man could
have been set free if he had not appealed to Cae-
sar."

Departure for Rome

27 1† When it was decided that we should
sail to Italy, they handed Paul and some
other prisoners over to a centurion named Julius
of the Cohort Augusta.† 2* We went on board a
ship from Adramyttium bound for ports in the
province of Asia and set sail. Aristarchus, a Mace-
donian from Thessalonica, was with us. 3 On the
following day we put in at Sidon where Julius
was kind enough to allow Paul to visit his friends
who took care of him. 4 From there we put out to
sea and sailed around the sheltered side of Cy-
prus because of the headwinds, 5 and crossing the
open sea off the coast of Cilicia and Pamphylia
we came to Myra in Lycia.

†

26:14 *In Hebrew:* see the note on 21:40. *It is hard for you to kick against the goad:* this proverb is commonly found in Greek literature and in this context signifies the senselessness and ineffectiveness of any opposition to the divine influence in his life.

26:16 The words of Jesus directed to Paul here reflect the dialogues between Christ and Ananias (9:15) and between Ananias and Paul (22:14–15) in the two previous accounts of Paul's conversion.

26:18 *To open their eyes:* though no mention is made of Paul's blindness in this account (cf 9:8–9, 12, 18; 22:11–13), the task he is commissioned to perform is the removal of other people's spiritual blindness.

26:22 *Saying nothing different from what the prophets and Moses foretold:* see the note on Lk 18:31.

26:23 *That the Messiah must suffer:* see the note on Lk 24:26.

26:26 *Not done in a corner:* for Luke, this Greek proverb expresses his belief that he is presenting a story about Jesus and the church that is already well known. As such, the entire history of Christianity is public knowledge and incontestable. Luke presents his story in this way to provide "certainty" to his readers about the instructions they have received (Lk 1:4).

26:27–28 If the Christian missionaries proclaim nothing different from what the Old Testament prophets had proclaimed (22–23), then the logical outcome for the believing Jew, according to Luke, is to become a Christian.

26:31–32 In recording the episode of Paul's appearance before Agrippa, Luke wishes to show that, when Paul's case was judged impartially, no grounds for legal action against him were found (see 23:29; 25:25).

27:1—28:16 Here Luke has written a stirring account of adventure on the high seas, incidental to his main purpose of showing how well Paul got along with his captors and how his prophetic influence saved the lives of all on board. The recital also establishes the existence of Christian communities in Puteoli and Rome. This account of the voyage and shipwreck also constitutes the final "we-section" in Acts (see the note on 16:10–17).

27:1 *Cohort Augusta:* the presence of a Cohort Augusta in Syria during the first century A.D. is attested in inscriptions. Whatever the historical background to this information given by Luke may be, the name Augusta serves to increase the prominence and prestige of the prisoner Paul whose custodians bear so important a Roman name.

*

26:13 Acts 9:3; 22:6.
26:14 Acts 9:4; 22:7.
26:15 Mt 25:40; Acts 9:5; 22:8.
26:16 Ez 2:1; Acts 9:6; 22:10.
26:17 Jer 1:7.
26:18 Is 42:7, 16; 61:1 LXX; Col 1:13.
26:21 Acts 21:31.
26:22–23 Acts 3:18; Lk 24:26–27, 44–47.
26:23 Is 42:6; 49:6; Lk 2:32; 1 Cor 15:20–23.
26:32 Acts 25:11–12.
27:2 Acts 19:29; 20:4.

Storm and Shipwreck

6 There the centurion found an Alexandrian
ship that was sailing to Italy and put us on board.
7 For many days we made little headway, arriv-
ing at Cnidus only with difficulty, and because
the wind would not permit us to continue our
course we sailed for the sheltered side of Crete off
Salmone. 8 We sailed past it with difficulty and
reached a place called Fair Havens, near which
was the city of Lasea.
9*† Much time had now passed and sailing
had become hazardous because the time of the
fast had already gone by, so Paul warned them,
10 "Men, I can see that this voyage will result in
severe damage and heavy loss not only to the
cargo and the ship, but also to our lives." 11 The
centurion, however, paid more attention to the
pilot and to the owner of the ship than to what
Paul said. 12 Since the harbor was unfavorably
situated for spending the winter, the majority
planned to put out to sea from there in the hope
of reaching Phoenix, a port in Crete facing west-
northwest, there to spend the winter.
13 A south wind blew gently, and thinking
they had attained their objective, they weighed
anchor and sailed along close to the coast of
Crete. 14 Before long an offshore wind of hurri-
cane force called a "Northeaster" struck. 15 Since
the ship was caught up in it and could not head
into the wind we gave way and let ourselves be
driven. 16 We passed along the sheltered side
of an island named Cauda and managed only
with difficulty to get the dinghy under control.
17 They hoisted it aboard, then used cables to
undergird the ship. Because of their fear that
they would run aground on the shoal of Syrtis,
they lowered the drift anchor and were carried
along in this way. 18 We were being pounded
by the storm so violently that the next day they
jettisoned some cargo, 19 and on the third day
with their own hands they threw even the ship's
tackle overboard. 20 Neither the sun nor the stars
were visible for many days, and no small storm
raged. Finally, all hope of our surviving was
taken away.
21 When many would no longer eat, Paul stood
among them and said, "Men, you should have
taken my advice and not have set sail from Crete
and you would have avoided this disastrous loss.
22 I urge you now to keep up your courage; not
one of you will be lost, only the ship. 23 For last
night an angel of the God to whom I belong
and whom I serve stood by me 24* and said, 'Do
not be afraid, Paul. You are destined to stand
before Caesar; and behold, for your sake, God
has granted safety to all who are sailing with
you.' 25 Therefore, keep up your courage, men; I
trust in God that it will turn out as I have been
told. 26 We are destined to run aground on some
island."
27 On the fourteenth night, as we were still
being driven about on the Adriatic Sea, toward
midnight the sailors began to suspect that they
were nearing land. 28 They took soundings and
found twenty fathoms; a little farther on, they
again took soundings and found fifteen fath-
oms. 29 Fearing that we would run aground on a

Pray It!

When the Waves Get Too Rough

It is not easy to be courageous when you face danger. When you find yourself in situations where things are beyond your control, like Paul caught in a storm at sea, turn to God. After all, isn't faith for the times when you feel the most helpless and out of control?

Help, Lord, I'm lost at sea! When I started this journey of life, I thought I knew where I was headed, but then a few waves started to rock the boat, and I became frightened.

Next, the wind picked up, and my fear turned into confusion. Then the night fell, and my confusion turned into despair. And now I am lost and need you to help calm the waves in my life and stand beside me until the night turns into day.

Help me to find my bearings again, Lord. And when this storm is over, gift me with the wisdom to learn from this experience—to go back and make right what was wrong, not to lose hope at the first sign of trouble, and to hang on to you, my anchor, when life gets rough. Amen.

Acts 27:21–25

† **27:9** *The time of the fast:* the fast kept on the occasion of the Day of Atonement (Lv 16:29–31), which occurred in late September or early October.

27:9 Lv 16:29–31. **27:24** Acts 23:11.

rocky coast, they dropped four anchors from the
stern and prayed for day to come. 30 The sailors
then tried to abandon ship; they lowered the
dinghy to the sea on the pretext of going to lay
out anchors from the bow. 31 But Paul said to the
centurion and the soldiers, "Unless these men
stay with the ship, you cannot be saved." 32 So
the soldiers cut the ropes of the dinghy and set
it adrift.

33 Until the day began to dawn, Paul kept urg-
ing all to take some food. He said, "Today is the
fourteenth day that you have been waiting, going
hungry and eating nothing. 34 I urge you, there-
fore, to take some food; it will help you survive.
Not a hair of the head of anyone of you will be
lost." 35 * † When he said this, he took bread, gave
thanks to God in front of them all, broke it, and
began to eat. 36 They were all encouraged, and
took some food themselves. 37 In all, there were
two hundred seventy-six of us on the ship. 38 Af-
ter they had eaten enough, they lightened the
ship by throwing the wheat into the sea.

39 When day came they did not recognize the
land, but made out a bay with a beach. They
planned to run the ship ashore on it, if they
could. 40 So they cast off the anchors and aban-
doned them to the sea, and at the same time they
unfastened the lines of the rudders, and hoisting
the foresail into the wind, they made for the
beach. 41 But they struck a sandbar and ran the
ship aground. The bow was wedged in and could
not be moved, but the stern began to break up
under the pounding [of the waves]. 42 The sol-
diers planned to kill the prisoners so that none
might swim away and escape, 43 but the centu-
rion wanted to save Paul and so kept them from
carrying out their plan. He ordered those who
could swim to jump overboard first and get to
the shore, 44 and then the rest, some on planks,
others on debris from the ship. In this way, all
reached shore safely.

Winter in Malta

28 1 Once we had reached safety we learned
that the island was called Malta. 2 The na-
tives showed us extraordinary hospitality; they
lit a fire and welcomed all of us because it had
begun to rain and was cold. 3 Paul had gathered
a bundle of brushwood and was putting it on
the fire when a viper, escaping from the heat, fas-
tened on his hand. 4 † When the natives saw the
snake hanging from his hand, they said to one
another, "This man must certainly be a murderer;
though he escaped the sea, Justice has not let him
remain alive." 5 But he shook the snake off into
the fire and suffered no harm. 6 * They were ex-
pecting him to swell up or suddenly to fall down
dead but, after waiting a long time and seeing
nothing unusual happen to him, they changed
their minds and began to say that he was a god.
7 In the vicinity of that place were lands belong-
ing to a man named Publius, the chief of the
island. He welcomed us and received us cordially
as his guests for three days. 8 It so happened that
the father of Publius was sick with a fever and
dysentery. Paul visited him and, after praying,
laid his hands on him and healed him. 9 After
this had taken place, the rest of the sick on the
island came to Paul and were cured. 10 They paid
us great honor and when we eventually set sail
they brought us the provisions we needed.

Arrival in Rome

11 † Three months later we set sail on a ship
that had wintered at the island. It was an Alex-
andrian ship with the Dioscuri as its figurehead.
12 We put in at Syracuse and stayed there three
days, 13 and from there we sailed round the coast
and arrived at Rhegium. After a day, a south
wind came up and in two days we reached Pu-
teoli. 14 There we found some brothers and were
urged to stay with them for seven days. And thus
we came to Rome. 15 The brothers from there
heard about us and came as far as the Forum of
Appius and Three Taverns to meet us. On seeing
them, Paul gave thanks to God and took courage.
16 † When he entered Rome, Paul was allowed to
live by himself, with the soldier who was guard-
ing him.

Testimony to Jews in Rome

17 * † Three days later he called together the
leaders of the Jews. When they had gathered
he said to them, "My brothers, although I had

---

† **27:35** *He took bread . . . :* the words recall the traditional language of the celebration of the Eucharist (see Lk 22:19).

28:4 *Justice:* in Greek mythology, the pursuing goddess of vengeance and justice.

28:11 *Dioscuri:* that is, the Twin Brothers, Castor and Pollux, the sons of Zeus and the patrons of the sailors.

28:16 With Paul's arrival in Rome, the programmatic spread of the word of the Lord to "the ends of the earth" (1:8) is accomplished. In Rome, Paul is placed under house arrest, and under this mild form of custody he is allowed to proclaim the word in the capital of the civilized world of his day.

28:17–22 Paul's first act in Rome is to learn from the leaders of the Jewish community whether the Jews of Jerusalem plan to pursue their case against him before the Roman jurisdiction. He is informed that no such plan is afoot, but that the Jews of Rome have heard the Christian teaching denounced. Paul's offer to explain it to them is readily accepted.

---

* **27:35** Mt 15:36; Mk 6:41; 8:6; Lk 22:19; 1 Cor 11:23–24. **28:6** Acts 14:11. **28:17** Acts 24:12–13; 25:8.

done nothing against our people or our ancestral
customs, I was handed over to the Romans as a
prisoner from Jerusalem. 18* After trying my case
the Romans wanted to release me, because they
found nothing against me deserving the death
penalty. 19* But when the Jews objected, I was
obliged to appeal to Caesar, even though I had
no accusation to make against my own nation.
20*† This is the reason, then, I have requested
to see you and to speak with you, for it is on
account of the hope of Israel that I wear these
chains." 21 They answered him, "We have re-
ceived no letters from Judea about you, nor has
any of the brothers arrived with a damaging re-
port or rumor about you. 22* But we should like
to hear you present your views, for we know that
this sect is denounced everywhere."

23 So they arranged a day with him and came to
his lodgings in great numbers. From early morn-
ing until evening, he expounded his position to
them, bearing witness to the kingdom of God
and trying to convince them about Jesus from
the law of Moses and the prophets. 24 Some were
convinced by what he had said, while others did
not believe. 25† Without reaching any agreement
among themselves they began to leave; then
Paul made one final statement. "Well did the
holy Spirit speak to your ancestors through the
prophet Isaiah, saying:

26* 'Go to this people and say:
You shall indeed hear but not understand.
You shall indeed look but never see.
27 Gross is the heart of this people;
they will not hear with their ears;
they have closed their eyes,
so they may not see with their eyes
and hear with their ears
and understand with their heart and be
converted,
and I heal them.'

28* Let it be known to you that this salvation of
God has been sent to the Gentiles; they will lis-
ten." [29]†

30† He remained for two full years in his lodg-
ings. He received all who came to him, 31 and
with complete assurance and without hindrance
he proclaimed the kingdom of God and taught
about the Lord Jesus Christ.

†

28:20 *The hope of Israel:* in the words of Paul (23:6), Luke has identified this hope as hope in the resurrection of the dead.

28:25–28 Paul's final words in Acts reflect a major concern of Luke's writings: how the salvation promised in the Old Testament, accomplished by Jesus, and offered first to Israel (13:26), has now been offered to and accepted by the Gentiles. Quoting Is 6:9–10, Paul presents the scriptural support for his indictment of his fellow Jews who refuse to accept the message he proclaims. Their rejection leads to its proclamation among the Gentiles.

28:29 The Western text has added here a verse that is not found in the best Greek manuscripts: "And when he had said this, the Jews left, seriously arguing among themselves."

28:30–31 Although the ending of Acts may seem to be abrupt, Luke has now completed his story with the establishment of Paul and the proclamation of Christianity in Rome. Paul's confident and unhindered proclamation of the gospel in Rome forms the climax to the story whose outline was provided in 1:8: "You will be my witnesses in Jerusalem . . . and to the ends of the earth."

28:18 Acts 23:29; 25:25; 26:31–32.
28:19 Acts 25:11.
28:20 Acts 23:6; 24:15, 21; 26:6–8.
28:22 Acts 24:5, 14.
28:26 Is 6:9–10; Mt 13:14–15; Mk 4:12; Lk 8:10; Jn 12:40; Rom 11:8.
28:28 Acts 13:46; 18:6; Ps 67:2; Is 40:5 LXX; Lk 3:6.

Introduction to the Letters and Revelation

Despite the popularity of e-mailing, writing letters with pen and paper is still alive today. In letters, people often express themselves more clearly than they do in person, and say things that are difficult to say face-to-face. Perhaps you've been lucky enough to receive some special letters. Letters between parents and children, engaged couples, and even pen pals are often saved to be read again and again. They are treasured for their stories, their advice, and their expressions of love. The next twenty-one books of the New Testament are also treasured letters. Their stories, their advice, and their confidence in God's loving guidance have inspired generations of Christians

In Depth

When you read someone else's mail, you see only one side of the conversation. So you have to do some reading between the lines to understand the issues being addressed. This is also true of the New Testament letters. But when you do this, they give you a firsthand look at the first Christian communities and what they believed. In fact, the letters written by Paul are the oldest Christian documents we have, written even before the four Gospels. Paul's earliest letter, First Thessalonians, was probably written around AD 50. That's just a little over twenty years after the death and Resurrection of Jesus!

These letters follow a common pattern. They usually begin with (1) a greeting from the sender to the receiver or receivers. Next is (2) a prayer, most often of thanksgiving. This is followed by (3) the body of the letter, which addresses whatever issues the author wants to discuss; often, it includes general advice about Christian living. The letters close with (4) greetings and instructions to specific people and a final blessing.

There are exceptions to this pattern. The Books of Hebrews and First John do not have all four of these features and are more like essays about faith. The Book of James has more of the features but reads like a good sermon rather than a letter.

Saint Paul was the most prolific writer of the letters. At one time, it was thought that he produced thirteen of the twenty-one. However, modern scholars believe that some of the letters traditionally attributed to Paul were actually written by associates or later followers. Scholars have reached this conclusion because of differences in writing style, vocabulary, and thought. Those associates or followers of Paul applied his teaching to new situations faced by the early Christian communities. Similarly, the letters bearing the names of James, Peter, and John were probably written by associates or later followers of those men.

To a modern person, that might seem like forgery. But in the ancient world, it was not uncommon for followers of an important person to write in the person's name after her or his death. It was a way of honoring the person and keeping her or his traditions alive.

Although the Book of Revelation is grouped together with the letters in this introduction, it really is not a letter at all. Revelation was written as a series of visions to a disciple named John. The visions are filled with dramatic imagery and events. Some people interpret them as prophecies about the way the world will end, but for the most part, they are really coded messages about events happening in John's own time. Ultimately, the Book of Revelation is a hopeful message to persecuted Christians that God is in control and that goodness and justice will triumph.

As you explore these letters and the Book of Revelation, you'll see the church at its best: the miraculous growth, the Spirit-filled enthusiasm, and the deep love the early Christians had for one another and for Jesus. You'll also see how the early church was threatened by intense disagreements, jealousy, and scandals. Through it all, the authors reveal a deep faith and missionary spirit. They focus again and again on the death and Resurrection of Jesus and on the mystery of the church as the living Body of Christ acting in the world through the power of the Holy Spirit. These letters had a specific audience in the first century AD, but because God inspired them, their words are for you too!

Other Background

- There are nine letters by Paul or his followers named for the communities in which the recipient churches were located: Romans, First and Second Corinthians, Galatians, Ephesians (called a captivity letter because it is attributed to Paul writing from jail), Philippians (also a captivity letter), Colossians (also a captivity letter), and First and Second Thessalonians.
- There are four letters by Paul or his followers named for the individuals to whom they were sent: First and Second Timothy and Titus (called pastoral letters), and Philemon (a captivity letter).
- Hebrews is named for the Christian Jews for whom it was intended.
- There are seven catholic letters named after their stated authors: James; First and Second Peter; First, Second, and Third John; and Jude. They are called catholic because they are general letters to all Christians.
- The Book of Revelation is not a letter. It is a collection of the prophecies and visions of John of Patmos, a Christian prophet.

The Letter to the

Romans

Have you ever wondered what it is like to be loved unconditionally? This was the message Saint Paul was trying to convey to the people of Rome—God loves us unconditionally. In his Letter to the Romans, Paul addresses some important questions of life and faith. Paul wanted to share his understanding that although we may not always do what is right, God still desires a relationship with us through Jesus. We are justified—made right with God—by faith in Jesus Christ.

In Depth

Many people consider the Letter to the Romans the deepest expression of Paul's thinking. This was the only letter Paul wrote to a community he had not yet visited. At the time, he was planning to go to Rome and was trying to prepare the way by explaining his teaching on justification (or righteousness) and faith. Paul's message is that only God can acquit humanity of its sin so it can be restored to right relationship with God. His ideas are summed up in a verse from the first chapter: "For I am not ashamed of the gospel. It is the power of God for the salvation of everyone who believes" (verse 16).

Romans is not easy reading. Paul often makes his case by using arguments that might seem strange to us today. Some of his main points are these:

- Justification (or being made right with God) is available to both Jews and Gentiles (non-Jews).
- Because all people have sinned, no one has "earned" justification.
- Justification and salvation come through faith in Jesus Christ, not through following the Jewish religious law.
- Even though the Gospel has come to the Gentiles, God has not abandoned the Jews.

The Letter to the Romans contains many wonderfully comforting words. It tells us that when we don't know how to pray, God prays for us "with inexpressible groanings" (8:26)! And it says that "all things work for good for those who love God" (verse 28). And it asks, "If God is for us, who can be against us?" (verse 31).

So as you read this powerful letter, let go of your fears. Even though you're not perfect, God will never leave you. As Paul says, "I am convinced that neither death, nor life, nor angels, nor principalities, nor present things, nor future things, nor powers, nor height, nor depth, nor any other creature will be able to separate us from the love of God in Christ Jesus our Lord" (verses 38–39).

At a Glance

I. **Address (1:1–15).**
II. **Humanity Lost Without the Gospel (1:16—3:20).**
III. **Justification Through Faith in Christ (3:21—5:21).**
IV. **Justification and the Christian Life (6:1—8:39).**
V. **Jews and Gentiles in God's Plan (9:1—11:36).**
VI. **The Duties of Christians (12:1—15:13).**
VII. **Conclusion (15:14—16:27).**

Quick Facts

Inspired Author: Paul
Date Written: from AD 56 to 58
Audience: Jewish and Gentile Christians in Rome

Romans

6:4

I: Address

Greeting†

1 [1]* Paul, a slave of Christ Jesus,† called to be
an apostle and set apart for the gospel of God,
2* which he promised previously through his
prophets in the holy scriptures, 3*† the gospel
about his Son, descended from David according
to the flesh, 4* but established as Son of God in
power according to the spirit of holiness through
resurrection from the dead, Jesus Christ our Lord.
5*† Through him we have received the grace of
apostleship, to bring about the obedience of faith,
for the sake of his name, among all the Gentiles,
6* among whom are you also, who are called to
belong to Jesus Christ; 7*† to all the beloved of
God in Rome, called to be holy. Grace to you and
peace from God our Father and the Lord Jesus
Christ.

Thanksgiving

8*† First, I give thanks to my God through
Jesus Christ for all of you, because your faith is

†

1:1–7 In Paul's letters the greeting or *praescriptio* follows a standard form, though with variations. It is based upon the common Greco-Roman epistolary practice, but with the addition of Semitic and specifically Christian elements. The three basic components are: name of sender; name of addressee; greeting. In identifying himself, Paul often adds phrases to describe his apostolic mission; this element is more developed in Romans than in any other letter. Elsewhere he associates co-workers with himself in the greeting: Sosthenes (1 Corinthians), Timothy (2 Corinthians; Philippians; Philemon), Silvanus (1–2 Thessalonians). The standard secular greeting was the infinitive *chairein*, "greetings." Paul uses instead the similar-sounding *charis*, "grace," together with the Semitic greeting *šālôm* (Greek *eirēnē*), "peace." These gifts, foreshadowed in God's dealings with Israel (see Nm 6:24–26), have been poured out abundantly in Christ, and Paul wishes them to his readers. In Romans the Pauline *praescriptio* is expanded and expressed in a formal tone; it emphasizes Paul's office as apostle to the Gentiles. Verses 3–4 stress the gospel or kerygma, v 2 the fulfillment of God's promise, and vv 1 and 5 Paul's office. On his call, see Gal 1:15–16; 1 Cor 9:1; 15:8–10; Acts 9:1–22; 22:3–16; 26:4–18.

1:1 *Slave of Christ Jesus:* Paul applies the term slave to himself in order to express his undivided allegiance to the Lord of the church, the Master of all, including slaves and masters. "No one can serve (i.e., be a slave to) two masters," said Jesus (Mt 6:24). It is this aspect of the slave-master relationship rather than its degrading implications that Paul emphasizes when he discusses Christian commitment.

1:3–4 Paul here cites an early confession that proclaims Jesus' sonship as messianic descendant of David (cf Mt 22:42; 2 Tm 2:8; Rv 22:16) and as Son of God by the resurrection. As "life-giving spirit" (1 Cor 15:45), Jesus Christ is able to communicate the Spirit to those who believe in him.

1:5 Paul recalls his apostolic office, implying that the Romans know something of his history. *The obedience of faith:* as Paul will show at length in chs 6–8 and 12–15, faith in God's justifying action in Jesus Christ relates one to God's gift of the new life that is made possible through the death and resurrection of Jesus Christ and the activity of the holy Spirit (see especially 8:1–11).

1:7 *Called to be holy:* Paul often refers to Christians as "the holy ones" or "the saints." The Israelite community was called a "holy assembly" because they had been separated for the worship and service of the Lord (see Lv 11:44; 23:1–44). The Christian community regarded its members as sanctified by baptism (6:22; 15:16; 1 Cor 6:11; Eph 5:26–27). Christians are called to holiness (1 Cor 1:2; 1 Thes 4:7), that is, they are called to make their lives conform to the gift they have already received.

1:8 In Greco-Roman letters, the greeting was customarily followed by a prayer. The Pauline letters usually include this element (except Galatians and Titus), expressed in Christian thanksgiving formulas and usually stating the principal theme of the letter. In 2 Corinthians

*

1:1 Gal 1:10; Phil 1:1; Jas 1:1 / Acts 9:15; 13:2; 1 Cor 1:1; Gal 1:15; Ti 1:1.
1:2 Rom 16:25–26; Ti 1:2.
1:3 Rom 9:5; 2 Sm 7:12; Mt 1:1; Mk 12:35; Jn 7:42; Acts 13:22–23; 2 Tm 2:8; Rv 22:16.
1:4 Rom 10:9; Acts 13:33; Phil 3:10.
1:5 Rom 15:15; Gal 2:7, 9 / Rom 15:18; Acts 9:15; 26:16–18; Gal 1:16; 2:7, 9.
1:6 1 Cor 1:9.
1:7 Nm 6:25–26; 1 Cor 1:2–3; 2 Cor 1:1–2.
1:8 Rom 16:19; 1 Thes 1:8.

heralded throughout the world. 9* God is my
witness, whom I serve with my spirit in pro-
claiming the gospel of his Son, that I remember
you constantly, 10*† always asking in my prayers
that somehow by God's will I may at last find
my way clear to come to you. 11* For I long to
see you, that I may share with you some spiri-
tual gift so that you may be strengthened, 12 that
is, that you and I may be mutually encouraged
by one another's faith, yours and mine. 13*† I
do not want you to be unaware, brothers, that
I often planned to come to you, though I was
prevented until now, that I might harvest some
fruit among you, too, as among the rest of the
Gentiles. 14† To Greeks and non-Greeks alike, to
the wise and the ignorant, I am under obligation;

the thanksgiving becomes a blessing, and in Ephesians it is preceded by a lengthy blessing. Sometimes the thanksgiving is blended into the body of the letter, especially in 1 Thessalonians. In Romans it is stated briefly.

1:10–12 Paul lays the groundwork for his more detailed statement in 15:22–24 about his projected visit to Rome.

1:13 *Brothers* is idiomatic for all Paul's "kin in Christ," all those who believe in the gospel; it includes women as well as men (cf 4:3).

1:14 *Greeks and non-Greeks:* literally, "Greeks and barbarians." As a result of Alexander's conquests, Greek became the standard international language of the Mediterranean world. *Greeks* in Paul's statement therefore means people who know Greek or who have been influenced by Greek culture. *Non-Greeks* were people whose cultures remained substantially unaffected by Greek influences. Greeks called such people "barbarians" (cf Acts 28:2), meaning people whose speech was foreign. Roman citizens would scarcely classify themselves as such, and Nero, who was reigning when Paul wrote this letter, prided himself on his admiration for Greek culture. *Under obligation:* Paul will expand on the theme of obligation in 13:8; 15:1, 27.

1:9 2 Cor 1:23; Eph 1:16; Phil 1:8; 1 Thes 1:2; 2:5, 10; 2 Tm 1:3.
1:10 Rom 15:23, 32; Acts 18:21; 1 Cor 4:19; 1 Thes 2:17.
1:11 1 Thes 2:17; 3:10.
1:13 Rom 15:22; Jn 15:16; Acts 19:21.

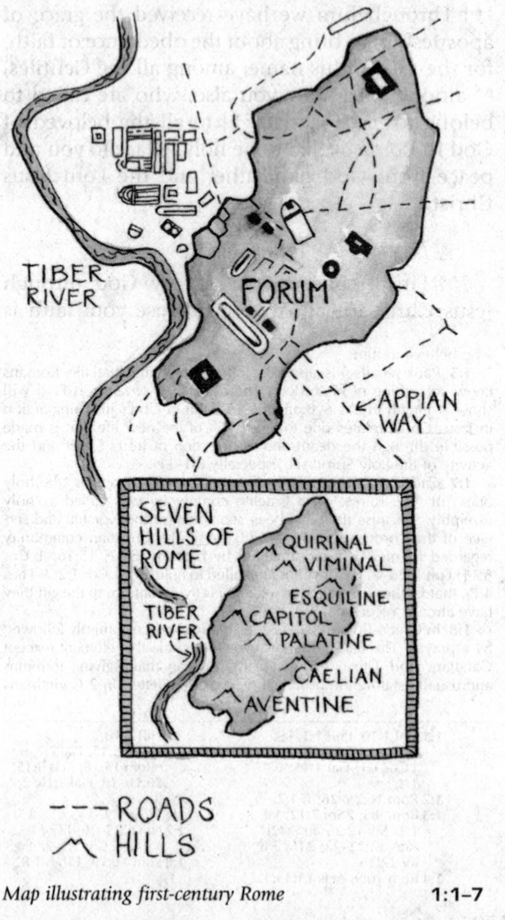

Map illustrating first-century Rome 1:1–7

Did You Know?

The Many Meanings of *Gospel*

The word *gospel* is the best translation of the Greek word *euangelion*, which was used in Romans 1:16. *Gospel* comes from the old English word *godspel*, which means "good news." From *euangelion*, we get the word *evangelize*, which means "to share the good news."

In the New Testament, the meaning of the word *Gospel* goes through an evolution. For Paul, whose writings are the earliest in the New Testament, *Gospel* referred to the good news of salvation for all who believe. Paul associated the Gospel directly with Jesus himself, centering on his death and Resurrection.

As Christian faith developed, the understanding of *Gospel* expanded to include the Reign (Kingdom) of God that Jesus preached. The Gospel was not just associated with Jesus' saving death and Resurrection, but included all his teachings, miracles, promises, and demands. After the original Apostles died or were killed, Christian communities desired a record of their teachings about Jesus, and the Gospel message was written down. So *Gospel* came also to refer to the writings named for Matthew, Mark, Luke, and John.

Rom 1:16

15* that is why I am eager to preach the gospel
also to you in Rome.

II: Humanity Lost Without the Gospel

God's Power for Salvation

16*† For I am not ashamed of the gospel. It
is the power of God for the salvation of every-
one who believes: for Jew first, and then Greek.
17*† For in it is revealed the righteousness of God
from faith to faith; as it is written, "The one who
is righteous by faith will live."

Punishment of Idolators

18*† The wrath† of God† is indeed being re-
vealed from heaven against every impiety and
wickedness of those who suppress the truth by
their wickedness. 19* For what can be known
about God is evident to them, because God
made it evident to them. 20* Ever since the cre-
ation of the world, his invisible attributes of
eternal power and divinity have been able to be
understood and perceived in what he has made.
As a result, they have no excuse; 21* for although
they knew God they did not accord him glory as
God or give him thanks. Instead, they became
vain in their reasoning, and their senseless minds
were darkened. 22* While claiming to be wise,
they became fools 23* and exchanged the glory of
the immortal God for the likeness of an image of
mortal man or of birds or of four-legged animals
or of snakes.

Did You Know?

Homosexuality and AIDS

In making his case that all people are in need of salvation, Paul talks about the sinfulness of humankind in Romans 1:18–32. As a specific example of what happens when people refuse to acknowledge God as God and Creator and instead worship created things, homosexual activity is discussed in verses 26–27.

Some people interpret these verses to mean that Paul is condemning homosexual persons. But this is a serious misinterpretation of Paul's words. Why? First, look at the context. After this specific example in verses 26–27, Paul lists all kinds of sinful behaviors in verses 28–32. He is not picking on homosexuals; rather, he is showing that all people are guilty of sin.

Most important, notice that Paul never condemns people; he condemns sinful behavior. The Catholic Church does the same. The Church teaches that homosexual orientation is not sinful, but it also states that any sexual activity outside of marriage is wrong.

Romans 1:18–32 has also been used wrongly against AIDS victims. Some of them have been told that their horrible disease is a result of God's vengeance against homosexual behavior. Our loving God would never use AIDS, or any other disease, to punish people.

▶ **Rom 1:18–32**

1:16–17 The principal theme of the letter is salvation through faith. *I am not ashamed of the gospel:* Paul is not ashamed to proclaim the gospel, despite the criticism that Jews and Gentiles leveled against the proclamation of the crucified savior; cf 1 Cor 1:23–24. Paul affirms, however, that it is precisely through the crucifixion and resurrection of Jesus that God's saving will and power become manifest. *Jew first* (cf 2:9–10) means that Jews especially, in view of the example of Abraham (ch 4), ought to be the leaders in the response of faith.

1:17 *In it is revealed the righteousness of God from faith to faith:* the gospel centers in Jesus Christ, in whom God's saving presence and righteousness in history have been made known. Faith is affirmation of the basic purpose and meaning of the Old Testament as proclamation of divine promise (2; 4:13) and exposure of the inability of humanity to effect its salvation even through covenant law. Faith is the gift of the holy Spirit and denotes acceptance of salvation as God's righteousness, that is, God's gift of a renewed relationship in forgiveness and power for a new life. Faith is response to God's total claim on people and their destiny. *The one who is righteous by faith will live:* see the note on Hb 2:4.

1:18—3:20 Paul aims to show that all humanity is in a desperate plight and requires God's special intervention if it is to be saved.

1:18–32 In this passage Paul uses themes and rhetoric common in Jewish-Hellenistic mission proclamation (cf Wis 13:1—14:31) to indict especially the non-Jewish world. The close association of idolatry and immorality is basic, but the generalization needs in all fairness to be balanced against the fact that non-Jewish Christian society on many levels displayed moral attitudes and performance whose quality would challenge much of contemporary Christian culture. Romans themselves expressed abhorrence over devotion accorded to animals in Egypt. Paul's main point is that the wrath of God does not await the end of the world but goes into action at each present moment in humanity's history when misdirected piety serves as a facade for self-interest.

1:18 *The wrath of God:* God's reaction to human sinfulness, an Old Testament phrase that expresses the irreconcilable opposition between God and evil (see Is 9:11, 16, 18, 20; 10:4; 30:27). It is not contrary to God's universal love for his creatures, but condemns Israel's turning aside from the covenant obligations. Hosea depicts Yahweh as suffering intensely at the thought of having to punish Israel (Hos 11:8–9). God's wrath was to be poured forth especially on the "Day of Yahweh" and thus took on an eschatological connotation (see Zep 1:15).

1:15 Acts 28:30–31.
1:16 Ps 119:46; 1 Cor 1:18, 24 / Rom 2:9; Acts 3:26; 13:46.
1:17 Rom 3:21–22; Hb 2:4; Gal 3:11; Heb 10:38.
1:18 Rom 2:5, 8–9; Is 66:15; Eph 5:6; Col 3:6.
1:19–32 Wis 13–19; Acts 14:15–17; 17:23–29.
1:20 Jb 12:7–9; Pss 8:4; 19:2; Sir 17:7–9; Is 40:26; Acts 14:17; 17:25–28.
1:21 Eph 4:17–18.
1:22 Wis 13:1–9; Is 5:21; Jer 10:14; Acts 17:29–30; 1 Cor 1:19–21.
1:23 Dt 4:15–19; Ps 106:20; Wis 11:15; 12:24; 13:10–19; Jer 2:11.

ROM

24*† Therefore, God handed them over to im-
purity through the lusts of their hearts for the
mutual degradation of their bodies. 25* They
exchanged the truth of God for a lie and revered
and worshiped the creature rather than the cre-
ator, who is blessed forever. Amen. 26 Therefore,
God handed them over to degrading passions.
Their females exchanged natural relations for un-
natural, 27* and the males likewise gave up nat-
ural relations with females and burned with lust
for one another. Males did shameful things with
males and thus received in their own persons
the due penalty for their perversity. 28 And since
they did not see fit to acknowledge God, God
handed them over to their undiscerning mind
to do what is improper. 29* They are filled with
every form of wickedness, evil, greed, and malice;
full of envy, murder, rivalry, treachery, and spite.
They are gossips 30 and scandalmongers and they
hate God. They are insolent, haughty, boastful,
ingenious in their wickedness, and rebellious
toward their parents. 31 They are senseless, faith-
less, heartless, ruthless. 32* Although they know
the just decree of God that all who practice such
things deserve death, they not only do them but
give approval to those who practice them.

God's Just Judgment

2 1*† Therefore, you are without excuse, every
one of you who passes judgment.† For by
the standard by which you judge another you
condemn yourself, since you, the judge, do the
very same things. 2 We know that the judgment of
God on those who do such things is true. 3* Do
you suppose, then, you who judge those who
engage in such things and yet do them yourself,
that you will escape the judgment of God? 4* Or
do you hold his priceless kindness, forbearance,
and patience in low esteem, unaware that the
kindness of God would lead you to repentance?
5* By your stubbornness and impenitent heart,
you are storing up wrath for yourself for the day
of wrath and revelation of the just judgment of
God, 6*† who will repay everyone according to
his works: 7 eternal life to those who seek glory,
honor, and immortality through perseverance in
good works, 8* but wrath and fury to those who
selfishly disobey the truth and obey wickedness.

Pray It!

Examination of Conscience

God of love and forgiveness, help me to be aware of those times when I begin to think I've earned the right to judge others. Paul reminds us that we are all guilty of sin. I have no right to judge others.

Direct me to turn my attention to examining my own conscience:

Have I been patient with those around me?

Have I offered forgiveness to those who have hurt me?

Have I had the courage to admit when I am wrong?

Have I treated my parents and siblings with respect?

Have I been sensitive to the feelings and needs of those around me?

Have I made an effort to become more aware of how my actions contribute to larger social problems such as hunger, poverty, and global warming?

Forgive me, God, for I have sinned. Help me to recognize the generosity of your forgiveness and love. Help me also to have the strength and courage to follow the ways of your Son Jesus. Amen.

▶ Rom 2:1–4

ROM

†

1:24 In order to expose the depth of humanity's rebellion against the Creator, *God handed them over to impurity through the lusts of their hearts.* Instead of curbing people's evil interests, God abandoned them to self-indulgence, thereby removing the facade of apparent conformity to the divine will. Subsequently Paul will show that the Mosaic law produces the same effect; cf 5:20; 7:13–24. The divine judgment expressed here is related to the theme of hardness of heart described in 9:17–18.

2:1—3:20 After his general indictment of the Gentile, Paul shows that in spite of special revelation Jews enjoy no advantage in moral status before God (3:1–8). With the entire human race now declared guilty before God (3:9–20), Paul will then be able to display the solution for the total problem: salvation through God's redemptive work that is revealed in Christ Jesus for all who believe (3:21–31).

2:1–11 As a first step in his demonstration that Jews enjoy no real moral supremacy over Gentiles, Paul explains that the final judgment will be a review of performance, not of privilege. From this perspective Gentiles stand on an equal footing with Jews, and Jews cannot condemn the sins of Gentiles without condemning themselves.

2:6 *Will repay everyone according to his works:* Paul reproduces the Septuagint text of Ps 62:12 and Prv 24:12.

*

1:24 Wis 12:25; 14:22–31; Acts 7:41–42; Eph 4:19.
1:25 Rom 9:5; Jer 13:25–27.
1:27 Lv 18:22; 20:13; Wis 14:26; 1 Cor 6:9; 1 Tm 1:10.
1:29–31 Rom 13:13; Mt 15:19; Mk 7:21–22; Gal 5:19–21; 2 Tm 3:2–4.
1:32 Acts 8:1; 2 Thes 2:12.
2:1 Mt 7:1–2.
2:3 Wis 16:15–16.
2:4 Rom 3:25–26; 9:22; Wis 11:23; 15:1; 2 Pt 3:9, 15.
2:5 Ex 33:3; Acts 7:51; Rv 6:17; 11:18.
2:6 Ps 62:12; Prv 24:12; Sir 16:14; Mt 16:27; Jn 5:29; 2 Cor 5:10.
2:8 2 Thes 1:8.

9 Yes, affliction and distress will come upon every
human being who does evil, Jew first and then
Greek. 10* But there will be glory, honor, and
peace for everyone who does good, Jew first and
then Greek. 11*† There is no partiality with God.

Judgment by the Interior Law

12*† All who sin outside the law will also per-
ish without reference to it, and all who sin under
the law will be judged in accordance with it.
13* For it is not those who hear the law who are
just in the sight of God; rather, those who ob-
serve the law will be justified. 14* For when the
Gentiles who do not have the law by nature ob-
serve the prescriptions of the law, they are a law
for themselves even though they do not have the
law. 15† They show that the demands of the law
are written in their hearts, while their conscience
also bears witness and their conflicting thoughts
accuse or even defend them 16* on the day when,
according to my gospel, God will judge people's
hidden works through Christ Jesus.

Judgment by the Mosaic Law

17*† Now if you call yourself a Jew and rely on
the law and boast of God 18* and know his will
and are able to discern what is important since you
are instructed from the law, 19* and if you are con-
fident that you are a guide for the blind and a light
for those in darkness, 20* that you are a trainer of
the foolish and teacher of the simple, because in
the law you have the formulation of knowledge
and truth— 21* then you who teach another, are
you failing to teach yourself? You who preach
against stealing, do you steal? 22 You who forbid
adultery, do you commit adultery? You who detest
idols, do you rob temples? 23 You who boast of the
law, do you dishonor God by breaking the law?
24*† For, as it is written, "Because of you the name
of God is reviled among the Gentiles."
25* Circumcision, to be sure, has value if
you observe the law; but if you break the law,
your circumcision has become uncircumcision.*

Did You Know?

Circumcision, the Law, and Faith

Circumcision is the surgical removal of the foreskin from a male's penis. It was the sign of the covenant (agreement) between Israel and God (see Gn 17:2). As Gentiles became Christians, many Jewish Christians claimed they had to live by Jewish religious laws, including circumcision.

Paul consistently insists that such rituals are not necessary for Gentile converts. He says that "circumcision is of the heart" (Rom 2:29), which leads to "faith working through love" (Gal 5:6). In Romans, chapter 4, Paul sheds further light on this by considering the case of Abraham. Abraham was considered the father of the Jewish faith. He was made righteous by God before he was circumcised (see verse 10). Why? Because of his strong and heroic faith in God. Christians are called to this kind of faith in God, whose plan of salvation is now fully revealed in Jesus Christ.

▶ **Rom 2:25–29**

26* Again, if an uncircumcised man keeps the
precepts of the law, will he not be considered
circumcised? 27 Indeed, those who are physically
uncircumcised but carry out the law will pass
judgment on you, with your written law and cir-
cumcision, who break the law. 28* One is not a
Jew outwardly. True circumcision is not outward,
in the flesh. 29* Rather, one is a Jew inwardly,
and circumcision is of the heart, in the spirit, not
the letter; his praise is not from human beings
but from God.

ROM

†

2:11 *No partiality with God:* this sentence is not at variance with the statements in vv 9–10. Since Jews are the first to go under indictment, it is only fair that they be given first consideration in the distribution of blessings. Basic, of course, is the understanding that God accepts no bribes (Dt 10:17).

2:12–16 Jews cannot reasonably demand from Gentiles the standard of conduct inculcated in the Old Testament since God did not address its revelation to them. Rather, God made it possible for Gentiles to know instinctively the difference between right and wrong. But, as Paul explained in 1:18–32, humanity misread the evidence of God's existence, power, and divinity, and "while claiming to be wise, they became fools" (1:22).

2:15 Paul expands on the thought of Jer 31:33; Wis 17:11.

2:17–29 Mere possession of laws is no evidence of virtue. By eliminating circumcision as an elitist moral sign, Paul clears away the last obstacle to his presentation of justification through faith without claims based on the receipt of circumcision and its attendant legal obligations.

2:24 According to Is 52:5 the suffering of Israel prompts her enemies to revile God. Paul uses the passage in support of his point that the present immorality of Israelites is the cause of such defamation.

*

2:10 Rom 1:16; 3:9.
2:11 Dt 10:17; 2 Chr 19:7; Sir 35:12–13; Acts 10:34; Gal 2:6; Eph 6:9; Col 3:25; 1 Pt 1:17.
2:12 Rom 3:19.
2:13 Mt 7:21; Lk 6:46–49; 8:21; Jas 1:22–25; 1 Jn 3:7.
2:14 Acts 10:35.
2:16 Acts 10:42; 17:31.
2:17 Is 48:1–2; Mi 3:11; Phil 3:4–6.
2:18 Phil 1:10.
2:19 Mt 15:14; Lk 6:39.
2:20 2 Tm 3:15.
2:21 Ps 50:16–21; Mt 23:3–4.
2:24 Is 52:5; Ez 36:20; 2 Pt 2:2.
2:25–29 Jer 4:4; 9:24–25.
2:25 1 Cor 7:19; Gal 5:3.
2:26 Gal 5:6.
2:28 Jn 7:24; 8:15, 39.
2:29 Dt 30:6; Jer 4:4; 9:25; Col 2:11 / 1 Cor 4:5; 2 Cor 10:18.

Live It!

The Law, Faith, and Justification

Throughout much of Romans, Paul is explaining the relationship between the law, faith, and justification (righteousness). At the end of Romans, chapter 2, and the beginning of chapter 3, he shows that the Jewish Law of the Old Testament cannot save us from the effect of sin. But he recognizes the value of the law (see 3:31). The law was the expression of the Jewish people's response of faith to God's Covenant. It expressed their covenant relationship with God and one another.

We often think of sin as breaking God's law. But at its core, sin is really breaking our relationship with God and distancing ourselves from God. Remember what Adam and Eve did after their first sin? They hid from God, ashamed of their action. Paul is clear that we are all guilty of sin. Separated from God, the source of all life, we would eventually perish without God's help. But God is always seeking us out. In the ultimate act of love, God sent Jesus to restore the break in our relationship caused by sin. Jesus' life, death, Resurrection, and Ascension show us that God's great love is far more powerful than any sin we can commit.

Paul uses the word *justification* (righteousness) to explain the process that brings us back into a good relationship with God. It is a state of being right with God, of not being separated from God.

How are we justified or considered righteous? Not by our ability to keep any laws but by God, as a free gift to those who have faith in Jesus Christ. God's gift of grace also helps us respond to his call to live the Gospel message. The effect of justification by God is opposite that of sin. Where sin creates distance, Christ draws us close. Where sin kills, Christ gives life. Where sin produces hate and misery, Christ brings love and peace.

▶ Rom 3:1–31

Answers to Objections

3 1† What advantage is there then in being a
Jew? Or what is the value of circumcision?
2* Much, in every respect. [For] in the first place,
they were entrusted with the utterances of God.
3* What if some were unfaithful? Will their infi-
delity nullify the fidelity of God? 4*† Of course
not! God must be true, though every human be-
ing is a liar, as it is written:

"That you may be justified in your words,
and conquer when you are judged."

5* But if our wickedness provides proof of God's
righteousness, what can we say? Is God unjust,
humanly speaking, to inflict his wrath? 6 Of
course not! For how else is God to judge the
world? 7 But if God's truth redounds to his glory
through my falsehood, why am I still being con-
demned as a sinner? 8* And why not say—as we
are accused and as some claim we say—that we
should do evil that good may come of it? Their
penalty is what they deserve.

Universal Bondage to Sin

9*† Well, then, are we better off? Not entirely,
for we have already brought the charge against
Jews and Greeks alike that they are all under the
domination of sin, 10* as it is written:

"There is no one just, not one,
11 there is no one who understands,
there is no one who seeks God.
12 All have gone astray; all alike are worthless;
there is not one who does good,
[there is not] even one.
13* Their throats are open graves;
they deceive with their tongues;

† **3:1–4** In keeping with the popular style of diatribe, Paul responds to the objection that his teaching on the sinfulness of all humanity detracts from the religious prerogatives of Israel. He stresses that Jews have remained the vehicle of God's revelation despite their sins, though this depends on the fidelity of God.

3:4 *Though every human being is a liar:* these words reproduce the Greek text of Ps 116:11. The rest of the verse is from Ps 51:6.

3:9–20 *Well, then, are we better off?:* this phrase can also be translated "Are we at a disadvantage?" but the latter version does not substantially change the overall meaning of the passage. Having explained that Israel's privileged status is guaranteed by God's fidelity, Paul now demonstrates the infidelity of the Jews by a catena of citations from scripture, possibly derived from an existing collection of *testimonia.* These texts show that all human beings share the common burden of sin. They are linked together by mention of organs of the body: throat, tongue, lips, mouth, feet, eyes.

3:2 Rom 9:4; Dt 4:7–8; Pss 103:7; 147:19–20.
3:3 Rom 9:6; 11:1, 29; Ps 89:30–37; 2 Tm 2:13.
3:4 Ps 116:11 / Ps 51:6.
3:5 Rom 9:14; Jb 34:12–17.
3:8 Rom 6:1.
3:9 Rom 1:18—2:25; 3:23; Sir 8:5.
3:10–11 Pss 14:1–3; 53:2–4; Eccl 7:20.
3:13 Pss 5:10; 140:4.

the venom of asps is on their lips;
14* their mouths are full of bitter cursing.
15* Their feet are quick to shed blood;
16 ruin and misery are in their ways,
17 and the way of peace they know not.
18* There is no fear of God before their eyes."

19*† Now we know that what the law says is
addressed to those under the law, so that every
mouth may be silenced and the whole world
stand accountable to God, 20*† since no human
being will be justified in his sight by observing
the law; for through the law comes conscious-
ness of sin.

III: Justification Through Faith in Christ

Justification apart from the Law†

21* But now† the righteousness of God has
been manifested apart from the law, though
testified to by the law and the prophets, 22* the
righteousness of God through faith in Jesus
Christ for all who believe. For there is no dis-
tinction; 23* all have sinned and are deprived
of the glory of God. 24* They are justified freely
by his grace through the redemption in Christ
Jesus, 25*† whom God set forth as an expiation,
through faith, by his blood, to prove his righ-
teousness because of the forgiveness of sins pre-
viously committed, 26 through the forbearance of
God—to prove his righteousness in the present
time, that he might be righteous and justify the
one who has faith in Jesus.

27*† What occasion is there then for boasting?
It is ruled out. On what principle, that of works?
No, rather on the principle of faith.† 28* For we
consider that a person is justified by faith apart
from works of the law. 29* Does God belong to
Jews alone? Does he not belong to Gentiles, too?
Yes, also to Gentiles, 30* for God is one and will
justify the circumcised on the basis of faith and
the uncircumcised through faith. 31*† Are we
then annulling the law by this faith? Of course
not! On the contrary, we are supporting the law.

Abraham Justified by Faith

4 1*† What then can we say that Abraham
found, our ancestor according to the flesh?
2† Indeed, if Abraham was justified on the basis
of his works, he has reason to boast; but this was
not so in the sight of God. 3*† For what does the
scripture say? "Abraham believed God, and it was
credited to him as righteousness." 4* A worker's

†

3:19 *The law:* Paul here uses the term in its broadest sense to mean all of the scriptures; none of the preceding texts is from the Torah or Pentateuch.

3:20 *No human being will be justified in his sight:* these words are freely cited from Ps 143:2. In place of the psalmist's "no living person," Paul substitutes "no human being" (literally "no flesh," a Hebraism), and he adds "by observing the law."

3:21–31 These verses provide a clear statement of Paul's "gospel," i.e., the principle of justification by faith in Christ. God has found a means of rescuing humanity from its desperate plight: Paul's general term for this divine initiative is the righteousness of God (21). Divine mercy declares the guilty innocent and makes them so. God does this not as a result of the law but apart from it (21), and not because of any merit in human beings but through forgiveness of their sins (24), in virtue of the redemption wrought in Christ Jesus for all who believe (22, 24–25). God has manifested his righteousness in the coming of Jesus Christ, whose saving activity inaugurates a new era in human history.

3:21 *But now:* Paul adopts a common phrase used by Greek authors to describe movement from disaster to prosperity. The expressions indicate that vv 21–26 are the consolatory answer to vv 9–20.

3:25 *Expiation:* this rendering is preferable to "propitiation," which suggests hostility on the part of God toward sinners. As Paul will be at pains to point out (5:8–10), it is humanity that is hostile to God.

3:27–31 People cannot boast of their own holiness, since it is God's free gift (27), both to the Jew who practices circumcision out of faith and to the Gentile who accepts faith without the Old Testament religious culture symbolized by circumcision (29–30).

3:27 *Principle of faith:* literally, "law of faith." Paul is fond of wordplay involving the term "law"; cf 7:21, 23; 8:2. Since "law" in Greek may also connote "custom" or "principle," his readers and hearers would have sensed no contradiction in the use of the term after the negative statement concerning law in v 20.

3:31 *We are supporting the law:* giving priority to God's intentions. God is the ultimate source of law, and the essence of law is fairness. On the basis of the Mosaic covenant, God's justice is in question if those who sinned against the law are permitted to go free (see 23–26). In order to rescue all humanity rather than condemn it, God thinks of an alternative: the law or "principle" of faith (27). What can be more fair than to admit everyone into the divine presence on the basis of forgiveness grasped by faith? Indeed, this principle of faith antedates the Mosaic law, as Paul will demonstrate in ch 4, and does not therefore mark a change in divine policy.

4:1–25 This is an expanded treatment of the significance of Abraham's faith, which Paul discusses in Gal 3:6–18; see the notes there.

4:2–5 Verse 2 corresponds to v 4, and v 3 to v 5. The Greek term here rendered *credited* means "made an entry." The context determines whether it is credit or debit. Verse 8 speaks of "recording sin" as a debit. Paul's repeated use of accountants' terminology in this and other passages can be traced both to the Old Testament texts he quotes and to his business activity as a tentmaker. The commercial term in Gn 15:6, "credited it to him," reminds Paul in vv 7–8 of Ps 32:2, in which the same term is used and applied to forgiveness of sins. Thus Paul is able to argue that Abraham's faith involved receipt of forgiveness of sins and that all believers benefit as he did through faith.

4:3 Jas 2:24 appears to conflict with Paul's statement. However, James combats the error of extremists who used the doctrine of justification through faith as a screen for moral self-determination. Paul discusses the subject of holiness in greater detail than does James and beginning with ch 6 shows how justification through faith introduces one to the gift of a new life in Christ through the power of the holy Spirit.

*

3:14 Ps 10:7.
3:15–17 Prv 1:16; Is 59:7–8.
3:18 Ps 36:2.
3:19 Rom 7:7.
3:20 Ps 143:2; Gal 2:16 / Rom 7:7.
3:21 Is 51:6–8; Acts 10:43.
3:22 Rom 1:17; Gal 2:16; Phil 3:9.
3:23 Rom 3:9; 5:12.
3:24 Eph 2:8; Ti 3:7 / Rom 5:1–2; Eph 1:7.
3:25 Lv 16:12–15; Acts 17:31; 1 Jn 4:10.
3:27 Rom 8:2; 1 Cor 1:29–31.
3:28 Rom 5:1; Gal 2:16.
3:29 Rom 10:12.
3:30 Dt 6:4; Gal 3:20; Jas 2:19 / Rom 4:11–12.
3:31 Rom 8:4; Mt 5:17.
4:1 Gal 3:6–9.
4:3 Gn 15:6; Gal 3:6; Jas 2:14, 20–24.
4:4 Rom 11:6.

ROM

wage is credited not as a gift, but as something due. 5 But when one does not work, yet believes in the one who justifies the ungodly, his faith is credited as righteousness. 6 So also David declares the blessedness of the person to whom God credits righteousness apart from works:

7* "Blessed are they whose iniquities are forgiven
and whose sins are covered.
8 Blessed is the man whose sin the Lord does
not record."

9*† Does this blessedness apply only to the circumcised, or to the uncircumcised as well? Now we assert that "faith was credited to Abraham as righteousness." 10 Under what circumstances was it credited? Was he circumcised or not? He was not circumcised, but uncircumcised. 11* And he received the sign of circumcision as a seal on the righteousness received through faith while he was uncircumcised. Thus he was to be the father of all the uncircumcised who believe, so that to them [also] righteousness might be credited, 12 as well as the father of the circumcised who not only are circumcised but also follow the path of faith that our father Abraham walked while still uncircumcised.

Inheritance through Faith

13* It was not through the law that the promise was made to Abraham and his descendants that he would inherit the world, but through the righteousness that comes from faith. 14* For if those who adhere to the law are the heirs, faith is null and the promise is void. 15*† For the law produces wrath; but where there is no law, neither is there violation. 16* For this reason, it depends on faith, so that it may be a gift, and the promise may be guaranteed to all his descendants, not to those who only adhere to the law but to those who follow the faith of Abraham, who is the father of all of us, 17* as it is written, "I have made you father of many nations." He is our father in the sight of God, in whom he believed, who gives life to the dead and calls into being what does not exist. 18* He believed, hoping against hope, that he would become "the father of many nations," according to what was said, "Thus shall your descendants be." 19* He did not weaken in faith when he considered his own body as [already] dead (for he was almost a hundred years old) and the dead womb of Sarah. 20† He did not doubt God's promise in unbelief; rather, he was empowered by faith and gave glory to God 21* and was fully convinced that what he had promised he was also able to do. 22* That is why "it was credited to him as righteousness." 23 But it was not for him alone that it was written that "it was credited to him"; 24* it was also for us, to whom it will be credited, who believe in the one who raised Jesus our Lord from the dead, 25* who was handed over for our transgressions and was raised for our justification.

Faith, Hope, and Love†

5 1* Therefore, since we have been justified by faith, we have peace† with God through our Lord Jesus Christ, 2* through whom we have gained access [by faith] to this grace in which we stand, and we boast in hope of the glory of God. 3 Not only that, but we even boast of our afflictions, knowing that affliction produces endurance, 4* and endurance, proven character, and proven character, hope, 5* and hope does not disappoint, because the love of God has been poured out into our hearts through the holy Spirit that has been given to us. 6 For Christ, while we were still helpless, yet died at the

R
O
M

†

4:9 *Blessedness:* evidence of divine favor.

4:15 Law has the negative function of bringing the deep-seated rebellion against God to the surface in specific sins; see the note on 1:18–32.

4:20 *He did not doubt God's promise in unbelief:* any doubts Abraham might have had were resolved in commitment to God's promise. Heb 11:8–12 emphasizes the faith of Abraham and Sarah.

5:1–11 Popular piety frequently construed reverses and troubles as punishment for sin; cf Jn 9:2. Paul therefore assures believers that God's justifying action in Jesus Christ is a declaration of peace. The crucifixion of Jesus Christ displays God's initiative in certifying humanity for unimpeded access into the divine presence. Reconciliation is God's gift of pardon to the entire human race. Through faith one benefits personally from this pardon or, in Paul's term, is justified. The ultimate aim of God is to liberate believers from the pre-Christian self as described in chs 1–3. Since this liberation will first find completion in the believer's resurrection, salvation is described as future in 5:10. Because this fullness of salvation belongs to the future it is called the Christian hope. Paul's Greek term for hope does not, however, suggest a note of uncertainty, to the effect: "I wonder whether God really means it." Rather, God's promise in the gospel fills believers with expectation and anticipation for the climactic gift of unalloyed commitment in the holy Spirit to the performance of the will of God. The persecutions that attend Christian commitment are to teach believers patience and to strengthen this hope, which will not disappoint them because the holy Spirit dwells in their hearts and imbues them with God's love (5).

5:1 *We have peace:* a number of manuscripts, versions, and church Fathers read "Let us have peace"; cf 14:19.

*

4:7–8 Ps 32:1–2.
4:9 Rom 4:3.
4:11 Gn 17:10–11; Gal 3:6–8.
4:13 Gn 12:7; 18:18; 22:17–18; Sir 44:21; Gal 3:16–18, 29.
4:14 Gal 3:18.
4:15 Rom 3:20; 5:13; 7:8; Gal 3:19.
4:16 Sir 44:19; Gal 3:7–9.
4:17 Gn 17:5; Heb 11:19 / Is 48:13.
4:18 Gn 15:5.
4:19–20 Gn 17:17; Heb 11:11.
4:21 Gn 18:14; Lk 1:37.
4:22 Gn 15:6.
4:24 Rom 10:9; 1 Pt 1:21.
4:25 Is 53:4–5, 12; 1 Cor 15:17; 1 Pt 1:3 / Rom 8:11.
5:1 Rom 3:24–28; Gal 2:16.
5:2 Eph 2:18; 3:12.
5:4 2 Cor 12:9–10; Jas 1:2–4; 1 Pt 1:5–7; 4:12–14.
5:5 Rom 8:14–16; Pss 22:5–6; 25:20.

appointed time for the ungodly. [7]† Indeed, only with difficulty does one die for a just person, though perhaps for a good person one might even find courage to die. [8]* But God proves his love for us in that while we were still sinners Christ died for us. [9]* How much more then, since we are now justified by his blood, will we be saved through him from the wrath. [10]* Indeed, if, while we were enemies, we were reconciled to God through the death of his Son, how much more, once reconciled, will we be saved by his life. [11] Not only that, but we also boast of God through our Lord Jesus Christ, through whom we have now received reconciliation.

Humanity's Sin through Adam

[12]*† Therefore, just as through one person sin entered the world, and through sin, death, and thus death came to all, inasmuch as all sinned†— [13]* for up to the time of the law, sin was in the world, though sin is not accounted when there is no law. [14]* But death reigned from Adam to Moses, even over those who did not sin after the pattern of the trespass of Adam, who is the type of the one who was to come.

Grace and Life through Christ

[15] But the gift is not like the transgression. For if by that one person's transgression the many died, how much more did the grace of God and the gracious gift of the one person Jesus Christ overflow for the many. [16] And the gift is not like the result of the one person's sinning. For after one sin there was the judgment that brought condemnation; but the gift, after many transgressions, brought acquittal. [17] For if, by the transgression of one person, death came to reign through that one, how much more will those who receive the abundance of grace and of the gift of justification come to reign in life through the one person Jesus Christ. [18]* In conclusion, just as through one transgression condemnation came upon all, so through one righteous act acquittal and life came to all. [19]* For just as through the disobedience of one person the many were made sinners, so through the obedience of one the many will be made righteous. [20]*† The law entered in so that transgression might increase but, where sin increased, grace overflowed all the more, [21]* so that, as sin reigned in death, grace also might reign through justification for eternal life through Jesus Christ our Lord.

Live It!

Trusting the Grace of God

A grandmother pushes her grandson out of the path of a speeding car, but she is hit by the car and dies. A stranger jumps into a surging river to save a young girl, but he loses his own life. A firefighter is killed battling a blaze to rescue three trapped people. Their concern for others leads these real-life heroes to make the ultimate sacrifice.

Like the grandson, the young girl, and the three trapped people, we too have been saved from death at a great cost—Jesus' loving sacrifice in obedience to God's will. Paul reminds us that our justification—our reconciliation and peace with God—is not a reward we deserve for being good. It is God's free gift of love despite our weakness and sin. And that is grace. Put your faith not in your own ability to please God, but in God's abundant grace. It is God's grace that will give you the strength you need to reach out in loving service to others.

▶ **Rom 5:1–11**

†

5:7 In the world of Paul's time the *good person* is especially one who is magnanimous to others.

5:12–21 Paul reflects on the sin of Adam (Gn 3:1–13) in the light of the redemptive mystery of Christ. Sin, as used in the singular by Paul, refers to the dreadful power that has gripped humanity, which is now in revolt against the Creator and engaged in the exaltation of its own desires and interests. But no one has a right to say, "Adam made me do it," for all are culpable (12): Gentiles under the demands of the law written in their hearts (2:14–15), and Jews under the Mosaic covenant. Through the Old Testament law, the sinfulness of humanity that was operative from the beginning (13) found further stimulation, with the result that sins were generated in even greater abundance. According to vv 15–21, God's act in Christ is in total contrast to the disastrous effects of the virus of sin that invaded humanity through Adam's crime.

5:12 *Inasmuch as all sinned:* others translate "because all sinned," and understand v 13 as a parenthetical remark. Unlike Wis 2:24, Paul does not ascribe the entry of death to the devil.

5:20 *The law entered in:* sin had made its entrance (12); now the law comes in alongside sin. See the notes on 1:18–32; 5:12–21. *Where sin increased, grace overflowed all the more:* Paul declares that grace outmatches the productivity of sin.

*

5:8 Jn 3:16; 1 Jn 4:10, 19.
5:9 Rom 1:18; 1 Thes 1:10.
5:10 Rom 8:7–8; 2 Cor 5:18; Col 1:21–22.
5:12 Gn 2:17; 3:1–19; Wis 2:24 / Rom 3:19, 23.
5:13 Rom 4:15.
5:14 1 Cor 15:21.
5:18 1 Cor 15:21–22.
5:19 Is 53:11; Phil 2:8–9.
5:20 Rom 4:15; 7:7–8; Gal 3:19.
5:21 Rom 6:23.

Pray It!

In Christ, We Receive New Life!

In chapter 6 of Romans, Paul tells us that we die to sin and receive new life in Jesus Christ—who died for the forgiveness of all sin and rose from the dead. By participating in the Paschal mystery (see "Dying for New Life," near Jn 12:24–26) through Baptism, we are no longer enslaved to sin.

The "end is eternal life. For the wages of sin is death, but the gift of God is eternal life in Christ Jesus our Lord" (Rom 6:22–23). Let the message of this passage fill you. Feel God's liberating grace in you. Never forget that God has already restored you to right relationship with him.

Loving God, I confess that I have sinned. My actions have at times hurt me and others. Help me to do better, to learn from my mistakes, and to model my life on the ways of Jesus. I pray that I may grow to understand more fully the many gifts you have offered me as a person of faith. Amen.

▶ **Rom 6:1–23**

IV: Justification and the Christian Life

Freedom from Sin; Life in God

6 1*† What then shall we say? Shall we persist
in sin that grace may abound? Of course not!
2* How can we who died to sin yet live in it? 3* Or
are you unaware that we who were baptized into
Christ Jesus were baptized into his death? 4* We
were indeed buried with him through baptism
into death, so that, just as Christ was raised from
the dead by the glory of the Father, we too might
live in newness of life.
5* For if we have grown into union with him
through a death like his, we shall also be united
with him in the resurrection. 6* We know that
our old self was crucified with him, so that our
sinful body might be done away with, that we
might no longer be in slavery to sin. 7 For a dead
person has been absolved from sin. 8* If, then,
we have died with Christ, we believe that we
shall also live with him. 9* We know that Christ,
raised from the dead, dies no more; death no
longer has power over him. 10* As to his death,
he died to sin once and for all; as to his life, he
lives for God. 11* Consequently, you too must
think of yourselves as [being] dead to sin and
living for God in Christ Jesus.
12*† Therefore, sin must not reign over your
mortal bodies so that you obey their desires.
13* And do not present the parts of your bodies
to sin as weapons for wickedness, but present
yourselves to God as raised from the dead to life
and the parts of your bodies to God as weapons
for righteousness. 14* For sin is not to have any
power over you, since you are not under the law
but under grace.
15* What then? Shall we sin because we are not
under the law but under grace? Of course not!
16* Do you not know that if you present yourselves to someone as obedient slaves, you are
slaves of the one you obey, either of sin, which
leads to death, or of obedience, which leads to
righteousness?* 17† But thanks be to God that,
although you were once slaves of sin, you have
become obedient from the heart to the pattern
of teaching to which you were entrusted. 18 Freed
from sin, you have become slaves of righteousness. 19 I am speaking in human terms because

†

6:1–11 To defend the gospel against the charge that it promotes moral laxity (cf 3:5–8), Paul expresses himself in the typical style of spirited diatribe. God's display of generosity or grace is not evoked by sin but, as stated in 5:8, is the expression of God's love, and this love pledges eternal life to all believers (5:21). Paul views the present conduct of the believers from the perspective of God's completed salvation when the body is resurrected and directed totally by the holy Spirit. Through baptism believers share the death of Christ and thereby escape from the grip of sin. Through the resurrection of Christ the power to live anew becomes reality for them, but the fullness of participation in Christ's resurrection still lies in the future. But life that is lived in dedication to God now is part and parcel of that future. Hence anyone who sincerely claims to be interested in that future will scarcely be able to say, "Let us sin so that grace may prosper" (cf 1).

6:12–19 Christians have been released from the grip of sin, but sin endeavors to reclaim its victims. The antidote is constant remembrance that divine grace has claimed them and identifies them as people who are alive only for God's interests.

6:17 In contrast to humanity, which was handed over to self-indulgence (1:24–32), believers are *entrusted* ("handed over") to God's *pattern of teaching,* that is, the new life God aims to develop in Christians through the productivity of the holy Spirit. Throughout this passage Paul uses the slave-master model in order to emphasize the fact that one cannot give allegiance to both God and sin.

*

6:1 Rom 3:5–8.
6:2 1 Pt 4:1.
6:3 Gal 3:27.
6:4 Col 2:12; 1 Pt 3:21–22.
6:5 Phil 3:10–11; 2 Tm 2:11.
6:6 Gal 5:24; 6:14; Eph 4:22–23.
6:8 1 Thes 4:17.
6:9 Acts 13:34; 1 Cor 15:26; 2 Tm 1:10; Rv 1:18.
6:10 Heb 9:26–28; 1 Pt 3:18.
6:11 2 Cor 5:15; 1 Pt 2:24.
6:12 Gn 4:7.
6:13 Rom 12:1; Eph 2:5 / 5:14; Col 3:5.
6:14 Gal 5:18; 1 Jn 3:6.
6:15 Rom 5:17, 21.
6:16 Jn 8:31–34; 2 Pt 2:19.
6:16–18 Jn 8:32–36.

of the weakness of your nature. For just as you
presented the parts of your bodies as slaves to
impurity and to lawlessness for lawlessness, so
now present them as slaves to righteousness for
sanctification. 20*† For when you were slaves of
sin, you were free from righteousness. 21* But
what profit did you get then from the things
of which you are now ashamed? For the end of
those things is death. 22*† But now that you have
been freed from sin and have become slaves of
God, the benefit that you have leads to sanctifica-
tion, and its end is eternal life. 23* For the wages
of sin is death, but the gift of God is eternal life
in Christ Jesus our Lord.

Freedom from the Law

7 1† Are you unaware, brothers (for I am speak-
ing to people who know the law), that the
law has jurisdiction over one as long as one lives?
2* Thus a married woman is bound by law to her
living husband; but if her husband dies, she is
released from the law in respect to her husband.
3 Consequently, while her husband is alive she
will be called an adulteress if she consorts with
another man. But if her husband dies she is free
from that law, and she is not an adulteress if she
consorts with another man.
4 In the same way, my brothers, you also were
put to death to the law through the body of
Christ, so that you might belong to another, to
the one who was raised from the dead in order
that we might bear fruit for God. 5* For when we
were in the flesh, our sinful passions, awakened
by the law, worked in our members to bear fruit
for death. 6* But now we are released from the
law, dead to what held us captive, so that we may
serve in the newness of the spirit and not under
the obsolete letter.

Acquaintance with Sin through the Law

7*† What then can we say? That the law is sin?
Of course not!† Yet I did not know sin except
through the law, and I did not know what it is
to covet except that the law said, "You shall not
covet." 8* But sin, finding an opportunity in the
commandment, produced in me every kind of
covetousness. Apart from the law sin is dead. 9 I
once lived outside the law, but when the com-
mandment came, sin became alive; 10* then I
died, and the commandment that was for life

†

6:20 *You were free from righteousness:* expressed ironically, for such freedom is really tyranny. The commercial metaphors in vv 21–23 add up only one way: sin is a bad bargain.

6:22 *Sanctification:* or holiness.

7:1–6 Paul reflects on the fact that Christians have a different understanding of the law because of their faith in Christ. Law binds the living, not the dead, as exemplified in marriage, which binds in life but is dissolved through death. Similarly, Christians who through baptism have died with Christ to sin (cf 6:2–4) are freed from the law that occasioned transgressions, which in turn were productive of death. Now that Christians are joined to Christ, the power of Christ's resurrection makes it possible for them to bear the fruit of newness of life for God.

7:7–25 In this passage Paul uses the first person singular in the style of diatribe for the sake of argument. He aims to depict the disastrous consequences when a Christian reintroduces the law as a means to attain the objective of holiness pronounced in 6:22.

7:7–12 The apostle defends himself against the charge of identifying the law with sin. Sin does not exist in law but in human beings, whose sinful inclinations are not overcome by the proclamation of law.

*

6:20 Jn 8:34.
6:21 Rom 8:6, 13; Prv 12:28; Ez 16:61, 63.
6:22 1 Pt 1:9.
6:23 Gn 2:17; Gal 6:7–9; Jas 1:15.
7:2 1 Cor 7:39.
7:5 Rom 6:21; 8:6, 13.
7:6 Rom 8:2; 2 Cor 3:6.
7:7 Rom 3:20; Ex 20:17; Dt 5:21.
7:8 Rom 5:13, 20; 1 Cor 15:56 / Rom 4:15.
7:10 Lv 18:5.

Pray It!

I'm Not Perfect

Some people today think, If God has already forgiven me, why should I be concerned about sinning? Evidently, some people in Paul's time thought that too (see Rom 6:15). Paul reminds them, and us, that faith in Christ should be a matter of the heart, not simply a mechanical commitment. Like a married couple's love calls them to commit to each other (see 7:2), so our love for Christ should make us want to live in the light, free from sin. Why would we want to return to the things that bring death to the soul (see 6:21)?

But even when we commit to follow Christ, sin is a constant challenge. Paul encourages us, in the face of temptation, to maintain our focus on God and refrain from sin.

Jesus, you experienced temptation throughout your ministry. Yet, you always made the decision to avoid sin and live in the light.

I have made the commitment to follow you. Give me the strength to overcome temptations and avoid sin. If in my weaknesses I allow my sin and passions to steer me in the wrong direction, please forgive me and help me to find the right path again.
Amen.

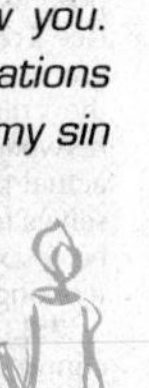

▶ **Rom 6:15—7:6**

Live It!

Our Inner Struggle

In Romans 7:15–16, Paul reveals his own struggle to do what is right. It seems there's a part of us that wants to do right, and another part that wants to do wrong. Even when we try to be good, "evil is at hand" (verse 21), ready to have its way.

Paul uses the words *spiritual* and *carnal* to describe this struggle. He says our flesh tempts us to do wrong, and our spirit wants us to do right. Paul does not mean that our physical bodies are evil and the source of sin; rather, he is warning us that it is difficult to always do good, and many things around us can lead us astray.

Sin is hard to resist at times. To do what is right requires us to stop and think clearly about our choices and actively select good over sin. The good news is that God, the understanding forgiver, is on our side in the struggle. Thanks be to God!

▶ Rom 7:13–25

turned out to be death for me. 11* For sin, seizing
an opportunity in the commandment, deceived
me and through it put me to death. 12* So then
the law is holy, and the commandment is holy
and righteous and good.

Sin and Death

13*† Did the good, then, become death for
me? Of course not! Sin, in order that it might be
shown to be sin, worked death in me through the
good, so that sin might become sinful beyond
measure through the commandment. 14* We
know that the law is spiritual; but I am carnal,
sold into slavery to sin. 15 What I do, I do not understand. For I do not do what I want, but I do
what I hate. 16 Now if I do what I do not want, I
concur that the law is good. 17 So now it is no
longer I who do it, but sin that dwells in me.
18* For I know that good does not dwell in me,
that is, in my flesh. The willing is ready at hand,
but doing the good is not. 19 For I do not do the
good I want, but I do the evil I do not want.
20 Now if [I] do what I do not want, it is no longer I who do it, but sin that dwells in me. 21 So,
then, I discover the principle that when I want
to do right, evil is at hand. 22 For I take delight in
the law of God, in my inner self, 23*† but I see in
my members another principle at war with the
law of my mind, taking me captive to the law of
sin that dwells in my members. 24 Miserable one
that I am! Who will deliver me from this mortal
body? 25* Thanks be to God through Jesus Christ
our Lord. Therefore, I myself, with my mind,
serve the law of God but, with my flesh, the law
of sin.

The Flesh and the Spirit

8 1† Hence, now there is no condemnation for
those who are in Christ Jesus. 2* For the law
of the spirit of life in Christ Jesus has freed you
from the law of sin and death. 3* For what the
law, weakened by the flesh, was powerless to do,
this God has done: by sending his own Son in the
likeness of sinful flesh and for the sake of sin, he
condemned sin in the flesh, 4* so that the righteous decree of the law might be fulfilled in us,
who live not according to the flesh but according
to the spirit. 5 For those who live according to the
flesh are concerned with the things of the flesh,
but those who live according to the spirit with
the things of the spirit. 6* The concern of the

†

7:13–25 Far from improving the sinner, law encourages sin to expose itself in transgressions or violations of specific commandments (see 1:24; 5:20). Thus persons who do not experience the justifying grace of God, and Christians who revert to dependence on law as the criterion for their relationship with God, will recognize a rift between their reasoned desire for the goodness of the law and their actual performance that is contrary to the law. Unable to free themselves from the slavery of sin and the power of death, they can only be rescued from defeat in the conflict by the power of God's grace working through Jesus Christ.

7:23 As in 3:27, Paul plays on the term *law,* which in Greek can connote custom, system, or *principle*.

8:1–13 After his warning in ch 7 against the wrong route to fulfillment of the objective of holiness expressed in 6:22, Paul points his addressees to the correct way. Through the redemptive work of Christ, Christians have been liberated from the terrible forces of sin and death. Holiness was impossible so long as the *flesh* (or our "old self"), that is, self-interested hostility toward God (7), frustrated the divine objectives expressed in the law. What is worse, sin used the law to break forth into all manner of lawlessness (8). All this is now changed. At the cross God broke the power of sin and pronounced sentence on it (3). Christians still retain the flesh, but it is alien to their new being, which is life in the spirit, namely the new self, governed by the holy Spirit. Under the direction of the holy Spirit Christians are able to fulfill the divine will that formerly found expression in the law (4). The same Spirit who enlivens Christians for holiness will also resurrect their bodies at the last day (11). Christian life is therefore the experience of a constant challenge to put to death the evil deeds of the body through life of the spirit (13).

*

7:11 Gn 3:13; Heb 3:13.
7:12 1 Tm 1:8.
7:13 Rom 4:15; 5:20.
7:14 Rom 8:7–8; Ps 51:7.
7:18 Gn 6:5; 8:21; Phil 2:13.
7:23 Gal 5:17; 1 Pt 2:11.
7:25 1 Cor 15:57.
8:2 Rom 7:23–24; 2 Cor 3:17.
8:3 Acts 13:38; 15:10 / Jn 3:16–17; 2 Cor 5:21; Gal 3:13; 4:4; Phil 2:7; Col 1:22; Heb 2:17; 4:15; 1 Jn 4:9.
8:4 Gal 5:16–25.
8:6 Rom 6:21; 7:5; 8:13; Gal 6:8.

Catholic Connection

The Holy Spirit

Do you allow the Holy Spirit to lead your life? The Letter to the Romans reminds us that through the gift of the Holy Spirit, we are all children of God, and as his children we are called to live a life of love according to God's will. The same Spirit that makes us children of God is the one that helps us to live out God's will individually and collectively as a Church.

On a personal level, God's Spirit is at work in many different ways in our lives. At Baptism we receive the Holy Spirit and become temples, or homes, for God's Spirit. As we grow in faith, the Holy Spirit is there guiding us and interceding for us when we pray. During the sacrament of Confirmation, the grace of Baptism is completed with a special outpouring of the Holy Spirit, giving us the gifts we need to live and spread the Gospel message.

Throughout the Scriptures, there are many symbols for the Holy Spirit that can help us to understand how the Spirit can guide us in our daily lives. For example:

- The Holy Spirit in the form of a **dove** recalls the end of the flood during the time of Noah (see Gn 8:8–12) and the descent of God's Spirit after Jesus was baptized (see Mt 3:16). It can serve as a reminder of our own Baptism and that we are called to live as followers of Christ.
- The Holy Spirit in the form of a **cloud**, who led the Israelites on their journey out of slavery toward the Promised Land (see Ex 40:34–38) and overshadowed Mary when the angel told her she would be the Mother of God's Son (see Lk 1:35), can remind us that God's Spirit can give us clarity when we have tough decisions to make and can guide us on our journey through life.
- The Holy Spirit in the form of **fire**, who descended on the disciples at Pentecost and transformed all who were present, can serve as a reminder that God's Spirit is present and is transforming our lives today (see Acts 2:3–12).

The same Spirit who is at work in our lives individually is also active in helping and guiding the Church. The Holy Spirit inspired the writing of the Scriptures and guides the Church in its understanding of them. God's Spirit continues to guide the Pope and bishops (the Magisterium) as they lead the Church and teach about the faith. (see "The Bible, Tradition, and Magisterium," near Lk 4:1–13.) And it is the Holy Spirit that unites us as the Body of Christ and empowers us to bring Christ's message to the world.

- How is the Holy Spirit present and actively working in your life? in the lives of your family and friends? in your community? in the world?

Rom 8:1–17

Catechism, nos. 683–747

flesh is death, but the concern of the spirit is life
and peace. 7* For the concern of the flesh is hos-
tility toward God; it does not submit to the law
of God, nor can it; 8* and those who are in the
flesh cannot please God. 9* But you are not in
the flesh; on the contrary, you are in the spirit, if
only the Spirit of God dwells
in you. Whoever does not
have the Spirit of Christ
does not belong to him.
10* But if Christ is in you,
although the body is dead
because of sin, the spirit is
alive because of righteous-
ness. 11 If the Spirit of the
one who raised Jesus from
the dead dwells in you, the
one who raised Christ from the dead will give
life to your mortal bodies also, through his Spirit
that dwells in you. 12 Consequently, brothers,
we are not debtors to the flesh, to live according
to the flesh. 13* For if you live according to the
flesh, you will die, but if by the spirit you put to
death the deeds of the body, you will live.

"We know that all things work for good for those who love God, who are called according to his purpose."
(Rom 8:28)

Children of God through Adoption

14*† For those who are led by the Spirit of God
are children of God. 15*† For you did not receive
a spirit of slavery to fall back into fear, but you
received a spirit of adoption, through which we
cry, "*Abba*, Father!" 16* The Spirit itself bears wit-
ness with our spirit that we are children of God,
17* and if children, then heirs, heirs of God and
joint heirs with Christ, if only we suffer with him
so that we may also be glorified with him.

Destiny of Glory

18*† I consider that the sufferings of this pres-
ent time are as nothing compared with the glory
to be revealed for us. 19 For creation awaits with
eager expectation the revelation of the children
of God; 20* for creation was made subject to
futility, not of its own accord but because of
the one who subjected it, in hope 21* that cre-
ation itself would be set free from slavery to
corruption and share in the
glorious freedom of the
children of God. 22* We
know that all creation is
groaning in labor pains
even until now; 23* and
not only that, but we our-
selves, who have the first-
fruits of the Spirit, we also
groan within ourselves as
we wait for adoption, the
redemption of our bodies. 24* For in hope we
were saved. Now hope that sees for itself is not
hope. For who hopes for what one sees? 25 But
if we hope for what we do not see, we wait with
endurance.

26 In the same way, the Spirit too comes to the
aid of our weakness; for we do not know how to
pray as we ought, but the Spirit itself intercedes
with inexpressible groanings. 27* And the one
who searches hearts knows what is the intention
of the Spirit, because it intercedes for the holy
ones according to God's will.

God's Indomitable Love in Christ

28*† We know that all things work for good for
those who love God,† who are called according
to his purpose. 29*† For those he foreknew he
also predestined to be conformed to the image of
his Son, so that he might be the firstborn among
many brothers. 30* And those he predestined he
also called; and those he called he also justified;
and those he justified he also glorified.

ROM

†

8:14–17 Christians, by reason of the Spirit's presence within them, enjoy not only new life but also a new relationship to God, that of adopted children and heirs through Christ, whose sufferings and glory they share.

8:15 *Abba:* see the note on Mk 14:36.

8:18–27 The glory that believers are destined to share with Christ far exceeds the sufferings of the present life. Paul considers the destiny of the created world to be linked with the future that belongs to the believers. As it shares in the penalty of corruption brought about by sin, so also will it share in the benefits of redemption and future glory that comprise the ultimate liberation of God's people (19–22). After patient endurance in steadfast expectation, the full harvest of the Spirit's presence will be realized. On earth believers enjoy the firstfruits, i.e., the Spirit, as a guarantee of the total liberation of their bodies from the influence of the rebellious old self (23).

8:28–30 These verses outline the Christian vocation as it was designed by God: *to be conformed to the image of his Son,* who is to *be the firstborn among many brothers* (29). God's redemptive action on behalf of the believers has been in process before the beginning of the world. Those whom God chooses are *those he foreknew* (29) or elected. Those who are *called* (30) are *predestined* or predetermined. These expressions do not mean that God is arbitrary. Rather, Paul uses them to emphasize the thought and care that God has taken for the Christian's salvation.

8:28 *We know that all things work for good for those who love God:* a few ancient authorities have God as the subject of the verb, and some translators render: "We know that God makes everything work for good for those who love God . . . ."

8:29 *Image:* while man and woman were originally created in God's image (Gn 1:26–27), it is through baptism into Christ, the image of God (2 Cor 4:4; Col 1:15), that we are renewed according to the image of the Creator (Col 3:10).

8:7 Rom 5:10; Jas 4:4.
8:8 1 Jn 2:16.
8:9 1 Cor 3:16.
8:10 Gal 2:20; 1 Pt 4:6.
8:13 Gal 5:24; 6:8; Eph 4:22–24.
8:14 Gal 5:18.
8:15 Mk 14:36; Gal 4:5–6; 2 Tm 1:7.
8:16 Jn 1:12; Gal 3:26–29.
8:17 Gal 4:7; 1 Pt 4:13; 5:1.
8:18 2 Cor 4:17.
8:20 Gn 3:17–19.
8:21 2 Pt 3:12–13; Rv 21:1.
8:22 2 Cor 5:2–5.
8:23 2 Cor 1:22; Gal 5:5.
8:24 2 Cor 5:7; Heb 11:1.
8:27 Ps 139:1; 1 Cor 4:5.
8:28–29 Eph 1:4–14; 3:11.
8:29 Eph 1:5; 1 Pt 1:2.
8:30 Is 45:25; 2 Thes 2:13–14.

31*† What then shall we say to this? If God is
for us, who can be against us? 32* He who did
not spare his own Son but handed him over for
us all, how will he not also give us everything
else along with him? 33* Who will bring a charge
against God's chosen ones? It is God who acquits
us. 34* Who will condemn? It is Christ [Jesus]
who died, rather, was raised, who also is at the
right hand of God, who indeed intercedes for us.
35 What will separate us from the love of Christ?
Will anguish, or distress, or persecution, or fam-
ine, or nakedness, or peril, or the sword? 36* As
it is written:

"For your sake we are being slain all the day;
we are looked upon as sheep to be
slaughtered."

37* No, in all these things we conquer overwhelm-
ingly through him who loved us. 38*† For I am
convinced that neither death, nor life, nor angels,
nor principalities, nor present things, nor future
things, nor powers, 39† nor height, nor depth, nor
any other creature will be able to separate us from
the love of God in Christ Jesus our Lord.

V: Jews and Gentiles in God's Plan†

Paul's Love for Israel†

9 1* I speak the truth in Christ, I do not lie;
my conscience joins with the holy Spirit in
bearing me witness 2 that I have great sorrow
and constant anguish in my heart. 3* For I could
wish that I myself were accursed and separated
from Christ for the sake of my brothers, my kin
according to the flesh. 4* They are Israelites;
theirs the adoption, the glory, the covenants, the
giving of the law, the worship, and the prom-
ises; 5*† theirs the patriarchs, and from them,
according to the flesh, is the Messiah. God who
is over all be blessed forever. Amen.

Pray It!

Absolutely Nothing!

God, what could separate me from your love?
Not a failed test or a broken promise or a hurtful word.
What could tear you from me?
Not the lure of power or immediate gratification or unnatural highs.
If you, God, are on my side, who could be against me?
Not a vengeful peer or an uncaring date or someone whose relationship with me has gone sour.
What situation could divide you and me, God?
Not depression over a loss or anger over being laughed at or guilt from being caught red-handed.
No, in all these things, I know that I am never alone, because you, God, conquered sin, despair, and even death itself through your endless love, a love that showed itself through your Son. I am convinced, Lord, that nothing, absolutely nothing, will ever separate me from your love . . . ever!
Amen.

Rom 8:31–39

†

8:31–39 The all-conquering power of God's love has overcome every obstacle to Christians' salvation and every threat to separate them from God. That power manifested itself fully when God's own Son was delivered up to death for their salvation. Through him Christians can overcome all their afflictions and trials.

8:38 *Present things* and *future things* may refer to astrological data. Paul appears to be saying that the gospel liberates believers from dependence on astrologers.

8:39 *Height, depth* may refer to positions in the zodiac, positions of heavenly bodies relative to the horizon. In astrological documents the term for "height" means "exaltation" or the position of greatest influence exerted by a planet. Since hostile spirits were associated with the planets and stars, Paul includes *powers* (38) in his list of malevolent forces.

9:1—11:36 Israel's unbelief and its rejection of Jesus as savior astonished and puzzled Christians. It constituted a serious problem for them in view of God's specific preparation of Israel for the advent of the Messiah. Paul addresses himself here to the essential question of how the divine plan could be frustrated by Israel's unbelief. At the same time, he discourages both complacency and anxiety on the part of Gentiles. To those who might boast of their superior advantage over Jews, he warns that their enjoyment of the blessings assigned to Israel can be terminated. To those who might anxiously ask, "How can we be sure that Israel's fate will not be ours?" he replies that only unbelief can deprive one of salvation.

9:1–5 The apostle speaks in strong terms of the depth of his grief over the unbelief of his own people. He would willingly undergo a curse himself for the sake of their coming to the knowledge of Christ (3; cf Lv 27:28–29). His love for them derives from God's continuing choice of them and from the spiritual benefits that God bestows on them and through them on all of humanity (4–5).

9:5 Some editors punctuate this verse differently and prefer the translation, "Of whom is Christ according to the flesh, who is God over all." However, Paul's point is that *God who is over all* aimed to use Israel, which had been entrusted with every privilege, in outreach to the entire world through the Messiah.

*

8:31 Ps 118:6; Heb 13:6.
8:32 Jn 3:16.
8:33–34 Is 50:8.
8:34 Ps 110:1; Heb 7:25; 1 Jn 2:1.
8:36 Ps 44:23; 1 Cor 4:9; 15:30; 2 Cor 4:11; 2 Tm 3:12.
8:37 1 Jn 5:4.
8:38–39 1 Cor 3:22; Eph 1:21; 1 Pt 3:22.
9:1 2 Cor 11:31; 1 Tm 2:7.
9:3 Ex 32:32.
9:4–5 Rom 3:2; Ex 4:22; Dt 7:6; 14:1–2.
9:5 Mt 1:1–16; Lk 3:23–38 / Rom 1:25; Ps 41:14.

God's Free Choice

6* But it is not that the word of God has
failed. For not all who are of Israel are Israel,
7* nor are they all children of Abraham because
they are his descendants; but "It is through Isaac
that descendants shall bear your name." 8* This
means that it is not the children of the flesh who
are the children of God, but the children of the
promise are counted as descendants. 9* For this
is the wording of the promise, "About this time I
shall return and Sarah will have a son." 10*† And
not only that, but also when Rebecca had con-
ceived children by one husband, our father
Isaac— 11 before they had yet been born or had
done anything, good or bad, in order that God's
elective plan might continue, 12* not by works
but by his call—she was told, "The older shall
serve the younger." 13*† As it is written:

"I loved Jacob
but hated Esau."

14*† What then are we to say? Is there injustice
on the part of God? Of course not! 15* For he
says to Moses:

"I will show mercy to whom I will,
I will take pity on whom I will."

16* So it depends not upon a person's will or ex-
ertion, but upon God, who shows mercy. 17* For
the scripture says to Pharaoh, "This is why I have
raised you up, to show my power through you
that my name may be proclaimed throughout
the earth." 18*† Consequently, he has mercy

Did You Know?

The Fate of Israel

In Romans, chapters 9–11, Paul takes on a difficult question: What will happen to Israel (the Jews), God's Chosen People, if they reject Jesus? For the early Jewish Christians, who probably had friends and maybe had family members who didn't believe in Jesus, this was an important question.

To respond, Paul makes several points. In the beginning of chapter 9, he affirms Israel's special place in God's plan of salvation. But the people's righteousness (see "The Law, Faith, and Justification," near Rom 3:1–31) is based on faith, not on fulfilling the law. In chapter 10, Paul notes that justification is available for all. The Jewish people are not left out if they call on the name of the Lord. But Israel's rejection of Jesus is good news for the Gentiles who have come to believe.

In chapter 11, Paul uses the analogy of grafting branches onto a tree. The Gentiles were grafted onto the original tree, which is Israel. Paul warns the Gentile Christians not to think they are better than the Jews. God grafted the Gentiles onto the tree; he can just as easily remove them. Paul says the Jews can be grafted back onto that tree (see verse 23). In fact, he ends with the hopeful promise that after the salvation of the Gentiles, all Israel will be saved (see verse 26)!

Christians recognize Jewish people as their spiritual ancestors. Christians have inherited from the Jews part of their Scriptures and a rich spiritual tradition. They respect the Jews' faith and their relationship with God. They pray for the Jews' salvation and their own, in the hope that Paul's promise will come to pass.

▶ **Romans, chapters 9–11**

† **9:10** *Children by one husband, our father Isaac:* Abraham had two children, Ishmael and Isaac, by two wives, Hagar and Sarah, respectively. In that instance Isaac, although born later than Ishmael, became the bearer of the messianic promise. In the case of twins born to Rebecca, God's elective procedure is seen even more dramatically, and again the younger, contrary to Semitic custom, is given the preference.

9:13 The literal rendering, *"Jacob I loved, but Esau I hated,"* suggests an attitude of divine hostility that is not implied in Paul's statement. In Semitic usage "hate" means to love less; cf Lk 14:26 with Mt 10:37. Israel's unbelief reflects the mystery of the divine election that is always operative within it. Mere natural descent from Abraham does not ensure the full possession of the divine gifts; it is God's sovereign prerogative to bestow this fullness upon, or to withhold it from, whomsoever he wishes; cf Mt 3:9; Jn 8:39. The choice of Jacob over Esau is a case in point.

9:14–18 The principle of divine election does not invite Christians to theoretical inquiry concerning the nonelected, nor does this principle mean that God is unfair in his dealings with humanity. The instruction concerning divine election is a part of the gospel and reveals that the gift of faith is the enactment of God's mercy (16). God raised up Moses to display that mercy, and Pharaoh to display divine severity in punishing those who obstinately oppose their Creator.

9:18 *The basic biblical principle is:* those who will not see or hear *shall* not see or hear. On the other hand, the same God who thus makes stubborn or hardens the heart can reconstruct it through the work of the holy Spirit.

*
9:6 Nm 23:19 / Mt 3:9.
9:7 Gn 21:12; Gal 3:29.
9:8 Gal 4:23, 28.
9:9 Gn 18:10, 14.
9:10 Gn 25:21.
9:12 Rom 11:5–6 / Gn 25:23–24.
9:13 Mal 1:3.
9:14 Dt 32:4.
9:15 Ex 33:19.
9:16 Eph 2:8; Ti 3:5.
9:17 Ex 9:16.
9:18 Rom 11:30–32; Ex 4:21; 7:3.

upon whom he wills, and he hardens whom he
wills.
19*† You will say to me then, "Why [then]
does he still find fault? For who can oppose his
will?" 20* But who indeed are you, a human be-
ing, to talk back to God? Will what is made say to
its maker, "Why have you created me so?" 21 Or
does not the potter have a right over the clay,
to make out of the same lump one vessel for a
noble purpose and another for an ignoble one?
22* What if God, wishing to show his wrath and
make known his power, has endured with much
patience the vessels of wrath made for destruc-
tion? 23 This was to make known the riches of his
glory to the vessels of mercy, which he has pre-
pared previously for glory, 24 namely, us whom
he has called, not only from the Jews but also
from the Gentiles.

Witness of the Prophets

25*† As indeed he says in Hosea:

"Those who were not my people I will call
'my people,'
and her who was not beloved I will call
'beloved.'
26* And in the very place where it was said to
them, 'You are not my people,'
there they shall be called children of the
living God."

27* And Isaiah cries out concerning Israel, "Though
the number of the Israelites were like the sand of
the sea, only a remnant will be saved; 28 for deci-
sively and quickly will the Lord execute sentence
upon the earth." 29* And as Isaiah predicted:

"Unless the Lord of hosts had left us
descendants,
we would have become like Sodom
and have been made like Gomorrah."

Righteousness Based on Faith

30*† What then shall we say? That Gentiles,
who did not pursue righteousness, have achieved
it, that is, righteousness that comes from faith;
31* but that Israel, who pursued the law of righ-
teousness, did not attain to that law? 32*† Why
not? Because they did it not by faith, but as if it
could be done by works. They stumbled over the
stone that causes stumbling, 33* as it is written:

"Behold, I am laying a stone in Zion
that will make people stumble
and a rock that will make them fall,
and whoever believes in him shall not be put
to shame."

10 1*† Brothers, my heart's desire and prayer
to God on their behalf is for salvation. 2* I
testify with regard to them that they have zeal
for God, but it is not discerning. 3* For, in their
unawareness of the righteousness that comes
from God and their attempt to establish their
own [righteousness], they did not submit to the
righteousness of God. 4*† For Christ is the end
of the law for the justification of everyone who
has faith.
5*† Moses writes about the righteousness that
comes from [the] law, "The one who does these
things will live by them." 6* But the righteous-
ness that comes from faith says, "Do not say in
your heart, 'Who will go up into heaven?' (that

†

9:19–29 The apostle responds to the objection that if God rules over faith through the principle of divine election, God cannot then accuse unbelievers of sin (19). For Paul, this objection is in the last analysis a manifestation of human insolence, and his "answer" is less an explanation of God's ways than the rejection of an argument that places humanity on a level with God. At the same time, Paul shows that God is far less arbitrary than appearances suggest, for God endures *with much patience* (22) a person like the Pharaoh of the Exodus.

9:25 *Beloved:* in Semitic discourse means "preferred" or "favorite" (cf 13). See Hos 2:1, which is transposed after Hos 3:5 in the NAB.

9:30–33 In the conversion of the Gentiles and, by contrast, of relatively few Jews, the Old Testament prophecies are seen to be fulfilled; cf 25–29. Israel feared that the doctrine of justification through faith would jeopardize the validity of the Mosaic law, and so they never reached their goal of righteousness that they had sought to attain through meticulous observance of the law (31). Since Gentiles, including especially Greeks and Romans, had a great regard for righteousness, Paul's statement concerning Gentiles in v 30 is to be understood from a Jewish perspective: quite evidently they had not been interested in "God's" righteousness, for it had not been revealed to them; but now in response to the proclamation of the gospel they respond in faith.

9:32 Paul discusses Israel as a whole from the perspective of contemporary Jewish rejection of Jesus as Messiah. The Old Testament and much of Jewish noncanonical literature in fact reflect a fervent faith in divine mercy.

10:1–13 Despite Israel's lack of faith in God's act in Christ, Paul does not abandon hope for her salvation (1). However, Israel must recognize that the Messiah's arrival in the person of Jesus Christ means the termination of the Mosaic law as the criterion for understanding oneself in a valid relationship to God. Faith in God's saving action in Jesus Christ takes precedence over any such legal claim (6).

10:4 The Mosaic legislation has been superseded by God's action in Jesus Christ. Others understand *end* here in the sense that Christ is the goal of the law, i.e., the true meaning of the Mosaic law, which cannot be correctly understood apart from him. Still others believe that both meanings are intended.

10:5–6 The subject of the verb *says* (6) is *righteousness* personified. Both of the statements in vv 5 and 6 derive from Moses, but Paul wishes to contrast the language of law and the language of faith.

*

9:19 Rom 3:7; Wis 12:12.
9:20–21 Wis 15:7; Is 29:16; 45:9; Jer 18:6.
9:22 Rom 2:4; Wis 12:20–21; Jer 50:25.
9:25 Hos 2:25.
9:26 Hos 2:1.
9:27–28 Is 10:22–23; Hos 2:1 / Rom 11:5 / Is 28:22.
9:29 Is 1:9; Mt 10:15.
9:30 Rom 10:4, 20.
9:31 Rom 10:3.
9:32 Is 8:14.
9:33 Is 28:16; 1 Pt 2:6–8.
10:1 Rom 9:1, 3.
10:2 Acts 22:3.
10:3 Rom 9:31–32; Phil 3:9.
10:4 Acts 13:38–39; 2 Cor 3:14; Heb 8:13.
10:5 Lv 18:5; Gal 3:12.
10:6 Dt 9:4; 30:12.

is, to bring Christ down) 7*† or 'Who will go
down into the abyss?' (that is, to bring Christ up
from the dead)." 8* But what does it say?

> "The word is near you,
> in your mouth and in your heart"

(that is, the word of faith that we preach),
9*† for, if you confess with your mouth that Jesus
is Lord and believe in your heart that God raised
him from the dead, you will be saved. 10 For one
believes with the heart and so is justified, and
one confesses with the mouth and so is saved.
11 *For the scripture says, "No one who believes
in him will be put to shame." 12* For there is no
distinction between Jew and Greek; the same
Lord is Lord of all, enriching all who call upon
him. 13* For "everyone who calls on the name of
the Lord will be saved."

14*† But how can they call on him in whom
they have not believed? And how can they be-
lieve in him of whom they have not heard? And
how can they hear without someone to preach?
15*† And how can people preach unless they are
sent? As it is written, "How beautiful are the feet
of those who bring [the] good news!" 16* But
not everyone has heeded the good news; for
Isaiah says, "Lord, who has believed what was
heard from us?" 17* Thus faith comes from what
is heard, and what is heard comes through the
word of Christ. 18* But I ask, did they not hear?
Certainly they did; for

> "Their voice has gone forth to all the earth,
> and their words to the ends of the world."

19* But I ask, did not Israel understand? First
Moses says:

> "I will make you jealous of those who are not
> a nation;
> with a senseless nation I will make you
> angry."

20* Then Isaiah speaks boldly and says:

> "I was found [by] those who were not
> seeking me;
> I revealed myself to those who were not
> asking for me."

Pray It!

Are Your Feet Beautiful?

Have you ever been drawn to buy something new after seeing a really clever commercial on TV? Companies trying to sell a product develop amazing ways of grabbing our attention. Without this effort, they will reach few people and fail in their mission.

The Church has undoubtedly the most important mission of all—to share with others the saving power that comes from faith in Jesus Christ. The promise in Romans 10:11–15 is that all who know and call on the name of Jesus will be saved. God is great!

How do others hear about this Good News? Paul says only through us. And he adds, "How beautiful are the feet of those who bring [the] good news!" (verse 15). In other words, action, not just words, is needed to spread the Gospel message.

In your prayer, reflect or journal on the following questions:

- Who are some of the people who first helped you to know Jesus and how did they do that?
- In what ways can you show others how important your faith is to you?
- Which of your friends need to hear this Good News about Jesus? How can you share your faith with them, perhaps through a message of hope, forgiveness, healing, or encouragement?

▶ **Rom 10:11–15**

ROM

† **10:7** Here Paul blends Dt 30:13 and Ps 107:26.

10:9–11 To confess Jesus as Lord was frequently quite hazardous in the first century (cf Mt 10:18; 1 Thes 2:2; 1 Pt 2:18–21; 3:14). For a Jew it could mean disruption of normal familial and other social relationships, including great economic sacrifice. In the face of penalties imposed by the secular world, Christians are assured that *no one who believes in Jesus will be put to shame* (11).

10:14–21 The gospel has been sufficiently proclaimed to Israel, and Israel has adequately understood God's plan for the messianic age, which would see the gospel brought to the uttermost parts of the earth. As often in the past, Israel has not accepted the prophetic message; cf Acts 7:51–53.

10:15 *How beautiful are the feet of those who bring [the] good news:* in Semitic fashion, the parts of the body that bring the messenger with welcome news are praised; cf Lk 11:27.

* **10:7** Dt 30:13; 1 Pt 3:19.
10:8 Dt 30:14.
10:9 1 Cor 12:3.
10:11 Rom 9:33; Is 28:16.
10:12 Rom 1:16; 3:22, 29; Acts 10:34; 15:9, 11; Gal 3:28; Eph 2:14.
10:13 Jl 3:5; Acts 2:21.
10:14 Acts 8:31.
10:15 Is 52:7; Na 2:1; Eph 6:15.
10:16 Is 53:1; Jn 12:38.
10:17 Jn 17:20.
10:18 Ps 19:5; Mt 24:14.
10:19 Rom 11:11, 14; Dt 32:21.
10:20–21 Rom 9:30; Is 65:1–2.

21 But regarding Israel he says, "All day long I
stretched out my hands to a disobedient and
contentious people."

The Remnant of Israel

11 1*† I ask, then, has God rejected his people?
Of course not! For I too am an Israelite, a
descendant of Abraham, of the tribe of Benja-
min.* 2 God has not rejected his people whom
he foreknew. Do you not know what the scrip-
ture says about Elijah, how he pleads with God
against Israel? 3* "Lord, they have killed your
prophets, they have torn down your altars, and
I alone am left, and they are seeking my life."
4* But what is God's response to him? "I have
left for myself seven thousand men who have
not knelt to Baal." 5* So also at the present time
there is a remnant, chosen by grace. 6* But if by
grace, it is no longer because of works; otherwise
grace would no longer be grace. 7* What then?
What Israel was seeking it did not attain, but the
elect attained it; the rest were hardened, 8* as it
is written:

"God gave them a spirit of deep sleep,
eyes that should not see
and ears that should not hear,
down to this very day."

9* And David says:

"Let their table become a snare and a trap,
a stumbling block and a retribution for
them;
10 let their eyes grow dim so that they may not see,
and keep their backs bent forever."

The Gentiles' Salvation

11*† Hence I ask, did they stumble so as to
fall? Of course not! But through their transgres-
sion salvation has come to the Gentiles, so as to
make them jealous. 12 Now if their transgression
is enrichment for the world, and if their dimin-
ished number is enrichment for the Gentiles,
how much more their full number.

13* Now I am speaking to you Gentiles. Inas-
much then as I am the apostle to the Gentiles, I
glory in my ministry 14 in order to make my race
jealous and thus save some of them. 15 For if their
rejection is the reconciliation of the world, what
will their acceptance be but life from the dead?
16*† If the firstfruits are holy, so is the whole
batch of dough; and if the root is holy, so are
the branches.

17* But if some of the branches were broken
off, and you, a wild olive shoot, were grafted in
their place and have come to share in the rich
root of the olive tree, 18* do not boast against
the branches. If you do boast, consider that you
do not support the root; the root supports you.
19 Indeed you will say, "Branches were broken
off so that I might be grafted in." 20* That is so.
They were broken off because of unbelief, but
you are there because of faith. So do not become
haughty, but stand in awe. 21* For if God did not
spare the natural branches, [perhaps] he will not
spare you either. 22* See, then, the kindness and
severity of God: severity toward those who fell,
but God's kindness to you, provided you remain
in his kindness; otherwise you too will be cut off.
23* And they also, if they do not remain in un-
belief, will be grafted in, for God is able to graft
them in again. 24 For if you were cut from what is
by nature a wild olive tree, and grafted, contrary
to nature, into a cultivated one, how much more
will they who belong to it by nature be grafted
back into their own olive tree.

God's Irrevocable Call

25*† I do not want you to be unaware of this
mystery, brothers, so that you will not become
wise [in] your own estimation: a hardening has

ROM

†

11:1–10 Although Israel has been unfaithful to the prophetic message of the gospel (10:14–21), God remains faithful to Israel. Proof of the divine fidelity lies in the existence of Jewish Christians like Paul himself. The unbelieving Jews, says Paul, have been blinded by the Christian teaching concerning the Messiah.

11:11–15 The unbelief of the Jews has paved the way for the preaching of the gospel to the Gentiles and for their easier acceptance of it outside the context of Jewish culture. Through his mission to the Gentiles Paul also hopes to fill his fellow Jews with jealousy. Hence he hastens to fill the entire Mediterranean world with the gospel. Once all the Gentile nations have heard the gospel, Israel as a whole is expected to embrace it. This will be tantamount to resurrection of the dead, that is, the reappearance of Jesus Christ with all the believers at the end of time.

11:16–24 Israel remains holy in the eyes of God and stands as a witness to the faith described in the Old Testament because of *the firstfruits* (or the first piece baked) (16), that is, the converted remnant, and *the root* that *is holy,* that is, the patriarchs (16). The Jews' failure to believe in Christ is a warning to Gentile Christians to be on guard against any semblance of anti-Jewish arrogance, that is, failure to recognize their total dependence on divine grace.

11:25–29 In God's design, Israel's unbelief is being used to grant the light of faith to the Gentiles. Meanwhile, Israel remains dear to God (cf 9:13), still the object of special providence, the mystery of which will one day be revealed.

*

11:1 2 Cor 11:22; Phil 3:5.
11:1–2 1 Sm 12:22; Ps 94:14.
11:3 1 Kgs 19:10, 14.
11:4 1 Kgs 19:18.
11:5 Rom 9:27.
11:6 Rom 4:4; Gal 3:18.
11:7 Rom 9:31.
11:8 Dt 29:3; Is 29:10; Mt 13:13–15; Acts 28:26–27.
11:9–10 Pss 69:23–24; 35:8.
11:11 Acts 13:46; 18:6; 28:28 / Rom 10:19; Dt 32:21.
11:13 Rom 1:5.
11:16 Nm 15:17–21; Ez 44:30; Neh 10:36–38.
11:17 Eph 2:11–19.
11:18 1 Cor 1:31.
11:20 Rom 12:16.
11:21 1 Cor 10:12.
11:22 Jn 15:2, 4; Heb 3:14.
11:23 2 Cor 3:16.
11:25 Prv 3:7 / Rom 12:16; Mk 13:10; Lk 21:24; Jn 10:16.

come upon Israel in part, until the full number
of the Gentiles comes in, 26* and thus all Israel
will be saved, as it is written:*

"The deliverer will come out of Zion,
he will turn away godlessness from Jacob;
27* and this is my covenant with them
when I take away their sins."

28* In respect to the gospel, they are enemies on
your account; but in respect to election, they are
beloved because of the patriarchs. 29* For the
gifts and the call of God are irrevocable.

Triumph of God's Mercy

30† Just as you once disobeyed God but
have now received mercy because of their
disobedience, 31 so they have now disobeyed in
order that, by virtue of the mercy shown to you,
they too may [now] receive mercy. 32* For God
delivered all to disobedience, that he might have
mercy upon all.

33*† Oh, the depth of the riches and wisdom
and knowledge of God! How inscrutable are his
judgments and how unsearchable his ways!

34*† "For who has known the mind of the Lord
or who has been his counselor?"
35*† "Or who has given him anything
that he may be repaid?"

36* For from him and through him and for him
are all things. To him be glory forever. Amen.

VI: The Duties of Christians

Sacrifice of Body and Mind

12 1*† I urge you therefore, brothers, by the
mercies of God, to offer your bodies as a
living sacrifice,† holy and pleasing to God, your
spiritual worship. 2* Do not conform yourself

Live It!

We Are the Body of Christ

According to Romans 12:1–8, we are the Body of Christ! Just thinking about this beautiful and powerful image fills us with energy. Imagine the power if all Christians really behaved as the living Body of Christ in their home, church, neighborhood, country, and world.

In verse 1, Paul calls us to present our bodies to God as a living, holy, and acceptable sacrifice. The best thing that we can offer to God is our whole life—all we are and all we do. When we worship God by doing this, our prayer and rituals are real and meaningful.

In verse 2, Paul calls us not to be conformed to this world but to be transformed. We are transformed by renewing our mind. We are intelligent people. God gave us the power to discern what is good and evil, true and false, in agreement with or against God's loving plan for humanity.

We must think and act according to the measure of faith and the different gifts we have received for the service of others (charisms). So we, who are many, may become one Body in Christ and be better collaborators in Jesus' mission.

▶ Rom 12:1–8

†

11:30–32 Israel, together with the Gentiles who have been handed over to all manner of vices (ch 1), has been *delivered . . . to disobedience*. The conclusion of v 32 repeats the thought of 5:20, "Where sin increased, grace overflowed all the more."

11:33–36 This final reflection celebrates the wisdom of God's plan of salvation. As Paul has indicated throughout these chapters, both Jew and Gentile, despite the religious recalcitrance of each, have received the gift of faith. The methods used by God in making this outreach to the world stagger human comprehension but are at the same time a dazzling invitation to abiding faith.

11:34 The citation is from the Greek text of Is 40:13. Paul does not explicitly mention Isaiah in this verse, nor Job in v 35.

11:35 Paul quotes from an old Greek version of Jb 41:3a, which differs from the Hebrew text (Jb 41:11a).

12:1—13:14 Since Christ marks the termination of the Mosaic law as the primary source of guidance for God's people (10:4), the apostle explains how Christians can function, in the light of the gift of justification through faith, in their relation to one another and the state.

12:1–8 The Mosaic code included elaborate directions on sacrifices and other cultic observances. The gospel, however, invites believers to present their *bodies as a living sacrifice* (1). Instead of being limited by specific legal maxims, Christians are liberated for the exercise of good judgment as they are confronted with the many and varied decisions required in the course of daily life. To assist them, God distributes a variety of gifts to the fellowship of believers, including those of prophecy, teaching, and exhortation (6–8). Prophets assist the community to understand the will of God as it applies to the present situation (6). Teachers help people to understand themselves and their responsibilities in relation to others (7). One who *exhorts* offers encouragement to the community to exercise their faith in the performance of all that is pleasing to God (8). Indeed, this very section, beginning with v 1, is a specimen of Paul's own style of exhortation.

*

11:26 Mt 23:39.
11:26–27 Ps 14:7; Is 59:20–21.
11:27 Is 27:9; Jer 31:33–34.
11:28 Rom 15:8; 1 Thes 2:15–16.
11:29 Rom 9:6; Nm 23:19; Is 54:10.
11:32 Gal 3:22; 1 Tm 2:4.
11:33 Jb 11:7–8; Ps 139:6, 17–18; Wis 17:1; Is 55:8–9.
11:34 Jb 15:8; Wis 9:13; Is 40:13; Jer 23:18; 1 Cor 2:11–16.
11:35 Jb 41:3; Is 40:14.
11:36 1 Cor 8:6; Col 1:16–17.
12:1 2 Cor 1:3 / Rom 6:13; 1 Pt 2:5.
12:2 Eph 4:17, 22–23; 1 Pt 1:14 / Eph 5:10, 17; Phil 1:10.

to this age but be transformed by the renewal of your mind, that you may discern what is the will of God, what is good and pleasing and perfect.

Many Parts in One Body

3* For by the grace given to me I tell everyone among you not to think of himself more highly than one ought to think, but to think soberly, each according to the measure of faith that God has apportioned. 4* For as in one body we have many parts, and all the parts do not have the same function, 5† so we, though many, are one body in Christ and individually parts of one another. 6*† Since we have gifts that differ according to the grace given to us, let us exercise them: if prophecy, in proportion to the faith; 7 if ministry, in ministering; if one is a teacher, in teaching; 8† if one exhorts, in exhortation; if one contributes, in generosity; if one is over others, with diligence; if one does acts of mercy, with cheerfulness.

Mutual Love

9* Let love be sincere; hate what is evil, hold on to what is good; 10* love one another with mutual affection; anticipate one another in showing honor. 11* Do not grow slack in zeal, be fervent in spirit, serve the Lord. 12* Rejoice in hope, endure in affliction, persevere in prayer. 13* Contribute to the needs of the holy ones, exercise hospitality. 14*† Bless those who persecute [you], bless and do not curse them.* 15* Rejoice with those who rejoice, weep with those who weep. 16* Have the same regard for one another; do not be haughty but associate with the lowly; do not be wise in your own estimation. 17* Do not repay anyone evil for evil; be concerned for what is noble in the sight of all. 18* If possible, on your part, live at peace with all. 19* Beloved, do not look for revenge but leave room for the wrath; for it is written, "Vengeance is mine, I will repay, says the Lord." 20* Rather, "if your enemy is hungry, feed him; if he is thirsty, give him something to drink; for by so doing you will heap burning coals upon his head." 21 Do not be conquered by evil but conquer evil with good.

Live It!

Becoming a Peacemaker

A common response when someone mistreats us is to seek revenge. But in Romans 12:17–19, Paul tells us we should never try to avenge wrong against us—God will take care of it in God's own time. He goes on to remind us of Jesus' teaching to treat our enemies with kindness. That is certainly easier said than done! It is difficult to respond with goodwill when we are hurt.

Nevertheless, real people have tried to embody the idea of living peaceably—Martin Luther King Jr., Mother Teresa, Bishop Desmond Tutu, and the Dalai Lama are some examples. But there are also countless unnamed persons in our world who respond to hurt with love, respond to assault with peace. Perhaps you know people in your own community who have made similar commitments.

- Think of the people you know. Who is a peacemaker in your life?
- What can you do to be a peacemaker in your family, school, or community?

▶ Rom 12:17–19

R O M

12:5 *One body in Christ:* on the church as the body of Christ, see 1 Cor 12:12–27.

12:6 Everyone has some gift that can be used for the benefit of the community. When the instruction on justification through faith is correctly grasped, the possesser of a gift will understand that it is not an instrument of self-aggrandizement. Possession of a gift is not an index to quality of faith. Rather, the gift is a challenge to faithful use.

12:8 *Over others:* usually taken to mean "rule over" but possibly "serve as a patron." Wealthier members in Greco-Roman communities were frequently asked to assist in public service projects. In view of the references to contributing *in generosity* and to *acts of mercy,* Paul may have in mind people like Phoebe (16:1–2), who is called a *benefactor* (or "patron") because of the services she rendered to many Christians, including Paul.

12:14–21 Since God has justified the believers, it is not necessary for them to take justice into their own hands by taking vengeance. God will ultimately deal justly with all, including those who inflict injury on the believers. This question of personal rights as a matter of justice prepares the way for more detailed consideration of the state as adjudicator.

12:3 Rom 15:15 / Phil 2:3 / 1 Cor 12:11; Eph 4:7.
12:4–5 1 Cor 12:12, 27; Eph 4:25.
12:6–8 1 Cor 12:4–11, 28–31; Eph 4:7–12; 1 Pt 4:10–11 / 2 Cor 9:7.
12:9 2 Cor 6:6; 1 Tm 1:5; 1 Pt 1:22 / Am 5:15.
12:10 Jn 13:34; 1 Thes 4:9; 1 Pt 2:17; 2 Pt 1:7 / Phil 2:3.
12:11 Acts 18:25.
12:12 Rom 5:2–3; Col 4:2; 1 Thes 5:17.
12:13 Heb 13:2; 1 Pt 4:9.
12:14–21 Mt 5:38–48; 1 Cor 4:12; 1 Pt 3:9.
12:14 Lk 6:27–28.
12:15 Ps 35:13; Sir 7:34; 1 Cor 12:26.
12:16 Rom 15:5; Phil 2:2–3 / Rom 11:20; Prv 3:7; Is 5:21.
12:17 Prv 3:4; 1 Thes 5:15; 1 Pt 3:9.
12:18 Heb 12:14.
12:19 Lv 19:18; Dt 32:35, 41; Mt 5:39; 1 Cor 6:6–7; Heb 10:30.
12:20 Prv 25:21–22; Mt 5:44.

Pray It!

A Real Love

Lord, why is it so hard to love? Love is mentioned so much in the Bible that it makes me wonder why we don't get it. It seems that we do a good job of talking love and a poor job of doing love. We can point out where there is no love, but it sure is hard to bring love to where it is needed.

Jesus, fill me with your love to share with others. The kind of love that changes people forever. The kind of love that breaks down barriers and overcomes fears. The love that gives without counting the costs. Amen.

▶ Rom 13:8–10

Obedience to Authority

13 1*† Let every person be subordinate to
the higher authorities, for there is no
authority except from God, and those that ex-
ist have been established by God. 2 Therefore,
whoever resists authority opposes what God has
appointed, and those who oppose it will bring
judgment upon themselves. 3* For rulers are not
a cause of fear to good conduct, but to evil. Do
you wish to have no fear of authority? Then do
what is good and you will receive approval from
it, 4* for it is a servant of God for your good. But
if you do evil, be afraid, for it does not bear the
sword without purpose; it is the servant of God
to inflict wrath on the evildoer. 5* Therefore, it
is necessary to be subject not only because of
the wrath but also because of conscience. 6 This
is why you also pay taxes, for the authorities
are ministers of God, devoting themselves to
this very thing. 7* Pay to all their dues, taxes to
whom taxes are due, toll to whom toll is due,
respect to whom respect is due, honor to whom
honor is due.

Love Fulfills the Law

8*† Owe nothing to anyone, except to love
one another; for the one who loves another has
fulfilled the law. 9* The commandments, "You
shall not commit adultery; you shall not kill;
you shall not steal; you shall not covet," and
whatever other commandment there may be, are
summed up in this saying, [namely] "You shall
love your neighbor as yourself." 10* Love does no
evil to the neighbor; hence, love is the fulfillment
of the law.

Awareness of the End of Time

11*† And do this because you know the time;
it is the hour now for you to awake from sleep.
For our salvation is nearer now than when we
first believed; 12* the night is advanced, the
day is at hand. Let us then throw off the works
of darkness [and] put on the armor of light;
13*† let us conduct ourselves properly as in the
day, not in orgies and drunkenness, not in pro-
miscuity and licentiousness, not in rivalry and
jealousy. 14* But put on the Lord Jesus Christ,
and make no provision for the desires of the
flesh.

†

13:1–7 Paul must come to grips with the problem raised by a message that declares people free from the law. How are they to relate to Roman authority? The problem was exacerbated by the fact that imperial protocol was interwoven with devotion to various deities. Paul builds on the traditional instruction exhibited in Wis 6:1–3, according to which kings and magistrates rule by consent of God. From this perspective, then, believers who render obedience to the governing authorities are obeying the one who is highest in command. At the same time, it is recognized that Caesar has the responsibility to make just ordinances and to commend uprightness; cf Wis 6:4–21. That Caesar is not entitled to obedience when such obedience would nullify God's prior claim to the believers' moral decision becomes clear in the light of the following verses.

13:8–10 When love directs the Christian's moral decisions, the interest of law in basic concerns, such as familial relationships, sanctity of life, and security of property, is safeguarded (9). Indeed, says Paul, the same applies to any *other commandment* (9), whether one in the Mosaic code or one drawn up by local magistrates under imperial authority. Love anticipates the purpose of public legislation, namely, to secure the best interests of the citizenry. Since Caesar's obligation is to punish the wrongdoer (4), the Christian who acts in love is free from all legitimate indictment.

13:11–14 These verses provide the motivation for the love that is encouraged in vv 8–10.

13:13 *Let us conduct ourselves properly as in the day:* the behavior described in 1:29–30 is now to be reversed. Secular moralists were fond of making references to people who could not wait for nightfall to do their carousing. Paul says that Christians claim to be people of the new day that will dawn with the return of Christ. Instead of planning for nighttime behavior they should be concentrating on conduct that is consonant with avowed interest in the Lord's return.

13:1 Prv 8:15–16; Wis 6:3; Jn 19:11; 1 Pt 2:13–17; Ti 3:1.
13:3 1 Pt 2:13–14; 3:13.
13:4 Rom 12:19.
13:5 1 Pt 2:19.
13:7 Mt 22:21; Mk 12:17; Lk 20:25.
13:8 Jn 13:34; Gal 5:14.
13:9 Ex 20:13–17 / Lv 19:18; Dt 5:17–21; Mt 5:43–44; 19:18–19; 22:39; Mk 12:31; Lk 10:27; Gal 5:14; Jas 2:8.
13:10 Mt 22:40; 1 Cor 13:4–7.
13:11 Eph 5:8–16; 1 Thes 5:5–7.
13:12 Jn 8:12; 1 Thes 5:4–8; 1 Jn 2:8 / 2 Cor 6:7; 10:4; Eph 5:11; 6:13–17.
13:13 Lk 21:34; Eph 5:18.
13:14 Gal 3:27; 5:16; Eph 4:24; 6:11.

To Live and Die for Christ

14 1*† Welcome anyone who is weak in faith,
but not for disputes over opinions.* 2* One
person believes that one may eat anything, while
the weak person eats only vegetables. 3* The
one who eats must not despise the one who ab-
stains, and the one who abstains must not pass
judgment on the one who eats; for God has wel-
comed him. 4* Who are you to pass judgment on
someone else's servant? Before his own master
he stands or falls. And he will be upheld, for the
Lord is able to make him stand. 5*† [For] one
person considers one day more important than
another, while another person considers all days
alike. Let everyone be fully persuaded in his own
mind. 6 Whoever observes the day, observes it for
the Lord. Also whoever eats, eats for the Lord,
since he gives thanks to God; while whoever ab-
stains, abstains for the Lord and gives thanks to
God. 7 None of us lives for oneself, and no one
dies for oneself. 8*† For if we live, we live for the
Lord, and if we die, we die for the Lord; so then,
whether we live or die, we are the Lord's. 9* For
this is why Christ died and came to life, that he
might be Lord of both the dead and the living.
10* Why then do you judge your brother? Or you,
why do you look down on your brother? For we
shall all stand before the judgment seat of God;
11* for it is written:

"As I live, says the Lord, every knee shall bend
before me,
and every tongue shall give praise to
God."

12* So [then] each of us shall give an account of
himself [to God].

Consideration for the Weak Conscience

13* Then let us no longer judge one another,
but rather resolve never to put a stumbling block
or hindrance in the way of a brother. 14* I know
and am convinced in the Lord Jesus that nothing
is unclean in itself; still, it is unclean for some-
one who thinks it unclean. 15* If your brother is
being hurt by what you eat, your conduct is no
longer in accord with love. Do not because of

Live It!

Respecting Differences

If you have traveled to different parts of the United States, you may have discovered that people call similar drinks and sandwiches by different names, depending on what city you are in. Some people talk about soda and others call it pop. Still others call it a soft drink. So too with sandwiches. You may order a hoagie in one town, but it's called a submarine sandwich or grinder in a different part of the country.

In the same way that people from different parts of our country disagree over the "best" names for their favorite food or drink, Christians have different ideas about what to believe and how to act. In this passage, Paul has heard that the Christians in Rome disagree about what to eat (see Rom 14:2) and what days to hold holy (see verse 5). He tells them not to quarrel over these differences. Whatever they do, they should do it "for the Lord" (verse 6). The Church would be shamed if these minor differences became a stumbling block to someone's faith.

The fullness of God's truth exists in a unique way in the Catholic Church, but we respect God's truth where it is found in other Christian Churches. Christians of all denominations should rejoice in their common faith, respect and learn from their differences, and work together "for the Lord."

▶ Rom 14:1–23

ROM

†

14:1—15:6 Since Christ spells termination of the law, which included observance of specific days and festivals as well as dietary instruction, the jettisoning of long-practiced customs was traumatic for many Christians brought up under the Mosaic code. Although Paul acknowledges that in principle no food is a source of moral contamination (14), he recommends that the consciences of Christians who are scrupulous in this regard be respected by other Christians (21). On the other hand, those who have scruples are not to sit in judgment on those who know that the gospel has liberated them from such ordinances (10). See 1 Cor 8 and 10.

14:5 Since the problem to be overcome was humanity's perverted mind or judgment (1:28), Paul indicates that the *mind* of the Christian is now able to function with appropriate discrimination (cf 12:2).

14:8 *The Lord:* Jesus, our Master. The same Greek word, *kyrios,* was applied to both rulers and holders of slaves. Throughout the Letter to the Romans Paul emphasizes God's total claim on the believer; see the note on 1:1.

*

14:1–23 1 Cor 8:1–13.
14:1 Rom 15:1, 7; 1 Cor 9:22.
14:2 Gn 1:29; 9:3; 1 Cor 8:1–13; 10:14–33.
14:3 Col 2:16.
14:4 Rom 2:1; Mt 7:11; Jas 4:11–12.
14:5 Gal 4:10.
14:8 Lk 20:38; 2 Cor 5:15; Gal 2:20; 1 Thes 5:10.
14:9 Acts 10:42.
14:10 Acts 17:31; 2 Cor 5:10.
14:11 Is 49:18 / Is 45:23; Phil 2:10–11.
14:12 Gal 6:5.
14:13 1 Cor 8:9, 13.
14:14 Mk 7:5, 20; Acts 10:15; 1 Cor 10:25–27; 1 Tm 4:4.
14:15 1 Cor 8:11–13.

your food destroy him for whom Christ died.
16* So do not let your good be reviled. 17* For
the kingdom of God is not a matter of food and
drink, but of righteousness, peace, and joy in
the holy Spirit; 18 whoever serves Christ in this
way is pleasing to God and approved by others.
19*† Let us then pursue what leads to peace and
to building up one another. 20* For the sake of
food, do not destroy the work of God. Everything
is indeed clean, but it is wrong for anyone to be-
come a stumbling block by eating; 21 it is good
not to eat meat or drink wine or do anything that
causes your brother to stumble. 22 Keep the faith
[that] you have to yourself in the presence of
God; blessed is the one who does not condemn
himself for what he approves. 23*† But whoever
has doubts is condemned if he eats, because this
is not from faith; for whatever is not from faith
is sin.

Patience and Self-Denial

15 1* We who are strong ought to put up with
the failings of the weak and not to please
ourselves; 2* let each of us please our neighbor
for the good, for building up. 3*† For Christ
did not please himself; but, as it is written, "The
insults of those who insult you fall upon me."
4* For whatever was written previously was writ-
ten for our instruction, that by endurance and
by the encouragement of the scriptures we might
have hope. 5*† May the God of endurance and
encouragement grant you to think in harmony
with one another, in keeping with Christ Jesus,
6 that with one accord you may with one voice
glorify the God and Father of our Lord Jesus
Christ.

God's Fidelity and Mercy

7*† Welcome one another, then, as Christ wel-
comed you, for the glory of God. 8* For I say that
Christ became a minister of the circumcised to
show God's truthfulness, to confirm the prom-
ises to the patriarchs, 9* but so that the Gentiles
might glorify God for his mercy. As it is written:

"Therefore, I will praise you among the
Gentiles
and sing praises to your name."

10*† And again it says:

"Rejoice, O Gentiles, with his people."

11* And again:

"Praise the Lord, all you Gentiles,
and let all the peoples praise him."

12* And again Isaiah says:

"The root of Jesse shall come,
raised up to rule the Gentiles;
in him shall the Gentiles hope."

13* May the God of hope fill you with all joy and
peace in believing, so that you may abound in
hope by the power of the holy Spirit.

VII: Conclusion

Apostle to the Gentiles

14† I myself am convinced about you, my
brothers, that you yourselves are full of good-
ness,† filled with all knowledge, and able to
admonish one another. 15* But I have written
to you rather boldly in some respects to remind
you, because of the grace given me by God 16* to
be a minister of Christ Jesus to the Gentiles in
performing the priestly service of the gospel of
God, so that the offering up of the Gentiles may
be acceptable, sanctified by the holy Spirit. 17 In
Christ Jesus, then, I have reason to boast in what

ROM

†

14:19 Some manuscripts, versions, and church Fathers read, "We then pursue . . ."; cf 5:1.

14:23 *Whatever is not from faith is sin:* Paul does not mean that all the actions of unbelievers are sinful. He addresses himself to the question of intracommunity living. *Sin* in the singular is the dreadful power described in 5:12–14.

15:3 Liberation from the law of Moses does not make the scriptures of the old covenant irrelevant. Much consolation and motivation for Christian living can be derived from the Old Testament, as in the citation from Ps 69:10. Because this psalm is quoted several times in the New Testament, it has been called indirectly messianic.

15:5 *Think in harmony:* a Greco-Roman ideal. Not rigid uniformity of thought and expression but thoughtful consideration of other people's views finds expression here.

15:7–13 True oneness of mind is found in pondering the ultimate mission of the church: to bring it about that God's name be glorified throughout the world and that Jesus Christ be universally recognized as God's gift to all humanity. Paul here prepares his addressees for the climactic appeal he is about to make.

15:10 Paul's citation of Dt 32:43 follows the Greek version.

15:14–33 Paul sees himself as apostle and benefactor in the priestly service of the gospel and so sketches plans for a mission in Spain, supported by those in Rome.

15:14 *Full of goodness:* the opposite of what humanity was filled with according to 1:29–30.

14:16 Rom 2:24; Ti 2:5.
14:17 1 Cor 8:8.
14:19 Rom 12:18 / Rom 15:2.
14:20–21 1 Cor 8:11–13; 10:28–29; Ti 1:15.
14:23 Ti 1:15; Jas 4:17.
15:1 Rom 14:1–2.
15:2 Rom 14:1, 19; 1 Cor 9:19; 10:24, 33.
15:3 Ps 69:10.
15:4 Rom 4:23–24; 1 Mc 12:9; 1 Cor 10:11; 2 Tm 3:16.
15:5 Rom 12:16; Phil 2:2; 4:2.
15:7 Rom 14:1.
15:8 Mt 15:24 / Mi 7:20; Acts 3:25.
15:9 Rom 11:30 / 2 Sm 22:50; Ps 18:50.
15:10 Dt 32:43.
15:11 Ps 117:1.
15:12 Is 11:10; Rv 5:5; 22:16.
15:13 Rom 5:1–2.
15:15 Rom 1:5; 12:3.
15:16 Rom 11:13; Phil 2:17.

pertains to God. 18* For I will not dare to speak of anything except what Christ has accomplished through me to lead the Gentiles to obedience by word and deed, 19† by the power of signs and wonders, by the power of the Spirit [of God], so that from Jerusalem all the way around to Illyricum I have finished preaching the gospel of Christ. 20*† Thus I aspire to proclaim the gospel not where Christ has already been named, so that I do not build on another's foundation, 21*† but as it is written:

"Those who have never been told of him shall see,
and those who have never heard of him shall understand."

Paul's Plans; Need for Prayers

22 That is why I have so often been prevented from coming to you. 23* But now, since I no longer have any opportunity in these regions and since I have desired to come to you for many years, 24* I hope to see you in passing as I go to Spain and to be sent on my way there by you, after I have enjoyed being with you for a time. 25*† Now, however, I am going to Jerusalem to minister to the holy ones. 26*† For Macedonia and Achaia have decided to make some contribution for the poor among the holy ones in Jerusalem; 27* they decided to do it, and in fact they are indebted to them, for if the Gentiles have come to share in their spiritual blessings, they ought also to serve them in material blessings. 28 So when I have completed this and safely handed over this contribution to them, I shall set out by way of you to Spain; 29 and I know that in coming to you I shall come in the fullness of Christ's blessing.

30* I urge you, [brothers,] by our Lord Jesus Christ and by the love of the Spirit, to join me in the struggle by your prayers to God on my behalf, 31 that I may be delivered from the disobedient in Judea, and that my ministry for Jerusalem may be acceptable to the holy ones, 32 so that I may come to you with joy by the will of God and be refreshed together with you. 33* The God of peace be with all of you. Amen.

Phoebe Commended

16 1*† I commend to you Phoebe our sister, who is [also] a minister† of the church at Cenchreae, 2 that you may receive her in the Lord in a manner worthy of the holy ones, and help her in whatever she may need from you, for she has been a benefactor to many and to me as well.

Paul's Greetings

3*† Greet Prisca and Aquila, my co-workers in Christ Jesus, 4 who risked their necks for my life, to whom not only I am grateful but also all the churches of the Gentiles; 5*† greet also the church at their house. Greet my beloved Epaenetus, who was the firstfruits in Asia for Christ. 6 Greet Mary, who has worked hard for you. 7† Greet Andronicus and Junia, my relatives and my fellow prisoners; they are prominent among the apostles and they were in Christ before me. 8 Greet Ampliatus, my beloved in the Lord. 9 Greet Urbanus, our co-worker in Christ, and my beloved Stachys.

---

†

15:19 *Illyricum:* Roman province northwest of Greece on the eastern shore of the Adriatic.

15:20 *I aspire:* Paul uses terminology customarily applied to philanthropists. Unlike some philanthropists of his time, Paul does not engage in cheap competition for public acclaim. This explanation of his missionary policy is to assure the Christians in Rome that he is also not planning to remain in that city and build on other people's foundations (cf 2 Cor 10:12–18). However, he does solicit their help in sending him on his way to Spain, which was considered the limit of the western world. Thus Paul's addressees realize that evangelization may be understood in the broader sense of mission or, as in Rom 1:15, of instruction within the Christian community that derives from the gospel.

15:21 The citation from Is 52:15 concerns the Servant of the Lord. According to Isaiah, the Servant is first of all Israel, which was to bring the knowledge of Yahweh to the nations. In chs 9–11 Paul showed how Israel failed in this mission. Therefore, he himself undertakes almost singlehandedly Israel's responsibility as the Servant and moves as quickly as possible with the gospel through the Roman empire.

15:25–27 Paul may have viewed the contribution he was gathering from Gentile Christians for the poor in Jerusalem (cf 2 Cor 8 and 9) as a fulfillment of the vision of Is 60:5–6. In confidence that the messianic fulfillment was taking place, Paul stresses in chs 14–16 the importance of harmonious relationships between Jews and Gentiles.

15:26 *Achaia:* the Roman province of southern Greece.

16:1–23 Some authorities regard these verses as a later addition to the letter, but in general the evidence favors the view that they were included in the original. Paul endeavors through the long list of greetings (3–16; 21–23) to establish strong personal contact with congregations that he has not personally encountered before. The combination of Jewish and Gentile names dramatically attests the unity in the gospel that transcends previous barriers of nationality, religious ceremony, or racial status.

16:1 *Minister:* in Greek, *diakonos;* see the note on Phil 1:1.

16:3 *Prisca and Aquila:* presumably the couple mentioned at Acts 18:2; 1 Cor 16:19; 2 Tm 4:19.

16:5 *The church at their house:* i.e., that meets there. Such local assemblies (cf 1 Cor 16:19; Col 4:15; Phlm 2) might consist of only one or two dozen Christians each. It is understandable, therefore, that such smaller groups might experience difficulty in relating to one another on certain issues. *Firstfruits:* cf 8:23; 11:16; 1 Cor 16:15.

16:7 The name Junia is a woman's name. One ancient Greek manuscript and a number of ancient versions read the name "Julia." Most editors have interpreted it as a man's name, Junias.

15:18 Acts 15:12; 2 Cor 12:12.
15:20 2 Cor 10:13–18.
15:21 Is 52:15.
15:23 Rom 1:10–13; Acts 19:21–22.
15:24 1 Cor 16:6.
15:25 Acts 19:21; 20:22.
15:26 1 Cor 16:1; 2 Cor 8:1–4; 9:2, 12.
15:27 Rom 9:4 / 1 Cor 9:11.
15:30 2 Cor 1:11; Phil 1:27; Col 4:3; 2 Thes 3:1.
15:33 Rom 16:20; 2 Cor 13:11; Phil 4:9; 1 Thes 5:23; 2 Thes 3:16; Heb 13:20.
16:1 Acts 18:18.
16:3 Acts 18:2, 18–26; 1 Cor 16:19; 2 Tm 4:19.
16:5 1 Cor 16:19; Col 4:15; Phlm 2 / 1 Cor 16:15.

ROM

Introducing...

Phoebe and Junia

In Romans 16:1–16, Paul greets almost thirty people and their families in Rome—more people than he greets in any of his other letters. It is thought that perhaps he is trying to establish a connection among the Christians in Rome by mentioning mutual acquaintances. About a third of the people he greets are women, highlighting the important role women played in Paul's ministry and in the leadership of the early Church.

Of particular interest are Paul's comments about Phoebe, whom he calls a deacon, and Junia (also called Julia), whom he declares "prominent among the apostles" (verse 7). In Paul's time, deacons were usually associated with a ministry of service, and apostles with a ministry of leadership. Even though women were not allowed to fill official positions in government or society, the early Church recognized them as being as important as men in service, leadership, and bringing the Gospel to others.

▶ Rom 16:1–16

10 Greet Apelles, who is approved in Christ. Greet those who belong to the family of Aristobulus. 11 Greet my relative Herodion. Greet those in the Lord who belong to the family of Narcissus. 12 Greet those workers in the Lord, Tryphaena and Tryphosa. Greet the beloved Persis, who has worked hard in the Lord. 13*† Greet Rufus, chosen in the Lord, and his mother and mine. 14 Greet Asyncritus, Phlegon, Hermes, Patrobas, Hermas, and the brothers who are with them. 15 Greet Philologus, Julia, Nereus and his sister, and Olympas, and all the holy ones who are with them. 16* Greet one another with a holy kiss. All the churches of Christ greet you.

Against Factions

17*† I urge you, brothers, to watch out for those who create dissensions and obstacles, in opposition to the teaching that you learned; avoid them. 18* For such people do not serve our Lord Christ but their own appetites, and by fair and flattering speech they deceive the hearts of the innocent. 19* For while your obedience is known to all, so that I rejoice over you, I want you to be wise as to what is good, and simple as to what is evil; 20*† then the God of peace will quickly crush Satan under your feet. The grace of our Lord Jesus be with you.

Greetings from Corinth

21* Timothy, my co-worker, greets you; so do Lucius and Jason and Sosipater, my relatives. 22 I, Tertius, the writer of this letter, greet you in the Lord. 23*† Gaius, who is host to me and to the whole church, greets you. Erastus, the city treasurer, and our brother Quartus greet you. [24]†

Doxology†

[25* Now to him who can strengthen you, according to my gospel and the proclamation of Jesus Christ, according to the revelation of the mystery kept secret for long ages† 26* but now manifested through the prophetic writings and, according to the command of the eternal God, made known to all nations to bring about the obedience of faith, 27* to the only wise God, through Jesus Christ be glory forever and ever. Amen.]

ROM

---

†

16:13 This Rufus cannot be identified to any degree of certainty with the Rufus of Mk 15:21.

16:17–18 Paul displays genuine concern for the congregations in Rome by warning them against self-seeking teachers. It would be a great loss, he intimates, if their obedience, which is known to all (cf 1:8), would be diluted.

16:20 This verse contains the only mention of Satan in Romans.

16:23 This Erastus is not necessarily to be identified with the Erastus of Acts 19:22 or of 2 Tm 4:20.

16:24 Some manuscripts add, similarly to v 20, "The grace of our Lord Jesus Christ be with you all. Amen."

16:25–27 This doxology is assigned variously to the end of chs 14:15, and 16 in the manuscript tradition. Some manuscripts omit it entirely. Whether written by Paul or not, it forms an admirable conclusion to the letter at this point.

16:25 Paul's gospel reveals *the mystery kept secret for long ages:* justification and salvation through faith, with all the implications for Jews and Gentiles that Paul has developed in the letter.

---

*

16:13 Mk 15:21.
16:16 1 Cor 16:20; 2 Cor 13:12; 1 Thes 5:26; 1 Pt 5:14.
16:17 Mt 7:15; Ti 3:10.
16:18 Phil 3:18–19; Col 2:4; 2 Pt 2:3.
16:19 Rom 1:8; Mt 10:16; 1 Cor 14:20.
16:20 Rom 15:33; Gn 3:15; Lk 10:19 / 1 Cor 16:23; 1 Thes 5:28; 2 Thes 3:18.
16:21 Acts 16:1–2; 19:22; 20:4; 1 Cor 4:17; 16:10; Phil 2:19–22; Heb 13:23.
16:23 Acts 19:29; 1 Cor 1:14 / 2 Tm 4:20.
16:25 1 Cor 2:7; Eph 1:9; 3:3–9; Col 1:26.
16:26 2 Tm 1:10 / Rom 1:5; Eph 3:4–5, 9; 1 Pt 1:20.
16:27 Rom 11:36; Gal 1:5; Eph 3:20–21; Phil 4:20; 1 Tm 1:17; 2 Tm 4:18; Heb 13:21; 1 Pt 4:11; 2 Pt 3:18; Jude 25; Rv 1:6.

The First Letter to the Corinthians

Churches have problems. Sometimes parishes harbor power struggles, sex scandals, troubled marriages, bitter disagreements, alcohol abuse, and even disorderly worship. Maybe you know of Christian communities that have had some of these difficulties. The early church in Corinth had them all. In his first letter to the Corinthians, Paul gave them guidance and encouragement. This letter can teach churches in all times to more faithfully follow Christ.

In Depth

Corinth was an important seaport city in what is now southern Greece. It was a center of commerce for people from many cultures. It also had quite a reputation for sexual immorality. Paul established the Christian church there around AD 51 and spent about eighteen months with its converts. After Paul left, a man named Apollos came to help the young church grow.

Later, when Paul was in Ephesus, he got a letter from the Corinthian church (see 1 Cor 7:1) and a report from others about them (see 1:11). The church there was having problems. The problems were natural in a young Christian community whose members included both Jewish Christians and Gentile (non-Jewish) converts. The community was divided into groups with different leaders. There were some disagreements on how to worship properly. And there were different opinions about eating meat that had been sacrificed to pagan idols. In addition, some of the wealthy Christians were ignoring those who were poorer. And those with certain spiritual gifts were claiming to be more important than other people.

In response to all these divisions and various questions, Paul gives the Corinthians good, practical advice. At the same time, he reminds them of what is truly important for Christian believers: the death and Resurrection of Jesus is central to faith; human wisdom is foolish when measured against God's wisdom; others' needs and concerns must always be put before their own; and love should be the primary focus in everything they do and say.

To this divided, confused community, Paul offers a picture of unity: we are all different parts of the same Body of Christ (see 12:12–26). Paul celebrates our diversity and insists on our unity. The advice and teaching he gives in this letter are good for Christians of any time or place to take to heart.

At a Glance

I. **Address (1:1–9).**

II. **Disorders in the Corinthian Community (1:10—6:20).**

III. **Answers to the Corinthians' Questions (7:1—11:1).**

IV. **Problems in Liturgical Assemblies (11:2—14:40).**

V. **The Resurrection (15:1–58).**

VI. **Conclusion (16:1–24).**

Quick Facts

Inspired Author: Paul
Date Written: AD 56
Audience: the mainly Gentile church at Corinth

1 Corinthians

11:23–26

I: Address†

Greeting

1 [1]* Paul, called to be an apostle of Christ Jesus
by the will of God,† and Sosthenes our brother,
[2]* to the church of God that is in Corinth, to you
who have been sanctified in Christ Jesus, called to
be holy, with all those everywhere who call upon
the name of our Lord Jesus Christ, their Lord and
ours. [3] Grace to you and peace from God our Father and the Lord Jesus Christ.

Thanksgiving

[4] I give thanks to my God always on your account for the grace of God bestowed on you in
Christ Jesus, [5] that in him you were enriched in every way, with all discourse and all knowledge, [6]† as
the testimony to Christ was confirmed among you,
[7]* so that you are not lacking in any spiritual gift as
you wait for the revelation of our Lord Jesus Christ.
[8]* He will keep you firm to the end, irreproachable
on the day of our Lord Jesus [Christ.] [9]* God is
faithful, and by him you were called to fellowship
with his Son, Jesus Christ our Lord.

II: Disorders in the Corinthian Community

A. Divisions in the Church

Groups and Slogans

[10]*† I urge you, brothers, in the name of our
Lord Jesus Christ, that all of you agree in what you
say, and that there be no divisions among you,
but that you be united in the same mind and in
the same purpose. [11] For it has been reported to
me about you, my brothers, by Chloe's people,
that there are rivalries among you. [12]*† I mean
that each of you is saying, "I belong to Paul," or

1:1–9 Paul follows the conventional form for the opening of a Hellenistic letter (cf Rom 1:1–7), but expands the opening with details carefully chosen to remind the readers of their situation and to suggest some of the issues the letter will discuss.

1:1 *Called . . . by the will of God:* Paul's mission and the church's existence are grounded in God's initiative. God's call, grace, and fidelity are central ideas in this introduction, emphasized by repetition and wordplays in the Greek.

1:6 *The testimony:* this defines the purpose of Paul's mission (see also 15:15 and the note on 2:1). The forms of his testimony include oral preaching and instruction, his letters, and the life he leads as an apostle.

1:10–4:21 The first problem Paul addresses is that of divisions within the community. Although we are unable to reconstruct the situation in Corinth completely, Paul clearly traces the divisions back to a false self-image on the part of the Corinthians, coupled with a false understanding of the apostles who preached to them (cf 4:6, 9; 9:1–5) and of the Christian message itself. In these chapters he attempts to deal with those underlying factors and to bring the Corinthians back to a more correct perspective.

1:12 *I belong to:* the activities of Paul and Apollos in Corinth are described in Acts 18. *Cephas* (i.e., "the Rock," a name by which Paul designates Peter also in 3:22; 9:5; 15:5 and in Gal 1:18; 2:9, 11, 14) may well have passed through Corinth; he could have baptized some members of the community either there or elsewhere. The reference to *Christ* may be intended ironically here.

1:1 Rom 1:1.
1:2 Acts 18:1–11.
1:7 Ti 2:13.
1:8 Phil 1:6.
1:9 1 Jn 1:3.
1:10 Phil 2:2.
1:12 1 Cor 3:4, 22; 16:12; Acts 18:24–28.

"I belong to Apollos," or "I belong to Cephas,"
or "I belong to Christ." 13† Is Christ divided? Was
Paul crucified for you? Or were you baptized in
the name of Paul? 14* I give thanks [to God] that
I baptized none of you except Crispus and Gaius,
15 so that no one can say you were baptized in my
name. 16* (I baptized the household of Stepha-
nas also; beyond that I do not know whether I
baptized anyone else.) 17*† For Christ did not
send me to baptize but to preach the gospel, and
not with the wisdom of human eloquence,† so
that the cross of Christ might not be emptied of
its meaning.

Paradox of the Cross

18* The message of the cross is foolishness
to those who are perishing, but to us who are
being saved it is the power of God. 19* For it is
written:

"I will destroy the wisdom of the wise,
and the learning of the learned I will set
aside."

20* Where is the wise one? Where is the scribe?
Where is the debater of this age? Has not God
made the wisdom of the world foolish? 21† For
since in the wisdom of God the world did not

† **1:13–17** The reference to baptism and the contrast with preaching the gospel in v 17a suggest that some Corinthians were paying special allegiance to the individuals who initiated them into the community.

1:17b–18 The basic theme of chs 1–4 is announced. Adherence to individual leaders has something to do with differences in rhetorical ability and also with certain presuppositions regarding wisdom, eloquence, and effectiveness (power), which Paul judges to be in conflict with the gospel and the cross.

1:17b *Not with the wisdom of human eloquence:* both of the nouns employed here involve several levels of meaning, on which Paul deliberately plays as his thought unfolds. *Wisdom* (*sophia*) may be philosophical and speculative, but in biblical usage the term primarily denotes practical knowledge such as is demonstrated in the choice and effective application of means to achieve an end. The same term can designate the arts of building (cf 3:10) or of persuasive speaking (cf 2:4) or effectiveness in achieving salvation. *Eloquence* (*logos*): this translation emphasizes one possible meaning of the term *logos* (cf the references to rhetorical style and persuasiveness in 2:1, 4). But the term itself may denote an internal reasoning process, plan, or intention, as well as an external word, speech, or message. So by his expression *ouk en sophia logou* in the context of gospel preaching, Paul may intend to exclude both human ways of reasoning or thinking about things and human rhetorical technique. *Human:* this adjective does not stand in the Greek text but is supplied from the context. Paul will begin immediately to distinguish between *sophia* and *logos* from their divine counterparts and play them off against each other.

1:21–25 True wisdom and power are to be found paradoxically where one would least expect them, in the place of their apparent negation. To human eyes the crucified Christ symbolizes impotence and absurdity.

* **1:14** Acts 18:8 / Rom 16:23.
1:16 1 Cor 16:15–17.
1:17 1 Cor 2:1, 4.
1:18 1 Cor 2:14 / Rom 1:16.
1:19 Is 29:14.
1:20 Is 19:12.

Live It!

Divisions in the Church

At a family reunion to honor his grandfather's eighty-fifth birthday, Tyrone brags about his school's victory over his cousin Martin's school in a recent football game. Martin counters that the referees overlooked a crucial penalty. Before long, the entire gathering is fighting about which team was the best. The birthday party is ruined.

This is similar to what happened to the Christians in Corinth. They were divided over which missionary was the best and which leaders to follow. Paul challenges them to get over this foolish division and focus on the important thing they share—the love of God and their salvation through the cross of Christ.

Christians today continue to struggle with Paul's challenge to be united. Even though the gift of unity has been given to the Church by Christ, the Church is called to work toward that unity by living holy lives, through public and private prayer, and in service to others. Knowing this, we look for those shared beliefs and practices that unite us, while respectfully talking about the sometimes significant differences that exist between different Christian Churches. In this way, all Catholics seek to build unity and communion with other Christians.

▶ 1 Cor 1:10–17

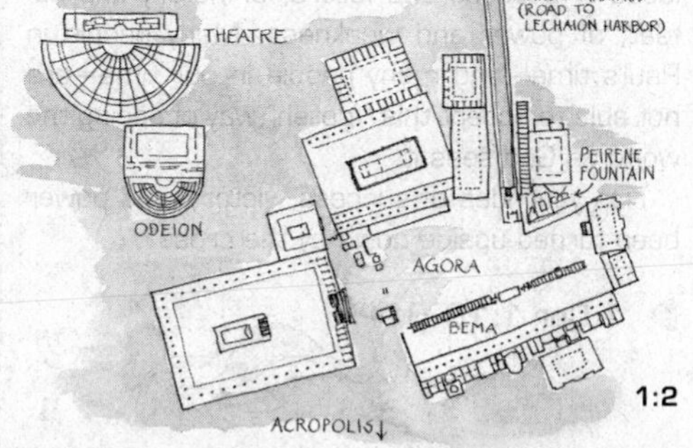

1:2

Artist's rendering of city plans for first-century Corinth

come to know God through wisdom, it was
the will of God through the foolishness of the
proclamation to save those who have faith.
22* For Jews demand signs and Greeks look for
wisdom, 23* but we proclaim Christ crucified,
a stumbling block to Jews and foolishness to
Gentiles, 24 but to those who are called, Jews
and Greeks alike, Christ the power of God
and the wisdom of God. 25 For the foolish-
ness of God is wiser than human wisdom, and
the weakness of God is stronger than human
strength.

Live It!

God's Wisdom and Ours

What is the difference between a smart person and a wise person? Many smart people excel in a subject in school or a skill at work. A person has to be very smart to run an illegal drug ring or to make a nuclear bomb. But being smart in these ways does not make a person wise in the ways of God.

Paul reminds the Corinthians that the central Christian message—that Christ was crucified for our salvation—seems foolish to many wise people of their time. The Greeks of this period pride themselves on their wisdom. And the Jews hope for signs of a kingly messiah who will make the nation strong. Both the Jews and the Greeks think the idea of a crucified messiah, or a god who can suffer and die, is foolish.

There is great mystery here: The foolishness of God is wiser than the greatest wisdom of the world. Our ways are not God's ways. Christ's hanging on a cross turns upside down the world's ideas of success and failure, of victory and defeat, of power and weakness. Many people in Paul's time—and many people in our time—are not able to accept this "foolish" way of seeing the world as God sees it.

Has your idea of success, victory, and power been turned upside down by the cross?

▶ **1 Cor 1:18–31**

The Corinthians and Paul

26† Consider your own calling, brothers. Not
many of you were wise by human standards, not
many were powerful, not many were of noble
birth. 27* Rather, God chose the foolish of the
world to shame the wise, and God chose the
weak of the world to shame the strong, 28 and
God chose the lowly and despised of the world,
those who count for nothing, to reduce to noth-
ing those who are something, 29*† so that no hu-
man being might boast before God. 30* It is due
to him that you are in Christ Jesus, who became
for us wisdom from God, as well as righteous-
ness, sanctification, and redemption, 31* so that,
as it is written, "Whoever boasts, should boast
in the Lord."

2 1*† When I came to you, brothers, proclaim-
ing the mystery of God, I did not come with
sublimity of words or of wisdom. 2* For I re-
solved to know nothing while I was with you ex-
cept Jesus Christ, and him crucified. 3† I came to
you in weakness and fear and much trembling,
4*† and my message and my proclamation were
not with persuasive [words of] wisdom, but with
a demonstration of spirit and power, 5* so that
your faith might rest not on human wisdom but
on the power of God.

†

1:26—2:5 The pattern of God's wisdom and power is exemplified in their own experience, if they interpret it rightly (1:26–31), and can also be read in their experience of Paul as he first appeared among them preaching the gospel (2:1–5).

1:29–31 "Boasting (about oneself)" is a Pauline expression for the radical sin, the claim to autonomy on the part of a creature, the illusion that we live and are saved by our own resources. "Boasting in the Lord" (31), on the other hand, is the acknowledgment that we live only from God and for God.

2:1 *The mystery of God:* God's secret, known only to himself, is his plan for the salvation of his people; it is clear from 1:18–25; 2:2, 8–10 that this secret involves Jesus and the cross. In place of *mystery*, other good manuscripts read "testimony" (cf 1:6).

2:3 The *weakness* of the crucified Jesus is reflected in Paul's own bearing (cf 2 Cor 10–13). *Fear and much trembling:* reverential fear based on a sense of God's transcendence permeates Paul's existence and preaching. Compare his advice to the Philippians to work out their salvation with "fear and trembling" (Phil 2:12), because God is at work in them just as his exalting power was paradoxically at work in the emptying, humiliation, and obedience of Jesus to death on the cross (Phil 2:6–11).

2:4 Among many manuscript readings here the best is either "not with the persuasion of wisdom" or "not with persuasive words of wisdom," which differ only by a nuance. Whichever reading is accepted, the inefficacy of human wisdom for salvation is contrasted with the power of the cross.

*

1:22 Mt 12:38; 16:1 / Acts 17:18–21.
1:23 1 Cor 2:2; Gal 3:1 / Gal 5:11.
1:27 Jas 2:5.
1:29 Eph 2:9.
1:30 Rom 4:17 / 1 Cor 6:11; Rom 3:24–26; 2 Cor 5:21 / Eph 1:7; Col 1:14; 1 Thes 5:23.
1:31 Jer 9:23; 2 Cor 10:17.
2:1 1 Cor 1:17.
2:2 1 Cor 1:23; Gal 6:14.
2:4 1 Cor 4:20; Rom 15:19; 1 Thes 1:5.
2:5 2 Cor 4:7.

The True Wisdom

6† Yet we do speak a wisdom to those who
are mature, but not a wisdom of this age, nor
of the rulers of this age who are passing away.
7† Rather, we speak God's wisdom, mysterious,
hidden, which God predetermined before the
ages for our glory, 8† and which none of the
rulers of this age knew; for if they had known it,
they would not have crucified the Lord of glory.
9* But as it is written:

> "What eye has not seen, and ear has not
> heard,
> and what has not entered the human heart,
> what God has prepared for those who love
> him,"

10* this God has revealed to us through the
Spirit.

For the Spirit scrutinizes everything, even the
depths of God. 11 Among human beings, who
knows what pertains to a person except the spirit
of the person that is within? Similarly, no one
knows what pertains to God except the Spirit
of God. 12 We have not received the spirit of the
world but the Spirit that is from God, so that
we may understand the things freely given us
by God. 13† And we speak about them not with
words taught by human wisdom, but with words
taught by the Spirit, describing spiritual realities
in spiritual terms.

14† Now the natural person does not accept
what pertains to the Spirit of God, for to him
it is foolishness, and he cannot understand it,
because it is judged spiritually. 15† The spiritual
person, however, can judge everything but is not
subject to judgment by anyone.

16* For "who has known the mind of the Lord,
so as to counsel him?" But we have the mind of
Christ.

3 1† Brothers, I could not talk to you as spir-
itual people, but as fleshly people,† as in-
fants in Christ. 2* I fed you milk, not solid food,
because you were unable to take it. Indeed, you
are still not able, even now, 3*† for you are still
of the flesh. While there is jealousy and rivalry
among you, are you not of the flesh and behav-
ing in an ordinary human way? 4* Whenever
someone says, "I belong to Paul," and another,
"I belong to Apollos," are you not merely hu-
man?

The Role of God's Ministers†

5 What is Apollos, after all, and what is Paul?
Ministers† through whom you became believers,
just as the Lord assigned each one. 6* I planted,

†

2:6—3:4 Paul now asserts paradoxically what he has previously been denying. To the Greeks who "are looking for wisdom" (1:22), he does indeed bring a wisdom, but of a higher order and an entirely different quality, the only wisdom really worthy of the name. The Corinthians would be able to grasp Paul's preaching as wisdom and enter into a wisdom-conversation with him if they were more open to the Spirit and receptive to the new insight and language that the Spirit teaches.

2:7–10a *God's wisdom:* his plan for our salvation. This was his own eternal secret that no one else could fathom, but in this new age of salvation he has graciously revealed it to us. For the pattern of God's secret, hidden to others and now revealed to the Church, cf also Rom 11:25–36; 16:25–27; Eph 1:3–10; 3:3–11; Col 1:25–28.

2:8 *The rulers of this age:* this suggests not only the political leaders of the Jews and Romans under whom Jesus was crucified (cf Acts 4:25–28) but also the cosmic powers behind them (cf Eph 1:20–23; 3:10). *They would not have crucified the Lord of glory:* they became the unwitting executors of God's plan, which will paradoxically bring about their own conquest and submission (15:24–28).

2:13 *In spiritual terms:* the Spirit teaches spiritual people a new mode of perception (12) and an appropriate language by which they can share their self-understanding, their knowledge about what God has done in them. The final phrase in v 13 can also be translated "describing spiritual realities to spiritual people," in which case it prepares for vv 14–16.

2:14 *The natural person:* see the note on 3:1.

2:15 *The spiritual person . . . is not subject to judgment:* since spiritual persons have been given knowledge of what pertains to God (11–12), they share in God's own capacity to judge. One to whom the mind of the Lord (and of Christ) is revealed (16) can be said to share in some sense in God's exemption from counseling and criticism.

3:1–4 The Corinthians desire a sort of wisdom dialogue or colloquy with Paul; they are looking for solid, adult food, and he appears to disappoint their expectations. Paul counters: if such a dialogue has not yet taken place, the reason is that they are still at an immature stage of development (cf 2:6).

3:1 *Spiritual people . . . fleshly people:* Paul employs two clusters of concepts and terms to distinguish what later theology will call the "natural" and the "supernatural." (1) The natural person (2:14) is one whose existence, perceptions, and behavior are determined by purely natural principles, the *psychē* (2:14) and the *sarx* (flesh, a biblical term that connotes creatureliness, 1, 3). Such persons are only infants (1); they remain on a purely human level (*anthrōpoi,* 4). (2) On the other hand, they are called to be animated by a higher principle, the *pneuma,* God's spirit. They are to become spiritual (*pneumatikoi,* 1) and mature (2:6) in their perceptions and behavior (cf Gal 5:16–26). The culmination of existence in the Spirit is described in 15:44–49.

3:3–4 Jealousy, rivalry, and divisions in the community are symptoms of their arrested development; they reveal the immaturity both of their self-understanding (4) and of the judgments about their apostles (21).

3:5—4:5 The Corinthians tend to evaluate their leaders by the criteria of human wisdom and to exaggerate their importance. Paul views the role of the apostles in the light of his theology of spiritual gifts (cf chs 12–14, where the charism of the apostle heads the lists). The essential aspects of all spiritual gifts (12:4–6 presents them as gifts of grace, as services, and as modes of activity) are exemplified by the apostolate, which is a gift of grace (3:10) through which God works (3:9) and a form of service (3:5) for the common good (elsewhere expressed by the verb "build up," suggested here by the image of the building, 3:9). The apostles serve the church, but their accountability is to God and to Christ (4:1–5).

3:5 *Ministers:* for other expressions of Paul's understanding of himself as minister or steward to the church, cf 4:1; 9:17, 19–27; 2 Cor 3:6–9; 4:1; 5:18; 6:3–4; and 11:23 (the climax of Paul's defense).

*

2:9 Is 64:3.
2:10 Mt 11:25; 13:11; 16:17.
2:16 Wis 9:13; Is 40:13; Rom 11:34.
3:2 Heb 5:12–14.
3:3 Jas 3:13–16.
3:4 1 Cor 1:12.
3:6 Acts 18:1–11, 24–28.

Apollos watered, but God caused the growth.
7Therefore, neither the one who plants nor the
one who waters is anything, but only God, who
causes the growth. 8The one who plants and the
one who waters are equal, and each will receive
wages in proportion to his labor. 9* For we are
God's co-workers; you are God's field, God's
building.
10† According to the grace of God given to me,
like a wise master builder I laid a foundation,
and another is building upon it. But each one
must be careful how he builds upon it, 11for
no one can lay a foundation other than the one
that is there, namely, Jesus Christ. 12If anyone
builds on this foundation with gold, silver, pre-
cious stones, wood, hay, or straw, 13*† the work
of each will come to light, for the Day will dis-
close it. It will be revealed with fire, and the fire
[itself] will test the quality of each one's work.
14If the work stands that someone built upon

† **3:10–11** There are diverse functions in the service of the community, but each individual's task is serious, and each will stand accountable for the quality of his contribution.

3:13 *The Day:* the great day of Yahweh, the day of judgment, which can be a time of either gloom or joy. *Fire* both destroys and purifies.

* **3:9** Eph 2:20–22; 1 Pt 2:5. **3:13** Mt 3:11–12; 2 Thes 1:7–10.

Live It!

We Are God's Servants, Who Share a Common Mission

Sometimes, Christians engage in destructive competition or are motivated by personal pride. Paul says clearly that all Christians are God's servants, should work together, and should have a common purpose—God's purpose. Whatever we do for the Gospel is part of Jesus' mission and has the same value for God. Paul uses two images to tell us this: "Therefore, neither the one who plants nor the one who waters is anything, but only God, who causes the growth" (1 Cor 3:7) and "Like a wise master builder I laid a foundation, and another is building upon it . . . for no one can lay a foundation other than the one that is there, namely, Jesus Christ" (verses 10–11).

- As a young person, how can you work cooperatively with other young people and with the adult community?
- Express your gratitude for the building of the Church done by previous generations of Christians. Pray that young Christians will embrace Jesus' mission with passion and with the global perspective needed at this time in history.

▶ 1 Cor 3:1–15

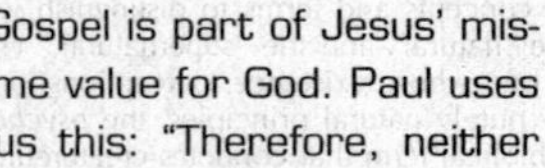

Pray It!

From the Bottom Up

The most important part of a building is its foundation. If the foundation is built well and with care, what is placed on it will last. And so it is with people. We all have before us a wide variety of construction materials—values, beliefs, and principles—to use in building the foundation of our lives. Initially, our foundation is built through our family, using the values taught in schools and churches. In our adolescent years, most of us discover that other materials are available and that we must choose which ones to add to our foundation.

In 1 Corinthians 3:10–17, Paul tells the people of Corinth that whatever they choose to use in building their foundation will show itself in the end. A poor foundation will lead to a poor end. He also reminds them that they are living temples of God, to be filled with the Holy Spirit. Even though Paul was referring to Christ as the foundation of the Church, each of us as individuals is also called to build our lives on Christ.

In your prayer, reflect or journal on the following questions:

- How is Christ the foundation you build your life on?
- What kind of person do you want to be remembered as when you are gone?
- What qualities, values, and virtues do you want to have? How can these be a sign of the Holy Spirit living within you?

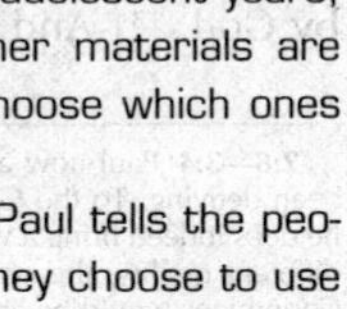

▶ 1 Cor 3:10–17

the foundation, that person will receive a wage.
15† But if someone's work is burned up, that one
will suffer loss; the person will be saved, but only
as through fire. 16* Do you not know that you
are the temple of God, and that the Spirit of God
dwells in you? 17† If anyone destroys God's tem-
ple, God will destroy that person; for the temple
of God, which you are, is holy.

18* Let no one deceive himself. If anyone
among you considers himself wise in this age, let
him become a fool so as to become wise. 19* For
the wisdom of this world is foolishness in the
eyes of God, for it is written:

"He catches the wise in their own ruses,"

20*and again:

"The Lord knows the thoughts of the wise,
that they are vain."

21*† So let no one boast about human beings, for
everything belongs to you, 22 Paul or Apollos or
Cephas, or the world or life or death, or the pres-
ent or the future: all belong to you, 23 and you to
Christ, and Christ to God.

4 1* Thus should one regard us: as servants of
Christ and stewards of the mysteries of God.
2 Now it is of course required of stewards that
they be found trustworthy. 3 It does not concern
me in the least that I be judged by you or any
human tribunal; I do not even pass judgment on
myself; 4* I am not conscious of anything against
me, but I do not thereby stand acquitted; the one
who judges me is the Lord. 5 Therefore, do not
make any judgment before the appointed time,
until the Lord comes, for he will bring to light
what is hidden in darkness and will manifest the
motives of our hearts, and then everyone will re-
ceive praise from God.

Pray It!

We Are God's Temple

We are God's temple.
We are rich, we are poor,
We are young, we are old,
We are male, we are female,
We are disabled, we are sick, we are healthy,
We are unborn,
We are all races and cultures.
O God,
Fill us with your spirit of unity.
Abolish the destructive forces of hate:
prejudice, racism, physical and verbal abuse,
abortion, murder, and euthanasia.
Break down the barriers that divide us.
Fill us with your loving spirit and an
appreciation for the value of each and
every life. Amen.

▶ 1 Cor 3:16–17

Paul's Life as Pattern†

6 I have applied these things to myself and
Apollos for your benefit, brothers, so that you
may learn from us not to go beyond what is
written,† so that none of you will be inflated
with pride in favor of one person over against
another. 7 Who confers distinction upon you?
What do you possess that you have not received?
But if you have received it, why are you boasting
as if you did not receive it? 8† You are already
satisfied; you have already grown rich; you have

†

3:15 *Will be saved:* although Paul can envision very harsh divine punishment (cf 17), he appears optimistic about the success of divine corrective means both here and elsewhere (cf 5:5; 11:32 [discipline]). The text of v 15 has sometimes been used to support the notion of purgatory, though it does not envisage this.

3:17 *Holy:* i.e., "belonging to God." The cultic sanctity of the community is a fundamental theological reality to which Paul frequently alludes (cf 1:2, 30; 6:11; 7:14).

3:21–23 These verses pick up the line of thought of 1:10–13. If the Corinthians were genuinely wise (18–20), their perceptions would be reversed, and they would see everything in the world and all those with whom they exist in the church in their true relations with one another. Paul assigns all the persons involved in the theological universe a position on a scale: God, Christ, church members, church leaders. Read from top to bottom, the scale expresses ownership; read from bottom to top, the obligation to serve. This picture should be complemented by similar statements such as those in 8:6 and 15:20–28.

4:6–21 This is an emotionally charged peroration to the discussion about divisions. It contains several exhortations and statements of Paul's purpose in writing (cf 6, 14–17, 21) that counterbalance the initial exhortation at 1:10.

4:6 *That you may learn from us not to go beyond what is written:* the words "to go" are not in the Greek, but have here been added as the minimum necessary to elicit sense from this difficult passage. It probably means that the Corinthians should avoid the false wisdom of vain speculation, contenting themselves with Paul's proclamation of the cross, which is the fulfillment of God's promises in the Old Testament (what is written). *Inflated with pride:* literally, "puffed up," i.e., arrogant, filled with a sense of self-importance. The term is particularly Pauline, found in the New Testament only in 1 Cor 4:6, 18–19; 5:2; 8:1; 13:4; Col 2:18 (cf the related noun at 2 Cor 12:20). It sometimes occurs in conjunction with the theme of "boasting," as in vv 6–7 here.

4:8 *Satisfied . . . rich . . . kings:* these three statements could also be punctuated as questions continuing the series begun in v 7. In

*

3:16 1 Cor 6:19; 2 Cor 6:16; Eph 2:20–22.
3:18 1 Cor 8:2; Is 5:21; Gal 6:3.
3:19 1 Cor 1:20 / Jb 5:13.
3:20 Ps 94:11.
3:21 1 Cor 4:6 / Rom 8:32.
4:1 Ti 1:7; 1 Pt 4:10.
4:4 2 Cor 1:12 / Rom 2:16; 2 Cor 5:10.

1 COR

become kings without us! Indeed, I wish that
you had become kings, so that we also might be-
come kings with you.
9*† For as I see it, God has exhibited us apos-
tles as the last of all, like people sentenced to
death, since we have become a spectacle to the
world, to angels and human beings alike. 10* We
are fools on Christ's account, but you are wise in
Christ; we are weak, but you are strong; you are
held in honor, but we in disrepute. 11* To this
very hour we go hungry and thirsty, we are poor-
ly clad and roughly treated, we wander about
homeless 12* and we toil, working with our own
hands. When ridiculed, we bless; when perse-
cuted, we endure; 13 when slandered, we respond
gently. We have become like the world's rubbish,
the scum of all, to this very moment.
14† I am writing you this not to shame you,
but to admonish you as my beloved children.
15* Even if you should have countless guides to
Christ, yet you do not have many fathers, for I
became your father in Christ Jesus through the
gospel. 16* Therefore, I urge you, be imitators of
me. 17* For this reason I am sending you Timo-
thy, who is my beloved and faithful son in the
Lord; he will remind you of my ways in Christ
[Jesus], just as I teach them everywhere in every
church.
18† Some have become inflated with pride, as
if I were not coming to you. 19 But I will come
to you soon, if the Lord is willing, and I shall
ascertain not the talk of these inflated people but
their power. 20* For the kingdom of God is not
a matter of talk but of power. 21* Which do you
prefer? Shall I come to you with a rod, or with
love and a gentle spirit?

B. Moral Disorders†

A Case of Incest†

5 1* It is widely reported that there is immo-
rality among you, and immorality of a kind
not found even among pagans—a man living
with his father's wife. 2† And you are inflated
with pride. Should you not rather have been
sorrowful? The one who did this deed should
be expelled from your midst. 3* I, for my part,
although absent in body but present in spirit,
have already, as if present, pronounced judg-
ment on the one who has committed this deed,
4 in the name of [our] Lord Jesus: when you have
gathered together and I am with you in spirit
with the power of the Lord Jesus, 5*† you are to
deliver this man to Satan for the destruction of
his flesh, so that his spirit may be saved on the
day of the Lord.
6*† Your boasting is not appropriate. Do you
not know that a little yeast leavens all the dough?

---

† any case these expressions reflect a tendency at Corinth toward an overrealized eschatology, a form of self-deception that draws Paul's irony. The underlying attitude has implications for the Corinthians' thinking about other issues, notably morality and the resurrection, that Paul will address later in the letter.

4:9–13 A rhetorically effective catalogue of the circumstances of apostolic existence, in the course of which Paul ironically contrasts his own sufferings with the Corinthians' illusion that they have passed beyond the folly of the passion and have already reached the condition of glory. His language echoes that of the beatitudes and woes, which assert a future reversal of present conditions. Their present sufferings ("to this very hour," 11) place the apostles in the class of those to whom the beatitudes promise future relief (Mt 5:3–11; Lk 6:20–23); whereas the Corinthians' image of themselves as "already" filled, rich, ruling (8), as wise, strong, and honored (10) places them paradoxically in the position of those whom the woes threaten with future undoing (Lk 6:24–26). They have lost sight of the fact that the reversal is predicted for the future.

4:14–17 *My beloved children:* the close of the argument is dominated by the tender metaphor of the father who not only gives his children life but also educates them. Once he has begotten them through his preaching, Paul continues to present the gospel to them existentially, by his life as well as by his word, and they are to learn, as children do, by imitating their parents (16). The reference to the *rod* in v 21 belongs to the same image-complex. So does the image of the *ways* in v 17: the ways that Paul teaches everywhere, "his ways in Christ Jesus," mean a behavior pattern quite different from the human ways along which the Corinthians are walking (3:3).

4:18–21 Verse 20 picks up the contrast between a certain kind of talk (*logos*) and true power (*dynamis*) from 1:17–18 and 2:4–5. The kingdom, which many of them imagine to be fully present in their lives (8), will be rather unexpectedly disclosed in the strength of Paul's encounter with them, if they make a powerful intervention on his part necessary. Compare the similar ending to an argument in 2 Cor 13:1–4, 10.

5:1—6:20 Paul now takes up a number of other matters that require regulation. These have come to his attention by hearsay (5:1), probably in reports brought by "Chloe's people" (1:11).

5:1–13 Paul first deals with the incestuous union of a man with his stepmother (1–8) and then attempts to clarify general admonitions he has given about associating with fellow Christians guilty of immorality (9–13). Each of these three brief paragraphs expresses the same idea: the need of separation between the holy and the unholy.

5:2 *Inflated with pride:* this remark and the reference to *boasting* in v 6 suggest that they are proud of themselves despite the infection in their midst, tolerating and possibly even approving the situation. The attitude expressed in 6:2, 13 may be influencing their thinking in this case.

5:5 *Deliver this man to Satan:* once the sinner is expelled from the church, the sphere of Jesus' lordship and victory over sin, he will be in the region outside over which Satan is still master. *For the destruction of his flesh:* the purpose of the penalty is medicinal: through affliction, sin's grip over him may be destroyed and the path to repentance and reunion laid open. With Paul's instructions for an excommunication ceremony here, contrast his recommendations for the reconciliation of a sinner in 2 Cor 2:5–11.

5:6 *A little yeast:* yeast, which induces fermentation, is a natural symbol for a source of corruption that becomes all-pervasive. The expression is proverbial.

---

* **4:9** 1 Cor 15:31; Rom 8:36; 2 Cor 4:8–12; 11:23 / Heb 10:33.
4:10 1 Cor 1:18; 3:18; 2 Cor 11:19 / 1 Cor 2:3; 2 Cor 13:9.
4:11 Rom 8:35; 2 Cor 11:23–27.
4:12 Acts 9:6–14; 18:3; 20:34; 1 Thes 2:9 / 1 Pt 3:9.
4:15 Gal 4:19; Phlm 10.
4:16 1 Cor 11:1; Phil 3:17; 4:9; 1 Thes 1:6; 2 Thes 3:7, 9.
4:17 1 Cor 16:10; Acts 19:22.
4:20 1 Cor 2:4; 1 Thes 1:5.
4:21 2 Cor 1:23; 10:2.
5:1 Lv 18:7–8; 20:11; Dt 27:20.
5:3 Col 2:5.
5:5 1 Tm 1:20.
5:6 Gal 5:9.

[7]*† Clear out the old yeast, so that you may be-
come a fresh batch of dough, inasmuch as you
are unleavened. For our paschal lamb, Christ,
has been sacrificed. [8]* Therefore, let us celebrate
the feast, not with the old yeast, the yeast of
malice and wickedness, but with the unleavened
bread of sincerity and truth.
[9]† I wrote you in my letter not to associate
with immoral people, [10]* not at all referring to
the immoral of this world or the greedy and
robbers or idolaters; for you would then have to
leave the world. [11]* But I now write to you not
to associate with anyone named a brother, if he
is immoral, greedy, an idolater, a slanderer, a
drunkard, or a robber, not even to eat with such
a person. [12] For why should I be judging outsid-
ers? Is it not your business to judge those within?
[13]* God will judge those outside. "Purge the evil
person from your midst."

Lawsuits before Unbelievers

6 [1]† How can any one of you with a case
against another dare to bring it to the unjust
for judgment instead of to the holy ones? [2]*† Do
you not know that the holy ones will judge the
world? If the world is to be judged by you, are
you unqualified for the lowest law courts? [3] Do
you not know that we will judge angels? Then
why not everyday matters? [4] If, therefore, you
have courts for everyday matters, do you seat as
judges people of no standing in the church? [5] I
say this to shame you. Can it be that there is not
one among you wise enough to be able to set-
tle a case between brothers? [6] But rather brother
goes to court against brother, and that before
unbelievers?
[7]* Now indeed [then] it is, in any case, a fail-
ure on your part that you have lawsuits against
one another. Why not rather put up with injus-
tice? Why not rather let yourselves be cheated?
[8] Instead, you inflict injustice and cheat, and this
to brothers. [9]*† Do you not know that the unjust
will not inherit the kingdom of God? Do not be
deceived; neither fornicators nor idolaters nor
adulterers nor boy prostitutes† nor sodomites
[10] nor thieves nor the greedy nor drunkards nor
slanderers nor robbers will inherit the kingdom
of God. [11]* That is what some of you used to be;
but now you have had yourselves washed, you
were sanctified, you were justified in the name
of the Lord Jesus Christ and in the Spirit of our
God.

Sexual Immorality†

[12]* "Everything is lawful for me,"† but not
everything is beneficial. "Everything is lawful for
me," but I will not let myself be dominated by
anything. [13] "Food for the stomach and the stom-
ach for food," but God will do away with both
the one and the other. The body, however, is not
for immorality, but for the Lord, and the Lord is
for the body; [14]* God raised the Lord and will
also raise us by his power.
[15]*† Do you not know that your bodies are

5:7–8 In the Jewish calendar, Passover was followed immediately by the festival of Unleavened Bread. In preparation for this feast all traces of old bread were removed from the house, and during the festival only unleavened bread was eaten. The sequence of these two feasts provides Paul with an image of Christian existence: Christ's death (the true Passover celebration) is followed by the life of the Christian community, marked by newness, purity, and integrity (a perpetual feast of unleavened bread). Paul may have been writing around Passover time (cf 16:5); this is a little Easter homily, the earliest in Christian literature.

5:9–13 Paul here corrects a misunderstanding of his earlier directives against associating with immoral fellow Christians. He concedes the impossibility of avoiding contact with sinners in society at large but urges the Corinthians to maintain the inner purity of their own community.

6:1–11 Christians at Corinth are suing one another before pagan judges in Roman courts. A barrage of rhetorical questions (1–9) betrays Paul's indignation over this practice, which he sees as an infringement upon the holiness of the Christian community. **6:2–3** The principle to which Paul appeals is an eschatological prerogative promised to Christians: they are to share with Christ the judgment of the world (cf Dn 7:22, 27). Hence they ought to be able to settle minor disputes within the community.

6:9–10 A catalogue of typical vices that exclude from the kingdom of God and that should be excluded from God's church. Such lists (cf 5:10) reflect the common moral sensibility of the New Testament period.

6:9 The Greek word translated as *boy prostitutes* may refer to catamites, i.e., boys or young men who were kept for purposes of prostitution, a practice not uncommon in the Greco-Roman world. In Greek mythology this was the function of Ganymede, the "cupbearer of the gods," whose Latin name was Catamitus. The term translated *sodomites* refers to adult males who indulged in homosexual practices with such boys. See similar condemnations of such practices in Rom 1:26–27; 1 Tm 1:10.

6:12–20 Paul now turns to the opinion of some Corinthians that sexuality is a morally indifferent area (12–13). This leads him to explain the mutual relation between the Lord Jesus and our bodies (13b) in a densely packed paragraph that contains elements of a profound theology of sexuality (15–20).

6:12–13 *Everything is lawful for me:* the Corinthians may have derived this slogan from Paul's preaching about Christian freedom, but they mean something different by it: they consider sexual satisfaction a matter as indifferent as food, and they attribute no lasting significance to bodily functions (13a). Paul begins to deal with the slogan by two qualifications, which suggest principles for judging sexual activity. *Not everything is beneficial:* cf 10:23, and the whole argument of chs 8–10 on the finality of freedom and moral activity. *Not let myself be dominated:* certain apparently free actions may involve in fact a secret servitude in conflict with the lordship of Jesus.

6:15b–16 *A prostitute:* the reference may be specifically to religious prostitution, an accepted part of pagan culture at Corinth and elsewhere; but the prostitute also serves as a symbol for any sexual relationship that conflicts with Christ's claim over us individually. *The two . . . will become one flesh:* the text of Gn 2:24 is applied positively to human marriage in Matthew and Mark, and in

---

5:7 Ex 12:1–13; Dt 16:1–2; 1 Pt 1:19.
5:8 Ex 12:15–20; 13:7; Dt 16:3.
5:10 1 Cor 10:27; Jn 17:15.
5:11 Mt 18:17; 2 Thes 3:6, 14; 2 Jn 10.
5:13 Dt 13:6; 17:7; 22:24.
6:2 Wis 3:8; Mt 19:28; Rv 20:4.
6:7 Mt 5:38–42; Rom 12:17–21; 1 Thes 5:15.
6:9 1 Cor 15:50; Gal 5:19–21; Eph 5:5.
6:11 Ti 3:3–7.
6:12 1 Cor 10:23.
6:14 Rom 8:11; 2 Cor 4:14.
6:15 1 Cor 12:27; Rom 6:12–13; 12:5; Eph 5:30.

members of Christ? Shall I then take Christ's
members and make them the members of a pros-
titute? Of course not! [16]* [Or] do you not know
that anyone who joins himself to a prostitute
becomes one body with her? For "the two," it
says, "will become one flesh." [17]* But whoever is
joined to the Lord becomes one spirit with him.
[18]† Avoid immorality. Every other sin a person
commits is outside the body, but the immoral
person sins against his own body. [19]*† Do you
not know that your body is a temple of the holy
Spirit within you, whom you have from God,
and that you are not your own? [20]* For you have
been purchased at a price. Therefore glorify God
in your body.

Live It!

Living Well

Some people think that God or the Christian religion is primarily interested in preventing us from doing fun things. They imagine the Bible as a book of thou-shalt-nots, and the church as a place where they are told to avoid enjoying themselves!

Paul helps us to understand that God's desire is for us to live well. All good gifts from God, including food and sexuality, are meant to be enjoyed to the fullest. But they also can be misused, and if they are, we miss out on the joy and purpose intended by God.

For example, in 1 Corinthians 6:12–20, Paul affirms that sexual intercourse is meant to bond a man and a woman for life. Fornication—sexual intercourse between people who are not married—defeats its true purpose. Fornication diminishes the full joy and beauty of sexual intimacy as intended by God.

God created our sexuality. Our sexual desires—felt keenly during adolescence!—are not sinful but a normal part of being human. As the author of our sexuality, God wants us not to be hurt by this gift but instead to experience its fullness in marriage.

► 1 Cor 6:12–20

III: Answers to the Corinthians' Questions

A. Marriage and Virginity†

Advice to the Married†

7 [1]† Now in regard to the matters about which
you wrote: "It is a good thing for a man
not to touch a woman," [2] but because of cases
of immorality every man should have his own
wife, and every woman her own husband. [3] The
husband should fulfill his duty toward his wife,
and likewise the wife toward her husband. [4] A
wife does not have authority over her own body,
but rather her husband, and similarly a husband
does not have authority over his own body, but
rather his wife. [5] Do not deprive each other,
except perhaps by mutual consent for a time,
to be free for prayer, but then return to one an-
other, so that Satan may not tempt you through
your lack of self-control. [6]† This I say by way of

† Eph 5:29–32: love of husband and wife reflect the love of Christ for his church. The application of the text to union with a prostitute is jarring, for such a union is a parody, an antitype of marriage, which does conflict with Christ's claim over us. This explains the horror expressed in 15b.

6:18 *Against his own body:* expresses the intimacy and depth of sexual disorder, which violates the very orientation of our bodies.

6:19–20 Paul's vision becomes trinitarian. *A temple:* sacred by reason of God's gift, his indwelling Spirit. *Not your own:* but "for the Lord," who acquires ownership by the act of redemption. *Glorify God in your body:* the argument concludes with a positive imperative to supplement the negative "avoid immorality" of v 18. Far from being a terrain that is morally indifferent, the area of sexuality is one in which our relationship with God (and his Christ and his Spirit) is very intimately expressed: he is either highly glorified or deeply offended.

7:1–40 Paul now begins to answer questions addressed to him by the Corinthians (7:1—11:1). The first of these concerns marriage. This chapter contains advice both to the married (1–16) and to the unmarried (25–38) or widowed (39–40); these two parts are separated by vv 17–24, which enunciate a principle applicable to both.

7:1–16 It seems that some Christians in Corinth were advocating asceticism in sexual matters. The pattern *it is a good thing . . . , but* occurs twice (1–2, 8–9; cf 26), suggesting that in this matter as in others the Corinthians have seized upon a genuine value but are exaggerating or distorting it in some way. Once again Paul calls them to a more correct perspective and a better sense of their own limitations. The phrase *it is a good thing* (1) may have been the slogan of the ascetic party at Corinth.

7:1–7 References to Paul's own behavior (7–8) suggest that his celibate way of life and his preaching to the unmarried (cf 25–35) have given some the impression that asceticism within marriage, i.e., suspension of normal sexual relations, would be a laudable ideal. Paul points to their experience of widespread immorality to caution them against overestimating their own strength (2); as individuals they may not have the particular gift that makes such asceticism feasible (7) and hence are to abide by the principle to be explained in vv 17–24.

7:6 *By way of concession:* this refers most likely to the concession mentioned in v 5a: temporary interruption of relations for a legitimate purpose.

6:16 Gn 2:24; Mt 19:5; Mk 10:8; Eph 5:31.
6:17 Rom 8:9–10; 2 Cor 3:17.
6:19 1 Cor 3:16–17; Rom 5:5.
6:20 1 Cor 3:23; 7:23; Acts 20:28 / Rom 12:1; Phil 1:20.

concession, however, not as a command. 7*† Indeed, I wish everyone to be as I am, but each has a particular gift from God, one of one kind and one of another.

8*† Now to the unmarried and to widows I say: It is a good thing for them to remain as they are, as I do, 9 but if they cannot exercise self-control they should marry, for it is better to marry than to be on fire. 10*† To the married, however, I give this instruction (not I, but the Lord): a wife should not separate from her husband 11—and if she does separate she must either remain single or become reconciled to her husband—and a husband should not divorce his wife.

12† To the rest I say (not the Lord): if any brother has a wife who is an unbeliever, and she is willing to go on living with him, he should not divorce her; 13 and if any woman has a husband who is an unbeliever, and he is willing to go on living with her, she should not divorce her husband. 14* For the unbelieving husband is made holy through his wife, and the unbelieving wife is made holy through the brother. Otherwise your children would be unclean, whereas in fact they are holy.

15† If the unbeliever separates, however, let him separate. The brother or sister is not bound in such cases; God has called you to peace. 16 For how do you know, wife, whether you will save your husband; or how do you know, husband, whether you will save your wife?

The Life That the Lord Has Assigned

17† Only, everyone should live as the Lord has assigned, just as God called each one. I give this order in all the churches. 18* Was someone called after he had been circumcised? He should not try to undo his circumcision. Was an uncircumcised person called? He should not be circumcised. 19* Circumcision means nothing, and uncircumcision means nothing; what matters is keeping God's commandments. 20 Everyone should remain in the state in which he was called.

Did You Know?

Strange Advice!?

First Corinthians, chapter 7, says people shouldn't marry, uncircumcised people shouldn't get circumcised, and slaves should remain slaves.

Why is Paul giving such strange advice? Because Paul thinks that Jesus will be returning soon to establish God's Reign for all time (see verse 31). So he advises the Corinthians to remain in whatever condition they were called, in order to keep their focus on preparing for Christ's return, rather than be distracted with other cares.

But Jesus didn't come back during Paul's time. In fact, we are still waiting for his return. When is Jesus going to come again? Don't try to figure it out. Jesus told us we will never know (see Mt 24:36–44). But whatever our state of life is, or will become, we would be wise to follow Paul's intent, which is to promote "propriety and adherence to the Lord without distraction" (1 Cor 7:35).

▶ 1 Corinthians, chapter 7

21 Were you a slave when you were called? Do not be concerned but, even if you can gain your freedom, make the most of it. 22* For the slave called in the Lord is a freed person in the Lord, just as the free person who has been called is a slave of Christ. 23* You have been purchased at a price. Do not become slaves to human beings. 24 Brothers, everyone should continue before God in the state in which he was called.

† **7:7** *A particular gift from God:* use of the term *charisma* suggests that marriage and celibacy may be viewed in the light of Paul's theology of spiritual gifts (chs 12–14).

7:8 Paul was obviously unmarried when he wrote this verse. Some interpreters believe that he had previously been married and widowed; there is no clear evidence either for or against this view, which was expressed already at the end of the second century by Clement of Alexandria.

7:10–11 *(Not I, but the Lord):* Paul reminds the married of Jesus' principle of nonseparation (Mk 10:9). This is one of his rare specific references to the teaching of Jesus.

7:12–14 *To the rest:* marriages in which only one partner is a baptized Christian. Jesus' prohibition against divorce is not addressed to them, but Paul extends the principle of nonseparation to such unions, provided they are marked by peacefulness and shared sanctification.

7:15–16 *If the unbeliever separates:* the basis of the "Pauline privilege" in Catholic marriage legislation.

7:17–24 On the ground that distinct human conditions are less significant than the whole new existence opened up by God's call, Paul urges them to be less concerned with changing their states of life than with answering God's call where it finds them. The principle applies both to the married state (1–16) and to the unmarried (25–38).

* **7:7** Mt 19:11–12.
7:8 1 Tm 5:11–16 / 1 Cor 9:5.
7:10–11 Mt 5:32; 19:9.
7:14 Rom 11:16.
7:18 1 Mc 1:15 / Acts 15:1–2.
7:19 Rom 2:25, 29; Gal 5:6; 6:15.
7:22 Eph 6:5–9; Col 3:11; Phlm 16.
7:23 1 Cor 6:20.

Advice to Virgins and Widows

25† Now in regard to virgins I have no commandment from the Lord, but I give my opinion as one who by the Lord's mercy is trustworthy. 26* So this is what I think best because of the present distress: that it is a good thing for a person to remain as he is. 27 Are you bound to a wife? Do not seek a separation. Are you free of a wife? Then do not look for a wife. 28 If you marry, however, you do not sin, nor does an unmarried woman sin if she marries; but such people will experience affliction in their earthly life, and I would like to spare you that.

29*† I tell you, brothers, the time is running out. From now on, let those having wives act as not having them, 30 those weeping as not weeping, those rejoicing as not rejoicing, those buying as not owning, 31 those using the world as not using it fully. For the world in its present form is passing away.

32 I should like you to be free of anxieties. An unmarried man is anxious about the things of the Lord, how he may please the Lord. 33* But a married man is anxious about the things of the world, how he may please his wife, 34* and he is divided. An unmarried woman or a virgin is anxious about the things of the Lord, so that she may be holy in both body and spirit. A married woman, on the other hand, is anxious about the things of the world, how she may please her husband. 35* I am telling you this for your own benefit, not to impose a restraint upon you, but for the sake of propriety and adherence to the Lord without distraction.

36† If anyone thinks he is behaving improperly toward his virgin, and if a critical moment has come† and so it has to be, let him do as he wishes. He is committing no sin; let them get married. 37 The one who stands firm in his resolve, however, who is not under compulsion but has power over his own will, and has made up his mind to keep his virgin, will be doing well. 38 So then, the one who marries his virgin does well; the one who does not marry her will do better.

39*† A wife is bound to her husband as long as he lives. But if her husband dies, she is free to be married to whomever she wishes, provided that it be in the Lord. 40* She is more blessed, though, in my opinion, if she remains as she is, and I think that I too have the Spirit of God.

B. Offerings to Idols†

Knowledge Insufficient

8 1* Now in regard to meat sacrificed to idols:† we realize that "all of us have knowledge"; knowledge inflates with pride, but love builds up. 2 If anyone supposes he knows something, he does not yet know as he ought to know. 3* But if one loves God, one is known by him.

4* So about the eating of meat sacrificed to idols: we know that "there is no idol in the world," and that "there is no God but one." 5 Indeed, even though there are so-called gods in heaven and on earth (there are, to be sure, many "gods" and many "lords"), 6*† yet for us there is

†

7:25–28 Paul is careful to explain that the principle of v 17 does not bind under sin but that present earthly conditions make it advantageous for the unmarried to remain as they are (28). These remarks must be complemented by the statement about "particular gifts" from v 7.

7:29–31 *The world . . . is passing away:* Paul advises Christians to go about the ordinary activities of life in a manner different from those who are totally immersed in them and unaware of their transitoriness.

7:36–38 The passage is difficult to interpret, because it is unclear whether Paul is thinking of a father and his unmarried daughter (or slave), or of a couple engaged in a betrothal or spiritual marriage. The general principles already enunciated apply: there is no question of sin, even if they should marry, but staying as they are is "better" (for the reasons mentioned in 28–35). Once again the *charisma* of v 7, which applies also to the unmarried (8–9), is to be presupposed.

7:36 *A critical moment has come:* either because the woman will soon be beyond marriageable age, or because their passions are becoming uncontrollable (cf 9).

7:39–40 Application of the principles to the case of widows. If they do choose to remarry, they ought to prefer Christian husbands.

8:1—11:1 The Corinthians' second question concerns meat that has been sacrificed to idols; in this area they were exhibiting a disordered sense of liberation that Paul here tries to rectify. These chapters contain a sustained and unified argument that illustrates Paul's method of theological reflection on a moral dilemma. Although the problem with which he is dealing is dated, the guidelines for moral decisions that he offers are of lasting validity. Essentially Paul urges them to take a communitarian rather than an individualistic view of their Christian freedom. Many decisions that they consider pertinent only to their private relationship with God have, in fact, social consequences. Nor can moral decisions be determined by merely theoretical considerations; they must be based on concrete circumstances, specifically on the value and needs of other individuals and on mutual responsibility within the community. Paul here introduces the theme of "building up" (*oikodomē*), i.e., of contributing by individual action to the welfare and growth of the community. This theme will be further developed in ch 14; see the note on 14:3b–5. Several years later Paul would again deal with the problem of meat sacrificed to idols in Rom 14:1—15:6.

8:1a *Meat sacrificed to idols:* much of the food consumed in the city could have passed through pagan religious ceremonies before finding its way into markets and homes. *"All of us have knowledge":* a slogan, similar to 6:12, which reveals the self-image of the Corinthians. Verse 4 will specify the content of this knowledge.

8:6 This verse rephrases the monotheistic confession of v 4 in such a way as to contrast it with polytheism (5) and to express our relationship with the one God in concrete, i.e., in personal and Christian terms. *And for whom we exist:* since the Greek contains no verb here and the action intended must be inferred from the preposition *eis,* another translation is equally possible: "toward whom we return." *Through whom all things:* the earliest reference in the New Testament to Jesus' role in creation.

*

7:26 1 Cor 7:8.
7:29 Rom 13:11.
7:33 Lk 14:20.
7:34 1 Tm 5:5.
7:35 Lk 10:39–42.
7:39 Rom 7:2.
7:40 1 Cor 7:25.
8:1 Rom 15:14 / 1 Cor 13:1–13; Rom 14:15, 19.
8:3 Rom 8:29; Gal 4:9.
8:4 1 Cor 10:19; Dt 6:4.
8:6 Mal 2:10 / Rom 11:36; Eph 4:5–6 / 1 Cor 1:2–3 / Jn 1:3; Col 1:16.

one God, the Father,
from whom all things are and for whom
we exist,
and one Lord, Jesus Christ,
through whom all things are and through
whom we exist.

Practical Rules

[7]* But not all have this knowledge. There are
some who have been so used to idolatry up until
now that, when they eat meat sacrificed to idols,
their conscience, which is weak, is defiled.
[8]*† Now food will not bring us closer to God.
We are no worse off if we do not eat, nor are we
better off if we do. [9]* But make sure that this
liberty of yours in no way becomes a stumbling
block to the weak. [10]If someone sees you, with
your knowledge, reclining at table in the temple
of an idol, may not his conscience too, weak
as it is, be "built up" to eat the meat sacrificed
to idols? [11]* Thus through your knowledge,
the weak person is brought to destruction, the
brother for whom Christ died. [12]When you sin in
this way against your brothers and wound their
consciences, weak as they are, you are sinning
against Christ. [13]*† Therefore, if food causes my
brother to sin, I will never eat meat again, so that
I may not cause my brother to sin.

Paul's Rights as an Apostle

9 [1]*† Am I not free? Am I not an apostle? Have
I not seen Jesus our Lord? Are you not my
work in the Lord? [2]Although I may not be an
apostle for others, certainly I am for you, for you
are the seal of my apostleship in the Lord.
[3]† My defense against those who would pass
judgment on me is this. [4]† Do we not have the
right to eat and drink? [5]Do we not have the right

† **8:8–9** Although the food in itself is morally neutral, extrinsic circumstances may make the eating of it harmful. *A stumbling block:* the image is that of tripping or causing someone to fall (cf 13; 9:12; 10:12, 32; 2 Cor 6:3; Rom 14:13, 20–21). This is a basic moral imperative for Paul, a counterpart to the positive imperative to "build one another up"; compare the expression "giving offense" as opposed to "pleasing" in 10:32–33.

8:13 His own course is clear: he will avoid any action that might harm another Christian. This statement prepares for the paradigmatic development in ch 9.

9:1–27 This chapter is an emotionally charged expansion of Paul's appeal to his own example in 8:13; its purpose is to reinforce the exhortation of 8:9. The two opening questions introduce the themes of Paul's freedom and his apostleship (1), themes that the chapter will develop in reverse order, vv 1–18 treating the question of his apostleship and the rights that flow from it, and vv 19–27 exploring dialectically the nature of Paul's freedom. The language is highly rhetorical, abounding in questions, wordplays, paradoxes, images, and appeals to authority and experience. The argument is unified by repetitions; its articulations are highlighted by inclusions and transitional verses.

9:3 *My defense against those who would pass judgment on me:* the reference to a defense (*apologia*) is surprising, and suggests that Paul is incorporating some material here that he has previously used in another context. The defense will touch on two points: the fact of Paul's rights as an apostle (4–12a and 13–14) and his nonuse of those rights (12b and 15–18).

9:4–12a Apparently some believe that Paul is not equal to the other apostles and therefore does not enjoy equal privileges. His defense on this point (here and in 13–14) reinforces the assertion of his apostolic character in v 2. It consists of a series of analogies from natural equity (7) and religious custom (13) designed to establish his equal right to support from the churches (4–6, 11–12a); these analogies are confirmed by the authority of the law (8–10) and of Jesus himself (14).

* **8:7** 1 Cor 10:28; Rom 14:23 / Rom 14:1; 15:1.
8:8 Rom 14:17.
8:9 Rom 14:13, 20–21.
8:11 Rom 14:15, 20.
8:13 Mt 18:6; Rom 14:20–21.
9:1 1 Cor 9:19 / 2 Cor 12:12 / 1 Cor 15:8–9; Acts 9:17; 26:16.

Live It!

Restrain Your Ego!

Maria's parents have stopped drinking alcohol. Not that they ever drank to excess. But for months, Maria bugged them, saying, "If I can't drink, then why do you?" Because she accepted none of their arguments, they agreed that they would stop until she reached legal age.

Crazy? Not according to Paul. He recommends something similar. Paul recognizes that it is not necessarily wrong for some members of the community of Christians in Corinth to eat meat sacrificed to idols, or pagan gods, because they don't believe in those gods. Still, he recommends that they not do it, because some members of the community find it upsetting. For Paul, paying attention to the welfare of everyone in the community is more important than always "being right."

Do you ever do things that aren't necessarily wrong just because it's your right? like whistle around a sibling who cannot stand it? or pick a sweater for the family picture that doesn't match anyone else's? or, when your younger brothers and sisters are around, watch a television show that's okay for you but not for them? When you find yourself doing something like this, think about Paul's advice. Are you making your ego more important than other people's feelings?

▶ 1 Cor 8:1–13

Live It!

Spiritual Perseverance

Did you know that Michael Jordan—once the points leader of the record-setting Chicago Bulls—had difficulty making his high school varsity basketball team the first year he tried out? He could have quit trying, but he set a goal for himself and made practicing a priority for his daily life. Not only did he finally make the team, he broke state scoring records and was named all-state. And that was just the beginning!

Perseverance means setting priorities, sticking to them even when you get discouraged, and trying over and over to accomplish your goals. For the next six months, set yourself a goal that will help you to grow closer to God. What will you have to do to accomplish it? What priorities must you establish? As 1 Corinthians 9:24–27 says, run your race by staying focused on your goal!

▶ 1 Cor 9:24–27

to take along a Christian wife, as do the rest of the apostles, and the brothers of the Lord, and Cephas? 6* Or is it only myself and Barnabas who do not have the right not to work? 7* Who ever serves as a soldier at his own expense? Who plants a vineyard without eating its produce? Or who shepherds a flock without using some of the milk from the flock? 8 Am I saying this on human authority, or does not the law also speak of these things? 9* It is written in the law of Moses, "You shall not muzzle an ox while it is treading out the grain." Is God concerned about oxen, 10* or is he not really speaking for our sake? It was written for our sake, because the plowman should plow in hope, and the thresher in hope of receiving a share. 11* If we have sown spiritual seed for you, is it a great thing that we reap a material harvest from you? 12*† If others share this rightful claim on you, do not we still more?

Reason for Not Using His Rights

Yet we have not used this right. On the contrary, we endure everything so as not to place an obstacle to the gospel of Christ. 13*† Do you not know that those who perform the temple services eat [what] belongs to the temple, and those who minister at the altar share in the sacrificial offerings? 14* In the same way, the Lord ordered that those who preach the gospel should live by the gospel.

15*† I have not used any of these rights, however, nor do I write this that it be done so in my case. I would rather die. Certainly no one is going to nullify my boast. 16* If I preach the gospel, this is no reason for me to boast, for an obligation has been imposed on me, and woe to me if I do not preach it! 17* If I do so willingly, I have a recompense, but if unwillingly, then I have been entrusted with a stewardship. 18* What then is my recompense? That, when I preach, I offer the gospel free of charge so as not to make full use of my right in the gospel.

All Things to All

19*† Although I am free in regard to all, I have made myself a slave to all so as to win over as many as possible. 20 To the Jews I became like a Jew to win over Jews; to those under the law I became like one under the law—though I myself am not under the law—to win over those under the law. 21 To those outside the law I became like one outside the law—though I am not outside God's law but within the law of Christ—to win over those outside the law. 22* To the weak I

†

9:12b It appears, too, that suspicion or misunderstanding has been created by Paul's practice of not living from his preaching. The first reason he asserts in defense of this practice is an entirely apostolic one; it anticipates the developments to follow in vv 19–22. He will give a second reason in vv 15–18.

9:13–14 The position of these verses produces an interlocking of the two points of Paul's defense. These arguments by analogy (13) and from authority (14) belong with those of vv 7–10 and ground the first point. But Paul defers them until he has had a chance to mention "the gospel of Christ" (12b), after which it is more appropriate to mention Jesus' injunction to his preachers and to argue by analogy from the sacred temple service to his own liturgical service, the preaching of the gospel (cf Rom 1:9; 15:16).

9:15–18 Paul now assigns a more personal motive to his nonuse of his right to support. His preaching is not a service spontaneously undertaken on his part but a stewardship imposed by a sort of divine compulsion. Yet to merit any reward he must bring some spontaneous quality to his service, and this he does by freely renouncing his right to support. The material here is quite similar to that contained in Paul's "defense" at 2 Cor 11:5–12; 12:11–18.

9:19–23 In a rhetorically balanced series of statements Paul expands and generalizes the picture of his behavior and explores the paradox of apostolic freedom. It is not essentially freedom *from* restraint but freedom *for* service–a possibility of constructive activity.

9:6 Acts 4:36–37; 13:1–2; Gal 2:1, 9, 13; Col 4:10.
9:7 2 Tm 2:3–4.
9:9 Dt 25:4; 1 Tm 5:18.
9:10 2 Tm 2:6.
9:11 Rom 15:27.
9:12 2 Cor 11:7–12; 12:13–18; 2 Thes 3:6–12.
9:13 Nm 18:8, 31; Dt 18:1–5.
9:14 Mt 10:10; Lk 10:7–8.
9:15 2 Cor 11:9–10.
9:16 Acts 26:14–18.
9:17 1 Cor 4:1; Gal 2:7.
9:18 2 Cor 11:7–12.
9:19 Mt 20:26–27.
9:22 1 Cor 10:33; Rom 15:1; 2 Cor 11:29.

became weak, to win over the weak. I have be-
come all things to all, to save at least some. 23 All
this I do for the sake of the gospel, so that I too
may have a share in it.
24*† Do you not know that the runners in the
stadium all run in the race, but only one wins
the prize? Run so as to win. 25* Every athlete ex-
ercises discipline in every way. They do it to win
a perishable crown, but we an imperishable one.
26 Thus I do not run aimlessly; I do not fight as
if I were shadowboxing. 27† No, I drive my body
and train it, for fear that, after having preached to
others, I myself should be disqualified.

Warning against Overconfidence

10 1*† I do not want you to be unaware,
brothers, that our ancestors were all under
the cloud and all passed through the sea, 2* and
all of them were baptized into Moses in the
cloud and in the sea. 3 All ate the same spiritual
food, 4*† and all drank the same spiritual drink,
for they drank from a spiritual rock that followed
them, and the rock was the Christ. 5* Yet God
was not pleased with most of them, for they were
struck down in the desert.
6*† These things happened as examples for us,
so that we might not desire evil things, as they
did. 7* And do not become idolaters, as some of
them did, as it is written, "The people sat down
to eat and drink, and rose up to revel." 8* Let us
not indulge in immorality as some of them did,
and twenty-three thousand fell within a single
day. 9*† Let us not test Christ as some of them
did, and suffered death by serpents. 10* Do not
grumble as some of them did, and suffered death

Live It!

Addictive Behavior

How do you spend the bulk of your free time? Talking with your friends on the phone? playing video games? listening to your favorite music? If you discover that you have become obsessed with a particular activity, maybe it has become addictive. Although perhaps your obsession is not a true addiction—like those caused by drugs, alcohol, gambling, or eating disorders—it still might have more control over your life than it should have.

Paul reminds the Corinthians that they should put God at the center of their lives. He points out that they will always be tempted to replace God with something else—which is called idolatry—like the ancient Israelites were tempted. Paul is also introducing his teaching on participation in the Eucharist as a way of turning one's back on this old way of life and committing oneself to a new way of life.

How about us today? We may not worship foreign gods or eat meat sacrificed to idols. But in many ways, our addictive behaviors are like idolatry. They consume our thoughts and time and can even lead us away from God.

Addictive behaviors are hard to break. And true addictions are very difficult to control. But you have the promise that God "will not let you be tried beyond your strength" (1 Cor 10:13). If you think you may have an addiction, talk to a parent or school counselor or minister. Participating in the Eucharist is also a good way to express your desire to live the life God is calling you to.

▶ 1 Cor 10:6–14

9:24–27 A series of miniparables from sports, appealing to readers familiar with Greek gymnasia and the nearby Isthmian games.

9:27 *For fear that . . . I myself should be disqualified:* a final paradoxical turn to the argument: what appears at first a free, spontaneous renunciation of rights (12–18) seems subsequently to be required for fulfillment of Paul's stewardship (to preach effectively he must reach his hearers wherever they are, 19–22), and finally is seen to be necessary for his own salvation (23–27). Mention of the possibility of disqualification provides a transition to ch 10.

10:1–5 Paul embarks unexpectedly upon a panoramic survey of the events of the Exodus period. The privileges of Israel in the wilderness are described in terms that apply strictly only to the realities of the new covenant ("baptism," "spiritual food and drink"); interpreted in this way they point forward to the Christian experience (1–4). But those privileges did not guarantee God's permanent pleasure (5).

10:4 *A spiritual rock that followed them:* the Torah speaks only about a rock from which water issued, but rabbinic legend amplified this into a spring that followed the Israelites throughout their migration. Paul uses this legend as a literary type: he makes the rock itself accompany the Israelites, and he gives it a spiritual sense. *The rock was the Christ:* in the Old Testament, Yahweh is the Rock of his people (cf Dt 32, Moses' song to Yahweh the Rock). Paul now applies this image to the Christ, the source of the living water, the true Rock that accompanied Israel, guiding their experiences in the desert.

10:6–13 This section explicitates the typological value of these Old Testament events: the desert experiences of the Israelites are examples, meant as warnings, to deter us from similar sins (idolatry, immorality, etc.) and from a similar fate.

10:9 *Christ:* to avoid Paul's concept of Christ present in the wilderness events, some manuscripts read "the Lord."

9:24 Heb 12:1.
9:25 2 Tm 2:5 / 2 Tm 4:7–8; Jas 1:12; 1 Pt 5:4.
10:1 Ex 13:21–22; 14:19–20 / Ex 14:21–22, 26–30.
10:2 Rom 6:3; Gal 3:27 / Ex 16:4–35.
10:4 Ex 17:1–7; Nm 20:7–11; Dt 8:15.
10:5 Nm 14:28–38; Jude 5.
10:6 Nm 11:4, 34.
10:7 Ex 32:6.
10:8 Nm 25:1–9.
10:9 Nm 21:5–9.
10:10 Nm 14:2–37; 16:1–35.

Cultural Connection

Food and Gratitude

Have you ever considered eating and drinking for the glory of God? Paul tells the Corinthians that it is more important to respect the conscience of their dining partners than to worry about where the meat came from. By appreciating what they have been given to eat, they show respect for the people who have prepared the food.

Native Americans have that same sense of appreciation—not just for the people they share meals with but for the animals and plants that provide the food. When they kill an animal to eat, they pray to its spirit for forgiveness. Everything from the animal is put to good use, because wasting any part of it would be an insult to its honor.

This Native American meal blessing is an expression of thanks:

Now that I am about to eat,
O great Spirit, give my thanks
to the beasts and birds whom
You have provided for my hunger, and pray deliver my sorrow that living things must make a sacrifice for my comfort and well-being. Let the feather of corn spring up in its time and let it not wither but make full grains for the fires of our cooking pots, now that I am about to eat.

▶ 1 Cor 10:23–33

by the destroyer. 11† These things happened to
them as an example, and they have been written
down as a warning to us, upon whom the end
of the ages has come. 12† Therefore, whoever
thinks he is standing secure should take care not
to fall. 13* No trial has come to you but what is
human. God is faithful and will not let you be
tried beyond your strength; but with the trial he
will also provide a way out, so that you may be
able to bear it.

Warning against Idolatry

14*† Therefore, my beloved, avoid idolatry.
15 I am speaking as to sensible people; judge
for yourselves what I am saying. 16* The cup of
blessing that we bless, is it not a participation
in the blood of Christ? The bread that we break,
is it not a participation in the body of Christ?
17* Because the loaf of bread is one, we, though
many, are one body, for we all partake of the
one loaf.
18* Look at Israel according to the flesh; are
not those who eat the sacrifices participants in
the altar? 19 So what am I saying? That meat sacrificed to idols is anything? Or that an idol is
anything? 20*† No, I mean that what they sacrifice, [they sacrifice] to demons, not to God, and
I do not want you to become participants with
demons. 21* You cannot drink the cup of the
Lord and also the cup of demons. You cannot
partake of the table of the Lord and of the table
of demons. 22* Or are we provoking the Lord to
jealous anger? Are we stronger than he?

Seek the Good of Others†

23* "Everything is lawful," but not everything
is beneficial.† "Everything is lawful," but not
everything builds up. 24* No one should seek

†

10:11 *Upon whom the end of the ages has come:* it is our period in time toward which past ages have been moving and in which they arrive at their goal.

10:12–13 *Take care not to fall:* the point of the whole comparison with Israel is to caution against overconfidence, a sense of complete security (12). This warning is immediately balanced by a reassurance, based, however, on God (13).

10:14–22 The warning against idolatry from v 7 is now repeated (14) and explained in terms of the effect of sacrifices: all sacrifices, Christian (16–17), Jewish (18), or pagan (20), establish communion. But communion with Christ is exclusive, incompatible with any other such communion (21). Compare the line of reasoning at 6:15.

10:20 *To demons:* although Jews denied divinity to pagan gods, they often believed that there was some nondivine reality behind the idols, such as the dead, or angels, or demons. The explanation Paul offers in v 20 is drawn from Dt 32:7: the power behind the idols, with which the pagans commune, consists of demonic powers hostile to God.

10:23—11:1 By way of peroration Paul returns to the opening situation (ch 8) and draws conclusions based on the intervening considerations (chs 9–10).

10:23–24 He repeats in the context of this new problem the slogans of liberty from 6:12, with similar qualifications. Liberty is not merely an individual perfection, nor an end in itself, but is to be used for the common good. The language of v 24 recalls the descriptions of Jesus' self-emptying in Phil 2.

*

10:13 Mt 6:13; Jas 1:13–14 / 1 Cor 1:9.
10:14 1 Jn 5:21.
10:16 Mt 26:26–29; Acts 2:42.
10:17 Rom 12:5; Eph 4:4.
10:18 Lv 7:6.
10:20 Dt 32:17.
10:21 2 Cor 6:14–18.
10:22 Dt 32:21 / Eccl 6:10.
10:23 1 Cor 6:12.
10:24 Rom 15:2; Phil 2:4, 21.

his own advantage, but that of his neighbor.
[25]† Eat anything sold in the market, without rais-
ing questions on grounds of conscience, [26]* for
"the earth and its fullness are the Lord's." [27]If
an unbeliever invites you and you want to go,
eat whatever is placed before you, without rais-
ing questions on grounds of conscience. [28]But
if someone says to you, "This was offered in
sacrifice," do not eat it on account of the one
who called attention to it and on account of
conscience; [29]I mean not your own conscience,
but the other's. For why should my freedom be
determined by someone else's conscience? [30]* If
I partake thankfully, why am I reviled for that
over which I give thanks?

[31]So whether you eat or drink, or whatever you
do, do everything for the glory of God. [32]† Avoid
giving offense, whether to Jews or Greeks or the
church of God, [33]* just as I try to please everyone
in every way, not seeking my own benefit but
that of the many, that they may be saved.

11 [1]* Be imitators of me, as I am of Christ.

IV: Problems in Liturgical Assemblies

[2]*† I praise you because you remember me in
everything and hold fast to the traditions, just as
I handed them on to you.

A. Women's Headdresses†

Man and Woman

[3]* But I want you to know that Christ is the
head of every man, and a husband the head of
his wife,† and God the head of Christ. [4]† Any
man who prays or prophesies with his head
covered brings shame upon his head. [5]But any
woman who prays or prophesies with her head
unveiled brings shame upon her head, for it is
one and the same thing as if she had had her
head shaved. [6]For if a woman does not have her
head veiled, she may as well have her hair cut
off. But if it is shameful for a woman to have her
hair cut off or her head shaved, then she should
wear a veil.

"Do everything for the glory of God."
(1 Cor 10:31)

[7]*† A man, on the other hand, should not
cover his head, because he is the image and glory
of God, but woman is the glory of man. [8]* For
man did not come from woman, but woman
from man; [9]* nor was man created for woman,
but woman for man; [10]† for this reason a woman
should have a sign of authority on her head,

†

10:25–30 A summary of specific situations in which the eating of meat sacrificed to idols could present problems of conscience. Three cases are considered. In the first (the marketplace, 25–26) and the second (at table, 27), there is no need to be concerned with whether food has passed through a pagan sacrifice or not, for the principle of 8:4–6 still stands, and the whole creation belongs to the one God. But in the third case (28), the situation changes if someone present explicitly raises the question of the sacrificial origin of the food; eating in such circumstances may be subject to various interpretations, some of which could be harmful to individuals. Paul is at pains to insist that the enlightened Christian conscience need not change its judgment about the neutrality, even the goodness, of the food in itself (29–30); yet the total situation is altered to the extent that others are potentially endangered, and this calls for a different response, for the sake of others.

10:32—11:1 In summary, the general rule of mutually responsible use of their Christian freedom is enjoined first negatively (32), then positively, as exemplified in Paul (33), and finally grounded in Christ, the pattern for Paul's behavior and theirs (11:1; cf Rom 15:1–3).

11:2—14:40 This section of the letter is devoted to regulation of conduct at the liturgy. The problems Paul handles have to do with the dress of women in the assembly (11:3–16), improprieties in the celebration of community meals (11:17–34), and the use of charisms or spiritual gifts (12:1—14:40). The statement in 11:2 introduces all of these discussions, but applies more appropriately to the second (cf the mention of praise in 11:17 and of tradition in 11:23).

11:3–16 Women have been participating in worship at Corinth without the head-covering normal in Greek society of the period. Paul's stated goal is to bring them back into conformity with contemporary practice and propriety. In his desire to convince, he reaches for arguments from a variety of sources, though he has space to develop them only sketchily and is perhaps aware that they differ greatly in persuasiveness.

11:3 *A husband the head of his wife:* the specific problem suggests to Paul the model of the head as a device for clarifying relations within a hierarchical structure. The model is similar to that developed later in greater detail and nuance in Eph 5:21–33. It is a hybrid model, for it grafts onto a strictly theological scale of existence (cf 3:21–23) the hierarchy of sociosexual relations prevalent in the ancient world: men, dominant, reflect the active function of Christ in relation to his church; women, submissive, reflect the passive role of the church with respect to its savior. This gives us the functional scale: God, Christ, man, woman.

11:4–6 From man's direct relation to Christ, Paul infers that his head should not be covered. But woman, related not directly to Christ on the scale but to her husband, requires a covering as a sign of that relationship. *Shameful . . . to have her hair cut off:* certain less honored classes in society, such as lesbians and prostitutes, are thought to have worn their hair close-cropped.

11:7–9 The hierarchy of v 3 is now expressed in other metaphors: the image (*eikōn*) and the reflected glory (*doxa*). Paul is alluding basically to the text of Gn 1:27, in which mankind as a whole, the male-female couple, is created in God's image and given the command to multiply and together dominate the lower creation. But Gn 1:24 is interpreted here in the light of the second creation narrative in Gn 2, in which each of the sexes is created separately (first the man and then the woman *from* man and *for* him, to be his helpmate, Gn 2:20–23), and under the influence of the story of the fall, as a result of which the husband rules over the woman (Gn 3:16). This interpretation splits the single image of God into two, at different degrees of closeness.

11:10 *A sign of authority:* "authority" (*exousia*) may possibly be due to mistranslation of an Aramaic word for "veil"; in any case, the

*

10:26 Pss 24:1; 50:12.
10:30 Rom 14:6; 1 Tm 4:3–4.
10:33 1 Cor 9:22; Rom 15:2.
11:1 1 Cor 4:16; Phil 3:17.
11:2 1 Cor 15:3; 2 Thes 2:15.
11:3 Eph 5:23.
11:7 Gn 1:26–27; 5:1.
11:8 Gn 2:21–23.
11:9 Gn 2:18.

Cultural Connection

Called to Share

In China and Singapore, when people meet up with friends, they ask whether the friends have eaten a meal yet. This custom dates back to the great famine of China in the 1950s, when there was so little food that people were starving and a friend's last meal might have been a day or two ago. So whatever food someone had, he or she shared it with friends. Such generosity is truly a sign of God's love and justice.

Paul had to remind the Corinthians about God's love and justice when they gathered in their homes to talk about their faith, share a meal, and celebrate the Eucharist. In 1 Corinthians 11:17–22, Paul tells the Corinthians that when the wealthy humiliate the poor by not allowing them to share equally in the meal, they are abusing the purpose of the Lord's Supper. To celebrate the Lord's Supper is to partake in the Body and Blood of Christ, and it is impossible to do this if they do not live out the values of Christ.

In your prayer, journal or reflect on the following questions:

- What might Paul say to your church community if he sat with you during Sunday Mass?
- How do you share with people who have little or nothing?
- What can you do in your community so that the celebration of the Lord's Supper is more truly a sign of generosity, justice, and love?

▶ 1 Cor 11:17–33

because of the angels. 11*† Woman is not inde-
pendent of man or man of woman in the Lord.
12* For just as woman came from man, so man is
born of woman; but all things are from God.
13† Judge for yourselves: is it proper for a
woman to pray to God with her head unveiled?
14 Does not nature itself teach you that if a
man wears his hair long it is a disgrace to him,
15 whereas if a woman has long hair it is her
glory, because long hair has been given [her] for
a covering? 16 But if anyone is inclined to be ar-
gumentative, we do not have such a custom, nor
do the churches of God.

B. The Lord's Supper

An Abuse at Corinth

17† In giving this instruction, I do not praise
the fact that your meetings are doing more harm
than good. 18* First of all, I hear that when you
meet as a church there are divisions among you,
and to a degree I believe it; 19† there have to be
factions among you in order that [also] those
who are approved among you may become
known. 20 When you meet in one place, then, it is
not to eat the Lord's supper, 21 for in eating, each
one goes ahead with his own supper, and one
goes hungry while another gets drunk. 22* Do
you not have houses in which you can eat and
drink? Or do you show contempt for the church
of God and make those who have nothing feel
ashamed? What can I say to you? Shall I praise
you? In this matter I do not praise you.

Tradition of the Institution

23*† For I received from the Lord what I also
handed on to you, that the Lord Jesus, on the
night he was handed over, took bread, 24 and,

connection with v 9 indicates that the covering is a sign of woman's subordination. *Because of the angels:* a surprising additional reason, which the context does not clarify. Presumably the reference is to cosmic powers who might inflict harm on women or whose function is to watch over women or the cult.

11:11–12 These parenthetical remarks relativize the argument from Gn 2–3. *In the Lord:* in the Christian economy the relation between the sexes is characterized by a mutual dependence, which is not further specified. And even in the natural order conditions have changed: the mode of origin described in Gn 2 has been reversed (12a). But the ultimately significant fact is the origin that all things have in common (12b).

11:13–16 The argument for conformity to common church practice is summed up and pressed home. Verses 14–15 contain a final appeal to the sense of propriety that contemporary Greek society would consider "natural" (cf 5–6).

11:17–34 Paul turns to another abuse connected with the liturgy, and a more serious one, for it involves neglect of basic Christian tradition concerning the meaning of the Lord's Supper. Paul recalls that tradition for them and reminds them of its implications.

11:19 *That . . . those who are approved among you may become known:* Paul situates their divisions within the context of the eschatological separation of the authentic from the inauthentic and the final revelation of the difference. The notion of authenticity-testing recurs in the injunction to self-examination in view of present and future judgment (28–32).

11:23–25 This is the earliest written account of the institution of

11:11 Gal 3:27–28.
11:12 1 Cor 8:6; Rom 11:36.
11:18 1 Cor 1:10–12; Gal 5:20.
11:22 Jas 2:1–7.
11:23 1 Cor 11:2; 15:3 / 1 Cor 10:16–17; Mt 26:26–29; Mk 14:22–25; Lk 22:14–20.

Catholic Connection

Real Presence

If Jesus were standing in the room, would you be acting any differently? Paul could have posed this question to the Church in Corinth. In his letter, Paul scolds the people for getting drunk while letting others continue to starve, all during the celebration of the Lord's Supper! The Corinthians had forgotten that Jesus Christ is really present during the Eucharistic celebration.

The Church teaches that Christ is present in various ways every time we celebrate the Mass. Christ is present in the word when it is proclaimed, in the assembly gathered, in the priest who is presiding, and, most important, in the consecrated bread and wine.

The Church teaches that Christ, his soul and divinity, is truly and completely present in the Eucharist. We call this "real presence." Through the power of Christ's words from the Last Supper and the workings of the Holy Spirit, the bread and wine become the Body and Blood of Christ. They may look and taste like bread and wine, but in substance they have been changed into Christ's Body and Blood. The Church calls this *transubstantiation*. The Church also teaches that Christ's Body cannot be divided and is therefore fully present in both the bread and the wine, even in the smallest crumb or drop of the Eucharist!

Through Christ's real presence in the Eucharist, we are able to celebrate and renew the new and everlasting covenant that Christ established with the sacrifice of his own Body and Blood. By celebrating the Eucharist, we as a community and as individuals are transformed to love others as Christ has loved us. So next time you are at Mass, reflect on the many ways Christ is making himself present to you and give thanks for the gift of his real presence that he is offering to you in the Eucharist. Then go forth to be Christ's presence in the world.

1 Cor 11:23–26

Catechism, nos. 1373–1377

after he had given thanks, broke it and said, "This
is my body that is for you. Do this in remem-
brance of me." 25* In the same way also the cup,
after supper, saying, "This cup is the new cov-
enant in my blood. Do this, as often as you drink
it, in remembrance of me." 26 For as often as you
eat this bread and drink the cup, you proclaim
the death of the Lord until he comes.

27† Therefore whoever eats the bread or drinks
the cup of the Lord unworthily will have to an-
swer for the body and blood of the Lord. 28† A
person should examine himself, and so eat the
bread and drink the cup. 29† For anyone who eats
and drinks without discerning the body, eats and
drinks judgment on himself. 30 That is why many
among you are ill and infirm, and a considerable
number are dying. 31 If we discerned ourselves,
we would not be under judgment; 32* but since
we are judged by [the] Lord, we are being disci-
plined so that we may not be condemned along
with the world.

33 Therefore, my brothers, when you come to-
gether to eat, wait for one another. 34 If anyone
is hungry, he should eat at home, so that your
meetings may not result in judgment. The other
matters I shall set in order when I come.

C. Spiritual Gifts

Unity and Variety

12 1† Now in regard to spiritual gifts, broth-
ers, I do not want you to be unaware.
2*† You know how, when you were pagans, you
were constantly attracted and led away to mute
idols. 3* Therefore, I tell you that nobody speak-
ing by the spirit of God says, "Jesus be accursed."
And no one can say, "Jesus is Lord," except by
the holy Spirit.

4*† There are different kinds of spiritual gifts
but the same Spirit; 5 there are different forms of
service but the same Lord; 6 there are different
workings but the same God who produces all of
them in everyone. 7 To each individual the man-
ifestation of the Spirit is given for some benefit.
8* To one is given through the Spirit the expres-
sion of wisdom; to another the expression of
knowledge according to the same Spirit; 9 to an-
other faith by the same Spirit; to another gifts of
healing by the one Spirit; 10* to another mighty
deeds; to another prophecy; to another discern-
ment of spirits; to another varieties of tongues; to
another interpretation of tongues. 11* But one
and the same Spirit produces all of these, distrib-
uting them individually to each person as he
wishes.

One Body, Many Parts

12*† As a body is one though it has many parts,
and all the parts of the body, though many, are
one body, so also Christ. 13* For in one Spirit we
were all baptized into one body, whether Jews
or Greeks, slaves or free persons, and we were all
given to drink of one Spirit.

14 Now the body is not a single part, but many.
15 If a foot should say, "Because I am not a hand
I do not belong to the body," it does not for this
reason belong any less to the body. 16 Or if an
ear should say, "Because I am not an eye I do

---

the Lord's Supper in the New Testament. The narrative emphasizes Jesus' action of self-giving (expressed in the words over the bread and the cup) and his double command to repeat his own action.

11:27 It follows that the only proper way to celebrate the Eucharist is one that corresponds to Jesus' intention, which fits with the meaning of his command to reproduce his action in the proper spirit. If the Corinthians eat and drink unworthily, i.e., without having grasped and internalized the meaning of his death for them, they *will have to answer for the body and blood,* i.e., will be guilty of a sin against the Lord himself (cf 8:12).

11:28 *Examine himself:* the Greek word is similar to that for "approved" in v 19, which means "having been tested and found true." The self-testing required for proper eating involves *discerning the body* (29), which, from the context, must mean understanding the sense of Jesus' death (26), perceiving the imperative to unity that follows from the fact that Jesus gives himself to all and requires us to repeat his sacrifice in the same spirit (18–25).

11:29–32 *Judgment:* there is a series of wordplays in these verses that would be awkward to translate literally into English; it includes all the references to judgment (*krima,* 29, 34; *krinō,* 31, 32), discernment (*diakrinō,* 29, 31), and condemnation (*katakrinō,* 32). The judgment is concretely described as the illness, infirmity, and death that have visited the community. These are signs that the power of Jesus' death is not yet completely recognized and experienced. Yet even the judgment incurred is an expression of God's concern; it is a medicinal measure meant to rescue us from condemnation with God's enemies.

12:1—14:40 Ecstatic and charismatic activity were common in early Christian experience, as they were in other ancient religions. But the Corinthians seem to have developed a disproportionate esteem for certain phenomena, especially tongues, to the detriment of order in the liturgy. Paul's response to this development provides us with the fullest exposition we have of his theology of the charisms.

12:2–3 There is an experience of the Spirit and an understanding of ecstatic phenomena that are specifically Christian and that differ, despite apparent similarities, from those of the pagans. It is necessary to discern which spirit is leading one; ecstatic phenomena must be judged by their effect (2). Verse 3 illustrates this by an example: power to confess Jesus as Lord can come only from the Spirit, and it is inconceivable that the Spirit would move anyone to curse the Lord.

12:4–6 There are some features common to all charisms, despite their diversity: all are *gifts* (*charismata*), grace from outside ourselves; all are *forms of service* (*diakoniai*), an expression of their purpose and effect; and all are *workings (energēmata),* in which God is at work. Paul associates each of these aspects with what later theology will call one of the persons of the Trinity, an early example of "appropriation."

12:12–26 The image of *a body* is introduced to explain Christ's relationship with believers (12). Verse 13 applies this model to the church: by baptism all, despite diversity of ethnic or social origins, are integrated into one organism. Verses 14–26 then develop the need for diversity of function among the parts of a body without threat to its unity.

11:25 Ex 24:8; 2 Cor 3:6; Heb 8:6–13.
11:32 Dt 8:5; Heb 12:5–11.
12:2 Eph 2:11–18.
12:3 Rom 10:9; 1 Jn 4:2–3.
12:4 Rom 12:6; Eph 4:7, 11.
12:8 1 Cor 2:6–13.
12:10 1 Cor 14:5, 26, 39; Acts 2:4.
12:11 1 Cor 7:7; Eph 4:7.
12:12 1 Cor 10:17; Rom 12:4–5; Eph 2:16; Col 3:15.
12:13 Gal 3:28; Eph 2:13–18; Col 3:11 / Jn 7:37–39.

Cultural Connection

The Body of Christ

As Christians we are called to work together within the Body of Christ. Read 1 Corinthians 12:12–31. Here Paul says that God has given us different gifts.

A long time ago, Booker T. Washington realized that everyone can make a contribution to the world, regardless of his or her status or possessions. He wrote, "No race can prosper till it learns that there is as much dignity in tilling a field as in writing a poem." This is the Kwanzaa principle of *umoja*, or unity (see "Kwanzaa as a Way of Life," near Dt 10:12–22).

Paul proclaims that each part of the Body of Christ—not only each person, but each diverse culture and race—is needed for the Church to function properly. Many look at the most visible people in the Church and conclude that they are more important than others. Remember that God sees differently. Often, important things are done by quiet people with little fanfare, but God always notices.

Can you focus on the success of the whole rather than on what you have or do not have?

Dear God, free me from excessive worry about what someone else has or is able to do. Place my mind on unity and community. Amen.

▶ 1 Cor 12:12–31

not belong to the body," it does not for this rea-
son belong any less to the body. [17]If the whole
body were an eye, where would the hearing be?
If the whole body were hearing, where would
the sense of smell be? [18]But as it is, God placed
the parts, each one of them, in the body as he in-
tended. [19]If they were all one part, where would
the body be? [20]But as it is, there are many parts,
yet one body. [21]The eye cannot say to the hand,
"I do not need you," nor again the head to the
feet, "I do not need you." [22]Indeed, the parts of
the body that seem to be weaker are all the more
necessary, [23]and those parts of the body that we
consider less honorable we surround with greater
honor, and our less presentable parts are treated
with greater propriety, [24]whereas our more pre-
sentable parts do not need this. But God has so
constructed the body as to give greater honor to a
part that is without it, [25]so that there may be no
division in the body, but that the parts may have
the same concern for one another. [26]If [one] part
suffers, all the parts suffer with it; if one part is
honored, all the parts share its joy.

Application to Christ

[27]*† Now you are Christ's body, and individu-
ally parts of it. [28]*† Some people God has desig-
nated in the church to be, first, apostles; second,
prophets; third, teachers; then, mighty deeds;
then gifts of healing, assistance, administra-
tion, and varieties of tongues. [29]Are all apostles?
Are all prophets? Are all teachers? Do all work
mighty deeds? [30]Do all have gifts of healing? Do
all speak in tongues? Do all interpret? [31]Strive
eagerly for the greatest spiritual gifts.

The Way of Love

But I shall show you a still more excellent way.

13 [1]*† If I speak in human and angelic
tongues† but do not have love, I am a re-
sounding gong or a clashing cymbal. [2]* And if

1 COR

†

12:27–30 Paul now applies the image again to the church as a whole and its members (27). The lists in vv 28–30 spell out the parallelism by specifying the diversity of functions found in the church (cf Rom 12:6–8; Eph 4:11).

12:28 *First, apostles:* apostleship was not mentioned in vv 8–10, nor is it at issue in these chapters, but Paul gives it pride of place in his listing. It is not just one gift among others but a prior and fuller gift that includes the others. They are all demonstrated in Paul's apostolate, but he may have developed his theology of charisms by reflecting first of all on his own grace of apostleship (cf 3:5—4:14; 9:1–27; 2 Cor 2:14—6:13; 10:1—13:30, esp. 11:23 and 12:12).

13:1–13 This chapter involves a shift of perspective and a new point. All or part of the material may once have been an independent piece in the style of Hellenistic eulogies of virtues, but it is now integrated, by editing, into the context of chs 12–14 (cf the reference to tongues and prophecy) and into the letter as a whole (cf the references to knowledge and to behavior). The function of ch 13 within the discussion of spiritual gifts is to relativize all the charisms by contrasting them with the more basic, pervasive, and enduring value that gives them their purpose and their effectiveness. The rhetoric of this chapter is striking.

13:1–3 An inventory of gifts, arranged in careful gradation: nei-

*

12:27 Rom 12:5–8; Eph 1:23; 4:12; 5:30; Col 1:18, 24.
12:28 Eph 2:20; 3:5; 4:11.
13:1 1 Cor 8:1; 16:14; Rom 12:9–10; 13:8–10.
13:2 1 Cor 4:1; 14:2 / 1 Cor 1:5; 8:1–3; 12:8 / Mt 17:20; 21:21; Col 2:3.

I have the gift of prophecy and comprehend all
mysteries and all knowledge; if I have all faith
so as to move mountains, but do not have love,
I am nothing. 3* If I give away everything I own,
and if I hand my body over so that I may boast
but do not have love, I gain nothing.
4*† Love is patient, love is kind. It is not jeal-
ous, [love] is not pompous, it is not inflated,
5* it is not rude, it does not seek its own inter-
ests, it is not quick-tempered, it does not brood
over injury, 6 it does not rejoice over wrongdoing
but rejoices with the truth. 7* It bears all things,
believes all things, hopes all things, endures all
things.
8† Love never fails. If there are prophecies,
they will be brought to nothing; if tongues, they
will cease; if knowledge, it will be brought to
nothing. 9 For we know partially and we proph-
esy partially, 10 but when the perfect comes, the
partial will pass away. 11 When I was a child, I
used to talk as a child, think as a child, reason
as a child; when I became a man, I put aside

† ther tongues (on the lowest rung), nor prophecy, knowledge, or faith, nor even self-sacrifice has value unless informed by love.

13:4–7 This paragraph is developed by personification and enumeration, defining love by what it does or does not do. The Greek contains fifteen verbs; it is natural to translate many of them by adjectives in English.

13:8–13 The final paragraph announces its topic, *Love never fails* (8), then develops the permanence of love in contrast to the charisms (9–12), and finally asserts love's superiority even over the other "theological virtues" (13).

13:3 Mt 6:2.
13:4 Eph 4:2 / 1 Cor 4:6, 18; 5:2; 8:1.
13:5 1 Cor 10:24, 33; Phil 2:4, 21; 1 Thes 5:15.
13:7 Prv 10:12; 1 Pt 4:8.

Pray It!

Loving Others

Read 1 Corinthians 13:1–13. It is a beautiful description of the spiritual gift Paul wants the Christian community to strive for—love. You may want to reflect in your journal upon some experiences you have had with the kind of love Paul speaks about:

- When have you seen a love that is patient and kind, and is not boastful or arrogant or resentful?
- Consider people you know who share their love in this way and imagine how you might grow to love others as Jesus loved us.

Often this passage is read at weddings as a model for the new couple and how they might love each other, but we are all invited to stretch in our capacity to love. Love is much more complicated and expansive than the kind of romantic love we most often hear about.

Dear Lord, help me to recognize the people in my life who share their love with me as you call us to do. Please help me to grow in my understanding of the fullness of love so that I may express this love to my family and friends, and most especially to those whom I often find most difficult to love. Amen.

▶ 1 Corinthians, chapter 13

Did You Know?

God's Love

Greek, the language of the New Testament, has several words for love. There are words for parental love, romantic love, and love between friends or relatives. The Greek word Paul uses in 1 Corinthians, chapter 13—*agape*—is reserved for a special kind of love.

Agape (ah-GAH-pay) is love without conditions or motivations. It is there no matter who you are or what you do. It willingly chooses to serve without expectation of service in return. The Bible tells us that God is *agape* (see 1 Jn 4:16). The source of *agape* is the unconditional love of God. God's *agape* is revealed to us in Jesus Christ. Through the Holy Spirit, we become a channel for communicating this wonderful love to others.

We are created in God's image. God wants us to love one another with the *agape* that Paul describes in chapter 13. It's a wonderful challenge!

▶ 1 Corinthians, chapter 13

childish things. 12* At present we see indistinctly,
as in a mirror, but then face to face. At present I
know partially; then I shall know fully, as I am
fully known. 13*† So faith, hope, love remain,
these three; but the greatest of these is love.

Prophecy Greater than Tongues

14 1*† Pursue love, but strive eagerly for the
spiritual gifts, above all that you may
prophesy. 2† For one who speaks in a tongue
does not speak to human beings but to God,
for no one listens; he utters mysteries in spirit.
3*† On the other hand, one who prophesies does
speak to human beings, for their building up,
encouragement, and solace. 4 Whoever speaks in
a tongue builds himself up, but whoever proph-
esies builds up the church. 5 Now I should like
all of you to speak in tongues, but even more to
prophesy. One who prophesies is greater than
one who speaks in tongues, unless he interprets,
so that the church may be built up.

6† Now, brothers, if I should come to you
speaking in tongues, what good will I do you if
I do not speak to you by way of revelation, or
knowledge, or prophecy, or instruction? 7 Like-
wise, if inanimate things that produce sound,
such as flute or harp, do not give out the tones
distinctly, how will what is being played on
flute or harp be recognized? 8 And if the bugle
gives an indistinct sound, who will get ready
for battle? 9 Similarly, if you, because of speak-
ing in tongues, do not utter intelligible speech,
how will anyone know what is being said? For
you will be talking to the air. 10 It happens that
there are many different languages in the world,
and none is meaningless; 11 but if I do not know
the meaning of a language, I shall be a foreigner
to one who speaks it, and one who speaks it a
foreigner to me. 12 So with yourselves: since you
strive eagerly for spirits, seek to have an abun-
dance of them for building up the church.

Need for Interpretation

13† Therefore, one who speaks in a tongue
should pray to be able to interpret. 14† [For] if
I pray in a tongue, my spirit is at prayer but my
mind is unproductive. 15* So what is to be done?
I will pray with the spirit, but I will also pray
with the mind. I will sing praise with the spirit,
but I will also sing praise with the mind. 16 Oth-
erwise, if you pronounce a blessing [with] the
spirit, how shall one who holds the place of the
uninstructed say the "Amen" to your thanksgiv-
ing, since he does not know what you are saying?
17 For you may be giving thanks very well, but the
other is not built up. 18 I give thanks to God that I
speak in tongues more than any of you, 19 but in
the church I would rather speak five words with
my mind, so as to instruct others also, than ten
thousand words in a tongue.

Functions of These Gifts

20*† Brothers, stop being childish in your
thinking. In respect to evil be like infants, but
in your thinking be mature. 21* It is written in
the law:

13:13 In speaking of love, Paul is led by spontaneous association to mention faith and hope as well. They are already a well-known triad (cf 1 Thes 1:3), three interrelated (cf 7) features of Christian life, more fundamental than any particular charism. *The greatest . . . is love:* love is operative even within the other members of the triad (7), so that it has a certain primacy among them. Or, if the perspective is temporal, love will remain (cf "never fails," 8) even when faith has yielded to sight and hope to possession.

14:1–5 Verse 1b returns to the thought of 12:31a and reveals Paul's primary concern. The series of contrasts in vv 2–5 discloses the problem at Corinth: a disproportionate interest in tongues, with a corresponding failure to appreciate the worth of prophecy. Paul attempts to clarify the relative values of those gifts by indicating the kind of communication achieved in each and the kind of effect each produces.

14:2–3a They involve two kinds of communication: tongues, private speech toward God in inarticulate terms that need interpretation to be intelligible to others (see 27–28); prophecy, communication with others in the community.

14:3b–5 They produce two kinds of effect. One who speaks in tongues *builds himself up;* it is a matter of individual experience and personal perfection, which inevitably recalls Paul's previous remarks about being inflated, seeking one's own good, pleasing oneself. But a prophet *builds up the church:* the theme of "building up" or "edifying" others, the main theme of the letter, comes to clearest expression in this chapter (3, 4, 5, 12, 17). It has been anticipated at 8:1 and 10:23, and by the related concept of "the beneficial" in 6:12; 10:23; 12:7; etc.

14:6–12 Sound, in order to be useful, must be intelligible. This principle is illustrated by a series of analogies from music (7–8) and from ordinary human speech (10–11); it is applied to the case at hand in v 9 and v 12.

14:13–19 The charism of interpretation lifts tongues to the level of intelligibility, enabling them to produce the same effect as prophecy (cf 5, 26–28).

14:14–15 *My spirit:* Paul emphasizes the exclusively ecstatic, nonrational quality of tongues. The tongues at Pentecost are also described as an ecstatic experience (Acts 2:4, 12–13), though Luke superimposes further interpretations of his own. *My mind:* the ecstatic element, dominant in earliest Old Testament prophecy as depicted in 1 Sm 10:5–13; 19:20–24, seems entirely absent from Paul's notion of prophecy and completely relegated to tongues. He emphasizes the role of reason when he specifies instruction as a function of prophecy (6, 19, 31). But he does not exclude intuition and emotion; cf references to encouragement and consolation (3, 31) and the scene describing the ideal exercise of prophecy (24–25).

14:20–22 The Corinthians pride themselves on tongues as a sign of God's favor, a means of direct communication with him (2, 28). To challenge them to a more mature appraisal, Paul draws from scripture a less flattering explanation of what speaking in tongues may signify. Isaiah threatened the people that if they failed to listen to their prophets, the Lord would speak to them (in punishment) through the lips of Assyrian conquerors (Is 28:11–12). Paul compresses Isaiah's text and makes God address his people directly. Equating tongues with foreign languages (cf 10–11), Paul concludes from Isaiah that *tongues are a sign not for those who believe,* i.e., not a mark of God's pleasure for those who listen to him but a mark of his displeasure with those in the community who are faithless, who have not heeded the message that he has sent through the prophets.

13:12 2 Cor 5:7; Heb 11:1 / 2 Tm 2:19; 1 Jn 3:2.
13:13 Col 1:4; 1 Thes 1:3; 5:8.
14:1 1 Cor 14:5, 12, 39.
14:3 1 Cor 14:4–5, 12, 17, 26; 3:9; 8:1, 10; 10:23.
14:15 Eph 5:19; Col 3:16.
14:20 Mt 10:16; Rom 16:19; Eph 4:14.
14:21 Is 28:11–12; Dt 28:49.

Catholic Connection

The Theological Virtues

Have you ever witnessed one group of students putting down another group of students for some reason? Well, Paul was addressing a similar problem in his Letter to the Corinthians. People in the community were claiming that their particular spiritual gift made them superior to others in the community. Paul challenges the Corinthians to be unified as one community and to respect their diversity of gifts. To put it all in perspective, Paul calls them to seek something even greater: faith, hope, and love.

Together faith, hope, and love (also called charity) are what the Church calls theological virtues. These virtues are attitudes or habits that direct our hearts and minds toward God and strengthen our relationship with God. They help open our hearts to living according to God's will and serve as a basis for all our actions. Ultimately, they help us to live as children of God.

Faith. Faith is the virtue that helps us to believe in God and all that God has revealed. Through faith we give over our lives to God and actively seek to do God's will. For our faith to be truly alive, it must be evident in the love we show others and in the good works we do. We are called to not only have and live faith but also to confidently share our faith in God with others.

Hope. Hope is the virtue that helps us to keep our hearts and minds focused on the goal, eternal life with God in heaven. Through hope our actions take on a new direction and purpose, namely building up the Reign of God. By placing our hope in God's plan for our lives, our daily struggles and sufferings take on new meaning. Hope gives us the strength to endure what previously seemed impossible. Jesus' teachings on the Beatitudes and the Lord's Prayer express the fullness of what is hoped for.

Love (charity). Paul leaves no doubt that love is the most important of the theological virtues. Love is the virtue that helps us to fulfill the two greatest commandments: to love God with our whole heart and to love others as we love ourselves. Jesus showed us just how much God loves us not only by his words and deeds but also by his dying for us despite our sinfulness. Jesus calls us to love God and one another with the same limitless love.

All three of these virtues are essential to our lives in Christ but, as Paul points out, without love everything else is worth nothing.

- Where in your life is God calling you to put your faith into action? be filled with hope? love others as God has loved you?

1 Cor 13:13

Catechism, nos. 1812–1841

"By people speaking strange tongues
and by the lips of foreigners
I will speak to this people,
and even so they will not listen to me,

says the Lord." 22 Thus, tongues are a sign not for those who believe but for unbelievers, whereas prophecy is not for unbelievers but for those who believe.

23*† So if the whole church meets in one place and everyone speaks in tongues, and then uninstructed people or unbelievers should come in, will they not say that you are out of your minds? 24 But if everyone is prophesying, and an unbeliever or uninstructed person should come in, he will be convinced by everyone and judged by everyone, 25* and the secrets of his heart will be disclosed, and so he will fall down and worship God, declaring, "God is really in your midst."

Rules of Order

26*† So what is to be done, brothers? When you assemble, one has a psalm, another an instruction, a revelation, a tongue, or an interpretation. Everything should be done for building up. 27 If anyone speaks in a tongue, let it be two or at most three, and each in turn, and one should interpret. 28 But if there is no interpreter, the person should keep silent in the church and speak to himself and to God.

29 Two or three prophets should speak, and the others discern. 30 But if a revelation is given to another person sitting there, the first one should be silent. 31 For you can all prophesy one by one, so that all may learn and all be encouraged. 32 Indeed, the spirits of prophets are under the prophets' control, 33† since he is not the God of disorder but of peace.

As in all the churches of the holy ones, 34* women should keep silent in the churches, for they are not allowed to speak, but should be subordinate, as even the law says. 35 But if they want to learn anything, they should ask their husbands at home. For it is improper for a woman to speak in the church. 36 Did the word of God go forth from you? Or has it come to you alone?

37 If anyone thinks that he is a prophet or a spiritual person, he should recognize that what I am writing to you is a commandment of the

Did You Know?

What's Going On?

In 1 Corinthians 14:34, Paul says women should be silent in church. Yet, in 11:5 he implies that women can pray and prophesy in church, and throughout his life, he supported and worked closely with many different women (see "Introducing Lydia and Priscilla," near Acts 16:14–15, 18:1–26, and "Introducing Phoebe and Junia," near Rom 16:1–16).

What explains Paul's turnaround? It appears that 1 Corinthians 14:34–36, was added to Paul's original letter by a later writer (see footnote 14:33b–36). Perhaps someone copying Paul's letters needed to show that Christianity was not a movement that would disrupt the social order by allowing women to speak in public. It is important to note that this cultural expectation in the ancient world is not directly transferable to our contemporary setting.

Like Paul, the Catholic Church today values women's participation in worship. Women are cantors, musicians, lectors, and Eucharistic ministers. But like the later editor of 1 Corinthians, chapter 14, the Church insists on a certain order in worship and limits women's roles because the Church seeks to remain faithful to Christ's original design of the ministry of the Apostles.

▶ **1 Cor 14:34–36**

†

14:23–25 Paul projects the possible missionary effect of two hypothetical liturgical experiences, one consisting wholly of tongues, the other entirely of prophecy. *Uninstructed* (*idiōtai*): the term may simply mean people who do not speak or understand tongues, as in v 16, where it seems to designate Christians. But coupled with the term "unbelievers" it may be another way of designating those who have not been initiated into the community of faith; some believe it denotes a special class of non-Christians who are close to the community, such as catechumens. *Unbelievers* (*apistoi*): he has shifted from the inner-community perspective of v 22; the term here designates non-Christians (cf 6:6; 7:15; 10:27).

14:26–33a Paul concludes with specific directives regarding exercise of the gifts in their assemblies. Verse 26 enunciates the basic criterion in the use of any gift: it must contribute to "building up."

14:33b–36 Verse 33b may belong with what precedes, so that the new paragraph would begin only with v 34. Verses 34–35 change the subject. These two verses have the theme of submission in common with ch 11, despite differences in vocabulary, and a concern with what is or is not becoming; but it is difficult to harmonize the injunction to silence here with ch 11, which appears to take it for granted that women do pray and prophesy aloud in the assembly (cf 11:5, 13). Hence the verses are often considered an interpolation, reflecting the discipline of later churches; such an interpolation would have to have antedated our manuscripts, all of which contain them, though some transpose them to the very end of the chapter.

14:23 Acts 2:6, 13.
14:25 1 Cor 4:5 / Is 45:14; Zec 8:23.
14:26 Eph 4:12.
14:34 1 Tm 2:11–15; 1 Pt 3:1.

Lord. [38] If anyone does not acknowledge this, he is not acknowledged. [39] So, [my] brothers, strive eagerly to prophesy, and do not forbid speaking in tongues, [40] but everything must be done properly and in order.

V: The Resurrection†

A. The Resurrection of Christ

The Gospel Teaching

15 [1]† Now I am reminding you, brothers, of the gospel I preached to you, which you indeed received and in which you also stand. [2] Through it you are also being saved, if you hold fast to the word I preached to you, unless you believed in vain. [3]*† For I handed on to you as of first importance what I also received: that Christ died for our sins in accordance with the scriptures; [4]* that he was buried; that he was raised on the third day in accordance with the scriptures; [5]* that he appeared to Cephas, then to the Twelve. [6] After that, he appeared to more than five hundred brothers at once, most of whom are still living, though some have fallen asleep. [7] After that he appeared to James, then to all the apostles. [8]* Last of all, as to one born abnormally, he appeared to me. [9]*† For I am the least of the apostles, not fit to be called an apostle, because I persecuted the church of God. [10] But by the grace of God I am what I am, and his grace to me has not been ineffective. Indeed, I have toiled harder than all of them; not I, however, but the grace of God [that is] with me. [11] Therefore, whether it be I or they, so we preach and so you believed.

B. The Resurrection of the Dead

Results of Denial

[12]† But if Christ is preached as raised from the dead, how can some among you say there is no resurrection of the dead? [13]* If there is no resurrection of the dead, then neither has Christ been raised. [14] And if Christ has not been raised, then empty [too] is our preaching; empty, too, your faith. [15]* Then we are also false witnesses to God, because we testified against God that he raised Christ, whom he did not raise if in fact the dead are not raised. [16] For if the dead are not raised, neither has Christ been raised, [17]† and if Christ has not been raised, your faith is vain; you are still in your sins. [18] Then those who have fallen asleep in Christ have perished. [19] If for this life only we have hoped in Christ, we are the most pitiable people of all.

Christ the Firstfruits†

[20]* But now Christ has been raised from the dead, the firstfruits† of those who have fallen asleep. [21]† For since death came through a human being, the resurrection of the dead came

---

† **15:1–58** Some consider this chapter an earlier Pauline composition inserted into the present letter. The problem that Paul treats is clear to a degree: some of the Corinthians are denying the resurrection of the dead (12), apparently because of their inability to imagine how any kind of bodily existence could be possible after death (35). It is plausibly supposed that their attitude stems from Greek anthropology, which looks with contempt upon matter and would be content with the survival of the soul, and perhaps also from an overrealized eschatology of gnostic coloration, such as that reflected in 2 Tm 2:18, which considers the resurrection a purely spiritual experience already achieved in baptism and in the forgiveness of sins. Paul, on the other hand, will affirm both the essential corporeity of the resurrection and its futurity. His response moves through three steps: a recall of the basic kerygma about Jesus' resurrection (1–11), an assertion of the logical inconsistencies involved in denial of the resurrection (12–34), and an attempt to perceive theologically what the properties of the resurrected body must be (35–58).

15:1–11 Paul recalls the tradition (3–7), which he can presuppose as common ground and which provides a starting point for his argument. This is the fundamental content of all Christian preaching and belief (1–2, 11).

15:3–7 The language by which Paul expresses the essence of the "gospel" (1) is not his own but is drawn from older credal formulas. This credo highlights Jesus' death for our sins (confirmed by his burial) and Jesus' resurrection (confirmed by his appearances) and presents both of them as fulfillment of prophecy. *In accordance with the scriptures:* conformity of Jesus' passion with the scriptures is asserted in Mt 16:1; Lk 24:25–27, 32, 44–46. Application of some Old Testament texts (Pss 2:7; 16:8–11) to his resurrection is illustrated by Acts 2:27–31; 13:29–39; and Is 52:13—53:12 and Hos 6:2 may also have been envisaged.

15:9–11 A persecutor may have appeared disqualified (*ouk . . . hikanos*) from apostleship, but in fact God's grace has qualified him. Cf the remarks in 2 Corinthians about his qualifications (2:16; 3:5) and his greater labors (11:23). These verses are parenthetical, but a nerve has been touched (the references to his abnormal birth and his activity as a persecutor may echo taunts from Paul's opponents), and he is instinctively moved to self-defense.

15:12–19 Denial of the resurrection (12) involves logical inconsistencies. The basic one, stated twice (13, 16), is that if there is no such thing as (bodily) resurrection, then it has not taken place even in Christ's case.

15:17–18 The consequences for the Corinthians are grave: both forgiveness of sins and salvation are an illusion, despite their strong convictions about both. Unless Christ is risen, their faith does not save.

15:20–28 After a triumphant assertion of the reality of Christ's resurrection (20a), Paul explains its positive implications and consequences. As a soteriological event of both human (20–23) and cosmic (24–28) dimensions, Jesus' resurrection logically and necessarily involves ours as well.

15:20 *The firstfruits:* the portion of the harvest offered in thanksgiving to God implies the consecration of the entire harvest to come. Christ's resurrection is not an end in itself; its finality lies in the whole harvest, ourselves.

15:21–22 Our human existence, both natural and supernatural, is corporate, involves solidarity. *In Adam . . . in Christ:* the Hebrew word *'adam* in Genesis is both a common noun for mankind and a proper noun for the first man. Paul here presents Adam as at least a literary type of Christ; the parallelism and contrast between them will be developed further in vv 45–49 and in Rom 5:12–21.

15:3 1 Cor 11:23 / 1 Pt 2:24; 3:18 / Is 53:4–12.
15:4 Acts 2:23–24 / Ps 16:8–11; Hos 6:1–2; Jon 2:1.
15:5 Mk 16:14; Mt 28:16–17; Lk 24:36; Jn 20:19.
15:8 1 Cor 9:1; Acts 9:3–6; Gal 1:16.
15:9 Acts 8:3; 9:1–2; Gal 1:23; Eph 3:8; 1 Tm 1:15.
15:13 1 Thes 4:14.
15:15 Acts 5:32.
15:20 Rom 8:11; Col 1:18; 1 Thes 4:14.

Cultural Connection: The First Creed and a Contemporary Creed

In 1 Corinthians 15:3–11 is an early creed written in the Scriptures. It expresses the fundamental aspects of the Christian faith and is made up of historic facts and faith statements such as the following:

- Christ died for our sins, according to the Scriptures (see Isaiah, chapter 53).
- Christ was buried.
- Christ rose on the third day.

Christians of all times have created creeds to express their shared beliefs (see also "I Believe! The Apostles' Creed," near Acts 4:5–12). Some Christian communities create their own particular creedal statements based on the foundations of the Christian faith and their experience of God. Here are some extracts from a credo created by Hispanics during their Third Encuentro Nacional de Pastoral, in 1985:

> *We believe in the most Holy Trinity,* God the Father, Son, and Holy Spirit. We sense his powerful work in our people, and we see it as a model to be followed. . . .
>
> *We believe in our identification with Christ,* as the suffering people we are. We believe, . . . as he did, in . . . liberation through love. . . .
>
> *We believe in the Catholic Church,* which is integrated in Christ by means of the communion we, as laity, share with bishops, priests, and men and women religious. . . .
>
> *We have faith in our people* because we know that God, who abides in a special manner and forever among us, has raised it [our people] up. . . .
>
> *We believe in the gift of being a prophetic voice* as something given by God to our people and as a means of promoting the unity and love that are necessary for the building of the Kingdom. . . .
>
> *We believe in Mary, our Mother,* who has taken our Hispanic culture under her protection, and who has accompanied us and will accompany us always in our journey as she works to carry the message of Jesus to the whole world. . . .
>
> Amen.

(Secretariat for Hispanic Affairs, *Prophetic Voices,* pp. 17–18)

▶ 1 Cor 15:3–11

also through a human being. [22]* For just as in
Adam all die, so too in Christ shall all be brought
to life, [23]* but each one in proper order: Christ
the firstfruits; then, at his coming, those who be-
long to Christ; [24]*† then comes the end, when he
hands over the kingdom to his God and Father,
when he has destroyed every sovereignty and ev-
ery authority and power. [25]* For he must reign
until he has put all his enemies under his feet.
[26]*† The last enemy to be destroyed is death,
[27]*† for "he subjected everything under his feet."
But when it says that everything has been sub-
jected, it is clear that it excludes the one who sub-
jected everything to him. [28]* When everything is
subjected to him, then the Son himself will [also]
be subjected to the one who subjected everything
to him, so that God may be all in all.

Practical Arguments†

[29]† Otherwise, what will people accomplish by

† **15:24–28** Paul's perspective expands to cosmic dimensions, as he describes the climax of history, *the end.* His viewpoint is still christological, as in vv 20–23. Verses 24 and 28 describe Christ's final relations to his enemies and his Father in language that is both royal and military; vv 25–28 insert a proof from scripture (Pss 110:1; 8:7) into this description. But the viewpoint is also theological, for God is the ultimate agent and end, and likewise soteriological, for we are the beneficiaries of all the action.

15:26 *The last enemy . . . is death:* a parenthesis that specifies the final fulfillment of the two Old Testament texts just referred to, Ps 110:1 and Ps 8:7. Death is not just one cosmic power among many, but the ultimate effect of sin in the universe (cf 56; Rom 5:12). Christ defeats death where it prevails, in our bodies. The destruction of the last enemy is concretely the "coming to life" (22) of "those who belong to Christ" (23).

15:27b–28 *The one who subjected everything to him:* the Father is the ultimate agent in the drama, and the final end of the process, to whom the Son and everything else is ordered (24, 28). *That God may be all in all:* his reign is a dynamic exercise of creative power, an outpouring of life and energy through the universe, with no further resistance. This is the supremely positive meaning of "subjection": that God may fully be God.

15:29–34 Paul concludes his treatment of logical inconsistencies with a listing of miscellaneous Christian practices that would be meaningless if the resurrection were not a fact.

15:29 *Baptized for the dead:* this practice is not further explained here, nor is it necessarily mentioned with approval, but Paul cites it as something in their experience that attests in one more way to belief in the resurrection.

15:22 Gn 3:17–19; Rom 5:12–19.
15:23 1 Thes 4:15–17.
15:24 Eph 1:22.
15:25 Ps 110:1.
15:26 Rom 6:9; 2 Tm 1:10; Rv 20:14; 21:4.
15:27 Ps 8:7; Eph 1:22; Phil 3:21.
15:28 Eph 4:6; Col 3:11.

Live It!

Life After Death

During childhood, reality and fantasy are often confused. We might believe in Santa Claus, the Easter Bunny, the Tooth Fairy, even a monster living under our bed. We may imagine heaven as having pearly gates, golden streets, and angels flying around with harps. As we grow older, some of us exchange this fantastic image for a more mature belief in the mystery of the Resurrection. But many adult Christians simply do not know what to believe about life after death.

Christians from Corinth also had problems with the concept of resurrection of the body. Common ideas influenced by Greek philosophy made it difficult for them to think of a body's returning to life after death. They believed body and soul were separate. The soul was immortal and continued living after the body died.

In contrast, the Hebrews saw a unity between the spiritual and material aspects of the human person. When the prophets, such as Daniel, envisaged a blessed life after death, they did not think in terms of a soul freed from the body but in terms of a body filled once more with life (see "Resurrection," near Dn 12:1–3).

Believing in the resurrection of the body is essential in the Christian faith. The Gospel writers describe the risen Jesus as different from the Jesus who died on the cross; the disciples did not recognize him at first sight; they knew him only through their faith.

Paul gets right to the point: Jesus' followers need to believe in their own resurrection of the body, otherwise the belief that Christ was raised from death is in vain. Paul explains that in the resurrection, our earthly body will be transformed—it will become a glorious, imperishable, and immortal body. We will not be disembodied spirits or souls when we have eternal life in communion with God. And we will be made alive in Christ, whether our mind can comprehend that idea or not. Our end is not death, but eternal life with Christ!

▶ 1 Cor 15:35–58

1 COR

having themselves baptized for the dead? If the
dead are not raised at all, then why are they having themselves baptized for them?
30*† Moreover, why are we endangering ourselves all the time? 31* Every day I face death;
I swear it by the pride in you [brothers] that I
have in Christ Jesus our Lord. 32* If at Ephesus I
fought with beasts, so to speak, what benefit was
it to me? If the dead are not raised:

"Let us eat and drink,
for tomorrow we die."

33 Do not be led astray:

"Bad company corrupts good morals."

34* Become sober as you ought and stop sinning.
For some have no knowledge of God; I say this
to your shame.

C. The Manner of the Resurrection†

35† But someone may say, "How are the dead
raised? With what kind of body will they come
back?"

The Resurrection Body

36*† You fool! What you sow is not brought to
life unless it dies. 37 And what you sow is not the
body that is to be but a bare kernel of wheat, perhaps, or of some other kind; 38* but God gives it
a body as he chooses, and to each of the seeds its
own body. 39† Not all flesh is the same, but there
is one kind for human beings, another kind of

† **15:30–34** A life of sacrifice, such as Paul describes in 4:9–13 and 2 Cor, would be pointless without the prospect of resurrection; a life of pleasure, such as that expressed in the Epicurean slogan of v 32, would be far more consistent. *I fought with beasts:* since Paul does not elsewhere mention a combat with beasts at Ephesus, he may be speaking figuratively about struggles with adversaries.

15:35–58 Paul imagines two objections that the Corinthians could raise: one concerning the manner of the resurrection (*how?*), the other pertaining to the qualities of the risen body (*what kind?*). These questions probably lie behind their denial of the resurrection (12), and seem to reflect the presumption that no kind of body other than the one we now possess would be possible. Paul deals with these objections in inverse order, in vv 36–49 and vv 50–58. His argument is fundamentally theological and its appeal is to the understanding.

15:35–49 Paul approaches the question of the nature of the risen body *(what kind of body?)* by means of two analogies: the seed (36–44) and the first man, Adam (45–49).

15:36–38 The analogy of the seed: there is a change of attributes from seed to plant; the old life-form must be lost for the new to emerge. By speaking about the seed as a *body* that dies and comes to life, Paul keeps the point of the analogy before the reader's mind.

15:39–41 The expression "its own body" (38) leads to a development on the marvelous diversity evident in bodily life.

* **15:30** 2 Cor 4:8–12; 11:23–27. **15:31** Ps 44:23; Rom 8:36. **15:32** 1 Cor 4:9; 2 Cor 4:10–11 / Wis 2:5–7; Is 22:13. **15:34** Mt 22:29; Mk 12:24. **15:36** Jn 12:24. **15:38** Gn 1:11.

flesh for animals, another kind of flesh for birds,
and another for fish. 40 There are both heavenly
bodies and earthly bodies, but the brightness of
the heavenly is one kind and that of the earthly
another. 41 The brightness of the sun is one kind,
the brightness of the moon another, and the
brightness of the stars another. For star differs
from star in brightness.
42† So also is the resurrection of the dead. It is
sown corruptible; it is raised incorruptible. 43* It
is sown dishonorable; it is raised glorious. It is
sown weak; it is raised powerful. 44 It is sown a
natural body; it is raised a spiritual body. If there
is a natural body, there is also a spiritual one.
45*† So, too, it is written, "The first man,
Adam, became a living being," the last Adam a
life-giving spirit. 46 But the spiritual was not first;
rather the natural and then the spiritual. 47 The
first man was from the earth, earthly; the second
man, from heaven. 48 As was the earthly one, so
also are the earthly, and as is the heavenly one,
so also are the heavenly. 49*† Just as we have
borne the image of the earthly one, we shall also
bear the image of the heavenly one.

The Resurrection Event

50*† This I declare, brothers: flesh and blood
cannot inherit the kingdom of God, nor does
corruption† inherit incorruption. 51*† Behold,
I tell you a mystery. We shall not all fall asleep,
but we will all be changed, 52* in an instant,
in the blink of an eye, at the last trumpet. For
the trumpet will sound, the dead will be raised
incorruptible, and we shall be changed. 53* For
that which is corruptible must clothe itself with
incorruptibility, and that which is mortal must
clothe itself with immortality. 54*† And when
this which is corruptible clothes itself with incor-
ruptibility and this which is mortal clothes itself
with immortality, then the word that is written
shall come about:

"Death is swallowed up in victory.
55* Where, O death, is your victory?
Where, O death, is your sting?"

56*† The sting of death is sin, and the power of
sin is the law. 57* But thanks be to God who gives
us the victory through our Lord Jesus Christ.
58 Therefore, my beloved brothers, be firm,
steadfast, always fully devoted to the work of the
Lord, knowing that in the Lord your labor is not
in vain.

VI: Conclusion

The Collection†

16 1* Now in regard to the collection† for the
holy ones, you also should do as I ordered
the churches of Galatia. 2 On the first day of the
week each of you should set aside and save what-
ever he can afford, so that collections will not
be going on when I come. 3 And when I arrive, I
shall send those whom you have approved with

†

15:42–44 The principles of qualitative difference before and after death (36–38) and of diversity on different levels of creation (39–41) are now applied to the human body. Before: a body animated by a lower, natural life-principle (*psychē*) and endowed with the properties of natural existence (corruptibility, lack of glory, weakness). After: a body animated by a higher life-principle (*pneuma;* cf 45) and endowed with other qualities (incorruptibility, glory, power, spirituality), which are properties of God himself.

15:45 The analogy of *the first man, Adam,* is introduced by a citation from Gn 2:7. Paul alters the text slightly, adding the adjective *first,* and translating the Hebrew *'ādām* twice, so as to give it its value both as a common noun (*man*) and as a proper name (*Adam*). Verse 45b then specifies similarities and differences between the two Adams. *The last Adam,* Christ (cf 21–22) has become *a . . . spirit* (*pneuma*), a life-principle transcendent with respect to the natural soul (*psychē*) of the first Adam (on the terminology here, cf the note on 3:1). Further, he is not just alive, but *life-giving,* a source of life for others.

15:49 *We shall also bear the image:* although it has less manuscript support, this reading better fits the context's emphasis on futurity and the transforming action of God; on future transformation as conformity to the image of the Son, cf Rom 8:29; Phil 3:21. The majority reading, "let us bear the image," suggests that the image of the heavenly man is already present and exhorts us to conform to it.

15:50–57 These verses, an answer to the first question of v 35, explain theologically how the change of properties from one image to another will take place: God has the power to transform, and he will exercise it.

15:50–53 *Flesh and blood . . . corruption:* living persons and the corpses of the dead, respectively. In both cases, the gulf between creatures and God is too wide to be bridged unless God himself transforms us.

15:51–52 *A mystery:* the last moment in God's plan is disclosed; cf the notes on 2:1, 7–10a. The final trumpet and the awakening of the dead are stock details of the apocalyptic scenario. *We shall not all fall asleep:* Paul expected that some of his contemporaries might still be alive at Christ's return; after the death of Paul and his whole generation, copyists altered this statement in various ways. *We will all be changed:* the statement extends to all Christians, for Paul is not directly speaking about anyone else. Whether they have died before the end or happen still to be alive, all must be transformed.

15:54–55 *Death is swallowed up in victory:* scripture itself predicts death's overthrow. *O death:* in his prophetic vision Paul may be making Hosea's words his own, or imagining this cry of triumph on the lips of the risen church.

15:56 *The sting of death is sin:* an explanation of Hosea's metaphor. Death, scorpion-like, is equipped with a sting, sin, by which it injects its poison. Christ defeats sin, the cause of death (Gn 3:19; Rom 5:12).

16:1–4 This paragraph contains our earliest evidence for a project that became a major undertaking of Paul's ministry. The collection for the church at Jerusalem was a symbol in his mind for the unity of Jewish and Gentile Christianity. Cf Gal 2:10; Rom 15:25–29; 2 Cor 8–9 and the notes to this last passage.

16:1 *In regard to the collection:* it has already begun in Galatia and Macedonia (cf 2 Cor 8), and presumably he has already instructed the Corinthians about its purpose.

*

15:43 Phil 3:20–21; Col 3:4.
15:45 Gn 2:7 / Jn 5:21–29; 2 Cor 3:6, 17.
15:49 Gn 5:3 / Rom 8:29; Phil 3:21.
15:50 Jn 3:3–6.
15:51 1 Thes 4:14–17.
15:52 Jl 2:1; Zec 9:14; Mt 24:31; Rv 11:15–18.
15:53 2 Cor 5:2–4.
15:54 Is 25:8; 2 Cor 5:4; 2 Tm 1:10; Heb 2:14–15.
15:55 Hos 13:14.
15:56 Rom 4:15; 7:7, 13.
15:57 Jn 16:33; 1 Jn 5:4.
16:1 Acts 24:17; Rom 15:25–32; 2 Cor 8–9; Gal 2:10.

letters of recommendation to take your gracious
gift to Jerusalem. 4† If it seems fitting that I
should go also, they will go with me.

Paul's Travel Plans

5*† I shall come to you after I pass through
Macedonia (for I am going to pass through Mac-
edonia), 6 and perhaps I shall stay or even spend
the winter with you, so that you may send me on
my way wherever I may go. 7* For I do not wish to
see you now just in passing, but I hope to spend
some time with you, if the Lord permits. 8*† I
shall stay in Ephesus until Pentecost, 9* because a
door has opened for me wide and productive for
work, but there are many opponents.
10* If Timothy comes, see that he is without
fear in your company, for he is doing the work of
the Lord just as I am. 11 Therefore, no one should
disdain him. Rather, send him on his way in
peace that he may come to me, for I am expect-
ing him with the brothers. 12* Now in regard to
our brother Apollos, I urged him strongly to go
to you with the brothers, but it was not at all his
will that he go now. He will go when he has an
opportunity.

Exhortation and Greetings

13 Be on your guard, stand firm in the faith, be
courageous, be strong. 14 Your every act should
be done with love.
15* I urge you, brothers—you know that the
household of Stephanas is the firstfruits of
Achaia and that they have devoted themselves to
the service of the holy ones— 16 be subordinate
to such people and to everyone who works and
toils with them. 17 I rejoice in the arrival of Steph-
anas, Fortunatus, and Achaicus, because they
made up for your absence, 18* for they refreshed
my spirit as well as yours. So give recognition to
such people.
19*† The churches of Asia send you greetings.
Aquila and Prisca together with the church at
their house send you many greetings in the Lord.
20* All the brothers greet you. Greet one another
with a holy kiss.
21* I, Paul, write you this greeting in my own
hand. 22*† If anyone does not love the Lord, let
him be accursed. *Marana tha.* 23* The grace of the
Lord Jesus be with you. 24 My love to all of you
in Christ Jesus.

---

†

16:4 *That I should go also:* presumably Paul delivered the collection on his final visit to Jerusalem; cf Rom 15:25–32; Acts 24:14.

16:5–12 The travel plans outlined here may not have materialized precisely as Paul intended; cf 2 Cor 1:8–2:13; 7:4–16.

16:8 *In Ephesus until Pentecost:* this tells us the place from which he wrote the letter and suggests he may have composed it about Easter time (cf 5:7–8).

16:19–24 These paragraphs conform to the normal epistolary conclusion, but their language is overlaid with liturgical coloration as well. The *greetings* of the Asian churches are probably to be read, along with the letter, in the liturgy at Corinth, and the union of the church is to be expressed by *a holy kiss* (19–20). Paul adds to this his own greeting (21) and blessings (23–24).

16:22 *Accursed:* literally, "anathema." This expression (cf 12:3) is a formula for exclusion from the community; it may imply here a call to self-examination before celebration of the Eucharist, in preparation for the Lord's coming and judgment (cf 11:17–34). *Marana tha:* an Aramaic expression, probably used in the early Christian liturgy. As understood here ("O Lord, come!"), it is a prayer for the early return of Christ. If the Aramaic words are divided differently (*Maran atha,* "Our Lord has come"), it becomes a credal declaration. The former interpretation is supported by what appears to be a Greek equivalent of this acclamation in Rv 22:20: "Amen. Come, Lord Jesus!"

---

*

16:5 Acts 19:21; Rom 15:26; 2 Cor 1:15–16.
16:7 Acts 18:21.
16:8 1 Cor 15:32; Acts 18:19; 19:1–10.
16:9 Acts 14:27; 2 Cor 2:12.
16:10 1 Cor 4:17; Acts 16:1; 19:22; Phil 2:19–23.
16:12 1 Cor 1:12; 3:4–6, 22; Acts 18:24–28.
16:15 1 Cor 1:16.
16:18 1 Thes 5:12–13.
16:19 Acts 18:2, 18, 26; Rom 16:3–5.
16:20 Rom 16:16; 2 Cor 13:12; 1 Thes 5:26; 1 Pt 5:14.
16:21 Gal 6:11; Col 4:18; 2 Thes 3:17.
16:22 1 Cor 12:3; Rom 9:3; Gal 1:8–9; Rv 22:20.
16:23 Rom 16:20.

Unfortunately, you probably know all too well what it's like to be criticized. It's no fun to be under attack. Our instinct is to get defensive and strike back. But in his Second Letter to the Corinthians, Paul shows us how God helps us rise above our instincts. Paul responds to personal attacks with directness and honesty. He demonstrates how to witness to Jesus—even when we are in the middle of conflict.

In Depth

The relationship between Paul and the Corinthians deteriorated after Paul wrote First Corinthians. Apparently, some other traveling missionaries came to Corinth and undermined Paul's credibility. They attacked him as a person (see 2 Cor 10:10), implied that he was mentally imbalanced (see 5:13), and criticized him as a speaker (see 10:10). They even suggested that Paul was not trustworthy about money (see 8:20–21).

As part of these attacks, some people claimed that Paul couldn't make up his mind about returning to visit Corinth; they said he kept changing between yes and no. In defending himself, Paul skillfully changes the focus and says that in Jesus, we always find a yes. In Jesus, every one of God's promises is a yes (see 1:19–20). And whereas Paul's opponents make boastful claims for themselves, Paul realizes that God's grace is all he needs. In fact, he says, "I will rather boast most gladly of my weaknesses, in order that the power of Christ may dwell with me" (12:9). Paul's decision not to return is also an attempt to avoid causing the community any more pain as a result of another conflict that happened within the Corinthian community (see 2:1–11).

With breathtaking insight, Paul puts all the conflicts into perspective. "From now on we regard no one according to the flesh. . . . So whoever is in Christ is a new creation" (5:16–17). Knowing Christ changes everything! Through Christ, we are reconciled with God, meaning God overcomes the sin and weakness that separate us from God's love. We should also become ambassadors for Christ, reconciling with one another and announcing to all that they are reconciled with God.

Scholars see evidence that several original letters were combined to form Second Corinthians. For example, Paul's concerns seem to be resolved in chapter 7, but then chapters 10–13 pick up those concerns again. And chapters 8 and 9 each describe a collection being taken up for the Christians in Jerusalem without making any connection between the two collections. Despite its uneven flow, the letter reveals a personal look into Paul's life and ministry.

At a Glance

I. Address (1:1–11).
II. The Crisis Between Paul and the Corinthians (1:12—7:16).
III. The Collection for Jerusalem (8:1—9:15).
IV. Paul's Defense of His Ministry (10:1—13:10).
V. Conclusion (13:11–13).

Quick Facts

Inspired Author: Paul
Date Written: around AD 57
Audience: the mainly Gentile (non-Jewish) church in Corinth

2 Corinthians

I: Address

Greeting

1 [1]*† Paul, an apostle of Christ Jesus by the will
of God, and Timothy our brother, to the
church of God that is in Corinth, with all the
holy ones throughout Achaia: [2]grace to you and
peace from God our Father and the Lord Jesus
Christ.

Thanksgiving

[3]*† Blessed be the God and Father of our Lord
Jesus Christ, the Father of compassion and God
of all encouragement, [4]* who encourages us in
our every affliction, so that we may be able to
encourage those who are in any affliction with
the encouragement with which we ourselves are
encouraged by God. [5]† For as Christ's suffer-
ings overflow to us, so through Christ does our
encouragement also overflow. [6]If we are afflicted,
it is for your encouragement and salvation; if we
are encouraged, it is for your encouragement,
which enables you to endure the same sufferings
that we suffer. [7]† Our hope for you is firm, for we
know that as you share in the sufferings, you also
share in the encouragement.

[8]*† We do not want you to be unaware, broth-
ers, of the affliction that came to us in the prov-
ince of Asia; we were utterly weighed down
beyond our strength, so that we despaired even of
life. [9]*† Indeed, we had accepted within ourselves
the sentence of death, that we might trust not in
ourselves but in God who raises the dead. [10]* He
rescued us from such great danger of death, and
he will continue to rescue us; in him we have put
our hope [that] he will also rescue us again, [11]* as
you help us with prayer, so that thanks may be
given by many on our behalf for the gift granted
us through the prayers of many.

†

1:1–11 The opening follows the usual Pauline form, except that the thanksgiving takes the form of a doxology or glorification of God (3). This introduces a meditation on the experience of suffering and encouragement shared by Paul and the Corinthians (4–7), drawn, at least in part, from Paul's reflections on a recent affliction (8–10). The section ends with a modified and delayed allusion to thanksgiving (11).

1:3 *God of all encouragement:* Paul expands a standard Jewish blessing so as to state the theme of the paragraph. The theme of "encouragement" or "consolation" (*paraklēsis*) occurs ten times in this opening, against a background formed by multiple references to "affliction" and "suffering."

1:5 *Through Christ:* the Father of compassion is the Father of our Lord Jesus (3); Paul's sufferings and encouragement (or "consolation") are experienced in union with Christ. Cf Lk 2:25: the "consolation of Israel" is Jesus himself.

1:7 *You also share in the encouragement:* the eschatological reversal of affliction and encouragement that Christians expect (cf Mt 5:4; Lk 6:24) permits some present experience of reversal in the Corinthians' case, as in Paul's.

1:8 *Asia:* a Roman province in western Asia Minor, the capital of which was Ephesus.

1:9–10 *The sentence of death:* it is unclear whether Paul is alluding to a physical illness or to an external threat to life. The result of the situation was to produce an attitude of faith in God alone. *God who raises the dead:* rescue is the constant pattern of God's activity; his final act of encouragement is the resurrection.

1:1 Eph 1:1; Col 1:1 / 2 Cor 1:19; Acts 16 / Rom 1:7; 1 Cor 1:2.
1:3 1 Cor 15:24; Eph 1:3; 1 Pt 1:3 / Rom 15:5.
1:4 2 Cor 7:6–7, 13; 1 Thes 3:6–8; 2 Thes 2:16.
1:8 Acts 20:18–19; 1 Cor 15:32.
1:9 2 Cor 4:7–11; Rom 4:17.
1:10 2 Tm 4:18.
1:11 2 Cor 4:15; 9:12.

II: The Crisis between Paul and the Corinthians

A. Past Relationships†

Paul's Sincerity and Constancy

[12]† For our boast is this, the testimony of our
conscience that we have conducted ourselves in
the world, and especially toward you, with the
simplicity and sincerity of God, [and] not by
human wisdom but by the grace of God. [13] For
we write you nothing but what you can read and
understand, and I hope that you will understand
completely, [14]* as you have come to understand
us partially, that we are your boast as you also are
ours, on the day of [our] Lord Jesus.

[15]† With this confidence I formerly intended
to come to you so that you might receive a dou-
ble favor, [16]* namely, to go by way of you to
Macedonia, and then to come to you again on
my return from Macedonia, and have you send
me on my way to Judea. [17]*† So when I intended
this, did I act lightly? Or do I make my plans
according to human considerations, so that with
me it is "yes, yes" and "no, no"? [18]† As God is
faithful, our word to you is not "yes" and "no."
[19]* For the Son of God, Jesus Christ, who was
proclaimed to you by us, Silvanus and Timo-
thy and me, was not "yes" and "no," but "yes"
has been in him. [20]* For however many are the

†

1:12—2:13 The autobiographical remarks about the crisis in Asia Minor lead into consideration of a crisis that has arisen between Paul and the Corinthians. Paul will return to this question, after a long digression, in 7:5–16. Both of these sections deal with travel plans Paul had made, changes in the plans, alternative measures adopted, a breach that opened between him and the community, and finally a reconciliation between them.

1:12–14 Since Paul's own conduct will be under discussion here, he prefaces the section with a statement about his habitual behavior and attitude toward the community. He protests his openness, single-mindedness, and conformity to God's grace; he hopes that his relationship with them will be marked by mutual understanding and pride, which will constantly increase until it reaches its climax at the judgment. Two references to boasting frame this paragraph (12, 14), the first appearances of a theme that will be important in the letter, especially in chs 10–13; the term is used in a positive sense here (cf the note on 1 Cor 1:29–31).

1:15 *I formerly intended to come:* this plan reads like a revision of the one mentioned in 1 Cor 16:5. Not until 1:23—2:1 will Paul tell us something his original readers already knew, that he has canceled one or the other of these projected visits.

1:17 *Did I act lightly?:* the subsequent change of plans casts suspicion on the original intention, creating the impression that Paul is vacillating and inconsistent or that *human considerations* keep dictating shifts in his goals and projects (cf the counterclaim of 12). *"Yes, yes" and "no, no":* stating something and denying it in the same or the next breath; being of two minds at once, or from one moment to the next.

1:18–22 *As God is faithful:* unable to deny the change in plans, Paul nonetheless asserts the firmness of the original plan and claims a profound constancy in his life and work. He grounds his defense in God himself, who is firm and reliable; this quality can also be predicated in various ways of those who are associated with him. Christ, Paul, and the Corinthians all participate in analogous ways in the constancy of God. A number of the terms here, which appear related only conceptually in Greek or English, would be variations of the same root, *'mn*, in a Semitic language, and thus naturally associated in a Semitic mind, such as Paul's. These include the words *yes* (17–20), *faithful* (18), *Amen* (20), *gives us security* (21), *faith, stand firm* (24).

*

1:14 Phil 2:16; 1 Thes 2:19–20.
1:16 1 Cor 16:5–9; Acts 19:21.
1:17 Mt 5:37; Jas 5:12.
1:19 Acts 16:1–3; 1 Thes 1:1; 2 Thes 1:1.
1:20 1 Cor 14:16; Rv 3:14.

Live It!

The Presence of God

Carlos is an undocumented worker at a chicken processing plant, that is until he and many others are apprehended by Immigration Services and brought to a detention center where they will be processed before being returned to Mexico. The workers' spirits are low. Many of them have children in school and in child care. They suffer uncertainty over knowing when they might be reunited with their families.

Then Carlos hears Marisol, a grandmother who works with him, call out to the group: "We are not alone, and we have not been abandoned. God has been with us every minute through this ordeal. I pray every morning and every night in thanksgiving for that presence. It is on my worst days that I most strongly feel the presence of God." Carlos finds consolation in Marisol's words.

When we are suffering, we too can feel alone and abandoned—sometimes even by God. But Paul emphasizes that God is always present, consoling us in our affliction. It is sometimes difficult to experience this presence because we are caught up in the pain and hurt of the situation, as Carlos was in his captivity. How do you experience God's presence or absence during times of pain and suffering?

Paul also says that the support of the Christian community can help us to get through our pain. The comfort of friends and relatives during difficult times can help us to recognize that God is with us. Is there someone you can comfort who is going through a hard time?

▶ 2 Cor 1:3–11

Cultural Connection

Yes, Yes, May We Not Fail

Paul ensures the people of Corinth that he has not wavered in his commitment to them. In a similar manner, Saint Andrew Dung-Lac and the Vietnamese martyrs were unwavering in their commitment to the Gospels. These martyrs consisted of 117 people who died for their faith in nineteenth-century Vietnam. Saint Andrew was a priest in Vietnam, and many of the other 117 martyrs were Catholic laypeople. Pope John Paul II made them all saints of the Church on June 19, 1988.

Vietnam is a country that has been rocked by many bloody wars, run by ruthless dictators, and overrun by rampant violence through many of the years of its history as a country. Despite such extreme social conditions, and in the midst of such horrible violence, these martyrs and many like them had the courage to preach the Gospel and live as disciples of Christ.

Take a few moments to reflect on the lives of these martyrs.

▶ 2 Cor 1:15–22

promises of God, their Yes is in him; therefore,
the Amen from us also goes through him to God
for glory. 21*† But the one who gives us security
with you in Christ and who anointed us is God;
22* he has also put his seal upon us and given the
Spirit in our hearts as a first installment.

Paul's Change of Plan

23*† But I call upon God as witness, on my
life, that it is to spare you that I have not yet gone
to Corinth. 24 Not that we lord it over your faith;
rather, we work together for your joy, for you
stand firm in the faith.

2 1 For I decided not to come to you again in
painful circumstances. 2 For if I inflict pain
upon you, then who is there to cheer me except
the one pained by me? 3† And I wrote as I did
so that when I came I might not be pained by
those in whom I should have rejoiced, confident
about all of you that my joy is that of all of you.
4 For out of much affliction and anguish of heart
I wrote to you with many tears, not that you
might be pained but that you might know the
abundant love I have for you.

The Offender

5† If anyone has caused pain, he has caused it
not to me, but in some measure (not to exaggerate) to all of you. 6 This punishment by the majority is enough for such a person, 7* so that on the
contrary you should forgive and encourage him
instead, or else the person may be overwhelmed
by excessive pain. 8 Therefore, I urge you to reaffirm your love for him. 9* For this is why I wrote,
to know your proven character, whether you
were obedient in everything. 10 Whomever you
forgive anything, so do I. For indeed what I have

†

1:21–22 The commercial terms *gives us security, seal, first installment* are here used analogously to refer to the process of initiation into the Christian life, perhaps specifically to baptism. The passage is clearly trinitarian. The Spirit is the *first installment* or "down payment" of the full messianic benefits that God guarantees to Christians. Cf Eph 1:13–14.

1:23–24 *I have not yet gone to Corinth:* some suppose that Paul received word of some affair in Corinth, which he decided to regulate by letter even before the first of his projected visits (cf 16). Others conjecture that he did pay the first visit, was offended there (cf 2:5), returned to Ephesus, and sent a letter (2:3–9) in place of the second visit. The expressions *to spare you* (23) and *work together for your joy* (24) introduce the major themes of the next two paragraphs, which are remarkable for insistent repetition of key words and ideas. These form two clusters of terms in the English translation: (1) cheer, rejoice, encourage, joy; (2) pain, affliction, anguish. These clusters reappear when Paul resumes treatment of this subject in 7:5–16.

2:3–4 *I wrote as I did:* we learn for the first time about the sending of a letter in place of the proposed visit. Paul mentions the letter in passing, but emphasizes his motivation in sending it: to avoid being saddened by them (cf 1), and to help them realize the depth of his love. Another motive will be added in 7:12: to bring to light their own concern for him. *With many tears:* it has been suggested that we may have all or part of this "tearful letter" somewhere in the Corinthian correspondence, either in 1 Cor 5 (the case of the incestuous man), or in 1 Corinthians as a whole, or in 2 Cor 10–13. None of these hypotheses is entirely convincing. See the note on 13:1.

2:5–11 The nature of the *pain* (5) is unclear, though some believe an individual at Corinth rejected Paul's authority, thereby scandalizing many in the community. In any case, action has been taken, and Paul judges the measures adequate to right the situation (6). The follow-up directives he now gives are entirely positive: forgive, encourage, love. *Overwhelmed* (7): a vivid metaphor (literally "swallowed") that Paul employs positively at 5:4 and in 1 Cor 15:54 (7). It is often used to describe satanic activity (cf 1 Pt 5:8); note the reference to Satan here in v 11.

1:21 1 Jn 2:20, 27.
1:22 Eph 1:13–14; 4:30 / 2 Cor 5:5; Rom 5:5; 8:16, 23.
1:23 2 Cor 13:2.
2:7 Col 3:13.
2:9 2 Cor 7:15.

forgiven, if I have forgiven anything, has been
for you in the presence of Christ, [11]* so that we
might not be taken advantage of by Satan, for we
are not unaware of his purposes.

Paul's Anxiety

[12]*† When I went to Troas for the gospel of
Christ, although a door was opened for me in the
Lord, [13]*† I had no relief in my spirit because I
did not find my brother Titus. So I took leave of
them and went on to Macedonia.

B. Paul's Ministry†

Ministers of a New Covenant

[14]† But thanks be to God,† who always leads
us in triumph in Christ† and manifests through
us the odor of the knowledge of him† in every
place. [15]* For we are the aroma of Christ for God
among those who are being saved and among
those who are perishing, [16]† to the latter an odor
of death that leads to death, to the former an
odor of life that leads to life. Who is qualified
for this? [17]* For we are not like the many who
trade on the word of God; but as out of sincerity,
indeed as from God and in the presence of God,
we speak in Christ.

3 [1]*† Are we beginning to commend ourselves
again? Or do we need, as some do, letters of
recommendation to you or from you? [2]† You are
our letter, written on our hearts, known and read
by all, [3]*† shown to be a letter of Christ admin-
istered by us, written not in ink but by the Spirit
of the living God, not on tablets of stone but on
tablets that are hearts of flesh.

[4]† Such confidence we have through Christ to-
ward God. [5]* Not that of ourselves we are qual-
ified to take credit for anything as coming from
us; rather, our qualification comes from God,
[6]*† who has indeed qualified us as ministers of
a new covenant, not of letter but of spirit; for the
letter brings death, but the Spirit gives life.

†

2:12–13 *I had no relief:* Paul does not explain the reason for his anxiety until he resumes the thread of his narrative at 7:5: he was waiting to hear how the Corinthians would respond to his letter. Since 7:5–16 describes their response in entirely positive terms, we never learn in detail why he found it necessary to defend and justify his change of plans, as in 1:15–24. Was this portion of the letter written before the arrival of Titus with his good news (7:6–7)?

2:13 *Macedonia:* a Roman province in northern Greece.

2:14—7:4 This section constitutes a digression within the narrative of the crisis and its resolution (1:12—2:13 and 7:5–16). The main component (2:14—6:10) treats the nature of Paul's ministry and his qualifications for it; this material bears some similarity to the defense of his ministry in chs 10–13, but it may well come from a period close to the crisis. This is followed by a supplementary block of material quite different in character and tone (6:14—7:1). These materials may have been brought together into their present position during final editing of the letter; appeals to the Corinthians link them to one another (6:11–13) and lead back to the interrupted narrative (7:2–4).

2:14—6:10 The question of Paul's adequacy (16; cf 3:5) and his credentials (3:1–2) has been raised. Paul responds by an extended treatment of the nature of his ministry. It is a ministry of glory (3:7—4:6), of life (4:7—5:10), of reconciliation (5:11—6:10).

2:14–16a The initial statement plunges us abruptly into another train of thought. Paul describes his personal existence and his function as a preacher in two powerful images (14) that constitute a prelude to the development to follow.

2:14a *Leads us in triumph in Christ:* this metaphor of a festive parade in honor of a conquering military hero can suggest either a positive sharing in Christ's triumph or an experience of defeat, being led in captivity and submission (cf 4:8–11; 1 Cor 4:9). Paul is probably aware of the ambiguity, as he is in the case of the next metaphor.

2:14b–16a *The odor of the knowledge of him:* incense was commonly used in triumphal processions. The metaphor suggests the gradual diffusion of the knowledge of God through the apostolic preaching. *The aroma of Christ:* the image shifts from the fragrance Paul diffuses to the aroma that he is. Paul is probably thinking of the "sweet odor" of the sacrifices in the Old Testament (e.g., Gn 8:21; Ex 29:18) and perhaps of the metaphor of wisdom as a sweet odor (Sir 24:15). *Death . . . life:* the aroma of Christ that comes to them through Paul is perceived differently by various classes of people. To some his preaching and his life (cf 1 Cor 1:17—2:6) are perceived as *death,* and the effect is death for them; others perceive him, despite appearances, as *life,* and the effect is life for them. This fragrance thus produces a separation and a judgment (cf the function of the "light" in John's gospel).

2:16b–17 *Qualified:* Paul may be echoing either the self-satisfied claims of other preachers or their charges about Paul's deficiencies. No one is really qualified, but the apostle contrasts himself with those who dilute or falsify the preaching for personal advantage and insists on his totally good conscience: his ministry is from God, and he has exercised it with fidelity and integrity (cf 3:5–6).

3:1 Paul seems to allude to certain preachers who pride themselves on their written credentials. Presumably they reproach him for not possessing similar credentials and compel him to spell out his own qualifications (4:2; 5:12; 6:4). The Corinthians themselves should have performed this function for Paul (5:12; cf 12:11). Since he is forced to find something that can recommend him, he points to them: their very existence constitutes his *letter* of recommendation (1–2). Others who engage in self-commendation will also be mentioned in 10:12–18.

3:2–3 Mention of "letters of recommendation" generates a series of metaphors in which Paul plays on the word "letter": (1) the community is Paul's letter of recommendation (2a); (2) they are a letter engraved on his affections for all to see and read (2b); (3) they are a letter from Christ that Paul merely delivers (3a); (4) they are a letter written by the Spirit on the tablets of human hearts (3b). One image dissolves into another.

3:3b This verse contrasts Paul's letter with those *written . . . in ink* (like the credentials of other preachers) and those *written . . . on tablets of stone* (like the law of Moses). These contrasts suggest that the other preachers may have claimed special relationship with Moses. If they were Judaizers zealous for the Mosaic law, that would explain the detailed contrast between the old and the new covenants (6; 4:7—6:10). If they were charismatics who claimed Moses as their model, that would explain the extended treatment of Moses himself and his glory (3:7—4:6). *Hearts of flesh:* cf Ezekiel's contrast between the heart of flesh that the Spirit gives and the heart of stone that it replaces (Ez 36:26); the context is covenant renewal and purification that makes observance of the law possible.

3:4–6 These verses resume 2:1—3:3. Paul's confidence (4) is grounded in his sense of God-given mission (2:17), the specifics of which are described in vv 1–3. Verses 5–6 return to the question of his qualifications (2:16), attributing them entirely to God. Verse 6 further spells out the situation described in v 3b and "names" it: Paul is living within *a new covenant,* characterized by the Spirit, which *gives life.* The usage of a *new covenant* is derived from Jer 31:31–33, a passage that also speaks of writing on the heart; cf 2.

3:6b This verse serves as a topic sentence for 3:7—6:10. For the contrast between *letter* and *spirit,* cf Rom 2:29; 7:5–6.

*

2:11 Eph 4:27.
2:12 Acts 16:8.
2:13 2 Cor 7:6; 1 Tm 1:3.
2:15 2 Cor 4:3; 1 Cor 1:18.
2:17 2 Cor 4:2; 1 Cor 5:8.
3:1 Acts 18:27; Rom 16:1; 1 Cor 16:3.
3:3 Ex 24:12; 31:18; 32:15–19 / Jer 31:33; Ez 11:19; 36:26–27.
3:5 Jn 3:27.
3:6 Eph 3:7 / Jer 31:31–34.

Live It!

Christ in Us

It is sometimes tempting to take ourselves a bit too seriously, to feel too self-important. When given a particular responsibility at school, home, or church, we may begin to act as though we are what is important, rather than the task.

The same is true when we accept our calling as a disciple of Christ. Feelings of self-righteousness or pride can creep in, leading to what friends might call a holier-than-thou attitude. Paul reminds us that "we do not preach ourselves but Jesus Christ as Lord" (2 Cor 4:5). We are simply fragile clay jars that hold a great treasure to be shared with all. What a wonderful and awesome responsibility we have been given: to share, with our lives and our words, what Jesus has done in us, giving him the glory and not seeking it for ourselves.

▶ 2 Cor 4:5–10

Contrast with the Old Covenant

7*† Now if the ministry of death,† carved in
letters on stone, was so glorious that the Israelites
could not look intently at the face of Moses be-
cause of its glory that was going to fade, 8† how
much more will the ministry of the Spirit be
glorious? 9 For if the ministry of condemnation
was glorious, the ministry of righteousness will
abound much more in glory. 10 Indeed, what was
endowed with glory has come to have no glory in
this respect because of the glory that surpasses it.
11 For if what was going to fade was glorious, how
much more will what endures be glorious.

12† Therefore, since we have such hope, we act
very boldly 13† and not like Moses, who put a
veil over his face so that the Israelites could not
look intently at the cessation of what was fading.
14† Rather, their thoughts were rendered dull,
for to this present day the same veil remains un-
lifted when they read the old covenant, because
through Christ it is taken away. 15* To this day,
in fact, whenever Moses is read, a veil lies over
their hearts, 16* but whenever a person turns to
the Lord the veil is removed. 17† Now the Lord
is the Spirit, and where the Spirit of the Lord
is, there is freedom. 18*† All of us, gazing with
unveiled face on the glory of the Lord, are being
transformed into the same image from glory to
glory, as from the Lord who is the Spirit.

†

3:7—4:6 Paul now develops the contrast enunciated in 3:6b in terms of the relative glory of the two covenants, insisting on the greater glory of the new. His polemic seems directed against individuals who appeal to the glorious Moses and fail to perceive any comparable glory either in Paul's life as an apostle or in the gospel he preaches. He asserts in response that Christians have a glory of their own that far surpasses that of Moses.

3:7 The *ministry of death:* from his very first words, Paul describes the Mosaic covenant and ministry from the viewpoint of their limitations. They lead to *death* rather than life (6–7; cf 4:7—5:10), to *condemnation* rather than reconciliation (9; cf 5:11—6:10). *Was so glorious:* the basic text to which Paul alludes is Ex 34:29–35, to which his opponents have undoubtedly laid claim. *Going to fade:* Paul concedes the glory of Moses' covenant and ministry, but grants them only temporary significance.

3:8–11 *How much more:* the argument "from the less to the greater" is repeated three times (8, 9, 11). Verse 10 expresses another point of view: the difference in glory is so great that only the new covenant and ministry can properly be called "glorious" at all.

3:12 *Such hope:* the glory is not yet an object of experience, but that does not lessen Paul's confidence. *Boldly:* the term *parrēsia* expresses outspoken declaration of Christian conviction (cf 4:1–2). Paul has nothing to hide and no reason for timidity.

3:13–14a *Not like Moses:* in Exodus Moses veiled his face to protect the Israelites from God's reflected glory. Without impugning Moses' sincerity, Paul attributes another effect to the veil. Since it lies between God's glory and the Israelites, it explains how they could fail to notice the glory disappearing. *Their thoughts were rendered dull:* the problem lay with their understanding. This will be expressed in vv 14b–16 by a shift in the place of the veil: it is no longer over Moses' face but over their perception.

3:14b–16 The parallelism in these verses makes it necessary to interpret corresponding parts in relation to one another. *To this present day:* this signals the shift of Paul's attention to his contemporaries; his argument is typological, as in 1 Cor 10. The Israelites of Moses' time typify the Jews of Paul's time, and perhaps also Christians of Jewish origin or mentality who may not recognize the temporary character of Moses' glory. *When they read the old covenant:* the lasting dullness prevents proper appraisal of Moses' person and covenant. When his writings are read in the synagogue, a veil still impedes their understanding. *Through Christ:* i.e., in the new covenant. *Whenever a person turns to the Lord:* Moses in Exodus appeared before God without the veil and gazed on his face unprotected. Paul applies that passage to converts to Christianity: when they turn to the Lord fully and authentically, the impediment to their understanding is removed.

3:17 *The Lord is the Spirit:* the "Lord" to whom the Christian turns (16) is the Spirit of whom Paul has been speaking, the life-giving Spirit of the living God (6, 8), the inaugurator of the new covenant and ministry, who is also the Spirit of Christ. *The Spirit of the Lord:* the Lord here is the living God (3), but there may also be an allusion to Christ as Lord (14, 16). *Freedom:* i.e., from the ministry of death (7) and the covenant that condemned (9).

3:18 Another application of the veil image. *All of us . . . with unveiled face:* Christians (Israelites from whom the veil has been removed) are like Moses, standing in God's presence, beholding and reflecting his glory. *Gazing:* the verb may also be translated "contemplating as in a mirror"; 4:6 would suggest that the mirror is Christ himself. *Are being transformed:* elsewhere Paul speaks of transformation, conformity to Jesus, God's image, as a reality of the end time, and even v 12 speaks of the glory as an object of hope. But the life-giving Spirit, the distinctive gift of the new covenant, is already present in the community (cf 1:22, the "first installment"), and the process of transformation has already begun. *Into the same image:* into the image of God, which is Christ (4:4).

3:7 Ex 34:29–35.
3:15 Rom 11:7–10.
3:16 Ex 34:34.
3:18 Rom 8:29–30; 12:2; Gal 4:19; Phil 3:10, 20–21 / 2 Cor 4:4–6; 1 Cor 15:49; Col 1:15; 3:9–11; 1 Jn 3:2.

Integrity in the Ministry

4 [1]† Therefore, since we have this ministry
through the mercy shown us, we are not dis-
couraged. [2]* Rather, we have renounced shame-
ful, hidden things; not acting deceitfully or
falsifying the word of God, but by the open
declaration of the truth we commend ourselves
to everyone's conscience in the sight of God.
[3]*† And even though our gospel is veiled, it is
veiled for those who are perishing, [4]* in whose
case the god of this age has blinded the minds of
the unbelievers, so that they may not see the light
of the gospel of the glory of Christ, who is the
image of God. [5]† For we do not preach ourselves
but Jesus Christ as Lord, and ourselves as your
slaves for the sake of Jesus. [6]*† For God who
said, "Let light shine out of darkness," has shone
in our hearts to bring to light the knowledge of
the glory of God on the face of [Jesus] Christ.

The Paradox of the Ministry

[7]† But we hold this treasure in earthen vessels,†
that the surpassing power may be of God and not
from us. [8]*† We are afflicted in every way, but
not constrained; perplexed, but not driven to
despair; [9] persecuted, but not abandoned; struck
down, but not destroyed; [10]*† always carrying
about in the body the dying of Jesus, so that the
life of Jesus may also be manifested in our body.
[11]* For we who live are constantly being given up
to death for the sake of Jesus, so that the life of
Jesus may be manifested in our mortal flesh.
[12]† So death is at work in us, but life in you.
[13]*† Since, then, we have the same spirit of
faith, according to what is written, "I believed,
therefore I spoke," we too believe and therefore

Pray It!

Hopeless and Hurting

Sometimes, life can be filled with despair and discouragement. We can get down in the dumps and feel like everything is a waste of our time and energy. Paul encourages us not to lose hope but to keep our hearts and minds very much alive. Paul connects our moments of despair to Jesus' suffering on the cross. Jesus never lost hope. He believed to the end and then was raised from the dead to new life to show the world that his suffering and death had a hopeful outcome. God promises us this same hopeful outcome of being raised up.

Try this exercise: Re-read 2 Corinthians 4:7–18 in a prayerful way, perhaps while listening to some reflective music. Then write a few thoughts of your own in a journal, or write your own prayer about suffering and despair. Don't forget to mention hope at the end of your prayer, because, ultimately, that was Jesus' message.

▶ **2 Cor 4:7–18**

†

4:1–2 A ministry of this sort generates confidence and forthrightness; cf 1:12–14; 2:17.

4:3–4 *Though our gospel is veiled:* the final application of the image. Paul has been reproached either for obscurity in his preaching or for his manner of presenting the gospel. But he confidently asserts that there is no veil over his gospel. If some fail to perceive its light, that is because of unbelief. The veil lies over their eyes (3:14), a blindness induced by Satan, and a sign that they are headed for destruction (cf 2:15).

4:5 *We do not preach ourselves:* the light seen in his gospel is the glory of Christ (4). Far from preaching himself, the preacher should be a transparent medium through whom Jesus is perceived (cf 10–11). *Your slaves:* Paul draws attention away from individuals as such and toward their role in relation to God, Christ, and the community; cf 1 Cor 3:5; 4:1.

4:6 Autobiographical allusion to the episode at Damascus clarifies the origin and nature of Paul's service; cf Acts 9:1–19; 22:3–16; 26:2–18. *"Let light shine out of darkness":* Paul seems to be thinking of Gn 1:3 and presenting his apostolic ministry as a new creation. There may also be an allusion to Is 9:1, suggesting his prophetic calling as servant of the Lord and light to the nations; cf Is 42:6, 16; 49:6; 60:1–2, and the use of light imagery in Acts 26:13–23. *To bring to light the knowledge:* Paul's role in the process of revelation, expressed at the beginning under the image of the odor and aroma (2:14–15), is restated now, at the end of this first moment of the development, in the imagery of light and glory (3–6).

4:7—5:10 Paul now confronts the difficulty that his present existence does not appear glorious at all; it is marked instead by suffering and death. He deals with this by developing the topic already announced in 3:3, 6, asserting his faith in the presence and ultimate triumph of life, in his own and every Christian existence, despite the experience of death.

4:7 *This treasure:* the glory that he preaches and into which they are being transformed. *In earthen vessels:* the instruments God uses are human and fragile; some imagine small terracotta lamps in which light is carried.

4:8–9 A catalogue of his apostolic trials and afflictions. Yet in these the negative never completely prevails; there is always some experience of rescue, of salvation.

4:10–11 Both the negative and the positive sides of the experience are grounded christologically. The logic is similar to that of 1:3–11. His sufferings are connected with Christ's, and his deliverance is a sign that he is to share in Jesus' resurrection.

4:12–15 His experience does not terminate in himself, but in others (12, 15; cf 1:4–5). Ultimately, everything is ordered even beyond the community, toward God (15; cf 1:11).

4:13–14 Like the Psalmist, Paul clearly proclaims his faith, affirming life within himself despite death (10–11) and the life-giving effect of his experience upon the church (12, 14–15). *And place us with you in his presence:* Paul imagines God presenting him and them to Jesus at the parousia and the judgment; cf 11:2; Rom 14:10.

*

4:2 2 Cor 2:17; 1 Thes 2:4–7.
4:3 2 Cor 2:15–16; 2 Thes 2:10.
4:4 Jn 12:31–36 / 1 Tm 1:11.
4:6 Gn 1:3; Is 9:1; Acts 26:13–23; Gal 1:15–16 / Jn 8:12; Heb 1:3.
4:8 2 Cor 6:4–10; 1 Cor 4:9–13.
4:10 Col 1:24.
4:11 Rom 8:36; 1 Cor 15:31.
4:13 Ps 116:10.

speak, 14* knowing that the one who raised
the Lord Jesus will raise us also with Jesus and
place us with you in his presence. 15* Everything
indeed is for you, so that the grace bestowed
in abundance on more and more people may
cause the thanksgiving to overflow for the glory
of God.
16*† Therefore, we are not discouraged;† rather,
although our outer self is wasting away, our in-
ner self is being renewed day by day. 17* For this
momentary light affliction is producing for us an
eternal weight of glory beyond all comparison,
18* as we look not to what is seen but to what is
unseen; for what is seen is transitory, but what is
unseen is eternal.

Our Future Destiny

5 1*† For we know that if our earthly dwelling,
a tent, should be destroyed, we have a build-
ing from God, a dwelling not made with hands,
eternal in heaven. 2*† For in this tent we groan,
longing to be further clothed with our heavenly
habitation 3† if indeed, when we have taken it
off, we shall not be found naked. 4*† For while
we are in this tent we groan and are weighed
down, because we do not wish to be unclothed
but to be further clothed, so that what is mortal

Pray It!

It's What's Inside That Counts

Television, magazines, and advertising show the ideal person as skinny, well developed, muscular, clear complexioned, tall, and with perfect features. Very few people fit that image. Many of those who don't fit that image feel insecure and inadequate. Some people try desperately to measure up to that standard with crash diets, workouts at fitness centers, weight training, steroids, or plastic surgery. Some people even end up with eating disorders like bulimia and anorexia.

In 2 Corinthians 5:1–5, Paul reminds us that our earthly body is a temporary dwelling. It is important for us to take care of this earthly "tent" with a healthy diet and regular exercise. But our desire for our heavenly dwelling should cause us to focus on our inner appearance more than our outer appearance.

In your prayer, reflect on the following questions:

- Are you satisfied with your physical appearance? Why or why not?
- Do you spend as much time working on your inner appearance—by developing virtues like compassion, generosity, mercy, and patience—as you do on your outer appearance?

Write a prayer asking God for the grace (gift) to feel secure in your outward appearance. Listen for God's response.

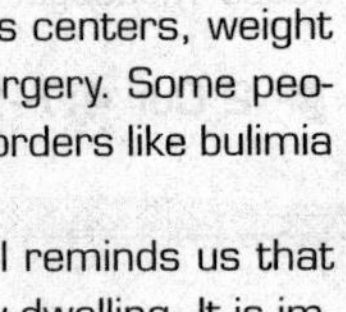

▶ 2 Cor 5:1–5

2 COR

4:16–18 In a series of contrasts Paul explains the extent of his faith in life. Life is not only already present and revealing itself (8–11, 16) but will outlast his experience of affliction and dying: it is eternal (17–18).

4:16 *Not discouraged:* i.e., despite the experience of death. Paul is still speaking of himself personally, but he assumes his faith and attitude will be shared by all Christians. *Our outer self:* the individual subject of ordinary perception and observation, in contrast to the interior and hidden self, which undergoes renewal. *Is being renewed day by day:* this suggests a process that has already begun; cf 3:18. The renewal already taking place even in Paul's dying is a share in the life of Jesus, but this is recognized only by faith (13, 18; 5:7).

5:1 *Our earthly dwelling:* the same contrast is restated in the imagery of a dwelling. The language recalls Jesus' saying about the destruction of the temple and the construction of another building *not made with hands* (Mk 14:58), a prediction later applied to Jesus' own body (Jn 2:20).

5:2–5 Verses 2–3 and 4 are largely parallel in structure. *We groan, longing:* see the note on 5:5. *Clothed with our heavenly habitation:* Paul mixes his metaphors, adding the image of the garment to that of the building. *Further clothed:* the verb means strictly "to put one garment on over another." Paul may desire to put the resurrection body on over his mortal body, without dying; vv 2 and 4 permit this meaning but do not impose it. Or perhaps he imagines the resurrection body as a garment put on over the Christ-garment first received in baptism (Gal 3:27) and preserved by moral behavior (Rom 13:12–14; Col 3:12; cf Mt 22:11–13). Some support for this interpretation may be found in the context; cf the references to baptism (5), to judgment according to works (10), and to present renewal (4:16), an idea elsewhere combined with the image of "putting on" a new nature (Eph 4:22–24; Col 3:1–5, 9–10).

5:3 *When we have taken it off:* the majority of witnesses read "when we have put it on," i.e., when we have been clothed (in the resurrection body), then we shall not be without a body (naked). This seems mere tautology, though some understand it to mean: whether we are "found" (by God at the judgment) clothed or naked depends upon whether we have preserved or lost our original investiture in Christ (cf the previous note). In this case to "put it on" does not refer to the resurrection body, but to keeping intact the Christ-garment of baptism. The translation follows the western reading (Codex Bezae, Tertullian), the sense of which is clear: to "take it off" is to shed our mortal body in death, after which we shall be clothed in the resurrection body and hence not "naked" (cf 1 Cor 15:51–53).

5:4 *We do not wish to be unclothed:* a clear allusion to physical death (4:16; 5:1). Unlike the Greeks, who found dissolution of the body desirable (cf Socrates), Paul has a Jewish horror of it. He seems to be thinking of the "intermediate period," an interval between death and resurrection. *Swallowed up by life:* cf 1 Cor 15:54.

4:14 Rom 4:24–25; 8:11; 1 Cor 6:14; 1 Thes 4:14.
4:15 2 Cor 1:11.
4:16 2 Cor 4:1.
4:17 Mt 5:11–12; Rom 8:18.
4:18 Rom 8:24–25; Heb 11:1.
5:1 Is 38:12 / Col 3:1–4 / Mk 14:58; Col 2:11; Heb 9:11, 24.
5:2 Rom 8:23 / 1 Cor 15:51–54.
5:4 Is 25:8; 1 Cor 15:54.

may be swallowed up by life. 5*† Now the one
who has prepared us for this very thing is God,
who has given us the Spirit as a first installment.
6† So we are always courageous, although we
know that while we are at home in the body we
are away from the Lord, 7 for we walk by faith, not
by sight. 8* Yet we are courageous, and we would
rather leave the body and go home to the Lord.
9 Therefore, we aspire to please him, whether we
are at home or away. 10*† For we must all appear
before the judgment seat of Christ, so that each
one may receive recompense, according to what
he did in the body, whether good or evil.

"So whoever is in Christ is a new creation."
(2 Cor 5:17)

The Ministry of Reconciliation

11*† Therefore, since we know the fear of
the Lord, we try to persuade others; but we are
clearly apparent to God, and I hope we are also
apparent to your consciousness. 12* We are not
commending ourselves to you again but giving
you an opportunity to boast of us, so that you
may have something to say to those who boast
of external appearance rather than of the heart.
13† For if we are out of our minds, it is for God;
if we are rational, it is for you. 14*† For the love
of Christ impels us, once we have come to the
conviction that one died for all; therefore, all
have died. 15* He indeed died for all, so that
those who live might no longer live for them-
selves but for him who for their sake died and
was raised.
16† Consequently, from now on we regard
no one according to the flesh; even if we once
knew Christ according to the flesh, yet now we
know him so no longer. 17* So whoever is in
Christ is a new creation: the old things have

Live It!

Ambassadors for Christ

The title *ambassador* is usually used by people who are authorized to represent their country while living as a resident in a foreign nation. For example, the U.S. ambassador to Mexico is an official representative of the United States who lives in Mexico and speaks for the U.S. government in Mexico.

Paul tells us that we are reconciled—that is, united—with God through Christ, and that God has now entrusted us with the ministry of helping others to be reconciled through Christ. This is our mission today. We are ambassadors for Christ! Of all the ways God could be made known in the world, God chooses to use us. We are authorized representatives. We are God's messengers.

That might sound a bit intimidating! We might naturally wonder how we, broken and imperfect people, are supposed to represent God, who is completely holy and just. The reality is that God wants to use us, flaws and all. God does not need perfect people—just willing people! Spend some time in prayer, and share with God your thoughts, feelings, and fears about being invited to take on this great role of ambassador for Christ.

▶ **2 Cor 5:17–21**

†

5:5 God has created us for resurrected bodily life and already prepares us for it by the gift of the Spirit in baptism. *The Spirit as a first installment:* the striking parallel to 5:1–5 in Rom 8:17–30 describes Christians who have received the "firstfruits" (cf "first installment" here) of the Spirit as "groaning" (cf 2, 4 here) for the resurrection, the complete redemption of their bodies. In place of clothing and building, Rom 8 uses other images for the resurrection: adoption and conformity to the image of the Son.

5:6–9 Tension between present and future is expressed by another spatial image, the metaphor of the country and its citizens. At present we are like citizens in exile or far away from home. The Lord is the distant homeland, believed in but unseen (7).

5:10 *We must all appear:* the verb is ambiguous: we are scheduled to "appear" for judgment, at which we will be "revealed" as we are (cf 11; 2:14; 4:10–11).

5:11–15 This paragraph is transitional. Paul sums up much that has gone before. Still playing on the term "appearance," he reasserts his transparency before God and the Corinthians, in contrast to the self-commendation, boasting, and preoccupation with externals that characterize some others (cf 1:12–14; 2:14; 3:1; 3:7—4:6). Verse 14 recalls 3:7—4:6, and sums up 4:7—5:10.

5:13 *Out of our minds:* this verse confirms that a concern for ecstasy and charismatic experience may lie behind the discussion about "glory" in 3:7—4:6. Paul also enjoys such experiences but, unlike others, does not make a public display of them or consider them ends in themselves. *Rational:* the Greek virtue *sōphrosynē,* to which Paul alludes, implies reasonableness, moderation, good judgment, self-control.

5:14–15 These verses echo 4:14 and resume the treatment of "life despite death" from 4:7—5:10.

5:16–17 *Consequently:* the death of Christ described in vv 14–15 produces a whole new order (17) and a new mode of perception (16). *According to the flesh:* the natural mode of perception, characterized as "fleshly," is replaced by a mode of perception proper to the Spirit.

*

5:5 2 Cor 1:22.
5:8 Phil 1:21–23.
5:10 Mt 16:27; 25:31–46; Rom 2:16; 14:10–11.
5:11 2 Cor 1:12–14.
5:12 2 Cor 3:1 / 2 Cor 1:14; Phil 1:26.
5:14 Rom 6:1–6.
5:15 Rom 4:25; 6:4–11; 14:9; Col 3:3–4.
5:17 Gal 6:15; Eph 2:15 / Is 43:18–21; Rv 21:5.

Cultural Connection

An "Anyway" God

We serve an "anyway" God. Impediments, hurdles, and obstacles are part of our inheritance, yet we excel anyway. Some of us were kidnapped from Africa, enslaved and shackled, stripped of our culture, robbed of our native language, and torn from our family, yet today, we thrive anyway.

Surely, the Lord was in the midst of the African Americans' past, ushering them on to a better day. The evidence that the Lord walked with them through horrific conditions is simply too great to deny. Yet, as a people, they can identify with Paul's words in 2 Corinthians 6:1–10—their struggles have only made them stronger.

Even today, life for most of us is no cakewalk, but our ability to walk at all comes from God, who conquers all. Can you recognize God's grace and mercy and celebrate the presence of God in your good and bad times?

Dear God, no matter how high the odds are stacked against me, I can overcome them with your grace and mercy, and survive. Amen.

▶ 2 Cor 6:1–10

passed away; behold, new things have come.
[18]† And all this is from God, who has reconciled us to himself through Christ and given us the ministry of reconciliation,
[19]* namely, God was reconciling the world to himself in Christ, not counting their trespasses against them and entrusting to us the message of reconciliation.
[20]* So we are ambassadors for Christ, as if God were appealing through us. We implore you on behalf of Christ, be reconciled to God.
[21]*† For our sake he made him to be sin who did not know sin, so that we might become the righteousness of God in him.

The Experience of the Ministry

6 [1]*† Working together, then, we appeal to you not to receive the grace of God in vain.†
[2]*† For he says:

> "In an acceptable time I heard you,
> and on the day of salvation I helped you."

Behold, now is a very acceptable time; behold, now is the day of salvation.
[3]*† We cause no one to stumble in anything, in order that no fault may be found with our ministry;
[4]*† on the

† Elsewhere Paul contrasts what Christ looks like according to the old criteria (weakness, powerlessness, folly, death) and according to the new (wisdom, power, life); cf vv 15, 21; 1 Cor 1:17—3:3. Similarly, he describes the paradoxical nature of Christian existence, e.g., in 4:10–11, 14. *A new creation:* rabbis used this expression to describe the effect of the entrance of a proselyte or convert into Judaism or of the remission of sins on the Day of Atonement. The new order created *in Christ* is the new covenant (3:6).

5:18–21 Paul attempts to explain the meaning of God's action by a variety of different categories; his attention keeps moving rapidly back and forth from God's act to his own ministry as well. *Who has reconciled us to himself:* i.e., he has brought all into oneness. *Not counting their trespasses:* the reconciliation is described as an act of justification (cf "righteousness," 21); this contrasts with the covenant that condemned (3:8). *The ministry of reconciliation:* Paul's role in the wider picture is described: entrusted with the message of reconciliation (19), he is Christ's ambassador, through whom God appeals (20a). In v 20b Paul acts in the capacity just described.

5:21 This is a statement of God's purpose, expressed paradoxically in terms of sharing and exchange of attributes. As Christ became our righteousness (1 Cor 1:30), we become God's righteousness (cf vv 14–15).

6:1–10 This paragraph is a single long sentence in the Greek, interrupted by the parenthesis of v 2. The one main verb is "we appeal." In this paragraph Paul both exercises his ministry of reconciliation (cf 5:20) and describes how his ministry is exercised: the "message of reconciliation" (5:19) is lived existentially in his apostolic experience.

6:1 *Not to receive . . . in vain:* i.e., conform to the gift of justification and new creation. The context indicates how this can be done concretely: become God's righteousness (5:21), not live for oneself (5:15), be reconciled with Paul (6:11–13; 7:2–3).

6:2 *In an acceptable time:* Paul cites the Septuagint text of Is 49:8; the Hebrew reads "in a time of favor"; it is parallel to "on the day of salvation." *Now:* God is bestowing favor and salvation at this very moment, as Paul is addressing his letter to them.

6:3 *Cause no one to stumble:* the language echoes that of 1 Cor 8–10, as does the expression "no longer live for themselves" in 5:15. *That no fault may be found:* i.e., at the eschatological judgment (cf 1 Cor 4:2–5).

6:4a This is the central assertion, the topic statement for the catalogue that follows. *We commend ourselves:* Paul's self-commendation is ironical (with an eye on the charges mentioned in 3:1–3) and paradoxical (pointing mostly to experiences that would not normally be considered points of pride but are perceived as such by faith). Cf also the self-commendation in 11:23–29. *As ministers of God:* the same Greek word, *diakonos,* means "minister" and "servant"; cf 11:23, the central assertion in a similar context, and 1 Cor 3:5.

* **5:19** Rom 5:10–11; Col 1:20.
5:20 Eph 6:20; Phlm 9.
5:21 Is 53:6–9; Gal 3:13 / Rom 3:24–26; 1 Cor 1:30; 1 Pt 2:24; 1 Jn 3:5–8.
6:1 1 Cor 3:9; 1 Thes 3:2.
6:2 Is 49:8.
6:3 1 Cor 9:12; 10:32 / 2 Cor 8:20–21.
6:4 2 Cor 4:8–11; 11:23–27; 1 Cor 4:9–13.

contrary, in everything we commend ourselves
as ministers of God, through much endurance,†
in afflictions, hardships, constraints, 5* beatings,
imprisonments, riots, labors, vigils, fasts; 6*† by
purity, knowledge, patience, kindness, in a holy
spirit, in unfeigned love, 7* in truthful speech,
in the power of God; with weapons of righ-
teousness at the right and at the left; 8† through
glory and dishonor, insult and praise. We are
treated as deceivers and yet are truthful; 9* as
unrecognized and yet acknowledged; as dying
and behold we live; as chastised and yet not put
to death; 10* as sorrowful yet always rejoicing; as
poor yet enriching many; as having nothing and
yet possessing all things.

11† We have spoken frankly to you, Corinthi-
ans; our heart is open wide. 12* You are not con-
strained by us; you are constrained by your own
affections. 13* As recompense in kind (I speak as
to my children), be open yourselves.

Call to Holiness

14† Do not be yoked with those who are dif-
ferent, with unbelievers.† For what partnership
do righteousness and lawlessness have? Or what
fellowship does light have with darkness? 15 What
accord has Christ with Beliar? Or what has a be-
liever in common with an unbeliever? 16*† What
agreement has the temple of God with idols? For
we are the temple of the living God; as God said:

"I will live with them and move among them,
 and I will be their God
  and they shall be my people.
17* Therefore, come forth from them
 and be separate," says the Lord,
"and touch nothing unclean;

Live It!

Shine Like a Star

Second Corinthians 6:14 makes a sudden transition; 6:14—7:1 may even be a fragment from another letter. We are not sure what kind of behavior or problem Paul is talking about here. But it does seem clear that Paul is cautioning the Corinthians against being too closely influenced by non-Christians—unbelievers. Paul doesn't want the Corinthians to return to sinful behaviors.

Christians in the United States are also surrounded by many unhealthy and unholy choices. Our words and behaviors should show that "we are the temple of the living God" (6:16). We must be careful of friendships and media influences that might tempt us to start thinking that wrong is right. This doesn't mean we should be arrogant and separate ourselves from others. Remember that Jesus sometimes hung around with sinners. But he didn't share in their sins. He was a light for them.

As Paul says in Philippians 2:15, we are "children of God" in a "perverse generation," where we shine "like lights in the world."

▶ **2 Cor 6:14–18**

†

6:4b–5 *Through much endurance:* this phrase functions as a subtitle; it is followed by an enumeration of nine specific types of trials endured.

6:6–7a A list of virtuous qualities in two groups of four, the second fuller than the first.

6:8b–10 A series of seven rhetorically effective antitheses, contrasting negative external impressions with positive inner reality. Paul perceives his existence as a reflection of Jesus' own and affirms an inner reversal that escapes outward observation. The final two members illustrate two distinct kinds of paradox or apparent contradiction that are characteristic of apostolic experience.

6:11–13 Paul's tone becomes quieter, but his appeal for acceptance and affection is emotionally charged. References to the heart and their mutual relations bring the development begun in 2:14—3:3 to an effective conclusion.

6:14—7:1 Language and thought shift noticeably here. Suddenly we are in a different atmosphere, dealing with a quite different problem. Both the vocabulary and the thought, with their contrast between good and evil, are more characteristic of Qumran documents or the Book of Revelation than they are of Paul. Hence, critics suspect that this section was inserted by another hand.

6:14–16a The opening injunction to separate from unbelievers is reinforced by five rhetorical questions to make the point that Christianity is not compatible with paganism. Their opposition is emphasized also by the accumulation of five distinct designations for each group. These verses are a powerful statement of God's holiness and the exclusiveness of his claims.

6:16c–18 This is a chain of scriptural citations carefully woven together. God's covenant relation to his people and his presence among them (16) is seen as conditioned on cultic separation from the profane and cultically impure (17); that relation is translated into the personal language of the parent-child relationship, an extension to the community of the language of 2 Sm 7:14 (18). Some remarkable parallels to this chain are found in the final chapters of Revelation. God's presence among his people (21:22) is expressed there, too, by applying 2 Sm 7:14 to the community (21:7). There is a call to separation (18:4) and exclusion of the unclean from the community and its liturgy (21:27). The title "Lord Almighty" (*Pantokratōr*) occurs in the New Testament only here in 18 and nine times in Revelation.

*

6:5 Acts 16:23.
6:6 Gal 5:22–23.
6:7 2 Cor 10:4; Rom 13:12; Eph 6:11–17.
6:9 2 Cor 4:10–11; Rom 8:36.
6:10 Rom 8:32; 1 Cor 3:21.
6:12 2 Cor 7:3.
6:13 Gal 4:19.
6:16 1 Cor 10:20–21 / 1 Cor 3:16–17; 6:19 / Ex 25:8; 29:45; Lv 26:12; Jer 31:1; 32:38; Ez 37:27.
6:17 Is 52:11; Ez 20:34, 41; Rv 18:4; 21:27.

then I will receive you
18* and I will be a father to you,
and you shall be sons and daughters to me,
says the Lord Almighty."

7 1 Since we have these promises, beloved, let us cleanse ourselves from every defilement of flesh and spirit, making holiness perfect in the fear of God.

2† Make room for us; we have not wronged anyone, or ruined anyone, or taken advantage of anyone. 3* I do not say this in condemnation, for I have already said that you are in our hearts, that we may die together and live together. 4 I have great confidence in you, I have great pride in you; I am filled with encouragement, I am overflowing with joy all the more because of all our affliction.

C. Resolution of the Crisis†

Paul's Joy in Macedonia

5*† For even when we came into Macedonia,† our flesh had no rest, but we were afflicted in every way—external conflicts, internal fears. 6* But God, who encourages the downcast, encouraged us by the arrival of Titus, 7 and not only by his arrival but also by the encouragement with which he was encouraged in regard to you, as he told us of your yearning, your lament, your zeal for me, so that I rejoiced even more. 8*† For even if I saddened you by my letter, I do not regret it; and if I did regret it ([for] I see that that letter saddened you, if only for a while), 9 I rejoice now, not because you were saddened, but because you were saddened into repentance; for you were saddened in a godly way, so that you did not suffer loss in anything because of us. 10 For godly sorrow produces a salutary repentance without regret, but worldly sorrow produces death. 11 For behold what earnestness this godly sorrow has produced for you, as well as readiness for a defense, and indignation, and fear, and yearning, and zeal, and punishment. In every way you have shown yourselves to be innocent in the matter. 12* So then even though I wrote to you, it was not on account of the one who did the wrong, or on account of the one who suffered the wrong, but in order that your concern for us might be made plain to you in the sight of God. 13† For this reason we are encouraged.

And besides our encouragement, we rejoice even more because of the joy of Titus, since his spirit has been refreshed by all of you. 14 For if I have boasted to him about you, I was not put to shame. No, just as everything we said to you was true, so our boasting before Titus proved to be the truth. 15* And his heart goes out to you all the more, as he remembers the obedience of all of you, when you received him with fear and trembling. 16 I rejoice, because I have confidence in you in every respect.

III: The Collection for Jerusalem†

Generosity in Giving

8 1*† We want you to know, brothers,† of the grace of God† that has been given to the

† **7:2–4** These verses continue the thought of 6:11–13, before the interruption of 6:14—7:1. Verse 4 serves as a transition to the next section: the four themes it introduces (confidence; pride or "boasting"; encouragement; joy in affliction) are developed in vv 5–16. All have appeared previously in the letter.

7:5–16 This section functions as a peroration or formal summing up of the whole first part of the letter, chs 1–7. It deals with the restoration of right relations between Paul and the Corinthians, and it is marked by fullness and intensity of emotion.

7:5–7 Paul picks up the thread of the narrative interrupted at 2:13 (5) and describes the resolution of the tense situation there depicted (6–7). Finally Titus arrives and his coming puts an end to Paul's restlessness (2:13; 7:5), casts out his fears, and reverses his mood. The theme of encouragement and affliction is reintroduced (cf 1:3–11); here, too, encouragement is traced back to God and is described as contagious (6). The language of joy and sorrow also reappears in v 7 (cf 1:23—2:1 and the note on 1:23–24).

7:5 *Macedonia:* see the note on 2:13.

7:8–12 Paul looks back on the episode from the viewpoint of its ending. The goal of their common activity, promotion of their joy (1:24), has been achieved, despite and because of the sorrow they felt. That sorrow was God-given. Its salutary effects are enumerated fully and impressively in vv 10–11; not the least important of these is that it has revealed to them the attachment they have to Paul.

7:13–16 Paul summarizes the effect of the experience on Titus: encouragement, joy, love, relief. Finally, he describes its effects on himself: encouragement, joy, confidence, pride or "boasting" (i.e., the satisfaction resulting from a boast that proves well-founded; cf 4; 1:12, 14).

8:1—9:15 Paul turns to a new topic, the collection for the church in Jerusalem. There is an early precedent for this project in the agreement mentioned in Gal 2:6–10. According to Acts, the church at Antioch had sent Saul and Barnabas to Jerusalem with relief (Acts 11:27–30). Subsequently Paul organized a project of relief for Jerusalem among his own churches. Our earliest evidence for it comes in 1 Cor 16:1–4, after it had already begun (see the notes there); by the time Paul wrote Rom 15:25–28 the collection was completed and ready for delivery. Chapters 8 and 9 contain what appear to be two letters on the subject. In them Paul gives us his fullest exposition of the meaning he sees in the enterprise, presenting it as an act of Christian charity and as an expression of the unity of the church, both present and eschatological. These chapters are especially rich in the recurrence of key words, on which Paul plays; it is usually impossible to do justice to these wordplays in the translation.

8:1–24 This is a letter of recommendation for Titus and two unnamed companions, written from Macedonia probably at least a year later than 1 Cor 16. The recommendation proper is prefaced by remarks about the ideals of sharing and equality within the Christian community (1–15). Phil 4:10–20 shows that Paul has reflected on his personal experience of need and relief in his relations with the community at Philippi; he now develops his reflections on the larger scale of relations between his Gentile churches and the mother church in Jerusalem.

8:1–5 The example of the Macedonians, a model of what ought to be happening at Corinth, provides Paul with the occasion for expounding his theology of "giving."

8:1 *The grace of God:* the fundamental theme is expressed by

6:18 2 Sm 7:14; Ps 2:7; Is 43:6; Jer 31:9; Rv 21:7 / Rv 4:8; 11:17; 15:3; 21:22.
7:3 2 Cor 6:11–13.
7:5 2 Cor 2:13.
7:6 2 Cor 7:13–14; 1 Thes 3:6–8.
7:8 2 Cor 2:2–4; Heb 12:11.
7:12 2 Cor 2:3, 9; 7:8.
7:15 2 Cor 2:9.
8:1 2 Cor 11:9; Rom 15:26.

Cultural Connection

Christians Share Their Money out of Solidarity

In chapters 8–9 of Second Corinthians, Paul encourages the Corinthians to give generously to a collection for the poor Christians of Jerusalem. In a similar way, Hispanics in the United States often generously collect and share the money they earn with their families in Latin America.

"I cannot fail my mother," Anita said. "I always try to send her at least a hundred dollars a month because she depends on me." Anita, who lives in Minneapolis with her husband and children, has been sending money to her mother in central Mexico since Anita came to the United States eight years ago. Anita and other Hispanics share the money they make in the United States with their families in Latin America in the spirit of solidarity. "It is something that we have to do," a Central American immigrant tells us. "It is part of our culture. It is the responsibility of all adult children to help our families, even if we don't make much money."

- How are you generous with your money? What financial sacrifices can you make this week for the sake of family members or others you know who are as poor or poorer than you?
- Ask the Holy Spirit for the gift of generosity for yourself and for other young Catholics. Pray that a willingness to share the resources God has blessed you with becomes a lifelong habit.

▶ 2 Corinthians, chapters 8–9

churches of Macedonia, [2]† for in a severe test of
affliction, the abundance of their joy and their
profound poverty overflowed in a wealth of gen-
erosity on their part. [3]† For according to their
means, I can testify, and beyond their means,
spontaneously, [4]* they begged us insistently for
the favor of taking part in the service to the
holy ones, [5]† and this, not as we expected, but
they gave themselves first to the Lord and to us
through the will of God, [6]*† so that we urged Ti-
tus that, as he had already begun, he should also
complete for you this gracious act also. [7]*† Now
as you excel in every respect, in faith, discourse,
knowledge, all earnestness, and in the love we
have for you, may you excel in this gracious act
also.
[8]I say this not by way of command, but to test
the genuineness of your love by your concern
for others. [9]*† For you know the gracious act of
our Lord Jesus Christ, that for your sake he be-
came poor although he was rich, so that by his
poverty you might become rich. [10]* And I am
giving counsel in this matter, for it is appropri-
ate for you who began not only to act but to act
willingly last year: [11]† complete it now, so that
your eager willingness may be matched by your

---

† the Greek noun *charis,* which will be variously translated throughout these chapters as "grace" (8:1; 9:8, 14), "favor" (8:4), "gracious act" (8:6, 7, 9) or "gracious work" (8:19), to be compared to "gracious gift" (1 Cor 16:3). The related term, *eucharistia,* "thanksgiving," also occurs at 9:11, 12. The wordplay is not superficial; various mutations of the same root signal inner connection between aspects of a single reality, and Paul consciously exploits the similarities in vocabulary to highlight that connection.

8:2 Three more terms are now introduced. *Test (dokimē):* the same root is translated as "to test" (8) and "evidence" (9:13); it means to be tried and found genuine. *Abundance:* variations on the same root lie behind "overflow" (8:2; 9:12), "excel" (8:7), "surplus" (8:14), "superfluous" (9:1), "make abundant" and "have an abundance" (9:8). These expressions of fullness contrast with references to need (8:14; 9:12). *Generosity:* the word *haplotēs* has nuances of both simplicity and sincerity; here and in 9:11, 13 it designates the singleness of purpose that manifests itself in generous giving.

8:3–4 Paul emphasizes the spontaneity of the Macedonians and the nature of their action. *They begged us insistently:* the same root is translated as "urge," "appeal," "encourage" (8:6, 17; 9:5). *Taking part:* the same word is translated "contribution" in 9:13 and a related term as "partner" in 8:23. *Service (diakonia):* this word occurs also in 9:1, 13 as "service"; in 9:12 it is translated "administration," and in 8:19, 20 the corresponding verb is rendered "administer."

8:5 *They gave themselves . . . to the Lord and to us:* on its deepest level their attitude is one of self-giving.

8:6 *Titus:* 1 Cor 16 seemed to leave the organization up to the Corinthians, but apparently Paul has sent Titus to initiate the collection as well; 8:16–17 will describe Titus' attitude as one of shared concern and cooperation.

8:7 The charitable service Paul is promoting is seen briefly and in passing within the perspective of Paul's theology of the charisms. *Earnestness (spoudē):* this or related terms occur also in v 22 ("earnest") and 8:8, 16, 17 ("concern").

8:9 The dialectic of Jesus' experience, expressed earlier in terms of life and death (5:15), sin and righteousness (5:21), is now rephrased in terms of poverty and wealth. Many scholars think this is a reference to Jesus' preexistence with God (his "wealth") and to his incarnation and death (his "poverty"), and they point to the similarity between this verse and Phil 2:6–8. Others interpret the wealth and poverty as succeeding phases of Jesus' earthly existence, e.g., his sense of intimacy with God and then the desolation and the feeling of abandonment by God in his death (cf Mk 15:34).

8:11 *Eager:* the word *prothymia* also occurs in 8:12, 19; 9:2.

---

* **8:4** Acts 24:17; Rom 15:31.
8:6 2 Cor 2:13; 7:6–7, 13–14; 8:16, 23; 12:18.
8:7 1 Cor 1:5.
8:9 2 Cor 6:10; Phil 2:6–8.
8:10 2 Cor 9:2; 1 Cor 16:1–4.

completion of it out of what you have. [12]† For if the eagerness is there, it is acceptable according to what one has, not according to what one does not have; [13]not that others should have relief while you are burdened, but that as a matter of equality [14]your surplus at the present time should supply their needs, so that their surplus may also supply your needs, that there may be equality. [15]* As it is written:

"Whoever had much did not have more,
and whoever had little did not have less."

Titus and His Collaborators

[16]† But thanks be to God who put the same concern for you into the heart of Titus, [17]for he not only welcomed our appeal but, since he is very concerned, he has gone to you of his own accord. [18]*† With him we have sent the brother who is praised in all the churches for his preaching of the gospel. [19]* And not only that, but he has also been appointed our traveling companion by the churches in this gracious work administered by us for the glory of the Lord [himself] and for the expression of our eagerness. [20]† This we desire to avoid, that anyone blame us about this lavish gift administered by us, [21]* for we are concerned for what is honorable not only in the sight of the Lord but also in the sight of others. [22]And with them we have sent our brother whom we often tested in many ways and found earnest, but who is now much more earnest because of his great confidence in you. [23]As for Titus, he is my partner and co-worker for you; as for our brothers, they are apostles of the churches, the glory of Christ. [24]† So give proof before the churches of your love and of our boasting about you to them.

God's Indescribable Gift

9 [1]† Now about the service to the holy ones, it is superfluous for me to write to you, [2]*† for I know your eagerness, about which I boast of you to the Macedonians, that Achaia has been ready since last year; and your zeal has stirred up most of them. [3]† Nonetheless, I sent the brothers so that our boast about you might not prove empty in this case, so that you might be ready, as I said, [4]for fear that if any Macedonians come with me and find you not ready we might be put to shame (to say nothing of you) in this conviction. [5]So I thought it necessary to encourage the brothers to go on ahead to you and arrange in advance for your promised gift, so that in this way it might be ready as a bountiful gift and not as an exaction.

[6]* Consider this: whoever sows sparingly will also reap sparingly, and whoever sows bountifully will also reap bountifully. [7]* Each must do as already determined, without sadness or compulsion, for God loves a cheerful giver. [8]† Moreover, God is able to make every grace abundant for you, so that in all things, always having all you need, you may have an abundance for every good work. [9]* As it is written:

"He scatters abroad, he gives to the poor;
his righteousness endures forever."

[10]* The one who supplies seed to the sower and bread for food will supply and multiply your seed and increase the harvest of your righteousness.

[11]† You are being enriched in every way for all generosity, which through us produces thanks-

†

8:12–15 Paul introduces the principle of *equality* into the discussion. The goal is not impoverishment but sharing of resources; balance is achieved at least over the course of time. In v 15 Paul grounds his argument unexpectedly in the experience of Israel gathering manna in the desert: equality was achieved, independently of personal exertion, by God, who gave with an even hand according to need. Paul touches briefly here on the theme of "living from God."

8:16–24 In recommending Titus and his companions, Paul stresses their personal and apostolic qualities, their good dispositions toward the Corinthians, and their authority as messengers of the churches and representatives of Christ.

8:18 *The brother:* we do not know the identity of this co-worker of Paul, nor of the third companion mentioned below in v 22.

8:20–22 *That anyone blame us:* 12:16–18 suggests that misunderstandings may indeed have arisen concerning Paul's management of the collection through the messengers mentioned here, but those same verses seem to imply that the Corinthians by and large would recognize the honesty of Paul's conduct in this area as in others (cf 6:3).

8:24 As Paul began by holding up the Macedonians as examples to be imitated, he closes by exhorting the Corinthians to show their love (by accepting the envoys and by cooperating as the Macedonians do), thus justifying the pride Paul demonstrates because of them before other churches.

9:1–15 Quite possibly this was originally an independent letter, though it deals with the same subject and continues many of the same themes. In that case, it may have been written a few weeks later than ch 8, while the delegation there mentioned was still on its way.

9:2 *Achaia:* see the note on Rom 15:26.

9:3 *I sent the brothers:* the Greek aorist tense here could be epistolary, referring to the present; in that case Paul would be sending them now, and ch 9 would merely conclude the letter of recommendation begun in ch 8. But the aorist may also refer to a sending that is past as Paul writes; then ch 9, with its apparently fresh beginning, is a follow-up message entrusted to another carrier.

9:8–10 The behavior to which he exhorts them is grounded in God's own pattern of behavior. God is capable of overwhelming generosity, as scripture itself attests (9), so that they need not fear being short. He will provide in abundance, both supplying their natural needs and increasing their righteousness. Paul challenges them to godlike generosity and reminds them of the fundamental motive for encouragement: God himself cannot be outdone.

9:11–15 Paul's vision broadens to take in all the interested parties in one dynamic picture. His language becomes liturgically colored and conveys a sense of fullness. With a final play on the words *charis* and *eucharistia* (see the note on 8:1), he describes a circle that closes

*

8:15 Ex 16:18.
8:18 2 Cor 12:18.
8:19 1 Cor 16:3–4.
8:21 Rom 12:17.
9:2 2 Cor 8:10; Rom 15:26.
9:6 Prv 11:24–25.
9:7 Prv 22:8 LXX.
9:9 Ps 112:9.
9:10 Is 55:10.

giving to God, 12 for the administration of this public service is not only supplying the needs of the holy ones but is also overflowing in many acts of thanksgiving to God. 13* Through the evidence of this service, you are glorifying God for your obedient confession of the gospel of Christ and the generosity of your contribution to them and to all others, 14 while in prayer on your behalf they long for you, because of the surpassing grace of God upon you. 15* Thanks be to God for his indescribable gift!

IV: Paul's Defense of His Ministry†

Accusation of Weakness†

10 1† Now I myself, Paul, urge you through the gentleness and clemency of Christ, I who am humble when face to face with you, but brave toward you when absent, 2*† I beg you that, when present, I may not have to be brave with that confidence with which I intend to act boldly against some who consider us as acting according to the flesh. 3† For, although we are in the flesh, we do not battle according to the flesh, 4* for the weapons of our battle are not of flesh but are enormously powerful, capable of destroying fortresses. We destroy arguments 5 and every pretension raising itself against the knowledge of God, and take every thought captive in obedience to Christ, 6* and we are ready to punish every disobedience, once your obedience is complete.

7*† Look at what confronts you. Whoever is confident of belonging to Christ should consider that as he belongs to Christ, so do we. 8* And even if I should boast a little too much of our authority, which the Lord gave for building you up and not for tearing you down, I shall not be put to shame. 9† May I not seem as one frightening you through letters. 10* For someone will say, "His letters are severe and forceful, but his bodily presence is weak, and his speech contemptible." 11* Such a person must understand that what we are in word through letters when absent, that we also are in action when present.

12*† Not that we dare to class or compare ourselves with some of those who recommend themselves. But when they measure themselves by one another and compare themselves with one another, they are without understanding. 13† But we will not boast beyond measure but will keep to the limits God has apportioned us, namely, to reach even to you. 14 For we are not overreaching ourselves, as though we did not reach you; we indeed first came to you with the gospel of Christ. 15 We are not boasting beyond

---

† on itself: the movement of grace overflowing from God to them and handed on from them through Paul to others is completed by the prayer of praise and thanksgiving raised on their behalf to God.

10:1—13:10 These final chapters have their own unity of structure and theme and could well have formed the body of a separate letter. They constitute an *apologia* on Paul's part, i.e., a legal defense of his behavior and his ministry; the writing is emotionally charged and highly rhetorical. In the central section (11:16—12:10), the *apologia* takes the form of a boast. This section is prepared for by a prologue (11:1–15) and followed by an epilogue (12:11–18), which are similar in content and structure. These sections, in turn, are framed by an introduction (10:1–18) and a conclusion (12:19—13:10), both of which assert Paul's apostolic authority and confidence and define the purpose of the letter. The structure that results from this disposition of the material is chiastic, i.e., the first element corresponds to the last, the second to the second last, etc., following the pattern *a b c b' a'*.

10:1–18 Paul asserts his apostolic authority and expresses the confidence this generates in him. He writes in response to certain opinions that have arisen in the community and certain charges raised against him and in preparation for a forthcoming visit in which he intends to set things in order. This section gives us an initial glimpse of the situation in Corinth that Paul must address; much of its thematic material will be taken up again in the finale (12:19—13:10).

10:1–2 A strong opening plunges us straight into the conflict. Contrasts dominate here: presence versus absence, gentleness-clemency-humility versus boldness-confidence-bravery. *Through the gentleness and clemency of Christ:* the figure of the gentle Christ, presented in a significant position before any specifics of the situation are suggested, forms a striking contrast to the picture of the bold and militant Paul (2–6); this tension is finally resolved in 13:3–4. *Absent . . . present:* this same contrast, with a restatement of the purpose of the letter, recurs in 13:10, which forms an inclusion with 10:1–2.

10:2b–4a *Flesh:* the Greek word *sarx* can express both the physical life of the body without any pejorative overtones (as in "we are in the flesh," 3) and also our natural life insofar as it is marked by limitation and weakness (as in the other expressions) in contrast to the higher life and power conferred by the Spirit; cf the note on 1 Cor 3:1. The wordplay is intended to express the paradoxical situation of a life already taken over by the Spirit but not yet seen as such except by faith. Lack of empirical evidence of the Spirit permits misunderstanding and misjudgment, but Paul resolutely denies that his behavior and effectiveness are as limited as some suppose.

10:3b–6 Paul is involved in combat. The strong military language and imagery are both an assertion of his confidence in the divine power at his disposal and a declaration of war against those who underestimate his resources. The threat is echoed in 13:2–3.

10:7–8 *Belonging to Christ . . . so do we:* these phrases already announce the pattern of Paul's boast in 11:21b–29, especially 11:22–23. *For building you up and not for tearing you down:* Paul draws on the language by which Jeremiah described the purpose of the prophetic power the Lord gave to him (Jer 1:9–10; 12:16–17; 24:6). Though Paul's power may have destructive effects on others (2–6), its intended effect on the community is entirely constructive (cf 13:10). *I shall not be put to shame:* his assertions will not be refuted; they will be revealed as true at the judgment.

10:9–10 Paul cites the complaints of some who find him lacking in personal forcefulness and holds out the threat of a personal *parousia* (both "return" and "presence") that will be forceful, indeed will be a demonstration of Christ's own power (cf 13:2–4).

10:12–18 Paul now qualifies his claim to boldness, indicating its limits. He distinguishes his own behavior from that of others, revealing those "others" as they appear to him: as self-recommending, immoderately boastful, encroaching on territory not assigned to them, and claiming credit not due to them.

10:13 *Will keep to the limits:* the notion of proper limits is expressed here by two terms with overlapping meanings, *metron* and *kanōn,* which are played off against several expressions denoting overreaching or expansion beyond a legitimate sphere.

---

* **9:13** 2 Cor 8:4; Rom 15:31.
9:15 Rom 5:15–16.
10:2 2 Cor 13:2, 10; 1 Cor 4:21.
10:4 2 Cor 6:7; 13:2–3; 1 Cor 1:25; Eph 6:10–14.
10:6 2 Cor 2:9.
10:7 1 Cor 1:12.
10:8 2 Cor 13:10.
10:10 1 Cor 2:3.
10:11 2 Cor 13:1–2.
10:12 2 Cor 3:1–2; 4:2; 5:12; 6:4; 10:18; 12:11.

measure, in other people's labors; yet our hope is
that, as your faith increases, our influence among
you may be greatly enlarged, within our proper
limits, [16]* so that we may preach the gospel
even beyond you, not boasting of work already
done in another's sphere. [17]*† "Whoever boasts,
should boast in the Lord." [18]*† For it is not the
one who recommends himself who is approved,
but the one whom the Lord recommends.

Preaching without Charge†

11 [1]*† If only you would put up with a little
foolishness from me! Please put up with
me. [2]*† For I am jealous of you with the jealousy
of God, since I betrothed you to one husband to
present you as a chaste virgin to Christ. [3]*† But
I am afraid that, as the serpent deceived Eve by
his cunning, your thoughts may be corrupted
from a sincere [and pure] commitment to Christ.
[4]*† For if someone comes and preaches another
Jesus than the one we preached, or if you receive
a different spirit from the one you received or a
different gospel from the one you accepted, you
put up with it well enough. [5]*† For I think that
I am not in any way inferior to these "super-
apostles." [6]*† Even if I am untrained in speaking,
I am not so in knowledge; in every way we have
made this plain to you in all things.
[7]*† Did I make a mistake when I humbled
myself so that you might be exalted, because
I preached the gospel of God to you without
charge? [8]I plundered other churches by ac-
cepting from them in order to minister to you.
[9]* And when I was with you and in need, I did
not burden anyone, for the brothers who came
from Macedonia supplied my needs. So I re-
frained and will refrain from burdening you in
any way. [10]* By the truth of Christ in me, this
boast of mine shall not be silenced in the regions
of Achaia. [11]*† And why? Because I do not love
you? God knows I do!
[12]And what I do I will continue to do, in order
to end this pretext of those who seek a pretext
for being regarded as we are in the mission of
which they boast. [13]† For such people are false
apostles, deceitful workers, who masquerade as

---

† **10:17** *Boast in the Lord:* there is a legitimate boasting, in contrast to the immoderate boasting to which vv 13 and 15 allude. God's work through Paul in the community is the object of his boast (13–16; 1:12–14) and constitutes his recommendation (3:1–3). Cf the notes on 1:12–14 and 1 Cor 1:29–31.

10:18 *Approved:* to be approved is to come successfully through the process of testing for authenticity (cf 13:3–7 and the note on 8:2). *Whom the Lord recommends:* self-commendation is a premature and unwarranted anticipation of the final judgment, which the Lord alone will pass (cf 1 Cor 4:3–5). Paul alludes to this judgment throughout chs 10–13, frequently in final or transitional positions; cf 11:15; 12:19a; 13:3–7.

11:1–15 Although these verses continue to reveal information about Paul's opponents and the differences he perceives between them and himself, 11:1 signals a turn in Paul's thought. This section constitutes a prologue to the boasting that he will undertake in 11:16—12:10, and it bears remarkable similarities to the section that follows the central boast, 12:11–18.

11:1 *Put up with a little foolishness from me:* this verse indicates more clearly than the general statement of intent in 10:13 the nature of the project Paul is about to undertake. He alludes ironically to the Corinthians' toleration for others. *Foolishness:* Paul qualifies his project as folly from beginning to end; see the note on 11:16—12:10.

11:2 Paul gives us a sudden glimpse of the theological values that are at stake. *The jealousy of God:* the perspective is that of the covenant, described in imagery of love and marriage, as in the prophets; cf 1 Cor 10:22. *I betrothed you:* Paul, like a father (cf 12:14), betroths the community to Christ as his bride (cf Eph 5:21–33) and will present her to him at his second coming. Cf Mt 25:1–13 and the nuptial imagery in Rv 21.

11:3 *As the serpent deceived Eve:* before Christ can return for the community Paul fears a repetition of the primal drama of seduction. Corruption of minds is satanic activity (see 2:11; 4:4). Satanic imagery recurs in 11:13–15, 20; 12:7b, 16–17; see the notes on these passages.

11:4 *Preaches another Jesus:* the danger is specified, and Paul's opponents are identified with the cunning serpent. The battle for minds has to do with the understanding of Jesus, the Spirit, the gospel; the Corinthians have flirted with another understanding than the one that Paul handed on to them as traditional and normative.

11:5 *These "superapostles":* this term, employed again in 12:11b, designates the opponents of whom Paul has spoken in ch 10 and again in 11:4. They appear to be intruders at Corinth. Their preaching is marked at least by a different emphasis and style, and they do not hesitate to accept support from the community. Perhaps these itinerants appeal to the authority of church leaders in Jerusalem and even carry letters of recommendation from them. But it is not those distant leaders whom Paul is attacking here. The intruders are "superapostles" not in the sense of the "pillars" at Jerusalem (Gal 2), but in their own estimation. They consider themselves superior to Paul as apostles and ministers of Christ, and they are obviously enjoying some success among the Corinthians. Paul rejects their claim to be apostles in any superlative sense (*hyperlian*), judging them bluntly as "false apostles," ministers of Satan masquerading as apostles of Christ (13–15). On the contrary, he himself will claim to be a superminister of Christ (*hyper egō*, 23).

11:6 Apparently found deficient in both rhetorical ability (cf 10:10) and knowledge (cf 10:5), Paul concedes the former charge but not the latter. *In every way:* in all their contacts with him revelation has been taking place. Paul, through whom God reveals the knowledge of himself (2:14), and in whom the death and life of Jesus are revealed (4:10–11; cf 6:4), also demonstrates his own role as the bearer of true knowledge. Cf 1 Cor 1:18—2:16.

11:7–10 Abruptly Paul passes to another reason for complaints: his practice of preaching without remuneration (cf 1 Cor 9:3–18). He deftly defends his practice by situating it from the start within the pattern of Christ's own self-humiliation (cf 10:1) and reduces objections to absurdity by rhetorical questions (cf 12:13).

11:11–12 Paul rejects lack of affection as his motive (possibly imputed to him by his opponents) and states his real motive, a desire to emphasize the disparity between himself and the others (cf 19–21). The topic of his gratuitous service will be taken up once more in 12:13–18. 1 Cor 9:15–18 gives a different but complementary explanation of his motivation.

11:13–15 Paul picks up again the imagery of v 3 and applies it to the opponents: they are false apostles of Christ, really serving another master. *Deceitful . . . masquerade:* deception and simulation, like cunning (3), are marks of the satanic. *Angel of light:* recalls the contrast between light and darkness, Christ and Beliar at 6:14–15. *Ministers of righteousness:* recalls the earlier contrast between the ministry of condemnation and that of righteousness (3:9). *Their end:* the section closes with another allusion to the judgment, when all participants in the final conflict will be revealed or unmasked and dealt with as they deserve.

---

* **10:16** Rom 15:20–21.
10:17 Jer 9:22–23; 1 Cor 1:31.
10:18 2 Cor 13:3–9.
11:1 2 Cor 11:21; 12:11.
11:2 Hos 2:21–22; Eph 5:26–27.
11:3 Gn 3:1–6.
11:4 Gal 1:6–9.
11:5 2 Cor 12:11.
11:6 1 Cor 1:5, 17; 2:1–5.
11:7 2 Cor 12:13–18; Acts 18:3; 1 Cor 9:6–18.
11:9 Phil 4:15, 18.
11:10 1 Cor 9:15.
11:11 2 Cor 12:15.

apostles of Christ. [14]And no wonder, for even Satan masquerades as an angel of light. [15]So it is not strange that his ministers also masquerade as ministers of righteousness. Their end will correspond to their deeds.

Paul's Boast: His Labors

[16]† I repeat, no one should consider me foolish;† but if you do, accept me as a fool, so that I too may boast a little.† [17]What I am saying I am not saying according to the Lord but as in foolishness, in this boastful state. [18]Since many boast according to the flesh, I too will boast. [19]For you gladly put up with fools, since you are wise yourselves. [20]† For you put up with it if someone enslaves you, or devours you, or gets the better of you, or puts on airs, or slaps you in the face. [21]† To my shame I say that we were too weak!

But what anyone dares to boast of (I am speaking in foolishness) I also dare. [22]*† Are they Hebrews? So am I. Are they Israelites? So am I. Are they descendants of Abraham? So am I. [23]*† Are they ministers of Christ? (I am talking like an insane person.)† I am still more, with far greater labors, far more imprisonments, far worse beatings, and numerous brushes with death. [24]* Five times at the hands of the Jews I received forty lashes minus one. [25]* Three times I was beaten with rods, once I was stoned, three times I was shipwrecked, I passed a night and a day on the deep; [26]on frequent journeys, in dangers from rivers, dangers from robbers, dangers from my own race, dangers from Gentiles, dangers in the city, dangers in the wilderness, dangers at sea, dangers among false brothers; [27]* in toil and hardship, through many sleepless nights, through hunger and thirst, through frequent fastings, through cold and exposure. [28]And apart from these things, there is the daily pressure upon me of my anxiety for all the churches. [29]* Who is weak, and I am not weak? Who is led to sin, and I am not indignant?

Paul's Boast: His Weakness

[30]† If I must boast, I will boast of the things that show my weakness. [31]† The God and Father of the Lord Jesus knows, he who is blessed forever, that I do not lie. [32]At Damascus, the governor under King Aretas guarded the city of Damascus, in order to seize me, [33]* but I was lowered in a basket through a window in the wall and escaped his hands.

12 [1]† I must boast; not that it is profitable, but I will go on to visions and revelations of the Lord. [2]I know someone in Christ who, fourteen years ago (whether in the body or out of the body I do not know, God knows), was caught up to the third heaven. [3]And I know that this person (whether in the body or out of the body I do not know, God knows) [4]* was caught up into Paradise and heard ineffable things, which no one may utter. [5]† About this person

---

† **11:16—12:10** Paul now accepts the challenge of his opponents and indulges in boasting similar to theirs, but with differences that he has already signaled in 10:12–18 and that become clearer as he proceeds. He defines the nature of his project and unmistakably labels it as folly at the beginning and the end (11:16–23; 12:11). Yet his boast does not spring from ignorance (11:21; 12:6) nor is it concerned merely with human distinctions (11:18). Paul boasts "in moderation" (10:13, 15) and "in the Lord" (10:17).

11:16–29 The first part of Paul's boast focuses on labors and afflictions, in which authentic service of Christ consists.

11:16–21 These verses recapitulate remarks already made about the foolishness of boasting and the excessive toleration of the Corinthians. They form a prelude to the boast proper.

11:20 Paul describes the activities of the "others" in terms that fill out the picture drawn in vv 3–4, 13–15. Much of the vocabulary suggests fleshly or even satanic activity. *Enslaves:* cf Gal 2:4. *Devours:* cf 1 Pt 5:8. *Gets the better:* the verb *lambanō* means "to take," but is used in a variety of senses; here it may imply financial advantage, as in the English colloquialism "to take someone." It is similarly used at 12:16 and is there connected with cunning and deceit. *Puts on airs:* the same verb is rendered "raise oneself" (10:5) and "be too elated" (12:7).

11:21 Paul ironically concedes the charge of personal weakness from 10:1–18 but will refute the other charge there mentioned, that of lack of boldness, accepting the challenge to demonstrate it by his boast.

11:22 The opponents apparently pride themselves on their "Jewishness." Paul, too, can claim to be a Jew by race, religion, and promise. *Descendants of Abraham:* elsewhere Paul distinguishes authentic from inauthentic heirs of Abraham and the promise (Rom 4:13–18; 9:7–13; 11:1; Gal 3:9, 27–29; cf Jn 8:33–47). Here he grants his opponents this title in order to concentrate on the principal claim that follows.

11:23a *Ministers of Christ . . . I am still more:* the central point of the boast (cf the note on 11:5). *Like an insane person:* the climax of his folly.

11:23b–29 Service of the humiliated and crucified Christ is demonstrated by trials endured for him. This rhetorically impressive catalogue enumerates many of the labors and perils Paul encountered on his missionary journeys.

11:30—12:10 The second part of Paul's boast, marked by a change of style and a shift in focus. After recalling the project in which he is engaged, he states a new topic: his weaknesses as matter for boasting. Everything in this section, even the discussion of privileges and distinctions, will be integrated into this perspective.

11:31–32 The episode at Damascus is symbolic. It aptly illustrates Paul's weakness but ends in deliverance (cf 4:7–11).

12:1–4 *In the body or out of the body:* he seemed no longer confined to bodily conditions, but he does not claim to understand the mechanics of the experience. *Caught up:* i.e., in ecstasy. *The third heaven . . . Paradise:* ancient cosmologies depicted a multitiered universe. Jewish intertestamental literature contains much speculation about the number of heavens. Seven is the number usually mentioned, but the Testament of Levi (2:7–10; 3:1–4) speaks of three; God himself dwelt in the third of these. Without giving us any clear picture of the cosmos, Paul indicates a mental journey to a nonearthly space, set apart by God, in which secrets were revealed to him. *Ineffable things:* i.e., privileged knowledge, which it was not possible or permitted to divulge.

12:5–7 *This person:* the indirect way of referring to himself has the effect of emphasizing the distance between that experience and his everyday life, just as the indirect *someone in Christ* (2) and all the passive verbs emphasize his passivity and receptivity in the experience. The revelations were not a personal achievement, nor were they meant to draw attention to any quality of his own.

11:22 Acts 22:3 / Rom 11:1; Phil 3:5–6.
11:23 2 Cor 6:5; Acts 16:22–24; 1 Cor 15:31–32.
11:24 Dt 25:2–3.
11:25 Acts 14:19; 27:43–44.
11:27 1 Cor 4:11.
11:29 1 Cor 9:22.
11:33 Acts 9:23–25.
12:4 Lk 23:43; Rv 2:7.

I will boast, but about myself I will not boast,
except about my weaknesses. [6]Although if I
should wish to boast, I would not be foolish, for
I would be telling the truth. But I refrain, so that
no one may think more of me than what he sees
in me or hears from me [7*†] because of the abun-
dance of the revelations. Therefore, that I might
not become too elated, a thorn in the flesh was
given to me, an angel of Satan, to beat me, to
keep me from being too elated. [8*†] Three times
I begged the Lord about this, that it might leave
me, [9*†] but he said to me, "My grace is sufficient
for you, for power is made perfect in weakness."
I will rather boast most gladly of my weak-
nesses,† in order that the power of Christ may
dwell with me. [10*†] Therefore, I am content with
weaknesses, insults, hardships, persecutions, and
constraints, for the sake of Christ; for when I am
weak, then I am strong.

Selfless Concern for the Church

[11*†] I have been foolish. You compelled me,
for I ought to have been commended by you. For
I am in no way inferior to these "superapostles,"
even though I am nothing. [12*†] The signs of an
apostle were performed among you with all en-
durance, signs and wonders, and mighty deeds.
[13*†] In what way were you less privileged than
the rest of the churches, except that on my part I
did not burden you? Forgive me this wrong!

Live It!

When I Am Weak, Then I Am Strong!

Sensible people go to a physician when they are suffering from an illness or injury. Smart students seek help from a teacher when they are stumped by an assignment. Honest people admit when they have failed. Humble people are not afraid to apologize. Admitting we are sick or need help with a problem or have failed or been wrong is a sign not of weakness but a sign of wisdom and maturity.

Paul mentions a mysterious affliction he had to suffer—a "thorn in the flesh" (2 Cor 12:7)—and how desperately he wanted to be rid of it. When he asked God to remove the "thorn," God chose to let it remain in Paul's life.

Paul wanted to be strong on his own, but his experience of struggling with this thorn reminded him that he needed to depend completely on the grace of God. Recognizing that we need God, admitting that we cannot make it on our own—that is a sign of true strength!

▶ **2 Cor 12:1–10**

†

12:7b *That I might not become too elated:* God assures that there is a negative component to his experience, so that he cannot lose proper perspective; cf 1:9; 4:7–11. *A thorn in the flesh:* variously interpreted as a sickness or physical disability, a temptation, or a handicap connected with his apostolic activity. But since Hebrew "thorn in the flesh," like English "thorn in my side," refers to persons (cf Nm 33:55; Ez 28:24), Paul may be referring to some especially persistent and obnoxious opponent. The language of vv 7–8 permits this interpretation. If this is correct, the frequent appearance of singular pronouns in depicting the opposition may not be merely a stylistic variation; the singular may be provoked and accompanied by the image of one individual in whom criticism of Paul's preaching, way of life, and apostolic consciousness is concentrated, and who embodies all the qualities Paul attributes to the group. *An angel of Satan:* a personal messenger from Satan; cf the satanic language already applied to the opponents in 11:3, 13–15, 20.

12:8 *Three times:* his prayer was insistent, like that of Jesus in Gethsemane, a sign of how intolerable he felt the thorn to be.

12:9 *But he said to me:* Paul's petition is denied; release and healing are withheld for a higher purpose. The Greek perfect tense indicates that Jesus' earlier response still holds at the time of writing. *My grace is sufficient for you:* this is not a statement about the sufficiency of grace in general. Jesus speaks directly to Paul's situation. *Is made perfect:* i.e., is given most fully and manifests itself fully.

12:9b–10a Paul draws the conclusion from the autobiographical anecdote and integrates it into the subject of this part of the boast. *Weaknesses:* the apostolic hardships he must endure, including active personal hostility, as specified in a final catalogue (10a). *That the power of Christ may dwell with me:* Paul pinpoints the ground for the paradoxical strategy he has adopted in his self-defense.

12:10b *When I am weak, then I am strong:* Paul recognizes a twofold pattern in the resolution of the weakness-power (and death-life) dialectic, each of which looks to Jesus as the model and is experienced in him. The first is personal, involving a reversal in oneself (Jesus, 13:4a; Paul, 1:9–10; 4:10–11; 6:9). The second is apostolic, involving an effect on others (Jesus, 5:14–15; Paul, 1:6; 4:12; 13:9). The specific kind of "effectiveness in ministry" that Paul promises to demonstrate on his arrival (13:4b; cf 10:1–11) involves elements of both; this, too, will be modeled on Jesus' experience and a participation in that experience (9; 13:3b).

12:11–18 This brief section forms an epilogue or concluding observation to Paul's boast, corresponding to the prologue in 11:1–15. A four-step sequence of ideas is common to these two sections: Paul qualifies his boast as folly (11:1; 12:11a), asserts his noninferiority to the "superapostles" (11:5; 12:11b), exemplifies this by allusion to charismatic endowments (11:6; 12:12), and finally denies that he has been a financial burden to the community (11:7–12; 12:13–18).

12:12 Despite weakness and affliction (suggested by the mention of *endurance*), his ministry has been accompanied by demonstrations of power (cf 1 Cor 2:3–4). *Signs of an apostle:* visible proof of belonging to Christ and of mediating Christ's power, which the opponents require as touchstones of apostleship (11; cf 13:3).

12:13–18 Paul insists on his intention to continue refusing support from the community (cf 11:8–12). In defending his practice and his motivation, he once more protests his love (cf 11:11) and rejects the suggestion of secret self-enrichment. He has recourse here again to language applied to his opponents earlier: "cunning" (11:3), "deceit" (11:13), "got the better of you" (see the note on 11:20), "take advantage" (2:11).

12:7 Nm 33:55; Jos 23:13; Ez 28:24.
12:8 Mt 26:39–44.
12:9 2 Cor 4:7.
12:10 2 Cor 6:4–5; Rom 5:3 / Phil 4:13.
12:11 2 Cor 11:5.
12:12 Rom 15:19; 1 Thes 1:5.
12:13 2 Cor 11:9–12.

14 Now I am ready to come to you this third
time. And I will not be a burden, for I want not
what is yours, but you. Children ought not to
save for their parents, but parents for their chil-
dren. 15 I will most gladly spend and be utterly
spent for your sakes. If I love you more, am I
to be loved less? 16* But granted that I myself
did not burden you, yet I was crafty and got the
better of you by deceit. 17 Did I take advantage
of you through any of those I sent to you? 18* I
urged Titus to go and sent the brother with him.
Did Titus take advantage of you? Did we not
walk in the same spirit? And in the same steps?

Final Warnings and Appeals†

19† Have you been thinking all along that we
are defending ourselves before you? In the sight
of God we are speaking in Christ, and all for
building you up, beloved. 20*† For I fear that
when I come I may find you not such as I wish,
and that you may find me not as you wish; that
there may be rivalry, jealousy, fury, selfishness,
slander, gossip, conceit, and disorder. 21† I fear
that when I come again my God may humiliate
me before you, and I may have to mourn over
many of those who sinned earlier and have not
repented of the impurity, immorality, and licen-
tiousness they practiced.

13 1*† This third time I am coming to you.
"On the testimony of two or three witnesses
a fact shall be established." 2† I warned those
who sinned earlier and all the others, and I warn
them now while absent, as I did when present
on my second visit, that if I come again I will not

†

12:19—13:10 This concludes the development begun in ch 10. In the chiastic arrangement of the material (see the note on 10:1—13:10), this final part corresponds to the opening; there are important similarities of content between the two sections as well.

12:19 This verse looks back at the previous chapters and calls them by their proper name, a defense, an *apologia* (cf 1 Cor 9:3). Yet Paul insists on an important distinction: he has indeed been speaking for their benefit, but the ultimate judgment to which he submits is God's (cf 1 Cor 4:3–5). This verse also leads into the final section, announcing two of its themes: judgment and building up.

12:20 *I fear that . . . :* earlier Paul expressed fear that the Corinthians were being victimized, exploited, seduced from right thinking by his opponents (11:3–4, 19–21). Here he alludes unexpectedly to moral disorders among the Corinthians themselves. The catalogue suggests the effects of factions that have grown up around rival apostles.

12:21 *Again:* one can also translate, "I fear that when I come my God may again humiliate me." Paul's allusion to the humiliation and mourning that may await him recall the mood he described in 2:1–4, but there is no reference here to any individual such as there is in 2:5–11. The crisis of ch 2 has happily been resolved by integration of the offender and repentance (7:4–16), whereas 12:21 is preoccupied with still unrepentant sinners. The sexual sins recall 1 Cor 5–7.

13:1 *This third time I am coming:* designation of the forthcoming visit as the "third" (cf 12:14) may indicate that, in addition to his founding sojourn in Corinth, Paul had already made the first of two visits mentioned as planned in 1:15, and the next visit will be the long-postponed second of these. If so, the materials in 1:12—2:13 plus 7:4–16 and chs 10–13 may date from the same period of time, presumably of some duration, between Paul's second and third visit, though it is not clear that they are addressing the same crisis. The chronology is too unsure and the relations between sections of 2 Corinthians too unclear to yield any certainty. The hypothesis that chs 10–13 are themselves the "tearful letter" mentioned at 2:3–4 creates more problems than it solves.

13:2 *I warned those who sinned earlier:* mention of unrepentant sinners (12:21 and here) and of an oral admonition given them on an earlier visit complicates the picture at the very end of Paul's development. It provides, in fact, a second explanation for the show of power that has been threatened from the beginning (10:1–6), but a different reason for it, quite unsuspected until now. It is not clear whether Paul is merely alluding to a dimension of the situation that he has not previously had occasion to mention, or whether some other community crisis, not directly connected with that behind chs 10–13, has influenced the final editing. *I will not be lenient:* contrast Paul's hesitation and reluctance to inflict pain in 1:23 and 2:1–4. The next visit will bring the showdown.

*

12:16 2 Cor 11:3, 13.
12:18 2 Cor 2:13; 8:16, 23.
12:20 1 Cor 1:11; 3:3.
13:1 Dt 19:15; Mt 18:16; Jn 8:17; Heb 10:28.

Live It!

A Spiritual Checkup

STOP! How often do you take a break from all the activities in your life to do a spiritual checkup on your relationships with God, other people, and yourself? In 2 Corinthians 13:5–7, Paul suggests that the Corinthians give themselves a spiritual self-check. This is good advice for us today as well.

A stop sign is a good guiding image for a spiritual checkup. It signals you to interrupt the motion of life and look at what's going on around you. Each letter of the sign can be a reminder to check a different area of your spiritual life:

- *S* can stand for "seek." Do you seek information, counsel, and help when facing difficult or confusing situations and choices?
- *T* can stand for "think." Do you honestly think about how your actions and behaviors affect you, others, and your relationship with God?
- *O* can stand for "others." Do you make it a priority to reach out and support others—particularly those in great need? Are you there for your family and friends?
- *P* can stand for "pray." Do you turn to God for guidance in your life? for the strength to do what is right? Do you thank God for your blessings and the struggles that make you stronger?

▶ 2 Cor 13:5–7

be lenient, 3† since you are looking for proof of
Christ speaking in me. He is not weak toward you
but powerful in you. 4 For indeed he was crucified
out of weakness, but he lives by the power of God.
So also we are weak in him, but toward you we
shall live with him by the power of God.
5† Examine yourselves to see whether you are
living in faith. Test yourselves. Do you not real-
ize that Jesus Christ is in you?—unless, of course,
you fail the test. 6 I hope you will discover that
we have not failed. 7 But we pray to God that
you may not do evil, not that we may appear to
have passed the test but that you may do what is
right, even though we may seem to have failed.
8 For we cannot do anything against the truth,
but only for the truth. 9 For we rejoice when we
are weak but you are strong. What we pray for is
your improvement.
10*† I am writing this while I am away, so that
when I come I may not have to be severe in vir-
tue of the authority that the Lord has given me to
build up and not to tear down.

V: Conclusion

11† Finally, brothers, rejoice. Mend your ways,
encourage one another, agree with one another,
live in peace, and the God of love and peace will
be with you. 12* Greet one another with a holy
kiss. All the holy ones greet you.
13* The grace of the Lord Jesus Christ and the
love of God and the fellowship of the holy Spirit
be with all of you.

†

13:3–4 Paul now gives another motive for severity when he comes, the charge of weakness leveled against him as an apostle. The motive echoes more closely the opening section (10:1–18) and the intervening development (especially 11:30—12:10). *Proof of Christ speaking in me:* the threat of 10:1–2 is reworded to recall Paul's conformity with the pattern of Christ, his insertion into the interplay of death and life, weakness and power (cf the note on 12:10b).

13:5–9 Paul turns the challenge mentioned in v 3 on them: they are to put themselves to the test to demonstrate whether Christ is in them. These verses involve a complicated series of plays on the theme of *dokimē* (testing, proof, passing and failing a test). Behind this stands the familiar distinction between present human judgment and final divine judgment. This is the final appearance of the theme (cf 10:18; 11:15; 12:19).

13:10 *Authority . . . to build up and not to tear down:* Paul restates the purpose of his letter in language that echoes 10:2, 8, emphasizing the positive purpose of his authority in their regard. This verse forms an inclusion with the topic sentence of the section (12:19), as well as with the opening of this entire portion of the letter (10:1–2).

13:11–13 These verses may have originally concluded chs 10–13, but they have nothing specifically to do with the material of that section. It is also possible to consider them a conclusion to the whole of 2 Corinthians in its present edited form. The exhortations are general, including a final appeal for peace in the community. The letter ends calmly, after its many storms, with the prospect of ecclesial unity and divine blessing. The final verse is one of the clearest trinitarian passages in the New Testament.

*

13:10 2 Cor 10:8.
13:12 Rom 16:16; 1 Cor 16:20 / Phil 4:22; 1 Thes 5:26; 1 Pt 5:14.
13:13 Rom 16:20; 1 Cor 16:23.

The Letter to the Galatians

Do you ever scan a letter before you start to read, to see what mood the writer was in? Try it with Galatians. Notice that Paul is angry and upset. He was weak and sick when he founded the church in Galatia. Now, everything is falling apart. He feels like a mother who has to give birth to her children all over again (see 4:12–20). Why? Paul is afraid the Galatians are trading in the true Gospel, based on faith in Jesus, for a false gospel based on Jewish rules and customs.

In Depth

Jesus, the disciples, and most of the first Christians were Jewish. When Gentiles (non-Jews) started to become Christians, a question came up that almost split the early Christian community: Do Gentiles have to become Jewish before they can become Christian? The whole debate soon centered around the Jewish ritual of circumcision. (Circumcision is the surgical removal of the foreskin of a male's penis, which for Jews is the mark of the covenant.)

Paul insisted that circumcision—and all the other Jewish ceremonial laws—had nothing to do with faith in Jesus and was unnecessary for Gentile Christians. At the Council of Jerusalem (see Acts of the Apostles, chapter 15), the other Apostles reluctantly agreed with Paul. But the argument wasn't over. Other Christian missionaries came to Galatia after Paul left the Christian community there. They implied that faith in Christ wasn't enough and insisted that Gentile Christians must be circumcised. The Galatian churches seemed to have agreed because they accepted this difficult teaching quickly.

When Paul heard of this, he was mad! In his Letter to the Galatians, he doesn't even include his typical thanksgiving at the end of his greeting but launches right into his concern. He starts by defending his apostleship. He goes on to tell how the other Apostles at the Council of Jerusalem had agreed with him that the Gentiles do not need to be circumcised. He states how he later challenged Peter personally when Peter allowed himself to be influenced by missionaries preaching something else.

In his fervor, Paul confronts the Galatians: "I am afraid on your account that perhaps I have labored for you in vain" (4:11). He condemns the false missionaries: "If anyone preaches to you a gospel other than the one that you received, let that one be accursed!" (1:9). Paul is defending the freedom of Gentile Christians from having to obey Jewish religious laws. He is writing the Christians' declaration of independence: "Christ set us free" (5:1).

At a Glance

I. Address (1:1–5).

II. Loyalty to the Gospel (1:6–10).

III. Paul's Defense of His Gospel and His Authority (1:11—2:21).

IV. Faith and Liberty (3:1—4:31).

V. Exhortation to Christian Living (5:1—6:10).

VI. Conclusion (6:11–18).

Quick Facts

Inspired Author: Paul
Date: from AD 54 to 55
Audience: Gentile Christian churches, probably in northern Galatia

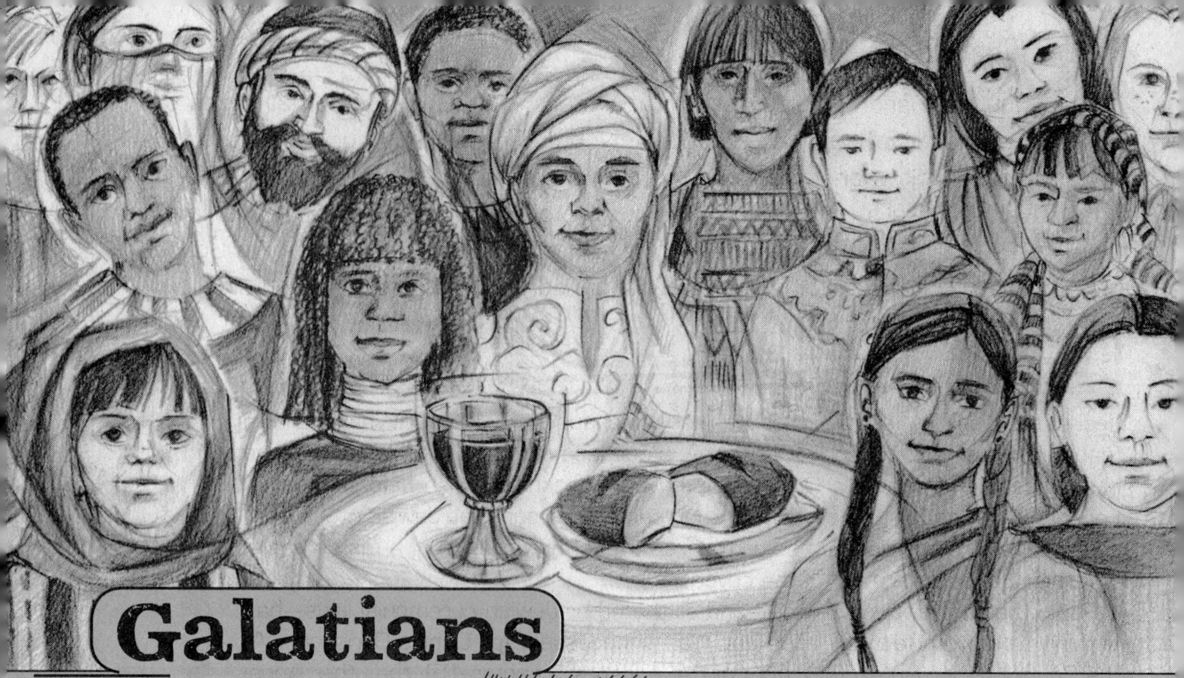

Galatians

3:28

I: Address

Greeting†

1 [1]*† Paul, an apostle not from human beings
nor through a human being but through Jesus
Christ and God the Father who raised him from
the dead,* [2]† and all the brothers who are with
me, to the churches of Galatia: [3]grace to you and
peace from God our Father and the Lord Jesus
Christ, [4]*† who gave himself for our sins that he
might rescue us from the present evil age in accord with the will of our God and Father, [5]* to
whom be glory forever and ever. Amen.

II: Loyalty to the Gospel†

[6]*† I am amazed that you are so quickly forsaking the one who called you by [the] grace [of
Christ] for a different gospel [7](not that there is
another). But there are some who are disturbing you and wish to pervert the gospel of Christ.
[8]*† But even if we or an angel from heaven should
preach [to you] a gospel other than the one that
we preached to you, let that one be accursed! [9]As
we have said before, and now I say again, if anyone preaches to you a gospel other than the one
that you received, let that one be accursed!

[10]*† Am I now currying favor with human beings or God? Or am I seeking to please people? If
I were still trying to please people, I would not be
a slave of Christ.

III: Paul's Defense of His Gospel and His Authority

His Call by Christ

[11]*† Now I want you to know, brothers, that
the gospel preached by me is not of human

†

1:1–5 See the note on Rom 1:1–7, concerning the greeting.

1:1 *Apostle:* because of attacks on his authority in Galatia, Paul defends his apostleship. He is not an apostle commissioned by a congregation (Phil 2:25; 2 Cor 8:23) or even by prophets (1 Tm 1:18 and 4:14) but *through Jesus Christ and God the Father.*

1:2 *All the brothers:* fellow believers in Christ, male and female; cf 3:27–28. Paul usually mentions the co-sender(s) at the start of a letter, but the use of *all* is unique, adding weight to the letter. *Galatia:* central Turkey more likely than the Roman province of Galatia; see Introduction.

1:4 The greeting in v 3 is expanded by a christological formula that stresses deliverance through the Lord Jesus from a world dominated by Satan; cf 2 Cor 4:4; Eph 2:2; 6:12.

1:6–10 In place of the usual thanksgiving (see the note on Rom 1:8), Paul, with little to be thankful for in the Galatian situation, expresses amazement at the way his converts are deserting the gospel of Christ for a perverted message. He reasserts the one gospel he has preached (7–9) and begins to defend himself (10).

1:6 *The one who called you:* God or Christ, though in actuality Paul was the divine instrument to call the Galatians.

1:8 *Accursed:* in Greek, *anathema;* cf Rom 9:3; 1 Cor 12:3; 16:22.

1:10 This charge by Paul's opponents, that he sought to conciliate people with flattery and to curry favor with God, might refer to his mission practices (cf 1 Cor 9:19–23) but the word *still* suggests it refers to his pre-Christian days (cf 14; Phil 3:6). The self-description *slave of Christ* is one Paul often uses in a greeting (Rom 1:1).

1:11—2:21 Paul's presentation on behalf of his message and of his apostleship reflects rhetorical forms of his day: he first narrates the facts about certain past events (1:12—2:14) and then states his contention regarding justification by faith as the gospel message (2:15–21).

1:1–3 Rom 1:1–7; 1 Cor 1:1–3.
1:1 Gal 1:11–12.
1:4 Gal 2:20; Eph 5:2; 1 Tm 2:6 / 1 Jn 5:19 / Rom 12:2; Eph 5:16; Heb 10:10.
1:5 Rom 16:27; 2 Tm 4:18.
1:6–7 Gal 5:8, 10; Acts 15:1, 24; 2 Cor 11:4.
1:8–9 1 Cor 16:22 / Gal 5:3, 21; 2 Cor 13:2.
1:10 2 Cor 5:11 / 1 Thes 2:4.
1:11–12 1 Cor 15:1 / Gal 1:1; Eph 3:3.

origin. 12† For I did not receive it from a human
being, nor was I taught it, but it came through a
revelation of Jesus Christ.
13*† For you heard of my former way of life
in Judaism, how I persecuted the church of God
beyond measure and tried to destroy it, 14* and
progressed in Judaism beyond many of my con-
temporaries among my race, since I was even
more a zealot for my ancestral traditions. 15* But
when [God], who from my mother's womb had
set me apart and called me through his grace,
was pleased 16*† to reveal his Son to me, so that
I might proclaim him to the Gentiles, I did not
immediately consult flesh and blood, 17† nor did
I go up to Jerusalem to those who were apostles
before me; rather, I went into Arabia and then
returned to Damascus.
18*† Then after three years† I went up to Jeru-
salem to confer with Cephas and remained with
him for fifteen days. 19*† But I did not see any
other of the apostles, only James the brother of
the Lord. 20* (As to what I am writing to you,
behold, before God, I am not lying.) 21* Then I
went into the regions of Syria and Cilicia. 22 And
I was unknown personally to the churches of
Judea that are in Christ; 23* they only kept hear-
ing that "the one who once was persecuting us
is now preaching the faith he once tried to de-
stroy." 24 So they glorified God because of me.

The Council of Jerusalem†

2 1* Then after fourteen years† I again went
up to Jerusalem with Barnabas, taking Titus
along also. 2*† I went up in accord with a reve-
lation, and I presented to them the gospel that I
preach to the Gentiles—but privately to those of
repute—so that I might not be running, or have
run, in vain. 3*† Moreover, not even Titus, who
was with me, although he was a Greek, was com-
pelled to be circumcised, 4*† but because of the
false brothers secretly brought in, who slipped
in to spy on our freedom that we have in Christ
Jesus, that they might enslave us— 5*† to them
we did not submit even for a moment, so that the
truth of the gospel might remain intact for you.
6* But from those who were reputed to be impor-
tant (what they once were makes no difference to
me; God shows no partiality)—those of repute

---

† Further arguments follow from both experience and scripture in chs 3 and 4, before he draws out the ethical consequences (5:1—6:10). The specific facts that he takes up here to show that his gospel is not a human invention (1:11) but *came through a revelation of Jesus Christ* (1:12) deal with his own calling as a Christian missionary (1:13–17), his initial relations with the apostles in Jerusalem (1:18–24), a later journey to Jerusalem (2:1–10), and an incident in Antioch involving Cephas and persons from James (2:11–14). The content of Paul's revealed gospel is then set forth in the heart of the letter (2:15–21).

1:12 Although Paul received his gospel *through a revelation* from Christ, this did not exclude his use of early Christian confessional formulations. See the note on 1:4.

1:13–17 Along with Phil 3:4–11, which also moves from autobiography to its climax in a discussion on justification by faith (cf Gal 2:15–21), this passage is Paul's chief account of the change from his *former way of life* (13) to service as a Christian missionary (16); cf Acts 9:1–22; 22:4–16; 26:9–18. Paul himself does not use the term "conversion" but stresses revelation (12, 16). In v 15 his language echoes the Old Testament prophetic call of Jeremiah. Unlike the account in Acts (cf 22:4–16), the calling of Paul here includes the mission to proclaim Christ *to the Gentiles* (16).

1:16 *Flesh and blood:* human authorities (cf Mt 16:17; 1 Cor 15:50). Paul's apostleship comes from God (1).

1:17 *Arabia:* probably the region of the Nabataean Arabs, east and south of Damascus.

1:18–24 Paul's first journey to Jerusalem as a Christian, according to Galatians (cf Acts 9:23–31 and the note on Acts 12:25). He is quite explicit about contacts there, testifying under oath (20). On returning to *Syria* (perhaps specifically Damascus, cf v 17) *and Cilicia* (including his home town Tarsus, cf Acts 9:30; 22:3), Paul most likely engaged in missionary work. He underscores the fact that Christians in Judea knew of him only by reputation.

1:18 *After three years:* two years and more, since Paul's call. To *confer with* Cephas may mean simply "pay a visit" or more specifically "get information from" him about Jesus, over a two-week period. *Cephas:* Aramaic name of Simon (Peter); cf Mt 16:16–18 and the notes there.

1:19 *James the brother of the Lord:* not one of the Twelve, but a brother of Jesus (see the note on Mk 6:3). He played an important role in the Jerusalem church (see the note on Gal 2:9), the leadership of which he took over from Peter (Acts 12:17). Paul may have regarded James as an apostle.

2:1–10 Paul's second journey to Jerusalem, according to Galatians, involved a private meeting with *those of repute* (2). At issue was a Gentile, Titus, and the question of circumcision, which *false brothers* (4) evidently demanded for him. Paul insists that the gospel he preaches (2; cf 1:9, 11) remained intact with no addition by those of repute (6); that *Titus* was not *compelled* to accept circumcision (3); and that he and the reputed *pillars* in Jerusalem agreed on how each would advance the missionary task (7–10). Usually, 1–10 is equated with the "Council of Jerusalem," as it is called, described in Acts 15. See the notes on Acts 15:6–12 and 15:13–35, the latter concerning the "decree" that Paul does not mention.

2:1 *After fourteen years:* thirteen or more years, probably reckoned from the return to Syria and Cilicia (1:21), though possibly from Paul's calling as a Christian (1:15). *Barnabas:* cf 9, 13; 1 Cor 9:6. A Jewish Christian missionary, with whom Paul worked (Acts 4:36–37; 11:22, 25, 30; 12:25; 13:1–3; 15:2). *Titus:* a missionary companion of Paul (2 Cor 2:13; 7:6, 13–15; 8:6, 16, 23; 12:18), non-Jewish (Gal 2:3), never mentioned in Acts.

2:2 *A revelation:* cf 1:1, 12. Paul emphasizes it was God's will, not Jerusalem authority, that led to the journey. Acts 15:2 states that the church in Antioch appointed Paul and Barnabas for the task. *Those of repute:* leaders of the Jerusalem church; the term, while positive, may be slightly ironic (cf 6, 9). *Run, in vain:* while Paul presents a positive picture in what follows, his missionary work in Galatia would have been to no purpose if his opponents were correct that circumcision is needed for complete faith in Christ.

2:3 *Not even* a Gentile Christian like Titus was compelled to receive the rite of circumcision. The Greek text could be interpreted that he voluntarily accepted circumcision, but this is unlikely in the overall argument.

2:4 *False brothers:* Jewish Christians who took the position that Gentile Christians must first become Jews through circumcision and observance of the Mosaic law in order to become Christians; cf Acts 15:1.

2:5 *The truth of the gospel:* the true gospel, in contrast to the false one of the opponents (1:6–9); the gospel of grace, used as a norm (14).

---

* **1:13** Acts 8:1–3; 9:1–2; 1 Cor 15:9. **1:14** Acts 26:4–5. **1:15** Is 49:1; Jer 1:4. **1:16** Gal 1:11–12; Rom 1:5; 1 Cor 15:10; Acts 9:3–9 / Gal 2:2, 7 / Mt 16:17. **1:18** Acts 9:26–30 / Jn 1:42. **1:19** Gal 2:9; Mt 13:55; Acts 12:17. **1:20** Rom 9:1; 2 Cor 11:31. **1:21** Acts 9:30. **1:23** Gal 1:13. **2:1** Acts 15:2. **2:2** Gal 1:11–12, 16 / Gal 1:16 / Phil 2:16. **2:3** 2 Cor 2:13; 7:6–7; 8:16–17; 12:18; Ti 1:4 / Gal 2:14; 6:12. **2:4** Gal 5:1; Acts 15:1, 24. **2:5** Gal 2:14; 4:16. **2:6** Dt 10:17; Rom 2:11.

GAL

made me add nothing. 7*† On the contrary, when they saw that I had been entrusted with the gospel to the uncircumcised, just as Peter to the circumcised, 8 for the one who worked in Peter for an apostolate to the circumcised worked also in me for the Gentiles, 9*† and when they recognized the grace bestowed upon me, James and Cephas and John, who were reputed to be pillars, gave me and Barnabas their right hands in partnership, that we should go to the Gentiles and they to the circumcised. 10*† Only, we were to be mindful of the poor, which is the very thing I was eager to do.

Peter's Inconsistency at Antioch†

11*† And when Cephas came to Antioch, I opposed him to his face because he clearly was wrong. 12*† For, until some people came from James, he used to eat with the Gentiles; but when they came, he began to draw back and separated himself, because he was afraid of the circumcised. 13*† And the rest of the Jews [also] acted hypocritically along with him, with the result that even Barnabas was carried away by their hypocrisy. 14*† But when I saw that they were not on the right road in line with the truth of the gospel, I said to Cephas in front of all, "If you, though a Jew, are living like a Gentile and not like a Jew, how can you compel the Gentiles to live like Jews?"

Faith and Works

15† We, who are Jews by nature and not sinners

Live It!

Consistent and Trustworthy

At the beginning of Galatians, chapter 2, Paul describes what went on at the Council of Jerusalem. The Council established that Gentile Christians do not have to become Jews by following certain Jewish laws, such as circumcision and dietary regulations, to gain admission to the Christian community. Paul emphasizes that a person is made right with God (justified) not through the law but through faith in Jesus Christ.

In Antioch, when Peter (Cephas) stops eating with Gentile Christians under pressure from Jewish Christians, Paul challenges him. He points out that Peter's behavior is not consistent with the truth of the Gospel and that this inconsistency is misleading and confusing to the Christian community.

A credible Christian seeks to be consistent in word and deed. Unfortunately, Peter's actions speak much louder than his words. And, like Peter, when our actions do not match our words, people stop trusting us. And then we too begin to feel like hypocrites and lose our self-esteem.

Take some time to reflect on how consistently your actions reflect your words. Consider ways you can improve. When your actions match your words, people will recognize you as a person of integrity and place their trust in you.

▶ Gal 2:11–14

2:7–9 Some think that actual "minutes" of the meeting are here quoted. Paul's apostleship to the Gentiles (1:16) is recognized alongside that of Peter to the Jews. Moreover, the right to proclaim the gospel without requiring circumcision and the Jewish law is sealed by a handshake. That Paul and colleagues *should go to the Gentiles* did not exclude his preaching to the Jews as well (Rom 1:13–16) or Cephas to Gentile areas.

2:9 *James and Cephas and John:* see the notes on 1:18 and 19; on Peter and John as leaders in the Jerusalem church, cf Acts 3:1 and 8:14. The order here, with James first, may reflect his prominence in Jerusalem after Peter (Cephas) departed (Acts 12:17).

2:10 *The poor:* Jerusalem Christians or a group within the church there (cf Rom 15:26). The collection for them was extremely important in Paul's thought and labor (cf Rom 15:25–28; 1 Cor 16:1–4; 2 Cor 8 and 9).

2:11–14 The decision reached in Jerusalem (3–7) recognized the freedom of Gentile Christians from the Jewish law. But the problem of table fellowship between Jewish Christians, who possibly still kept kosher food regulations, and Gentile believers was not yet settled. When Cephas first came to the racially mixed community of Jewish and Gentile Christians in Antioch (12), he ate with non-Jews. Pressure from persons arriving later from Jerusalem caused him and Barnabas to draw back. Paul therefore publicly rebuked Peter's inconsistency toward the gospel (14). Some think that what Paul said on that occasion extends through v 16 or v 21.

2:11 *Clearly was wrong:* literally, "stood condemned," by himself and also by Paul. His action in breaking table fellowship was especially grievous if the eating involved the meal at the Lord's supper (cf 1 Cor 11:17–25).

2:12 *Some people came from James:* strict Jewish Christians (cf Acts 15:1, 5; 21:20–21), either sent by James (1:19; 2:9) or claiming to be from the leader of the Jerusalem church. *The circumcised:* presumably Jewish Christians, not Jews.

2:13 *The Jews:* Jewish Christians, like Barnabas. *Hypocrisy:* literally, "pretense," "play-acting"; moral insincerity.

2:14 *Compel the Gentiles to live like Jews:* that is, conform to Jewish practices, such as circumcision (3–5) or regulations about food (12).

2:15–21 Following on the series of incidents cited above, Paul's argument, whether spoken to Cephas at Antioch or only now articulated, is pertinent to the Galatian situation, where believers were having themselves circumcised (6:12–13) and obeying other aspects of Jewish law (4:9–10; 5:1–4). He insists that salvation is by faith in Christ, not by works of the law. His teaching on the gospel concerns justification by faith (16) in relation to sin (17), law (19), life in Christ (19–20), and grace (21).

2:7 Gal 1:15–16; Acts 9:15; 15:12; 22:21; Rom 1:5.
2:9 Rom 15:15 / Gal 1:18–19; Jn 1:42; Acts 12:17 / Gal 2:1.
2:10 Acts 11:29–30; Rom 15:25–28; 1 Cor 16:1–4; 2 Cor 8:9.
2:11 Gal 1:18 / Acts 11:19–30; 15:1–2.
2:12 Acts 10:15, 28; 11:3.
2:13 Gal 2:1, 9.
2:14 Gal 2:5 / Gal 1:18; 2:9 / Gal 2:3.

from among the Gentiles, 16*† [yet] who know
that a person is not justified by works of the law
but through faith in Jesus Christ, even we have
believed in Christ Jesus that we may be justified
by faith in Christ and not by works of the law,
because by works of the law no one will be justi-
fied. 17† But if, in seeking to be justified in Christ,
we ourselves are found to be sinners, is Christ
then a minister of sin? Of course not! 18† But if
I am building up again those things that I tore
down, then I show myself to be a transgressor.
19*† For through the law I died to the law, that
I might live for God. I have been crucified with
Christ; 20* yet I live, no longer I, but Christ lives
in me; insofar as I now live in the flesh, I live by
faith in the Son of God who has loved me and
given himself up for me. 21* I do not nullify the
grace of God; for if justification comes through
the law, then Christ died for nothing.

IV: Faith and Liberty

Justification by Faith†

3 1*† O stupid Galatians! Who has bewitched
you, before whose eyes Jesus Christ was
publicly portrayed as crucified? 2*† I want to
learn only this from you: did you receive the
Spirit from works of the law, or from faith in
what you heard? 3*† Are you so stupid? After
beginning with the Spirit, are you now end-
ing with the flesh? 4† Did you experience so
many things in vain?—if indeed it was in vain.
5* Does, then, the one who supplies the Spirit to
you and works mighty deeds among you do so
from works of the law or from faith in what you
heard? 6*† Thus Abraham "believed God, and it
was credited to him as righteousness."
7*† Realize then that it is those who have
faith who are children of Abraham. 8* Scripture,
which saw in advance that God would justify the
Gentiles by faith, foretold the good news to Abra-
ham, saying, "Through you shall all the nations
be blessed." 9* Consequently, those who have
faith are blessed along with Abraham who had
faith. 10*† For all who depend on works of the

Did You Know?

Justified in Christ

Throughout Galatians, Paul speaks about the difference between being justified by faith and being justified through the law. Christians believe they are justified—made right with God—not through a perfect keeping of religious laws, but through God's free gift to those who have faith in Christ. Christ's saving sacrifice alone will set them free from their sin. Their trust must be in him and not in their own ability to please God. God gives us the grace needed to live as children of God.

▶ **Gal 3:1—4:7**

2:16 *No one will be justified:* Ps 143:2 is reflected.

2:17 *A minister of sin:* literally, "a servant of sin" (cf Rom 15:8), an agent of sin, one who promotes it. This is possibly a claim by opponents that justification on the basis of faith in Christ makes Christ an abettor of sin when Christians *are found to be sinners.* Paul denies the conclusion (cf Rom 6:1–4).

2:18 To return to observance of the law as the means to salvation would entangle one not only in inevitable transgressions of it but also in the admission that it was wrong to have abandoned the law in the first place.

2:19 *Through the law I died to the law:* this is variously explained: the law revealed sin (Rom 7:7–9) and led to death and then to belief in Christ; or, the law itself brought the insight that law cannot justify (16; Ps 143:2); or, the "law of Christ" (6:2) led to abandoning the Mosaic law; or, the law put Christ to death (cf 3:13) and so provided a way to our salvation, through baptism into Christ, through which we die (*crucified with Christ;* see Rom 6:6). Cf also 3:19–25 on the role of the law in reference to salvation.

3:1–14 Paul's contention that justification comes not through the law or the works of the law but by faith in Christ and in his death (2:16, 21) is supported by appeals to Christian experience (1–5) and to scripture (6–14). The gift of God's Spirit to the Galatians came from the gospel received in faith, not from doing what the law enjoins. The story of Abraham shows that faith in God brings *righteousness* (6; Gn 15:6). The promise to Abraham (8; Gn 12:3) extends to the Gentiles (14).

3:1 *Stupid:* not just senseless, for they were in danger of deserting their salvation.

3:2 *Faith in what you heard:* Paul's message received with faith. The Greek can also mean "the proclamation of the faith" or "a hearing that comes from faith."

3:3 On the contrast of *Spirit* and *flesh,* cf Rom 8:1–11. Having received the Spirit, they need not be circumcised now.

3:4 *Experience so many things:* probably the *mighty deeds* of v 5 but possibly the experience of sufferings.

3:6 *Abraham . . . righteousness:* see Gn 15:6; Rom 4:3. The Galatians like Abraham heard with faith and experienced justification. This first argument forms the basis for the further scriptural evidence that follows.

3:7–9 *Faith* is what matters, for *Abraham* and the *children of Abraham,* in contrast to the claims of the opponents that circumcision and observance of the law are needed to bring the promised blessing of Gn 12:3; cf Gn 18:18; Sir 44:21; Acts 3:25.

3:10–14 Those *who depend* not on promise and faith but *on works of the law are under a curse* because they do *not persevere in doing all the things written in the book of the law* (10; Dt 27:26) in order to gain life (12; Lv 18:5; cf Rom 10:5). But scripture teaches that *no one is justified before God by the law* (11; Hb 2:4, adapted from the Greek version of Habakkuk; cf Rom 1:17; Heb 10:38). Salvation, then, depends on faith in Christ who died on the cross

---

2:16 Gal 3:2, 11; Ps 143:1–2; Rom 3:20, 28; 4:5; 11:6; Eph 2:8–9; Phil 3:9.
2:19 Gal 6:14; Rom 6:6, 8, 10; 7:6.
2:20 Gal 1:4; Rom 8:10–11; Col 3:3–4.
2:21 Gal 5:2.
3:1 Gal 5:7; 1 Cor 1:23.
3:2 Gal 2:16 / Gal 3:14; Rom 10:17.
3:3 Gal 5:16–18.
3:5 Gal 2:16.
3:6 Gn 15:6; Rom 4:3; Jas 2:23.
3:7 Gal 3:29; Rom 4:11–12 / Sir 44:19–21.
3:8 Gn 12:3; 18:17–19; Acts 3:25.
3:9 Rom 4:16.
3:10 Dt 27:26; Jas 2:10.

law are under a curse; for it is written, "Cursed be everyone who does not persevere in doing all the things written in the book of the law." 11* And that no one is justified before God by the law is clear, for "the one who is righteous by faith will live." 12* But the law does not depend on faith; rather, "the one who does these things will live by them." 13* Christ ransomed us from the curse of the law by becoming a curse for us, for it is written, "Cursed be everyone who hangs on a tree," 14* that the blessing of Abraham might be extended to the Gentiles through Christ Jesus, so that we might receive the promise of the Spirit through faith.

"There is neither Jew nor Greek, there is neither slave nor free person, there is not male and female; for you are all one in Christ Jesus."
(Gal 3:28)

The Law Did Not Nullify the Promise

15*† Brothers, in human terms I say that no one can annul or amend even a human will once ratified. 16*† Now the promises were made to Abraham and to his descendant. It does not say, "And to descendants," as referring to many, but as referring to one, "And to your descendant," who is Christ. 17*† This is what I mean: the law, which came four hundred and thirty years afterward, does not annul a covenant previously ratified by God, so as to cancel the promise. 18*† For if the inheritance comes from the law, it is no longer from a promise; but God bestowed it on Abraham through a promise.

19*† Why, then, the law? It was added for transgressions, until the descendant† came to whom the promise had been made; it was promulgated by angels at the hand of a mediator. 20* Now there is no mediator when only one party is involved, and God is one. 21* Is the law then opposed to the promises [of God]? Of course not! For if a law had been given that could bring life, then righteousness would in reality come from the law. 22* But scripture confined all things under the power of sin, that through faith in Jesus Christ the promise might be given to those who believe.

What Faith Has Brought Us

23*† Before faith came, we were held in custody under law, confined for the faith that was to be revealed. 24*† Consequently, the law was our disciplinarian for Christ, that we might be justified by faith. 25* But now that faith has come, we are no longer under a disciplinarian. 26*† For through faith you are all children of God in Christ Jesus. 27*† For all of you who were

---

† (13), taking upon himself a curse found in Dt 21:23 (about executed criminals hanged in public view), to free us from *the curse of the law* (13). That the Gentile Galatians have received the promised Spirit (14) by faith and in no other way returns the argument to the experience cited in vv 1–5.

3:15–18 A third argument to support Paul's position that salvation is not through the law but by promise (1–14) comes from legal practice and scriptural history. A legal agreement or *human will,* duly *ratified,* is unalterable (15). God's *covenant* with *Abraham* and its repeated promises (Gn 12:2–3, 7; 13:15; 17:7–8; 22:16–18; 24:7) is not superseded by *the law,* which came much later, in the time of Moses. *The inheritance* (of the Spirit and the blessings) is by promise, not by law (18). Paul's argument hinges on the fact that the same Greek word, *diathēkē,* can be rendered as *will* or testament (15) and as *covenant* (17).

3:16 *Descendant:* literally, "and to his seed." The Hebrew, as in Gn 12:7; 15:18; 22:17–18, is a collective singular, traditionally rendered as a plural, *descendants,* but taken by Paul in its literal number to refer to *Christ* as descendant of Abraham.

3:17 *Four hundred and thirty years afterward:* follows Ex 12:40 in the Greek (Septuagint) version, in contrast to Gn 15:13 and Acts 7:6, for chronology.

3:18 This refutes the opponents' contention that the promises of God are fulfilled only as a reward for human observance of the law.

3:19–22 A digression: if the Mosaic law, then, does not save or *bring life,* why was it given? Elsewhere, Paul says the law served to show what sin is (Rom 3:20; 7:7–8). Here the further implication is that the law in effect served to produce transgressions. Moreover, it was received at second hand *by angels,* through a *mediator,* not directly from God (19). The law does not, however, oppose God's purposes, for it carries out its function (22), so that *righteousness* comes by *faith* and *promise,* not by human works of the law.

3:19 *The descendant:* Christ (16). *By angels:* Dt 33:2–4 stressed their presence as enhancing the importance of the law; Paul uses their role to diminish its significance (cf Acts 7:38, 53). *A mediator:* Moses. But in a covenant of promise, where all depends on the one God, no mediator is needed (20).

3:23–29 Paul adds a further argument in support of righteousness or justification by faith and through God's promise rather than by works of the law (2:16; 3:22): as *children of God, baptized into Christ,* the Galatians are all *Abraham's descendant* and *heirs* of the *promise* to Abraham (8, 14, 16–18, 29). The teaching in 23–25, that since *faith* (Christianity) *has come, we are no longer under* the law, could be taken with the previous paragraph on the role of the Mosaic law, but it also fits here as a contrast between the situation *before faith* (23) and the results after faith has come (25–29).

3:24–25 *Disciplinarian:* the Greek *paidagōgos* referred to a slave who escorted a child to school but did not teach or tutor; hence, a guardian or monitor. Applying this to the law fits the role of the law described in vv 19–25.

3:26 *Children of God:* literally "sons," in contrast to the young child under the disciplinarian in vv 24–25. The term includes males and females (28).

3:27–28 Likely a formula used at baptism that expresses racial, social-economic, and sexual equality in Christ (cf Col 3:11).

---

* **3:11** Gal 2:16; Hb 2:4; Rom 1:17.
3:12 Lv 18:5; Rom 10:5.
3:13 Dt 21:23; Rom 8:3; 2 Cor 5:21.
3:14 Gal 3:2–3, 5; Is 44:3; Jl 3:1–2; Acts 2:33.
3:15 Rom 3:5 / Heb 9:16–17.
3:16 Gn 12:7; 13:15; 17:8; 22:17; 24:7; Mt 1:1.
3:17 Ex 12:40.
3:18 Rom 4:16; 11:6.
3:19 Rom 4:15; 5:20; 7:7, 13 / Acts 7:38, 53.
3:20 Dt 6:4.
3:21 Rom 7:7, 10; 8:2–4.
3:22 Rom 3:9–20, 23; 11:32.
3:23 Gal 4:3–5; 5:18.
3:24 Gal 2:16.
3:25 Rom 10:4.
3:26 Gal 4:5–7; Jn 1:12; Rom 8:14–17.
3:27 Rom 6:3; 13:14; Eph 4:24.

Catholic Social Teaching

Radical Equality

Galatians 3:28 may have been an early baptismal formula. In it Paul makes a radical statement: The source of our equality as humans is Jesus Christ! (Note that the word *radical* means both "root" and "extreme"—and that Paul's statement is both fundamental to Christian belief and a great expression of that belief.)

This passage is a source of hope for all who have at times been made to feel as if they are not fully human. In Baptism we become one in Christ and, as part of the Christian community, are called to respect the equality of all living persons. This may not seem like a radical idea in our contemporary culture, but throughout history people have not always been treated as full human persons. Even today in many parts of the world there are people who find themselves treated as "less than" because of their race, ethnic background, religion, or gender.

The principles of Catholic social teaching call us to respect the dignity of all human persons and to be in solidarity with others, especially those who live on the margins. Being in solidarity means that we help to create a world in which basic human needs like food, housing, healthcare, and religious freedom are met and justice and peace are available to all.

Is Paul's vision of equality a reality in the world around you? Are all the people in your school or community regarded as equally valuable? What can you do to help create a world where all people live in solidarity?

Gal 3:28

Solidarity

baptized into Christ have clothed yourselves
with Christ.† 28* There is neither Jew nor Greek,
there is neither slave nor free person, there is not
male and female; for you are all one in Christ
Jesus. 29* And if you belong to Christ, then you
are Abraham's descendant, heirs according to the
promise.

God's Free Children in Christ†

4 1† I mean that as long as the heir is not of
age, he is no different from a slave, although
he is the owner of everything, 2 but he is under
the supervision of guardians and administrators
until the date set by his father. 3*† In the same
way we also, when we were not of age, were
enslaved to the elemental powers of the world.
4* But when the fullness of time had come, God
sent his Son, born of a woman, born under the
law, 5* to ransom those under the law, so that we
might receive adoption. 6*† As proof that you are
children, God sent the spirit of his Son into our
hearts, crying out, "Abba, Father!" 7* So you are
no longer a slave but a child, and if a child then
also an heir, through God.

Do Not Throw This Freedom Away†

8*† At a time when you did not know God,
you became slaves to things that by nature are
not gods; 9* but now that you have come to
know God, or rather to be known by God, how
can you turn back again to the weak and desti-
tute elemental powers? Do you want to be slaves

†

3:27 *Clothed yourselves with Christ:* literally, "have put on Christ"; cf Rom 13:14; Eph 4:24; Col 3:10. Baptismal imagery, traceable to the Old Testament (Jb 29:14; Is 59:17) but also found in pagan mystery cults.

4:1–7 What Paul has argued in 3:26–29 is now elaborated in terms of the Christian as *the heir* (1, 7; cf 3:18, 29) freed from control by others. Again, as in 3:2–5, the proof that Christians are children of God is the gift of the Spirit of Christ relating them intimately to God.

4:1, 3 *Not of age:* an infant or minor.

4:3 *The elemental powers of the world:* while the term can refer to the "elements" like earth, air, fire, and water or to elementary forms of religion, the sense here is more likely that of celestial beings that were thought in pagan circles to control the world; cf 8; Col 2:8, 20.

4:6 *Children:* see the note on 3:26; here in contrast to the infant or young person *not of age* (1, 3). *Abba:* cf Mk 14:36 and the note; Rom 8:15.

4:8–11 On the basis of the arguments advanced from 3:1 through 4:7, Paul now launches his appeal to the Galatians with the question, *how can you turn back* to the slavery of the law (9)? The question is posed with reference to bondage to the *elemental powers* (see the note on 4:3) because the Galatians had originally been converted to Christianity from paganism, not Judaism (8). The use of the direct question is like 3:3–5.

4:8 *Things that by nature are not gods:* or "gods that by nature do not exist."

*

3:28 Rom 10:12; 1 Cor 12:13; Col 3:11.
3:29 Gal 3:7, 14, 16, 18; Rom 4:16–17; 9:7 / Gal 4:1, 7; Rom 4:13–14; 8:17; Heb 6:12; Jas 2:5.
4:3 Gal 3:23 / Gal 4:9; Col 2:20.
4:4 Mk 1:15.
4:5 Gal 3:13, 26.
4:6 Gal 3:26; Rom 8:15.
4:7 Gal 3:29; Rom 8:16–17.
4:8 1 Cor 12:2.
4:9 Gal 4:3; Col 2:20.

to them all over again? 10*† You are observing
days, months, seasons, and years. 11† I am afraid
on your account that perhaps I have labored for
you in vain.

Appeal to Former Loyalty†

12*† I implore you, brothers, be as I am, be-
cause I have also become as you are. You did me
no wrong; 13† you know that it was because of
a physical illness that I originally preached the
gospel to you, 14 and you did not show disdain or
contempt because of the trial caused you by my
physical condition, but rather you received me as
an angel of God, as Christ Jesus. 15† Where now
is that blessedness of yours? Indeed, I can testify
to you that, if it had been possible, you would
have torn out your eyes and given them to me.
16 So now have I become your enemy by telling
you the truth? 17*† They show interest in you,
but not in a good way; they want to isolate you,
so that you may show interest in them. 18 Now
it is good to be shown interest for good reason
at all times, and not only when I am with you.
19* My children, for whom I am again in labor
until Christ be formed in you! 20 I would like to
be with you now and to change my tone, for I am
perplexed because of you.

An Allegory on Christian Freedom

21† Tell me, you who want to be under the law,
do you not listen to the law? 22* For it is written
that Abraham had two sons, one by the slave
woman and the other by the freeborn woman.
23* The son of the slave woman was born natu-
rally, the son of the freeborn through a promise.
24* Now this is an allegory. These women rep-
resent two covenants. One was from Mount
Sinai, bearing children for slavery; this is Hagar.
25† Hagar represents Sinai, a mountain in Ara-
bia; it corresponds to the present Jerusalem, for
she is in slavery along with her children. 26* But
the Jerusalem above is freeborn, and she is our
mother. 27*† For it is written:

"Rejoice, you barren one who bore no children;
break forth and shout, you who were not in
labor;
for more numerous are the children of the
deserted one
than of her who has a husband."

28* Now you, brothers, like Isaac, are children of
the promise. 29 But just as then the child of the
flesh persecuted the child of the spirit, it is the
same now. 30* But what does the scripture say?

"Drive out the slave woman and her son!
For the son of the slave woman shall not
share the inheritance with the son"

of the freeborn. 31* Therefore, brothers, we are
children not of the slave woman but of the free-
born woman.

V: Exhortation to Christian Living

The Importance of Faith†

5 1*† For freedom Christ set us free; so stand
firm and do not submit again to the yoke of
slavery.

†

4:10 This is likely a reference to ritual observances from the Old Testament, promoted by opponents: sabbaths or Yom Kippur, new moon, Passover or Pentecost, sabbatical years.

4:11 Cf 2:2. If the Galatians become *slaves . . . all over again* to the law (9), Paul will have worked in vain among them.

4:12–20 A strongly personal section. Paul appeals to past ties between the Galatians and himself. He speaks sharply of the opponents (17–18) and pastorally to the Galatians (19–20).

4:12 *Because I have also become as you are:* a terse phrase in Greek, meaning "Be as I, Paul, am," i.e., living by faith, independent of the law, for, in spite of my background in Judaism (1:13), I have become as you Galatians are now, a brother in Christ.

4:13 *Physical illness:* because its nature is not described, some assume an eye disease (15); others, epilepsy; some relate it to 2 Cor 12:7–9. *Originally:* this may also be translated "formerly" or "on the first (of two) visit(s)"; cf Acts 16:6; 18:23.

4:15 *That blessedness of yours:* possibly a reference to the Galatians' initial happy reception of Paul (14) and of his gospel (1:6; 3:1–4) and their felicitation at such blessedness, but the phrase could also refer ironically to earlier praise by Paul of the Galatians, no longer possible when they turn from the gospel to the claims of the opponents (17–18; 1:7). If the word is a more literal reference to a beatitude, Gal 3:26–28 may be in view.

4:17 *Isolate you:* that is, from the blessings of the gospel and/or from Paul.

4:21–31 Paul supports his appeal for the gospel (9; 1:6–9; 2:16; 3:2) by a further argument from scripture (cf 3:6–18). It involves the relationship of *Abraham* (3:6–16) to his wife, Sarah, the *freeborn woman,* and to Hagar, *the slave woman,* and the contrast between the sons born to each, *Isaac,* child of promise, and Ishmael, son of Hagar (Gn 16 and 21). Only through Isaac is the promise of God preserved. This *allegory* (24), with its equation of the Sinai covenant and Mosaic law with slavery and of the promise of God with freedom, Paul uses only in light of previous arguments. His quotation of Gn 21:10 at v 30 suggests on a scriptural basis that the Galatians should expel those who are troubling them (1:7).

4:25 *Hagar represents Sinai . . . :* some manuscripts have what seems a geographical note, "For Sinai is a mountain in Arabia."

4:27 Is 54:1 in the Septuagint translation is applied to Sarah as the *barren one* (in Gn 15) who ultimately becomes the mother not only of Isaac but now of numerous children, i.e., of all those who believe, the *children of the promise* (28).

5:1–6 Paul begins the exhortations, continuing through 6:10, with an appeal to the Galatians to side with freedom instead of slavery (1). He reiterates his message of justification or righteousness by faith instead of law and circumcision (2–5); cf 2:16; 3:3. Faith, not circumcision, is what counts (6).

5:1 *Freedom:* Paul stresses as the conclusion from the allegory in 4:21–31 this result of Christ's work for us. It is a principle previously

4:10 Col 2:16–20.
4:12 1 Cor 11:1.
4:17 Gal 1:7; 6:12; Acts 20:30.
4:19 1 Cor 4:14–15; 2 Cor 6:13; 1 Thes 2:7–8.
4:22 Gn 16:15; 21:2–3.
4:23 Gn 17:16; Rom 4:19–20; 9:7–9.
4:24 Gal 3:17 / Ex 19:20 / Gn 16:1.
4:26 Heb 12:22; Rv 21:2.
4:27 Is 54:1.
4:28 Rom 9:8.
4:30 Gn 21:10.
4:31 Gal 3:29; Jn 8:35.
5:1 Gal 2:4; 4:5, 9; Jn 8:32, 36.

2* It is I, Paul, who am telling you that if you
have yourselves circumcised, Christ will be of
no benefit to you. 3*† Once again I declare to
every man who has himself circumcised that
he is bound to observe the entire law. 4 You are
separated from Christ, you who are trying to
be justified by law; you have fallen from grace.
5* For through the Spirit, by faith, we await
the hope of righteousness. 6*† For in Christ
Jesus, neither circumcision nor uncircumcision
counts for anything, but only faith working
through love.

Be Not Misled†

7† You were running well; who hindered you
from following [the] truth? 8*† That enticement
does not come from the one who called you. 9* A
little yeast leavens the whole batch of dough.
10* I am confident of you in the Lord that you
will not take a different view, and that the one
who is troubling you will bear the condemna-
tion, whoever he may be. 11*† As for me, broth-
ers, if I am still preaching circumcision, why am I
still being persecuted? In that case, the stumbling
block of the cross has been abolished. 12† Would
that those who are upsetting you might also cas-
trate themselves!

Freedom for Service†

13* For you were called for freedom, brothers.
But do not use this freedom as an opportunity
for the flesh; rather, serve one another through
love.† 14*† For the whole law is fulfilled in one
statement, namely, "You shall love your neigh-
bor as yourself." 15 But if you go on biting and
devouring one another, beware that you are not
consumed by one another.
16*† I say, then: live by the Spirit and you
will certainly not gratify the desire of the flesh.
17* For the flesh has desires against the Spirit,

mentioned (2:4), the responsible use of which v 13 will emphasize.

5:3 Cf 3:10–12. Just as those who seek to live by the law must carry out all its contents, so those who have faith and live by promise must stand firm in their freedom (1, 13).

5:6 Cf Rom 2:25–26; 1 Cor 7:19; Gal 6:15. The Greek for *faith working through love* or "faith expressing itself through love" can also be rendered as "faith energized by (God's) love."

5:7–12 Paul addresses the Galatians directly: with questions (7, 11), a proverb (9), a statement (8), and biting sarcasm (12), seeking to persuade the Galatians to break with those trying to add law and circumcision to Christ as a basis for salvation.

5:7 *Running well:* as in an athletic contest; cf 2:2; 1 Cor 9:24–26; Phil 2:16; 3:14.

5:8 *The one who called you:* see the note on 1:6.

5:11 *Preaching circumcision:* this could refer to Paul's pre-Christian period (possibly as a missionary for Judaism); more probably it arose as a charge from opponents, based perhaps on the story in Acts 16:1–3 that Paul had circumcised Timothy "on account of the Jews." Unlike the Gentile Titus in Gal 2:3, Timothy was the son of a Jewish mother. *The stumbling block of the cross:* cf 1 Cor 1:23.

5:12 A sarcastic half-wish that their knife would go beyond mere circumcision; cf Phil 3:2 and the note there.

5:13–26 In light of another reminder of the freedom of the gospel (13; cf 1), Paul elaborates on what believers are called to do and be: they fulfill the law by love of neighbor (14–15), walking in the Spirit (16–26), as is illustrated by concrete *fruit of the Spirit* in their lives.

5:13 *Serve . . . through love:* cf v 6.

5:14 Lv 19:18, emphasized by Jesus (Mt 22:39; Lk 10:27); cf Rom 13:8–10.

5:16–25 *Spirit . . . flesh:* cf 3:3 and the note on Rom 8:1–13.

5:19–23 Such lists of vices and virtues (cf Rom 1:29–31; 1 Cor 6:9–10) were common in the ancient world. Paul contrasts *works of the flesh* (19) with *fruit* (not "works") *of the Spirit* (22). Not law, but the Spirit, leads to such traits.

5:2 Gal 2:21; Acts 15:1–29.
5:3 Gal 3:10; Rom 2:25; Jas 2:10.
5:5 Rom 8:23, 25.
5:6 Gal 3:28; 6:15; 1 Cor 7:19.
5:8 Gal 1:6.
5:9 1 Cor 5:6.
5:10 Gal 1:7.
5:11 Gal 6:12, 14; 1 Cor 1:23.
5:13 Gal 5:1 / Rom 6:18; 1 Cor 8:9; 1 Pt 2:16.
5:14 Lv 19:18; Mt 22:39; Rom 13:8–10.
5:16 Gal 5:24–25; Rom 8:5.
5:17 Rom 7:15, 23; 8:6.

Pray It!

Fill Me, Lord

Fill me with the fruits of your Spirit, Lord.
Fill me with love, *so that I seek to understand and appreciate the rich variety and diversity of life that surrounds me.*
Fill me with joy, *so that I celebrate your presence in each and every moment I am on this earth.*
Fill me with peace, *so that I know how to ease those angry and sometimes violent urges that well up inside of me.*
Fill me with patience, *so that I stop rushing long enough to witness your miraculous work taking place all around me (and within me!).*
Fill me with kindness, *so that I take the extra time to help the one in need, even when it isn't convenient for me.*
Fill me with faithfulness, *so that I place my mind, heart, and all that I do in the service of your Gospel.*
Fill me with gentleness, *so that others know that I believe in a God who loves and cares for all people.*
Fill me with self-control, *so that I act not on my impulses and urges, but rather on my beliefs and values, which are rooted in you.*
Fill me with these fruits of your spirit, Lord! Amen.

▶ **Gal 5:22–26**

GAL

Cultural Connection

The Principle of *Imani*

> Be not discouraged. There is a future for you. . . . The resistance encountered now predicates hope. . . . Only as we rise . . . do we encounter opposition.

These words by Frederick Douglass in 1892 encouraged African Americans not to abandon their struggle for equality. It seemed that the more they struggled, the more pain was inflicted on them. In the face of certain suffering, Douglass urged them to look toward the promise of living as equals under the law.

They knew that God was their liberator and justice giver. God made them brave in the face of danger and capable of dying for the cause they embraced. They looked to God and saw their future. They took the words of Galatians 6:9 seriously: "Let us not grow tired of doing good."

Today, we don't face slave masters and live on plantations as servants in fetters, but we do endure other situations equally as dangerous. Let us not grow weary or lose heart. We must practice the Kwanzaa principle of *imani*, or "faith" (see "Kwanzaa as a Way of Life," near Dt 10:12–22). Our God is still in the saving business.

Dear God, my future is in your hands. Lead me to it with your power. Amen.

▶ Gal 6:9

and the Spirit against the flesh; these are opposed to each other, so that you may not do what you want. 18* But if you are guided by the Spirit, you are not under the law. 19*† Now the works of the flesh are obvious: immorality, impurity, licentiousness, 20* idolatry, sorcery, hatreds, rivalry, jealousy, outbursts of fury, acts of selfishness, dissensions, factions, 21† occasions of envy, drinking bouts, orgies, and the like. I warn you, as I warned you before, that those who do such things will not inherit the kingdom of God. 22* In contrast, the fruit of the Spirit is love, joy, peace, patience, kindness, generosity, faithfulness, 23* gentleness, self-control. Against such there is no law. 24* Now those who belong to Christ [Jesus] have crucified their flesh with its passions and desires. 25* If we live in the Spirit, let us also follow the Spirit. 26* Let us not be conceited, provoking one another, envious of one another.

Life in the Community of Christ

6 1*† Brothers, even if a person is caught in some transgression, you who are spiritual should correct that one in a gentle spirit, looking to yourself, so that you also may not be tempted. 2*† Bear one another's burdens, and so you will fulfill the law of Christ. 3* For if anyone thinks he is something when he is nothing, he is deluding himself. 4† Each one must examine his own work, and then he will have reason to boast with regard to himself alone, and not with regard to someone else; 5* for each will bear his own load.

6*† One who is being instructed in the word should share all good things with his instructor. 7 Make no mistake: God is not mocked, for a person will reap only what he sows, 8* because the one who sows for his flesh will reap corruption from the flesh, but the one who sows for the

†

5:21 *Occasions of envy:* after the Greek word *phthonoi*, "envies," some manuscripts add a similar sounding one, *phonoi*, "murders."

6:1–10 The ethical exhortations begun at 5:1 continue with a variety of admonitions to the community (*brothers:* see the note on 1:2). Nearly every sentence contains a separate item of practical advice; the faith and freedom of the gospel underlie each maxim. Tensions and temptation within communal life have previously been addressed in 5:15, 26, and v 1 continues with a case in which *a person is caught in some transgression* such as those in 5:19–21; cf 2:17.

6:2 *The law of Christ:* cf Rom 8:2; 1 Cor 9:21; Gal 5:14. The principle of love for others is meant. To *bear one another's burdens* is to "serve one another through love" (5:13).

6:4–5 Self-examination is the cure for self-deception. Compare what you are with what you were before, and give the glory to God; cf Rom 6:19–22. *Load:* used elsewhere of a soldier's pack. Correcting one's own conduct avoids burdening others with it.

6:6 Implies oral instruction in the faith by catechists; these are to be remunerated for their service; cf Rom 15:27.

*

5:18 Rom 6:14; 8:14.
5:19–21 Rom 1:29–31; 1 Cor 6:9–10; Col 3:5–6, 8.
5:20 Rv 22:15.
5:22 Eph 5:9 / 1 Cor 13:4–7; 2 Cor 6:6; 1 Tm 4:12; 2 Pt 1:6.
5:23 1 Tm 1:9.
5:24 Gal 2:19; Rom 6:6; 8:13.
5:25 Gal 5:16.
5:26 Phil 2:3.
6:1 Mt 18:15; Jas 5:19 / 1 Cor 10:12–13.
6:2 Col 3:13 / 1 Cor 9:21.
6:3–4 1 Cor 3:18; 8:2; 2 Cor 12:11.
6:5 Rom 14:12.
6:6 1 Cor 9:14.
6:8 Prv 11:18; Rom 8:6, 13.

spirit will reap eternal life from the spirit. [9]* Let us not grow tired of doing good, for in due time we shall reap our harvest, if we do not give up. [10]*† So then, while we have the opportunity, let us do good to all, but especially to those who belong to the family of the faith.

VI: Conclusion

Final Appeal†

[11]*† See with what large letters I am writing to you in my own hand! [12]*† It is those who want to make a good appearance in the flesh who are trying to compel you to have yourselves circumcised, only that they may not be persecuted for the cross of Christ. [13]† Not even those having themselves circumcised observe the law themselves; they only want you to be circumcised so that they may boast of your flesh. [14]*† But may I never boast except in the cross of our Lord Jesus Christ, through which the world has been crucified to me, and I to the world. [15]*† For neither does circumcision mean anything, nor does uncircumcision, but only a new creation. [16]*† Peace and mercy be to all who follow this rule and to the Israel of God.

[17]*† From now on, let no one make troubles for me; for I bear the marks of Jesus on my body. [18]* The grace of our Lord Jesus Christ be with your spirit, brothers. Amen.

†

6:10 *The family of the faith:* the Christian household or church. Doing good has a universal object (*to all*), but the local community makes specific the reality of those to be served.

6:11–18 A postscript in Paul's own hand, as was his practice (see 1 Cor 16:21; 2 Thes 3:17). Paul summarizes his appeal against his opponents (12–13), then returns to his message of glorying in the cross, not in circumcision, as the means of salvation (14–15; cf 5:11). A benediction follows at v 16. In the polemical spirit that the attack on his apostleship called forth (1:11—2:21), Paul reasserts his missionary credentials (17) before giving a final benediction (18).

6:11 *Large letters:* in contrast to the finer hand of the scribe who wrote the letter up to this point. The larger Greek letters make Paul's message even more emphatic. Some find a hint of poor eyesight on Paul's part. See the note on 4:13.

6:12–15 The Jewish Christian opponents wished *not to be persecuted,* possibly by Jews. But since Judaism seems to have had a privileged status as a religion in the Roman empire, circumcised Christians might, if taken as Jews, thereby avoid persecution from the Romans. In any case, Paul instead stresses conformity with *the cross of our Lord Jesus Christ;* cf 2:19–21; 5:11.

6:13 *Those having themselves circumcised:* other manuscripts read, "those who have had themselves circumcised."

6:14 *Through which:* or "through whom."

6:15 *New creation:* or "new creature"; cf 2 Cor 5:17.

6:16 *This rule:* the principle in vv 14 and 15. *The Israel of God:* while the church may be meant (the phrase can be translated "to all who follow this rule, even the Israel of God"; cf 10; 1 Cor 10:18), the reference may also be to God's ancient people, Israel; cf Pss 125:5; 128:6.

6:17 *The marks of Jesus:* slaves were often branded by marks (*stigmata*) burned into their flesh to show to whom they belonged; so also were devotees of pagan gods. Paul implies that instead of outdated circumcision, his body bears the scars of his apostolic labors (2 Cor 11:22–31), such as floggings (Acts 16:22; 2 Cor 11:25) and stonings (Acts 14:19), that mark him as belonging to the Christ who suffered (cf Rom 6:3; 2 Cor 4:10; Col 1:24) and will protect his own.

*

6:9 2 Thes 3:13; Heb 12:1–3.
6:10 1 Thes 5:15.
6:11 1 Cor 16:21.
6:12 Gal 5:2, 11.
6:14 Gal 2:20; 1 Cor 2:2.
6:15 Gal 5:6; 1 Cor 7:19 / 2 Cor 5:17.
6:16 Pss 125:5; 128:6.
6:17 2 Cor 4:10.
6:18 Phil 4:23; 2 Tm 4:22; Phlm 25.

The Letter to the Ephesians

What's the purpose of life? Why am I alive? What's the point of it all anyway? You may have asked questions like these out of simple curiosity, or during a time when life wasn't going so well. In either case, God has an answer for you tucked away inside the Letter to the Ephesians. This letter talks about God's plan to save us for a life in union with God and one another, both now and for all eternity!

In Depth

Three times in the poetic opening chapter, the writer of Ephesians tells us that we are here because we have been chosen by God! In this beautiful prayer of praise for the Father (see verses 3–6), the Son (see verse 12), and the Holy Spirit (see verses 13–14), we are told that that's why we're alive!

This letter has hardly any of the personal greeting you'd expect in a communication to a specific group of people. Also, the reference to Ephesus in the first verse doesn't appear in some of the earliest copies we have of the letter. For these reasons, many scholars believe that this letter was intended to be circulated among various churches and that the author was addressing the universal church with Christ as its head, unlike Paul who talks about the individual or local church. Most scholars also believe that the Letter to the Colossians was used as a pattern for this letter.

Ephesians emphasizes unity among Christians. It especially emphasizes that Gentile (non-Jewish) Christians are one with Jewish Christians, for Christ has "made both one and broke down the dividing wall" (2:14). It explains that it is the early Christians' job—as it is our job—to treat one another with love, "striving to preserve the unity" (4:3). The image of the church as Christ's body is used here, as it is in 1 Corinthians, chapter 12, to emphasize our unity (see 4:15–16).

Ephesians also talks about the place of good works in the life of a Christian. Good works can be thought of as living a moral life, or as following moral rules. The author of this letter has made clear that we are not saved by the law. So, does this mean we can do anything we want? The letter explains that we are saved not *by doing* good works but *in order to do* good works. Both faith and service are necessary.

The letter ends with some practical advice for living out the faith on a daily basis. There are rules for moral living. There are instructions for Christian family life. There is an analogy for putting on the "armor of God" to resist evil in all its forms. As long as we keep in mind that this letter is written for a culture that was different from ours, the advice will serve us well too!

At a Glance

I. **Address (1:1–14).**

II. **Unity of the Church in Christ (1:15—2:22).**

III. **World Mission of the Church (3:1—4:24).**

IV. **Daily Conduct, an Expression of Unity (4:25—6:20).**

V. **Conclusion (6:21–24).**

Quick Facts

Inspired Author: a follower of Paul (see "Introduction to the Letters and Revelation")

Date Written: after Paul's death, from AD 90 to 100

Audience: Gentile churches, possibly in Asia Minor

Ephesians

5:21–33

I: Address

Greeting†

1 1*† Paul, an apostle of Christ Jesus by the will
of God, to the holy ones who are [in Ephesus]
faithful in Christ Jesus: 2* grace to you and peace
from God our Father and the Lord Jesus Christ.

The Father's Plan of Salvation

3*† Blessed be the God and Father of our
Lord Jesus Christ, who has blessed us in Christ
with every spiritual blessing in the heavens,†
4* as he chose us in him, before the foundation
of the world, to be holy and without blemish
before him. In love 5* he destined us for adop-
tion to himself through Jesus Christ, in accord
with the favor of his will, 6* for the praise of
the glory of his grace that he granted us in the
beloved.

Fulfillment through Christ

7* In him we have redemption by his blood,
the forgiveness of transgressions, in accord with
the riches of his grace 8* that he lavished upon
us. In all wisdom and insight, 9*† he has made
known to us the mystery of his will in accord with
his favor that he set forth in him 10* as a plan
for the fullness of times, to sum up all things in
Christ, in heaven and on earth.

1:1–2 For the epistolary form used at the beginning of letters, see the note on Rom 1:1–7. Twenty-two of the thirty Greek words in vv 1–2 also occur in Col 1:1–2.

1:1 *[In Ephesus:]* the phrase is lacking in important early witnesses such as P46 (3rd cent.), and Sinaiticus and Vaticanus (4th cent.), appearing in the latter two as a fifth-century addition. Basil and Origen mention its absence from manuscripts. See Introduction. Without the phrase, the Greek can be rendered, as in Col 1:2, "to the holy ones and faithful brothers in Christ."

1:3–14 While a Pauline letter usually continues after the greeting with a prayer of thanksgiving, as in 15–23 below, Ephesians first inserts a blessing of God for the blessings Christians have experienced, as in 2 Cor 1:3–4 and 1 Pt 1:3–12. The blessing here, akin to a Jewish *berakah,* is rich in images almost certainly drawn from hymns and liturgy. Many ideas here are also found in Col 1:3–23. Certain phrases are frequently repeated, such as *in Christ* (3, 10, 12) or *in him* (4, 7, 9, 11, 13) or *in the beloved* (6) and *(for) the praise of (his) glory* (6, 12, 14). Some terms like *chose* (4) and *destined* (5) reflect Old Testament theology (Dt 7:7; 9:4–6; 23:5) or Pauline themes (*redemption,* 7, 14; *grace,* 6, 7) or specific emphases in Colossians (*forgiveness,* Col 1:14). A triadic structure is discernible in vv 3–14: *God* the *Father* (3–6, 8, 11), *Christ* (3, 5, 7–10, 12), and the *Spirit* (13–14). The spiritual blessings Christians have received through Christ (3) are gratefully enumerated: the call to holiness (4; cf Col 1:22); the gift of divine *adoption* establishing a unique spiritual relationship with God the Father through Christ (5; cf Gal 4:5); liberation from sin through Christ's sacrificial death (7); revelation of God's plan of salvation in Christ (9; cf 3:3–4; Rom 16:25); the gift of election and faith in Christ bestowed upon Jewish Christians (see the note on 12, *we who first hoped in Christ*); and finally, the same gift granted to Gentiles (13, *you also*). In the Christ-centered faith and existence of the Christian communities the apostle sees the predetermined *plan* of God to bring all creation under the final rule of Christ (4–5, 9–10) being *made known* (9) and carried through, to God's *glory* (6, 12, 14).

1:3 *In the heavens:* literally, "in the heavenlies" or "in the heavenly places," a term in Ephesians for the divine realm.

1:9 *Mystery:* as in Rom 16:25; Col 1:26, 27 and elsewhere, a secret of God now revealed in the *plan* to save and *sum up all things in Christ* (10); cf 3:3–6.

1:1 Rom 1:7; 1 Cor 1:1–2; Col 1:1.
1:2 Col 1:2.
1:3 Eph 2:6; 2 Cor 1:3.
1:4 Eph 5:27; Jn 15:16; 17:24; Rom 8:29; 2 Thes 2:13.
1:5 Jn 1:12; 1 Jn 3:1.
1:6 Mt 3:17; Col 1:13.
1:7 Eph 2:7–13; Rom 3:24; Col 1:14, 20.
1:8 Col 1:9.
1:9 Eph 3:3, 9; Rom 16:25.
1:10 Gal 4:4; Col 1:16, 20.

1:1

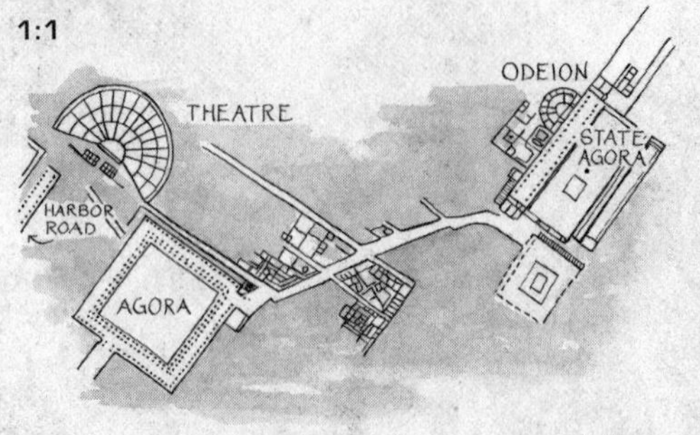

Artist's rendition of the city plan for first-century Ephesus

Pray It!

I Give God Thanks for You!

Think of people in your family, community, school, and church who are living out the Gospel message. Who is honestly striving to live her or his Christian faith? A parent or guardian? a friend? a neighbor? a teacher? a minister?

Hold this person in your heart as you read Ephesians 1:15–23. Meditate on how this person has influenced you as a Christian. How has he or she helped you on your faith journey? Consider writing your own prayer of thanks to God for this person's example. If it seems appropriate, share your prayer with this person.

▶ **Eph 1:15–23**

Inheritance through the Spirit

[11]* In him we were also chosen, destined in
accord with the purpose of the One who accom-
plishes all things according to the intention of
his will, [12]† so that we might exist for the praise
of his glory, we who first hoped in Christ. [13]*† In
him you also, who have heard the word of truth,
the gospel of your salvation, and have believed
in him, were sealed with the promised holy
Spirit, [14]*† which is the first installment of our
inheritance toward redemption as God's posses-
sion, to the praise of his glory.

II: Unity of the Church in Christ

The Church as Christ's Body†

[15]*† Therefore, I, too, hearing of your faith
in the Lord Jesus and of your love for all the
holy ones, [16]* do not cease giving thanks for
you, remembering you in my prayers, [17]* that
the God of our Lord Jesus Christ, the Father of
glory, may give you a spirit of wisdom and rev-
elation resulting in knowledge of him. [18]* May
the eyes of [your] hearts be enlightened, that
you may know what is the hope that belongs
to his call, what are the riches of glory in his
inheritance among the holy ones, [19]* and what
is the surpassing greatness of his power for us
who believe, in accord with the exercise of his
great might, [20]* which he worked in Christ, rais-
ing him from the dead and seating him at his
right hand in the heavens, [21]* far above every
principality, authority, power, and dominion,
and every name that is named not only in this
age but also in the one to come. [22]* And he put
all things beneath his feet and gave him as head
over all things to the church, [23]*† which is his
body, the fullness of the one who fills all things
in every way.

†

1:12 *We who first hoped:* probably Jewish Christians (contrast 13, *you,* the Gentiles); possibly the people of Israel, "we who already enjoyed the hope of Christ," or perhaps present hope in contrast to future redemption (cf 14).

1:13 *Sealed:* by God, in baptism; cf 4:30; 2 Cor 1:22.

1:14 *First installment:* down payment by God on full salvation, as at 2 Cor 1:22.

1:15–23 See the note on Rom 1:8 for the thanksgiving form in a letter. Much of the content parallels thoughts in Col 1:3–20. The prayer moves from God and Christ (17, 20–21) to the Ephesians (17–19) and the church (22–23). Paul asks that the blessing imparted by God the Father (3) to the Ephesians will be strengthened in them through the message of the gospel (13, 17–19). Those blessings are seen in the context of God's *might* in establishing the sovereignty of Christ over all other creatures (19–21) and in appointing him *head* of the church (22–23). For the allusion to angelic spirits in v 21, see Rom 8:38 and Col 1:16. Here, as in 1 Cor 15:24–25 and Col 2:15, every such *principality* and *power* is made subject to Christ.

1:15 *Your faith . . . your love:* some manuscripts omit the latter phrase, but cf Col 1:4.

1:23 *His body:* the church (22); cf the note on Col 1:18. Only in Ephesians and Colossians is Christ the *head* of the *body,* in contrast to the view in 1 Cor 12 and Rom 12:4–8 where Christ is equated with the entire body or community. *Fullness:* see the note on Col 1:19. Some take *the one who fills* as God, others as Christ (cf 4:10). If in Christ "dwells the fullness of the deity bodily" (Col 2:9), then, as God "fills" Christ, Christ in turn fills the church and the believer (3:19; 5:18). But the difficult phrases here may also allow the church to be viewed as the "complement" of Christ who is "being filled" as God's plan for the universe is carried out through the church (cf 3:9–10).

*

1:11 Is 46:10; Rom 8:28; Col 1:12; Rv 4:11.
1:13 Eph 4:30; Acts 2:33; Col 1:5–6.
1:14 2 Cor 1:22; 5:5.
1:15 Col 1:3–4; Phlm 4–5.
1:16 Col 1:3, 9.
1:17 Eph 3:14, 16; Col 1:9–10; 1 Jn 5:20.
1:18 Eph 4:4; Col 1:12, 27.
1:19 2 Cor 13:4; Col 1:11; 2:12.
1:20 Ps 110:1; Heb 1:3.
1:21 Phil 2:9; Col 1:16; 1 Pt 3:22.
1:22 Eph 4:15; Ps 8:7; Mt 28:18; Col 1:18.
1:23 Eph 4:10, 12; Rom 12:5; 1 Cor 12:27; Col 1:19.

Generosity of God's Plan†

2 1*† You were dead in your transgressions
and sins† 2*† in which you once lived fol-
lowing the age of this world, following the ruler
of the power of the air, the spirit that is now at
work in the disobedient. 3* All of us once lived
among them in the desires of our flesh, follow-
ing the wishes of the flesh and the impulses, and
we were by nature children of wrath, like the
rest. 4 But God, who is rich in mercy, because of
the great love he had for us, 5*† even when we
were dead in our transgressions, brought us to
life with Christ (by grace you have been saved),
6* raised us up with him, and seated us with him
in the heavens in Christ Jesus, 7* that in the ages
to come he might show the immeasurable riches
of his grace in his kindness to us in Christ Jesus.
8* For by grace you have been saved through
faith, and this is not from you; it is the gift of
God; 9* it is not from works, so no one may
boast. 10* For we are his handiwork, created in
Christ Jesus for the good works that God has pre-
pared in advance, that we should live in them.

One in Christ

11† Therefore, remember that at one time you,
Gentiles in the flesh, called the uncircumcision
by those called the circumcision, which is done
in the flesh by human hands, 12*† were at that
time without Christ, alienated from the com-
munity of Israel and strangers to the covenants
of promise, without hope and without God in
the world. 13* But now in Christ Jesus you who
once were far off have become near by the blood
of Christ.
14*† For he is our peace, he who made both

Did You Know?

Faith Versus Good Works

Ephesians 2:1–10 deals with the question of faith versus good works (good works are moral living and Gospel-motivated works of service, justice, courage, and so on). This issue has divided Christians since the early Church and was a major issue at the time of the Protestant Reformation. Some say we are saved by our good works. Others say that good works are irrelevant and that we are saved only through our faith in Christ.

The writer of Ephesians makes it clear that both those statements are incomplete. The core Christian belief is this: We are saved by God's grace through faith in Jesus Christ. We were saved not *by doing* good works but *in order to do* good works. Our salvation is God's gift to us; how we live is our gift to God.

► Eph 2:1–10

2:1–22 The gospel of *salvation* (1:13) that God *worked in Christ* (1:20) is reiterated in terms of what God's *great love* (4), expressed in Christ, means for us. The passage sometimes addresses *you,* Gentiles (1–2, 8, 11–13, 19, 22), but other times speaks of *all of us* who believe (3–7, 10, 14, 18). In urging people to *remember* their grim past when they were *dead* in sins (1–3, 11–12) and what they are *now in Christ* (4–10, 13), the author sees both Jew and Gentile reconciled with God, now *one new person,* a new humanity, *one body, the household of God, a temple* and *dwelling place* of God's Spirit (15–16, 19–22). The presentation falls into two parts, the second stressing more the meaning for the church.

2:1–10 The recipients of Paul's letter have experienced, in their redemption from *transgressions and sins,* the effect of Christ's supremacy over the power of the devil (1–2; cf 6:11–12), who rules not from the netherworld but from the *air* between God in heaven and human beings on earth. Both Jew and Gentile have experienced, through Christ, God's free gift of salvation that already marks them for a future heavenly destiny (3–7). The language *dead, raised us up,* and *seated us . . . in the heavens* closely parallels Jesus' own passion and Easter experience. The terms in vv 8–9 describe salvation in the way Paul elsewhere speaks of justification: by grace, through faith, the gift of God, not from works; cf Gal 2:16–21; Rom 3:24–28. Christians are a newly created people in Christ, fashioned by God for a life of goodness (10).

2:1–7 These verses comprise one long sentence in Greek, the main verb coming in v 5, God *brought us to life,* the object you/us *dead in . . . transgressions* being repeated in 1 and 5; cf Col 2:13.

2:2 *Age of this world:* or "aeon," a term found in gnostic thought, possibly synonymous with *the rulers of this world,* but also reflecting the Jewish idea of "two ages," this present evil age and "the age to come"; cf 1 Cor 3:19; 5:10; 7:31; Gal 1:4; Ti 2:12. *The disobedient:* literally, "the sons of disobedience," a Semitism as at Is 30:9.

2:5 Our relation through baptism *with Christ,* the risen Lord, is depicted in terms of realized eschatology, as already exaltation, though v 7 brings in the future aspect too.

2:11–22 The Gentiles lacked Israel's messianic expectation, lacked the various *covenants* God made with *Israel,* lacked *hope* of salvation and knowledge of the true *God* (11–12); but through Christ all these religious barriers between Jew and Gentile have been transcended (13–14) by the abolition of the Mosaic covenant-law (15) for the sake of uniting Jew and Gentile into a single religious community (15–16), imbued with the same holy *Spirit* and worshiping the same *Father* (18). The Gentiles are now included in God's *household* (19) as it arises upon the *foundation* of *apostles* assisted by those endowed with the prophetic gift (3:5), the preachers of Christ (20; cf 1 Cor 12:28). With Christ as the *capstone* (20; cf Is 28:16; Mt 21:42), they are being built into the holy *temple* of God's people where the divine presence dwells (21–22).

2:12 *The community of Israel:* or "commonwealth"; cf 4:18. *The covenants:* cf Rom 9:4: with Abraham, with Moses, with David.

2:14–16 The elaborate imagery here combines pictures of Christ as *our peace* (Is 9:5), his crucifixion, the ending of the Mosaic law (cf Col 2:14), reconciliation (2 Cor 5:18–21), and the destruction of *the dividing wall* such as kept people from God in the temple or a barrier in the heavens.

2:1 Col 1:21; 2:13.
2:2 Eph 6:12; Jn 12:31; Col 1:13.
2:3 Col 3:6–7.
2:5 Rom 5:8; 6:13; Col 2:13.
2:6 Rom 8:10–11; Phil 3:20; Col 2:12.
2:7 Eph 1:7.
2:8 Rom 3:24; Gal 2:16.
2:9 1 Cor 1:29.
2:10 Eph 4:24; Ti 2:14.
2:12 Rom 9:4; Col 1:21, 27.
2:13 Eph 2:17; Is 57:19; Col 1:20.
2:14 Gal 3:28.

Cultural Connection

Rooted in Love

Read the prayer in Ephesians 3:14–21. Then reflect on the prayer below from Christians in the Philippines, which also talks about roots and love.

Lord,
make us realize that our Christianity is like a rice field:
when it is newly planted the paddies are prominent,
but as the plants take root and grow taller,
these divided paddies gradually vanish,
and soon there appears only one vast continuous field.
So give us roots that love,
and help us grow in Christian fellowship and service,
that thy will be done in our lives,
through our Savior, Jesus Christ.

(From *Your Will Be Done*, p. 145)

Finally, personalize the prayer in 3:14–21 by changing *you* to *I* or *we*, and *your* to *my* or *our*. Kneel and pray this prayer, knowing that God is indeed listening to you at this very moment.

▶ **Eph 3:14–21**

one and broke down the dividing wall of enmity, through his flesh, 15*† abolishing the law with its commandments and legal claims, that he might create in himself one new person in place of the two, thus establishing peace, 16* and might reconcile both with God, in one body, through the cross, putting that enmity to death by it. 17* He came and preached peace to you who were far off and peace to those who were near, 18* for through him we both have access in one Spirit to the Father.

19* So then you are no longer strangers and sojourners, but you are fellow citizens with the holy ones and members of the household of God, 20*† built upon the foundation of the apostles and prophets, with Christ Jesus himself as the capstone. 21* Through him the whole structure is held together and grows into a temple sacred in the Lord; 22* in him you also are being built together into a dwelling place of God in the Spirit.

III: World Mission of the Church

Commission to Preach God's Plan†

3 1*† Because of this, I, Paul, a prisoner of Christ [Jesus] for you Gentiles— 2*† if, as I suppose, you have heard of the stewardship of God's grace that was given to me for your benefit, 3*† [namely, that] the mystery was made known to me by revelation, as I have written briefly earlier. 4 When you read this you can understand my insight into the mystery of Christ, 5* which was not made known to human beings in other generations as it has now been revealed to his holy apostles and prophets by the Spirit, 6* that the Gentiles are coheirs, members of the same body, and copartners in the promise in Christ Jesus through the gospel.

7* Of this I became a minister by the gift of God's grace that was granted me in accord with the exercise of his power. 8* To me, the very

2:15 *One new person:* a corporate body, the Christian community, made up of Jews and Gentiles, replacing ancient divisions; cf Rom 1:16.

2:20 *Capstone:* the Greek can also mean cornerstone or keystone.

3:1–13 Paul reflects on his mission to the Gentiles. He alludes to his call and appointment to the apostolic office (2–3) and how his *insight* through revelation, as well as that of the other apostles and charismatic prophets in the church (4–5), has deepened understanding of God's plan of salvation in Christ. Paul is the special herald (7) of a new *promise* to the *Gentiles* (6): that the divine plan includes them in the spiritual benefits promised to Israel. Not only is this unique apostolic role his; Paul also has been given the task of explaining to all the divine *plan* of salvation (8–9), once *hidden*. Through *the church,* God's plan to save through Christ is becoming manifest to angelic beings (10; cf 1:21), in accord with God's *purpose* (11). The fulfillment of the plan in Christ gives the whole church more *confidence* through *faith* in God (12). The readers of this letter are also thereby encouraged to greater confidence despite Paul's imprisonment (13).

3:1 *A prisoner of Christ:* see Introduction. Paul abruptly departs from his train of thought at the end of v 1, leaving an incomplete sentence.

3:2 *Stewardship:* the Greek is the same term employed at 1:10 for the *plan* that God administers (Col 1:25) and in which Paul plays a key role.

3:3–4 *The mystery:* God's resolve to deliver Gentiles along with Israel through Christ; cf the notes on 1:10; 3:9.

2:15 2 Cor 5:17; Col 2:14.
2:16 Col 1:20, 22.
2:17 Is 57:19; Zec 9:10.
2:18 Eph 3:12.
2:19 Heb 12:22–23.
2:20 Is 28:16; Rv 21:14.
2:21 1 Cor 3:16; Col 2:19.
2:22 1 Pt 2:5.
3:1 Phil 1:7, 13; Col 1:24–29; 4:18; Phlm 9; 2 Tm 2:9.
3:2 Col 1:25.
3:3 Eph 1:9–10; Col 1:26.
3:5 Col 1:26.
3:6 Eph 2:13, 18–19.
3:7 Rom 15:15; Col 1:25, 29.
3:8 1 Cor 15:8–10; Gal 1:16; 2:7–9.

least of all the holy ones, this grace was given, to
preach to the Gentiles the inscrutable riches of
Christ, 9*† and to bring to light [for all] what is
the plan of the mystery hidden from ages past in
God who created all things, 10*† so that the
manifold wisdom of God might now
be made known through the church
to the principalities and author-
ities in the heavens. 11 This was
according to the eternal pur-
pose that he accomplished in
Christ Jesus our Lord, 12* in
whom we have boldness of
speech and confidence of
access through faith in him.
13* So I ask you not to lose heart
over my afflictions for you; this is
your glory.

"One body and one Spirit, as you were also called to the one hope of your call; one Lord, one faith, one baptism; one God and Father of all."

(Eph 4:4–6)

Prayer for the Readers†

14† For this reason I kneel before the Father,
15 from whom every family in heaven and on
earth is named, 16* that he may grant you in
accord with the riches of his glory to be strength-
ened with power through his Spirit in the inner
self, 17* and that Christ may dwell in your hearts
through faith; that you, rooted and grounded in
love, 18* may have strength to comprehend with
all the holy ones what is the breadth and length
and height and depth, 19* and to know the love
of Christ that surpasses knowledge, so that you
may be filled with all the fullness of God.
20* Now to him who is able to accomplish far
more than all we ask or imagine, by the power at
work within us, 21 to him be glory in the church
and in Christ Jesus to all generations, forever and
ever. Amen.

Unity in the Body

4 1*† I, then, a prisoner for the Lord,
urge you to live in a manner
worthy of the call you have re-
ceived, 2* with all humility and
gentleness, with patience, bear-
ing with one another through
love, 3* striving to preserve
the unity of the spirit through
the bond of peace: 4*† one
body and one Spirit, as you
were also called to the one
hope of your call; 5* one Lord,
one faith, one baptism; 6* one
God and Father of all, who is over
all and through all and in all.

Diversity of Gifts

7* But grace was given to each of us according
to the measure of Christ's gift. 8*† Therefore, it
says:

"He ascended on high and took prisoners
captive;
he gave gifts to men."

9 What does "he ascended" mean except that he
also descended into the lower [regions] of the
earth? 10 The one who descended is also the one
who ascended far above all the heavens, that he
might fill all things.
11*† And he gave some as apostles, others as

EPH

3:9 *[For all]:* while some think this phrase was added so as to yield the sense "to enlighten all about the plan . . . ," it is more likely that some manuscripts and Fathers omitted it accidentally or to avoid the idea that *all* conflicted with Paul's assignment to preach to *the Gentiles* (8) specifically.

3:10 *Principalities and authorities:* see the note on 1:15–23 regarding v 21.

3:14–21 The apostle prays that those he is addressing may, like the rest of the church, deepen their understanding of God's plan of salvation in Christ. It is a plan that affects the whole universe (15) with *the breadth and length and height and depth* of God's love in Christ (18) or possibly the universe in all its dimensions. The apostle prays that they may perceive the redemptive love of Christ for them and be completely immersed in the fullness of God (19). The prayer concludes with a doxology to God (20–21).

3:14–15 *Every family:* in the Greek there is wordplay on the word for *the Father (patria, patēr).* The phrase could also mean "God's whole family" (cf 2:21).

4:1–16 A general plea for unity in the church. Christians have been fashioned through the *Spirit* into a single harmonious religious community (*one body*, 4, 12; cf 16), belonging to a single *Lord* (in contrast to the many gods of the pagan world), and by one way of salvation through *faith,* brought out especially by the significance of *baptism* (1–6; cf Rom 6:1–11). But Christian unity is more than adherence to a common belief. It is manifested in the exalted Christ's gifts to individuals to serve so as to make the community more Christlike (11–16). This teaching on Christ as the source of the gifts is introduced in v 8 by a citation of Ps 68:18, which depicts Yahweh triumphantly leading Israel to salvation in Jerusalem. It is here understood of Christ, ascending *above all the heavens,* the *head* of the church; through his redemptive death, resurrection, and ascension he has become the source of the church's spiritual gifts. The "descent" of Christ (9–10) refers more probably to the incarnation (cf Phil 2:6–8) than to Christ's presence after his death in the world of the dead (cf 1 Pt 3:19).

4:4–6 The "seven unities" (church, *Spirit, hope; Lord, faith* in Christ [Eph 1:13], *baptism; one God*) reflect the triune structure of later creeds in reverse.

4:8–10 While the emphasis is on an ascension and gift-giving by Christ, there is also a reference in taking *prisoners captive* to the aeons and powers mentioned at 1:21; 2:2; 3:10; and 6:12.

4:11 Concerning this list of ministers, cf 1 Cor 12:28 and Rom 12:6–8. *Evangelists:* missionary preachers (cf Acts 21:8 and 2 Tm 4:5), not those who wrote gospels. *Pastors and teachers:* a single group in the Greek, shepherding congregations.

3:9 Rom 16:25; Col 1:26–27.
3:10 1 Pt 1:12.
3:12 Rom 5:1–2; Heb 4:16.
3:13 Col 1:22, 24; 2 Tm 2:10.
3:16 Eph 6:10; Rom 7:22; 2 Cor 4:16; Col 1:11.
3:17 Jn 14:23; Col 1:23; 2:7.
3:18 Col 2:2.
3:19 Col 2:3, 9.
3:20 Rom 16:25–27; Col 1:29.
4:1 Eph 3:1; Col 1:10.
4:2 Col 3:12–13.
4:3 Col 3:14–15.
4:4 Rom 12:5; 1 Cor 10:17; 12:12–13.
4:5 1 Cor 8:6.
4:6 1 Cor 12:6.
4:7 Rom 12:3, 6; 1 Cor 12:28.
4:8 Ps 68:19; Col 2:15.
4:11 1 Cor 12:28.

Cultural Connection

Weave for Us a Garment

The prayer in Ephesians 4:1–6 is a prayer of unity, a prayer for us to live as one—one faith, one Baptism, one God, one body, one Spirit, one hope. This Native American prayer is also a prayer of unity, a prayer for us to live in a world where all people, all creation, are woven into one garment. May we walk in such a world. May we be part of creating such a world.

Weave for us a garment of brightness;
May the warp be the white light of morning,
May the weft be the red light of evening,
May the fringes be the falling rain,
May the border be the standing rainbow.
Thus weave for us a garment of brightness,
That we may walk fittingly where birds sing,
That we may walk fittingly where grass is green,
O our Mother the Earth, O our Father the Sky.

► Eph 4:1–6

prophets, others as evangelists, others as pastors and teachers, [12]† to equip the holy ones for the work of ministry, for building up the body of Christ, [13]*† until we all attain to the unity of faith and knowledge of the Son of God, to mature manhood, to the extent of the full stature of Christ, [14]* so that we may no longer be infants, tossed by waves and swept along by every wind of teaching arising from human trickery, from their cunning in the interests of deceitful scheming. [15]*† Rather, living the truth in love, we should grow in every way into him who is the head, Christ, [16]* from whom the whole body, joined and held together by every supporting ligament, with the proper functioning of each part, brings about the body's growth and builds itself up in love.

Renewal in Christ

[17]*† So I declare and testify in the Lord that you must no longer live as the Gentiles do, in the futility of their minds; [18]* darkened in understanding, alienated from the life of God because of their ignorance, because of their hardness of heart, [19]* they have become callous and have handed themselves over to licentiousness for the practice of every kind of impurity to excess. [20]That is not how you learned Christ, [21] assuming that you have heard of him and were taught in him, as truth is in Jesus, [22]* that you should put away the old self of your former way of life, corrupted through deceitful desires, [23]* and be renewed in the spirit of your minds, [24]*† and put on the new self, created in God's way in righteousness and holiness of truth.

IV: Daily Conduct, an Expression of Unity

Rules for the New Life

[25]*† Therefore, putting away falsehood, speak the truth, each one to his neighbor, for we are members one of another. [26]*† Be angry but do not sin; do not let the sun set on your anger, [27]* and do not leave room for the devil. [28]*† The thief must no longer steal, but rather labor,

†

4:12 The ministerial leaders in v 11 are to equip the whole people of God for their *work of ministry*.

4:13 *Mature manhood:* literally, "a perfect man" (cf Col 1:28), possibly the "one new person" of 2:15, though there *anthrōpos* suggests humanity, while here *anēr* is the term for male. This personage becomes visible in the church's growing to its fullness in the unity of those who believe in Christ.

4:15–16 *The head, Christ:* cf Col 1:18 and contrast 1 Cor 12:12–27 and Rom 12:4–5 where Christ is identified with the whole body, including the head. The imagery may derive from ancient views in medicine, the *head* coordinating and caring for the body, each *ligament* (perhaps the ministers of v 11) supporting the whole. But as at 2:19–22, where the temple is depicted as a growing organism, there may also be the idea here of growing toward the capstone, Christ.

4:17–24 Paul begins to indicate how the new life in Christ contrasts with the Gentiles' old way of existence. Literally, *the old self* (22) and *the new self* (24) are "the old man" and "the new man" (*anthrōpos,* person), as at 2:15; cf the note on 4:13.

4:24 *Put on:* in baptism. See the note on Gal 3:27.

4:25—6:20 For similar exhortations to a morally good life in response to God's gift of faith, see the notes on Rom 12:1—13:14 and Gal 5:13–26.

4:26 If angry, seek reconciliation that day, not giving the devil (6:11) opportunity to lead into sin.

4:28 *Honest work:* literally, "the good." *His [own] hands:* some manuscripts have the full phrase as in 1 Cor 4:12.

*

4:13 Col 1:28.
4:14 1 Cor 14:20; Col 2:4, 8; Heb 13:9; Jas 1:6.
4:15 1 Cor 11:3; Col 1:18; 2:19.
4:16 Col 2:19.
4:17 Rom 1:21.
4:18 Col 1:21; 1 Pt 1:14.
4:19 Col 3:5.
4:22 Rom 8:13; Gal 6:8; Col 3:9.
4:23 Rom 12:2.
4:24 Gn 1:26–27; Col 3:10.
4:25 Zec 8:16.
4:26 Ps 4:5 LXX; Mt 5:22.
4:27 2 Cor 2:11.
4:28 1 Thes 4:11.

Cultural Connection

Prophets of Hope, Youth on a Mission

Ephesians 4:17–32 has some teachings about the Christian way of life that uses baptismal imagery. Those who are trying to follow Jesus want to be prophets of hope, as expressed in this song written for Hispanic youth:

We're Prophets of Hope, youth on a mission,
spreading the Gospel of Christ.
We're Prophets of Hope, issuing the challenge:
to build the Reign of God.

Pilgrims on a journey, marching towards our goal.
Led by the Spirit, strengthened by the Lord.
We bear each other's burdens and give each
other hope.
Following our savior we press on towards our
goal.

We come from towns and cities.
We are immigrants and natives,
laborers and students who want a better life.
We want to be successful, but not at any cost.
Unless we work for justice humanity is lost.

We face discrimination, poverty and drugs.
The values of our culture are all under attack.
But we have faith in Jesus; he will give us
strength.
Together we will struggle to build a better world.

The Gospel is our road map, the Church is our
guide.
We're Catholic Latinos, youth who take a stand.
Leaders in our churches, reflecting as we go.
Learning from our set-backs, we never give up
hope.

(Jose Antonio Rubio)

Eph 4:17–32

doing honest work with his [own] hands, so that
he may have something to share with one in
need. 29* No foul language should come out of
your mouths, but only such as is good for needed
edification, that it may impart grace to those who
hear. 30† And do not grieve the holy Spirit of
God, with which you were sealed for the day of
redemption. 31* All bitterness, fury, anger, shout-
ing, and reviling must be removed from you,
along with all malice. 32* [And] be kind to one
another, compassionate, forgiving one another
as God has forgiven you in Christ.

5 1*† So be imitators of God, as beloved chil-
dren, 2* and live in love, as Christ loved us
and handed himself over for us as a sacrificial
offering to God for a fragrant aroma. 3* Immo-
rality or any impurity or greed must not even be
mentioned among you, as is fitting among holy
ones, 4* no obscenity or silly or suggestive talk,
which is out of place, but instead, thanksgiving.
5* Be sure of this, that no immoral or impure or
greedy person, that is, an idolater, has any inher-
itance in the kingdom of Christ and of God.

Duty to Live in the Light

6*† Let no one deceive you with empty argu-
ments, for because of these things the wrath of
God is coming upon the disobedient. 7 So do not
be associated with them. 8* For you were once
darkness, but now you are light in the Lord.
Live as children of light, 9* for light produces
every kind of goodness and righteousness and
truth. 10* Try to learn what is pleasing to the
Lord. 11* Take no part in the fruitless works of
darkness; rather expose them, 12 for it is shame-
ful even to mention the things done by them in
secret; 13* but everything exposed by the light be-
comes visible, 14*† for everything that becomes
visible is light. Therefore, it says:

"Awake, O sleeper,
and arise from the dead,
and Christ will give you light."

†
4:30 See the note on 1:13.
5:1 *Imitators of God:* in forgiving (4:32) and in loving (as exhibited in how *Christ loved us*).
5:6 See the note on 2:2.
5:14 An early Christian hymn, possibly from a baptismal liturgy. For the content compare 2:5–6; 3:9 and Is 60:1.

4:29 Eph 5:4; Col 3:16; 4:6.
4:31 Col 3:8.
4:32 Mt 6:14; Col 3:12–13.
5:1 Mt 5:45, 48.
5:2 Ex 29:18; Ps 40:7; Gal 2:20; 1 Jn 3:16.
5:3 Gal 5:19; Col 3:5.
5:4 Eph 4:29; Col 3:8.
5:5 1 Cor 6:9–10; Gal 5:21; Col 3:5.
5:6 Rom 1:18; Col 2:4, 8.
5:8 Eph 2:11–13; Jn 12:36; Col 1:12–13.
5:9 Gal 5:22.
5:10 Rom 12:2.
5:11 Rom 13:12.
5:13 Jn 3:20–21.
5:14 Is 26:19; 60:1.

15*† Watch carefully then how you live, not as
foolish persons but as wise, 16 making the most
of the opportunity, because the days are evil.
17 Therefore, do not continue in ignorance, but
try to understand what is the will of the Lord.
18* And do not get drunk on wine, in which lies
debauchery, but be filled with the Spirit, 19* ad-
dressing one another [in] psalms and hymns and
spiritual songs, singing and playing to the Lord
in your hearts, 20* giving thanks always and for
everything in the name of our Lord Jesus Christ
to God the Father.

Wives and Husbands

21*† Be subordinate to one another out of rever-
ence for Christ.† 22* Wives should be subordinate

†

5:15–16, 19–20 The wording is similar to Col 4:5 and 3:16–17.

5:21—6:9 Cf the notes on Col 3:18—4:1 and 1 Pt 2:18—3:7 for a similar listing of household duties where the inferior is admonished first (*wives,* 5:22; *children,* 6:1; *slaves,* 6:5), then the superior (*husbands,* 5:25; *fathers,* 6:4; *masters,* 6:9). Paul varies this pattern by an emphasis on mutuality (see 5:20); use of Old Testament material about *father and mother* in 6:2; the judgment to come for slave-owners (*you have a Master in heaven,* 6:9); and above all the initial principle of subordination *to one another* under *Christ,* thus effectively undermining exclusive claims to domination by one party. Into the section on *wives* and *husbands* an elaborate teaching on *Christ* and *the church* has been woven (5:22–33).

5:21–33 The apostle exhorts married Christians to a strong mutual love. Holding with Gn 2:24 that marriage is a divine institution (31), Paul sees Christian marriage as taking on a new meaning symbolic of the intimate relationship of love between Christ and the church. The wife should serve her husband in the same spirit as that of the church's service to Christ (22, 24), and the husband should care for his wife with the devotion of Christ to the church (25–30). Paul gives

5:15–16 Col 4:5.
5:18 Prv 23:31 LXX; Lk 21:34.
5:19 Ps 33:2–3; Col 3:16.
5:20 Col 3:17.
5:21 1 Pt 5:5.
5:22 Col 3:18—4:1; 1 Pt 3:1–7.

Live It!

Alcohol

The author of Ephesians 5:10–20 does not mince words. This passage encourages the early Christians, and us, to wake up and find out what pleases God. It calls them to avoid participating in actions they would be ashamed of if the actions were exposed in the light. Its tone is not of scolding but rather of passionate encouragement, wanting the best for each of us.

Although the use of alcohol is singled out in this passage, drinking is not the only substance abuse issue young people face during adolescence. Many young people are pressured by friends, the media, or family members to participate in drinking, smoking, and using drugs. Abuse of these substances prevents us from being filled with the Spirit. As the author of Ephesians advises, making wise choices about these substances is important.

Take some time to reflect on your own life.

- What temptations do you face in this regard?
- What choices can you make that would please God and allow you to enjoy the fullness of life in the Spirit?
- Who can help you to make the correct decisions and help you to stick to them?

▶ Eph 5:10–20

Live It!

Family Relationships

When Ephesians 5:21—6:4 comes up in the Sunday readings, it sometimes causes confusion. People wonder how the Bible can teach that a wife should be subject to her husband. This is another case where we must take into account the cultural context of the biblical writer in order to properly interpret the passage. At the time the Letter to the Ephesians was written, males were dominant in society. Wives and children were considered men's property. The letter's challenge to a man to love his wife and to treat his children respectfully was probably viewed as a radical statement by people at the time.

Our culture is different. Just as we should not interpret 6:5–9 as giving permission to own slaves, we should not interpret 5:21—6:4 as commanding submissive behavior of married women today. Understanding this, we can appreciate the passage as it was intended: a practical guide for a family life where love is the rule (see "The Christian Family," near Col 3:18—4:1).

▶ Eph 5:21—6:4

to their husbands as to the Lord. 23* For the husband is head of his wife just as Christ is head of the church, he himself the savior of the body. 24 As the church is subordinate to Christ, so wives should be subordinate to their husbands in everything. 25* Husbands, love your wives, even as Christ loved the church and handed himself over for her 26* to sanctify her, cleansing her by the bath of water with the word, 27* that he might present to himself the church in splendor, without spot or wrinkle or any such thing, that she might be holy and without blemish. 28 So [also] husbands should love their wives as their own bodies. He who loves his wife loves himself. 29 For no one hates his own flesh but rather nourishes and cherishes it, even as Christ does the church, 30* because we are members of his body.

31* "For this reason a man shall leave [his] father
and [his] mother
and be joined to his wife,
and the two shall become one flesh."

32* This is a great mystery, but I speak in reference to Christ and the church. 33 In any case, each one of you should love his wife as himself, and the wife should respect her husband.

Children and Parents

6 1* Children, obey your parents [in the Lord], for this is right. 2* "Honor your father and mother." This is the first commandment with a promise, 3 "that it may go well with you and that you may have a long life on earth." 4* Fathers, do not provoke your children to anger, but bring them up with the training and instruction of the Lord.

Slaves and Masters

5* Slaves, be obedient to your human masters with fear and trembling, in sincerity of heart, as to Christ, 6* not only when being watched, as currying favor, but as slaves of Christ, doing the will of God from the heart, 7 willingly serving the Lord and not human beings, 8 knowing that each will be requited from the Lord for whatever good he does, whether he is slave or free. 9* Masters, act in the same way toward them, and stop bullying, knowing that both they and you have a Master in heaven and that with him there is no partiality.

Pray It!

The "Peace Prayer" of Saint Francis of Assisi

Ephesians 6:10–17 is a poetic passage encouraging us to resist evil. The "Peace Prayer" of Saint Francis of Assisi tells us how to do this—without using the imagery of warfare. After you read each line of this powerful prayer, close your eyes to meditate on its meaning for your life. What is one way you can live out each line of this prayer?

Lord, make me an instrument of your
peace;
where there is hatred, let me sow love;
where there is injury, pardon;
where there is doubt, faith;
where there is despair, hope;
where there is darkness, light;
and where there is sadness, joy.
Grant that I may not so much seek
to be consoled as to console;
to be understood as to understand,
to be loved as to love;
for it is in giving that we receive,
it is in pardoning that we are pardoned,
and it is in dying that we
are born to eternal life.

Eph 6:10–17

Battle against Evil

10† Finally, draw your strength from the Lord and from his mighty power. 11* Put on the armor of God so that you may be able to stand firm against the tactics of the devil. 12* For our struggle is not with flesh and blood but with the principalities, with the powers, with the world rulers of this present darkness, with the evil

to the Genesis passage its highest meaning in the light of the union of Christ and the church, of which Christlike loyalty and devotion in Christian marriage are a clear reflection (31–33).

6:10–20 A general exhortation to courage and prayer. Drawing upon the imagery and ideas of Is 11:5; 59:16–17; and Wis 5:17–23, Paul describes the Christian in terms of the dress and equipment of Roman soldiers. He observes, however, that the Christian's readiness for combat is not directed against human beings but against the spiritual powers of evil (10–17; cf 1:21; 2:2; 3:10). Unique importance is placed upon prayer (18–20).

5:23 1 Cor 11:3; Col 1:18.
5:25 Col 3:19; 1 Tm 2:6.
5:26 Rom 6:4; Ti 3:5–7.
5:27 2 Cor 11:2; Col 1:22.
5:30 Rom 12:5; 1 Cor 6:15.
5:31 Gn 2:24; Mt 19:5; Mk 10:7–8.
5:32 Rv 19:7.
6:1 Prv 6:20; Sir 3:1–6; Col 3:20.
6:2–3 Ex 20:12; Dt 5:16.
6:4 Col 3:21–22.
6:5 Col 3:22–25; 1 Tm 6:1–2; Ti 2:9–10.
6:6 1 Pt 2:18.
6:9 Col 4:1.
6:11 Rom 13:12; 2 Cor 6:7; 10:4; Jas 4:7.
6:12 Eph 1:21; 2:2; Col 1:13.

spirits in the heavens. 13* Therefore, put on the
armor of God, that you may be able to resist on
the evil day and, having done everything, to hold
your ground. 14* So stand fast with your loins
girded in truth, clothed with righteousness as a
breastplate, 15* and your feet shod in readiness
for the gospel of peace. 16* In all circumstances,
hold faith as a shield, to quench all [the] flaming
arrows of the evil one. 17* And take the helmet
of salvation and the sword of the Spirit, which is
the word of God.

Constant Prayer

18* With all prayer and supplication, pray at
every opportunity in the Spirit. To that end, be
watchful with all perseverance and supplication
for all the holy ones 19* and also for me, that
speech may be given me to open my mouth, to
make known with boldness the mystery of the gos-
pel 20* for which I am an ambassador in chains, so
that I may have the courage to speak as I must.

V: Conclusion

A Final Message

21*† So that you also may have news of me
and of what I am doing, Tychicus, my beloved
brother and trustworthy minister in the Lord,
will tell you everything. 22* I am sending him
to you for this very purpose, so that you may
know about us and that he may encourage your
hearts.

23 Peace be to the brothers, and love with faith,
from God the Father and the Lord Jesus Christ.
24* Grace be with all who love our Lord Jesus
Christ in immortality.

---

† **6:21–24** *Tychicus:* the bearer of the letter; see the note on Col 4:7. Verses 21–22 parallel Col 4:7–8, often word for word. If Ephesians is addressed to several Christian communities (see Introduction), it is understandable that no greetings to individual members of these communities should have been included in it.

---

* **6:13** Rom 13:12.
6:14 Wis 5:17–20; Is 11:5; Lk 12:35; 1 Thes 5:8.
6:15 Is 52:7.
6:16 1 Pt 5:9.
6:17 Is 59:17; 1 Thes 5:8.
6:18 Mt 26:41; Col 4:2–3.
6:19 Acts 4:29; Col 4:3; 2 Thes 3:1.
6:20 2 Cor 5:20; Col 4:4.
6:21 Acts 20:4; Col 4:7; 2 Tm 4:12.
6:22 Col 4:8.
6:24 1 Pt 1:8.

"To be, or not to be: that is the question." In this line from Shakespeare's *Hamlet,* Hamlet wonders which is better for him—to live or to die. He doesn't want to live and suffer, but he's afraid the "sleep of death" may be worse. Either way, he loses. In the Letter to the Philippians, Paul struggles with a similar question. But Paul wants to die to be with God. His desire to stay is to later serve the church.

The Letter to the Philippians

In Depth

When Paul wrote this letter, he was imprisoned facing a charge that might end in his death. He wrote it either near the end of his life when he was under house arrest in Rome or, more likely, during an earlier imprisonment in Ephesus (see 1 Cor 15:32, 2 Cor 1:8).

Like Hamlet, Paul is torn: "I am caught between" life and death (Phil 1:23). But unlike Hamlet, Paul feels he'll win either way: "For to me life is Christ, and death is gain" (verse 21). In addition, Paul believes this imprisonment will not end with his death, because he is still needed to support the new churches he helped start.

Incredibly, even in prison, Paul exhibits a spirit of hope and encouragement. In this short letter, he uses the words *rejoice* and *joy* fifteen times! Living in Christ doesn't mean everything will always go wonderfully. But it does mean that God can get you through the good times and the difficult times with joy.

In this letter, Paul asks the Philippians—and us—to imitate Christ. Imitating Christ is to think and act as Christ did even when things aren't going our way. Paul quotes an early Christian song (see 2:6–11) to the Philippians to show what imitating Christ means. The song praises our Lord Jesus, who chose to humble himself, chose to become a servant, and was "obedient to death" (verse 8). Therefore God exalted him above all things.

It is clear from this letter that Paul had a close relationship with the Philippians. No doubt, they were upset for him. Paul wanted them to rejoice in Christ and in their suffering, and to stop worrying (see 4:4–6). He encouraged them to present their concerns—all of them—to God in prayer. And he pointed out that if they did so, "the peace of God that surpasses all understanding will guard your hearts and minds in Christ Jesus" (verse 7). What marvelous advice and comfort for people of all times and ages.

At a Glance

I. **Address (1:1–11).**
II. **Progress of the Gospel (1:12–26).**
III. **Instructions for the Community (1:27—2:18).**
IV. **Travel Plans of Paul and His Assistants (2:19—3:1).**
V. **Polemic: Righteousness and the Goal in Christ (3:2–21).**
VI. **Instructions for the Community (4:1–9).**
VII. **Gratitude for the Philippians' Generosity (4:10–20).**
VIII. **Farewell (4:21–23).**

Quick Facts

Inspired Author: Paul
Date Written: AD 55 if from Ephesus, from AD 59 to 63 if from Rome
Audience: the church in Philippi

2:10–11

Philippians

I: Address

Greeting†

1 [1]* Paul and Timothy, slaves† of Christ Jesus, to
all the holy ones in Christ Jesus who are in Phi-
lippi, with the overseers and ministers: [2]*† grace
to you and peace from God our Father and the
Lord Jesus Christ.

Thanksgiving

[3]*† I give thanks to my God at every remem-
brance of you, [4]praying always with joy in my
every prayer for all of you, [5]because of your part-
nership for the gospel from the first day until
now. [6]*† I am confident of this, that the one who
began a good work in you will continue to com-
plete it until the day of Christ Jesus. [7]It is right
that I should think this way about all of you, be-
cause I hold you in my heart, you who are all part-
ners with me in grace, both in my imprisonment
and in the defense and confirmation of the gos-
pel. [8]* For God is my witness, how I long for all
of you with the affection of Christ Jesus. [9]* And
this is my prayer: that your love may increase ever
more and more in knowledge and every kind of

†

1:1–2 See the note on Rom 1:1–7, concerning the greeting.

1:1 *Slaves:* Paul usually refers to himself at the start of a letter as an apostle. Here he substitutes a term suggesting the unconditional obligation of himself and Timothy to the service of Christ, probably because, in view of the good relationship with the Philippians, he wishes to stress his status as a co-servant rather than emphasize his apostolic authority. Reference to Timothy is a courtesy: Paul alone writes the letter, as the singular verb throughout shows (3–26), and the reference (2:19–24) to Timothy in the third person. *Overseers:* the Greek term *episkopos* literally means "one who oversees" or "one who supervises," but since the second century it has come to designate the "bishop," the official who heads a local church. In New Testament times this office had not yet developed into the form that it later assumed, though it seems to be well on the way to such development in the Pastorals; see 1 Tm 3:2 and Ti 1:7, where it is translated *bishop.* At Philippi, however (and at Ephesus, according to Acts 20:28), there was more than one *episkopos,* and the precise function of these officials is uncertain. In order to distinguish this office from the later stages into which it developed, the term is here translated as *overseers. Ministers:* the Greek term *diakonoi* is used frequently in the New Testament to designate "servants," "attendants," or "ministers." Paul refers to himself and to other apostles as "ministers of God" (2 Cor 6:4) or "ministers of Christ" (2 Cor 11:23). In the Pastorals (1 Tm 3:8, 12) the *diakonos* has become an established official in the local church; hence the term is there translated as *deacon.* The *diakonoi* at Philippi seem to represent an earlier stage of development of the office; we are uncertain about their precise functions. Hence the term is here translated as *ministers.* See Rom 16:1, where Phoebe is described as a *diakonos (minister)* of the church of Cenchreae.

1:2 The gifts come *from* Christ the Lord, not simply through him from the Father; compare the christology in 2:6–11.

1:3–11 As in Rom 1:8–15 and all the Pauline letters except Galatians, a thanksgiving follows, including a direct prayer for the Philippians (9–11); see the note on Rom 1:8. On their *partnership for the gospel* (5), cf 29–30; 4:10–20. Their devotion to the faith and to Paul made them his pride and joy (4:1). The characteristics thus manifested are evidence of the community's continuing preparation for the Lord's parousia (6, 10). Paul's especially warm relationship with the Philippians is suggested here (7, 8) as elsewhere in the letter. The eschatology serves to underscore a concern for ethical growth (9–11), which appears throughout the letter.

1:6 *The day of Christ Jesus:* the parousia or triumphant return of Christ, when those loyal to him will be with him and share in his eternal glory; cf 10; 2:16; 3:20–21; 1 Thes 4:17; 5:10; 2 Thes 1:10; 1 Cor 1:8.

*

1:1 Rom 1:1; 2 Cor 1:1; 1 Thes 1:1; Phlm 1 / 1 Tm 3:1–13.
1:2 Rom 1:7; Gal 1:3; Phlm 3.
1:3 Rom 1:8; 1 Cor 1:4; 1 Thes 1:2.
1:6 Phil 2:13 / Phil 1:10; 2:16; 1 Cor 1:8.
1:8 Rom 1:9; 2 Cor 1:23; 1 Thes 2:5.
1:9 Eph 3:14–19; Col 1:9–10; Phlm 6.

perception, 10* to discern what is of value, so that
you may be pure and blameless for the day of
Christ, 11* filled with the fruit of righteousness
that comes through Jesus Christ for the glory and
praise of God.

II: Progress of the Gospel

12*† I want you to know, brothers, that my
situation has turned out rather to advance the
gospel, 13*† so that my imprisonment has be-
come well known in Christ throughout the
whole praetorium and to all the rest, 14† and so
that the majority of the brothers, having taken
encouragement in the Lord from my imprison-
ment, dare more than ever to proclaim the word
fearlessly.
15 Of course, some preach Christ from envy
and rivalry, others from good will. 16 The latter
act out of love, aware that I am here for the de-
fense of the gospel; 17 the former proclaim Christ
out of selfish ambition, not from pure motives,
thinking that they will cause me trouble in
my imprisonment. 18*† What difference does it
make, as long as in every way, whether in pre-
tense or in truth, Christ is being proclaimed? And
in that I rejoice.
Indeed I shall continue to rejoice, 19*† for I
know that this will result in deliverance for me†
through your prayers and support from the Spirit
of Jesus Christ. 20* My eager expectation and
hope is that I shall not be put to shame in any
way, but that with all boldness, now as always,
Christ will be magnified in my body, whether by
life or by death. 21* For to me life is Christ, and
death is gain. 22* If I go on living in the flesh, that
means fruitful labor for me. And I do not know
which I shall choose. 23* I am caught between
the two. I long to depart this life and be with
Christ, [for] that is far better. 24 Yet that I remain

Friendship

In Philippians 1:3–11, Paul writes beautifully of his love for and friendship with the people living in Philippi. We need to remember that Paul—and the other people who wrote the inspired words of the Scriptures—was a real person with problems and needs. He had some dear friends in Philippi, and his words to them provide a great model of true friendship: sharing the ups and downs, being committed to one another, being thankful for one another, and wanting the best for one another. Friendship in Christ is like that!

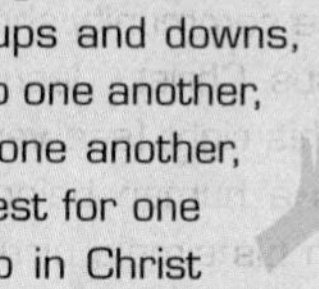

Who are true friends for you? To whom are you a true friend? How can you keep Christ at the center of your friendships?

▶ **Phil 1:3–11**

[in] the flesh is more necessary for your benefit.
25 And this I know with confidence, that I shall
remain and continue in the service of all of you
for your progress and joy in the faith, 26 so that
your boasting in Christ Jesus may abound on
account of me when I come to you again.

III: Instructions for the Community

Steadfastness in Faith

27*† Only, conduct yourselves in a way worthy
of the gospel of Christ, so that, whether I come
and see you or am absent, I may hear news of

†

1:12–26 The body of the letter begins with an account of Paul's present *situation,* i.e., his *imprisonment* (12–13; see Introduction), and then goes on with advice for the Philippians (1:27—2:18). The *advance of the gospel* (12) and the *progress* of the Philippians *in the faith* (25) frame what is said.

1:13 *Praetorium:* either the praetorian guard in the city where Paul was imprisoned or the governor's official residence in a Roman province (cf Mk 15:16; Acts 23:35). See Introduction on possible sites.

1:14–18 Although Paul is imprisoned, Christians there nonetheless go on preaching Christ. But they do so with varied motives, *some* with personal hostility toward Paul, others out of personal ambition.

1:18 *Rejoice:* a major theme in the letter; see Introduction.

1:19–25 Paul earnestly debates his prospects of martyrdom or continued missionary labor. While he may *long to depart this life* and thus *be with Christ* (23), his overall and final expectation is that he will be delivered from this imprisonment and *continue in the service* of the Philippians and of others (19, 25; 2:24). In either case, Christ is central (20, 21); if to live means Christ for Paul, death means to be united with Christ in a deeper sense.

1:19 *Result in deliverance for me:* an echo of Jb 13:16, hoping that God will turn suffering to ultimate good and deliverance from evil.

1:27–30 Ethical admonition begins at this early point in the letter, emphasizing steadfastness and congregational unity in the face of possible suffering. The *opponents* (28) are those in Philippi, probably pagans, who oppose the gospel cause. *This is proof . . .* (28) may refer to the whole outlook and conduct of the Philippians, turning out for their salvation but to the judgment of the opponents (cf 2 Cor 2:15–16), or possibly the sentence refers to the opinion of the opponents, who hold that the obstinacy of the Christians points to the destruction of such people as defy Roman authority (though in reality, Paul holds, such faithfulness leads to salvation).

*

1:10 Rom 2:18; 12:2 / Phil 1:6.
1:11 Jn 15:8.
1:12–13 Eph 3:1; 6:20; 2 Tm 2:9; Phlm 9.
1:13 Phil 4:22.
1:18 Phil 4:10.
1:19 Jb 13:16 / 2 Cor 1:11.
1:20 1 Cor 6:20; 1 Pt 4:16.
1:21 Gal 2:20.
1:22 Rom 1:13.
1:23 2 Cor 5:8.
1:27 Eph 4:1; Col 1:10; 1 Thes 2:12 / Phil 4:3.

Live It!

Divine Humility, Cosmic Glory

Mention the name Jesus, or the title Christ, and many images spring to mind. That is good, because no single image can capture Jesus' true nature completely.

In Philippians 2:6–11, borrowing from a hymn sung in the earliest days of the Church, Paul explains how the community should be of the same mind as Jesus Christ. Jesus gave up equality with God as his right (see verse 6) and entered our world as a human being. He lived in utter humility, from his simple birth to his Crucifixion. Because of his humility and obedience, Jesus' name is exalted by God so that Jesus Christ is now Lord of all and worshiped by all creation!

To be the loving people God calls us to be, we must imitate Christ's humility in our love for one another. Most of us are used to seeing those who are "powerful" in this world being served by others. But Paul reminds us it is the nature of Jesus to serve. Christians are called to be powerful in a radically different way—to see humble service as their basic call and the path to true glory—with the "same attitude that is also yours in Christ Jesus" (verse 5).

▶ **Phil 2:1–11**

you, that you are standing firm in one spirit, with
one mind struggling together for the faith of the
gospel, 28 not intimidated in any way by your
opponents. This is proof to them of destruction,
but of your salvation. And this is God's doing.
29* For to you has been granted, for the sake of
Christ, not only to believe in him but also to suf-
fer for him. 30*† Yours is the same struggle as you
saw in me and now hear about me.

Plea for Unity and Humility

2 1† If there is any encouragement in Christ,
any solace in love, any participation in the
Spirit, any compassion and mercy, 2* complete
my joy by being of the same mind, with the same
love, united in heart, thinking one thing. 3* Do
nothing out of selfishness or out of vainglory;
rather, humbly regard others as more important
than yourselves, 4* each looking out not for his
own interests, but [also] everyone for those of
others.

5† Have among yourselves the same attitude
that is also yours in Christ Jesus,

6*† Who, though he was in the form of God,
did not regard equality with God
something to be grasped.†
7*† Rather, he emptied himself,
taking the form of a slave,
coming in human likeness;
and found human in appearance,
8*† he humbled himself,
becoming obedient to death,
even death on a cross.
9*† Because of this, God greatly exalted him

1:30 A reference to Paul's earlier imprisonment in Philippi (Acts 16:19–24; 1 Thes 2:2) and to his present confinement.

2:1–11 The admonition to likemindedness and unity (2–5) is based on the believers' threefold experience with Christ, God's love, and the Spirit. The appeal to humility (3) and to obedience (12) is rooted in christology, specifically in a statement about Christ Jesus (6–11) and his humbling of self and obedience to the point of death (8).

2:5 *Have . . . the same attitude that is also yours in Christ Jesus:* or, "that also Christ Jesus had." While it is often held that Christ here functions as a model for moral imitation, it is not the historical Jesus but the entire Christ event that vv 6–11 depict. Therefore, the appeal is to have in relations among yourselves that same relationship you have in Jesus Christ, i.e., serving one another as you serve Christ (4).

2:6–11 Perhaps an early Christian hymn quoted here by Paul. The short rhythmic lines fall into two parts, vv 6–8 where the subject of every verb is Christ, and vv 9–11 where the subject is God. The general pattern is thus of Christ's humiliation and then exaltation. More precise analyses propose a division into six three-line stanzas (6; 7abc; 7d–8; 9; 10; 11) or into three stanzas (6–7ab; 7cd–8; 9–11). Phrases such as *even death on a cross* (8c) are considered by some to be additions (by Paul) to the hymn, as are vv 10c and 11c.

2:6 Either a reference to Christ's preexistence and those aspects of divinity that he was willing to give up in order to serve in human form, or to what the man Jesus refused to grasp at to attain divinity. Many see an allusion to the Genesis story: unlike Adam, Jesus, *though . . . in the form of God* (Gn 1:26–27), did not reach out for *equality with God,* in contrast with the first Adam in Gn 3:5–6.

2:7 *Taking the form of a slave, coming in human likeness:* or ". . . taking the form of a slave. // Coming in human likeness, and found human in appearance." While it is common to take vv 6 and 7 as dealing with Christ's preexistence and v 8 with his incarnate life, so that lines 7b and c are parallel, it is also possible to interpret so as to exclude any reference to preexistence (see the note on 2:6) and to take vv 6–8 as presenting two parallel stanzas about Jesus' human state (6–7b; 7cd–8); in the latter alternative, *coming in human likeness* begins the second stanza and parallels 6a to some extent.

2:8 There may be reflected here language about the servant of the Lord, Is 52:13—53:12, especially 53:12.

2:9 *The name:* "Lord" (11), revealing the true nature of the one who is named.

1:29 Mt 5:10; 10:38; Mk 8:34; Acts 5:41.
1:30 Phil 1:13; Acts 16:22–24.
2:2 Rom 15:5; 1 Cor 1:10.
2:3 Rom 12:3, 10; Gal 5:26.
2:4 1 Cor 10:24, 33; 13:5.
2:6 Jn 1:1–2; 17:5; Col 2:9; Heb 1:3.
2:7 Is 53:3, 11; Jn 1:14; Rom 8:3; 2 Cor 8:9; Gal 4:4; Heb 2:14, 17.
2:8 Mt 26:39; Jn 10:17; Heb 5:8; 12:2.
2:9 Acts 2:33; Mt 23:12; Eph 1:20–21; Heb 1:3–4.

and bestowed on him the name
that is above every name,
10*† that at the name of Jesus
every knee should bend,
of those in heaven and on earth and under
the earth,
11*† and every tongue confess that
Jesus Christ is Lord,
to the glory of God the Father.

Obedience and Service in the World†

12* So then, my beloved, obedient as you have
always been, not only when I am present but all
the more now when I am absent, work out your
salvation with fear and trembling.† 13* For God
is the one who, for his good purpose, works in
you both to desire and to work. 14* Do everything
without grumbling or questioning, 15*† that you
may be blameless and innocent, children of God
without blemish in the midst of a crooked and
perverse generation, among whom you shine
like lights in the world, 16* as you hold on to
the word of life, so that my boast for the day of
Christ may be that I did not run in vain or labor
in vain. 17*† But, even if I am poured out as a
libation upon the sacrificial service of your faith,
I rejoice and share my joy with all of you. 18* In
the same way you also should rejoice and share
your joy with me.

IV: Travel Plans of Paul and His Assistants†

Timothy and Paul

19*† I hope, in the Lord Jesus, to send Timothy
to you soon, so that I too may be heartened by
hearing news of you. 20 For I have no one com-
parable to him for genuine interest in whatever
concerns you. 21* For they all seek their own
interests, not those of Jesus Christ. 22 But you
know his worth, how as a child with a father he
served along with me in the cause of the gos-
pel. 23 He it is, then, whom I hope to send as
soon as I see how things go with me, 24† but I
am confident in the Lord that I myself will also
come soon.

Epaphroditus

25*† With regard to Epaphroditus, my brother
and co-worker and fellow soldier, your mes-
senger and minister in my need, I consider
it necessary to send him to you. 26 For he has
been longing for all of you and was distressed
because you heard that he was ill. 27 He was in-
deed ill, close to death; but God had mercy on
him, not just on him but also on me, so that I
might not have sorrow upon sorrow. 28 I send
him therefore with the greater eagerness, so
that, on seeing him, you may rejoice again, and
I may have less anxiety. 29* Welcome him then
in the Lord with all joy and hold such people
in esteem, 30 because for the sake of the work of
Christ he came close to death, risking his life to
make up for those services to me that you could
not perform.

Concluding Admonitions

3 1*† Finally, my brothers, rejoice in the Lord.
Writing the same things to you is no burden
for me but is a safeguard for you.

†

2:10–11 *Every knee should bend . . . every tongue confess:* into this language of Is 45:23 there has been inserted a reference to the three levels in the universe, according to ancient thought, *heaven, earth, under the earth.*

2:11 *Jesus Christ is Lord:* a common early Christian acclamation; cf 1 Cor 12:3; Rom 10:9. But doxology to God the Father is not overlooked here (11c) in the final version of the hymn.

2:12–18 Paul goes on to draw out further ethical implications for daily life (14–18) from the salvation God works in Christ.

2:12 *Fear and trembling:* a common Old Testament expression indicating awe and seriousness in the service of God (cf Ex 15:16; Jdt 2:28; Ps 2:11; Is 19:16).

2:15–16 *Generation . . . as you hold on to . . . :* or ". . . generation. Among them shine like lights in the world because you hold the word of life . . . ."

2:17 *Libation:* in ancient religious ritual, the pouring out on the ground of a liquid offering as a sacrifice. Paul means that he may be facing death.

2:19—3:1 The plans of Paul and his assistants for future travel are regularly a part of a Pauline letter near its conclusion; cf Rom 15:22–29; 1 Cor 16:5–12.

2:19 *Timothy:* already known to the Philippians (Acts 16:1–15; cf 1 Cor 4:17; 16:10).

2:24 *I myself will also come soon:* cf 1:19–25 for the significance of this statement.

2:25 *Epaphroditus:* sent by the Philippians as their *messenger* (literally, "apostle") to aid Paul in his imprisonment, he had fallen seriously ill; Paul commends him as he sends him back to Philippi.

3:1 *Finally . . . rejoice:* the adverb often signals the close of a letter; cf 4:8; 2 Cor 13:11. While the verb could also be translated "good-bye" or "farewell," although it is never so used in Greek epistolography, the theme of joy has been frequent in the letter (1:18; 2:2, 18); note also 4:4 and the addition of "always" there as evidence for the meaning "rejoice." To write *the same things* may refer to what Paul has previously taught in Philippi or to what he has just written or to what follows.

*

2:10 Is 45:23; Jn 5:23; Rom 14:11; Rv 5:13.
2:11 Acts 2:36; Rom 10:9; 1 Cor 12:3.
2:12 Ps 2:11; 1 Cor 2:3; 2 Cor 7:15.
2:13 Phil 1:6; 1 Cor 12:6; 15:10; 2 Cor 3:5.
2:14 1 Cor 10:10; 1 Pt 4:9.
2:15 1 Thes 3:13 / Dt 32:5; Mt 10:16; Acts 2:40 / Dn 12:3; Mt 5:14, 16; Eph 5:8.
2:16 1 Thes 2:19 / Is 49:4; 65:23; Gal 2:2.
2:17 Rom 15:16; 2 Tm 4:6.
2:18 Phil 3:1; 4:4.
2:19 Acts 16:1–3; 17:14–15; 1 Cor 4:17; 16:10.
2:21 1 Cor 13:5; 2 Tm 4:10.
2:25 Phil 4:10–11, 15–16, 18.
2:29 1 Cor 16:18.
3:1 Phil 2:18; 4:4.

Live It!

Commitment to the Ultimate Goal

In what ways have you become more mature in the last five years? How do other people recognize that you are maturing?

In Philippians 3:12–16, Paul describes one measure of maturity—the ability to keep a commitment to the ultimate goal of God's call in Christ Jesus. Mature people—whether sixteen or sixty—are always striving to perfect themselves in pursuit of their goals.

Paul says the goal that guides his life is "to know [Christ] and the power of his resurrection" (verse 10). Is knowing Christ and the power of his Resurrection the goal that guides your life?

▶ Phil 3:12–16

PHIL

V: Polemic: Righteousness and the Goal in Christ†

Against Legalistic Teachers

2*† Beware of the dogs! Beware of the evil-work-
ers! Beware of the mutilation!† 3*† For we are the
circumcision, we who worship through the Spirit
of God, who boast in Christ Jesus and do not put
our confidence in flesh, 4* although I myself have
grounds for confidence even in the flesh.

Paul's Autobiography

If anyone else thinks he can be confident in
flesh, all the more can I. 5*† Circumcised on
the eighth day, of the race of Israel, of the tribe
of Benjamin, a Hebrew of Hebrew parentage,
in observance of the law a Pharisee, 6* in zeal I
persecuted the church, in righteousness based on
the law I was blameless.

Righteousness from God

7*† [But] whatever gains I had, these I have
come to consider a loss because of Christ. 8 More
than that, I even consider everything as a loss
because of the supreme good of knowing Christ
Jesus my Lord. For his sake I have accepted the
loss of all things and I consider them so much
rubbish, that I may gain Christ 9* and be found
in him, not having any righteousness of my own
based on the law but that which comes through
faith in Christ, the righteousness from God, de-
pending on faith 10* to know him and the power
of his resurrection and [the] sharing of his suf-
ferings by being conformed to his death, 11* if
somehow I may attain the resurrection from the
dead.

Forward in Christ†

12*† It is not that I have already taken hold of
it or have already attained perfect maturity, but I
continue my pursuit in hope that I may possess
it, since I have indeed been taken possession of
by Christ [Jesus]. 13 Brothers, I for my part do not
consider myself to have taken possession. Just
one thing: forgetting what lies behind but strain-
ing forward to what lies ahead, 14* I continue
my pursuit toward the goal, the prize of God's

†

3:2–21 An abrupt change in content and tone, either because Paul at this point responds to disturbing news he has just heard about a threat to the faith of the Philippians in the form of false teachers, or because part of another Pauline letter was inserted here; see Introduction. The chapter describes these teachers in strong terms as *dogs.* The persons meant are evidently different from the rival preachers of 1:14–18 and the opponents of 1:28. Since vv 2–4 emphasize Jewish terms like *circumcision* (2–3, 5), some relate them to the "Judaizers" of the Letter to the Galatians. Other phrases make them appear more like the false teachers of 2 Cor 11:12–15, the *evil-workers.* The latter part of the chapter depicts the *many* who are *enemies* of Christ's cross in terms that may sound more Gentile or even "gnostic" than Jewish (18–19). Accordingly, some see two groups of false teachers in ch 3, others one group characterized by a claim of having attained "perfect maturity" (12–15).

3:2–11 Paul sets forth the Christian claim, especially using personal, autobiographical terms that are appropriate to the situation. He presents his own experience in coming to know Christ Jesus in terms of *righteousness* or justification (cf Rom 1:16–17; 3:21—5:11; Gal 2:5–11), contrasting *the righteousness from God* through faith and that of one's own *based on the law* as two exclusive ways of pleasing God.

3:2 *Beware of the mutilation:* literally, "incision," an ironic wordplay on "circumcision"; cf Gal 5:12. There may be an association with the self-inflicted mutilations of the prophets of Baal (1 Kgs 18:28) and of devotees of Cybele who slashed themselves in religious frenzy.

3:3 *We are the circumcision:* the true people of God, seed and offspring of Abraham (Gal 3:7, 29; 6:15). *Spirit of God:* some manuscripts read "worship God by the Spirit."

3:5 *Circumcised on the eighth day:* as the law required (Gn 17:12; Lv 12:3).

3:7 *Loss:* his knowledge of Christ led Paul to reassess the ways of truly pleasing and serving God. His reevaluation indicates the profound and lasting effect of his experience of the meaning of Christ on the way to Damascus some twenty years before (Gal 1:15–16; Acts 9:1–22).

3:12–16 To be *taken possession of by Christ* does not mean that one has already arrived at perfect spiritual maturity. Paul and the Philippians instead press on, trusting in God.

3:12 *Attained perfect maturity:* possibly an echo of the concept in the mystery religions of being an initiate, admitted to divine secrets.

*

3:2 Ps 22:17, 21; Rv 22:15 / 2 Cor 11:13 / Gal 5:6, 12.
3:3 Rom 2:28–29; Col 2:11.
3:4 2 Cor 11:18, 21–23.
3:5 Lk 1:59; 2:21 / Acts 22:3; 23:6; 26:5.
3:6 Acts 8:3; 22:4; 26:9–11.
3:7 Mt 13:44, 46; Lk 14:33.
3:9 Rom 3:21–22.
3:10 Rom 6:3–5; 8:17; Gal 6:17.
3:11 Jn 11:23–26; Acts 4:2; Rv 20:5–6.
3:12 1 Tm 6:12, 19.
3:14 1 Cor 9:24–25; 2 Tm 4:7.

upward calling, in Christ Jesus. 15 Let us, then, who are "perfectly mature" adopt this attitude. And if you have a different attitude, this too God will reveal to you. 16† Only, with regard to what we have attained, continue on the same course.

Wrong Conduct and Our Goal†

17*† Join with others in being imitators of me, brothers, and observe those who thus conduct themselves according to the model you have in us. 18* For many, as I have often told you and now tell you even in tears, conduct themselves as enemies of the cross of Christ. 19* Their end is destruction. Their God is their stomach; their glory is in their "shame." Their minds are occupied with earthly things. 20*† But our citizenship is in heaven, and from it we also await a savior, the Lord Jesus Christ. 21* He will change our lowly body to conform with his glorified body by the power that enables him also to bring all things into subjection to himself.

"Rejoice in the Lord always. I shall say it again: rejoice!" (Phil 4:4)

VI: Instructions for the Community

Live in Concord

4 1*† Therefore, my brothers, whom I love and long for, my joy and crown, in this way stand firm in the Lord, beloved.

2† I urge Euodia and I urge Syntyche to come to a mutual understanding in the Lord. 3*† Yes, and I ask you also, my true yokemate, to help them, for they have struggled at my side in promoting the gospel, along with Clement and my other co-workers, whose names are in the book of life.

Joy and Peace

4*† Rejoice in the Lord always. I shall say it again: rejoice! 5*† Your kindness should be known to all. The Lord is near. 6* Have no anxiety at all, but in everything, by prayer and petition, with thanksgiving, make your requests known to God. 7* Then the peace of God that surpasses all understanding will guard your hearts and minds in Christ Jesus.

8*† Finally, brothers, whatever is true, whatever is honorable, whatever is just, whatever is pure, whatever is lovely, whatever is gracious, if there is any excellence and if there is anything worthy of praise, think about these things. 9*† Keep on doing what you have learned and received and heard and seen in me. Then the God of peace will be with you.

PHIL

VII: Gratitude for the Philippians' Generosity

10*† I rejoice greatly in the Lord that now at last you revived your concern for me. You were, of course, concerned about me but lacked an opportunity. 11* Not that I say this because of need, for I have learned, in whatever situation I find myself, to be self-sufficient. 12 I know indeed how to live in humble circumstances; I know also how to live with abundance. In every

†

3:16 Some manuscripts add, probably to explain Paul's cryptic phrase, "thinking alike."

3:17–21 Paul and those who live a life centered in Christ, envisaging both his suffering and resurrection, provide a model that is the opposite of opponents who reject Christ's cross (cf 1 Cor 1:23).

3:17 *Being imitators of me:* not arrogance, but humble simplicity, since all his converts know that Paul is wholly dedicated to imitating Christ (1 Cor 11:1; cf also Phil 4:9; 1 Thes 1:6; 2 Thes 3:7, 9; 1 Cor 4:6).

3:20 *Citizenship:* Christians constitute a colony of heaven, as Philippi was a *colonia* of Rome (Acts 16:12). The hope Paul expresses involves the final coming of Christ, not a status already attained, such as the opponents claim.

4:1–9 This series of ethical admonitions rests especially on the view of Christ and his coming (cf 5) in 3:20–21. Paul's instructions touch on unity within the congregation, joy, prayer, and the Christian outlook on life.

4:2 *Euodia . . . Syntyche:* two otherwise unknown women in the Philippian congregation; on the advice to them, cf 2:2–4.

4:3 *Yokemate:* or "comrade," although the Greek *syzygos* could also be a proper name. *Clement:* otherwise unknown, although later writers sought to identify him with Clement, bishop of Rome (Eusebius, *Ecclesiastical History* 3, 15, 1).

4:4 *Rejoice:* see the note on 3:1.

4:5 *Kindness:* considerateness, forbearance, fairness. *The Lord is near:* most likely a reference to Christ's parousia (1:6, 10; 3:20–21; 1 Cor 16:22), although some sense an echo of Ps 119:151 and the perpetual presence of the Lord.

4:8 The language employs terms from Roman Stoic thought.

4:9 Cf the note on 3:17.

4:10–20 Paul, more directly than anywhere else in the letter (cf 1:3–5), here thanks the Philippians for their gift of money sent through Epaphroditus (2:25). Paul's own policy was *to be self-sufficient* as a missionary, supporting himself by his own labor (1 Thes 2:5–9; 1 Cor 9:15–18; cf Acts 18:2–3). In spite of this reliance on self and on God to provide (11–13), Paul accepted gifts from the Philippians *not only once but more than once* (16) when he was in Thessalonica (Acts 17:1–9), as he does now, in prison (*my distress,* 14). While commercial terms appear in the passage, like *an account of giving and receiving* (15) and *received full payment* (18), Paul is most concerned about the spiritual growth of the Philippians (10, 17, 19); he emphasizes that God will care for their needs, through Christ.

*

3:17 1 Cor 4:16; 11:1; 1 Thes 1:7; 1 Pt 5:3.
3:18 1 Cor 1:17, 23; Gal 6:12.
3:19 Rom 8:5–6; 16:18.
3:20 Eph 2:6, 19; Col 3:1–3; Heb 12:22.
3:21 Rom 8:23, 29; 1 Cor 15:42–57; 2 Cor 3:18; 5:1–5 / 1 Cor 15:27–28.
4:1 1 Thes 2:19–20.
4:3 Ex 32:32–33; Ps 69:29; Dn 12:1; Lk 10:20; Rv 3:5; 13:8; 17:8; 20:12, 15; 21:27.
4:4 Phil 2:18; 3:1.
4:5 Ti 3:2 / Ps 145:18; Heb 10:37; Jas 5:8–9.
4:6 Mt 6:25–34; 1 Pt 5:7 / Col 4:2.
4:7 Jn 14:27; Col 3:15.
4:8 Rom 12:17.
4:9 1 Thes 4:1 / Rom 15:33; 16:20; 1 Cor 14:33; 1 Thes 5:23.
4:10 Phil 1:18; 2:25; 1 Cor 9:11; 2 Cor 11:9.
4:11–12 1 Cor 4:11; 2 Cor 6:10; 11:27 / 2 Cor 12:9–10.

Cultural Connection

The Beauty of Creation

Paul ends his message to the Philippians by encouraging them to keep their minds on things that are true, humble, just, pure, lovely, and gracious. This would certainly include the wonder and beauty of creation, something Native Americans are deeply aware of. Let this Navajo prayer in praise of creation inspire you to keep focused on the beauty God has provided in the world around us:

I walk with beauty before me
I walk with beauty behind me
I walk with beauty above me
I walk with beauty below me
Beauty has been restored
from the East
Beauty has been restored
from the South
Beauty has been restored
from the West
Beauty has been restored
from the North
Beauty has been restored
from the sky-top
Beauty has been restored
from the earth-bottom
Beauty has been restored
from all around me

(From Michael F. Steltenkamp, *The Sacred Vision*, p. 92)

▶ Phil 4:8–9

PHIL

circumstance and in all things I have learned the
secret of being well fed and of going hungry, of
living in abundance and of being in need. 13* I
have the strength for everything through him
who empowers me. 14 Still, it was kind of you to
share in my distress.
15† You Philippians indeed know that at the
beginning of the gospel, when I left Macedonia,
not a single church shared with me in an account
of giving and receiving, except you alone. 16 For
even when I was at Thessalonica you sent me
something for my needs, not only once but more
than once. 17 It is not that I am eager for the gift;
rather, I am eager for the profit that accrues to
your account. 18*† I have received full payment
and I abound. I am very well supplied because
of what I received from you through Epaphrodi-
tus, "a fragrant aroma," an acceptable sacrifice,
pleasing to God. 19* My God will fully supply
whatever you need, in accord with his glorious
riches in Christ Jesus. 20* To our God and Father,
glory forever and ever. Amen.

VIII: Farewell

21† Give my greetings to every holy one in
Christ Jesus. The brothers who are with me send
you their greetings; 22*† all the holy ones send
you their greetings, especially those of Caesar's
household. 23 The grace of the Lord Jesus Christ
be with your spirit.

†

4:15 *The beginning of the gospel:* it was at Philippi that Paul first preached Christ in Europe, going on from there to Thessalonica and Beroea (Acts 16:9—17:14).

4:18 *Aroma . . . sacrifice:* Old Testament cultic language (cf Gn 8:21; Ex 29:18, 25, 41; Lv 1:9, 13; Ez 20:41) applied to the Philippians' gift; cf Eph 5:2; 2 Cor 2:14–16.

4:21–23 On the usual greetings at the conclusion of a letter, see the note on 1 Cor 16:19–24. Inclusion of greetings from *all the holy ones* in the place from which Paul writes would involve even the Christians of 1:14–18 who had their differences with Paul.

4:22 *Those of Caesar's household:* minor officials or even slaves and freedmen, found in Ephesus or Rome, among other places.

*

4:13 Col 1:29; 2Tm 4:17.
4:18 Gn 8:21; Ex 29:18; Eph 5:2; Heb 13:16.
4:19 1 Thes 3:11, 13.
4:20 Rom 16:27; Eph 5:20.
4:22 Phil 1:13.

Every now and then, we hear about some latest secular fads being applied to Christianity. It is not unusual to hear of a minister of some megachurch applying an entertainment model to ministry or preaching that Christians will be rewarded with prosperity, reflecting the comfort and ease of contemporary suburban life. Although those fads may be popular, they do not accurately reflect the Christian message. This is not a new phenomenon, even in first-century Colossae. There was a group who was applying pagan religious practices and beliefs from Greek philosophy to the Christian community. The author's advice in the Letter to the Colossians is pretty direct: Stay focused on Christ and the authentic Gospel message!

In Depth

This letter attacks a group that was teaching a weird mixture of ideas. It insisted on Jewish rituals (see 2:16) and regulations (see verse 22), severe treatment of one's own body (see verse 23), and a philosophy that included "the elemental powers of the world" (verse 8) mixed with pagan religious practices. These teachers probably had Jewish roots, because they observed the Sabbath and other Jewish feasts (see verse 16). But it appears they were teaching that Jesus was a firstborn creature, although lower than the angels.

Against the backdrop of all this thinking, the author—who may not have been Paul but a disciple of Paul—declares the supreme mystery of Christ. Quoting a Christian hymn (see 1:15–20), the writer says Christ is honored not only as the firstborn of creation but also as the one through whom everything was created and who holds everything together. He is above everything that is!

Christians believe Jesus is more than just a great teacher; they believe Jesus is God, who chose to become human and live with us. This letter gives us an early statement of that belief: "In [Christ] dwells the whole fullness of the deity bodily" (2:9).

The Letter to the Colossians also offers comforting words about our God. God has given us life and forgiveness. God erased the record of our sins and set it aside, "nailing it to the cross" (verse 14). Unlike those teachers who burden their followers with guilt and impossible rules, our God frees us from guilt and gives us life! As you read this letter, you will find these and many other words to live by: "God's chosen ones . . . forgiving one another . . . put on love . . . And let the peace of Christ control your hearts" (3:12–15).

At a Glance

I. **Address (1:1–14).**
II. **The Preeminence of Christ (1:15—2:3).**
III. **Warnings Against False Teachers (2:4–23).**
IV. **The Ideal Christian Life in the World (3:1—4:6).**
V. **Conclusion (4:7–18).**

Quick Facts

Inspired Author: Paul or more likely a follower of Paul (see "Introduction to the Letters and Revelation")

Date Written: around AD 61 if by Paul; if by a follower, approximately AD 80

Audience: the Christian community at Colossae

Colossians

3:15–16

I: Address

Greeting

1 [1]*† Paul, an apostle of Christ Jesus by the will
of God, and Timothy our brother, [2] to the holy
ones and faithful brothers in Christ in Colossae:
grace to you and peace from God our Father.

Thanksgiving

[3]*† We always give thanks to God, the Father
of our Lord Jesus Christ, when we pray for you,
[4] for we have heard of your faith in Christ Jesus
and the love that you have for all the holy ones
[5]* because of the hope reserved for you in heaven.
Of this you have already heard through the word
of truth, the gospel, [6] that has come to you. Just as
in the whole world it is bearing fruit and growing,
so also among you, from the day you heard it and
came to know the grace of God in truth, [7]*† as
you learned it from Epaphras our beloved fellow
slave, who is a trustworthy minister of Christ on
your behalf [8] and who also told us of your love
in the Spirit.

Prayer for Continued Progress

[9]*† Therefore, from the day we heard this,
we do not cease praying for you and asking that
you may be filled with the knowledge of his will
through all spiritual wisdom and understanding
[10] to live in a manner worthy of the Lord, so as to
be fully pleasing, in every good work bearing fruit
and growing in the knowledge of God, [11] strength-
ened with every power, in accord with his glori-
ous might, for all endurance and patience, with
joy [12]*† giving thanks to the Father, who has

†

1:1–2 For the epistolary form used by Paul at the beginning of his letters, see the note on Rom 1:1–7. On *holy ones* or "God's people," see the note on Rom 1:7. Awareness of their calling helps this group to be *faithful brothers* and sisters *in Christ,* i.e., dedicated to the tasks implied in their calling.

1:3–8 On thanksgiving at the start of a letter, see the note on Rom 1:8. The apostle, recalling his own prayers for them and the good report about them he has received (3–4), congratulates the Colossians upon their acceptance of Christ and their faithful efforts to live the gospel (3:6–8). To encourage them he mentions the success of the gospel elsewhere (6) and assures them that his knowledge of their community is accurate, since he has been in personal contact with Epaphras (7–8), who likely had evangelized Colossae and other cities in the Lycus Valley of Asia Minor (cf 4:12, 13; Phlm 23). On *faith, love,* and *hope* (4, 5, 8), see the note on 1 Cor 13:13; cf 1 Thes 1:3; 5:8.

1:7 *Epaphras:* now with Paul but a Colossian, founder of the church there.

1:9–14 Moved by Epaphras' account, the apostle has prayed and continues to pray fervently for the Colossians that, in their response to the gospel, they *may be filled with the knowledge of* God's *will* (9; cf 3:10). Paul expects a mutual interaction between their life according to the gospel and this knowledge (10), yielding results (*fruit;* 10; cf 6) *in every good work:* growth, strength, *endurance, patience, with joy* (11), and the further giving of thanks (12).

1:12–14 A summary about *redemption* by *the Father* precedes the statement in vv 15–20 about the *beloved Son* who is God's love in person (13). Christians share *the inheritance . . . in light* with *the holy ones,* here probably the angels (12). The imagery reflects the Exodus (*delivered . . . transferred*) and Jesus' theme of the *kingdom. Redemption* is explained as *forgiveness of sins* (cf Acts 2:38; Rom 3:24–25; Eph 1:7).

1:1 Eph 1:1.
1:3 Eph 1:15–16; Phlm 4–5.
1:5 Eph 1:13, 18; 1 Pt 1:4.
1:7 Phlm 23.
1:9 Eph 1:15–17; 5:17; Phil 1:9.
1:12 Col 3:17; Jn 8:12; Acts 26:18; 1 Tm 6:16; 1 Pt 2:9.

made you fit to share in the inheritance of the
holy ones in light. 13 He delivered us from the
power of darkness and transferred us to the king-
dom of his beloved Son, 14* in whom we have
redemption, the forgiveness of sins.

II: The Preeminence of Christ

His Person and Work

15*† He is the image† of the invisible God,
the firstborn of all creation.
16*† For in him were created all things in heaven
and on earth,
the visible and the invisible,
whether thrones or dominions or
principalities or powers;
all things were created through him and for
him.
17 He is before all things,
and in him all things hold together.
18*† He is the head of the body, the church.
He is the beginning, the firstborn from the
dead,
that in all things he himself might be
preeminent.
19† For in him all the fullness was pleased to dwell,
20*† and through him to reconcile all things for
him,
making peace by the blood of his cross
[through him], whether those on earth or
those in heaven.

21*† And you who once were alienated and hos-
tile in mind because of evil deeds 22 he has now
reconciled in his fleshly body through his death,
to present you holy, without blemish, and ir-
reproachable before him, 23 provided that you
persevere in the faith, firmly grounded, stable,
and not shifting from the hope of the gospel
that you heard, which has been preached to ev-
ery creature under heaven, of which I, Paul, am
a minister.

Live It!

The Image of God

It is possible to describe God by naming certain characteristics. We can say God is all-powerful, all-knowing, and eternal. But knowing about God is not the same as knowing God. So how can we really understand the mysterious, invisible, eternal God?

The author of Colossians gives us a clue. This writer calls Jesus "the image of the invisible God" (Col 1:15). If we want to know about God, who is hidden from us in mystery, we look at Christ. Christ has existed for all eternity; through Christ, all things were created; and in Christ, all things continue to "hold together" (verse 17). God chose to use Christ as the way in which all creation would be reconciled to God (see verse 20).

Is there still the unknown? Yes. We cannot comprehend God completely. But we can understand more about God by getting to know more about Jesus Christ.

▶ **Col 1:15–20**

†

1:15–20 As the poetic arrangement indicates, these lines are probably an early Christian hymn, known to the Colossians and taken up into the letter from liturgical use (cf Phil 2:6–11; 1 Tm 3:16). They present Christ as the mediator of creation (15–18a) and of redemption (18b–20). There is a parallelism between *firstborn of all creation* (15) and *firstborn from the dead* (18). While many of the phrases were at home in Greek philosophical use and even in gnosticism, the basic ideas also reflect Old Testament themes about Wisdom found in Prv 8:22–31; Wis 7:22—8:1; and Sir 1:4. See also the notes on what is possibly a hymn in Jn 1:1–18.

1:15 *Image:* cf Gn 1:27. Whereas the man and the woman were originally created in the image and likeness of God (see also Gn 1:26), Christ as image (2 Cor 4:4) of *the invisible God* (Jn 1:18) now shares this new nature in baptism with those redeemed (cf 3:10–11).

1:16–17 Christ (though not mentioned by name) is preeminent and supreme as God's agent in the creation of *all things* (cf Jn 1:3), as prior to *all things* (17; cf Heb 1:3).

1:18 *Church:* such a reference seemingly belongs under "redemption" in the following lines, not under the "creation" section of the hymn. Stoic thought sometimes referred to the world as "the body of Zeus." Pauline usage is to speak of the church as the body of Christ (1 Cor 12:12–27; Rom 12:4–5). Some think that the author of Colossians has inserted the reference to the church here so as to define "head of the body" in Paul's customary way. See v 24. *Preeminent:* when Christ was raised by God as *firstborn from the dead* (cf Acts 26:23; Rv 1:5), he was placed over the community, the church, that he had brought into being, but he is also indicated as crown of the whole new creation, over *all things*. His further role is to *reconcile all things* (20) for God or possibly "to himself."

1:19 *Fullness:* in gnostic usage this term referred to a spiritual world of beings above, between God and the world; many later interpreters take it to refer to *the fullness of the deity* (2:9); the reference could also be to the fullness of grace (cf Jn 1:16).

1:20 *The blood of his cross:* the most specific reference in the hymn to redemption through Christ's death, a central theme in Paul; cf 2:14–15; 1 Cor 1:17, 18, 23. *[Through him]:* the phrase, lacking in some manuscripts, seems superfluous but parallels the reference to reconciliation through Christ earlier in the verse.

1:21–23 Paul, in applying this hymn to the Colossians, reminds them that they have experienced the reconciling effect of Christ's death. He sees the effects of the cross in the redemption of human beings, not of cosmic powers such as those referred to in vv 16 and 20 (*all things*). Paul also urges adherence to Christ in faith and begins to point to his own role as minister (23), sufferer (24), and proclaimer (27–28) of this gospel.

*

1:14 Eph 1:7.
1:15 Ps 89:28; Jn 1:3, 18; 2 Cor 4:4.
1:16 1 Cor 8:6; Eph 1:10, 21.
1:18 1 Cor 11:3; 12:12, 27; 15:20; Eph 1:22–23; Rv 1:5.
1:20 2 Cor 5:18–19; Eph 1:10.
1:21 Eph 2:14–16.

Pray It!

Where Are Your Roots?

What is one thing that motivates you, that keeps you going? Is it a special friendship or a close family? the drive to succeed or to be the best? Maybe it's having a car or holding down a job.

Colossians 2:7 says that we should be "rooted in [Christ] and built upon him." Where you have your roots is where you get your nourishment to keep going. Think again about what motivates you. Is it enough to nourish a full, rich life?

In your prayer, journal or reflect on the following questions:

- What things are most important in your life right now? Where is God in each of those things?
- What do you need to reorder so that Christ "might be preeminent" (1:18) in your life?

▶ **Col 2:6–7**

Christ in Us†

24† Now I rejoice in my sufferings for your
sake, and in my flesh I am filling up what is
lacking in the afflictions of Christ on behalf of
his body, which is the church, 25 of which I am
a minister in accordance with God's stewardship
given to me to bring to completion for you the
word of God, 26* the mystery hidden from ages
and from generations past. But now it has been
manifested to his holy ones, 27* to whom God
chose to make known the riches of the glory of
this mystery among the Gentiles; it is Christ in
you, the hope for glory. 28* It is he whom we
proclaim, admonishing everyone and teaching
everyone with all wisdom, that we may present
everyone perfect in Christ. 29* For this I labor
and struggle, in accord with the exercise of his
power working within me.

2 1† For I want you to know how great a strug-
gle I am having for you and for those in
Laodicea and all who have not seen me face to
face, 2* that their hearts may be encouraged as
they are brought together in love, to have all the
richness of fully assured understanding, for the
knowledge of the mystery of God, Christ, 3* in
whom are hidden all the treasures of wisdom
and knowledge.

III: Warnings against False Teachers

A General Admonition

4*† I say this so that no one may deceive
you by specious arguments. 5* For even if I am
absent in the flesh, yet I am with you in spirit,
rejoicing as I observe your good order and the
firmness of your faith in Christ. 6 So, as you
received Christ Jesus the Lord, walk in him,
7* rooted in him and built upon him and estab-
lished in the faith as you were taught, abound-
ing in thanksgiving. 8*† See to it that no one

---

† **1:24—2:3** As the community at Colossae was not personally known to Paul (see Introduction), he here invests his teaching with greater authority by presenting a brief sketch of his apostolic ministry and sufferings as they reflect those of Christ on behalf of the church (24). The preaching of God's word (25) carries out the divine plan (*the mystery,* 26) to make Christ known to the Gentiles (27). It teaches the God-given wisdom about Christ (28), whose power works mightily in the apostle (29). Even in those communities that do not know him personally (2:1), he can increase the perception of God in Christ, unite the faithful more firmly in love, and so bring encouragement to them (2). He hopes that his apostolic authority will make the Colossians perceive more readily the defects in the teaching of others who have sought to delude them, the next concern in the letter.

1:24 *What is lacking:* although variously interpreted, this phrase does not imply that Christ's atoning death on the cross was defective. It may refer to the apocalyptic concept of a quota of "messianic woes" to be endured before the end comes; cf Mk 13:8, 19–20, 24 and the note on Mt 23:29–32. Others suggest that Paul's mystical unity with Christ allowed him to call his own *sufferings the afflictions of Christ.*

2:1 *Laodicea:* chief city in Phrygia, northwest of Colossae; cf 4:13, 16; Rv 3:14–22.

2:4–23 In face of the threat posed by false teachers (4), the Colossians are admonished to adhere to the gospel as it was first preached to them (6), steeping themselves in it with grateful hearts (7). They must reject religious teachings originating in any source except the gospel (8) because in Christ alone will they have access to God, *the deity* (9). So fully has Christ enlightened them that they need no other source of religious knowledge or virtue (10). They do not require *circumcision* (11), for *in baptism* their whole being has been affected by Christ (12) through forgiveness of sin and resurrection to a new life (13; cf 3:1 and Rom 6:1–11).

On the cross Christ canceled the record of the debt that stood against us with all its claims (14), i.e., he eliminated the law (cf Eph 2:15) that human beings could not observe—and that could not save them. He forgave sins against the law (14) and exposed as false and misleading (15) all other powers (cf 1:16) that purport to offer salvation. Therefore, the Colossians are not to accept judgments from such teachers on *food and drink* or to keep certain religious festivals or engage in certain cultic practices (16), for the Colossians would thereby risk severing themselves from Christ (19). If, when they accepted the gospel, they believed in Christ as their savior, they must be convinced that their salvation cannot be achieved by appeasing ruling spirits through dietary practices or through a wisdom gained simply by means of harsh asceticism (20–23).

2:8 *Elemental powers of the world:* see the note on Gal 4:3.

---

* **1:26** Rom 16:25–26; 1 Cor 2:7; Eph 3:3, 9. **1:27** Col 3:4; Rom 8:10. **1:28** Eph 4:13. **1:29** Col 2:1; 4:12; Phil 4:13. **2:2** Col 1:26–27; Eph 3:18–19. **2:3** Prv 2:4–5; Is 45:3; Rom 11:33; 1 Cor 1:30. **2:4** Eph 4:14. **2:5** 1 Cor 5:3; Phil 1:27. **2:7** Eph 2:20–22; 3:17. **2:8** Gal 4:3; Eph 5:6.

captivate you with an empty, seductive philosophy according to human tradition, according to the elemental powers of the world and not according to Christ.

Sovereign Role of Christ

9*† For in him dwells the whole fullness of the deity bodily, 10 and you share in this fullness in him, who is the head of every principality and power. 11*† In him you were also circumcised with a circumcision not administered by hand, by stripping off the carnal body, with the circumcision of Christ. 12* You were buried with him in baptism, in which you were also raised with him through faith in the power of God, who raised him from the dead. 13* And even when you were dead [in] transgressions and the uncircumcision of your flesh, he brought you to life along with him, having forgiven us all our transgressions; 14*† obliterating the bond against us, with its legal claims, which was opposed to us, he also removed it from our midst, nailing it to the cross; 15*† despoiling the principalities and the powers, he made a public spectacle of them, leading them away in triumph by it.

Practices Contrary to Faith

16*† Let no one, then, pass judgment on you in matters of food and drink or with regard to a festival or new moon or sabbath. 17* These are shadows of things to come; the reality belongs to Christ. 18*† Let no one disqualify you, delighting in self-abasement and worship of angels, taking his stand on visions, inflated without reason by his fleshly mind, 19* and not holding closely to the head, from whom the whole body, supported and held together by its ligaments and bonds, achieves the growth that comes from God.

20 If you died with Christ to the elemental powers of the world, why do you submit to regulations as if you were still living in the world? 21 "Do not handle! Do not taste! Do not touch!" 22* These are all things destined to perish with use; they accord with human precepts and teachings. 23 While they have a semblance of wisdom in rigor of devotion and self-abasement [and] severity to the body, they are of no value against gratification of the flesh.

IV: The Ideal Christian Life in the World

Mystical Death and Resurrection

3 1*† If then you were raised with Christ, seek what is above, where Christ is seated at the right hand of God. 2 Think of what is above, not of what is on earth. 3* For you have died, and your life is hidden with Christ in God. 4 When Christ your life appears, then you too will appear with him in glory.

Renunciation of Vice†

5*† Put to death, then, the parts of you that are earthly: immorality, impurity, passion, evil desire, and the greed that is idolatry. 6*† Because of these the wrath of God is coming [upon the disobedient]. 7 By these you too once conducted yourselves, when you lived in that way. 8*† But now you must put them all away: anger, fury, malice, slander, and obscene language out of your mouths. 9* Stop lying to one another, since you have taken off the old self with its practices 10*† and have put on the new self, which is

2:9 *Fullness of the deity:* the divine nature, not just attributes; see the note on 1:19.

2:11 A description of baptism (12) in symbolic terms of the Old Testament rite for entry into the community. The false teachers may have demanded physical circumcision of the Colossians.

2:14 The elaborate metaphor here about how God canceled the legal claims against us through Christ's cross depicts not Christ being nailed to the cross by men but *the bond . . . with its legal claims* being nailed to the cross by God.

2:15 The picture derives from the *public spectacle* and *triumph* of a Roman emperor's victory parade, where captives marched in subjection. *The principalities and the powers* are here conquered, not reconciled (cf 1, 16, 20). An alternate rendering for *by it* (the cross) is "by him" (Christ).

2:16 *Festival or new moon or sabbath:* yearly, monthly, and weekly observances determined by religious powers associated with a calendar set by the heavenly bodies, sun, moon, and stars (cf 8).

2:18 Ascetic practices encouraged by the false teachers included subjection of self humbly to their rules, worship of angels, and cultivation of visions, though exact details are unclear.

3:1–4 By retaining the message of the gospel that the risen, living Christ is the source of their salvation, the Colossians will be free from false religious evaluations of the things of the world (1–2). They have died to these; but one day *when Christ . . . appears,* they will live with Christ in the presence of God (3–4).

3:5–17 In lieu of false asceticism and superstitious festivals, the apostle reminds the Colossians of the moral life that is to characterize their response to God through Christ. He urges their participation in the liturgical hymns and prayers that center upon God's plan of salvation in Christ (16).

3:5, 8 The two lists of five vices each are similar to enumerations at Rom 1:29–31 and Gal 5:19–21.

3:6 *The wrath of God:* see the note on Rom 1:18. Many manuscripts add, as at Eph 5:6, "upon the disobedient."

3:8–10 *Put . . . away; have taken off; have put on:* the terms may reflect baptismal practice, taking off garments and putting on new ones after being united with Christ, here translated into ethical terms.

3:10 *Image:* see the note on 1:15.

2:9 Col 1:19; Eph 3:19.
2:11 Col 1:22; Jer 4:4; Rom 2:25–29; Phil 3:3.
2:12 Rom 6:3–4.
2:13 Eph 2:1, 5.
2:14 Eph 2:14–15.
2:15 Col 1:16, 20; 2 Cor 2:14; Eph 1:21.
2:16 Rom 14:3–4; 1 Tm 4:3.
2:17 Heb 8:5; 10:1.
2:18 Col 2:23; Mt 24:4.
2:19 Eph 2:21–22; 4:16.
2:22 Is 29:13.
3:1 Col 2:12; Ps 110:1; Phil 3:20; Eph 2:6.
3:3 Rom 6:2–5.
3:5 Mt 15:19; Rom 1:29–30; Gal 5:19–21; Eph 5:3, 5.
3:6 Rom 1:18.
3:8 Eph 4:22, 25, 31.
3:9 Rom 6:4, 6; Eph 4:22–25; Heb 12:1; 1 Pt 2:1; 4:2.
3:10 Gn 1:26–27.

being renewed, for knowledge, in the image of
its creator. 11*† Here there is not Greek and Jew,
circumcision and uncircumcision, barbarian,
Scythian, slave, free; but Christ is all and in all.
12* Put on then, as God's chosen ones, holy
and beloved, heartfelt compassion, kindness, hu-
mility, gentleness, and patience, 13* bearing with
one another and forgiving one another, if one
has a grievance against another; as the Lord has
forgiven you, so must you also do. 14* And over
all these put on love, that is, the bond of perfec-
tion. 15* And let the peace of Christ control your
hearts, the peace into which you were also called
in one body. And be thankful. 16* Let the word
of Christ dwell in you richly, as in all wisdom
you teach and admonish one another, singing
psalms, hymns, and spiritual songs with grat-
itude in your hearts to God. 17* And whatever
you do, in word or in deed, do everything in the
name of the Lord Jesus, giving thanks to God the
Father through him.

The Christian Family

18*† Wives, be subordinate to your husbands,
as is proper in the Lord. 19 Husbands, love your
wives, and avoid any bitterness toward them.
20* Children, obey your parents in everything,
for this is pleasing to the Lord. 21* Fathers, do
not provoke your children, so they may not be-
come discouraged.

Slaves and Masters

22*† Slaves, obey your human masters in every-
thing, not only when being watched, as currying
favor, but in simplicity of heart, fearing the Lord.
23 Whatever you do, do from the heart, as for the
Lord and not for others, 24 knowing that you will
receive from the Lord the due payment of the in-
heritance; be slaves of the Lord Christ. 25* For the
wrongdoer will receive recompense for the wrong
he committed, and there is no partiality.

4 1 Masters, treat your slaves justly and fairly,
realizing that you too have a Master in
heaven.

Prayer and Apostolic Spirit

2* Persevere in prayer, being watchful in it
with thanksgiving; 3* at the same time, pray
for us, too, that God may open a door to us for
the word, to speak of the mystery of Christ, for

Live It!

A Top-Shelf Life

In stores, the best product is often put on the top shelf, for all to see. It is also usually priced higher than other products, and therefore is not purchased by everyone. Colossians 3:1 calls us to "seek what is above, where Christ is seated at the right hand of God"—in other words, to live a top-shelf life.

Living a top-shelf life means living a moral life, free from sin. It means ridding ourselves of "anger, fury, malice, slander, and obscene language out of your mouths" (verse 8). It means avoiding "immorality, impurity, licentiousness, idolatry, sorcery, hatreds, rivalry, jealousy, outbursts of fury, acts of selfishness, dissensions, factions, occasions of envy, drinking bouts, orgies, and the like" (Gal 5:19–21). It also means living with "compassion, kindness, humility, gentleness, and patience," and forgiving one another and clothing ourselves with love (Col 3:12–14). Paul and the other authors of the letters focus on moral living because it is what God wants for us. How could we claim to have faith in Jesus Christ and choose to live in sin?

Living a moral life, a top-shelf life, isn't always easy. But it is the way to true happiness, holiness, and health. This is the witness of the Church and generations of Christian believers. Why settle for less?

▶ **Col 3:1–4**

3:11 *Scythian:* a barbarous people from north of the Black Sea.

3:18—4:6 After general recommendations that connect family life and the social condition of slavery with the service of Christ (3:18—4:1), Paul requests prayers for himself, especially in view of his imprisonment (2–3), and recommends friendly relations and meaningful discussions of Christian teaching with *outsiders,* i.e., non-Christians (5–6). See the note on Eph 5:21—6:9.

3:22–25 *Slaves:* within this table of duties in family and societal relations, involving wives and husbands, children and parents (18–21), such as also appears in Eph 5:22—6:9, slaves here receive special attention because of the case of Onesimus the slave returning to his master (4:9; Phlm 10–12).

3:11 1 Cor 12:13; Gal 3:27–28.
3:12 Eph 4:1–2, 32; 1 Thes 5:15.
3:13 Mt 6:14; 18:21–35; Eph 4:32.
3:14 Rom 13:8–10.
3:15 Rom 12:5; 1 Cor 12:12; Eph 2:16; 4:3–4; Phil 4:7.
3:16 Eph 5:19–20.
3:17 1 Cor 10:31.
3:18 Eph 5:22; Ti 2:5; 1 Pt 3:1.
3:20 Eph 6:1.
3:21 Eph 6:4.
3:22 Eph 6:5; 1 Tm 6:1; Ti 2:9–10; 1 Pt 2:18.
3:25 Rom 2:11.
4:2 Lk 18:1; Rom 12:12; Eph 6:18–20; 1 Thes 5:17.
4:3 Rom 15:30; 1 Cor 16:9; Eph 6:19; 2 Thes 3:1.

Catholic Social Teaching

The Christian Family

The rules for Christian families in chapter 3 of Colossians seem a little strange in our culture. But Colossians is simply calling families to be rooted in loving relationships (see also "Family Relationships," near Eph 5:21—6:4). A family is God's gift. It is a community where an atmosphere of mutual love and respect exists between its members, both young and old. It is a community we can turn to for comfort and support. The Catholic Church calls families the domestic church, meaning that they are the primary place where people learn about God and God's love. Catholic social teaching says that the family is the foundation on which communal life is built.

Being the domestic church doesn't just happen, however. Every member of a family must make an effort. That means taking time to listen to one another, to help one another out, and to respect each person in the family. Sometimes, selfishness gets in the way of making God's love real. At those times, family members must try even harder. Taking time to pray together, and to read and talk about the Bible together, can help a family focus on God's presence in their lives. The bishops understand that families face many challenges today, and they invite all of us to help families find the support they need to stay together as loving communities.

How is your family life? Is love the guiding rule? Does everyone take time to pray together? Do you support and participate in family activities and chores willingly? How does your parish or community serve as a source of support for your family?

Col 3:18—4:1

Call to Family, Community, and Participation

COL

which I am in prison, 4 that I may make it clear,
as I must speak. 5* Conduct yourselves wisely
toward outsiders, making the most of the op-
portunity. 6 Let your speech always be gracious,
seasoned with salt, so that you know how you
should respond to each one.

V: Conclusion†

Tychicus and Onesimus

7*† Tychicus, my beloved brother, trustworthy
minister, and fellow slave in the Lord, will tell
you all the news of me. 8 I am sending him to
you for this very purpose, so that you may know
about us and that he may encourage your hearts,
9* together with Onesimus, a trustworthy and
beloved brother, who is one of you. They will tell
you about everything here.

From Paul's Co-Workers

10*† Aristarchus, my fellow prisoner, sends
you greetings, as does Mark the cousin of Bar-
nabas (concerning whom you have received
instructions; if he comes to you, receive him),
11† and Jesus, who is called Justus, who are
of the circumcision; these alone are my co-
workers for the kingdom of God, and they
have been a comfort to me. 12*† Epaphras
sends you greetings; he is one of you, a slave
of Christ [Jesus], always striving for you in his
prayers so that you may be perfect and fully as-
sured in all the will of God. 13† For I can testify
that he works very hard for you and for those
in Laodicea and those in Hierapolis. 14*† Luke
the beloved physician sends greetings, as does
Demas.

†

4:7–18 Paul concludes with greetings and information concerning various Christians known to the Colossians.

4:7 *Tychicus:* Acts 20:4 mentions his role in the collection for Jerusalem; Eph 6:21 repeats what is said here; see also 2 Tm 4:12; Ti 3:12.

4:10 *Aristarchus:* a Thessalonian who was with Paul at Ephesus and Caesarea and on the voyage to Rome (Acts 19:29; 20:4; 27:2). *Mark:* also referred to at Phlm 24 and 2 Tm 4:11 and, as "John Mark," in Acts (12:12, 25; 13:13; 15:37–40). See also 1 Pt 5:13 and the note there. Traditionally the author of the second gospel.

4:11 *Jesus:* a then common Jewish name, the Greek form of Joshua.

4:12 *Epaphras:* see the notes on 1:3–8 and 1:7.

4:13 *Laodicea:* see the note on 2:1. *Hierapolis:* a city northeast of Laodicea and northwest of Colossae.

4:14 *Luke:* only here described as a medical doctor; cf Phlm 24 and 2 Tm 4:11. Traditionally the author of the third gospel. *Demas:* cf Phlm 24; he later deserted Paul (2 Tm 4:10).

*

4:5 Eph 5:15–16.
4:7 Acts 20:4; Eph 6:21–22; Phil 1:12.
4:9 Phlm 10–11.
4:10 Acts 19:29; 20:4; 27:2 / Acts 12:12, 25; 13:13; 15:37, 40; 2 Tm 4:11; Phlm 24; 1 Pt 5:13.
4:12 Col 1:7; Rom 15:30.
4:14 Phlm 24; 2 Tm 4:10–11.

A Message for the Laodiceans

15† Give greetings to the brothers in Laodi-
cea and to Nympha and to the church in her
house. 16† And when this letter is read before
you, have it read also in the church of the
Laodiceans, and you yourselves read the one
from Laodicea. 17*† And tell Archippus, "See
that you fulfill the ministry that you received
in the Lord."

18*† The greeting is in my own hand, Paul's.
Remember my chains. Grace be with you.

†

4:15 *Nympha and . . . her house:* some manuscripts read a masculine for the house-church leader, "Nymphas and . . . his house."

4:16 *The one from Laodicea:* either a letter by Paul that has been lost or the Letter to the Ephesians (cf the note on Eph 1:1, *in Ephesus*).

4:17 *Fulfill the ministry:* usually taken to mean that *Archippus,* the son of Philemon and Apphia (Phlm 1–2), is "pastor" at Colossae. An alternate interpretation is that Archippus, not Philemon, is the owner of the slave Onesimus and that Paul is asking Archippus to complete the service he has received in the Lord by sending Onesimus back to minister to Paul in his captivity (cf Phlm 20).

4:18 *My own hand:* a postscript in Paul's own hand was his custom; cf Gal 6:11–18 and 2 Thes 3:17–18.

*

4:17 Phlm 2.
4:18 1 Cor 16:21; Gal 6:11; Eph 3:1; 2 Thes 3:17.

You're about to read what is probably the oldest book in the New Testament. It was written a little over twenty years after Jesus' death and Resurrection, by a man named Paul. It is the very first Christian letter that we still have! In it, Paul answers some questions that were on people's minds back then. Even though it was written so long ago, you might have some of the same questions.

The First Letter to the Thessalonians

At a Glance

I. Address (1:1–10).

II. Previous Relations with the Thessalonians (2:1—3:13).

III. Specific Exhortations (4:1—5:25).

IV. Final Greeting (5:26–28).

Quick Facts

Inspired Author: Paul
Date Written: AD 51
Audience: the mainly Gentile church in Thessalonica

In Depth

Thessalonica was the capital of a Roman province called Macedonia. Today, that area is in northern Greece (see map 8, "Paul's First and Second Journeys"). Acts of the Apostles, chapter 17, tells us that Paul spent three weeks in Thessalonica preaching about Jesus Christ. Because of his preaching, many people, mainly Gentiles (non-Jews), became Christians. After Paul left the city, he worried about the new Christian community, so he sent his coworker Timothy back to check things out. When Timothy rejoined Paul, he had some great news. Even though the Thessalonians were being persecuted, they were staying strong in their "faith and love" (1 Thes 3:6).

When you read this letter, you can tell that Paul is thankful that the church is thriving! Four different times he expresses his gratitude. But he also apparently feels the need to defend himself against some critics. So he reminds everyone that he has been genuine and has cared for them "as a nursing mother cares for her children" (2:7).

After reassuring the Thessalonians that the persecution they are suffering is to be expected (see 3:3–4), Paul takes the time to answer some questions about the coming of the Lord at the end of time. Apparently, some of the Thessalonians are concerned about their friends who have already died. Will they join the living when Christ returns again?

Paul tells them they don't have to worry about those who die before Jesus returns; the dead will be raised first and join the living, to "always be with the Lord" (4:17). When will that happen? they ask. No one knows, Paul says, but Christians don't have to be afraid of that day. Their job is to stay alert and clothe themselves with "faith and love and . . . hope" (5:8).

1 Thessalonians

4:16–17

I: Address

Greeting

1 1*† Paul, Silvanus, and Timothy to the church
of the Thessalonians in God the Father and the
Lord Jesus Christ: grace to you and peace.

Thanksgiving for Their Faith

2* We give thanks to God always for all of you,
remembering you in our prayers, unceasingly
3† calling to mind your work of faith and labor
of love and endurance in hope of our Lord Jesus
Christ, before our God and Father, 4* knowing,
brothers loved by God, how you were chosen.
5* For our gospel did not come to you in word
alone, but also in power and in the holy Spirit
and [with] much conviction. You know what sort
of people we were [among] you for your sake.
6† And you became imitators of us and of the
Lord, receiving the word in great affliction, with
joy from the holy Spirit, 7* so that you became
a model for all the believers in Macedonia and
in Achaia. 8* For from you the word of the Lord
has sounded forth not only in Macedonia and
[in] Achaia, but in every place your faith in God
has gone forth, so that we have no need to say
anything. 9* For they themselves openly declare
about us what sort of reception we had among
you, and how you turned to God from idols to
serve the living and true God 10* and to await
his Son from heaven, whom he raised from [the]
dead, Jesus, who delivers us from the coming
wrath.

II: Previous Relations with the Thessalonians

Paul's Ministry Among Them

2 1 For you yourselves know, brothers, that our
reception among you was not without effect.
2* Rather, after we had suffered and been inso-
lently treated, as you know, in Philippi, we drew
courage through our God to speak to you the
gospel of God with much struggle. 3 Our exhor-
tation was not from delusion or impure motives,
nor did it work through deception. 4*† But as we
were judged worthy by God to be entrusted with

1:1 On the address, see the note on Rom 1:1–7.

1:3 *Faith . . . love . . . hope:* this, along with 5:8, is the earliest mention in Christian literature of the three "theological virtues" (see 1 Cor 13:13). The order here stresses eschatological hope, in line with the letter's emphasis on the Lord's second, triumphal coming, or parousia (10; 2:12, 19; 3:13; 4:13—5:11; 5:23).

1:6 *Imitators:* the Pauline theme of "imitation" (see 2:14; 1 Cor 4:16; 11:1; 2 Thes 3:9) is rooted in Paul's view of solidarity in Christ through sharing in Jesus' cross and in the Spirit of the risen Lord.

2:4 *Judged worthy:* Paul regards "worthiness" not as grounded in one's own talent or moral self-righteousness but in God's discernment of genuinely selfless attitudes and actions (see 2 Cor 10:17–18).

1:1 Acts 15:40; 16:1–3, 19; 17:14–15; 2 Thes 1:1–2.
1:2 2 Thes 1:3.
1:4 2 Thes 2:13.
1:5 Acts 13:52; 17:1–9.
1:7 2 Thes 1:4; 1 Cor 4:16; 11:1 / 1 Thes 2:14; Phil 3:17.
1:8 Rom 1:8.
1:9 Acts 14:15; Gal 4:8 / 1 Thes 4:5.
1:10 Rom 2:1–16; 5:9; 13:4 / 1 Thes 5:9.
2:2 Acts 16:19—17:10.
2:4 Gal 1:10.

the gospel, that is how we speak, not as trying to please human beings, but rather God, who judges our hearts. 5 Nor, indeed, did we ever appear with flattering speech, as you know, or with a pretext for greed—God is witness— 6* nor did we seek praise from human beings, either from you or from others, 7† although we were able to impose our weight as apostles of Christ. Rather, we were gentle among you, as a nursing mother cares for her children. 8 With such affection for you, we were determined to share with you not only the gospel of God, but our very selves as well, so dearly beloved had you become to us. 9* You recall, brothers, our toil and drudgery. Working night and day in order not to burden any of you, we proclaimed to you the gospel of God. 10 You are witnesses, and so is God, how devoutly and justly and blamelessly we behaved toward you believers. 11* As you know, we treated each one of you as a father treats his children, 12* exhorting and encouraging you and insisting that you conduct yourselves as worthy of the God who calls you into his kingdom and glory.

Further Thanksgiving

13 And for this reason we too give thanks to God unceasingly, that, in receiving the word of God from hearing us, you received not a human word but, as it truly is, the word of God, which is now at work in you who believe. 14† For you, brothers, have become imitators of the churches of God that are in Judea in Christ Jesus. For you suffer the same things from your compatriots as they did from the Jews, 15*† who killed both the Lord Jesus and the prophets and persecuted us; they do not please God, and are opposed to everyone, 16* trying to prevent us from speaking to the Gentiles that they may be saved, thus constantly filling up the measure of their sins. But the wrath of God has finally begun to come upon them.

Paul's Recent Travel Plans

17* Brothers, when we were bereft of you for a short time, in person, not in heart, we were all the more eager in our great desire to see you in person. 18* We decided to go to you—I, Paul, not only once but more than once—yet Satan thwarted us. 19* For what is our hope or joy or crown to boast of in the presence of our Lord Jesus at his coming if not you yourselves? 20 For you are our glory and joy.

3 1* That is why, when we could bear it no longer, we decided to remain alone in Athens 2* and sent Timothy, our brother and co-worker

Pray It!

Encouragement

Sometimes, we feel alone in our faith. We wonder if anyone feels, thinks, or prays the way we do. As a first missionary of the faith, Paul must have experienced his share of dark days when he wondered if the people would really accept the Good News. He must have been so encouraged when Timothy returned to tell him of the "faith and love" of the Thessalonians (1 Thes 3:6).

The Christian faith is never meant to be held privately. We don't grow in our faith, hope, and love by being isolated from other people. Like Paul, we need the encouragement and challenge of other people: our family, friends, and the entire Christian community.

In your prayer, reflect or journal on the following questions:

- How do you encourage others to grow in Christ?
- How do others encourage or challenge you to grow in faith, hope, and love?

▶ 1 Thes 3:6–13

2:7 *Gentle:* many excellent manuscripts read "infants" *(nēpioi)*, but "gentle" *(ēpioi)* better suits the context here.

2:14 Luke's picture of the persecutions at Philippi (by Gentiles) and in Thessalonica and Beroea (by Jews) seems to be considerably schematized (Acts 16:11–40; 17:1–15). Paul pictures the Thessalonian community as composed of converts from paganism (1:9) and speaks here of persecution by their (pagan) compatriots rather than by Jews.

2:15–16 Paul is speaking of historical opposition on the part of Palestinian Jews in particular and does so only some twenty years after Jesus' crucifixion. Even so, he quickly proceeds to depict the persecutors typologically, in apocalyptic terms. His remarks give no grounds for anti-Semitism to those willing to understand him, especially in view of Paul's pride in his own ethnic and religious background (Rom 9:1–5; 10:1; 11:1–3; Phil 3:4–6). Sinful conduct (16) is itself an anticipation of the ultimate wrath or judgment of God (Rom 1:18—2:5), whether or not it is perceived as such.

2:6 Jn 5:41, 44; 1 Cor 10:31; 2 Cor 4:17.
2:9 Acts 20:34; 1 Cor 4:12; 9:3–18; 2 Thes 3:7–9.
2:11 Acts 20:31.
2:12 1 Pt 5:10 / 1 Thes 4:7; 2 Thes 2:14.
2:15 Acts 2:23; 7:52.
2:16 Gn 15:16; 2 Mc 6:14 / Rom 1:18; 2:5–6.
2:17 1 Thes 3:10; Rom 1:10–11.
2:18 Rom 15:22.
2:19 2 Cor 1:14; Phil 2:16; 4:1.
3:1 Acts 17:14.
3:2 Acts 16:1–2; 1 Cor 3:5–9.

Live It!

True Love Waits

The Church has taught from its beginning that fornication, including premarital sex, is wrong. Paul's teaching in 1 Thessalonians 4:1–8 clearly explains why. If we get involved in a sexual relationship outside of marriage, we are exploiting another person (see verse 6)—even if that person is a willing partner. God intends sexual intercourse to create a lifelong bond between a man and a woman for the creation of a family. Sexual expression outside of marriage diminishes the beautiful purpose of sexual intimacy.

Paul reminds the Thessalonians to live in ways pleasing to God. To behave contrary to God's purpose is to say no to the gift of the Holy Spirit and to the holiness God wants for us. In our culture, sex is often portrayed as a recreational activity, violating the gift of sexuality God created within us! God's message in the Bible and the Church calls us to take a stand that is unpopular with some people—to support sexual abstinence until marriage.

Valuing our gift of sexuality and expressing it as God intended is not always easy. However, this old idea has a new slogan and campaign today: True love waits. Think about it!

▶ 1 Thes 4:1–8

for God in the gospel of Christ, to strengthen and
encourage you in your faith, 3† so that no one be
disturbed in these afflictions. For you yourselves
know that we are destined for this. 4* For even
when we were among you, we used to warn you
in advance that we would undergo affliction,
just as has happened, as you know. 5 For this
reason, when I too could bear it no longer, I sent
to learn about your faith, for fear that somehow
the tempter had put you to the test and our toil
might come to nothing.
6 But just now Timothy has returned to us from
you, bringing us the good news of your faith and
love, and that you always think kindly of us and
long to see us as we long to see you. 7 Because of
this, we have been reassured about you, brothers, in our every distress and affliction, through
your faith. 8 For we now live, if you stand firm
in the Lord.

Concluding Thanksgiving and Prayer

9† What thanksgiving, then, can we render to
God for you, for all the joy we feel on your account before our God? 10 Night and day we pray
beyond measure to see you in person and to
remedy the deficiencies of your faith. 11 Now may
God himself, our Father, and our Lord Jesus direct our way to you, 12* and may the Lord make
you increase and abound in love for one another
and for all, just as we have for you, 13* so as to
strengthen your hearts, to be blameless in holiness before our God and Father at the coming of
our Lord Jesus with all his holy ones. [Amen.]

III: Specific Exhortations

General Exhortations

4 1 Finally, brothers, we earnestly ask and exhort you in the Lord Jesus that, as you
received from us how you should conduct yourselves to please God—and as you are conducting
yourselves—you do so even more. 2† For you
know what instructions we gave you through the
Lord Jesus.

Holiness in Sexual Conduct

3† This is the will of God, your holiness: that
you refrain from immorality, 4 that each of you

3:3 *We are destined:* the Greek phraseology and the context suggest Paul's concern to alert his readers to difficulties he knew they would necessarily face and to enable them to see their present experience in the light of what he warned them would happen in the future. This line of thought is followed in 2 Thes 2:1–15.

3:9–10 The tension between Paul's optimism concerning the Thessalonians' faith and his worries about their perseverance remains unresolved. Perhaps this is accounted for not only by the continuing harassment but also by the shortness of his own stay in Thessalonica (even if that were over twice as long as the conventional three weeks that Luke assigns to it, Acts 17:2).

4:2 *Instructions:* these include specific guidelines on the basis of the Lord's authority, not necessarily sayings Jesus actually uttered. More profoundly, as v 8 implies, the instructions are practical principles that Paul worked out in accordance with his understanding of the role of the Spirit.

4:3–8 Many think that this passage deals with a variety of moral regulations (fornication, adultery, sharp business practices). It can be more specifically interpreted as bringing general norms to bear on a specific problem, namely, marriage within degrees of consanguinity (as between uncle and niece) forbidden in Jewish law but allowed according to a Greek heiress law, which would insure retention of an inheritance within the family and perhaps thereby occasion divorce. In that case, "immorality" (3) should be rendered as "unlawful marriage" and "this matter" (6) as "a lawsuit." The phrase in v 4, "acquire a wife for himself," has often been interpreted to mean "control one's body."

3:4 Acts 14:22; 2 Thes 2:5–7; 2 Tm 3:12.
3:12 1 Thes 4:9–10; 2 Thes 1:3.
3:13 1 Thes 5:23; 1 Cor 1:8.

Cultural Connection

Iroquois Prayer of Thanksgiving

This Iroquois prayer—although clearly not addressed to the one God who is creator of all—is still a beautiful expression of thankfulness for the wonders of the natural world. It can remind us of Paul's instruction to the Thessalonians (1 Thes 5:16–24) to give thanks without ceasing.

We return thanks to our mother,
the earth, which sustains us.
We return thanks to the rivers and streams,
which supply us with water.
We return thanks to all herbs,
which furnish medicines for the cure to our diseases.
We return thanks to the corn, and to her sisters,
the beans and squashes,
which give us life.
We return thanks to the bushes and trees,
which provide us with fruit.
We return thanks to the wind,
which, moving in the air, has banished diseases.
We return thanks to the moon and stars,
which have given to us their light
when the sun was gone.
We return thanks to our grandfather Hé-no,
that he has protected his grandchildren
from witches and reptiles,
and has given to us his rain.
We return thanks to the sun,
that he has looked upon the earth
with a beneficent eye.
Lastly, we return thanks to the Great Spirit,
in whom is embodied all goodness,
and who directs all things
for the good of his children.

▶ 1 Thes 5:16–24

know how to acquire a wife for himself in holi-
ness and honor, 5* not in lustful passion as do
the Gentiles who do not know God; 6 not to take
advantage of or exploit a brother in this matter,
for the Lord is an avenger in all these things, as
we told you before and solemnly affirmed. 7 For
God did not call us to impurity but to holiness.
8* Therefore, whoever disregards this, disregards
not a human being but God, who [also] gives his
holy Spirit to you.

Mutual Charity

9* On the subject of mutual charity you have
no need for anyone to write you, for you your-
selves have been taught by God to love one an-
other. 10* Indeed, you do this for all the brothers
throughout Macedonia. Nevertheless we urge
you, brothers, to progress even more, 11 and to
aspire to live a tranquil life, to mind your own
affairs, and to work with your [own] hands,
as we instructed you, 12 that you may conduct
yourselves properly toward outsiders and not de-
pend on anyone.

Hope for the Christian Dead

13 We do not want you to be unaware, broth-
ers, about those who have fallen asleep, so that
you may not grieve like the rest, who have no
hope. 14* For if we believe that Jesus died and
rose, so too will God, through Jesus, bring with
him those who have fallen asleep. 15*† Indeed,
we tell you this, on the word of the Lord, that
we who are alive, who are left until the com-
ing of the Lord, will surely not precede those
who have fallen asleep. 16* For the Lord him-
self, with a word of command, with the voice
of an archangel and with the trumpet of God,
will come down from heaven, and the dead
in Christ will rise first. 17† Then we who are
alive, who are left, will be caught up together
with them in the clouds to meet the Lord in
the air. Thus we shall always be with the Lord.

† **4:15** *Coming of the Lord:* Paul here assumes that the second coming, or parousia, will occur within his own lifetime but insists that the time or season is unknown (5:1–2). Nevertheless, the most important aspect of the parousia for him was the fulfillment of union with Christ. His pastoral exhortation focuses first on hope for the departed faithful, then (5:1–3) on the need of preparedness for those who have to achieve their goal.

4:17 *Will be caught up together:* literally, snatched up, carried off; cf 2 Cor 12:2; Rv 12:5. From the Latin verb here used, *rapiemur,* has come the idea of "the rapture," when believers will be transported away from the woes of the world; this construction combines this verse with Mt 24:40–41 (see the note there) // Lk 17:34–35 and passages from Revelation in a scheme of millennial dispensationalism.

* **4:5** Ps 79:6; Jer 10:25; 2 Thes 1:8; 1 Pt 3:7.
4:8 Lk 10:16.
4:9 Jn 6:45; 13:34; 1 Jn 2:20–21, 27; 4:7.
4:10 2 Thes 3:6–12.
4:14 1 Cor 15:3–4, 12, 20.
4:15 1 Cor 15:51; Rv 14:13; 20:4–6.
4:16 Mt 24:31; 1 Cor 15:23, 52.

Cultural Connection

Give Thanks at All Times

Gratitude is an essential element of the Christian faith for Hispanic people. We turn to the Scriptures and Tradition for examples of gratitude in all things. Mary, the mother of Jesus, personified this gratitude when she accepted the responsibility of bearing the Son of God in her womb. Paul continually promoted gratitude in his letters to the first Christians.

To be grateful, we must humbly open up to receiving and acknowledging God's many gifts to us. When we do this, we express our gratitude for God's gifts by loving God and neighbor. Expressing love is an automatic response for someone who is grateful.

Juan Diego, a sixteenth-century Mexican man, opened up to the love and message of Our Lady of Guadalupe, who appeared to him on Tepeyac Hill, today located within Mexico City. In the spirit of gratitude, Juan Diego wanted to share the news of this loving appearance. After persistently speaking about it and eventually providing proof of the appearance to his local bishop, he was finally listened to and believed. For hundreds of years, a church, which is now a basilica, has stood on Tepeyac Hill. Mary had asked Juan Diego to see that a church was built there.

Juan Diego's message and Mary's message to him continue to be spread today in the lives of Mexicans and Mexican Americans. Because Juan Diego's gratitude was so great and because he shared his gratitude with so many others, Pope John Paul II declared him a saint on July 31, 2002.

▶ 1 Thes 5:18

18 Therefore, console one another with these words.

Vigilance

5 1* Concerning times and seasons, brothers, you have no need for anything to be written to you. 2* For you yourselves know very well that the day of the Lord will come like a thief at night. 3 When people are saying, "Peace and security," then sudden disaster comes upon them, like labor pains upon a pregnant woman, and they will not escape.

4* But you, brothers, are not in darkness, for that day to overtake you like a thief. 5† For all of you are children of the light and children of the day. We are not of the night or of darkness. 6* Therefore, let us not sleep as the rest do, but let us stay alert and sober. 7 Those who sleep go to sleep at night, and those who are drunk get drunk at night. 8* But since we are of the day, let us be sober, putting on the breastplate of faith and love and the helmet that is hope for salvation. 9 For God did not destine us for wrath, but to gain salvation through our Lord Jesus Christ, 10† who died for us, so that whether we are awake or asleep we may live together with him. 11* Therefore, encourage one another and build one another up, as indeed you do.

Church Order

12 We ask you, brothers, to respect those who are laboring among you and who are over you in the Lord and who admonish you, 13 and to show esteem for them with special love on account of their work. Be at peace among yourselves.

14 We urge you, brothers, admonish the idle, cheer the fainthearted, support the weak, be patient with all. 15* See that no one returns evil for evil; rather, always seek what is good [both] for each other and for all. 16 Rejoice always. 17 Pray without ceasing. 18* In all circumstances give thanks, for this is the will of God for you in Christ Jesus. 19† Do not quench the Spirit. 20 Do

†

5:5 *Children of the light:* that is, belonging to the daylight of God's personal revelation and expected to achieve it (an analogous development of imagery that appears in Jn 12:36).

5:10 Characteristically, Paul plays on words suggesting ultimate and anticipated death and life. Union with the crucified and risen Lord at his parousia is anticipated in some measure in contrasted states of our temporal life. The essential element he urges is our indestructible personal union in Christ's own life (see Rom 5:1–10).

5:19–21 Paul's buoyant encouragement of charismatic freedom sometimes occasioned excesses that he or others had to remedy (see 1 Cor 14; 2 Thes 2:1–15; 2 Pt 3:1–16).

*

5:1 Mt 24:36–45.
5:2 2 Pt 3:10.
5:4 Eph 5:8–9.
5:6 Mt 24:42; Rom 13:12–13; 1 Pt 5:8.
5:8 Is 59:17; Rom 13:11–14; Eph 6:11, 14–17.
5:11 Rom 15:2; 1 Cor 8:1; 14:12, 26; Eph 4:29.
5:15 Prv 20:22; Mt 5:38–42; Rom 12:17.
5:18 Eph 5:20.

not despise prophetic utterances. 21 Test
everything; retain what is good. 22 Re-
frain from every kind of evil.

Concluding Prayer

23*† May the God of peace
himself make you perfectly holy
and may you entirely, spirit, soul,
and body, be preserved blameless
for the coming of our Lord Jesus
Christ. 24 The one who calls you is
faithful, and he will also accomplish it.
25 Brothers, pray for us [too].

"Test everything; retain what is good. Refrain from every kind of evil."
(1 Thes 5:21–22)

IV: Final Greeting

26† Greet all the brothers
with a holy kiss. 27 I adjure you
by the Lord that this letter be
read to all the brothers. 28 The
grace of our Lord Jesus Christ be
with you.

†

5:23 Another possible translation is, "May the God of peace himself make you perfectly holy and sanctify your spirit fully, and may both soul and body be preserved blameless for the coming of our Lord Jesus Christ." In either case, Paul is not offering an anthropological or philosophical analysis of human nature. Rather, he looks to the wholeness of what may be called the supernatural and natural aspects of a person's service of God.

5:26 *Kiss:* the holy embrace (see Rom 16:16; 1 Cor 16:20; 2 Cor 13:12; 1 Pt 5:14) was a greeting of respect and affection, perhaps given during a liturgy at which Paul's letter would have been read.

5:23 2 Thes 3:16.

The Second Letter to the

Thessalonians

Has a parent or other adult ever said to you, "You know, when I was your age . . ." and launched into some story about how hard it was in the "good old days"? It seems all past generations, including those who lived in biblical times, had their struggles and challenges. When the Thessalonians were going through some really tough times, Paul's second letter to them promised that if they continued to trust God and endure, they would give glory to God and receive salvation.

At a Glance

I. **Address (1:1–12).**

II. **Warning Against Deception Concerning the Parousia (2:1–17).**

III. **Concluding Exhortations (3:1–16).**

IV. **Final Greetings (3:17–18).**

Quick Facts

Inspired Author: possibly Paul, but more likely a disciple of Paul (see "Introduction to the Letters and Revelation")

Date Written: after AD 51 if by Paul, from AD 90 to 100 if by a disciple

Audience: the mainly Gentile (non-Jewish) church in Thessalonica

In Depth

From the short Second Letter to the Thessalonians, it appears the Thessalonians were experiencing two problems. First, they were being persecuted by non-Christians. Second, some of them were becoming confused over "the coming of our Lord Jesus Christ" (2:1), sometimes called the second coming. Word was being spread that Jesus had already come again (see verse 2)! They were becoming fearful that they hadn't seen the signs of the end times or properly interpreted them.

This letter speaks to the Thessalonians, using apocalyptic language (see "Apocalyptic Literature," near Daniel, chapters 7–10, and the introduction to Revelation), which means it is rich in cosmic symbolism. It tells the Thessalonians to have peace and not let themselves be deceived, because "all who have not believed the truth but have approved wrongdoing may be condemned" (2:12). It also tells them to have hope because at the end time, Christ will overcome all evil and will destroy the lawless one (see 2:8).

This letter is not as warm and personal as First Thessalonians. Perhaps that's because it's filled with the sobering awareness that more suffering is to come before the end time. In such an environment, the letter advises the Thessalonians—and us—to "stand firm and hold fast to the traditions that you were taught" (2:15).

2 Thessalonians

I: Address

Greeting

1 1*† Paul, Silvanus, and Timothy to the church
of the Thessalonians in God our Father and the
Lord Jesus Christ: 2 grace to you and peace from
God [our] Father and the Lord Jesus Christ.

Thanksgiving

3*† We ought to thank God always for you,
brothers, as is fitting, because your faith flour-
ishes ever more, and the love of every one of
you for one another grows ever greater. 4 Accord-
ingly, we ourselves boast of you in the churches
of God regarding your endurance and faith in
all your persecutions and the afflictions you
endure.
5* This is evidence of the just judgment of
God, so that you may be considered worthy of
the kingdom of God for which you are suffering.
6 For it is surely just on God's part to repay with
afflictions those who are afflicting you, 7 and to
grant rest along with us to you who are undergo-
ing afflictions, at the revelation of the Lord Jesus
from heaven with his mighty angels, 8* in blazing
fire, inflicting punishment on those who do not
acknowledge God and on those who do not obey
the gospel of our Lord Jesus. 9* These will pay
the penalty of eternal ruin, separated from the
presence of the Lord and from the glory of his
power, 10*† when he comes to be glorified among
his holy ones and to be marveled at on that day
among all who have believed, for our testimony
to you was believed.

Prayer

11* To this end, we always pray for you, that
our God may make you worthy of his calling and
powerfully bring to fulfillment every good pur-
pose and every effort of faith, 12*† that the name
of our Lord Jesus may be glorified in you, and you
in him, in accord with the grace of our God and
Lord Jesus Christ.

1:1–2 On the address, see the note on Rom 1:1–7 and cf 1 Thes 1:1.

1:3–12 On the thanksgiving, see the note on Rom 1:8 and cf 1 Thes 1:2–10. Paul's gratitude to God for the faith and love of the Thessalonians (3) and his Christian pride in their faithful endurance (4–5) contrast with the condemnation announced for those who afflict them, a judgment to be carried out at the parousia (6–10), which is described in vivid language drawn from Old Testament apocalyptic. A prayer for the fulfillment of God's purpose in the Thessalonians (11–12) completes the section, as is customary in a Pauline letter (cf 1 Thes 1:2–3).

1:10 *Among his holy ones:* in the Old Testament, this term can refer to an angelic throng (cf also Jude 14), but here, in parallel with *among all who have believed,* it can refer to the triumphant people of God.

1:12 *The grace of our God and Lord Jesus Christ:* the Greek can also be translated, "the grace of our God and of the Lord Jesus Christ."

1:1 1 Thes 1:1.
1:3 1 Cor 1:4; 1 Thes 1:2; 3:12.
1:5 Phil 1:28; 1 Thes 2:12.
1:8 Ps 79:5–6; Is 66:15; Jer 10:25.
1:9 Is 2:10, 19, 21.
1:10 Ps 89:8; Dn 7:18–22, 27; 1 Thes 3:13.
1:11 1 Thes 1:2–3.
1:12 Is 66:5.

II: Warning against Deception Concerning the Parousia

Christ and the Lawless One

2 [1]*† We ask you, brothers, with regard to the
coming of our Lord Jesus Christ and our as-
sembling with him, [2]*† not to be shaken out of
your minds suddenly, or to be alarmed either by
a "spirit," or by an oral statement, or by a letter
allegedly from us to the effect that the day of the
Lord is at hand. [3]† Let no one deceive you in any
way. For unless the apostasy comes first and the
lawless one is revealed, the one doomed to perdi-
tion, [4]*† who opposes and exalts himself above
every so-called god and object of worship, so as
to seat himself in the temple of God, claiming
that he is a god— [5] do you not recall that while I
was still with you I told you these things? [6]† And
now you know what is restraining, that he may

2:1–17 The Thessalonians have been *shaken* by a message purporting to come from Paul himself that *the day of the Lord* is already present. He warns against this deception in eschatology by citing a scenario of events that must first occur (3–12) before the end will come. The overall point Paul makes is the need to reject such lies as Satan sends; he also reaffirms the Thessalonians in their calling (13–14). They are to uphold what Paul himself has taught (15). There is a concluding prayer for their strengthening (16–17). As in 1:8–10, the Old Testament provides a good deal of coloring; cf especially Is 14:13–14; 66:15, 18–21; Ez 28:2–9; Dn 11:36–37. The contents of 2:3b–8 may come from a previously existing apocalypse. The details have been variously interpreted.

An alternative to the possibilities noted below understands that an oracular utterance, supposedly coming from a prophetic spirit (2–3a), has so disrupted the community's thinking that its effects may be compared to those of the mania connected with the worship of the Greek god Dionysus. On this view, the writer seems to allude in vv 6–8 to Dionysiac "seizure," although, of course, ironically, somewhat as Paul alludes to witchcraft ("an evil eye") in Gal 3:1 in speaking of the threat to faith posed by those disturbing the Galatians (Gal 1:6–7; 5:10b). On this view of 2 Thes 2, the Greek participles *katechon* (rendered above as *what is restraining*) and *katechōn* (*the one who restrains*) are to be translated "the seizing power" in v 6 and "the seizer" in v 7. They then allude to a pseudocharismatic force or spirit of Dionysiac character that has suddenly taken hold of the Thessalonian community (see 2). The addressees *know* (6) this force or spirit because of the problem it is causing. This pseudocharismatic force or spirit is a kind of anticipation and advance proof of the ultimate, climactic figure (*the lawless one* or the rebel, 3), of which the community has been warned (see the note on 1 Thes 3:3). It is, however, only the beginning of the end that the latter's manifestation entails; the end is not yet. For in the course of *the mystery of lawlessness* (7), false prophetism, after it ceases in the Thessalonian community, will be manifested in the world at large (8–12), where it will also be eliminated in turn by the Lord Jesus.

2:2 *"Spirit":* a Spirit-inspired utterance or ecstatic revelation. *An oral statement:* literally, a "word" or pronouncement, not necessarily of ecstatic origin. *A letter allegedly from us:* possibly a forged letter, so that Paul calls attention in 3:17 to his practice of concluding a genuine letter with a summary note or greeting in his own hand, as at Gal 6:11–18 and elsewhere.

2:3b–5 This incomplete sentence (anacoluthon, 4) recalls what the Thessalonians had already been taught, an apocalyptic scenario depicting, in terms borrowed especially from Dn 11:36–37 and related verses, human self-assertiveness against God in *the temple of God* itself. *The lawless one* represents the climax of such activity in this account.

2:4 *Seat himself in the temple of God:* a reflection of the language in Dn 7:23–25; 8:9–12; 9:27; 11:36–37; and 12:11 about the attempt of Antiochus IV Epiphanes to set up a statue of Zeus in the Jerusalem temple and possibly of the Roman emperor Caligula to do a similar thing (Mk 13:14). Here the imagery suggests an attempt to install someone in the place of God, *claiming that he is a god* (cf Ez 28:2). Usually, it is the Jerusalem temple that is assumed to be meant; on the alternative view sketched above (see the note on 2:1–17), *the temple* refers to the Christian community.

2:6–7 *What is restraining . . . the one who restrains:* neuter and masculine, respectively, of a force and person holding back the lawless one. The Thessalonians know what is meant (6), but the terms, seemingly found only in this passage and in writings dependent on it, have been variously interpreted. Traditionally, v 6 has been applied to the Roman empire and v 7 to the Roman emperor (in Paul's day, Nero) as bulwarks holding back chaos (cf Rom 13:1–7). A second interpretation suggests that cosmic or angelic powers are binding Satan (9) and so restraining him; some relate this to an anti-Christ figure (1 Jn 2:18) or to Michael the archangel (Rv 12:7–9; 20:1–3). A more recent view suggests that it is the preaching of the Christian gospel that restrains the end, for in God's plan the end cannot come until the gospel is preached to all nations (Mk 13:10); in that case, Paul as missionary preacher par excellence is "the one who restrains," whose removal (death) will bring the end (7). On the alternative view (see the note on 2:1–17), the phrases should be referred to that which and to him who seizes (a prophet) in ecstasy so as to have him speak pseudo-oracles.

2:1 1 Thes 4:13–17. **2:2** Mt 24:6; 1 Cor 14:26, 32–33; 1 Thes 5:1–2. **2:4** Dn 11:36–37; Ez 28:2.

Did You Know?

The Parousia

After Jesus' death and Resurrection, the early Christians start to wait for his Second Coming, also called the Parousia. They think Jesus will return soon in glory to judge the living and the dead and to bring to complete fulfillment the Reign of God. They even see some signs of his imminent arrival and express an urgent call to be prepared. Paul seems to expect Christ's return in the near future but insists that nobody can predict when. He emphasizes the importance of living the Gospel and always being prepared for "our assembling with him" (2 Thes 2:1).

The important message for us today is that our history has meaning and purpose and that Christ ultimately triumphs over sin and death. The various descriptions of the signs preceding the end time are intended not to predict the future but rather to encourage us to live the Gospel as we wait in hope for Christ's glorious return.

▶ 2 Thes 1:5—2:17

Catholic Connection

Revelation and the Apostolic Tradition

What are some of your favorite family traditions? The traditions you celebrate when you gather with your relatives say something about who you are as a family. The same is true for Christianity. The Second Letter to the Thessalonians emphasizes the importance of the traditions about Jesus Christ that had been handed on to the church in Thessalonica through the Apostles' preaching and written letters (see 2 Thes 2:15).

Like the Thessalonians, we too are called by God to know Jesus Christ. Yet even before the coming of Christ, God had been slowly revealing himself through words, as when God spoke to Moses out of the burning bush (see Ex 3:1–22) and deeds, as when God led the Israelites across the Red Sea (see Ex 14:1–31). These words and deeds laid the foundation for the ultimate and final revelation of God in the Word made flesh, Jesus Christ. It is through knowing Jesus Christ, the Son of God, that we come to know God the Father and find salvation.

The Church teaches that, through the guidance of the Holy Spirit, the Apostles went forth as Jesus commanded and spread the Gospel, in both written and spoken word. The writings of the Apostles were preserved for the benefit of all generations in Sacred Scripture. The spoken words and actions of the Apostles, which reflect the growth and development of the Church's understanding and teachings about Jesus Christ, have also been preserved in what is known as the Apostolic Tradition. Both Sacred Scripture and Tradition have the same goal, yet they are distinct from one another (see "The Bible, Tradition, and Magisterium," near Lk 4:1–13). As successors to the Apostles, bishops have been entrusted with handing on the Apostolic Tradition through the Church's doctrines, worship, and life.

The Apostolic Tradition, big-T Tradition, should not be confused with what is called ecclesial tradition, small-t tradition. Small-t traditions are the customs and rituals that help Catholics live out their faith in their own particular time and locale. These traditions are influenced by history and culture and account for the rich variety of faith expressions in the Universal Church. They can also be changed or eliminated over time. Ecclesial traditions are important and good, as long as they help us to live out the mission and teachings of Jesus embodied in Sacred Scripture and Tradition.

- What big-T Traditions or small-t traditions of the Church have been important to you?
- Ask the same question of a parent, a grandparent, or someone from a previous generation and compare your answers.

2 Thes 2:13–17
Catechism, nos. 74–83

Live It!

Laziness

How well do you balance work—the things you are expected to do in your home, school, job, or community—with leisure? Workaholics find it hard to relax and just do nothing. Others find it easy to loosen up and recreate, and need a little push to get back to their responsibilities.

Evidently, some of the early Thessalonians are determined to avoid work altogether (see 2 Thes 3:6) because they thought the end time had already come. The author of Second Thessalonians sees this idleness as destructive for the Church. His answer is simple: no work, no food (see verse 10).

Christ invites us not to a life of laziness, where we take advantage of the kindness of others, but to an active life. Our work ought to be an expression of who we are and should contribute something meaningful and positive to the world.

▶ 2 Thes 3:6–13

be revealed in his time. 7*† For the mystery of
lawlessness is already at work. But the one who
restrains is to do so only for the present, until
he is removed from the scene. 8* And then the
lawless one will be revealed, whom the Lord
[Jesus] will kill with the breath of his mouth
and render powerless by the manifestation of his
coming, 9* the one whose coming springs from
the power of Satan in every mighty deed and in
signs and wonders that lie, 10 and in every wicked
deceit for those who are perishing because they
have not accepted the love of truth so that they
may be saved. 11 Therefore, God is sending them
a deceiving power so that they may believe the
lie, 12 that all who have not believed the truth but
have approved wrongdoing may be condemned.
13*† But we ought to give thanks to God for you
always, brothers loved by the Lord, because God
chose you as the firstfruits for salvation through
sanctification by the Spirit and belief in truth.
14* To this end he has [also] called you through
our gospel to possess the glory of our Lord Jesus
Christ. 15† Therefore, brothers, stand firm and
hold fast to the traditions that you were taught,
either by an oral statement or by a letter of ours.
16 May our Lord Jesus Christ himself and God
our Father, who has loved us and given us ever-
lasting encouragement and good hope through
his grace, 17 encourage your hearts and strengthen
them in every good deed and word.

III: Concluding Exhortations

Request for Prayers

3 1*† Finally, brothers, pray for us, so that the
word of the Lord may speed forward and be
glorified, as it did among you, 2 and that we may
be delivered from perverse and wicked people,
for not all have faith. 3* But the Lord is faithful;
he will strengthen you and guard you from the
evil one. 4* We are confident of you in the Lord
that what we instruct you, you [both] are doing
and will continue to do. 5 May the Lord direct
your hearts to the love of God and to the endur-
ance of Christ.

Neglect of Work

6† We instruct you, brothers, in the name of
[our] Lord Jesus Christ, to shun any brother who

2:7–12 *The lawless one* and *the one who restrains* are involved in an activity or process, *the mystery of lawlessness,* behind which *Satan* stands (9). The action of the *Lord [Jesus]* in overcoming the lawless one is described in Old Testament language (*with the breath of his mouth;* cf Is 11:4; Jb 4:9; Rv 19:15). *His coming* is literally the Lord's "parousia." The biblical concept of the "holy war," eschatologically conceived, may underlie the imagery.

2:13 *As the firstfruits:* there is also strong manuscript evidence for the reading, "God chose you from the beginning," thus providing a focus on God's activity from beginning to end; *firstfruits* is a Pauline term, however; cf Rom 8:23; 11:16; 16:5, among other references.

2:15 Reference to *an oral statement* and *a letter* (2) and the content here, including a formula of conclusion (cf 1 Cor 16:13; Gal 5:1), suggest that vv 1–15 or even 1–17 are to be taken as a literary unit, notwithstanding the incidental thanksgiving formula in v 13.

3:1–18 The final chapter urges the Thessalonians to pray for Paul and his colleagues (1–2) and reiterates confidence in the Thessalonians (3–5), while admonishing them about a specific problem in their community that has grown out of the intense eschatological speculation, namely, not to work but to become instead disorderly busybodies (6–15). A benediction (16) and postscript in Paul's own hand round out the letter. On vv 17–18, cf the note on 2:2.

3:6 Some members of the community, probably because they regarded the parousia as imminent or the new age of the Lord to be already here (2:2), had apparently ceased to work for a living. The disciplinary problem they posed could be rooted in distorted thinking about Paul's own teaching (cf 1 Thes 2:16; 3:3–4; 5:4–5) or, more likely, in a forged letter (2:2) and the type of teaching dealt with in 2:1–15. The apostle's own moral teaching, reflected in his selfless labors for others, was rooted in a deep doctrinal concern for the gospel message (cf 1 Thes 2:3–10).

2:7 Mt 13:36–43; Acts 20:29; Gal 5:10; 2 Pt 2:1; Rv 22:11.
2:8 Is 11:4; Rv 19:15.
2:9 Mt 24:24; Rv 13:13.
2:13 1 Thes 2:13; 5:9.
2:14 Rom 5:1–10; 8:29–30; 1 Thes 4:7; 5:9.
3:1 Eph 6:19; Col 4:3.
3:3 1 Thes 5:24 / 1 Cor 16:13 / Mt 6:13.
3:4 2 Cor 7:16; 1 Thes 4:1–2.

conducts himself in a disorderly way and not
according to the tradition they received from us.
7 For you know how one must imitate us. For
we did not act in a disorderly way among you,
8* nor did we eat food received free from anyone.
On the contrary, in toil and drudgery, night and
day we worked, so as not to burden any of you.
9* Not that we do not have the right. Rather, we
wanted to present ourselves as a model for you,
so that you might imitate us. 10* In fact, when we
were with you, we instructed you that if anyone
was unwilling to work, neither should that one
eat. 11* We hear that some are conducting themselves among you in a disorderly way, by not
keeping busy but minding the business of others.
12 Such people we instruct and urge in the Lord
Jesus Christ to work quietly and to eat their own
food. 13 But you, brothers, do not be remiss in
doing good. 14 If anyone does not obey our word
as expressed in this letter, take note of this person
not to associate with him, that he may be put to
shame. 15* Do not regard him as an enemy but
admonish him as a brother. 16* May the Lord of
peace himself give you peace at all times and in
every way. The Lord be with all of you.

IV: Final Greetings

17* This greeting is in my own hand, Paul's.
This is the sign in every letter; this is how I write.
18 The grace of our Lord Jesus Christ be with all
of you.

3:8 1 Thes 2:9.
3:9 Mt 10:10; Phil 3:17.
3:10 1 Thes 4:11.
3:11 1 Thes 5:14.
3:15 2 Cor 2:7; Gal 6:1.
3:16 Jn 14:27; Rom 15:33.
3:17 1 Cor 16:21; Gal 6:11.

The Pastoral Letters

Imagine you are a bishop writing a letter to the new priests, deacons, and lay ministers in your diocese. How do you encourage them? What do you warn them about? The two Letters to Timothy and the Letter to Titus are such letters, written to give good, practical advice to the leaders of the early church.

In Depth

The Letters to Timothy and Titus are called the pastoral letters because they were written to church leaders, or pastors. These letters sound as if they were written by Paul. But a great deal of evidence suggests they may have been written by later disciples of Paul, adapting Paul's teaching and advice to the situation of the churches a generation later.

The First Letter to Timothy addresses practical issues the churches needed to deal with in order to achieve stability and respond to new challenges as Christianity became more visible in society: How should the churches deal with people teaching false beliefs? What qualities should church leaders have? Who deserves financial help from the community? How should Christians view success?

The Second Letter to Timothy presents Paul as being close to his execution. As you read this letter, you will experience his sadness at death, hear his reflections on his life and ministry, and see a man who feels deserted by many. This letter tells Timothy—who stands for all faithful Christians—that he needs to endure suffering with hope. Doing the right thing often means more pain than popularity. But even when other people desert us, God "remains faithful, / for he cannot deny himself" (2:13).

The Letter to Titus gives advice for elders, bishops, older men, older women, slaves, younger men, and younger women. It also offers repeated warnings to guard against temptations and false teachings and to be self-controlled.

The pastoral letters give us a picture of the church moving into a new phase. The church seems to have more structure, leadership roles are becoming more defined, and the people are more concerned about its public appearance. Like Christians today, the early Christians struggled to be faithful in applying the Gospel of Jesus Christ to their culture and time.

At a Glance

I. **Address (1 Tm 1:1–2).**

II. **Sound Teaching (1 Tm 1:3–20).**

III. **Problems of Discipline (1 Tm 2:1—4:16).**

IV. **Duties Toward Others (1 Tm 5:1—6:2a).**

V. **False Teaching and True Wealth (1 Tm 6:2b–19).**

VI. **Final Recommendation and Warning (1 Tm 6:20–21).**

I. **Address (2 Tm 1:1–5).**

II. **Exhortations to Timothy (2 Tm 1:6—2:13).**

III. **Instructions Concerning False Teaching (2 Tm 2:14—4:8).**

IV. **Personal Requests and Final Greetings (2 Tm 4:9–22).**

I. **Address (Ti 1:1–4).**

II. **Pastoral Charge (Ti 1:5–16).**

III. **Teaching the Christian Life (Ti 2:1—3:15).**

Quick Facts

Inspired Author: followers of Paul (see "Introduction to the Letters and Revelation")
Date Written: around AD 100
Audience: leaders of the early churches

1 Timothy

6:6–10, 17–19

I: Address

Greeting

1 1*† Paul, an apostle of Christ Jesus by com-
mand of God our savior and of Christ Jesus our
hope, 2* to Timothy, my true child in faith: grace,
mercy, and peace from God the Father and Christ
Jesus our Lord.

II: Sound Teaching

Warning against False Doctrine

3*† I repeat the request I made of you when I
was on my way to Macedonia, that you stay in
Ephesus to instruct certain people not to teach
false doctrines 4*† or to concern themselves with
myths and endless genealogies, which promote
speculations rather than the plan of God that is to
be received by faith. 5* The aim of this instruction
is love from a pure heart, a good conscience,
and a sincere faith. 6* Some people have devi-
ated from these and turned to meaningless talk,
7 wanting to be teachers of the law, but without
understanding either what they are saying or what
they assert with such assurance.

8*† We know that the law is good, provided
that one uses it as law, 9 with the understanding
that law is meant not for a righteous person but
for the lawless and unruly, the godless and sin-
ful, the unholy and profane, those who kill their
fathers or mothers, murderers, 10*† the unchaste,
sodomites, kidnappers, liars, perjurers, and what-
ever else is opposed to sound teaching, 11* ac-
cording to the glorious gospel of the blessed God,
with which I have been entrusted.

Gratitude for God's Mercy

12*† I am grateful to him who has strengthened
me, Christ Jesus our Lord, because he considered

†

1:1–2 For the Pauline use of the conventional epistolary form, see the note on Rom 1:1–7.

1:3–7 Here Timothy's initial task *in Ephesus* (cf Acts 20:17–35) is outlined: to suppress the idle religious speculations, probably about Old Testament figures (3–4, but see the note on 6:20–21), which do not contribute to the development of love within the community (5) but rather encourage similar useless conjectures (6–7).

1:4 The *plan of God that is to be received by faith:* the Greek may also possibly mean "God's trustworthy plan" or "the training in faith that God requires."

1:8–11 Those responsible for the speculations that are to be suppressed by Timothy do not present the Old Testament from the Christian viewpoint. The Christian values the Old Testament not as a system of law but as the first stage in God's revelation of his saving plan, which is brought to fulfillment in the good news of salvation through faith in Jesus Christ.

1:10 *Sodomites:* see 1 Cor 6:9 and the note there.

1:12–17 Present gratitude for the Christian apostleship leads Paul to recall an earlier time when he had been a fierce persecutor of the Christian communities (cf Acts 26:9–11) until his conversion by intervention of divine mercy through the appearance of Jesus. This and his subsequent apostolic experience testify to the saving purpose of Jesus' incarnation. The fact of his former ignorance of the truth has not kept the apostle from regarding himself as having been the worst of sinners (15). Yet he was chosen to be an apostle, that God might manifest his firm will to save sinful humanity through Jesus Christ (16). The recounting of so great a mystery leads to a spontaneous outpouring of adoration (17).

*

1:1 1 Tm 2:3; Lk 1:47; Ti 1:3; 2:10 / Col 1:27.
1:2 2 Tm 1:2; Ti 1:4.
1:3 Acts 20:1.
1:4 1 Tm 4:7; Ti 1:14; 3:9; 2 Pt 1:16.
1:5 Rom 13:10.
1:6 1 Tm 6:4, 20; Ti 1:10.
1:8 Rom 7:12, 16.
1:10 1 Tm 4:6; 6:3; 2 Tm 4:3; Ti 1:9; 2:1.
1:11 Ti 1:3.
1:12 Phil 4:13 / Acts 9:15; Gal 1:15–16.

me trustworthy in appointing me to the minis-
try. 13* I was once a blasphemer and a persecutor
and an arrogant man, but I have been mercifully
treated because I acted out of ignorance in my
unbelief. 14* Indeed, the grace of our Lord has
been abundant, along with the faith and love
that are in Christ Jesus. 15*† This saying is trust-
worthy and deserves full acceptance: Christ Jesus
came into the world to save sinners. Of these
I am the foremost. 16 But for that reason I was
mercifully treated, so that in me, as the foremost,
Christ Jesus might display all his patience as an
example for those who would come to believe in
him for everlasting life. 17*† To the king of ages,
incorruptible, invisible, the only God, honor and
glory forever and ever. Amen.

Responsibility of Timothy†

18* I entrust this charge to you, Timothy, my
child, in accordance with the prophetic words
once spoken about you.† Through them may you
fight a good fight 19* by having faith and a good
conscience. Some, by rejecting conscience, have
made a shipwreck of their faith, 20*† among them
Hymenaeus and Alexander, whom I have handed
over to Satan to be taught not to blaspheme.

III: Problems of Discipline

Prayer and Conduct

2 1*† First of all, then, I ask that supplica-
tions, prayers, petitions, and thanksgivings
be offered for everyone, 2 for kings and for all in
authority, that we may lead a quiet and tranquil

Live It!

Conscience: God in the Gut

Do you ever wonder where God is during those really difficult moments of decision? Like when you're with some friends and someone proposes you all do something exciting but dangerous, and you feel caught in the middle. Or when an entire group is taking advantage of a teacher who has left the room during a test. Or when a new kid trips and falls in the cafeteria and no one makes a move to help.

One of the best places to look for God's direction is that feeling in the center of your stomach when you are faced with life's dilemmas. That feeling may be a sign of your conscience prompting you to act.

In 1 Timothy 1:19, Timothy is told to have "faith and a good conscience." A good conscience is based on reason and love and is developed through a commitment to make good and thoughtful moral decisions. It also means acting in a way that is true to your faith. In other words, Timothy is supposed to be a model of sound teaching and moral action that corresponds to it.

Take time to develop your conscience by studying moral issues and the Church's teaching on them. The more you develop your conscience, the more you will experience God's speaking to you and the more you will be empowered to live your faith.

▶ **1 Tm 1:18–19**

1:15 *This saying is trustworthy:* this phrase regularly introduces in the Pastorals a basic truth of early Christian faith; cf 3:1; 4:9; 2 Tm 2:11; Ti 3:8.

1:17 *King of ages:* through Semitic influence, the Greek expression could mean "everlasting king"; it could also mean "king of the universe."

1:18–20 Timothy is to be mindful of his calling, which is here compared to the way Barnabas and Saul were designated by Christ as prophets for missionary service; cf Acts 13:1–3. Such is probably the sense of the allusion to the prophetic words (18). His task is not to yield, whether in doctrine or in conduct, to erroneous opinions, taking warning from what has already happened at Ephesus in the case of Hymenaeus and Alexander (19–20).

1:18 *The prophetic words once spoken about you:* the Greek may also be translated, "the prophecies that led (me) to you." It probably refers to testimonies given by charismatic figures in the Christian communities. *Fight a good fight:* this translation preserves the play on words in Greek. The Greek terms imply a lengthy engagement in battle and might well be translated "wage a good campaign."

1:20 *Hymenaeus:* mentioned in 2 Tm 2:17 as saying that the resurrection has already taken place (in baptism). *Alexander:* probably the Alexander mentioned in 2 Tm 4:14 as the coppersmith who "did me a great deal of harm." *Whom I have handed over to Satan:* the same terms are used in the condemnation of the incestuous man in 1 Cor 5:5.

2:1–7 This marked insistence that the liturgical prayer of the community concern itself with the needs of all, whether Christian or not, and especially of those in authority, may imply that a disposition existed at Ephesus to refuse prayer for pagans. In actuality, such prayer aids the community to achieve peaceful relationships with non-Christians (2) and contributes to salvation, since it derives its value from the presence within the community of Christ, who is the one and only savior of all (3–6). The vital apostolic mission to the Gentiles (7) reflects Christ's purpose of universal salvation. Verse 5 contains what may well have been a very primitive creed. Some interpreters have called it a Christian version of the Jewish *shema:* "Hear, O Israel, the LORD is our God, the LORD alone . . ." (Dt 6:4–5). The assertion in v 7, "I am speaking the truth, I am not lying," reminds one of similar affirmations in Rom 9:1; 2 Cor 11:31; and Gal 1:20.

1:13 Acts 8:3; 9:1–2; 1 Cor 15:9; Gal 1:13.
1:14 Rom 5:20; 2 Tm 1:13.
1:15 Lk 15:2; 19:10.
1:17 Rom 16:27.
1:18 1 Tm 4:14 / 1 Tm 6:12; 2 Tm 4:7; Jude 3.
1:19 1 Tm 3:9.
1:20 2 Tm 2:17; 4:14 / 1 Cor 5:5.
2:1 Eph 6:18; Phil 4:6.

life in all devotion and dignity. 3* This is good
and pleasing to God our savior, 4* who wills ev-
eryone to be saved and to come to knowledge of
the truth.

5* For there is one God.
There is also one mediator between God and
the human race,
Christ Jesus, himself human,
6*† who gave himself as ransom for all.

This was the testimony at the proper time. 7* For
this I was appointed preacher and apostle (I am
speaking the truth, I am not lying), teacher of the
Gentiles in faith and truth.
8† It is my wish, then, that in every place the
men should pray, lifting up holy hands, without
anger or argument. 9* Similarly, [too], women
should adorn themselves with proper conduct,
with modesty and self-control, not with braided
hairstyles and gold ornaments, or pearls, or ex-
pensive clothes, 10* but rather, as befits women
who profess reverence for God, with good deeds.
11* A woman must receive instruction silently
and under complete control. 12† I do not per-
mit a woman to teach or to have authority over
a man. She must be quiet. 13* For Adam was
formed first, then Eve. 14* Further, Adam was
not deceived, but the woman was deceived and
transgressed. 15* But she will be saved through
motherhood, provided women persevere in faith
and love and holiness, with self-control.

Qualifications of Various Ministers

3 1*† This saying is trustworthy:† whoever as-
pires to the office of bishop desires a noble

2:6 *The testimony:* to make sense of this overly concise phrase, many manuscripts supply "to which" (or "to whom"); two others add "was given." The translation has supplied "this was."

2:8–15 The prayer of the community should be unmarred by internal dissension (8); cf Mt 5:21–26; 6:14; Mk 11:25. At the liturgical assembly the dress of women should be appropriate to the occasion (9); their chief adornment is to be reputation for good works (10). Women are not to take part in the charismatic activity of the assembly (11–12; cf 1 Cor 14:34) or exercise authority; their conduct there should reflect the role of man's helpmate (13; cf Gn 2:18) and not the later relationship of Eve to Adam (14; cf Gn 3:6–7). As long as women perform their role as wives and mothers in faith and love, their salvation is assured (15).

2:12 *A man:* this could also mean "her husband."

3:1–7 The passage begins by commending those who aspire to the office of bishop (*episkopos;* see the note on Phil 1:1) within the community, but this first sentence (1) may also imply a warning about the great responsibilities involved. The writer proceeds to list the qualifications required: personal stability and graciousness; talent for teaching (2); moderation in habits and temperament (3); managerial ability (4); and experience in Christian living (5–6). Moreover, the candidate's previous life should provide no grounds for the charge that he did not previously practice what he now preaches. No list of qualifications for presbyters appears in 1 Timothy. The presbyter-bishops here and in Titus (see the note on Ti 1:5–9) lack certain functions reserved here for Paul and Timothy.

3:1 *This saying is trustworthy:* the saying introduced is so unlike others after this phrase that some later Western manuscripts read, "This saying is popular." It is understood by some interpreters as concluding the preceding section (2:8–15). *Bishop:* literally, "overseer"; see the note on Phil 1:1.

2:3 1 Tm 1:1; 4:10.
2:4 2 Tm 3:7; 2 Pt 3:9.
2:5 1 Cor 8:6; Heb 8:6; 9:15; 12:24 / Rom 5:15.
2:6 Mk 10:45; Gal 1:4; 2:20; Eph 5:25; Ti 2:14.
2:7 Acts 9:15; 1 Cor 9:1; Gal 2:7–8.
2:9 1 Pt 3:3–5.
2:10 1 Tm 5:10; 1 Pt 3:1.
2:11–12 1 Cor 14:34–35.
2:13 Gn 1:27; 2:7, 22; 1 Cor 11:8–9.
2:14 Gn 3:6, 13; 2 Cor 11:3.
2:15 1 Tm 5:14.
3:1–7 Ti 1:6–9.

Did You Know?

Women and Cultural Roles

A modern person reading 1 Timothy 2:8–15 may be shocked by the teaching there. A passage like this can be easily misunderstood and even misused against women. It is very important to realize that it is a reflection of women's roles in the ancient world. Whatever her religious background—Jewish, Christian, or pagan—a woman's place was in the home. Women generally married young, had no education, and were not allowed to hold a position of public authority.

The earliest Christian communities gathered in members' homes. In this less public arena, women taught and performed other ministries. As Christianity became more widely accepted, concern for how the Church appeared to outsiders grew—including concern about drunken bishops, immodest dress, and women teaching in public. That is probably why the author of First Timothy says, "I do not permit a woman to teach" (2:12).

Are things different for women in contemporary Christianity? Yes! Society has changed. Today, people in the United States are not scandalized if a woman manages a business, runs for public office, or leads a private foundation. Today, if you ask people to name influential Church leaders, Mother Teresa almost always comes up. Think of women you know who are involved in Church life. In your own parish or community, for example, there are probably women who are religious education directors, coordinators of youth ministry, or pastoral ministers.

▶ 1 Tm 2:8–15

3:1–13

task. 2 Therefore, a bishop must be irreproachable, married only once, temperate, self-controlled, decent, hospitable, able to teach, 3* not a drunkard, not aggressive, but gentle, not contentious, not a lover of money. 4 He must manage his own household well, keeping his children under control with perfect dignity; 5 for if a man does not know how to manage his own household, how can he take care of the church of God? 6† He should not be a recent convert, so that he may not become conceited and thus incur the devil's punishment. 7* He must also have a good reputation among outsiders, so that he may not fall into disgrace, the devil's trap.

8† Similarly, deacons must be dignified, not deceitful, not addicted to drink, not greedy for sordid gain, 9 holding fast to the mystery of the faith with a clear conscience. 10 Moreover, they should be tested first; then, if there is nothing against them, let them serve as deacons. 11*† Women, similarly, should be dignified, not slanderers, but temperate and faithful in everything. 12 Deacons may be married only once and must manage their children and their households well. 13 Thus those who serve well as deacons gain good standing and much confidence in their faith in Christ Jesus.

The Mystery of Our Religion

14† I am writing you about these matters, although I hope to visit you soon. 15* But if I should be delayed, you should know how to behave in the household of God, which is the church of the living God, the pillar and foundation of truth. 16*† Undeniably great is the mystery of devotion,

Who was manifested in the flesh,
vindicated in the spirit,
seen by angels,
proclaimed to the Gentiles,
believed in throughout the world,
taken up in glory.

False Asceticism

4 1*† Now the Spirit explicitly says that in the last times some will turn away from the faith by paying attention to deceitful spirits and demonic instructions 2 through the hypocrisy of liars with branded consciences. 3* They forbid marriage and require abstinence from foods that God created to be received with thanksgiving by those who believe and know the truth. 4* For everything created by God is good, and nothing is to be rejected when received with thanksgiving,

1 TM

†

3:6 *The devil's punishment:* this phrase could mean the punishment once incurred by the devil (objective genitive) or a punishment brought about by the devil (subjective genitive).

3:8–13 Deacons, besides possessing the virtue of moderation (8), are to be outstanding for their faith (9) and well respected within the community (10). Women in the same role, although some interpreters take them to mean wives of deacons, must be dignified, temperate, dedicated, and not given to malicious talebearing (11). Deacons must have shown stability in marriage and have a good record with their families (12), for such experience prepares them well for the exercise of their ministry on behalf of the community (13). See further the note on Phil 1:1.

3:11 *Women:* this seems to refer to women deacons but may possibly mean wives of deacons. The former is preferred because the word is used absolutely; if deacons' wives were meant, a possessive "their" would be expected. Moreover, they are also introduced by the word "similarly," as in v 8; this parallel suggests that they too exercised ecclesiastical functions.

3:14–16 In case there is some delay in the visit to Timothy at Ephesus planned for the near future, the present letter is being sent on ahead to arm and enlighten him in his task of preserving sound Christian conduct in the Ephesian church. The care he must exercise over this community is required by the profound nature of Christianity. It centers in Christ, appearing in human flesh, vindicated by the holy Spirit; the mystery of his person was revealed to the angels, announced to the Gentiles, and accepted by them in faith. He himself was taken up (through his resurrection and ascension) to the divine glory (16). This passage apparently includes part of a liturgical hymn used among the Christian communities in and around Ephesus. It consists of three couplets in typical Hebrew balance: flesh-spirit (contrast), seen-proclaimed (complementary), world-glory (contrast).

3:16 *Who:* the reference is to Christ, who is himself "the mystery of our devotion." Some predominantly Western manuscripts read "which," harmonizing the gender of the pronoun with that of the Greek word for mystery; many later (eighth/ninth century on), predominantly Byzantine manuscripts read "God," possibly for theological reasons.

4:1–5 Doctrinal deviations from the true Christian message within the church have been prophesied, though the origin of the prophecy is not specified (1–2); cf Acts 20:29–30. The letter warns against a false asceticism that prohibits marriage and regards certain foods as forbidden, though they are part of God's good creation (3).

*

3:3 Heb 13:5.
3:7 2 Cor 8:21; 2 Tm 2:26.
3:11 Ti 2:3.
3:15 Eph 2:19–22.
3:16 Jn 1:14; Rom 1:3–4.
4:1 2 Tm 3:1; 4:3; 2 Pt 3:3; Jude 18.
4:3 Gn 9:3; Rom 14:6; 1 Cor 10:30–31.
4:4 Gn 1:31; Acts 10:15.

Catholic Connection

The Incarnation

Being new at something can be difficult, and it helps to have someone experienced show you the way. This is what Paul was doing for Timothy in his first letter. Timothy was new at leading his local church and was apparently facing some difficulties with people promoting false beliefs about Jesus Christ. To help, Paul provides Timothy with a brief summary of beliefs and acknowledges that faith in Christ involves mystery, or things that go beyond understanding. In this brief summary, Paul mentions that Jesus "was manifested in the flesh" (1 Tm 3:16). This verse points to the mystery that Jesus is both fully divine and fully human.

Similar to the challenges that Timothy faced, the Church has also had to address those who preached false beliefs. During its first five hundred years, the Church struggled to clarify and explain the mystery of the relationship between Jesus' divinity and humanity. Some falsely said Jesus was created by God and therefore only semi-divine. Others falsely said the two natures remained totally separate in Jesus. And still others falsely claimed Jesus' human nature ceased to exist once it was assumed by Christ when he came in the flesh.

The Scriptures provide evidence of the presence and role of both a divine and human nature united in one person, Jesus Christ. We see that Jesus is truly human, for he had to learn and grow (see Lk 2:52), he experienced emotions (see Jn 11:28–37), and he faced temptations just like we do (see Mt 4:1–11). We also see that Jesus is truly divine, for he could read the heart of those he encountered (see Jn 4:5–42) and performed many miracles (see Mt 9:18–26).

After much effort, this mysterious relationship is now understood through the Church's teaching called the Incarnation. The Incarnation is the belief that Jesus is truly divine and assumed a truly human nature when he became man. The Church teaches that, with the exception of sinning, Jesus is just like each one of us in every way. By becoming human, Jesus showed us how God would live and act. He showed us how to live totally obedient to the Father's will. Through his love and service to others, he showed us how much God loves us and how much we should love others. By becoming human, Jesus revealed to us our true nature as sons and daughters of God.

▶ 1 Tm 3:14–16

Catechism, nos. 456–483

Live It!

Training for Christ

We spend countless hours in training to become better athletes, musicians, scientists, teachers, electricians; you name it, we train for it if we want to be good at it. Paul says the soul needs that same kind of training.

In your journal or on a piece of paper, make two columns—one to list the ways you train for your sporting event or other activity and the other to list ways you might train your soul to become a more loving person, in the image of Jesus. Once you have completed your lists, put them in a place where you can see them every day. Use them as a guide and as a reminder to continue in your efforts to train for Christ. You may also find that you need to keep adding to your soul-training list as your training starts to pay off!

▶ 1 Tm 4:6–10

5† for it is made holy by the invocation of God
in prayer.

Counsel to Timothy

6† If you will give these instructions to the
brothers, you will be a good minister of Christ
Jesus, nourished on the words of the faith and of
the sound teaching you have followed. 7* Avoid
profane and silly myths. Train yourself for devo-
tion, 8* for, while physical training is of limited
value, devotion is valuable in every respect, since
it holds a promise of life both for the present
and for the future. 9* This saying is trustworthy
and deserves full acceptance. 10*† For this we
toil and struggle, because we have set our hope
on the living God, who is the savior of all, espe-
cially of those who believe.

11† Command and teach these things. 12*† Let
no one have contempt for your youth, but set an
example for those who believe, in speech, con-
duct, love, faith, and purity. 13† Until I arrive,
attend to the reading, exhortation, and teaching.
14*† Do not neglect the gift you have, which was
conferred on you through the prophetic word
with the imposition of hands of the presbyter-
ate. 15 Be diligent in these matters, be absorbed
in them, so that your progress may be evident
to everyone. 16 Attend to yourself and to your
teaching; persevere in both tasks, for by doing
so you will save both yourself and those who
listen to you.

IV: Duties toward Others

5 1*† Do not rebuke an older man, but appeal
to him as a father. Treat younger men as
brothers, 2 older women as mothers, and younger
women as sisters with complete purity.

Rules for Widows

3 Honor widows who are truly widows. 4 But
if a widow has children or grandchildren, let
these first learn to perform their religious duty

†

4:5 *The invocation of God in prayer:* literally, "the word of God and petition." The use of "word of God" without an article in Greek suggests that it refers to the name of God being invoked in blessing rather than to the "word of God" proclaimed to the community.

4:6–10 Timothy is urged to be faithful, both in his teaching and in his own life, as he looks only to God for salvation.

4:10 *Struggle:* other manuscripts and patristic witnesses read "suffer reproach."

4:11–16 Timothy is urged to preach and teach with confidence, relying on the gifts and the mission that God has bestowed on him.

4:12 *Youth:* some commentators find this reference a sign of pseudepigraphy. Timothy had joined Paul as a missionary already in A.D. 49, some fifteen years before the earliest supposed date of composition.

4:13 *Reading:* the Greek word refers to private or public reading. Here, it probably designates the public reading of scripture in the Christian assembly.

4:14 *Prophetic word:* this may mean the utterance of a Christian prophet designating the candidate or a prayer of blessing accompanying the rite. *Imposition of hands:* this gesture was used in the Old Testament to signify the transmission of authority from Moses to Joshua (Nm 27:18–23; Dt 34:9). The early Christian community used it as a symbol of installation into an office: the Seven (Acts 6:6) and Paul and Barnabas (Acts 13:3). *Of the presbyterate:* this would mean that each member of the college of presbyters imposed hands and appears to contradict 2 Tm 1:6, in which Paul says that he imposed hands on Timothy. This latter text, however, does not exclude participation by others in the rite. Some prefer to translate "for the presbyterate," and thus understand it to designate the office into which Timothy was installed rather than the agents who installed him.

5:1–16 After a few words of general advice based on common sense (1–2), the letter takes up, in its several aspects, the subject of widows. The first responsibility for their care belongs to the family circle, not to the Christian community as such (3–4, 16). The widow left without the aid of relatives may benefit the community by her prayer, and the community should consider her material sustenance its responsibility (5–8). Widows who wish to work directly for the Christian community should not be accepted unless they are well beyond the probability of marriage, i.e., sixty years of age, married only once, and with a reputation for good works (9–10). Younger widows are apt to be troublesome and should be encouraged to remarry (11–15).

*

4:7 1 Tm 1:4; 2 Tm 2:16; Ti 1:14.
4:8 1 Tm 6:6.
4:9 1 Tm 1:15; 2 Tm 2:11; Ti 3:8.
4:10 1 Tm 2:4; Ti 2:11.
4:12 1 Cor 16:11; Ti 2:15 / Phil 3:17.
4:14 1 Tm 5:22; Acts 6:6; 8:17; 2 Tm 1:6.
5:1 Lv 19:32; Ti 2:2.

to their own family and to make recompense to their parents, for this is pleasing to God. 5* The real widow, who is all alone, has set her hope on God and continues in supplications and prayers night and day. 6 But the one who is self-indulgent is dead while she lives. 7 Command this, so that they may be irreproachable. 8 And whoever does not provide for relatives and especially family members has denied the faith and is worse than an unbeliever.

9 Let a widow be enrolled if she is not less than sixty years old, married only once, 10* with a reputation for good works, namely, that she has raised children, practiced hospitality, washed the feet of the holy ones, helped those in distress, involved herself in every good work. 11 But exclude younger widows, for when their sensuality estranges them from Christ, they want to marry 12 and will incur condemnation for breaking their first pledge. 13* And furthermore, they learn to be idlers, going about from house to house, and not only idlers but gossips and busybodies as well, talking about things that ought not to be mentioned. 14* So I would like younger widows to marry, have children, and manage a home, so as to give the adversary no pretext for maligning us. 15 For some have already turned away to follow Satan. 16† If any woman believer has widowed relatives, she must assist them; the church is not to be burdened, so that it will be able to help those who are truly widows.

"Let no one have contempt for your youth, but set an example for those who believe, in speech, conduct, love, faith, and purity."
(1 Tm 4:12)

Rules for Presbyters

17*† Presbyters who preside well deserve double honor, especially those who toil in preaching and teaching. 18* For the scripture says, "You shall not muzzle an ox when it is threshing," and, "A worker deserves his pay." 19* Do not accept an accusation against a presbyter unless it is supported by two or three witnesses. 20* Reprimand publicly those who do sin, so that the rest also will be afraid. 21 I charge you before God and Christ Jesus and the elect angels to keep these rules without prejudice, doing nothing out of favoritism. 22* Do not lay hands too readily on anyone, and do not share in another's sins. Keep yourself pure. 23 Stop drinking only water, but have a little wine for the sake of your stomach and your frequent illnesses.

24 Some people's sins are public, preceding them to judgment; but other people are followed by their sins. 25 Similarly, good works are also public; and even those that are not cannot remain hidden.

Rules for Slaves

6 1*† Those who are under the yoke of slavery must regard their masters as worthy of full respect, so that the name of God and our teaching† may not suffer abuse. 2*† Those whose masters are believers must not take advantage of them because they are brothers but must give better service because those who will profit from their work are believers and are beloved.

V: False Teaching and True Wealth

Teach and urge these things. 3* Whoever teaches something different and does not agree

†

5:16 *Woman believer:* some early Latin manuscripts and Fathers have a masculine here, while most later manuscripts and patristic quotations conflate the two readings, perhaps to avoid unfair restriction to women.

5:17–25 The function of presbyters is not exactly the same as that of the *episkopos,* "bishop" (3:1); in fact, the relation of the two at the time of this letter is obscure (but cf the note on Ti 1:5–9). The Pastorals seem to reflect a transitional stage that developed in many regions of the church into the monarchical episcopate of the second and third centuries. The presbyters possess the responsibility of preaching and teaching, for which functions they are supported by the community (17–18). The realization that their position subjects them to adverse criticism is implied in the direction to Timothy (19–20) to make sure of the truth of any accusation against them before public reproof is given. He must be as objective as possible in weighing charges against presbyters (21), learning from his experience to take care in selecting them (22). Some scholars take v 22 as a reference not to ordination of presbyters but to reconciliation of public sinners. The letter now sounds an informal note of personal concern in its advice to Timothy not to be so ascetic that he even avoids wine (23). Judgment concerning the fitness of candidates to serve as presbyters is easy with persons of open conduct, more difficult and prolonged with those of greater reserve (24–25).

6:1–2 Compare the tables for household duties, such as that of Col 3:18—4:1. Domestic relationships derive new meaning from the Christian faith.

6:1 *Our teaching:* this refers to the teaching of the Christian community.

6:2b–10 Timothy is exhorted to maintain steadfastly the position outlined in this letter, not allowing himself to be pressured into any other course. He must realize that false teachers can be discerned by their pride, envy, quarrelsomeness, and greed for material gain. Verse 6 is rather obscure and is interpreted, and therefore translated, variously. The suggestion seems to be that the important gain that religion brings is spiritual, but that there is material gain, too, up to the point of what is needed for physical sustenance (cf 17–19).

*

5:5 Jer 49:11; Lk 2:37; 18:7.
5:10 Jn 13:14; Heb 13:2.
5:13 2 Thes 3:11.
5:14 1 Cor 7:9.
5:17 1 Cor 16:18; Phil 2:29.
5:18 Dt 25:4; 1 Cor 9:8 / Mt 10:10; Lk 10:7.
5:19 Dt 17:6; 19:15; Mt 18:16; 2 Cor 13:1.
5:20 Gal 2:14; Eph 5:11; 2 Tm 4:2; Ti 1:9, 13.
5:22 1 Tm 4:14; 2 Tm 1:6.
6:1 Eph 6:5; Ti 2:9–10.
6:2 Phlm 16.
6:3 Gal 1:6–9; 2 Tm 1:13; Ti 1:1.

Live It!

Dangers of Money

We live in a culture that glorifies material things, money, and consumption. People are generally thought to be successful if they have great riches and all the luxury items to prove it to their neighbors. There is a bumper sticker that reads, "The one who dies with the most toys wins!" Even when individuals or families have the essential things to live comfortably, many are driven to acquire more.

An important truth found many places in the Scriptures (see, for example, Lk 12:20) is repeated here: You can't take it with you. The Scriptures warn about something that most of us know deep down but often ignore: "The love of money is the root of all evils" (1 Tm 6:10). In our eagerness to become financially rich, we can lose sight of God and become entangled in all kinds of senseless distractions.

All of us need the basic stuff of life: food, clothing, and shelter. God wants us to have these things—and more! Ultimately, real riches or success will not be measured by bank accounts or material things, but by the love and generosity with which we have lived. How rich are you becoming in these things?

▶ **1 Tm 6:6–10**

with the sound words of our Lord Jesus Christ
and the religious teaching [4]is conceited, under-
standing nothing, and has a morbid disposition
for arguments and verbal disputes. From these
come envy, rivalry, insults, evil suspicions,
[5]* and mutual friction among people with cor-
rupted minds, who are deprived of the truth,
supposing religion to be a means of gain.
[6]*† Indeed, religion with contentment is a great
gain. [7]* For we brought nothing into the world,
just as we shall not be able to take anything out
of it. [8]* If we have food and clothing, we shall
be content with that. [9]* Those who want to be
rich are falling into temptation and into a trap
and into many foolish and harmful desires,
which plunge them into ruin and destruction.
[10]For the love of money is the root of all evils,
and some people in their desire for it have
strayed from the faith and have pierced them-
selves with many pains.

Exhortations to Timothy†

[11]* But you, man of God,† avoid all this.
Instead, pursue righteousness, devotion, faith,
love, patience, and gentleness. [12]* Compete
well for the faith. Lay hold of eternal life, to
which you were called when you made the
noble confession in the presence of many wit-
nesses. [13]* I charge [you] before God, who gives
life to all things, and before Christ Jesus, who
gave testimony under Pontius Pilate for the
noble confession, [14]to keep the commandment
without stain or reproach until the appearance
of our Lord Jesus Christ [15]* that the blessed
and only ruler will make manifest at the proper
time, the King of kings and Lord of lords,
[16]* who alone has immortality, who dwells in
unapproachable light, and whom no human
being has seen or can see. To him be honor and
eternal power. Amen.

Right Use of Wealth

[17]*† Tell the rich in the present age not to be
proud and not to rely on so uncertain a thing as
wealth but rather on God, who richly provides
us with all things for our enjoyment. [18]Tell them
to do good, to be rich in good works, to be gen-
erous, ready to share, [19]* thus accumulating as
treasure a good foundation for the future, so as
to win the life that is true life.

†

6:6 *Contentment:* the word *autarkeia* is a technical Greek philosophical term for the virtue of independence from material goods (Aristotle, Cynics, Stoics).

6:11–16 Timothy's position demands total dedication to God and faultless witness to Christ (11–14) operating from an awareness, through faith, of the coming revelation in Jesus of the invisible God (15–16).

6:11 *Man of God:* a title applied to Moses and the prophets (Dt 33:1; 1 Sm 2:27; 1 Kgs 12:22; 13:1; etc.).

6:17–19 Timothy is directed to instruct the rich, advising them to make good use of their wealth by aiding the poor.

*

6:5 2 Tm 3:8; 4:4; Ti 1:14.
6:6 1 Tm 4:8; Phil 4:11–12; Heb 13:5.
6:7 Jb 1:21; Eccl 5:14.
6:8 Prv 30:8.
6:9 Prv 23:4; 28:22.
6:11 2 Tm 2:22.
6:12 1 Cor 9:26; 2 Tm 4:7.
6:13 Jn 18:36–37; 19:11.
6:15 2 Mc 13:4; Rv 17:14.
6:16 Ex 33:20; Ps 104:2.
6:17 Ps 62:11; Lk 12:20.
6:19 Mt 6:20.

VI: Final Recommendation and Warning

[20]*† O Timothy, guard what has been en-
trusted to you. Avoid profane babbling and
the absurdities of so-called knowledge. [21]* By
professing it, some people have deviated from
the faith.

Grace be with all of you.

6:20–21 A final solemn warning against the heretical teachers, with what seems to be a specific reference to gnosticism, the great rival and enemy of the church for two centuries and more (the Greek word for "knowledge" is *gnōsis*). If gnosticism is being referred to here, it is probable that the warnings against "speculations" and "myths and genealogies" (cf especially 1:4; Ti 3:9) involve allusions to that same kind of heresy. Characteristic of the various gnostic systems of speculation was an elaborate mythology of innumerable superhuman intermediaries, on a descending scale ("genealogies"), between God and the world. Thus would be explained the emphasis upon Christ's being the *one* mediator (as in 2:5). Although fully developed gnosticism belonged to the second and later centuries, there are signs that incipient forms of it belonged to Paul's own period.

6:20 2Tm 1:14 / 1Tm 4:7. **6:21** 1Tm 1:6; 2Tm 2:18.

For background on this letter, see the introduction to the pastoral letters, before 1 Timothy.

2 Timothy

I: Address

Greeting†

1 1* Paul, an apostle of Christ Jesus by the will of God for the promise of life in Christ Jesus,† 2 to Timothy, my dear child: grace, mercy, and peace from God the Father and Christ Jesus our Lord.

Thanksgiving

3*† I am grateful to God, whom I worship with a clear conscience as my ancestors did, as I remember you constantly in my prayers, night and day. 4† I yearn to see you again, recalling your tears, so that I may be filled with joy, 5* as I recall your sincere faith that first lived in your grandmother Lois and in your mother Eunice and that I am confident lives also in you.

II: Exhortations to Timothy

The Gifts Timothy Has Received

6*† For this reason, I remind you to stir into flame the gift of God that you have through the imposition of my hands. 7* For God did not give us a spirit of cowardice but rather of power and love and self-control. 8*† So do not be ashamed of your testimony to our Lord, nor of me, a prisoner for his sake; but bear your share of hardship for the gospel with the strength that comes from God.

9*† He saved us and called us to a holy life, not according to our works but according to his own design and the grace bestowed on us in Christ Jesus before time began, 10* but now made manifest through the appearance of our savior Christ Jesus, who destroyed death and brought life and immortality to light through the gospel, 11*† for which I

1:1–2 For the formula of address and greeting, see the note on Rom 1:1–7.

1:1 *The promise of life in Christ Jesus:* that God grants through union with Christ in faith and love; cf Col 3:4; 1 Tm 4:8.

1:3 *As my ancestors did:* this emphasizes the continuity of Judaism and Christianity; for a similar view, see Rom 9:3–5; Phil 3:4–6.

1:4–5 Purportedly written from prison in Rome (8, 17; 4:6–8) shortly before the writer's death, the letter recalls the earlier sorrowful parting from Timothy, commending him for his faith and expressing the longing to see him again.

1:6 *The gift of God:* the grace resulting from the conferral of an ecclesiastical office. *The imposition of my hands:* see the note on 1 Tm 4:14.

1:8 *Do not be ashamed of your testimony to our Lord:* i.e., of preaching and suffering for the sake of the gospel.

1:9–10 Redemption from sin and the call to holiness of life are not won by personal deeds but are freely and graciously bestowed according to God's eternal plan; cf Eph 1:4.

1:11 *Teacher:* the overwhelming majority of manuscripts and Fathers read "teacher of the nations," undoubtedly a harmonization with 1 Tm 2:7.

1:1 1 Tm 4:8.
1:3 1 Tm 3:9 / Phil 3:5.
1:5 1 Tm 1:5 / Acts 16:1.
1:6 1 Tm 4:14; 5:22 / Acts 6:6; 8:17.
1:7 Rom 5:5; 8:15; 1 Cor 2:4.
1:8 2 Tm 2:3, 15; Rom 1:16.
1:9 Eph 2:8–9; Ti 3:5 / Eph 1:4; Ti 1:2.
1:10 Rom 16:26; 1 Pt 1:20 / 1 Tm 6:14 / Phil 3:20; Ti 1:4; 2:13; 2 Pt 1:11 / 1 Cor 15:54–55; Heb 2:14 / 1 Cor 15:53–54.
1:11 1 Tm 2:7.

was appointed preacher and apostle and teacher.
12*† On this account I am suffering these things;
but I am not ashamed, for I know him in whom
I have believed and am confident that he is able
to guard what has been entrusted to me until that
day. 13* Take as your norm the sound words that
you heard from me, in the faith and love that are
in Christ Jesus. 14* Guard this rich trust with the
help of the holy Spirit that dwells within us.

Paul's Suffering

15*† You know that everyone in Asia deserted
me, including Phygelus and Hermogenes. 16*† May
the Lord grant mercy to the family of Onesiphorus
because he often gave me new heart and was not
ashamed of my chains. 17 But when he came to
Rome, he promptly searched for me and found
me. 18*† May the Lord grant him to find mercy
from the Lord on that day. And you know very
well the services he rendered in Ephesus.

Timothy's Conduct

2 1† So you, my child, be strong in the grace
that is in Christ Jesus. 2 And what you heard
from me through many witnesses entrust to
faithful people who will have the ability to teach
others as well. 3* Bear your share of hardship
along with me like a good soldier of Christ Jesus.
4* To satisfy the one who recruited him, a sol-
dier does not become entangled in the business
affairs of life. 5* Similarly, an athlete cannot
receive the winner's crown except by compet-
ing according to the rules. 6* The hardworking
farmer ought to have the first share of the crop.
7* Reflect on what I am saying, for the Lord will
give you understanding in everything.
8*† Remember Jesus Christ, raised from the
dead, a descendant of David: such is my gospel,
9* for which I am suffering, even to the point of
chains, like a criminal. But the word of God is
not chained. 10* Therefore, I bear with everything
for the sake of those who are chosen, so that they
too may obtain the salvation that is in Christ
Jesus, together with eternal glory. 11* This saying
is trustworthy:

Live It!

Do Not Be Ashamed

Terry is a popular guy in the senior class. He is on the basketball and track teams and served on student council. He is extremely friendly and never says anything bad about anyone. Everyone likes him.

Terry is also very active in his church's youth group. He is not afraid to let others know that church is important to him. He never preaches religion, but he lets people know that church and Jesus are central to his life.

The author of Second Timothy encourages today's readers, "Do not be ashamed of your testimony to our Lord" (1:8). You do not have to announce your faith from mountaintops or from street corners, but like Terry, you should not be afraid to admit that God is important to you. You will likely discover that others admire you for your faith and commitment.

▶ 2 Tm 1:6–18

1:12 *He is able to guard . . . until that day:* the intervening words can also be translated "what I have entrusted to him" (i.e., the fruit of his ministry) as well as "what has been entrusted to me" (i.e., the faith). The same difficult term occurs in v 14, where it is modified by the adjective "rich" and used without a possessive.

1:15 Keen disappointment is expressed, here and later (4:16), that the Christians of the province of Asia, especially Phygelus and Hermogenes, should have abandoned the writer and done nothing to defend his case in court.

1:16–18 *The family of Onesiphorus because he . . . of my chains:* Onesiphorus seems to have died before this letter was written. His family is mentioned twice (here and in 4:19), though it was Onesiphorus himself who was helpful to Paul in prison and rendered much service to the community of Ephesus. Because the apostle complains of abandonment by all in Asia during his second imprisonment and trial, the assistance of Onesiphorus seems to have been given to Paul during his first Roman imprisonment (A.D. 61–63).

1:18 *Lord . . . Lord:* the first "Lord" here seems to refer to Christ, the second "Lord" to the Father.

2:1–7 This passage manifests a characteristic deep concern for safeguarding the faith and faithfully transmitting it through trustworthy people (1–2; cf 1:14; 1 Tm 6:20; Ti 1:9). Comparisons to the soldier's detachment, the athlete's sportsmanship, and the farmer's arduous work as the price of recompense (4–6) emphasize the need of singleness of purpose in preaching the word, even at the cost of hardship, for the sake of Christ (3).

2:8–13 The section begins with a sloganlike summary of Paul's gospel about Christ (8) and concludes with what may be part of an early Christian hymn (11b–12a; most exegetes include the rest of v 12 and all of v 13 as part of the quotation). The poetic lines suggest that through baptism Christians die spiritually with Christ and hope to live with him and reign with him forever, but the Christian life includes endurance, witness, and even suffering, as the final judgment will show and as Paul's own case makes clear; while he is imprisoned for preaching the gospel (9), his sufferings are helpful to the elect for obtaining the salvation and glory available in Christ (10), who will be true to those who are faithful and will disown those who deny him (12–13).

1:12 1 Pt 4:16 / 1 Tm 1:10–11.
1:13 1 Tm 1:14.
1:14 1 Tm 6:20 / Rom 8:11.
1:15 2 Tm 4:16.
1:16 2 Tm 4:19.
1:18 Jude 21.
2:3 2 Tm 1:8; 4:5; Phlm 2.
2:4 1 Cor 9:6.
2:5 1 Cor 9:25.
2:6 1 Cor 9:7–10.
2:7 Prv 2:6.
2:8 Rom 1:3; 1 Cor 15:4, 20 / Rom 2:16; Gal 1:11; 2:2.
2:9 Phil 1:12–14.
2:10 Col 1:24; 1 Tm 1:15.
2:11 Rom 6:8.

Live It!

Teaching Others

Have you ever tried to explain to someone something about your faith? That can be challenging. Second Timothy 2:22–26 contains some tips on sharing faith with others: live a good moral life, do good works, and have a pure heart. Be kind, patient, and gentle. And be an apt teacher, someone who is qualified or prepared.

Imagine that you are helping to teach a group of younger people about their faith. What do you want to say about God? How do you explain Jesus' love? How do you show your patience and gentleness? If you can answer these questions, maybe you should volunteer to help with your church's religious education program!

▶ **2 Tm 2:22–26**

If we have died with him
we shall also live with him;
12* if we persevere
we shall also reign with him.
But if we deny him
he will deny us.
13* If we are unfaithful
he remains faithful,
for he cannot deny himself.

III: Instructions Concerning False Teaching

Warning against Useless Disputes

14*† Remind people of these things and charge
them before God† to stop disputing about
words. This serves no useful purpose since it
harms those who listen. 15* Be eager to present
yourself as acceptable to God, a workman who
causes no disgrace, imparting the word of truth
without deviation. 16* Avoid profane, idle talk,
for such people will become more and more
godless, 17* and their teaching will spread like
gangrene. Among them are Hymenaeus and
Philetus, 18* who have deviated from the truth
by saying that [the] resurrection has already
taken place and are upsetting the faith of some.
19* Nevertheless, God's solid foundation stands,
bearing this inscription, "The Lord knows those
who are his"; and, "Let everyone who calls upon
the name of the Lord avoid evil."
20 In a large household there are vessels not
only of gold and silver but also of wood and
clay, some for lofty and others for humble use.
21* If anyone cleanses himself of these things, he
will be a vessel for lofty use, dedicated, benefi-
cial to the master of the house, ready for every
good work. 22*† So turn from youthful desires
and pursue righteousness, faith, love, and peace,
along with those who call on the Lord with
purity of heart. 23* Avoid foolish and ignorant
debates, for you know that they breed quarrels.
24* A slave of the Lord should not quarrel, but
should be gentle with everyone, able to teach,
tolerant, 25* correcting opponents with kindness.
It may be that God will grant them repentance
that leads to knowledge of the truth, 26*† and
that they may return to their senses out of the
devil's snare, where they are entrapped by him,
for his will.

The Dangers of the Last Days

3 1*† But understand this: there will be terri-
fying times in the last days. 2* People will
be self-centered and lovers of money, proud,
haughty, abusive, disobedient to their parents,
ungrateful, irreligious, 3 callous, implacable, slan-
derous, licentious, brutal, hating what is good,
4 traitors, reckless, conceited, lovers of pleasure

†

2:14–19 For those who dispute about mere words (cf 23–24) and indulge in irreligious talk to the detriment of their listeners (16–19), see the notes on 1 Tm 1:3–7; 6:20–21. Hymenaeus and Philetus (17), while accepting the Christian's mystical death and resurrection in Christ through baptism, claimed that baptized Christians are already risen with Christ in this life and thus that there is no future bodily resurrection or eternal glory to come. The first quotation in v 19 is from Nm 16:5; the other quotation is from some unidentified Jewish or Christian writing.

2:14 *Before God:* many ancient manuscripts read "before the Lord."

2:22 *Those who call on the Lord:* those who believe in Christ and worship him as Lord, i.e., Christians (Acts 9:14–16, 20–21; Rom 10:12–13; cf 19, literally, "Everyone who names the name of the Lord").

2:26 Some interpreters would render this passage, "Thus they may come to their senses and, forced to do his (i.e., God's) will, may escape the devil's trap." This interpretation of the Greek is possible, but the one accepted in the text seems more likely.

3:1–9 The moral depravity and false teaching that will be rampant in the last days are already at work (1–5). The frivolous and su-

2:12 Mt 10:22, 33; Lk 12:9.
2:13 Nm 23:19; Rom 3:3–4; 1 Cor 10:13; Ti 1:2.
2:14 1 Tm 6:4.
2:15 2 Tm 1:8; 2 Cor 6:7; Eph 1:13; Col 1:5.
2:16 1 Tm 4:7.
2:17 1 Tm 1:20.
2:18 2 Thes 2:2.
2:19 Is 28:16; 1 Cor 3:10–15 / Nm 16:5; Jn 10:14.
2:21 2 Tm 3:17.
2:22 Gal 5:22; 1 Tm 6:11 / Rom 10:13; 1 Cor 1:2.
2:23 1 Tm 1:4; 4:7; 6:4; Ti 3:9.
2:24 1 Tm 3:2–3.
2:25 2 Tm 3:7; 1 Tm 2:4.
2:26 1 Tm 3:7.
3:1 1 Tm 4:1; 2 Pt 3:3; Jude 18.
3:2–4 Rom 1:29–31.

Pray It!

For Those Who Walk with Us

We pray, Lord, for those who formed us in our faith.
We pray for our families who first spoke your name to us and shared our journey of faith from the beginning.
We pray for our friends who shared their faith and continue to walk with us in our journey.
We pray for the teachers, priests, youth ministers, and other members of our church who took the time to recognize us as individuals and who showed us that faith can be both fun and challenging.
Thank you, God, for sending these people into our lives and for their gifts of faith, love, and patience. May we honor them by sharing our faith with a new generation of believers. We pray this in Jesus' name. Amen.

▶ **2 Tm 3:12–14**

rather than lovers of God, 5* as they make a pretense of religion but deny its power. Reject them. 6* For some of these slip into homes and make captives of women weighed down by sins, led by various desires, 7* always trying to learn but never able to reach a knowledge of the truth. 8* Just as Jannes and Jambres opposed Moses, so they also oppose the truth—people of depraved mind, unqualified in the faith. 9 But they will not make further progress, for their foolishness will be plain to all, as it was with those two.

Paul's Example and Teaching

10† You have followed my teaching, way of life, purpose, faith, patience, love, endurance, 11* persecutions, and sufferings, such as happened to me in Antioch, Iconium, and Lystra, persecutions that I endured. Yet from all these things the Lord delivered me. 12* In fact, all who want to live religiously in Christ Jesus will be persecuted. 13 But wicked people and charlatans will go from bad to worse, deceivers and deceived. 14* But you, remain faithful to what you have learned and believed, because you know from whom you learned it, 15* and that from infancy you have known [the] sacred scriptures, which are capable of giving you wisdom for salvation through faith in Christ Jesus. 16*† All scripture is inspired by God and is useful for teaching, for refutation, for correction, and for training in righteousness,† 17* so that one who belongs to God may be competent, equipped for every good work.

"All scripture is inspired by God and is useful for teaching, for refutation, for correction, and for training in righteousness."
(2 Tm 3:16)

Solemn Charge

4 1*† I charge you in the presence of God and of Christ Jesus, who will judge the living and the dead, and by his appearing and his kingly power: 2* proclaim the word; be persistent whether it is convenient or inconvenient; convince, reprimand, encourage through all patience

---

perficial, too, devoid of the true spirit of religion, will be easy victims of those who pervert them by falsifying the truth (6–8), just as Jannes and Jambres, Pharaoh's magicians of Egypt (Ex 7:11–12, 22), discredited the truth in Moses' time. Exodus does not name the magicians, but the two names are widely found in much later Jewish, Christian, and even pagan writings. Their origins are legendary.

3:10–17 Paul's example for Timothy includes persecution, a frequent emphasis in the Pastorals. Timothy is to be steadfast to what he has been taught and to scripture. The scriptures are the source of wisdom, i.e., of belief in and loving fulfillment of God's word revealed in Christ, through whom salvation is given.

3:16 *All scripture is inspired by God:* this could possibly also be translated, "All scripture inspired by God is useful for . . . ." In this classic reference to inspiration, God is its principal author, with the writer as the human collaborator. Thus the scriptures are the word of God in human language. See also 2 Pt 1:20–21.

3:16–17 *Useful for teaching . . . every good work:* because as God's word the scriptures share his divine authority. It is exercised through those who are ministers of the word.

4:1–5 The gravity of the obligation incumbent on Timothy to preach the word can be gauged from the solemn adjuration: in the presence of God, and of Christ coming as universal judge, and by his appearance and *his kingly power* (1). Patience, courage, constancy, and endurance are required despite the opposition, hostility, indifference, and defection of many to whom the truth has been preached (2–5).

3:5 Rom 2:20–22; Ti 1:16.
3:6 Ti 1:11.
3:7 2 Tm 2:25.
3:8 Ex 7:11, 22; 1 Tm 6:5.
3:11 Acts 13:50; 14:5, 19 / Ps 34:20.
3:12 Jn 15:20; Acts 14:22.
3:14 2 Tm 2:2.
3:15 Jn 5:39.
3:16 Rom 15:4; 2 Pt 1:19–21.
3:17 2 Tm 2:21.
4:1 1 Tm 5:21; 6:14 / Acts 10:42; Rom 14:9–10; 1 Pt 4:5.
4:2 Acts 20:20, 31; 1 Tm 5:20.

Live It!

Misleading Messages

Sticking with something can be difficult. When things get tough, many people are tempted to quit or walk away. If swim practice is boring, they drop off the team. If homework is too complicated, they just don't finish it. If one of their friends starts to annoy them, they stop hanging around with her or him. We are surrounded by messages like "If it feels good, do it" and "You should have whatever your heart desires," and "Life will be great if you wear these clothes" or "Drink this beverage" or "Hang out with these people."

But reaching this worthy goal often requires hard choices and hard work. Second Timothy 4:1–5 warns us against being taken in by deceptive messages that suit our own desires—like cultural teachings that life should always be easy and pleasurable. Such messages water down the real challenge of living as a follower of Jesus Christ! If we are not finding life to be challenging, maybe we have tuned in to these misleading messages.

▶ 2 Tm 4:1–5

and teaching. 3*† For the time will come when
people will not tolerate sound doctrine but, following their own desires and insatiable curiosity,
will accumulate teachers 4* and will stop listening to the truth and will be diverted to myths.
5 But you, be self-possessed in all circumstances; put up with hardship; perform the work of an evangelist; fulfill your ministry.

Reward for Fidelity

6*† For I am already being poured out like a libation, and the time of my departure is at
hand. 7*† I have competed well; I have finished the race; I have kept the faith. 8*† From now on
the crown of righteousness awaits me, which the Lord, the just judge, will award to me on that day, and not only to me, but to all who have longed for his appearance.

IV: Personal Requests and Final Greetings

Paul's Loneliness

9† Try to join me soon, 10*† for Demas, enamored of the present world, deserted me and went to Thessalonica, Crescens to Galatia, and Titus to
Dalmatia. 11* Luke is the only one with me. Get Mark and bring him with you, for he is helpful
to me in the ministry. 12* I have sent Tychicus to
Ephesus. 13* When you come, bring the cloak I left with Carpus in Troas, the papyrus rolls, and especially the parchments.

14*† Alexander the coppersmith did me a great deal of harm; the Lord will repay him according
to his deeds. 15 You too be on guard against him, for he has strongly resisted our preaching.

16* At my first defense no one appeared on my behalf, but everyone deserted me. May it not be
held against them! 17* But the Lord stood by me and gave me strength, so that through me the proclamation might be completed and all the Gentiles might hear it. And I was rescued from
the lion's mouth. 18* The Lord will rescue me

† **4:3** *Insatiable curiosity:* literally, "with itching ears."

4:6 The apostle recognizes his death through martyrdom to be imminent. He regards it as an act of worship in which his blood will be poured out in sacrifice; cf Ex 29:38–40; Phil 2:17.

4:7 At the close of his life Paul could testify to the accomplishment of what Christ himself foretold concerning him at the time of his conversion, "I will show him what he will have to suffer for my name" (Acts 9:16).

4:8 When the world is judged at the parousia, all who have eagerly looked for the Lord's appearing and have sought to live according to his teachings will be rewarded. The crown is a reference to the laurel wreath placed on the heads of victorious athletes and conquerors in war; cf 2:5; 1 Cor 9:25.

4:9–13 Demas either abandoned the work of the ministry for worldly affairs or, perhaps, gave up the faith itself (10). Luke (11) may have accompanied Paul on parts of his second and third missionary journeys (Acts 16:10–12; 20:5–7). Notice the presence of the first personal pronoun "we" in these Acts passages, suggesting to some that Luke (or at least some traveling companion of Paul's) was the author of Acts. Mark, once rejected by Paul (Acts 13:13; 15:39), is now to render him a great service (11); cf Col 4:10; Phlm 24. For Tychicus, see Eph 6:21; cf also Acts 20:4; Col 4:7.

4:10 *Galatia:* some manuscripts read "Gaul" or "Gallia."

4:14–18 *Alexander:* an opponent of Paul's preaching (14–15), perhaps the one who is mentioned in 1 Tm 1:20. Despite Paul's abandonment by his friends in the province of Asia (cf 1:15–16), the divine assistance brought this first trial to a successful issue, even to the point of making the gospel message known to those who participated in or witnessed the trial (16–17).

* **4:3** 1 Tm 4:1.
4:4 1 Tm 1:4; 4:7; Ti 1:14.
4:6 Phil 2:17.
4:7 1 Tm 1:18; 6:12; Jude 3 / Acts 20:24; 1 Cor 9:24; Heb 12:1.
4:8 2 Tm 2:5; Wis 5:16; 1 Cor 9:25; Phil 3:14; Jas 1:12; 1 Pt 5:4; Rv 2:10.
4:10 Col 4:14; Phlm 24 / 2 Cor 2:13; 7:6–7; 8:23; Gal 2:3; Ti 1:4.
4:11 Col 4:14; Phlm 24 / Col 4:10; Phlm 24.
4:12 Acts 20:4; Eph 6:21; Col 4:7.
4:13 Acts 16:8; 20:6.
4:14 1 Tm 1:20 / 2 Sm 3:39; Pss 28:4; 62:12; Prv 24:12; Rom 2:6.
4:16 2 Tm 1:15.
4:17 Acts 23:11; 27:23; Phil 4:13 / 1 Mc 2:60; Ps 22:22; Dn 6:23.
4:18 2 Cor 1:10 / Rom 16:27.

from every evil threat and will bring me safe to
his heavenly kingdom. To him be glory forever
and ever. Amen.

Final Greeting

19*† Greet Prisca and Aquila and the family of
Onesiphorus. 20*† Erastus remained in Corinth,
while I left Trophimus sick at Miletus. 21† Try to
get here before winter. Eubulus, Pudens, Linus,
Claudia, and all the brothers send greetings.
22* The Lord be with your spirit. Grace be with
all of you.

4:19 *Prisca and Aquila:* they assisted Paul in his ministry in Corinth (Acts 18:2–3) and Ephesus (Acts 18:19, 26; 1 Cor 16:19). They risked death to save his life, and all the Gentile communities are indebted to them (Rom 16:3–5).

4:20 *Erastus:* he was the treasurer of the city of Corinth (Rom 16:24); cf also Acts 19:22. *Trophimus:* from the province of Asia, he accompanied Paul from Greece to Troas (Acts 20:4–5).

4:21 *Linus:* Western tradition sometimes identified this Linus with the supposed successor of Peter as bishop of Rome, and Claudia as the mother of Linus (*Apostolic Constitutions,* fourth century).

4:19 Acts 18:2; Rom 16:3; 1 Cor 16:19 / 2 Tm 1:16.
4:20 Acts 19:22; Rom 16:24 / Acts 20:4; 21:29.
4:22 Gal 6:18; Phil 4:23; Col 4:18; 1 Tm 6:21; Ti 3:15.

Titus

For background on this letter, see the introduction to the pastoral letters, before 1 Timothy.

I: Address

Greeting

1 1*† Paul, a slave of God and apostle of Jesus
Christ for the sake of the faith of God's chosen
ones and the recognition of religious truth, 2* in
the hope of eternal life that God, who does not
lie, promised before time began, 3* who indeed
at the proper time revealed his word in the proc-
lamation with which I was entrusted by the com-
mand of God our savior, 4* to Titus, my true child
in our common faith: grace and peace from God
the Father and Christ Jesus our savior.

II: Pastoral Charge

Titus in Crete

5† For this reason I left you in Crete so that
you might set right what remains to be done
and appoint presbyters in every town, as I
directed you, 6* on condition that a man be
blameless, married only once, with believing
children who are not accused of licentiousness
or rebellious. 7 For a bishop as God's steward
must be blameless, not arrogant, not irritable,
not a drunkard, not aggressive, not greedy for
sordid gain, 8 but hospitable, a lover of good-
ness, temperate, just, holy, and self-controlled,
9* holding fast to the true message as taught so
that he will be able both to exhort with sound
doctrine and to refute opponents. 10† For there
are also many rebels, idle talkers and deceivers,
especially the Jewish Christians.† 11 It is impera-
tive to silence them, as they are upsetting whole
families by teaching for sordid gain what they
should not. 12† One of them, a prophet of their
own, once said, "Cretans have always been li-
ars, vicious beasts, and lazy gluttons." 13* That
testimony is true. Therefore, admonish them
sharply, so that they may be sound in the faith,
14* instead of paying attention to Jewish myths

1:1–4 On the epistolary form, see the note on Rom 1:1–7. The apostolate is the divinely appointed mission to lead others to the true faith and through it to eternal salvation (1–3).

1:5–9 This instruction on the selection and appointment of presbyters, substantially identical with that in 1 Tm 3:1–7 on a bishop (see the note there), was aimed at strengthening the authority of Titus by apostolic mandate; cf 2:15. In vv 5, 7 and Acts 20:17, 28, the terms *episkopos* and *presbyteros* ("bishop" and "presbyter") refer to the same persons. Deacons are not mentioned in Titus. See also the note on Phil 1:1.

1:10–16 This adverse criticism of the defects within the community is directed especially against certain Jewish Christians, who busy themselves with useless speculations over persons mentioned in the Old Testament, insist on the observance of Jewish ritual purity regulations, and thus upset whole families by teaching things they have no right to teach; cf 3:9; 1 Tm 1:3–10.

1:10 *Jewish Christians:* literally, "those of the circumcision."

1:12 *Cretans . . . gluttons:* quoted from Epimenides, a Cretan poet of the sixth century B.C.

1:1 1 Tm 2:4; 4:3; 2 Tm 2:25; 3:7; Heb 10:26.
1:2 Ti 3:7; 2 Tm 1:1; 1 Jn 2:25.
1:3 Ti 2:10; 3:4; Ps 24:5; 1 Tm 1:1; 2:3; 4:10; Jude 25.
1:4 Ti 2:13; 3:6; Phil 3:20; 2 Tm 1:10; 2 Pt 1:1, 11; 2:20; 3:2, 18.
1:6–7 1 Tm 3:2–7; 2 Tm 2:24–26.
1:9 Ti 1:13; 2:1–2, 8; 1 Tm 1:10; 6:3; 2 Tm 1:13; 4:3.
1:13 Ti 1:9.
1:14 Ti 3:9; 1 Tm 1:4; 4:7; 2 Tm 4:4; 2 Pt 1:16.

and regulations of people who have repudiated the truth. 15* To the clean all things are clean, but to those who are defiled and unbelieving nothing is clean; in fact, both their minds and their consciences are tainted. 16 They claim to know God, but by their deeds they deny him. They are vile and disobedient and unqualified for any good deed.

III: Teaching the Christian Life

Christian Behavior

2 1*† As for yourself, you must say what is consistent with sound doctrine, namely, 2 that older men should be temperate, dignified, self-controlled, sound in faith, love, and endurance. 3 Similarly, older women should be reverent in their behavior, not slanderers, not addicted to drink, teaching what is good, 4 so that they may train younger women to love their husbands and children, 5* to be self-controlled, chaste, good homemakers, under the control of their husbands, so that the word of God may not be discredited.

6 Urge the younger men, similarly, to control themselves, 7 showing yourself as a model of good deeds in every respect, with integrity in your teaching, dignity, 8 and sound speech that cannot be criticized, so that the opponent will be put to shame without anything bad to say about us.

9* Slaves are to be under the control of their masters in all respects, giving them satisfaction, not talking back to them 10* or stealing from them, but exhibiting complete good faith, so as to adorn the doctrine of God our savior in every way.

Transformation of Life

11*† For the grace of God has appeared, saving all 12 and training us to reject godless ways and worldly desires and to live temperately, justly, and devoutly in this age, 13*† as we await the blessed hope, the appearance of the glory of the great God and of our savior Jesus Christ, 14* who gave himself for us to deliver us from all lawlessness and to cleanse for himself a people as his own, eager to do what is good.

15* Say these things. Exhort and correct with all authority. Let no one look down on you.

Live It!

Christian Leadership

Leadership is an esteemed but difficult calling. Church leaders in particular must earn the respect of others through the integrity of their lifestyle and their commitment and service to the values of Jesus Christ. Good leaders also know how to motivate others to grow and to serve.

Maybe you too possess leadership qualities and wish to pursue a leadership position in the Church or in another field. Make a list of the values you think a leader should have. How closely does your list match the characteristics of a good leader in Titus 1:5–9? When you are ready to lead, review the list from verses 5–9, and remember the importance of living a life of character and leading others to positions of leadership.

As you discern your own leadership potential, look to others who you feel possess good leadership qualities. Which leaders in your school or youth program do you admire the most? What qualities make them good leaders? How do these leaders stack up against the good-leader characteristics you listed?

▶ **Ti 1:5–9**

†

2:1–10 One of Titus' main tasks in Crete is to become acquainted with the character of the Cretans and thereby learn to cope with its deficiencies (see 1:12). The counsel is not only for Titus himself but for various classes of people with whom he must deal: older men and women (2–4), younger women and men (4–7), and slaves (9–10); cf Eph 6:1–9; Col 3:18—4:1.

2:11–15 Underlying the admonitions for moral improvement in 1–10 as the moving force is the constant appeal to God's revelation of salvation in Christ, with its demand for transformation of life.

2:13 *The blessed hope, the appearance:* literally, "the blessed hope and appearance," but the use of a single article in Greek strongly suggests an epexegetical, i.e., explanatory sense. *Of the great God and of our savior Jesus Christ:* another possible translation is "of our great God and savior Jesus Christ."

1:15 Mk 7:18–23; Acts 10:15; Rom 14:14–23.
2:1 Ti 1:9, 13; 2:8; 1 Tm 1:10; 6:3; 2 Tm 1:13; 4:3.
2:5 1 Cor 11:3; 14:34; Eph 5:22–24; Col 3:18; 1 Tm 2:11–15; 1 Pt 3:1–6.
2:9 1 Cor 7:21–22; Eph 6:5–8; Col 3:22–25; 1 Tm 6:1–2; 1 Pt 2:18.
2:10 Ti 1:3; 3:4; Ps 24:5; 1 Tm 1:1; 2:3; 4:10; Jude 25.
2:11 1 Tm 2:4; 4:10.
2:13 1 Cor 1:7; Phil 3:20; 1 Thes 1:10 / 2 Tm 1:10 / Ti 1:4; 3:6; 2 Pt 1:11; 2:20; 3:2, 18.
2:14 Gal 1:4; 2:20; Eph 5:2, 25; 1 Tm 2:6; 1 Pt 1:18–19 / Ps 130:8.
2:15 1 Tm 4:12.

Cultural Connection

Sioux Prayer for Transformation

I come before thee as one of thy many children. See, I am small and weak; I need thy strength and wisdom.
Grant me to walk in beauty and that my eyes may ever behold the crimson sunset. May my hands treat with respect the things which thou hast created, may my ears hear thy voice!
Make me wise, that I may understand the things which thou hast taught my people, which thou hast hidden in every leaf and every rock.
I long for strength, not in order that I may overreach my brother but to fight my greatest enemy—myself.
Make me ever ready to come to thee with pure hands and candid eyes, so that my spirit, when life disappears like the setting sun, may stand unashamed before thee.

Ti 3:3–7

3 1*† Remind them to be under the control
of magistrates and authorities,† to be obe-
dient, to be open to every good enterprise.
2 They are to slander no one, to be peace-
able, considerate, exercising all graciousness
toward everyone. 3* For we ourselves were
once foolish, disobedient, deluded, slaves to
various desires and pleasures, living in malice
and envy, hateful ourselves and hating one
another.

4* But when the kindness and generous love
of God our savior appeared,
5* not because of any righteous deeds we had
done
but because of his mercy,
he saved us through the bath of rebirth
and renewal by the holy Spirit,
6* whom he richly poured out on us
through Jesus Christ our savior,
7* so that we might be justified by his grace
and become heirs in hope of eternal life.

8*† This saying is trustworthy.

Advice to Titus

I want you to insist on these points, that those
who have believed in God be careful to devote
themselves to good works; these are excellent
and beneficial to others. 9*† Avoid foolish argu-
ments, genealogies, rivalries, and quarrels about
the law, for they are useless and futile. 10* After a
first and second warning, break off contact with
a heretic, 11 realizing that such a person is per-
verted and sinful and stands self-condemned.

Directives, Greetings, and Blessing

12*† When I send Artemas to you, or Tychicus,
try to join me at Nicopolis, where I have decided
to spend the winter. 13* Send Zenas the lawyer
and Apollos on their journey soon, and see to it
that they have everything they need. 14* But let
our people, too, learn to devote themselves to
good works to supply urgent needs, so that they
may not be unproductive.
15* All who are with me send you greetings.
Greet those who love us in the faith.
Grace be with all of you.

3:1–8 The list of Christian duties continues from 2:9–10, undergirded again as in 2:11–13 by appeal to what God in Christ has done (4–7; cf 2:11–14). The spiritual renewal of the Cretans, signified in God's merciful gift of baptism (4–7), should be reflected in their improved attitude toward civil authority and in their Christian relationship with all (1–3).

3:1 *Magistrates and authorities:* some interpreters understand these terms as referring to the principalities and powers of the heavenly hierarchy. *To be open to every good enterprise:* this implies being good citizens. It could also be translated "ready to do every sort of good work" (as Christians); cf 14.

3:8–11 In matters of good conduct and religious doctrine, Titus is to stand firm.

3:9 See the note on 1 Tm 6:20–21.

3:12–15 *Artemas* or *Tychicus* (2 Tm 4:12) is to replace Titus, who will join Paul in his winter sojourn at Nicopolis in Epirus, on the western coast of Greece.

3:1 Rom 13:1–7; 1 Tm 2:1–2; 1 Pt 2:13–14.
3:3 1 Cor 6:9–11; Eph 2:1–3; 5:8; Col 3:5–7; 1 Pt 4:3.
3:4 Ti 1:3; 2:10; Ps 24:5; 1 Tm 1:1; 2:3; 4:10; Jude 25.
3:5 Dt 9:5; Eph 2:4–5, 8–9; 2 Tm 1:9.
3:6 Ti 1:4; 2:13; Phil 3:20; 2 Tm 1:10; 2 Pt 1:1, 11; 2:20; 3:2, 18.
3:7 Ti 1:2; 2 Tm 1:1; 1 Jn 2:25.
3:8 1 Tm 1:15; 3:1; 4:9; 2 Tm 2:11.
3:9 1 Tm 1:4; 4:7; 2 Tm 2:23.
3:10 Mt 18:15–18; Rom 16:17; 1 Cor 5:11; 2 Thes 3:6, 14–15.
3:12 Acts 20:4; Eph 6:21; Col 4:7; 2 Tm 4:12.
3:13 Acts 18:24–26; 1 Cor 1:12; 3:4–6, 22; 4:6; 16:12.
3:14 Ti 2:14; 3:8; Heb 10:24; 1 Pt 3:13.
3:15 Heb 13:25.

The Letter to Philemon

The brief Letter to Philemon is about slavery. It may surprise you that it doesn't condemn slavery outright. In fact, other parts of the Bible take the idea of human slavery for granted! How can the Bible not challenge something we think is wrong? Seeking to understand this puzzling question gives us a key to understanding God's Revelation in the Bible.

In Depth

One key to understanding God's message in the Bible is to understand the beliefs of the authors and the first readers. The Letter to Philemon is addressed to a slave owner named Philemon, a woman named Apphia, and a soldier named Archippus, who all lived in Colossae. Philemon's slave, Onesimus, ran away, wound up in prison with Paul, and became a Christian. Now, Paul is sending him back to Philemon, as the law requires. That same law gives Philemon the right to punish Onesimus for escaping. But Paul asks—indirectly, but clearly enough—for Onesimus's freedom. Paul also asks for something far more challenging—that Philemon, Apphia, and Archippus accept Onesimus as "a brother, beloved" (verse 16) in Christ.

We see in this letter the beginning of a new attitude toward slavery. Recall Paul's basic statement on Christian freedom in Galatians 3:28: "There is neither Jew nor Greek, there is neither slave nor free person, there is not male and female; for you are all one in Christ Jesus." However, slavery was an integral part of life during Paul's time. This is probably why he never directly challenged the institution of slavery.

Paul may not have been a social revolutionary by our standards, but he did believe the Christian community ought to live by a higher standard than other people. This letter is a masterpiece of persuasion as it urges Philemon and the church community in Colossae to accept Onesimus as a beloved brother in Christ. It uses flattery (see verses 4–7), a veiled reference to Paul's authority (see verses 8–9), Paul's personal relationship with everyone involved (see verses 12–17), and maybe even a little guilt in Paul's offer to pay for anything Onesimus stole (see verses 18–19). Paul's message to the household of Philemon and to us is this: We must get beyond whatever cultural boundaries prevent us from treating one another as brothers and sisters in Christ!

At a Glance

I. **Greeting and Thanksgiving (verses 1–7).**
II. **Plea for Onesimus (verses 8–22).**
III. **Final Greetings (verses 23–25).**

Quick Facts

Inspired Author: Paul

Date Written: from AD 54 to 56 if from Ephesus, from AD 61 to 63 if from Rome

Audience: Philemon and his household

Philemon

Address and Greeting

1*† Paul, a prisoner for Christ Jesus, and Tim-
othy our brother, to Philemon, our beloved and
our co-worker, 2*† to Apphia our sister, to Archip-
pus our fellow soldier, and to the church at your
house. 3*† Grace to you and peace from God our
Father and the Lord Jesus Christ.

Thanksgiving

4*† I give thanks to my God always, remember-
ing you in my prayers, 5† as I hear of the love and
the faith you have in the Lord Jesus and for all
the holy ones, 6*† so that your partnership in the
faith may become effective in recognizing every
good there is in us that leads to Christ.

Plea for Onesimus

7*† For I have experienced much joy and en-
couragement from your love, because the hearts
of the holy ones have been refreshed by you,
brother. 8† Therefore, although I have the full
right in Christ to order you to do what is proper,
9*† I rather urge you out of love, being as I am,
Paul, an old man, and now also a prisoner for
Christ Jesus. 10* I urge you on behalf of my child
Onesimus, whose father I have become in my
imprisonment, 11† who was once useless to you
but is now useful to [both] you and me. 12 I am
sending him, that is, my own heart, back to you.
13*† I should have liked to retain him for myself,
so that he might serve me on your behalf in my

1 *Prisoner:* as often elsewhere (cf Romans, 1 Corinthians, Galatians especially), the second word in Greek enunciates the theme and sets the tone of the letter. Here it is the prisoner appealing rather than the apostle commanding.

2 *Apphia our sister:* sister is here used (like brother) to indicate a fellow Christian. *The church at your house: your* here is singular. It more likely refers to Philemon than to the last one named, Archippus; Philemon is then the owner of the slave Onesimus (10). An alternate view is that the actual master of the slave is Archippus and that the one to whom the letter is addressed, Philemon, is the most prominent Christian there; see the note on Col 4:17.

3 *Grace . . . and peace:* for this greeting, which may be a combination of Greek and Aramaic epistolary formulae, see the note on Rom 1:1–7.

4 *In my prayers:* literally, "at the time of my prayers."

5 *Holy ones:* a common term for members of the Christian community (so also 7).

6 *In us:* some good ancient manuscripts have *in you* (plural). *That leads to Christ: leads to* translates the Greek preposition *eis,* indicating direction or purpose.

7 *Encouragement:* the Greek word *paraklēsis* is cognate with the verb translated "urge" in vv 9, 10, and serves as an introduction to Paul's plea. *Hearts:* literally, "bowels," expressing in Semitic fashion the seat of the emotions, one's "inmost self." The same Greek word is used in v 12 and again in v 20, where it forms a literary inclusion marking off the body of the letter.

8 *Full right:* often translated "boldness," the Greek word *parrēsia* connotes the full franchise of speech, as the right of a citizen to speak before the body politic, claimed by the Athenians as their privilege (Euripides).

9 *Old man:* some editors conjecture that Paul here used a similar Greek word meaning "ambassador" (cf Eph 6:20). This conjecture heightens the contrast with "prisoner" but is totally without manuscript support.

11 *Useless . . . useful:* here Paul plays on the name Onesimus, which means "useful" or "beneficial." The verb translated "profit" in v 20 is cognate.

13 *Serve:* the Greek *diakoneō* could connote a ministry.

1 Phlm 9; Eph 3:1; 4:1; Phil 1:7, 13.
2 Col 4:17.
3 Rom 1:7; Gal 1:3; Phil 1:2.
4–5 Rom 1:8–9; Eph 1:15–16.
6 Phil 1:9; Col 1:9.
7 2 Cor 7:4.
9 Phlm 1; Eph 3:1; 4:1; Phil 1:7, 13.
10 1 Cor 4:14–15; Gal 4:19; Col 4:9.
13 Phil 2:30.

imprisonment for the gospel, [14]* but I did not
want to do anything without your consent, so
that the good you do might not be forced but
voluntary. [15]† Perhaps this is why he was away
from you for a while, that you might have him
back forever, [16]*† no longer as a slave but more
than a slave, a brother, beloved especially to me,
but even more so to you, as a man and in the
Lord. [17] So if you regard me as a partner, welcome
him as you would me. [18]† And if he has done
you any injustice or owes you anything, charge
it to me. [19]* I, Paul, write this in my own hand: I
will pay. May I not tell you that you owe me your
very self. [20] Yes, brother, may I profit from you in
the Lord. Refresh my heart in Christ.
[21] With trust in your compliance I write to
you, knowing that you will do even more than
I say. [22]* At the same time prepare a guest room
for me, for I hope to be granted to you through
your prayers.

Final Greetings

[23]*† Epaphras, my fellow prisoner in Christ
Jesus, greets you, [24]* as well as Mark, Aristarchus,
Demas, and Luke, my co-workers. [25] The grace of
the Lord Jesus Christ be with your spirit.

15 *Was away from:* literally, "was separated from," but the same verb means simply "left" in Acts 18:1. It is a euphemism for his running away.

16 *As a man:* literally, "in the flesh." With this and the following phrase, Paul describes the natural and spiritual orders.

18–19 *Charge it to me . . . I will pay:* technical legal and commercial terms in account keeping and acknowledgment of indebtedness.

23–24 *Epaphras:* a Colossian who founded the church there (Col 1:7) and perhaps also in Laodicea and Hierapolis (Col 2:1; 4:12–13). *Aristarchus:* a native of Thessalonica and fellow worker of Paul (Acts 19:29; 20:4; 27:2). For Mark, Demas, and Luke, see 2 Tm 4:9–13 and the note there.

Live It!

Rethinking Social Structures

In sending Onesimus back to Philemon, Paul asked Philemon not only to forgive his runaway slave but to rethink his relationship with him. Paul's plea to Philemon and the Church in Colossae to look on Onesimus as a brother in Christ was radical for the time. People expected runaway slaves to be punished severely. Accepting Onesimus as a Christian would be a sign that Paul truly intended that his notion of the Church as one body in Christ should be lived out in concrete ways!

- What commonly accepted social structures in our day might need a fresh look?
- Might any privileges that we take for granted actually prevent true equality in Christ?

▶ Philemon, verses 8–21

PHLM

14 2 Cor 9:7; 1 Pt 5:2.
16 1 Tm 6:2.
19 Gal 6:11; 2 Thes 3:17.
22 Heb 13:19.
23 Col 1:7; 4:12–13.
24 Acts 12:12, 15; 13:13; 15:37–39; 19:29; 20:4; 27:2; Col 4:10, 14; 2 Tm 4:10–13.

Have you ever wondered why it makes sense to believe that Jesus is the Savior of all humanity? It's an honest question. Evidently, some early Christians asked it. The Letter to the Hebrews is a sermon—to them and to us—to strengthen our faith and belief in Jesus Christ, the Son of God and our "great high priest" (4:14).

The Letter to the

Hebrews

At a Glance

I. **Introduction (1:1–4).**
II. **The Son Higher Than the Angels (1:5—2:18).**
III. **Jesus, Faithful and Compassionate High Priest (3:1—5:10).**
IV. **Jesus' Eternal Priesthood and Eternal Sacrifice (5:11—10:39).**
V. **Examples, Discipline, Disobedience (11:1—12:29).**
VI. **Final Exhortation, Blessing, Greetings (13:1–25).**

Quick Facts

Inspired Author: unknown
Date Written: from approximately AD 80 to 90
Audience: Hellenistic (Greek-speaking) Christians and possibly Jewish Christians

In Depth

The Letter to the Hebrews gives us almost no information about its author and the community it is addressed to. But it appears that some members of the community are in danger of giving up their faith—and this is happening after the group has already survived a period of persecution. The letter encourages them to be strong in their faith and seeks to give a sound foundation for believing in Jesus Christ. It is a statement on the saving power of Christ's sacrificial death and his unique role as High Priest of the New Covenant.

The letter presents Christ as the divine Son of God, through whom the world was created, superior to any angel, and the culmination of all the promises and expectations of the Old Testament. In explaining Christ's importance, the letter uses a type of argument called "from the lesser to the greater." This type of argument is based on the idea that if you accept something as true in a lesser situation, then it is certainly true in a greater situation. The author uses it to show that Christ's sacrifice is far greater than the sacrifices offered by the priests in the Temple. As the perfect high priest, Christ offers the perfect sacrifice—his death on the cross—through which God saves us once and for all from sin.

This letter reads like one long sermon made up of interconnecting parts. Begin by reading the whole thing out loud to truly appreciate its power and wording. Then look up some of its references to people and events in the Old Testament to better appreciate its inspired explanation of Christ's nature and mission.

Hebrews

I: Introduction

1 [1]† In times past, God spoke in partial and var-
ious ways to our ancestors through the proph-
ets; [2]* in these last days, he spoke to us through
a son, whom he made heir of all things and
through whom he created the universe,

3* who is the refulgence of his glory,
the very imprint of his being,
and who sustains all things by his mighty word.
When he had accomplished purification from
sins,
he took his seat at the right hand of the
Majesty on high,
4* as far superior to the angels
as the name he has inherited is more excellent
than theirs.

II: The Son Higher Than the Angels

Messianic Enthronement

5*† For to which of the angels did God ever
say:

"You are my son; this day I have begotten you"?

Or again:

"I will be a father to him, and he shall be a
son to me"?

1:1–4 The letter opens with an introduction consisting of a reflection on the climax of God's revelation to the human race in his Son. The divine communication was initiated and maintained during Old Testament times in fragmentary and varied ways through *the prophets* (1), including Abraham, Moses, and all through whom God spoke. But now *in these last days* (2), the final age, God's revelation of his saving purpose is achieved *through a son,* i.e., one who is Son, whose role is redeemer and mediator of creation. He was made *heir of all things* through his death and exaltation to glory, yet he existed before he appeared as man; through him God *created the universe.* Verses 3–4, which may be based upon a liturgical hymn, assimilate the Son to the personified Wisdom of the Old Testament as *refulgence of* God's *glory* and *imprint of his being* (3; cf Wis 7:26). These same terms are used of the Logos in Philo. The author now turns from the cosmological role of the preexistent Son to the redemptive work of Jesus: he brought about purification from sins and has been exalted to the right hand of God (see Ps 110:1). The once-humiliated and crucified Jesus has been declared God's Son, and this name shows his superiority to the angels. The reason for the author's insistence on that superiority is, among other things, that in some Jewish traditions angels were mediators of the old covenant (see Acts 7:53; Gal 3:19). Finally, Jesus' superiority to the angels emphasizes the superiority of the new covenant to the old because of the heavenly priesthood of Jesus.

1:5–14 Jesus' superiority to the angels is now demonstrated by a series of seven Old Testament texts. Some scholars see in the stages of Jesus' exaltation an order corresponding to that of enthronement ceremonies in the ancient Near East, especially in Egypt, namely, elevation to divine status (5–6); presentation to the angels and proclamation of everlasting lordship (7–12); enthronement and conferral of royal power (13). The citations from the Psalms in vv 5 and 13 were traditionally used of Jesus' messianic sonship (cf Acts 13:33) through his resurrection and exaltation (cf Acts 2:33–35); those in vv 8 and 10–12 are concerned with his divine kingship and his creative function. The central quotation in v 7 serves to contrast the angels with the Son. The author quotes it according to the Septuagint translation, which is quite different in meaning from that of the Hebrew ("You make the winds your messengers, and flaming fire your ministers"). The angels are only *sent to serve . . . those who are to inherit salvation* (14).

1:2 Is 2:2; Jer 23:20; Ez 38:16; Dn 10:14 / Jn 3:17; Rom 8:3; Gal 4:4 / Prv 8:30; Wis 7:22; Jn 1:3; 1 Cor 8:6; Col 1:16.
1:3 Wis 7:26; 2 Cor 4:4; Col 1:15 / Heb 8:1; 10:12; 12:2; Mk 16:19; Acts 2:33; 7:55–56; Rom 8:34; Eph 1:20; Col 3:1; 1 Pt 3:22.
1:4 Eph 1:21; Phil 2:9–11.
1:5 Ps 2:7 / 2 Sm 7:14.

Live It!

"The Very Imprint"

Throughout history there have been many opinions about who Jesus of Nazareth was. Some have called him a great teacher, some a prophet, some a charismatic preacher, and others a worker of miracles. Christians believe Jesus was all of these and more—much more.

The Letter to the Hebrews makes a bold claim about Jesus. It says the historical human being from Nazareth named Jesus is the perfect human image of God. Jesus reflects God's glory and is "the very imprint of [God's] being" (1:3). In other words, although a human being like us, Jesus is God.

This astonishing claim is central to the Christian faith. If you accept it as true, it will change your life. And if you are to believe it, you need to know the whole story behind it and all the evidence that supports it. The best place to start is with the book in your hands right now. Read on!

▶ **Heb 1:1–14**

6* † And again, when he leads the first-born into the world, he says:

"Let all the angels of God worship him."

7* Of the angels he says:

"He makes his angels winds
and his ministers a fiery flame";

8* † but of the Son:

"Your throne, O God, stands forever and ever;
and a righteous scepter is the scepter of
your kingdom.
9 You loved justice and hated wickedness;
therefore God, your God, anointed you
with the oil of gladness above your
companions";

10* and:

"At the beginning, O Lord, you established
the earth,
and the heavens are the works of your hands.
11 They will perish, but you remain;
and they will all grow old like a garment.
12 You will roll them up like a cloak,
and like a garment they will be changed.
But you are the same, and your years will
have no end."

13* But to which of the angels has he ever said:

"Sit at my right hand
until I make your enemies your footstool"?

14* Are they not all ministering spirits sent to serve, for the sake of those who are to inherit salvation?

Exhortation to Faithfulness

2 1† Therefore, we must attend all the more
to what we have heard, so that we may not
be carried away. 2* For if the word announced
through angels proved firm, and every transgres-
sion and disobedience received its just recom-
pense, 3* how shall we escape if we ignore so great
a salvation? Announced originally through the
Lord, it was confirmed for us by those who had
heard. 4* God added his testimony by signs, won-
ders, various acts of power, and distribution of the
gifts of the holy Spirit according to his will.

Exaltation through Abasement

5† For it was not to angels that he subjected
the world to come, of which we are speaking.
6* Instead, someone has testified somewhere:

1:6 *And again, when he leads:* the Greek could also be translated "And when he again leads" in reference to the parousia.

1:8–12 *O God:* the application of the name "God" to the Son derives from the preexistence mentioned in vv 2–3; the psalmist had already used it of the Hebrew king in the court style of the original. See the note on Ps 45:7. It is also important for the author's christology that in vv 10–12 an Old Testament passage addressed to God is redirected to Jesus.

2:1–4 The author now makes a transition into exhortation, using an a fortiori argument (as at 7:21–22; 9:13–14; 10:28–29; 12:25). The *word announced through angels* (2), the Mosaic law, is contrasted with the more powerful word that Christians have received (3–4). Christ's supremacy strengthens Christians against being *carried away* from their faith.

2:5–18 The humanity and the suffering of Jesus do not constitute a valid reason for relinquishing the Christian faith. Ps 8 (6–7) is also applied to Jesus in 1 Cor 15:27; Eph 1:22; and probably 1 Pt 3:22. This christological interpretation, therefore, probably reflects a common early Christian tradition, which may have originated in the expression *the son of man* (6). The psalm contrasts God's greatness with man's relative insignificance but also stresses the superiority of man to the rest of creation, of which he is lord. Hebrews applies

1:6 Dt 32:43 LXX; Ps 97:7.
1:7 Ps 104:4 LXX.
1:8 Ps 45:7–8.
1:10–12 Ps 102:26–28.
1:13 Ps 110:1.
1:14 Ps 91:11; Dn 7:10.
2:2 Acts 7:38, 53; Gal 3:19.
2:3 Heb 10:29; 12:25.
2:4 Mk 16:20; Acts 14:3; 19:11.
2:6 Ps 8:5–7.

"What is man that you are mindful of him,
or the son of man that you care for him?
7 You made him for a little while lower than
the angels;
you crowned him with glory and honor,
8* subjecting all things under his feet."

In "subjecting" all things [to him], he left noth-
ing not "subject to him." Yet at present we do not
see "all things subject to him," 9* but we do see
Jesus "crowned with glory and honor" because
he suffered death, he who "for a little while" was
made "lower than the angels," that by the grace
of God he might taste death for everyone.
10* For it was fitting that he, for whom and
through whom all things exist, in bringing many
children to glory, should make the leader to their
salvation perfect through suffering. 11 He who
consecrates and those who are being consecrated
all have one origin. Therefore, he is not ashamed
to call them "brothers," 12* saying:

"I will proclaim your name to my brothers,
in the midst of the assembly I will praise
you";

13* and again:

"I will put my trust in him";

and again:

"Behold, I and the children God has
given me."

14* Now since the children share in blood and
flesh, he likewise shared in them, that through
death he might destroy the one who has the power
of death, that is, the devil, 15 and free those who
through fear of death had been subject to slavery all
their life. 16 Surely he did not help angels but rather
the descendants of Abraham; 17* therefore, he had
to become like his brothers in every way, that he
might be a merciful and faithful high priest before
God to expiate the sins of the people. 18 Because he
himself was tested through what he suffered, he is
able to help those who are being tested.

III: Jesus, Faithful and Compassionate High Priest

Jesus, Superior to Moses

3 1† Therefore, holy "brothers," sharing in a
heavenly calling, reflect on Jesus, the apostle
and high priest of our confession, 2* who was
faithful to the one who appointed him, just as
Moses was "faithful in [all] his house." 3* But
he is worthy of more "glory" than Moses, as the
founder of a house has more "honor" than the
house itself. 4 Every house is founded by some-
one, but the founder of all is God. 5 Moses was
"faithful in all his house" as a "servant" to testify
to what would be spoken, 6*† but Christ was

HEB

this christologically: Jesus lived a truly human existence, *lower than the angels,* in the days of his earthly life, particularly in his suffering and death; now, *crowned . . . with glory and honor,* he is raised above all creation. The author considers all things as already *subject to him* because of his exaltation (8–9), though *we do not see* this yet. The reference to Jesus as *leader* (10) sounds the first note of an important leitmotif in Hebrews: the journey of the people of God to the sabbath rest (4:9), the heavenly sanctuary, following Jesus, their "forerunner" (6:20). It was fitting that God should make him *perfect through suffering,* consecrated by obedient suffering. Because he is perfected as high priest, Jesus is then able to consecrate his people (11); access to God is made possible by each of these two consecrations. If Jesus is able to help human beings, it is because he has become one of us; we are his "brothers." The author then cites three Old Testament texts as proofs of this unity between ourselves and the Son. Psalm 22:23 is interpreted so as to make Jesus the singer of this lament, which ends with joyful praise of the Lord in the assembly of "brothers." The other two texts are from Is 8:17, 18. The first of these seems intended to display in Jesus an example of the trust in God that his followers should emulate. The second curiously calls these followers "children"; probably this is to be understood to mean children of Adam, but the point is our solidarity with Jesus. By sharing human nature, including the ban of death, Jesus broke the power of the devil over death (14); the author shares the view of Hellenistic Judaism that death was not intended by God and that it had been introduced into the world by the devil. The *fear of death* (15) is a religious fear based on the false conception that death marks the end of a person's relations with God (cf Ps 115:17–18; Is 38:18). Jesus deliberately allied himself with the *descendants of Abraham* (16) in order to be a *merciful and faithful high priest.* This is the first appearance of the central theme of Hebrews, Jesus the great high priest expiating the *sins of the people* (17), as one who experienced the same tests as they (18).

3:1–6 The author now takes up the two qualities of Jesus mentioned in 2:17, but in inverse order: faithfulness (3:1—4:13) and mercy (4:14—5:10). Christians are called *holy "brothers"* because of their common relation to him (2:11), the *apostle,* a designation for Jesus used only here in the New Testament (cf Jn 13:16; 17:3), meaning one sent as God's final word to us (1:2). He is compared with Moses probably because he is seen as mediator of the new covenant (9:15) just as Moses was of the old (9:19–22, including his sacrifice). But when the author of Hebrews speaks of Jesus' sacrifice, he does not consider Moses as the Old Testament antitype, but rather the high priest on the Day of Atonement (9:6–15). Moses' faithfulness *"in [all] his house"* refers back to Nm 12:7, on which this section is a midrashic commentary. In vv 3–6, the author does not indicate that he thinks of either Moses or Christ as the founder of the household. *His house* (2, 5, 6) means God's house, not that of Moses or Christ; in the case of Christ, compare v 6 with 10:21. The *house* of v 6 is the Christian community; the author suggests its continuity with Israel by speaking not of two houses but of only one. Verse 6 brings out the reason why Jesus is superior to Moses: the latter was the faithful *servant* laboring *in* the house founded by God, but Jesus is God's *son,* placed *over* the house.

3:6 The majority of manuscripts add "firm to the end," but these words are not found in the three earliest and best witnesses and are probably an interpolation derived from v 14.

2:8 Mt 28:18; 1 Cor 15:25–28; Eph 1:20–23; Phil 3:21; 1 Pt 3:22.
2:9 Phil 2:6–11.
2:10 Heb 12:2; Is 53:4 / Rom 11:36; 1 Cor 8:6.
2:12 Ps 22:23.
2:13 Is 8:17, 18.
2:14 Is 25:8; Hos 13:14; Jn 12:31; Rom 6:9; 1 Cor 15:54–55; 2 Tm 1:10; Rv 12:10.
2:17 Heb 4:15; 5:1–3.
3:2 Nm 12:7.
3:3 2 Cor 3:7–8.
3:6 Heb 10:21; Eph 2:19; 1 Tm 3:15; 1 Pt 4:17.

faithful as a son placed over his house. We are his
house, if [only] we hold fast to our confidence
and pride in our hope.

Israel's Infidelity a Warning

7*† Therefore, as the holy Spirit says:

"Oh, that today you would hear his voice,
8 'Harden not your hearts as at the rebellion
in the day of testing in the desert,
9* where your ancestors tested and tried me
and saw my works 10 for forty years.
Because of this I was provoked with that
generation
and I said, "They have always been of
erring heart,
and they do not know my ways."
11 As I swore in my wrath,
"They shall not enter into my rest." ' "

12 Take care, brothers, that none of you may have
an evil and unfaithful heart, so as to forsake the
living God. 13 Encourage yourselves daily while
it is still "today," so that none of you may grow
hardened by the deceit of sin. 14* We have be-
come partners of Christ if only we hold the be-
ginning of the reality firm until the end, 15* for
it is said:

"Oh, that today you would hear his voice:
'Harden not your hearts as at the rebellion.' "

16* Who were those who rebelled when they
heard? Was it not all those who came out of
Egypt under Moses? 17* With whom was he "pro-
voked for forty years"? Was it not those who had
sinned, whose corpses fell in the desert? 18* And
to whom did he "swear that they should not
enter into his rest," if not to those who were dis-
obedient? 19 And we see that they could not enter
for lack of faith.

The Sabbath Rest

4 1 Therefore, let us be on our guard while the
promise of entering into his rest remains,
that none of you seem to have failed. 2 For in fact
we have received the good news just as they did.
But the word that they heard did not profit them,
for they were not united in faith with those who
listened. 3* For we who believed enter into [that]
rest, just as he has said:

"As I swore in my wrath,
'They shall not enter into my rest,' "

and yet his works were accomplished at the
foundation of the world. 4* For he has spoken
somewhere about the seventh day in this man-
ner, "And God rested on the seventh day from
all his works"; 5* and again, in the previously
mentioned place, "They shall not enter into my
rest." 6 Therefore, since it remains that some will
enter into it, and those who formerly received
the good news did not enter because of disobe-
dience, 7* he once more set a day, "today," when
long afterwards he spoke through David, as al-
ready quoted:

"Oh, that today you would hear his voice:
'Harden not your hearts.' "

8* Now if Joshua had given them rest, he would
not have spoken afterwards of another day.
9 Therefore, a sabbath rest still remains for the
people of God. 10 And whoever enters into God's
rest, rests from his own works as God did from
his. 11 Therefore, let us strive to enter into that
rest, so that no one may fall after the same exam-
ple of disobedience.
12* Indeed, the word of God is living and
effective, sharper than any two-edged sword,
penetrating even between soul and spirit, joints

† **3:7—4:13** The author appeals for steadfastness of faith in Jesus, basing his warning on the experience of Israel during the Exodus. In the Old Testament the Exodus had been invoked as a symbol of the return of Israel from the Babylonian exile (Is 42:9; 43:16–21; 51:9–11). In the New Testament the redemption was similarly understood as a new exodus, both in the experience of Jesus himself (Lk 9:31) and in that of his followers (1 Cor 10:1–4). The author cites Ps 95:7–11, a salutary example of hardness of heart, as a warning against the danger of growing weary and giving up the journey. To call God *living* (12) means that he reveals himself in his works (cf Jos 3:10; Jer 10:10). The *rest* (11) into which Israel was to enter was only a foreshadowing of that rest to which Christians are called. They are to remember the example of Israel's revolt in the desert that cost a whole generation the loss of the promised land (15–19; cf Nm 14:20–29). In 4:1–11, the symbol of *rest* is seen in deeper dimension: because the promise to the ancient Hebrews foreshadowed that given to Christians, it is *good news;* and because the promised land was the place of rest that God provided for his people, it was a share in his own rest, which he enjoyed after he had finished his creative work (3–4; cf Gn 2:2). The author attempts to read this meaning of God's rest into Ps 95:7–11 (6–9). The Greek form of the name of Joshua, who led Israel into the promised land, is Jesus (8). The author plays upon the name but stresses the superiority of Jesus, who leads his followers into heavenly rest. Verses 12 and 13 are meant as a continuation of the warning, for the word of God brings judgment as well as salvation. Some would capitalize *the word of God* and see it as a personal title of Jesus, comparable to that of Jn 1:1–18.

3:7–11 Ps 95:7–11.
3:9 Ex 17:7; Nm 20:2–5.
3:14 Rom 8:17.
3:15 Ps 95:7–8.
3:16–19 Nm 14:1–38; Dt 1:19–40.
3:17 Nm 14:29.
3:18 Nm 14:22–23; Dt 1:35.
4:3 Heb 3:11; Ps 95:11.
4:4 Gn 2:2.
4:5 Ps 95:11.
4:7 Heb 3:7–8, 15; Ps 95:7–8.
4:8 Dt 31:7; Jos 22:4.
4:12 Wis 18:15–16; Is 49:2; Eph 6:17; Rv 1:16; 2:12.

and marrow, and able to discern reflections and thoughts of the heart. 13* No creature is concealed from him, but everything is naked and exposed to the eyes of him to whom we must render an account.

"The word of God is living and effective."
(Heb 4:12)

Jesus, Compassionate High Priest

14*† Therefore, since we have a great high priest who has passed through the heavens, Jesus, the Son of God, let us hold fast to our confession. 15* For we do not have a high priest who is unable to sympathize with our weaknesses, but one who has similarly been tested in every way, yet without sin. 16* So let us confidently approach the throne of grace to receive mercy and to find grace for timely help.

5 1† Every high priest is taken from among men and made their representative before God, to offer gifts and sacrifices for sins.† 2† He is able to deal patiently with the ignorant and erring, for he himself is beset by weakness 3* and so, for this reason, must make sin offerings for himself as well as for the people. 4* No one takes this honor upon himself but only when called by God, just as Aaron was. 5* In the same way, it was not Christ who glorified himself in becoming high priest, but rather the one who said to him:

"You are my son;
 this day I have begotten you";

Live It!

Approach God Boldly!

Have you ever believed you did something God could never forgive? Or do you ever have thoughts that make you feel so ashamed you do not dare talk with God about them?

Hebrews 4:14–16 reminds us of a remarkable truth: Jesus, though fully divine, was also fully human. And though he never sinned, this Scripture passage tells us that he was tempted, as we are, in every respect. Think about that! Jesus was once fourteen years old. He was once seventeen. He was once twenty-two. There is no temptation that you have considered that Jesus cannot understand. And that is why you can approach him in any circumstance—even your deepest trouble—and find compassion and grace.

Remember: (1) you cannot hide from God, and (2) you don't have to!

▶ Heb 4:14–16

6*† just as he says in another place:

"You are a priest forever
 according to the order of Melchizedek."

7*† In the days when he was in the flesh, he

4:14–16 These verses, which return to the theme first sounded in 2:16—3:1, serve as an introduction to the section that follows. The author here alone calls Jesus *a great high priest* (14), a designation used by Philo for the Logos; perhaps he does so in order to emphasize Jesus' superiority over the Jewish high priest. He has *been tested in every way, yet without sin* (15); this indicates an acquaintance with the tradition of Jesus' temptations, not only at the beginning (as in Mk 1:13) but throughout his public life (cf Lk 22:28). Although the reign of the exalted Jesus is a theme that occurs elsewhere in Hebrews, and Jesus' throne is mentioned in 1:8, *the throne of grace* (16) refers to the throne of God. The similarity of v 16 to 10:19–22 indicates that the author is thinking of our confident access to God, made possible by the priestly work of Jesus.

5:1–10 The true humanity of Jesus (see the note on 2:5–18) makes him a more rather than a less effective high priest to the Christian community. In Old Testament tradition, the high priest was identified with the people, guilty of personal sin just as they were (1–3). Even so, the office was of divine appointment (4), as was also the case with the sinless Christ (5). For v 6, see the note on Ps 110:4. Although Jesus was Son of God, he was destined as a human being to learn obedience by accepting the suffering he had to endure (8). Because of his perfection through this experience of human suffering, he is the cause of salvation for all (9), a *high priest according to the order of Melchizedek* (10; cf 6 and 7:3).

5:1 *To offer gifts and sacrifices for sins:* the author is thinking principally of the Day of Atonement rite, as is clear from 9:7. This ritual was celebrated to atone for "all the sins of the Israelites" (Lv 16:34).

5:2 *Deal patiently:* the Greek word *metriopathein* occurs only here in the Bible; this term was used by the Stoics to designate the golden mean between excess and defect of passion. Here it means rather the ability to sympathize.

5:6–8 The author of Hebrews is the only New Testament writer to cite v 4 of Ps 110, here and in 7:17, 21, to show that Jesus has been called by God to his role as priest. Verses 7–8 deal with his ability to sympathize with sinners, because of his own experience of the trials and weakness of human nature, especially fear of death. In his present exalted state, weakness is foreign to him, but he understands what we suffer because of his previous earthly experience.

5:7 *He offered prayers . . . to the one who was able to save him from death:* at Gethsemane (cf Mk 14:35), though some see a broader reference (see the note on Jn 12:27).

4:13 Jb 34:21–22; Pss 90:8; 139:2–4.
4:14 Heb 9:11, 24.
4:15 Heb 2:17–18; 5:2.
4:16 Heb 8:1; 10:19, 22, 35; 12:2; Eph 3:12.
5:3 Lv 9:7; 16:15–17, 30, 34.
5:4 Ex 28:1.
5:5 Ps 2:7.
5:6 Ps 110:4.
5:7 Mt 26:38–44; Mk 14:34–40; Lk 22:41–46; Jn 12:27.

offered prayers and supplications with loud cries
and tears to the one who was able to save him
from death, and he was heard because of his
reverence. 8*† Son though he was, he learned
obedience from what he suffered; 9* and when
he was made perfect, he became the source of
eternal salvation for all who obey him, 10* de-
clared by God high priest according to the order
of Melchizedek.

IV: Jesus' Eternal Priesthood and Eternal Sacrifice

Exhortation to Spiritual Renewal

11† About this we have much to say, and it is
difficult to explain, for you have become sluggish
in hearing. 12* Although you should be teachers
by this time, you need to have someone teach
you again the basic elements of the utterances of
God. You need milk, [and] not solid food. 13 Ev-
eryone who lives on milk lacks experience of the
word of righteousness, for he is a child. 14 But
solid food is for the mature, for those whose
faculties are trained by practice to discern good
and evil.

6 1* Therefore, let us leave behind the basic
teaching about Christ and advance to matu-
rity, without laying the foundation all over again:
repentance from dead works and faith in God,
2*† instruction about baptisms and laying on of
hands, resurrection of the dead and eternal judg-
ment. 3 And we shall do this, if only God permits.

† **5:8** *Son though he was:* two different though not incompatible views of Jesus' sonship coexist in Hebrews, one associating it with his exaltation, the other with his preexistence. The former view is the older one (cf Rom 1:4).

5:11—6:20 The central section of Hebrews (5:11—10:39) opens with a reprimand and an appeal. Those to whom the author directs his teaching about Jesus' priesthood, which is *difficult to explain,* have become *sluggish in hearing* and forgetful of even *the basic elements* (5:12). But rather than treating of basic teachings, the author apparently believes that the challenge of more advanced ones may shake them out of their inertia (*therefore,* 6:1). The six examples of *basic teaching* in 6:1–3 are probably derived from a traditional catechetical list. No effort is made to address apostates, for their very hostility to the Christian message cuts them off completely from Christ (6:4–8). This harsh statement seems to rule out repentance after apostasy, but perhaps the author deliberately uses hyperbole in order to stress the seriousness of abandoning Christ. With 6:9 a milder tone is introduced, and the criticism of the community (6:1–3, 9) is now balanced by an expression of confidence that its members are living truly Christian lives, and that God will justly reward their efforts (10). The author is concerned especially about their persevering (11–12), citing in this regard the achievement of Abraham, who relied on God's promise and on God's oath (13–18; cf Gn 22:16), and proposes to them as a firm anchor of Christian hope the high priesthood of Christ, who is now living with God (19–20).

6:2 *Instruction about baptisms:* not simply about Christian baptism but about the difference between it and similar Jewish rites, such as proselyte baptism, John's baptism, and the washings of the Qumran sectaries. *Laying on of hands:* in Acts 8:17; 19:6 this rite effects the infusion of the holy Spirit; in Acts 6:6; 13:3; 1 Tm 4:14; 5:22; 2 Tm 1:6 it is a means of conferring some ministry or mission in the early Christian community.

5:8 Rom 5:19; Phil 2:8.
5:9 Heb 7:24–25, 28.
5:10 Heb 6:20; Ps 110:4.
5:12 1 Cor 3:1–3.
6:1 Heb 9:14.
6:2 Heb 9:10; Mk 7:4 / Acts 6:6; 8:17; 13:3; 19:6; 1 Tm 4:14; 5:22; 2 Tm 1:6.

Did You Know?

The Priesthood and Christ's Sacrifice

In the Old Testament, the priesthood evolved after Israel became a nation, and it underwent a long process of development. Priests were not ordained; the priesthood was considered hereditary within the tribe of Levi. After the Exile, three classes of clergy emerged: high priests, priests, and Levites. Priestly functions included maintaining religion as the center of Israel's life, taking care of the Temple of Jerusalem, and interpreting and teaching the Scriptures. In a special way, the priests of Israel represented the people before God by offering prayer and sacrifices for the forgiveness of sin. Their sacrifices foreshadowed the sacrifice of Jesus, the only sacrifice truly capable of reconciling a broken relationship with God caused by sin.

In the New Testament, Christ made the Apostles co-ministers in his saving mission, including a special participation in his high priesthood—the high priesthood described in Hebrews 4:14—5:10. Today, the bishops, as successors of the Apostles, continue the Apostolic Tradition. They ordain priests to assist in their responsibilities as pastors of the faithful, preachers of God's word, and celebrants of Christian worship (see "Holy Orders," near Mk 3:13–19).

Catholic bishops and priests exercise their special participation in Christ's priesthood while presiding at the Eucharist. Acting in Christ's name and in communion with the assembly, they celebrate a memorial of Jesus' life, death, and Resurrection. In the celebration of the Eucharist, Christ's sacrifice on the cross is "re-presented"—that is, Jesus' sacrifice for the forgiveness of sins is made real and present.

► Heb 4:14—5:10

Cultural Connection

Anchor of the Soul

Something mighty powerful kept a smile on my mother's face every day when I was a little girl. I never knew she was in pain. All I saw was a woman with a demeanor of hope and a purpose in life.

I did not know it back then, but she was enduring racial harassment at her job. There was unceasing verbal hate toward African Americans. As I have matured, I have learned that her harassment was not unique. It was a common experience for many African Americans in this country.

When faced with oppressive situations, let us be thankful for a God who continuously fills us with hope. Without hope, oppression is lethal. Hope keeps us moving forward when we are about to give up. Hope makes us smile at tomorrow, even though today is a bitter pill.

Hope is "an anchor of the soul, sure and firm" (Heb 6:19). A hopeless soul is a major threat to our faith. Is your hope anchored in the Lord?

Dear God, give me hope when I face oppression. Amen.

▶ **Heb 6:19–20**

4* † For it is impossible in the case of those who have once been enlightened and tasted the heavenly gift and shared in the holy Spirit 5† and tasted the good word of God and the powers of the age to come, 6* † and then have fallen away, to bring them to repentance again, since they are recrucifying the Son of God for themselves and holding him up to contempt. 7* Ground that has absorbed the rain falling upon it repeatedly and brings forth crops useful to those for whom it is cultivated receives a blessing from God. 8* But if it produces thorns and thistles, it is rejected; it will soon be cursed and finally burned.

9 But we are sure in your regard, beloved, of better things related to salvation, even though we speak in this way. 10 For God is not unjust so as to overlook your work and the love you have demonstrated for his name by having served and continuing to serve the holy ones. 11* We earnestly desire each of you to demonstrate the same eagerness for the fulfillment of hope until the end, 12* † so that you may not become sluggish, but imitators of those who, through faith and patience, are inheriting the promises.

God's Promise Immutable

13* † When God made the promise to Abraham, since he had no one greater by whom to swear, "he swore by himself," 14* and said, "I will indeed bless you and multiply" you. 15* † And so, after patient waiting, he obtained the promise. 16 Human beings swear by someone greater than themselves; for them an oath serves as a guarantee and puts an end to all argument. 17* So when God wanted to give the heirs of his promise an even clearer demonstration of the immutability of his purpose, he intervened with an oath, 18* † so that by two immutable things, in which it was impossible for God to lie, we who have taken refuge might be strongly encouraged to hold fast to the hope that lies before us. 19* † This we have as an anchor of the soul, sure and firm,

†

6:4 *Enlightened and tasted the heavenly gift:* this may refer to baptism and the Eucharist, respectively, but more probably means the neophytes' enlightenment by faith and their experience of salvation.

6:5 *Tasted the good word of God and the powers of the age to come:* the proclamation of the *word of God* was accompanied by signs of the Spirit's power (1 Thes 1:5; 1 Cor 2:4).

6:6 *They are recrucifying the Son of God for themselves:* a colorful description of the malice of apostasy, which is portrayed as again crucifying and deriding the Son of God.

6:12 *Imitators of those . . . inheriting the promises:* the author urges the addressees to imitate the faith of the holy people of the Old Testament, who now possess the promised goods of which they lived in hope. This theme will be treated fully in ch 11.

6:13 *He swore by himself:* God's promise to Abraham, which he confirmed by an oath ("I swear by myself," Gn 22:16) was the basis for the hope of all Abraham's descendants.

6:15 *He obtained the promise:* this probably refers not to Abraham's temporary possession of the land but to the eschatological blessings that Abraham and the other patriarchs have now come to possess.

6:18 *Two immutable things:* the promise and the oath, both made by God.

6:19 *Anchor . . . into the interior behind the veil:* a mixed metaphor.

6:4 Heb 10:26, 32; Ps 34:6; 2 Cor 4:6.
6:6 2 Pt 2:21.
6:7 Gn 1:11–12; Dt 11:11.
6:8 Gn 3:17–18; Mt 7:16; 13:7; Mk 4:7; Lk 8:7.
6:11 Heb 3:14.
6:12 Heb 5:11; Gal 3:14; Eph 1:13–14.
6:13 Gn 22:16.
6:14 Gn 22:17.
6:15 Heb 6:12; Rom 4:20.
6:17 Heb 6:12.
6:18 Nm 23:19; 1 Sm 15:29; Jn 8:17; 2 Tm 2:13.
6:19 Heb 10:20; Ex 26:31–33; Lv 16:2.

which reaches into the interior behind the veil, 20* where Jesus has entered on our behalf as forerunner, becoming high priest forever according to the order of Melchizedek.

Melchizedek, a Type of Christ

7 1*† This "Melchizedek, king of Salem and priest of God Most High,"† "met Abraham as he returned from his defeat of the kings" and "blessed him." 2† And Abraham apportioned to him "a tenth of everything." His name first means righteous king, and he was also "king of Salem," that is, king of peace. 3*† Without father, mother, or ancestry, without beginning of days or end of life, thus made to resemble the Son of God, he remains a priest forever.

4*† See how great he is to whom the patriarch "Abraham [indeed] gave a tenth" of his spoils. 5* The descendants of Levi who receive the office of priesthood have a commandment according to the law to exact tithes from the people, that is, from their brothers, although they also have come from the loins of Abraham. 6 But he who was not of their ancestry received tithes from Abraham and blessed him who had received the promises. 7† Unquestionably, a lesser person is blessed by a greater. 8 In the one case, mortal men receive tithes; in the other, a man of whom it is testified that he lives on. 9† One might even say that Levi himself, who receives tithes, was tithed through Abraham, 10 for he was still in his father's loins when Melchizedek met him.

11*† If, then, perfection came through the levitical priesthood, on the basis of which the people received the law, what need would there still have been for another priest to arise according to the order of Melchizedek, and not reckoned according to the order of Aaron? 12 When there is a change of priesthood, there is necessarily a change of law as well. 13† Now he of whom these things are said belonged to a different tribe, of which no member ever officiated at the altar. 14*† It is clear that our Lord arose from Judah, and in regard to that tribe Moses said nothing about priests. 15† It is even more obvious if another priest is raised up after the likeness of Melchizedek, 16† who has become so, not by a law expressed in a commandment concerning physical descent but by the power of a life that cannot be destroyed. 17* For it is testified:

"You are a priest forever
 according to the order of Melchizedek."

18* On the one hand, a former commandment is annulled because of its weakness and uselessness,

†

The Holy of Holies, beyond the veil that separates it from the Holy Place (Ex 26:31–33), is seen as the earthly counterpart of the heavenly abode of God. This theme will be developed in ch 9.

7:1–3 Recalling the meeting between Melchizedek and Abraham described in Gn 14:17–20, the author enhances the significance of this priest by providing the popular etymological meaning of his name and that of the city over which he ruled (2). Since Genesis gives no information on the parentage or the death of Melchizedek, he is seen here as a type of Christ, representing a priesthood that is unique and eternal (3).

7:1 The author here assumes that Melchizedek was a priest of the God of Israel (cf Gn 14:22 and the note there).

7:2 In Gn 14, the Hebrew text does not state explicitly who gave tithes to whom. The author of Hebrews supplies Abraham as the subject, according to a contemporary interpretation of the passage. This supports the argument of the midrash and makes it possible to see in Melchizedek a type of Jesus. The messianic blessings of righteousness and peace are foreshadowed in the names "Melchizedek" and "Salem."

7:3 *Without father, mother, or ancestry, without beginning of days or end of life:* this is perhaps a quotation from a hymn about Melchizedek. The rabbis maintained that anything not mentioned in the Torah does not exist. Consequently, since the Old Testament nowhere mentions Melchizedek's ancestry, birth, or death, the conclusion can be drawn that he *remains . . . forever.*

7:4–10 The tithe that Abraham gave to Melchizedek (4), a practice later followed by the levitical priesthood (5), was a gift (6) acknowledging a certain superiority in Melchizedek, the foreign priest (7). This is further indicated by the fact that the institution of the levitical priesthood was sustained by hereditary succession in the tribe of Levi, whereas the absence of any mention of Melchizedek's death in Genesis implies that his personal priesthood is permanent (8). The levitical priesthood itself, through Abraham, its ancestor, paid tithes to Melchizedek, thus acknowledging the superiority of his priesthood over its own (9–10).

7:7 *A lesser person is blessed by a greater:* though this sounds like a principle, there are some examples in the Old Testament that do not support it (cf 2 Sm 14:22; Jb 31:20). The author may intend it as a statement of a liturgical rule.

7:9 *Levi:* for the author this name designates not only the son of Jacob mentioned in Genesis but the priestly tribe that was thought to be descended from him.

7:11–14 The levitical priesthood was not typified by the priesthood of Melchizedek, for Ps 110:4 speaks of a priesthood of a new order, the order of Melchizedek, to arise in messianic times (11). Since the levitical priesthood served the Mosaic law, a new priesthood (12) would not come into being without a change in the law itself. Thus Jesus was not associated with the Old Testament priesthood, for he was a descendant of the tribe of Judah, which had never exercised the priesthood (13–14).

7:13 *He of whom these things are said:* Jesus, the priest "according to the order of Melchizedek." According to the author's interpretation, Ps 110 spoke prophetically of Jesus.

7:14 *Judah:* the author accepts the early Christian tradition that Jesus was descended from the family of David (cf Mt 1:1–2, 16, 20; Lk 1:27; 2:4; Rom 1:3). The Qumran community expected two Messiahs, one descended from Aaron and one from David; Hebrews shows no awareness of this view or at least does not accept it. Our author's view is not attested in contemporaneous Judaism.

7:15–19 Jesus does not exercise a priesthood through family lineage but through his immortal existence (15–16), fulfilling Ps 110:4 (17; cf 3). Thus he abolishes forever both the levitical priesthood and the law it serves, because neither could effectively sanctify people (18) by leading them into direct communication with God (19).

7:16 *A life that cannot be destroyed:* the life to which Jesus has attained by virtue of his resurrection; it is his exaltation rather than his divine nature that makes him priest. The Old Testament speaks of the Aaronic priesthood as eternal (see Ex 40:15); our author does not explicitly consider this possible objection to his argument but implicitly refutes it in vv 23–24.

*

6:20 Heb 5:10; Ps 110:4.
7:1 Gn 14:17–20.
7:3 Heb 4:14; 6:6; 10:29.
7:4 Gn 14:20.
7:5 Nm 18:21 / Gn 35:11.
7:11 Heb 5:6; Ps 110:4.
7:14 Gn 49:10; Is 11:1; Mt 1:1–2, 16, 20; 2:6; Lk 1:27; 2:4; Rom 1:3; Rv 5:5.
7:17 Heb 5:6; Ps 110:4.
7:18 Heb 10:1.

19† for the law brought nothing to perfection; on the other hand, a better hope is introduced, through which we draw near to God. 20† And to the degree that this happened not without the taking of an oath†—for others became priests without an oath, 21* but he with an oath, through the one who said to him:

> "The Lord has sworn, and he will not repent:
> 'You are a priest forever' "—

22*† to that same degree has Jesus [also] become the guarantee of an [even] better covenant. 23 Those priests were many because they were prevented by death from remaining in office, 24* but he, because he remains forever, has a priesthood that does not pass away. 25*† Therefore, he is always able to save those who approach God through him, since he lives forever to make intercession for them.

26*† It was fitting that we should have such a high priest: holy, innocent, undefiled, separated from sinners, higher than the heavens.† 27*† He has no need, as did the high priests, to offer sacrifice day after day, first for his own sins and then for those of the people; he did that once for all when he offered himself. 28* For the law appoints men subject to weakness to be high priests, but the word of the oath, which was taken after the law, appoints a son, who has been made perfect forever.

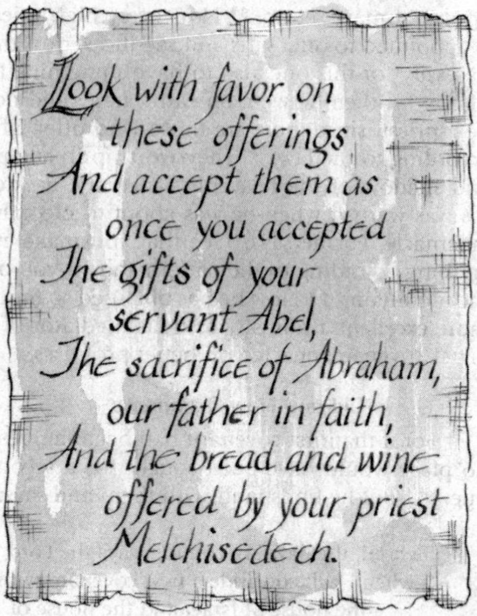

(Roman Missal)

Heavenly Priesthood of Jesus

8 1*† The main point of what has been said is this: we have such a high priest, who has taken his seat at the right hand of the throne of the Majesty in heaven, 2*† a minister of the

---

7:19 *A better hope:* this hope depends upon the sacrifice of the Son of God; through it we "approach the throne of grace" (4:16); cf 6:19, 20.

7:20–25 As was the case with the promise to Abraham (6:13), though not with the levitical priesthood, the eternal priesthood of the order of Melchizedek was confirmed by God's oath (20–21); cf Ps 110:4. Thus Jesus becomes the guarantee of a permanent covenant (22) that does not require a succession of priests as did the levitical priesthood (23) because his high priesthood is eternal and unchangeable (24). Consequently, Jesus is able to save all who draw near to God through him since he is their ever-living intercessor (25).

7:20 *An oath:* God's oath in Ps 110:4.

7:22 *An [even] better covenant:* better than the Mosaic covenant because it will be eternal, like the priesthood of Jesus upon which it is based. Verse 12 argued that a change of priesthood involves a change of law; since "law" and "covenant" are used correlatively, a new covenant is likewise instituted.

7:25 *To make intercession:* the intercession of the exalted Jesus, not the sequel to his completed sacrifice but its eternal presence in heaven; cf Rom 8:34.

7:26–28 Jesus is precisely the high priest whom the human race requires, holy and sinless, installed far above humanity (26); one having no need to offer sacrifice daily for sins but making a single offering of himself (27) once for all. The law could only appoint high priests with human limitations, but the fulfillment of God's oath regarding the priesthood of Melchizedek (Ps 110:4) makes the Son of God the perfect priest forever (28).

7:26 This verse with its list of attributes is reminiscent of v 3 and is perhaps a hymnic counterpart to it, contrasting the exalted Jesus with Melchizedek.

7:27 Such daily sacrifice is nowhere mentioned in the Mosaic law; only on the Day of Atonement is it prescribed that the high priest must *offer sacrifice . . . for his own sins and then for those of the people* (Lv 16:11–19). *Once for all:* this translates the Greek words *ephapax/hapax* that occur eleven times in Hebrews.

8:1–6 The Christian community has in Jesus the kind of high priest described in 7:26–28. In virtue of his ascension Jesus has taken his place at God's right hand in accordance with Ps 110:1 (1), where he presides over the heavenly sanctuary established by God himself (2). Like every high priest, he has his offering to make (3; cf 9:12, 14), but it differs from that of the levitical priesthood in which he had no share (4) and which was in any case but a shadowy reflection of the true offering in the heavenly sanctuary (5). But Jesus' ministry in the heavenly sanctuary is that of mediator of a superior covenant that accomplishes what it signifies (6).

8:2 *The sanctuary:* the Greek term could also mean "holy things" but bears the meaning "sanctuary" elsewhere in Hebrews (9:8, 12, 24, 25; 10:19; 13:11). *The true tabernacle:* the heavenly tabernacle *that the Lord . . . set up* is contrasted with the earthly tabernacle that Moses set up in the desert. *True* means "real" in contradistinction to a mere "copy and shadow" (5); compare the Johannine usage (e.g., Jn 1:9; 6:32; 15:1). The idea that the earthly sanctuary is a reflection of a heavenly model may be based upon Ex 25:9, but probably also derives from the Platonic concept of a real world of which our observable world is merely a shadow.

7:21 Ps 110:4.
7:22 Heb 8:6–10; 9:15–20; 10:29; 12:24; 13:20.
7:24 Heb 5:6; 13:8.
7:25 Rom 8:34; 1 Jn 2:1; Rv 1:18.
7:26 Heb 4:14, 15.
7:27 Heb 5:3; 9:12, 25–28; 10:11–14; Ex 29:38–39; Lv 16:6, 11, 15–17; Nm 28:3–4; Is 53:10; Rom 6:10.
7:28 Heb 5:1, 2, 9.
8:1 Heb 1:3; 4:14; 7:26–28.
8:2 Heb 9:11; Ex 33:7; Nm 24:6 LXX.

sanctuary and of the true tabernacle that the Lord, not man, set up. 3* Now every high priest is appointed to offer gifts and sacrifices; thus the necessity for this one also to have something to offer. 4* If then he were on earth, he would not be a priest, since there are those who offer gifts according to the law. 5* They worship in a copy and shadow of the heavenly sanctuary, as Moses was warned when he was about to erect the tabernacle. For he says, "See that you make everything according to the pattern shown you on the mountain." 6* Now he has obtained so much more excellent a ministry as he is mediator of a better covenant, enacted on better promises.

Old and New Covenants

7† For if that first covenant had been faultless, no place would have been sought for a second one. 8*† But he finds fault with them and says:

"Behold, the days are coming, says the Lord,
when I will conclude a new covenant with the house of Israel and the house of Judah.
9 It will not be like the covenant I made with their fathers
the day I took them by the hand to lead them forth from the land of Egypt;
for they did not stand by my covenant
and I ignored them, says the Lord.
10* But this is the covenant I will establish with the house of Israel
after those days, says the Lord:
I will put my laws in their minds
and I will write them upon their hearts.
I will be their God,
and they shall be my people.
11 And they shall not teach, each one his fellow citizen
and kinsman, saying, 'Know the Lord,'
for all shall know me,
from least to greatest.
12 For I will forgive their evildoing
and remember their sins no more."

13*† When he speaks of a "new" covenant, he declares the first one obsolete. And what has become obsolete and has grown old is close to disappearing.

The Worship of the First Covenant

9 1† Now [even] the first covenant had regulations for worship and an earthly sanctuary. 2*† For a tabernacle was constructed, the outer one, in which were the lampstand, the table, and the bread of offering; this is called the Holy Place. 3*† Behind the second veil was the tabernacle called the Holy of Holies, 4*† in which were the gold altar of incense and the ark of the covenant entirely covered with gold. In it were the gold jar containing the manna, the staff of Aaron that had sprouted, and the tablets of the covenant. 5*† Above it were the cherubim of glory overshadowing the place of expiation. Now is not the time to speak of these in detail.

6*† With these arrangements for worship, the priests, in performing their service, go into the outer tabernacle repeatedly, 7*† but the high

†

8:7–13 Since the first covenant was deficient in accomplishing what it signified, it had to be replaced (7), as Jeremiah (31:31–34) had prophesied (8–12). Even in the time of Jeremiah, the first covenant was antiquated (13). In 7:22–24, the superiority of the new covenant was seen in the permanence of its priesthood; here the superiority is based on better promises, made explicit in the citation of Jer 31 (LXX: 38), 31–34, namely, in the immediacy of the people's knowledge of God (11) and in the forgiveness of sin (12).

8:8–12 In citing Jeremiah the author follows the Septuagint; some apparent departures from it may be the result of a different Septuagintal text rather than changes deliberately introduced.

8:13 *Close to disappearing:* from the prophet's perspective, not that of the author of Hebrews.

9:1–10 The regulations for worship under the old covenant permitted all the priests to enter the Holy Place (2, 6), but only the high priest to enter the Holy of Holies and then only once a year (3–5, 7). The description of the sanctuary and its furnishings is taken essentially from Ex 25–26. This exclusion of the people from the Holy of Holies signified that they were not allowed to stand in God's presence (8) because their offerings and sacrifices, which were merely symbols of their need of spiritual renewal (10), could not obtain forgiveness of sins (9).

9:2 *The outer one:* the author speaks of *the outer tabernacle* (6) and *the inner one* (7) rather than of one Mosaic tabernacle divided into two parts or sections.

9:3 *The second veil:* what is meant is the veil that divided the Holy Place from the Holy of Holies. It is here called *the second,* because there was another veil at the entrance to the Holy Place, or "outer tabernacle" (Ex 26:36).

9:4 *The gold altar of incense:* Ex 30:6 locates this altar in the Holy Place, i.e., the first tabernacle, rather than in the Holy of Holies. Neither is there any Old Testament support for the assertion that the jar of manna and the staff of Aaron were in the ark of the covenant. For the tablets of the covenant, see Ex 25:16.

9:5 *The place of expiation:* the gold "mercy seat" (Greek *hilastērion,* as in Rom 3:25), where the blood of the sacrificial animals was sprinkled on the Day of Atonement (Lv 16:14–15). This rite achieved "expiation" or atonement for the sins of the preceding year.

9:6 *In performing their service:* the priestly services that had to be performed regularly in the Holy Place or *outer tabernacle* included burning incense on the incense altar twice each day (Ex 30:7), replacing the loaves on the table of the bread of offering once each week (Lv 24:8), and constantly caring for the lamps on the lampstand (Ex 27:21).

9:7 *Not without blood:* blood was essential to Old Testament sacrifice because it was believed that life was located in the blood. Hence blood was especially sacred, and its outpouring functioned as a meaningful symbol of cleansing from sin and reconciliation with God. Unlike Hebrews, the Old Testament never says that the blood is "offered." The author is perhaps retrojecting into his description of Mosaic ritual a concept that belongs to the New Testament antitype,

8:3 Heb 5:1.
8:4 Heb 7:13.
8:5 Heb 9:23; Ex 25:40; Acts 7:44; Col 2:17.
8:6 Heb 7:22; 9:15.
8:8 Jer 31:31–34.
8:10 Heb 10:16–17.
8:13 Rom 10:4.
9:2 Ex 25:23–30.
9:3 Ex 26:31–34.
9:4 Ex 16:32–34; 25:10, 16, 21; 30:1–10; Lv 16:12–13; Nm 17:2–7, 16–26.
9:5 Ex 25:16–22; 26:34; Lv 16:14–15.
9:6 Ex 27:21; 30:7; Lv 24:8.
9:7 Ex 30:10; Lv 16:1–14.

priest alone goes into the inner one once a year, not without blood that he offers for himself and for the sins of the people. [8]In this way the holy Spirit shows that the way into the sanctuary had not yet been revealed while the outer tabernacle still had its place. [9]† This is a symbol of the present time, in which gifts and sacrifices are offered that cannot perfect the worshiper in conscience [10]* but only in matters of food and drink and various ritual washings: regulations concerning the flesh, imposed until the time of the new order.

Sacrifice of Jesus

[11]*† But when Christ came as high priest of the good things that have come to be,† passing through the greater and more perfect tabernacle not made by hands, that is, not belonging to this creation, [12]* he entered once for all into the sanctuary, not with the blood of goats and calves but with his own blood, thus obtaining eternal redemption. [13]*† For if the blood of goats and bulls and the sprinkling of a heifer's ashes can sanctify those who are defiled so that their flesh is cleansed, [14]*† how much more will the blood of Christ, who through the eternal spirit offered himself unblemished to God, cleanse our consciences from dead works to worship the living God.

[15]*† For this reason he is mediator of a new covenant: since a death has taken place for deliverance from transgressions under the first covenant, those who are called may receive the promised eternal inheritance. [16]† Now where there is a will, the death of the testator must be established. [17]For a will takes effect only at death; it has no force while the testator is alive. [18]Thus not even the first covenant was inaugurated without blood. [19]*† When every commandment had been proclaimed by Moses to all the people according to the law, he took the blood of calves [and goats], together with water and crimson wool and hyssop, and sprinkled both the book itself and all the people, [20]* saying, "This is 'the blood of the covenant which God has enjoined upon you.' " [21]*† In the same way, he sprinkled also the tabernacle and all the vessels of worship with blood. [22]*† According to the law almost everything is purified by blood, and without the shedding of blood there is no forgiveness.

[23]*† Therefore, it was necessary for the copies of the heavenly things to be purified by these rites, but the heavenly things themselves by better sacrifices than these. [24]* For Christ did not enter into a sanctuary made by hands, a copy of

---

† as Paul does when he speaks of the Israelites' passage through the sea as a "baptism" (1 Cor 10:2).

9:9 *The present time:* this expression is equivalent to the "present age," used in contradistinction to the "age to come."

9:11–14 Christ, the high priest of the spiritual blessings foreshadowed in the Old Testament sanctuary, has actually entered the true sanctuary of heaven that is not of human making (11). His place there is permanent, and his offering is his own blood that won eternal redemption (12). If the sacrifice of animals could bestow legal purification (13), how much more effective is the blood of the sinless, divine Christ who spontaneously offered himself to purge the human race of sin and render it fit for the service of God (14).

9:11 *The good things that have come to be:* the majority of later manuscripts here read "the good things to come"; cf 10:1.

9:13 *A heifer's ashes:* ashes from a red heifer that had been burned were mixed with water and used for the cleansing of those who had become ritually defiled by touching a corpse; see Nm 19:9, 14–21.

9:14 *Through the eternal spirit:* this expression does not refer either to the holy Spirit or to the divine nature of Jesus but to the life of the risen Christ, "a life that cannot be destroyed" (7:16).

9:15–22 Jesus' role as *mediator of a new covenant* is based upon his sacrificial *death* (cf 8:6). His death has effected *deliverance from transgressions,* i.e., deliverance from sins committed under the old covenant, which the Mosaic sacrifices were incapable of effacing. Until this happened, the *eternal inheritance* promised by God could not be obtained (15). This effect of his work follows the human pattern by which a last will and testament becomes effective only with the death of the testator (16–17). The Mosaic covenant was also associated with death, for Moses made use of blood to seal the pact between God and the people (18–21). In Old Testament tradition, guilt could normally not be remitted without the use of blood (22; cf Lv 17:11).

9:16–17 *A will . . . death of the testator:* the same Greek word *diathēkē,* meaning "covenant" in vv 15 and 18, is used here with the meaning *will.* The new covenant, unlike the old, is at the same time a will that requires the *death of the testator.* Jesus as eternal Son is the one who established the new covenant together with his Father, author of both covenants; at the same time he is the testator whose death puts his *will* into effect.

9:19–20 A number of details here are different from the description of this covenant rite in Ex 24:5–8. Exodus mentions only calves ("young bulls," NAB), not goats (but this addition in Hebrews is of doubtful authenticity), says nothing of the use of *water and crimson wool and hyssop* (these features probably came from a different rite; cf Lv 14:3–7; Nm 19:6–18), and describes Moses as splashing blood on the altar, whereas Hebrews says he sprinkled it on the book (but both book and altar are meant to symbolize the agreement of God). The words of Moses are also slightly different from those in Exodus and are closer to the words of Jesus at the Last Supper in Mk 14:24 // Mt 26:28.

9:21 According to Exodus, the tabernacle did not yet exist at the time of the covenant rite. Moreover, nothing is said of sprinkling it with blood at its subsequent dedication (Ex 40:9–11).

9:22 *Without the shedding of blood there is no forgiveness:* in fact, ancient Israel did envisage other means of obtaining forgiveness; the Old Testament mentions contrition of heart (Ps 51:19), fasting (Jl 2:12), and almsgiving (Sir 3:29). The author is limiting his horizon to the sacrificial cult, which did always involve the shedding of blood for its expiatory and unitive value.

9:23–28 Since the blood of animals became a cleansing symbol among Old Testament prefigurements, it was necessary that the realities foreshadowed be brought into being by a shedding of blood that was infinitely more effective by reason of its worth (23). Christ did not simply prefigure the heavenly realities (24) by performing an annual sacrifice with a blood not his own (25); he offered the single sacrifice of himself as the final annulment of sin (26). Just as death is the unrepeatable act that ends a person's life, so Christ's offering of himself for all is the unrepeatable sacrifice that has once for all achieved redemption (27–28).

9:10 Heb 13:9; Lv 11; 14:8; Nm 19:11–21; Col 2:16.
9:11 Heb 4:14; 10:1, 20.
9:12 Heb 7:27; Mt 26:28.
9:13 Heb 10:4; Lv 16:6–16; Nm 19:9, 14–21.
9:14 Heb 10:10; Rom 5:9; 1 Tm 3:9; Ti 2:14; 1 Pt 1:18–19; 1 Jn 1:7; Rv 1:5.
9:15 1 Tm 2:5.
9:19 Heb 9:12–13.
9:20 Ex 24:3–8; Mt 26:28; Mk 14:24.
9:21 Ex 40:9; Lv 8:15, 19.
9:22 Lv 17:11.
9:23 Jb 15:15.
9:24 Heb 7:25; Rom 8:34; 1 Jn 2:1–2.

Did You Know?

The Perfect Sacrifice

The author of the Letter to the Hebrews uses the "from the lesser to the greater" argument again to explain that Christ's sacrifice on the cross is greater than any sacrifice that could ever be offered in the Temple. Even though perfect animals are offered over and over, they never take away sins (see Heb 10:1–4). The sacrifice of Christ takes away sins because it is the perfect sacrifice, offered only once for the sins of all (see verses 12–14). After Christ's death, there is no longer any need for anyone else to offer a sacrifice for the forgiveness of sins.

▶ **Heb 10:1–18**

the true one, but heaven itself, that he might now
appear before God on our behalf. 25 Not that
he might offer himself repeatedly, as the high
priest enters each year into the sanctuary with
blood that is not his own; 26*† if that were so,
he would have had to suffer repeatedly from the
foundation of the world. But now once for all he
has appeared at the end of the ages to take away
sin by his sacrifice. 27* Just as it is appointed
that human beings die once, and after this the
judgment, 28*† so also Christ, offered once to
take away the sins of many, will appear a second
time, not to take away sin but to bring salvation
to those who eagerly await him.

One Sacrifice instead of Many

10 1*† Since the law has only a shadow of the
good things to come,† and not the very im-
age of them, it can never make perfect those who
come to worship by the same sacrifices that they
offer continually each year. 2 Otherwise, would
not the sacrifices have ceased to be offered, since
the worshipers, once cleansed, would no longer
have had any consciousness of sins? 3* But in
those sacrifices there is only a yearly remembrance
of sins, 4* for it is impossible that the blood of
bulls and goats take away sins. 5*† For this reason,
when he came into the world, he said:

"Sacrifice and offering you did not desire,
but a body you prepared for me;
6 holocausts and sin offerings you took no
delight in.
7 Then I said, 'As is written of me in the scroll,
Behold, I come to do your will, O God.' "

8*† First he says, "Sacrifices and offerings, holo-
causts and sin offerings, you neither desired nor
delighted in." These are offered according to the
law. 9* Then he says, "Behold, I come to do your
will." He takes away the first to establish the sec-
ond. 10* By this "will," we have been consecrated
through the offering of the body of Jesus Christ
once for all.

11*† Every priest stands daily at his ministry,
offering frequently those same sacrifices that can

9:26 *At the end of the ages:* the use of expressions such as this shows that the author of Hebrews, despite his interest in the Platonic concept of an eternal world above superior to temporal reality here below, nevertheless still clings to the Jewish Christian eschatology with its sequence of "the present age" and "the age to come."

9:28 *To take away the sins of many:* the reference is to Is 53:12. Since the Greek verb *anapherō* can mean both "to take away" and "to bear," the author no doubt intended to play upon both senses: Jesus took away sin by bearing it himself. See the similar wordplay in Jn 1:29. *Many* is used in the Semitic meaning of "all" in the inclusive sense, as in Mk 14:24. *To those who eagerly await him:* Jesus will appear *a second time* at the parousia, as the high priest reappeared on the Day of Atonement, emerging from the Holy of Holies, which he had entered *to take away sin.* This dramatic scene is described in Sir 50:5–11.

10:1–10 Christian faith now realizes that the Old Testament sacrifices did not effect the spiritual benefits to come but only prefigured them (1). For if the sacrifices had actually effected the forgiveness of sin, there would have been no reason for their constant repetition (2). They were rather a continual reminder of the people's sins (3). It is not reasonable to suppose that human sins could be removed by the blood of animal sacrifices (4). Christ, therefore, is here shown to understand his mission in terms of Ps 40:6–8, cited according to the Septuagint (5–7). Jesus acknowledged that the Old Testament sacrifices did not remit the sins of the people and so, perceiving the will of God, offered his own body for this purpose (8–10).

10:1 *A shadow of the good things to come:* the term *shadow* was used in 8:5 to signify the earthly counterpart of the Platonic heavenly reality. But here it means a prefiguration of what is to come in Christ, as it is used in the Pauline literature; cf Col 2:17.

10:5–7 A passage from Ps 40:7–9a is placed in the mouth of the Son at his incarnation. As usual, the author follows the Septuagint text. There is a notable difference in v 5 (Ps 40:7b), where the Masoretic text reads "ears you have dug for me" ("ears open to obedience you gave me," NAB), but most Septuagint manuscripts have "a body you prepared for me," a reading obviously more suited to the interpretation of Hebrews.

10:8 *Sacrifices and offerings, holocausts and sin offerings:* these four terms taken from the preceding passage of Ps 40 (with the first two changed to plural forms) are probably intended as equivalents to the four principal types of Old Testament sacrifices: peace offerings (Lv 3, here called *sacrifices*); cereal offerings (Lv 2, here called *offerings*); *holocausts* (Lv 1); and *sin offerings* (Lv 4–5). This last category includes the guilt offerings of Lv 5:14–26.

10:11–18 Whereas the levitical priesthood offered daily sacrifices that were ineffectual in remitting sin (11), Jesus offered a single sacrifice that won him a permanent place at God's right hand. There he has only to await the final outcome of his work (12–13; cf Ps 110:1). Thus he has brought into being in his own person the new covenant prophesied by Jeremiah (31:33–34) that has rendered meaningless all other offerings for sin (14–18).

9:26 Heb 7:27; Jn 1:29; Gal 4:4.
9:27 Gn 3:19.
9:28 Heb 10:10; Is 53:12.
10:1 Heb 8:5; Col 2:17.
10:3 Lv 16:21; Nm 5:15 LXX.
10:4 Is 1:11; Mi 6:6–8.
10:5–7 Ps 40:7–9.
10:8 Heb 10:5–6; Ps 40:7.
10:9 Heb 7; Ps 40:8; Mt 26:39; Mk 14:36; Lk 22:42; Jn 6:38.
10:10 Heb 9:12, 14.
10:11 Heb 7:27; Dt 10:8; 18:7.

never take away sins. 12* But this one offered one
sacrifice for sins, and took his seat forever at the
right hand of God; 13† now he waits until his
enemies are made his footstool. 14* For by one
offering he has made perfect forever those who
are being consecrated. 15† The holy Spirit also
testifies to us, for after saying:

16* "This is the covenant I will establish with
them after those days, says the Lord:
'I will put my laws in their hearts,
and I will write them upon their minds,' "

17*† he also says:

"Their sins and their evildoing
I will remember no more."

18 Where there is forgiveness of these, there is no
longer offering for sin.

Recalling the Past

19*† Therefore, brothers, since through the
blood of Jesus we have confidence of entrance
into the sanctuary 20*† by the new and living
way he opened for us through the veil, that is, his
flesh, 21*† and since we have "a great priest over
the house of God," 22*† let us approach with
a sincere heart and in absolute trust, with our
hearts sprinkled clean from an evil conscience
and our bodies washed in pure water. 23* Let
us hold unwaveringly to our confession that
gives us hope, for he who made the promise is
trustworthy. 24 We must consider how to rouse
one another to love and good works. 25*† We
should not stay away from our assembly, as is
the custom of some, but encourage one another,
and this all the more as you see the day drawing
near.

26*† If we sin deliberately after receiving
knowledge of the truth, there no longer remains
sacrifice for sins 27* but a fearful prospect of
judgment and a flaming fire that is going to con-
sume the adversaries. 28*† Anyone who rejects
the law of Moses is put to death without pity on
the testimony of two or three witnesses. 29* Do
you not think that a much worse punishment is
due the one who has contempt for the Son of
God, considers unclean the covenant-blood by
which he was consecrated, and insults the spirit
of grace? 30* We know the one who said:

"Vengeance is mine; I will repay,"

and again:

"The Lord will judge his people."

31* It is a fearful thing to fall into the hands of
the living God.

HEB

10:13 *Until his enemies are made his footstool:* Ps 110:1 is again used; the reference here is to the period of time between the enthronement of Jesus and his second coming. The identity of the *enemies* is not specified; cf 1 Cor 15:25–27.

10:15–17 The testimony of the scriptures is now invoked to support what has just preceded. The passage cited is a portion of the new covenant prophecy of Jer 31:31–34, which the author previously used in 8:8–12.

10:17 *He also says:* these words are not in the Greek text, which has only *kai,* "also," but the expression *after saying* in v 15 seems to require such a phrase to divide the Jeremiah text into two sayings. Others understand "the Lord says" of v 16 (here rendered *says the Lord*) as outside the quotation and consider v 16b as part of the second saying. Two ancient versions and a number of minuscules introduce the words "then he said" or a similar expression at the beginning of v 17.

10:19–39 Practical consequences from these reflections on the priesthood and the sacrifice of Christ should make it clear that Christians may now have direct and confident access to God through the person of Jesus (19–20), who rules God's house as high priest (21). They should approach God with sincerity and faith, in the knowledge that through baptism their sins have been remitted (22), reminding themselves of the hope they expressed in Christ at that event (23). They are to encourage one another to Christian love and activity (24), not refusing, no matter what the reason, to participate in the community's assembly, especially in view of the parousia (25; cf 1 Thes 4:13–18). If refusal to participate in the assembly indicates rejection of Christ, no sacrifice exists to obtain forgiveness for so great a sin (26); only the dreadful judgment of God remains (27). For if violation of the Mosaic law could be punished by death, how much worse will be the punishment of those who have turned their backs on Christ by despising his sacrifice and disregarding the gifts of the holy Spirit (28–29). Judgment belongs to the Lord, and he enacts it by his living presence (30–31). There was a time when the spirit of their community caused them to welcome and share their sufferings (32–34). To revitalize that spirit is to share in the courage of the Old Testament prophets (cf Is 26:20; Hb 2:3–4), the kind of courage that must distinguish the faith of the Christian (35–39).

10:20 *Through the veil, that is, his flesh:* the term *flesh* is used pejoratively. As the temple veil kept people from entering the Holy of Holies (it was rent at Christ's death, Mk 15:38), so the flesh of Jesus constituted an obstacle to approaching God.

10:21 *The house of God:* this refers back to 3:6, "we are his house."

10:22 *With our hearts sprinkled clean from an evil conscience:* as in 9:13 (see the note there), the sprinkling motif refers to the Mosaic rite of cleansing from ritual impurity. This could produce only an external purification, whereas sprinkling with the blood of Christ (9:14) cleanses the *conscience. Washed in pure water:* baptism is elsewhere referred to as a washing; cf 1 Cor 6:11; Eph 5:26.

10:25 *Our assembly:* the liturgical *assembly* of the Christian community, probably for the celebration of the Eucharist. *The day:* this designation for the parousia also occurs in the Pauline letters, e.g., Rom 2:16; 1 Cor 3:13; 1 Thes 5:2.

10:26 *If we sin deliberately:* verse 29 indicates that the author is here thinking of apostasy; cf 3:12; 6:4–8.

10:28 *Rejects the law of Moses:* evidently not any sin against the law, but idolatry. Dt 17:2–7 prescribed capital punishment for idolaters who were convicted on the testimony of two or three witnesses.

10:12–13 Ps 110:1.
10:14 Heb 9:28.
10:16 Heb 8:10; Jer 31:33.
10:17 Heb 8:12; Jer 31:34.
10:19 Heb 3:6; 4:16; 6:19–20; Eph 1:7; 3:12.
10:20 Jn 14:6 / Heb 6:19–20; 9:8, 11–12; Mt 27:51; Mk 15:38; Lk 23:45.
10:21 Heb 3:6.
10:22 Heb 9:13–14; Ez 36:25; 1 Cor 6:11; Ti 3:5; 1 Pt 3:21.
10:23 Heb 3:1, 6; 4:14; 1 Cor 10:13.
10:25 Rom 13:12; 1 Cor 3:13.
10:26 Heb 3:12; 6:4–8.
10:27 Heb 10:31; 9:27; Is 26:11 LXX; Zep 1:18.
10:28 Dt 17:6.
10:29 Heb 6:6.
10:30 Dt 32:35, 36; Rom 12:19.
10:31 Heb 10:27; Mt 10:28; Lk 12:4–5.

32*† Remember the days past when, after you
had been enlightened, you endured a great con-
test of suffering. 33* At times you were publicly
exposed to abuse and affliction; at other times
you associated yourselves with those so treated.
34* You even joined in the sufferings of those in
prison and joyfully accepted the confiscation of
your property, knowing that you had a better and
lasting possession. 35* Therefore, do not throw
away your confidence; it will have great recom-
pense. 36* You need endurance to do the will of
God and receive what he has promised.

37*† "For, after just a brief moment,
he who is to come shall come;
he shall not delay.
38* But my just one shall live by faith,
and if he draws back I take no pleasure in
him."

39 We are not among those who draw back and
perish, but among those who have faith and will
possess life.

V: Examples, Discipline, Disobedience

Faith of the Ancients†

11 1* Faith is the realization of what is hoped
for and evidence† of things not seen. 2 Be-
cause of it the ancients were well attested. 3*† By
faith we understand that the universe was ordered
by the word of God, so that what is visible came
into being through the invisible. 4*† By faith Abel
offered to God a sacrifice greater than Cain's.
Through this he was attested to be righteous, God
bearing witness to his gifts, and through this,
though dead, he still speaks. 5* By faith Enoch was
taken up so that he should not see death, and "he
was found no more because God had taken him."
Before he was taken up, he was attested to have
pleased God. 6*† But without faith it is impossible
to please him, for anyone who approaches God
must believe that he exists and that he rewards
those who seek him. 7* By faith Noah, warned
about what was not yet seen, with reverence built
an ark for the salvation of his household. Through
this he condemned the world and inherited the
righteousness that comes through faith.
8* By faith Abraham obeyed when he was
called to go out to a place that he was to receive
as an inheritance; he went out, not knowing
where he was to go. 9* By faith he sojourned in
the promised land as in a foreign country, dwell-
ing in tents with Isaac and Jacob, heirs of the
same promise; 10* for he was looking forward to
the city with foundations, whose architect and
maker is God. 11* By faith he received power
to generate, even though he was past the nor-
mal age—and Sarah herself was sterile—for he
thought that the one who had made the promise
was trustworthy. 12* So it was that there came

†

10:32 *After you had been enlightened:* "enlightenment" is an ancient metaphor for baptism (cf Eph 5:14; Jn 9:11), but see 6:4 and the note there.

10:37–38 In support of his argument, the author uses Hb 2:3–4 in a wording almost identical with the text of the Codex Alexandrinus of the Septuagint but with the first and second lines of v 4 inverted. He introduces it with a few words from Is 26:20: *after just a brief moment.* Note the Pauline usage of Hb 2:4 in Rom 1:17; Gal 3:11.

11:1–40 This chapter draws upon the people and events of the Old Testament to paint an inspiring portrait of religious faith, firm and unyielding in the face of any obstacles that confront it. These pages rank among the most eloquent and lofty to be found in the Bible. They expand the theme announced in 6:12, to which the author now returns (10:39). The material of this chapter is developed chronologically. Verses 3–7 draw upon the first nine chapters of Genesis; vv 8–22, upon the period of the patriarchs; vv 23–31, upon the time of Moses; vv 32–38, upon the history of the judges, the prophets, and the Maccabean martyrs. The author gives the most extensive description of faith provided in the New Testament, though his interest does not lie in a technical, theological definition. In view of the needs of his audience he describes what authentic faith does, not what it is in itself. Through faith God guarantees the blessings to be hoped for from him, providing evidence in the gift of faith that what he promises will eventually come to pass (1). Because they accepted in faith God's guarantee of the future, the biblical personages discussed in vv 3–38 were themselves commended by God (2). Christians have even greater reason to remain firm in faith since they, unlike the Old Testament men and women of faith, have perceived the beginning of God's fulfillment of his messianic promises (39–40).

11:1 *Faith is the realization . . . evidence:* the author is not attempting a precise definition. There is dispute about the meaning of the Greek words *hypostasis* and *elenchos,* here translated *realization* and *evidence,* respectively. *Hypostasis* usually means "substance," "being" (as translated in 1:3), or "reality" (as translated in 3:14); here it connotes something more subjective, and so *realization* has been chosen rather than "assurance" (RSV). *Elenchos,* usually "proof," is used here in an objective sense and so translated *evidence* rather than the transferred sense of "(inner) conviction" (RSV).

11:3 *By faith . . . God:* this verse does not speak of the faith of the Old Testament men and women but is in the first person plural. Hence it seems out of place in the sequence of thought.

11:4 The "Praise of the Ancestors" in Sir 44:1—50:21 gives a similar list of heroes. The Cain and Abel narrative in Gn 4:1–16 does not mention Abel's faith. It says, however, that God "looked with favor on Abel and his offering" (Gn 4:4); in view of v 6 the author probably understood God's favor to have been activated by Abel's faith. *Though dead, he still speaks:* possibly because his blood "cries out to me from the soil" (Gn 4:10), but more probably a way of saying that the repeated story of Abel provides ongoing witness to faith.

11:6 One must believe not only that God *exists* but that he is concerned about human conduct; the Old Testament defines folly as the denial of this truth; cf Ps 52:2.

10:32 Heb 6:4.
10:33 1 Cor 4:9.
10:34 Heb 13:3; Mt 6:19–20; Lk 12:33–34.
10:35 Heb 4:16.
10:36 Lk 21:19.
10:37 Is 26:20; Hb 2:3.
10:38 Hb 2:4; Rom 1:17; Gal 3:11.
11:1 Heb 1:3; 3:14; Rom 8:24; 2 Cor 4:18.
11:3 Gn 1:3; Ps 33:6; Wis 9:1; Jn 1:3.
11:4 Heb 12:24; Gn 4:4, 10.
11:5 Gn 5:24; Sir 44:16.
11:6 Wis 4:10.
11:7 Gn 6:8–22; Sir 44:17–18; Mt 24:37–39; Lk 17:26–27; 1 Pt 3:20; 2 Pt 2:5.
11:8 Gn 12:1–4; 15:7–21; Sir 44:19–22; Acts 7:2–8; Rom 4:16–22.
11:9 Gn 12:8; 13:12; 23:4; 26:3; 35:27.
11:10 Heb 12:22; 13:14; Rv 21:10–22.
11:11 Gn 17:19; 21:2; Rom 4:19–21 / 1 Cor 10:13.
11:12 Gn 15:5; 22:17; 32:13; Ex 32:13; Dt 10:22; Dn 3:36.

forth from one man, himself as good as dead, de-
scendants as numerous as the stars in the sky and
as countless as the sands on the seashore.
13* All these died in faith. They did not receive
what had been promised but saw it and greeted
it from afar and acknowledged themselves to be
strangers and aliens on earth, 14 for those who
speak thus show that they are seeking a home-
land. 15 If they had been thinking of the land
from which they had come, they would have had
opportunity to return. 16* But now they desire a
better homeland, a heavenly one. Therefore, God
is not ashamed to be called their God, for he has
prepared a city for them.
17* By faith Abraham, when put to the test,
offered up Isaac, and he who had received the
promises was ready to offer his only son, 18* of
whom it was said, "Through Isaac descendants
shall bear your name." 19*† He reasoned that
God was able to raise even from the dead, and
he received Isaac back as a symbol. 20*† By faith
regarding things still to come Isaac blessed Jacob
and Esau. 21* By faith Jacob, when dying, blessed
each of the sons of Joseph and "bowed in worship,
leaning on the top of his staff." 22* By faith Joseph,
near the end of his life, spoke of the Exodus of the
Israelites and gave instructions about his bones.
23* By faith Moses was hidden by his parents
for three months after his birth, because they saw
that he was a beautiful child, and they were not
afraid of the king's edict. 24*† By faith Moses,
when he had grown up, refused to be known
as the son of Pharaoh's daughter; 25 he chose
to be ill-treated along with the people of God
rather than enjoy the fleeting pleasure of sin.
26 He considered the reproach of the Anointed
greater wealth than the treasures of Egypt, for
he was looking to the recompense. 27* By faith
he left Egypt, not fearing the king's fury, for he
persevered as if seeing the one who is invisible.
28* By faith he kept the Passover and sprinkled
the blood, that the Destroyer of the firstborn
might not touch them. 29* By faith they crossed
the Red Sea as if it were dry land, but when
the Egyptians attempted it they were drowned.
30* By faith the walls of Jericho fell after being
encircled for seven days. 31* By faith Rahab the
harlot did not perish with the disobedient, for
she had received the spies in peace.
32* What more shall I say? I have not time
to tell of Gideon, Barak, Samson, Jephthah, of
David and Samuel and the prophets, 33* who
by faith conquered kingdoms, did what was
righteous, obtained the promises; they closed
the mouths of lions, 34* put out raging fires, es-
caped the devouring sword; out of weakness they
were made powerful, became strong in battle,
and turned back foreign invaders. 35* Women
received back their dead through resurrection.
Some were tortured and would not accept deliv-
erance, in order to obtain a better resurrection.
36* Others endured mockery, scourging, even
chains and imprisonment. 37* They were stoned,
sawed in two, put to death at sword's point; they
went about in skins of sheep or goats, needy, af-
flicted, tormented. 38* The world was not worthy
of them. They wandered about in deserts and on
mountains, in caves and in crevices in the earth.
39 Yet all these, though approved because of
their faith, did not receive what had been prom-
ised. 40† God had foreseen something better for
us, so that without us they should not be made
perfect.

God our Father

12 1† Therefore, since we are surrounded by
so great a cloud of witnesses, let us rid our-
selves of every burden and sin that clings to us†

†

11:19 *As a symbol:* Isaac's "return from death" is seen as a *symbol* of Christ's resurrection. Others understand the words *en parabolē* to mean "in figure," i.e., the word *dead* is used figuratively of Isaac, since he did not really die. But in the one other place that *parabolē* occurs in Hebrews, it means symbol (9:9).

11:20–22 Each of these three patriarchs, Isaac, Jacob, and Joseph, had faith in the future fulfillment of God's promise and renewed this faith when near death.

11:24–27 The reason given for Moses' departure from Egypt differs from the account in Ex 2:11–15. The author also gives a christological interpretation of his decision to share the trials of his people.

11:40 *So that without us they should not be made perfect:* the heroes of the Old Testament obtained their recompense only after the saving work of Christ had been accomplished. Thus they already enjoy what Christians who are still struggling do not yet possess in its fullness.

12:1–13 Christian life is to be inspired not only by the Old Testament men and women of faith (1) but above all by Jesus. As the architect of Christian faith, he had himself to endure the cross before receiving the glory of his triumph (2). Reflection on his sufferings should give his followers courage to continue the struggle, if necessary even to the shedding of blood (3–4). Christians should regard their own sufferings as the affectionate correction of the Lord, who loves them as a father loves his children.

12:1 *That clings to us:* the meaning is uncertain, since the Greek word *euperistatos,* translated *cling,* occurs only here. The papyrus P46 and one minuscule read *euperispastos,* "easily distracting," which also makes good sense.

*

11:13 Gn 23:4; Ps 39:13.
11:16 Heb 13:14; Ex 3:6.
11:17 Gn 22:1–10; Sir 44:20; 1 Mc 2:52; Jas 2:21.
11:18 Gn 21:12 LXX; Rom 9:7.
11:19 Rom 4:16–22.
11:20 Gn 27:27–40.
11:21 Gn 27:38–40; 47:31 LXX; 48:15–16.
11:22 Gn 50:24–25.
11:23 Ex 2:2; Acts 7:20.
11:24–25 Ex 2:10–15; Acts 7:23–29.
11:27 Ex 2:15; Acts 7:29.
11:28 Ex 12:21–23; Wis 18:25; 1 Cor 10:10.
11:29 Ex 14:22–28.
11:30 Jos 6:12–21.
11:31 Jos 2:1–21; 6:22–25; Jas 2:25.
11:32 Jgs 4:6–22; 6:11—8:32; 11:1—12:7.
11:33 Dn 6:23.
11:34 Dn 3:22–25, 49–50.
11:35 1 Kgs 17:17–24; 2 Kgs 4:18–37; 2 Mc 6:18—7:42.
11:36 2 Chr 36:16; Jer 20:2; 37:15.
11:37 2 Chr 24:21.
11:38 1 Mc 2:28–30.

and persevere in running the race that lies before
us 2* while keeping our eyes fixed on Jesus, the
leader and perfecter of faith. For the sake of the
joy that lay before him he endured the cross,
despising its shame, and has taken his seat at
the right of the throne of God. 3 Consider how
he endured such opposition from sinners, in or-
der that you may not grow weary and lose heart.
4 In your struggle against sin you have not yet
resisted to the point of shedding blood. 5* You
have also forgotten the exhortation addressed to
you as sons:

"My son, do not disdain the discipline of the
Lord
or lose heart when reproved by him;
6 for whom the Lord loves, he disciplines;
he scourges every son he acknowledges."

7* Endure your trials as "discipline"; God treats
you as sons. For what "son" is there whom his
father does not discipline? 8 If you are with-
out discipline, in which all have shared, you
are not sons but bastards. 9* Besides this, we
have had our earthly fathers to discipline us,
and we respected them. Should we not [then]
submit all the more to the Father of spirits and
live? 10 They disciplined us for a short time as
seemed right to them, but he does so for our
benefit, in order that we may share his ho-
liness. 11* At the time, all discipline seems a
cause not for joy but for pain, yet later it brings
the peaceful fruit of righteousness to those
who are trained by it.

12* So strengthen your drooping hands and
your weak knees. 13* Make straight paths for
your feet, that what is lame may not be dislo-
cated but healed.

Penalties of Disobedience

14* Strive for peace with everyone, and for that
holiness without which no one will see the Lord.
15*† See to it that no one be deprived of the grace
of God, that no bitter root spring up and cause
trouble, through which many may become defiled,
16* that no one be an immoral or profane person
like Esau, who sold his birthright for a single meal.
17* For you know that later, when he wanted to in-
herit his father's blessing, he was rejected because
he found no opportunity to change his mind, even
though he sought the blessing with tears.

18*† You have not approached that which
could be touched and a blazing fire and gloomy
darkness and storm† 19* and a trumpet blast
and a voice speaking words such that those who
heard begged that no message be further ad-
dressed to them, 20* for they could not bear to
hear the command: "If even an animal touches
the mountain, it shall be stoned." 21* Indeed,
so fearful was the spectacle that Moses said, "I
am terrified and trembling." 22* No, you have
approached Mount Zion and the city of the liv-
ing God, the heavenly Jerusalem, and countless
angels in festal gathering, 23*† and the assembly
of the firstborn enrolled in heaven, and God the
judge of all, and the spirits of the just made per-
fect, 24*† and Jesus, the mediator of a new cov-
enant, and the sprinkled blood that speaks more
eloquently than that of Abel.

25* See that you do not reject the one who
speaks. For if they did not escape when they re-
fused the one who warned them on earth, how
much more in our case if we turn away from the
one who warns from heaven. 26* His voice shook
the earth at that time, but now he has prom-
ised, "I will once more shake not only earth but

†

12:15–17 Esau serves as an example in two ways: his *profane* attitude illustrates the danger of apostasy, and his inability to secure a blessing afterward illustrates the impossibility of repenting after falling away (see 6:4–6).

12:18–29 As a final appeal for adherence to Christian teaching, the two covenants, of Moses and of Christ, are compared. The Mosaic covenant, the author argues, is shown to have originated in fear of God and threats of divine punishment (18–21). The covenant in Christ gives us direct access to God (22), makes us members of the Christian community, God's children, a sanctified people (23), who have Jesus as mediator to speak for us (24). Not to heed the voice of the risen Christ is a graver sin than the rejection of the word of Moses (25–26). Though Christians fall away, God's kingdom in Christ will remain and his justice will punish those guilty of deserting it (28–29).

12:18–24 This remarkably beautiful passage contrasts two great assemblies of people: that of the Israelites gathered at Mount Sinai for the sealing of the old covenant and the promulgation of the Mosaic law, and that of the followers of Jesus gathered at *Mount Zion, the heavenly Jerusalem,* the assembly of the *new covenant.* This latter scene, marked by the presence of *countless angels* and of *Jesus* with his redeeming *blood,* is reminiscent of the celestial liturgies of the Book of Revelation.

12:23 *The assembly of the firstborn enrolled in heaven:* this expression may refer to the angels of v 22, or to the heroes of the Old Testament (see ch 11), or to the entire assembly of the new covenant.

12:24 *Speaks more eloquently:* the blood of Abel, the first human blood to be shed, is contrasted with that of Jesus. Abel's blood cried out from the earth for vengeance, but the blood of Jesus has opened the way for everyone, providing cleansing and access to God (10:19).

12:2 Heb 2:10; Ps 110:1; Phil 2:6–8.
12:5–6 Prv 3:11–12 / Dt 8:5; 1 Cor 11:32.
12:7 Prv 13:24; Sir 30:1.
12:9 Nm 16:22; 27:16 LXX.
12:11 2 Cor 4:17; Phil 1:11; Jas 3:18.
12:12 Is 35:3; Sir 25:23; Jb 4:3–4.
12:13 Prv 4:26 LXX.
12:14 Rom 12:18; 14:19.
12:15 Dt 29:18 (17 LXX).
12:16 Gn 25:33.
12:17 Gn 27:34–38.
12:18 Ex 19:12–14; Dt 4:11; 5:22–23.
12:19 Ex 19:16, 19; 20:18–19.
12:20 Ex 19:12–13.
12:21 Dt 9:19.
12:22 Gal 4:26; Rv 21:2.
12:23 Lk 10:20; Rv 5:11.
12:24 Heb 7:22; 8:6; 9:15 / Heb 11:4; Gn 4:10.
12:25 Ex 20:19.
12:26 Ex 19:18; Jgs 5:4–5; Ps 68:9; Hg 2:6.

heaven." 27* That phrase, "once more," points to [the] removal of shaken, created things, so that what is unshaken may remain. 28* Therefore, we who are receiving the unshakable kingdom should have gratitude, with which we should offer worship pleasing to God in reverence and awe. 29* For our God is a consuming fire.

VI: Final Exhortation, Blessing, Greetings

13 1† Let mutual love continue. 2* Do not neglect hospitality, for through it some have unknowingly entertained angels. 3* Be mindful of prisoners as if sharing their imprisonment, and of the ill-treated as of yourselves, for you also are in the body. 4* Let marriage be honored among all and the marriage bed be kept undefiled, for God will judge the immoral and adulterers. 5* Let your life be free from love of money but be content with what you have, for he has said, "I will never forsake you or abandon you." 6* Thus we may say with confidence:

"The Lord is my helper,
[and] I will not be afraid.
What can anyone do to me?"

7 Remember your leaders who spoke the word of God to you. Consider the outcome of their way of life and imitate their faith. 8* Jesus Christ is the same yesterday, today, and forever.

9*† Do not be carried away by all kinds of strange teaching. It is good to have our hearts strengthened by grace and not by foods, which do not benefit those who live by them. 10† We have an altar from which those who serve the tabernacle have no right to eat. 11* The bodies of the animals whose blood the high priest brings into the sanctuary as a sin offering are burned outside the camp. 12* Therefore, Jesus also suffered outside the gate, to consecrate the people by his own blood. 13 Let us then go to him outside the camp, bearing the reproach that he bore. 14* For here we

Live It!

Entertaining Angels

The subject of angels has always fascinated the media, especially filmmakers and television show producers. They often develop stories around the idea from the Letter to the Hebrews that people sometimes encounter angels and that angels are sent to rescue people caught in dire or tragic circumstances.

We know God has created a category of beings that is made up of pure spirits without bodies. These beings act as God's messengers and serve as spiritual guardians for humans. Their mission is to bring God's word to those who are open to hear it and respond to it with faith and humility.

Will we ever have the opportunity to entertain angels in human disguise? We may never know the answer to this question, but we should entertain this truth in our hearts and minds: God guides the world and has sent messengers and guardians—angels—whose mysterious presence offers support, protection, and intercession for those who believe in God and seek the face of God.

▶ **Heb 13:1–5**

have no lasting city, but we seek the one that is to come. 15* Through him [then] let us continually offer God a sacrifice of praise, that is, the fruit of lips that confess his name. 16* Do not neglect to do good and to share what you have; God is pleased by sacrifices of that kind.

17† Obey your leaders and defer to them, for

13:1–16 After recommendations on social and moral matters (1–6), the letter turns to doctrinal issues. The fact that the original leaders are dead should not cause the recipients of this letter to lose their faith (7), for Christ still lives and he remains always the same (8). They must not rely for their personal sanctification on regulations concerning foods (9), nor should they entertain the notion that Judaism and Christianity can be intermingled (10; cf the notes on Gal 2:11–14 and 2:15–21). As Jesus died separated from his own people, so must the Christian community remain apart from the religious doctrines of Judaism (11–14). Christ must be the heart and center of the community (15–16).

13:9 *Strange teaching:* this doctrine about *foods* probably refers to the Jewish food laws; in view of v 10, however, the author may be thinking of the Mosaic sacrificial banquets.

13:10 *We have an altar:* this does not refer to the Eucharist, which is never clearly mentioned in Hebrews, but to the sacrifice of Christ.

13:17–25 Recommending obedience to the leaders of the community, the author asks for prayers (17–19). The letter concludes with a blessing (20–21), a final request for the acceptance of its message (22), information regarding Timothy (23), and general greetings (24–25).

12:27 Is 66:22; Mt 24:35; Mk 13:31; Lk 21:33.
12:28 Dn 7:14, 18 / Rom 1:9.
12:29 Dt 4:24; Is 33:14.
13:2 Gn 18:3; 19:2–3; Jgs 6:11–22; Tb 5:4.
13:3 Mt 25:36.
13:4 1 Cor 5:13; Eph 5:5.
13:5 Dt 31:6, 8; Jos 1:5.
13:6 Pss 27:1–3; 118:6.
13:8 Heb 1:12; 7:24; Rv 1:17.
13:9 Rom 14:17; 1 Cor 8:8; Eph 4:14; Col 2:16.
13:11 Ex 29:14; Lv 16:27.
13:12 Mt 21:39; Mk 12:8; Lk 20:15; Jn 19:17.
13:14 Heb 11:10, 14.
13:15 Hos 14:3.
13:16 Phil 4:18.

they keep watch over you and will have to give
an account, that they may fulfill their task with
joy and not with sorrow, for that would be of no
advantage to you.
[18] Pray for us, for we are confident that we have
a clear conscience, wishing to act rightly in every
respect. [19] I especially ask for your prayers that I
may be restored to you very soon.
[20]* † May the God of peace, who brought up
from the dead the great shepherd of the sheep
by the blood of the eternal covenant, Jesus our
Lord, [21] furnish you with all that is good, that you
may do his will. May he carry out in you what is
pleasing to him through Jesus Christ, to whom
be glory forever [and ever]. Amen.
[22] Brothers, I ask you to bear with this message
of encouragement, for I have written to you rather
briefly. [23]* I must let you know that our brother
Timothy has been set free. If he comes soon, I shall
see you together with him. [24] Greetings to all your
leaders and to all the holy ones. Those from Italy
send you greetings. [25]* Grace be with all of you.

† **13:20–21** These verses constitute one of the most beautiful blessings in the New Testament. The resurrection of Jesus is presupposed throughout Hebrews, since it is included in the author's frequently expressed idea of his exaltation, but this is the only place where it is explicitly mentioned.

* **13:20** Is 63:11; Zec 9:11; Jn 10:11; Acts 2:24; Rom 15:33.
13:23 Acts 16:1.
13:25 Ti 3:15.

Have you ever noticed how a kite strains at the string as it soars in the sky? It seems to want to be free of the string that ties it down, free to fly on its own. But if that string does break, the kite flounders and crashes. The kite has the freedom to fly only as long as it's tied to something. That's the way we are under the New Covenant in Christ. We may think we're free to do whatever we want, but if we break from a faithful response to God's love for us, we flounder and crash. The Letter of James provides guidance for living "the perfect law of freedom" (1:25), which leads to real freedom.

At a Glance

I. **Address (1:1).**

II. **The Value of Trials and Temptation (1:2–18).**

III. **Exhortations and Warnings (1:19—5:12).**

IV. **The Power of Prayer (5:13–20).**

Quick Facts

Inspired Author: possibly James the relative of Jesus, but most likely a later admirer of James
Date Written: from AD 57 to 62 if by James, from AD 70 to 110 if by a later admirer
Audience: Christians in Palestine, Syria, or Rome

In Depth

Defining the literary form (structure) of James is a little difficult. It opens like the other letters but lacks the typical closing. In ways, it is similar to the wisdom literature of the Old Testament. It provides practical advice for how wise people ought to live. It is also similar to Greek moral teaching, which used famous people as models for how we ought to live. This has led scholars to think the book might have been written by an educated Jewish Christian, possibly living in Jerusalem. The author could have been an admirer of James, the first leader of the early church in Jerusalem.

The letter addresses several issues in Christian living. It warns that rich people should not discriminate against poor people. It insists that Christians' actions must reflect their beliefs. It cautions against careless speech and a poorly controlled tongue. It encourages believers to patiently endure suffering.

James also addresses a misunderstanding of Paul's teaching that "a person is justified by faith apart from works of the law" (Rom 3:28). Using Abraham and Rahab as examples, the author of James declares, "A person is justified by works and not by faith alone" (Jas 2:24). After all, "faith of itself, if it does not have works, is dead" (2:17). To say you love Jesus, and then do unloving things, makes no sense; it's just plain hypocritical.

But, if we act on God's word and live our faith intensely from the heart, as the Letter of James instructs, we will keep from floundering and be able to soar in the freedom of God's love!

The Letter of James

James

3:5–10

I: Address

1 [1]* † James, a slave of God and of the Lord Jesus
Christ, to the twelve tribes in the dispersion,
greetings.

II: The Value of Trials and Temptation

Perseverance in Trial

[2]* † Consider it all joy, my brothers, when you
encounter various trials, [3]† for you know that the
testing of your faith produces perseverance. [4]And
let perseverance be perfect, so that you may be
perfect and complete, lacking in nothing. [5]* † But
if any of you lacks wisdom, he should ask God
who gives to all generously and ungrudgingly,
and he will be given it. [6]* But he should ask in
faith, not doubting, for the one who doubts is
like a wave of the sea that is driven and tossed
about by the wind. [7]For that person must not
suppose that he will receive anything from the
Lord, [8]since he is a man of two minds, unstable
in all his ways.

[9]* † The brother in lowly circumstances should
take pride in his high standing, [10]* and the rich
one in his lowliness, for he will pass away "like
the flower of the field." [11]For the sun comes up
with its scorching heat and dries up the grass, its
flower droops, and the beauty of its appearance
vanishes. So will the rich person fade away in the
midst of his pursuits.

Temptation

[12]* † Blessed is the man who perseveres in
temptation, for when he has been proved he will
receive the crown of life that he promised to those

1:1 *James, a slave of God and of the Lord Jesus Christ:* a declaration of the writer's authority for instructing the Christian communities; cf Rom 1:1. Regarding the identity of the author, see Introduction. *Dispersion:* see Introduction.

1:2 *Consider it all joy . . . various trials:* a frequent teaching of the New Testament derived from the words and sufferings of Jesus (Mt 5:10–12; Jn 10:11; Acts 5:41).

1:3–8 The sequence of testing, perseverance, and being perfect and complete indicates the manner of attaining spiritual maturity and full preparedness for the coming of Christ (5:7–12; cf 1 Pt 1:6–7; Rom 5:3–5). These steps require wisdom (5).

1:5 *Wisdom:* a gift that God readily grants to all who ask in faith and that sustains the Christian in times of trial. It is a kind of knowledge or understanding not accessible to the unbeliever or those who doubt, which gives the recipient an understanding of the real importance of events. In this way a Christian can deal with adversity with great calm and hope (cf 1 Cor 2:6–12).

1:9–11 Throughout his letter (see 2:5; 4:10, 13–16; 5:1–6), the author reaffirms the teaching of Jesus that worldly prosperity is not necessarily a sign of God's favor but can even be a hindrance to proper humility before God (cf Lk 6:20–25; 12:16–21; 16:19–31).

1:12 *Temptation:* the Greek word used here is the same one used for "trials" in v 2. *The crown of life:* in ancient Palestine, crowns or wreaths of flowers were worn at festive occasions as signs of joy and honor. In the Hellenistic world, wreaths were given as a reward to great statesmen, soldiers, athletes. *Life:* here means eternal life. *He promised:* some manuscripts read "God" or "the Lord," while the best witnesses do not specify the subject of "promised."

1:1 Jn 7:35; 1 Pt 1:1.
1:2 Rom 5:3–5; 1 Pt 1:6; 4:13–16.
1:5 Prv 2:2–6; Wis 9:4, 9–12.
1:6 Mt 7:7; Mk 11:24.
1:9 Jas 2:5.
1:10 Is 40:6–7.
1:12 1 Cor 9:25; 2 Tm 4:8; 1 Pt 5:4; Rv 2:10.

who love him. 13*† No one experiencing tempta-
tion should say, "I am being tempted by God";
for God is not subject to temptation to evil, and
he himself tempts no one. 14 Rather, each person
is tempted when he is lured and enticed by his
own desire. 15 Then desire conceives and brings
forth sin, and when sin reaches maturity it gives
birth to death.

16† Do not be deceived, my beloved brothers:
17† all good giving and every perfect gift is from
above, coming down from the Father of lights,
with whom there is no alteration or shadow
caused by change. 18*† He willed to give us birth
by the word of truth that we may be a kind of
firstfruits of his creatures.

III: Exhortations and Warnings

Doers of the Word

19*† Know this, my dear brothers: everyone
should be quick to hear, slow to speak, slow
to wrath, 20* for the wrath of a man does not
accomplish the righteousness of God. 21* There-
fore, put away all filth and evil excess and hum-
bly welcome the word that has been planted in
you and is able to save your souls.

22* Be doers of the word and not hearers
only, deluding yourselves. 23 For if anyone is
a hearer of the word and not a doer, he is like
a man who looks at his own face in a mirror.
24 He sees himself, then goes off and promptly
forgets what he looked like. 25*† But the one
who peers into the perfect law of freedom and
perseveres, and is not a hearer who forgets but
a doer who acts, such a one shall be blessed in
what he does.

26*† If anyone thinks he is religious and does
not bridle his tongue but deceives his heart,† his
religion is vain. 27*† Religion that is pure and un-
defiled before God and the Father is this: to care
for orphans and widows in their affliction and to
keep oneself unstained by the world.

Pray It!

Meditation on the Walk of Faith

Relax. Clear your mind. Read and reflect on this meditation:

Imagine yourself on your favorite stretch of road. Look back along the road as if it represents your life so far. You have traveled this road all your life to get to where you are standing right now. What obstacles and temptations to your faith have you encountered? Which ones have you stumbled over? Which ones have you overcome?

You see a figure approaching. You strain to see who it is. It gets close enough to recognize. It is Jesus! Jesus sits down with you and asks about the trials you have encountered on your journey. Talk to Jesus about how they have given you the opportunity to grow. Talk to him about the many choices you have made, the good and the bad.

Leave with Jesus to continue forward on the journey. With Jesus, you can joyfully accept the tests of faith that lie ahead, knowing that each is an opportunity to build endurance "so that you may be perfect and complete, lacking in nothing" (Jas 1:4).

▶ **Jas 1:2–18**

JAS

†

1:13–15 It is contrary to what we know of God for God to be the author of human temptation (13). In the commission of a sinful act, one is first beguiled by passion (14), then consent is given, which in turn causes the sinful act. When sin permeates the entire person, it incurs the ultimate penalty of death (15).

1:16–18 The author here stresses that God is the source of all good and of good alone, and the evil of temptation does not come from him.

1:17 *All good giving and every perfect gift* may be a proverb written in hexameter. *Father of lights:* God is here called the Father of the heavenly luminaries, i.e., the stars, sun, and moon that he created (Gn 1:14–18). Unlike orbs moving from nadir to zenith, he never changes or diminishes in brightness.

1:18 Acceptance of the gospel message, *the word of truth,* constitutes new birth (Jn 3:5–6) and makes the recipient the *first-fruits* (i.e., the cultic offering of the earliest grains, symbolizing the beginning of an abundant harvest) of a new creation; cf 1 Cor 15:20; Rom 8:23.

1:19–25 *To be quick to hear* the gospel is to accept it readily and to act in conformity with it, removing from one's soul whatever is opposed to it, so that it may take root and effect salvation (19–21). To listen to the gospel message but not practice it is failure to improve oneself (22–24). Only conformity of life to the perfect law of true freedom brings happiness (25).

1:25 *Peers into the perfect law:* the image of a person doing this is paralleled to that of hearing God's word. The *perfect law* applies the Old Testament description of the Mosaic law to the gospel of Jesus Christ that brings freedom.

1:26–27 A practical application of v 22 is now made.

1:26 For control of the tongue, see the note on 3:1–12.

1:27 In the Old Testament, orphans and widows are classical examples of the defenseless and oppressed.

*

1:13 Sir 15:11–20; 1 Cor 10:13.
1:18 Jn 1:12–13; 1 Pt 1:23.
1:19 Prv 14:17; Sir 5:11.
1:20 Eph 4:26.
1:21 Col 3:8.
1:22 Mt 7:26; Rom 2:13.
1:25 Jas 2:12; Ps 19:8; Rom 8:2.
1:26 Jas 3:2; Ps 34:14.
1:27 Ex 22:21.

Catholic Social Teaching

Playing Favorites

Many of us have had the experience of watching someone else receive special treatment. It doesn't seem fair when a person gets singled out because of his or her looks, money, athletic ability, or some other reason. Too often it makes others feel hurt and diminished. In James 2:1–13, the author clearly spells out where God stands on the issue of favoritism and partiality. God's response is to turn things upside down by raising up the poor and the lowly (see verse 5). The Catholic Church refers to this response as a preferential option or love for the poor, which means always giving priority to the needs of those who are poor and vulnerable when setting policies, providing benefits, and so on.

In our world, there is a big difference between rich and poor, top and bottom, included and excluded. God needs us to respond to this injustice by recognizing that we have a special responsibility to care for those who are struggling the most just to live. If we do not give those living in poverty opportunities to live in justice and equality, and if we do not challenge the people in power to live according to God's justice, who will? And if we don't reach out to those students at school who seem to be the least popular or least favorite, who will?

Jas 2:1–13
Option for the Poor and Vulnerable

JAS

Sin of Partiality

2 [1]† My brothers, show no partiality as you
adhere to the faith in our glorious Lord Jesus
Christ. [2]For if a man with gold rings on his fingers
and in fine clothes comes into your assembly, and
a poor person in shabby clothes also comes in,
[3]and you pay attention to the one wearing the fine
clothes and say, "Sit here, please," while you say
to the poor one, "Stand there," or "Sit at my feet,"
[4]† have you not made distinctions among yourselves and become judges with evil designs?
[5]*† Listen, my beloved brothers. Did not God
choose those who are poor in the world to be rich
in faith and heirs of the kingdom that he promised to those who love him? [6]But you dishonored the poor person. Are not the rich oppressing
you? And do they themselves not haul you off to
court? [7]* Is it not they who blaspheme the noble
name that was invoked over you? [8]*† However,
if you fulfill the royal law according to the scripture, "You shall love your neighbor as yourself,"
you are doing well. [9]* But if you show partiality,
you commit sin, and are convicted by the law as
transgressors. [10]* For whoever keeps the whole
law, but falls short in one particular, has become
guilty in respect to all of it. [11]* For he who said,
"You shall not commit adultery," also said, "You
shall not kill." Even if you do not commit adultery but kill, you have become a transgressor of
the law. [12]*† So speak and so act as people who
will be judged by the law of freedom. [13]* For the
judgment is merciless to one who has not shown
mercy; mercy triumphs over judgment.

Faith and Works

[14]*† What good is it, my brothers, if someone
says he has faith but does not have works? Can

† **2:1–13** In the Christian community there must be no discrimination or favoritism based on status or wealth (2–4; cf Mt 5:3; 11:5; 23:6; 1 Cor 1:27–29). Divine favor rather consists in God's election and promises (5). The rich who oppress the poor blaspheme the name of Christ (6–7). By violating one law of love of neighbor, they offend against the whole law (8–11). On the other hand, conscious awareness of the final judgment helps the faithful to fulfill the whole law (12).

2:4 When Christians show favoritism to the rich they are guilty of the worst kind of prejudice and discrimination. The author says that such Christians set themselves up as judges who judge not by divine law but by the basest, self-serving motives.

2:5 The poor, "God's poor" of the Old Testament, were seen by Jesus as particularly open to God for belief in and reliance on him alone (Lk 6:20). God's law cannot tolerate their oppression in any way (9).

2:8 *Royal:* literally, "kingly"; because the Mosaic law came from God, the universal king. There may be an allusion to Jesus' uses of this commandment in his preaching of the kingdom of God (Mt 22:39; Mk 12:31; Lk 10:27).

2:12–13 The law upon which the last judgment will be based is the law of freedom. As Jesus taught, mercy (which participates in God's own loving mercy) includes forgiveness of those who wrong us (see Mt 6:12, 14–15).

2:14–26 The theme of these verses is the relationship of faith and works (deeds). It has been argued that the teaching here contradicts that of Paul (see especially Rom 4:5–6). The problem can only be understood if the different viewpoints of the two authors are

* **2:5** 1 Cor 1:26–28; Rv 2:9.
* **2:7** 1 Pt 4:4.
* **2:8** Lv 19:18; Mt 22:39; Rom 13:9.
* **2:9** Dt 1:17.
* **2:10** Gal 3:10.
* **2:11** Ex 20:13–14; Dt 5:17–18.
* **2:12** Jas 1:25; Rom 8:2.
* **2:13** Mt 5:7; 6:14–15; 18:32–33.
* **2:14** Mt 25:31–46; Gal 5:6.

that faith save him? 15 If a brother or sister has nothing to wear and has no food for the day, 16* and one of you says to them, "Go in peace, keep warm, and eat well," but you do not give them the necessities of the body, what good is it? 17 So also faith of itself, if it does not have works, is dead.

18 Indeed someone may say, "You have faith and I have works." Demonstrate your faith to me without works, and I will demonstrate my faith to you from my works. 19 You believe that God is one. You do well. Even the demons believe that and tremble. 20 Do you want proof, you ignoramus, that faith without works is useless? 21* Was not Abraham our father justified by works when he offered his son Isaac upon the altar? 22 You see that faith was active along with his works, and faith was completed by the works. 23* Thus the scripture was fulfilled that says, "Abraham believed God, and it was credited to him as righteousness," and he was called "the friend of God." 24 See how a person is justified by works and not by faith alone. 25* And in the same way, was not Rahab the harlot also justified by works when she welcomed the messengers and sent them out by a different route? 26 For just as a body without a spirit is dead, so also faith without works is dead.

Power of the Tongue

3 1† Not many of you should become teachers, my brothers, for you realize that we will be judged more strictly, 2* for we all fall short in many respects. If anyone does not fall short in speech, he is a perfect man, able to bridle his whole body also. 3 If we put bits into the mouths of horses to make them obey us, we also guide their whole bodies. 4 It is the same with ships: even though they are so large and driven by fierce winds, they are steered by a very small rudder wherever the pilot's inclination wishes. 5 In the same way the tongue is a small member and yet has great pretensions.

Consider how small a fire can set a huge forest ablaze. 6 The tongue is also a fire. It exists among our members as a world of malice, defiling the whole body and setting the entire course of our lives on fire, itself set on fire by Gehenna. 7 For every kind of beast and bird, of reptile and sea creature, can be tamed and has been tamed by the human species, 8* but no human being can tame the tongue. It is a restless evil, full of deadly poison. 9 With it we bless the Lord and Father, and with it we curse human beings who are made in the likeness of God. 10 From the same mouth come blessing and cursing. This need not be so, my brothers. 11 Does a spring gush forth from the same opening both pure and brackish water? 12* Can a fig tree, my brothers, produce olives, or a grapevine figs? Neither can salt water yield fresh.

Live It!

Faith and Works

A person who insists that faith alone is necessary for our salvation might think: "I don't have to demonstrate my faith with action at all. I just have to believe in Jesus, and then I can do anything I want." Such an attitude isn't very faithful, mature, or helpful.

Yet a person who insists that particular actions alone are necessary for our salvation might think: "I don't have to really believe in what I'm doing. I'll just go through the motions of faith, and that way I'll play it safe." This attitude is not very faithful, mature, or helpful either.

James is saying, "Show me a person who has real faith, and I will show you a person doing good works."

Faith and works are discussed at length in two letters from Paul: Romans 3:21–31 (see also "The Law, Faith, and Justification," near Rom 3:1–31) and Galatians 2:15—3:14 (see also "Justified in Christ," near Gal 3:1—4:7).

▶ Jas 2:14–26

JAS

† seen. Paul argues against those who claim to participate in God's salvation because of their good deeds as well as because they have committed themselves to trust in God through Jesus Christ (Paul's concept of faith). Paul certainly understands, however, the implications of true faith for a life of love and generosity (see Gal 5:6, 13–15). The author of James is well aware that proper conduct can only come about with an authentic commitment to God in faith (18, 26). Many think he was seeking to correct a misunderstanding of Paul's view.

3:1–12 The use and abuse of the important role of teaching in the church (1) are here related to the good and bad use of the tongue (9–12), the instrument through which teaching was chiefly conveyed (see Sir 5:11—6:1; 28:12–26).

* **2:16** 1 Jn 3:17.
2:21 Gn 22:9–12; Heb 11:17.
2:23 Gn 15:6; Rom 4:3; Gal 3:6 / 2 Chr 20:7; Is 41:8.
2:25 Jos 2:1–21.
3:2 Jas 1:26; Prv 13:3; Sir 28:12–26.
3:8 Ps 140:4.
3:12 Mt 7:16–17.

JAS

Live It!

The Tongue: Friend or Foe?

Sometimes, we are advised to hold it. Other times, we are ordered to bite it. Try as we might to keep this counsel, our tongue often proves to be much stronger than our will to control it.

All of us have said things we have later regretted. Frequently against our better judgment, we find ourselves speaking in ways that hurt or offend others and God. People are injured by what others say to—or about—them far more often than by physical attack. The scars left by hurtful words can last a lifetime, destroying families and ruining friendships.

Have you spoken words that are hurtful to another person, directly or behind the person's back? How might you use your tongue to begin to heal someone's hurts? Apologies, compliments, and affirmations—the tongue can utter these things too! It is a mark of maturity and confidence when we are able to ask forgiveness or affirm others. Christians are called to this kind of courage and maturity.

Use your tongue to speak positively to others today!

► Jas 3:1–12

True Wisdom

[13]* † Who among you is wise and understand-
ing? Let him show his works by a good life in the
humility that comes from wisdom. [14] But if you
have bitter jealousy and selfish ambition in your
hearts, do not boast and be false to the truth.
[15] Wisdom of this kind does not come down
from above but is earthly, unspiritual, demonic.
[16] For where jealousy and selfish ambition exist,
there is disorder and every foul practice. [17]* But
the wisdom from above is first of all pure, then
peaceable, gentle, compliant, full of mercy and
good fruits, without inconstancy or insincerity.
[18]* And the fruit of righteousness is sown in
peace for those who cultivate peace.

Causes of Division

4 [1]* † Where do the wars and where do the con-
flicts among you come from? Is it not from
your passions† that make war within your mem-
bers? [2] You covet but do not possess. You kill and
envy but you cannot obtain; you fight and wage
war. You do not possess because you do not ask.
[3] You ask but do not receive, because you ask
wrongly, to spend it on your passions. [4]* † Adul-
terers! Do you not know that to be a lover of
the world means enmity with God? Therefore,
whoever wants to be a lover of the world makes
himself an enemy of God. [5]† Or do you suppose
that the scripture speaks without meaning when
it says, "The spirit that he has made to dwell in
us tends toward jealousy"? [6]* † But he bestows a
greater grace; therefore, it says:

"God resists the proud,
but gives grace to the humble."

[7]* So submit yourselves to God. Resist the devil,
and he will flee from you. [8]* Draw near to God,
and he will draw near to you. Cleanse your
hands, you sinners, and purify your hearts, you
of two minds. [9] Begin to lament, to mourn, to
weep. Let your laughter be turned into mourning
and your joy into dejection. [10]* Humble your-
selves before the Lord and he will exalt you.

†

3:13–18 This discussion of true wisdom is related to the previous reflection on the role of the teacher as one who is in control of his speech. The qualities of the wise man endowed from above are detailed (17–18; cf Gal 5:22–23), in contrast to the qualities of earthbound wisdom (14–16; cf 2 Cor 12:20).

4:1–12 The concern here is with the origin of conflicts in the Christian community. These are occasioned by love *of the world,* which *means enmity with God* (4). Further, the conflicts are bound up with failure to pray properly (cf Mt 7:7–11; Jn 14:13; 15:7; 16:23), that is, not asking God at all or using God's kindness only for one's pleasure (2–3). In contrast, the proper dispositions are submission to God, repentance, humility, and resistance to evil (7–10).

4:1 *Passions:* the Greek word here (literally, "pleasures") does not indicate that pleasure is evil. Rather, as the text points out (2–3), it is the manner in which one deals with needs and desires that determines good or bad. The motivation for any action can be wrong, especially if one does not pray properly but seeks only selfish enjoyment (3).

4:4 *Adulterers:* a common biblical image for the covenant between God and his people is the marriage bond. In this image, breaking the covenant with God is likened to the unfaithfulness of adultery.

4:5 The meaning of this saying is difficult because the author of James cites, probably from memory, a passage that is not in any extant manuscript of the Bible. Other translations of the text with a completely different meaning are possible: "The Spirit that he (God) made to dwell in us yearns (for us) jealously," or, "He (God) yearns jealously for the spirit that he has made to dwell in us." If this last translation is correct, the author perhaps had in mind an apocryphal religious text that echoes the idea that God is zealous for his creatures; cf Ex 20:5; Dt 4:24; Zec 8:2.

4:6 The point of this whole argument is that God wants the happiness of all, but that selfishness and pride can make that impossible. We must work with him in humility (10).

*

3:13 Eph 4:1–2.
3:17 Jas 1:17; Wis 7:22–23.
3:18 Mt 5:9.
4:1 Rom 7:23; 1 Pt 2:11.
4:4 Mt 6:24; Lk 16:13; Rom 8:7; 1 Jn 2:15–16.
4:6 Jb 22:29; Prv 3:34; Mt 23:12; 1 Pt 5:5.
4:7 1 Pt 5:8–9.
4:8 Zec 1:3; Mal 3:7.
4:10 Jb 5:11; Mt 23:12; Lk 14:11; 18:14; 1 Pt 5:6.

11† Do not speak evil of one another, brothers.
Whoever speaks evil of a brother or judges his
brother speaks evil of the law and judges the law.
If you judge the law, you are not a doer of the law
but a judge. 12* There is one lawgiver and judge
who is able to save or to destroy. Who then are
you to judge your neighbor?

"Draw near to God, and he will draw near to you."
(Jas 4:8)

Warning against Presumption

13† Come now, you who say, "Today or tomorrow
we shall go into such and such a town,
spend a year there doing business, and make a
profit"— 14*† you have no idea what your life
will be like tomorrow. You are a puff of smoke
that appears briefly and then disappears. 15† Instead
you should say, "If the Lord wills it, we
shall live to do this or that." 16 But now you are
boasting in your arrogance. All such boasting is
evil. 17*† So for one who knows the right thing
to do and does not do it, it is a sin.

Warning to the Rich

5 1*† Come now, you rich, weep and wail over
your impending miseries. 2* Your wealth has
rotted away, your clothes have become moth-
eaten, 3* your gold and silver have corroded, and
that corrosion will be a testimony against you; it
will devour your flesh like a fire. You have stored
up treasure for the last days. 4* Behold, the wages
you withheld from the workers who harvested
your fields are crying aloud, and the cries of the
harvesters have reached the ears of the Lord of
hosts. 5* You have lived on earth in luxury and
pleasure; you have fattened your hearts for the
day of slaughter. 6*† You have condemned; you
have murdered the righteous one; he offers you
no resistance.

Live It!

Justice for Those Who Are Poor

Warnings to the rich are common in the Bible and should be of concern for Christians living in a wealthy nation like the United States. Here are two tough questions to consider: First, in what do we put our trust—the comfort and pleasure that can be had in wealth and material possessions, or God? And second, how does our lifestyle—including the way we spend money, the choices we make about our future work, and the way we use our time—affect the poor people of this world?

God's justice requires that Christians care about the abuse of poor people for the benefit of rich people. God does not want us to become paralyzed with guilt because we are wealthy compared with the poorest of the earth. But the Scriptures remind us that the life choices we make matter, and that those choices may either contribute to a more just world, or support a status quo that keeps rich people comfortable and poor people down. To make good life choices, we must educate ourselves about the situations that cause poverty, examine how our own lifestyle or beliefs might unintentionally contribute to the misery of those who are poor, and actively work to alleviate the suffering of others. That is hard work—perhaps work we would rather avoid. But ignoring the plight of poor people is exactly what the Scriptures warn us against! Money in itself is not evil; it's what we do (or don't do) with it that can be sinful.

▶ Jas 5:1–6

4:11 Slander of a fellow Christian does not break just one commandment but makes mockery of the authority of law in general and therefore of God.

4:13–17 The uncertainty of life (14), its complete dependence on God, and the necessity of submitting to God's will (15) all help one know and do what is right (17). To disregard this is to live in pride and arrogance (16); failure to do what is right is a sin (17).

4:14 Some important Greek manuscripts here have, "You who have no idea what tomorrow will bring. Why, what is your life?"

4:15 *If the Lord wills it:* often in piety referred to as the *"conditio Jacobaea,"* the condition James says we should employ to qualify all our plans.

4:17 *It is a sin:* those who live arrogantly, forgetting the contingency of life and our dependence on God (13–16), are guilty of sin.

5:1–6 Continuing with the theme of the transitory character of life on earth, the author points out the impending ruin of the godless. He denounces the unjust rich, whose victims cry to heaven for judgment on their exploiters (4–6). The decay and corrosion of the costly garments and metals, which symbolize wealth, prove them worthless and portend the destruction of their possessors (2–3).

5:6 The author does not have in mind any specific crime in his readers' communities but rather echoes the Old Testament theme of the harsh oppression of the righteous poor (see Prv 1:11; Wis 2:10, 12, 20).

4:12 Mt 7:1; Rom 2:1; 14:4.
4:14 Prv 27:1 / Ps 39:6–7.
4:17 Lk 12:47.
5:1 Lk 6:24.
5:2 Mt 6:19.
5:3 Ps 21:10; Prv 11:4; Jdt 16:17.
5:4 Lv 19:13; Dt 24:14–15; Mal 3:5.
5:5 Jer 12:3; Lk 16:19–25.
5:6 Wis 2:10–20.

Catholic Connection

Anointing of the Sick

Have you or a loved one ever been seriously ill? It can be a scary time. Yet, it is in the midst of fear and suffering that Jesus' followers are called to bring compassion and healing. In the Letter of James, the author talks about how Christians are called to care for those who are sick by praying over them and anointing them with oil. As a result, the sick will be helped and strengthened by Christ and have their sins forgiven.

Caring for those who are ill, as expressed in the Letter of James, is still practiced in the Catholic Church today through the sacrament of the Anointing of the Sick. Through prayers and anointing with sacred oil, those who are seriously ill are entrusted to God's merciful love and the physical and spiritual struggles that their illness brings are addressed. Physically, the sick are strengthened by the sacrament and, if God wills, find healing. Spiritually, the sick receive special graces from the Holy Spirit. These graces help the sick unite their own sufferings with those of Christ, free them from their sins, and give them the courage they need to face the challenges and fear illness brings.

The sacrament may be celebrated within Mass or outside of Mass, with a large group of those who are ill or with an individual sick person. No matter how it is celebrated, it is always administered by a priest or bishop and has the same three basic parts. During the first part, **the prayer of faith**, the priest, family, friends, and others from the community who are gathered confidently ask God to help those who are sick. The second part is the **laying on of hands**, where the priest, like Jesus often did, lays his hands upon those who are sick. Through this gesture, the priest shows that the prayers the community is offering are directed toward the sick. It is a sign of blessing as the community prays for God's healing grace so those who are sick can be healed and strengthened. The laying on of hands is also a plea for the Holy Spirit to descend upon those who are ill. The third part is the **anointing with oil**. The sacred oil signifies the presence of the Holy Spirit, whose power can bring strength and healing both physically and spiritually.

So, if you or a loved one is faced with a serious illness, remember that the Church is there to relieve your fears and suffering through the sacrament of the Anointing of the Sick.

► **Jas 5:13–15**

Catechism, nos. 1499–1532

Patience and Oaths

[7]† Be patient, therefore, brothers, until the
coming of the Lord. See how the farmer waits for
the precious fruit of the earth, being patient with
it until it receives the early and the late rains.†
[8]* You too must be patient. Make your hearts
firm, because the coming of the Lord is at hand.
[9] Do not complain, brothers, about one another,
that you may not be judged. Behold, the Judge is
standing before the gates. [10] Take as an example
of hardship and patience, brothers, the prophets
who spoke in the name of the Lord. [11]* Indeed
we call blessed those who have persevered. You
have heard of the perseverance of Job, and you
have seen the purpose of the Lord, because "the
Lord is compassionate and merciful."
[12]*† But above all, my brothers, do not swear,
either by heaven or by earth or with any other oath,
but let your "Yes" mean "Yes" and your "No" mean
"No," that you may not incur condemnation.

IV: The Power of Prayer

Anointing of the Sick

[13] Is anyone among you suffering? He should
pray. Is anyone in good spirits? He should
sing praise. [14]*† Is anyone among you sick? He
should summon the presbyters of the church,
and they should pray over him and anoint [him]
with oil in the name of the Lord, [15]† and the
prayer of faith will save the sick person, and the
Lord will raise him up. If he has committed any
sins, he will be forgiven.

Confession and Intercession

[16] Therefore, confess your sins to one another
and pray for one another, that you may be healed.
The fervent prayer of a righteous person is very
powerful. [17]* Elijah was a human being like us;
yet he prayed earnestly that it might not rain, and
for three years and six months it did not rain upon
the land. [18]* Then he prayed again, and the sky
gave rain and the earth produced its fruit.

Pray It!

The Making of a Prayer

Have you ever been in a prayer rut? It happens when you get stuck on saying the same prayer every time, no matter what the situation. It becomes a habit, and like all habits, after a while, you may stop thinking about why you are even doing it.

James offers some advice in 5:13–18 that can help you to get out of such a rut and back on track with your prayer life. This passage says to think about the needs and feelings you have at any given moment of the day and turn them into a prayer. Feeling down? Tell God about it. Just had the best day of your life? Share it with God. Want to get even with a person who hurt you? Let God know about it. In fact, there is nothing you can't tell God—even if you are mad and God is the one you are mad at.

Get in touch with what is occupying your mind the most right now—good, bad, or ordinary—and turn it into a prayer by sharing it with the God who is always ready to hear what you have to say.

▶ **Jas 5:13–18**

Conversion of Sinners

[19]* My brothers, if anyone among you should
stray from the truth and someone bring him
back, [20]*† he should know that whoever brings
back a sinner from the error of his way will save
his soul from death and will cover a multitude
of sins.

---

† **5:7–11** Those oppressed by the unjust rich are reminded of the need for patience, both in bearing the sufferings of human life (9) and in their expectation of the coming of the Lord. It is then that they will receive their reward (7–8, 10–11; cf Heb 10:25; 1 Jn 2:18).

5:7 *The early and the late rains:* an expression related to the agricultural season in ancient Palestine (see Dt 11:14; Jer 5:24; Jl 2:23).

5:12 This is the threat of condemnation for the abuse of swearing oaths (cf Mt 5:33–37). *By heaven or by earth:* these words were substitutes for the original form of an oath, to circumvent its binding force and to avoid pronouncing the holy name of God (see Ex 22:10).

5:14 In case of sickness a Christian should ask for the presbyters of the church, i.e., those who have authority in the church (cf Acts 15:2, 22–23; 1 Tm 5:17; Ti 1:5). They are to pray over the person and anoint with oil; oil was used for medicinal purposes in the ancient world (see Is 1:6; Lk 10:34). In Mk 6:13, the Twelve anoint the sick with oil on their missionary journey. *In the name of the Lord:* by the power of Jesus Christ.

5:15 The results of the prayer and anointing are physical health and forgiveness of sins. The Roman Catholic Church (Council of Trent, Session 14) declared that this anointing of the sick is a sacrament "instituted by Christ and promulgated by blessed James the apostle."

5:20 When a Christian is instrumental in the conversion of a sinner, the result is forgiveness of sins and a reinstatement of the sinner to the life of grace.

---

* **5:8** Lk 21:19; Heb 10:36 / Heb 10:25; 1 Pt 4:7.
5:11 Ex 34:6; Ps 103:8.
5:12 Mt 5:34–37.
5:14 Mk 6:13.
5:17 1 Kgs 17:1; Lk 4:25.
5:18 1 Kgs 18:45.
5:19 Mt 18:15; Gal 6:1.
5:20 Prv 10:12; 1 Pt 4:8.

JAS

The First Letter of Peter

Close friends refuse to speak to you after you challenge them about shoplifting. Students make fun of classmates who are trying to start a prayer group before school. Citizens break windows in the homes of Christian leaders who have spoken out publicly against racist attitudes. It's enough to make some Christians ask, Is living our faith worth this persecution and separation? This is a major concern addressed by the First Letter of Peter.

At a Glance

Quick Facts

Inspired Author: possibly Peter, but most likely a later disciple of Peter
Date Written: from AD 60 to 63 if by Peter, from AD 70 to 90 if by a later disciple
Audience: a Gentile (non-Jewish) Christian community

In Depth

The First Letter of Peter was written to a Christian community that was alienated and persecuted because of its Christian lifestyle. Its members were ridiculed, treated as evildoers, and insulted by unbelieving neighbors who did not understand their faith or their moral code of behavior. The author—who may have been Peter but was more likely a later disciple of his—wants to console them and help them make sense of what they're going through.

The author of the First Letter of Peter says that Christ suffered, and therefore we should expect to suffer too. The writer also says that suffering purifies our faith and makes it more genuine (see 1 Pt 1:7). When we suffer, we are united with all the world's people who are suffering (see 5:9). And no matter how great our suffering is, we should be hopeful, and we should be willing to witness to our hope. Then our persecutors will be ashamed and will repent of their wrongdoing (see 3:14–16). We cannot avoid suffering, but when we follow in the footsteps of Jesus, we can make it result in something good.

Despite all this attention to suffering, First Peter is a hope-filled letter. It offers constant reminders of the wonderful things God has done—and will do—for us. When you are going through a hard time, turn to this letter for hope and encouragement. "The God of all grace who called you to his eternal glory through Christ [Jesus] will himself restore, confirm, strengthen, and establish you after you have suffered a little" (5:10).

1 Peter

2:25

I: Address

Greeting

1 1*† Peter, an apostle of Jesus Christ, to the cho-
sen sojourners of the dispersion† in Pontus,
Galatia, Cappadocia, Asia, and Bithynia, 2* in the
foreknowledge of God the Father, through sanc-
tification by the Spirit, for obedience and sprin-
kling with the blood of Jesus Christ: may grace
and peace be yours in abundance.

II: The Gift and Call of God in Baptism

Blessing

3*† Blessed be the God and Father of our Lord
Jesus Christ, who in his great mercy gave us a new
birth to a living hope through the resurrection of
Jesus Christ from the dead, 4* to an inheritance
that is imperishable, undefiled, and unfading,
kept in heaven for you 5 who by the power of
God are safeguarded through faith, to a salva-
tion that is ready to be revealed in the final time.
6*† In this you rejoice, although now for a little
while you may have to suffer through various
trials, 7* so that the genuineness of your faith,
more precious than gold that is perishable even
though tested by fire, may prove to be for praise,
glory, and honor at the revelation of Jesus Christ.
8* Although you have not seen him you love him;
even though you do not see him now yet believe
in him, you rejoice with an indescribable and glo-
rious joy, 9 as you attain the goal of [your] faith,
the salvation of your souls.
10† Concerning this salvation, prophets who
prophesied about the grace that was to be yours
searched and investigated it, 11* investigating the
time and circumstances that the Spirit of Christ
within them indicated when it testified in advance

---

†

1:1–2 The introductory formula names *Peter* as the writer (but see Introduction). In his comments to the presbyters (5:1), the author calls himself a "fellow presbyter." He addresses himself to the Gentile converts of Asia Minor. Their privileged status as a *chosen* and sanctified people makes them worthy of God's *grace* and *peace*. In contrast is their actual existence as aliens and *sojourners,* scattered among pagans, far from their true country.

1:1 *Dispersion:* literally, *diaspora;* see Jas 1:1 and Introduction to that letter. *Pontus . . . Bithynia:* five provinces in Asia Minor, listed in clockwise order from the north, perhaps in the sequence in which a messenger might deliver the letter.

1:3–5 A prayer of praise and thanksgiving to God who bestows the gift of new life and hope in baptism (*new birth,* 3) *through the resurrection of Jesus Christ from the dead.* The new birth is a sign of an *imperishable inheritance* (4), of *salvation* that is still in the future (*to be revealed in the final time,* 5).

1:6–9 As the glory of Christ's resurrection was preceded by his sufferings and death, the new life of faith that it bestows is to be subjected to many *trials* (6) while achieving its goal: the glory of the fullness of *salvation* (9) at the coming of Christ (7).

1:10–12 The *Spirit of Christ* (11) is here shown to have been present in the prophets, moving them to search, investigate, and prophesy about the *grace* of *salvation* that was to come (10), and in the apostles impelling them to preach the fulfillment of salvation in the message of Christ's sufferings and glory (12).

---

*

1:1 Jas 1:1.
1:2 Rom 8:29.
1:3 Ti 3:5.
1:4 Mt 6:19–20.
1:6 Jas 1:2–3.
1:7 1 Cor 3:13.
1:8 2 Cor 5:6–7.
1:11 Is 52:13—53:12; Dn 9:24.

Cultural Connection

Saint Lucy

December 13 marks the feast day of Saint Lucy. Little is known about Saint Lucy except that she was martyred in Sicily early in the fourth century.

In Scandinavia, however, Saint Lucy is a very important part of the Christmas celebration. By tradition, the feast of Santa Lucia marks the longest night of the year. And keep in mind that winter nights are very long there because of the northern location.

The tradition goes that the oldest daughter in each home dresses in white with a red ribbon tied around her waist and wears on her head a wreath with candles. She then rises early in the morning to serve the family hot chocolate and cinnamon rolls. This is done in commemoration of the legend that Saint Lucy brought food and water to the early Christians who were hiding from their Roman persecutors. Despite the risk of suffering and persecution, Lucy was committed to living her faith by serving others.

This Scandinavian tradition is a beautiful reminder of how, even in the midst of darkness, Christians can bring the light of hope and nourishment to one another. To whom can you bring the light of hope today?

▶ 1 Pt 1:3–9

to the sufferings destined for Christ and the glories to follow them. 12 It was revealed to them that they were serving not themselves but you with regard to the things that have now been announced to you by those who preached the good news to you [through] the holy Spirit sent from heaven, things into which angels longed to look.

Obedience

13† Therefore, gird up the loins of your mind,† live soberly, and set your hopes completely on the grace to be brought to you at the revelation of Jesus Christ. 14† Like obedient children, do not act in compliance with the desires of your former ignorance 15* but, as he who called you is holy, be holy yourselves in every aspect of your conduct, 16* for it is written, "Be holy because I [am] holy."

Reverence

17* Now if you invoke as Father him who judges impartially according to each one's works, conduct yourselves with reverence during the time of your sojourning, 18* realizing that you were ransomed from your futile conduct, handed on by your ancestors, not with perishable things like silver or gold 19*† but with the precious blood of Christ as of a spotless unblemished lamb. 20 He was known before the foundation of the world but revealed in the final time for you, 21 who through him believe in God who raised him from the dead and gave him glory, so that your faith and hope are in God.

Mutual Love

22*† Since you have purified yourselves by obedience to the truth for sincere mutual love, love one another intensely from a [pure] heart. 23*† You have been born anew, not from perishable but from imperishable seed, through the living and abiding word of God, 24* for:

"All flesh is like grass,
and all its glory like the flower of the field;
the grass withers,
and the flower wilts;

†

1:13–25 These verses are concerned with the call of God's people to holiness and to mutual love by reason of their redemption through the blood of Christ (18–21).

1:13 *Gird up the loins of your mind:* a figure reminiscent of the rite of Passover when the Israelites were in flight from their oppressors (Ex 12:11), and also suggesting the vigilance of the Christian people in expectation of the parousia of Christ (Lk 12:35).

1:14–16 The *ignorance* here referred to (14) was their former lack of knowledge of God, leading inevitably to godless conduct. Holiness (15–16), on the contrary, is the result of their call to the knowledge and love of God.

1:19 Christians have received the redemption prophesied by Isaiah (52:3), through the blood (Jewish symbol of life) of the spotless lamb (Is 53:7, 10; Jn 1:29; Rom 3:24–25; cf 1 Cor 6:20).

1:22–25 The new birth of Christians (23) derives from Christ, the *imperishable seed* or sowing that produces a new and lasting existence in those who accept the gospel (24–25), with the consequent duty of loving *one another* (22).

1:23 *The living and abiding word of God:* or, "the word of the living and abiding God."

*

1:15 Mt 5:48; 1 Jn 3:3.
1:16 Lv 11:44; 19:2.
1:17 1 Pt 2:11.
1:18 Is 52:3; 1 Cor 6:20.
1:19 Ex 12:5; Jn 1:29; Heb 9:14.
1:22 Rom 12:10.
1:23 1 Jn 3:9.
1:24 Is 40:6–8.

25 but the word of the Lord remains forever."
This is the word that has been proclaimed to
you.

God's House and People

2 1*† Rid yourselves of all malice and all deceit,
insincerity, envy, and all slander; 2 like new-
born infants, long for pure spiritual milk so that
through it you may grow into salvation, 3*† for
you have tasted that the Lord is good. 4*† Come
to him, a living stone, rejected by human beings
but chosen and precious in the sight of God,
5*† and, like living stones, let yourselves be built
into a spiritual house to be a holy priesthood to
offer spiritual sacrifices acceptable to God through
Jesus Christ. 6* For it says in scripture:

"Behold, I am laying a stone in Zion,
a cornerstone, chosen and precious,
and whoever believes in it shall not be put to
shame."

7* Therefore, its value is for you who have faith,
but for those without faith:

"The stone which the builders rejected
has become the cornerstone,"

8* and

"A stone that will make people stumble,
and a rock that will make them fall."

They stumble by disobeying the word, as is their
destiny.
9*† But you are "a chosen race, a royal priest-
hood, a holy nation, a people of his own, so that
you may announce the praises" of him who called
you out of darkness into his wonderful light.

Pray It!

Live the Belief

Holy God,
You invite me to live the Gospel message,
not just hear and accept it. It is not enough
to say I believe. I am called to live that belief.
I want to lovingly serve you, God, and all my
brothers and sisters.
I want to seek knowledge of your word and
follow it faithfully.
I want to exercise self-control and avoid
temptations.
I want to build endurance to stand firm against
life's trials.
I want to value truth and goodness.
Provide me with the fruits of your Spirit
to sustain me for my journey, as
I work to imitate your Son, Jesus
Christ. Amen.

▶ 1 Pt 1:13–25

10* Once you were "no people"
but now you are God's people;
you "had not received mercy"
but now you have received mercy.

III: The Christian in a Hostile World

Christian Examples

11*† Beloved, I urge you as aliens and sojourn-
ers to keep away from worldly desires that wage

1 PT

† **2:1–3** Growth toward salvation is seen here as two steps: first, stripping away all that is contrary to the new life in Christ; second, the nourishment *(pure spiritual milk)* that the newly baptized have received.

2:3 *Tasted that the Lord is good:* cf Ps 34:9.

2:4–8 Christ is the cornerstone (cf Is 28:16) that is the foundation of the spiritual edifice of the Christian community (5). To unbelievers, Christ is an obstacle and a stumbling block on which they are destined to fall (8); cf Rom 11:11.

2:5 *Let yourselves be built:* the form of the Greek word could also be indicative passive, "you are being built" (cf 9).

2:9–10 The prerogatives of ancient Israel mentioned here are now more fully and fittingly applied to the Christian people: "a chosen race" (cf Is 43:20–21) indicates their divine election (Eph 1:4–6); "a royal priesthood" (cf Ex 19:6) to serve and worship God in Christ, thus continuing the priestly functions of his life, passion, and resurrection; "a holy nation" (Ex 19:6) reserved for God, a people he claims for his own (cf Mal 3:17) in virtue of their baptism into his death and resurrection. This transcends all natural and national divisions and unites the people into one community to glorify the one who led them from the darkness of paganism to the light of faith in Christ. From being "no people" deprived of all mercy, they have become the very people of God, the chosen recipients of his mercy (cf Hos 1:9; 2:25).

2:11—3:12 After explaining the doctrinal basis for the Christian community, the author makes practical applications in terms of the virtues that should prevail in all the social relationships of the members of the community: good example to Gentile neighbors (2:11–12); respect for human authority (2:13–17); obedience, patience, and endurance of hardship in domestic relations (2:18–25); Christian behavior of husbands and wives (3:1–7); mutual charity (3:8–12).

2:11 *Aliens and sojourners:* no longer signifying absence from one's native land (Gn 23:4), this image denotes rather their estrangement from the world during their earthly pilgrimage (see also 1:1, 17).

* **2:1–2** Jas 1:21.
2:3 Ps 34:9.
2:4 Ps 118:22; Mt 21:42; Acts 4:11.
2:5 Eph 2:21–22.
2:6 Is 28:16.
2:7 Ps 118:22; Mt 21:42; Lk 20:17; Acts 4:11.
2:8 Is 8:14; Rom 9:33.
2:9 Ex 19:6; Is 61:6; Rv 1:6; 20:6.
2:10 Hos 1:9; 2:25 / Hos 1:6.
2:11 Gal 5:24.

war against the soul. 12 Maintain good conduct
among the Gentiles, so that if they speak of you
as evildoers, they may observe your good works
and glorify God on the day of visitation.

"You are 'a chosen race, a royal priesthood, a holy nation, a people of his own.' "
(1 Pt 2:9)

Christian Citizens

13*† Be subject to every human institution for
the Lord's sake, whether it be to the king as su-
preme 14 or to governors as sent by him for the
punishment of evildoers and the approval of
those who do good. 15 For it is the will of God
that by doing good you may silence the igno-
rance of foolish people. 16* Be free, yet without
using freedom as a pretext for evil, but as slaves
of God. 17* Give honor to all, love the commu-
nity, fear God, honor the king.

Christian Slaves

18*† Slaves, be subject to your masters with all
reverence, not only to those who are good and
equitable but also to those who are perverse.
19 For whenever anyone bears the pain of unjust
suffering because of consciousness of God, that
is a grace. 20 But what credit is there if you are
patient when beaten for doing wrong? But if you
are patient when you suffer for doing what is
good, this is a grace before God. 21*† For to this
you have been called, because Christ also suf-
fered for you, leaving you an example that you
should follow in his footsteps.

22*† "He committed no sin,
and no deceit was found in his mouth."
23* When he was insulted, he returned no insult;
when he suffered, he did not threaten; instead,

†

2:13–17 True Christian freedom is the result of being servants of God (16; see the note on 2:18–23). It includes reverence for God, esteem for every individual, and committed love for fellow Christians (17). Although persecution may threaten, subjection to human government is urged (13, 17) and concern for the impact of Christians' conduct on those who are not Christians (12, 15).

2:18–21 Most of the labor in the commercial cities of first-century Asia Minor was performed by a working class of slaves. The sense of freedom contained in the gospel undoubtedly caused great tension among Christian slaves: witness the special advice given concerning them here and in 1 Cor 7:21–24; Eph 6:5–8; Col 3:22–25; Philemon. The point made here does not have so much to do with the institution of slavery, which the author does not challenge, but with the nonviolent reaction (20) of slaves to unjust treatment. Their patient suffering is compared to that of Jesus (21), which won righteousness for all humanity.

2:21 *Suffered:* some ancient manuscripts and versions read "died" (cf 3:18).

2:22–25 After the quotation of Is 53:9b, the passage describes Jesus' passion with phrases concerning the Suffering Servant from Is 53:4–12, perhaps as employed in an early Christian confession of faith; cf 1:18–21 and 3:18–22.

*

2:13 Rom 13:1–7.
2:16 Gal 5:13.
2:17 Prv 24:21; Mt 22:21.
2:18 Eph 6:5.
2:21 Mt 16:24.
2:22 Is 53:9.
2:23 Mt 5:39.

Did You Know?

The Priesthood of the Faithful

In the New Testament, the only person, other than the Jewish priests, who is actually called a priest is Jesus. In the Letter to the Hebrews, the efficacy, or effectiveness, of Jesus as High Priest is proclaimed—a new priesthood has been born in Christ, one that surpasses the priesthood of the Old Testament.

Did you know that every baptized Christian shares in Christ's priesthood as well? Although it is different from hierarchical or ordained priesthood, the priesthood of each baptized person is recognized in their participating in the mission of Christ. Every Christian is to offer her or his life as a living sacrifice and to intercede on behalf of the Church and the world with the Father.

The priesthood of the faithful is part of our baptismal responsibility to proclaim what God has done for his people and to live a life consecrated by faith and hope in Christ crucified and risen. Because we share in the priesthood of the Son through Baptism, we have access to the divine through him. We are consecrated, put aside for the work of salvation.

We live this priesthood by offering ourselves to God. When we do so, we align ourselves to the way of Christ and live as lights for the world. We live for others and thus become instruments in the hand of God. Remember the words of 1 Peter 2:9: "You are 'a chosen race, a royal priesthood, a holy nation, a people of [God's] own.' "

▶ 1 Pt 2:1–10

he handed himself over to the one who judges
justly. 24* He himself bore our sins in his body
upon the cross, so that, free from sin, we might
live for righteousness. By his wounds you have
been healed. 25*† For you had gone astray like
sheep, but you have now returned to the shep-
herd and guardian of your souls.

Christian Spouses

3 1† Likewise, you wives should be subordinate
to your husbands so that, even if some dis-
obey the word, they may be won over without
a word by their wives' conduct 2* when they ob-
serve your reverent and chaste behavior. 3* Your
adornment should not be an external one: braid-
ing the hair, wearing gold jewelry, or dressing in
fine clothes, 4 but rather the hidden character of
the heart, expressed in the imperishable beauty
of a gentle and calm disposition, which is pre-
cious in the sight of God. 5 For this is also how
the holy women who hoped in God once used to
adorn themselves and were subordinate to their
husbands; 6 thus Sarah obeyed Abraham, calling
him "lord." You are her children when you do
what is good and fear no intimidation.

7*† Likewise, you husbands should live with
your wives in understanding, showing honor to
the weaker female sex, since we are joint heirs of
the gift of life, so that your prayers may not be
hindered.

Christian Conduct

8† Finally, all of you, be of one mind, sympa-
thetic, loving toward one another, compassionate,
humble. 9* Do not return evil for evil, or insult
for insult; but, on the contrary, a blessing, be-
cause to this you were called, that you might
inherit a blessing. 10* For:

"Whoever would love life
  and see good days
must keep the tongue from evil
  and the lips from speaking deceit,
11 must turn from evil and do good,
  seek peace and follow after it.
12 For the eyes of the Lord are on the righteous
  and his ears turned to their prayer,
but the face of the Lord is against evildoers."

Pray It!

Part of the Family

All of us come from and belong to a family. Some families are large and some small, some have two parents and others one, and some include aunts, uncles, or grandparents. Every family is unique.

Christians belong to a family that extends well beyond the relationships of blood or adoption. As followers of Christ, they make up a "royal priesthood" and a "holy nation," and are called "a people of [God's] own" (1 Pt 2:9). That is pretty lofty language! What does it mean?

First, it means that our faith is not just between us and God but is shared with others. Yes, there is something personal about our relationship with the Lord, but in addition, we are called by God into a community of disciples who share a common faith. Second, God has chosen us to live together in such a way that others who see our example will see something so good that they want to be a part of it.

In your prayer, reflect or journal on the following questions:

- How connected do you feel to the Christian family?
- What kind of support would you like to receive from other believers? What kind of support can you give?

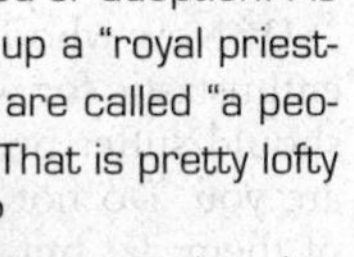

▶ 1 Pt 2:9–17

† **2:25** *The shepherd and guardian of your souls:* the familiar shepherd and flock figures express the care, vigilance, and love of God for his people in the Old Testament (Ps 23; Is 40:11; Jer 23:4–5; Ez 34:11–16) and of Jesus for all humanity in the New Testament (Mt 18:10–14; Lk 15:4–7; Jn 10:1–16; Heb 13:20).

3:1–6 The typical marital virtues of women of the ancient world, obedience, reverence, and chastity (1–2), are outlined here by the author, who gives them an entirely new motivation: Christian wives are to be virtuous so that they may be instrumental in the conversion of their husbands. In imitation of *holy women* in the past (5) they are to cultivate the interior life (4) instead of excessive concern with their appearance (3).

3:7 Husbands who do not respect their wives will have as little success in prayer as those who, according to Paul, have no love: their prayers will be "a resounding gong or a clashing cymbal" (1 Cor 13:1). Consideration for others is shown as a prerequisite for effective prayer also in Mt 5:23–24; 1 Cor 11:20–22; Jas 4:3. After all, whatever the social position of women in the world and in the family, they are equal recipients of the gift of God's salvation. Paul is very clear on this point, too (see 1 Cor 11:11–12; Gal 3:28).

3:8–12 For the proper ordering of Christian life in its various aspects as described in 2:11—3:9, there is promised the blessing expressed in Ps 34:13–17. In the Old Testament this refers to longevity and prosperity; here, it also refers to eternal life.

* **2:24** Is 53:4, 12/ Is 53:5.
2:25 Is 53:6.
3:2 1 Cor 7:12–16; Eph 5:22–24; Col 3:18; 1 Tm 2:9–15.
3:3 1 Tm 2:9–10.
3:7 Eph 5:25–33; Col 3:19.
3:9 Mt 5:44; Lk 6:28; Rom 12:14.
3:10–12 Ps 34:13–17.

Cultural Connection

Living Gospel Values Even If It Demands Suffering

Many Hispanic teenagers and young adults in the United States send money to parents in Latin America. Others work to sustain the education of younger brothers and sisters here. Many times they are criticized because they are unable to continue their own studies and advance in society.

Other young people, of any culture, also suffer for living the Gospel. Those who want to leave a gang are harassed by gang members. Young women and men who want to maintain their virginity are made fun of. Young people who start participating in church programs are not understood by their friends. The commitment of young leaders sometimes is misinterpreted by their parents as a way of escaping their duties at home.

These behaviors cause suffering because Gospel values are conflicting with the mainstream culture within our society. In today's First World, particularly in the United States, blending into the surrounding society is pushed by the media and is almost an ideal set by society.

- How does a true Christian lifestyle cause conflict with mainstream culture within our society? How can young Hispanics keep their values of love, generosity, and solidarity with their families while continuing their own personal development?
- Think of Peter's advice to the early Christian communities. Remember Jesus' suffering, and offer yours together with his so that you and all young people may share Christ's new life.

▶ 1 Pt 3:13–22

Christian Suffering

13† Now who is going to harm you if you are enthusiastic for what is good? 14 But even if you should suffer because of righteousness, blessed are you. Do not be afraid or terrified with fear of them, 15* but sanctify Christ as Lord in your hearts. Always be ready to give an explanation to anyone who asks you for a reason for your hope, 16 but do it with gentleness and reverence, keeping your conscience clear, so that, when you are maligned, those who defame your good conduct in Christ may themselves be put to shame. 17 For it is better to suffer for doing good, if that be the will of God, than for doing evil.

18*† For Christ also suffered for sins once, the righteous for the sake of the unrighteous, that he might lead you to God. Put to death in the flesh, he was brought to life in the spirit. 19† In it he also went to preach to the spirits in prison, 20* who had once been disobedient while God patiently waited in the days of Noah during the building of the ark, in which a few persons, eight in all, were saved through water. 21*† This prefigured baptism, which saves you now. It is not a removal of dirt from the body but an appeal to God for a clear conscience, through the resurrection of Jesus Christ, 22* who has gone into heaven and is at the right hand of God, with angels, authorities, and powers subject to him.

Christian Restraint

4 1† Therefore, since Christ suffered in the flesh, arm yourselves also with the same

---

3:13–22 This exposition, centering on v 17, runs as follows: by his suffering and death Christ the righteous one saved the unrighteous (18); by his resurrection he received new life in the spirit, which he communicates to believers through the baptismal bath that cleanses their consciences from sin. As Noah's family was saved *through water,* so Christians are saved through the waters of baptism (19–22). Hence they need not share the fear of sinners; they should rather rejoice in suffering because of their hope in Christ. Thus their innocence disappoints their accusers (13–16; cf Mt 10:28; Rom 8:35–39).

3:18 *Suffered:* very many ancient manuscripts and versions read "died." *Put to death in the flesh:* affirms that Jesus truly died as a human being. *Brought to life in the spirit:* that is, in the new and transformed existence freed from the limitations and weaknesses of natural human life (cf 1 Cor 15:45).

3:19 *The spirits in prison:* it is not clear just who these spirits are. They may be the spirits of the sinners who died in the flood, or angelic powers, hostile to God, who have been overcome by Christ (cf 22; Gn 6:4; Enoch 6–36, especially 21:6; 2 Enoch 7:1–5).

3:21 *Appeal to God:* this could also be translated "pledge," that is, a promise on the part of Christians to live with a good conscience before God, or a pledge from God of forgiveness and therefore a good conscience for us.

4:1–6 Willingness to suffer with Christ equips the Christian with the power to conquer sin (1). Christ is here portrayed as the judge to whom those guilty of pagan vices must render an account (5; cf Jn 5:22–27; Acts 10:42; 2 Tm 4:1).

3:15 Is 8:12.
3:18 1 Cor 15:45.
3:20 Gn 7:7, 17; 2 Pt 2:5.
3:21 Eph 5:26; Heb 10:22.
3:22 Eph 1:20–21.

attitude (for whoever suffers in the flesh has broken with sin), 2 so as not to spend what remains of one's life in the flesh on human desires, but on the will of God. 3* For the time that has passed is sufficient for doing what the Gentiles like to do: living in debauchery, evil desires, drunkenness, orgies, carousing, and wanton idolatry. 4 They are surprised that you do not plunge into the same swamp of profligacy, and they vilify you; 5* but they will give an account to him who stands ready to judge the living and the dead. 6† For this is why the gospel was preached even to the dead that, though condemned in the flesh in human estimation, they might live in the spirit in the estimation of God.

Christian Charity

7† The end of all things is at hand. Therefore, be serious and sober for prayers. 8*† Above all, let your love for one another be intense, because love covers a multitude of sins. 9* Be hospitable to one another without complaining. 10* As each one has received a gift, use it to serve one another as good stewards of God's varied grace. 11*† Whoever preaches, let it be with the words of God; whoever serves, let it be with the strength that God supplies, so that in all things God may be glorified through Jesus Christ, to whom belong glory and dominion forever and ever. Amen.

IV: Advice to the Persecuted

Trial of Persecution

12*† Beloved, do not be surprised that a trial by fire is occurring among you, as if something strange were happening to you. 13* But rejoice to the extent that you share in the sufferings of Christ, so that when his glory is revealed you may also rejoice exultantly. 14* If you are insulted for the name of Christ, blessed are you, for the Spirit of glory and of God rests upon you. 15 But let no one among you be made to suffer as a murderer, a thief, an evildoer, or as an intriguer. 16 But whoever is made to suffer as a Christian should not be ashamed but glorify God because of the name. 17* For it is time for the judgment to begin with the household of God; if it begins with us, how will it end for those who fail to obey the gospel of God?

Shout for Joy!

No healthy person likes to suffer. Yet, when we suffer for resisting evil and doing good—like being identified as a follower of Christ or defending someone who is under attack by others—First Peter calls us blessed. God notices when we are mocked or ridiculed for our faith. We are challenged to rejoice when we experience such treatment, rather than take it as a sign of failure. Didn't Christ suffer for doing good? Won't he be with us when we suffer for his name? The Gospel has a strange way of turning things upside down—it says that instead of causing suffering, these things should bring us joy!

The Bible has a lot more to say on the topic of suffering. See the "Life and Faith Issues" index to locate other passages.

▶ 1 Pt 4:12–19

4:6 *The dead:* these may be the sinners of the flood generation who are possibly referred to in 3:19. But many scholars think that there is no connection between these two verses, and that *the dead* here are Christians who have died since hearing the preaching of the gospel.

4:7–11 The inner life of the eschatological community is outlined as *the end* (the parousia of Christ) and the judgment draws near in terms of seriousness, sobriety, prayer, and love expressed through hospitality and the use of one's gifts for the glory of God and of Christ.

4:8 *Love covers a multitude of sins:* a maxim based on Prv 10:12; see also Ps 32:1; Jas 5:20.

4:11 Some scholars feel that this doxology concludes the part of the homily addressed specifically to the newly baptized, begun in 1:3; others that it concludes a baptismal liturgy. Such doxologies do occur within a New Testament letter, e.g., Rom 9:5. Some propose that v 11 was an alternate ending, with 4:12—5:14 being read in places where persecution was more pressing. But such doxologies usually do not occur at the end of letters (the only examples are 2 Pt 3:18, Jude 25, and Rom 16:27, the last probably a liturgical insertion).

4:12–19 The suffering to which the author has already frequently referred is presented in more severe terms. This has led some scholars to see these verses as referring to an actual persecution. Others see the heightening of the language as only a rhetorical device used at the end of the letter to emphasize the suffering motif.

4:3 Eph 2:2–3; 4:17–19; Col 3:7; Ti 3:3.
4:5 Acts 10:42; 2 Tm 4:1.
4:8 Prv 10:12; Jas 5:20.
4:9 Heb 13:2.
4:10 Rom 12:6–8; 1 Cor 12:4–11.
4:11 1 Cor 10:31.
4:12 1 Pt 1:6–7; 3:14, 17.
4:13 Rom 5:3–5; 8:17; 2 Tm 2:12.
4:14 Acts 5:41 / Is 11:2.
4:17 Lk 23:31; 2 Thes 1:8.

18* "And if the righteous one is barely saved,
where will the godless and the sinner
appear?"

19 As a result, those who suffer in accord with God's will hand their souls over to a faithful creator as they do good.

Advice to Presbyters†

5 1 So I exhort the presbyters among you, as a fellow presbyter† and witness to the sufferings of Christ and one who has a share in the glory to be revealed. 2* Tend the flock of God in your midst, [overseeing] not by constraint but willingly, as God would have it, not for shameful profit but eagerly. 3 Do not lord it over those assigned to you, but be examples to the flock. 4*† And when the chief Shepherd is revealed, you will receive the unfading crown of glory.

Advice to the Community†

5* Likewise, you younger members,† be subject to the presbyters. And all of you, clothe yourselves with humility in your dealings with one another, for:

"God opposes the proud
but bestows favor on the humble."

6* So humble yourselves under the mighty hand of God, that he may exalt you in due time. 7* Cast all your worries upon him because he cares for you.

8* Be sober and vigilant. Your opponent the devil is prowling around like a roaring lion looking for [someone] to devour. 9 Resist him, steadfast in faith, knowing that your fellow believers throughout the world undergo the same sufferings. 10* The God of all grace who called you to his eternal glory through Christ [Jesus] will himself restore, confirm, strengthen, and establish you after you have suffered a little. 11 To him be dominion forever. Amen.

V: Conclusion

12† I write you this briefly through Silvanus, whom I consider a faithful brother, exhorting you and testifying that this is the true grace of God. Remain firm in it. 13† The chosen one at Babylon sends you greeting, as does Mark, my son. 14* Greet one another with a loving kiss. Peace to all of you who are in Christ.

†

5:1–4 In imitation of Christ, the chief shepherd, those entrusted with a pastoral office are to tend the flock by their care and example.

5:1 *Presbyters:* the officially appointed leaders and teachers of the Christian community (cf 1 Tm 5:17–18; Ti 1:5–8; Jas 5:14).

5:4 See the note on 2:25.

5:5–11 The community is to be subject to the presbyters and to show humility toward one another and trust in God's love and care (5–7). With sobriety, alertness, and steadfast faith they must resist the evil one; their sufferings are shared with Christians everywhere (8–9). They will be strengthened and called to eternal glory (10–11).

5:5 *Younger members:* this may be a designation for officeholders of lesser rank.

5:12 *Silvanus:* the companion of Paul (see 2 Cor 1:19; 1 Thes 1:1; 2 Thes 1:1). Jews and Jewish Christians, like Paul, often had a Hebrew name (Saoul, Silas) and a Greek or Latin name (Paul, Silvanus). On Silvanus's possible role as amanuensis, see Introduction.

5:13 *The chosen one:* feminine, referring to the Christian community *(ekklēsia)* at *Babylon,* the code name for Rome in Rv 14:8; 17:5; 18:2. *Mark, my son:* traditionally a prominent disciple of Peter and co-worker at the church in Rome, perhaps the John Mark referred to in Acts 12:12, 25; 13:5, 13; and in 15:37–39, a companion of Barnabas. Perhaps this is the same Mark mentioned as Barnabas's cousin in Col 4:10, a co-worker with Paul in Phlm 24 (see also 2 Tm 4:11).

*

4:18 Prv 11:31 LXX.
5:2 Acts 20:28; Ti 1:7.
5:4 Wis 5:15–16; 1 Cor 9:25; 2 Tm 4:8; Jas 1:12.
5:5 Prv 3:34.
5:6 Jb 22:29; Jas 4:10.
5:7 Ps 55:23; Mt 6:25–33; Lk 12:22–31; Phil 4:6.
5:8 1 Thes 5:6.
5:10 Rom 8:18; 2 Cor 4:17.
5:14 Rom 16:16; 1 Cor 16:20; 2 Cor 13:12.

What happens to us when we die? What is Heaven like? Does God even care what happens to us? Many people believe there is no Heaven, no hell, and no God. Some say that when we die, our bodies simply decay and we no longer exist in any form. They say there is no life after death, no punishment, and no reward. But the Bible tells us differently. Second Peter was written to reassure believers that God does indeed care, and that they will be rewarded for leading faithful and virtuous lives.

At a Glance

I. Address (1:1–2).

II. Exhortation to Christian Virtue (1:3–21).

III. Condemnation of the False Teachers (2:1–22).

IV. The Delay of the Second Coming (3:1–16).

V. Final Exhortation and Doxology (3:17–18).

Quick Facts

Inspired Author: an unknown person writing in Peter's name

Date Written: from approximately AD 100 to 125

Audience: a community of both Jewish and Gentile (non-Jewish) Christians

In Depth

Bible scholars have convincing evidence that Second Peter is one of the latest books in the New Testament. The letter appears to have been written by someone who is appealing to the authority of the dead Apostle Peter (see "Introduction to the Letters and Revelation"). At the time of its writing—perhaps as much as one hundred years after Jesus' death and Resurrection—some Christians were starting to wonder if what they believed was true. People were even teaching that there would be no reward or punishment after death. So why not live any way you wanted to?

The author of the Second Letter of Peter is arguing against these false teachers. This writer uses famous examples from the Old Testament to remind readers how God has acted through history. And the author promises that those who have chosen to separate themselves from God in their lifetime will experience the fullness of separation from God in death—a separation that Christians call hell. Those who have stayed faithful to God's calling will enjoy eternal life in union with God—a life that Christians call Heaven. Why? Because God is good and just.

Tied to this argument is another concern. Many of the earliest Christians believed Christ would return soon after his Resurrection, probably within their lifetime, to establish God's Reign once and for all (see "The Parousia," near 2 Thes 1:5—2:17). When generations had passed and Christ had not yet returned, false teachers claimed he would never return. The author of Second Peter reminds readers that God's time is not our time—Christ is simply waiting so more people have a chance to repent of their sins before he comes for judgment (see 2 Pt 3:9).

2 Peter

I: Address

Greeting

1 1† Symeon Peter, a slave and apostle of Jesus Christ, to those who have received a faith of equal value to ours through the righteousness of our God and savior Jesus Christ: 2† may grace and peace be yours in abundance through knowledge of God and of Jesus our Lord.

II: Exhortation to Christian Virtue

The Power of God's Promise

3*† His divine power has bestowed on us everything that makes for life and devotion, through the knowledge of him who called us by his own glory and power.† 4* Through these, he has bestowed on us the precious and very great promises, so that through them you may come to share in the divine nature, after escaping from the corruption that is in the world because of evil desire. 5*† For this very reason, make every effort to supplement your faith with virtue, virtue with knowledge, 6 knowledge with self-control, self-control with endurance, endurance with devotion, 7 devotion with mutual affection, mutual affection with love. 8 If these are yours and increase in abundance, they will keep you from being idle or unfruitful in the knowledge of our Lord Jesus Christ. 9* Anyone who lacks them is blind and shortsighted, forgetful of the cleansing of his past sins. 10† Therefore, brothers, be all the more eager to make your call and election firm, for, in doing so, you will never stumble. 11 For, in this way, entry into the eternal kingdom of our Lord and savior Jesus Christ will be richly provided for you.

Apostolic Witness

12† Therefore, I will always remind you of these things, even though you already know them and

†

1:1 *Symeon Peter:* on the authorship of 2 Peter, see Introduction; on the spelling here of the Hebrew name *Šim'ôn,* cf Acts 15:14. The greeting is especially similar to those in 1 Peter and Jude. The words translated *our God and savior Jesus Christ* could also be rendered "our God and the savior Jesus Christ"; cf 11; 2:20; 3:2, 18.

1:2 *Knowledge:* a key term in the letter (3, 8; 2:20; 3:18), perhaps used as a Christian emphasis against gnostic claims.

1:3–4 Christian life in its fullness is a gift of divine power effecting a knowledge of Christ and the bestowal of divine promises (3:4, 9). *To share in the divine nature,* escaping from a corrupt world, is a thought found elsewhere in the Bible but expressed only here in such Hellenistic terms, since it is said to be accomplished through knowledge (3); cf 2; 2:20; but see also Jn 15:4; 17:22–23; Rom 8:14–17; Heb 3:14; 1 Jn 1:3; 3:2.

1:3 *By his own glory and power:* the most ancient papyrus and the best codex read "through glory and power."

1:5–9 Note the climactic gradation of qualities (5–7), beginning with faith and leading to the fullness of Christian life, which is love; cf Rom 5:3–4; Gal 5:6, 22 for a similar series of "virtues," though the program and sense here are different than in Paul. The fruit of these is knowledge of Christ (8) referred to in v 3; their absence is spiritual blindness (9).

1:10–11 Perseverance in the Christian vocation is the best preventative against losing it and the safest provision for attaining its goal, the kingdom. *Kingdom of . . . Christ,* instead of "God," is unusual; cf Col 1:13 and Mt 13:41, as well as the *righteousness of . . . Christ* (1).

1:12–19 The purpose in writing is to call to mind the apostle's witness to the truth, even as he faces the end of his life (12–15), his eyewitness testimony to Christ (16–18), and the true prophetic message (19) through the Spirit in scripture (20–21), in contrast to what

1:3 2 Cor 4:6; 1 Pt 2:9.
1:4 2 Cor 7:1; 1 Jn 2:15.
1:5–7 Gal 5:22–23.
1:9 1 Jn 2:9, 11.

are established in the truth you have. 13† I think it right, as long as I am in this "tent," to stir you up by a reminder, 14* since I know that I will soon have to put it aside, as indeed our Lord Jesus Christ has shown me. 15 I shall also make every effort to enable you always to remember these things after my departure.

16*† We did not follow cleverly devised myths when we made known to you the power and coming of our Lord Jesus Christ, but we had been eyewitnesses of his majesty. 17*† For he received honor and glory from God the Father when that unique declaration came to him from the majestic glory, "This is my Son, my beloved, with whom I am well pleased." 18† We ourselves heard this voice come from heaven while we were with him on the holy mountain. 19* Moreover, we possess the prophetic message that is altogether reliable. You will do well to be attentive to it, as to a lamp shining in a dark place, until day dawns and the morning star rises in your hearts. 20† Know this first of all, that there is no prophecy of scripture that is a matter of personal interpretation, 21 for no prophecy ever came through human will; but rather human beings moved by the holy Spirit spoke under the influence of God.

III: Condemnation of the False Teachers

False Teachers

2 1*† There were also false prophets among the people, just as there will be false teachers among you, who will introduce destructive heresies and even deny the Master who ransomed them, bringing swift destruction on themselves. 2* Many will follow their licentious ways, and because of them the way of truth will be reviled. 3* In their greed they will exploit you with fabrications, but from of old their condemnation has not been idle and their destruction does not sleep.

Lessons from the Past

4*† For if God did not spare the angels when they sinned, but condemned them to the chains of Tartarus† and handed them over to be kept for judgment; 5*† and if he did not spare the ancient world, even though he preserved Noah, a herald of righteousness, together with seven others, when he brought a flood upon the godless world; 6* and if he condemned the cities of Sodom and Gomorrah [to destruction], reducing them to ashes, making them an example for the godless [people] of what is coming; 7 and if he rescued Lot, a righteous man oppressed by the licentious conduct of unprincipled people 8 (for day after day that righteous man living among them was tormented in his righteous soul at the lawless deeds that he saw and heard), 9* then the Lord knows how to rescue the devout from trial and to keep the unrighteous under punishment for the day of judgment, 10*† and especially those who follow the flesh with its depraved desire and show contempt for lordship.

†

false teachers are setting forth (ch 2).

1:13 *Tent:* a biblical image for transitory human life (Is 38:12), here combined with a verb that suggests not folding or packing up a tent but its being discarded in death (cf 2 Cor 5:1–4).

1:16 *Coming:* in Greek *parousia,* used at 3:4, 12 of the second coming of Christ. The word was used in the extrabiblical writings for the visitation of someone in authority; in Greek cult and Hellenistic Judaism it was used for the manifestation of the divine presence. What the apostles *made known* has been interpreted to refer to Jesus' transfiguration (17) or to his entire first coming or to his future coming in power (ch 3).

1:17 The author assures the readers of the reliability of the apostolic message (including Jesus' power, glory, and coming; cf the note on 1:16) by appeal to the transfiguration of Jesus in glory (cf Mt 17:1–8 and parallels) and by appeal to the prophetic message (19; perhaps Nm 24:17). Here, as elsewhere, the New Testament insists on continued reminders as necessary to preserve the historical facts about Jesus and the truths of the faith; cf 3:1–2; 1 Cor 11:2; 15:1–3. *My Son, my beloved:* or, "my beloved Son."

1:18 *We:* at Jesus' transfiguration, referring to Peter, James, and John (Mt 17:1).

1:20–21 Often cited, along with 2 Tm 3:16, on the "inspiration" of scripture or against private interpretation, these verses in context are directed against the false teachers of ch 2 and clever tales (16). The prophetic word in scripture comes admittedly through *human beings* (21), but *moved by the holy Spirit,* not from their own interpretation, and is a matter of what the author and Spirit intended, not the *personal interpretation* of false teachers. Instead of *under the influence of God,* some manuscripts read "holy ones of God."

2:1–3 The pattern of *false prophets* among the Old Testament people of God will recur through *false teachers* in the church. Such destructive opinions of heretical sects bring loss of faith in Christ, contempt for the way of salvation (cf 21), and immorality.

2:4–6 The false teachers will be punished just as surely and as severely as were the fallen *angels* (4; cf Jude 6; Gn 6:1–4), the sinners of Noah's day (5; Gn 7:21–23), and the inhabitants of the cities of the Plain (6; Jude 7; Gn 19:25). Whereas there are three examples in Jude 5–7 (Exodus and wilderness; rebellious angels; Sodom and Gomorrah), 2 Peter omitted the first of these, has inserted a new illustration about Noah (5) between Jude's second and third examples, and listed the resulting three examples in their Old Testament order (Gn 6; 7; 19).

2:4 *Chains of Tartarus:* cf Jude 6; other manuscripts in 2 Peter read "pits of Tartarus." *Tartarus:* a term borrowed from Greek mythology to indicate the infernal regions.

2:5–10a Although God did not spare the sinful, he kept and saved the righteous, such as *Noah* (5) and *Lot* (7), and he *knows how to rescue the devout* (9), who are contrasted with the false teachers of the author's day. On Noah, cf Gn 5:32—9:29, especially 7:1. On Lot, cf Gn 13 and 19.

2:10b–22 Some take 10b and 11 with the preceding paragraph. Others begin the new paragraph with 10a, supplying from v 9 *The Lord knows how . . . to keep . . . under punishment,* with reference to God and probably specifically Christ (1). The conduct of the false teachers is described and condemned in language similar to that of Jude 8–16. This arrogance knows no bounds; animal-like, they are due to be caught and destroyed. They seduce even those who have knowledge of Christ (20).

*

1:14 Is 38:12; Jn 21:18–19.
1:16 Lk 9:28–36; Jn 1:14.
1:17 Ps 2:7; Mt 17:4–6.
1:19 Lk 1:78–79; Rv 2:28.
2:1 Mt 24:11, 24; 1 Tm 4:1; Jude 4.
2:2 Is 52:5.
2:3 Rom 16:18.
2:4 Jude 6.
2:5 Gn 8:15–19; Heb 11:7.
2:6 Gn 19:24–25; Jude 7.
2:9 1 Cor 10:13; Rv 3:10.
2:10 Jude 8.

Did You Know?

Identifying False Prophets

Many times throughout history, people have misled others in the name of God. Adolf Hitler is probably the best known such leader in the twentieth century. Some of these leaders have even convinced their followers to commit mass suicide as part of their beliefs. These extreme examples show how people can be misguided by false prophets.

In 2 Peter 2:1–3, the author gives guidelines for identifying false prophets, explaining that false prophets use secrets, propose destructive opinions, deny God's teachings, twist the truth to their needs, and exploit their followers. Beware of any leader, religious or nonreligious, who uses these techniques. As Second Peter says, they malign the way of truth.

▶ 2 Pt 2:1–3

False Teachers Denounced

Bold and arrogant, they are not afraid to revile glorious beings, 11*† whereas angels, despite their superior strength and power, do not bring a reviling judgment against them from the Lord. 12* But these people, like irrational animals born by nature for capture and destruction, revile things that they do not understand, and in their destruction they will also be destroyed, 13*† suffering wrong as payment for wrongdoing. Thinking daytime revelry a delight, they are stains and defilements as they revel in their deceits while carousing with you. 14 Their eyes are full of adultery and insatiable for sin. They seduce unstable people, and their hearts are trained in greed. Accursed children! 15*† Abandoning the straight road, they have gone astray, following the road of Balaam, the son of Bosor, who loved payment for wrongdoing, 16* but he received a rebuke for his own crime: a mute beast spoke with a human voice and restrained the prophet's madness.

17* These people are waterless springs and mists driven by a gale; for them the gloom of darkness has been reserved. 18*† For, talking empty bombast, they seduce with licentious desires of the flesh those who have barely escaped from people who live in error. 19* They promise them freedom, though they themselves are slaves of corruption, for a person is a slave of whatever overcomes him. 20* For if they, having escaped the defilements of the world through the knowledge of [our] Lord and savior Jesus Christ, again become entangled and overcome by them, their last condition is worse than their first. 21*† For it would have been better for them not to have known the way of righteousness than after knowing it to turn back from the holy commandment handed down to them. 22*† What is expressed in the true proverb has happened to them, "The dog returns to its own vomit," and "A bathed sow returns to wallowing in the mire."

IV: The Delay of the Second Coming

Denial of the Parousia

3 1† This is now, beloved, the second letter I am writing to you; through them by way of reminder I am trying to stir up your sincere disposition, 2* to recall the words previously spoken by the holy prophets and the commandment of the Lord and savior through your apostles. 3*† Know this first of all, that in the

---

2:10b *Glorious beings:* literally, "glories"; cf Jude 8. While some think that illustrious personages are meant or even political officials behind whom (fallen) angels stand, it is more likely that the reference is to glorious angelic beings (cf Jude 9).

2:11 *From the Lord:* some manuscripts read "before the Lord"; cf Jude 9.

2:13 *Suffering wrong:* some manuscripts read "receiving a reward." *In their deceits:* some manuscripts read "in their love feasts" (Jude 12).

2:15 *Balaam, the son of Bosor:* in Nm 22:5, Balaam is said to be the son of Beor, and it is this name that turns up in a few ancient Greek manuscripts by way of "correction" of the text. Balaam is not portrayed in such a bad light in Nm 22. His evil reputation and his *madness* (16), and possibly his surname Bosor, may have come from a Jewish tradition about him in the first/second century, of which we no longer have any knowledge.

2:18 *Barely escaped:* some manuscripts read "really escaped."

2:21 *Commandment handed down:* cf 3:2 and Jude 3.

2:22 The second proverb is of unknown origin, while the first appears in Prv 26:11.

3:1–4 The false teachers not only flout Christian morality (cf Jude 8–19); they also deny the second coming of Christ and the judgment (4; cf 7). They seek to justify their licentiousness by arguing that the promised return of Christ has not been realized and the world is the same, no better than it was before (3–4). The author wishes to strengthen the faithful against such errors by reminding them in this *second letter* of the instruction in 1 Peter and of the teaching of the *prophets* and of Christ, conveyed through the *apostles* (1–2; cf Jude 17); cf 1 Pt 1:10–12, 16–21, especially 16–21; Eph 2:20.

3:3 *Scoffers:* cf Jude 18, where, however, only the passions of the scoffers are mentioned, not a denial on their part of Jesus' parousia.

2:11 Jude 9.
2:12 Ps 49:13–15; Jude 10.
2:13 Jude 12.
2:15 Nm 31:16; Jude 11.
2:16 Nm 22:28–33.
2:17 Jude 12–13.
2:18 Jude 16.
2:19 Jn 8:34; Rom 6:16–17.
2:20 Mt 12:45.
2:21 Ez 3:20.
2:22 Prv 26:11.
3:2 Jude 17.
3:3 1 Tm 4:1; 2 Tm 3:1; Jude 18.

last days scoffers will come [to] scoff, living
according to their own desires 4*† and saying,
"Where is the promise of his coming? From the
time when our ancestors fell asleep, everything
has remained as it was from the beginning
of creation." 5*† They deliberately ignore the
fact that the heavens existed of old and earth
was formed out of water and through water by
the word of God; 6*† through these the world
that then existed was destroyed, deluged with
water. 7* The present heavens and earth have
been reserved by the same word for fire, kept
for the day of judgment and of destruction of
the godless.
8*† But do not ignore this one fact, beloved,
that with the Lord one day is like a thousand
years and a thousand years like one day. 9* The
Lord does not delay his promise, as some re-
gard "delay," but he is patient with you, not
wishing that any should perish but that all
should come to repentance. 10*† But the day
of the Lord will come like a thief, and then the
heavens will pass away with a mighty roar and
the elements will be dissolved by fire, and the
earth and everything done on it will be found
out.

Exhortation to Preparedness

11*† Since everything is to be dissolved in this
way, what sort of persons ought [you] to be,
conducting yourselves in holiness and devotion,
12*† waiting for and hastening the coming of the
day of God, because of which the heavens will be
dissolved in flames and the elements melted by
fire. 13*† But according to his promise we await
new heavens and a new earth in which righteous-
ness dwells.

Live It!

Seeing God

A frustrated and frazzled New York City tour guide is trying to get her group through a maze of homeless people and panhandlers outside the great Saint Patrick's Cathedral. After the group has safely entered the cathedral, she exclaims, with arms outstretched, "God is definitely here!" A young girl whose gaze lingers on the people outside asks, with all seriousness, "Why won't they let him out?"

The early readers of Second Peter were confused that Jesus Christ had not yet returned again (see "The Parousia," near 2 Thes 1:5—2:17). They wondered, "Where is God?" The author reminds them not to apply human limits to God's response.

Sometimes, when we pray for something, it seems like God keeps us waiting for an eternity. We want something to happen quickly—but God is on a different schedule. You might say the only limits we have in seeing God's actions are the ones we establish. What prevents you from seeing God in your life?

▶ 2 Pt 3:9

14 Therefore, beloved, since you await these
things, be eager to be found without spot or

† **3:4–7** The false teachers tried to justify their immorality by pointing out that the promised *coming* (*parousia*) of the Lord has not yet occurred, even though early Christians expected it in their day. They thus insinuate that God is not guiding the world's history anymore, since nothing has changed and the first generation of Christians, *our ancestors* (4) has all died by this time. The author replies that, just as God destroyed the earth by water in the flood (5–6, cf 2:5), so he will destroy it along with the false teachers on judgment day (7). *The word of God,* which called the world into being (Gn 1; Ps 33:6) and *destroyed* it by the waters of a flood, will destroy it again by fire on *the day of judgment* (5–7).

3:5 *Formed out of water and through water:* Gn 1:2, 6–8 is reflected as well as Greek views that water was the basic element from which all is derived.

3:6 *Destroyed, deluged with water:* cf 2:5; Gn 7:11—8:2.

3:8–10 The scoffers' objection (4) is refuted also by showing that delay of the Lord's second coming is not a failure to fulfill his word but rather a sign of his patience: God is giving time for repentance before the final judgment (cf Wis 11:23–26; Ez 18:23; 33:11).

3:8 Cf Ps 90:4.

3:10 *Like a thief:* Mt 24:43; 1 Thes 5:2; Rv 3:3. *Will be found out:* cf 1 Cor 3:13–15. Some few versions read, as the sense may demand, "will not be found out"; many manuscripts read "will be burned up"; there are further variants in other manuscripts, versions, and Fathers. Total destruction is assumed (11).

3:11–16 The second coming of Christ and the judgment of the world are the doctrinal bases for the moral exhortation to readiness through vigilance and a virtuous life; cf Mt 24:42, 50–51; Lk 12:40; 1 Thes 5:1–11; Jude 20–21.

3:12 *Flames . . . fire:* although this is the only New Testament passage about a final conflagration, the idea was common in apocalyptic and Greco-Roman thought. *Hastening:* eschatology is here used to motivate ethics (11), as elsewhere in the New Testament. Jewish sources and Acts 3:19–20 assume that proper ethical conduct can help bring the promised day of the Lord; cf 9. Some render the phrase, however, "desiring it earnestly."

3:13 *New heavens and a new earth:* cf Is 65:17; 66:22. The divine promises will be fulfilled after the day of judgment will have passed. The universe will be transformed by the reign of God's *righteousness* or justice; cf Is 65:17–18; Acts 3:21; Rom 8:18–25; Rv 21:1.

*
3:4 Is 5:19.
3:5 Gn 1:2, 6, 8; Ps 24:2.
3:6 Gn 7:21.
3:7 Is 51:6; Mt 3:12.
3:8 Ps 90:4.
3:9 Ez 18:23; 1 Tm 2:4.
3:10 Is 66:15–16; Mt 24:29.
3:11 Acts 3:19–21.
3:12 Is 34:4; Heb 10:27.
3:13 Is 65:17; 66:22; Rom 8:21; Rv 21:1, 27.

blemish before him, at peace. 15* And consider
the patience of our Lord as salvation, as our
beloved brother Paul, according to the wisdom
given to him, also wrote to you, 16† speaking
of these things as he does in all his letters.
In them there are some things hard to understand that the ignorant and unstable distort to
their own destruction, just as they do the other
scriptures.

3:16 *These things:* the teachings of this letter find parallels in Paul, e.g., God's will to save (Rom 2:4; 9:22–23; 1 Cor 1:7–8), the coming of Christ (1 Thes 4:16–17; 1 Cor 15:23–52), and preparedness for the judgment (Col 1:22–23; Eph 1:4–14; 4:30; 5:5–14). *Other scriptures:* used to guide the faith and life of the Christian community. The letters of Paul are thus here placed on the same level as books of the Old Testament. Possibly other New Testament writings could also be included.

V: Final Exhortation and Doxology

17*† Therefore, beloved, since you are forewarned, be on your guard not to be led into the
error of the unprincipled and to fall from your own
stability. 18* But grow in grace and in the knowledge of our Lord and savior Jesus Christ. To him be
glory now and to the day of eternity. [Amen.]

3:17–18 To avoid the dangers of *error* and loss of *stability*, Christians are *forewarned* to be *on your guard* and to *grow in grace and . . . knowledge* (1:2) of Christ. The doxology (18) recalls 1 Pt 4:11. Some manuscripts add Amen.

3:15 Rom 8:19; Jude 24.
3:17 Mk 13:5; Heb 2:1.
3:18 Rom 16:27.

Betrayal is painful. Unfortunately, most of us have experienced it at one time or another. It often begins with a misunderstanding. Sometimes harsh words are exchanged, and people part ways feeling sad and bitter. The community addressed by the Letters of John had experienced sharp division and conflict. It is impossible to avoid the author's feeling of betrayal as you read these letters.

The First, Second, and Third Letters of John

In Depth

All three Letters of John were probably written by the same person, the elder referred to in the second and third letters. This writer probably belonged to the community for which the Gospel of John was written. He saw himself and his community as being faithful to the true meaning of John's Gospel. Now, others who had once belonged to this community had abandoned it in its time of need. They too read the Gospel of John, but they interpreted it very differently. The disagreement between these two groups resulted in a bitter conflict.

Even after careful study of the first letter, it is difficult to determine exactly what the disagreement was about. One issue seems to have been the proper understanding of Jesus' humanity. Apparently, the deceivers did not fully believe in Jesus' humanity and its connection to salvation through Jesus' death and Resurrection. To emphasize Jesus' humanity, the author several times mentions that Jesus came "in the flesh" and comments on the saving power of the "blood of Jesus."

The author also challenges the deceivers' claims that they were free to do anything they wanted and still love God. If they truly loved God, they would also love their brothers and sisters and would not have abandoned the community.

The Second Letter of John is brief and seems to be a follow-up to the first letter addressed to the same community. The Third Letter of John is also brief. It is addressed to a man named Gaius, and in it the elder is complaining about a church leader named Diotrephes who refused to provide hospitality to some missionaries sent by the elder.

Through these letters, God reminds today's Christians that believers will inevitably have profoundly different understandings about what they believe. Conflict and disagreement will occur even within the Christian community. Can Christians handle such discord with love and respect?

At a Glance

- I. Prologue (1 Jn 1:1–4).
- II. God as Light (1 Jn 1:5—3:10).
- III. Love for One Another (1 Jn 3:11—5:12).
- IV. Epilogue (1 Jn 5:13–21).
- I. The Second Letter of John.
- I. The Third Letter of John.

Quick Facts

Inspired Author: an unknown person associated with the community that produced the Gospel of John

Date Written: approximately AD 100

Audience: Christians who were suffering from a split in their community

1 John

4:7

I: Prologue

The Word of Life

1 [1]* † What was from the beginning,
what we have heard,
what we have seen with our eyes,
what we looked upon
and touched with our hands
concerns the Word of life—
2* for the life was made visible;
we have seen it and testify to it
and proclaim to you the eternal life
that was with the Father and was made
visible to us—
3* what we have seen and heard
we proclaim now to you,
so that you too may have fellowship with us;
for our fellowship is with the Father
and with his Son, Jesus Christ.
4* We are writing this so that our joy may be
complete.

II: God As Light

God is Light

[5]† Now this is the message that we have heard
from him and proclaim to you: God is light, and
in him there is no darkness at all. [6]* If we say,
"We have fellowship with him," while we con-
tinue to walk in darkness, we lie and do not act in
truth. [7]* But if we walk in the light as he is in the
light, then we have fellowship with one another,
and the blood of his Son Jesus cleanses us from
all sin. [8]*† If we say, "We are without sin," we de-
ceive ourselves, and the truth is not in us. [9]* If we
acknowledge our sins, he is faithful and just and
will forgive our sins and cleanse us from every
wrongdoing. [10]* If we say, "We have not sinned,"
we make him a liar, and his word is not in us.

Christ and His Commandments

2 [1]* † My children, I am writing this to you so
that you may not commit sin. But if anyone

1:1–4 There is a striking parallel to the prologue of the gospel of John (Jn 1:1–18), but the emphasis here is not on the preexistent Word but rather on the apostles' witness to the incarnation of life by their experience of the historical Jesus. He is *the Word of life* (1; cf Jn 1:4), *the eternal life that was with the Father and was made visible* (2; cf Jn 1:14), and was *heard, seen, looked upon,* and *touched* by the apostles. The purpose of their teaching is to share that *life,* called *fellowship . . . with the Father and with his Son, Jesus Christ,* with those who receive their witness (3; Jn 1:14, 16).

1:5–7 *Light* is to be understood here as truth and goodness; *darkness* here is error and depravity (cf Jn 3:19–21; 17:17; Eph 5:8). To *walk* in light or darkness is to live according to truth or error, not merely intellectual but moral as well. Fellowship with God and with one another consists in a life according to the truth as found in God and in Christ.

1:8–10 Denial of the condition of sin is self-deception and even contradictory of divine revelation; there is also the continual possibility of sin's recurrence. Forgiveness and deliverance from sin through Christ are assured through acknowledgment of them and repentance.

2:1 *Children:* like the term "beloved," this is an expression of pastoral love (cf Jn 13:33; 21:5; 1 Cor 4:14). *Advocate:* for the use of

1:1 1 Jn 2:13; Jn 1:1, 14; 20:20, 25, 27.
1:2 Jn 15:27; 17:5.
1:3 Jn 17:21; Acts 4:20.
1:4 Jn 15:11; 2 Jn 12.
1:6 Jn 12:35.
1:7 Mt 26:28; Rom 3:24–25; Heb 9:14; 1 Pt 1:19; Rv 1:5.
1:8 2 Chr 6:36; Prv 20:9.
1:9 Prv 28:13; Jas 5:16.
1:10 1 Jn 5:10.
2:1 Jn 14:16; Heb 7:25.

does sin, we have an Advocate with the Father, Jesus Christ the righteous one. 2* He is expiation for our sins, and not for our sins only but for those of the whole world. 3*† The way we may be sure that we know him is to keep his commandments. 4* Whoever says, "I know him," but does not keep his commandments is a liar, and the truth is not in him. 5* But whoever keeps his word, the love of God is truly perfected in him. This is the way we may know that we are in union with him: 6 whoever claims to abide in him ought to live [just] as he lived.

The New Commandment

7*† Beloved, I am writing no new commandment to you but an old commandment that you had from the beginning. The old commandment is the word that you have heard. 8*† And yet I do write a new commandment to you, which holds true in him and among you, for the darkness is passing away, and the true light is already shining. 9* Whoever says he is in the light, yet hates his brother, is still in the darkness. 10* Whoever loves his brother remains in the light, and there is nothing in him to cause a fall. 11 Whoever hates his brother is in darkness; he walks in darkness and does not know where he is going because the darkness has blinded his eyes.

Members of the Community

12*† I am writing to you, children, because your sins have been forgiven for his name's sake.†

13* I am writing to you, fathers, because you know him who is from the beginning.

I am writing to you, young men, because you have conquered the evil one.

14 I write to you, children, because you know the Father.

I write to you, fathers, because you know him who is from the beginning.

I write to you, young men, because you are strong and the word of God remains in you, and you have conquered the evil one.

15*† Do not love the world or the things of the world. If anyone loves the world, the love of the Father is not in him. 16† For all that is in the world, sensual lust, enticement for the eyes, and a pretentious life, is not from the Father but is from the world. 17* Yet the world and its enticement are passing away. But whoever does the will of God remains forever.

Antichrists

18*† Children, it is the last hour; and just as you heard that the antichrist was coming, so now many antichrists have appeared. Thus we know

Live It!

Live in the Light

Do you ever find it hard to decide whether something is right or wrong? Instead of the sharp distinction between light and darkness described in First John, you might see a lot of shades of gray. But be careful; you might simply be seeing what you want to see! Remember, "If we say, 'We are without sin,' we deceive ourselves" (1 Jn 1:8). There are times when our choices aren't clear, but usually they are. Listen to your inner voice of honesty and integrity, and courageously choose to live in the light!

▶ **1 Jn 1:5–10**

† the term, see Jn 14:16. Forgiveness of sin is assured through Christ's intercession and expiation or "offering"; the death of Christ effected the removal of sin.

2:3–6 *The way we may be sure:* to those who claim, "I have known Christ and therefore I know him," our author insists on not mere intellectual knowledge but obedience to God's commandments in a life conformed to the example of Christ; this confirms our knowledge of him and is *the love of God . . . perfected.* Disparity between moral life and the commandments proves improper belief.

2:7–11 The author expresses the continuity and freshness of mutual charity in Christian experience. Through Christ the commandment of love has become the *light* defeating the *darkness* of evil in a new age. All hatred as darkness is incompatible with the light and Christian life. Note also the characteristic Johannine polemic in which a positive assertion is emphasized by the negative statement of its opposite.

2:8 *Which holds true in him and among you:* literally, "a thing that holds true in him and in you."

2:12–17 The Christian community that has experienced the grace of God through forgiveness of sin and knowledge of Christ is armed against the evil one.

2:12 *For his name's sake:* because of Christ our sins are forgiven.

2:15 *The world:* all that is hostile toward God and alienated from him. Love of the *world* and love of God are thus mutually exclusive; cf Jas 4:4.

2:16 *Sensual lust:* literally, "the lust of the flesh," inordinate desire for physical gratification. *Enticement for the eyes:* literally, "the lust of the eyes," avarice or covetousness; the eyes are regarded as the windows of the soul. *Pretentious life:* literally, "pride of life," arrogance or ostentation in one's earthly style of life that reflects a willful independence from God and others.

2:18 *It is the last hour:* literally, "a last hour," the period between the death and resurrection of Christ and his second coming. *The antichrist:* opponent or adversary of Christ; the term appears only in 1–2 John, but "pseudochrists" (translated "false messiahs") in Mt 24:24

2:2 1 Jn 4:10.
2:3 Jn 14:15; 15:10.
2:4 1 Jn 4:20.
2:5 Jn 14:23.
2:7 1 Jn 3:11; Dt 6:5; Mt 22:37–40.
2:8 Jn 13:34 / Jn 1:5; Rom 13:12.
2:9 Jn 8:12.
2:10 Eccl 2:14; Jn 11:10.
2:12 1 Cor 6:11.
2:13 1 Jn 1:1; Jn 1:1.
2:15 Rom 8:7–8; Jas 4:4; 2 Pt 1:4.
2:17 Is 40:8; Mt 7:21; 1 Cor 7:31; 1 Pt 4:2.
2:18 1 Tm 4:1.

Cultural Connection

Be Reconciled

Sometimes, it's hardest to show your love to the people you are closest to. Maybe you get along great with all your friends but are always arguing with your brother or sister. Or in your youth group, you are always tense around that one person with whom you had angry words several months ago.

The author of First John tells us we cannot ignore a relationship with a brother or sister in the Lord who has been upset. The Hmong culture has the same tradition. If you frighten or hurt or offend someone, you have created an imbalance of spirits. It is your responsibility to go back and seek to re-establish harmony. It is the Hmong custom to go to a shaman (an elder of the community, a holy person) for advice and to perform a ritual for reconciliation.

The Catholic Tradition has the sacrament of Penance and Reconciliation for the same purpose: to admit that the imbalance in a relationship has been caused by sin, discuss ways to make things right, express sorrow, and celebrate God's forgiveness and love.

▶ 1 Jn 2:7–11

this is the last hour. [19]† They went out from us, but they were not really of our number; if they had been, they would have remained with us. Their desertion shows that none of them was of our number. [20]*† But you have the anointing that comes from the holy one, and you all have knowledge. [21]* I write to you not because you do not know the truth but because you do, and because every lie is alien to the truth. [22]*† Who is the liar? Whoever denies that Jesus is the Christ. Whoever denies the Father and the Son, this is the antichrist. [23]* No one who denies the Son has the Father, but whoever confesses the Son has the Father as well.

Life from God's Anointing

[24]*† Let what you heard from the beginning remain in you. If what you heard from the beginning remains in you, then you will remain in the Son and in the Father. [25]* And this is the promise that he made us: eternal life. [26] I write you these things about those who would deceive you. [27] As for you, the anointing that you received from him remains in you, so that you do not need anyone to teach you. But his anointing teaches you about everything and is true and not false; just as it taught you, remain in him.

Children of God

[28]† And now, children, remain in him, so that when he appears we may have confidence and not be put to shame by him at his coming. [29] If you consider that he is righteous, you also know that everyone who acts in righteousness is begotten by him.

3 [1]*† See what love the Father has bestowed on us that we may be called the children of God. Yet so we are. The reason the world does not know us is that it did not know him. [2]*† Beloved, we are God's children now; what we shall be has not yet been revealed. We do know that when it is revealed we shall be like him, for we shall see him as he is. [3]* Everyone who has this

---

† and Mk 13:22, and Paul's "lawless one" in 2 Thes 2:3, are similar figures. *Many antichrists:* Matthew, Mark, and Revelation seem to indicate a collectivity of persons, here related to the false teachers.

2:19 *Not really of our number:* the apostate teachers only proved their lack of faith by leaving the community.

2:20 *The anointing that comes from the holy one:* this anointing is in the Old Testament sense of receiving the Spirit of God. The *holy one* probably refers to Christ. True knowledge is the gift of the Spirit (cf Is 11:2), and the function of the Spirit is to lead Christians to the truth (Jn 14:17, 26; 16:13).

2:22–23 Certain gnostics denied that the earthly Jesus was the Christ; to deny knowledge of the Son is to deny the Father, since only through the Son has God been fully revealed (Jn 1:18; 14:8–9).

2:24 Continuity with the apostolic witness as proclaimed in the prologue is the safeguard of right belief.

2:28–29 Our confidence at his judgment is based on the daily assurance of salvation. Our actions reflect our true relation to him.

3:1–3 The greatest sign of God's love is the gift of his Son (Jn 3:16) that has made Christians true children of God. This relationship is a present reality and also part of the life to come; true knowledge of God will ultimately be gained, and Christians prepare themselves now by virtuous lives in imitation of the Son.

3:2 *When it is revealed:* or "when he is revealed" (the subject of the verb could be Christ).

---

* **2:20** Jn 14:26.
2:21 1 Jn 3:19; 2 Pt 1:12.
2:22 2 Thes 2:4.
2:23 Jn 14:7–9.
2:24 Jn 14:23.
2:25 Jn 5:24; 10:28; 17:2.
3:1 Jn 1:12; Eph 1:5 / Jn 15:21; 17:25.
3:2 Phil 3:21.
3:3 1 Jn 2:6.

hope based on him makes himself pure, as he is pure.

Avoiding Sin

4† Everyone who commits sin commits lawlessness, for sin is lawlessness. 5* You know that he was revealed to take away sins, and in him there is no sin. 6 No one who remains in him sins; no one who sins has seen him or known him. 7 Children, let no one deceive you. The person who acts in righteousness is righteous, just as he is righteous. 8* Whoever sins belongs to the devil, because the devil has sinned from the beginning. Indeed, the Son of God was revealed to destroy the works of the devil. 9† No one who is begotten by God commits sin, because God's seed remains in him; he cannot sin because he is begotten by God. 10 In this way, the children of God and the children of the devil are made plain; no one who fails to act in righteousness belongs to God, nor anyone who does not love his brother.

III: Love for One Another

11*† For this is the message you have heard from the beginning: we should love one another, 12* unlike Cain who belonged to the evil one and slaughtered his brother. Why did he slaughter him? Because his own works were evil, and those of his brother righteous. 13* Do not be amazed, [then,] brothers, if the world hates you. 14* We know that we have passed from death to life because we love our brothers. Whoever does not love remains in death. 15* Everyone who hates his brother is a murderer, and you know that no murderer has eternal life remaining in him. 16* The way we came to know love was that he laid down his life for us; so we ought to lay down our lives for our brothers. 17* If someone who has worldly means sees a brother in need and refuses him compassion, how can the love of God remain in him? 18* Children, let us love not in word or speech but in deed and truth.

"Let us love not in word or speech but in deed and truth."
(1 Jn 3:18)

Confidence before God

19† [Now] this is how we shall know that we belong to the truth and reassure our hearts before him 20 in whatever our hearts condemn, for God is greater than our hearts and knows everything. 21 Beloved, if [our] hearts do not condemn us, we have confidence in God 22* and receive from him whatever we ask, because we keep

Pray It!

Love in Action

Clear your mind of all thoughts and concerns. Help your body and mind relax with some deep breaths. Now read 1 John 3:18 several times until you can say it by heart. Reflect on its meaning. Think about how you have lived and acted during this past week. Have you shown love in truth and action? by word or speech?

Ask God to forgive you for any situations in which you failed to act lovingly. Pray for the gift of being able to put your love in action in your daily life. Throughout the remainder of this day, remind yourself of this prayer by calling to mind verse 18.

▶ **1 Jn 3:18**

1 JN

3:4 *Lawlessness:* a reference to the activity of the antichrist, so it is expressed as hostility toward God and a rejection of Christ. The author goes on to contrast the states of sin and righteousness. Christians do not escape sin but realize that when they sin they cease to have fellowship with God. Virtue and sin distinguish the children of God from the children of the devil.

3:9 A habitual sinner is a child of the devil, while a child of God, who by definition is in fellowship with God, cannot sin. *Seed:* Christ or the Spirit who shares the nature of God with the Christian.

3:11–18 Love, even to the point of self-sacrifice, is the point of the commandment. The story of Cain and Abel (12–15; Gn 4:1–16) presents the rivalry of two brothers, in a contrast of evil and righteousness, where envy led to murder. For Christians, proof of deliverance is love toward others, after the example of Christ. This includes concrete acts of charity, out of our material abundance.

3:19–24 Living a life of faith in Jesus and of Christian love assures us of abiding in God no matter what our feelings may at times tell us. Our obedience gives us confidence in prayer and trust in God's judgment. This obedience includes our belief in Christ and love for one another.

3:19b–20 This difficult passage may also be translated "we shall be at peace before him in whatever our hearts condemn, for . . ." or "and before God we shall convince our hearts, if our hearts condemn us, that God is greater than our hearts."

3:5 Is 53:9; Jn 1:29; 8:46; 1 Pt 2:22.
3:8 Jn 8:44; 12:31–32.
3:11 1 Jn 2:7; Jn 13:34; 15:12, 17.
3:12 Gn 4:8; Jude 11.
3:13 Mt 24:9; Jn 15:18; 17:14.
3:14 Lv 19:17; Jn 5:24.
3:15 Jn 8:44.
3:16 Mt 20:28; Jn 10:11; 15:13.
3:17 Dt 15:7, 11; Jas 2:15–16.
3:18 Jas 1:22.
3:22 1 Jn 5:15; Mt 7:7–11; 21:22; Jn 14:13–14.

Live It!

Testing Spirits

Ancient peoples believed in different kinds of spirits that could affect the way things happened in the world. The First Letter of John talks about two kinds of spirit: that which comes from God and that which does not come from God. This letter gives us two ways for testing whether something comes from God: The first has to do with whether our actions reflect love for God and love for our brothers and sisters (see 1 Jn 3:18). The second has to do with our beliefs about Jesus Christ. To understand this, let's look closer at the controversy that prompted the author of this letter to offer these two tests.

The author of First John says of those who left their community—he calls them antichrists—that they do not believe that Jesus is the Christ and they do not confess the Father and the Son (see 2:22). But this cannot be the end of the story because they are Jesus' followers just like the author. The key to the problem is 1 John 4:2, but the meaning of this verse in its original Greek language is not clear. Even Bible scholars don't know how to translate it. Luckily they could go to Second John, verse 7, where the letter writes more clearly about the same issue. These deceivers do not believe that Jesus Christ came in the flesh. They believe in Jesus Christ and that he came to live among us, but they do not believe he actually became one of us and suffered and died like we do. After all, who could possibly imagine God doing such a thing? But this is what the author of First John believed and what Christians today believe. This is what we mean when we talk about the Incarnation—God takes on flesh and becomes like us.

You can apply this letter's two tests to just about any spiritual idea or practice you come across. Ask yourself: Does this help me to love God and other people? Does this support the Christian belief that Jesus Christ is fully God and fully human, and that faith in him is necessary for salvation? If you cannot answer yes to both of these questions, stay away!

▶ 1 Jn 4:1–21

his commandments and do what pleases him.
23* And his commandment is this: we should
believe in the name of his Son, Jesus Christ,
and love one another just as he commanded us.
24* Those who keep his commandments remain
in him, and he in them, and the way we know
that he remains in us is from the Spirit that he
gave us.

Testing the Spirits

4 1*† Beloved, do not trust every spirit but
test the spirits to see whether they belong
to God, because many false prophets have gone
out into the world. 2* This is how you can know
the Spirit of God: every spirit that acknowledges
Jesus Christ come in the flesh belongs to God,
3*† and every spirit that does not acknowledge
Jesus does not belong to God. This is the spirit
of the antichrist that, as you heard, is to come,
but in fact is already in the world. 4 You belong
to God, children, and you have conquered them,
for the one who is in you is greater than the one
who is in the world. 5* They belong to the world;
accordingly, their teaching belongs to the world,
and the world listens to them. 6* We belong to
God, and anyone who knows God listens to us,
while anyone who does not belong to God refuses to hear us. This is how we know the spirit
of truth and the spirit of deceit.

God's Love and Christian Life

7† Beloved, let us love one another, because
love is of God; everyone who loves is begotten
by God and knows God. 8 Whoever is without
love does not know God, for God is love. 9* In
this way the love of God was revealed to us: God
sent his only Son into the world so that we might
have life through him. 10* In this is love: not that
we have loved God, but that he loved us and sent

†

4:1–6 Deception is possible in spiritual phenomena and may be tested by its relation to Christian doctrine (cf 1 Cor 12:3): those who fail to acknowledge Jesus Christ in the flesh are false prophets and belong to the antichrist. Even though these false prophets are well received in the world, the Christian who belongs to God has a greater power in the truth.

4:3 *Does not acknowledge Jesus:* some ancient manuscripts add "Christ" and/or "to have come in the flesh" (cf 2), and others read "every spirit that annuls (or severs) Jesus."

4:7–12 Love as we share in it testifies to the nature of God and to his presence in our lives. One who loves shows that one is a child of God and knows God, for God's very being is love; one without love is without God. The revelation of the nature of God's love is found in the free gift of his Son to us, so that we may share life with God and be delivered from our sins. The love we have for one another must be of the same sort: authentic, merciful; this unique Christian love is our proof that we know God and can "see" the invisible God.

3:23 Jn 13:34; 15:17.
3:24 1 Jn 4:13; Jn 14:21–23.
4:1 1 Jn 2:18; Mt 24:24.
4:2 1 Cor 12:3; 1 Thes 5:21.
4:3 1 Jn 3:22.
4:5 Jn 15:19.
4:6 Jn 8:47; 10:16.
4:9 Jn 3:16.
4:10 Rom 5:8.

his Son as expiation for our sins. [11] Beloved, if
God so loved us, we also must love one another.
[12]* No one has ever seen God. Yet, if we love
one another, God remains in us, and his love is
brought to perfection in us.
[13]† This is how we know that we remain in
him and he in us, that he has given us of his
Spirit. [14] Moreover, we have seen and testify that
the Father sent his Son as savior of the world.
[15] Whoever acknowledges that Jesus is the Son of
God, God remains in him and he in God. [16] We
have come to know and to believe in the love
God has for us.
God is love, and whoever remains in love re-
mains in God and God in him. [17]* In this is love
brought to perfection among us, that we have
confidence on the day of judgment because as
he is, so are we in this world. [18] There is no fear
in love, but perfect love drives out fear because
fear has to do with punishment, and so one who
fears is not yet perfect in love. [19] We love because
he first loved us. [20]*† If anyone says, "I love
God," but hates his brother, he is a liar; for who-
ever does not love a brother whom he has seen
cannot love God whom he has not seen. [21]* This
is the commandment we have from him: who-
ever loves God must also love his brother.

Live It!

Understanding Love

Some of the most beautiful prose and poetry written about love are contained in the Bible. First John 4:7–21 is a particularly eloquent piece that captures the heart of the Good News: God has loved us in Christ Jesus, who came as the Savior of the world. Now, we have been given the Spirit of God, and we are commanded to love others as we have been loved by God.

It is easy to say we love God. But First John tells us that our love for God is shown in our love for one another. Loving one another is much harder than simply saying, "I love God." What does this love for God look like? It is not the romantic love or sentimental affection the world usually presents to us. Read Matthew 25:31–36 or 1 Corinthians, chapter 13, for some ideas.

▶ 1 Jn 4:7–21

Faith is Victory over the World

5 [1]*† Everyone who believes that Jesus is the
Christ is begotten by God, and everyone who
loves the father loves [also] the one begotten
by him. [2] In this way we know that we love the
children of God when we love God and obey his
commandments. [3]* For the love of God is this,
that we keep his commandments. And his com-
mandments are not burdensome, [4]* for whoever
is begotten by God conquers the world. And
the victory that conquers the world is our faith.
[5]* Who [indeed] is the victor over the world
but the one who believes that Jesus is the Son
of God?
[6]*† This is the one who came through water
and blood, Jesus Christ, not by water alone, but
by water and blood. The Spirit is the one that
testifies, and the Spirit is truth. [7] So there are
three that testify, [8]* the Spirit, the water, and the
blood, and the three are of one accord. [9]* If we
accept human testimony, the testimony of God
is surely greater. Now the testimony of God is
this, that he has testified on behalf of his Son.
[10]* Whoever believes in the Son of God has this
testimony within himself. Whoever does not
believe God has made him a liar by not believ-
ing the testimony God has given about his Son.
[11]* And this is the testimony: God gave us eter-
nal life, and this life is in his Son. [12] Whoever

†

4:13–21 The testimony of the Spirit and that of faith join the testimony of love to confirm our knowledge of God. Our love is grounded in the confession of Jesus as the Son of God and the example of God's love for us. Christian life is founded on the knowledge of God as love and on his continuing presence that relieves us from fear of judgment (16–18). What Christ is gives us confidence, even as we live and love in this world. Yet Christian love is not abstract but lived in the concrete manner of love for one another.

4:20 *Cannot love God:* some ancient manuscripts read "how can he love . . . ?"

5:1–5 Children of God are identified not only by their love for others (4:7–9) and for God (5:1–2) but by their belief in the divine sonship of Jesus Christ. Faith, the acceptance of Jesus in his true character and the obedience in love to God's commands (3), is the source of the Christian's power in the world and conquers the world of evil (4–5), even as Christ overcame the world (Jn 16:33).

5:6–12 *Water and blood* (6) refers to Christ's baptism (Mt 3:16–17) and to the shedding of his blood on the cross (Jn 19:34). *The Spirit* was present at the baptism (Mt 3:16; Mk 1:10; Lk 3:22; Jn 1:32, 34). *The testimony* to Christ as the Son of God is confirmed by divine witness (7–9), greater by far than the two legally required human witnesses (Dt 17:6). To deny this is to deny God's truth; cf Jn 8:17–18. The gist of the divine witness or *testimony* is that *eternal life* (11–12) is given in Christ and nowhere else. To *possess the Son* is not acceptance of a doctrine but of a person who lives now and provides life.

*

4:12 Jn 1:18; 1 Tm 6:16.
4:17 1 Jn 2:28.
4:20 1 Jn 2:4.
4:21 Jn 13:34; 14:15, 21; 15:17.
5:1 Jn 8:42; 1 Pt 1:23.
5:3 Jn 14:15.
5:4 Jn 16:33.
5:5 1 Cor 15:57.
5:6 Jn 15:26; 19:34.
5:8 Jn 5:32, 36; 15:26.
5:9 Jn 5:32, 37.
5:10 1 Jn 3:33.
5:11 1 Jn 1:2; Jn 1:4; 5:21, 26; 17:3.

possesses the Son has life; whoever does not pos-
sess the Son of God does not have life.

IV: Epilogue

Prayer for Sinners

13*† I write these things to you so that you
may know that you have eternal life, you who
believe in the name of the Son of God. 14* And
we have this confidence in him, that if we ask
anything according to his will, he hears us. 15 And
if we know that he hears us in regard to whatever
we ask, we know that what we have asked him
for is ours. 16* If anyone sees his brother sinning,
if the sin is not deadly, he should pray to God
and he will give him life. This is only for those
whose sin is not deadly. There is such a thing as
deadly sin, about which I do not say that you
should pray. 17 All wrongdoing is sin, but there is
sin that is not deadly.
18 We know that no one begotten by God sins;
but the one begotten by God he protects, and the
evil one cannot touch him. 19 We know that we
belong to God, and the whole world is under the
power of the evil one. 20* We also know that the
Son of God has come and has given us discern-
ment to know the one who is true. And we are in
the one who is true, in his Son Jesus Christ. He is
the true God and eternal life. 21 Children, be on
your guard against idols.

† **5:13–21** As children of God we have confidence in prayer because of our intimate relationship with him (14–15). In love, we pray (16–17) for those who are in *sin,* but not in *deadly sin* (literally, "sin unto death"), probably referring to apostasy or activities brought on under the antichrist; cf Mk 3:29; Heb 6:4–6; 10:26–31. Even in the latter case, however, prayer, while not enjoined, is not forbidden. The letter concludes with a summary of the themes of the letter (18–20). There is a sharp antithesis between the children of God and those belonging to the world and to the evil one. The Son reveals the God of truth; Christians dwell in the true God, *in his Son,* and have eternal life. The final verse (21) voices a perennial warning about *idols,* any type of rival to God.

* **5:13** Jn 1:12; 20:31. **5:14** 1 Jn 3:21–22; Mt 7:7; Jn 14:13–14. **5:16** Mt 12:31. **5:20** Jer 24:7; Jn 17:3; Eph 1:17.

1 JN

For background on this letter, see the introduction to 1, 2, and 3 John, before 1 John.

2 John

1*† The Presbyter to the chosen Lady and to her
children whom I love in truth—and not only I
but also all who know the truth— 2 because of the
truth that dwells in us and will be with us forever.
3† Grace, mercy, and peace will be with us from
God the Father and from Jesus Christ the Father's
Son in truth and love.
4*† I rejoiced greatly to find some of your
children walking in the truth just as we were
commanded by the Father. 5* But now, Lady, I
ask you, not as though I were writing a new com-
mandment but the one we have had from the
beginning: let us love one another. 6*† For this
is love, that we walk according to his command-
ments; this is the commandment, as you heard
from the beginning, in which you should walk.
7*† Many deceivers have gone out into the
world, those who do not acknowledge Jesus
Christ as coming in the flesh; such is the deceit-
ful one and the antichrist. 8† Look to yourselves
that you do not lose what we worked for but may
receive a full recompense. 9*† Anyone who is so
"progressive" as not to remain in the teaching of
the Christ does not have God; whoever remains
in the teaching has the Father and the Son. 10*† If
anyone comes to you and does not bring this

---

1 *The chosen Lady:* literally "elected"; this could also be translated "Kyria (a woman's name) chosen (by God)" or "the lady Electa" or "Electa Kyria." The adjective "chosen" is applied to all Christians at the beginning of other New Testament letters (1 Pt 1:1; Ti 1:1). The description is of a specific community with "children" who are its members. *The truth:* the affirmation of Jesus in the flesh and in contrast to false teaching (7).

3 *Grace, mercy, and peace:* like 1 and 2 Timothy this letter adds *mercy* to the terms used frequently in a salutation to describe Christian blessing; it appears only here in the Johannine writings. The author also puts the blessing in relation to *truth* and *love,* the watchwords of the Johannine teaching. *The Father's Son:* the title that affirms the close relationship of Christ to God; similar variations of this title occur elsewhere (Jn 1:14; 3:35), but the precise wording is not found elsewhere in the New Testament.

4 *Some of your children:* this refers to those whom the Presbyter has recently encountered, but it may also indicate the presence of false doctrine in the community: the Presbyter encourages those who have remained faithful. *Walking in the truth:* an expression used in the Johannine writings to describe a way of living in which the Christian faith is visibly expressed; cf 1 Jn 1:6–7; 2:6, 11; 3 Jn 3.

6 *His commandments:* cf 1 Jn 2:7–8; 3:23; 4:21; obedience to the commandment of faith and love includes all others.

7 *The antichrist:* see 1 Jn 2:18–19, 22; 4:3.

8 *You* (plural): it is not certain whether this means the Christians addressed or includes the Presbyter, since some of the ancient Greek manuscripts and Greek Fathers have "we."

9 *Anyone who is so "progressive":* literally, "Anyone who goes ahead." Some gnostic groups held the doctrine of the Christ come in the flesh to be a first step in belief, which the more advanced and spiritual believer surpassed and abandoned in his knowledge of the spiritual Christ. The author affirms that fellowship with God may be gained only by holding to the complete doctrine of Jesus Christ (1 Jn 2:22–23; 4:2; 5:5–6).

10–11 At this time false teachers were considered so dangerous and divisive as to be shunned completely. From this description they seem to be wandering preachers. We see here a natural suspicion of early Christians concerning such itinerants and can envisage the problems faced by missionaries such as those mentioned in 3 Jn 10.

---

1 Jn 8:32; 3 Jn 1.
4 3 Jn 3.
5 Jn 13:34; 15:12; 1 Jn 4:7.
6 Jn 13:34; 14:15; 1 Jn 5:3.
7 1 Jn 2:22; 4:2.
9 Jn 8:31; 1 Jn 2:23; 4:15.
10 Rom 16:17; 2 Thes 3:6.

Live It!

Unwelcome Guests

The author of Second John is warning a Christian community—called the chosen Lady and her children—about the false message of some "deceivers" (see the introduction to First, Second, and Third John, before First John). The author cautions the community not to have anything to do with such people, not even to let them into their homes (see 2 John, verses 10–11). Although the words sound harsh, the reasoning is sound.

Every day, we could be letting people with false messages into our homes "virtually" through television, books, music, the Internet, and magazines. Their false messages promote values and behaviors that are contrary to a healthy and holy way of life. Can these "guests" affect our attitudes and choices? They sure can, especially if we welcome them blindly without thinking about the impact of their messages.

- On a piece of paper or in your journal, identify the television shows, magazines, radio stations, and Internet sites that regularly visit your home. List the positive values and behaviors these guests display. Now list the negative ones. How do the lists compare?
- How can you manage your media exposure wisely in order to resist its negative influence?

doctrine, do not receive him in your house or
even greet him; 11 for whoever greets him shares
in his evil works.
12*† Although I have much to write to you,
I do not intend to use paper and ink. Instead,
I hope to visit you and to speak face to face so
that our joy may be complete. 13† The children of
your chosen sister send you greetings.

† **12** *Our joy:* a number of other Greek manuscripts read "your joy."

13 *Chosen sister:* the community of which the Presbyter is now a part greets you (singular), the community of the Lady addressed.

* **12** Jn 15:11; 1 Jn 1:4; 3 Jn 13.

3 John

For background on this letter, see the introduction to 1, 2, and 3 John, before 1 John.

1*† The Presbyter to the beloved Gaius whom
I love in truth.
2 Beloved, I hope you are prospering in every
respect and are in good health, just as your soul
is prospering. 3*† I rejoiced greatly when some of
the brothers came and testified to how truly you
walk in the truth. 4* Nothing gives me greater joy
than to hear that my children are walking in the
truth.
5*† Beloved, you are faithful in all you do for
the brothers, especially for strangers; 6*† they
have testified to your love before the church.
Please help them in a way worthy of God to con-
tinue their journey. 7† For they have set out for
the sake of the Name and are accepting nothing
from the pagans. 8 Therefore, we ought to support

Verses 2–8

Live It!

Supporting the Ministry of Others

Gaius was a man of faith who opened his home to missionaries who were passing through his city. Though Gaius did not personally know these missionaries, he provided hospitality for them because he knew they were helping to spread the Good News. In Third John, the elder appeals to him to welcome his messenger, Demetrius, even when others refuse to do so.

Christians find many needs they cannot respond to by themselves. The story of Gaius shows how you can become a co-missionary with Christians who are ministering in some way you cannot. These may be ministers in your own parish or diocese, or a religious group that sends missionaries to other countries. You can offer them your hospitality, support them financially, or promote their work in your parish or community. Consider talking with your family about a specific ministry or missionary activity you can support together.

†

1 *Beloved Gaius:* a frequent form of address for fellow Christians in New Testament epistolary literature.

3 *The brothers:* in this letter, the term may refer to Christians who have been missionaries and received hospitality from Gaius (5–6). *Walk in the truth:* the common Johannine term to describe Christian living; this description presents Gaius as following the teachings of the Presbyter in contrast to Diotrephes.

5 *You are faithful in all you do:* Gaius's aid to the missionaries is a manifestation of his true Christian faith.

6 *Help them . . . to continue their journey:* the Presbyter asks Gaius not only to continue to welcome the missionaries to his community but also to equip them for further travels.

7 *The Name:* of Jesus Christ (cf Acts 5:41; 1 Jn 2:12; 3:23; 5:13). *Accepting nothing:* not expecting support from the pagans to whom they preach the gospel, so that they will not be considered as beggars; they required support from other Christians; cf Paul's complaints to the Corinthians (1 Cor 9:3–12).

*

1 2 Jn 1.
3 3 Jn 5; Gal 6:10; 2 Jn 4.
4 1 Thes 2:11–12; 1 Tm 1:2; 2 Tm 1:2; 1 Jn 2:1; 2 Jn 4.
5 Rom 12:13; Gal 6:10; Heb 13:2.
6 Acts 15:3; Col 1:10; 1 Thes 2:12.

such persons, so that we may be co-workers in
the truth.
9† I wrote to the church, but Diotrephes, who
loves to dominate, does not acknowledge us.
10† Therefore, if I come, I will draw attention to
what he is doing, spreading evil nonsense about
us. And not content with that, he will not receive
the brothers, hindering those who wish to do so
and expelling them from the church.
11*† Beloved, do not imitate evil but imitate
good. Whoever does what is good is of God;
whoever does what is evil has never seen God.
12*† Demetrius receives a good report from all,
even from the truth itself. We give our testimoni-
al as well, and you know our testimony is true.
13* I have much to write to you, but I do not
wish to write with pen and ink. 14 Instead, I hope
to see you soon, when we can talk face to face.
15*† Peace be with you. The friends greet you;
greet the friends there each by name.

†

9 *Who loves to dominate:* the Presbyter does not deny Diotrephes' place as leader but indicates that his ambition may have caused him to disregard his letter and his influence.

10 *If I come:* the Presbyter may visit the community to challenge the actions of Diotrephes toward himself and the missionaries. *Will not receive the brothers:* Diotrephes may have been critical of the teachings of the Presbyter and sought to maintain doctrinal purity; cf 1 Jn 2:19 and 2 Jn 10–11.

11 *Do not imitate evil:* Gaius should not be influenced by the behavior of Diotrephes.

12 *Demetrius:* because of the fear of false teachers, Demetrius, perhaps the bearer of the letter, is provided with a recommendation from the Presbyter; cf 2 Cor 3:1; Rom 16:1. *Even from the truth itself:* this refers probably to the manner of Demetrius's life that testifies to his true belief; cf Gaius above (v 3).

15 *Friends:* although a Johannine term for Christians (Jn 15:15), the word here may refer to those in the community loyal to the Presbyter and to Gaius.

*

11 1 Jn 2:29; 3:6, 10.
12 Jn 19:35; 21:24; 1 Tm 3:7.
13 2 Jn 12.
15 Jn 20:19, 21, 26; Eph 6:23; 1 Pt 5:14.

They pretend to be part of your group, but all they really do is cause trouble. They claim to have all the right answers, but they won't listen to other people's opinions. They flatter people to get what they want, but then they grumble and complain behind people's backs. They cause division wherever they go. Do you know people like this? Maybe you even find yourself acting like them sometimes. The Letter of Jude has some things to say about "these people."

At a Glance

I. Address and Greeting (verses 1–2).

II. Occasion for Writing, False Teachers, and Exhortations (verses 3–23).

III. Doxology (verses 24–25).

Quick Facts

Inspired Author: unknown, traditionally thought to be Jude, the brother of James

Date Written: maybe from AD 80 to 90

Audience: unknown

In Depth

The purpose of the Letter of Jude is to warn churches about false teachers who come into the Christian community with lies and tricks, making trouble wherever they go. The author recalls stories from the past in which God punished such people: stories about the Egyptians who opposed God's plan to bring the Hebrew people to the Promised Land; the immoral people of Sodom and Gomorrah; the angels who revolted against God; and Cain, who killed his brother. The author also encourages people to build themselves in the faith. Finally, the author cautions Christians to ignore ungodly people—unless those people truly want to change, in which case, Christians should be examples of the mercy of Jesus Christ.

Notice that this letter includes some terms that are unfamiliar to modern Christians or that have different meanings today. For instance, the term *holy ones* refers to the members of the Christian community, and a *love feast* is a celebration of the Eucharist.

The message of the Letter of Jude is difficult to understand for many reasons. We know almost nothing about who wrote it, to whom it was written, when it was written, and what it is really addressing—except from hints in the letter itself. Tradition says that the author is Jude, the brother of James and Jesus as mentioned in Mark 6:3 (the name Jude is a form of Judas). The word *brother* was used to express the relationship between a close sibling, a cousin, or other clan member, and even a spiritual relationship with someone of the same religion.

Jude

Verse 6

Address and Greeting

1*† Jude, a slave of Jesus Christ and brother of
James, to those who are called, beloved in God
the Father and kept safe for Jesus Christ: 2* may
mercy, peace, and love be yours in abundance.

Occasion for Writing

3*† Beloved, although I was making every ef-
fort to write to you about our common salvation,
I now feel a need to write to encourage you to
contend for the faith that was once for all handed
down to the holy ones. 4* For there have been
some intruders, who long ago were designated for
this condemnation, godless persons, who pervert
the grace of our God into licentiousness and who
deny our only Master and Lord, Jesus Christ.

The False Teachers

5*† I wish to remind you, although you know
all things, that [the] Lord who once saved a peo-
ple from the land of Egypt later destroyed those
who did not believe. 6*† The angels too, who
did not keep to their own domain but deserted
their proper dwelling, he has kept in eternal
chains, in gloom, for the judgment of the great
day. 7*† Likewise, Sodom, Gomorrah, and the
surrounding towns, which, in the same manner
as they, indulged in sexual promiscuity and prac-
ticed unnatural vice, serve as an example by un-
dergoing a punishment of eternal fire.
8† Similarly, these dreamers nevertheless also
defile the flesh, scorn lordship, and revile glori-
ous beings. 9*† Yet the archangel Michael, when

†

1 *Jude . . . brother of James:* for the identity of the author of this letter, see Introduction. *To those who are called:* the vocation to the Christian faith is God's free gift to those whom he loves and whom he safely protects in Christ until the Lord's second coming.

3–4 *Our common salvation:* the teachings of the Christian faith derived from the apostolic preaching and to be kept by the Christian community.

5 For this first example of divine punishment on those who had been saved but did not then keep faith, see Nm 14:28–29 and the note there. Some manuscripts have the word "once" (*hapax* as at 3) after "you know"; some commentators have suggested that it means "knowing one thing" or "you know all things once for all." Instead of "[the] Lord" manuscripts vary, having "Jesus," "God," or no subject stated.

6 This second example draws on Gn 6:1–4 as elaborated in the apocryphal Book of Enoch (cf 14): heavenly beings came to earth and had sexual intercourse with women. God punished them by casting them out of heaven into darkness and bondage.

7 *Practiced unnatural vice:* literally, "went after alien flesh." This example derives from Gn 19:1–25, especially 4–11, when the towns-men of Sodom violated both hospitality and morality by demanding that Lot's two visitors (really messengers of Yahweh) be handed over to them so that they could abuse them sexually. *Unnatural vice:* this refers to the desire for intimacies by human beings with angels (the reverse of the example in 6). Sodom (whence "sodomy") and Gomorrah became proverbial as object lessons for God's punishment on sin (Is 1:9; Jer 50:40; Am 4:11; Mt 10:15; 2 Pt 2:6).

8 *Dreamers:* the writer returns to the false teachers of v 4, applying charges from the three examples in vv 5, 6, 7. This may apply to claims they make for revelations they have received by night (to the author, hallucinations). *Defile the flesh:* this may mean bodily pollutions from the erotic dreams of sexual license (7). *Lordship . . . glorious beings:* these may reflect the Lord (5; Jesus, 4) whom they spurn and the angels (6; cf the note on 2 Pt 2:10, here, as there, literally, "glories").

9 *The archangel Michael . . . judgment:* a reference to an incident in the apocryphal Assumption of Moses. Dt 34:6 had said of Moses,

*

1 Mt 13:55; Mk 6:3; Acts 12:17; Rom 1:7.
2 Gal 6:16; 1 Tm 1:2; 2 Pt 1:2.
3 Jude 17, 20; 1 Tm 6:12.
4 Gal 2:4; 2 Tm 3:6; 2 Pt 2:1.
5 Nm 14:35; 1 Cor 10:5; Heb 3:16, 17.
6 2 Pt 2:4, 9.
7 Dt 29:22–24; Mt 25:41; 2 Thes 1:8–9; 2 Pt 2:6; 3:7.
9 Dn 10:21; 12:1.

he argued with the devil in a dispute over the
body of Moses, did not venture to pronounce a
reviling judgment upon him but said, "May the
Lord rebuke you!" 10* But these people revile
what they do not understand and are destroyed
by what they know by nature like irrational ani-
mals. 11*† Woe to them! They followed the way
of Cain, abandoned themselves to Balaam's error
for the sake of gain, and perished in the rebellion
of Korah. 12*† These are blemishes on your love
feasts, as they carouse fearlessly and look after
themselves. They are waterless clouds blown
about by winds, fruitless trees in late autumn,
twice dead and uprooted. 13 They are like wild
waves of the sea, foaming up their shameless
deeds, wandering stars for whom the gloom of
darkness has been reserved forever.
14*† Enoch, of the seventh generation from
Adam, prophesied also about them when he
said, "Behold, the Lord has come with his count-
less holy ones 15 to execute judgment on all and
to convict everyone for all the godless deeds that
they committed and for all the harsh words god-
less sinners have uttered against him." 16* These
people are complainers, disgruntled ones who
live by their desires; their mouths utter bombast
as they fawn over people to gain advantage.

Exhortations

17* But you, beloved, remember the words
spoken beforehand by the apostles of our Lord
Jesus Christ, 18*† for they told you, "In [the]
last time there will be scoffers who will live ac-
cording to their own godless desires." 19* These
are the ones who cause divisions; they live on
the natural plane, devoid of the Spirit. 20* But
you, beloved, build yourselves up in your most
holy faith; pray in the holy Spirit. 21* Keep
yourselves in the love of God and wait for
the mercy of our Lord Jesus Christ that leads
to eternal life. 22† On those who waver, have
mercy; 23† save others by snatching them out
of the fire; on others have mercy with fear,
abhorring even the outer garment stained by
the flesh.

Doxology

24*† To the one who is able to keep you from
stumbling and to present you unblemished
and exultant, in the presence of his glory, 25* to
the only God, our savior, through Jesus Christ
our Lord be glory, majesty, power, and author-
ity from ages past, now, and for ages to come.
Amen.

literally in Greek, "they buried him" or "he (God?) buried him" (taken to mean "he was buried"). The later account tells how Michael, who was sent to bury him, was challenged by the devil's interest in the body. Our author draws out the point that if an archangel refrained from reviling even the devil, how wrong it is for mere human beings to revile glorious beings (angels).

11 *Cain . . . Balaam . . . Korah:* examples of rebellious men and of the punishment their conduct incurred; cf Gn 4:8–16; Nm 16:1–35; 31:16. See the note on 2 Pt 2:15.

12 *Blemishes on your love feasts:* or "hidden rocks" or "submerged reefs" (cf 13). The opponents engaged in scandalous conduct in connection with community gatherings called *love feasts* (agape meals), which were associated with eucharistic celebrations at certain stages of early Christian practice; cf 1 Cor 11:18–34 and the note on 2 Pt 2:13.

14–15 Cited from the apocryphal Book of Enoch 1:9.

18 This is the substance of much early Christian preaching rather than a direct quotation of any of the various New Testament passages on this theme (see Mk 13:22; Acts 20:30; 1 Tm 4:1–3; 2 Pt 3:3).

22 *Have mercy:* some manuscripts read "convince," "confute," or "reprove." Others have "even though you waver" or "doubt" instead of *who waver.*

23 *With fear:* some manuscripts connect the phrase "with fear" with the imperative "save" or with the participle "snatching." Other manuscripts omit the phrase "on others have mercy," so that only two groups are envisioned. Rescue of those led astray and caution in the endeavor are both enjoined. *Outer garment stained by the flesh:* the imagery may come from Zec 3:3–5, just as that of *snatching . . . out of the fire* comes from Zec 3:2; the very garments of the godless are to be abhorred because of their contagion.

24–25 With this liturgical statement about the power of God to keep the faithful from stumbling, and praise to him through Jesus Christ, the letter reaches its conclusion by returning to the themes with which it began (1–2).

10 2 Pt 2:12.
11 Gn 4:8–16; 1 Jn 3:12 / Nm 31:15–16; 2 Pt 2:15; Rv 2:14 / Nm 16:19–35.
12 2 Pt 2:13, 17.
14–15 Mt 16:27; Heb 12:22–23.
16 Jude 18; 1 Cor 10:10; 2 Pt 2:10, 18.
17 Heb 2:3; 2 Pt 3:2.
18 1 Tm 4:1; 2 Tm 3:1–5; 2 Pt 3:3.
19 1 Cor 2:14; Jas 3:15.
20 Jude 2; Eph 6:18; Col 2:7.
21 Ti 2:13.
24 2 Cor 4:14; 1 Pt 4:13.
25 Rom 11:36; 1 Tm 1:17.

The Revelation to John

Have you ever shown people a text message from a friend and they just couldn't seem to understand it? You may understand it perfectly, but others cannot because they weren't part of your conversation. Similarly, it is also hard to understand the message in the Book of Revelation. The symbols and visions that appear in this book are not always clear. Some people mistakenly think it is a frightening book about the end of the world. However, for the early Christian community and the Church today, the Book of Revelation is a message of hope that proclaims God's ultimate triumph over evil in history.

At a Glance

I. Prologue (1:1–3).

II. Letters to the Churches of Asia (1:4—3:22).

III. God and the Lamb in Heaven (4:1—5:14).

IV. The Seven Seals, Trumpets, and Plagues, with Interludes (6:1—16:21).

V. The Punishment of Babylon and the Destruction of Pagan Nations (17:1—20:15).

VI. The New Creation (21:1—22:5).

VII. Epilogue (22:6–21).

Quick Facts

Inspired Author: a Jewish-Christian prophet named John

Date: probably from AD 92 to 96

Audience: Christian churches in Asia Minor during a time of Roman persecution

In Depth

This book is unique in that the author, who calls himself John, received a series of visions from God that form most of the content. The recorded visions take the form of apocalyptic literature (see "Apocalyptic Literature," near Daniel, chapters 7–10) and are full of symbols. These symbols are like the language of a secret club. You use it when you want to keep people who do not belong to your club from understanding what you are saying.

Why was it important that the meaning of the visions be known to the Christian communities only? Because the Christians still remembered their persecution under the Roman emperor Nero Caesar (AD 54–68) and were suffering a new persecution under the Roman emperor Domitian (AD 81–96). This "coded language" allowed John to criticize the Roman emperor and empire without necessarily putting his readers at risk of persecution or even death. John himself was exiled to an island off Asia Minor for preaching the Gospel (see Rv 1:9).

Once the symbols are understood, it is clear that the Book of Revelation offers hope to a church under persecution. It expresses belief in God's justice and God's victory over evil—an evil that at John's time was embodied in the Roman Empire. But it also expresses the great Christian belief that God will ultimately be victorious, at the end of time, when Christ will come again in his full glory and power. It is a mistake for Christians to try to decipher Revelation as a prediction as to when and how that final coming will occur. But they can take great joy and hope in the promise of a new world where God will wipe away every tear, and suffering and death will be no more (see 21:4).

Revelation

5:1—6:11

I: Prologue

1 1*† The revelation of Jesus Christ, which God
gave to him, to show his servants what must
happen soon. He made it known by sending his
angel to his servant John, 2 who gives witness to
the word of God and to the testimony of Jesus
Christ by reporting what he saw. 3*† Blessed is the
one who reads aloud and blessed are those who
listen to this prophetic message and heed what is
written in it, for the appointed time is near.

II: Letters to the Churches of Asia

Greeting†

4* John, to the seven churches in Asia:† grace to
you and peace from him who is and who was and
who is to come, and from the seven spirits before
his throne, 5*† and from Jesus Christ, the faithful
witness, the firstborn of the dead and ruler of the
kings of the earth. To him who loves us and has
freed us from our sins by his blood, 6* who has
made us into a kingdom, priests for his God and
Father, to him be glory and power forever [and
ever]. Amen.

7* Behold, he is coming amid the clouds,
and every eye will see him,
even those who pierced him.
All the peoples of the earth will lament him.
Yes. Amen.

8*† "I am the Alpha and the Omega," says the
Lord God, "the one who is and who was and who
is to come, the almighty."

The First Vision†

9 I, John, your brother, who share with you
the distress, the kingdom, and the endurance we

†

1:1–3 This prologue describes the source, contents, and audience of the book and forms an inclusion with the epilogue (22:6–21), with its similar themes and expressions.

1:3 *Blessed is the one:* this is the first of seven beatitudes in this book; the others are in 14:13; 16:15; 19:9; 20:6; 22:7, 14. *This prophetic message:* literally, "the words of the prophecy"; so 22:7, 10, 18, 19 by inclusion. *The appointed time:* when Jesus will return in glory; cf 1:7; 3:11; 22:7, 10, 12, 20.

1:4–8 Although Revelation begins and ends (22:21) with Christian epistolary formulae, there is nothing between chs 4 and 22 resembling a letter. The author here employs the standard word order for greetings in Greek letter writing: "N. to N., greetings . . ."; see the note on Rom 1:1.

1:4 *Seven churches in Asia:* Asia refers to the Roman province of that name in western Asia Minor (modern Turkey); these representative churches are mentioned by name in v 11, and each is the recipient of a message (2:1—3:22). *Seven* is the biblical number suggesting fullness and completeness; thus the seer is writing for the whole church.

1:5 *Freed us:* the majority of Greek manuscripts and several early versions read "washed us"; but "freed us" is supported by the best manuscripts and fits well with Old Testament imagery, e.g., Is 40:2.

1:8 *The Alpha and the Omega:* the first and last letters of the Greek alphabet. In 22:13 the same words occur together with the expressions "the First and the Last, the Beginning and the End"; cf 17; 2:8; 21:6; Is 41:4; 44:6.

1:9–20 In this first vision, the seer is commanded to write what he

•

1:1 Rv 22:6–8, 20; Dn 2:28 / Rv 19:10.
1:3 Rv 22:7 / Lk 11:28.
1:4 Rv 1:8; 4:8; 11:17; 16:5; Ex 3:14.
1:5 Rv 3:14; 1 Cor 15:20; Col 1:18 / Heb 9:14; 1 Pt 1:19; 1 Jn 1:7.
1:6 Ex 19:6; 1 Pt 2:9.
1:7 Dn 7:13 / Zec 12:10; Mt 24:30; Jn 19:37.
1:8 Rv 17; 21:6; 22:13; Is 41:4; 44:6; 48:12.

RV

have in Jesus, found myself on the island called
Patmos† because I proclaimed God's word and
gave testimony to Jesus. 10† I was caught up in
spirit on the Lord's day and heard behind me
a voice as loud as a trumpet, 11† which said,
"Write on a scroll what you see and send it to the
seven churches: to Ephesus, Smyrna, Pergamum,
Thyatira, Sardis, Philadelphia, and Laodicea."
12† Then I turned to see whose voice it was that
spoke to me, and when I turned, I saw seven
gold lampstands 13*† and in the midst of the
lampstands one like a son of man, wearing an
ankle-length robe, with a gold sash around his
chest. 14† The hair of his head was as white as
white wool or as snow, and his eyes were like a
fiery flame. 15† His feet were like polished brass
refined in a furnace, and his voice was like the
sound of rushing water. 16*† In his right hand he
held seven stars. A sharp two-edged sword came
out of his mouth, and his face shone like the sun
at its brightest.
17*† When I caught sight of him, I fell down
at his feet as though dead. He touched me with
his right hand and said, "Do not be afraid. I am
the first and the last, 18† the one who lives. Once
I was dead, but now I am alive forever and ever.
I hold the keys to death and the netherworld.
19† Write down, therefore, what you have seen,
and what is happening, and what will happen
afterwards. 20† This is the secret meaning of the
seven stars you saw in my right hand, and of

Pray It!

The Alpha and the Omega

In the first chapter of Revelation, John introduces God's message to the seven churches in Asia. After explaining that he received the message through a vision and that an angel instructed him to communicate it to them, John describes a vision of Christ.

A vision is like a dream. It cannot be interpreted literally; we must seek its deep meaning and be open to its message. For example, in the vision of Revelation 1:12–16, a magnificently robed Christ stands amid seven lampstands. The deeper meaning is that the resurrected Jesus in all his glory and power is watching over the seven churches. Here's another example: Revelation 1:8 has God saying, "I am the Alpha and the Omega." In the Greek alphabet, *alpha* is the first letter, and *omega* is the last letter. This passage is telling us that God and Jesus are in control of all history, from its beginning to its end.

In your prayer, think of any current event that frightens you or any harassments you experience because of your faith or moral principles. See the image of the risen Christ described by John. Feel Jesus lovingly touching your head. Hear Jesus telling you that history is always in God's hands. Let God strengthen your faith and renew your hope with this wonderful revelation of God's love.

▶ **Rv 1:7–20**

†

sees to the seven churches (9–11). He sees Christ in glory, whom he depicts in stock apocalyptic imagery (12–16), and hears him describe himself in terms meant to encourage Christians by emphasizing his victory over death (17–20).

1:9 *Island called Patmos:* one of the Sporades islands in the Aegean Sea, some fifty miles south of Ephesus, used by the Romans as a penal colony. *Because I proclaimed God's word:* literally, "on account of God's word."

1:10 *The Lord's day:* Sunday. *As loud as a trumpet:* the imagery is derived from the theophany at Sinai (Ex 19:16, 19; cf Heb 12:19 and the trumpet in other eschatological settings in Is 27:13; Jl 2:1; Mt 24:31; 1 Cor 15:52; 1 Thes 4:16).

1:11 *Scroll:* a papyrus roll.

1:12–16 A symbolic description of Christ in glory. The metaphorical language is not to be understood literally; cf Introduction.

1:13 *Son of man:* see the note on Mk 8:31. *Ankle-length robe:* Christ is priest; cf Ex 28:4; 29:5; Wis 18:24; Zec 3:4. *Gold sash:* Christ is king; cf Ex 28:4; 1 Mc 10:89; 11:58; Dn 10:5.

1:14 *Hair . . . as white as white wool or as snow:* Christ is eternal, clothed with the dignity that belonged to the "Ancient of Days"; cf 18; Dn 7:9. *His eyes were like a fiery flame:* Christ is portrayed as all-knowing; cf 2:23; Ps 7:10; Jer 17:10; and similar expressions in 2:18; 19:12; cf Dn 10:6.

1:15 *His feet . . . furnace:* Christ is depicted as unchangeable; cf Ez 1:27; Dn 10:6. The Greek word translated "refined" is unconnected grammatically with any other word in the sentence. *His voice . . . water:* Christ speaks with divine authority; cf Ez 1:24.

1:16 *Seven stars:* in the pagan world, Mithras and the Caesars were represented with seven stars in their right hand, symbolizing their universal dominion. *A sharp two-edged sword:* this refers to the word of God (cf Eph 6:17; Heb 4:12) that will destroy unrepentant sinners; cf 2:16; 19:15; Wis 18:15; Is 11:4; 49:2. *His face . . . brightest:* this symbolizes the divine majesty of Christ; cf 10:1; 21:23; Jgs 5:31; Is 60:19; Mt 17:2.

1:17 It was an Old Testament belief that for sinful human beings to see God was to die; cf Ex 19:21; 33:20; Jgs 6:22–23; Is 6:5.

1:18 *Netherworld:* Greek Hades, Hebrew Sheol, the abode of the dead; cf 20:13–14; Nm 16:33.

1:19 *What you have seen, and what is happening, and what will happen afterwards:* the three parts of the Book of Revelation, the vision (10–20), the situation in the seven churches (chs 2–3), and the events of chs 6–22.

1:20 *Secret meaning:* literally, "mystery." *Angels:* these are the presiding spirits of the seven churches. Angels were thought to be in charge of the physical world (cf 7:1; 14:18; 16:5) and of nations (Dn 10:13; 12:1), communities (the seven churches), and individuals (Mt 18:10; Acts 12:15). Some have seen in the "angel" of each of the seven churches its pastor or a personification of the spirit of the congregation.

1:13 Dn 7:13; 10:5.
1:16 Heb 4:12.
1:17 Dn 8:18 / Rv 1:8.

the seven gold lampstands: the seven stars are
the angels of the seven churches, and the seven
lampstands are the seven churches.

To Ephesus

2 1† "To the angel of the church† in Ephesus,†
write this:
" 'The one who holds the seven stars in his
right hand and walks in the midst of the seven
gold lampstands says this: 2† "I know your
works, your labor, and your endurance, and that
you cannot tolerate the wicked; you have tested
those who call themselves apostles but are not,
and discovered that they are impostors. 3 More-
over, you have endurance and have suffered for
my name, and you have not grown weary. 4 Yet I
hold this against you: you have lost the love you
had at first. 5 Realize how far you have fallen.
Repent, and do the works you did at first. Other-
wise, I will come to you and remove your lamp-
stand from its place, unless you repent. 6† But
you have this in your favor: you hate the works
of the Nicolaitans, which I also hate.
7*† " ' "Whoever has ears ought to hear what
the Spirit says to the churches. To the victor I will
give the right to eat from the tree of life that is in
the garden of God." '

To Smyrna†

8 "To the angel of the church in Smyrna,† write
this:
" 'The first and the last, who once died but came
to life, says this: 9*† "I know your tribulation
and poverty, but you are rich. I know the slan-
der of those who claim to be Jews and are not,
but rather are members of the assembly of Satan.
10 Do not be afraid of anything that you are going
to suffer. Indeed, the devil will throw some of you
into prison, that you may be tested, and you will
face an ordeal for ten days. Remain faithful until
death, and I will give you the crown of life.
11*† " ' "Whoever has ears ought to hear what
the Spirit says to the churches. The victor shall
not be harmed by the second death." '

Did You Know?

The Seven Churches

The messages addressed to the seven churches in Asia Minor (modern Greece and Turkey) are not predictions of the future. Like the prophets of the Old Testament who called Israel to return to the covenant, John calls these communities to deeper faith. Two churches are praised (Smyrna and Philadelphia), two are scolded (Sardis and Laodicea), and the remaining three receive both praise and criticism. The churches are scolded because they have tolerated leaders whose teaching contradicts the true Gospel message and because their faith has become "lukewarm," lacking the devotion it had when they first became Christians.

If the author of Revelation wrote such a prophecy to your local church, what would he praise and what would he criticize? Is your community on fire in living the Gospel, or is it lukewarm in its commitment?

▶ Rv 2:1—3:22

†

2:1–3:22 Each of the seven letters follows the same pattern: address; description of the exalted Christ; blame and/or praise for the church addressed; threat and/or admonition; final exhortation and promise to all Christians.

2:1–7 The letter to Ephesus praises the members of the church there for their works and virtues, including discerning false teachers (2–3), but admonishes them to repent and return to their former devotion (4–5). It concludes with a reference to the Nicolaitans (see the note on 6) and a promise that the victor will have access to eternal life (7).

2:1 *Ephesus:* this great ancient city had a population of ca. 250,000; it was the capital of the Roman province of Asia and the commercial, cultural, and religious center of Asia. The other six churches were located in the same province, situated roughly in a circle; they were selected for geographical reasons rather than for the size of their Christian communities. *Walks in the midst of the seven gold lampstands:* this signifies that Christ is always present in the church; see the note on 1:4.

2:2 *Who call themselves . . . impostors:* this refers to unauthorized and perverse missionaries; cf Acts 20:29–30.

2:6 *Nicolaitans:* these are perhaps the impostors of v 2; see the note on vv 14–15. There is little evidence for connecting this group with Nicolaus, the proselyte from Antioch, mentioned in Acts 6:5.

2:7 *Victor:* referring to any Christian individual who holds fast to the faith and does God's will in the face of persecution. *The tree of life that is in the garden of God:* this is a reference to the tree in the primeval paradise (Gn 2:9); cf 22:2, 14, 19. The decree excluding humanity from the tree of life has been revoked by Christ.

2:8–11 The letter to Smyrna encourages the Christians in this important commercial center by telling them that although they are impoverished, they are nevertheless rich, and calls those Jews who are slandering them members of the assembly of Satan (9). There is no admonition; rather, the Christians are told that they will suffer much, even death, but the time of tribulation will be short compared to their eternal reward (10), and they will thus escape final damnation (11).

2:8 *Smyrna:* modern Izmir, ca. thirty miles north of Ephesus, and the chief city of Lydia, with a temple to the goddess Roma. It was renowned for its loyalty to Rome, and it also had a large Jewish community very hostile toward Christians.

2:9–10 The church in Smyrna was materially poor but spiritually rich. Accusations made by Jewish brethren there occasioned the persecution of Christians; cf Acts 14:2, 19; 17:5, 13.

2:11 *The second death:* this refers to the eternal death, when sinners will receive their final punishment; cf 20:6, 14–15; 21:8.

*

2:7 Rv 2:11, 17, 29; 3:6, 13, 22; 13:9; Mt 11:15.
2:9 Jas 2:5.
2:11 Rv 20:6, 14; 21:8.

To Pergamum†

12 "To the angel of the church in Pergamum,† write this:

" 'The one with the sharp two-edged sword says this: 13† "I know that you live where Satan's throne is, and yet you hold fast to my name and have not denied your faith in me, not even in the days of Antipas, my faithful witness, who was martyred among you, where Satan lives. 14*† Yet I have a few things against you. You have some people there who hold to the teaching of Balaam, who instructed Balak to put a stumbling block before the Israelites: to eat food sacrificed to idols and to play the harlot. 15 Likewise, you also have some people who hold to the teaching of [the] Nicolaitans. 16 Therefore, repent. Otherwise, I will come to you quickly and wage war against them with the sword of my mouth.

17*† " ' "Whoever has ears ought to hear what the Spirit says to the churches. To the victor I shall give some of the hidden manna; I shall also give a white amulet upon which is inscribed a new name, which no one knows except the one who receives it." '

To Thyatira†

18 "To the angel of the church in Thyatira,† write this:

" 'The Son of God, whose eyes are like a fiery flame and whose feet are like polished brass, says this: 19 "I know your works, your love, faith, service, and endurance, and that your last works are greater than the first. 20† Yet I hold this against you, that you tolerate the woman Jezebel, who calls herself a prophetess, who teaches and misleads my servants to play the harlot and to eat food sacrificed to idols. 21 I have given her time to repent, but she refuses to repent of her harlotry. 22 So I will cast her on a sickbed and plunge those who commit adultery with her into intense suffering unless they repent of her works. 23*† I will also put her children to death. Thus shall all the churches come to know that I am the searcher of hearts and minds and that I will give each of you what your works deserve. 24† But I say to the rest of you in Thyatira, who do not uphold this teaching and know nothing of the so-called deep secrets of Satan: on you I will place no further burden, 25 except that you must hold fast to what you have until I come.

26*† " ' "To the victor, who keeps to my ways†
until the end,
I will give authority over the nations.
27 He will rule them with an iron rod.
Like clay vessels will they be smashed,

28 just as I received authority from my Father. And to him I will give the morning star.

29 " ' "Whoever has ears ought to hear what the Spirit says to the churches." '

To Sardis†

3 1 "To the angel of the church in Sardis,† write this:

---

† **2:12–17** The letter to Pergamum praises the members of the church for persevering in their faith in Christ even in the midst of a pagan setting and in face of persecution and martyrdom (13). But it admonishes them about members who advocate an unprincipled morality (14; cf 2 Pt 2:15; Jude 11) and others who follow the teaching of the Nicolaitans (15; see the note there). It urges them to repent (16) and promises them the hidden manna and Christ's amulet (17).

2:12 *Pergamum:* modern Bergama, ca. forty-five miles northeast of Smyrna, a center for various kinds of pagan worship. It also had an outstanding library (the word *parchment* is derived from its name).

2:13 *Satan's throne:* the reference is to emperor worship and other pagan practices that flourished in Pergamum, perhaps specifically to the white marble altar erected and dedicated to Zeus by Eumenes II (197–160 B.C.).

2:14–15 Like Balaam, the biblical prototype of the religious compromiser (cf Nm 25:1–3; 31:16; 2 Pt 2:15; Jude 11), the Nicolaitans in Pergamum and Ephesus (6) accommodated their Christian faith to paganism. They abused the principle of liberty enunciated by Paul (1 Cor 9:19–23).

2:17 *The hidden manna:* this is the food of life; cf Ps 78:24–25. *White amulet:* literally, "white stone," on which was written a magical name, whose power could be tapped by one who knew the secret name. It is used here as a symbol of victory and joy; cf 3:4–5. *New name:* this is a reference to the Christian's rebirth in Christ; cf 3:12; 19:12; Is 62:2; 65:15.

2:18–29 The letter to Thyatira praises the progress in virtue of this small Christian community (19) but admonishes them for tolerating a false prophet who leads them astray (20). Her fate is sealed, but there is hope of repentance for her followers (21–22). Otherwise, they too shall die (23). They are warned against Satanic power or knowledge (24–25). Those who remain faithful will share in the messianic reign, having authority over nations (26–27), and will in fact possess Christ himself (28).

2:18 *Thyatira:* modern Akhisar, ca. forty miles southeast of Pergamum, a frontier town famous for its workers' guilds (cf Acts 16:14), membership in which may have involved festal meals in pagan temples.

2:20 The scheming and treacherous Jezebel of old (cf 1 Kgs 19:1–2; 21:1–14; 2 Kgs 9:22, 30–34) introduced pagan customs into the religion of Israel; this new Jezebel was doing the same to Christianity.

2:23 *Children:* spiritual descendants.

2:24 *The so-called deep secrets of Satan:* literally, "the deep things of Satan," a scathing reference to the perverse teaching of the Nicolaitans (15).

2:26–28 The Christian who perseveres in faith will share in Christ's messianic authority (cf Ps 2:8–9) and resurrection victory over death, symbolized by the morning star; cf 22:16.

2:26 *Who keeps to my ways:* literally, "who keeps my works."

3:1–6 The letter to Sardis does not praise the community but admonishes its members to watchfulness, mutual support, and repentance (2–3). The few who have remained pure and faithful will share Christ's victory and will be inscribed in the book of life (4–5).

3:1 *Sardis:* this city, located ca. thirty miles southeast of Thyatira, was once the capital of Lydia, known for its wealth at the time of Croesus (6th century B.C.). Its citadel, reputed to be unassailable, was captured by surprise, first by Cyrus and later by Antiochus. The church is therefore warned to be on guard.

---

* **2:14** Nm 22–24; 25:1–3; 31:16; 2 Pt 2:15; Jude 11.
2:17 Is 62:2; 65:15.
2:23 1 Sm 16:7; Jer 11:20; 17:10.
2:26 Rv 12:5; Ps 2:8–9.

" 'The one who has the seven spirits of God
and the seven stars says this: "I know your
works, that you have the reputation of be-
ing alive, but you are dead. 2 Be watchful and
strengthen what is left, which is going to die,
for I have not found your works complete in the
sight of my God. 3* Remember then how you
accepted and heard; keep it, and repent. If you
are not watchful, I will come like a thief, and
you will never know at what hour I will come
upon you. 4* However, you have a few people
in Sardis who have not soiled their garments;
they will walk with me dressed in white, be-
cause they are worthy.
5*† " ' "The victor will thus be dressed in
white, and I will never erase his name from the
book of life but will acknowledge his name in
the presence of my Father and of his angels.
6 " ' "Whoever has ears ought to hear what the
Spirit says to the churches." '

To Philadelphia†

7* "To the angel of the church in Philadel-
phia,† write this:

" 'The holy one, the true,
who holds the key of David,
who opens and no one shall close,
who closes and no one shall open,

says this:
8† " ' "I know your works (behold, I have
left an open door before you, which no one
can close). You have limited strength, and yet
you have kept my word and have not denied
my name. 9* Behold, I will make those of the
assembly of Satan who claim to be Jews and
are not, but are lying, behold I will make them
come and fall prostrate at your feet, and they
will realize that I love you. 10† Because you have
kept my message of endurance, I will keep you
safe in the time of trial that is going to come to
the whole world to test the inhabitants of the
earth. 11* I am coming quickly. Hold fast to
what you have, so that no one may take your
crown.
12*† " ' "The victor I will make into a pillar
in the temple of my God, and he will never
leave it again. On him I will inscribe the name
of my God and the name of the city of my
God, the new Jerusalem, which comes down
out of heaven from my God, as well as my new
name.
13 " ' "Whoever has ears ought to hear what the
Spirit says to the churches." '

Live It!

Opening the Door

The image in Revelation 3:20 inspired an artist to depict our relationship with Christ in a popular painting. The painting shows a door overgrown with vines. The door obviously has not been opened in a long time. As you examine it, you realize it has no outside latch or knob—it can be opened only from the inside. At the door stands Jesus, knocking—not pounding, just knocking patiently.

What is your relationship with Christ like right now? Is the door of your life open to let Christ in, or has it been closed for a while? Jesus will not force his way into your life. Jesus seeks a close friendship with you, and real friendship—real love—always involves a free choice. No one can choose to open the door but you.

▶ **Rv 3:14–22**

† **3:5** *In white:* white is a sign of victory and joy as well as resurrection; see the note on 2:17. *The book of life:* the roll in which the names of the redeemed are kept; cf 13:8; 17:8; 20:12, 15; 21:27; Phil 4:3; Dn 12:1. They will be acknowledged by Christ in heaven; cf Mt 10:32.

3:7–13 The letter to Philadelphia praises the Christians there for remaining faithful even with their limited strength (8). Members of the assembly of Satan are again singled out (9; see 2:9 above). There is no admonition; rather, the letter promises that they will be kept safe at the great trial (10–11) and that the victors will become pillars of the heavenly temple, upon which three names will be inscribed: God, Jerusalem, and Christ (12).

3:7 *Philadelphia:* modern Alasehir, ca. thirty miles southeast of Sardis, founded by Attalus II Philadelphus of Pergamum to be an "open door" (8) for Greek culture; it was destroyed by an earthquake in A.D. 17. Rebuilt by money from the Emperor Tiberius, the city was renamed Neo-Caesarea; this may explain the allusions to "name" in v 12. *Key of David:* to the heavenly city of David (cf Is 22:22), "the new Jerusalem" (12), over which Christ has supreme authority.

3:8 *An open door:* opportunities for sharing and proclaiming the faith; cf Acts 14:27; 1 Cor 16:9; 2 Cor 2:12.

3:10 *My message of endurance:* this does not refer to a saying of Jesus about patience but to the example of Christ's patient endurance. *The inhabitants of the earth:* literally, "those who live on the earth." This expression, which also occurs in 6:10; 8:13; 11:10; 13:8, 12, 14; 17:2, 8, always refers to the pagan world.

3:12 *Pillar:* this may be an allusion to the rebuilding of the city; see the note on v 7. *New Jerusalem:* it is described in 21:10—22:5.

* **3:3** Mt 24:42–44; Mk 13:33; 1 Thes 5:2; 2 Pt 3:10.
3:4 Rv 7:13–14.
3:5 Ps 69:29; Dn 12:1 / Mt 10:32.
3:7 Is 22:22; Mt 16:19.
3:9 Rv 2:9 / Is 45:14; 60:14.
3:11 Rv 2:25; 22:7, 20.
3:12 Rv 21:2–3; Ez 48:35 / Rv 19:13.

To Laodicea†

14*† "To the angel of the church in Laodicea,
write this:
" 'The Amen, the faithful and true witness, the
source of God's creation, says this: 15† "I know
your works; I know that you are neither cold nor
hot. I wish you were either cold or hot. 16† So,
because you are lukewarm, neither hot nor cold,
I will spit you out of my mouth. 17*† For you
say, 'I am rich and affluent and have no need
of anything,' and yet do not realize that you are
wretched, pitiable, poor, blind, and naked. 18† I
advise you to buy from me gold refined by fire
so that you may be rich, and white garments to
put on so that your shameful nakedness may not
be exposed, and buy ointment to smear on your
eyes so that you may see. 19* Those whom I love,
I reprove and chastise. Be earnest, therefore, and
repent.
20† " ' "Behold, I stand at the door and knock. If
anyone hears my voice and opens the door, [then]
I will enter his house and dine with him, and he
with me. 21* I will give the victor the right to sit
with me on my throne, as I myself first won the
victory and sit with my Father on his throne.
22 " ' "Whoever has ears ought to hear what the
Spirit says to the churches." ' "

Live It!

Jesus Christ Is the Lord of History

After the messages to the churches in Asia, John presents several visions that reveal God's action in history. Read Revelation 4:1–11. The vision of God's throne is the background of the whole Book of Revelation. It symbolizes God's authority over history. The vision is enhanced by a heavenly worship in which God is proclaimed and praised:

"Holy, holy, holy is the Lord God almighty,
who was, and who is, and who is to come."
(Rv 4:8)

Read 5:1–14. The vision continues. Two symbols stand out: a sealed scroll and a lamb. God holds a scroll, whose meaning was hidden to the Christian communities in their persecution. A lamb appears. It is the risen Jesus, carrying in his body the signs of his Passion. He receives the scroll from God. He is the only one who can open the scroll and reveal the mystery of death and life.

Read both visions again and experience the honor, glory, and power of Christ. Let these visions reinforce your faith and renew your hope every time you wonder about the meaning of an event you cannot make sense of.

▶ Revelation, chapters 4–5

III: God and the Lamb in Heaven

Vision of Heavenly Worship†

4 1 After this I had a vision of an open door†
to heaven, and I heard the trumpetlike voice
that had spoken to me before, saying, "Come
up here and I will show you what must happen
afterwards." 2*† At once I was caught up in spirit.

3:14–22 The letter to Laodicea reprimands the community for being lukewarm (15–16), but no particular faults are singled out. Their material prosperity is contrasted with their spiritual poverty, the violet tunics that were the source of their wealth with the white robe of baptism, and their famous eye ointment with true spiritual perception (17–18). But Christ's chastisement is inspired by love and a desire to be allowed to share the messianic banquet with his followers in the heavenly kingdom (19–21).

3:14 *Laodicea:* ca. forty miles southeast of Philadelphia and ca. eighty miles east of Ephesus, a wealthy industrial and commercial center, with a renowned medical school. It exported fine woolen garments and was famous for its eye salves. It was so wealthy that it was proudly rebuilt without outside aid after the devastating earthquake of A.D. 60/61. *The Amen:* this is a divine title (cf Hebrew text of Is 65:16) applied to Christ; cf 2 Cor 1:20. *Source of God's creation:* literally, "the beginning of God's creation," a concept found also in Jn 1:3; Col 1:16–17; Heb 1:2; cf Prv 8:22–31; Wis 9:1–2.

3:15–16 Halfhearted commitment to the faith is nauseating to Christ; cf Rom 12:11.

3:16 *Spit:* literally, "vomit." The image is that of a beverage that should be either hot or cold. Perhaps there is an allusion to the hot springs of Hierapolis across the Lycus river from Laodicea, which would have been lukewarm by the time they reached Laodicea.

3:17 Economic prosperity occasioned spiritual bankruptcy.

3:18 *Gold . . . fire:* God's grace. *White garments:* symbol of an upright life; the city was noted for its violet/purple cloth. *Ointment . . . eyes:* to remove spiritual blindness; one of the city's exports was eye ointment (see the note on 3:14).

3:20 Christ invites all to the messianic banquet in heaven; cf Is 25:6; Lk 14:15; 22:30.

4:1–11 The seer now describes a vision of the heavenly court in worship of God enthroned. He reverently avoids naming or describing God but pictures twenty-four elders in priestly and regal attire (4) and God's throne and its surroundings made of precious gems and other symbols that traditionally express the majesty of God (5–6). Universal creation is represented by the four living creatures (6–7). Along with the twenty-four elders, they praise God unceasingly in humble adoration (8–11).

4:1 The ancients viewed heaven as a solid vault, entered by way of actual doors.

4:2–8 Much of the imagery here is taken from Ez 1 and 10.

3:14 Rv 1:5. **3:17** Prv 13:7; Lk 12:21. **3:19** Prv 3:11–12; 1 Cor 11:32; Heb 12:5–11. **3:21** Lk 22:28–30; Mt 19:28. **4:2–3** Is 6:1 / Ez 1:26–28.

A throne was there in heaven, and on the throne
sat 3 one whose appearance sparkled like jasper
and carnelian. Around the throne was a halo
as brilliant as an emerald. 4*† Surrounding the
throne I saw twenty-four other thrones on which
twenty-four elders sat, dressed in white garments
and with gold crowns on their heads. 5† From the
throne came flashes of lightning, rumblings, and
peals of thunder. Seven flaming torches burned
in front of the throne, which are the seven spirits
of God. 6*† In front of the throne was something
that resembled a sea of glass like crystal.
In the center and around the throne, there
were four living creatures covered with eyes in
front and in back. 7† The first creature resembled
a lion, the second was like a calf, the third had a
face like that of a human being, and the fourth
looked like an eagle in flight. 8*† The four living

†

4:4 *Twenty-four elders:* these represent the twelve tribes of Israel and the twelve apostles; cf 21:12–14.

4:5 *Flashes of lightning, rumblings, and peals of thunder:* as in other descriptions of God's appearance or activity; cf 8:5; 11:19; 16:18; Ex 19:16; Ez 1:4, 13. *The seven spirits of God:* the seven "angels of the presence" as in 8:2 and Tb 12:15.

4:6 *A sea of glass like crystal:* an image adapted from Ez 1:22–26. *Four living creatures:* these are symbols taken from Ez 1:5–21; they are identified as cherubim in Ez 10:20. *Covered with eyes:* these suggest God's knowledge and concern.

4:7 *Lion . . . calf . . . human being . . . eagle:* these symbolize, respectively, what is noblest, strongest, wisest, and swiftest in creation. *Calf:* traditionally translated "ox," the Greek word refers to a heifer or young bull. Since the second century, these four creatures have been used as symbols of the evangelists Mark, Luke, Matthew, and John, respectively.

4:8 *Six wings:* like the seraphim of Is 6:2.

*

4:4 Is 24:23.
4:6 Ex 24:10.
4:8 Is 6:2–3 / Rv 1:4, 8; 11:17; 16:5.

Pray It!

Enthusiastic Praise!

Over and over in John's vision of heaven, we find enthusiastic praise being offered to God, or to the Lamb of God, who is Christ Jesus. There are angels, incense, fantastic creatures, jewels, gold, elders, white-robed martyrs, and a crowd too great to number. The scenes of this vision inspire us to add our voice to theirs, to praise the majesty of God and the saving sacrifice of Jesus Christ.

In some Christian traditions, including some Catholic traditions, loud, spontaneous praise of God is common. However, for other Catholics and Christians, praise is also expressed through more solemn prayers and music. Whatever our expression, we should be enthusiastic with our praise!

How does the vision of the "countless in number" crying out "in a loud voice" in Revelation 5:11–12 encourage you to be more bold in your praise of God? Can you sing out more loudly in Mass? Can you participate more from your heart in saying common prayers with others? In your private prayer, can you praise God without asking for anything or using memorized prayers?

► **Rv 4:1—5:14**

Did You Know?

Symbolic Numbers and Colors

To understand the Book of Revelation, we need to understand the symbolism of its numbers and colors. The numbers seven and twelve symbolize fullness or perfection. The number four symbolizes universality (as in the four compass directions). The number one thousand symbolizes a multitude or a quantity too big to count. Thus, the twenty-four elders (see Rv 4:4) represent the perfection of the twelve Tribes of Israel and the Twelve Apostles. The Lamb with horns and eyes (see 5:6) represents the risen Christ, who has the fullness of power (seven horns) and perfect knowledge (seven eyes). The 144,000 who will be saved (see 7:4) represent a chosen multitude too big to count, because 144,000 equals 12 times 12 times 1,000.

The color white symbolizes victory, and red symbolizes bloodshed. Thus, the people who are slaughtered and given white robes (see 6:9–11) are the martyrs, who gave up their lives for their faith. They are victorious in martyrdom because God raised them to eternal life.

► **Rv 4:1—7:17**

creatures, each of them with six wings, were cov-
ered with eyes inside and out. Day and night they
do not stop exclaiming:

"Holy, holy, holy is the Lord God almighty,
who was, and who is, and who is to come."

9 Whenever the living creatures give glory and
honor and thanks to the one who sits on the
throne, who lives forever and ever, 10 the twenty-
four elders fall down before the one who sits on
the throne and worship him, who lives forever
and ever. They throw down their crowns before
the throne, exclaiming:

11* "Worthy are you, Lord our God,
to receive glory and honor and power,
for you created all things;
because of your will they came to be and
were created."

The Scroll and the Lamb†

5 1* I saw a scroll† in the right hand of the
one who sat on the throne. It had writing
on both sides and was sealed with seven seals.
2 Then I saw a mighty angel who proclaimed in
a loud voice, "Who is worthy to open the scroll
and break its seals?" 3 But no one in heaven or
on earth or under the earth was able to open
the scroll or to examine it. 4 I shed many tears
because no one was found worthy to open the
scroll or to examine it. 5*† One of the elders said
to me, "Do not weep. The lion of the tribe of Ju-
dah, the root of David, has triumphed, enabling
him to open the scroll with its seven seals."
6*† Then I saw standing in the midst of the
throne and the four living creatures and the el-
ders a Lamb that seemed to have been slain. He
had seven horns and seven eyes; these are the
[seven] spirits of God sent out into the whole
world. 7 He came and received the scroll from
the right hand of the one who sat on the throne.
8 When he took it, the four living creatures and
the twenty-four elders fell down before the
Lamb. Each of the elders held a harp and gold
bowls filled with incense, which are the prayers
of the holy ones. 9 They sang a new hymn:

"Worthy are you to receive the scroll
and to break open its seals,
for you were slain and with your blood you
purchased for God
those from every tribe and tongue, people
and nation.
10* You made them a kingdom and priests for
our God,
and they will reign on earth."

11*† I looked again and heard the voices of many
angels who surrounded the throne and the living
creatures and the elders. They were countless in
number, 12 and they cried out in a loud voice:

"Worthy is the Lamb that was slain
to receive power and riches, wisdom and
strength,
honor and glory and blessing."

13 Then I heard every creature in heaven and on
earth and under the earth and in the sea, every-
thing in the universe, cry out:

"To the one who sits on the throne and to the
Lamb
be blessing and honor, glory and might,
forever and ever."

14 The four living creatures answered, "Amen,"
and the elders fell down and worshiped.

IV: The Seven Seals, Trumpets, and Plagues, with Interludes†

The First Six Seals†

6 1† Then I watched while the Lamb broke
open the first of the seven seals, and I heard

---

† **5:1–14** The seer now describes a papyrus roll in God's right hand (1) with seven seals indicating the importance of the message. A mighty angel asks who is worthy to open the scroll, i.e., who can accomplish God's salvific plan (2). There is despair at first when no one in creation can do it (3–4). But the seer is comforted by an elder who tells him that Christ, called the lion of the tribe of Judah, has won the right to open it (5). Christ then appears as a Lamb, coming to receive the scroll from God (6–7), for which he is acclaimed as at a coronation (8–10). This is followed by a doxology of the angels (11–12) and then finally by the heavenly church united with all of creation (13–14).

5:1 *A scroll:* a papyrus roll possibly containing a list of afflictions for sinners (cf Ez 2:9–10) or God's plan for the world. *Sealed with seven seals:* it is totally hidden from all but God. Only the Lamb (7–9) has the right to carry out the divine plan.

5:5 *The lion of the tribe of Judah, the root of David:* these are the messianic titles applied to Christ to symbolize his victory; cf 22:16; Gn 49:9; Is 11:1, 10; Mt 1:1.

5:6 Christ is the Paschal Lamb without blemish, whose blood saved the new Israel from sin and death; cf Ex 12; Is 53:7; Jn 1:29, 36; Acts 8:32; 1 Pt 1:18–19. This is the main title for Christ in Revelation, used twenty-eight times. *Seven horns and seven eyes:* Christ has the fullness (see the note on 1:4) of power (horns) and knowledge (eyes); cf Zec 4:10. *[Seven] spirits:* as in 1:4; 3:1; and 4:5.

5:11 *Countless:* literally, "100,000,000 plus 1,000,000," used by the author to express infinity.

6:1—16:21 A series of seven disasters now begins as each seal is broken (6:1—8:1), followed by a similar series as seven trumpets sound (8:2—11:19) and as seven angels pour bowls on the earth causing plagues (15:1—16:21). These gloomy sequences are inter-

---

4:11 Rom 4:17; 16:27.
5:1 Is 29:11.
5:5 Is 11:1, 10; Rom 15:12.
5:6 Jn 1:29.
5:10 Rv 1:6; Ex 19:6; Is 61:6.
5:11 Dn 7:10; Jude 14–15.

one of the four living creatures cry out in a voice
like thunder, "Come forward." 2*† I looked, and
there was a white horse, and its rider had a bow.
He was given a crown, and he rode forth victori-
ous to further his victories.
3 When he broke open the second seal, I heard
the second living creature cry out, "Come for-
ward." 4*† Another horse came out, a red one.
Its rider was given power to take peace away from
the earth, so that people would slaughter one an-
other. And he was given a huge sword.
5† When he broke open the third seal, I heard
the third living creature cry out, "Come forward."
I looked, and there was a black horse, and its rider
held a scale in his hand. 6*† I heard what seemed
to be a voice in the midst of the four living crea-
tures. It said, "A ration of wheat costs a day's pay,
and three rations of barley cost a day's pay. But do
not damage the olive oil or the wine."
7 When he broke open the fourth seal, I heard
the voice of the fourth living creature cry out,
"Come forward." 8*† I looked, and there was
a pale green horse. Its rider was named Death,
and Hades accompanied him. They were given
authority over a quarter of the earth, to kill with
sword, famine, and plague, and by means of the
beasts of the earth.
9† When he broke open the fifth seal, I saw

† rupted by longer or shorter scenes suggesting the triumph of God and his witnesses (e.g., chs 7, 10, 11, 12, 13, 14).

6:1–17 This chapter provides a symbolic description of the contents of the sealed scroll. The breaking of the first four seals reveals four riders. The first rider (of a white horse) is a conquering power (1–2), the second (red horse) a symbol of bloody war (3–4), the third (black horse) a symbol of famine (5–6), the fourth (pale green horse) a symbol of Death himself, accompanied by Hades (the netherworld) as his page (7–8). Verse 8b summarizes the role of all four riders. The breaking of the fifth seal reveals Christian martyrs in an attitude of sacrifice as blood poured out at the foot of an altar begging God for vindication, which will come only when their quota is filled; but they are given a white robe symbolic of victory (9–11). The breaking of the sixth seal reveals typical apocalyptic signs in the sky and the sheer terror of all people at the imminent divine judgment (12–17).

6:1–8 The imagery is adapted from Zec 1:8–10; 6:1–8.

6:2 *White horse . . . bow:* this may perhaps allude specifically to the Parthians on the eastern border of the Roman empire. Expert in the use of the bow, they constantly harassed the Romans and won a major victory in A.D. 62; see the note on 9:13–21. But the Old Testament imagery typifies the history of oppression of God's people at all times.

6:4 *Huge sword:* this is a symbol of war and violence; cf Ez 21:14–17.

6:5 *Black horse:* this is a symbol of famine, the usual accompaniment of war in antiquity; cf Lv 26:26; Ez 4:16–17. The *scale* is a symbol of shortage of food with a corresponding rise in price.

6:6 *A day's pay:* literally, "a denarius," a Roman silver coin that constitutes a day's wage in Mt 20:2. Because of the famine, food was rationed and sold at an exorbitant price. A liter of flour was considered a day's ration in the Greek historians Herodotus and Diogenes Laertius. *Barley:* food of the poor (Jn 6:9, 13; cf 2 Kgs 7:1, 16, 18); it was also used to feed animals; cf 1 Kgs 5:8. *Do not damage:* the olive and the vine are to be used more sparingly in time of famine.

6:8 *Pale green:* symbol of death and decay; cf Ez 14:21.

6:9 *The altar:* this altar corresponds to the altar of holocausts in the temple in Jerusalem; see also 11:1. *Because of the witness . . . word of God:* literally, "because of the word of God and the witness they had borne."

* **6:2** Zec 1:8–10; 6:1–3. **6:4** Ez 21:14–16. **6:6** Lv 26:26; Ez 4:16–17. **6:8** Ez 14:21.

Did You Know?

The Seven Seals and Seven Trumpets

The vision continues. In chapters 6–8 of Revelation, the Lamb opens the seven seals on the scroll and thus reveals the great forces in salvation history. The opening of the first four seals reveals the four horses of the apocalypse that bring conquest, strife, famine, and plagues. These are the things that throughout history have made people yearn for God's salvation.

The opening of the fifth seal reveals the souls of the martyrs, who demand justice. Their white robes indicate that they are already with the risen Christ. They are waiting for other martyrs, but this stage will end soon.

The opening of the sixth seal reveals how God will get justice for the martyrs. History will change, and all people, even the powerful, will suffer. The visions of the census and of the great crowd in 7:1–17 reveal the destiny of Christians. The vision contains many reminders of the Exodus story. After this, a multitude that cannot be counted, from all nations, tribes, peoples, and languages, will experience God's salvation and sing of God's glory.

Finally, the Lamb opens the last seal. Seven more trumpets are revealed. When they are blown by angels, a new series of plagues is released (see 8:6—9:21). One-third of the people are destroyed by these plagues so that those remaining might repent. But in spite of these warnings, many people do not change.

Apocalyptic writing, as in the Book of Revelation, used symbolic language because it was addressed to Christians who were being persecuted. Its meaning could not be taken at face value but held a deeper meaning for those who believed. This vision tells us that no matter what evil besets us, God saves the faithful.

▶ **Revelation, chapters 6–9**

underneath the altar the souls of those who had been slaughtered because of the witness they bore to the word of God. 10† They cried out in a loud voice, "How long will it be, holy and true master, before you sit in judgment and avenge our blood on the inhabitants of the earth?" 11 Each of them was given a white robe, and they were told to be patient a little while longer until the number was filled of their fellow servants and brothers who were going to be killed as they had been.

12*† Then I watched while he broke open the sixth seal, and there was a great earthquake; the sun turned as black as dark sackcloth† and the whole moon became like blood. 13† The stars in the sky fell to the earth like unripe figs shaken loose from the tree in a strong wind. 14*† Then the sky was divided like a torn scroll curling up, and every mountain and island was moved from its place. 15† The kings of the earth, the nobles, the military officers, the rich, the powerful, and every slave and free person hid themselves in caves and among mountain crags. 16* They cried out to the mountains and the rocks, "Fall on us and hide us from the face of the one who sits on the throne and from the wrath of the Lamb, 17† because the great day of their wrath has come and who can withstand it?"

The 144,000 Sealed

7 1*† After this I saw four angels standing at the four corners of the earth,† holding back the four winds of the earth so that no wind could blow on land or sea or against any tree. 2† Then I saw another angel come up from the East, holding the seal of the living God. He cried out in a loud voice to the four angels who were given power to damage the land and the sea, 3* "Do not damage the land or the sea or the trees until we put the seal on the foreheads of the servants of our God." 4*† I heard the number of those who had been marked with the seal, one hundred and forty-four thousand marked from every tribe of the Israelites: 5† twelve thousand were marked from the tribe of Judah, twelve thousand from the tribe of Reuben, twelve thousand from the tribe of Gad, 6 twelve thousand from the tribe of Asher, twelve thousand from the tribe of Naphtali, twelve thousand from the tribe of Manasseh, 7 twelve thousand from the tribe of Simeon, twelve thousand from the tribe of Levi, twelve thousand from the tribe of Issachar, 8 twelve thousand from the tribe of Zebulun, twelve thousand from the tribe of Joseph, and twelve thousand were marked from the tribe of Benjamin.

Triumph of the Elect

9† After this I had a vision of a great multitude, which no one could count, from every nation, race, people, and tongue. They stood before the throne and before the Lamb, wearing white robes and holding palm branches in their hands. 10† They cried out in a loud voice:

"Salvation comes from our God, who is
seated on the throne,
and from the Lamb."

11 All the angels stood around the throne and around the elders and the four living creatures. They prostrated themselves before the throne, worshiped God, 12 and exclaimed:

6:10 *Holy and true master:* Old Testament usage as well as the context indicates that this is addressed to God rather than to Christ.

6:12–14 Symbolic rather than literal description of the cosmic upheavals attending the day of the Lord when the martyrs' prayer for vindication (10) would be answered; cf Am 8:8–9; Is 34:4; 50:3; Jl 2:10; 3:3–4; Mt 24:4–36; Mk 13:5–37; Lk 21:8–36.

6:12 *Dark sackcloth:* for mourning, sackcloth was made from the skin of a black goat.

6:13 *Unripe figs:* literally, "summer (or winter) fruit."

6:14 *Was divided:* literally, "was split," like a broken papyrus roll torn in two, each half then curling up to form a roll on either side.

6:15 *Nobles:* literally, "courtiers," "grandees." *Military officers:* literally, "commanders of 1,000 men," used in Josephus and other Greek authors as the equivalent of the Roman *tribunus militum.* The listing of various ranks of society represents the universality of terror at the impending doom.

6:17 *Their:* this reading is attested in the best manuscripts, but the vast majority read "his" in reference to the wrath of the Lamb in the preceding verse.

7:1–17 An interlude of two visions precedes the breaking of the seventh seal, just as two more will separate the sixth and seventh trumpets (ch 10). In the first vision (1–8), the elect receive the seal of the living God as protection against the coming cataclysm; cf 14:1; Ez 9:4–6; 2 Cor 1:22; Eph 1:13; 4:30. The second vision (9–17) portrays the faithful Christians before God's throne to encourage those on earth to persevere to the end, even to death.

7:1 *The four corners of the earth:* the earth is seen as a table or rectangular surface.

7:2 *East:* literally, "rising of the sun." The east was considered the source of light and the place of paradise (Gn 2:8). *Seal:* whatever was marked by the impression of one's signet ring belonged to that person and was under his protection.

7:4–9 *One hundred and forty-four thousand:* the square of twelve (the number of Israel's tribes) multiplied by a thousand, symbolic of the new Israel (cf 14:1–5; Gal 6:16; Jas 1:1) that embraces people *from every nation, race, people, and tongue* (9).

7:5–8 Judah is placed first because of Christ; cf "the Lion of the tribe of Judah" (5:5). Dan is omitted because of a later tradition that the antichrist would arise from it.

7:9 *White robes . . . palm branches:* symbols of joy and victory; see the note on 3:5.

7:10 *Salvation comes from:* literally, "(let) salvation (be ascribed) to." A similar hymn of praise is found at the fall of the dragon (12:10) and of Babylon (19:1).

6:12 Jl 3:4; Mt 24:29.
6:14 Is 34:4 / Rv 16:20.
6:16 Is 2:19; Hos 10:8; Lk 23:30.
7:1 Jer 49:36; Zec 6:5.
7:3 Ex 12:7–14; Ez 9:4; 2 Cor 1:22; Eph 1:13; 4:30.
7:4 Rv 14:1.

Catholic Connection

The Communion of Saints

What do you do when things get really difficult? John is answering that question for his readers. John describes a looming ordeal and how the faithful will be marked on the forehead as a sign of God's protection. This sign does not remove them from the trials ahead but calls them to trust in God during the trials. John then describes a multitude in heaven that have already survived the ordeal and remained faithful to God. The important message for John's audience is how those in heaven survived. The angel says that they were made pure through the blood of the Lamb. That is, they united their lives with the Passion, death, and Resurrection of Jesus Christ and remained faithful throughout.

It is the union of those on earth facing life's ordeals and those already in heaven, along with those who have died and are being purified, that make up the Church. The Church refers to this body of believers as the communion of saints. As a communion of saints, we are all united to one another, and the good that any one of us does benefits all of us. Therefore, our prayers for the dead are effective, just as the prayers of those in heaven help us on earth.

As a Church, we often ask for the prayers of those in heaven, especially the saints—those who have been canonized or officially recognized by the Church. These women and men lived extraordinary, often heroic, lives of faith. The process of canonization can take many years, even centuries. During the process, the Church investigates the individual's life, writings, and any miracles attributed to her or him. If there is sufficient evidence of the person's holiness, the Church beatifies the individual, which is an intermediate step toward canonization. Then over time, if there are more confirmed miracles, the Church may then decide to canonize the person, making her or him an official saint.

The saints also serve as models for how we are to face trials and remain faithful throughout our lives. Just like the saints and the faithful in John's vision, we too are called to resist sin and offer our lives to God, even if it means facing the discipline of suffering. We are called to be the new generation of witnesses—the saints of our day whose example calls and strengthens others on the journey.

▶ **Rv 7:2–14**

Catechism, nos. 946–962

Pray It!

Sing God's Glory

The Book of Revelation contains beautiful prayers of praise. Among them are the hymn to the Lamb (see 5:9–14), the hymn of the multitude from every nation (see 7:10–17), the song of the Lamb (see 15:3–4), and the victory song (see 19:1–8).

In your prayer, read these prayers slowly and carefully. Imagine the awe-inspiring scenes of God's glory they describe. Quietly reflect on how you have experienced the glory and power of God in your life. Look at the events you experience day to day; can you find the extraordinary in the ordinary? End your reflection by letting these songs inspire your own prayer of praise to God.

▶ **Rv 7:10–17**

"Amen. Blessing and glory, wisdom and
thanksgiving,
honor, power, and might
be to our God forever and ever. Amen."

13 Then one of the elders spoke up and said to
me, "Who are these wearing white robes, and
where did they come from?" 14*† I said to him,
"My lord, you are the one who knows." He said
to me, "These are the ones who have survived
the time of great distress; they have washed their
robes and made them white in the blood of the
Lamb.

15 "For this reason they stand before God's
throne
and worship him day and night in his
temple.
The one who sits on the throne will shelter
them.
16* They will not hunger or thirst anymore,
nor will the sun or any heat strike them.
17*† For the Lamb who is in the center of the
throne will shepherd them
and lead them to springs of life-giving water,
and God will wipe away every tear from
their eyes."

The Seven Trumpets

8 1*† When he broke open the seventh seal,
there was silence in heaven† for about half
an hour. 2* And I saw that the seven angels who
stood before God were given seven trumpets.

The Gold Censer

3*† Another angel came and stood at the altar,
holding a gold censer. He was given a great quan-
tity of incense to offer, along with the prayers of
all the holy ones, on the gold altar that was be-
fore the throne. 4 The smoke of the incense along
with the prayers of the holy ones went up before
God from the hand of the angel. 5* Then the an-
gel took the censer, filled it with burning coals
from the altar, and hurled it down to the earth.
There were peals of thunder, rumblings, flashes
of lightning, and an earthquake.

The First Four Trumpets

6* The seven angels who were holding the
seven trumpets prepared to blow them.
7† When the first one blew his trumpet, there
came hail and fire mixed with blood, which was
hurled down to the earth. A third of the land was
burned up, along with a third of the trees and all
green grass.
8*† When the second angel blew his trumpet,
something like a large burning mountain was
hurled into the sea. A third of the sea turned to
blood, 9† a third of the creatures living in the sea
died, and a third of the ships were wrecked.

7:14 *Time of great distress:* fierce persecution by the Romans; cf Introduction.

7:17 *Life-giving water:* literally, "the water of life," God's grace, which flows from Christ; cf 21:6; 22:1, 17; Jn 4:10, 14.

8:1–13 The breaking of the seventh seal produces at first silence and then seven symbolic disasters, each announced by a trumpet blast, of which the first four form a unit as did the first four seals. A minor liturgy (3–5) is enclosed by a vision of seven angels (2, 6). Then follow the first four trumpet blasts, each heralding catastrophes modeled on the plagues of Egypt affecting the traditional prophetic third (cf Ez 5:12) of the earth, sea, fresh water, and stars (7–12). Finally, there is a vision of an eagle warning of the last three trumpet blasts (13).

8:1 *Silence in heaven:* as in Zep 1:7, a prelude to the eschatological woes that are to follow; cf Introduction.

8:3 *Altar:* there seems to be only one altar in the heavenly temple, corresponding to the altar of holocausts in 6:9, and here to the altar of incense in Jerusalem; cf also 9:13; 11:1; 14:18; 16:7.

8:7 This woe resembles the seventh plague of Egypt (Ex 9:23–24); cf Jl 3:3.

8:8–11 The background of these two woes is the first plague of Egypt (Ex 7:20–21).

8:9 *Creatures living in the sea:* literally, "creatures in the sea that had souls."

7:14 Mt 24:21.
7:16 Is 49:10.
7:17 Rv 21:4; Is 25:8.
8:1 Hb 2:20; Zep 1:7; Zec 2:17.
8:2 Rv 4:5; Tb 12:15.
8:3 Ps 141:2; Tb 12:12.
8:5 Ez 10:2; Ps 11:6 / Rv 4:5; 11:19; 16:18.
8:6 Rv 16:1–21.
8:8 Ex 7:20.

10* When the third angel blew his trumpet, a large star burning like a torch fell from the sky. It fell on a third of the rivers and on the springs of water. 11*† The star was called "Wormwood," and a third of all the water turned to wormwood. Many people died from this water, because it was made bitter.

12* When the fourth angel blew his trumpet, a third of the sun, a third of the moon, and a third of the stars were struck, so that a third of them became dark. The day lost its light for a third of the time, as did the night.

13† Then I looked again and heard an eagle flying high overhead cry out in a loud voice, "Woe! Woe! Woe to the inhabitants of the earth from the rest of the trumpet blasts that the three angels are about to blow!"

The Fifth Trumpet†

9 1*† Then the fifth angel blew his trumpet, and I saw a star that had fallen from the sky to the earth. It was given the key for the passage to the abyss. 2* It opened the passage to the abyss, and smoke came up out of the passage like smoke from a huge furnace. The sun and the air were darkened by the smoke from the passage. 3*† Locusts came out of the smoke onto the land, and they were given the same power as scorpions of the earth. 4 They were told not to harm the grass of the earth or any plant or any tree, but only those people who did not have the seal of God on their foreheads. 5† They were not allowed to kill them but only to torment them for five months; the torment they inflicted was like that of a scorpion when it stings a person. 6* During that time these people will seek death but will not find it, and they will long to die but death will escape them.

7*† The appearance of the locusts was like that of horses ready for battle. On their heads they wore what looked like crowns of gold; their faces were like human faces, 8* and they had hair like women's hair. Their teeth were like lions' teeth, 9 and they had chests like iron breastplates. The sound of their wings was like the sound of many horse-drawn chariots racing into battle. 10 They had tails like scorpions, with stingers; with their tails they had power to harm people for five months. 11† They had as their king the angel of the abyss, whose name in Hebrew is Abaddon and in Greek Apollyon.

12 The first woe has passed, but there are two more to come.

The Sixth Trumpet†

13* Then the sixth angel blew his trumpet, and I heard a voice coming from the [four]† horns of the gold altar before God, 14† telling the sixth angel who held the trumpet, "Release the four angels who are bound at the banks of the great river Euphrates." 15 So the four angels were released, who were prepared for this hour, day, month, and year to kill a third of the human race. 16 The number of cavalry troops was two hundred million; I heard their number. 17*† Now in my vision this is how I saw the horses and their riders. They wore red, blue, and yellow breastplates, and the horses' heads were like heads of lions, and out of their mouths came fire, smoke, and sulfur. 18 By these three plagues of fire, smoke, and sulfur that came out of their mouths a third of the human race was killed. 19 For the power of the horses is in their mouths and in their tails; for their tails are like snakes, with heads that inflict harm.

20*† The rest of the human race, who were

---

†

8:11 *Wormwood:* an extremely bitter and malignant plant symbolizing the punishment God inflicts on the ungodly; cf Jer 9:12–14; 23:15.

8:13 *Woe! Woe! Woe:* each of the three woes pronounced by the angel represents a separate disaster; cf 9:12; 11:14. The final woe, released by the seventh trumpet blast, includes the plagues of ch 16.

9:1–12 The fifth trumpet heralds a woe containing elements from the eighth and ninth plagues of Egypt (Ex 10:12–15, 21–23) but specifically reminiscent of the invasion of locusts in Jl 1:4—2:10.

9:1 *A star:* late Judaism represented fallen powers as stars (Is 14:12–15; Lk 10:18; Jude 13), but a comparison with 1:20 and 20:1 suggests that here it means an angel. *The passage to the abyss:* referring to Sheol, the netherworld, where Satan and the fallen angels are kept for a thousand years, to be cast afterwards into the pool of fire; cf 20:7–10. The abyss was conceived of as a vast subterranean cavern full of fire. Its only link with the earth was a kind of passage or mine shaft, which was kept locked.

9:3 *Scorpions:* their poisonous sting was proverbial; Ez 2:6; Lk 11:12.

9:5 *For five months:* more or less corresponding to the life-span of locusts.

9:7–10 Eight characteristics are listed to show the eschatological and diabolical nature of these locusts.

9:11 *Abaddon:* Hebrew (more precisely, Aramaic) for destruction or ruin. *Apollyon:* Greek for the "Destroyer."

9:13–21 The sixth trumpet heralds a woe representing another diabolical attack symbolized by an invasion by the Parthians living east of the Euphrates; see the note on 6:2. At the appointed time (15), the frightful horses act as God's agents of judgment. The imaginative details are not to be taken literally; see Introduction and the note on 6:12–14.

9:13 *[Four]:* many Greek manuscripts and versions omit the word. The horns were situated at the four corners of the altar (Ex 27:2; 30:2–3); see the note on 8:3.

9:14–15 *The four angels:* they are symbolic of the destructive activity that will be extended throughout the universe.

9:17 *Blue:* literally, "hyacinth-colored." *Yellow:* literally, "sulfurous."

9:20 *The works of their hands:* i.e., the gods their hands had made.

---

*

8:10 Is 14:12.
8:11 Jer 9:14.
8:12 Ex 10:21–23.
9:1 Rv 20:1.
9:2 Gn 19:28.
9:3 Ex 10:12–15; Wis 16:9.
9:6 Jb 3:21.
9:7 Jl 2:4.
9:8 Jl 1:6.
9:13 Ex 30:1–3.
9:17 Jb 41:10–13.
9:20 Ps 135:15–17; Is 17:8; Dn 5:4.

not killed by these plagues, did not repent of
the works of their hands, to give up the worship
of demons and idols made from gold, silver,
bronze, stone, and wood, which cannot see or
hear or walk. 21 Nor did they repent of their mur-
ders, their magic potions, their unchastity, or
their robberies.

The Angel with the Small Scroll

10 1† Then I saw another mighty angel come
down from heaven wrapped in a cloud,
with a halo around his head;† his face was like
the sun and his feet were like pillars of fire. 2† In
his hand he held a small scroll that had been
opened. He placed his right foot on the sea and
his left foot on the land, 3* and then he cried out
in a loud voice as a lion roars. When he cried
out, the seven thunders raised their voices, too.
4 When the seven thunders had spoken, I was
about to write it down; but I heard a voice from
heaven say, "Seal up what the seven thunders
have spoken, but do not write it down." 5 Then
the angel I saw standing on the sea and on the
land raised his right hand to heaven 6*† and
swore by the one who lives forever and ever, who
created heaven and earth and sea and all that is
in them, "There shall be no more delay. 7*† At
the time when you hear the seventh angel blow
his trumpet, the mysterious plan of God shall
be fulfilled, as he promised to his servants the
prophets."

8 Then the voice that I had heard from heaven
spoke to me again and said, "Go, take the scroll
that lies open in the hand of the angel who is
standing on the sea and on the land." 9† So I
went up to the angel and told him to give me the
small scroll. He said to me, "Take and swallow
it. It will turn your stomach sour, but in your
mouth it will taste as sweet as honey." 10* I took
the small scroll from the angel's hand and swal-
lowed it. In my mouth it was like sweet honey,
but when I had eaten it, my stomach turned sour.
11† Then someone said to me, "You must proph-
esy again about many peoples, nations, tongues,
and kings."

The Two Witnesses

11 1*† Then I was given a measuring rod like
a staff and I was told, "Come and measure
the temple of God and the altar, and count those
who are worshiping in it. 2† But exclude the
outer court of the temple; do not measure it, for
it has been handed over to the Gentiles, who will
trample the holy city for forty-two months. 3† I
will commission my two witnesses to prophesy
for those twelve hundred and sixty days, wearing
sackcloth." 4*† These are the two olive trees and
the two lampstands that stand before the Lord
of the earth. 5† If anyone wants to harm them,
fire comes out of their mouths and devours their
enemies. In this way, anyone wanting to harm
them is sure to be slain. 6* They have the power
to close up the sky so that no rain can fall during
the time of their prophesying. They also have
power to turn water into blood and to afflict the
earth with any plague as often as they wish.

7*† When they have finished their testimony,
the beast that comes up from the abyss will wage

10:1—11:14 An interlude in two scenes (10:1–11 and 11:1–14) precedes the sounding of the seventh trumpet; cf 7:1–17. The first vision describes an angel astride sea and land like a colossus, with a small scroll open, the contents of which indicate that the end is imminent (ch 10). The second vision is of the measuring of the temple and of two witnesses, whose martyrdom means that the kingdom of God is about to be inaugurated.

10:1–4 *The seven thunders:* God's voice announcing judgment and doom; cf Ps 29:3–9, where thunder, as the voice of Yahweh, is praised seven times.

10:2 *He placed . . . on the land:* this symbolizes the universality of the angel's message, as does the figure of the small scroll open to be read.

10:6 *Heaven and earth and sea:* the three parts of the universe. *No more delay:* cf Dn 12:7; Hb 2:3.

10:7 *The mysterious plan of God:* literally, "the mystery of God," the end of the present age when the forces of evil will be put down (17:1—19:4, 11–21; 20:7–10; cf 2 Thes 2:6–12; Rom 16:25–26), and the establishment of the reign of God when all creation will be made new (21:1—22:5).

10:9–10 The small scroll was sweet because it predicted the final victory of God's people; it was sour because it also announced their sufferings. Cf Ez 3:1–3.

10:11 This further prophecy is contained in chs 12–22.

11:1 The temple and altar symbolize the new Israel; see the note on 7:4–9. The worshipers represent Christians. The measuring of the temple (cf Ez 40:3—42:20; 47:1–12; Zec 2:5–6) suggests that God will preserve the faithful remnant (cf Is 4:2–3) who remain true to Christ (14:1–5).

11:2 *The outer court:* the Court of the Gentiles. *Trample . . . forty-two months:* the duration of the vicious persecution of the Jews by Antiochus IV Epiphanes (Dn 7:25; 12:7); this persecution of three and a half years (half of seven, counted as 1260 days in 3; 12:6) became the prototype of periods of trial for God's people; cf Lk 4:25; Jas 5:17. The reference here is to the persecution by the Romans; cf Introduction.

11:3 The two witnesses, wearing sackcloth symbolizing lamentation and repentance, cannot readily be identified. Do they represent Moses and Elijah, or the Law and the Prophets, or Peter and Paul? Most probably they refer to the universal church, especially the Christian martyrs, fulfilling the office of witness (two because of Dt 19:15; cf Mk 6:7; Jn 8:17).

11:4 *The two olive trees and the two lampstands:* the martyrs who stand in the presence of the Lord; the imagery is taken from Zec 4:1–3, 11–14, where the olive trees refer to Zerubbabel and Joshua.

11:5–6 These details are derived from stories of Moses, who turned *water into blood* (Ex 7:17–20), and of Elijah, who called down fire from heaven (1 Kgs 18:36–40; 2 Kgs 1:10) and closed up the sky for three years (1 Kgs 17:1; cf 18:1).

11:7 *The beast . . . from the abyss:* the Roman emperor Nero, who symbolizes the forces of evil, or the antichrist (13:1, 8; 17:8); cf Dn 7:2–8, 11–12, 19–22 and Introduction.

10:3 Ps 29:3–9; Jer 25:30; Am 3:8.
10:6 Dt 32:40; Dn 12:7 / Ez 12:28.
10:7 Am 3:7.
10:10 Ez 3:1–3.
11:1 Ez 40:3–5 / Zec 2:5–9.
11:4 Zec 4:3, 14.
11:6 Ex 7:17.
11:7 Dn 7:21.

war against them and conquer them and kill
them. 8† Their corpses will lie in the main street
of the great city, which has the symbolic names
"Sodom" and "Egypt," where indeed their Lord
was crucified. 9† Those from every people, tribe,
tongue, and nation will gaze on their corpses for
three and a half days, and they will not allow
their corpses to be buried. 10 The inhabitants
of the earth will gloat over them and be glad
and exchange gifts because these two prophets
tormented the inhabitants of the earth. 11* But
after the three and a half days, a breath of life
from God entered them. When they stood on
their feet, great fear fell on those who saw them.
12* Then they heard a loud voice from heaven
say to them, "Come up here." So they went up
to heaven in a cloud as their enemies looked on.
13† At that moment there was a great earthquake,
and a tenth of the city fell in ruins. Seven thou-
sand people were killed during the earthquake;
the rest were terrified and gave glory to the God
of heaven.

14 The second woe has passed, but the third is
coming soon.

The Seventh Trumpet

15† Then the seventh angel blew his trumpet.
There were loud voices in heaven, saying, "The
kingdom of the world now belongs to our Lord
and to his Anointed, and he will reign forever
and ever." 16 The twenty-four elders who sat on
their thrones before God prostrated themselves
and worshiped God 17 and said:

"We give thanks to you, Lord God almighty,
who are and who were.
For you have assumed your great power
and have established your reign.
18* The nations raged,
but your wrath has come,
and the time for the dead to be judged,
and to recompense your servants, the prophets,
and the holy ones and those who fear your name,
the small and the great alike,
and to destroy those who destroy the earth."

19 Then God's temple in heaven was opened, and
the ark of his covenant could be seen in the tem-
ple. There were flashes of lightning, rumblings,
and peals of thunder, an earthquake, and a vio-
lent hailstorm.

The Woman and the Dragon

12 1*† A great sign appeared in the sky, a
woman† clothed with the sun, with the

Live It!

God in Control

The world is a wonderful place, full of life and hope. At the same time, it is full of pain and suffering, illness and death. It can seem frightening and out of control. Wars break out, a drought threatens the lives of millions, a friend dies in a senseless car accident, terrorists attack and kill innocent people, global warming threatens the existence of life as we know it. We can be left wondering why God allows such things.

The Book of Revelation was written to encourage the people of John's time that despite the evil that happens, God is in control. It can do the same for us too. The song in 11:15–18 reminds us that there will come a time when the just will be rewarded and the wicked punished. And although God's Reign is not yet fully realized, as members of God's family, we are called to be people of justice, peace, and hope to a world desperately seeking these things.

▶ **Rv 11:15–18**

†

11:8 *The great city:* this expression is used constantly in Revelation for Babylon, i.e., Rome; cf 14:8; 16:19; 17:18; 18:2, 10, 21. *"Sodom" and "Egypt":* symbols of immorality (cf Is 1:10) and oppression of God's people (cf Ex 1:11–14). *Where indeed their Lord was crucified:* not the geographical but the symbolic Jerusalem that rejects God and his witnesses, i.e., Rome, called Babylon in chs 16–18; see the note on 17:9 and Introduction.

11:9–12 Over the martyrdom (7) of the two witnesses, now called prophets, the ungodly rejoice *for three and a half days,* a symbolic period of time; see the note on v 2. Afterwards they go in triumph to heaven, as did Elijah (2 Kgs 2:11).

11:13 *Seven thousand people:* a symbolic sum to represent all social classes (seven) and large numbers (thousands); cf Introduction.

11:15–19 The seventh trumpet proclaims the coming of God's reign after the victory over diabolical powers; see the note on 10:7.

12:1—14:20 This central section of Revelation portrays the power of evil, represented by a dragon, in opposition to God and his people. First, the dragon pursues the woman about to give birth, but her son is saved and "caught up to God and his throne" (12:5). Then Michael and his angels cast the dragon and his angels out of heaven (12:7–9). After this, the dragon tries to attack the boy indirectly by attacking members of his church (12:13–18). A beast, symbolizing the Roman empire, then becomes the dragon's agent, mortally wounded but restored to life and worshiped by all the world (13:1–10). A second beast arises from the land, symbolizing the antichrist, which leads

*

11:11 Ez 37:5, 10.
11:12 2 Kgs 2:11.
11:18 Ps 2:1, 5 / Am 3:7.
12:1 Gn 37:9.

Did You Know?

The Woman and the Dragon

The vision in chapter 12 of Revelation symbolizes the great battle between Christ and Satan. In the opening scene, the pregnant woman represents Israel, from which the Messiah will come. The dragon waiting to devour her child is a symbol for Satan (see verse 9). This child, who will rule all the nations, is the Messiah, Jesus Christ. Therefore, the woman has also been equated with Mary, the mother of Jesus.

The conflict moves from heaven to earth when Satan fails to devour the child and is thrown down from his place in heaven. The dragon continues his pursuit of the woman on earth. The woman now represents the Church. The "rest of her offspring" (verse 17) represent its members whom the dragon angrily persecutes because he did not succeed in devouring her child. In this vision, John is telling the persecuted Christians of his time to have hope because in the end, Christ will totally and completely destroy Satan (see also 20:1–10).

Rv 12:1–18

moon under her feet, and on her head a crown
of twelve stars. 2† She was with child and wailed
aloud in pain as she labored to give birth.
3*† Then another sign appeared in the sky; it
was a huge red dragon, with seven heads and
ten horns, and on its heads were seven diadems.
4* Its tail swept away a third of the stars in the
sky and hurled them down to the earth. Then
the dragon stood before the woman about to
give birth, to devour her child when she gave
birth. 5*† She gave birth to a son, a male child,
destined to rule all the nations with an iron rod.
Her child was caught up to God and his throne.
6† The woman herself fled into the desert where
she had a place prepared by God, that there she
might be taken care of for twelve hundred and
sixty days.
7† Then war broke out in heaven; Michael†
and his angels battled against the dragon. The
dragon and its angels fought back, 8 but they did
not prevail and there was no longer any place
for them in heaven. 9*† The huge dragon, the
ancient serpent, who is called the Devil and Satan, who deceived the whole world, was thrown
down to earth, and its angels were thrown down
with it.
10† Then I heard a loud voice in heaven say:

"Now have salvation and power come,
and the kingdom of our God
and the authority of his Anointed.
For the accuser of our brothers is cast out,
who accuses them before our God day and night.
11 They conquered him by the blood of the Lamb
and by the word of their testimony;
love for life did not deter them from death.
12 Therefore, rejoice, you heavens,
and you who dwell in them.
But woe to you, earth and sea,
for the Devil has come down to you in great fury,
for he knows he has but a short time."

13* When the dragon saw that it had been

† people astray by its prodigies to idolize the first beast (13:11–18). This is followed by a vision of the Lamb and his faithful ones, and the proclamation of imminent judgment upon the world in terms of the wine of God's wrath (14:1–20).

12:1–6 The woman adorned with the sun, the moon, and the stars (images taken from Gn 37:9–10) symbolizes God's people in the Old and the New Testament. The Israel of old gave birth to the Messiah (5) and then became the new Israel, the church, which suffers persecution by the dragon (6, 13–17); cf Is 50:1; 66:7; Jer 50:12. This corresponds to a widespread myth throughout the ancient world that a goddess pregnant with a savior was pursued by a horrible monster; by miraculous intervention, she bore a son who then killed the monster.

12:2 Because of Eve's sin, the woman gives birth in distress and pain (Gn 3:16; cf Is 66:7–14).

12:3 *Huge red dragon:* the Devil or Satan (cf 9; 20:2), symbol of the forces of evil, a mythical monster known also as Leviathan (Ps 74:13–14) or Rahab (Jb 26:12–13; Ps 89:11). *Seven diadems:* these are symbolic of the fullness of the dragon's sovereignty over the kingdoms of this world; cf Christ with many diadems (19:12).

12:5 *Rule . . . iron rod:* fulfilled in 19:15; cf Ps 2:9. *Was caught up to God:* reference to Christ's ascension.

12:6 God protects the persecuted church in the desert, the traditional Old Testament place of refuge for the afflicted, according to the typology of the Exodus; see the note on 11:2.

12:7–12 Michael, mentioned only here in Revelation, wins a victory over the dragon. A hymn of praise follows.

12:7 *Michael:* the archangel, guardian and champion of Israel; cf Dn 10:13, 21; 12:1; Jude 9. In Hebrew, the name Michael means "Who can compare with God?"; cf 13:4.

12:9 *The ancient serpent:* who seduced Eve (Gn 3:1–6), mother of the human race; cf 20:2; Eph 6:11–12. *Was thrown down:* allusion to the expulsion of Satan from heaven; cf Lk 10:18.

12:10 *The accuser:* the meaning of the Hebrew word "Satan," found in v 9; Jb 1–2; Zec 3:1; 1 Chr 21:1; he continues to accuse Christ's disciples.

* **12:3** Dn 7:7.
* **12:4** Dn 8:10.
* **12:5** Is 66:7 / Ps 2:9.
* **12:9** Gn 3:1–4 / Lk 10:18.
* **12:13** Gn 3:15.

Cultural Connection

Mary Has a Vital Mission in Salvation History

The New Testament links Mary's mission intimately to the mystery of Christ. In Luke 1:38, Mary's yes to the angel Gabriel allows the Son of God to enter the world as a human being. At a wedding in Cana (see Jn 2:1–11), Mary is a model for the Church as she intercedes before Jesus, has faith in him, points to him as the source of life, and leads others to follow his words. Jesus' words to Mary and the Beloved Disciple at the cross (see Jn 19:26–27) name Mary mother of the universal Church, which is symbolized by the Beloved Disciple.

Over the centuries, some Christians have seen in the unnamed woman mentioned in chapter 12 of Revelation representations of Mary and the Church, who both share in Jesus' messianic mission. For Catholics on the feast of the Assumption, this passage is one of the readings that celebrates Mary's entrance into heaven as the first disciple. Mary is a symbol of the triumphant Church that awaits and intercedes for us, the pilgrim Church.

Catholics of Latino origin have a long tradition of linking Mary to their history of salvation. She is their companion on their journey of faith and a very dear member of their community. Hispanic popular piety draws strength from Mary's example in daily life, in situations of need and suffering, and in times of celebration.

Reflect on the ways Mary teaches us to be servants of the Reign of God. Pray that we are as willing to fulfill our mission in salvation history as she is.

▶ Revelation, chapter 12

thrown down to the earth, it pursued the
woman who had given birth to the male child.
14*† But the woman was given the two wings
of the great eagle, so that she could fly to her
place in the desert, where, far from the serpent,
she was taken care of for a year, two years, and
a half-year. 15† The serpent, however, spewed
a torrent of water out of his mouth after the
woman to sweep her away with the current.
16 But the earth helped the woman and opened
its mouth and swallowed the flood that the
dragon spewed out of its mouth. 17*† Then the
dragon became angry with the woman and went
off to wage war against the rest of her offspring,
those who keep God's commandments and bear
witness to Jesus. 18† It took its position on the
sand of the sea.

The First Beast

13 1*† Then I saw a beast come out of the sea
with ten horns and seven heads; on its horns
were ten diadems, and on its heads blasphemous
name[s]. 2*† The beast I saw was like a leopard,
but it had feet like a bear's, and its mouth was
like the mouth of a lion. To it the dragon gave its
own power and throne, along with great author-
ity. 3† I saw that one of its heads seemed to have
been mortally wounded, but this mortal wound
was healed. Fascinated, the whole world followed
after the beast. 4† They worshiped the dragon be-
cause it gave its authority to the beast; they also
worshiped the beast and said, "Who can compare
with the beast or who can fight against it?"
5*† The beast was given a mouth uttering

†

12:14 *Great eagle:* symbol of the power and swiftness of divine help; cf Ex 19:4; Dt 32:11; Is 40:31.

12:15 The serpent is depicted as the sea monster; cf 13:1; Is 27:1; Ez 32:2; Ps 74:13–14.

12:17 Although the church is protected by God's special providence (16), the individual Christian is to expect persecution and suffering.

12:18 *It took its position:* many later manuscripts and versions read "I took my position," thus connecting the sentence to the following paragraph.

13:1–10 This wild beast, combining features of the four beasts in Dn 7:2–28, symbolizes the Roman empire; the seven heads represent the emperors; see the notes on 17:10 and 17:12–14. The blasphemous names are the divine titles assumed by the emperors.

13:2 Satan (12:9), the prince of this world (Jn 12:31), commissioned the beast to persecute the church (5–7).

13:3 This may be a reference to the popular legend that Nero would come back to life and rule again after his death (which occurred in A.D. 68 from a self-inflicted stab wound in the throat); cf v 14; 17:8. Domitian (A.D. 81–96) embodied all the cruelty and impiety of Nero. Cf Introduction.

13:4 *Worshiped the beast:* allusion to emperor worship, which Domitian insisted upon and ruthlessly enforced. *Who can compare with the beast:* perhaps a deliberate parody of the name Michael; see the note on 12:7.

13:5–6 Domitian, like Antiochus IV Epiphanes (Dn 7:8, 11, 25), demanded that he be called by divine titles such as "our lord and god" and "Jupiter." See the note on 11:2.

12:14 Ex 19:4; Dn 7:25; 12:7.
12:17 Gn 3:15.
13:1 2 Thes 2:3–12.
13:2 Dn 7:3–6.
13:5 Dn 7:8, 11, 25; 8:14; 9:27; 11:36; 12:7.

proud boasts and blasphemies, and it was given
authority to act for forty-two months.† 6 It
opened its mouth to utter blasphemies against
God, blaspheming his name and his dwelling
and those who dwell in heaven. 7* It was also
allowed to wage war against the holy ones and
conquer them, and it was granted authority over
every tribe, people, tongue, and nation. 8* All the
inhabitants of the earth will worship it, all whose
names were not written from the foundation of
the world in the book of life, which belongs to
the Lamb who was slain.

9* Whoever has ears ought to hear these
words.
10* Anyone destined for captivity goes into
captivity.
Anyone destined to be slain by the sword
shall be slain by the sword.

Such is the faithful endurance of the holy ones.

The Second Beast

11† Then I saw another beast come up out
of the earth; it had two horns like a lamb's but
spoke like a dragon. 12 It wielded all the authority
of the first beast in its sight and made the earth
and its inhabitants worship the first beast, whose
mortal wound had been healed. 13* It performed
great signs, even making fire come down from
heaven to earth in the sight of everyone. 14 It de-
ceived the inhabitants of the earth with the signs
it was allowed to perform in the sight of the first
beast, telling them to make an image for the
beast who had been wounded by the sword and
revived. 15* It was then permitted to breathe life
into the beast's image, so that the beast's image
could speak and [could] have anyone who did
not worship it put to death. 16* It forced all the
people, small and great, rich and poor, free and
slave, to be given a stamped image on their right
hands or their foreheads, 17 so that no one could
buy or sell except one who had the stamped im-
age of the beast's name or the number that stood
for its name.

18*† Wisdom is needed here; one who under-
stands can calculate the number of the beast, for
it is a number that stands for a person. His num-
ber is six hundred and sixty-six.

Did You Know?

The Number of the Beast

The vision of the two beasts in chapter 13 of Revelation is a continuation of the vision about the woman and the dragon in chapter 12. The beasts represent the Roman Empire and its emperor, which at the time threatened the true practice of Christianity. Roman leaders expected all citizens, including Christians, to offer sacrifices to the Roman gods and to worship the emperor as though he were a god. This may have been especially true in the cities in Asia Minor, which were trying to prove their loyalty to the Roman emperor.

In Revelation 13:18, we are told that the number of the second beast is 666. Most scholars believe that this stands for Nero Caesar, who was the emperor of Rome from AD 54 to 68. Their reasoning is that when you convert the Greek letters for Nero's name and title into Hebrew letters, which also stand for numbers, and then add them up, you get the number 666. Six is one less than seven, the perfect number, so 666 represents something less than perfect or evil itself. Nero was responsible for some especially vicious attacks on Christians in Rome. The Book of Revelation was written after Nero committed suicide, but many people thought that he had not died and had come out of hiding in the East to lead this new wave of persecution against Christians (see verse 3).

▶ **Revelation, chapter 13**

†

13:5 *Forty-two months:* this is the same duration as the profanation of the holy city (11:2), the prophetic mission of the two witnesses (11:3), and the retreat of the woman into the desert (12:6, 14).

13:11–18 The second beast is described in terms of the false prophets (cf 16:13; 19:20; 20:10) who accompany the false messiahs (the first beast); cf Mt 24:24; Mk 13:22; 2 Thes 2:9; cf also Dt 13:2–4. Christians had either to worship the emperor and his image or to suffer martyrdom.

13:18 Each of the letters of the alphabet in Hebrew as well as in Greek has a numerical value. Many possible combinations of letters will add up to 666, and many candidates have been nominated for this infamous number. The most likely is the emperor Caesar Nero (see the note on 13:3), the Greek form of whose name in Hebrew letters gives the required sum. (The Latin form of this name equals 616, which is the reading of a few manuscripts.) Nero personifies the emperors who viciously persecuted the church. It has also been observed that "6" represents imperfection, falling short of the perfect number "7," and is represented here in a triple or superlative form.

*

13:7 Dn 7:21.
13:8 Rv 3:5; 17:8; 20:12.
13:9 Mt 13:9.
13:10 Jer 15:2.
13:13 Dt 13:2–4; Mt 24:24; 2 Thes 2:9–10.
13:15 Dn 3:5–7, 15.
13:16 Rv 14:9; 16:2; 19:20; 20:4.
13:18 Rv 17:9.

The Lamb's Companions†

14 1* Then I looked and there was the Lamb
standing on Mount Zion,† and with him
a hundred and forty-four thousand who had
his name and his Father's name written on their
foreheads. 2 I heard a sound from heaven like the
sound of rushing water or a loud peal of thun-
der. The sound I heard was like that of harpists
playing their harps. 3* They were singing [what
seemed to be] a new hymn before the throne,
before the four living creatures and the elders.
No one could learn this hymn except the hun-
dred and forty-four thousand who had been
ransomed from the earth. 4*† These are they
who were not defiled with women; they are vir-
gins and these are the ones who follow the Lamb
wherever he goes. They have been ransomed as
the firstfruits of the human race for God and
the Lamb. 5*† On their lips no deceit has been
found; they are unblemished.

The Three Angels†

6 Then I saw another angel flying high overhead,
with everlasting good news† to announce to those
who dwell on earth, to every nation, tribe, tongue,
and people. 7* He said in a loud voice, "Fear God
and give him glory, for his time has come to sit in
judgment. Worship him who made heaven and
earth and sea and springs of water."
8*† A second angel followed, saying:

"Fallen, fallen is Babylon the great,
that made all the nations drink
the wine of her licentious passion."

9 A third angel followed them and said in a loud
voice, "Anyone who worships the beast or its
image, or accepts its mark on forehead or hand,
10† will also drink the wine of God's fury, poured
full strength into the cup of his wrath, and will be
tormented in burning sulfur before the holy an-
gels and before the Lamb. 11* The smoke of the
fire that torments them will rise forever and ever,
and there will be no relief day or night for those
who worship the beast or its image or accept the
mark of its name." 12*† Here is what sustains the
holy ones who keep God's commandments and
their faith in Jesus.
13*† I heard a voice from heaven say, "Write
this: Blessed are the dead who die in the Lord
from now on." "Yes," said the Spirit, "let them
find rest from their labors, for their works ac-
company them."

The Harvest of the Earth

14*† Then I looked and there was a white
cloud, and sitting on the cloud one who looked
like a son of man, with a gold crown on his head
and a sharp sickle in his hand. 15* Another an-
gel came out of the temple, crying out in a loud
voice to the one sitting on the cloud, "Use your
sickle and reap the harvest, for the time to reap
has come, because the earth's harvest is fully
ripe." 16 So the one who was sitting on the cloud
swung his sickle over the earth, and the earth was
harvested.
17 Then another angel came out of the temple
in heaven who also had a sharp sickle. 18† Then
another angel [came] from the altar, [who] was in
charge of the fire, and cried out in a loud voice to
the one who had the sharp sickle, "Use your sharp
sickle and cut the clusters from the earth's vines,
for its grapes are ripe." 19* So the angel swung his

14:1–5 Now follows a tender and consoling vision of the Lamb and his companions.

14:1 *Mount Zion:* in Jerusalem, the traditional place where the true remnant, the Israel of faith, is to be gathered in the messianic reign; cf 2 Kgs 19:30–31; Jl 3:5; Ob 17; Mi 4:6–8; Zep 3:12–20. *A hundred and forty-four thousand:* see the note on 7:4–9. *His Father's name . . . foreheads:* in contrast to the pagans who were marked with the name or number of the beast (13:16–17).

14:4 *Virgins:* metaphorically, because they never indulged in any idolatrous practices, which are considered in the Old Testament to be adultery and fornication (2:14–15, 20–22; 17:1–6; cf Ez 16:1–58; 23:1–49). The parallel passages (7:3; 22:4) indicate that the 144,000 whose foreheads are sealed represent all Christian people.

14:5 *No deceit:* because they did not deny Christ or do homage to the beast. Lying is characteristic of the opponents of Christ (Jn 8:44), but the Suffering Servant spoke no falsehood (Is 53:9; 1 Pt 2:22). *Unblemished:* a cultic term taken from the vocabulary of sacrificial ritual.

14:6–13 Three angels proclaim imminent judgment on the pagan world, calling all peoples to worship God the creator. Babylon (Rome) will fall, and its supporters will be tormented forever.

14:6 *Everlasting good news:* that God's eternal reign is about to begin; see the note on 10:7.

14:8 This verse anticipates the lengthy dirge over Babylon (Rome) in 18:1—19:4. The oracle of Is 21:9 to Babylon is applied here.

14:10–11 *The wine of God's fury:* image taken from Is 51:17; Jer 25:15–16; 49:12; 51:7; Ez 23:31–34. Eternal punishment in the fiery pool of burning sulfur (or "fire and brimstone"; cf Gn 19:24) is also reserved for the Devil, the beast, and the false prophet (19:20; 20:10; 21:8).

14:12 In addition to *faith in Jesus,* the seer insists upon the necessity and value of works, as in 2:23; 20:12–13; 22:12; cf Mt 16:27; Rom 2:6.

14:13 See the note on 1:3. According to Jewish thought, people's actions followed them as witnesses before the court of God.

14:14–20 The reaping of the harvest symbolizes the gathering of the elect in the final judgment, while the reaping and treading of the grapes symbolizes the doom of the ungodly (cf Jl 4:12–13; Is 63:1–6) that will come in 19:11–21.

14:18 *Altar:* there was only one altar in the heavenly temple; see the notes above on 6:9; 8:3; 11:1.

14:1 Jl 3:5; Ob 17; Acts 2:21.
14:3 Pss 33:3; 96:1; 98:1; Is 42:10.
14:4 Jer 2:2; Jas 1:18.
14:5 Zep 3:13.
14:7 Rv 2:10; Mt 10:28.
14:8 Rv 18:2–3; Is 21:9; Jer 51:8 / Is 51:17; Jer 25:15–17.
14:11 Rv 19:3.
14:12 Rv 12:17.
14:13 Mt 11:28–29; 2 Thes 1:7; Heb 4:10.
14:14 Rv 1:7; Dn 7:13.
14:15 Jl 4:13; Mt 13:36–43.
14:19 Rv 19:15; Is 63:1–6.

sickle over the earth and cut the earth's vintage. He threw it into the great wine press of God's fury. 20† The wine press was trodden outside the city and blood poured out of the wine press to the height of a horse's bridle for two hundred miles.

The Seven Last Plagues

15 1† Then I saw in heaven another sign,† great and awe-inspiring: seven angels with the seven last plagues, for through them God's fury is accomplished.

2*† Then I saw something like a sea of glass mingled with fire. On the sea of glass were standing those who had won the victory over the beast and its image and the number that signified its name. They were holding God's harps, 3*† and they sang the song of Moses, the servant of God, and the song of the Lamb:

"Great and wonderful are your works,
Lord God almighty.
Just and true are your ways,
O king of the nations.
4* Who will not fear you, Lord,
or glorify your name?
For you alone are holy.
All the nations will come
and worship before you,
for your righteous acts have been revealed."

5† After this I had another vision. The temple that is the heavenly tent of testimony† opened, 6* and the seven angels with the seven plagues came out of the temple. They were dressed in clean white linen, with a gold sash around their chests. 7 One of the four living creatures gave the seven angels seven gold bowls filled with the fury of God, who lives forever and ever. 8* Then the temple became so filled with the smoke from God's glory and might that no one could enter it until the seven plagues of the seven angels had been accomplished.

The Seven Bowls

16 1† I heard a loud voice speaking from the temple to the seven angels, "Go and pour out the seven bowls of God's fury upon the earth."

2† The first angel went and poured out his bowl on the earth. Festering and ugly sores broke out on those who had the mark of the beast or worshiped its image.

3† The second angel poured out his bowl on the sea. The sea turned to blood like that from a corpse; every creature living in the sea died.

4* The third angel poured out his bowl on the rivers and springs of water. These also turned to blood. 5* Then I heard the angel in charge of the waters say:

"You are just, O Holy One,
who are and who were,
in passing this sentence.
6* For they have shed the blood of the holy ones
and the prophets,
and you [have] given them blood to drink;
it is what they deserve."
7* Then I heard the altar cry out,
"Yes, Lord God almighty,
your judgments are true and just."

8 The fourth angel poured out his bowl on the sun. It was given the power to burn people with fire. 9* People were burned by the scorching heat and blasphemed the name of God who had power over these plagues, but they did not repent or give him glory.

10*† The fifth angel poured out his bowl on the throne of the beast. Its kingdom was plunged into darkness, and people bit their tongues in pain 11* and blasphemed the God of heaven because of their pains and sores. But they did not repent of their works.

---

†

14:20 *Two hundred miles:* literally sixteen hundred stades. The *stadion,* a Greek unit of measurement, was about 607 feet in length, approximately the length of a furlong.

15:1—16:21 The seven bowls, the third and last group of seven after the seven seals and the seven trumpets, foreshadow the final cataclysm. Again, the series is introduced by a heavenly prelude, in which the victors over the beast sing the canticle of Moses (15:2–4).

15:1–4 A vision of the victorious martyrs precedes the vision of woe in 15:5—16:21; cf 7:9–12.

15:2 *Mingled with fire:* fire symbolizes the sanctity involved in facing God, reflected in the trials that have prepared the victorious Christians or in God's wrath.

15:3 *The song of Moses:* the song that Moses and the Israelites sang after their escape from the oppression of Egypt (Ex 15:1–18). The martyrs have escaped from the oppression of the Devil. *Nations:* many other Greek manuscripts and versions read "ages."

15:5–8 Seven angels receive the bowls of God's wrath.

15:5 *Tent of testimony:* the name of the meeting tent in the Greek text of Ex 40. Cf 2 Mc 2:4–7.

16:1–21 These seven bowls, like the seven seals (6:1–17; 8:1) and the seven trumpets (8:2—9:21; 11:15–19), bring on a succession of disasters modeled in part on the plagues of Egypt (Ex 7–12). See the note on 6:12–14.

16:2 Like the sixth Egyptian plague (Ex 9:8–11).

16:3–4 Like the first Egyptian plague (Ex 7:20–21). The same woe followed the blowing of the second trumpet (8:8–9).

16:10 *The throne of the beast:* symbol of the forces of evil. *Darkness:* like the ninth Egyptian plague (Ex 10:21–23); cf 9:2.

---

*

15:2 Rv 7:9, 14; 13:15–18.
15:3 Pss 92:6; 98:1 / Dt 32:4; Ps 145:17.
15:4 Ps 86:9–10; Jer 10:7.
15:6 Rv 19:8.
15:8 1 Kgs 8:10; Is 6:4.
16:4 Ex 7:14–24.
16:5 Rv 1:4.
16:6 Ez 35:6; Mt 23:34–35.
16:7 Dn 3:27; Tb 3:2.
16:9 Am 4:6.
16:10 Ex 10:21–23.
16:11 Ex 9:8–11 / Jer 5:3.

12† The sixth angel emptied his bowl on the
great river Euphrates. Its water was dried up to
prepare the way for the kings of the East. 13*† I
saw three unclean spirits like frogs come from
the mouth of the dragon, from the mouth of the
beast, and from the mouth of the false prophet.
14* These were demonic spirits who performed
signs. They went out to the kings of the whole
world to assemble them for the battle on the
great day of God the almighty. 15*† ("Behold, I
am coming like a thief." Blessed is the one who
watches and keeps his clothes ready, so that he
may not go naked and people see him exposed.)
16† They then assembled the kings in the place
that is named Armageddon in Hebrew.

17* The seventh angel poured out his bowl
into the air. A loud voice came out of the temple
from the throne, saying, "It is done." 18* Then
there were lightning flashes, rumblings, and
peals of thunder, and a great earthquake. It was
such a violent earthquake that there has never
been one like it since the human race began on
earth. 19† The great city was split into three parts,
and the gentile cities fell. But God remembered
great Babylon, giving it the cup filled with the
wine of his fury and wrath. 20† Every island fled,
and mountains disappeared. 21* Large hailstones
like huge weights came down from the sky on
people, and they blasphemed God for the plague
of hail because this plague was so severe.

V: The Punishment of Babylon and the Destruction of Pagan Nations

Babylon the Great

17 1*† Then one of the seven angels who were
holding the seven bowls came and said to
me, "Come here. I will show you the judgment on
the great harlot† who lives near the many waters.
2*† The kings of the earth have had intercourse
with her, and the inhabitants of the earth became
drunk on the wine of her harlotry." 3*† Then he
carried me away in spirit to a deserted place where
I saw a woman seated on a scarlet beast that was
covered with blasphemous names, with seven
heads and ten horns. 4*† The woman was wearing
purple and scarlet and adorned with gold, pre-
cious stones, and pearls. She held in her hand a
gold cup that was filled with the abominable and
sordid deeds of her harlotry. 5 On her forehead
was written a name, which is a mystery, "Babylon
the great, the mother of harlots and of the abomi-
nations of the earth." 6† I saw that the woman was
drunk on the blood of the holy ones and on the
blood of the witnesses to Jesus.

Meaning of the Beast and Harlot

When I saw her I was greatly amazed. 7 The
angel said to me, "Why are you amazed? I will
explain to you the mystery of the woman and
of the beast that carries her, the beast with the
seven heads and the ten horns. 8*† The beast that
you saw existed once but now exists no longer.
It will come up from the abyss and is headed for
destruction. The inhabitants of the earth whose
names have not been written in the book of
life from the foundation of the world shall be
amazed when they see the beast, because it ex-
isted once but exists no longer, and yet it will
come again. 9*† Here is a clue for one who has
wisdom. The seven heads represent seven hills
upon which the woman sits. They also represent
seven kings: 10† five have already fallen, one still
lives, and the last has not yet come, and when
he comes he must remain only a short while.
11† The beast that existed once but exists no lon-
ger is an eighth king, but really belongs to the
seven and is headed for destruction. 12*† The ten

†

16:12 *The kings of the East:* Parthians; see the notes on 6:2 and 17:12–13. *East:* literally, "rising of the sun," as in 7:2.

16:13 *Frogs:* possibly an allusion to the second Egyptian plague (Ex 7:26—8:11). *The false prophet:* identified with the two-horned second beast (13:11–18 and the note there).

16:15 *Like a thief:* as in 3:3 (cf Mt 24:42–44; 1 Thes 5:2). *Blessed:* see the note on 1:3.

16:16 *Armageddon:* in Hebrew, this means "Mountain of Megiddo." Since Megiddo was the scene of many decisive battles in antiquity (Jgs 5:19–20; 2 Kgs 9:27; 2 Chr 35:20–24), the town became the symbol of the final disastrous rout of the forces of evil.

16:19 *The great city:* Rome and the empire.

16:20–21 See the note on 6:12–14. *Hailstones:* as in the seventh Egyptian plague (Ex 9:23–24); cf 8:7. *Like huge weights:* literally, "weighing a talent," about one hundred pounds.

17:1—19:10 The punishment of Babylon is now described as a past event and, metaphorically, under the image of the great harlot who leads people astray into idolatry.

17:1–6 Babylon, the symbolic name (5) of Rome, is graphically described as "the great harlot."

17:2 *Intercourse . . . harlotry:* see the note on 14:4. The pagan kings subject to Rome adopted the cult of the emperor.

17:3 *Scarlet beast:* see the note on 13:1–10. *Blasphemous names:* divine titles assumed by the Roman emperors; see the note on 13:5–6.

17:4 Reference to the great wealth and idolatrous cults of Rome.

17:6b–18 An interpretation of the vision is here given.

17:8 Allusion to the belief that the dead Nero would return to power (11); see the note on 13:3.

17:9 *Here is a clue:* literally, "Here a mind that has wisdom." *Seven hills:* of Rome.

17:10 There is little agreement as to the identity of the Roman emperors alluded to here. The number seven (9) suggests that all the emperors are meant; see the note on 1:4.

17:11 *The beast:* Nero; see the note on v 8.

17:12–13 *Ten kings who have not yet been crowned:* perhaps Parthian satraps who are to accompany the revived Nero (the beast) in his march on Rome to regain power; see the note on 13:3. In 19:11–21, the Lamb and his companions will conquer them.

*

16:13 Ex 8:2–3.
16:14 1 Cor 1:8.
16:15 Mt 24:42–44 / Rv 3:17.
16:17 Is 66:6.
16:18 Mk 13:19.
16:21 Ex 9:22–26.
17:1 Jer 50:38; 51:13.
17:2 Jer 51:7.
17:3 Rv 13:1.
17:4 Rv 18:16.
17:8 Rv 13:3–4 / Rv 3:5; 13:8; 20:12.
17:9 Rv 13:18.
17:12 Dn 7:24.

horns that you saw represent ten kings who have
not yet been crowned; they will receive royal au-
thority along with the beast for one hour. 13 They
are of one mind and will give their power and
authority to the beast. 14* They will fight with the
Lamb, but the Lamb will conquer them, for he is
Lord of lords and king of kings, and those with
him are called, chosen, and faithful."

Live It!

The Sins of Empires

In John's coded language, the whore called Babylon in chapter 17 is Rome, a city built on seven hills. She is dressed in colors that symbolize her royalty (purple) and her obscene and immoral behavior (scarlet). Her gold and pearls are signs of her wealth and excessive luxury. The blasphemous names on her forehead are the titles that should be given to God but are given to the emperor instead. By calling her Babylon, John is creating a tie with the capital of another evil empire from the Old Testament (see "The Fall of Jerusalem," near 2 Kgs 25:1–21).

The whore is drunk on the blood of the saints she killed because of their faith. John indicates that her evil is caused by her unrestrained desire for wealth and luxury and her abuse of power (see Rv 18:3–19). He tells his Christian readers that they can be hopeful, even amid so much suffering, because in the end, the Lamb (Christ) will conquer the beast (see 17:14).

Since Revelation was written, many other countries have abused their power, including the United States. Consider, for example, its treatment of Native Americans, practice of slavery, and lack of care for the environment.

Reflect for a moment.

- In what areas does your country need to take more responsibility to ensure justice for all people? Where has the desire for wealth and luxury gone too far?
- What can you do locally to take greater responsibility in these areas?

▶ **Revelation, chapter 17**

15 Then he said to me, "The waters that you saw
where the harlot lives represent large numbers
of peoples, nations, and tongues. 16*† The ten
horns that you saw and the beast will hate the
harlot; they will leave her desolate and naked;
they will eat her flesh and consume her with fire.
17 For God has put it into their minds to carry out
his purpose and to make them come to an agree-
ment to give their kingdom to the beast until the
words of God are accomplished. 18 The woman
whom you saw represents the great city that has
sovereignty over the kings of the earth."

The Fall of Babylon

18 1*† After this I saw another angel coming
down from heaven, having great authority,
and the earth became illumined by his splendor.
2*† He cried out in a mighty voice:

"Fallen, fallen is Babylon the great.
She has become a haunt for demons.
She is a cage for every unclean spirit,
a cage for every unclean bird,
[a cage for every unclean] and disgusting
[beast].
3*† For all the nations have drunk
the wine of her licentious passion.
The kings of the earth had intercourse with
her,
and the merchants of the earth grew rich
from her drive for luxury."

4*† Then I heard another voice from heaven
say:

"Depart from her, my people,
so as not to take part in her sins
and receive a share in her plagues,
5* for her sins are piled up to the sky,

† **17:16–18** *The ten horns:* the ten pagan kings (12) who unwittingly fulfill God's will against harlot Rome, the great city; cf Ez 16:37.

18:1—19:4 A stirring dirge over the fall of Babylon-Rome. The perspective is prophetic, as if the fall of Rome had already taken place. The imagery here, as elsewhere in this book, is not to be taken literally. The vindictiveness of some of the language, borrowed from the scathing Old Testament prophecies against Babylon, Tyre, and Nineveh (Is 23; 24; 27; Jer 50–51; Ez 26–27), is meant to portray symbolically the inexorable demands of God's holiness and justice; cf Introduction. The section concludes with a joyous canticle on the future glory of heaven.

18:2 Many Greek manuscripts and versions omit *a cage for every unclean . . . beast.*

18:3–24 Rome is condemned for her immorality, symbol of idolatry (see the note on 14:4), and for persecuting the church; cf 19:2.

18:4 *Depart from her:* not evacuation of the city but separation from sinners, as always in apocalyptic literature.

17:14 Rv 19:11–21; 2 Mc 13:4; 1 Tm 6:15 / Rom 1:6; 1 Pt 2:9; Jude 1.
17:16 Ez 16:37–41; 23:25–29.
18:1 Ez 43:2.
18:2 Rv 14:8; Is 21:9; Jer 50:2–3; 51:8.
18:3 Rv 17:2; Jer 51:7.
18:4 Is 48:20; Jer 50:8.
18:5 Jer 51:9.

and God remembers her crimes.
6* Pay her back as she has paid others.
Pay her back double for her deeds.
Into her cup pour double what she poured.
7* To the measure of her boasting and
wantonness
repay her in torment and grief;
for she said to herself,
'I sit enthroned as queen;
I am no widow,
and I will never know grief.'
8 Therefore, her plagues will come in one day,
pestilence, grief, and famine;
she will be consumed by fire.
For mighty is the Lord God who judges her."

9 The kings of the earth who had intercourse with
her in their wantonness will weep and mourn
over her when they see the smoke of her pyre.
10 They will keep their distance for fear of the tor-
ment inflicted on her, and they will say:

"Alas, alas, great city,
Babylon, mighty city.
In one hour your judgment has come."

11† The merchants of the earth will weep and
mourn for her, because there will be no more
markets for their cargo: 12 their cargo of gold, sil-
ver, precious stones, and pearls; fine linen, pur-
ple silk, and scarlet cloth; fragrant wood of every
kind, all articles of ivory and all articles of the
most expensive wood, bronze, iron, and marble;
13† cinnamon, spice, incense, myrrh, and frank-
incense; wine, olive oil, fine flour, and wheat;
cattle and sheep, horses and chariots, and slaves,
that is, human beings.

14* "The fruit you craved
has left you.
All your luxury and splendor are gone,
never again will one find them."

15 The merchants who deal in these goods, who
grew rich from her, will keep their distance for
fear of the torment inflicted on her. Weeping and
mourning, 16* they cry out:

"Alas, alas, great city,
wearing fine linen, purple and scarlet,
adorned [in] gold, precious stones, and
pearls.
17 In one hour this great wealth has been ruined."

Every captain of a ship, every traveler at sea, sail-
ors, and seafaring merchants stood at a distance
18 and cried out when they saw the smoke of her
pyre, "What city could compare with the great
city?" 19* They threw dust on their heads and
cried out, weeping and mourning:

"Alas, alas, great city,
in which all who had ships at sea
grew rich from her wealth.
In one hour she has been ruined.
20* Rejoice over her, heaven,
you holy ones, apostles, and prophets.
For God has judged your case against her."

21* A mighty angel picked up a stone like a huge
millstone and threw it into the sea and said:

"With such force will Babylon the great city
be thrown down,
and will never be found again.
22* No melodies of harpists and musicians,
flutists and trumpeters,
will ever be heard in you again.
No craftsmen in any trade
will ever be found in you again.
No sound of the millstone
will ever be heard in you again.
23* No light from a lamp
will ever be seen in you again.
No voices of bride and groom
will ever be heard in you again.
Because your merchants were the great ones
of the world,
all nations were led astray by your magic
potion.
24* In her was found the blood of prophets and
holy ones
and all who have been slain on the earth."

19

1† After this I heard what sounded like the
loud voice of a great multitude in heaven,
saying:

"Alleluia!
Salvation, glory, and might belong to our God,

---

† **18:11** Ironically, the merchants weep not so much for Babylon-Rome, but for their lost markets; cf Ez 27:36.

18:13 *Spice:* an unidentified spice plant called in Greek *amōmon.*

19:1, 3, 4, 6 *Alleluia:* found only here in the New Testament, this frequent exclamation of praise in the Hebrew psalms was important in Jewish liturgy.

18:6 Jer 50:15 / Jer 16:18.
18:7 Is 47:8–9.
18:14 Hos 10:5 / Am 6:7.
18:16 Rv 17:4.
18:19 Ez 27:27–32.
18:20 Rv 19:1–2; Dt 32:43.
18:21 Jer 51:63–64; Ez 26:21.
18:22 Is 24:8; Ez 26:13.
18:23 Jer 7:34; 16:9; 25:10.
18:24 Rv 16:6.

2* for true and just are his judgments.
He has condemned the great harlot
who corrupted the earth with her harlotry.
He has avenged on her the blood of his
servants."

3*They said a second time:

"Alleluia! Smoke will rise from her forever
and ever."

4The twenty-four elders and the four living crea-
tures fell down and worshiped God who sat on
the throne, saying, "Amen. Alleluia."

The Victory Song

5*† A voice coming from the throne said:

"Praise our God, all you his servants,
[and] you who revere him, small and
great."

6Then I heard something like the sound of a
great multitude or the sound of rushing water or
mighty peals of thunder, as they said:

"Alleluia!
The Lord has established his reign,
[our] God, the almighty.
7*† Let us rejoice and be glad
and give him glory.
For the wedding day of the Lamb has come,
his bride has made herself ready.
8*† She was allowed to wear
a bright, clean linen garment."

(The linen represents the righteous deeds of the
holy ones.)
9*† Then the angel said to me, "Write this:
Blessed are those who have been called to the
wedding feast of the Lamb." And he said to me,
"These words are true; they come from God."
10*† I fell at his feet to worship him. But he said
to me, "Don't! I am a fellow servant of yours
and of your brothers who bear witness to Jesus.
Worship God. Witness to Jesus is the spirit of
prophecy."

The King of Kings

11*† Then I saw the heavens opened, and there
was a white horse; its rider was [called] "Faithful
and True." He judges and wages war in righteous-
ness. 12*† His eyes were [like] a fiery flame, and on
his head were many diadems. He had a name in-
scribed that no one knows except himself. 13*† He
wore a cloak that had been dipped in blood, and
his name was called the Word of God. 14* The ar-
mies of heaven followed him, mounted on white
horses and wearing clean white linen. 15*† Out of
his mouth came a sharp sword to strike the na-
tions. He will rule them with an iron rod, and he
himself will tread out in the wine press the wine
of the fury and wrath of God the almighty. 16* He
has a name written on his cloak and on his thigh,
"King of kings and Lord of lords."
17† Then I saw an angel standing on the sun.
He cried out [in] a loud voice to all the birds fly-
ing high overhead, "Come here. Gather for God's
great feast, 18* to eat the flesh of kings, the flesh
of military officers, and the flesh of warriors, the
flesh of horses and of their riders, and the flesh
of all, free and slave, small and great." 19Then I
saw the beast and the kings of the earth and their
armies gathered to fight against the one riding
the horse and against his army. 20*† The beast
was caught and with it the false prophet who had
performed in its sight the signs by which he led
astray those who had accepted the mark of the
beast and those who had worshiped its image.
The two were thrown alive into the fiery pool

†

19:5–10 A victory song follows, sung by the entire church, celebrating the marriage of the Lamb, the union of the Messiah with the community of the elect.

19:7 *The wedding day of the Lamb:* symbol of God's reign about to begin (21:1—22:5); see the note on 10:7. *His bride:* the church; cf 2 Cor 11:2; Eph 5:22–27. Marriage is one of the biblical metaphors used to describe the covenant relationship between God and his people; cf Hos 2:16–22; Is 54:5–6; 62:5; Ez 16:6–14. Hence, idolatry and apostasy are viewed as adultery and harlotry (Hos 2:4–15; Ez 16:15–63); see the note on 14:4.

19:8 See the note on 14:12.

19:9 *Blessed:* see the note on 1:3.

19:10 *The spirit of prophecy:* as the prophets were inspired to proclaim God's word, so the Christian is called to give witness to the Word of God (13) made flesh; cf 1:2; 6:9; 12:17.

19:11–16 Symbolic description of the exalted Christ (cf 1:13–16) who together with the armies of heaven overcomes the beast and its followers; cf 17:14.

19:12 *A name:* in Semitic thought, the name conveyed the reality of the person; cf Mt 11:27; Lk 10:22.

19:13 *Had been dipped in:* other Greek manuscripts and versions read "had been sprinkled with"; cf v 15. *The Word of God:* Christ is the revelation of the Father; cf Jn 1:1, 14; 1 Jn 2:14.

19:15 The treading of the wine press is a prophetic symbol used to describe the destruction of God's enemies; cf Is 63:1–6; Jl 4:13.

19:17–21 The certainty of Christ's victory is proclaimed by an angel, followed by a reference to the mustering of enemy forces and a fearsome description of their annihilation. The gruesome imagery is borrowed from Ez 39:4, 17–20.

19:20 *Beast . . . false prophet:* see the notes on ch 13. *The fiery pool . . . sulfur:* symbol of God's punishment (14:10; 20:10, 14–15), different from the abyss; see the note on 9:1.

*

19:2 Dn 3:27 / Jer 51:48–49.
19:3 Rv 14:11; Is 34:10.
19:5 Rv 11:18; Ps 115:13.
19:7 Mt 22:9; Eph 5:27.
19:8 Rv 15:6; Is 61:10; Mt 22:11–12.
19:9 Mt 8:11; Lk 14:15.
19:10 Rv 22:8–9.
19:11 Is 11:4.
19:12 Rv 1:14–16; 2:18 / Lk 10:22.
19:13 Is 63:1 / Jn 1:1.
19:14 Rv 15:6; 19:8.
19:15 Rv 14:20; Is 63:3.
19:16 Rv 17:14; 2 Mc 13:4.
19:18 Ez 39:17–20.
19:20 Rv 14:10.

burning with sulfur. 21 The rest were killed by the
sword that came out of the mouth of the one rid-
ing the horse, and all the birds gorged themselves
on their flesh.

The Thousand-year Reign

20 1*† Then I saw an angel come down
from heaven, holding in his hand the
key to the abyss† and a heavy chain. 2*† He
seized the dragon, the ancient serpent, which
is the Devil or Satan, and tied it up for a thou-
sand years 3 and threw it into the abyss, which
he locked over it and sealed, so that it could no
longer lead the nations astray until the thousand
years are completed. After this, it is to be released
for a short time.
4*† Then I saw thrones; those who sat on them
were entrusted with judgment. I also saw the
souls of those who had been beheaded for their
witness to Jesus and for the word of God, and
who had not worshiped the beast or its image
nor had accepted its mark on their foreheads or
hands. They came to life and they reigned with
Christ for a thousand years. 5 The rest of the dead
did not come to life until the thousand years
were over. This is the first resurrection. 6† Blessed
and holy is the one who shares in the first res-
urrection. The second death has no power over
these; they will be priests of God and of Christ,
and they will reign with him for [the] thousand
years.
7† When the thousand years are completed,
Satan will be released from his prison. 8*† He
will go out to deceive the nations at the four
corners of the earth, Gog and Magog, to gather
them for battle; their number is like the sand
of the sea. 9*† They invaded the breadth of the
earth and surrounded the camp of the holy ones
and the beloved city. But fire came down from
heaven and consumed them. 10 The Devil who
had led them astray was thrown into the pool

†

20:1–6 Like the other numerical values in this book, the thousand years are not to be taken literally; they symbolize the long period of time between the chaining up of Satan (a symbol for Christ's resurrection-victory over death and the forces of evil) and the end of the world. During this time God's people share in the glorious reign of God that is present to them by virtue of their baptismal victory over death and sin; cf Rom 6:1–8; Jn 5:24–25; 16:33; 1 Jn 3:14; Eph 2:1.

20:1 *Abyss:* see the note on 9:1.

20:2 *Dragon . . . serpent . . . Satan:* see the notes on 12:3, 9, 10, 15.

20:4 *Beast . . . mark:* see ch 13 and its notes.

20:6 *Blessed:* see the note on 1:3. *Second death:* see the note on 2:11. *Priests:* as in 1:6; 5:10; cf 1 Pt 2:9.

20:7–10 A description of the symbolic battle to take place when Satan is released at the end of time, when the thousand years are over; see the note on vv 1–6.

20:8 *Gog and Magog:* symbols of all pagan nations; the names are taken from Ez 38:1—39:20.

20:9 *The breadth of the earth:* Palestine. *The beloved city:* Jerusalem; see the note on 14:1.

*

20:1 Rv 9:1.
20:2 Gn 3:1.
20:4 Mt 19:28.
20:8 Ez 38:2, 9, 16.
20:9 Ez 38:22.

Live It!

The New Jerusalem

The last three chapters of Revelation contain John's visions of the Reign of God, the end of history, and eternal life. In chapter 20, Satan is alive but has limited power. This is symbolized by the dragon's thousand-year imprisonment, during which the martyrs reign with Christ. The thousand-year reign has been interpreted in many different ways over the centuries, but no one knows its true significance. At the end of the thousand years, Satan is defeated, and Christ sits in final judgment over all the dead.

In chapter 21, John describes a new heaven and a new earth. The Bible begins in Genesis with the story of the creation of a world in which everything is good. It ends in Revelation with a new creation where God's goodness again overflows. A holy city, the New Jerusalem, comes down out of heaven. The New Jerusalem is described as a beautiful bride who is preparing to marry Jesus Christ. John tells his Christian readers that they should look forward to the time of this new city with joy, because when it comes, God and Christ will live in their midst. The whole city will be God's temple. The sun will always shine, a river of living water will flow from God's throne, and the trees will produce fruit year-round recalling the Garden of Eden where Adam and Eve lived before their sin. The New Jerusalem is a symbol for the new world that God will establish when evil is destroyed and suffering is banished.

These visions helped Christians at the end of the first century to maintain their hope by focusing on the glorious victory of God in history. They can also help us to renew our commitment to Christ and keep our hope alive, especially when we are misunderstood or harassed because of our faith.

▶ **Rv 20:1—22:5**

of fire and sulfur, where the beast and the false
prophet were. There they will be tormented day
and night forever and ever.

The Large White Throne

11*† Next I saw a large white throne and the
one who was sitting on it. The earth and the sky
fled from his presence and there was no place
for them. 12*† I saw the dead, the great and the
lowly, standing before the throne, and scrolls
were opened. Then another scroll was opened,
the book of life. The dead were judged accord-
ing to their deeds, by what was written in the
scrolls. 13† The sea gave up its dead; then Death
and Hades gave up their dead. All the dead were
judged according to their deeds. 14*† Then Death
and Hades were thrown into the pool of fire.
(This pool of fire is the second death.) 15 Anyone
whose name was not found written in the book
of life was thrown into the pool of fire.

VI: The New Creation†

The New Heaven and the New Earth

21 1* Then I saw a new heaven and a new
earth. The former heaven and the former
earth had passed away, and the sea was no more.†
2*† I also saw the holy city, a new Jerusalem,
coming down out of heaven from God, prepared
as a bride adorned for her husband. 3* I heard a
loud voice from the throne saying, "Behold, God's
dwelling is with the human race. He will dwell
with them and they will be his people† and God
himself will always be with them [as their God].†
4* He will wipe every tear from their eyes, and
there shall be no more death or mourning, wail-
ing or pain, [for] the old order has passed away."
5*† The one who sat on the throne said, "Be-
hold, I make all things new." Then he said, "Write
these words down, for they are trustworthy and
true." 6*† He said to me, "They are accomplished.
I [am] the Alpha and the Omega, the beginning
and the end. To the thirsty I will give a gift from
the spring of life-giving water. 7*† The victor will
inherit these gifts, and I shall be his God, and he
will be my son. 8*† But as for cowards, the un-
faithful, the depraved, murderers, the unchaste,
sorcerers, idol-worshipers, and deceivers of every
sort, their lot is in the burning pool of fire and
sulfur, which is the second death."

The New Jerusalem†

9 One of the seven angels who held the seven
bowls filled with the seven last plagues came and
said to me, "Come here. I will show you the bride,
the wife of the Lamb."† 10* He took me in spirit to
a great, high mountain and showed me the holy
city Jerusalem coming down out of heaven from
God. 11* It gleamed with the splendor of God.
Its radiance was like that of a precious stone, like
jasper, clear as crystal. 12 It had a massive, high
wall, with twelve gates where twelve angels were
stationed and on which names were inscribed,
[the names] of the twelve tribes of the Israelites.
13* There were three gates facing east, three north,
three south, and three west. 14*† The wall of the
city had twelve courses of stones as its foundation,
on which were inscribed the twelve names of the
twelve apostles of the Lamb.

15† The one who spoke to me held a gold mea-
suring rod to measure the city, its gates, and its
wall. 16† The city was square, its length the same
as [also] its width. He measured the city with
the rod and found it fifteen hundred miles in

†

20:11–15 A description of the final judgment. After the intermediate reign of Christ, all the dead are raised and judged, thus inaugurating the new age.

20:12 *The book of life:* see the note on 3:5. *Judged . . . scrolls:* see the note on 14:12.

20:13 *Hades:* the netherworld; see the note on 1:18.

20:14 *Second death:* see the note on 2:11.

21:1—22:5 A description of God's eternal kingdom in heaven under the symbols of a new heaven and a new earth; cf Is 65:17–25; 66:22; Mt 19:28.

21:1 *Sea . . . no more:* because as home of the dragon it was doomed to disappear; cf Jb 7:12.

21:2 *New Jerusalem . . . bride:* symbol of the church (Gal 4:26); see the note on 19:7.

21:3 *People:* other ancient manuscripts read a plural, "peoples."

21:3–4 Language taken from Ez 37:27; Is 25:8; 35:10; cf 7:17.

21:5 *The one . . . on the throne:* God himself; cf 4:1–11.

21:6 *They are accomplished:* God's reign has already begun; see the note on 20:1–6. *Alpha . . . Omega:* see the note on 1:8. *Life-giving water:* see the note on 7:17.

21:7 *The victor:* over the forces of evil; see the conclusions of the seven letters (2:7, 11, 17, 26; 3:5, 12, 21). *He will be my son:* the victorious Christian enjoys divine affiliation by adoption (Gal 4:4–7; Rom 8:14–17); see the note on 2:26–28.

21:8 *Cowards:* their conviction is so weak that they deny Christ in time of trial and become traitors. *Second death:* see the note on 2:11.

21:9—22:5 Symbolic descriptions of the new Jerusalem, the church. Most of the images are borrowed from Ez 40–48.

21:9 *The bride, the wife of the Lamb:* the church (2), the new Jerusalem (10); cf 2 Cor 11:2.

21:14 *Courses of stones . . . apostles:* literally, "twelve foundations"; cf Eph 2:19–20.

21:15–17 The city is shaped like a gigantic cube, a symbol of perfection (cf 1 Kgs 6:19–20). The measurements of the city and its wall are multiples of the symbolic number twelve; see the note on 7:4–9.

21:16 *Fifteen hundred miles:* literally, twelve thousand stades, about 12,000 furlongs (see the note on 14:20); the number is symbolic: twelve (the apostles as leaders of the new Israel) multiplied by 1,000 (the immensity of Christians); cf Introduction. *In length and width and height:* literally, "its length and width and height are the same."

*

20:11 2 Pt 3:7, 10, 12.
20:12 Rom 2:6.
20:14 1 Cor 15:26, 54–55.
21:1 Is 65:17; 66:22; Rom 8:19–23; 2 Pt 3:13.
21:2 Rv 19:7–9.
21:3 Ez 37:27.
21:4 Rv 7:17; Is 25:8; 35:10.
21:5 Is 43:19; 2 Cor 5:17.
21:6 Rv 22:17; Ps 36:8–9; Is 55:1.
21:7 2 Sm 7:14.
21:8 Rv 22:15; Rom 1:29–32.
21:10 Ez 40:2.
21:11 Heb 11:10.
21:13 Ez 48:31–35.
21:14 Eph 2:20.

length and width and height. 17† He also mea-
sured its wall: one hundred and forty-four cubits
according to the standard unit of measurement
the angel used. 18† The wall was constructed
of jasper, while the city was pure gold, clear as
glass. 19* The foundations of the city wall were
decorated with every precious stone; the first
course of stones was jasper, the second sapphire,
the third chalcedony, the fourth emerald, 20 the
fifth sardonyx, the sixth carnelian, the seventh
chrysolite, the eighth beryl, the ninth topaz, the
tenth chrysoprase, the eleventh hyacinth, and the
twelfth amethyst. 21 The twelve gates were twelve
pearls, each of the gates made from a single
pearl; and the street of the city was of pure gold,
transparent as glass.
22*† I saw no temple in the city, for its temple
is the Lord God almighty and the Lamb. 23*† The
city had no need of sun or moon to shine on it,
for the glory of God gave it light, and its lamp
was the Lamb. 24*† The nations will walk by its
light, and to it the kings of the earth will bring
their treasure. 25 During the day its gates will
never be shut, and there will be no night there.
26 The treasure and wealth of the nations will be
brought there, 27* but nothing unclean will enter
it, nor any[one] who does abominable things or
tells lies. Only those will enter whose names are
written in the Lamb's book of life.

22 1*† Then the angel showed me the river
of life-giving water, sparkling like crystal,
flowing from the throne of God and of the Lamb
2† down the middle of its street. On either side of
the river grew the tree of life that produces fruit
twelve times a year, once each month; the leaves
of the trees serve as medicine for the nations.
3 Nothing accursed will be found there anymore.
The throne of God and of the Lamb will be in it,
and his servants will worship him. 4† They will
look upon his face, and his name will be on their
foreheads. 5* Night will be no more, nor will
they need light from lamp or sun, for the Lord
God shall give them light, and they shall reign
forever and ever.

Live It!

Come, Lord Jesus!

Most young children want immediate gratification. Waiting for Christmas or a birthday is nearly impossible. Saving a piece of candy for after dinner is downright torture. And a long trip in a car produces a familiar and persistent question: Are we there yet?

The Bible tells us that Jesus will return. In the creed, Christians proclaim, "He will come again in glory to judge the living and the dead and his kingdom will have no end" (Roman Missal). When will this happen? Like impatient children, some people have tried to predict the Lord's Second Coming. "But of that day and hour no one knows, . . . but the Father alone" (Mt 24:36).

Can we say, with John, "Amen! Come, Lord Jesus!" (Rv 22:20) and really hope that Jesus will come today? We may hesitate, wanting to hang on to the life we know here and now. Yet, the coming of Christ will be the most glorious event imaginable for those who have put their trust in God. So keep preparing and praying for the return of Christ!

▶ **Rv 22:7–21**

VII: Epilogue

6*† And he said to me, "These words are
trustworthy and true, and the Lord, the God of
prophetic spirits, sent his angel to show his ser-
vants what must happen soon." 7* "Behold, I am
coming soon."† Blessed† is the one who keeps
the prophetic message of this book.

21:17 *One hundred and forty-four cubits:* the cubit was about eighteen inches in length. *Standard unit of measurement the angel used:* literally, "by a human measure, i.e., an angel's."

21:18–21 The gold and precious gems symbolize the beauty and excellence of the church; cf Ex 28:15–21; Tb 13:16–17; Is 54:11–12.

21:22 Christ is present throughout the church; hence, no temple is needed as an earthly dwelling for God; cf Mt 18:20; 28:20; Jn 4:21.

21:23 *Lamp . . . Lamb:* cf Jn 8:12.

21:24–27 All men and women of good will are welcome in the church; cf Is 60:1, 3, 5, 11. *The . . . book of life:* see the note on 3:5.

22:1, 17 *Life-giving water:* see the note on 7:17.

22:2 *The tree of life:* cf v 14; see the note on 2:7. *Fruit . . . medicine:* cf Ez 47:12.

22:4 *Look upon his face:* cf Mt 5:8; 1 Cor 13:12; 1 Jn 3:2.

22:6–21 The book ends with an epilogue consisting of a series of warnings and exhortations and forming an inclusion with the prologue by resuming its themes and expressions; see the note on 1:1–3.

22:7, 12, 20 *I am coming soon:* Christ is the speaker; see the note on 1:3.

22:7, 14 *Blessed:* see the note on 1:3.

21:19 Is 54:11–12.
21:22 Jn 2:19–20.
21:23 Is 60:1–2, 19–20.
21:24 Is 60:11.
21:27 Is 35:8; 52:1; Zec 13:2/ Rv 3:5; 20:12.
22:1 Ez 47:1–12.
22:5 Is 60:20.
22:6 Rv 1:1.
22:7 Rv 22:12, 20 / Rv 1:3.

RV

AMEN!

In Hebrew, *amen* means "so be it" or "yes, it is true." So saying "Amen" in your prayers is the same as saying, "Yes, I believe!" It is an appropriate way to conclude the last book of the Bible, and it should not be said lightly. Are you able to say "Amen" to all you have read, prayed, and reflected on in this Bible? Have the stories and the poems, the teachings and the parables, the songs and the sayings led you to believe in a God who is with you every step of your journey, every minute of the day and night?

Each of us is invited to join the great Amen, to say: "Yes, I believe in a loving God who is father and mother to us all! Yes, I believe in God's Son, Jesus Christ, who is my Lord and Savior! Yes, I believe in the Holy Spirit, who will help me to continue Jesus' mission of justice, reconciliation, and love!" But these words remain just words until people with courage and conviction take the risk to live them out in their own corner of the world. Take the risk; heaven awaits you! Amen!

▶ **Rv 22:20**

8 It is I, John, who heard and saw these things,
and when I heard and saw them I fell down to
worship at the feet of the angel who showed
them to me. 9* But he said to me, "Don't! I am a
fellow servant of yours and of your brothers the
prophets and of those who keep the message of
this book. Worship God."
10† Then he said to me, "Do not seal up the
prophetic words of this book, for the appointed
time is near. 11 Let the wicked still act wickedly,
and the filthy still be filthy. The righteous must
still do right, and the holy still be holy."
12* "Behold, I am coming soon. I bring with me
the recompense I will give to each according to his
deeds. 13*† I am the Alpha and the Omega, the
first and the last, the beginning and the end."
14*† Blessed are they who wash their robes so
as to have the right to the tree of life and enter the
city through its gates. 15* Outside are the dogs, the
sorcerers, the unchaste, the murderers, the idol-
worshipers, and all who love and practice deceit.
16*† "I, Jesus, sent my angel to give you this
testimony for the churches. I am the root and off-
spring of David, the bright morning star."
17*† The Spirit and the bride say, "Come." Let
the hearer say, "Come." Let the one who thirsts
come forward, and the one who wants it receive
the gift of life-giving water.
18 I warn everyone who hears the prophetic
words in this book: if anyone adds to them,
God will add to him the plagues described in
this book, 19* and if anyone takes away from the
words in this prophetic book, God will take away
his share in the tree of life and in the holy city
described in this book.
20*† The one who gives this testimony says, "Yes,
I am coming soon." Amen! Come, Lord Jesus!
21 The grace of the Lord Jesus be with all.

†

22:10 *The appointed time:* see the note on 1:3.
22:13 Christ applies to himself words used by God in 1:8.
22:14 *The city:* heavenly Jerusalem; see the note on 21:2.
22:16 *The root . . . of David:* see the note on 5:5. *Morning star:* see the note on 2:26–28.
22:17 *Bride:* the church; see the note on 21:2.
22:20 *Come, Lord Jesus:* a liturgical refrain, similar to the Aramaic expression *Marana tha*—"Our Lord, come!"—in 1 Cor 16:22; cf the note there. It was a prayer for the coming of Christ in glory at the parousia; see the note on 1:3.

*

22:9 Rv 19:10.
22:12 Rv 22:7, 20 / Ps 62:12; 2 Tm 4:14.
22:13 Rv 1:8; 21:6; Is 41:4; 44:6.
22:14 Rv 7:14–15; 22:2.
22:15 Rv 21:8; Rom 1:29–32.
22:16 Rv 1:1, 11–12; 22:6 / Rv 2:28.
22:17 Rv 21:6; Is 55:1.
22:19 Dt 4:2.
22:20 Rv 22:7, 12 / Acts 3:20–21; 1 Cor 15:23; 16:22.

Where Do I Find It?

Events, People, and Teachings

Old Testament Stories

These stories are listed in the order in which they first appear in the Bible.

Creation, *Gn, chs 1–2*
original sin and its punishment, *Gn, ch 3*
Cain and Abel, *Gn 4:1–16*
Noah and the Great Flood, *Gn, chs 6–9*
God's covenant with Abraham, *Gn 17:1—18:15*
God's command to sacrifice Isaac, *Gn 22:1–19*
Isaac's blessing of Jacob, *Gn 27:1–29*
Jacob's dream, *Gn 28:10–22*
Joseph and his brothers, *Gn, chs 37–46*
birth and youth of Moses, *Ex 2:1–10*
Moses at the burning bush, *Ex 3:1–12*
plagues on Egypt, *Ex, chs 7–12*
Passover and the Exodus, *Ex, chs 12–14*
Ten Commandments, *Ex 20:1–17*
destruction of Jericho, *Jos 5:13—6:27*
Gideon and the sign of the fleece, *Jgs 6:36–40*
Samson, *Jgs, chs 13–16*
Samuel's birth and calling, *1 Sm, chs 1–3*
David and Goliath, *1 Sm, ch 17*
David and Bathsheba, *2 Sm, ch 11*
Solomon's wisdom, *1 Kgs, ch 3*
Elijah's triumph over the priests of Baal, *1 Kgs 18:20–40*
miracles of Elisha, *2 Kgs 4:1—6:23*
end of the Babylonian captivity, *Ezra, ch 1*
battles of Judas Maccabeus, *1 Mc, chs 3–5*
Ezekiel and the valley of dry bones, *Ez 37:1–14*
Daniel, *Dn, chs 1–6*
Jonah and the Ninevites, *Jon, chs 1–3*

New Testament Stories

These stories are listed in the order in which they first appear in the Bible.

birth of Jesus, *Mt 1:18—2:12; Lk, chs 1–2*
baptism of Jesus, *Mt 3:13–17; Mk 1:9–11; Lk 3:21–22*
temptation of Jesus, *Mt 4:1–11; Mk 1:12–13; Lk 4:1–13*
Peter's declaration about Jesus, *Mt 16:13–20; Mk 8:27–30; Lk 9:18–20*
Transfiguration of Jesus, *Mt 17:1–13; Mk 9:2–13; Lk 9:28–36*
Jesus' triumphal entry into Jerusalem, *Mt 21:1–11; Mk 11:1–11; Lk 19:28–40; Jn 12:12–19*
Jesus in the Temple, *Mt 21:12–17; Mk 11:15–19; Lk 19:45–48; Jn 2:13–16*
Judas's betrayal of Jesus, *Mt 26:14–16,47–56; Mk 14:10–11,43–52; Lk 22:1–53; Jn 13:21–30; 18:1–5*
Last Supper, *Mt 26:17–30; Mk 14:12–25; Lk 22:7–38; 1 Cor 11:23–26*
Jesus at Gethsemane, *Mt 26:36–56; Mk 14:32–52; Lk 22:39–53*
Peter's denial of Christ, *Mt 26:69–75; Mk 14:66–72; Lk 22:54–62; Jn 18:15–18,25–27*
Crucifixion, *Mt 27:32–56; Mk 15:21–41; Lk 23:26–49; Jn 19:16–37*
Resurrection and appearances, *Mt, ch 28; Mk, ch 16; Lk, ch 24; Jn, chs 20–21; Acts 1:1–11*
Jesus washing his disciples' feet, *Jn 13:1–17*
Holy Spirit at Pentecost, *Acts 2:1–42*
stoning of Stephen, *Acts, chs 6–7*
conversion of Saul, *Acts 9:1–31*
Peter's escape from prison, *Acts 12:1–19*
Paul and Silas's escape from prison, *Acts 16:16–40*
Paul's journey to Rome for his trial, *Acts, chs 27–28*

People

Each person is followed by the page number that will lead you to an "Introducing . . ." article. For other articles on these and other Bible people see the Article Subject Index.

Prayers

These prayers are listed in the order in which they first appear in the Bible.

Miracles of Jesus

These miracle stories are listed in the order in which they first appear in the Bible.

Healing Individuals

Controlling Nature

walking on water, *Mt 14:22–33; Mk 6:45–52; Jn 6:16–21*
feeding four thousand, *Mt 15:32–39; Mk 8:1–10*
fish with a coin, *Mt 17:24–27*
fig tree withers, *Mt 21:18–22; Mk 11:12–14,20–25*
huge catch of fish, *Lk 5:1–11; Jn 21:1–11*
turning water into wine, *Jn 2:1–11*

Raising the Dead
Jairus's daughter, *Mt 9:18–19,23–26; Mk 5:21–24,35–43; Lk 8:40–42,49–56*
widow's son at Nain, *Lk 7:11–17*
Lazarus, *Jn 11:1–44*

Parables of Jesus

These parables are listed in alphabetical order.

barren fig tree, *Lk 13:6–9*
canceled debts, *Lk 7:41–43*
cost of discipleship, *Lk 14:25–33*
dishonest manager, *Lk 16:1–8*
faithful or unfaithful slave, *Mt 24:45–51; Lk 12:42–48*
fig tree, *Mt 24:32–35; Mk 13:28–31; Lk 21:29–33*
good Samaritan, *Lk 10:30–37*
great dinner, *Lk 14:16–24*
growing seed, *Mk 4:26–29*
hidden treasure and pearl, *Mt 13:44–46*
honor at a banquet, *Lk 14:7–14*
laborers in the vineyard, *Mt 20:1–16*
light of the world, *Mt 5:14–16*
lost coin, *Lk 15:8–10*
lost sheep, *Mt 18:12–14; Lk 15:3–7*
mustard seed, *Mt 13:31–32; Mk 4:30–32; Lk 13:18–19*
net, *Mt 13:47–50*
new wine in old wineskins, *Mt 9:16–17; Mk 2:21–22; Lk 5:36–39*
persistent friend, *Lk 11:5–8*
persistent widow, *Lk 18:2–8*
Pharisee and the tax collector, *Lk 18:10–14*
prodigal son, *Lk 15:11–32*
rich fool, *Lk 12:16–21*
rich man and Lazarus, *Lk 16:19–31*
salt, *Mt 5:13; Mk 9:50; Lk 14:34–35*
sheep and the goats, *Mt 25:31–46*
sower, *Mt 13:3–8,18–23; Mk 4:3–9,14–20; Lk 8:5–8,11–15*
talents, *Mt 25:14–30*
ten bridesmaids, *Mt 25:1–13*
ten pounds, *Lk 19:11–27*
two sons, *Mt 21:28–31*
unforgiving servant, *Mt 18:23–35*
watchful slaves, *Lk 12:35–40*
wedding banquet, *Mt 22:1–14*
weeds among the wheat, *Mt 13:24–30,36–43*
wicked tenants, *Mt 21:33–44; Mk 12:1–12; Lk 20:9–18*
wise and foolish builders, *Mt 7:24–27; Lk 6:47–49*
worthless slaves, *Lk 17:7–10*
yeast, *Mt 13:33; Lk 13:20–21*

Teachings of Jesus

These teachings are listed in alphabetical order.

Beatitudes, *Mt 5:1–12; Lk 6:20–26*
born from above, *Jn 3:1–21*
bread of life, *Jn 6:25–59*
children, *Mk 10:13–16*
discipleship, *Lk 14:25–33*
do not worry, *Mt 6:19–21,25–34; Lk 12:22–34*
golden rule, *Mt 7:12; Lk 6:31*
good shepherd, *Jn 10:1–21*
greatest commandment, *Mt 22:34–40; Mk 12:28–34; Lk 10:25–28*
living water, *Jn 4:1–26*
Lord's Prayer, *Mt 6:9–13; Lk 11:2–4*
mission of the twelve Apostles, *Mt 10:1–15*
paying taxes, *Mt 22:15–22; Mk 12:13–17; Lk 20:20–26*
rich young man, *Mt 19:16–30; Mk 10:17–31; Lk 18:18–30*
Sermon on the Mount, *Mt, chs 5–7*
Sermon on the Plain, *Lk 6:17–49*
vine and branches, *Jn 15:1–17*
"the way, the truth, and the life," *Jn 14:1–14*
"where two or three are gathered," *Mt 18:20*

Catholic Connections

Creed

Morality

Prayer

Sacraments

Sacrament Connections

These are some passages that can help us understand God's action in the sacraments. It is not meant to be a complete list of all the biblical connections for all seven sacraments.

Baptism

Is 43:1
Mt 3:13–17; 28:19–20
Mk 1:9–11
Lk 3:21–22
Jn 1:29–34; 3:5
Acts 2:37–41
Rom 6:3–4

Confirmation

Is 11:2; 61:1
Mt 3:13–17
Jn 1:33–34; 14:15–31; 16:5–15
Acts 2:1–4; 8:14–17
2 Cor 1:21–22
Gal 5:22–23

Eucharist

Gn 14:17–20
Ex 12:1–28; 24:1–8
Mt 14:13–21; 26:17–29
Mk 6:30–44; 14:12–25
Lk 9:10–17; 22:14–20; 24:13–35
Jn 6:1–13,25–59
1 Cor 11:17–34

Reconciliation (penance)

Gn 45:1–15
Jl 2:12–13
Mt 5:21–26,38–48; 18:23–35
Mk 2:1–12
Lk 15:11–32
Jn 20:19–23
Rom, ch 6

Anointing

Ps 23
Mk 6:7–13
Lk 13:10–13
2 Tm 2:11–12
Jas 5:14–16

Holy Orders

Dt 18:1–5
Ps 110:1–4
Mt 10:1–4
Mk 3:14–19
Lk 6:12–16
Jn 13:1–14
Rom 12:1–8
1 Tm 3:1–13
Ti 1:5–9
Heb 4:14—5:10

Marriage

Gn 2:18–25
Song 8:6–7
Mt 19:1–12
Mk 10:2–12
Jn 2:1–11
1 Cor, ch 13
Eph 5:21–33
1 Jn 4:4–16

Seven Themes of Catholic Social Teaching

Here is an index to articles on seven significant themes that summarize much of Catholic social teaching, which is rooted in the Scriptures and Tradition and should be woven into the biblical principles that every disciple lives by. For a fuller description/ see page C24.

Life and Faith Issues

Here are some passages that can give you comfort or direction. There are many other passages in the Bible that also address these and other topics.

Anger
Mt 5:21–24
Jn 2:13–17
Eph 4:25–27,31–32
Jas 1:19–21

Call
Gn 12:1–9
1 Sm, chs 1–3
Is 6:1–8
Jer 1:4–10
Mt 4:18–22; 28:16–20
Mk 1:16–20
Lk 5:1–11

Commitment
Nm 30:2–4
Dt 6:1–9; 11:8–9
Jos 24:14–15
Mk 8:34–38

Courage
Jos 1:9
1 Sm, ch 17
Ps 31

Discipleship
Mk 8:34–38
Lk 9:1–6
Jn 4:1–42

Family
Gn 4:9; 12:10–20
Sir 3:1–16
Eph 5:21—6:4

Fear
Ps 27, 91
Zep 3:14–20
Mt 14:22–33
Mk 4:35–41
Lk 22:54–62

Forgiveness
Gn 33:1–17
Ps 51
Mt 18:21–35
Lk 6:27–36; 23:34
Jn 8:2–11

Friendship
Ruth 1:1–19
1 Sm, ch 20
Sir 6:5–17
Jn 15:12–17

Friendship with God
Gn 28:10–22
Mi 6:8
Jn 15:12–17

Giving
2 Chr 31:2–10
Ezr 1:6–11
Mk 12:41–44
Lk 21:1–4

Happiness
Sir 25:1–11
Lk 12:22–34
Phil 4:4–9

Honesty with God
Gn 18:22–33
Jer 12:1–16
Mk 14:32–42

Hope
Eccl 3:1–8
Lam 3:22–26
Rom 8:18–30

Hypocrisy
Mt 6:1–6; 23:1–36
Lk 18:9–14
Jas 1:22—2:4

Images of God
Gn 1:26–27; 32:22–32
Ps 23
Jer 18:1–11

Judgment of Others
Mt 7:1–5
Rom 14:1–12
Gal 3:26–28

Loneliness and Abandonment
Ps 22:1–12
Mk 15:33–34
2 Tm 4:9–18

Love
Song 8:6–7
Mt 5:43–48
Mk 12:28–34
1 Cor, ch 13

Peace
Is 11:1–9
Mi 4:1–5
Jn 14:25–31

Persistence
Lk 11:5–8; 18:1–8

Popularity
Mk 9:33–37
1 Cor 3:1–9
Phil 2:1–11

Presence of God
Gn 15:7
Ex 3:1–6; 33:17–23
Mt 18:20

Promises of God
Ex 6:1–9
Jer 29:11
Lk 4:14–30

Repentance
1 Chr 21:1–17
Jl 2:12–18
Lk 15:11–32

Responsibility
Sir 15:11–20
Ez, ch 18

Service
Is 42:1–6
Mt 20:20–28; 25:31–46
Mk 10:35–45
Jn 13:1–17

Sexuality
Gn 1:26–31
Tb 8:4–9
Song of Songs
Eph 5:1–14
1 Thes 4:3–8

Suffering
Jb 1:13–21
Ps 22
Mt 5:1–12
1 Pt 3:13–18

Temptation
Gn, ch 3
Mt 4:1–11
Mk 1:12–13; 7:14–23
Lk 4:1–13

Trust in God
Ps 62
Is 43:1–5
Mt 11:28–30
Mk 10:46–52

Vocation (*See* call; discipleship)

Wisdom
2 Chr 1:7–13
Prv 8:1–21
Wis, ch 7

Acknowledgments

Third edition focus group members: Jane Angha, Kelsey Denzer, Jacob DeMarais, Elizabeth Kilkus, Rebecca Otte, Elizabeth Perkins, Margaret Scannell, Larry Schatz, FSC; Sarah Schrupp, James Spillman, Jocelyn Stage, Dan Streefland

Second edition writers: Tony Tamberino, Victor Valenzuela, Larry Schatz, FSC, Lisa-Marie Calderone-Stewart, and Vikki Shepp

First Edition article and introduction writers: Eduardo Arnouil; Lisa-Marie Calderone-Stewart; Carmen Maria Cervantes; Catherine Cory; Gary Dreier; Karen Emmerich; Carole Goodwin; Ron Kenney; Edward P. Kunzman; Judi Lanciotti; Joseph A. Morris, CM; Daniel Ponsetto; Rosa Sanchez; Larry Schatz, FSC; Valerie Shields; Brian Singer-Towns; and Michael Theisen

Consultants: Barbara Allaire, Mary Lee Becker, Philip J. Calderone, Brian K. Johnson, Carl Koch, Stephan Nagel, Pheme Perkins, and Kevin Schneider

The Catholic Youth Bible NRSV Publishing Team: Brian Singer-Towns, general editor; Carmen María Cervantes, Shirley Kelter, and Robert P. Stamschror, consulting editors; Lynn Riska Dahdal, production editor; Cheryl Drivdahl and Mary Duerson, copy editors; Hollace Storkel, article typesetter; Auto-Graphics, Scripture typesetters; Peachtree Editorial and Proofreading Service, Scripture proofreaders; Maurine R. Twait, art director; Stephan Nagel, art director and cover designer; Sue Campbell, Carol Evans-Smith, Kent Linder, and Cindi Ramm, designers; Alan S. Hanson, prepress specialist; Gary J. Boisvert and Alan S. Hanson, illustration colorizers; Michael O. McGrath, illustrator

The Catholic Youth Bible NAB Publishing team: Steven Roe development editor; Beverly DeGeorge, managing editor; Don Curtin, marketing coordinator; Bill Northam, printing coordinator; Stephan Nagel and Brian Singer-Towns, consulting editors; Cindi Ramm, consulting cover designer; Lynn Riska, consultant for typesetting and project management; Gabrielle Koenig and Brooke E. Saron, editorial assistance; Genevieve Nagel, photo and illustration acquisition editor; James Koenig and Alan S. Hanson, technical assistance; Cären Yang, contributing graphic designer; The Livingstone Corporation, article and Scripture typesetter, copy editor, cover design adaptation, and project management; Peachtree Editorial and Proofreading Service, Scripture and article proofreaders; Michael O. McGrath, illustrator

The Catholic Youth Bible, Revised, Publishing Team: Steven Roe and Brian Singer-Towns, development editors; Heather Sutton, marketing director; Bill Northam, printing coordinator; Jim Gurley and Cären Yang, production editors; Andy Palmer, designer; Lynn Riska, consultant for typesetting; Brooke E. Saron and Paul Grass, FSC, copy editors; Genevieve Nagel, photo and illustration acquisitions editor; James Koenig, technical consultant; Alan S. Hanson, prepress specialist; The Livingstone Corporation, article and Scripture typesetter and project management; Peachtree Editorial and Proofreading Service, Scripture and article proofreaders. We extend a special thank-you to our student article reviewers, for their time, enthusiasm, invaluable comments, and recommendations. The student article review team included Renea Carlson, Neal Frantzen, Joshua Hamann, Aubrey Hollnagel, William Jaspers, Benjamin Leist, Megan Leopold, Kendall Marsden, and Brenda Maurer.

A special thank-you to the members of the original *Catholic Youth Bible* focus group: Catherine Cory; Carole Goodwin; Maryann Hakowski; Shirley Kelter; Marilyn Kielbasa; Joseph A. Morris, CM; Daniel Ponsetto; Pat Rinker; Virginia Smith; Carleen Suttman; and especially Robert P. Stamschror for his work in starting this project.

Finally, we are very grateful for the many young people, youth leaders, and teachers who helped as reviewers and consultants through the duration of this project.

The excerpts marked *Catechism* and *CCC* are from the English translation of the *Catechism of the Catholic Church* for use in the United States of America, second edition, number 2308. Copyright © 1994 by the United States Catholic Conference, Inc.—Libreria Editrice Vaticana. English translation of the *Catechism of the Catholic Church: Modifications from the Editio Typica* copyright © 1997 by the United States Catholic Conference, Inc.—Libreria Editrice Vaticana.

The quotation by Pope Benedict XVI on the back cover and page C9 is from "Message of the Holy Father Benedict XVI to the Young People of the World on the Occasion of the 21st World Youth Day, 2006," at *www.vatican.va/holy_father/benedict_xvi/messages/youth/documents/hf_ben-xvi_mes_20060222_youth_en.html*, accessed February 25, 2009. Copyright © 2006 by Libreria Editrice Vaticana.

The quotation on page 102 is from *He Is Risen*, by Thomas Merton (Allen, TX: RCL Enterprises, 1975), page 22. Copyright © 1975 by RCL Enterprises. Used with permission of the Merton Legacy Trust.

The poems "God Is Rice" on page 117 and "Living Water" on page 1484 are by Masao and Fumiko Takenaka, as quoted in *Gifts of Many Cultures: Worship Resources for the Global Community*, edited by Maren C. Tirabassi and Kathy Wonson Eddy (Cleveland: United Church Press, 1995), pages 186 and 144. Copyright © 1995 by United Church Press.

The Lakota code on page 238 is from *Sacred Ground: Reflections on Lakota Spirituality and the Gospel*, by Ron Zeilinger (Chamberlain, SD: Tipi Press, no date), pages 74–75. Used with permission of the author.

The quotations on pages 271 and 1045 and the creed on page 1631 are from *Prophetic Voices: The Document on the Process of the Third Encuentro Nacional Hispano de Pastoral*, by the Secretariat for Hispanic Affairs, of the United States Catholic Conference (USCCB) and the National Conference of Catholic Bishops (Washington, DC: USCCB, 1986), pages 23, 6, and 17–18, respectively. Copyright © 1986 by the USCCB. The excerpt on page 1200 is from page 12, quoting *Working Document for the Third Encuentro Nacional Hispano de Pastoral*, August 1985, number 9, page 105. Used with permission of the USCCB. All rights reserved.

The words of John Paul II on page 319 are from *A Reconciliation Sourcebook*, edited by Kathleen Hughes and Joseph A. Favazza (Chicago: Archdiocese of Chicago, Liturgy Training Publications, 1997), page 4. Copyright © 1997 by the Archdiocese of Chicago, Liturgy Training Publications.

The quotations on pages 511, 973, 1314, 1432, and 1813 are from the English translation of The Roman Missal © 2010, International Commission on English in the Liturgy (ICEL). All rights reserved. Used with permission of the ICEL.

The haiku on page 548 is from *My Haiku of Hiroshima*, by Yasuhiko Shigemoto (Hiroshima, Japan: Keisuisha Company Ltd, 1995), page 14. Copyright © 1995 by Yasuhiko Shigemoto. Used with permission of the author.

The poem on page 655 and the prayers on pages 1029 and 1670 are reprinted from *Your Will Be Done* (Hong Kong: Christian Conference of Asia, 1984), pages 42, 95, and 145, respectively. Copyright © 1984 CCA Youth, Christian Conference of Asia. Used with permission of the Christian Conference of Asia.

The lyrics from "On Eagle's Wings" on page 771 are by Jan Michael Joncas. Copyright © 1979 by Jan Michael Joncas. Published by OCP Publications, 5536 N.E. Hassalo, Portland, OR 97213. All rights reserved. Used with permission of OCP Publications.

The lyrics from "Blest Be the Lord" on page 771 are by Dan Schutte. Copyright © 1976 by OCP Publications, 5536 N.E. Hassalo, Portland, OR 97213. All rights reserved. Used with permission of OCP Publications.

The passage on page 857 is from *Tao te Ching: A New English Version*, translated by Stephen Mitchell (New York: HarperPerennial, 1988), number 29. Translation copyright © 1988 by Stephen Mitchell.

The Cherokee poem "You Are Part of Me" on page 868 is by Lloyd Carl Owle, and is reprinted from *American Indian Prayers and Poetry*, edited by J. Ed Sharpe (Cherokee, NC: Cherokee Publications, 1985), page 9. Copyright © 1985 by Cherokee Publications. Used with permission of Cherokee Publications.

The quotations on pages 889 and 891 are Richard Wood's English translations of portions of *Huehuehtlahtolli: Testimonios de la Antigua Palabra*, by Miguel León-Portilla and Librado Silva Galeana (Mexico: Secretaría de Educación Pública and Fondo de Cultura Económica, 1991), pages 49, 53, 79, 86, 91–92, and 95–97, respectively. Copyright © Secretaría de Educación Pública; copyright © Fondo de Cultura Económica.

The lyrics from "Be Not Afraid" on page 1012 are by Bob Dufford, SJ. Copyright © 1975, 1978 by Robert J. Dufford, SJ, and OCP Publications, 5536 N.E. Hassalo, Portland, OR 97213. All rights reserved. Used with permission of OCP Publications.

The prayer on page 1214, Elizabeth S. Tapia's "Earth Credo," is from *A Time to Speak*. Copyright © 1993, published through the efforts of the General Board of Global Ministries of the United Methodist Church and Youth and Young Adults Ministries, in coordination with the United Methodist Youth Fellowship in the Philippines and the Methodist Youth Fellowship in Korea, Manila, Philippines, 18. Used with permission of the author.

The quotations in the article on page 1308 are from the English translation of the *Rite of Christian Initiation of Adults*, copyright ©1985 by the ICEL, numbers 226 and 228, and the quotation on page 1529 is from the English translation of the *Rite of Confirmation*, second edition, © 1975 by the ICEL, number 27, as found in the *Rites of the Catholic Church*, volume one, prepared by the ICEL, a Joint Commission of Catholic Bishops' Conferences (Collegeville, MN: The Liturgical Press, 1990). Copyright © 1990 by the Order of Saint Benedict, Collegeville, MN. Used with permission of the ICEL.

The prayer on page 1493 is from *The Sacred Pipe: Black Elk's Account of the Seven Rites of the Oglala Sioux*, by Joseph Epes Brown. Copyright © 1953 by the University of Oklahoma Press. Used with permission of the University of Oklahoma Press.

The quotation on page 1518 is from *A Handbook on Guadalupe: Our Lady Patroness of the Americas* (Stockton, CA: Office of Religious Education, Department of Catechesis, 1974), pages 148 and 152. Copyright © 1974 by Franciscan Marytown Press, Kenosha, Wisconsin.

The song lyrics on page 1673 were written by Jose Antonio Rubio. Used with permission.

The Navajo prayer on page 1684 is from *The Sacred Vision: Native American Religion and Its Practice Today*, by Michael F. Steltenkamp (New York: Paulist Press, 1982), page 82. Copyright © 1982 by Michael Steltenkamp. Used with permission of the author.

The excerpt on page 1737 is from the English translation of The Roman Missal © 1973, ICEL (New York: Catholic Book Publishing Company, 1985), page 546. Illustrations and arrangement © 1985-1974 by the Catholic Book Publishing Company, New York.

The information on the "Study It!" insert on pages C1–C8 is adapted from three *Saint Mary's Press® Essential Quick Charts*: *Bible Basics* © 2007, *Salvation History* © 2007, and *Interpreting the Bible* © 2009, by Saint Mary's Press, Winona, MN. All rights reserved.

The "Pray It!" insert on C9–C16 is adapted from the *Personal Journey Bible: The Catholic Youth Bible New Testament and Psalms* (Winona, MN: Saint Mary's Press, 2009), pages c1–c8. Copyright © 2009 by Saint Mary's Press. All rights reserved.

The quotation by Pope Benedict XVI on page C17 is from "Message of the Holy Father Benedict XVI to the Young People of the World on the Occasion of the XXIII World Youth Day, 2008," number 7, at *www.vatican.va/holy_father/benedict_xvi/messages/youth/documents/hf_ben-xvi_mes_20070720_youth_en.html*, accessed February 25, 2009. Copyright © 2007 by Libreria Editrice Vaticana.

The Catholic social teaching themes described on page C24 are adapted from "Themes of Catholic Social Teaching," by the USCCB, at *www.usccb.org/sdwp/projects/socialteaching/excerpt.shtml*, accessed February 25, 2009. Copyright © 2005 by the USCCB, Washington, DC. All rights reserved.

The information on the "Catholic Practices and Prayers" insert on pages C33–C40 is taken from *Catholic Quick View*, second edition, by Brian Singer-Towns, Marilyn Kielbasa, and Robert Feduccia Jr. (Winona, MN: Saint Mary's Press, 2008), pages 6–17, 20–22, and 25–27, respectively. Copyright © 2008 by Saint Mary's Press. All rights reserved.

During this book's preparation, all citations, facts, figures, names, addresses, telephone numbers, Internet URLs, and other pieces of information cited within were verified for accuracy. The authors and Saint Mary's Press staff have made every attempt to reference current and valid sources, but we cannot guarantee the content of any source, and we are not responsible for any changes that may have occurred since our verification. If you find an error in, or have a question or concern about, any of the information or sources listed within, please contact Saint Mary's Press.

To view copyright terms and conditions for Internet materials cited here, log on to the home pages for the referenced Web sites.

Maps.com grants no license or rights, expressly or otherwise, beyond the rights of Saint Mary's Press and Thomas Nelson Publishers. Maps.com revised the maps on pages C41, C42, C44, C46, C47, and C48. Contact www.maps.com for all your mapping needs.

published through the efforts of the General Board of Global Ministries of the United Methodist Church and Youth and Young Adults Ministries, in cooperation with the United Methodist Youth Fellowship in the Philippines and the Methodist Youth Fellowship in Santa Mesa, Manila, Philippines, vs. Used with permission of the author.

The quotations in the article on page 1308 are from the English translation of the *Rite of Christian Initiation of Adults*, copyright © 1985 by the ICEL, numbers 226 and 228, and the quotation on page 1529 is from the English translation of the *Rite of Confirmation*, second edition, © 1975 by the ICEL, number 27, as found in *The Rites of the Catholic Church*, volume one, prepared by the ICEL, a Joint Commission of Catholic Bishops Conferences (Collegeville, MN: The Liturgical Press, 1990). Copyright © 1990 by the Order of Saint Benedict, Collegeville, MN. Used with permission of the ICEL.

The prayer on page 1493 is from *The Sacred Pipe: Black Elk's Account of the Seven Rites of the Oglala Sioux*, by Joseph Epes Brown. Copyright © 1953 by the University of Oklahoma Press. Used with permission of the University of Oklahoma Press.

The quotation on page 1518 is from *A Handbook for Catechists: Our Catechumenate of the Americas* (Stockton, CA: Office of Religious Education, Department of Catechesis, 1974), pages 148 and 152. Copyright © 1974 by Franciscan Marytown Press, Kenosha, Wisconsin.

The song lyrics on page 1673 were written by Jose Antonio Rubio. Used with permission.

The Navajo prayer on page 1652 is from *The Sacred Vision: Native American Religion and Its Practice Today*, by Michael F. Steltenkamp (New York: Paulist Press, 1982), page 82. Copyright © 1982 by Michael F. Steltenkamp. Used with permission of the author.

The excerpt on page 1237 is from the English translation of the Roman Missal © 1973, ICEL (New York: Catholic Book Publishing Company, 1985), page 546. Illustrations and arrangement © 1964–1974 by the Catholic Book Publishing Company, New York.

The information on the "Study It" insert on pages C1–C8 is adapted from three Saint Mary's Press® Essential Quick Charts: *Bible Basics* © 2002, *Salvation History* © 2005, and *Interpreting the Bible* © 2009, by Saint Mary's Press, Winona, MN. All rights reserved.

The "Pray It" insert on C9–C16 is adapted from the *Personal Journal Bible, The Catholic Youth Bible New Testament and Psalms* (Winona, MN: Saint Mary's Press, 2008), pages 1–38. Copyright © 2008 by Saint Mary's Press. All rights reserved.

The quotation by Pope Benedict XVI on page C17 is from "Message of the Holy Father Benedict XVI to the Young People of the World on the Occasion of the XXIII World Youth Day 2008," number 7, at *www.vatican.va/holy_father/benedict_xvi/messages/youth/documents/hf_ben-xvi_mes_20070720_youth_en.html*, accessed February 25, 2009. Copyright © 2007 by Libreria Editrice Vaticana.

The Catholic social teaching themes described on page C24 are adapted from "Themes of Catholic Social Teaching," by the USCCB, at *www.usccb.org/sdwp/projects/socialteaching/excerpt.shtml*, accessed February 25, 2009. Copyright © 2005 by the USCCB, Washington, DC. All rights reserved.

The information on the "Catholic Practices and Prayers" insert on pages C33–C40 is taken from *Catholic Quick View*, second edition, by Brian Singer-Towns, Marilyn Kielbasa, and Robert Feduccia Jr. (Winona, MN: Saint Mary's Press, 2008), pages 6–17, 20–22, and 25–27, respectively. Copyright © 2008 by Saint Mary's Press. All rights reserved.

During this book's preparation, all citations, facts, figures, names, addresses, telephone numbers, Internet URLs, and other pieces of information cited within were verified for accuracy. The authors and Saint Mary's Press staff have made every attempt to reference current and valid sources, but we cannot guarantee the content of any source, and we are not responsible for any changes that may have occurred since our verification. If you find an error in, or have a question or concern about, any of the information or sources listed within, please contact Saint Mary's Press.

To view copyright terms and conditions for Internet materials cited here, log on to the home pages for the referenced Web sites.

Maps.com grants no license or rights, expressly or otherwise, beyond the rights of Saint Mary's Press and Thomas Nelson Publishers. Maps.com created the maps on pages C41, C42, C43, C46, C47, and C48. Contact www.maps.com for all your mapping needs.

Study Aids

The Church Year

The Feast Days and Holy Days celebrated by Catholics and other Christians follow a yearly pattern. This pattern is called the liturgical year; it is different from the calendar year. Here is a description of the major seasons in the liturgical year. It might help you if you also take a look at the circular diagram of the liturgical year, found on the following page.

Advent begins the liturgical year four Sundays before Christmas. It is a time of preparation for the coming of Christ. The Advent season can be found on the liturgical year wheel in November and December. It is represented by the small graphic of an Advent wreath.

The **Christmas** season lasts twelve days, beginning with Christmas Day and concluding with the feast of the Baptism of the Lord. This season is found at the top part of the liturgical year wheel. The cross reminds us that the wood of the manger becomes the wood of the cross.

Lent begins with Ash Wednesday and lasts forty days. It is a solemn time of fasting, prayer, and almsgiving in preparation for Easter. The small picture of the palms and cross in the liturgical year wheel symbolizes all of Lent as a journey toward Palm Sunday, when the same crowd that waves palms and yells "Hosanna!" ends up waving angry fists and shouting "Crucify him!"

The **Easter Triduum** is the celebration of Holy Thursday, Good Friday, and the Easter Vigil on Holy Saturday. At this one, continuous, three-day liturgy, Christians remember the Lord's Supper, Christ's Passion and death, and his Resurrection. These feasts are at the heart of the liturgical year. They are represented by the picture of the Easter candle, which makes its appearance in the darkness of the Easter Vigil. The vestments and altar cloths seen are red on Good Friday and white on the other two days.

The **Easter** Season lasts fifty days, beginning with Easter Sunday and ending with the feast of Pentecost. The symbol of the lamb represents Jesus, the innocent sacrificial lamb of God. The symbol of the Holy Spirit reminds us that the Holy Spirit came to the disciples, in the rush of wind and tongues of fire. The altar cloths and vestments are white throughout the Easter season, and then red on Pentecost. Red is the color of the Holy Spirit (as in Confirmation Mass) and of the celebration of feast days associated with martyrs, people killed for their faith (such as the feast of Saints Peter and Paul).

The season of **Ordinary Time** is made up of the days between Christmas and Lent, and the days between Easter and Advent. The bread and wine show us that the main focus of Ordinary Time is the ministry of Jesus, represented by the grapes and bread of communion. There are some special feast days during Ordinary Time that are not celebrated with green vestments and altar cloths, such as Trinity Sunday and the Feast of the Body and Blood of Christ, the first two Sundays after Pentecost, and the Feast of Christ the King, the last Sunday before Advent. You'll see white on all three of those days. The particular dates and days these feasts fall upon vary from year to year.

Christmas is always December 25, so counting backwards four Sundays shows the four Sundays of Advent. Sometimes Advent includes Thanksgiving weekend, and sometimes it doesn't, depending on which day of the week Christmas is.

Easter is always the first Sunday after the first full moon in the spring. Counting backwards six Sundays and then one Wednesday shows when Ash Wednesday and Lent begin. Sometimes Easter is in March, and sometimes it is in April.

On page 1838, you will find a Bible reading plan that corresponds to the readings of the Bible heard on Sundays throughout these seasons. That is an excellent way to get to know the Bible and the liturgical year at the same time.

December
January
February
March
April
May
June
July
August
September
October
November
Christmas
Advent
Ordinary Time
Lent
Easter Triduum
Easter
Pentecost
Ordinary Time

Sunday Readings

Reading the Bible with the Church

This reading plan lists the Sunday readings for the liturgical year. The Scripture passages listed in the following table reflect those found in the official Catholic Lectionary for Mass, *which uses the New American Bible translation.*

Advent and Christmas

	Year A 2010, 2013, 2016	Year B 2011, 2014, 2017	Year C 2009, 2012, 2015
The First Sunday of Advent	Is 2:1–5 Rom 13:11–14 Mt 24:37–44	Is 63:16–17; 64:1–8 1 Cor 1:3–9 Mk 13:33–37	Jer 33:14–16 1 Thes 3:12—4:2 Lk 21:25–28,34–36
The Second Sunday of Advent	Is 11:1–10 Rom 15:4–9 Mt 3:1–12	Is 40:1–5,9–11 2 Pt 3:8–14 Mk 1:1–8	Bar 5:1–9 Phil 1:4–6,8–11 Lk 3:1–6
The Third Sunday of Advent	Is 35:1–6,10 Jas 5:7–10 Mt 11:2–11	Is 61:1–2,10–11 1 Thes 5:16–24 Jn 1:6–8,19–28	Zep 3:14–18 Phil 4:4–7 Lk 3:10–18
The Fourth Sunday of Advent	Is 7:10–14 Rom 1:1–7 Mt 1:18–24	2 Sm 7:1–5,8–11,14,16 Rom 16:25–27 Lk 1:26–38	Mi 5:2–4 Heb 10:5–10 Lk 1:39–45
Midnight Mass *(25 December, every year, readings are the same for all cycles)*	Is 9:2–7 Ti 2:11–14 Lk 2:1–14	Is 9:2–7 Ti 2:11–14 Lk 2:1–14	Is 9:2–7 Ti 2:11–14 Lk 2:1–14
Feast of the Holy Family	Sir 3:2–7,12–14 Col 3:12–21 Mt 2:13–15,19–23	Sir 3:2–7,12–14 Col 3:12–21 Lk 2:22–40	Sir 3:2–7,12–14 Col 3:12–21 Lk 2:41–52
Solemnity of Mary, Mother of God *(1 January, every year, readings are the same for all cycles)*	Nm 6:22–27 Gal 4:4–7 Lk 2:16–21	Nm 6:22–27 Gal 4:4–7 Lk 2:16–21	Nm 6:22–27 Gal 4:4–7 Lk 2:16–21
Epiphany *(readings are the same for all cycles)*	Is 60:1–6 Eph 3:2–3,5–6 Mt 2:1–12	Is 60:1–6 Eph 3:2–3,5–6 Mt 2:1–12	Is 60:1–6 Eph 3:2–3,5–6 Mt 2:1–12
Baptism of the Lord	Is 42:1–4,6–7 Acts 10:34–38 Mt 3:13–17	Is 42:1–4,6–7 Acts 10:34–38 Mk 1:7–11	Is 42:1–4,6–7 Acts 10:34–38 Lk 3:15–16,21–22

Lent and Easter

	Year A 2011, 2014, 2017	Year B 2012, 2015, 2018	Year C 2010, 2013, 2016
Ash Wednesday *(readings are the same for all cycles)*	Jl 2:12–18 2 Cor 5:20—6:2 Mt 6:1–6,16–18	Jl 2:12–18 2 Cor 5:20—6:2 Mt 6:1–6,16–18	Jl 2:12–18 2 Cor 5:20—6:2 Mt 6:1–6,16–18

Lent and Easter *(continued)*

	Year A 2011, 2014, 2017	Year B 2012, 2015, 2018	Year C 2010, 2013, 2016
The First Sunday of Lent			
	Gn 2:7–9; 3:1–7	Gn 9:8–15	Dt 26:4–10
	Rom 5:12–19	1 Pt 3:18–22	Rom 10:8–13
	Mt 4:1–11	Mk 1:12–15	Lk 4:1–13
The Second Sunday of Lent			
	Gn 12:1–4	Gn 22:1–2,9,10–13,15–18	Gn 15:5–12,17–18
	2 Tm 1:8–10	Rom 8:31–34	Phil 3:17—4:1
	Mt 17:1–9	Mk 9:2–10	Lk 9:28–36
The Third Sunday of Lent			
	Ex 17:3–7	Ex 20:1–17	Ex 3:1–8,13–15
	Rom 5:1–2,5–8	1 Cor 1:22–25	1 Cor 10:1–6,10–12
	Jn 4:5–42	Jn 2:13–25	Lk 13:1–9
The Fourth Sunday of Lent			
	1 Sm 16:1,6–7,10–13	2 Chr 36:14–17,19–23	Jos 5:9,10–12
	Eph 5:8–14	Eph 2:4–10	2 Cor 5:17–21
	Jn 9:1–41	Jn 3:14–21	Lk 15:1–3,11–32
The Fifth Sunday of Lent			
	Ez 37:12–14	Jer 31:31–34	Is 43:16–21
	Rom 8:8–11	Heb 5:7–9	Phil 3:8–14
	Jn 11:1–45	Jn 12:20–33	Jn 8:1–11
Passion Sunday (Palm Sunday)			
	Is 50:4–7	Is 50:4–7	Is 50:4–7
	Phil 2:6–11	Phil 2:6–11	Phil 2:6–11
	Mt 26:14—27:66	Mk 14:1—15:47	Lk 22:14—23:56
Holy Thursday *(readings are the same for all cycles)*			
	Ex 12:1–8,11–14	Ex 12:1–8,11–14	Ex 12:1–8,11–14
	1 Cor 11:23–26	1 Cor 11:23–26	1 Cor 11:23–26
	Jn 13:1–15	Jn 13:1–15	Jn 13:1–15
Good Friday *(readings are the same for all cycles)*			
	Is 52:13—53:12	Is 52:13—53:12	Is 52:13—53:12
	Heb 4:14–16; 5:7–9	Heb 4:14–16; 5:7–9	Heb 4:14–16; 5:7–9
	Jn 18:1—19:42	Jn 18:1—19:42	Jn 18:1—19:42
Easter Sunday *(readings are the same for all cycles)*			
	Acts 10:34,37–43	Acts 10:34,37–43	Acts 10:34,37–43
	Col 3:1–4 or 1 Cor 5:6–8	Col 3:1–4 or 1 Cor 5:6–8	Col 3:1–4 or 1 Cor 5:6–8
	Jn 20:1–9	Jn 20:1–9	Jn 20:1–9
Second Sunday of Easter			
	Acts 2:42–47	Acts 4:32–35	Acts 5:12–16
	1 Pt 1:3–9	1 Jn 5:1–6	Rev 1:9–19
	Jn 20:19–31	Jn 20:19–31	Jn 20:19–31
Third Sunday of Easter			
	Acts 2:14,22–28	Acts 3:13–19	Acts 5:27–32,40–41
	1 Pt 1:17–21	1 Jn 2:1–5	Rev 5:11–14
	Lk 24:13–35	Lk 24:35–48	Jn 21:1–19
Fourth Sunday of Easter			
	Acts 2:14,36–41	Acts 4:8–12	Acts 13:14,43–52
	1 Pt 2:20–25	1 Jn 3:1–2	Rev 7:9,14–17
	Jn 10:1–10	Jn 10:11–18	Jn 10:27–30
Fifth Sunday of Easter			
	Acts 6:1–7	Acts 9:26–31	Acts 14:21–27
	1 Pt 2:4–9	1 Jn 3:18–24	Rev 21:1–5
	Jn 14:1–12	Jn 15:1–8	Jn 13:31–35
Sixth Sunday of Easter			
	Acts 8:5–8,14–17	Acts 10:25–26,34–35,44–48	Acts 15:1–2,22–29
	1 Pt 3:15–18	1 Jn 4:7–10	Rev 21:10–14,22–23
	Jn 14:15–21	Jn 15:9–17	Jn 14:23–29

Lent and Easter *(continued)*

	Year A 2011, 2014, 2017	Year B 2012, 2015, 2018	Year C 2010, 2013, 2016
Seventh Sunday of Easter			
	Acts 1:12–14	Acts 1:15–17,20–26	Acts 7:55–60
	1 Pt 4:13–16	1 Jn 4:11–16	Rev 22:12–14,16–17,20
	Jn 17:1–11	Jn 17:11–19	Jn 17:20–26
Pentecost Sunday *(readings are the same for all cycles)*			
	Acts 2:1–11	Acts 2:1–11	Acts 2:1–11
	1 Cor 12:3–7,12–13	1 Cor 12:3–7,12–13	1 Cor 12:3–7,12–13
	Jn 20:19–23	Jn 20:19–23	Jn 20:19–23

Ordinary Time

	Year A 2011, 2014, 2017	Year B 2012, 2015, 2018	Year C 2010, 2013, 2016
The First Sunday in Ordinary Time *(see the Feast of the Baptism of the Lord under "Advent and Christmas")*			
The Second Sunday in Ordinary Time			
	Is 49:3,5–6	1 Sm 3:3b–10,19	Is 62:1–5
	1 Cor 1:1–3	1 Cor 6:13c–15a,17–20	1 Cor 12:4–11
	Jn 1:29–34	Jn 1:35–42	Jn 2:1–11
The Third Sunday in Ordinary Time			
	Is 8:23—9:3	Jon 3:1–5,10	Neh 8:2–4a,5–6,8–10
	1 Cor 1:10–13,17	1 Cor 7:29–31	1 Cor 12:12–30
	Mt 4:12–23	Mk 1:14–20	Lk 1:1–4; 4:14–21
The Fourth Sunday in Ordinary Time			
	Zep 2:3; 3:12–13	Dt 18:15–20	Jer 1:4–5,17–19
	1 Cor 1:26–31	1 Cor 7:32–35	1 Cor 12:31—13:13
	Mt 5:1–12a	Mk 1:21–28	Lk 4:21–30
The Fifth Sunday in Ordinary Time			
	Is 58:7–10	Jb 7:1–4,6–7	Is 6:1–2a,3–8
	1 Cor 2:1–5	1 Cor 9:16–19,22–23	1 Cor 15:1–11
	Mt 5:13–16	Mk 1:29–39	Lk 5:1–11
The Sixth Sunday in Ordinary Time			
	Sir 15:15–20	Lv 13:1–2,45–46	Jer 17:5–8
	1 Cor 2:6–10	1 Cor 10:31—11:1	1 Cor 15:12,16–20
	Mt 5:17–37	Mk 1:40–45	Lk 6:17,20–26
The Seventh Sunday in Ordinary Time			
	Lv 19:1–2,17–18	Is 43:18–19,21–22,24b–25	1 Sm 26:2,7–9,12–13,22–23
	1 Cor 3:16–23	2 Cor 1:18–22	1 Cor 15:45–49
	Mt 5:38–48	Mk 2:1–12	Lk 6:27–38
The Eighth Sunday in Ordinary Time			
	Is 49:14–15	Hos 2:16b,17b,21–22	Sir 27:4–7
	1 Cor 4:1–5	2 Cor 3:1b–6	1 Cor 15:54–58
	Mt 6:24–34	Mk 2:18–22	Lk 6:39–45
The Ninth Sunday in Ordinary Time			
	Dt 11:18,26–28,32	Dt 5:12–15	1 Kgs 8:41–43
	Rom 3:21–25a,28	2 Cor 4:6–11	Gal 1:1–2,6–10
	Mt 7:21–27	Mk 2:23—3:6	Lk 7:1–10
The Tenth Sunday in Ordinary Time			
	Hos 6:3–6	Gn 3:9–15	1 Kgs 17:17–24
	Rom 4:18–25	2 Cor 4:13—5:1	Gal 1:11–19
	Mt 9:9–13	Mk 3:20–35	Lk 7:11–17
The Eleventh Sunday in Ordinary Time			
	Ex 19:2–6a	Ez 17:22–24	2 Sm 12:7–10,13
	Rom 5:6–11	2 Cor 5:6–10	Gal 2:16,19–21
	Mt 9:36—10:8	Mk 4:26–34	Lk 7:36—8:3

Ordinary Time *(continued)*

	Year A 2011, 2014, 2017	Year B 2012, 2015, 2018	Year C 2010, 2013, 2016
The Twelfth Sunday in Ordinary Time			
	Jer 20:10–13	Jb 38:1,8–11	Zec 12:10–11; 13:1
	Rom 5:12–15	2 Cor 5:14–17	Gal 3:26–29
	Mt 10:26–33	Mk 4:35–41	Lk 9:18–24
The Thirteenth Sunday in Ordinary Time			
	2 Kgs 4:8–11,14–16a	Wis 1:13–15; 2:23–24	1 Kgs 19:16b,19–21
	Rom 6:3–4,8–11	2 Cor 8:7,9,13–15	Gal 5:1,13–18
	Mt 10:37–42	Mk 5:21–43	Lk 9:51–62
The Fourteenth Sunday in Ordinary Time			
	Zec 9:9–10	Ez 2:2–5	Is 66:10–14c
	Rom 8:9,11–13	2 Cor 12:7–10	Gal 6:14–18
	Mt 11:25–30	Mk 6:1–6	Lk 10:1–12,17–20
The Fifteenth Sunday in Ordinary Time			
	Is 55:10–11	Am 7:12–15	Dt 30:10–14
	Rom 8:18–23	Eph 1:3–14	Col 1:15–20
	Mt 13:1–23	Mk 6:7–13	Lk 10:25–37
The Sixteenth Sunday in Ordinary Time			
	Wis 12:13,16–19	Jer 23:1–6	Gn 18:1–10a
	Rom 8:26–27	Eph 2:13–18	Col 1:24–28
	Mt 13:24–43	Mk 6:30–34	Lk 10:38–42
The Seventeenth Sunday in Ordinary Time			
	1 Kgs 3:5,7–12	2 Kgs 4:42–44	Gn 18:20–32
	Rom 8:28–30	Eph 4:1–6	Col 2:12–14
	Mt 13:44–52	Jn 6:1–15	Lk 11:1–13
The Eighteenth Sunday in Ordinary Time			
	Is 55:1–3	Ex 16:2–4,12–15	Eccl 1:2; 2:21–23
	Rom 8:35,37–39	Eph 4:17,20–24	Col 3:1–5,9–11
	Mt 14:13–21	Jn 6:24–35	Lk 12:13–21
The Nineteenth Sunday in Ordinary Time			
	1 Kgs 19:9a,11–13a	1 Kgs 19:4–8	Wis 18:6–9
	Rom 9:1–5	Eph 4:30—5:2	Heb 11:1–2,8–19
	Mt 14:22–33	Jn 6:41–51	Lk 12:32–48
The Twentieth Sunday in Ordinary Time			
	Is 56:1,6–7	Prv 9:1–6	Jer 38:4–6,8–10
	Rom 11:13–15,29–32	Eph 5:15–20	Heb 12:1–4
	Mt 15:21–28	Jn 6:51–58	Lk 12:49–53
The Twenty-First Sunday in Ordinary Time			
	Is 22:19–23	Jos 24:1–2a,15–17,18b	Is 66:18–21
	Rom 11:33–36	Eph 5:21–32	Heb 12:5–7,11–13
	Mt 16:13–20	Jn 6:60–69	Lk 13:22–30
The Twenty-Second Sunday in Ordinary Time			
	Jer 20:7–9	Dt 4:1–2,6–8	Sir 3:17–18,20,28–29
	Rom 12:1–2	Jas 1:17–18,21b–22,27	Heb 12:18–19,22–24a
	Mt 16:21–27	Mk 7:1–8,14–15,21–23	Lk 14:1,7–14
The Twenty-Third Sunday in Ordinary Time			
	Ez 33:7–9	Is 35:4–7a	Wis 9:13–18b
	Rom 13:8–10	Jas 2:1–5	Phlm 9–10,12–17
	Mt 18:15–20	Mk 7:31–37	Lk 14:25–33
The Twenty-Fourth Sunday in Ordinary Time			
	Is 55:6–9	Is 50:5–9a	Ex 32:7–11,13–14
	Rom 14:7–9	Jas 2:14–18	1 Tm 1:12–17
	Mt 18:21–35	Mk 8:27–35	Lk 15:1–32
The Twenty-Fifth Sunday in Ordinary Time			
	Acts 2:14,22–28	Wis 2:12,17–20	Am 8:4–7
	Phil 1:20c–24,27a	Jas 3:16—4:3	1 Tm 2:1–8
	Mt 20:1–16a	Mk 9:30–37	Lk 16:1–13

Ordinary Time *(continued)*

	Year A 2011, 2014, 2017	Year B 2012, 2015, 2018	Year C 2010, 2013, 2016
The Twenty-Sixth Sunday in Ordinary Time			
	Ez 18:25–28	Nm 11:25–29	Am 6:1a,4–7
	Phil 2:1–11	Jas 5:1–6	1 Tm 6:11–16
	Mt 21:28–32	Mk 9:38–43,45,47–48	Lk 16:19–31
The Twenty-Seventh Sunday in Ordinary Time			
	Is 5:1–7	Gn 2:18–24	Hb 1:2–3; 2:2–4
	Phil 4:6–9	Heb 2:9–11	2 Tm 1:6–8,13–14
	Mt 21:33–43	Mk 10:2–16	Lk 17:5–10
The Twenty-Eighth Sunday in Ordinary Time			
	Is 25:6–10a	Wis 7:7–11	2 Kgs 5:14–17
	Phil 4:12–14,19–20	Heb 4:12–13	2 Tm 2:8–13
	Mt 22:1–14	Mk 10:17–30	Lk 17:11–19
The Twenty-Ninth Sunday in Ordinary Time			
	Is 45:1,4–6	Is 52:10–11	Ex 17:8–13
	1 Thes 1:1–5b	Heb 4:14–16	2 Tm 3:14—4:2
	Mt 22:15–21	Mk 10:35–45	Lk 18:1–8
The Thirtieth Sunday in Ordinary Time			
	Ex 22:20–26	Jer 31:7–9	Sir 35:12–14,16–18
	1 Thes 1:5c–10	Heb 5:1–6	2 Tm 4:6–8,16–18
	Mt 22:34–40	Mk 10:46–52	Lk 18:9–14
The Thirty-First Sunday in Ordinary Time			
	Mal 1:14b—2:2b,8–10	Dt 6:2–6	Wis 11:22—12:2
	1 Thes 2:7b–9,13	Heb 7:23–28	2 Thes 1:11—2:2
	Mt 23:1–12	Mk 12:28b–34	Lk 19:1–10
The Thirty-Second Sunday in Ordinary Time			
	Wis 6:12–16	1 Kgs 17:10–16	2 Mc 7:1–2,9–14
	1 Thes 5:1–6	Heb 9:24–28	2 Thes 2:16—3:5
	Mt 25:14–30	Mk 12:38–44	Lk 20:27–38
The Thirty-Third Sunday in Ordinary Time			
	Prv 31:10–13,19–20,30–31	Dn 12:1–3	Mal 3:19–20a
	Rom 8:35,37–39	Heb 10:11–14,18	2 Thes 3:7–12
	Mt 14:13–21	Mk 13:24–32	Lk 21:5–19
The Thirty-Fourth Sunday in Ordinary Time (*The Solemnity of Our Lord Jesus Christ the King*)			
	Ez 34:11–12,15–17	Dn 7:13–14	2 Sm 5:1–3
	1 Cor 15:20–26,28	Rev 1:5–8	Col 1:12–20
	Mt 25:31–46	Jn 18:33b–37	Lk 23:35–43

Glossary

A

abba
From Aramaic—a language spoken in Palestine at the time of Jesus—*abba,* meaning "father," was used by children in addressing their fathers. Jesus used the word *abba* to express his relationship with God (see Mk 14:36) and taught his disciples to pray to God as a loving and loveable parent.

Adam
Related to the Hebrew *adamah,* meaning "ground," this name signifies "one formed from the earth." According to the Book of Genesis, Adam was the first man to be formed; he was the husband of Eve and the father of Cain and Abel. Christ is sometimes called the "new Adam" or the "second Adam," as Christ initiated the new or second creation by restoring the divine friendship that had been lost by original sin.

allegory
This is a literary form in which something is said to be like something else. Allegories are often used to communicate a hidden or symbolic meaning commonly understood by the people it is addressed to. The Bible often uses allegories to explain spiritual reality. For example, Jesus is called the Lamb of God (see Jn 1:29), an allegory symbolizing that Jesus was the sacrifice for our sins.

alleluia
From the Hebrew meaning "praise to Yahweh" or "praise to God," *alleluia* is an exclamation that is used in the Christian liturgy as a way of praising God, especially during the Easter season.

amen
This Hebrew word means "let it be so" or "let it be done." As a conclusion to prayer, it represents the agreement by the person praying to what has been said in the prayer.

angel
This word is based on a word meaning "messenger," a personal and immortal creature, with intelligence and free will, who constantly glorifies God and serves as a messenger of God to humans in order to carry out God's saving plan.

anointing
This word (from the Latin *inungere,* meaning "to smear" or "rub on" oil or ointment for medicinal purposes) refers to an act of applying oil in a religious ceremony or as part of a blessing. In the Old Testament, kings, priests, and prophets were anointed as sign of their divine mission. Today, anointing is part of the sacraments of Baptism, Confirmation, Holy Orders, and Anointing of the Sick.

Antichrist
This word from the Greek literally means "against Christ," thus an adversary of Christ. In the New Testament, the Antichrist is a deceitful figure associated with the mystery of iniquity that is to precede the Second Coming of Christ. In modern usage, the term Antichrist describes both those who falsely claim to speak in the name of Christ and those who are enemies of Christ.

apocalypse
This word (from the Greek *apocalypses,* meaning "revelation" or "unveiling" or "uncovering"), in a general sense, refers to the end of the world when God will destroy the forces of evil. In the Scriptures, the Apocalypse or Book of Revelation, which is the last book of the New Testament, describes the conflict between good and evil, the end of the world and heaven.

apocalyptic literature
Having roots in both Jewish and Christian tradition, this genre of literature appears in the books of Ezekiel, Daniel, and Revelation. It is associated with the end-times or the last things and anticipates the time of Last Judgment when Jesus returns and the world as we know it disappears. Frequently referred to as "crisis literature," it generally appears in the context of historical, political, or religious turmoil and is characterized by symbols and images used to communicate a message to the intended audience while preventing the enemies of faith from understanding its true meaning.

Apocryphal Books
In the first centuries of Christianity, a great number of books and letters written by Christians did not become part of the Bible. These writings were not included in the New Testament because they were not in complete agreement theologically with the Apostolic Tradition. They are called apocryphal writings, and they

include such works as the gospels of Thomas, Peter, and Mary Magdalene, the Epistle of Barnabas, the Acts of John and Paul, and the Shepherd of Hermas.

Some of the images in apocryphal writings are quite beautiful, some are Gnostic (an early Christian heresy), and some are just strange. With the exception of Thomas, most were written in the second through the fourth centuries AD. Apocryphal writings provide a resource that helps scholars reconstruct and understand the diversity of the early Christian period, but they are not inspired Scripture, and they are theologically in error. See *canon of Scripture, deuterocanonical books.*

apostle
The general term *apostle* means "one who is sent" and can be used in reference to any missionary of the Church during the New Testament period. In reference to the twelve companions chosen by Jesus, also known as "the Twelve," the term refers to those special witnesses of Jesus on whose ministry the early Church was built, and whose successors are the bishops.

Apostolic Tradition
See *Tradition*.

ark of the Covenant
In the Old Testament, this sacred chest housed the holy presence of God. The Book of Exodus contains the details of its construction (see 25:10–22, 37:1–9, 39:16–21). In the time of Moses, the ark was carried during the desert wanderings (1250 BC) and kept in the Tent of Meeting. In the period of the kings (about 1000 BC), it was placed in the holy of holies in the Temple (see 1 Kgs 8:6–8). It held the tablets of the Law of Moses, manna from heaven, and the rod of Aaron. It was also called the ark of God (see 1 Sm 3:3).

Ascension
This is the "going up" into heaven of the risen Christ forty days after his Resurrection (see Mk 16:19, Lk 24:50–53).

B

Baal
This generic Semitic word means "master," "owner," "husband," or "lord." The word could be used to refer to Yahweh or to the master of a slave (see Hos 2:16). However, in the Scriptures, the word Baal most often refers to the practices of idolatry or the worship of gods other than Yahweh. Baal was both the name of a specific god and a generic title that could refer to any number of gods such as Baal Peor or Baal of Hermon. Often, the religion included the use of Temple prostitutes and even demanded human sacrifice, especially of infants. The worshipers of Baal were generally seen as the enemies of the Israelites (see 1 Kgs 18:20–40).

Babylonian captivity
Babylon pillaged Judah three times, eventually causing the demise of the holy city, Jerusalem. In 587 BC, King Nebuchadnezzar murdered thousands of Israelites, destroyed the Temple, stole anything of value, burned Jerusalem to the ground, and enslaved a large portion of the population, sending them into exile in Babylon.

The captivity resulted in the deaths of multitudes, destruction of the land, devastation of the nation, loss of national identity, and infliction of hopelessness. The captivity lasted an entire generation (586–539 BC) until Cyrus the Persian, the king of Elam, conquered the Babylonians and let the Israelite people return home to Jerusalem (see Ezra, chapter 1). See *Diaspora, exile.*

ban, the
This was God's command that the Israelites destroy all the inhabitants, animals, and material possessions of the towns that they conquered. The ban first appears in the Book of Deuteronomy and is included partly as a warning to God's people against taking up the immoral practices of other religions, which included Temple prostitution and human sacrifice.

Beatitudes
The Beatitudes are the blessings enunciated by Jesus as part of the Sermon on the Mount (see Mt 5:3–12) and as part of the Sermon on the Plain (see Lk 6:20–26). The Beatitudes are often considered to represent the heart of the preaching of Jesus.

Bible
This word (derived from the Greek *biblia*, meaning "books") refers to the collection of Jewish and Christian writings that are considered inspired and normative for belief. The Hebrew Bible contains many of the works of what Christians call the Old Testament; the Christian Bible also includes writings known as the New Testament. See *New Testament, Old Testament.*

biblical criticism
This term (from the Greek *kritikos*, meaning "able to judge") refers to two different approaches to studying the Bible: (1) "lower criticism" attempts to reconstruct the original biblical text (because none of the original manuscripts have survived), and (2) "higher criticism" compares this reconstructed text with other documents of the time.

biblical interpretation
This kind of Scripture study looks at not only what the human authors intended to say but also at what God reveals to humans through their words. Criteria for

interpreting the Scriptures are (1) considering the kind of writing—that is, the literary form—in which a particular passage appears, (2) considering the context of each author's historical time and the presumptions the author and the audience shared, and (3) considering the context of the process of revelation that occurred over time. Early insights often represent one step in understanding a mystery, not the fullness of revelation. The Scriptures should be read and understood within the living Tradition of the Church.

C

canon of Scripture

The canon of Scripture is the official list of the books of the Bible regarded as sacred because they are inspired; the list of books accepted by Catholic and Orthodox Churches includes some books and parts of books not accepted as inspired by most Protestant Churches.

Chosen People

According to the Old Testament, God chose Abraham and his descendants to be the recipients of Divine Revelation and so to play a unique role in salvation history; thus, their descendants, the Jewish people, are God's Chosen People.

Christian

According to the Acts of the Apostles (see 11:26), the disciples of Jesus were first called Christians in Antioch. In accord with the Greek word *christos* (meaning the "anointed one"), a Christian is a person who has been anointed at Baptism and Confirmation. In contemporary usage, all those who profess to follow Christ are called Christians.

church

In common Christian usage, the term *church* is used in three related ways: (1) to mean the entire people of God throughout the world, (2) to mean the diocese, which is also known as the local church, and (3) to mean the assembly of believers gathered for celebration of the liturgy, especially the Eucharist. In the creed, the Church is recognized as one, holy, catholic, and apostolic—traits that together are referred to as "marks of the Church."

circumcision

This is the act of surgically removing the foreskin of males; according to Jewish Law, males are to be circumcised eight days after birth (see Gn 17:12–14, Lv 12:3).

cities of refuge

These are cities that were designated as safe places where an individual who had accidentally caused the death of another could seek protection from the victim's family members who were seeking revenge for the killing. Initially the accused would seek safety by clinging to the horns of the altar in the sanctuary. Later on, various cities in strategic locations were set aside as safe havens. Offering sanctuary was a humanitarian effort to protect people who were falsely accused and prevent blood feuds between families that would continue until one family was completely annihilated. Still practiced today, sanctuary is often in the form of aid to the homeless and persecuted.

Commandments of God

The Commandments of God are the ten laws, or Decalogue, given by God to Moses on Mount Sinai (see Ex 20:2–17, Dt 5:6–21) as the fundamental rules of conduct for the Chosen People. These commandments, also called the Law of Moses, were given in the books of Exodus, Leviticus, Numbers, and Deuteronomy. The first three of the Ten Commandments concern the love of God; the other seven commandments concern the love of neighbor.

contextualist

A contexualist is a person who interprets biblical passages by considering the literary and historical context and the whole process of revelation in order to correctly understand what the Bible is teaching.

council of the Church

An official assembly of Church leaders, this body gathers often for the purpose of discernment and decision making about particular issues. When represented by and concerned with the entire Church, it is called ecumenical, from a word meaning "the whole wide world." Councils can also be regional or local. The Jerusalem Council in chapter 15 of the Acts of the Apostles is considered the first council of the Church.

covenant

In general, a covenant is a solemn agreement between human beings or between God and a human being in which mutual commitments are recognized. A covenant can also be called a testament. In the Bible, two covenants are central: (1) the covenant between God and the ancient people of Israel established in God's Sinai Covenant with Moses, also called the Old Testament or Old Covenant; and (2) the New Covenant established by Jesus through his sacrificial death and Resurrection, also called the New Testament. The term testament has come to be associated primarily with the

Sacred Scriptures that record the history and meaning of the two biblical covenants.

Creation accounts
Genesis, the first book of the Bible presents two different accounts of God's Creation of all things (see 1:1—2:4, 2:4—3:24). Although different in their details, both accounts present Creation as a divine action that affirms the goodness of all creatures; in particular, humans were created in the image of God (see Gn 1:27) and called to live in mutual and life-giving friendships (see 2:18–22).

D

Day of Judgment
This is the biblical name for the time when God's justice will prevail, also known as the Day of the Lord or the Day of Wrath. In the Old Testament, the prophets proclaimed a Day of the Lord, in which all of humanity will share the bounty of the earth and "beat their swords into plowshares" and make war no more (Is 2:2–4). The prophets also declared that the Day of the Lord was a time when God's wrath would be brought against those who practiced idolatry and injustice (see Zep 2:1–3).

In the New Testament, the Day of Judgment came to mean the Last Judgment, when Jesus Christ will judge each person (see Mt 10:15; 12:36).

Dead Sea Scrolls
From the time of King David (1000 BC), Jewish rebels and refugees sought shelter in the caves cut into the limestone cliffs along the left bank of the Dead Sea. The site had been a ruin since the Romans destroyed Jerusalem in AD 68–70. In the spring of 1947, Bedouin shepherds found clay jars filled with ancient writings hidden by a group we call the Essenes. The find included the Dead Sea Scrolls, a Hebrew canon of Scripture (except Esther) from 250 BC, older than any Old Testament in existence by one thousand years. The Dead Sea Scroll collection also included Essene writings in Hebrew, Aramaic, and Greek. See *Essenes*.

deuterocanonical books
These are seven books that are part of the Catholic Old Testament but are not included in many Protestant Bibles. The deuterocanonical books were part of a Greek-language collection of the Jewish Scriptures called the Septuagint. The Catholic Church uses this collection of the Jewish Scriptures as the basis for the Old Testament. The seven deuterocanonical books in the Old Testament canon are Tobit, Judith, First Maccabees, Second Maccabees, Sirach, Baruch, and Wisdom of Solomon, along with parts of Esther and Daniel. Catholics believe them to be the inspired word of God.

deuteronomist
This term is used for the person or group responsible for writing the histories contained in the Old Testament books of Deuteronomy through Second Kings. The deuteronomist emphasized that God's just punishment occurred whenever the people sinned and broke their covenant with God. The deuteronomist also emphasized that if the people repented and returned to obedience to the Law of Moses, God's favor would return.

devil; demon
A devil or demon is a fallen angel—one created naturally good but who has sinned against God by refusing to accept God's Reign. The term devil refers to Satan, Lucifer, or the Evil One, the chief of the fallen angels; demon refers to an agent of the Evil One.

Diaspora
This word (from the Greek *diaspeirein*, meaning "to scatter") refers to a community of people who live in exile from their native land. In the Old Testament, the Diaspora of the Jewish people began in 587 BC when the Temple in Jerusalem was destroyed and many Jews were taken into exile in Babylon.

disciple
A disciple is a follower of Christ. It is based on a word for "pupil" or "student" and is used to designate both those who learned from and followed Jesus in New Testament times (the disciples) as well as those who commit to follow him today.

dispersion
See *Diaspora*.

E

Elohim
Elohim is one of the names for God in the Old Testament. Some scholars translate the word in the plural to mean "divinities" or "host of heaven"; other scholars consider Elohim a "majestic plural."

Elohist
The scribes who wrote of Elohim were the Elohists. They lived in seventh to sixth centuries BC. Later writers edited the Elohists' writings into sections of the Pentateuch. The scribes portray God as a humanlike figure who appears in person at different events and who is capable of regret. This is referred to by scholars as the E Tradition.

Emmanuel
This word from the Hebrew means "God with us." Matthew's Gospel calls Jesus by the name Emmanuel (see 1:23).

epistle
This word refers to the letters written by Church leaders in the first two centuries AD, especially those letters that are included in the New Testament and read during the celebration of the Mass and other sacraments.

Essenes
The Essenes were a group of pious, ultraconservative Jews who left the Temple of Jerusalem and began a community beside the Dead Sea that was known as Qumran. Originating in 100 BC, the Essenes thrived until AD 70, when the Romans violently put down a Jewish rebellion. The Essene community copied, wrote, and preserved the library of texts known today as the Dead Sea Scrolls.

E Tradition
See *Elohist*.

Eucharist, the
Also called the Mass or Lord's Supper, the term Eucharist is based on a word for "thanksgiving." It is the central Christian liturgical celebration, established by Jesus at the Last Supper. In the Eucharist, the sacrificial death and Resurrection of Jesus are both remembered ("Do this in memory of me") and renewed ("This is my body, given for you"). The Sunday celebration of the Eucharist is considered the heart of the Church's life and worship, and participation in it is expected of all Catholics of the age and ability to do so.

evangelist
Based on a word for "good news," evangelist describes anyone who actively works to spread the Gospel of Jesus; more commonly and specifically, evangelist refers to one of the persons traditionally recognized as an author of the four Gospels, Matthew, Mark, Luke, and John.

Eve
This name (related to the Hebrew *hawwah*, meaning "a living being") was given to the first woman, who was the partner of Adam and the mother of Cain and Abel. Mary is sometimes called the "new Eve" or the "second Eve," because, as mother of God, she was instrumental in initiating the new or second creation.

exegesis
The writers and editors of the Bible lived in various countries and cultures, wrote in several different languages, and wrote about events that spanned thousands of years. Faithful scholars have dedicated their lives to understanding the languages, symbols, culture, history, and meanings intended by those who wrote the Bible. The search into the Scriptures is called by the Greek word *exegesis*, which means "to draw out" or "to explain." The work of scholars assists Church leaders in their interpretation. Catholics interpret the Scriptures in union with the Tradition and the Magisterium of the Church.

Modern scholars use a number of methods to deepen understanding of the Bible. These methods are often called criticisms, not in the sense of being critically negative, but in the sense of taking a disciplined approach to the Bible as literature. See *form criticism, historical critical method, literary criticism, redaction criticism, source criticism, textual criticism*.

exile
This word (from the Latin *exilium*, meaning "banishment") refers to an absence from one's native land; sometimes this separation is forced, but other times it is self-imposed or voluntary. The Babylonian Exile (587–539 BC) was a particularly symbolic part of Jewish history; the Church today considers itself in exile until the coming of the risen Lord. See *Babylonian captivity, Diaspora*.

Exodus
This Greek word meaning "going out" is the name given the second book of the Bible, which describes the departure of the Israelites from Egypt under the leadership of Moses. The Exodus is celebrated at Passover as the liberation of the Chosen People.

F

Fall, the
Also called the fall from grace, the Fall is the biblical revelation about the origins of sin and evil in the world, expressed figuratively in the story of Adam and Eve in Genesis. See *Original Sin*.

Father
Like many other religions, Christianity looks upon God as a Father. Jesus called God abba (Father) and taught his disciples to pray to God as "Our Father."

form criticism
Form criticism is a method of studying the literary forms of a document in order to ascertain the background of a particular passage. For example, biblical form criticism studies such forms as parables, proverbs, and poems in order to discover the origin and history of a particular scriptural text.

fundamentalism
This is an interpretation of the Bible and Christian doctrine that is based on the literal meaning of the words and without regard to the historical setting in which the writings or teachings were first developed. A person who holds such a perspective is called a fundamentalist.

G

Gehenna

This word (from the Hebrew *Ge Hinnom*, meaning the "Valley of Hinnom") is the name of the place where children were once sacrificed to *Moloch (Baal)* (see Jer 19:5); Jesus spoke of Gehenna as a place of punishment for those who refused to repent and be converted.

genre

A genre is a category of literature, art, or music. Genres in the Scriptures include prose, poetry, myth, law codes, historical narrative, didactic (teaching) narrative, parable, and miracle stories. The first step in correctly interpreting a Scripture passage is to know its genre.

Gentile

This word (from the Latin *gens*, meaning "race" or "clan") is usually used in the New Testament to designate a person who is not Jewish; sometimes the word is used to refer to a person who is not Christian.

Gospel

Most basically, *Gospel* means "the Good News" of the Revelation of God in and through Jesus Christ, proclaimed initially by him, then by the Apostles, and now by the Church. The term also refers to those four books of the New Testament that focus on the person, life, teachings, death, and Resurrection of Jesus.

H

heaven

From the Old English meaning "home of God," *heaven* has various meanings: (1) in the ancient world, heaven was often identified with the sky or firmament and considered the dwelling place of the divine; (2) in Judaism, because of the reluctance to pronounce the name of God, heaven was sometimes used as a substitute for God's name; (3) among Christians, heaven represents the final goal of all Christians, where they are definitively united with God and reunited with their fellow Christians.

Hebrew

This word of Hebrew origin seemingly meant "one from the other side" or possibly "immigrant." The term *Hebrew* can refer to either the Israelite people or their language.

Hebrew Scriptures

See *Old Testament*.

hermeneutics

This word (from the Greek *hermeneus*, meaning "interpreter") refers to the study of the interpretation of texts, especially the study of the theory and method of biblical interpretation.

high place

Both the Hebrews and the Canaanites established places of worship on high ground (see Gn 12:7–8, 1 Kgs 13:32). The Canaanite high places often included practices of the fertility rites and human sacrifices offered to Baal Molech and Asherah. Over the centuries, the Hebrews destroyed the high places of the Canaanites (see Dt 12:2–3).

historical books

These writings make up a continuous narrative of Israel's history from the conquest of the land of Canaan to the rebuilding of Jerusalem after the Babylonian Exile. They include the books of Joshua, Judges, Ruth, First and Second Samuel, First and Second Kings, First and Second Chronicles, Ezra, Nehemiah, Tobit, Judith, Esther, and First and Second Maccabees.

historical critical method

This term (from the Greek *historia*, meaning "record" or "account," and *kritikos*, meaning "able to judge") refers to a method of studying texts, especially the Bible. The historical critical method considers the historical context, the philosophical presuppositions, and the theological perspective of a particular passage. See *biblical criticism*.

Holiness Code

This is a collection of teachings found in the Book of Leviticus, chapters 17–26, that remind God's people that true worship is more than following prescribed rituals or saying the right prayers. Love of God is demonstrated in the just and compassionate ways others are treated. Many of the precepts show great sensitivity to those who are poor and to the understanding of social justice.

holy of holies

The holy of holies, the innermost part of the Temple in Jerusalem, was the repository for the ark of the Covenant. Only the high priest was permitted to enter the holy of holies and then only once a year.

Holy Spirit

This word (from the Latin *spiritus*, meaning "breath" or "soul") refers to the third person of the Trinity, the Paraclete divinely sent to teach and guide the Church to the end of times. See *Paraclete*.

I

I AM

"I AM WHO AM" was the name God called himself when talking to Moses from the burning bush (see Ex 3:14). It expressed that God simply is, God has no beginning and no end, and everything else exists because of God. Yahweh, the most common name for God in the Old Testament, was probably based on that phrase.

The New Testament contained suggestions of this title in connection with Jesus. Jesus asked Peter, "Who do you say that I am?" And Peter said, "You are the Messiah, the Son of the living God" (Mt 16:16).

idolatry
Idolatry is worship of other beings, creatures, or material goods in a way that is fitting for God alone. It is a violation of the first commandment (see Ex 20:3, Dt 5:7).

Incarnation, the
Based on words meaning "in flesh," the Incarnation refers to the mystery and Church dogma that the Son of God assumed human nature and "became flesh" in the person of Jesus of Nazareth (Jn 1:14). The Incarnation means that Jesus, the Son of God and second person of the Trinity, is both fully God and fully human.

inerrancy
This term, as related to the Scriptures, means that the books of the Bible are free from error regarding the spiritual and religious truth that God wishes to reveal through them for the sake of our salvation. See also *inspiration, biblical; Tradition*.

inspiration, biblical
This term refers to the guidance of the Holy Spirit in the development of the Scriptures, whereby the Spirit guided the human authors to teach without error those truths of God that are necessary for our salvation. It is on the basis of inspiration that we can call the Bible the word of God.

Israel
This name comes from Jacob's experience of "wrestling with God" (see Gn 32:28) and is used in different ways: (1) the twelve Tribes of Israel as descendants of the twelve sons of Jacob, (2) the Chosen People or Jewish People as a whole, (3) the northern kingdom (Israel) in contrast to the southern kingdom (Judah), (4) the modern nation of Israel.

Israelites
The Israelites were the Chosen People of God; members of the twelve Tribes of Israel descended from Jacob, who inhabited the land of Israel during biblical times.

J

Jesus Christ
In Hebrew *Jesus* means "God saves" and was the name given the historical Jesus at the Annunciation. Christ comes from the Greek *christos*, meaning the "anointed one" and translates the Hebrew word *messiah*. In the Old Testament, kings, priests, and prophets were anointed; in giving Jesus the title *Christ*, the New Testament indicates that Jesus fulfilled the messianic hope of Israel through his threefold office of king, prophet, and priest.

J Tradition
See *Yahwist*.

jubilee
This word comes from the sound of the ram's horn trumpet, the shofar. When blown, the shofar's sound signified the heavens' opening and the presence of God made near. According to the Law of Moses, every fiftieth year was proclaimed a jubilee, a year of repentance, and the people were to place their focus on the redistribution of wealth and property to the poor and dispossessed. During the jubilee, the land was to rest. Only gleaning of the fields was permitted. All landed property was returned to its original owners, slaves were set free, and all debts were erased (see Lv 25:8–55). The jubilee created a society of justice in which the bounty and the land were shared. It prevented abject poverty and erased lines between rich and poor. It corrected societal injustices and restored God's intended equality to human relationships.

Judah, Judea
These words come from the Hebrew word *Yehudah*, meaning "praise the Lord." Judah was a son of Jacob and Leah, a patriarch and founder of one of the twelve Tribes of Israel. The tribe of Judah became the most powerful of the twelve Tribes of Israel. Judah became a place-name of the southern territory of Palestine. Judah and its capital city, Jerusalem, were the headquarters for the administration of the nation of Israel, the location of religious life via the Temple, and dwelling place of the royal family of David. After the civil war at the end of Solomon's reign, the northern tribes separated and became known as the kingdom of Israel, and the southern tribes became known as the kingdom of Judah. For centuries the Temple priests and Judean kings ruled Judah. In the time of Roman rule, the area was called Judea.

Judaism
This word, which has been traced to Judah, the fourth son of Jacob and the tribe descended from him, refers to the monotheistic religion of the Jewish people who trace their origin to Abraham and whose religious observance is based on the Torah and the Talmud.

judge
Judges were men and women who served the Hebrew people as tribal leaders and military commanders. The judges settled disputes and proclaimed the will

of God. They were not judges as we understand that role today, presiding over legal cases. Instead, they were charismatic leaders whom the Holy Spirit inspired to lead the Israelites when they were a loosely knit federation of tribes (1200–1000 BC). The judges were clan heroes who empowered the faith of the people in times of crisis and focused their attention on the promises of the covenant.

K

Kingdom of God
Also referred to as the Reign of God, this term refers to the reign or rule of God over the hearts of people and, as a consequence of that, the development of a new social order based on unconditional love.

kingdom of heaven
The Gospel of Matthew uses this phrase, which seemingly reflects the Jewish custom of not speaking directly about God or the Kingdom of God.

L

Last Supper
During the Jewish celebration of Passover, this was the last meal Jesus shared with his disciples before being handed over for Crucifixion. It is remembered by Catholics as the occasion of the first Eucharist and is commemorated by believers on Holy Thursday.

law (biblical)
The Law, or Torah, which consists of the first five books of the Bible, is contrasted with the books of the prophets and the other writings. In the New Testament, Jesus often referred to "the Law and the Prophets." See *Tanak*.

Law (New)
This is the law of the Gospel of Jesus Christ, a law of love, grace, and freedom. It is distinguished from the Old Law, or the Law of Moses.

Law (Old)
This is the Law of Moses, the Ten Commandments. It contrasts the New Law of the Gospel. See *Torah, Pentatuech, law (biblical)*.

lectio divina
This is a form of meditative prayer, usually focused on a passage from the Scriptures, that involves repetitive readings and periods of reflection. Lectio divina can serve as either private or communal prayer.

Levi, Levite
Levi was one of Leah's sons fathered by Jacob (see Gn 29:34). He became a patriarch of Israel and the head of the tribe that carried his name, the Levites. Moses and Aaron were descendants of Levi (see Ex 2:1). According to the command of God, only Aaron and his sons could serve as priests (see 28:1). Thus, the Levites became the tribe entrusted with sacred ministries, the caretakers of the tabernacle and the Temple (see Nm 1:48–54). See *priest, sacrifice*.

literal sense
This term (from the Latin *litera*, meaning "letter") refers to a form of biblical interpretation that translates a text word-for-word and emphasizes the explicit meaning of biblical texts. See *senses of the Scriptures*.

literary criticism
This term refers to a method of studying the Scriptures that looks at the text and seeks to understand it as a work of literature. Literary criticism considers what literary form (poetry, letter, story, and so on) or device (pun, parable, exaggeration, and so on) was used and how the particular literary forms or devices function in an ancient society. See *exegesis*.

literary forms
Literary forms are categories of smaller units of text that can be used within a particular genre. For example, the newspaper genre contains many literary forms, including national news stories, editorials, obituaries, sports stories, and classified ads.

Lord
This is the Old Testament name for God that in speaking or reading aloud was automatically substituted for the name Yahweh, which was considered too sacred to be spoken. In the New Testament, Lord is used for both God the Father and, on occasion, for Jesus, to reflect awareness of Jesus' identity as the Son of God.

M

Maccabees
This refers to a family whose real name was the Hasmoneans but became known after the most famous son, Judas Maccabeus. Maccabeus was probably his nickname, meaning "the hammer." The Maccabees became the political and religious leaders of the Jewish people in the second and first centuries before Christ.

Magisterium
This is the name given the official teaching authority of the Church, whose task is to interpret and preserve the truths of the Church revealed in both the Scriptures and Tradition.

messiah
This word comes from the Hebrew *mashah*, meaning "anoint" and was later translated into Greek as *christos* and into English as *Christ*. Many of the Jewish contemporaries of Jesus were awaiting the arrival of a messiah to deliver them from oppression.

metaphor
This word (from the Greek *metaphora,* meaning "transfer") refers to a literary comparison that compares and contrasts two things that are basically different. The parables of Jesus, for example, describe the Kingdom of God by using human examples that are different from, but simultaneously suggest the uniqueness of, the Kingdom.

monotheism
This is the belief in and worship of one true God. The Israelites were unique in their monotheism; other peoples in biblical times were polytheistic, believing in many gods and goddesses.

Mosaic Law
See *Law (Old)*.

Mount Zion
This is the hill on which the citadel of David and the city of Jerusalem stood. On Zion, David built his palace, and Solomon later built the Temple of Jerusalem. The city of Jerusalem came to represent the people and faith of Israel (see Pss 87:2, 149:2). In the Scriptures, the use of the phrase "virgin Zion" represents the ideal, pure relationship between the people of Israel and God (see 2 Kgs 19:21, Lam 2:13–22). During the Babylonian captivity (586–539 BC), the prophets promised a time when God would make his home again in Zion (see Zec 2:10–11). In the Book of Revelation, Jesus Christ, the lamb of God, appears on Mount Zion (see 14:1).

myth
This word (from the Greek *mythos,* meaning "story" or "speech") is used in a variety of ways: (1) originally a myth was a story about the gods or heavenly beings and usually taught a moral lesson, (2) theologians sometimes contrast fact and myth understood as a story that is not factual but artificially contrived to teach a lesson, (3) myth has been understood as a story of ultimate significance that treats the origin, purpose, and end of creatures and creation.

N

natural law
This is our God-given instinct to be in right relationship with God, other people, the world, and ourselves. The basis for natural law is our participation in God's wisdom and goodness because we are created in the divine likeness. The fundamental expressions of natural law remain fixed and unchanging, which is why natural law is the foundation for both personal morality and civil norms.

New Covenant
This term refers to the covenant or law established by God in order to fulfill and perfect the Old Covenant or Mosaic Law. The Second Vatican Council emphasized that the New Covenant does not replace the Old Covenant, much less does it oppose the Old Covenant; rather it brings the Old Covenant to completion. See *Law (New), Law (Old), Old Covenant.*

New Testament
This is the name of the twenty-seven books of the Bible written during the early years of the Church in response to the life, mission, death, and Resurrection of Jesus. It is also another name for the New Covenant established between God and humanity by Jesus.

northern kingdom
See *Israel.*

O

Old Covenant
This term refers to the covenant or law that was given by God to Moses on Mount Sinai for the Chosen People. Although Christians consider the Old Law a preparation for the New Covenant or New Law given by Christ, the Old Covenant has never been revoked. See *Law (New), Law (Old), New Covenant.*

Old Testament
This is the name of the forty-six books of the Bible that record the history of salvation from Creation, through the story of ancient Israel, and up to the time of Jesus. It also refers to the Old Covenant established between God and the people of Israel in God's encounter with Moses on Mount Sinai. See *Septuagint, Tanak.*

oral tradition
In the ancient world, storytellers preserved the sacred wisdom, parables, regulations, and rules of life revealed to the ancestors and passed down across the ages. By telling these stories around campfires and at religious festivals, the sacred wisdom was passed from one generation to the next, until later scribes wrote it down. Many of the stories and teachings in both the Old and New Testaments were passed on by oral tradition for a generation or more before they were written down.

original sin
This term refers to the sin of the first human beings who disobeyed God's command and thereby lost their original holiness and became subject to death. Original sin affects every person born into the world.

P

parable
A parable is a story intended to convey a religious truth or particular teaching through the use of metaphors. Parables are a

central feature of Jesus' teaching ministry.

Paraclete
This is a name for the Holy Spirit, based on a word for "helper" or "advocate." See *Holy Spirit*.

paradise
This word refers both to the Garden of Eden in the Book of Genesis and also to the New Jerusalem in the Book of Revelation. It has come to be identified with heaven.

Parousia
This is the Second Coming of Christ, when his Kingdom will be fully established and his triumph over evil will be complete.

Paschal lamb
This is a name for Jesus, whose death and Resurrection redeemed humanity. The name is associated with Passover, a commemoration of the deliverance of the Jewish people from Egypt. To avoid the slaughter of firstborn sons by the Egyptian army, the Jews sprinkled the blood of a lamb on their doorposts. See *Passover; Eucharist, the.*

Passion of Christ
This term refers to the sufferings of Jesus during the final days in his life: his agony in the garden at Gethsemane, his trial, and his Crucifixion. Contemporary theologians often relate the Passion of Christ to the present-day suffering of people, especially those who are needy and marginalized.

Passover
This is the Jewish feast that memorializes the Exodus from Egypt when the Hebrews sacrificed a lamb; smeared its blood on their doorposts; prepared unleavened bread, bitter herbs, and the wine of blessing; and shared the sacred seder meal as family. That night the Lord passed over the houses of Egypt, and in all the houses not marked with the blood of the lamb, the firstborn children and animals died (see Ex 21:29–30). Pharaoh sent the Israelites away. They crossed the Red Sea and became a free people.

The Passover festival, with its seder meal and its Paschal lamb, commemorates the creation of a new people, a society of justice based on a sacred trust between Yahweh and Israel. Passover honors a God who heard the cries of his people and responded with miraculous power to free them from a terrible oppressor. Jesus gathered his disciples together on Passover to celebrate the seder and offer them the bread of life (see Mt 26:17–30; Mk 14:12–26; Lk 22:7–23; 1 Cor 10:1, 11:23–26). See *Eucharist, the; Exodus; Last Supper; Paschal lamb.*

patriarch (Old Testament)
This word (from the Greek *patriarches,* meaning "chief" or "head of a family") is a title given to the fathers of the Old Testament, such as Abraham, Isaac, and Jacob, who were divinely selected to guide the Chosen People.

Pentateuch
This word (from the Greek *pente,* meaning "five," and *teuchos,* meaning "vessels" or "containers for scrolls") is a name given to the Torah, the first five books of the Hebrew Scriptures: Genesis, Exodus, Leviticus, Numbers, and Deuteronomy. See *Old Testament, Torah.*

Pentecost
This is the biblical event that followed the Resurrection and Ascension of Jesus at which the Holy Spirit was poured out on his disciples. The first Pentecost is often identified as the birth of the Church (see Acts 2:1–13). In the Christian liturgical year, the feast of Pentecost recalls the biblical event and is celebrated fifty days after Easter.

People of God
This is the biblical image for the Church, referring to those who share in Christ's mission as priest, prophet, and king.

Pharisees
The Pharisees were a Jewish sect during the time of Jesus. They were known for their strict adherence to the law and their concern with superficial matters.

priest
This word (from the Greek *presbyter,* meaning "elder") in the Scriptures designates one who offers sacrifice to God on behalf of the people. The first priestly man in the Hebrew tradition was Melchizedek of Salem. With Abraham he offered bread and wine and was a "priest of God Most High" (Gn 14:18). As part of the Sinai Covenant, God instituted an order of priests that began with Aaron and his sons. Because they were of the tribe of Levi, the Levites became known as the priestly class. As the Israelites settled Palestine, they built local temples at which the priests led the community in prayer and offered required animal sacrifices.

Once the Temple was built in Jerusalem, religious observances became centered there. All local temples were destroyed, and the priests were all moved to Jerusalem, where they assisted with worship and sacrifice in the Temple. The high priest was the chief priest and led all the major religious rituals in the Temple. The priesthood of Christ fulfills the expectations of the Old Testament priesthood through Christ's perfect sacrifice on the cross (see Heb 7:1–28). See *Levi, Levite.*

Priestly Tradition
This particular theological tradition present in the Pentateuch is the work of priestly scribes who hoped to restore the memory of the divided kingdoms of Israel and Judah and restore focus on the Sinai Covenant. Commonly known by scholars as the P Tradition, this tradition involved the scribes' blending the sacred names from northern Israel and southern Judah into a unified title for the Holy, which in English translates as "LORD God." God is portrayed as transcendent and distant, thus the need for priestly intercession.

Promised Land
This term refers to the land that God promised to the descendants of Abraham (see Genesis, chapter 12), the land of Canaan or Palestine.

prophet
This word (from the Greek *prophetes*, meaning "interpreter" or "spokesperson") refers to a person chosen by God to communicate a salvific message. A biblical prophet was primarily a communicator of a divine message of repentance to the Chosen People and not necessarily a person who predicted the future. Prophecy refers to the messages communicated by prophets on behalf of God. Seventeen prophets had books in the Bible named after them. Known as the prophetic books, they include Isaiah, Jeremiah, Baruch, Ezekiel, Daniel, Hosea, Joel, Amos, Obadiah, Jonah, Micah, Nahum, Habakkuk, Zephaniah, Haggai, Zechariah, and Malachi. The author of the book of Lamentations is unknown. The prophecies of other prophets, such as Moses, Deborah, Nathan, Elijah, Elisha, and Anna, were recorded in other books. Isaiah, Jeremiah, and Ezekiel are called the major prophets because so much of their prophecies were written down.

proverb
This word (from the Latin *proverbium*, meaning "common saying") refers to any short saying that has been orally passed down as advice from generation to generation. The Book of Proverbs in the Old Testament contains many examples of such wisdom sayings, which provide an understanding of human experience from a religious perspective.

psalm, psalter
The word *psalm* refers to a hymn or song of prayer that expresses praise, thanksgiving, petition, lamentation, or a historical memory of God's actions on behalf of the Chosen People. The word *psalter* refers to the Book of Psalms in the Old Testament that contains 150 psalms.

P Tradition
See *Priestly Tradition*.

R

redaction criticism
This refers to the process of editing or revising a text. Redaction criticism is the technical effort to determine the editorial history of a particular text, especially in biblical studies.

redemption, Redeemer
Redemption is the process by which we are "bought back" (the meaning of *redeem*) from slavery to sin into a right relationship with God. We are redeemed by the grace of God and through the life, death, and Resurrection of Jesus Christ. As the agent of redemption, Jesus is called the Redeemer.

Reign of God
See *Kingdom of God*.

Resurrection of Christ
This is the passage of Jesus from death to life "on the third day" after his Crucifixion. This is the heart of the Paschal mystery and the basis of our hope in the resurrection of the dead.

resurrection of the dead
This is the Christian dogma that all those deemed righteous by God will be raised and will live forever with God in heaven. It is the conviction that not only our souls but also our transformed bodies will live on after death ("I believe in the resurrection of the body").

revelation
This is God's self-communication and disclosure of the divine plan to humankind through creation, events, persons, and, most fully, in Jesus Christ.

S

Sabbath, *Shabbath*
In the Old Testament, this is the "seventh day" on which God rested after the work of Creation was completed. In Jewish Law, this is the weekly day of rest to remember God's work through private prayer, communal worship, and spiritual disciplines such as fasting. For Catholics, this is Sunday, the day on which Jesus was raised, which we are to observe with participation in the Eucharist in fulfillment of the commandment to "keep holy the Sabbath."

sacrifice
This word (from the Latin *sacer*, meaning "sacred," and *facere*, meaning "to make") refers to an offering made to God by a priest on behalf of the people as a sign of adoration, thanksgiving, petition, and communion (see Leviticus, chapters 1–7). In the Old Testament, a sacrifice was needed as atonement—that

is, a healing rite that restored holiness by cleansing the people from infractions of the law. Sacrifices also reconciled their covenant relationship with God (see Ps 51:1–17). The only perfect sacrifice is that offered by Christ on the cross (see Heb 7:22–28).

salvation
Salvation is liberation from sin and eternal union with God in heaven. Salvation is accomplished by God alone through the Paschal mystery—the dying and rising of Jesus Christ.

salvation history
The pattern of events in human history that exemplify God's presence and saving actions. In Catholic thought, all of history is salvation history, even though God's presence may not be recognized.

Samaria
This territory, whose name comes from Shemer, the owner of the hill on which the town was originally constructed (see 1 Kgs 16:24), consisted, at the time of Jesus, of the region south of Galilee and north of Judea—that is, the region between Nazareth and Jerusalem.

Samaritans
This term refers to the inhabitants of Samaria. The Samaritans rejected the Jerusalem Temple and worshiped at Mount Gerizim. The New Testament describes the Jewish rejection of Samaritans in both the parable of the good Samaritan (see Lk 10:29–37) and the account of Jesus' speaking with the Samaritan woman at the well (see Jn 4:1–42).

Satan
This Hebrew word, meaning "adversary," refers to the fallen angel or spirit of evil, who is the enemy of God and a continuing instigator of temptation and sin in the world.

Savior
This word (from the Latin *salvator*, meaning "saver" or "preserver") is a title appropriately given to Jesus, whose Hebrew name means "God saves."

scribes
In Jewish history, these were government officials and scholars of the Law of Moses. They enforced the requirements of the law.

Scriptures
In general this is the term for any sacred writing. For Christians it refers to the Old and New Testaments that make up the Bible and are recognized as the word of God.

Semitic
The ancient language, culture, and various racial groups that make up the Middle East all have a common Semitic ancestry. The Hebrew, Aramaic, Arabic, and Akkadian languages, as well as the lost Hyksos language of Egypt, all have a Semitic source or root.

senses of the Scriptures
This term indicates that every text is open to a variety of interpretations or senses. In the history of Christian biblical interpretation, the following meanings or senses of the Scriptures have been proposed: (1) the literal sense seeks the word-for-word meaning of a text, (2) the allegorical sense seeks the symbolic meaning behind the text, (3) the anagogical sense seeks the spiritual meaning of a text, (4) the tropological sense searches for the ethical implications of a text, (5) the typological sense shows how the Old Testament prefigured the New Testament.

Septuagint
This term (from the Latin *septuaginta*, meaning "seventy") is the name given to the Greek translation of the Hebrew Bible that was widely used among Hellenized Jews at the time of Jesus. According to a popular legend, a group of seventy (or seventy-two) Jewish scholars, working independently, produced the identically same translation in seventy (or seventy-two) days; hence the name Septuagint (seventy). See *Old Testament, Torah*.

Shema
The prayer known as the Shema has been said by observant Jews three times a day for thousands of years to honor the unity of God. In essence, it calls the faithful across the centuries to "Hear, O Israel! The LORD [Yahweh] is our God [Elohim], the LORD alone" (Dt 6:4). It leads the faithful to love the Lord with a whole heart, mind, and soul, and to love others as one loves oneself (see 6:5, 11:13–21). Jesus used the Shema to summarize the law and the faith of Moses into the two great commandments (see Mt 22:36–40).

source criticism
This term refers to the method of studying the Scriptures that identifies other writings outside of the Scriptures known in the ancient cultures that influenced the writer of a specific passage. It considers whether the writers build on an existing story, myth, or other literature as a basis for their work and whether the theology or justice ethic of the biblical version varies from that of the cultural source. See *exegesis*.

southern kingdom
See *Judah*.

suffering servant
The prophets revealed that the people of Israel were God's suffering servant who endured the pain of alienation and grief across history. Yet, the prophets also proclaimed that one to

come, the promised one of God, would suffer as a result of his compassion for humanity. He was to be Emmanuel—God with us. The suffering servant of Yahweh would be one with the people and would be one who knew suffering. He would bear our sufferings and bring us redemption (see Is 52:13—53:12).

synagogue
This Greek word, meaning "meeting" or "assembly," refers to the worship assemblies of Jews, who lived outside of Jerusalem, to celebrate the Sabbath. Jesus is depicted in the Gospel of Luke (see 4:14–30) as beginning his Galilean ministry in the synagogue at Nazareth.

synoptic Gospels
This term (from the Greek *syn*, meaning "seen together") refers to the fact that the Gospels of Matthew, Mark, and Luke follow a similar pattern in both their overall structure and their individual narratives.

T

tabernacle
The receptacle in a church in which the consecrated bread and wine of the Eucharist is reserved for Communion for the sick and dying. The tabernacle is sometimes the focus of private and communal prayer and adoration. It was originally the portable Dwelling carried by the Israelites in their wilderness wandering (see Ex 25:8–9).

Talmud
This Hebrew word meaning "instruction" refers to the collection of rabbinic writings that constitute the basic religious authority in Judaism.

Tanak
This word is an acronym that refers to the major divisions of the Hebrew Scriptures: Torah (Law–T), Nebi'im (Prophets–N), and Ketubim (Writings–K).

temples
This biblical term refers to the various temples mentioned in the Old Testament. The Jewish people built temples on Mount Moriah, which is believed to be the place where Abraham went to sacrifice Isaac (see Genesis, chapter 22). The so-called First Temple period (1006–586 BC) began with David's occupation of Jerusalem and was followed by Solomon's building the First Temple. This period ended with the Babylonian Exile. The Second Temple period (536 BC–AD 70) began with the return of the Jewish exiles and culminated in the building of a new Temple by Herod shortly before the birth of Jesus. This Temple was destroyed by the Romans about four decades after the death of Jesus.

Ten Commandments
See *Commandments of God.*

testament
This word (from the Latin *testamentum*, meaning "will") describes the two parts of the Bible, the Old Testament and the New Testament, both of which are covenants offered by God.

textual criticism
This term refers to a method of studying the Scriptures that compares and contrasts various translations of the Scriptures to more clearly understand the meaning of a given passage. It considers whether the modern translations are in union with the oldest versions of the Scriptures available. See *exegesis.*

Torah
This word (from the Hebrew *torah*, meaning "law" or "instruction") refers to the Pentateuch or the Mosaic Law, which includes the first five books of the Hebrew Scriptures: Genesis, Exodus, Leviticus, Numbers, and Deuteronomy. See *Old Testament, Tanak.*

Tradition
Based on a word meaning "to hand on," Tradition is the central content of Catholic faith contained in both the Scriptures and in Church doctrines and dogmas, as well as the process by which that content is faithfully passed on from generation to generation, under the guidance of the Holy Spirit.

twelve Tribes
The twelve Tribes were a confederation of twelve Hebrew tribes that traced their origin to the patriarch Jacob. The Pentateuch stories tell how God renewed with Jacob the promises of the covenant he had originally made with Abraham (see Gn 28:10–17). Jacob then went on to have twelve sons by his two wives, Leah and Rachel, and their two maidservants, Zilpah and Bilhah. Leah bore six sons—Reuben, Simeon, Levi, Judah, Issachar, and Zebulun—and one daughter, Dinah. Leah's slave Zilpah bore Gad and Asher. Rachel, Jacob's beloved, gave birth to Joseph and Benjamin. Rachel's slave Bilhah mothered two more sons. Rachel named them Dan and Naphtali (see Gn 35:22–26).

After Jacob's first eleven sons were born, God renamed Jacob Israel (see Gn 32:28). Thus, the descendants of Jacob / Israel's sons became the Israelites, God's Chosen People. Their names came to symbolize the twelve Tribes that settled in the Promised Land.

W

wisdom

This word (from the Old English "aware" or "cunning") has several meanings: (1) Wisdom is one of the books of the Old Testament; (2) in the Hebrew Scriptures, wisdom is depicted as the action of God in the world; (3) in Christian theology, wisdom is one of the seven gifts of the Holy Spirit and enables a person to know God's divine plan of salvation.

wisdom literature

This is a genre of ancient literature that extolled the virtue of wisdom and gave practical advice on what it meant to be wise. In the Old Testament, the books of Proverbs, Job, Ecclesiastes, Sirach, and the Wisdom of Solomon are wisdom literature. Sections of other books (see Genesis, chapters 37–50) and certain psalms (see Psalm 37) also have traits of wisdom literature. The Song of Songs, a collection of love songs, is also included with the wisdom books. Typical themes in these books were the value of wisdom, self-control, patience, honesty, diligence, and respect for elders. A theme in several of the books was wisdom personified as a woman, Lady Wisdom (see Prv 1:1–36, Wis 6:12–25).

Wisdom literature in the Bible has certain characteristics. There is little mention of Israelite history, the Law of Moses, or the covenant. The emphasis is on what can be learned by experience and applied in daily life. The writing is often somewhat poetic; an idea is stated and then repeated in a slightly different way in the next line. See *wisdom*.

word of God

God's word is the power through which God created all that is (see Ps 33:6). The Bible is called the word of God because it has the power to create new life within the soul, to renew spirits, to teach, and to give hope (see 2 Tm 3:14–16). The Revelation contained in the Bible is inspired by the Holy Spirit to be without error in teaching the religious truth people need for salvation.

Jesus is also called the Word of God—the *Logos* in Greek (see Jn 1:1, Rev 19:13). This title describes the divine nature of Christ: "The Word was with God, and the Word was God" (Jn 1:1). See *Bible*.

Y

Yahweh

This word represents the four consonants, usually transcribed YHWH, used in the Hebrew Scriptures to indicate the name for God. Modern biblical scholars have reconstructed the word as *Yahweh*, though some have transcribed the Hebrew letters as JHVH and pronounce the name as "Jehovah." The meaning of YHWH is often translated as "I am who am" (Ex 3:14).

Yahwist

This is a particular school of writing woven throughout the Pentateuch, attributed to the Yahwist authors or Yahwist school. This is the oldest literary source in the Pentateuch. It is sometimes called the J Tradition because the scholars who first noticed this were German, and in German, Yahweh is spelled *Jahweh*. This J Tradition was probably written by unknown scribes from Judah who, in 950 BC, wrote sections of the books of Genesis through Numbers. God to the Yahwist had human, or anthropomorphic, qualities. This God walked in the Garden (see Gn 3:8), sculpted humanity with divine hands (see 2:7), planted groves of trees (see 2:8), and grieved at the human beings who were lost among the trees or idols.

Yom Kippur

Yom Kippur is a Jewish holy day that is also referred to as the Day of Atonement, which falls on the tenth day of Tishri and is observed with prayer and fasting in accord with Leviticus (see chapter 16).

Z

zealots

This word refers to a Jewish group at the beginning of the first century AD who sought religious and political independence from the Romans and rose up in open rebellion. After their defeat, they carried on guerrilla warfare against the Romans.

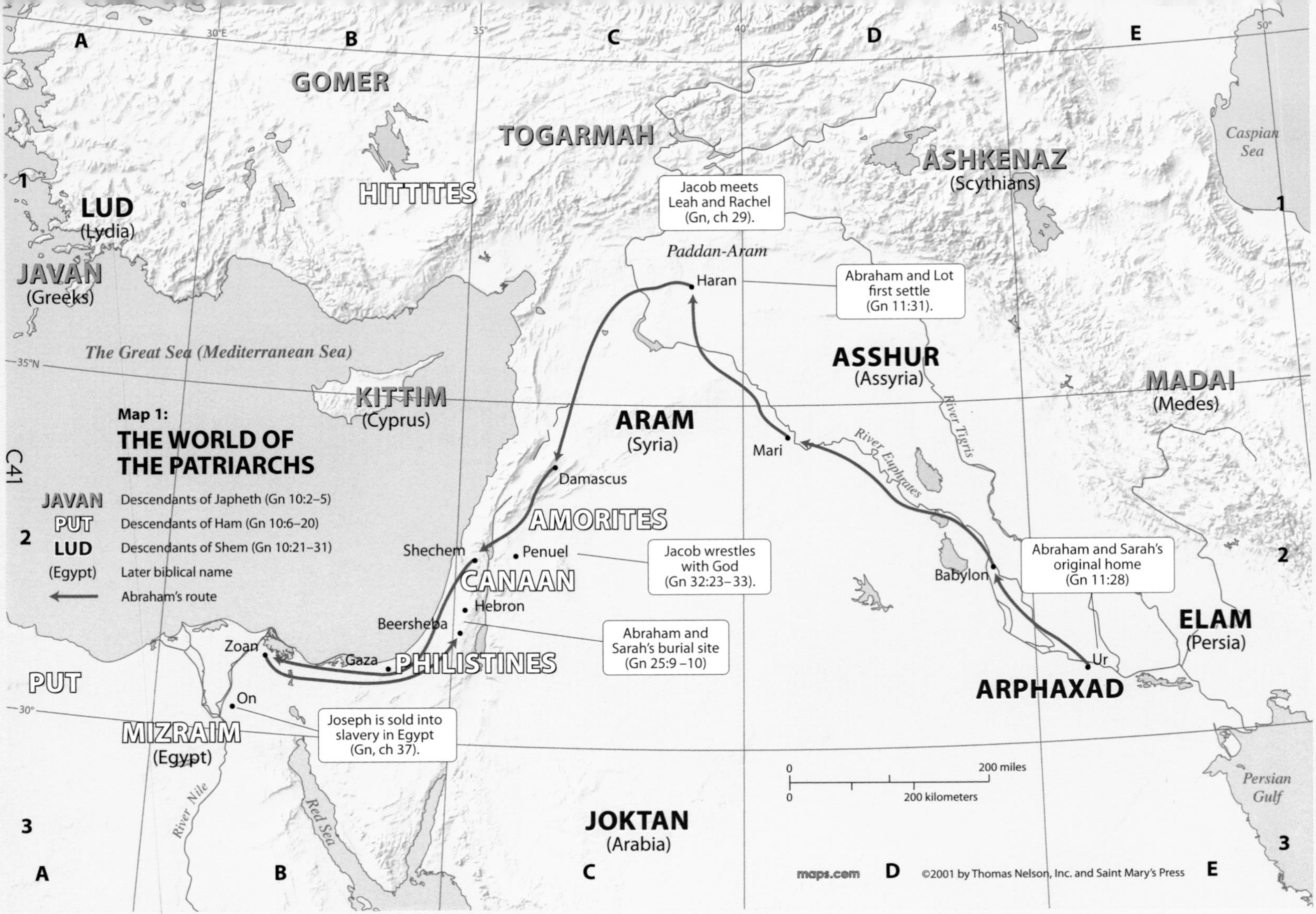
Map 1:
THE WORLD OF THE PATRIARCHS
JAVAN Descendants of Japheth (Gn 10:2–5)
PUT Descendants of Ham (Gn 10:6–20)
LUD Descendants of Shem (Gn 10:21–31)
(Egypt) Later biblical name
Abraham's route
A
B
C
D
E
1
2
3
30°E
35°
40°
45°
50°
35°N
30°
GOMER
TOGARMAH
ASHKENAZ
(Scythians)
HITTITES
LUD
(Lydia)
JAVAN
(Greeks)
The Great Sea (Mediterranean Sea)
KITTIM
(Cyprus)
Caspian Sea
Jacob meets Leah and Rachel (Gn, ch 29).
Paddan-Aram
Haran
Abraham and Lot first settle (Gn 11:31).
ASSHUR
(Assyria)
MADAI
(Medes)
ARAM
(Syria)
Mari
River Tigris
River Euphrates
Damascus
AMORITES
Shechem
Penuel
CANAAN
Jacob wrestles with God (Gn 32:23–33).
Hebron
Beersheba
Abraham and Sarah's burial site (Gn 25:9–10)
Zoan
Gaza
PHILISTINES
Babylon
Abraham and Sarah's original home (Gn 11:28)
ELAM
(Persia)
Ur
ARPHAXAD
PUT
On
MIZRAIM
(Egypt)
Joseph is sold into slavery in Egypt (Gn, ch 37).
River Nile
Red Sea
JOKTAN
(Arabia)
0 200 miles
0 200 kilometers
Persian Gulf
maps.com
©2001 by Thomas Nelson, Inc. and Saint Mary's Press

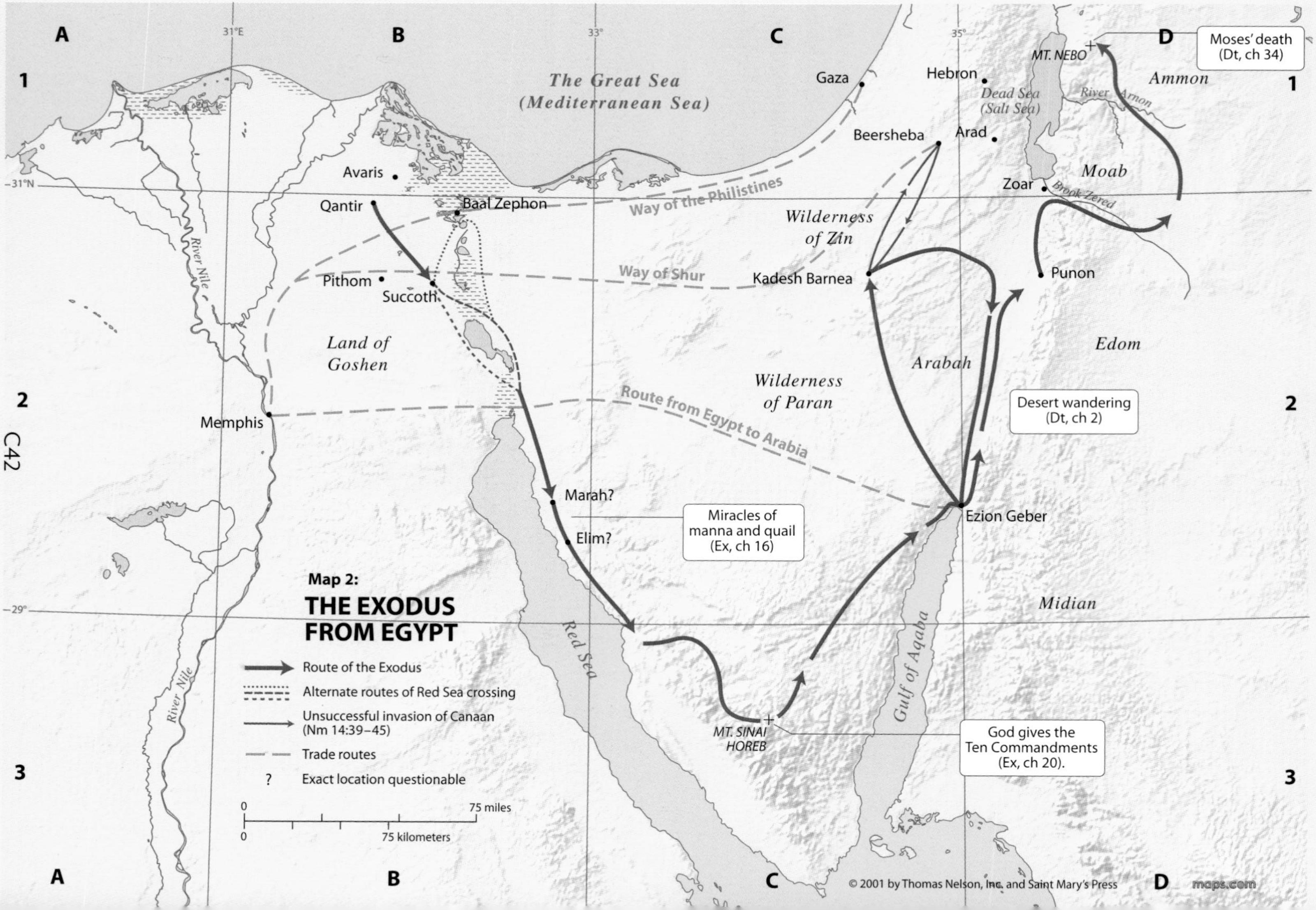

Map 2:
THE EXODUS FROM EGYPT
Route of the Exodus
Alternate routes of Red Sea crossing
Unsuccessful invasion of Canaan (Nm 14:39–45)
Trade routes
? Exact location questionable
0 75 miles
0 75 kilometers
A
B
C
D
1
2
3
31°E
33°
35°
31°N
29°
The Great Sea (Mediterranean Sea)
Avaris
Qantir
Baal Zephon
Pithom
Succoth
Land of Goshen
Memphis
River Nile
Way of the Philistines
Way of Shur
Route from Egypt to Arabia
Marah?
Elim?
Miracles of manna and quail (Ex, ch 16)
Red Sea
MT. SINAI HOREB
God gives the Ten Commandments (Ex, ch 20).
Gulf of Aqaba
Ezion Geber
Wilderness of Paran
Wilderness of Zin
Kadesh Barnea
Gaza
Beersheba
Hebron
Arad
Dead Sea (Salt Sea)
Zoar
Brook Zered
Arabah
Desert wandering (Dt, ch 2)
Punon
Edom
Moab
River Arnon
Ammon
MT. NEBO
Moses' death (Dt, ch 34)
Midian
© 2001 by Thomas Nelson, Inc. and Saint Mary's Press
maps.com

Map 3:
JACOB'S CHILDREN IN PALESTINE

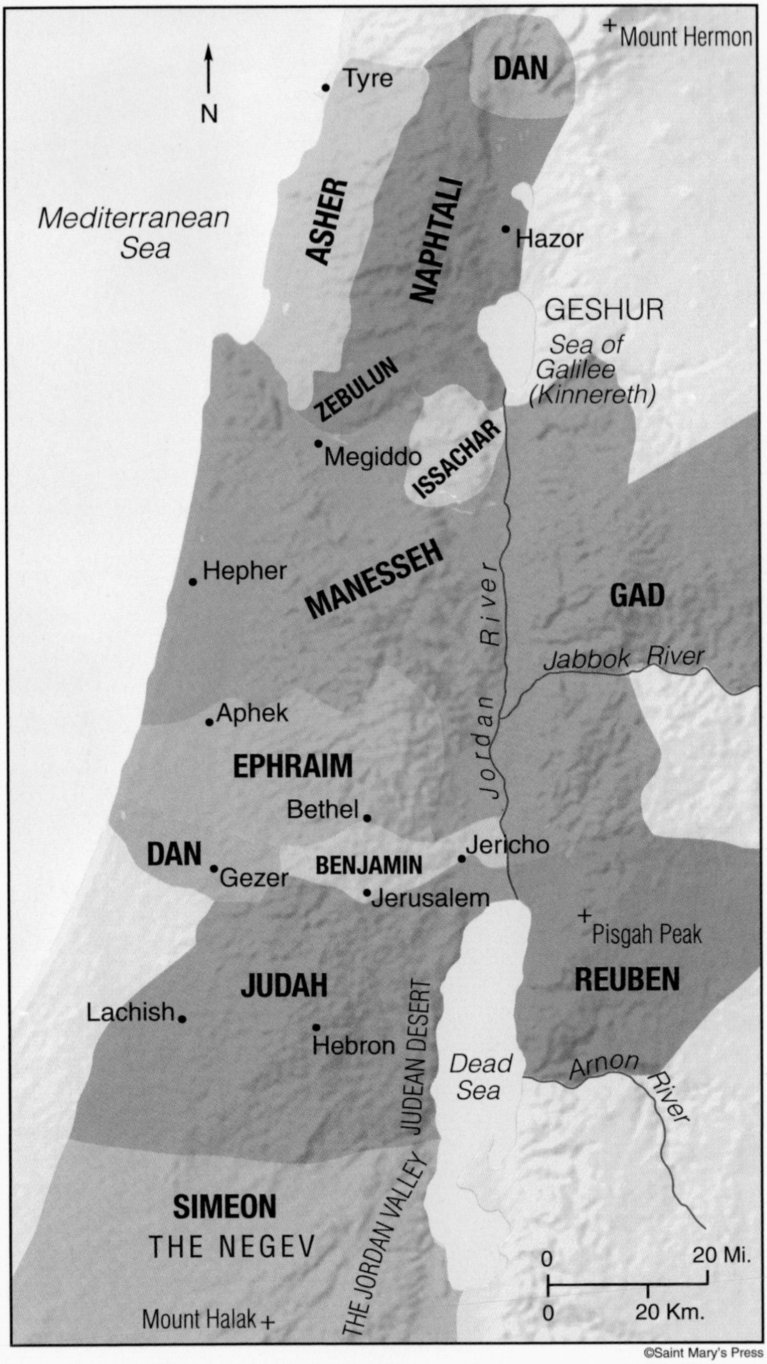

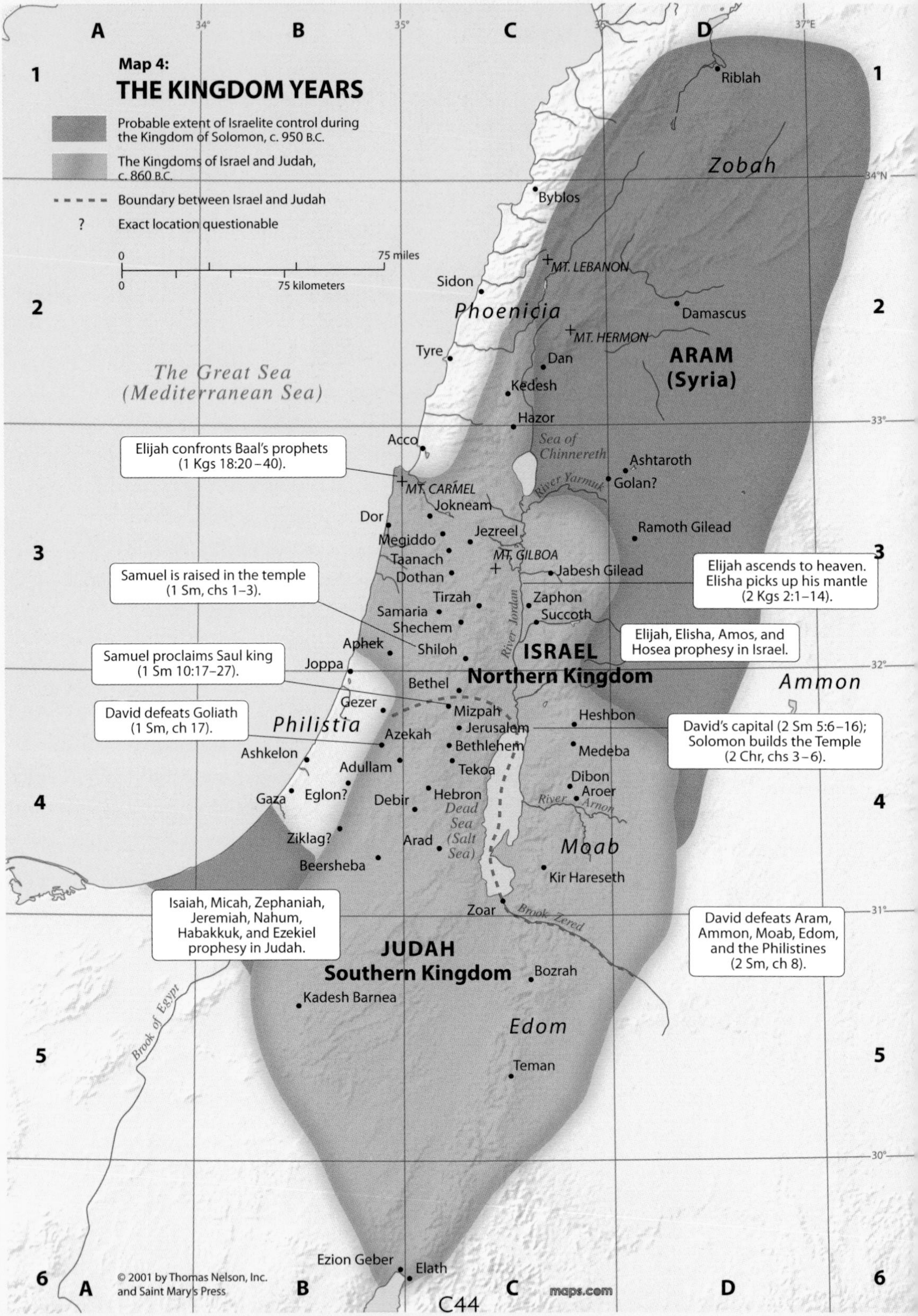

Map 4:
THE KINGDOM YEARS
Probable extent of Israelite control during the Kingdom of Solomon, c. 950 B.C.
The Kingdoms of Israel and Judah, c. 860 B.C.
Boundary between Israel and Judah
? Exact location questionable
0
75 miles
0
75 kilometers
A
B
C
D
1
2
3
4
5
6
34°
35°
36°
37°E
34°N
33°
32°
31°
30°
The Great Sea (Mediterranean Sea)
Riblah
Zobah
Byblos
MT. LEBANON
Sidon
Phoenicia
Damascus
MT. HERMON
Tyre
Dan
ARAM (Syria)
Kedesh
Hazor
Acco
Sea of Chinnereth
Ashtaroth
Golan?
River Yarmuk
Elijah confronts Baal's prophets (1 Kgs 18:20–40).
MT. CARMEL
Jokneam
Dor
Jezreel
Ramoth Gilead
Megiddo
Taanach
MT. GILBOA
Dothan
Jabesh Gilead
Elijah ascends to heaven. Elisha picks up his mantle (2 Kgs 2:1–14).
Samuel is raised in the temple (1 Sm, chs 1–3).
Tirzah
Zaphon
Samaria
Succoth
Shechem
River Jordan
Aphek
Shiloh
ISRAEL
Northern Kingdom
Elijah, Elisha, Amos, and Hosea prophesy in Israel.
Samuel proclaims Saul king (1 Sm 10:17–27).
Joppa
Bethel
Ammon
Gezer
Mizpah
Heshbon
David defeats Goliath (1 Sm, ch 17).
Philistia
Jerusalem
David's capital (2 Sm 5:6–16); Solomon builds the Temple (2 Chr, chs 3–6).
Azekah
Bethlehem
Medeba
Ashkelon
Tekoa
Adullam
Dibon
Aroer
Gaza
Eglon?
Debir
Hebron
River Arnon
Dead Sea (Salt Sea)
Ziklag?
Arad
Moab
Beersheba
Kir Hareseth
Isaiah, Micah, Zephaniah, Jeremiah, Nahum, Habakkuk, and Ezekiel prophesy in Judah.
Zoar
Brook Zered
David defeats Aram, Ammon, Moab, Edom, and the Philistines (2 Sm, ch 8).
JUDAH
Southern Kingdom
Bozrah
Kadesh Barnea
Brook of Egypt
Edom
Teman
Ezion Geber
Elath
© 2001 by Thomas Nelson, Inc. and Saint Mary's Press
maps.com

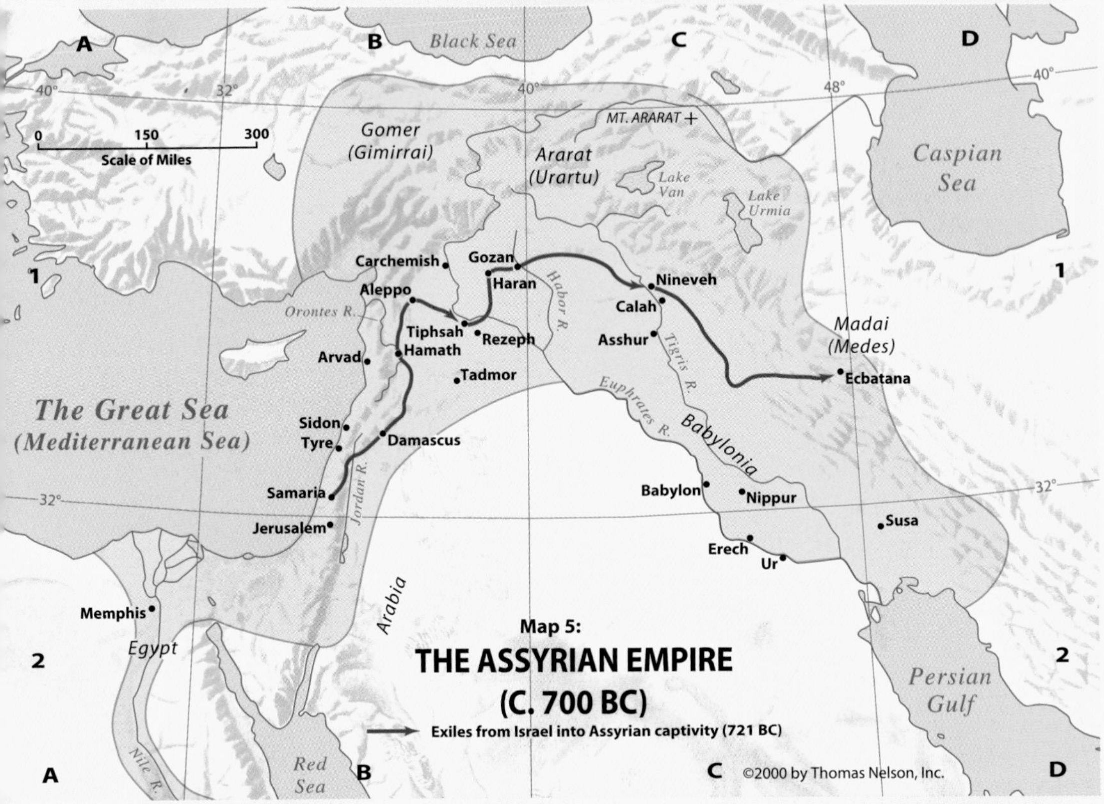

Map 5:

THE ASSYRIAN EMPIRE (C. 700 BC)

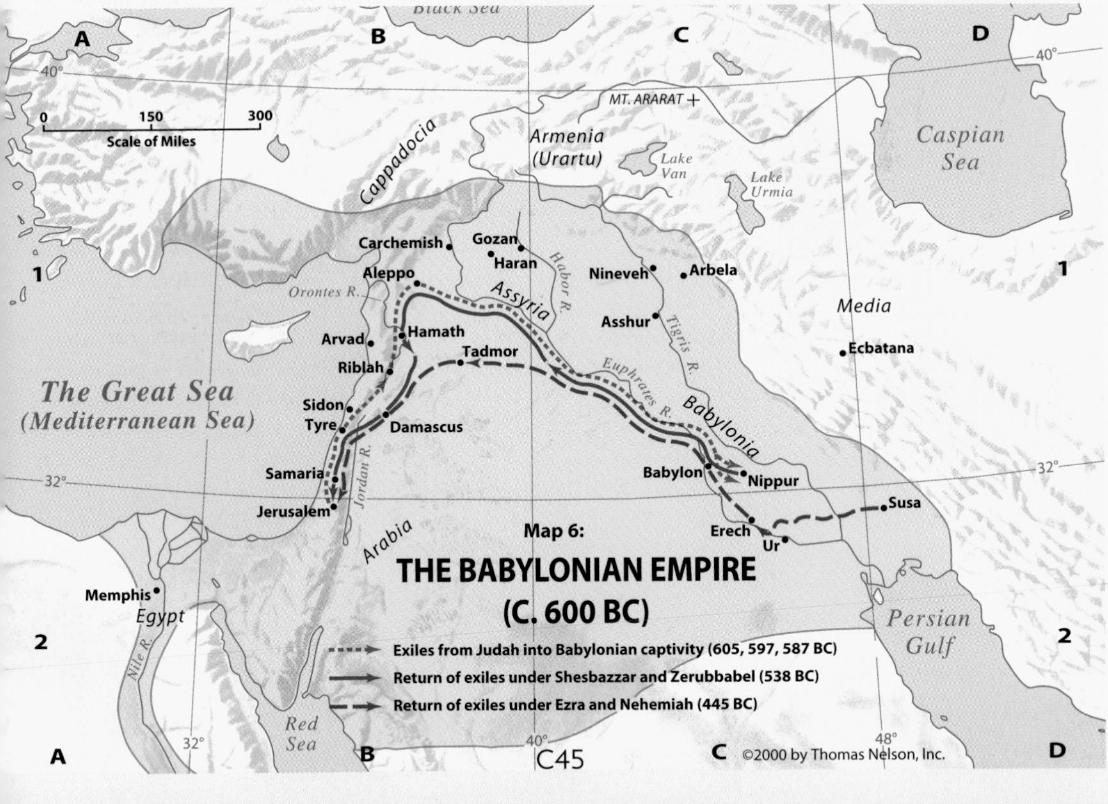

Map 6:

THE BABYLONIAN EMPIRE (C. 600 BC)

Map 7:
THE MINISTRY OF JESUS
(1,742) Elevation, in feet
? Exact location questionable
0 30 miles
0 30 kilometers
34°30′E
35°00′
35°30′
36°00′
33°30′N
33°00′
32°30′
32°00′
31°30′
A
B
C
D
1
2
3
4
5
Sidon
Damascus
Zarephath
MT. LEBANON (11,000)
MT. HERMON (9,200)
Iturea
Tyre
Phoenicia
Panias (Caesarea Philippi)
Trachonitis
Galilee
Ptolemais
Chorazin
Bethsaida?
Feeds five thousand (Lk 9:10–17)
Heals centurion's servant (Mt 8:5–13) and a paralytic (Mt 9:2–8), and raises Jairus's daughter (Mt 9:18–26)
Capernaum
MT. CARMEL (1,742)
Magdala
Sea of Galilee
Gergesa
Cana
Tiberias
Calms the storm (Mk 4:35–41); walks on water (Mt 14:22–33)
Performs wedding feast miracle (Jn 2:1–11)
River Kishon
River Yarmuk
Nazareth
MT. TABOR (1,843)
Gadara?
Nain
Grows up in Nazareth (Lk 2:39–40)
Esdraelon
River Jezreel
Transfiguration? (Mt 17:1–13)
Caesarea
Scythopolis
Raises widow's son (Lk 7:11–17)
MT. GILBOA (1,696)
The Great Sea (Mediterranean Sea)
Decapolis
Samaria
Talks to Samaritan woman (Jn 4:4–42)
Samaria
Sychar
Gerasa
River Jabbok
River Jordan
MT. GERIZIM (2,890)
Antipatris
Perea
Joppa
Arimathea
Gadara?
Ephraim
Philadelphia
Lydda
Crucifixion and Resurrection
Heals Bartimaeus (Mk 10:46–52); calls Zacchaeus (Lk 19:1–10)
Appears to two disciples after Resurrection (Lk 24:13–35)
Emmaus
Jericho
Kirjath Jearim
Jerusalem
Bethabara
Jesus' baptism? (Mk 1:9–11)
Beth Haccerem
Bethany
Qumran
Azotus
Bethlehem
Raises Lazarus (Jn 11:1–44)
Medeba
Ashkelon
Herodium
Judea
Jesus' birth (Lk 2:1–7)
Machaerus
Hebron
Gaza
Dead Sea (Salt Sea) (-1,300)
River Arnon
Masada
Idumea
Beersheba
C46
maps.com
© 2001 by Thomas Nelson, Inc. and Saint Mary's Press

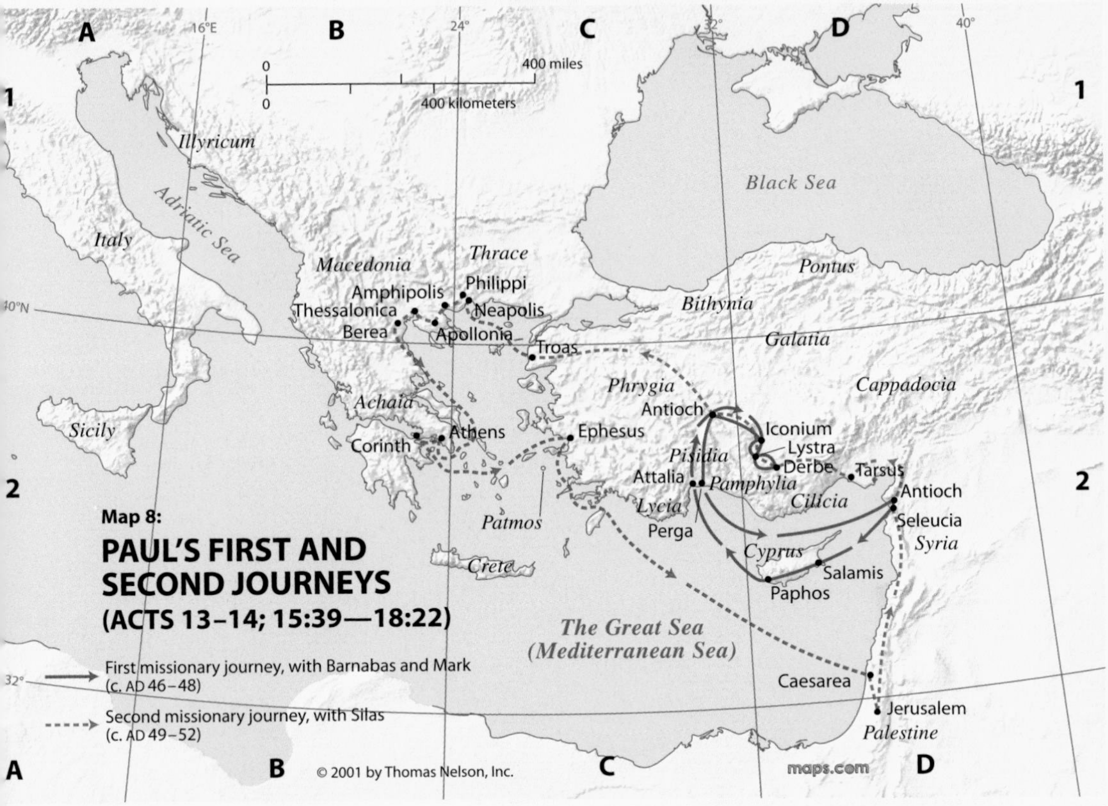

Map 8:

PAUL'S FIRST AND SECOND JOURNEYS (ACTS 13–14; 15:39—18:22)

First missionary journey, with Barnabas and Mark (c. AD 46–48)

Second missionary journey, with Silas (c. AD 49–52)

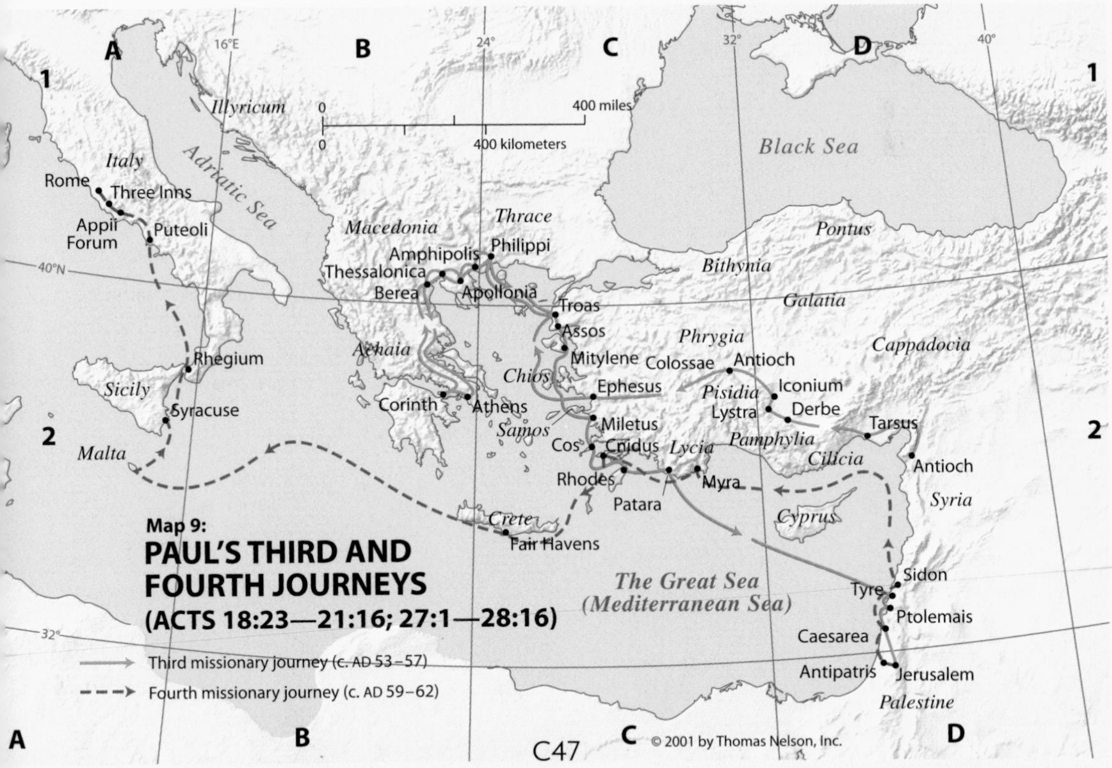

Map 9:

PAUL'S THIRD AND FOURTH JOURNEYS (ACTS 18:23—21:16; 27:1—28:16)

Third missionary journey (c. AD 53–57)

Fourth missionary journey (c. AD 59–62)

Map 10:
THE HOLY LAND IN MODERN TIMES
Area occupied by Israel since June 1967
0
75 miles
0
75 kilometers
A
B
C
D
E
1
2
3
4
5
6
34°
35°
36°
37°E
34°N
33°
32°
31°
30°
LEBANON
SYRIA
JORDAN
EGYPT
SAUDI ARABIA
ISRAEL
Tripoli
Beirut
BEKAA VALLEY
LEBANON MOUNTAINS
ANTI-LEBANON MOUNTAINS
Sidon
Damascus
Tyre
Dan
Qiryat Shemona
Quneitra
GOLAN HEIGHTS
1973 Line
1967 Cease-Fire Line
The Great Sea (Mediterranean Sea)
Nahariyya
Akko
Safad
Haifa
Tiberias
Sea of Galilee
Nazareth
Afula
Beth Shean
Dera
Ramtha
Hadera
Netanya
Tulkarm
Nablus
Jarash
Herzliyya
Tel Aviv
Yafo
Petah Tiqwa
WEST BANK
River Jordan
Rishon le Zion
Lod
Ramla
Ramalah
Amman
Ashdod
Jericho
Jerusalem
Bethlehem
Madaba
Ashqelon
Qiryat Gat
Gaza
Hebron
Dhiban
GAZA STRIP
En Gedi
Dead Sea (Salt Sea)
Beersheba
Karak
Al-Arish
Negev
Arabah
Sinai
Elat
Aqaba
maps.com

Old Testament Figures and Events

Adam and Eve

(See Gn 3:1–24) By Jan Brueghel the Younger, Flemish 17th century. In this painting Adam and Eve are being escorted from the Garden of Eden by an angel. In contrast to the beauty and richness of God's creation all around them, Adam and Eve have clothed themselves in an attempt to hide their shame in having disobeyed God. In what ways do people today still try to cover up and hide their sinfulness?

Noah's Ark

(See Gn 5:32—9:29), by the contemporary American artist Laura James. The artist captures the energy of Noah's family as they load the ark with supplies. The Book of Genesis has many stories about families. When has your family worked together to accomplish an important goal?

Rachel at the well

(See Gn 29:1–30), by Harry Mileham, England, 1903. Jacob fell in love with Rachel at the well and served her father for fourteen years in order to marry her. Notice how young they look. What would you do for someone you loved?

Moses with the Tablets of the Law

(See Ex 20:1–21, 32:15–20) This depiction of Moses holding a stone tablet on top of Mount Sinai appears in the chapel of Moses in the Church of the Transfiguration on Mount Tabor. The tablets always symbolize the Ten Commandments. Do you think images of the tablets should be allowed in public places?

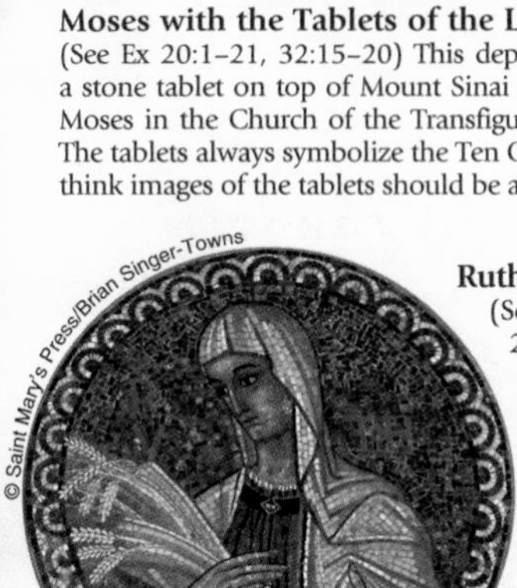

Ruth Gleaning the Field

(See Ruth, chapter 2; Lv 23:22) This depiction of Ruth holding a sheaf of grain is one of six women from the Old Testament surrounding Jesus in a mosaic that appears in the Church of the Dormition on Mount Zion in Jerusalem. Ruth is a foreigner from the land of Moab who becomes the great-grandmother of King David, an ancestor of Jesus.

David and Goliath

(See 1 Sm 17:1–51) This statue, which stands in the Tower of David Museum in the Old City of Jerusalem, depicts David's victory over Goliath, a Philistine warrior who challenged God's People to a fight and threatened to enslave them. David's faith in God helped him defeat the giant. In your life, what Goliaths do you need God's help to face?

New Testament Figures and Events

Mary Greets Elizabeth
(See Lk 1:39–56) This statue of Mary greeting her cousin Elizabeth appears in the courtyard of the Church of the Visitation on the hillside of Ein Kerem in Jerusalem. When Elizabeth heard Mary's greeting, the child within her leapt for joy. How do you react when hearing the Good News of the Gospel?

Wise Men from the East
(See Mt 2:1–12) By Iranian artist Agha Behzad, 1958. This painting, from Iran, of the Nativity does not contain images of angels or the star of Bethlehem. Why do some paintings emphasize the human nature of Jesus' birth while other paintings emphasize his divine nature?

The Escape to Egypt and the Slaughter of the Innocents
(See Mt 2:13–18) This mural, found in the Orthodox Church of the Annunciation in Nazareth, depicts the flight of the Holy Family into Egypt when King Herod threatened to destroy the child Jesus and ordered the massacre of all boys two years old and younger. Who or what threatens the lives of innocent people today?

Calming the Storm
(See Mt 8:23–27, Mk 4:35–41, Lk 8:22–25), by the contemporary American artist Laura James. The artist reflects both the humanity of the Apostles and the divinity of Jesus. Imagine being on that boat.

Jesus' Body is Removed from the Cross
(See Mt 27:57–61, Mk 15:42–47, Lk 23:50–55, Jn 19:38–42) This painting of Jesus' family and friends removing his body from the cross is from the Church of the Holy Sepulcher in Jerusalem, built on what is believed to be the site of Jesus' tomb. Imagine the sorrow Jesus' family and friends must have been feeling. How would you have reacted to Jesus' death?

Encounters with Jesus

Madonna and Child
This mosaic of Mary holding the child Jesus is from Japan and hangs in the Basilica of the Annunciation in Nazareth. Why do you think it is important to view images of Christ from different cultural perspectives?

Jesus Teaches the Crowds
(See Mt 5:1–11, Lk 6:20–26) By French artist James Tissot, 1836–1902. This painting depicts Jesus teaching the crowds. One of the most important teachings Jesus shared with his followers was the Beatitudes, rules for living that will bring true happiness. What has given you true happiness?

Jesus prays in the Garden at Gethsemane
(See Mt 26:36–46, Mk 14:32–42, Lk 22:39–46), from the Mafa Life of Jesus series, late twentieth century. This painting reflects the West-African vision of a garden. Notice how rocky it is and how short the trees are. How do you envision the Garden at Gethsemane?

Jesus Holding the Word
(See Jn 6:60–69) This mosaic of Jesus holding the word is in the Church of the Dormition on Mount Zion in Jerusalem. Jesus offers his followers the words of eternal life. Will you believe and follow?

Lamb of God
(See Jn 1:29; Rev 5:1–14) Found in the Church of the Visitation in Jerusalem, this mosaic of the Lamb of God symbolizes Jesus' sacrifice in redeeming the sins of the world. What sacrifice are you willing to make for others?

Cro-Magnon people appear. (35,000)

Humans live in permanent settlements. (10,000)

35,000 | 10,000 | 9000

BC

Timeline of Human History

Expanded Timeline of Biblical History

BC

PREHISTORY | 2000 | 1900 | 1800 | 1700

Note: All dates are approximate.

Also, the solid orange and blue sections of the *Timeline of Human History* on pages C54 and C55 correspond to the entire *Timeline of Biblical History* on all four pages.

Jacob's descendants settle in Egypt. (1750)

Abraham and Sarah arrive in Canaan. (1850)

BIBLICAL PREHISTORY

Important Biblical Figures
Adam and Eve
Cain and Abel
Noah

TIME OF THE PATRIARCHS AND MATRIARCHS

Important Biblical Figures
Abraham and Sarah
Isaac and Rebekah
Jacob, Leah, and Rachel
Joseph and Asenath

Last glacial period ends. (8200)

Farming villages form; goats, sheep, and oxen are domesticated. (7000)

8000 | 7000 | 6000 | 5000

BC

Timeline of Human History

Expanded Timeline of Biblical History

BC

1600 | 1500 | 1400 | 1300 | 1200 | 1100

Moses leads Exodus from Egypt. (1290)

Joshua invades Canaan. (1250)

Judges lead Israelite tribes in Canaan. (1200)

TIME IN EGYPT AND THE EXODUS

Important Biblical Figures

Moses
Aaron
Miriam

TIME OF THE JUDGES

Important Biblical Figures

Deborah
Gideon
Samson
Samuel

City-states and river-valley civilizations begin with Bronze Age. **(3800)**

First pharaohs rule Egypt. Hieroglyphic writing is invented. **(3000)**

Great Pyramids are built. **(2500)**

Abraham and Sarah arrive in Canaan. **(1850)**

Hammurabi develops code of law in Babylon. **(1792)**

Canaanites invent alphabet. **(1550)**

4000 3000 2000 1000

BC

Timeline of Human History

Biblical History

Expanded Timeline of Biblical History

PROPHETS Prominent Kings of Israel Prominent Kings of Judah

BC

1000 900 800 700 600 500

Saul is named first king of Israel. **(1020)**

David unites kingdom, takes Jerusalem as capital. **(1000)**

Solomon rules kingdom, builds Temple. **(961)**

Kingdom divides into Israel and Judah. **(922)**

Assyrians capture Samaria, ending the kingdom of Israel. **(721)**

Babylonians take Jerusalem. Exile of Judah begins. **(587)**

Cyrus of Persia frees Jews to return to Judah. **(538)**

People of Judah rebuild Temple. **(515)**

ELIJAH (865)

ELISHA (850)

AMOS (783)

HOSEA (760)

FIRST ISAIAH (740)

MICAH (720)

NAHUM (663)

ZEPHANIAH (630)

JEREMIAH (626)

HABAKKUK (609)

EZEKIEL (593)

OBADIAH (586)

SECOND ISAIAH (540)

ZECHARIAH (520)

HAGGAI (520)

TIME OF THE KINGS AND PROPHETS

UNITED KINGDOM — DIVIDED KINGDOM — PERSIAN DOMINATION

Saul David Solomon

Jeroboam I (922) Ahab (869) Ahaziah (850) Jeroboam II (786) Hoshea (732)

Rehoboam (922) Ahaziah (842) Jehoash (837) Uzziah (783) Hezekiah (715) Josiah (640) Jehoiachin (598) Zedekiah (597)

Buddha is born in India.
(563)

Confucius is born in China.
(551)

Greece has golden age.
(400)

Roman Empire is established.
(43 BC)

Jesus is crucified in Palestine.
(AD 30)

Roman Empire falls.
(476)

Muhammad founds Islam in Arabia.
(622)

Crusades begin.
(1096)

Gutenberg invents printing press.
(1450)

Columbus sails to America.
(1492)

Luther starts Protestant Reformation.
(1517)

Declaration of Independence is signed.
(1776)

Dominion of Canada is created.
(1867)

World War II begins.
(1939)

Personal computers become available.
(1972)

0 1000 2000

AD

Biblical History

Timeline of Human History

Expanded Timeline of Biblical History

New Testament Books

BC AD

400 300 200 100 0 100

Revolt against Greeks by Maccabees begins.
(166)

Romans conquer Holy Land.
(63)

Greeks conquer Holy Land.
(332)

Temple is rededicated.
(165)

Jesus is born.
(5 BC)

Ezra brings Torah to Jerusalem.
(398)

Jesus is crucified.
(AD 30)

Simon, Jonathan's brother, establishes Hasmonean dynasty.
(142)

Saul is converted.
(31)

Nehemiah becomes governor of Judah, starts renewal.
(445)

James is martyred.
(61)

Nero persecutes Christians. Peter and Paul are martyred.
(64–68)

Romans destroy Jerusalem Temple.
(70)

Domitian persecutes Christians.
(95)

1 Thes (51), Paul's major letters (mid- to late 50s)

Colossians, Philemon (early 60s)

Gospel of Mark (mid-60s)

Gospels of Matthew and Luke, Acts of the Apostles, Hebrews (70s to 80s)

Gospel of John; 1, 2, and 3 John; and Revelation (90s); 2 Peter (after 100)

MALACHI (458)

JOEL (400)

TIME OF FOREIGN DOMINATION

TIME OF NEW TESTAMENT

GREEK DOMINATION

HASMONEAN DYNASTY
(FREE FROM FOREIGN DOMINATION)

ROMAN DOMINATION

Nehemiah Ezra The Maccabees

Alphabetical List of Bible Books and Abbreviations

All scripture is inspired by God and is useful for teaching, for refutation, for correction, and for training in righteousness, so that one who belongs to God may be competent, equipped for every good work.
(2 Tm 3: 16–17)